AMERICAN MEN & WOMEN OF SCIENCE

PHYSICAL AND BIOLOGICAL SCIENCES

15TH EDITION
VOLUME VII
T-Z

EDITED BY
JAQUES CATTELL PRESS

R. R. BOWKER COMPANY
NEW YORK & LONDON 1982

Published by R.R. Bowker Co.
1180 Avenue of the Americas, New York, N.Y. 10036

International Standard Book Number
Set: 0-8352-1413-3
Volume I: 0-8352-1414-1
Volume II: 0-8352-1416-8
Volume III: 0-8352-1417-6
Volume IV: 0-8352-1418-4
Volume V: 0-8352-1419-2
Volume VI: 0-8352-1420-6
Volume VII: 0-8352-1421-4
International Standard Serial Number: 0192-8570
Library of Congress Catalog Card Number: 6-7326

CONTENTS

Advisory Committee vi

Preface vii

Abbreviations ix

Biographies 1

ADVISORY COMMITTEE

Dr. Dael L. Wolfle, Committee Chairman
Professor Emeritus,
Graduate School of Public Affairs
University of Washington

Dr. Carl D. Douglass
Director,
Division of Research Grants
National Institutes of Health

Mr. Alan Fechter
Head,
Scientific and Technical Personnel Studies
National Science Foundation

Dr. Harold S. Ginsberg
Professor & Chairman,
Department of Microbiology
College of Physicians and Surgeons
Columbia University

Dr. Allen L. Hammond
Editor, *Science '81*,
American Association for the Advancement of Science

Dr. Anna J. Harrison
Professor,
Department of Chemistry
Mt. Holyoke College

Dr. William C. Kelly
Executive Director,
Office of Scientific and Engineering Personnel
National Research Council

Dr. H. William Koch
Director,
American Institute of Physics

Dr. Robert Krauss
Executive Director,
Federation of American Societies for Experimental Biology

Dr. William J. LeVeque
Executive Director,
American Mathematical Society

Dr. Raymond P. Mariella
Executive Director,
American Chemical Society

Dr. James H. Mulligan, Jr.
Professor,
Department of Electrical Engineering
University of California, Irvine

Dr. Kenneth Prewitt
President,
Social Science Research Council

Dr. Helen M. Ranney
Professor & Chairman,
Department of Medicine
University of California, San Diego

Dr. Matthias Stelly
Executive Vice President,
American Society of Agronomy

Mr. William E. Zimmie
President,
Zimmite Corporation

PREFACE

American Men and Women of Science is without peer as a chronicle of North American scientific endeavor and achievement. It has recorded the careers of over 280,000 scientists and engineers since the first edition appeared in 1906, and continues to provide current information on the leaders in America's research and academic communities.

The Fifteenth Edition contains the biographies of 130,000 women and men; 7,500 appear for the first time. The names of new entrants were submitted for consideration at the editors' request by current entrants and by persons in charge of academic, government and private research programs. All of those included meet the following criteria:

1. Achievement, by reason of experience and training of a stature in scientific work equivalent to that associated with the doctoral degree, coupled with presently continued activity in such work;

   or

2. Research activity of high quality in science as evidenced by publication in reputable scientific journals; or, for those whose work cannot be published because of governmental or industrial security, research activity of high quality in science as evidenced by the judgment of the individual's peers;

   or

3. Attainment of a position of substantial responsibility requiring scientific training and experience to the extent described for (1) and (2).

This edition profiles living scientists in the physical and biological fields as well as public health scientists, engineers, mathematicians, statisticians, and computer scientists. The information is collected by means of direct communication whenever possible. Forms are sent to all entrants for corroboration and updating, and those whose biographies are appearing for the first time receive verification proofs before publication. The information submitted by entrants is included as completely as possible within the boundaries of editorial and space restrictions. Full entries are repeated for former listees who do not return forms but whose current location can be verified in secondary sources. References to the previous edition are given for those who do not return forms and cannot be located, but who are presumed to be still active in science or engineering. A notation is made when an entrant from the previous edition is known to be deceased. Non-citizens of the Americas are included if working in the United States or Canada for a reasonable duration. Information on former entrants who have entered fields other than science and engineering, or who have been retired for ten years and are no longer professionally active has been omitted.

American Men and Women of Science has experienced many changes in its long history, and this edition is no exception. Following the suggestion of the advisory committee, and based on the recommendation of a user survey, the geographic and discipline indexes have been discontinued in printed form. The Fifteenth Edition will be available for on-line searching, however, through BRS, DIALOG and the Jaques Cattell Press. All elements of an entry, including field of interest, experience and location, can be accessed by the use of key words. Although *American Men and Women of Science* is on a three year publication cycle, the on-line database will be updated at more frequent intervals. Previous users of the directory will be pleased to find that the type size has been enlarged in response to many requests.

The Social and Behavioral Sciences section of *American Men and Women of Science* was last published in 1978. The limited acceptance of this section caused the postponement of subsequent editions. Realizing the importance of maintaining current data on the disciplines, the publishers are considering several possibilities for the future. One is the inclusion of selected, appropriate fields in the *Directory of American Scholars,* also a Bowker/Cattell publication. Another plan under consideration is the systematic addition of social and behavioral scientists to the on-line database for eventual publication in an all-inclusive *American Men and Women of Science.*

The editors take this opportunity to thank the Fifteenth Edition advisory committee for their guidance, encouragement and support. Appreciation is expressed to the many scientific societies who provided their membership lists for the purpose of locating former entrants whose addresses had changed.

Comments and suggestions on any aspect of the Fifteenth Edition are encouraged and should be directed to The Editors, *American Men and Women of Science,* P.O. Box 25001, Tempe, Arizona 85282.

Martha Cargill, *Editor*
Renee Lautenbach, *Managing Editor*
Terence Basom, *General Manager*
JAQUES CATTELL PRESS

August, 1982

ABBREVIATIONS

AAAS—American Association for the Advancement of Science
abnorm—abnormal
abstr—abstract(s)
acad—academic, academy
acct—account, accountant, accounting
acoust—acoustic(s), acoustical
ACTH—adrenocorticotrophic hormone
actg—acting
activ—activities, activity
addn—addition(s), additional
Add—Address
adj—adjunct, adjutant
adjust—adjustment
Adm—Admiral
admin—administration, administrative
adminr—administrator(s)
admis—admission(s)
adv—adviser(s), advisory
advan—advance(d), advancement
advert—advertisement, advertising
AEC—Atomic Energy Commission
aerodyn—aerodynamic(s)
aeronaut—aeronautic(s), aeronautical
aerophys—aerophysical, aerophysics
aesthet—aesthetic(s)
AFB—Air Force Base
affil—affiliate(s), affiliation
agr—agricultural, agriculture
agron—agronomic, agronomical, agronomy
agrost—agrostologic, agrostological, agrostology
agt—agent
AID—Agency for International Development
Ala-Alabama
allergol—allergological, allergology
alt—alternate
Alta—Alberta
Am—America, American
AMA—American Medical Association
anal—analysis, analytic, analytical
analog—analogue
anat—anatomic, anatomical, anatomy
anesthesiol—anesthesiology
angiol—angiology
Ann—Annal(s)
ann—annual
anthrop—anthropological, anthropology
anthropom—anthropometric, anthropometrical, anthropometry
antiq—antiquary, antiquities, antiquity
antiqn—antiquarian
apicult—apicultural, apiculture
APO—Army Post Office
app—appoint, appointed
appl—applied
appln—application
approx—approximate(ly)
Apr—April
apt—apartment(s)
aquacult—aquaculture
arbit—arbitration
arch—archives
archaeol—archaeological, archaeology
archit—architectural, architecture
Arg—Argentina, Argentine
Ariz—Arizona
Ark—Arkansas
artil—artillery
asn—association
assoc(s)—associate(s), associated
asst(s)—assistant(s), assistantship(s)
Assyriol—Assyriology
astrodyn—astrodynamics
astron—astronomical, astronomy
astronaut—astronautical, astronautics
astronr—astronomer
astrophys—astrophysical, astrophysics
attend—attendant, attending
atty—attorney
audiol—audiology
Aug—August
auth—author
AV—audiovisual
Ave—Avenue
avicult—avicultural, aviculture

b—born
bact—bacterial, bacteriologic, bacteriological, bacteriology
BC—British Columbia
bd—board
behav—behavior(al)
Belg—Belgian, Belgium
bibl—biblical
bibliog—bibliographic, bibliographical, bibliography
bibliogr—bibliographer
biochem—biochemical, biochemistry
biog—biographical, biography
biol—biological, biology
biomed—biomedical, biomedicine
biomet—biometric(s), biometrical, biometry
biophys—biophysical, biophysics
bk(s)—book(s)
bldg—building
Blvd—Boulevard
Bor—Borough
bot—botanical, botany
br—branch(es)
Brig—Brigadier
Brit—Britain, British
Bro(s)—Brother(s)
byrol—byrology
Bull—Bulletin
bur—bureau
bus—business
BWI—British West Indies

c—children
Calif—California
Can—Canada, Canadian
cand—candidate
Capt—Captain
cardiol—cardiology
cardiovasc—cardiovascular
cartog—cartographic, cartographical, cartography
cartogr—cartographer
Cath—Catholic
CEngr—Corps of Engineers
cent—central
Cent Am—Central America
cert—certificate(s), certification, certified
chap—chapter
chem—chemical(s), chemistry
chemother—chemotherapy
chmn—chairman
citricult—citriculture
class—classical
climat—climatological, climatology
clin(s)—clinic(s), clinical
cmndg—commanding
Co—Companies, Company
coauth— coauthor
co-dir—co-director
co-ed—co-editor
coeduc—coeducation, coeducational
col(s)—college(s), collegiate, colonel
collab—collaboration, coloborative
collabr—collaborator
Colo—Colorado
com—commerce, commercial

ABBREVIATIONS

Comdr—Commander
commun—communicable, communication(s)
comn(s)—commission(s), commissioned
comnr—commissioner
comp—comparative
compos—composition
comput—computation, computer(s), computing
comt(s)—committee(s)
conchol—conchology
conf—conference
cong—congress, congressional
Conn—Connecticut
conserv—conservation, conservatory
consol—consolidated, consolidation
const—constitution, constitutional
construct—construction, constructive
consult(s)—consult, consultant(s) consultantship(s), consultation, consulting
contemp—contemporary
contrib—contribute, contributing, contribution(s)
contribr—contributor
conv—convention
coop—cooperating, cooperation, cooperative
coord—coordinate(d), coordinating, coordination
coordr—coordinator
corp—corporate, corporation(s)
corresp—correspondence, correspondent, corresponding
coun—council, counsel, counseling
counr—councilor, counselor
criminol—criminological, criminology
cryog—cryogenic(s)
crystallog—crystallographic, crystallograpiical, crystallography
crystallogr—crystallographer
Ct—Court
Ctr—Center
cult—cultural, culture
cur—curator
curric—curriculum
cybernet—cybernetic(s)
cytol—cytological, cytology
Czech—Czechoslovakia

DC—District of Columbia
Dec—December
Del—Delaware
deleg—delegate, delegation
delinq—delinquency, delinquent
dem—democrat(s), democratic
demog—demographic, demography
demogr—demographer
demonstr—demonstrator
dendrol—dendrologic, dendrological, dendrology
dent—dental, dentistry
dep—deputy
dept—department(al)
dermat—dermatologic, dermatological, dermatology
develop—developed, developing, development, developmental
diag—diagnosis, diagnostic
dialectol—dialectological, dialectology
dict—dictionaries, dictionary
Dig—Digest
dipl—diploma, diplomate
dir(s)—director(s), directories, directory
dis—disease(s), disorders
Diss Abstr—Dissertation Abstracts
dist—district
distrib—distributed, distribution, distributive
distribr—distributor(s)
div—division, divisional, divorced
DNA—deoxyribonucleic acid
doc—document(s), documentary, documentation
Dom—Dominion
Dr—Drive

e—east
ecol—ecological, ecology
econ(s)—economic(s), economical, economy
economet—econometric(s)
ECT—electroconvulsive or electroshock therapy
ed—edition(s), editor(s), editorial
ed bd—editorial board
educ—education, educational
educr—educator(s)
EEG—electroencephalogram, electroencephalographic, electroencephalography
Egyptol—Egyptology
EKG—electrocardiogram
elec—electric, electrical, electricity
electrochem—electrochemical, electrochemistry
electrophys—electrophysical, electrophysics
elem—elementary
embryol—embryologic, embryological, embryology
emer—emeriti, emiritus
employ—employment
encour—encouragement
encycl—encyclopedia
endocrinol—endocrinologic, endocrinology
eng—engineering
Eng—England, English
engr(s)—engineer(s)
enol—enology
Ens—Ensign
entom—entomological, entomology
environ—environment(s), environmental
enzym—enzymology
epidemiol—epidemiologic, epidemiological, epidemiology
equip—equipment
ESEA—Elementary & Secondary Education Act
espec—especially
estab—established, establishment(s)
ethnog—ethnographic, ethnographical, ethnography
ethnogr—ethnographer
ethnol—ethnologic, ethnological, ethnology
Europ—European
eval—evaluation
evangel—evangelical
eve—evening
exam—examination(s), examining
examr—examiner
except—exceptional
exec(s)—executive(s)
exeg—exegeses, exegesis, exegetic, exegetical
exhib(s)—exhibition(s), exhibit(s)
exp—experiment, experimental
exped(s)—expedition(s)
explor—exploration(s), exploratory
expos—exposition
exten—extension

fac—faculty
facil—facilities, facility
Feb—February
fed—federal
fedn—federation
fel(s)—fellow(s), fellowship(s)
fermentol—fermentology
fertil—fertility, fertilitization
Fla—Florida
floricult—floricultural, floriculture
found—foundation
FPO—Fleet Post Office
Fr—French
Ft—Fort

Ga—Georgia
gastroenterol—gastroenterological, gastroenterology
gen—general
geneal—genealogical, genealogy
geod—geodesy, geodetic
geog—geographic, geographical, geography
geogr—geographer
geol—geologic, geological, geology
geom—geometric, geometrical, geometry
geomorphol—geomorphologic, geomorphology
geophys—geophysical, geophysics
Ger—German, Germanic, Germany
geriat—geriatric(s)
geront—gerontological, gerontology
glaciol—glaciology
gov—governing, governor(s)
govt—government, governmental
grad—graduate(d)
Gt Brit—Great Britain
guid—guidance
gym—gymnasium
gynec—gynecologic, gynecological, gynecology

handbk(s)—handbook(s)
helminth—helminthology
hemat—hematologic, hematological, hematology
herpet—herpetologic, herpetological, herpetology
Hisp—Hispanic, Hispania
hist—historic, historical, history
histol—histological, histology
HM—Her Majesty
hochsch—hochschule
homeop—homeopathic, homeopathy
hon(s)—honor(s), honorable, honorary
hort—horticultural, horticulture
hosp(s)—hospital(s), hospitalization
hq—headquarters
HumRRO—Human Resources Research Office
husb—husbandry
Hwy—Highway
hydraul—hydraulic(s)
hydrodyn—hydrodynamic(s)
hydrol—hydrologic, hydrological, hydrology
hyg—hygiene, hygienic(s)
hypn—hypnosis

ichthyol—ichthyological, ichthyology
Ill—Illinois
illum—illuminating, illumination
illus—illustrate, illustrated, illustration
illusr—illustrator
immunol—immunologic, immunological, immunology

Imp—Imperial
improv—improvement
Inc—Incorporated
in-chg—in charge
incl—include(s), including
Ind—Indiana
indust(s)—industrial, industries, industry
inf—infantry
info—information
inorg—inorganic
ins—insurance
inst(s)—institute(s), institution(s)
instnl—institutional(ized)
instr(s)—instruct, instruction, instructor(s)
instrnl—instructional
int—international
intel—intelligence
introd—introduction
invert—invertebrate
invest(s)—investigation(s)
investr—investigator
irrig—irrigation
Ital—Italian

J—Journal
Jan—January
Jct—Junction
jour—journal, journalism
jr—junior
jurisp—jurisprudence
juv—juvenile

Kans—Kansas
Ky—Kentucky

La—Louisiana
lab(s)—laboratories, laboratory
lang—language(s)
laryngol—laryngological, laryngology
lect—lecture(s)
lectr—lecturer(s)
legis—legislation, legislative, legislature
lett—letter(s)
lib—liberal
libr—libraries, library
librn—librarian
lic—license(d)
limnol—limnological, limnology
ling—linguistic(s), linguistical
lit—literary, literature
lithol—lithologic, lithological, lithology
Lt—Lieutenant
Ltd—Limited

m—married
mach—machine(s), machinery
mag—magazine(s)
maj—major
malacol—malacology
mammal—mammalogy
Man—Manitoba
Mar—March
Mariol—Mariology
Mass—Massachusetts
mat—material(s)
mat med—materia medica
math—mathematic(s), mathematical
Md—Maryland
mech—mechanic(s), mechanical
med—medical, medicinal, medicine
Mediter—Mediterranean
Mem—Memorial
mem—member(s), membership(s)
ment—mental(ly)
metab—metabolic, metabolism
metall—metallurgic, metallurgical, metallurgy
metallog—metallographic, metallography
metallogr—metallographer
metaphys—metaphysical, metaphysics
meteorol—meteorological, meteorology
metrol—metrological, metrology
metrop—metropolitan
Mex—Mexican, Mexico
mfg—manufacturing
mfr(s)—manufacture(s), manufacturer(s)
mgr—manager
mgt—management
Mich—Michigan
microbiol—microbiological, microbiology
micros—microscopic, microscopical, microscopy
mid—middle
mil—military
mineral—mineralogical, mineralogy
Minn—Minnesota
Miss—Mississippi
mkt—market, marketing
Mo—Missouri
mod—modern
monogr—monograph
Mont—Montana
morphol—morphological, morphology
Mt—Mount
mult—multiple
munic—municipal, municipalities
mus—museum(s)
musicol—musicological, musicology
mycol—mycologic, mycology

n—north
NASA—National Aeronautics & Space Administration
nat—national, naturalized
NATO—North Atlantic Treaty Organization
navig—navigation(al)
NB—New Brunswick
NC—North Carolina
NDak—North Dakota
NDEA—National Defense Education Act
Nebr—Nebraska
nematol—nematological, nematology
nerv—nervous
Neth—Netherlands
neurol—neurological, neurology
neuropath—neuropathological, neuropathology
neuropsychiat—neuropsychiatric, neuropsychiatry
neurosurg—neurosurgical, neurosurgery
Nev—Nevada
New Eng—New England
New York—New York City
Nfld—Newfoundland
NH—New Hampshire
NIH—National Institutes of Health
NIMH—National Institute of Mental Health
NJ—New Jersey
NMex—New Mexico
nonres—nonresident
norm—normal
Norweg—Norwegian
Nov—November
NS—Nova Scotia
NSF—National Science Foundation
NSW—New South Wales
numis—numismatic(s)
nutrit—nutrition, nutritional
NY—New York State
NZ—New Zealand

observ—observatories, observatory
obstet—obstetric(s), obstetrical
occas—occasional(ly)
occup—occupation, occupational
oceanog—oceanographic, oceanographical, oceanography
oceanogr—oceanographer
Oct—October
odontol—odontology
OEEC—Organization for European Economic Cooperation
off—office, official
Okla—Oklahoma
olericult—olericulture
oncol—oncologic, oncology
Ont—Ontario
oper(s)—operation(s), operational, operative
ophthal—ophthalmologic, ophthalmological, ophthalmology
optom—optometric, optometrical, optometry
ord—ordnance
Ore—Oregon
org—organic
orgn—organization(s), organizational
orient—oriental
ornith—ornithological, ornithology
orthod—orthodontia, orthodontic(s)
orthop—orthopedic(s)
osteop—osteopathic, osteopathy
otol—otological, otology
otolaryngol—otolaryngological, otolaryngology
otorhinol—otorhinologic, otorhinology

Pa—Pennsylvania
Pac—Pacific
paleobot—paleobotanical, paleobotany
paleont—paleontological, paleontology
Pan-Am—Pan-American
parasitol—parasitology
partic—participant, participating
path—pathologic, pathological, pathology
pedag—pedagogic(s), pedagogical, pedagogy
pediat—pediatric(s)
PEI—Prince Edward Islands
penol—penological, penology
periodont—periodontal, periodontic(s), periodontology
petrog—petrographic, petrographical, petrography
petrogr—petrographer
petrol—petroleum, petrologic, petrological, petrology
pharm—pharmacy
pharmaceut—pharmaceutic(s), pharmaceutical(s)
pharmacog—pharmacognosy
pharamacol—pharmacologic, pharmacological, pharmacology
phenomenol—phenomenologic(al), phenomenology
philol—philological, philology
philos—philosophic, philosophical, philosophy
photog—photographic, photography
photogeog—photogeographic, photogeography

ABBREVIATIONS

photogr—photographer(s)
photogram—photogrammetric, photogrammetry
photom—photometric, photometrical, photometry
phycol—phycology
phys—physical
physiog—physiographic, physiographical, physiography
physiol—physiological, physiology
Pkwy—Parkway
Pl—Place
polit—political, politics
polytech—polytechnic(al)
pomol—pomological, pomology
pontif—pontifical
pop—population
Port—Portugal, Portuguese
postgrad—postgraduate
PQ—Province of Quebec
PR—Puerto Rico
pract—practice
practr—practitioner
prehist—prehistoric, prehistory
prep—preparation, preparative, preparatory
pres—president
Presby—Presbyterian
preserv—preservation
prev—prevention, preventive
prin—principal
prob(s)—problem(s)
proc—proceedings
proctol—proctologic, proctological, proctology
prod—product(s), production, productive
prof—professional, professor, professorial
Prof Exp—Professional Experience
prog(s)—program(s), programmed, programming
proj—project(s), projection(al), projective
prom—promotion
protozool—protozoology
prov—province, provincial
psychiat—psychiatric, psychiatry
psychoanal—psychoanalysis, psychoanalytic, psychoanalytical
psychol—psychological, psychology
psychomet—psychometric(s)
psychopath—psychopathologic, psychopathology
psychophys—psychophysical, psychophysics
psychophysiol—psychophysiological, psychophysiology
psychosom—psychosomatic(s)
psychother—psychotherapeutic(s), psychotherapy
Pt—Point
pub—public
publ—publication(s), publish(ed), publisher, publishing
pvt—private

Qm—Quartermaster
Qm Gen—Quartermaster General
qual—qualitative, quality
quant—quantitative
quart—quarterly

radiol—radiological, radiology
RAF—Royal Air Force
RAFVR—Royal Air Force Volunteer Reserve
RAMC—Royal Army Medical Corps
RAMCR—Royal Army Medical Corps Reserve
RAOC—Royal Army Ordnance Corps
RASC—Royal Army Service Corps
RASCR—Royal Army Service Corps Reserve
RCAF—Royal Canadian Air Force
RCAFR—Royal Canadian Air Force Reserve
RCAFVR—Royal Canadian Air Force Volunteer Reserve
RCAMC—Royal Canadian Army Medical Corps
RCAMCR—Royal Canadian Army Medical Corps Reserve
RCASC—Royal Canadian Army Service Corps
RCASCR—Royal Canadian Army Service Corps Reserve
RCEME—Royal Canadian Electrical & Mechanical Engineers
RCN—Royal Canadian Navy
RCNR—Royal Canadian Naval Reserve
RCNVR—Royal Canadian Naval Volunteer Reserve
Rd—Road
RD—Rural Delivery
rec—record(s), recording
redevelop—redevelopment
ref—reference(s)
refrig—refrigeration
regist—register(ed), registration
registr—registrar
regt—regiment(al)
rehab—rehabilitation
rel(s)—relation(s), relative
relig—religion, religious
REME—Royal Electrical & Mechanical Engineers
rep—represent, representative
repub—republic
req—requirements
res—research, reserve
rev—review, revised, revision
RFD—Rural Free Delivery
rhet—rhetoric, rhetorical
RI—Rhode Island
Rm—Room
RM—Royal Marines
RN—Royal Navy
RNA—ribonucleic acid
RNR—Royal Naval Reserve
RNVR—Royal Naval Volunteer Reserve
roentgenol—roentgenologic, roentgenological, roentgenology
RR—Railroad, Rural Route
rte—route
Russ—Russian
rwy—railway

s—south
SAfrica—South Africa
SAm—South America, South American
sanit—sanitary, sanitation
Sask—Saskatchewan
SC—South Carolina
Scand—Scandinavia(n)
sch(s)—school(s)
scholar—scholarship
sci—science(s), scientific
SDak—South Dakota
SEATO—Southeast Asia Treaty Organization
sec—secondary
sect—section
secy—secretary
seismog—seismograph, seismographic, seismography
seismogr—seismographer
seismol—seismological, seismology
sem—seminar, seminary
sen—senator, senatorial
Sept—September
ser—serial, series
serol—serologic, serological, serology
serv—service(s), serving
silvicult—silvicultural, silviculture
soc(s)—societies, society
soc sci—social science
sociol—sociologic, sociological, sociology
Span—Spanish
spec—special
specif—specification(s)
spectrog—spectrograph, spectrographic, spectography
spectrogr—spectrographer
spectrophotom—spectrophotometer, spectrophotometric, spectrophotometry
spectros—spectroscopic, spectroscopy
speleol—speleological, speleology
Sq—Square
sr—senior
St—Saint, Street(s)
sta(s)—station(s)
stand—standard(s), standardization
statist—statistical, statistics
Ste—Sainte
steril—sterility
stomatol—stomatology
stratig—stratigraphic, stratigraphy
stratigr—stratigrapher
struct—structural, structure(s)
stud—student(ship)
subcomt—subcommittee
subj—subject
subsid—subsidiary
substa—substation
super—superior
suppl—supplement(s), supplemental, supplementary
supt—superintendent
supv—supervising, supervision
supvr—supervisor
supvry—supervisory
surg—surgery, surgical
surv—survey, surveying
survr—surveyor
Swed—Swedish
Switz—Switzerland
symp—symposia, symposium(s)
syphil—syphilology
syst(s)—system(s), systematic(s), systematical

taxon—taxonomic, taxonomy
tech—technical, technique(s)
technol—technologic(al), technology
tel—telegraph(y), telephone
temp—temporary
Tenn—Tennessee
Terr—Terrace
Tex—Texas
textbk(s)—textbook(s)
text ed—text edition
theol—theological, theology
theoret—theoretic(al)
ther—therapy
therapeut—therapeutic(s)

thermodyn—thermodynamic(s)
topog—topographic, topographical, topography
topogr—topographer
toxicol—toxicologic, toxicological, toxicology
trans—transactions
transl—translated, translation(s)
translr—translator(s)
transp—transport, transportation
treas—treasurer, treasury
treat—treatment
trop—tropical
tuberc—tuberculosis
TV—television
Twp—Township

UAR—United Arab Republic
UK—United Kingdom
UN—United Nations
undergrad—undergraduate
unemploy—unemployment
UNESCO—United Nations Educational Scientific & Cultural Organization
UNICEF—United Nations International Childrens Fund
univ(s)—universities, university
UNRRA—United Nations Relief & Rehabilitation Administration
UNRWA—United Nations Relief & Works Agency
urol—urologic, urological, urology
US—United States
USA—US Army
USAAF—US Army Air Force
USAAFR—US Army Air Force Reserve
USAF—US Air Force
USAFR—US Air Force Reserve
USAR—US Army Reserve
USCG—US Coast Guard
USCGR—US Coast Guard Reserve
USDA—US Department of Agriculture
USMC—US Marine Corps
USMCR—US Marine Corps Reserve
USN—US Navy
USNAF—US Naval Air Force
USNAFR—US Naval Air Force Reserve
USNR—US Naval Reserve
USPHS—US Public Health Service
USPHSR—US Public Health Service Reserve
USSR—Union of Soviet Socialist Republics
USWMC—US Women's Marine Corps
USWMCR—US Women's Marine Corps Reserve

Va—Virginia
var—various
veg—vegetable(s), vegetation
vent—ventilating, ventilation
vert—vertebrate
vet—veteran(s), veterinarian, veterinary
VI—Virgin Islands
vinicult—viniculture
virol—virological, virology
vis—visiting
voc—vocational
vocab—vocabulary
vol(s)—voluntary, volunteer(s), volume(s)
vpres—vice president
vs—versus
Vt—Vermont

w—west
WAC—Women's Army Corps
Wash—Washington
WAVES—Women Accepted for Voluntary Emergency Service
WHO—World Health Organization
WI—West Indies
wid—widow, widowed, widower
Wis—Wisconsin
WRCNS—Women's Royal Canadian Naval Service
WRNS—Women's Royal Naval Service
WVa—West Virginia
Wyo—Wyoming

yearbk(s)—yearbook(s)
YMCA—Young Men's Christian Association
YMHA—Young Men's Hebrew Association
yr(s)—year(s)
YWCA—Young Women's Christian Association
YWHA—Young Women's Hebrew Association

zool—zoological, zoology

AMERICAN MEN & WOMEN OF SCIENCE

T

TAAGEPERA, MARE, b Narva, Estonia, May 16, 38; US citizen; m 61; c 3. PHYSICAL ORGANIC CHEMISTRY. *Educ:* Univ Del, BS, 60, MS, 63; Univ Pa, PhD(chem), 70. *Prof Exp:* Chemist, E I du Pont de Nemours & Co, Inc, 62-64; FEL CHEM, UNIV CALIF, IRVINE, 71- *Mem:* Am Chem Soc; Sigma Xi; Asn Advan Baltic Studies. *Res:* Mechanisms of organic reactions; rate and equilibrium studies; mass and ion cyclotron resonance spectroscopy. *Mailing Add:* Dept Chem Univ Calif Irvine CA 92717

TAAM, RONALD EVERETT, b New York, NY. HYDRODYNAMICS, STELLAR STRUCTURE & EVOLUTION. *Educ:* Polytech Inst Brooklyn BS, 69; Columbia Univ, MA, 71, PhD(astron), 73. *Prof Exp:* Fel, Univ Calif, Santa Cruz, 73-76, vis prof astron, Berkeley, 76-78; ASST PROF PHYSICS & ASTRON, NORTHWESTERN UNIV, 79- *Mem:* Am Astron Soc; Royal Astron Soc. *Res:* Application of fluid mechanics, radiation transfer, and nuclear physics to astrophysical problems; structure and evolution of close binary stars. *Mailing Add:* Dept Physics & Astron Northwestern Univ Evanston IL 60201

TABACHNICK, IRVING I A, b New York, NY, July 20, 24; m 51; c 2. PHARMACOLOGY. *Educ:* Harvard Univ, AB, 48; Yale Univ, PhD(pharmacol), 53. *Prof Exp:* Pharmacologist & statistician, Baxter Labs, 53-55; pharmacologist, 55-58, sr pharmacologist, 58-60, sect head, 60-61, head dept biochem pharm, 61-64, head dept physiol & biochem, 64-68, assoc dir biol res div, 68-70, dir, 70-72, sr dir biol res & develop, Schering Corp, 72-77, VPRES, DRUG SAFETY & METAB, SCHERING-PLOUGH CORP, 77- *Mem:* AAAS; Am Soc Pharmacol & Exp Therapeut; Soc Exp Biol & Med; NY Acad Sci; Am Acad Allergy. *Res:* Histamine; diabetes; insulin; catecholamines; adrenergic receptors; anti-hormones; Toxicology; drug metabolism. *Mailing Add:* Schering Plough Corp 86 Orange St Bloomfield NJ 07003

TABACHNICK, JOSEPH, b New York, NY, May 14, 19; m 61; c 2. RADIOIMMUNOASSAY. *Educ:* Univ Calif, Berkeley, BS, 42, MS, 47, PhD(comp biochem), 50. *Prof Exp:* Res asst food technol, Univ Calif, Berkeley, 46-51, lab instr, 47-49; res chemist, Turner Hall Corp, NJ, 51-52; res biochemist, 52-59, SR RES BIOCHEMIST & ASSOC MEM, DIV OF LABS & HEAD, LAB EXP DERMAT, ALBERT EINSTEIN MED CTR, 59- *Concurrent Pos:* Adj assoc prof, NY Med Col, 73-; head, Dept Chem, Ria Lab, 78- *Mem:* AAAS; Soc Invest Dermat; Am Soc Exp Path; Am Chem Soc; Radiation Res Soc. *Res:* Estrogen and progesterone receptors in human breast cancer; radiation biology and biochemistry of the skin; cytokinetics of repair in beta-irradiated skin; formation and metabolism of pyroglutamic acid and free amino acid in skin; suppression of radiation fibrosis. *Mailing Add:* Lab of Exp Dermat Albert Einstein Med Ctr Philadelphia PA 19141

TABACHNICK, MILTON, b New York, NY, June 25, 22; m 52. BIOCHEMISTRY. *Educ:* Univ Calif, AB, 47, MA, 49, PhD(biochem), 53. *Prof Exp:* Asst, Univ Calif, 49-52; Am Cancer Soc res fel biochem, Sch Med, Duke Univ, 52-53; instr, Inst Indust Med, Post-Grad Med Sch, NY Univ, 53-55; vis investr, Div Nutrit & Physiol, Pub Health Res Inst of City New York, 55-57; res assoc chem, Mt Sinai Hosp, 57-59; res assoc, NY State Psychiat Inst, 59-60; from asst prof to assoc prof, 61-69, dean Grad Sch Basic Med Sci, 71-80, PROF BIOCHEM, NEW YORK MED COL, 69- *Mem:* Am Soc Biol Chem; Am Chem Soc; Endocrine Soc; Am Thyroid Asn; AAAS. *Res:* Protein chemistry; transport and mechanism of action of thyroid hormone; purification and characterization of thyroxing-binding globulin. *Mailing Add:* Dept of Biochem New York Med Col Valhalla NY 10595

TABACHNICK, WALTER J, b Brooklyn, NY, June 14, 47. POPULATION GENETICS, EVOLUTIONARY BIOLOGY. *Educ:* Brooklyn Col, City Univ New York, BS, 68; Rutgers Univ, MS, 71, PhD(zool), 74. *Prof Exp:* Asst prof genetics, Univ Wis, Parkside, 73-75; NIH fel, Yale Univ, 75-78; lectr biol & genetics, Univ Calif, Los Angeles, 78-79; RES ASSOC GENETICS, YALE UNIV, 79- *Concurrent Pos:* Nat Defense Educ Act Title IV fel, Rutgers Univ, 70-73; prin investr, Yale Univ & NIH res grant, 80- *Mem:* AAAS; Sigma Xi; Am Soc Study Evolution; Genetics Soc Am; Am Soc Trop Med & Hyg. *Res:* Studying the genetics and evolution of insect disease vectors with the goal of using this information to understand and control human disease. *Mailing Add:* Yale Dept Biol 260 Whitney Ave PO Box 6666 New Haven CT 06511

TABAK, DANIEL, b Wilna, Poland, June 16, 34; US citizen; m 60; c 2. AUTOMATIC CONTROL SYSTEMS, COMPUTER ENGINEERING. *Educ:* Israel Inst Technol, BS, 59, MS, 63; Univ Ill, Urbana, PhD(elec eng), 67. *Prof Exp:* Asst nuclear sci, Israel Inst Technol, 61-63; elec engr, Univ Ill, Urbana, 63-66; guid & control systs engr, Missile & Space Div, Gen Elec Co, Pa, 66-68; sr consult, Wolf Res & Develop Corp, Md, 68-70; assoc prof systs eng, Rensselaer Polytech Inst, 70-72; assoc prof elec eng, 72-76, chmn, Indust Eng Dept, 73-74, chmn, Elec Eng Dept, 76-77, PROF ELEC ENG, BEN-GURION UNIV OF THE NEGEV, ISRAEL, 76- *Concurrent Pos:* Consult, Missile & Space Div, Gen Elec Co, 66, Wolf Res & Develop Corp, 70-72; assoc ed, J Automatica, Int Fedn Automatic Control, 72-; on leave, NRC sr res assoc, NASA Langley Res Ctr, 77-78 & vis prof elec eng, Univ Tex, Austin, 78-79. *Mem:* Sr mem Inst Elec & Electronics Engrs; Opers Res Soc Am. *Res:* Computational methods of optimal control; digital systems; computer architecture. *Mailing Add:* Dept Elec Eng Ben-Gurion Univ of the Negev Beer-Sheva Israel

TABAK, MARK DAVID, b Philadelphia, Pa, Dec 2, 37; m 61; c 2. SOLID STATE PHYSICS, ELECTRICAL ENGINEERING. *Educ:* Univ Pa, BS, 59; Princeton Univ, MA, 62, PhD(elec eng), 65. *Prof Exp:* Instr, Princeton Univ, 62-63; scientist xerographic sci, Res Labs Div, 65-70, area mgr, 70-72, sect mgr, 72-73, mgr, Imaging Sci Lab, 73-77, mgr, Advan Marking Prog, Corp Res & Develop Group, 77-78, VPRES & MGR, WEBSTER RES CTR, XEROX CORP, 78- *Mem:* Am Phys Soc; Inst Elec & Electronics Engrs. *Res:* Electrophotographic materials and systems; photoconductivity; electronic transport and photogeneration; amorphous semiconductors. *Mailing Add:* Webster Res Ctr W105 Xerox Sq Rochester NY 14644

TABAKIN, BURTON SAMUEL, b Philadelphia, Pa, July 6, 21; m 72; c 5. MEDICINE. *Educ:* Univ Pa, AB, 43, MD, 47; Am Bd Internal Med, dipl, 55. *Prof Exp:* Fel physiol, Univ Vt & Trudeau Found, 51-52; from instr to assoc prof, 54-67, actg chmn dept, 74-76, dir Cardiol Univ, 72-80, PROF MED, COL MED, UNIV VT, 67- DIR CARDIOPULMONARY LAB, 54- *Concurrent Pos:* Attend physician, Mary Fletcher Hosp & DeGoesbriand Mem Hosp, Burlington, Vt, 60-66; fel coun clin cardiol, Am Heart Asn. *Mem:* Fel Am Col Physicians; Am Heart Asn; Am Col Chest Physicians; Am Fedn Clin Res; fel Am Col Cardiol. *Res:* Clinical cardiopulmonary and exercise physiology; echocardiography. *Mailing Add:* Med Ctr Hosp of Vt Burlington VT 05401

TABAKIN, FRANK, b Newark, NJ, Sept 20, 35; m 63; c 2. THEORETICAL PHYSICS. *Educ:* Queens Col, NY, BS, 56; Mass Inst Technol, PhD(physics), 63. *Prof Exp:* Res assoc physics, Columbia Univ, 63-65; from asst prof to assoc prof, 65-74, PROF PHYSICS, UNIV PITTSBURGH, 74- *Concurrent Pos:* Res visitor, Oxford Univ, 70. *Mem:* Am Phys Soc. *Res:* Nuclear forces and matter; three-body problems; properties of nuclei; meson physics; meson photoproduction. *Mailing Add:* Dept of Physics Univ of Pittsburgh Pittsburgh PA 15260

TABAKOFF, BORIS, b Tien-Tsin, China, Sept 27, 42. NEUROPHARMACOLOGY, ALCOHOLISM. *Educ:* Univ Colo, Boulder, BA & BPh, 66, PhD(pharmacol), 70. *Prof Exp:* Asst prof biochem, Chicago Med Sch, 71-73, assoc prof, 73-75; assoc prof, 75-78, PROF DEPT PHYSIOL, UNIV ILL MED CTR, 78- *Concurrent Pos:* Bd trustees res award, Chicago Med Sch, 73; Hoffman LaRoche Found award & NIH-Swiss NSF award, 75; res award, Interstate Postgrad Med Asn NAm, 76; mem, NIH/Alcohol, Drug Abuse & Ment Health Admin Study Sect, Nat Inst Alcohol Abuse & Alcoholism, 78-81; res scientist, West Side Vet Admin Med Ctr, Chicago, 79-; dir, Alcohol & Drug Abuse Res & Training Prog, Univ Ill Med Ctr, 80- *Mem:* Am Soc Pharmacol & Exp Therapeut; Am Soc Neurochem; Soc Neurosci; Res Soc Alcoholism; Int Soc Biomed Res Alcoholism. *Res:* Neurochemical and behavioral effects of alcohol and their contribution to development of tolerance and physical dependence; development of therapies to ameliorate tolerance and physical dependence. *Mailing Add:* Dept Physiol & Biophys Univ Ill Med Ctr PO Box 6998 Chicago IL 60612

TABAKOFF, WIDEN, b Stakevzi, Bulgaria, Dec 14, 19; US citizen; m 43; c 2. PROPULSION, GAS DYNAMICS. *Educ:* Prague Tech Univ, MS, 42; Univ Berlin, MS, 46, PhD(sci), 45. *Prof Exp:* Asst technician, Univ Berlin, 42-46; designer, Aerotallers Argentinos, 48-50; tech dir prod, Helamet, Arg, 50-56; supvr res, Knapsack Grisheim, Ger, 56-58; from instr to assoc prof, 58-66, PROF AEROSPACE ENG & APPL MECH, UNIV CINCINNATI, 67- *Concurrent Pos:* Consult indust & govt, 54- *Mem:* Fel Am Inst Aeronaut & Astronaut; Am Soc Eng Educ; Am Soc Mech Engrs; Am Asn Univ Prof; Am Soc Testing & Mat. *Res:* Turbomachinery components, inlets, compressors, combustion chambers, turbine nozzles and exhaust engine nozzles; ramjet components; aerodynamic heating for hypersonic vehicles; internal gas dynamics flows; erosion problems in propulsion systems. *Mailing Add:* Dept of Aerospace Eng & Appl Mech Univ of Cincinnati Cincinnati OH 45221

TABARROK, B(EHROUZ), b Tehran, Iran, June 16, 38; m 63; c 3. MECHANICAL ENGINEERING. *Educ:* Wolverhampton & Staffordshire Col Technol, BSc, 62; Oxford Univ, PhD(struct dynamics), 65. *Prof Exp:* Ford Found fel mech eng, 65-66, asst prof, 66-71, assoc prof, 71-77, PROF MECH ENG, UNIV TORONTO, 77- *Concurrent Pos:* Alexander von Humboldt fel, Hannover Tech Univ, 69; sr res fel, Sci Res Coun, UK, 74. *Mem:* Can Soc Mech Engrs; Brit Inst Mech Engrs; fel Eng Inst Can. *Res:* Applied mechanics, particularly in dynamics of structures. *Mailing Add:* Dept of Mech Eng Univ of Toronto Toronto ON M5S 1A1 Can

TABATA, SUSUMU, b Steveston, BC, Dec 9, 25; m 59; c 3. PHYSICAL OCEANOGRAPHY. *Educ:* Univ BC, BA, 50, MA, 54; Univ Tokyo, DSc, 65. *Prof Exp:* Phys oceanogr, Pac Oceanog Group, Fisheries Res Bd Can, 52-70; res phys oceanogr, Offshore Oceanog Group, 71-75, RES SCIENTIST, INST OCEAN SCI, 75- *Concurrent Pos:* Asst scientist, Pac Oceanog Group, Fisheries Res Bd Can, 52-58, assoc scientist, 59-65, sr scientist, 66-70. *Mem:* Am Soc Limnol & Oceanog; Am Meteorol Soc; Am Geophys Union; fel Royal Meteorol Soc; Oceanog Soc Japan. *Res:* Circulation of inshore and offshore waters; processes affecting water properties; variability in the oceans; large-scale air-sea interactions; interpretation of satellite imagery. *Mailing Add:* Inst of Ocean Sci Patricia Bay PO Box 6000 Sidney BC V8L 4B2 Can

TABATABAI, LOUISA BRAAL, b Oostvoorne, Neth, Dec 18, 39; US citizen; m 62; c 3. BIOCHEMISTRY. *Educ:* Univ Calif, Berkeley, BA, 62; Iowa State Univ, MS, 66, PhD(biochem), 76. *Prof Exp:* Res assoc food technol, Iowa State Univ, 64-70, res assoc muscle biochem, 71-74, assoc biochem, 76-77; RES CHEMIST BIOCHEM, NAT ANIMAL DIS CTR, 77- *Concurrent Pos:* Nat Res Coun fel, Nat Animal Dis Ctr, 77-78. *Mem:* Am Chem Soc; Am Soc Microbiol; AAAS. *Res:* Virulence and pathogenicity of Brucella organisms; biochemical immunological properties of Brucella cell surface proteins, mechanism of action on host tissues. *Mailing Add:* Nat Animal Dis Ctr PO Box 70 Ames IA 50010

TABATABAI, M ALI, b Karbala, Iraq, Feb 25, 34; US citizen; m 62; c 3. SOIL CHEMISTRY, SOIL BIOCHEMISTRY. *Educ:* Univ Baghdad, BS, 58; Okla State Univ, MS, 60; Iowa State Univ, PhD(soil chem), 65. *Prof Exp:* Res assoc soil biochem, 66-72, from asst prof to assoc prof, 72-78, PROF SOIL CHEM & BIOCHEM, IOWA STATE UNIV, 78- *Concurrent Pos:* Consult, Elec Power Res Inst, Palo Alto, Calif, 78- *Mem:* Am Soc Agron; Am Chem Soc; Am Soc Microbiol; AAAS; Int Soc Soil Sci. *Res:* Soil enzymology and chemistry of sulfur, nitrogen and phosphorus in soils; nutrient cycling in the environment. *Mailing Add:* Dept of Agron Iowa State Univ Ames IA 50011

TABATABAIAN, ALI MOHAMMAD, mathematics, see previous edition

TABB, DAVID LEO, b Louisville, Ky, Feb 8, 46; m 66; c 2. POLYMER SCIENCE. *Educ:* Univ Louisville, BChE, 69; Case Western Reserve Univ, MS, 72, PhD(polymer sci), 74. *Prof Exp:* Res eng chem eng, 69-70, SR RES ENGR, POLYMER PRODS DEPT, ELASTOMERS DIV, E I DU PONT DE NEMOURS & CO, INC, 74- *Res:* Characterization of polymer structure and correlation to physical properties; thermoset and thermoplastic elastomers; polymer blends; polymer processing technology; Fourier transform infrared spectroscopy. *Mailing Add:* Polymer Prods Dept/ Elastomers Div Chestnut Run E I du Pont de Nemours & Co Wilmington DE 19898

TABBERT, ROBERT L, b Ripon, Wis, Sept 6, 28; m 52; c 2. GEOLOGY. *Educ:* Univ Wis, BS, 52, MSc, 54. *Prof Exp:* Micropaleontologist, Magnolia Petrol Co, 54-59; micropaleontologist, Socony Mobil's Field Res Lab, 59-62; palynologist, 62-67, supvr palynology group, 67-73, dir struct & stratig res, 73-75, sr res assoc, Geol Sci Group, 75-76, EXPLOR GEOLOGIST, ATLANTIC RICHFIELD CO, 76- *Mem:* Soc Econ Paleont & Mineral; Am Asn Petrol Geologists; Am Asn Stratig Palynologists; Geol Soc Am; Asn Prof Geol Scientists. *Res:* Biostratigraphy of Cretaceous-Tertiary sediments of Alaska; regional correlations in Mesozoic and Tertiary sediments of Arctic; structural geology, stratigraphy and petroleum exploration of Arctic; exploration and geothermal energy of Western United States. *Mailing Add:* PO Box 2819 Dallas TX 75221

TABBUTT, FREDERICK DEAN, b Philadelphia, Pa, Dec 28, 31; m 56; c 4. COMPUTER SIMULATIONS, CATASTROPHE THEORY. *Educ:* Haverford Col, BS, 53; Harvard Univ, MA, 55, PhD(chem), 58. *Prof Exp:* Instr, Reed Col, 57-59, asst prof chem, 59-63, assoc prof, 63-67, prof, 67-70; MEM FAC CHEM, EVERGREEN STATE COL, 70- *Concurrent Pos:* NSF fac fel, Southhampton Univ, UK, 63-64, Univ Warwick, 74-75. *Mem:* Am Chem Soc. *Res:* Oscillating chemical reactions, particularly the Belousov-Zhabotinsky reaction; applications of castastrophe theory to oscillating systems; gas phase kinetics of unimolecular reactions. *Mailing Add:* 3213 Cove Lane NW Olympia WA 98502

TABER, CHARLES ALEC, b Texanna, Okla, Dec 10, 37; m 70. ICHTHYOLOGY. *Educ:* Northeastern State Col, BS, 61; Univ Okla, PhD(zool), 69. *Prof Exp:* Asst prof biol, 69-77, ASSOC PROF LIFE SCI, SOUTHWEST MO STATE UNIV, 77- *Mem:* Am Soc Ichthyologists & Herpetologists; Am Fisheries Soc. *Res:* Natural history and ecology of fishes. *Mailing Add:* Dept of Life Sci Southwest Mo State Univ Springfield MO 65802

TABER, DAVID, b New York, NY, July 14, 22; m 48; c 3. BIOMEDICAL ENGINEERING, ORGANIC CHEMISTRY. *Educ:* NY Univ, AB, 48; Polytech Inst Brooklyn, PhD(chem), 53. *Prof Exp:* Jr chemist, Air Reduction Co, Inc, 48-49; res assoc indust med, Postgrad Med Sch, NY Univ, 53-55; chemist, Gen Aniline & Film Corp, 55-58; sr chemist, Koppers Co, Inc, 58-63; sect head, Org Chem, Armour Grocery Prod Co, 63-65, res mgr new chem, Household Prod Res & Develop Dept, 65-68, mgr biol & med progs, Armour-Dial, Inc, 68-69, asst res dir, 69-75; vpres & dir tech serv, Hollister, Inc, 75-77; DIR REGULATORY AFFAIRS, WESLEY-JESSEN INC, 77-; CONSULT, DAVID TABER & ASSOC, 78- *Mem:* Am Chem Soc; Soc Cosmetic Chemists. *Res:* Organic synthesis, germicides, microbiology; product safety; regulatory affairs; clinical testing; medical and hospital devices; quality assurance. *Mailing Add:* 200 Barton Ave Evanston IL 60202

TABER, ELSIE, b Columbia, SC, May 3, 15. EMBRYOLOGY, REPRODUCTIVE PHYSIOLOGY. *Educ:* Univ SC, BS, 35; Stanford Univ, MA, 36; Univ Chicago, PhD(zool), 47. *Prof Exp:* Teacher biol, Greenwood High Sch, SC, 36-38; instr, Lander Col, 38-41; instr, Univ Chicago, 44-48, asst dean students, Div Biol Sci, 47-48; from asst prof to assoc prof, 48-65, PROF ANAT, MED UNIV SC, 65- *Mem:* AAAS; Am Soc Zool; Am Asn Anatomists; Am Inst Biol Sci; Soc Study Reproduction. *Res:* Developmental biology; endocrinology of reproductive systems. *Mailing Add:* Dept of Anat Med Univ of SC Charleston SC 29403

TABER, HARRY WARREN, b Longview, Wash, Oct 30, 35; c 3. MICROBIOLOGY, MOLECULAR BIOLOGY. *Educ:* Reed Col, BA, 57; Univ Rochester, PhD(biochem), 63. *Prof Exp:* AEC fel, Univ Rochester, 62-64; USPHS fel, Nat Inst Neurol Dis & Stroke, Bethesda, Md, 64-66; USPHS spec fel, Ctr Molecular Genetics, Gif-sur-Yvette, France, 66-67; asst prof microbiol, Sch Med, Univ Rochester, 68-73, assoc prof, 73-80; MEM FAC, DEPT MICROBIOL & IMMUNOL, ALBANY MED COL OF UNION UNIV, 80- *Concurrent Pos:* NIH res career develop award, 74. *Mem:* Am Soc Microbiol; Soc Gen Microbiol; Am Soc Photobiol; NY Acad Sci; Am Asn Univ Prof. *Res:* Genetic regulation of membrane structure and function; antibiotic transport by bacteria; biosynthesis of vitamin K. *Mailing Add:* Dept Microbiol & Immunol Albany Med Col of Union Univ Albany NY 12208

TABER, JOSEPH JOHN, b Adena, Ohio, Feb 6, 20; m 47; c 4. PHYSICAL CHEMISTRY, PETROLEUM ENGINEERING. *Educ:* Muskingum Col, BS, 42; Univ Pittsburgh, PhD, 55. *Prof Exp:* Asst prof naval sci, Ohio State Univ, 46; instr chem, Washington & Jefferson Col, 46-50; sr proj chemist, Gulf Res & Develop Co, 54-64; from asst prof to assoc prof chem, 64-72, adj assoc prof petrol eng, 67-72, prof chem, grad fac, 72-76, officer, Admin Dept, 64-76, prof petrol eng, 72-77, DIR NMEX PETRO RECOVERY RES CTR, NMEX INST MINING & TECHNOL, 76- *Mem:* Am Chem Soc; Am Inst Mining, Metall & Petrol Eng; AAAS. *Res:* Surface chemistry; liquid-liquid and liquid-solid interfaces; effect of interfacial energies on capillarity and fluid flow in porous media; new methods of petroleum recovery. *Mailing Add:* NMex Inst Mining & Technol NMex Petrol Recovery Res Ctr Socorro NM 87801

TABER, RICHARD DOUGLAS, b San Francisco, Calif, Nov 22, 20; m 46; c 3. WILDLIFE ECOLOGY. *Educ:* Univ Calif, AB, 42, PhD, 51; Univ Wis, MS, 49. *Prof Exp:* Wildlife researcher & asst specialist, Univ Calif, 51-55, actg asst prof zool, 55-56; actg asst prof forestry, Univ Mont, 56-57, from assoc prof to prof, 58-68, assoc dir, Mont Forest & Conserv Exp Sta, 64-68; PROF FOREST ZOOL, UNIV WASH, 68- *Concurrent Pos:* US specialist forest-wildlife rels, Ger & Czech, 60 & Poland, 60 & 64; Fulbright res scholar, West Pakistan, 63-64; Guggenheim fel, 64; mem comn threatened deer, Int Union Conserv Nature, 73- *Mem:* Wildlife Soc; Ecol Soc Am; Am Soc Mammal. *Res:* Biology and conservation of free-living birds and mammals; wildlife and human culture; ungulate biology and effects on ecosystem. *Mailing Add:* Col of Forest Resources Univ of Wash Seattle WA 98195

TABER, RICHARD LAWRENCE, b Pontiac, Mich, Nov 9, 35; m 57; c 2. BIO-ORGANIC CHEMISTRY. *Educ:* Colo State Col, AB, 58; Univ NMex, PhD(org chem), 63. *Prof Exp:* From asst prof to assoc prof, 63-75, PROF CHEM, COLO COL, 75- *Honors & Awards:* Meritorious Serv Award, Am Chem Soc, 69. *Mem:* Am Chem Soc; Sigma Xi. *Res:* Enzymology of dihydroorotate dehydrogenase; organic liquid scintillation solutes. *Mailing Add:* Chem Dept Colo Col Colorado Springs CO 80903

TABER, ROBERT IRVING, b Perth Amboy, NJ, June 28, 36; m 60; c 3. PSYCHOPHARMACOLOGY, NEUROPHARMACOLOGY. *Educ:* Rutgers Univ, BS, 58; Med Col Va, PhD(pharmacol), 63. *Prof Exp:* Pharmacologist, 62-66, sr pharmacologist, 66-71, mgr pharmacol, 71-74, dir biol res, 74-77, SR DIR BIOL RES, SCHERING CORP, BLOOMFIELD, 77- *Mem:* AAAS; assoc Am Col Neuropsychopharmacol; Am Soc Pharmacol & Exp Therapeut; Acad Pharmaceut Sci; Am Pharmaceut Asn. *Res:* Analgesics; drug effects on learning and memory. *Mailing Add:* 60 Orange Bloomfield NJ 07003

TABER, STEPHEN, III, b Columbia, SC, Apr 17, 24; m 45; c 5. APICULTURE. *Educ:* Univ Wis, BS, 49. *Prof Exp:* Apiculturist, USDA, La, 50-65, apiculturist, Ariz, 65-79; RES DIR, TABER APIARIES, 79- *Mem:* AAAS; Entom Soc Am; Am Genetic Asn; Bee Res Asn. *Res:* Bee behavior and genetics. *Mailing Add:* Taber Apiaries 7052 Plesants Vally Rd Vacaville CA 95688

TABER, WILLARD ALLEN, b Marshalltown, Iowa, Feb 18, 25; m 50; c 3. MICROBIOLOGY. *Educ:* Univ Iowa, AB, 49, MS, 51; Rutgers Univ, PhD(microbiol), 54. *Prof Exp:* Asst, Univ Iowa, 49-51; fel, Rutgers Univ, 54-55; asst res officer, Prairie Regional Lab, Nat Res Coun Can, 55-61, sr res officer, 61-63; PROF BIOL, TEX A&M UNIV, 63- *Concurrent Pos:* NIH consult, 67-70. *Mem:* Am Soc Microbiologists; Soc Indust Microbiol. *Res:* Antifungal antibiotics; ecology of soil fungi; morphogenesis of fungi; metabolism of nonsugar carbon sources; mycology; secondary metabolism; transport in fungi, mycorrhizae, streptomyces. *Mailing Add:* Dept Biol Tex A&M Univ College Station TX 77843

TABI, RIFAT, b Simferopol, Crimea, of Turkish descent, June 5, 38; US citizen; m 67; c 1. MECHANICAL ENGINEERING. *Educ:* Aachen Tech Univ, BSME, 61, MSME, 62; Vienna Tech Univ, Dr Eng Sci (mech eng), 65; State Univ NY, PE, 72. *Prof Exp:* Sci res asst, Testing & Res Inst Mat, Vienna Tech Univ, 62-65; proj engr, Tech Ctr, Gen Motors Corp, Mich, 65-66; asst prof mech eng technol, 66-67, assoc prof, 67-70, prof, 70-72, PROF MECH, INDUST & AEROSPACE ENG & CHMN DEPT, NY INST TECHNOL, 72-, ASSOC DIR, CTR TECHNOL, 80- *Concurrent Pos:* Consult, private practice, 67-; qualified fallout shelter analyst & instr, Univ Hawaii, 68. *Res:* Materials-mechanics; fracture mechanics of materials and failure analysis. *Mailing Add:* Dept of Mech Indust & Aerospace Eng 268 Wheatley Rd Old Westbury NY 11568

TABIBIAN, RICHARD, b Detroit, Mich, June 1, 29; m 55; c 3. POLYMER CHEMISTRY. *Educ:* Wayne State Univ, BS, 51, MS, 54, PhD(chem), 56. *Prof Exp:* CHEMIST, E I DU PONT DE NEMOURS & CO, INC, 55- *Mem:* Am Chem Soc. *Res:* Colloid chemistry; elastomers. *Mailing Add:* Elastomers Dept Exp Sta E I du Pont de Nemours & Co Inc Wilmington DE 19898

TABISZ, GEORGE CONRAD, b New York, NY, Aug 28, 39; Can citizen; m 66; c 2. MOLECULAR PHYSICS. *Educ:* Univ Toronto, BASc, 61, MA, 63, PhD(physics), 68. *Prof Exp:* Nat Res Coun Can fel, High Pressure Lab, Nat Ctr Sci Res, France, 68-70; asst prof physics, 70-75, assoc prof, 75-80, PROF PHYSICS, UNIV MANITOBA, 80- *Mem:* Optical Soc Am; Can Asn Physicists. *Res:* Molecular interactions in gases and liquids; visible and infrared absorption spectroscopy; laser raman scattering. *Mailing Add:* Dept of Physics Univ of Manitoba Winnipeg MB R3T 2N2 Can

TABITA, F ROBERT, b Bronx, NY, Oct 1, 43. MICROBIAL BIOCHEMISTRY, PHOTOSYNTHETIC METABOLISM. *Educ:* St Johns Univ, BS, 65, MS, 67; Syracuse Univ, PhD(microbiol), 71. *Prof Exp:* NIH fel biochem, Wash State Univ, 71-73; asst prof, 73-78, ASSOC PROF MICROBIOL, UNIV TEX AUSTIN, 78- *Concurrent Pos:* Panel mem, Biochem Study Sect, NIH, 76-77; mem, Competitive Res Grants Panel, USDA, 81; asst dir, Ctr Appl Microbiol, Univ Tex Austin, 81- *Mem:* Am Soc Biol Chemists; Am Chem Soc; Am Soc Microbiol; AAAS; Sigma Xi. *Res:* Molecular basis and biochemistry of carbon dioxide fixation; regulation of biological nitrogen fixation; protection of nitrogenase from oxygen inactivation in vivo. *Mailing Add:* Dept Microbiol & Ctr Appl Microbiol Univ Tex Austin TX 78712

TABLER, KENNETH AMBROSE, mathematical statistics, analytical statistics, see previous edition

TABLER, RONALD DWIGHT, b Denver, Colo, May 18, 37; m 64; c 2. HYDROLOGY. *Educ:* Colo State Univ, BS, 59, PhD(watershed mgt), 65. *Prof Exp:* RES HYDROLOGIST, ROCKY MOUNTAIN FOREST & RANGE EXP STA, US FOREST SERV, 59-, PROJ LEADER WATERSHED MGT, 64- *Concurrent Pos:* Lectr, Univ Wyo; consult, Wyo State Hwy Dept; Japanese Govt Award for Foreign Specialists, 80-81. *Honors & Awards:* D Grant Mickle Award, Nat Acad Sci, 79. *Mem:* AAAS; Soc Am Foresters; Am Geophys Union; Soil Conserv Soc; Am Water Resources Asn. *Res:* Physics of snow transport by wind; design of snow fence systems for highway protection; management of snow in windswept areas to increase water yields; watershed management. *Mailing Add:* US Forest Serv 222 S 22nd St Laramie WY 82070

TABOADA, JOHN, b Tampico, Mex, Sept 8, 43; US citizen; m 68; c 1. PHYSICAL OPTICS, APPLIED PHYSICS. *Educ:* Trinity Univ, BA, 66; Tex A&M Univ, MS, 68, PhD(physics), 73. *Prof Exp:* Asst physics, Tex A&M Univ, 66-68; RES PHYSICIST, RADIATION SCI DIV, US AIR FORCE SCH AEROSPACE MED, 68-, RES PHYSICIST, DATA SCI DIV, 80- *Concurrent Pos:* Mem comt laser measurements, Am Nat Standards Inst, 76- *Honors & Awards:* Outstanding Tech Achievement Award, US Air Force Systs Command, 71, Outstanding Sci Achievement Award, 75. *Mem:* Am Phys Soc; Optical Soc Am. *Res:* Biophysics of ultrashort pulsed lasers; laser spectroscopy; nonlinear optics; applied optics. *Mailing Add:* 12530 Elm Country San Antonio TX 78230

TABOR, CELIA WHITE, b Boston, Mass, Nov 15, 18; m 46; c 4. BIOCHEMISTRY. *Educ:* Radcliffe Col, BA, 40; Columbia Univ, MD, 43. *Prof Exp:* Intern med, Mass Gen Hosp, Boston, 44-45; asst resident, Univ Hosp, Vanderbilt Univ, 45-46; res assoc pharmacol, George Washington Univ, 47-49; MEM STAFF, LAB BIOCHEM PHARMACOL, NAT INST ARTHRITIS, METAB & DIGESTIVE DIS & USPHS, 52- *Mem:* AAAS; Am Soc Biol Chemists; Am Soc Pharmacol & Exp Therapeut. *Res:* Biochemistry; enzymatic and metabolic studies of the polyamines. *Mailing Add:* Bldg 4 Rm 112 Nat Inst Arthritis Metab & Digestive Dis Bethesda MD 20205

TABOR, CHRISTOPHER ALAN, b Frederick, Md, Jan 1, 37; m 59; c 1. PLANT PHYSIOLOGY. *Educ:* NC State Univ, BS, 59, MS, 65. *Prof Exp:* Mem staff bioprod res & develop, Dow Chem Co, 64-65; res forester, 67-77, PLANT PHYSIOLOGIST, FOREST SERV, USDA, 77- *Mem:* Am Soc Plant Physiologists; Bot Soc Am; Scand Soc Plant Physiol; Soc Am Foresters; Int Asn Plant Tissue Cult. *Res:* Physiology of differentiation, growth and development in plants; emphasis on the control of morphogenesis in woody plants. *Mailing Add:* Forest Physiol Lab Agr Res Cent-West Bldg 011-19 Beltsville MD 20705

TABOR, EDWARD, b Washington, DC, Apr 30, 47; m 70; c 3. BLOOD, HEPATITIS. *Educ:* Harvard Univ, BA, 69; Columbia Univ, MD, 73. *Prof Exp:* Intern pediat, Columbia-Presby Med Ctr, New York, 73-74, resident, 74-75; res investr, 75-81, SR MED INVESTR HEPATITIS, BUR BIOLOGICS, FOOD & DRUG ADMIN, 81- *Concurrent Pos:* Clin asst prof pediat, Georgetown Univ Hosp, 80-; mem, scientific working group, Coord Comt Viral Hepatitis, NIH, 78- *Mem:* Fel Infectious Dis Soc Am; Am Asn Study Liver; Am Soc Microbiol. *Res:* Development of animal model for human non-A and non-B hepatitis; epidemiology of hepatitis A and B with special interest in infections during childhood; developing procedures to inactivate hepatitis viruses in blood and blood products. *Mailing Add:* Bur of Biologics 8800 Rockville Pike Bethesda MD 20205

TABOR, HERBERT, b New York, NY, Nov 28, 18; m 46; c 4. PHARMACOLOGY, BIOCHEMISTRY. *Educ:* Harvard Univ, AB, 37, MD, 41. *Prof Exp:* Biochem researcher, Harvard Med Sch, 41-42; intern med, New Haven Hosp, Conn, 42; USPHS, 43-, CHIEF LAB BIOCHEM PHARMACOL, NAT INST ARTHRITIS, METAB & DIGESTIVE DIS, 61- *Concurrent Pos:* Field ed, J Pharmacol & Exp Therapeut, 60-68; assoc ed, J Biol Chem, 68-71, ed-in-chief, 71- *Mem:* Nat Acad Sci; Am Soc Pharmacol & Exp Therapeut; Am Soc Biol Chem; Am Chem Soc; Am Acad Arts & Sci. *Res:* Biochemistry of amino acids and amines. *Mailing Add:* Bldg 4 Rm 110 Nat Inst Arthritis Metab & Digestive Dis Bethesda MD 20014

TABOR, ROWLAND WHITNEY, b Denver, Colo, June 10, 32; m 57, 70; c 2. GEOLOGY. *Educ:* Stanford Univ, BS, 54; Univ Wash, MS, 58, PhD(geol), 61. *Prof Exp:* Teaching asst geol, Univ Wash, 57-61; GEOLOGIST, US GEOL SURV, 61- *Mem:* fel Geol Soc Am. *Res:* Field mapping northwestern Washington, stratigraphy, igneous andmetamorphic petzology and structure of Olympic and North Cascade Mountains; emphasis on geologic history and hazards; KAr geochromology; popular science writing. *Mailing Add:* U S Geol Surv 345 Middlefield Rd Menlo Park CA 94025

TABOR, SAMUEL LYNN, b Tylertown, Miss, June 10, 45. NUCLEAR PHYSICS. *Educ:* Tulane Univ, BS, 67; Stanford Univ, MS, 68, PhD(physics), 72. *Prof Exp:* Res assoc nuclear physics, Univ Pa, 72-75 & Argonne Nat Lab, 75-77; sr res assoc nuclear physics, Univ Md, 77-79; ASST PROF, FLA STATE UNIV, 79- *Mem:* Am Phys Soc; Sigma Xi. *Res:* Nuclear structure and reactions. *Mailing Add:* Dept Physics Fla State Univ Tallahassee FL 32306

TABOR, THEODORE EMMETT, b Great Falls, Mont, Dec 28, 40; m 60; c 3. ORGANIC CHEMISTRY. *Educ:* Univ Mont, BA, 62; Kans State Univ, PhD(org chem), 67. *Prof Exp:* Res chemist, Spec Assignment Prog, Dow Chem Co, 67, res chemist, Prod Dept Lab, 67-72; res specialist, Halogens Res Lab, 72-75, mgr acad educ, 75-78, res leader org chem dept, 78-81; MGR, TECHNOL ACQUISITION, 81- *Concurrent Pos:* Adj prof, Cent Mich Univ, Mt Pleasant, 79-83. *Mem:* Am Chem Soc. *Res:* Mechanisms of epoxide rearrangements; solvent processing of textiles; fire retardant chemicals for textiles and plastics; specialty organic chemicals product development. *Mailing Add:* Technol Acquisition Dow Chem Co, Zozo Dow Ctr Midland MI 48640

TABOR, WILLIAM JOSEPH, b Rockfall, Conn, Mar 22, 31; m 59; c 2. MAGNETISM. *Educ:* Rensselaer Polytech Inst, BS, 53; Harvard Univ, AM, 54, PhD(chem physics), 57. *Prof Exp:* MEM TECH STAFF, BELL LABS, INC, 59- *Res:* Microwave spectroscopy of gases and paramagnetic solids; quantum electronics; ferromagnetic solids; magneto-optics; magnetic bubble device technology. *Mailing Add:* Bell Labs Inc Murray Hill NJ 07974

TABORSKY, GEORGE, b Budapest, Hungary, Feb 12, 28; nat US; m 53; c 2. BIOCHEMISTRY. *Educ:* Brown Univ, BS, 51; Yale Univ, PhD(biochem), 56. *Prof Exp:* Am Cancer Soc fel, Carlsberg Lab, Denmark, 56-57; from instr to assoc prof biochem, Yale Univ, 57-70, dir grad studies in biochem, 64-67; assoc prof biochem, 70-72, chmn dept, 73-78, PROF BIOCHEM, UNIV CALIF, SANTA BARBARA, 72- *Mem:* Am Chem Soc; Biophys Soc; Am Soc Biol Chemists; Am Inst Chemists; NY Acad Sci. *Res:* Biochemistry of phosphoproteins; protein chemistry; biochemistry of egg yolk; phosphoprotein-metal interactions. *Mailing Add:* Dept of Biol Sci Univ of Calif Santa Barbara CA 93106

TACHIBANA, DORA K, b Cupertino, Calif, Dec 19, 34. IMMUNOLOGY, MEDICAL MICROBIOLOGY. *Educ:* San Jose State Col, BA, 56; Stanford Univ, MA, 62, PhD(immunol), 64. *Prof Exp:* Pub health microbiologist trainee, Calif State Dept Pub Health, 56-57; clin lab technician trainee, San Jose Hosp, Calif, 57; pub health microbiologist, Santa Clara County Pub Health, 57-59; NIH fel immunol, Czech Acad Sci, 64-65; lab instr & res asst, Stanford Univ, 65-66; asst prof microbiol & immunol, San Francisco State Col, 66-69; res assoc med, Sch Med, Stanford Univ, 70; assoc prof, 70-75, PROF IMMUNOL & MICROBIOL, CALIF COL PODIATRIC MED, 75- *Concurrent Pos:* Fac res award, San Francisco State Col, 68-69; clin lab dir, Calif Podiatry Hosp, San Francisco, 70-79; consult, Bur Med Devices-Immunol Div, Food & Drug Admin, 80-81. *Mem:* Am Soc Microbiol; Am Asn Immunol; Sigma Xi; Am Asn Univ Professors; AAAS. *Res:* Microbial flora of the foot. *Mailing Add:* Dept of Basic Sci Calif Col of Podiat Med San Francisco CA 94115

TACHIBANA, HIDEO, b Los Altos, Calif, June 30, 25; m 64; c 2. PLANT PATHOLOGY. *Educ:* Univ Calif, Davis, BS, 57; Wash State Univ, PhD(plant path), 63. *Prof Exp:* RES PLANT PATHOLOGIST, USDA, 63- *Mem:* Am Phytopath Soc; Int Soc Plant Path; Crop Sci Soc Am; AAAS. *Res:* Soybean diseases; brown stem rot; breeding and screening for disease resistance; gene and pest management. *Mailing Add:* 4024 Quebec Ames IA 50010

TACHMINDJI, ALEXANDER JOHN, b Athens, Greece, Feb 16, 28; US citizen; m 65. HYDRODYNAMICS. *Educ:* Durham Univ, BSc, 49, BSc(hons), 50; Mass Inst Technol, SM, 51. *Prof Exp:* With Swann, Hunter & W Richardson, Eng, 45-46; res assoc naval archit, Mass Inst Technol,

50-51; mem res staff, Ship Div, David W Taylor Model Basin, US Navy, 51-54, head res & propeller br, 54-59; head tactical warfare group, weapons syst eval div, Inst Defense Anal, 59-64, asst dir res & eng support div, 64-67, dep dir sci technol div, 67-69, dir systs eval div, 69-72; dir tactical technol off, Defense Advan Res Proj Agency, Dept Defense, 72-73, dep dir, Defense Advan Res Proj Agency, 73-75; chief scientist, 75-76, vpres, 76-79, VPRES & GEN MGR, WASHINGTON C3 OPER, MITRE CORP, 79- *Concurrent Pos:* Consult, Am Bur Shipping, 56-59, Anti-Submarine Warfare Comt, Defense Sci Bd, 65-70 & Naval Surface Warfare Panel, 75; ed, J Defense Res, 69-; mem publ comt, Am Inst Aeronaut & Astronaut. *Mem:* Fel AAAS; Soc Naval Architects & Marine Engrs; assoc fel Am Inst Aeronaut & Astronaut; Opers Res Soc Am; fel Royal Inst Naval Architects. *Res:* Cavitation; super cavitation; potential theory; ship vibration and noise; systems analyses; hydroelasticity. *Mailing Add:* Mitre Corp Westgate Res Park McLean VA 22101

TACHOVSKY, THOMAS GREGORY, b Los Angeles, Calif, Feb 1, 47; m 68; c 2. IMMUNOLOGY, VIROLOGY. *Educ:* Gonzaga Univ, BS, 68; Univ Rochester, PhD(microbiol), 74. *Prof Exp:* Lab technician microbiol, Sch Med, Univ Rochester, 71-74; fel immunol, 74-76, res asst, 76-77, ASST PROF IMMUNOL, WISTAR INST, 77- *Mem:* Sigma Xi; Am Soc Microbiol; AAAS. *Res:* Neuroimmunology; multiple sclerosis; immunopathology of central nervous system diseases; neurovirology. *Mailing Add:* Wistar Inst 36th & Spruce Sts Philadelphia PA 19104

TACK, PETER ISAAC, b Marion, NY, Apr 15, 11; m 37; c 2. FISH BIOLOGY. *Educ:* Cornell Univ, BS, 34, PhD(agr), 39. *Prof Exp:* Asst biologist, State Conserv Dept, NY, 39-40, biologist, 40; instr zool, 40-43, asst prof & res asst, 43-46, assoc prof & res assoc, 46-50, prof fisheries & wildlife, 50-70, chmn dept, 50-69, prof fisheries, wildlife & zool, 70-78, EMER PROF FISHERIES & WILDLIFE, MICH STATE UNIV, 77- *Concurrent Pos:* Mem, Governor's Botulism Control Comn, 64-65. *Mem:* Am Soc Limnol & Oceanog; Am Fisheries Soc; Am Soc Ichthyologists & Herpetologists. *Res:* Pond fish culture; population fluctuations of whitefish in Northern Lake Michigan and effects of pumped storage generating facility on Lake Michigan ecology. *Mailing Add:* 314 Brittany Dr Lansing MI 48906

TACKER, EDGAR CARROLL, systems science, electrical engineering, see previous edition

TACKER, MARTHA MCCLELLAND, b Mineral Wells, Tex, Jan 16, 43; m 67; c 3. BIOCHEMISTRY, SCIENCE WRITING. *Educ:* Baylor Col Med, PhD(biochem), 69. *Prof Exp:* Res assoc biochem, Baylor Col Med, 69-70; res asst gastroenterol, Mayo Grad Sch Med, Univ Minn & Mayo Found, 70-71; instr physiol, Baylor Col Med, 71-74; SCI WRITING & EDITING, 74- *Mem:* AAAS; Sigma Xi; fel Am Med Writers Asn; Coun Biol Ed. *Mailing Add:* 2901 Wilshire Ave West Lafayette IN 47906

TACKER, WILLIS ARNOLD, JR, b Tyler, Tex, May 24, 42; m 67; c 3. CARDIOVASCULAR PHYSIOLOGY, MEDICAL EDUCATION. *Educ:* Baylor Univ, BS, 64, MD & PhD(physiol), 70. *Prof Exp:* Intern med, Mayo Clin, 70-71; mem fac physiol, Baylor Col Med, 71-74; MEM FAC BIOMED ENG, PURDUE UNIV, WEST LAFAYETTE, 74- *Mem:* Am Physiol Soc; Asn Advan Med Instrumentation. *Res:* Life-threatening arrhythmia therapy; new teaching techniques and devices; diagnostic and therapeutic devices development. *Mailing Add:* Biomed Eng Ctr Purdue Univ West Lafayette IN 47906

TACKETT, JAMES EDWIN, JR, b Los Angeles, Calif, Oct 8, 37; m 62; c 3. ANALYTICAL CHEMISTRY. *Educ:* Occidental Col, BA, 60; Univ Calif, Riverside, PhD(chem), 64. *Prof Exp:* Chemist, Union Carbide Corp, WVa, 64-65; sr res chemist, 65-77, MGR ANAL DEPT, DENVER RES CTR, MARATHON OIL CO, 77- *Mem:* Am Chem Soc; Sigma Xi. *Res:* Applied spectroscopy; thermal analysis; analytical separations. *Mailing Add:* Marathon Oil Co Denver Res Ctr PO Box 269 Littleton CO 80160

TACKETT, JESSE LEE, b Dublin, Tex, Sept 20, 35; m 55; c 3. SOIL PHYSICS. *Educ:* Tex A&M Univ, BS, 57; Auburn Univ, MS, 61, PhD(soil physics), 63. *Prof Exp:* Instr agron, Tarleton State Col, 57-59; asst, Tex A&M Univ, 59-60; res soil scientist, Soil & Water Conserv Res Div, Agr Res Serv, USDA, 63-65; assoc prof agr, 65-70, PROF AGR & DEAN SCH AGR & BUS, TARLETON STATE UNIV, 70- *Mem:* Am Soc Agron; Soil Sci Soc Am. *Res:* Soil aeration and strength; plant growth relations. *Mailing Add:* Sch of Agr & Bus Tarleton State Univ Stephenville TX 76402

TACKETT, STANFORD L, b Virgie, Ky, Sept 5, 30; m 51; c 4. ANALYTICAL CHEMISTRY. *Educ:* Ohio State Univ, BS, 57, PhD(chem), 62. *Prof Exp:* Instr chem, Ohio State Univ, 61-62; asst prof, Ariz State Univ, 62-66; assoc prof, 66-69, PROF CHEM, INDIANA UNIV PA, 69-, CHMN DEPT, 74- *Concurrent Pos:* Consult, Off Res Anal, Holloman AFB, 63; NIH res grant, 64-66. *Mem:* AAAS; Am Chem Soc; Meteoritical Soc. *Res:* Analytical chemistry and electro-analytical techniques; chemistry of meteorites; chemistry of cyanocobalamin; pollution of streams by acid coal mine waste. *Mailing Add:* Dept of Chem Indiana Univ of Pa Indiana PA 15701

TACKLE, DAVID, silviculture, see previous edition

TADE, WILLIAM HOWARD, b Hillsboro, Iowa, Sept 6, 23; m 46; c 4. PATHOLOGY, PHYSIOLOGY. *Educ:* Univ Iowa, BA, 50, DDS, 54, MS, 60, PhD(physiol), 61. *Prof Exp:* From asst prof to assoc prof, 61-71, PROF ORAL PATH, COL DENT, UNIV IOWA, 71- *Mem:* AAAS; Am Acad Oral Path; Am Dent Asn; Int Asn Dent Res. *Res:* Histochemistry of dental pulp; keratinization of mucosa. *Mailing Add:* Dept Oral Path Univ Iowa Col Dent Iowa City IA 52242

TADJERAN, HAMID, b Tehran, Nov 30, 52. NUMERICAL ANALYSIS. *Educ:* Am Univ Beirut, BS, 74; Univ Colo Boulder, MS, 78, PhD(appl math), 80. *Prof Exp:* NSF res asst, Univ Colo, 78-80, US Geol Surv res assoc, 80; lectr math & comput sci, Univ Calif, Davis, 80-81; ASST PROF COMPUT SCI & MATH, UNIV NC, WILMINGTON, 81- *Mem:* Soc Indust & Appl Math; Am Math Soc. *Res:* Numerical solution of differential equations; step size control. *Mailing Add:* Math Sci Dept Univ NC PO Box 3725 Wilmington NC 28406

TADROS, MAHER EBEID, b Egypt, July 25, 43; m 72; c 1. SURFACE CHEMISTRY. *Educ:* Univ Assiut, BSc, 63; Ain Shams Univ, Cairo, MSc, 66; Clarkson Col Technol, MS, 71, PhD(inorg chem), 72. *Prof Exp:* Instr chem, Ain Shams Univ, Cairo, 63-68; res assoc surface chem, Univ Southern Calif, 72-74; RES SCIENTIST CHEM, MARTIN MARIETTA LAB, 74-, MGR RES, 80- *Mem:* Am Chem Soc. *Res:* Colloid and surface chemistry; suspension stability; microemulsions; catalysis; corrosion protection. *Mailing Add:* Martin Marietta Lab 1450 S Rolling Rd Baltimore MD 21227

TAFF, LAURENCE GORDON, b New York City, NY, Feb 5, 47; m 82; c 1. ASTROMETRY, CELESTIAL MECHANICS. *Educ:* City Col NY, BS, 67, MA, 68; Univ Rochester, PhD(physics & astron), 73. *Prof Exp:* Lectr physics, City Col NY, 67; res assoc, Dept Physics & Astron, Univ Rochester, 73; res assoc, Dept Physics, Univ Pittsburgh, 73-75; PROF STAFF, LINCOLN LAB, MASS INST TECHNOL, 75- *Concurrent Pos:* Prin investr, Lincoln Lab, Mass Inst Technol, 81. *Mem:* Am Phys Soc; Am Astron Soc; Astron Soc Pac; Royal Astron Soc. *Res:* Celestial mechanics and gravitation including local applications (artificial satellites to clusters of galaxies); applied mathematics and astrometry. *Mailing Add:* Lincoln Lab Mass Inst Technol Boston MA 02173

TAFFE, WILLIAM JOHN, b Albany, NY, Feb 3, 43; m 65; c 2. COMPUTER SCIENCE. *Educ:* Le Moyne Col, NY, BS, 64; Univ Chicago, SM, 67, PhD(geophys), 68. *Prof Exp:* Res physicist, Air Force Cambridge Res Labs, 68-69; asst prof physics, Colby Col, 69-71; asst prof natural sci, 71-75, ASSOC PROF NATURAL SCI, PLYMOUTH STATE COL, 75- *Mem:* Asn Comput Mach; Sigma Xi; Am Asn Physics Teachers. *Res:* Computer modeling and simulation; computer aided instruction. *Mailing Add:* Dept Comput Sci Plymouth State Col Plymouth NH 03264

TAFT, BRUCE A, b San Francisco, Calif, Jan 29, 30; m 61; c 1. PHYSICAL OCEANOGRAPHY. *Educ:* Stanford Univ, BS, 51; Univ Calif, San Diego, MS, 61, PhD(oceanog), 65. *Prof Exp:* Statistician, US Fish & Wildlife Serv, Calif, 55-58; grad res oceanogr, Scripps Inst, Univ Calif, 58-59; res asst, Johns Hopkins Univ, 59-60; grad res oceanogr, Scripps Inst Oceanog, Univ Calif, 60-65, asst res oceanogr, 65-68, asst prof oceanog, 68-73; res assoc prof, 73-81, RES PROF OCEANOG, UNIV WASH, 81- *Concurrent Pos:* NSF grant, US-Japan Coop Sci Prog, 66-; supvr oceanogr, Pac Marine Environ Lab, Nat Ocean & Atmospheric Admin. *Mem:* AAAS; Am Geophys Union; Oceanog Soc Japan. *Res:* Description of large scale oceanic circulation; velocity structure and distribution of properties in ocean currents. *Mailing Add:* Dept of Oceanog Univ of Wash Seattle WA 98195

TAFT, CHARLES KIRKLAND, b Cleveland, Ohio, July 24, 28; m 51; c 3. CONTROL ENGINEERING. *Educ:* Amherst Col, BA, 51; Mass Inst Technol, BS, 53; Case Inst Technol, MS, 56, PhD(feedback control systs), 60. *Prof Exp:* Spec apprentice to res engr, Warner & Swasey, 53-58, chief servo engr, 60-61; from asst prof to assoc prof eng, Case Inst Technol, 61-67; PROF MECH ENG, UNIV NH, 67- *Honors & Awards:* Charles Strosacker Award, Case Inst Technol, 66; Achievement Award, Nat Fluid Power Asn, 66. *Mem:* Am Soc Mech Engrs; Inst Elec & Electronics Engrs; Instrument Soc Am. *Res:* Feedback systems; control system synthesis; digital and discontinuous control and fluidic systems. *Mailing Add:* Dept of Mech Eng Univ of NH Durham NH 03824

TAFT, CLARENCE EGBERT, b Romeo, Mich, Nov 13, 06; m 30; c 2. BOTANY. *Educ:* Mich State Norm Col, AB, 29; Univ Okla, MS, 31; Ohio State Univ, PhD(bot), 34. *Prof Exp:* Asst bot, Univ Okla, 29-31; asst bot, 31-33, chief lab asst, 33-35, from instr to assoc prof, 35-54, prof bot,54-77,EMER PROF, OHIO STATE UNIV, 77- *Concurrent Pos:* Exchange prof, Cornell Univ, 37; consult city algologist, Columbus, 42- *Mem:* Assoc Bot Soc Am; assoc Am Micros Soc (vpres, 47 & 48, pres, 49); Int Phycol Soc; Phycol Soc Am. *Res:* Freshwater algae; biological control of microorganisms in industrial and drinking water. *Mailing Add:* Dept Bot Col Biol Sci Ohio State Univ 1735 Neil Ave Columbus OH 43210

TAFT, DAVID DAKIN, b Cleveland, Ohio, Mar 27, 38; m 61; c 3. POLYMER CHEMISTRY, ORGANIC CHEMISTRY. *Educ:* Kenyon Col, AB, 60; Mich State Univ, PhD(org chem), 63. *Prof Exp:* Sr res chemist, Archer Daniels Midland Co, 64-67; group leader, Resins, Ashland Chem Co, 67-70, mgr polymer chem, Ashland Oil, Inc, 70-72; vpres & gen mgr, Oxyplast, Inc, 74; dir com develop, Gen Mills Chem, Inc, 72-73, asst to pres, 72-74, dir res & develop, 74-76, vpres, 77-78, GROUP VPRES CONSUMER & SPEC PROD, WENKEL CORP, 78- *Mem:* Am Chem Soc; Indust Res Inst; Fedn Socs Paint Technol; Com Develop Asn. *Res:* Acrylic, polyester, epoxy, urethane coating and adhesive systems; water soluble coating and adhesive polymers; functional monomers; powder coatings; non-yellowing isocyanates; nylon polymers; hydrophilic polymers; surface active agents; specialty chemicals for cosmetics; consumer adhesive products. *Mailing Add:* Gen Mills Chem Inc 4620 W 77th St Minneapolis MN 55435

TAFT, EARL J, b New York, NY, Aug 27, 31; m 59; c 2. ALGEBRA. *Educ:* Amherst Col, BA, 52; Yale Univ, MA, 53, PhD(math), 56. *Prof Exp:* Instr math, Columbia Univ, 56-59; from asst prof to assoc prof, 59-66, PROF MATH, RUTGERS UNIV, 66- *Concurrent Pos:* NSF res grants, 63-67, 70-71 & 73 & 76; exec ed, Commun in Algebra, 74-, Monographs & Lectr Roles Math, Marcel Denner Inc, New York. *Mem:* Am Math Soc; Math Asn Am. *Res:* Nonassociative algebras; Hopf algebras; rings; groups. *Mailing Add:* Dept Math Rutgers Univ New Brunswick NJ 08903

TAFT, EDGAR BRECK, b New Haven, Conn, Nov 16, 16; m 43. PATHOLOGY. *Educ:* Yale Univ, MD, 42; Univ Kans, MS, 50. *Prof Exp:* Nat Res Coun fel, Univ Kans, 48-49; Runyon clin res fel, Univ Kans & Univ Stockholm, 49-50; from asst pathologist to assoc pathologist, 52-60, PATHOLOGIST, MASS GEN HOSP, 61-; ASSOC CLIN PROF PATH, HARVARD MED SCH, 63- *Mem:* AAAS; Histochem Soc; Soc Develop Biol; AMA; Am Asn Pathologists. *Res:* Liver disease; methods of histochemistry and cytochemistry. *Mailing Add:* Dept of Path Mass Gen Hosp Boston MA 02114

TAFT, HORACE DWIGHT, b Cincinnati, Ohio, Apr 2, 25; m 52; c 3. PHYSICS. *Educ:* Yale Univ, BA, 50; Univ Chicago, MS, 53, PhD, 55. *Prof Exp:* From instr to assoc prof physics, 56-65, master, Davenport Col, 66-71, dean, Yale Col, 71-78, PROF PHYSICS, YALE UNIV, 65- *Res:* High energy physics. *Mailing Add:* Dept Physics Yale Univ New Haven CT 06520

TAFT, JAY LESLIE, b Rockville Centre, NY, Mar 19, 44. BIOLOGICAL OCEANOGRAPHY. *Educ:* Lafayette Col, BA, 67; Johns Hopkins Univ, MA, 73, PhD(biol oceanog), 74. *Prof Exp:* Res assoc, 74, ASSOC RES SCIENTIST BIOL OCEANOG, CHESAPEAKE BAY INST, 74- *Mem:* AAAS; Am Soc Limnol & Oceanog; Phycol Soc Am; Estuarine Res Fedn. *Res:* Production and utilization of dissolved organic matter in estuaries and coastal ocean; nutrient cycling in estuaries. *Mailing Add:* Chesapeake Bay Inst Johns Hopkins Univ Baltimore MD 21218

TAFT, KINGSLEY ARTER, JR, b Cleveland, Ohio, Nov 17, 30; m 55; c 3. FORESTRY, GENETICS. *Educ:* Amherst Col, AB, 53; Univ Mich, BS, 57; NC State Univ, MS, 62, PhD(forestry, genetics), 66. *Prof Exp:* Forester, Nebo Oil Co, La, 57-59; res asst forestry, NC State, 59-63; forest geneticist, Div Forestry, 63-74, chief, Forest & Wildlife Resources Br, Fisheries & Wildlife Develop, 74-79, SPEC PROJS COORDR & ASST TO DIR, DIV LAND & FOREST RESOURCES, TENN VALLEY AUTHORITY, 79- *Mem:* Soc Am Foresters. *Res:* Hardwood tree improvement and genetics. *Mailing Add:* Div Land & Forest Resources Tenn Valley Authority Norris TN 37828

TAFT, ROBERT WHEATON, JR, b Lawrence, Kans, Dec 17, 22; m 44; c 3. PHYSICAL CHEMISTRY, ORGANIC CHEMISTRY. *Educ:* Univ Kans, BS, 44, MS, 46; Ohio State Univ, PhD(chem), 49. *Prof Exp:* Lab asst chem, Univ Kans, 44-46; asst, Ohio State Univ, 46-49; res assoc, Columbia Univ, 49-50; from asst prof to prof, Pa State Univ, 50-65; PROF CHEM, UNIV CALIF, IRVINE, 65- *Concurrent Pos:* Sloan fel, 55-57; Guggenheim fel, Harvard Univ, 58; consult, Sun Oil Co, 58- *Mem:* Am Chem Soc. *Res:* Kinetics; effect of molecular structure on reactivity; mechanisms of organic reactions; rate and equilibrium studies; fluorine nuclear magnetic resonance shielding. *Mailing Add:* Dept of Chem Univ of Calif Irvine CA 92664

TAFURI, JOHN FRANCIS, b St Barbara, Italy, Aug 4, 24; nat US; m 58; c 3. ENTOMOLOGY. *Educ:* Fordham Univ, BS, 44, MS, 48, PhD, 51. *Prof Exp:* Lab instr comp anat, Fordham Univ, 47-48, lab instr entom, 48, instr comp anat, Sch Educ, 50-51; from instr to assoc prof biol, 51-68, PROF BIOL, XAVIER UNIV, OHIO, 68- *Concurrent Pos:* Asst, Dept Animal Behavior, Am Mus Natural Hist, NY, 48-51. *Mem:* AAAS; Sigma Xi. *Res:* Electrical changes in tissues; social behavior in insects; aging in cells and tissues. *Mailing Add:* Dept of Biol Xavier Univ Cincinnati OH 45207

TAG, PAUL MARK, b Meyersdale, Pa, Sept 8, 45. METEOROLOGY, ATMOSPHERIC NUMERICAL MODELING. *Educ:* Pa State Univ, BS, 66, MS, 68, PhD(meteorol), 77. *Prof Exp:* Res meteorologist, Navy Weather Res Facil, 68-71; RES METEOROLOGIST, NAVAL ENVIRON PREDICTION RES FACIL, 71- *Mem:* Am Meteorol Soc; Sigma Xi. *Res:* Numerical weather prediction; cloud physics; atmospheric turbulence; boundary layer; atmospheric numerical modeling. *Mailing Add:* Naval Environ Prediction Res Facil Monterey CA 93940

TAGER, IRA BRUCE, US citizen. CLINICAL EPIDEMIOLOGY, INFECTIOUS DISEASES. *Educ:* Colgate Univ, AB, 65; Univ Rochester, MD, 69; Harvard Med Sch, MPH, 73. *Prof Exp:* Res fel infectious dis, 72-73, instr med, 73-76, ASST PROF MED, HARVARD MED SCH, 76- *Concurrent Pos:* Edward Elliot Trudeau fel, Am Lung Asn, 77-81; consult, Dept Health, Div Epidemiol, State of RI, 78- *Mem:* Am Thoracic Soc; Am Soc Microbiol; fel Infectious Dis Soc Am; fel Am Col Epidemiolgy. *Res:* Epidemiology chronic lung disease and identification of determinants; determinants interventions for hospital acquired infections. *Mailing Add:* Channing Lab 180 Longwood Ave Boston MA 02115

TAGGART, GEORGE BRUCE, b Philadelphia, Pa, Apr 8, 42. CONDENSED MATTER THEORY, PHYSICAL METALLURGY. *Educ:* Col William & Mary, BS, 64; Temple Univ, PhD(physics), 71. *Prof Exp:* Instr physics, Drexel Univ, 70; vis asst prof, Temple Univ, 70-71; asst prof, 71-76, ASSOC PROF PHYSICS, VA COMMONWEALTH UNIV, 76- *Concurrent Pos:* Consult, Temple Univ, 74, res assoc, 75; res assoc, Oak Ridge Nat Lab, 74; vis prof, Dept Theoret Physics, Oxford Univ, 78; vis assoc prof physics, Univ Ill, Urbana-Champaign, 78-79; guestworker, Thermophysics Div, Nat Bur Standards, Gaithersburg, Md, 78-; Vis prof physics, Fed Univ Pernambuco, Brazil, 80. *Mem:* AAAS; Am Phys Soc; Fedn Am Scientists. *Res:* Theory of Ising systems as applied to magnetism, alloys, and surfaces. *Mailing Add:* Dept of Physics Va Commonwealth Univ Richmond VA 23284

TAGGART, JOHN VICTOR, b Brigham, Utah, Aug 29, 16; m 59. PHYSIOLOGY, MEDICINE. *Educ:* Univ Southern Calif, MD, 41. *Prof Exp:* Intern, Los Angeles County Hosp, Calif, 40-41; asst resident med, Clins, Univ Chicago, 41-42; res resident, Goldwater Mem Hosp, New York, 42-43; from asst & instr to prof med, Col Physicians & Surgeons, Columbia Univ, 46-82, Dalton prof physiol & chmn dept, 62-82. *Concurrent Pos:* Nat Res Coun Welch fel internal med, 46-52; consult, Comn on Growth, Nat Res Coun, 53-54; Nathanson mem lectr, Univ Southern Calif, 55; consult, USPHS, 55-60; mem bd dirs, Russell Sage Inst Path, 55-, pres, 59-72; career investr, Am Heart Asn, 58-62; mem exec comt, Health Res Coun, City of New York, 63-70, vchmn, 67-70; mem res career award comt, NIH, 66-69, chmn, 67-69; mem bd sci counselors, Nat Heart & Lung Inst, 69-72. *Mem:* Am Physiol Soc; Am Soc Clin Invest; Harvey Soc (pres, 69); Asn Am Physicians. *Res:* Metabolic aspects of renal transport mechanisms; biochemistry; enzymology. *Mailing Add:* Dept Physiol Columbia Univ New York NY 10032

TAGGART, KEITH ANTHONY, b Cleveland, Ohio, July 10, 44; m 68; c 3. PHYSICS, COMPUTATIONAL PHYSICS. *Educ:* Case Inst Technol, BS, 66, MS, 68; Case Western Reserve Univ, PhD(physics), 70. *Prof Exp:* Staff scientist plasma physics, Air Force Weapons Lab, 70-72; fel, Plasma Physics Lab, Princeton Univ, 73; STAFF MEM LASER FUSION, LOS ALAMOS SCI LAB, 73- *Mem:* Am Phys Soc. *Res:* Laser fusion target simulation on digital computers. *Mailing Add:* Los Alamos Sci Lab MS-531 Los Alamos NM 87545

TAGGART, RAYMOND, b Bradford, Eng, July 9, 22; m 49. MECHANICAL ENGINEERING. *Educ:* Univ London, BSc, 48; Queen's Univ, Belfast, PhD, 56. *Prof Exp:* Eng draftsman, Harland & Wolffe, Ltd, N Ireland, 38-43; instr mech eng, Col Technol, Belfast, 43-48, sr lectr, 48-56; lectr, Queen's Univ, Belfast, 56-57; Nat Res Coun Can fel metall, Univ Alta, 57-58, res assoc, 58-59; from asst prof to assoc prof, 59-68, PROF MECH ENG, UNIV WASH, 68- *Concurrent Pos:* Blair fel, London County Coun, London, 57-58. *Mem:* Am Soc Metals; Brit Inst Mech Engrs; Sigma Xi. *Res:* Fatigue of metals with reference to crack propagation; effects of microstructural changes and precipitate morphology on properties of materials, especially crack propagation; relation of constitution to mechanical properties in binary alloys; superconducting properties of zirconium and titanium base alloys. *Mailing Add:* Dept of Mech Eng FU10 Univ of Wash Seattle WA 98195

TAGUE, B(YRL) DALE, b Farmersburg, Ind, July 4, 18; m 43; c 2. ELECTRICAL ENGINEERING. *Educ:* Purdue Univ, BSEE, 40, MSEE, 55. *Prof Exp:* Elec tester, Westinghouse Elec Corp, 40-42; electronic engr, Naval Avionics Facil, US Dept Navy, 46-50, head spec components br, 50-59, chief tech develop staff, Exp Res Div, 59-63, tech consult, appl res staff, 63-80; TECH CONSULT, 80- *Mem:* Sr mem Inst Elec & Electronics Engrs. *Res:* Naval airborne electronic equipment for fire control, navigation and missile systems; electromechanical devices, servo-systems and transistor circuitry; radar; microelectronics; thin films. *Mailing Add:* 6417 Brokenhurst Rd Indianapolis IN 46220

TAHA, HAMDY ABDELAZIZ, b Egypt, Apr 19, 37; US citizen; m 65; c 3. OPERATIONS RESEARCH. *Educ:* Univ Alexandria, BS, 58; Stanford Univ, MS, 62; Ariz State Univ, PhD(indust eng), 64. *Prof Exp:* Instr elec eng, Univ Assiut, 58-59; mgr planning, Suez Oil Co, Egypt, 64-67; asst prof indust eng, Univ Okla, 67-69; assoc prof, 69-75, PROF INDUST ENG, UNIV ARK, FAYETTEVILLE, 75- *Concurrent Pos:* Lectr, Cairo Univ, 64-67; consult, Tenneco Oil Co, Okla, 67, Sun Oil Co, Tex, 70, Ford Found, 72, Petromin, Saudi Arabia, 75 & Hylsa, SA, Puebla, Mex, 77-78; vis prof, Univ Americas, Puebla, Mex, 77-78. *Mem:* Am Inst Indust Engrs; Inst Mgt Sci; Opers Res Soc Am. *Res:* Mathematical programming with emphasis on integer programming. *Mailing Add:* 406 Lake Rd Springdale AR 72764

TAHAN, THEODORE WAHBA, b Alexandria, Egypt, Jan 22, 36; m 62; c 1. RADIATION ONCOLOGY. *Educ:* Alexandria Univ, MBBCh, 61, DMR&E, 64, MD & PhD(radiother), 69. *Prof Exp:* Resident radiother, Alexandria Univ Hosps, 62-64, clin demonstr, Fac Med, 64-69, lectr, 69-71; asst prof, 72-75, assoc prof, 75-79, PROF RADIATION ONCOL & CHMN, FAC MED, SHERBROOKE UNIV, 79- *Concurrent Pos:* Consult radiother, Hotel Dieu Hosp, St Vincent Hosp & Sherbrooke Hosp, Sherbrooke, 73. *Mem:* Can Radiol Asn; Can Oncol Soc; Egyptian Cancer Soc; Egyptian Radiol Soc; Radiol Soc NAm. *Res:* Elemental diet in irradiated patients; bronchial carcinoma, carcinoma of the bilharzial bladder, tongue and nasopharynx. *Mailing Add:* Radiother Dept Cent Hosp Univ of Sherbrooke Sherbrooke PQ 51K 2R1 Can

TAHIR-KHELI, RAZA ALI, b Hazara, West Pakistan, May 1, 36; m 62; c 1. THEORETICAL MAGNETISM. *Educ:* Oxford Univ, BA, 58, DPhil(physics), 62. *Prof Exp:* Res assoc physics, Univ Pa, 62-64; sr scientific officer, Pakistan Atomic Energy Comn, 64-66; from asst prof to assoc prof, 66-71, PROF PHYSICS, TEMPLE UNIV, 71- *Concurrent Pos:* Assoc, Exp Sta, E I du Pont de Nemours & Co, Del, 67-70. *Mem:* Am Phys Soc. *Res:* Solid state physics; many body physics; magnetism; order-disorder phenomena; random magnetism; atomic diffusion; non-equilibrium thermodynamics. *Mailing Add:* Dept of Physics Temple Univ Col Lib Arts Philadelphia PA 19122

TAI, CHEN-TO, b Soochow, China, Dec 30, 15; US citizen; m 41; c 5. ELECTRICAL ENGINEERING. *Educ:* Tsinghua Univ, China, BS, 37; Harvard Univ, DSc(commun), 47. *Prof Exp:* Res fel elec eng, Harvard Univ, 47-49; sr res engr, Stanford Res Inst, 49-54; assoc prof elec eng, Ohio State Univ, 54-56; prof electronics, Tech Inst Aeronaut, Brazil, 56-60; prof elec eng, Ohio State Univ, 60-64; PROF ELEC ENG, UNIV MICH, ANN ARBOR, 64- *Concurrent Pos:* Mem, Comn B, Int Union Radio Sci, 62- *Mem:* Fel Inst Elec & Electronics Engrs. *Res:* Electromagnetic and antenna theories. *Mailing Add:* Radiation Lab Univ of Mich Ann Arbor MI 48109

TAI, CHRISTINE YIU-KAM, b Vietnam, June 2, 43; nat US; m 70; c 2. ORGANIC CHEMISTRY. *Educ:* Chung Chi Col Hong Kong, dipl, 64; Case Western Reserve Univ, MS, 68, PhD(org chem), 70. *Prof Exp:* Fel chem, Cornell Univ, 70-71 & Ariz State Univ, 71-72; instr, Univ Ky, 73-74, res assoc vet sci, 74-75; ASST PROF CHEM, JACKSON STATE UNIV, 78- *Mem:* Am Chem Soc. *Res:* Organic synthesis of pharmaceutically important compounds. *Mailing Add:* Dept of Chem Jackson State Univ Jackson MS 39217

TAI, CLEMENT LEO, b Shanghai, China, Oct 19, 15; US citizen; m 46; c 2. APPLIED MECHANICS, APPLIED MATHEMATICS. *Educ:* Nat Cent Univ, China, BS, 41; Univ Colo, MS, 48; Polytech Inst Brooklyn, PhD(appl mech), 61. *Prof Exp:* Asst engr, Pub Health Admin, Repub China, 41-44, assoc engr, Ministry Commun, 44-46; sr designer struct eng, Devenco, Inc, 48-50; engr, Hardesty & Hanover, 50; struct engr, Chem Construct Corp, 50-61; res specialist struct dynamics, 61-63, sr tech specialist fluid, Space & space & struct dynamics, 63-66, proj engr, 66-67, MEM TECH STAFF, SPACE DIV, NAM ROCKWELL CORP, 67- *Mem:* Am Inst Aeronaut & Astronaut; Am Soc Mech Eng; Chinese Inst Eng. *Res:* Transient dynamics of orbiting space stations; cable dynamics; longitudinal oscillations of large liquid launch vehicles; oscillations of fluid in elastic containers; wave propagations in propellent lines; rotation of changing bodies. *Mailing Add:* Rockwell Int Corp Space Div 12214 Lakewood Blvd Downey CA 90241

TAI, DOUGLAS L, b Hong Kong, Nov 6, 40; m 70. RADIOLOGICAL PHYSICS. *Educ:* Chinese Univ Hong Kong, BSc, 64; Cornell Univ, PhD(chem), 69. *Prof Exp:* Res assoc phys chem, Cornell Univ, 69-71; fac res assoc solid state chem, Ariz State Univ, 71-72, asst prof, 72-73; instr, Dept Chem, Univ Ky, 73-74, instr, Dept Physics & Astron, 75-77; instr & radiol physicist, Dept Radiol, Univ Miss Med Ctr, 77-79, asst prof & radiol physicist, 79-81; ASST PROF & RADIOL PHYSICIST, DEPT RADIOL, UNIV TENN CTR HEALTH SCI, 81- *Concurrent Pos:* Res assoc, Dept Radiation Med, Albert B. Chandler Med Ctr, Univ Ky, 75- *Mem:* Am Asn Physiol Med; Health Physics Soc; Soc Photo-Optical Instrumentation Engrs. *Res:* Teletherapy and intracavitary dosimetry. *Mailing Add:* Dept Radiol Univ Tenn Ctr Health Sci Memphis TN 38163

TAI, HAN, b Yang Chow, China, Mar 20, 24; m 61; c 2. ANALYTICAL CHEMISTRY. *Educ:* Nanking Univ, BS, 49; Emory Univ, MS, 55, PhD(chem), 58. *Prof Exp:* Asst geol, Nat Taiwan Univ, Formosa, 51-54; res chemist, A E Staley Mfg Co, 58-66, head instrumental anal lab, 66-67, group leader anal labs, 67-70, SUPVR PESTICIDES MONITORING LAB, ENVIRON PROTECTION AGENCY, 70- *Mem:* Am Chem Soc; NY Acad Sci; Soc Appl Spectros. *Res:* Chemical analysis of rocks and minerals, carbohydrates, polymers, pesticides; infrared spectroscopy; chromatography; environmental monitoring on inorganic and organic pollutants and pesticide residues. *Mailing Add:* Pesticides Monitoring Lab Environ Protection Agency Bay St Louis MS 39529

TAI, JULIA CHOW, b Shanghai, China. CHEMISTRY. *Educ:* Nat Taiwan Univ, BS, 57; Univ Okla, MS, 59; Univ Ill, Urbana, PhD(chem), 63. *Prof Exp:* Fels, Wayne State Univ, 63-68; asst prof, 69-73, assoc prof, 73-79, PROF CHEM, UNIV MICH, DEARBORN, 79- *Mem:* Am Chem Soc. *Res:* Quantum mechanical calculations of electronic spectra of molecules; structure of molecules. *Mailing Add:* Dept Natural Sci Univ of Mich Dearborn MI 48128

TAI, KING LIEN, b Shanghai, China, Feb 24, 40; US citizen; m 67; c 3. METALLURGY, PHYSICS. *Educ:* Stevens Inst Technol, MS, 67, PhD(metall), 76. *Prof Exp:* Assoc mem tech staff, 67-76, MEM TECH STAFF THIN FILMS, BELL LABS, 76- *Res:* Inorganic resist systems; fine line lithography; electron beam lithography; electromigration in thin films; diffusion in thin films. *Mailing Add:* Bell Labs 600 Mountain Ave Murray Hill NJ 07974

TAI, PETER YAO-PO, b Chutung, Taiwan, July 6, 37; US citizen; m 64; c 2. PLANT BREEDING. *Educ:* Nat Taiwan Univ, BS, 61; Tex A&M Univ, MS, 66; Okla State Univ, PhD(crop sci), 72. *Prof Exp:* Res assoc, 72-75, instr plant breeding, Agr Exp Sta, Univ Ga, 75-77; RES GENETICIST PLANT, SCI & EDUC ADMIN-AGR RES, USDA, 77- *Mem:* Am Soc Agron; Crop Sci Soc Am; Am Soc Sugar Cane Technol; AAAS. *Res:* Development of new breeding lines of sugarcane (Saccharum sp), improvement of cold tolerance in sugarcane and selection methodology. *Mailing Add:* Sugarcane Field Station Star Rte Box 8 Canal Point FL 33438

TAI, WILLIAM, b Yangzhow, China, Mar 9, 34; m 63; c 4. CYTOGENETICS, CROP BREEDING. *Educ:* Nat Chung Hsing Univ, BSc, 56; Utah State Univ, MSc, 64; Univ Utah, PhD(genetics), 67. *Prof Exp:* NIH fel biol sci, Stanford Univ, 67-69; asst prof bot & plant path, Mich State Univ, 69-72, assoc prof, 72-78, prof, 79-82; PROF PLANT SCI, UNIV MAN, 82- *Concurrent Pos:* Vis prof, Nat Chung-Hsing Univ, 75-76; vis prof, Genetic Inst, Acad Sinica, Beijing, China; hon prof, Acad Sci China. *Mem:* AAAS; Am Inst Biol Sci; Am Soc Cell Biol; Am Soc Agron; Crop Sci Soc Am. *Res:* Plant cytogenetics; cytotaxonomy; plant breeding. *Mailing Add:* Dept Plant Sci Univ Manitoba Winnipeg MB R3T 2N2 Can

TAIBLESON, MITCHELL H, b Oak Park, Ill, Dec 31, 29; m 49; c 3. MATHEMATICS. *Educ:* Univ Chicago, SM, 60, PhD(math), 62. *Prof Exp:* From asst prof to assoc prof math, 62-69, chmn dept, 70-73, res prof, Dept Psychiat, Med Sch, 73-75, PROF MATH, WASHINGTON UNIV, 69- *Concurrent Pos:* Mem, Inst Advan Study, 66-67. *Mem:* Am Math Soc; Math Asn Am. *Res:* Several dimensional harmonic analysis on real and local fields; Lipschitz and potential spaces; special functions; mathematical models in medical and behavioral science. *Mailing Add:* Dept of Math Washington Univ St Louis MO 63130

TAICHMAN, NORTON STANLEY, b Toronto, Ont, May 27, 36; m 58; c 5. PATHOLOGY, IMMUNOLOGY. *Educ:* Univ Toronto, DDS, 61, PhD(immunopath), 67; Harvard Univ, dipl periodont, 64. *Prof Exp:* Assoc dent, Fac Dent, Univ Toronto, 65-68, from lectr to asst prof path, 67-71; PROF PATH & CHMN DEPT, SCH DENT MED, UNIV PA, 72- *Concurrent Pos:* Assoc prof dent, Fac Dent, Univ Toronto, 68-72, assoc prof path, 71-72, mem, Inst Immunol, 70-72. *Mem:* Am Soc Exp Path; Am Soc Microbiol; Reticuloendothel Soc; Int Asn Dent Res. *Res:* Inflammation, immunopathology, periodontal disease; immune deficiency syndromes; polymorphonuclear-leukocytes; platelets; lysosomes. *Mailing Add:* Dept Path Univ Pa Sch Dent Med Philadelphia PA 19174

TAIGANIDES, E PAUL, agricultural & environmental engineering, see previous edition

TAIGEN, THEODORE LEE, b Seattle, Wash, Nov 22, 52; m 73; c 2. PHYSIOLOGICAL ECOLOGY. *Educ:* Colo State Univ, BS, 76, MS, 78; Cornell Univ, PhD(ecol), 81. *Prof Exp:* ASST PROF ECOL, UNIV CONN, 81- *Mem:* Am Soc Ichthyologists & Herpetologists; Am Ornithologists Union; Am Soc Zoologists; Ecol Soc Am; Sigma Xi. *Res:* Ecological and behavioral correlates of metabolic characteristics of terrestrial vertebrates; physiological variables, including resting and activity metabolism, are analyzed for their association with foraging strategies, habitat selection, predator avoidance mechanisms and modes of locomotion. *Mailing Add:* Ecol Sect Biol Sci Group Univ Conn Storrs CT 06268

TAIMUTY, SAMUEL ISAAC, b West Newton, Pa, Dec 20, 17; m 53; c 2. PHYSICS. *Educ:* Carnegie Inst Technol, BS, 40; Univ Southern Calif, PhD(physics), 51. *Prof Exp:* Asst res physicist, Am Soc Heat & Ventilating Eng Lab, 40-42; physicist, Philadelphia Naval Shipyard, 42-44 & Long Beach Naval Shipyard, 44-46; sr physicist, US Naval Radiol Defense Lab, 50-52 & Stanford Res Inst, 52-72; SR PHYSICIST, LOCKHEED MISSILES & SPACE CO, 72- *Mem:* Am Phys Soc; Sigma Xi. *Res:* Heat transmission; magnetism; nuclear and radiation physics; radiation effects in solids; radiation dosimetry; industrial applications of radiation, ferroelectricity, thin films and organic dielectrics. *Mailing Add:* 3346 Kenneth Dr Palo Alto CA 94303

TAINITER, MELVIN, b Brooklyn, NY, Apr 24, 36; m 59; c 3. APPLIED MATHEMATICS. *Educ:* Brooklyn Col, BS, 58; NY Univ, MS, 61; Johns Hopkins Univ, PhD(statist), 65. *Prof Exp:* Mathematician, Thomas J Watson Res Ctr, Int Bus Mach Corp, 59-63; res assoc appl math, Carlyle Barton Lab, Johns Hopkins Univ, 63-65; mathematician, Brookhaven Nat Lab, 65-72; ASSOC PROF MATH, CITY COL NEW YORK, 72- *Mem:* Math Asn Am; Soc Indust & Appl Math; Am Math Soc. *Res:* Algebraic combinatorial theory; sequential decision theory. *Mailing Add:* Dept of Math City Col of New York New York NY 10031

TAINTER, FRANKLIN HUGH, forest pathology, see previous edition

TAIT, JAMES SIMPSON, b Charlottetown, PEI, Feb 25, 30; m 58; c 2. FISH BIOLOGY. *Educ:* Dalhousie Univ, BSc, 50, MSc, 52; Univ Toronto, PhD(zool), 59. *Prof Exp:* Res scientist, Res Br, Ont Dept Lands & Forests, 58-64; asst prof biol, 64-70, ASSOC PROF BIOL, YORK UNIV, 70- *Concurrent Pos:* Consult, Res Br, Ont Dept Lands & Forests, 64-70. *Mem:* Am Fisheries Soc; Can Soc Zool. *Res:* Physiology of fish, particularly temperature and depth relations and swimbladder function; selective breeding of salmonid hybrids; effects of pesticides on fish. *Mailing Add:* Dept of Biol York Univ Downsview ON M3J 1P3 Can

TAIT, JOHN CHARLES, b Vancouver, BC, Sept 23, 45. NUCLEAR WASTE MANAGEMENT. *Educ:* Univ BC, BSc, 67, PhD(chem), 74. *Prof Exp:* Fel phys chem, Nat Res Coun Can, 74-77; res assoc, Univ BC, 77-78; RES CHEMIST PHYS CHEM, ATOMIC ENERGY CAN, LTD, 78- *Res:* Kinetics and dissolution properties of glasses for nuclear waste disposal; surface adsorption; surface analysis by secondary ion mass spectrometry, electros spectroscopy for chemical analysis; glass melt viscosity; hydrothermal alteration of glasses. *Mailing Add:* Atomic Energy Can Ltd Whiteshell Nuclear Res Estab Pinawa MB R0E 1L0 Can

TAIT, KEVIN S, b New York, NY, Nov 24, 33; m 59; c 4. APPLIED MATHEMATICS. *Educ:* Princeton Univ, AB, 55; Harvard Univ, PhD(appl math), 65. *Prof Exp:* Res staff mem, Sperry Rand Res Ctr, 64-67; assoc prof math, Boston Univ, 67-74; mem staff, Aerodyne Res, 74-75; STAFF ANALYST, THE ANAL SCI CORP, 75- *Mem:* Soc Indust & Appl Math. *Res:* Optimal control and estimation; mathematical programming; numerical analysis. *Mailing Add:* The Anal Sci Corp 1 Jacob Way Reading MA 01867

TAIT, ROBERT MALCOLM, agriculture, animal husbandry, see previous edition

TAIT, WILLIAM CHARLES, b Waterloo, Iowa, Feb 9, 32; m 54; c 4. THEORETICAL SOLID STATE PHYSICS. *Educ:* Wabash Col, BA, 54; Cornell Univ, MA, 58; Purdue Univ, PhD, 62. *Prof Exp:* Teaching asst, Cornell Univ, 54-58; physicist, Res Lab, Bendix Corp, 58; instr physics, Wabash Col, 58-61; sr physicist, Cent Res, 62-66, res specialist, 67-68, supvr, 69-70, mgr cent res, 71-72, MGR DUPLICATING PROD, MINN MINING & MFG CO, 72- *Mem:* Am Phys Soc. *Res:* Solid state and quantum field theory; semiconductor lasers; photoconductors; electrophotography. *Mailing Add:* 14452 N 57th St Stillwater MN 55082

TAIZ, LINCOLN, b Philadelphia, Pa, Nov 5, 42; m 63; c 1. PLANT PHYSIOLOGY. *Educ:* Univ Utah, BS, 67; Univ Calif, Berkeley, PhD(bot), 71. *Prof Exp:* Actg asst prof bot, Univ Calif, Berkeley, 72-73; ASST PROF BIOL, UNIV CALIF, SANTA CRUZ, 73- *Concurrent Pos:* NSF grant, 75. *Mem:* Am Soc Plant Physiologists; Bot Soc Am. *Res:* The role of cell wall metabolism in plant growth and secretion; DNA metabolism in nondividing plant cells. *Mailing Add:* Dept Biol Univ Calif Santa Cruz CA 95064

TAJBL, DANIEL G(EORGE), chemical engineering, see previous edition

TAJIMA, TOSHIKI, b Ngoya, Japan, Jan 18, 48; c 2. PLASMAS PHYSICS. *Educ:* Univ Tokyo, BS, 71, MS, 73; Univ Calif, Irvine, PhD(physics), 75. *Prof Exp:* Asst res physicist, Univ Calif, Los Angeles, 76-80, assoc res physicist, 80; ASST PROF PHYSICS, UNIV TEX, AUSTIN, 80- *Concurrent Pos:* Consult, TRW, Inc, 78-81, Jaycor, 78-79, Toshiba, 79-80 & Western Res Inc, 78-; prin investr, NSF, 81-; mem, Int Sci Radio Union/Nat Security Coun; fel, Japan Soc Prom Sci. *Mem:* Am Physiol Soc; Am Geophys Union. *Res:* Physics of nuclear fusion, plasma physics, astrophysics and particle accelerators by means of analysis and computer simulations. *Mailing Add:* Physics Dept Univ Tex Austin TX 78712

TAKAGI, SHOZO, b Nishinomiya, Japan, Apr 2, 43; m 67; c 2. CRYSTALLOGRAPHY. *Educ:* Kwansei Gakuin Univ, BSc, 66; Univ Pittsburgh, PhD(crystallog), 71. *Prof Exp:* Res assoc chem, Vanderbilt Univ, 71-75; res assoc, Dept Chem, Brookhaven Nat Lab, 75-78; RES ASSOC, AM DENT ASN HEALTH FOUND RES UNIT, NAT BUR STANDARDS, 78- *Mem:* Int Asn Dent Res; Am Crystallog Asn. *Res:* To determine structures of components of importance to dental health by x-ray and neutron diffraction techniques. *Mailing Add:* Am Dent Asn Health Found Res Unit Nat Bur Standards Washington DC 20234

TAKAGI, SHUNSUKE, b Fukuoka, Japan, Mar 22, 19; m 43; c 3. THERMAL PHYSICS. *Educ:* Univ Tokyo, BAgE, 43; Hokkaido Univ, DSc(physics), 56. *Prof Exp:* Asst prof math & mech, Tokyo Univ Agr & Technol, 47-60; contract scientist, 60-66, PHYS RES SCIENTIST, US ARMY COLD REGIONS RES & ENG LAB, 66- *Concurrent Pos:* Army Res Off-Durham grant, 71-73. *Honors & Awards:* Agr Eng Soc Japan Award, 59. *Mem:* Am Soc Civil Eng; Am Acad Mechanics; Soc Eng Sci; Japan Soc Civil Eng. *Res:* Mathematical analysis of frost heaving; mathematical analysis of ice mechanics. *Mailing Add:* 17 Dresden Rd Hanover NH 03755

TAKAHASHI, AKIO, b Tokyo, Japan, Apr 15, 31; m 64; c 4. POLYMER CHEMISTRY. *Educ:* Tokyo Col Sci, BS, 57; Tokyo Inst Technol, MS, 60, PhD(polymer chem), 63. *Prof Exp:* Sr chemist, Mitsui Chem Indust, Inc, 63-65; sr chemist, Gaylord Assocs, Inc, NJ, 65-67, sect mgr, 67-70; res assoc polymer chem, Hooker Chem & Plastics Co, 70-73, sr res assoc, 73-75, scientist & discipline/prog leader, 75-78; RES MGR, AM CAN CO, 78- *Mem:* Am Chem Soc; Japanese Soc Polymer Sci. *Res:* Polymer-organic chemistry; polymerization by free radical, Ziegler-Natta and ionic catalysts; polymerization through charge-transfer complexes; polybutadiene; polyvinyl chloride; polyethers; graft copolymers. *Mailing Add:* Box 277 Comfort Rd Solebury PA 18963

TAKAHASHI, ELLEN SHIZUKO, b Berkeley, Calif. PHYSIOLOGICAL OPTICS, OPTOMETRY. *Educ:* Univ Calif, Berkeley, BS, 52, MOpt, 53, PhD(physiol optics), 68. *Prof Exp:* Optometrist in pvt pract, 53-56; optometrist orthoptics, Stanford Univ Hosps, 56-62; clin instr & actg asst prof optom, Univ Calif, 62-67; NIH fel visual neurophysiol, Australian Nat Univ, 68-70; asst prof, 70-72, assoc prof, 72-81 dir grad studies, Sch Optom, 74-76, PROF PHYSIOL OPTICS, UNIV ALA, 81- *Mem:* Am Acad Optom; Asn Res Vision & Ophthal; Soc Neurosci. *Res:* Visual neurophysiology and anatomy; binocular vision. *Mailing Add:* Sch Optom Med Ctr Univ Ala Birmingham AL 35294

TAKAHASHI, FRANCOIS IWAO, b Hakodate, Japan, Dec 12, 25; Can citizen; div; c 2. MICROBIAL GENETICS. *Educ:* Hakodate Fisheries Col, BA, 45; Kyushu Univ, MAS, 49; Univ Montreal, PhD(bact), 55. *Prof Exp:* Fel microbiol, Nat Res Coun Can, 56-58; res officer, Microbiol Res Inst, Can Dept Agr, Ottawa, 58-60, head genetics & taxon sect, 60-63; assoc prof biol, 64-67, PROF BIOL, McMASTER UNIV, 67- *Mem:* Am Soc Microbiol; Can Soc Microbiol; Can Soc Biochem. *Res:* Molecular biology of bacterial sporulation; transducing bacteriophage. *Mailing Add:* Dept of Biol McMaster Univ Hamilton ON L8S 4K1 Can

TAKAHASHI, HIRONORI, b Tokyo, Japan, June 5, 42. PLASMA PHYSICS. *Educ:* Keio Univ, Japan, BEng, 65; Mass Inst Technol, MS, 67, DSc(aeronaut & astronaut), 70. *Prof Exp:* Fel plasma physics, Univ Stuttgart, 71-72, guest lectr, 72-73; res assoc, Plasma Physics Lab, Princeton Univ, 73-75, res staff mem, 75-79; GROUP LEADER & CO-PRIN INVESTR, NAT MAGNETIC LAB, MASS INST TECHNOL, 79- *Res:* Plasma physics in connection with controlled thermonuclear fusion research; plasma waves, wave heating, tokamaks. *Mailing Add:* Francis Bitter Nat Magnetic Lab Mass Inst of Technol Cambridge MA 02139

TAKAHASHI, MARK T, b Holtville, Calif, Feb 26, 36; m 61; c 2. PHYSICAL BIOCHEMISTRY. *Educ:* Oberlin Col, BA, 58; Univ Wis-Madison, PhD(phys chem), 63. *Prof Exp:* Res biochemist, Battelle Mem Inst, 64-67; asst prof, 70-77, ASSOC PROF PHYSIOL, RUTGERS MED SCH, COL MED & DENT NJ, 77- *Concurrent Pos:* NIH fel, Univ Mass, Amherst, 67-70. *Mem:* AAAS; Biophys Soc; Am Soc Biol Chemists; Am Chem Soc. *Res:* Physical enzymology; membranes. *Mailing Add:* Dept of Physiol Rutgers Med Sch Piscataway NJ 08854

TAKAHASHI, PATRICK KENJI, b Honolulu, Hawaii, Sept 6, 40; m 62. CHEMICAL ENGINEERING, ENERGY. *Educ:* Stanford Univ, BS, 62; La State Univ, Baton Rouge, MS, 69, PhD(chem eng), 71. *Prof Exp:* Sugar processing engr, C Brewer, 62-67; proj engr computerized optimization, Hawaiian Sugar Planters Asn, 67-68; asst prof eng, 71-75, ASSOC PROF CIVIL ENG, UNIV HAWAII, 75-, ACTG ASSOC DEAN ENG, 76-, ACAD ASST CHANCELLOR, 78- *Concurrent Pos:* Consult, Lawrence Livermore Lab, Gen Tel & Electronics Corp, 77-; spec asst energy to Sen Spark Matsunaga, 79-82. *Mem:* Am Chem Soc; Am Inst Chem Engrs. *Res:* Energy (biomass, geothermal, wind, solar); laser applications. *Mailing Add:* Dept Civil Eng Univ Hawaii Honolulu HI 96822

TAKAHASHI, TARO, b Tokyo, Japan, Nov 15, 30; US citizen; m 66; c 2. GEOCHEMISTRY, GEOPHYSICS. *Educ:* Univ Tokyo, BEng, 53; Columbia Univ, PhD(geol), 57. *Prof Exp:* Res scientist, Lamont Geol Observ, 57-59, res assoc, 59-77, ADJ PROF DEPT GEOL SCI, COLUMBIA UNIV, 77-, SR RES ASSOC, LAMONT-DOHERTY GEOL OBSERV, 77-, ASSOC DIR, 81- *Concurrent Pos:* Lectr, Queens Col, NY, 58; res chemist, Scripps Inst Oceanog, Univ Calif, 59; asst prof, State Univ NY Col Ceramics, Alfred, 59-62, vis prof, 63; assoc prof, Univ Rochester, 62-70, prof, 70; vis asst prof, Columbia Univ, 66; vis assoc prof, Calif Inst Technol, 71; distinguished prof, Queens Col, NY, 71-77. *Mem:* Am Geophys Union; Geol Soc Am; Geochemical Soc (secy, 81-). *Res:* Thermodynamic and physical properties of metal oxides under extremely high pressures and temperatures; geochemistry of carbon dioxid- in the ocean atmosphere system; thermodynamics of ore forming minerals. *Mailing Add:* 350 Hennessy St Haworth NJ 07641

TAKAHASHI, YASUNDO, b Nagoya-shi, Japan, June 12, 12; m 39; c 1. MECHANICAL ENGINEERING. *Educ:* Tokyo Imp Univ, BSc, 35; Univ Tokyo, DrEng, 46. *Hon Degrees:* Dr, Nat Polytech Inst, France, 78. *Prof Exp:* Asst engr, Govt Rwys, Japan, 35-37; asst prof heat power systs, Yokohama Tech Col, 37-40 & Nagoya Imp Univ, 40-44; from asst prof to prof automatic control, Univ Tokyo, 44-58; vis prof, 55-56, PROF AUTOMATIC CONTROL, UNIV CALIF, BERKELEY, 58- *Concurrent Pos:* Fulbright res scholar & vis fel, Mass Inst Technol, 54-55; consult, Mitsubishi Heavy Industs, Japan, 56-57, Ajinomoto Co, 56-57 & Nucleonics Div, Aerojet Gen Corp, 59-60; vis prof, Polytech Inst Grenoble, France, 65 & 70, Tokyo Inst Technol, 65 & 70, Nat Polytech Inst, Mex, 72, 75 & 78, Univ LaPlata, Arg, 73 & Keio Univ, Japan, 77. *Mem:* Am Soc Mech Engrs; Instrument Soc Am; Japanese Soc Mech Engrs; Japanese Instrument Soc. *Res:* Theory of automatic control; dynamical systems design; digital control algorithms. *Mailing Add:* Dept of Mech Eng Rm 5118 EH Univ of Calif Berkeley CA 94720

TAKAHASHI, YASUSHI, b Osaka, Japan, Dec 12, 24; m 59; c 2. THEORETICAL PHYSICS. *Educ:* Nagoya Univ, BSc, 51, DSc(physics), 54. *Prof Exp:* Nat Res Coun Can fel, 54-55; res assoc physics, Iowa State Univ, 55-57; res scholar, Dublin Inst Advan Studies, 57, from asst prof to prof, 57-68; PROF PHYSICS, UNIV ALTA, 68-, DIR THEORET PHYSICS INST, 69- *Mem:* Am Phys Soc; Royal Irish Acad. *Res:* Quantization of relativistic fields; quantum electrodynamics and field theory; many-body theory. *Mailing Add:* Dept of Physics Univ of Alta Edmonton AB T6G 2S1 Can

TAKANO, MASAHARU, b Tainan, Taiwan, Jan 20, 35; nat US; m 65; c 3. PHYSICAL CHEMISTRY, APPLIED PHYSICS. *Educ:* Hokkaido Univ, BSc, 57; Univ Tokyo, MSc, 59, DrSc(rheol), 63. *Prof Exp:* Nat Res Coun fel, McGill Univ, 63-65, fel, 65-67; res specialist, Corp Res Dept, 67-75, SR RES SPECIALIST & TECH TRANSLATOR, NUTRIT CHEM DIV, MONSANTO INDUST CHEM CO, 75- *Mem:* Soc Rheol; Am Chem Soc; AAAS; Am Phys Soc; Am Inst Chemists. *Res:* Rheology and physical chemistry of polymers and disperse systems; polymer solid physics and commposites technologies; industrial process technologies; crystallization, solvent extraction and reaction kinetics. *Mailing Add:* Monsanto Indust Chem Co 800 N Lindbergh Blvd St Louis MO 63167

TAKARO, TIMOTHY, b Budapest, Hungary, Aug 30, 20; US citizen; m 49; c 4. MEDICINE. *Educ:* Dartmouth Col, BA, 41; NY Univ, MD, 43; Univ Minn, MS, 50. *Prof Exp:* Dir surg, Wanless Tuberc Sanatorium, India, Presby Bd Foreign Missions, 54-57; dir res & resident educ, 57-60, chief cardiovasc surg sect, 60-62, CHIEF SURG SERV, VET ADMIN MED CTR, 62-, SR PHYSICIAN, 71- *Concurrent Pos:* Exchange scientist, US-USSR Exchange Agreement, Moscow, 62; co-chmn, Vet Admin Coop Study of Surg for Coronary Arterial Occlusive Dis, 68-; assoc clin prof surg, Duke Univ Med Ctr, 68-80, clin prof, 80-; chmn, Cardiac Surg Adv Group, Vet Admin Cent Off, 70-; assoc ed, Annals Thoracic Surg, 70- *Mem:* Fel Am Col Surgeons; Am Asn Thoracic Surg; Soc Thoracic Surgeons; Soc Vascular Surg. *Res:* Pulmonary emphysema; coronary arterial occlusive disease. *Mailing Add:* Vet Admin Med Ctr Asheville NC 28805

TAKASHIMA, SHIRO, b Japan, May 12, 23; m 53; c 2. PHYSICAL BIOCHEMISTRY, NEUROPHYSIOLOGY. *Educ:* Univ Tokyo, BS, 47, PhD(biochem), 55. *Prof Exp:* Res fel phys chem, Univ Minn, 55-57; res assoc biomed eng, Univ Pa, 57-59; from assoc prof to prof protein res, Osaka Univ, 59-62; vis scientist, Walter Reed Med Ctr, 62-63; res assoc biomed eng, 63-64, asst prof, 64-70, assoc prof, 70-76, PROF BIOMED ENG, UNIV PA, 76- *Mem:* Biophys Soc; Inst Elec & Electronics Engrs; NY Acad Sci; AAAS. *Res:* Dielectric relaxation of desoxyribonucleic acid; synthetic polynucleotides; polyamino acids and proteins; theory of dielectric relaxation; quantum chemistry of hydrogen bonds; electrical properties of excitable membranes; brain function. *Mailing Add:* Dept of Bioeng D2 Univ of Pa Philadelphia PA 19104

TAKASUGI, MITSUO, b Tacoma, Wash, Jan 28, 28; m 54; c 4. CANCER, IMMUNOLOGY. *Educ:* Univ Calif, Los Angeles, BA, 52, PhD(immunogenetics), 68; Univ Ore, MS, 62. *Prof Exp:* Sci teacher, Los Angeles City Schs, 53-64; fel, 53-64; Dept Tumor Biol, Karolinska Inst, Stockholm, Sweden, 68-69; RESEARCHER CANCER, DEPT SURG, UNIV CALIFORNIA, LOS ANGELES, 69- *Mem:* AAAS; Am Asn Cancer Res; Am Asn Immunologists; Transplantation Soc. *Res:* Investigations into the cellular and humoral immune response to cancer. *Mailing Add:* Dept of Surg Sch Med Univ of Calif Los Angeles CA 90024

TAKATS, STEPHEN TIBOR, b West Englewood, NJ, May 24, 30; m 60; c 3. CYTOLOGY, GENETICS. *Educ:* Cornell Univ, BS, 52; Univ Wis, MS, 54, PhD(genetics), 58. *Prof Exp:* Asst genetics, Univ Wis, 52-55; res collabr & USPHS res fel, Biol Dept, Brookhaven Nat Lab, 57-60; USPHS res fel biochem, Univ Glasgow, 60-61, Med Res Coun grant, 61; from asst prof to assoc prof biol, 61-69, chmn dept, 69-75, PROF BIOL, TEMPLE UNIV, 69- *Mem:* Bot Soc Am; Am Soc Plant Physiol; Genetics Soc Am; Am Soc Cell Biol. *Res:* Biochemical cytology; control of DNA synthesis in plant development. *Mailing Add:* Dept of Biol Temple Univ Philadelphia PA 19122

TAKAYAMA, KUNI, b Wapato, Wash, Feb 28, 32; m 59; c 2. BIOCHEMISTRY, MICROBIOLOGY. *Educ:* Ore State Univ, BS, 56; Univ Idaho, MS, 61, PhD(biochem), 64. *Prof Exp:* NIH grant, Inst Enzyme Res, Univ Wis-Madison, 64-65; proj assoc biochem of mycobact, Vet Admin Hosp, Madison, Wis, 65-67, res chemist, Tuberc Res Lab, 67-71, actg chief chemist, 68-69, chief chemist, 71-74, CHIEF RES CHEMIST, TUBERC RES LAB, VET ADMIN HOSP, MADISON, WIS, 74- *Concurrent Pos:* Proj assoc, Inst Enzyme Res, Univ Wis-Madison, 65-67, asst prof, 67-; NSF grants, Vet Admin Hosp & Univ Wis-Madison, 69-72, NIH grant, 73- *Mem:* AAAS; Am Soc Microbiol; Am Soc Biol Chem; Am Soc Cell Biol; Am Inst Biol Sci. *Res:* Biochemistry of mycobacteria; biosynthesis of mannophospholipids; synthesis of lipids; mode of action of isoniazid. *Mailing Add:* 2500 Overlook Terrace Madison WI 53705

TAKEDA, YASUHIKO, b Nagano, Japan, Mar 16, 27; m 57; c 4. PHYSIOLOGY, CLINICAL PATHOLOGY. *Educ:* Shinshu Univ, 46-48; Chiba Univ, MD, 52; Am Bd Path, dipl, 70. *Prof Exp:* From instr to asst prof, 63-69, assoc prof, 69-78, PROF, MED CTR, UNIV COLO, DENVER, 79- *Concurrent Pos:* Res fel, Div Lab Med, Med Ctr, Univ Colo, 58-60; Nat Res Coun Can res fel, McGill Univ, 60-63; Colo Heart Asn sr res fel med, Med Ctr, Univ Colo, Denver, 63-64, Am Heart Asn advan res fel, 64-66; NIH career develop award, 67-72; mem coun thrombosis, Am Heart Asn. *Mem:* AAAS; Am Physiol Soc; Am Soc Clin Path; Int Soc Thrombosis & Hemorrhagic Dis; Col Am Pathologists. *Res:* Regulation of plasma protein metabolism in health and disease; dynamics of thrombus formation and dissolution. *Mailing Add:* Dept of Med Univ of Colo Med Ctr Denver CO 80220

TAKEMORI, AKIRA EDDIE, b Stockton, Calif, Dec 9, 29; m 58; c 2. PHARMACOLOGY. *Educ:* Univ Calif, AB, 51, MS, 53; Univ Wis, PhD(pharmacol), 58. *Prof Exp:* Res asst pharmacol, Univ Calif, 51-53; res asst, Univ Wis, 55-57, Am Cancer Soc fel, Enzyme Inst, 58-59; instr pharmacol, State Univ NY Upstate Med Ctr, 59-61, asst prof, 61-63; from asst prof to assoc prof, 63-69, PROF PHARMACOL, HEALTH SCI CTR, UNIV MINN, MINNEAPOLIS, 69- *Concurrent Pos:* Mem pharmacol A study sect, NIH, 70-74. *Honors & Awards:* Vis Scientist Award, Japan Soc Promotion Sci, 71; Alan Gregg Fellow Med Educ, China Med Bd NY, 71. *Mem:* AAAS; Am Soc Pharmacol & Exp Therapeut; Soc Exp Biol & Med; Am Asn Univ Prof; Am Chem Soc. *Res:* Mechanism of action of narcotic analgesics and narcotic antagonists; transport of drugs to the central nervous system. *Mailing Add:* Dept Pharmacol 105 Millard Hall Univ Minn Minneapolis MN 55455

TAKEMOTO, DOLORES JEAN, b Indianapolis, Ind, May 5, 49; m 73; c 1. CYCLIC NUCLEOTIDE METABOLISM, DRUG DEVELOPMENT. *Educ:* Ball State Univ, BS, 71; Colo State Univ, MS, 73; Univ Southern Calif, PhD(molecular biol), 79. *Prof Exp:* Sr res technician physiol, Colo State Univ, 73-75; asst molecular biol, Univ Southern Calif, 75-79; res assoc, 79-81, VIS ASST PROF BIOCHEM, KANS STATE UNIV, 81- *Concurrent Pos:* Prin investr, Nat Cancer Inst grant, 80-83; mem, Kans State Ctr Basic Cancer Res, 80- *Mem:* Asn Res Vision & Opthalmol. *Res:* Cyclic nucleotide metabolism in leukemic vs normal human lymphocytes; anti-leukemic drugs aimed at controlling cyclic nucleotide levels in leukemic cells. *Mailing Add:* Dept Biochem Willard Hall Kans State Univ Manhattan KS 66506

TAKEMOTO, JON YUTAKA, b Chicago, Ill, Sept 13, 44; m 73; c 2. MICROBIAL PHYSIOLOGY, BIOCHEMISTRY. *Educ:* Univ Calif, Los Angeles, BS, 67, PhD(microbiol), 73. *Prof Exp:* Fel biol & Maria Moor Cabot fel, Harvard Univ, 73-74; asst prof, 75-80, ASSOC PROF BIOL, UTAH STATE UNIV, 80- *Concurrent Pos:* NIH fel, Harvard Univ, 74; staff mem, Utah Agr Exp Sta, Logan, 75-; prin investr, NSF grants, Utah State Univ, 76- *Mem:* Am Soc Microbiol; Sigma Xi; AAAS. *Res:* Structure, function and assembly of photosynthetic prokaryotic membranes; chlorophyll biosynthesis. *Mailing Add:* Dept Biol UMC 3 Utah State Univ Logan UT 84322

TAKEMOTO, KENNETH KANAME, b Hawaii, Sept 26, 20; m 51; c 2. VIROLOGY. *Educ:* George Washington Univ, BS, 49, MS, 50, PhD(virol), 53. *Prof Exp:* USPHS res fel virol, Nat Microbiol Inst, 53-54; VIROLOGIST, NAT INST ALLERGY & INFECTIOUS DIS, 54- *Mem:* Am Soc Microbiol; Am Asn Immunologists; Soc Exp Biol & Med. *Res:* Anti-viral substances; tumor viruses; cell biology. *Mailing Add:* Nat Inst Allergy & Infect Dis Bethesda MD 20014

TAKEMURA, KAZ HORACE, b San Juan Bautista, Calif, Nov 2, 21; m 59; c 7. ORGANIC CHEMISTRY. *Educ:* Univ Calif, Los Angeles, BS, 47; Univ Ill, MS, 48, PhD(chem), 50. *Prof Exp:* Res fel chem, Ohio State Univ, 50-52; res chemist, Univ Calif, Berkeley, 52-53; chemist southern regional res lab, USDA, La, 53-56; asst prof chem, Loyola Univ, La, 56-58 & Univ Tulsa, 58-59; chemist, Sahyun Labs, 59-60; from asst prof to assoc prof chem, 60-66, chmn dept, 70-73, PROF CHEM, CREIGHTON UNIV, 66- *Mem:* Chem Soc London; Am Chem Soc. *Res:* Organic synthesis and mechanisms. *Mailing Add:* Dept of Chem Creighton Univ Omaha NE 68178

TAKESAKI, MASAMICHI, b Sendai, Japan, July 18, 33; m 59; c 1. MATHEMATICS. *Educ:* Tohoku Univ, Japan, MS, 58, DSc(math), 65. *Prof Exp:* Res asst math, Tokyo Inst Technol, 58-63; assoc prof, Tohoku Univ, Japan, 63-70; PROF MATH, UNIV CALIF, LOS ANGELES, 70- *Concurrent Pos:* Fel, Sakkokai Found, 65-68; vis assoc prof, Univ Pa, 68-69 & Univ Calif, Los Angeles, 69-70; vis prof, Univ Aix-Marseille, 73-74 & Univ Bielefeld, 75-76. *Mem:* Am Math Soc; Math Soc Japan; Math Soc France. *Res:* Functional analysis; operator algebras; mathematical physics. *Mailing Add:* Dept of Math Univ of Calif Los Angeles CA 90024

TAKESHITA, TSUNEICHI, b Tokyo, Japan, Sept 13, 26; m 56; c 3. PHYSICAL ORGANIC CHEMISTRY. *Educ:* Waseda Univ, Japan, BSEng, 50; Univ Del, PhD(org chem), 62. *Prof Exp:* Chemist, Cent Res Inst, Japan Monopoly Corp, Tokyo, 50-64; assoc prof catalysis, Res Inst Catalysis, Hokkaido Univ, 64-66; chemist, Elastomer Chem Dept, E I Du Pont de Nemours & Co, Inc, Wilmington, 66-80. *Mem:* Am Chem Soc; NY Acad Sci; Chem Soc Japan; Sigma Xi. *Res:* Catalytic studies in organic chemistry; polymer chemistry. *Mailing Add:* 5 Hillock Ln Chadds Ford PA 19317

TAKETA, FUMITO, b Waimea Kauai, Hawaii, Mar 10, 26. BIOCHEMISTRY. *Educ:* Washington Univ, AB, 50; Univ Wis, PhD(biochem), 57. *Prof Exp:* Proj asst biochem, Univ Wis, 56-57, proj assoc, 57-58; from instr to assoc prof, Marquette Univ, 58-70; assoc prof, 70-72, PROF BIOCHEM, MED COL WIS, 72- *Concurrent Pos:* Fogarty sr int fel & vis prof biochem, King's Col, Univ London, 75-76. *Mem:* AAAS; Am Chem Soc; Am Soc Biol Chemists. *Res:* Protein and sulfhydryl chemistry; development of red blood cell; biosynthesis, structure and function of hemoglobin; metabolic and molecular control mechanisms. *Mailing Add:* Med Col Wis 8701 Watertown Plank Rd Milwaukee WI 53226

TAKETO, MAKOTO, b Ishikawa, Japan, July 8, 48; m 78. EMBRYOLOGY, GENETICS. *Educ:* Kyoto Univ, MD, 73, PhD(biochem), 78. *Prof Exp:* Assoc molecular biol, Rockefeller Univ, 78-81; FEL DEVELOP BIOL, ROCH INST MOLECULAR BIOL, 81- *Res:* Cell biology of embryonal carcinoma; molecular biology of gene expression control. *Mailing Add:* Dept Cell Biol Roche Inst Molecular Biol Nutley NJ 07110

TAKETOMO, YASUHIKO, b Tokyo, Japan; US citizen; m; c 2. PSYCHIATRY. *Educ:* First Col, Tokyo, BA, 42; Osaka Univ, MD, 45, DMedSc, 49; Columbia Univ, cert psychoanal med, 59; Univ State New York, MD, 81. *Prof Exp:* Spec res fel, Ministry Educ, Japanese Govt, Med Sch, Osaka Univ, 45-47, asst biochem & neuropsychiat, 47-50; asst resident neuropsychiat, Albany Med Col, 50-51; resident/asst res psychiatrist, Worcester State Hosp, 51-52; res psychiatrist/sr res scientist, Res Facil, Rockland State Hosp, 52-64; res assoc neurol & psychiat, St Vincent's Hosp & Med Ctr, 64-67; asst prof psychiat, New York Med Col, 68-69; asst prof, 70-73, assoc prof psychiat, 73-77, ASSOC CLIN PROF, ALBERT EINSTEIN COL MED, 77-; SR PHYCHIATRIST & ASSOC DIR, ALBERT EINSTEIN PSYCHIAT RESIDENCY PROG, BRONX PSYCHIAT CTR, 79- *Concurrent Pos:* Garioa scholar, US State Dept, Albany Med Col & Worcester State Hosp, 50-52; from res asst to res assoc, Col Physicians & Surgeons, Columbia Univ, 52-64; lectr, Med Sch, Osaka Univ, 54; vis scientist, NIH, 56; assoc, New York Sch Psychiat, 62-67; New York City Health Res Coun career scientist award, St Vincent's Hosp & New York Med Col, 64-69; mem acad fac, State Conn Dept Ment Health, 65-67; symp assoc, Ctr Res Math, Morphol & Psychol, 67-73; consult, Asn for Help of Retarded Children, 73-76; consult, Sch Med, Uniformed Serv Univ, 78. *Mem:* Am Psychiat Asn; fel Am Acad Psychoanal; Asn Psychoanal Med; Am Psychoanal Asn. *Res:* Psychopathology and treatment of psychiatric disorders of mental retardation; communicational behavior; cognitive and semiotic psychiatry; phenomenology of adaptational and existential crises; methodology of psychiatric research, especially the issue of temporality; transcultural psychiatry. *Mailing Add:* Dept of Psychiat Albert Einstein Col Med Bronx NY 10461

TAKEUCHI, KENJI, b Tokyo, Japan, Dec 11, 34; m 64; c 3. ENGINEERING SCIENCE, PHYSICS. *Educ:* Tokyo Inst Technol, BS, 58; Univ Mich, PhD(nulcear eng), 67. *Prof Exp:* Res assoc, Argonne Nat Lab, 66-70; res fel, Univ Manchester, 70-73; FEL ENGR REACTOR SAFETY, WESTINGHOUSE ELEC CORP, 73- *Mem:* Am Phys Soc; Am Nuclear Soc. *Res:* Analysis methods development of fluid structural interactions for the purpose of nuclear reactor safety evaluation; theoretical nuclear physics. *Mailing Add:* Westinghouse Elec Corp MNC Bay 328 Box 355 Pittsburgh PA 15230

TAKEUTI, GAISI, b Isikawa, Japan, Jan 25, 26; m 47; c 2. MATHEMATICAL LOGIC. *Educ:* Univ Tokyo, PhD(math logic), 56. *Prof Exp:* Instr math, Univ Tokyo, 49-50; from asst prof to prof, Tokyo Univ Educ, 50-66; PROF MATH, UNIV ILL, URBANA, 66- *Concurrent Pos:* Mem, Inst Advan Study, 59-60 & 66-68. *Mem:* Am Math Soc; Asn Symbolic Logic; Math Soc Japan; Japan Asn Philos Sci. *Res:* Proof-theory; set-theory. *Mailing Add:* Dept of Math 375 Altgeld Hall Univ of Ill Urbana IL 61801

TAKMAN, BERTIL HERBERT, b Stockholm, Sweden, Aug 15, 21; m 43; c 5. CHEMISTRY. *Educ:* Univ Stockholm, PhD(org chem), 63. *Prof Exp:* Head chem sect, Astra Pharmaceut Prod, 58-77, INTERNAL CONSULT, ASTRA RES LABS, 77- *Concurrent Pos:* Guest prof med chem, Northeastern Univ, 73- *Mem:* Am Chem Soc; NY Acad Sci. Medicinal and organic chemistry. *Res:* Chemistry of local anesthetics and locl anesthesia; chemical interactions. *Mailing Add:* Astra Res Labs Framingham MA 01701

TAKRURI, HARUN, b Hebron, Palestine, Aug 15, 42; US citizen. PHARMACY. *Educ:* Am Univ Beirut, BSc, 63, Univ Ill, MS, 66, PhD(pharm), 69. *Prof Exp:* Asst prof pharm, Col Pharm, Univ Ill Med Ctr, 69-70; SR PHARMACEUT CHEMIST, ELI LILLY & CO, 70- *Mem:* AAAS; Sigma Xi. *Res:* Colloid and polydisperse systems; mechanisms of drug release and absorption. *Mailing Add:* Res Lab M-745 Eli Lilly & Co Indianapolis IN 46206

TAKVORIAN, KENNETH BEDROSE, b Philadelphia, Pa, Aug 24, 43; m 66; c 2. POLYMER CHEMISTRY, TEXTILE CHEMISTRY. *Educ:* Philadelphia Col Textiles & Sci, BS, 65; Clemson Univ, MS, 67, PhD(chem), 69. *Prof Exp:* RES CHEMIST, TEXTILE RES LAB, E I DU PONT DE NEMOURS & CO, INC, 69- *Mem:* Am Chem Soc; Am Asn Textile Chemists & Colorists. *Res:* All areas of textile chemistry; dyeing, finishing, and textile technology; polymer synthesis and morphology; metal chelates and organic synthesis and mechanisms. *Mailing Add:* 72 Westcliff Rd Wilmington DE 19803

TALAAT, MOSTAFA E(ZZAT), b Cairo, Egypt, May 16, 24; nat US; m 51; c 5. ELECTRICAL ENGINEERING. *Educ:* Cairo Univ, BSc, 46, MSc, 47; Univ Pa, PhD(elec eng), 51. *Prof Exp:* Asst, Mass Inst Technol, 47-49; instr, Univ Pa, 51; proj engr, Westinghouse Elec Corp, 51-52; spec mach designer, Star Kimble Motor Div, Miehle Press, 53; sr res engr, Elliott Co Div, Carrier Corp, 53-59; mgr energy conversion & asst dir eng res, Nuclear Div, Martin-Marietta Corp, 59-64; prof energy conversion, 64-76, PROF MECH ENG, COL ENG, UNIV MD, COLLEGE PARK, 76- *Concurrent Pos:* Consult. *Honors & Awards:* Inst Elec & Electronics Engrs Awards, 56-58; Awards, Martin-Marietta Corp, 60-63. *Mem:* AAAS; Inst Elec & Electronics Engrs; Am Phys Soc; Am Inst Aeronaut & Astronaut. *Res:* Energy conversion, including megnetoplasma-dynamics, thermionic, thermoelectric and fuel cell energy conversion as well as biological power sources. *Mailing Add:* Dept of Mech Eng Univ of Md College Park MD 20742

TALALAY, PAUL, b Berlin, Ger, Mar 31, 23; nat US; m 53; c 4. MOLECULAR PHARMACOLOGY. *Educ:* Mass Inst Technol, SB, 44; Yale Univ, MD, 48. *Hon Degrees:* DSc, Acadia Univ, 74. *Prof Exp:* Intern & asst resident, Surg Serv, Mass Gen Hosp, 48-50; asst prof, Ben May Lab Cancer Res, Univ Chicago, 50-57, from assoc prof to prof, Lab & Dept Biochem & Med, Univ, 57-63; John Jacob Abel prof pharmacol & exp therapeut & dir dept pharmacol, 63-75, JOHN JACOB ABEL DISTINGUISHED SERV PROF PHARMACOL & EXP THERAPEUT, SCH MED, JOHNS HOPKINS UNIV, 75- *Concurrent Pos:* Am Cancer Soc scholar, 54-58; Charles Hayden Found prof, 58-63; mem pharm B study sect, NIH, 63-67; mem, Nat Adv Cancer Coun, 67-71; ed-in-chief, Molecular Pharm, 68-71; mem bd sci consults, Sloan-Kettering Inst, 71-80; mem bd sci adv, Jane Coffin Childs Mem Fund for Med Res, 71-80; Guggenheim Mem fel, 73-74; Am Cancer Soc prof, 77- *Honors & Awards:* Theobold Smith Award, AAAS, 57. *Mem:* Fel AAAS; fel Am Acad Arts & Sci; Am Soc Biol Chemists; Am Soc Pharmacol & Exp Therapeut; Am Soc Clin Invest. *Res:* Molecular pharmacology; biochemistry; metabolism and mechanism of action of steroid hormones; amino acids; conformation and chemoteherapeutic activity; chemoprotection against cancer. *Mailing Add:* Dept Pharmacol Sch Med Johns Hopkins Univ Baltimore MD 21205

TALAMO, BARBARA LISANN, b Washington, DC, May 30, 39; m 58; c 3. NEUROBIOLOGY, BIOCHEMISTRY. *Educ:* Radcliffe Col, AB, 60; Harvard Univ, PhD(biochem), 72. *Prof Exp:* Tutor biochem sci, Harvard Med Sch, 71-74; asst prof neurol & physiol chem, Med Sch, Johns Hopkins Univ, 74-80; ASST PROF NEUROL & PHYSIOL, MED SCH, TUFTS UNIV, 80- *Concurrent Pos:* NSF fel neurobiol, Harvard Med Sch, 72-74; mem study sect, NIH, 79- *Mem:* Soc Neurosci; Am Soc Neurochem; Int Soc Neurochem. *Res:* regulation and mechanism of neurotransmitter sensitivity; developmental regulation of mechanisms of secretion. *Mailing Add:* Dept Neurol Tufts Med Sch 136 Harrison Ave Boston MA 02111

TALASH, ALVIN WESLEY, b Caldwell, Tex, Mar 31, 32; m 54; c 3. PETROLEUM ENGINEERING. *Educ:* Tex A&M Univ, BS, 56, MS, 60, PhD(petrol eng), 65. *Prof Exp:* Assoc res technologist, Tex Petrol Res Comt, Tex A&M Univ, 58-64; SR RES ENGR, FIELD RES LABS, MOBIL OIL CORP, 64- *Mem:* Sigma Xi; Am Soc Petrol Engrs. *Res:* Fluid flow in porous media; oil recovery processes. *Mailing Add:* 407 Peacock Way Duncanville TX 75131

TALATY, ERACH R, b Nagpur, India, Oct 20, 26; nat US; m 60. ORGANIC CHEMISTRY, ELECTROCHEMISTRY. *Educ:* Univ Nagpur, BSc(honors), 48, MSc, 49, PhD(electrochem), 54; Ohio State Univ, PhD(org chem), 57. *Prof Exp:* Lectr chem, Col Sci, Univ Nagpur, 48-54; asst, Ohio State Univ, 56-57; sr res chemist, Columbia-Southern Chem Corp, 57-61; sr res chemist, Bridesburg Labs, Rohm and Haas Co, Pa, 61; fel, Harvard Univ, 61-62; assoc prof, Univ SDak, 62-64; res assoc, Iowa State Univ, 64-66; asst prof chem, La State Univ, New Orleans, 66-69; RES PROF CHEM, WICHITA STATE UNIV, 69- *Mem:* Am Chem Soc; Royal Soc Chem; Indian Chem Soc. *Res:* Isomerization of azobenzenes; electrodeposition of metals; phosgene chemistry; reactions of chloroformates and carbonates; addition and condensation polymers; acid chlorides; electron spin resonance; steroids; natural products; small-ring compounds; theoretical studies. *Mailing Add:* Dept Chem Wichita State Univ Wichita KS 67208

TALBERT, GEORGE BRAYTON, b Ripon, Wis, July 21, 21; m 47; c 2. AGING, ANATOMY. *Educ:* Univ NDak, BS, 41; Univ Wis, MA, 42, PhD(zool), 50. *Prof Exp:* From res assoc to assoc prof, 50-68, PROF ANAT & CELL BIOL, COL MED, STATE UNIV NY DOWNSTATE MED CTR, 68- *Concurrent Pos:* USPHS spec fel anat, Univ Birmingham, 63-64; USPHS res grant, Nat Inst Child Health & Human Develop, 66-76. *Mem:* Endocrine Soc; Am Asn Anatomists; Brit Soc Fertil; Geront Soc; Soc Study Reproduction. *Res:* Pituitary-gonadal relationship; sexual maturation; longevity; aging of reproductive system. *Mailing Add:* Dept of Anat & Cell Biol State Univ of NY Downstate Med Ctr Brooklyn NY 11203

TALBERT, JAMES LEWIS, b Cassville, Mo, Sept 26, 31; m 58; c 2. PEDIATRIC SURGERY, THORACIC SURGERY. *Educ:* Vanderbilt Univ, BA, 53, MD, 57. *Prof Exp:* Intern surg, Johns Hopkins Hosp, 56-57, resident, 59-60 & 62-64, resident pediat surg, 64-65, instr surg, Sch Med, Johns Hopkins Univ, 65-66, asst prof surg & pediat surg, 66-67; assoc prof, 67-70, PROF SURG & PEDIAT, COL MED, UNIV FLA, 70- *Concurrent Pos:* Sr asst surgeon, Nat Heart Inst, 60-62; Garrett scholar pediat surg, Sch Med, Johns Hopkins Univ, 65-66; consult surg, Univ Hosp Jacksonville & Vet Admin Hosp, Gainesville, 72- *Mem:* Am Surg Asn; Soc Pediat Res; Soc Univ Surgeons; Am Pediat Surg Asn; Am Pediat Soc. *Res:* Congenital anomalies; cancer in childhood; metabolic responses to surgical stress in infants and children. *Mailing Add:* Dept Surg Univ Fla Col Med Gainesville FL 32610

TALBERT, LUTHER M, b Abingdon, Va, Dec 30, 26; m 49; c 3. OBSTETRICS & GYNECOLOGY. *Educ:* Emory & Henry Col, BA, 49; Univ Va, MD, 53; Am Bd Obstet & Gynec, dipl. *Prof Exp:* From instr to assoc prof, 58-69, PROF OBSTET & GYNEC, SCH MED, UNIV NC, CHAPEL HILL, 69- *Mem:* Endocrine Soc; Soc Gynec Invest; Am Gynec Soc; Am Asn Obstet & Gynec; Am Fertil Soc; Am Col Obstet & Gynec. *Res:* Reproductive endocrinology and infertility. *Mailing Add:* Dept Obstet/Gynec Univ NC 4012 Old Clinic Bldg 226H Chapel Hill NC 27514

TALBERT, NORWOOD K(EITH), b Felixville, La, July 29, 21; m 51; c 3. CHEMICAL ENGINEERING, PHYSICAL CHEMISTRY. *Educ:* Tex A&M Univ, BS, 49. *Prof Exp:* Chem engr, Exp Sta, E I du Pont de Nemours & Co, Del, 49-55; group leader & staff specialist, Chem Res Dept, Spencer Chem Co, 55-60, mgr new prod develop, Chemetron Corp, 60-63; mgr com develop, Texas City Refinery, 63-66, mgr nitrogen ctr, 66-67, mgr nitrogen div, 67-71, DIR ENVIRON QUAL, AGWAY INC, 71- *Mem:* Am Chem Soc; Am Inst Chem Engrs. *Res:* Chemical process studies and engineering development; economic evaluation and market appraisal; product and commercial development; management. *Mailing Add:* Agway Inc PO Box 4933 Syracuse NY 13221

TALBERT, PRESTON TIDBALL, b Washington, DC, Feb 17, 25; m 56. ORGANIC CHEMISTRY. *Educ:* Howard Univ, BS, 50, MS, 52; Washington Univ, PhD(chem), 55. *Prof Exp:* Asst, Washington Univ, 51-52; res assoc, Univ Wash, 55-56, res instr, 56-59, NIH fel, 57-59; from asst prof to assoc prof bio-org chem, 59-70, PROF BIO-ORG CHEM, HOWARD UNIV, 70-, ASSOC CHMN DEPT, 66- *Concurrent Pos:* Mem postdoc fel panel, Nat Res Coun, 80. *Mem:* Fel AAAS; fel Am Inst Chemists; Am Chem Soc; NY Acad Sci. *Res:* Mechanism of function, synthesis and degradation of biologically important compounds, especially nucleic, nucleosides, proteins and vitamins; enzyme function and mechanism of action. *Mailing Add:* Dept Chem Howard Univ Washington DC 20059

TALBERT, RONALD EDWARD, b Toulon, Ill, May 20, 36; m 55; c 3. AGRONOMY, WEED SCIENCE. *Educ:* Univ Mo, BS, 58, MS, 60, PhD(field crops), 63. *Prof Exp:* Instr field crops, Univ Mo, 60-63; from asst prof to assoc prof agron, 63-73, PROF AGRON, UNIV ARK, FAYETTEVILLE, 73- *Mem:* AAAS; Weed Sci Soc Am; Am Soc Agron. *Res:* Use of herbicides in crops; behavior of herbicides in soils; physiological selectivity and action of herbicides. *Mailing Add:* Althiemer Lab Univ of Ark Rte 11 Box 83 Fayetteville AR 72701

TALBERT, WILLARD LINDLEY, JR, b Casper, Wyo, Mar 8, 32; m 52; c 4. NUCLEAR PHYSICS. *Educ:* Univ Colo, BA, 54; Iowa State Univ, PhD(physics), 60. *Prof Exp:* Res physicist, Ohio Oil Co, 59-62; from asst prof to prof physics, Iowa State Univ, 62-76; STAFF MEM, LOS ALAMOS NAT LAB, 76-, GROUP LEADER, 77- *Concurrent Pos:* Prog dir nuclear sci, Ames Lab, US Energy Res & Develop Admin, 74- *Mem:* Fel Am Phys Soc. *Res:* Experimental nuclear spectroscopy, especially shortlived isotopes using on-line isotope separator; critical experiments and diagnostics. *Mailing Add:* 2 La Flora Ct Los Alamos NM 87544

TALBOT, BERNARD, b New York, NY, Oct 6, 37; m 63; c 2. MEDICAL SCIENCES. *Educ:* Columbia Col, BA, 58; Columbia Univ, MD, 62; Mass Inst Technol, PhD(biol), 67. *Prof Exp:* Fel, Mass Inst Technol, 67-69 & Univ Rome, 69-70; grants assoc, NIH, 70-71, med officer, Nat Cancer Inst, 71-75, special asst intramural affairs, 75-78, special asst to dir, 78-81, DEP DIR, NAT INST ALLERGY & INFECTIOUS DIS, NIH, 81- *Mailing Add:* NIH Bldg 31 Rm 7A03 Bethesda MD 20205

TALBOT, DONALD R(OY), b Bridgeport, Conn, Jan 23, 31; m 53; c 5. NUCLEAR ENGINEERING. *Educ:* State Univ NY, BS, 52. *Prof Exp:* Test engr, Gen Elec Co, 52, engr, Knolls Atomic Power Lab, 53-56, proj engr, Atomic Power Equip Dept, 56-57, shift supvr, Vallecitos Atomic Lab, 57-58; mgr eng labs, Nuclear Div, Martin Co, 58-62, proj dir, Floating Nuclear Power Plant, 62-67, dir water resources progs, Chem Div, Martin Marietta Corp, NY, 67-69, dir spec studies, Corp Hq, 68-70, dir environ progs, Corp Res Lab, Md, 70-74, DIR ENVIRON TECHNOL CTR, MARTIN MARIETTA CORP, 74- *Concurrent Pos:* Mem natural resources comt, US Chamber of Com, 68-; chmn environ steering comt, Ctr Int Mgt Studies, 73-; mem bus & indust adv comt, Orgn Econ Coop & Develop, 73-; mem directorate, man & biosphere, UNESCO, 77-79; consult, Nat Comn Air Qual, 79-80. *Honors & Awards:* Dept Defense Antarctica Serv Medal. *Mem:* Water Pollution Control Fedn; Air Pollution Control Asn; Nat Asn Mfrs. *Mailing Add:* Corp Res Lab 1450 S Rolling Rd Baltimore MD 21227

TALBOT, EUGENE L(EROY), b Ogden, Utah, Jan 18, 21; m 42; c 4. METALLURGY, MATERIALS ENGINEERING. *Educ:* La State Univ, BS, 44; Univ Utah, BS, 47, MS, 48, PhD(metall), 50. *Prof Exp:* Chemist, Tri State Oil & Refining Co, 41-42; explosives, Ogden Ord Depot, 42; proj leader, Minn Mining & Mfg Co, 50-59, inorg applns leader, 59-63; supt mat develop, 63-75, MAT SPECIALIST, HERCULES INC, 75- *Concurrent Pos:* Lectr, Brigham Young Univ, 65 & Univ Utah, 67; adj prof, Univ Utah, 69- *Mem:* Soc Advan Mat & Process Eng (nat vpres, 73-75, nat pres, 75-76); Am Soc Metals. *Res:* Materials research; high temperature insulation; graphite; metals; stress corrosion; fractography; protective coatings; surface chemistry; adhesives; sealers; composite structures; ceramics; rocket motor systems. *Mailing Add:* Hercules Inc PO Box 98 Magna UT 84044

TALBOT, FRANK DAVID FREDERICK, b Pasqua, Sask, Dec 5, 28; m 57; c 3. CHEMICAL ENGINEERING. *Educ:* Univ Sask, BE, 50, MSc, 51; Univ Toronto, PhD(chem eng), 66. *Prof Exp:* Design engr, Eng Div, Imperial Oil Ltd, 55-65; from asst prof to assoc prof, 65-72, PROF CHEM ENG, UNIV OTTAWA, 72- *Mem:* Can Soc Chem Engrs. *Res:* Process dynamics and control; application of process knowledge to the control of chemical processes; digital control of chemical engineering processes. *Mailing Add:* Dept of Chem Eng Univ of Ottawa Ottawa ON K1N 6N5 Can

TALBOT, JAMES LAWRENCE, b Epsom, Eng, Sept 6, 32; div; c 3. GEOLOGY, STRUCTURAL. *Educ:* Cambridge Univ, BA, 54; Univ Calif, Berkeley, MA, 57; Univ Adelaide, PhD(geol), 63. *Prof Exp:* Lectr struct geol, Univ Adelaide, 58-63, sr lectr, 63-67; assoc prof geol, Lakehead Univ, 67-70; prof geol & chmn dept, 70-75, actg acad vpres, Univ Mont, 75-76; PROF GEOL & VPRES ACAD AFFAIRS, WESTERN WASH UNIV, 76- *Concurrent Pos:* Alexander von Humboldt Found fel, Univ Bonn, 63-64. *Mem:* Geol Soc Am. *Res:* Structural analysis of basementcover complexes; analysis of strain in metamorphic rocks; studies on rock cleavage and mylonites. *Mailing Add:* Western Wash Univ Bellingham WA 98225

TALBOT, JOHN MAYO, b Sebastopol, Calif, May 8, 13; m 46; c 3. AEROSPACE MEDICINE, RADIOBIOLOGY. *Educ:* Univ Ore, AB, 35, MD, 38; Univ Calif, PhD(radiobiol), 48. *Prof Exp:* Med officer, US Army & US Air Force, 39-73; dir sci commun div, George Washington Univ Med Ctr, 73-74; CONSULT BIOMED RES, LIFE SCI RES OFF, FEDN AM SOCS EXP BIOL, 74- *Concurrent Pos:* Consult aerospace med, NASA, 73-76; med consult, Environ Protection Agency, 73-75; pvt consult occup med, 78- *Honors & Awards:* Theodore C Lyster Award, Aerospace Med Asn, 67. *Mem:* Aerospace Med Asn; Int Acad Astronaut; Am Col Prev Med; Pan Am Med Asn. *Res:* Biology and nutrition. *Mailing Add:* 2509 Carrollton Rd Annapolis MD 21403

TALBOT, LAWRENCE, b Brooklyn, NY, Dec 30, 25; m 59; c 2. MECHANICAL ENGINEERING. *Educ:* Univ Mich, PhD(eng mech), 52. *Prof Exp:* Asst prof mech eng, 52-58, assoc prof aeronaut sci, 58-63, vchmn dept, 70-74, PROF MECH ENG, UNIV CALIF, BERKELEY, 63- *Concurrent Pos:* Lectr & consult, Adv Group Aeronaut Res & Develop, Europe, 56-57 & 67-68; Guggenheim fel & vis res fel, All Souls Col, Oxford Univ, 67-68. *Mem:* Am Phys Soc; Am Inst Aeronaut & Astronaut. *Res:* Fluid mechanics; rarefied gas dynamics; physiological fluid mechanics. *Mailing Add:* Dept of Mech Eng Univ of Calif Col of Eng Berkeley CA 94720

TALBOT, LEE MERRIAM, b New Beford, Mass, Aug 2, 30; m 59; c 1. ECOLOGY. *Educ:* Univ Calif, AB, 53, MA & PhD(geog range & vert ecol), 63. *Prof Exp:* Field biologist, Arctic Res Lab, Alaska, 51; staff ecologist, UNESCO-Int Union Conserv, Belg, 54-56; ecologist & dir EAfrican wildlife & wild land res proj, Nat Acad Sci-Nat Res Coun, Rockefeller Found, NY Zool Soc & Govt Kenya, 59-63; dir SE Asia proj, UNESCO-Int Union Conserv, 64-65; field rep int affairs ecol & conserv & res ecologist, Smithsonian Inst, 66-70, sci coordr conserv sect, Int Biol Prog, 66-70; sr scientist, President's Coun on Environ Qual, 70-75, asst to chmn int & sci affairs, President's Coun Environ Qual, 75-78; DIR CONSERV & SPEC SCI ADV, WORLD WILDLIFE FUND INT & SR SCI ADV CONSERV & NATURAL RESOURCES, INT COUN SCI UNIONS, 78- *Concurrent Pos:* UNESCO lectr, Southeast Asia, 55, consult, 65-; leader, African wildlife exp, Wildlife Mgt Inst & Am Comt Int Wildlife Protection, 56; Taussig traveling fel, Univ Calif, 58-59; Pop Ref Bur consult, Govt Kenya & Tanganyika, 59-63, Hong Kong, 63, Philippines, 64, Indonesia & Thailand, 64-65 & Malaya, Sabah & Sarawak, 65; wildlife adv, UN Spec Fund & EAfrican Agr & Forestry Res Orgn, 63-64; assoc ecol, US Nat Zool Park, 66-; spec adv, Mus Natural Hist, Smithsonian Inst, 67-, res assoc, 74-; overseas consult, Fauna Preservation Soc, 67-; consult, UN Spec Fund, 63, Pac Sci Bd, Nat Acad Sci-Nat Res Coun, 64-65, Peace Corps, 66, Int Comn Nat Parks, 66-, Nat Park Serv, 68 & AID, 69; chmn, Am Comt Int Conserv, 74-; vpres, Int Union Conserv Nature & Natural Resources, 75- *Honors & Awards:* Wildlife Soc Award, 63; Albert Schweitzer Medal, Animal Welfare Inst, 75; Distinguished Serv Award, Am Inst Biol Sci, 79. *Mem:* Fel AAAS; Am Soc Mammal; Soc Range Mgt; Asn Am Geog; Wildlife Soc. *Res:* International conservation; wildlife, especially ecology and management; tropical land use and savannah ecology; conservation of renewable natural resources; methodology of ecological research and survey; environmental impact analysis; endangered species. *Mailing Add:* World Wildlife Fund Int 1110 Morges Switzerland

TALBOT, NATHAN BILL, b Boston, Mass, Nov 25, 09; m 34; c 2. PEDIATRICS. *Educ:* Harvard Univ, AB, 32, MD, 36. *Prof Exp:* Intern, Children's Hosp, 36-38; from asst to assoc prof, 39-62, Charles Wilder Prof Pediat & head dept, 62-80, EMER PROF, HARVARD MED SCH, 80- *Concurrent Pos:* Asst resident, Children's Hosp, 39-40, asst physician, 41-42; res fel pediat, Harvard Med Sch, 40-41; from asst physician to physician, Mass Gen Hosp, 42-62; consult, Children's Hosp Med Ctr, Boston Lying-In Hosp & Cambridge City Hosp. *Honors & Awards:* Mead Johnson Award & Borden Award, Am Acad Pediat. *Mem:* Fel Am Acad Arts & Sci; fel Am Soc Clin Invest; fel Am Pediat Soc; fel Soc Pediat Res; fel Endocrine Soc. *Res:* Interplay of physical, biologic, social, psychologic and behavioral factors on human development, health and disease. *Mailing Add:* 176 Warren St Brookline MA 02146

TALBOT, PRUDENCE, b Mass, June 9, 44; m 68. REPRODUCTIVE PHYSIOLOGY, CELL BIOLOGY. *Educ:* Wilson Col, BA, 66; Wellesley Col, MA, 68; Univ Houston, PhD(cell biol), 72. *Prof Exp:* Res assoc mammalian fertil, Univ Houston, 72-77; asst prof, 77-81, ASSOC PROF BIOL, UNIV CALIF, RIVERSIDE, 81- *Mem:* Am Soc Cell Biol; Am Soc Zoologists; Soc Study Reprod; Sigma Xi. *Res:* Morphology, physiology and biochemistry of mammalian fertilization and the mechanism of mammalian ovulation. *Mailing Add:* Dept Biol Univ Calif Riverside CA 92521

TALBOT, RAYMOND JAMES, JR, b Portsmouth, Va, Sept 17, 41; m 68. IMAGE PROCESSING, ASTROPHYSICS. *Educ:* Mass Inst Technol, SB, 63, PhD(physics), 69. *Prof Exp:* Res assoc, Space Sci Physics & Astron, Rice Univ, 69-71, asst prof, 71-76, assoc prof, 76-81; MEM TECH STAFF, AEROSPACE CORP, 81- *Mem:* Am Astron Soc; Sigma Xi. *Res:* Evolution of stars and galaxies; nucleosynthesis; image processing. *Mailing Add:* 1927 Curtis Ave Houston TX 77001

TALBOT, T(HOMAS) F, b Birmingham, Ala, July 31, 30; m 57; c 3. MECHANICAL ENGINEERING, METALLURGY. *Educ:* Auburn Univ, BME, 52; Calif Inst Technol, MSME, 53; Ga Inst Technol, PhD(mech eng), 64. *Prof Exp:* Sr practice man, Tenn Coal & Iron Div, US Steel Corp, 56-58; asst prof mech eng, Ga Inst Technol, 58-65; assoc prof mat sci & mech design, Vanderbilt Univ, 65-67; from assoc prof to prof eng, 67-79, dir continuing eng educ, 72-79, PROF MECH ENG, UNIV ALA, BIRMINGHAM, 79- *Concurrent Pos:* Consult, Humble Oil & Refining Co, 59, Chicago Bridge & Iron Co, 65 & Rust Eng Co, 66; chmn bd dirs, Am Alloy Prods, 77- *Mem:* Am Soc Metals; Am Soc Mech Engrs; Am Soc Eng Educ; Am Welding Soc; Soc Automotive Engrs. *Res:* Machine design; materials processing; design aspects of automobile safety; design aspects of product liability. *Mailing Add:* 3837 Brook Hollow Lane Birmingham AL 35243

TALBOT, TIMOTHY RALPH, JR, b Berkeley, Calif, July 14, 16; m 43; c 5. RESEARCH ADMINISTRATION. *Educ:* Univ Pa, AB, 37, MD, 41. *Prof Exp:* Instr med, Sch Med, Boston Univ, 46-48; instr, Med Col, Cornell Univ, 48-51; assoc, 51-54, asst prof, 54-66, ASSOC PROF MED, SCH MED, UNIV PA, 66-; VCHMN BD FOX CHASE CANCER CTR, 80- *Concurrent Pos:* Asst, Sloan-Kettering Inst Cancer Res & asst attend physician, Mem Hosp, New York, 48-51; ward physician & mem hemat sect, Hosp Univ Pa, 51-; Nat Cancer Inst fel, Chester Beatty Res Inst, London, Eng, 56-57; dir, Inst Cancer Res, 57-76, pres, 72-76; dir, Fox Chase Ctr Cancer & Med Sci, 71-74, pres, 74-80. *Mem:* AAAS; Asn Am Cancer Insts; Am Fedn Clin Res; Am Asn Cancer Res; Am Clin & Climat Asn. *Res:* Hematology and cancer. *Mailing Add:* Fox Chase Cancer Ctr 7701 Burholme Ave Philadelphia PA 19111

TALBOT, WILLIAM HENRY, neurophysiology, see previous edition

TALBOTT, RICHARD LLOYD, b Chicago, Ill, July 15, 35; m 58; c 3. ORGANIC CHEMISTRY. *Educ:* DePauw Univ, BA, 57; Univ Ill, PhD(org chem), 60. *Prof Exp:* NSF fel org chem, Mass Inst Technol, 60-61; sr chemist, Cent Res Dept, 61-66, sr chemist, Indust Tape Div, 66-68, supvr adhesives res, 68-74, RES MGR, PACKAGING SYSTS DIV, 3M CO, 74- *Mem:* Am Chem Soc. *Res:* Pressure-sensitive adhesives chemistry; chemistry of fluorinated oxidants and fluorinated peroxides; oriented plastic films. *Mailing Add:* 3M Co 230-2E 3M Center St Paul MN 55101

TALBOTT, TED DELWYN, b Sudan, Tex, Oct 18, 29; m 55; c 2. ANALYTICAL CHEMISTRY. *Educ:* NTex State Col, BS, 51, MS, 55. *Prof Exp:* Indust chemist, E I du Pont de Nemours & Co, 55-57; anal chemist, Res Ctr, US Rubber Co, 57-64; SR RES CHEMIST, ANAL RES SECT, AGR DIV, MOBAY CHEM CORP, 64- *Mem:* Am Chem Soc; Soc Appl Spectros. *Res:* Methods development for various pesticides which include organic phosphorus compounds, Carbamates and nitrogen hetercyclics utilizing various chromatographic and spectographic techniques; high pressure and gas liquid chromatography. *Mailing Add:* Anal Res Sect Agr Div Box 4913 Hawthorne Rd Kansas City MO 64120

TALENT, LARRY GENE, b Cerrogordo, Ark, May 4, 46; m 65; c 2. ECOLOGY, ZOOLOGY. *Educ:* Calif State Univ, Fresno, BA, 70, MA, 73; Ore State Univ, PhD(wildlife), 80. *Prof Exp:* Instr biol, Hartnell Community Col, 73-74; ASST PROF ZOOL, OKLA STATE UNIV, 80- *Mem:* Wildlife Soc; Wilson Ornith Soc; Am Ornithologists Union; Cooper Ornith Soc; Herpetologists League. *Res:* Vertebrate ecology; habitat use and competitive interactions of sympatric species. *Mailing Add:* Dept Zool Okla State Univ Stillwater OK 74078

TALESNIK, JAIME, b Santiago, Chile, May 18, 16; m 41; c 2. PHARMACOLOGY, PHYSIOLOGY. *Educ:* Univ Chile, MD, 41. *Prof Exp:* Second chief instr physiol, Sch Med, Univ Chile, 41-49, asst prof, 50-58, assoc prof physiopath, 58-61, interim prof physiopath & dir dept exp med, 61-63; vis prof, 67-69, PROF PHARMACOL, FAC MED, UNIV TORONTO, 69- *Concurrent Pos:* Rockefeller Found grant, Banting & Best Dept Med Res, Univ Toronto, 46-47; Brit Coun grant, Nat Inst Med Res, London, Eng, 52. *Mem:* Chilean Biol Soc; Brit Physiol Soc; Am Soc Pharmacol & Exp Therapeut; Pharmacol Soc Can; NY Acad Sci. *Res:* Physiopharmacology of the coronary circulation; central modulation of cardiovascular reflexes. *Mailing Add:* Dept of Pharmacol Univ of Toronto Fac of Med Toronto ON M5S 1A8 Can

TALHAM, ROBERT J, b Cohoes, NY, May 27, 29; m 56; c 4. APPLIED MATHEMATICS, ACOUSTICS. *Educ:* State Univ NY Albany, BA, 55, MS, 56; Rensselaer Polytech Inst, PhD(appl math), 60. *Prof Exp:* Nat Acad Sci-Nat Res Coun res fel, Naval Res Lab, DC, 60-61; mem tech staff, Bell Tel Labs, NJ, 61-64; mgr undersea defense systs eng, Heavy Mil Electronics Dept, 64-77, MGR OPER PLANNING, GEN ELEC CO, 77- *Mem:* Am Math Soc; Soc Indust & Appl Math; Acoust Soc Am. *Res:* Sonar systems; underwater acoustics; sound propagation in non-homogeneous medium; acoustic array design and development; signal processing. *Mailing Add:* General Elec Co HMES FRPI-A5 Farrell Rd Plant Syracuse NY 13201

TALIAFERRO, CHARLES M, b Leon, Okla, Mar 1, 40; m 60; c 2. PLANT BREEDING, PLANT GENETICS. *Educ:* Okla State Univ, BS, 62; Tex A&M Univ, MS, 65, PhD(plant breeding & genetics), 66. *Prof Exp:* Res agronomist, Agr Res Serv, USDA, 65-68; asst prof, 68-72, assoc prof, 72-76, PROF FORAGE BREEDING & GENETICS, OKLA STATE UNIV, 76- *Mem:* Am Soc Agron; Am Genetic Asn. *Res:* Basic genetic and breeding studies involving forage crops. *Mailing Add:* Dept of Agron Okla State Univ Stillwater OK 74075

TALIAFERRO, H(AROLD) R(ICHARD), b Effingham, Kans, Feb 14, 16; m 44; c 3. CHEMICAL ENGINEERING. *Educ:* Univ Kans, BS, 38. *Prof Exp:* Lab control chemist, Lever Bros Co, 38-39, asst process foreman, Edible Div, 39-40; chem eng, Res Dept, Standard Oil Co, Ind, 40-46, group leader, 46-50, sect leader, 50-58, dir, Automotive Res Div, 58-60 & Res & Develop Dept, 60-62, asst dir fuels res, 62-67 & coord automotive emmissions res, 67-77, DIR FUELS RES, AM OIL CO, 77 *Mem:* Am Chem Soc; Soc Automotive Engrs. *Res:* Automotive emissions research and development. *Mailing Add:* Res & Develop Dept Am Oil Co PO Box 400 Warrenville Rd Naperville IL 60540

TALIAFERRO, STEVEN DOUGLAS, b Honolulu, Hawaii, Apr 4, 49; US citizen. MATHEMATICS. *Educ:* San Diego State Univ, BS, 71; Stanford Univ, PhD(math), 76. *Prof Exp:* Teaching asst math, Stanford Univ, 72-76; ASST PROF MATH, TEX A&M UNIV, 76- *Mem:* Am Math Soc. *Res:* Asymptotic behavior and stability of solutions of ordinary differential equations. *Mailing Add:* Dept of Math Tex A&M Univ College Station TX 77843

TALKE, FRANK E, b Dresden, Ger, Sept 16, 39; m 70. MECHANICAL ENGINEERING. *Educ:* Univ Stuttgart, Dipl Ing, 65; Univ Calif, Berkeley, MSc, 66, PhD(fluid mech), 68. *Prof Exp:* Mgr mech & fluid mech, 68 - 74, MGR DEVICE MECH, IBM, 75- *Concurrent Pos:* Lectr, Univ Santa Clara, 69-77. *Mem:* Am Soc Mech Engrs. *Res:* Magnetic recording technology; ink jet technology; tribology; mechanics and fluid mechanics. *Mailing Add:* 5600 Cottle Rd San Jose CA 95193

TALLAL, PAULA, b Austin, Tex, May 12, 47; m 72. EXPERIMENTAL PSYCHOLOGY, SPEECH SCIENCE. *Educ:* NY Univ, BA, 69; Cambridge Univ, PhD(exp psychol), 73. *Prof Exp:* Instr pediat, Sch Med, Johns Hopkins Univ, 74-75, asst prof neurol, 75-79; asst prof, 79-80, ASSOC PROF PSYCHIAT, SCH MED, UNIV CALIF, SAN DIEGO, 80- *Concurrent Pos:* Prin investr, Nat Inst Neurol Dis, 76-79. *Honors & Awards:* Distinguished Young Scientist of the Year, Md Acad Sci, 76. *Mem:* Int Neuropsychol Soc; Acoustical Soc Am. *Res:* Sensory, perceptual and cognitive functioning of individuals with or without delayed language development or language disorders; neural processing of nonverbal and verbal information in various sensory modalities. *Mailing Add:* Dept of Psychiat M-003 Univ Calif at San Diego La Jolla CA 92093

TALLAN, HARRIS H, b New York, NY, July 9, 24; c 3. BIOCHEMISTRY. *Educ:* NY Univ, BA, 47; Yale Univ, PhD(biochem), 50. *Prof Exp:* Asst, Rockefeller Inst, 50-53, asst prof biochem, 53-59; biochemist, Res Labs, Geigy Chem Corp, 59-68; RES SCIENTIST V, DEPT HUMAN DEVELOP, NY STATE INST BASIC RES IN DEVELOP DISABILITIES, 68- *Concurrent Pos:* NIH spec fel, Oxford Univ, 57-58. *Mem:* Am Soc Biol Chemists; NY Acad Sci. *Res:* Enzymology; amino acid metabolism; inborn errors of metabolism; neurochemistry. *Mailing Add:* Dept of Human Develop, NY State Inst Basic Res in Develop Disabilities Staten Island NY 10314

TALLAN, IRWIN, b New York, NY, June 26, 27; m 59. GENETICS. *Educ:* Rutgers Univ, BA, 49; Ind Univ, PhD(genetics), 57. *Prof Exp:* Technician to H J Muller, Ind Univ, 50, asst to T M Sonneborn, 50-53; lectr zool, 56-58, from asst prof to assoc prof, 58-74, PROF ZOOL, UNIV TORONTO, 74- *Mem:* Am Soc Zool; Brit Soc Gen Microbiol. *Res:* Genetics; nucleo-cytoplasmic interactions in protozoans; infectivity of kappa and other plasmids. *Mailing Add:* Dept of Zool Univ of Toronto Toronto ON M5S 1A1 Can

TALLAN, NORMAN M, b Newark, NJ, Sept 24, 32; m 58; c 4. MATERIALS SCIENCE, CERAMICS. *Educ:* Rutgers Univ, BSc, 54; Ohio State Univ, MS, 55; Alfred Univ, PhD(solid state ceramics), 59. *Prof Exp:* Res physicist, Aerospace Res Labs, 59-61, supvr ceramic res, 61-70, dir, Metall & Ceramics Res Lab, 70-76, chief processing & high temperature mat br, Air Force Mat Lab, 76-77, actg chief metals & ceramics div, 77-78, CHIEF SCIENTIST, AIR FORCE MAT LAB, WRIGHT-PATTERSON AFB, 78- *Concurrent Pos:* Res asst, Israel Inst Technol, 66-67. *Honors & Awards:* Ross Coffin Purdy Award, 69. *Mem:* Fel Am Ceramic Soc; Am Phys Soc. *Res:* Equilibrium point defect structure and the transport of charge and mass in metal oxides at high temperatures; physical and mechanical properties of ceramic materials. *Mailing Add:* Mat Lab AFWAL/MS Wright-Patterson AFB Dayton OH 45433

TALLARIDA, RONALD JOSEPH, b Philadelphia, Pa, May 26, 37; m 58; c 3. BIOMATHEMATICS, PHARMACOLOGY. *Educ:* Drexel Inst, BS, 59, MS, 63; Temple Univ, PhD(pharmacol), 67. *Prof Exp:* Coop student, Philco Corp-Drexel Inst, 55-59; jr engr, Philco Corp, 59-60; from instr to asst prof math, Drexel Inst, 60-67; asst prof, 67-71, assoc prof pharmacol, 71-78, mem fac, 78-79, PROF PHARMACOL, TEMPLE UNIV, 79- *Concurrent Pos:* Lectr, Philadelphia Col Pharm, 60, PMC Col, 61-62 & cardiovascular training grant prog, Med Sch, Temple Univ, 63-64; consult, Drexel Inst, 67- *Mem:* AAAS; Math Asn Am; Am Soc Pharmacol & Exp Therapeut. *Res:* Mathematical models for application to biology and medicine; drug receptor theory; pharmacology of vascular smooth muscle; pharmacology of morphine; drug induced disease. *Mailing Add:* Dept of Pharmacol Temple Univ Sch of Med Philadelphia PA 19140

TALLEDO, OSCAR EDUARDO, b Sullana, Peru, Aug 1, 29; US citizen; m 59; c 3. OBSTETRICS & GYNECOLOGY. *Educ:* San Marcos Univ, Lima, BS, 48, MD, 55; Am Bd Obstet & Gynec, spec cert div gynec oncol, 75. *Prof Exp:* Intern, San Marcos Univ, Lima, 54-55; intern, Crawford W Long Hosp, Emory Univ, 56-57, resident obstet & gynec, 57-58; resident, 58-60, fel, 60-61, from instr to assoc prof, 61-71, PROF OBSTET & GYNEC, MED COL GA, 71-, CHIEF GYNEC SERV, 74- *Concurrent Pos:* Nat Heart Inst grant obstet & gynec, Med Col Ga, 65, NIH grant, 68, dir obstet/gynec residency training prog, 74-; consult, Cent State Hosp, Macon City Hosp, Greenville Mem Hosp & Mem Med Ctr. *Mem:* Fel Am Col Obstet & Gynec; Soc Gynec Invest; AMA; Am Fertil Soc. *Res:* Physiology of pregnancy; vascular reactivity in pregnancy; fetal electrocardiography; uterine contractility studies; amniotic fluid. *Mailing Add:* Dept of Obstet & Gynec Med Col of Ga Augusta GA 30902

TALLENT, WILLIAM HUGH, b Akron, Ohio, May 28, 28; m 52; c 3. ORGANIC CHEMISTRY, BIOCHEMISTRY. *Educ:* Univ Tenn, BS, 49, MS, 50; Univ Ill, PhD(biochem), 53. *Prof Exp:* Asst, Univ Tenn, 49-50 & Univ Ill, 50-53; asst scientist, Nat Heart Inst, 53-57; res chemist, G D Searle & Co, 57-64; invests leader, Northern Regional Res Ctr, 64-69, chief indust crops res, 69-75, DIR NORTHERN REGIONAL RES CTR, AGR RES SERV, USDA, 75- *Concurrent Pos:* Assoc ed, J Am Oil Chemists Soc, 70- *Mem:* Am Chem Soc; Am Oil Chemists Soc; Soc Econ Bot. *Res:* Application of chromatographic and spectroscopic methods to analysis, isolation and structure determination of terpenes, plant lipids, natural insecticides; plant enzymes; useful derivatives and synthetic modifications of natural products; research management. *Mailing Add:* Northern Regional Res Ctr Agr Res Serv USDA Peoria IL 61604

TALLER, ROBERT ARTHUR, physical organic chemistry, see previous edition

TALLERICO, PAUL JOSEPH, b New York, NY, Nov 30, 38; m 62; c 2. ELECTRICAL ENGINEERING. *Educ:* Mass Inst Technol, BS & MS, 61; Univ Mich, PhD(elec eng), 68. *Prof Exp:* Staff mem, Int Bus Mach Res Labs, 62-63; ASSOC GROUP LEADER, LOS ALAMOS NAT LAB, 68- *Concurrent Pos:* Consult, various orgns, 79 & 80. *Mem:* Sigma Xi; Inst Elec & Electronics Engrs. *Res:* Microwave generation and amplification especially as applied to accelerator power sources. *Mailing Add:* Los Alamos Nat Lab M/S 827 PO Box 1663 Los Alamos NM 87545

TALLEY, CHARLES PETER, b New York, NY, Aug 15, 41; m 68; c 3. ANALYTICAL CHEMISTRY. *Educ:* St Peter's Col, NJ, BS, 63; Polytech Inst New York, PhD(phys & org chem), 74. *Prof Exp:* Sr res chemist, Merck Sharp & Dohme Res Labs, Div Merck & Co, 68-72; res chemist, Anal Chem Div, Nat Bur Standards, 73; sr group leader anal res, Calgon Corp, Subsid Merck & Co, Inc, 73-78; DIR RES & DEVELOP, GAF CORP, 79- *Mem:* Am Chem Soc; AAAS. *Res:* Gas and high pressure liquid chromatography, especially as applied to the analysis of trace organics in biological, environmental and polymeric matrices. *Mailing Add:* GAF Corp 1361 Alps Rd Wayne NJ 07470

TALLEY, EUGENE ALTON, b Glenn Allen, Va, June 5, 11; m 44; c 2. AGRICULTURAL CHEMISTRY. *Educ:* Col William & Mary, BCh, 36; Univ Richmond, MS, 38; Ohio State Univ, PhD(org chem), 42. *Prof Exp:* Asst chemist carbohydrate div, Eastern Regional Res Lab, Bur Agr & Indust Chem, 42-44, chemist, 44-53, sr chemist, 53-80, EMER PROTEIN CHEMIST, PLANT PROD LAB, EASTERN REGIONAL RES LAB, AGR RES SERV, USDA, 80- *Mem:* Am Chem Soc; Am Potato Asn. *Res:* Synthesis of oligosaccharides; preparation of starch esters and ethers; nitrogen compounds in plants; glycoalkaloids. *Mailing Add:* 3100 Quarry Lane Lafayette Hill PA 19444

TALLEY, HARRY E, b Blue Springs, Mo, Aug 8, 24; m 43; c 2. ELECTRICAL ENGINEERING. *Educ:* Rockhurst Col, BS, 49; Univ Kans, MS, 53, PhD(physics), 54. *Prof Exp:* Mem tech staff, Bell Tel Labs, 54-64; assoc prof, 64-69, PROF ELEC ENG, UNIV KANS, 69- *Concurrent Pos:* Vis prof, Lehigh Univ, 61-62. *Mem:* Inst Elec & Electronics Engrs. *Res:* Semiconductor device theory; semiconductor surface phenomena and related devices; properties of semiconductor materials. *Mailing Add:* Rte 2 Box 139 Lawrence KS 66044

TALLEY, JOHN HERBERT, b Wilmington, Del, Jan 16, 44; m 67; c 2. GROUND-WATER GEOLOGY. *Educ:* Univ Del, BA, 69; Franklin & Marshall Col, MS, 74. *Prof Exp:* Eng geologist, Geo-Del, Ltd, 71-72; proj geologist, 72-74, SCIENTIST & HYDROGEOLOGIST, DEL GEOL SURV, 74- *Mem:* Asn Eng Geologists; Nat Waterwell Asn; Soc Econ Paleontologists & Mineralogists. *Res:* Geologic mapping; subsurface stratigraphy and structural interpretation; hydrologic mapping; ground water exploration; ground water-surface water relationships; borehole geophysics. *Mailing Add:* Del Geol Surv Univ Del Newark DE 19711

TALLEY, ROBERT MORRELL, b Erwin, Tenn, Mar 13, 24; m 48; c 2. INFRARED DETECTORS. *Educ:* Univ SC, BS, 45; Univ Tenn, MS, 48, PhD(physics), 50. *Prof Exp:* Chief infrared br, US Naval Ord Lab, 51-57, chief solid state div, 57-58; vpres & mgr labs, 58-76, PRES, SANTA BARBARA RES CTR, 76- *Mem:* Am Phys Soc; Optical Soc Am. *Res:* Infrared spectroscopy; intermetallic semiconductors; energy bands in solids; photodetectors; military infrared systems. *Mailing Add:* Santa Barbara Res Ctr 75 Coromar Dr Goleta CA 93017

TALLEY, SPURGEON MORRIS, b Atkins, Ark, May 6, 18; m 48; c 1. ANIMAL NUTRITION. *Educ:* Agr, Mech & Norm Col, Ark, BSA, 47; Kas State Univ, MS, 53, PhD(nutrit), 66. *Prof Exp:* Asst prof poultry sci & prod mgr, 54-66, assoc prof animal nutrit, 66-77, PROF ANIMAL SCI, LINCOLN UNIV, MO, 77- *Mem:* Poultry Sci Asn; Am Soc Animal Sci. *Res:* Monogastric animals; nutrition of poultry and swine; plant proteins as sources of protein for the avian species; level of dietary protein and phase feeding on esophagoulcerogenesis of market swine; metabolizable energy requirements of market-type swine. *Mailing Add:* Dept of Agr Lincoln Univ Jefferson City MO 65101

TALLEY, THURMAN LAMAR, b Portales, NMex, July 26, 37; m 62; c 2. PHYSICS. *Educ:* Eastern NMex Univ, BS, 59, MS, 60; Fla State Univ, PhD(physics), 68. *Prof Exp:* Instr eng sci, Fla State Univ, 64-65; MEM STAFF, LOS ALAMOS NAT LAB, UNIV CALIF, 66- *Concurrent Pos:* Chmn, Joint AEC-Dept Defense Working Group Safeguard Sprint Nuclear Vulnerability & Effects, 68-71. *Mem:* Am Phys Soc. *Res:* Nuclear reaction theory; nuclear weapons design; nuclear weapons effects; computer simulation of complex physical phenomena. *Mailing Add:* Los Alamos Nat Lab PO Box 1663 Los Alamos NM 87544

TALLEY, WILSON K(INTER), b St Louis, Mo, Jan 27, 35; m 81; c 3. NUCLEAR ENGINEERING, APPLIED MATHEMATICS. *Educ:* Univ Calif, Berkeley, BS, 56, PhD(nuclear eng), 63; Univ Chicago, SM, 57. *Prof Exp:* Physicist, Lawrence Radiation Lab, 59; from asst prof to assoc prof appl sci, 63-72, vchmn dept appl sci, 66-67, actg chmn, 68-69, PROF APPL SCI, UNIV CALIF, DAVIS, 72- *Concurrent Pos:* Consult, Lawrence Livermore Lab, 63-, leader, Theoret Physics Div, 71 & Governor's Select Comt, NY, 66-68; mem, Stanford Res Inst, 67-70; White House fel, Dept Health, Educ & Welfare, 69-70; consult, Hazardous Mat Adv Comt, Environ Protection Agency, 71-74; asst vpres acad planning, Univ Calif, 71-74; pres, Fannie & John Hertz Found, 72-; study dir, Comn Critical Choices Am, 74; asst admin res & develop, US Environ Protection Agency, Washington, DC, 74-77; mem, US Army Sci Bd, 78- *Mem:* Am Nuclear Soc; Am Phys Soc. *Res:* Linear transport theory; peaceful uses of nuclear explosives; applications of radioisotopes; energy and environmental policy. *Mailing Add:* One Clipper Hill Oakland CA 94618

TALLIAN, TIBOR E(UGENE), b Budapest, Hungary, Oct 18, 20; nat US; m 50; c 2. MECHANICAL ENGINEERING, MECHANICS. *Educ:* Budapest Tech Univ, ME, 43. *Prof Exp:* Supvr eng & res, Ball Bearing Factories, Hungary, 52-56; supvr metrology, 57-58, mgr res lab, 58-68, vpres res, 68-73, VPRES TECHNOL SERV, SKF INDUSTS, INC, 73- *Honors & Awards:* Nat Award, Am Soc Lubrication Engrs, 75. *Mem:* Fel Am Soc Lubrication Engrs; fel Am Soc Mech Engrs. *Res:* Fatigue of metals; applied mechanics of bearings; surface geometry and vibrations of rolling systems; mathematical statistics; random processes; electromechanical instrumentation. *Mailing Add:* SKF Industs Inc 1100 First Ave King of Prussia PA 19406

TALLITSCH, ROBERT BOYDE, b Oak Park, Ill, June 3, 50; m 71. PHYSIOLOGY. *Educ:* NCent Col, BA, 71; Univ Wis-Madison, MS, 72, PhD(physiol), 75. *Prof Exp:* Res fel, Wis Heart Asn, 74-75; ASST PROF BIOL, AUGUSTANA COL, 75- *Concurrent Pos:* Vis scientist, Geront Res Ctr, Nat Inst Aging, NIH, 81. *Mem:* Assoc Am Physiol Soc. *Res:* Ion transport in skeletal and cardiac muscle cells. *Mailing Add:* Dept of Biol Augustana Col Rock Island IL 61201

TALLMADGE, J(OHN) A(LLEN), b Allentown, Pa, Feb 19, 28; m 54; c 3. CHEMICAL ENGINEERING, ENVIRONMENTAL SCIENCE. *Educ:* Lehigh Univ, BS, 48; Carnegie-Mellon Univ, MS, 50, PhD(chem eng), 54. *Prof Exp:* Res engr process develop, E I du Pont de Nemours & Co, 53-56; asst prof chem eng, Yale Univ, 56-62, assoc prof eng & appl sci, 62-65; sr vis, Imp Col, Univ London, 65; actg head dept, 67 & 73-74, PROF CHEM ENG, DREXEL UNIV, 66- *Concurrent Pos:* Fulbright prof, Univ NSW, Australia, 74. *Mem:* Am Chem Soc; Am Soc Eng Educ; Water Pollution Control Fedn; Am Inst Chem Engrs; Am Powder Metall Inst. *Res:* Fluid dynamics; heat transfer, powder metallurgical atomization; industrial water pollution; mass transfer; packed beds; ion exchange; coating processes. *Mailing Add:* Dept of Chem Eng Drexel Univ Philadelphia PA 19104

TALLMAN, DENNIS EARL, b Bellefontaine, Ohio, Apr 23, 42; m 63; c 2. ANALYTICAL CHEMISTRY, LABORATORY COMPUTERS. *Educ:* Ohio State Univ, BSc, 64, PhD(anal chem), 68. *Prof Exp:* NIH fel chem, Cornell Univ, 68-70; asst prof anal chem, 70-73, assoc prof, 73-78, PROF ANAL CHEM, NDAK STATE UNIV, 78-, CHMN DEPT, 77- *Concurrent Pos:* Res Corp grant, NDak State Univ, 71-73; Off Water Resources res grants, 71-79; NIH res grant, 74-76; EPA res grant, 75-81. *Mem:* Soc Appl Spectros; AAAS; Am Chem Soc. *Res:* Electroanalytical chemistry; high-performance liquid chromatography; environmental chemistry; laboratory applications of small computers; solution dynamics. *Mailing Add:* Dept Chem NDak State Univ Fargo ND 58105

TALLMAN, J(OHN) C(ORNWELL), b Auburn, NY, June 12, 18; m 41; c 4. CHEMICAL ENGINEERING. *Educ:* Cornell Univ, BCh, 39, ChemE, 40. *Prof Exp:* Jr Res engr, Ammonia Dept, Exp Sta, E I du Pont de Nemours & Co, Del, 40-41, WVa, 41-46, asst tech supt, 46-47, res engr, 47-52, econ studies supvr, Textile Fibers Dept, 52-56, indust mkt analyst, Develop Dept, 56-62, mgr mkt res, Latin Am Div, Int Dept, 62-69, mgr develop, Du Pont Do Brasil, 69-71, tech investr, Tech Div, Int Dept, 71-76, sr bus analyst, Finance Div, 77-81; RETIRED. *Concurrent Pos:* Abstractor, Chem Abstr, 47-75, sect ed, 59-62. *Mem:* Am Chem Soc; Chem Mkt Res Asn; Am Inst Chem Engrs. *Res:* Plastics; synthetic fibers; economic studies; market research; foreign exchange. *Mailing Add:* 119 Marcella Rd Webster Farm Wilmington DE 19803

TALLMAN, JOHN GARY, b Sistersville, WVa, Mar 20, 50. GENETICS, BIOCHEMISTRY. *Educ:* West Liberty State Col, AB, 71; WVa Univ, PhD(genetics), 76. *Prof Exp:* Found fel genetics, WVa Univ, 71-75, Gulf Oil Found fel, 75-76; res assoc biochem, Kans State Univ, 76-78; asst prof, 78-80, PROF BIOL & GENETICS, PEPPERDINE UNIV, 80- *Mem:* Am Genetic Asn; Am Chem Soc; AAAS. *Res:* Heterosis; chromatin structure and function; transcription; DNA tumor viruses; plant protoplasting and tissue culture; stomatol isolation and biochemistry. *Mailing Add:* Div Nat Sci Pepperdine Univ Malibu CA 90265

TALLMAN, RALPH COLTON, b Cedar Rapids, Iowa, Oct 6, 05; m 29; c 1. ORGANIC CHEMISTRY. *Educ:* Cornell Col, Iowa, AB, 27; Cornell Univ, PhD(org chem), 31. *Prof Exp:* Instr org chem, Cornell Univ, 30-35; dir res, Schieffelin & Co, 35-43; proj leader cent res lab, Allied Chem & Dye Corp, 43-50; mgr planning & surv dept, Lion Oil Co Div, Monsanto Co, 50-51, dir res, 51-61, dir hydrocarbons div, 61-65, assoc dir res, Hydrocarbons & Polymers Div, 65-70; CONSULT, ENG DYNAMICS INT, 72- *Mem:* Emeritus mem Am Chem Soc. *Res:* Drugs and pharmaceuticals; organic and industrial chemicals; administrative research. *Mailing Add:* Eng Dynamics Int 8420 Delmar Blvd St Louis MO 63124

TALLMAN, RICHARD LOUIS, b Wheeling, WVa, Apr 24, 31; m 56; c 3. CHEMISTRY, CORROSION. *Educ:* Kenyon Col, AB, 53; Univ Wis, PhD(phys chem), 60. *Prof Exp:* Sr chemist, Res Labs, Westinghouse Elec Corp, 59-73; sr res chemist, Gen Motors Res Labs, 73-76; assoc scientist, 77-80, SCIENTIST, EG&G IDAHO INC, 80- *Mem:* Am Chem Soc. *Res:* Corrosion; metal oxidation; combustion; crystallography; microscopy; gravimetry; radwaste leaching. *Mailing Add:* 1653 Halsey Idaho Falls ID 83401

TALMAGE, DAVID WILSON, b Kwangju, Korea, Sept 15, 19; US citizen; m 44; c 5. TRANSPLANTATION, CANCER. *Educ:* Davidson Col, BS, 41; Washington Univ, MD, 44. *Hon Degrees:* DSc, Bueno Vista Col, 69, Colo State Univ, 80. *Prof Exp:* USPHS res fel, Washington Univ, 50-51; asst res prof path, Sch Med, Univ Pittsburgh, 51-52; from asst prof to assoc prof med, Sch Med, Univ Chicago, 52-59; chmn, Dept Microbiol, 63-66, assoc dean fac, 66-68, actg dean, 68-69, dean, 69-71, PROF MED, SCH MED, UNIV COLO, 59-, PROF MICROBIOL, 60-, DIR, WEBB-WARING LUNG INST, 73- *Concurrent Pos:* Markle scholar med sci, 55-60; consult, Vet Admin Hosp, 59-71; ed, J Allergy, 63-67. *Mem:* Nat Acad Sci; AAAS; Am Soc Clin Invest; Am Asn Immunologists (pres, 78); Am Acad Allergy (pres, 65). *Res:* Effect of oxygen during culture on survival of mouse throid allografts; immunological tolerance in animals bearing cultured allografts. *Mailing Add:* Webb-Waring Lung Inst Univ Colo Health Sci Ctr 4200 E Ninth Ave Denver CO 80262

TALMAGE, ROY VAN NESTE, b Moppo, Korea, Feb 9, 17; US citizen; m 42; c 3. PHYSIOLOGY. *Educ:* Maryville Col, AB, 38; Univ Richmond, MA, 40; Harvard Univ, PhD(endocrinol), 47. *Prof Exp:* Instr biol, Univ Richmond, 40-41; asst, Harvard Univ, 41-42 & 46-47; from instr to prof, Rice Univ, 47-70, chmn dept, 56-64, master, Wiess Col, 57-70; DIR ORTHOP RES & PROF SURG & PHARMACOL, SCH MED, UNIV NC, CHAPEL HILL, 70- *Concurrent Pos:* NIH res fel, State Univ Leiden, 64; mem, NIH Study Sects, 64-68 & 70-; gen chmn & co-chmn parathyroid confs, Houston, 60, Leiden, 64, Montreal, 67, Chapel Hill, 71, Oxford, Eng, 74, Vancouver, 77 & Denver, 80; staff biochemist, AEC, 69-70, mem nat adv dent res coun, Nat Inst Dent Res, 74-77; pres, Inst Conf Calcium Regulatory Hormones, 79-81. *Mem:* AAAS; Orthop Res Soc; Am Soc Zoologists; Soc Exp Biol & Med; Am Physiol Soc; Endocrine Soc. *Res:* Calcium regulating hormones and ion transport processes in bone. *Mailing Add:* Orthop Res Labs Univ of NC Chapel Hill NC 27514

TALMAN, JAMES DAVIS, b Toronto, Ont, July 24, 31; m 57; c 4. THEORETICAL PHYSICS. *Educ:* Univ Western Ont, BA, 53, MSc, 54; Princeton Univ, PhD, 59. *Prof Exp:* Instr physics, Princeton Univ, 57-59; asst prof, Am Univ Beirut, 59-60; from asst prof to prof math, 60-67, PROF APPL MATH, UNIV WESTERN ONT, 67- *Concurrent Pos:* Res asst, Univ Calif, Davis, 63-64; vis, Niels Bohr Inst, Copenhagen, Denmark, 69-70; vis prof physics & aeronomy, Univ Fla, Gainesville, 78-79. *Mem:* Am Phys Soc; Can Asn Physicists. *Res:* Quantal many-body problem; atomic structure theory; numerical methods. *Mailing Add:* Dept of Appl Math Univ of Western Ont London ON N6A 5B8 Can

TALMAN, RICHARD MICHAEL, b Toronto, Ont, Sept 24, 34; m 57; c 4. PHYSICS. *Educ:* Univ Western Ont, BA, 56, MA, 57; Calif Inst Technol, PhD(physics), 63. *Prof Exp:* From asst prof to assoc prof, 62-71, PROF PHYSICS, CORNELL UNIV, 71- *Mem:* Am Phys Soc. *Res:* Elementary and experimental particle physics; accelerator physics. *Mailing Add:* Dept of Physics Cornell Univ Ithaca NY 14850

TALNER, NORMAN STANLEY, b Mt Vernon, NY, Sept 28, 25; m 50; c 3. PEDIATRICS, CARDIOLOGY. *Educ:* Univ Mich, Ann Arbor, BS, 45; Yale Univ, MD, 49. *Hon Degrees:* MA, Yale Univ, 69. *Prof Exp:* Intern & resident pediat, Kings County Hosp, State Univ NY, 49-51; resident, Univ Hosp, Univ Mich, 51-52, instr, Med Sch, 54-56, Mich Heart Asn fel pediat cardiol, Hosp, 56-58, asst prof pediat, Univ, 58-60; from asst prof to assoc prof, 60-69, PROF PEDIAT, SCH MED, YALE UNIV, 69- *Concurrent Pos:* Attend physician, Yale-New Haven Hosp, 60-; USPHS career develop award, 62-72; examr, Sub-Bd Pediat Cardiol, Am Bd Pediat, 69-74; prog chmn, Am Heart Asn, 69-72; consult, Vet Admin, 72- *Mem:* Soc Pediat Res (mem secy, 69-72); Am Pediat Soc; Am Col Cardiol (asst secy, 72-74); cor mem Asn Europ Pediat Cardiol. *Res:* Cardiopulmonary physiology in infants and children. *Mailing Add:* Dept of Pediat Yale Univ Sch of Med New Haven CT 06510

TALPEY, THOMAS E(DWIN), b Auburn, NY, Mar 20, 25; m 48; c 2. ELECTRICAL ENGINEERING, UNDERWATER ACOUSTICS. *Educ:* Cornell Univ, BEE, 46; Univ Mich, MSE, 48, PhD(elec eng), 54; Univ Grenoble, DUniv, 52. *Prof Exp:* Instr elec eng, Univ Mich, 46-53; mem tech staff, Bell Tel Labs, Inc, 53-60; res assoc, Cornell Univ, Arecibo Radio Observ, PR, 60-63; MEM TECH STAFF, BELL TEL LABS, INC, 63- *Mem:* Inst Elec & Electronics Engrs. *Res:* Underwater acoustics; low noise, wide-band amplifiers; radar receiver and data handling system design. *Mailing Add:* Bell Tel Labs, Inc Whippany NJ 07981

TALSO, PETER JACOB, b Ishpeming, Mich, Sept 22, 21; m 43; c 4. MEDICINE. *Educ:* Wayne State Univ, BA, 43, MD, 45; Am Bd Internal Med, dipl, 54. *Prof Exp:* From instr to asst prof med, Univ Chicago, 50-52; from asst prof to prof med, Stritch Sch Med, Loyola Univ Chicago, 53-71, chmn dept, 63-70; MED DIR, LITTLE COMPANY OF MARY HOSP, 71- *Concurrent Pos:* Consult, Hines Vet Admin Hosp, Maywood, 59-71; attend physician, Cook County Hosp, 59-66, consult, 66-71. *Mem:* Fel Am Col Cardiol; fel Am Col Physicians; Sigma Xi; Am Fedn Clin Res; fel Am Col Physicians. *Res:* Electrolyte and water metabolism; hypertension renal disease. *Mailing Add:* Little Company of Mary Hosp 2800 W 95th St Evergreen Park IL 60642

TALWANI, MANIK, b India, Aug 22, 33; m 58; c 3. GEOPHYSICS. *Educ:* Univ Delhi, BSc, 51, MSc, 53; Columbia Univ, PhD(geol), 59. *Hon Degrees:* PhD, Univ Oslo, Norway. *Prof Exp:* Dir, 73-81, MEM STAFF, LAMONT-DOHERTY GEOL OBSERV, COLUMBIA UNIV, 57-, PROF GEOL, UNIV, 70- *Concurrent Pos:* Mem ocean affairs bd & exec comt, Joint Oceanog Inst Deep Earth Sampling; mem, Ocean Policy Comt, Nat Acad Sci & Bd Gov Joint Oceanog Inst, Inc; Fulbright-Hays Fel, 73; Guggenheim fel, 74. *Honors & Awards:* Indian Geophys Union First Krishnan Medal, 65; James B Macelwane Award, Am Geophys Union, 67; NASA Exceptional Sci Achievement Award, 73; Maurice Ewing Award, Am Geophys Union, 81. *Mem:* Am Soc Explor Geophys; fel Am Geophys Union; Seismol Soc Am; fel Geol Soc Am; fel Royal Astron Soc. *Res:* Marine geophysics; oceanography, geodesy. *Mailing Add:* Gulf Res & Develop Co PO Drawer 2038 Pittsburgh PA 15230

TAM, ANDREW CHING, b Canton, China, Oct 13, 44; m 70; c 1. ATOMIC PHYSICS, MOLECULAR PHYSICS. *Educ:* Univ Hong Kong, BSc, 68, MSc, 70; Columbia Univ, PhD(physics), 75. *Prof Exp:* Fac fel physics, Columbia Radiation Lab, Columbia Univ, 70-72, preceptor, 71-72, res asst physics, 72-74, res assoc, 75-77; mem tech staff, Bell Labs, 78-80; MEM STAFF, IBM RES LAB, 80- *Mem:* Am Phys Soc; Sigma Xi. *Res:* Atomic and molecular spectroscopy; optical pumping; excimer lasers; laser interaction with atomic and molecular systems; laser-induced isotope separation. *Mailing Add:* Dept K46-282 IBM Res Labs San Jose CA 95193

TAM, CHRISTOPHER K W, US citizen. FLUIDS, NOISE. *Educ:* McGill Univ, BEng, 62; Calif Inst Technol, MSc, 63, PhD(appl mech), 66. *Prof Exp:* Res fel, Calif Inst Technol, 66-67; asst prof, Mass Inst Technol, 67-71; assoc prof, 71-76, PROF MATH, FLA STATE UNIV, 76- *Mem:* Acoust Soc Am; Soc Indust & Appl Math; Am Inst Aeronaut & Astronaut; Am Phys Soc; Am Geophys Union. *Res:* Physics of noise generation and propagation in aeroacoustics, including jet noise, airframe noise and duct acoustics; turbulence and hydrodynamic stability theory; applied mathematics. *Mailing Add:* Dept of Math Fla State Univ Tallahassee FL 32306

TAM, JAMES PINGKWAN, b Hong Kong, Mar 25, 47; m 72; c 2. MEDICINAL CHEMISTRY, BIOCHEMISTRY. *Educ:* Univ Wis, BS, 71, PhD(pharm), 76. *Prof Exp:* fel, 76-77, res assoc, 77-79, ASST PROF BIOCHEM, ROCKEFELLER UNIV, 80- *Mem:* Am Chem Soc; NY Acad Sci. *Res:* New synthetic methods; solution and solid phase peptide syntheses; hormonol, immunological peptides and enzyme inhibitors. *Mailing Add:* Rockefeller Univ 1230 York Ave New York NY 10021

TAM, KWOK KUEN, b Hong Kong, Oct 30, 38; m 64; c 2. APPLIED MATHEMATICS. *Educ:* Univ Toronto, BASc, 62, MA, 63, PhD(appl math), 65. *Prof Exp:* Asst prof, 65-69, assoc prof, 70-79, PROF APPL MATH, MCGILL UNIV, 80- *Concurrent Pos:* Res fel, Harvard Univ, 71-72. *Mem:* Can Math Cong. *Res:* Fluid mechanics; construction of approximate solutions to some nonlinear boundary value problems. *Mailing Add:* Dept of Math McGill Univ Montreal PQ H3A 2K6 Can

TAM, KWOK-WAI, b Hong Kong, Mar 16, 38; US citizen; m 68; c 3. MATHEMATICAL ANALYSIS, OPERATIONS RESEARCH. *Educ:* Univ Wash, BS, 60, PhD(math), 67. *Prof Exp:* Teaching asst math, Univ Wash, 61-66; asst prof, 66-75, ASSOC PROF MATH, PORTLAND STATE UNIV, 75- *Mem:* Am Math Soc. *Res:* Mathematical programming. *Mailing Add:* Dept of Math Portland State Univ Portland OR 97201

TAM, WING-GAY, Can citizen. PHYSICS. *Educ:* Hong Kong Univ, BSc, 60; Univ BC, MSc, 64, PhD(physics), 67. *Prof Exp:* Nat Res Coun overseas fel theoret physics, Univ Nijmegan, Neth, 67-69; res assoc molecular physics, Laval Univ, Can, 69-72, asst prof, 72-74; DEFENSE SCIENTIST OPTICAL PHYSICS, DEFENSE RES ESTAB, VALCARTIER, QUE, 74- *Mem:* Optical Soc Am. *Res:* Atmospheric propagation of electromagnetic waves; energy transfer in molecular systems; atmospheric aerosols. *Mailing Add:* Def Res Estab Valcartier PO Box 880 Courcelette PQ G0A 1R0 Can

TAMAKI, GEORGE, b Los Angeles, Calif, Mar 20, 31; m 56; c 2. ENTOMOLOGY. *Educ:* Univ Calif, Berkeley, BS, 60, PhD(entom), 65. *Prof Exp:* ENTOMOLOGIST, ENTOM RES DIV, USDA, 65- *Mem:* Entom Soc Am. *Res:* Insect population dynamics; insect ecology and biological control. *Mailing Add:* 3706 Nob Hill Blvd Yakima WA 98902

TAMAOKI, TAIKI, b Miki, Hyogo-Ken, Japan, Dec 3, 28; m 61; c 4. BIOCHEMISTRY, PLANT PATHOLOGY. *Educ:* Univ Tokyo, BSc, 51; Purdue Univ, MS, 58; Univ Wis, PhD(plant path), 60. *Prof Exp:* Fel oncol, McArdle Lab, Univ Wis, 61-64; asst prof biochem, Cancer Res Unit, Univ Alta, 68-80; WITH SOUTHERN ALBERTA CANCER CTR, 80- *Mem:* AAAS; Am Chem Soc; Am Soc Biol Chem; Am Asn Cancer Res; Can Biochem Soc. *Res:* Regulation of protein and RNA synthesis in mammalian cells. *Mailing Add:* Southern Alberta Cancer Ctr 2104 Second St SW Calgary AB T2S 1S5 Can

TAMAR, HENRY, b Vienna, Austria, Sept 15, 29; nat US; m 55; c 3. PROTOZOOLOGY, PHYSIOLOGY. *Educ:* NY Univ, AB, 49, MS, 51; Fla State Univ, PhD(physiol), 57. *Prof Exp:* Researcher, Lebanon Hosp, New York, 51; asst physiol, Fla State Univ, 51-55; asst prof biol, Am Int Col, 55-57; prof & head div, Pembroke State Col, 57-62; assoc prof, 62-77, PROF ZOOL, IND STATE UNIV, TERRE HAUTE, 77- *Concurrent Pos:* Vis prof, Stephen F Austin State Col, 59, NC State Col, 61-62 & Marine Biol Labs, Woods Hole, 65, 72 & 74, Marine Sci Ctr, Santa Catalina Island, 81. *Mem:* Am Micro Soc; Soc Protozool. *Res:* Principles of sensory physiology; locomotion, responses and structure of ciliates; jumping ciliates and their forward avoidance reactions. *Mailing Add:* Dept of Life Sci Ind State Univ Terre Haute IN 47809

TAMARI, DOV, b Fulda, Ger, Apr 29, 11; m 48; c 3. MATHEMATICS. *Educ:* Hebrew Univ, Israel, MSc, 39; Univ Paris, Dr es Sc(math), 51. *Prof Exp:* Res fel math, Nat Ctr Sci Res, Paris, France, 49-53; sr lectr, Israel Inst Technol, 53-55, assoc prof, 55-59; prof, Univ Rochester, 59-60; mem, Inst Advan Study, 60-61; Orgn Am States vis prof, Univ Brazil, 61-62; res assoc, Univ Utrecht, 62; prof, Univ Caen, 62-63; chmn dept math, 64-67, PROF MATH, STATE UNIV NY BUFFALO, 63- *Concurrent Pos:* Vis prof, Hebrew Univ, Israel, 53-59; mem, Inst Advan Study, 67-68; vis prof, Israel Inst Technol, 73. *Mem:* Am Math Soc; Math Asn Am; Asn Symbolic Logic. *Res:* Algebra; semi-group, group and ring theory; embedding and word problems; topological semi-groups, groups and fields; mathematical logic; binary relations; partial algebras; combinatorial analysis. *Mailing Add:* Dept of Math Diefendorf Hall Buffalo NY 14214

TAMARIN, ARNOLD, b Chicago, Ill, Mar 27, 23; m 45; c 2. ORAL BIOLOGY, HISTOLOGY. *Educ:* Univ Ill, BS, 49, DDS, 51; Univ Wash, MSD, 60. *Prof Exp:* Assoc prof, 66-69, PROF ORAL BIOL, UNIV WASH, 69-, ADJ PROF, DEPT BIOL STRUCT, 74- *Mem:* Fel Royal Micros Soc; Am Asn Anatomists; fel Zool Soc, London; Am Soc Cell Biol. *Res:* Comparative odontology; cell kinematics in the exocrine secretory process; exocrine collagen secretion in mytilus; ultrastructural morphology; embryological morphogenesis. *Mailing Add:* Dept Oral Biol Univ Wash Seattle WA 98195

TAMARIN, ROBERT HARVEY, b Brooklyn, NY, Dec 14, 42; m 68. GENETICS, ECOLOGY. *Educ:* Brooklyn Col, BS, 63; Ind Univ, PhD(zool), 68. *Prof Exp:* Comt Instnl Coop traveling scholar, Univ Wis, 67-68; USPHS fel genetics, Univ Hawaii, 68-70; Ford Found fel, Princeton Univ, 70-71; asst prof, 71-77, ASSOC PROF BIOL, BOSTON UNIV, 77- *Concurrent Pos:* NIH & NSF res grants. *Mem:* AAAS; Sigma Xi; Am Soc Mammal; Am Soc Naturalists; Ecol Soc Am. *Res:* Population biology, including genetics, demography, reproductive physiology, behavior and general ecology of insular and mainland field mice to understand population regulation; tropical and radiation studies of field mice. *Mailing Add:* Dept of Biol Boston Univ Boston MA 02215

TAMARKIN, PAUL, physics, research management, see previous edition

TAMASHIRO, MINORU, b Hilo, Hawaii, Sept 16, 24; m 52. INSECT PATHOLOGY. *Educ:* Univ Hawaii, BS, 51, MS, 54; Univ Calif, PhD, 60. *Prof Exp:* Asst entom, 51-54, jr entomologist, 54-55, from asst prof entom & asst entomologist to assoc prof entom & assoc entomologist, 57-73, PROF ENTOM & ENTOMOLOGIST, UNIV HAWAII, 73- *Concurrent Pos:* WHO consult, 63; NIH fel, 64-65. *Mem:* Entom Soc Am. *Res:* Microbial control; effect of pathogens and insecticides on biological control; termites, biology, ecology, control. *Mailing Add:* Dept of Entom Univ of Hawaii Honolulu HI 96822

TAMBASCO, DANIEL JOSEPH, b Amsterdam, NY, Mar 10, 36; m 66; c 2. THEORETICAL PHYSICS. *Educ:* Union Col, BS, 58; Univ Iowa, PhD(physics), 65. *Prof Exp:* Asst prof, 65-69, ASSOC PROF PHYSICS, MERRIMACK COL, 69- *Mem:* Am Phys Soc. *Res:* Field theory theory; statistical mechanics. *Mailing Add:* Dept of Physics Merrimack Col North Andover MA 01845

TAMBORSKI, CHRIST, b Buffalo, NY, Nov 12, 26; m 49; c 7. ORGANIC CHEMISTRY, FLUORINE CHEMISTRY. *Educ:* Univ Buffalo, BA, 49, PhD(org chem), 53. *Prof Exp:* Fel, Univ Buffalo, 53; SR SCIENTIST, AIR FORCE MAT LAB, WRIGHT-PATTERSON AFB, 55- *Concurrent Pos:* Consult, Childrens Hosp Res Found, 74- *Honors & Awards:* Jacobowitz Award, 52. *Mem:* Am Chem Soc; Sigma Xi. *Res:* High temperature stable fluids and elastomers for advanced aerospace applications; synthesis of organometallic compounds, heterocyclic compounds, organoaliphatic and aromatic fluorine compounds, anti-oxidants. *Mailing Add:* 5016 Georgian Dr Dayton OH 45429

TAMBURIN, HENRY JOHN, b Passaic, NJ, July 24, 44; m 68; c 2. INDUSTRIAL ORGANIC CHEMISTRY, DYESTUFF CHEMISTRY. *Educ:* Seton Hall Univ, BS, 66; Univ Md, College Park, PhD(org chem), 71. *Prof Exp:* From teaching asst to instr org chem, Univ Md, College Park, 66-72; res & develop chemist, Toms River Chem Corp, 72-75, sr develop chemist, 75-77, actg group leader, 78-79, sr prod chemist, 79-81, GROUP LEADER, CIBA-GEIGY CORP, 81- *Mem:* Am Chem Soc. *Res:* The introduction of modern chemical and processing technology in the dyestuff manufacturing process. *Mailing Add:* Bldg 200 Ciba-Geigy Corp PO Box 71 Toms River NJ 08753

TAMBURINO, LOUIS ANTHONY, b Pittsburgh, Pa, May 9, 36; m 58; c 1. MATHEMATICAL PHYSICS. *Educ:* Carnegie Inst Technol, BS, 57; Univ Pittsburgh, PhD(physics), 62. *Prof Exp:* Res assoc, Syracuse Univ, 63-64; res physicist, Aerospace Res Labs, 64-72, MATH PHYSICIST, AIR FORCE AVIONICS LAB, US AIR FORCE, 72- *Mem:* Asn Comput Mach; Inst Elec & Electronic Engrs; Sigma Xi; Am Phys Soc. *Res:* General relativity; airborne electronic terrain map and display systems; inertial navigation; pattern recognition; optics; image processing; cybernetics. *Mailing Add:* Systs Avionics Div Air Force Avionics Lab Bldg 620 Wright-Patterson AFB OH 45433

TAMBURRO, CARLO HORACE, b Caserta, Italy, Jan 20, 36; US citizen; m 71; c 4. INTERNAL MEDICINE, HEPATOLOGY. *Educ:* Georgetown Univ, BS, 58; Seton Hall Univ, MD, 62. *Prof Exp:* Intern med, Jersey City Med Ctr, NJ, 62-63, resident, 63-64; asst, Sch Med, Tufts Univ, 64-65; instr med, NJ Med Sch, 67-68; asst prof, Col Med & Dent NJ, Newark, 69-74; assoc prof, NJ Med Sch, 74; assoc prof med, Sch Med, 74-77, assoc oncol, Cancer Ctr, chief, Div Digestive Dis & Nutrit, & dir, Vinyl Chloride Proj, 74-80, PROF MED & ASSOC PEIDAT, SCH MED, UNIV LOUISVILLE, 77-, DIR, LIVER REFERENCE LAB, 80-, PROF COMMUN HEALTH, 81-, CHIEF, DIV OCCUPATIONAL HEALTH, 81- *Concurrent Pos:* Resident med, New Eng Ctr Hosp, Boston, 64-65; NIH fel hepatic dis, 65-68. *Mem:* Int Asn Study Liver; Am Asn Study Liver Dis; Am Soc Human Genetics; Am Col Toxicol; Am Fedn Clin Res. *Res:* Hepatic cancer; industrial chemical carcinogenesis, vinyl monomer; clinical toxicology; alcoholism, drug addiction, and withdrawal syndromes; viral hepatitis; liver disease and nutrition; vitamin metabolism and deficiency; liver regeneration and metabolism; hepatic collagen formation; immunology and liver injury. *Mailing Add:* Div of Digestive Dis & Nutrit Univ of Louisville Sch of Med Louisville KY 40232

TAMBURRO, KATHLEEN O'CONNELL, b New York, NY, Oct 30, 42; m 71; c 4. PROTOZOOLOGY. *Educ:* Marymount Manhattan Col, BA, 64; Fordham Univ, MS, 65, PhD(biol, protozool), 68. *Prof Exp:* From res asst to res assoc biochem & physiol of protozoa, Haskins Labs, 65-74; admin assoc & grant coordr-med/ed, Div Digestive Dis & Nutrit, 76-80, SR MED ED & ADMIN ASSOC, DIV OCCUP DIS, SCH MED, UNIV LOUISVILLE, 80- *Mem:* AAAS; Sigma Xi; Soc Protozool; Am Soc Trop Med & Hyg; Am Soc Microbiologists. *Res:* Protozoa as pharmacological tools; chemotherapy of trypanosomatid parasites; nutrition; biochemistry and physiology of Trypanosomatidae. *Mailing Add:* 512 Brandon Rd Louisville KY 40207

TAMHANE, AJIT CHINTAMAN, b Bhiwandi, India, Nov 12, 46; m 75. APPLIED STATISTICS, MATHEMATICAL STATISTICS. *Educ:* Indian Inst Technol, Bombay, BTech(Hon), 68; Cornell Univ, MS, 73, PhD(statist), 75. *Prof Exp:* Jr engr design, Larsen & Toubro Ltd, Bombay, 68-70; asst prof, 75-79, ASSOC PROF INDUST ENG & MGT SCI, NORTHWESTERN UNIV, 79- *Concurrent Pos:* Statist consult. *Mem:* Inst Math Statist; Am Statist Asn; Biometrics Soc. *Res:* Ranking and selection procedures; multiple comparisons; design of experiments; biostatistics. *Mailing Add:* Dept of Indust Eng Technol Inst Northwestern Univ Evanston IL 60201

TAMIMI, HAMDI AHMAD, microbiology, infectious diseases, see previous edition

TAMIMI, YUSUF NIMR, b Nablus, Jordan, Nov 15, 31; m 63; c 3. SOIL CHEMISTRY. *Educ:* Purdue Univ, BS, 57; NMex State Univ, MS, 60; Univ Hawaii, PhD(soil chem), 64. *Prof Exp:* Asst agronomist, Univ, 63-70, assoc soil scientist, 70-75, PROF SOIL SCI, AGR EXP STA, UNIV HAWAII, 75- *Mem:* Am Soc Agron; Int Soc Soil Sci. *Res:* Chemistry of soil phosphorous; field crops, tropical pasture fertilization and forest tree nutrition; forest soils. *Mailing Add:* Agr Exp Sta Univ Hawaii 461 W Lani Kaula Hilo HI 96720

TAMIR, HADASSAH, neuroscience, biochemistry, see previous edition

TAMIR, THEODOR, b Bucharest, Roumania, Sept 17, 27; m 49; c 2. ELECTROPHYSICS, ELECTRICAL ENGINEERING. *Educ:* Israel Inst Technol, BS, 53, Dipl Ing, 54, MS, 58; Polytech Inst Brooklyn, PhD(electrophys), 62. *Prof Exp:* Res engr, Sci Dept, Ministry Defense, Israel,

53-56; instr elec eng, Israel Inst Technol, 56-58; res assoc, 58-62, from asst prof to assoc prof, 62-69, PROF ELECTROPHYS, POLYTECH INST NEW YORK, 69- *Concurrent Pos:* Consult indust & govt labs; co-ed, Springer Series in Optical Sciences, 79-; adv ed, Optics Commun, 75-; head, Dept Elec Eng, Polytech Inst NY, 74-79. *Honors & Awards:* Citation Distinguished Res, Polytech Chap, Sigma Xi, 78. *Mem:* Fel Inst Elec & Electronics Engrs; Brit Inst Elec Eng; Int Union Radio Sci; fel Optical Soc Am. *Res:* Electromagnetic wave propagation in non-uniform media and periodic structures; radiation and diffraction phenomena; properties of configurations supporting surface, leaky, lateral and other wave types; elastic and optical waves. *Mailing Add:* Dept of Elec Eng & Electrophys Polytech Inst of New York Brooklyn NY 11201

TAMM, IGOR, b Tapa, Estonia, Apr 27, 22; nat US; m 53; c 3. VIROLOGY, MEDICINE. *Educ:* Yale Univ, MD, 47. *Prof Exp:* Intern med, Grace-New Haven Community Hosp Univ Serv, 47-48, asst resident, 48-49; from asst to assoc prof, 49-64, PROF MED & VIROL & SR PHYSICIAN, HOSP, ROCKEFELLER UNIV, 64- *Concurrent Pos:* Asst, Sch Med, Yale Univ, 47-49; from asst physician to physician, Rockefeller Univ Hosp, 49-64; assoc mem comn acute respiratory dis, Armed Forces Epidemiol Bd, 61-73; mem virol & rickettsiology study sect, NIH, 64-68; mem bd sci consults, Sloan-Kettering Inst Cancer Res, 66-73; centennial lectr, Univ Ill, 68; mem study panel allergy & infectious dis, Health Res Coun City of New York, 68-75; mem adv comt, Am Cancer Soc, 69-72; gen chmn, task force virol, Nat Insts Allergy & Infectious Dis, NIH, 76-78. *Honors & Awards:* Alfred Benzon Prize, 67; Sarah L Poiley Award, NY Acad Sci, 77. *Mem:* Nat Acad Sci; Am Soc Cell Biol; Asn Am Physicians. *Res:* Viral replication and virus-induced alterations in cells; biosynthesis of nucleic acids and proteins; interaction of viruses with mucoproteins; actions of benzimidazoles and interferons on cells. *Mailing Add:* Dept of Virol Rockefeller Univ New York NY 10021

TAMM, PAUL WHITFIELD, chemical engineering, see previous edition

TAMMEMAGI, HANS YNGVE, geophysics, see previous edition

TAMOR, STEPHEN, b New York, NY, Nov 29, 25; m 49; c 4. THEORETICAL PHYSICS. *Educ:* City Col New York, BS, 44; Univ Rochester, PhD, 50. *Prof Exp:* Physicist, Oak Ridge Nat Lab, 50-52; physicist, Radiation Lab, Univ Calif, 52-55; physicist, Res Lab, Gen Elec Co, NY, 55-66, Space Sci Lab, Pa, 66-71; PHYSICIST, SCI APPLN, INC, 71- *Concurrent Pos:* Guggenheim fel, 63-64. *Mem:* Am Phys Soc. *Res:* Meson theory; nuclear and plasma physics; reactor theory. *Mailing Add:* Sci Appln Inc PO Box 2351 La Jolla CA 92037

TAMORRIA, CHRISTOPHER RICHARD, b Washington, DC, June 20, 32; m 61; c 1. CHEMISTRY. *Educ:* Georgetown Univ, BS, 54, MS, 58; Univ Md, PhD(med chem), 61. *Prof Exp:* Asst org chem, Georgetown Univ, 54-55; chemist, Food & Drug Admin, 55-56; asst org chem, Georgetown Univ, 56-57; asst inorg chem, Univ Md, 57-58; org chemist, Pharmaceut Prod Develop Sect, Lederle Labs, Am Cyanamid Co, 60-68, mgr regulatory agencies & info processing, Med Res Div, Cyanamid Int, 68-70; sr tech assoc, US Pharmacopeia, Md, 70-73; dir sci commun, Purdue Frederick Co & Affil, 73-77; mgr tech info, Toxicol Sect, Lederle Labs, 77; sr regulatory assoc, Drug Regulatory Affairs, Ayerst Labs, 78-80; DEP DIR, DRUG REGULATORY AFFAIRS, STERLING DRUG INC, 80- *Honors & Awards:* Gold Medal, Am Inst Chemists, 54. *Mem:* Am Chem Soc; Am Pharmaceut Asn; fel Am Found Pharmaceut Educ; Am Inst Chemists; Regulatory Affairs Prof Soc. *Res:* Partial synthesis of steroids; correlation of structure and biological activity, especially in the synthesis of new steroid homologs and tetracycline antibiotics. *Mailing Add:* 27 Maymont Lane Trumbull CT 06611

TAMPAS, JOHN PETER, b Burlington, Vt, May 18, 29; m 62; c 4. RADIOLOGY. *Educ:* Univ Vt, BS, 51, MD, 54. *Prof Exp:* Teaching fel pediat radiol, Children's Hosp of Los Angeles, Univ Southern Calif, 60-61; NIH res fel cardiovasc radiol, Nat Heart Inst, 61-62; from asst prof to assoc prof, 62-69, PROF RADIOL & CHMN DEPT, UNIV VT, 70- *Concurrent Pos:* James Picker Found scholar radiol res, Univ Vt, 62-65; from asst attend radiologist to attend radiologist, Mary Fletcher Hosp & DeGoesbriand Mem Hosp, 62-; physician-in-residence, Vet Admin Hosp, 72- *Mem:* AMA; fel Am Col Radiol; Soc Pediat Radiol; Am Roentgen Ray Soc; Radiol Soc NAm. *Res:* Basic and clinical problems in radiology; pediatric and cardiovascular radiology. *Mailing Add:* Dept Radiol Mary Fletcher Unit Med Ctr Hosp Vt Burlington VT 05401

TAMPICO, JOSEPH, b Baltimore, Md, Apr 28, 16; div; c 3. ELECTRICAL ENGINEERING. *Educ:* Johns Hopkins Univ, BE, 37, Dr Eng, 41. *Prof Exp:* Mem staff, Lab Appl Physics, Johns Hopkins Univ, 45-54 & Hycon Mfg Co, 54-55; vpres, Assoc Missile Prod Corp, Am Mach & Foundry Co, 55-58; mgr independent res & develop, Marquardt Corp, 59-65; mgr bus planning, Spacecraft Dept, 65-72, mgr oper planning, Locomotive Dept, 72-76, strategic planning analyst, Locomotive Opers, 77-81, MGR MKT ANAL, LOCOMOTIVE MKT, MKT DIV, GEN ELEC CO, 81- *Mem:* Assoc fel Am Inst Aeronaut & Astronaut; sr mem Inst Elec & Electronics Engrs. *Res:* Properties of dielectrics; resistance welding; jet propulsion engines; interfacial contact resistance; electronic test equipment; research administration; aerospace business planning. *Mailing Add:* 5946 Jodie Lane Apt 13 Erie PA 16509

TAMRES, MILTON, b Warsaw, Poland, Mar 12, 22; US citizen; m 60; c 2. PHYSICAL INORGANIC CHEMISTRY. *Educ:* Brooklyn Col, BA, 43; Northwestern Univ, PhD(phys chem), 49. *Prof Exp:* Anal chemist, Celanese Corp Am, Md, 43-44; asst, Northwestern Univ, 44-47; from instr to asst prof chem, Univ Ill, 48-53; from asst prof to assoc prof, 53-63, PROF CHEM, UNIV MICH, ANN ARBOR, 63- *Concurrent Pos:* Guggenheim fel, 59-60; mem, Adv Coun Col Chem, 62-66; Am Chem Soc-Petrol Res Fund int fel, 66-67; vis scholar, Univ Tokyo, 74. *Mem:* Fel AAAS; Am Chem Soc; fel Am Inst Chemists. *Res:* Electron donor-acceptor interactions; basicities of cyclic compounds. *Mailing Add:* Dept of Chem Univ of Mich Ann Arbor MI 48109

TAMSITT, JAMES RAY, b Big Spring, Tex, Nov 22, 28. ZOOLOGY, MAMMALIAN SYSTEMATICS. *Educ:* Univ Tex, BA, 51, MA, 53, PhD(vert ecol), 58. *Prof Exp:* Lectr zool, Univ Man, 57-58; instr biol, ETex State Univ, 58-59; prof zool, Univ of the Andes, Colombia, 59-65; NIH fel med zool, Sch Med, Univ PR, San Juan, 65-67; assoc cur, Dept Mammal, 67-73, ASSOC PROF ZOOL, UNIV TORONTO, 69-, CUR, ROYAL ONT MUS, 73- *Concurrent Pos:* Vis prof biol, Pontificia Univ Javeriana, Colombia, 75; sr Fulbright-Hays fel, 75. *Mem:* Fel AAAS; Am Soc Mammalogists; Soc Study Evolution; Asn Trop Biol. *Res:* Ecology, natural history, taxonomy and ectoparasites of Neotropical mammals. *Mailing Add:* Dept of Mammal 100 Queen's Park Toronto ON M5S 2C6 Can

TAMSKY, MORGAN JEROME, b St Louis, Mo, July 26, 42; m 66. PHYSICAL CHEMISTRY. *Educ:* Washington Univ, BA, 64; Univ Kans, PhD(chem), 70. *Prof Exp:* Sr chemist, 69-74, RES SPECIALIST, 3M CO, 74-, SUPVR POLYMER PHYSICS, CENT RES LABS, 77- *Mem:* Soc Rheology; Am Chem Soc. *Res:* Surface phenomenon; adhesion; polymer physics. *Mailing Add:* 1920 Baynard Ave St Paul MN 55116

TAMURA, TSUNEO, b Hawaii, Nov 15, 25; div; c 3. SOILS, WASTE MANAGEMENT. *Educ:* Univ Hawaii, BS, 48; Univ Wis, MS, 51, PhD(soils), 52. *Prof Exp:* From asst soil scientist to assoc soil scientist, Conn Agr Exp Sta, 52-57; chemist, Westinghouse Elec Corp, 57; sr res staff mem, 57-77, EARTH SCI SECT HEAD, OAK RIDGE NAT LAB, 77- *Mem:* Fel AAAS; fel Am Soc Agron; Am Chem Soc; Sigma Xi; fel Soil Sci Soc Am. *Res:* Soil chemistry and genesis; soil clay mineralogy; radioactive waste disposal; health physics; toxic metals in environment. *Mailing Add:* 206 Elmhurst Dr No 35 Oak Ridge TN 37830

TAN, AGNES W H, b Epin, China, March 16, 42. BIOCHEMISTRY. *Educ:* Viterbo Col, Wis, BA, 63; Univ Minn, PhD(biochem), 67. *Prof Exp:* Fel biochem, Harvard Med Sch, 67-68, Univ Minn, 68-69; instr, Rutgers Med Sch, New Brusnwick, 69-70, Temple Med Sch, Pa, 70-72; RES CHEMIST, VET ADMIN MED CTR, MINNEAPOLIS, 72- *Concurrent Pos:* Asst prof, Dept Biochem, Med Sch, Univ Minn, 78- *Mem:* Am Chem Soc; Am Soc Biol Chemists. *Res:* Mechanism of enzyme regulation by hormones and metabolites in mammalian systems including enzymes involved in the glycogen metabolic pathway. *Mailing Add:* Va Med Ctr 618-111G 54th St & 48th Ave S Minneapolis MN 55417

TAN, AH-TI CHU, b Amoy, China, Sept 24, 35; Can citizen. CHEMISTRY, BIOCHEMISTRY. *Educ:* Mapua Inst Technol, BSChem, 57; Adamson Univ, Manila, BSChE, 58; McGill Univ, MSc, 62, PhD(chem kinetics), 66. *Prof Exp:* Lectr phys chem, Adamson Univ, Manila, 58-60; res chemist, Bathurst Paper Co, 65-66; assoc biochem, Col Med, Univ Vt, 66-68, vis asst prof, 68-69; asst prof ophthal, Fac Med, McGill Univ, 69-72, asst prof anesthesia, 72-78; assoc prof, Fac Med, Univ Manitoba, 78-79; ASSOC PROF, FAC MED, UNIV MONTREAL, 80- *Concurrent Pos:* NIH grant biochem, Col Med, Univ Vt, 66-68; Que Med Res Coun grant ophthal, Fac Med, McGill Univ, 69-72; prof assoc anaesthesia res, McGill Univ, 72- *Mem:* Am Chem Soc; Chem Inst Can; Can Biochem Soc; Soc Neurosci; AAAS. *Res:* Physicochemical studies of proteins; brain cell membranes; neurotransmitters; molecular mechanism of synaptic transmission; neuroendocrinology; molecular mechanism of depression. *Mailing Add:* Apt 703 1436 Mackay St Montreal PQ H3G 2H8 Can

TAN, BARRIE S P, b Ipoh, Perak, Oct 7, 53. CHEMICAL TOXICOLOGY, PHARMACOLOGY. *Educ:* Univ Otago, NZ, BS, 76, PhD(anal chem), 79. *Prof Exp:* Res assoc fel environ toxicol, Auburn Univ, Ala, 79-81; ASST PROF ANAL CHEM, UNIV MASS, AMHERST, 81- *Mem:* Am Chem Soc. *Res:* Use of gigahertz and high pressure liquid chromatography for analyses of environmental organic pollutants; bioanalytical techniques in cancer research (detection of carcinogens and mutagens); chemical carcinogenesis, biochemical toxicology; solution calorimetry-clincial, pharmaceutical and biochemical analyses; enzyme immobilization. *Mailing Add:* Dept Chem Univ Mass Amherst MA 01003

TAN, CELINE G L, biochemistry, molecular biology, see previous edition

TAN, CHARLES HUA-MIN, internal medicine, biochemistry, see previous edition

TAN, CHARLOTTE, b Kiang-Si, China, Apr 19, 23; US citizen; m 59; c 1. CANCER. *Educ:* Hsiang-Ya Med Col, China, MD, 47; Am Bd Pediat, dipl, 54. *Prof Exp:* Resident internal med, Nanking Cent Hosp, China, 47-48; intern & resident, St Barnabas Hosp, Newark, NJ, 48-49; res resident hemat & pediat resident, Children's Hosp Philadelphia, 50-51; res fel chemother, 52-54, res assoc, 55-57, asst, 57-62, assoc, 60-62, ASSOC MEM, SLOAN-KETTERING INST, 62-; assoc prof, 70-78, PROF PEDIAT, MED COL, CORNELL UNIV, 78- *Concurrent Pos:* Spec fel med, Memorial Ctr, New York, 52-55, spec fel pediat, 55-57, clin asst, Pediat Serv, 57-58; instr med, Sloan-Kettering Div, Grad Sch Med Sci, Med Col, Cornell Univ, 54-55, instr med, Med Col, 55-57, instr pediat, 58 & 62-70; clin asst pediatrician, James Ewing Hosp, 57-58, asst vis pediatrician, 58-62, assoc vis pediatrician, 62-; from asst attend pediatrician to assoc attend pediatrician, Memorial Hosp, 58-70, attend pediatrician, 70-, assoc chmn chemother, 74-80, pediat, 74-, assoc develop therapeut, 80-; vis prof, Nat Taiwan Univ Med Col, 66-67. *Mem:* Am Acad Pediat; Am Asn Cancer Res; Am Fedn Clin Res; AMA; Am Soc Clin Oncol. *Mailing Add:* Sloan-Kettering Cancer Ctr 44 E 68th St New York NY 10021

TAN, CHOR-WENG, b Canton, China, Apr 20, 36; US citizen; m 63; c 2. MECHANICAL ENGINEERING. *Educ:* Evansville Col, BS, 59; Univ Ill, MS, 61, PhD(mech eng), 63. *Prof Exp:* PROF MECH ENG, COOPER UNION, 63-, DEAN, SCH ENG, 76- *Concurrent Pos:* Exec dir, Cooper Union Res Found; dir bd, Tround Int, Inc. *Mem:* Am Soc Mech Engrs; Am Soc Eng Educ. *Res:* Thermodynamic and transport properties of partially ionized gases; magnetohydrodynamics; electrogasdynamics; environmental engineering. *Mailing Add:* Sch Eng Cooper Union 51 Astor Pl New York NY 10003

TAN, ENG M, b Malaysia, Aug 26, 26; US citizen; m 62; c 2. IMMUNOLOGY. *Educ:* Johns Hopkins Univ, AB, 52, MD, 56. *Prof Exp:* Asst prof med, Washington Univ, 65-67; assoc mem, Dept Exp Path, Scripps Clin & Res Found, 67-70, head div allergy & immunol, 70-77; HEAD DIV RHEUMATIC DIS, UNIV COLO MED CTR, 77- *Concurrent Pos:* Nesbitt vis prof, Minneapolis, 79; Donlop-Dottridge lectr, Can Rheumatism Asn, Ottawa, 80; McLaughlin lectr, Galveston, 81; chmn, Allergy, Immunol & Transplantation Res Comt, NIH, 81; Macy Found fac scholar, 81. *Mem:* Asn Am Physicians; Am Soc Clin Invest; Am Asn Immunologists; Am Asn Pathologists. *Res:* Autoimmune diseases; immunological aspects of rheumatic diseases; antinuclear and other autoantibodies in systemic lupus erythematosis, rheumatoid arthritis, Sjogren's syndrome, scleroderma, dermatomyositis and polymyositis. *Mailing Add:* Div Rheumatic Dis 4200 E Ninth Ave Denver CO 80262

TAN, FRANCIS C, b Manila, Philippines, Sept 21, 39; m 71. CHEMICAL OCEANOGRAPHY. *Educ:* Cheng Kung Univ, Taiwan, BSc, 61; McGill Univ, MSc, 65; Pa State Univ, PhD(geochem), 69. *Prof Exp:* NSF fel, Pa State Univ, 69-70; geochemist, Minn Geol Surv, Univ Minn, 70-71; RES SCIENTIST, ATLANTIC OCEANOG LAB, BEDFORD INST OCEANOG, CAN DEPT FISHERIES & OCEANS, 72- *Mem:* Geochem Soc; Am Geophys Union. *Res:* Stable isotope oceanography, marine geochemistry. *Mailing Add:* Atlantic Oceanog Lab Bedford Inst Oceanog Dartmouth NS B2Y 4A2 Can

TAN, HENRY HARRY, b Sukabumi, Indonesia, Dec 15, 24; US citizen; m 59; c 5. ORGANIC CHEMISTRY. *Educ:* Hope Col, AB, 55; Univ Mich, Ann Arbor, MS, 58, PhD(chem), 62. *Prof Exp:* Res chemist, 62-64, tech field rep, Appl Chem & Mkt, 64-68, res chemist, 68-73, mem tech serv & develop staff, 73-81, DEVELOP SPEC GEOTEXTILES, E I DU PONT DE NEMOURS & CO, INC, 81- *Mem:* Am Chem Soc; Am Soc Testing & Mat. *Res:* Organic syntheses; applied chemistry; political, social and economic affairs of Asia. *Mailing Add:* 103 Colorado Ave Shipley Heights Wilmington DE 19803

TAN, HENRY S I, b Bandung, Indonesia, Mar 26, 32; US citizen. PHARMACEUTICAL CHEMISTRY, ANALYTICAL CHEMISTRY. *Educ:* Univ Indonesia, BSPharm, 54, MSPharm, 56; Univ Ky, PhD(pharmaceut sci), 71. *Prof Exp:* Instr & assoc prof, Bandung Inst Technol, 57-66; asst prof, 71-76, ASSOC PROF PHARM, UNIV CINCINNATI, 76- *Mem:* Am Pharmaceut Asn; Acad Pharmaceut Sci; Am Asn Col Pharm; Asn Anal Chem. *Res:* Developmental analysis procedures of drugs in dosage forms, biological fluids and animal feed. *Mailing Add:* Univ of Cincinnati Cincinnati OH 45267

TAN, JAMES CHIEN-HUA, b Nanchang, China, Oct 8, 35; m 65; c 2. GENETICS, STATISTICS. *Educ:* Chung-Shing Univ, Taiwan, BS, 57; Mont State Univ, MS, 61; NC State Univ, PhD(genetics), 68. *Prof Exp:* Asst prof biol, Slippery Rock State Col, 65-66; from asst prof to assoc prof, 66-78, PROF BIOL, VALPARAISO UNIV, 78-, UNIV RES PROF, 80- *Concurrent Pos:* Res fel, Roswell Park Mem Inst,77; fel, O P Kretzemann Mem Wheat Ridge Found. *Mem:* AAAS; Am Genetics Soc; Environ Mutagen Soc; Genetics Soc Can. *Res:* Cytogenetics and statistical biology; mutagenicity and carcinogenicity testing. *Mailing Add:* Dept of Biol Valparaiso Univ Valparaiso IN 46383

TAN, JULIA S, b Taipei, Taiwan; US citizen. POLYMER SCIENCE, PHYSICAL CHEMISTRY. *Educ:* Nat Taiwan Univ, BA, 61; Wesleyan Univ, MA, 63; Yale Univ, PhD(chem), 66. *Prof Exp:* Asst prof chem, Wesleyan Univ, 66-69; res assoc biophys, Univ Rochester, 69-70; res chemist, 70-77, RES ASSOC, RES LABS, EASTMAN KODAK CO, 77- *Mem:* Am Chem Soc. *Res:* Solution properties of polyelectrolytes. *Mailing Add:* B-81 Res Labs Eastman Kodak Co Rochester NY 14650

TAN, KIM H, b Djakarta, Indonesia, Mar 24, 26; US citizen; m 57; c 1. TROPICAL AGRICULTURE, SOIL CHEMISTRY. *Educ:* Univ Indonesia, MSc, 55, PhD(soil sci), 58. *Prof Exp:* Assoc prof soil sci fac agr, Univ Indonesia, 58-64, prof fac agr & agr acad, 64-67, head dept soil sci, 65-67; technician soil anal nitrogen lab, Agr Res Serv, USDA, Colo, 67-68; asst prof soil sci, Dept Agron, 68-73, assoc prof agron, 73-77, PROF AGRON, UNIV GA, 77- *Concurrent Pos:* Rockefeller Found grant/fel, NC State Univ, 60-61 & Cornell Univ, 61; mem comt VIII, Southern Regional Coop Soil Surv, Soil Conserv Serv, USDA, 72- *Mem:* Clay Mineral Soc Am; Am Soc Agron; Soil Sci Soc Am; Int Soc Soil Sci. *Res:* Pedology: genesis and characterization of soils and organic matter in soils; effect of organic matter on soil properties and plant growth; chemistry and mineralogy of soils. *Mailing Add:* Dept of Agron Univ of Ga Athens GA 30602

TAN, KOK-KEONG, b Shanghai, China, June 1, 43; m 69; c 4. MATHEMATICS. *Educ:* Nanyang Univ, BSc, 66; Univ BC, PhD(Math), 70. *Prof Exp:* Teacher high sch, Malaysia, 66; asst prof, 70-76, ASSOC PROF MATH, DALHOUSIE UNIV, 76- *Concurrent Pos:* Vis res prof, Nat Tsing Hua Univ, Taiwan, 80-81; vis res expert, Acad Sinica, Taiwan, 81. *Mem:* Am Math Soc; Math Asn Am; Can Math Soc. *Res:* Functional analysis and topology, in particular, fixed point theorems. *Mailing Add:* Dept of Math Dalhousie Univ Halifax NS B3H 3J5 Can

TAN, LIAT, b Semarang, Java, Apr 1, 29; m 63; c 2. BIOCHEMISTRY, ORGANIC CHEMISTRY. *Educ:* Univ Amsterdam, BSc, 53; Univ Münster, MSc, 55; Univ Freiburg, Dr rer nat, 58. *Prof Exp:* Res chemist, Steroid Res Lab, Leo Pharmaceut Prod, Denmark, 59-60; sr res chemist, Union Chimique Belge SA, 60-62; res fel org chem, Laval Univ, 62-63; examr steroid chem, Can Patent Off, 63-66; Welch res fel & instr biochem & nutrit, Med Br, Univ Tex, 66-67; from asst prof to assoc prof, 67-80, PROF BIOCHEM, UNIV SHERBROOKE, 80- *Concurrent Pos:* Vis scientist, Hormone Res Lab, Univ Calif, 76-77. *Mem:* AAAS; Am Chem Soc; Chem Soc Belg; NY Acad Sci; Can Biochem Soc. *Res:* Synthesis and biochemistry of steroids; steroidases, specificity and mechanism of action; microbiological transformations; chemical endocrinology; physiologically active natural products; mechanism of biological oxidations at inactive sites in steroids; biosynthesis jof neuropeptides. *Mailing Add:* Dept of Biochem Univ of Sherbrooke Sherbrooke PQ J1H 5N4 Can

TAN, MENG HEE, b Kuala Pilah, Malaysia, Mar 30, 42; Can citizen; m 70; c 3. INTERNAL MEDICINE, MEDICAL SCIENCES. *Educ:* Dalhousie Univ, BSc, 65, MD, 69; FRCP(C), 75. *Prof Exp:* Lectr, 74-75, asst prof, 75-78, ASSOC PROF MED, DALHOUSIE UNIV, 78- *Concurrent Pos:* Res fel, Harvard Med Sch, 71-73; res fel, Med Coun Can, 71-74, centennial fel, 74-75; res fel, Cardiovasc Res Inst, San Francisco, 73-75. *Mem:* Am Col Physicians; Am Diabetes Asn; Am Fedn Clin Res; Royal Col Physicians & Surgeons Can. *Res:* Roles of lipoprotein lipase and apoproteins in triglyceride metabolism in diabetes mellitus; insulin receptors. *Mailing Add:* 5849 University Ave Halifax NS B3H 1W3 Can

TAN, OWEN T(IONGOEN), b Indramaju, Indonesia, Aug 30, 31; US citizen; m 56; c 3. ELECTRICAL ENGINEERING. *Educ:* Bandung Technol Faculty, MSc, 55; Eindhoven Technol Univ, PhD(elec eng), 61. *Prof Exp:* Res & develop engr, Willem Smit & Co, Neth, 56-62; lectr elec eng, Bandung Technol Inst, 62-64, sr lectr, 64-66; from asst prof to assoc prof, 67-78, PROF ELEC ENG, LA STATE UNIV, BATON ROUGE, 78- *Concurrent Pos:* Res fels, Siemens Schuckert, WGer, 62 & Eindhoven Univ Technol, 77. *Mem:* Inst Elec & Electronics Engrs; Neth Royal Inst Eng. *Res:* Energy conversion; power systems; control theory. *Mailing Add:* Dept Elec Eng La State Univ Baton Rouge LA 70803

TAN, PETER CHING-YAO, b Canton, China, Nov 1, 23; Can citizen; m. MATHEMATICAL STATISTICS, CIVIL ENGINEERING. *Educ:* Sun Yat-Sen Univ, BSc, 43; Luther Col, BA, 57; Univ Sask, MA, 59; Univ Toronto, PhD(math), 68. *Prof Exp:* Instr math, Univ Sask, 59-60; lectr, Univ Toronto, 62-65; spec lectr, Univ Sask, Regina Campus, 66-68; vis asst prof statist, Stanford Univ, 68-69; asst prof math, 69-73, ASSOC PROF MATH, CARLETON UNIV, 73- *Concurrent Pos:* Vis lectr, Univ Guyana, 75-76. *Mem:* Can Statist Asn; Can Math Cong; Math Asn Am; Inst Math Statist; Am Statist Asn. *Res:* Statistical inference; mathematical and statistical methods in civil engineering. *Mailing Add:* Dept of Math Carleton Univ Colonel By Drive Ottawa ON K1S 5B6 Can

TAN, SWIE-IN, b Djakarta, Indonesia, Feb 8, 34; US citizen; m 63; c 3. ENGINEERING, MATERIALS SCIENCE. *Educ:* Univ Calif, Los Angeles, BS, 58, MS, 60, PhD(eng), 65. *Prof Exp:* MEM RES STAFF, THOMAS J WATSON RES CTR, IBM CORP, 64- *Mem:* Electrochem Soc. *Res:* Dielectric breakdown studies of insulating films for magnetic recording heads and bubble devices; magnetic and insulating film deposition by evaporation and sputtering, studies of its properties and deposition parameters; semiconductor device packaging and interconnections; infrared temperature measurements and instrumentations; development of advanced instrumentations and measurements for manufacturing. *Mailing Add:* 44 S Church Bedford Hills NY 10507

TAN, VICTOR, b Manila, Philippines, Aug 8, 44; m 76. POLYMER ENGINEERING, MATERIAL SCIENCE. *Educ:* Adamson Univ, BS, 67; Univ Pittsburgh, MS, 70; Stevens Inst Technol, PhD(chem eng), 75. *Prof Exp:* Fel, 74-76, RES ASSOC CHEM ENG, MCGILL UNIV, 78- *Mem:* Soc Plastics Engrs. *Res:* Polymer characterization and polymer processing; computer simulation of polymer processing; polymer physics. *Mailing Add:* Dept of Chem Eng 3480 University St Montreal PQ H3A 2A7 Can

TAN, WAI-YUAN, b China, Aug 14, 34; m 64; c 2. STATISTICS. *Educ:* Taiwan Prov Col Agr, BA, 55; Nat Taiwan Univ, MS, 59; Univ Wis, MS(math) & MS(statist), 63, PhD(statist), 64. *Prof Exp:* Asst res fel biostatist, Inst Bot, Acad Sinica, Taiwan, 59-61, assoc res fel, 64-67 & res fel, 67-68; assoc prof statist, Nat Taiwan Univ, 65-67; assoc prof biostatist, Biol Res Ctr, Taiwan, 65-67, prof, 67-68; asst prof statist, Univ Wis-Madison, 68-72; assoc prof math, Wash State Univ, 73-75; PROF MATH, MEMPHIS STATE UNIV, 75- *Concurrent Pos:* Vis assoc prof, Tsing Hua Univ, Taiwan, 65-67; statist adv, Joint Inst Indust Res, Taiwan, 65-67. *Mem:* Am Statist Asn; Biomet Soc; Inst Math Statist; Royal Statist Soc. *Res:* Statistical inferences; multivariate analysis; mathematical genetics and quantitative genetics; robust statistics; biostatistics; statistical methods for mutagenicity and carcinogenesis. *Mailing Add:* Dept Math Memphis State Univ Memphis TN 38152

TAN, Y H, b Singapore, Sept 2, 42; c 2. MOLECULAR BIOLOGY, GENETICS. *Educ:* Univ Singapore, BSc Hons, 65; Univ Man, PhD(biochem), 69. *Prof Exp:* Med Res Coun Can fel biochem & virol, Univ Pittsburgh, 69-71; Med Res Coun Can fel somatic cell genetics, Yale Univ, 72-74; asst prof pediat, Johns Hopkins Univ, 74-75; ASSOC PROF, DIV MED BIOCHEM, UNIV CALGARY, 75- *Concurrent Pos:* Sect chief molecular genetics, Lab Cellular Comp Physiol, Nat Inst Aging, 74-75; Nat Cancer Inst scholar, 76-80. *Mem:* Am Soc Microbiol; Can Biochem Soc. *Res:* Regulation of human interferon genes; molecular genetics of host cell-virus interaction; charactensation of mercury resistant gene; gene transfer in mammalian and plant cells. *Mailing Add:* Div of Med Biochem Univ of Calgary Fac of Med Calgary AB T2N 1N4 Can

TAN, YEN T, b Hong Kong, Feb 12, 40. SOLID STATE PHYSICS, SURFACE PHYSICS. *Educ:* Columbia Univ, BS, 62; Yale Univ, PhD(chem), 66. *Prof Exp:* RES ASSOC, RES LABS, EASTMAN KODAK CO, 66- *Concurrent Pos:* Adj prof, Rochester Inst Technol, 74-75. *Mem:* Am Chem Soc; Am Inst Mining, Metall & Petrol Eng; Am Vacuum Soc. *Res:* Surface properties of solids; transport phenomena; thermodynamics. *Mailing Add:* Res Labs B-81 Eastman Kodak Co Rochester NY 14650

TAN, ZOILO CHENG-HO, b Bulan, Philippines, Oct 18, 40; m 67; c 2. PHOTOGRAPHIC CHEMISTRY. *Educ:* Cheng Kung Univ, Taiwan, BS, 63; Univ Ark, Fayetteville, MS, 66; Mass Inst Technol, PhD(nuclear chem), 69. *Prof Exp:* Res asst chem, Univ Ark, Fayetteville, 63-65 & Mass Inst Technol, 65-69; SR RES CHEMIST, RES LABS, EASTMAN KODAK CO, 69- *Res:* Solvent extraction from molten salts; electron exchange reaction in mixed solvents; solubility and complex formation of silver with halides and thiol compounds; photographic research; electron and x-ray resists. *Mailing Add:* 171 Chimney Hill Rd Rochester NY 14612

TANABE, MASATO, b Stockton, Calif, Jan 18, 25; m 55; c 3. ORGANIC CHEMISTRY. *Educ:* Univ Calif, BS, 47, PhD(chem), 51. *Prof Exp:* Chemist, US Naval Radiation Defense Lab, 47-48; res chemist, Riker Labs, Inc, 51-57; sr org chemist, 57-72, DIR DEPT BIO-ORG CHEM, SRI INT, MENLO PARK, 72- *Concurrent Pos:* Fulbright res fel, Japan, 54-55. *Mem:* Am Chem Soc. *Res:* Medicinal chemistry; steroids; alkaloids; natural products; biosynthesis. *Mailing Add:* 972 Moreno Ave Palo Alto CA 94303

TANABE, MICHAEL JOHN, b Keaau, Hawaii, Sept 15, 47. HORTICULTURE, PLANT PHYSIOLOGY. *Educ:* Univ Hawaii, Manoa, BS, 69, MS, 72, PhD(hort), 76. *Prof Exp:* ASST PROF HORT, COL AGR, UNIV HAWAII, HILO, 75- *Mem:* Am Soc Hort Sci; Sigma Xi. *Res:* Phenylalanine ammonia lyase activity as it affects anthocyanin production. *Mailing Add:* Univ of Hawaii Col Agr PO Box 1357 Hilo HI 96720

TANABE, TSUNEO Y, b Blackfoot, Idaho, Nov 17, 18; m 66; c 2. PHYSIOLOGY. *Educ:* Iowa State Col, BS, 42; Cornell Univ, MS, 45; Univ Wis, PhD(physiol of reprod), 48. *Prof Exp:* Asst prof, 49-50, 52-68, ASSOC PROF DAIRY PHYSIOL, PA STATE UNIV, UNIVERSITY PARK, 68- *Concurrent Pos:* Gosney fel, Calif Inst Technol, 51. *Mem:* AAAS; Am Soc Animal Sci; Am Dairy Sci Asn. *Res:* Embryology; dairy physiology; endocrinology. *Mailing Add:* Dept of Dairy & Animal Sci Pa State Univ University Park PA 16802

TANADA, TAKUMA, b Honolulu, Hawaii, Oct 30, 19; m 47; c 2. PLANT PHYSIOLOGY. *Educ:* Univ Hawaii, BS, 42, MS, 44; Univ Ill, PhD(bot), 50. *Prof Exp:* Asst soil chemist, Agr Exp Sta, Univ Hawaii, 42-44; sci consult natural resources sect, Supreme Comdr Allied Powers, US Army, Tokyo, 46-47; plant physiologist, Agr Res Serv, USDA, 50-57; agron res adv, Int Coop Admin, Ceylon, 57-60; RES PLANT PHYSIOLOGIST, SCI & EDUC ADMIN-AGR RES, USDA, 60- *Mem:* Am Soc Plant Physiol; Am Inst Biol Sci. *Res:* Photobiology; photosynthesis; mineral nutrition. *Mailing Add:* 12920 Moray Rd Silver Spring MD 20906

TANADA, YOSHINORI, b Puuloa, Oahu, Hawaii, June 8, 17; m 49; c 2. INSECT PATHOLOGY. *Educ:* Univ Hawaii, BS, 40, MS, 45; Univ Calif, PhD(entom), 53. *Prof Exp:* Asst zool, Univ Hawaii, 43-45, jr entomologist exp sta, 45-53, asst entomologist, 53-56, asst prof zool & entom, 54-56, assoc prof & assoc entomologist, 56; asst insect pathologist, Lab Insect Path, 56-59, assoc insect pathologist, 59-64, lectr, 61-65, chmn div invert path, 64-65, INSECT PATHOLOGIST, EXP STA, UNIV CALIF, BERKELEY, 64-, PROF ENTOM, UNIV, 65- *Concurrent Pos:* Consult, US Army, Okinawa, 50, SPac Comn, Pac Sci Bd, Nat Res Coun, 59, UN Develop Prog, Western Samoa, 71 & Food & Agr Orgn, UN, Thailand, 71; Fulbright res scholar, Japan, 62-63; spec vis prof, Univ Tokyo, 80. *Mem:* Fel AAAS; Entom Soc Am; Soc Protozool; Soc Invert Path; Am Inst Biol Scientists. *Res:* General insect pathology; epizootiology of diseases of insects; resistance of insects to diseases; microbial and biological control; economic entomology. *Mailing Add:* Div Entom & Parasitol Univ Calif Berkeley CA 94720

TANAKA, FRED SHIGERU, b Shoshone, Idaho, Aug 1, 37; m 66; c 3. PESTICIDE CHEMISTRY. *Educ:* Ore State Univ, BS, 59, PhD(org chem), 66. *Prof Exp:* Chief chemist, Wash State Dept Health, 66-67; RES CHEMIST USDA, 67- *Concurrent Pos:* Japanese Govt Res Award, Foreign Specialists, 77. *Mem:* Am Chem Soc. *Res:* Organic microsynthesis of radiochemically labeled compounds; photochemical degradation of pesticides; identification of biological metabolites; organic and biological reaction mechanisms. *Mailing Add:* Metab & Radiation Res Lab State Univ Sta PO Box 5674 Fargo ND 58105

TANAKA, JOHN, b San Diego, Calif, June 18, 24; m 59; c 2. INORGANIC CHEMISTRY. *Educ:* Univ Calif, Los Angeles, BA, 51; Iowa State Univ, PhD, 56. *Prof Exp:* From asst prof to assoc prof chem, SDak State Univ, 56-63; NASA fel, Univ Pittsburgh, 63-65; from asst prof to assoc prof chem, 65-75, PROF CHEM, UNIV CONN, 75-, DIR HONORS PROG, 71- *Mem:* Am Chem Soc; Royal Soc Chem; Inst Elec & Electronics Engrs. *Res:* Synthesis and properties of ternary hydrides; materials for electrical insulation; reactions of boron hydrides; vacuum line syntheses. *Mailing Add:* Dept of Chem Univ of Conn Storrs CT 06268

TANAKA, KATSUMI, b San Francisco, Calif, Mar 1, 25; m 53; c 1. PHYSICS. *Educ:* Univ Calif, AB, 49, PhD(physics), 52. *Prof Exp:* Assoc physicist, Argonne Nat Lab, 52-64; PROF PHYSICS, OHIO STATE UNIV, 64- *Concurrent Pos:* Vis prof, Univ Naples, 60-61. *Mem:* Fel Am Phys Soc. *Res:* Elementary particle physics. *Mailing Add:* Dept Physics Ohio State Univ Columbus OH 43210

TANAKA, KOUICHI ROBERT, b Fresno, Calif, Dec 15, 26; m 65; c 3. MEDICINE, HEMATOLOGY. *Educ:* Wayne State Univ, BS, 49, MD, 52. *Prof Exp:* Intern, Los Angeles County Gen Hosp, 52-53; resident path, Detroit Receiving Hosp, Mich, 53-54, resident med, 54-57; instr med & jr res hematologist, 57-59, asst prof med, Sch Med & asst res hematologist, Med Ctr, 59-61, assoc prof med, Sch Med, 61-68, PROF MED, SCH MED, UNIV CALIF, LOS ANGELES, 68-, ATTEND PHYSICIAN, MED CTR, 58-; CHIEF DIV HEMAT, HARBOR GEN HOSP, 61-, ASSOC CHMN DEPT MED, 71- *Concurrent Pos:* Consult, US Naval Hosp, Long Beach. *Mem:* AAAS; fel Am Col Physicians; Asn Am Physicians; Am Soc Hemat; Am Soc Clin Invest; Am Fedn Clin Res. *Res:* Internal medicine; red cell metabolism. *Mailing Add:* Dept Med Harbor-UCLA Med Ctr Torrance CA 90509

TANAKA, NOBUYUKI, b Tokyo, Japan, May 12, 37; US citizen. NUCLEAR PHYSICS, NUCLEAR ENGINEERING. *Educ:* Harvard Univ, AB, 62; Tufts Univ, PhD(physics), 69. *Prof Exp:* Res asst physics, Tufts Univ, 65-69; STAFF MEM PHYSICS, LOS ALAMOS SCI LAB, UNIV CALIF, 69- *Res:* Intermediate-energy nuclear research using high resolution proton and pion spectrometers; improving the existing spectrometers and associated equipment. *Mailing Add:* 6 Verano Lane Santa Fe NM 87501

TANAKA, TOYOICHI, b Nagaoka, Japan, Jan 4, 46; m 70; c 2. BIOPHYSICS. *Educ:* Univ Tokyo, BS, 68, MA, 70, DSc(physics), 72. *Prof Exp:* Fel biophys, 72-75, from asst prof to assoc prof, 75-82, PROF PHYSICS, MASS INST TECHNOL, 82- *Concurrent Pos:* Res assoc med physics, Retina Found, 73- *Mem:* Am Phys Soc; Phys Soc Japan; Biophys Soc Japan. *Res:* Laser scattering spectroscopy; critical phenomena of macromolecular solutions with applications to cataract disease; critical phenomena of gels. *Mailing Add:* Rm 13-2009 Mass Inst of Technol 77 Massachusetts Ave Cambridge MA 02139

TANAKA, YASUOMI, b Tokyo, Japan, Dec 5, 39; m 74; c 2. FOREST ECOLOGY. *Educ:* Tokyo Univ Educ, BS, 62; Duke Univ, MF, 67, PhD(forest ecol), 70. *Prof Exp:* Silviculturist, Agr Farm Monte D'Este, Brazil, 62-63; res fel forestry, Univ Sao Paulo, Brazil, 64-65; instr, Univ Parana, Brazil, 65-66; res assoc ecol, Ecol Sci Div, Oak Ridge Nat Lab, 70-71; FOREST NURSERY ECOLOGIST, WEYERHAEUSER FORESTRY RES CTR, 71- *Mem:* Japanese Forestry Soc; Soc Am Foresters. *Res:* Physiological and ecological aspect of seedling production; seedling dormancy, growth, nutrition in the greenhouse and openbed nursery; seed technology. *Mailing Add:* 505 N Pearl St Weyerhaeuser Forestry Res Ctr Centralia WA 98531

TANANBAUM, HARVEY DALE, b Buffalo, NY, July 17, 42; m 64; c 2. ASTROPHYSICS. *Educ:* Yale Univ, BA, 64; Mass Inst Technol, PhD(physics), 68. *Prof Exp:* Staff scientist, Am Sci & Eng, Inc, 68-73; ASTROPHYSICIST, SMITHSONIAN INST ASTROPHYS OBSERV, 73- *Concurrent Pos:* Assoc astron, Harvard Col Observ, Harvard Univ, 73-, lectr, Dept Astron, 80-; assoc dir, Harvard/Smithsonian Ctr Astrophys, 81- *Mem:* AAAS; Am Astron Soc. *Res:* X-ray astronomy, especially discrete cosmic x-ray sources with satellite payloads. *Mailing Add:* Ctr for Astrophys 60 Garden St Cambridge MA 02138

TANCRELL, ROGER HENRY, b Whitinsville, Mass, Feb 17, 35. PHYSICS, ELECTRICAL ENGINEERING. *Educ:* Worcester Polytech Inst, BS, 56; Mass Inst Technol, MS, 58; Harvard Univ, PhD(appl physics), 68. *Prof Exp:* Mem staff digital electronics, Lincoln Labs, Mass Inst Technol, 56-60; PRIN SCIENTIST MED ELECTRONICS, RAYTHEON RES, 68- *Mem:* Inst Elec & Electronics Engrs; Am Inst Ultrasound Med; Am Asn Physicists Med. *Res:* Medical imaging systems including ultrasound, x-ray and nuclear; surface acoustic wave devices for filters and analog signal processing; sonar (naval) transducers. *Mailing Add:* Raytheon Res 28 Seyon St Waltham MA 02154

TANCZOS, FRANK I, b Northampton, Pa, Jan 2, 21. CHEMICAL PHYSICS. *Educ:* Moravian Col, BS, 39; Cath Univ, PhD(physics), 56. *Prof Exp:* Res chemist cent labs, Lehigh Portland Cement Co, Pa, 39-43; phys chemist, Bur Ord, 46-59, tech dir supporting res, Bur Naval Weapons, 59-66, TECH DIR RES & TECHNOL, AIR SYSTS COMMAND, DEPT NAVY, 66- *Concurrent Pos:* Mem, NASA res adv comts, Chem Energy Processes, 59-60, mem chem energy systs, 60-61 & air-breathing propulsion systs, 62-; lectr grad sch eng, Cath Univ, 60-61. *Mem:* Am Chem Soc; Am Phys Soc; assoc fel Am Inst Aeronaut & Astronaut. *Res:* New cement composition chemistry; molecular vibrational relaxation theory; energy conversion; propellant chemistry and thermodynamics; rocket and air-breathing jet propulsion principles; hypersonic air-breathing propulsion principles. *Mailing Add:* 1500 Massachusetts Ave NW Washington DC 20005

TANDBERG-HANSSEN, EINAR ANDREAS, b Bergen, Norway, Aug 6, 21; US citizen; m 51; c 2. ASTRONOMY, PHYSICS. *Educ:* Univ Oslo, PhD(astron), 60. *Prof Exp:* Res assoc astrophys, Univ Oslo, 50-57; mem sr res staff solar physics, High Altitude Observ, Boulder, Colo, 57-74; SR RES SCIENTIST SOLAR PHYSICS, NASA MARSHALL SPACE FLIGHT CTR, 74- *Mem:* Int Astron Union; Am Astron Soc; Norwegian Geophys Soc. *Res:* Solar physics, particularly flare and prominence research; solar corona and interplanetary space; solar-terrestrial relationships. *Mailing Add:* ESOI NASA Marshall Space Flight Ctr Huntsville AL 35812

TANDLER, BERNARD, b Brooklyn, NY, Feb 18, 33; m 55; c 2. CYTOLOGY, ELECTRON MICROSCOPY. *Educ:* Brooklyn Col, BS, 55; Columbia Univ, AM, 57; Cornell Univ, PhD(cytol), 61. *Prof Exp:* Res fel, Sloan-Kettering Inst, 61-62; instr anat, Sch Med, NY Univ, 62-63; assoc biol, Sloan-Kettering Inst Cancer Res, Cornell Univ, 63-67, asst prof, Grad Sch, Sloan-Kettering Div, 66-67; assoc prof oral biol & med, 67-72, assoc prof anat, 67-79, PROF ORAL BIOL & MED, SCH DENT, CASE WESTERN RESERVE UNIV, 72-, PROF ANAT, SCH MED, 79- *Concurrent Pos:* Lectr, Brooklyn Col, 61-63; vis prof anat, Univ Copenhagen, 73; vis assoc prof, Sch Med, Stanford Univ, 75 & Col Med, Northeastern Ohio Univ, 81. *Mem:* Am Soc Cell Biol; Am Asn Anatomists; Electron Micros Soc Am; Int Asn Dent Res. *Res:* Mitochondrial biogenesis; ultrastructure of normal and neoplastic salivary glands; pumonary ultrastructure. *Mailing Add:* Dept Anat Sch Dent Case Western Reserve Univ Cleveland OH 44106

TANEJA, VIDAY SAGAR, b India, Sept 7, 31; m 62; c 2. MATHEMATICAL STATISTICS. *Educ:* Panjab Univ India, BA, 50, MA, 52; Univ Minn, MA, 63; Univ Conn, PhD(statist), 66. *Prof Exp:* Lectr math, Doaba Col, 53-59; instr, Univ Minn, Morris, 64-65; asst prof math statist, NMex State Univ, 66-70; assoc prof, 70-74, PROF MATH STATIST, WESTERN ILL UNIV, 74- *Concurrent Pos:* Vis prof, Ohio State Univ, 77-78. *Mem:* Inst Math Statist; Opers Res Soc Am; Am Statist Asn; Sigma Xi. *Res:* Statistical methodology, statistical analysis, time series, operations research and optimization. *Mailing Add:* Dept of Math Western Ill Univ Macomb IL 61455

TANENBAUM, BASIL SAMUEL, b Providence, RI, Dec 1, 34; m 56; c 3. IONOSPHERIC PHYSICS. *Educ:* Brown Univ, BS, 56; Yale Univ, MS, 57, PhD(physics), 60. *Prof Exp:* Staff physicist res div, Raytheon Co, 60-63; prof eng, Case Western Reserve Univ, 63-75; DEAN FAC, HARVEY MUDD COL, 75- *Concurrent Pos:* Vis scientist, Arecibo Observ, 67-68; Sigma Xi Res Award, 69; sci adv comt, Nat Astron & Ionospheric Ctr, 72-77. *Mem:* Am Phys Soc; AAAS; Am Soc Eng Educ; Inst Elec & Electronic Eng; Am Asn

Univ Professors. *Res:* Sound propagation; theory of turbulence; ionospheric physics; waves in plasmas; radiation in a plasma; kinetic theory of gas mixtures and plasmas; shock wave theory; energy conversion; solar energy. *Mailing Add:* Dean Fac Harvey Mudd Col Claremont CA 91711

TANENBAUM, MORRIS, b Huntington, WVa, Nov 10, 28; m 50; c 2. CHEMICAL PHYSICS, METALLURGY. *Educ:* Johns Hopkins Univ, AB, 49; Princeton Univ, Am, 51, PhD(phys chem), 52. *Prof Exp:* Asst, Princeton Univ, 49-50, instr, 50-51; mem tech staff, Bell Tel Labs, 52-56, subdept head, 56-60, asst metall dir, 60-62, dir solid state devices lab, 62-64; dir res & develop, Western Elec Co, Inc, 64-68, gen mgr eng, 68-71, vpres eng, 71-72, vpres, Transmission Equip Div, 72-75; exec vpres systems eng & develop, Bell Labs, 75-76; vpres eng & network serv, Am Tel & Tel Co, 76-78; pres, NJ Bell Tel Co, 78-80; EXEC VPRES, AM TEL & TEL CO, 80- *Concurrent Pos:* Mem mat adv bd, Nat Res Coun-Nat Acad Sci; consult, Dept Defense, NASA & Nat Bur Standards; mem vis comts, Mass Inst Technol, Princeton Univ, Carnegie Inst Technol, Univ Pa & Lehigh Univ. *Mem:* Nat Acad Eng; Am Chem Soc; fel Am Phys Soc; Am Inst Mining, Metall & Petrol Engrs; Inst Elec & Electronics Engrs. *Res:* Chemistry and physics of solids; solid-state device physics; engineering research in manufacturing processes. *Mailing Add:* Am Tel & Tel Co 195 Broadway New York NY 10007

TANENBAUM, STUART WILLIAM, b New York, NY, July 15, 24; m 62; c 2. BIOCHEMISTRY, MICROBIOLOGY. *Educ:* City Col New York, BS, 44; Columbia Univ, PhD, 51. *Prof Exp:* Instr chem, City Col New York, 48; Am Cancer Soc fel, Stanford Univ, 51-52; lectr bact, Univ Calif, 52; res assoc biol, Stanford Univ, 52-53; from res assoc to prof microbiol, Col Physicians & Surgeons, Columbia Univ, 53-73; DEAN SCH BIOL CHEM & ECOL, STATE UNIV NY COL ENVIRON SCI & FORESTRY, 73-; ADJ PROF MICROBIOL, STATE UNIV NY UPSTATE MED CTR, 73- *Concurrent Pos:* Mem panel molecular biol, NSF, 62-63 & 72-73, resident prog dir molecular biol sect, 71-72; State Univ NY fac exchange scholar, 74-77; trustee, Forestry Found, Syracuse, NY, 74-; mem competitive res, NSF, 80- *Mem:* Am Soc Biol Chemists; Brit Biochem Soc; Am Soc Microbiol; Am Chem Soc. *Res:* Fungal metabolism; antibiotic biosynthesis; bacterial physiology; immunochemistry; cell and molecular biology. *Mailing Add:* Sch of Biol Chem & Ecol SUNY Col Environ Sci & Forestry Syracuse NY 13210

TANFORD, CHARLES, b Halle, Ger, Dec 29, 21; nat US; div; c 3. MEMBRANES & TRANSPORT. *Educ:* NY Univ, BA, 43; Princeton Univ, MA, 44, PhD(phys chem), 47. *Prof Exp:* Asst, Princeton Univ, 43-44; chemist, Tenn Eastman Corp, 44-45; asst, Princeton Univ, 45-46; Lalor fel phys chem, Harvard Med Sch, 47-49; from asst prof to prof, Univ Iowa, 49-60; prof, 60-71, JAMES B DUKE PROF, DUKE UNIV, MED CTR, 71- *Concurrent Pos:* Guggenheim fel, Yale Univ, 56-57; consult, USPHS, 59-63; USPHS res career award, 62; vis prof, Harvard Univ, 66; mem, Whitehead Med Res Inst, 77-; George Eastman vis prof, Univ Oxford, 77-78; Walker-Ames prof, Univ Washington, 79; Reilly lectr, Univ Notre Dame, 79. *Mem:* Nat Acad Sci; Am Acad Arts & Sci; AAAS; Am Chem Soc; Biophys Soc (pres, 79-80). *Res:* Physical chemistry of proteins, especially transport proteins and related substances; structure and function of membranes. *Mailing Add:* Dept of Physiology Duke Univ Med Ctr Durham NC 27710

TANG, ALFRED SHO-YU, b Shanghai, China, Sept 9, 34; US citizen; m 69; c 2. ALGEBRA. *Educ:* Univ Hong Kong, BSc, 56; Univ SC, MS, 60; Univ Calif, Berkeley, PhD(math), 69. *Prof Exp:* Assoc prof, 66-80, PROF MATH, SAN FRANCISCO STATE UNIV, 80- *Mem:* AAAS; Am Math Soc; Math Asn Am. *Mailing Add:* Def Math San Francisco State Univ San Francisco CA 94132

TANG, ANDREW H, b Canton, China, Feb 10, 36; US citizen; m 64; c 2. PHARMACOLOGY. *Educ:* Howard Col, BS, 60; Purdue Univ, MS, 62, PhD(pharmacol), 64. *Prof Exp:* Res assoc, 64-70, SR RES SCIENTIST PHARMACOL, UPJOHN CO, 70- *Mem:* AAAS; Am Soc Pharmacol & Exp Therapeut. *Res:* Pharmacology of the central nervous system; spinal cord physiology; behavioral pharmacology. *Mailing Add:* Upjohn Co Kalamazoo MI 49001

TANG, CHUNG LIANG, b Shanghai, China, May 14, 34; US citizen; m 58; c 3. PHYSICS. *Educ:* Univ Wash, BS, 55; Calif Inst Technol, MS, 56; Harvard Univ, PhD(appl physics), 60. *Prof Exp:* Res staff mem, Raytheon Co, 60-61, sr res scientist, 61-63, prin res scientist, 63-64; assoc prof elec eng, 64-68, PROF ELEC ENG, CORNELL UNIV, 68-; PRES, ITHACA RES CORP. *Concurrent Pos:* Consult res div, Raytheon Co, 64-72; assoc ed, J Quantum Electronics, Inst Elec & Electronics Eng, 69- *Mem:* Fel Inst Elec & Electronics Engrs; fel Am Phys Soc. *Res:* Quantum electronics; electromagnetic theory. *Mailing Add:* Dept of Elec Eng Cornell Univ Ithaca NY 14850

TANG, CHUNG-MUH, b Tungkang, Taiwan, Oct 20, 36; m 65; c 2. METEOROLOGY. *Educ:* Nat Taiwan Univ, BS, 59; Univ Calif, Los Angeles, MA, 65, CPhil, 69, PhD(meteorol), 70. *Prof Exp:* Res asst, Taiwan Rain Stimulation Res Inst, 61-62; NSF grant & asst res meteorologist, Univ Calif, Los Angeles, 70; Defense Dept grant & res staff meteorologist, Yale Univ, 70-75; ASST PROF PHYSICS & ATMOSPHERIC SCI, DREXEL UNIV, 75- *Mem:* AAAS; Am Meteorol Soc; Meteorol Soc Japan. *Res:* Theoretical studies of large scale atmospheric motions. *Mailing Add:* Dept Physics & Atmospheric Sci Drexel Univ Philadelphia PA 19104

TANG, CHUNG-SHIH, b China, Jan 8, 38; m 65; c 2. PLANT CHEMISTRY. *Educ:* Taiwan Univ, BS, 60, MS, 62; Univ Calif, Davis, PhD(agr chem), 67. *Prof Exp:* Res chemist, Univ Calif, Davis, 67-68; asst prof agr biochem, 68-73, assoc prof, 73-77, ASST PROF AGR BIOCHEM, UNIV HAWAII, 77- *Mem:* AAAS; Am Chem Soc; Am Soc Plant Physiol. *Res:* Volatile compounds of tropical fruit; naturally occurring isothiocyanates. *Mailing Add:* Dept Agr Biochem Univ of Hawaii Honolulu HI 96822

TANG, DER-HUA EDWARD, water resources, applied mathematics, see previous edition

TANG, DONALD T(AO-NAN), b China, May 9, 32; m 62; c 2. ELECTRICAL ENGINEERING. *Educ:* Nat Taiwan Univ, BS, 53; Univ Ill, PhD(elec eng), 60. *Prof Exp:* Instr elec eng, Univ Ill, 55-60; MEM RES STAFF, IBM CORP, 60- *Mem:* Inst Elec & Electronics Engrs. *Res:* Network theory, communication theory and information theory with applications to filter design, pattern recognition, error-correcting codes and data compaction. *Mailing Add:* 49 Fox Den Rd Mount Kisco NY 10549

TANG, EDWARD LUNHAN, b Kwangtung, China, Nov 21, 29; m 63; c 2. NUCLEAR SCIENCE, ENGINEERING. *Educ:* Univ Taiwan, BS, 53, MS, 59; Univ Mich, MS, 62, PhD(nuclear sci), 65. *Prof Exp:* Instr mech eng, Univ Taiwan, 53-57; res asst nuclear eng, Univ Mich, 62-64; asst prof, 64-68, ASSOC PROF PHYSICS, UNIV DETROIT, 68- *Mem:* Am Nuclear Soc; Am Phys Soc. *Res:* Perturbed gamma-gamma angular correlations; power reactor dynamics; nuclear bound state problems. *Mailing Add:* Dept of Physics Univ of Detroit Detroit MI 48221

TANG, HOMER H(O), b Kwangtung, China, Apr 4, 34; m 60; c 2. PHYSICAL SCIENCE, AERONAUTICAL ENGINEERING. *Educ:* Taiwan Prov Cheng-Kung Univ, BS, 56; Okla State Univ, MS, 61, PhD(aeronaut eng), 64. *Prof Exp:* Instr mech eng, Okla State Univ, 63; res engr, Douglas Aircraft Co, 63-64, sr scientist 64-68, SECT CHIEF, GAS DYNAMICS, McDONNEL DOUGLAS CORP, 68- *Mem:* Am Inst Aeronaut & Astronaut. *Res:* Jet mixing and separated flow; blastwave interaction and nuclear gasdynamics; missile and re-entry vehicle technology. *Mailing Add:* McDonnell Douglas Astronaut Co 5301 Bolsa Blvd Huntington Beach CA 92647

TANG, IGNATIUS NING-BANG, b Nanking, China, July 7, 33; m 62; c 2. CHEMICAL ENGINEERING, APPLIED MATHEMATICS. *Educ:* Nat Taiwan Univ, BS, 55; Univ NDak, MS, 60; State Univ NY Stony Brook, MS, 75. *Prof Exp:* Asst engr, Taiwan Fertilizer Corp, Formosa, 56-58; CHEMIST, BROOKHAVEN NAT LAB, 64- *Mem:* AAAS. *Res:* Kinetics and thermodynamics of ion-molecule reactions and free radical reactions; mechanisms of gas-to-particle conversion and atmospheric nucleation phenomena; condensational growth and light scattering of atmospheric aerosols; applied inverse problems. *Mailing Add:* Brookhaven Nat Lab Bldg 815 Upton NY 11973

TANG, JAMES JUH-LING, b Tientsin, China, Mar 8, 37; US citizen; m 65; c 2. APPLIED MECHANICS, HEAT TRANSFER. *Educ:* Nat Taiwan Univ, BS, 59; Univ Mo-Rolla, MS, 63; Yale Univ, PhD(appl mech), 70. *Prof Exp:* Engr, Weiskopf & Pickworth, 63-65; sr res engr, Am Can Co, Princeton, NJ, 70-75, res assoc, 75-77, supvr machine design, 77-78, SUPVR DEVELOP ENG, AM CAN CO, BARRINGTON, ILL, 78- *Mem:* Am Soc Mech Engrs; Soc Rheology; Am Inst Physics. *Res:* Elastic-plastic material behavior; heat transfer of industrial processes; computerized process control; finite element analysis. *Mailing Add:* 833 S Elm St Palatine IL 60067

TANG, JORDAN J N, b Foochow, China, Mar 23, 31; m 58; c 2. BIOCHEMISTRY. *Educ:* Taiwan Prov Col, BS, 53; Okla State Univ, MS, 57; Univ Okla, PhD(biochem), 61. *Prof Exp:* Res asst biochem, Okla State Univ, 55-57; res asst, 57-58, biochemist, 61-63, assoc biochem, 63-65, assoc prof, 65-69, head neurosci sect & actg head, Found, 70-71, HEAD LAB PROTEIN STUDIES, OKLA MED RES FOUND, 71-; PROF BIOCHEM, SCH MED, UNIV OKLA, 71- *Concurrent Pos:* Res assoc biochem, Sch Med, Univ Okla, 62-63, asst prof & asst head dept, 63-67, assoc prof, 67-70; vis scientist, Lab Molecular Biol, Cambridge, Eng, 65-66. *Mem:* AAAS; Am Chem Soc; Am Soc Biol Chemists. *Res:* Structure and function of proteins; structure of gastric and lysosomal proteolytic enzymes. *Mailing Add:* Okla Med Res Found 825 NE 13th St Oklahoma City OK 73104

TANG, KWONG-TIN, b Feb 24, 36; US citizen. PHYSICS, PHYSICAL CHEMISTRY. *Educ:* Univ Wash, BS, 58, MA, 59; Columbia Univ, PhD(physics), 65. *Prof Exp:* Res assoc chem, Columbia Univ, 65-66; physicist, Collins Radio Co, 66-67; from asst prof to assoc prof, 67-72, chmn dept, 72-77, PROF PHYSICS, PAC LUTHERAN UNIV, 72- *Concurrent Pos:* Consult, Boeing Co, 70 & 72; vis lectr, Univ Wash, 71; Res Corp grant, Pac Lutheran Univ, 71-74. *Mem:* Am Phys Soc; Am Asn Physics Teachers. *Res:* Atomic and molecular collision; scattering theory; reaction rates; intermolecular forces; optical dispersion; lattice vibration. *Mailing Add:* Dept of Physics Pac Lutheran Univ Tacoma WA 98447

TANG, LILY C, neuroscience, neuropharmacology, see previous edition

TANG, PEI CHIN, b Hupei, China, Sept 14, 14; nat US; m; c 6. NEUROPHYSIOLOGY, NEUROANATOMY. *Educ:* Tsing Hua Univ, China, BS, 42; Univ Wash, PhD(physiol), 53. *Prof Exp:* Instr physiol, Med Sch, Peking Univ, 45-48; instr pharmacol, Univ Wash, 52-55; asst prof anat, Univ Tex Southwestern Med Sch Dallas, 55-56; neurophysiologist, Air Force Sch Aviation Med, 56-60; chief neurophysiol br, Civil Aeromed Res Inst, Fed Aviation Agency, Okla, 60-66; chief physiol sci div, Res Dept, Naval Aerospace Med Inst, 66-70; assoc prof, 70-77, PROF PHYSIOL, CHICAGO MED SCH, 77- *Mem:* Am Physiol Soc; Am Asn Anat; Aerospace Med Asn; Soc Exp Biol & Med. *Res:* Central nervous control of respiration, micturition and vasomotor activity. *Mailing Add:* Dept Physiol Chicago Med Sch 3333 Green Bay Rd North Chicago IL 60064

TANG, RUEN CHIU, b Kiangsu, China, Oct 31, 34; m 60; c 3. FOREST PRODUCTS. *Educ:* Nat Chung-Hsin Univ, Taiwan, BS, 57; NC State Univ, PhD(wood sci), 68. *Prof Exp:* Teacher, Kung Hua Sch Elec Technol, 56-57; wood technologist, Taiwan Forest Bur, 59-63; res asst, US Naval Res, NC State Univ, 63-66; teaching asst wood mech, Univ Wash, 66-67; State of Ky & US Air Force res assoc, Inst Theoret & Appl Mech, Univ Ky, 68, State of Ky res assoc wood mech, Univ, 69, from asst prof to assoc prof wood sci, 74-77; PROF WOOD SCI, AUBURN UNIV, 78- *Mem:* Soc Wood Sci & Technol; Soc Exp Stress Anal; Forest Prod Res Soc; Soc Am Foresters; Am Soc Testing & Mat. *Res:* Anisotropic elasticity; composite materials; fiber mechanics; noise control; reliability in structural design; math modeling. *Mailing Add:* Dept Forestry Auburn Univ Auburn AL 36830

TANG, SAM, b Hong Kong, May 7, 31; m 60; c 2. SOLID MECHANICS. *Educ:* Taiwan Univ, BS, 56; Ill Inst Technol, MS, 58; NY Univ, PhD(aeronaut), 65. *Prof Exp:* Asst prof eng, State Univ NY Buffalo, 64-66; res scientist, Lockheed Missiles & Space Co, Lockheed Aircraft Corp, 66-70; vis assoc prof eng sci, Univ Wis-Parkside, 70-71, from assoc prof to prof, 71-74; SR ENGR, GRUMMAN AEROSPACE CORP, 74- *Mem:* Am Acad Mech; Am Soc Mech Engrs. *Res:* Wave propagations in initially-stressed solids; instability of elastic solids; thermal stresses analyses in aerospace structures; buckling of plates; mechanics of superplasticity; creep in laminated anisotropic plates and shells; mechanics of composite materials. *Mailing Add:* Grumman Aerospace Corp Bethpage NY 11714

TANG, STEPHEN SHIEN-PU, b Changsha, China, Nov 13, 35; m 72; c 2. SYSTEMS ENGINEERING. *Educ:* Nat Taiwan Univ, BS, 59; Univ Cailf, Berkeley, MS, 64; Princeton Univ, PhD(aerosci), 69. *Prof Exp:* Res assoc molecular beams, Dept Appl Sci, Yale Univ, 68-71; vis assoc prof fluid mech, Nat Univ Taiwan, 71-72, vis assoc prof molecular beams, Tech Univ Hannover, Ger, 72-74; res scientist chem laser, Defense & Space Syst Group, TRW, Inc, 74-80; PROJ ENGR SPACE TECHNOL PLANNING, AEROSPACE CORP, LOS ANGELES, 80- *Mem:* Am Inst Aeronaut & Astronaut; Am Phys Soc; Sigma Xi. *Res:* Molecular beams; gasdynamics and fluid mechanics; gas phase kinetics; gas-solid interactions; space technology planning; high power lasers; high beam energy particle beams; satellite systems and technologies. *Mailing Add:* 1611 Toscanini Dr San Pedro CA 90732

TANG, TERRY CHU, microbiology, see previous edition

TANG, TING-WEI, b Taiwan, China, May 27, 34; m 63; c 2. ELECTRICAL ENGINEERING, PLASMA PHYSICS. *Educ:* Taiwan Univ, BSEE, 57; Brown Univ, MS, 61, PhD(eng), 64. *Prof Exp:* Teaching asst elec eng, Taiwan Univ, 57-59; res asst eng, Brown Univ, 59-63; instr elec eng, Univ Conn, 63-64, asst prof aerospace eng, 64-68; assoc prof elec eng, 68-74, PROF ELEC & COMPUT ENG, UNIV MASS, AMHERST, 74- *Concurrent Pos:* NSF res initiation grant, 65-66, res grants, 66-68, 70-72, 74-76 & 76-78. *Mem:* Inst Elec & Electronics Engrs; Am Phys Soc. *Res:* Electromagnetic theory; nonlinear wave interactions in plasmas; antenna design; solid-state device modeling. *Mailing Add:* Dept of Elec & Comput Eng Univ of Mass Amherst MA 01003

TANG, VICTOR KUANG-TAO, b Peiping, China, Mar 13, 29; US citizen; m 63. STATISTICS, MATHEMATICS. *Educ:* Nat Taiwan Univ, BA, 56; Univ Wash, MA, 63; Iowa State Univ, PhD(statist), 71. *Prof Exp:* Assoc prof, 72-76, PROF MATH, HUMBOLDT STATE UNIV, 76- *Mem:* Inst Math Statist; Int Asn Survey Statisticians; Royal Statist Soc; Am Statist Asn. *Res:* Applied and mathematical statistics. *Mailing Add:* Dept Math Humboldt State Univ Arcata CA 95521

TANG, WALTER KWEI-YUAN, b Wusih, China, Aug 8, 29; US citizen; m 58; c 3. CHEMICAL ENGINEERING, POLYMER CHEMISTRY. *Educ:* Univ Wis-Madison, BS, 55, MS, 56, PhD(chem eng), 64. *Prof Exp:* Staff engr chem eng, Aqua-Chem, Inc, 56-59; chem engr polymer chem, Forest Prod Lab, Forest Serv, USDA, 59-64; SR MEM RES STAFF CHEM & POLYMER ENG, E I DU PONT DE NEMOURS & CO, INC, 64- *Mem:* Am Inst Chem Engrs; Am Chem Soc; Soc Plastics Engrs; Sigma Xi. *Res:* Catalysis; synthesis processes; kinetics; polymer finishing; rheology; mass transfer; polymer compounding processes and polymer properties. *Mailing Add:* 2211 Greenstone Rd Wilmington DE 19810

TANG, Y(U) S(UN), b Nanking, China, Oct 24, 22; US citizen; m 50; c 3. HEAT TRANSFER, NUCLEAR ENGINEERING. *Educ:* Nat Cent Univ, China, BSME, 44; Univ Wis, MS, 48; Univ Fla, PhD(chem eng), 52. *Prof Exp:* Sr process engr, Gen Chem Div, Allied Chem & Dye Corp, 52-54, sr proj engr, 54-56; sr develop engr, Steam Div, Westinghouse Elec Corp, 56-59; group leader heat transfer, Allison Div, Gen Motors Corp, 59-64, prin scientist, 64-66; adv engr, Astronuclear Lab, 66-71, ADV ENGR, ADVAN REACTORS DIV, WESTINGHOUSE ELEC CORP, 71- *Concurrent Pos:* Lectr, Univ Pittsburgh, 67-68. *Mem:* Fel Am Inst Chem Engrs; Am Nuclear Soc. *Res:* Heat transfer and fluid flow; liquid metal boiling and two-phase flow; space power generation; liquid-metal fast breed reactor thermal analysis. *Mailing Add:* 1552 Holly Hill Dr Bethel Park PA 15102

TANG, YAU-CHIEN, b China, Aug 7, 28; nat US; m 60; c 2. PHYSICS. *Educ:* Univ Ill, PhD(physics), 58. *Prof Exp:* Res assoc, Fla State Univ, 58-62 & Brookhaven Nat Lab, 62-64; assoc prof, 64-70, PROF PHYSICS, UNIV MINN, MINNEAPOLIS, 70- *Mem:* Am Phys Soc. *Res:* Low energy nuclear physics. *Mailing Add:* Dept of Physics & Astron Univ of Minn Minneapolis MN 55455

TANG, YEIH-PING, b Peiping, China, Mar 27, 30; US citizen; m 54; c 2. CHEMICAL ENGINEERING, MATHEMATICS. *Educ:* Taiwan Prov Col Eng, BS, 52; Univ Tex, Austin, MS, 62, PhD(chem eng), 64. *Prof Exp:* Process engr, Chinese Petrol Corp, 53-59; sr engr, Chem & Plastics Opers Div, 64-73, group leader, 73-80, COMPUT CONSULT, SCI APPLN, BUS SERV, UNION CARBIDE CORP, 73-, MGR, 80- *Concurrent Pos:* Lectr, WVa Univ, 67-68. *Mem:* Soc Indust & Appl Math; Inst Mgt Sci. *Res:* Application of modern mathematical and management science techniques to develop systems for process simulation, operations planning and production scheduling. *Mailing Add:* Union Carbide Corp PO Box 4488 Charleston WV 25304

TANG, YI-NOO, b Hunan, China, Feb 28, 38; m 64; c 2. PHYSICAL CHEMISTRY, RADIOCHEMISTRY. *Educ:* Chung Chi Col, Hong Kong, BA, 59; Univ Kans, PhD(chem), 64. *Prof Exp:* Fel, Univ Kans, 64-65; fel, Univ Calif, Irvine, 65-66, instr chem, 66-67; asst prof, 67-69, ASSOC PROF CHEM, TEX A&M UNIV, 69- *Mem:* Am Chem Soc; Am Inst Physics. *Res:* Hot atom chemistry; unimolecular reactions; photochemistry; carbene chemistry; gas chromatography; silicon chemistry. *Mailing Add:* Dept of Chem Tex A&M Univ College Station TX 77843

TANGEL, O(SCAR) F(RANK), b Philadelphia, Pa, Jan 11, 10; m 36; c 3. METALLURGY. *Educ:* Lafayette Col, BS, 32; Mont Sch Mines, MS, 34. *Prof Exp:* Mill supt & metall engr, Mont Coal & Iron Co, 35; metall engr, New Bononza Mine, Nev, 36; mill supt & metall engr, Ambassador Gold Mines, Ltd, Nev, 36 & Goldfields of Am, Ltd, 36-37; metall engr, Fresnillo Co, Mex, 37-40, asst mill supt, 40-41; res engr, Battelle Mem Inst, 41-42, asst supvr, 45-53, div chief, 53-65, tech adv, 65-66; consult, Newmont Mining Corp, 66-67, chief metall engr, 68-71, vpres res & develop, 72-77; PVT CONSULT, 78- *Concurrent Pos:* Plant shift boss, Lakeview Gold Mines, Mont, 35; assayer, King Solomon Gold Mines, Calif, 35-36; metall engr, Pan-Am Eng Co, Calif, 37; dir, Atlantic Cement Co, 67-, Idarado Mining Co, 69-78, Newmont Explor Ltd, 69-, Foote Mineral Co, 74- & Magma Copper Co, 75-78; vpres, Newmont Explor Ltd, 69-78. *Mem:* Am Inst Mining, Metall & Petrol Engrs; Can Inst Mining & Metall. *Res:* Beneficiation of metallic and non-metallic ores. *Mailing Add:* 25 Thunder Mountain Rd Greenwich CT 06830

TANGHERLINI, FRANK R, b Boston, Mass, Mar 14, 24; m 60; c 4. PHYSICS. *Educ:* Harvard Univ, BS, 48; Univ Chicago, MS, 52; Stanford Univ, PhD(physics), 59. *Prof Exp:* NSF fel physics, Niels Bohr Inst, Copenhagen, Denmark, 58-59 & Sch Theoret & Nuclear Physics, Naples, Italy, 59-60; res assoc, Univ NC, Chapel Hill, 60-61; asst prof, Duke Univ, 61-64; assoc prof, George Washington Univ, 64-66; sci assoc space res, Ion Lab, Tech Univ Denmark & Danish Space Res Inst, 66-67; ASSOC PROF PHYSICS, COL HOLY CROSS, 67- *Concurrent Pos:* Sr res engr, Gen Dynamics/Convair, 52-55; lectr, Univ NC, Chapel Hill, 61; vis scientist, Int Ctr Theoret Physics, 73-74; mem, Int Comt Gen Relativity. *Mem:* Am Phys Soc; Sigma Xi. *Res:* Mathematical biology; cybernetics; high energy physics; foundations of special relativity; general relativity and gravitation; dimensionality of space; classical electron theory; ionosphere and space physics; theoretical physics; elementary particles; cosmology; relativity and quantum optics. *Mailing Add:* Dept of Physics Col of the Holy Cross Worcester MA 01610

TANGNEY, JOHN FRANCIS, b Evanston, Ill, Aug 4, 49. HUMAN PATTERN RECOGNITION, VISUAL PSYCHOPHYSICS. *Educ:* Loyola Univ Chicago, BS, 71; State Univ NY Buffalo, PhD(psychol), 78. *Prof Exp:* Res asst, Parmly Hearing Inst, 73-74; res asst, Psychol Dept, State Univ NY Buffalo, 74-78; fac res asst, 79-80, FAC RES ASSOC, UNIV MD, COLLEGE PARK, 81- *Concurrent Pos:* Co-prin investr, NIH grants, 80- *Mem:* Asn Res Vision & Ophthal; AAAS; Am Asn Univ Professors; Optical Soc Am; Bipolar Soc. *Res:* Visual psychophysical experiments--to discriminate between models of human pattern recognition and to describe the dynamics and the interaction of neural structures that underlie vision. *Mailing Add:* Psychol Dept Univ Md College Park MD 20742

TANGONAN, GREGORY LIGOT, b Springfield, Mass, Oct 26, 47. APPLIED PHYSICS, PHYSICS. *Educ:* Ateneo Manila Univ, BS, 69; Calif Inst Technol, MS, 72, PhD(appl physics), 75. *Prof Exp:* Mem tech staff, 71-78, HEAD INTEGRATED OPTICS SECT, HUGHES RES LABS, HUGHES AIRCRAFT CO, 78- *Mem:* Sigma Xi; Optical Soc Am. *Res:* Development of optical circuits for use in high speed optical data processing with emphasis on development of new fabrication techniques for optical waveguide devices. *Mailing Add:* Hughes Res Labs Malibu CA 90265

TANGORA, MARTIN CHARLES, b New York, NY, June 21, 36; m 73. TOPOLOGY. *Educ:* Calif Inst Technol, BS, 57; Northwestern Univ, MS, 58, PhD(math), 66. *Prof Exp:* Instr math, Northwestern Univ, 66-67 & Univ Chicago, 67-69; temp lectr, Univ Manchester, 69-70; asst prof, 70-72, ASSOC PROF MATH, UNIV ILL, CHICAGO CIRCLE, 72- *Concurrent Pos:* Sr vis fel, Univ Oxford, 73-74. *Mem:* Am Math Soc; Math Asn Am. *Res:* Algebraic topology; homotopy theory; cohomological methods. *Mailing Add:* Dept of Math PO Box 4348 Chicago IL 60680

TANGUAY, A(RMAND) R(ENE), b Can, Feb 1, 24; nat US; m 48; c 3. ELECTRICAL ENGINEERING. *Educ:* Univ Mass, BS, 50; Mass Inst Technol, MS, 51. *Prof Exp:* Asst comput lab, Mass Inst Technol, 50-51; sect head systs anal, Cornell Aeronaut Lab, Inc, 51-57; dept head systs res, Res Div, Radiation, Inc, Fla, 57-60; dir advan systs, Ryan Aerolab, Aerolab Develop Co, 60-61; assoc mgr advan electronics & info systs div, Electro-Optical Systs, Inc, 61-63, mgr, 63, mgr energy conversion div, 64, mgr info systs div, 65-67; div mgr med diag opers, Xerox Corp, 67-70, mgr, Micrographics Progs Res & Eng Div, 70-71, mgr strategic tech planning info technol group, 72-80; ASST PROF, DEPT ELEC ENG, UNIV SOUTHERN CALIF, 80- *Mem:* Sr mem Inst Elec & Electronics Engrs. *Res:* Systems and technology development and engineering in information sciences; automation; control systems; technical planning and program management; technology and systems planning and development management in digital and graphical information processing and management with specialties in micrographics and office information automation. *Mailing Add:* Dept Elec Eng Univ Southern Calif Los Angeles CA 90007

TANI, SMIO, b Tokyo, Japan, Feb 24, 25; US citizen; m 58; c 3. THEORETICAL PHYSICS. *Educ:* Univ Tokyo, BS, 46, ScD, 55. *Prof Exp:* Res assoc, Kyoto Univ, 51-54, Tokyo Univ Educ, 54-57, Case Western Reserve Univ, 57-59 & Wash Univ, 59-60; from res scientist to sr res scientist physics, NY Univ, 60-65; assoc prof, 65-68, PROF PHYSICS, MARQUETTE UNIV, 68- *Mem:* Am Phys Soc; Am Asn Physics Teachers. *Res:* Theory of scattering; canonical transformation in classical and quantum mechanics; atomic physics; elementary particle physics. *Mailing Add:* Dept Physics Marquette Univ Milwaukee WI 53233

TANIGAKI, NOBUYUKI, b Tokyo, Japan, Oct 22, 29; m. CANCER. *Educ:* Tokyo Univ, MD, 56. *Prof Exp:* Res fel path, Sch Med, Hokkaido Univ, 57-61, asst, 61-63, asst, Inst Cancer Immunopath, 63-66, instr, 66-67; asst prof, Cancer Res Inst, Kanazawa Univ, 67-68; sr cancer res scientist, Dept Biochem Res, 69-72, assoc cancer res scientist, 72-75, PRIN CANCER RES SCIENTIST, ROSWELL PARK MEM INST, 75- *Concurrent Pos:* Sloan-Kettering Inst Cancer Res fel, 63-64; cancer res scientist, Dept Biochem Res, Roswell Park Mem Inst, 64-66. *Mem:* Japanese Cancer Asn; Japanese Path Soc; Am Asn Immunologists. *Mailing Add:* 10 Chateau Terr Snyder NY 14226

TANIKELLA, MURTY SUNDARA SITARAMA, b Amalapuram, India, Dec 5, 38; m 67. PHYSICAL CHEMISTRY, POLYMER CHEMISTRY. *Educ:* Osmania Univ, India, BSc, 57, MSc, 59; Princeton Univ, MA, 64; Univ Pittsburgh, PhD(phys, physico-org chem), 67. *Prof Exp:* Lectr chem, Osmania Univ, India, 59-62; fel with Prof K S Pitzer, Rice Univ, 67-68; fel, Nat Res Coun Can, 68-69; Nat Res Coun Can fel, Univ Calgary, 69-70; res chemist, Carothers Res Lab, 70-74, sr res chemist, 74-76, SR RES CHEMIST, CHATTANOOGA NYLON TECH, E I DU PONT DE NEMOURS & CO, INC, 77- *Concurrent Pos:* Fulbright travel grant, 62. *Mem:* Am Chem Soc. *Res:* Thermodynamics of hydrogen bonding; spectroscopy; structure of water; problems in textile fibers chemistry. *Mailing Add:* Tech Sect E I du Pont de Nemours & Co Inc Chattanooga TN 37401

TANIMOTO, TAFFEE TADASHI, b Kobe, Japan, Dec 15, 17; nat US; m 46; c 4. MATHEMATICS, GEOMETRY. *Educ:* Univ Calif, Los Angeles, AB, 42; Univ Chicago, MS, 46; Univ Pittsburgh, PhD(math), 50. *Prof Exp:* Instr math, Ill Inst Technol, 46-49; instr math, Allegheny Col, 49-51, asst prof, 51-54; mathematician, Int Bus Mach Corp, 54-61; head pattern recognition lab, Melpar, Inc, 61-63; staff mathematician, Honeywell, Inc, 63-65; PROF MATH & CHMN DEPT, UNIV MASS, BOSTON, 65-, DIR GRAD PROGS, 75- *Mem:* Am Math Soc; Math Asn Am. *Res:* Geometry and analysis. *Mailing Add:* Dept of Math Univ of Mass Harbor Campus Boston MA 02125

TANIS, ELLIOT ALAN, b Grand Rapids, Mich, Apr 23, 34; m; c 3. COMPUTER ART, COMPUTERS IN EDUCATION. *Educ:* Cent Col, Iowa, BA, 56; Univ Iowa, MS, 60, PhD(math), 63. *Prof Exp:* Lectr math, Univ Iowa, 63; asst prof math statist, Univ Nebr, 63-65; assoc prof math, 65-71, PROF MATH & CHMN DEPT, HOPE COL, 71- *Mem:* Am Math Soc; Sigma Xi; Math Asn Am; Inst Math Statist; Am Statist Asn. *Res:* Writing educational materials in statistics-testbooks and computer based laboratory materials; developing computer programs for drawing artistic designs and repeating pattern; use of the computer in statistics. *Mailing Add:* Dept of Math Hope Col Holland MI 49423

TANIS, JAMES IRAN, b Zeeland, Mich, Oct 8, 34; m 70; c 1. EXPLORATION GEOPHYSICS. *Educ:* Mich Technol Univ, BS, 57, MS, 58; Univ Utah, PhD(geophys), 63. *Prof Exp:* Geophysicist, Shell Oil Co, 62-70; GEOPHYSICIST, CONTINENTAL OIL CO, 70- *Mem:* Soc Explor Geophysicists. *Res:* Crustal studies. *Mailing Add:* Continental Oil Co Box 1267 Ponca City OK 74601

TANIS, STEVEN PAUL, b Newport, RI, Sept 1, 52; m 79. SYNTHETIC ORGANIC CHEMISTRY. *Educ:* Rutgers Univ, BA, 74; Columbia Univ, MA, 77, MPhil, 78, PhD(chem), 80. *Prof Exp:* NIH fel, Calif Inst Technol, 79-80; ASST PROF ORG CHEM, MICH STATE UNIV, 80- *Mem:* Am Chem Soc. *Res:* Isolation; structure determination; synthesis of biologically active natural products. *Mailing Add:* Dept Chem Mich State Univ East Lansing MI 48823

TANK, PATRICK WAYNE, b Charlotte, Mich, Jan 9, 50; m 73. PATTERN FORMATION, REGENERATION. *Educ:* Western Mich Univ, BS, 72; Univ Mich, Ann Arbor, MS, 73, PhD(anat), 76. *Prof Exp:* Fel develop biol, Univ Calif, Irvine, 76-78; ASST PROF ANAT, UNIV ARK MED SCI, 78- *Mem:* Am Asn Anatomists; Soc Develop Biol; Sigma Xi. *Res:* Morphogenesis during development and regeneration in vertebrates; pattern formation during regeneration of the limbs of urodele amphibians; larval and embryonic systems. *Mailing Add:* Dept Anat 510 Univ Ark Med Sci 4301 W Marhkam Little Rock AR 72205

TANK, RONALD W, geology, see previous edition

TANKERSLEY, ROBERT WALKER, JR, b Watsonville, Calif, June 18, 27; m 51; c 3. VIROLOGY, BACTERIOLOGY. *Educ:* Stanford Univ, AB, 52, MA, 54, PhD(med microbiol), 56. *Prof Exp:* Instr virol, Med Sch, Univ Minn, 56-58, instr bact & virol, 58-60; from asst prof to assoc prof microbiol, Med Col Va, 60-68; dir microbiol res, 68-80, DIR MOLECULAR BIOL, A H ROBINS PHARMACEUT CO, 80- *Concurrent Pos:* USPHS fel, Med Sch, Univ Minn, 56-58. *Mem:* Am Soc Microbiol. *Res:* Antiviral chemotherapy; cell-virus relationships. *Mailing Add:* 1211 Sherwood Ave Richmond VA 23220

TANKIN, RICHARD S, b Baltimore, Md, July 14, 24; m 56; c 3. FLUID MECHANICS. *Educ:* Johns Hopkins Univ, AB, 48, BS, 50; Mass Inst Technol, MS, 53; Harvard Univ, PhD(mech eng), 60. *Prof Exp:* Asst prof civil eng, Univ Del, 60-61; from asst prof to assoc prof mech eng, 61-69, chmn dept, 72-77, PROF MECH ENG, NORTHWESTERN UNIV, EVANSTON, 77- *Mem:* Am Soc Mech Engrs. *Res:* Hydrodynamic stability; plasma properties; combustion; two phase flow. *Mailing Add:* Dept Mech Eng Northwestern Univ Evanston IL 60201

TANKINS, EDWIN S, b Midland, Pa, Sept 12, 27; m 55; c 3. PHYSICAL METALLURGY. *Educ:* Univ Wis, BS, 54; Univ Pa, MS, 57. *Prof Exp:* Jr engr air mat lab, Naval Air Eng Ctr, 54-55, res asst, 56-59, res metallurgist, 59, mat engr, 59-61, res metallurgist, 61-67, asst to chief scientist, 66-67, RES PHYS METALLURGIST, MAT LAB, AIRCRAFT & CREW SYSTS TECHNOL DIRECTORATE, NAVAL AIR DEVELOP CTR, 67- *Mem:* AAAS; Am Soc Metals; Am Inst Mining, Metall & Petrol Engrs; Am Chem Soc; Sigma Xi. *Res:* Chemical metallurgy; neutron activation studies; yield and fracture stress of refractory metals as a function of temperature, grain, size and strain rate; equilibria of hydrogen and oxygen in iron group metals; binary and ternary alloys related to thermodynamic studies; gas analysis in metals; applied mathematics. *Mailing Add:* Mat Lab Naval Air Develop Ctr Warminster PA 18974

TANNAHILL, MARY MARGARET, b Weatherford, Tex, Apr 30, 44. POLYMER CHEMISTRY. *Educ:* Tex Tech Univ, BS, 66; Mich State Univ, PhD(phys chem), 73. *Prof Exp:* Asst chem, Mich State Univ, 66-72; trainee physiol, Univ Tex Med Br, Galveston, 72-73; res chemist, Union Carbide Corp, 74-75; dir mats control, High Density Polyethylene, Gulf Oil Chem Co, 75-79; sr res chemist res & develop, 79, PROD & QUAL SUPVR, MOBIL CHEM CO, 80- *Mem:* Am Chem Soc; Soc Plastics Engrs. *Res:* Product development for polypropylene; catalyst preparation and testing; high density polyethylene. *Mailing Add:* Mobil Chem Co PO Box 2295 Beaumont TX 77704

TANNEN, RICHARD L, b New York, NY, Aug 31, 37; m 65; c 3. INTERNAL MEDICINE, NEPHROLOGY. *Educ:* Univ Tenn, MD, 60. *Prof Exp:* Asst Med, Harvard Med, Sch, Boston, 65-66; asst prof & co-dir nephrology, Univ Vt, Burlington, 69-73, assoc prof & dir, 73-78, actg assoc chmn, Dept Med, 75-76; vis scientist clin biochem, Radcliffe Infirmary, Oxford, Eng, 76-77; PROF & DIR NEPHROL, UNIV MICH, 78- *Concurrent Pos:* Estab investr, Am Heart Asn; actg chief nephrology, Vet Admin Med Ctr, Mich, 78-82; sci adv bd, Nat Kidney Found, 81-; exec comt, Coun Kidney Dis, Am Heart Asn, 82- *Mem:* Fel Am Col Physicians; Am Fedn Clin Res; Am Soc Nephrology; Int Soc Nephrology; Am Soc Clin Invest. *Res:* Acid-base physiology; renal ammonia metabolism; potassium regulation. *Mailing Add:* Div Nephrology D3238 Box 19 Med Sch Univ Mich Ann Arbor MI 48109

TANNENBAUM, CARL MARTIN, b New York, NY, Apr 1, 40. BIOCHEMISTRY. *Educ:* City Col New York, BS, 60; Univ Ariz, MS, 68; Univ Nebr, PhD(chem), 74. *Prof Exp:* Chemist, Ciba Pharmaceut Co, 61-64; fel physiol, Med Sch, Yale Univ, 72-75; asst prof biochem, Swiss Fed Inst Technol, 75-78; RES BIOLOGIST, PROCTER & GAMBLE CO, 78- *Mem:* Am Chem Soc. *Res:* Epithelial membrane transport of sugars and amino acids; characterization of the factors involved in transport. *Mailing Add:* Procter & Gamble Co Box 39175 Cincinnati OH 45247

TANNENBAUM, HAROLD E, b New York, NY, Dec 31, 14; m 37; c 2. SCIENCE EDUCATION. *Educ:* Columbia Univ, MA, 37, EdD, 50. *Prof Exp:* Teacher, Park Sch, Ohio, 37-42; head sci dept, Elisabeth Irwin High Sch, NY, 44-52; prof sci educ, State Univ NY Teachers Col, New Paltz, 52-61; chmn div curric & instruct, Grad Sch Educ, Yeshiva Univ, 61-64; prof, 64-78, chmn dept curric & teaching, 68-72, EMER PROF SCI EDUC, HUNTER COL, 78- *Concurrent Pos:* Sci Manpower Comt fel, Columbia Univ, 58-59; consult, State Educ Depts, NH, Va, NDak & NY. *Mem:* AAAS; Nat Sci Teachers Asn. *Mailing Add:* Box 295 Phoenicia NY 12464

TANNENBAUM, HARVEY, b New York, NY, June 26, 23; m 46; c 3. PHYSICAL CHEMISTRY. *Educ:* NY Univ, BS, 48. *Prof Exp:* Mem staff, 49-65, CHIEF REMOTE SENSING, CB DETECTION & ALARMS DIV, CHEM SYSTS LAB, EDGEWOOD ARSENAL, 65- *Concurrent Pos:* Partic, NATO Experts Panel Laser Remote Sensing of Atmosphere, 75-; mem, Joint Army Navy NASA Air Force Comt Propulsion Hazards, 75- *Mem:* Optical Soc Am; Sigma Xi. *Res:* Infrared physics; trace gas detection; pollution monitoring instrumentation; remote sensing instrumentation; electro-optical systems; spectroscopy. *Mailing Add:* CB Detection & Alarms Div Chem Systs Lab Aberdeen Proving Ground MD 21010

TANNENBAUM, IRVING ROBERT, b Spring Lake, NJ, Feb 24, 26; m 51; c 4. PHYSICAL CHEMISTRY. *Educ:* Va Polytech Inst, BS, 46, MS, 48; Univ Ill, PhD(phys chem), 51. *Prof Exp:* Instr math, Va Polytech Inst, 46-47; asst phys chem, Univ Ill, 47-50; mem staff chem res, Los Alamos Sci Lab, Univ Calif, 51-56; sr phys chemist, Atomics Int Div, NAm Aviation, Inc, 56-61; scientist, Electro-Optical Systs, Inc, 61-63; sr scientist, Heliodyne Corp, 63-65; PRES & TECH DIR CHEMATICS RES CORP, RESEDA, 65-; PROF CHEM, WEST LOS ANGELES COL, 79- *Concurrent Pos:* Adj prof, Univ Calif, Los Angeles, 58- *Mem:* Am Chem Soc. *Res:* Theory of liquid mixtures; inorganic and plutonium chemistry; hydrides; x-ray crystallography; chemical kinetics; re-entry physics. *Mailing Add:* 8354 Etiwanda Ave Northridge CA 91324

TANNENBAUM, MICHAEL J, b Bronx, NY, Mar 10, 39; m 73; c 2. HIGH ENERGY PHYSICS. *Educ:* Columbia Univ, AB, 59, MA, 60, PhD(physics), 65. *Prof Exp:* Vis scientist, Europ Orgn Nuclear Res, 65-66; from asst prof to assoc prof physics, Harvard Univ, 66-71; assoc prof physics, Rockefeller Univ, 71-80; HEAD PLANNING & ANAL, ISABELLE MAGNET DIV, BROOKHAVEN NAT LAB, 80- *Concurrent Pos:* Ernest Kempton Adams traveling fel from Columbia Univ, 65-66; NSF fel, 66; Alfred P Sloan Found fel, 67-69; mem prog adv comt, Fermi Nat Lab, 72-75; attache sci, Europ Orgn Nuclear Res, 73-80. *Mem:* Fel Am Phys Soc; AAAS; NY Acad Sci; Sigma Xi. *Res:* Muon elastic and inelastic scattering; muon g-2; muon tridents; photoproduction with a tagged beam; single leptons, lepton pairs and high transverse momentum phenomena in proton-proton interactions; superconductive magnetics. *Mailing Add:* Bldg 902A Isabelle Brookhaven Nat Lab Upton NY 11973

TANNENBAUM, STANLEY, b New York, NY, Mar 1, 25; m 47; c 4. INORGANIC CHEMISTRY. *Educ:* City Col New York, BS, 46; Ohio State Univ, PhD(chem), 49. *Prof Exp:* Res chemist, Nat Adv Comt Aeronaut, 50-53; res chemist reaction motors div, Thiokol Chem Corp, 53-59, sect head, 59-66, prod mgr, 66-69; mgr tech serv, Ronson Metals Corp, 69-76; SR SCIENTIST, HAZARD RES CORP, 76- *Mem:* Am Chem Soc. *Res:* Synthesis of silicon and boron containing chemicals; physical and thermochemical properties of materials; alteration of properties of rocket propellants; determination of fire and explosive hazards of chemicals and chemical processes. *Mailing Add:* 18 A Celtis Plaza Cranbury NJ 08512

TANNENBAUM, STEVEN ROBERT, b Brooklyn, NY, Feb 23, 37; m 59; c 2. FOOD CHEMISTRY. *Educ:* Mass Inst Technol, BS, 58, PhD(food sci), 62. *Prof Exp:* Res assoc food technol, 62-63, from instr to assoc prof food sci, 63-74, prof food chem, 74-81, PROF TOXICOLOGY & FOOD CHEM,

MASS INST TECHNOL, 81- *Concurrent Pos:* Consult, US Food & Drug Admin, 71-73; mem, Expert Panel Food Safety & Nutrit, Inst Food Technologists, 71-73, co-chmn, 76-77, chmn, 77-78; mem spec prog adv comt, Nat Cancer Inst, 79-82. *Honors & Awards:* Samuel Cate Prescott Award, Inst Food Technologists, 70, Tanner Award, 76, Babcock Hart Award, 80. *Mem:* Am Chem Soc; Inst Food Technologists; Am Inst Nutrit; Brit Nutrit Soc; fel Brit Inst Food Sci & Technol. *Res:* Chemistry of nitrates, nitrites and nitrosamines; chemistry and biochemistry of pyrolysis products of foods; analysis of cancer risk in human populations. *Mailing Add:* Dept Nutrit & Food Sci Rm 16-209 Mass Inst Technol Cambridge MA 02139

TANNENWALD, LUDWIG MAX, b Frankfurt, Ger, Feb 21, 28; nat US; m 63; c 2. OPTICAL PHYSICS. *Educ:* Univ Chicago, BS, 46, MS, 49, PhD(physics), 51. *Prof Exp:* Physicist, US Naval Ord Test Sta, 51-55, assoc res scientist, 55-56, res scientist, 56-58, group leader, 58-59, staff scientist, 59-72, STAFF SCIENTIST, LOCKHEED MISSILE & SPACE CO, 72- *Concurrent Pos:* Res physicist, Univ Calif, Berkeley, 71-72. *Mem:* Am Phys Soc. *Res:* Quantum mechanical calculations of collision processes and statistical mechanics. *Mailing Add:* Lockheed Missile & Space Co 3251 Hanover Palo Alto CA 94304

TANNENWALD, PETER ERNEST, b Kiel, Ger, Mar 30, 26; nat US. PHYSICS. *Educ:* Univ Calif, AB, 47, PhD(physics), 52. *Prof Exp:* Asst physics, Univ Calif, 47-51, Radiation Lab, 50-52; physicist, 52-59, asst group leader, 59-62, group leader, 62-63, asst head, 63-65, assoc head, 65-74, SR SCIENTIST, SOLID STATE DIV, LINCOLN LAB, MASS INST TECHNOL, 74- *Mem:* Fel Am Phys Soc. *Res:* Solid state physics and quantum electronics; microwave resonance in ferrites; spin wave resonance in magnetic films; masers; millimeter waves; microwave ultrasonics; lasers; Raman and Brillouin spectroscopy; far infrared quantum electronics and submillimeter wave technology. *Mailing Add:* Solid State Div Lincoln Lab Mass Inst of Technol Lexington MA 02173

TANNER, ALAN ROGER, b Port Lavaca, Tex, Jan 2, 41; m 69; c 2. INDUSTRIAL ORGANIC CHEMISTRY, ELECTROCHEMISTRY. *Educ:* Univ Tex, Austin, BS, 64, PhD(org chem), 69. *Prof Exp:* Appln res chemist, Jefferson Chem Co, 69-71; RES & DEVELOP CHEMIST, SOUTHWESTERN ANAL CHEM, INC, 71- *Concurrent Pos:* Instr org chem, St Edward's Univ, 74-75. *Mem:* Am Chem Soc. *Res:* Conventional and electrochemical synthetic approaches to new and existing marketable products. *Mailing Add:* Southwestern Anal Chem Inc 821 E Woodward Austin TX 78704

TANNER, ALLAN BAIN, b New York, NY, May 27, 30; m 80; c 3. GEOPHYSICS, GEOCHEMISTRY. *Educ:* Mass Inst Technol, SB, 52. *Prof Exp:* Geophysicist theoret geophys br, US Geol Surv, DC, 54-69, GEOPHYSICIST ISOTOPE GEOL BR, US GEOL SURV, 69- *Concurrent Pos:* Comt mem, Nat Coun Radiation Protection & Measurements, 73-74. *Mem:* Soc Explor Geophys; Am Geophys Union. *Res:* Behavior of radon isotopes in natural environments; nuclear geophysics and geochemistry; x-ray fluorescence; isotope geology; gamma-ray spectrometry; in situ neutron activation analysis; health physics. *Mailing Add:* US Geol Surv 990 Nat Ctr Reston VA 22092

TANNER, CHAMP BEAN, b Idaho Falls, Idaho, Nov 16, 20; m 41; c 5. MICROCLIMATOLOGY, SOIL PHYSICS. *Educ:* Brigham Young Univ, BS, 42; Univ Wis, PhD(soils), 50. *Prof Exp:* From instr to assoc prof soils, 50-61, prof soil sci & meterol, 61-80, EMIL TRUOG PROF SOIL SCI, UNIV WIS-MADISON, 80- *Mem:* AAAS; Soil Sci Soc Am; Am Soc Agron; Am Geophys Union; Am Meteorol Soc. *Res:* Evapotranspiration; plant environment; soil moisture and structure. *Mailing Add:* Dept of Soil Sci Univ of Wis Madison WI 53706

TANNER, CHARLES E, b Preston, Cuba, Sept 10, 32; Can citizen; m 57; c 2. IMMUNOLOGY, PARASITOLOGY. *Educ:* Purdue Univ, BS, 53; McGill Univ, MS, 56, PhD, 57. *Prof Exp:* Teaching fel bact & immunol, McGill Univ, 55-57; Nat Res Coun Can overseas fel, 57-58; from asst prof to assoc prof parasitol, 58-71, PROF PARASITOL, INST PARASITOL, MACDONALD COL, McGILL UNIV, 71-, ASSOC MEM MICROBIOL, FAC AGR, UNIV, 73- *Concurrent Pos:* Mem, Int Comn Trichinellosis, 73-; mem, Nat Res Ctr Parasitol. *Mem:* AAAS; Am Soc Parasitologists; Can Soc Microbiol; Can Soc Immunol; Can Soc Zool. *Res:* Immunology of host-parasite relations; immunochemistry of parasite antigens. *Mailing Add:* Inst Parasitol PO Box 231 Macdonald Col McGill Univ Ste Anne de Bellevue PQ H9X 1C0 Can

TANNER, DAVID, b Brooklyn, NY, Aug 7, 28; m 53; c 4. POLYMER CHEMISTRY. *Educ:* NY Univ, BA, 50; Brooklyn Polytech Inst, PhD(polymer chem), 54. *Prof Exp:* Res asst polymer chem, Univ Ill, 53-54; res chemist exp sta, Nylon Res Div, 54-59, res assoc, 59-62, supvr res, 62-63, sr supvr technol, Nylon Tech Div, 63-65, res mgr, Orlon-Lycra Res Div, 65-68, lab dir, Benger Lab, 68-69, tech mgr, Dacron Div, 70-72, tech mgr, Orlon-Acetate-Lycra Div, 72-76, res dir, Textile Fibers Dept, 76-80, MGR, STRATEGIC PLANNING DIV, E I DU PONT DE NEMOURS & CO, INC, 80- *Mem:* Am Chem Soc; Asn Res Dirs; NAm Planning Soc. *Res:* Organic synthesis; radiation chemistry; fiber technology including polyesters, polyamides, acrylics, elastomers and high temperature fibers. *Mailing Add:* Textile Fibers Dept Nemours Bldg E I du Pont de Nemours & Co Inc Wilmington DE 19898

TANNER, DAVID JOHN, b Redfield, SDak, May 7, 42; m 61; c 2. LOW TEMPERATURE PHYSICS, MICROCOMPUTER APPLICATIONS. *Educ:* Univ Chicago, SB, 60, SM, 61, PhD, 66. *Prof Exp:* Asst prof physics, Wayne State Univ, 65-70, lead programmer, 70-72; PHYSICIST-PROGRAMMER, KMS FUSION, INC, 72- *Mem:* Am Phys Soc. *Res:* Ions in liquid helium; laser-plasma interaction. *Mailing Add:* KMS Fusion Inc PO Box 1567 3621 S State Rd Ann Arbor MI 48106

TANNER, DENNIS DAVID, b Montreal, Que, Mar 6, 30; US citizen; m 60; c 2. ORGANIC CHEMISTRY. *Educ:* Univ Calif, Los Angeles, BSc, 53; Stanford Univ, MSc, 57; Univ Colo, PhD(chem), 61. *Prof Exp:* Asst, Stanford Univ, 56-57 & Univ Colo, 57-60; res fel chem, Columbia Univ, 61-63; annual asst prof, 63-65, from asst prof to assoc prof, 65-75, PROF CHEM, UNIV ALTA, 75- *Mem:* Am Chem Soc; Chem Inst Can. *Res:* Mechanisms of free radical reactions; free radical and ionic rearrangement mechanisms. *Mailing Add:* Dept of Chem Univ of Alta Edmonton AB T5H 0Z8 Can

TANNER, EARL C, b Providence, RI, Nov 16, 19; m 57; c 2. FUSION ENERGY. *Educ:* Brown Univ, AB, 41, AM, 47, ScM, 59; Harvard Univ, PhD(hist), 51. *Prof Exp:* Asst to dir, Plasma Physics Lab, Princeton Univ, 58-64, asst dir, 64-77, asst dir spec projs, 77-81. *Mem:* Am Phys Soc. *Res:* Role of fusion in world energy scenrios. *Mailing Add:* Plasma Physics Lab Princeton Univ PO Box 451 Princeton NJ 08540

TANNER, GARY DALE, b Cherokee, Okla, Oct 27, 42; m 65; c 3. ENTOMOLOGY, BIOLOGY. *Educ:* Bob Jones Univ, BS, 64; Clemson Univ, MS, 66; Va Polytech Inst & State Univ, PhD(entom), 71. *Prof Exp:* Res asst entom, Clemson Univ, 64-66; asst chief eval sect, Aedes Aegypti Eradication Prog, Nat Ctr Dis Control, Dept Health, Educ & Welfare, Ga, 66-68; ASST PROF BIOL, GRACE COL, 71- *Mem:* AAAS; Entom Soc Am; Am Mosquito Control Asn. *Res:* Host preferences and feeding activities of Culicoides biting gnats. *Mailing Add:* Dept of Biol Grace Col Winona Lake IN 46590

TANNER, GEORGE ALBERT, b Vienna, Austria, Aug 2, 38; US citizen; m 62; c 2. PHYSIOLOGY. *Educ:* Cornell Univ, AB, 59; Harvard Univ, PhD(physiol), 64. *Prof Exp:* Nat Heart Inst res trainee physiol, Med Col, Cornell Univ, 64-67; from asst prof to assoc prof, 67-78, PROF PHYSIOL, SCH MED, IND UNIV, INDIANAPOLIS, 78- *Concurrent Pos:* Vis prof, Heidelberg Univ, 74-75. *Mem:* Am Heart Asn; Soc Exp Biol & Med; Int Soc Nephrology; Am Soc Nephrology; Am Physiol Soc. *Res:* Renal function. *Mailing Add:* Dept of Physiol Ind Univ Med Ctr Indianapolis IN 46223

TANNER, JAMES GORDON, geophysics, see previous edition

TANNER, JAMES MERVIL, b Jesup, Ga, Dec 29, 34; m 56; c 3. THEORETICAL PHYSICS. *Educ:* Ga Inst Technol, BS, 56, MS, 61, PhD(physics), 64. *Prof Exp:* Assoc scientist, Westinghouse Elec Corp, 56-58; instr physics, Ga Inst Technol, 58-62, asst prof, 64-65; assoc prof, Univ NC, Charlotte, 65-67; ASSOC PROF PHYSICS, GA INST TECHNOL, 67- *Mem:* Am Phys Soc; Am Asn Physics Teachers. *Res:* Mathematical physics. *Mailing Add:* Dept of Physics Ga Inst of Technol Atlanta GA 30332

TANNER, JAMES TAYLOR, b Homer, NY, Mar 6, 14; m 41; c 3. ANIMAL ECOLOGY. *Educ:* Cornell Univ, BS, 35, MS, 36, PhD(ornith), 40. *Prof Exp:* Asst prof biol, Tenn State Teachers Col, Johnson City, 40-42 & ETenn State Col, 46; from asst prof to assoc prof zool, 47-63, dir grad prog ecol, 69-74, prof, 63-79, EMER PROF ZOOL, UNIV TENN, KNOXVILLE, 79- *Mem:* AAAS; Ecol Soc Am; Am Ornith Union. *Res:* Ecological and population studies of animals. *Mailing Add:* Dept of Zool Univ of Tenn Knoxville TN 37996

TANNER, JAMES THOMAS, b Franklin, Ky, Apr 23, 39; m 64. RADIOCHEMISTRY. *Educ:* Eastern Ky State Col, BS, 61; Univ Ky, PhD(radiochem), 66. *Prof Exp:* Res chemist, Carnegie-Mellon Univ, 66-68, lectr chem, 68-69; res chemist, 69-79, CHIEF, NUTRIENT SURVEILLANCE BR, FOOD & DRUG ADMIN, 79- *Mem:* Fel AAAS; fel Meteoritical Soc; Am Chem Soc; Sigma Xi. *Res:* Neutron activation analysis; trace elements in meteorites; trace element distribution in foods, drugs and consumer products; nutrient content of foods. *Mailing Add:* HFF-266 Food & Drug Admin Washington DC 20204

TANNER, JOHN EYER, JR, b Cleveland, Ohio, Apr 30, 30; m 66; c 3. PHYSICAL CHEMISTRY. *Educ:* Oberlin Col, AB, 51; Ind Univ, MS, 54; Univ Wis, PhD(phys chem), 66. *Prof Exp:* Res asst phys chem, Am Found Biol Res, Wis, 59-62; res fel, Pa State Univ, 66-68; res asst, Max Planck Inst Med Res, Ger, 68-69; fel, Sci Res Staff, Ford Motor Co, Mich, 69-71; res chemist, Naval Weapons Support Ctr, 71-79; SR RES ENGR, EXXON NUCLEAR IDAHO CO, 79- *Mem:* Am Chem Soc; Biophys Soc; Am Phys Soc. *Res:* Nuclear magnetic resonance; emission and absorption spectroscopy; thermodynamics. *Mailing Add:* Tech Dept Exxon Nuclear Idaho Co Idaho Falls ID 83401

TANNER, LEE ELLIOT, b Brooklyn, NY, May 28, 31; m 56; c 2. PHYSICAL METALLURGY. *Educ:* NY Univ, BS, 53; Univ Pa, MS, 58. *Prof Exp:* Res asst phys metall, Armour Res Found, 53, assoc metallurgist, 56-59; sr metallurgist, ManLabs, Inc ManLabs, Inc, 59-63; sr res metallurgist, Ledgemont Lab, Kennecott Copper Corp, 63-73; staff metallurgist, Mat Res Ctr, Allied Chem Corp, 73-78; SR METALLURGIST, MANLABS, INC, 78- *Mem:* AAAS; Am Soc Metals; Am Inst Mining, Metall & Petrol Engrs; Am Inst Physics; Electron Micros Soc Am. *Res:* Electron microscopy; metals and alloys; crystalline and amorphous; phase transformations, precipitation, ordering; relationships of microstructure top to physical properties. *Mailing Add:* ManLabs Inc 21 Erie St Cambridge MA 02139

TANNER, LLOYD GEORGE, b Cozad, Nebr, Oct 3, 18; c 4. GEOLOGY. *Educ:* Univ Nebr, BS, 51, MS, 56. *Prof Exp:* Field asst & party leader, Univ Nebr State Mus, 38-39 & 51-75, field supvr, Works Progress Admin, 39-40, asst cur vert paleontol, 51-56, assoc cur, 56-77, asst prof geol, Univ Nebr, 71-73, res assoc vert paleontol, 73-78, ASSOC PROF MUS & GEOL, UNIV NEBR, 78-, COORDR SYST COLLECTIONS, UNIV NEBR STATE MUSEUM, 70- & CUR VERT PALEONT, 77- *Concurrent Pos:* Co-prin investr fauna & stratig sequence, Big Bone Lick, Ky, 62-66; mem, Yale Peabody Mus Egyptian Expeds, 62-66; fac fel, Univ Nebr, 71-; mem, Duke Univ Egyptian Expeds, 77-81. *Res:* Vertebrate paleontology; stratigraphy; Pleistocene geology. *Mailing Add:* Rm W-436 Nebraska Hall Univ of Nebr Lincoln NE 68588

TANNER, NOALL STEVAN, b Ogden, Utah, Sept 21, 34; m 55; c 2. PHARMACOLOGY, PHARMACOGNOSY. *Educ:* Univ Utah, BS, 56, PhD(pharmacog), 66. *Prof Exp:* Asst prof pharmacog, Col Pharm, Butler Univ, 63-66; ASSOC PROF PHARMACOL, COL PHARM, NDAK STATE UNIV, 67- *Mem:* Am Pharmaceut Asn; Acad Pharmaceut Sci; Soc Hosp Pharmacists. *Res:* Biopharmaceutical sciences; environmental study of Veratrum californicum; relation of neurotransmitter to behavior in rats; study and screening of natural products. *Mailing Add:* Dept of Pharmacol NDak State Univ Fargo ND 58102

TANNER, RAYMOND LEWIS, b Memphis, Tenn, Dec 11, 31; m 68; c 3. RADIOLOGICAL PHYSICS, HEALTH PHYSICS. *Educ:* Memphis State Univ, BS, 53; Vanderbilt Univ, MS, 55; Univ Calif, Los Angeles, PhD(med physics), 67. *Prof Exp:* Asst prof physics, Memphis State Univ, 55-62; vis physicist, Harbor Gen Hosp, Torrance, Calif, 63-64; assoc prof, 67-70, PROF MED PHYSICS, CTR HEALTH SCI, UNIV TENN, MEMPHIS, 70-, ASST TO CHANCELLOR FOR FACIL PLANNING, 77- *Concurrent Pos:* Consult self-radiation protection, 55- *Mem:* Am Asn Physicists in Med (pres, 73-74); Health Physics Soc; Am Col Radiol; Radiol Soc NAm (vpres, 80-81); Sigma Xi. *Res:* Radiation dosimetry. *Mailing Add:* Ctr for Health Sci Univ of Tenn Memphis TN 38163

TANNER, ROBERT DENNIS, b Detroit, Mich, Jan 17, 39; m 63; c 2. CHEMICAL ENGINEERING, BIOCHEMICAL ENGINEERING. *Educ:* Univ Mich, BSE, 61 & 62, MSE, 63; Case Western Reserve Univ, PhD(chem eng), 67. *Prof Exp:* Engr, Diamond Shamrock Corp, 63; eng assoc res, Merck & Co, Inc, 67-72; asst prof, 72-77, ASSOC PROF CHEM ENG, VANDERBILT UNIV, 77- *Concurrent Pos:* vis prof, Eidgenössische Technische Hochschule, Zürich, 81-82. *Mem:* Am Inst Chem Engrs; Am Chem Soc. *Res:* Fermentation modeling; enzyme kinetics; yeast technology; ethanol biosynthesis and recovery; utilization of kudzu. *Mailing Add:* Dept of Chem Eng Vanderbilt Univ Nashville TN 37235

TANNER, ROBERT MICHAEL, b Spanish Fork, Utah, Mar 22, 46; m 65; c 2. INFORMATION SCIENCES. *Educ:* Stanford Univ, BS, 66, MS, 67, PhD(elec eng), 71. *Prof Exp:* Asst prof elec eng, Tenn State Univ, 70-71; asst prof, 71-78, ASSOC PROF INFO SCI, UNIV CALIF, SANTA CRUZ, 78- *Concurrent Pos:* Consult, Technol Commun Int, 71- *Mem:* Inst Elec & Electronics Engrs. *Res:* Information theory, coding and complexity. *Mailing Add:* 523A Riverview Dr Capitola CA 95010

TANNER, ROGER IAN, b Wells, Eng, July 25, 33; m 57; c 5. ENGINEERING. *Educ:* Bristol Univ, BSc, 56; Univ Calif, Berkeley, MS, 58; Manchester Univ, PhD(sci), 61. *Prof Exp:* Tech asst engr, Bristol-Siddeley Aero Engines Ltd, UK, 57-58; asst lectr mech eng, Univ Manchester, 58-59, lectr, 59-61; sr lectr, Sydney Univ, 61-64, reader, 64-66; from assoc prof to prof eng, Brown Univ, 66-75; P N RUSSELL PROF, SYDNEY UNIV, 75- *Honors & Awards:* David Medal, Royal Soc NSW, 67. *Mem:* Soc Rheol; Brit Soc Rheol; Australian Acad Sci; assoc mem Am Soc Mech Eng. *Res:* Flow of non-newtonian fluids; solar energy. *Mailing Add:* Dept Mech Eng Univ Sydney Sydney NSW 2006 Australia

TANNER, ROGER LEE, b Union City, Pa, Sept 17, 43; c 4. ANALYTICAL CHEMISTRY, ATMOSPHERIC CHEMISTRY. *Educ:* Pa State Univ, BS, 64; Univ Ill, Urbana, PhD(anal chem), 69. *Prof Exp:* Temp asst prof chem, Portland State Univ, 68-69; asst prof chem, Univ Okla, 69-71; res assoc chem, Univ Ill, Urbana, 72-73; asst chemist atmospheric chem, 73-75, assoc chemist, 75-77, CHEMIST ATMOSPHERIC CHEM, BROOKHAVEN NAT LAB, 77- *Concurrent Pos:* Consult, Sci Adv Bd, Environ Protection Agency, 77- *Mem:* Am Chem Soc; AAAS. *Res:* Trace analytical chemistry of environmental samples; derivatization chromatography; atmospheric chemistry of sulfur and nitrogen compounds; chemical speciation of aerosols; real-time air monitoring instrumentation. *Mailing Add:* Brookhaven Nat Lab Bldg 426 Upton NY 11973

TANNER, WARD DEAN, JR, b Jacksonville, Fla, Dec 6, 18. WILDLIFE MANAGEMENT, ECOLOGY. *Educ:* Univ Minn, BS, 41; Pa State Univ, MS, 48; Iowa State Univ, PhD(zool), 53. *Prof Exp:* Asst wildlife mgt, Pa State Univ, 41, 46-48; refuge mgr, Bombay Hook Nat Wildlife Refuge, US Fish & Wildlife Serv, 48-50; from instr to assoc prof biol, 53-74, PROF BIOL, GUSTAVUS ADOLPHUS COL, 74- *Mem:* Wildlife Soc. *Res:* Ecology of wildlife and ruffed grouse; botany; forestry; fisheries management. *Mailing Add:* Dept of Biol Gustavus Adolphus Col St Peter MN 56082

TANNER, WILLIAM FRANCIS, JR, b Milledgeville, Ga, Feb 4, 17; m 38; c 3. SEDIMENT TRANSPORT, PALEOGEOGRAPHY. *Educ:* Baylor Univ, BA, 37; Tex Tech Col, MA, 39; Univ Okla, PhD(geol), 53. *Prof Exp:* Asst geol, Baylor Univ, 35-37; oil ed, Amarillo Times, 39-41 & 45-46; asst prof geol & journalism, Okla Baptist Univ, 46-51; spec instr, Univ Okla, 51-54; vis lectr geol, 54-56, from assoc prof to prof, 56-74, REGENTS PROF GEOL, FLA STATE UNIV, 74- *Concurrent Pos:* Geologist, Shell Oil Co, 54; ed, Coastal Res, 62-; NSF vis scientist, 65-66. *Mem:* Fel AAAS; fel Geol Soc Am; Soc Econ Paleontologists & Mineralogists; Int Asn Sedimentology; Am Geophys Union. *Res:* Sedimentology; stratigraphy; geomorphology; hydrodynamics; beach and shore processes; structural, areal, field and subsurface geology; rheology and deformation of materials; circular statistics; paleogeography; paleoclimatology; petroleum exploration and resources; other energy sources. *Mailing Add:* Dept of Geol Fla State Univ Tallahassee FL 32306

TANQUARY, ALBERT CHARLES, b Columbus, Kans, Mar 9, 29; m 49; c 5. POLYMER SCIENCE. *Educ:* Kans State Col, Pittsburg, BS, 50; Okla State Univ, MS, 52, PhD(chem), 54. *Prof Exp:* Sr chemist cent res dept, Minn Mining & Mfg Co, 54-55, group supvr, 55-58, res mgr fibers dept, 59-61, mgr, 62-63; group leader res & develop div, Union Camp Corp, 63-65; ASSOC DIR SOUTHERN RES INST, 66- *Mem:* Am Chem Soc; Am Asn Textile Chemists & Colorists; Fiber Soc; Soc Plastics Engrs; Tech Asn Pulp & Paper Indust. *Res:* Polymer and textile chemistry; mechanical properties of polymers, fibers and films; fiber spinning; biomaterials research; biomedical engineering. *Mailing Add:* Gulf Res Inst New Orleans Lab PO Box 26518 New Orleans LA 70186

TANSEY, MICHAEL RICHARD, b Oakland, Calif, Mar 27, 43; m 63; c 2. MYCOLOGY. *Educ:* Univ Calif, Berkeley, BA, 65, PhD(bot), 70. *Prof Exp:* NSF fel & res assoc microbiol, 70-71, asst prof, 71-77, ASSOC PROF BIOL, IND UNIV, BLOOMINGTON, 78- *Mem:* AAAS; Am Soc Microbiol; Bot Soc Am; Mycol Soc Am; Brit Mycol Soc. *Res:* Biology of thermophilic fungi; cellulose biodegradation; heated habitats. *Mailing Add:* Dept Biol Ind Univ Bloomington IN 47405

TANSEY, ROBERT PAUL, SR, b Newark, NJ, Apr 27, 14; m 41; c 4. PHARMACY. *Educ:* Rutgers Univ, BS, 38, MS, 50. *Prof Exp:* Control pharmacist, Res & Develop Labs, Burroughs Wellcome Co, Inc, 40-43; asst dept head prod & control, E R Squibb & Sons, 43-45; head, Pharmaceut Res & Develop Lab, Maltbie Labs, 45-50; assoc dept head, Merck & Co, 50-53; sect leader, Schering Co, Inc, 53-58; res coordr, Strong Cobb Arner Co, Inc, 58-62; regist pharmacist, Saywell Pharm, Ohio, 62-63; TECH DIR, VET LABS, INC, 63- *Mem:* Animal Health Inst; Am Pharmaceut Asn. *Res:* Pharmaceutical development; formulation and methods analysis; production processing techniques and control methods; pharmaceutical plant and equipment design; development of special techniques for control and sustained release medicinal forms; plant management. *Mailing Add:* 11141 Glen Arbor Rd Kansas City MO 64114

TANSY, MARTIN F, b Wilkes Barre, Pa, Mar 8, 37; m 64; c 3. PHYSIOLOGY. *Educ:* Wilkes Col, BA, 59; Jefferson Med Col, MS, 61, PhD(physiol), 64. *Prof Exp:* Res asst physiol, Jefferson Med Col, 59-61, fel, 62-64; from asst prof to assoc prof, 64-72, PROF PHYSIOL, SCHS DENT, PHARM & ALLIED HEALTH PROF, TEMPLE UNIV, 72-, CHMN DEPT, 64-, BASIC SCI COORDR, 79- *Mem:* Fel Am Col Nutrit; Soc Exp Biol & Med; Am Physiol Soc; Am Pharmaceut Asn; Am Fedn Clin Res. *Res:* Gastrointestinal and radiation physiology. *Mailing Add:* Dept of Physiol & Biophys Temple Univ Dent Sch Philadelphia PA 19140

TANTRAPORN, WIROJANA, b Chonburi, Thailand, Apr 17, 31; m 53; c 1. SOLID STATE PHYSICS. *Educ:* Univ Denver, BS, 52; Univ Mich, MS, 53, PhD(physics), 58. *Prof Exp:* Lectr physics, Univ Mich, 58-59; physicist electronics lab, 59-62, PHYSICIST, RES & DEVELOP CTR, GEN ELEC CO, 62- *Res:* Thin films; semiconductors; insulators; solid state microwave devices; electron devices; computer simulations. *Mailing Add:* Gen Elec Res & Develop Ctr Schenectady NY 12301

TANTRAVAHI, RAMANA V, b Samalkot, India, Dec 1, 35; m 62; c 2. HUMAN GENETICS, CYTOGENETICS. *Educ:* Andhra Univ, BS(Hons), 56, MS, 57; Harvard Univ, PhD(biol & plant genetics), 67. *Prof Exp:* Lectr bot, Andhra Univ, 58-62; res fel biol, Harvard Univ, 67-69; Govt India pool officer plant genetics, Agr Univ, Bangalore, 69-70; res assoc plant genetics, Suburban Exp Sta, Univ Mass, 70-73; RES ASSOC HUMAN GENETICS, COLUMBIA UNIV MED CTR, 73- *Res:* Mammalian cytogenetics and mouse cytogenetics; gene mapping by cytogenetic and somatic cell genetic techniques; evolutionary aspects of animal and plant communities. *Mailing Add:* Dept of Human Genetics & Develop Columbia Univ Med Ctr New York NY 10032

TANTTILA, WALTER H, b Sax, Minn, Nov 21, 22; m 51; c 3. PHYSICS. *Educ:* Univ Minn, BChE, 48, MA, 50; Univ Wash, PhD(physics), 55. *Prof Exp:* Instr physics, Minn State Teachers Col, Winona, 50-51; res physicist, Minneapolis-Honeywell Regulator Co, 51-52; asst physics, Univ Wash, 52-55; asst prof, Mich State Univ, 55-58; from asst prof to assoc prof, 58-62, PROF PHYSICS, UNIV COLO, BOULDER, 62- *Mem:* Am Phys Soc. *Res:* Glass, solid and liquid properties; low temperature phenomena. *Mailing Add:* Dept of Physics Univ of Colo Boulder CO 80309

TAN-WILSON, ANNA LI, b Manila, Philippines, Mar 16, 46. BIOCHEMISTRY, IMMUNOLOGY. *Educ:* Univ Philippines, BS, 66; Univ Col London, MSc, 67; State Univ NY, Buffalo, PhD(biochem), 73. *Prof Exp:* Instr chem, Univ Philippines, 67-69; res assoc biochem & immunol, State Univ NY, Buffalo, 73-75; res assoc biochem, Purdue Univ, 75-76; ASST PROF BIOL, STATE UNIV NY, BINGHAMTON, 76- *Concurrent Pos:* Fel State Univ NY Res Found grant, 77-79 & 78-80; co prin investr, NSF grant. *Mem:* Am Soc Zoologists; Biophys Soc; AAAS; Am Chem Soc. *Res:* Immunochemical and biochemical alalysis of plant proteinase inhibitor metabolism. *Mailing Add:* Dept Biol Sci State Univ of NY Binghamton NY 13901

TANZ, RALPH, b New York, NY, Oct 10, 25; m 52; c 3. PHARMACOLOGY, PHYSIOLOGY. *Educ:* Univ Rochester, BA, 48; Harvard Med Sch, 49-52; Univ Colo, PhD(pharmacol), 58. *Prof Exp:* Asst pharmacol, Sch Med, Univ Colo, 54-57; instr, Med Units, Univ Tenn, 57-59; sr instr, Sch Med, Western Reserve Univ, 59-62; asst prof pharmacol, New York Med Col, 62-63; head cardiovasc sect, Dept Pharmacol, Geigy Res Labs, NY, 63-69; assoc prof, 69-80, PROF PHARMACOL, SCH MED, ORE HEALTH SCI UNIV, 80- *Concurrent Pos:* NIH career develop award, 61; chmn sect, Gordon Res Conf, 66; Fogarty sr int fel, Heart Res Labs, Dept Med, Univ Cape Town Med Sch, SAfrica, 76-77. *Mem:* AAAS; Am Soc Pharmacol & Exp Therapeut; Cardiac Muscle Soc (pres, 64); Am Heart Asn; Int Heart Res Soc. *Res:* Isolated cardiac tissue; effect of cardiac glycosides and catecholamines on cardiac muscle; antihypertensives; physiological and biochemical correlates of arrhythmogenesis and antiarrhythinic drugs. *Mailing Add:* Dept Pharmacol Sch Med Ore Health Sci Univ Portland OR 97201

TANZER, CHARLES, b New York, NY, Dec 4, 12; m 58. SCIENCE EDUCATION, MEDICAL MICROBIOLOGY. *Educ:* Long Island Univ, BS, 33; NY Univ, MS, 36, PhD(bact), 41. *Hon Degrees:* LHD, Long Island Univ, 80. *Prof Exp:* Asst bact, Col Med, NY Univ, 34-38; instr, Bronx High Sch Sci, 38-43 & Dewitt Clinton High Sch, 45-49; chmn sci dept, Seward Park High Sch, 49-57; prin jr high schs, New York, 57-65; prof & coordr sci, Teacher Educ Prog, 65-73, EMER PROF TEACHER EDUC PROG, HUNTER COL, 73- *Concurrent Pos:* Adj assoc prof, Long Island Univ,

51-65; Ford Found fel, 57. *Honors & Awards:* Meritorious Serv Award, Am Cancer Soc, 73. *Mem:* AAAS; Sigma Xi; Am Cancer Soc; Nat Asn Biol Teachers. *Res:* Serology; parasitology; intestinal parasites. *Mailing Add:* 600 W 218th St New York NY 10034

TANZER, JASON MICHAEL, dentistry, microbial physiology, see previous edition

TANZER, MARVIN LAWRENCE, b New York, NY, Jan 26, 35; m 54; c 4. BIOCHEMISTRY. *Educ:* Mass Inst Technol, SB, 55; NY Univ, MD, 59. *Prof Exp:* Intern med, Johns Hopkins Hosp, Baltimore, 59-60, asst resident, 60-61; res fel, Mass Gen Hosp-Harvard Med Sch, 61-62 & 64-65, asst biologist, 65-68, assoc, 67-68; from asst prof to assoc prof, 68-75, PROF BIOCHEM, HEALTH CTR, UNIV CONN, 75-, PROF ORTHOP SURG & DIR ORTHOP LABS, 78- *Concurrent Pos:* Arthritis Found fel, Mass Gen Hosp, Boston, 61-62, Am Heart Asn fel, 64-66; Am Heart Asn estab investr, Mass Gen Hosp, Boston, 66-68 & Med Sch, Univ Conn, 68-71; investr, Marine Biol Lab, Woods Hole, 66-71; tutor biochem sci, Harvard Univ, 67-68; Josiah Macy, Jr Found fac scholar award, 74-75; vis prof dermat, Univ Liege, Belg, 74-75; NIH Study Sect, Biophys & Biophys Chem B, 76-80; vis prof, Univ Calif, Los Angeles, Bone Res Lab, 76; vis prof, Jap Soc Promotion Sci, Tokyo, 77 & Univ Lund, Sweden, 81. *Mem:* Am Soc Bone & Mineral Res; Orthop Res Soc; Am Soc Cell Biol; Am Chem Soc; Am Soc Biol Chemists. *Res:* Properties, function and synthesis of connective tissue components. *Mailing Add:* Dept of Biochem Univ of Conn Health Ctr Farmington CT 06032

TANZER, RADFORD CHAPPLE, b Little Falls, NY, Sept 16, 05; m 43. MEDICINE. *Educ:* Dartmouth Col, BS, 25; Harvard Med Sch, MD, 29. *Prof Exp:* Instr anat, 39-42, from instr to asst prof surg, 42-49, from asst prof surg to prof plastic surg, 49-71, EMER PROF PLASTIC SURG, DARTMOUTH MED SCH, 71- *Concurrent Pos:* Consult, Vet Admin. *Mem:* Am Soc Plastic & Reconstruct Surg; Am Soc Surg of the Hand; Am Asn Plastic Surg (pres, 71-72). *Res:* Surgery of the hand; ear reconstruction. *Mailing Add:* 8 N Balch St Hanover NH 03755

TAO, FRANK F, b Chang Sha, China; US citizen; c 2. SYNTHETIC FUEL, LUBRICATION. *Educ:* Univ Mo, MS, 57; Univ Mo-Rolla, PhD(chem eng), 64. *Prof Exp:* Res engr, Dorr-Oliver Inc, 57-62; instr, Univ Mo-Rolla, 62-64; sr res engr, 64-71, eng assoc, 72-81, SR ENG ASSOC, EXXON RES & ENG CO, 82- *Honors & Awards:* Arch T Colwell Award, Soc Automobile Engrs, 75. *Mem:* Am Inst Chem Engrs; Sigma Xi. *Res:* Fluidification; lubrication; synthetic fuel (coal liquefaction). *Mailing Add:* 5110 Ashwood Dr Baytown TX 77521

TAO, KAR-LING JAMES, b Canton, China, Aug 20, 41; m 69; c 2. PLANT PHYSIOLOGY. *Educ:* New Asia Col, dipl, 64; Tuskegee Inst, MSc, 68; Univ Wis, PhD(hort & bot), 71. *Prof Exp:* Sec educ teacher sci, Tsung Tsin Mid Sch, 65-66; assoc plant biochem, Cornell Univ, 71-72; res assoc plant physiol, NY State Agr Exp Sta, 72-76; PLANT PHYSIOLOGIST, USDA, 76- *Concurrent Pos:* USDA off escort to Chinese Cotton Deleg, 80; vis scientist, Ministry Agr, China, 81. *Mem:* Am Soc Plant Physiol; AAAS; Crop Sci Soc Am; Am Soc Agron. *Res:* Plant hormones, seed dormancy and seed germination; protein and RNA synthesis in plants; seed deteiolation and seed vigor. *Mailing Add:* Seed Standardization Br USDA Bldg 306 BARC Beltsville MD 20705

TAO, L(UH) C(HENG), b Wusih, China, Feb 6, 22; m 50; c 4. CHEMICAL ENGINEERING. *Educ:* Univ Nanking, China, BS, 46; Univ Wis, MS, 49, PhD, 52. *Prof Exp:* Asst, Univ Nanking, 46-47; chem process engr, Singh Co, Ill, 52-55; res engr, Titanium Metals Corp Am, Nev, 55-59; from assoc prof to prof, 59-70, HOWARD S WILSON PROF CHEM ENG, UNIV NEBR-LINCOLN, 70-, CHMN DEPT, 78- *Mem:* AAAS; Am Chem Soc; Am Inst Chem Engrs; Am Soc Eng Educ. *Res:* Heat and mass transfer; phase equilibrium. *Mailing Add:* Dept of Chem Eng Univ of Nebr Lincoln NE 68508

TAO, LIANG NENG, b China, June 27, 27; nat US; m 57; c 3. ENGINEERING. *Educ:* Chiao Tung Univ, BS, 49; Univ Ill, MS, 50, PhD(mech eng), 53. *Prof Exp:* Res engr, Worthington Corp, 53-55; from asst prof to assoc prof, 55-61, PROF MECH, ILL INST TECHNOL, 61- *Concurrent Pos:* Consult, Armour Res Found Am. *Mem:* Soc Eng Educ; Am Soc Mech Engrs; Am Inst Aeronaut & Astronaut; Am Asn Univ Professors; Sigma Xi (chap pres, 65-66). *Res:* Engineering sciences; applied mathematics; fluid mechanics; heat transfer; thermodynamics; lubrication; magnetohydrodynamics. *Mailing Add:* 6950 N Kilpatrick Ave Lincolnwood IL 60646

TAO, ROBERT CHI-MEI, nutrition, see previous edition

TAO, SHU-JEN, b Soochow, China, Oct 7, 28; m 58; c 3. NUCLEAR SCIENCE, PHYSICAL CHEMISTRY. *Educ:* Amoy Univ, BSc, 49; Univ NSW, MEngSc, 61, PhD(nuclear chem), 64. *Prof Exp:* Scientist, Taiwan Rain Stimulation Res Inst, 51-59; res fel nuclear & radiation chem, Australian AEC, 60-61; SR STAFF SCIENTIST, NEW ENG INST MED RES, 65- *Mem:* AAAS; Am Phys Soc; Am Chem Soc; NY Acad Sci. *Res:* Positron physics; positronium chemistry; fast timing electronic instruments; applied statistics. *Mailing Add:* 12 Woodchuck Lane Wilton CT 06897

TAOKA, GEORGE TAKASHI, b Honolulu, Hawaii, Feb 19, 35. ENGINEERING MECHANICS, CIVIL ENGINEERING. *Educ:* Ore State Univ, BS, 58; Univ Ill, MS, 60, PhD(mech), 64. *Prof Exp:* Struct engr, NAm Aviation, 58-59; instr mech, Univ Ill, 60-64; tech staff mech, Sandia Corp, 64-65; PROF CIVIL ENG, UNIV HAWAII, 65- *Concurrent Pos:* NASA fel, Jet Propulsion Lab, 68; vis fel, Princeton Univ, 72-73; vis prof, Tokyo Inst Technol, 74. *Mem:* Am Acad Mech; Am Soc Civil Engrs; Soc Exp Stress Anal; Inst Transp Engrs. *Res:* Traffic accident analysis; structural dynamics. *Mailing Add:* Dept of Civil Eng 2540 Dole St Honolulu HI 96822

TAPE, GERALD FREDERICK, b Ann Arbor, Mich, May 29, 15; m 39; c 3. SCIENCE ADMINISTRATION. *Educ:* Eastern Mich Univ, AB, 35; Univ Mich, MS, 36, PhD(physics), 40. *Hon Degrees:* DSc, Eastern Mich Univ, 64. *Prof Exp:* Asst physics, Eastern Mich Univ, 33-35 & Univ Mich, 36-39; instr, Cornell Univ, 39-42; staff mem radiation lab, Mass Inst Technol, 42-46; from asst prof to assoc prof physics, Univ Ill, 46-50; asst to dir, Brookhaven Nat Lab, 50-51, dep dir, 51-62; from vpres to pres, Assoc Univs, Inc, 62-63; comnr, US AEC, 63-69; pres, 69-80, SPEC ASST TO PRES, ASSOC UNIVS, INC, 80- *Concurrent Pos:* Mem, President's Sci Adv Comn, 69-73; mem high energy adv panel, US AEC, 69-74, sr tech adv Geneva IV, 71; mem, Defense Sci Bd, 70-74, chmn, 70-73; mem bd dirs, Atomic Indust Forum, 70-73; bd trustees, Sci Serv, 70-; mem sci adv comt, Int Atomic Energy Agency, 72-74, US rep, 73-77; mem gen adv comt, US Energy Res & Develop Admin, 75-77; mem adv coun, Elec Power Res Inst, 78- *Honors & Awards:* Cert Appreciation, Army-Navy, 47 & Dept of State, 69; Meritorious Civilian Serv Medal, Secy of Defense, 69; Distinguished Pub Serv Medal, Dept of Defense, 73; Henry DeWolf Smyth Nuclear Statesman Award, 78; Comndr Order of Leopold II, Belgium. *Mem:* Fel AAAS; fel Am Phys Soc; fel Am Nuclear Soc; Am Astron Soc. *Res:* Nuclear physics; particle physics; accelerator development; reactor development; applications of atomic energy; radioastronomy. *Mailing Add:* Assoc Univs Inc 1717 Massachusetts Ave NW Washington DC 20036

TAPER, CHARLES DANIEL, b PEI, Aug 18, 11. HORTICULTURE. *Educ:* Univ Man, PhD(bot), 53. *Prof Exp:* Chmn, Dept Hort, McGill Univ, 71-80; RETIRED. *Mem:* Agr Inst Can; Can Hort Soc. *Res:* Malus tissue culture studies. *Mailing Add:* 22 Maple Ave Apt 21 Ste Anne de Bellevue PQ H9X 2E6 Can

TAPIA, FERNANDO, b Panama, Apr 8, 22; m 47; c 3. PSYCHIATRY. *Educ:* Univ Iowa, BA, 44, MD, 47; Am Bd Psychiat & Neurol, dipl psychiat, 60, dipl child psychiat, 66. *Prof Exp:* Intern, Santo Thomas Hosp, Panama, 48; dir, Boquette Sanit Unit-Panama, 48-54; resident psychiat, Barnes Hosp, Wash Univ, 54-57; asst dir out-patient clin, Malcolm Bliss Ment Health Ctr, 57-58; chief psychiatrist, Child Guid Clin, St Louis County Health Ctr, 58-59, dir ment health div, 59-61; from asst prof to prof psychiat, Sch Med, Univ Mo-Columbia, 61-72, chief sect child psychiat, 61-72; PROF PSYCHIAT & BEHAV SCI, COL MED, UNIV OKLA, 72- CHIEF MENT HEALTH SERV, UNIV HOSP & CLINS, 72- *Concurrent Pos:* Instr, Wash Univ, 57-61; consult, St Louis County Juv Court, 57-61 & Convent of the Good Shepherd, 57-61; dir children's serv, Mid-Mo Ment Health Ctr, 66-72. *Mem:* Fel Am Psychiat Asn. *Mailing Add:* Univ of Okla Health Sci Ctr PO Box 26901 Oklahoma City OK 73190

TAPIA, M(OIEZ) A(HMEDALE), b Surat, India, Nov 17, 35; m 72. ELECTRICAL ENGINEERING. *Educ:* Univ Poona, BE, 60; Univ Ill, Urbana, MS, 62; Univ Notre Dame, PhD(elec eng), 66. *Prof Exp:* Asst lectr elec eng, Polytech Inst, India, 60-61; asst prof, Ga Inst Technol, 66-67 & Univ Miami, 67-68; asst prof, Ga Inst Technol, 68-76; ASST PROF ELEC ENG, UNIV MIAMI, 76- *Concurrent Pos:* Jr engr, Koyna Elec, India, 60-61; Am Soc Eng Educ-Ford Found resident fel, NASA-Langley Res Ctr, 72-73; NASA grant fel prog comput sci, 72- *Mem:* Inst Elec & Electronics Engrs. *Res:* Computer engineering and science; network topology; communications; linear systems. *Mailing Add:* Univ of Miami Box 248294 Coral Gables FL 33134

TAPIA, RICHARD, b Santa Monica, Calif, Mar 25, 39; m 60; c 2. NUMERICAL ANALYSIS. *Educ:* Univ Calif, Los Angeles, BA, 61, MA, 66, PhD(math), 67. *Prof Exp:* Mathematician, Todd Shipyards, Calif, 61-63 & Int Bus Mach Corp, 63-65; actg asst prof math, Univ Calif, Los Angeles, 67-68; vis asst prof, US Army Math Res Ctr, Univ Wis-Madison, 68-70; from asst prof to assoc prof, 70-76, PROF MATH SCI, RICE UNIV, 76- *Mem:* Soc Indust & Appl Math; Inst Math Statist; Soc Advan Chicano & Native Am Scientists; Am Math Soc. *Mailing Add:* Dept of Math Sci Rice Univ Houston TX 77001

TAPIA, SANTIAGO, b Santiago, Chile, Nov 13, 39. ASTROPHYSICS. *Educ:* Univ Chile, Lic, 65; Univ Ariz, PhD(astron), 75. *Prof Exp:* Lab asst crystallog, Univ Chile, 61-62, teaching asst physics, 63-65, res asst astron, 66-69; res assoc astron, 75-79, ASST ASTRONR, UNIV ARIZ, 80- *Concurrent Pos:* Lectr astron, Tech Sch Aeronaut, Chilean Air Force, 69. *Mem:* Am Astron Soc. *Res:* Observational study of optical properties of BL Lacertae objects and their relation to quasi-stellar objects; observational study of optical polarization in am herculis type objects and x-ray binary sources. *Mailing Add:* Steward Observ Univ Ariz Tucson AZ 85721

TAPLEY, BYRON D(EAN), b Charleston, Miss, Jan 16, 33; m 59; c 2. AEROSPACE ENGINEERING, ASTRODYNAMICS. *Educ:* Univ Tex, BS, 56, MS, 58, PhD(eng mech), 60. *Prof Exp:* Asst prof aerospace eng & eng mech, 60-64, assoc prof, 64-66, assoc prof aerospace eng, 66-68, chmn dept, 66-77, prof, 68-75, W R WOOLRICH PROF, AEROSPACE ENG & ENG MECH, UNIV TEX, AUSTIN, 76- *Concurrent Pos:* Ford Found fel, Univ Tex, 61-62; mem adv comt guid, control & navig, NASA, 65-66; mem, Geophys Res Bd, Nat Res Coun, Aeronautics & Space Eng Bd & chmn, Comt Geodesy, 80- *Mem:* Am Soc Mech Engrs; Am Astronaut Soc; fel Am Inst Aeronaut & Astronaut; Soc Eng Sci; Inst Elec & Electronics Engrs. *Res:* Theory of the guidance and navigation of continuous powered space vehicles including the development and application of methods in numerical optimization theory of stochastic processes and orbit determination theory. *Mailing Add:* Dept of Aerospace Eng & Eng Mech Univ of Tex Austin TX 78712

TAPLEY, DONALD FRASER, b Woodstock, NB, May 19, 27; nat US; m 57; c 3. INTERNAL MEDICINE. *Educ:* Acadia Univ, BSc, 48; Univ Chicago, MD, 52. *Prof Exp:* Intern & asst resident, Presby Hosp, New York, 52-54; fel physiol chem, Johns Hopkins Univ, 54-56; from asst prof to assoc prof, 56-72, actg dean fac med, 73-74, PROF MED, COL PHYSICIANS & SURGEONS, COLUMBIA UNIV, 72-, ASSOC DEAN FAC AFFAIRS, 70-, DEAN FAC

MED, 74- *Concurrent Pos:* Fel physiol chem, Oxford Univ, 56-57; from asst attend physician to attend, Presby Hosp, 57- *Mem:* Am Soc Clin Invest; Am Thyroid Asn; Endocrine Soc; Harvey Soc. *Res:* Intermediary metabolism; thyroid physiology. *Mailing Add:* Col of Physicians & Surgeons 630 W 168th St New York NY 10032

TAPLEY, NORAH DUVERNET, medicine, see previous edition

TAPLIN, DAVID MICHAEL ROBERT, b Chesterfield, Eng, July 19, 39; c 4. PHYSICAL METALLURGY, MECHANICAL ENGINEERING. *Educ:* Univ Aston, BSc, 61, DSc, 79; Oxford Univ, DPhil(metall), 64. *Prof Exp:* Metallurgist, Imp Chem Industs, Birmingham, Eng, 57-61; lectr phys metall, Univ Melbourne, 64-68; res fel metall, Banaras Hindu Univ, 67-68; assoc prof, 68-72, PROF MECH ENG & PHYSICS, UNIV WATERLOO, 72- *Concurrent Pos:* Mem coun, Int Cong Fracture, 69-77, dir & vpres, 77-81, pres, 81-; pres, Can Fracture Corp, 76-; dir, Pergamon Press of Can, 78-; ed-in-chief, Int Conf on Fracture, 77. *Honors & Awards:* Kamani Gold Medal, Indian Inst Metals, 71. *Mem:* Fel Brit Inst Metall; fel Royal Soc Arts; Am Inst Mining, Metall & Petrol Engrs; hon fel, Int Cong Fracture. *Res:* Creep and creep fracture in metals; fatigue at elevated temperatures; superplasticity; grain boundary sliding and intergranular fracture; thermal cycling; ductile-brittle transition; grain size effects on mechanical behavior; fracture maps. *Mailing Add:* Dept of Mech Eng Univ of Waterloo Waterloo ON N2L 3G1 Can

TAPLIN, LAEL BRENT, b Blackwell, Okla, Jan 5, 27; m 51; c 4. MECHANICAL ENGINEERING, ELECTRICAL ENGINEERING. *Educ:* Ore State Col, BS, 48; Univ Ill, MS, 51. *Prof Exp:* Test engr, Gen Elec Co, 48-49; res asst theoret & appl mech, Univ, Ill, 49-50, res assoc, 50-51; sr engr, Vickers Inc, Sperry Rand Corp, 51-55, proj engr, 55-58; proj engr, Res Labs Div, Bendix Corp, 58-61, dept head, Lab Flight Controls, 61-64, mgr energy conversion & dynamic controls, 64-66, dir mech sci & controls lab, 66-74, consult scientist, Res Labs, 74-80; WITH ENG-ADVAN TECH & SYST, SPERRY VICKERS, 80- *Concurrent Pos:* Instr, Wayne State Univ, 57-58. *Mem:* Inst Elec & Electronics Engrs. *Res:* Dynamics of fluid power servovalves, motors and control systems; hot gas servos; pneumatic controls; gas generators and controls; pneumatic flight controls; fluidic elements, sensors and systems; fluidic circuit analysis; fuel management; electronic fuel injection; emissions control. *Mailing Add:* 1401 Crooks Rd Sperry Vickers Troy MI 48084

TAPP, CHARLES MILLARD, b Memphis, Tenn, Nov 9, 36; m 55, 78; c 3. ENGINEERING. *Educ:* Union Univ, BA, 58; Memphis State Univ, BS, 60; Univ Va, MS, 62, PhD(physics), 64. *Prof Exp:* Staff mem radiation calibration, Nat Bur Standards, 60, 62; tech staff mem radiation damage, 64-66, div supvr vacuum tube physics & technol, 66-69, dept mgr vacuum tube devices, 69-71, dept mgr microelectronic components, 71-77, mgr info systs dept, 77-80, MGR ELECTRONIC INSTRUMENTATION DEPT SANDIA NAT LABS, 80- *Concurrent Pos:* Ed, Transactions Components, Hybrids & Mfg Technol & gen chmn, Electronic Components Conf, Inst Elec & Electronics Engrs, 74- *Mem:* Inst Elec & Electronics Engrs; Am Phys Soc. *Res:* Solid state electronics and circuits; microelectronic thin and thick film processes; vacuum tube design, development; radiation effects in devices; neutron sources. *Mailing Add:* Orgn 8460 Sandia Nat Labs Livermore CA 94550

TAPP, WILLIAM JOUETTE, b Quincy, Ill, July 26, 18; m 46; c 1. ORGANIC CHEMISTRY. *Educ:* Univ Ill, BS, 39; Cornell Univ, PhD(org chem), 43. *Prof Exp:* Asst chem, Cornell Univ, 40-41 & 41-43, Nat Defense Res Comt fel, 40-41; res & develop chemist, Union Carbide Corp, 43-46, proj leader, 46-54, staff asst, 55-56, patent adminr, 57-66, asst dir pharmaceut tech, 66-67, mgr admin, 67-81; CONSULT, 81- *Mem:* Am Chem Soc. *Res:* Organic nitrogen and sulfur compounds; synthetic lubricants; industrial organic synthesis. *Mailing Add:* W Lane Revonah Woods Stamford CT 06905

TAPPAN, DONALD VESTER, b Orestes, Ind, May 5, 25; m 49; c 5. BIOCHEMISTRY. *Educ:* Purdue Univ, BS, 49; Univ Wis, MS, 51, PhD(biochem), 53. *Prof Exp:* Res assoc, Andean Inst Biol, Lima, 53-55; proj assoc oncol, McArdle Mem Lab, Univ Wis, 55-56; from asst prof to assoc prof biochem, Univ Maine, 56-59; chief biochem sect, 69-70, HEAD BIOCHEM DIV SUBMARINE MED RES LAB, US NAVAL SUBMARINE BASE, 71- *Mem:* AAAS; Am Chem Soc; fel Am Inst Chemists; NY Acad Sci. *Res:* Metabolic influences of environmental factors; endocrine control of metabolism; hyperbaric biochemistry; nutrition. *Mailing Add:* Biochem Div Submarine Med Res Lab US Naval Submarine Base Groton CT 06340

TAPPEINER, JOHN CUMMINGS, II, b Los Angeles, Calif, Dec 15, 34; m 65; c 2. FOREST ECOLOGY, SILVICULTURE. *Educ:* Univ of Calif, Berkeley, BS, 57, MS, 61, PhD(forestry), 66. *Prof Exp:* Forester, US Forest Serv, 59-63; res asst forest ecol, Univ Calif, Berkeley, 63-66; Ford Found teaching fel forestry, Agr Univ Minas Gerais, 66-67; from asst prof to assoc prof, Forest Res Ctr, Univ Minn, St Paul, 68-73; regional sivliculturist, US Forest Serv, 73-81; ASSOC PROF FORESTRY, SILVICULTURE & FOREST ECOL, ORE STATE UNIV, 81- *Mem:* Soc Am Foresters; Ecol Soc Am. *Res:* Natural regeneration of Sierra Nevada Douglas fir and ponderosa pine; ecology of hazel and understory vegetation; biomass and nutrient content of shrubs and herbs; effect of mechanized harvesting of forest soils; ecology of shrubs and hardwood in forests of southwest Oregon. *Mailing Add:* Dept Forest Mgt Ore State Univ Corvallis OR 97331

TAPPEL, ALOYS LOUIS, b St Louis, Mo, Nov 21, 26; m 51; c 6. BIOCHEMISTRY. *Educ:* Iowa State Univ, BS, 48; Univ Minn, PhD(biochem), 51. *Prof Exp:* From instr to assoc prof, 51-61, PROF FOOD SCI & BIOCHEMIST, UNIV CALIF DAVIS, 61- *Concurrent Pos:* Guggenheim fel, 65-66. *Honors & Awards:* Borden Award, Am Inst Nutrit, 73. *Mem:* Am Chem Soc; Am Oil Chem Soc; Am Soc Biol Chem; Am Inst Nutrit. *Res:* Oxidant molecular damage and biological protection systems. *Mailing Add:* Dept Food Sci & Technol Univ Calif Davis CA 95616

TAPPEN, NEIL CAMPBELL, b Jacksonville, Fla, Feb 26, 20; m 52; c 2. PHYSICAL ANTHROPOLOGY, PRIMATOLOGY. *Educ:* Univ Fla, AB, 41; Univ Chicago, MA, 49, PhD(anthrop), 52. *Prof Exp:* Res assoc human biol, Univ Mich, 51-52; from assoc anthrop to instr, Univ Pa, 52-54; from instr anat to asst prof, Emory Univ, 54-59; assoc prof phys anthrop, Tulane Univ, 59-65; prof anthrop, 65-69, EARNEST A HOOTON PROF ANTHROP, UNIV WIS, MILWAUKEE, 69- *Concurrent Pos:* NIH grants, Emory Univ, 55-59, Tulane Univ, 60-65 & Univ Wis, Milwaukee, 65-71; Fulbright sr res scholar, Makerere Col, Uganda, 56-57; NSF grant, Univ Wis, Milwaukee, 71-76. *Mem:* AAAS; Am Anthrop Asn; Am Asn Phys Anthropologists; Am Anat Asn; Int Primatological Soc. *Res:* Organization of bone; non-human primates and their relationship to human evolution; structure of bone in fossil hominids; problems of human evolution. *Mailing Add:* Dept Anthrop Univ Wis Milwaukee WI 53201

TAPPER, DANIEL NAPHTALI, b Philadelphia, Pa, Dec 5, 29; m 59. NEUROPHYSIOLOGY. *Educ:* Rutgers Univ, BS, 51; Univ Pa, VMD, 55; Cornell Univ, PhD(physiol), 59. *Prof Exp:* Asst physiol, 55-59, res assoc radiation biol, 59-61, from asst prof to assoc prof, 61-69, PROF, CORNELL UNIV, 69- *Concurrent Pos:* NIH spec fel, Stockholm, 65-66; NIH spec fel, 72-73, adj prof, Rockefeller Univ, 73-74. *Mem:* AAAS; Soc Neurosci; Am Physiol Soc. *Res:* Behavior; receptor physiology; neurophysiology of skin sensibility. *Mailing Add:* Sect of Physiol Cornell Univ Ithaca NY 14853

TAPPERT, FREDERICK DRACH, b Philadelphia, Pa, Apr 21, 40. PHYSICS. *Educ:* Pa State Univ, BS, 62; Princeton Univ, PhD(physics), 67. *Prof Exp:* Mem tech staff, Bell Labs, 67-73; sr res scientist, Courant Inst Math Sci, NY Univ, 74-78; PROF OCEAN ENG & PHYSICS, 78- *Concurrent Pos:* Vis staff mem, Los Alamos Sci Lab, 74-; consult, Sci Applns, Inc, 74-; consult, Nat Oceanog & Atmospheric Admin, US Govt, 80- *Mem:* Am Phys Soc; AAAS; Soc Indust & Appl Math; Am Geophys Union; Acoustical Soc Am. *Res:* Theory and numerical simulation of wave propagation effects in plasmas, gases, liquids and solids. *Mailing Add:* Univ of Miami Coral Gables FL 33124

TAPPHORN, RALPH M, b Grinnell, Kans, July 26, 44; m 69; c 2. NUCLEAR PHYSICS. *Educ:* Ft Hays Kans State Col, BS, 66; Kans State Univ, PhD(physics), 70. *Prof Exp:* Res assoc nuclear physics, Ballistics Res Lab, Aberdeen Proving Ground, Md, 70-72; sr scientist nuclear physics, Schlumberger-Doll Res Ctr, 72-77; SR MEM TECH STAFF, BALL AEROSPACE SYSTS DIV, 77- *Mem:* Am Phys Soc; Sigma Xi. *Res:* Aerospace instrumentation of gamma-ray spectrometers for astrophysical studies; geophysical exploration with gamma-ray spectroscopy; nuclear detectors and instrumentation; radiation damage investigations. *Mailing Add:* Ball Aerospace Systs Div PO Box 1062 Boulder CO 80306

TAPPMEYER, WILBUR PAUL, b Owensville, Mo, May 19, 22; m 47; c 5. INORGANIC CHEMISTRY. *Educ:* Southeast Mo State Col, AB, 45; Univ Mo, BS, 47, PhD(inorg chem), 61. *Prof Exp:* Teacher high sch, Mo, 44-45; asst chem, Mo Sch Mines, 45-46; prof, Southwest Baptist Col, 47-60; from asst prof to assoc prof, 60-66, PROF CHEM, UNIV MO, ROLLA, 66- *Mem:* Am Chem Soc. *Res:* Solid phase extraction of metal chelates; dimeric and polymeric properties of certain metal acetates and other alkonates. *Mailing Add:* Dept of Chem Univ of Mo Rolla MO 65401

TAPSCOTT, ROBERT EDWIN, b Terre Haute, Ind, June 10, 38; m 67; c 1. CHEMISTRY. *Educ:* Univ Colo, BS, 64; Univ Ill, Urbana, PhD, 68. *Prof Exp:* Asst prof, 68-72, ASSOC PROF CHEM, UNIV NMEX, 72- *Mem:* Sigma Xi; AAAS; Royal Soc Chem; Am Chem Soc. *Res:* Stereoselective effects in transition metal complexes; geometry and structure of coordination compounds. *Mailing Add:* Dept of Chem Univ of NMex Albuquerque NM 87131

TARAGIN, MORTON FRANK, b Washington, DC, Feb 1, 44; m 68; c 4. SOLID STATE PHYSICS. *Educ:* George Washington Univ, BS, 65, MPh, 69, PhD(physics), 70. *Prof Exp:* ASSOC PROF PHYSICS, GEORGE WASHINGTON UNIV, 70- *Concurrent Pos:* Consult comput prog, APL. *Mem:* Am Phys Soc. *Res:* Mössbauer effect; spectroscopy studies of glass structure. *Mailing Add:* Dept of Physics George Washington Univ Washington DC 20052

TARANIK, JAMES VLADIMIR, b Los Angeles, Calif, Apr 23, 40; m 71; c 2. EXPLORATION GEOLOGY, PHOTOGEOLOGY. *Educ:* Stanford Univ, BS, 64; Colo Sch Mines, PhD(geol), 74. *Prof Exp:* Chief remote sensing, Iowa Geol Surv, 71-74; prin remote sensing scientist, Earth Resources Observ Syst Data Ctr, US Geol Surv, 75-78; CHIEF NON-RENEWABLE RESOURCES BR, NASA HQ, WASHINGTON, DC, 79- *Concurrent Pos:* Adj prof geol, Univ Iowa, 71-; vis prof civil eng, Iowa State Univ, 72-74; consult, Earth Resources Technol Satellite Follow on Eval Panel Geol, Goddard Space Flight Ctr, NASA, Synchronous Observ Satellite Prog Eval, Geol Applns, Active microwave Syst Eval Workshop Earth-Land Panel, Geol Landuse Water, Johnson Space Ctr, 74; adj prof Earth Sci, Univ SDak, 76-79; chmn working group on instrumentation for remote sensor data processing & anal, Int Soc Photogrammetry, 77-80; chmn, working group non-renewable resources, Int Soc Photogram & Remote Sensing; mem adv comt comp planetology, Int Union Geol Sci; scientist, various space shuttle progs; govt liasion mem, Geol Sci Bd, Nat Acad Sci. *Mem:* Fel Geol Soc Am; Am Asn Petrol Geologists; Am Inst Aeronaut & Astronaut; Am Inst Prof Geologists; Soc Explor Geophysicists. *Res:* Development of applications of remote sensing technology to mineral and mineral fuel exploration; assessment of environmental and engineering geologic aspects of mineral resource development; engineering geology and geohydrology of civil works site selection. *Mailing Add:* Resource Observ Div NASA Hq Code ERS-2 Washington DC 20546

TARANTINE, FRANK J(AMES), b Youngstown, Ohio, May 27, 35; m 57; c 4. MECHANICAL ENGINEERING. *Educ:* Youngstown Univ, BE, 57; Univ Akron, MS, 61; Carnegie Inst Technol, PhD(fluid dynamics), 65. *Prof Exp:* From instr to assoc prof, 57-70, PROF MECH ENG, YOUNGSTOWN STATE UNIV, 70- *Mem:* Am Soc Mech Engrs; Am Soc Eng Educ; Sigma Xi. *Res:* Vibrations and experimental stress analysis; mechanical design; acoustics. *Mailing Add:* 1221 Cherokee Dr Youngstown OH 44511

TARANTINO, LAURA M(ARY), b Exeter, Pa, Feb 6, 47. BIOCHEMISTRY. *Educ:* Col Misericordia, BS, 68; Cornell Univ, PhD(biochem), 75. *Prof Exp:* Assoc res scientist med, Col Physicians & Surgeons, Columbia Univ & Roosevelt Hosp, 75-78; ASST PROF BIOCHEM, EASTERN VA MED SCH, 79- *Mem:* AAAS; Sigma Xi; NY Acad Sci; Am Chem Soc. *Res:* Enzyme regulation in the central nervous system; role and control of hexosemonophosphate shunt in cells; metabolic effects of insulin; diabetes. *Mailing Add:* Dept Biochem PO Box 1980 Norfolk VA 23501

TARANTO, MICHAEL VINCENT, b Brooklyn, NY, Nov 3, 50; m 70; c 2. FOOD SCIENCE, BIOCHEMISTRY. *Educ:* Pa State Univ, BS, 72; Tex A&M Univ, MS, 74, PhD(food sci), 78. *Prof Exp:* Res asst food sci, Tex A&M Univ, 72-78; asst prof food sci, Univ Ill, 78-81; CHEMIST, ITT CONTINENTAL BAKING CO, 81- *Concurrent Pos:* Res fel, Ralston Purina Food Sci, 74-77. *Mem:* Inst Food Technologists; Sigma Xi; Am Oil Chemists; Am Asn Cereal Chemists. *Res:* Tomato processing; oilseed processing; food biochemistry; microscopy of foods and foods ingredients; food rheology; baking science and technology. *Mailing Add:* Res Lab ITT Continental Baking Co Rye NY 10580

TARAPCHAK, STEPHEN J, b Staten Island, NY, Mar 20, 42; m 65. LIMNOLOGY, PHYCOLOGY. *Educ:* Clarion State Col, BS, 64; Ohio Univ, MS, 66; Univ Minn, PhD(ecol), 73. *Prof Exp:* Res fel, Limnol Res Ctr, Univ Minn, Minneapolis, 73-74; RES SCIENTIST BIOL OCEANOG, GT LAKES ENVIRON RES LAB, NAT OCEANIC & ATMOSPHERIC ADMIN, 74- *Concurrent Pos:* Consult, Environ Statements Syst Div, Argonne Nat Lab, 73-74. *Mem:* Am Phycol Soc; Am Soc Limnol & Oceanog; Int Limnol Soc. *Res:* Phytoplankton ecology; ecology. *Mailing Add:* Gt Lakes Environ Res Lab 2300 Washtenaw Ave Ann Arbor MI 48104

TARAS, MICHAEL ANDREW, b Olyphant, Pa, Sept 6, 21; m 48; c 4. FOREST PRODUCTS, WOOD TECHNOLOGY. *Educ:* Pa State Univ, BS, 42, MF, 48; NC State Univ, PhD(wood technol), 65. *Prof Exp:* Forest prod technologist, Forest Prod Lab, US Forest Serv, 48-54, forest prod technologist, Southeastern Forest Exp Sta, Forestry Sci Lab, 54-79; PROF FORESTRY, CLEMSON UNIV, 79- *Mem:* Forest Prod Res Soc; Soc Wood Sci & Technol; Int Asn Wood Anat. *Res:* Forestry; wood anatomy related to wood identification, quality, seasoning and moisture movement through wood; in log and tree classification systems and wood weight-volume relationships; forest tree biomass prediction and evaluation. *Mailing Add:* Forestry Dept Col Forest & Recreation Clemson Univ Clemson SC 29631

TARAS, PAUL, b Tunisia, May 12, 41; m 63; c 2. NUCLEAR PHYSICS. *Educ:* Univ Toronto, BScEng Phys, 62, MSc, 63, PhD(nuclear physics), 65. *Prof Exp:* Asst prof, 65-70, assoc prof, 70-76, PROF PHYSICS, UNIV MONTREAL, 76- *Mem:* Am Phys Soc; Can Asn Physicists. *Res:* Nuclear spectroscopy and reaction mechanisms induced reactions. *Mailing Add:* Dept of Physics Univ of Montreal Montreal PQ H3C 3J7 Can

TARASUK, JOHN DAVID, b St Walburg, Sask, Dec 24, 36; m 61; c 3. THERMODYNAMICS, MECHANICAL ENGINEERING. *Educ:* Univ Toronto, BASc, 59, MASc, 61; Univ Sask, PhD(mech eng), 69. *Prof Exp:* Demonstr thermodyn, Univ Toronto, 59-61; res & develop engr, John Inglis, Toronto, 61-62; asst prof heat transfer, NS Tech Col, 62-65; lectr thermodyn & heat transfer, Univ Sask, 65-68; MEM FAC MECH ENG, UNIV WESTERN ONT, 68- *Concurrent Pos:* Consult, G Graner & Assoc, Toronto, 58-64; NSF grants, Okla State Univ, 63 & Univ Calif, Los Angeles, 64. *Res:* Natural convection; natural and forced convection; thermodynamic properties of engineering fluids. *Mailing Add:* 101 Rollingwood Circle London ON N6G 1R1 Can

TARASZKA, ANTHONY JOHN, b Wallington, NJ, Feb 19, 35; m 60. ANALYTICAL CHEMISTRY, PHARMACEUTICAL CHEMISTRY. *Educ:* Rutgers Univ, BS, 56, MS, 58; Univ Wis, PhD(pharmaceut chem), 62. *Prof Exp:* Res assoc anal res & develop, 62-63, head dept, 63-66, mgr control res & develop, 66-70, dir control, 70-74, VPRES CONTROL, UPJOHN CO, 74- *Mem:* Am Chem Soc; Am Pharmaceut Asn. *Res:* Trace component analysis; separation techniques; reaction mechanisms. *Mailing Add:* The Upjohn Co 7171 Portage Rd Kalamazoo MI 49001

TARBELL, DEAN STANLEY, b Hancock, NH, Oct 19, 13; m 42; c 3. ORGANIC CHEMISTRY. *Educ:* Harvard Univ, AB, 34, MA, 35, PhD(org chem), 37. *Prof Exp:* Asst, Radcliffe Col, 36-37; fel, Univ Ill, 37-38; from instr to prof org chem, Univ Rochester, 38-60, Houghton prof chem, 60-66, chmn dept, 64-66; Harvie Branscom distinguished prof, 75-76, DISTINGUISHED PROF CHEM, VANDERBILT UNIV, 67- *Concurrent Pos:* Guggenheim fels, Oxford Univ, 46-47 & Stanford Univ, 61-62; Fuson lectr, Univ Nev, 72; mem, NIH study sects; consult, Walter Reed Army Inst Res, 72- *Honors & Awards:* C H Herty Medal, Am Chem Soc, 73. *Mem:* Nat Acad Sci; Am Chem Soc; Am Acad Arts & Sci; The Chem Soc; Hist Sci Soc. *Res:* Reaction phenolic ethers; organic sulfur compounds; structure and synthesis of natural products; structural and theoretical organic chemistry; structure of antibiotics; history of organic chemistry in the United States. *Mailing Add:* Dept of Chem Vanderbilt Univ Nashville TN 37235

TARBET, WILLARD J, b Grace, Idaho, Nov 13, 33; m 54; c 7. DENTISTRY, BIOCHEMISTRY. *Educ:* Northwestern Univ, DDS, 58, PhD(biochem), 64. *Prof Exp:* Asst prof biochem, Sch Dent Med, Univ Pittsburgh, 64-69; asst dir clin res, 69-70, dir dept dent res, 70-72, dir oral hyg & dent res, 72-78, DIR DENT SCI, VICK DIV RES, RICHARDSON MERRELL INC, 78- *Concurrent Pos:* Adj prof biochem, NY Univ Dent Sch, 70-72. *Mem:* Am Asn Dent Res. *Res:* Methodology for testing products used in oral cavity; development of new products related to oral discomfort and disease. *Mailing Add:* Vick Div Res One Bradford Rd Mt Vernon NY 10553

TARBY, STEPHEN KENNETH, b Braddock, Pa, July 15, 34; m 58; c 2. METALLURGICAL ENGINEERING. *Educ:* Carnegie Inst Technol, BS, 56, MS, 59, PhD(metall eng), 62. *Prof Exp:* Asst prof metall eng, 61-62, from asst prof to assoc prof, 63-76, PROF METALL & MAT SCI, LEHIGH UNIV, 76- *Mem:* Am Inst Mining, Metall & Petrol Engrs; Metall Soc. *Res:* Kinetics of slag-metal reactions; thermodynamics of liquid metals and alloys; computer applications to metallurgical processes. *Mailing Add:* Dept of Metall & Mat Sci Whitaker Lab Lehigh Univ Bethlehem PA 18015

TARBY, THEODORE JOHN, b Auburn, NY, May 9, 41; m 64; c 1. ANATOMY, NEUROPHYSIOLOGY. *Educ:* Calif Inst Technol, BS, 64; Univ Calif, Los Angeles, PhD(anat), 68. *Prof Exp:* Asst prof anat, Med Ctr, Univ Colo, Denver, 68-80. *Concurrent Pos:* Milhelm Found Cancer Res grant, Med Ctr, Univ Colo, Denver, 71- *Mem:* AAAS; Am Asn Anat. *Res:* Cerebral tissue impedance and extracellular space; blood-brain barrier; olfactory function in normal salmon; glial physiology. *Mailing Add:* 11988 Charter House Lane St Louis MO 63141

TARDIFF, ROBERT G, b Lowell, Mass, Feb 1, 42; m 70; c 3. TOXICOLOGY, ENVIRONMENTAL HEALTH. *Educ:* Merrimack Col, BA, 64; Univ Chicago, PhD(toxicol & pharmacol), 68. *Prof Exp:* Res toxicologist org contaminants, USPHS, 68-70; br chief toxicol assessments, Environ Protection Agency, 70-77; EXEC DIR TOXICOL & ENVIRON HEALTH, NAT ACAD SCI, 77- *Concurrent Pos:* USPHS fel, 64-68; assoc prof, Med Col Va, 79- *Mem:* Am Col Toxicol; Soc Toxicol; Environ Mutagen Soc; NY Acad Sci; Soc Risk Anal. *Res:* Hazard assessment; interactions; metabolism; organic compounds in drinking water; mutagens; carcinogens. *Mailing Add:* Nat Acad of Sci 2101 Constitution Ave Washington DC 20481

TAREN, JAMES A, b Toledo, Ohio, Nov 10, 24. NEUROSURGERY. *Educ:* Univ Toledo, BS, 48; Univ Mich, MD, 52; Am Bd Neurol Surg, dipl, 60. *Prof Exp:* Intern surg, Univ Hosp, Univ Mich, 52-53, resident, 53-54; teaching fel neurosurg, Harvard Med Sch, 54-55; resident, 55-57, from instr to assoc prof, 57-69, dir Neurobehav Sci Prog, 75-78, PROF NEUROSURG, MED SCH, UNIV MICH, ANN ARBOR, 69-, ASSOC DEAN EDUC & STUDENT AFFAIRS, 78- *Concurrent Pos:* Res fel, Boston Children's Hosp, 54-55; asst surg, Peter Bent Brigham Hosp, Boston, 54-55; actg chief neurosurg, Vet Admin Hosp, Ann Arbor, 58-73; chief neurosurg, Wayne County Gen Hosp, 58-72; vis fel, Karolimskz Inst, Stockholm, 81. *Mem:* AAAS; Asn Am Med Cols; Cong Neurol Surg; NY Acad Sci. *Res:* Central nervous system; stereotoxic neurosurgery. *Mailing Add:* Sect Neurosurg Univ Mich 1405 E Ann St Ann Arbor MI 48109

TARESKI, VAL GERARD, b Bottineau, NDak, Dec 20, 41; m 66; c 3. COMPUTER SCIENCE, ELECTRICAL ENGINEERING. *Educ:* NDak State Univ, BS, 63, MS, 69; Univ Ill, Urbana, PhD(comput sci), 73. *Prof Exp:* Engr, Collins Radio, 62; tech writer, AC Electronics Div, Gen Motors Corp, 63; asst elec eng, NDak State Univ, 63-64, instr, 64-67; res asst comput sci, Univ Ill, Urbana, 67-69 & 70-71; asst prog dir, NSF, 71-72, assoc prog dir, 72-74; ASST PROF, NDAK STATE UNIV, 71- *Concurrent Pos:* Instr, Moorhead State Col, 67 & NDak State Univ, 67-71; assoc prof, Univ Nebr, 72. *Mem:* Inst Elec & Electronics Engrs; Asn Comput Mach; Sigma Xi; Soc Indust & Appl Math. *Res:* Computer architecture; computer systems; software engineering. *Mailing Add:* NDak State Univ Fargo ND 58105

TARG, RUSSELL, b Chicago, Ill, Apr 11, 34; m 58; c 3. PHYSICS, PARAPSYCHOLOGY. *Educ:* Queens Col, NY, BS, 54. *Prof Exp:* Res asst physics, Columbia Univ, 54-56; engr, Sperry Gyroscope Co, 56-59; res assoc plasmas, Polytech Inst Brooklyn, 59; physicist, TRG, Inc, 59-62; eng specialist, Sylvania Elec Co, 62-72; SR RES PHYSICIST, RADIO PHYSICS LAB, STANFORD RES INST, 72- *Mem:* Am Phys Soc; Parapsychology Asn; Inst Elec & Electronics Engrs. *Res:* Extra sensory perception, electron beam-plasma interactions; gas laser research; laser detection; modulation and frequency control; research in extra sensory perception. *Mailing Add:* Stanford Res Inst K 1027 Menlo Park CA 94025

TARGETT, NANCY MCKEEVER, b Pittsburgh, Pa, Dec 23, 50. CHEMICAL ECOLOGY. *Educ:* Univ Pittsburgh, BS, 72; Univ Miami, MS, 75; Univ Maine, PhD(oceanog), 79. *Prof Exp:* Res assoc, 80-82, ASST RES PROF, SKIDAWAY INST OCEANOG, 82- *Mem:* Am Chem Soc; Phycol Soc Am; Am Soc Limnol & Oceanog; Asn Women Sci. *Res:* Chemical ecology, specifically the role of secondary metabolites in chemical-biological interactions among marine organisms; agricultural and pharmaceutical applications of marine natural products. *Mailing Add:* Skidaway Inst Oceanog PO Box 13687 Savannah GA 31406

TARGETT, TIMOTHY ERWIN, b Farmington, Maine, Aug 1, 50; m 75. FISH COMMUNITY ECOLOGY, ENERGETICS. *Educ:* Univ Maine, BS, 72, PhD(zool), 79; Univ Miami, MS, 75. *Prof Exp:* ASST RES PROF, SKIDAWAY INST OCEANOG, 80- *Concurrent Pos:* Adj asst prof, Dept Zool, Univ Ga, 81- *Mem:* Am Soc Ichthyologists & Herpetologists; Am Fisheries Soc. *Res:* Ecology of marine fish communities: community dynamics, trophic ecology and energetics processes (pathways and efficiencies of energy flow) within communities as well as in individual fishes. *Mailing Add:* Skidaway Inst Oceanog PO Box 13687 Savannah GA 31406

TARGOWSKI, STANISLAW P, b Nagorzyce, Poland, Nov 13, 40; m 70. IMMUNOLOGY, VETERINARY MICROBIOLOGY. *Educ:* Univ Warsaw, DVM, 63; Univ Wis, MS, 69, PhD(immunol), 72. *Prof Exp:* Resident vet, Kroplewo Stud Farm, 63-66; res asst vet sci, Pa State Univ, 66-67; res asst vet microbiol, Univ Wis, 67-72; res assoc, Purdue Univ, 72-74; asst prof microbiol, State Univ NY, Buffalo, 74-78, PROF DEPT VET PREV MED & DIR CENT LAB ANIMAL RESOURCE, OHIO STATE UNIV,

COLUMBUS, 78- *Mem:* Am Soc Microbiol; Am Vet Med Asn; Am Asn Immunologists; Am Col Vet Microbiologists; NY Acad Sci. *Res:* Bacteriology, virology and immunology with particular emphasis on immunity in neoplastic and infectious diseases, diagnostic microbiology and clinical immunology. *Mailing Add:* Dept of Vet Prev Med Ohio State Univ Columbus OH 43210

TARICA, RONALD RICHARD, b Chicago, Ill, Mar 18, 43; m 67; c 2. CHEMICAL ENGINEERING, COMPUTER SCIENCE. *Educ:* Ill Inst Technol, BS, 64; Northwestern Univ, Evanston, MS, 67, PhD(chem eng), 69. *Prof Exp:* Teaching asst, Northwestern Univ, Evanston, 67-69; res engr comput applns chem eng, Chevron Res Co, 69-76, SR ANALYST COMPUT APPLNS, STANDARD OIL CO CALIF, 76- *Mem:* Am Inst Chem Engrs; Am Prod & Inventory Control Soc. *Res:* Computer applications to chemical process engineering calculations and control and petroleum retinery planning and information systems; mathematical and computer modeling of physiological systems and biomedical engineering. *Mailing Add:* Standard Oil Co of Calif PO Box 3069 San Francisco CA 94119

TARIKA, E(LIO) E(LIAKIM), b Cairo, Egypt, July 21, 26; nat US; m 49; c 3. CHEMICAL ENGINEERING. *Educ:* Univ Ill, BSChE, 49; Newark Col Eng, MS, 51; Univ Chicago, MS, 60. *Prof Exp:* Proj chem engr, Colgate-Palmolive Peet Co, 49-51; supvr develop cellulose casings, Visking Corp, 51-60, opers mgr food casings, Union Carbide Corp, 60-64, exec vpres food prod div, 64-67, div pres, 67-71, asst to pres, 71-72, corp vpres, 72-77, SR VPRES, UNION CARBIDE CORP, 77- *Mem:* Am Inst Chem Engrs. *Mailing Add:* Union Carbide Corp Old Ridgebury Rd Danbury CT 06817

TARJAN, ARMEN CHARLES, b Chambridge, Mass, Dec 10, 20; m 45; c 2. PLANT NEMATOLOGY. *Educ:* Rutgers Univ, BS, 47; Univ Md, MS, 49, PhD(plant path), 51. *Prof Exp:* Asst nematologist, USDA, Md, 50-51; asst res prof plant path, Univ RI, 51-55; PROF NEMATOL, AGR RES & EDUC CTR, UNIV FLA, 55- *Mem:* Soc Nematol. *Res:* Chemical control of plant nematodes; taxonomic studies of nematodes; biological control of nematodes; nematophagus fungi. *Mailing Add:* Agr Res & Educ Ctr Univ of Fla Lake Alfred FL 33850

TARJAN, GEORGE, b Zsolna, Hungary, June 18, 12; US citizen; m 41; c 2. PSYCHIATRY. *Educ:* Pazmany Peter Univ, Hungary, MD, 35. *Prof Exp:* Resident physician, Mercy Hosp, Janesville, Wis, 40-41; asst physician, Utah State Hosp, Provo, 41-43; dir clin serv, Peoria State Hosp, Ill, 46-47; dir clin serv, Pac State Hosp, Pomona, Calif, 47-49, supt & med dir, 49-65; from asst clin prof to clin prof, 53-65, clin prof, Sch Pub Health, 61-65, prof psychiat sch pub health, 65-76, PROF PSYCHIAT, SCH MED & PUB HEALTH, UNIV CALIF, LOS ANGELES, 65-, PROG DIR MENT RETARDATION & CHILD PSYCHIAT, NEUROPSYCHIAT INST, 65- *Concurrent Pos:* Mem, President's Panel Ment Retardation, 61-62 & President's Comt, 66-71, consult, 71- *Honors & Awards:* Int Award Distinguished Leadership in Field Ment Retardation, Kennedy Found, 71; Am Asn Ment Deficiency Leadership Award, 70; President's Comt Ment Retardation Award Merit, 72; Am Psychiat Asn Distinguished Serv Award, 73; Seymour Vestermark Award & Agnes Purcell McGavin Award, Am Psychiat Asn, 78. *Mem:* Am Psychiat Asn; Am Asn Ment Deficiency (pres, 58-59); AMA; Am Acad Child Psychiat; Group Advan Psychiat (pres, 71-73). *Res:* Child psychiatry; mental retardation. *Mailing Add:* Neuropsychiat Inst 760 Westwood Plaza Los Angeles CA 90024

TARJAN, ROBERT ENDRE, b Pomona, Calif, Apr 30, 48; m 78. COMPUTER SCIENCE. *Educ:* Calif Inst Technol, BS, 69; Stanford Univ, MS, 71, PhD(comput sci), 72. *Prof Exp:* Asst prof, Cornell Univ, 72-74; asst prof, 74-77, ASSOC PROF COMPUT SCI, STANFORD UNIV, 77- *Concurrent Pos:* Miller fel, Univ Calif, Berkeley, 73-75; Guggenheim fel, Stanford Univ, 78-79. *Mem:* Soc Indust & Appl Math; Asn Comput Mach; Math Asn Am. *Res:* Analysis of algorithms; computational complexity; combinatorics. *Mailing Add:* Dept of Comput Sci Stanford Univ Stanford CA 94305

TARLE, GREGORY, b New York, NY, June 13, 51; m 72. ASTROPHYSICS, NUCLEAR PHYSICS. *Educ:* Calif Inst Technol, BS, 72; Univ Calif, Berkeley, PhD(physics), 78. *Prof Exp:* ASST RES PHYSICIST, SPACE SCI LAB, UNIV CALIF, BERKELEY, 78- *Mem:* Am Phys Soc. *Res:* The isotopic composition of primary cosmic radiation; energy loss of heavily charged particles in matter; gamma rays from nuclear collisions; development of new particle detectors. *Mailing Add:* Dept of Physics 329 Le Conte Berkeley CA 94720

TARLETON, GADSON JACK, JR, b Sumter, SC, Apr 29, 20; m 49; c 2. RADIOLOGY. *Educ:* Morris Col, AB, 39; Meharry Med Col, MD, 44. *Prof Exp:* Resident radiol & orthop, Hubbard Hosp & Meharry Med Col, 44, resident radiol, 45-48; assoc prof, Meharry Med Col, 49-52, chmn dept & dir tumor clin, 49-78, prof radiol, 52-78; ASST CHIEF, DEPT RADIOL, VET ADMIN MED CTR, NASHVILLE, 79- *Concurrent Pos:* Fel radiother, Bellevue Hosp, New York, 48-49; vis scholar, Columbia Presby Hosp, New York, 49; guest examr, Am Bd Radiol, 71-76 & 78-81. *Mem:* Radiol Soc NAm; AMA; Nat Med Asn; fel Am Col Radiol. *Mailing Add:* 1714 Windover Dr Nashville TN 37208

TARLOV, ALVIN R, b South Norwalk, Conn, July 11, 29; m 56; c 5. INTERNAL MEDICINE, BIOCHEMISTRY. *Educ:* Dartmouth Col, BA, 51; Univ Chicago, MD, 56. *Prof Exp:* Intern, Philadelphia Gen Hosp, 56-57; resident med, Univ Chicago, 57-58, res assoc, 58-62; res assoc biochem, Harvard Med Sch, 62-64; from asst prof to assoc prof, 64-70, PROF MED & CHMN DEPT, UNIV CHICAGO, 70- *Concurrent Pos:* USPHS res career develop award, 62-69; Markle scholar, 66-71; chmn, Fed Coun Int Med; chmn grad med educ nat adv comt. *Mem:* Asn Prof Med (pres-elect); Am Fedn Clin Res. *Res:* Metabolism of red blood cells; inherited disorders of red cell metabolism; biochemistry of red cell membranes; health manpower, supply, productivity, needs. *Mailing Add:* Dept of Internal Med Univ of Chicago Chicago IL 60637

TARN, TZYH-JONG, b Szechwan, China, Nov 16, 37; m 67; c 2. MATHEMATICAL SYSTEMS THEORY. *Educ:* Cheng Kung Univ, Taiwan, BSc, 59; Stevens Inst Technol, MEng, 65; Washington Univ, DSc(control systs), 68. *Prof Exp:* Res assoc control theory, 68-69, asst prof chem eng, 69-72, assoc prof control systs, 72-77, PROF CONTROL SYSTS, WASHINGTON UNIV, 77- *Concurrent Pos:* NSF grant, 70-81. *Mem:* Soc Indust & Appl Math; Inst Elec & Electronics Engrs. *Res:* Control theory; stochastic systems; process optimization. *Mailing Add:* Box 1040 Washington Univ St Louis MO 63130

TARNEY, ROBERT EDWARD, b Hammond, Ind, Jan 8, 31; m 66; c 3. ORGANIC CHEMISTRY. *Educ:* Purdue Univ, BS, 52; Univ Wis, PhD, 58. *Prof Exp:* RES CHEMIST, E I DU PONT DE NEMOURS & CO, INC, 57- *Res:* Synthesis of monomers for and polymers of elastomeric materials. *Mailing Add:* 6 Summit Dr Berkeley Ridge DE 19707

TARONE, ROBERT ERNEST, b Modesto, Calif, Sept 11, 46; m 76; c 2. SURVIVAL ANALYSIS, CATEGORICAL DATA ANALYSIS. *Educ:* Univ Calif, Davis, BS, 68, MS, 69, PhD(math), 74. *Prof Exp:* MATH STATISTICIAN, NAT CANCER INST, 74- *Concurrent Pos:* Assoc ed, Am Statist Asn, 78- *Mem:* Am Statist Asn; Biomet Soc. *Res:* Analysis methods for censored survival data; categorical data analysis; empirical bayes methods for frequency data; multiple comparisons problems; methods for analyzing epidemiologic studies. *Mailing Add:* Nat Cancer Inst Landon Bldg Rm 5C25 Bethesda MD 20205

TARPLEY, ANDERSON RAY, JR, b New Orleans, La, Sept 19, 44; m 69. PHYSICAL CHEMISTRY, SPECTROSCOPY. *Educ:* Ga Inst Technol, BS, 66; Emory Univ, MS, 70, PhD(phys chem), 71; Ga State Univ, MBA, 72. *Prof Exp:* Res chemist, Eastman Kodak Co, NY, 66-67; instr res, Emory Univ, 71-72; SR CHEMIST ANAL SERV, TENN EASTMAN CO, EASTMAN KODAK CO, 72- *Concurrent Pos:* NIH fel med chem, Emory Univ, 71. *Mem:* AAAS; Am Chem Soc; Am Inst Chem; Am Mgt Asn. *Res:* Nuclear magnetic resonance spectroscopy; technical management; uses of computers in science; molecular orbital calculations; mass spectrometry. *Mailing Add:* Anal Serv Lab Org Chem Div Tenn Eastman Co Kingsport TN 37662

TARPLEY, JERALD DAN, b Lubbock, Tex, July 13, 42; m 65; c 2. ATMOSPHERIC PHYSICS, REMOTE SENSING. *Educ:* Tex Technol Col, BS, 64; Univ Colo, PhD(astrogeophys), 69. *Prof Exp:* Advan Study Prog fel, Nat Ctr Atmospheric Res, 69-70, physicist, Environ Res Labs, 70-73, PHYSICIST, NAT EARTH SATELLITE SERV, NAT OCEANIC & ATMOSPHERIC ADMIN, 73- *Mem:* Am Geophys Union; Am Meteorol Soc. *Res:* Physics of upper atmosphere and ionosphere; geomagnetism; remote sensing of the environment. *Mailing Add:* Nat Earth Satellite Serv Nat Oceanic & Atmospheric Admin Washington DC 20233

TARPLEY, WALLACE ARMELL, b Norwood, Ga, Feb 13, 34; m 59; c 2. INSECT ECOLOGY. *Educ:* Univ Ga, BSEd, 54, PhD(zool), 67; Clemson Univ, MS, 56. *Prof Exp:* Asst prof entom, Va Polytech Inst & State Univ, 60-64; ASSOC PROF BIOL, E TENN STATE UNIV, 64- *Mem:* AAAS; Entom Soc Am; Ecol Soc Am. *Res:* Ecological terminology, specifically the preparation of an ecological glossary; history of ecological terms; ecology of fresh water insects. *Mailing Add:* Dept of Biol E Tenn State Univ Johnson City TN 37601

TARQUIN, ANTHONY JOSEPH, b Follansbee, WVa, July 10, 41; m 65; c 1. SANITARY ENGINEERING, ENVIRONMENTAL ENGINEERING. *Educ:* WVa Univ, BSIE, 64, MSE, 65, PhD(environ eng), 69. *Prof Exp:* Asst prof environ eng, 69-73, asst dean eng, 76-79, ASSOC PROF CIVIL ENG, UNIV TEX, EL PASO, 73- *Concurrent Pos:* Nat Sci Found & Environ Protection Agency grants. *Mem:* Water Pollution Control Fedn; Am Soc Civil Engrs. *Res:* Combined disposal of liquid and solid wastes; solar energy; land disposal of wastewater and sludges. *Mailing Add:* Dept Civil Eng Univ Tex El Paso TX 79968

TARR, BETTY R, b Milwaukee, Wis, Oct 10, 13; m 42. CHEMISTRY. *Educ:* Toledo Univ, BS, 35, MS, 37; Univ Ill, PhD(chem), 41. *Prof Exp:* Tech asst, Patent Dept, Phillips Petrol Co, Okla, 41-54, mgr tech info sect, Res & Develop Dept, 54-55; res librn, Technicolor Corp, 55-65; sr res chemist, Bell & Howell Res Labs, Calif, 65-68; asst prof, 68-71, ASSOC PROF CHEM, LOS ANGELES SOUTHWEST COL, 71- *Mem:* AAAS; Am Chem Soc. *Mailing Add:* Los Angeles Southwest Col Los Angeles CA 90047

TARR, CHARLES EDWIN, b Johnstown, Pa, Jan 14, 40; m 77. PHYSICS. *Educ:* Univ NC, Chapel Hill, BS, 61, PhD(physics), 66. *Prof Exp:* Asst physics, Univ NC, Chapel Hill, 62-66, res assoc, summer 66 & Univ Pittsburgh, 66-68; from asst prof to assoc prof physics, 68-78, assoc dean, Col Arts & Sci, 79-81, PROF PHYSICS, UNIV MAINE, ORONO, 78-, ACTG DEAN, GRAD SCH, 81- *Mem:* Am Phys Soc. *Res:* Nuclear magnetic resonance; electron paramagnetic resonance; instrumentation for nuclear magnetic resonance. *Mailing Add:* Dept of Physics Univ of Maine Orono ME 04473

TARR, DONALD ARTHUR, b Norfolk, Nebr, Aug 1, 32; m 57; c 2. INORGANIC CHEMISTRY. *Educ:* Doane Col, AB, 54; Yale Univ, MS, 56, PhD(chem), 59. *Prof Exp:* From instr to asst prof chem, Col Wooster, 58-65; asst prof, 65-67, ASSOC PROF CHEM, ST OLAF COL, 67- *Concurrent Pos:* Danforth teaching fel, 58-; res assoc, Univ Colo, 64-65; vis res fel, Univ Kent, 72-73. *Mem:* Fed Am Scientists; Am Asn Univ Prof; AAAS; Am Chem Soc. *Res:* Structure and stability of metal complexes; kinetics and mechanism of reaction of coordination compounds. *Mailing Add:* Dept of Chem St Olaf Col Northfield MN 55057

TARR, JOEL ARTHUR, b Jersey City, NJ, May 8, 34. HISTORY OF TECHNOLOGY. *Educ:* Rutgers Univ, BS, 56, MA, 57; Northwestern Univ, PhD(hist), 63. *Prof Exp:* Asst prof hist, Calif State Univ, Long Beach, 61-66; vis asst prof, Univ Calif, Santa Barbara, 66-67; PROF HIST TECHNOL,

CARNEGIE-MELLON UNIV, 67- *Mem:* AAAS; Soc Hist Technol. *Res:* The city and technology, interaction of the processes of urbanization and technological innovation; transportation systems; wastewater systems; communication systems; heating, lighting and air conditioning; energy systems; retrospective technology assessment. *Mailing Add:* Prog in Technol & Soc Schenley Park Pittsburgh PA 15213

TARRANT, PAUL, b Birmingham, Ala, Nov 1, 14; m 37, 72; c 3. CHEMISTRY. *Educ:* Howard Col, BS, 36; Purdue Univ, MS, 38; Duke Univ, PhD(chem), 44. *Prof Exp:* Instr, Ala Bd Educ, 38-40; chemist, Shell Develop Co, Calif, 40-41; asst, Duke Univ, 41-44; res chemist, Am Cyanamid Co, Conn, 44-46; from instr to assoc prof, 46-57, PROF CHEM, UNIV FLA, 57- *Concurrent Pos:* Chief investr, Off Naval Res Proj, 47-50 & 53-56; dir, Off Qm Gen Res Proj, 51-67, US Air Force Res Proj, 54-66 & 72-74, NSF, 68-71, NASA, 69-71 & Mass Inst Technol, 69-71; dir res, PCR, 53-66, vpres, 66-68; consult, Redstone Arsenal, US Dept Army & Naval Ord Lab, Calif; adv, Cotton Chem Lab, USDA; ed, Fluorine Chem Rev. *Mem:* Am Chem Soc. *Res:* Preparations and reactions of fluorine containing organic compounds and inert polymers. *Mailing Add:* Dept of Chem Univ of Fla Gainesville FL 32601

TARRANTS, WILLIAM EUGENE, b Liberty, Mo, Dec 9, 27; div; c 2. SAFETY ENGINEERING, HUMAN FACTORS ENGINEERING. *Educ:* Ohio State Univ, BIE, 51, MSc, 59; NY Univ, PhD(indust safety), 63. *Prof Exp:* Chief, Ground Safety Div, US Air Force, 51-57; instr indust eng, Ohio State Univ, 58-59; instr & res assoc indust safety, NY Univ, 59-63, asst prof, 63-64; chief div accident res, Bur Labor Statist, US Dept Labor, 65-67; chief manpower develop div, 67-80, CHIEF SCIENTIST, OFF PROG & DEMON EVALUATION, HWY SAFETY, US DEPT TRANSP, 80- *Concurrent Pos:* Consult evaluation res, Indust Comn Ohio, 59; mem safety standards bd, Am Nat Standards Inst, 67-69; mem res proj comt, Nat Safety Coun, 73-76; chmn sci & tech info adv bd, Nat Hwy Traffic Safety Admin, 73-; mem comt planning & admin transp safety, Nat Acad Sci, 74- *Mem:* AAAS; fel Am Soc Safety Engrs (pres, 77-78); sr mem Am Inst Indust Engrs; Human Factors Soc; Evaluation Research Soc. *Res:* Measurement of safety performance; accident causation; psychological factors in accidents; risk acceptance; highway traffic safety. *Mailing Add:* Nat Hwy Traffic Safety Admin US Dept of Transp NTS-40 Washington DC 20590

TARSHIS, IRVIN BARRY, b Portland, Ore, May 12, 14; m 44; c 2. PARASITOLOGY, ZOOLOGY. *Educ:* Ore State Col, BA, 38; Univ Calif, Berkeley, PhD(parasitol), 53. *Prof Exp:* Res scientist, State Dept Fish & Game, Calif, 48-51; agr res scientist, USDA, Ga, 53-54; sect dep chief & med entomologist, Ft Detrick, Md, 54-57; asst prof entom, Univ Calif, Los Angeles, 57-63; RES PARASITOLOGIST, PATUXENT WILDLIFE RES CTR, 64-, RES ZOOLOGIST, 76- *Concurrent Pos:* Scripps res fel, Zool Soc San Diego, 60-61; consult, Israel, 60-61; del, Int Cong Entom, Montreal, Can, 56, Vienna, Austria, 60, Canberra, Australia, 72; del Int Cong Trop Med & Malaria, Rio de Janeiro, Brazil, 63. *Honors & Awards:* Gorgas Mem Award, 34; Animal Care Panel Res Award, 63. *Mem:* Fel AAAS; Sigma Xi; Entom Soc Am. *Res:* Biology and epidemiology of arthropods affecting man and animal; host-parasite relationships; transmission of arthropod-borne diseases to wildlife; biology of Simuliidae; membrane feeding haematophagous arthropods; uptake and depuration of petroleum hydrocarbons by aquatic organisms; accumulation and elimination of heavy metals by terrestrial arthropods. *Mailing Add:* 17219 Emerson Dr Silver Spring MD 20904

TARSKI, ALFRED, b Warsaw, Poland, Jan 14, 20; nat US; m 29; c 2. MATHEMATICS. *Educ:* Univ Warsaw, PhD(math), 23. *Prof Exp:* Instr logic, Pedagog Inst, Fical, Warsaw, 22-25; docent & adj prof math & logic, Univ Warsaw, 25-39; res assoc math, Harvard Univ, 39-41; Guggenheim fel, 41-42 & 55-56; mem, Inst Advan Study, 42; lectr, 42-45, from assoc prof to prof, 45-68, res prof, Inst Basic Res in Sci, 58-60, EMER PROF MATH, UNIV CALIF, BERKELEY, 68- *Concurrent Pos:* Prof, Zeromski's Lycee, Warsaw, 25-39; Rockefeller Found fel, 35; vis prof, City Col New York, 40; Sherman mem lectr, Univ Col, Univ London, 50, 66; lectr, Sorbonne, 55; vis prof, US Dept State Smith-Mundt grant, Nat Univ Mex, 57; vis Flint prof philos, Univ Calif, Los Angeles, 67; pres, Int Union Hist & Philos Sci, 57, chmn, US Nat Comt, 62-63. *Honors & Awards:* Alfred Jurzykowski Found Award, 66. *Mem:* Nat Acad Sci; Am Math Soc; Asn Symbolic Logic (pres, 44-46); Royal Neth Acad Sci; hon mem Neth Math Soc. *Res:* Mathematical logic and meta-mathematics; set theory; measure theory; general algebra. *Mailing Add:* 462 Michigan Ave Berkeley CA 94707

TARTAGLIA, PAUL EDWARD, b New York, NY, Sept 30, 44; m 71; c 1. ENGINEERING. *Educ:* Univ Detroit, BME, 67, DEng, 70; Northwestern Univ, Evanston, MS, 68. *Prof Exp:* Engr, Space Div, Chrysler Corp, La, 64-65; test engr, Elec Boat Div, Gen Dynamics Corp, Conn, 65; proj engr, Eng Off, Chrysler Corp, Mich, 69-70; asst prof mech eng, Univ Mass, Amherst, 70-75; proj engr, Rodney Hunt Co, 75-76; chief engr, Computerized Biomech Anal, Inc, 76-77; ASSOC HEAD DEPT ENG & TECHNOL, NORWICH UNIV, 77- *Concurrent Pos:* Nat Sci Found, Norton Co & Kollmorgen, Inc grants, Univ Mass, Amherst, 72-73. *Mem:* Am Soc Mech Engrs; Am Soc Eng Educ. *Res:* Mechanical engineering; transportation; engineering systems design; automatic control systems; sports equipment design and analysis; biomechanics of sports. *Mailing Add:* Dept Eng & Technol Norwich Univ Northfield VT 05663

TARTAR, VANCE, b Corvallis, Ore, Sept 15, 11; m S0; c 3. EXPERIMENTAL MORPHOLOGY. *Educ:* Univ Wash, Seattle, BS, 33, MS, 34; Yale Univ, PhD(zool), 38. *Prof Exp:* Seessel fel, Yale Univ, 39; instr zool, Univ Vt, 39-42 & Yale Univ, 42; asst aquatic biologist, US Fish & Wildlife Serv, 42; biologist, Wash State Dept Fisheries, 43-50; res assoc prof, 51-61, RES PROF ZOOL, UNIV WASH, 61- *Mem:* Am Soc Zool; Soc Protozool; Soc Develop Biol. *Res:* Oyster and cell biology; experimental morphogenesis in ciliates; protozoology; cell biology; the biology of Stentor. *Mailing Add:* Univ of Wash Field Lab Ocean Park WA 98640

TARTER, CURTIS BRUCE, b Louisville, Ky, Sept 26, 39; div; c 1. ASTROPHYSICS, THEORETICAL PHYSICS. *Educ:* Mass Inst Technol, SB, 61; Cornell Univ, PhD(astrophys), 67. *Prof Exp:* Sr scientist, Aeronutronic Div, Philco-Ford Corp, 67; physicist, 67-69, group leader, 69-73, dep div leader, 73-78, DIV LEADER, THEORET PHYSICS, LAWRENCE LIVERMORE LAB, 78- *Concurrent Pos:* Lectr, Dept Appl Sci, Univ Calif, Davis, 71- *Mem:* Int Astron Union; Am Phys Soc; Am Astron Soc. *Res:* Theoretical description of the properties of matter at high temperatures and densities; theoretical astrophysics, particularly x-ray astronomy and the dynamical phases of stellar evolution. *Mailing Add:* Lawrence Livermore Lab PO Box 808 L-71 Livermore CA 94550

TARTER, DONALD CAIN, b Somerset, Ky, July 22, 36; m 60; c 3. ZOOLOGY. *Educ:* Georgetown Col, Ky, BS, 58; Miami Univ, Ohio, MAT, 62; Univ Louisville, PhD(zool), 68. *Prof Exp:* Teacher chem biol, Bradford High Sch, Ohio, 58-60 & Tipp City High Sch, Ohio, 60-64; teacher biol, Ky Southern Col, 64-68; instr zool, 68-81, ASSOC PROF BIOL, MARSHALL UNIV, 81- *Mem:* Am Fisheries Soc; Am Entom Soc; Sigma Xi; Am Soc Ichthyologists & Herpetologists. *Res:* Taxonomy and ecology of fishes and aquatic insects. *Mailing Add:* Dept of Biol Sci Marshall Univ Huntington WV 25705

TARTER, MICHAEL E, b New York, NY, Dec 20, 38; m 61; c 2. BIOSTATISTICS. *Educ:* Univ Calif, Los Angeles, AB, 59, MA, 61, PhD(biostatist), 64. *Prof Exp:* From asst prof to assoc prof biostatist, Univ Mich, Ann Arbor, 64-67; assoc prof, 68-78, PROF BIOSTATIST, DEPT MED & MATH, UNIV CALIF, IRVINE, 78-; assoc prof, 70-76, PROF, UNIV CALIF, BERKELELY, 77- *Concurrent Pos:* Consult, Upjohn Drug Co, Med Diag Corp, Regional Med Asn, Pac Med Ctr & Presch & Adolescent Proj; Calif State Health Dept, NIH Cancer & Heart, Lung & Blood Insts. *Mem:* Fel Am Statist Asn; Asn Comput Mach; Int Statist Inst. *Res:* Graphical biometry; computational aspects of statistical procedures; biostatistical consultation training; nonparametric density estimation; programmed and computer assisted instruction; sorting theory. *Mailing Add:* 32 Warren Hall Univ Calif Berkeley CA 94720

TARTOF, KENNETH D, b Detroit, Mich, Dec 30, 41; m 67. GENETICS. *Educ:* Univ Mich, BS, 63, PhD(genetics), 68. *Prof Exp:* NIH res fel, 68-70, res assoc, 70-71, asst mem, 71-76, MEM, INST CANCER RES, 76- *Mem:* AAAS; Genetics Soc Am. *Res:* Structure and function of genes; genetic control of gene redundancy; regulation of DNA and RNA metabolism. *Mailing Add:* Inst for Cancer Res 7701 Burholme Ave Philadelphia PA 19111

TARVER, FRED RUSSELL, JR, b Knoxville, Tenn, Mar 7, 25; m 50; c 3. FOOD TECHNOLOGY, BACTERIOLOGY. *Educ:* Univ Tenn, BSA, 50, MA, 54; Univ Ga, PhD(food technol, bact), 63. *Prof Exp:* Mem staff, Security Mills, Inc, Tenn, 50-54; instr poultry, Univ Tenn, 54-56; asst prof, Univ Fla, 56-60, 62-63; exten assoc prof, 63-75, EXTEN PROF FOOD SCI, NC STATE UNIV, 75. *Mem:* Inst Food Technol; Poultry Sci Asn; World Poultry Sci Asn. *Res:* Product development and marketing of new poultry and egg products; sanitation in processing plants, with emphasis on ecology; 4-H club activities connected with poultry and egg products. *Mailing Add:* Dept Food Sci 129-D Schaub Hall NC State Univ Raleigh NC 27650

TARVER, HAROLD, b Wigan, Eng, June 7, 08; nat US; m; c 2. BIOCHEMISTRY, MEDICAL & HEALTH SCIENCES. *Educ:* Univ Alta, BS, 32, MSc, 35; Univ Calif, PhD(biochem), 39. *Prof Exp:* Asst, Univ Alta, 32-35; asst, Sch Med, Univ Calif, Berkeley, 36-39, fel, 39-41; from instr to prof biochem, 41-75, EMER PROF BIOCHEM, SCH MED, UNIV CALIF, SAN FRANCISCO, 75- *Mem:* AAAS; Am Soc Biol Chem; Soc Exp Biol & Med. *Res:* Metabolism of sulfur and protein-isotopic studies. *Mailing Add:* 1715 Wawona St San Francisco CA 94116

TARVER, JAMES H, JR, b Birmingham, Ala, Aug 17, 41; m 63; c 2. CLINICAL DRUGS. *Educ:* Talladega Col, BA, 63; Howard Univ, PhD(pharmacol), 73; Kean Col, MA, 80. *Prof Exp:* Chemist, NIH, 65-68; asst biochemist, Roche Inst Molecular Biol, 68-72; sr learning partner chem technol, State Univ NY, Albany, 72-74; sr scientist, Hoffmann La Roche, 74-78, assoc mgr technol training, 78-81; ASSOC SR INVESTR, SMITH KLINE BECKMAN CORP, 81- *Concurrent Pos:* Vis mem staff, Roche Inst Molecular Biol, 72-73; consult, Off Pub Defender, Albany, NY, 73-74; vis prof, Sch Pharm, Fla A&M Univ, 74-; adj prof, Dept Chem, Bergen County Community Col, 80-81. *Mem:* AAAS; Soc Neurosci; NY Acad Sci. *Mailing Add:* 1004 W 66th Ave Philadelphia PA 19126

TARVER, MAE-GOODWIN, b Selma, Ala, Aug 9, 16. STATISTICS. *Educ:* Univ Ala, BS, 39, MS, 40. *Prof Exp:* Res engr, Continental Can Co, Inc, 41-48, proj engr statist, 48-54, res statistician & internal qual control consult res & develop dept, 54-77; PRIN CONSULT, QUEST ASSOCS, 78- *Concurrent Pos:* Instr, Ill Inst Technol, 57-62, adj assoc prof, 63- *Honors & Awards:* Lisy Award, Am Soc Qual Control, 61; Edward J Oakley Award, Am Soc Qual Control, 75. *Mem:* Am Statist Asn; fel Am Soc Qual Control; sr mem Soc Women Engrs; Inst Food Technol. *Res:* Multivariate statistical analysis of industrial research data; statistical and information theory appraisal of sensory tests; quality engineering applied to container fabrication and packaging of food products. *Mailing Add:* c/o Quest Assocs 130-26th St Park Forest IL 60466

TARVIN, JEFFREY A, b Cincinnati, Ohio, Nov 15, 51; m; c 1. CONDENSED MATTER PHYSICS, PHYSICAL OPTICS. *Educ:* Thomas More Col, AB, 71; Mass Inst Technol, PhD(physics), 76. *Prof Exp:* Res asst physics, Mass Inst Technol, 74-76; res assoc neutron scattering, Brookhaven Nat Lab, 76-78; RES SCIENTIST ADVAN PHYS CHARACTERIZATION, CRYOGENICS & LASER-FUSION TARGET DESIGN, KMS FUSION, INC, SUBSID KMS INDUSTS, INC, 78- *Mem:* Am Phys Soc. *Res:* Cryogenics, including the properties of liquid helium; physics of condensed matter as studied by thermal neutron scattering; techniques for physical characterization of materials; optics, lasers and laser-plasma interactions. *Mailing Add:* KMS Fusion Inc PO Box 1567 Ann Arbor MI 48106

TARVIN, ROBERT FLOYD, b Montezuma, Iowa, Feb 20, 42; m 61; c 3. POLYMER SYNTHESIS, ORGANIC CHEMISTRY. *Educ:* Univ Northern Iowa, BA, 65; Univ Iowa, PhD(org chem), 72. *Prof Exp:* Res asst drug interaction, Univ Iowa, 65-67; NAS vis prof liquid crystalline polymers, Univ Rio de Janeiro, 72-74; proj leader water treating & mining chem, 74-80, MGR PAPER CHEM, CHEM RES DIV, AM CYANAMID CO, 80- *Mem:* Am Chem Soc; Sigma Xi. *Res:* Organic polymer synthesis; water treating chemicals; slow release drug delivery; liquid crystalline polymers; paper chemicals. *Mailing Add:* Am Cyanamid Co 1937 W Main St Stamford CT 06904

TARWATER, JAN DALTON, b Ft Worth, Tex, Sept 30, 37; m 58; c 3. ALGEBRA. *Educ:* Tex Tech Col, BS, 59; Univ NMex, MA, 61, PhD(math), 65. *Prof Exp:* Asst prof math, Western Mich Univ, 65-67 & NTex State Univ, 67-68; from asst prof to assoc prof, 68-73, assoc chmn dept, 72-73, chmn dept, 73-78, PROF MATH, TEX TECH UNIV, 73- *Mem:* Math Asn Am; Am Math Soc; Soc Indust & Appl Math. *Res:* Algebra, especially Abelian groups and homological algebra; graph theory; history of mathematics. *Mailing Add:* Dept of Math Tex Tech Univ Lubbock TX 79409

TARWATER, OLIVER REED, b Chattanooga, Tenn, Mar 12, 44; m 66. SYNTHETIC ORGANIC CHEMISTRY, POLYMER CHEMISTRY. *Educ:* Maryville Col, BS, 66; Purdue Univ, Lafayette, MS, 69, PhD(med chem), 70. *Prof Exp:* Res chemist, Personal Care Div, Gillette Co, Chicago, 70-74; sr chemist, Southern Res Inst, Birmingham, 74-76; sr chemist, 76-80, RES SCIENTIST, LILLY RES LABS, GREENFIELD, IND, 81- *Mem:* Am Chem Soc; Controlled Release Soc. *Res:* Controlled release of bioactive materials, especially pesticides and animal health drugs; formulation of agrichemicals; agricultural and food chemistry. *Mailing Add:* Lilly Res Labs Greenfield IN 46140

TARZWELL, CLARENCE MATTHEW, b Deckerville, Mich, Sept 29, 07; m 38; c 3. WATER POLLUTION, POLLUTION BIOLOGY. *Educ:* Univ Mich, AB, 30, MS, 32, PhD(aquatic biol, fisheries mgt), 36. *Hon Degrees:* ScD, Baldwin-Wallace Col, 67. *Prof Exp:* Stream improv supvr, Mich State Dept Conserv, 33-34; asst aquatic biologist, US Bur Fisheries, 34; asst range examr, US Forest Serv, NMex, 35, 36-38; from asst aquatic biologist to assoc aquatic biologist, Tenn Valley Authority, Ala, 38-43; asst & sr sanitarian, USPHS, Ga, 43-46, sr biologist, Tech Develop Div, 46-48, chief aquatic biol sect, Environ Health Ctr, Cincinnati, Ohio, 48-53, sci dir, Robert A Taft Sanit Eng Ctr, 53-65; dir, Nat Marine Water Qual Lab, Environ Protection Agency, RI, 65-72; sr res advr, Environ Protection Agency Nat Environ Res Ctr, Corvallis Ore, 72-75; ENVIRON CONSULT, 75- *Concurrent Pos:* Mem aquatic life adv comt, Ohio River Valley Sanit Compact, 52-68; chmn & mem comt on stand bioassay methods, Water Pollution Control Fedn, 56-75; mem adv comt control stream temperatures, Pa Sanit Water Bd, 59-62; mem adv comt water qual criteria, Calif State Water Pollution Control Bd, 61-63; mem subcomt res, comt pest control & wildlife rels, Nat Acad Sci-Nat Res Coun, 61-63; US deleg int meetings sci res water pollution, Orgn Econ Coop & Develop, Paris, France, 61-62, chmn int comt on toxic mat in aquatic environ, 62-67; mem expert adv panel environ health, WHO, 62-65; actg dir nat water qual lab, Fed Water Pollution Control Admin, Duluth, Minn, 64-67; adj prof, Col Resource Develop, Univ RI, 65-75, vis prof, 76-79; chmn nat tech adv comt water qual req fish, other aquatic life & wildlife, Secy Interior, 67-68; mem comt power plant siting, Nat Acad Eng-Nat Acad Sci, 71-72; mem nat temperature comt, Environ Protection Agency, 71-72; mem, NAm Game Policy Comt, 71-73; mem regional task force, New Eng River Basin Comn, 72-75. *Honors & Awards:* Conservationist of the Yr Award, State of Ohio, 61; Prof Conservationist Award, Am Motors Corp, 62; Aldo Leopold Medal, Wildlife Soc, 63; USPHS Meritorious Serv Medal, 64; Distinguished Career Award, Environ Protection Agency, 73 & Commendable Serv Medal, 74; Award of Excellence, Am Fisheries Soc, 74. *Mem:* Hon mem Am Fisheries Soc; hon mem Wildlife Soc; Am Soc Ichthyol & Herpet; Am Soc Limnol & Oceanog; Atlantic Estuarine Res Soc. *Res:* Water pollution control; determination of water quality criteria and standards for aquatic life; standard bioassay methods; environmental improvement and management; toxicity of wastes to aquatic life; aquatic biology and ecology. *Mailing Add:* Rte 5 Box 159 Old Post Rd Wakefield RI 02879

TASAKI, ICHIJI, b Fukushim-Ken , Japan, Oct 21, 10; nat US; m; c 2. NEUROPHYSIOLOGY. *Educ:* Keio Univ, Japan, MD, 38. *Hon Degrees:* DS, Uppsala Univ, 72. *Prof Exp:* Privat-docent physiol, Keio Univ, 38-42, privat-docent physics & prof physiol, Med Col, 42-51; prof physiol, Nihon Univ, Tokyo, 51; res assoc, Cent Inst Deaf, St Louis, Mo, 51-53; chief spec senses sect, Lab Neurophysiol, Nat Inst Neurol Dis & Blindness, 53-61; mem staff, 61-66, CHIEF LAB NEUROBIOL, NIMH, 66- *Concurrent Pos:* Mem, Marine Biol Lab, Woods Hole, Mass. *Mem:* Am Acad Neurol; Physiol Soc Japan. *Res:* Nerve and sense organs; electrophysiology. *Mailing Add:* Lab of Neurobiol Rm ID-02 Bldg 36 NIMH Bethesda MD 20014

TASCH, AL FELIX, JR, b Corpus Christi, Tex, May 12, 41; m 63; c 2. SOLID STATE PHYSICS. *Educ:* Univ Tex, Austin, BS, 63; Univ Ill, Urbana, MS, 65, PhD(physics), 69. *Prof Exp:* RES SCIENTIST, SOLID STATE PHYSICS, CENT RES LABS, TEX INSTRUMENTS, INC, 69- *Mem:* Am Phys Soc. *Res:* Solid state device physics and processing technology; recombination-generation and trapping in semiconductors; metal-oxide-silicon field effect transistors; microwave transistors; charge-coupled devices. *Mailing Add:* MS 134 Cent Res Labs Tex Instruments Inc PO Box 5936 Dallas TX 75222

TASCH, PAUL, b New York, NY, Nov 28, 10. PALEOBIOLOGY, GEOLOGY. *Educ:* City Col New York, BS, 48; Pa State Col, MS, 50; Iowa State Univ, PhD(geol), 52. *Prof Exp:* Instr geol, Pa State Col, 48-49; instr, Univ Conn, 52-53; asst prof, NDak Agr Col, 53-54; assoc prof, Moorhead State Univ, 54-55; PROF GEOL, WICHITA STATE UNIV, 55-, DISTINGUISHED PROF NAT SCI, 77- *Concurrent Pos:* Chief investr earth sci grant, NSF, 56-73 & off polar progs, 66-76 & 77- *Honors & Awards:* Antarctic Serv Medal, US Cong, 70. *Mem:* Paleont Soc; fel Geol Soc Am; fel AAAS; fel Geol Soc India; fel Geol Soc London. *Res:* Non-marine fossil biotas of Antarctica and other Gondwana continents, especially conchostracans palynomorphs and spoor; geomicrobiology; evaporites; branchiopoda, fossil and living; history of science. *Mailing Add:* Dept of Geol Wichita State Univ Wichita KS 67208

TASCHDJIAN, CLAIRE LOUISE, b Berlin, Ger, Jan 7, 14; nat US; m 44; c 1. MEDICINE, MYCOLOGY. *Educ:* Catholic Univ, Peking, China, BSc, 45; Wagner Col, MS, 60. *Prof Exp:* Asst, Cenozoic res lab, Peking Union Med Col, China, 40-41; teacher, Peking Am High Sch, China, 45-48; mycologist, Sect Dermat, Dept Med, Univ Chicago, 49-52; clin asst dermat & syphilol, Postgrad Med Sch, NY Univ, 52-56; asst prof biol, St Francis Col, NY, 64-69, assoc prof, 69-79; RES ASSOC PEDIAT, MAIMONIDES MED CTR, 56- *Concurrent Pos:* Lectr, State Univ NY Downstate Med Ctr, 63-75; vis prof, Dept Path, Univ Ulm, 70-71. *Mem:* Med Mycol Soc Am; Am Soc Microbiol; NY Acad Sci; Int Soc Human & Animal Mycol. *Res:* Immunologic, immunochemical and histochemical factors in candidiasis; epidemiology, serology, pathogenesis and serodiagnosis of systemic candidiasis; physiology of Candida albicans in vivo and in vitro; writing; evolution. *Mailing Add:* 109-50 117th St S Ozone Park Sta Jamaica NY 11420

TASCHEK, RICHARD FERDINAND, b Chicago, Ill, June 5, 15; m 42; c 4. PHYSICS. *Educ:* Univ Wis, BA, 36, PhD(physics), 41; Univ Fla, MS, 38. *Prof Exp:* Teaching asst, Univ Wis, 38-40; res physicist, Oldbury Electro-Chem Co, NY, 41-42; Nat Defense Res Comt physicist, Princeton Univ, 42-43; physicist, 43-62, div leader exp physics, 62-70, asst dir res, 71-72, ASSOC DIR RES, LOS ALAMOS NAT LAB, 72- *Concurrent Pos:* Mem nuclear cross sect adv group, AEC, 48-57, chmn, 53-57, mem tripartite nuclear cross sect comt, 56-61, chmn, 61; mem Euro-Am nuclear data comt, 57-72, chmn, 60-62; mem int nuclear data working group, 63-72; adv, Int Nuclear Data Comt, 63-73, ex-officio mem, 72-74; mem standing comt controlled thermonuclear reactions & ad hoc adv comt on Los Alamos meson proj; co-chmn, Vis Comt Lab Nuclear Sci, Mass Inst Technol, 67; mem adv comt neutron physics, Oak Ridge Nat Lab; mem Nuclear Physics Panel, Physics Surv Comt, Div Phys Sci, Nat Res Coun; mem Off Stand Ref Data Eval Panel, Nat Bur Stand, & Inst Basic Stand Eval Panel, 71-75; mem, Ctr Radiation Res, Nat Bur Stand Panel, 71-76, chmn, 72-; mem adv comt, Univ Alaska Geophys Inst, 73-76; mem, Numerical Data Adv Bd, US Nat Comt for CODATA, 73-, chmn, 74- *Mem:* Fel AAAS; fel Am Phys Soc; fel Am Nuclear Soc; Am Geophys Union. *Res:* Nuclear reactions and scattering; nuclear properties; neutron physics; accelerators and detectors; space physics; Vela satellite program; controlled thermonuclear reactions. *Mailing Add:* Mail Stop 102 Box 1663 Los Alamos Nat Lab Los Alamos NM 87545

TASHIAN, RICHARD EARL, b Cranston, RI, Oct 7, 22; m 68; c 1. BIOCHEMICAL GENETICS. *Educ:* Univ RI, BS, 47; Purdue Univ, MS, 49, PhD(zool), 51. *Prof Exp:* Asst, Purdue Univ, 48-51; asst prof biol, Long Island Univ, 51-54, actg chmn dept, 54; sci assoc, Dept Trop Res, NY Zool Soc, 54-55; res assoc, Inst Study Human Variation, Columbia Univ, 56-57; from res assoc to assoc prof, 57-70, PROF HUMAN GENETICS, MED SCH, UNIV MICH, ANN ARBOR, 70- *Concurrent Pos:* Vis scientist, Dept Chem, Carlsberg Lab, Copenhagen, Denmark, 68-69. *Mem:* Fel AAAS; Am Soc Human Genetics; Am Soc Biol Chemists; Brit Biochem Soc. *Res:* Biochemical genetics and molecular evolution; evolution of structure-function relationships of carbonic anhydrase isozymes; organization, structure and evolution of carbonic anhydrase genes. *Mailing Add:* Dept Human Genetics Univ Mich Med Sch Ann Arbor MI 48109

TASHIRO, HARUO, b Selma, Calif, Mar 24, 17; m 42; c 3. ENTOMOLOGY. *Educ:* Wheaton Col, BS, 45; Cornell Univ, MS, 46, PhD(entom), 50. *Prof Exp:* Asst entom, Cornell Univ, 47-50; entomologist, USDA, 50-67; PROF ENTOM, AGR EXP STA, CORNELL UNIV, 67- *Concurrent Pos:* Assoc prof, Cornell Univ, 58-63; res assoc, Univ Calif, Riverside, 63-67. *Mem:* Entom Soc Am; Sigma Xi. *Res:* Biology; biological and chemical control of turf insects; insects, ornamental plants, permanent plantings; insect pathology. *Mailing Add:* Dept Entom Agr Exp Sta Cornell Univ Geneva NY 14456

TASHJIAN, ARMEN H, JR, b Cleveland, Ohio, May 2, 32; m 55; c 3. ENDOCRINOLOGY, PHARMACOLOGY. *Educ:* Yale Univ, 50-53; Harvard Univ, MD, 57. *Prof Exp:* Intern med, Harvard Serv, Boston City Hosp, 57-58, asst resident, 58-59; clin res assoc, Metab Dis Br, Nat Inst Arthritis & Metab Dis, 59-61; Nat Found res fel, 61-63, from instr to assoc prof, 63-70, prof pharmacol, Sch Dent Med & Sch Med, 70-78, PROF TOXICOL, SCH PUB HEALTH & PROF PHARMACOL, SCH MED, HARVARD UNIV, 78- *Concurrent Pos:* Assoc ed, Cancer Res, 80- *Honors & Awards:* H B Van Dyke Mem Award & lectr, Columbia Univ, 77; Edwin B Astwood lectr, Endocrine Soc, 77. *Mem:* AAAS; Am Soc Pharmacol & Exp Therapeut; Endocrine Soc; Am Soc Cell Biol; Tissue Cult Asn. *Res:* Purification, bioassay, immunoassay and immunochemistry, structure-function interrelationships and mechanism of action of protein and peptide hormones; cell biology; establishment, control of function and growth, and immunology of differentiated, clonal strains of animal cells in culture; toxicology; mechinsm of action of tumor promoters; toxicology. *Mailing Add:* Lab Toxicol Harvard Sch Pub Health 665 Huntington Ave Boston MA 02115

TASHJIAN, DAVID REITLER, b Kalamazoo, Mich, June 22, 11; m 38; c 4. ELECTRONIC ENGINEERING, PHYSICS. *Educ:* Univ Mich, BSE, 32; Mass Inst Technol, MS, 34; Western Mich Univ, BA, 36, DSc, 59. *Hon Degrees:* DSc, Western Mich Univ, 59. *Prof Exp:* Res engr mech design, Clarage Fan Co, 36-41; design engr electronics, Westinghouse Elec Crop, 41-44, sect mgr, 44-50, sub div mgr, 50-55, engr mgr mil equip, 55-63; consult engr aerospace, Lockheed Missiles & Space Co, 63-76; consult engr, 76-78; RETIRED. *Mem:* Inst Elec & Electronics Engrs; Am Inst Aeronaut & Astronaut. *Mailing Add:* 6168 Montgomery Place San Jose CA 95135

TASHJIAN, ROBERT JOHN, b Worcester, Mass, Feb 4, 30. VETERINARY MEDICINE. *Educ:* Clark Univ, AB, 51; Univ Pa, VMD, 56. *Hon Degrees:* DSc, Hartwick Col, 68. *Prof Exp:* Staff vet, Animal Med Ctr, New York, 56-58, head med, 58-62, chief of staff, 62-63, dir, 63-74; PRES, NEW ENGLAND INST COMP MED, WEST BOYLSTON, MASS, 74- *Concurrent Pos:* Res assoc, Vet Admin Hosp, Bronx, NY, 60-64; instr, Sch Vet Med, Univ Pa, 61-63; prin investr, Nat Heart Inst grant, 62-66, sponsor grant, 66-69; lectr animal sci & mem grad fac, Univ Maine, Orono, 67-, vis prof, 74-; affil prof, Colo State Univ, 67-; adj prof, Univ Mass, Amherst, 69-70; dir, Duke Farms, Somerville, NJ, 71-74; consult to bd trustees, Animal Med Ctr, New York, 74-; mem coun clin cardiol, Am Heart Asn. *Mem:* AAAS; Am Asn Lab Animal Sci; Am Asn Vet Clinicians; Am Vet Med Asn; Am Vet Radiol Soc. *Res:* Internal medicine, especially comparative cardiovascular disease. *Mailing Add:* 405 Prospect St West Boylston MA 01583

TASHLICK, IRVING, b New York, NY, July 5, 28; m 50. ORGANIC CHEMISTRY, POLYMER CHEMISTRY. *Educ:* City Col New York, BS, 49; Polytech Inst Brooklyn, MS, 53, PhD(org chem), 58. *Prof Exp:* Chemist, Plastics Div, Monsanto Co, 58-60, group leader, 60-62; mgr chem res, Res & Eng Div, Int Pipe & Ceramics Corp, 62-66; vpres, Wharton Industs, Inc, 68-72; PRES, ALVA-TECH INC, 73- *Mem:* Am Chem Soc; Soc Plastics Eng. *Res:* Long term properties of plastics, coatings and adhesives; polyurethanes. *Mailing Add:* 311 Newark Ave Bradley Beach NJ 07720

TASI, JAMES, b New York, NY, Dec 6, 33; m 60; c 3. MECHANICS. *Educ:* NY Univ, BCE, 55; Univ Ill, MS, 56; Columbia Univ, PhD(mech), 62. *Prof Exp:* Engr, Martin Co, Md, 57-58, assoc res scientist, Colo, 61-65; fel mech, Johns Hopkins Univ, 65-66; assoc prof, 66-72, PROF MECH, STATE UNIV NY STONY BROOK, 72- *Mem:* Am Soc Mech Engrs. *Res:* Acoustic vibrations of structures; thermoelastic dissipation in crystalline solids; wave propagation; stability; mechanical properties of solids; shock response of crystal lattices. *Mailing Add:* Dept of Mech Eng State Univ of NY Stony Brook NY 11790

TASKER, CLINTON WALDORF, b Syracuse, NY, Sept 14, 18; m 41; c 3. CHEMISTRY. *Educ:* Syracuse Univ, BSc, 41, MSc, 44; McGill Univ, PhD(cellulose chem), 47. *Prof Exp:* Res chemist, Sylvania Indust Corp, Va, 41-43; lab asst pulp & paper technol, State Univ NY Col Forestry, Syracuse Univ, 43-44; lab demonstr org & inorg chem, McGill Univ, 44-46; sr res chemist, Sylvania Div, Am Viscose Corp, 47-53, tech supt, 53-59, mgr supt, 59-61; dir tech res & develop, 61-65, vpres res & develop, 65-68, vpres & gen mgr, Filer Mill, Paperboard Div, 68-73, VPRES CORP RES & DEVELOP, PACKAGING CORP AM, TENNECO INC, 73- *Mem:* Am Inst Chemists; NY Acad Sci; Am Chem Soc; Tech Asn Pulp & Paper Indust. *Res:* Alkaline chemical pulping processes; chemistry and structure of cellulose ethers; synthesis of plasticizers for cellulose; tosyl and iodo derivatives of some hydroxyethyl ethers. *Mailing Add:* 3075 Baker Park Dr SE Grand Rapids MI 49508

TASKER, JOHN B, b Concord, NH, Aug 28, 33; m 61; c 3. VETERINARY MEDICINE, CLINICAL PATHOLOGY. *Educ:* Cornell Univ, DVM, 57, PhD(vet path), 63. *Prof Exp:* Am Vet Med Asn fel, Cornell Univ, 61-63; from asst prof to assoc prof vet med, Colo State Univ, 63-67; assoc prof vet path, NY State Vet Col, Cornell Univ, 67-69, prof clin path, 69-78; PROF CLIN PATH & ASSOC DEAN, SCH VET MED, LA STATE UNIV, 78- *Mem:* Am Vet Med Asn; Am Soc Vet Clin Path. *Res:* Veterinary clinical pathology. *Mailing Add:* Off of Dean Sch of Vet Med Baton Rouge LA 70803

TASKER, RONALD REGINALD, b Toronto, Ont, Dec 18, 27; m 55; c 4. NEUROSURGERY. *Educ:* Univ Toronto, BA, 48, MD, 52, MA, 54; FRCS(C), 59. *Prof Exp:* Asst physiol, Banting & Best Dept Med Res, 48-52, mem clin & res staff, 61-66, ASST PROF SURG, FAC MED, UNIV TORONTO, 66-; PROF NEUROSURG, TORONTO GEN HOSP, 78- *Concurrent Pos:* Resident fel neurosurg, Fac Med, Univ Toronto, 58-59; McLaughlin traveling fel, Mass Gen Hosp, 59 & Univ Wis, 60; mem clin & res staff, Toronto Gen Hosp, 61-66, asst prof neurosurg, 66-73, assoc prof, 73-78. *Mem:* Am Asn Neurol Surg; Can Neurosurg Soc; Can Med Asn; Am Acad Neurol Surg; Am Soc Res Stereoencephalotomy. *Res:* Hyperkinetic disorders; dyskinesias and stereotatic surgery; sensory physiology and pain. *Mailing Add:* Rm 124 Toronto Gen Hosp Toronto ON M5S 1A1 Can

TASLITZ, NORMAN, b New York, NY, Feb 12, 29; m 56; c 3. NEUROANATOMY. *Educ:* NY Univ, BS, 51; Univ Pa, cert phys ther, 52; Stanford Univ, PhD(anat), 63. *Prof Exp:* Physical therapist, Univ Wis Hosps, Madison, 52-54 & Wis Neurol Found, Madison, 54-58; asst prof anat, Sch Phys Ther, Case Western Reserve Univ, 63-71, from instr to sr instr, Dept Anat, 63-67, asst prof anat, 67-77; ASSOC PROF ANAT & PROG DIR HUMAN ANAT, NORTHEASTERN OHIO UNIVS COL MED, 77- *Mem:* Am Asn Anatomists; Sigma Xi; AAAS; Am Asn Univ Prof. *Res:* Development of biological models to demonstrate the hemodynamic, metabolic and electrophysiologic performance of intact central nervous system tissue under control conditions, at various subnormal temperature levels and following trauma or periods of circulatory arrest. *Mailing Add:* Northeastern Ohio Univs Col of Med Rootstown OH 44272

TASMAN, WILLIAM S, US citizen; m; c 3. OPHTHALMOLOGY. *Educ:* Haverford Col, BA, 51; Temple Univ, MD, 55. *Prof Exp:* ASSOC RETINA SERV, RETINOVITREOUS ASSOC, 62- *Concurrent Pos:* Heed fel, 61-62; Retina Found fel, 62. *Mem:* Am Col Physicians; Am Col Surg; Am Ophthal Soc. *Res:* Retinal diseases in children; retinal detachment surgery. *Mailing Add:* Retinovitreous Assoc 187 E Evergreen Ave Philadelphia PA 19118

TASSAVA, ROY A, b Ironwood, Mich, July 5, 37; m 61; c 3. DEVELOPMENTAL BIOLOGY, COMPARATIVE ENDOCRINOLOGY. *Educ:* Northern Mich Univ, BS, 59; Brown Univ, MAT, 65; Mich State Univ, PhD(zool), 68. *Prof Exp:* Pub sch teacher, 59-64; NIH res fel zool, Mich State Univ, 68-69; asst prof, 69-73, assoc prof, 73-76, PROF ZOOL, OHIO STATE UNIV, 76- *Concurrent Pos:* Sigma Xi res award, 68. *Mem:* Am Inst Biol Sci; Am Soc Zoologists. *Res:* Role of hormones and nerves in amphibian limb regeneration; pituitary, thyroid and adrenal hormone physiology in amphibians. *Mailing Add:* Dept of Zool Ohio State Univ Columbus OH 43210

TASSINARI, SILVIO JOHN, b New York, NY, June 2, 22; m 52; c 2. NUCLEAR MEDICINE, RADIOCHEMISTRY. *Educ:* St Michael's Col, Vt, BS, 42, MS, 47; Int Univ, PhD(chem, nuclear med), 77. *Prof Exp:* Supv radiochemist, Brookhaven Nat Lab, 51-71; supv radiochemist, Brooklyn, 71-72, SUPV RADIOCHEMIST NUCLEAR MED, VET ADMIN MED CTR, NORTHPORT, 72- *Concurrent Pos:* Consult, Cath Med Ctr Brooklyn & Queens, 73-; adj instr & consult, J F Kennedy Med Ctr, 74- *Mem:* Fel Am Inst Chemists; Radiation Res Soc; Health Physics Soc; Soc Nuclear Med; Am Soc Radiologic Technologists. *Res:* Diagnostic nuclear medicine using new and innovative radioisotopes and radiopharmaceuticals; investigation of new procedures in organ and system dianosis. *Mailing Add:* 47 Moriches Rd Nissequogue St James NY 11780

TASSONI, JOSEPH PAUL, entomology, see previous edition

TASSOUL, JEAN-LOUIS, b Brussels, Belg, Nov 1, 38; m 66. ASTROPHYSICS. *Educ:* Free Univ Brussels, LSc, 61, DSc, 64. *Prof Exp:* Res fel, Nat Found Sci Res, Belg, 65-66; res assoc, Univ Chicago, 66-67 & Princeton Univ, 67-68; from asst prof to assoc prof, 68-75, PROF PHYSICS, UNIV MONTREAL, 75- *Mem:* Int Astron Union. *Res:* Rotating stars and nonlinear instabilities. *Mailing Add:* Dept of Physics Univ Montreal PO Box 6128 Montreal PQ H3C 3J7 Can

TASSOUL, MONIQUE, b Brussels, Belg, Sept 23, 42; m 66. ASTROPHYSICS. *Educ:* Univ Brussels, Belg, LSc, 63; Univ Montreal, PhD(physics), 74. *Prof Exp:* RESEARCHER ASTROPHYSICS, UNIV MONTREAL, 74- *Mem:* Int Astron Union. *Res:* Stellar structure and stability. *Mailing Add:* Dept of Physics PO Box 6128 Montreal PQ H3C 3J7 Can

TASWELL, HOWARD FILMORE, b Paterson, NJ, July 21, 28; m 52; c 6. IMMUNOHEMATOLOGY, LABORATORY MEDICINE. *Educ:* Harvard Col, AB, 49; New York Univ, MD, 53; Univ Minn, MS, 61; Am Bd Path, cert, anat & clin path, 61 & blood banking & immuno hemat, 73. *Prof Exp:* Asst prof path, Hahnemann Med Sch, 61-63; from instr to asst prof clin path, 63-73, assoc prof lab med, 73-77, PROF LAB MED, MAYO MED SCH, UNIV MINN, 77- *Concurrent Pos:* Assoc pathologist, Harrisburg Hosp, Pa, 61-63; NIH prin & co-investr, Nat Inst Arthritis & Metab Dis, 63-67, 66-71, 71-74 & 75-; pres, Minn Asn Blood Banks, 69-70 & Minn Soc Clin Pathologists, 72-73; consult, Food & Drug Admin, Bur Biologics, 74-75; dir blood bank, Mayo Clin, Rochester, Minn, 63- *Mem:* Am Asn Blood Banks; Am Soc Clin Pathologists; Am Blood Comn. *Res:* Clinical aspects of immuno hematology, blood banking, blood transfusion and transfusion reactions; post-transfusion hepatitis; blood resource management and quality control; histocompatibility testing for tissue transplantation. *Mailing Add:* Mayo Clin Blood Bank & Transfusion Serv Rochester MN 55901

TATARCZUK, JOSEPH RICHARD, b Portland, Maine, June 15, 36; m 64; c 4. NUCLEAR PHYSICS, COMPUTER ENGINEERING. *Educ:* Col of the Holy Cross, BS, 58; Rensselaer Polytech Inst, MS, 61, PhD(physics), 65. *Prof Exp:* Res asst nuclear physics, Rennselaer Polytech Inst, 59-65; res assoc, Nuclear Physics Div, Max Planck Inst Chem, 65-66; res assoc neutron physics, 66-70, ASST TO DIR LINAC OPERS & SUPPORT SERV, LINEAR ACCELERATOR LAB, RENNSELAER POLYTECH INST, 70-; ASSOC PROF, ALBANY MED COL, 74- *Concurrent Pos:* Chief physicist, Nuclear Med Serv, Albany Vet Admin Hosp, 72-; adj prof nuclear eng & sci, Renneslaer Polytech Inst, 76-79, adj prof biomed eng, 80- *Mem:* Am Phys Soc. *Res:* Neutron physics; gamma ray spectroscopy; nuclear, accelerator and computer instrumentation. *Mailing Add:* Physicist & Comput Syst Mgr Vet Admin Med Ctr Albany NY 12208

TATE, BRYCE EUGENE, b Girard, Ill, Apr 15, 20; m 59; c 2. ORGANIC CHEMISTRY. *Educ:* Univ Ill, BS, 42; Univ Wis, MS, 44, PhD(chem), 50. *Prof Exp:* Res fel chem, Harvard Univ, 53-55; chemist, Chas Pfizer & Co, 55-59, proj leader, 59-61, group supvr, 61-68, mgr chem prod res, 68-77, ASST DIR INDUST SPECIALTY CHEM DEPT, PFIZER INC, 77- *Mem:* Am Chem Soc; Soc Petrol Engrs. *Res:* Synthetic organic chemistry; mechanism of organic reactions; polymer chemistry. *Mailing Add:* Cent Res Pfizer Inc Eastern Point Rd Groton CT 06340

TATE, CHARLES LUTHER, pathology, veterinary medicine, see previous edition

TATE, CHARLOTTE ANNE, b Mt Clemens, Mich, Sept 15, 44. EXERCISE PHYSIOLOGY, CARDIOVASCULAR SCIENCES. *Educ:* Tex Woman's Univ, BS, 69; Southwest Tex State Univ, MA, 72; Univ Tex, Austin, PhD(phys educ & exercise physiol), 76. *Prof Exp:* Teacher adaptive phys educ, Northeast ISD, 69-72; teaching asst, Univ Tex, Austin, 72-76; res physiologist biochem, Inst Environ Stress, 76-77; fel biochem res muscle, 77-79, instr, 79-80, ASST PROF, BAYLOR COL MED, 80- *Concurrent Pos:* Res asst, Univ Res Coun, Univ Tex, Austin, 74-75; NIH trainee, Inst Environ Stress, 76-77 & NIH fel, Baylor Col Med, 77-79. *Mem:* Am Heart Asn; Am Col Sports Med; Am Physiol Soc; AAAS; NY Acad Sci. *Res:* Calcium fluxes in subcellular organelles of cardiac and skeletal muscle in normal and diseased states; biochemical adaptations to exercise and fatique in muscle. *Mailing Add:* Dept of Med Baylor Col of Med Houston TX 77030

TATE, DAVID PAUL, b Chicago, Ill, Dec 10, 31; m 53; c 3. ORGANIC & POLYMER CHEMISTRY. *Educ:* Hamline Univ, BS, 53; Purdue Univ, MS, 55, PhD, 58. *Prof Exp:* Sr chemist, Stand Oil Co, Ohio, 57-63; mgr polymerization, 63-71, asst dir res, 71-80, RES ASSOC, FIRESTONE TIRE & RUBBER CO, 80- *Mem:* Am Chem Soc. *Res:* Lithium amine reductions; phosphorous compounds; organometallic chemistry; elastomer synthesis; inorganic polymers, phosphazene polymers. *Mailing Add:* Firestone Tire & Rubber Co Akron OH 44317

TATE, FRED ALONZO, organic chemistry, information science, deceased

TATE, JAMES LEROY, JR, ecology, see previous edition

TATE, JOHN T, b Minneapolis, Minn, Mar 13, 25; m 56; c 3. MATHEMATICS. *Educ:* Harvard Univ, BA, 46; Princeton Univ, PhD(math), 50. *Prof Exp:* PROF MATH, HARVARD UNIV, 60- *Honors & Awards:* Cole Prize, Am Math Soc, 56. *Mem:* Nat Acad Sci; Am Math Soc; Math Asn Am. *Res:* Algebra; algebraic number theory; diophantine algebraic geometry. *Mailing Add:* Dept of Math Harvard Univ Sci Ctr Cambridge MA 02138

TATE, LAURENCE GRAY, b Cambridge, Eng, Feb 10, 45; US citizen. INSECT TOXICOLOGY, INSECT PHYSIOLOGY. *Educ:* Limestone Col, BS, 66; Univ SC, MS, 68, PhD(biol), 71. *Prof Exp:* USPHS res assoc insect toxicol, NC State Univ, 71-74; asst prof, 74-77, ASSOC PROF BIOL, UNIV S ALA, 77- *Mem:* Sigma Xi. *Res:* Metabolism of xenobiotics in tissues of marine organisms; carbohydrate metabolism in insects. *Mailing Add:* Dept of Biol Sci Univ of S Ala Mobile AL 36688

TATE, R(OGER) W(ALLACE), b Chicago, Ill, Jan 31, 25; m 58; c 3. CHEMICAL ENGINEERING. *Educ:* Ill Inst Technol, BS, 48; Univ Wis, MS, 48, PhD(chem eng), 50. *Prof Exp:* Chem engr, Standard Oil Develop Co, NJ, 50-54; staff engr, Kearney & Trecker Corp, Wis, 54-57; DIR RES, DELAVAN CORP, 57- *Concurrent Pos:* Adj prof, Newark Col Eng, 51-53. *Mem:* Am Chem Soc; Am Inst Chem Engrs; Am Soc Testing & Mat. *Res:* Atomization and spray analysis; development of fuel injectors and spray nozzles. *Mailing Add:* Delavan Corp 811 Fourth St Des Moines IA 50265

TATE, ROBERT FLEMMING, b Oakland, Calif, Dec 15, 21. MATHEMATICAL STATISTICS. *Educ:* Univ Calif, AB, 44, PhD(math statist), 52; Univ NC, MS, 49. *Prof Exp:* Lectr, Univ Calif, 51-53; from instr to assoc prof math, Univ Wash, Seattle, 53-65; assoc prof, 65-67, PROF MATH, UNIV ORE, 67- *Concurrent Pos:* Mem, Math Inst & Inst Statist, Univ Vienna, 64. *Mem:* Sigma Xi; fel Inst Math Statist (assoc secy, 63-73); Am Statist Asn. *Res:* Theory of correlation and of estimation. *Mailing Add:* Dept Math Univ Ore Eugene OR 97403

TATE, ROBERT LEE, III, b Victoria, Tex, Dec 1, 44; m 71; c 2. SOIL MICROBIOLOGY. *Educ:* Univ Ariz, BS, 66, MS, 67; Univ Wis-Madison, PhD(bact), 70. *Prof Exp:* Scholar bact, Univ Calif, Los Angeles, 70-72, res assoc, Dept Agron, Cornell Univ, 72-75; asst prof microbiol, Agr Res & Educ Ctr, Univ Fla, 75-80, assoc prof, 80-81; ASST PROF SOIL MICROBIOL, DEPT SOILS & CROPS, RUTGERS UNIV, 81- *Mem:* Am Soc Microbiol; Soil Sci Soc Am; Am Soc Agron. *Res:* Microbial interactions with soil organic matter; reactions involved with the subsidence of these soils and the products produced during this oxidation; denitrification and soil factors controlling the denitrifier; nitrification; soil enzymes. *Mailing Add:* Dept Soils & Crops Cook Col PO Box 231 Rutgers Univ New Brunswick NJ 08903

TATELMAN, MAURICE, b Omaha, Nebr, Dec 6, 17; m 61; c 2. MEDICINE. *Educ:* Univ Nebr, AB, 40, MD, 42. *Prof Exp:* From asst prof to assoc prof, 50-61, PROF RADIOL, COL MED, WAYNE STATE UNIV, 61- *Concurrent Pos:* Chmn dept radiol, Sinai Hosp Detroit, 68-; consult, Wayne County Gen Hosp, Darborn Vet Admin Hosp, Detroit Mem Hosp & Highland Park Gen Hosp. *Mem:* Fel Am Col Radiol; Am Roentgen Ray Soc; Radiol Soc NAm; sr mem Am Soc Neuroradiol; Am Soc Head & Neck Radiol. *Res:* Clinical diagnostic radiology; neuroradiology. *Mailing Add:* 6767 W Outer Dr Detroit MI 48235

TATEOSIAN, LOUIS HAGOP, b Chelsea, Mass, Mar 23, 37; m 62; c 2. DENTAL MATERIALS. *Educ:* Case Western Reserve Univ, BS, 59; Univ Md, MS, 62. *Prof Exp:* Res chemist, Naval Res Lab, 62-65; CHIEF CHEMIST, DENTSPLY INT, INC, 65- *Mem:* Am Chem Soc; Am Asn Dent Res; Soc Plastic Engrs. *Res:* Fluorinated epoxy resin synthesis; acrylic polymer preparation; adhesives and coatings; radiation polymerization; hydrogels. *Mailing Add:* Cent Res Lab Dentsply Int Inc 570 W College Ave PO Box 872 York PA 17405

TATINI, SITA RAMAYYA, b Mortha, India, Oct 6, 35; m 54; c 3. MICROBIOLOGY, FOOD SCIENCE. *Educ:* Univ Madras, BVSc, 57; Univ Minn, MS, 66, PhD(food sci & indust), 69. *Prof Exp:* Vet asst surgeon, Andhra Animal Husb Dept, State of Andhra Pradesh, India, 58-61; res fel, 69, NIH-Food & Drug Admin res grant, 71-74, asst prof food microbiol, 69-77, PROF FOOD SCI & NUTRIT, UNIV MINN, ST PAUL, 77- *Mem:* AAAS; Inst Food Technol; Am Soc Microbiol; Am Dairy Sci Asn; Int Asn Milk, Food & Environ Sanit. *Res:* Growth, survival and production of enterotoxins by staphylococci in food products; developing rapid methods for assessment of psychrophilic bacteria in milk. *Mailing Add:* Dept of Food Sci & Nutrit Univ of Minn St Paul MN 55101

TATLOW, RICHARD H(ENRY), III, b Denver, Colo, May 27, 06; m 32; c 2. CIVIL ENGINEERING. *Educ:* Univ Colo, BS, 27, CE, 32. *Prof Exp:* Jr hwy engr, US Bur Pub Rds, DC, 27-29; engr, Harrington & Cortelyou, Mo, 29-34, partner, DC, 34-41; CHMN, ABBOTT, MERKT & CO, 46-, CHMN BD, ABBOTT, MERKT INT INC, 72- *Concurrent Pos:* Mem comt supersonic transport-sonic boom, Nat Acad Sci, 64; mem, Mayor's Sci & Tech Adv Comt, New York, 66-; dir, NUS Corp. *Mem:* Nat Acad Eng; Am Soc Civil Engrs (pres, 68); Am Soc Mech Engrs; Am Inst Consult Engrs. *Res:* Structural engineering; design of industrial buildings and department stores. *Mailing Add:* 630 Third Ave New York NY 10017

TATOMER, HARRY NICHOLAS, b Jersey City, NJ, Feb 13, 13; m 40; c 4. CHEMICAL ENGINERRING. *Educ:* Univ Ill, BS, 37. *Prof Exp:* Develop engr, Olin Mathieson Chem Corp, 37-40, asst proj supvr, 40-43, proj supvr, 43-46, mgr pilot opers, 46-52, process develop, 52-57, tech asst prod, Energy Div, 57-60; tech asst prod, Chem Div, Union Carbide Corp, 60-64, admin assoc to dir rocket propulsion & staff coordr res & develop admin, South Charleston Tech Ctr, 64-77, chem eng, 77-78; RETIRED. *Mem:* Am Chem Soc; Am Inst Chem Engrs. *Res:* Pilot plant development of sodium chlorite; chlorine dioxide generation; sodium amalgam processes; hydrazine and derivatives; boron hydrides; high energy fuels; rocket propellants; government contract administration; research administration. *Mailing Add:* 2018 Weberwood Dr Charleston WV 25303

TATOR, CHARLES HASKELL, b Toronto, Ont, Aug 24, 36; m 60; c 2. NEUROSURGERY. *Educ:* Univ Toronto, MD, 61, MA, 63, PhD(neuropath), 65. *Prof Exp:* From assoc to asst prof, 69-74, assoc prof, 74-80, PROF SURG, UNIV TORONTO, 80-; SURGEON, DIV NEUROSURG, SUNNYBROOK MED CTR, 69- *Res:* Brain tumor research and spinal cord injury research. *Mailing Add:* Div of Neurosurg Sunnybrook Med Ctr 2075 Bayview Ave Toronto ON M4N 3M5 Can

TATRO, CLEMENT A(USTIN), b Kingman Co, Kans, May 16, 24; m 46; c 2. MECHANICS. *Educ:* Friends Univ, BA, 49; Purdue Univ, MS, 51, PhD(physics), 56. *Prof Exp:* Res asst, Purdue Univ, 49-56; asst prof appl mech, Mich State Univ, 56-60, assoc prof metall, mech & mat sci, 60-62; prof mech eng, Tulane Univ, 62-66; head mat eng sect, Dept Mech Eng, 66-77, RES & ADVAN DEVELOP ENGR, LAWRENCE LIVERMORE LAB, UNIV CALIF, 77- *Mem:* Am Soc Testing & Mat; Am Phys Soc; Soc Exp Stress Anal; Am Soc Nondestructive Testing; Inst Environ Sci (pres, 80-81). *Res:* Acoustic emission; wave propagation in solids; experimental stress analysis; material dynamics. *Mailing Add:* Lawrence Livermore Lab PO Box 808 Livermore CA 94550

TATRO, MAHLON CHARLES, b Enosburg Falls, Vt, Aug 29, 22; m 52; c 3. ENVIRONMENTAL SCIENCES. *Educ:* Univ Mo, BA, 49; Univ Mass, MS, 51, PhD(food tech), 52. *Prof Exp:* Control chemist, Linde Air Prod Co Div, Union Carbide & Carbon Chem Co, 48-49; anal chemist, State Bur Labs, Vt, 52-54; chief chemist, Loma Linda Food Co, Calif, 54-56; agr chemist, Agr & Natural Resources Div, Int Coop Admin, 56-58, agr prog officer, 58-62; res assoc prof, Natural Resources Inst, Univ Md & dir seafood processing lab, 63-74; ASSOC PROF, CTR ENVIRON & ESTUARINE STUDIES, UNIV MD, 74- *Concurrent Pos:* Lab dir, Edward W McCready Mem Hosp, 68-74. *Res:* Studies on home sewage disposal systems utilizing Evapo-transpiration beds including modifications of same; chemical characteristics of ground water from the Pleistoncene aquifer. *Mailing Add:* Box 775 Univ of Md Ctr Environ & Estuarine Studies Cambridge MD 21613

TATRO, PETER RICHARD, b Winthrop, Mass, Jan 20, 36; m 57; c 3. PHYSICAL OCEANOGRAPHY, ACOUSTICS. *Educ:* Ga Inst Technol, BME, 57; Mass Inst Technol, PhD(oceanog), 66. *Prof Exp:* Res oceanogr, Fleet Numerical Weather Ctr, Calif, 66-69; spec asst for ocean sci, Off Naval Res, Washington, DC, 69-72, head, Acoust Environ Support Detachment, Arlington, 72-75, spec asst oceanogr of the Navy, 75-76; mgr, Ocean Sci Div, 77-80, VPRES, OCEAN SCI DEPT, SCI APPLICATIONS INC, MCLEAN, VA, 80- *Concurrent Pos:* Consult, Int Decade Ocean Explor, NSF, 72-75. *Honors & Awards:* Navy Achievement Medal; Navy Expeditionary Medal. *Res:* Application of advanced digital technology to the problem of predicting the acoustic characteristics of the oceans. *Mailing Add:* 2604 Ryegate Lane Alexandria VA 22308

TATSUMOTO, MITSUNOBU, b Junsho, Japan, Mar 19, 23; m 48; c 2. GEOCHEMISTRY, GEOCHRONOLOGY. *Educ:* Tokyo Bunrika Univ, BS, 48, DSc(inorg chem), 57. *Hon Degrees:* Dr, Univ Paris VII, 75. *Prof Exp:* Res asst chem, Tokyo Kyoiku Univ, 48-57, lectr, 57; res fel oceanog, Scripps Inst, Calif, 57-58; Welch Found fel, 59; res fel oceanog, Tex A&M Univ, 59; res fel geochem, Calif Inst Technol, 59-62; CHEMIST, US GEOL SURV, 62- *Concurrent Pos:* Vis prof, Inst Geophys, Univ Paris VI, 71 & 74; adj prof dept geol sci, Univ Rochester, NY, 78- *Mem:* Geochem Soc; Am Geophys Union. *Res:* Isotope geochemistry; natural radioactivity; meteorite and lunar chronology; marine geochemistry. *Mailing Add:* Isotope Geol Br US Geol Surv MS 963 Box 25046 Denver CO 80225

TATTAR, TERRY ALAN, b Port Chester, NY, May 9, 43; m 69; c 2. FOREST PATHOLOGY, SHADE TREE PATHOLOGY. *Educ:* Northeastern Univ, BA, 67; Univ New Hampshire, PhD(bot), 71. *Prof Exp:* Plant pathologist forest path, USDA Forest Serv, 71-73; asst prof, 73-79, ASSOC PROF FOREST PATH, UNIV MASS, 79- *Mem:* Am Phytopath Soc; Sigma Xi. *Res:* Determining the effects of vascular wilt pathogens on trees; developing diagnostic techniques for early detection of diseases of trees. *Mailing Add:* Shade Tree Lab Univ Mass Amherst MA 01003

TATTER, DOROTHY, b Chicago, Ill, Apr 11, 22; m 49; c 3. MEDICINE. *Educ:* Rosary Col, BS, 43; Univ Ill, MD, 47. *Prof Exp:* From instr to asst prof, 49-70, ASSOC PROF PATH, SCH MED, UNIV SOUTHERN CALIF, 70- *Concurrent Pos:* Resident path, Los Angeles County Gen Hosp, 49-52, head physician, Autopsy Dept Labs, 52- *Mem:* AMA. *Res:* Pathology. *Mailing Add:* Dept Labs & Path Univ of Southern Calif Med Ctr Los Angeles CA 90033

TATTERSALL, IAN MICHAEL, b Paignton, Devon, Eng, May 10, 45. PHYSICAL ANTHROPOLOGY, PRIMATOLOGY. *Educ:* Cambridge Univ, BA, 67, MA, 70; Yale Univ, MPhil, 70, PhD(geol), 71. *Prof Exp:* Asst cur, 71-76, assoc cur, 76-81, CUR PHYS ANTHROP, AM MUS NATURAL HIST, 81- *Concurrent Pos:* Vis lectr, Grad Fac, New Sch Social Res, 71-72; adj asst prof, Lehman Col, City Univ New York, 71-74; adj assoc prof, Columbia Univ, 78-79. *Mem:* Am Asn Phys Anthropologists; Soc Vert Paleont; Am Soc Primatology; Int Primatology Soc; AAAS. *Res:* Evolution, functional anatomy, ecology and behavior of the primates, particularly of the Malagasy lemurs; human evolution; primate systematics; evolutionary theory in relation to phylogenetic reconstruction and other systematic applications. *Mailing Add:* Dept Anthrop Am Mus Natural Hist Cent Park W at 79th St New York NY 10024

TATUM, CHARLES MARIS, b Philadelphia, Pa, Oct 10, 47; m 70; c 2. BIOCHEMISTRY, ORGANIC CHEMISTRY. *Educ:* Amherst Col, BA, 69; Pa State Univ, PhD(org chem), 76. *Prof Exp:* Biochemist clin chem, Gen Rose Mem Hosp, 70-72; asst prof chem, Middlebury Col, 76-79; SR SCIENTIST, ROHM & HAAS CO, 79- *Mem:* Am Chem Soc. *Res:* Strategic planning, agricultural applications of genetic engineering and pesticide biochemistry. *Mailing Add:* Res Labs Rohm & Haas Co Spring House PA 19477

TATUM, F(INLEY) W(OMACK), b Kent, Tex, July 9, 14; m 38; c 1. ELECTRICAL ENGINEERING. *Educ:* Columbia Univ, BSEE, 35, MSEE, 46; Tex A&M Univ, PhD(elec eng), 63. *Prof Exp:* Eng supvr, Am Dist Tel Co, NY, 35-47; assoc prof elec eng, Southern Methodist Univ, 47-51, chmn dept, 47-74, prof, 51-80; PROF ELEC ENG, UNIV TEX, ARLINGTON, 80- *Concurrent Pos:* Mem tech staff, Bell Tel Labs, Inc, 52-54. *Mem:* Am Soc Eng Educ; Nat Soc Prof Engrs; fel Inst Elec & Electronics Engrs. *Res:* Switching and digital systems; control systems. *Mailing Add:* Dept Elec Eng Univ Tex Box 19016 Arlington TX 76019

TATUM, FREEMAN A(RTHUR), b Mansfield, La, Apr 8, 21; m 46. PHYSICAL ELECTRONICS, MATHEMATICS. *Educ:* Agr & Mech Col, Tex, BS, 48, MS, 49, PhD, 51. *Prof Exp:* Instr physics & math, Kilgore Col, 41-42; asst mass spectrometry, Res Found, Agr & Mech Col, Tex, 48-49; res engr, Douglas Aircraft Co, 51-55; phys scientist, Rand Corp, 55-78; RETIRED. *Concurrent Pos:* Consult, Rand Corp, 78- *Res:* Analysis of military weapons systems, especially electronic and electronic countermeasure aspects of warfare. *Mailing Add:* 1083 Vista Grande Dr Hemet CA 92343

TATUM, JAMES PATRICK, b Dallas, Tex, July 6, 38. PHYSICAL CHEMISTRY. *Educ:* Rice Univ, BA, 61; Fla State Univ, PhD(phys chem), 66. *Prof Exp:* Res assoc chem, Univ Ill, 66-68; asst prof, 68-77, ASSOC PROF CHEM, IND STATE UNIV, TERRE HAUTE, 77- *Concurrent Pos:* Vis prof quantum theory proj, Univ Fla, Gainesville, 78. *Mem:* Am Phys Soc. *Res:* Theoretical chemistry. *Mailing Add:* Dept Chem Ind State Univ Terre Haute IN 47809

TATUM, WILLIAM EARL, b Ft Payne, Ala, Sept 13, 33; m 52; c 4. ORGANIC CHEMISTRY. *Educ:* Chattanooga Univ, BS, 55; Univ Tenn, PhD(chem), 58. *Prof Exp:* Res chemist, Exp Sta, 58-61, tech rep, Venture Develop Sect, 61-63, staff scientist, Yerkes Res Lab, 63-64, res supvr, Circleville Res Lab, Ohio, 64-67, develop supvr, Circleville Plant, 67-68, tech supt, Florence Plant, SC, 68-70, cellophane prod mgr, Del, 70-71, dir prod & tech div, 71-73, venture mgr, 73-74, dir specialty mkt div, 75-76, dir packaging films div, 76-78, dir, Fluoropolymers Div, Polymer Prod Dept, 78-80, dir environ affairs, 80-81, DIR SAFETY, HEALTH & ENVIRON AFFAIRS, E I DU PONT DE NEMOURS & CO INC, DEL, 81-, GEN MGR, ENERGY & MAT DEPT, 81- *Mem:* Am Chem Soc; Am Phys Soc; Am Inst Chem Engrs. *Res:* Polymer chemistry and engineering; synthetic organic chemistry. *Mailing Add:* Energy & Mat Dept E I du Pont de Nemours & Co Inc Wilmington DE 19898

TAUB, ABRAHAM, b New York, NY, Sept 21, 01. PHARMACEUTICAL CHEMISTRY. *Educ:* Columbia Univ, BS, 22, AM, 27. *Hon Degrees:* ScD, Columbia Univ, 76. *Prof Exp:* From instr to prof chem, 22-65, distinguished serv prof, 65-69, EMER DISTINGUISHED SERV PROF CHEM, COL PHARMACEUT SCI, COLUMBIA UNIV, 69- *Concurrent Pos:* Asst, Revision Comt, US Pharmacopeia, 20-30; consult chemist, 22-; asst, Nat Formulary, 37; consult, Nat Asn Pharmaceut Mfrs, 70- *Honors & Awards:* Rusby Award, 62; Man of Year Award, Nat Asn Pharmaceut Mfrs, 72. *Mem:* AAAS; Am Chem Soc; Am Pharmaceut Asn; fel Am Inst Chem; NY Acad Sci. *Res:* Quantitative color standards; deterioration of medicinals; development of analytical methods; stability of parenteral solutions; chromatography; radioisotope tracer techniques. *Mailing Add:* 1080 Fifth Ave New York NY 10028

TAUB, ABRAHAM HASKEL, b Chicago, Ill, Feb 1, 11; m 33; c 3. MATHEMATICS. *Educ:* Univ Chicago, BS, 31; Princeton Univ, PhD(math physics), 35. *Prof Exp:* Asst, Princeton Univ, 34-35 & Inst Adv Study, 35-36 & 40-41; from instr to prof math, Univ Wash, Seattle, 36-48; res prof appl math, Univ Ill, Urbana, 48-64, head digital comput lab, 61-64; dir comput ctr, 64-68, prof, 64-78, EMER PROF MATH, UNIV CALIF, BERKELEY, 78- *Concurrent Pos:* Theoret physicist, Div 2, Nat Defense Res Comt, Princeton Univ, 42-45; mem, Guggenheim Post-Serv, 47-48 & Guggenheim fel, 53 & 58; mem, Appl Math Adv Coun, Nat Bur Stand, 49-54, chmn adv panel, Appl Math Div, 51-60; mem comt on training & res in math, Nat Res Coun, 52-54; mem rev comt, Appl Math Div, Argonne Nat Lab, 60-62. *Mem:* Fel AAAS (vpres, sect A, 68-69); Am Math Soc; fel Am Phys Soc; Math Asn Am; fel Am Acad Arts & Sci. *Res:* Relativity; interaction of shock waves; digital computers; numerical analysis. *Mailing Add:* Dept of Math Univ of Calif Berkeley CA 94720

TAUB, ARTHUR, b New York, NY, Jan 4, 32; m 63; c 1. NEUROPHYSIOLOGY, NEUROLOGY. *Educ:* Yeshiva Univ, BA, 52; Mass Inst Technol, SM, 53, PhD(neurophysiol), 64; Yale Univ, MD, 57; Am Bd Psychiat Neurol, dipl, 75. *Prof Exp:* NIH fel neurophysiol, Mass Inst Technol, 64-66, res assoc, 66-68; dir neurosurg res lab, 69-75, dir pain clin, 71-75, asst prof, 68-72, assoc prof neurophysiol & neurol, 72-75, PROF CLIN ANESTHESIOL & DIR SECT STUDY & TREATMENT OF PAIN, DEPT ANESTHESIOL, SCH MED, YALE UNIV, 75-, CLIN PROF ANESTHESIOL, 76- *Concurrent Pos:* NIH res career develop award, Mass Inst Technol & Yale Univ, 66-73; resident neurol, Sch Med, Yale Univ, 69-72; assoc neurologist, Yale New Haven Hosp, 71-75, attend neurologist, 75-; Royal Soc Med Found traveling fel, UK, 72. *Mem:* AAAS; Am Acad Neurol; Sigma Xi; Soc Neurosci; Int Asn Study Pain. *Res:* Pain; application of basic scientific approach to modalities for control; neuropharmacology; computer simulation; clinical control by medical and surgical means; anesthesiology. *Mailing Add:* 60 Temple St New Haven CT 06510

TAUB, DAVID, b New York, NY, Nov 13, 19; m 44; c 2. ORGANIC CHEMISTRY. *Educ:* City Col New York, BS, 40; Harvard Univ, AM, 46, PhD, 50. *Prof Exp:* Chemist, Manhattan Proj, Kellex Corp, 42-46; USPHS fel, Harvard Univ, 49-51; sr chemist, 51-65, sect head process res, 65-68, sr res fel, 68-77, SR INVESTR, MERCK SHARP & DOHME RES LABS, 77- *Mem:* Am Chem Soc; Royal Soc Chem. *Res:* Organic synthesis; natural products; synthetic medicinals. *Mailing Add:* Merck Sharp & Dohme Res Labs Rahway NJ 07065

TAUB, EDWARD, b Brooklyn, NY, Oct 22, 31; m 59. PHYSIOLOGICAL PSYCHOLOGY. *Educ:* Brooklyn Col, BA, 53; Columbia Univ, MA, 59; NY Univ, PhD(psychol), 70. *Prof Exp:* Res asst neuropsychol, Columbia Univ, 56; res asst, Dept Exp Neurol, Jewish Chronic Dis Hosp, 57-60, res assoc, 60-68; CHIEF, BEHAV BIOL CTR, INST BEHAV RES, 68- *Concurrent Pos:* Asst prof, Sch Med, Johns Hopkins Univ, 70- *Mem:* Fel Am Psychol Asn; Soc Neurosci; Biofeedback Res Soc; Psychonomic Soc; Am Physiol Soc. *Res:* The role of somatosensory feedback and spinal reflexes in movement and learning; fetal surgery; transcendental meditation as a therapy for alcoholism; biofeedback and self-regulation of human hand temperature. *Mailing Add:* Behav Biol Ctr Inst Behav Res 2429 Linden Lane Silver Spring MD 20910

TAUB, FRIEDA B, b Newark, NJ, Oct 11, 34; m 54; c 1. ECOLOGY, POLLUTION. *Educ:* Rutgers Univ, BA, 55, MA, 57, PhD(zool), 59. *Prof Exp:* Fisheries biologist, 59-61, instr food sci, 61-62, from res asst prof to res assoc prof, 62-71, PROF FISHERIES, COL FISHERIES, UNIV WASH, 71- *Concurrent Pos:* Res grants, 61-78. *Mem:* Fel AAAS; Ecol Soc Am; Am Soc Limnol & Oceanog; Am Soc Ichthyologists & Herpetologists; Am Fisheries Soc. *Res:* Aquatic food chains; ecosystems. *Mailing Add:* Col of Fisheries WH-10 Univ of Wash Seattle WA 98195

TAUB, HERBERT, b New York, NY, Dec 23, 18; m 43; c 3. ELECTRICAL ENGINEERING. *Educ:* City Col New York, BS, 40; Columbia Univ, MA, 43, PhD, 49. *Prof Exp:* Tutor, Dept Physics, City Col New York, 40-43; elec engr, Nat Defense Res Proj, Princeton Univ, 43-44; tutor, 44-46, from instr to assoc prof, 47-59, PROF ELEC ENG, CITY COL NEW YORK, 60- *Concurrent Pos:* Elec engr, Allen B Du Mont, Inc, NJ, 41; consult, Gen Tel & Electronics, Inc, NY, 69-70 & Bell Labs, 72- *Mem:* Sr mem Inst Elec & Electronics Engrs; Sigma Xi. *Res:* Determination of nuclear magnetic moments by molecular beam methods; electronics, especially pulse circuitry. *Mailing Add:* Dept Elec Eng Convent Ave & 139th St New York NY 10031

TAUB, IRWIN A(LLEN), b Brooklyn, NY, July 18, 34; m 59; c 2. FOOD STABILITY, FOOD IRRADIATION. *Educ:* Queens Col, NY, BS, 55; Univ Minn, PhD(inorg chem), 61. *Prof Exp:* Resident res assoc, Argonne Nat Lab, 61-63; fel, Carnegie-Mellon Univ, 63-69; supvry chemist & chief, Cobalt Br, Radiation Sources Div, 69-80, CHIEF PLANT PROD GROUP, FOOD TECHNOL DIV, US NATICK RES & DEVELOP LABS, 80- *Mem:* Am Chem Soc; Sigma Xi. *Res:* Radiation chemistry; kinetics and spectra of free radicals and intermediates by pulse radiolysis; food irradiation; inorganic fast reactions; protein and lipid radicals; myoglobin radiolysis; autoxidation; vitamin, protein and lipid stability; reactions in frozen state. *Mailing Add:* 24 Oak Crest Dr Framingham MA 01701

TAUB, JESSE J, b New York, NY, Apr 27, 27; m 55; c 3. ELECTRICAL ENGINEERING, PHYSICS. *Educ:* City Col New York, BEE, 48; Polytech Inst Brooklyn, MEE, 49. *Prof Exp:* Engr, US Naval Mat Lab, 49-51, group leader, 51-55; engr, 55-58, group leader, 58, sect head, 58-60, dept consult, 60-66, div consult, 66-75, CHIEF SCIENTIST, AIL DIV, CUTLER HAMMER INC, 75- *Concurrent Pos:* Mem staff, Grad Sch, City Col New York, 59-61. *Mem:* Fel Inst Elec & Electronics Engrs. *Res:* Microwave device development; millimeter and submillimeter techniques; mixers and mixer diodes; multimode power measurements; microwave network synthesis. *Mailing Add:* AIL Div Walt Whitman Rd Melville NY 11746

TAUB, JOHN MARCUS, b Chicago, Ill, July 26, 47. PSYCHOPHYSIOLOGY. *Educ:* Univ Calif, Santa Cruz, AB, 69, MS & PhD(biopsychol), 72. *Prof Exp:* Res biophysicist, Univ Calif, Santa Cruz, 72-73; fel neurosci, Brain Res Inst, Univ Calif, Los Angeles, 73-75; dir, Sleep & Dream Lab & asst prof psychiat & physiol, Sch Med, Univ Va, 75-80; MEM FAC, SLEEP & PERFORMANCE RES LAB, ST LOUIS UNIV, 80- *Concurrent Pos:* NIH res fel, 73. *Mem:* AAAS; Asn Psychophysiol Study Sleep; Soc Neurosci. *Res:* Investigations on the behavioral and psychophysiological effects of acute and chronic variations in the length and time of sleep in young adults. *Mailing Add:* Sleep & Performance Res Lab St Louis Univ 221 N Grand Blvd St Louis MO 63103

TAUB, ROBERT NORMAN, b Brooklyn, NY, Apr 21, 36; m 68; c 1. ONCOLOGY, HEMATOLOGY. *Educ:* Yeshiva Univ, AB, 57; Yale Univ, MD, 61; Univ London, PhD(biol), 69. *Prof Exp:* Intern med, New Eng Med Ctr Hosps, Boston, 61-62; intern path, Sch Med, Yale Univ, 62-63; clin & res fel hemat, New Eng Med Ctr Hosps, 63-65, asst resident med, 65-66; NIH res fel immunol, Nat Inst Med Res, London, 66-68; assoc hemat, Mt Sinai Sch Med, 68-69, asst prof med, 69-72, assoc prof med, 72-76, head transplantation immunol lab, Mt Sinai Hosp, 70-76; prof & chmn, Med Col Va, Richmond, 76-81, assoc dir, Va Commonwealth Univ Cancer Ctr, 77-81; PROF CLIN MED, COL PHYSICIANS & SURGEONS, COLUMBIA UNIV, 81- *Concurrent Pos:* Res fel path, Sch Med, Yale Univ, 62-63; Leukemia Soc Am scholar award, 68-73; attend physician, Mt Sinai Hosp, 69-70; USPHS res career develop award, 75-; Am Cancer Soc prof clin oncol, 77-; co-dir, Columbia Comprehensive Cancer Ctr, 81- *Honors & Awards:* Emil Conason Mem Res Award, Mt Sinai Sch Med, 71. *Mem:* Transplantation Soc; Am Soc Clin Invest; Am Soc Hemat; Am Asn Immunologists; Am Soc Exp Path. *Res:* Cancer cell biology; immunology of cancer and leukemia. *Mailing Add:* Col Physicians & Surgeons Columbia Univ New York NY 10027

TAUB, STEPHEN ROBERT, b Jamaica, NY, Nov 30, 33; m 63; c 2. GENETICS. *Educ:* Rochester Univ, AB, 55; Univ Ind, PhD(zool), 60. *Prof Exp:* Instr biol, Harvard Univ, 60-63; asst prof, Princeton Univ, 63-69; from asst prof to assoc prof, Richmond Col, City Univ New York, 69-74; chmn dept, 74-77, PROF BIOL, GEORGE MASON UNIV, FAIRFAX, 74- *Mem:* AAAS; Genetics Soc Am; Am Soc Cell Biol. *Res:* Extra-chromosomal and developmental genetics. *Mailing Add:* Dept of Biol George Mason Univ Fairfax VA 22030

TAUBE, HENRY, b Neudorf, Sask, Nov 30, 15; nat US; m 40, 52; m 4. INORGANIC CHEMISTRY. *Educ:* Univ Sask, BS, 35, MS, 37; Univ Calif, PhD(chem), 40. *Prof Exp:* Instr chem, Univ Calif, 40-41; from instr to asst prof, Cornell Univ, 41-46; res assoc, Nat Defense Res Comt, 44-45; from asst prof to prof chem, Univ Chicago, 46-61, chmn dept, 55-59; chmn dept, 72-74, PROF CHEM, STANFORD UNIV, 61- *Concurrent Pos:* Guggenheim fel, 49 & 55. *Honors & Awards:* Award, Am Chem Soc, 55, Howe Award, 60; Chandler Award, Columbia Univ, 64; Kirkwood Award, Yale Univ & Am Chem Soc, 66, Monsanto Co, 81; Nat Medal Sci, 77. *Mem:* Nat Acad Sci; Am Chem Soc; Am Acad Arts & Sci. *Res:* Chemistry of complex ions; new aquo ions, nitrogen as a ligand; mechanism of electron transfer; mixed valence molecules. *Mailing Add:* Dept of Chem Stanford Univ Stanford CA 94305

TAUBENECK, WILLIAM HARRIS, b Marshall, Ill, Aug 27, 33. PETROLOGY. *Educ:* Ore State Col, BS, 49, MS, 50; Columbia Univ, PhD(geol), 55. *Prof Exp:* From instr to assoc prof, 51-65, PROF GEOL, ORE STATE UNIV, 65- *Concurrent Pos:* NSF fel, 59-61; Guggenheim fel, 63-64. *Mem:* AAAS; Geol Soc Am; Mineral Soc Am. *Res:* Layering in igneous rocks; petrogenesis of granite rocks; Columbia River basalt; thermal metamorphism; rock forming minerals; general geology of northeastern Oregon and western Idaho; evolution of the Pacific Northwest. *Mailing Add:* Dept of Geol Ore State Univ Corvallis OR 97331

TAUBER, ARTHUR, b New York, NY, June 2, 28; m 56; c 3. CHEMISTRY, MAGNETISM. *Educ:* NY Univ, BA, 51, MA, 52; Polytech Inst Brooklyn, MS, 59, PhD, 72. *Prof Exp:* Phys chemist, Sig Corps Eng Labs, 52-56, res phys scientist, Electronics Res & Develop Labs, 56-63, RES PHYS SCIENTIST, ELECTRONICS COMMAND, US ARMY, 63- *Honors & Awards:* Meritorious Civilian Serv Medal, US Dept Army, 63. *Mem:* Am Chem Soc; Inst Elec & Electronic Engrs; Am Crystallog Asn; Am Asn Crystal Growth. *Res:* Synthesize and characterize polycrystalline and single crystal microwave/millimeter wave ferrites; samarium cobalt permanent magnets; amorphous magnetics; intermetallic hydrogen absorbers. *Mailing Add:* US Army Electronics 927 Woodgate Ave Elberon Long Branch NJ 07740

TAUBER, GERALD ERICH, b Vienna, Austria, Oct 31, 22; nat US; m 56; c 3. THEORETICAL PHYSICS. *Educ:* Univ Toronto, BA, 46; Univ Minn, MA, 47, PhD(theoret physics), 51. *Prof Exp:* Asst physics, Univ Minn, 46-50; lectr, McMaster Univ, 50-52; fel, Nat Res Coun Can, 52-54; from asst prof to prof physics, Case Western Reserve Univ, 54-68; vis prof, 65-68, PROF PHYSICS, TEL AVIV UNIV, 68- *Concurrent Pos:* Vis prof, Nat Res Coun Can, 55; consult, Franklin Inst, 56-; vis prof, Israel Inst Technol, 59-60. *Mem:* Am Phys Soc; Can Asn Physicists; Israeli Phys Soc; Int Soc Gen Relativity & Gravitation. *Res:* Independent particle model in nuclear physics; atomic physics; cosmology; astrophysics; general relativity; cosmological models; field theory; transport phenomena; elementary particles in relativity; collective motion; relativistic astrophysics. *Mailing Add:* Dept of Phys & Astron Tel Aviv Univ Tel Aviv Israel

TAUBER, MAURICE JESSE, b Cracow, Can, Oct 21, 37; m 66; c 3. ENTOMOLOGY. *Educ:* Univ Man, BS, 58, MS, 59; Univ Calif, Berkeley, PhD, 66. *Prof Exp:* Asst mgr, Tauber, Good & Assocs, 57-59, gen mgr, 61-62; PROF ENTOM, CORNELL UNIV, 66-, CHMN DEPT, 81- *Mem:* Fel AAAS; Am Soc Zool; Animal Behav Soc; Ecol Soc Am; Am Inst Biol Sci. *Res:* Insect behavior; biological control; insect phenology. *Mailing Add:* Dept of Entomol Cornell Univ Ithaca NY 14853

TAUBER, SELMO, b Shanghai, China, Aug 24, 20; nat US; m 50; c 1. APPLIED MATHEMATICS. *Educ:* Beirut Sch Eng, Lebanon, dipl, 43; Univ Lyons, France, Lic es sc, 47; Univ Vienna, Austria, DrPhil, 50. *Prof Exp:* Head sci dept, High Sch, Lebanon, 51-55; design engr, 56-57; assoc prof, 57-63, PROF MATH, PORTLAND STATE UNIV, 63- *Concurrent Pos:* From instr to asst prof, Univ Kans, 57-59. *Mem:* Am Math Soc; Soc Indust & Appl Math; Math Asn Am. *Res:* Engineering structural problems; finite differences; differential equations; combinatorial analysis; system analysis; mathematical models in air pollution; mathematical models in physiology. *Mailing Add:* Dept of Math Portland State Univ Portland OR 97207

TAUBERT, KATHRYN ANNE, b Lufkin, Tex, Jan 3, 45. CARDIOVASCULAR PHYSIOLOGY. *Educ:* Stephen F Austin State Univ, BS, 65, MS, 66; Univ Tex Southwestern Med Sch, PhD(physiol), 75. *Prof Exp:* Res asst cardiol, Univ Tex Southwestern Med Sch, 66-68; physiologist, Dallas Vet Admin Hosp, 68-75; instr, Univ Tex Southwestern Med Sch, 75-77; asst prof physiol, Univ Calif, Riverside, 77-80; ASSOC PROF PHYSIOL & PHARMACOL, SCH PHARM, UNIV PAC, 80- *Concurrent Pos:* Fel, Univ Tex Health Sci Ctr, 75; NIH investr, Univ Calif, Riverside, 77-80; prin investr, Calif Heart Asn, 78-81. *Mem:* Am Heart Asn; Am Fedn Clin Res; Am Physiol Soc; Int Soc Heart Res. *Res:* Actions of cardiac glycosides on the heart, especially in circumstances similar to those seen in patients with ischemic heart disease or myocardial infarctions; effects of hypertension on cardiac muscle mechanics. *Mailing Add:* Univ Pac Sch Med 751 Brookside Rd Stockton CA 95207

TAUBLER, JAMES H, b Cokeville, Pa, Mar 30, 35; m 59; c 1. MICROBIOLOGY. *Educ:* St Vincent Col, BA, 57; Cath Univ, MS, 59, PhD(microbiol), 65. *Prof Exp:* Microbiologist, Philadelphia Gen Hosp, 59-69; asst prof, 69-71, PROF BIOL, ST VINCENT COL, 71- *Concurrent Pos:* Lectr, Holy Family Col, Pa, 66-; dir, Delmont Labs, Swarthmore, 66-; Environ Protection Agency grant, 75-77. *Mem:* AAAS; Am Soc Microbiol; Brit Soc Gen Microbiol. *Res:* Staphylococcal alpha toxin and its relationship to pathogenesis; delayed hypersensitivity and its effects in staphylococcal infections. *Mailing Add:* Dept of Biol St Vincent Col Latrobe PA 15650

TAUBMAN, MARTIN ARNOLD, b New York, NY, July 10, 40; m 65; c 1. IMMUNOLOGY, ORAL BIOLOGY. *Educ:* Brooklyn Col, BS, 61; Columbia Univ, DDS, 65; State Univ NY Buffalo, PhD(oral biol), 70. *Prof Exp:* Sr staff mem & head immunol dept, Forsyth Dent Ctr, 70-76; asst clin prof, 76-80, ASSOC CLIN PROF, DEPT ORAL BIOL & PATHOPHYSIOL, HARVARD UNIV SCH DENT MED, BOSTON, 80- & HEAD, IMMUNOL DEPT, FORSYTH DENT CTR, 70- *Concurrent Pos:* Nat Inst Dent Res grant, Forsyth Dent Ctr, 72-, NIH career develop award, 72-77. *Mem:* AAAS; Am Asn Immunologists; Int Asn Dent Res. *Res:* Secretory immunoglobulins; effect of secretory antibodies on oral microorganisms. *Mailing Add:* Forsyth Dent Ctr 140 Fenway Boston MA 02115

TAUBMAN, ROBERT EDWARD, b New York, NY, Jan 12, 21; m 43; c 3. PSYCHIATRY, PSYCHOLOGY. *Educ:* City Col New York, BA, 41; Columbia Univ, MS, 42, PhD(psychol), 48; Univ Nebr, MD, 60. *Prof Exp:* Chief psychol serv, Hastings State Hosp, Nebr, 52-56; resident physician psychiat, Ore State Hosp, Salem, 61-64; assoc prof, 64-70, PROF PSYCHIAT, MED SCH, UNIV ORE, 70- *Concurrent Pos:* NIMH fel ment retardation, Letchworth Village, Thiells, NY, 62; consult, Ore Fairview Home, Div Voc Rehab, Marion County Juv Dept, 62-64; pvt pract, 64-; attend physician, Vet Admin Hosp, Portland, Ore, 64-; psychiat dir, Physicians Inst, Ore Acad Family Physicians, 65- *Mem:* Am Pyschiat Asn; AMA; Soc Teachers Family Med. *Res:* Aging; dying; death; self growth among physicians and other professionals; emotional components of life-threatening diseases; psychiatry for non-psychiatric physicians. *Mailing Add:* Dept of Psychiat Ore Univ Med Sch Portland OR 97201

TAUBMAN, SHELDON BAILEY, b Cleveland, Ohio, Oct 8, 36; m 60; c 2. IMMUNOLOGY, PATHOLOGY. *Educ:* Northwestern Univ, Evanston, BA, 58; Case Western Reserve Univ, PhD(biochem), 64, MD, 66. *Prof Exp:* Asst prof path, 68-77, ASST PROF LAB MED, HEALTH CTR, UNIV CONN, 77- *Concurrent Pos:* NIH fel, 64-66, fel path, NY Univ, 66-68 & grant, Health Ctr, Univ Conn. *Mem:* AAAS; Harvey Soc; Am Asn Path & Bact. *Res:* Biochemical mechanisms of inflammation. *Mailing Add:* Dept of Lab Med Univ of Conn Health Ctr Farmington CT 06032

TAUC, JAN, b Pardubice, Czech, Apr 15, 22; m 47; c 2. SOLID STATE PHYSICS. *Educ:* Czech Inst Technol, IngDr, 49; Czech Acad Sci, DrSc(physics), 56; Charles Univ, Prague, RNDr, 56. *Prof Exp:* Scientist microwave res, Sci & Tech Res Inst, Tanvald & Prague, Czech, 49-52; dept head inst solid state physics, Czech Acad Sci, 53-69; prof exp physics, Charles Univ, Prague, 64-69, dir inst physics, 68-69; mem tech staff, Bell Labs, 69-70; PROF ENG & PHYSICS, BROWN UNIV, 70- *Concurrent Pos:* UNESCO res fel, Harvard Univ, 61-62; vis prof, Univ Paris, 69; consult, Bell Labs, 70-78; vis prof, Stanford Univ, 77; Alexander von Humboldt US sr scientist award, 81. *Honors & Awards:* Nat Prize for Sci, Czech Govt, 55 & 69; Isakson Prize, Am Phys Soc, 82. *Mem:* Fel Am Phys Soc; found mem Europ Phys Soc; fel AAAS. *Res:* Optical properties of crystalline and amorphous solids; electronic states; lattice vibrations; picoscond spectroscopy of amorphous semiconductors. *Mailing Add:* Div of Eng Brown Univ Providence RI 02912

TAUCHERT, THEODORE R, b New York, NY, Sept 3, 35; m 58; c 5. SOLID MECHANICS. *Educ:* Princeton Univ, BSE, 57; Yale Univ, MEng, 60, DEng(solid mech), 64. *Prof Exp:* Struct engr, Sikorsky Aircraft Div, United Aircraft Corp, 57-61; res assoc & lectr solid mech, Princeton Univ, 64-65, asst prof, 65-70; assoc prof, 70-76, PROF SOLID MECH, UNIV KY, 76-, CHMN DEPT ENG MECH, 80- *Mem:* Am Soc Eng Educ; Sigma Xi; Am Soc Civil Engrs; Am Soc Mech Engrs; Soc Eng Sci. *Res:* Composite materials; pressure vessels; thermal stresses. *Mailing Add:* Dept of Eng Mech Univ of Ky Lexington KY 40506

TAUER, KENNETH J, b Minn, Apr 5, 23; m 44; c 4. PHYSICAL CHEMISTRY, CHEMICAL PHYSICS. *Educ:* Univ Minn, PhD, 51. *Prof Exp:* Researcher, Gen Elec Co, Wash, 51-53; asst prof chem, Boston Col, 53-56; MEM RES STAFF, MAT RES AGENCY LAB, US ARMY MAT & MECH RES CTR, 57- *Mem:* Am Chem Soc; Am Phys Soc. *Res:* Electronics structure of transition metals and alloys; magnetism; electronic transport; magnetoresistance; Hall effect. *Mailing Add:* US Army Mat & Mech Res Amra Bldg 292 Watertown MA 02172

TAULBEE, CARL D(ONALD), b Detroit, Mich, Oct 18, 28; div; c 2. MECHANICAL ENGINEERING, NUCLEAR ENGINEERING. *Educ:* Wayne State Univ, BSME, 53, MSME, 59. *Prof Exp:* Engr, Studebaker-Packard Corp, 53-56; supvry engr, Res Lab Div, Bendix Corp, 56-73; spec projs mgr, Door-Man Mfg Co, 73-79; PRES, AM INDUST DOORS, 79- *Mem:* Am Welding Soc; Am Nuclear Soc; Am Soc Mech Engrs; Am Soc Qual Control. *Res:* Nuclear power plant products; earth resources; radiation effects; nuclear power and propulsion and gas turbine technologies. *Mailing Add:* 26 Oakland Park Blvd Pleasant Ridge MI 48069

TAULBEE, DALE B(RUCE), b Detroit, Mich, Nov 17, 36; m 58; c 2. AEROSPACE & ENGINEERING SCIENCE. *Educ:* Mich State Univ, BS, 58, MS, 60; Univ Ill, PhD(appl mech), 64. *Prof Exp:* Asst prof aerospace eng, 63-70, ASSOC PROF ENG SCI, STATE UNIV NY BUFFALO, 70- *Concurrent Pos:* Tech consult, Bell Aerosysts Co, 66- *Mem:* Am Inst Aeronaut & Astronaut; Am Soc Mech Engrs. *Res:* Fluid mechanics, laminar and turbulent boundary layers; gas dynamics, high speed viscous flows. *Mailing Add:* Dept of Eng Sci State Univ of NY Buffalo NY 14214

TAULBEE, ORRIN EDISON, b Taulbee, Ky, Oct 18, 27; m 55; c 4. COMPUTER SCIENCE. *Educ:* Berea Col, BA, 50; Mich State Univ, MA, 51, PhD(math), 57. *Prof Exp:* Res mathematician, Univac Div, Sperry Rand Corp, 55-58; math specialist, Lockheed Aircraft Corp, 58-59; assoc prof math, Mich State Univ, 59-61; mgr info sci, Goodyear Aerospace Corp, 61-66; dir mgt info systs & comput ctr, 66-70, PROF COMPUT SCI & CHMN DEPT, UNIV PITTSBURGH, 66- *Concurrent Pos:* Consult, US Air Force, 66-71, Pittsburgh Bd Educ, 67-72 & Pa Dept Educ, 72-78; ed bd, Encycl Libr & Info

Sci, 65- & J Info Systs, 73-; lectr, Asn Comput Mach, 67-68, chmn, Comput Sci Conf Comt, mem, Conf & Symp Comt & dir, Comput Sci Employment Register, 74-; vis scientist, Nat Bur Standards, 71; mem, Comput Sci Bd, 74-, vchmn, 77, chmn, 78. *Mem:* Am Math Soc; Math Asn Am; Asn Comput Mach; Am Soc Info Sci; NY Acad Sci. *Res:* Computer networking; applications of computers; pattern recognition; classification theory; computer performance measurement; instructional computing; computing resources management; management information systems; information processing systems. *Mailing Add:* Dept Comput Sci Univ Pittsburgh Pittsburgh PA 15260

TAUNTON, JOHN WILLIAM, chemical engineering, see previous edition

TAUNTON-RIGBY, ALISON, b Barnsley, Eng, Apr 23, 44; m 66; c 3. CHEMISTRY, BIOCHEMISTRY. *Educ:* Bristol Univ, BSc, 65, PhD(chem), 68. *Prof Exp:* SR RES CHEMIST, COLLAB RES INC, 68-, HEAD, CHEM RES, PROD DIV, 70-, PROJ LEADER, 70-, DIR, NUCLEIC ACIDS, 74- *Mem:* AAAS; Am Chem Soc. *Res:* Nucleic acid chemistry and biochemistry; recombinant DNA; immunology; psychoactive drugs; carcinogens; pteridines; enzymology. *Mailing Add:* Chem Res Lab Collab Res Inc 1365 Main St Waltham MA 02154

TAURINS, ALFRED, b Dauguli, Latvia, Aug 20, 04; Can citizen; m 30; c 2. ORGANIC CHEMISTRY. *Educ:* Univ Latvia, ChEng, 30, DrChem, 36. *Prof Exp:* Instr chem, Univ Latvia, Riga, 30-38, privat-docent, Org Chem, 38-39; prof chem, Latvian Agr Acad, Yelgava, 39-44; from assoc prof to prof, 49-72, EMER PROF ORG CHEM, McGILL UNIV, 72- *Concurrent Pos:* Morberg fel, Univ Latvia, 39. *Mem:* Am Chem Soc; Chem Inst Can; fel Royal Soc Can. *Res:* Synthesis and spectra of heterocyclic compounds; thiazoloisoquinolines, isothiazolopyridines, naphthyridines. *Mailing Add:* Dept Chem McGill Univ Montreal PQ H3A 2K6 Can

TAUROG, ALVIN, b St Louis, Mo, Dec 5, 15; m 40; c 2. BIOCHEMISTRY, PHYSIOLOGY. *Educ:* Univ Calif, Los Angeles, BA, 37, MA, 39; Univ Calif, Berkeley, PhD(physiol), 43. *Prof Exp:* Asst chem, Univ Calif, Los Angeles, 37-38; asst physiol, Univ Calif, Berkeley, 42-43, chemist, Radiation Lab, 44-45, res assoc physiol, 46-59; assoc prof, 59-63, PROF PHARMACOL, UNIV TEX HEALTH SCI CTR DALLAS, 63- *Concurrent Pos:* Career res award, US Pub Health Serv, 63. *Mem:* AAAS; Am Chem Soc; Am Soc Biol Chem; Endocrine Soc; Am Thyroid Asn. *Res:* Thyroid physiology and biochemistry; iodine metabolism. *Mailing Add:* Dept of Pharmacol Univ of Tex Health Sci Ctr Dallas TX 75235

TAUSSIG, ANDREW, b Budapest, Hungary, Dec 6, 29; Can citizen; m 59; c 3. MICROBIOLOGY, BIOCHEMISTRY. *Educ:* McGill Univ, BSc, 52, PhD(biochem), 55. *Prof Exp:* Res fel biochem, McGill Univ, 55-61; from asst bacteriologist to bacteriologist, Jewish Gen Hosp, 61-67; vis scientist, Dept Biochem, McGill Univ, 67-70; BACTERIOLOGIST, MICROBIOL LAB, 69- *Concurrent Pos:* Bacteriologist, Bellechasse Hosp, Montreal, 73-, Jewish Convalescent Hosp, Chomedey & Mt Sinai Hosp, St Agathe, Que; dir labs, Mt Sinai Hosp, St Agathe, Que, 74- *Mem:* Am Soc Microbiol; Asn Microbiol Que; Can Soc Microbiol. *Res:* Nucleic acids of bacteria and bacteriophage; induced enzyme synthesis in bacteria; diagnostic bacteriology. *Mailing Add:* Microbiol Lab 5845 Cote de Neiges Rd Montreal PQ H3C 1T1 Can

TAUSSIG, HELEN BROOKE, b Cambridge, Mass, May 24, 98. MEDICINE. *Educ:* Univ Calif, AB, 21; Johns Hopkins Univ, MD, 27. *Hon Degrees:* Twenty from various int cols & univs, 48-78. Prof from assoc prof to prof pediat, Johns Hopkins Univ, 46-63, EMER PROF PEDIAT, JOHNS HOPKINS UNIV, 63-, PHYSICIAN-IN-CHGE CARDIAC CLIN, HARRIET LANE HOME, JOHNS HOPKINS HOSP, 30- *Concurrent Pos:* Thomas River Mem res fel award, 63-69; mem bd, Int Cardiol Found, 67- *Honors & Awards:* Chevalier Legion d'Honneur, France, 47; Mead-Johnson Award, 48; Passano Award, 48; Lasker Award, 54; Feltrinelli Prize, Rome, Italy, 54; Gardner Award, 59; Gold Heart Award, Am Heart Asn, 63; Medal of Freedom, 64; Founders Award, Radcliffe Col, 66; John Phillips Mem Award, Am Col Physicians, 66; Carl Ludwig Medal of Honor, Ger, 67; Distinguished Serv Award, Wilson Col, 68; William F Faulkes Award, Nat Rehab Asn, 71; Howland Award, Am Pediat Soc, 71; Milton S Eisenhower Award, Johns Hopkins Univ, 77. *Mem:* Nat Acad Sci; master Am Col Physicians; Am Pediat Soc; Soc Pediat Res. *Res:* Congenital malformations of the heart; blue babies. *Mailing Add:* Apt 158 Crosslands Kennett Square PA 19348

TAUSSIG, ROBERT TRIMBLE, plasma physics, see previous edition

TAUSSIG, STEVEN J, b Timisoara, Rumania, June 2, 14; US citizen; m 65; c 1. INDUSTRIAL MICROBIOLOGY, ENZYMOLOGY. *Educ:* Univ Prague, Czech, Chem Eng, 37; Bucharest Polytech Inst, PhD(biochem), 58. *Prof Exp:* Chemist, Solventul SA, Timisoara, 37-48; asst prof, Polytech Inst Timisoara, 48-57; res fel, Agr Res Inst, Timisoara, 57-59; mgr plant & equip sales, Int Chem Corp, NY, 60-61; tech dir, Pac Labs, Inc, Honolulu, 61-62 & Pac Enzyme Prod, 62-63; res biochemist, Dole Co, Inc, 63-64, dir lab serv, 64-73; PRES, CHEM CONSULTS INT INC, HONOLULU, 73- *Concurrent Pos:* Tech consult, Pac Labs, Inc & Pac Biochem Co, 63- & Monsanto Co, Mo, 64-65. *Mem:* AAAS; Am Chem Soc; Soc Indust Microbiol; Inst Food Technologists. *Res:* Fermentations; bacterial and other hydrolytic enzymes; chemical equilibria in esterification reactions; cancer research; study of effects of Bromelain on cancer. *Mailing Add:* 469 Ena Rd Apt 3205 Honolulu HI 96815

TAUTVYDAS, KESTUTIS JONAS, b Telsiai, Lithuania, Jan 1, 40; US citizen; m 62; c 4. WEED SCIENCE. *Educ:* Univ Md, BS, 63; Cornell Univ, MS, 65; Yale Univ, PhD(cell & molecular develop biol), 69. *Prof Exp:* Res assoc cell biol, Univ Colo, 69-71; asst prof plant physiol, Marquette Univ, 71-79; SUPVR BIOL SCREENING & BIOCHEM, 3M CO, 79- *Mem:* Am Soc Plant Physiol; AAAS; Am Soc Hort Sci; Weed Sci Soc Am; Plant Molecular Biol Asn. *Res:* Mode action of agricultural chemicals in plants; biochemistry of plant growth regulators; control of plant growth and development. *Mailing Add:* 3M Ctr Bldg 203-1N 3M Co St Paul MN 55144

TAUXE, WELBY NEWLON, b Knoxville, Tenn, May 24, 24; c 4. NUCLEAR MEDICINE, CLINICAL PATHOLOGY. *Educ:* Univ Tenn, Knoxville, BS, 44, MD, 50; Univ Minn, Minneapolis, MS, 58. *Prof Exp:* Mayo Found fel, Mayo Clin, 54-58, chief nuclear med dept, 58-72; prof nuclear med & clin path, 72-77, PROF DIAG RADIOL & PATH, COL MED, UNIV ALA, BIRMINGHAM, 77- *Concurrent Pos:* Consult, AEC, 62-70; treas, Am Bd Nuclear Med, 71; consult, Am Nat Standards Inst, 72. *Mem:* Am Soc Clin Path; Soc Nuclear Med. *Res:* Copper kinetics in Wilson's disease; use of radioactive materials in diagnosis. *Mailing Add:* Dept of Path Univ of Ala Sch of Med Birmingham AL 35294

TAVANO, DONALD C, b Newark, NY, Aug 26, 36; m 58; c 2. PUBLIC HEALTH EDUCATION, MEDICAL EDUCATION. *Educ:* State Univ NY Col Cortland, BS, 60; Univ Ill, MS, 61; Univ Mich, MPH, 63; Mich State Univ, PhD(educ), 71. *Prof Exp:* Instr health educ, State Univ NY Col Cortland, 61-62; dir health educ, Saginaw City & County Health Depts, 63-65; consult health educ, Mich Dept Pub Health, 65-66; asst prof, 66-72, ASSOC PROF COMMUNITY MED, MICH STATE UNIV, 72- *Concurrent Pos:* Vis lectr, Sch Pub Health, Univ Mich, 72; consult, Mich Dept Educ, 66-, Gov Off Health & Med Affairs & Nat Bd Examrs Osteop Physicians & Surgeons Inc, 75. *Mem:* Soc Pub Health Educ; Am Pub Health Asn; Asn Behav Sci Med Educ; Asn Teachers Prev Med. *Res:* Patient education; the impact of patient education on health care cost containment, patient compliance and treatment outcomes. *Mailing Add:* Dept of Community Med Mich State Univ East Lansing MI 48824

TAVARES, DONALD FRANCIS, b East Providence, RI, Apr 1, 31; m 66; c 2. ORGANIC CHEMISTRY. *Educ:* Brown Univ, AB, 53; Yale Univ, MSc, 55, PhD(org chem), 59. *Prof Exp:* Teaching asst chem, Yale Univ, 53-55 & 56-59; teacher, Prospect Sch, Conn, 55-56; res assoc, Univ Ill, Urbana, 59-60 & Duke Univ, 60-61; res assoc chem, Univ Alta, 61-62; asst prof, 62-69, asst dean arts & sci, 67-70, ASSOC PROF CHEM, UNIV CALGARY, 69- *Honors & Awards:* Schering Found Prize, Yale Univ, 59. *Mem:* Sigma Xi; Am Chem Soc; Chem Inst Can; Royal Soc Chem. *Res:* Study of organic reaction mechanisms; carbanions; organic photochemistry; chemistry of epoxides; chemistry of organic sulfur compounds. *Mailing Add:* Dept of Chem Univ of Calgary Calgary AB T2N 1N4 Can

TAVARES, ISABELLE IRENE, b Merced, Calif, Oct 6, 21. MYCOLOGY, LICHENOLOGY. *Educ:* Univ Calif, PhD(bot), 59. *Prof Exp:* Sr lab technician protozool, 49-52, from herbarium botanist to sr herbarium botanist, 52-68, ASSOC SPECIALIST BOT, UNIV CALIF, BERKELEY, 68- *Mem:* Bot Soc Am; Mycol Soc Am; Am Bryological & Lichenological Soc. *Res:* Laboulbeniales; Usnea. *Mailing Add:* Dept of Bot Univ of Calif Berkeley CA 94720

TAVARES, STAFFORD EMANUEL, b Kingston, Jamaica, WI, May 11, 40; Can citizen. ELECTRICAL ENGINEERING. *Educ:* McGill Univ, BEng, 62, PhD(elec eng), 68; Calif Inst Technol, MS, 64. *Prof Exp:* Jr res off elec eng, Nat Res Coun Can Labs, Ottawa, 62-65, asst res off, 65-70; asst prof, 70-74, assoc prof, 74-80, PROF ELEC ENG, QUEEN'S UNIV, ONT, 80- *Concurrent Pos:* Lectr, Carleton Univ, 68-70; Natural Sci & Eng Res Coun Can res grants, Queen's Univ, Ont, 71-; vis assoc prof, Stanford Univ, 77-78. *Mem:* Inst Elec & Electronics Engrs. *Res:* Computer communications; digital communications; error-correcting codes; data encryption and security in computer communications networks. *Mailing Add:* Dept of Elec Eng Queen's Univ Kingston ON K7L 3N6 Can

TAVASSOLI, MEHDI, b Tehran, Iran, Mar 30, 33; US citizen; m 66; c 3. HEMATOLOGY. *Educ:* Tehran Univ Sch Med, MD, 61. *Prof Exp:* Intern, Cambridge City Hosp, Mass, 61-62; resident, Cook County Hosp, Chicago, 63-64 & Carney Hosp, Boston, 64-66; hematologist, Tufts-New Eng Med Ctr, 66-72 & from instr to asst prof med, Sch Med, Tufts Univ, 69-72; hematologist, Scripps Clin & Res Found, 72-81; PROF MED, SCH MED, UNIV WIS, 81-; CHIEF HEMAT-ONCOL & DIR CELL BIOL LAB, VET ADMIN HOSP, JACKSON, MISS, 81- *Concurrent Pos:* Charlton fel, Tufts Univ, 68; res fel, The Med Found, Boston, 70; vis investr anat, Med Sch, Johns Hopkins Univ, 70-71; consult hemat, Vet Admin Hosp & Univ Calif, San Diego, 73- *Honors & Awards:* John Larkin Award, The Guild of St Luke, 66. *Mem:* Am Soc Hemat; Am Col Physicians; Int Soc Exp Hemat; Am Asn Cancer Res; Am Soc Clin Oncol. *Res:* Structural basis of hemopoiesis and the function of microenvironmental factor in immunohemopoiesis; membrane structure and function. *Mailing Add:* Dept Res Vets Admin Med Ctr 1500 E Woodrow Wilson Dr Jackson MS 39216

TAVE, DOUGLAS, b Oxford, Eng, Dec 13, 49; US citien; m 78. AQUACULTURE, FISH BREEDING. *Educ:* Coe Col, BA, 71; Univ Ill, MS, 73; Auburn Univ, PhD(aquacult), 79. *Prof Exp:* Fel fish breeding, Dept Fisheries & Allied Aquacultures, Auburn Univ, 74-80, asst prof, 80-81; ASST PROF AQUACULT, DEPT ENTOM, FISHERIES & WILDLIFE, UNIV MINN, 81- *Mem:* Sigma Xi; Am Fisheries Soc. *Res:* Quantitative and mendelian genetic research on tropical and temperate food fish: tilapia and catfishes. *Mailing Add:* Dept Entom Fisheries & Wildlife Univ Minn St Paul MN 55108

TAVEL, MORTON, b Brooklyn, NY, June 14, 39; m 69; c 1. THEORETICAL PHYSICS. *Educ:* City Col New York, BS, 60; Stevens Inst Technol, MS, 62; Yeshiva Univ, PhD(physics), 64. *Prof Exp:* Res assoc, Brookhaven Nat Lab, 64-66, asst scientist, 66-67; asst prof, 67-70, assoc prof, 70-74, PROF PHYSICS, VASSAR COL, 74- *Mem:* AAAS; Am Phys Soc. *Res:* Quantum field theory; plasma physics; transport theory. *Mailing Add:* Dept of Physics Vassar Col Poughkeepsie NY 12601

TAVERAS, JUAN M, b Dom Repub, Sept 27, 19; nat US; m 47; c 3. RADIOLOGY. *Educ:* Norm Sch Santiago, Dom Repub, BS, 37; Univ Santo Domingo, MD, 43; Univ Pa, MD, 49. *Prof Exp:* Instr radiol, Col Physicians & Surgeons, Columbia Univ, 50-52, from asst prof to prof, 52-65; prof radiol & chmn dept, Sch Med, Wash Univ, radiologist-in-chief, Barnes & Allied

Hosps, Univ Med Ctr & dir, Mallinckrodt Inst Radiol, 65-71; RADIOLOGIST-IN-CHIEF, MASS GEN HOSP, BOSTON, 71-, PROF RADIOL, HARVARD MED SCH, 76- *Concurrent Pos:* Dir radiol, Neurol Inst, New York, 52-65; from asst to attend radiologist, Presby Hosp, New York, 50-65; mem neurol study sect, Nat Inst Neurol Dis & Stroke, 64-68; consult, US Marine Hosp, Staten Island, NY, Bronx Vet Admin Hosp, St Barnabas Hosp Chronic Dis, New York, Morristown Mem Hosp, NJ, St Louis City Hosp & Jewish Hosp, St Louis, 65-71. *Mem:* AMA; Am Neurol Asn; fel Am Col Radiol; Am Roentgen Ray Soc; Am Soc Neuroradiol (pres, 62-64). *Res:* Radiologic aspect of neurological science, especially cerebral angiography and cerebral vascular disease. *Mailing Add:* Mass Gen Hosp Boston MA 02114

TAVES, DONALD R, b Aberdeen, Idaho, July 22, 26; m 51; c 4. MEDICINE, RADIOBIOLOGY. *Educ:* Washington Univ, BS, 49, MD, 53; Univ Calif, MPH, 57; Univ Rochester, PhD(radiation biol), 63. *Prof Exp:* Health officer, Shasta County Health Dept, 57-60; USPHS fel, 60-63; asst prof radiation biol & biophys, 63-67, ASSOC PROF PHARMACOL, TOXICOL, RADIATIONBIOL & BIOPHYSICS, SCH MED, UNIV ROCHESTER, 67- *Mem:* Soc Toxicol; Am Soc Pharmacol & Exp Therapeut. *Res:* Pharmacology and toxicology of fluoride. *Mailing Add:* Dept of Pharmacol Univ of Rochester Sch of Med Rochester NY 14642

TAVES, MILTON ARTHUR, b Aberdeen, Idaho, Aug 14, 25; m 45; c 2. ORGANIC CHEMISTRY. *Educ:* Univ Utah, BS, 45; Mass Inst Technol, PhD(org chem), 48. *Prof Exp:* Lab asst chem, Univ Utah, 43-45; asst, Mass Inst Technol, 45-46; res chemist, Res Ctr, Hercules, Inc, 48-54, res supvr, 54-60 & 62-64, tech asst to dir res, 60-62, res mgr, Synthetic Res Div, 64-77, new technol coordr, 77-81; ASSOC, MONKMAN, RUMSEY, INC, 81- *Concurrent Pos:* Consult, 81- *Mem:* Am Chem Soc. *Res:* Heterocyclics; hydrogen peroxide; hydroperoxide chemistry; auto-oxidation and catalytic oxidation of organic compounds; terpenes; condensation polymers; resins; plasticizers; chemicals via fermentation; immobilized enzyme technology; process development; agricultural chemicals. *Mailing Add:* 210 N Spring Valley Rd Wilmington DE 19807

TAVILL, ANTHONY SYDNEY, b Manchester, Eng, July 15, 36; m 59; c 3. GASTROENTEROLOGY. *Educ:* Univ Manchester, MB & ChB, 60, MD, 70; Royal Col Physicians London, MRCP, 63, FRCP, 78. *Prof Exp:* Med Res Coun travelling fel med, Albert Einstein Col Med, 66-68; lectr, Royal Free Hosp, Sch Med, Univ London, 68-71; sr clin scientist, Div Clin Invest, Med Res Coun Clin Res Ctr, Eng, 71-72, consult gastroenterol & liver dis, 72-75; HEAD GASTROENTEROL & PROF MED, CASE WESTERN RESERVE UNIV, CLEVELAND METROP GEN HOSP, 75- *Mem:* Med Res Soc Gt Brit; Brit Soc Gastroenterol; Europ Soc Clin Invest; Am Asn Study Liver Dis; Int Asn Study Liver. *Res:* Control mechanisms in hepatic protein metabolism in gastrointestinal and renal disease, homeostasis of plasma transport proteins and metabolic interrelationships between iron transport and storage proteins of the liver. *Mailing Add:* Dept of Gastroenterol Cleveland Metrop Gen Hosp Cleveland OH 44109

TAVIS, MICHAEL T, b Chicago, Ill, June 1, 41; m 74; c 2. THEORETICAL PHYSICS. *Educ:* Ill Inst Technol, BS, 63; Univ Calif, Riverside, MA, 65, PhD(physics), 68. *Prof Exp:* MEM TECH STAFF, AEROSPACE CORP, 66- *Res:* Applied physics in the area of gallium arsenide laser (phase locking of multiple devices and amplifier theory); linear optical propagation. *Mailing Add:* Aerospace Corp PO Box 92957 Los Angeles CA 90009

TAVLARIDES, LAWRENCE LASKY, b Wilkinsburg, Pa, Jan 8, 42; m 65; c 2. CHEMICAL ENGINEERING. *Educ:* Univ Pittsburgh, BSChE, 63, MS, 64, PhD(chem eng), 68. *Prof Exp:* Engr, Mobay Chem Co, 62; chem engr, Gulf Res & Develop Co, 64-66 & 68; fel photochem reactions, Delft Univ Technol, 68-69; asst prof, 69-75, assoc prof, 75-81, PROF CHEM ENG, ILL INST TECHNOL, 81- *Concurrent Pos:* Consult, CPC Int, Inc, 70- & Res Inst, Ill Inst of Technol, 73-; NSF Found res grants, 71-72, 75, 77 & 78. *Mem:* AAAS; Am Inst Chem Engrs. *Res:* Metal extraction in liquid dispersions; droplet rate processes in liquid dispersions; mixing in liquid dispersions; kinetics of metal extraction; Fischer-Tropsch kinetics; chemical reaction engineering. *Mailing Add:* Dept of Chem Eng 3300 S Federal St Chicago IL 60616

TAX, ANNE, b New York, NY, May 7, 44; m 68; c 2. IMMUNOLOGY. *Educ:* Rutgers Univ, BA, 66; Cornell Univ, PhD(microbiol), 71. *Prof Exp:* Head radioimmunoassay lab, Meloy Labs, 71-73; ASST PROF TUMOR IMMUNOL, WISTAR INST, 73- *Mem:* AAAS. *Res:* Immunology; to produce and utilize monoclonal antibodies to detect cell surface antigens. *Mailing Add:* Wistar Inst 36th & Spruce Sts Philadelphia PA 19104

TAYA, MINORU, b Yokosuka, Japan, Sept 19, 44; m 76; c 2. APPLIED MECHANICS, MATERIALS SCIENCE. *Educ:* Univ Tokyo, BS, 68; Northwestern Univ, MS, 73, PhD(ductile fracture), 77. *Prof Exp:* Design engr stress anal, Sumitomo Heavy Industs Co Ltd, Japan, 68-71 & 73-76; fel mech property of porous media, Northwestern Univ, 77-78; ASST PROF MECH ENG, UNIV DEL, 78- *Mem:* Soc Naval Architects Japan; Am Acad Mechanics; Am Soc Mech Engrs. *Res:* Plasticity of a porous material; thermo-mechanical properties of composite materials; manufacturing process of composite materials; ductile fracture of two-phase alloys. *Mailing Add:* Dept Mech & Aerospace Eng Univ Del Newark DE 19711

TAYAMA, HARRY K, b Los Angeles, Calif, May 26, 35; m 61; c 2. HORTICULTURE, FLORICULTURE. *Educ:* Univ Ill, BS, 58, MS, 59; Ohio State Univ, PhD(hort), 63. *Prof Exp:* Asst prof hort, Pa State Univ, 63-64; from asst prof to assoc prof, 64-71, asst prof hort, Ohio Agr Res & Develop Ctr, 66-67, PROF HORT, OHIO AGR RES & DEVELOP CTR, OHIO STATE UNIV, 71- *Concurrent Pos:* Ed, Ohio Florists' Asn Bull, 77- *Honors & Awards:* Kenneth Post Award, 66. *Mem:* Am Soc Hort Sci. *Res:* Ecological factors affecting growth and flowering of florist crops; plant growth regulators. *Mailing Add:* Dept of Hort Ohio State Univ 2001 Fyffe Ct Columbus OH 43210

TAYBACK, MATTHEW, b Tarrytown, NY, June 30, 19; m 45; c 3. PUBLIC HEALTH. *Educ:* Harvard Univ, AB, 39; Columbia Univ, AM, 40; Johns Hopkins Univ, ScD(biostatist), 53. *Prof Exp:* Res assoc, NY State Psychiat Inst, 40-42; res statistician, NY State Health Dept, 46-48, dir bur biostatist, Baltimore, 48-53, dir statist sect, 53, asst comnr health, 57-63, dep comnr health, 63-69, asst secy health & ment hyg & sci affairs, 69-73; from asst prof to assoc prof, 52-65, PROF HYG & PUB HEALTH, SCH MED, UNIV MD, BALTIMORE CITY, 65-; STATE DIR ON AGING, 74- *Concurrent Pos:* Lectr, Johns Hopkins Univ, 51-; vis prof, Univ Philippines, 57; consult, US Army, 57-, WHO, 60- & USAID, 61-; vchmn, State Comn on Aging, Md, 61-75; chmn, State Adv Bd Price Comn, 72-74; chmn, State Emp Ret Rev Bd, 74-; hon prof community med, Pahlavi Univ, Iran, 78. *Mem:* Am Pub Health Asn. *Res:* Epidemiology; demography; health services administration. *Mailing Add:* State Dir Aging State Off Bldg 301 W Preston St Baltimore MD 21201

TAYLOR, ALAN NEIL, b Franklin, NY, Sept 10, 34; m 55; c 2. PHYSIOLOGY, BIOCHEMISTRY. *Educ:* Ohio State Univ, BS, 57; Cornell Univ, MS, 60, PhD(phys biol), 69. *Prof Exp:* Res assoc mineral metab, NY State Vet Col, Cornell Univ, 60-66, NIH traineeship, 66-69, sr res assoc membrane transport, 69-75; ASSOC PROF, BAYLOR COL DENT, DALLAS, 76-; ASSOC PROF, GRAD SCH, BAYLOR UNIV, 77- *Mem:* AAAS; Am Inst Nutrit; Am Asn Anatomists; Soc Exp Biol & Med. *Res:* Mineral metabolism; membrane transport; mechanisms of vitamin D action. *Mailing Add:* Dept of Microanat Baylor Col Dent 3302 Gaston Ave Dallas TX 75246

TAYLOR, ALBERT CECIL, b Hopei, China, Aug 15, 05; US citizen; m 35; c 2. BIOLOGY. *Educ:* Taylor Univ, BA, 30; Univ Ky, MA, 34; Univ Chicago, PhD(zool), 42. *Prof Exp:* Teacher biol acad, Chicago Evangel Inst, 30-32; teacher sci, Asheland Jr High Sch, Louisville, 34-35; teacher zool, NC State Teachers Col, Asheville, 35-39; asst zool, Univ Chicago, 42-43; res assoc, 43-45; asst prof anat, Col Dent, NY Univ, 45-49, assoc prof, Col Dent & Grad Sch, 49-55; assoc, Rockefeller Inst, 55-58, assoc prof develop biol, 58-65; prof anat, Univ Tex Dent Br Houston & Grad Sch Biomed Sci & mem dent sci inst, Houston, 65-74; RETIRED. *Mem:* Soc Exp Biol & Med; Am Asn Anatomists; Am Soc Cell Biol; Soc Develop Biol; Soc Cryobiol. *Res:* Development nervous system; freezing and freeze-drying of tissues; cell interactions in development; cell contact and adhesion; lysis of tissue collagen. *Mailing Add:* 3202 Bluebonnet Houston TX 77025

TAYLOR, ALBERT LEE, b Florence, Colo, Nov 30, 01; m 28; c 1. NEMATOLOGY. *Educ:* George Washington Univ, BS, 34. *Prof Exp:* Nematologist, USDA, 35-46; technologist, Shell Chem Corp, 46-49; nematologist, USDA, 49-56, leader, Nematol Invests, 56-64; consult nematologist, Food & Agr Orgn, UN, Cyprus, 64-65 & Thailand, 65; nematologist, USDA, Fla, 66-67 & Food & Agr Orgn, Fiji, 67-68, nematologist & proj mgr, Thailand, 68-72; chief nematologist, Div Plant Indust, Fla Dept Agr & Consumer Serv, 72-75; ADJ PROF, INST FOOD & AGR SCI, UNIV FLA, 72- *Concurrent Pos:* Consult, AID Int Meloidogyne Prof, NC State Univ, 77-78. *Honors & Awards:* Geigy Award, Soc Nematologists. *Mem:* Soc Nematologists; Orgn Tropical Am Nematologists. *Res:* Plant nematology; chemical control of plant nematodes. *Mailing Add:* 2620 SW 14th Dr Gainesville FL 32608

TAYLOR, ALLEN, b New York, NY, Jan 11, 46; m 77; c 1. BIOCHEMISTRY, ORGANIC CHEMISTRY. *Educ:* City Col New York, BS, 67; Rutgers Univ, PhD(org chem), 73. *Prof Exp:* Teaching asst, Rutgers Univ, 68-71, teaching intern, 71-72; fel, Univ Calif, Berkeley, 73-75, vis scientist, 75-77; ASST PROF CHEM & BIOCHEM, WILLIAMS COL, MASS, 77- *Concurrent Pos:* Lectr dept biochem, Univ Calif, Berkeley, 73, 74 & 76; NIH fel, 74, res grant, 78-82; vis scientist, Harvard Univ, 81-82. *Mem:* Am Chem Soc; Sigma Xi; AAAS; Asn Res Vision Ophthal. *Res:* Eye lens cataractogenesis; processes involved in cholesterol absorption in the gut; role of proteasis in lens metabolism; uses of proteasis in anticataract therapy; structure and mechanism of action of aminopeptidase. *Mailing Add:* Dept Chem Williams Col Williamstown MA 01267

TAYLOR, ANDREW RONALD ARGO, b Ottawa, Ont, July 6, 21; m 47; c 4. BOTANY. *Educ:* Univ Toronto, BA, 43, PhD(bot), 55. *Prof Exp:* Asst bot, Univ Toronto, 43-46; from asst prof to assoc prof biol, 46-62, actg dean sci, 74-75, PROF BOT, UNIV NB, FREDERICTON, 62- *Concurrent Pos:* Asst biologist, Fisheries Res Bd Can, 48-60; hon lectr, Univ St Andrews, 60-61, 76; vis prof, Univ Adelaide, 75-76. *Mem:* Int Phycol Soc (treas, 77-82); Phycol Soc Am; Can Bot Asn; Brit Phycol Soc. *Res:* Developmental morphology, ecology and taxonomy of north Atlantic marine algae and zostera. *Mailing Add:* Dept of Biol Univ of NB Fredericton NB E3B 5A3 Can

TAYLOR, ANGUS ELLIS, b Craig, Colo, Oct 13, 11; m 36; c 3. MATHEMATICS. *Educ:* Harvard Univ, SB, 33; Calif Inst Technol, PhD(math), 36. *Prof Exp:* Instr math, Calif Inst Technol, 36-37; Nat Res Coun fel, Princeton Univ, 37-38; from instr to prof math, Univ Calif, Los Angeles, 38-66; vpres acad affairs, Univ Calif Systemwide Admin, 65-75, Univ provost, 75-77; univ provost & chancellor, Univ Calif, Santa Cruz, 76-77, EMER PROF, UNIV CALIF, LOS ANGELES & BERKELEY, EMER UNIV PROVOST & EMER CHANCELLOR, SANTA CRUZ, 77- *Concurrent Pos:* Fulbright res fel, Univ Mainz, 55. *Mem:* Am Math Soc; Math Asn Am. *Res:* Theory of functions; linear operators and spectral theory; history of mathematics. *Mailing Add:* 82 Norwood Ave Berkeley CA 94707

TAYLOR, ANNA NEWMAN, b Vienna, Austria, Oct 28, 33; US citizen; m 59. PHYSIOLOGY, ANATOMY. *Educ:* Western Reserve Univ, AB, 55, PhD(physiol), 61. *Prof Exp:* Am Heart Asn res fel physiol, Western Reserve Univ, 61-63, instr, 62-63; Am Heart Asn adv res fel, Lab Neurophysiol, Henri-Rousselle Hosp, Paris, France, 63-64; asst prof physiol, Western Reserve Univ, 64-65; asst prof anat, Dept Anat & Psychiat, Col Med, Baylor Univ, 65-67; asst res anatomist, 67-68, from asst prof to assoc prof, 68-79, PROF ANAT, UNIV CALIF, LOS ANGELES, 79-; CHIEF, ALCOHOL

RES LAB, US VET ADMIN, BRENTWOOD, LOS ANGELES, 79- *Concurrent Pos:* USPHS fel, 61; res specialist, Houston State Psychiat Inst, 65-67; NIMH res scientist develop award, 72-77; mem biomed panel, Nat Insts Drug Abuse Res Review Comt, 77-81; US Vet Admin Alcohol res award, 79-81. *Mem:* Fel AAAS; Am Physiol Soc; Endocrine Soc; Am Asn Anat; Soc Neurosci. *Res:* Neuroendocrinology; central nervous system regulation of pituitary-adrenal function; central actions of hormones; developmental and long-term effects of perinatal exposure to hormones, drugs of abuse and alcohol. *Mailing Add:* Dept of Anat Univ Calif Sch Med Los Angeles CA 90024

TAYLOR, ARDELL NICHOLS, b Terral, Okla, Jan 19, 17; m 43; c 2. PHYSIOLOGY. *Educ:* Tex Tech Col, BS, 39; Univ Tex, MA, 41, PhD(zool sci), 43. *Hon Degrees:* DSc, Lincoln Col, 71. *Prof Exp:* Tutor zool, Univ Tex, 39-42, from instr to asst prof physiol, Sch Med, 43-46; from asst prof to assoc prof, Sch Med, Univ Okla, 46-51, prof, chmn dept & assoc dean, 51-60; assoc secy, Coun Med Educ & dir, Dept Allied Med Prof & Serv, AMA, 60-67; dean sch related health sci, Chicago Med Sch, 67-69, pres, 69-76, EMER PRES, UNIV HEALTH SCI-CHICAGO MED SCH, 76- *Mem:* Soc Exp Biol & Med; Am Physiol Soc. *Res:* Nucleic acid metabolism on ova; nerve conduction and facilitation; hypertension; experimental vascular physiology; dynamics of circulation; medical education. *Mailing Add:* 503 Hawthorn Winnetka IL 60093

TAYLOR, ARTHUR CANNING, JR, b Bridgeport, Conn, Aug 8, 23; m 48; c 2. ENGINEERING. *Educ:* Va Mil Inst, BS, 47; Ohio State Univ, MS, 52, PhD, 64. *Prof Exp:* Instr mech, 49-53, asst prof, 53-56, assoc prof mech & thermodyn, 56-69, PROF MECH & THERMODYN, VA MIL INST, 69-, HEAD DEPT MECH ENG, 56- *Concurrent Pos:* Fel, Va Mil Inst, 51, 55; mem coop proj, State Dept Hwys, Va, 55-59; res contracts, US Weather Bur & Harry Diamond Labs, 64- *Mem:* Am Soc Eng Educ; Am Soc Civil Engrs; Am Soc Mech Engrs. *Res:* Mechanics; thermodynamics. *Mailing Add:* Dept of Mech Eng Va Mil Inst Lexington VA 24450

TAYLOR, AUBREY ELMO, b El Paso, Tex, June 4, 33; m 54; c 3. PHYSIOLOGY, BIOPHYSICS. *Educ:* Tex Christian Univ, AB, 60; Univ Miss, PhD(physiol, biophys), 64. *Prof Exp:* Res asst learning theory, Bell Helicopter Co, Tex, 59-60; prof math, Exten Ctr, Univ Miss, 60-65, from asst prof physiol & biophys to prof, Med Ctr, 71-77; PROF PHYSIOL & CHMN DEPT, UNIV S ALA, 77- *Concurrent Pos:* Fel, Harvard Med Sch Biophysics Lab, 64-67; assoc ed, J Applied Physiol; NIH fel. *Mem:* AAAS; Am Math Soc; Am Heart Asn; Biophys Soc; Am Physiol Soc. *Res:* Irreversible thermodynamics and membrane biophysics to mammalian physiology, especially in fields of cardio-pulmonary, intestinal dynamics and capillary exchange; author or coauthor of over 300 publications. *Mailing Add:* Dept of Physiol Univ of S Ala Mobile AL 36688

TAYLOR, AUSTIN LAURENCE, b Vancouver, BC, Jan 23, 32; US citizen; m 56; c 2. BACTERIAL GENETICS, BACTERIOPHAGE GENETICS. *Educ:* Western Md Col, BS, 54; Univ Calif, Berkeley, PhD(bact), 61. *Prof Exp:* Res assoc bact genetics, Brookhaven Nat Lab, 61-62; res microbiologist, NIH, 62-65; asst prof, 65-70, ASSOC PROF MICROBIOL, SCH MED, UNIV COLO, DENVER, 70- *Concurrent Pos:* Prin investr, USPHS res grant, 66- *Mem:* AAAS; Genetics Soc Am; Am Soc Microbiol. *Res:* Molecular genetic studies on the mechanism of bacteriophage Mu DNA replication and transportation. *Mailing Add:* Dept Microbiol Box B175 Med Ctr Univ Colo 4200 E 9th Ave Denver CO 80262

TAYLOR, BARNEY EDSEL, b Elizabethton, Tenn, Dec 10, 51; m 71. EXPERIMENTAL SOLID STATE PHYSICS. *Educ:* ETenn State Univ, BS, 73; Clemson Univ, PhD(physics), 78. *Prof Exp:* Asst prof physics, Denison Univ, 78-79; ASST PROF PHYSICS, JACKSON STATE UNIV, 79- *Mem:* Am Phys Soc; Am Asn Physics Teachers. *Res:* Transport studies in ionic solids by means of electrical conductivity; ionic thermocurrents and radiotracer diffusion. *Mailing Add:* Dept Physics Jackson State Univ Jackson MS 39217

TAYLOR, BARRIE FREDERICK, b Nottingham, Eng, Nov 21, 39; m 65; c 2. MARINE MICROBIOLOGY. *Educ:* Univ Leeds, BSc, 62, PhD(biochem), 65. *Prof Exp:* NSF grant bact, Rutgers Univ, 65-67; res assoc microbiol, Univ Tex, Austin, 67-69; asst prof marine sci, Biol & Living Resources Div, Sch Marine & Atmospheric Sci, Univ Miami, 70-74, assoc prof, 74-77; assoc prof biol & living resources, Univ Miami, Coral Gables, 77-80; PROF MARINE & ATMOSPHERIC CHEM DIV, ROSENSTIEL SCH MARINE & ATMOSPHERIC SCI, UNIV MIAMI, 80- *Concurrent Pos:* NSF res grants, 70-72 & 73-81; NIH grant, 74-77 & 81-82. *Mem:* AAAS; Am Soc Microbiol; Am Soc Limnol & Oceanog. *Res:* Microbial biochemistry; autotrophic and lithotrophic micro-organisms; aromatic degradation by microbes. *Mailing Add:* Div Marine & Atmospheric Chem Univ Miami Rosenstiel Sch Marine & Atmospheric Sci Miami FL 33149

TAYLOR, BARRY EDWARD, b Potsdam, NY, July 7, 47; m 68; c 1. SOLID STATE CHEMISTRY. *Educ:* State Univ NY Col Fredonia, BS, 69; Brown Univ, PhD(chem), 74. *Prof Exp:* Teaching asst chem, State Univ NY Col Fredonia, 66-67, res asst, 68-69; teaching assoc chem, Brown Univ, 69-73; chemist, 73-74, res chemist, exp sta, 74-78, sr res chemist, 78-81, RES ASSOC, PHOTO EMD, E I DU PONT DE NEMOURS & CO, INC, NIAGARA FALLS, NY, 81- *Mem:* Am Chem Soc; AAAS; Int Soc Hybrid Microelectronics; Electrochem Soc; Am Ceramic Soc. *Res:* Preparative solid state chemistry; crystallographic and physical properties of oxides, halides and sulfides; chemistry of alkali metal compounds; study of ionic conductivity in solids; thick film technology of resistors, conductors, dielectrics and solder compositions. *Mailing Add:* Photo-EMD E I du Pont de Nemours & Co Inc Niagara Falls NY 14302

TAYLOR, BARRY NORMAN, b Philadelphia, Pa, Mar 27, 36; m 58; c 3. FUNDAMENTAL CONSTANTS, ELECTRICAL METROLOGY. *Educ:* Temple Univ, AB, 57; Univ Pa, MS, 60, PhD(physics), 63. *Prof Exp:* From instr to asst prof physics, Univ Pa, 63-66; physicist, RCA Labs, NJ, 66-70; chief, Absolute Elec Measurements Sect, 70-74, chief elec div, 74-78, CHIEF ELEC MEASUREMENTS & STANDARDS DIV, NAT BUR STANDARDS, 78- *Concurrent Pos:* Consult, Philco Corp, 64-65; instr math, Rider Col, 69-70; mem, Nat Acad Sci-Nat Res Coun-Nat Acad Eng Adv Comt Fundamental Constants, 69-, mem adv panel to Elec Div of Inst Basic Standards, Nat Bur Standards, 69, mem Comt Data Sci & Technol Task Group on Fundamental Constants, 76-; co-chmn, Orgn Int de Metrologie Legale, 75-; Nat Bur Standards deleg, 14th Session Comt Consult Elec, Comt Int Poids & Mesures, Paris, France, 75, deleg 15th session, 78; ed, Metrologia, 76-; tech adv & chmn, Measurement of Elec & Magnetic Quantities, 77-; mem, NSF Interagency Atomic & Molecular Physics Group, 76-; mem comt definitions of elec terms, Am Nat Standards Inst, 78- *Honors & Awards:* RCA Outstanding Achievement Award in Sci, 69; John Price Wetherill Medal, Franklin Inst, Philadelphia & Silver Medal Award, Dept Com, Washington, 75. *Mem:* Fel Am Phys Soc; fel Inst Elec & Electronics Eng. *Res:* Precision measurements and fundamental constants; absolute electrical measurements; superconductivity; electron tunneling; Josephson effects; percision measurements. *Mailing Add:* Rm B258 Bldg 220 Nat Bur Stand Washington DC 20234

TAYLOR, BENJAMIN JOSEPH, b Pasadena, Calif, July 5, 42; m 70; c 6. PHYSICS, ASTRONOMY. *Educ:* Pasadena City Col, AA, 62; Univ Calif, Berkeley, BA, 64, PhD(astron), 69. *Prof Exp:* Res assoc, Princeton Univ, 69-71; res assoc, Univ Wash, 71-73, instr astron, 74; Nat Res Coun assoc, Ames Res Ctr, NASA, 74-76, assoc, 77-80; ASST PROF PHYSICS & ASTRON, BRIGHAM YOUNG UNIV, 80- *Concurrent Pos:* Inst physics & astron, San Jose State Univ, 77-80. *Mem:* Astron Soc Pac. *Res:* Spectrophotometry of secondary standards and solar analogs; differential broad-band photometry of clusters for blanketing analyses; spectrophotometry of K giants for abundance analyses. *Mailing Add:* Dept Physics & Astron Brigham Young Univ Provo UT 84602

TAYLOR, BEVERLEY ANN PRICE, b Kingsport, Tenn, Nov 24, 51; m 71. PHYSICS, QUANTUM FIELD THEORY. *Educ:* ETenn State Univ, BS, 73; Clemson Univ, PhD(physics), 78. *Prof Exp:* asst prof physics, Denison Univ, 78-79; ASST PROF PHYSICS, JACKSON STATE UNIV, 79- *Mem:* Am Phys Soc; Am Asn Phys Teachers. *Res:* Intrinsically nonlinear quantum field theories; solitary wave solutions of such field equations. *Mailing Add:* Dept of Physics & Astron Jackson State Univ Jackson MS 39217

TAYLOR, BILLY G, b Booneville, Miss, Aug 11, 24; m 49; c 2. ONCOLOGY, SURGERY. *Educ:* Harvard Med Sch, MD, 48. *Prof Exp:* From intern to resident surg, Grady Mem Hosp, Atlanta, Ga, 48-50; resident, Hosp, Emory Univ, 50-51; resident, Mem Ctr Cancer & Allied Dis, New York, 53-57; instr surg, 57-61, assoc prof clin surg, 64-72, assoc prof surg, 72-74, PROF SURG, LA STATE UNIV MED CTR, NEW ORLEANS, 74- *Concurrent Pos:* Spec fel head & neck surg with Dr Hayes Martin, Mem Ctr Cancer & Allied Dis, New York, 57; chief surg, Vet Admin Hosp, New Orleans, 64-, sr physician, 72-; consult, USPHS Hosp, New Orleans, 64-81; active staff, Touro Infirmary, New Orleans, 64-; sr vis surgeon, Charity Hosp, New Orleans, 64- *Mem:* James Ewing Soc; Soc Head & Neck Surg; AMA; fel Am Col Surg; Am Thoracic Soc. *Res:* Oncologic and head and neck surgery; physical and chemical properties of human cadaver blood; clincial studies of ameloblastoma of the mandible and carotid body tumors; clinical studies on carcinoma of the male breast, the parotid salivary gland and the larynx. *Mailing Add:* Vet Admin Hosp 1601 Perdido St New Orleans LA 70146

TAYLOR, BRUCE CAHILL, b Cleveland, Ohio, June 5, 42; div; c 4. BIOMEDICAL ENGINEERING, INSTRUMENTATION. *Educ:* Hiram Col, BA, 64; Kent State Univ, MA, 66, PhD(physiol), 71. *Prof Exp:* Assoc dir res, Vascular Res Lab, Akron City Hosp, 71-75; sr res scientist, Abcor, Inc, 75-76; mem staff, Ambur Systs, 76-78; DIR DEPT MED ENG, AKRON CITY HOSP, 78-; ASSOC PROF BIOENG, UNIV AKRON, 81- *Concurrent Pos:* Biomed consult, Midgard Electronics, 75-80; consult, Norton Co, 78- *Mem:* Am Soc Artifical Internal Organs; Asn Advan Med Instrumentation; Inst Elec & Electronics Engrs; Eng Med & Biol Soc. *Res:* Design and development of new types of medical instrumentation and new techniques for biomaterials development; blood pressure monitoring. *Mailing Add:* Dept of Med Eng Akron City Hosp Akron OH 44309

TAYLOR, C(HARLES) E(DWIN), b West Lafayette, Ind, Mar 24, 24; m 46; c 2. MECHANICS. *Educ:* Purdue Univ, BSME, 46, MS, 48; Univ Ill, PhD(theoret & appl mech), 53. *Prof Exp:* Instr eng mech, Purdue Univ, 46-48; instr theoret & appl mech, Univ Ill, 48-51, asst prof, 51-52; struct res engr, David Taylor Model Basin, DC, 52-54; asst prof theoret & appl mech, 54-55, assoc prof, 55-57, PROF THEORET & APPL MECH, UNIV ILL, URBANA, 57- *Concurrent Pos:* Vis prof, India, 66, 69 & Univ Calif, Berkeley, 68. *Honors & Awards:* M M Frocht Award, Soc Exp Stress Anal, 69 & M Hetenyi Award, 70. *Mem:* Nat Acad Eng; Am Soc Mech Engrs; Am Soc Eng Educ; Am Soc Eng Sci. *Res:* Three-dimensional photoelasticity; applications of lasers to experimental mechanics; shell theory; holography. *Mailing Add:* 3321 Kimberly Dr Champaign IL 61820

TAYLOR, C PAT(RICK) S(TIRLING), b Toronto, Ont, May 11, 30; m 55; c 4. BIOPHYSICS. *Educ:* Univ BC, BA, 52; Oxford Univ, BA, 54, MA, 57; Univ Pa, PhD(biophys), 60. *Prof Exp:* Childs Mem Fund fel biophys, Cambridge Univ, 60-61; asst prof physics, Univ BC, 61-67; assoc prof, 68-74, PROF BIOPHYS, UNIV WESTERN ONT, 74- *Mem:* Sigma Xi; Biophys Soc; Can Soc Cell Biol; Am Soc Photobiol. *Res:* Electron paramagnetic resonance of cytochromes including canformation effects; saturations transfer spectroscopy. *Mailing Add:* Dept Biophys Univ Western Ont London ON N6A 5B8 Can

TAYLOR, CARL ERNEST, b Mussoorie, India, July 26, 16; m 43; c 3. PREVENTIVE MEDICINE, EPIDEMIOLOGY. *Educ:* Muskingum Col, BS, 37; Harvard Univ, MD, 41, MPH, 51, DrPH, 53; FRCP(C), 45. *Hon Degrees:* DSc, Muskingum Col, 62; DHL, Towson State Univ, Baltimore, 78. *Prof Exp:* Med officer, Gorgas Hosp, 41-44; chief med serv, USPHS Marine Hosp, Pittsburgh, 44-46; hosp supt, Fatehgarh, India, 47-50; instr, Sch Pub Health, Harvard Univ, 51-53; prof prev med, Christian Med Col, India, 53-56; assoc prof prev med & pub health & dir prog for teachers, Sch Pub Health, Harvard Univ, 56-61; PROF & CHMN DEPT INT HEALTH, SCH HYG & PUB HEALTH, JOHNS HOPKINS UNIV, 61- *Mem:* Inst Med-Nat Acad Sci; Asn Teachers Prev Med; Am Pub Health Asn; Royal Soc Trop Med & Hyg; Am Soc Trop Med & Hyg. *Res:* International health; health planning in developing countries; population dynamics; medical education; epidemiology of leprosy and nutrition and infections; integration of health and family planning. *Mailing Add:* Dept Int Health Sch Hyg & Pub Health Johns Hopkins Univ Baltimore MD 21205

TAYLOR, CHARLES ARTHUR, JR, b Ithaca, NY, July 28, 13; m 37, 69; c 2. PLANT TAXONOMY. *Educ:* Cornell Univ, BS, 35, MS, 39. *Prof Exp:* Assoc prof bot, SDak State Univ, 49-67, prof, 67-80, cur, Herbarium, 49-80. *Mem:* AAAS; Am Soc Plant Taxon; Int Asn Plant Taxon. *Res:* Flora of South Dakota, monographic studies in Poaceae. *Mailing Add:* 201 17th Ave Brookings SD 57006

TAYLOR, CHARLES BRUCE, b Hecla, SDak, Feb 6, 15; m 38; c 2. PATHOLOGY. *Educ:* Univ Minn, BS, 38, MB, 40, MD, 41. *Prof Exp:* Intern, Univ Hosp, Univ Minn, 40-41, fel physiol, 41-42; res assoc & asst prof path, Col Med, Univ Ill, 46-51, assoc prof, 54-59; assoc prof, Univ NC, 51-54; prof, Med Sch, Northwestern Univ, 69-70; prof, Med Ctr, Univ Ala, Birmingham, 70-72; PROF PATH, ALBANY MED COL, 72-; dir res, Vet Admin Hosp, Albany, 72-80; PROF PATH, MED COL UNION UNIV, 80- *Concurrent Pos:* Res assoc, Presby Hosp, Chicago, 46-51, attend pathologist, 54-59; chmn dept path, Evanston Hosp, Ill, 59-70; mem coun arteriosclerosis, Am Heart Asn. *Mem:* Am Physiol Soc; Am Soc Exp Path; Am Heart Asn; Am Asn Path & Bact; AMA. *Res:* Arteriosclerosis and its pathogenesis; human metabolism of cholesterol; degenerative pulmonary diseases; pathogenesis of gall stones. *Mailing Add:* Dept Path Med Col Union Univ Albany NY 12208

TAYLOR, CHARLES ELLETT, b Chicago, Ill, Sept 9, 45; m 69. POPULATION GENETICS. *Educ:* Univ Calif, Berkeley, AB, 68; State Univ NY, Stony Brook, PhD(ecol & evolution), 73. *Prof Exp:* asst prof biol, Univ Calif, Riverside, 74-79; ASSOC PROF BIOL, UNIV CALIF, LOS ANGELES, 80- *Mem:* Genetics Soc Am; Soc Study Evolution; Am Ecol Soc; Am Soc Naturalists. *Res:* Population genetics and ecology. *Mailing Add:* Dept Biol Univ Calif Los Angeles CA 90024

TAYLOR, CHARLES EMERY, b White Plains, NY, Mar 2, 40; m 70. NUCLEAR MAGNETIC RESONANCE. *Educ:* Williams Col, BA, 61, MA, 63; Mich State Univ, PhD(physics), 67. *Prof Exp:* Asst prof, 67-73, ASSOC PROF PHYSICS, ANTIOCH COL, 73- *Mem:* Am Phys Soc; Int Solar Energy Asn; Am Asn Physics Teachers. *Res:* Nuclear spin lattice relaxation in antiferromagnetics; holography; holaesthetics; solar energy and alternative energy sources. *Mailing Add:* Dept of Physics Antioch Col Yellow Springs OH 45387

TAYLOR, CHARLES JOEL, b Portland, Ore, Apr 12, 19; m 52; c 3. PHYSICS. *Educ:* Univ Ill, BS, 40, MS, 48, PhD(physics), 51. *Prof Exp:* Asst nuclear physics, Univ Ill, 50-51; physicist, NAm Aviation, Inc, 51-52; tech mgt systs anal nuclear weapons, 75-81, PHYSICIST, LAWRENCE LIVERMORE NAT LAB, UNIV CALIF, 52-, ASST ASSOC DIR, 81- *Concurrent Pos:* Consult US Deleg, conf disarmament, Geneva, Switz, 79, 80. *Mem:* Am Phys Soc. *Res:* Scintillation counters; neutron physics; nuclear weapons design; systems analysis. *Mailing Add:* Lawrence Livermore Nat Lab Univ of Calif Livermore CA 94550

TAYLOR, CHARLES RICHARD, b Phoenix, Ariz, Sept 8, 39. COMPARATIVE PHYSIOLOGY, ENVIRONMENTAL PHYSIOLOGY. *Educ:* Occidental Col, BA, 60; Harvard Univ, MA, 62, PhD(biol), 63. *Prof Exp:* Res fel mammal, Mus Comp Zool, Harvard Univ, 64-67; res assoc zool, Duke Univ, 68-70; assoc prof, 70-74, PROF BIOL, HARVARD UNIV, 74-, ALEXANDER AGASSIZ PROF ZOOL, 74-, DIR CONCORD FIELD STA, 70- *Concurrent Pos:* Hon lectr, Univ Col, Nairobi, Kenya & attached res officer, EAfrican Vet Res Orgn, 64-67; res assoc, Mus Comp Zool, Harvard Univ, 68-; vis prof, Univ Nairobi, 77; Guggenheim fel, 77. *Mem:* AAAS; Am Soc Mammal; Am Physiol Soc; Am Soc Zool; NY Acad Sci. *Res:* Water metabolism; temperature regulation; respiratory and exercise physiology; physiology of wild and domestic ruminants. *Mailing Add:* Concord Field Sta Harvard Univ Old Causeway Rd Bedford MA 01730

TAYLOR, CHARLES WILLIAM, b Duluth, Minn, Sept 26, 30; m 53; c 4. ORGANIC CHEMISTRY. *Educ:* Univ Minn, BA, 52; Univ Wis, PhD(chem), 57. *Prof Exp:* Sr chemist, 57-72, res specialist, 72-81, SR RES SPECIALIST, MED PROD DIV, CENT RES DEPT, 3M CO, 81- *Mem:* Am Chem Soc; Sigma Xi. *Res:* Fluorocarbon chemistry; biomedical materials; thermosetting acrylics; pressure sensitive adhesives. *Mailing Add:* 3M Co 3M Ctr Bldg 230-3G St Paul MN 55101

TAYLOR, CLAYBORNE D, b Kokomo, Miss, July 15, 38; m 63; c 3. ELECTROMAGNETICS. *Educ:* Miss State Univ, BS, 61; NMex State Univ, MS, 64, PhD(physics), 65. *Prof Exp:* Staff mem, Sandia Corp, 65-67; from asst prof to assoc prof physics, Miss State Univ, 67-71; prof elec eng, Univ Miss, 71-72; prof elec eng, 72-74, PROF ELEC ENG & PHYSICS, MISS STATE UNIV, 74- *Concurrent Pos:* Assoc mem US Nat Comt, Int Union Radio Sci. *Mem:* Am Phys Soc; Inst Elec & Electronics Engrs. *Res:* Field and antenna theories; electromagnetic boundary value problems. *Mailing Add:* Dept of Physics Miss State Univ Mississippi State MS 39762

TAYLOR, CLIVE ROY, b Cambridge, Eng, July 24, 44; m 67; c 4. PATHOLOGY. *Educ:* Cambridge Univ, MBBChem, 69, MD, 80; Oxford Univ, PhD(immunol), 74. *Prof Exp:* Lectr path, Univ Oxford, 70-75; fel cancer res, UK Res Coun, 75-76; PROF IMMUNOPATH, UNIV SOUTHERN CALIF, LOS ANGELES, 76- *Res:* Immunopathology, immunohistology and cancer diagnosis, with particular reference to leukemia & lymphoma. *Mailing Add:* Dept Path Univ Southern Calif 2025 Zonal Ave Los Angeles CA 90033

TAYLOR, CONSTANCE ELAINE SOUTHERN, b Washington, DC, Nov 14, 37; m 59; c 3. ECOLOGY, SYSTEMATIC BOTANY. *Educ:* Univ Okla, BS, 59, MS, 61, PhD(plant ecol & syst bot), 75. *Prof Exp:* Teacher pub schs, Okla, 63-64; instr, 70-74, asst prof, 74-78, ASSOC PROF BIOL, SOUTHEASTERN OKLA STATE UNIV, 78- *Mem:* Am Soc Plant Taxonomists; Nat Wildlife Fedn. *Res:* The genus Solidago, or goldenrods, Oklahoma vascular plants and chemotaxonomy of bacteria. *Mailing Add:* Dept of Biol Southeastern Okla State Univ Durant OK 74701

TAYLOR, D DAX, b Chicago, Ill, Oct 10, 37; m 61; c 3. ANATOMIC PATHOLOGY, CLINICAL PATHOLOGY. *Educ:* Amherst Col, AB, 59; Univ Mo-Columbia, MD, 63; Am Bd Path, dipl & cert anat path & clin path, 68. *Prof Exp:* Resident path, Sch Med, Univ Mo-Columbia, 63-68, instr, 68-69, asst prof path & asst dean sch med, 69-72; assoc prof & assoc dean med educ, Southern Ill Univ, Springfield, 72-76, prof path & assoc dean acad affairs, Sch Med, 76-79, exec assoc dean, 79-80; VPRES EVALUATION PROG, NAT BD MED EXAMINERS, 80- *Mem:* Asn Am Med Cols; Am Soc Clin Path. *Res:* Medical education, student and curriculum evaluation; platelet patho-physiology. *Mailing Add:* 3930 Chestnut St Nat Bd Med Examiners Philadelphia PA 19104

TAYLOR, D LANSING, b Baltimore, Md, Dec 26, 46; m 69; c 3. CELL BIOLOGY. *Educ:* Univ Md, BS, 68; State Univ NY, Albany, PhD(biol), 73. *Prof Exp:* Fel biophysics, Marine Biol Labs, 73-74; asst prof biol, Harvard Univ, 74-78, assoc prof, 78-82; PROF BIOL, CARNEGIE-MELLON UNIV, 82- *Concurrent Pos:* Ed, J Cell Biol & J Cell Motility, 81- *Mem:* Am Soc Cell Biol; Biophys Soc; NY Acad Sci. *Res:* Molecular basis of amoebiod movements, utilizing biochemical, cell biological and biophysical approaches and fluorescence spectroscopy. *Mailing Add:* Dept Biol Sci Carnegie-Mellon Univ Pittsburgh PA 15213

TAYLOR, DALE FREDERICK, b Evansville, Ind, June 16, 44; m 67; c 2. ELECTROCHEMISTRY. *Educ:* Univ Toronto, BSc, 66, MSc, 68, PhD(chem), 70. *Prof Exp:* Staff scientist battery res, 70-73, mgr personnel admin, 74, STAFF SCIENTIST, MAT SCI & ENG SECTOR, GEN ELEC CORP RES & DEVELOP, 75- *Mem:* Electrochem Soc. *Res:* Crevice corrosion and stress corrosion cracking of boiling water reactor structural materials. *Mailing Add:* Gen Elec Res & Develop Ctr PO Box 8 Schenectady NY 12301

TAYLOR, DALE L, b Studley, Kans, Sept 30, 36; m 58; c 3. ECOLOGY. *Educ:* Kans State Univ, BS, 58, MS, 60; Univ Wyo, PhD(ecol), 69. *Prof Exp:* Instr zool, Kans State Univ, 60-61; instr biol, Augustana Col, 61-64; instr zool, Univ Wyo, 64-68; asst prof, Millikin Univ, 68-70; assoc prof & head biol, Sterling Col, 70-77; res biologist, South Fla Ctr Res, Everglades Nat Park, 77-81; FIRE ECOLOGIST, ALASKA STATE OFF, BUR LAND MGT, ANCHORAGE, 81- *Concurrent Pos:* Collabr, Nat Park Serv, 70-74, res biologist, 74-77. *Mem:* Ecol Soc Am; Am Inst Biol Sci; Am Soc Mammal. *Res:* Biotic succession following prescribed, natural and wildfire. *Mailing Add:* Alaska State Off Bur Land Mgt Anchorage AK 99513

TAYLOR, DAVID COBB, b Portland, Maine, June 7, 39; m 71. ANALYTICAL CHEMISTRY. *Educ:* Bowdoin Col, AB, 61; Wesleyan Univ, MA, 63; Univ Conn, PhD(chem), 70. *Prof Exp:* Asst prof, 68-72, ASSOC PROF CHEM, SLIPPERY ROCK STATE COL, 72- *Concurrent Pos:* Consult anal methods & environ systs eng. *Mem:* AAAS; Am Chem Soc; fel Am Inst Chemists; Nat Sci Teachers Asn. *Res:* Electroanalytical chemistry and multicomponent systems. *Mailing Add:* Dept Chem Slippery Rock State Col Slippery Rock PA 16057

TAYLOR, DAVID NEELY, b Ann Arbor, Mich, July 31, 48; m 80. INFECTIOUS DISEASES. *Educ:* Kenyon Col, BA, 70; Dartmouth Med Sch, DMS, 72; Harvard Med Sch, MD, 74; London Sch Hygiene & Trop Med, MSc, 78. *Prof Exp:* Med resident, State Univ NY, Buffalo, 74-77; res fel geographic med, Sch Med, Johns Hopkins Univ, 78-80; EPIDEMIOLOGIST ENTERIC DIS, CTR DIS CONTROL, WALTER REED ARMY INST RES, 80- *Concurrent Pos:* Consult, Gorga's Hosp, Panama, 78-80. *Mem:* Am Soc Microbiol; Am Soc Trop Med & Hyg. *Res:* Epidemiologic studies in infectious causes of diaphreal disease, including studies in salmonella, typhoid, campylobacter and intestinal parasites; development of rapid diagnostic methods to detect enteric disease agents. *Mailing Add:* Dept Bacterial Dis Walter Reed Army Inst Res Washington DC 20012

TAYLOR, DAVID WARD, b Chesterfield, Eng, Aug 18, 38; m 65; c 2. THEORETICAL PHYSICS, SOLID STATE PHYSICS. *Educ:* Oxford Univ, BA, 61, MA, 65, PhD(physics), 65. *Prof Exp:* Mem tech staff, Bell Tel Labs, NJ, 64-67; from asst prof to assoc prof, 67-77, assoc chmn, Physics Dept, 80-82, PROF THEORET SOLID STATE PHYSICS, MCMASTER UNIV, 77- *Mem:* Can Phys Soc; Am Phys Soc. *Res:* Dynamics of disordered crystals; calculations of phonons and phonon dependent properties of metals and alloys. *Mailing Add:* Dept Physics McMaster Univ Hamilton ON L8S 4L8 Can

TAYLOR, DERMOT BROWNRIGG, b Ireland, Mar 30, 15; US citizen; m 45, 65; c 1. PHARMACOLOGY. *Educ:* Trinity Col, Dublin, MD, 37, MB, BCh & BAO, 38. *Prof Exp:* Asst physiol, Trinity Col, Dublin, 38-39; lectr, King's Col, Univ London, 39-45, lectr pharmacol, 45-50; assoc prof, Univ Calif, San Francisco, 50-53; chmn dept, 53-68, PROF PHARMACOL, UNIV CALIF, LOS ANGELES, 53- *Concurrent Pos:* Univ London traveling fel, Yale Univ,

48. *Mem:* Am Soc Pharmacol & Exp Therapeut; Brit Physiol Soc; Royal Soc Chem; Brit Biochem Soc; Brit Pharmacol Soc. *Res:* Mode of action of neuromuscular blocking agents. *Mailing Add:* 6982 Wildlife Malibu CA 90265

TAYLOR, DIANE WALLACE, b Covina, Calif. TROPICAL MEDICINE, HYBRIDOMA TECHNOLOGY. *Educ:* Univ Hawaii, BA, 68, MS, 70, PhD(zool), 75. *Prof Exp:* Instr biol, Sch Med, Univ Hawaii, 70-73, fel trop med, 75-78; FEL IMMUNOL, LAB MICROBIOL IMMUNOL, NIH, 78- *Mem:* Am Soc Trop Med Hyg; Sigma Xi; Am Soc Microbiologists; Am Soc Primatol. *Res:* Immune studies of parasitic infections with special emphasis on malaria. *Mailing Add:* Lab of Microbial Immunity NIH Bethesda MD 20205

TAYLOR, DONALD CURTIS, b London, Ky, June 16, 39; m 67; c 1. MATHEMATICS. *Educ:* Univ Ky, BS, 61, MS, 64, PhD(math), 67. *Prof Exp:* Elec eng, Westinghouse Elec Corp, 61-62; assoc prof math, Univ Mo-Columbia, 67-73; assoc prof, 73-77, PROF MATH, MONT STATE UNIV, 77- *Concurrent Pos:* Fel, La State Univ, Baton Rouge, 69-70. *Mem:* Am Math Soc. *Res:* Functional analysis. *Mailing Add:* Dept of Math Mont State Univ Bozeman MT 59715

TAYLOR, DONALD FULTON, pathobiology, biochemistry, see previous edition

TAYLOR, DONALD JAMES, b Dayton, Ohio, Mar 6, 33; m 55; c 2. ASTRONOMY. *Educ:* Calif Inst Technol, BS, 55, MS, 58; Univ Wis, PhD(astron), 63. *Prof Exp:* Proj assoc space astron lab, Univ Wis, 63-65; asst prof astron, Univ Ariz, 65-71; ASSOC PROF PHYSICS, UNIV NEBR, LINCOLN, 71- *Mem:* Int Astron Union; Am Astron Soc; Astron Soc Pac. *Res:* Planetary astronomy; astronomical instrumentation; pulsars; applications of area scanning to astronomical problems. *Mailing Add:* Behlen Lab of Physics Univ of Nebr Lincoln NE 68588

TAYLOR, DOROTHY JANE, b Waco, Tex. BIOLOGY. *Educ:* Rice Univ, BA, 43; Iowa State Univ, MS, 47; George Washington Univ, PhD(biol), 57. *Prof Exp:* Tech asst, Synthetic Rubber Lab, Humble Oil Co, 43-45; lab instr zool, biol & physiol, Iowa State Univ, 45-47; parasitologist, Lab Trop Dis, NIH, 47-58; head endocrine-related tumor syst sect, Cancer Chemother Nat Serv Ctr, 58-69, head, Gen Lab & Clin, 64-73; head exp biol proj sect, Breast Cancer Prog Coord Br, 73-75, CHIEF, BREAST CANCER PROG COORD BR, DIV CANCER BIOL & DIAG & EXEC SECY, BREAST CANCER TASK FORCE COMT, NAT CANCER INST, NIH, 75- *Mem:* Fel AAAS; Am Asn Cancer Res; Sigma Xi. *Res:* Experimental biology of breast cancer; malaria and amebiasis; in vitro cultivation; experimental chemotherapy; nutritional aspects; endocrine tumors; host-tumor biology and therapy. *Mailing Add:* Breast Cancer Coord Br NCI Landow Bldg NIH Bethesda MD 20014

TAYLOR, DOUGLAS HIRAM, b Doddsville, Miss, Dec 15, 39; m 61. ETHOLOGY, ECOLOGY. *Educ:* Univ Dayton, BS, 66, MS, 68; Miss State Univ, PhD(zool), 70. *Prof Exp:* NSF fel, Univ Notre Dame, 70-71; asst prof, 71-74, ASSOC PROF ZOOL, MIAMI UNIV, 74- *Mem:* AAAS; Am Soc Zoologists; Animal Behav Soc; Ecol Soc Am. *Res:* Animal behavior, ecology and orientation; agonistic behavior; behavioral aspects of ecology of vertebrates. *Mailing Add:* Dept of Zool Miami Univ Oxford OH 45056

TAYLOR, DUANE FRANCIS, b Iowa City, Iowa, Sept 30, 25; m 50; c 7. DENTAL MATERIALS. *Educ:* Univ Mich, BSE, 49, MSE, 50; Georgetown Univ, PhD(biochem), 61. *Prof Exp:* Head dept dent mat, Sch Dent, Wash Univ, St Louis, 50-54; phys metallurgist, Dent Sect, Nat Bur Stand, 54-61; dir mat res, CMP Industs, 61-63; prof dent, Sch Dent, 63-74, PROF OPER DENT-DENT SCI, DENT RES CTR, UNIV NC, CHAPEL HILL, 74- *Concurrent Pos:* Consult, US Army, 67- & NIH, 69- *Mem:* AAAS; Am Soc Metals; Int Asn Dent Res. *Res:* Dental amalgams; cobalt-chromium alloys; denture base materials; polymerization mechanisms; properties of multiphase solids; materials for implant prosthesis. *Mailing Add:* Dent Res Ctr Univ of NC Chapel Hill NC 27514

TAYLOR, DUNCAN PAUL, b Bremerton, Wash, Feb 4, 49; c 1. NEUROPHARMACOLOGY. *Educ:* Calif Inst Technol, BS, 71; Ore State Univ, PhD(biochem), 77. *Prof Exp:* Technician, Anal Serv, Carnation Co Res Labs, 67-70; volunteer, US Peace Corps, 71-73; res asst, Dept Biochem & Biophysics, Ore State Univ, 73-77; res assoc, Sect Biochem & Pharmacol, Nat Inst Mental Health, 77-79; scientist & neuropharmacologist, 79-80, res assoc & neuropharmacologist, 80, SR SCIENTIST & NEUROPHARMACOLOGIST BIOL RES, PHARMACEUT DIV, MEAD JOHNSON & CO, 80- *Concurrent Pos:* Res fel, Comt Advan Sci Training, NSF, 65 & 70; teaching asst, Dept Biochem & Biophysics, Ore State Univ, 74; Partic, Advan Study Inst Cyclic Nucleotides, NATO, 77; Nat Res Serv Award, Nat Inst Drub Abuse, 77-79. *Mem:* Am Chem Soc; AAAS; Am Soc Neurochem; Soc Exp Biol & Med; Sigma Xi. *Res:* Receptors in nervous tissue membranes; receptor coupling to second messengers; linkage of changes in receptors to pathology behavior; author or coauthor of over 50 publications. *Mailing Add:* 112 Ryan Lane Evansville IN 47712

TAYLOR, DWIGHT WILLARD, b Pasadena, Calif, Jan 18, 32. INVERTEBRATE ZOOLOGY. *Educ:* Univ Mich, BS, 53; Univ Calif, MA, 54, PhD, 57. *Prof Exp:* Geologist, US Geol Surv, DC, 55-67; assoc prof zool, Ariz State Univ, 67-69; res assoc malacol, San Diego Mus Natural Hist, 69-74; prof zool, Pac Marine Sta, Univ Pac, 74-77; PROF ZOOL, TIBURON CTR ENVIRON STUDIES, SAN FRANCISCO STATE UNIV, 77- *Mem:* AAAS; Soc Syst Zool; Am Malacol Union. *Res:* Freshwater mollusks, ecology, taxonomy and distribution; biogeography. *Mailing Add:* Tiburon Ctr for Environ Studies PO Box 855 Tiburon CA 94920

TAYLOR, EDWARD CURTIS, b Springfield, Mass, Aug 3, 23; m 46; c 2. ORGANIC CHEMISTRY. *Educ:* Cornell Univ, AB, 46, PhD(org chem), 49. *Hon Degrees:* DSc, Hamilton Col, 69. *Prof Exp:* Merck fel, Zurich Tech Univ, 49-50; Du Pont fel, Univ Ill, 50-51, instr chem, 51-53, asst prof org chem, 53-54; from asst prof to assoc prof, 54-64, chmn dept chem, 74-79, PROF CHEM, PRINCETON UNIV, 64-, A BARTON HEPBURN PROF ORG CHEM, 66- *Concurrent Pos:* Consult, Procter & Gamble Co, 52-; NSF sr fac fel, Harvard Univ, 59; Fulbright scholar, 60; vis prof inst org chem, Stuttgart Tech Univ, 60; vis lectr, Weizmann Inst, 60; mem, Chem Adv Comt, Air Force Off Sci Res, 62-70; consult, Eastman Kodak Co, 65-; distinguished vis prof, Univ Buffalo, 69; ed org chem, Wiley Intersci, Inc, 69-; vis prof, Univ E Anglia, 69 & 72; consult, Eli Lilly & Co, 70- & Tenn Eastman Co, 71-; H J Backer lectr, Univ Groningen, 71; ed, Advances in Org Chem; co-ed, Gen Heterocyclic Chem & Chem of Heterocyclic Compounds; mem ed adv bd, J Org Chem, Synthetic Commun, Heterocycles & Chem Substruct Index, 73-; Guggenheim Mem fel, 79-80. *Honors & Awards:* Res Awards, Smith Kline & French Found, 55, Hoffmann-La Roche Found, 64 & 65, S B Penick Found, 69, 70, 71 & 72 & Ciba Pharmaceut Co, 71; Creative Work Award, Am Chem Soc, 74; Distinguished Hamilton Award, Hamilton Col, 78. *Mem:* AAAS; Am Chem Soc; fel NY Acad Sci; Royal Soc Chem; Ger Chem Soc. *Res:* Organic synthesis; heterocyclic chemistry, particularly pyrimidines, purines and pteridines; organothallium chemistry; natural products; photochemistry. *Mailing Add:* Frick Chem Lab Princeton Univ Princeton NJ 08540

TAYLOR, EDWARD DONALD, b Clifton, Tex, Sept 30, 40; m 65; c 1. PHYSICAL CHEMISTRY. *Educ:* Univ Tex, Austin, BS, 63; Tex Tech Univ, PhD(chem), 67. *Prof Exp:* Asst prof & fel chem, Fla State Univ, 67-68; PROF CHEM, ODESSA COL, 68- *Concurrent Pos:* Fel, Tex A&M Univ, 71. *Honors & Awards:* Eastman Fel, Eastman Kodak Co, 68. *Mem:* Am Chem Soc. *Res:* Investigations of thermoluminescence via electron paramagnetic resonance to understand the mechanism of the process. *Mailing Add:* Odessa Col 201 W Univ Odessa TX 79762

TAYLOR, EDWARD MORGAN, b Rapid City, SDak, Dec 27, 33; m 58; c 2. GEOLOGY, PETROLOGY. *Educ:* Ore State Univ, BS, 57, MS, 60; Wash State Univ, PhD(geol), 67. *Prof Exp:* Instr geol, Ore State Univ, 62-63 & Wash State Univ, 64-65; asst prof, 66-71, ASSOC PROF GEOL, ORE STATE UNIV, 71- *Mem:* Geol Soc Am; Mineral Soc Am. *Res:* Volcanic petrology of Cascade Range of California, Oregon and Washington. *Mailing Add:* Dept of Geol Ore State Univ Corvallis OR 97331

TAYLOR, EDWARD S(TORY), b New York, NY, Jan 26, 03; m 31, 54; c 2. ENGINEERING. *Educ:* Mass Inst Technol, BS, 24. *Prof Exp:* Engr, Pub Serv of NJ, 24-25 & Wright Aero Corp, 25-27; from instr to assoc prof automotive eng, 27-42, prof aircraft engines, 42-68, EMER PROF AIRCRAFT ENGINES & SR LECTR, MASS INST TECHNOL, 68- *Concurrent Pos:* Consult, Wright Aero Corp, 36-40, 42-58 & Off Prod Mgt, 40-42; mem power plants comt, Nat Adv Comt Aeronaut, 40-56; sci adv bd, US Dept Air Force, 56-59; tech adv bd, Reaction Motors, 57-62. *Honors & Awards:* Reed Prize, 36; Robert Hutchings Goddard Award, 73. *Mem:* Soc Automotive Engrs; fel Am Soc Mech Engrs; fel Am Inst Aeronaut & Astronaut; fel Am Acad Arts & Sci. *Res:* Internal combustion engines; gas turbines; jet engines; compressors; turbines. *Mailing Add:* 16 Tabor Hill Rd Lincoln MA 01773

TAYLOR, EDWARD STEWART, b Hecla, SDak, Aug 20, 11; m 40; c 3. OBSTETRICS & GYNECOLOGY. *Educ:* Univ Iowa, BA, 33, MD, 36; Am Bd Obstet & Gynec, dipl, 46. *Prof Exp:* Prof obstet & gynec & head dept, 47-76, dir, Am Bd Obstet & Gynec, 60-69, CLIN PROF OBSTET & GYNEC, MED CTR, UNIV COLO, DENVER, 77- *Concurrent Pos:* Consult Surgeon Gen, US Dept Air Force; ed, Obstet & Gynec Surv J; coun mem, Nat Inst Child Health & Human Develop; Ed, Obstet & Gynec Surv, 67-, Beck's Obstet Pract, 8th, 9th & 10th edition & Essentials Gynec, 1st, 2nd, 3rd & 4th edition. *Mem:* Am Gynec Soc; Am Asn Obstet & Gynec; Am Col Surg; Am Col Obstet & Gynec. *Res:* Cancer of the cervix; physiology of pregnancy. *Mailing Add:* Dept of Obstet & Gynec Univ of Colo Med Ctr Denver CO 80220

TAYLOR, EDWARD WYLLYS, b Richmond, Va, Mar 1, 27; m 50; c 3. CHEMISTRY, PSYCHOLOGY. *Educ:* Hampden-Sydney Col, BS, 49. *Prof Exp:* Res chemist, Va-Carolina Chem Corp, 49-55, asst plant supt, 55-58, asst plant mgr, 58-59, proj mgr, 59-61; exec vpres, Gulf Design Corp, 61-72; pres, Conserv, Inc, 72-74, PRES, PINE-LAKE CHEM CORP, 74- *Mem:* NY Acad Sci; Am Inst Chem; Am Inst Chem Eng; Am Chem Soc. *Res:* Fluorine recovery and utilization; phosphate processing; uranium recovery; fertilizer manufacturing; air pollution control; plant design, engineering and construction. *Mailing Add:* Pine Lake Chem Corp Number 1 Lone Palm Pl Lakeland FL 33801

TAYLOR, EDWIN FLORIMAN, b Oberlin, Ohio, June 22, 31; m 55; c 3. PHYSICS. *Educ:* Oberlin Col, AB, 53; Harvard Univ, MA, 54, PhD(physics), 58. *Prof Exp:* Asst prof physics, Wesleyan Univ, 56-64; vis assoc prof, Educ Res Ctr, Mass Inst Technol, 64-66, sr res scientist, 66-73; ed, Am JPhysics, 73-78; DIR, EDUC VIDEO RESOURCES, MASS INST TECHNOL, 79- *Mem:* Am Phys Soc; Am Asn Physics Teachers. *Res:* Solid state physics; educational writing and research in mechanics, special relativity and quantum physics; computer-assisted learning. *Mailing Add:* Dept Physics Rm 9-315 Mass Inst Technol Cambridge MA 02139

TAYLOR, EDWIN WILLIAM, b Toronto, Ont, June 8, 29; m 56; c 3. BIOPHYSICS. *Educ:* Univ Toronto, BA, 52; McMaster Univ, MSc, 55; Univ Chicago, PhD(biophys), 57. *Prof Exp:* Instr physics, Ont Agr Col, 52-53; res assoc biol, Mass Inst Technol, 57-59; from instr to prof biophys, 59-74, PROF BIOPHYS & THEORET BIOL, UNIV CHICAGO, 74-, MASTER BIOL SCI COL DIV & ASSOC DEAN COL, 76- *Mem:* Biophys Soc. *Res:* Mechanochemical systems; muscle; flagella; protoplasmic streaming; mechanism of cell division; physical protein chemistry. *Mailing Add:* Dept of Biophys Univ of Chicago 5640 Ellis Ave Chicago IL 60637

TAYLOR, ELIZABETH BEAMAN HESCH, b Sumter, SC, Oct 27, 21; m 48, 77; c 2. MATHEMATICS. *Educ:* Winthrop Col, BA, 43; Duke Univ, MA, 46; Columbia Univ, PhD, 55. *Prof Exp:* Instr math, Winthrop Col, 43; teacher pub schs, SC, 43-45; asst prof, Radford Col, 46-52 & Westhampton Col, 52-70; assoc prof, 70-78, PROF MATH, UNIV RICHMOND, 78- *Mem:* Math Asn Am. *Res:* Nature of mathematical evidence and its significance for the teaching of secondary school mathematics. *Mailing Add:* 2431 Swathmore Rd Richmond VA 23235

TAYLOR, ELLA RICHARDS, analytical chemistry, see previous edition

TAYLOR, ELLISON HALL, physical chemistry, see previous edition

TAYLOR, ELMORE HECTOR, pharmacognosy, phytochemistry, see previous edition

TAYLOR, EUGENE M, b Cheyenne, Wyo, Dec 25, 32; m 78; c 3. PHYSIOLOGY. *Educ:* Idaho State Col, BS, 58; Univ Wash, MS, 59, PhD(physiol & psychol), 64. *Prof Exp:* Asst prof psychol, Ariz State Univ, 64-72; res asst prof rehab med, Sch Med, Univ Wash, 72-74; investr physiol, Va Mason Res Ctr, 74-77, assoc mem sci staff physiol, 77-81; LECTR PSYCHOLOGY, UNIV WASHINGTON, 81- *Concurrent Pos:* Consult, Vet Admin Hosp, Phoenix, Ariz, 68-72; assoc dir, Exotic Environ Lab, Ariz State Univ, 69-72; fel, Dept Bioeng, Univ Wash, 71-72, affil assoc prof, Dept Otolaryngol, 76-, res affil, Regional Primate Res Ctr, 77-; affil investr, Virginia Mason Res Ctr, 71-74. *Mem:* Am Soc Primatologists; Int Primatological Soc. *Res:* Pathophysiology of disorders of infancy; neurophysiology; biologic effects of electromagnetic radiation. *Mailing Add:* 2640 Perkins Lane W Seattle WA 98199

TAYLOR, FLETCHER BRANDON, JR, b Aug 24, 29; m 54; c 4. INTERNAL MEDICINE. *Educ:* Stanford Univ, BS, 52; Univ Calif, San Francisco, MD, 56. *Hon Degrees:* MS, Univ Pa, 71. *Prof Exp:* Intern, Southern Pac Hosp, San Francisco, 56-57, resident surg, 57-58; res assoc protein chem, London Hosp, Eng, 58-59; mem res staff thrombosis, Cardiovasc Res Inst, San Francisco, 59-65; from asst prof to assoc prof med, Hosp Univ Pa, Philadelphia, 65-74, co-chmn div allergy & immunol, 68-74; PROF PATH & MED & DIR DIV EXP PATH & MED, HEALTH SCI CTR, UNIV OKLA, 74- *Concurrent Pos:* Resident med, Univ Calif Hosp, San Francisco, 59-62; consult hemat, NASA Manned Space Flight Ctr, 68-; mem thrombosis coun, Am Heart Asn, 71-; head, Am Acad Allergy Post-Graduate Educ Comt; clin prof res med, Okla Univ Health Sci Ctr, prof res biochem, head sect exp path & med; dir clin hemat serv, Univ Hosp, Oklahoma City; dir, Oklahoma City Children's Mem Hosp Coagulation Lab. *Honors & Awards:* Cochems Prize Cardiovasc Res, 68; Louis Pasteur Lectr Award, Univ Paris, 69. *Mem:* Int Soc Thrombosis & Haemostasis; Am Asn Immunol; Am Soc Clin Invest; Am Physiol Soc; Am Fedn Clin Res. *Res:* Thrombosis and protein chemistry. *Mailing Add:* PO Box 26901 Oklahoma City OK 73190

TAYLOR, FLOYD HECKMAN, b North Versailles, Pa, May 6, 26; m 55; c 2. MATHEMATICS. *Educ:* Bucknell Univ, BS, 49; Univ Pittsburgh, MS, 53, ScD, 63. *Prof Exp:* Asst proj engr math, Sperry Gyroscope Co, NY, 53-54; instr, Hood Col, 54-56; mathematician, Atlantic Div, Aerojet Gen Corp Div, Gen Tire & Rubber Co, 56-57 & US Army Biol Labs, 57-64; asst prof biostatist, Grad Sch Pub Health & asst prof prev med, Sch Med, 64-70, assoc prof community med, 70-75, RES PROF COMMUNITY MED, SCH MED, UNIV PITTSBURGH, 75- *Concurrent Pos:* Instr, Frederick Community Col, 57-61. *Mem:* Sigma Xi; Am Statist Soc; Biomet Soc. *Res:* Numerical analysis; applications of mathematics to digital computers; mathematical models as applied to biology; biostatistics. *Mailing Add:* Sch of Med Univ of Pittsburgh Pittsburgh PA 15261

TAYLOR, FRANCIS B, b New York, NY, June 15, 25. MATHEMATICS. *Educ:* Manhattan Col, AB, 44; Columbia Univ, AM, 47, PhD(math educ), 59. *Prof Exp:* From instr to assoc prof, 47-65, head dept, 64-72, PROF MATH, MANHATTAN COL, 65- *Concurrent Pos:* Lectr, Col Mt St Vincent, 53-56; NSF fac fel, 57-58; lectr, Sch Gen Studies, Hunter Col, 59-60. *Mem:* Math Asn Am; Am Statist Asn; Inst Math Statist; Nat Coun Teachers Math; Sigma Xi. *Res:* Mathematical statistics. *Mailing Add:* Dept of Math Manhattan Col Bronx NY 10471

TAYLOR, FRANK EUGENE, b Richmond, Va, Apr 1, 42; m 68; c 2. EXPERIMENTAL HIGH ENERGY PHYSICS. *Educ:* Mich State Univ, BS, 64; Cornell Univ, PhD(exp high energy physics), 70. *Prof Exp:* Res assoc exp high energy physics, Lab Nuclear Studies, Cornell Univ, 70-71, Deutsches Elektronen Synchrotron-Hamburg, Ger, 71-72; asst prof, 72-77, ASSOC PROF EXP HIGH ENERGY PHYSICS, NORTHERN ILL UNIV, 77- *Concurrent Pos:* Prin physicist, Dept of Energy grant, 78- *Mem:* Am Phys Soc. *Res:* Experiment and phenomenology of inclusive reactions in strong interactions; experimental high energy neutrino physics. *Mailing Add:* Dept of Physics Northern Ill Univ De Kalb IL 60115

TAYLOR, FRANK JOHN RUPERT (MAX), b Cairo, Egypt, July 17, 39; m 63. MARINE BIOLOGY. *Educ:* Univ Cape Town, BSc, 59, Hons, 60, PhD(marine bot), 65. *Prof Exp:* Res asst marine phytoplankton, Inst Oceanog, Univ Cape Town, 60-64; from asst prof to assoc prof, 65-75, PROF BIOL & OCEANOG, INST OCEANOG, UNIV BC, 75- *Concurrent Pos:* Can-France Exchange fel, France, 72; vis scientist, Phuket Marine Biol Ctr, Thailand, 73; res assoc, Int Develop Res Ctr, Bellairs Res Inst, Barbados, 79-80. *Mem:* Soc Evolutionary Protistology (pres, 79-81). *Res:* Taxonomy and distributional ecology of unicellular marine organisms, principally diatoms and dinoflagellates; undergraduate biology; marine phytoplankton ecology; red tides; intracellular symboisis; evolution. *Mailing Add:* Inst of Oceanog Univ of BC Vancouver BC V6T 1W5 Can

TAYLOR, FRED M, b Chanute, Kans, Aug 21, 19; m 42; c 5. PEDIATRICS. *Educ:* Stanford Univ, AB, 41, MD, 44. *Prof Exp:* From instr to prof pediat, Baylor Col Med, 48-69; prof, Univ Tex Med Sch San Antonio, 69-72, from asst dean to assoc dean acad develop, 69-72; dir, Off Continuing Educ, 72-78, spec asst to exec vpres & dean, 78-80, PROF PEDIAT, BAYLOR COL MED, 72-, EXEC ASST TO PRES, 80- *Mem:* AAAS; Am Acad Pediat; Soc Res Child Develop. *Res:* Infant nutrition and feeding; developmental behavior of infants, children and adolescents. *Mailing Add:* Off Pres Baylor Col Med Houston TX 77030

TAYLOR, FRED WILLIAM, b Springcreek, WVa, Jan 17, 32; m 54; c 4. WOOD SCIENCE & TECHNOLOGY. *Educ:* Va Polytech Inst, BS, 53; NC State Col, MWT, 54, PhD(wood sci & technol), 65. *Prof Exp:* Asst prof forestry, Univ Vt, 54-55; asst timber buyer, J B Belcher Lumber Co, 55-56; wood technologist, Pulaski Veneer & Furniture Co, 56-59; res asst, NC State Univ, 59-62; wood utilization exten specialist, Univ Mo, 63-65; PROF WOOD SCI & TECHNOL & ASST DIR, MISS FORESTRY PROD UTILIZATION LAB, MISS STATE UNIV, 65- *Concurrent Pos:* Coun Sci & Indust Res grant, SAfrica, 71-72. *Mem:* Forest Prod Res Soc; Soc Wood Sci & Technol; Int Asn Wood Anatomists; Inst Wood Sci. *Res:* Natural variation in the anatomical structure of angiosperm xylem, especially genetic implications of property variations. *Mailing Add:* Miss Forest Prod Lab Mississippi State MS 39762

TAYLOR, FREDRIC WILLIAM, b Amble, Eng, Sept 24, 44; m 69. ATMOSPHERIC PHYSICS. *Educ:* Univ Liverpool, BSc, 66; Oxford Univ, DPhil(atmos physics), 70. *Prof Exp:* RES SCIENTIST TECH STAFF ATMOS PHYSICS, JET PROPULSION LAB, CALIF INST TECHNOL, 71- *Mem:* Fel Royal Meteorol Soc; Am Meteorol Soc; Optical Soc Am; assoc Am Astron Asn. *Res:* Physics of the atmospheres of the Earth and planets, specializing in atmospheric radiation, remote sensing techniques and infrared observational methods. *Mailing Add:* Jet Propulsion Lab 4800 Oak Grove Dr Pasadena CA 91103

TAYLOR, FREDRICK JAMES, b Wisconsin Rapids, Wis, Apr 28, 40; m 68; c 3. ELECTRICAL ENGINEERING, COMPUTER SCIENCE. *Educ:* Milwaukee Sch Eng, BS, 65; Univ Colo, MS, 66, PhD(elec eng), 69. *Prof Exp:* Researcher elec eng, Tex Instruments, Dallas, 69-70; assoc prof, Univ Tex, El Paso, 70-75; PROF ELEC ENG, UNIV CINCINNATI, 75- *Concurrent Pos:* Prin investr, US Army Atmospheric Sci Lab grant, 73-75, Eng Found grant, 77-78 & NSF grant, 78- *Mem:* Inst Elec & Electronics Engrs. *Res:* Digital systems; digital signal processing; medical signal analysis; ultrasound; finite mathematics. *Mailing Add:* Dept Elec & Comput Eng Univ Cincinnati Cincinnati OH 45221

TAYLOR, G JEFFREY, b Port Jefferson, NY, June 27, 44; m 65; c 5. PLANETARY SCIENCE. *Educ:* Colgate Univ, AB, 66; Rice Univ, MA, 68, PhD(geol), 70. *Prof Exp:* Smithsonian Res Found res fel, lunar mineral & petrol, Smithsonian Astrophys Observ, 70-72, res assoc, 72-73; asst prof, Wash Univ, 73-76; SR RES ASSOC, INST METEORITICS, UNIV NMEX, 76- *Concurrent Pos:* Assoc, Harvard Univ, 70-; vis scientist, Lunar Sci Inst, 74-76. *Honors & Awards:* Nininger Meteorite Prize, Ctr Meteorite Studies, Ariz State Univ, 69. *Mem:* Am Geo- phys Union; Geochem Soc; Meteoritical Soc; AAAS. *Res:* Petrologic and chemical nature of the moon, meteorites and earth, with emphasis on their origins and thermal histories. *Mailing Add:* Dept of Geol Univ of NMex Albuquerque NM 87131

TAYLOR, GARY, b London, Eng, Sept 23, 52. PLASMA PHYSICS, LASER PHYSICS. *Educ:* Univ Manchester, BSc, 74; Oxford Univ, MSc, 75, DPhil(plasma physics), 77. *Prof Exp:* Res assoc, 7-79, STAFF RES PHYSICIST, PLASMA PHYSICS LAB, PRINCETON UNIV, 79- *Mem:* Am Phys Soc. *Res:* Application of laser Thomson scattering to high temperature plasma diagnostics in Tokamak fusion machines; investigation on nuclear radiation damage to materials in fusion research devices. *Mailing Add:* Princeton Plasma Physics Lab Princeton Univ PO Box 451 Princeton NJ 08544

TAYLOR, GARY N, b Plainfield, NJ, Oct 19, 42; m 64; c 3. ORGANIC CHEMISTRY. *Educ:* Princeton Univ, BA, 64; Yale Univ, MS, 66, PhD(org chem), 68. *Prof Exp:* Air Force Off Sci Res fel, Calif Inst Technol, 68-69; MEM TECH STAFF, BELL LABS, 69-, SUPVR, 79- *Mem:* Am Chem Soc; Electrochem Soc. *Res:* Synthetic organic chemistry; photochemistry; polymer chemistry; radiation chemistry; lithography; plasma chemistry. *Mailing Add:* Bell Labs 1D247 Murray Hill NJ 07974

TAYLOR, GENE WARREN, b Abilene, Tex, Nov 9, 36; m 64; c 2. PHYSICAL CHEMISTRY, MATERIALS SCIENCE. *Educ:* Tex Western Col, BS, 63; NMex State Univ, PhD(phys chem), 69. *Prof Exp:* Mem staff chem, El Paso Natural Gas Prod, 63-65; teacher math, Ysleta Independent Schs, 64-65; mem fac chem, Kans State Univ, 69-72; ASST GROUP LEADER CHEM, LOS ALAMOS NAT LAB, 72- *Concurrent Pos:* Mem staff, Schlesinger Res Found, 64-65; fel, Kans State Univ, 69-72. *Mem:* Am Chem Soc. *Res:* Rare gas, metastable atom flowing afterglow reactions for chemical analysis; gas phase chemical kinetics, and solid phase thermal decomposition reaction kinetics; composite materials. *Mailing Add:* Los Alamos Nat Lab PO Box 1663 Los Alamos NM 87545

TAYLOR, GEORGE ALLAN, b Hinton, Okla, June 18, 37; m 60; c 2. PLANT BREEDING, GENETICS. *Educ:* Utah State Univ, MS, 65; Iowa State Univ, PhD(plant breeding), 67. *Prof Exp:* Assoc secy, Crop Qual Coun, 67-69; Mont Wheat Res & Mkt Comt grant, 69-76, ASSOC PROF AGRON & GENETICS, MONT STATE UNIV, 69- *Mem:* Am Soc Agron; Crop Sci Soc Am; Am Inst Biol Sci. *Res:* Plant breeding, genetics and plant physiology as related to improvement of plant species. *Mailing Add:* Dept of Plant & Soil Sci Mont State Univ Bozeman MT 59715

TAYLOR, GEORGE EVANS, JR, b Richmond, Va, June 3, 49; m 72; c 1. EVOLUTIONARY BIOLOGY. *Educ:* Randolph-Macon Col, BS, 71; Emory Univ, PhD(biol), 76. *Prof Exp:* Instr biol, Agnes Scott Col, 76-77; res assoc bot, Nat Acad Sci, Nat Res Coun, 77-80; MEM STAFF, OAK RIDGE NAT LAB, 80- *Mem:* Soc Study Evolution; Bot Soc Am; Am Soc Naturalists; AAAS; Sigma Xi. *Res:* Evolutionary biology of plant populations including genetics, physiological ecology and population biology; rapid microevolutionary events in response to man generated stresses. *Mailing Add:* Environ Sci Div Oak Ridge Nat Lab Oak Ridge TN 37830

TAYLOR, GEORGE RUSSELL, b Pittsburgh, Pa, Aug 31, 23; m 48; c 1. PHYSICAL CHEMISTRY. *Educ:* Carnegie Inst Technol, DSc(chem), 51. *Prof Exp:* Group leader, Goodyear Synthetic Rubber Plant, Tex, 48-49; fel, Mellon Inst, 49-50, sr fel, 51-55; adv scientist, supvry engr & mgr chem, Atomic Power Dept, 55-66, MGR CHEM, ADV REACTORS DIV, WESTINGHOUSE ELEC CORP, 67- *Mem:* AAAS; Am Chem Soc; Am Nuclear Soc; Am Soc Testing & Mat. *Res:* Quantum chemistry; elastomers; birefringence; crystallization, viscoelasticity and strength; colloid chemistry; systems analysis; high temperature water chemistry; liquid sodium chemistry. *Mailing Add:* Advan Reactors Div Westinghouse Elec Corp Madison PA 15663

TAYLOR, GEORGE STANLEY, b Jackson, NC, Nov 29, 20; m 47; c 3. SOIL PHYSICS. *Educ:* NC State Col, BS, 43, MS, 48; Iowa State Univ, PhD(soil physics), 50. *Prof Exp:* Asst, NC State Col, 47-48 & Iowa State Univ, 49-50; from asst prof to assoc prof, 51-61, PROF AGRON, OHIO STATE UNIV, 61- *Concurrent Pos:* Vis assoc prof, Univ Calif, 58-59; consult, US Agency Int Develop, Punjab, India, 68 & 70. *Mem:* Am Soc Agron; Am Soc Agr Engr; Am Geophys Union; Soil Sci Soc Am. *Res:* Water flow in porous media; land drainage; two-dimensional modeling of heat and water flow in porous media by numerical techniques; disposal wastes in soil. *Mailing Add:* Dept Agron Ohio State Univ 2021 Coffey Rd Columbus OH 43210

TAYLOR, GEORGE THOMAS, b Asheboro, NC, July 18, 35. DEVELOPMENTAL BIOLOGY, ZOOLOGY. *Educ:* Guilford Col, AB, 57; Univ NC, Chapel Hill, MA, 64; Univ Mass, Amherst, PhD(zool), 70. *Prof Exp:* Instr zool, Atlantic Christian Col, 62-65; asst prof human anat, Col Osteop Med & Surg, 69-73; asst prof physiol, Southern Ill Univ, 73-77; ASST PROF DEPT BIOL SCI & DIR ELECTRON MICROS LAB, FLA INT UNIV, 77- *Mem:* AAAS; Am Soc Cell Biol; Am Soc Zoologists; Soc Develop Biol; Am Ornithologists Union. *Res:* Cytochemical and cytological aspects of oocyte differentiation and early development in marine invertebrates; special interest in changes in subcellular morphology and function during embryonic cytodifferentiation. *Mailing Add:* Dept of Biol Sci Tamiami Campus Fla Int Univ Miami FL 33199

TAYLOR, GEORGE WILLIAM, b Perth, Australia, June 16, 34; US citizen; m 57; c 4. SOLID STATE PHYSICS, ELECTRICAL ENGINEERING. *Educ:* Western Australia Univ, BE, 57, DEng, 81; London Univ, PhD(ferroelec), 61. *Prof Exp:* Group engr, telecommun, Australian Post Off, 61; lectr elec eng, Sydney Univ, 61-62; mem tech staff comput res, RCA Corp Labs, 62-70; vpres res & eng, Princeton Mat Sci Inc, 71-75, PRES, PRINCETON RESOURCES INC, 75- *Concurrent Pos:* Ed, Int J, Ferroelectrics, 70-; prof elec eng, Rutgers Univ, 76-77. *Honors & Awards:* RCA Labs Achievement Award, 66. *Mem:* Sr mem Inst Elec & Electronics Engrs; fel Australian Inst Eng; Am Phys Soc; fel Brit Inst Elec Eng. *Res:* Properties, synthesis, applications of ferroelectric materials; computer memories; displays and electro-optics. *Mailing Add:* Princeton Resources Inc Box 211 Princeton NJ 08540

TAYLOR, GERALD C, b Oregon, Mo, Sept 10, 19; m 50; c 4. BACTERIOLOGY, VIROLOGY. *Educ:* Univ Kans, BA, 49, MA, 51, PhD(bact), 55. *Prof Exp:* Lab instr bact & virol, Univ Kans, 50-52, asst rickettsiae, 52-55; asst, Lab Br, Commun Dis Ctr, USPHS, 55-57, lab supvr & unit chief, Tissue Cult Unit, 57-71, LAB SUPVR & UNIT CHIEF, LAB BR & CHIEF CELL CULT & MEDIA SECT, SCI SERV DIV, CTR DIS CONTROL, USPHS, 71- *Honors & Awards:* Presidential Citation, 64; Commendation Medal, USPHS, 72. *Mem:* AAAS; Am Soc Microbiol; Sigma Xi. *Res:* Human and animal virology; development of tissue culture in the field of virology. *Mailing Add:* Cell Cult & Media Sect Ctr Dis Control 1600 Clifton Rd Atlanta GA 30333

TAYLOR, GERALD REED, JR, b Bloxom, Va, Apr 17, 37; m 60; c 2. PHYSICS. *Educ:* Va Polytech Inst & State Univ, BS, 59, MS, 61; Univ Va, PhD(physics), 67. *Prof Exp:* Assoc physicist, Texaco Exp Inc, 60-62; res physicist solid state physics, Linde Div, Union Carbide Corp, 67-69; assoc prof physics, Madison Col, 69-80, PROF PHYSICS, JAMES MADISON UNIV, HARRISONBURG, VA, 80- *Concurrent Pos:* dir, Vis Scientists Prog, Va Acad Sci, 77-79. *Honors & Awards:* J Shelton Horsley Res Award, Va Acad Sci, 62. *Mem:* Am Phys Soc; Am Asn Physics Teachers. *Res:* Low Temperature solid state physics; ferromagnetism; magneto-thermal conductivity; resistivity; physics education and instruction; plasma physics and plasma diagnostics. *Mailing Add:* Dept of Physics James Madison Univ Harrisonburg VA 22807

TAYLOR, GORDON STEVENS, b Danbury, Conn, Nov 12, 21; m 46; c 1. PLANT PATHOLOGY. *Educ:* Univ Conn, BS, 47; Iowa State Col, MS, 49, PhD(corn stalk rot), 52. *Prof Exp:* Asst corn leaf blight & stalk rot, Iowa State Col, 48-52; asst agr scientist, 52-53, assoc agr scientist, Valley Lab, 53-55, agr scientist, 55-60, CHIEF AGR SCIENTIST, VALLEY LAB, CONN AGR EXP STA, 60- *Mem:* AAAS; Am Phytopath Soc; Am Inst Biol Sci; Air Pollution Control Asn. *Res:* Helminthosporium leaf blight of corn; stalk rot of corn in relation to the corn borer; verticillium wilt of potatoes; tobacco diseases; canker disease on maples; nematodes; effects of air pollution on plants. *Mailing Add:* Conn Agr Exp Sta Valley Lab PO Box 248 Windsor CT 06095

TAYLOR, HAROLD ALLISON, JR, b Richmond, Va, Oct 18, 42; m 65; c 2. HUMAN GENETICS, BIOCHEMISTRY. *Educ:* Univ Tenn, BS, 65, MS, 67, PhD(zool), 71. *Prof Exp:* Fel pediat, Sch Med, Johns Hopkins Univ, 71-73, instr, 73-75; asst dir, Genetics Lab, John F Kennedy Inst, Baltimore, 73-75; DIR LABS, GREENWOOD GENETIC CTR, 75- *Mem:* AAAS; Am Soc Human Genetics. *Res:* Lysosomal storage diseases; inborn errors of metabolism; genetics of mental retardation. *Mailing Add:* Greenwood Genetics Ctr Genet Lab 1020 Spring St at Ellenberg Greenwood SC 29646

TAYLOR, HAROLD EVANS, b Philadelphia, Pa, Sept 13, 39; m 64; c 4. PLASMA PHYSICS, SPACE PHYSICS. *Educ:* Haverford Col, BA, 61; Mass Inst Technol, MS, 62; Univ Iowa, PhD(physics), 66. *Prof Exp:* Res assoc physics, Univ Iowa, 66; Nat Acad Sci assoc, Goddard Spaceflight Ctr, NASA, 66-68; res assoc plasma physics, Princeton Univ, 68-71; asst prof, 71-77, ASSOC PROF ASTROPHYS, STOCKTON STATE COL, 77- *Concurrent Pos:* Consult, Los Alamos Sci Labs, vis prof mech eng, Univ Pa, 78. *Mem:* AAAS; Fedn Am Sci; Int Solar Energy Soc; Am Phys Soc. *Res:* Space plasma physics, including physics of the magnetosphere; physics of the interplanetary medium; cosmic rays; solar and wind energy devices. *Mailing Add:* Fac Natural Sci & Math Stockton State Col Pomona NJ 08240

TAYLOR, HAROLD LELAND, b Cambridge, Kans, May 3, 20; m 43; c 1. BIOCHEMISTRY. *Educ:* Southwestern Col, Kans, AB, 42; Univ Kans, PhD(biochem), 55. *Hon Degrees:* DSc, Southwestern Col, Kans, 73. *Prof Exp:* Res assoc, Harvard Univ, 42-46; biochemist, State Health Dept, Mich, 46-51 & 53-56; mgr immunochem dept, Pitman-Moore Div, Dow Chem Co, 56-63, tech asst to dir biol labs, 63-64, res chemist, Dow Res Labs, Zionsville, 64-72, clin monitor, Med Dept, 72-74, CLIN INVESTR, MERRELL DOW PHARMACEUT, 74- *Mem:* Am Chem Soc; Sigma Xi; NY Acad Sci; Am Soc Clin Pharmacol & Therapeut. *Res:* Fractionation of human blood plasma; physiological effects of antithyroid drugs in rats; isolation of immune fraction from hyperimmune canine plasma; control of biologicals production; drug metabolism; serum cholesterol lowering drugs. *Mailing Add:* Merrell Dow Pharmaceut PO Box 68511 Indianapolis IN 46268

TAYLOR, HAROLD LEROY, b East Chicago, Ind, Mar 2, 29; m 52; c 4. MECHANICAL ENGINEERING. *Educ:* Purdue Univ, Lafayette, BSEME, 51, MS, 52, PhD(eng), 55. *Prof Exp:* Asst educ, Purdue Univ, Lafayette, 51-55; res metallurgist, Res Labs, 55-56, supvr field develop, 56-59, chief res engr, 59-62, asst mgr prod develop, 62-64, assoc mgr develop dept, 64-68, prod eng, 68-72, dir res planning & admin, 72-77, SR ADV RES, INLAND STEEL CO, 77- *Concurrent Pos:* Chmn metrication planning comt, Am Iron & Steel Inst, 78- *Mem:* Am Soc Mech Engrs; Am Soc Metals; Am Inst Mining, Metall & Petrol Engrs. *Res:* Process development for new steel production processes, energy conservation, and new carbon steel products; product application research in area of high strength carbon sheet steels. *Mailing Add:* Inland Steel Res Labs 3001 E Columbus Dr East Chicago IN 46312

TAYLOR, HAROLD NATHANIEL, b Baltimore, Md, May 18, 21; m 42; c 3. CHEMISTRY. *Educ:* Johns Hopkins Univ, BE, 42, MS, 45; Cornell Univ, PhD(phys chem), 49. *Prof Exp:* Jr chem engr, Tenn Valley Authority, Wilson Dam, Ala, 42-43; jr instr chem eng, Johns Hopkins Univ, 43-44, asst, Off Rubber Reserve, 44 & Manhattan Proj, SAM Labs, Columbia Univ, 44-45; res chemist, Manhattan Proj, Carbide & Carbon Chem Co, 45-46 & Ammonia Dept, Exp Sta, E I du Pont de Nemours & Co, 49-53; PRES, HAGERSTOWN LEATHER GOODS CO, 53- *Concurrent Pos:* Dir, Cent Chem Co, 70- & Antietam Bank Co, 74- *Mem:* AAAS; Am Chem Soc. *Res:* Polymer chemistry; polymerization; plastic applications. *Mailing Add:* 1877 Fountain Head Rd Hagerstown MD 21740

TAYLOR, HARRY ELMER, b Easton, Pa, July 1, 31; m 53; c 3. ELECTRICAL ENGINEERING. *Educ:* Okla State Univ, BS, 57, MS, 58. *Prof Exp:* Mem tech staff, 58-68, SUPVR INTEGRATED CIRCUIT DESIGN GROUP, BELL TEL LABS, 68- *Res:* Transistor applications in Bell System use; consult and advise circuit designers desiring custom integrated circuits for Bell System use. *Mailing Add:* 926 Bradford Bethlehem PA 18018

TAYLOR, HARRY WILLIAM, b Saskatchewan, Can, Sept 28, 25; m 49; c 2. NUCLEAR PHYSICS. *Educ:* Univ Man, BSc, 51, MSc, 52, PhD(physics), 54. *Prof Exp:* Lectr physics, Univ Man, 52-53; fel, Cosmic Ray Sect, Nat Res Coun Can, 54-55; asst prof physics, Queen's Univ, Ont, 55-61; assoc prof, Univ Alta, 61-65; assoc prof, 65-69, PROF PHYSICS, UNIV TORONTO, 69- *Mem:* Fel AAAS; fel Am Phys Soc; fel Brit Inst Physics; fel Inst Nuclear Eng. *Res:* Gamma-ray spectroscopy; angular correlations of successive gamma-rays; distribution of fallout in Arctic plants. *Mailing Add:* Dept of Physics Univ of Toronto Toronto ON L5L 1C6 Can

TAYLOR, HENRY LONGSTREET, b St Paul, Minn, Feb 2, 12; m 41; c 3. PHYSIOLOGY. *Educ:* Harvard Univ, AB, 35; Univ Minn, PhD(physiol), 42. *Prof Exp:* Asst, 40-42, res assoc, 42-44, from asst prof to assoc prof, 44-56, actg dir lab physiol hyg, 51-52, PROF PHYSIOL HYG, UNIV MINN, MINNEAPOLIS, 56- *Concurrent Pos:* Mem coun arteriosclerosis, Am Heart Asn. *Mem:* AAAS; Am Physiol Soc; Soc Exp Biol & Med; Geront Soc; Am Heart Asn. *Res:* Exercise; nutrition; semi-starvation; cardiovascular function in man; epidemiology of heart disease. *Mailing Add:* Dept of Physiol Hyg Sch of Pub Health Univ of Minn Minneapolis MN 55455

TAYLOR, HERBERT LYNDON, b Van Alstyne, Tex, Aug 11, 31; m 56; c 2. PHYSICS, ELECTRICAL ENGINEERING. *Educ:* Austin Col, BA, 51; Rice Inst, MA, 52, PhD(physics), 55. *Prof Exp:* Mem tech staff res & develop, Tex Instruments Inc, 55-63; vis lectr, Univ Tex, Austin, 63-65, assoc prof, 65-80; failure analyst, Mostev, 80-81; CONSULT ENGR, 81- *Mem:* Am Phys Soc; Inst Elec & Electronics Engrs; Am Vacuum Soc; Electrochem Soc. *Res:* Semiconductors; solid state devices; solid surfaces and interfaces; reconfigurable computer structures; optical systems. *Mailing Add:* 4228 Hanover St Dallas TX 75225

TAYLOR, HOWARD CANNING, JR, b New York, NY, Feb 17, 00; m 24; c 3. OBSTETRICS & GYNECOLOGY. *Educ:* Yale Univ, PhB, 20; Columbia Univ, MD, 24. *Hon Degrees:* DSc, NY Univ, 55. *Prof Exp:* From asst to assoc prof gynec & obstet, Col Med, NY Univ, 35-39; prof gynec, Sch Med, Univ Pa, 39-40; from assoc to prof gynec & obstet & chmn, Col Med, NY Univ, 40-46; prof obstet & gynec & chmn dept, 46-65, dir, Int Inst Study Human Reprod, 65-70, EMER PROF OBSTET & GYNEC, COL PHYSICIANS & SURGEONS, COLUMBIA UNIV, 65- *Concurrent Pos:* From asst to attend gynecologist, Roosevelt Hosp, New York, 27-46; from asst to attend surgeon, Mem Hosp, 27-39 & 40-46; assoc & attend obstetrician & gynecologist, Bellevue Hosp, 35-39 & 40-46; dir, Sloane Hosp Women, 46-65; ed-in-chief, Am J Obstet & Gynec, 59-69; sr consult, Pop Coun New York, 70-77. *Mem:* Fel Am Gynec Soc (secy, 41-46, pres, 57-58); Harvey Soc; Am Cancer Soc (pres, 54); fel Am Pub Health Asn; fel Am Col Obstet & Gynec (pres, 66-67). *Res:* Cancer of female reproductive organs; physiology of pregnancy. *Mailing Add:* Box 328 Southport CT 06430

TAYLOR, HOWARD EDWARD, b Ft Worth, Tex, Feb 1, 22; m 44; c 3. MATHEMATICS. *Educ:* Rice Inst, BA, 42, MA, 48, PhD(math), 50; Calif Inst Technol, MS, 43. *Prof Exp:* Instr meteorol, Calif Inst Technol, 43-44; asst math, Rice Inst, 46-50; from instr to assoc prof, Fla State Univ, 50-69; CALLAWAY PROF MATH, WGA COL, 69- *Concurrent Pos:* Vis assoc prof, Univ Chicago, 57-58; assoc chmn dept math, Fla State Univ, 64-69; mem comt math exam, Col Entrance Exam Bd, 70-, chmn, 75-, mem math adv comt, 76- *Mem:* Am Math Soc; Am Meteorol Soc; Math Asn Am; Nat Coun Teachers Math. *Res:* Functions of a complex variable; analysis. *Mailing Add:* Dept of Math WGa Col Carrollton GA 30118

TAYLOR, HOWARD LAWRENCE, b Kansas City, Mo, May 23, 38; c 2. APPLIED MATHEMATICS, RESEARCH ADMINISTRATION. *Educ:* Austin Col, AB, 59; Univ Kans, MA, 62, PhD(math), 68. *Prof Exp:* Lab asst physics, Austin Col, 57-59; asst math, Univ Kans, 59-67; mathematician, 60-70, mgr res, 70-77, MGR GEOPHYSICS, SUN OIL CO, 77- *Mem:* Math Asn Am; Soc Indust & Appl Math; Soc Petrol Engrs; Soc Explor Geophysicists. *Res:* Development of mathematical methods to analyze geophysical data and solve reservoir engineering problems; simulation models and inverse problems. *Mailing Add:* Sun Oil Co 503 N Cent Expressway Richardson TX 75080

TAYLOR, HOWARD MELVIN, b Pride, Tex, Jan 20, 24; m 48; c 2. SOIL SCIENCE. *Educ:* Tex Tech Col, BS, 49; Univ Calif, PhD, 57. *Prof Exp:* Soil scientist, Soil Conserv Serv, USDA, 49-54; res asst irrig, Univ Calif, 55-57, instr, 57; soil scientist, Agr Res Serv, USDA, 57-80; PROF AGRON, IOWA STATE UNIV, 80- *Concurrent Pos:* FAO Andre Mayer fel, Australia, 65-66. *Mem:* Fel AAAS; fel Am Soc Agron; fel Soil Sci Soc Am; Am Soc Agr Eng; Soil Conserv Soc Am. *Res:* Soil physics, particularly soil-plant water relations and effects of soil compaction on plant growth. *Mailing Add:* Dept Agron Iowa State Univ Ames IA 50010

TAYLOR, HOWARD MILTON, III, b Baltimore, Md, May 9, 37; m 64. APPLIED MATHEMATICS, STATISTICS. *Educ:* Cornell Univ, BME, 60, MIndustEng, 61; Stanford Univ, PhD(math, statist), 65. *Prof Exp:* Res assoc & lectr appl probability, Stanford Univ, 64-65; from asst prof to assoc prof appl probability, 65-74, assoc prof oper res, 74-80, PROF OPER RES, CORNELL UNIV, 80- *Concurrent Pos:* NSF fel & vis asst prof, Univ Calif, Berkeley, 68-69; on leave at Math Inst, Oxford Univ, 72-73; grad fac rep, Cornell Univ, 74-77. *Mem:* Inst Math Statist. *Res:* Applied probability; Markov sequential decision processes; optimal stopping problems; quality control. *Mailing Add:* Dept of Indust Eng & Oper Res Col of Eng Cornell Univ Ithaca NY 14853

TAYLOR, HOWARD S, b New York, NY, Sept 17, 35; m 59; c 2. CHEMISTRY, PHYSICS. *Educ:* Columbia Univ, BA, 56; Univ Calif, Berkeley, PhD(chem), 59. *Prof Exp:* NSF fel chem, Free Univ Brussels, 59-61; from asst prof to prof, 61-74, Humboldt prof, 74-75, PROF CHEM & PHYSICS, UNIV SOUTHERN CALIF, 75- *Concurrent Pos:* Consult, Jet Propulsion Lab, Calif Inst Technol, 60- & NAm Aviation, Inc, 65-66; guest prof, Univ Freiburg, 67; staff scientist, Los Alamos Nat Lab, 73. *Mem:* Am Chem Soc; Am Phys Soc; The Chem Soc. *Mailing Add:* Dept of Chem Univ of Southern Calif Univ Park Los Angeles CA 90007

TAYLOR, HUGH ALAN, analytical chemistry, see previous edition

TAYLOR, HUGH P, JR, b Holbrook, Ariz, Dec 27, 32; m 59. PETROLOGY, GEOCHEMISTRY. *Educ:* Calif Inst Technol, BS, 54, PhD(geochem), 59; Harvard Univ, AM, 55. *Prof Exp:* Asst prof geol, Calif Inst Technol, 59-61; asst prof geochem, Pa State Univ, 61-62; from asst prof to assoc prof, 62-69, PROF GEOL, CALIF INST TECHNOL, 69- *Mem:* AAAS; Geol Soc Am; Am Geophys Union; Mineral Soc Am. *Res:* Oxygen, hydrogen, carbon and silicon isotopic compositions of igneous and metamorphic minerals and rocks, meteorites and the moon; ore deposits and hydrothermal alteration; ultramafic rocks of southeast Alaska. *Mailing Add:* Div of Geol & Planetary Sci Calif Inst of Technol Pasadena CA 91125

TAYLOR, IAIN EDGAR PARK, b Chester, Eng, Aug 18, 38; m 67. PLANT PHYSIOLOGY, PLANT BIOCHEMISTRY. *Educ:* Univ Liverpool, BSc, 61, PhD(bot), 64. *Prof Exp:* Teacher, Blundell's Sch, Tiverton, Eng, 64-66; res assoc bot, Univ Tex, Austin, 67-68, vis asst prof, 68; asst prof, 68-71, ASSOC PROF BOT, UNIV BC, 71- *Mem:* Am Soc Plant Physiol; Can Bot Asn; Can Soc Plant Physiol; Brit Biochem Soc; Brit Inst Biol. *Res:* Plant cell walls and cell wall associated proteins; gibberellins in algae; plant glycoprotein structure. *Mailing Add:* Dept of Bot Univ of BC Vancouver BC V6T 1W5 Can

TAYLOR, ISAAC MONTROSE, b Morganton, NC, June 15, 21; m 46; c 5. MEDICINE. *Educ:* Univ NC, AB, 42; Harvard Univ, MD, 45. *Prof Exp:* Intern, Mass Gen Hosp, 45-46, resident physician, 47; asst med adv, Harvard Med Sch, 48; chief med res, Mass Gen Hosp, 51; from asst prof to assoc prof, Sch Med, Univ NC, Chapel Hill, 52-64, dean sch med, 64-71, prof med, 64-78, res prof dept community med, 78-80; ASSOC DIR ADMIN, HUBERT H HUMPHREY CANCER RES CTR, BOSTON UNIV, 80-, ADJ PROF MED, SCH MED, 81- *Concurrent Pos:* Nat Res Coun fel, Harvard Med Sch, 48-50; Markle scholar, 54-61; manpower consult, Tristate Regional Med Prog, 71-72, assoc dir manpower, 72-74. *Mem:* Soc Exp Biol & Med; AMA; Am Fedn Clin Res. *Res:* Metabolism of electrolytes. *Mailing Add:* 9 Charles River Sq Boston MA 02114

TAYLOR, J(AMES) HERBERT, b Corsicana, Tex, Jan 14, 16; m 46; c 3. BIOLOGY. *Educ:* Southeastern State Col, BS, 39; Univ Okla, MS, 41; Univ Va, PhD(biol), 44. *Prof Exp:* Teacher high sch, Okla, 39-40; asst prof plant sci, Univ Okla, 46-47; assoc prof bot, Univ Tenn, 47-51; from asst prof to assoc prof, Columbia Univ, 51-58, prof cell biol, 58-64; assoc dir, 72-80, PROF BIOL SCI, FLA STATE UNIV, 64-, DIR, INST MOLECULAR BIOPHYS, 80- *Concurrent Pos:* Guggenheim Found fel, Calif Inst Technol, Pasadena, 58-59. *Mem:* Am Soc Cell Biol (pres, 70-71); Genetics Soc Am; Biophys Soc. *Res:* Autoradiographic studies of nucleic acid and protein synthesis at the cellular level; chromosome duplication and structure; mechanisms of DNA replication in chromosomes; molecular organization of chromosomes; cloning origins of replication and modifications of DNA (methylation). *Mailing Add:* Inst Molecular Biophys Fla State Univ Tallahassee FL 32306

TAYLOR, JACK CROSSMAN, b Washington, DC, Nov 9, 24; m 52; c 2. ANIMAL HUSBANDRY. *Educ:* Va Polytech Inst, BS, 50, MS, 57. *Prof Exp:* Instr, Agr Exp Sta, Univ Va, 51-57; asst prof animal husb, Miss State Univ, 57-63; res geneticist, Swine Res Br, Animal Husb Res Div, Agr Res Serv, USDA, 63-67; SUPVR ANIMAL HUSB, FOOD & DRUG ADMIN, 67- *Mem:* Am Soc Animal Sci. *Res:* Evaluation of data for animal safety and efficacy of new animal drugs; development of standards and regulations for animal feed ingredients derived from animal, human & industrial wastes. *Mailing Add:* HFV 136 5600 Fishers Ln Rockville MD 20857

TAYLOR, JACK ELDON, b Emporia, Kans, Jan 16, 26; m 48; c 2. PHYSICS. *Educ:* Univ Wis, PhB, 46, MS, 49, PhD(physics), 51. *Prof Exp:* Asst physics, Univ Wis, 47-51; res assoc, Gen Elec Co, 51-61; sr res staff mem, Gen Dynamics/Electronics, 61-71; PRIN ENGR, STROMBERG CARLSON CORP, 71- *Mem:* Am Phys Soc; Inst Elec & Electronics Eng; Optical Soc Am; Sigma Xi. *Res:* Ultra high vacuum techniques; gas lasers; optical communication systems; atmospheric optical transmission; solid state devices; LSI logic arrays; switching matrices; material and manufacturing problems. *Mailing Add:* 31 Old Pond Rd Rochester NY 14625

TAYLOR, JACK HOWARD, b Memphis, Tenn, July 7, 22; m 44; c 4. PHYSICS. *Educ:* Southwestern at Memphis, BS, 44; Johns Hopkins Univ, PhD(physics), 52. *Prof Exp:* Physicist, US Naval Res Lab, 44-46; instr physics, Southwestern at Memphis, 46-47; asst, Radiation Lab, Johns Hopkins Univ, 48-50; physicist, Exp Sta, E I du Pont de Nemours & Co, 52-53; asst prof physics, Univ of the South, 53-54; consult infrared, US Naval Res Lab, 54-56; assoc prof, 56-60, PROF PHYSICS, SOUTHWESTERN AT MEMPHIS, 60-, PRIN INVESTR INFRARED, AIR FORCE CAMBRIDGE RES CTR CONTRACT, 59-, DIR LAB ATMOSPHERIC & OPTICAL PHYSICS, 64- *Concurrent Pos:* Consult, Electro-Optics Group, Pan Am World Airways, Inc & Patrick Air Force Base, Fla, 63- *Mem:* Fel AAAS; Am Phys Soc; fel Optical Soc Am; Am Asn Physics Teachers. *Res:* Physics and military applications of infrared; atmospheric physics and transmission in infrared; time-dependent infrared phenomena and infrared techniques. *Mailing Add:* Dept of Physics Southwestern at Memphis Memphis TN 38112

TAYLOR, JACK NEEL, b Jacksonville, Fla, Aug 15, 18; div; c 2. UROLOGY. *Educ:* Ohio State Univ, AB, 40; Harvard Univ, MD, 43; Am Bd Urol, dipl, 54. *Prof Exp:* Asst prof genito-urinary surg, 51-66, ASSOC PROF UROL, COL MED, OHIO STATE UNIV, 66- *Mem:* AMA; Am Urol Asn; fel Am Col Surgeons. *Res:* Clinical urology. *Mailing Add:* 1275 Olentagy River Rd Columbus OH 43212

TAYLOR, JACKSON JOHNSON, b Winnabow, NC, Nov 20, 18; m 51; c 3. PHYSICS. *Educ:* Univ Richmond, BS, 42; Cornell Univ, MS, 48. *Prof Exp:* From instr to assoc prof, 48-69, chmn div sci, 57-72, chmn dept physics, 51-54, 55-58 & 63-69, PROF PHYSICS, UNIV RICHMOND, 69- *Concurrent Pos:* Assoc prof, Sch Pharm, Med Col Va, 51-61. *Mem:* Am Phys Soc; Am Asn Physics Teachers. *Res:* Evaporation of chlorine atoms from silver chloride crystals; teaching undergraduate physics, especially lecture demonstrations and curriculum development; computer-assured instruction in introductory physics. *Mailing Add:* Dept of Physics Univ of Richmond Richmond VA 23173

TAYLOR, JAMES A, JR, b Woonsocket, RI, 1939; m 60; c 3. BIOCHEMISTRY, PHARMACOLOGY. *Educ:* Providence Col, BS, 60; Purdue Univ, MS, 63, PhD(biochem), 66. *Prof Exp:* Resident res assoc, Div Biol & Med, Argonne Nat Lab, 65-67; sr res scientist, Med Res Labs, Pfizer Inc, 67-75, liaison officer, Food & Drug Admin, Pfizer Cent Res, 75-79; mgr, New Drug Affairs, ICI Americas, 79-80; DIR, DRUG REGULATORY AFFAIRS DEPT, STUART PHARMACEUT, 80- *Mem:* Am Soc Pharmacol & Exp Therapeut; Sigma Xi; Regulatory Affairs Prof Soc; Drug Info Asn. *Res:* Drug metabolism and pharmacokinetics. *Mailing Add:* Drug Regulatory Affairs Dept Stuart Pharmaceut Wilmington DE 19897

TAYLOR, JAMES EARL, b Beverly, Ohio, Sept 7, 16; m 45; c 3. RESEARCH ADMINISTRATION. *Educ:* Western Reserve Univ, AB, 38, MS, 40; Univ Pa, PhD(physics), 43. *Prof Exp:* Asst physics, Western Reserve Univ, 38-40 & Univ Pa, 40-42; physicist, Norden Labs Corp, 43-44, head res & develop sect, 44-50; from supvr electronics group & dir exp lab to lab dir, M Ten Bosch, Inc, 50-63; mem tech planning dept, 63-66, mgr res, Tech Planning Off, 66-69 & commun & educ, 69-70, tech staff specialist, 70-74, MGR RES TECH STAFF, XEROX CORP, 74- *Mem:* Am Phys Soc. *Res:* Ultrasonic studies; mass spectroscopy; isotope separation; ordnance research and development; research and development management; education. *Mailing Add:* Xerox Corp 105 Phillips Rd Webster NY 14580

TAYLOR, JAMES H(OBERT), b Tishomingo, Miss, Jan 28, 29; m 51; c 2. AGRICULTURAL ENGINEERING. *Educ:* Miss State Univ, BS, 51; Auburn Univ, PhD(agr eng), 64. *Prof Exp:* Jr engr, Int Harvester Co, 51-52, asst zone mgr farm equip, 54-59; asst agr eng, Auburn Univ, 59-62; res agr engr, 62-72, RES LEADER, TRACTION RES, NAT TILLAGE MACH LAB, AGR RES, US DEPT AGR, 72- *Concurrent Pos:* Res lectr, Grad Fac, Auburn Univ, 68- *Mem:* Am Soc Agr Engrs; Int Soc Terrain-Vehicle Systs; Soc Automotive Engrs; Am Soc Testing & Mat. *Res:* Terrain vehicle systems; off-road-locomotion; soil-machine systems; mobility; force-deformation relationships; systems analysis; soil dynamics. *Mailing Add:* Nat Tillage Mach Lab US Dept Agr Box 792 Auburn AL 36830

TAYLOR, JAMES HUGH, b San Jose, Calif, June 21, 40; m 63; c 4. NONLINEAR SYSTEMS THEORY, STOCHASTIC SYSTEMS. *Educ:* Univ Rochester, BSc, 63, MSc, 64; Yale Univ, MPh, 68, PhD(eng & appl sci), 69. *Prof Exp:* Vis asst prof elec eng, Indian Inst Sci, Bangalore, India, 69-72; sr engr & proj leader systs eng, The Anal Sci Corp, Reading, Mass, 73-78; assoc prof mech & aerospace eng, Okla State Univ, 78-81; SYSTS ENGR, GEN ELEC CORP RES & DEVELOP, 81- *Concurrent Pos:* Consult, Syst Eng Tech Assoc Corp, Stillwater, Okla, 79-81. *Mem:* Am Soc Mech Engrs; Inst Elec & Electronics Engrs; Sigma Xi. *Res:* Nonlinear system theory, especially analysis and design using describing function methods and stability criteria; stochastic systems theory, especially nonlinear estimation and control; modeling; simulation. *Mailing Add:* Gen Elec Corp Res & Develop Schenectady NY 12345

TAYLOR, JAMES KENNETH, b Fall River, Mass, July 28, 29; m 53; c 2. ECOLOGY. *Educ:* State Teachers Col Bridgewater, BScEd, 51; Columbia Univ, MA, 55. *Prof Exp:* Teacher pub schs, Mass, 51-56; from instr to asst prof, 56-64, ASSOC PROF BIOL, WESTFIELD STATE COL, 64-, CHMN DEPT BIOL, 74- *Concurrent Pos:* Consult, Rand-McNally Publ Co, 72-80; chmn, Westfield Conserv Comn, 62- *Mem:* AAAS; Nat Asn Biol Teachers; Ecol Soc Am; Nat Sci Teachers Asn; Am Forestry Asn. *Res:* Ecological basis of conservation; dissemination of ecological principles and their applications to solution of local problems. *Mailing Add:* Dept Biol Westfield State Col Westfield MA 01085

TAYLOR, JAMES LEE, b Berkey, Ohio, Jan 6, 31; m 58; c 2. HORTICULTURE. *Educ:* Ohio State Univ, BS, 53; Mich State Univ, MS, 57; Univ Ill, PhD(bot), 60. *Prof Exp:* PROF HORT & EXTEN SPECIALIST, MICH STATE UNIV, 60- *Concurrent Pos:* Mem bd trustees & treas, Nat Jr Hort Found, Inc. *Mem:* Am Hort Soc; Am Soc Hort Sci; Nat Jr Hort Asn. *Res:* Nut tree culture and physiology. *Mailing Add:* Dept of Hort Mich State Univ East Lansing MI 48824

TAYLOR, JAMES ROBERT, b Dubuque, Iowa, Apr 3, 23; m 44; c 3. ANALYTICAL CHEMISTRY. *Educ:* Univ Dubuque, BS, 47. *Prof Exp:* Chemist, 48-52, res chemist, 52-65, supvr routine chem, 65-69, res chemist, 69-73, sect head, 73-78, GROUP LEADER, ANAL SERV, SWIFT & CO, 78- *Mem:* Am Oil Chemists Soc; Am Chem Soc; Am Soc Testing & Mat. *Res:* Development of new analytical methods for food products and improving existing methods; thin layer chromatography, gas chromatography and atomic absorption spectroscopy. *Mailing Add:* Swift & Co 1919 Swift Dr Oak Brook IL 60521

TAYLOR, JAMES VANDIGRIFF, b New York, NY, Dec 27, 31; m 55; c 1. FORENSIC ANTHROPOLOGY. *Educ:* Columbia Univ, BS, 57, PhD(anthrop), 68. *Prof Exp:* Lectr anthrop, Hunter Col, City Univ New York, 64-65; lectr anthrop, New York Univ, 66-67; asst prof, 67-71, ASSOC PROF ANTHROP, LEHMAN COL, CITY UNIV NEW YORK, 71- *Concurrent Pos:* Prin investr res award, City Univ New York, 75-76, co-prin investr, 80-81, prin investr, 79-; dir Metrop Forensic Anthrop Team, Lehman Col, City Univ New York, 79- *Res:* Identification of human skeletal and dental remains in a forensic context. *Mailing Add:* Dept Anthrop Lehman Col City Univ New York New York NY 10468

TAYLOR, JAMES WELCH, b Newton, Miss, Sept 17, 35; m 57; c 2. ANALYTICAL CHEMISTRY. *Educ:* Vanderbilt Univ, BA, 56; Ga Inst Technol, MS, 58; Univ Ill, Urbana, PhD(chem), 64. *Prof Exp:* Develop chemist, Mobil Oil Co, 58-61; asst prof chem, Tulane Univ, La, 64-66; from asst prof to assoc prof, 66-70, PROF CHEM, UNIV WIS-MADISON, 70- *Mem:* Am Chem Soc; The Chem Soc. *Res:* Photoionization mass spectrometry; photoelectron spectroscopy; isotope kinetics; rates and mechanisms of reactions; analytical instrumentation. *Mailing Add:* Dept of Chem Univ of Wis 1101 University Ave Madison WI 53706

TAYLOR, JAVIN MORSE, b Lancaster, Wis, Jan 20, 36; m 59; c 4. ELECTRICAL ENGINEERING, COMPUTER SCIENCE. *Educ:* Univ Ill, Urbana, BS, 57; Univ Southern Calif, MS, 62; Univ Wyo, PhD(elec eng), 70. *Prof Exp:* Field engr, Hughes Aircraft Co, 57-59; engr, Ramo-Wooldridge Div, TRW, Inc, 59-61, TRW Comput Div, 61-62; eng specialist, Guid & Control Systs Div, Litton Industs, 62-66; instr & res engr, Natural Resources Res Inst, Univ Wyo, 66-69; res engr, Autonetics Div, NAm Rockwell, Inc, 69-70; from asst prof to assoc prof elec eng, Univ Mo-Rolla, 70-77; ASSOC PROF ELEC & COMPUT ENG, NMEX STATE UNIV, 77- *Concurrent Pos:* Consult, TRW Comput Div, TRW, Inc, 63, Guid & Control Systs Div, Litton Industs, 66-68 & John S Bereman & Co Eng Consult, 68-69; lectr, Calif State Univ, Los Angeles, 70; vis assoc prof elec & comput eng, NMex State Univ, 76-77; consult, Instrumentation Directorate, White Sands Missile Range, 77-80. *Mem:* Inst Elec & Electronics Engrs; Asn Comput Mach. *Res:* Computer architecture, distributed computing, microprocessors, real-time computing. *Mailing Add:* Dept Elec & Comput Eng NMex State Univ Las Cruces NM 88003

TAYLOR, JAY EUGENE, b Stayton, Ore, Feb 2, 18; m 48; c 4. CHEMISTRY. *Educ:* Ore State Col, BA, 40; Univ Wis, MS, 43; Purdue Univ, PhD, 47. *Prof Exp:* Instr chem, Univ Wis, 46-48; asst prof chem, Miami Univ, 48-52; fel phys chem, Ohio State Univ, 52-54; asst prof, Univ Nebr, 54-60; assoc prof phys-org chem, 60-63, PROF CHEM, KENT STATE UNIV, 63- *Mem:* Am Chem Soc. *Res:* Mechanisms of oxidation and decomposition reactions; flow techniques applied to kinetic studies of both liquid and gaseous systems; homogeneous versus heterogeneous gas-phase pyrolysis studies using wall-less and homogeneous front reactors. *Mailing Add:* Dept Chem Kent State Univ Kent OH 44242

TAYLOR, JEAN ELLEN, b San Mateo, Calif, Sept 17, 44; m 73; c 3. MATHEMATICS. *Educ:* Mt Holyoke Col, BA, 66; Univ Calif, Berkeley, MSc, 68 & Univ Warwick, 71; Princeton Univ, PhD(math), 73. *Prof Exp:* Instr math, Mass Inst Technol, 72-73; asst prof, 73-77, ASSOC PROF MATH, RUTGERS UNIV, 77- *Concurrent Pos:* Prin investr, NSF grant, 73-; mem, Inst Adv Study, 74-75 & 77-78; Alfred P Sloan Found fel, 76-78; mem comt appl math training, Nat Acad Sci/Nat Res Coun, 77-78; vis, Princeton Univ, 80-81. *Mem:* Am Math Soc; Math Asn Am; Asn Women Math; AAUP. *Res:* Geometric measure theory, in particular mathematical models for surface phenomena. *Mailing Add:* Dept Math Rutgers Univ New Brunswick NJ 08903

TAYLOR, JEAN MARIE, b Protection, NY, Nov 21, 32. TOXICOLOGY, PHARMACOLOGY. *Educ:* Keuka Col, BA, 54; Univ Rochester, MS, 56, PhD(pharm), 59. *Prof Exp:* Res assoc pharm, Atomic Energy Proj, Univ Rochester, 54-59; pharmacologist, 59-71, ACTG CHIEF, CHRONIC TOXICOL BR, DIV TOXICOL, US FOOD & DRUG ADMIN, 71- *Mem:* Soc Toxicol. *Res:* Toxicity of flavoring agents; hepatotoxins. *Mailing Add:* 1299 Delaware Ave SW Washington DC 20024

TAYLOR, JERRY DUNCAN, b Plumerville, Ark, June 5, 38; m 64; c 3. MATHEMATICS. *Educ:* State Col Ark, BA, 60; Univ Ark, MS, 64; Fla State Univ, PhD(math educ), 69. *Prof Exp:* ASSOC PROF MATH, CAMPBELL COL, NC, 62- *Mem:* Math Asn Am. *Res:* New methods of extending the field of rational numbers to the field of real numbers. *Mailing Add:* Dept of Math Campbell Col Buies Creek NC 27506

TAYLOR, JOCELYN MARY, b Portland, Ore, May 30, 31; m 72. ZOOLOGY. *Educ:* Smith Col, BA, 52; Univ Calif, Berkeley, MA, 53, PhD(zool), 59. *Prof Exp:* Asst zool, Conn Col, 53-54; Fulbright grantee, Australia, 54-55; assoc zool, Univ Calif, 59; from instr to asst prof, Wellesley Col, 59-65; assoc prof, 65-74, PROF ZOOL, UNIV BC, 74- *Concurrent Pos:* Sigma Xi grant, 61-62; Lalor Found grant, 62-63; NSF grants, 63-71 & Australia, 63-64 & 65; Nat Res Coun Can res grants, 66-80, travel grant, Div Animal Physiol, Commonwealth Sci & Indust Res Orgn, Australia, 71-72; Killiam Sr res fel, 78-79; assoc ed, J Mammalog, 81-; mem rodent specialist group, endangered species, Int Union Conserv Nature & Natural resources, 80- *Mem:* AAAS; Am Soc Mammalogists (vpres, 78-82); Soc Study Reprod; Am Soc Zool; Australian Soc Mammal. *Res:* Reproductive biology of mammals; evolution of Australasian murid rodents; marsupial placentation. *Mailing Add:* 2718 SW Old Orchard Rd Portland OR 97201

TAYLOR, JOHN BRYAN, b Beverly, Eng, Apr 13, 33; Can citizen; m 56; c 3. CRYSTAL CHEMISTRY, THERMODYNAMICS. *Educ:* Univ Manchester, BSc, 53, MSc, 54, PhD(chem), 56. *Prof Exp:* Fel chem, Nat Res Coun, Can, 56-58; develop engr float glass, Pilkington Bros, Eng, 58-61; PRIN RES OFF CHEM, NAT RES COUN, CAN, 62- *Concurrent Pos:* Energy prog coord, Div Energy Res & Develop, 77- *Mem:* Int Asn Hydrogen Energy; Am Chem Soc. *Res:* Crystallography and crystal chemistry of binary; intermetallic compounds of rare earth elements with As, Sb and Bi, intermetallic compound hydrides; thermal energy storage. *Mailing Add:* Div of Chem Montreal Rd Ottawa ON K1A 0R9 Can

TAYLOR, JOHN CHRISTOPHER, b Chelmsford, Eng, Jan 17, 36; Can citizen; m 69; c 3. MATHEMATICS. *Educ:* Acadia Univ, BSc, 55; Queen's Univ, Ont, MA, 57; McMaster Univ, PhD(math), 60. *Prof Exp:* J F Ritt instr math, Columbia Univ, 60-63; from asst prof to assoc prof, 63-74, PROF MATH, MCGILL UNIV, 74- *Mem:* Am Math Soc; Can Math Cong. *Res:* Analysis; potential theory. *Mailing Add:* Dept of Math McGill Univ 805 Shetbrooke St W Montreal PQ H3A 2K6 Can

TAYLOR, JOHN DIRK, b Mecca, Calif, Mar 31, 39; m 63; c 2. DEVELOPMENTAL BIOLOGY. *Educ:* Univ Ariz, BS, 62, PhD(biol), 67. *Prof Exp:* NSF, US-Japan Coop Sci Prog fel biol, Keio Univ, Japan, 67-68; from asst prof to assoc prof, 68-75, assoc prof comp med, 72-75, PROF BIOL, WAYNE STATE UNIV, 75-, PROF COMP MED, SCH MED, 75-, CHMN DEPT BIOL, 74- *Concurrent Pos:* Asian Found guest lectr, Univs in Seoul, Korea, 68. *Mem:* AAAS; Am Soc Cell Biol; Am Soc Zool; Soc Develop Biol. *Res:* Biochemical and ultrastructural aspects of developmental processes with particular emphasis on cell differentiation and cell death in embryonic development and cell renewal in adult organisms. *Mailing Add:* Dept of Biol Wayne State Univ Detroit MI 48207

TAYLOR, JOHN EDGAR, b Cheyenne, Wyo, Oct 17, 31; m 54; c 3. RANGE SCIENCE, PLANT ECOLOGY. *Educ:* Idaho State Univ, BS, 58 & Wash State Univ, 60; Mont State Univ, MS, 67; NDak State Univ, PhD(bot & plant ecol), 76. *Prof Exp:* Instr, 63-67, asst prof, 67-76, ASSOC PROF RANGE SCI, MONT STATE UNIV, 76- *Mem:* Soc Range Mgt; Ecol Soc Am; Am Soc Photogram. *Res:* Rangeland analysis and measurements; remote sensing of natural resources data; ecological effects of energy development on native grassland systems. *Mailing Add:* Dept of Animal & Range Sci Mont State Univ Bozeman MT 59717

TAYLOR, JOHN F(REDERICK), b Columbus, Ohio, Sept 30, 26; m 53; c 4. TECHNICAL MANAGEMENT. *Educ:* La State Univ, 45; Univ Ill, MS, 48, PhD(chem eng), 50. *Prof Exp:* Asst fluid dynamics, Univ Ill, 46-50; engr, Shell Develop Co, 50-53; Pine Bluff Arsenal, Chem Corps, US Dept Army, 53-55; chem engr, Esso Res & Eng Co, 55-61, asst dir appl math, 61-64, mgr, Europ Tech Serv Off, Neth, 64-65, dir chem processes eng, 65-66, gen mgr, Eng Chem Dept, 66-70, chief exec, Essochem Australia, 70-73, mgr light hydrocarbons div, Exxon Corp, 73-75, Brent Gas Mgr, Esso Europe, 75-76,

GEN PROJ MGR, FLAGS, ESSO EUROPE INC, 77- *Concurrent Pos:* Mem staff, Esso Petrol Co, Ltd, 59-60. *Mem:* Am Inst Chem Engrs. *Res:* Engineering management. *Mailing Add:* Esso Europe Inc 5 Hanover Square London England

TAYLOR, JOHN FULLER, b Jamestown, NY, June 10, 12; m 35; c 2. BIOCHEMISTRY. *Educ:* Cornell Univ, AB, 33; Johns Hopkins Univ, PhD(physiol chem), 37; Am Bd Clin Chem, dipl. *Prof Exp:* Nat Res Coun fel med sci, Harvard Med Sch, 37-39, teaching fel biol chem, 39-41; biochemist, Lederle Labs, Inc, 41-43; asst prof biol chem, Sch Med, Washington Univ, 43-52; chmn dept, 52-72, prof, 52-78, EMER PROF BIOCHEM, SCH MED, UNIV LOUISVILLE, 78- *Concurrent Pos:* Vis prof, Univ Oslo, 55; Commonwealth Fund fel, Cambridge, Eng & Rome, Italy, 61-62. *Mem:* Am Chem Soc; Am Soc Biol Chemists; Soc Exp Biol & Med; Biophys Soc; Brit Biochem Soc. *Res:* Hemoglobin; enzyme proteins; quinones; hemochromogens; oxidation-reduction potentials of biological systems; sulfhydryl groups of proteins; physical chemistry of proteins and polysaccharides; ultracentrifugation. *Mailing Add:* Dept Biochem Health Sci Ctr Univ Louisville Louisville KY 40292

TAYLOR, JOHN GARDINER VEITCH, b Toronto, Ont, Sept 22, 26; m 55. PHYSICS. *Educ:* McMaster Univ, BSc, 50; Univ Sask, MSc, 52. *Prof Exp:* Res physicist photonuclear reactions, Univ Sask, 53; res physicist atomic mass measurements, McMaster Univ, 54-55; res physicist radioactivity standards, 56-76, HEAD, COUNTER DEVELOP SECT, ATOMIC ENERGY CAN, LTD, 76- *Mem:* Am Phys Soc; Can Asn Physicists. *Res:* Radioactivity; radiation detectors. *Mailing Add:* Physics Div Atomic Energy of Can Ltd Chalk River ON K0J 1J0 Can

TAYLOR, JOHN HALL, b Greenfield, Mass, Feb 18, 22; m 48; c 4. VISION. *Educ:* Wesleyan Univ, AB, 47; Univ Mich, MA, 50, PhD(psychol), 52. *Prof Exp:* Asst psychol, Univ Mich, 48-52, res assoc, 52-54; asst res psychologist, Scripps Inst Oceanog, 54-60, assoc res psychologist, 60-65, res psychologist, Visibility Lab, 65-72 & Inst Pure & Appl Phys Sci, 72-74, RES PSYCHOLOGIST, UNIV CALIF SAN DIEGO, 75- *Concurrent Pos:* Mem exec coun, Comt Vision, Armed Forces-Nat Res Coun, 71-72, staff sci adv, 72-75; consult, Int Comn Illum, 72- *Mem:* AAAS; Optical Soc Am; Asn Res Vision & Ophthal; Int Acad Astronaut. *Res:* Psychophysiology of vision sensory psychology; visual problems of space exploration; vision underwater; vision problems in underground mining; visual sensitivity in humans; photic responses of marine forms; ultraviolet photobiology of marine fishes. *Mailing Add:* Dept Psychol (C-009) Univ Calif San Diego La Jolla CA 92093

TAYLOR, JOHN JACOB, b Dayton, Ohio, June 26, 28. MICROBIOLOGY. *Educ:* Heidelberg Col, BS, 50; Univ Ohio, MS, 52; Ohio State Univ, PhD, 57. *Prof Exp:* Instr bot, Univ Ohio, 50-52; res specialist toxicol, Nat Cash Register Co, 52-54; asst, Res Found, Ohio State Univ, 56-57; from asst prof to assoc prof, 57-69, PROF MICROBIOL, UNIV MONT, 69- *Mem:* Mycol Soc Am; Med Mycol Soc of the Americas; Can Soc Microbiol. *Res:* Morphology and physiology of fungi; host parasite relationships; antibiotic resistance in pathogenic fungi. *Mailing Add:* Dept of Microbiol Univ of Mont Missoula MT 59801

TAYLOR, JOHN JOSEPH, b Hackensack, NJ, Feb 27, 22; m 43; c 2. MATHEMATICS. *Educ:* St John's Univ, NY, AB, 42; Univ Notre Dame, MS, 47. *Hon Degrees:* DSc, St John's Univ, NY, 74. *Prof Exp:* Appl mathematician, Bendix Aviation Corp, 46-47; scientist, Physics Dept, Kellex Corp, NY, 47-50; scientist, Bettis Atomic Power Lab, Westinghouse Elec Corp, 50-52, mgr shielding physics, 52-55 & surface ship proj, Physics Dept, 55-58, mgr reactor develop, 58-65 & mat develop, 65-67, mgr eng, Atomic Power Div, 67, eng mgr, PWR Plant Div, 67-70, gen mgr, Breeder Reactor Div, 70-74; vpres, Advan Nuclear Systs, 74-76, vpres, Water Reactor Div, 76-81; DIR NUCLEAR POWER DIV, ELEC POWER RES INST, 81- *Concurrent Pos:* Consult, US Govt Acct Off, 74-; mem subcomt sci & pub policy, Nat Res Coun, 75- *Honors & Awards:* Westinghouse Award of Merit, 57. *Mem:* Nat Acad Eng; AAAS; Am Phys Soc; Int Platform Asn; Am Nuclear Soc. *Res:* Nuclear reactors; shielding and reactors for atomic submarines; digital computer techniques in reactor design; nuclear fuel development. *Mailing Add:* PO Box 10412 Elec Power Res Inst Palo Alto CA 94303

TAYLOR, JOHN JOSEPH, b Westhampton Beach, NY, May 15, 25; m 46; c 2. ANATOMY. *Educ:* Hofstra Col, BA, 53; Cornell Univ, MS, 56; Univ Buffalo, PhD(anat), 59. *Prof Exp:* Asst to Dr G N Papanicolaou, Med Col, Cornell Univ, 50-53, asst anat, 54-56; from asst to instr, Sch Med, Univ Buffalo, 56-60; from asst prof to assoc prof, Sch Med, Univ NDak. 60-66; ASSOC PROF ANAT, SCH MED, ST LOUIS UNIV, 66-, ASSOC PROF NEUROANAT IN NEUROL, 67- *Concurrent Pos:* Lectr, Drexel Inst, 62-64. *Mem:* Soc Neurosci; Am Asn Anatomists; Electron Micros Soc Am; Am Soc Cell Biol; Am Asn Hist Med. *Res:* Electron microscopy and histochemistry of connective tissue and central nervous system. *Mailing Add:* Dept of Anat St Louis Univ Sch of Med St Louis MO 63104

TAYLOR, JOHN KEENAN, b Mt Rainier, Md, Aug 14, 12; m 38; c 2. PHYSICAL CHEMISTRY, ANALYTICAL CHEMISTRY. *Educ:* George Washington Univ, BS, 34; Univ Md, MS, 38, PhD(chem), 41. *Prof Exp:* Sci aide, 29-36, chemist, 36-40, asst chemist, 40-42, assoc chemist, 42-44, chemist, 44-61, chief microchem anal sect, 61-73, chief, Air & Water Pollution Anal Sect, 73-77, chief, gas & Particulate Sci Div, 77-80, QUALITY ASSURANCE & VOL STANDARDS COORDR, NAT BUR STANDARDS, 80- *Concurrent Pos:* Adj prof, Am Univ. *Honors & Awards:* Rosa Award Stand Activ, Nat Bur Standards, 74. *Mem:* Am Chem Soc; Electrochem Soc; Air Pollution Control Soc. *Res:* Preparation of pure platinum metals; electrochemistry of solutions; standard electrode potentials; separation of isotopes; polarography; coulometry; microchemical and environmental analysis; development of analytical methods and standard reference materials for air and water pollution analysis; quality assurance procedures for chemical analysis. *Mailing Add:* A309 Chem Bldg Nat Bur of Standards Washington DC 20234

TAYLOR, JOHN LANGDON, JR, b Brooklyn, NY, Nov 3, 28; m 61. MEDICAL EDUCATION. *Educ:* Univ Chicago, PhB, 50; Univ Calif, Los Angeles, PhD(physiol), 57. *Prof Exp:* Grad res anatomist, Univ Calif, Los Angeles, 56-57, grad res physiologist, 57, asst res physiologist, 57-59; from instr to asst prof physiol, Col Med, Univ Ill, 59-65; assoc prof biol, Wayne State Univ, 65-68; assoc prof physiol & asst to dean, Col Osteop Med, Mich State Univ, 69-71, assoc prof med educ, & asst dean student affairs, Col Osteop Med, 71-72, assoc prof acad affairs, Col Osteop Med, 72-75; assoc dean student affairs, 75-79, PROF OSTEOP MED, COL OSTEOP MED, OHIO UNIV, 75- *Mem:* AAAS; Am Educ Res Asn; Nat Coun Measurement in Educ; Soc Gen Physiol; Biophys Soc. *Res:* Neuro-regulatory mechanism; biological rhythms; test scoring methods; career choices in the health professions; computer assisted instruction. *Mailing Add:* Col of Osteop Med Ohio Univ Athens OH 45701

TAYLOR, JOHN MARSTON, b Melbourne, Australia, Sept 10, 41; m 60; c 2. VIROLOGY. *Educ:* Univ Melbourne, BSc, 62, MSc, 64; Univ Toronto, PhD(cell biol), 68. *Prof Exp:* MEM STAFF, INST CANCER RES, 74- *Res:* Virus replication; cell biology; carcinogenesis. *Mailing Add:* Inst Cancer Res 7701 Burholme Ave Philadelphia PA 19111

TAYLOR, JOHN ROBERT, b London, Eng, Feb 2, 39; m 62; c 2. THEORETICAL PHYSICS. *Educ:* Cambridge Univ, BA, 60; Univ Calif, Berkeley, PhD(physics), 63. *Prof Exp:* NATO fel physics, Cambridge Univ, 62-64; instr, Princeton Univ, 64-66; from asst prof to assoc prof, 66-72, PROF PHYSICS, UNIV COLO, BOULDER, 72- *Mem:* Am Phys Soc. *Res:* Quantum theory; quantum theory of scattering. *Mailing Add:* 3290 Heidelberg Dr Boulder CO 80303

TAYLOR, JOHN WILLIAM, b Austin, Tex, Dec 14, 46; m 68; c 2. ANALYTICAL & PHARMACEUTICAL CHEMISTRY. *Educ:* Univ Cincinnati, BS, 69; Duke Univ, PhD(anal chem), 78. *Prof Exp:* REVIEWING CHEMIST Rx DRUGS, DIV GENERIC DRUG MONOGRAPHS, BUR DRUGS, FOOD & DRUG ADMIN, HEW, 74- *Mem:* Sigma Xi; Asn Off Anal Chemists; Am Chem Soc. *Res:* Prediction of ion exchange selectivities in mixed solvents; isotope separations; polymorphism and bioavailability. *Mailing Add:* 1001 Paul Dr Rockville MD 20851

TAYLOR, JOSEPH HOOTON, JR, b Philadelphia, Pa, Mar 29, 41; m 63; c 2. ASTRONOMY. *Educ:* Haverford Col, BA, 63; Harvard Univ, PhD(astron), 68. *Prof Exp:* Lectr astron & res assoc, Harvard Col Observ, Harvard Univ, 68-69; from asst prof to assoc prof astron, Univ Mass, 69-76, prof, 76-81; PROF PHYSICS, PRINCETON UNIV, 81- *Concurrent Pos:* Grant, Res Corp, Univ Mass, 68-69, NSF, 69-82 & NASA, 71-72; consult, Mass Gen Hosp, 71-73. *Mem:* Am Astron Soc; Int Union Radio Sci; Int Astron Union; Am Phys Soc. *Res:* Radio astronomy; pulsars; design and development of radio telescopes and information processing systems. *Mailing Add:* Dept Physics Princeton Univ Princeton NJ 08544

TAYLOR, JOSEPH LAWRENCE, b Apr 7, 41; US citizen; m 59; c 3. MATHEMATICAL ANALYSIS. *Educ:* La State Univ, BS, 63, PhD(math), 64. *Prof Exp:* Instr math, Harvard Univ, 64-65; from asst prof to assoc prof, 65-71, PROF MATH, UNIV UTAH, 71- *Concurrent Pos:* Sloan fel. *Honors & Awards:* Steele Prize, Am Math Soc, 75. *Mailing Add:* Dept Math Univ Utah Salt Lake City UT 84112

TAYLOR, JULIUS DAVID, b Erie, Pa, Dec 18, 13; m 38; c 1. BIOCHEMISTRY, TOXICOLOGY. *Educ:* Univ Pittsburgh, BS, 36; Univ Rochester, PhD(biochem), 40. *Prof Exp:* Instr biochem, Sch Med & Dent, Univ Rochester, 40-41; res org chemist, Distillation Prod, Inc, NY, 41-43; res biochemist, Eaton Labs, Inc, 43-47; chem pharmacologist, Abbott Labs, 48-60, from asst dept head to dept head pharmacol, 60-64, drug eval specialist, Dept Drug Regist, 65-69 & Div Regulatory Affairs, 69-70, data specialist, Dept Exp Biomet, 70-77, control record coordr, 78-79; RETIRED. *Concurrent Pos:* Lectr, Med Sch, Northwestern Univ, Chicago, 59-62; prof, Sch Med, Univ Chicago, 62- *Mem:* AAAS; Am Chem Soc; Soc Exp Biol & Med; Am Soc Pharmacol & Exp Therapeut; Drug Info Asn. *Res:* Drug enzymology, metabolism and kinetics; pharmacology; toxicology; bionics; simulation. *Mailing Add:* Apt A8 905 Baldwin Ave Waukegan IL 60085

TAYLOR, KATHLEEN C, b Cambridge, Mass, Mar 16, 42. PHYSICAL CHEMISTRY. *Educ:* Rutgers Univ, New Brunswick, AB, 64; Northwestern Univ, Evanston, PhD(phys chem), 68. *Prof Exp:* Fel, Univ Edinburgh, 68-70; assoc sr res chemist, 70-74, sr res chemist, 74-75, ASST DEPT HEAD, RES LABS, GEN MOTORS CORP, 75- *Mem:* Am Chem Soc; Catalysis Soc; Royal Chem Soc; Mat Res Soc; Soc Automotive Engrs. *Res:* Surface chemistry; heterogeneous catalysis; catalytic control of automobile exhaust emissions. *Mailing Add:* Phys Chem Dept Gen Motors Res Labs 12 Mile & Mound Roads Warren MI 48090

TAYLOR, KEITH EDWARD, b Toronto, Ont, Dec 21, 46; m 68; c 2. BIOCHEMISTRY. *Educ:* Univ Toronto, BSc, 69; PhD(bioorg chem), 74. *Prof Exp:* Fel enzymatic stereochem, Lab Org Chem, Swiss Fed Inst Technol, 73-76; fel protein chem, Harvard Univ, 76; ASST PROF BIOCHEM, UNIV WINDSOR, 76- *Mem:* Am Chem Soc; Chem Inst Can; Can Biochem Soc. *Res:* Chemical probes of membrane protein organization; protein chemistry enzymology. *Mailing Add:* Dept Chem Univ of Windsor Windsor ON N9B 3P4 Can

TAYLOR, KEITH MAR, b Thatcher, Ariz, Nov 15, 22; m 46; c 3. ORGANIC CHEMISTRY. *Educ:* Univ Ariz, BS, 45, MS, 47; Purdue Univ, PhD(chem), 50. *Prof Exp:* Instr chem, Univ Ariz, 45-46; asst instr, Purdue Univ, 47-48; res sect leader, 52-53, res group leader, 53-78, SR SPECIALIST, RES CTR, MONSANTO CO, 78- *Res:* Natural products, composition of tree fractions; fluorinated organic nitrogen compounds; petrochemicals. *Mailing Add:* Monsanto Co 800 N Lindburgh Rd St Louis MO 63166

TAYLOR, KENNETH BOIVIN, b Columbus, Ohio, Aug 7, 35; m 58; c 2. BIOCHEMISTRY, ENZYMOLOGY. *Educ:* Oberlin Col, AB, 57; Case Western Reserve Univ, MD, 61; Mass Inst Technol, PhD, 67. *Prof Exp:* Res assoc, Mass Inst Technol, 64-67, asst prof biol, 67-70; ASSOC PROF BIOCHEM, UNIV ALA, BIRMINGHAM, 70- *Res:* Enzyme mechanism specifically applied to oxygenases of the central nervous system and their relationships with behavioral states; kinetics; stereochemistry and isotope effects on dehydrogenases and transferases. *Mailing Add:* Dept Biochem Univ Ala Birmingham AL 35294

TAYLOR, KENNETH GRANT, b Paterson, NJ, May 12, 36; m 61; c 3. ORGANIC CHEMISTRY. *Educ:* Calvin Col, AB, 57; Wayne State Univ, PhD(org chem), 63. *Prof Exp:* Res assoc, Mass Inst Technol, 63-64; sr res assoc chem, Wayne State Univ, 64-66; from asst prof to assoc prof, 66-73, PROF CHEM, UNIV LOUISVILLE, 73-, CHMN DEPT, 78- *Concurrent Pos:* Assoc prof, Univ Nancy I, France, 74-75. *Mem:* Am Chem Soc; AAAS. *Res:* Synthesis of strained carbocyclic and heterocyclic compounds; carbohydrate chemistry; chemical carcinogenesis; cycloaddition reactions. *Mailing Add:* Dept Chem Univ Louisville Louisville KY 40292

TAYLOR, KIRMAN, b Yorkshire, Eng, Sept 30, 20; nat US; m 41; c 2. ANALYTICAL CHEMISTRY, CLINICAL CHEMISTRY. *Educ:* Queen's Col, NY, BS, 41; Polytech Inst Brooklyn, MS, 43. *Prof Exp:* Instr, Polytech Inst Brooklyn, 46; res chemist, Celotex Corp, 47-48; res chemist & group leader, Westvaco Chem Div, Food Machinery & Chem Corp, 48-52; res assoc, George Washington Univ, 52-54; group leader, Diamond Alkali Co, 54-65, proj mgr, 65-67, assoc dir res dept, 68-75, DIR RES ADMIN, RES CTR, DIAMOND SHAMROCK CORP, 76- *Concurrent Pos:* Lectr, Wagner Col, 49-52 & Lake Erie Col, 60-67. *Mem:* Am Chem Soc; NY Acad Sci; AAAS. *Res:* Building materials technology; inorganic phosphates; coordination compounds; inorganic polymers; plastic and metal coatings; nuclear fuels; water chemistry; electroless and electrolytic plating; research administration; hydrometallurgy; management of analytical environmental chemical facilities. *Mailing Add:* 512 Whisperwood Dr Greenville TN 37743

TAYLOR, LARRY THOMAS, b Woodruff, SC, Dec 31, 39; m 60; c 2. INORGANIC POLYMER CHEMISTRY, COAL CHEMISTRY. *Educ:* Clemson Univ, BS, 62, PhD(chem), 65. *Prof Exp:* Res assoc chem, Ohio State Univ, 65-67; from asst prof to assoc prof, 67-78, PROF CHEM, VA POLYTECH INST & STATE UNIV, 78- *Mem:* Am Chem Soc; Sigma Xi. *Res:* Coordination chemistry; small molecule reactivity with metal complexes; liquid chromatography; multi element analyses; modification of polymers by metal ion addition. *Mailing Add:* Dept of Chem Va Polytech Inst & State Univ Blacksburg VA 24061

TAYLOR, LAURISTON SALE, b Brooklyn, NY, June 1, 02; m 25; c 2. MEDICAL PHYSICS. *Educ:* Cornell Univ, AB, 26. *Hon Degrees:* DSc, Univ Pa, 60 & St Procopius Col, 65. *Prof Exp:* Asst, Heckscher Found, Cornell Univ, 24-27; from asst physicist to assoc physicist, Nat Bur Standards, 27-35, sr physicist & chief, X-ray Sect, 35-41, chief proving ground group, 42-43, chief x-ray sect, 42-43, 46-49, asst chief, Atomic Physics Div, 47-51, chief, Radiol Physics Lab, 49-51, Atomic & Radiation Physics Div, 51-60, Radiation Physics Div, 60-62, assoc dir, 62-64; spec asst to pres, Nat Acad Sci, 65-69, exec dir adv comt emergency planning, 65-71; pres, 64-77, HON PRES, NAT COUN RADIATION PROTECTION & MEASUREMENTS, 77-; RADIATION PHYSICS CONSULT, 77- *Concurrent Pos:* Mem, Int Comn Radiol Protection, 28-69, secy, 37-50, emer mem, 69-; mem, Int Comn Radiol Units & Measurements 28-69, secy, 34-50, chmn, 53-69, hon chmn & emer mem, 69-; chmn, Nat Coun Radiation Protection & Measurements, 29-64, chmn subcomt regulation of radiation exposure, 53-57, subcomt permissible exposure under emergency conditions, 55-59; dir Pan-Am Cancer Union, 39; mem sect E, div A, Nat Defense Res Comt, Off Sci Res & Develop, 42; nuclear comt Z-54, safety code, indust use of radiation, Am Nat Stand Comt, 42-46, nuclear stand bd, 56-; consult, Air Force Opers Anal Div, Dept Defense, 47-52, mem, guided missiles countermeasures panel, Res & Develop Bd, 47-52, adv comt radiol defense, 48-51, comt weapons systs eval with Nat Acad Sci, 53-55, consult, Weapons Systs Eval Group, Joint Chiefs of Staff, 54-65, mem interagency comt biomed weapons effects tests, 57, consult, Inst Defense Anal, 57-67, mem ad hoc sci adv comt, Armed Forces Radiobiol Res Facil & chmn panel radiol instruments, 62-65, mem nuclear weapons effects res med adv group, 65-71, chmn rev comt, Armed Forces Radiobiol Res Inst, 66; chief biophys br, AEC, 48-49; mem subcomt radiobiol, Comt Nuclear Sci, Nat Acad Sci-Nat Res Coun, 49-54, consult comt med & surg, 54, comt radiol, 54, mem adv comt civil defense, 54-65, chmn, 57-65; sr consult, Civil Serv Bd Expert Exam, Civil Serv Comn, 52-58, chmn, 62-65. *Honors & Awards:* Landauer award, Am Asn Physicists Med & Health Physics Soc, 79; Sievert award, Int Radiol Protection Asn, 79; Antoine Beclere Prize & Gold Medal, Int Soc Radiol, 81. *Mem:* hon mem Nippon Soc Radiologica 20814

TAYLOR, LAWRENCE AUGUST, b Paterson, NJ, Sept 14, 38; m 60; c 2. GEOCHEMISTRY, PETROLOGY. *Educ:* Ind Univ, Bloomington, BS, 61, MS, 63; Lehigh Univ, PhD(geochem), 68. *Prof Exp:* Instr geol, Univ Del, 63-64; fel geochem, Geophys Lab, Carnegie Inst Washington, 68-70; Fulbright fel, Max Planck Inst Nuclear Physics, Heidelberg, 70-71; asst prof, Purdue Univ, West Lafayette, 71-73; mem fac, Dept Geol Sci, 73, PROF GEOL SCI, UNIV TENN, KNOXVILLE, 73-; DISCIPLINE SCIENTIST & PROG MGR, SOLAR SYST EXPLOR, NASA, WASHINGTON, DC, 81- *Concurrent Pos:* Res grants, Geochem Sect, NSF; prin investr, Lunar Sample Prog, NASA, 72-; co-investr, Max Planck Inst Nuclear Physics; prin investr, NASA Planetary Mat Prog, NASA Meteorite Prog, mem, Lunar Sample Rev Panel, 74-75, Lunar & Planetary Rev Panel, 75-76, Lunar Sample Anal Prog Team, 76-78, Lunar & Planetary Sample Team, 78-80 & meteorite steering comt, 81- *Mem:* Mineral Soc Am; Mineral Asn Can; Am Geophys Union; Meteoritical Soc; Int Mineral Asn. *Res:* Experimental geochemistry and petrology into the stability relations of sulfide, oxide and silicate compounds at low and high pressures and application of these data to natural minerals and rocks; kinetics of melt crystallization and cooling rates of rock formation; geochemistry of lunar rocks, meteorites and ore deposits. *Mailing Add:* Dept of Geol Sci Univ of Tenn Knoxville TN 37916

TAYLOR, LAWRENCE DOW, b Boston, Mass, Oct 6, 32; m 55; c 2. GLACIOLOGY, GEOMORPHOLOGY. *Educ:* Dartmouth Col, BA, 54, MA, 58; Ohio State Univ, PhD(geol), 62. *Prof Exp:* Geologist, US Geol Surv, Greenland, 54-55; res assoc, Northwest Greenland Glaciol, Dartmouth Col & Air Force Cambridge Res Labs, 57-58; res assoc, Southeast Alaska Glaciol, Inst Polar Studies, Ohio State Univ, 59-62; chief glaciologist, SPole Traverse, US Antarctic Res Prog, NSF, 62-63; asst prof geol, Col Wooster, 63-64; asst prof, 64-70, assoc prof, 70-76, PROF GEOL, ALBION COL, 77-, CHMN DEPT, 64- *Concurrent Pos:* NSF res grants, 60-61 & 62-63, field inst grant, Can Rockies, 68; Kellogg Found res & teaching grant, 71-72. *Mem:* AAAS; fel Geol Soc Am; Am Polar Soc; Nat Asn Geol Teachers; Arctic Inst NAm. *Res:* Glacial geology of Michigan; structure of lake ice, Greenland; structure and flow of Alaskan glaciers; snow stratigraphy, Antarctica; microparticles in Antarctic ice. *Mailing Add:* Dept of Geol Sci Albion Col Albion MI 49224

TAYLOR, LEIGHTON ROBERT, JR, b Glendale, Calif, Nov 17, 40; m 63; c 2. ICHTHYOLOGY. *Educ:* Occidental Col, BA, 62; Univ Hawaii, MS, 65; Scripps Inst Oceanog, Univ Calif, San Diego, PhD(marine biol), 72. *Prof Exp:* Res asst, Scripps Inst Oceanog, 69-71, mus cur, Scripps Aquarium-Mus, La Jolla, Calif, 71-72; asst leader res, Hawaii Coop Fishery Res Unit, 72-75; DIR, WAIKIKI AQUARIUM, UNIV HAWAII, 75- *Concurrent Pos:* Mem grad fac, Dept Zool, Univ Hawaii, 72-; res assoc, Calif Acad Sci & B P Bishop Mus; pres, Phoenix Sci Ctr. *Mem:* Am Soc Ichthyologists & Herpetologists; Am Fisheries Soc; Am Soc Zoologists; Sigma Xi. *Res:* Taxonomy and ecology of tropical marine fishes and sharks. *Mailing Add:* Waikiki Aquarium 2777 Kalakaua Ave Honolulu HI 96815

TAYLOR, LEONARD S, b Brooklyn, NY, Dec 28, 28; m 54; c 2. ELECTRICAL ENGINEERING, BIOELECTRO-MAGNETICS. *Educ:* Harvard Univ, AB, 51; NMex State Univ, MS, 56, PhD(physics), 60. *Prof Exp:* Electronics engr, Raytheon Mfg Co, 51-54; electronics scientist, White Sands Missile Range, 54-59; theoret physicist, Gen Elec Co, 60-64; assoc prof eng, Case Western Reserve Univ, 64-67; PROF ELEC ENG, UNIV MD, COLLEGE PARK, 67- *Concurrent Pos:* Sr Fulbright lectr, Univ Madrid, 62-63; consult, Ford Found & vis prof, Ford Found prog, Ctr Adv Res & Studies, Nat Polytech Inst, Mex, 64-65; mem, Comn VI, US Nat Comt/Int Union Radio Sci, 71- & US Nat Comn, Int Sci Radio Union, 78-82. *Mem:* fel Inst Elec & Electronics Engrs; Am Phys Soc. *Res:* Optical and radio communication systems; remote sensing; microwave engineering; biological effects of microwaves; microwave diathermy and hyperthermia. *Mailing Add:* 706 Apple Grove Rd Silver Spring MD 20904

TAYLOR, LINCOLN HOMER, b Wolsey, SDak, Oct 26, 20; m 46; c 5. AGRONOMY. *Educ:* SDak State Col, BS, 42; Iowa State Univ, MS, 49, PhD, 51. *Prof Exp:* From asst prof to assoc prof agron, Univ Maine, 51-55; PROF AGRON, VA POLYTECH INST & STATE UNIV, 55- *Mem:* Crop Sci Soc Am; Am Soc Agron. *Res:* Forage crop and turfgrass breeding; genetics. *Mailing Add:* Dept of Agron Va Polytech Inst & State Univ Blacksburg VA 24061

TAYLOR, LLOYD DAVID, b Boston, Mass, Jan 11, 33; m 57; c 3. CHEMISTRY. *Educ:* Boston Col, BS, 54; Mass Inst Technol, PhD(org chem), 58. *Prof Exp:* Res assoc, Mass Inst Technol, 57-58; scientist, 58-65, res group leader, 65-68, mgr polymer res lab, 68-78, tech dir polymer sci, 78-80, DIR CHEM RES & SR RES FEL, POLAROID CORP, CAMBRIDGE, 80- *Mem:* AAAS; Am Chem Soc; Am Inst Chem; Soc Photog Sci & Eng. *Res:* Polymer chemistry; photographic chemistry; syntheses of novel monomers and polymers; plastics; solubility and diffusional phenomena; critical temperature behaviour and mixing. *Mailing Add:* One Maureen Rd Lexington MA 02173

TAYLOR, LYLE HERMAN, b Paton, Iowa, Oct 23, 36; m 59; c 3. LASERS. *Educ:* Iowa State Univ, BS, 58; NMex State Univ, MS, 61; Univ Kans, PhD(physics), 68. *Prof Exp:* Asst physicist, White Sands Missile Range, 58-61; assoc physicist, Midwest Res Inst, 61-64, tech consult, 64-67; SR SCIENTIST, WESTINGHOUSE RES LABS, 67- *Mem:* Am Phys Soc. *Res:* Phonon-phonon interactions; physical adsorption; cleavage energies; F-center wave functions; spin-spin interactions; rare earth fluorescence; crystal field theory; laser pumps; holographic strain analysis; gas laser computer simulation. *Mailing Add:* 3317 Benden Dr Murreysville PA 15668

TAYLOR, LYNN JOHNSTON, b Akron, Ohio, June 10, 36; m 61; c 2. ORGANIC CHEMISTRY, POLYMER CHEMISTRY. *Educ:* Harvard Univ, AB, 58; Mass Inst Technol, PhD(org chem), 63. *Prof Exp:* Sr res chemist, Agr Div, Monsanto Co, 63-65; res scientist, Okemos Res Lab, 66-70, sr res scientist, Owens-Ill, Inc, 70-74, chief plastics mat res, 74-79; GROUP LEADER, ASHLAND CHEMICAL CO, 79- *Mem:* Am Chem Soc; Am Inst Chem; The Chem Soc. *Res:* Kinetics and mechanisms of organic chemical reactions; polymer synthesis, modification and degradation; thermal analysis of polymers. *Mailing Add:* Ashland Chemical Co PO Box 2219 Columbus OH 43216

TAYLOR, M(AURICE) E(UGENE), electrical engineering, see previous edition

TAYLOR, MALCOLM HERBERT, b Annapolis, Md, Apr 7, 42; m 65; c 4. ENVIRONMENTAL PHYSIOLOGY, ENDOCRINOLOGY. *Educ:* Franklin & Marshall Col, BA, 64; Johns Hopkins Univ, PhD(physiol), 69. *Prof Exp:* NIH fel physiol, Med Sch, Univ Pittsburgh, 69-71; res assoc marine sci, Col Marine Studies, 71-73, asst prof biol sci, 73-79, ASSOC PROF LIFE & HEALTH SCI, UNIV DEL, 79- *Concurrent Pos:* Joint appt, Col Marine Studies, Univ Del, 77- *Mem:* AAAS; Am Soc Zoologists; Atlantic Estuarine Res Soc. *Res:* Environmental control of reproduction and adrenal stress responses in fish; biological clocks in fish reproduction. *Mailing Add:* Sch Life & Health Sci Univ Del Newark DE 19711

TAYLOR, MARVIN, b Brooklyn, NY, Apr 30, 25; m; c 4. MECHANICAL ENGINEERING. *Educ:* Cooper Union, BME, 47. *Prof Exp:* Designer, Kennedy Van-Saun Mfg & Eng Corp, Pa, 47; engr, Etched Prod Co, 48, Alexander Smith, 51-52 & Monroe Bus Mach, Inc, 52-53; engr design & develop, Arma Div, Ambac Industs, Inc, Garden City, 49-50, 54-59, sect head, 59-65, mgr inertial equip, 65-77; prof engr, Western Elec Co, 77-80; MEM STAFF, LINCOLN LAB, MASS INST TECHNOL, 80- *Mem:* Am Inst Aeronaut & Astronaut; Am Inst Navig; Inst Elec & Electronics Engrs. *Res:* Inertial gyroscopes; gyro compasses; navigation equipment; business machines; textile machinery. *Mailing Add:* Lincoln Lab Mass Inst Technol 244 Wood St Lexington MA 02173

TAYLOR, MARY LOWELL BRANSON, b Coeur d'Alene, Idaho, Nov 24, 32; m 55; c 2. MICROBIAL PHYSIOLOGY. *Educ:* Univ Idaho, BS, 54; Univ Ill, PhD(bact), 59. *Prof Exp:* Asst, Univ Ill, 54-57; res assoc, Emory Univ, 57-59; USPHS fel, Oak Ridge Nat Lab, 59-61; res assoc biol, 61-77, ASSOC PROF ENVIRON SCI & RESOURCES, PORTLAND STATE UNIV, 77- *Mem:* Am Soc Microbiol; Am Soc Plant Physiol. *Res:* Bacterial physiology; carbohydrate synthesis and dissimilation; alcohol oxidation; natural products oxidation; enzyme biosynthesis; role of metals and metaloids in microbial metabolism biological oxidation aj as. *Mailing Add:* Dept of Biol Portland State Univ PO Box 751 Portland OR 97207

TAYLOR, MARY MARSHALL, b Swarthmore, Pa, Jan 9, 29; m 50, 71; c 3. MICROBIOLOGY. *Educ:* Bryn Mawr Col, BA, 50, PhD(biol), 64. *Prof Exp:* Sr scientist, Sci Info Dept, Smith Kline & French Labs, 64-68; instr microbiol, Med Col Pa, 68-69; teacher, Baldwin Sch, Pa, 69-71; asst prof microbiol & biol, 72-75, dir acad serv, 75-78, assoc prof, 75-79, PROF BIOL SCI, MONTGOMERY COUNTY COMMUNITY COL, 79- *Mem:* AAAS. *Res:* Gastrointestinal effects of bacterial endotoxins; normal flora of intestine and oral cavity. *Mailing Add:* Dept of Sci Montgomery County Community Col 340 DeKalb Pike Blue Bell PA 19422

TAYLOR, MERLIN GENE, b Zanesville, Ohio, May 11, 36; m 63; c 2. PHYSICS. *Educ:* Muskingum Col, BS, 58; Brown Univ, MSc, 65, PhD(physics), 67. *Prof Exp:* Res asst, High Energy Physics Lab, Brown Univ, 58-66; asst prof physics, Wilkes Col, 66-67 & Am Univ Cairo, 67-69; asst prof, 69-71, assoc prof, 71-81, PROF PHYSICS, BLOOMSBURG STATE COL, 81- *Mem:* Am Phys Soc; Am Asn Physics Teachers. *Res:* Use of computers in physics teaching; nuclear physics; activation analysis. *Mailing Add:* Dept of Physics Bloomsburg State Col Bloomsburg PA 17815

TAYLOR, MICHAEL ALAN, b New York, NY, Mar 6, 40; m 63; c 2. NEUROPSYCHIATRY. *Educ:* Cornell Univ, BA, 61; New York Med Col, MD, 65. *Prof Exp:* Residency psychiat, New York Med Col, 69, asst prof & chief acute treatment univ, 71-73; assoc prof & dir residency training, State Univ NY, Stony Brook, 73-76; PROF PSYCHIAT & BEHAV SCI, CHMN DEPT & DIR RESIDENCY TRAINING, CHICAGO MED SCH, UNIV HEALTH SCI, 76-, PROF PSYCHOL, 77- *Concurrent Pos:* Consult, Pilgrim Psychiat Ctr, West Brentwood, NY, 73-76, Kings Park Psychiat Ctr, Kings Park, NY, 74-76, South Oaks Hosp, Amityville, NY, 74-76 & Psychiat Serv, North Chicago Vet Admin Hosp, North Chicago, Ill, 76-; mem res subcomt, Prov Ment Health Adv Coun, Alberta, Can, 76-80; mem psychiat adv bd, Ill Dept Ment Health & Deviation Dis, Springfield, Ill, 77-; actg chmn, Dept Psychol, Sch Grad & Postdoctoral Studies, Chicago Med Sch, Univ Health Sci, 77-80. *Honors & Awards:* A E Bennett Clin Res Award, Soc Biol Psychiat, 69; First Prize Clin Res, NY Acad Med, 69; Morris L Parker Award, Chicago Med Sch, Univ Health Sci, 78. *Mem:* Am Psychiat Asn; Am Psychopath Asn; Psychiat Res Soc; AAAS; Int Neuropsychol Soc. *Res:* Validity of diagnoses of schizophrenia and manic depressive illness by relating clinical phenomenology of these groups to demographic, family illness, cerebral latoralization of cortical dysfunction, neuropsychological and treatment response variables; functional relationships between neuronal groups and behavior utilizing neuropsychological techniques; genetics of major psyches. *Mailing Add:* Dept of Psychiat Univ Health Sci Bldg 50 North Chicago IL 60064

TAYLOR, MICHAEL DEE, b New York, NY, Dec 17, 40; m 70. MATHEMATICS. *Educ:* Univ Fla, BA, 63; Fla State Univ, MS, 65, PhD(math), 69. *Prof Exp:* Asst prof, 68-72, ASSOC PROF MATH, FLA TECHNOL UNIV, 72- *Mem:* Math Asn Am; Am Math Soc. *Res:* Topology of 3-manifolds and probabilistic metric spaces. *Mailing Add:* Dept of Math Sci Fla Technol Univ Orlando FL 32816

TAYLOR, MICHAEL GERARD, b Toronto, Ont, July 17, 53. MAGNETIC RESONANCE. *Educ:* McMaster Univ, BSc, 77; Univ Ottawa, PhD(chem), 82. *Prof Exp:* INDUST FEL, XEROX RES CTR CAN, 81- *Res:* Solid state nuclear magnetic resonance of natural and synthetic macromolecules; structure and dynamics in liquid crystals and biomembranes. *Mailing Add:* Xerox Res Ctr Can 2480 Dunwin Dr Mississauga ON L5L 1J9 Can

TAYLOR, MICHAEL LEE, b Rockville, Ind, May 27, 41; m 65; c 2. ANALYTICAL CHEMISTRY, MEDICINAL CHEMISTRY. *Educ:* Purdue Univ, Lafayette, BS, 63, MS, 65, PhD(med chem), 67. *Prof Exp:* Nat Res Coun resident res assoc, Chem Lab, Aerospace Res Labs, Wright-Patterson AFB, Ohio, 70-71, res scientist anal mass spectros, 71-75; RES ASSOC PROF CHEM, WRIGHT STATE UNIV, 75-, ASSOC PROF PHARMACOL & ASSOC DIR, BREHM LAB, 78- *Concurrent Pos:* Mem bd dirs, Spectronics, Inc, 74- *Mem:* Am Soc Mass Spectrometry; Am Chem Soc. *Res:* Use of ultrasensitive mass spectral techniques to assess relationships between molecular structure and elicited toxicological and pharmacological response and to determine environmental distribution and the fate of toxic chemicals. *Mailing Add:* Brehm Lab Wright State Univ Dayton OH 45431

TAYLOR, MILTON WILLIAM, b Glasgow, Scotland, Dec 10, 31; US citizen; m 57; c 2. GENETICS, MOLECULAR BIOLOGY. *Educ:* Cornell Univ, BS, 61; Stanford Univ, PhD(biol), 66. *Prof Exp:* NIH fel virol, Univ Calif, Irvine, 66-67; from asst prof to assoc prof, 67-75, PROF MICROBIOL & GENETICS, IND UNIV, BLOOMINGTON, 75- *Mem:* AAAS; Am Soc Microbiol; Am Soc Biol Chemists; Tissue Cult Asn; Genetics Soc Am. *Res:* Cancer research; viral oncolysis; recombinant DNA and gene cloning; somatic cell genetics; purine metabolism; microbiology. *Mailing Add:* Dept of Biol Ind Univ Bloomington IN 47401

TAYLOR, MORRIS CHAPMAN, b Fulton, Ky, May 28, 39; m 60; c 2. INSTRUMENTATION. *Educ:* Univ Tenn, BS, 62; Univ Calif, Los Angeles, MS, 64; Rice Univ, MA, 66, PhD(physics), 68. *Prof Exp:* Lab technician, Oak Ridge Nat Lab, 61-62; mem tech staff, Hughes Aircraft Co, 62-64; asst prof physics, St Louis Univ, 68-69; mem staff, Columbia Sci Res Inst, Houston, 69-71; AEC & State of Tex joint sr fel, Rice Univ & Univ Tex M D Anderson Hosp & Tumor Inst, 71; chief scientist, 72-76, DIR ENG, COLUMBIA SCI INDUSTS, 76- *Mem:* Am Soc Testing & Mat; Air Pollution Control Asn; Instrument Soc Am; Am Phys Soc. *Res:* Experimental nuclear physics; radiological physics; air quality monitoring; nondestructive elemental analysis. *Mailing Add:* Dept of Eng Columbia Sci Industs PO Box 9908 Austin TX 78766

TAYLOR, MORRIS D, b Mitchell, Ind, Apr 14, 34; m 56; c 3. SCIENCE EDUCATION, PHYSICAL CHEMISTRY. *Educ:* Purdue Univ, BS, 56, PhD(sci educ), 66. *Prof Exp:* Instr physics & educ, Purdue Univ, 60-63; from asst prof to prof chem & educ, 63-70, PROF CHEM, EASTERN KY UNIV, 70- *Mem:* AAAS; Nat Sci Teachers Asn. *Mailing Add:* Dept of Chem Eastern Ky Univ Richmond KY 40475

TAYLOR, MURRAY EAST, b Casselton, NDak, Apr 14, 15; m 50; c 1. ANALYTICAL CHEMISTRY. *Educ:* Univ Wash, BS, 48, MS, 52, PhD(chem), 60. *Prof Exp:* Microchemist, Univ Wash, 48-52, res instr chemother, 52-58; res chemist, Boeing Airplane Co, 58-63; assoc staff scientist, Missile Div, Chrysler Corp, 63-64; prin engr, 64-80, SR PRIN ENGR, BOEING CO, SEATTLE, 80- *Mem:* AAAS; Am Chem Soc; NY Acad Sci. *Res:* Instrumental analysis; microchemistry; thermochemistry; radiation effects on materials; polymer chemistry. *Mailing Add:* 4401 138th Ave SE Bellevue WA 98006

TAYLOR, NORMAN FLETCHER, b Newcastle Upon Tyne, Eng, Mar 4, 28; m 48; c 2. BIOCHEMISTRY. *Educ:* Univ Oxford, BA, 53, MA, 56, DPhil(biochem), 56; FRSC. *Prof Exp:* Exchange vis scientist, Dept Pharmacol, Univ Calif, Los Angeles, 57-59; Sci Res Coun fel, Dept Biochem, Univ Oxford, 59-60; sr lectr chem, Bristol Col Sci & Technol, Eng, 62-65; reader & head biochem, Univ Bath, Eng, 65-73; PROF BIOCHEM, UNIV WINDSOR, 73- *Concurrent Pos:* Vis prof, Dept Chem, Temple Univ, 67; fel, Canterbury Col, Ont, 74- *Mem:* Am Soc Biol Chemists; Can Biochem Soc; Brit Biochem Soc; Brit Chem Soc. *Res:* Microbial and mammalian metabolism of synthetic fluorinated carbohydrates and related compounds; mechanism of transport across biological membranes; insect biochemistry. *Mailing Add:* Dept Chem Univ Windsor Windsor ON N9B 3P4 Can

TAYLOR, NORMAN LINN, b Augusta, Ky, July 18, 26; m 51; c 5. AGRONOMY. *Educ:* Univ Ky, BS, 49, MS, 51; Cornell Univ, PhD(plant breeding), 53. *Prof Exp:* Asst agronomist, 53-56, assoc prof, 56-66, ASSOC AGRONOMIST, UNIV KY, 56-, PROF AGRON, 66- *Honors & Awards:* Cert of Merit, Am Forage & Grasslands Coun, 72. *Mem:* AAAS; Crop Sci Soc Am; fel Am Soc Agron; Am Genetic Asn; Genetics Soc Can. *Res:* Forage crops genetics and breeding; interspecific hybridization in the genus Trifolium. *Mailing Add:* Dept Agron Univ Ky Lexington KY 40506

TAYLOR, OLIVER CLIFTON, b Hallett, Okla, Nov 29, 18; m 40; c 3. HORTICULTURE. *Educ:* Okla Agr & Mech Col, MS, 51; Mich State Col, PhD, 53. *Prof Exp:* Asst county agent, Okla Exten Serv, 47-49; instr agr, Northeast Okla Agr & Mech Col, 50-51; horticulturist, 53, lectr plant sci, 74-76, HORTICULTURIST, STATEWIDE AIR POLLUTION RES CTR, UNIV CALIF, RIVERSIDE, 53-, PROF PLANT SCI, 76- *Mem:* AAAS; Air Pollution Control Asn; Am Soc Hort Sci. *Res:* Citriculture; biological effects of air pollutants and plant physiological responses to air pollutants. *Mailing Add:* Statewide Air Pollution Res Ctr Univ of Calif Riverside CA 92521

TAYLOR, PALMER WILLIAM, b Stevens Point, Wis, Oct 3, 38; m 65; c 2. PHARMACOLOGY. *Educ:* Univ Wis-Madison, BS, 60, PhD(pharm), 64. *Prof Exp:* Res assoc pharmacol, NIH, Bethesda, Md, 64-68; NIH vis fel, Molecular Pharmacol Res Unit, Cambridge Univ, 68-70; assoc prof, 74-78, PROF & HEAD, DIV PHARMACOL, SCH MED, UNIV CALIF, SAN DIEGO, 78- *Concurrent Pos:* NIH grant pharmacol, Sch Med, Univ Calif, San Diego, 70- *Mem:* Am Soc Biol Chemists; Am Soc Pharmacol & Exp Therapeut. *Res:* Drug-protein interactions; kinetic and physical-chemical studies. *Mailing Add:* Div Pharmacol Sch Med Univ Calif San Diego La Jolla CA 92093

TAYLOR, PATRICK TIMOTHY, b Mt Vernon, NY, Mar 20, 38. GEOPHYSICS. *Educ:* Mich State Univ, BS, 60; Pa State Univ, MS, 62; Stanford Univ, PhD(geophys), 65. *Prof Exp:* Res asst marine geophys, Lamont-Doherty Geol Observ, Columbia Univ, 65-66; geophysicist, US Naval Oceanog Off, 66-76 & Naval Ocean Res & Develop Activity, 76-78, GEOPHYSICIST, GEOPHYS BR, GODDARD SPACE FLIGHT CTR, NASA, 78- *Concurrent Pos:* Assoc prof lectr, George Washington Univ. *Honors & Awards:* Kaminiski Award, Sci Res Soc Am, 70. *Mem:* Am Geophys Union; Geol Soc Am; Soc Explor Geophys. *Res:* Interpretation of satellite derived and marine geophysical data, such as gravity, magnetics, seismic and heat flow, with supporting geophysical and geological information, for example petrological and remotely sensed photographs. *Mailing Add:* Code 922 NASA Greenbelt MD 20771

TAYLOR, PAUL DUANE, b Warren, Ohio, July 8, 40; m 65; c 4. CHEMISTRY. *Educ:* Ind Inst Technol, BS, 62; Long Island Univ, MS, 64; Univ Cincinnati, PhD(inorg chem), 69. *Prof Exp:* Teaching asst, Long Island Univ, 62-64; res chemist, Res & Eng Develop Dept, M W Kellogg Co, 64-66; teaching asst, Univ Cincinnati, 66-68; from res chemist to sr res chemist,

Celanese Res Co, 69-74, res supvr, 74-77, sect leader, Celanese Chem Co, Tex, 77-78; res mgr, Oxirane Int, 78-81; MGR CATALYSIS DEVELOP, ARCO CHEM CO, PA, 81- *Mem:* NY Acad Sci; Am Chem Soc. *Res:* Research and management of homogeneous and heterogeneous catalysis. *Mailing Add:* ARCO Chem Co 3801 W Chester Pike Newtown Square PA 19073

TAYLOR, PAUL JOHN, b Chicago, Ill, Jan 30, 39; m 60; c 1. ANALYTICAL CHEMISTRY. *Educ:* Northern Ill Univ, BS, 64, PhD(anal chem), 71. *Prof Exp:* US AEC fel, Purdue Univ, Lafayette, 70-72; from asst prof to assoc prof chem, Wright State Univ, 72-78; lectr, 78-81, PROF, UNIV WIS-LACROSSE, 81- *Mem:* Am Chem Soc. *Res:* Coordination compounds and their analytical applications, gas chromatography; computers and their applications to analytical chemistry; liquid crystals and mass spectroscopy. *Mailing Add:* Dept Chem Univ Wis Lacrosse WI 54601

TAYLOR, PAUL M, b Baltimore, Md, June 26, 27; m 55; c 4. PEDIATRICS, PHYSIOLOGY. *Educ:* Johns Hopkins Univ, AB, 47, MD, 51. *Prof Exp:* Res fel, 54-56, from instr to assoc prof, 56-71, PROF PEDIAT, OBSTET & GYNEC, SCH MED, UNIV PITTSBURGH, 71- *Concurrent Pos:* USPHS fel, Nuffield Inst Med Res, Oxford Univ, 59-60; dir div neonatology & chief dept pediat, Magee-Women's Hosp, 65-; vis prof, Inst Path, Univ Geneva, 71-72. *Mem:* Soc Pediat Res; Am Physiol Soc. *Res:* Physiology of the newborn infant; development of parent-infant attachment. *Mailing Add:* Dept of Pediat Magee-Women's Hosp Pittsburgh PA 15213

TAYLOR, PAUL OWEN, b Young, Australia, May 24, 45. PHYSICS, ASTRONOMY. *Educ:* Univ NSW, BSc, 65; Univ Colo, PhD(physics), 72. *Prof Exp:* Sr res assoc physics, Univ Newcastle, Eng, 72-74; res assoc, Joint Inst Lab Astrophys, Univ Colo, Nat Bur Standards, 74-76; PHYSICIST ASTRON, CTR ASTROPHYS, 76- *Res:* X-ray spectroscopy; fusion diagnostics; x-ray astronomy; atomic collisions experiments. *Mailing Add:* Ctr for Astrophys 60 Garden St Cambridge MA 02138

TAYLOR, PAUL PEAK, b Childress, Tex, May 11, 21; m 45; c 2. PEDODONTICS. *Educ:* Baylor Univ, DDS, 44; Univ Mich, MS, 51. *Prof Exp:* PROF GRAD PEDODONTICS & CHMN DEPT, COL DENT, BAYLOR UNIV, 60-; DIR TRAINING & ASST CHIEF DENT SERV, CHILDREN'S MED CTR, 60-, DIR DENT, 66- *Concurrent Pos:* Staff, Tex Scottish Rite Hosp for Crippled Children, Dallas, Tex, 60- & Denton State Sch, 64-; proctor, Am Bd Pedodont, 66; exam mem, Am Bd Pedodont, 77- *Mem:* Fel Am Col Dent; Am Acad Pedodont; Am Dent Asn; Am Soc Dent for Children. *Res:* Physiological responses of pulp tissues and the testing of patient responses to dental stimuli. *Mailing Add:* Dept Pedodont Col Dent Baylor Univ Dallas TX 75246

TAYLOR, PETER, b Warkworth, Eng, Sept 12, 49; m 73; c 1. INORGANIC CHEMISTRY, CRYSTALLOGRAPHY. *Educ:* Univ Birmingham, BSc, 69, PhD(inorg chem), 72. *Prof Exp:* Fel struct inorg chem, Univ NB, 72-75; fel, 75-77, ASSOC RES OFFICER STRUCT INORG CHEM, RES CHEM BR, WHITESHELL NUCLEAR RES ESTAB, ATOMIC ENERGY CAN LTD, 77- *Mem:* Chem Inst Can; Am Ceramic Soc. *Res:* Structural chemistry and phase relations in inorganic oxide systems; radioactive waste management. *Mailing Add:* Res Chem Br Whiteshell Nuclear Res Estab Pinawa MB R0E 1LD Can

TAYLOR, PETER ANTHONY, b Liverpool, Eng, June 9, 32; m 68; c 2. PHYSICAL CHEMISTRY, TEXTILE ENGINEERING. *Educ:* Liverpool Col Technol, Eng, ARIC, 56; Univ Manchester, PhD(chem), 63. *Prof Exp:* Jr asst analyst, Liverpool City Pub Health Dept, 49-52; analyst, Distillers Co (Biochem), Ltd, 52-56, res chemist, 58-60 & Fibers Div, Allied Chem Corp, 63-66; PROJ MGR, PHILLIPS FIBERS CORP, 66- *Mem:* Royal Inst Chem; Am Chem Soc. *Res:* Polymerization kinetics, free radical and condensation; man-made fiber rheology, processing and dyeing; polymer pigmentation; textile and fiber finishing; spin finish development. *Mailing Add:* Res Dept Phillips Fibers Corp PO Box 66 Greenville SC 29602

TAYLOR, PETER BERKLEY, b Yonkers, NY, Dec 1, 33; m 58; c 3. MARINE ECOLOGY. *Educ:* Cornell Univ, BS, 55; Univ Calif, Los Angeles, MS, 60; Univ Calif, San Diego, PhD(marine biol), 64. *Prof Exp:* NSF res fel, 63-64; asst prof oceanog, Univ Wash, 64-71; MEM FAC, EVERGREEN STATE COL, 71- *Res:* Coastal and estuarine benthic ecology; ecology of marine fishes; venomous marine animals. *Mailing Add:* Evergreen State Col Olympia WA 98505

TAYLOR, PHILIP CRAIG, b Paterson, NJ, Mar 17, 42; m; c 2. SOLID STATE PHYSICS. *Educ:* Carleton Col, AB, 64; Brown Univ, PhD(physics), 69. *Prof Exp:* Fel physics, Nat Res Coun, NAS, 69-71; RES PHYSICIST SOLID STATE PHYSICS, NAVAL RES LAB, 71- *Mem:* Am Phys Soc; AAAS; Am Ceramic Soc. *Res:* Crystalline and amorphous semiconductors. *Mailing Add:* Code 5273 Naval Res Lab Washington DC 20375

TAYLOR, PHILIP LIDDON, b London, Eng, Oct 17, 37; m 66. SOLID STATE PHYSICS. *Educ:* Univ London, BSc, 59; Cambridge Univ, PhD(physics), 62. *Prof Exp:* Magnavox res fel mat sci, 62-64, from asst prof to assoc prof, 64-74, PROF PHYSICS, CASE WESTERN RESERVE UNIV, 74-, PROF MACROMOLECULAR SCI, 77- *Concurrent Pos:* Mem, comt recommendations for US Army basic sci res, Nat Res Coun Assembly Math & Phys Sci. *Res:* Theoretical solid state physics. *Mailing Add:* Dept of Physics Case Western Res Univ Univ Circle Cleveland OH 44106

TAYLOR, PHILIP SEYFANG, b Minneapolis, Minn, Dec 16, 21; m 42. ENTOMOLOGY. *Educ:* Univ Minn, BS, 48, MS, 52. *Prof Exp:* Lab technician, Univ Minn, 47-48, asst, 48-52; cur zool & ed supt, 52-58, DIR, SCI MUS MINN, ST PAUL INST, 58- *Concurrent Pos:* Dir, Urban Lab, Inc, 75- *Mem:* Am Inst Biol Sci; Int Coun Mus; Am Asn Mus; Nat Asn Biol Teachers. *Res:* Biology and ecology of insects; indentification of zoological remains associated with archaeological sites; science education. *Mailing Add:* Sci Mus of Minn 30 ETenth St St Paul MN 55101

TAYLOR, RALPH E, b Lykens, Ohio, Sept 25, 05; m 34; c 1. GEOLOGY. *Educ:* Univ Mich, AB, 27, MS, 28; La State Univ, PhD(geol), 38. *Prof Exp:* Field geologist, Ark Natural Gas Co, La, Tex, Kans & Nebr, 29-32 & USDA, 33-34; asst, La State Univ, 34-37; explor geologist, Freeport Sulphur Co, US, Can, Cuba, Mex & Africa, 37-49; sr staff geologist, Humble Oil & Refining Co, 49-67; CONSULT GEOLOGIST, 67- *Concurrent Pos:* Dir & mgr explor, Phelan Sulphur Co, 68-71; vpres & dir, Frontier Petrol Co, Inc & Frontier Sulphur Co, Inc, NY, 68-71; vpres, Transworld Minerals Australia, Australia & SEAsia, 70-72; consult geologist, var co & individuals in Australia & NZ, 73. *Mem:* Geol Soc Am; Soc Econ Geol; Mineral Soc Am; Am Inst Mining, Metall & Petrol Eng; Australian Geol Soc. *Res:* Geology of cap rock and salt of salt domes; limestones; economic geology of petroleum, sulphur, salt, manganese, nickel, iron, potash, phosphates and uranium; North and South America, Africa, Europe, Australia and the Middle and Far East. *Mailing Add:* PO Drawer A La Porte TX 77571

TAYLOR, RALPH EDWARD, b Hickory, NC, Nov 28, 23; m 48; c 2. ELECTRONIC ENGINEERING, PHYSICS. *Educ:* George Washington Univ, BA, 51. *Prof Exp:* Radio engr, US Naval Res Lab, 42-48; supvry electronic engr, Nat Bur Standards, 48-51, ord div, 51-53; proj leader, Diamond Ord Fuze Labs, US Army Ord Corps, 53-57, proj supvr, 57-60; sect head, Goddard Space Flight Ctr, NASA, 60-71, tech mgr, Navig & Data Collection Br, 71-81. *Honors & Awards:* Achievement Award, Inst Elec & Electronics Engrs, 77 & 81. *Mem:* Fel Inst Elec & Electronics Engrs. *Res:* Aerospace communications and navigation systems; aerospace radio frequency tracking receiving systems; radio frequency interference; telemetry systems for guided missiles; guided missile radar fuzes; antennas; microwave equipment. *Mailing Add:* Code 974 NASA Goddard Space Flight Ctr Greenbelt MD 20771

TAYLOR, RALPH WILSON, b Whitesburg, Ky, June 1, 37. FIELD BIOLOGY, VERTEBRATE ZOOLOGY. *Educ:* Murray State Univ, BS, 60; Univ Louisville, MS, 68, PhD(herpet), 72. *Prof Exp:* Pub sch teacher biol, Durrett High Sch, Louisville, Ky, 69-70; instr, Spalding Col, 69-70; asst prof, 72-80, ASSOC PROF BIOL, MARSHALL UNIV, 80- *Mem:* Soc Study Amphibians & Reptiles; Am Malacological Union; Sigma Xi. *Res:* Ecology, taxonomy, and distribution of amphibians, reptiles and freshwater; terrestrial mollusks of West Virginia and surrounding states. *Mailing Add:* Dept of Biol Sci Marshall Univ Huntington WV 25701

TAYLOR, RAYMOND DEAN, b Okemah, Okla, Aug 18, 28; m 61; c 2. LOW TEMPERATURE PHYSICS. *Educ:* Kans State Col, Pittsburg, BS, 50; Rice Inst, PhD(phys chem), 54. *Prof Exp:* Asst, Rice Inst, 51-52; mem staff, 54-73, ASSOC GROUP LEADER, LOS ALAMOS NAT LAB, 73- *Mem:* Am Chem Soc; Am Phys Soc. *Res:* Low temperature calorimetry; cryogenics; transport and state properties of liquid helium; Mössbauer effect; superconductivity; magnetism; direct current superconducting power transmission lines. *Mailing Add:* Los Alamos Nat Lab Box 1663 MS764 Los Alamos NM 87545

TAYLOR, RAYMOND JOHN, b Ada, Okla, Jan 20, 30; m 59; c 3. PLANT TAXONOMY. *Educ:* ECent State Col, BSEd, 54; Univ Okla, MNS, 61, PhD(plant ecol), 67. *Prof Exp:* Teacher high sch, Okla, 54-55 & Okla City Pub Sch Syst, 55-61; asst prof biol, Southeastern State Col, 61-63; asst bot, Univ Okla, 63-65; assoc prof, 65-74, PROF BIOL, SOUTHEASTERN STATE UNIV, 74- *Concurrent Pos:* Grants, Southeastern State Col Res Found, 68 & NIH, 72. *Mem:* Am Soc Plant Taxonomists. *Res:* Dauphine Island, Oklahoma, Alaska, Costa Rica and Alabama plants; aquatic microphytes; endangered plant species. *Mailing Add:* Dept of Biol Southeastern State Univ Durant OK 74701

TAYLOR, RAYMOND L, b Providence, RI, July 3, 30; m 55; c 5. LASERS, CHEMICAL PHYSICS. *Educ:* Brown Univ, ScB, 55; Calif Inst Technol, PhD(chem), 60. *Prof Exp:* Asst, Calif Inst Technol, 55-59; prin res scientist, Avco Everett Res Lab, Inc, 59-73; prin scientist & mem bd dirs, Phys Sci Inc, 73-78, mgr laser devices, 78-80; MEM STAFF, RES & LASER TECH INC, 80- *Concurrent Pos:* Chmn atomic physics res comt, Avco Everett Res Lab, Inc, 70-73; mem, Dept Transp Comt Stratospheric Chem, 73-75. *Honors & Awards:* Silver Combustion Medal, Combustion Inst, 68. *Mem:* Am Chem Soc; Am Phys Soc; Combustion Inst; Sigma Xi. *Res:* Radiation and energy transfer processes in gases; optical experiments and instrumentation; molecular gas laser device research and development; laser applications. *Mailing Add:* 6 Frank St Res & Laser Tech Inc Rockport MA 01966

TAYLOR, RICHARD EDWARD, b Medicine Hat, Alta, Nov 2, 29; m 50; c 1. HIGH ENERGY PHYSICS. *Educ:* Univ Alta, BSc, 50, MSc, 52; Stanford Univ, PhD(physics), 62. *Hon Degrees:* Dr, Univ Paris, 80. *Prof Exp:* Physicist, Lawrence Radiation Lab, Univ Calif, 61-62; staff mem, 62-68, assoc prof, 68-70, PROF PHYSICS, STANFORD LINEAR ACCELERATOR CTR, STANFORD UNIV, 70- *Concurrent Pos:* Guggenheim fel, 71; Alexander von Humboldt award, 82. *Mem:* Am Phys Soc; Can Asn Physicists. *Res:* High energy physics, interactions of electrons and photons with matter; high energy electron scattering. *Mailing Add:* Stanford Linear Accelerator Ctr Stanford Univ PO Box 4349 Stanford CA 94305

TAYLOR, RICHARD MELVIN, b Salt Lake City, Utah, Aug 19, 29; m 55; c 4. AGRONOMY, PLANT PHYSIOLOGY. *Educ:* Utah State Univ, BS, 58, MS, 59; Iowa State Univ, PhD(agron, plant physiol), 64. *Prof Exp:* Instr agron, Iowa State Univ, 59-64; ASST AGRONOMIST, TEX A&M UNIV, 64- *Mem:* Am Soc Agron; Crop Sci Soc Am. *Res:* Effects of soluble salts and temperature upon the germination and emergence of seeds and fruiting patterns of cotton; production and management; root physiology, native plants and vegetable domestication. *Mailing Add:* Tex Agr Res Ctr 10601 NLoop Rd El Paso TX 79927

TAYLOR, RICHARD TIMOTHY, b Coatesville, Pa, June 12, 50. ORGANIC CHEMISTRY. *Educ:* Univ Del, BS, 72; Ohio State Univ, PhD(chem), 77. *Prof Exp:* Asst chem, Ohio State Univ, 73-75, fel, 75-77; NIH fel org chem, Cornell Univ, 77-78; ASST PROF ORG CHEM, MIAMI UNIV, 78- *Mem:* Am Chem Soc. *Res:* Synthetic aspects of organosilicon chemistry; synthesis of strained ring compounds. *Mailing Add:* 616 S College Ave Apt 63 Oxford OH 45056

TAYLOR, ROBERT BURNS, JR, b Downingtown, Pa, Oct 13, 20; m 45, 71; c 1. ORGANIC CHEMISTRY, INFORMATION SCIENCE. *Educ:* Swarthmore Col, AB, 41; Ohio State Univ, MSc, 42; Pa State Col, PhD(org chem), 45. *Prof Exp:* Instr chem, Pa State Col, 45-46; res chemist, 46-53, res supvr, 53-56, sr patent chemist, 56-60, from supvr to sr supvr textile fibers patent div, 60-71, mgr cent patent index, 71-76, ASST TO DIV MGR, INFO SYST DEPT, E I DU PONT DE NEMOURS & CO, INC, 76- *Mem:* Sigma Xi. *Res:* Synthetic antimalarials; synthetic fibers; patents. *Mailing Add:* 1450 Nemours Bldg E I du Pont de Nemours & Co Inc Wilmington DE 19898

TAYLOR, ROBERT CLEMENT, b Mankato, Minn, Dec 2, 35; m 57; c 6. PHYSIOLOGY, ZOOLOGY. *Educ:* Mankato State Col, BS, 57; Univ SDak, MS, 61; Univ Ariz, PhD(physiol), 66. *Prof Exp:* Asst prof, 66-76, ASSOC PROF ZOOL, UNIV GA, 77- *Mem:* AAAS; Am Soc Zoologists. *Res:* Comparative physiology; neurophysiology. *Mailing Add:* Dept of Zool Univ of Ga Athens GA 30602

TAYLOR, ROBERT COOPER, b Colorado Springs, Colo, May 5, 17; m 42; c 2. PHYSICAL CHEMISTRY, MOLECULAR SPECTROSCOPY. *Educ:* Kalamazoo Col, AB, 41; Brown Univ, PhD(phys chem), 47. *Prof Exp:* Asst chem, Brown Univ, 41-42, res chemist, Manhattan Proj, 42-46, instr phys chem, 47-49; from instr to assoc prof, 49-62, actg chmn, 66, PROF CHEM, UNIV MICH, ANN ARBOR, 62-, ASSOC CHMN, 67- *Concurrent Pos:* Consult, W J Barrow Res Lab, 74-77; vis staff mem, Los Alamos Sci Lab, 75-; Nat Res Coun fel, 46-47. *Mem:* AAAS; Am Chem Soc; Am Phys Soc. *Res:* Molecular spectroscopy and structure; boron hydride derivatives; Lewis complexes; liquid ammonia solutions; hydrogen bonded substances; uranium chemistry. *Mailing Add:* Dept of Chem Univ of Mich Ann Arbor MI 48109

TAYLOR, ROBERT CRAIG, b Franklin, Pa, Jan 26, 39; m 66; c 1. INORGANIC CHEMISTRY. *Educ:* Col Wooster, BA, 60; Princeton Univ, MA, 62, PhD(chem), 64. *Prof Exp:* NATO fel, Imp Col, Univ London, 64-65; asst prof chem, Univ Ga, 65-72; ASSOC PROF CHEM, OAKLAND UNIV, 72- *Mem:* Am Chem Soc; Royal Soc Chem; Sigma Xi; Am Asn Univ Professors; NY Acad Sci. *Res:* Transition metal chemistry; organophosphorous chemistry; lanthanide shift reagents; transition metal catalyzed stereospecific polymerizations of diolefins; transition metal complexes as antitumor agents; role of molybdenum in enzymes; Nuclear magnetic resonance and electrochemistry of metal clusters. *Mailing Add:* Dept of Chem Oakland Univ Rochester MI 48063

TAYLOR, ROBERT E, b Havelock, Nebr, July 24, 20; m 47; c 3. PHYSIOLOGY, BIOPHYSICS. *Educ:* Univ Ill, BS, 42; Univ Rochester, PhD(physiol), 50. *Prof Exp:* Mem staff, Radiation Lab, Off Sci Res & Develop, Mass Inst Technol, 42-45; Merck fel physiol, Univ Chicago, 50-51, Nat Heart Inst fel, 51-52; asst prof neurophysiol, Col Med, Univ Ill, 52-53; NSF fel, Physiol Lab, Cambridge Univ, 53-54, Nat Inst Neurol Dis & Blindness fel, 54-55 & Univ Col, Univ London, 55-56; PHYSIOLOGIST, LAB BIOPHYS, NAT INST NEUROL & COMMUN DISORDERS & STROKE, 56- *Mem:* Am Physiol Soc; Biophys Soc; NY Acad Sci; Soc Gen Physiol; hon mem Chilean Biol Soc. *Res:* Properties of natural excitable membranes; muscle contraction activation. *Mailing Add:* Bldg 36 Rm 2A31 Nat Inst Neurol & Commun Disorders & Stroke Bethesda MD 20205

TAYLOR, ROBERT EMERALD, JR, b Polk City, Fla, Aug 21, 30; m 51; c 4. PHYSIOLOGY. *Educ:* Southern Col Pharm, BS, 58; Univ Fla, MS, 61, PhD(physiol), 63. *Prof Exp:* NIH fel pharmacol, Univ Vt, 63-65; from asst prof to prof physiol & biophys, Sch Med, Univ Ala, Birmingham, 65-73, coord correlated basic med sci educ, 71-73, assoc dir off undergrad med educ, 72-73; PROF PHYSIOL & BIOPHYS & ASSOC DEAN GRAD SCH MED SCI, UNIV TENN CTR HEALTH SCI, MEMPHIS, 73- *Mem:* Biophys Soc; Am Soc Zool; Endocrine Soc; Am Physiol Soc. *Res:* Experimental endocrinology; control of water and electrolyte balance; active ion transport; developmental physiology. *Mailing Add:* Col of Basic Med Sci Univ of Tenn Ctr for Health Sci Memphis TN 38163

TAYLOR, ROBERT FRANKLIN, b Wartrace, Tenn, Aug 5, 25; m 51; c 2. DENTISTRY. *Educ:* Univ Tenn, Knoxville, BSc, 49, DDS, 50; Univ Wash, Seattle, MSD, 54. *Prof Exp:* Dent surgeon, USPHS, 50-52; instr orthod, 54-60, orthod consult, Dept Pedodontics, 66-69, PROF & CHMN ORTHOD, UNIV TENN, MEMPHIS, 78- *Concurrent Pos:* Consult, Dent Div, Vet Admin Med Ctr, Memphis, 78- *Res:* Biometric description of growth, development and treatment. *Mailing Add:* Col Dent Univ Tenn Rm S-301 875 Union Ave Memphis TN 38163

TAYLOR, ROBERT GAY, b Cleveland, Ohio, July 8, 40. MICROBIOLOGY, ENVIRONMENTAL SCIENCES. *Educ:* Wittenberg Univ, BS, 63; John Carroll Univ, MS, 66; Tex A&M Univ, PhD(environ studies), 69. *Prof Exp:* Sr bacteriologist, Cleveland Dept Pub Health, 63-65; asst prof, 69-73, ASSOC PROF MICROBIOL, EASTERN NMEX UNIV, 73-, DIR, SCH NATURAL SCI, 77- *Concurrent Pos:* Dept Interior, Water Resources Res Inst grant, Eastern NMex Univ, 71-72; vis scientist, Lawrence Berkeley Lab, Univ Calif, 72; consult, Dept Civil Eng, Univ Tex, El Paso, 72- *Honors & Awards:* Outstanding Res Award, Nat Air Pollution Control Asn, 67. *Mem:* AAAS; Am Chem Soc. *Res:* Biomedical biochemical mechanisms; environmental microbiology with respect to water treatment and contamination. *Mailing Add:* PO Box 2296 Portales NM 88130

TAYLOR, ROBERT JOE, b Pomona, Calif, May 1, 45; m 67; c 2. POPULATION ECOLOGY. *Educ:* Stanford Univ, AB, 67; Univ Calif, Santa Barbara, MS, 70, PhD(biol), 72. *Prof Exp:* Res assoc ecol, Princeton Univ, 71-72; asst prof ecol, Univ Minn, St Paul, 72-78; ASSOC PROF ZOOL, CLEMSON UNIV, 78- *Mem:* Ecol Soc Am; Brit Ecol Soc; Soc Pop Ecol. *Res:* The influence of predatory behavior upon population in space and time; patterns of species diversity on peninsulas. *Mailing Add:* Dept Zool Clemson Univ Clemson SC 29631

TAYLOR, ROBERT JOSEPH, b Salt Lake City, Utah, Dec 10, 41; m 67; c 4. PHYSICS, ELECTROMAGNETISM. *Educ:* Univ Utah, BA, 67; Cornell Univ, PhD(appl physics), 71. *Prof Exp:* Scientist metall, Res Ctr, Kennecott Copper Co, 67; scientist acoust, Interand Corp, 71-72; PHYSICIST, JOHNS HOPKINS UNIV APPL PHYSICS LAB, 72- *Mem:* Am Phys Soc. *Res:* Electromagnetic wave propagation through the ionosphere for global dissemination of submicrosecond time from satellites; systems studies for determining the lowest cost energy conversion systems. *Mailing Add:* 10105 Pasture Gate Lane Columbia MD 21044

TAYLOR, ROBERT LEE, b Palmer, Nebr, July 17, 25; m 45. MEDICAL MYCOLOGY. *Educ:* Nebr Wesleyan Univ, AB, 47; Univ Nebr, MA, 50; Duke Univ, PhD(microbiol), 54; Am Bd Microbiol, dipl. *Prof Exp:* Asst chief bact & chief mycol sect, Lab Serv, Fitzsimons Army Hosp, Med Serv Corp, US Army, Colo, 50-55, chief bact sect, Med Res & Develop Unit, 55-58 & mycol sect, Middle Am Res Unit, Ancon, CZ, 58-61, mycologist, Walter Reed Army Inst Res, 61-63, chief mycol sect, 63-65, chief dept bact & mycol, SEATO Med Res Lab, Bangkok, Thailand, 65-67; dep chmn dept, 72-78, PROF MICROBIOL, UNIV TEX HEALTH SCI CTR, SAN ANTONIO, 68-, . *Mem:* Fel Am Acad Microbiol; Am Soc Microbiol; Mycol Soc Am; Am Thoracic Soc; Med Mycol Soc Am. *Mailing Add:* Dept Microbiol Univ Tex Health Sci Ctr San Antonio TX 78284

TAYLOR, ROBERT LEE, b Tenn, July 23, 43; m 68. MATHEMATICS, STATISTICS. *Educ:* Univ Tenn, Knoxville, BS, 66; Fla State Univ, MS, 69, PhD(statist), 70. *Prof Exp:* Teaching asst math, Univ Tenn, Knoxville, 66-67; asst prof, 71-74, assoc prof math, 74-80, PROF MATH & STATIST, UNIV SC, 80- *Mem:* Math Asn Am; Am Statist Asn; Inst Math Statist. *Res:* Probability; probabilistic functional analysis and statistical applications. *Mailing Add:* Dept Math & Statist Univ of SC Columbia SC 29208

TAYLOR, ROBERT MORGAN, b Orange, NJ, May 13, 41; m 65; c 2. ANALYTICAL CHEMISTRY, ELECTROCHEMISTRY. *Educ:* Williams Col, BA, 63; Pa State Univ, PhD(chem), 68; Drexel Univ, MBA, 74. *Prof Exp:* From scientist to sr scientist, 68-70, PRIN SCIENTIST, TECH CTR, LEEDS & NORTHRUP CO, 70- *Mem:* Am Chem Soc; Electrochem Soc; Mat Res Soc. *Res:* Potentiometric and voltammetric analysis; high temperature electrochemistry; molten and solid electrolytes; thermometric analysis; chemical instrumentation. *Mailing Add:* Leeds & Northrup Co Sumneytown Pike North Wales PA 19454

TAYLOR, ROBERT THOMAS, b Harrison, Ark, Sept 14, 36; m 58; c 2. BIOCHEMISTRY. *Educ:* Univ Calif, Los Angeles, BA, 59; Univ Calif, Berkeley, PhD(biochem), 64. *Prof Exp:* USPHS res fel, Nat Heart Inst, 64-66, staff res fel, 66-68; RES BIOCHEMIST, BIOMED SCI DIV, LAWRENCE LIVERMORE NAT LAB, 68- *Mem:* Inter-Am Photochem Soc; Soc Environ Geochem & Health; Am Soc Biol Chem; AAAS; Environ Mutagen Soc. *Res:* Enzymology, one-carbon enzymes, B-12 methyltransferases, folate coenzyme metabolism; heavy metal methylation; alkyl-metal cellular toxicity; mammmalial cell mutagenesis. *Mailing Add:* Biomed Sci Div Lawrence Livermore Nat Lab L-452 Livermore CA 94550

TAYLOR, ROBERT TIECHE, b San Diego, Calif, June 29, 32; m 64; c 2. MEDICAL ENTOMOLOGY. *Educ:* Okla State Univ, BS, 54, MS, 57, PhD(entom), 60. *Prof Exp:* Asst prev med officer, US Army, Ft Stewart, Ga, 54-56; malaria specialist, Pan Am Health Orgn, 60-61; spec asst wood preserv & entom, Are Pub Works Off, Chesapeake, US Navy, 61-63; malaria specialist, Malaria Eradication Prog, Port-au-Prince, Haiti, 63-65; sr scientist, 65-72, SCIENTIST DIR ENTOM, PARASITIC DIS DIV, CTR INFECTIOUS DIS, USPHS, 72- *Concurrent Pos:* Consult, WHO, Pan Am Health Orgn & USAID. *Mem:* Am Soc Trop Med & Hyg; Royal Soc Trop Med & Hyg; Entom Soc Am; Am Mosquito Control Asn. *Res:* Conducting and supervising investigations on chemical control of mosquitoes, triatomidae and simuliidae. *Mailing Add:* Parasitic Dis Div C-23 Ctr for Dis Control Atlanta GA 30333

TAYLOR, ROBERT WILLIAM, b Dallas, Tex, Feb 10, 32; m 55; c 3. COMPUTER SCIENCE, RESEARCH MANAGEMENT. *Educ:* Univ Tex, Austin, BA, 57, MA, 64. *Prof Exp:* Res scientist psychoacoustics, Defense Res Lab, Univ Tex, Austin, 55-59; teacher math, Howey Acad, Fla, 59-60; systs engr systs design, Martin Co, Fla, 60-61; sr res scientist man-mach systs res, ACF Electronics, Md, 61-62; res mgr electronics & control, Off Advan Res & Technol, NASA Hq, Washington, DC, 62-65; res dir comput sci, Advan Res Projs Agency, Off Secy Defense, 65-69; res dir, Info Res Lab, Univ Utah, 69-70; prin scientist & assoc mgr, 70-80, MGR, COMPUT SCI LAB, XEROX PALO ALTO RES CTR, 80- *Concurrent Pos:* Mem comts vision & bioacoust, Nat Res Coun, 62-65; mem comput sci & eng bd, Nat Acad Sci, 67-69; mem electronic data processing adv bd, Dept Defense, 68-69; mem comput sci adv bd, Stanford Univ, 71-81 & chmn, 78-79, lectr, 75- & mem comput sci adv comt, Nat Sci Found, 78-81 & Univ Cal, Berkeley, 80- *Honors & Awards:* Cert Appreciation, Advan Res Projs Agency, Off Secy Defense, 69. *Mem:* Asn Comput Mach; Inst Elec & Electronics Engrs. *Res:* Interactive information processing and communications systems; central nervous system; computer graphics; artificial intelligence; research and development management. *Mailing Add:* Comput Sci Lab Xerox Palo Alto Res Ctr 3333 Coyote Hill Rd Palo Alto CA 94304

TAYLOR, ROGER, b Horsham, Eng, May 21, 40; Can citizen; m 62; c 3. SOLID STATE PHYSICS. *Educ:* Bishop's Univ, BSc, 60; McMaster Univ, PhD(physics), 65. *Prof Exp:* Fel, 65-67, from asst res officer to assoc res officer, 67-78, SR RES OFFICER PHYSICS, NAT RES COUN, CAN, 78- *Mem:* Can Asn Physicists; Am Phys Soc. *Res:* Electron-phonon interaction, interionic potentials and properties of defects in metals; theory of one- and two-component plasmas. *Mailing Add:* Physics Div Nat Res Coun Ottawa ON K1A 1R6 Can

TAYLOR, RONALD, b Victor, Idaho, Oct 16, 32; m 55; c 2. BOTANY, GENETICS. *Educ:* Idaho State Univ, BS, 56; Univ Wyo, MS, 60; Wash State Univ, PhD(bot, genetics), 64. *Prof Exp:* Asst prof bot, 64-68, assoc prof biol, 68-72, PROF BIOL, WESTERN WASH UNIV, 72- *Concurrent Pos:* Environ consult, Northwest Pollution Authority, 74- *Mem:* AAAS; Bot Soc Am; Genetics Soc Am; Am Soc Plant Taxon; Sigma Xi. *Res:* Chemotaxonomy and evolution of selected higher plant taxa; biosystematics and ecology of Picea; biosystematics of Castilleja. *Mailing Add:* Dept of Biol Western Wash Univ Bellingham WA 98225

TAYLOR, RONALD CHARLES, b Port Huron, Mich, Nov 28, 32; m 64; c 1. METEOROLOGY. *Educ:* Univ Calif, Los Angeles, BA, 59; Univ Hawaii, PhD(meteorol), 68. *Prof Exp:* Asst prof meteorol, St Louis Univ, 68-69, Univ Hawaii, 69-74 & State Univ NY, Brockport, 75; assoc prof meteorol, Inst Fluid Dynamics, Univ Md, College Park, 75-77; PROG DIR, ATMOSPHERE RES SECT, NAT SCI FOUND, 78- *Concurrent Pos:* Res contract, US Navy Weather Res Facility, Norfolk, Va, 69- *Mem:* AAAS; Am Meteorol Soc; Am Geophys Union; Meteorol Soc Japan. *Res:* Tropical meteorology air-sea interaction; polar meteorology, Antarctic, synoptic and physical. *Mailing Add:* Atmosphere Res Sect Nat Sci Found Washington DC 20550

TAYLOR, ROSCOE L, b Wolsey, SDak, Dec 1, 23; m 52; c 8. AGRONOMY. *Educ:* SDak State Col, BS, 48; Iowa State Col, MS, 50. *Prof Exp:* Agronomist, 51-56, head agron dept, 56-67, RES AGRONOMIST, AGR EXP STA, UNIV ALASKA, 67- *Mem:* Crop Sci Soc Am; Am Soc Agron; Biomet Soc. *Res:* Cereal and forage crop breeding; genetics and speciation in naturally occuring grass and legume plant populations. *Mailing Add:* Inst of Agr Sci Box AE Palmer AK 99645

TAYLOR, ROY JASPER, b Salvisa, Ky, Nov 1, 18; m 46; c 3. CHEMICAL ENGINEERING, CHEMISTRY. *Educ:* Purdue Univ, Lafayette, BSChE, 42; Polytech Inst Brooklyn, PhD(chem), 70. *Prof Exp:* Res engr, Com Solvents Corp, 42-44; chem engr, Allegany Ballistics Lab, 44-45; chem engr, 45-47, supvr process develop, 47-52, mgr, 52-61, dir chem prod & develop, 61-64, MGR PROD PROCESS DEVELOP, CHEM DIV, PFIZER, INC, 64- *Mem:* Am Chem Soc; NY Acad Sci. *Res:* Processes for separation and purification; chemical reaction kinetics; reverse osmosis; ultrafiltration; mass transfer kinetics. *Mailing Add:* Pfizer Inc Eastern Point Rd Groton CT 06340

TAYLOR, ROY LEWIS, b Olds, Alta, Apr 12, 32. PLANT TAXONOMY. *Educ:* Sir George Williams Univ, BSc, 57; Univ Calif, Berkeley, PhD(bot), 62. *Prof Exp:* Teaching bot, Univ Calif, Berkeley, 58-60, assoc, 61-62; res officer, Plant Res Inst, Can Dept Agr, 62-65, chief taxon sect, 65-68; PROF PLANT SCI & DIR BOT GARDEN, UNIV BC, 68- *Concurrent Pos:* Mem exec comt & coun, Pac Sci Asn, 79-83; mem gov bd, Biol Coun Can, 66-69, secy, 69-72, from vpres to pres, 72-74. *Mem:* Int Orgn Biosyst; Am Soc Plant Taxon; fel Linnean Soc London; Can Bot Asn (secy, 65-66, vpres, 66-67, pres, 67-68); Am Asn Bot Gardens & Arboretums (vpres, 73-75, pres, 75-77). *Res:* Systematic botany of western North American vascular plants; systematics and cytotaxonomy of the vascular plants of British Columbia. *Mailing Add:* Bot Garden Univ of BC Vancouver BC V6T 1W5 Can

TAYLOR, RUSSELL JAMES, JR, b Rockville, Conn, Mar 8, 35. CLINICAL PHARMACOLOGY. *Educ:* Bates Col, BS, 57; Ohio State Univ, MSc, 62, PhD(biochem), 64. *Prof Exp:* Res chemist, Parke, Davis & Co, Mich, 57-59; asst biochem, Ohio State Univ, 59-64; res biochemist, Lederle Labs, Am Cyanamid Co, NY, 64-69; sr res biochemist, McNeil Labs, Inc, 69-70, group leader biochem, 70-79, asst dir med res, 79-80; SR MED ASSOC, MILES PHARMACEUT, 80- *Mem:* AAAS; Am Chem Soc; NY Acad Sci. *Res:* Intermediary metabolism and enzymology of amino acids, catecholamines, serotonin and histamine; coenzymes; enzyme inhibitors. *Mailing Add:* Miles Pharmaceut 400 Morgan Lane West Haven CT 06516

TAYLOR, SAMUEL EDWIN, b Tuskegee, Ala, Oct 19, 41; m 61; c 2. PHARMACOLOGY. *Educ:* Univ Ala, Tuscaloosa, BS, 63; Univ Ala, Birmingham, PhD(pharmacol) , 71. *Prof Exp:* NIH trainee pharmacol, Univ Tenn Med Units, 71-72; asst prof pharmacol, Sch Dent, Univ Ore Health Sci Ctr, 72-80; MEM FAC, PHARMACOL DEPT, BAYLOR COL MED, 80- *Res:* Autonomic/cardiovascular pharmacology; effects of autonomic agents on bronchial and vascular smooth muscle; differentiation of autonomic receptors; cardiovascular shock. *Mailing Add:* Pharmacol Dept Baylor Col Dent 3302 Gaston Ave Dallas TX 75246

TAYLOR, SAMUEL G, III, b Elmhurst, Ill, Sept 2, 04; m 38; c 3. ONCOLOGY. *Educ:* Yale Univ, BA, 27; Univ Chicago, MD, 32. *Prof Exp:* Dir steroid tumor clin, Univ Ill, 47-71; dir cancer ctr planning, Rush Presby-St Luke's Med Ctr, 72-75, assoc dir, Rush Cancer Ctr, 75-78, prof, 71-78, EMER PROF MED, RUSH UNIV, 78- *Concurrent Pos:* Assoc attend physician, Presby Hosp, 48-60; from asst prof to prof, Univ Ill Col Med, 48-72; rep dept med, Tumor Coun, Univ Ill, 48-72; mem consult staff, Lake Forest Hosp, 54-61; from attend physician to sr attend physician, Presby-St Luke's Hosp, Chicago, 61-78, head sect oncol, 61-71, consult, Sect Oncol, 71-; consult, Cancer Control Prog, USPHS, 59-63; dir, Ill Cancer Coun Comprehensive Cancer Ctr, 73-78. *Mem:* Endocrine Soc; Am Asn Cancer Res; Am Col Physicians; Am Radium Soc; Soc Surg Oncol. *Res:* Systematic therapy for cancer. *Mailing Add:* Rush Univ 1725 W Harrison Chicago IL 60612

TAYLOR, SNOWDEN, b New York, NY, June 25, 24; m 49; c 6. HIGH ENERGY PHYSICS, PARTICLE PHYSICS. *Educ:* Stevens Inst Technol, ME, 50; Columbia Univ, AM, 57, PhD(physics), 59. *Prof Exp:* Asst & lectr physics, Columbia Univ, 52-58; from instr to assoc prof, 58-66, PROF PHYSICS, STEVENS INST TECHNOL, 66- *Honors & Awards:* Ottens Res Award, 63; STEP Award, 75. *Mem:* Am Phys Soc; Sigma Xi. *Res:* Strong and weak interaction physics, primarily using bubble chamber techniques; technical education for minority and disadvantaged students. *Mailing Add:* Dept of Physics Stevens Inst of Technol Hoboken NJ 07030

TAYLOR, STEPHEN KEITH, b Los Angeles, Calif, Mar 28, 44; m 69; c 2. INDUSTRIAL CHEMISTRY, ORGANIC CHEMISTRY. *Educ:* Pasadena Col, BA, 69; Univ Nev, Reno, PhD(org chem), 74. *Prof Exp:* Res chemist, E I du Pont de Nemours & Co, Inc, 73-78, sr res chemist, 78; asst prof, 78-80, ASSOC PROF CHEM, OLIVET NAZARENE COL, 80- *Mem:* Am Chem Soc; Sigma Xi; Soc Photog Scientist & Engrs. *Res:* Influence of metal ions in organic reactions; reactions of epoxides; polymer crosslinking reactions. *Mailing Add:* Dept of Chem Olivet Nazarene Col Kankakee IL 60901

TAYLOR, STERLING ELWYNN, agricultural meteorology, ecology, see previous edition

TAYLOR, STEVE L, b Portland, Ore, July 19, 46; m 73. FOOD SCIENCE, TOXICOLOGY. *Educ:* Ore State Univ, BS, 68, MS, 69; Univ Calif, Davis, PhD, 73. *Prof Exp:* Res assoc, Dept Food Sci, Univ Calif, Davis, 73-74, fel toxicol, 74-76; res chemist food toxicol, Dept Nutrit, Letterman Army Inst Res, 76-78; ASST PROF, FOOD RES INST, UNIV WIS, 78- *Concurrent Pos:* Fel, Nat Inst Environ Health Sci, 74-76. *Mem:* Inst Food Technologists; Am Chem Soc. *Res:* Toxicological evaluation of food chemicals and products including improved analytical methods, evaluation of relative hazard, analysis of toxin levels in foods; food allergy studies. *Mailing Add:* Food Res Inst 1925 Willow Dr Madison WI 53706

TAYLOR, STUART ROBERT, b Brooklyn, NY, July 15, 37; m 63; c 3. PHYSIOLOGY, BIOPHYSICS. *Educ:* Cornell Univ, BA, 58; Columbia Univ, MA, 61; NY Univ, PhD(physiol), 66. *Prof Exp:* Lab asst zool, Columbia Univ, 59-60, lectr, 60-61; res asst physiol, Inst Muscle Dis, Inc, 62-67; Dept Health, Educ & Welfare rehab res fel, Univ Col, Univ London, 67-69; from instr to asst prof pharmacol, State Univ NY Downstate Med Ctr, 69-71; assoc prof, 75-78, PROF PHYSIOL & BIOPHYS, PHARMACOL, MAYO MED SCH, UNIV MINN, 78-, CONSULT, 71- *Concurrent Pos:* Mem res allocations comt, Minn Heart Asn, 72-74, mem bd dirs, 73-75; mem physiol study sect, Div Res Grants, NIH, 73-77; estab investr, Am Heart Asn, 74-79. *Mem:* Am Physiol Soc; Biophys Soc; Brit Biophys Soc; assoc Brit Physiol Soc; Soc Gen Physiol. *Res:* Physiology of stimulus-response coupling in contractile cells. *Mailing Add:* Mayo Grad Sch Med Mayo Found Rochester NY 55905

TAYLOR, SUSAN SEROTA, b Racine, Wis, June 20, 42; m 65; c 2. BIOCHEMISTRY. *Educ:* Univ Wis-Madison, BA, 64; Johns Hopkins Univ, PhD(biochem), 68. *Prof Exp:* NIH fel, Med Res Coun Lab Molecular Biol, Cambridge Univ, 68-70; NIH fel, 71-72, ASST PROF CHEM, UNIV CALIF, SAN DIEGO, 72- *Concurrent Pos:* NIH career develop award & res grant, Univ Calif, San Diego, 72-77. *Mem:* Am Soc Biol Chemists; Am Chem Soc. *Res:* Protein chemistry; cAMP-dep protein kinase; LDH; amino acid sequencing. *Mailing Add:* 352 Chem Res Bldg Univ of Calif San Diego La Jolla CA 92093

TAYLOR, TERRY MAC, ruminant nutrition, see previous edition

TAYLOR, THEODORE BREWSTER, b Mexico City, Mex, July 11, 25; nat US; m 48; c 5. APPLIED PHYSICS. *Educ:* Calif Inst Technol, BS, 45; Cornell Univ, PhD(theoret physics), 54. *Prof Exp:* Physicist, Radiation Lab, Univ Calif, 46-49, theoret physicist, Los Alamos Sci Lab, 49-56; nuclear physicist, High Energy Fluid Dynamics Dept & chmn, Gen Atomic Div, Gen Dynamics Corp, 56-64; dep dir, Defense Atomic Support Agency, 64-66; chmn bd, Int Res & Tech Corp, 67-76; PROF MECH & AEROSPACE ENG, PRINCETON UNIV, 76- *Concurrent Pos:* Consult, Govt & Indust, 56-; lectr, San Diego State Col, 57. *Honors & Awards:* Lawrence Mem Award, AEC, 65; Meritorious Civilian Serv Medal, Secy Defense, 66. *Mem:* AAAS; Am Phys Soc; Solar Energy Soc. *Res:* Solar energy systems; controlled environment agriculture; international control and development of nuclear energy; nuclear explosives and effects of nuclear explosions; space propulsion; pollution control; technology assessment. *Mailing Add:* 10325 Bethesda Church Rd Damascus MD 20750

TAYLOR, THOMAS NEWTON, b Cedar Rapids, Iowa, June 21, 44. SURFACE PHYSICS. *Educ:* Iowa State Univ, BS, 66; Brown Univ, MS & PhD(physics), 73. *Prof Exp:* Fel surface physics, Lawrence Berkeley Lab & Lawrence Livermore Lab, 73-75; STAFF PHYSICIST, LOS ALAMOS NAT LAB, 75- *Mem:* Am Chem Soc; Am Vacuum Soc. *Res:* Surface properties of actinide elements and their compounds; emphasis on catalysis and corrosion; low energy electron diffraction, Auger electron spectroscopy and allied techniques. *Mailing Add:* Los Alamos Nat Lab CMB-8 MS-734 PO Box 1663 Los Alamos NM 87545

TAYLOR, THOMAS NORWOOD, b Lakewood, Ohio, June 14, 37; m 59; c 5. PALEOBOTANY. *Educ:* Miami Univ, AB, 60; Univ Ill, Urbana, PhD(bot), 64. *Prof Exp:* NSF res fel, Yale Univ, 64-65; from asst prof to prof biol sci, Univ Ill, Chicago Circle, 65-72, dir scanning electron microscope lab, 67-72; prof bot, Ohio Univ, 72-74; chmn dept, 74-78, PROF BOT, OHIO STATE UNIV, 74-, PROF, DEPT TEOLOGY & MINERAL, 79- *Concurrent Pos:* NSF res grants, 64-; NSF res grants paleobot, 65-78; res assoc, Geol Dept, Field Mus Natural Hist, Chicago, 67-; Ill Acad Sci res grants, 70-72; assoc ed, Rev Palaeobot Polynol, Paleobiol. *Mem:* Bot Soc Am; Brit Paleont Asn; Int Orgn Paleobot; Int Asn Plant Taxon; fel Linnean Soc London. *Res:* Structure and evolution of Paleozoic vascular plants; electron microscopy of fossil pollen and spores; morphology of extant vascular plants. *Mailing Add:* Dept Bot Ohio State Univ 1735 Neil Ave Columbus OH 43210

TAYLOR, THOMAS TALLOTT, b Montpelier, Ind, Apr 18, 21; m 58; c 2. PHYSICS. *Educ:* Purdue Univ, BS, 42; Calif Inst Technol, MS, 53, PhD(physics), 58. *Prof Exp:* Engr, Gen Elec Co, 42-46; res physicist, Hughes Aircraft Co, 46-54; asst prof physics, Univ Calif, Riverside, 58-63; from asst prof to prof physics, 63-80, chmn dept, 67-77, EMER PROF PHYSICS, LOYOLA MARYMOUNT UNIV, LOS ANGELES, 80- *Concurrent Pos:* Instr, Engr Exten, Univ Calif, Los Angeles, 47-50 & 57-58. *Honors & Awards:* Best Paper Award, Inst Elec & Electronics Engrs, 60. *Mem:* Am Phys Soc; fel Inst Elec & Electronics Engrs; Am Asn Physics Teachers. *Res:* Electromagnetic theory; antennas; lattice sums in crystals. *Mailing Add:* 6622 W87th St Los Angeles CA 90045

TAYLOR, TIMOTHY H, b Sawyer, Ky, July 4, 18; m 45; c 2. AGRONOMY. *Educ:* Univ Ky, BS, 48, MS, 50; Pa State Univ, PhD(agron), 55. *Prof Exp:* Asst agronomist, Va Agr Exp Sta, 49-55; assoc agronomist, Agr Exp Sta, 55-60, assoc prof, 60-66, PROF AGRON, UNIV KY, 67- *Concurrent Pos:* Consult, 59-; vis scientist, Am Soc Agron; vis biologist, Am Inst Biol Sci. *Honors & Awards:* Outstanding Educator Am Award, 75. *Mem:* Fel Am Soc Agron; Crop Sci Soc Am; Brit Grassland Soc; Am Forage & Grassland Coun; Sigma Xi. *Res:* Ecology of humid temperate grasslands; forage crop ecology and physiology; ecology of cultivated grasslands. *Mailing Add:* Dept Agron Univ Ky Lexington KY 40506

TAYLOR, WALTER FULLER, b Boston, Mass, Dec 5, 40; m 67. MATHEMATICS. *Educ:* Swarthmore Col, AB, 62; Harvard Univ, MA, 63, PhD(math), 68. *Prof Exp:* From asst prof to assoc prof, 67-77, NSF grants, 69-74 & 76-79, PROF MATH, UNIV COLO, 77- *Concurrent Pos:* Fulbright Found sr res fel, Univ New SWales, Australia, 75; vis prof, Univ Hawaii, 77-78; ed, Algebra Universalis, 77- *Mem:* Am Math Soc. *Res:* Model theory, universal algebra and topology. *Mailing Add:* Dept of Math Univ of Colo Boulder CO 80309

TAYLOR, WALTER HERMAN, JR, b Laurens, SC, July 5, 31; m 55; c 2. MICROBIAL PHYSIOLOGY. *Educ:* Duke Univ, MA, 54; Univ Ill, PhD(bact), 59. *Prof Exp:* Asst bact, Univ Ill, 54-57 & Emory Univ, 57-59; res assoc biol div, Oak Ridge Nat Lab, 59, USPHS fel, 59-61; from asst prof to assoc prof, 61-69, PROF BIOL & HEAD DEPT, PORTLAND STATE UNIV, 69- *Mem:* AAAS; Am Soc Microbiol; Brit Soc Gen Microbiol; Am Chem Soc. *Res:* Bacterial physiology; carbohydrate metabolism; protein biosynthesis; pyrimidine metabolism in microorganisms. *Mailing Add:* Dept of Biol Portland State Univ PO Box 751 Portland OR 97207

TAYLOR, WALTER KINGSLEY, b Calhoun, Ky, Nov 12, 39; m 68. ORNITHOLOGY, VERTEBRATE ECOLOGY. *Educ:* Murray State Univ, BS, 62; La Tech Inst, MS, 64; Ariz State Univ, PhD(zool), 67. *Prof Exp:* Asst, La Tech Univ, 62-64 & Ariz State Univ, 64-67; asst prof biol, 69-71, ASSOC PROF BIOL, UNIV CENT FLA, 71- *Mem:* Am Ornith Union; Wilson Ornith Soc; Cooper Ornith Soc; Sigma Xi. *Res:* Breeding biology; migratory biology; population ecology of birds. *Mailing Add:* Dept Biol Univ Cent Fla Orlando FL 32816

TAYLOR, WALTER ROWLAND, b Baltimore, Md, Dec 31, 18; m 44; c 2. OCEANOGRAPHY. *Educ:* Wash Col, Md, BS, 40; Univ Wis, MS, 47, PhD(biochem), 49. *Prof Exp:* Asst chem, Ga Inst Technol, 40-41; asst biochem, Univ Wis, 46-49; res assoc chem, Univ Ill, 49-51; instr physiol chem, Sch Med, 51-56, res assoc, Chesapeake Bay Inst, 56-74, from asst prof to assoc prof oceanog, 58-68, assoc prof earth & planetary sci, 68-74, asst dir res, 75-78, actg dir, 78-81, PRIN RES SCIENTIST, CHESAPEAKE BAY INST, JOHNS HOPKINS UNIV, 74-, DIR, 81- *Concurrent Pos:* Instr marine ecol, Marine Biol Lab, Woods Hole, Mass, 60-70, instr-in-chg, 63-67. *Mem:* AAAS; Am Soc Limnol & Oceanog; Phycol Soc Am; Ecol Soc Am; Int Phycol Soc. *Res:* Primary production and nutrient recycling in marine and estuarine environments; physiology and ecology of marine organisms. *Mailing Add:* Chesapeake Bay Inst Johns Hopkins Univ Shady Side MD 20764

TAYLOR, WARREN EGBERT, b Colorado Springs, Colo, Nov 15, 20; m 47; c 3. METROLOGY. *Educ:* Kalamazoo Col, BA, 47; Ohio State Univ, PhD(physics), 52. *Prof Exp:* Mem tech staff, 52-70, PROJ LEADER, VACUUM METROLOGY GROUP, SANDIA NAT LABS, 70- *Mem:* Am Phys Soc; Am Vacuum Soc. *Res:* Vacuum technology; nuclear radiation measurements; health physics. *Mailing Add:* Div 2551 Sandia Labs Albuquerque NM 87185

TAYLOR, WELTON IVAN, b Birmingham, Ala, Nov 12, 19; m 45; c 2. MICROBIOLOGY. *Educ:* Univ Ill, Urbana, AB, 41, MS, 47, PhD(bact), 48; Am Bd Med Microbiol, dipl. *Prof Exp:* From instr to asst prof bact, Univ Ill Col Med, 48-54; res bacteriologist, Swift & Co, 54-59; supvr clin microbiol, Children's Mem Hosp, 59-64; bacteriologist in chief, West Suburban Hosp, Oak Park, Ill, 64-69; ASSOC PROF MICROBIOL, UNIV ILL MED CTR, 69- *Concurrent Pos:* Consult, Chicago Park Dist, 49 & Inst Gas Technol, Ill Inst Technol, 60; Nat Inst Allergy & Infectious Dis spec res fel, Inst Pasteur, France & Cent Pub Health Lab, Eng, 61-62; consult microbiologist, Northwest Community Hosp, Arlington Heights, Ill, 63-70, Jackson Park & Englewood Hosps, Chicago, 64-, Armour & Co, 66-68, Resurrection Hosp, Chicago, 67-, Grant Hosp, Chicago, 69-75, St Mary of Nazareth Hosp Ctr, Chicago, 73- & Swedish Covenant Hosp, Chicago, 74-80; Nat Commun Dis Ctr res grant, 66-68; Dept Army res contract, 71-73. *Mem:* Am Soc Microbiol; fel Am Acad Microbiol. *Res:* Detection of Vibrio parahemolyticus in routine stool analysis; methods for detection of Salmonella and Shigella with minimal laboratory facilities; rapid identification procedures for non-enteric pathogens. *Mailing Add:* 7621 S Prairie Ave Chicago IL 60619

TAYLOR, WENDELL HERTIG, b Uniontown, Pa, June 15, 05. CHEMISTRY. *Educ:* Princeton Univ, BS, 26, AM, 30, PhD(chem), 33. *Prof Exp:* Res chemist, Exp Sta, E I du Pont de Nemours & Co, 26-29; asst chem, Princeton Univ, 29-31 & 32-33, from instr to asst prof, 33-43; chmn dept sci, 43-70, EMER CHMN DEPT SCI, LAWRENCEVILLE SCH, 70- *Concurrent Pos:* Mem chem bond approach comt, NSF, 59- *Mem:* Am Chem Soc. *Res:* Organic sulfur compounds; phenolaldehyde condensations; hydramides; history of science. *Mailing Add:* 122 Patton Ave Princeton NJ 08540

TAYLOR, WESLEY GORDON, b Melfort, Sask, Mar 29, 47; m 69. MEDICINAL CHEMISTRY, PESTICIDE CHEMISTRY. *Educ:* Univ Sask, BSP, 69; PhD(pharm), 73. *Prof Exp:* Fel pharm, Dept Med Chem & Pharmacog, Sch Pharm & Pharm Sci, Purdue Univ, 73-75; RES SCIENTIST PESTICIDE CHEM, RES BR, RES STA, AGR CAN, 76- *Mem:* Am Chem Soc; Am Pharmaceut Asn; Chem Inst Can. *Res:* Biological alkylating agents; organic synthesis; drug metabolism; pesticide toxicology. *Mailing Add:* Res Sta Agr Can Lethbridge AB TIJ 4B1 Can

TAYLOR, WILLIAM CLYNE, b Aberdeen, Scotland, Mar 26, 24; Can citizen; m 54; c 3. PEDIATRICS. *Educ:* Aberdeen Univ, MB & ChB, 45; Univ London, DCH, 50; FRCP(C), 58. *Prof Exp:* PROF PEDIAT, UNIV ALTA, 57- *Concurrent Pos:* Mead Johnson res fel, Univ Alta, 58-59; Schering traveling fel, Africa, Australia & NZ, 66-67; Brit Commonwealth grant, UK, 66. *Mem:* Can Soc Clin Invest; Am Acad Pediat; Can Pediat Soc. *Res:* Evaluation of undergraduate and postgraduate medical education; delivery of health care in the Northwest Territories of Canada. *Mailing Add:* Dept of Pediat Univ of Alta Edmonton AB T6G 2E1 Can

TAYLOR, WILLIAM DANIEL, b Cardiff, Gt Brit, May 25, 34. DNA REPAIR, MUTAGENESIS. *Educ:* Univ Manchester, BSc, 56, PhD(phys chem), 59. *Prof Exp:* Fel physics, Pa State Univ, 59-61; res fel chem, Univ Manchester, 61-63; asst prof biophysics, 63-68, assoc prof, 68-71, head dept, 71-75, PROF BIOPHYSICS, PA STATE UNIV, UNIVERSITY PARK, 71- *Mem:* AAAS; Radiol Res Soc; Biophys Soc; Fedn Am Sci; The Chem Soc. *Res:* Biophysical chemistry; chemical carcinogenesis; nucleic acids; radiation biology. *Mailing Add:* Dept of Biochem & Biophys 106 Althouse Lab Pa State Univ University Park PA 16802

TAYLOR, WILLIAM EDWIN, materials science, see previous edition

TAYLOR, WILLIAM F, b Cincinnati, Ohio, Oct 14, 21; m 43, 81; c 3. BIOSTATISTICS. *Educ:* Univ Calif, PhD(math statist), 51. *Prof Exp:* Instr biostatist, Univ Calif, 50-51; chief dept biometrics, Sch Aviation Med, US Air Force, 51-58; assoc prof biostatist, Sch Pub Health, Univ Calif, Berkeley, 58-63, prof, 63-67; head med res statist sect, 67-76, MEM FAC DEPT MED STATIST & EPIDEMIOL, MAYO CLIN, 76- *Mem:* Biomet Soc; fel Am Pub Health Asn; fel Am Statist Asn. *Res:* Design of clinical trials; sequential analysis in medicine; reference value problems. *Mailing Add:* Dept Med Statist & Epidemiol Mayo Clin Rochester MN 55901

TAYLOR, WILLIAM FRANCIS, b Washington, DC, Apr 20, 31; m 61; c 3. FUEL TECHNOLOGY, PETROLEUM ENGINEERING. *Educ:* Cath Univ Am, BChE, 53; Ohio State Univ, MS, 57; Rutgers Univ, MS, 62; Stevens Inst Technol, ScD(chem eng), 67. *Prof Exp:* Chem engr, Goodyear Tire & Rubber Co, Ohio, 53-54; res engr, 57-71, sr res engr, 71-75, ENG ASSOC, EXXON RES & ENG CO, 75- *Mem:* Am Inst Chem Engrs; Am Chem Soc; Catalysis Soc; Sigma Xi. *Res:* Synthetic fuels; fuel storage and thermal stability; jet fuel product quality; heterogeneous kinetics and catalysis. *Mailing Add:* Exxon Res & Eng Co PO Box 51 Linden NJ 07036

TAYLOR, WILLIAM H, II, b Philadelphia, Pa, Dec 17, 38; m 57; c 2. SOLID STATE PHYSICS. *Educ:* Johns Hopkins Univ, BES, 60; Princeton Univ, MSE, 61, AM, 61, PhD(solid state sci), 64. *Prof Exp:* Staff mem, Redstone Arsenal Res Div, Rohm and Haas Co, Ala, 63-64; chief, Solid State Br, Explosives Lab, Picatinny Arsenal, 66-68; vpres, Data Sci Ventures, Inc, 68-72; vpres, White, Weld & Co, Inc, 72-73; vpres, Crocker Capital Corp, 73-79; VPRES, TAYLOR & TURNER, VENTURE CAPITAL, 79- *Mem:* Am Phys Soc. *Res:* Investment banking, venture capital financing of technology companies; point defects in solids; properties of solid explosives; soft contact lens materials. *Mailing Add:* Crocker Capital Corp Rm 600 111 Sutter St San Francisco CA 94104

TAYLOR, WILLIAM IRVING, b NZ, July 23, 23; m 52; c 3. ORGANIC CHEMISTRY. *Educ:* Univ Auckland, PhD(chem), 48, DSc, 68. *Prof Exp:* Nat Res Coun scholar, Switz, 48-49; Nat Res Coun Can fel, 50; Imp Chem Industs fel, Cambridge Univ, 51-52; assoc prof chem, Univ NB, 52-55; chemist, Ciba Pharmaceut Co, 55-62, dir natural prod, 63-67, dir biochem res, 67-68; dir fragrance res, 68-71, VPRES RES & DEVELOP, INT FLAVORS & FRAGRANCES, INC, 71-, DIR CHEM SYNTHESIS & DEVELOP, 72-, VPRES, 78- *Concurrent Pos:* Guest investr, Rockefeller Univ, 66-67. *Mem:* Am Chem Soc; Am Soc Pharmacog; NY Acad Sci; fel The Chem Soc. *Res:* Synthesis and structural elucidation of natural products, especially in field of flavor and aroma chemicals. *Mailing Add:* Int Flavors & Fragrances Inc 1515 Hwy 36 Union Beach NJ 07735

TAYLOR, WILLIAM JAPE, b Bonneville, Miss, Sept 5, 24; m 48; c 4. INTERNAL MEDICINE, CARDIOLOGY. *Educ:* Yale Univ, BS, 44; Harvard Med Sch, MD, 47. *Prof Exp:* Intern, Second Harvard Med Serv, Boston City Hosp, 47-48; asst resident med, Duke Univ, 48-50, instr, Sch Med & Hosp, 54-55; instr, Sch Med, Univ Pittsburgh, 55-58; chief, Div Cardiol, 58-74, from asst prof to assoc prof, 58-64, prof med, 64-74, DISTINGUISHED SERV PROF MED, COL MED, UNIV FLA, 74- *Concurrent Pos:* Fel coun clin cardiol, Am Heart Asn; Am Col Physicians res fel med, Duke Univ, 50-51, univ res fel, Sch Med & Hosp, 51-52, USPHS res fel, 54-55; vis prof med, Fac Health Sci, Univ Ife, Ile-Ife, Nigeria, 74-75. *Mem:* Am Fedn Clin Res; Asn Univ Cardiol; fel Am Col Cardiol; fel Am Col Physicians. *Mailing Add:* Dept Med Univ Fla Col Med Gainesville FL 32601

TAYLOR, WILLIAM JOHNSON, b Chengtu, China, Dec 3, 16; US citizen; m 49; c 4. PHYSICAL CHEMISTRY, THEORETICAL CHEMISTRY. *Educ:* Denison Univ, AB, 37; Ohio State Univ, PhD(phys chem), 42. *Prof Exp:* Instr chem, Univ Calif, Berkeley, 41-42; res assoc, Thermochem Sect, Nat Bur Standards, 42-47; spectros & low-temperature res, Cryogenic Lab, 47-50, from asst prof to assoc prof chem, 50-61, PROF CHEM, OHIO STATE UNIV, 61- *Mem:* Am Chem Soc; Am Phys Soc. *Res:* Statistical and quantum mechanics; statistics of long-chain molecules; molecular vibrations; dipole moments; localized molecular orbitals; configuration interaction method and correlation energy; quantum integrals; applications of group theory. *Mailing Add:* Dept of Chem Ohio State Univ 140 W 18th Ave Columbus OH 43210

TAYLOR, WILLIAM L, b Corsicana, Tex, Oct 17, 26; m 50; c 3. METEOROLOGY, ELECTROMAGNETISM. *Educ:* Okla State Univ, BS, 50. *Prof Exp:* Physicist, Nat Bur Standards, Washington, DC, 50-51, Alaska, 51-52 & Colo, 52-65; physicist, Inst Telecommun Sci & Aeronomy, Environ Sci Serv Admin, 65-70, PHYSICIST, ENVIRON RES LABS, NAT

OCEANIC & ATMOSPHERIC ADMIN, US DEPT COM, 70- *Mem:* AAAS; Am Geophys Union; Sigma Xi; Int Union Radio Sci; Am Meteorol Soc. *Res:* Radio propagation between the earth and ionosphere in the lower frequency bands, using lightning discharges as the source; measurement of radio noise from severe thunderstorms and tornadoes; lightning discharge characteristics at all radio frequencies; relationships between thunderstorm precipitation, windfields, turbulence and lightning. *Mailing Add:* Nat Severe Storms Lab 1313 Halley Circle Norman OK 73069

TAYLOR, WILLIAM RALPH, b Spring Hill, Kans, Aug 29, 19; c 6. ICHTHYOLOGY. *Educ:* Univ Kans, AB, 47; Univ Mich, MS, 51, PhD(zool), 55. *Prof Exp:* Asst mus natural hist, Univ Kans, 38-41; asst, Div Fishes, Mus Zool, Univ Mich, 47-51; biologist, Inst Fisheries Res, State Dept Conserv, Mich, 52-53; aquatic biologist, State Wildlife & Fisheries Comn, La, 54-56; assoc cur, 56-79, EMER CUR FISHES, NAT MUS NATURAL HIST, 79- *Mem:* Soc Syst Zool (treas, 70-72); Am Fisheries Soc; Am Soc Ichthyologists & Herpetologists; Am Soc Limnol & Oceanog. *Res:* Taxonomy and distribution of fishes; fishery biology; vertebrate zoology. *Mailing Add:* Div Fishes Nat Mus Natural Hist Washington DC 20560

TAYLOR, WILLIAM RANDOLPH, b Philadelphia, Pa, Dec 21, 95; m 26; c 2. BOTANY. *Educ:* Univ Pa, BS, 16, MS, 17, PhD(bot), 20. *Prof Exp:* Asst bot, Univ Pa, 15-17, from instr to asst prof, 18-27, prof, 27-30; prof, 30-66, CUR ALGAE, UNIV MICH, ANN ARBOR, 30-, EMER PROF BOT, 66- *Concurrent Pos:* Res assoc, Acad Natural Sci Philadelphia, 25- & Farlow Herbarium, Harvard Univ, 62-; mem corp, Woods Hole Marine Biol Lab, 25-, trustee, 39-, chmn libr comt, 47-53; mem, Hancock Exped, Galapagos Islands, SAm & Cent Am, 33-34 & Cent Am & Caribbean, 39; mem corp, Bermuda Biol Sta, 35-, trustee, 53-; mem adv comn, Charles Darwin Biol Sta, Galapagos, Ecuador; sr biologist, Oceanog Sect, Bikini Exped, Crossroads, 46; mem expeds to Jamaica, 56, Lesser Antilles, 66, 67 & 68 & Bermuda; corresp, Royal Flemish Acad Sci, Belg, Inst France & Venezuelan Acad Natural Sci. *Honors & Awards:* Retzius Medal, Univ Lund, 48; Russel lectr, Univ Mich, 64. *Mem:* AAAS; Am Soc Naturalists (secy, 43-46); Bot Soc Am (vpres, 56); Phycol Soc Am (pres, 48); Brit Phycol Soc. *Res:* Fresh water algae; North Atlantic marine algae, marine algae of the tropical Americas, Falkland Islands and Magellan Strait, Galapagos Islands, Pacific and Indian Oceans. *Mailing Add:* Dept of Bot Univ of Mich Ann Arbor MI 48109

TAYLOR, WILLIAM ROBERT, b Borger, Tex, Oct 25, 39; m 59; c 2. ENGINEERING, APPLIED STATISTICS. *Educ:* Okla State Univ, BS, 63; Univ Ark, Fayetteville, MS, 67, PhD(eng), 69. *Prof Exp:* Indust engr, Southwestern Bell Tel Co, Okla, 63-65; teaching asst, Univ Ark, Fayetteville, 68-69; asst prof, 69-77, ASSOC PROF INDUST & MGT ENG, MONT STATE UNIV, 77-, US FOREST SERV GRANT, 71- *Concurrent Pos:* Consult, Morrison-Knudsen Co, Inc, 72- *Mem:* Am Inst Indust Engrs; Am Soc Eng Educ. *Res:* Operations research applications for harvesting timber; application of management science principles to hospital systems; application of engineering principles in designing disease diagnostic equipment. *Mailing Add:* Dept of Indust Eng Mont State Univ Bozeman MT 59717

TAYLOR, WILLIAM WALLER, b Rochester, NY, Nov 20, 50; c 1. LIMNOLOGY, FISHERIES BIOLOGY. *Educ:* Hartwick Col, BA, 72; WVa Univ, MS, 75; Ariz State Univ, PhD(zool), 78. *Prof Exp:* Asst prof fisheries, Univ Mo-Columbia, 78-80; ASST PROF, DEPT FISHERIES & WILDLIFE, MICH STATE UNIV, 80- *Concurrent Pos:* Vis scientist, Hydrobiol Inst, Lake Ohrid, Yugoslavia, Smithsonian Inst, 76- *Mem:* AAAS; Am Fisheries Soc; Am Soc Limnol & Oceanog; Int Asn Theoret & Appl Limnol; Sigma Xi. *Res:* Biological limnology; population dynamics and production of heterotrophs; ecosystem structure and function. *Mailing Add:* Dept Fish & Wildlife Mich State Univ East Lansing MI 48824

TAYLOR, WILLIAM WEST, b Northampton Co, NC, Dec 4, 23; m 53; c 4. PHARMACY. *Educ:* Univ NC, BS, 47, PhD(pharm), 62. *Prof Exp:* Intern hosp pharm, Duke Hosp, Durham, NC, 46-47, staff pharmacist, 48; chief pharmacist, Strong Mem Hosp, Rochester, NY, 48; inst, 52-62, ASST PROF HOSP PHARM, DIV PHARMACEUT, UNIV NC, CHAPEL HILL, 62- *Concurrent Pos:* Chief pharmacist, NC Mem Hosp, 52-68, assoc dir, Div Pharm Serv, 68-74, special formulations pharmacist, 75- *Mem:* Am Pharmaceut Asn; Am Soc Hosp Pharmacists; Am Asn Cols Pharm. *Res:* Hospital pharmacy; drug control; special compounding and dosage preparation; purification and formulation of dyes for clinical purposes. *Mailing Add:* Rte 2 Whitfield Rd Chapel Hill NC 27514

TAYLOR-MAYER, RHODA E, b Hartford City, Ind, Feb 20, 36; m 57, 81; c 2. MARINE BIOLOGY, REPRODUCTIVE ENDOCRINOLOGY. *Educ:* Asbury Col, BA, 57; Purdue Univ, MS, 63, PhD(physiol), 65. *Prof Exp:* Asst prof biol, Ind Univ, Kokomo, 65-67; assoc prof, 67-80, PROF BIOL, SLIPPERY ROCK STATE COL, 80- *Concurrent Pos:* Cong affairs specialist, Intergovt Personnel Agreement, Appt Nat Oceanic & Atmospheric Admin, 80-; NSF pre-col teacher develop sci prog grants, 79 & 80. *Mem:* AAAS; Am Soc Zool; Am Inst Biol Sci; Sigma Xi; Nat Marine Educ Asn. *Res:* Maternal behavior; reproductive physiology and behavior. *Mailing Add:* Dept Biol Slippery Rock State Col Slippery Rock PA 16057

TAYLORSON, RAYMOND BRIERLY, b Providence, RI, June 10, 32; m 56; c 2. PLANT PHYSIOLOGY, HORTICULTURE. *Educ:* Univ RI, BS, 54; Univ Wis, PhD(hort, bot), 58. *Prof Exp:* Plant physiologist, Ga Coastal Plain Exp Sta, 65, PLANT PHYSIOLOGIST, BELTSVILLE AGR RES CTR, SCI & EDUC ADMIN-AGR RES, USDA, 66- *Mem:* Am Soc Plant Physiol; Weed Sci Soc Am; Am Soc Hort Sci. *Res:* Natural and synthetic growth regulators; weed biology; weed seed germination; weed control. *Mailing Add:* Weed Sci Lab Beltsville Agr Res Ctr-West Beltsville MD 20705

TAYMOR, MELVIN LESTER, b Brockton, Mass, Feb 10, 19; m 42; c 3. OBSTETRICS & GYNECOLOGY. *Educ:* Johns Hopkins Univ, AB, 40; Tufts Univ, MD, 43; Am Bd Surg, dipl, 54. *Prof Exp:* From instr to assoc prof, 56-81, CLIN PROF OBSTET & GYNEC, HARVARD MED SCH, 81-; CHIEF DIV INFERTILITY & REPRODUCTIVE ENDOCRINOL, BETH ISRAEL HOSP, BOSTON, 77- *Concurrent Pos:* USPHS fel, 50-51; NIH fel, 50-51; mem, Pop Coun, 58-60; chief gynec, Peter Bent Brigham Hosp, 70-77. *Mem:* Am Fertil Soc (treas, 61-66); Endocrine Soc; Soc Gynec Invest; Am Col Obstet & Gynec; Am Gynec Soc. *Res:* Gonadotropins in reproductive physiology. *Mailing Add:* Beth Israel Hosp 330 Brookline Ave Boston MA 02215

TAYSOM, ELVIN DAVID, b Rockland, Idaho, Aug 5, 17; m 39; c 3. ANIMAL HUSBANDRY. *Educ:* Univ Idaho, BS, 40; Utah State Univ, MS, 50; Wash State Univ, PhD, 61. *Prof Exp:* Asst animal sci, Utah State Univ, 49-50; asst, Wash State Univ, 50-53, sheep specialist, 53; from asst prof to assoc prof, 53-62, PROF ANIMAL SCI, ARIZ STATE UNIV, 69- *Mem:* Am Soc Animal Sci. *Res:* Mineral metabolism and its relation to the formation to urinary calculi and hormone functions in the body. *Mailing Add:* Div Agr Ariz State Univ Tempe AZ 85281

TAZUMA, JAMES JUNKICHI, b Seattle, Wash, July 17, 24; m 54; c 2. CHEMISTRY. *Educ:* Univ Wash, BSc, 48, PhD(org chem), 53. *Prof Exp:* Parke Davis Co fel, Wayne State Univ, 52-53; res chemist, Henry Ford Hosp, 53-54 & Food Mach & Chem Corp, NJ, 55-58; sr res chemist, 58-65, sect head spec assignment, 65-79, RES SCIENTIST, GOODYEAR TIRE & RUBBER CO, 79- *Mem:* Am Chem Soc. *Res:* Petroleum chemistry; catalysis; reaction mechanism; process development; polymer additives; monomers; rubber chemicals development. *Mailing Add:* Goodyear Tire & Rubber Co 142 Goodyear Blvd Akron OH 44316

TCHAO, RUY, b China. CELL BIOLOGY. *Educ:* Univ Nottingham, BSc, 60; Univ Manchester, PhD(biochem), 64. *Prof Exp:* Res fel, Inst Cancer Res, Chester Beatty Inst, London, 64-66, from mem res staff to sr biochemist, 66-72; asst prof path, 72-76, ASSOC PROF PATH, MED COL PA, 76- *Concurrent Pos:* Vis assoc prof, Med Col, Nat Taiwan Univ, 69; vis prof, Institut fur Zellforschungszentrum, Heidelberg, Ger, 77; res fel, Int Agency Res Cancer, Lyon, France, 80-81. *Mem:* Int Soc Differentiation; Europ Tissue Culture Asn; NY Acad Sci. *Res:* Tumor cell differentiation, invasion. *Mailing Add:* Dept of Path 3300 Henry Ave Philadelphia PA 19129

TCHEN, TCHE TSING, b Peiping, China, Oct 1, 24; nat US; m 60. BIOCHEMISTRY. *Educ:* Aurora Univ, China, ChemE, 48; Univ Chicago, PhD(biochem), 54. *Prof Exp:* Asst, Univ Chicago, 51-54, res assoc, 54-55; res fel, Harvard Univ, 55-58; assoc prof biochem, 58-61, PROF BIOCHEM, WAYNE STATE UNIV, 61-, ADJ PROF BIOL, 80- *Concurrent Pos:* Am Cancer Soc scholar, 56-58; mem, Physiol Chem Study Sect, USPHS, 60-64; mem res comt, Am Heart Asn, 66-71; ed, Arch Biochem & Biophys, 68-72, J Biol Chem, Am Soc Biol Chem, 68-72 & Endocrine Res Commun, 74- *Mem:* Am Chem Soc; Am Soc Biol Chem. *Res:* Cellular differentiation; mechanism of cell death; action of ACTH and MSH; pigment cells. *Mailing Add:* 435 Dept of Chem Wayne State Univ Detroit MI 48202

TCHERTKOFF, VICTOR, b Lausanne, Switz, Aug 7, 19; US citizen; m 42; c 2. PATHOLOGY. *Educ:* City Col New York, BS, 40; New York Med Col, MD, 43; Am Bd Path, dipl anat, 61. *Prof Exp:* Asst pathologist, Metrop Hosp, New York, 57-60; assoc prof, 61-67, PROF PATH, NEW YORK MED COL, 67-; DIR PATH LABS, METROP HOSP, 67- *Concurrent Pos:* Pathologist-in-chg, Metrop Hosp, 61-66. *Mem:* Col Am Path; Am Soc Clin Path; Int Acad Path; Pan-Am Med Asn; Am Soc Contemporary Med & Surg. *Mailing Add:* Off of Dir of Labs Metrop Hosp 1901 First Ave New York NY 10029

TCHEUREKDJIAN, NOUBAR, b Beirut, Lebanon, Jan 4, 37; m 71; c 2. PHYSICAL CHEMISTRY. *Educ:* Ill Inst Technol, BS, 58; Lehigh Univ, MS, 60, PhD(phys chem), 63. *Prof Exp:* Sr res chemist, 63-80, RES ASSOC, S C JOHNSON & SON, INC, 80- *Mem:* Am Chem Soc; Soc Rheology; Sigma Xi. *Res:* Colloid and surface chemistry; personal care; chemical specialties; aerosol technology. *Mailing Add:* Dermal Res S C Johnson & Son Inc Racine WI 53403

TCHIR, MORRIS FREDERICK, chemistry, see previous edition

TCHOBANOGLOUS, GEORGE, b Patterson, Calif, May 24, 35; m 57; c 3. ENVIRONMENTAL ENGINEERING. *Educ:* Univ of the Pac, BS, 58; Univ Calif, Berkeley, MS, 60; Stanford Univ, PhD(sanit eng), 69. *Prof Exp:* Res engr, Univ Calif, Berkeley, 60-62 & Water Resources Engrs, Inc, 62-63; actg asst prof sanit eng, Stanford Univ, 66-70; assoc prof, 70-76, PROF CIVIL ENG, UNIV CALIF, DAVIS, 76- *Concurrent Pos:* Consult, Metcalf & Eddy Engrs, Inc, 65- *Mem:* AAAS; Water Pollution Control Fedn; Am Soc Civil Engrs; Am Geophys Union; Am Water Works Asn. *Res:* Physical processes in water and wastewater treatment; operation of treatment systems; solid waste management. *Mailing Add:* Dept of Civil Eng Univ of Calif Davis CA 95616

TCHOLAKIAN, ROBERT KEVORK, b Jerusalem, Palestine, Apr 26, 38; US citizen; c 1. BIOCHEMISTRY, REPRODUCTIVE BIOLOGY. *Educ:* Berea Col, BS, 58; Fla State Univ, MS, 63; Med Col Ga, PhD(physiol, biochem), 67. *Prof Exp:* NIH fels, Steroid Biochem Inst, Univ Utah, 67-68 & Univ Southern Calif, 68-69; instr reprod, Univ Southern Calif, 69-70; asst prof endocrinol, M D Anderson Hosp & Tumor Inst, 70-71; asst prof, 71-81, ASSOC PROF REPROD MED & BIOL, MED SCH, UNIV TEX, HOUSTON, 81- *Mem:* AAAS; Am Soc Zoologists; Soc Study Reprod; Am Soc Archology. *Res:* Comparative endocrinology, primarily sexual differentiation; reproductive biology and steroid biochemistry as related to action of hormones. *Mailing Add:* Dept of Reprod Med & Biol Univ of Tex Med Sch Houston TX 77025

TEABEAUT, JAMES ROBERT, II, b Fayetteville, NC, Aug 27, 24. PATHOLOGY. *Educ:* Duke Univ, MD, 47; Am Bd Path, dipl, 53. *Prof Exp:* Intern path, Duke Hosp, Durham, NC, 48, intern internal med, 49; Rockefeller res fel legal med, Harvard Med Sch, 49-51; chief div forensic path,

Armed Forces Inst Path, 51-54; asst prof path, Sch Med, Univ Tenn, 54-59; coroner, Shelby County, Tenn, 55-59; assoc prof, 59-69, PROF PATH, MED COL GA, 69- *Concurrent Pos:* Lederle med fac award, 54-55; Med examr, State of Ga, 59-; consult, Vet Admin Hosp, Augusta, Ga, 59- & US Army Hosp, Ft Gordon, Ga, 60-, lectr, Mil Police Sch, 63-, hon mem staff, 66- *Mem:* Col Am Path; Am Soc Clin Path; AMA; Int Acad Path; Int Acad Forensic Sci. *Res:* Forensic pathology; pathology of human cardiovascular disease. *Mailing Add:* Dept of Path Med Col of Ga Augusta GA 30902

TEACH, EUGENE GORDON, b Hayward, Calif, Oct 27, 26; m 54; c 1. ORGANIC CHEMISTRY. *Educ:* St Mary's Col, Calif, BS, 51; Univ Notre Dame, PhD(chem), 53. *Prof Exp:* Res assoc, Univ Calif, Los Angeles, 53-54, res chemist, USDA, 54-57; RES ASSOC, STAUFFER CHEM CO, 57-, SUPVR, 74- *Mem:* AAAS; Am Chem Soc; Royal Soc Chem. *Res:* Actylene-allene chemistry; high temperature polymers; fluorine chemistry; agricultural chemistry. *Mailing Add:* Richmond Res Ctr 1200 S 47th St Richmond CA 94804

TEAFORD, MARGARET ELAINE, b Union Star, Mo, Feb 2, 28. BIOCHEMISTRY, CLINICAL CHEMISTRY. *Educ:* Northwest Mo State Col, BS, 50; Univ Mo-Columbia, MS, 59, PhD(biochem), 64; Am Bd Clin Chemists, dipl. *Prof Exp:* Med technologist, Methodist Hosp, St Joseph, Mo, 51-52, chief med technol, 52-56; NIH traineeship, Univ Wash, 64-66; TECH DIR LAB MED, ALLEN MED LABS, LTD, 66- *Mem:* AAAS; Am Asn Clin Chemists; Asn Clin Sci. *Res:* Methodology in clinical chemistry and establishing normal values for the various biochemical parameters in the human. *Mailing Add:* 1964 Dougherty Ferry St Louis MO 63122

TEAGER, HERBERT MARTIN, b Canton, Ohio, Mar 20, 30; m 53; c 2. ELECTRICAL ENGINEERING, BIOMEDICAL ENGINEERING. *Educ:* Mass Inst Technol, SB, 52, ScD(control eng), 55. *Prof Exp:* From asst prof to assoc prof, 59-66, LECTR ELEC ENG, MASS INST TECHNOL & RES PROF MED & CHIEF BIOMED ENG, SCH MED, BOSTON UNIV, 66- *Concurrent Pos:* Consult, President's Sci Adv, Sprague Elec Co, Elec Boat Div, Gen Dynamics Corp, Am Optical Co & Compagnie Europeene D'Automatisme Electronique. *Mem:* AAAS; sr mem Inst Elec & Electronics Engrs; Asn Comput Mach; NY Acad Sci; Am Soc Acoust. *Res:* Application of information processing techniques to the collection and analysis of diagnostic information from machine perceived sonic, tactile and visual information; instrumentation; computer design and man-machine interaction; physiology and pathology of speech production and hearing; diagnostic uses of sound (passive) and vibration; speech recognition. *Mailing Add:* Boston Univ Med Ctr 750 Harrison Ave Boston MA 02118

TEAGUE, ABNER F, b Gainesville, Tex, May 25, 19; m 71; c 3. CHEMICAL ENGINEERING. *Educ:* Tex Tech Col, BS, 43; Univ Southern Calif, MS, 69. *Prof Exp:* Chemist, Naval Ord Test Sta, 46-48, res chemist, 48-51; unit head, Bur Ord, US Navy, Washington, DC, 51-56; proj engr, Astrodyn, McGregor, Tex, 56-58; engr, TRW Space Tech Labs, 59-63, proj mgr, TRW Systs, Inc, 63-65, proj engr, 65-67, mgr propulsion subproj, TRW, Inc, 67-71; engr, Naval Weapons Eng Support Activ for Navy Space Projs-Fleet Commun Satellite Proj, Naval Electronic Systs Command, 71-77, HEAD, MECH SYSTS BR & DIR MISSLE DEVELOP, JOINT CRUISE MISSILE PROJS OFF CRUISE MISSILE, NAVY MAT COMMAND, WASHINGTON, DC, 77- *Mem:* NY Acad Sci; Am Inst Chem Engrs; Nat Geog Soc. *Res:* Developing hydrazine propulsion systems for satellite attitude control and station keeping; development and processing of solid propellant rockets; cruise missile mechanical systems including booster and pyrotechnic systems. *Mailing Add:* 8072 Fairfax Rd Alexandria VA 22308

TEAGUE, CLAUDE EDWARD, JR, b Sanford, NC, Sept 9, 24; div; c 3. CHEMISTRY. *Educ:* Univ NC, AB, 47, PhD(chem), 50. *Prof Exp:* Res chemist, Am Viscose Corp, 50-51; res chemist, 52-60, mgr chem res, 60-70, asst dir res, 70-75, planning mgr, 76-77, DIR CORP RES, R J REYNOLDS INDUST, 78- *Mem:* Am Chem Soc. *Res:* Synthetic organic chemistry; research planning; polymers and synthetic fibers; tobacco chemistry. *Mailing Add:* R J Reynolds Indust Corp Res Dept 115 Chestnut St SE Winston-Salem NC 27102

TEAGUE, DAVID BOYCE, b Franklin, NC, May 17, 37; m 64; c 2. APPLIED MATHEMATICS. *Educ:* NC State Col, BSEE, 59, MS, 61; NC State Univ, PhD(appl math), 65. *Prof Exp:* Instr math, NC State Univ, 64-65; asst prof, Univ NC, Charlotte, 65-68; ASSOC PROF MATH, WESTERN CAROLINA UNIV, 68- *Concurrent Pos:* Vis assoc prof comput sci, 82. *Res:* Elasticity; mathematical theory of elasticity; mixed boundary value problems in elasticity; computer science; operating systems. *Mailing Add:* Dept of Math Western Carolina Univ Cullowhee NC 28723

TEAGUE, HAROLD JUNIOR, b Fayetteville, NC, Nov 5, 41; m 70. ORGANIC CHEMISTRY. *Educ:* Methodist Col, NC, BS, 64; NC State Univ, MS, 67, PhD(org chem), 70. *Prof Exp:* Assoc prof, 70-77, PROF CHEM, PEMBROKE STATE UNIV, 77- *Mem:* Am Chem Soc. *Res:* Mechanistic rearrangement studies of sulfur containing ring compounds. *Mailing Add:* Dept of Chem Pembroke State Univ Pembroke NC 28372

TEAGUE, HOWARD STANLEY, b Rockville, Ind, Jan 16, 22; m 43; c 4. NUTRITION, REPRODUCTIVE PHYSIOLOGY. *Educ:* Univ Nebr, BS, 48, MS, 49; Univ Minn, PhD, 52. *Prof Exp:* From asst prof to prof animal sci, Ohio Agr Res & Develop Ctr, 52-72; mem staff, Animal Sci Res Div, US Meat Animal Res Ctr, 72-76; MEM STAFF COOP RES, SCI & EDUC, USDA, 76- *Mem:* Am Soc Animal Sci; Am Inst Nutrit; Soc Study Reproduction. *Res:* Nutrition and physiology relative to growth and reproductive processes in domestic animals. *Mailing Add:* Coop State Res Serv Sci & Educ USDA Washington DC 20250

TEAGUE, KEFTON HARDING, b Siler City, NC, Sept 30, 20; m 43; c 2. ECONOMIC GEOLOGY. *Educ:* NC State Col, BS, 41. *Prof Exp:* JR assoc geologist, Tenn Valley Authority, 42-51; geologist, US Geol Surv, 51-55; geologist, 55-62, chief div geologist, 62-73, SR GEOLOGIST GROUP, INT MINERALS & CHEM CORP, 73- *Mem:* Geol Soc Am; Soc Econ Geol; Clay Minerals Soc. *Res:* Areal and structural geology of Georgia; mica pegmatites; sillimanite; kyanite; talc; feldspar; olivine; barite; bentonite; quartz. *Mailing Add:* Int Min & Chem Co 666 Garland Pl Des Plaines IL 60016

TEAGUE, MARION WARFIELD, b Arkadelphia, Ark, July 6, 41; m 62; c 3. PHYSICAL INORGANIC CHEMISTRY. *Educ:* Ouachita Baptist Col, BS, 63; Purdue Univ, MS, 68, PhD(chem), 71. *Prof Exp:* Res chemist, Aberdeen Res & Develop Ctr, 68-70; ASSOC PROF CHEM, HENDRIX COL, 70- *Mem:* AAAS; Am Chem Soc. *Res:* Non-coplanar aromatic systems; electron transfer mechanism. *Mailing Add:* Dept of Chem Hendrix Col Conway AR 72032

TEAGUE, PERRY OWEN, b Marshall, Tex, July 13, 36; m 64; c 2. IMMUNOLOGY. *Educ:* NTex State Univ, BA, 58, MA, 61; Univ Okla, PhD(immunol), 66. *Prof Exp:* Res assoc immunol, Univ Southern Calif, 66; res fel, Univ Minn, 66-68; asst prof, 68-73, ASSOC PROF PATH, MED SCH, UNIV FLA, 73- *Concurrent Pos:* NIH fel pediat, Univ Minn, 67-68. *Mem:* Am Asn Immunol; Soc Exp Biol & Med; assoc Am Soc Clin Path. *Res:* Age-associated and early decline of thymus dependent lymphocyte function; diagnostic clinical immunology. *Mailing Add:* Dept of Path Univ of Fla Col of Med Gainesville FL 32610

TEAGUE, PEYTON CLARK, b Montgomery, Ala, June 26, 15; m 37; c 1. ORGANIC CHEMISTRY. *Educ:* Auburn Univ, BS, 36; Pa State Univ, MS, 37; Univ Tex, PhD(org chem, biochem), 42. *Prof Exp:* Res chemist, Am Agr Chem Co, NJ, 37-39; instr chem, Auburn Univ, 41-42; res chemist, US Naval Res Lab, DC, 42-45; asst prof chem, Univ Ga, 45-48 & Univ Ky, 48-50; assoc prof chem, 50-56, assoc dean grad sch, 66-68, PROF CHEM, UNIV SC, 56- *Concurrent Pos:* Vis prof, Univ Col, Dublin, 63-74 & 77. *Mem:* Am Chem Soc; Phytochem Soc NAm (pres, 69-70). *Res:* Chemistry and stereochemistry of flavonoids. *Mailing Add:* Dept of Chem Univ of SC Columbia SC 29208

TEAGUE, ROBERT STERLING, pharmacology, endocrinology, deceased

TEAGUE, TOMMY KAY, b Crossett, Ark, July 11, 43; m 65; c 1. PERFORMANCE EVALUATION, GROUP THEORY. *Educ:* Hendrix Col, AB, 65; Univ Kans, MA, 67; Mich State Univ, PhD(math), 71. *Prof Exp:* Asst prof math, Gustavus Adolphus Col, 71; asst prof math, Hendrix Col, 71-76, coordr comput syst & serv, 75-76; systs rep, 76-77, sr syst rep, 77-79, systs specialist, 79-80, SR SYSTS SPECIALIST, BURROUGHS CORP, 80- *Mem:* Am Math Soc; Math Asn Am. *Res:* Varieties of groups; embeddings of groups; computer science. *Mailing Add:* Burroughs Corp 2900 Woodcock Blvd 100 Atlanta GA 30341

TEAL, GORDON KIDD, b Dallas, Tex, Jan 10, 07; m 31; c 3. PHYSICAL CHEMISTRY. *Educ:* Baylor Univ, AB, 27; Brown Univ, ScM, 28, PhD(chem), 31. *Hon Degrees:* LLD, Baylor Univ, 69; ScD, Brown Univ, 69. *Prof Exp:* Res chemist, Bell Tel Labs, Inc, 30-53; asst vpres & dir mat & components res, Tex Instruments, Inc, 53-55, asst vpres & dir res, 55-61, asst vpres res & eng, 61-63, int tech dir, 63-65; dir, Inst Mat Res, Nat Bur Standards, 65-67; asst vpres in charge tech develop, Equip Group, Tex Instruments, Inc, 67-68, vpres & chief scientist for corp develop, 68-72; CONSULT, 72- *Concurrent Pos:* Res assoc, Columbia Univ, 32-35; consult, Dept Defense, NASA, Nat Acad Sci-Nat Acad Eng & Nat Bur Standards, 56-64 & 70-; mem panel selenium, Nat Acad Sci-Nat Res Coun, 56, mem panel semiconductors, 57, mem mat adv bd, 60-64, mem ad hoc comt mat & processes for electronic devices, 70-71; mem mat panel, Adv Group Electronic Parts, Off Asst Secy Defense, 56-59; dir at large, Inst Radio Eng, 59 & 62; mem adv panel to Inst Appl Technol, Nat Bur Standards, 69-75, mem comt electronic technol issues study, 72-74, chmn panel to evaluate electronic technol div, 72-75; mem, US-India Nat Acad Sci Workshop Indust Res Mgt, 70; chmn US Nat Acad Sci deleg to Ceylon, Indust Res Mgt Workshop, 70; mem aeronaut & space eng bd, Nat Acad Eng, 70-72; mem, Nat Acad Eng Comn Int Activ, 70-71; chmn bd comt comput in educ, Brown Univ, 71-75, mem, 76-, trustee, 69-74, emer trustee, 74-; mem adv coun, Arts & Sci, 72-79, Col Natural Sci, 79-, Univ Tex, Austin; contribr, Comt Surv Mat Sci & Eng, Nat Acad Sci, 72; mem US Nat Acad Sci deleg to Joint Repub China-US Workshop Indust Innovation & Prod Develop, 75; chmn, Nat Acad Sci-Nat Res Coun panel res facil & sci opportunities in use of low energy neutrons, 77-78. *Honors & Awards:* Inventor of the Year Award, Patent, Trademark & Copyright Res Inst, George Washington Univ, 66; Golden Plate Award, Am Acad Achievement, 67; Cert Appreciation & Honor Scroll, Nat Bur Standards & US Dept Com, 67; Medal of Honor, Inst Elec & Electronics Eng, 68; Creative Invention Award, Am Chem Soc, 70. *Mem:* Nat Acad Engr; fel AAAS (vpres & chmn indust sci sect, 69 & 70); fel Inst Elec & Electronics Engr; fel Am Inst Chem; Am Chem Soc. *Res:* Raman spectra deuterium isotopic effects; photoelectric and secondary emission phenomena; pyrolytically deposited hard or semiconducting films; microwave attenuator materials; silicon carbide varistors; germanium and silicon single crystals; transistors; junction transistor. *Mailing Add:* 5222 Park Ln Dallas TX 75220

TEAL, JOHN MOLINE, b Omaha, Nebr, Nov 9, 29; m 50, 79; c 2. MARINE BIOLOGY, ECOLOGY. *Educ:* Harvard Univ, AB, 51, MA, 52, PhD, 55. *Prof Exp:* Asst prof zool, Marine Inst, Univ Ga, 55-59; asst zool & oceanog, Inst Oceanog, Dalhousie Univ, 59-61; assoc scientist, 61-71, SR SCIENTIST, WOODS HOLE OCEANOG INST, 71- *Mem:* AAAS; Am Soc Limnol & Oceanog; Ecol Soc Am. *Res:* Ecology, chemical cycling, productivity of coastal wetlands; hydrocarbon biogeochemistry; coastal pollution. *Mailing Add:* Woods Hole Oceanog Inst Woods Hole MA 02543

TEANEY, DALE T, b Monrovia, Calif, May 19, 33; m; c 3. SOLID STATE PHYSICS, ACOUSTICS. *Educ:* Pomona Col, BA, 55; Univ Calif, Berkeley, PhD(physics), 60. *Prof Exp:* Res assoc physics, Atomic Energy Res Estab, Eng, 60-62; RES STAFF MEM, WATSON RES CTR, IBM CORP, 62- *Concurrent Pos:* Staff scientist, Nat Acad Sci Phys Surv Comt, 70-71; hon res fel, Univ Col, London, 80-81. *Mem:* AAAS; fel Am Phys Soc; NY Acad Sci. *Res:* Magnetic resonance; calorimetry; liquid crystals; lipid bilayers; acoustic spectroscopy. *Mailing Add:* IBM Watson Res Ctr PO Box 218 Yorktown Heights NY 10598

TEARE, B(ENJAMIN) R(ICHARD), JR, b Menomonie, Wis, Jan 12, 07; m 32; c 1. ELECTRICAL ENGINEERING. *Educ:* Univ Wis, BS, 27, MS, 28; Yale Univ, DE, 37. *Hon Degrees:* DSc, Tri-State Col, 65; DEng, Cleveland State Univ, 70 & Carnegie Mellon Univ, 77. *Prof Exp:* Mem gen eng dept, Gen Elec Co, NY, 29-33; from instr to asst prof elec eng, Yale Univ, 33-39; univ prof eng, 39-75, Buhl prof, 43-54, head, Dept Elec Eng, 44-52, dean grad studies, 50-53, assoc dean, Col Eng & Sci, 52-53, dean, 53-66, EMER PROF ENG, CARNEGIE-MELLON UNIV, 75- *Concurrent Pos:* Educ consult, World Bank & other orgns. *Honors & Awards:* Westinghouse Award, Am Soc Eng Educ, 47 & Lamme Award, 63; Education Medal, Inst Elec & Electronics Engrs, 64. *Mem:* Fel AAAS; hon mem Am Soc Eng Educ (vpres, 53-55, pres, 59-60); fel Am Inst Elec Engrs (pres, 62); fel Inst Elec & Electronics Engrs (vpres, 63). *Res:* Hysteresis motors; current distribution at high frequencies; circuits; engineering education. *Mailing Add:* 1344 Denniston Ave Pittsburgh PA 15217

TEARE, FREDERICK WILSON, b Lacombe, Alta, June 9, 25; m 50; c 4. PHARMACEUTICAL CHEMISTRY, RADIOPHARMACY. *Educ:* Univ Alta, BSc, 49, MSc, 51; Univ NC, PhD(pharmaceut chem), 55. *Prof Exp:* Res pharmacist, Chas Pfizer Co, NY, 55-57; asst prof pharmaceut chem, 57-64, assoc prof, 64-77, PROF PHARMACEUT CHEM, UNIV TORONTO, 77- *Concurrent Pos:* Sabbatical, Drugs Metab Labs, Ciba Ltd, Switz, 69-70. *Mem:* Can Pharmaceut Asn; Soc Nuclear Med; Can Inst Chem; Radiopharmaceut Sci Coun; Asn Fac Pharm Can. *Res:* Toxicology; radiopharmaceutics; quantitative analysis of drugs and metabolites in products and in biological media; drug metabolism; electrochemical and chemical radiocodination of various drugs (or substrates) used as potential diagnstic agents or to study and/or optimize parameters for their synthesis; separation and purification; characteriztion and stability of new compounds. *Mailing Add:* Fac of Pharm Univ of Toronto Toronto ON M5S 1A1 Can

TEARE, IWAN DALE, b Moscow, Idaho, July 24, 31; m 52; c 4. CROP PHYSIOLOGY. *Educ:* Univ Idaho, BS, 53; Wash State Univ, MS, 59; Purdue Univ, PhD(crop physiol, ecol), 63. *Prof Exp:* County agent, Idaho, 56-57; instr agron, Purdue Univ, 61-63; asst prof, Wash State Univ, 63-69; assoc prof agron, Kans State Univ, 69-77, prof, 77-79; PROF & DIR, AGR RES & EDUC CTR, UNIV FLA, QUINCY-MARIANNA, 79- *Mem:* Crop Sci Soc Am; Am Soc Agron; Sigma Xi. *Res:* Crop water relations; modeling the plant canopy in relation to the evapotranspiration process; assessing the interrelationships in the soil-plant-air continuum; effect of phytoclimate on physiological processes of plants in relation to predicting water stress, irrigation scheduling and maximization of crop yield. *Mailing Add:* Evapotranspiration Lab Kans State Univ Manhattan KS 66506

TEAS, DONALD CLAUDE, b San Antonio, Tex, 1927; m 56; c 3. PHYSIOLOGICAL PSYCHOLOGY. *Educ:* Univ Tex, BA, 50, MA, 51, PhD(psychol), 54. *Prof Exp:* Res scientist, Defense Res Lab & instr, Univ Tex, 54-56; asst prof psychol, Drake Univ, 56-58; res assoc, Cent Inst Deaf, St Louis, Mo, 58-61; fel, Res Lab Electronics, Mass Inst Technol, 61-62; asst res prof otolaryngol, Sch Med, Univ Pittsburgh, 62-66, assoc res prof, 67; assoc prof psychol, speech & biomed, 67-71, PROF PSYCHOL, SPEECH & BIOMED, INST ADVAN STUDY COMMUN PROCESSES, UNIV FLA, 71- *Concurrent Pos:* Nat Inst Neurol Dis & Blindness spec fel, 58-62, career res develop award, 62-67. *Mem:* AAAS; Acoust Soc Am; Psychonomic Soc; Soc Neurosci. *Res:* Physiological acoustics; cochlear processes; extracellular recording acoustic-evoked neural activity. *Mailing Add:* Inst Advan Study Commun Process Univ of Fla Gainesville FL 32601

TEAS, HOWARD JONES, b Rolla, Mo, Sept 4, 20; m 42; c 4. GENETICS. *Educ:* La State Univ, AB, 42; Stanford Univ, MA, 46; Calif Inst Technol, PhD(genetics), 47. *Prof Exp:* Asst genetics, Carnegie Inst, 42-43; biologist, Oak Ridge Nat Lab, 47-48; res fel, Calif Inst Technol, 48-49, sr res fel, 50-53; plant physiologist, USDA, 53-56; assoc prof biochem, Univ Fla, 56-60; head agr bio-sci div, Nuclear Ctr, Univ PR, 60-62; prog dir, NSF, 62-64; chmn div biol sci, Univ Ga, 64-67; PROF BIOL, UNIV MIAMI, 67- *Concurrent Pos:* Mem bd dirs, Orgn Trop Studies, 67-72. *Mem:* AAAS; Ecol Soc Am; Am Soc Plant Physiol; Am Soc Biol Chem; Radiation Res Soc. *Res:* Plant physiology; tropical biology; physiological ecology. *Mailing Add:* 6700 SW 130th Terr Miami FL 33156

TEASDALE, JOHN G, b Utah, June 11, 13; m 42; c 3. PHYSICS. *Educ:* Univ Calif, Los Angeles, AB, 36, PhD(physics), 50. *Prof Exp:* Physicist, US Navy Radio & Sound Lab, 41 & Manhattan Proj, Radiation Lab, Univ Calif, 42-45; res fel, Calif Inst Technol, 50-52, sr res fel, 52-56; from asst prof to assoc prof physics, 56-62, PROF PHYSICS, SAN DIEGO STATE UNIV, 62- *Concurrent Pos:* Consult, Convair Div, Gen Dynamics Corp, 60. *Mem:* Am Phys Soc; Am Inst Physics; Am Asn Physics Teachers; Sigma Xi. *Res:* Nuclear physics. *Mailing Add:* Dept of Physics San Diego State Univ San Diego CA 92182

TEASDALE, WILLIAM BROOKS, b Brownsville, Pa, July 19, 39; m 63; c 2. ORGANIC CHEMISTRY. *Educ:* Geneva Col, BS, 61. *Prof Exp:* Prod chemist, 61-62, develop chemist, 62-73, sr develop chemist, 73-76 & Dept Tech Staff, 76-77, SR DEVELOP CHEMIST, DIV TECH STAFF, EASTMAN KODAK CO, 77- *Mem:* Am Chem Soc; Soc Photog Scientists & Engrs. *Res:* Research and development of organic chemical processes to be used in the production of photographic chemicals. *Mailing Add:* Bldg 151 Kodak Park Rochester NY 14650

TEASDALL, ROBERT DOUGLAS, b London, Ont, Dec 9, 20; m 48; c 2. NEUROLOGY. *Educ:* Univ Western Ont, MD, 46, PhD, 50; Am Bd Psychiat & Neurol, dipl, 57. *Prof Exp:* Asst res neurol, Baltimore City Hosps, 52-53; asst, Johns Hopkins Hosp, 53-54, from instr to assoc prof neurol med, Sch Med, Johns Hopkins Univ, 54-73; chief div neurol, 74-79, STAFF NEUROLOGIST, HENRY FORD HOSP, 79-; CLIN PROF NEUROL, UNIV MICH, ANN ARBOR, 75- *Mem:* Am Physiol Soc; AMA; Am Neurol Asn; Am Acad Neurol. *Res:* Neurophysiology. *Mailing Add:* Dept Neurol Henry Ford Hosp Detroit MI 48202

TEASEL, RICHARD C(HESTER), b Sandusky, Ohio, May 10, 22; m 46; c 1. MECHANICAL ENGINEERING. *Educ:* Univ Chicago, BS, 44; Univ Detroit, BME, 48; Purdue Univ, MSME, 49. *Prof Exp:* Engr trainee, Parke, Davis & Co, 42-43; instr eng math, Univ Detroit, 46-47, draftsman, Aeronaut Eng Dept, 47-48; engr, Proj Squid, Off Naval Res, Purdue Univ, 48-49; proj engr, Res Dept, 49-55, dir res, 55-69, VPRES RES & DEVELOP, CHAMPION SPARK PLUG CO, 69- *Res:* Ignition devices and instrumentation for internal combustion engines. *Mailing Add:* Champion Spark Plug Co 900 Upton Ave PO Box 910 Toledo OH 43661

TEATE, JAMES LAMAR, b Moultrie, Ga, Mar 4, 32; m 53; c 3. FOREST ECOLOGY. *Educ:* Univ Ga, BS, 54, MF, 56; NC State Univ, PhD(forestry, ecol), 67. *Prof Exp:* Info & educ forester, Fla Forest Serv, 56-58; instr forestry & res asst, Auburn Univ, 58-60; instr & asst forester, Miss State Univ, 60-62; assoc prof forestry, Wis State Univ-Stevens Point, 65-67; assoc prof forest recreation, Okla State Univ, 67-76; res specialist, Okla Agr Exp Sta, 67-76; DIR & PROF, SCH FORESTRY, LA TECH UNIV, 76- *Concurrent Pos:* Proj consult statewide comprehensive outdoor recreation plant, Okla Indust Develop & Parks Dept, 69-70. *Mem:* Soc Am Foresters; Forest Farmers Asn; Sigma Xi; Am Forestry Asn. *Mailing Add:* Sch of Forestry La Tech Univ Ruston LA 71272

TEATER, ROBERT WOODSON, b Ky, Feb 27, 27; m 52; c 4. AGRONOMY. *Educ:* Univ Ky, BS, 51; Ohio State Univ, MS, 55, PhD(agron), 57. *Prof Exp:* Asst prof agron, Ohio State Univ & Agr Exp Sta, 57; exec asst to dir, Ohio Dept Natural Resources, 61-63, asst dir, 63-69; dir, Sch Natural Resources, 71-74, chmn & prof, Dept Natural Resources & prof agron, 73-74, ASSOC DEAN, COL AGR & HOME ECON, OHIO STATE UNIV, 69-; DIR, OHIO DEPT NATURAL RESOURCES, 75- *Mem:* Am Soc Agron; Soil Conserv Soc Am. *Res:* Soil fertility; plant nutrition; conservation; natural resources; nature conservancy; environmental science. *Mailing Add:* Ohio Dept of Natural Resources Fountain Sq Columbus OH 43224

TEBBE, DENNIS LEE, b St Louis, Mo, Oct 21, 42; m 64. ELECTRICAL ENGINEERING, STATISTICS. *Educ:* Univ Mo-Columbia, BS, 64, MS, 65, PhD(elec eng, statist), 68. *Prof Exp:* Asst prof elec eng, Univ Mo-Columbia, 68-74; SCIENTIST, GEOMETRIC DATA, DIV OF SMITHKLINE CORP, 74- *Mem:* Inst Elec & Electronics Engrs; Pattern Recognition Soc; Am Statist Asn; AAAS. *Res:* Pattern recognition; information theory and multivariate data analysis; medical instrumentation. *Mailing Add:* Geometric Data Div 999 W Valley Rd Wayne PA 19087

TE BEEST, DAVID ORIEN, b Baldwin, Wis, Nov 9, 46; m 73; c 2. PLANT PATHOLOGY. *Educ:* Univ Wis-Stevens Point, BS, 68, Univ Wis-Madison, MS, 71, PhD(plant path), 74. *Prof Exp:* Res asst plant path, Univ Wis-Madison, 68-74; res assoc, 75-78, ASST PROF UNIV ARK, FAYETTEVILLE, 78- *Mem:* Am Phytopath Soc; Int Soc Plant Path; Sigma Xi. *Res:* Biological control of weeds with plant pathogens; pesticide physiology of fungi; physiology of plant disease; biological control of plant diseases. *Mailing Add:* Dept of Plant Path Univ of Ark Fayetteville AR 72701

TEBO, HEYL GREMMER, b Atlanta, Ga, Oct 17, 16; m 40. ANATOMY. *Educ:* Oglethorpe Univ, AB, 37, MA, 39; Emory Univ, DDS, 47. *Prof Exp:* Instr anat, Oglethorpe Univ, 38-39; teaching fel oral surg & anat, Univ Tex Dent Br Houston, 47-48, instr anat & surg, 48-50; asst prof diag & radiol, Sch Dent, Univ Ala, Birmingham, 50-52; asst chief dent serv, Vet Admin Hosp, Houston, Tex, 52-61; PROF ANAT, UNIV TEX DENT BR HOUSTON, 62-, PROF ANAT, MED SCH, 74-, CHMN GROSS ANAT, DENT BR, 78- *Concurrent Pos:* Clin assoc prof, Univ Tex Dent Br Houston, 52-61; consult, Vet Admin Hosp, Houston, Tex, 62- *Mem:* Fel AAAS; Am Asn Anat; Int Asn Dent Res; Am Acad Dent Radiol; Am Asn Phys Anthrop. *Res:* Osteology of head; radiographic anatomy; personality characteristics of patients; oral pathology related to radiography of head. *Mailing Add:* Dept of Anat Univ of Tex Dent Br PO Box 20068 Houston TX 77025

TEBO, PAUL VINSON, chemical engineering, see previous edition

TECHO, ROBERT, b New York, NY, Jan 1, 31; m 55; c 3. INFORMATION SCIENCE, DATA COMMUNICATIONS. *Educ:* Ga Inst Technol, BChE, 53, MS, 58, PhD(chem eng), 61. *Prof Exp:* Sr res engr, Eng Exp Sta, Ga Inst Technol 59-65; assoc prof info systs, Ga State Univ, 69-74; CONSULT, CHEM ENG & COMPUT ANAL, 65-; PROF INFO SYSTS, GA STATE UNIV, 74- *Mem:* Am Chem Soc; Am Inst Chem Eng; Asn Comput Mach; AAAS. *Res:* Computer applications of engineering problems, including systems analysis for pipeline operations and hydraulic transients; computer science, including teleprocessing information systems, data communications design and computer communication networks. *Mailing Add:* Ga State Univ University Plaza Atlanta GA 30303

TECKLENBURG, HARRY, b Seattle, Wash, Nov 3, 27; m 51; c 2. CHEMICAL ENGINEERING. *Educ:* Mass Inst Technol, BS, 50; Univ Wash, MS, 52. *Prof Exp:* Chem engr, Procter & Gamble Co, 52-54, group leader soap process develop, 54-57, sect leader res & develop, 57-60, dir paper prod develop, 60-61, mgr paper mfg & prod develop, 61-67, dir res & develop, 67-69, mgr, 69-70, vpres, 70-76, SR V PRES RES & DEVELOP, PROCTER & GAMBLE CO, 76- *Mem:* AAAS; Am Inst Chem Engrs; Am Chem Soc; Tech Asn Pulp & Paper Indust. *Res:* Research administration. *Mailing Add:* Procter & Gamble Co Winton Hill Tech Ctr Cincinnati OH 45224

TECOTZKY, MELVIN, b Chicago, Ill, Feb 17, 24; m 56; c 2. INORGANIC CHEMISTRY. *Educ:* Univ Ill, BS, 48, PhD(chem), 53. *Prof Exp:* Res asst inorg chem, Univ Ill, 51-53, fel, 53-54; res chemist, Diversey Corp, 54-56; sr chemist, W R Grace & Co, 56-59; res chemist & proj leader, FMC Corp, 59-61; staff scientist, Missiles & Space Div, Lockheed Aircraft Corp, Calif, 61-68; dir res, Chem Prod Div, Radium Corp, 68-80; VPRES, OPTONIX INC, HACKETTSTOWN, NJ, 80- *Mem:* Am Chem Soc; Am Phys Soc; Electrochem Soc; The Chem Soc. *Res:* Rare earths; solid state chemistry; luminescence; chelates; thorium; uranium; sulfides; hydrazine; phosphates; transition elements; electronic materials; magnetic materials; non-aqueous solvents. *Mailing Add:* 27 N Linden Ln Mendham NJ 07945

TEDESCHI, DAVID HENRY, b Newark, NJ, Feb 20, 30. PHARMACOLOGY. *Educ:* Rutgers Univ, BSc, 52; Univ Utah, PhD, 55. *Prof Exp:* Asst pharmacol, Univ Utah, 52-54; assoc dir pharmacol, Smith Kline & French Labs, Pa, 55-68; dir pharmacol, Geigy Pharmaceut, NY, 68-70, dir pharmacol & dep dir biol res, Ciba-Geigy Corp, 70-72; dir cent nerv syst dis ther, Res Sect, Lederle Labs Div, Am Cyanamid Co, 72-77; staff div neurol, Henry Ford Hosp, Detroit, 78-80; DIR BIOSCI RES LABS, 3M CO, 80- *Honors & Awards:* Am Pharmaceut Asn Found Award in Pharmacodynamics, 69. *Mem:* Am Col Neuropsychopharmacol; Am Soc Pharmacol & Exp Therapeut; Soc Exp Biol & Med; Int Col Neuropsychopharmacol; Int Soc Biochem Pharmacol. *Res:* Neuropsychopharmacology; site and mechanism of action of drugs on central nervous system. *Mailing Add:* 3M CO 3M Ctr Cent Res Labs PO Box 33221 St Paul MN 55133

TEDESCHI, HENRY, b Novara, Italy, Feb 3, 30; nat US; m 57; c 3. PHYSIOLOGY. *Educ:* Univ Pittsburgh, BS, 50; Univ Chicago, PhD(physiol), 55. *Prof Exp:* Res assoc & instr, Univ Chicago, 55-57, asst prof, 57-60; from asst prof to assoc prof physiol, Univ Ill Col Med, 60-65; PROF BIOL, STATE UNIV NY ALBANY, 65- *Concurrent Pos:* NIH sr res fel, Oxford Univ, 71-72. *Mem:* Biophys Soc; Am Soc Cell Biol; Am Physiol Soc; Soc Gen Physiol; Am Soc Biol Chem. *Res:* Cell physiology; structural and functional organization of the cell; intracellular membranes. *Mailing Add:* Dept Biol Sci State Univ NY Albany NY 12222

TEDESCHI, RALPH EARL, b Newark, NJ, Nov 20, 27; m 51; c 2. PHARMACOLOGY. *Educ:* Rutgers Univ, BS, 51; Med Col Va, PhD(pharmacol), 54. *Prof Exp:* Resident pharmacol, Oxford Univ, 54-55; res assoc, Div Metab Res, Jefferson Med Col, 55-56; assoc dir pharmacol, Smith Kline & French Labs, 56-69; head dept pharmacol, Wm S Merrell Co, Ohio, 69-71; head dept, 71-72, dir clin pharmacol, 72-73, dir develop, 73-74, tech asst to dir pharmaceut res & develop, 74-75, TECH ASST TO MED DIR, HUMAN HEALTH RES & DEVELOP LABS, DOW CHEM CO, ZIONSVILLE, 75- *Mem:* Am Soc Pharmacol & Exp Therapeut; Acad Pharmaceut Sci; Am Pharmaceut Asn; Soc Exp Biol & Med. *Res:* Neuropharmacology; pharmacology of the autonomic nervous system; cardiovascular pharmacology. *Mailing Add:* 7850 Holly Creek Lane Indianapolis IN 46240

TEDESCHI, ROBERT JAMES, b Woodside, NY, July 25, 21; m 52; c 3. ORGANIC CHEMISTRY. *Educ:* Cornell Univ, AB, 44, MS, 45, PhD(org chem), 47. *Prof Exp:* Microanal chemist, Wyeth Inst, Pa, 46; res chemist, Calco Chem Div, Am Cyanamid Co, NJ, 47-53; sect head, Cent Res Labs, Air Reduction Co, 53-59, proj leader, Air Prod & Chem Co, 59-64, supvr chem div, Airco Chem & Plastics Div, 64-69, supvr org chem, 69-71, dir res & develop, Acetylenic Chem Div, 71-74, assoc dir res, Acetylenic Chem Div, Middlesex, 74-79; PRES, TEDESCHI & ASSOCS, 80- *Mem:* Am Chem Soc; fel Am Inst Chem; NY Acad Sci. *Res:* Acetylene chemistry; high pressure synthesis; catalytic reactions; organic chemicals development; industrial applications for acetylenic chemicals; organo metallics; chelates and complexes; corrosion inhibitors; perfumery intermediates; agricultural chemicals; acetylenic surfactants; specialty monomers and polymers. *Mailing Add:* RD 2 Box 143 Whitehouse Station NJ 08889

TEDESCO, THOMAS ALBERT, b York, Pa, Dec 5, 35. HUMAN GENETICS, BIOCHEMICAL GENETICS. *Educ:* Franklin & Marshall Col, BS, 60; Univ Pa, PhD(biol, genetics), 69. *Prof Exp:* Res technician pediat, Hosp, 60-61, res asst, 61-62, res assoc genetics, 62-65, from instr to asst prof pediat, Sch Med, Univ Pa, 65-72, asst prof pediat & med genetics, 72-74; asst prof, 74-81, ASSOC PROF PEDIAT, COL MED, UNIV SOUTH FLA, 81-, DIR PEDIAT LABS, 74- *Concurrent Pos:* Prin investr, NIH grant; prog dir, Nat Found-March Dimes Med Serv grant; co-dir, Regional Genetics Prog, Children's Med Serv, Dept Health & Rehab Serv, State Fla. *Mem:* NY Acad Sci; AAAS; Am Soc Human Genetics. *Res:* Inborn errors in metabolism; enzyme deficiency disease; cytogenetics. *Mailing Add:* Dept Pediat Col Med Univ South Fla Tampa FL 33612

TEDESKO, ANTON, b Gruenberg, Ger, May 25, 03; nat US; m 38; c 2. STRUCTURAL ENGINEERING. *Educ:* Inst Technol, Vienna, Austria, CE, 26, DSc, 51; Univ Berlin, dipl eng, 30. *Hon Degrees:* DEng, Lehigh Univ, 66; DTechSc, Univ Vienna, 78. *Prof Exp:* Construct engr, Vienna, 26; mem staff, Fairbanks-Morse Co, Chicago, 27 & Miss Valley Struct Steel Co, Melrose Park, Ill, 27-28; asst prof, Inst Technol, Vienna, 29; designer dams, bridges, shells and indust struct, Dyckerhoff & Widmann, Wiesbaden, Ger, 30-32; mem staff, Roberts & Schaefer Co, Engrs, Chicago, 32-43, eng mgr, Washington, DC, 43-44, struct mgr, Chicago, 44-54, mgr, New York, 55, vpres, 56-67; CONSULT ENG, 67- *Concurrent Pos:* Consult, Hq US Air Force, 55-70; dir, Thompson-Starrett Co, 60-61; struct eng Apollo rocket assembly & launch facil, Kennedy Space Ctr, 62-66; mem exec comt, Reinforced Concrete Res Coun, 71-; mem, Res Coun Performance Struct; mem metric comn, Engrs Joint Coun. *Honors & Awards:* Alfred Lindau Award, 61; Arthur J Boase Award, Reinforced Concrete Res Coun, 78. *Mem:* Nat Acad Eng; hon mem Am Soc Civil Engrs; hon mem Int Asn Shell & Spatial Struct; Int Asn Bridge & Struct Eng; hon mem Am Concrete Inst. *Res:* Design of construction of arenas, air terminals, bridges, toll roads, industrial structures, ballistic missile and space rocket launching facilities, wide-span hangars and shell structures; shell concrete structures of long span. *Mailing Add:* 26 Brookside Circle Bronxville NY 10708

TEDFORD, RICHARD HALL, b Los Angeles, Calif, Apr 25, 29; m 54. VERTEBRATE PALEONTOLOGY, STATRIGRAPHY. *Educ:* Univ Calif, Los Angeles, BS, 51; Univ Calif, Berkeley, PhD(paleont), 60. *Prof Exp:* Instr geol, Univ Calif, Riverside, 59-60, lectr, 60-61, from asst prof to assoc prof, 61-66; assoc curator vert paleont, 66-69, CURATOR VERT PALEONT, AM MUS NATURAL HIST, 69-, CHMN DEPT, 77- *Mem:* Soc Study Evolution; Australian Mammal Soc; Soc Vert Paleont; Paleont Soc; Am Soc Mammal. *Res:* Phylogeny, geographic distribution and paleoecology of Carnivora, Marsupials and other mammals; stratigraphy and chronology of Cenozoic rocks. *Mailing Add:* Am Mus Natural Hist Central Park W at 79th St New York NY 10024

TEDMON, CRAIG SEWARD, JR, b Pueblo, Colo, Jan 19, 39; m 59; c 3. METALLURGY, ELECTROCHEMISTRY. *Educ:* Mass Inst Technol, SB, 61, MS, 62, ScD(metall), 64. *Prof Exp:* Instr metall, Mass Inst Technol, 63-64; res metallurgist, 64-70, MGR SURFACES & REACTIONS BR, GEN ELEC RES & DEVELOP CTR, GEN ELEC CO, 70- *Concurrent Pos:* Mem adj staff, Union Col NY, 66- *Mem:* AAAS; Electrochem Soc; Am Soc Metals; Am Inst Mining, Metall & Petrol Engrs; Brit Inst Metals. *Res:* Metallurgy of high-field superconductors; high-temperature oxidation; diffusion in metals and oxides; high temperature electrochemistry. *Mailing Add:* 37 Sunny Ridge Rd Easton CT 06425

TEDROW, JOHN CHARLES FREMONT, b Rockwood, Pa, Apr 21, 17; m 43; c 2. SOILS. *Educ:* Pa State Univ, BS, 39; Mich State Univ, MS, 40; Rutgers Univ, PhD, 50. *Prof Exp:* Jr soil surveyor, Soil Conserv Serv, USDA, 41, soil scientist, 46-47; from instr to assoc prof, 48-57, PROF SOILS, RUTGERS UNIV, NEW BRUNSWICK, 57- *Concurrent Pos:* Sr pedologist, Arctic Soil Invests, 53; consult indust & govt; prin investr, Arctic Inst NAm, 55-67; Antarctic pedologic investr, NSF, 61-63; ed in chief, Soil Sci, 69-79; Lindback res award, Rutgers Univ. *Mem:* Fel Soil Sci Soc Am; Am Polar Soc; Am Arbit Asn; Am Geophys Union; fel Am Soc Agron. *Res:* Soil morphology; genesis and survey; soils of the Arctic and Alpine regions. *Mailing Add:* Dept Soils Lipman Hall Rutgers Univ New Brunswick NJ 08903

TEDROW, PAUL MULLER, b Ware, Mass, Apr 5, 40. LOW TEMPERATURE PHYSICS. *Educ:* Mass Inst Technol, SB, 61; Cornell Univ, PhD(physics), 66. *Prof Exp:* Fel physics, Cornell Univ, 66-67; MEM STAFF, FRANCIS BITTER NAT MAGNET LAB, MASS INST TECHNOL, 67- *Mem:* Fel Am Phys Soc. *Res:* Superconductivity; ferromagnetism. *Mailing Add:* Francis Bitter Nat Magnet Lab Mass Inst Technol Cambridge MA 02139

TEEBOR, GEORGE WILLIAM, b Vienna, Austria, July 22, 35; US citizen; m 58; c 3. CARCINOGENESIS, DNA REPAIR MECHANISMS. *Educ:* Yale Univ, BS, 56; Yeshiva Univ, MD, 61. *Prof Exp:* ASSOC PROF PATH, NY UNIV MED CTR, 65- *Mem:* Am Asn Cancer Res; Am Asn Pathologists. *Res:* Mammalian DNA repair enzymology; characterization of DNA damage. *Mailing Add:* NY Univ Med Ctr 550 1st St New York NY 10016

TEEGARDEN, BONNARD JOHN, b Elizabeth, NJ, Aug 23, 40; m 62; c 2. ASTROPHYSICS. *Educ:* Mass Inst Technol, BS, 62; Univ Md, PhD(physics), 67. *Prof Exp:* PHYSICIST ASTROPHYSICS, NASA GODDARD SPACE FLIGHT CTR, 63- *Mem:* Am Phys Soc; Am Astron Soc. *Res:* Gamma-ray astronomy. *Mailing Add:* NASA Goddard Space Flight Ctr Code 661 Greenbelt MD 20771

TEEGARDEN, DAVID MORRISON, b Dayton, Ohio, Jan 10, 41; m 66; c 3. ORGANIC CHEMISTRY, POLYMER CHEMISTRY. *Educ:* Ohio Wesleyan Univ, AB, 63; Univ Mich, MS, 65, PhD(org chem), 72. *Prof Exp:* Asst prof chem, Univ Wis-Platteville, 69-73; asst prof chem, St John Fisher Col, 73-79, assoc prof, 79-82; MEM RES STAFF, XEROX WEBSTER RES CTR, 80- *Concurrent Pos:* Fel, Xerox Webster Res Ctr, 79-80. *Mem:* Am Chem Soc. *Res:* Stereochemistry and mechanisms of reactions of bicyclic compounds; synthesis of functional monomers and polymers; mechanism of anionic polymerizations; polymer supported reactions. *Mailing Add:* 159 Village Lane Rochester NY 14610

TEEGARDEN, KENNETH JAMES, b Chicago, Ill, May 13, 28; m 59. PHYSICS. *Educ:* Univ Chicago, AB, 47, BS, 50; Univ Ill, MS, 51, PhD, 54. *Prof Exp:* Res assoc, 54-58, asst prof, 58-59, sr res assoc, 60-61, assoc prof, 61-66, PROF OPTICS, INST OPTICS, UNIV ROCHESTER, 66- *Concurrent Pos:* Alfred P Sloan Found fel, Univ Rochester, 59-63. *Mem:* Fel Am Phys Soc; Optical Soc Am. *Res:* Electronic properties of ionic solids and the solid rare gases. *Mailing Add:* Dept of Optics Univ of Rochester Rochester NY 14627

TEEGUARDEN, DENNIS EARL, b Gary, Ind, Aug 21, 31; m 54; c 2. FORESTRY ECONOMICS. *Educ:* Mich Tech Univ, BS, 53; Univ Calif, Berkeley, MF, 58, PhD(agr econ), 64. *Prof Exp:* Res asst, Pac Southwest Forest & Range Exp Sta, US Forest Serv, Berkeley, Calif, 57; asst specialist, Agr Exp Sta, 58-63, actg asst prof, Sch Forestry, 63, from asst prof to assoc prof, 64-73, PROF FORESTRY, SCH FORESTRY, UNIV CALIF, BERKELEY, 73-, CHMN DEPT FORESTRY & RESOURCE MGT, 78- *Mem:* Soc Am Foresters; Am Econ Asn. *Res:* Application of operations research techniques to problems of resource allocation in public and private forestry enterprises. *Mailing Add:* Dept of Forestry & Conserv Univ of Calif Berkeley CA 94720

TEEKELL, ROGER ALTON, b Elmer, La, Mar 3, 30; m 53; c 4. METABOLISM, BIOCHEMISTRY. *Educ:* La State Univ, BS, 51, MS, 55, PhD(nutrit, biochem), 58. *Prof Exp:* Asst, La State Univ, 54-58; res scientist, Agr Res Lab, Univ Tenn-AEC, 58-61; res chemist, Dow Chem Co, Tex, 61-63; from assoc prof to prof physiol, La State Univ, Baton Rouge, 63-67, prof poultry sci, 67-76; head, Dept Poultry Sci, 76-79, ASSOC DEAN, GRAD SCH, VA POLYTECH INST & STATE UNIV, BLACKSBURG, 79- *Mem:* Am Inst Biol Sci; Sigma Xi; Poultry Sci Asn; World Poultry Sci Asn. *Res:* Intermediary metabolism of amino acids and lipids using labeled compounds. *Mailing Add:* Dept Poultry Sci Va Polytech Inst & State Univ Blacksburg VA 24061

TEERI, ARTHUR EINO, b Dover, NH, July 29, 16; m 41; c 2. BIOCHEMISTRY. *Educ:* Univ NH, BS, 37, MS, 40; Rutgers Univ, PhD(biochem), 43. *Prof Exp:* Asst physiol chem, Univ NH, 38-40; res fel biochem, Res Labs, US Dept Interior, 40-41; asst prof, 43-53, PROF BIOCHEM, UNIV NH, 53- *Mem:* Fel AAAS; Am Chem Soc; Am Inst Nutrit; NY Acad Sci. *Res:* Physiological chemistry; animal and human nutrition; vitamins; clinical methods. *Mailing Add:* Dept of Biochem Univ of NH Durham NH 03824

TEERI, JAMES ARTHUR, b Exeter, NH, Feb 28, 44; m 67. ECOLOGY, POLAR BIOLOGY. *Educ:* Univ NH, BS, MS, 68; Duke Univ, PhD(bot), 72. *Prof Exp:* ASST PROF BIOL, UNIV CHICAGO, 72- *Concurrent Pos:* Assoc ed, Paleobiol, 74-; mem, Comn Optical Radiation Measurement, 74; actg chmn, Comt Evol Biol, 78. *Mem:* AAAS; Sigma Xi; Ecol Soc Am; Am Inst Biol Sci; Arctic Inst NAm. *Res:* Evolution of plant growth responses to environmental fluctuation; evolutionary biology. *Mailing Add:* Dept Biol Univ Chicago Chicago IL 60637

TEETER, JAMES WALLIS, b Hamilton, Ont, Mar 14, 37; m 60; c 3. MICROPALEONTOLOGY, PALEOECOLOGY. *Educ:* McMaster Univ, BSc, 60, MSc, 62; Rice Univ, PhD(paleont), 66. *Prof Exp:* From asst prof to assoc prof, 65-76, PROF GEOL, UNIV AKRON, 76- *Concurrent Pos:* Faculty res grants, Univ Akron, 69, 73, 74 & 78. *Mem:* Paleont Soc; Sigma Xi; Geol Soc Am; Int Oceanog Found; Soc Econ Paleont & Mineral. *Res:* Post Pleistocene depositional history, San Salvador Island, Bahamas; Key Largo limestone facies; Ordovician Nautiloid touchmarks; Ostracoda and environments of Caloosahatchee Formation; living Pelecypod behavior; marine Ostracoda dispersal. *Mailing Add:* Dept of Geol Univ of Akron Akron OH 44325

TEETER, MARTHA MARY, b Boston, Mass, Oct 15, 44. PROTEIN CRYSTALLOGRAPHY. *Educ:* Wellesley Col, BA, 66; Pa State Univ, PhD(inorg chem), 73. *Prof Exp:* Prog dir, Rohm and Haas, 73-74; Nat Cancer Inst fel, Dept Biol, Mass Inst Technol, 74-76, Naval Res Lab, 76-77; vis asst prof phys chem, 77-78, instr life sci chem, 78-80, RES ASST PROF, DEPT CHEM, BOSTON UNIV, 80- *Concurrent Pos:* Vis scientist, Dept Biol, Mass Inst Technol, 77- *Mem:* Am Chem Soc; Am Crystallog Asn; Biophys Soc; AAAS. *Res:* High resolution protein crystal structure determination (x-ray and neutron) as well as molecular dynamics; structure/function in membrane-active plant toxins; spectroscopy and lipid binding as well as crystallography. *Mailing Add:* Dept Chem Boston Univ 685 Commonwealth Ave Boston MA 02215

TEETER, RICHARD MALCOLM, b Berkeley, Calif, Feb 24, 26; m 49, 68; c 2. MASS SPECTROMETRY. *Educ:* Univ Calif, BS, 49; Univ Wash, PhD(chem), 54. *Prof Exp:* Res chemist, 54-64, sr res chemist, 64-68, SR RES ASSOC, CHEVRON RES CO, 68- *Mem:* Am Chem Soc; Am Soc Mass Spectrometry. *Res:* Analytical mass spectrometry; preparation of derivatives to aid analysis; reaction mechanisms in mass spectrometry; application of computers to mass spectrometry. *Mailing Add:* Chevron Res Co 576 Standard Ave Richmond CA 94802

TEETERS, WILLIAM DALE, b Englewood, NJ, May 4, 42; m 61; c 2. THEORETICAL HIGH ENERGY PHYSICS, THEORETICAL PHYSICS. *Educ:* Univ Iowa, BA, 64, MS, 66, PhD(physics), 68. *Prof Exp:* Asst prof physics, Chicago State Univ, 68-73, assoc prof, 73-77, prof, 77-81; DIR TECH SUPPORT, SPEAKEASY COMPUT CORP, 81- *Concurrent Pos:* Staff mem, Physics Div, Argonne Nat Lab, 75-76; consult, Argonne Nat Lab, 76- *Mem:* Am Phys Soc. *Res:* Elementary particle theory with emphasis on weak interactions; nuclear theory; relativistic treatment of bound states and applications to quark model. *Mailing Add:* Speakeasy Comput Corp 222 W Adams Chicago IL 60606

TEFFT, MELVIN, b Dec 15, 32; US citizen. RADIOTHERAPY. *Educ:* Harvard Univ, AB, 54; Boston Univ, MD, 58; Am Bd Radiol, dipl, 63. *Prof Exp:* Intern med, Boston City Hosp, 58-59; resident radiol, Mass Mem Hosp, 59-62; asst, Harvard Med Sch, 62-65, instr, 66-67, clin assoc, 67-69, asst prof, 69-70, from asst prof to assoc prof radiation ther, 70-73; prof radiol, Cornell Univ, 73-75; PROF RADIATION MED, BROWN UNIV, 75-; RADIOTHERAPIST, DEPT RADIATION ONCOL & ASSOC MEM, DEPT PEDIAT, RI HOSP, 75- *Concurrent Pos:* Asst radiol, Children's Hosp Med Ctr, 62-64, radiotherapist, Med Ctr & Tumor Ther Div, 64-70, chief, Div Radiother & Nuclear Med, 67-69, radiotherapist-in-chief, Dept Radiation Ther, 69-70; consult radiol, Lemuel Shattuck Hosp, 62-68, Mass Gen Hosp, 64-71 & Boston Lying-In Hosp, 66-74; consult radiother, Lemuel Shattuck Hosp, 66-70; consult, Dept Radiother, Tufts Med Sch at Lemuel Shattuck Hosp, 69-70; mem, Children's Cancer Chemother Group A, 69-; consult, Dept Radiation Ther, Mem Hosp, New York, 72-74; asst radiol, Sch Med, Boston Univ, 62-68; NIH clin fel radiation ther, Mass Gen Hosp, 63-64; assoc radiol, Peter Bent Brigham Hosp, 66-70; assoc prof therapeut radiol, Med Sch, Tufts Univ, 69-70; assoc attend radiotherapist, Mem Hosp, 70-71, attend radiotherapist, 73-75, dir med educ, Dept Radiation Ther, 73-75; assoc mem, Sloan-Kettering Inst, 70-71; assoc radiotherapist, Mass Gen Hosp, 71-73; attend radiologist, New York Hosp, 73-75. *Mem:* Fel Am Col Radiol; Am Soc Therapeut Radiologists; Am Radium Soc; Int Soc Pediat Oncol; AMA. *Res:* Pediatric oncology, combined radiation therapy and chemotherapy to enhance local control and disease-free survival; evaluation of normal tissue sensitivity by combined modalities of treatment. *Mailing Add:* Dept of Radiation Oncol RI Hosp Providence RI 02902

TEGGE, B(RUCE) R(OBERT), b Haddon Heights, NJ, May 31, 17; m 40; c 4. CHEMICAL ENGINEERING. *Educ:* Pa State Univ, BS, 38, MS, 40, PhD(chem eng), 42. *Prof Exp:* Asst petrol ref, Pa State Col, 40; SR ENG ASSOC, EXXON RES & ENG CO, 42- *Mem:* Am Textile Inst; Am Inst Chem Engrs; Am Chem Soc; Soc Plastics Engrs. *Res:* Equilibrium relationships between sulfur dioxide and pure binary hydrocarbon mixtures; performance of solvent extraction equipment; butyl rubber; paraxylene; petroleum resins; synthetic polymer plants; polypropylene; synthetic textile fibers; synthetic fertilizers; organic fungicides; polyesters; mastics and polyisobutylenes; detergents. *Mailing Add:* 68 Prospect St Madison NJ 07940

TEGGINS, JOHN E, b Wallasey, Eng, Jan 6, 37; m 60; c 3. INORGANIC CHEMISTRY. *Educ:* Univ Sheffield, BSc, 58; Boston Univ, AM, 60, PhD(chem), 65. *Prof Exp:* Res chemist, Courtaulds Can, Ltd, 60-62; res assoc radiochem, Iowa State Univ, 65-66; from asst prof to assoc prof, 66-75, PROF CHEM, AUBURN UNIV, MONTGOMERY, 75-, HEAD DEPT, 81- *Mem:* Am Chem Soc; sr mem Chem Inst Can. *Res:* Determination of thermodynamic and kinetic data for coordination complexes in aqueous solution. *Mailing Add:* 4425 Shamrock Ln Montgomery AL 36106

TEGNER, MIA JEAN, b Santa Monica, Calif, July 7, 47. MARINE & DEVELOPMENTAL BIOLOGY. *Educ:* Univ Calif, San Diego, BA, 69, PhD(marine biol), 74. *Prof Exp:* Res asst develop biol, 71-74, res biologist marine biol, 74-77, ASST RES BIOLOGIST MARINE BIOL, SCRIPPS INST OCEANOG, UNIV CALIF, SAN DIEGO, 77- *Concurrent Pos:* Researcher, Sea Grant, 74-, Develop Multispecies Mgt Kelp Bed Resources, 77-81 & Exp Abalone Enhancement Prog, 77-; chairperson, Joint Univ Calif Sea Grant Col & Calif Dept Fish & Game Exp Abalone Enhancement Prog, 77-81. *Mem:* AAAS; Am Soc Limnol & Oceanog; Am Soc Zoologists. *Res:* Kelp bed community ecology; living marine resources of the nearshore environment; how man's activities have affected the structure and dynamics of this community. *Mailing Add:* Scripps Inst of Oceanog La Jolla CA 92093

TEGTMEYER, CHARLES JOHN, b Hamilton, NY, July 25, 39; m 63. ANGIOGRAPHY & INTERVENTIONAL RADIOLOGY. *Educ:* Colgate Univ, BA, 61; George Washington Univ Sch Med, MD, 65. *Prof Exp:* Intern, George Washington Univ Hosp, 65-66, residency surg, 66-68, diagnostic radiol, 68-71; fel, Peter Bent Brigham Hosp, Harvard, 71-72; asst prof radiol, 72-75, asst prof anat, 73-77, assoc prof radiol, 75-78, ASSOC PROF ANAT, UNIV VA MED CTR, 77-, PROF RADIOL, 78-, DIR ANGIOGRAPHY & SPECIAL PROCEDURES, 74- *Concurrent Pos:* Founder & coordr, Sch Special Procedure, Univ Va Med Ctr, 72, dir, radiol med students, 72-81, bus mgr, Radiol Dept, 80-; mem adv coun radiol, Minn Mining & Manufacturing Co, 78; examiner, Am Bd Radiol, 79, 81; course dir, New Dimensions Tech Space Processes, 80 & 81; vis prof, radiol dept, WVa Univ, 80, Southwestern Med Sch, 82, vis staff, Martha Jefferson Hosp, 81- *Mem:* Soc Cardiovasc Radiol; fel Am Col Radiol; Am Roentgen Ray Soc; Radiol Soc NAm; Sigma Xi. *Res:* Angiography, arthrography, lymphography and other specialized invasive radiographic procedures including interventional radiology. *Mailing Add:* Dept Radiol Univ Va Med Ctr Charlottesville VA 22908

TEH, HUNG-SIA, b Telok Anson, Malaysia, Oct 2, 45; Can citizen; m 69; c 2. IMMUNOLOGY. *Educ:* Univ Alta, BSc, 69, PhD(biochem), 75. *Prof Exp:* Res fel immunol, Ont Cancer Inst, Toronto, 75-77; ASST PROF MICROBIOL, UNIV BC, VANCOUVER, 77- *Concurrent Pos:* Mem, Basel Inst Immunol, 81-82. *Mem:* Can Soc Immunol; Am Asn Immunologists. *Res:* Cellular immunology. *Mailing Add:* Dept Microbiol Univ BC Vancouver BC V6T 1W5 Can

TEHON, STEPHEN WHITTIER, b Shenandoah, Iowa, Oct 20, 20; m 42; c 5. ELECTRICAL ENGINEERING. *Educ:* Univ Ill, BS, 42, MS, 47, PhD(elec eng), 58. *Prof Exp:* Sr engr, Curtiss-Wright Corp, 47; instr elec eng, Univ Ill, 47-52; engr, Electronics Lab, Gen Elec Co, 52-60, consult engr, 60-66; res elec engr, Res Lab, Tecumseh Prod Co, 66-67; consult scientist, 67-80, PRIN STAFF SCIENTIST, ELECTRONICS LAB, GEN ELEC CO, 80- *Concurrent Pos:* Adj prof, Univ Mich, 66-67 & Syracuse Univ, 76-; vis prof, Clarkson Col Technol, Potsdam, NY, 79. *Mem:* Fel Inst Elec & Electronics Engrs. *Res:* Ultrasonic transducers; nondestructive testing; ultrasonic medical imaging; digital sensors. *Mailing Add:* 6056 Pine Grove Rd Clay NY 13041

TEICH, ABRAHAM HIRSH, b Winnipeg, Man, Dec 2, 33; m 56; c 3. PLANT BREEDING. *Educ:* Univ Man, BSA, 60, MSc, 62; Iowa State Univ, PhD(plant breeding), 65. *Prof Exp:* Tree breeder, Can Forestry Serv, 65-74; WHEAT BREEDER, CAN DEPT AGR, 74- *Res:* Winter wheat breeding. *Mailing Add:* 2886 Orion Circle Harrow ON N0R 1G0 Can

TEICH, MALVIN CARL, b New York, NY, May 4, 39. QUANTUM ELECTRONICS. *Educ:* Mass Inst Technol, SB, 61; Stanford Univ, MS, 62; Cornell Univ, PhD(quantum electronics), 66. *Prof Exp:* Res scientist, Lincoln Lab, Mass Inst Technol, 66-67; chmn, Dept Elec Eng & Comput Sci, 78-80, PROF ENG SCI, COLUMBIA UNIV, 67- *Concurrent Pos:* NSF res grant, 68-; John Simon Guggenheim Mem fel, 73. *Honors & Awards:* Browder J Thompson Mem Prize Award, Inst Elec & Electronics Engrs, 69. *Mem:* Am Phys Soc; Inst Elec & Electronics Engrs; Optical Soc Am; NY Acad Sci; Acoustical Soc Am. *Res:* Optical and infrared detection; lightwave communications; sensory perception. *Mailing Add:* Dept of Elec Eng & Comput Sci Columbia Univ New York NY 10027

TEICHER, HARRY, b Middle Village, NY, Jan 11, 27; m 51; c 3. FOOD SCIENCE & TECHNOLOGY. *Educ:* Queens Col, NY, BS, 48; Syracuse Univ, MS, 50, PhD(chem), 53. *Prof Exp:* Asst chem, Syracuse Univ, 49-53; res chemist, 53-56, res group leader, 56-81, RES MGR, RES & DEVELOP DEPT, MONSANTO CO, 81- *Mem:* AAAS; Am Chem Soc; Sigma Xi; Am Asn Cereal Chemists; Inst Food Technol. *Res:* Silica. *Mailing Add:* Monsanto Co Res & Develop Dept 800 N Lindbergh Blvd St Louis MO 63167

TEICHER, HENRY, b Jersey City, NJ, July 9, 22. MATHEMATICAL STATISTICS. *Educ:* Univ Iowa, BA, 46; Columbia Univ, MA, 47, PhD(math statist), 50. *Prof Exp:* Asst prof math, Univ Del, 50-51; from asst prof to prof math statist, Purdue Univ, 51-67; vis prof, Columbia Univ, 67-68; PROF MATH STATIST, RUTGERS UNIV, NEW BRUNSWICK, 68- *Concurrent Pos:* Vis asst prof, Stanford Univ, 55-56; vis assoc prof & mem inst math sci, NY Univ, 60-61. *Mem:* Am Math Soc; fel Inst Math Statist. *Res:* Probability and mathematical statistics, especially stopping rules, limit distributions and mixtures of distributions. *Mailing Add:* Statist Ctr Rutgers Univ New Brunswick NJ 08903

TEICHER, JOSEPH D, b New York, NY, Aug 1, 17; m 42; c 2. PSYCHIATRY. *Educ:* City Col New York, BS, 33; Columbia Univ, MA, 34; NY Univ, MD, 40; NY Psychoanal Inst, cert, 51. *Prof Exp:* Consult, Pub Schs, Bronxville, NY, 46-52; assoc clin prof psychiat, 53-60, PROF PSYCHIAT & BEHAV SCI, SCH MED, UNIV SOUTHERN CALIF, 60- *Concurrent Pos:* Dir child guid clin, St Luke's Hosp, New York, 47-52; dir, Child Guid Clin Los Angeles, 52-; chief psychiat, Children's Hosp, 53-58; mem fac, Southern Calif Psychoanal Inst, 54- *Mem:* Fel Am Psychiat Asn; Am Psychoanal Asn. *Res:* Normal and atypical child development; communication with the elderly; studies in attempted suicide; alcoholism and drug abuse. *Mailing Add:* 152 S Lasky Dr Beverly Hills CA 90212

TEICHLER-ZALLEN, DORIS, b New York, NY; c 2. CELL BIOLOGY, GENETICS. *Educ:* Brooklyn Col, BS, 61; Harvard Univ, AM, 63, PhD(biol), 66. *Prof Exp:* NIH fel biol, Univ Rochester, 66-69, asst prof, 69-70; ASST PROF BIOL, NAZARETH COL ROCHESTER, 77- *Concurrent Pos:* Fel pediat & genetics, Sch Med, Univ Rochester, 77- *Mem:* AAAS; Am Soc Plant Physiologists; Sigma Xi. *Res:* Development of new methods of prenatal detection of genetic disorders; analysis of the genetic and biochemical basis of chloroplast development. *Mailing Add:* Nazareth Col Rochester 4245 E Ave Rochester NY 14610

TEICHMAN, ROBERT, b Berlin, Ger, June 22, 23; nat US; m 62; c 2. BIOSTATISTICS. *Educ:* Univ Conn, BS, 51, MS, 53; NC State Univ, PhD(animal sci), 67. *Prof Exp:* Asst animal nutrit, Univ Conn, 50-58, asst exp statist, NC State Univ, 58-60, asst statistician, 60-61; mgr res statist dept, Ralson Purina Co, 61-67; assoc prof exp statist, NC State Univ, 67-69; mgr biostatist, ICI Americas Inc, 69-81; CONSULT BIOSTATIST & DATA MGT, 82- *Mem:* Am Statist Asn; Biomet Soc; Am Soc Pharmacol & Exp Therapeut. *Res:* Design and analysis of biological experiments; research in statistical procedures. *Mailing Add:* 1100 Brantin Rd Wilmington DE 19803

TEICHMANN, THEODOR, b Königsberg, Ger, Sept 16, 23; nat US; m 53; c 2. APPLIED PHYSICS. *Educ:* Univ Cape Town, BSc, 43, MSc, 45; Princeton Univ, Am, 47, PhD(physics), 49. *Prof Exp:* Jr lectr elec eng, Univ Cape Town, 44-46; res assoc physics, Princeton, 50-52; res physicist, Res & Develop Labs, Hughes Aircraft Co, 52-55; mgr systs anal & simulation, Missiles & Space Div, Lockheed Aircraft Corp, 55-56, mgr nuclear physics, 56-57, sci asst to dir res, 57-60; consult scientist satellite systs, 60; mem res & develop staff, Spec Nuclear Effects Lab, Gen Atomic Div, Gen Dynamics Corp, 60-68; prin scientist, KMS Technol Ctr, Calif, 68-72, prin scientist, KMS Fusion Inc, Ann Arbor, 72-75; consult, Phys Dynamics, Inc, 75-77; PHYSICIST, BROOKHAVEN NAT LAB, 78- *Mem:* AAAS; Am Phys Soc; Am Math Soc; Soc Indust & Appl Math. *Res:* Operations research; continuum mechanics; energy conversion; systems analysis; application of inertially confined fusion to energy production on both electric and gas sectors; energy systems analysis. *Mailing Add:* PO Box 424 Upton NY 11973

TEICHNER, VICTOR JEROME, b New York, NY, Oct 22, 26; m 55; c 1. PSYCHIATRY, PSYCHOANALYSIS. *Educ:* Temple Univ, MD, 49; Columbia Univ, cert psychoanal med, 63. *Prof Exp:* Sr psychiatrist, Bellevue Psychiat Hosp, New York, 54-59; DIR DEPT PSYCHIAT, METROP HOSP CTR, 72-; PROF CLIN PSYCHIAT, NY MED COL, 73- *Concurrent Pos:* Ed, Bull Asn Psychoanal Div, 71-75, consult ed, 75-78; asst ed, J Am Acad Psychoanal, 72- *Mem:* Fel Am Acad Psychoanal; fel Am Psychiat Asn. *Res:* Psychotherapy; psychiatric administration. *Mailing Add:* 145 E 84th St New York NY 10028

TEICHROEW, DANIEL, b Can, Jan 5, 25; nat US; m 50; c 1. MATHEMATICS. *Educ:* Univ Toronto, BA, 48, MA, 49; Univ NC, PhD(statist), 53. *Prof Exp:* Res assoc, Univ NC, 51-52; mathematician, Nat Bur Stand, DC & Inst Numerical Anal, Univ Calif, Los Angeles, 52-55; sr electronics appln specialist, Nat Cash Register Co, 55, spec rep prod develop, 55-56, head bus systs anal, 56-57; from assoc prof to prof mgt, Grad Sch Bus, Stanford Univ, 57-64; prof orgn sci & head div, Case Western Reserve Univ, 64-68; chmn dept, 68-73, PROF INDUST ENG, UNIV MICH, ANN ARBOR, 68- *Concurrent Pos:* Lectr, Sch Bus Admin, Univ Southern Calif, 56-57; ed sci & bus appln sect, Communications, Asn Comput Mach, 63- *Mem:* Asn Comput Mach; Inst Mgt Sci (vpres, 67-); Opers Res Soc Am; Inst Math Statist; Am Math Soc. *Res:* Development and application of scientific techniques to organizational problems, particularly operations research, management science and computer techniques. *Mailing Add:* Dept of Indust Eng 231 W Eng Bldg Univ of Mich Ann Arbor MI 48109

TEIGER, MARTIN, b New York, Dec 30, 36; m 64; c 1. PHYSICS, ASTRONOMY. *Educ:* Columbia Univ, AB, 58, MA, 60, PhD(physics), 65. *Prof Exp:* Lectr physics, City Col New York, 61-65, instr, 65-66; from asst prof to assoc prof, 66-75, chmn dept, 69-79, PROF PHYSICS, LONG ISLAND UNIV, 75- *Mem:* AAAS; Am Phys Soc; Am Pub Health Asn; NY Acad Sci. *Res:* Planetary atmospheres and surface environments; radiative transfer theory; numerical methods for computers; environmental management. *Mailing Add:* Dept of Physics Long Island Univ Brooklyn NY 11201

TEIN, JOHN KAI, b China, June 4, 40; US citizen. METALLURGY, MATERIALS SCIENCE. *Educ:* Worcester Polytech Inst, BSME, 62; Yale Univ, MEng, 64; Carnegie-Mellon Univ, MS, 67, PhD(metall), 69. *Prof Exp:* Proj supvr, Chase Brass & Copper Co, Conn, 64-65; res assoc metall & mat sci, Adv Mat Res & Develop Lab, Pratt & Whitney Aircraft, 67-71; assoc prof, 71-76, PROF METALL, COLUMBIA UNIV, 76- *Mem:* Am Inst Mining, Metall & Petrol Engrs. *Res:* Effects of solidification and heat treating conditions on the microstructure and properties of materials; the migrational characteristics of interfaces; the effect of stress on particle coarsening; energetics of reaction processes; creep; fatigue, oxidation; alloy design. *Mailing Add:* Dept of Metall Columbia Univ New York NY 10027

TEIPEL, JOHN WILLIAM, b Covington, Ky, Feb 17, 43; m 66; c 2. BIOCHEMISTRY, IMMUNOASSAYS. *Educ:* Rockhurst Col, BA, 64; Duke Univ, PhD(biochem), 68. *Prof Exp:* Am Cancer Soc fel biochem, Univ Calif, Berkeley, 68-70; asst prof chem & biochem, Univ Ill, Urbana, 70-72; scientist, 72-74, sr scientist, 74-75, prin scientist, 75-76, RES DIR, ORTHO DIAG SYSTS, INC, 76- *Res:* Physical biochemistry of proteins and enzymes; labelled immunoassays; immunochemistry. *Mailing Add:* Dept of Immunosci Ortho Diag Systs Inc Raritan NJ 08869

TEITEL, ROBERT J(ERRELL), b Indianapolis, Ind, Aug 4, 22. METALLURGY. *Educ:* Purdue Univ, BS, 44; Mass Inst Technol, ScD(metall), 48. *Prof Exp:* Assoc metallurgist, Brookhaven Nat Labs, 48-53, metallurgist, 53-55; group leader, Nuclear & Basic Res Lab, Dow Chem Co, Mich, 55-60; sr tech specialist, Rocketdyne Div, NAm Aviation, Inc, 60-61; prin scientist, Douglas Aircraft Co, 61-72; head mat eng dept, KMS Fusion, Inc, Ann Arbor, Mich, 72-76; PRES, ROBERT J TEITEL ASSOCS, 76- *Concurrent Pos:* Civilian with AEC, 44. *Mem:* AAAS; Am Soc Metals; fel Am Nuclear Soc. *Res:* Material sciences; nuclear fission and fusion reactor materials and design; nuclear fuel cycles; missile materials; space nuclear power plants; hydrogen production and storage systems; fossil fuel systems; metallurgical thermodynamics; liquid metal corrosion; alloy phase diagrams. *Mailing Add:* Robert J Teitel Assocs PO Box 81921 San Diego CA 92138

TEITEL, SIDNEY, medicinal chemistry, see previous edition

TEITELBAUM, CHARLES LEONARD, b Brooklyn, NY, June 14, 25; m 50. ANALYTICAL CHEMISTRY. *Educ:* Brooklyn Col, BA, 45; Purdue Univ, MS, 48, PhD(org chem), 51. *Prof Exp:* Res chemist, Heyden Chem Corp, 50-53; prin chemist, Battelle Mem Inst, 53-58; chemist, Coty, Inc Div, Chas Pfizer & Co, 58-65 & Florasynth, Inc, 65-66; RES SPECIALIST, GEN FOODS CORP, 66- *Mem:* Am Chem Soc. *Res:* Analysis of natural products relating to odor and flavor. *Mailing Add:* 225 W 11th St New York NY 10014

TEITELBAUM, DANIEL THAU, b New York, NY, May 26, 35. TOXICOLOGY, MEDICINE. *Educ:* Hamilton Col, AB, 56; Jewish Theol Seminary Am, MHL, 60; Albert Einstein Col Med, MD, 64. *Prof Exp:* Asst prof med & toxicol, Univ Colo Med Ctr, 68-70; pres, Poisonlab, Inc, 70-73; pres, Poisonlab-Enbionics, Chemed Corp, 73-78; med dir toxicol, Poison Lab-Enbionics, Metpath Co, 78-80; WITH CTR TOXICOL, MAN & ENVIRON, 80- *Concurrent Pos:* WHO travelling fel, Geneva, 68; asst clin prof med & prev med, Univ Colo Med Ctr, 70-; chief, Poisoning Treatment Ctr, St Anthony Hosp, Denver, 70-; chmn, Toxicol Diag Prod, Adv Comt, US Food & Drug Admin, Washington DC, 75-78; special consult, Occup Safety & Health Admin, Dept Labor, Washington DC, 76- *Mem:* Am Col Clin Pharmacol; Am Acad Clin Toxicol (secy treas, 68-70); Am Soc Clin Pathologists; Am Indust Hygiene Asn; Occupational Med Asn. *Res:* Clinical and environmental toxicology. *Mailing Add:* Ctr Toxicol Man & Environ 6825 E Tennesse Ave Suite 365 Denver CO 80224

TEITELBAUM, PHILIP, b Brooklyn, NY, Oct 9, 28; c 3. NEUROSCIENCE. *Educ:* City Col New York, BS, 50; Johns Hopkins Univ, MA, 52, PhD, 54. *Prof Exp:* Asst prof physiol psychol, Harvard Univ, 56-59; assoc prof, Univ Pa, 59-63, prof, 63-73; PROF PSYCHOL, UNIV ILL, CHAMPAIGN, 73-, PROF, CTR ADVAN STUDY, 80- *Concurrent Pos:* Fel behav sci, Ctr Advan Study, Stanford Univ, 75-76; Fulbright fel, Dept Zool, Tel Aviv Univ, 78-79. *Mem:* Nat Acad Sci; Am Physiol Soc; Am Psychol Asn (pres, 77); Am Physiol Soc. *Mailing Add:* Dept Psychol Univ Ill 603 E Daniel St Champaign IL 61820

TEITLER, SIDNEY, b New York, NY, July 1, 30. PHYSICS. *Educ:* Long Island Univ, BS, 51; Univ Ill, MS, 53; Syracuse Univ, PhD(physics), 57. *Prof Exp:* PHYSICIST, US NAVAL RES LAB, 57- *Mailing Add:* Code 1405 US Naval Res Lab Washington DC 20375

TEIXEIRA, ARTHUR ALVES, b Fall River, Mass, Jan 30, 44; m 66; c 2. FOOD ENGINEERING, AGRICULTURAL ENGINEERING. *Educ:* Univ Mass, BS, 66, MS, 68, PhD(food eng), 71. *Prof Exp:* Proj leader res, Ross Div, Abbott Labs, 71-73, group leader mgt, 73-77; PROJ LEADER CONSULT, ARTHUR D LITTLE, INC, 77- *Honors & Awards:* Presidential Award, Ross Div, Abbott Labs, 75. *Mem:* Inst Food Technologists; Am Soc Agr Engrs; Sigma Xi. *Res:* Thermal processing of canned foods; food product and process development; applications of energy-saving technologies in food processing. *Mailing Add:* Arthur D Little Inc Acorn Park Cambridge MA 02140

TEJA, AMYN SADRUDDIN, b Zanzibar, Tanzania, May 11, 46; UK citizen; m 71; c 2. PHASE EQUILIBRIA, CRITICAL PROPERTIES. *Educ:* Imp Col London, BSc, & ACGI, 68, PhD(chem eng) & DIC, 72. *Prof Exp:* Vis assoc prof chem eng, Ohio State Univ, 80; res fel, Loughborough Univ, Eng, 71-74, lectr, 74-80; vis assoc prof, Univ Del, 78-79; ASSOC PROF CHEM ENG, GA INST TECHNOL, 80- *Concurrent Pos:* Assoc ed, Chem Eng J, 73- *Mem:* Am Inst Chem Engrs. *Res:* Measurement, correlation and prediction of the thermodynamic and transport properties of mixtures with emphasis on the critical region and on mixtures of technological interest. *Mailing Add:* Sch Chem Eng Ga Inst Technol Atlanta GA 30332

TEJA, EDWARD RAY, b Ft Bragg, NC, Feb 22, 48; m 69; c 2. ELECTRONICS, ECONOMICS. *Educ:* Calif State Univ, Fullerton, BA, 77. *Prof Exp:* Electronic eng test equip, Anaconda Telecommunications, 76-78; WESTERN ED COMPUT, EDN MAG, CAHNER'S PUBL CO, 78- *Mem:* AAAS. *Res:* Microcomputer software and hardware; voice input and output. *Mailing Add:* EDN Mag 1220 N Ventura St Anaheim CA 92801

TEJWANI, COPI ASSUNDOMAL, b Dadu, India, March 1, 46; m 73; c 1. METABOLIC REGULATION, DRUGS. *Educ:* Nagpur Univ, India, BS, 66, MS, 68; All-India Inst Med Sci, PhD(biochem), 73. *Prof Exp:* Fel enzyme, Sch Med, St Louis Univ, 73-74 & Roche Inst Molecular Biol, 74-76; clin asst prof, 76-78, ASST PROF PHARMACOL, COL MED, OHIO STATE

UNIV, 78- *Concurrent Pos:* Vis prof, Univ Sao Paulo, Brazil, 78 & Moscow State Univ, 81; Lectr, Univ Chile, 78, Univ Wroclaw, Poland, 81 & Univ Ioannina, Greece, 81; consult, Ortho Pharmaceut Corp, NJ, 80; prin investr, numerous res grants biochem pharmacol, 78- *Mem:* Am Asn Clin Chem; AAAS. *Res:* Regulation of key enzymes involved in glycolysis and gluconegenesis; mechanism of action of ethanol, tumor-promoters and retinoids; role of endorphins in obesity and cardiovascular diseases; energy metabolism in human platelets, effect of carcinogens on cyclic nucleotides. *Mailing Add:* Dept Pharmacol Col Med Ohio State Univ 333 W 10th Ave Columbus OH 43210

TEK, MEHMET RASIN, b Istanbul, Turkey, Jan 6, 27; nat US; m 52; c 3. CHEMICAL ENGINEERING, PETROLEUM ENGINEERING. *Educ:* Univ Mich, BSE, 48, MSE, 49, PhD(mech eng), 53. *Prof Exp:* Test engr, Int Gen Elec Co, 50-51; res asst, eng res inst, Univ Mich, 51-53, res engr, 53-56, res group leader, 56-57; sect mgr, Phillips Petrol, 57; from asst prof to assoc prof, 57-65, PROF CHEM ENG, UNIV MICH, ANN ARBOR, 65- *Concurrent Pos:* Consult to over 50 petrol, natural gas & pipeline co in 6 countries, UN, Dept of Energy & Exec Off of President. *Mem:* Soc Petrol Engrs; Am Soc Mech Engrs; Am Inst Chem Engrs. *Res:* Fluid dynamics; petroleum production and reservoir engineering; multiphase flow; natural gas storage. *Mailing Add:* Dept Chem Eng Univ Mich Ann Arbor MI 48104

TEKEL, RALPH, b New York, NY, May 27, 20; m 60; c 2. ORGANIC CHEMISTRY. *Educ:* Polytech Inst NY, BS, 41; Purdue Univ, MS, 47, PhD(chem), 49. *Prof Exp:* Asst tech dir, Vitamins, Inc, Ill, 48-49; res assoc, Carter Prod, NJ, 49-51; mgr pilot plant, Nat Drug Co, 51-60; asst to mgr chem div, Wyeth Labs, 60-63; dir org res, Betz Lab, 63-65; from asst prof to assoc prof org chem, 65-74, ASSOC PROF CHEM, LA SALLE COL, 74- *Concurrent Pos:* Lectr, Holy Family Col, Pa, 66-67; consult, Am Electronic Labs, 66- *Mem:* AAAS; fel Am Inst Chem; Am Chem Soc. *Res:* Medicinals; biochemicals; halogen chemicals; pilot plant development; continuous thin layer chromatography. *Mailing Add:* Dept of Chem La Salle Col Philadelphia PA 19141

TEKELI, SAIT, b Samsun, Turkey, June 14, 32; m 59; c 1. VETERINARY MEDICINE, PATHOLOGY. *Educ:* Univ Ankara, DVM, 54, PhD(path), 58; Univ Wis-Madison, MS, 62, PhD(avian leukosis), 64. *Prof Exp:* Dist vet, Dept Agr, Samsun, Turkey, 54-55; res asst animal path, Univ Ankara, 55-60; res asst vet sci, Univ Wis-Madison, 60-64, res asst bovine leukosis, 66-67; res pathologist, Norwich Pharmacal Corp, 67-69; PATHOLOGIST, ABBOTT LABS, 69- *Mem:* Soc Toxicol; Int Acad Path; Soc Pharmacol & Environ Path. *Res:* Drug toxicity; drug-induced lesions as well as chemical carcinogens. *Mailing Add:* Dept of Path Abbott Labs North Chicago IL 60064

TELANG, VASANT G, b Kumta, India, July 18, 35. MEDICINAL CHEMISTRY. *Educ:* Univ Bombay, BS, 56, MS, 64; Univ RI, PhD(pharmaceut chem), 68. *Prof Exp:* Lab instr pharmaceut chem, Univ Bombay, 59-62, asst prof pharm, 62-63; teaching asst pharmaceut chem, Col Pharm, Univ RI, 63-68; NIH res specialist, Col Pharm, Univ Minn, Minneapolis, 68-74; mem staff, Col Pharm, 74-80, ASSOC PROF BIOMED CHEM, HOWARD UNIV, 80-, ASSOC DEAN, SCH PHARM, 80- *Concurrent Pos:* Consult, Suneeta Labs, India, 70- *Mem:* Indian Pharmaceut Asn; Am Chem Soc. *Res:* Mechanism of action of narcotic analgesics and their antagonists. *Mailing Add:* 1010 Palmer Rd Oxion Hill MD 20022

TELEGDI, VALENTINE LOUIS, b Budapest, Hungary, Jan 11, 22; nat US; m 50. PHYSICS. *Educ:* Univ Lausanne, MSc, 46; Swiss Fed Inst Technol, PhD(physics), 50. *Prof Exp:* Asst physics, Swiss Fed Inst Technol, 47-50; from instr to prof, 50-71, ENRICO FERMI DISTINGUISHED SERV PROF PHYSICS, UNIV CHICAGO, 71- *Concurrent Pos:* Vis mem, H H Wills Lab, Univ Bristol, 48; lectr, Northwestern Univ, 53-54; vis res fel, Calif Inst Technol, 53; Ford fel & NSF vis scientist, Europ Orgn Nuclear Res, Geneva, 59; Loeb vis prof, Harvard Univ, 66; univ lectr, NY Univ, 67. *Mem:* Am Phys Soc. *Res:* Nuclear emulsion technique; experiment and theory of interaction of nuclei with photons; Compton effect of proton; symmetry properties of weak interactions; muon decay and absorption; decay of free neutron; magnetic properties of the muon; hypernuclei; long-lived strange particles. *Mailing Add:* Dept of Physics Univ of Chicago 5640 Ellis Ave Chicago IL 60637

TELETZKE, GERALD H(OWARD), b Beaver Dam, Wis, Mar 22, 28; m 52; c 2. SANITARY ENGINEERING. *Educ:* Univ Wis, BSCE, 52, MSCE, 53, PhD(sanit eng), 56. *Prof Exp:* Instr civil eng, Univ Wis, 54-55; asst prof sanit eng, Purdue Univ, 56-58, assoc prof, 58-59; dir sanit eng res, Eimco Corp, 59-61; sanitary engr, Zimpro Inc, Sterling Drug Inc, 61-65, exec vpres, 65-69, pres, 69-76, V PRES, STERLING DRUG INC, 76-; DIR, GEN TEL & ELECTRON, WIS, 76- *Concurrent Pos:* Dir, River Valley State Bank, Rothschild, Wis, 73- *Res:* Water, sewage, industrial waste treatment and solids disposal. *Mailing Add:* Sterling Drug Inc Military Rd Rothschild WI 54474

TELFAIR, WILLIAM BOYS, b Richmond, Ind, Apr 8, 47; m 69; c 2. PHYSICS, COMPUTER SCIENCE. *Educ:* Pa State Univ, MS, 72, PhD(physics), 74. *Prof Exp:* Physicist, Wilks Sci Corp, 74-77; physicist indust res instrument, 77-80, MGR, FOXBORO/WILKS, INC, 80- *Honors & Awards:* Indust Res 100 Award, 77. *Mem:* Am Asn Physics Teachers; Optical Soc Am. *Res:* Development of infrared instrumentation to yield higher precise line strength and absorbance measurements; microcomputer equipment to control and automatically reduce the data. *Mailing Add:* Foxboro/Wilks Inc 140 Water St South Norwalk CT 06856

TELFER, NANCY, b San Francisco, Calif, Apr 15, 30. MEDICINE, NUCLEAR MEDICINE. *Educ:* Stanford Univ, AB, 51; Med Col Pa, MD, 56; Am Bd Internal Med, dipl, 63 & 77; Am Bd Nuclear Med, dipl, 72. *Prof Exp:* Intern, Los Angeles County-Univ Southern Calif Med Ctr, 56-57, resident internal med, 57-60; instr med, Ctr Health Sci, Univ Calif, Los Angeles, 60-61, asst prof, 62-67; asst prof, 67-69, ASSOC PROF RADIOL & MED, LOS ANGELES COUNTY-UNIV SOUTHERN CALIF MED CTR, 69- *Concurrent Pos:* Los Angeles County Heart Asn res fel, Isotope Lab Med, Cantonal Hosp, Geneva, Switz, 61-62; Kate Meade Hurd fel, Woman's Med Col Pa, 61-62. *Mem:* Am Fedn Clin Res; fel Am Col Physicians; Soc Nuclear Med; fel Am Col Nuclear Physicians. *Res:* Body electrolyte composition using radioactive tracers and the dilution principle; computer analysis of radionuclide cardiac and pulmonary function studies; soft tissue deposition of 99m technetium diphorphonate; red blood cell 86rubidium uptake. *Mailing Add:* LAC-USC Med Ctr 1200 N State St Box 772 Los Angeles CA 90033

TELFER, WILLIAM HARRISON, b Seattle, Wash, June 21, 24; m 50; c 2. REPRODUCTIVE BIOLOGY, DEVELOPMENTAL BIOLOGY. *Educ:* Reed Col, BA, 48; Harvard Univ, MS, 49, PhD(biol), 52. *Prof Exp:* Jr fel, Harvard Soc Fels, 52-54; from asst prof to prof biol, 54-73, chmn grad group, 60-70, prof zool & chmn dept biol, 73-77, PROF BIOL, UNIV PA, 78- *Concurrent Pos:* Guggenheim fel, Stanford Univ, 60-61; NSF sr fel, Univ Miami, 68-69; staff mem, NIH training prog in fertilization & gamete physiology, Marine Biol Lab, Woods Hole, Mass, 71-; res assoc biochem, Univ Ariz, 81-82. *Mem:* Am Soc Zool; Soc Devleop Biol. *Res:* Physiology and developmental aspects of egg formation and blood proteins in insects. *Mailing Add:* Dept of Biol Univ of Pa Philadelphia PA 19174

TELFORD, IRA ROCKWOOD, b Idaho Falls, Idaho, May 6, 07; m 33; c 4. ANATOMY. *Educ:* Univ Utah, AB, 31, AM, 33; George Washington Univ, PhD(anat), 42. *Prof Exp:* Sch teacher, Idaho, 33-37; instr anat, Sch Med, George Washington Univ, 41-43, from asst prof to assoc prof, 43-47; prof & chmn dept, Sch Dent, Univ Tex, 47-53; prof & chmn dept, Sch Med, George Washington Univ, 53-72; prof anat, Schs Med & Dent, Georgetown Univ, 72-78. *Concurrent Pos:* Vis prof anat, Uniformed Serv Univ, 78- *Mem:* Soc Exp Biol & Med; Am Asn Anat; Am Acad Neurol. *Res:* Histology, muscle and nerve studies in vitamin E deficiency; vitamins; cancer in dietary deficiencies; muscular dystrophy. *Mailing Add:* Dept of Anat Georgetown Univ Schs Med & Dent Washington DC 20007

TELFORD, JAMES WARDROP, b Merbein, Australia, Aug 16, 27; m 54; c 3. ATMOSPHERIC PHYSICS, COMPUTER SCIENCE. *Educ:* Univ Melbourne, BSc, 50, DSc(atmospheric convection), 70; Univ Sydney, dipl numerical anal automatic comput, 62. *Prof Exp:* Sr res scientist, Radiophys Div, Commonwealth Sci & Indust Res Orgn, 50-65; vis scientist, Dept Cloud Physics, Imp Col, Univ London, 65-66; sr res scientist, Radiophys Div, Commonwealth Sci & Indust Res Orgn, 66-67; dep dir lab atmospheric physics & res prof, 67-78, DIR AIR MOTION LAB & RES PROF, DESERT RES INST, UNIV NEV SYST, RENO, 78- *Concurrent Pos:* Dept Defense res contract, Atmospheric Sci Ctr, Desert Res Inst, Reno, 67-81, NSF res grants, 70-81, lectr, Univ Nev, Reno, 78. *Mem:* Fel Am Meteorol Soc; fel Royal Meteorol Soc; Sigma Xi; AAAS. *Res:* Experimental and theoretical work on coalescence mechanisms in clouds; theory of stochastic coalescence in warm clouds; theory of clear air and cloudy air convection; airborne air motion measuring system; thunderstorm theory. *Mailing Add:* Atmospheric Sci Ctr Stead Campus Univ Nev Syst Reno NV 89507

TELFORD, SAM ROUNTREE, JR, b Winter Haven, Fla, Aug 25, 32; m 57; c 3. EPIZOOTIOLOGY. *Educ:* Univ Va, BA, 55; Univ Fla, MS, 61; Univ Calif, Los Angeles, PhD(zool), 64. *Prof Exp:* Lectr zool, Univ Calif, Los Angeles, 64-65; Nat Inst Allergy & Infectious Dis res fel parasitol, Inst Infectious Dis, Univ Tokyo, 65-67; mem staff, Gorgas Mem Lab, CZ, 67-70; int assoc cur, 70, asst cur, 70-73, asst prof biol sci & zool, 70-73, FIELD RES ASSOC, FLA STATE MUS, UNIV FLA, 73- *Concurrent Pos:* Med Zoologist, WHO, Geneva, Switz, 73, Chagas Dis Vector Res Unit, Acarigua, Venezuela, 73-75 & Vertebrate Pest Control Ctr, Karachi, Pakistan, 75-77; WHO Spec Prog for Res & Training in Trop Dis-Div Malaria, Geneva, Switz, 77-78; Rodent Control Demonstration Unit, WHO, Rangoon, Burma, 78-80; proj leader, Denmark-Tanzania Rodent Control, Morogoro, 81- *Mem:* Am Soc Ichthyologists & Herpetologists; Am Soc Parasitol; Soc Protozool; Soc Study Amphibians & Reptiles. *Res:* Herpetology; parasitology; ecology; population dynamics of reptilian host-parasite associations; lower vertebrate parasitology; ecology and systematics of reptiles and amphibians; saurian malaria; zoonotic disease. *Mailing Add:* Fla State Mus Univ Fla Gainesville FL 32601

TELFORD, WILLIAM MURRAY, b Ottawa, Ont, Aug 7, 17; m 42; c 2. PHYSICS, GEOPHYSICS. *Educ:* McGill Univ, BSc, 39, MSc, 41, PhD(physics), 49. *Prof Exp:* Engr, Res Enterprises, Ont, 41-45; from asst prof to assoc prof geophys, 60-75, RES ASSOC PHYSICS, McGILL UNIV, 45-, PROF GEOPHYS, 75- *Res:* Radar; high energy accelerators; applied geophysics. *Mailing Add:* Dept of Mining & Metall Eng McGill Univ Montreal PQ H3A 2K6 Can

TELIONIS, DEMETRI PYRROS, b Athens, Greece, Mar 17, 41; m 67. AERODYNAMICS, APPLIED MATHEMATICS. *Educ:* Nat Tech Univ Athens, dipl, 64; Cornell Univ, MS, 69, PhD(aerospace eng), 70. *Prof Exp:* Mech engr, Royal Greek Navy Shipyards, 64-67; asst prof aerospace eng, 70-74, assoc prof eng mech, 74-78, PROF ENG MECH, VA POLYTECH INST & STATE UNIV, 78- *Concurrent Pos:* Consult, Commun Orgn of Greece, 67 & Hellenic Air Force, 77- *Mem:* Assoc fel Am Inst Aeronaut & Astronaut; Sigma Xi; Tech Chamber Greece. *Res:* Incompressible and compressible aerodynamics; viscous flows; boundary-layer theory; acoustics; applied mechanics; turbulent flows; unsteady aerodynamics; experimental fluid mechanics. *Mailing Add:* Dept Eng Sci & Mech Va Polytech Inst & State Univ Blacksburg VA 24061

TELKES, MARIA, b Budapest, Hungary, Dec 12, 00; nat US. SOLAR ENERGY CONVERSION, THERMAL ENERGY STORAGE. *Educ:* Univ Budapest, BA, 20, PhD(phys chem), 24. *Hon Degrees:* DSc, St Joseph Col, Conn, 57. *Prof Exp:* Instr physics, Univ Budapest, 23-24; biophysicist, Cleveland Clin Found, 26-37; engr, Res Dept, Westinghouse Elec & Mfg Co, 37-39; res assoc, Mass Inst Technol, 39-53; proj dir solar energy prog, Res

Div, NY Univ, 53-58; res dir, Solar Energy Lab, Curtiss-Wright Corp, 58-60; dir res, Cryo-Therm, Inc, Pa, 60-64; mgr thermodyn lab, Melpar Inc, Westinghouse Air Brake Co, 64-69; sr res specialist, Nat Ctr Energy Mgt & Power, Univ Pa, 69-72; sr scientist, Inst Energy Conversion, Univ Del, 72-77; dir solar thermal storage develop, Am Technol Univ, 77-80; CONSULT, 80- *Mem:* Am Chem Soc; Solar Energy Soc; Am Soc Heating, Refrigerating & Air-Conditioning Engr; Soc Women Engrs. *Res:* Solar-thermal storage materials used in solar heated and cooled buildings; thermoelectric generators; semiconductors; phase-change thermal control of terrestrial and space applications. *Mailing Add:* Suite 821 10500 Rockville Pike Rockville MD 20852

TELL, BENJAMIN, b Philadelphia, Pa, Dec 11, 36; m 66; c 2. PHYSICS. *Educ:* Columbia Univ, BA, 58; Univ Mich, Ann Arbor, MS, 60, PhD(physics), 63. *Prof Exp:* Mem tech staff, Bell Tel Labs, 63-77; mem staff, Philips Industs N V Philips Res Lab, Eindhoven Holland, 78-80. *Mem:* Am Phys Soc. *Res:* Optical and electrical properties of semiconductors. *Mailing Add:* Crawford Corner Rd Holmdel NJ 07733

TELLE, JOHN MARTIN, b Akron, Ohio, Nov 3, 47; m 68; c 3. LASERS. *Educ:* Univ Colo, BS, 69; Cornell Univ, MS, 72, PhD(physics), 75. *Prof Exp:* RES SCIENTIST LASER PHYSICS, LOS ALAMOS NAT LAB,75- *Mem:* Am Phys Soc. *Res:* Optically pumped infrared gas lasers. *Mailing Add:* 210 Garver Lane White Rock NM 87544

TELLER, DANIEL MYRON, b Nashville, Tenn, Feb 10, 30; m 58; c 2. ORGANIC CHEMISTRY. *Educ:* Northwestern Univ, BS, 52; Loyola Univ, Ill, MS, 54; Mich State Univ, PhD(org chem), 59. *Prof Exp:* Res chemist, Fabrics & Finishes Dept, E I du Pont de Nemours & Co, 59-60; RES SCIENTIST, WYETH LABS, INC, PHILADELPHIA, 60- *Mem:* Am Chem Soc. *Res:* Thiophene derivatives; steroid synthesis; medicinal chemistry. *Mailing Add:* 824 Devon State Rd Devon PA 19333

TELLER, DAVID CHAMBERS, b Wilkes-Barre, Pa, July 25, 38; m 60; c 1. PHYSICAL BIOCHEMISTRY. *Educ:* Swarthmore Col, BA, 60; Univ Calif, Berkeley, PhD(biochem), 65. *Prof Exp:* Asst prof, 65-70, ASSOC PROF BIOCHEM, UNIV WASH, 70- *Concurrent Pos:* Consult, Spinco Div, Beckman Instruments, 66. *Mem:* Am Soc Biol Chem. *Res:* Physical chemistry and equilibria of proteins; non-covalent association. *Mailing Add:* Dept of Biochem Univ of Wash Seattle WA 98195

TELLER, DAVID NORTON, b New York, NY, Oct 1, 36; m 59. NEUROCHEMISTRY, PSYCHOPHARMACOLOGY. *Educ:* Brooklyn Col, BS, 57; NY Univ, MS, 60, PhD(cytochem), 64. *Prof Exp:* Biologist, Fine Organics, Inc, 56-57; res asst hemat & nutrit, New York Med Col, 57-59; sr res scientist, NY State Ment Hyg, Manhattan State Hosp, NY State Res Inst, 59-66, assoc res scientist, 66-76; ASSOC PROF, DEPT PSYCHIAT & BEHAV SCI, MED SCH, UNIV LOUISVILLE, 76- *Concurrent Pos:* Lectr, Dept Psychiat, New York Med Col, 66-67 & Grad Div, Fairleigh Dickinson Univ, 68-71. *Mem:* Am Chem Soc; Am Soc Neurochem; Am Soc Pharmacol & Exp Therapeut; Am Soc Test & Mat; Int Col Neuropsychopharmacol. *Res:* Drug binding and transport; subcellular particle preparation; molecular pharmacology. *Mailing Add:* Univ Louisville Med Sch PO Box 35260 Louisville KY 40232

TELLER, DAVIDA YOUNG, b Yonkers, NY, July 25, 38; m 60; c 2. VISION, VISUAL DEVELOPMENT. *Educ:* Swarthmore Col, BA, 60; Univ Calif, Berkeley, PhD(psychol), 65. *Prof Exp:* Res asst prof psychol, 65-67, actg asst prof, 67-68, from asst prof to assoc prof psychol & physiol, 68-74, PROF PSYCHOL & PHYSIOL, UNIV WASH, 74- *Concurrent Pos:* Nat Inst Neurol Dis & Blindness res grant, 68-71; Nat Eye Inst res grants, 71-74 & 75-; mem comt vision, Nat Res Coun, 71-; mem vision res & training comt, Nat Eye Inst, 72-76; affil, Regional Primate Res Ctr, 73- & Child Develop & Ment Retardation Ctr, 75-; NSF res grant, 75. *Mem:* AAAS; fel Optical Soc Am; Asn Res Vision & Opthal. *Res:* Philosophical aspects of visual sciences; development of vision in human and monkey infants; statistical properties of psychophysical techniques. *Mailing Add:* Dept of Psychol NI-25 Univ of Wash Seattle WA 98195

TELLER, EDWARD, b Budapest, Hungary, Jan 15, 08; nat US; m 34; c 2. PHYSICS. *Educ:* Univ Leipzig, PhD, 30. *Hon Degrees:* Many from various cols & univ in US, 54-64. *Prof Exp:* Res assoc, Univ Leipzig, 29-31 & Univ Göttingen, 31-33; Rockefeller fel, Copenhagen, 34; lectr, Univ London, 34-35; prof physics, George Washington Univ, 35-41 & Columbia Univ, 41-42; physicist, Manhattan Eng Dist, Univ Chicago, 42-43 & Los Alamos Sci Lab, 43-46; prof physics, Univ Chicago, 46-52; prof, 53-60, univ prof, 60-75, EMER PROF PHYSICS, UNIV CALIF, BERKELEY, 75-; SR RES FEL, HOOVER INST WAR, PEACE & REVOLUTION, STANFORD UNIV, 75- *Concurrent Pos:* Asst dir, Los Alamos Sci Lab, 49-52; consult, Lawrence Radiation Lab, Livermore, 52-53, dir, 58-60, assoc dir, Lawrence Livermore Lab, Univ Calif, 54-58, assoc dir, 72-; mem sci adv bd, US Air Force; gen adv comt, USAEC; dir, Thermo Electron Corp; mem, President's Foreign Intel Adv Bd; consult, Comn Critical Choices of Americans, 74-; mem, White House Sci Coun. *Honors & Awards:* Priestley Mem Award, Dickinson Col, 57; Einstein Award, 59; Gen Donovan Mem Award, 59; Award, Midwest Res Inst, 60; Living Hist Award, Res Inst Am, 60; Golden Plate Award, 61; White & Fermi Awards, 62; Robins Award Am, 63; Harvey Prize, The Technion, Haifa, Israel, 75. *Mem:* Nat Acad Sci; fel Am Nuclear Soc; fel Am Phys Soc; Am Ord Asn; Am Acad Arts & Sci. *Res:* Chemical, molecular and nuclear physics; quantum theory. *Mailing Add:* Hoover Inst Stanford Univ Stanford CA 94305

TELLER, JAMES TOBIAS, b Evanston, Ill, Aug 1, 40; m 63; c 2. GEOLOGY. *Educ:* Univ Cincinnati, BS, 62, PhD(geol), 70; Ohio State Univ, MS, 64. *Prof Exp:* Field geologist, Inst Polar Studies, 64-65; petrol geologist, Atlantic Richfield Co, 65-67; from asst prof to assoc prof, 70-81, PROF GEOL, UNIV MAN, 81- *Concurrent Pos:* Nat Res Coun Can grants, Univ Man, 70-75 & 77-83, Geol Surv Can grant, 71-72, 81-; geol consult sand, gravel & petrol, 75-; vis assoc prof geol, Univ Cincinnati, 76; res fel, Australian Nat Univ, 77. *Mem:* Am Asn Quaternary Res; Soc Econ Paleont & Mineral. *Res:* Glacial and lacustrine sedimentation and stratigraphy. *Mailing Add:* Dept of Earth Sci Univ of Man Winnipeg MB R3T 2N2 Can

TELLER, JOHN ROGER, b Cincinnati, Ohio, June 30, 32; m 60; c 2. ALGEBRA. *Educ:* Univ Cincinnati, BS, 55, MA, 59; Tulane Univ, PhD(math), 64. *Prof Exp:* Asst prof math, Univ NH, 64-65; ASSOC PROF MATH, GEORGETOWN UNIV, 65- *Mem:* Am Math Soc; Math Asn Am. *Res:* Mathematical research in partially ordered groups. *Mailing Add:* Dept of Math Georgetown Univ Washington DC 20057

TELLER, MORRIS N, b New York, NY, Jan 18, 15; m 42; c 3. CANCER. *Educ:* Brooklyn Col, BS, 40; Univ Minn, MS, 46, PhD(plant path), 48. *Prof Exp:* Asst plant path, Univ Minn, 44-48; assoc res microbiologist, Parke, Davis & Co, 48-52, head microbiol sect, 52-54; asst, Div Steroid Biol, Sloan-Kettering Inst Cancer Res, 54-56, assoc & head rat host studies sect, Div Human Tumor Exp Chemother, 54-60, assoc mem, 60-81, head cancerigenesis & chemother sect, 60-64, sect head, Div Exp Chemother, 63-81; prof, 58-81, EMER PROF BIOL, SLOAN-KETTERING DIV, MED COL, CORNELL UNIV, 81- *Mem:* AAAS; Am Asn Cancer Res; Am Asn Immunol; Geront Soc. *Res:* Experimental chemotherapy; aging, immunity and cancer; carcinogenesis. *Mailing Add:* Walker Lab Sloan-Kettering Inst Rye NY 10580

TELLINGHUISEN, JOEL BARTON, b Cedar Falls, Iowa, May 27, 43; m 72; c 2. MOLECULAR SPECTROSCOPY, MOLECULAR PHYSICS. *Educ:* Cornell Univ, AB, 65; Univ Calif, Berkeley, PhD(chem), 69. *Prof Exp:* Res assoc chem, Univ Canterbury, 69-71; res assoc physics, Univ Chicago, 71-73; Nat Res Coun res assoc, Nat Oceanic & Atmospheric Admin, Boulder, Co, 73-75; asst prof, 75-80, ASSOC PROF CHEM, VANDERBILT UNIV, 80- *Mem:* Am Chem Soc; Am Phys Soc. *Res:* Molecular and atomic physics; optical spectroscopy; lasers. *Mailing Add:* Dept of Chem Vanderbilt Univ Nashville TN 37240

TELSCHOW, KENNETH LOUIS, b St Paul, Minn, Jan 4, 47; m 74; c 1. PHYSICS, MATERIALS SCIENCE. *Educ:* Univ Calif, Los Angeles, BS, 69, PhD(physics), 73. *Prof Exp:* Adj asst prof physics, Univ Calif, Los Angeles, 74-75; lectr physics, Univ Mass, Amherst, 75-77; ASST PROF PHYSICS, SOUTHERN ILL UNIV, 77- *Concurrent Pos:* Teaching fel physics, Univ Calif, Los Angeles, 69-73; fel physics, Univ Mass, Amherst, 75-77; prin investr, Res Corp res grant, 77-79; prin investr, NSF res grant, 79-81. *Mem:* Am Phys Soc; Acoust Soc Am. *Res:* Low temperature physics; liquid helium; acoustics; quantum fluids and solids. *Mailing Add:* Dept of Physics & Astron Southern Ill Univ Carbondale IL 62901

TELSER, ALVIN GILBERT, b Chicago, Ill, May 11, 39; m 67; c 2. BIOCHEMISTRY, CELL BIOLOGY. *Educ:* Univ Chicago, BS, 61, PhD(biochem), 68. *Prof Exp:* Helen Hay Whitney Found fel develop biol, Brandeis Univ, 68-70; Helen Hay Whitney Found fel cell biol, Yale Univ, 70-71; asst prof, 71-77, ASSOC PROF ANAT & CELL BIOL, MED SCH, NORTHWESTERN UNIV, CHICAGO, 77- *Mem:* AAAS; Soc Develop Biol; Am Soc Cell Biol; NY Acad Sci; Sigma Xi. *Res:* Biochemical aspects of differentiation and development in eukaryotic systems with emphasis on understanding regulatory mechanisms at a molecular level. *Mailing Add:* Dept of Anat Northwestern Univ Med Sch Chicago IL 60611

TEMES, CLIFFORD LAWRENCE, b Jersey City, NJ, Feb 4, 30; m 63; c 3. ELECTRICAL ENGINEERING. *Educ:* Cooper Union, BEE, 51; Case Inst Technol, MS, 54; Columbia Univ, EE, 60; Polytech Inst Brooklyn, PhD(elec eng), 65. *Prof Exp:* Electronic scientist instrumentation, Nat Adv Comt Aeronaut, 51-54; lab supvr radar systs, Electronics Res Lab, Columbia Univ, 56-60; sr proj engr elec eng, Fed Sci Corp, 60-65; mem tech staff, Gen Res Corp, 65-74; mem dept staff, Mitre Corp, 74-77; HEAD SEARCH RADAR BR, NAVAL RES LAB, 77- *Concurrent Pos:* Consult, Electronics Res Lab, Columbia Univ, 60-65; reviewer, Inst Elec & Electronics Engrs, 60-75, Prentice-Hall, 68-69. *Honors & Awards:* Qual Award, Naval Res Lab, 78. *Mem:* Sigma Xi; sr mem Inst Elec & Electronics Engrs. *Res:* Radar systems and technology; signal processing and wave form design; surveillance and tracking radar; clutter rejection; pulse compression and high resolution systems. *Mailing Add:* Naval Res Lab 4555 Overlook Ave SW Washington DC 20375

TEMES, GABOR CHARLES, b Budapest, Hungary, Oct 14, 29; Can citizen; m 54; c 2. ELECTRICAL ENGINEERING, COMPUTER SCIENCES. *Educ:* Budapest Tech Univ, Dipl Ing, 52; Eötvös Lorand Univ, Budapest, dipl phys, 54; Univ Ottawa, PhD(elec eng), 61. *Prof Exp:* Asst prof elec eng, Budapest Tech Univ, 52-56; proj engr, Measurement Eng Ltd, 57-59; dept head networks, Northern Elec Co Ltd, 59-64; group leader light electronics, Stanford Linear Accelerator Ctr, 64-66; corp consult networks, Ampex Corp, Calif, 66-69; PROF ELEC ENG, UNIV CALIF, LOS ANGELES, 69-, CHMN DEPT ELEC SCI & ENG, 75- *Concurrent Pos:* Ed, Trans on Circuit Theory, 69-71; consult, TRW, Rockwell Int, 75- & Am Microsysts, Inc, 78- *Honors & Awards:* Darlington Award, Inst Elec & Electronics Engrs, Circuits & Systs Soc, 69. *Mem:* Fel Inst Elec & Electronics Engrs. *Res:* Circuit design, filters and digital signal processing. *Mailing Add:* Rm 7732 Boelter Hall Univ of Calif Los Angeles CA 90024

TEMIN, HOWARD MARTIN, b Philadelphia, Pa, Dec 10, 34; m 62; c 2. ONCOLOGY, VIROLOGY. *Educ:* Swarthmore Col, BA, 55; Calif Inst Technol, PhD(biol), 59. *Hon Degrees:* Dr, Swarthmore Col, 72; Dr, New York Med Col, 72. *Prof Exp:* Asst prof, 60-64, assoc prof, 64-69, PROF ONCOL, UNIV WIS-MADISON, 69-, WIS ALUMNI RES FOUND PROF CANCER RES, 71-, AM CANCER SOC PROF VIRAL ONCOL & CELL BIOL, 74- *Concurrent Pos:* Mem virol & rickettsiol study sect, NIH, 71-75; assoc ed, J Cell Physiol, 66-77 & Cancer Res, 71-74. *Honors & Awards:* Warren Triennial Prize, Mass Gen Hosp, 71 (shared); Pap Award, Pap Inst Miami, 72; Bertner Award, Univ Tex M D Anderson Hosp & Tumor Inst

Houston, 72; US Steel Award, Nat Acad Sci, 72; Award Enzyme Chem, Am Chem Soc, 73; Award Distinguished Achievement, Mod Med, 73; Griffuel Prize, Asn Develop Res Cancer, Villejuif, France, 73; Dyer Lectr Award, NIH, 74; Clowes Lectr Award, Am Asn Cancer Res, 74; Int Award, Gaindner Found, Toronto, 74 (shared); Albert Lasker Award Basic Med Sci, 74; Nobel Prize in Physiol or Med, 75 (shared); Lucy Wortham James Award, Soc Surg Oncologists, 76; Lila Gruber Res Awardee, Am Acad Dermat, 81. *Mem:* Nat Acad Sci; Am Philos Soc; fel Am Acad Arts & Sci; Am Soc Microbiol; Am Asn Cancer Res. *Res:* Replication of and mechanism of neoplastic transformation by RNA tumor viruses; RNA-directed DNA synthesis and protoviruses; control of multiplication of cultured cells. *Mailing Add:* McArdle Lab Univ of Wis Madison WI 53706

TEMIN, RAYLA GREENBERG, b New York, NY, May 4, 36; m 62; c 2. GENETICS. *Educ:* Brooklyn Col, BS, 56; Univ Wis, MS, 58, PhD(genetics), 63. *Prof Exp:* Proj assoc, 63-72, ASST SCIENTIST MED GENETICS & GENETICS, UNIV WIS-MADISON, 72- *Mem:* NY Acad Sci; Genetics Soc Am. *Res:* Studies of the segregation distorter gene in natural populations of drosophila melanogaster; teaching of undergraduate genetics. *Mailing Add:* Dept Genetics Univ of Wis Madison WI 53706

TEMIN, SAMUEL CANTOR, b Washington, DC, Nov 4, 19; m 47; c 2. POLYMER CHEMISTRY. *Educ:* Wilson Teachers Col, BS, 39; Univ Md, MS, 43, PhD(org chem), 49. *Prof Exp:* Res chemist, Army Chem Ctr, Md, 42-44; asst gen org chem & biochem, Univ Md, 46-48; res chemist, Indust Rayon Corp, Ohio, 49-53, res supvr, 53-58; mgr polymer chem group, Explor Sect, Koppers Co, Inc, 58-65; asst dir, Fabric Res Labs, Inc, Mass, 65-72; SECT HEAD POLYMER CHEM, LEXINGTON LAB, KENDALL CO, COLGATE-PALMOLIVE CO, LEXINGTON, 72- *Concurrent Pos:* Lectr, Pa State Univ, 63-65 & Northeastern Univ, 66- *Mem:* Am Chem Soc; Fiber Soc; Int Asn Dent Res; Soc Plastics Engr. *Res:* Polymer synthesis and structural relationships, adhesives, dental materials, monomer synthesis. *Mailing Add:* 22 Trout Pond Ln Needham MA 02192

TEMKIN, AARON, b Morristown, NJ, Aug 15, 29; m 58; c 2. ATOMIC PHYSICS. *Educ:* Rutgers Univ, BS, 51; Mass Inst Technol, PhD(physics), 56. *Prof Exp:* Fulbright fel, Ger, 56-57; physicist, US Naval Res Lab, 57-58; physicist, Nat Bur Standards, 58-60; HEAD ATOMIC PHYSICS OFF, LAB FOR ASTRON & SOLAR PHYSICS, GODDARD SPACE FLIGHT CTR, NASA, 60- *Mem:* Fel Am Phys Soc. *Res:* Scattering of electrons from atoms, polarized orbitals, nonadiabatic theory; oxygen, hydrogen; threshold law for electron-atom impact ionization; symmetric Euler angle decomposition of three body problem; calculation of autoionization states; quasiprojection operators; fixed-nuclei, adiabatic-nuclei and hybrid theories of electron-molecule scattering. *Mailing Add:* Code 680 NASA-Goddard Space Flight Ctr Greenbelt MD 20771

TEMKIN, OWSEI, b Minsk, Russia, Oct 6, 02; US citizen; m 32; c 2. HISTORY OF MEDICINE & SCIENCE. *Educ:* Univ Leipzig, MD, 27. *Hon Degrees:* LLD, Johns Hopkins Univ, 73; DSc, Med Col Ohio, 75. *Prof Exp:* Intern, St Jacob Hosp, Leipzig, Ger, 27-28; asst hist of med, Univ Leipzig, 28-32, privat dozent, 31-33; assoc, 32-35, from assoc prof to prof, 35-58, William H Welch prof & dir dept, 58-68, EMER WILLIAM H WELCH PROF HIST OF MED, JOHNS HOPKINS UNIV, 68- *Concurrent Pos:* Actg ed & ed, Bull Hist of Med, 48-68; Hideyo Noguchi lectr, Johns Hopkins Univ, 69; Messenger lectr, Cornell Univ, 70. *Honors & Awards:* William H Welch Medal, Am Asn Hist of Med, 52; Sarton Medal, Hist of Sci Soc, 60; Distinguished Scholar in Humanities Prize, Am Coun Learned Socs, 62. *Mem:* Nat Acad Sci; Am Philos Soc; Am Acad Arts & Sci; Am Asn Hist of Med (pres, 58-60); Hist of Sci Soc. *Res:* History of irritability; life and work of Hippocrates and Galen. *Mailing Add:* 419 Alabama Rd Baltimore MD 21204

TEMKIN, RICHARD JOEL, b Boston, Mass, Jan 8, 45; m 72; c 3. LASERS, PLASMA PHYSICS. *Educ:* Harvard Col, BA, 66; Mass Inst Technol, PhD(physics), 71. *Prof Exp:* Res fel physics, Harvard Univ, 71-74; staff mem physsics, Francis Bitter Nat Magnet Lab, 74-79, asst group leader, 79, GROUP LEADER, PLASMA FUSION CTR, MASS INST TECHNOL, 80- *Concurrent Pos:* IBM Corp fel, 72-74; assoc ed, Int J Infrared & Millimeter Waves. *Mem:* Am Phys Soc; Fusion Power Asn. *Res:* Submillimeter lasers, both theory and experiment; laser breakdown and heating of gases; optical and submillimeter diagnostics of plasmas; plasma heating; cyclotron resonance masers. *Mailing Add:* Plasma Fusion Ctr NW16-254 Mass Inst Technol 170 Albany St Cambridge MA 02139

TEMKIN, SAMUEL, b Mexico City, Mex, Jan 10, 36; m 65; c 2. FLUID DYNAMICS, ACOUSTICS. *Educ:* Univ Nuevo Leon, ME, 60; Brown Univ, ScM, 64, PhD(eng), 66. *Prof Exp:* Sr scientist acoust, Bolt Beranek & Newman, Inc, 66-67; from asst prof to assoc prof eng, 67-73, PROF MECH ENG, RUTGERS UNIV, NEW BRUNSWICK, 73-, GRAD PROG DIR MECH & AEROSPACE ENGR, 76-, CHMN DEPT MECH & AEROSPACE ENG, 80- *Concurrent Pos:* Consult, US Army Ballistic Res Labs, 69-73; Lady Davis Trust Fund fel, 74-75. *Mem:* AAAS; Am Phys Soc; Acoust Soc Am; Am Soc Mech Engrs. *Res:* Acoustic wave propagation; fluid dynamics of aerosols; droplet dynamics. *Mailing Add:* Dept Mech Eng Rutgers Univ New Brunswick NJ 08903

TEMME, DONALD H(ENRY), b Winside, Nebr, Jan 12, 28; m 55; c 2. ELECTRICAL ENGINEERING. *Educ:* Univ Nebr, BS, 49; Mass Inst Technol, MS, 55. *Prof Exp:* Asst physics, Univ Nebr, 49-51; assoc group leader, 58-76, GROUP LEADER, LINCOLN LAB, MASS INST TECHNOL, 76- *Mem:* Inst Elec & Electronics Engrs. *Res:* Phased array radar components. *Mailing Add:* Lincoln Lab PO Box 73 Lexington MA 02139

TEMMER, GEORGES MAXIME, b Vienna, Austria, Apr 10, 22; nat US; m 43. NUCLEAR PHYSICS. *Educ:* Queens Col, NY, BS, 43; Univ Calif, MA, 44, PhD(physics), 49. *Prof Exp:* Asst physics, Univ Calif, 43-44 & 46-49; res assoc, Univ Rochester, 49-51; physicist, Nat Bur Standards, S1-53; mem staff terrestrial magnetism, Carnegie Inst, 53-63; PROF PHYSICS & DIR, NUCLEAR PHYSICS LAB, RUTGERS UNIV, NEW BRUNSWICK, 63- *Concurrent Pos:* Guest investr, Cryogenic Sect, Nat Bur Standards, 53-55; Guggenheim Mem fel, Paris & Copenhagen, 56-57; vis prof, Univ Md, 59; prof, Fla State Univ, 60-63; Rutgers Res Coun fac fel, 68-69 & 75; Nat Acad Sci sr exchange scholar, People's Repub China, 80. *Honors & Awards:* Lindback Award for Excellence in Res, Rutgers Univ, 73. *Mem:* Fel Am Phys Soc. *Res:* Nuclear reaction mechanisms; very short lifetimes; scattering; angular correlation; low temperature nuclear alignment; gamma-ray spectroscopy; Coulomb excitation; polarized particle sources; electron channeling radiation; beam-foil spectroscopy. *Mailing Add:* Dept of Physics Rutgers Univ New Brunswick NJ 08903

TEMPELIS, CONSTANTINE H, b Superior, Wis, Aug 27, 27; m 55; c 2. IMMUNOLOGY. *Educ:* Univ Wis, Superior, BS, 50; Univ Wis-Madison, MS, 53, PhD(med microbiol), 55. *Prof Exp:* Proj assoc immunol, Univ Wis, 55-57; instr microbiol, Sch Med, Univ WVa, 57-58; from asst res immunologist to assoc res immunologist, 58-66, lectr, 60-66, assoc prof-in-residence immunol, 67-70, assoc prof, 70-72, PROF IMMUNOL, SCH PUB HEALTH, UNIV CALIF, BERKELEY, 72- *Concurrent Pos:* NIH career develop award, 65-70; vis scientist, Wellcome Res Labs, Eng, 77-78; Fogarty Sr Int Fel, 77-78. *Mem:* AAAS; Am Asn Immunol; NY Acad Sci; Sigma Xi; Fedn Am Soc Exp Biol. *Res:* Production of immunologic tolerance in chickens to soluble protein antigens; immunologic approaches to study of feeding habits of arthropod vectors. *Mailing Add:* Sch of Pub Health Univ of Calif Berkeley CA 94720

TEMPELMAN-KLUIT, DIRK JACOB, b Macassar, Indonesia, June 14, 39; Can citizen; m 64; c 2. STRUCTURAL GEOLOGY. *Educ:* Univ BC, BASc, 62, MASc, 64; McGill Univ, PhD(geol), 66. *Prof Exp:* Res scientist geol, Geol Surv Can, 67-80; chief geologist, Dept Indian Affairs & Develop Northern, 80-82; RES SCIENTIST GEOL, GEOL SURV CAN, 82- *Mem:* Geol Asn Can. *Res:* Regional geology of Yukon Territory including regional tectonics, metallogeny, evolution of physiography and stratigraphy. *Mailing Add:* 15 Sunset Dr N Whitehorse YT Y1A 4M7 Can

TEMPERLEY, JUDITH KANTACK, b Meriden, Conn, Feb 12, 36; m 56. WEAPONS SYSTEMS ANALYSIS. *Educ:* Univ Rochester, BS, 57; Univ Ore, MS, 59, PhD(physics), 65. *Prof Exp:* RES PHYSICIST, US ARMY NUCLEAR DEFENSE LAB & US ARMY BALLISTIC RES LABS, 65- *Mem:* Am Phys Soc; Sigma Xi. *Res:* Engineering analysis and effectiveness studies of new concepts in weapon systems. *Mailing Add:* USAARRADCOM Ballistic Res lab Aberdeen Proving Ground MD 21005

TEMPEST, BRUCE DEAN, b Catasauqua, Pa, Nov 3, 35; m 59; c 3. INFECTIOUS DISEASES. *Educ:* Lafayette Col, AB, 57; Univ Pa, MD, 61; Am Bd Internal Med, cert, 68 & 74. *Prof Exp:* Resident med, Philadelphia Gen Hosp, 61-65; fel allergy & immunol, Univ Pa Hosp, 65-67; chief internal med, Dept Health, Educ & Welfare, USPHS, Tuba City, 67-70, Gallup Indian Med Ctr, 70-71, CLIN DIR, SURVEILLANCE PROJ, GALLUP INDIAN MED CTR, 71-; clin dir, Pneumococcal Surveillance Proj, 71-75, DEP CHIEF INTERNAL MED, GALLUP INDIAN MED CTR, 75- *Concurrent Pos:* Clin asst prof, Dept Med, Sch Med, Univ NMex, 73-78, assoc prof, 78- *Mem:* Fel Am Col Physicians. *Res:* Epidemiology of pneumonia, especially pneumococcal pneumonia and the study of clinical manifestations; efficacy of vaccines in pneumonia prevention. *Mailing Add:* 1603 Monterey Dr Gallup NM 87301

TEMPLE, AUSTIN LIMIEL, (JR), b Leesville, La, Nov 3, 40; m 62; c 2. APPLIED MATHEMATICS. *Educ:* Centenary Col La, BS, 62; La State Univ, Baton Rouge, MA, 64; George Peabody Col, PhD(math), 71. *Prof Exp:* Instr math, Northwestern State Univ, 64-65, asst prof, 67-69; instr, Vanderbilt Univ, 69-70; asst prof, 70-75, ASSOC PROF MATH, NORTHWESTERN STATE UNIV, 75- *Mem:* Math Asn Am. *Res:* Mathematics education, in-service curriculum for elementary school teachers; develop and standardize tests for college freshmen math courses; develop computer statistical library. *Mailing Add:* Dept of Math Northwestern State Univ Natchitoches LA 71457

TEMPLE, CARROLL GLENN, b Hickory, NC, Mar 7, 32:; m 56; c 2. ORGANIC CHEMISTRY, MEDICINAL CHEMISTRY. *Educ:* Lenoir-Rhyne Col, BS, 54; Birmingham-Southern Col, MS, 58; Univ NC, PhD(org chem), 62. *Prof Exp:* Assoc chemist, 55-59, res chemist, 60-64, sr chemist, 64-80, HEAD, PHARMACEUT CHEM DIV, SOUTHERN RES INST, 81- *Mem:* Am Chem Soc. *Res:* Synthesis of potential antimalarian and anticancer drugs. *Mailing Add:* Southern Res Inst PO Box 3307-A Birmingham AL 35255

TEMPLE, DAVIS LITTLETON, JR, b Tupelo, Miss, June 10, 43; m 66. MEDICINAL CHEMISTRY. *Educ:* Univ Miss, BS, 66, PhD(med chem), 69. *Prof Exp:* Res assoc, La State Univ, New Orleans, 69-70; sr investr, 70-80, DIR CHEM RES, MEAD JOHNSON & CO, DIV BRISTOL-MYERS CO, 80- *Concurrent Pos:* Mem, Bio-Org & Nat Prod Study Sect, NIH, 81; adv bd, Advan Develop Chem Series, Am Chem Soc. *Mem:* AAAS; Am Chem Soc; Soc Neurosci; hon mem British Brain Asn; NY Acad Sci. *Res:* Central nervous system, cardiovascular and respiratory drugs; chemistry and biology. *Mailing Add:* Chem Res Mead Johnson & Co Evansville IN 47721

TEMPLE, KENNETH LOREN, b St Paul, Minn, Mar 22, 18; m 43; c 3. GEOENVIRONMENTAL SCIENCE. *Educ:* Middlebury Col, AB, 40; Univ Wis, MS, 42; Rutgers Univ, PhD(microbiol), 48. *Prof Exp:* Chemist, US Naval Res Lab, DC, 42-45; instr bact, Univ RI, 48; assoc res specialist, Eng Exp Sta, WVa Univ, 48-53; microbiologist, Tex Co, 53-55; assoc prof microbiol, Agr Exp Sta, Mont State Univ, 55-61; sr res specialist, Commonwealth Sci &

Indust Res Orgn, Australia, 61-63; PROF MICROBIOL, MONT STATE UNIV, 64- *Mem:* Am Soc Microbiol; Am Acad Microbiol. *Res:* Autotrophic bacteria; microbiology of thermal waters; coal mines; geomicrobiology. *Mailing Add:* Dept Microbiol Mont State Univ Bozeman MT 59715

TEMPLE, PETER LAWRENCE, b Springfield, Mass, Dec 13, 46; m 78; c 1. SOLAR ENERGY. *Educ:* Dartmouth Col, AB, 69. *Prof Exp:* Instr physics, Mount Holyoke Col, 70-73; instr physics eng, Holyoke Community Col, 76-77; SR RES ENGR, RES & DEVELOP SOLAR ENERGY, TOTAL ENVIRON ACTION, INC, 77- *Concurrent Pos:* Tech ed, Solar Age, Solar Vision Inc, 77- *Mem:* Int Solar Energy Soc. *Res:* Solar energy system design; building energy analysis; solar materials science; appropriate technology for developing countries; innovative solar product development; photovoltaics; passive solar systems. *Mailing Add:* The Island Harrisville NH 03450

TEMPLE, ROBERT DWIGHT, b Des Moines, Iowa, July 1, 41; m 65; c 4. ORGANIC CHEMISTRY. *Educ:* Clemson Col, BS, 62; Fla State Univ, PhD(chem), 66. *Prof Exp:* Chemist, E I du Pont de Nemours & Co, 62; RES CHEMIST, PROCTER & GAMBLE CO, 66-, SECT HEAD, 72- *Mem:* Am Chem Soc; Am Oil Chemists Soc. *Res:* Physical organic chemistry. *Mailing Add:* Procter & Gamble Co Miami Valley Labs Cincinnati OH 45239

TEMPLE, ROBERT JAY, internal medicine, see previous edition

TEMPLE, STANLEY, b New York, NY, Aug 17, 30; c 2. ORGANIC CHEMISTRY. *Educ:* NY Univ, AB, 52, PhD(org chem), 58. *Prof Exp:* Res fel cancer steroids, Med Sch, Univ Va, 58-60; res chemist, Plant Tech Sect, Org Chem Dept, 60, res chemist, Process Dept, 60-61, res chemist, Res & Develop Div, Org Chem Dept, 61-74, SR RES CHEMIST, JACKSON LABS, CHAMBERS WORKS, E I DU PONT DE MOURS & CO, INC, 74- *Mem:* AAAS; Sigma Xi; Am Chem Soc; Lepidopterists' Soc; Royal Soc Chem. *Res:* Fluorochemicals; fluorinated polymers; surface active agents; bio-organic chemistry; cosmetics; environmental chemistry; pollution control; water treatment; food processing. *Mailing Add:* Jackson Lab E I du Pont de Nemours & Co Inc Wilmington DE 19898

TEMPLE, STANLEY A, b Cleveland, Ohio, Sept 26, 46; m 69, 80. ECOLOGY, CONSERVATION. *Educ:* Cornell Univ, BSc, 68, MSc, 70, PhD(ecol), 73. *Prof Exp:* Teaching asst ecol, Cornell Univ, 68-73; res biologist, World Wildlife Fund, 73-75; res assoc ornith, Cornell Univ, 75-76; asst prof, 76-80, ASSOC PROF WILDLIFE ECOL, UNIV WIS-MADISON, 80-, BEERS-BASCOM PROF CONSERV, 80- *Concurrent Pos:* Dir, Int Coun Bird Preserv, 76-78, secy, 78-, dir, 80-; dir, Raptor Res Found, 77- *Mem:* Am Ornithologists Union; Ecol Soc Am; Wildlife Soc; Wilson Ornith Soc; AAAS. *Res:* Ornithology; wildlife management; endangered species; physiology; behavior. *Mailing Add:* Dept of Wildlife Ecol Univ of Wis Madison WI 53706

TEMPLE, VICTOR ALBERT KEITH, b Winnipeg, Man, Apr 3, 44. SOLID STATE PHYSICS. *Educ:* Univ Man, BSc, 67; MacMaster Univ, MEng, 68, PhD(physics), 72. *Prof Exp:* PHYSICIST, RES & DEVELOP CTR, GEN ELEC, 74- *Concurrent Pos:* Nat Adv Coun fel, MacMaster Univ, 72-74. *Mem:* Inst Elec & Electronic Engrs. *Res:* Physics of power semiconductor carriers and the design; fabrication and development of new and improved power semiconductor devices. *Mailing Add:* 1 River Rd Schenectady NY 12301

TEMPLE, WADE JETT, b Petersburg, Va, Feb 8, 33. MOLECULAR PHYSICS. *Educ:* Randolph-Macon Col, BS, 54; Univ WVa, MS, 60, PhD(physics), 64. *Prof Exp:* Instr physics, Randolph-Macon Col, 55-58; from instr to asst, Univ WVa, 60-64; assoc prof, 64-71, PROF PHYSICS, RANDOLPH-MACON COL, 71- *Mem:* Am Asn Physics Teachers; Am Phys Soc. *Res:* Electron spin resonance; microwave spectroscopy of free radicals. *Mailing Add:* Dept of Physics Randolph-Macon Col Ashland VA 23005

TEMPLEMAN, GARETH J, b Little Falls, NY, Apr 21, 37; m 70; c 1. PHYSICAL CHEMISTRY, ANALYTICAL CHEMISTRY. *Educ:* Ohio Wesleyan Univ, BA, 60; State Univ NY Buffalo, PhD(chem), 70. *Prof Exp:* Res fel phys org chem, State Univ NY Buffalo, 69-70; scientist, Pillsbury Co, 70-71, group leader instrumentation, Corp Res, 71-78; mgr appl res, Pepsico Inc, 78-80; WITH STANDARD BRANDS INC, 80- *Mem:* Am Chem Soc; Inst Food Technologists. *Res:* Nuclear magnetic resonance; mass spectrometry; electrochemistry; flavors; perception; food chemistry; microwave heating; fats and oils; thermal chemistry; beverage technology; emulsions; surface chemistry; chemical kinetics; food chemistry. *Mailing Add:* Standard Brands Inc 15 River Rd Wilton CT 06897

TEMPLEMAN, WILFRED, b Bonavista, Nfld, Feb 22, 08; m 37; c 4. MARINE BIOLOGY, FISHERIES. *Educ:* Dalhousie Univ, BSc, 30; Univ Toronto, MA, 31, PhD(marine biol), 33; Mem Univ, DSc, 76. *Prof Exp:* Sci asst zool, Biol Bd Can, 30-33; lectr zool, McGill Univ, 33-36; from assoc prof to prof biol, Mem Univ Nfld, 36-44, head dept, 36-44; dir, Nfld Govt Lab, 44-49; dir, St John's Biol Sta, Fisheries Res Bd Can, 49-72; J L PATON PROF MARINE BIOL & FISHERIES, MEM UNIV NFLD, 72- *Concurrent Pos:* Vis prof, Mem Univ Nfld, 57-72; fisheries adv, Govt Nfld, 73-75; mem fisheries & oceans res adv comt, Can, 81- *Mem:* Am Fishers Soc; Am Soc Ichthyologists & Herpetologists; Can Soc Zoologists; fel Royal Soc Can; Marine Biol Asn UK. *Res:* Life history of lobster, capelin, dogfish, cod, haddock and redfish; distribution, systematics and life history of fish species in western North Atlantic. *Mailing Add:* 12 Darling St St John's NF A1B 1V6 Can

TEMPLER, DAVID ALLEN, b Chicago, Ill, July 23, 42; m 65. POLYMER CHEMISTRY. *Educ:* Northwestern Univ, Evanston, BS, 64; Ind Univ, Bloomington, PhD(org chem), 68. *Prof Exp:* Sr chemist, 68-75, lab head, Latin Am oper, 75-78, RES & DEVELOP MGR, INDUST CHEMS, LATIN AM REGION, TECH SERV LAB, ROHM AND HAAS, 78- *Mem:* AAAS; Am Chem Soc; Royal Soc Chem. *Res:* Polymer synthesis and characterization with regard to applications in the area of organic coatings; medicinal chemistry; leather chemistry; textile chemistry; ion exchange. *Mailing Add:* Rohm and Haas Latin Am Oper 12906 SW 89th Ct Miami FL 33156

TEMPLETON, ARCH W, b Madison, Wis, Mar 30, 32; m 55; c 4. MEDICINE, RADIOLOGY. *Educ:* Univ Omaha, BA, 54; Univ Nebr, MD, 57. *Prof Exp:* Asst prof med, Wash Univ, 63-64; assoc prof, Univ Mo, 64-68; PROF RADIOL & CHMN DEPT, MED CTR, UNIV KANS, 68- *Mem:* Radiol Soc NAm; AMA; Asn Univ Radiol. *Res:* Computer research in medicine; vascular radiology. *Mailing Add:* Dept of Radiol Univ of Kans Med Ctr Kansas City MO 66103

TEMPLETON, CHARLES CLARK, b Houston, Tex, Oct 4, 21; m 44; c 4. PHYSICAL CHEMISTRY. *Educ:* La Polytech Inst, BS, 42; Univ Wis, MS, 47, PhD(chem), 48. *Prof Exp:* Jr res chemist, Shell Oil Co, 42; res chemist, Univ Wis, 46-48; instr, Univ Mich, 48-50; staff res chemist, Bellaire Res Ctr, Shell Develop Co, 50-80. *Mem:* Am Chem Soc; Am Inst Mining, Metall & Petrol Eng. *Res:* Solvent extraction; phase equilibria; electrochemistry; multiphase fluid flow; petroleum production. *Mailing Add:* 6119 Reamer St Houston TX 77074

TEMPLETON, DAVID HENRY, b Houston, Tex, Mar 2, 20; m 48; c 2. PHYSICAL CHEMISTRY. *Educ:* La Polytech Inst, BS, 41; Univ Tex, MA, 43; Univ Calif, PhD(chem), 47. *Hon Degrees:* Fil Dr, Univ Uppsala, 77. *Prof Exp:* Instr chem, Univ Tex, 42-44; res chemist, Metall Lab, Univ Chicago, 44-46; res chemist, Radiation Lab, 46-47, from instr to assoc prof, Univ, 47-58, dean col chem, 70-75, PROF CHEM, UNIV CALIF, BERKELEY, 58- *Concurrent Pos:* Guggenheim Mem fel, 53. *Mem:* AAAS; Am Chem Soc; Am Crystallog Asn. *Res:* Properties of radioactive isotopes; nuclear reactions; structures of crystals. *Mailing Add:* Dept of Chem Univ of Calif Berkeley CA 94720

TEMPLETON, FREDERIC EASTLAND, b Portland, Ore, May 11, 05; m 36, 75; c 2. RADIOLOGY. *Educ:* Washington Univ, BS, 27; Univ Ore, MD, 31. *Prof Exp:* Univ Chicago fel radiol, Univ Stockholm, 33-34; from instr to assoc prof roentgenol, Univ Chicago, 35-43; head dept radiol, Cleveland Clin, 43-45; prof & exec officer, 47-53, clin prof, 53-68, prof, 68-75, EMER PROF RADIOL, MED SCH, UNIV WASH, 75- *Mem:* Am Gastroenterol Asn; Am Roentgen Ray Soc (1st vpres, 54); fel AMA; Radiol Soc NAm; hon mem Mex Soc Radiol & Phys Ther. *Res:* Radiologic gastroenterology. *Mailing Add:* Univ Hosp Univ of Wash Med Sch Seattle WA 98195

TEMPLETON, GEORGE EARL, b Little Rock, Ark, June 27, 31; m 58; c 4. PLANT PATHOLOGY. *Educ:* Univ Ark, BS, 53, MS, 54; Univ Wis, PhD(plant path), 58. *Prof Exp:* Asst, Univ Wis, 56-58; from asst prof to assoc prof, 58-67, PROF PLANT PATH, UNIV ARK, FAYETTEVILLE, 67- *Mem:* Am Phytopath Soc; Mycol Soc Am. *Res:* Physiology of parasitism; diseases of rice; biological control of weeds with plant pathogen. *Mailing Add:* Dept of Plant Path Univ of Ark Fayetteville AR 72701

TEMPLETON, GORDON HUFFINE, b Edowah, Tenn, July 17, 40; m 64; c 1. PHYSIOLOGY. *Educ:* Univ Tenn, Knoxville, BS, 63; Southern Methodist Univ, MS, 68; Univ Tex Southwestern Med Sch Dallas, PhD(biophys), 70. *Prof Exp:* Instrumentation engr, Gen Dynamics Corp, Tex, 63-66; instr, 70-71, asst prof, 71-77, ASSOC PROF PHYSIOL, UNIV TEX SOUTHWESTERN MED SCH DALLAS, 78- *Mem:* Am Heart Asn; Inst Elec & Electronics Engrs; Am Fedn Clin Res; Am Physiol Soc. *Res:* Muscle diffractometry. *Mailing Add:* Dept of Physiol Univ of Tex Southwestern Med Sch Dallas TX 75235

TEMPLETON, IAN M, b Rugby, Eng, July 31, 29; m 56; c 2. METAL PHYSICS, LOW TEMPERATURE PHYSICS. *Educ:* Oxford Univ, MA, 50, DPhil(physics), 53. *Prof Exp:* Fel physics, Nat Res Coun Can, 53-54; mem staff, Res Lab, Assoc Elec Industs, Rugby, 55-57; asst res officer,57-60, assoc res officer, 60-64, sr res officer, 64-71, PRIN RES OFFICER PHYSICS DIV, NAT RES COUN CAN, 71- *Concurrent Pos:* Chmn, Nat Comt, Int Union Pure & Appl Physics. *Mem:* Fel Brit Inst Physics; fel Royal Soc Can; Am Phys Soc; Can Asn Physicists. *Res:* Noise in semiconductors; superconductive devices; thermoelectricity; Fermi surfaces. *Mailing Add:* Nat Res Coun Physics Div Ottawa ON K1A 0R6 Can

TEMPLETON, JOE WAYNE, b Loraine, Tex, July 18, 41; m 62; c 1. IMMUNOLOGY, GENETICS. *Educ:* Abilene Christian Col, BS, 64; Ore State Univ, PhD(genetics), 68. *Prof Exp:* Res fel genetics, Ore State Univ, 65-68; asst prof med genetics, Med Sch, Univ Ore, 68-75; asst prof microbiol & immunol, Baylor Col Med, Houston, 75-78; ASSOC PROF VET MED & SURG, COL VET MED, TEX A&M UNIV, 75- *Mem:* Genetics Soc Am; Am Genetic Asn. *Res:* Immunogenetics of organ transplantation, especially in the dog; general canine genetics. *Mailing Add:* 3017 Adrienne College Station TX 77840

TEMPLETON, JOHN CHARLES, b Buffalo, NY, June 7, 43; m 67; c 2. INORGANIC CHEMISTRY. *Educ:* Col Wooster, BA, 65; Wesleyan Univ, MA, 67; Univ Colo, Boulder, PhD(inorg chem), 70. *Prof Exp:* asst prof, 70-76, ASSOC PROF CHEM, WHITMAN COL, 76- *Concurrent Pos:* NSF grant, Whitman Col, 71-73. *Mem:* Am Chem Soc; Sigma Xi (vpres, 72-73, pres, 73-74). *Res:* Studies of transition-metal complex ions in concentrated acid solutions, correlations with acidity functions; reaction kinetics and mechanisms; ultraviolet-visible spectroscopy. *Mailing Add:* Dept of Chem Whitman Col Walla Walla WA 99362

TEMPLETON, JOHN Y, III, b Portsmouth, Va, July 1, 17; m 43; c 4. SURGERY. *Educ:* Davidson Col, BS, 37; Jefferson Med Col, MD, 41. *Prof Exp:* Clin prof surg, Jefferson Med Col, 57-64; prof, Univ Pa, 65-67; Samuel D Gross prof & head dept, 67-70, PROF SURG, JEFFERSON MED COL, 70- *Concurrent Pos:* Am Cancer Soc clin fel, Jefferson Hosp, 50-51, Runyon fel, 51-52. *Mem:* Am Surg Asn; Soc Thoracic Surg; Am Col Surg; Soc Vascular Surg; Int Soc Surg. *Res:* General, cardiac and gastrointestinal surgery. *Mailing Add:* Dept of Surg Jefferson Med Col Philadelphia PA 19107

TEMPLETON, JOSEPH LESLIE, b Knoxville, Iowa, Nov 3, 48; m 71; c 2. EARLY TRANSITION METALS, METAL CLUSTERS. *Educ:* Calif Inst Technol, BS, 71; Iowa State Univ, PhD(inorg), 75. *Prof Exp:* NATO fel, Imperial Col Sci & Technol, 75-76; asst prof, 76-81, ASSOC PROF INORG, UNIV NC, 81- *Mem:* Am Chem Soc. *Res:* Early transition metal organometallic chemistry; ligand pi donation in electron deficient complexes; metal cluster chemistry; organometallic reaction mechanisms. *Mailing Add:* Dept Chem Univ NC Chapel Hill NC 27514

TEMPLETON, MCCORMICK, b Cincinnati, Ohio, May 12, 23; m 54; c 2. ANATOMY. *Educ:* Columbia Univ, AB, 48; Univ Kans, PhD(anat), 58. *Prof Exp:* Asst zool, Columbia Univ, 48-49, asst oncol & path, Med Ctr, Univ Kans, 49-51, instr anat, 51-54, asst neuroembryol, 54-57; instr anat, Med Sch, Northwestern Univ, 57-65; asst prof, 65-69, actg chmn dept, 71-76, ASSOC PROF ANAT, SCH DENT, UNIV SOUTHERN CALIF, 69-, CHMN DEPT, 76-, CO-DIR TEMPOROMANDIBULAR JOINT AND OROFACIAL PAIN CLIN, 78- *Mem:* AAAS; Am Asn Anat; Biol Stain Comn; Am Soc Cell Biol. *Res:* Medical anatomy; histochemistry and microchemistry of nervous system of embryo and adult vertebrates; electrophoresis of esterases in blood and digestive tract. *Mailing Add:* Dept of Anat Univ of Southern Calif Los Angeles CA 90007

TEMPLETON, WILLIAM CHELCY, JR, b Ackerman, Miss, June 14, 18; m 46; c 1. AGRONOMY. *Educ:* Miss State Univ, BS, 38; Univ Ill, MS, 39; Purdue Univ, PhD, 60. *Prof Exp:* Instr, 39-42, from asst prof to prof agron, Univ Ky, 46-77; DIR US REGIONAL PASTURE RES LAB, 77- *Mem:* Am Soc Agron. *Res:* Forage crop production and utilization; physiology and ecology of pasture plants; techniques of measuring grassland productivity; forage plant-grazing animal complex. *Mailing Add:* US Regional Pasture Res Lab Curtin Rd University Park PA 16802

TEMPLETON, WILLIAM LEES, b London, Eng, Apr 15, 26; m 52; c 3. RADIATION ECOLOGY, MARINE ECOLOGY. *Educ:* Univ St Andrews, BSc, 50, Hons, 51. *Prof Exp:* Sr biologist, UK Atomic Energy Authority, Windscale, Eng, 51-65; sr res scientist radioecol, 65-68, mgr aquatic ecol, 68-69, ASSOC DEPT MGR ECOSYSTS, PAC NORTHWEST LABS, BATTELLE MEM INST, 69- *Concurrent Pos:* Consult, Int Atomic Energy Agency, 60-; mem panel radioactivity in marine environ, Nat Acad Sci-Nat Res Coun, 68-72, mem panel energy & environ, 75-78. *Mem:* Fel AAAS; Marine Biol Asn UK; Am Soc Limnol & Oceanog; Brit Ecol Soc; Brit Freshwater Biol Asn. *Res:* Waste management practice as related to radioecology and limnology of fresh and marine waters; effects of low level chronic pollution by heavy metal, radiation and oil. *Mailing Add:* Pac Northwest Labs Ecosyst Dept Battelle Mem Inst PO Box 999 Richland WA 99352

TEMPLIN, ROBERT JAMES, b Toronto, Can, Dec 9, 27; m 50; c 3. TECHNICAL MANAGEMENT. *Educ:* Rensselaer Polytech Inst, BChE, 47. *Prof Exp:* Var engr, 57-65, asst chief engr, Cadillac Motor Car Div, 65-69, tech dir, Res Labs, 69-70, gen proj mgr, Special Prod Develop, 70-72, spec asst to pres, 72-73, CHIEF ENGR, CADILLAC MOTOR CAR DIV, GM CORP, 73- *Concurrent Pos:* Vpres, Rensselaer Coun, 80-82. *Mem:* Soc Automotive Engrs; Coord Res Coun. *Res:* Automobile design and development; internal combustion engine design and development; emissions technology development. *Mailing Add:* 2860 Clark Detroit MI 48232

TEMS, ROBIN DOUGLAS, b London, UK, Nov 28, 52. STRESS CORROSION ENGINEERING. *Educ:* Univ Newcastle, UK, BSc, 74, PhD(stress corrosion), 78. *Prof Exp:* Jr res assoc, Univ Newcastle upon Tyne, 74-77, res assoc, 77-78; res engr, Pedco Environ, Inc, 78-79; SR STAFF METALLURGIST, MOBIL RES & DEVELOP CORP, 80- *Mem:* Inst Melallurgists; Nat Asn Corrosion Engrs. *Res:* Corrosion and stress corrosion research and development in the fields of pollution control, gas transmission and oil and gas exploration and production. *Mailing Add:* Mobil Field Res Lab MRDC PO Box 900 Dallas TX 75221

TENAZA, RICHARD REUBEN, b San Mateo, Calif, Mar 22, 39. ETHOLOGY, ECOLOGY. *Educ:* San Francisco State Univ, BA, 64; Univ Calif, Davis, PhD(zool), 74. *Prof Exp:* Asst prof biol, Univ of the Pac, 75-76; res scientist wildlife biol, Sci Applns, Inc, 76-77; ASST PROF BIOL, UNIV OF THE PAC, 77- *Concurrent Pos:* Consult wildlife biol, Sci Applns, Inc, 77- *Mem:* AAAS. *Res:* Primatology; behavioral ecology; animal communication; marine birds and mammals; environmental impacts of oil development. *Mailing Add:* Dept of Biol Univ of the Pac Stockton CA 95211

TEN BRINK, NORMAN WAYNE, b Shelby, Mich, May 17, 43; m 67; c 2. QUATERNARY GEOLOGY. *Educ:* Univ Mich, Ann Arbor, BS, 66; Franklin & Marshall Col, MS, 68; Univ Wash, PhD(geol), 71. *Prof Exp:* Contract geologist, Geol Surv Greenland, 69-71; res fel geol, Inst Polar Studies & Dept Geol, Ohio State Univ, 71-72, asst dir, Inst Polar Studies, 72-73; ASSOC PROF GEOL, COL ARTS & SCI, GRAND VALLEY STATE COLS, 73- *Concurrent Pos:* Field leader NSF grant, Univ Wash, 70-71; prin investr NSF grants, Ohio State Univ, 72-74 & 73-75; consult geohydrologist, Environ Protection Agency, 76-77; Nat Park Serv & Nat Geog grants, Grand Valley State Col & Univ Alaska, 77- *Mem:* AAAS; Am Quaternary Asn; Arctic Inst NAm; Geol Asn Can; Geol Soc Am. *Res:* Glacial geology and geomorphology of Arctic, Antarctic and alpine areas. *Mailing Add:* Dept of Geol Col Arts & Sci Grand Valley State Cols Allendale MI 49401

TENBROEK, BERNARD JOHN, b Grand Rapids, Mich, Mar 29, 24; m 48; c 4. ZOOLOGY. *Educ:* Calvin Col, BA, 49; Univ Colo, MA, 55, PhD(zool), 60. *Prof Exp:* From instr to assoc prof, 55-66, chmn dept, 61-73, PROF BIOL, CALVIN COL, 66- *Mem:* AAAS; Am Soc Zool. *Res:* Studies on thyroid and pituitary function in neotenic forms of Ambystoma tigrinum. *Mailing Add:* Dept of Biol Calvin Col Grand Rapids MI 49506

TENCA, JOSEPH IGNATTIUS, b Bay Shore, NY, Apr 6, 29; m 55; c 3. ENDODONTICS. *Educ:* Holy Cross Col, AB, 50; Georgetown Univ, DDS, 57; George Washington Univ, MA, 74; Am Bd Endodontics, dipl. *Prof Exp:* Captain dent, US Navy, 53-75; ASSOC PROF & CHMN ENDODONTICS DEPT, SCH DENT MED, TUFTS UNIV, 75- *Concurrent Pos:* Dir, secy-treas, Am Bd Endodontics, 79-; chmn & dir grad educ, Nat Naval Dent Ctr, Md, 71-75; prof & lectr oral biol, Grad Sch George Washington Univ, 71-75; consult, Nat Naval Dent Ctr, 76- & Comn Dent Accreditation, Am Dent Asn, 80- *Mem:* Int Asn Dent Res; Am Asn Endodontists; Am Dent Asn; Am Asn Dent Schs; fel Int Col Dentists. *Res:* Clinical endodontics, more specifically in radiographic interpretation and reliability of various endodontic instruments, filling materials and medications. *Mailing Add:* Endodontics Dept Sch Dent Med Tufts Univ One Kneeland St Boston MA 02111

TEN CATE, ARNOLD RICHARD, b Accrington, Eng, Oct 21, 33; m 56; c 3. ANATOMY, DENTISTRY. *Educ:* Univ London, BDS, 60, BSc, 55, PhD(anat), 58. *Prof Exp:* Sr lectr dent sci, Royal Col Surgeons Eng, 61-63; sr lectr anat in dent, Guy's Hosp Med Sch, Univ London, 63-68; prof anat & dent, 68-71, chmn div, 71-77, PROF BIOL SCI & DEAN FAC DENT, UNIV TORONTO, 77- *Honors & Awards:* Colyer Prize, Royal Soc Med, 62; Milo Hellman Award, Am Asn Orthod, 75; Isaac Schour Mem Award, Int Asn Dent Res, 78. *Mem:* Int Asn Dent Res. *Res:* Dental histology; development of periodontium and connective tissue remodeling. *Mailing Add:* Fac of Dent Univ of Toronto 124 Edward St Toronto ON M5G 1G6 Can

TENCH, DENNIS MORGAN, US citizen. ELECTROCHEMISTRY, PHYSICAL CHEMISTRY. *Educ:* WVa Inst Technol, BS, 65; Western Reserve Univ, MS, 67; Case Western Reserve Univ, PhD(phys chem), 70. *Prof Exp:* Sr res chemist, Standard Oil Co, Ohio, 70-71; staff scientist, Gould, Inc, 71-72; fel, Fritz-Haber-Inst der Max-Planck-Gesellschaft, Berlin, WGer, 72-73; sr res scientist, Ford Motor Co, 74-75; mem tech staff, 75-76, MGR, ELECTROCHEM PROCESSES, ROCKWELL INT MICROELECTRONICS RES & DEVELOP CTR, 76- *Mem:* Electrochem Soc; Am Electroplaters Soc. *Res:* Electrodeposition; semiconductor electrochemistry; photoelectrochemistry; electrochemical solar cells; electrochemical photocapacitance spectroscopy. *Mailing Add:* Rockwell Int Microelectronics Res & Develop Ctr 1049 Camino Dos Rios Thousand Oaks CA 91360

TENCZA, THOMAS MICHAEL, b Wallington, NJ, July 8, 32; m 59. ORGANIC CHEMISTRY. *Educ:* Columbia Univ, AB, 54; Seton Hall Univ, MS, 64, PhD(chem), 66; Fairleigh Dickenson Univ, MBA, 71. *Prof Exp:* Res chemist, S B Penick Co, 57-60; DIR RES & DEVELOP COORD, BRISTOL-MYERS CO, HILLSIDE, 60- *Mem:* Am Chem Soc; Am Pharmaceut Asn; Am Mgt Asn; Soc Cosmetic Chemists. *Res:* Research and development management; product development; rearrangement reactions of small ring compounds; botanical drugs. *Mailing Add:* 31 Wagner Ave Wallington NJ 07057

TENCZAR, FRANCIS J, pathology, see previous edition

TENDAM, DONALD JAN, b Hamilton, Ohio, May 28, 16; m 39; c 3. NUCLEAR PHYSICS. *Educ:* Miami Univ, AB, 40; Purdue Univ, MS, 42, PhD(physics), 49. *Prof Exp:* Asst, 40-42, from instr to assoc prof, 42-60, PROF PHYSICS, PURDUE UNIV, WEST LAFAYETTE, 60-, ASSOC HEAD DEPT, 66- *Mem:* AAAS; Am Phys Soc; Am Asn Physics Teachers. *Res:* Particle accelerators; radioactive tracers; nuclear reactions; deuteron-bombarded semiconductors. *Mailing Add:* Dept Physics Purdue Univ West Lafayette IN 47906

TENDLER, MOSES DAVID, b New York, NY, Aug 7, 26; m 48; c 8. MICROBIOLOGY. *Educ:* NY Univ, BA, 47, MA, 51; Columbia Univ, PhD, 57. *Prof Exp:* From instr to assoc prof, 52-63, asst dean, 56-59, PROF BIOL, YESHIVA UNIV, 63- *Concurrent Pos:* Consult, Eli Lilly & Co, 59-61 & Hoffmann-La Roche Inc, 63-; res dir, Thermobios Pharmaceut Corp, 63-; mem res adv coun, NY Cancer Res Inst, 65-71. *Mem:* AAAS; Am Soc Microbiol; Torrey Bot Club; Am Soc Clin Pharmacol & Therapeut; NY Acad Sci. *Res:* Nutrition of thermophilic actinomycetes; antibiotic and antitumor agents proliferated by thermophilic organisms; physiological problems of thermophily; discoverer of Anthramycin, an antitumor antibiotic. *Mailing Add:* Dept of Biol Yeshiva Univ 500 W 185th St New York NY 10033

TEN EICK, ROBERT EDWIN, b Portchester, NY, Oct 14, 37; m 62; c 2. CELLULAR ELECTROPHYSIOLOGY, PHARMACOLOGY. *Educ:* Columbia Univ, BS, 63, PhD(pharmacol), 68. *Prof Exp:* Guest investr cardiac electrophysiol, Rockefeller Univ, 68; asst prof, 68-74, assoc prof, 74-81, PROF PHARMACOL, MED SCH, NORTHWESTERN UNIV, CHICAGO, 81- *Concurrent Pos:* NIH trainee cardiac electrophysiol, Rockefeller Univ, 68; Chicago Heart Asn res rev comt; vis prof II, Physiol Inst, Univ Saarland, WGer, 74-75; NIH res career develop award, 75-80. *Mem:* Am Physiol Soc; Am Heart Asn; Am Soc Pharmacol & Exp Therapeut; Cardiac Muscle Soc. *Res:* Cellular electrophysiological basis of cardiac dysrhythmias associated with heart disease; cellular electrophysiology of the heart; myocardial membrane currents and their relation to cardiac electrical activity and cardiac contraction. *Mailing Add:* Dept Pharmacol Northwestern Univ Med Sch Chicago IL 60611

TENENBAUM, JOEL, b Brooklyn, NY, Dec 17, 40; m 67; c 3. DYNAMIC METEOROLOGY. *Educ:* Calif Inst Technol, BS, 62; Harvard Univ, AM, 63, PhD(physics), 69. *Prof Exp:* Res assoc physics, Stanford Linear Accelerator Ctr, 68-71; asst prof, 71-76, actg dean, Natural Sci, 78 & 79, ASSOC PROF PHYSICS, STATE UNIV NY COL PURCHASE, 76- *Concurrent Pos:* Consult, Inst Space Studies, NASA Goddard Space Flight Ctr, 72-75; vis assoc prof meteorol, Mass Inst Technol, 80-82; vis scholar meteorol, Harvard, 80-82. *Mem:* AAAS; Am Phys Soc; Am Asn Physics Teachers. *Res:* Modeling of large scale processes in dynamic meteorology; elementary particle physics. *Mailing Add:* Div Natural Sci State Univ NY Col Purchase NY 10577

TENENBAUM, MICHAEL, b St Paul, Minn, July 23, 14; m 41; c 2. METALLURGY. *Educ:* Univ Minn, BS, 36, MS, 37, PhD(metall, phys chem), 40. *Hon Degrees:* DSc, Northwestern Univ, 74. *Prof Exp:* Raw mat res TC&I RR, 39-40; metallurgist, Metall Dept, 41-50, asst supt qual control, 50-56, supt metall dept, 56-59, asst gen mgr tech serv, 59-61, gen mgr res & qual control, 61-66, vpres res, 66-68, vpres, Steel Mfg, 68-71, PRES, INLAND STEEL CO, 71- *Concurrent Pos:* Dir, Blast Furnace Res, Inc, 64-69; US rep, Int Iron & Steel Inst. *Honors & Awards:* Nat Open Hearth Comt Award, Am Inst Mining, Metall & Petrol Eng, 47 & 48, Raymond Award, 49, Hunt Award, 50 & Fairless Award, 75. *Mem:* Distinguished mem Am Inst Mining, Metall & Petrol Eng (pres, 68); Am Iron & Steel Inst; distinguished mem Am Soc Metals; Asn Iron & Steel Engrs. *Res:* Metallurgy and chemistry of iron and steel manufacture. *Mailing Add:* Inland Steel Co 30 W Monroe St Chicago IL 60603

TENENBAUM, SAUL, b New York, NY, Nov 3, 17; m; c 3. MICROBIOLOGY. *Educ:* Wash State Univ, BS, 43; Long Island Univ, MS, 64. *Prof Exp:* Jr seafood inspector, US Food & Drug Admin, 42-44; asst chemist, US Maritime Comn, 44-45; sr biochemist, Standard Brands, 45-46; bacteriologist, Atlantic Yeast Co, 46-48; chief bacteriologist, Premo Pharmaceut Lab, 48-57; group leader, 57-65, mgr, 65-67, asst dir microbiol, 67-79, DIR RES MICROBIOL, REVLON RES CTR, 79- *Concurrent Pos:* Lectr, Fairleigh-Dickinson Univ, 51-56; adj assoc prof pharmaceut sci, Sch Pharm, St John Univ, 73-; course dir, Ctr Continuing Educ, 77- *Mem:* Soc Indust Microbiol; Am Soc Microbiol; Soc Cosmetic Chemistry; NY Acad Sci. *Res:* Development and evaluation of biostatic and biocidal agents; pseudomonads; preservation; microbial content; skin microbiology; immunology; hypersensitive state and agents; analytical immunological technics; mutagenicity, topical and ocular infection; clinical evaluation of irritants and allergens. *Mailing Add:* 86-22 155th Ave Howard Beach NY 11414

TENENHOUSE, ALAN M, b Montreal, Que, Aug 8, 35; m 61; c 2. BIOCHEMISTRY, ENDOCRINOLOGY. *Educ:* McGill Univ, BSc, 55, PhD(biochem), 59, MD & CM, 62. *Prof Exp:* Asst prof, 68-77, ASSOC PROF PHARMACOL & THERAPEUT, McGILL UNIV, 78- *Concurrent Pos:* Fel biochem, Univ Wis, 63-65; NIH fel, 64-66; fel biochem, Univ Pa, 65-68; Univ Pa plan scholar, 66-68. *Mem:* Endocrine Soc; Can Biochem Soc; Can Pharmacol Soc. *Res:* Mechanism of hormone action with emphasis on role of 3' 5' AMP and calcium in hormone action; biochemistry and physiology of parathyroid hormone and calcitonin. *Mailing Add:* Dept of Pharmacol & Therapeut McGill Univ McIntyre Med Ctr Montreal PQ H3A 2T5 Can

TENER, GORDON MALCOLM, b Vancouver, BC, Nov 24, 27. BIOCHEMISTRY. *Educ:* Univ BC, BA, 49; Univ Wis, MS, 51, PhD(biochem), 53. *Prof Exp:* Rockefeller fel biochem, Inst Phys-Chem Biol, Paris, France, 53-54; res scientist, BC Res Coun, Vancouver, 54-60; from asst prof to assoc prof, 60-67, PROF BIOCHEM, UNIV BC, 67- *Concurrent Pos:* Merck Sharp & Dohme Award, Chem Inst Can, 64. *Mem:* Am Chem Soc; Am Soc Biol Chem; Can Biochem Soc; The Chem Soc. *Res:* Nucleotide and oligonucleotide synthesis and isolation; purification and properties of transfer ribonucleic acids; gene localization in Drosophila; gene structure; recombinant DNA. *Mailing Add:* Dept of Biochem Univ of BC Vancouver BC V6T 1W5 Can

TEN EYCK, DAVID RODERICK, b Portland, Ore, Oct 24, 29. MEDICINE, PUBLIC HEALTH. *Educ:* Occidental Col, AB, 51; Univ Southern Calif, MD, 55; Johns Hopkins Univ, MPH, 67, DPH, 73. *Prof Exp:* Med officer, Med Corps, US Navy, 55-69, dep dir, US Naval Med Res Unit 3, Addis Ababa, Ethiopia, 69-71, cmndg officer, US Naval Med Res Unit 1, Univ Calif, Berkeley, 71-75, cmndg officer, Naval Health Res Ctr, San Diego, 75; PVT PRACT, 75- *Mem:* AMA; Am Pub Health Asn. *Res:* Tropical medicine and epidemiology; serologic diagnosis of parasitic diseases; diagnosis and prevention of coccidioidomycosis. *Mailing Add:* 17412 Hart St Van Nuys CA 91406

TEN EYCK, EDWARD H(ANLON), JR, b Pearl River, NY, Sept 6, 23; m 52; c 2. CHEMICAL ENGINEERING. *Educ:* Syracuse Univ, BChE, 43; Polytech Inst Brooklyn, MChE, 48, DChE, 50. *Prof Exp:* Chem engr, Johns Manville Corp, 44; from asst tech supt to lab adminr, 49-71, prog mgr, 71-76, MFG MGR, PLASTICS DEVELOP, E I DU PONT DE NEMOURS CO, INC, WILMINGTON, 76- *Mem:* Am Chem Soc; Am Inst Chem Engrs. *Res:* Polymerization and plasticizers; phase relations of petroleum hydrocarbons; process development; organic chemicals. *Mailing Add:* PO Box 3656 Greenville DE 19807

TENFORDE, TOM SEBASTIAN, b Middletown, Ohio, Dec 15, 40; m 79; c 1. BIOPHYSICS. *Educ:* Harvard Univ, AB, 62; Univ Calif, Berkeley, PhD(biophysics), 69. *Prof Exp:* Fel, Univ Calif, Berkeley, 69-73; BIOPHYSICIST, LAWRENCE BERKELEY LAB, UNIV CALIF, BERKELEY, 73-, DEP GROUP LEADER, RADIATION BIOPHYSICS GROUP, BIOL & MED DIV, 81- *Concurrent Pos:* mem, Comt SC-67, Nat Coun Radiation Protection & Measurements, 81-; mem bd dir, Bioelectromagnetics Soc, 81- *Mem:* AAAS; Bioelectromagnetics Soc; Biophys Soc; NY Acad Sci; Radiation Res Soc. *Res:* Tumor radiobiology studies with accelerated charged-particle beams; biological effects of high magnetic fields; surface chemistry of normal and cancer cells. *Mailing Add:* Biol & Med Div Bldg 934 Rm 6 Lawrence Berkeley Lab No 1 Cyclotron Rd Berkeley CA 94720

TENG, CHING SUNG, b Amoy, Fukien, Nov 20, 37; US citizen; m 64; c 2. REPRODUCTIVE BIOLOGY, BIOCHEMISTRY. *Educ:* Tunghai Univ, Taiwan, BS, 60; Univ Tex, Austin, MS, 64, PhD(biochem), 67. *Prof Exp:* Res assoc biochem, Univ Tex, Austin, 67-69; guest investr, Rockefeller Univ, 69-71; asst prof develop biol, State Univ NY Stony Brook, 71-73; assoc prof cell biol, Baylor Col Med, 73-80; PROF ANAT & PHYSIOL, NC STATE UNIV, 81- *Concurrent Pos:* NIH res fel, Cancer Inst, 69-70, NIH spec res fel, 70-71, NIH grant award, 73- *Mem:* Am Soc Cell Biol; Endocrine Soc; Sigma Xi. *Res:* Steroid hormone-controlled sex organ differentiation. *Mailing Add:* Dept Ant & Physiol Grinnels Lab Box 5658 NC State Univ Raleigh NC 27650

TENG, CHOJAN, b Taipei, Taiwan, Aug 31, 47; m 71; c 1. ELECTRICAL ENGINEERING, COMPUTER SCIENCES. *Educ:* Nat Taiwan Univ, BS, 69; Wash State Univ, MS, 72; Univ Wis-Madison, MS, 76, PhD(elec eng), 78. *Prof Exp:* MEM TECH STAFF RADAR SYST, DIGITAL SIGNAL PROCESSING & WAVE PROPAGATION, MITRE CORP, 78- *Mem:* Inst Elec & Electronics Engrs; Sigma Xi. *Res:* Electromagnetic wave propagation; communication; digital signal processing; numerical analysis; applied mathematics. *Mailing Add:* MITRE Corp PO Box 208 Bedford MA 01730

TENG, CHRISTINA WEI-TIEN TU, b Kuming, Yunnan, China, July 23, 42; m 64; c 2. CELL BIOLOGY, BIOCHEMISTRY. *Educ:* Tunghai Univ, Taiwan, BS, 63; Univ Tex, Austin, PhD(biol), 69. *Prof Exp:* Guest investr cell biol, Rockefeller Univ, 69-71; sr res assoc med, Brookhaven Nat Lab, 71-73; asst prof cell biol, Baylor Col Med, 73-81; RES SCIENTIST, NC STATE UNIV, 81- *Mem:* Am Soc Cell Biol; Sigma Xi. *Res:* Hormone controlled sex organ differentiation; study of the regulatory mechanism for gene activation in mammalian system. *Mailing Add:* Dept Anatomy NC State Univ Raleigh NC 27650

TENG, EVELYN LEE, b Chungking, China, Feb 8, 38; m 63; c 2. PSYCHOBIOLOGY. *Educ:* Taiwan Univ, BS, 59; Stanford Univ, MA, 60, PhD(psychol), 63. *Prof Exp:* Res fel psychobiol, Calif Inst Technol, 63-69, sr res fel, 69-72; asst prof neurol, 72-75, ASSOC PROF NEUROL, SCH MED, UNIV SOUTHERN CALIF, 75- *Mem:* Am Psychol Asn. *Res:* Functional relationship between brain and behavior, especially higher cognitive functions in man. *Mailing Add:* 1474 Rose Villa St Pasadena CA 91106

TENG, JAMES, b Hong Kong, Dec 4, 29; US citizen; m 57; c 2. CHEMISTRY. *Educ:* Tri-State Col, BS, S2; Case Western Reserve Univ, MS, 61, PhD(org chem), 67. *Prof Exp:* Chem engr, Radio Receptor Co, 52-53; process engr, Nylonge Corp, 53-56, res supvr, 56-61, tech supvr, 61-66; fel, Purdue Univ, 66-67; res proj mgr, 68-75, res mgr advan prod, 75-78, MGR, PROCESS OPTIMIZATION CTR, ANHEUSER BUSCH INC, 78- *Mem:* AAAS; Am Inst Chem; NY Acad Sci; Am Chem Soc. *Res:* Carbohydrate chemistry; regenerated cellulose; cellulose derivatives; starch derivatives; carbohydrates in brewing. *Mailing Add:* Cent Res Dept Anheuser Busch Inc St Louis MO 63118

TENG, JON IE, b Kienow, China, Oct 19, 30; m 58; c 2. STEROID CHEMISTRY, NATURAL PRODUCTS CHEMISTRY. *Educ:* Nat Taiwan Univ, BS, 55; SDak State Univ, MS, 62; Univ Fla, PhD(agr biochem), 65. *Prof Exp:* Agr scientist, Taiwan Sugar Corp, Inc, 56-60; res assoc nitrogen metab in hort plants, Univ Ill, Urbana, 65-66; res chemist, Am Crystal Sugar Co, 66-68; NIH fel steroid biochem, Med Sch, Univ Minn, 68-69, res assoc pharmacol, 69-70; res biochemist, 70-75, RES SCIENTIST, UNIV TEX MED BR GALVESTON, 75- *Mem:* Am Chem Soc; Inst Am Chemists. *Res:* Steroid biosynthesis and metabolism; drug metabolism; plant nutrition and biochemistry; steroid biochemistry; cholesterol metabolism in mammalian liver, kidney, brain and aortal tissues. *Mailing Add:* Dept of Biochem Hendrix Bldg Univ of Tex Med Br Galveston TX 77550

TENG, LEE CHANG-LI, b Peiping, China, Sept 5, 26; nat US; m 61; c 1. ELEMENTARY PARTICLE PHYSICS. *Educ:* Fu Jen Univ, China, BS, 46; Univ Chicago, MS, 48, PhD(physics), 51. *Prof Exp:* Cyclotron asst, Univ Chicago, 49-51; lectr physics, Univ Minn, 51-52, asst prof, 52-53; assoc prof, Univ Wichita, 53-55; assoc physicist, Particle Accelerator Div, Argonne Nat Lab, 55-61, head theory group, 56-62, sr physicist, 61-67, dir, 62-67; head accelerator theory sect, 67-72, head adv proj sect, 72-75, ASSOC HEAD, ACCELERATOR DIV, FERMI NAT ACCELERATOR LAB, 75- *Mem:* Fel Am Phys Soc. *Res:* High energy accelerators and instrumentation; high energy and nuclear physics. *Mailing Add:* Fermi Nat Accelerator Lab PO Box 500 Batavia IL 60510

TENG, LINA CHEN, b Fukien, China, Dec 8, 39; US citizen; m 65. DRUG METABOLISM. *Educ:* Nat Taiwan Univ, BS, 63; Utah State Univ, PhD(org chem), 67. *Prof Exp:* Res chemist, Philip Morris Inc, 67-71; sr res chemist, 73-78, RES ASSOC, A H ROBINS CO, INC, 78- *Mem:* Am Chem Soc; Sigma Xi; AAAS. *Res:* Studies of the metabolism, mainly isolation and identification of the metabolites, of the existing or research drugs in animals and human beings; synthesis of radiolabelled compounds for drug research. *Mailing Add:* 7638 Redbud Rd Richmond VA 23235

TENG, TA-LIANG, b China, July 3, 37; m 63; c 2. GEOPHYSICS. *Educ:* Univ Taiwan, BS, 59; Calif Inst Technol, PhD(geophys, appl math), 66. *Prof Exp:* Res fel geophys, Seismol Lab, Calif Inst Technol, 66-67; from asst prof to assoc prof geophys, 67-74, assoc prof, 74-77, PROF GEOL SCI, UNIV SOUTHERN CALIF, 78- *Mem:* AAAS; Am Geophys Union; Seismol Soc Am. *Res:* Elastic wave propagations; observational and theoretical seismology; elastic and anelastic properties of the earth and planetary interiors. *Mailing Add:* Dept of Geol Sci Univ of Southern Calif Los Angeles CA 90007

TENG, WAYNE C, b Chengtu, China, Dec 11, 20; m 49; c 2. CIVIL ENGINEERING. *Educ:* Nat Cent Univ, China, BS, 42; Univ Ill, Urbana, MS, 47, PhD(eng), 49. *Prof Exp:* Distinguished prof asst, Univ Ill, Urbana, 46-49; struct engr, Skidmore, Owings & Merrill, Architects & Engrs, 49-52, asst chief struct eng, 55-58; struct engr, Sargent & Lundy, Engrs, 52-55; chief struct engr, Meissner Engrs, 58-59; PRES, TENG & ASSOCS, INC, 59- *Concurrent Pos:* Lectr, Ill Inst Technol, 53-55; vis prof, Univ Ill, Chicago Circle, 69-70. *Mem:* Am Rwy Eng Asn; fel Am Soc Civil Engrs; Am Concrete Inst. *Res:* Structural and foundation engineering. *Mailing Add:* Teng & Assocs Inc 220 S State St Chicago IL 60604

TENGERDY, ROBERT PAUL, b Budapest, Hungary, Dec 17, 30; US citizen; m 53; c 2. IMMUNOCHEMISTRY, MICROBIOLOGY. *Educ:* Budapest Tech Univ, Dipl Chem Eng, 53; St John's Univ, NY, PhD(microbial biochem), 61. *Prof Exp:* Asst prof biochem eng, Budapest Tech Univ, 53-56; res biochemist, Chas Pfizer & Co, NY, 57-61; asst prof chem & microbiol, 61-

64, assoc prof biochem & microbiol, 64-71, PROF MICROBIOL, COLO STATE UNIV, 71- *Concurrent Pos:* Europ Molecular Biol Orgn fel, Pasteur Inst Paris, 68; Humboldt fel, Max Planck Inst, Univ Göettingen, 68. *Mem:* AAAS; Am Asn Immunol; Am Soc Microbiol. *Res:* Stress immunology; nutritional aspects of immunology; applied microbiology; waste conversion by microbes. *Mailing Add:* Dept of Microbiol Colo State Univ Ft Collins CO 80523

TENHOVER, MICHAEL ALAN, b Cincinnati, Ohio, Nov 9, 53. CATALYSIS. *Educ:* Univ Cincinnati, BS, 76; Calif Inst Technol, MS, 78, PhD(appl physics), 81. *Prof Exp:* SR RES PHYSICIST, DEPT RES, STANDARD OIL CO, 81- *Mem:* Am Phys Soc. *Res:* Atomic and electronic structure of amorphous metals and semiconductors; high fluid superconductivity; nuclear spectroscopy; oxidation catalysis. *Mailing Add:* Dept Res Warrensville Res Ctr Standard Oil Co Warrensville Heights OH 44128

TENNANKORE, KANNAN NAGARAJAN, b Madras, India, Oct 30, 46; m 71; c 1. CHEMICAL ENGINEERING. *Educ:* Univ Madras, BSc, 65; Indian Inst Technol, Madras, BTech, 68, MTech, 70; Univ NB, PhD(chem eng), 75. *Prof Exp:* Asst eng design & develop distillation columns, Engrs India Ltd, India, 70-71; fel combustion, Univ NB, 75-77, res assoc dispersion of aerial sprays, 77-78; ENG RES ANALYST FLOW MASS & HEAT TRANSFER ENCLOSURES, WHITESHELL NUCLEAR RES ESTAB, ATOMIC ENERGY CAN LTD, 78- *Res:* Experimental study and modeling of flow, heat and mass transfer in enclosures. *Mailing Add:* 13 Stanley St Pinawa MB R0E 1L0 Can

TENNANT, BUD C, b Burbank, Calif, Nov 10, 33; m 63; c 3. VETERINARY MEDICINE, GASTROENTEROLOGY. *Educ:* Univ Calif, BS , 57, DVM, 59. *Prof Exp:* Intern, Sch of Vet Med, Univ Calif, 59, from asst prof to assoc prof, 62-72; res assoc, Dept Surg, Albert Einstein Col Med, 62; res fel, Gastrointestinal Unit, Mass Gen Hosp, 6869; PROF COMP GASTROENTEROL, NY STATE COL VET MED, CORNELL UNIV, 72- *Mem:* Am Col Vet Internal Med; Am Gastroenterol Asn; Am Inst Nutrit; Am Vet Med Asn; Soc Exp Biol in Med. *Res:* Diseases of the gastrointestinal tract and liver of domestic animals; pathogenesis of neonatal enteric infections; influence of microorganisms on intestinal function. *Mailing Add:* NY State Col of Vet Med Cornell Univ Ithaca NY 14853

TENNANT, DONALD L, b Mt Gilead, Ohio, Jan 27, 27; m 56; c 3. FISH BIOLOGY, LIMNOLOGY. *Educ:* Ohio State Univ, BS, 52. *Prof Exp:* Fish mgt supvr, Ohio Div Wildlife, 52-57; fishery res biologist, 57-59, fishery biologist, 59-67, FISH & WILDLIFE BIOLOGIST, US FISH & WILDLIFE SERV, 67- *Honors & Awards:* Fisheries Scientist Award, Am Fisheries Soc, 68. *Mem:* Am Fisheries Soc; Fel Am Inst Fishery Res Biologists. *Res:* In stream flow regimens for fish, wildlife, recreation and related environmental resources; reservoir, lake and pond limnology and management; artificial propagation of muskellunge and fish hybridization. *Mailing Add:* US Fish & Wildlife Serv Fed Bldg Rm 3025 Billings MT 59101

TENNANT, JUDITH R, b Sioux City, Iowa, Apr 3, 19; m 68, 77. VIROLOGY. *Educ:* Ohio Wesleyan Univ, BA, 40; Univ Minn, Minneapolis, MS, 57, PhD(virol, cancer biol), 61. *Prof Exp:* Fel, Jackson Lab, 61-63; res assoc, Sloan-Kettering Inst Cancer Res, 64-67, assoc, 67-72; ASSOC EXEC ED, J CELL BIOL, ROCKEFELLER UNIV, 73- *Mem:* Am Asn Immunol; Coun Biol Ed; Am Asn Cancer Res; NY Acad Sci. *Res:* Cancer biology, etiology, natural resistance, genetic factors and immuno-therapy in leukemogenesis. *Mailing Add:* Rockefeller Univ 1230 York Ave New York NY 10021

TENNANT, RAYMOND WALLACE, b West Frankfort, Ill, Sept 19, 37; m 60; c 4. MICROBIOLOGY, VIROLOGY. *Educ:* Univ Notre Dame, MS, 61; Georgetown Univ, PhD(microbiol), 63. *Prof Exp:* Virologist, Dept Virus Res, Microbiol Assocs, Inc, Md, 61-65; USPHS fel replication of DNA viruses, Albert Einstein Med Ctr, 65-66; sr staff scientist, Biol Div, Oak Ridge Nat Lab, 66-80; CHIEF, CELLULAR & GENETIC TOXICOL BR, NAT TOXICOL PROG, NAT INST ENVIRON HEALTH SCI, RESEARCH TRIANGLE PARK, NC, 80- *Concurrent Pos:* mem adv comt, Am Cancer Soc. *Mem:* AAAS; Am Asn Cancer Res; Am Soc Microbiol. *Res:* Epizoology of murine viruses; replication of DNA containing viruses; murine leukemia; RNA tumor virus cell biology and genetics; cellular transformation; cancer biology; genetic toxicology. *Mailing Add:* 4916 Larchmont Dr Raleigh NC 27612

TENNANT, WILLIAM EMERSON, b Washington, DC, Oct 8, 45; m 68; c 3. SOLID STATE PHYSICS. *Educ:* Harvard Univ, AB, 67; Univ Calif, Berkeley, PhD(solid state physics), 74. *Prof Exp:* Mem tech staff physics, 73-79, MGR, INFRARED DETECTOR MAT GROUP, ROCKWELL INT SCI CTR, 79- *Res:* Infrared detectors and imagers; semiconductor devices; collective excitations in solids; optical nondestructive evaluation methods; low frequency excitations of organic compounds; radiation damage; crystal alloys and defects; solar energy collection. *Mailing Add:* Rockwell Int Sci Ctr 1049 Camino Dos Rios Thousand Oaks CA 91360

TENNEBAUM, JAMES I, b Cincinnati, Ohio, Aug 21, 32; m 59; c 4. ALLERGY. *Educ:* Univ Cincinnati, BS, 54, MD, 58. *Prof Exp:* From instr to assoc prof, 65-74, CLIN PROF MED, COL MED, OHIO STATE UNIV, 74-, DIR DIV ALLERGY, 71- *Concurrent Pos:* Teaching fel, Nat Trudeau Asn, 60-61; ed sect allergy, J Comtemp Therapy, 74- *Mem:* Fel Am Acad Allergy; fel Am Col Physicians; Am Asn Immunologists; Am Fedn Clin. *Res:* fel Am Asn Clin Immunol & Allergy. Res: Allergic antibody; pharmacokinetics of aminophylline. *Mailing Add:* 456 Clin Dr Ohio State Univ Hosp Clin Columbus OH 43210

TENNENT, DAVID MADDUX, b Bryn Mawr, Pa, Oct 2, 14; m 45; c 4. BIOCHEMISTRY. *Educ:* Yale Univ, AB, 36, PhD(org chem), 40. *Prof Exp:* Asst appl physiol, Yale Univ, 40-42; biochemist, Merck Inst Therapeut Res, 42-60; asst dir res, Hess & Clark Div, Richardson-Merrell Inc, 60-63, dir res & develop, 63-69, vpres & dir res & develop, 69-75; consult, Vet Affairs, Rhodia Inc, 75-79; RETIRED. *Concurrent Pos:* Fel, Coun Arteriosclerosis, Am Heart Asn. *Mem:* Fel AAAS; Am Chem Soc; Am Soc Biol Chem; Soc Exp Biol & Med. *Res:* Pharmacology of drugs; bacterial pyrogens; cholesterol metabolism and experimental atherosclerosis; medications to improve performance and health of production animals; FDA applications. *Mailing Add:* 981 Forest Lane Ashland OH 44805

TENNENT, HOWARD GORDON, b Quebec, Que, Feb 29, 16; US citizen; m 48; c 4. ORGANOMETALLIC CHEMISTRY. *Educ:* Rensselaer Polytech Inst, BS, 37, MS, 39; Univ Wis, PhD(phys chem), 42. *Prof Exp:* Res chemist, Hercules, Inc, 42-47, mgr res div cellulose prod, 47-51, exp sta, 52, cent res div, 53-57, res assoc, 58-66, sr res assoc, 66-81; RETIRED. *Mem:* Am Chem Soc; Sci Res Soc Am. *Res:* Surface modification for electrocatalysis. *Mailing Add:* Chandler Mill Rd Kennett Square PA 19348

TENNER, THOMAS EDWARD, JR, b Pittsburgh, Pa, June 2, 49; m 72; c 2. CARDIOVASCULAR PHARMACOLOGY, SUPERSENSITIVITY PHENOMENA. *Educ:* Univ Dallas, BA, 71; Univ Tex Health Sci Ctr, PhD(pharmacol), 76. *Prof Exp:* Fel, Fac Pharmaceut Sci, Univ BC, 76-78; ASST PROF, DEPT PHARMACOL, TEX TECH UNIV HEALTH SCI CTR, 78- *Res:* Drug-induced modulation of sensitivity and responsiveness of the cardiovascular systems in particular reserpine and propranolol withdrawal induced supersensitivity phenomena. *Mailing Add:* Tex Tech Univ Health Sci Ctr 3601 4th St Lubbock TX 79430

TENNESSEN, KENNETH JOSEPH, b Ladysmith, Wis, June 10, 46; m 67; c 2. FRESH WATER ECOLOGY. *Educ:* Univ Wis, BS, 68; Univ Fla, MS, 73, PhD(entom), 75. *Prof Exp:* BIOLOGIST ECOLOGICAL EFFECTS AQUATIC INSECTS, TENN VALLEY AUTHORITY, 75- *Mem:* Entom Soc Am; NAm Benthological Soc; Int Soc Odontol. *Res:* Investigation of effects of heated discharge and toxic substances from electric generating plants on the survival, growth, reproductive capacity and distribution of aquatic insects in the Tennessee River Valley. *Mailing Add:* Aquatic Biol Sect Tenn Valley Authority Muscle Shoals AL 35660

TENNEY, AGNES, b Boston, Mass. THEORETICAL PHYSICAL CHEMISTRY. *Educ:* Regis Col, AB, 68; Ind Univ, PhD(chem), 75. *Prof Exp:* Assoc instr chem, Ind Univ, 68-73, syst analyst comput sci, 73-76, vis asst prof, 76-77; ASST PROF CHEM, UNIV PORTLAND, 77- *Concurrent Pos:* Fac res grant, Univ Portland, 78-79. *Mem:* Am Chem Soc; Am Phys Soc; Int Asn Hydrogen. *Res:* Theory, particularly, electron atom molecule scattering in the intermediate energy range; renewable energy storage via hydrogen; computer controlled experiments. *Mailing Add:* Dept of Chem Univ of Portland Portland OR 97203

TENNEY, ALBERT SEWARD, III, b Lakewood, NJ, Mar 31, 43; m 66; c 2. PHYSICAL CHEMISTRY. *Educ:* Rutgers Univ, AB, 65, PhD(phys chem), 71. *Prof Exp:* Phys chemist mat sci, Gen Elec Co, 69-74; group leader solar cells, SES, Inc, 74-76; prin scientist temp measurement, 76-80, PRIN SCIENTIST SENSOR DEVELOP, LEEDS & NORTHRUP CO, 80- *Mem:* Am Chem Soc; Instrument Soc Am. *Res:* Materials research on molten salts, thin films, glasses and semiconductors; temperature measurement; development of light-emitting diodes, solar cells, temperature measuring instruments and analytical sensors. *Mailing Add:* Leeds & Northrup Co Dickerson Rd North Wales PA 19454

TENNEY, DARREL RAY, b Buckhannon, WVa, May 1, 42; m 61; c 3. METALLURGICAL ENGINEERING. *Educ:* WVa Wesleyan Col, BS, 64; Va Polytech Inst & State Univ, PhD(mat eng sci), 69. *Prof Exp:* Res asst metall eng, Va Polytech Inst & State Univ, 64-69, asst prof, 69-77; MEM STAFF, MAT RES BR, NASA-LANGLEY RES CTR, 77- *Concurrent Pos:* NSF res initiation grant, Va Polytech Inst & State Univ, 70-72, NASA res grant, 71-73; tech consult, KDI Electro-Tec Corp, 72. *Mem:* Am Soc Metals; Am Inst Mining, Metall & Petrol Engrs; Analog/Hybrid Comput Educ Soc. *Res:* Physical metallurgy, oxidation of metals; diffusion, x-ray diffraction; mathematical modeling of metallurgical process; computer control of processes. *Mailing Add:* MD Mat Res Br NASA-Langley Res Ctr Hampton VA 23665

TENNEY, GEROLD H, b Ebersdorf, Austria, Jan 19, 09; nat US; m 41. ENGINEERING. *Educ:* Univ Vienna, Dipl eng, 35. *Prof Exp:* Asst, Electropath Dept, Univ Vienna, 35-38; instr physics & in chg dept, Eastern Sch Physicians Aides, 39-43; group leader, Los Alamos Sci Lab, 44-66, tech adv nondestructive testing, 66-70; CONSULT, 70- *Concurrent Pos:* Leader, Int Conf Nondestructuve Testing, Belg, 55, admin chmn, US, 57; mem, Arg Nondestructive Testing Ctr, US del, Int Comn Nondestructive Testing. *Honors & Awards:* Gold Medal, Japan, 60; Du Pont Award, Am Soc Nondestructive Testing, 64. *Mem:* Fel AAAS; hon mem Am Soc Nondestructive Testing (pres, 54); fel Am Soc Metals; Am Soc Testing & Mat; Nondestructive Testing Soc Gt Brit. *Res:* Radiology; electron microscopy; use of radioactive isotopes in industrial radiography; microradiography. *Mailing Add:* 704 47th St Los Alamos NM 87544

TENNEY, MARK W, b Chicago, Ill, Dec 10, 36; m 74; c 2. ENVIRONMENTAL HEALTH ENGINEERING, CIVIL ENGINEERING. *Educ:* Mass Inst Technol, SB, 58, SM, 59, ScD(civil & sanit eng), 65; Environ Eng Intersoc, dipl. *Prof Exp:* Design engr, Greeley & Hansen Eng, 59-61; from asst prof to assoc prof civil eng, Univ Notre Dame, 65-73; PRES, TENECH ENVIRON ENGRS, INC, 69- *Honors & Awards:* Harrison Prescott Eddy Medal, Water Pollution Control Fedn, 73. *Mem:* Fel Am Soc Civil Engrs; Am Water Works Asn; Water Pollution Control Fedn; Nat Soc Prof Engrs; Am Acad Environ Engrs. *Res:* Sanitary engineering. *Mailing Add:* TenEch Environ Engrs Inc 744 W Washington Ave South Bend IN 46601

TENNEY, ROBERT IMBODEN, b Decatur, Ill, Nov 15, 10; m 35; c 3. MICROBIOLOGY. *Educ:* Univ Ill, BS, 32. *Prof Exp:* Master brewer, Rockford Brewing Co, 32-34; chief chemist, Best Malt Prod Co, 34-35; chemist & instr, Wahl-Henius Inst, 35-38, tech dir, 38-42, pres, 42-58; pres, Sassy Int, 56-66; VPRES & SECY, OZONE, INC, 71- *Concurrent Pos:* Tech dir, Fleischmann Malting Co, 58-61, vpres, 61-64, exec vpres, 64-66; consult to food & fermentation industs. *Mem:* AAAS; Am Soc Qual Control; Am Soc Brewing Chemists (pres, 67-68); Am Chem Soc; Inst Food Technol. *Res:* Brewing; production of foods through fermentations or enzymes; sterilization by ozonation; ozone treatment of waste materials. *Mailing Add:* PO Box 123 Winnetka IL 60093

TENNEY, STEPHEN MARSH, b Bloomington, Ill, Oct 22, 22; m 47; c 3. PHYSIOLOGY. *Educ:* Dartmouth Col, AB, 43; Cornell Univ, MD, 46. *Prof Exp:* Asst prof physiol, Dartmouth Med Sch, 51-54; asst prof physiol & med, Sch Med & Dent, Univ Rochester, 52-56, assoc prof, 56; chmn dept, 56-77, prof physiol, 56-74, NATHAN SMITH PROF PHYSIOL, DARTMOUTH MED SCH, 74- *Concurrent Pos:* Markle scholar, 54-59. *Mem:* Am Physiol Soc; Am Acad Arts & Sci; Nat Inst Med; Am Soc Clin Invest. *Res:* Physiology of circulation and respiration. *Mailing Add:* Dept of Physiol Dartmouth Med Sch Hanover NH 03755

TENNEY, WILTON R, b Buckhannon, WVa, July 2, 28; m 51. PLANT PATHOLOGY. *Educ:* WVa Wesleyan Col, BS, 50; Univ WVa, MS, 52, PhD(plant path), 55. *Prof Exp:* Plant scientist, Chem Res & Develop Labs, Army Chem Ctr, Md, 57; from asst prof to assoc prof, 57-71, PROF BIOL, UNIV RICHMOND, 71- *Res:* Physiology of fungi; host-parasite relations in fungus diseases of plants; toxicity of freshwater bryozoans. *Mailing Add:* Dept of Biol Univ of Richmond Richmond VA 23173

TENNILLE, AUBREY W, b Baker Co, Ga, Feb 4, 29; m 53; c 2. SOIL FERTILITY, SOIL MICROBIOLOGY. *Educ:* Univ Ga, BSA, 50; Okla State Univ, MSA, 55; Univ Fla, PhD(soils), 59. *Prof Exp:* Lab asst soil microbiol, Univ Fla, 58-59; asst county agent, Coop Exten, Univ Ga, 59-60, exten specialist, 60-62; from asst prof to assoc prof, 62-66, PROF AGRON, ARK STATE UNIV, 66- *Mem:* Am Soc Agron; Soil Sci Soc Am; Soil Conserv Soc Am. *Res:* Fertility research on zinc and manganese of rice soils of Arkansas and soil salt problems of eastern Arkansas. *Mailing Add:* Dept of Agron Ark State Univ State University AR 72467

TENNILLE, NEWTON BRIDGEWATER, b South Richmond, Va, Mar 15, 08; m 35; c 3. VETERINARY RADIOLOGY. *Educ:* Ohio State Univ, DVM, 33. *Prof Exp:* Vet, WToledo Animal Hosp, 36-48; assoc prof vet med & surg, 49-53, prof vet med & surg & head radiol div, 53-73, EMER PROF RADIOL, COL VET MED, OKLA STATE UNIV, 73- *Mem:* Am Vet Radiol Soc (pres, 57-58); Am Vet Med Asn; Soc Nuclear Med; Am Animal Hosp Asn. *Res:* Improved methods for diagnosis and therapy; use of radioisotopes in animals. *Mailing Add:* 603 Arapaho Dr Stillwater OK 74074

TENNISON, ROBERT L, b Cleburne, Tex, July 12, 33; m 58; c 3. MATHEMATICS. *Educ:* Howard Payne Col, BA, 54, MEd, 57; Okla State Univ, MS, 59, PhD(math), 64. *Prof Exp:* Asst prof math, ECent State Univ, 59-61, assoc prof, 64-65; asst prof, 65-67, ASSOC PROF MATH, UNIV TEX, ARLINGTON, 67- *Mem:* Math Asn Am. *Res:* Convexity; linear geometry. *Mailing Add:* Dept of Math Univ of Tex Arlington TX 76010

TENNISSEN, ANTHONY CORNELIUS, b Akron, Ohio, Feb 14, 20; m 52; c 2. GEOLOGY. *Educ:* Univ Tulsa, BS, 50; Syracuse Univ, MS, 52; Univ Mo-Rolla, PhD(geol), 63. *Prof Exp:* Geologist, US AEC, 52-54; head geologist, Ideal Cement Co, 54-57; geologist, Mo Geol Surv, 59-63; from asst prof to assoc prof, 63-74, prof, 74-80, REGENTS PROF GEOL, LAMAR UNIV, 80- *Mem:* Mineral Soc Am; Am Crystallog Asn. *Res:* Characterization of minerals and inorganic compounds by x-ray analysis; crystal-structure analysis of minerals and other compounds. *Mailing Add:* Dept of Geol Lamar Univ Beaumont TX 77710

TENNY, FUAD MIKHAIL, b Zahle, Lebanon, Jan 17, 29; US citizen; m 56; c 6. AGRICULTURAL CHEMISTRY, FOOD TECHNOLOGY. *Educ:* Lewis & Clark Col, BS, 53; Ore State Univ, MS, 56. *Prof Exp:* Chemist agr chem, Ore State Univ, 56-61; environ chemist, Wash State Dept Health, 61-66; RES CHEMIST ANAL CHEM, NAT OCEANIC & ATMOSPHERIC ADMIN, NAT MARINE FISHERIES SERV, US DEPT COM, 66- *Honors & Awards:* Super Performance Award, US Dept of Interior, Bur of Com Fisheries, 70. *Res:* Trace metal analysis in foods, particularly in fish and fishery products. *Mailing Add:* US Dept of Com 2725 Montlake Blvd E Seattle WA 98112

TENNYSON, MARILYN ELIZABETH, b Pittsburgh, Pa, June 17, 48. STRUCTURAL GEOLOGY, TECTONICS. *Educ:* Middlebury Col, AB, 70; Univ Wash, MS, 72, PhD(geol), 74. *Prof Exp:* Asst prof geol, Whittier Col, 74-77; asst prof geol, Carleton Col, 77-80; WITH PHILLIPS PETROL CO, 80- *Mem:* Geol Soc Am; Am Geophys Union. *Res:* Cordilleran tectonics, particularly Mesozoic history of the Pacific Northwest. *Mailing Add:* 1312 Brookside Parkway Bartlesville OK 74003

TENNYSON, R(ODERICK) C(LARENCE), mechanics, materials science, see previous edition

TENNYSON, RICHARD HARVEY, b Minneapolis, Minn, Oct 11, 21; m 45; c 9. ORGANIC CHEMISTRY. *Educ:* St Mary's Col, Minn, BS, 46; Univ Ill, PhD(org chem), 52. *Prof Exp:* Res chemist, Corn Prod Co, 50-55, anal res supvr, 56-61; sect leader, Qual Control Dept, 61-68, dir nutrit qual control, 68-76, V PRES QUAL ASSURANCE, MEAD JOHNSON & CO, 76- *Mem:* Am Chem Soc; Inst Food Technol; Am Soc Qual Control; Sigma Xi. *Res:* Quality control administration; analytical methods development; physical, chemical, biological and microbiological control; nutritionals and pharmaceuticals. *Mailing Add:* 1365 Mesker Park Dr Evansville IN 47712

TENORE, KENNETH ROBERT, b Boston, Mass, Mar 22, 43. BIOLOGICAL OCEANOGRAPHY. *Educ:* St Anselm Col, AB, 65; NC State Univ, MS, 67, PhD(zool), 70. *Prof Exp:* Investr biol oceanog, Woods Hole Oceanog Inst, 70-72, asst scientist, 72-75; asst prof biol oceanog, Skidaway Inst Oceanog, 75-77; adj prof, Grad Sch Oceanog, Univ RI, 78-80; MEM FAC, SKIDAWAY INST OCEANOG, UNIV GA, 80- *Mem:* Am Soc Limnol & Oceanog; Estuarine Res Fedn; Ecol Soc Am; AAAS. *Res:* Bioenergetics of detrital food chains in marine benthic communities. *Mailing Add:* Skidaway Inst Oceanog Univ Ga PO Box 13687 Savannah GA 31406

TENOSO, HAROLD JOHN, US citizen. IMMUNOLOGY, MEDICAL MICROBIOLOGY. *Educ:* Univ Calif, Los Angeles, BA, 60, PhD, 66. *Prof Exp:* From sr biologist to mgr microbiol, Aerojet Med & Biol Syst, Aerojet-Gen Corp, 66-72, mgr biol oper, 72-74; dir biol oper, 74-76, dir res & develop, Organon Diag, 76-80, GEN MGR, DIAG DIV, ORGANON INC, 80- *Mem:* Am Asn Clin Chem; Am Soc Microbiol; AAAS. *Res:* Clinical chemistry; immunology and infectious disease, especially as it relates to immunoassays and early disease detection. *Mailing Add:* Organon Diag PO Box 5850 El Monte CA 91734

TENSMEYER, LOWELL GEORGE, b Pocatello, Idaho, Feb 21, 28; m 54; c 4. PHYSICAL CHEMISTRY. *Educ:* Univ Utah, BA, 52, PhD(combustion), 57. *Prof Exp:* Asst prof chem, Ohio Univ, 56-57 & Utah State Univ, 57-59; Petrol Inst fel ceramics, Pa State Univ, 59; res scientist, Linde Div, Union Carbide Corp, 60-63; SR PHYS CHEMIST, ELI LILLY & CO, 63- *Mem:* Am Chem Soc; Am Phys Soc; Coblentz Soc. *Res:* Molecular spectroscopy; adsorption; crystal growth and purification; lasers; photochemistry and photobiology. *Mailing Add:* 35 W 59th St Indianapolis IN 46208

TENZER, RUDOLF KURT, b Jena, Ger, Oct 9, 20; nat US; m 47; c 4. PHYSICS. *Educ:* Univ Frankfort, Dipl & Dr rer nat, 50. *Prof Exp:* Scientist radiation temperature measurements, Hartmann & Braun Co, Ger, 48-53; scientist magnetics; Ind Gen Corp, 53-69, mgr res, 66-69; mgr res, 69-74, mgr res & mfg eng, 74-76, TECH DIR, IGC DIV, ELECTRONIC MEMORIES & MAGNETICS CORP, 76- *Mem:* Inst Elec & Electronics Engrs; Am Phys Soc. *Res:* Permanent magnets; magnetization process; domain theory; ferrites; high temperature properties; temperature measurements by radiation; color pyrometers. *Mailing Add:* 1643 Brookdale Dr Martinsville NJ 08836

TEODORO, ROSARIO REYES, b Philippines, Sept 24, 13; nat US; m 32; c 2. BACTERIOLOGY. *Educ:* Univ Mich, PhD(bact), 45. *Prof Exp:* Bacteriologist, Western Condensing Co, 45-51; res bacteriologist, Henry Ford Hosp, 52-53; from asst prof to assoc prof bact, 53-74, ASSOC PROF BIOL, WAYNE STATE UNIV, 74- *Concurrent Pos:* NSF fac fel, Oxford Univ, 59. *Mem:* AAAS; Am Soc Microbiol. *Res:* Growth factors and metabolism of butyl alcohol organisms; beta-propiolactone and other virucidal agents; riboflavin production by microorganisms. *Mailing Add:* Dept of Biol Wayne State Univ Detroit MI 48202

TEPAS, DONALD IRVING, b Buffalo, NY, Apr 7, 33; m; c 2. PHYSIOLOGICAL PSYCHOLOGY, NEUROSCIENCE. *Educ:* Univ Buffalo, BA, 55; State Univ NY Buffalo, PhD(psychol), 63. *Prof Exp:* Instr psychol, Univ Buffalo, 58-59; res scientist neuropsychiat, Walter Reed Army Inst Res, 59-62; sr res scientist human factors, Honeywell, Inc, 62-66; prof psychol, St Louis Univ, 66-78; chmn dept, 78-81, PROF PSYCHOL, ILL INST TECHNOL, 78- *Concurrent Pos:* Asst prof ophthal res, Univ Minn, 63-66; prin investr, US Air Force, NSF, NIMH, Nat Inst Occup Safety & Health grants, exchange scientist, Nat Acad Sci, Czechoslovakia, 67; pres, Nat Conf Use On-Line Comput in Psychol, 72-73. *Mem:* Fel Am Psychol Asn; fel AAAS; Psychonomic Soc; Asn Psychophysiol Study Sleep; Soc Neurosci. *Res:* Human sleep; computer applications in psychology; psychophysiology of the auditory and visual systems; human electrophysiology. *Mailing Add:* Dept Psychol IIT Ctr LS 252 Chicago IL 60616

TE PASKE, EVERETT RUSSELL, b Sheldon, Iowa, Sept 15, 30; m 51; c 4. BIOLOGY, ANIMAL BEHAVIOR. *Educ:* Westmar Col, AB, 51; State Col Iowa, MA, 57; Okla State Univ, PhD(zool), 63. *Prof Exp:* Teacher pub schs, Iowa, 52-61; from asst prof to assoc prof, 63-71, PROF BIOL UNIV NORTHERN IOWA, 71- *Mem:* AAAS; Animal Behav Soc; Am Inst Biol Sci; Poultry Sci Asn. *Res:* Morphology and taxonomy of Chiroptera; breeding behavior in the Japanese quail; social behavior in chickens. *Mailing Add:* Dept Biol Univ Northern Iowa Cedar Falls IA 50613

TEPE, JOHN BRIGHT, chemical engineering, see previous edition

TEPFER, SANFORD SAMUEL, b Brooklyn, NY, Mar 24, 18; m 42; c 4. PLANT MORPHOLOGY. *Educ:* City Col New York, BS, 38; Cornell Univ, MS, 39; Univ Calif, PhD(bot), 50. *Prof Exp:* Asst bot, Univ Calif, 47-50; instr, Univ Ariz, 50-53, res assoc agr, 53-54; instr biol, Ore Col Educ, 54-55; from asst prof to assoc prof, 55-67, co-chmn dept, 68-71, head dept, 72-78, PROF BIOL, UNIV ORE, 67- *Concurrent Pos:* NSF sci fac fel, 65; Fulbright lectr, Univ Paris, 71-72, vis prof, 71-72 & 78-79. *Mem:* AAAS; Bot Soc Am; Int Soc Plant Morphol. *Res:* Developmental studies of shoot apex and flowers; culture of floral buds; floral morphogenesis. *Mailing Add:* Dept of Biol Univ of Ore Eugene OR 97403

TEPHLY, THOMAS R, b Norwich, Conn, Feb 1, 36; m 60; c 2. PHARMACOLOGY. *Educ:* Univ Conn, BS, 57; Univ Wis, PhD(pharmacol), 62; Univ Minn, MD, 65. *Prof Exp:* Instr pharmacol, Univ Wis, 62; from asst prof to assoc prof, Univ Mich, Ann Arbor, 65-71; PROF PHARMACOL & DIR TOXICOL CTR, UNIV IOWA, 71- *Concurrent Pos:* Am Cancer Soc res scholar, 62-65. *Honors & Awards:* John J Abel Award, Am Soc Pharmacol & Exp Therapeut, 71. *Mem:* Am Soc Pharmacol & Exp Therapeut; Am Soc Biol Chem; Soc Toxicol. *Res:* Biochemical pharmacology and toxicology; drug metabolism; methanol and ethanol metabolism; heme biosynthesis. *Mailing Add:* Dept Pharmacol Univ Iowa Iowa City IA 52240

TEPLEY, NORMAN, b Denver, Colo, Dec 14, 35; m 68; c 3. MEDICAL PHYSICS, SOLID STATE PHYSICS. *Educ:* Mass Inst Technol, SB, 57, PhD(physics), 63. *Prof Exp:* Asst prof physics, Wayne State Univ, 63-69; assoc prof, 69-77, PROF PHYSICS, OAKLAND UNIV, 77- *Concurrent Pos:* Vis prof, Dept Physics, Univ Lancaster, 70. *Mem:* AAAS; Am Phys Soc. *Res:* Magnetic fields arising from living systems; magnetocardiography, neuromagnetism; physics of metals; ultrasonic studies of Fermi surfaces; electronic structures of metals; properties of superconductors. *Mailing Add:* Dept Physics Oakland Univ Rochester MI 48063

TEPLICK, JOSEPH GEORGE, b Philadelphia, Pa, Sept 29, 11; m 37; c 3. MEDICINE, RADIOLOGY. *Educ:* Univ Pa, AB, 31, MS, 32, MD, 36, MSc, 42. *Prof Exp:* Assoc radiol, Jefferson Med Col, 43-48; chief & dir radiol, Kensington Hosp, 49-63; clin assoc prof radiol, 63-69, clin assoc prof diag radiol, 69-71, PROF RADIOL, HAHNEMANN MED COL, 71-, DIR DIV GEN DIAG, 74- *Concurrent Pos:* Dir, Curtis X-ray Dept, Jefferson Med Col, 45-48; chief radiol, Albert Einstein Med Ctr, 50-53; vis radiologist, Philadelphia Gen Hosp, 60-; assoc, Sch Med, Univ Pa, 60-; mem staff, Hahnemann Hosp, 63- *Mem:* Fel Am Col Radiol; Radiol Soc N Am; Roentgen Ray Soc; Am Thoracic Soc; NY Acad Sci. *Res:* Hapato-splenography; intravenous and parenteral radiopaque emulsions. *Mailing Add:* Dept Diag Radiol Hahnemann Med Col Philadelphia PA 19102

TEPLITZ, VIGDOR LOUIS, b Cambridge, Mass, Feb 5, 37; m 61. HIGH ENERGY PHYSICS. *Educ:* Mass Inst Technol, SB, 58; Univ Md, PhD(physics), 62. *Prof Exp:* Physicist, Lawrence Radiation Lab, Univ Calif, Berkeley, 62-64; NATO fel physics, Europ Orgn Nuclear Res, 64-65; asst prof, Mass Inst Technol, 65-69, assoc prof, 69-73; head dept, 73-77, PROF PHYSICS, VA POLYTECH INST & STATE UNIV, 73- *Concurrent Pos:* Coun mem, Fedn Am Scientists, 72-76; coun mem forum on physics & soc, Am Phys Soc, 77-79; phys sci officer, US Army Control & Disarmament Agency, Washington, DC, 78-80. *Mem:* Fel Am Phys Soc; Fedn Am Sci. *Res:* Elementary particle theory; S-matrix theory; weak interaction models; phenomenology and data analysis; applications of particle theory to cosmology. *Mailing Add:* Dept of Physics Va Polytech Inst & State Univ Blacksburg VA 24061

TEPLY, LESTER JOSEPH, b Muscoda, Wis, Apr 22, 20; m 50; c 3. BIOCHEMISTRY. *Educ:* Univ Wis, BA, 40, MS, 44, PhD(biochem), 45. *Prof Exp:* Asst biochem, Univ Wis, 40-45; tech secy, Food Composition Comt, Nutrit Biochemist Coord, Nat Res Coun, 45; biochemist, USPHS, 45-46; res biochemist, Columbia Univ, 46-48; res biochemist, Enzyme Inst, Univ Wis, 48-51, asst dir labs, Wis Alumni Res Found, 51-55, dir lab projs, 55-60; SR NUTRITIONIST, UNICEF, NY, 60- *Concurrent Pos:* Chmn, Int Vitamin A Consult Group. *Mem:* AAAS; Am Chem Soc; Am Inst Food Tech; Am Pub Health Asn; Am Inst Nutrit. *Res:* Nutrition; vitamins; enzymes; animal nutrition; microbiological nutrition and metabolism; B-complex vitamins; food technology. *Mailing Add:* United Nations Children's Fund United Nations Bldg New York NY 10017

TEPLY, MARK LAWRENCE, b Lincoln, Nebr, Jan 11, 42; m 68; c 1. ALGEBRA. *Educ:* Univ Nebr, BA, 63, MA, 65, PhD(math), 68. *Prof Exp:* Asst prof, 68-73, assoc prof, 73-81, PROF MATH, UNIV FLA, 81- *Concurrent Pos:* Ed, Commun in Algebra, 81- *Mem:* Am Math Soc; Math Asn Am. *Res:* Noncommutative rings and their modules; torsion theories; filters of ideals; direct sum decompositions of modules; idealizer subrings; semigroup rings. *Mailing Add:* Dept Math Univ Fla Gainesville FL 32611

TEPPER, BYRON SEYMOUR, b New Bedford, Mass, Apr 12, 30; m 55; c 2. MICROBIOLOGY. *Educ:* Northeastern Univ, BS, 51; Univ Mass, MS, 53; Univ Wis, PhD(microbiol), 57. *Prof Exp:* Res assoc biochem, Univ Ill Col Med, 57-59; asst prof, 60-68, assoc prof pathobiol, Sch Hyg, 68-77, ASSOC PROF ENVIRON HEALTH, JOHNS HOPKINS UNIV, 78-, EXEC SECY, COMT USE INFECT AGENTS & BIOHAZARDOUS MATS, 78- *Concurrent Pos:* Assoc biochemist, Leonard Wood Mem Leprosy Res Lab, Baltimore, 59-65, microbiologist, 65-74; biohazards safety officer, Johns Hopkins Med Insts, 74-77. *Mem:* AAAS; Am Soc Microbiol; Soc Gen Microbiol; Int leprosy Asn; Am Acad Microbiol. *Res:* Host dependent microorganisms; human and murine leprosy; mycobacterial physiology; photobiology. *Mailing Add:* Dept of Environ Health Johns Hopkins Med Insts Baltimore MD 21205

TEPPER, FREDERICK, b Brooklyn, NY, Apr 9, 34; m 54; c 2. PHYSICAL CHEMISTRY, METALLURGY. *Educ:* NY Univ, BA, 54; Brooklyn Col, MA, 57. *Prof Exp:* Chemist, Turner-Hall Corp, 54-55; phys chemist, Radiation Res Corp, 55-56; metallurgist, Atomic Energy Div, Sylvania-Elec Corp, 56-57; phys chemist, Mine Safety Appliances Res Corp, 57-60, sect head mat res, 60-69, dir res, 69-70, GEN MGR, CATALYST RES CORP DIV, MINE SAFETY APPLIANCE CO, 70-, VPRES, 71- *Mem:* Am Soc Metals; Electrochem Soc; Am Ord Asn. *Res:* Alkali metals; physical, thermodynamic and chemical properties; phase diagrams; production and purification techniques; corrosive effects on structural materials; gas sorption phenomena by activated carbon, metal oxides and ion exchange resins; molten salt electrochemistry; batteries. *Mailing Add:* Catalyst Res Corp 1421 Clarkview Rd Baltimore MD 21209

TEPPER, HERBERT BERNARD, b Brooklyn, NY, Dec 25, 31; m 59; c 2. PLANT ANATOMY. *Educ:* State Univ NY Col Forestry, Syracuse Univ, BS, 53, MS, 58; Univ Calif, Davis, PhD(bot), 62. *Prof Exp:* Res asst forest bot, State Univ NY Col Forestry, Syracuse Univ, 56-58; res forester, US Forest Serv, 58-59; res asst, Univ Calif, Davis, 59-62; from instr to assoc prof, 62-67, PROF FOREST BOT, STATE UNIV NY COL ENVIRON SCI & FORESTRY, SYRACUSE, 67- *Mem:* AAAS; Bot Soc Am; Int Soc Plant Morphol. *Res:* Morphogenesis in the shoot apex; seed germination; bud and cambial reactivation. *Mailing Add:* Dept of Forest Bot & Path Environ Sci & Forestry Syracuse NY 13210

TEPPER, LLOYD BARTON, b Los Angeles, Calif, Dec 21, 31; m 57; c 2. TOXICOLOGY, OCCUPATIONAL HEALTH. *Educ:* Dartmouth Col, AB, 54; Harvard Univ, MD, 57, MIH, 60, ScD(occup med), 62; Am Bd Prev Med, dipl, 64. *Prof Exp:* Fel, Mass Gen Hosp, 58-60; fel, Mass Inst Technol, 59-61; physician, Eastman Kodak Co, 61-62 & AEC, 62-65; assoc dir occup med & inst environ health, Kettering Lab, Univ Cincinnati, 65-72, assoc prof environ health, Univ, 65-71, prof, 71-72, assoc prof med, 69-72; assoc comnr sci, Food & Drug Admin, 72-76; CORP MED DIR, AIR PROD & CHEM, INC, 76-, ADJ PROF ENVIRON MED, UNIV PA, 77- *Concurrent Pos:* Ed, J Occup Med, 79- *Mem:* Am Acad Occup Med (pres, 80-81); Am Occup Med Asn. *Res:* Industrial and environmental toxicology, especially as related to toxicology of beryllium, lead and other industrial metals; environmental and medical standards. *Mailing Add:* Air Prod & Chem Inc PO Box 538 Allentown PA 18105

TEPPER, MORRIS, b Palestine, Mar 1, 16; nat US; m; c 2. METEOROLOGY, SCIENCE ADMINISTRATION. *Educ:* Brooklyn Col, BA, 36, MA, 38; Johns Hopkins Univ, PhD(fluid mech), 52. *Prof Exp:* Qualifications analyst & chief, Phys Sci Unit, US Civil Serv Comn, 39-43; chief, Severe Local Storms Res Unit, US Weather Bur, 46-59; dir meteorol prog, NASA, 59-65, dep dir space applications progs & dir meteorol, 66-69, dep dir earth observs progs & dir meteorol, 69-78, head, Spec Proj Off, Goddard Space Flight Ctr, 78-79; PROF MATH PHYSICS, CAPITOL INST TECHNOL, MD, 79- *Concurrent Pos:* Mem staff, USDA Grad Sch, 52-; mem, US Nat Comt Int Hydrol Decade & chmn work group remote sensing in hydrol, Nat Acad Sci, 71-75, liaison rep, US Comt Global Atmospheric Res Prog, mem, Comt Int Environ Progs, US Interagency Comts; chmn, Working Group 6, Comt Space Res, Int Coun Sci Unions; mem, Int Comn Space Sci Bd. *Honors & Awards:* Meissinger Award, Am Meteorol Soc, 50; Except Serv Medal, NASA, 66; Gold Medal, Nat Ctr Space Studies, France, 72; Am Meteorol Soc Spec Award, 78; Nordberg Mem Award, Comt Space Res, 79. *Mem:* Fel Am Meteorol Soc; AAAS. *Res:* Satellite meteorology; mesometeorology; severe local storms; space applications; earth observation satellites; remote sensing; global atmospheric research; climate; education. *Mailing Add:* 107 Bluff Terr Silver Spring MD 20902

TEPPERMAN, BARRY LORNE, b Toronto, Ont, Jan 29, 47; m 72; c 1. MEDICAL SCIENCES. *Educ:* Univ Toronto, BSc, 69, MSc, 72; Univ Calgary, PhD(physiol), 75. *Prof Exp:* Fel physiol, Univ Tex, Houston, 75-77; asst prof physiol, Univ Western Ont, 77- *Mem:* Am Gastroenterol Asn; Can Physiol Asn. *Res:* Factors regulating the integrity of gastrointestinal mussa, specifically prostaglandins and prostaglandin receptors as salivary gland factors; role of gastrointestinal peptides of central origin in the regulation of gastrointestinal function. *Mailing Add:* Dept Physiol Health Sci Ctr Univ Western Ont London ON N6A 5C1 Can

TEPPERMAN, HELEN MURPHY, b Hartford, Conn, Jan 9, 17; m 43; c 3. PHYSIOLOGICAL CHEMISTRY. *Educ:* Mt Holyoke Col, BA, 38; Yale Univ, PhD(physiol chem), 42. *Prof Exp:* Asst, Mem Hosp, NY, 42-43 & Yale Univ, 43-44; pharmacologist, Med Res Lab, Edgewood Arsenal, Md, 44-45; from instr to assoc prof, 46-72, PROF PHARMACOL, STATE UNIV NY UPSTATE MED CTR, 72- *Mem:* Am Physiol Soc; Endocrine Soc. *Res:* Endocrinology and metabolism. *Mailing Add:* Dept of Pharmacol 766 Irving Ave State Univ NY Upstate Med Ctr Syracuse NY 13210

TEPPERMAN, JAY, b Newark, NJ, Mar 23, 14; m 43; c 3. MEDICINE. *Educ:* Univ Pa, AB, 33; Columbia Univ, MD, 38. *Prof Exp:* Intern, Bassett Hosp, NY, 38-40; hon fel, Sch Med, Yale Univ, 40-41, Coxe fel, 41-42, asst, Aeromed Unit, Dept Physiol, 42-44; assoc prof pharmacol, 46-53, PROF EXP MED, COL MED, STATE UNIV NY UPSTATE MED CTR, 53- *Concurrent Pos:* Mem metab study sect, NIH & physiol comt, Nat Bd Med Examr, 63-67, mem pharmacol comt, 72-75; consult, Vet Admin, DC, 64-67 & Food & Drug Admin, 69-; fac exchange scholar, State Univ NY. *Honors & Awards:* Purkinje Medalist, Czech Med Soc. *Mem:* Soc Exp Biol & Med; Am Physiol Soc; Endocrine Soc; Am Soc Pharmacol & Exp Therapeut; Am Soc Biol Chem. *Res:* Endocrinology and metabolism. *Mailing Add:* Dept Pharmacol Col Med State Univ NY Syracuse NY 13210

TEPPERT, WILLIAM ALLAN, SR, b Oshkosh, Nebr, Oct 10, 15; m 39; c 2. PHARMACOLOGY. *Educ:* Univ Ill, BS, 43 & 48, MS, 47; Univ Iowa, PhD(zool), 58. *Prof Exp:* Asst mammalian physiol, Univ Ill, 42-43 & 46-48; from instr to asst prof biol, 48-57, from asst prof to assoc prof pharmacol, 49-64, PROF PHARMACOL, COL PHARM, DRAKE UNIV, 64- *Mem:* Sigma Xi. *Res:* Cell physiology and pharmacology; cellular neuropharmacology; convulsive disorders; geriatric medication. *Mailing Add:* Col of Pharm Drake Univ Des Moines IA 50311

TEPPING, BENJAMIN JOSEPH, b Philadelphia, Pa, Jan 29, 13; m 40; c 2. MATHEMATICAL STATISTICS, APPLIED STATISTICS. *Educ:* Ohio State Univ, BA, 33, MA, 35, PhD(math), 39. *Prof Exp:* Math statistician, US Bur Census, 40-55; mathematician, Nat Analysts, Inc, 55-60; chief statist adv group, Surv & Res Corp, Korea, 60-63; chief, Res Ctr Measurement Methods, US Bur Census, 63-73; STATIST CONSULT, 73- *Concurrent Pos:* Lectr, USDA Grad Sch, 41-52, Am Univ, 43 & Univ Mich, 48-53; adj assoc prof, Univ Pa, 56-60; assoc ed, J Am Statist Asn, 64-66; mem vis lectr prog, Inst Math Statist, 69-72. *Honors & Awards:* Meritorious Serv Award, Dept Com, 50; Cult Medal, Repub Korea, 63. *Mem:* Fel AAAS; fel Am Statist Asn; Am Math Soc; Inst Math Statist; Int Statist Inst. *Res:* Sampling theory and methods; measurement problems in censuses and surveys; problems of matching lists. *Mailing Add:* 401 Apple Grove Rd Silver Spring MD 20904

TERADA, KAZUJI, b Honolulu, Hawaii, Jan 4, 27. INORGANIC CHEMISTRY. *Educ:* Univ Hawaii, BA, 52, MS, 54; Univ Utah, PhD, 61. *Prof Exp:* CHEMIST, RES & DEVELOP, ROCKY FLATS DIV, ROCKWELL INT, GOLDEN, 60- *Mem:* Am Chem Soc. *Mailing Add:* 161 Linden Ave Boulder CO 80302

TERANGO, LARRY, b Clarksburg, WVa, Nov 30, 25; m 51; c 2. SPEECH PATHOLOGY, AUDIOLOGY. *Educ:* Kent State Univ, BA, 50, MA, 54; Case Western Reserve Univ, PhD(speech path & audiol), 66. *Prof Exp:* Clinician, Painesville City Schs, 52-59; instr speech path & audiol, Kent State Univ, 61-62; asst prof, San Jose State Col, 62-63; instr speech path & audiol, Kent State Univ, 63-64; instr speech & dir speech & hearing clin, Ohio State Univ, 64-66; assoc prof speech & dir speech & hearing clin, Univ Wyo, 66-68; prof, chmn dept spec educ & dir speech & hearing clin, ETenn State Univ, 68-74; prof health sci & dir speech & hearing ctr, Western Carolina Univ, 74-78; PROF SPEC EDUC & COORDR COMMUN PROG, EASTERN KY UNIV, 78- *Concurrent Pos:* Vpres, Wyo Cleft Palate Eval Team, 66-68. *Mem:* Am Speech & Hearing Asn; Coun Except Children; Nat Educ Asn; Am Cleft Palate Asn. *Res:* Vocal characteristics in the male voice; language dysfunction; multidisciplinary approach to study of neurological disturbances. *Mailing Add:* Eastern Ky Univ PO Box 457 Richmond KY 40475

TERANISHI, ROY, b Stockton, Calif, Aug 1, 22; m 44; c 1. ORGANIC CHEMISTRY. *Educ:* Univ Calif, BS, 50; Ore State Col, PhD, 54. *Prof Exp:* Instr chem, Portland State Col, 53-54; RES CHEMIST, USDA, 54- *Mem:* Am Chem Soc. *Res:* Gas chromatography; flavor chemistry. *Mailing Add:* 89 Kingston Rd Kensington CA 94707

TERASAKI, PAUL ICHIRO, b Los Angeles, Calif, Sept 10, 29; m 56; c 4. IMMUNOLOGY. *Educ:* Univ Calif, Los Angeles, BA, 50, MA, 52, PhD(zool), 56. *Prof Exp:* Res asst zool, 52-54, res asst, Atomic Energy Proj, 54-55, res zoologist, Dept Surg, 55-56, jr res zoologist, 56-57, asst res zoologist, 58-61, assoc res zoologist, 61-62, assoc prof surg, 62-66, PROF SURG, CTR HEALTH SCI, UNIV CALIF, LOS ANGELES, 66- *Concurrent Pos:* Res fel zool with Prof P B Medawar, Univ Col, Univ London, 57-58; USPHS career develop award, 63-; mem transplantation & immunol adv comt, NIH, 67-70; mem nomenclature comt leukocyte antigens, WHO. *Honors & Awards:* Modern Med Award Distinguished Achievement. *Mem:* Am Soc Cell Biol; Am Asn Immunol; Soc Cryobiol; Am Soc Immunol; Int Transplantation Soc. *Res:* Transplantation immunology; homotransplantation; leucocyte typing. *Mailing Add:* Dept of Surg Univ of Calif Ctr for Health Sci Los Angeles CA 90024

TERASAWA, EI, b Ihda City, Japan, Apr 8, 38; m 75; c 1. NEUROENDOCRINOLOGY, REPRODUCTIVE PHYSIOLOGY. *Educ:* Univ Tokyo, BS, 61; Yokohama City Univ, PhD(physiol), 66. *Prof Exp:* Res physiologist anat, Dept Physiol, Univ Calif, Berkeley, 66-67; res fel physiol, Dept Anat, Univ Calif, Los Angeles, 67-68; instr, Dept Physiol, Med Sch, Yokohama City Univ, 68-70, asst prof, 70-73; assoc scientist, 73-80, SR SCIENTIST, PHYSIOL, PRIMATE RES CTR, UNIV WIS-MADISON, 80- *Mem:* Soc Study Reproduction; AAAS; Soc Neurosci; Am Physiol Soc; Endocrine Soc. *Res:* Integral function of the hypothalamus in control of the pituitary-gonadal system; control mechamisms of the Lutenizing-hormone releasing hormone neuronal system, which may serve as a model of peptidergic neurons in the mammalian hypothalamus. *Mailing Add:* Regional Primate Res Ctr Univ Wis 1233 Capitol Ct Madison WI 53715

TERASMAE, JAAN, b Estonia, May 28, 26; nat Can; m 54. GEOLOGY, PALYNOLOGY. *Educ:* Univ Uppsala, Fil Kand, 51; McMaster Univ, PhD, 55. *Prof Exp:* Asst, Palynological Lab Stockholm, 50-51; geologist, Geol Surv Can, 55-68; chmn dept geol sci, 69-75, PROF GEOL, BROCK UNIV, 68- *Mem:* AAAS; Int Glaciol Soc; Int Limnol Soc; Int Peat Soc; Soc Environ Geochem & Health. *Res:* Pleistocene chronology, geology and stratigraphy; paleobotany of Pleistocene deposits. *Mailing Add:* Dept Geol Sci Brock Univ St Catherines ON L2S 3A1 Can

TERBORGH, JOHN J, b Washington, DC, Apr 16, 36. POPULATION BIOLOGY, PLANT PHYSIOLOGY. *Educ:* Harvard Univ, AB, 58, AM, 60, PhD(biol), 63. *Prof Exp:* Staff scientist, Tyco Labs, Inc, 63-65; asst prof bot, Univ Md, 65-71; assoc prof, 71-80, PROF BIOL, PRINCETON UNIV, 80- *Concurrent Pos:* Res grants, Am Philos Soc, Am Mus Natural Hist & Nat Geog Soc, 64-67; NSF res grants, 68- *Mem:* AAAS; Am Soc Naturalists; Soc Study Evolution; Ecol Soc Am. *Res:* Tropical ecology; population biology of birds. *Mailing Add:* Dept of Biol Princeton Univ Princeton NJ 08540

TERDIMAN, JOSEPH FRANKLIN, b New York, NY, Feb 14, 40; m 65; c 2. BIOMEDICAL ENGINEERING. *Educ:* Cornell Univ, BEngPhys, 61; NY Univ, MD, 65; Univ Ill Med Ctr, PhD(physiol), 72. *Prof Exp:* Res scientist pop exposure studies, Nat Ctr Radiol Health, 67-69; med info scientist, Kaiser Found Res Inst, 69-79; ASST TO DIR, MED METHODS RES, KAISER-PERMANENTE, 80- *Concurrent Pos:* Lectr, Univ Ill, Chicago Circle, 65-67 & Sch Optom, Univ Calif, Berkeley, 69-78; NIH special fel, 67-69; clin asst prof, Sch Optom, Univ Calif, Berkeley, 79- *Mem:* AAAS; Soc Advan Med Systs; Biomed Eng Soc. *Res:* Development of medical information systems for hospital automation; patient monitoring, diagnosis and therapy; integration of computers and engineering methods with classical neurophysiological techniques; neurophysiology. *Mailing Add:* Kaiser Hosp 3700 Broadway Oakland CA 94611

TERENZI, JOSEPH F, b Marlboro, NY, Aug 21, 32; m 54; c 3. PLASTICS ENGINEERING, CHEMICAL ENGINEERING. *Educ:* Rensselaer Polytech Inst, BS, 53; Princeton Univ, MS, 55, PhD, 58. *Prof Exp:* Mem stafff res & develop, 58-65, tech mgr plastics div, 65-71, mgr mfg, 71-75, mgr, 75-80, DIR MFG TECHNOL & ENVORON, AM CYANAMID CO, 80- *Concurrent Pos:* Mem fac, Dept Chem Eng, Univ Conn, 64; lectr, Princeton Univ, Columbia Univ, Pa State Univ & Lowell Tech Inst. *Mailing Add:* 688 King Rd Franklin Lakes NJ 07417

TERESA, GEORGE WASHINGTON, b Osceola, Ark, Nov 23, 23; m 54. BACTERIOLOGY. *Educ:* Ark Agr & Mech Col, BS, 52; Univ Ark, MS, 55; Kans State Univ, PhD(microbiol), 59. *Prof Exp:* Asst prof bact, Auburn Univ, 59-61 & Univ RI, 61-62; assoc prof biol, Wichita State Univ, 62-68; from asst prof to assoc prof bact & biochem, 68-81, PROF BACT, UNIV IDAHO, 81- *Mem:* AAAS; Am Soc Microbiol. *Res:* Immunology and pathogenic bacteriology; immunology and pathogenic mechanism of Gram anaerobes. *Mailing Add:* Dept of Bacteriol & Biochem Univ of Idaho Moscow ID 83843

TERESHKOVICH, GEORGE, b New York, NY, Mar 18, 30; m 55; c 1. HORTICULTURE. *Educ:* La Polytech Inst, BS, 52; Univ Ga, MS, 57; La State Univ, PhD(hort, agron), 63. *Prof Exp:* Res asst, Univ Ga, 52-54, asst prof hort, 56-60; res assoc, La State Univ, 60-63; asst prof, Univ Ga, 63-68; assoc prof hort, 68-74, PROF & ASSOC CHAIRPERSON DEPT PLANT & SOIL SCI, TEX TECH UNIV, 75- *Mem:* Am Soc Hort Sci; Sigma Xi. *Res:* Cultural and adaptability studies with vegetable and ornamental crops. *Mailing Add:* Dept Plant & Soil Sci Tex Tech Univ Lubbock TX 79409

TERESI, JOSEPH DOMINIC, b San Jose, Calif, Aug 18, 15; m 47; c 6. BIOCHEMISTRY, HEALTH PHYSICS. *Educ:* San Jose State Col, AB, 38; Univ Wis, PhD(biochem), 43. *Prof Exp:* Res assoc, Manhattan Proj, Chicago, 43, Clinton Labs, Tenn, 44, & Univ Chicago, 45; res assoc, Stanford Univ, 47-51, actg instr, 48-50, actg asst prof, 50-51; chemist, US Naval Radiol Defense Lab, 51-69; sr biochemist, Stanford Res Inst, 69-71; sr scientist, San Francisco Bay Marine Res Ctr, 71-73; res assoc div nuclear med, Stanford Univ, 73-74; sr eng, Advan Reactor Systs Dept, Gen Elec Co, 74-80; RETIRED. *Mem:* Fel AAAS; Am Chem Soc; Health Physics Soc; Am Nuclear Soc. *Res:* Analysis of radionuclides in biological materials; radiation effects; aerospace nuclear safety; radiation protection; radiation ecology and internal emitters; bay sediment analysis; radiological assessment; nuclear reactor safety analysis. *Mailing Add:* 1395 Villa Dr Los Altos CA 94022

TERESINE (LEWIS), MARY, b St Louis, Mo, July 6, 08. MATHEMATICS. *Educ:* Fontbonne Col, AB, 38; Cath Univ, MA, 44, PhD(math), 47. *Prof Exp:* Instr high sch, Colo, 38-43; asst math, Cath Univ, 43-44 & 46-47; from instr to prof, 47-74, dean women, 51-66, EMER PROF MATH, FONTBONNE COL, 74- *Mem:* Am Math Soc; Math Asn Am. *Res:* Number theory; theory of congruences; construction and application of magic rectangles. *Mailing Add:* Dept Math Fontbonne Col 6800 Wydown Blvd St Louis MO 63105

TERHAAR, CLARENCE JAMES, toxicology, see previous edition

TER HAAR, GARY L, b Zeeland, Mich, May 2, 36; m 56; c 2. INORGANIC CHEMISTRY. *Educ:* Hope Col, BA, 58; Univ Mich, MS, 60, PhD(chem), 62. *Prof Exp:* Res assoc, 62-76, DIR TOXICOL & INDUST HYG, ETHYL CORP, 76- *Mem:* Am Chem Soc. *Res:* Environmental research. *Mailing Add:* Ethyl Corp 451 Florida Ave Baton Rouge LA 70801

TERHUNE, ROBERT WILLIAM, b Detroit, Mich, Feb 7, 26; m 47; c 2. QUANTUM ELECTRONICS. *Educ:* Univ Mich, BS, 47, PhD(physics), 57; Dartmouth Col, MA, 48. *Prof Exp:* Supvr, Digital Comput & Logic Des Sect, Willow Run Labs, Univ Mich, 51-54, res physicist, 54-59, mgr, Solid State Physics Lab, 59-60; res physicist, Sci Lab, Ford Motor Co, Dearborn, Mich, 60-65, mgr, Physics Electronics Dept, 65-75; vis scholar, Stanford Univ, 75-76; SR STAFF SCIENTIST, ENG & RES STAFF, FORD MOTOR CO, 76- *Concurrent Pos:* Ed, Optics Letters J, Optical Soc Am, 77- *Honors & Awards:* Sci & Eng Award, Drexel Inst Technol, 64. *Mem:* Optical Soc Am; Am Phys Soc; Inst Elec & Electronic Engrs. *Res:* Quantum electronics; nonlinear optics; optical properties of solids and surfaces; molecular spectroscopy; advanced instrumentation. *Mailing Add:* 1645 Chalmers Ann Arbor MI 48104

TERICHOW, OLEG, b Kikinda, Yugoslavia, Dec 27, 22; US citizen; m 55; c 2. MINING ENGINEERING. *Educ:* Univ Ill, BS, 54; Pa State Univ, MS, 58. *Prof Exp:* Mining methods res engr, US Bur Mines, Minneapolis, 60-66, mining res engr, Marine Minerals Tech Ctr, Tiburon, Calif, 66-69, minerals engr, Metall Res Ctr, Tuscaloosa, 69-72; minerals engr, Marine Minerals Tech Ctr, Nat Oceanic & Atmospheric Admin, 72-73; SR ENGR, BECHTEL CORP, 73- *Concurrent Pos:* Rochester-Pittsburgh grant, 57-58. *Mem:* Am Inst Mining, Metall & Petrol Engrs. *Res:* Mineral processing methods; mineral resources from sea; methods of marine mining and of mineral beneficiation; plant design; coal processing and conversion; resource evaluation and development. *Mailing Add:* Bechtel Corp 50 Beale St San Francisco CA 94119

TERKLA, LOUIS GABRIEL, b Anaconda, Mont, Mar 24, 25; m 49; c 2. DENTISTRY. *Educ:* Univ Ore, DMD, 52. *Hon Degrees:* DSc, Georgetown Univ, 79. *Prof Exp:* From instr to assoc prof, 52-61, asst to dean dent sch, 60-66, asst dean acad affairs, 66-67, PROF DENT, DENT SCH, UNIV ORE, 61-, DEAN DENT SCH, 67- *Mem:* AAAS; Am Dent Asn; Int Asn Dent Res; fel Am Col Dent (pres, 73-74); Am Asn Dent Schs (pres, 75-76). *Res:* Clinical behavior of dental materials; cavity preparation design; testing to predict technical performance of dental students. *Mailing Add:* Univ of Ore Dent Sch 611 SW Campus Dr Portland OR 97201

TERMAN, CHARLES RICHARD, b Mansfield, Ohio, Sept 8, 29; m 51; c 2. ANIMAL ECOLOGY, ANIMAL BEHAVIOR. *Educ:* Albion Col, AB, 52; Mich State Univ, MS, 54, PhD(behav pop dynamics), 59. *Prof Exp:* Assoc prof biol, Taylor Univ, 61-63, actg dir res, 62-63; from asst prof to assoc prof, 63-69, PROF BIOL, COL WILLIAM & MARY, 69- *Concurrent Pos:* Nat Inst Ment Health fel, Sch Hyg & Pub Health, Johns Hopkins Univ, 59 & Penrose Res Lab, 59-61; NATO sr sci fel, Eng & exchange scientist, US & Polish Nat Acads Sci, 74; NIH career develop award, 70-74. *Mem:* Fel AAAS; Animal Behav Soc; Am Sci Affil; Am Soc Mammal; Am Soc Nat. *Res:* Population dynamics; socio-biological factors influencing the growth and physiology of populations; reproductive physiology; behavioral ecology. *Mailing Add:* Lab of Endocrinol & Pop Ecol Dept Biol Col of William & Mary Williamsburg VA 23185

TERMAN, FREDERICK E(MMONS), b English, Ind, June 7, 00; m 28; c 3. ELECTRONIC ENGINEERING. *Educ:* Stanford Univ, AB, 20, EE, 22; Mass Inst Technol, ScD(elec eng), 24. *Hon Degrees:* ScD, Harvard Univ, 45, Univ BC, 50, Syracuse Univ, 55 & Southern Methodist Univ, 77; LHD, John F Kennedy Univ, 78. *Prof Exp:* From instr to assoc prof elec eng, 25-37, prof & exec head dept, 37-45, dean sch eng, 45-58, provost, 55-65, vpres, 59-65, EMER PROF ELEC ENG, STANFORD UNIV, 65- *Concurrent Pos:* Mem divs 14 & 15, Nat Defense Res Comt, 41-45; dir, Radio Res Lab, Harvard

Univ, 42-45; mem eng div, Nat Res Coun, 43-46; chmn fel bd, Radio Corp Am, 47-50; mem adv comt contractual & admin procedures res & develop, US Dept Army, 48; mem spec tech adv group, US Dept Defense, 50-53; mem comt tests of battery additives, Nat Acad Sci, 53-54, chmn eng sect, 53-56, mem coun, 56-59; mem res & develop adv comt, Signal Corps, 54-62, adv coun electronics proving ground, 54-57; mem math, physics & eng sci div, NSF, 55-59, chmn, 58-59; mem, US Naval Res Adv Comt, 56-64, chmn, 57-58; mem, Defense Sci Bd, 57-58; consult, President's Sci Adv Comt, 59-63 & 70-73; mem bd foreign scholars, US Dept State, 60-65; mem, US Off Educ Mission to USSR, 65; pres, Found Sci & Eng, Southern Methodist Univ, 65-74; party leader, USAID Team to Korea, 70; dir, Watkins-Johnson Co & Granger Assocs; emer dir, Hewlett-Packard Co; trustee, Inst Defense Anal. *Honors & Awards:* Decoration, Brit Govt, 46; Medal of Honor, Inst Elec & Electronic Engrs, 50, Educ Medal, 56, Founders Award, 62; Presidential Medal for Merit, 58; Wema Medal of Achievement, 63; Lamme Medal, Am Soc Eng Educ, 64, Hall of Fame, 68; Order of Civil Merit, Repub of Korea, 75; Nat Medal of Sci, 76. *Mem:* Nat Acad Sci; Nat Acad Eng; hon mem Am Soc Eng Educ (vpres, 49-51); fel Inst Elec & Electronics Engrs (vpres, 40, pres, 41); Sigma Xi (pres, 75). *Res:* Long distance transmission of electrical power; resonant transmission lines; electronic circuits, tubes, electron warfare, measurements; microwaves. *Mailing Add:* Rm 174 McCullough Bldg Stanford Univ Stanford CA 94305

TERMAN, GILBERT LEROY, agronomy, deceased

TERMAN, LEWIS MADISON, b San Francisco, Calif, Aug 26, 35; m 58. ELECTRONICS. *Educ:* Stanford Univ, BS, 56, MS, 58, PhD(elec eng), 61. *Prof Exp:* Res staff mem, 61-63, mgr read only storage res, 63-65, mgr integrated memory circuit res, 65-70, mgr semiconductor storage-circuits & systs, 70-75, mem staff, 75-79, mem, Dir Res Tech Planning Staff, 79-80, MGR, VERY-LARGE-SCALE INTEGRATION CIRCUITS, IBM CORP, 80- . *Concurrent Pos:* Ed, J Solid State Circuits, 74-77. *Mem:* Fel AAAS; fel Inst Elec & Electrical Engrs. *Res:* Integrated circuits, memory systems and semiconductor device research and development. *Mailing Add:* Res Ctr IBM Corp PO Box 218 Yorktown Heights NY 10598

TERMAN, MAX R, b Mansfield, Ohio, Apr 15, 45; m 68. ECOLOGY, ETHOLOGY. *Educ:* Spring Arbor Col, BA, 67; Mich State Univ, MS, 69, PhD(zool), 73. *Prof Exp:* PROF BIOL, TABOR COL, 69- *Mem:* Ecol Soc Am; Am Soc Mammalogists; Animal Behav Soc; Am Inst Biol Sci; Sigma Xi. *Res:* Interspecific competition between rodents; ecosystem ecology; rodent population dynamics; behavior of rodents. *Mailing Add:* RR 2 Box 79 Hillsboro KS 67063

TERMINE, JOHN DAVID, b Brooklyn, NY, Sept 25, 38; m 61; c 4. BIOCHEMISTRY. *Educ:* St John's Univ, NY, BS, 60; Univ Md, MS, 63; Cornell Univ, PhD(biochem), 66. *Prof Exp:* Teaching asst chem, Univ Md, 60-63; asst res scientist, Hosp Spec Surg, New York, 63-66; from instr to asst prof biochem, Med Col, Cornell Univ, 66-70; spec res fel, 70-73, res biochemist, Molecular Struct Sect, 73-80, CHIEF, SKELETAL MATRIX BIOCHEM SECT, LAB BIOL STRUCT, NAT INST DENT RES, NIH, 80- *Mem:* AAAS; Int Asn Dent Res; Am Chem Soc; Biophys Soc; Am Soc Biol Chemists. *Res:* Calcification biochemistry; physical biochemistry; protein biochemistry; spectroscopy. *Mailing Add:* Lab Biol Struct Nat Inst Dent Res NIH Bethesda MD 20014

TERMINIELLO, LOUIS, b New York, NY, Sept 22, 30; m 53; c 5. ENZYMOLOGY. *Educ:* Fordham Univ, BS, 52, MS, 54, PhD, 57. *Prof Exp:* Proj leader, Nat Dairy Res Labs, Nat Dairy Prods Corp, 57-58; res assoc, 58-62, res biologist, 62-69, group leader, 69-78, SR RES BIOLOGIST, STERLING-WINTHROP RES INST, 78- *Mem:* NY Acad Sci. *Res:* Isolation and characterization of proteins and enzymes; mechanism of enzyme action; chemical modification of enzymes and the relationship of structure to activity; therapeutic application of enzymes; fibrinolysis; fibrinolytic enzymes; isolation of natural products. *Mailing Add:* Sterling-Winthrop Res Inst Rennselaer NY 12144

TERNAY, ANDREW LOUIS, JR, b New York, NY, Aug 29, 39; m 61; c 2. ORGANIC CHEMISTRY. *Educ:* City Col New York, BS, 59; NY Univ, MS, 62, PhD(chem), 63. *Prof Exp:* NSF fel & res assoc chem, Univ Ill, 63-64; instr, Case Western Reserve Univ, 64-65, asst prof, 65-69; assoc prof, 70-76, PROF CHEM, UNIV TEX, ARLINGTON, 77- *Concurrent Pos:* Grants, Nat Cancer Inst, Dept Chem, Case Western Reserve Univ, 66-69 & Welch Found, Univ Tex, 72-; consult, Arbrook, Inc, 71-; adj prof med chem, Univ Houston, 81. *Mem:* AAAS; Am Chem Soc; Royal Soc Chem. *Res:* Drug design; molecular spectroscopy; application of stereochemistry to synthesis of new drugs, especially psychoactive materials. *Mailing Add:* Dept Chem Box 19065 Univ Tex Arlington TX 76019

TERNBERG, JESSIE L, b Corning, Calif, May 28, 24. SURGERY. *Educ:* Grinnell Col, AB, 46; Univ Tex, PhD(biochem), 50; Washington Univ, MD, 53. *Hon Degrees:* DSc, Univ Mo-St Louis. *Prof Exp:* From instr to assoc prof, 59-71, PROF PEDIAT SURG, SCH MED, WASHINGTON UNIV, 71- *Honors & Awards:* Horatio Alger Award. *Res:* Free radicals in biological systems as studies by electron spin resonance spectrometer. *Mailing Add:* Dept of Surg 4960 Audubon Ave St Louis MO 63110

TERNER, CHARLES, b Lublin, Poland, Apr 30, 16; nat US; m 45; c 3. BIOCHEMISTRY. *Educ:* Univ London, BSc, 44, DSc(biochem), 69; Univ Sheffield, PhD(biochem), 49. *Prof Exp:* Mem staff, Med Res Coun Unit for Res Cell Metab, Dept Biochem, Univ Sheffield, 47-50; sr sci officer, Dept Physiol, Nat Inst Res in Dairying, Eng, 50-55; mem staff, Worcester Found Exp Biol, 55-59; PROF BIOL, BOSTON UNIV, 59- *Concurrent Pos:* Vis scientist, Pop Coun, Rockefeller Univ, 72. *Mem:* AAAS; Am Soc Biol Chem; Biochem Soc (Gt Brit); Soc Exp Biol & Med; Soc Study Reproduction. *Res:* Biochemistry of male reproductive tissues; control of male fertility; embryonic development of fish. *Mailing Add:* Biol Sci Ctr 2 Cummington St 2 Cummington St Boston Univ Boston MA 02215

TER-POGOSSIAN, MICHEL MATHEW, b Berlin, Ger, Apr 21, 25; nat US. MEDICAL PHYSICS. *Educ:* Univ Paris, BA, 42; Washington Univ, MS, 48, PhD(nuclear physics), 50. *Prof Exp:* From instr to prof radiation sci, 50-71, PROF RADIOL, SCH MED, WASHINGTON UNIV, 71- *Mem:* Fel Am Phys Soc; Am Nuclear Soc; Am Radium Soc; Radiation Res Soc; hon fel Am Col Radiol. *Res:* Medical applications of short-lived isotopes; gamma ray spectroscopy; scintillation counters; radiation dosimetry; radiobiology; lasers in biology; reconstructive tomography in radiologic imaging; positron emission imaging. *Mailing Add:* Div of Radiation Sci Washington Univ Sch of Med St Louis MO 63110

TERRACIO, LOUIS, histology, see previous edition

TERRAGLIO, FRANK PETER, b Portland, Ore, May 19, 28; m 64. ENVIRONMENTAL SCIENCE, CHEMISTRY. *Educ:* Univ Portland, BS, 49; Rutgers Univ, MS, 62, PhD(environ sci), 64. *Prof Exp:* Chemist, Ore State Bd Health, 49-50 & Ore Air Pollution Authority, 52-56; asst instr air pollution, Rutgers Univ, 56-63; res chemist, Calif Dept Pub Health, 63-64; asst prof civil eng, Ore State Univ, 64-66; from asst prof to assoc prof, 66-72, PROF APPL SCI, PORTLAND STATE UNIV, 72- *Mem:* Am Chem Soc; Air Pollution Control Asn; Am Water Works Asn; Water Pollution Control Fedn; Am Indust Hyg Asn. *Res:* Reactions of atmospheric sulfur dioxide. *Mailing Add:* Dept of Appl Sci & Eng Portland State Univ Portland OR 97207

TERRANOVA, ANDREW CHARLES, b Cleveland, Ohio, Aug 29, 35. ENTOMOLOGY, TOXICOLOGY. *Educ:* Ohio State Univ, BSc, 60, MSc, 61, PhD(entom), 65. *Prof Exp:* Insect physiologist, Metab & Radiation Res Lab, 65-76, RES ENTOMOLOGIST, SCI & EDUC ADMIN-AGR RES, USDA, 76- *Mem:* AAAS; Entom Soc Am; Am Chem Soc. *Res:* Metabolism and mode of action of insect chemosterilants; biochemistry and physiology of insect reproduction. *Mailing Add:* Pee Dee Exp Sta Box 271 Florence SC 29501

TERRANT, SELDON W, b Cleveland, Ohio, Nov 17, 18; div; c 1. CHEMISTRY, INFORMATION SCIENCE. *Educ:* Ohio Univ, BS, 40; Case Inst Technol, MS, 48, PhD(chem), 50. *Prof Exp:* Anal chemist, Carbide & Carbon Chem Corp, 40-42; instr chem, Case Inst Technol, 49-52; res chemist, E I du Pont de Nemours & Co, NC, 52-57; tech dir, Stand Prod Co, Ohio, 57-59; asst ed, Chem Abstr Serv, 59-60, assoc ed, 60-62; sr scientist, Southern Res Inst, Ala, 62-63; assoc ed, Chem Abstr Serv, 63-64, managing ed spec publ & serv, 64-68, sr staff adv, 68-72; HEAD RES & DEVELOP, BKS & JOURS DIV, AM CHEM SOC, 72- *Mem:* Am Chem Soc; Am Soc Info Sci; Spec Libr Asn; Soc Tech Commun. *Res:* Polarography; stereoisomerism of polymers; textile fibers; rubber processing; chemical literature. *Mailing Add:* Bks & Jours Div Am Chem Soc 1155 16th St NW Washington DC 20036

TERRAS, AUDREY ANNE, b Wash, DC, Sept 10, 42; div. NUMBER THEORY. *Educ:* Univ Md, College Park, BS, 64; Yale Univ, MA, 66, PhD(math), 70. *Prof Exp:* Instr math, Univ Ill, Urbana, 68-70; asst prof Univ PR, Mayaguez, 70-71 & Brooklyn Col, 71-72; asst prof, 72-76, ASSOC PROF MATH, UNIV CALIF, SAN DIEGO, 76- *Concurrent Pos:* NSF grant, 74- *Mem:* Am Math Soc; Math Asn Am; Am Women in Math; Soc Indust & Appl Math; AAAS. *Res:* Zeta functions; automorphic forms of matrix argument; harmonic analysis on homogeneous spaces. *Mailing Add:* Dept Math C-012 Univ Calif San Diego La Jolla CA 92093

TERREAULT, BERNARD J E J, b Montreal, Que, Mar 29, 40; m 68; c 2. SURFACE PHYSICS, THERMONUCLEAR FUSION TECHNOLOGY. *Educ:* Univ Montreal, BSc, 60, MSc, 62; Univ Ill, Urbana-Champaign, PhD(physics), 68. *Prof Exp:* Fel, Lab High Energy Physics, Polytech Sch, Paris, 69-70; res assoc high energy physics, Ohio Univ, 70-71, asst prof, 71-72; assoc prof, 72-77, PROF NUCLEAR SCI, ENERGY CTR, NAT INST SCI RES, UNIV QUE, 77- *Mem:* Am Phys Soc; AAAS; Can Asn Physicists; Am Vacuum Soc. *Res:* Radiation effects in nuclear materials of interest in controlled thermonuclear fusion, mainly low-energy light-ion bombardment on surfaces. *Mailing Add:* Energy Ctr Nat Inst Sci Res Univ Que CP 1020 Varennes PQ J0L 2P0 Can

TERREL, RONALD LEE, b Klamath Falls, Ore, Sept 2, 36; m 59, 81; c 3. CIVIL ENGINEERING, ENGINEERING GEOLOGY. *Educ:* Purdue Univ, Lafayette, BSCE, 60, MSCE, 61; Univ Calif, Berkeley, PhD(civil eng), 67. *Prof Exp:* Estimator, J H Pomeroy & Co, Inc, 55-56; mat engr, US Bur Reclamation, Denver, 61-64; proj engr, J H Pomeroy & Co, Inc, 64-65; res asst, Univ Calif, Berkeley, 65-67; from asst prof to assoc prof civil eng & head transp, Construct & Geometronics Div, Univ Wash, 67-75, prof, 75-78; PRES, PAVEMENT SYSTA, INC, 72-; DIR, WASH STATE TRANSP CTR, 81- *Concurrent Pos:* Chmn, Triaxial Inst Struct Pavement Design, 71-73; mem trans res bd, Nat Acad Sci; consult eng res & develop, gov & private indust, States, Fed Hwy Admin, United Nations. *Honors & Awards:* Construction Man of Year Award, Eng-News-Record, 73. *Mem:* Asn Asphalt Paving Technol; Am Soc Civil Engrs; Am Soc Testing & Mat; Am Rd & Transp Builders Asn; Asn Eng Geologists. *Res:* Pavement and construction materials technology including asphalt, concrete, aggregates, waste materials such as sulphur, lignin, ash, and recycled pavement materials for highway and airports; construction engineering and management. *Mailing Add:* Dept of Civil Eng FX-10 Univ of Wash Seattle WA 98195

TERRELL, C(HARLES) W(ILLIAM), b Louisville, Ky, May 10, 27; m 52; c 2. NUCLEAR ENGINEERING, ENGINEERING EDUCATION. *Educ:* Purdue Univ, BSEE, 52, PhD(nuclear eng), 70; NC State Univ, Raleigh, BS, 54, MS, 55. *Prof Exp:* Eng asst electronics, Sentinel Radio & TV Corp, Ill, 47-50; res engr, Bendix Res Labs, Mich, 52-54; mem res & teaching staff physics, NC State Univ, Raleigh, 54-57; supvr reactor opers, Armour Res Found, 57-59, supvr reactor res, 59-61, mgr nuclear res, 61-63; asst dir physics res, IIT Res Inst, 63-65, dir physics res div, 65-67; assoc prof nuclear eng & supvr comput opers, Purdue Univ, 69-70; dist mgr appl sci & mkt support, Comput Sci Corp, Ill, 70-72; pres, Ind Inst Technol, 72-77; PROF

NUCLEAR ENG, UNIV OKLA, 77- *Mem:* Am Nuclear Soc; Am Soc Eng Educ. *Res:* Higher education administration; nuclear engineering education; computer applications; computer science. *Mailing Add:* Sch Aerospace Mech & Nuclear Eng Univ Okla Norman OK 73019

TERRELL, EDWARD EVERETT, b Wilmington, Ohio, Oct 6, 23; m 50; c 3. PLANT TAXONOMY. *Educ:* Wilmington Col, AB, 47; Cornell Univ, MS, 49; Univ Wis, PhD, 52. *Prof Exp:* Muellhaupt scholar bot, Ohio State Univ, 52-53; assoc prof biol & head dept sci, Pembroke State Col, 54-56; assoc prof biol, Guilford Col, 56-60; BOTANIST, AGR RES SERV, USDA, 60- *Mem:* AAAS; Bot Soc Am; Am Soc Plant Taxon; Torrey Bot Club; Int Asn Plant Taxon. *Res:* Plant taxonomy and ecology; taxonomy of Houstonia; taxonomy of grasses. *Mailing Add:* Agr Res Ctr West Beltsville MD 20705

TERRELL, GLEN EDWARD, b Humble, Tex, Nov 17, 39; m 59; c 2. NUCLEAR PHYSICS. *Educ:* Univ Tex, Austin, BS, 62, MA, 64, PhD(physics), 66. *Prof Exp:* Asst prof, 66-74, ASSOC PROF PHYSICS, UNIV TEX, ARLINGTON, 74- *Mem:* Am Phys Soc. *Res:* Computer-assisted instruction; low energy nuclear physics; polarization of protons elastically scattered by several nuclei; gamma ray directional correlation. *Mailing Add:* Dept of Physics Univ of Tex Arlington TX 76010

TERRELL, MARVIN PALMER, b Pine Bluff, Ark, May 19, 34; m 59; c 2. INDUSTRIAL ENGINEERING, OPERATIONS RESEARCH. *Educ:* Univ Ark, Fayetteville, BSIE, 57, MSIE, 60; Univ Tex, Austin, PhD(opers res), 66. *Prof Exp:* Instr indust eng, Univ Ark, Fayetteville, 57-60; mfg engr, Gen Elec Co, 60-63; indust engr, Tex Instruments Co, 63-64; asst eng & Ford Found & Alcoa fels, Univ Tex, Austin, 64-66, Nat Tau Beta Pi-Ford fel, 65-66; from asst prof to assoc prof, 66-77, PROF INDUST ENG, OKLA STATE UNIV, 77- *Concurrent Pos:* Consult, Continental Oil Co, 67, NAm Rockwell Corp, 68-69 & Phillips Petrol Co, 72 & Bray Truck Lines, 79-82. *Mem:* Am Inst Indust Engrs; Opers Res Soc Am; Inst Mgt Sci; Am Soc Eng Educ. *Res:* Mathematical programming; optimization theory; combinatorics; operations modeling and analysis; management science; quality control and reliability. *Mailing Add:* Dept of Indust Eng Okla State Univ Stillwater OK 74074

TERRELL, NELSON JAMES, JR, b Houston, Tex, Aug 15, 23; m 45; c 3. PHYSICS, ASTROPHYSICS. *Educ:* Rice Univ, BA, 44, MA, 47, PhD(physics), 50. *Prof Exp:* Res asst physics, Rice Univ, 50; asst prof, Case Western Reserve Univ, 50-51; MEM STAFF, LOS ALAMOS NAT LAB, UNIV CALIF, 51- *Concurrent Pos:* USAEC fel, 48-50. *Mem:* Fel AAAS; fel Am Phys Soc; Am Astron Soc; Sigma Xi. *Res:* Astrophysics; relativity; fission; diffraction; Fourier analysis; x-ray astronomy. *Mailing Add:* Los Alamos Nat Lab Mail Stop 436 Box 1663 Univ Calif Los Alamos NM 87545

TERRELL, ROSS CLARK, b Oneonta, NY, Sept 22, 25; m 56. ORGANIC CHEMISTRY. *Educ:* Hartwick Col, BS, 50; Columbia Univ, PhD(org chem), 55. *Prof Exp:* Res chemist, Shulton Inc, 55-59; sr chemist, Air Reduction Co, Inc, 59-67, supvr chem res, Ohio Med Prods, 67-75, MGR PHARMACEUT RES, OHIO MED ANESTHETICS, DIV OF AIRCO INC, 75- *Concurrent Pos:* Hon vis res fel, Univ Birmingham, 66-67. *Res:* Organic synthesis; terpenes; surfactants; anesthetics; fluorine chemistry; pharmaceuticals. *Mailing Add:* Ohio Med Anesthetics 100 Mountain Ave Murray Hill NJ 07974

TERRELL, TERRY LEE TICKHILL, b Wheeling, WVa, Nov 23, 49. AQUATIC ECOLOGY. *Educ:* Ohio State Univ, BS, 71; Univ Ga, PhD(zool), 76. *Prof Exp:* Instr bot, Univ Wyo, 75-76, guest lectr bot, 76, asst prof, 76; AQUATIC ECOLOGIST, US FISH & WILDLIFE SERV, 77- *Concurrent Pos:* Aquatic ecologist, Res Eval Tech Prog, US Forest Serv, 79-81; leader Aquatic Classification Tech Working Group, Five-Way Interagency Agreement Comt Nat Assessments, 79-81. *Mem:* Phycol Soc Am; Am Soc Limnol & Oceanog; Int Soc Limnol; AAAS. *Res:* Classification, inventory and analysis of aquatic ecosystems in relation to natural resource management; most emphasis on such management perturbations as mining and hydroelectric development; classical limnological studies and their application to natural resources management; lake trophic dynamics. *Mailing Add:* Naval Support Act Bldg 204 Nat Fishery Res Ctr Seattle WA 98115

TERRES, GERONIMO, b Santa Barbara, Calif, July 1, 25; m 47; c 5. IMMUNOBIOLOGY. *Educ:* Univ Calif, BA, 50; Stanford Univ, MA, 51; Calif Inst Technol, PhD(biol), 56. *Prof Exp:* Asst, Calif Inst Technol, 52-55; assoc scientist microbiol, Brookhaven Nat Lab, 55-60; asst prof human physiol, Sch Med, Stanford Univ, 60-69; assoc prof, 69-78, PROF PHYSIOL, SCH MED, TUFTS UNIV, 78- *Concurrent Pos:* NIH sr res fel, 60-62; USPHS res career develop award, 62-69; vis asst prof, Harvard Med Sch, 67-68; vis scientist, Md Inst Technol, 75-76; vis assoc, Calif Inst Technol, 81; Yamagiwa-Yoshida fel award, 79. *Mem:* AAAS; Am Asn Immunol; Soc Exp Biol & Med; Am Physiol Soc; Radiation Res Soc. *Res:* Immune degradation; tumor (leukemias) cell rejection; T cell hybridization; acquired immune tolerance in mice; initiation and control of the immune response. *Mailing Add:* Dept of Physiol Tufts Univ Sch of Med Boston MA 02111

TERRIERE, LEON C, b Stone, Idaho, June 17, 20; m 44; c 3. BIOCHEMSITRY, INSECT TOXICOLOGY. *Educ:* Univ Idaho, BS, 43; Ore State Col, PhD(chem), 50. *Prof Exp:* From asst prof to assoc prof, Agr Exp Sta, 50-61, PROF INSECT TOXICOL, AGR CHEM & ENTOM, ORE STATE UNIV, 60- *Concurrent Pos:* Vis prof, Univ Sydney, Australia, 80. *Mem:* Entom Soc Am; Am Chem Soc; AAAS. *Res:* Chemistry of insecticides; insect toxicology; detoxication mechanisms in insects; biochemistry of insect resistance to insecticides; insect host plant relationships; toxicology of pesticides in the environment; residues in foods; insecticide metabolism. *Mailing Add:* Dept of Entom Ore State Univ Corvallis OR 97331

TERRIERE, ROBERT T, b Seattle, Wash, July 17, 26; m 58; c 2. GEOLOGY. *Educ:* Calif Inst Technol, BS, 49; Pa State Col, MS, 51; Univ Tex, PhD(geol), 60. *Prof Exp:* Geologist, US Geol Surv, 51-58; res geologist, Cities Serv Oil Co, 58-70, res assoc, 70-78, sr geol assoc, 78-80, REGION EXPLOR GEOLOGIST, CITIES SERV CO-PETROL EXPLOR, 80- *Mem:* Fel Geol Soc Am; Am Asn Petrol Geol. *Res:* Physical stratigraphy; sedimentary petrography; petroleum geology. *Mailing Add:* 2618 S Allison St Denver CO 80227

TERRILE, RICHARD JOHN, b New York, NY, Mar 22, 51; m 81. PLANETARY SCIENCE. *Educ:* State Univ NY, Stony Brook, BS, 72; Calif Inst Technol, MS, 73, PhD(planetary sci), 78. *Prof Exp:* Res asst, Calif Inst Technol, 72-78, assoc scientist, 78; physicist, Trend Western Tech Corp, 78-80, sr scientist, 80-81, MEM TECH STAFF, JET PROPULSION LAB, 81- *Concurrent Pos:* mem, Voyager Target Selection Working Group, 78-; planetary astron prin investr, NASA grant, 78-, planetary atmospheres prin investr, 79-; guest investr, Voyager Imaging Sci Team, 78-80. *Mem:* Am Astron Soc; Am Geophys Union; Int Astron Union; Sigma Xi. *Res:* Ground-based planetary astromony; planetary atmospheres; comparative geology; photographic interpretation of spacecraft data and the study of planetary ring systems. *Mailing Add:* Jet Propulsion Lab MS 183-301 Pasadena CA 91109

TERRILL, CLAIR ELMAN, b Rippey, Iowa, Oct 27, 10; m 32; c 2. ANIMAL BREEDING. *Educ:* Iowa State Col, BS, 32; Univ Mo, PhD, 36. *Prof Exp:* Asst animal husb, Univ Mo, 32-36; asst animal husbandman, Exp Sta, Univ Ga, 36; asst animal husbandman, Sheep Exp Sta, Bur Animal Indust, Idaho, 36-37, assoc animal husbandman, Western Sheep Breeding Lab & Sheep Exp Sta, Agr Res Serv, 53-55, chief sheep & fur animal res br, Animal Husb Res Div, 55-72, NAT PROG STAFF SCIENTIST FOR SHEEP & OTHER ANIMALS, AGR RES SERV, USDA, 72- *Concurrent Pos:* Dir, Am Forage & Grass Land Coun, 63-65; mem, World Asn Animal Prod Coun, 63- *Honors & Awards:* Achievement Award, Ital Exp Inst & Ital Soc Advan Zootech; Distinguished Achievement Award, Sheep Indust Develop. *Mem:* AAAS; Genetics Soc Am; hon fel Am Soc Animal Sci (secy-treas, 60-62, vpres, 63, pres, 64); Am Meat Sci Asn; Am Genetic Asn (vpres, 69, pres, 70). *Res:* Animal genetics; reproductive physiology; sheep, goat and fur animal breeding and production. *Mailing Add:* Nat Prog Staff Agr Res Ctr-West Agr Res Serv USDA Beltsville MD 20705

TERRILL, THOMAS ROBERT, plant breeding, genetics, see previous edition

TERRIS, MILTON, b New York, NY, Apr 22, 15; m 41, 71; c 2. EPIDEMIOLOGY. *Educ:* Columbia Col, AB, 35; NY Univ, MD, 39; Johns Hopkins Univ, MPH, 44. *Prof Exp:* Intern, Harlem Hosp, New York, 39-41 & Bellevue Psychiat Hosp, New York, 41-42; apprentice epidemiologist, State Dept Health, NY, 42-43, asst dist health officer, 44-46; med assoc subcomt on med care, Am Pub Health Asn, 46-48, staff dir, 48-51; assoc prev med & pub health, Sch Med, Univ Buffalo, 52-54, from asst prof to assoc prof, 54-58; prof epidemiol, Sch Med, Tulane Univ, 58-60; head chronic dis unit, Div Epidemiol, Pub Health Res Inst New York, 60-64; PROF PREV MED, NEW YORK MED COL, 64-, CHMN DEPT COMMUNITY & PREV MED, 68- *Concurrent Pos:* Asst dean post-grad educ, Univ Buffalo, 51-58. *Mem:* Am Pub Health Asn (pres, 66-67); Soc Epidemiol Res (pres, 67-69); Am Epidemiol Soc; Asn Teachers Prev Med (pres, 61-62); Int Epidemiol Asn. *Res:* Epidemiology of cancer; cirrhosis of liver; prematurity; heart disease. *Mailing Add:* Dept of Community & Prev Med NY Med Col Fifth Ave & 106th St New York NY 10029

TERRY, DAVID LEE, b Burkley, Ky, Mar 22, 36; div; c 3. SOIL SCIENCE. *Educ:* Univ Ky, BS, 58, MS, 61; NC State Univ, PhD(soil sci), 68. *Prof Exp:* Agronomist, Univ Ky, 59-60; from instr to asst prof soil sci, NC State Univ, 71-74; COORDR FERTILIZER REGULATORY PROG, UNIV KY, 74- *Mem:* Asn Am Plant Food Control Officials; Am Soc Agron. *Res:* Soil fertility; fertilizer control in state of Kentucky. *Mailing Add:* Regulatory Serv Univ of Ky Lexington KY 40506

TERRY, FRED HERBERT, b Bedford, Ind, July 29, 40; m 63; c 2. ELECTRICAL ENGINEERING, BIOENGINEERING. *Educ:* Rose-Hulman Inst Technol, BS, 62, MS, 64; Case Western Reserve Univ, PhD(eng), 67. *Prof Exp:* Asst prof, 67-69, head elec eng, 69-72, assoc prof, 70-80, PROF ELEC ENG, CHRISTIAN BROS COL, 80-, CHMN DEPT ENG, 72- *Concurrent Pos:* Instr med units, Univ Tenn, 67-; gen res eng, Memphis Vet Admin Hosp, 75-78. *Mem:* Inst Elec & Electronics Engrs; Am Soc Eng Educ; Nat Soc Prof Engrs. *Res:* Computer acquisition and analysis of electrophysiological data; linear electrical properties of canine purkinje tissue; modeling of cardiac conduction abnormalities; electroacoustic analysis of heart sounds. *Mailing Add:* Dept of Eng Christian Bros Col Memphis TN 38104

TERRY, HERBERT, b New York, NY, Jan 30, 22; m 57; c 2. OPERATIONS RESEARCH. *Educ:* City Col New York, BS, 42; Polytech Inst Brooklyn, BChE, 46. *Prof Exp:* Group leader, Foster D Snell, Inc, 42-46; tech serv mgr, Shawinigan Resins Corp, 47-63; tech mgr coatings div, Hooker Chem Corp, 63-67; res dir polymer appln, Foster D Snell, Inc, Subsidiary Booz, Allen & Hamilton, Inc, 67-69, res dir, 69-71, vpres, 71-74; PRES, DECISIONEX, INC, 74- *Mem:* Am Chem Soc; Opers Res Soc Am; Inst Mgt Sci. *Res:* Applications of decision theory and operations research to computer programming for financial analysis. *Mailing Add:* Decisionex Inc 1200 Post Rd E Westport CT 06880

TERRY, IRA A(NDERSON), b Ogden, Utah, Oct 31, 03; m 26; c 2. ELECTRICAL ENGINEERING, MECHANICAL ENGINEERING. *Educ:* Univ Utah, BSEE, 25; Union Col, MSEE, 29. *Prof Exp:* Student engr, Gen Elec Co, Mass, 25-27, engr, 27-33, asst engr, 33-40, asst to mgr, 40-42, asst to vpres apparatus design eng, 42-46, works engr, 46-47, asst mgr eng, 47-48, mgr, 48-62, mgr dent health res, 62-67; RES AFFIL, FORSYTH

DENT CTR, BOSTON, 67- *Concurrent Pos:* Pres, Calif North Mission, Church of Jesus Christ of Latter-Day Saints, 69-72. *Mem:* Fel Inst Elec & Electronics Engrs (vpres, Inst Elec Eng); Am Soc Mech Engrs; assoc Am Dent Asn; fel Am Pub Health Asn; Int Asn Dent Res. *Res:* Turbines; motors; synchronous motors and generators; direct current motors and generators; clocks; timers; timing motors. *Mailing Add:* 151 Gayland Apt 48 Escondido CA 92027

TERRY, JAMES LAYTON, b Peoria, Ill, Apr 8, 51. ATOMIC & HIGH TEMPERATURE PHYSICS. *Educ:* Denison Univ, BS, 73; Johns Hopkins Univ, MA, 75, PhD(physics), 78. *Prof Exp:* RES STAFF PHYSICS, MASS INST TECHNOL, 78- *Mem:* Am Phys Soc. *Res:* Diagnostics of high temperature plasmas. *Mailing Add:* Mass Inst Technol NW16-282 Cambridge MA 02139

TERRY, LUTHER LEONIDAS, b Red Level, Ala, Sept 15, 11; m 40; c 3. MEDICINE. *Educ:* Birmingham-Southern Col, BS, 31; Tulane Univ, MD, 35; Am Bd Internal Med, dipl, 43. *Hon Degrees:* DSc, Birmingham-Southern Col, 61, Jefferson Med Col, 62, Tulane Univ, 64, Union Col, 64, Univ RI, 64, Rose Polytech Inst, 65, McGill Univ, 66 & Univ Ala, 66; Dr Med Sci, Woman's Med Col Pa, 64; LLD, Univ Alaska, 64, Calif Col Med, 65 & Marquette Univ, 68. *Prof Exp:* Intern, Hillman Hosp, Birmingham, Ala, 35-36; asst resident med, Univ Hosp, Cleveland, Ohio, 36-37; resident City Hosp, 37-38, intern path & asst admitting officer, 38-39; instr med, Washington Univ, 39-40; from instr to assoc prof med, prev med & pub health, Univ Tex, 40-42; mem med serv staff, USPHS Hosp, Baltimore, Md, 42-43, chief med serv, 43-53, asst dir, Nat Heart Inst, 58-61, Surgeon Gen, USPHS, 61-65; vpres med affairs, Univ Pa, 65-71, prof med & community med, 65-76; CORP VPRES, MED AFFAIRS, ARA SERV, INC, 80- *Concurrent Pos:* Adj prof, Univ Tex, 42-46; instr, Sch Med, Johns Hopkins Univ, 44-53, asst prof, 53-61; mem med div, Strategic Bombing Surv, Japan, 45-46; staff mem, Subcomt Invest Malmedy Atrocities, Senate Comt Mil Affairs, 49; chief cardiovasc clin, USPHS Hosp, Baltimore, Md, 50-53, chief gen med & exp therapeut, Nat Heart Inst, 50-58; mem cardiovasc study sect, NIH, 50-55, chmn med bd, Clin Ctr, 53-55, mem, 53-58, dir residency training prog, Nat Heart Inst, 53-61, chmn cardiovasc res training comt, 57-61, mem comt civilian health requirements, USPHS, 56-58, mem adv comt nutrit, Indian Health Serv, 57-61; chmn, Nat Interagency Coun Smoking & Health, 67-69; chmn adv comt vet med res & educ, Nat Acad Sci, 69-71; spec consult, Am Cancer Soc, 72-75; pub trustee, Nutrit Found; dir, Med Alert Found, chmn bd, 75; dir, Elwyn Inst; Nat Health & Safety Comt, BSA; chmn, State Adv Comt Health for Appalachia, Pa; mem expert comt cardiovasc dis, WHO, 74-; res fel pneumonia, Washington Univ, 39-40. *Honors & Awards:* Bruce Award, Am Col Physicians, 65; Hilleboe Prize lect, NY State Annual Health Conf, 65; Distinguished Serv Med, USPHS, 65. *Mem:* Hon fel Am Col Chest Physicians; hon mem Am Hosp Asn; hon fel Am Col Dent; fel & hon master Am Col Physicians; hon fel Royal Soc Health. *Res:* Experimental therapeutics; cardiovascular diseases. *Mailing Add:* 2035 Delancey Pl Philadelphia PA 19103

TERRY, MAURICE ERNEST, b Tooele, Utah, Mar 28, 44; m 70; c 2. PLANT PHYSIOLOGY. *Educ:* Sacramento State Univ, BS, 71; Univ Calif, Davis, MS, 74, PhD(bot), 78. *Prof Exp:* Res botanist, Univ Calif, Berkeley, 78-80; res assoc, Plant Res Lab, Mich State Univ, 80-81; ASST PROF, DEPT PLANT PATH & CROP PHYSIOL, LA STATE UNIV, 81- *Mem:* Am Soc Plant Physiologists; Plant Growth Regulator Soc Am. *Res:* Improving the productivity of sugar cane, especially the role growth regulators play in either increasing the early growth of sugar cane, or decreasing growth prior to harvest. *Mailing Add:* Dept Plant Path & Crop Physiol 302 Life Sci Bldg La State Univ Baton Rouge LA 70803

TERRY, MILTON EVERETT, b Windham, Conn, June 14, 16; m 37; c 3. MATHEMATICAL STATISTICS. *Educ:* Acadia Univ, BSc, 37; Univ NC, PhD(math statist), 51. *Prof Exp:* Instr math & French, Cascadilla, 37-39; asst prof math, Blue Ridge Col, 39-41; instr, Randolph-Macon Woman's Col, 46; assoc prof statist, Va Polytech Inst & State Univ, 49-52; statistician, 52-60, head dept statist, 60-63, asst dir traffic studies, 63-64, dir opers res & comput, 64-65, dir comput projs res ctr, 65-71, HEAD STATIST COMPUT RES, BELL TEL LABS, INC, 71- *Concurrent Pos:* Adj prof, Rutgers Univ, 55-62; vis prof, Inst Statist Studies & Res, Univ Cairo, 69-71; mem adv coun, Qm Food & Container Inst; mem subcomt adv bd, Nat Res Coun. *Mem:* Fel Am Soc Qual Control; fel Am Statist Asn; Inst Math Statist. *Res:* Use of electronic computer systems; design of management information and analytic systems. *Mailing Add:* Bell Telephone Labs Room 7C502 Murry Hill NJ 07974

TERRY, NORMAN, b Maidstone, Eng, Sept 5, 39; m 68; c 3. PLANT PHYSIOLOGY. *Educ:* Southampton Univ, BSc, 61; Nottingham Univ, MSc, 63, PhD(plant physiol), 66. *Prof Exp:* Res fel plant physiol, Div Biosci, Nat Res Coun Can, 66-68; asst specialist plant physiol, Dept Soils & Plant Nutrit, 68-72, asst prof, 72-78, ASSOC PROF ENVIRON PLANT PHYSIOL, UNIV CALIF, BERKELEY, 78- *Mem:* Am Soc Plant Physiologists; AAAS; Crop Sci Soc Am; Brit Soc Exp Biol. *Res:* Environmental and internal factors involved in the regulation of photosynthesis; physiology of trace elements. *Mailing Add:* Dept of Soils & Plant Nutrit Univ of Calif Berkeley CA 94720

TERRY, ONA JOY, b Houston, Tex, Nov 13, 21; m 46; c 1. ORGANIC CHEMISTRY. *Educ:* Univ Houston, BS, 42, MS, 45. *Prof Exp:* Asst prof chem, Tarleton State Univ, 58, assoc prof, 58-79; MEM STAFF, QUAL CONTROL INSTRUMENTATION, COMANCHE PEAK STEAM ELEC STA, TEX, 79- *Mem:* Am Chem Soc; Am Asn Univ Profs. *Res:* Freshman chemistry; organic preparation. *Mailing Add:* Dept of Phys Sci Tarleton State Univ Tarleton Station TX 76402

TERRY, ORVILLE WHITFIELD, b Orient, NY, Apr 12, 14; m 50. MARINE PLANT ECOLOGY. *Educ:* Cornell Univ, BS, 35, MS, 37; State Univ NY Stony Brook, PhD(biol sci), 70. *Prof Exp:* Res asst agr, Cornell Univ, 46; teacher high schs, NY, 61-63; res assoc marine sci, 70-76, ASSOC RES PROF MARINE SCI, MARINE SCI RES CTR, STATE UNIV NY STONY BROOK, 76- *Concurrent Pos:* Sci ed, NY Sea Grant Inst, State Univ NY-Cornell Univ, 72-76; adj prof marine sci, C W Post Ctr, Long Island Univ, 77- *Mem:* AAAS; World Mariculture Soc; Ecol Soc Am; Phycol Soc Am; Am Soc Agr Engrs. *Res:* Physiology, ecology and culture of seaweeds; mariculture of shellfish; environmental management. *Mailing Add:* Marine Sci Res Ctr State Univ NY Stony Brook NY 11794

TERRY, PAUL H, b Fall River, Mass, June 22, 28. ORGANIC CHEMISTRY. *Educ:* Southeastern Mass Univ, BS, 51; Univ Mass, MS, 59, PhD(org chem), 63. *Prof Exp:* Chemist, Dept Geront, Wash Univ, 52-53; RES CHEMIST, INSECT CHEMOSTERILANTS LAB, AGR ENVIRON QUAL INST, AGR RES SERV, USDA, 63- *Mem:* AAAS; Am Chem Soc; Am Inst Chem. *Res:* Synthesis and mode of action of insect chemosterilants; phosphorus chemistry, especially phosphoramides. *Mailing Add:* Insect Chemosterilants Lab Inst Agr Res Ctr Beltsville MD 20705

TERRY, RAYMOND DOUGLAS, b Southampton, NY, Apr 19, 45; m 81. MATHEMATICS. *Educ:* State Univ NY, Stony Brook, BS, 66; Mich State Univ, MS, 68, PhD(math), 72. *Prof Exp:* Teaching asst math, Mich State Univ, 66-72; instr math, Ga Inst Technol, 72-74; asst prof, 74-78, ASSOC PROF MATH, CALIF POLYTECH STATE UNIV, SAN LUIS OBISPO, 78- *Concurrent Pos:* Vis assoc prof, Mich State Univ, 81-82. *Mem:* Am Math Soc; Math Asn Am; Soc Indust & Appl Math. *Res:* Higher-order delay and functional differential equations. *Mailing Add:* Dept of Math Calif Polytech State Univ San Luis Obispo CA 93407

TERRY, RICHARD D, b Salt Lake City, Utah, Jan 29, 24; m 48; c 1. OCEANOGRAPHY, SPACE SCIENCES. *Educ:* Univ Southern Calif, AB, 50, MS, 56, PhD, 65. *Prof Exp:* Res asst oceanog, Allan Hancock Found, Univ Southern Calif, 50-55, res assoc, 55-60; res specialist, Autonetics Div, NAm Aviation Inc, 60-64, dir ocean eng, Gen Off, 64-65, spec asst oceanology, Ocean Systs Oper & Mgr, Earth Resources Group, 66-68; pres, Seaonics Int Inc, 68-70; PRES, RICHARD TERRY & ASSOCS/ENVIRON SCI & SERV, 70- *Concurrent Pos:* Consult oceanog, marine geology, 55-, Dep Asst Secy Defense, 64 & US Dept Navy, 64-68; mem, Community Regional & Natural Resources Develop Group Comt, US Chamber Commerce, 66-67; prog dir, Nat Oceanog Govt & Indust Report, 64-65; chmn bd, Red Sea Enterprises Co, Ltd, 70- *Mem:* Am Geophys Union; Geol Soc Am. *Res:* Marine geology; submarine topography; sediment; physical and chemical oceanography; ocean engineering; deep submergence technology; oceanography from space science; environmental sciences; basic and applied research in environmental sciences. *Mailing Add:* 3903 Calle Abril San Clemente CA 92672

TERRY, RICHARD ELLIS, b Rigby, Idaho, Feb 8, 49; m 72; c 3. SOIL BIOCHEMISTRY, SOIL MICROBIOLOGY. *Educ:* Brigham Young Univ, BS, 72; Purdue Univ, MS, 74, PhD(soil Sci), 76. *Prof Exp:* Asst soil sci, Purdue Univ, 74-75, res asst, 72-76; asst prof soil bioche, Univ Fla, 77-80; ASSOC PROF AGRON, BRIGHAM YOUNG UNIV, 80- *Mem:* Am Soc Agron; Soil Sci Soc Am. *Res:* Microbial oxidation of soil organic matter; subsidence of organic soils; nitrogen transformations in soils and sediments; denitrification in terrestrial and aquatic systems; recycling of sewage wastes on land. *Mailing Add:* Dept Agron Brigham Young Univ Provo FL 33430

TERRY, ROBERT DAVIS, b Hartford, Conn, Jan 13, 24; m 52; c 1. NEUROPATHOLOGY. *Educ:* Williams Col, Mass, BA, 46; Union Univ, NY, MD, 50. *Prof Exp:* Asst neuropathologist, Montefiore Hosp, New York, 55-59; PROF PATH, ALBERT EINSTEIN COL MED, 59-, CHMN DEPT, 70- *Mem:* Am Asn Path & Bact; Am Neurol Asn; Am Asn Neuropath (pres, 69-70); Am Acad Neurol. *Res:* Electron microscope studies of pathology of the nervous system; biologic studies of aging brain. *Mailing Add:* Dept of Path Albert Einstein Col of Med Bronx NY 10461

TERRY, ROBERT JAMES, b Crockett, Tex, May 1, 22; m 48; c 1. ZOOLOGY, DEVELOPMENTAL BIOLOGY. *Educ:* Tex Southern Univ, BS, 46; Univ Atlanta, MS, 49; Univ Iowa, PhD(zool, bact), 54. *Prof Exp:* Instr biol, 48-49, asst prof biol & bact, 50-52, assoc prof biol & actg head dept, 53-54, head dept, 54-76, dean col arts & sci, 69-71, PROF BIOL, TEX SOUTHERN UNIV, 54-, DEAN FACULTIES, 71-, VPRES ACAD AFFAIRS, 74- *Concurrent Pos:* Consult, State Teachers Asn Tex, 55; vis scientist, Tex Acad Sci, 60-66; sci consult, Govt India, 65; NSF consult, 67; mem gen res support prog adv comt, NIH, 72-76. *Mem:* Am Soc Zoologists; Nat Inst Sci. *Res:* Neurobiology, particularly regeneration of central nervous tissue in amphibia and in mice; influence of thyroxine on development of specific tissues in amphibians. *Mailing Add:* Sch of Arts & Sci Tex Southern Univ Houston TX 77004

TERRY, ROBERT LEE, b Mt Holly, NJ, Aug 7, 18; m 43; c 2. CELL PHYSIOLOGY. *Educ:* Earlham Col, AB, 39; Univ Pa, PhD(zool), 48. *Prof Exp:* Instr biol, Philadelphia Col Pharm, 46-47; asst instr zool, Univ Pa, 47-48; asst prof biol, Union Col, NY, 48-51; asst prof zool, Iowa State Col, 51-52; assoc prof biol, 52-67, chmn div natural sci, 73-76, PROF BIOL, COLBY COL, 67- *Concurrent Pos:* Chmn, Comt Med Prep, 57-79. *Mem:* AAAS; Am Soc Zool; Sigma Xi. *Res:* Granular components of frog eggs; ionic requirements of bacteria; surface properties of myxomycete plasmodia. *Mailing Add:* Dept of Biol Colby Col Waterville ME 04901

TERRY, ROGER, b Waterville, NY, May 8, 17; m 42; c 2. SURGICAL PATHOLOGY. *Educ:* Colgate Univ, AB, 39; Univ Rochester, MD, 44. *Prof Exp:* Intern path, Med Ctr, Univ Rochester, 44-45, instr, Univ, 45-51, from asst prof to prof, 51-69; PROF PATH, MED CTR, UNIV SOUTHERN CALIF, 69-, HEAD SURG PATHOLOGIST, LOS ANGELES COUNTY-UNIV SOUTHERN CALIF MED CTR, 69- *Concurrent Pos:* Actg pathologist, Park Ave Hosp, Rochester, NY, 45-47; resident, Med Ctr, Univ Rochester, 45-51; actg pathologist, Genesee Hosp, Rochester, 47-50 & Highland Hosp, 49-51; co-exec dir, Calif Tumor Tissue Registry, Los Angeles, 69. *Mem:* Am Soc Exp Path; Am Soc Clin Path; Am Asn Pathologists; Am Geriat Soc; Int Acad Path. *Res:* Metabolic bone diseases. *Mailing Add:* 2841 Shakespeare Dr San Marino CA 91108

TERRY, SAMUEL MATTHEW, b Nashville, Tenn, Jan 23, 15; m 43; c 2. CHEMISTRY. *Educ:* Vanderbilt Univ, BA, 43. *Prof Exp:* Jr chemist, Winthrop Chem Co, NY, 43-44; chemist, Publicker Industs, Inc, 44-46; res engr, Battelle Mem Inst, 46-51; res fel, Mellon Inst, 51-54; res chemist, Pittsburgh Plate Glass Co, 54-56; mgr prod develop, Reynolds Chem Prods Co, 56-66; vpres & tech dir, Atlantis Chem Corp, 66-67; tech dir, Hoover Chem Prod Div, Hovver Ball & Bearing Co, 67-81; RETIRED. *Mem:* Am Chem Soc. *Res:* Physical, organic and polymer chemistry. *Mailing Add:* 1560 Marian Ave Ann Arbor MI 48103

TERRY, STUART LEE, b Chicago, Ill, Apr 8, 42; m 80; c 4. POLYMER CHEMISTRY, APPLICATIONS TECHNOLOGY. *Educ:* Cornell Univ, BChemE, 65, PhD(chem eng), 69; Rensselaer Polytech Inst, MS, 74. *Prof Exp:* NSF trainee polymer chem, Cornell Univ, 64-68 & asst, 65-68; sr res chemist, 68-75, group leader polymer synthesis, 75-78, GROUP LEADER PROD DEVELOP, MONSANTO CO, 78- *Res:* Identification of product opportunities and preparation of polymeric materials with morphologies required for industrial and consumer end use performance. *Mailing Add:* Monsanto Co 730 Worcester St Indian Orchard MA 01151

TERRY, THOMAS MILTON, b Knoxville, Tenn, Apr 2, 39; m 64; c 2. BIOPHYSICS, MICROBIOLOGY. *Educ:* Yale Univ, BA, 61, MS, 63, PhD(molecular biophys), 67. *Prof Exp:* USPHS fel biophys, Univ Geneva, 67; asst prof microbiol, Albert Einstein Col Med, 68-69; asst prof microbiol & biol, 77-81, ASSOC PROF BIOL, UNIV CONN, 81- *Mem:* AAAS; Am Soc Microbiol. *Res:* Biological membrane structure and function; molecular biology of mycoplasma; ultrastructure of bacteria; bacteriophage development. *Mailing Add:* Dept of Microbiol Univ of Conn Storrs CT 06268

TERRY, WILLIAM DAVID, b New York, NY, Oct 22, 33; m 66; c 4. IMMUNOLOGY. *Educ:* Cornell Univ, BA, 54; State Univ NY Downstate Med Ctr, MD, 58. *Prof Exp:* Intern, Jewish Hosp Brooklyn, NY, 58-59, asst resident, 59-61; NIH trainee, Sch Med, Univ Calif, San Francisco, 61-62; res assoc, Immunol Sect, Gen Labs & Clins, 62-64, sr investr, 64-71, ASSOC DIR IMMUNOL, DIV CANCER BIOL & DIAG, NAT CANCER INST, 73-, BR CHIEF, 71- *Concurrent Pos:* Adminr, Cancer Ctrs Prog, Nat Cancer Inst, 78-81, Cancer Control Prog, 79-80, ctrs & community activ, Div Resources, 80-81. *Mem:* Am Asn Immunol; Am Fedn Clin Res; Am Soc Clin Invest; Am Asn Cancer Res. *Res:* Nature of the immune response, particularly as it relates to the recognition of and reaction against tumors by the tumor bearing host. *Mailing Add:* Div of Cancer Biol & Diag Nat Cancer Inst Bethesda MD 20014

TERSHAK, DANIEL R, b Wilkes-Barre, Pa, Nov 19, 36; m 67; c 2. VIROLOGY, MICROBIOLOGY. *Educ:* King's Col, Pa, BS, 58; Yale Univ, PhD(virol), 62. *Prof Exp:* Fel, Yale Univ, 62-63, instr microbiol, 63-64; asst prof, 64-69, ASSOC PROF MICROBIOL, PA STATE UNIV, 69- *Concurrent Pos:* USPHS grant, 65-; actg head microbiol & cell biol, Pa State Univ, 78-80; sabbatical leave, Virus Res Inst, Pirbright, Eng, 82- *Mem:* Am Soc Microbiol; NY Acad Sci; Am Soc Virol. *Res:* Nucleic acid and protein synthesis; biochemical genetics; regulation of cell protein synthesis by polio virus; guandidine inhibition of polio virus growth; polio virus polymerase; defective interfering particles of polio virus; phosphorylation of proteins during polio infection. *Mailing Add:* Microbiol Prog S-101 Frear Bldg Pa State Univ University Park PA 16802

TERSHAKOVEC, GEORGE ANDREW, b Lviv, Ukraine, May 6, 14; nat US; m 54; c 2. BIOCHEMISTRY. *Educ:* Lviv Univ, MD, 39. *Prof Exp:* Sr asst biochem, Sch Med, Lviv Univ, 39-41; biochemist & biologist pharmaceut mfg, Laokoon, Lviv, 41-44; asst physiol chem, Sch Med, Univ Vienna, 45-49; instr path, Med Res Unit, 50-52, from instr to assoc prof, 52-60, prof, 60-80, EMER PROF BIOCHEM, SCH MED, UNIV MIAMI, 80- *Mem:* AAAS; Am Chem Soc; Sigma Xi; Shevchenko Sci Soc. *Res:* Carbohydrate metabolism in muscle and liver; enzymatic synthesis of adenosine-5'-phosphate and adenosine triphosphate from adenosine; dynamics of inflammation and repair; clinical biochemistry; gerontology. *Mailing Add:* Dept of Biochem Sch of Med Univ of Miami PO Box 016129 Miami FL 33101

TERSS, ROBERT H, b East St Louis, Ill, Sept 13, 25; m 55. ORGANIC CHEMISTRY. *Educ:* Wash Univ, AB, 49; Univ Kans, PhD(chem), 53. *Prof Exp:* Asst instr chem, Univ Kans, 49-51; res chemist, Dept Org Chem, 53-57, res supvr dyes, 57-58, head div dyes, 59-63, patents & intel, 63-65, photochem, 65-70, supt dyes & chem qual control, 70-71, supt dye mfg, 71-73, div head dyes process, 73-75, div head patents, 76-77, mem, Res & Develop Staff Serv, 76-79, MEM, PERSONNEL DEVELOP, EMPLOYEE RELATIONS DEPT, E I DU PONT DE NEMOURS & CO, INC, 80- *Mem:* Am Chem Soc. *Res:* Dyes; heterocycles; photochemistry; information handling systems; photographic materials. *Mailing Add:* E I Du Pont de Nemours & Co Inc 1007 Market St Wilmington DE 19898

TERWEDOW, HENRY ALBERT, JR, b Hoboken, NJ, July 22, 46; m 67; c 3. MEDICAL ENTOMOLOGY, AGRICULTURAL ENTOMOLOGY. *Educ:* Univ Notre Dame, BS, 68, PhD(biol), 74; Montclair State Col, MA, 69. *Prof Exp:* Res assoc entom, Sch Med, Univ Md, 73-75; fel entom, Univ Calif, Berkeley, 75-77; res entomologist, Celanese Res Co, 77-80; WITH VELSICOL CHEM CORP, 80- *Mem:* Entom Soc Am; Am Soc Trop Med & Hyg; Am Soc Parasitologists; Genetics Soc Am; Am Mosquito Control Asn. *Res:* Vectorial capacity and genetic control of mosquito species involved in the transmission of filariae and arboviruses; entomological aspects of insecticidal improvement. *Mailing Add:* Velsicol Chem Corp 341 E Ohio St Chicago IL 60611

TERWILLIGER, CHARLES, JR, plant ecology, range science, see previous edition

TERWILLIGER, DON WILLIAM, b Klamath Falls, Ore, Mar 27, 42; m 70. COMPUTER SCIENCE. *Educ:* Calif Inst Technol, BS, 64; Univ Ore, MA, 66, PhD(physics), 70. *Prof Exp:* Asst prof physics, Middlebury Col, 70-75; MGR COMPUT RES, TEKTRONIX LABS, 76- *Mem:* Inst Elec & Electronic Engrs; Comput Soc; Comput Applns & Instrumentation. *Res:* Low temperature physics; electron scattering from imperfections in metals; Fermi surface studies. *Mailing Add:* Tektronix Inc PO Box 500 Beaverton OR 97077

TERWILLIGER, JAMES PAUL, b Miami Beach, Fla, Feb 25, 43; m 65; c 2. CHEMICAL ENGINEERING. *Educ:* Rensselaer Polytech Inst, BChE, 65, MChE, 66, PhD(chem eng), 69. *Prof Exp:* Sr res chemist, 69-74, res assoc, 74-75, res lab head, 75-80, ASST DIV DIR, EASTMAN KODAK CO, 80- *Mem:* Am Inst Chem Engrs; Instrument Soc Am; Soc Photog Scientists & Engrs. *Res:* Heat and mass transfer; reaction kinetics; process control; crystallization. *Mailing Add:* 109 Dorian Lane Eastman Kodak Co Kodak Park Rochester NY 14626

TERWILLIGER, KENT MELVILLE, b San Jose, Calif, June 17, 24; m 51; c 4. HIGH ENERGY PHYSICS. *Educ:* Calif Inst Technol, BS, 49; Univ Calif, Berkeley, PhD(physics), 52. *Prof Exp:* From instr to assoc prof, 52-65, PROF PHYSICS, UNIV MICH, ANN ARBOR, 65- *Concurrent Pos:* John Simon Guggenheim fel, 64-65; mem high energy physics adv panel, AEC, 68-71; vis scientist, Europ Orgn Nuclear Res, 72. *Mem:* Am Asn Univ Prof; AAAS; Am Phys Soc. *Res:* Elementary particle scattering experiments; high energy accelerators. *Mailing Add:* Dept of Physics Univ of Mich Ann Arbor MI 48109

TERZAGHI, MARGARET, b Boston, Mass, May 7, 41. CANCER. *Educ:* Boston Univ, AB, 64, MS, 69; Harvard Univ, MS, 70, DSc(radiation biol, physiol), 74. *Prof Exp:* Res asst cancer res, Harvard Univ, 70-75, res assoc, 75; RES ASSOC CANCER RES, OAK RIDGE NAT LAB, 75- *Res:* An examination of possible in vitro models of in vivo carcinogenesis induced by chemical carcinogens and/or radiation. *Mailing Add:* Biol Div Carcinogenesis Group Oak Ridge Nat Lab PO Box Y Oak Ridge TN 37830

TERZIAN, YERVANT, b Feb 9, 39; m 66; c 2. ASTRONOMY. *Educ:* Am Univ Cairo, BSc, 60; Univ Ind, MA, 63, PhD(astron), 65. *Prof Exp:* Res assoc radio astron, Cornell Univ Ctr Radiophysics & Space Res & Arecibo Ionospheric Observ, 65-67, from asst prof to assoc prof, 67-77, asst dir, Ctr Radiophysics & Space Res, 68-74, grad fac rep, 74-79, PROF ASTRON, CORNELL UNIV, 77-, CHMN, DEPT ASTRON, 79- *Mem:* Int Union Radio Sci; Int Astron Union; Am Astron Soc. *Res:* Radio astronomical studies of interstellar matter; radio properties of extragalactic nebulae and other radio sources; radio emission from planetary nebulae; pulsars. *Mailing Add:* Dept of Astron Cornell Univ Ithaca NY 14853

TERZUOLI, ANDREW JOSEPH, b Brooklyn, NY, Oct 5, 14; m 42; c 4. MATHEMATICS. *Educ:* Brooklyn Col, BA, 36; NY Univ, MS, 48. *Prof Exp:* PROF MATH, POLYTECH INST BROOKLYN, 46- *Concurrent Pos:* Consult statist. *Mem:* AAAS; Am Math Soc; Am Meteorol Soc; Math Asn Am; Inst Math Statist. *Res:* Probability; mathematical statistics. *Mailing Add:* Dept Math Polytech Inst Brooklyn 333 Jay St Brooklyn NY 11201

TERZUOLO, CARLO A, b Acqui, Italy, Sept 2, 25; nat US; m 54; c 1. PHYSIOLOGY. *Educ:* Univ Turin, MD, 49. *Prof Exp:* Asst, Univ Turin, 48-49; Ital Res Coun fel, 50-51; asst prof, Free Univ Brussels, 51-53; asst, Univ Calif, Los Angeles, 54-56, res assoc, 57-59; dir lab neurophysiol, 71-76, PROF PHYSIOL, UNIV MINN, MINNEAPOLIS, 59- *Concurrent Pos:* Multiple Sclerosis Soc fel, 56-57; Fulbright res fel, Univ Pisa, 67-68. *Mem:* Am Physiol Soc; Biophys Soc; Soc Neurosci. *Res:* Nerve cell and receptor physiology; dynamic characteristics of neuronal systems controlling movements; vestibular, cerebellar and segmental reflex mechanisms; models of brain functions. *Mailing Add:* Lab Neurophysiol Univ Minn Minneapolis MN 55455

TESAR, DELBERT, b Beaver Crossing, Nebr, Sept 2, 35; m 57; c 4. MECHANICAL ENGINEERING. *Educ:* Univ Nebr, BSc, 58, MSc, 60; Ga Inst Technol, PhD(mech eng), 64. *Prof Exp:* Instr eng mech, Univ Nebr, 57-59 & appl mech, Kans State Univ, 59-61; lectr mech eng, Ga Inst Technol, 61-64; assoc prof, 64-69, PROF MECH ENG & ENG SCI, UNIV FLA, 69- *Concurrent Pos:* Chief investr, US Army Res Off res grant, 61; NSF res grants, 64, 69-71 & 72-74; NSF-NATO fel, Vienna Tech Univ, 64-65; consult, Procter & Gamble Co, Ohio, 66-; vis prof, Wash State Univ, 67; consult, Wayne S Colony Co, Fla, 71- & Deering Milliken Res Corp, SC, 72-; vis res prof, Liverpool Polytech, Eng, 71-72; mem, Sci Adv Bd Air Force, 82-; dir & founder, Ctr Intelligent Machines & Robotics. *Mem:* Am Soc Eng Educ; Am Soc Mech Engrs. *Res:* Kinematic synthesis; dynamic analysis and synthesis; vibrations; machine design; lubrication; experimental stress analysis; strength of materials; continuum mechanics. *Mailing Add:* Dept of Mech Eng Univ of Fla Gainesville FL 32601

TESAR, MILO, b Nebr, Apr 7, 20; m 44; c 4. AGRONOMY. *Educ:* Univ Nebr, BS, 41; Univ Wis, MS, 47, PhD(agron), 49. *Prof Exp:* From asst prof to assoc prof, 49-58, actg chmn dept, 64-66, PROF CROP SCI, MICH STATE UNIV, 58- *Concurrent Pos:* NATO fel, Grassland Res Inst, Eng, 59-60; consult, Univ Ryukus, 67 & Univ Federale Rio Grande du Sul, Brazil, 76; mem, Int Grassland Cong, Australia, 70, Russia, 74; mem, USSR Forage Surv, 74 & AID, Somalia Mission, 78. *Mem:* Crop Sci Soc Am; Am Soc Agron. *Res:* Forage physiology and digestibility; legume seeding establishment; pasture renovation; recycling waste water through forage. *Mailing Add:* 509 Kedzie Dr East Lansing MI 48823

TESCHAN, PAUL E, b Milwaukee, Wis, Dec 15, 23; m 48; c 2. MEDICINE. *Educ:* Univ Minn, BS, 46, MD & MS, 48; Am Bd Internal Med, dipl, 55. *Prof Exp:* Intern, Res & Educ Hosp, Univ Ill, 48-49, resident internal med, Presby Hosp, Chicago, 49-50, ward officer, Metab Ward, Dept Hepatic & Metab Dis, Walter Reed Army Inst Res, 50-53, resident internal med, Barnes Hosp, St

Louis, Mo, 53-54, chief renal br, Surg Res Unit, Brooke Army Med Ctr, Ft Sam Houston, Tex, 54-60, asst commandant, Walter Reed Army Inst Res, Walter Reed Army Med Ctr, 60-63, dep dir div basic surg res, 64-65, dep dir div surg, 65-66, chief dept metab & dir div med, 66-69; ASSOC PROF MED & UROL, VANDERBILT UNIV, 69- *Concurrent Pos:* Med Corps, US Army, 48-69; fel cardiorenal dis, Peter Bent Brigham Hosp, Boston, 50; chief renal insufficiency ctr, Korea, 52-53; consult, Surgeon Gen, US Army, 60-69; chief dept surg physiol, Walter Reed Army Inst Res, Walter Reed Army Med Ctr, 61-66, dep dir div basic surg res, 62-63, chief renal-metab serv, Walter Reed Gen Hosp, 66-69; chief US Army med res team, Vietnam, 63-64; dir, Tenn Mid-South Regional Med Prog, 69-72. *Mem:* Am Fedn Clin Res; fel Am Col Physicians; Soc Artificial Internal Organs; Am Physiol Soc; Int Soc Nephrol. *Res:* Pathogenesis and prevention of acute renal failure; prophylactic dialysis; uremia. *Mailing Add:* Dept of Med & Urol Vanderbilt Univ Sch of Med Nashville TN 37232

TESCHE, FREDERICK RUTLEDGE, b San Jose, Calif, Aug 11, 21; m 42; c 5. PHYSICS. *Educ:* Univ Calif, BA, 43; Univ Calif, Los Angeles, MA, 49, PhD(physics), 51. *Prof Exp:* Engr, Consol Vultee Aircraft, 46-51; mem staff, Los Alamos Sci Lab, 51-57, group leader, 57-65, assoc div leader, 65-68; dep dir mil appln, AEC, US Dept Energy, 68-71, sci rep, London, 71-72, spec asst to dir, Div Controlled Thermonuclear Res, 72-73, sci adv to mgr, San Francisco Opers Off, 73-80; RETIRED. *Concurrent Pos:* Consult prof, Univ NMex, 57-61. *Mem:* Sr mem Inst Elec & Electronics Engrs. *Res:* Electromagnetism; flash radiography; accelerator development. *Mailing Add:* 135 Sharlene Lane Apt 12 Lafayette CA 94549

TESH, ROBERT BRADFIELD, b Wilmington, Del, Jan 22, 36; m 60; c 2. EPIDEMIOLOGY. *Educ:* Franklin & Marshall Col, BS, 57; Jefferson Med Col, MD, 61; Tulane Univ, MS, 67. *Prof Exp:* Intern, San Francisco Gen Hosp, Calif, 61-62; resident pediat, Gorgas Hosp, 62-63; physician, USPHS, Peace Corps, Recife, Brazil, 63-65; NIH fel infectious dis, Depts Pediat & Epidemiol, Sch Med, Tulane Univ, 65-67; epidemiologist, Mid Am Res Unit, NIH, 67-72, Pac Res Sect, 72-80; MEM STAFF, DEPT EPIDEMIOL & PUB HEALTH, YALE ARBOVIRUS RES UNIT, SCH MED, YALE UNIV, 80- *Mem:* AAAS; Am Soc Trop Med & Hyg; Am Soc Microbiol; Royal Soc Trop Med & Hyg. *Res:* Entomology; microbiology; public health; virology. *Mailing Add:* Sch Med Yale Univ PO Box 3333 New Haven CT 06510

TESK, JOHN A, b Chicago, Ill, Oct 19, 34; m. DENTAL RESEARCH. *Educ:* Northwestern Univ, BS, 57, MS, 60, PhD(mat sci), 63. *Prof Exp:* Asst prof metall, Univ Ill, Chicago, 64-68; asst metallurgist, Metall Div, Argonne Nat Lab, 68-70; asst mgr res & develop, How-Medica, Inc, Chicago, 70-71, dir res & develop, Dent Div, 71-77; dir educ serv, Div, How-Medica, Inc, Chicago, 71-80 & Inst Gas Technol, 77-80; WITH NAT BUR STANDARDS, 80- *Concurrent Pos:* Consult, Argonne Nat Lab, 64-67; dent res, 77- *Honors & Awards:* Grainger Award, Univ Ill, Chicago, 64. *Mem:* Int Asn Dent Res; Am Soc Prev Dent; Am Inst Mining & Metall Engrs; Am Soc Metals; Am Soc Eng Educ. *Res:* Radiation damage in metals at low temperature; point defects in metals; dental and medical materials and devices; biomaterials. *Mailing Add:* Bldg 224 Rm A 141 Nat Bur Standards Washington DC 20234

TESKA, WILLIAM REINHOLD, b Chicago, Ill, Oct 11, 50. ECOLOGY, MAMMALOGY. *Educ:* Univ Idaho, BS, 72; Mich State Univ, MSc, 74, PhD(zool), 78. *Prof Exp:* ASST PROF BIOL, FURMAN UNIV, 77- *Mem:* Am Soc Mammalogists; Ecol Soc Am; Wildlife Soc; Sigma Xi. *Res:* Mammalian ecology; population ecology; vertebrate ecology. *Mailing Add:* Dept of Biol Furman Univ Greenville SC 29613

TESKE, RICHARD GLENN, b Cleveland, Ohio, Aug 16, 30. ASTRONOMY. *Educ:* Bowling Green State Univ, BS, 52; Ohio State Univ, MA, 56; Harvard Univ, PhD, 61. *Prof Exp:* From instr to assoc prof, McMath-Hulbert Observ, 61-77, PROF ASTRON, UNIV MICH, ANN ARBOR, 77- *Mem:* AAAS; Int Astron Union; Am Astron Soc. *Res:* Astronomical and solar spectroscopy; solar physics; solar x-radiation. *Mailing Add:* Dept of Astron Univ of Mich Ann Arbor MI 48109

TESKE, RICHARD H, b Christiansburg, Va, July 22, 39; m 61; c 2. VETERINARY MEDICINE, TOXICOLOGY. *Educ:* Va Polytech Inst, BA, 62; Univ Ga, DVM, 65; Univ Fla, MS, 66; Am Bd Vet Toxicol, dipl. *Prof Exp:* Asst prof vet sci, Univ Fla, 67; dir toxicol, Hill Top Res, Inc, Ohio, 67-70; VET MED OFFICER, DIV VET MED RES, BUR VET MED, FOOD & DRUG ADMIN, 70- *Mem:* Fel Am Col Vet Toxicol; fel Am Acad Vet Pharm & Toxicol. *Res:* Comparative pharmacology and toxicology. *Mailing Add:* Div Vet Med Res Bur Vet Med 5600 Fishers Lane Rockville MD 20857

TESKEY, HERBERT JOSEPH, b Grande Prairie, Alta, June 9, 28; m 53; c 2. ENTOMOLOGY, SYSTEMATICS. *Educ:* Univ Alta, BSc, 51; Univ Toronto, MSA, 56; Cornell Univ, PhD(entom), 67. *Prof Exp:* Res scientist entom, Can Dept Agr, Guelph, 51-67; RES SCIENTIST ENTOM, BIOSYST RES INST, AGR CAN, 67- *Mem:* Entom Soc Can. *Res:* Systematics of the Diptera, especially of the lower Brachycera and of the immature stages of Diptera. *Mailing Add:* 569 Brierwood Ottawa ON K2A 2H6 Can

TESMER, IRVING HOWARD, b Buffalo, NY, May 31, 26; m 64; c 2. STRATIGRAPHY, PALEONTOLOGY. *Educ:* Univ Buffalo, BA, 46, MA, 48; Syracuse Univ, PhD(geol), 54. *Prof Exp:* From instr to asst prof geol, Univ NH, 50-55; instr, Rutgers Univ, 55-57; from asst prof to assoc prof, 57-63, chmn dept, 66-69, PROF GEOL, STATE UNIV NY COL BUFFALO, 63- *Concurrent Pos:* Mem, Paleont Res Inst. *Mem:* Fel AAAS; fel Geol Soc Am; Am Asn Petrol Geol; Paleont Soc. *Res:* Devonian stratigraphy and paleontology; geology of western New York. *Mailing Add:* Dept of Geosci 1300 Elmwood Ave State Univ of NY Col at Buffalo Buffalo NY 14222

TESMER, JOSEPH RANSDELL, b Lafayette, Ind, Sept 9, 39; m 62; c 2. EXPERIMENTAL NUCLEAR PHYSICS. *Educ:* Purdue Univ, BS, 62; Univ Wash, PhD(nuclear physics), 71. *Prof Exp:* Engr, Boeing Co, 62-64; res assoc nuclear physics, Purdue Univ, 71-73; asst scientist physics, Univ Wis, 73-75; STAFF MEM NUCLEAR PHYSICS, LOS ALAMOS NAT LAB, 75- *Mem:* Am Phys Soc; AAAS. *Res:* Stripping of high energy negative hydrogen beams, and negative hydrogen beam production; accelerator development; accelerator based mass spectrometry. *Mailing Add:* Los Alamos Nat Lab PO Box 1663 MS 480 Los Alamos NM 87545

TESORIERO, JOHN VINCENT, b Brooklyn, NY, Feb 10, 41; m 64; c 2. CELL BIOLOGY, BIOLOGY OF AGING. *Educ:* Fairfield Univ, BS, 63; Adelphi Univ, MS, 68; State Univ NY, Downstate Med Sch, PhD(anat), 76. *Prof Exp:* ASST PROF, NJ MED SCH, UNIV MED & DENT NJ, 75- *Mem:* Am Asn Anatomists; Am Soc Cell Biol. *Res:* Cell biology of mammalian oogenesis with particular emphasis on age related changes in maturing oocytes; age related changes of the tubulin-microtubular sytem in mammalian oocytes. *Mailing Add:* Dept Anat NJ Med Sch Univ Med & Dent NJ 100 Bergen St Newark NJ 07103

TESORO, GIULIANA C, b Venice, Italy, June 1, 21; nat US; m 43; c 2. ORGANIC POLYMER CHEMISTRY. *Educ:* Yale Univ, PhD(org chem), 43. *Prof Exp:* Res chemist, Calco Chem Co, NJ, 34-44; res chemist, Onyx Oil & Chem Co, 44-46, head org synthesis dept, 46-55, asst dir res, 55-57, assoc dir, 57-58; asst dir org res, Cent Res Lab, J P Stevens & Co, Inc, 58-68; sr scientist, Textile Res Inst, NJ, 68-69; sr scientist, Burlington Industs, Inc, 69-71, dir chem res, 71-72. *Concurrent Pos:* Vis prof, Mass Inst Technol, 72-76, adj prof & sr res scientist, 76-; mem comt on fire safety aspects of polymeric materials, Nat Acad Sci, 72-78, mem nat mat adv bd, 76-78; mem comt military personnel supplies, Nat Res Coun, 79- *Mem:* Am Chem Soc; Am Asn Textile Chem & Colorists; Fiber Soc (pres, 74); Am Inst Chemists; AAAS. *Res:* Synthesis of pharmaceuticals; textile chemicals; germicides; polymers; chemical modification of fibers; synthesis and rearrangement of glycols in the hydrogenated naphthalene series; polymer flammability and flame retardants. *Mailing Add:* 278 Clinton Ave Dobbs Ferry NY 10522

TESS, ROY WILLIAM HENRY, b Chicago, Ill, Apr 25, 15; m 44; c 2. POLYMER CHEMISTRY. *Educ:* Univ Ill, BS, 39; Univ Minn, PhD(org chem), 44. *Prof Exp:* Lab asst, Underwriters Labs, Inc, Ill, 36-37; asst chem, Univ Minn, 39-44; chemist, Shell Develop Co, 44-59, res supvr, Shell Chem Co, 59-62 & 64-67, Royal Dutch Shell Plastics Lab, Holland, 62-63, tech planning supvr, Coatings, Shell Chem NY, 67-70, Tex, 70-73, tech supvr solvents bus ctr, 73-78, consult solvents & resin prod, 78-80. *Concurrent Pos:* Trustee, Paint Res Inst, 71-, pres, 73-76. *Mem:* Fedn Soc Paint Technol; Soc Cosmetic Chem; Am Chem Soc (chmn div organic coatings & plastic chem, 78); fel Am Inst Chem; Am Oil Chem Soc. *Res:* Epoxy, allyl, alkyd, polyester and hydrocarbon resins; surface coatings; varnishes and drying oils; polyols; polar and hydrocarbon solvents; high polymer latices; atmospheric chemistry. *Mailing Add:* PO Box 577 Fallbrook CA 92028

TESSEL, RICHARD EARL, b Cincinnati, Ohio, June 9, 44. NEUROPHARMACOLOGY, PSYCHOPHARMACOLOGY. *Educ:* Univ Calif, Los Angeles, BA, 66; Univ Ill, Chicago Circle, MA, 69; Univ Mich, PhD(pharmacol), 74. *Prof Exp:* Nat Inst Drug Abuse fel pharmacol, Sch Med, Univ Colo, 74-75; ASST PROF PHARMACOL, SCH PHARM, UNIV KANS, 75-, ASSOC TOXICOL, 81- *Res:* Role of biogenic amine disposition in brain in modulating the reinforcing, locomotor-stimulant, stereotypic and operant-schedule effects of amphetamines and its congeners. *Mailing Add:* Dept of Pharmacol & Toxicol Sch of Pharm Univ of Kans Lawrence KS 66045

TESSER, HERBERT, b Jersey City, NJ, Mar 25, 39; m 61; c 2. PHYSICS. *Educ:* Polytech Inst Brooklyn, BS, 60; Stevens Inst Technol, MS, 63, PhD(physics), 68. *Prof Exp:* Metrol engr, Kearfott Corp, 60-62; res asst physics, Stevens Inst Technol, 64-67; assoc prof, 67-81, PROF PHYSICS, PRATT INST, 81- *Concurrent Pos:* Res consult, NRA, Inc, 71-72, Procedyne, 73-74 & Stevens Inst, 75-78. *Mem:* Am Phys Soc. *Res:* Electrodynamics; statistical mechanics; relativity; plasma physics. *Mailing Add:* Dept of Physics Pratt Inst Brooklyn NY 11205

TESSIERI, JOHN EDWARD, b Vineland, NJ, Sept 3, 20; m 43; c 3. RESEARCH ADMINISTRATION. *Educ:* Pa State Univ, BS, 42, MS, 47; Stanford Univ, PhD(org chem), 50. *Prof Exp:* Chemist & asst to asst dir res, Texaco, Inc, NY, 49, group leader, 55, asst supvr lubricants res, 55, Tex, 55-56, supvr chem res, 56-57, asst dir res, 57-60, dir fuels & chem res, 60-62, vpres, Texaco Exp Inc, Va, 62-63, exec vpres, 63-65, pres, 65-66, mgr sci planning, Texaco Inc, 67-68, asst to pres, 68-69, staff coordr strategic planning group exec off, 69-70, gen mgr strategic planning, 70-71, VPRES RES ENVIRON & SAFETY DEPT, TEXACO INC, 71- *Mem:* Am Chem Soc; Indust Res Inst; AAAS; Sci Res Soc Am; Dirs Indust Res. *Res:* Product and process development, including petrochemicals, fuels and lubricants; exploration and production research; coal beneficiation, gasification and liquefaction. *Mailing Add:* Texaco Inc PO Box 509 Beacon NY 12508

TESSLER, ARTHUR NED, b New York, NY, Feb 21, 27; m 53; c 4. UROLOGY. *Educ:* NY Univ, AB, 48, MD, 52; Am Bd Urol, dipl. *Prof Exp:* Investr, USPHS grant, 59-62, PROF CLIN UROL, SCH MED, NY UNIV, 72- *Concurrent Pos:* Consult, Vet Admin Hosp, NY, 70- *Honors & Awards:* Carl Hartman Award, Am Fertil Soc, 63. *Mem:* AMA; Am Fertil Soc; Am Col Surg. *Mailing Add:* 566 First Ave New York NY 10016

TESSLER, GEORGE, b Brooklyn, NY, Mar 7, 36; m 69. PHYSICS. *Educ:* Brooklyn Col, BS, 57; Univ Pa, MS, 59, PhD(physics), 64. *Prof Exp:* SR SCIENTIST, BETTIS ATOMIC POWER LAB, WESTINGHOUSE ELEC CORP, 63- *Mem:* Am Phys Soc; AAAS; NY Acad Sci. *Res:* Acquisition of neutron cross section data for use in reactor design; nondestructive assay of irradiated reactor fuel rods. *Mailing Add:* Bettis Atomic Power Lab Westinghouse Elec Corp PO Box 79 West Mifflin PA 15122

TESSLER, MARTIN MELVYN, b Brooklyn, NY, Sept 12, 37; m 62; c 2. ORGANIC CHEMISTRY, POLYSACCHARIDE CHEMISTRY. *Educ:* Brooklyn Col, BS, 58; Univ Kans, PhD(chem), 62. *Prof Exp:* Chemist, Enjay Chem Intermediates Lab, Esso Res & Eng Co, 65-68; proj supvr, 68-72, res assoc, 72-76, sr res assoc, 76-81, SR RES SCIENTIST, NAT STARCH & CHEM CORP, BRIDGEWATER, 81- *Mem:* AAAS; Am Chem Soc; Am Asn Cereal Chemists. *Res:* Starch chemistry. *Mailing Add:* 507 Darwin Blvd Edison NJ 08820

TESSMAN, ETHEL S, b New York, NY, Apr 11, 29; m 49; c 1. MOLECULAR BIOLOGY. *Educ:* Bryn Mawr Univ, BA, 50; Yale Univ, MS, 52, PhD(biophysics), 54. *Prof Exp:* Res assoc molecular biol, Purdue Univ, 61-70, Univ Calif, Irvine, 70-73; SR RES SCIENTIST MOLECULAR BIOL, PURDUE UNIV, 73- *Res:* Single stranded DNA phages; SOS repair system of bacteria. *Mailing Add:* Dept of Biol Sci Purdue Univ West Lafayette IN 47907

TESSMAN, IRWIN, b New York, NY, Nov 24, 29; m 49; c 1. BIOPHYSICS, MOLECULAR BIOLOGY. *Educ:* Cornell Univ, AB, 50; Yale Univ, MS, 51, PhD(physics), 54. *Prof Exp:* NSF fel, Cornell Univ, 54-55, Am Cancer Soc fel, 55-57; fel, Mass Inst Technol, 57-58, res assoc biol, 58-59; assoc prof biophys, 59-62, PROF BIOL, PURDUE UNIV, 62- *Concurrent Pos:* NSF sr fel, Harvard Med Sch, 67; prof molecular biol, Univ Calif, 69-72. *Honors & Awards:* Gravity Res Found Prize, 53; Sigma Xi Res Award, Purdue Univ, 66. *Mem:* Am Soc Biol Chemists; AAAS; Genetics Soc Am; Am Soc Microbiol. *Res:* Radiocarbon dating; ionization by charged particles; molecular genetics; reproduction of bacterial viruses; molecular studies of replication, mutation, recombination and function of genetic material. *Mailing Add:* Dept Biol Sci Purdue Univ Lafayette IN 47907

TESSMAN, JACK ROBERT, b New York, NY, May 5, 19; m 63; c 2. PHYSICS. *Educ:* City Col New York, BS, 38; Univ Calif, Berkeley, MA, 50, PhD(physics), 52. *Prof Exp:* Tutorial fel, City Col New York, 39; physicist, Mat Div, Wright-Patterson Air Force Base, 39-46; asst, Univ Calif, Berkeley, 46-50; asst prof physics, Pa State Univ, 52-56; from asst prof to assoc prof, 56-72, vis lectr, 55-56, PROF PHYSICS, TUFTS UNIV, 72- *Concurrent Pos:* Vis assoc prof, Univ Calif, 61; lectr, Mass Inst Technol, 64-65, staff mem sci teaching ctr, 62-65; NSF Sci Fac fel, 62-63. *Mem:* AAAS; Am Phys Soc; Am Asn Physics Teachers. *Res:* Solid state physics; magnetic phenomena; electromagnetism; science education. *Mailing Add:* Dept of Physics Tufts Univ Medford MA 02155

TESSMER, CARL FREDERICK, b North Braddock, Pa, May 28, 12; m 39; c 2. PATHOLOGY. *Educ:* Univ Pittsburgh, BS, 33, MD, 35; Am Bd Path, dipl, 41. *Prof Exp:* Resident path, Presby Hosp, Pittsburgh, 36-37; fel, Mayo Clin, 37-38; resident pathologist, Queen's Hosp, Honolulu, Hawaii, 39-40; chief lab, Tripler Gen Hosp, Honolulu, Med Corps, US Army, 42-45, chief radiologic safety, Bikini, 46, pathologist, US Naval Med Res Inst, 46-48, dir atomic bomb casualty comn, Nat Res Coun, 48-51, commanding officer, Army Med Res Lab, Ft Knox, Ky, 51-54, chief basic sci div & radiation path br, Armed Forces Inst Path, Walter Reed Army Med Ctr, DC, 54-60, commanding officer, 406th Med Gen Lab, Japan, 60-62, pathologist, Walter Reed Army Inst Res, 62-63; chief exp path sect, Univ Tex M D Anderson Hosp & Tumor Inst Houston, 63-71, prof path, 63-73; CHIEF LAB SERV, VET ADMIN CTR, TEMPLE, TEX, 73- *Concurrent Pos:* Hektoen lect, 60; Armed Forces Inst Path Centennial lect, 62; mem grad fac, Univ Tex Grad Sch Biomed Sci, 63-73, path coordr, Univ Tex Med Sch Houston, 71-73; consult, Walter Reed Army Med Ctr, 64-; mem, USPHS Adv Comt, Collab Radiol Health Animal Res Lab, 65-70; mem, subcomt 34, Nat Comt Radiation Protection, 70-76; consult, Radiation Bioeffects & Epidemiol Adv Comn, Food & Drug Admin, Dept Health, Educ & Welfare, 72-75. *Mem:* Fel Am Soc Clin Path; Radiation Res Soc; Am Asn Path & Bact; fel Col Am Path; Int Acad Path. *Res:* Morphologic and experimental radiation pathology; trace elements; copper metabolism. *Mailing Add:* Lab Serv Vet Admin Ctr Temple TX 76501

TEST, CHARLES EDWARD, b Indianapolis, Ind, Jan 10, 16; m 38; c 4. MEDICINE. *Educ:* Princeton Univ, AB, 37; Univ Chicago, MD, 41. *Prof Exp:* Instr med, Univ Chicago, 49-51; from asst prof to assoc prof, 53-63, PROF MED, SCH MED, IND UNIV, INDIANAPOLIS, 63- *Mem:* Endocrine Soc; Am Diabetes Asn; fel Am Col Physicians. *Res:* Endocrinology; metabolism. *Mailing Add:* 4430 N Meridan St Indianapolis IN 46208

TEST, FREDERICK L(AURENT), b Philadelphia, Pa, June 15, 25; m 47; c 3. MECHANICAL ENGINEERING. *Educ:* Mass Inst Technol, SB, 45, SM, 47; Pa State Univ, PhD(mech eng), 56. *Prof Exp:* Res engr, Mass Inst Technol, 47-48; instr mech eng, Northeastern Univ, 48-49; from instr to assoc prof, 49-72, chmn dept, 72-76, PROF MECH ENG, UNIV RI, 72- *Concurrent Pos:* NSF fac fel, 59-60; consult, US Navy, 60-66; Fulbright res fel, Neth, 66-67. *Mem:* Am Soc Mech Engrs; Am Inst Aeronaut & Astronaut. *Mailing Add:* 88 Pine Hill Rd Wakefield RI 02879

TESTA, ANTHONY CARMINE, b New York, NY, Nov 19, 33; m 62. PHYSICAL CHEMISTRY, PHOTOCHEMISTRY. *Educ:* City Col New York, BS, 55; Columbia Univ, MA, 58, PhD(chem), 61. *Prof Exp:* Res chemist, Cent Res Div, Lever Bros Co, 61-63; from asst prof to assoc prof, 63-71, PROF CHEM, ST JOHN'S UNIV, NY, 71- *Concurrent Pos:* Res leave, Max-Planck Inst Spectros, Göttingen, 70-71. *Mem:* NY Acad Sci; Am Chem Soc. *Res:* Photochemistry and flash photolysis of molecules in solution; luminescence spectroscopy; fluorescence and phosphorescence. *Mailing Add:* Dept of Chem St John's Univ Jamaica NY 11439

TESTA, RAYMOND THOMAS, b New Haven, Conn, Dec 21, 37; m 62; c 3. MICROBIOLOGY, BIOCHEMISTRY. *Educ:* Providence Col, BS, 59; Syracuse Univ, MS, 64, PhD(microbiol), 66. *Prof Exp:* Res asst microbiol, Syracuse Univ, 64-66; scientist, Schering Corp, 66-68, sr scientist, 68-72, prin microbiologist, 72-74, mgr, antibiotics screening & fermentation dept, 74-77; MEM STAFF, AM CYANAMID CO, 77- *Mem:* AAAS; Am Soc Microbiol; Soc Indust Microbiol; NY Acad Sci. *Res:* Antibiotics; factors affecting the production and biosynthesis of antibiotic; spore formation. *Mailing Add:* Am Cyanamid Co Lederle Lab Pear River NY 10965

TESTA, RENE B(IAGGIO), b Montreal, Can, May 30, 37; m 59; c 4. CIVIL ENGINEERING, ENGINEERING MECHANICS. *Educ:* McGill Univ, BEng, 59; Columbia Univ, MS, 60, Eng ScD(eng mech), 63. *Prof Exp:* From asst prof to assoc prof, 63-75, PROF CIVIL ENG & ENG MECH, COLUMBIA UNIV, 75-, DIR, ROBERT A W CARLETON MAT LAB, 65- *Concurrent Pos:* Consult var govt & indust orgns. *Mem:* Am Soc Mech Engrs; Am Soc Civil Engrs; Am Soc Testing & Mat; Struct Stability Res Coun. *Res:* Solid mechanics; experimental mechanics of materials and structures; mechanical properties of coated fabrics. *Mailing Add:* Sch of Eng & Appl Sci Columbia Univ New York NY 10027

TESTARDI, LOUIS RICHARD, b Philadelphia, Pa, Sept 23, 30; m 57; c 4. SOLID STATE PHYSICS. *Educ:* Univ Calif, Berkeley, AB, 56; Univ Pa, MS, 60, PhD(physics), 63. *Prof Exp:* Res physicist, Elec Storage Battery Co, 57-58 & Franklin Inst Labs, 58-62; res asst, Univ Pa, 63; res physicist, Bell Tel Labs, 63-80; MEM STAFF, NASA HQ, 80- *Mem:* Am Phys Soc. *Res:* Transport, optical, magnetic and ultrasonic properties of solids; low temperature physics; superconductivity. *Mailing Add:* Code EN-1 NASA Hq Washington DC 20546

TESTER, CECIL FRED, b Boone, NC, May 23, 38; m 67; c 2. BIOCHEMISTRY, ENVIRONMENTAL MANAGEMENT. *Educ:* Appalachian State Univ, BS, 60; Univ Ga, PhD(biochem), 67. *Prof Exp:* Teacher city schs, NC, 60-61; res asst biochem, Univ Ga, 64-65, teaching asst, 65-66; AEC fel, Purdue Univ, Lafayette, 67-68; res chemist & USDA grant, NC State Univ, 68-75; RES CHEMIST, BELTSVILLE AGR RES CTR, WEST, SCI & EDUC ADMIN-AGR RES, USDA, 75- *Mem:* Am Soc Agron; Soil Sci Soc; Crop Sci Soc. *Res:* Biological waste management and plant interactions. *Mailing Add:* 11402 Westview Ct Beltsville MD 20705

TESTER, JEFFERSON WILLIAM, b New York, NY, Mar 27, 45; m 67. CHEMICAL ENGINEERING, PHYSICAL CHEMISTRY. *Educ:* Cornell Univ, BS, 66, MS, 67; Mass Inst Technol, PhD(chem eng), 71. *Prof Exp:* Fel, Los Alamos Sci Lab, Univ Calif, 71-72; asst prof chem eng & dir, Sch Chem Eng Pract at Oak Ridge Nat Lab, Mass Inst Technol, 72-74; group leader-geothermal technol, Los Alamos Sci Lab, 74-80; ASSOC PROF CHEM ENG & DIR, SCH CHEM ENG PRACT, MASS INST TECHNOL, 80- *Concurrent Pos:* Vis staff mem, Los Alamos Sci Lab, Univ Calif, 72-74; adj prof chem eng, Univ NMex, 75-80. *Mem:* Am Inst Chem Engrs; Am Chem Soc; Soc Petrol Engrs. *Res:* Applied thermodynamics; surface chemistry and physics; chemical kinetics; heat and mass transfer; computer simulation and interactive graphics; electrochemistry; geothermal energy, reservoir engineering. *Mailing Add:* Chem Eng Dept Rm 66-305 Mass Inst Technol Cambridge MA 02139

TESTER, JOHN ROBERT, b New Ulm, Minn, Nov 18, 29; m 60; c 2. ECOLOGY. *Educ:* Univ Minn, BS, 51; Colo State Univ, MS, 53; Univ Minn, PhD(wildlife ecol), 60. *Prof Exp:* Res asst wildlife biol, Colo Game & Fish Dept, 51-53; game biologist, Minn Div Game & Fish, 54-56; asst scientist ecol, Mus Natural Hist, 56-60, from instr to assoc prof, 60-70, head dept, 73-76, PROF ECOL & BEHAV BIOL, UNIV MINN, MINNEAPOLIS, 70- *Concurrent Pos:* NSF fel, Aschoff Div, Max Planck Inst Physiol of Behav & Aberdeen Univ, 69-70; mem behav sci training comt, NIH; Nat Acad Sci exchange scientist, 82. *Mem:* Fel AAAS; Ecol Soc Am; Am Soc Mammal; Wildlife Soc. *Res:* Population ecology; biotelemetry; wildlife management; animal behavior. *Mailing Add:* Dept Ecol & Behav Biol Univ Minn Minneapolis MN 55455

TESTERMAN, JACK DUANE, b Marietta, Okla, Dec 13, 33; m 53; c 3. STATISTICS, COMPUTER SCIENCE. *Educ:* Okla State Univ, BS, 55, MS, 57; Univ Tex, PhD, 72. *Prof Exp:* Res statistician, Jersey Prod Res Co, 57-63 & Phillips Petrol Co, 63; assoc prof, 63-69, registr, 65-70, PROF MATH & STATIST, UNIV SOUTHWESTERN LA, 69-, DIR INSTNL RES, 70-, VPRES UNIV RELATIONS, 73- *Concurrent Pos:* Chmn inst studies & opers anal comt, Am Asn Col Registrars & Admissions Officers, 74-; chmn ad hoc comt ways & means, Am Statist Asn, 75- *Mem:* Am Statist Asn; Asn Comput Mach; Asn Instnl. *Res:* Application of statistics; data analysis and use of computers. *Mailing Add:* Univ of Southwestern La PO Box 42331 Lafayette LA 70504

TESTERMAN, JOHN KENDRICK, b Galveston, Tex, Feb 25, 45; m 66; c 1. COMPARATIVE PHYSIOLOGY. *Educ:* Loma Linda Univ, BA, 67; Univ Calif, Irvine, PhD(biol), 71. *Prof Exp:* ASST PROF BIOL, LOMA LINDA UNIV, LA SIERRA CAMPUS, 71- *Mem:* AAAS; Am Soc Zoologists. *Res:* Organic compounds in sea water and their significance to marine organisms; comparative physiology of marine invertebrates; effects of pollutants on marine life. *Mailing Add:* Dept of Biol Loma Linda Univ La Sierra Campus Riverside CA 92505

TESTERMAN, M(AURICE) K(ENDALL), instrumentation, physical chemistry, see previous edition

TETENBAUM, MARVIN, b Brooklyn, NY, June 27, 21; m 54; c 3. PHYSICAL CHEMISTRY. *Educ:* NY Univ, BChE, 42; Polytech Inst Brooklyn, MChE, 47, PhD(chem), 54. *Prof Exp:* Res asst, Metall Lab, Univ Chicago, 42-43; res engr sam labs, Columbia Univ, 43-44; chem engr, Ballistics Res Lab, Ord Dept, US Dept Army, 47-48; radio chemist, US Naval Res Lab, 48-56; sr engr, Aircraft Nuclear Propulsion Dept, Gen Elec Co, Ohio, 56-59; CHEMIST, ARGONNE NAT LAB, 59- *Concurrent Pos:* Mem staff, Atomic Energy Res Estab, Harwell, Eng, 66-67. *Mem:* Am Nuclear Soc; Am Ceramic Soc; AAAS; Am Chem Soc; Sci Res Soc Am. *Res:* High temperature chemistry. *Mailing Add:* Chem Eng Div Argonne Nat Lab 9700 S Cass Ave Argonne IL 60439

TETENBAUM, SIDNEY JOSEPH, electromagnetism, see previous edition

TETER, NORMAN C, agricultural engineering, see previous edition

TETERIS, NICHOLAS JOHN, b Martins Ferry, Ohio, Jan 14, 29; m 61; c 2. OBSTETRICS & GYNECOLOGY. *Educ:* Washington & Jefferson Col, BA, 50; Ohio State Univ, MD, 54, MSc, 61; Am Bd Obstet & Gynec, dipl, 65. *Prof Exp:* Asst prof, 65-67, assoc prof & asst dean col med, 67-70, PROF OBSTET & GYNEC, COL MED, OHIO STATE UNIV, 70- *Concurrent Pos:* Cancer fel obstet & gynec, Col Med, Ohio State Univ, 62-64; consult, US Air Force Hosps, Wright-Patterson & Lockborne Air Force Bases, 62; asst dir, Ohio State Univ Hosps, 62- *Mem:* AMA; Am Col Obstet & Gynec; Am Col Surg. *Res:* Fetology; gynecologic cancer; obstetrical emergencies. *Mailing Add:* 473 W 12th Ave Columbus OH 43210

TETLOW, NORMAN JAY, b Downs, Kans, Dec 9, 34; m 57; c 2. CHEMICAL ENGINEERING. *Educ:* Kans State Univ, BS, 57, MS, 59; Tex A&M Univ, PhD(chem eng), 66. *Prof Exp:* Chem engr, Mason & Hanger, Silas Mason Co, 57-58 & 59-60; res & develop engr, Dow Chem Co, 60-63 & Tex Instruments, Inc, 66-68; process syst specialist, 68-79, PROCESS ENG MGR, TEX DIV, DOW CHEM CO, 79- *Mem:* Am Inst Chem Engrs; Am Chem Soc. *Res:* Application of computers and numerical methods to chemical process engineering and process control. *Mailing Add:* APB Bldg Dow Chem Co Freeport TX 77541

TETRAULT, ROBERT CLOSE, b Walhalla, NDak, Nov 25, 33; m 58; c 4. ENTOMOLOGY. *Educ:* NDak State Univ, BS, 58, MS, 63; Univ Wis, PhD(entom), 67. *Prof Exp:* Asst prof, 65-71, ASSOC PROF ENTOM, PA STATE UNIV, UNIVERSITY PARK, 71- *Mem:* Entom Soc Am. *Res:* Taxonomy of Coleoptera, especially the family Helodidae. *Mailing Add:* Dept of Entom Pa State Univ University Park PA 16802

TETREAULT, FLORENCE G, b Detroit, Mich. STATISTICS. *Educ:* Univ Detroit, BS; Univ Mich, MA; Iowa State Univ, PhD(statist), 65. *Prof Exp:* Instr statist, Iowa State Univ, 60-64; assoc prof, 64-72, PROF MATH, UNIV DETROIT, 72- *Mailing Add:* Dept of Math Univ of Detroit Detroit MI 48154

TETTENHORST, RODNEY TAMPA, b St Louis, Mo, Feb 1, 34; m 60; c 1. MINERALOGY. *Educ:* Wash Univ, BS, 55, MA, 57; Univ Ill, Urbana, PhD(mineral), 60. *Prof Exp:* From asst prof to assoc prof, 60-75, PROF MINERAL, OHIO STATE UNIV, 75- *Mem:* Clay Minerals Soc; Mineral Soc Am; Mineral Soc Gt Brit & Ireland. *Res:* Clay mineralogy. *Mailing Add:* Dept of Mineral & Geol Ohio State Univ Columbus OH 43210

TEUBER, LARRY ROSS, b Prescott, Ariz, July 8, 51. PLANT BREEDING, GENETICS. *Educ:* NMex State Univ, BS, 73, MS, 74; Univ Minn, PhD(plant breeding), 78. *Prof Exp:* ASST PROF PLANT BREEDING, UNIV CALIF, DAVIS, 77- *Concurrent Pos:* Asst agronomist, Calif Agr Exp Sta, 77- *Mem:* Crop Sci Soc Am; Am Soc Agron; Int Comn Bee Bot; Sigma Xi. *Res:* Alfalfa breeding and genetics; nectar and seed production, dormacy, insect and disease resistance including: aphids, nematodes, phytophthora root rot, anthracnose, phoma, stagnospora and stemphylium. *Mailing Add:* Dept of Agron & Range Sci Univ of Calif Davis CA 95616

TEUKOLSKY, SAUL ARNO, b Johannesburg, SAfrica, Aug 2, 47; m 71; c 2. THEORETICAL ASTROPHYSICS, GENERAL RELATIVITY. *Educ:* Univ Witwatersrand, BSc Hons(physics) & BSc Hons(appl math), 70; Calif Inst Technol, PhD(physics), 73. *Prof Exp:* Res assoc physics, Calif Inst Technol, 73-74; asst prof, 74-77, ASSOC PROF PHYSICS, CORNELL 77- *Concurrent Pos:* Alfred P Sloan Found res fel, 75-77. *Mem:* Am Phys Soc; Am Astron Soc. *Res:* General relativity and relativistic astrophysics. *Mailing Add:* Lab of Nuclear Studies Cornell Univ Ithaca NY 14853

TEUMAC, FRED N, b Little Ferry, NJ, Feb 2, 31; m 57; c 3. THERMODYNAMICS. *Educ:* Rutgers Univ, BS, 52; Univ Fla, MS, 58, PhD(chem), 61. *Prof Exp:* Chemist, Burry Biscuit Co, 54-56; res asst, Univ Fla, 56-61; sr res chemist, Dow Chem Co, 61-65; sr prog engr, Fiber Indust, 65-66; tech dir, Wica Chem Co, 66-68; develop mgr, Uniroyal Inc, 68-78; RES DIR, REEVES BROS INC, 78- *Res:* Modifying galvanic reactions that occur in the cleaning or protection of metal surfaces. *Mailing Add:* Reeves Bros Inc PO Box 26596 Charlotte NC 28213

TEUSCHER, GEORGE WILLIAM, b Chicago, Ill, Jan 11, 08; m 34; c 2. DENTISTRY. *Educ:* Northwestern Univ, DDS, 29, MSD, 36, MA, 40, PhD(educ), 42. *Hon Degrees:* ScD, NY Univ, 65. *Prof Exp:* From instr to assoc prof, 31-45, dean, Dent Sch, 53-72, PROF PEDODONTICS, DENT SCH, NORTHWESTERN UNIV, 45- *Concurrent Pos:* Regent, Nat Libr Med; ed, J Am Soc Dent for Children, 68- *Mem:* Am Soc Dent for Children; Am Dent Asn; Am Acad Pedodontics; fel Am Col Dent; Int Asn Dent Res. *Res:* Dental caries; reactions of dental pulp in children; sodium fluoride; prevention in clinical dentistry for children; principles of dental education. *Mailing Add:* Am Soc Dent for Children 211 E Chicago Ave Chicago IL 60611

TEVAULT, DAVID EARL, b Evansville, Ind, July 23, 48; m 73; c 2. INORGANIC CHEMISTRY. *Educ:* Univ Evansville, BA, 70; Univ Va, PhD(chem), 74. *Prof Exp:* Fel chem, Marquette Univ, 74-76; FEL CHEM, NAVAL RES LAB, 76-78. *Mem:* Am Chem Soc; Sigma Xi. *Res:* Mechanisms and kinetics of atmospheric, combustion related, heterogeneous catalysis, and infrared laser promoted chemical reactions by cryogenic spectroscopic methods. *Mailing Add:* 5530 Crossrail Ct Burke VA 22015

TEVEBAUGH, ARTHUR DAVID, b Knox Co, Ind, Nov 25, 17; m 43; c 2. PHYSICAL CHEMISTRY. *Educ:* Purdue Univ, BS, 40; Iowa State Univ, PhD(phys chem), 47. *Prof Exp:* Asst chem, Iowa State Univ, 40-42; res chemist, Manhattan Proj, 42-47; res chemist, Knolls Atomic Power Lab, Gen Elec Co, 47-55; supvr reactor chem unit, 50-54, actg mgr chem & chem eng sect, 54-55, sr res chemist, Res & Develop Lab, 55-63; sr chemist & sect mgr chem eng div, Argonne Nat Lab, 63-69, assoc dir div, 69-72, dir lab prog planning off, 72-73, dir coal progs, 73-77, assoc dir chem div, 77-81. *Mem:* Am Chem Soc; Am Nuclear Soc. *Res:* Analytical, radio and soil chemistry; production and handling of fluorine; chemical problems related to development and operation of nuclear reactors and reactor fuel reprocessing; polymer research; thermoelectric materials; fuel cells and batteries; electrochemistry; reactor safety. *Mailing Add:* 5 Park Rd Hatfield PA 19440

TEVETHIA, MARY JUDITH (ROBINSON), b Ft Wayne, Ind, Feb 25, 39; m 65; c 2. MOLECULAR BIOLOGY, GENETICS. *Educ:* Mich State Univ, BS, 60, MS, 62, PhD(microbiol), 64. *Prof Exp:* Fel microbiol, Emory Univ, 64-65; fel biol, Univ Tex, M D Anderson Hosp & Tumor Inst, Houston, 65-72, asst biologist & asst prof biol, 72-73; ASST PROF PATH, SCH MED, TUFTS UNIV, 73- *Concurrent Pos:* NIH fels, 64-65, 65- *Mem:* Am Soc Microbiol. *Res:* Genetic studies on simian papova virus SVAO. *Mailing Add:* Dept of Path Tufts Univ Sch of Med Boston MA 02111

TEVETHIA, SATVIR S, b Buland Shahr, India, Aug 5, 36; m 65; c 1. VIROLOGY, IMMUNOLOGY. *Educ:* Agra Univ, BSc, 54, BVSc, 58; Mich State Univ, MS, 62, PhD(microbiol), 64. *Prof Exp:* Vet asst surg, Indian Govt, 58-59; res asst microbiol, Mich State Univ, 60-64; from asst prof to assoc prof virol, Baylor Col Med, 71-73; assoc prof path, Sch Med, Tufts Univ, 73-77, prof, 77-78; PROF MICRO BIOL, COL MED, PA STATE UNIV, 78- *Concurrent Pos:* Fel virol, Baylor Col Med, 64-66; Nat Cancer Inst res career develop award, 67-71. *Mem:* AAAS; Am Soc Microbiol; Transplantation Soc; Am Soc Cell Biol; Am Asn Cancer Res. *Res:* Tumor viruses and immunology. *Mailing Add:* Dept of Microbiol Pa State Univ Col of Med Hershey PA 17033

TEVIOTDALE, BETH LUISE, b Long Beach, Calif, July 17, 40; div. PHYTOPATHOLOGY. *Educ:* Pomona Col, BA, 62; Univ Calif, Davis, MS, 70, PhD(plant path), 74. *Prof Exp:* Lab technician bot, Calif Inst Technol, 62-63; lab technician immunol, Univ Calif, Los Angeles, 65-68; EXTEN SPECIALIST PLANT PATH, SAN JOAQUIN VALLEY RES & EXTEN CTR, UNIV CALIF, 75- *Mem:* Sigma Xi. *Res:* Vegetable and tree crops, with major emphasis on disease-free potatoes for seed and deep bark canker of walnuts. *Mailing Add:* San Joaquin Valley Res & Exten Ctr Univ Calif 9240 S Riverbend Rd Parlier CA 93648

TEW, JOHN GARN, b Mapleton, Utah, Oct 26, 40; m 65; c 6. IMMUNOLOGY, MICROBIOLOGY. *Educ:* Brigham Young Univ, BS, 66, MS, 67, PhD(microbiol), 70. *Prof Exp:* NIH fel, Case Western Reserve Univ, 70-72; asst prof, 72-76, ASSOC PROF MICROBIOL, VA COMMONWEALTH UNIV, 76- *Mem:* Am Soc Microbiol; Am Asn Immunologists; Reticuloendothelial Soc. *Res:* Role of persisting antigen in the induction maintenance and regulation of the humoral immune response; role of beta-lysin in innate immunity; immunobiology of periodontal disease. *Mailing Add:* Dept Microbiol Med Col Va Sta Richmond VA 23298

TEW, RICHARD WILCOX, b Chicago, Ill, May 10, 27; m 50; c 3. MICROBIOLOGY. *Educ:* Harvard Univ, BA, 49, MA, 51; Univ Wis, PhD(bot, bact), 59. *Prof Exp:* Res chemist, Prod Res Dept, Oscar Mayer & Co, 53-56; instr biol, Univ Wis-Green Bay, 56-59; asst prof microbiol, Miss State Univ, 59-60; scientist, Aerojet-Gen Corp, 60-65; var defense assignments, 65-69; ASSOC PROF BIOL, UNIV NEV, LAS VEGAS, 69- *Mem:* Am Soc Microbiol. *Res:* Microbial ecology; aquatic microbiology; aerobiology. *Mailing Add:* Dept of Biol Univ of Nev Las Vegas NV 89154

TEWARI, GAYATRI P, agronomy, see previous edition

TEWARI, PARAM HANS, b Gorakhpur, India, Jan 31, 29; m; c 2. SURFACE CHEMISTRY, COLLOID CHEMISTRY. *Educ:* Lucknow Univ, India, BS, 50, MS, 52, PhD(chem), 59. *Prof Exp:* Asst prof chem, Lucknow Univ, India, 58-59; asst prof & reader, Gorakhpur Univ, India, 59-62; res assoc, Univ Md, College Park, 62-65, Univ Southern Calif, 66 & Univ Alta, 67-68; res officer, Atomic Energy Can, Whiteshell Nuclear Res Estab, 69-80; WITH EXXON ENTERPRISES INC, 80- *Mem:* Am Chem Soc; Chem Inst Can. *Res:* High temperature chemistry of metal oxides-water interfaces, surface and colloid chemistry of filtration, particle deposition, and corrosion of metal oxides and sulfides. *Mailing Add:* Exxon Enterprises Inc 328 Gibraltar Dr Sunnyvale CA 94086

TEWARI, SUJATA, b Murshidabad, India, July 1, 38; m 64; c 2. MOLECULAR BIOLOGY, NEUROCHEMISTRY. *Educ:* Agra Univ, BSc, 55; Univ Lucknow, MS, 57; McGill Univ, PhD(biochem), 62. *Prof Exp:* Neurochemist co-investr brain protein synthesis & neurotransmitters, Vet Admin Hosp, City of Hope, Sepulveda, Calif, 66-70; asst researcher neurochemist step III ethanol & cent nervous syst protein synthesis, 70-72, asst researcher neurochemist step IV, 72, asst prof res III, 72-76, asst prof res IV, 76-78, ASSOC PROF RES ETHANOL & CENT NERVOUS SYST PROTEIN SYNTHESIS, DEPT PSCYHIAT & HUMAN BEHAV, UNIV CALIF, IRVINE, 78- *Concurrent Pos:* Fel biochem, Lucknow Univ, India, 63-64; NSF res proj grant, 75; prin investr, Nat Inst Alcohol Abuse & Alcoholism, 76-, NIMH grant, 78-; mem, Pub Comt Alcoholism, Clin & Exp Res, 77- & biomed panel Calif state supported ctr, 78-; sponsor, Nat Inst Alcohol Abuse & Alcoholism, Ronald L Alkana & Eugene Fleming fel, 78-; sci dir, Nat Inst Alcohol Abuse & Alcoholism, Alcohol Res Ctr grant, 78- *Mem:* AAAS; Biochem Soc; Int Soc Neurochem; Res Soc Alcoholism; Int Soc Biomed Res on Alcoholism. *Res:* Neurobiology combining the disciplines of molecular biology, biochemistry, neurochemistry and neuropharmacology; biomedical research in alcoholism and psychoactive drugs. *Mailing Add:* Dept Psychiat & Human Behav Univ Calif Irvine CA 92717

TEWARSON, ARCHIBALD, fuel technology, physical chemistry, see previous edition

TEWARSON, REGINALD P, b Pauri, India, Nov 17, 30; m 60; c 2. APPLIED MATHEMATICS, COMPUTER SCIENCE. *Educ:* Univ Lucknow, BSc, 50; Agra Univ, MSc, 52; Boston Univ, PhD(appl math), 61. *Prof Exp:* Lectr physics, Messmore Col, India, 50-51; lectr math, Univ Lucknow, 52-57; sr mathematician, Honeywell Inc, 60-64; from asst prof to assoc prof, 64-69, PROF APPL MATH, STATE UNIV NY STONY BROOK, 69- *Concurrent Pos:* Vis prof, Oxford Univ, 70-71. *Mem:* Am Math Soc; Soc Indust & Appl Math; Asn Comput Mach; Soc Math Biol; Int Asn Math Modelling. *Res:* Sparse matrices; linear algebra; numerical analysis; mathematical modelling in biology. *Mailing Add:* Dept of Appl Math & Statist State Univ of NY Stony Brook NY 11794

TEWES, HOWARD ALLAN, b Los Angeles, Calif, May 1, 24; m 53; c 3. PHYSICAL CHEMISTRY. *Educ:* Univ Calif, Los Angeles, BS, 48, MS, 50, PhD(chem), 52. *Prof Exp:* Asst chem, Univ Calif, Los Angeles, 49-52; chemist, Calif Res & Develop Co, 52-53; CHEMIST, LAWRENCE LIVERMORE NAT LAB, UNIV CALIF, 53- *Mem:* AAAS; Am Chem Soc; Am Phys Soc. *Res:* Proton induced reactions of thorium; spallation reactions; high energy neutron induced nuclear reactions; industrial applications of nuclear explosives; analysis of environmental impacts of advanced energy resource recovery technologies; nuclear waste isolation technology. *Mailing Add:* Lawrence Livermore Nat Lab PO Box 808 Livermore CA 94550

TEWHEY, JOHN DAVID, b Lewiston, Maine, Feb 14, 43; m 65; c 3. PETROLOGY. *Educ:* Colby Col, BA, 65; Univ SC, MS, 68; Brown Univ, PhD(geol), 75. *Prof Exp:* geologist, Lawrence Livermore Lab, Univ, Calif, 74-80, proj leader, Synroc Proj, 79-80; MGR EARTH SCI, JORDAN GORRILL ASSOCS, 81- *Concurrent Pos:* Mem geosci fac, Chabot Col, Livermore, Calif, 73-80. *Mem:* Geol Soc Am; Am Geophys Union; Soc Mining Engrs. *Res:* Evaluation of the geochemical controls of mineral equilibria in contact metamorphic environments; geothermal geology; radionuclide migration in porous media; geological applications to engineering. *Mailing Add:* Jordan Gorrill Assocs PO Box 7050 Portland ME 04112

TEWKSBURY, CHARLES ISAAC, b Portsmouth, NH, Feb 26, 25; m 49; c 3. RUBBER CHEMISTRY. *Educ:* Univ NH, BS, 48, MS, 49; Princeton Univ, PhD(chem), 53. *Prof Exp:* Lab asst, Univ NH, 48-49; asst, Princeton Univ, 49-53; phys chemist, Nat Res Corp, 53-54, proj mgr, 54-57, sr chemist, 57-59; res chemist, Monsanto Chem Co, 59; group leader, Cabot Corp, 59-61; asst assoc dir new prod res, 61-63; RES DIR, ODELL CO, 63-; TREAS, FAY SPECIALTIES, INC, 71-, PRES, 74- *Mem:* Am Chem Soc. *Res:* Gas kinetics; hydrocarbon oxidation; heterogeneous catalysis; metals; high temperature phenomena; radiation chemistry; polymerization; polymer characterization; elastomers; adhesives. *Mailing Add:* Odell Co 60 Acton St PO Box 201 Watertown MA 02172

TEWKSBURY, DUANE ALLAN, b Osceola, Wis, Oct 4, 36; m 58; c 2. BIOCHEMISTRY. *Educ:* St Olaf Col, BA, 58; Univ Wis, MS, 60, PhD(biochem), 64. *Prof Exp:* res biochemist, 64-80, SR RES BIOCHEMIST, MARSHFIELD MED FOUND, 80- *Mem:* Am Chem Soc; NY Acad Sci; Am Soc Biol Chemists. *Res:* Biochemical studies of peptide hormone systems; isolation and characterization of the protein components of the renin-angiotension system. *Mailing Add:* Marshfield Med Found 510 N St Joseph Ave Marshfield WI 54449

TEWS, JEAN KRING, b Ogdensburg, NY, May 21, 28; m 56; c 1. BIOCHEMISTRY. *Educ:* St Lawrence Univ, BS, 49; Univ Wis, MS, 52, PhD(biochem), 54. *Prof Exp:* Asst biochem, Univ Wis, 50-54; biochemist, Galesburg State Res Hosp, 54-55; proj assoc physiol, 55-62, res assoc, 63-66, res assoc biochem, 67-77, ASSOC SCIENTIST BIOCHEM, UNIV WIS-MADISON, 77- *Mem:* Int Soc Neurochem; Am Inst Nutrit; Am Soc Neurochem. *Res:* Enzyme activities and nutrition; neurochemistry; factors influencing chemical components of brain; amino acids; amino acid transport. *Mailing Add:* Dept of Biochem Univ of Wis Madison WI 53706

TEWS, LEONARD L, b Rush Lake, Wis, May 28, 34; m 60; c 4. BOTANY, MYCOLOGY. *Educ:* Wis State Univ, Oshkosh, BS, 56; Ind Univ, MA, 58; Univ Wis, PhD(bot, mycol), 65. *Prof Exp:* Teaching asst bot, Ind Univ, 56-58; teacher high sch, 58-61; res asst mycol, Univ Wis, 61-63; from instr to assoc prof, 64-75, PROF BIOL, UNIV WIS-OSHKOSH, 75- *Concurrent Pos:* Water Resources res grant, Water Resources Ctr, 69-70. *Mem:* Mycol Soc Am; Brit Mycol Soc. *Res:* Effects of soil fumigants and fungicides on microfungi of a marsh; microfungi of lakes and cattail marshes; lignin decomposition. *Mailing Add:* Dept of Biol Univ Wis Oshkosh WI 54901

TEXON, MEYER, b New York, NY, Apr 23, 09; m 41; c 2. MEDICINE. *Educ:* Harvard Univ, AB, 30; NY Univ, MD, 34; Am Bd Internal Med & Am Bd Cardiovasc Dis, dipl, 44. *Prof Exp:* Asst prof, 57-73, ASSOC PROF FORENSIC MED, POST-GRAD MED SCH, NY UNIV, 73- *Concurrent Pos:* Asst med examr, City of New York, 57-; assoc physician, French Hosp & New York Infirmary; attend physician, Manhattan Eye, Ear & Throat Hosp; consult cardiovasc dis, Bur Hearings & Appeals, Social Security Agency, Dept Health, Educ & Welfare; fel coun clin cardiol & coun atherosclerosis, Am Heart Asn; attend physician, Doctors Hosp. *Honors & Awards:* Hektoen Silver Medal, AMA, 58. *Mem:* AMA; Am Heart Asn; Am Col Physicians; fel Am Col Cardiol; NY Acad Med. *Res:* Cardiovascular disease; internal medicine; atherosclerosis; hemodynamics; heart disease and industry; role of vascular dynamics in the development of atherosclerosis. *Mailing Add:* 3 E 68th St New York NY 10021

TEXTER, E CLINTON, JR, b Detroit, Mich, June 12, 23; m 49; c 3. MEDICAL EDUCATION, GASTROENTEROLOGY. *Educ:* Mich State Univ, BA, 43; Wayne State Univ, MD, 46. *Prof Exp:* Asst resident, Goldwater Mem Hosp, NY Univ, 50-51; instr, Sch Med, Duke Univ, 51-53; assoc, Med Sch, Northwestern Univ, Chicago, 53-56, asst chief gastroenterol clins, 53-55, dir training prog in gastroenterol, 55-63, from asst prof to assoc prof med, 58-68; chmn dept clin physiol, Olen B Culbertson Res Ctr, Scott & White Clin, Temple, Tex, 68-72; asst dean, Col Health Related Prof, Med Ctr, 72-73, assoc dean, 73-75, PROF MED PHYSIOL & BIOPHYS, COL MED, UNIV ARK, LITTLE ROCK, 72-, DIR, DIV GASTROENTEROL, 73- *Concurrent Pos:* Res fel med, Col Med, Cornell Univ, 48-50; attend physician, Passavant Mem Hosp, 53-68; ed, Am J Digestive Dis, 56-68; chief gastroenterol sect, Vet Admin Res Hosp, 59-63; consult, US Naval Hosp, Great Lakes, 63-68; attend physician, Cook County Hosp, Ill, 66-68; mem sr staff, Scott & White Mem Hosp, Temple Univ, 68-72; consult, Santa Fe Hosp, Vet Admin Ctr, Temple, 68-72; William Beaumont Hosp, Dept Army, El Paso, 68-, consult to Surgeon Gen, US Army, 70; lectr, Univ Fla, 69; adj prof physiol, Univ Tex Southwestern Med Sch Dallas, 69-72; fac coordr allied health training prog, Temple Jr Col, 69-72; attend physician, Univ Hosp, Univ Ark, Little Rock, 72-; assoc chief of staff for educ & actg chief gastroenterol, Vet Admin Hosp, 72-75. *Mem:* Am Physiol Soc; Am Gastroenterol Asn; fel Am Col Physicians; Am Fedn Clin Res; Am Med Writers' Asn (pres, 73-74). *Res:* Gastrointestinal physiology and pathophysiology; health care delivery systems. *Mailing Add:* Univ Ark Med Sci 4301 W Markham #567 Little Rock AR 72205

TEXTOR, ROBIN EDWARD, b Detroit, Mich, Mar 19, 43; m 65; c 2. MATHEMATICS. *Educ:* Tenn Polytech Inst, BS, 64; Univ Tenn, Knoxville, MS, 68; Drexel Univ, PhD(math), 72. *Prof Exp:* Comput appln programmer, Comput Technol Ctr, Union Carbide Corp, Tenn, 64-69; asst prof math, Univ SC, 71-72; COMPUT APPLN ANALYST, OAK RIDGE NAT LAB, UNION CARBIDE CORP, 72-, SECT HEAD, 73- *Mem:* Math Asn Am; Am Math Soc; Soc Indust & Appl Math. *Res:* Singular hyperbolic partial differential equations; numerical solution of fluid flow problems and partial differential equations. *Mailing Add:* Comput Sci Div Union Carbide Corp PO Box P Oak Ridge TN 31830

TEXTORIS, DANIEL ANDREW, b Cleveland, Ohio, Jan 19, 36; m 59; c 3. GEOLOGY. *Educ:* Case Western Reserve Univ, BA, 58; Ohio State Univ, MS, 60; Univ Ill, PhD(geol), 63. *Prof Exp:* Asst prof geol, Univ Ill, 63-65; from asst prof to assoc prof, 65-73, asst dean res admin, 68-74, PROF GEOL, UNIV NC, CHAPEL HILL, 73-, ASSOC DEAN RES ADMIN, 74- *Concurrent Pos:* Geologist, Diamond Alkali Co, 57-60; consult, Southern Ill-Pa Coal, 61-65; coord NSF sci develop prog, 67-74; consult, Carbonate Dredging, 68-70; sr assoc, Dept of Energy, 78-, consult, 79-81. *Mem:* AAAS; Geol Soc Am; Soc Econ Paleont & Mineral; Am Asn Petrol Geol; Nat Coun Univ Res Adminrs. *Res:* Sedimentary geology; carbonate petrography; diagenesis of sediments; petrology and geochemistry of volcanic tuff; interpretation of ancient carbonate environments; paleoecology; geology of fossil fuels. *Mailing Add:* Dept Geol Univ NC Chapel Hill NC 27514

TEYLER, TIMOTHY JAMES, b Portland, Ore, Nov 25, 42; m 66; c 1. NEUROSCIENCES. *Educ:* Ore State Univ, BS, 64; Univ Ore, MS, 68, PhD(psychol), 69. *Prof Exp:* Asst prof psychol, Univ Southern Calif, 68-69; lectr psychobiol, Univ Calif, Irvine, 69-72, assoc res psychobiologist, 73-74; lectr psychol, Harvard Univ, 74-75, assoc prof, 75-77; assoc prof, 77-81, PROF NEUROBIOL, COL MED, NORTHEASTERN OHIO UNIV, 81- *Concurrent Pos:* NIMH fel, Univ Calif, Irvine, 70-72; NSF sr fel & Fulbright scholar, Inst Neurophysiol, Univ Oslo, 73-74. *Mem:* Soc Neurosci; Psychonomic Soc. *Res:* Neurobiological correlates of behavioral plasticity; neurolinguistics; magnetoencephalography; neuroendocrinology. *Mailing Add:* Neurobiol Prog Col Med Northeastern Ohio Univ Rootstown OH 44272

THACH, WILLIAM THOMAS, b Oklahoma City, Okla, Jan 3, 37; m 63; c 3. NEUROPHYSIOLOGY, NEUROLOGY. *Educ:* Princeton Univ, AB, 59; Harvard Med Sch, MD, 64. *Prof Exp:* Intern & resident med & neurol, Mass Gen Hosp, 64-66, 69-71; staff assoc neurophysiol, NIMH, 66-69; from asst prof to assoc prof physiol & neurol, Med Sch, Yale Univ, 71-75; ASSOC PROF NEUROBIOL & NEUROL, SCH MED, WASHINGTON UNIV, 75- *Concurrent Pos:* Prin investr, Nat Inst Neurol Dis & Stroke res grant, 71-; assoc neurologist, Barnes Hosp, St Louis City Hosp, 75- *Mem:* Soc Neurosci; Am Physiol Soc; Am Acad Neurol. *Res:* Physiology of behavior; cerebellar control of posture and movement. *Mailing Add:* Dept of Anat & Neurobiol 660 S Euclid Ave St Louis MO 63110

THACHER, HENRY CLARKE, JR, b New York, NY, Aug 8, 18; m 42; c 5. COMPUTER SCIENCE, NUMERICAL ANALYSIS. *Educ:* Yale Univ, AB, 40; Harvard Univ, MA, 42; Yale Univ, PhD(phys chem), 49. *Prof Exp:* Instr chem, Yale Univ, 46-48; asst prof, Ind Univ, 49-54; task scientist, Aeronaut Res Lab, Wright Air Develop Ctr, US Air Force, Ohio, 54-58; assoc chemist, Argonne Nat Lab, 58-66; prof comput sci, Univ Notre Dame, 66-71; PROF COMPUT SCI, UNIV KY, 71- *Concurrent Pos:* Consult, Argonne Nat Lab, 66-77. *Mem:* AAAS; Soc Indust & Appl Math; NY Acad Sci. *Res:* Numerical approximation and computer programming; computation and approximation of special functions. *Mailing Add:* Dept Comput Sci Univ Ky Lexington KY 40506

THACHER, PHILIP DURYEA, b Palo Alto, Calif, Jan 13, 37; m 63; c 2. SOLID STATE PHYSICS. *Educ:* Calif Inst Technol, BS, 58; Cornell Univ, PhD(physics), 65. *Prof Exp:* STAFF MEM, SANDIA LABS, 65- *Mem:* AAAS; Am Phys Soc; Inst Elec & Electronics Eng. *Res:* Optical effects in ferroelectric ceramics and crystals; laser energy; radiometry; 14 MeV neutron detection. *Mailing Add:* Div 2552 Sandia Labs Albuquerque NM 87185

THACKER, HARRY B, b Pittsburgh, Pa, May 4, 47; m 76; c 1. HIGH ENERGY PHYSICS, PARTICLE PHYSICS. *Educ:* Calif Inst Technol, BS, 68; Univ Calif, Los Angeles, MS, 71, PhD(particle physics theory), 73. *Prof Exp:* Res assoc, State Univ NY Stony Brook, 73-76; THEORET PHYSICIST PARTICLE PHYSICS, FERMI NAT ACCELERATOR LAB, 76- *Res:* Quantum field theory; gauge theories of quarks and leptons; connections between statistical mechanics and quantum field theory. *Mailing Add:* Fermi Nat Accelerator Lab Batavia IL 60510

THACKER, JAMES DOUGLAS, b Palmerton, Pa, July 25, 49. ORGANIC CHEMISTRY. *Educ:* NC State Univ, BS, 77, PhD(org chem), 82. *Prof Exp:* CHEMIST, BOLL WEEVIL RES LAB, NC STATE UNIV, USDA, 82- *Concurrent Pos:* Vis asst prof, Delta State Univ, 82- *Mem:* AAAS; Am Chem Soc. *Res:* Isolation, structure, determination, and synthesis of natural products that illicit a behavioral response in phytophagus insects in order to determine a chemical rationale for the host plant selection process. *Mailing Add:* Dept Chem NC State Univ Raleigh NC 27650

THACKER, JOHN CHARLES, b Clinton, Okla, Oct 29, 43; m 68; c 2. STATISTICAL ANALYSIS. *Educ:* Cornell Univ, BS, 66; Brown Univ, PhD(appl math), 74. *Prof Exp:* MEM TECH STAFF STATIST, AEROSPACE CORP, 74- *Mem:* Am Math Soc; Inst Math Statist; Am Statist Asn; Soc Indust & Appl Math. *Res:* Statistical inference on stochastic processes; time series analysis; stochastic point processes; application of statistical techniques to air and water pollution problems. *Mailing Add:* Aerospace Corp PO Box 92957 Los Angeles CA 90009

THACKER, RAYMOND, b Ashton-U-Lyne, UK, May 9, 32. ELECTROCHEMISTRY, PHYSICAL CHEMISTRY. *Educ:* Univ Manchester, BSc, 52, MSc, 53, PhD(phys chem), 55. *Prof Exp:* Sci officer, UK Atomic Energy Auth Indust Group, 55-58; res assoc electrode kinetics, Univ Pa, 58-60; SR RES CHEMIST, RES LABS, GEN MOTORS CORP, 60- *Mem:* Electrochem Soc; Royal Soc Chem. *Res:* Thermodynamic properties of nonelectrolyte solutions; electrochemistry of surfaces; fuel cell electrode processes; batteries. *Mailing Add:* Gen Motors Corp Res Labs 12 Mile & Mound Rds Warren MI 48090

THACKER, WILLIAM CARLISLE, fluid dynamics, see previous edition

THACKRAY, ARNOLD, b Eng, July 30, 39; c 3. HISTORY & PHILOSPHY OF SCIENCE. *Educ:* Bristol Univ, Eng, BSc, 60; Cambridge Univ, Eng, MA, 65, PhD(hist sci), 66. *Prof Exp:* Res fel, Churchill Col, Cambridge Univ, 65-68; chmn, 70-77, PROF HIST & SOCIOL SCI, UNIV PA, 68- *Concurrent Pos:* Vis lectr, Harvard Univ, 67-68, Nat lectr, Sigma Xi, 76; ed, Isis, 78- *Mem:* fel AAAS; fel Royal Hist Soc; fel Royal Soc Chem; Soc Social Studies Sci (pres, 82-84); Hist Sci Soc. *Mailing Add:* Dept Hist & Sociol Sci E F Smith Hall D6 Univ Pa Philadelphia PA 19104

THACKSTON, EDWARD LEE, b Nashville, Tenn, Apr 29, 37; m 61; c 2. ENVIRONMENTAL ENGINEERING, WATER RESOURCES ENGINEERING. *Educ:* Vanderbilt Univ, BE, 61, PhD(environ & water resources eng), 66; Univ Ill, Urbana, MS, 63. *Prof Exp:* City engr, Lebanon, Tenn, 58-59; design engr, City of Nashville, 61-62; from asst prof to assoc prof sanit & water resources eng, 66-76, prof environ & water resources eng, 76-80, PROF CIVIL & ENVIRON ENG & CHMN DEPT, VANDERBILT UNIV, 80- *Concurrent Pos:* Consult engr, Vanderbilt Univ, 66-; on leave as staff asst environ affairs to Gov State of Tenn, 72-73. *Mem:* Am Soc Civil Engrs; Am Water Works Asn; Water Pollution Control Fedn; Asn Environ Eng Prof; Am Acad Environ Engrs. *Res:* Mixing and reaeration in streams; effects of impoundments on water quality; industrial waste treatment; environmental policy; civil engineering. *Mailing Add:* 2010 Priest Rd Nashville TN 37215

THACORE, HARSHAD RAI, b Ahemdabad, India, Dec 1, 39; US citizen; m 65; c 1. VIROLOGY. *Educ:* Univ Lucknow, BSc, 58, MSc, 60; Duke Univ, PhD(microbiol), 65. *Prof Exp:* Fel virol, Ohio State Univ, 65-67; res assoc, Univ Pittsburgh, 67-69, instr, 69-71, asst res prof, 71-74; asst prof, 74-79, ASSOC PROF VIROL, STATE UNIV NY BUFFALO, 79- *Mem:* Am Soc Microbiol. *Res:* Interferon, especially mechanism and induction of; rescue of interferon sensitive virus by poxviruses; persistent viral infections, especially initiation and maintenance of. *Mailing Add:* Dept Microbiol Sch Med State Univ NY Buffalo NY 14214

THADDEUS, PATRICK, b June 6, 32; US citizen; m 63; c 2. PHYSICS, ASTROPHYSICS. *Educ:* Univ Del, BSc, 53; Oxford Univ, MA, 55; Columbia Univ, PhD(physics), 60. *Prof Exp:* Res physicist, Radiation Lab, Columbia Univ, 60-61; Nat Acad Sci fel astrophys, 61-64, RES PHYSICIST, GODDARD INST, SPACE STUDIES, 64- *Concurrent Pos:* Adj asst prof, Columbia Univ, 64-66, adj prof, 71-; adj assoc prof, NY Univ, 63-; vis assoc prof, State Univ NY Stony Brook, 66-; mem, Space Sci Adv Comt, NASA, 79, Astron Surv Comt, 78-80. *Mem:* Am Phys Soc; Am Astron Soc; Sigma Xi. *Res:* Radio and optical astronomy; interstellar molecules; microwave spectroscopy; masers. *Mailing Add:* Goddard Inst for Space Studies 2880 Broadway New York NY 10025

THAELER, CHARLES SCHROPP, JR, b Philadelphia, Pa, Jan 9, 32; m 57; c 3. ZOOLOGY. *Educ:* Earlham Col, AB, 54; Univ Calif, Berkeley, MA, 60, PhD(zool), 64. *Prof Exp:* Actg instr zool, Univ Calif, Berkeley, 63-64, actg asst cur, Mus Vert Zool, 63-64; asst prof zool, South Bend Campus, Ind Univ, 64-66; from asst prof to assoc prof, 66-74, PROF BIOL, NMEX STATE UNIV, 74- *Concurrent Pos:* NSF res grants, 68-70 & 72-74. *Mem:* Fel AAAS; Am Soc Mammal; Soc Study Evolution; Ecol Soc Am; Soc Syst Zool. *Res:* Mammalian systematics and cytogenetics; evolution and ecology, especially taxonomy; evolution, cytogenetics and distribution of geomyids; taxonomy of microtine rodents. *Mailing Add:* Dept of Biol NMex State Univ Las Cruces NM 88003

THAEMERT, JONA CARL, b Sylvan Grove, Kans, May 25, 22; m 47; c 2. ANATOMY. *Educ:* Univ Denver, BS, 50, MA, 52; Univ Colo, PhD(anat), 59. *Prof Exp:* Instr zool, Univ Denver, 50-52; instr biol, Ft Lewis Col, 52-55; asst prof anat, Sch Med, Univ Mo, 59-61; asst prof, Univ Colo, 61-66; head sect electron micros, Congenital Heart Dis Res & Training Ctr, Hektoen Inst Med Res, 66-74; ASSOC PROF ANAT, CHICAGO MED SCH, 74- *Concurrent Pos:* Assoc prof anat, Sch Med, Northwestern Univ, Chicago, 66-71. *Mem:* Sigma Xi; Am Asn Anat; Am Soc Cell Biol; Electron Micros Soc Am. *Res:* Cytology of muscle and nerve; electron microscopy. *Mailing Add:* Dept Anat 3333 Green Bay Rd Chicago Med Sch North Chicago IL 60064

THAKAR, JAY H, b Bombay, India, Dec 4, 40; Can citizen; m 73; c 2. PSYCHOPHARMACOLOGY. *Educ:* Univ Bombay, BSc Hons, 62, MSc, 64; Univ Manitoba, PhD(biochem), 73. *Prof Exp:* Sci officer, Bhabha Atomic Res Ctr, Bombay, India, 64-68; fel animal sci, Univ Cailf, Davis, 74-76; prof asst biochem, Univ Western Ont, 76-78; clin chemist, Civic Hosp, Ottawa, 78-80; CHIEF, NEUROPHARMACOL LAB, ROYAL OTTAWA HOSP, 80- *Res:* Neuropsychopharmacology of psychiatric disorders; normal and abnormal functions of muscle organelle; animal models of muscular dystrophy. *Mailing Add:* Neuropharmacol Lab Royal Ottawa Hosp 1145 Carling Ave Ottawa ON K1Z 7K4 Can

THAKKAR, ARVIND LAVJI, b Karachi, Pakistan, Apr 19, 39; m 73; c 3. PHYSICAL PHARMACY. *Educ:* Univ Bombay, BPharm, 61; Columbia Univ, MS, 64; Univ Wash, PhD(phys pharm), 67. *Prof Exp:* Teaching asst col pharm, Columbia Univ, 61-63; col pharm, Univ Wash, 64-66; sr pharmaceut chemist, 67-75, RESEARCH SCIENTIST, RES LABS, ELI LILLY & CO, 75- *Mem:* Am Pharmaceut Asn; Acad Pharmaceut Sci; NY Acad Sci. *Res:* Surface activity of drugs; micellar solubilization; complex formation; polymorphism; solubility. *Mailing Add:* Lilly Res Labs Indianapolis IN 46285

THAKOR, NITISH VYOMESH, b Bombay, India, Feb 19, 52. BIOMEDICAL COMPUTING, MEDICAL INSTRUMENTATION. *Educ:* Indian Inst Technol, BTech, 74; Univ Wis, Masison, MS, 78, PhD(elec eng), 81. *Prof Exp:* Electronics engr instrument design & mkt, Philips India, Ltd, 74-76; res asst biomed eng, Univ Wis, Madison, 77-81; ASST PROF MICROCOMPUT & BIOMED COMPUT, NORTHWESTERN UNIV, 81- *Mem:* Inst Elec & Electronics Engrs Comput Soc; Inst Elec & Electronics Engrs Biomed Soc. *Res:* Medical instrumentation and computer applications in medical care, including microprocessors, very large scale integrations, signal processing and pattern recognition in medicine. *Mailing Add:* Dept Elec Eng & Comput Sci Northwestern Univ Evanston IL 60201

THALACKER, VICTOR PAUL, b Muscatine, Iowa, Apr 21, 41; m 70; c 2. ORGANIC CHEMISTRY. *Educ:* Wis State Univ-Stevens Point, BS, 63; Univ Ariz, PhD(org chem), 68. *Prof Exp:* Sr chemist org chem, 67-77, res supvr, 77-80, TECH MGR, 3M CO, 80- *Mem:* Am Chem Soc. *Res:* Radiation curing; radiation curable coatings and adhesives; ultraviolet curable inks and polymers; insect attractants, pheromones; polymer processing; water based adhesives; plant culture; printing technology. *Mailing Add:* 3M Co Bldg 208-1 3M Ctr St Paul MN 55119

THALE, THOMAS RICHARD, b Indianapolis, Ind, June 4, 15; m 41; c 5. PSYCHIATRY. *Educ:* Loyola Univ Chicago, BSM, 38, MD, 39. *Prof Exp:* Resident psychiat, Manteno State Hosp, Ill, 39 & Norwich State Hosp, Conn, 39-43; instr psychol, Univ Conn, 42-45; instr psychiat & pub health, Yale Univ, 43-45; instr psychiat, Wash Univ, 45-50; from instr to assoc prof, 50-69, PROF PSYCHIAT, MED SCH & ASSOC PROF SOCIAL WORK, SCH SOCIAL SERV, ST LOUIS UNIV, 70- *Concurrent Pos:* Med adv, Bur Hearings & Appeals, Social Security Admin, 67-; consult, Family & Childrens Soc Greater St Louis & Vet Admin Asn Retarded Children. *Mem:* AMA; fel Am Psychiat Asn; Am Group Psycotherapy Asn. *Res:* Psychological evaluation chemotherapy. *Mailing Add:* 11 S Meramec Clayton MO 63105

THALER, ALVIN ISAAC, b New York, NY, Aug 26, 38; m 59; c 2. ALGEBRA, NUMBER THEORY. *Educ:* Columbia Univ, AB, 59; Johns Hopkins Univ, PhD(math), 66. *Prof Exp:* Assoc math appl physics lab, Johns Hopkins Univ, 62-64; instr, Col Notre Dame, Md, 64-66; asst prof, Univ Md, 66-71; prog dir algebra & number theory, 71-81, PROG DIR SPEC PROJS MATH SCI, NSF, 81- *Mem:* Am Math Soc; Math Asn Am. *Res:* Algebraic number theory; algebraic geometry. *Mailing Add:* Math Sci Sect NSF Washington DC 20550

THALER, G(EORGE) J(ULIUS), b Baltimore, Md, Mar 15, 18; m 44; c 4. ELECTRICAL ENGINEERING. *Educ:* Johns Hopkins Univ, BE, 40, DrEng, 47. *Prof Exp:* Instr & asst elec eng, Johns Hopkins Univ, 42-47; asst prof, Univ Notre Dame, 47-51; from asst prof to prof, 51-76, DISTINGUISHED PROF ELEC ENG, NAVAL POSTGRAD SCH, 76- *Mem:* Am Soc Eng Educ; Inst Elec & Electronics Engrs. *Res:* Theory of automatic control, particularly discontinuous and nonlinear systems. *Mailing Add:* Dept of Elec Eng Naval Postgrad Sch Monterey CA 93940

THALER, JON JACOB, b Richland, Wash, Feb 3, 47; m 68; c 1. EXPERIMENTAL HIGH ENERGY PHYSICS. *Educ:* Columbia Univ, BA, 67, MA, 69, PhD(physics), 72. *Prof Exp:* From instr to asst prof physics, Princeton Univ, 71-77; ASST PROF PHYSICS, UNIV ILL, URBANA, 77- *Mem:* Am Phys Soc. *Res:* Investigation of high energy processes as tests of the Quark-Parton model, scaling, and the possible existence of new quantum numbers. *Mailing Add:* Dept of Physics Univ of Ill Urbana IL 61820

THALER, M MICHAEL, Can citizen; m 66; c 2. PEDIATRICS, DEVELOPMENTAL BIOLOGY. *Educ:* Univ Toronto, MD, 58. *Prof Exp:* Intern, Mt Zion Hosp, San Francisco, 58-59; jr pediat resident, Children's Hosp, Detroit, 59-60; sr resident, Boston City Hosp, Mass, 60-61; asst resident path, Hosp for Sick Children, Toronto, 61-62; res fel pediat path, Univ Toronto, 62; vis resident, Hosp St Antoine, Paris, 63; res fel path chem, Hosp for Sick Children, Toronto, 63-65; res fel develop biochem, Harvard Med Sch, 65-67; from instr to asst prof, 67-72, assoc prof, 72-76, PROF PEDIAT, SCH MED, UNIV CALIF, SAN FRANCISCO, 77- *Concurrent Pos:* Vis scientist, Wash Univ, 64; Josiah Macy Jr Found fac scholar, 74-75; vis scientist, Weizmann Inst Sci, Israel. *Mem:* Soc Pediat Res; Am Soc Clin Invest; Am Soc Biol Chemists; Am Asn Study Liver Dis; Int Asn Study Liver. *Res:* Liver disease of newborn infants; perinatal and developmental aspects of hepatic metabolism; bilirubin metabolism; pediatric gastrointestinal function and pathology. *Mailing Add:* Dept of Pediat Univ of Calif Med Sch San Francisco CA 94143

THALER, OTTO FELIX, b Vienna, Austria, June 17, 23; US citizen; m 47; c 3. PSYCHIATRY, PSYCHOANALYSIS. *Educ:* Univ Rochester, MD, 49; State Univ NY Downstate Med Ctr, cert psychoanal, 66. *Prof Exp:* PROF PSYCHIAT, SCH MED, UNIV ROCHESTER, 55- *Mem:* Am Psychiat Asn. *Mailing Add:* Dept Psychiat Univ Rochester Sch Med Rochester NY 14642

THALER, RAPHAEL MORTON, b Brooklyn, NY, May 19, 25; m 52; c 4. THEORETICAL PHYSICS. *Educ:* NY Univ, AB, 47; Brown Univ, ScM, 49, PhD(physics), 50. *Prof Exp:* Res assoc theoret physics, Yale Univ, 50-52; mem staff, Los Alamos Sci Lab, 53-60; assoc prof, 60-64, PROF PHYSICS, CASE WESTERN RESERVE UNIV, 64-, VCHMN DEPT, 67- *Concurrent Pos:* Res assoc, Mass Inst Technol, 57-58; consult, Argonne Nat Lab & Lewis Res Lab, NASA. *Mem:* Fel Am Phys Soc; Ital Phys Soc. *Res:* Nuclear and elementary particle physics. *Mailing Add:* Dept of Physics Case Western Reserve Univ Cleveland OH 44106

THALER, WARREN ALAN, b New York, NY, Jan 7, 34; m 56; c 1. ORGANIC CHEMISTRY. *Educ:* City Col New York, BS, 56; Columbia Univ, MA, 58, PhD(chem), 61. *Prof Exp:* Res assoc, 60-77, SR CORP RES LAB, EXXON RES & ENG CO, 77- *Mem:* Am Chem Soc. *Res:* Free radical chemistry; sulfur chemistry; additive substitution reactions; stereochemistry of free radical reactions; cationic polymerization; elastomer chemistry. *Mailing Add:* Corp Res Lab Exxon Res & Eng Co Linden NJ 07036

THALER, WILLIAM JOHN, b Baltimore, Md, Dec 4, 25; m 51; c 2. PHYSICS. *Educ:* Loyola Col, BS, 47; Cath Univ, MS, 49, PhD(physics), 51. *Prof Exp:* Physicist, Baird Assocs, Inc, 47; instr physics, Cath Univ, 47-48, asst, 48-51; PHYSICIST, US OFF NAVAL RES, 51-; PROF PHYSICS, GEORGETOWN UNIV, 60- *Concurrent Pos:* Chief scientist, Off Telecommun Policy, Exec Off President, 76-77, dir, 77-78. *Mem:* Am Phys Soc; Acoust Soc Am. *Res:* Ultrasonic studies of relaxation phenomena in gases; propagation of shock waves in liquids, solids and gases; effects of ultrasonics on biological media; laser research. *Mailing Add:* 5532 Summit St Centreville VA 22020

THALL, PETER FRANCIS, b Stillwater, Okla, Aug 5, 49. MATHEMATICAL STATISTICS, PROBABILITY. *Educ:* Mich State Univ, BS, 71; Fla State Univ, MS, 73, PhD(statist & probability), 75. *Prof Exp:* Biomet trainee statist, Fla State Univ, 71-75; asst prof statist, Univ Tex, Dallas, 75-80; ASST PROF STATIST, GEORGE WASHINGTON UNIV, WASHINGTON, DC, 80- *Mem:* Am Statist Asn; Inst Math Statist. *Res:* Statistical consulting; probability information theory; stochastic point processes and random measures; reliability theory. *Mailing Add:* Dept Statist Bldg C Rm 315 George Washington Univ Washington DC 20052

THALMANN, ROBERT H, b San Antonio, Tex, Nov 14, 39. NEUROSCIENCE. *Educ:* Univ Tex, BA, 61; Univ Mich, MA, 64, PhD(psychol), 67. *Prof Exp:* USPHS fel, Emory Univ, 67-69; ASST PROF ANAT, BAYLOR COL MED, 69- *Mem:* Soc Neuroscience; AAAS. *Res:* Neurophysiology of neurotransmitters. *Mailing Add:* Dept of Cell Biol Baylor Col of Med Houston TX 77025

THAM, MIN JACK, b Shanghai, China, Apr 14, 35; US citizen; m 69. CHEMICAL ENGINEERING. *Educ:* Univ Rangoon, BScEng, 59; Univ Fla, MSEng, 64, PhD(chem eng), 68. *Prof Exp:* Chief engr, Ngwe Zin Yaw Flour Mills, 60-63; engr, Shell Develop Co, 68-77, RES ENGR, SHELL OIL CO, 77- *Mem:* Am Inst Chem Engrs; Am Chem Soc; Soc Petrol Engrs; Am Inst Mining, Metall & Petrol Engrs. *Res:* Thermodynamics; transport properties; computer applications in reservoir simulations; process and engineering design. *Mailing Add:* Shell Oil Co Entex Bldg Box 991 Houston TX 77001

THAM, MIN KWAN, b Rangoon, Burma, July 29, 39; US citizen; m 70; c 2. CHEMICAL ENGINEERING, PHYSICAL CHEMISTRY. *Educ:* Rangoon Univ, BSc, 62; Univ Fla, MSE, 68, PhD(chem eng), 70. *Prof Exp:* Asst lectr chem eng, Rangoon Inst Technol, 63-66; fel, Univ Fla, 70-72, res assoc, 72-74, asst engr, 74-76; CHEM ENGR, BARTLESVILLE ENERGY TECHNOL CTR, US DEPT ENERGY, 76- *Mem:* Am Chem Soc; Am Inst Chem Engrs; Soc Petrol Engrs. *Res:* Statistical thermodynamics; fuel cells and batteries research; physical and chemical aspects of tertiary oil recovery; interfacial phenomena, adsorptions, mass transfer. *Mailing Add:* Bartlesville Energy Technol Ctr PO Box 1398 Bartlesville OK 74003

THAMER, B(URTON) J(OHN), b Kitchener, Ont, June 22, 21; nat US. NUCLEAR ENGINEERING, CHEMISTRY. *Educ:* Univ Calif, BS, 43; Iowa State Col, PhD(chem), 50; Univ Ariz, MS, 73. *Prof Exp:* Asst chemist, Manhattan Proj Calif, 43-44, Clinton Labs, 44 & Hanford Eng Works, 44-45; asst chem, Inst Atomic Res, Iowa State Univ, 46-50; mem staff, Los Alamos Sci Lab, NMex, 50-71; metallurgist, Magma Copper Co, Ariz, 73-77; NUCLEAR ENGR, FORD, BACON & DAVIS, UTAH, 77- *Mem:* Am Chem Soc; Am Nuclear Soc. *Res:* Chemistry of nuclear reactors, management of radioactive waste, chemical equilibria; diffusion of radon. *Mailing Add:* Ford Bacon & Davis PO Box 8009 Salt Lake City UT 84108

THAMES, HOWARD DAVIS, JR, b Monroe, La, Aug 3, 41; m 66; c 2. BIOMATHEMATICS. *Educ:* Rice Univ, BA, 63, PhD(chem), 70. *Prof Exp:* Proj investr, 70-71, asst prof biomath, 71-78, ASSOC PROF BIOMATH, UNIV TEX M D ANDERSON HOSP & TUMOR INST, HOUSTON, 78- *Mem:* Radiation Res Soc; Soc Math Biol. *Res:* Modeling and data analysis in radiobiology. *Mailing Add:* Dept of Biomath M D Anderson Hosp & Tumor Inst Houston TX 77025

THAMES, JOHN LONG, b Richmond, Va, Sept 29, 24; m 48; c 4. WATERSHED MANAGEMENT. *Educ:* Univ Fla, BSF, 50; Univ Miss, MS, 59; Univ Ariz, PhD, 66. *Prof Exp:* Res forester, US Forest Serv, 50-67; assoc prof watershed hydrol, 67-69, PROF WATERSHED HYDROL, UNIV ARIZ, 69-, PROG CHMN WATERSHED HYDROL, 75- *Concurrent Pos:* Coordr, Int Biol Prog; consult, Argonne Nat Lab, Am Smelting & Refining Co & Shelly Loy. *Mem:* Soil Sci Soc Am; Soc Am Foresters; Sigma Xi; Am Geophys Union. *Res:* Plant-soil-water relations; hydrologic modeling; decision analyses; hydrology of surface mined lands. *Mailing Add:* Sch of Renewable Natural Resources Univ of Ariz Tucson AZ 85721

THAMES, SHELBY FRELAND, b Hattiesburg, Miss, Aug 10, 36; m 54; c 3. POLYMER CHEMISTRY, ORGANIC CHEMISTRY. *Educ:* Univ Southern Miss, BS, 59, MS, 61; Univ Tenn, PhD(org chem), 64. *Prof Exp:* From instr to assoc prof chem, 60-70, dean col sci, 71-74, dean col sci & technol, 74-77, PROF POLYMER SCI, UNIV SOUTHERN MISS, 70-, VPRES ADMIN & REGIONAL CAMPUSES, 77-; DIR SOUTHERN INST SURFACE COATINGS, 68- *Concurrent Pos:* Res grants, Walter Reed Inst Res, 64-68, Diamond-Shamrock Corp, 66-68, Inst Copper Res Asn, NASA, Masonite Corp & Stand Paint & Varnish Co; Petrol Res Fund fel award, 68-69. *Mem:* Am Chem Soc; Am Inst Chem. *Res:* Organosilicon, synthetic organic and organometallic chemistry. *Mailing Add:* Univ of Southern Miss Hattiesburg MS 39401

THAMES, WALTER HENDRIX, JR, b Richmond, Va, July 29, 18; m 43; c 2. NEMATOLOGY. *Educ:* Univ Fla, BSA, 47, MS, 48, PhD, 59. *Prof Exp:* Asst entomologist, Everglades Exp Sta, Univ Fla, 48-55, asst soil microbiol, 57-59; assoc prof, 59-68, prof, 68-80, EMER PROF PLANT NEMATOL, TEX A&M UNIV, 80- *Mem:* Soc Nematol. *Res:* Biology and control of nematodes; plant nematology. *Mailing Add:* 705 Pershing St College Station TX 77840

THAMM, RICHARD C, JR, b Danville, Va, Jan 6, 30; m 67; c 2. ORGANIC CHEMISTRY. *Educ:* Wash State Univ, BS, 53; Univ Ill, PhD(org chem), 56. *Prof Exp:* chemist, Elastomer Chem Dept, 56-79, CHEMIST, POLYMER PROD DEPT, E I DU PONT DE NEMOURS & CO, INC, 79- *Mem:* Am Chem Soc. *Res:* Organic chemistry as related to synthetic elastomers. *Mailing Add:* E I Du Pont de Nemours & Co Inc 1007 Market St Wilmington DE 19898

THANASSI, JOHN WALTER, b St Louis, Mo, Oct 2, 37; m 64; c 3. BIOCHEMISTRY. *Educ:* Lafayette Col, BA, 59; Yale Univ, PhD(biochem), 63. *Prof Exp:* Fel chem, Cornell Univ, 63-64; fel, Univ Calif, Santa Barbara, 64-65; staff fel, Lab Chem, NIH, 65-67; asst prof, 67-72, assoc prof biochem, 72-78, PROF BIOCHEM, COL MED, UNIV VT, 78- *Concurrent Pos:* USPHS res grants, 68-71, 72-76 & 78-, NASA res grant, 74-75. *Mem:* AAAS; Am Chem Soc; Am Soc Biol Chem; Am Inst Nutrit; Am Asn Univ Professors. *Res:* Vitamin B6 metabolism. *Mailing Add:* Dept Biochem Univ Vt Col Med Burlington VT 05401

THANIGASALAM, KANDIAH, b Jaffna, Ceylon, Oct 26, 39. NUMBER THEORY. *Educ:* Univ Ceylon, BS, 60; Univ London, MS, 64; Pa State Univ, PhD(math), 70. *Prof Exp:* Asst lectr math, Univ Ceylon, 60-62; lectr math, Lanchester Col Technol, Eng, 65-67; sr lectr math, Constantine Col Technol, Eng, 67-68; asst prof math, Fordham Univ, 70-71; asst prof math, Pa State Univ, Beaver, 71-80. *Res:* Analytic theory of numbers, with special interest in Waring's problem and its generalizations. *Mailing Add:* 659 3rd St Beaver PA 15009

THANOS, ANDREW, b Canton, Ohio, June 12, 22; m 43; c 2. MICROBIOLOGY, PLANT PATHOLOGY. *Educ:* Kent State Univ, AB, 47; Univ WVa, MS, 48; Mich State Univ, PhD(plant path, mycol, bact), 52. *Prof Exp:* Teaching asst bot mycol & plant path, Mich State Univ, 48-50, instr bot & plant path, 50-51; sr res microbiologist, Eli Lilly & Co, 52-61; head microbiol, NAm Aviation, Inc, 62-67; dir microbiol, RPC Corp, 67-73; pres, Lume Corp, 73-74; owner, Polychrome Spec, 74-75; CONSULT, INDUST MICROBIOL, 73- *Concurrent Pos:* Lectr, Butler Univ, 58-60; invest counselor, 78- *Mem:* AAAS; Am Soc Microbiol; Soc Indust Microbiol; Mycol Soc Am. *Res:* Development of rapid biochemical detection systems utilizing microorganisms as sensors; microbiological deterioration of materials; microbiological desalination of sea water; fungal physiology; marine microbiology; rapid detection of air-borne pathogens. *Mailing Add:* PO Box 821 El Segundo CA 90245

THAPAR, MANGAT RAI, b Khanna, India, Apr 4, 39; m 68; c 1. SEISMOLOGY, GEOPHYSICS. *Educ:* Indian Sch Mines, Dhanbad, BSc, 61, MSc & AISM, 62; Univ Western Ont, PhD(geophys), 68. *Prof Exp:* Sr sci officer seismol, Coun Sci & Indust Res, New Delhi, 62-64; teaching fel seismol & geophys, Univ Western Ont, 68-71; NSF res fel seismol, Univ Pittsburgh, 71-72; chief res engr, Seismograph Serv Corp, 72; analyst seismol, Phillips Petrol Co, 72-74; geophys assoc, 74-80, SR GEOPHYS ASSOC, CITIES SERV CO, 80- *Concurrent Pos:* Lectr, Univ Pittsburgh, 71-72. *Mem:* Am Geophys Union; Soc Exp Geophys; Indian Soc Earthquake Technol. *Res:* Applied geophysics; experimental, theoretical, model earthquake and lunar seismology; digital data processing techniques; geophysical exploration techniques; seismic interpretation research; seismic wave propagation; 2-dimensional digital seismic modeling; color processing of seismic data. *Mailing Add:* Cities Serv Co Geophys Data Ctr PO Box 300 Tulsa OK 74102

THAPAR, NIRWAN TILAK, b Raikot, India, Jan 26, 38; US citizen; m 67; c 2. VETERINARY PATHOLOGY, VETERINARY MEDICINE. *Educ:* Punjab State Vet Col, India, BVScAH, 61; Univ SDak, Brookings, MS, 64. *Prof Exp:* Instr & res assoc, Punjab State Vet Col, Hissar, India, 61-62; res asst, SDak State Univ, 62-64, Univ Wis-Madison, 64-66; vet clin res, Div Vet Res, Norwich Pharmaceut Co, Eatons Labs, 66-68; vet pathol, Toxicol Sect, Wis Alumni Res Found, 68-69; teaching asst pathol, Med Sch, Univ Wis, 72; vet pathologist, County of San Diego, 72-77; CONSULT PATH FELINE PRACT, 73-, CANINE PRACT, 74-; DIR, ANIMAL HEALTH DIAG LAB, MD STATE DEPT AGR, 77- *Concurrent Pos:* Chmn regional exam bd, mem bd dir, Am Asn for Lab Animal Sci, San Diego County Vet Med Asn; partner Emergency Animal Clin, 73-; chmn rabies & libr comt, San Diego County Vet Med Asn, 76-77; consult, Bio-vet Labs, Inc, Annapolis, 81- *Mem:* Sigma Xi; Am Vet Med Asn; Soc Pharmacol & Environ Pathologists. *Res:* Experimental pathology; diagnostic and toxicologic pathology. *Mailing Add:* State Animal Health Lab Box 145 Rte 1 Centreville MD 21617

THARIN, JAMES COTTER, b West Palm Beach, Fla, Mar 22, 31; m 55; c 2. GEOLOGY. *Educ:* St Joseph's Col, Ind, BS, 54; Univ Ill, Urbana, MS, 58, PhD(geol), 60. *Prof Exp:* Instr phys sci, Univ Ill, Urbana, 59-61; petrol geologist, Chevron Oil Co, 61-63; asst prof geol, Wesleyan Univ, 63-67; assoc prof, 67-74, chmn dept, 67-80, PROF GEOL, HOPE COL, 74- *Mem:* AAAS; Geol Soc Am; Soc Econ Geol; Soc Econ Paleont & Mineral; Sigma Xi. *Res:* Sedimentation; Pleistocene geology; glacial geology and clay mineralogy; textural studies of glacial drift in northwestern Pennsylvania, Calgary area, Alberta and Connecticut Valley; petroleum exploration in Mississippi Delta. *Mailing Add:* Dept Geol Hope Col Holland MI 49423

THARP, A G, b Franklinton, Ky, Jan 6, 27. INORGANIC CHEMISTRY. *Educ:* Univ Ky, BS, 51; Purdue Univ, PhD, 57. *Prof Exp:* Asst, Purdue Univ, 51-54; asst res engr, Univ Calif, 54-55, res engr, 59; res chemist, Oak Ridge Nat Lab, 56-59; from asst prof to prof inorg chem, 59-74, PROF CHEM, CALIF STATE UNIV, LONG BEACH, 74- *Mem:* Am Chem Soc. *Res:* Structural investigations of high melting silicides, germanides and carbides; thermodynamic properties of high melting inorganic compounds. *Mailing Add:* Dept of Chem Calif State Univ Long Beach CA 90840

THARP, EDWARD LEON, civil engineering, see previous edition

THARP, GERALD D, b Wahoo, Nebr, Aug 9, 32; m 57; c 4. VERTEBRATE PHYSIOLOGY. *Educ:* Univ Nebr, BS, 58, MS, 61; Univ Iowa, PhD(physiol), 65. *Prof Exp:* Instr physiol, Univ Iowa, 64-65; asst prof, Wis State Univ, Oshkosh, 65-67; asst prof, 67-72, assoc prof, 72-76, PROF PHYSIOL, UNIV NEBR, LINCOLN, 76- *Mem:* Am Physiol Soc; Am Col Sports Med. *Res:* Exercise and stress physiology especially the effects of training. *Mailing Add:* Sch of Life Sci Univ of Nebr Lincoln NE 68588

THARP, VERNON LANCE, b Hemlock, Ohio, Mar 13, 17; m 40; c 6. VETERINARY MEDICINE. *Educ:* Ohio State Univ, DVM, 40. *Prof Exp:* Field vet, US Bur Animal Indust, 40-42; instr vet surg & clin, 42-47, from asst prof to assoc prof vet med, 47-55, dir vet clin, 47-71, chmn dept vet clin sci, 60-71, dir equine res ctr, 65-71, dir food animal res ctr, 70-71, PROF VET MED, COL VET MED, OHIO STATE UNIV, 55-; ASSOC DEAN, 72- *Concurrent Pos:* Harness Tracks Am, NY Racing Asn & New York Jockey Club grants equine res col vet med, Ohio State Univ, 65-72. *Mem:* Am Vet Soc Study Breeding Soundness; Am Asn Bovine Practitioners; Am Vet Med Asn (pres, 78-79); Am Asn Vet Clinicians (secy-treas, 62). *Res:* Funding, administration and performance of research in environmental health, nutrition and diseases of domestic and laboratory animals. *Mailing Add:* Col of Vet Med Ohio State Univ 1900 Coffey Rd Columbus OH 43210

THATCHER, C(HARLES) M(ANSON), b Milwaukee, Wis, Apr 4, 22; m 46; c 2. CHEMICAL ENGINEERING. *Educ:* Univ Mich, BSE, 43, MSE, 50, PhD(chem eng), 55. *Prof Exp:* Instr chem eng, Univ Mich, 47-54, asst prof chem eng & metall eng, 55-58; prof chem eng & chmn dept, Pratt Inst, 58-63, dean, Sch Eng & Sci, 63-70; DISTINGUISHED PROF CHEM ENG, UNIV ARK, FAYETTEVILLE, 70- *Honors & Awards:* Western Elec Award, 67. *Mem:* Am Chem Soc; Am Inst Chem Engrs; Nat Soc Prof Engrs; NY Acad Sci. *Res:* Computer systems programming and data processing; mathematical modelling and computer simulation; educational methods. *Mailing Add:* Dept of Chem Eng Univ of Ark Fayetteville AR 72701

THATCHER, EVERETT WHITING, b Jefferson, Ohio, Jan 24, 04; m 28; c 2. PHYSICS. *Educ:* Oberlin Col, AB, 26, AM, 27; Univ Mich, PhD(physics), 31. *Prof Exp:* Asst physics, Purdue Univ, 26-27; instr, Univ Nebr, 27-29; instr, Univ Mich, 29-31; from asst prof to assoc prof, Union Univ, NY, 31-46, instr aerodyn, meteorol & radio civilian pilot training prog, 39-43, coordr, 40-43, instr electronics eng defense training, 40-41; head res dept, US Naval Electronics Lab, 46-53, head spec res div, 53-65; CHMN SPACE SCI & MEM EXEC COUN & ADV COMT, COMN EDUC RESOURCES, 65- *Concurrent Pos:* Res assoc, Princeton Univ, 43; sci liaison officer, OSRD, Washington, London & Europe, 44-45; dep tech dir joint task force I, Washington, DC & Bikini, 46. *Mem:* AAAS; fel Am Phys Soc; Inst Elec & Electronics Eng; Am Geophys Union. *Res:* Propagation of radio waves; statistical fluctuations in electron currents under space charge; thermal agitation of electric charge in conductors; multiple space-charge; properties of monomolecular films. *Mailing Add:* 3808 Liggett Dr San Diego CA 92106

THATCHER, JAMES W, b Schenectady, NY, Mar 25, 36; c 3. COMPUTER SCIENCE, MATHEMATICS. *Educ:* Pomona Col, BA, 58; Univ Mich, MA, 61, PhD(commun sci), 64. *Prof Exp:* Assoc engr, Convair Astronaut, 58-59; staff programmer comput ctr, Univ Mich, 59-60, res assoc automata logic of comput group, 62-63; STAFF MEM, THOMAS J WATSON RES CTR, IBM CORP, 63- *Concurrent Pos:* Lectr, NY Univ, 65; asst prof, Fisk Univ, 65-66; sr vis fel, Sch Artificial Intel, Edinburgh Univ, 72-73. *Mem:* Am Math Soc; Asn Symbolic Logic; Asn Comput Mach. *Res:* Programming theory; theoretical computer science; mathematical semantics. *Mailing Add:* Thomas J Watson Res Ctr IBM Corp Box 218 Yorktown Heights NY 10598

THATCHER, ROBERT CLIFFORD, b Boonville, NY, Jan 11, 29; m 49; c 4. FOREST ENTOMOLOGY. *Educ:* State Univ NY, BS, 53, MS, 54; Auburn Univ, PhD, 71. *Prof Exp:* Biol aide, Southern Forest Exp Sta, La, 54, entomologist, 54-68, asst br chief forest insects, 68-73, proj leader, Southern Forest Exp Sta, 73-74, PROG MGR, OFF OF SECY, USDA SOUTHERN PINE BEETLE PROG, US FOREST SERV, 74- *Concurrent Pos:* Instr, Stephen F Austin State Univ, 57 & 63. *Mem:* Soc Am Foresters. *Res:* Forest ecology; interdisciplinary research and development activities relating to southern pine beetle pest management. *Mailing Add:* 518 Welwyn Way Alexandria LA 71301

THATCHER, VERNON EVERETT, zoology, parasitology, see previous edition

THATCHER, WALTER EUGENE, b Evanston, Ill, Jan 22, 27; m 49; c 11. ANALYTICAL CHEMISTRY. *Educ:* Northwestern Univ, BS, 50; Univ Ill, PhD(chem), 55. *Prof Exp:* RES SPECIALIST, CENT RES LABS, 3M CO, 54- *Mem:* Am Chem Soc; Am Crystallog Asn. *Res:* Analytical chemistry in x-ray diffraction and fluorescence. *Mailing Add:* Cent Res Labs 3M Ctr 201-1E PO Box 3321 St Paul MN 55133

THATCHER, WAYNE RAYMOND, b Montreal, Que, May 23, 42; m 78. SEISMOLOGY. *Educ:* McGill Univ, BSc, 64; Calif Inst Technol, MS, 67, PhD(geophys), 72. *Prof Exp:* GEOPHYSICIST, OFF EARTHQUAKE STUDIES, US GEOL SURV, 71- *Concurrent Pos:* Vis prof, Stanford Univ, 72-76; mem, Nat Acad Sci comt on geodesy, 76-78. *Mem:* Am Geophys Union; Seismol Soc Am. *Res:* Aspects of earthquake source mechanism; crustal deformation and earthquake prediction; seismic surface wave propagation; crustal structure; microearthquakes. *Mailing Add:* Off Earthquake Studies MS 77 US Geol Surv 345 Middlefield Rd Menlo Park CA 94025

THATCHER, WILLIAM WATTERS, b Baltimore, Md, Jan 12, 42; m 62; c 3. REPRODUCTIVE PHYSIOLOGY, REPRODUCTION ENDOCRINOLOGY. *Educ:* Univ Md, BS, 63, MS, 65; Mich State Univ, PhD(dairy sci), 68. *Prof Exp:* NIH fel, Mich State Univ, 68-69; asst prof, 69-74, assoc prof, 74-78, PROF REPRODUCTIVE PHYSIOL & ENDOCRINOL, UNIV FLA, 78- *Mem:* Am Dairy Sci Asn; Soc Study Reproduction; Am Soc Animal Sci. *Mailing Add:* Dept of Dairy Sci Univ of Fla Gainesville FL 32611

THAU, FREDERICK E, b Bronx, NY, Dec 2, 38; m 62; c 2. ELECTRICAL ENGINEERING. *Educ:* NY Univ, BEE, 59, MEE, 61, DEngSc(modern control theory), 64. *Prof Exp:* Mem tech staff digital systs, Bell Labs, NY, 59-65; sr staff scientist modern control theory, Kearfott Div, Singer Co, NJ, 65-69; asst prof, City Col New York, 69-76; assoc prof, 76-78, PROF, DEPT ELEC ENG, CITY COL NEW YORK, 78- *Concurrent Pos:* City Univ New York fac res grant, 70-71. *Mem:* Inst Elec & Electronics Engrs. *Res:* Modern control theory and applications to process control; biological control problems; power systems; large space structures; adaptive signal processing. *Mailing Add:* City Col New York NY 10033

THAU, MARCUS, chemistry, engineering, deceased

THAU, ROSEMARIE B ZISCHKA, b Vienna, Austria, Mar 15, 36; m 70. BIOCHEMISTRY, ENDOCRINOLOGY. *Educ:* Univ Vienna, BS, 54, PhD(chem), 63. *Prof Exp:* Res assoc exp surg med ctr, Duke Univ, 63-65; instr pediat, State Univ NY Downstate Med Ctr, 67-70, asst prof, 67-72; SCIENTIST, POP COUN, ROCKEFELLER UNIV, 72- *Mem:* Sigma Xi; Endocrine Soc; Am Chem Soc; NY Acad Sci; AAAS. *Res:* Endocrinology of reproduction, contraceptive development, steroid and proteinhormone metabolism in reproductive physiology. *Mailing Add:* Pop Coun Rockefeller Univ York Ave & 66th St New York NY 10021

THAW, RICHARD FRANKLIN, b Denver, Colo, Nov 13, 20; m 42; c 1. BOTANY, NATURAL HISTORY. *Educ:* Ore State Col, BS, 43, MEd, 47, MS, 53, EdD(gen sci, sci educ), 58. *Prof Exp:* Teacher high sch, Ore, 47-58; sci coordr, San Diego County Schs, Calif, 58-59; assoc prof biol & natural sci, 59-68, PROF BIOL & NATURAL SCI, SAN JOSE STATE UNIV, 68- *Concurrent Pos:* Crown-Zellerbach fel, 54. *Honors & Awards:* Achievement Award, Nat Sci Teachers Asn, 56. *Mem:* Nat Sci Teachers Asn; Nat Audubon Soc. *Res:* Plant taxonomy; science teaching methods. *Mailing Add:* Dept of Natural Sci San Jose State Univ San Jose CA 95192

THAWLEY, DAVID GORDEN, b Hastings, NZ, Oct 4, 46; m 71; c 2. EPIDEMIOLOGY, VETERINARY MEDICINE. *Educ:* Massey Univ, NZ, BVSc, 70; Univ Guelph, PhD(vet prevent med), 75; Am Col Vet Prev Med, dipl, 78. *Prof Exp:* Vet pvt pract, Huntly Vet Club, 69-70, Morrinsville Club, 70-71; asst vet med, Univ Guelph, 71-75; clin teaching fel, Massey Univ, 75; asst prof, 76-79, ASSOC PROF VET MED, UNIV MO, 80- *Concurrent Pos:* Coop investr epidemiologist, US Dept Agr, 78-; prin investr, USPHS-NIH, 78-80, Mo Pork Producers & Nat Pork Producers, 78- *Mem:* Am Vet Med Asn; US Animal Health Asn; Am Acad Vet Prev Med; Asn Teachers Vet Pub Health & Prev Med. *Res:* Investigation of pseudorabies epidemiology and means of control; investigation of interactions among heavy metals and the resulting toxicities produced; general infectious disease epidemiology. *Mailing Add:* Dept of Vet Microbiol Univ of Mo Columbia MO 65211

THAXTON, GEORGE DONALD, b Richmond, Va, Feb 28, 31; m 54; c 4. NUCLEAR PHYSICS, SOLID STATE PHYSICS. *Educ:* Richmond Univ, BS, 59; Univ NC, PhD(physics), 65. *Prof Exp:* Res assoc physics, Fla State Univ, 64-66; asst prof, 66-77, ASSOC PROF PHYSICS, AUBURN UNIV, 77- *Mem:* Am Phys Soc; Am Asn Physics Teachers. *Res:* Theory of direct nuclear reactions; theory of band structure of solids. *Mailing Add:* Dept of Physics Auburn Univ Auburn AL 36830

THAXTON, JAMES PAUL, b Longview, Miss, Sept 6, 41; m 65; c 3. AVIAN PHYSIOLOGY. *Educ:* Miss State Univ, BS, 64, MS, 66; Univ Ga, PhD(physiol), 71. *Prof Exp:* Instr biol, Northeast La Univ, 66-67; asst prof poultry sci, 71-73, assoc prof, 73-78, PROF POULTRY SCI, NC STATE UNIV, 78- *Concurrent Pos:* Consult, Nat Inst Environ Health Sci, 74- *Honors & Awards:* Poultry Sci Assoc Res Award, Poultry Sci Asn, 74. *Mem:* AAAS; Poultry Sci Asn; World Poultry Sci Asn; Sigma Xi. *Res:* Effects of environmental parameters, such as temperatures, toxins and heavy metals, on the immunological responsiveness of the avian species. *Mailing Add:* Dept of Poultry Sci PO Box 5703 NC State Univ Raleigh NC 27650

THAYER, CHARLES WALTER, b Springfield, Vt, May 18, 44; m 67. INVERTEBRATE PALEONTOLOGY, PALEOECOLOGY. *Educ:* Dartmouth Col, BA, 66; Yale Univ, MPhil, 69, PhD(geol), 72. *Prof Exp:* Asst prof, 71-78, ASSOC PROF GEOL, UNIV PA, 78- *Mem:* AAAS; Paleont Soc. *Res:* Adaptation and functional morphology of invertebrates, especially brachiopods and bivalves; paleozoic communities; sedimentary environments. *Mailing Add:* Dept of Geol Univ of Pa Philadelphia PA 19104

THAYER, CHESTER ARTHUR, b Stillwater, Okla, July 30, 48; m 69; c 2. MOLECULAR PHOTOPHYSICS, LASER ISOTOPE SEPARATION. *Educ:* Okla State Univ, BS, 70; Univ Ill, PhD(phys chem), 74. *Prof Exp:* Res chemist, Victoria, Tex, 74-78, asst div supt, 78-80, RES SUPVR, SAVANNAH RIVER LAB, E I DU PONT DE NEMOURS, INC, 80-*Concurrent Pos:* Instr, Victoria Col, 77-80. *Mem:* Am Chem Soc; Sigma Xi. *Res:* Laser isotope separation methods for separating the isotopes of uranium and transuranic elements; photophysics of laser excited molecules; industrial synthesis of nylon intermediates. *Mailing Add:* Savannah River Lab E I du Pont de Nemours Co Inc Aiken SC 29808

THAYER, DONALD WAYNE, microbiology, biochemistry, see previous edition

THAYER, DUANE M, b Kingsford, Mich, June 15, 34; m 57; c 5. METALLURGICAL ENGINEERING. *Educ:* Mich Tech Univ, BS, 59, MS, 62. *Prof Exp:* From instr to assoc prof, 59-70, PROF METALL ENG, MICH TECHNOL UNIV, 70-, ADMIN ASST, 66- *Mem:* Am Inst Mining, Metall & Petrol Engrs. *Res:* Mineral processing; flotation and agglomeration of iron oxides; fine particle flotation; reclamation of industrial wastes. *Mailing Add:* Dept of Metall Eng Mich Technol Univ Houghton MI 49931

THAYER, GORDON WALLACE, b Weymouth, Mass, Feb 28, 40; m 63; c 2. ECOLOGY. *Educ:* Gettysburg Col, BA, 62; Oberlin Col, MA, 64; NC State Univ, PhD(zool), 69. *Prof Exp:* Fishery biologist, Southeast Fisheries Ctr, 68-77, BR LEADER, BEAUFORT LAB, NAT MARINE FISHERIES SERV, NAT OCEANIC & ATMOSPHERIC ADMIN, 77- *Mem:* Am Soc Limnol & Oceanog; Ecol Soc Am; Estuarine Res Fedn; Sigma Xi. *Res:* Ecology of seagrass; communities; dynamics of zooplankton and estuarine fishery populations; influence of detritus in invertebrate and vertebrate food webs; ecology of benthic communities. *Mailing Add:* Beaufort Lab Beaufort NC 28516

THAYER, HAROLD E(UGENE), b Rochester, NY, Mar 3, 12; m 38; c c 1. CHEMICAL ENGINEERING. *Educ:* Mass Inst Technol, BS, 34. *Hon Degrees:* DSc, St Louis Col Pharm, 63, Wash Univ, St Louis, 81. *Prof Exp:* Engr, Tech Sales Dept, Calco Div, Am Cyanamid Co, 34-39; mem staff sales res & develop, 39-41, War Prod Bd coordr, 41-43, proj mgr AEC plants, 43-52, 55-58, develop dir, 52-55, vpres, 50-60, exec vpres, 59-60, pres, 60-71, chief exec off, 65-81, DIR, MALLINCKRODT, INC, 56-, CHMN BD, 65-, CHMN EXEC COMT, 81- *Concurrent Pos:* Technol adv, US State Dept, Second Int Conf Peaceful Uses Atomic Energy, Geneva, Switz, 58 & Nat Asn Mfrs rep, Nat Conf Air Pollution, Washington, DC, 66; dir, Carboline Co, 65, Curlee Clothing Co, 70, First Union, Inc, 71 & Alvey, Inc, 72; pres, Arts & Educ Coun Greater St Louis, 71; mem bd trustees, Jefferson Nat Expansion Mem; trustee, Govt Res Inst; dir, First Nat Bank St Louis, Gen Am Life Ins Co, Laclede Gas Co, Mallinckrodt Chem Works, Ltd & Nat Asn Mfrs. *Honors & Awards:* Chem Indust Medal, Soc Chem Indust, 76. *Mem:* Am Chem Soc; Am Inst Chem Engrs. *Mailing Add:* Mallinckrodt Inc 675 McDonnell Blvd St Louis MO 63134

THAYER, JOHN STEARNS, b Glen Ridge, NJ, Apr 1, 38. INORGANIC CHEMISTRY, ORGANOMETALLIC CHEMISTRY. *Educ:* Cornell Univ, BA, 60; Univ Wis, PhD(chem), 64. *Prof Exp:* Asst prof chem, Ill Inst Technol, 64-66; asst prof, 66-79, ASSOC PROF CHEM, UNIV CINCINNATI, 79-*Concurrent Pos:* Frederick Gardner Cottrell grant, 67-73; vis res assoc prof, Chesapeake Biol Lab, 80-81. *Mem:* AAAS; Am Chem Soc. *Res:* Transmethylation of metals in aqueous media; biological aspects of organometallic chemistry; organometallic compounds of silicon, germanium, platinum and palladium; history of organometallics. *Mailing Add:* Dept of Chem Univ of Cincinnati Cincinnati OH 45221

THAYER, KEITH EVANS, b Lime Springs, Iowa, Feb 5, 28; m 53; c 4. DENTISTRY. *Educ:* Cornell Col, BA, 51; Univ Iowa, DDS, 55, MS, 56. *Prof Exp:* From instr to assoc prof, 56-63, head dept, 60-80, PROF FIXED PROSTHODONTICS, COL DENT, UNIV IOWA, 63- *Concurrent Pos:* Attend dentist, Vet Admin Hosp, Iowa City; vis Fulbright prof, Univ Singapore, 68-69; consult, Am Dent Asn Vietnam Educ Proj, 72; consult, Vet Admin Hosp. *Mem:* Int Dent Fedn; Int Asn Dent Res; Am Dent Asn. *Res:* Rubber base and silicone impression materials; gingival retraction agents and their effect on oral tissues; occlusion. *Mailing Add:* Univ of Iowa Col of Dent Iowa City IA 52240

THAYER, PAUL ARTHUR, b New York, NY, Apr 30, 40; m 66; c 1. MARINE GEOLOGY, SEDIMENTOLOGY. *Educ:* Rutgers Univ, BA, 61; Univ NC, PhD(geol), 67. *Prof Exp:* Develop geologist, Calif Co Div, Chevron Oil Co, 67-68; asst prof geol, Tex A&I Univ, 68-70; asst prof, 70-76, ASSOC PROF MARINE SCI RES, UNIV NC, WILMINGTON, 76- *Concurrent Pos:* Tex A&I Univ fac res grants, 68-69 & 69-70; Soc Sigma Xi grant, 69; petrol geologist, BP Alaska Explor Inc, 75-; instrnl sci equipment prog award, NSF, 72-74 & 75-77; res grant, AEC, 74. *Mem:* AAAS; Geol Soc Am; Int Asn Sedimentol; Soc Econ Paleont & Mineral; Am Asn Petrol Geol. *Res:* Petrology of clastic sedimentary rocks; reconstruction of depositional environments within ancient sedimentary rocks; Triassic nonmarine stratigraphy; provenance, dispersal and origin of modern and ancient sediments; sedimentology of modern carbonate sediments. *Mailing Add:* Dept Marine Sci Res Univ NC Wilmington NC 28401

THAYER, PAUL LOYD, b Centralia, WVa, Feb 25, 28; m 53; c 3. PLANT PATHOLOGY. *Educ:* Marietta Col, BS, 52; Ohio State Univ, MS, 55, PhD, 58. *Prof Exp:* Asst plant pathologist, Everglades Exp Sta, Univ Fla, 58-65; plant pathologist, 65-72, northeastern regional plant sci res mgr, 72-80, HEAD CROP PROTECTION RES, ELI LILLY & CO, GREENFIELD, 80-*Mem:* Am Phytopath Soc. *Res:* Bacterial and fungus diseases of vegetable crops; fungicide and nematocide evaluation. *Mailing Add:* Lilly Res Labs PO Box 708 Greenfield IN 46140

THAYER, PHILIP STANDISH, b Pelham, Mass, Oct 1, 23; div; c 3. MICROBIOLOGY. *Educ:* Amherst Col, BA, 48, MA, 49; Calif Inst Technol, PhD(biochem), 52. *Prof Exp:* Merck fel bact, Univ Calif, 51-53; instr chem, Univ Calif, Los Angeles, 53-55; mem staff biol, Arthur D Little, Inc, 55-81, vpres, 72-81. *Res:* Tissue culture; chemotherapy, radiation biology, toxicology and carcinogenesis. *Mailing Add:* 55 St Germain St Boston MA 02115

THAYER, ROLLIN HAROLD, b St Francis Mission, SDak, Dec 30, 16; m 44; c 1. POULTRY NUTRITION. *Educ:* Okla State Univ, BS, 40; Univ Nebr, MS, 42; Wash State Univ, PhD, 55. *Prof Exp:* From asst prof to prof poultry sci, 43-55, prof poultry sci & nutrit, 55-80, EMER PROF POULTRY SCI & NUTRIT, OKLA STATE UNIV, 80- *Mem:* AAAS; Am Poultry Sci Asn; Am Inst Nutrit; World Poultry Sci Asn. *Res:* Estrogens in poultry fattening; layer breeder hen requirements; nutritive requirements for breeder turkeys. *Mailing Add:* 105 N Stallard Stillwater OK 74074

THAYER, WALTER RAYMOND, JR, b Providence, RI, Apr 16, 29; m 55; c 3. MEDICINE, GASTROENTEROLOGY. *Educ:* Providence Col, BS, 50; Tufts Univ, MD, 54. *Hon Degrees:* MA, Brown Univ, 66. *Prof Exp:* Resident gastroenterol, Sch Med, Yale Univ, 61-62, instr med, 60-62, asst prof, 62-66; assoc prof, 66-70, PROF MED, BROWN UNIV, 70-; CHIEF GASTROENTEROL, RI HOSP, 66- *Concurrent Pos:* Fel clin gastroenterol, Sch Med, Yale Univ, 59-60; NSF fel, Wenner-Gren Inst, Stockholm, 71-72. *Mem:* Am Soc Clin Invest; Am Gastroenterol Asn. *Res:* Immunology in gastrointestinal diseases; gastric secretion. *Mailing Add:* Dept of Med Brown Univ Providence RI 02912

THAYNE, WILLIAM V, b Binghamton, NY, July 23, 41; m 63; c 3. ANIMAL BREEDING, STATISTICS. *Educ:* Cornell Univ, BS, 63; Univ Ill, MS, 67, PhD(dairy sci), 71. *Prof Exp:* Res asst dairy sci, Univ Ill, 63-67; instr animal sci, 67-70, asst prof statist & comput sci, 73-75, asst prof animal sci, 70-75, ASSOC PROF STATIST & COMPUT SCI, WVA UNIV, 75- *Mem:* Am Dairy Sci Asn; Biomet Soc; Am Genetic Asn. *Res:* Dairy cattle genetics. *Mailing Add:* 1016 AS WVA Univ Morgantown WV 26505

THEDFORD, ROOSEVELT, b Greene Co, Ala, Apr 16, 37; m 60; c 5. ORGANIC BIOCHEMISTRY, MOLECULAR BIOLOGY. *Educ:* Clark Col, BS, 59; Univ Buffalo, MA, 62; State Univ NY Buffalo, PhD(biochem), 73. *Prof Exp:* Cancer res scientist, Roswell Park Mem Inst, 61-69 & 72-74; ASSOC PROF CHEM, CLARK COL, 74- *Mem:* Am Chem Soc; Sigma Xi. *Res:* Study of the physicochemical and biological properties of alkylated synthetic homopoly ribonucleotides and determination of the functions of strategically located modified nucleosides as found in transfer RNA. *Mailing Add:* Dept of Chem Clark Col 240 Chestnut St SW Atlanta GA 30314

THEDFORD, WILLIAM ANDREW, b Okla City, Okla, Nov 15, 39; m 62; c 2. TOPOLOGY, ALGEBRA. *Educ:* Okla State Univ, BS, 62, MS, 64; NMex State Univ, PhD(math), 70. *Prof Exp:* Asst prof math sci, Va Commonwealth Univ, 70-77; MATHEMATICIAN, FED AVIATION ADMIN, 77- *Mem:* Am Math Soc; Math Asn Am Inst Aeronaut & Astronaut; Inst Navigation. *Res:* RF modeling and collison avoidance system design. *Mailing Add:* Appl Math Sect ANA-751 Fed Aviation Admin Dept Transp Atlantic City NJ 08405

THEEUWES, FELIX, b Duffel, Belgium, May 25, 37; m 62; c 3. PHYSICAL CHEMISTRY, PHARMACY. *Educ:* Cath Univ Louvain, Licentiaat physics, 61, DrSc(physics), 66. *Prof Exp:* Res assoc chem, Univ Kans, 66-68, asst prof, 68-70; res scientist pharm chem, 70-74, PRIN SCIENTIST, ALZA CORP, 74-, VPRES PROD, RES & DEVELOP, 80- *Concurrent Pos:* High sch teacher, St Vincent Sch, Westerlo, Belgium, 61-64. *Honors & Awards:* Louis Busse lectr, Dept Pharmacol, Univ Wis, 81. *Mem:* Acad Pharmaceut Sci; NY Acad Sci; Am Chem Soc. *Res:* Osmosis, diffusion; solid state physics; cryogenics; high pressure; thermodynamics; pharmacology; pharmacokinetics; calorimetry. *Mailing Add:* Alza Corp 950 Page Mill Rd Palo Alto CA 94304

THEIL, ELIZABETH, b Jamaica, NY, Mar 29, 36; m 57; c 2. BIOCHEMISTRY, DEVELOPMENTAL BIOLOGY. *Educ:* Cornell Univ, BS, 57; Columbia Univ, PhD(biochem), 62. *Prof Exp:* Res asst genetics of microorganisms, State Univ NY Downstate Med Ctr, 57-58; res assoc chem, Fla State Univ, 64-66; res assoc animal sci & biochem, 67-69, from instr to assoc prof, 69-79, PROF BIOCHEM, NC STATE UNIV, 79- *Mem:* Sigma Xi; Am Chem Soc; Soc Develop Biol; Am Soc Biol Chemists. *Res:* Biochemistry of development; regulation of protein synthesis particularly in erythroid cells; iron metabolism, iron storage and copper toxicity; structure and function of ferritin. *Mailing Add:* Dept of Biochem 339 Polk Hall NC State Univ Raleigh NC 27650

THEIL, MICHAEL HERBERT, b Brooklyn, NY, Nov 2, 33; m 57; c 2. POLYMER CHEMISTRY. *Educ:* Cornell Univ, AB, 54; Polytech Inst Brooklyn, PhD(chem), 63. *Prof Exp:* Sr res chemist, Res Ctr of Tex, US Chem Co, 62-64; res assoc chem, Fla State Univ, 64-66; asst prof, 66-73, assoc prof, 73-80, PROF TEXTILE CHEM, NC STATE UNIV, 80- *Mem:* Am Chem Soc; Am Phys Soc; Sigma Xi; Fiber Soc. *Res:* Phase transitions of polymers; polymerization mechanisms; copolymer statistics. *Mailing Add:* Dept of Textile Chem NC State Univ Raleigh NC 27650

THEILEN, ERNEST OTTO, b Columbus, Nebr, June 4, 23. INTERNAL MEDICINE. *Educ:* Univ Nebr, BA, 45, MD, 47; Am Bd Internal Med, dipl, 55; Am Bd Cardiovasc Dis, dipl, 65. *Prof Exp:* Instr med, 51-52, assoc, 52, from asst prof to assoc prof internal med, 55-63, PROF INTERNAL MED, COL MED, UNIV IOWA, 63- *Concurrent Pos:* Fel coun clin cardiol & coun circulation, Am Heart Asn. *Mem:* AMA; Am Fedn Clin Res; Am Col Cardiol; Am Soc Int Med; Am Col Physicians. *Res:* Cardiovascular physiology; electrocardiography; clinical cardiology. *Mailing Add:* Dept of Med Univ Hosps Iowa City IA 52242

THEILEN, GORDON H, b Montevideo, Minn, May 29, 28; m 53; c 3. VETERINARY MEDICINE. *Educ:* Univ Calif, BS, 53, DVM, 55. *Prof Exp:* Pvt pract, Ore, 55-56; lectr vet med, 56-57, from instr to asst prof, 57-62, from asst prof to prof clin sci, 62-74, PROF SURG, SCH VET MED, UNIV CALIF, DAVIS, 74- *Concurrent Pos:* Spec fel, Leukemia Prog, Nat Cancer Inst, 64-65; NY Cancer Res Inst fel tumor immunol, with Chester Beatty, Univ London, 72-73; mem sci & rev comt & bd dirs, Leukemia Soc Am, 71-76. *Honors & Awards:* alexander von Humboldt sr scientist Award, WGer Govt, 79-80. *Mem:* Am Vet Med Asn; Am Asn Cancer Res; Am Asn Vet Clin. *Res:* Leukemia-sarcoma and myeloproliferative disease complex and subjects dealing with clinical oncology, particularly tumor biology. *Mailing Add:* Dept Surg Sch Vet Med Univ Calif Davis CA 95616

THEILHEIMER, FEODOR, b Gunzenhausen, Ger, June 18, 09; nat US; m 48; c 1. MATHEMATICS. *Educ:* Berlin Univ, PhD(math), 36. *Prof Exp:* From instr to asst prof math, Trinity Col, 42-48; mathematician naval ord lab, 48-53, mathematician, Naval Ship Res & Develop Ctr US Dept Navy, Bethesda, Md, 53-78; RETIRED. *Mem:* Am Math Soc; Math Asn Am; Soc Indust & Appl Math; Asn Comput Mach. *Res:* Numerical analysis; fluid dynamics. *Mailing Add:* 2608 Spencer Rd Chevy Chase MD 20815

THEILHEIMER, WILLIAM, b Augsburg, Ger, Oct 11, 14; nat US; m 56; c 1. ORGANIC CHEMISTRY. *Educ:* Basel Univ, PhD(org chem), 40. *Prof Exp:* Asst to Prof Erlenmeyer, Basel Univ, 40-47; consult, 48-59, lit chemist sci info dept, 59-63, RESIDENT CONSULT, HOFFMANN-LA ROCHE, INC, 64- *Concurrent Pos:* Ed, Synthetic Methods Org Chem, 44-81. *Mem:* Am Chem Soc. *Res:* Synthetic methods. *Mailing Add:* 318 Hillside Ave Nutley NJ 07110

THEIMER, EDGAR E, b Newark, NJ, June 29, 15; m 58; c 1. ANALYTICAL CHEMISTRY, PHARMACEUTICAL CHEMISTRY. *Educ:* Polytech Inst Brooklyn, BChE, 36; NY Univ, MS, 39. *Prof Exp:* Chief chemist, Metrop Labs, Inc, 40-58; chief chemist, Pharmich Div, Mich Chem Corp, 58-61; staff chemist, Int Flavors & Fragrances, Inc, 61-64; head anal chem sect res & develop, Smith, Miller & Patch, Inc, 64-72; head anal chem sect prod develop, Cooper Labs, Inc, 72-78; SR SCI ASSOC, US PHARMACOPEIAL CONV, INC, ROCKVILLE, MD, 78- *Mem:* Am Chem Soc. *Res:* Analytical methods development. *Mailing Add:* 3919 Brooke Meadow Lane Olney MD 20832

THEIMER, OTTO, b Vienna, Austria, Feb 22, 18; m 45; c 2. PHYSICS. *Educ:* Univ Vienna, BS, 39; Munich Tech Univ, MS, 43, Dr rer nat (chem physics), 45. *Prof Exp:* Asst physics, Graz Tech Univ, 46-52, privat docent, 49-52; asst prof, Univ BC, 52-55; assoc prof, Univ Okla, 55-59; RES PROF RES CTR, NMEX STATE UNIV, 59- *Concurrent Pos:* Fel, Edinburgh Univ, 51; vis staff mem, Los Alamos Sci Labs, 65-73. *Honors & Awards:* Humboldt Award, 72. *Mem:* Fel AAAS; fel Am Phys Soc; Am Asn Physics Teachers. *Res:* Molecular spectroscopy; light scattering; physical adsorption of gases; quantum chemistry; statistical mechanis; solid state physics; atomic physics; chemical physics; electrodynamics; plasma physics; atmospheric physics. *Mailing Add:* NMex State Univ Res Ctr Las Cruces NM 88003

THEINE, ALICE, b Menomonee, Wis, Feb 23, 38. ORGANIC CHEMISTRY. *Educ:* Alverno Col, BA, 59; Marquette Univ, MS, 65; La State Univ, PhD(chem), 72. *Prof Exp:* Teacher sci & math, St Boniface High Sch, Iowa, 59-63 & St Joseph High Sch, Wis, 63-66; instr, 66-70, asst prof, 72-80, ASSOC PROF CHEM, ALVERNO COL, 80- *Mem:* Am Chem Soc; Sigma Xi. *Res:* Development of improved methods of competence-based instruction in undergraduate chemistry courses; investigation of cationic intermediates in oxidative decarboxylation reactions by product analysis studies. *Mailing Add:* 3401 S 39th St Milwaukee WI 53215

THEINER, MICHA, b Rehovoth, Israel, May 6, 36; m 63; c 2. BIOCHEMISTRY. *Educ:* Israel Inst Technol, BSc, 58; Univ Pittsburgh, PhD(biochem), 63. *Prof Exp:* Res assoc food safety, Mass Inst Technol, 63-66; asst prof biochem, Carnegie-Mellon Univ, 66-69; asst prof, 69-75, ASSOC PROF BIOCHEM, SCH DENT MED, UNIV PITTSBURGH, 75- *Mem:* Am Chem Soc; Inst Food Technol; Int Asn Dent Res; NY Acad Sci. *Res:* Dental biochemistry; gas chromatography; clinical chemistry; clinical nutrition and counseling; educational techniques. *Mailing Add:* Dept of Biochem 528 Salk Hall Univ of Pittsburgh Sch Dent Med Pittsburgh PA 15261

THEIS, GAIL ANN, b New York, NY, Mar 7, 33; m 61; c 2. IMMUNOLOGY. *Educ:* Cornell Univ, BA, 54; NY Univ, MS, 57; Univ Pa, PhD(biol), 61. *Prof Exp:* Instr path, Sch Med, NY Univ, 70-72; ASST PROF PATH, NEW YORK MED COL, 72- *Concurrent Pos:* Arthritis Found fel, NY Univ, 69-72; Leukemia Soc Am spec fel, New York Med Col, 72-74, USPHS res career develop award, 74- *Mem:* Am Asn Immunol. *Mailing Add:* Dept of Microbiol New York Med Col Valhalla NY 10595

THEIS, JEROLD HOWARD, b Richmond, Calif, July 29, 38; m 67; c 1. MEDICAL MICROBIOLOGY, PARASITOLOGY. *Educ:* Univ Calif, Berkeley, AB, 60; Univ Calif, Davis, DVM, 64, PhD(comp path), 72. *Prof Exp:* Asst res vet, George Williams Hooper Found, Univ Calif, San Francisco Med Ctr & Repub Singapore, 64-67; asst prof, 70-77, ASSOC PROF MED MICROBIOL, SCH MED, UNIV CALIF, DAVIS, 77- *Concurrent Pos:* USPHS fel, Univ Calif, Davis, 67-69; consult, Sacramento Med Ctr, Calif, 71- & Primate Res Ctr, Davis, 72- *Honors & Awards:* Grand Prize, Int Med Film Festival, Brussels, Belg, 72. *Mem:* Am Vet Med Asn. *Res:* Mechanisms of transmission of arthropod borne disease agents at the host-arthropod interface. *Mailing Add:* Dept of Med Microbiol Univ of Calif Sch of Med Davis CA 95616

THEIS, RICHARD JAMES, b Cincinnati, Ohio, Nov 30, 37; m 61; c 3. ORGANIC POLYMER CHEMISTRY. *Educ:* Xavier Univ, BS, 60, MS, 62; Univ Cincinnati, PhD(chem), 66. *Prof Exp:* Res chemist, 66-72, STAFF SCIENTIST FILM DEPT, E I DU PONT DE NEMOURS & CO, INC, 73- *Mem:* Am Chem Soc. *Res:* Barrier coatings for films; films for packaging uses; adherable films; filled films; polyester films for capacitors. *Mailing Add:* E I du Pont de Nemours & Co Inc PO Box 89 Circleville OH 43113

THEISEN, CHARLES THOMAS, b Appleton, Wis, June 2, 47; m 69, 81; c 3. ANATOMY, EMBRYOLOGY. *Educ:* Univ Wis, BA, 70; Univ Cincinnati, PhD(anat), 74. *Prof Exp:* From instr to asst prof, 74-80, ASSOC PROF, UNIV MINN, DULUTH, 80- *Concurrent Pos:* Prin investr, NIH Animal Resource Improv grant, 77-78. *Mem:* Teratology Soc. *Res:* Developmental neurobiology; differentiation; thalidomide teratogenicity. *Mailing Add:* Dept of Biomed Anat 2205 E Fifth St Duluth MN 55812

THEISEN, CYNTHIA THERES, b Dearborn, Mich. ORGANIC CHEMISTRY. *Educ:* Siena Heights Col, BS, 60; Purdue Univ, Lafayette, MS, 63; St John's Univ, PhD(org chem), 67. *Prof Exp:* Assoc ed org chem, 67-75, sr assoc ed, 75-81, SR ED ORG CHEM, CHEM ABSTR SERV, 81- *Mem:* Am Chem Soc. *Mailing Add:* Dept 51 Chem Abstr Serv Columbus OH 43210

THEISEN, WILFRED ROBERT, b Sept 5, 29; US citizen. HISTORY OF SCIENCE, PHYSICS. *Educ:* St John's Univ, BA, 52; Univ Colo, MS, 63; Univ Wis, PhD(hist of sci), 72. *Prof Exp:* ASST PROF PHYSICS & HIST OF SCI, ST JOHN'S UNIV, MINN, 55- *Res:* Medieval optical manuscripts of Euclid. *Mailing Add:* St John's Univ Collegeville MN 56321

THEISS, JEFFREY CHARLES, b Stamford, Conn, Aug 29, 46; m 68; c 2. PHARMACOLOGY. *Educ:* Univ RI, BS, 68; Brown Univ, PhD(med sci), 73. *Prof Exp:* Res assoc biochem pharmacol, Roger Williams Gen Hosp & Brown Univ, 71-73; res fel biochem pharmacol, Univ Calif, San Diego & L C Strong Res Found, 73-75; asst res sci pharmacol & toxicol, Univ Calif, San Diego, 75-77, asst prof res community med, 75-80; MEM FAC, SCH PUB HEALTH, UNIV TEX, 80- *Mem:* Sigma Xi; AAAS. Mechanistic studies in chemical carcinogenesis and cocarcinogenesis; screening of chemicals for carcinogenic potency by the A mouse lung tumor bioassay. *Mailing Add:* Sch Pub Health Univ Tex PO Box 20186 Houston TX 77025

THEKDI, ARVIND C, b Ahmedabad, India, Aug 5, 41; US citizen. COMBUSTION ENGINEERING, HEAT TRANSFER. *Educ:* Gujarat Univ, India, BS, 63; Indian Inst Sci, Bangalore, MS, 65; Pa State Univ, PhD(fuel sci), 70. *Prof Exp:* Res engr, Surface Combustion, 70-73, mgr thermal systs, 73-77, mgr thermal & mech eng, 78-80, ASST DIR DEVELOP, TECH CTR, MIDLAND-ROSS CORP, 80- *Concurrent Pos:* Res asst, Pa State Univ, 67-70; instr, Toledo Univ, 72-74. *Mem:* Am Soc Mech Eng; Combustion Inst; Air Pollution Control Asn. *Res:* Energy conservation and conversion; combustion heat transfer; heat recovery; process development in carbon and graphite industry. *Mailing Add:* Midland-Ross Corp 900 N Westwood Toledo OH 43691

THEKKEKANDAM, JOSEPH THOMAS, b Kerala, India, May 14, 38; m 70. ORGANIC CHEMISTRY. *Educ:* Univ Kerala, BSc, 59; Univ India, MS, 62; Univ Detroit, PhD(chem), 70. *Prof Exp:* Asst lectr chem, MS, Univ India, 62-66; teaching asst, Univ Detroit, 66-70; Coun Tobacco Res fel, A&T State Univ, NC, 70-71; CHEMIST-IN-CHARGE RES & DEVELOP, KAY CHEM CO, 71- *Concurrent Pos:* Fulbright travel grant, Inst Int Educ, India, 66. *Mem:* Am Chem Soc. *Res:* Photochemistry of ammonium azides and amines; pesticide metabolism; synthetic detergents. *Mailing Add:* Res & Develop Kay Chem Co Greensboro NC 27409

THELEN, CHARLES JOHN, b Cedar Rapids, Nebr, Mar 2, 21; m 47; c 1. ORGANIC CHEMISTRY, AEROSPACE TECHNOLOGY. *Educ:* Univ Iowa, BS, 42, PhD(org chem), 49. *Prof Exp:* Chemist, B F Goodrich Co, 42; asst, Univ Iowa, 47-49; fel, Univ Calif, Los Angeles, 49-50; res chemist, US Naval Ord Test Sta, 50-58, head explosives & pyrotech div, 58-60, head propellants div, 60-68, MISSILE PROPULSION TECHNOL ADMINR, NAVAL WEAPONS CTR, 69- *Concurrent Pos:* Navy mem exec comt, Joint Army, Navy, NASA, Air Force Interagency Propulsion Comt, 74-; Michelson Lab fel mgt, Naval Weapons Ctr, 72. *Mem:* Am Chem Soc; Sigma Xi. *Res:* Missile propulsion technology and high polymers. *Mailing Add:* Naval Weapons Ctr Code 3205 China Lake CA 93555

THELEN, EDMUND, b Berkeley, Calif, May 8, 13; m 65; c 2. MATERIALS SCIENCE, INDUSTRIAL CHEMISTRY. *Educ:* Univ Calif, Berkeley, BS, 34. *Prof Exp:* Asst chemist, Certain-teed Prod Corp, 34-36; res chemist, OC Field Gasoline Corp, 36-41; asst to exec engr Eclipse-Pioneer Div, Bendix Aviation Corp, 46-47; sr res engr, 47-51, mgr colloids & polymers lab, 51-74, co-dir dent mat sci ctr, 69-74, dir phys & life sci dept, 74-76, SECY COMT SCI & ARTS, FRANKLIN INST, 76- *Concurrent Pos:* Instr, Hahnemann Med Col, 64-74. *Res:* Nonmetallic materials; materials and processes to promote health, safety, energy conservation and environment; porous pavements; dental materials; solar applications. *Mailing Add:* Franklin Inst 20th & & Parkway Philadelphia PA 19103

THELEN, THOMAS HARVEY, b Albany, Minn, Aug 11, 41; m 64; c 2. GENETICS. *Educ:* St John's Univ, Minn, BS, 64; Univ Minn, PhD(genetics), 69. *Prof Exp:* Cytogeneticist, Minn Dept Health, 69-70; asst prof, 70-74, ASSOC PROF BIOL, CENT WASH UNIV, 74- *Res:* Behavioral genetics, human genetics, and related areas. *Mailing Add:* Dept of Biol Cent Wash Univ Ellensburg WA 98926

THELIN, JACK HORSTMANN, b Kearny, NJ, Aug 15, 12; m 39; c 2. CHEMISTRY. *Educ:* Maryville Col, BA, 38; Univ Tenn, MS, 39; Rutgers Univ, PhD(phys chem), 43. *Prof Exp:* Res chemist, Calco Chem Co Div, Am Cyanamid Co, 36-41, develop chemist, 41-45, asst chief develop chemist dye intermediates div, 45-46, chief develop chemist, 46-53, res chemist, Res Div, 53-77; RETIRED. *Mem:* Am Soc Testing & Mat; Am Chem Soc. *Res:* Sulfonation; nitration and alkylation; system ammonium sulfamate; sodium nitrate; ammonium nitrate; polymer physical testing equipment; polymer tribology. *Mailing Add:* 126 E Spring St Somerville NJ 08876

THELMAN, JOHN PATRICK, b Richmond Hill, NY, Dec 25, 42; m 65; c 3. PAPER CHEMISTRY. *Educ:* State Univ NY Stony Brook, BS, 64; State Univ NY Buffalo, PhD(org chem), 69. *Prof Exp:* Res chemist, 68-71, res group leader acetate sect, ITT Rayonnier Inc, Whippany, NJ, 71-74, res supvr acetate sect, Eastern Res Div, 74-77; chief res proj chemist, 77-81, RES SCIENTIST, SCOTT PAPER CO, PHILADELPHIA, 81- *Mem:* Am Chem Soc; Tech Asn Pulp & Paper Indust. *Res:* Papermaking; product development. *Mailing Add:* 974 Jefferis Bridge Dr West Chester PA 19380

THEMELIS, NICKOLAS JOHN, chemical engineering, see previous edition

THENEN, SHIRLEY WARNOCK, b San Mateo, Calif; m 62; c 2. OBESITY, VITAMINS. *Educ:* Univ Calif, Berkeley, AB, 57, PhD(nutrit), 70. *Prof Exp:* Res fel hemat & med, Harvard Med Sch & Mass Gen Hosp, 70-72; asst prof, 72-80, ASSOC PROF NUTRIT, SCH PUB HEALTH, HARVARD UNIV, 80- *Concurrent Pos:* NIH res career develop award, 75-80. *Mem:* Am Inst Nutrit; Soc Exp Biol & Med; Geront Soc Am; NY Acad Sci; Soc Nutrit Ed. *Res:* Significance of folic acid and vitamin B-12 metabolism in hemopoiesis and during pregnancy; mechanisms of biochemical and endocrine abnormalities in obesity and diabetes; insulin resistance in aging; vitamin C interactions. *Mailing Add:* Dept of Nutrit Harvard Univ Sch of Pub Health Boston MA 02115

THEOBALD, CHARLES EDWIN, JR, b Hackensack, NJ, Aug 14, 27; m 52; c 3. ELECTRICAL ENGINEERING, OPERATIONS RESEARCH. *Educ:* Columbia Univ, AB, 47, AM, 48; Mass Inst Technol, SM, 59. *Prof Exp:* Aerodynamicist, Curtiss-Wright Corp, NJ, 49-56; sr aerodynamicist, Kaman Aircraft Corp, Conn, 56-58; teaching asst instrumentation & control, Mass Inst Technol, 58-59; sr scientist, Syst Develop Corp, 59-67; prin engr, Systs Electronics Lab, Raytheon Co, 67-74; ENG CONSULT, 74- *Res:* Adaptive learning and optimal control; statistical decision theory; queueing theory; reliability theory; stability and control of fixed and rotary wing aircraft; public transit operations; railroad track dynamics and geometry. *Mailing Add:* 37 Old Billerica Rd Bedford MA 01730

THEOBALD, J KARL, b Prescott, Ariz, Feb 18, 21; m 42, 67. PHYSICS. *Educ:* Univ Calif, PhD(physics), 52. *Prof Exp:* Physicist, Los Alamos Sci Lab, 52-76; PHYSICIST, EG&G, INC, 76- *Mem:* Optical Soc Am; Am Geophys Union. *Res:* Fiber optics; radiation effects. *Mailing Add:* 130 Robin Hill Rd Goleta CA 93017

THEOBALD, JOHN J(ACOB), b New York, NY, Sept 8, 04; m 28; c 2. ENGINEERING. *Educ:* Columbia Univ, AB, 25, BS, 26, CE, 28, PhD(polit sci), 35. *Hon Degrees:* LLD, Columbia Univ, 54, Syracuse Univ, 56, Long Island Univ & Hofstra Col, 58; LHD, St John's Univ, NY, 56; hon DSc, Wagner Col, 56; hon EngD, Polytech Inst Brooklyn, 57; DLitt, Del Valley Col, 74. *Prof Exp:* Supt pub works, Lawrence, NY, 29-31; from instr to prof civil eng, City Col New York, 31-49, dean admin, 46-49; pres, Queen Col, NY, 49-58; exec vpres, 66-74, DEAN GRAD STUDIES, NY INST TECHNOL, 74-; EMER PRES, QUEENS COL, NY, 58- *Concurrent Pos:* Consult engr, 29-39; consult admin, 33-35 & 39-41; adj prof, Sch Eng & Sch Archit, Columbia Univ, 43-49; dep mayor, New York, 56-58, supt schs, 58-62; vpres, US Indust, Inc, 62-66 & dir educ & training, 65-66; cluster dir, Doctoral Prog Public Admin, Nova Univ, 77-; mem bd, Ford Fac Fel Prog. *Mem:* Am Soc Civil Engrs; Soc Naval Architects & Marine Engrs; Soc Small Craft Designers; Am Mus Natural Hist. *Res:* City planning; engineering administration; municipal engineering. *Mailing Add:* NY Inst of Technol Wheatley Rd Old Westbury NY 11568

THEOBALD, WILLIAM L, b New York, NY, Feb 12, 36. SYSTEMATIC BOTANY, HORTICULTURE. *Educ:* Rutgers Univ, BS, 58, MS, 59; Univ Calif, Los Angeles, PhD(bot), 63. *Prof Exp:* Lectr biol, Univ Calif, Santa Barbara, 63-65; NSF fel, Jodrell Lab, Royal Bot Gardens, Kew, Eng, 65-66; fel, Evolutionary Biol, Gray Herbarium, Harvard Univ, 66-67; asst prof biol, Occidental Col, 67-71; assoc prof bot, Univ Hawaii, 71-75; DIR, PAC TROP BOT GARDEN, LAWAI, HAWAII, 75- *Concurrent Pos:* Res assoc bot, Univ Hawaii & Bishop Mus, 75- *Mem:* Bot Soc Am; Am Soc Plant Taxon; fel Linnean Soc London; Int Asn Plant Taxon; Am Asn Bot Gardens & Arboreta. *Res:* Flora of Hawaii, Pacific Islands and Ceylon; systematics of Gesneriaceae, Acanthaceae, Araliaceae, Bignoniaceae, Umbelliferae; trichome anatomy and classification in angiosperms; comparative anatomical studies. *Mailing Add:* Pac Trop Bot Garden PO Box 340 Lawai Kauai HI 96765

THEODORE, JOHN G(EORGE), b Boston, Mass, June 15, 23; m 48; c 4. CHEMICAL ENGINEERING, MECHANICAL METALLURGY. *Educ:* Fenn Col, BS, 49. *Prof Exp:* Engr res & develop, Brush Wellman Co, 49-53, staff engr, 53-55, sect supvr, 55-58, div mgr, 58-73; mgr process eng, 73-75, dir process eng & control, 75-76, DIR QUAL ASSURANCE, S K WELLMAN INC, 76- *Mem:* Am Ord Asn; Am Power Metall Inst. *Res:* Extractive metallurgy of beryllium and zirconium; solid state reactions; ceramics and powder metallurgy; high temperature materials development and evaluation; micromeritics; product, process and fabrication development in powdered materials, process engineering and quality control of organic and inorganic friction materials and product lines. *Mailing Add:* Dir of Qual Assurance S K Wellman Inc Bedford OH 44146

THEODORE, JOSEPH M, JR, b Fall River, Mass, Apr 29, 31; m 55; c 5. PHARMACY. *Educ:* New Eng Col Pharm, BS, 55; Univ Wis, MS, 58; Mass Col Pharm, PhD(pharm), 65. *Prof Exp:* Instr pharm, New Eng Col Pharm, 58-61; from instr to asst prof, Northeastern Univ, 62-66; assoc prof, 66-74, PROF PHARM, OHIO NORTHERN UNIV, 74- *Mem:* Am Pharmaceut Asn; Am Col Apothecaries; Am Soc Hosp Pharmacists. *Res:* Spectrofluorometric analysis of drugs; solid state reactions occurring in certain tablet formulations. *Mailing Add:* Dept of Pharm Ohio Northern Univ Ada OH 45810

THEODORE, LOUIS, chemical engineering, see previous edition

THEODORE, TED GEORGE, b Los Angeles, Calif, Aug 19, 37; m 61; c 2. ECONOMIC GEOLOGY. *Educ:* Univ Calif, Los Angeles, AB, 61, PhD(geol), 67. *Prof Exp:* GEOLOGIST, US GEOL SURV, 67- *Mem:* AAAS; Geol Soc Am; Soc Econ Geol. *Res:* Genesis of porphyrytype, molybdenum and copper deposits; geochemistry of base-metal ore deposits; fabrics of metamorphic terranes. *Mailing Add:* US Geol Surv 345 Middlefield Rd Menlo Park CA 94025

THEODORE, THEODORE SPIROS, b Braddock, Pa, Nov 6, 33; m 57; c 3. MICROBIAL PHYSIOLOGY. *Educ:* Univ Pitteburgh, BSc, 55, MSc, 57, PhD(bact), 62. *Prof Exp:* Asst bact, Univ Pittsburgh, 57-62; staff fel, NIH, 62-65, res microbiologist, 65-76; MEM STAFF, LAB STEPOCOCCAL DIS, NAT INST ALLERGY & INFECTIOUS DIS, NIH, 76- *Mem:* AAAS; Am Soc Microbiol. *Res:* Bacterial physiology and nutrition; intermediary and mineral metabolism; biochemical genetics. *Mailing Add:* 1136 Pipestem Place Rockville MD 20854

THEODORIDES, VASSILIOS JOHN, b Konstantia, Greece, Feb 20, 31; US citizen; m 58; c 3. VETERINARY PARASITOLOGY. *Educ:* Univ Thessaloniki, DVM, 56; Boston Univ, MA, 60, PhD(parasitol), 63. *Prof Exp:* Asst to prof clins vet sch, Univ Thessaloniki, 56-57; teaching fel microbiol, Boston Univ, 58-62; lectr micros anat, 62-63; res parasitologist, Charles Pfizer & Co, Inc, 63-65; sr microbiologist parasitologist, Smith Kline & French Labs, 65-66, group leader microbiol, 66-68, group leader animal health dept, 68, assoc dir res chemother, 68-73, MGR PARASITOL, SMITH KLINE CORP, 73- *Concurrent Pos:* Adj prof, Sch Vet Med, Univ Pa, 72- *Mem:* Am Soc Microbiol; Am Vet Med Asn; Am Soc Parasitol; Am Soc Trop Med & Hyg; NY Acad Sci. *Res:* Morphology, physiology and electron microscopy of Trichomonas; development of chemotherapeutic agents for the control of gastrointestinal nematodes of domestic animals. *Mailing Add:* 1621 Margo Lane West Chester PA 19380

THEODORIDIS, GEORGE CONSTANTIN, b Braila, Romania, Dec 3, 35; US citizen; m 75; c 1. BIOMEDICAL ENGINEERING. *Educ:* Nat Tech Univ Athens, dipl elec eng, 59; Mass Inst Technol, ScD(nuclear eng), 64. *Prof Exp:* Res assoc biol, Mass Inst Technol, 64; sr scientist space res, Am Sci Eng, Mass, 64-68; assoc prof physiol optics, Univ Calif, Berkeley, 68-70; ASSOC PROF BIOMED ENG, UNIV VA, 70- *Concurrent Pos:* Prof, Univ Patras, Greece, 76-; consult, Food & Drug Admin, 77-78 & Appl Physics Lab, Johns Hopkins Univ, 78. *Mem:* Biomed Eng Soc; Am Phys Soc; Inst Elec & Electronics Engrs; Am Geophys Union; NY Acad Sci. *Res:* Speech perception; evolution; space physics. *Mailing Add:* Dept of Biomed Eng Univ of Va Charlottesville VA 22908

THEOFANOUS, THEOFANIS GEORGE, b Athens, Greece, May 21, 42; m 69; c 2. NUCLEAR ENGINEERING. *Educ:* Nat Tech Univ Athens, dipl, 65; Univ Minn, Minneapolis, PhD(chem eng), 69. *Prof Exp:* Instr chem eng, Univ Minn, Minneapolis, 68-69; from asst prof to assoc prof chem eng, 69-74, assoc prof, 74-76, PROF NUCLEAR ENG, PURDUE UNIV, 77- *Concurrent Pos:* Consult, Adv Comt on Reactor Safeguards, 71; vpres, FGH&T Ltd, Multiphase Flow Applications, 77-81; mem, CSNI Group of Experts on Fuel Coolant Interactions of the Sci of Vapor Explosions, 77; pres, Theofanous & Co Inc, 81-; mem nuclear regulatory res, Spec Rev Comt on Liquid Metal Fast Breeder Reactor Safety Res, 81- *Mem:* AAAS; Am Soc Eng Educ; Am Nuclear Soc; Am Inst Chem Engrs. *Res:* Transport phenomena in turbulent and multiphase systems with particular emphasis on nuclear and chemical reactor safety applications. *Mailing Add:* Sch of Nuclear Eng Purdue Univ West Lafayette IN 47907

THEOHAROUS, LEWIS, b Sayre, Pa, June 6, 23; m 55; c 3. CHEMICAL ENGINEERING. *Educ:* Northeastern Univ, BS, 45; Mass Inst Technol, MS, 49. *Prof Exp:* Proj engr & group leader, 49-55, sect head, Process Develop Dept, 55-65, assoc dir, Tech Serv Dept, 66-68, assoc dir process develop, Packaged Soap Div, 68-70, ASSOC DIR ENVIRON WATER QUAL RES DEPT, PROCTER & GAMBLE CO, 70- *Res:* Process development of synthetic detergents and related products. *Mailing Add:* 320 Ardon Lane Cincinnati OH 45215

THEOKRITOFF, GEORGE, b Eng, Apr 7, 24; Can citizen. PALEONTOLOGY. *Educ:* Univ London, BSc, 45, MSc, 48, PhD(geol), 61. *Prof Exp:* Instr geol, Mt Holyoke Col, 54-56 & Bucknell Univ, 56-60; asst prof geol, Univ NH, 60-61; assoc prof geol, St Lawrence Univ, 64-67; ASSOC PROF GEOL, RUTGERS UNIV, NEWARK, 67- *Mem:* Geol Soc Am; Geol Soc London; Paleont Soc. *Res:* Cambrian paleontology and stratigraphy, including morphology, taxonomy and evolution of Cambrian trilobites; ecology of Cambrian organisms; biogeography and biostratigraphy of North Atlantic region. *Mailing Add:* Dept Geol Rutgers Univ Newark NJ 07102

THEOLOGIDES, ATHANASIOS, b Ptolemais, Greece, Feb 5, 31; US citizen; m 65; c 2. INTERNAL MEDICINE, ONCOLOGY. *Educ:* Aristoteles Univ, MD, 55; Univ Minn, Minneapolis, PhD(med & biochem), 67. *Prof Exp:* From instr to assoc prof, 65-74, Nat Cancer Inst grant, Med Ctr, 69-75, PROF MED, MED SCH, UNIV MINN, MINNEAPOLIS, 74- *Mem:* Am Asn Cancer Res; Am Fedn Clin Res; Am Soc Clin Oncol; Soc Exp Biol & Med; Am Soc Hemat. *Res:* Medical oncology; tumor-host metabolic interrelationships; hematology. *Mailing Add:* Dept of Med Univ of Minn Med Ctr Minneapolis MN 55455

THERIOT, EDWARD DENNIS, JR, b Baton Rouge, La, Mar 19, 38; m 60; c 2. PHYSICS. *Educ:* Duke Univ, BS, 60; Yale Univ, MS, 61, PhD(physics), 67. *Prof Exp:* NATO vis scientist fel physics, Europ Orgn Nuclear Res, Geneva, Switz, 67-68; res fel, Los Alamos Sci Lab, 68-69; head neutrino dept, 76-78, PHYSICIST, FERMI NAT ACCELERATOR LAB, 69- *Mem:* Am Phys Soc. *Res:* Elementary particle physics, particularly relating to weak and electromagnetic interactions; neutrino interactions; hyperon decays; particle production; positronium; proton-antiproton colliding beams. *Mailing Add:* Fermi Nat Accelerator Lab PO Box 500 Batavia IL 60510

THERIOT, LEROY JAMES, b Port Arthur, Tex, Apr 11, 35; m 58; c 3. INORGANIC CHEMISTRY. *Educ:* Southwestern La Univ, BS, 57; Tulane Univ, PhD(chem), 62. *Prof Exp:* Chemist, Ethyl Corp, 62-63; fel, Harvard Univ, 63-64 & Univ Tex, 64-65; asst prof, 65-70, assoc prof, 70-80, PROF CHEM, NTEX STATE UNIV, 80- *Mem:* Am Chem Soc. *Res:* Preparation and electronic structure of metal complexes. *Mailing Add:* Dept of Chem NTex State Univ Denton TX 76203

THERRIAULT, DONALD G, b Claremont, NH, June 14, 27; m 52; c 4. BIOCHEMISTRY. *Educ:* Univ Ottawa, BSc, 50; Univ NH, MS, 52; Univ Louisville, PhD, 60. *Prof Exp:* Asst biochem, Ind Univ, 52-54; res biochemist, US Army Med Res Lab, 54-62, res biochemist, US Army Res Inst Environ Med, 62-66, chief biochem & pharmacol div, 66-72; health scientist adminr, Thrombosis & Hemorrrhagic Dis Br, Nat Heart & Lung Inst, 72-80; ASST ADMINR, DEPT HUMAN NUTRIT, SCI EDUC ADMIN, USDA, 80- *Mem:* AAAS; Am Soc Biol Chem; fel Am Inst Chem; fel NY Acad Sci; Am Oil Chem Soc. *Res:* Application of physicochemical methods to the problem of interaction of calcium ions and phospholipids with purified plasma proteins involved in blood coagulation. *Mailing Add:* Dept Human Nutrit USDA Sci & Educ Admin Bldg 005 Rm 28A Bethesda MD 20014

THERRIEN, CHESTER DALE, b Coos Bay, Ore, June 18, 36; m 60; c 2. MYCOLOGY, CYTOCHEMISTRY. *Educ:* St Ambrose Col, BA, 62; Univ Tex, PhD(bot), 66. *Prof Exp:* Asst prof biol, 65-70, ASSOC PROF BIOL, PA STATE UNIV, 70- *Mem:* Bot Soc Am; Genetics Soc Am. *Res:* Nucleic acids and nucleoproteins is the plasmodial slime molds. *Mailing Add:* Dept Biol 208 Mueller Lab Pa State Univ University Park PA 16802

THEUER, RICHARD CHARLES, b Hoboken, NJ, June 15, 39; m 62; c 3. NUTRITION. *Educ:* St Peter's Col, NJ, BS, 60; Univ Wis, Madison, MS, 62, PhD(biochem), 65; Ind State Univ, MBA, 73. *Prof Exp:* Res asst biochem, Univ Wis, 60-62 & 64-65; sr scientist, Mead Johnson Res Ctr, 65-67, group leader, 67-68, sect leader, 68-70, dir dept nutrit res, 70-75; DIR NUTRIT RES, INT DIV, BRISTOL-MYERS CO, 76- *Mem:* AAAS; Am Chem Soc; Am Inst Nutrit; Sigma Xi. *Res:* Infant nutrition; research and development of nutritional specialty products. *Mailing Add:* Bristol-Myers Co Int Div 345 Park Ave New York NY 10022

THEUER, WILLIAM JOHN, b New York, NY, Nov 27, 35; m 61; c 3. ORGANIC CHEMISTRY. *Educ:* Queens Col, BS, 57; Univ Del, PhD(chem), 65. *Prof Exp:* Sr scientist, Sandoz Pharmaceut, 65-67; res chemist, Celanese Res Co, 67-68, sr res chemist, Celanese Fibers Co, 68-71, group leader, Celanese Fibers Mkt Co, 71-74, tech mgr, 74-76, prod mgr, 76-77, tech dir resins, 78, TECH DIR EMULSIONS, CELANESE POLYMER/SPECIALTIES CO, 79- *Mem:* Am Chem Soc; Am Asn Textile Chemists & Colorists; Int Disposable & Nonwoven Asn. *Res:* Heterocyclic chemistry; photochemistry; cellulose and fiber chemistry; spinning research; pharmaceutical chemistry; industrial uses of fibers; textile polymer chemistry. *Mailing Add:* Celanese Plastics & Specs Co PO Box 32190 Louisville KY 40232

THEURER, CLARK BRENT, b Logan, Utah, Oct 17, 34; m 56; c 4. ANIMAL NUTRITION. *Educ:* Utah State Univ, BS, 56; Iowa State Univ, MS, 60, PhD(animal nutrit), 62. *Prof Exp:* Asst prof animal sci, Va Polytech Inst, 62-64; assoc prof, 64-71, PROF ANIMAL SCI, UNIV ARIZ, 71-, ANIMAL SCIENTIST, AGR EXP STA, 74- *Mem:* Am Soc Animal Sci; Am Dairy Sci Asn; Am Inst Nutrit; Soc Range Mgt. *Res:* Regulation of voluntary feed intake in ruminants; techniques in range livestock nutrition; starch, protein and volatile fatty acid metabolism in ruminants. *Mailing Add:* Dept of Animal Sci Univ of Ariz Tucson AZ 85721

THEURER, JESSOP CLAIR, b Logan, Utah, Sept 4, 28; m 53; c 4. PLANT GENETICS, PLANT BREEDING. *Educ:* Utah State Univ, BS, 53, MS, 57; Univ Minn, PhD(plant genetics), 62. *Prof Exp:* Res fel oats radiation, Univ Minn, 61-62; res agronomist, 62-63, GENETICIST, CROPS RES DIV, AGR RES SERV, USDA, 63- *Concurrent Pos:* Int farm youth exchange student, Lebanon & Syria, 52; assoc ed, Crop Sci Soc Am, 70-72. *Mem:* Am Soc Agron; Am Soc Sugar Beet Technol. *Res:* Agronomy; cytology; plant pathology; breeding, genetics and disease resistance of sugar beets; potential of sugar beets and fodder beets for fuel alcohol production. *Mailing Add:* Crops Res Lab Utah State Univ UMC63 Logan UT 84322

THEUSCH, COLLEEN JOAN, b Milwaukee, Wis, Dec 18, 32. NUMBER THEORY, OPERATIONS RESEARCH. *Educ:* Dominican Col, Wis, BEd, 61; Univ Detroit, MA, 66; Mich State Univ, PhD(math), 71. *Prof Exp:* Instr math, Col Racine, 70-71; MATHEMATICIAN, RES & DEVELOP DEPT, RICHMAN BROS CO, 71- *Mem:* Am Math Soc. *Res:* Development of grading and marker making system and numerically controlled cutting via laser cutters in men's clothing manufacturing. *Mailing Add:* 1376 Lakeland Ave Lakewood OH 44107

THEWALT, MICHAEL LUDWIG WOLFGANG, optics, semiconductors, see previous edition

THEWS, ROBERT LEROY, b Fairmont, Minn, June 13, 39; c 2. THEORETICAL PHYSICS. *Educ:* Mass Inst Technol, SB, 62, PhD(physics), 66. *Prof Exp:* Physicist, Lawrence Berkeley Lab, Univ Calif, 66-68; res assoc & asst prof physics, Univ Rochester, 68-70; asst prof, 70-75, assoc prof, 75-80, PROF PHYSICS, UNIV ARIZ, 80- *Mem:* Am Phys Soc. *Res:* Theoretical high energy elementary particle physics. *Mailing Add:* Dept Physics Univ Ariz Tucson AZ 85721

THEYS, JOHN C, astrophysics, see previous edition

THIBAULT, ROGER EDWARD, b Salem, Mass, June 28, 47; m 70. ECOLOGY. *Educ:* Univ Wis, BS, 69; Univ Conn, PhD(ecol), 74. *Prof Exp:* NDEA fel ecol, Univ Conn, 71-74; instr zool, Iowa State Univ, 74-75; ASST PROF BIOL, BOWLING GREEN STATE UNIV, 75- *Mem:* Am Soc Ichthyol & Herpet; Ecol Soc Am; Soc Study Evolution; Sigma Xi; AAAS. *Res:* Aquatic ecology; aquatic entomology and ichthyology; evolution of unisexual vertebrates. *Mailing Add:* Dept of Biol Sci Bowling Green State Univ Bowling Green OH 43402

THIBAULT, THOMAS DELOR, b Claremont, NH, Aug 14, 42; m 69; c 4. ORGANIC CHEMISTRY. *Educ:* Providence Col, BS, 64; Mass Inst Technol, PhD(org chem), 69. *Prof Exp:* Sr org chemist, 69-74, RES SCIENTIST, ELI LILLY & CO, 74- *Mem:* Am Chem Soc. *Res:* Synthesis of biologically active structures; reaction mechanisms; new synthetic reactions. *Mailing Add:* Eli Lilly & Co Box 708 Greenfield IN 46140

THIBEAULT, JACK CLAUDE, b Lowell, Mass, June 23, 46; m 66; c 1. COLLOID CHEMISTRY, COATINGS TECHNOLOGY. *Educ:* Lowell Technol Inst, BS, 67; Calif Inst Technol, PhD(inorg chem), 72. *Prof Exp:* Fel theoret chem, Cornell Univ, 72-74; RES CHEMIST, ROHM AND HAAS CO, 74- *Mem:* Am Chem Soc. *Res:* Physical chemistry of coatings. *Mailing Add:* 6529 Timothy Ct Cornwells Heights PA 19020

THIBERT, ROGER JOSEPH, b Tecumseh, Ont, Aug 29, 29; m 54; c 2. CHEMISTRY. *Educ:* Univ Western Ont, BA, 51; Univ Detroit, MS, 54; Wayne State Univ, PhD(biochem), 58. *Prof Exp:* Lectr chem, 53-56, from asst prof to assoc prof, 57-67, assoc dean arts & sci, 64-70, PROF CHEM, UNIV WINDSOR, 67- *Concurrent Pos:* Instr sch nursing, Grace Hosp, 54-73; res assoc sch med, Wayne State Univ, 71-72, prof path, 72-; assoc div head clin chem lab, Detroit Gen Hosp, Mich, 71- *Mem:* Fel AAAS; Am Chem Soc; fel Chem Inst Can; Am Soc Biol Chem; Am Asn Clin Chem. *Res:* Clinical biochemistry. *Mailing Add:* Dept Chem Univ Windsor Windsor ON N9B 3P4 Can

THIBODAUX, JOSEPH G, chemical engineering, see previous edition

THIBODEAU, GARY ARTHUR, b Sioux City, Iowa, Sept 26, 38; m 64; c 2. PHYSIOLOGY, PHARMACOLOGY. *Educ:* Creighton Univ, BS, 62; SDak State Univ, MS, 67, MS, 70, PhD(physiol), 71. *Prof Exp:* Mem prof serv staff, Baxter Labs, Inc, 63-65; from asst prof to assoc prof entom-zool, 65-80, PROF BIOL, SDAK STATE UNIV, 80-, VPRES, 80- *Mem:* AAAS; Am Inst Biol Sci; Am Pub Health Asn. *Res:* Animal physiology; pharmacology of hypolipedemic agents; pathological dyslipemias; thyroid physiology; vascular morphology. *Mailing Add:* Dept of Entom-Zool SDak State Univ Brookings SD 57006

THIBODEAUX, LOUIS J, b Church Point, La, Nov 14, 39; m 59; c 2. ENGINEERING. *Educ:* La State Univ, BS, 62, MS, 66, PhD(ionic diffusion), 68. *Prof Exp:* Engr, E I du Pont de Nemours & Co, 62-64, Uniroyal, Inc, 64 & Nat Coun Air Stream Improv, 64-68; from asst prof to assoc prof, 68-76, PROF CHEM ENG, UNIV ARK, FAYETTEVILLE, 76- *Concurrent Pos:* Res grant, 68-69, 72-73; consult, Ga Kraft Co, 69 & Int Paper Co, 70- *Mem:* AAAS; Am Inst Chem Engrs; Am Chem Soc; Sigma Xi (pres, 77-78). *Res:* Movement of chemicals in the environment, environmental chemistry and interphase mass transfer; fate, life-time, transport rates, direction of movement, chemodynamics of trace chemicals in the natural environment. *Mailing Add:* Dept of Chem Eng Col of Eng Univ of Ark Fayetteville AR 72701

THICH, JOHN ADONG, b London, Eng, Nov 16, 48; US citizen; m 74. AEROSPACE LUBRICANTS. *Educ:* Temple Univ, Pa, BA, 70; Rutgers Univ, NJ, PhD(inorg chem), 75. *Prof Exp:* Res fel chem, Calif Inst Technol, 75-77; scientist, Rohm and Haas Co, Pa, 77-79; GROUP LEADER CHEM, ROYAL LUBRICANTS CO, INC, NJ, 79- *Mem:* Am Chem Soc; Am Soc Lubrication Engrs; Am Soc Testing & Mat; Nat Asn Corrosion Engrs. *Res:* Development of high performance fluids and lubricants for the aerospace industry and the United States military. *Mailing Add:* 210 William St Boonton NJ 07005

THICKSTUN, WILLIAM RUSSELL, JR, b Washington, DC, Oct 14, 22; m 54. MATHEMATICS. *Educ:* Univ Md, BSc, 47, MA, 49, PhD, 52. *Prof Exp:* Mathematician, US Naval Ord Lab, Md, 53-68; assoc prof math, Clarkson Col Technol, 68-76 & Univ Petrol & Mineral, Saudi Arabia, 76-78; ASSOC PROF MATH, ST LAWRENCE UNIV, 76- *Mem:* Am Math Soc; Soc Indust & Appl Math; Am Inst Aeronaut & Astronaut. *Res:* Applied mathematics; fluid dynamics. *Mailing Add:* Dept of Math St Lawrence Univ Canton NY 13617

THIE, JOSEPH ANTHONY, b Indianapolis, Ind, Dec 15, 27. REACTOR PHYSICS. *Educ:* Univ Notre Dame, BS, 47, PhD(physics), 51. *Prof Exp:* Instr physics, Univ Dayton, 47-48; AEC fel, Cornell Univ, 51-52; assoc physicist, Argonne Nat Lab, 53-60; partner & consult, McLain Rodger Assocs, 60-61; INDEPENDENT NUCLEAR REACTOR CONSULT, 61- *Mem:* Am Nuclear Soc. *Res:* Reactor safety; reactor random fluctuation phenomena; heavy water exponential experiments. *Mailing Add:* PO Box 517 Barrington IL 60010

THIEBAUX, HELEN JEAN, b Washington, DC, Aug 17, 35; m 62; c 4. APPLIED STATISTICS. *Educ:* Reed Col, BA, 57; Univ Ore, MA, 60; Stanford Univ, PhD(statist), 64. *Prof Exp:* Res asst econ & indust, Ivan Block & Assoc, Econ & Indust Consult, 58; statist analyst, Med Sch, Univ Ore, summer 60; asst pub health analyst, Calif Dept Pub Health, summer 61; asst prof statist, Univ Conn, 64-65; asst prof, Univ Mass, Amherst, 65-66 & 67-71; lectr, Univ Colo, Boulder, 72-73; consult & vis scientist, Nat Ctr Atmospheric Res, 72-74; assoc prof, 75-81, PROF MATH, DALHOUSIE UNIV, 81- *Concurrent Pos:* Assoc ed, Can J Statist. *Mem:* Fel Royal Meteorol Soc; Statist Soc Can; Can Meteorol & Oceanog Soc. *Res:* Statistical modelling and estimation for spatially coherent systems; applications to meteorology and oceanography. *Mailing Add:* Dept Math Statist Comput Sci Dalhousie Univ Halifax NS B3H 4H8 Can

THIEBERGER, PETER, b Vienna, Austria, Sept 19, 35; m 63; c 1. EXPERIMENTAL NUCLEAR PHYSICS. *Educ:* Balseiro Inst Physics, Argentina, MS, 59; Univ Stockholm, Fil lic, 61, Fil Dr(physics), 62. *Prof Exp:* Physicist, Bariloche Atomic Ctr, Argentine AEC, 62-65; res asst, 65-67, from asst physicist to assoc physicist, 67-70, physicist, 70-74, head, Tandem Van De Graaff Facil Opers, 71-75, SR PHYSICIST, BROOKHAVEN NAT LAB, 74-, GROUP LEADER TANDEM VAN DE GRAAF FACIL OPERS & DEVELOP GROUP, 75- *Concurrent Pos:* Asst prof, Balseiro Inst Physics, 62-63, prof, 63-65; vis scientist, Res Inst Physics, Stockholm, Sweden, 68-69; consult, Tennelec Instrument Co, 67-71, Arg Atomic Energy Comn, 77- & Techint SACI, Arg, 78-80; NSF grants for coop res with Latin Am, 76- *Mem:* Fel Am Phys Soc. *Res:* Nuclear structure; measurements of half-lives and g-factors of nuclear states; development of nuclear instruments and methods; nuclear reactions with heavy ions; molecular ion structure measurements; accelerator development and operation. *Mailing Add:* Physics Dept Brookhaven Nat Lab Upton NY 11973

THIEDE, EDWIN CARL, b Richland Co, Wis, Nov 11, 37; m 64. ELECTRICAL ENGINEERING. *Educ:* Univ Wis-Madison, BS, 59; Univ Calif, Los Angeles, MS, 64; Stanford Univ, PhD(elec eng), 68. *Prof Exp:* Dynamics engr, Gen Dynamics/Astronaut, 59-62; tech staff engr, Hughes Aircraft Co, 63-65; res asst radar astron, Stanford Electronics Lab, 65-68; asst prof elec eng, Univ Minn, Minneapolis, 68-73; SR PRIN SCIENTIST, HONEYWELL, SYSTS & RES CTR, MINNEAPOLIS, 73- *Concurrent Pos:* Consult, Univac Defense Systs Div, Sperry Rand Corp, 72-; instr, Hennepin County Vo-Tech, 74- *Mem:* Inst Elec & Electronics Engrs. *Res:* Statistical communication theory, target detection and classification, radar signal processing in avionics and guided missiles, digital filtering, optimal filtering. *Mailing Add:* Honeywell Systs & Res Ctr 2600 Ridgway Pkwy Minneapolis MN 55413

THIEDE, HENRY A, b Rochester, NY, Oct 2, 26; m 51; c 2. OBSTETRICS & GYNECOLOGY. *Educ:* Univ Buffalo, MD, 49. *Prof Exp:* Intern surg, Buffalo Gen Hosp, 49-50; asst resident obstet & gynec, Genesee & Strong Mem Hosps, Rochester, 52-54; resident, Genesee Hosp, 54-56; from instr to assoc prof, Sch Med, Univ Rochester, 57-66; prof obstet & gynec & chmn dept, Sch Med, Univ Miss, 67-77, asst dean, Sch Med, 70-73, assoc dean, 73-77; PROF & CHMN DEPT OBSTET & GYNEC, OBSTETRICIAN & GYNECOLOGIST-IN-CHIEF, UNIV ROCHESTER MED SCH, 77- *Mem:* Am Col Obstet & Gynec; Soc Gynec Invest; Am Gynec & Obstet Soc; Am Gynec Club; Am Fertil Soc. *Res:* Biology of reproduction and reproduction wastage. *Mailing Add:* Dept of Obstet & Gynec Univ of Rochester Med Sch Rochester NY 14642

THIEL, FRANK L(OUIS), b Buffalo, NY, July 22, 42; m 63; c 2. FIBER OPTICS, OPTICAL WAVEGUIDES. *Educ:* Rensselaer Polytech Inst, BEE, 64, MEE, 65, PhD(electrophys), 69. *Prof Exp:* Instr elec eng, Rensselaer Polytech Inst, 65-69; sr physicist, Corning Glass Works, 69-71, sr res physicist, 71-75, mgr, 75-81; CHIEF ENGR & TECH MGR, OPTICAL FIBRES, DEESIDE, CLWYD, WALES, UK, 81- *Concurrent Pos:* Lectr optical waveguide courses, Univ Colo, 74-76 & George Washington Univ, 74-75. *Mem:* Inst Elec & Electronics Engrs; Am Phys Soc. *Res:* Electronic materials; physical electronics; opto-electronics; optical waveguides and associated components and processes. *Mailing Add:* Optical Fibres Second Ave Deeside Indust Park Deeside CH5 2NX Wales

THIEL, THOMAS J, b Upper Sandusky, Ohio, Dec 31, 28; m 55; c 4. SOIL PHYSICS, HYDROLOGY. *Educ:* Ohio State Univ, BS, 56, MS, 59. *Prof Exp:* Soil scientist, 57-63, soil scientist & asst adminr, 63-72, PROG ANALYST, PROG PLANNING & REV, AGR RES SERV, USDA, 72- *Honors & Awards:* Commendation Award, Soil Conserv Soc. *Mem:* Am Soc Agron; Soil Sci Soc Am; Soil Conserv Soc; Asn Comput Mach. *Res:* Analog, numerical, model and field studies on the drainage of agricultural lands, specifically on drainage of heavy-clay lake-bed soils, sloping fragipan soils and peat soils under artesian pressure; computer and systems analysis and information retrieval; program and administrative management especially in the area of soil and water conservation. *Mailing Add:* USDA Agr Res Serv NCent Region 2000 W Pioneer Pkwy Peoria IL 61615

THIELE, ELIZABETH HENRIETTE, b Portland, Ore, Apr 26, 20. BIOCHEMISTRY. *Educ:* Univ Wash, BS, 42; Univ Pa, MS, 43, PhD(bact), 51. *Prof Exp:* Technician, Merck Sharp & Dohme, 43-44, res assoc, Merck Inst Therapeut Res, 44-78; RETIRED. *Mem:* Am Soc Microbiol; Reticuloendothelial Soc. *Res:* Enzymology; immunology. *Mailing Add:* 17389 Plaza Dolores San Diego CA 92128

THIELE, GARY ALLEN, b Cleveland, Ohio, May 5, 38; m 60; c 3. ELECTRICAL ENGINEERING, ELECTROMAGNETISM. *Educ:* Purdue Univ, BSEE, 60; Ohio State Univ, MSc, 64, PhD(elec eng), 68. *Prof Exp:* Elec engr, Gen Elec Co, 60-61; res assoc, 63-68, asst prof, 68-75, ASSOC PROF ELEC ENG, OHIO STATE UNIV, 75- *Concurrent Pos:* Consult, Lockheed Missiles & Space Co, 71 & Nat Elec Coil, 78- *Honors & Awards:* NATO Res Award, 77. *Mem:* Int Union Radio Sci; Inst Elec & Electronics Engrs. *Res:* Electromagnetics; radiation and scattering problems via numerical methods; microwave techniques; propagation of electromagnetic waves; antennas. *Mailing Add:* Dept of Elec Eng Ohio State Univ 2015 Neil Ave Columbus OH 43210

THIELE, VICTORIA FLORENCE, b New York, NY, Oct 22, 33. NUTRITION. *Educ:* Hunter Col, BA, 55, MS, 57; Univ Maine, Orono, PhD(biochem), 65. *Prof Exp:* Instr chem, Univ Maine, Orono, 60-61; PROF NUTRIT, SYRACUSE UNIV, 64- *Mem:* Am Inst Nutrit; Soc Nutrit Educ; Am Dietetic Asn; Am Chem Soc; Nutrit Today Soc. *Res:* Vitamin B6; nutritional status surveys; nutrition education. *Mailing Add:* Dept of Human Nutrit 200 Slocum Hall Syracuse Univ Syracuse NY 13210

THIELEN, LAWRENCE EUGENE, b Chicago, Ill, Sept 2, 21; m 50; c 2. ORGANIC CHEMISTRY. *Educ:* Loyola Univ, Ill, BS, 42. *Prof Exp:* Chemist, Kankakee Ord Works, E I du Pont de Nemours & Co, 42; res chemist, Pure Oil Co, 43 & 46, G D Searle & Co, 46-56, Nalco Chem Co, 56-58 & Abbott Labs, 58-62; group leader polymer & org chem, R R Donnelley & Sons Co, 62-76; SAFETY & HEALTH DIR, PRINTING INK TECHNOL, INMONT CORP, CHICAGO, 76- *Mem:* Am Chem Soc. *Res:* Pharmaceuticals; synthesis of plastics and pharmaceuticals; inks; coatings; printing process technology. *Mailing Add:* 110 E Madison St Villa Park IL 60181

THIELGES, BART A, b Chicago, Ill, June 16, 38; m 60; c 3. FOREST GENETICS. *Educ:* Southern Ill Univ, BS, 63; Yale Univ, MF, 64, MPhil, 67, PhD(forest genetics), 67. *Prof Exp:* Res asst plant anat, Southern Ill Univ, 62-63; res asst forest genetics, Yale Univ, 63-67; asst prof, Ohio Agr Res & Develop Ctr, 67-71; assoc prof, Sch Forestry & Wildlife Mgt, La State Univ, Baton Rouge, 71-76; proj leader, US Forest Serv, Starkville, Miss, 76-77; PROF & CHMN DEPT FORESTRY, UNIV KY, 77- *Mem.* Soc Am Foresters. *Res:* Breeding of forest trees; natural variation studies; experimental taxonomy; biochemical systematics and genetics. *Mailing Add:* Dept of Forestry Univ of Ky Lexington KY 40546

THIELMAN, LEROY OSWALD, lasers, see previous edition

THIELMANN, VERNON JAMES, b Hastings, Minn, June 4, 37; m 63; c 2. ANALYTICAL CHEMISTRY. *Educ:* Northern State Col, BS, 63; Univ SDak, MNS, 68; Baylor Univ, PhD(chem), 74. *Prof Exp:* Teacher pub schs, SDak & Iowa, 63-69; asst prof chem, Morningside Col, 69-72; asst prof, 74-77, ASSOC PROF CHEM, SOUTHWEST MO STATE UNIV, 77- *Mem:* Am Chem Soc; Sigma Xi. *Res:* Preparation of complex cation exchanged montmorillonite clays and subsequent study of their structure, thermal stability, surface area and effectiveness for use as gas chromatographic packing materials. *Mailing Add:* Dept of Chem Southwest Mo State Univ Springfield MO 65802

THIEME, CORNELIS LEO HANS, b Arnhem, Netherlands, Dec 7, 48. SUPERCONDUCTORS, COMPOSITE MATERIALS. *Educ:* Twente Univ Technol, Netherlands, BEngSc, 73, MEngSc, 75. *Prof Exp:* res staff, Twente Univ Technol, Netherlands, 75-80; RES STAFF MAT SCI, MASS INST TECHNOL, 81- *Mem:* Netherlands Ceramic Soc. *Res:* Development of multifilamentary ductile superconductor materials. *Mailing Add:* NW 14th 3115 Mass Inst Technol Cambridge MA 02139

THIEME, MELVIN T, b Decatur, Ind, Oct 27, 25; m 49; c 3. SHOCK HYDRODYNAMICS, COMPUTER SCIENCE. *Educ:* Purdue Univ, BS, 49, MS, 51, PhD(nuclear physics), 55. *Prof Exp:* Staff mem, Los Alamos Nat Lab, 55-63 & Lawrence Livermore Lab, 63-64; staff mem, 64-72, asst group leader, 72-76, STAFF MEM, LOS ALAMOS NAT LAB, 76- *Mem:* Am Phys Soc. *Res:* Beta-ray spectroscopy; nuclear weapon design and development with specialization in shock hydrodynamics. *Mailing Add:* 79 Mesa Verde Dr Los Alamos NM 87544

THIEN, LEONARD B, evolution, systematics, see previous edition

THIEN, STEPHEN JOHN, b Clarence, Iowa, Apr 11, 44; m 66; c 2. AGRONOMY. *Educ:* Iowa State Univ, BS, 66; Purdue Univ, Lafayette, MS, 68, PhD(agron), 71. *Prof Exp:* Asst agron, Purdue Univ, 66-70; from asst prof to assoc prof, 70-81, PROF AGRON, KANS STATE UNIV, 81- *Concurrent Pos:* Danforth assoc. *Mem:* Am Soc Agron; Soil Sci Soc Am. *Res:* Soil fertility; plant nutrition and physiology; soil management; soil biochemistry. *Mailing Add:* Dept Agron Throckmorton Hall Kans State Univ Manhattan KS 66506

THIENE, PAUL G(EORGE), b Pasadena, Calif, Dec 10, 19; m 46; c 3. PHYSICAL ELECTRONICS. *Educ:* Calif Inst Technol, BS, 43, PhD(phys electronics), 52. *Prof Exp:* Asst physicist, Calif Inst Technol, 43-45, res engr, Jet Propulsion Lab, 46-47; dep chief & res adminr, Western Div, Off Sci Res, US Air Force, 52-55, consult, Air Tech Intel Ctr, 55-57; sr physicist, Res Lab, Giannini Plasmadyne Corp, 58-62; sr staff scientist, MHD Res Inc, 62-66; SUPVR, OPTICAL PHYSICS SECT, RES LAB, AERONUTRONIC DIV, PHILCO-FORD CORP, 66- *Concurrent Pos:* Consult, Litech, Inc, P W Webster Co, Surg Mech Res, Inc & Curt Deckert Assocs, 73- *Mem:* Am Phys Soc. *Res:* Electromedical technology, laser technology; semiconductor devices; superconductivity; plasma physics; magneto gas dynamics; electro-optics; microwave spectroscopy and radiometry. *Mailing Add:* 401 Ledroit Lane Laguna Beach CA 92651

THIER, SAMUEL OSIAH, b Brooklyn, NY, June 23, 37; m 58; c 3. MEDICINE. *Educ:* State Univ NY, Syracuse, MD, 60; Am Bd Internal Med, dipl, 67, recert, 74. *Prof Exp:* Instr med, Harvard Med Sch, 67, assoc, 67-68, asst prof, 69; from assoc prof to prof, Sch Med, Univ Pa, 69-74; PROF INTERNAL MED & CHMN DEPT, SCH MED, YALE UNIV, 75-, CHIEF MED, YALE-NEW HAVEN HOSP, 75- *Concurrent Pos:* Asst med & chief renal unit, Mass Gen Hosp, 67-69; assoc dir med serv, Univ Pa Hosp, 69-74; vchmn med, Sch Med, Univ Pa, 71-74; bd dirs, Hospice Inc, 76- & Yale-New Haven Hosp, 78- *Mem:* Inst Med-Nat Acad Sci; fel Am Col Physicians; Am Fedn Clin Res; Asn Am Med Cols; Am Bd Internal Med. *Res:* Amino acid transport in the kidney. *Mailing Add:* Dept Internal Med Yale Univ Sch Med New Haven CT 06510

THIERET, JOHN WILLIAM, b Chicago, Ill, Aug 1, 26; m 50; c 5. BOTANY. *Educ:* Utah State Univ, BS, 50, MS, 51; Univ Chicago, PhD(bot), 53. *Prof Exp:* Cur econ bot, Field Mus Natural Hist, 53-62; from assoc prof to prof biol, Univ Southwestern La, 62-73, Edwin Lewis Stephens prof sci, 72-73; chmn, Dept Biol Sci, 73-80, PROF BOT, NORTHERN KY UNIV, 73- *Concurrent Pos:* Adv, Encycl Britannica, 59- *Mem:* Soc Econ Bot. *Res:* Flora of central and southeastern United States; taxonomy of Scrophulariaceae and Gramineae; seed and fruit classification and morphology; economic botany. *Mailing Add:* Dept Biol Sci Northern Ky Univ Highland Heights KY 41076

THIERMANN, ALEJANDRO BORIES, b Valparaiso, Chile, July 15, 47; US citizen; m 73. VETERINARY MEDICINE, EPIDEMIOLOGY. *Educ:* Univ Chile, Santiago, DVM, 71; Wayne State Univ, PhD(microbiol, immunol), 79. *Prof Exp:* Vet small animals, pvt pract, 71-72; med ecologist pub health, Lockheed Elec Co, NASA, Houston, 72-73; instr, Lab Animal Med, Sch Med, Wayne State Univ, 73-80; WITH NAT ANIMAL DIS LAB, 80- *Concurrent Pos:* Mem, Am Leptospirosis Res Conf, 74-, chmn epidemiol sect, 77-; mem biohazards comt, Wayne State Univ, mem recombinant DNA subcomt, 77- *Mem:* Am Soc Microbiologists; Sigma Xi; Vet Med Asn Chile; Am Soc Parasitologists. *Res:* Leptospirosis, its epidemiology, and urban incidence; zoonotic diseases of concern in urban areas; use of laboratory animals as models for research of infectious diseases. *Mailing Add:* Nat Animal Dis Lab PO Box 70 Ames IA 50010

THIERRIN, GABRIEL, b Surpierre, Switz, Dec 22, 21; m 51; c 2. MATHEMATICS, COMPUTER SCIENCE. *Educ:* Univ Fribourg, DSc, 51; Univ Paris, DSc, 54. *Prof Exp:* Sci assoc, Nat Ctr Sci Res, France, 52-54 & Nat Found Sci Res, Switz, 54-57; prof math, Inst Higher Studies, Tunisia, 57-58 & Univ Montreal, 58-70; PROF MATH, UNIV WESTERN ONT, 70- *Mem:* Asn Comput Mach; Am Math Soc; Can Math Soc; Can Info Processing Soc. *Res:* Algebra; theories of rings and semi-groups; systems theory; theory of automata and languages. *Mailing Add:* Dept of Math Univ of Western Ont London ON N6A 5B8 Can

THIERS, HARRY DELBERT, b Ft McKavett, Tex, Jan 22, 19; m 53; c 1. MYCOLOGY. *Educ:* Schreiner Inst, AB, 38; Univ Tex, BA, 41, MA, 47; Univ Mich, PhD, 55. *Prof Exp:* Asst, Univ Tex, 39-41, tutor bot, 45-47, instr bot & mycol, Tex A&M Univ, 47-50, asst biol, 50-55, assoc prof, 55-59; assoc prof, 59-63, PROF BIOL, SAN FRANCISCO STATE UNIV, 63- *Concurrent Pos:* Assoc plant pathologist, USDA, 48. *Mem:* Bot Soc Am; Mycol Soc Am; Am Bryol & Lichenological Soc. *Res:* Taxonomy of fleshy fungi of California and West Coast of North America. *Mailing Add:* Dept of Biol San Francisco State Univ San Francisco CA 94132

THIERSTEIN, GERALD E, b Whitewater, Kans, Apr 30, 31; m 76. AGRICULTURAL ENGINEERING. *Educ:* Kans State Univ, BS, 57, MS, 63. *Prof Exp:* Asst prof agr eng, WVa Univ, 62-67; res assoc, McGill Univ, 67-71; sr lectr, Makerere Univ, Kampala, 71-73; vis assoc prof, Am Univ-Beirut, 73-76; PRIN SCIENTIST AGR ENG, INT CROPS RES INST SEMI-ARID TROPICS, 76- *Mem:* Am Soc Agr Engrs; Indian Soc Agr Engrs. *Res:* Farm machinery management; tillage; post-harvest technology. *Mailing Add:* Int Crop Res Inst for the Semi-Arid Tropics Icrisat Patancheru PO Andhra Pradesh 502324 India

THIERSTEIN, HANS RUDOLF, b Zürich, Switz, May 27, 44; m 69; c 2. GEOLOGY, MICROPALEONTOLOGY. *Educ:* Univ Zürich, dipl geol, 69, DrPhil, 72. *Prof Exp:* Teaching asst geol, Eidgenoessische Tech Hochschule, Zürich, Switz, 69-71, res asst, 71-73; fel, Swiss Nat Sci Found, 73-76; asst prof, 76-80, ASSOC PROF GEOL, SCRIPPS INST OCEANOG, UNIV CALIF, SAN DIEGO, 80- *Mem:* Geol Soc Am; Swiss Geol Soc; Am Geophys Union. *Res:* Paleoceanography, calcareous nannoplankton, biostratigraphy, sedimentology, geochemistry. *Mailing Add:* Scripps Inst Oceanog Univ Calif San Diego La Jolla CA 92093

THIES, RICHARD WILLIAM, b Detroit, Mich, Sept 16, 41; m 76; c 3. ORGANIC CHEMISTRY. *Educ:* Univ Mich, BS, 63; Univ Wis, PhD(org chem), 67. *Prof Exp:* NIH fel org chem, Univ Calif, Los Angeles, 67-68; asst prof, 68-75, ASSOC PROF ORG CHEM, ORE STATE UNIV, 75- *Concurrent Pos:* NATO sr scientists fel, 79-80. *Mem:* Am Chem Soc; Royal Soc Chem. *Res:* Medium sized ring chemistry; carbonium ion chemistry; thermal rearrangements; synthesis of hormone analogs. *Mailing Add:* Dept Chem Ore State Univ Corvallis OR 97331

THIES, ROGER E, b Bronxville, NY, June 30, 33; m 71; c 2. PHYSIOLOGY. *Educ:* Bates Col, BS, 55; Harvard Univ, AM, 57; Rockefeller Univ, PhD(physiol), 61; Univ Okla, MA, 75. *Prof Exp:* Guest investr neurophysiol & NIH fel, Rockefeller Univ, 60-61; from instr to asst prof physiol, Sch Med, Wash Univ, 61-65; lectr, Makerere Univ Col, Uganda, 65-67; ASSOC PROF PHYSIOL & BIOPHYS, MED CTR, UNIV OKLA, 67-, ASSOC PROF BIOL PSYCHOL, HEALTH SCI CTR, 72- *Concurrent Pos:* Hon res asst & NIH spec fel, Univ Col, Univ London, 64-65. *Mem:* Am Physiol Soc; Guild Struct Integration. *Res:* Mammalian neuromuscular transmission; effect of vagal activity on relay of cardiac pain to the brain; manipulation of jaw muscles for relief of tension; effective education and innovative teaching ways of health professionals caring for themselves. *Mailing Add:* Univ Okla Health Sci Ctr PO Box 26901 Oklahoma City OK 73190

THIESFELD, VIRGIL ARTHUR, b Glencoe, Minn, Oct 26, 37; m 59; c 2. BOTANY, PLANT PHYSIOLOGY. *Educ:* Luther Col, Iowa, BA, 59; Univ SDak, Vermillion, MA, 63; Univ Okla, PhD(bot), 65. *Prof Exp:* Teacher high sch, Iowa, 59-60 & Minn, 60-62; res asst bot, Univ Okla, 63-65; asst prof, 65-68, assoc prof biol, 68-76, CHMN DEPT, 68-, PROF BIOL, UNIV WIS-STEVENS POINT, 76- *Concurrent Pos:* Res grant, Univ Wis-Stevens Point, 68-69. *Mem:* Am Soc Plant Physiol. *Res:* Plant growth regulators. *Mailing Add:* Dept of Biol Univ of Wis Stevens Point WI 54481

THIESSEN, ALBERT RONALD, b San Francisco, Calif, Feb 21, 32. PHYSICS. *Educ:* Calif State Univ, BA, 71. *Prof Exp:* PHYSICIST, LAWRENCE LIVERMORE NAT LAB, UNIV CALIF, 60- *Res:* Inertial confinement fusion. *Mailing Add:* 934 Lucille Livermore CA 94550

THIESSEN, HENRY ARCHER, b Teaneck, NJ, Nov 8, 40; m 62; c 1. PHYSICS. *Educ:* Calif Inst Technol, BS, 61, MS, 62, PhD(physics), 67. *Prof Exp:* STAFF MEM MEDIUM ENERGY PHYSICS, LOS ALAMOS NAT LAB, 66- *Mem:* Am Phys Soc. *Res:* Experimental medium energy physics. *Mailing Add:* Mail Stop 841 Los Alamos Nat Lab Los Alamos NM 87544

THIESSEN, REINHARDT, JR, b Kiel, Wis, Oct 20, 13; m 38; c 2. BIOCHEMISTRY. *Educ:* Univ Pittsburgh, BS, 34. *Prof Exp:* Asst, Univ Pittsburgh, 35-37; head chemist res & control lab, Repub Yeast Corp, NJ, 37-41; proj leader cent labs, 42-46, head biol sect, 46-48, head nutrit sect, 48-55, from asst lab dir to lab dir, 55-62, sr res specialist, Tech Ctr, 62-69, res assoc & area mgr nutrit sci, 69-72, corp res mgr, 72-81, PRIN SCIENTIST NUTRIT SCI, TECH CTR, GEN FOODS CORP, 81- *Mem:* AAAS; Am Pub Health Asn; Am Chem Soc; Inst Food Technol; Am Inst Nutrit. *Res:* Nutrition; toxicology; bacteriology; protein nutrition; carbohydrate nutrition; cacao chemistry; tracers in nutrition and toxicology; food chemistry; dental caries. *Mailing Add:* 586 Gilbert Ave Pearl River NY 10965

THIESSEN, WILLIAM ERNEST, b Kansas City, Mo, Sept 17, 34; m 60; c 1. ORGANIC CHEMISTRY. *Educ:* Univ Calif, Berkeley, BS, 56, PhD(chem), 60. *Prof Exp:* Instr chem, Univ Wash, 60-62; asst prof, Univ Calif, Davis, 62-68; NIH spec fel, Chem Div, Oak Ridge Nat Lab, 68-70, RES CHEMIST, CHEM DIV, OAK RIDGE NAT LAB, 70- *Mem:* Am Chem Soc; Am Crystallog Asn. *Res:* Structure elucidation of complex natural products and accurate molecular geometry of organic compounds by x-ray and neutron diffraction. *Mailing Add:* 233 W Tennessee Ave Oak Ridge TN 37830

THIGPEN, J(OSEPH) J(ACKSON), b Ruston, La, Feb 4, 17; m 41; c 2. MECHANICAL ENGINEERING. *Educ:* La Polytech Inst, BS, 36; US Mil Acad, BS, 41; Univ Tex, MS, 51, PhD(mech eng), 59. *Prof Exp:* From asst prof to prof mech eng, 47-75, head dept, 53-75, assoc dean, 76, DEAN COL ENG, LA TECH UNIV, 76- *Concurrent Pos:* Consult, Opers Res Off, Johns Hopkins Univ, 48-50. *Mem:* Am Soc Mech Engrs; Am Soc Eng Educ; Nat Soc Prof Engrs. *Res:* Thermodynamics; heat transfer. *Mailing Add:* Col of Eng La Tech Univ Box 4875 Tech Sta Ruston LA 71272

THILENIUS, OTTO G, b Bad Soden, Ger, July 7, 29; US citizen; m 56; c 3. PEDIATRIC CARDIOLOGY, PHYSIOLOGY. *Educ:* Univ Frankfurt, MD, 53; Univ Chicago, PhD(physiol), 62. *Prof Exp:* Resident, 57-59, instr, 61-62, asst prof pediat & physiol, 64-69, assoc prof pediat, 69-72, PROF PEDIAT, UNIV CHICAGO, 72- *Concurrent Pos:* USPHS fel physiol, Univ Chicago, 59-61; fel cardiol, Harvard Univ, 62-64. *Mem:* Am Heart Asn; Am Acad Pediat; Am Col Cardiol; Soc Pediat Res. *Mailing Add:* Dept of Pediat Univ of Chicago Chicago IL 60637

THILL, DONALD CECIL, b Colfax, Wash, Aug 30, 50; m 71; c 4. WEED SCIENCE, PLANT PROTECTION. *Educ:* Wash State Univ, BS, 72, MS, 76; Ore State Univ, PhD(crop sci), 79. *Prof Exp:* Plant physiologist, Agr Res Serv, USDA, 75-79; biochem field specialist, PPG Industs, Inc, 79-80; ASST PROF WEED SCI, UNIV IDAHO, 80- *Concurrent Pos:* Prin investr, Weed Control Systs, Univ Idaho, 81- *Mem:* Weed Sci Soc Am; Am Soc Agron. *Res:* Develop cultural and herbicidal weed control tactics for use in small grains; herbicide mode and mechanism of action experiments. *Mailing Add:* Dept Plant & Soil Sci Univ Idaho Moscow ID 83843

THILL, RONALD E, b Tonopah, Nev, Oct 22, 44; m 66; c 2. RANGE-WILDLIFE INTERACTIONS. *Educ:* Humboldt State Col, Calif, BS, 67; SDak State Univ, MS, 69; Univ Ariz, PhD(range mgt), 81. *Prof Exp:* RANGE SCIENTIST, FOREST EXP STA, FOREST SERV, USDA, SOUTHERN REGION, 77- *Mem:* Soc Range Mgt; Wildlife Soc. *Res:* Deer and cattle interactions as influenced by cattle stocking, season of use and prescribed burning on southern forest range; forest management practices (spacing and site preparation) on cattle and deer forage resources. *Mailing Add:* 405 Highland Dr Pineville LA 71360

THIMANN, KENNETH VIVIAN, b Ashford, Eng, Aug 5, 04; nat US; m 29; c 3. PLANT PHYSIOLOGY, PLANT HORMONES. *Educ:* Univ London, BSc, 24, PhD(biochem), 28. *Hon Degrees:* AM, Harvard Univ, 38; PhD, Univ Basel, 60; Dr, Univ Clermont-Ferrand, 61. *Prof Exp:* Instr bact, Univ London, 26-28, Beit fel, 29-30; instr biochem, Calif Inst Technol, 30-35; lectr bot, 35-36, asst prof plant physiol, 36-39, tutor, 36-42, assoc prof, 39-46, dir biol labs, 46-50, prof, 46-62, Higgins prof biol, 62-65, EMER HIGGINS PROF BIOL, HARVARD UNIV, 65-; prof biol, 65-78, EMER PROF, UNIV CALIF, SANTA CRUZ, 78- *Concurrent Pos:* Guggenheim fel, 50-51 & 58; exchange prof, France, 54-55; provost, Crown Col, Univ Calif, Santa Cruz, 65-72; pres, Int Bot Cong, Seattle, 69 & Int Plant Growth Substance Cong, Tokyo, 73; mem exec comt, Assembly Life Sci, Nat Res Coun, 73-; vis prof, Univ Mass, Amherst, 74. *Honors & Awards:* Hales Prize, Am Soc Plant Physiol, 36. *Mem:* Fel Nat Acad Sci; Am Soc Naturalists (pres, 54); Bot Soc Am (pres, 60); Am Soc Plant Physiol (pres, 50); Soc Gen Physiol (pres, 49). *Res:* Physiology of bacteria, protozoa and fungi; growth, auxins and correlation in plants; anthocyanins; senescence of leaves. *Mailing Add:* Thimann Labs Univ Calif Santa Cruz CA 95064

THIO, ALAN POO-AN, b Jatinegara, Indonesia, Jan 17, 31; US citizen; m 57; c 3. MEDICINAL CHEMISTRY, PESTICIDE CHEMISTRY. *Educ:* Univ Indonesia, BS, 54, MS, 57; Univ Ky, PhD(org chem), 61. *Prof Exp:* Assoc prof orgc chem, Bandung Inst Technol, 60-67; assoc med chem, Col Pharm, 67-70, REGULATORY SPECIALIST, DIV REGULATORY SERV, UNIV KY, 70- *Concurrent Pos:* Abstractor, Chem Abstr Serv, 66- *Mem:* Am Chem Soc; Asn Offs Anal Chemists. *Res:* Development of analytical procedures for the quantitative determination of pesticide residues in feeds, fertilizers and soil. *Mailing Add:* Div of Regulatory Serv Univ of Ky Lexington KY 40546

THIRGOOD, JACK VINCENT, b Northumberland, Eng, Apr 5, 24; m 49; c 3. FORESTRY. *Educ:* Univ Wales, BSc, 50; Univ BC, MF, 61; Ore State Univ, MF, 65; State Univ NY Col Forestry, Syracuse, PhD, 71. *Prof Exp:* With, UK Forestry Comn, 40-44, silviculture asst, Res Br, 50-54; silviculturist, Cyprus Forest Serv, 54-56; adv & dir Nat Forest Res Inst Iraq, Food & Agr Orgn, UN, 56-57; forestry consult, UK, 57-58; forester, BC Forest Serv, 58; res forester, Celgar Ltd, BC, 59; asst prof silviculture, State Univ NY Col Forestry, Syracuse, 60-62; prof silviculture & forest bot & head dept, Univ Liberia, Found Mutual Asst in Africa & UK Ministry Overseas

Develop, 62-64; forestry consult & area dir, Tilhill Forestry & Adv Ltd, Eng, 64-67; assoc prof, 68-80, PROF SILVICULTURE & FOREST POLICY, UNIV BC, 80- *Concurrent Pos:* Consult indust land reclamation. *Mem:* Can Land Reclamation Asn; Sigma Xi; Can Inst Forestry. *Res:* Silviculture, forest management, history and policy; temperate, tropical and arid zone forestry; industrial land reclamation. *Mailing Add:* Fac of Forestry Univ of BC Vancouver BC V6T 1W5 Can

THIRION, JEAN PAUL JOSEPH, b Metz, France, July 30, 39; Can citizen; m 67; c 2. SOMATIC CELL GENETICS, RECOMBINANT DNA. *Educ:* Univ Nancy, France, BS, 60; Univ Wis-Madison, PhD(biochem), 66; Pastuer's Inst, France, Doct d'etat, 69. *Prof Exp:* Attache genetics, Nat Ctr Sci Res, Pasteur's Inst, 67-68, charge, 68-72; asst prof, 72-76, ASSOC PROF MICROBIOL, UNIV SHERBROOKE, 76- *Mem:* Am Genetics Soc. *Res:* Genetic analysis of gene reproduction. *Mailing Add:* Dept Microbiol Chu-Univ Sherbrooke Sherbrooke PQ J1H 5N4 Can

THIRKILL, JOHN D, b Soda Springs, Idaho, Apr 26, 29; m 50; c 3. CHEMICAL ENGINEERING. *Educ:* State Col Wash, BS, 53. *Prof Exp:* Chem engr, E I du Pont de Nemours & Co, 53; proj engr, Thiokol Chem Corp, Md, 55-58, dept head rocket eng, Wasatch Div, 58-60, preliminary design & anal, 60-63, div mgr, 63-64, proj eng, 64-67, dir eng, 67-68, div mgr, 68-71, dep dir space shuttle prog, 72-78, DIR ENG, THIOKOL CHEM CORP, 78- *Concurrent Pos:* Adv, NASA Internal Comt Design Criteria for Chem Propulsion, 66-68. *Mem:* Am Ord Asn; Am Inst Aeronaut & Astronaut. *Res:* Rocket propulsion, design and development of solid propellant propulsion systems. *Mailing Add:* 545 E Sixth N Brigham City UT 84302

THIRUGNANAM, MUTHUVELU, b India, July 20, 40; m 74. PLANT NEMATOLOGY, ENTOMOLOGY. *Educ:* Annamalai Univ, India, BS, 62, MS, 65; Rutgers Univ, PhD(nematol), 73. *Prof Exp:* Instr entom, Annamalai Univ, India, 62-65, lectr, 66-69; asst prof, Rutgers Univ, 73-75; ENTOMOLOGIST, ROHM AND HAAS CO RES LABS, 75- *Mem:* Entom Soc Am; Soc Nematologists. *Res:* Development of insecticides and nematicides; culture procedure for insects and nematodes; studies on the structure-activity relationship in insecticidal compounds. *Mailing Add:* Rohm and Haas Res Labs Norristown & McKean Rds Spring House PA 19477

THIRUVATHUKAL, JOHN VARKEY, b Shertallay, India, Aug 4, 39; m 71. GEOPHYSICS, OCEANOGRAPHY. *Educ:* St Louis Univ, BS, 61; Mich State Univ, MS, 63; Ore State Univ, PhD(geophys), 68. *Prof Exp:* Res asst geophys, Ore State Univ, 63-67; from instr to asst prof geol, DePauw Univ, 67-70; asst prof geol, 70-79, ASSOC PROF, MONTCLAIR STATE COL, 79- *Concurrent Pos:* Consult, Off Earth Sci, Nat Acad Sci, 69-; adj prof, Fairleigh Dickinson Univ. *Mem:* Am Geophys Union; Soc Explor Geophys. *Mailing Add:* Dept of Phys-Geosci Montclair State Col Upper Montclair NJ 07043

THIRUVATHUKAL, KURIAKOSE V, b Shertallay, Kerala, India, May 1, 25; m 65; c 3. ZOOLOGY, MORPHOLOGY. *Educ:* Univ Kerala, BSc, 53; Boston Col, MS, 56; St Louis Univ, PhD(biol, histol), 60. *Prof Exp:* Instr zool, anat, histol & animal tech, Duquesne Univ, 59-60; asst prof zool & histol, Aquinas Col, 60-62; asst prof biol, Gonzaga Univ, 62-65 & Canisius Col, 65-68; chmn dept, 68-71, PROF BIOL, LEWIS UNIV, 68- *Mem:* Am Micros Soc; Soc Syst Zool; Indian Soc Animal Morphol & Physiol; Am Soc Zoologists; Am Asn Univ Profs (secy, 75-). *Res:* Histology and morphology of reptiles; vertebrate zoology; coelacanth morphology; research in reptilia and coelacanth. *Mailing Add:* 2213 Arden Place Joliet IL 60435

THIRUVENGADA, SESHAN, polymer chemistry, physical chemistry, see previous edition

THIRUVENGADAM, ALAGU PILLAI, b Madurai, India, Aug 16, 35; US citizen; m 61; c 3. MECHANICAL ENGINEERING, SYSTEMS DESIGN. *Educ:* Univ Madras, BE, 57; Indian Inst Sci, MSc, 59, PhD(eng), 61. *Prof Exp:* Govt India sr res scholar, 58-60; Univ Grants Comn sr res fel, 60-62; res scientist, Hydronautics Inc, 62-65, sr res scientist, 65-67, prin res scientist, 67-69; from assoc prof to prof mech eng, Cath Univ Am, 69-75; CHMN BD, DAEDALEAN ASSOCS, INC, 72- *Concurrent Pos:* Lectr, Cath Univ Am, 65-69, prof, 69-78; fel, Fac Arts & Sci, Johns Hopkins Univ, 67-69; consult, Hydronautics Inc, 69-, Brookhaven Nat Lab, 69-71, Waukesha Motors, Wis, 71- & Naval Ship Res & Develop Ctr, 71-; chmn bd, Comser Corp, 78- *Honors & Awards:* Hess Award, Am Soc Mech Engrs, 63, Award of Merit, 76; Outstanding engr, Eng Joint Coun & Archit Socs, Nat Acad Sci, 64. *Mem:* Am Soc Mech Engrs; Am Soc Testing & Mat. *Res:* Dynamic response of materials; cavitation erosion, wet steam erosion, rain erosion, stress corrosion; corrosion fatigue; modeling erosion; open channel flow; fluid mechanics of turbomachinery; fluid dynamics; material engineering; power systems; materials science. *Mailing Add:* 10509 William Tell Lane Columbia MD 21044

THISTLE, DAVID, biological oceanography, meiofaunal ecology, see previous edition

THODE, E(DWARD) F(REDERICK), b New York, NY, May 31, 21; m 44; c 3. CHEMICAL ENGINEERING. *Educ:* Mass Inst Technol, SB, 42, SM, 43, ScD(chem eng), 47. *Prof Exp:* Chem engr, Boston Woven Hose & Rubber Co, Mass, 43-45; from asst prof to assoc prof chem eng, Univ Maine, 47-54; chem engr, Cent Res Dept, Minn Mining & Mfg Co, 54-55; res assoc phys chem, Inst Paper Chem, 55-57; chem eng, 57-59, chief pulping & papermaking sect, 59-60, adminr eng & tech sect, 60-61, coordr info processing, 61-63; prof chem eng & head dept, 63-74, assoc dir eng exp sta, 65-66, actg dir, Ctr Bus Res & Serv, 77, PROF MGT, N MEX STATE UNIV, 74- *Concurrent Pos:* Vis staff mem, Los Alamos Sci Lab, 65-; consult, Gen Elec Co, 64-66 & Bell Tel Labs, 66-70. *Mem:* Acad Mgt; Am Inst Decision Sci; Am Inst Chem Engrs; Am Soc Eng Educ. *Res:* Technico-economic studies of energy alternatives; environmental control technology; management science; production/operations management. *Mailing Add:* 2275 Avalon Dr Las Cruces NM 88005

THODE, LESTER ELSTER, b Alameda, Calif, Apr 8, 43; m 67; c 3. PLASMA PHYSICS, CHARGED PARTICLE BEAM PHYSICS. *Educ:* Univ Calif, Berkeley, BS, 69; Cornell Univ, PhD(appl physics), 74. *Prof Exp:* Staff mem, 73-78, alt group leader, 78-79, GROUP LEADER INTENSE PARTICLE BEAM PHYSICS, LOS ALAMOS NAT LAB, 79- *Mem:* Am Phys Soc. *Res:* Collective behavior of particle beams. *Mailing Add:* Intense Particle Beam Group Los Alamos Nat Lab Los Alamos NM 87545

THODOS, GEORGE, b Chicago, Ill, Sept 15, 15. CHEMICAL ENGINEERING. *Educ:* Armour Inst Technol, BS, 38, MS, 39; Univ Wis, PhD(chem eng), 43. *Prof Exp:* Jr chem engr, Standard Oil Co Ind, 39-40 & Phillips Petrol Co, Okla, 40-41, chem engr, 43-46; chem engr, Pure Oil Co, Ill, 46-47; from asst prof to prof chem eng, 47-77, WALTER P MURPHY PROF, TECH INST NORTHWESTERN UNIV, EVANSTON, 77- *Mem:* Am Chem Soc; Am Inst Chem Engrs. *Res:* Petroleum processing; mass transfer studies; vapor pressures and critical constants of hydrocarbons; transport properties of substances; vapor-liquid equilibrium studies. *Mailing Add:* Dept of Chem Eng Sheridan & Noyes Evanston IL 60201

THOE, ROBERT STEVEN, b Pensacola, Fla, Aug 19, 45; m 68; c 1. ATOMIC PHYSICS. *Educ:* Baylor Univ, BS, 68; Univ Conn, MS, 70, PhD(physics), 73. *Prof Exp:* Asst res prof physics, Univ Tenn, 73-76, asst prof, 76-80. *Concurrent Pos:* Consult, Union Carbide Corp, Oak Ridge Nat Lab, 75- *Mem:* Am Phys Soc. *Res:* The study of atomic collision phenomena, primarily by the detection and measurement of the non-characteristic radiations emitted during violent ion-atom collisions. *Mailing Add:* 1543 Oslo Ct Livermore CA 94550

THOENE, JESS GILBERT, b Bakersfield, Calif, Aug 4, 42; m 65. CLINICAL BIOCHEMICAL GENETICS. *Educ:* Stanford Univ, BS, 64; Johns Hopkins Univ, MD, 68. *Prof Exp:* Asst clin prof pediat, Univ Calif, San Diego, 75-77; asst prof, 77-81, ASSOC PROF PEDIAT, UNIV MICH, 81- *Concurrent Pos:* Dir, Mich Dept Ment Health Genetic Screening Lab, 77- *Mem:* Soc Pediat Res; Soc Inherited Metab Disorders; Am Soc Human Genetics; Am Chem Soc. *Res:* Inborn errors of aminoacid, organic acid and vitamin metabolism. *Mailing Add:* Dept Pediat Kresge II R6032 Sch Med Univ Mich Ann Arbor MI 48109

THOLEN, ALBERT DAVID, b Philadelphia, Pa, Aug 23, 27; m 56; c 4. CIVIL ENGINEERING, METROLOGY. *Educ:* Drexel Univ, BSCE, 49. *Prof Exp:* Vpres opers res, Gen Res Corp, 62-77; dep dir standards anal div, 77, CHIEF, OFF WEIGHTS & MEASURES, NAT BUR STANDARDS, US DEPT COM, 77- *Concurrent Pos:* Adv comt mem, Int Legal Metrol, US Dept of Com, 78- *Mem:* AAAS; Opers Res Soc Am. *Res:* Measurement science; electronics; microprocessing. *Mailing Add:* Off Weights & Measures US Dept of Com Washington DC 20234

THOM, KARLHEINZ, b Altena, Ger, May 14, 20; US citizen. PHYSICS. *Educ:* Univ Bonn, PhD(physics), 49. *Prof Exp:* Res engr, NASA Langley Res Ctr, 58-62, prog mgr plasma physics, NASA Hq, 62-72, chief, Appl Physics Br, NASA & Atomic Energy Comn Space Nuclear Systs Off, 72-76, prog mgr, NASA Hq, 76-78; RETIRED. *Concurrent Pos:* Vis prof, Univ Fla, 71- *Mem:* Am Inst Aeronaut & Astronaut; Am Nuclear Soc. *Res:* Plasma physics; nuclear engineering. *Mailing Add:* Ubierstrasse 49 Bonn 5300 West Germany

THOMA, GEORGE EDWARD, b Dayton, Ohio, Aug 9, 22; m 49; c 8. INTERNAL MEDICINE, NUCLEAR MEDICINE. *Educ:* Univ Dayton, BS, 43; St Louis Univ, MD, 47. *Prof Exp:* From instr to assoc prof internal med, 51-76, head, Sect Nuclear Med, 59-73, asst to vpres, 62-67, asst vpres, Med Ctr, 67-73, PROF INTERNAL MED, ST LOUIS UNIV, 76-, VPRES, MED CTR, 73- *Concurrent Pos:* Dir radioisotopes lab, Med Ctr, St Louis Univ, 49-51 & 54-73; consult, Health Physics Div, Oak Ridge Nat Lab, 54-, Lockheed Aircraft Corp, 54-, US Army, 56-, Med Div, Oak Ridge Inst Nuclear Studies, 58-, Div Radiol Health, USPHS, 60-, Div Compliance, US Nuclear Res Coun, 62- & Am Pub Health Asn, 62-; ed, J Nuclear Med, 59-70. *Mem:* Soc Nuclear Med; Radiation Res Soc; Health Physics Soc; Am Thyroid Asn; Am Soc Internal Med. *Res:* Radiobiology; thyroid function; clinical application of radioisotopes. *Mailing Add:* Dept of Internal Med St Louis Univ Med Ctr St Louis MO 63104

THOMA, GEORGE RANJAN, b India, Mar 1, 44; US citizen. ELECTRICAL ENGINEERING, COMMUNICATIONS ENGINEERING. *Educ:* Swarthmore Col, BS, 65; Univ Pa, MS, 67, PhD(elec eng), 71. *Prof Exp:* Ford Found fel, 65-67; res assoc, Moore Sch Elec Eng, Univ Pa, 68-71; systs engr, All Systs, Moorestown, NJ, 71-73, Gen Elec Co, 73-74; SR ELECTRONICS ENGR & ACTG CHIEF COMMUN ENG, NAT LIBR MED, HUNTINGTON HEALTH SERV, 74- *Mem:* Inst Elec & Electronics Engrs; Am Soc Info Sci; Soc Photo-Optical & Instrumentation Engrs. *Res:* Telecommunications; signal processing; estimation theory; satellite aided video and voice communications; satellite aided radio navigation. *Mailing Add:* Nat Libr Med 8600 Rockville Pike Bethesda MD 20209

THOMA, GEORGE WILLIAM, pathology, see previous edition

THOMA, JOHN ANTHONY, b Springfield, Ill, Dec 6, 32; m 58; c 4. BIOCHEMISTRY. *Educ:* Bradley Univ, AB, 54; Iowa State Univ, PhD(biochem), 58. *Prof Exp:* Asst prof, Ind Univ, 60-66; PROF CHEM, UNIV ARK, 70- *Concurrent Pos:* Vis fel, Univ Sydney, 72; vis scholar, Univ Calif, Los Angeles, 77-78. *Mem:* Am Chem Soc; Sigma Xi; Am Asn Biol Chemists. *Res:* Anti-viral substances; mechanism tritium cell billing; enzymology; theory and practice of chromatography. *Mailing Add:* Dept Chem Univ Ark Fayetteville AR 72701

THOMA, RICHARD WILLIAM, b Milwaukee, Wis, Dec 7, 21; m 52; c 4. INDUSTRIAL MICROBIOLOGY. *Educ:* Univ Wis, BSc, 47, MSc, 49, PhD(biochem), 51. *Prof Exp:* Res assoc sect microbiol, Squibb Inst Med Res, 51-61, res supvr microbiol develop, 62-68, asst dir biol process develop, 68-79, SR RES FEL, BIOL PROCESS DEVELOP, E R SQUIBB & SONS, 79-

Mem: AAAS; Am Inst Biol Sci; Soc Indust Microbiol; Brit Soc Gen Microbiol; Soc Fermentation Technol Japan. *Res:* Fermentation process research and development. *Mailing Add:* 1831 Mountain Top Rd Bridgewater NJ 08807

THOMA, ROY E, b San Antonio, Tex, May 12, 22; m 53; c 2. INORGANIC CHEMISTRY, PHYSICAL CHEMISTRY. *Educ:* Univ Tex, MA, 48. *Prof Exp:* Assoc prof, Sam Houston State Col, 48-51; asst prof, Tex Tech Col, 51-52; chemist, 52-60, proj chemist molten salt reactor progs, 67-71, task group dir, 71-78, TECH ASST TO ASSOC DIR ADMIN, OAK RIDGE NAT LAB, 78- *Concurrent Pos:* Mem bd dirs, Environ Systs Corp, 73-77. *Mem:* Am Chem Soc; Sigma Xi; fel Am Ceramic Soc; Am Nuclear Soc; fel AAAS. *Res:* Physical chemistry of inorganic fused salts, particularly determinations of phase equilibria and interrelationships of crystal structures in condensed systems of these materials; nuclear power stations, especially floating nuclear power plants. *Mailing Add:* Oak Ridge Nat Lab Oak Ridge TN 37830

THOMAN, CHARLES J, b Wilkes-Barre, Pa, Nov 4, 28. ORGANIC CHEMISTRY. *Educ:* Spring Hill Col, BS, 53; Fordham Univ, MS, 56; Woodstock Col, STB, 59, STM, 60; Univ Mass, Amherst, PhD(org chem), 66. *Prof Exp:* Instr chem, Univ Scranton, 53-55; res asst with L A Carpino, Univ Mass, 66; asst prof, 66-69, assoc prof, 69-73, PROF CHEM, UNIV SCRANTON, 73-, CHMN DEPT, 78- *Mem:* AAAS; fel Am Inst Chem; Am Chem Soc; Am Asn Jesuit Sci. *Res:* N-nitrosoketimines; chemistry of sydnones; nucleic acid antimetabolites. *Mailing Add:* Dept of Chem Univ of Scranton Scranton PA 18510

THOMANN, ROBERT V, b New York, NY, Sept 1, 34; m 57; c 7. CIVIL ENGINEERING, OCEANOGRAPHY. *Educ:* Manhattan Col, BCE, 56; NY Univ, MCE, 60, PhD(oceanog), 63. *Prof Exp:* Engr, Delaware River & Bay Study, USPHS, 56-59, engr in charge Narragansett Bay Study, 59-60; tech dir estuary water qual mgt, Fed Water Pollution Control Admin, 62-66; PROF CIVIL ENG, MANHATTAN COL, 66- *Concurrent Pos:* Consult. *Mem:* AAAS; Am Geophys Union; Am Soc Civil Engrs; Water Pollution Control Fedn. *Res:* Interrelationships of environment on waste water discharge, water quality and water use. *Mailing Add:* Dept Environ Eng & Sci Manhattan Col Bronx NY 10471

THOMAS, ALBERT LEE, JR, b Auburn, Ala, Sept 4, 23; m 49; c 5. ELECTRONICS. *Educ:* Cornell Univ, BEE, 49. *Prof Exp:* Res assoc, Ala Polytech Inst, 49; res engr, 49-53, head, instrument develop sect, 53-62, HEAD ENG PHYSICS DIV, SOUTHERN RES INST, 62- *Mem:* Instrument Soc Am; Inst Elec & Electronics Engrs. *Res:* Electro-optical instrumentation. *Mailing Add:* 2345 Tenton Rd Birmingham AL 35216

THOMAS, ALEXANDER, b New York, NY, Jan 11, 14; m 38; c 4. PSYCHIATRY. *Educ:* City Col New York, BS, 32; NY Univ, MD, 36; Am Bd Psychiat & Neurol, dipl, 48. *Prof Exp:* From instr to assoc prof, 48-66, PROF PSYCHIAT, SCH MED, NY UNIV, 66- *Concurrent Pos:* Assoc attend psychiatrist, Bellevue & Univ Hosps, 58-68, attend psychiatrist, 68-; dir psychiat div, Bellevue Hosp, New York, 68-78. *Honors & Awards:* Ittleson Award, Am Psychiat Asn; Baum Award, NY Ment Health Asn. *Mem:* Fel Am Psychiat Asn. *Res:* Longitudinal study of child development; psychosomatic medicine. *Mailing Add:* Dept of Psychiat NY Univ Sch of Med New York NY 10016

THOMAS, ALEXANDER EDWARD, III, b Chicago, Ill, May 3, 30; m 56; c 3. ORGANIC CHEMISTRY, ANALYTICAL CHEMISTRY. *Educ:* Univ Ill, BS, 55; DePaul Univ, MS, 61. *Prof Exp:* Res chemist, Cent Org Res Lab, Glidden Co, 55-58, sect head anal chem, Durkee Foods Group, 58-66, mgr chem res dept, 66-71, mgr chem res, Dwight P Joyce Res Ctr, 71-78, mgr applns res, Glidden-Durkee Div, 71-78, ASSOC DIR APPL SCI, DWIGHT P JOYCE RES CTR, DURKEE DIV, SCM CORP, 78- *Mem:* Am Chem Soc; Am Oil Chem Soc. *Res:* Analytical chemistry of glycerides, surfactants and protective coatings; chromatographic and instrumental methods; synthesis of organic azides. *Mailing Add:* 16335 Ramona Dr Middleburg Heights OH 44130

THOMAS, ALFORD MITCHELL, b Bunnlevel, NC, July 24, 42; m 70. MEDICINAL CHEMISTRY. *Educ:* Campbell Col, NC, BA, 64; Univ NC, Chapel Hill, PhD(org chem), 69. *Prof Exp:* NIH fel, Univ Va, 69-71, res assoc org chem, 71-72; SR CHEMIST, ABBOTT LABS, 72- *Mem:* Am Chem Soc; The Chem Soc; AAAS; Sigma Xi. *Res:* Synthesis of biological peptides. *Mailing Add:* Dept 482 Res Div Abbott Labs North Chicago IL 60064

THOMAS, ALVIN DAVID, JR, b Gary, Ind, Nov 3, 28; m 52; c 3. PHYSICAL METALLURGY. *Educ:* Case Inst Technol, BS, 40; Purdue Univ, MS, 59, PhD(metall eng), 61. *Prof Exp:* Res engr, Repub Steel Res Ctr, 60-63; asst prof mech eng, Univ Tex, 63-67; head mat res sect, Tracor, Inc, 67-72, dep dir, Environ & Phys Sci Div, 72-76; DIR, MAT SCI DIV, RADIAN CORP, 76- *Mem:* Am Inst Mining, Metall & Petrol Engrs; Am Soc Metals; Am Soc Testing & Mat. *Res:* Mechanisms in precipitation hardening; strengthening mechanisms in steels; properties of Invar and Elinvar type alloys; resistance welding; composite materials; failure analysis and accident prevention. *Mailing Add:* 6807 Shoal Creek Blvd Austin TX 78731

THOMAS, ANTHONY, b May 3, 31; US citizen. MECHANICAL ENGINEERING, ENGINEERING PHYSICS. *Educ:* Univ Mich, BS, 54, MS, 63. *Prof Exp:* Res proj engr aerial photog, Chicago Aerial Industs, 57-61; group leader bubble chamber, 61-78, PROG MGR OCEAN THERMAL ENERGY CONVERSION, ARGONNE NAT LAB, 78- *Concurrent Pos:* Mem, US Bubble Chamber Working Group, 77-78. *Res:* Design and operation of cryogenic devices; devices for the generation, conversion and enhancement of energy efficiency. *Mailing Add:* Argonne Nat Lab 9700 S Cass Ave Argonne IL 60439

THOMAS, ARTHUR L, b New York, NY, July 24, 28; m 77. CHEMISTRY. *Educ:* Columbia Col, AB, 51; Princeton Univ, PhD, 56. *Prof Exp:* Engr photo prod, E I du Pont de Nemours & Co, Inc, 55-58, res supvr, 58-59; chem engr, Standard Ultramarine & Color Co, 60-65 & MHD, Inc & Plasmachem Inc, 65-68; from instr to asst prof chem, Calif State Polytech Col, San Luis Obispo, 69-72; vis asst prof immunochem, Columbia Univ, 73; sci ed, Ronald Press Co, 74-77; ED, CHEM MKT RES, HULL & CO, 78- *Mem:* AAAS; Am Chem Soc. *Res:* Pigments; high temperature reactions. *Mailing Add:* 20 Brookside Dr 3D Greenwich CT 06830

THOMAS, ARTHUR NORMAN, b Los Angeles, Calif, Jan 27, 31; m 50; c 5. SURGERY, THORACIC SURGERY. *Educ:* Stanford Univ, BS, 53; Univ BC, MD, 57. *Prof Exp:* Intern surg, San Francisco Gen Hosp, 57-58, resident, 58-59; resident, Univ Hosp, 60-62, clin instr, Sch Med, 63-68, asst prof, 68-73, ASSOC PROF SURG, SCH MED, UNIV CALIF, SAN FRANCISCO, 73-; CHIEF THORACIC SURG, SAN FRANCISCO GEN HOSP, 70- *Concurrent Pos:* NIH res fel, Univ Hosp, Univ Calif, San Francisco, 59-60, NIH fel, Cardiovasc Res Inst, 63-65; asst chief surg, Vet Admin Hosp, San Francisco, 66-70, attend physician thoracic surg, 70- *Mem:* Soc Thoracic Surg; Samson Thoracic Surg Soc; Am Asn Thoracic Surg. *Res:* Thoracic surgery; cardiopulmonary research. *Mailing Add:* 1101 Potrero Ave San Francisco Gen Hosp San Francisco CA 94110

THOMAS, AUBREY STEPHEN, JR, b Wolfeboro, NH, Nov 4, 33; m 56. PLANT PHYSIOLOGY & ECOLOGY. *Educ:* Keene State Col, BEd, 62; Univ NH, MS, 64, PhD(bot, plant physiol), 67. *Prof Exp:* Asst prof, 67-70, ASSOC PROF BIOL, MERRIMACK COL, 70-, CHMN DEPT, 75- *Mem:* AAAS; Am Soc Plant Physiol; Bot Soc Am; Am Soc Photobiol; Ecol Soc Am. *Res:* Plant physiological ecology; effect of light, radiation, electrical fields and other environmental factors upon the growth and development of the plant and its physiology; plant allelopathy. *Mailing Add:* Dept of Biol Merrimack Col North Andover MA 01845

THOMAS, BARBARA SMITH, see Smith-Thomas, Barbara

THOMAS, BARRY, b Eng, Dec 31, 41; US citizen. ZOOLOGY, ENVIRONMENTAL EDUCATION. *Educ:* Calif State Univ, Fullerton, BA, 67, MA, 68; Univ BC, PhD(zool), 71. *Prof Exp:* Lectr ecol, Univ Calgary, 71-72; asst prof, 72-75, PROF ENVIRON EDUC, CALIF STATE UNIV, FULLERTON, 75- *Concurrent Pos:* Pres, BioReCon, 71-; dir, Tucker Wildlife Sanctuary, 72- *Mem:* Am Soc Mammal; Audubon Soc. *Res:* Karyotaxonomy of island rodents; urbanization effects on wild animal populations; biological impact statements. *Mailing Add:* Dept of Sci Educ Calif State Univ Fullerton CA 92634

THOMAS, BARRY HOLLAND, b Lancaster, Eng, June 1, 39; m 66; c 2. BIOCHEMISTRY, PHARMACOLOGY. *Educ:* Univ Liverpool, BSc, 62, PhD(pharmacol), 65. *Prof Exp:* Asst lectr pharmacol, Univ Liverpool, 65-67, lectr, 67-69; RES SCIENTIST, HEALTH PROTECTION BR, DEPT NAT HEALTH & WELFARE CAN, 69- *Concurrent Pos:* Assoc ed, Can J Physiol Pharmacol, 80- *Mem:* Soc Toxicol Can; Brit Pharmacol Soc; Pharmacol Soc Can. *Res:* Role of drug metabolism in the toxicity of drugs; toxicity of drug interactions. *Mailing Add:* Kars ON K0A 2E0 Can

THOMAS, BERT O, b Lead, SDak, May 15, 26; m 49; c 2. ZOOLOGY. *Educ:* Colo State Univ, BS, 50, MS, 52; Univ Minn, PhD, 59. *Prof Exp:* Biologist, Hydrol Surv, US Fish & Wildlife Serv, 50; asst zool, Univ Minn, 52-57; biologist, State Dept Health, Minn, 57-59; from asst prof to prof zool & chmn dept biol sci, 59-74, prof biol, 74-77, PROF ZOOL, UNIV NORTHERN COLO, 77- *Concurrent Pos:* NSF lectr, Univ Colo, 59-61; tech adv, Continental Mach, Inc, 55-57; consult, Wilkie Found, 57-59. *Mem:* AAAS; Am Soc Limnol & Oceanog. *Res:* Plankton communities; ichthyology; radio ecology; aquatic biology. *Mailing Add:* Dept of Biol Sci Univ of Northern Colo Greeley CO 80631

THOMAS, BERWYN BRAINERD, b Iowa City, Iowa, Apr 6, 19; m 50; c 3. CHEMISTRY. *Educ:* Univ Ariz, BS, 40; Lawrence Univ, PhD(paper chem), 44. *Prof Exp:* Res chemist, Olympic Res Div, ITT Rayonier Inc, 47-60, group leader, 60-72, tech info specialist, 72-80. *Mem:* Am Chem Soc; Tech Asn Pulp & Paper Indust. *Res:* Preparation and use of cellulose in chemical conversion processes and paper manufacture; methods of evaluation; information retrieval. *Mailing Add:* E 2370 Highway 3 Shelton WA 98584

THOMAS, BILLY SEAY, b Tenn, Dec 31, 26; m 53; c 1. THEORETICAL PHYSICS. *Educ:* Wayne State Univ, BS, 53; Vanderbilt Univ, MS, 55, PhD(physics), 59. *Prof Exp:* Nat Res Coun fel, Argonne Nat Lab, 58-59; asst prof physics, Vanderbilt Univ, 59-60; asst prof, 60-77, ASSOC PROF PHYSICS, UNIV FLA, 77- *Mem:* Am Phys Soc. *Res:* Atomic and molecular scattering; elementary particle physics. *Mailing Add:* Dept of Physics Univ of Fla Gainesville FL 32601

THOMAS, BRUCE ROBERT, b Guthrie Center, Iowa, Jan 1, 38; m 60; c 3. EXPERIMENTAL PHYSICS. *Educ:* Grinnell Col, BA, 60; Cornell Univ, PhD(theoret physics), 65. *Prof Exp:* Asst prof physics, Grinnell Col, 65-67; asst prof, 67-70, assoc prof, 70-77, PROF PHYSICS, CARLETON COL, 77- *Mem:* Am Phys Soc; Am Asn Physics Teachers. *Mailing Add:* Dept of Physics Carleton Col Northfield MN 55057

THOMAS, BYRON HENRY, b Oakland, Calif, Oct 9, 97; m 22; c 3. NUTRITION, BIOCHEMISTRY. *Educ:* Univ Calif, BS, 22; Univ Wis, MS, 24, PhD(animal nutrit), 29. *Prof Exp:* Instr animal husb, Univ Calif, 22-23; asst, Univ Wis, 24-25; dir nutrit, Walker-Gordon Lab Co, NJ, 29-31; prof animal husb & head animal nutrit & chem, Exp Sta, 31-49, PROF BIOCHEM, IOWA STATE UNIV, 49- *Mem:* Am Chem Soc; Am Soc Animal Sci; Soc Exp Biol & Med; Am Dairy Sci Asn; Am Inst Nutrit. *Res:* Irregularities in nutrition in the production of congenital abnormalities in mammals, and their effect on the nutrition, embryology, and histology of affected fetuses. *Mailing Add:* Dept of Biochem & Biophys Iowa State Univ Ames IA 50010

THOMAS, CARL H(ENRY), b Holly Hill, SC, Apr 4, 25; m 52; c 4. AGRICULTURAL ENGINEERING. *Educ:* Clemson Col, BS, 50; La State Univ, MS, 57; Mich State Univ, PhD, 69. *Prof Exp:* Asst agr eng, Agr Exp Sta, 50-51, res assoc, 51-53, asst agr engr, 53-58, assoc prof, 58-69, head dept, 69-76, PROF AGR ENG, LA STATE UNIV, BATON ROUGE, 69- *Mem:* Am Soc Agr Engrs. *Res:* Mechanization of harvesting of peppers and sweet potatoes; parameters that influence the harvesting of peppers; development of harvest equipment then utilizes these data. *Mailing Add:* Dept of Agr Eng La State Univ Baton Rouge LA 70803

THOMAS, CARLTON EUGENE (SANDY), b Cleveland, Ohio, Dec 16, 39; m 31; c 4. ELECTRICAL ENGINEERING, LASER FUSION. *Educ:* Univ Mich, BS, 61, MS, 63, PhD(elec eng), 71. *Prof Exp:* Res asst infrared, Inst Sci & Technol, Univ Mich, 61-62; dept head coherent optics, Conductron Corp, 62-67 & KMS Technol Ctr, 67-72; DIR LASER & OPTICS DIV, KMS FUSION, KMS INDUST, 72- *Mem:* Optical Soc Am; Inst Elec & Electronics Engrs; Sigma Xi. *Res:* Optics and laser systems for scientific demonstration of laser fusion; advanced laser system development for inertial confinement fusion reactor drivers. *Mailing Add:* KMS Fusion 3941 Research Park Dr Ann Arbor MI 48106

THOMAS, CAROLYN EYSTER, b Toledo, Ohio, July 14, 28; m 53. NEUROANATOMY, HISTOLOGY. *Educ:* Univ Toledo, BS, 48; Northwestern Univ, Chicago, MS, 51, PhD(anat), 53. *Prof Exp:* Instr anat, Med Sch, Northwestern Univ, Chicago, 53-58, asst prof, 58-66; asst prof, 66-68, ASSOC PROF ANAT, CHICAGO MED SCH-UNIV HEALTH SCI, 68- *Mem:* Am Asn Anat; Am Soc Zool. *Res:* Electrophysiological studies of cat cerebellum; spinal cord structure; muscular architecture of the heart; electron microscope studies of the spleen. *Mailing Add:* Dept Anat 3333 Green Bay Rd Chicago Med Sch-Univ Health Sci North Chicago IL 60064

THOMAS, CAROLYN MARGARET, b Brownville, Maine, Feb 25, 41. ANALYTICAL CHEMISTRY. *Educ:* Univ Maine, BA, 63; Northeastern Univ, PhD(anal chem), 68. *Prof Exp:* Teaching fel anal chem, Northeastern Univ, 63-67, lectr, Lincoln Col, 67-68; res chemist, US Army Natick Labs, 67-68; asst prof, 68-73, assoc prof, 73-77, PROF ANAL CHEM, WAYNESBURG COL, 77- *Mem:* Am Chem Soc; Sigma Xi. *Res:* Molten salts; electrochemistry; stability of foods; atomic absorption and emission spectroscopy applied to water pollution. *Mailing Add:* Dept Chem Waynesburg Col Waynesburg PA 15370

THOMAS, CECIL OWEN, JR, b East Cleveland, Ohio, Sept 6, 42; m 68; c 1. NUCLEAR ENGINEERING. *Educ:* Univ Tenn, Knoxville, BS, 64, MS, 66, PhD(nuclear eng), 71. *Prof Exp:* Res technician biomed res, Mem Res Ctr & Hosp, Univ Tenn, Knoxville, 63-64, asst, Univ, 67-68; Oak Ridge fel, Savannah River Lab, E I du Pont de Nemours & Co, Inc, 68-71; nuclear engr, Nuclear Eng Br, Tenn Valley Authority, 71-75; MEM STAFF, NUCLEAR REGULATORY COMN, 75- *Mem:* Am Nuclear Soc. *Res:* Nuclear power plant safety; nuclear instrumentation and control systems. *Mailing Add:* Nuclear Regulatory Comn 1717 H St NW Washington DC 20555

THOMAS, CHARLES ALLEN, b Scott Co, Ky, Feb 15, 00; m 26; c 4. CHEMISTRY. *Educ:* Transylvania Univ, BA, 20; Mass Inst Technol, Ms, 24; Transylvania Univ, DSc(org chem), 33; Hobart Col, LLD, 50; Univ Mo-Rolla, DEng, 65; Simpson Col, DSc, 67. *Hon Degrees:* DSc, Wash Univ, 47. *Prof Exp:* Res chemist, Gen Motors Res Corp, 23-24 & Ethyl Gasoline Corp, 24-25; res chemist, Thomas & Hochwalt Labs, Inc, 26-28, pres, 28-36; cent res dir, Monsanto Co, Ohio, 36-45, vpres & tech dir, Mo, 45-46, exec vpres, 47-50, pres, 51-60, chmn bd, 60-65, chmn finance comt, 65-68; RETIRED. *Concurrent Pos:* Cur, Transylvania Univ; mem corp, Mass Inst Technol; chmn bd trustees, Wash Univ. *Honors & Awards:* US Medal for Merit, 46; Medal, Indust Res Inst, 47; Gold Medal, Am Inst Chemists, 48; Perkin Medal, Soc Chem Indust, 53; Priestley Medal, Am Chem Soc, 55. *Mem:* Emer mem Nat Acad Eng; Nat Acad Sci; Soc Chem Indust; Electrochem Soc; Am Chem Soc (pres, 58). *Res:* Development of tetraethyl lead; bromine from sea water; effect of alkali metals on combustion; synthetic resins; synthetic styrene and rubber; rocket propellants; plutonium. *Mailing Add:* 7701 Forsyth Blvd St Louis MO 63105

THOMAS, CHARLES ALLEN, JR, b Dayton, Ohio, July 7, 27; m 51; c 2. BIOPHYSICAL CHEMISTRY. *Educ:* Princeton Univ, AB, 50; Harvard Univ, PhD(phys chem), 54. *Prof Exp:* Res scientist, Eli Lilly & Co, Ind, 54-55; Nat Res Coun fel physics, Univ Mich, 55-56 , instr, 56-57; from asst prof to prof biophys, Johns Hopkins Univ, 57-67; prof biol chem, Harvard Med Sch, 67-77; MEM & CHMN DEPT CELLULAR BIOL, SCRIPPS CLIN & RES FOUND, 77- *Concurrent Pos:* NSF sr fel, Weizmann Inst, 65. *Mem:* Am Acad Arts & Sci. *Res:* Molecular anatomy of viral and bacterial chromosomes; genetic recombination, organization and function of higher chromosomes. *Mailing Add:* Scripps Clin & Res Found 10666 N Torrey Pines Rd La Jolla CA 92037

THOMAS, CHARLES CARLISLE, JR, b Rochester, NY, Aug 18, 25; m 46; c 4. NUCLEAR MATERIALS SAFEGUARDS, NUCLEONICS. *Educ:* Univ Iowa, BS, 47; Univ Rochester, MS, 50; Am Inst Chemists, cert; Inst Nuclear Mat Mgt, cert. *Prof Exp:* Nuclear chemist, US Bur Mines, Okla, 50-51; sr engr, Bausch & Lomb Optical Co, NY, 51-52; tech engr, Aircraft Nuclear Propulsion Dept, Gen Elec Co, Ohio, 52-53; prin chemist, Battelle Mem Inst, 53-55; fel engr, Westinghouse Elec Corp, Pa, 55-60; proj leader radiation chem, Quantum, Inc, 60-62; res mgr, Western NY Nuclear Res Ctr, Inc, 62-72; actg dir, State Univ NY Buffalo, 72-74, dir nuclear sci & technol fac, 74-78; STAFF MEM, LOS ALAMOS NAT LAB, UNIV CALIF, 78- *Concurrent Pos:* Int Atomic Energy Agency vis prof, Tsing Hua, China, 64-65; adj assoc prof eng sci, aerospace & nuclear eng, State Univ NY Buffalo, 73-78. *Mem:* AAAS; Am Chem Soc; Am Nuclear Soc; fel Am Inst Chemists; Inst Nuclear Mat Mgt. *Res:* Neutron activation analysis; dosimetry of high intensity radiation; reactor technology; environmental analysis; radiation effects on materials. *Mailing Add:* 3373 La Avenida de San Marcas Santa Fe NM 87501

THOMAS, CHARLES GOMER, mathematics, computer sciences, see previous edition

THOMAS, CHARLES HILL, b Dexter, Ga, Jan 31, 22; m 45; c 1. POULTRY SCIENCE, GENETICS. *Educ:* Univ Ga, BSA, 52, MSA, 53; NC State Univ, PhD(genetics), 56. *Prof Exp:* Asst prof poultry husb, Miss State Univ & asst poultry husbandman, Agr Exp Sta, 56-58, assoc prof & assoc poultry husbandman, 58-66, PROF POULTRY SCI, MISS STATE UNIV & POULTRY GENETICIST, AGR EXP STA, 66-, PROF SCI BASIC TO MED, COL VET MED, 77- *Mem:* Am Poultry Sci Asn; Am Genetic Asn. *Res:* Inheritance of resistance to insecticides in Drosophila melanogaster. *Mailing Add:* Dept Poultry Sci Miss State Univ Box 298 Mississippi State MS 39762

THOMAS, CHARLES LAWRENCE, b South Plainfield, NJ, July 9, 29; m 56; c 3. CHEMISTRY, CHEMICAL ENGINEERING. *Educ:* Tusculum Col, BA, 52. *Prof Exp:* Res investr, 53-63, sect head res & develop, 63-78, SUPVR SPEC PROJS, ASARCO INC, 79- *Mem:* Sigma Xi (vpres, 65); Tech Asn Pulp & Paper Indust; Am Soc Test & Mat. *Res:* Gas instrument and analysis; method development; development of worldwide licensed processes for melting and casting copper; overseas engineering, commissioning and development of company licensed processes. *Mailing Add:* Central Res 901 Oak Tree Rd South Plainfield NJ 07080

THOMAS, CLAUDEWELL SIDNEY, b New York, NY, Oct 5, 32; m 68; c 3. PSYCHIATRY, PUBLIC HEALTH. *Educ:* Columbia Univ, BA, 52; State Univ NY Downstate Med Ctr, MD, 56; Am Bd Psychiat, dipl, 62; Yale Univ, MPH, 64. *Prof Exp:* Chief emergency treatment serv, Ment Health Ctr, New Haven, Conn, 65-67; educ dir psychiat emergency serv, Yale Univ, 67-68, dir social & community psychiat training, 68-73; dir div ment health prog, NIMH, 73-74; CHMN DEPT PSYCHIAT, COL MED & DENT, NJ MED SCH, 74- *Concurrent Pos:* Consult, Compass Club, New Haven, 63-65; consult psychiatrist, Div Alcoholism, State of Conn, 63-65; vol consult, Caribbean Fed Ment Health, New York, 64; dir Hill-West Haven div & chief unit III, Conn Ment Health Ctr, 67-68; mem ad hoc comt minority admin, Yale Univ, 68-70; soc sci mem, Nat Paterson; mem assembly behav & soc sci, Nat Acad Sci. Health Serv Res & Develop, 69-70; consult, Wash Sch Psychiat, A K Rice Inst Wash; prof sociol, Rutgers Univ; attend psychiatrist, Harrison Martland Hosp, Newark; consult, Carrier Clin Belle Mead, St Joseph's Hosp, Patterson. *Mem:* Fel Am Psychiat Asn; fel Am Pub Health Asn; fel Royal Soc Health; fel NY Acad Med; fel NY Acad Sci. *Res:* Application of theory and concepts in the areas of social and community psychiatry to further the understanding of mental health needs of individuals and groups. *Mailing Add:* Dept Psychiat NJ Med Sch Newark NJ 07103

THOMAS, CLAYTON LAY, b Metropolis, Ill, Dec 23, 21; m 50; c 4. MEDICINE. *Educ:* Univ Ky, BS, 44; Med Col Va, MD, 46; Harvard Univ, MPH, 58. *Prof Exp:* Intern med, Montreal Gen Hosp, 46-47; instr, US Naval Sch Aviation Med, 53-54; instr, Col Med, Univ Utah, 54-56; med dir, 58-70, VPRES MED AFFAIRS, TAMPAX INC, 69- *Concurrent Pos:* Clin asst, Harvard Med Serv, Boston City Hosp, 56-57; res fel path, Mallory Inst Path, 56-57; consult, Flight Safety Found, 57-58 & Parachutes, Inc, Mass, 60; consult, Dept Pop Sci, Sch Pub Health, Harvard Univ, fel epidemiol, 57-59; mem med & training serv comt, US Olympic Comt, 66-73; pres, Balloon Sch Mass, Inc, 70-; Fed Aviation Admin pilot exam-lighter-than-air-free balloon, 72-; pres, Pop Res Found, 74-; mem med dept vis comt, Mass Inst Technol, 75-78; mem med & training serv comt, US Olympic Coun Sports Med, 78-80. *Mem:* Am Fertil Soc; Am Sch Health Asn; Am Col Health Asn; Aerospace Med Asn; NY Acad Sci. *Res:* Medical ecology; physiology of menstruation; bacteriuria; medical aspects of sport parachuting and hot air ballooning; aerospace medicine; epidemiology; medical lexicography; sports medicine; health and sex education; physiology of reproduction. *Mailing Add:* Festiniog Farm Dingley Dell Palmer MA 01069

THOMAS, COLIN GORDON, JR, b Iowa City, Iowa, July 25, 18; m 46; c 4. SURGERY. *Educ:* Univ Chicago, BS, 40, MD, 43. *Prof Exp:* Assoc surg, Col Med, Univ Iowa, 50-51, asst prof, 51-52; from asst prof to assoc prof, 52-61, PROF SURG, SCH MED, UNIV NC, CHAPEL HILL, 61-, CHMN DEPT, 66- *Mem:* Am Col Surgeons; Am Asn Cancer Res; Am Thyroid Asn; Am Surg Asn; Soc Surg Alimentary Tract. *Res:* Thyroid cancer; gastrointestinal disorders; biological characeristics of thyroid neoplasms s related to the influence of Thyroid-Stimulating Hormone on their genesis, growth, function and management. *Mailing Add:* Dept of Surg 136 Clin Sci Bldg Chapel Hill NC 27514

THOMAS, DAN ANDERSON, b Ooltewah, Tenn, Oct 1, 22; m 44; c 2. PHYSICS. *Educ:* Univ Chattanooga, BS, 45; Vanderbilt Univ, PhD(physics), 52. *Prof Exp:* Asst prof physics, Univ of the South, 49-51; res physicist, US Naval Ord Lab, 51-52; from assoc prof to prof physics, Rollins Col, 52-63; prof physics & dean faculties, 63-80, vpres, 67-80, TRUSTEE PROF PHYSICS, JACKSONVILLE UNIV, 80- *Concurrent Pos:* Consult, US Naval Underwater Sound Reference Lab, 53-63. *Mem:* Fel AAAS; Am Phys Soc; Acoustical Soc Am; Am Asn Physics Teachers. *Res:* Beta ray spectroscopy; underwater acoustics; wave motion in solids; vibration of plates. *Mailing Add:* Dept Physics Jacksonville Univ Jacksonville FL 32211

THOMAS, DAVID ALDEN, b Baltimore, Md, Sept 8, 30; m 56; c 3. MATERIALS SCIENCE. *Educ:* Cornell Univ, BMetE, 53; Mass Inst Technol, ScD(metall), 58. *Prof Exp:* From instr to assoc prof metall, 53-63; chief mat sci res, Ingersoll-Rand Co, 63-68; assoc prof metall & mat sci, 68-70, PROF METALL & MAT SCI, LEHIGH UNIV, 70-, ASSOC DIR, MAT RES CTR, 68- *Mem:* AAAS; Am Soc Metals; Am Inst Mining, Metall & Petrol Engrs. *Res:* Structure and mechanical properties of metals, polymers and composites; materials applications; electro microscopy. *Mailing Add:* Dept of Metall & Mat Sci Lehigh Univ Bethlehem PA 18015

THOMAS, DAVID BARTLETT, b Butte, Mont, Sept 8, 37; m 61; c 2. MEDICINE, EPIDEMIOLOGY. *Educ:* Univ Washington, MD, 63; Johns Hopkins Univ, DrPH(epidemiol), 72. *Prof Exp:* From asst prof to assoc prof epidemiol, Johns Hopkins Univ, 71-75; assoc prof, 75-81, PROF EPIDEMIOL, UNIV WASH, 81- *Concurrent Pos:* Assoc mem epidemiol,

Fred Hutchinson Cancer Res Ctr, 75-; mem breast cancer task force, Nat Cancer Inst, 76-78; consult epidemiol, WHO, 78-79. *Mem:* Soc Epidemiol Res; Am Pub Health Asn; AAAS; Am Epidemiol Soc. *Res:* Epidemiologic studies of the etiology of cancers of the breast and cervix; studies of the potential carcinogenic effects of steroid contraceptives. *Mailing Add:* Dept of Epidemiol Univ of Wash Seattle WA 98195

THOMAS, DAVID DALE, b Lansing, Mich, Sept 18, 49; m 75. MOLECULAR BIOPHYSICS. *Educ:* Stanford Univ, BS, 71, PhD(biophys), 76. *Prof Exp:* Res asst physics, High Energy Physics Lab, Stanford Univ, 70; res asst, Dept Genetics, Stanford Univ, 71, student biophys, Dept Biol Sci, 71-75; fel biophys, dept muscle res, Boston Biomed Res Inst, 76-77; mem fac, Dept Biophysics, Stanford Univ, 77-80; ASST PROF BIOCHEM, DEPT BIOL, SCH MED, UNIV MINN, 80. *Concurrent Pos:* NSF fel, 71; fel, Muscular Dystrophy Asns Am, Inc, 76-77. *Mem:* AAAS; Fedn Am Scientists; Biophys Soc. *Res:* Molecular dynamics in muscle contraction as studied by spectroscopic probe methods; electron paramagnetic resonance studies of spin-labeled muscle proteins, such as actin and myosin. *Mailing Add:* Dept Biol Sch Med Univ Minn Minneapolis MN 55455

THOMAS, DAVID GILBERT, b London, Eng, Aug 4, 28; US citizen; m 57; c 2. TELECOMMUNICATION TRANSMISSION. *Educ:* Oxford Univ, BA, 49, MA, 50, & DPhil(chem), 52. *Prof Exp:* Head semiconductor electronics res lab, 62-68, dir electron device process & battery lab, 68-69, exec dir electronic device, Process Mat Div, Murray Hills, NJ, 69-76, EXEC DIR TRANSMISSION SYSTS, BELL LABS, HOLMDEL, NJ, 76- *Honors & Awards:* Oliver E Buckley Solid State Physics Award, Am Phys Soc, 69. *Mem:* Fel Am Phys Soc; fel Inst Elec & Electronics Engrs; AAAS. *Res:* Optical and electrical properties of semiconductors. *Mailing Add:* Bell Labs Holmdel NJ 07733

THOMAS, DAVID GLEN, b St Clairsville, Ohio, July 21, 26; m 59. HYDRODYNAMICS, CHEMICAL ENGINEERING. *Educ:* Ohio State Univ, BChE, 47, MSc, 48, PhD(chem eng), 53. *Prof Exp:* Res engr, Battelle Mem Inst, 48-50; res engr, 52-77, PROG MGR, OAK RIDGE NAT LAB, 77-, FORD FOUND PROF FLUID MECH, UNIV TENN, KNOXVILLE, 64- *Concurrent Pos:* NSF sr fel, Cambridge Univ, 60-61; consult, Aerojet-Gen Nucleonics Div, Gen Tire & Rubber Co, 62-63. *Mem:* AAAS; Am Inst Chem Engrs; Am Chem Soc; Sigma Xi; Soc Rheol. *Res:* Transport characteristics and non-Newtonian characteristics of suspensions; heat and mass transfer enhancement; vortex interactions; natural convection; turbulence promotion; reverse osmosis. *Mailing Add:* 113 Morningside Dr Oak Ridge TN 37830

THOMAS, DAVID LAURENCE, ichthyology, ecology, see previous edition

THOMAS, DAVID LEE, b Dodgeville, Wis, May 22, 49; m 71; c 3. ANIMAL BREEDING, ANIMAL PRODUCTION. *Educ:* Univ Wis-Madison, BS, 71; Okla State Univ, Stillwater, MS, 75, PhD(animal breeding), 77. *Prof Exp:* Asst prof, Ore State Univ, 77-81; ASST PROF ANIMAL SCI, UNIV ILL, 81- *Concurrent Pos:* With US Peace Corps, Kenya, 71-73. *Mem:* Am Soc Animal Sci; Am Genetic Asn; Sigma Xi. *Res:* Animal breeding research with sheep and sheep production with primary emphasis on improvement of reproductive efficiency. *Mailing Add:* 1912 Galen Dr Champaign IL 61820

THOMAS, DAVID PHILLIP, b Wasco, Ore, July 7, 18; m 43; c 3. FORESTRY. *Educ:* Univ Wash, BSF, 41, MF, 47. *Prof Exp:* Res assoc, Eng Exp Sta, Univ Wash, 46, assoc forestry, Col Forestry, 46-47; instr wood technol, State Univ NY Col Forestry, Syracuse, 47-50; from asst prof to assoc prof wood sci & technol, 50-66, spec asst to provost, 64-72, dir inst forest products, 66-72, assoc dean col, 73-75, chmn, Forest Mgt & Soc Sci Div, 75-80, PROF FOREST RESOURCES, COL FOREST RESOURCES, UNIV WASH, 66- *Concurrent Pos:* Mem, King Co Environ Develop Comn, 73-78 & State of Wash Forest Pract Adv Comt, 74-; trustee, Keep Wash Green, 75-; mem, Wilderness & Recreation Comt, King County Policy Develop Comt, 76-78; pres, Foresters' Alumni Asn, Univ Wash, 78-79. *Mem:* Soc Am Foresters; Forest Prod Res Soc; Am Forestry Asn. *Res:* Economics and technology of utilizing forest crops; forest practices and their impact on environmental quality. *Mailing Add:* Col Forest Resources AR-10 Univ Wash Seattle WA 98195

THOMAS, DAVID TIPTON, b Barnesville, Ohio, Dec 13, 37; m 66; c 2. ELECTRICAL ENGINEERING. *Educ:* Carnegie Inst Technol, BS, 59, MS, 60; Ohio State Univ, PhD(elec eng), 62. *Prof Exp:* Res assoc elec eng, Antenna Labs, Ohio State Univ, 61-62, assoc supvr & asst prof, 62-63; asst prof elec eng, Carnegie-Mellon Univ, 63-68; mem tech staff, Radio Transmission Lab, Bell Tel Labs, 68-73; prin engr, 73-78, MGR ANTENNA & MICROWAVE ENG, ELECTROMAGNETIC SYSTS DIV, ELECTROMAGNETIC SYSTS DIV, RAYTHEON CORP, 78- *Concurrent Pos:* NSF grant, Carnegie-Mellon Univ, 66-68. *Mem:* Inst Elec & Electronics Engrs. *Res:* Electromagnetic field theory; computer solutions in electromagnetics; scattering, antennas and radiation. *Mailing Add:* 1165 Camino Palomera Santa Barbara CA 93111

THOMAS, DON WYLIE, b Spanish Fork, Utah, Aug 8, 23; m 52; c 6. VETERINARY SCIENCE, ANIMAL SCIENCE. *Educ:* Utah State Univ, BS, 49; Iowa State Univ, DVM, 53. *Prof Exp:* Vet pathologist, Calif State Dept Agr, 53-54; PROF VET & ANIMAL SCI & EXTEN VET, UTAH STATE UNIV, 54- *Concurrent Pos:* State del nat plans conf, USDA, 56, 58 & 62; vchmn, Utah Herd Health & Mastitis Comt, 58- *Mem:* Am Asn Exten Vet; Am Asn Vet Nutritionists. *Res:* Prevention of diseases in cattle, sheep, horses and poultry. *Mailing Add:* Dept of Animal Sci Utah State Univ Logan UT 84322

THOMAS, DONALD CHARLES, b Cincinnati, Ohio, Sept 26, 36; m 57; c 3. MICROBIOLOGY, PATHOLOGY. *Educ:* Xavier Univ, BS, 57; Univ Cincinnati, MS, 59; St Louis Univ, PhD(microbiol & virol), 68. *Prof Exp:* Asst dir, Dept Surg, Surg Bact Labs, Univ Cincinnati, 59-61; instr, Dept Biol, Villa Madonna Col, 61-63; grad student, Dept Microbiol & Molecular Virol Inst, St Louis Univ, 63-68; instr, Dept Med Microbiol & Pediat, Col Med, Ohio State Univ, 68-69, asst prof, 69-72, assoc dir, Prog Develop Asst Div, 72-77; dir contracts & grants mgt,77-78, asst dean res, Sch Grad Studies, 79-80, ACTG DEAN & ASSOC DEAN RES, SCH GRAD STUDIES, DIR, UNIV RES SERV & ASSOC PROF, DEPT PATH & ASSOC PROF, PROG MICROBIOL & IMMUNOL, SCH MED & COL SCI & ENG, WRIGHT STATE UNIV, 80- *Concurrent Pos:* Adj asst prof, Dept Med Microbiol & Pediat, Col Med, Ohio State Univ, 72-77; admin adv, Nat Reyes Syndrome Found, Ohio, 75-; lab consult, Vet Admin Ctr, Ohio, 78-; fed liaison rep, Am Coun Educ, Wright State Univ, 79- *Mem:* Am Soc Microbiol; AAAS; Fedn Am Scientists; Licensing Execs Soc. *Res:* diagnostic virology; molecular aspects of virus replication, pathogenesis of virus diseases and developments in tumor viruses. *Mailing Add:* Sch Grad Studies Wright State Univ Dayton OH 45435

THOMAS, DONALD E(ARL), b Pittsburgh, Pa, Oct 27, 18; m 42; c 3. MATERIALS SCIENCE ENGINEERING. *Educ:* Carnegie Inst Technol, BS, 42, MS, 49; DSc, 50. *Prof Exp:* Asst phys metall, Carnegie Inst Technol, 46-47; supvry scientist corrosion & phys metall, Atomic Power Div, 49-58, mgr naval reactor metall, 58-59, mgr mat dept, Astronuclear Lab, 59-66, eng mgr systs & technol, 66-71, CONSULT SCIENTIST, RES LABS, WESTINGHOUSE ELEC CORP, 71- *Concurrent Pos:* Instr, Carnegie Inst Technol, 51-52. *Honors & Awards:* Eng Mat Achievement Award, Am Soc Metals, 72. *Mem:* Fel Am Nuclear Soc; Am Inst Mining, Metall & Petrol Engrs; fel Am Soc Metals; Brit Metals Soc. *Res:* Materials research and development. *Mailing Add:* 317 Old Farm Rd Pittsburgh PA 15228

THOMAS, DONALD H(ARVEY), b Phoenixville, Pa, Dec 1, 33; div; c 2. ENGINEERING, MEDICAL SCIENCE. *Educ:* Drexel Inst, BSME, 56, MSME, 59; Case Inst Technol, PhD(med eng), 65. *Prof Exp:* From instr to asst prof, 56-61, chmn curriculum, 70-73, ASSOC PROF MECH ENG, DREXEL UNIV, 65-, ASSOC DIR, CTR TEACHING INNOVATION, 74-, ASSOC DEAN ENG, 80- *Concurrent Pos:* Consult, 59- *Honors & Awards:* Lindback Award Distinguished Teaching, Christian R Lindbach Found, 78. *Mem:* Sigma Xi; Am Soc Mech Engrs; Am Soc Eng Educ; Inst Elec & Electronics Engrs. *Res:* Medical engineering; innovative teaching in engineering; biomechanics; product design liability; system dynamics and control; vehicle dynamics. *Mailing Add:* Col Eng Drexel Univ Philadelphia PA 19104

THOMAS, DONALD HENRY, b Detroit, Mich, Feb 25, 37; m 62; c 3. APPLIED MATHEMATICS, APPLIED STATISTICS. *Educ:* Wayne State Univ, BS, 59, MA, 64, PhD(math), 70. *Prof Exp:* Res mathematician, Gen Motors Res Labs, 60-68; asst prof math, Univ Detroit, 68-69; RES MATHEMATICIAN, GEN MOTORS RES LABS, 69- *Mem:* Soc Indust & Appl Math; Inst Math Statist. *Res:* Numerical analysis, approximation theory and statistics with special emphasis on spline approximations in one and several variables to problems of computer-aided design and automation. *Mailing Add:* Math Dept Gen Motors Res Labs Warren MI 48090

THOMAS, DUDLEY WATSON, b Los Angeles, Calif, Apr 14, 20; m 46; c 2. BIOCHEMISTRY. *Educ:* Univ Calif, AB, 42; Calif Inst Technol, MS, 47, PhD(org chem), 51. *Prof Exp:* Chemist, US Rubber Co, 42-43; biochemist, Rohm & Haas Co, 51-60; res fel chem, Calif Inst Technol, 60-62; asst prof biochem, Sch Dent, Univ Southern Calif, 62-67; asst prof zool, 67-76, chmn dept biol, 71-76, PROF BIOL, CALIF STATE UNIV, LOS ANGELES, 76- *Mem:* AAAS; Am Chem Soc; NY Acad Sci. *Res:* Enzymes; structural-biological activity relationships; connective tissue metabolism. *Mailing Add:* 1460 Linda Ridge Rd Pasadena CA 91103

THOMAS, E LLEWELLYN, b Salisbury, Eng, Dec 15, 17; m 47. MEDICINE, ELECTRICAL ENGINEERING. *Educ:* Univ London, BSc, 51; McGill Univ, MD & CM, 55. *Prof Exp:* Jr engr, Brit Broadcasting Co, 37-39; asst controller telecommun, Govt Malaya, 45-51; res assoc, Med Col, Cornell Univ, 56-58; sci officer, Defence Res Med Labs, Toronto, 58-60; PROF PHARMACOL, UNIV TORONTO, 61-, ASSOC DEAN MED, 74- *Concurrent Pos:* Prof psychol, Univ Waterloo, 62-64. *Mem:* Nat Soc Prof Eng; Inst Elec & Electronics Eng; fel Royal Soc Arts; Can Med Asn; fel Royal Soc Can. *Mailing Add:* Fac of Med Univ of Toronto Toronto ON M5S 1A1 Can

THOMAS, EDWARD DONNALL, b Mart, Tex, Mar 15, 20; m 42; c 3. INTERNAL MEDICINE, ONCOLOGY. *Educ:* Univ Tex, BA, 41, MA, 43; Harvard Med Sch, MD, 46; Am Bd Internal Med, dipl, 53. *Prof Exp:* From intern to sr asst resident med, Peter Bent Brigham Hosp, Boston, 46-52, chief med res, 52-53, hematologist, 53; res assoc, Cancer Res Found, Children's Med Ctr, 53-55; hematologist & asst physician, Mary Imogene Bassett Hosp, 55-56; assoc clin prof med, Col Physicians & Surgeons, Columbia Univ, 56-63; PROF MED, SCH MED, UNIV WASH, 63- *Concurrent Pos:* Fel med, Mass Inst Technol, 50-51; instr, Harvard Med Sch, 53; physician-in-chief, Mary Imogene Bassett Hosp, 56-63; clin prof, Albany Med Col, 58-63; mem, Fred Hutchinson Cancer Res Ctr, Seattle, 63- *Honors & Awards:* Nat Award Basic Sci, Am Cancer Soc, 80. *Mem:* Am Soc Clin Invest; Am Asn Cancer Res; Am Soc Hemat; Exp Hemat Soc; Transplantation Soc. *Res:* Marrow biochemistry and transplantation; irradiation effects; hematology. *Mailing Add:* Div Oncol Univ Wash Sch Med Seattle WA 98195

THOMAS, EDWARD SANDUSKY, JR, b Kansas City, Mo, Jan 11, 38; m 60. MATHEMATICS. *Educ:* Whittier Col, BA, 59; Univ Wash, MS, 61; Univ Calif, Riverside, PhD(math), 64. *Prof Exp:* Asst prof math, Univ Mich, Ann Arbor, 65-69; assoc prof, 69-75, chmn dept math & statist, 78-81, PROF MATH, STATE UNIV NY ALBANY, 75- *Mem:* Am Math Soc. *Res:* Topology, dynamical systems; differential equations. *Mailing Add:* Dept of Math State Univ of NY Albany NY 12203

THOMAS, EDWARD WILFRID, b Croydon, Eng, May 9, 40. PHYSICS. *Educ:* Univ London, BSc, 61, PhD(physics), 64. *Prof Exp:* Asst res physicist, 64-65, from asst prof to assoc prof, 65-73, PROF PHYSICS, GA INST TECHNOL, 73- *Concurrent Pos:* Consult, Oak Ridge Nat Lab, 65- *Mem:* Am Phys Soc; Optical Soc Am; Brit Inst Physics. *Res:* Collisions between atomic, ionic and molecular systems, particularly on the formation of excited states; development of photon and particle detection techniques. *Mailing Add:* Sch of Physics Ga Inst of Technol Atlanta GA 30332

THOMAS, EDWIN LEE, b Sandusky, Ohio, Nov 30, 43. BIOCHEMISTRY. *Educ:* Miami Univ, BA, 65; Univ Mich, PhD(biochem), 70. *Prof Exp:* Fel biochem, Roche Inst Molecular Biol, 70-72; ASSOC MEM STAFF BIOCHEM, ST JUDE CHILDREN'S HOSP & ASST PROF, UNIV TENN, 72- *Concurrent Pos:* Prin investr, Dent Res Inst, NIH, 76- *Mem:* Am Soc Microbiol; AAAS; Am Soc Biol Chemists. *Res:* Biological membrane structure and function; mechanisms of resistance to infection. *Mailing Add:* Dept of Biochem 332 N Lauderdale Memphis TN 38101

THOMAS, EDWIN LORIMER, b Attleboro, Mass, June 14, 47. POLYMER SCIENCE, MATERIALS ENGINEERING. *Educ:* Univ Mass, BS, 69; Cornell Univ, PhD(mat sci), 73. *Prof Exp:* Asst prof chem eng, Univ Minn, 73-77; ASSOC PROF POLYMER SCI & ENG, UNIV MASS, 77- *Concurrent Pos:* Vis prof, Univ Freiburg, Ger, 81; Humbolt fel, 81. *Mem:* Am Phys Soc; Am Chem Soc; Electron Micros Soc Am; Soc Rheol; Royal Micros Soc. *Res:* Polymer physics and engineering; application of electron microscopy; electron and x-ray diffraction to materials characterization; structure property relationships. *Mailing Add:* Dept Polymer Sci & Eng Univ Mass Amherst MA 01003

THOMAS, ELIZABETH WADSWORTH, b Washington, DC, May 23, 44; m 70; c 1. ANALYTICAL CHEMISTRY. *Educ:* ECarolina Univ, AB, 66; Univ Va, PhD(phys & org chem), 70. *Prof Exp:* Res assoc pharmacol, Med Sch, Univ Va, 70-72; lectr, Univ Wis, Parkside & Barat Col, 73-74; ANAL CHEMIST, ABBOTT LABS, 75- *Mem:* Am Chem Soc; Sigma Xi. *Res:* Development of analytical methodology for the analysis of new pharmaceutical products and new consumer products; solution of unusual complaints about current marketed products. *Mailing Add:* 3925 Dorchester Ave Gurnee IL 60031

THOMAS, ELLIDEE DOTSON, b Huntsville, Ark, July 20, 26; m 60; c 1. NEUROLOGY. *Educ:* Univ Ark, BA, 47, BSM, 58, MD, 58; Univ Tex Med Br, cert, 48. *Prof Exp:* Asst prof child neurol, Sch Med, 65-68, assoc prof, 70-75, PROF CHILD DEVELOP NEUROL, UNIV OKLA HEALTH SCI CTR, 75-, DIR, CHILD STUDY CTR, 69-, CHIEF SECT DEVELOP PEDIAT, 80- *Mem:* Child Neurol Soc; Am Acad Neurol; Am Acad Pediat; Am Acad Cerebral Palsy & Develop Med. *Res:* Normal and abnormal development in early life and the impact of a handicapped child on parents individually, family relationships and impact on siblings. *Mailing Add:* Child Study Ctr 1100 NE 13th St Oklahoma City OK 73177

THOMAS, ELMER LAWRENCE, b Springfield, Ohio, Jan 18, 16; m 41; c 3. FOOD SCIENCE. *Educ:* Ohio State Univ, BSc, 41; Univ Minn, MSc, 43, PhD, 50. *Prof Exp:* Res asst, 41-45, instr dairy prod, 46-50, asst prof dairy technol, 51-54, assoc prof dairy indust, 54-60, prof, 61-81, EMER PROF FOOD SCI, UNIV MINN, ST PAUL, 81- *Concurrent Pos:* Consult food indust, 50- *Mem:* Am Dairy Sci Asn; Inst Food Technologists. *Res:* Physical, chemical and engineering aspects of dairy products processing; sensory testing of foods. *Mailing Add:* 1987 N Aldine St Roseville MN 55113

THOMAS, ELVIN ELBERT, b Osceola, Iowa, Nov 23, 44; m 69; c 3. RUMINANT NUTRITION, ANIMAL NUTRITION. *Educ:* Iowa State Univ, BS, 68, MS, 74, PhD(animal nutrit), 77. *Prof Exp:* Voc agr instr, Newell Providence Community Schs, 68-71; instr animal sci, Iowa State Univ, 73-76; ASST PROF ANIMAL SCI, AUBURN UNIV, 77- *Res:* Improvement of the efficiency of feedstuff utilization by ruminants with emphasis on protein utilization and metabolism. *Mailing Add:* Dept of Animal & Dairy Sci Auburn Univ Auburn AL 36830

THOMAS, ESTES CENTENNIAL, III, b Plaquemine, La, Dec 13, 40; m 64; c 3. PETROPHYSICS. *Educ:* La State Univ, Baton Rouge, BS, 62; Stanford Univ, PhD(phys chem), 66. *Prof Exp:* Fel, Princeton Univ, 66-67; chemist, Shell Develop Co, 67-72, sr engr, 72-75, STAFF ENGR, SHELL OIL CO, 75- *Mem:* Soc Prof Well Log Analysts; Soc Petrol Eng; Sigma Xi. *Res:* Physical characteristics and transport of energy through interstices of subterranean earthen formations, particularly those containing hydrocarbons. *Mailing Add:* PO Box 481 Shell Oil Co Houston TX 77001

THOMAS, FLOYD W, JR, b Columbia, SC, Apr 7, 38. MECHANICAL ENGINEERING. *Educ:* Univ SC, BS, 61; NC State Univ, MS, 63, PhD(mech eng), 67. *Prof Exp:* Mem tech staff, Bell Tel Labs, 61-64; TRW Systs, 67-68; sr eng scientist, McDonnell Douglas Astronautics, 68-69; assoc prof eng & chmn mech aerospace eng, 69-76, PROF ENG, CALIF STATE UNIV, FULLERTON, 76- *Mem:* Am Soc Mech Engrs; Am Soc Eng Educ. *Res:* Thermodynamics of spacecraft propellant tank pressurization; curriculum development in engineering education. *Mailing Add:* Sch of Eng Calif State Univ Fullerton CA 92634

THOMAS, FORREST DEAN, II, b Provo, Utah, Dec 27, 30; m 52; c 2. INORGANIC CHEMISTRY. *Educ:* Brigham Young Univ, BS, 55; Pa State Univ, PhD(chem), 59. *Prof Exp:* From asst prof to assoc prof, 59-73, PROF CHEM, UNIV MONT, 73- *Mem:* Am Chem Soc. *Res:* Organic and inorganic synthesis; preparation of coordination compounds. *Mailing Add:* Dept of Chem Univ of Mont Missoula MT 59801

THOMAS, FRANK BANCROFT, b Camden, Del, June 14, 22; m 60; c 2. HORTICULTURE, FOOD TECHNOLOGY. *Educ:* Univ Del, BS, 48; Pa State Univ, MS, 49, PhD(hort), 55. *Prof Exp:* From instr to asst prof hort, Pa State Univ, 49-58; food processing exten specialist, 58-61, exten assoc prof, 61-66, EXTEN PROF FOOD SCI, NC STATE UNIV, 66- *Concurrent Pos:* Vis fel food technol, Mass Inst Technol, 54-55; consult cryogenic foods, 63-64; mem NC Gov Comn Com Fisheries, 64-65, mem Com & Sport Fisheries Adv Comt, 75-76; sabbatical, Dept Food Sci & Technol, Univ Hawaii, 68; partic, Food & Agr Orgn Conf Fish Qual & Inspection, Halifax, Can, 69 & Conf Fishery Prod Technol, Japan, 73; prog leader Food Sci Seafood Adv Serv, NC Sea Grant Prog, 70- *Mem:* Inst Food Technologists. *Res:* Post-harvest physiology of fruits and vegetables; food processing; chemical and microbiological changes in seafoods; flavor and color evaluation; extension and applied research on seafood utilization. *Mailing Add:* Dept of Food Sci NC State Univ Raleigh NC 27607

THOMAS, FRANK HARRY, b Alamo, Ga, Oct 16, 32; m 52; c 3. SOILS, INORGANIC CHEMISTRY. *Educ:* Univ Ga, BSA, 54, MS, 56, PhD(soil phosphorus), 59. *Prof Exp:* Asst chemist, Everglades Exp Sta, 59-66; assoc chemist, 66-68, prof chem & chmn div sci-math, 68-75, asst acad dean, 73-75, ACAD DEAN, ABRAHAM BALDWIN AGR COL, 75- *Mem:* Am Chem Soc; AAAS; Am Soc Allied Health Professions. *Mailing Add:* Off of Acad Dean Abraham Baldwin Agr Col Tifton GA 31793

THOMAS, FRANK J(OSEPH), b Pocatello, Idaho, Apr 15, 30; m 49; c 4. ENGINEERING, NUCLEAR PHYSICS. *Educ:* Univ Idaho, BS, 52; Univ Calif, Berkeley, MS, 57. *Prof Exp:* Staff mem advan studies, Sandia Corp, 52-56; prog mgr mobile reactors, Aerojet-Gen Nucleonics Div, 57-61, mgr eng, 61-63, dep mgr appl sci div, 63-64; staff specialist res & eng, Off Secy Defense, 64-65, asst dir res & eng, Nuclear Progs, 65-67; phys scientist, Rand Corp, Calif, 67-71; PRES, PAC-SIERRA RES CORP, SANTA MONICA, 71- *Concurrent Pos:* Lectr, Exten Div, Univ Calif, Berkeley, 57-58; adv, Sci Adv Comt, Defense Intel Agency, 66-73; consult, US Arms Control & Disarmament Agency, 72-76. *Honors & Awards:* Master Design Award, Prod Eng Mag, 63; Meritorious Civilian Serv Award, Secy Defense, 67. *Mem:* Am Inst Aeronaut & Astronaut; AAAS. *Res:* National security and energy issues. *Mailing Add:* 21442 Paseo Portola Malibu CA 90265

THOMAS, GARETH, b Maesteg, Gt Brit, Aug 9, 32; m 60; c 1. PHYSICAL METALLURGY, MATERIALS SCIENCE. *Educ:* Univ Wales, BSc, 52; Cambridge Univ, PhD(metall), 56, ScD, 69. *Prof Exp:* Res fel metall, Cambridge Univ, 55-58, Imp Chem Industs fel, 58-60; from asst prof to assoc prof, 60-67, assoc dean, Grad Div, 68-69, asst chancellor & actg vchancellor acad affairs, 69-72, Guggenheim fel, 72, PROF METALL, UNIV CALIF, BERKELEY, 67- *Concurrent Pos:* Consult, Exxon. *Honors & Awards:* McGraw Res Award, Am Soc Eng Educ; Stoughton Teaching Award, Am Soc Metals, 65, Grossman Pub Award, 66; Electron Micros Soc Am Prize, 65; Rosenhain Medal, Brit Metals Soc, 77; E O Lawrence Award, President & US Dept Energy, 78. *Mem:* Am Soc Metals; Electron Micros Soc Am; Am Phys Soc; Am Inst Mining, Metall & Petrol Engrs; Brit Inst Metals. *Res:* Electron microscopy; inveestigations of relation of structure to properties in materials using transmission electron microscopy and diffraction; alloy design. *Mailing Add:* Dept of Mat Sci & Eng Univ of Calif Berkeley CA 94720

THOMAS, GARLAND LEON, b Topeka, Kans, Aug 29, 20; m 48; c 3. PHYSICS. *Educ:* Drury Col, BS, 42; Univ Mo, AM, 48, PhD(physics), 54. *Prof Exp:* Fel engr, atomic power dept, Westinghouse Elec Corp, 53-59; assoc prof physics, Drury Col, 59-66 & Fla Inst Technol, 66-71; mem staff, Fla Planning Dept, Brevard County, 71-79; PRIN ENG, PLANNING RES CORP, KENNEDY SPACE CTR, FLA, 79- *Mem:* Biophys Soc; Am Phys Soc; Am Asn Physics Teachers; Am Nuclear Soc. *Res:* Remote sensing; nuclear reactor physics; ultrasonic cavitation. *Mailing Add:* 200 E Southgate Blvd Melbourne FL 32901

THOMAS, GARTH JOHNSON, b Pittsburgh, Kans, Sept 8, 16; m 45; c 2. BEHAVIORAL NEUROBIOLOGY. *Educ:* Kans State Teachers Col Pittsburg, AB, 38; Univ Kans, MA, 40; Harvard Univ, AM, 43, PhD(exp psychol), 48. *Prof Exp:* Asst instr, Univ Kans, 38-41; tutor, Harvard Univ, 41-43 & 47-48; from instr to asst prof psychol, Univ Chicago, 48-54; res assoc & assoc prof, Neuropsychiat Inst, Col Med, Univ Ill, 54-57, res prof, Biophys Res Lab, Dept Elec Eng & Dept Physiol & Biophys, 57-66; dir, Ctr Brain Res, 70-77, PROF, CTR BRAIN RES, UNIV ROCHESTER, 66- *Concurrent Pos:* Dept Defense NIMH & NSF res grants, Univ Chicago, Univ Ill & Univ Rochester, 51-77; mem psychol sci fel rev panel, NIMH, 64-69 & psychobiol rev panel NSF, 68-71; consult ed, McGraw-Hill Encycl Sci & Technol, 64-, Contemp Psychol, 64-73 & Sinauer Assocs Press, 68-; assoc ed, J Comp & Physiol Psychol, 69-74, ed, 75- *Mem:* AAAS; Am Physiol Soc; Psychonomic Soc; Soc Exp Psychol; Soc Neurosci. *Res:* Brain function; studies of behavioral effects of central nervous system lesions; spatial behavior; psychophysiology of sensation. *Mailing Add:* Ctr for Brain Res Box 605 Med Ctr Univ of Rochester Rochester NY 14642

THOMAS, GARY E, b Lookout, WVa, Oct 25, 34; m 61; c 2. ATMOSPHERIC PHYSICS. *Educ:* NMex State Univ, BS, 57; Univ Pittsburgh, PhD(physics), 63. *Prof Exp:* Res assoc, Aeronomy Serv, Nat Ctr Sci Res, France, 62-63; mem tech staff space physics lab, Aerospace Corp, 65-67; assoc prof astro-geophys, 67-74, PROF ASTRO-GEOPHYS, UNIV COLO, BOULDER, 74- *Mem:* AAAS; Am Geophys Union. *Res:* Theoretical study of upper atmosphere; radiative transfer; application of spectroscopic remote sensing data to study of atmospheric structure; measurement techniques and theoretical study of interplanetary medium; study of radiative and photochemical processes in the stratosphere and mesosphere. *Mailing Add:* Lab for Atmos & Space Physics Univ of Colo Boulder CO 80302

THOMAS, GARY LEE, b Willows, Calif, May 12, 37; m 77; c 3. ELECTRICAL ENGINEERING, SOLID STATE PHYSICS. *Educ:* Univ Calif, Berkeley, BSc, 60, MA, 62, PhD(elec eng), 67. *Prof Exp:* Ed officer elec sci, Accra Polytech Inst, 62-64; instr elec eng, Univ Calif, Berkeley, 67; from asst prof to prof elec eng, State Univ NY, Stony Brook, 67-79, chmn dept, 75-79; VPRES ACAD AFFAIRS, NJ INST TECHNOL, 80- *Concurrent Pos:* NSF grants, 72-; AAAS cong fel, 74-75; mem mat prog, Off Technol Assessment, 74-75. *Mem:* Am Phys Soc; Inst Elec & Electronics Engrs; AAAS; Am Asn Univ Professors. *Res:* Solid state electronics; laser annealing; magnetoelastic surface wave. *Mailing Add:* VPres Acad Affairs NJ Inst Technol Newark NJ 07102

THOMAS, GARY LEE, b El Paso, Tex, Feb 27, 47; m 71; c 3. POPULATION DYNAMICS, BIOMATHEMATICS. *Educ:* Calif Western Univ, BA, 70; San Diego State Univ, MS, 73; Univ Wash, PhD(fisheries), 78. *Prof Exp:* Res assoc, Scripps Inst, Univ Calif, 71-73; res asst, 73-78, biologist, 78-79, RES FAC, COL FISHERIES, UNIV WASH, 79-, RES SCIENTIST, APPL PHYSICS LAB, 80- *Concurrent Pos:* Prin investr, Fisheries Res Inst, 79- *Mem:* Am Fisheries Soc; Pac Fisheries Biologists; Am Fedn Inst Res Biologists. *Res:* Hydroacoustic measurement technology and its application to fish population dynamics. *Mailing Add:* Univ Wash WH-10 Seattle WA 98195

THOMAS, GEORGE BRINTON, JR, b Boise, Idaho, Jan 11, 14; m 36, 80; c 3. MATHEMATICS. *Educ:* State Col Wash, AB, 34, AM, 36; Cornell Univ, PhD(math), 40. *Prof Exp:* Instr math, Cornell Univ, 37-40; from instr to assoc prof, 44-60, asst elec eng, 43-45, exec officer dept math, 50-59, PROF MATH, MASS INST TECHNOL, 60-; RETIRED. *Mem:* Am Math Soc; Math Asn Am (1st vpres, 58-59). *Mailing Add:* Old Salem Path Magnolia MA 01930

THOMAS, GEORGE E, b Bloomington, Ill, July 18, 21; m 44; c 2. EXPERIMENTAL NUCLEAR PHYSICS. *Educ:* Ill Wesleyan Univ, BS, 43. *Prof Exp:* Jr physicist, 43-66, SCI ASSOC EXP NUCLEAR PHYSICS, ARGONNE NAT LAB, 66- *Mem:* Am Phys Soc; Int Nuclear Target Develop Soc. *Res:* Research, development and production of thin film targets used particularly at tandem and dynamatron accelerators, and nuclear physics experiments associated with these targets. *Mailing Add:* Argonne Nat Labs 9700 S Cass Ave Argonne IL 60439

THOMAS, GEORGE HOWARD, b Minerva, Ohio, Apr 27, 36; m 60; c 3. PEDIATRICS. *Educ:* Western Md Col, AB, 59; Univ Md, PhD, 63. *Prof Exp:* Instr biochem, Sch Med, Univ Md, 63; asst pediat, Sch Med, 65-67, instr, 67-68, asst prof pediat & med, Sch Med & dir genetics lab, John F Kennedy Inst, 68-76, ASSOC PROF PEDIAT, JOHNS HOPKINS HOSP, JOHNS HOPKINS UNIV, 76- *Mem:* AAAS; Am Soc Human Genetics; Soc Inherited Metab Dis; Soc Pediat Res. *Res:* Human genetics. *Mailing Add:* J F Kennedy Inst Genetics Lab 707 N Broadway Baltimore MD 21205

THOMAS, GEORGE JOSEPH, JR, b New Bedford, Mass, Dec 24, 41; m 66; c 3. BIOPHYSICAL CHEMISTRY, BIOMOLECULAR STRUCTURE & FUNCTION. *Educ:* Boston Col, BS, 63; Mass Inst Technol, PhD(phys chem), 67. *Prof Exp:* Asst prof, 68-70, assoc prof, 71-73, head dept, 74-80, PROF CHEM, SOUTHEASTERN MASS UNIV, 74- *Concurrent Pos:* Sr res fel, US-Japan Coop Sci Prog, Inst Protein Res Osaka Univ, Japan, 75-76; mem adv comt, NIH, 79-83. *Honors & Awards:* Coblentz Award, Coblentz Soc & Soc Appl Spectros. *Mem:* Biophys Soc; AAAS; Sigma Xi. *Res:* Raman and infrared spectroscopy; structure and function of biological molecules. *Mailing Add:* Southeastern Mass Univ North Dartmouth MA 02747

THOMAS, GEORGE RICHARD, b Bethlehem, Pa, Feb 1, 20; m 55; c 4. ORGANIC CHEMISTRY. *Educ:* Bowdoin Col, BS, 41; Northwestern Univ, PhD(chem), 48; Harvard Univ, adv mgt prog, 62. *Prof Exp:* Res fel, Univ Ill, 48-49 & Harvard Univ, 49-50; proj dir, Boston Univ, 50-54; dyestuffs res sect, Qm Res & Eng Command, Natick Labs, 54-56, asst chief res & develop, Chem & Plastics Div, 56-58, chief, 58-62, assoc dir & dir res, Clothing & Org Mat Lab, 62-68, chief, Mat Res Labs, 68-72, CHIEF, ORG MAT LAB, ARMY MAT & MECH RES CTR, US ARMY, 72- *Concurrent Pos:* Pres, Thomason Chem, Inc, 54-60; vis prof, Boston Univ, 63-65; sr exec fel, Kennedy Sch Gov, Harvard Univ, 80. *Mem:* Fel Am Inst Chemists; AAAS; Am Chem Soc; Sigma Xi. *Res:* Military applications of polymers as fibers, films, foams, elastomers and rigid and reinforced plastics; materials research; polymer research; operations and management research; business administration. *Mailing Add:* Org Mat Lab Army Mat & Mech Res Ctr Watertown MA 02172

THOMAS, GERALD ANDREW, b Birmingham, Ala, Oct 8, 11; m 40; c 4. RADIOCHEMISTRY. *Educ:* Birmingham-Southern Col, BS & MS, 32; Univ Fla, PhD(chem), 52. *Prof Exp:* Teacher pub schs, Ala, 32-39; asst, Johns Hopkins Univ, 39-40; res chemist, Niagara Alkali Co, 40-45; from instr to assoc prof chem, Univ Fla, 46-57; chmn div sci, math & eng, San Francisco State Univ, 57-63, prof chem, 57-77; RETIRED. *Concurrent Pos:* NSF fel, 54-56; lectr & scientist, US AEC Latin-Am Prog, Atoms in Action, 65-68; consult, Oak Ridge Assoc Univs, 63-80. *Mem:* Am Chem Soc; Am Nuclear Soc. *Res:* Physical properties of organic compounds; nucleonics; radioisotopes. *Mailing Add:* 410 Hillcrest Blvd Millbrae CA 94030

THOMAS, GERALD H, b Salt Lake City, Utah, Sept 3, 42; m 64; c 1. SOFTWARE SYSTEMS, THEORETICAL PHYSICS. *Educ:* Calif Inst Technol, BS, 64; Univ Calif, Los Angeles, MS, 66, PhD(physics), 69. *Prof Exp:* NATO fel physics, Europ Orgn Nuclear Res, 69-70; res assoc, Univ Helsinki, 70-71; postdoctoral physicist, Argonne Nat Lab, 71-73, asst physicist, 73-75, physicist, 75-81; MEM TECH STAFF, BELL LABS, 81- *Mem:* Am Phys Soc. *Res:* Planning of large software systems. *Mailing Add:* 6K-311 Bell Lab Naperville-Wheaton Rd Naperville IL 60566

THOMAS, GORDON ALBERT, b Kingston, Pa, June 8, 43; m 66; c 1. EXPERIMENTAL SOLID STATE PHYSICS. *Educ:* Brown Univ, ScB, 65; Univ Rochester, PhD(physics), 71. *Prof Exp:* Fel physics, Univ Rochester, 71-72; MEM TECH STAFF PHYSICS, BELL LABS, 72- *Mem:* Am Phys Soc. *Res:* Studies of transport properties and spectroscopy that probe the metal-insulator transition in liquids and solids. *Mailing Add:* Bell Labs Murray Hill NJ 07974

THOMAS, GORDON W, b Calgary, Alta, Jan 20, 31; m 60; c 4. PETROLEUM ENGINEERING & MATHEMATICS. *Educ:* Pa State Univ, BS, 54, MS, 57; Stanford Univ, PhD(petrol eng), 63. *Prof Exp:* Asst proj engr, Sinclair Res, Inc, 57-59, consult, 59-62, res scientist, 62-65; sr res scientist, Res Dept, Sinclair Oil & Gas Co, Okla, 65-68; lectr, 66-68, PROF PETROL ENG, UNIV TULSA, 68- *Mem:* Am Soc Petrol Engrs; Soc Indust & Appl Math. *Res:* Theoretical aspects of thermal recovery methods of petroleum; mathematical simulation of petroleum reservoirs; theoretical studies of underground retorting of oil shale. *Mailing Add:* Dept Petrol Eng Univ Tulsa Tulsa OK 74104

THOMAS, GRANT WORTHINGTON, b Washington, DC, Feb 23, 31; m 51; c 5. SOIL CHEMISTRY. *Educ:* Brigham Young Univ, BS, 53; NC State Univ, MS, 56, PhD(soils), 58. *Prof Exp:* Asst prof agron, Va Polytech Inst, 58-60, assoc prof, 60-64; prof soils, Tex A&M Univ, 64-68; PROF AGRON, UNIV KY, 68- *Concurrent Pos:* Vis prof, Univ Calif, Riverside, 62-63; vis fel, St Cross Col, Univ Oxford, 76. *Mem:* Fel Am Soc Agron; fel Soil Sci Soc Am. *Res:* Reactions and movement of solutes in soils and no-tillage cropping. *Mailing Add:* Dept Agron Univ Ky Lexington KY 40506

THOMAS, GUSTAVE DANIEL, b Bay St Louis, Miss, Aug 4, 40; m 60; c 4. ENTOMOLOGY. *Educ:* Miss State Univ, 62, MS, 64; Univ Mo-Columbia, PhD(entom), 67. *Prof Exp:* RES ENTOMOLOGIST, BIOL CONTROL INSECTS RES LAB, N CENT REGION, SCI & AGR ADMIN-AGR RES, USDA, 67- *Concurrent Pos:* Res assoc, Univ Mo, 67- *Mem:* Entom Soc Am; Int Orgn Biol Control. *Res:* Population dynamics; economic thresholds; relationships of parasites and predators to their hosts. *Mailing Add:* Biol Contr Insects Res Lab Agr Res USDA Box A Columbia MO 65205

THOMAS, H RONALD, b Auburn, Ind, June 9, 42. PHOTOELECTON SPECTROSCOPY, SURFACE CHEMISTRY. *Educ:* Univ Durham, MSc, 75, PhD(surface chem), 77. *Prof Exp:* Chemist, Xerox Webster Res Ctr, 67-74, assoc scientist, 77-79, scientist, 79-82; SR RES SCIENTIST, MINERALS, PIGMENTS & METALS DIV, PFIZER, INC, 82- *Concurrent Pos:* Instr, Intensive Short Course Photoelectron Spectros, 79-; adj prof chem eng, Univ Wash, 82- *Mem:* Am Chem Soc; Am Phys Soc; Am Vacuum Soc. *Res:* Surface studies on organic polymeric and metallic materials using photoelectron spectroscopy; radio frequency plasma chemistry; laser assisted chemical vapor deposition; interface studies; conducting and semiconducting polymers. *Mailing Add:* Pfizer Inc 640 N 13th St PO Box 548 Easton PA 18042

THOMAS, HAROLD A(LLEN), JR, b Terre Haute, Ind, Aug 14, 13; m 35; c 3. CIVIL ENGINEERING, SANITARY ENGINEERING. *Educ:* Carnegie Inst Technol, BS, 35; Harvard Univ, MS, 37, ScD(sanit eng), 38. *Prof Exp:* From instr to assoc prof sanit eng, 38-56, GORDON McKAY PROF CIVIL & SANIT ENG, HARVARD UNIV, 56- *Concurrent Pos:* Consult, Nat Acad Sci-Nat Res Coun, 43-, Dept Health, Educ & Welfare, 49- & US Dept Defense, 52-58. *Honors & Awards:* R E Horton Medal, Am Geophys Union, 78. *Mem:* Nat Acad Eng; fel Am Acad Arts & Sci; Am Geophys Union; Am Soc Civil Engrs. *Res:* Fluid mechanics; hydrology; mathematical statistics; water supply and treatment; systems analysis for water resource development. *Mailing Add:* Harvard Univ 120 Pierce Hall Cambridge MA 02138

THOMAS, HAROLD LEE, b Westphalia, Kans, July 2, 34; m 56; c 3. MATHEMATICS, STATISTICS. *Educ:* Kans State Col Pittsburg, BS, 58, MS, 59; Okla State Univ, PhD(statist), 64. *Prof Exp:* Instr math, Kans State Col Pittsburg, 59-60; asst, Okla State Univ, 60-64; from asst prof to assoc prof, 64-69, PROF MATH, PITTSBURG STATE UNIV, 69- *Mem:* Math Asn Am; Am Statist Asn. *Res:* Factorial experiments in experimental designs. *Mailing Add:* Dept of Math Pittsburg State Univ Pittsburg KS 66762

THOMAS, HAROLD TODD, b Seattle, Wash, Feb 3, 42; c 1. PHOTOCHEMISTRY, OPTICAL DISC MATERIALS. *Educ:* Calif Inst Technol, BS, 64; Wesleyan Univ, MA, 66; Princeton Univ, PhD(chem), 70. *Prof Exp:* Res chem, Bell Tel Labs, 69-70; sr res chemist, 70-79, RES ASSOC, EASTMAN KODAK CO, 79- *Mem:* Am Chem Soc. *Res:* Photochemistry of ordered systems; spectroscopy and photochemistry of adsorbed molecules; photoresists; optical disc materials. *Mailing Add:* 60 Wintergreen Way Rochester NY 14618

THOMAS, HAZEL JEANETTE, b Birmingham, Ala, Jan 19, 32. ORGANIC CHEMISTRY, MEDICINAL CHEMISTRY. *Educ:* Birmingham Southern Col, BS, 53, MS, 58. *Prof Exp:* SR CHEMIST, RES SOUTHERN RES INST, 53- *Mem:* Am Chem Soc (secy, 76-77). *Res:* Synthesis of potential anticancer agents; nucleosides and nucleotides. *Mailing Add:* Southern Res Inst 2000 Ninth Ave South Birmingham AL 35255

THOMAS, HENRY COFFMAN, b Sacramento, Ky, Dec 29, 18; m 44; c 1. PHYSICS. *Educ:* Western Ky State Col, BS, 43; Vanderbilt Univ, MS & PhD, 49. *Prof Exp:* From asst to assoc prof physics, Miss State Col, 49-55; assoc prof & head dept, Bradley Univ, 55-58; chmn dept, 58-74, assoc dean arts & sci, 74-76, PROF PHYSICS, TEX TECH UNIV, 58- *Mem:* Am Phys Soc. *Res:* Low energy nuclear physics. *Mailing Add:* Dept of Physics Tex Tech Univ Col of Arts & Sci Lubbock TX 79409

THOMAS, HERIBERTO VICTOR, b Panama City, Repub Panama, Mar 17, 17; US citizen; m 50; c 2. PREVENTIVE MEDICINE. *Educ:* Univ Southern Calif, AB, 50, MS, 60; Univ Calif, Los Angeles, MPH, 64; Univ Calif, Berkeley, PhD, 68. *Prof Exp:* Res fel pharmacol & biochem, Univ Southern Calif, 53-56, res assoc, Sch Med, 57-61; res assoc physiol & biochem, St Joseph Hosp, Burbank, 61-64; res chemist, Calif State Dept Health, 64-66, res specialist, 66-72, coordr, Sickle Cell Anemia Prog, 72-74, chief genetic dis, 74-80; SR LECTR, HEALTH & MED SCI, UNIV CALIF, BERKELEY, 73-; CONSULT, 80- *Concurrent Pos:* Reviewer & consult sci, AAAS & NSF, 72- & Nat Heart, Lung & Blood Inst, NIH, Rev Br, 75-; mem, Med Qual Rev Comt #5, State Bd Med Qual Assurance, 80- *Honors & Awards:* Macgee Award, Am Oil Chem Soc, 63. *Mem:* AAAS; Am Chem Soc; Am Soc Human Genetics; NY Acad Sci; Sigma Xi. *Res:* Physiological chemistry of air pollutants and their health effects; lipid metabolism; structural changes in lung tissue as a consequence of adverse ambient conditions; prenatal diagnosis of disabling genetic diseases; genetic counseling as a method of prevention. *Mailing Add:* PO Box 9062 Berkeley CA 94709

THOMAS, HERMAN HOIT, b Raleigh, NC, Dec 26, 31; m 57; c 2. ISOTOPE GEOCHEMISTRY, TRACE ELEMENT GEOCHEMISTRY. *Educ:* Lincoln Univ, Pa, BA, 58; Univ Pa, PhD(geochem), 73. *Prof Exp:* Chemist, US Geol Surv, 58-64, Fairchild-Hiller Corp, 64-65 & Melpar Corp, 65-66; SPACE SCIENTIST GEOCHEM, GODDARD SPACE FLIGHT CTR, NASA, 66- Mem; Am Geophys Union. *Res:* Composition of the Earth; geophysical analysis of earth's lithosphere; composition and age of the solar system. *Mailing Add:* Code 922 Goddard Space Flight Ctr NASA Greenbelt MD 20771

THOMAS, HOWARD MAJOR, b Elwood, Nebr, Feb 14, 18; m 43; c 6. PHYSICAL CHEMISTRY. *Educ:* Nebr State Teachers Col, 42; Univ Iowa, PhD(chem), 49. *Prof Exp:* Asst prof chem & head dept, St Ambrose Col, 49-52; from assoc prof to prof, Univ SDak, 53-58; chmn dept, 58-79, PROF CHEM, UNIV WIS-SUPERIOR, 58- *Concurrent Pos:* Vis prof, Univ Wis, 64-65; Fulbright lectr phys chem, Univ Col Cape Coast, Ghana, 68-69. *Mem:* AAAS; Am Chem Soc. *Res:* Chemical kinetics; azeotropic solution; audio-visual aids for chemistry teaching. *Mailing Add:* Dept Chem Univ Wis Superior WI 54880

THOMAS, HUBERT JON, b Philadelphia, Pa, June 14, 40; m 81. DIGITAL SYSTEM SIMULATION, CONTROL SYSTEM ANALYSIS. *Educ:* Pa State Univ, BS, 62, MS, 64, PhD(elec eng), 69. *Prof Exp:* Asst prof elec eng, Rochester Inst Technol, 69-71; asst prof eng, Calif State Univ, Los Angeles, 71-73; res engr, Zenith Radio Corp, 73-77; SR ENG SPECIALIST, LITTON GUID & CONTROL, 77- *Mem:* Inst Elec & Electronics Engrs. *Res:* Analog and hybrid computation; logical design and switching theory; system simulation and identification; stochastic optimal controls. *Mailing Add:* Litton Systs 5500 Canoga Ave M/S 91 Woodland Hills CA 91364

THOMAS, J(EREMIAH) L(INDSAY), JR, b Lynchburg, Va, June 25, 19; m 45; c 3. CHEMICAL ENGINEERING. *Educ:* Univ Va, BChE, 41; NY Univ, MChE, 47. *Prof Exp:* Res chemist, E I du Pont de Nemours & Co, Inc, Pa, 41-43; chem engr, Div War Res, Manhattan Proj, Columbia Univ, 43-45; engr, Exp Sta, 45-48, res engr, 48-49, tech group leader, Nylon Plant, Tenn, 50-52, tech supvr, 52-57, process supvr, Textile Fibers Dept, 57-60, sr supvr, 60-70, mgr environ control, 71-75, ENVIRON AFFAIRS COORDR, E I DU PONT DE NEMOURS & CO, INC, 75- *Res:* Synthetic fibers; environmental control. *Mailing Add:* E I du Pont de Nemours & Co Inc PO Box 27001 Richmond VA 23261

THOMAS, JACK WARD, b Ft Worth, Tex, Sept 7, 34; m 57; c 2. WILDLIFE BIOLOGY. *Educ:* Tex A&M Univ, BS, 57; WVa Univ, MS, 69; Univ Mass, PhD, 73. *Prof Exp:* Biologist, Tex Game & Fish Comn, 57-62; res biologist, Tex Parks & Wildlife Dept, 62-67; asst prof wildlife mgt, WVa Univ & wildlife res biologist, Forestry Sci Lab, Northeastern Forest Exp Sta, US Forest Serv, 67-71, proj dir environ forestry res, Pinchot Inst Environ Forestry, 71-73, PROJ LEADER, RANGE & WILDLIFE HABITAT RES, PAC NORTHWEST FOREST EXP STA, US FOREST SERV, 73-, CHIEF RES BIOLOGIST, 80- *Concurrent Pos:* Adj prof, Wash State Univ, Ore State Univ, Univ Idaho & Eastern Ore State Col. *Mem:* Sigma Xi; Wildlife Soc; Wilson Ornith Soc; Am Ornith Union; Am Soc Mammal. *Res:* Mobility and home range management of deer and turkeys; population dynamic of deer; disease impact on deer and antelope populations; wildlife habitat research; sociobioeconomic implications of game habitat manipulation; habitat requirements for wildlife in urbanizing areas; relationships of wild and domestic ungulates to forested ranges; non-consumptive utilization of wildlife; forestry/wildlife relationships. *Mailing Add:* US Forest Serv Range & Wildlife Habitat Lab La Grande OR 97850

THOMAS, JAMES ARTHUR, b International Falls, Minn, Apr 22, 38; m 61; c 2. BIOCHEMISTRY. *Educ:* St Olaf Col, BA, 60; Univ Wis, MS, 63, PhD(biochem), 66. *Prof Exp:* USPHS fel biochem, Univ Minn, 67-69; asst prof, 69-75, ASSOC PROF BIOCHEM, IOWA STATE UNIV, 75- *Mem:* AAAS; Am Chem Soc; Am Soc Biol Chemists. *Res:* Enzymology of glycogen metabolism and protein phosphorylation-dephosphorylation. *Mailing Add:* Dept of Biochem & Biophys Iowa State Univ Ames IA 50010

THOMAS, JAMES DOUGLAS, b Franklin Mine, Mich, July 19, 19; m 47; c 2. ELECTROCHEMISTRY, CHEMICAL ENGINEERING. *Educ:* Mich Technol Univ, BS, 41, MS, 46. *Prof Exp:* Res engr, Chem Eng, 46-62, ASST DEPT HEAD ELECTROCHEM, GEN MOTORS RES LAB, 62- *Mem:* Am Electroplaters Soc; hon mem Am Electroplater's Soc. *Res:* Fundamental electrochemistry; plating, corrosion of plated coatings; resource recovery of plant effluents; structures and properties of plated metals and of substrates. *Mailing Add:* 807 Lincoln Rd Grosse Pointe MI 48230

THOMAS, JAMES E, b Marshall, Mo, May 17, 26; m 52; c 2. PHYSICS. *Educ:* Mo Valley Col, BS, 50; Univ Mo-Rolla, MS, 55; Univ Mo-Columbia, PhD(physics), 63. *Prof Exp:* Teacher high sch, Mo, 50-52; instr math, Univ Mo-Rolla, 52-55; assoc prof physics, Mo Valley Col, 55-61; assoc prof, 63-65, PROF PHYSICS, PITTSBURG STATE UNIV, 65- *Mem:* Am Phys Soc; Am Asn Physics Teachers. *Res:* Small angle x-ray diffraction; particle size and structure determination, solid state; radiation damage in perfect crystals. *Mailing Add:* Dept of Physics Pittsburg State Univ Pittsburg KS 66764

THOMAS, JAMES H, b Cardston, Alta, Jan 9, 36; m 59; c 4. PLANT BREEDING, GENETICS. *Educ:* Utah State Univ, BSc, 61, MS, 63; Univ Alta, PhD(genetics), 66. *Prof Exp:* Res asst agron, Utah State Univ, 60-63; teacher sci, Taber Sch Div, Alta, 63-64; res asst genetics, Univ Alta, 64-66; res officer, Can Dept Agr, 66-67 & Rudy Patrick Seed Co, 67-69; seed specialist & adv, Utah State Univ-AID, Bolivia, 69-72, ASSOC PROF PLANT SCI & INT PROGS, UTAH STATE UNIV, 72- *Mem:* Am Soc Agron; Crop Sci Soc Am; Am Inst Biol Sci. *Res:* Administrator international programs. *Mailing Add:* Dept of Plant Sci UMC 83 Utah State Univ Logan UT 84322

THOMAS, JAMES POSTLES, b Washington, DC, July 28, 39; m 65; c 3. ZOOLOGY, ECOLOGY. *Educ:* Univ NC, Chapel Hill, AB, 62; Univ Ga, MS, 66, PhD(zool), 70. *Prof Exp:* Ga Power Co fel aquatic ecol, Univ Ga, 70; res assoc biol oceanog, Univ Wash, 70-72, NSF grant, 71-72; SUPVRY FISHERIES BIOLOGIST & INVESTS CHIEF BIOL OCEANOG, NAT MARINE FISHERIES SERV, 72- *Mem:* Am Soc Limnol & Oceanog; Estuarine Res Fedn. *Res:* Energy flow and cycling of carbon in marine and estuarine ecosystems; primary productivity and the release, assimilation and oxidation of phytoplankton-derived dissolved organic matter in marine waters; seabed oxygen consumption and plankton respiration primary productivity; remote sensing of coastal, shelf and slope waters of United States between Cape Hatteras and Nova Scotia using both aircraft and satellites. *Mailing Add:* US Dept Com Sandy Hook Lab Nat Marine Fisheries Serv Highlands NJ 07732

THOMAS, JAMES WILLIAM, b Ironwood, Mich, Nov 11, 41; m 67; c 1. MATHEMATICS. *Educ:* Mich Technol Univ, BS, 63; Univ Ariz, MS, 65, PhD(math), 67. *Prof Exp:* Asst prof math, Univ Wyo, 67-72; assoc prof, 72-77, PROF MATH, COLO STATE UNIV, 77- *Concurrent Pos:* NSF sci develop grant, Univ Ariz, 70-71. *Mem:* Am Math Soc. *Res:* Applied mathematics; hydrodynamics; nonlinear functional analysis; applications of nonlinear functional analysis. *Mailing Add:* Dept of Math Colo State Univ Ft Collins CO 80521

THOMAS, JEROME FRANCIS, b Chicago, Ill, Jan 8, 22; m; c 3. AIR POLLUTION, WATER POLLUTION. *Educ:* DePaul Univ, BS, 43; Univ Calif, PhD(chem), 50. *Prof Exp:* Res chemist, 50-55, assoc prof, 55-72, PROF SANIT ENG, UNIV CALIF, BERKELEY, 72-, CHMN, DIV HYDRAUL & SANIT ENG, 73- *Concurrent Pos:* Consult, Energy Res Develop Agency 69-; adj prof, Environ Protection Agency, 70-; consult, Nat Acad Sci, 73- *Mem:* Am Chem Soc; Am Soc Eng Educ; Soc Appl Spectros; Am Water Works Asn. *Res:* Sanitary chemistry; chemical aspects applied to air, water pollution and quality control. *Mailing Add:* Div Hydraul & Sanit Eng 631 Davis Hall Univ Calif Berkeley CA 94720

THOMAS, JOAB LANGSTON, b Holt, Ala, Feb 14, 33; m 54. BOTANY. *Educ:* Harvard Univ, AB, 55, AM, 57, PhD, 59. *Prof Exp:* Cytotaxonomist, Arnold Arboretum Harvard Univ, 59-61; from asst prof to prof biol, Univ Ala, 61-76, asst dean, Col Arts & Sci, 65, dean students & vpres students affairs, 65-76; CHANCELLOR, NC STATE UNIV, RALEIGH, 76-; PRES, UNIV ALA, 81- *Concurrent Pos:* Dir, Herbarium, Univ Ala, 61-76, dir arboretum, 64-76. *Mem:* Am Soc Plant Taxon; Bot Soc Am; Int Asn Plant Taxon. *Res:* Systematics and cytogenetics of higher plants. *Mailing Add:* Off of the Chancellor NC State Univ Raleigh NC 27607

THOMAS, JOE ED, b Moran, Tex, Oct 3, 37; m 58; c 3. ELECTRICAL ENGINEERING. *Educ:* Univ Wyo, BS, 60; Univ Idaho, MS, 62; Univ Denver, PhD(elec eng), 70. *Prof Exp:* Res engr seismic propagation, Standard Oil Co Calif, 60-61 & Denver Res Inst, 62-66; from asst prof to assoc prof, 66-77, PROF ELEC ENG & CHMN DEPT, UNIV IDAHO, 77- *Concurrent Pos:* NSF grant, Univ Idaho, 67-, Nat Oceanic & Atmospheric Admin grant, 71- *Mem:* Am Geophys Soc; Inst Elec & Electronics Engrs. *Res:* Acoustics, particularly acoustic-gravity wave propagation and acoustic sources. *Mailing Add:* Dept of Elec Eng Univ of Idaho Moscow ID 83843

THOMAS, JOHN, b Rome, Ga, May 13, 18; m 44; c 2. MEDICINE. *Educ:* Morris Brown Col, BA, 40; Meharry Med Col, MD, 44. *Prof Exp:* From instr to prof med, Meharry Med Col, 70-80, prof internal med, 70-80, dir, Cardiovasc Dis Clin Res Ctr, 61-80; RETIRED. *Concurrent Pos:* Fel med & cardiol, Meharry Med Col, 45-46, Nat Heart Inst trainee, 49-52; res collabr, Brookhaven Nat Lab, 61-62. *Mem:* Fel Am Col Physicians; Nat Med Asn. *Res:* Cardiovascular disease; hypertension and myocardial infarction. *Mailing Add:* Meharry Med Col Nashville TN 37208

THOMAS, JOHN A, b La Crosse, Wis, Apr 6, 33; m 57; c 2. PHARMACOLOGY. *Educ:* Univ Wis-La Crosse, BS, 56; Univ Iowa, MA, 58, PhD(physiol), 61. *Prof Exp:* Instr physiol, Univ Iowa, 60-61; asst prof pharmacol, Sch Med, Univ Va, 61-64; assoc prof, Sch Med, Creighton Univ, 64-67; asst dean, 73-75, PROF PHARMACOL, SCH MED, WVA UNIV, 67-, ASSOC DEAN, 75- *Mem:* Am Soc Pharmacol & Exp Therapeut; Endocrine Soc; Soc Toxicol. *Res:* Endocrine pharmacology, mechanism of action of androgens; prostate gland neoplasms; pesticides and reproduction; reproductive toxicology; phthalate acid esters. *Mailing Add:* Dept of Pharmacol WVa Univ Med Ctr Morgantown WV 26506

THOMAS, JOHN ALVA, b Berwyn, Ill, May 9, 40; m 65; c 2. BIOCHEMISTRY. *Educ:* DePauw Univ, AB, 62; Univ Ill, Urbana, PhD(biochem), 68. *Prof Exp:* NIH fel, Univ Pa, 68-70; asst prof, 70-77, ASSOC PROF BIOCHEM, SCH MED, UNIV SDAK, 78- *Concurrent Pos:* Vis prof, Cornell Univ, 77-78. *Mem:* AAAS; Biophys Soc; Am Chem Soc; Am Soc Biol Chemists. *Res:* Mechanism of action peroxidases and catalases; biological halogenation reactions; bioenergetics and oxidative phosphorylation; enzyme kinetics; intracellular pH. *Mailing Add:* Dept of Biochem Univ of SDak Sch of Med Vermillion SD 57069

THOMAS, JOHN B(OWMAN), b New Kensington, Pa, July 14, 25; m 44; c 6. ELECTRICAL ENGINEERING. *Educ:* Gettysburg Col, AB, 44; Johns Hopkins Univ, BS, 52; Stanford Univ, MS, 53, PhD(elec eng), 55. *Prof Exp:* Elec engr, Koppers Co, Inc, 46-51, asst chief engr, 51-52; from asst prof to assoc prof, 55-62, PROF ELEC ENG, PRINCETON UNIV, 62- *Concurrent Pos:* NSF sr fel, 67-68. *Mem:* Fel Inst Elec & Electronics Engrs. *Res:* Communication and information theory; random processes; corona discharge; high voltage rectification. *Mailing Add:* Dept of Elec Eng Princeton Univ Princeton NJ 08544

THOMAS, JOHN EUGENE, b Youngstown, Ohio, July 5, 14; m 42; c 3. PHYTOPATHOLOGY. *Educ:* Ohio State Univ, BSc, 41; Univ Wis, PhD(plant path), 47. *Prof Exp:* From instr to asst prof plant path, Univ Wis, 45-50; assoc prof, 50-57, prof & head dept, 67-80, EMER PROF PLANT PATH, OKLA STATE UNIV, 80- *Mem:* Am Inst Biol Sci; Am Phytopath Soc; Mycol Soc Am. *Res:* Diseases of trees. *Mailing Add:* Dept Plant Path Okla State Univ Stillwater OK 74074

THOMAS, JOHN HOWARD, b Chicago, Ill, Apr 9, 41; m 62; c 2. FLUID DYNAMICS, SOLAR PHYSICS. *Educ:* Purdue Univ, BS, 62, MS, 64, PhD(eng sci), 66. *Prof Exp:* NATO fel appl math, Cambridge Univ, 66-67; asst prof mech & aerospace sci, 67-73, assoc prof, 73-81, PROF MECH & AEROSPACE SCI & ASSOC DEAN GRAD STUDIES, COL ENG & APPL SCI, UNIV ROCHESTER, 81-, ASSOC, C E K MEES OBSERV, 72- *Concurrent Pos:* Vis scientist, Max Planck-Inst Physics & Astrophysics, Munich, 73-74. *Mem:* Am Phys Soc; Am Astron Soc; Int Astron Union; Am Geophys Union; Am Soc Mech Engrs. *Res:* Geophysical and astrophysical fluid dynamics; magnetohydrodynamics; solar physics; physical oceanography and limnology. *Mailing Add:* Dept Mech Eng Univ Rochester River Campus Rochester NY 14627

THOMAS, JOHN HUNTER, b Beuthen, Ger, Mar 26, 28; US citizen; m 53 & 66. PLANT SYSTEMATICS. *Educ:* Calif Inst Technol, BS, 49; Stanford Univ, AM, 49, PhD, 59. *Prof Exp:* Asst, Stanford Univ, 49-51 & 53-55, curatorial asst, 55-56; instr, Occidental Col, 56-58; from asst cur to cur, 58-72, assoc prof, 69-77, DIR DUDLEY HERBARIUM, STANFORD UNIV, 72-, PROF BIOL SCI, UNIV, 77- *Concurrent Pos:* Cur, Dept Bot, Calif Acad Sci, 69- *Mem:* Am Soc Plant Taxon; Bot Soc Am; Soc Study Evolution; Am Fern Soc. *Res:* Flora of central and lower California and Alaska; management of systematic collections; information storage and retrieval in systematic collections; botanical history. *Mailing Add:* Dept Biol Sci Stanford Univ Stanford CA 94305

THOMAS, JOHN JENKS, b Boston, Mass, Dec 15, 36; m 65. GEOLOGY. *Educ:* Williams Col, BA, 61; Northwestern Univ, MS, 65; Univ Kans, PhD(geol), 68. *Prof Exp:* Asst prof, 68-75, ASSOC PROF GEOL, SKIDMORE COL, 75- *Mem:* AAAS; Geol Soc Am; Am Geophys Union. *Res:* Structural geology; tectonics; metamorphic petrology. *Mailing Add:* Dept of Geol Skidmore Col Saratoga Springs NY 12866

THOMAS, JOHN KERRY, b Llanelly, South Wales, Gt Brit, May 16, 34; m 59; c 3. PHYSICAL CHEMISTRY. *Educ:* Univ Manchester, BSc, 54, PhD(chem), 57, DSc, 69. *Prof Exp:* Nat Res Coun Can fel chem, 57-58; sci off, Atomic Energy Res Estab, Eng, 58-60; res assoc, Argonne Nat Lab, 60-62, assoc chemist, 62-70; PROF CHEM, UNIV NOTRE DAME, 70- *Mem:* Radiation Res Soc; Am Chem Soc; Royal Soc Chem. *Res:* Polymer and radiation chemistry; photochemistry; colloid chemistry. *Mailing Add:* Dept Chem Univ Notre Dame Notre Dame IN 46556

THOMAS, JOHN M, b Wilmar, Calif, Sept 17, 36; m 57; c 3. BIOMETRICS, ECOLOGY. *Educ:* Calif State Polytech Col, BS, 58; Wash State Univ, MS, 60; Univ Ariz, PhD(biochem, nutrit), 65. *Prof Exp:* Instr avian physiol, Calif State Polytech Col, 60-61; res assoc biochem, Univ Ariz, 61-65; sr res scientist, Pac Northwest Labs, Battelle Mem Inst, 61-71; gen ecologist, Div Biol & Med, Energy Res & Develop Admin, 71-72; res assoc, 72-76, MEM STAFF, SCI ECOSYST DEPT, PAC NORTHWEST DIV, BATTELLE MEM INST, 76- *Concurrent Pos:* Mem task group, Int Comt Radiation Protection, 74-; adj prof & coordr biol prog, Wash State Univ, 77- *Mem:* AAAS; Am Statist Asn; Biomet Soc. *Res:* Biology and ecology; methods development for field surveys and the prediction of effects of various insults on humans based on laboratory and field animal data; ecological effect; environmental impact. *Mailing Add:* Ecosyst Dept PO Box 999 Richland WA 99352

THOMAS, JOHN MARTIN, b Omaha, Nebr, Oct 17, 10; m 36; c 4. PEDIATRICS. *Educ:* Grinnell Col, AB, 32; Yale Univ, MD, 37. *Prof Exp:* From instr to asst prof pediat, Col Med, Creighton Univ, 40-49; from asst prof to assoc prof, 49-58, PROF PEDIAT, UNIV NEBR MED CTR, OMAHA, 58-, ASST PROF REHAB, 66- *Mem:* AMA; Am Acad Pediat. *Mailing Add:* Swanson Prof Ctr 8601 W Dodge Rd Omaha NE 68114

THOMAS, JOHN OWEN, b Los Angeles, Calif, Nov 1, 46; c 2. BIOPHYSICAL CHEMISTRY, ELECTRON MICROSCOPY. *Educ:* San Diego State Univ, BS, 68; Cornell Univ, PhD(biochem), 72. *Prof Exp:* Fel, Biochem Dept, Stanford Univ, 72-75; ASST PROF BIOCHEM, MED SCH, NEW YORK UNIV, 75- *Concurrent Pos:* Fel, Damon Runyon Mem Fund, 72-74; Am Cancer Soc Sr Fel, 74-75. *Res:* Nucleic acid-protein interactions; structures of large nucleoprotein complexes; electron microscopy of macromolecules. *Mailing Add:* Dept Biochem Med Sch New York Univ 550 First Ave New York NY 10016

THOMAS, JOHN PAUL, b Kokomo, Ind, June 29, 33; m 61; c 2. PHYSICAL INORGANIC CHEMISTRY. *Educ:* Purdue Univ, BS, 54, PhD(phys chem), 62. *Prof Exp:* Res assoc phys chem, Univ Minn, 62-63; asst prof phys inorg chem, Ill Inst Technol, 63-69; assoc prof, 69-72, actg chmn, Div Sci & Math, 72-73, PROF CHEM, SOUTHWEST MINN STATE UNIV, 72- *Mem:* Am Chem Soc; Royal Soc Chem. *Res:* Spectroscopic studies of chemical bonding; infrared, visible-ultraviolet and electron paramagnetic resonance spectroscopy. *Mailing Add:* Chem Prog Southwest Minn State Univ Marshall MN 56258

THOMAS, JOHN PELHAM, b Ashby, Ala, Apr 18, 22; m 45; c 6. MATHEMATICS. *Educ:* Auburn Univ, BS, 46; Univ Va, MAT, 61; Univ SC, PhD(math), 65. *Prof Exp:* Asst county agt, Agr Exten Serv, Auburn, 46-53; farmer, 53-54; jr & high sch teacher, Ala, 55-60; asst prof math, Univ NC, 64-67; head dept, 67-75, PROF MATH, WESTERN CAROLINA UNIV, 67- *Mem:* Math Asn Am. *Res:* Maximal topological spaces; separation axioms; properties preserved under strengthening and weakening of topologies. *Mailing Add:* Dept of Math Western Carolina Univ Cullowhee NC 28723

THOMAS, JOHN RICHARD, b Anchorage, Ky, Aug 26, 21; m 44; c 2. PHYSICAL CHEMISTRY. *Educ:* Univ Calif, BS, 43, PhD(phys chem), 47. *Prof Exp:* Asst Nat Defense Res Comt, Univ Calif, 43-44, Manhattan Dist, 44-47; res assoc, US AEC Contract, Gen Elec Co, 47-48; res chemist, Calif Res Corp, 48-49; asst chief chem br, US AEC, 49-51; sr res scientist, Calif Res Corp, 51-67, mgr res & develop, Ortho Div, Chevron Chem Co, 67-68, asst secy, Stand Oil Co Calif, 68-70, PRES, CHEVRON RES CO, 70- *Res:* Free radicals; oxidation kinetics; electron spin resonance; petroleum technology; synthetic fuels. *Mailing Add:* Chevron Res Co Richmond CA 94802

THOMAS, JOHN WILLIAM, b Spanish Fork, Utah, Mar 25, 18; m 45; c 4. ANIMAL NUTRITION, DAIRY SCIENCE. *Educ:* Utah State Univ, BS, 40; Cornell Univ, PhD(nutrit), 46. *Prof Exp:* Res assoc, Nat Defense Res Comt, Northwestern Univ, 42-45 & Carnegie Inst Technol, 45; nutritionist & biochemist, Bur Dairy Indust, USDA, 46-53 & dairy husb res br, 53-60; PROF DAIRY SCI, MICH STATE UNIV, 60- *Concurrent Pos:* Exten specialist dairy, 79- *Honors & Awards:* Am Feed Mfrs Asn Award, 53; USDA Superior Serv Award, 59; Borden Award, Am Dairy Sci Asn, 74. *Mem:* Fel AAAS; Am Chem Soc; Am Soc Animal Sci; Am Dairy Sci Asn; Am Inst Nutrit. *Res:* Mineral and vitamin requirements and functions in feeding of dairy cattle; forage evaluation and preservation; thyroid active stimulants for cattle; rumen functions; calf nutrition. *Mailing Add:* Dept Animal Sci Mich State Univ East Lansing MI 48824

THOMAS, JOHN XENIA, JR, b Birmingham, Ala, July 25, 50; m 74. PHYSIOLOGY. *Educ:* Birmingham-Southern Col, BS, 72; Univ Miss Med Ctr, PhD(physiol), 76. *Prof Exp:* Res assoc, Dept Physiol & Biophys, Univ Miss, 72-76; res assoc, 76-78, ASST PROF DEPT PHYSIOL, LOYOLA UNIV CHICAGO, STRITCH SCH MED, 78- *Concurrent Pos:* Res fel, Chicago Heart Asn, 77-78; instr nursing physiol, Hinds Jr Col, 75-76; Schweppe Found career develop award, 78-82. *Mem:* Am Heart Asn; Am Physiol Soc; AAAS. *Res:* Cardiac metabolism; cardiac dynamics; coronary circulation; nervous control of circulation. *Mailing Add:* Dept Physiol 2160 S First Ave Maywood IL 60153

THOMAS, JOHNNY RAY, plant breeding, agronomy, see previous edition

THOMAS, JON CHARLES, b Ft Wayne, Ind, Apr 23, 48. ASTRONOMY. *Educ:* Ind Univ, Bloomington, BS, 70; Univ Mich, Ann Arbor, MS, 72, PhD(astron), 75. *Prof Exp:* MOREHEAD FEL & LECTR ASTRON, UNIV NC, CHAPEL HILL, 75- *Mem:* Am Astron Soc. *Res:* Empirical mass determination for O stars; radio clusters of galaxies. *Mailing Add:* 71 Laurel Ridge Apts Chapel Hill NC 27514

THOMAS, JOSEPH CALVIN, b Churubusco, Ind, May 2, 33; m 55; c 1. SCIENCE EDUCATION, ORGANIC CHEMISTRY. *Educ:* Asbury Col, AB, 54; Univ Ky, MA, 55, EdD(sci educ, chem), 61. *Prof Exp:* Instr chem, Asbury Col, 54-59 & Jessamine County High Sch, 59-60; asst prof sci, 61-65, chmn dept chem, 63-74, assoc dean, Sch Arts & Sci, 79-81, PROF CHEM, UNIV NORTH ALA, 65-, DEAN, SCH ARTS & SCI, 81- *Concurrent Pos:* Sci consult local pub sch systs, 63- *Mem:* AAAS; Am Chem Soc; Nat Sci Teachers Asn. *Res:* Preparation and continued education of secondary school science teachers, particularly their preparation in the physical sciences. *Mailing Add:* Dept of Chem Univ of N Ala Florence AL 35630

THOMAS, JOSEPH CHARLES, b Mt Union, Pa, Oct 16, 45; m 65; c 2. MATHEMATICS. *Educ:* Shippensburg State Col, BS, 66; Pa State Univ, MA, 68; Kent State Univ, PhD(math), 75. *Prof Exp:* Instr, 68-70, ASST PROF MATH, LOCK HAVEN STATE COL, 72- *Res:* Torsion theories generated by ideals; global dimension of associative rings with identity. *Mailing Add:* Dept Math & Comput Sci Lock Haven State Col Lock Haven PA 17745

THOMAS, JOSEPH FRANCIS, JR, b Chicago, Ill, Feb 29, 40; m 67; c 3. MATERIALS ENGINEERING, MATERIALS PROCESSING. *Educ:* Cornell Univ, BEP, 63; Univ Ill, Urbana, MS, 65, PhD(physics), 68. *Prof Exp:* Asst prof physics, Univ Va, 67-72; asst prof, 72-75, ASSOC PROF ENG & PHYSICS, WRIGHT STATE UNIV, 75-, PROG DIR, MAT SCI & ENG, 76- *Mem:* Am Soc Metals; Am Phys Soc; Metall Soc; Am Inst Metall Engrs. *Res:* Plastic deformation; applications to metal forming; material constitutive equations; physics of metals and alloys. *Mailing Add:* Dept Eng Wright State Univ Dayton OH 45435

THOMAS, JOSEPH JAMES, b Columbia, Pa, Sept 10, 09; m 32, 51; c 7. BIOCHEMISTRY. *Educ:* Pa State Univ, BS, 30, MS, 32, PhD(biochem), 35. *Prof Exp:* Asst res, NY Exp Sta, Geneva, 30; instr agr biochem, Pa State Univ, 31-36; biochemist, Rohm and Haas, 36-41; from asst dir to dir res, S D Warren Co, 42-68, vpres res, 68-72; tech consult, Edward C Jordan Co, Inc, 73-76; TECH PULP, PAPER & CHEM CONSULT, 73- *Mem:* Am Chem Soc; Tech Asn Pulp & Paper Indust. *Res:* Synthetic resins; functional uses of pulp and paper. *Mailing Add:* 16234 N 111th Ave Sun City AZ 85351

THOMAS, JOSEPHUS, JR, b Linton, Ind, Nov 28, 27; m 50; c 3. ANALYTICAL CHEMISTRY. *Educ:* Ind State Univ, BS, 53; Univ Ill, PhD(anal chem), 57. *Prof Exp:* Asst anal chem, Univ Ill, 53-56; res chemist, E I du Pont de Nemours & Co, Inc, 57-62; PHYS CHEMIST, ILL STATE GEOL SURV, 62- *Mem:* Am Chem Soc; Clay Minerals Soc. *Res:* Surfaces, sintering, x-ray and electron diffraction; instrumental methods of analysis; thermal analysis; phase transformations in solids. *Mailing Add:* Ill State Geol Surv 305 Natural Resources Bldg Urbana IL 61801

THOMAS, JULIAN EDWARD, SR, b Yazoo City, Miss, Aug 1, 37; m 56; c 3. MICROBIAL PHYSIOLOGY. *Educ:* Fisk Univ, AB, 59; Atlanta Univ, MS, 67, PhD(biol), 71; Southern Univ, MST, 68. *Prof Exp:* Teacher pub schs, Ga, 59-65; instr biol & chem, SC State Col, 67-69; fel microgenetics, Argonne Nat Lab, 71-73; assoc prof, 73-77, PROF BIOL, TUSKEGEE INST, 77-, HEAD, BIOL DEPT, 79-, ASSOC DIR, CARVER RES FOUND, 79- *Concurrent Pos:* Consult, Argonne Ctr Educ Affairs, 75-76. *Mem:* Sigma Xi;

Fedn Am Scientists; AAAS; Am Soc Microbiol. *Res:* Involvement of transfer RNA in the regulation of enzyme synthesis by repression, and derepression, control. *Mailing Add:* Dept of Biol Tuskegee Inst Tuskegee Institute AL 36088

THOMAS, KEITH SKELTON, b Tallahassee, Fla, Aug 29, 36; m 63; c 3. PHYSICS. *Educ:* Tulane Univ, BS, 58; Johns Hopkins Univ, PhD(physics), 64. *Prof Exp:* Instr physics, Johns Hopkins Univ, 63-64; staff mem, 64-75, GROUP LEADER, LOS ALAMOS NAT LAB, UNIV CALIF, 75- *Res:* Crystal spectroscopy of rare earth chlorides; high density and high temperature plasmas with emphasis on diagnostic techniques. *Mailing Add:* 340 Venado Los Alamos NM 87545

THOMAS, KENNETH EUGENE, III, b Hammond, La, Jan 31, 54; m 79. INORGANIC CHEMICAL SEPARATIONS. *Educ:* Southeastern La Univ, BS, 75; Univ Calif, Berkeley, PhD(chem), 80. *Prof Exp:* Resident, 79-80, MEM STAFF, LOS ALAMOS NAT LAB, 80- *Mem:* Am Chem Soc. *Res:* Production and isolation of large quantities of various radionuclides for use in the fields of medicine, chemistry, and physics; development of chemical separation processes applicable to hot cell handling of highly radioactive target materials. *Mailing Add:* CNC3/MS E514 Los Alamos Nat Lab Los Alamos NM 87545

THOMAS, KIMBERLY W, b Albany, NY, July 3, 52; m 79. NUCLEAR CHEMISTRY, RADIOBIOLOGY. *Educ:* Middlebury Col, AB, 73; Univ Calif, Berkeley, MBioradiol, 78, PhD(nuclear chem), 78. *Prof Exp:* STAFF SCIENTIST CHEM,LOS ALAMOS NAT LAB, 78- *Mem:* Am Chem Soc; Asn Women Sci. *Res:* Radiochemistry; radioactive waste management; isotope synthesis and isolation; applications of radiochemistry to biology and medicine. *Mailing Add:* Los Alamos Nat Lab MS-514 CNC-11 Los Alamos NM 87545

THOMAS, KURIAN K, b Kottayam, India, May 5, 34; m 65; c 2. PHYSIOLOGY, BIOCHEMISTRY. *Educ:* Univ Kerala, BSc, 54, MSc, 56; Univ Fla, PhD(zool), 64. *Prof Exp:* Lectr zool, C M S Col, Univ Kerala, 56-61; res assoc biol, Northwestern Univ, 65-68; asst prof, 68-72, assoc prof, 72-81, PROF BIOL, ST MARY'S UNIV, NS, 81- *Mem:* AAAS; Am Soc Zoologists. *Res:* Lipids and lipoprotein metabolism in insects. *Mailing Add:* Dept of Biol St Mary's Univ Halifax NS B3H 3C3 Can

THOMAS, LARRY EMERSON, b Indianapolis, Ind, Dec 27, 43. APPLIED MATHEMATICS. *Educ:* Rose Polytech Inst, BS, 66; Rensselaer Polytech Inst, MS, 68, PhD(math), 70. *Prof Exp:* Asst prof, 70-72, ASSOC PROF MATH, ST PETER'S COL, NJ, 72-, COORDR PRE-ENG PROG, 76- *Mem:* Math Asn Am; Soc Indust & Appl Math. *Res:* Differential equations. *Mailing Add:* Dept of Math St Peter's Col Jersey City NJ 07306

THOMAS, LAZARUS DANIEL, b Toledo, Ohio, Oct 21, 25; m 50; c 5. PHYSICAL CHEMISTRY. *Educ:* Univ Mich, BS, 48, MS, 49. *Prof Exp:* Teaching fel, Univ Mich, 49-50; RES SUPVR, LIBBEY-OWENS-FORD CO, 51- *Mem:* Electrochem Soc; Am Electroplaters Soc; Am Chem Soc; Am Ceramic Soc. *Res:* Films on glass; semiconductors; surface chemistry of glass; electrochemistry. *Mailing Add:* Libbey-Owens-Ford Co 1701 E Broadway Toledo OH 43605

THOMAS, LEE W(ILSON), b Boswell, Pa, Oct 31, 26; m 50; c 2. CHEMICAL ENGINEERING. *Educ:* Univ Pittsburgh, BS, 49. *Prof Exp:* Chem analyst, Jones & Laughlin Steel Co, 49-50; process engr, Bethlehem Steel Co, 50-52; field engr, Eng Dept, 52-63, res engr, Pigments Dept, 63-67, sr res engr, Newport, 67-72, TECH SERV REP, PIGMENTS DEPT, E I DU PONT DE NEMOURS & CO, INC, 72- *Mem:* Am Inst Chem Engrs. *Res:* Development work in particle processes including extreme temperature ranges. *Mailing Add:* 1107 Market St E I du Pont de Nemours & Co Inc Wilmington DE 09898

THOMAS, LEO ALVON, b Gifford, Idaho, Mar 19, 22; c 2. PARASITOLOGY, MEDICAL MICROBIOLOGY. *Educ:* Univ Idaho, BS, 49; Univ Mich, MS, 50; Tulane Univ, PhD(parasitol, med microbiol), 55. *Prof Exp:* With virus labs, Rockefeller Found, NY, 55-57; med bacteriologist, 57-80, RES MICROBIOLOGIST, ROCKY MOUNTAIN LAB, USPHS, 80- *Res:* Ecology and classification of arthropod-borne viruses; biological and chemical characterization of Coxiella burnetii antigens. *Mailing Add:* USPHS Rocky Mountain Lab Hamilton MT 59840

THOMAS, LEO JOHN, JR, b St Paul, Minn, Oct 30, 36; m 58; c 4. CHEMICAL ENGINEERING. *Educ:* Univ Minn, BS, 58; Univ Ill, MS, 60, PhD(chem eng), 62. *Prof Exp:* Res chemist, Color Photog Div, Res Labs, 61-67, head, Color Physics & Eng Lab, 67-70, asst div head, 70-72, tech asst to dir, 72-75, asst dir, Res Labs, 75-77, vpres, 77-78, DIR RES LABS, EASTMAN KODAK CO, 77-, SR VPRES, 78- *Mem:* Am Inst Chem Engrs; Soc Photog Sci & Engrs; Soc Motion Picture & TV Engrs; Directors Indust Res; AAAS. *Res:* Photographic science; mass transport; chemical engineering kinetics. *Mailing Add:* Res Labs Eastman Kodak Co Rochester NY 14650

THOMAS, LEWIS, b Flushing, NY, Nov 25, 13; m 43; c 3. INTERNAL MEDICINE, PATHOLOGY. *Educ:* Princeton Univ, BS, 33; Harvard Univ, MD, 37. *Hon Degrees:* MA, Yale Univ, 69; ScD, Univ Rochester, 74, Princeton Univ, 76, Med Col Ohio, 76, Columbia Univ, 78; LLD, Johns Hopkins Univ, 76; LHD, Duke Univ, 76, Reed Col, 77. *Prof Exp:* Intern, Boston City Hosp, 37-39; intern, Neurol Inst, New York, 39-41; Tilney Mem fel, Thorndike Lab, Boston City Hosp, 41-42; vis investr, Rockefeller Inst, 42-46; asst prof pediat, Sch Med, Johns Hopkins Univ, 46-48; from assoc prof to prof med, Sch Med, Tulane Univ, 48-50; prof pediat & med & dir pediat res labs, Heart Hosp, Univ Minn, 50-54; prof path & chmn dept, Sch Med, NY Univ, 54-58, prof med & chmn dept, 58-66, dean, 66-69; prof path & chmn dept, Sch Med Yale Univ, 69-72, dean sch med, 72-73; pres & chief exec officer 73-80, CHANCELLOR, MEM SLOAN-KETTERING CANCER CTR, 80-; PROF MED & PATH, MED SCH, CORNELL UNIV, 73-, CO-DIR, GRAD SCH MED SCI, 74- *Concurrent Pos:* Consult, Surgeon Gen, US Dept Army, 52; mem path study sect, Path Training Comt, NIH, 54-58, Nat Adv Health Coun, 58-62 & Nat Adv Child Health & Human Develop Coun, 63-67; mem comn streptococcal dis, Armed Forces Epidemiol Bd, NIH, 54 & 58; consult, Manhattan Vet Admin Hosp, 54-69; mem, Bd Health, New York, 56-69; dir third & fourth med divs, Bellevue Hosp, 58-66, pres med bd, 63-66, dir med, Univ Hosp, 58-66; mem bd sci consult, Sloan-Kettering Inst Cancer Res, 66-72; mem, President's Sci Adv Comt, 67-70; consult, Surgeon Gen, USPHS; mem bd dirs, Pub Health Res Inst, New York; mem med adv comt, Ctr Biomed Educ, City Univ New York, 72-; prof biol, SKI Div, Grad Sch Med Sci, Cornell Univ, 73-; mem comt educ, Div Biol & Med Sci, Brown Univ, 74-76; mem sci adv comt, Inst Cancer Res, Fox Chase, 74-; mem comt health professions of bd trustees, Sch Med, Univ Pittsburgh, 74-76; mem med adv comt, Irvington House Inst, New York, 74-; adj prof, Rockefeller Univ, 75-; trustee, Rockefeller Univ, 75-, John Simon Guggenheim Mem Found, 75-, Mt Sinai Med Sch, 78- & Draper Lab, 81-; mem bd dirs, Josiah Macy Jr Found, 75-; mem bd overseers, Harvard Univ, 76-82. *Mem:* Nat Acad Sci; Am Acad Arts & Sci; fel NY Acad Sci; Practitioners Soc; Am Soc Clin Oncol. *Res:* Infectious disease; hypersensitivity; pathogenicity of mycoplasmas. *Mailing Add:* Mem Sloan-Kettering Cancer Ctr 1275 York Ave New York NY 10021

THOMAS, LEWIS EDWARD, b Lima, Ohio, May 18, 13; m 40; c 4. ORGANIC CHEMISTRY. *Educ:* Ohio Northern Univ, BS, 35; Purdue Univ, MS, 37. *Prof Exp:* Asst chem, Purdue Univ, 35-39; from instr to asst prof, Va Mil Inst, 40-45; develop engr, 45-50, tech serv & lab supvr, 50-70, asst mgr lab, 70-73, mgr lab, Sun Oil Co, 74-78; RETIRED. *Concurrent Pos:* Vis scientist, Ohio Acad Sci, NSF vchmn bd trustees, Univ Toledo & Toledo-Lucas County Libr Syst. *Mem:* Nat Soc Prof Engrs; Am Chem Soc; Am Inst Chem Engrs. *Res:* Chlorination of aliphatic hydrocarbons; selective solvents for olefin and diolefin purification; pyrolysis of chlorinated aliphatic hydrocarbons; esterification of alcohol ethers. *Mailing Add:* 4148 Deepwood Lane Toledo OH 43614

THOMAS, LEWIS JONES, JR, b Philadelphia, Pa, Dec 13, 30; m 55; c 2. BIOMEDICAL COMPUTING. *Educ:* Haverford Col, BS, 53; Washington Univ, MD, 57; Am Bd Anesthesiol, dipl, 63. *Prof Exp:* Intern med, Bronx Munic Hosp, NY, 57-58; USPHS res fel, Sch Med, Washington Univ, 58-60; resident anesthesiol, Barnes Hosp, St Louis, Mo, 60-62; staff anesthesiologist, Clin Ctr, NIH, 62-64; asst prof anesthesiol, 64-74, asst prof physiol & biophys, 70-74, assoc dir biomed comput lab, 72-75, ASSOC PROF ANESTHESIOL, PHYSIOL & BIOPHYS, & BIOMED ENG, SCH MED, WASHINGTON UNIV, 74-, DIR BIOMED COMPUT LAB, 75-, ASSOC PROF ELEC ENG, 78- *Concurrent Pos:* USPHS res career develop award, 66. *Honors & Awards:* Borden Award, Asn Am Med Cols, 57. *Mem:* AAAS; Am Physiol Soc; AMA; NY Acad Sci. *Res:* Respiratory physiology; biomedical computer applications; anesthesia. *Mailing Add:* Biomed Comput Lab 700 S Euclid Washington Univ Sch of Med St Louis MO 63110

THOMAS, LLEWELLYN HILLETH, b London, Eng, Oct 21, 03; nat US; m 33; c 3. PHYSICS. *Educ:* Cambridge Univ, BA, 24, PhD(theoret physics), 27, MA, 28, DSc, 65. *Prof Exp:* From asst prof to prof physics, Ohio State Univ, 29-43; physicist & ballistician, Ballistic Res Lab, Aberdeen Proving Ground, Md, 43-45; prof physics, Ohio State Univ, 45-46; mem sr staff, Watson Sci Comput Lab, Columbia Univ, 46-48, prof physics, Univ, 50-68, EMER PROF PHYSICS, COLUMBIA UNIV, 68- *Concurrent Pos:* prof physics, NC State Univ, 68-76, emer prof, 76- *Mem:* Nat Acad Sci; AAAS; fel Am Phys Soc; Royal Astron Soc. *Res:* Theoretical astrophysics; atomic physics; relativity theory; nuclear, atomic and molecular structure; field theory; computational methods. *Mailing Add:* Dept Physics NC State Univ Raleigh NC 27607

THOMAS, LLYWELLYN MURRAY, b Detroit, Mich, Sept 23, 22; m 47; c 6. NEUROSURGERY. *Educ:* Wayne State Univ, BA, 49, MD, 52. *Prof Exp:* Assoc prof, 65-68, asst chmn dept, 65-70, assoc dean hosp affairs, 72-81, PROF NEUROSURG & CHMN DEPT, SCH MED, WAYNE STATE UNIV, 70- *Concurrent Pos:* Sr attend, Detroit Gen Hosp, 65- & Grace Hosp, Detroit, 70-; consult, Harper Hosp, 71- & Children's Hosp Mich, 71- *Mem:* Am Asn Neurol Surg; Am Col Surg; AMA; Cong Neurol Surg. *Res:* Head injury. *Mailing Add:* Dept of Neurosurg Wayne State Univ Sch of Med Detroit MI 48202

THOMAS, LOUIS BARTON, b Medicine Lodge, Kans, June 8, 19; m 44; c 3. PATHOLOGY. *Educ:* Col Idaho, AB, 40; Univ Chicago, MD, 45; Am Bd Path, dipl, 52. *Prof Exp:* Resident path, Univ Minn, 48-51; spec fel neuropath, Mayo Clin, 51-52; resident, Mem Ctr Cancer & Allied Dis, New York, 52-53; head surg path & post-mortem serv, Clin Ctr, NIH, 53-69; CHIEF LAB PATH, NAT CANCER INST, 69- *Concurrent Pos:* Clin prof, Schs Med & Dent, Georgetown Univ, 72- *Mem:* Am Asn Path & Bact; fel Col Am Path; Am Asn Cancer Res; Am Soc Exp Path; Int Acad Path. *Res:* Diagnostic and research pathology, particularly cancer; leukemia and malignant lympomas. *Mailing Add:* Lab of Path Rm 2A-29 Clin Ctr Nat Cancer Inst Bethesda MD 20014

THOMAS, LOWELL PHILLIP, b Miami, Fla, Dec 2, 33; div; c 3. BIOLOGICAL OCEANOGRAPHY. *Educ:* Univ Miami, BS, 55, MS, 59, PhD(marine biol), 65. *Prof Exp:* Res aide marine biol, 58-59, from instr to assoc prof, 60-75, PROF MARINE BIOL, ROSENTIEL INST, MARINE & ATMOSPHERIC SCI, UNIV MIAMI, 75- *Concurrent Pos:* Vis lectr, Fla State Univ, 63; mem staff, Orgn Trop Studies, Costa Rica, 67, Bermuda, Biol Sta, 68 & Fairleigh-Dickinson Field Sta, St Croix, 69 & 70. *Mem:* Marine Biol Asn UK; Sigma Xi. *Res:* Systematics and developmental anatomy of echinoderms; ecology and behavior of marine animals. *Mailing Add:* 6830 SW 52nd St Miami FL 33155

THOMAS, LUCIUS PONDER, b Easley, SC, June 30, 25; m 52; c 2. ELECTRONIC ENGINEERING. *Educ:* Clemson Univ, BS, 47. *Prof Exp:* Engr, 47-61, leader eng TV, 61-69, mgr advan prod develop, 69-71, mgr black & white TV, 71-78, MGR ENG PROD SAFETY, RCA CORP, 78- *Mem:* Sr mem Inst Elec & Electronics Engrs. *Res:* Design, development and supervision in television receiver development. *Mailing Add:* 7311 N Lesley Ave Indianapolis IN 46250

THOMAS, LYELL JAY, JR, b Madison, Wis, Apr 17, 25; m 48; c 2. PHARMACOLOGY. *Educ:* Oberlin Col, AB, 48; Univ Pa, PhD(zool), 53. *Prof Exp:* Instr pharmacol, Woman's Med Col, Pa, 52-55; asst prof biol, 55-60, assoc prof, 60-62, ASSOC PROF PHARMACOL, UNIV SOUTHERN CALIF, 62- *Mem:* Am Physiol Soc; Soc Gen Physiol; Cardiac Muscle Soc. *Res:* Cellular physiology and pharmacology of heart muscle; excitation contraction coupling in heart muscle; mechanism of insulin secretion. *Mailing Add:* Dept of Pharmacol Univ of Southern Calif Med Sch Los Angeles CA 90033

THOMAS, MCCALIP JOSEPH, b Yazoo City, Miss, Jan 1, 14; m 59; c 2. CHEMISTRY. *Educ:* Miss State Col, BS, 36; Vanderbilt Univ, MS, 38, PhD(org chem), 41. *Prof Exp:* Asst chemist, Exp Sta, Miss State Col, 36-37; Glidden-Upjohn-Abbott fel, Northwestern Univ, 41-42; from res chemist to sr res chemist, A E Staley Mfg Co, 42-48, asst to mgr, Mkt Develop Dept, 48-52, asst mgr, 52-61; mem staff, Applns Res Dept, Nat Cash Register Co, 61-67, sci liaison & mem staff tech support, 67-68; exec vpres, Hill Top Res, Inc, 68-73, DIR MKT, HILL TOP TESTING SERV, INC DIV, AM BIOMED CORP, 73-, V PRES MKT, 76- *Concurrent Pos:* Mem indust adv comt soup & gravy bases, Qm Food & Container Inst, 54 & task group, Res & Develop, 55. *Mem:* Am Chem Soc; Sigma Xi; Am Pharmaceut Asn; Inst Food Technol; fel Am Inst Chemists. *Res:* Research, development and testing in the biological, toxicological, chemical, medical and microbiological fields. *Mailing Add:* Hill Top Res Inc Am Biomed Corp Miamisville OH 45147

THOMAS, MARTHA JANE BERGIN, b Boston, Mass, Mar 13, 26; m 55; c 4. ANALYTICAL CHEMISTRY, PHYSICAL CHEMISTRY. *Educ:* Radcliffe Col, AB, 45; Boston Univ, AM, 50, PhD(chem), 52; Northeastern Univ, MBA, 81. *Prof Exp:* Sr engr in chg chem lab, 45-59, group leader lamp mat eng labs, Lighting Prod Div, 59-66, sect head chem & phosphor lab, Sylvania Lighting Ctr, 66-72, mgr tech asst labs, GTE sylvania lighting prod group, Sylvania Elec Prod, Inc, 72-81, TECH DIR, TECH SERV LABS, GEN TEL & ELECTRONICS CORP, DANVERS, 81- *Concurrent Pos:* Instr eve div, Boston Univ, 52-70; adj prof chem, Univ RI, 74- *Honors & Awards:* Nat Achievement Award, Soc Women Engrs, 65; Golden Plate, Am Acad Achievement, 66; Centennial Alumni Award, Boston Latin Acad, 78. *Mem:* Am Chem Soc; Electrochem Soc; fel Am Inst Chemists; Soc Women Engrs. *Res:* Phosphors; photoconductors; ion exchange membranes; complex ions; instrumental analysis. *Mailing Add:* Gen Tel & Electronics Lighting Prod Danvers MA 01923

THOMAS, MARTIN LEWIS HALL, b Feb 9, 35; Can citizen; m 56; c 2. BIOLOGY. *Educ:* Univ Durham, BSc, 56; Univ Toronto, MSA, 62; Dalhousie Univ, PhD, 70. *Prof Exp:* Assoc scientist, Biol Sta, Fisheries Res Bd Can, Ont, 56-62, scientist, Biol Sub-Sta, 62-70; asst prof, 70-74, assoc prof, 70-79, PROF BIOL, UNIV NB, ST JOHN, 79- *Concurrent Pos:* Mem, Int Oceanog Found, 55-; bd dir, Huntsman Marine Lab, 77- *Mem:* Hon mem NY Acad Sci; Nat Shellfisheries Asn; Marine Biol Asn UK; Brit Ecol Soc. *Res:* Ecology of larval lampreys; estuarine ecology; marine benthic ecology; ecology of freshwater bivalve molluscs; marine pollution. *Mailing Add:* Dept of Biol Univ of NB St John NB E3B 5A3 Can

THOMAS, MARY BETH, b Sewanee, Tenn, Mar 2, 41. CELL BIOLOGY, DEVELOPMENTAL BIOLOGY. *Educ:* Agnes Scott Col, BA, 63; Univ NC, Chapel Hill, MA, 70, PhD(zool), 71. *Prof Exp:* Vis asst prof biol, Wake Forest Univ, 71-72, asst prof, 72-76, assoc prof, 76-79; PROF BIOL, UNIV NC, CHARLOTTE, 80- *Mem:* Soc Develop Biol; AAAS; Am Soc Cell Biol. *Res:* Biological motility; spermiogenesis in flatworms; invertebrate embryology and cytology. *Mailing Add:* Dept of Biol Univ NC Charlotte NC 28223

THOMAS, MICHAEL DAVID, b Merthyr Tydfil, Wales, Jan 2, 42. GEOPHYSICS. *Educ:* Univ Wales, BS, 64, PhD(geol), 68. *Prof Exp:* Fel magnetic interpretation, Geol Surv Can, 68-69; geophysicist, Survair Ltd, 69-71; RES SCIENTIST GRAVITY INTERPRETATION, EARTH PHYSICS BR, DEPT ENERGY, MINES & RESOURCES, CAN, 72- *Mem:* Geol Asn Can; Can Geophys Union. *Res:* Geological interpretation of gravity anomalies within the Canadian Precambrian shield with emphasis on the anomalies along the structural province boundaries and over anorthositic-gabbroic intrusions and complexes. *Mailing Add:* Gravity & Geodyn Div Dept of Energy Mines & Resources Ottawa ON K1A 0Y3 Can

THOMAS, MICHAEL E(DWARD), b Monahans, Tex, May 10, 37; m 59; c 3. OPERATIONS RESEARCH. *Educ:* Univ Tex, BS, 60, MS, 63; Johns Hopkins Univ, PhD(opers res), 65. *Prof Exp:* Prod engr, Union Carbide Corp, 60-61; res asst optimization, Univ Tex, 61-62; jr instr chem eng, Johns Hopkins Univ, 62-63, res asst opers res, 63-64, instr, 64-65; from asst prof to assoc prof indust & systs eng, Univ Fla, 65-69, prof, 69-78, chairperson dept, 73-78; PROF & DIR, SCH INDUST & SYSTS ENG, GA INST TECHNOL, 78- *Concurrent Pos:* Consult, US Army Corps Engrs, 70-77, MAPS, Inc, 74-78 & Hewlett Packard, Inc, 80-81; opers res analyst, Nat Bur Sci, 71-72. *Mem:* Opers Res Soc Am (secy, 80-); Inst Mgt Sci; Am Inst Indust Engrs; Sigma Xi. *Res:* Optimization techniques, including decomposition techniques for nonlinear programming problems and optimal control theory. *Mailing Add:* Dept Indust & Systs Eng Ga Inst Technol Atlanta GA 30332

THOMAS, MICHAEL JOSEPH, organic chemistry, photochemistry, see previous edition

THOMAS, MIRIAM MASON HIGGINS, b Chicago, Ill, June 22, 20; m 47; c 1. NUTRITION. *Educ:* Bennett Col, NC, BS, 40; Univ Chicago, MS, 42. *Prof Exp:* Res assoc food chem, Div Biol Sci, Univ Chicago, 42-45; RES CHEMIST NUTRIT, SCI & ADV TECH LAB, BIOL SCI DIV, US ARMY NATICK RES & DEVELOP LABS, 45- *Concurrent Pos:* Vis fac lectr, Dept Nutrit & Food Sci, Mass Inst Technol, 74-; Dept Defense Sec Army fel, 75. *Mem:* AAAS; Soc Nutrit Educ; Asn Vitamin Chemists; Inst Food Technol; Sigma Xi. *Res:* Chemical aspects of protein and amino acid metabolism; bioavailability of nutrients; effects of processing and storage on the nutritive quality of military rations and vitamin fortification of ration components. *Mailing Add:* Sci & Adv Tech Lab US Army Natick Res & Develop Lab Natick MA 01760

THOMAS, MITCHELL, b Terre Haute, Ind, Nov 25, 36; m 64; c 3. PHYSICS, ENGINEERING. *Educ:* Harvard Univ, AB, 58; Univ Ill, Urbana, MS, 59; Calif Inst Technol, PhD(radiative transfer), 64. *Prof Exp:* Engr, McDonnell Douglas Corp, 59-61, eng consult, 62, sect chief appl res, 64-68, br chief, Advan Systs & Technol, 68-75; dir res & develop, 75-76, PRES, L'GARDE, INC, 76- *Mem:* Am Inst Aeronaut & Astronaut; AAAS. *Res:* Ablation, reentry and midcourse physics, especially radiative transfer through gases; calculation of transport properties of high-temperature gases. *Mailing Add:* L'Garde Inc 1555 Placentia Ave Newport Beach CA 92663

THOMAS, MONTCALM TOM, b Brooklyn, Conn, Feb 5, 36; m 62; c 1. PHYSICS. *Educ:* Univ Conn, BA, 57, MS, 59; Brown Univ, PhD(physics), 66. *Prof Exp:* Mem tech staff, Bell Tel Labs, NJ, 65-68; asst prof physics, Wash State Univ, 68-74; MEM STAFF, BATTELLE PAC NORTHWEST LABS, 74- *Mem:* Am Phys Soc; Am Vacuum Soc. *Res:* Solid state, atomic and molecular physics; surface structure and kinetics of solids; thin films in solid state physics; photoelectric phenomena; low energy electron diffraction; high vacuum techniques. *Mailing Add:* Battelle Pac Northwest Labs PO Box 999 Richland WA 99352

THOMAS, MORLEY KEITH, b Middlesex Co, Ont, Aug 19, 18; m 42; c 2. METEOROLOGY, CLIMATOLOGY. *Educ:* Univ Western Ont, BA, 41; Univ Toronto, MA, 49. *Prof Exp:* Meteorologist, Atmospheric Environ Serv, Can, 41-51 & div bldg res, Nat Res Coun Can, 51-53; supt climat opers, 53-72, dir meteorol applns br, 72-75, dir gen, Cent Servs, 76-80, DIR GEN, CAN CLIMATE CTR, ATMOSPHERIC ENVIRON SERV, 80- *Concurrent Pos:* Assoc comt snow & ice mech, Nat Res Coun Can, 59-65 & subcomt meteorol & atmospheric sci, 67-70; mem working group on climatic atlases, World Meteorol Orgn, 60-65, chmn, 65-69; mem, Nat Adv Comt Geog Res, 65-70; pres Comn Climatol & Appln Meteorol, World Meteorol Orgn, 78-82. *Mem:* Fel Am Meteorol Soc; Royal Meteorol Soc (treas, Can Br, 50-51, secy, 64-66, vpres, 66-67); Can Meteorol Soc (vpres, 67-68, pres, 68-70); Can Asn Geog. *Res:* Atlases; urban climates; climatic change; climatological services; meteorological applications. *Mailing Add:* Atmospheric Environ Serv Dufferin St Downsview ON M3A 5T4 Can

THOMAS, NORMAN RANDALL, b Caerphilly, Wales, Dec 22, 32; m 54; c 5. DENTISTRY, PHYSIOLOGY. *Educ:* Bristol Univ, BDS, 57, BSc, 60, PhD(dent), 65. *Prof Exp:* Med Res Coun sci asst path res, Royal Col Surgeons, Eng, 60-62; lectr dent med, Bristol Univ, 62-66, lectr anat, 66-68; PROF DENT & HONS PROF MED, UNIV ALTA, 68- *Mem:* Can Dent Asn; Can Asn Anat; Anat Soc Gt Brit & Ireland; Int Asn Dent Res. *Res:* Collagen formation and maturation in tooth eruption; neurophysiology of orofacial complex. *Mailing Add:* 5412 142 St Edmonton AB T6H 4B8 Can

THOMAS, OSCAR OTTO, b Aline, Okla, Feb 16, 19; m 49; c 3. ANIMAL NUTRITION. *Educ:* Okla State Univ, BS, 41; Wash State Univ, MS, 48; Okla State Univ, PhD(animal nutrit), 52. *Prof Exp:* From asst prof to assoc prof, 51-59, actg head dept, 79-81, PROF ANIMAL NUTRIT & ANIMAL NUTRITIONIST, EXP STA, MONT STATE UNIV, 59- *Concurrent Pos:* Mem subcomt prenatal & postnatal mortality bovines & comt animal health, Nat Res Coun. *Mem:* Fel AAAS; Am Soc Animal Sci; Sigma Xi. *Res:* Nutritive requirements of range livestock; energy, protein and phosphorus; utilization of barley in cattle fattening; growth stimulants. *Mailing Add:* Dept of Animal & Range Sci Mont State Univ Bozeman MT 59715

THOMAS, OWEN PESTELL, b Middelburg, SAfrica, Apr 28, 33; m 67; c 1. POULTRY NUTRITION. *Educ:* Univ Natal, BSc, 54, MSc, 62; Univ Md, College Park, PhD(poultry nutrit), 66. *Prof Exp:* Nutritionist, United Oil & Cake Mills Ltd, 55-61; asst, Univ Md, College Park, 64-66, res assoc, 66-68; nutritionist, United Oil & Cake Mills Ltd, 68-70; from asst prof to assoc prof, 70-77, PROF POULTRY SCI, UNIV MD, COLLEGE PARK, 77- CHMN DEPT, 71- *Mem:* Poultry Sci Asn. *Res:* Protein and amino acid requirements of broilers; body composition and pigmentation of broilers. *Mailing Add:* Dept of Poultry Sci Univ of Md College Park MD 20742

THOMAS, P(AUL) D(ANIEL), b Vaughnsville, Ohio, Jan 13, 05; m 35; c 3. METALLURGY. *Educ:* Ohio Wesleyan Univ, AB, 27. *Prof Exp:* Metallurgist, Jones & Laughlin Steel Corp, Pa, 27-33, foreman, 33-35, supvr tube invest & develop div, 35-49; mat engr, Asiatic Petrol Corp, 49-67; staff mat eng, Shell Oil Co, NY, 67-70; independent consult metallurgist, 70-74; staff metallurgist, Alyeska Pipeline Serv Co, 74-78; INDEPENDENT CONSULT METALLURGIST, 78- *Concurrent Pos:* Instr exten courses, Pa State Univ, 34-42. *Mem:* Am Petrol Inst; Soc Metals; Welding Soc; Asn Corrosion Engrs; NY Acad Sci. *Res:* Metallurgical and inspection phases in production of seamless and welded steel pipe and tubes; leak resistance of threaded joints; corrosion fatigue; ordnance tubing; high strength threaded joints and steels for pipe; welding metallurgy. *Mailing Add:* 9847 Warwana Rd Houston TX 77080

THOMAS, PAUL A V, b Guernsey, Channel Islands, Europ, Oct 6, 25; m 53; c 3. ELECTRICAL ENGINEERING. *Educ:* London Univ, BSc, 50; Glasgow Univ, PhD(elec eng), 61. *Prof Exp:* Res asst mech, Royal Col Sci & Technol, Scotland, 50-53; lectr, Glasgow Univ, 53-62; from assoc prof to prof elec eng, Univ Windsor, 75, head dept, 64-68; dept chmn, 75-78, PROF COMPUT SCI & INFO PROCESSING, BROCK UNIV, 75- *Mem:* Sr mem Inst Elec & Electronics Engrs; Brit Comput Soc; Brit Inst Elec Eng. *Res:* Electronic computers and graphics systems. *Mailing Add:* Dept of Comput Sci & Info Processing Brock Univ St Catharines ON L2S 3A1 Can

THOMAS, PAUL CLARENCE, b Watsonville, Calif, Nov 26, 28; m 56; c 1. PLANT BREEDING, VEGETABLE CROPS. *Educ:* Col Agr, Univ Calif, BS, 50. *Prof Exp:* Veg breeder, W Atlee Burpee Co, 50-58; DIR RES, PETOSEED CO, INC, 58- *Mem:* Am Soc Hort Sci. *Res:* Development of processing tomatoes, fresh market tomatoes, Open Pollinated and F-1 hybrids, bedding plant hybrid vegetables; quality studies for processing and fresh market. *Mailing Add:* Petoseed Res Ctr Rte 4 Box 1255 Woodland CA 95695

THOMAS, PAUL DAVID, b Bellwood, Pa, Mar 8, 26; m 51; c 4. ORGANIC CHEMISTRY. *Educ:* Rutgers Univ, BA, 49; Univ Ill, PhD(org chem), 54. *Prof Exp:* Chemist, Fries Bros Chem Mfg Co, 49-51; res chemist, Tidewater Assoc Oil Co, 51; res chemist, 54-71, res supvr org chem res & develop, 71-73, REGISTERED PATENT AGENT, CHAS PFIZER & CO, INC, 78- *Mem:* Am Chem Soc; Inst Food Technol. *Res:* Food additives and flavors. *Mailing Add:* 271 Plant St Groton CT 06340

THOMAS, PAUL EMERY, b Phoenix, Ariz, Feb 15, 27; m 58; c 2. TOPOLOGY. *Educ:* Oberlin Col, BA, 50; Oxford Univ, BA, 52; Princeton Univ, PhD(math), 55. *Prof Exp:* Res instr, Columbia Univ, 55-56; from asst prof to assoc prof, 56-63, chmn, 72-73, PROF MATH, UNIV CALIF, BERKELEY, 63- *Concurrent Pos:* NSF fel, 58-59; Guggenheim Mem Found fel, 61; prof, Miller Inst, 66-67; ed, Proc, Am Math Soc, 68-71; mem div math sci, Nat Res Coun, 70-72. *Mem:* Am Math Soc. *Res:* Algebraic topology; homotopy theory; differentiable manifolds. *Mailing Add:* Dept of Math Univ of Calif Berkeley CA 94720

THOMAS, PAUL MILTON, b Sligo, Pa, Dec 1, 29; m 51; c 1. IMMUNOBIOLOGY, ICHTHYOLOGY. *Educ:* Allegheny Col, BS, 58; Univ Mich, MA, 59, MS, 62, PhD(sci admin, ichthyol), 64; Drew Univ, DMin, 80. *Prof Exp:* Instr biol, Houghton Col, 59-62; teacher high sch, Mich, 62-64; from asst prof to assoc prof biol, Pasadena Col, 64-67; res fel, Calif Inst Technol, 67-68; PROF BIOL, EDINBORO STATE COL, 68-, CHMN DEPT, 69- *Concurrent Pos:* Res fel radiation biol, Cornell Univ, 66-67. *Mem:* Soc Ichthyologists & Herpetologists; Am Fisheries Soc. *Res:* Fish anesthetics; effects of industrial pollution of fish; radiation effects on elasmobranch antibody response; sexual dimorphism in fish; artificial fish shelters; administrative effects on science education; gamma globulin synthesis in fish; Lake Erie fishery; death education. *Mailing Add:* Dept of Biol Edinboro State Col Edinboro PA 16444

THOMAS, PERCY LEROY, b Rimbey, Alta, July 4, 40; m 65; c 2. GENETICS, MYCOLOGY. *Educ:* Univ Alta, BSc, 63, MSc, 65; Australian Nat Univ, PhD(genetics), 70. *Prof Exp:* RES SCIENTIST MICROBIAL GENETICS, RES BR, CAN DEPT AGR, 65- *Mem:* Genetics Soc Can. *Res:* Genetics of virulence of cereal diseases. *Mailing Add:* Res Sta Can Dept Agr 25Dafoe Rd Winnipeg MB R3T 2M9 Can

THOMAS, PETER, b Bridgend, UK, Apr 25, 46; m 80; c 1. GLYCOPROTEIN METABOLISM, CANCER MARKERS. *Educ:* Univ Wales, BSc, 67, PhD(biochem), 71. *Prof Exp:* A K fel chem, Inst Cancer Res, 71-79; SR RES ASSOC, MALLORY GASTROINTESTINAL RES LAB, MALLORY INST PATH, BOSTON CITY HOSP, 79-; ASSOC MED, HARVARD MED SCH, 79- *Mem:* Biochem Soc. *Res:* The metabolism of glycoproteins especially carcinoembryonic antigen; interactions between the kupfler cell and hepatocyte in glycoprotein handeling; mechanism of transfer of proteins from blood to bite. *Mailing Add:* Gastrointestinal Res Lab Mallory Inst Path Boston City Hosp Boston MA 02118

THOMAS, QUENTIN VIVIAN, b Glendale, Calif, Apr 13, 49; m 69; c 1. ANALYTICAL CHEMISTRY, MASS SPECTROMETRY. *Educ:* Ore State Univ, BS, 71; Purdue Univ, MS, 74, PhD(chem), 76. *Prof Exp:* Appln chemist mass spectrometry, Finnigan Instrument Div, 76-78, sr instr anal chem, 78-80, MGR TRAINING, FINNIGAN INST, 80- *Mem:* Am Chem Soc; Am Soc Mass Spectrometry. *Res:* Negative ion mass spectrometry; application of computers in the chemical laboratory. *Mailing Add:* Finnigan Inst 11 Triangle Park Dr Cincinnati OH 45246

THOMAS, R(OLAND) E(VERETT), b Austin, Tex, Apr 12, 30; m 51; c 3. ELECTRICAL ENGINEERING. *Educ:* NMex State Univ, BS, 51 & 52; Stanford Univ, MS, 53; Univ Ill, PhD(elec eng), 59. *Prof Exp:* Consult engr, Wright Air Develop Ctr, US Air Force, 53-57, from instr to prof astronaut, US Air Force Acad, 59-64, prof elec eng & head dept, 66-79; SR RES SCIENTIST, KAMAN SCI CORP, COLORADO SPRINGS, 79- *Mem:* Inst Elec & Electronics Engrs. *Res:* Control system analysis and synthesis; active network synthesis; linear systems synthesis; servomechanism analysis and synthesis. *Mailing Add:* 7226 Bell Dr Colorado Springs CO 80918

THOMAS, RALPH EDWARD, b Dayton, Ohio, Mar 14, 24; m 48, 65; c 4. OPERATIONS RESEARCH, STATISTICS. *Educ:* Ohio Wesleyan Univ, BA, 48; Ohio State Univ, MA, 50; Case Western Reserve Univ, PhD(opers res), 66. *Prof Exp:* Mathematician, Battelle Mem Inst, 52-55 & NAm Aviation, Inc, 55-57; math statistician, 57-63, chief appl statist, 63-66, chief statist & math modeling, 67-77, RES LEADER, BATTELLE MEM INST, 77- *Concurrent Pos:* Consult statist, 55-57; lectr, Ohio State Univ, 58-59 & Case Western Reserve Univ, 65-66. *Mem:* Am Math Soc; Math Asn Am; Inst Math Statist. *Res:* Development of statistical and mathematical models for applications to physical and human systems. *Mailing Add:* 2023 Concord Rd Columbus OH 43212

THOMAS, RALPH HAROLD, b Reading, Eng, Nov 27, 32; m 58; c 3. HEALTH PHYSICS. *Educ:* Univ London, BSc, 55, PhD(nuclear physics), 59 ,DSc, 79; Am Bd Health Physics, cert, 69; Univ Calif Sch Pub Health, MPH, 82. *Prof Exp:* Res physicist, Assoc Elec Industs, UK, 58-59; prin sci officer, Rutherford High Energy Lab, Sci Res Coun, UK, 59-68; sr health physicist, Stanford Univ, 68-70; ASST HEALTH & SAFETY, LAWRENCE BERKELEY LAB, UNIV CALIF, 70- *Concurrent Pos:* Lectr, Reading Col Technol, 55-63; vis scientist, Lawrence Berkeley Lab, Univ Calif, 63-65, Europ Orgn Nuclear Res, Geneva, Switz, 66, Brookhaven Nat Lab, 70 & KEK Nat Lab High-Energy Physics, Oho-Machi, Japan, 77; mem working group, Int Comn Radiol Protection, 66-70; chmn adv panel accelerator radiation safety, US Atomic Energy Comn, 69-72; mem, Comt High Energy & Space Disimetry, Int Comn Radiation Units, 73-78; mem comt 3, Int Comn Radiol Protection, 78-85; mem int comn, Radiation Units & Measurements Group, Dose Equivalent Determination, 80-; mem, Comt Int Systs Units, Nat Coun Res & Planning, 79- *Mem:* Health Physics Soc (treas, 77-79); Radiol Res Soc; fel Brit Inst Physics. *Res:* Accelerator radiation problems; high energy dosimetry; cosmic-ray produced neutrons; heavy ion radiobiology. *Mailing Add:* Dept of Health Physics Lawrence Berkeley Lab Univ Calif Berkeley CA 94720

THOMAS, RAYE EDWARD, b Cross Creek, NB, June 5, 38; m 63; c 2. SOLID STATE ELECTRONICS, ELECTRICAL ENGINEERING. *Educ:* Univ NB, BScEE, 61; Imp Col, Univ London, PhD(elec eng), 66. *Prof Exp:* Mem sci staff solid state devices, Res & Develop Labs, Northern Elec Co Ltd, 66-69, mgr physics devices, 69; from asst prof to assoc prof, 69-77, PROF ENG, CARLETON UNIV, 77- *Concurrent Pos:* Consult, Microsysts Int Ltd, 69-70 & Bell-Northern Res, 73- *Mem:* Sr mem Inst Elec & Electronics Engrs. *Res:* Solid state device physics; discrete device and integrated circuit design, fabrication and characterization; device modeling; solar energy conversion-photovoltaics. *Mailing Add:* Dept of Electronics Carleton Univ Ottawa ON K1S 5B6 Can

THOMAS, REYNOLD, JR, b Burlington, Twp, NJ, May 17, 30; m 52; c 4. SYSTEMS ENGINEERING, SYSTEMS ARCHITECTURE. *Educ:* US Mil Acad, BS, 52; Purdue Univ, MSEE, 60. *Prof Exp:* Systs engr, Nat Mil Command Syst, Defense Commun Agency, 66-74; STAFF ASST, OFF SECY DEFENSE, 74- *Concurrent Pos:* Instr, Univ Md Far East Div, 60-61; consult, NEO Corp, 64-66; task force secy, Defense Sci Bd, 78-79. *Mem:* Sr mem Inst Elec & Electronics Engrs. *Res:* Systems engineering with emphasis on measurement of effectiveness of complex computer systems; applications of models to transportation and communications systems; design of survivable national level command and control systems. *Mailing Add:* Off Secy Defense Pentagon Washington DC 20301

THOMAS, (JOHN) (PAUL) RICHARD, b Jacksonville, Fla, May 2, 38. VERTEBRATE SYSTEMATICS. *Educ:* Univ SFla, BA, 69; La State Univ, PhD(zool), 76. *Prof Exp:* ASST PROF BIOL, UNIV PR, 76- *Concurrent Pos:* Prin investr, NSF, 77-79. *Mem:* Am Soc Ichthyologists & Herpetologists; Herpetologists League; Soc Study Amphibians & Reptiles; Soc Study Evolution; Soc Syst Zoologists. *Res:* Systematics, biogeography and ecology of neotropical amphibians and reptiles, especially those of the Antillean region. *Mailing Add:* Dept of Biol Univ of PR Rio Piedras PR 00931

THOMAS, RICHARD ALAN, b Smithville, Mo, Mar 14, 48. LOW TEMPERATURE PHYSICS. *Educ:* William Jewell Col, BA, 70; Stanford Univ, PhD(appl phys), 77. *Prof Exp:* Asst physicist, 77-80, PHYSICS ASSOC I, BROOKHAVEN NAT LAB, 80- *Mem:* Am Phys Soc; Inst Elec & Electronics Engrs. *Res:* Superconducting power transmission, polymeric insulation, dielectric properties of helium, automatic monitoring and control of large-scale low-temperature systems, quantum mechanical tunneling in dielectrics. *Mailing Add:* Bldg 815 Brookhaven Nat Lab Upton NY 11973

THOMAS, RICHARD CHARLES, b Syracuse, NY, July 22, 49; m 71. ORGANIC CHEMISTRY, MEDICINAL CHEMISTRY. *Educ:* Univ Rochester, BS, 71; Univ Calif, Los Angeles, PhD(chem), 76. *Prof Exp:* Fel chem, Mass Inst Technol, 76-77; RES SCIENTIST CHEM, UPJOHN CO, 77- *Mem:* Am Chem Soc. *Res:* Chemical synthesis and modification of antibiotics. *Mailing Add:* Upjohn Co 7254-25-6 301 Henrietta St Kalamazoo MI 49001

THOMAS, RICHARD DEAN, b Payson, Utah, Feb 14, 47; m 70; c 3. TOXICOLOGY, MEDICINAL CHEMISTRY. *Educ:* Utah State Univ, BS, 71; Colo State Univ, PhD(chem), 74. *Prof Exp:* Sr metab chemist agr chem, Biochem Dept, Agr Div, Ciba-Geigy Corp, 74-76; toxicologist & criteria doc mgr, Ctr Occup & Environ Safety & Health, Stanford Res Inst, 76-78; sr environ systs scientist toxicol, Dept Environ Chem & Biol, Metrek Div, The Mitre Corp, 78-80; WITH BORRISTON LABS INC, 80- *Mem:* Am Chem Soc; AAAS; Am Inst Chemists; Am Soc Appl Spectros. *Res:* Investigation into the toxicology, metabolism and environmental impact of chemicals; physiological impairment and potential for cancer and disease production related to chemical exposure; setting tolerances as they relate to health and regulation of chemicals. *Mailing Add:* Borriston Labs Inc 5050 Beech Place Temple Hills MD 20031

THOMAS, RICHARD EUGENE, b Logan, Ohio, Dec 29, 25; m 50; c 3. AEROSPACE ENGINEERING. *Educ:* Ohio State Univ, BAeroE, 51, BA, 53, MS, 56, PhD(aerodyn), 64. *Prof Exp:* Aeronaut engr, Air Tech Intel Ctr, Wright-Patterson AFB, Ohio, 51-52; res assoc aerodyn, Ohio State Univ, 52-56, res assoc & instr, 56-61, asst supvr & instr, 61-64; assoc prof, Tex A&M Univ, 64-66, prof, 66-69; head dept aerospace eng, Univ Md, College Park, 69-71; prof eng, 71-77, actg dean, 77-79, DIR CTR STRATEGIC TECHNOL, TEX A&M UNIV, 79- . *Concurrent Pos:* Consult, Dept Aviation, Ohio State Univ, 63-64, NAm Aviation, Inc, 64, NSF, 76-80 & Comput Aided Mfg Comt, USAF, 77-81; vis distinguished prof, Am Univ, Cairo, 78-81. *Mem:* Am Inst Aeronaut & Astronaut. *Res:* Aerodynamics; gas dynamics; aerothermochemistry; flight dynamics. *Mailing Add:* Ctr Strategic Technol Tex A&M Univ College Station TX 77840

THOMAS, RICHARD GARLAND, b Houston, Tex, June 23, 23; m 71. PHYSICS. *Educ:* Hampton Inst, BS, 43; Columbia Univ, MA, 50; Univ Calif, Berkeley, PhD(physics), 59. *Prof Exp:* Sr scientist physics, Gen Elec Co, 59-63 & Lawrence Livermore Lab, 63-68; PROF PHYSICS & HEAD DEPT, PRAIRIE VIEW AGR & MECH COL, 68- *Mem:* AAAS; Am Phys Soc; Am Asn Physics Teachers. *Res:* Low energy nuclear physics; x-ray spectroscopy. *Mailing Add:* Dept of Physics Prairie View Agr & Mech Col Prairie View TX 77445

THOMAS, RICHARD JOSEPH, b Wilkes-Barre, Pa, Nov 29, 28; m 51; c 2. WOOD TECHNOLOGY. *Educ:* Pa State Univ, BS, 54; NC State Univ, MWT, 55; Duke Univ, DF, 67. *Prof Exp:* Tech rep, Nat Casein NJ, 55-57, sales mgr, 57; from asst prof to assoc prof wood & paper sci, 57-71, PROF WOOD & PAPER SCI, SCH FOREST RESOURCES, NC STATE UNIV, 71-, HEAD DEPT, 78- *Concurrent Pos:* Sci fac fel, NSF. *Mem:* Forest Prods Res Soc; Int Asn Wood Anat; Soc Wood Sci & Technol (pres elect, 81, pres, 82). *Res:* Study of wood ultrastructure, particularly relationships of ultrastructure to physical properties and function within the plant; investigations of differentiation of cell wall and cell wall markings; distribution of major chemical constituents throughout cell wall. *Mailing Add:* Dept Wood & Paper Sci NC State Univ PO Box 5488 Raleigh NC 27650

THOMAS, RICHARD NELSON, b Omaha, Nebr, Mar 3, 21; m 45; c 1. ASTROPHYSICS. *Educ:* Harvard Univ, BS, 42, PhD(astron), 48. *Prof Exp:* Ballistician, Ballistic Res Lab, Aberdeen Proving Ground, Md, 42-45; Jewett fel, Inst Advan Study, 48-49; assoc prof astron, Univ Utah, 48-53; vis lectr, Harvard Univ, 52-53, lectr observ, 53-57; consult astrophys to dir, Boulder Labs, Nat Bur Stand, 57-62; fel, Joint Inst Lab Astrophys, 62-74, ADJOINT PROF ASTROPHYS, UNIV COLO, BOULDER, 62- *Concurrent Pos:* Mem bd dirs, Annual Rev, Inc; vis prof, Col de France, Paris, 73-75 & Univ Paris, 61, 75-76. *Mem:* Int Astron Union; Am Astron Soc; Am Phys Soc. *Res:* Stellar atmospheres; solar physics; astroballistics; non-equilibrium thermodynamics. *Mailing Add:* Dept of Astrogeophys Univ of Colo Boulder CO 80302

THOMAS, RICHARD SANBORN, b Madison, Wis, June 14, 27; m 57; c 2. BIOPHYSICS, ELECTRON MICROSCOPY. *Educ:* Oberlin Col, BA, 49; Univ Calif, Berkeley, PhD(biophys), 55. *Prof Exp:* Am Cancer Soc fel cancer res & NSF fel cytochem, Carlsberg Lab, Denmark, 55-57; asst res biophysicist, Virus Lab, Univ Calif, Berkeley, 58-60; RES PHYSICIST, WESTERN REGIONAL RES CTR, USDA, 60- *Concurrent Pos:* USPHS spec fel, Dept Gen Botany, Swiss Fed Inst Technol, 67-68; consult microscopy & biosci appln plasma chem, Tegal Corp, Richmond, Calif, 72- *Mem:* AAAS; Electron Micros Soc Am; Am Soc Cell Biol; Biophys Soc; Microbeam Anal Soc. *Res:* Biological ultrastructure and fine cytochemistry; development of techniques for electron microscopic cytochemistry and electron probe microanalysis, especially by plasma etching; intracellular mineral deposits, bacterial spores, keratin, microfibrillar proteins, virus particles; plant tissues; cereal products. *Mailing Add:* Western Regional Res Ctr USDA Albany CA 94710

THOMAS, ROBERT, b Atlanta, Ga, Aug 27, 34; m 69. CRYSTALLOGRAPHY, PHYSICAL CHEMISTRY. *Educ:* Boston Univ, AB, 55, PhD(phys chem), 65. *Prof Exp:* NIH res assoc chem, Univ Colo, 64-66; AEC res assoc, 66-68, assoc scientist chem, 68-77, SCIENTIST CHEM, BROOKHAVEN NAT LAB, 77- *Mem:* Sigma Xi; Am Crystallog Asn; Am Chem Soc. *Res:* Crystal structure determination by x-ray development of computer controlled, parallel, single crystal x-ray data collection systems. *Mailing Add:* Dept of Chem Brookhaven Nat Lab Upton NY 11973

THOMAS, ROBERT E, b Salineville, Ohio, Feb 17, 36; m 62; c 2. PHYSIOLOGY, BIOCHEMISTRY. *Educ:* Kent State Univ, BS, 61, MA, 63, PhD(biol sci), 66. *Prof Exp:* Instr biol sci, Kent State Univ, 63-64; from asst prof to assoc prof, 66-74, PROF BIOL SCI, CALIF STATE UNIV, CHICO, 74- *Mem:* AAAS; Am Inst Biol Sci; Sigma Xi. *Res:* Sublethal effects of water soluble oil fractions on fish metabolism. *Mailing Add:* Dept of Biol Sci Calif State Univ Chico CA 95926

THOMAS, ROBERT EUGENE, b Iowa, Oct 15, 19; m 43; c 4. PSYCHIATRY. *Educ:* Univ Southern Calif, AB, 42, MD, 51; Johns Hopkins Univ, MPH, 55. *Prof Exp:* Intern, Santa Fe Coastlines Hosp, Los Angeles, Calif, 50-51; psychiat resident, Vet Admin Hosp, Perry Point & Baltimore, Md, 51-53; chief div ment health, Wash County Dept Health, Hagerstown, 53; from instr to asst prof pub health admin, Sch Hyg, Johns Hopkins Univ, 54-58; regional ment health adminr, Calif Dept Ment Hyg, 58-68, regional ment health dir, div local progs, 68-69; DIR, HEMET VALLEY COMMUNITY MENT HEALTH CTR, 69- *Concurrent Pos:* Chief div ment health, State Dept Health, Md, 53-55; mem, Gov Comn Ment Health, 54; lectr, Sch Pub Health & asst clin prof, Dept Psychiat, Sch Med, Univ Calif, Los Angeles, 60-70; psychiat resident ment health admin in pub health, Sch Hyg, Johns Hopkins Univ; assoc clin prof, Dept Psychiat, Loma Linda Sch Med. *Mem:* Fel Am Psychiat Asn; AMA; fel Am Pub Health Asn; fel Am Orthopsychiat Asn. *Res:* Mental health administration in public health; administration of alcoholism programs. *Mailing Add:* 1116 E Lathan Ave Hemet CA 92343

THOMAS, ROBERT GLENN, b Watertown, NY, Oct 9, 26; m 49; c 3. RADIOBIOLOGY, BIOPHYSICS. *Educ:* St Lawrence Univ, BS, 49; Univ Rochester, PhD(radiation biol), 55. *Prof Exp:* From instr to asst prof radiation biol, Univ Rochester, 55-61; from sect head to dept head radiobiol, Lovelace Found Med Educ & Res, 61-74; group leader mammalian biol, 74-79, HEALTH DIV OFF, LOS ALAMOS NAT LAB, 79- *Concurrent Pos:* Mem task group, Biol Effects Radiation on Lung Comt 1, Int Comn Radiol Protection, 68-; ed, Health Physics J, 81- *Mem:* Am Radiation Res Soc; Health Physics Soc; Reticuloendothelial Soc; Am Indust Hyg Asn; AAAS. *Res:* Toxicity of inhaled radioactive materials; application of experimental results to practical hazards evaluation in nuclear industry; toxicity of inhaled fossil fuel products. *Mailing Add:* 18 Timber Ridge Los Alamos NM 87544

THOMAS, ROBERT HAYNE, b Martins Ferry, Ohio, Jan 14, 21; m 43; c 2. CERAMICS ENGINEERING, PHYSICAL CHEMISTRY. *Educ:* Ohio State Univ, BCerE, 42, MSc, 46; Rutgers Univ, PhD, 49. *Prof Exp:* Asst prof ceramics, Rutgers Univ, 49-50; vpres, Falls Welding & Mfg Co, 50-56; vprovost & dir res admin, 56-67, VPROVOST SCI & TECHNOL, CASE WESTERN RESERVE UNIV, 67- *Concurrent Pos:* Mem bd dirs, Digital Gen Corp, 68-, vpres & treas, 69-71; mem bd dirs, Consults Comput Technol, 70- *Mem:* Am Soc Eng Educ. *Res:* Phase equilibrium of high temperature oxide systems. *Mailing Add:* 7200 Crawford Bldg Case Western Reserve Univ Cleveland OH 44106

THOMAS, ROBERT JAMES, b Flint, Mich, July 5, 49. BOTANY, DEVELOPMENTAL PHYSIOLOGY. *Educ:* Univ Mich, Flint, AB, 71; Univ Calif, Santa Cruz, PhD(biol), 75. *Prof Exp:* asst prof, 75-80, ASSOC PROF BIOL, BATES COL, 80- *Concurrent Pos:* Proj dir, NSF Instr Sci Equip Prog grant, 78-81, res corp grant, 80-82. *Mem:* Bot Soc Am; Am Soc Plant Physiologists; Am Bryol & Lichenol Soc; Brit Bryol Soc. *Res:* Plant growth and development; physiology, biochemistry and development of bryophytes. *Mailing Add:* Dept Biol Bates Col Lewiston ME 04240

THOMAS, ROBERT JAY, b Harvey, Ill, Mar 30, 30; m 53; c 2. COMPUTER SCIENCES. *Educ:* Oberlin Col, BA, 52; Ind Univ, MS, 54; Univ Ill, MS, 58, PhD(math), 64. *Prof Exp:* Dir recreational ther, Cent State Ment Hosp, Indianapolis, Ind, 54-55; adv, 3-2 combined eng prog, 62-72, dir comput ctr, 63-66, from instr to assoc prof math, 58-71, PROF MATH, DePAUW UNIV, 71-, PROF COMPUT SCI, 76- *Concurrent Pos:* Pace res appointment, Argonne Nat Lab, 67, comput consult, 67-71. *Mem:* AAAS; Asn Comput Mach; Am Asn Sex Educrs & Counrs. *Res:* Pattern recognition; determination of cell motility by computer; human sexuality. *Mailing Add:* Dept of Math DePauw Univ Greencastle IN 46135

THOMAS, ROBERT JOSEPH, b Lowell, Mass, July 13, 12; m 42; c 4. CHEMISTRY. *Educ:* Lowell Textile Inst, BTC, 34; Univ Notre Dame, MS, 37, PhD(org chem), 39. *Prof Exp:* Textile chemist, Apponaug Co, RI, 34-36; res chemist, Tech Lab, E I du Pont de Nemours & Co, Inc, 39-42, Jackson Lab, 42-43, Manhattan Proj, Chambers Works, 43-44 & Tech Lab, 44-50, supvr dyeing develop div, 50-65, interdept liaison, Tech Lab, 65-77; consult textile chem & dyeing, 77-80; RETIRED. *Concurrent Pos:* Adj prof textiles, Clemson Univ, 77-80. *Mem:* Am Chem Soc; Am Asn Textile Chem & Colorists. *Res:* Dye application to textile fibers; textile chemistry; interdepartmental relations. *Mailing Add:* 10 Sack Ave Penns Grove NJ 08069

THOMAS, ROBERT L, b Dover-Foxcroft, Maine, Oct 10, 38; m 62; c 1. SOLID STATE PHYSICS. *Educ:* Bowdoin Col, AB, 60; Brown Univ, PhD(physics), 65. *Prof Exp:* Res asst physics, Brown Univ, 60-65; res assoc, 65-66, from asst prof to assoc prof, 66-76, PROF PHYSICS, WAYNE STATE UNIV, 76- *Concurrent Pos:* Sr vis fel, Bedford Col, Univ London, 73-74. *Mem:* Am Phys Soc; Sigma Xi. *Res:* Ultrasonics; photoacoustic microscopy. *Mailing Add:* Dept of Physics Wayne State Univ Detroit MI 48202

THOMAS, ROBERT SPENCER DAVID, b Toronto, Ont, July 29, 41; m 65. MATHEMATICS, APPLICATIONS. *Educ:* Univ Toronto, BSc, 64; Univ Waterloo, MA, 65; Univ Southampton, PhD(math), 68. *Prof Exp:* Lectr math, Univ Waterloo, 65-66 & Univ Zambia, 68-70; from asst prof to assoc prof comput sci, 70-78, ASSOC PROF APPL MATH, UNIV MAN, 78- *Concurrent Pos:* Managing ed, Utilitas Math, 71- *Mem:* Can App Math Soc; Inst Math & Appln; Can Soc Hist & Philos Math. *Res:* Application of mathematics. *Mailing Add:* Dept of Appl Math Univ of Man Winnipeg MB R3T 2N2 Can

THOMAS, ROGER DAVID KEEN, b Maidstone, Kent, Eng, Oct 5, 42; m 70; c 2. PALEONTOLOGY, EVOLUTIONARY BIOLOGY. *Educ:* Imp Col Univ London, BSc, 63, ARCS, 63; Harvard Univ, AM, 65, PhD(geol), 70. *Prof Exp:* Asst prof geol, Harvard Univ, 70-75; asst prof, 75-80, ASSOC PROF GEOL, FRANKLIN & MARSHALL COL, 80- *Concurrent Pos:* Allston Burr sr tutor, Quincy House, Harvard Univ, 70-75, asst cur invert paleont, Mus Comp Zool, Harvard Univ, 70-75; Wissenschaftlich Angestellte Palokologie Universitat Tubingen, 73-74; prin investr, NSF grant, 77-79. *Mem:* Paleont Soc; Int Palaeont Asn; Geol Soc Am; Geol Soc London; AAAS. *Res:* Paleobiology of fossil bivalves; interaction of mechanical function, growth patterns and evolutionary history in the determination of organic form; paleoecology, functional morphology and the evolution of diversity. *Mailing Add:* Dept of Geol Franklin & Marshall Col Lancaster PA 17604

THOMAS, ROGER JERRY, b Detroit, Mich, July 3, 42; m 66; c 1. SOLAR PHYSICS, ASTROPHYSICS. *Educ:* Univ Mich, Ann Arbor, BS, 64, MS, 66, PhD(astron), 70. *Prof Exp:* Nat Acad Sci-Nat Res Coun resident res assoc solar physics, 70-71, ASTROPHYSICIST, GODDARD SPACE FLIGHT CTR, NASA, 71- *Concurrent Pos:* Proj scientist orbiting solar observ satellite prog, Goddard Space Flight Ctr, NASA, 75- *Mem:* Int Astron Union; Am Astron Soc. *Res:* Solar x-ray and extreme ultraviolet astronomy; solar activity; solar flares; solar corona. *Mailing Add:* Code 682 Goddard Space Flight Ctr NASA Greenbelt MD 20771

THOMAS, RONALD EMERSON, b Ont, Can, Apr 19, 30; m 62; c 3. MATHEMATICAL STATISTICS, OPERATIONS RESEARCH. *Educ:* Queen's Univ, Ont, BA, 52, MA, 58; Univ NC, PhD(math statist), 62. *Prof Exp:* Actuarial asst, Excelsior Life Inst Co, 52-57; mem tech staff, 62-68, supvr appl probability group, 68-75, opers res methods, 75-80, SUPVR, FIELD PERFORMANCE STUDIES, BELL LABS, 80- *Concurrent Pos:* Adj prof, Fairleigh Dickinson Univ, 64-65. *Mem:* Opers Res Soc Am; Am Statist Asn. *Res:* Mathematical studies of probability; statistical methodology; graph theory and network design. *Mailing Add:* Quality Assurance Ctr Bldg HP 1A-246 Bell Labs Holmdel NJ 07733

THOMAS, RONALD LESLIE, b Edmonton, Alta, Can, June 29, 35; m 59; c 3. AGRONOMY. *Educ:* Univ Alta, BSc, 57, MSc, 59; Ohio State Univ, PhD(soils), 63. *Prof Exp:* From asst prof to assoc prof, 63-71, PROF SOIL SCI, UNIV GUELPH, 71- *Mem:* Am Soc Agron; Agr Inst Can; Can Soc Soil Sci. *Res:* Soil organic matter chemistry, the reactions, nature and importance of organic matter and its decomposition. *Mailing Add:* Dept Land Resource Sci Univ Guelph Guelph ON N1G 2W1 Can

THOMAS, ROY DALE, b Sevier Co, Tenn, Nov 12, 36; m 59; c 3. PLANT TAXONOMY. *Educ:* Carson-Newman Col, BS, 58; Southeastern Baptist Theol Sem, BD, 62; Univ Tenn, PhD(plant taxon), 66. *Prof Exp:* Assoc prof, 66-76, PROF BIOL, NORTHEASTERN LA UNIV, 76-, CUR HERBARIUM, 74- *Mem:* Am Soc Plant Taxon; Bot Soc Am; Int Soc Plant Taxon; Soc Econ Bot; Am Fern Soc. *Res:* Vegetation and flora of Chilhowee Mountain in east Tennessee; flora of northeast Louisiana; Ophioglossaceae of the Gulf South. *Mailing Add:* Dept of Biol Northeast La Univ Monroe LA 71209

THOMAS, ROY ORLANDO, b Oneida, Tenn, Dec 15, 21; m 45; c 1. ANIMAL NUTRITION, DAIRY HUSBANDRY. *Educ:* Berea Col, BS, 46; Univ Tenn, MS, 52; Mich State Univ, PhD(animal nutrit), 64. *Prof Exp:* Teacher, Lewis County, Ky Bd Educ, 46 & Scott County, Tenn Bd Educ, 46-51; cow tester exten serv, Univ Tenn, 52; fieldman, Nashville Milk Producers, Inc, 52-53; asst dairy husbandman, Univ Tenn, 53-61; res asst animal nutrit, Mich State Univ, 61-64; asst prof, 64-72, ASSOC PROF DAIRY SCI & DAIRY SCIENTIST, W VA UNIV, 72- *Mem:* AAAS; Am Dairy Sci Asn; Am Soc Animal Sci. *Res:* Evaluation of feed materials, methods of feeding and the effect of these materials and methods on production and well-being of animals. *Mailing Add:* Div of Animal & Vet Sci WVa Univ Morgantown WV 26506

THOMAS, RUTH BEATRICE, b Ringgold, La. BOTANY. *Educ:* Northwestern State Col, La, BS, 40; George Peabody Col, MA, 44; Vanderbilt Univ, PhD(biol), 51. *Prof Exp:* Pub sch teacher, La, 40-44; instr, Sullins Col, 44-46; instr, George Peabody Col, 46-48; asst prof biol, Millikin Univ, 51-54; prof, Eastern NMex Univ, 54-63; assoc prof, 64-70, PROF BIOL, SAM HOUSTON STATE UNIV, 70- *Mem:* Fel AAAS; Bot Soc Am; Nat Asn Biol Teachers. *Res:* Gymnosperm gametophyte development; descriptive morphology. *Mailing Add:* Dept of Biol Sam Houston State Univ Huntsville TX 77340

THOMAS, SARAH NELL, b Gainesville, Ga. PHYSIOLOGY, RADIATION BIOLOGY. *Educ:* Brenau Col, BA, 48; Univ Denver, MS, 57; Tex Woman's Univ, PhD(radiation biol), 70. *Prof Exp:* Teacher & head dept sci, Pub Schs, Ga, 48-60; assoc prof biol & chmn dept, Brenau Col, 60-67; instr, Tex Woman's Univ, 70; assoc prof, 70-81, PROF BIOL & CHMN DEPT, LANGSTON UNIV, 81- *Concurrent Pos:* NSF traineeship, 67-69. *Mem:* AAAS; Am Inst Biol Sci. *Res:* Gonad development in male rats irradiated the first day of postnatal life. *Mailing Add:* PO Box 902 Guthrie OK 73044

THOMAS, STANISLAUS S(TEPHEN), b Barberton, Ohio, Nov 1, 19; m 46; c 5. MECHANICAL ENGINEERING, INDUSTRIAL ENGINEERING. *Educ:* Univ Akron, BME, 50; Cornell Univ, MS, 55; Purdue Univ, PhD, 67. *Prof Exp:* Chief resident inspector, Pittsburgh Chem Warfare Procurement Dist, Pa, 40-45; sr draftsman, Goodyear Tire & Rubber Co, Ohio, 46-51; engr, Army Chem Ctr, Md, 51-52; instr mach design, Sibley Sch Mech Eng, Cornell Univ, 52-55; asst prof mech eng, Notre Dame Univ, 55-60; mech engr, Midwestern Univs Res Asn, 60-61; instr, Sch Civil Eng, Purdue Univ, 61-66; eng mgr, Midwest Appl Sci Corp, Ind, 67-71; ASST CHMN DEPT INDUST & MGT ENG, NJ INST TECHNOL, 71- *Concurrent Pos:* Assoc fac, Grad Sch Med Agement, Rutgers Univ. *Mem:* Am Soc Mech Engrs; Am Soc Eng Educ; Am Soc Metals; Am Inst Ind Eng; Int Mat Handling Soc. *Res:* Design of mechanisms and machines; quality control in manufacturing processes; reliability of engineering systems. *Mailing Add:* Dept of Indust & Mgt Eng NJ Inst Technol 323 High St Newark NJ 07102

THOMAS, TELFER LAWSON, b Montreal, Que, June 1, 32; m 56; c 2. ORGANIC CHEMISTRY. *Educ:* McGill Univ, BS, 53, PhD(org chem), 57. *Prof Exp:* Res chemist, Imp Oil Ltd, 57-59 & Gen Aniline & Film Co, 59-62; PRIN INVESTR PHARMACEUT DIV, PENNWALT CORP, 62- *Mem:* Am Chem Soc; AAAS. *Res:* Synthesis of new compounds for discovery of useful drugs. *Mailing Add:* Pharm Div 755 Jefferson Rd Pennwalt Corp Rochester NY 14623

THOMAS, THEODOR W(ILLIAM), b St Paul, Minn, Aug 20, 04; m 33; c 6. CIVIL ENGINEERING. *Educ:* Univ Minn, BCE, 28, MCE, 39. *Prof Exp:* Design engr, Toltz King & Day, Inc, 28-30 & Ellerbe & Co, 30-31; res engr, State Dept Hwys, Minn, 32-47; from asst prof to prof civil eng, 47-70, EMER PROF CIVIL ENG & HYDRAUL, UNIV MINN, MINNEAPOLIS, 70- *Concurrent Pos:* Consult, State Dept Hwys, Minn, 48-49 & NCent Light Weight Aggregate Co, Inc, 59. *Mem:* Am Soc Civil Engrs; Asn Asphalt Paving Technol; Am Concrete Inst. *Res:* Durability of concrete, aggregate, asphalt and asphalt pavements. *Mailing Add:* 2075 Juno Ave St Paul MN 55116

THOMAS, THOMAS DARRAH, b Glen Ridge, NJ, Apr 8, 32; m 56; c 4. NUCLEAR CHEMISTRY, PHYSICAL CHEMISTRY. *Educ:* Haverford Col, BS, 54; Univ Calif, PhD(chem), 57. *Prof Exp:* From instr to asst prof chem, Univ Calif, 57-59; vis assoc chemist, Brookhaven Nat Lab, 59-60, assoc chemist, 60-61; from asst prof to assoc prof chem, Princeton Univ, 61-71; chmn, 81, PROF CHEM, ORE STATE UNIV, 71- *Concurrent Pos:* Consult, Los Alamos Sci Lab, 65; Guggenheim fel, Univ Calif, Berkeley, 69. *Mem:* Fel AAAS; Am Chem Soc; Am Phys Soc. *Res:* electron spectroscopy. *Mailing Add:* Dept Chem Ore State Univ Corvallis OR 97331

THOMAS, TIMOTHY FARRAGUT, b Cleveland, Ohio, June 15, 38; m 63; c 3. PHYSICAL CHEMISTRY, CHEMICAL DYNAMICS. *Educ:* Oberlin Col, AB, 60; Univ Ore, PhD(chem kinetics), 64. *Prof Exp:* Res assoc chem, Brandeis Univ, 64-66; asst prof, 66-73, ASSOC PROF CHEM, UNIV MO-KANSAS CITY, 73- *Concurrent Pos:* Nat Res Coun sr res assoc, Air Force Cambridge Res Lab, 75-76; univ resident res prog vis prof, Air Force Geophys Lab, 81- *Mem:* Am Chem Soc; Am Phys Soc; Am Soc Mass Spectrom; Royal Soc Chem; Inter-Am Photochem Soc. *Res:* Unimolecular reaction kinetics; photochemistry of gases; fluorescence lifetimes and quantum yields; mass spectrometry; photodissociation spectra of gaseous ions. *Mailing Add:* Dept of Chem Univ of Mo Kansas City MO 64110

THOMAS, TRACY YERKES, b Alton, Ill, Jan 8, 99; m 28; c 1. MATHEMATICS. *Educ:* Rice Inst, AB 21; Princeton Univ, AM, 22, PhD(math), 23. *Prof Exp:* Nat Res Coun fel physics, Univ Chicago, 23-24; Nat Res Coun fel math, Univ Zurich, 24-25 & Harvard Univ & Princeton Univ, 25-26; from asst prof to assoc prof math, Princeton Univ, 26-38; prof, Univ Calif, Los Angeles, 38-44, fac res lectr, 43; prof & chmn dept, 44-54, head grad inst appl math, 50-54, dir grad inst math & mech, 54-56, distinguished serv prof math, 56-69, EMER PROF MATH, IND UNIV, BLOOMINGTON, 69- *Concurrent Pos:* Consult appl math staff, US Naval Res Lab, 51-68 & Rand Corp, Santa Monica, Calif, 60-69; vis prof, Dept Math, Univ Calif, San Diego, 62-63 & Sch Eng, Univ Calif, Los Angeles, 65-66, 67-68 & 69-70; ed, J Math & Mech. *Mem:* Nat Acad Sci; AAAS; Am Math Soc (vpres, 40-42); Math Asn Am; Soc Eng Sci. *Res:* Tensor analysis and differential geometry; theory of relativity; supersonic flow and shock wave theory; plasticity theory; cosmology; gas dynamics; fracture; extended theory of conditions for discontinuities over moving surfaces. *Mailing Add:* Boelter Hall Rm 5732 Sch of Eng Univ of Calif Los Angeles CA 90024

THOMAS, TUDOR LLOYD, b Utica, NY, Apr 23, 21; m 44; c 4. PHYSICAL CHEMISTRY. *Educ:* Univ Mich, BS, 43, MS, 46, PhD(chem), 49. *Prof Exp:* Res chemist, 49-56, develop supvr, 56-58, from asst mgr to mgr molecular sieve develop, 58-63, mgr molecular sieve prod, 63-67, GEN MGR MOLECULAR SIEVE DEPT, LINDE DIV, UNION CARBIDE CORP, 67-, V PRES, 77- *Mem:* AAAS; Am Chem Soc; Am Mgt Asn. *Res:* Adsorption; catalysis. *Mailing Add:* 111 Hawthorne Pl Briarcliff Manor NY 10510

THOMAS, VERA, b Prague, Czech, May 2, 28; US citizen; m 67. CHEMISTRY, TOXICOLOGY. *Educ:* Charles Univ, Prague, MS, 52; Czech Acad Sci, PhD(chem), 62. *Prof Exp:* Res assoc indust toxicol, Inst Indust Hyg & Occup Dis, Prague, Czech, 49-67; asst prof, 67-77, assoc prof, 77-81, PROF DRUG METAB, SCH MED, UNIV MIAMI, 81- *Concurrent Pos:* Secy comt maximum allowable concentration toxic compounds, Czech Ministry Health, 62-67; consult, WHO, Chile & Venezuela, 67. *Mem:* NY Acad Sci; Am Conf Govt Indust Hygienists. *Res:* Uptake, distribution, metabolism and excretion of drugs, especially of volatile compounds; pesticides distribution. *Mailing Add:* 145 SE 25 Rd Miami FL 33129

THOMAS, VIRGINIA LEE, b Traer, Iowa, Sept 22, 16. MICROSCOPY. *Prof Exp:* Spectrographer & x-ray diffractionist, Rock Island Arsenal, 42-45; in charge electron micros res labs, US Rubber Co, 45-54; chief spectrographer, Driver-Harris Co, 54-56; group leader, Cent Res Labs, Interchem Corp, 56-62; res scientist, Res Div, Am Radiator-Stand Sanit Corp, NJ, 62-68; SUPVR ELECTRON MICROS & LECTR, DEPT MICROBIOL, RUTGERS MED SCH, COL MED & DENT NJ, 68- *Mem:* AAAS; Electron Micros Soc Am. *Res:* Use of electron microscopy in the graphic arts; microscopy of inks, pigment dispersions, fibers, plastics, ceramics, glasses and enamels; whiteware; microscopy of viruses; tissue culture; antibody-antigen reactions. *Mailing Add:* Dept of Microbiol Rutgers Med Sch Col Med & Dent NJ Piscataway NJ 08854

THOMAS, VIRGINIA LYNN, b Graham, Tex, Mar 29, 43. MEDICAL MICROBIOLOGY. *Educ:* Baylor Univ, BSc, 65, MSc, 67; Univ Tex Med Sch, San Antonio, PhD(microbiol), 73. *Prof Exp:* Teaching fel biol, Baylor Univ, 65-66, res asst & technician microbiol, Col Dent & Med Ctr, Dallas, 66-68; sr res & teaching asst microbiol, Univ Tex Med Sch, San Antonio, 68-70, teaching fel, 70-73; instr, 73-75, asst prof, 75-79, ASSOC PROF MICROBIOL, UNIV TEX HEALTH SCI CTR, SAN ANTONIO, 79- *Mem:* Am Soc Microbiol; Sigma Xi; AAAS. *Res:* Host-parasite relationships in bacterial diseases; immunologic aspects of urinary tract infection; immunofluorescence procedure for localizing the site of urinary tract infection. *Mailing Add:* Rte 4 Box 4014 Boerne TX 78006

THOMAS, WALTER DILL, JR, b St Louis, Mo, July 3, 18; m 39; c 2. PHYTOPATHOLOGY. *Educ:* Colo State Univ, BS, 39; Univ Minn, MS, 43, PhD(phytopath), 47. *Prof Exp:* Instr bot, Colo State Univ, 39-41; asst phytopath, Univ Minn, 41-44, 46; from asst prof plant path & asst plant pathologist to prof & plant pathologist, Agr Exp Sta, 46-54; dir res, Arboriculture Serv & Supply Co, Colo, 54-55; lead res biologist, Ortho Div, Chevron Chem Co, 55-66, tech asst to mgr res & develop, 66-67, forestry specialist, 67-70; pres, Forest & Environ Protection Serv, 70-71; vpres, Natural Resouces Mgt Corp & mem bd dir, Environ Home & Garden Serv, 72-74; PRES, FOREST-AGR ENVIRON PROTECTION SERV, 74- *Mem:* Am Phytopath Soc; fel AAAS; Soc Am Foresters; Asn Consult Foresters; Am Soc Consult Arborists. *Res:* Disease of potatoes, beans, onions and ornamental plants; forest diseases; agricultural pesticides; mycorrhizae; air pollution damage to plants; remote sensing of forest diseases and insects. *Mailing Add:* Forest-Agr Environ Protection Serv Suite 210 3483 Golden Gate Bx 745 Lafayette CA 94549

THOMAS, WALTER E, b West Lafayette, Ind, Dec 19, 22; m 43; c 4. MANUFACTURING ENGINEERING, ENGINEERING TECHNOLOGY. *Educ:* Purdue Univ, Lafayette, BSME, 48, MSIE, 53. *Prof Exp:* Instr, Sch Eng, Purdue Univ, Lafayette, 48-53; design supvr, Chrysler Grad Inst, Mich, 53-54; asst prof, Sch Eng, Univ Mich, Ann Arbor, 54-57; asst chief draftsman, Fla Res & Develop Ctr, Pratt & Whitney Aircraft, 57-62; mgr eng serv, Atlantic Res Corp, Va, 62-63; sr design engr, Fla Res & Develop Ctr, Pratt & Whitney Aircraft, 63-64; prof mech eng & head dept, Mfg Technol, Purdue Univ, Lafayette, 64-73; prof & assoc dean, Sch Technol, Fla Int Univ, 73-76; PROF & DEAN, SCH TECHNOL & APPL SCI, WESTERN CAROLINA UNIV, 76- *Concurrent Pos:* Design engr, HydroPower Inc, Ohio, 50-52; consult, Altamil Corp, Ind, 70-; chmn eng technol comt, Engrs Coun Prof Develop, 77-78. *Mem:* Soc Mfg Engrs; Am Soc Eng Educ. *Res:* Updating of manufacturing processes in the machine tool area and in the foundry area. *Mailing Add:* Sch of Technol & Appl Sci Western Carolina Univ Cullowhee NC 28723

THOMAS, WALTER IVAN, b Elwood, Nebr, Mar 27, 19; m 41; c 1. AGRONOMY, GENETICS. *Educ:* Iowa State Univ, BS, 49, MS, 53, PhD(plant breeding genetics), 55. *Prof Exp:* Res asst agron, Iowa State Univ, 49-50, 53-55, asst prof, 55-59; from assoc prof to prof, Pa State Univ, University Park, 59-79, head dept, 64-69, assoc dean res, Col Agr & assoc dir, Agr Exp Sta, 69-79; dep dir, Sci & Educ Admin-Coop Res, 79-81, ADMINR, COOP STATE RES SERV, USDA, 81- *Mem:* Fel AAAS; fel Am Soc Agron; Sigma Xi; fel Soil Sci Soc. *Res:* Plant breeding, genetics and pathology. *Mailing Add:* Off of the Adminr Coop State Res Serv USDA Washington DC 20250

THOMAS, WALTER WILLIAM, organic chemistry, deceased

THOMAS, WARREN H(AFFORD), b Portsmouth, Ohio, July 15, 33; m 57; c 2. INDUSTRIAL ENGINEERING, OPERATIONS RESEARCH. *Educ:* Case Inst Technol, BSME, 55; Purdue Univ, MSIE, 61, PhD(indust eng), 64. *Prof Exp:* Instr indust eng, Purdue Univ, 62-63; from asst prof to assoc prof, 63-77, DISTINGUISHED PROF INDUST ENG, STATE UNIV NY BUFFALO, 77-, CHMN DEPT, 69- *Concurrent Pos:* Vis sr res fel, Dept Oper Res, Univ Lancaster, 70-71; vis prof, Univ Nottingham, 81. *Mem:* Am Inst Indust Engrs; Opers Res Soc Am. *Res:* Health and educational systems; computer simulation; design of production control systems. *Mailing Add:* Dept of Indust Eng SUNY 342 Bell Hall Buffalo NY 14260

THOMAS, WILBUR ADDISON, b Louisville, Miss, June 26, 22; m 49; c 2. PATHOLOGY. *Educ:* Univ Miss, BA, 41; Univ Tenn, MD, 46; Am Bd Path, dipl. *Prof Exp:* Intern, Baptist Hosp, Memphis, Tenn, 46-47, asst resident path, 49-50; asst resident & resident, Mass Gen Hosp, Boston, 50-52; instr, Harvard Med Sch, 52-53; from instr to assoc prof, Sch Med, Wash Univ, 53-59; CYRUS STRONG MERRILL PROF PATH & CHMN DEPT, ALBANY MED COL, 59- *Mem:* Am Soc Exp Path; Am Asn Path & Bact; AMA; Col Am Path. *Res:* Arteriosclerosis. *Mailing Add:* Dept of Path Albany Med Col Albany NY 12208

THOMAS, WILLIAM A(LBERT), b Willoughby, Ohio, June 12, 08; m 34, 65; c 3. ELECTRICAL ENGINEERING. *Educ:* Case Western Reserve Univ, BS, 29, MS, 33; Yale Univ, DEng, 36. *Prof Exp:* Jr test engr, Gen Elec Co, 29-30; instr elec eng, Case Western Reserve Univ, 30-33, assoc prof, 48-52; asst, Yale Univ, 33-36; asst prof, Antioch Col, 36-37; Iowa State Col, 37-41; elec engr, E I du Pont de Nemours & Co, Del, 41-48; elec engr, Diamond Alkali Co, 49-51; chief engr, Elec Prod Co, 52-56, vpres eng, 56-59; mgr res & develop, Square D Co, 59-61; asst mgr new prod res, Addressograph-Multigraph Co, 61-64; assoc prof elec eng, Cuyahoga Community Col, 64-70, prof, 70-76; RETIRED. *Mem:* Inst Elec & Electronics Engrs. *Res:* Development and design of electrical equipment, including motors, generators, transformers, control and distribution systems. *Mailing Add:* 7050 Chillicothe Rd Mentor OH 44060

THOMAS, WILLIAM ANDREW, b Berea, Ky, July 23, 36; m 57; c 2. GEOLOGY. *Educ:* Univ Ky, BS, 56, MS, 57; Va Polytech Inst, PhD(geol), 60. *Prof Exp:* Geologist, Calif Co, 59-63; from assoc prof to prof geol, Birmingham-Southern Col, 63-70, chmn dept, 67-70; assoc prof, Queens Col, NY, 70-72, chmn dept, 71-72; prof geol & chmn dept, Ga State Univ, 72-79; PROF GEOL, UNIV ALA, 79- *Mem:* Geol Soc Am; Am Asn Petrol Geol; Soc Econ Paleontologists & Mineralogists. *Res:* Tectonics and tectonic framework of sedimentation; stratigraphic and structural continuity of Appalachian and Ouachita mountains; stratigraphy of Gulf Coastal Plain; Appalachian structure and stratigraphy; Mississippian stratigraphy. *Mailing Add:* Dept Geol Univ Ala University AL 35486

THOMAS, WILLIAM CLARK, JR, b Bartow, Ga, Apr 7, 19; m 46. INTERNAL MEDICINE, ENDOCRINOLOGY. *Educ:* Univ Fla, BS, 40; Cornell Univ, MD, 43. *Prof Exp:* Intern med, New York Hosp, 44, asst resident med, 46-49; pvt pract, 49-54; NIH fels, Johns Hopkins Univ, 54-57; asst prof med & chief div postgrad educ, 57-60, chief endocrine div, 57-70, assoc prof med, 60-63, dir clin res ctr, 62-68, PROF MED, COL MED, UNIV FLA, 63- *Concurrent Pos:* Chief med serv, Vet Admin Hosp, Gainesville, Fla, 68-73, assoc chief of staff for res, 73-; hon res fel, Univ Manchester, 69-70. *Mem:* AAAS; Am Clin & Climat Asn; Am Diabetes Asn; Endocrine Soc; Am Fedn Clin Res. *Res:* Mineral metabolism; clinical research; factors affecting renal calculus formation. *Mailing Add:* Med Serv Vet Admin Hosp Gainesville FL 32601

THOMAS, WILLIAM G, b Ipswich, SDak, July 11, 17; m 40; c 2. PHYSICAL CHEMISTRY. *Educ:* SDak State Col, BS, 39; Univ Mich, MS, 48; Mich State Univ, PhD(chem), 54. *Prof Exp:* Instr chem, SDak State Col, 46; asst prof & mem bd examrs, Mich State Univ, 49-53; from asst prof to prof chem, Cent Mich Univ, 53-59; PROF CHEM, EASTERN NMEX UNIV, 59-, DIR, DIV NATURAL SCI, 76-, DEAN COL ARTS & SCI, 80- *Mem:* Fel AAAS; Am Chem Soc. *Res:* Structure and properties of matter; x-ray crystallography, primarily binary crystalline fluorides; electrochemistry, primarily conductivity of fluoride solutions. *Mailing Add:* Dept of Chem Eastern NMex Univ Portales NM 88130

THOMAS, WILLIAM GRADY, b Charlotte, NC, Mar 21, 34; m 55; c 3. AUDIOLOGY. *Educ:* Appalachian State Univ, BS, 57; Wash Univ, MA, 61; Univ Fla, PhD(auditory physiol), 68. *Prof Exp:* From instr to asst prof, 61-70, ASSOC PROF DIV SPEECH & HEARING SCI, MED SCH, UNIV NC, CHAPEL HILL, 70-, DIR HEARING & SPEECH, 61-, DIR AUDITORY RES LAB, 68- *Concurrent Pos:* Fac res grant, Univ NC, Chapel Hill, 68-69, Off Naval Res grants, 69-79, NIH grant, 72-75; consult, Exp Diving Unit, Dept Navy, 69- & Nat Inst Environ Health Sci, 72-; Rockefeller Found grant, 75-80; NIH grant, 75-80; res scientist, Child Develop Inst, 76-; adj prof, Dept Commun & Theater, Univ NC, Greensboro, 81- *Honors & Awards:* Cert of Recognition, Am Speech & Hearing Asn, 69. *Mem:* fel Am Speech & Hearing Asn; Acoust Soc Am. *Res:* Auditory physiology and psychoacoustics, particularly the effects of drugs and environmental conditions on the ear; basic electrophysiology of the auditory system. *Mailing Add:* Dept of Surg Univ of NC Sch of Med Chapel Hill NC 27514

THOMAS, WILLIAM HEWITT, b Riverside, Calif, Dec 25, 26; m 56; c 2. BIOLOGICAL OCEANOGRAPHY. *Educ:* Pomona Col, BA, 49; Univ Md, MS, 52, PhD, 54. *Prof Exp:* Lab asst, Regional Salinity Lab, USDA, 46-47, lab asst plant physiol, 48; lab asst plant physiol, Citrus Exp Sta, Univ Calif, 49-50 & Univ Md, 51-54; jr res biologist, 54-56, asst res biologist, 56-64, assoc res biologist, 64-75, RES BIOLOGIST, SCRIPPS INST OCEANOG, UNIV CALIF, SAN DIEGO, 75- *Mem:* AAAS; Am Soc Limnol & Oceanog; Phycol Soc Am. *Res:* Mineral nutrition and nitrogen metabolism of algae; primary production in the ocean; cultural requirements of marine phytoplankton; marine pollution. *Mailing Add:* Scripps Inst of Oceanog Univ of Calif at San Diego La Jolla CA 92093

THOMAS, WILLIAM ROBB, b Toronto, Kans, Dec 17, 26; m 54; c 1. FOOD SCIENCE, DAIRY BACTERIOLOGY. *Educ:* Okla State Univ, BSc, 50; Ohio State Univ, MSc, 52; Iowa State Univ, PhD(dairy bact), 61. *Prof Exp:* Asst dairy tech, Ohio State Univ, 50-52; mem sanit stand staff, Evaporated Milk Asn, Ill, 52-53; asst prof dairy mfg, Univ Wyo, 53-59; res asst, Iowa State Univ, 59-61; assoc prof dairy mfg, Univ Wyo, 61-65; exten food technologist, Univ Calif, Davis, 65-68; ASSOC DEAN & DIR RESIDENT INSTR, COL AGR SCI, COLO STATE UNIV, 69- *Concurrent Pos:* Appointee, Int Sci & Educ Coun, 74-77. *Mem:* Nat Asn Col & Teachers Agr (pres, 75-76); Am Dairy Sci Asn; Inst Food Technol; Int Asn Milk, Food & Environ Sanit. *Res:* Dairy technology; thermoduric bacteria; lipolytic enzymes of milk; consumer and market analysis of dairy products; dairy plant operation analysis. *Mailing Add:* Col Agr Sci Colo State Univ Ft Collins CO 80523

THOMAS, WINFRED, b Geneva, Tex, June 6, 20; m 43; c 1. AGRONOMY. *Educ:* Prairie View State Col, BS, 43; Cornell Univ, MS, 47; Ohio State Univ, PhD(agron), 54. *Prof Exp:* Instr agron, Ala Agr & Mech Col, 47-51; asst, Ohio State Univ, 51-53; agronomist, 53-81, PROF AGRON, ALA A&M UNIV, 81-, DEAN, SCH AGR & ENVIRON SCI, 73- *Mem:* Am Soc Agron; Soil Sci Soc Am. *Res:* Effect of foliar applied fertilizers on growth and composition of corn; plant population-nitrogen relationships of corn; nitrogen-sulfur-protein relationships of corn. *Mailing Add:* Sch of Agr Environ Sci & Home Econ Ala A&M Univ Box 202 Normal AL 35762

THOMASIAN, ARAM JOHN, b Boston, Mass, Aug 12, 24; m 53; c 3. ELECTRICAL ENGINEERING, STATISTICS. *Educ:* Brown Univ, BSc, 49; Harvard Univ, MA, 51; Univ Calif, PhD(math statist), 56. *Prof Exp:* PROF ELEC ENG & STATIST, UNIV CALIF, BERKELEY, 56- *Res:* Information theory; probability; electroencephatography. *Mailing Add:* Dept of Elec Eng Univ of Calif Berkeley CA 94720

THOMASON, BERENICE MILLER, b Birmingham, Ala, Mar 10, 24; m 44; c 1. MICROBIOLOGY. *Educ:* Ga State Col, BS, 60. *Prof Exp:* Med technologist, Sta Hosp, Ft Benning, Ga, 43-45 & Thayer Gen Hosp, Nashville, Tenn, 45; pub health technologist, Muscogee County Health Dept, Columbus, Ga, 48-51; bacteriologist, Commun Dis Ctr, Atlanta, Ga, 51-53 & Third Army Labs, Ft McPherson, Ga, 53-54; bacteriologist, 54-63, RES MICROBIOLOGIST, CTR DIS CONTROL, USPHS, 63- *Mem:* Am Soc Microbiol; Sigma Xi. *Res:* Development and application of fluorescent antibody technic for rapid detection of pathogenic bacteria. *Mailing Add:* Anal Bacteriol Br Ctr for Dis Control Atlanta GA 30333

THOMASON, DAVID MORTON, b Martinsville, Va, May 28, 47; m 77. POULTRY SCIENCE. *Educ:* Va Polytech Inst, BS, 69, MS, 71, PhD(genetics), 74. *Prof Exp:* Res asst, Va Polytech Inst, 69-73; res assoc, Duck Res Lab, Cornell Univ, 74-76; exten poultry scientist, Coop Exten Serv, Univ Ga, 76-79; tech training dir, Mathtech, Inc, 79-81; DIR TECH SERV, AM SOYBEAN ASN, 81- *Concurrent Pos:* Adj assoc prof genetics, Southampton Col Long Island Univ, 75; consult, Delight Menues, Baltimore Md, 78, Pinecrest Duck Farm, 78, Govt Egypt thru Mathtec, 79, Int Develop Assoc, 81 & Poultry & Egg Facs, 81. *Mem:* AAAS; Poultry Sci Asn; World Poultry Sci. *Res:* Practical poultry processing technology; economical and physiological evaluation of the reproductive performance of turkeys under different environmental conditions. *Mailing Add:* Am Soybean Asn PO Box 27300 St Louis MO 63141

THOMASON, IVAN J, b Burney, Calif, June 27, 25; m 50; c 5. PLANT NEMATOLOGY, PLANT PATHOLOGY. *Educ:* Univ Calif, BS, 50; Univ Wis, MS, 52, PhD(plant path), 54. *Prof Exp:* Res asst plant path, Univ Wis, 50-54; jr nematologist, Citrus Res Ctr, Agr Exp Sta, 54-56, from asst nematologist to assoc nematologist, 54-67, chmn dept nematol, 63-70, prof nematol, 67-73, PROF NEMATOL & PLANT PATH, UNIV CALIF, RIVERSIDE, 73-, NEMATOLOGIST, CITRUS RES CTR, AGR EXP STA, 67- *Concurrent Pos:* Mem subcomt nematodes, Agr Bd, Nat Acad Sci-Nat Res Coun, 64-67; mem Univ Calif-AID Pest Mgt Study Team, Southeast Asia, 71; mem agr pest control adv comt, Calif State Dept Agr, 72- & Pest Control Advisors Comt, Dir Adv Comt on APCA, Calif Dept Food & Agr, 74-76; asst dir, Pest & Dis Mgt Prog, Coop Exten, Univ Calif, 76-, asst dir, Agr Exp Sta & dir, Statewide Pest Mgt Proj, 78- *Mem:* Am Phytopath Soc; Soc Nematol (pres, 75-76); Soc Europ Nematol. *Res:* Biology and control of nematodes attacking sugarbeets and dry beans; efficacy and mode of action of nematicides. *Mailing Add:* 4686 Holyoke Pl Riverside CA 92507

THOMASON, STEVEN KARL, b Salem, Ore, June 2, 40; m 60; c 2. MATHEMATICAL LOGIC. *Educ:* Univ Ore, BS, 62; Cornell Univ, PhD, 66. *Prof Exp:* From asst prof to assoc prof, 66-78, PROF MATH, SIMON FRASER UNIV, 78- *Concurrent Pos:* Vis asst prof, Univ Calif, Berkeley, 68-69. *Mem:* Am Math Soc; Can Math Cong; Am Philos Asn; Asn Symbolic Logic. *Res:* Nonclassical logic, especially modal logic. *Mailing Add:* Dept of Math Simon Fraser Univ Burnaby BC V5A 1S6 Can

THOMASON, WILLIAM HUGH, b Hampton, Ark, Apr 4, 45; m 69; c 1. PHYSICAL CHEMISTRY, CORROSION. *Educ:* Hendrix Col, BA, 67; La State Univ, Baton Rouge, PhD(phys chem), 75. *Prof Exp:* res scientist, 75-80, RES GROUP LEADER PHYS CHEM & CORROSION RES & DEVELOP, CONOCO, INC, 80- *Mem:* Am Chem Soc; Soc Petrol Engrs; Nat Asn Corrosion Engrs. *Res:* Corrosion problems in oil production, particularly those caused by hydrogen sulfide; water treating and scale problems. *Mailing Add:* Conoco Inc PO Drawer 1267 Ponca City OK 74601

THOMASSEN, KEITH I, b Harvey, Ill, Nov 22, 36; m 57; c 2. PLASMA PHYSICS. *Educ:* Chico State Col, BS, 58; Stanford Univ, MS, 60, PhD(elec eng), 63. *Prof Exp:* Res assoc plasma physics, Stanford Univ, 62-63, NATO fel, 63-64, res assoc, 64-65, lectr, 64-68, res physicist, 65-68; from asst prof to assoc prof elec eng, Mass Inst Technol, 68-73; asst ctr div leader, Los Alamos Sci Lab, 73-74, assoc ctr div leader, 74-76; FAC MEM, UNIV CALIF, LIVERMORE, 76- *Concurrent Pos:* Consult, Lincoln Labs, Lexington, Mass, 68-74. *Mem:* Am Phys Soc; Am Nuclear Soc. *Res:* Fusion reactor design; component development; plasma research, energy storage and transfer. *Mailing Add:* 9030 Doubletree Lane Livermore CA 94550

THOMASSEN, ROBERT WILLIAM, b Newman Grove, Nebr, June 2, 31; m 58; c 3. VETERINARY PATHOLOGY. *Educ:* Colo State Univ, BS, 55, DVM, 56. *Prof Exp:* Instr anat, Colo State Univ, 56-57; asst chief path sect, US Army Med Res & Nutrit Lab, 57-60; chief path sect, US Army Trop Res Med Lab, 60-63; pathologist, Armed Forces Inst Path, 63-66 & US Army Med Unit, Ft Detrick, Md, 66-67; chief, Path Sect, Collab Radiol Health Lab, Colo State Univ, 67-78; PRIN PATHOLOGIST, STAUFFER CHEM CO, 78- *Concurrent Pos:* Affil fac, Colo State Univ, 70-78. *Mem:* Am Col Vet Pathologists; Int Acad Path; Am Vet Med Asn. *Res:* Toxicology; experimental pathology. *Mailing Add:* Stauffer Chem Co 400 Farmington Ave Farmington CT 06032

THOMASSON, CLAUDE LARRY, b Blue Grass, Va, Mar 6, 32; m 57; c 3. PHARMACY. *Educ:* Univ Cincinnati, BS, 54; Univ Fla, PhD(pharm), 57. *Prof Exp:* Assoc prof pharm, Southern Col Pharm, Mercer, 57-61, prof & chmn dept, 61-64; assoc prof, WVa Univ, 64-66; ASSOC PROF PHARM, AUBURN UNIV, 66- *Mem:* Am Pharmaceut Asn; Acad Pharmaceut Sci; AAAS. *Res:* Dispensing and clinical pharmacy. *Mailing Add:* 251 Carter Auburn AL 36830

THOMASSON, MAURICE RAY, b Columbia, Mo, Sept 3, 30; m 56; c 3. GEOLOGY. *Educ:* Univ Mo, BA, 53, MA, 54; Univ Wis, PhD(geol), 59. *Prof Exp:* Geologist, Shell Oil Co, La, 59-68, mgr geol dept, Shell Develop Co, Tex, 68-70, div explor mgr, Shell Oil Co, La, 70-72, mgr forecasting, planning & econ, 72-74, mem staff, Shell Int Petrol Co, Ltd, London, 74-76, chief geologist, Shell Oil Co, Houston, 76-77; V PRES EXPLOR, McCORMICK OIL & GAS CORP, 77- *Mem:* Geol Soc Am; Soc Econ Paleont & Mineral; Am Asn Petrol Geol. *Res:* Paleogeography and sedimentation of western North America; paleocurrent and basin studies; general stratigraphy and stratigraphic paleontology. *Mailing Add:* McCormick Oil & Gas Corp 3600 Two Allen Center Houston TX 77002

THOME, FREDERICK A, b Union, NJ, Oct 27, 34; m 61; c 1. ANALYTICAL CHEMISTRY. *Educ:* Upsala Col, BS, 57; Ohio Univ, MS, 59. *Prof Exp:* Sr chemist, Standard Oil Co, Ohio, 61-64; RES CHEMIST, R J REYNOLDS TOBACCO CO, 64- *Mem:* Am Chem Soc; Sigma Xi. *Res:* Gas chromatography-mass spectrometry coupling; mass spectrometry of natural products; field desorption/field ionization mass spectrometry. *Mailing Add:* R J Reynolds Tobacco Co Res Dept 115 Chestnut St SE Winston-Salem NC 27102

THOME, GEORGE DURST, b Detroit, Mich, Feb 15, 36; m 60; c 3. RADIOPHYSICS, GEOPHYSICS. *Educ:* Antioch Col, BS, 59; Cornell Univ, MS, 62, PhD(elec eng), 66. *Prof Exp:* Engr radio physics, Raytheon Corp, 59-61; res assoc ionospheric physics, Cornell Univ, 66-68; SCIENTIST & CONSULT RADIO PHYSICS, RAYTHEON CORP, 68- *Concurrent Pos:* Mem comn III, Union Radio Sci. *Mem:* Am Geophys Union. *Res:* Man-made and natural ionospheric disturbances and radar techniques for studying them; traveling ionospheric disturbances; auroral irregularities; chemical releases; antenna arrays; computer graphics. *Mailing Add:* 218 Willis Rd Sudbury MA 01776

THOMEIER, SIEGFRIED, b Aussig, Czech, Dec 19, 37; Ger citizen; m 61; c 2. MATHEMATICS, TOPOLOGY. *Educ:* Univ Frankfurt, Dipl Math, 62, Dr Phil Nat(math), 65. *Prof Exp:* Sci asst math, Frankfurt Univ, 63-65; assoc prof, Math Inst, Aarhus, Denmark, 65-68; PROF MATH, MEM UNIV NFLD, 68- *Concurrent Pos:* Nat Res Coun Can res grant, Mem Univ Nfld, 69-; vis prof math, Univ Konstanz, Ger, 75-76. *Mem:* Can Math Soc; Am Math Soc; London Math Soc; Ger Math Soc; NY Acad Sci. *Res:* Homotopy theory; homotopy groups of special topological spaces; homology theory; homological and categorical algebra; fixed point theory; applications of topology. *Mailing Add:* Dept of Math Mem Univ of Nfld St John's NF A1B 3X7 Can

THOMERSON, JAMIE E, b Ft McKavett, Tex, May 7, 35; m 57; c 2. ICHTHYOLOGY, ZOOLOGY. *Educ:* Univ Tex, BS, 57; Tex Tech Col, MS, 61; Tulane Univ, PhD(zool), 65. *Prof Exp:* High sch teacher, 58-59; from asst prof to assoc prof, 65-77, PROF ZOOL, SOUTHERN ILL UNIV, EDWARDSVILLE, 77- *Mem:* Am Soc Ichthyologists & Herpetologists; Am Fisheries Soc; Asn Trop Biol; Soc Syst Zool. *Res:* Fish systematics, ecology, behavior and genetics. *Mailing Add:* Dept of Biol Sci Southern Ill Univ Edwardsville IL 62025

THOMFORDE, C(LIFFORD) J(OHN), b Crookston, Minn, Dec 15, 17; m 41; c 3. ELECTRICAL ENGINEERING. *Educ:* Univ NDak, BS, 41; Iowa State Univ, MSEE, 51. *Prof Exp:* Engr, Fed Commun Comn, 41-42 & Collins Radio Co, 42-47; asst prof elec eng, 47-55, chmn dept, 55-75, PROF ELEC ENG, UNIV N DAK, 55- *Mem:* Am Soc Eng Educ; Inst Elec & Electronics Engrs. *Res:* Radio communications, particularly in the field of radio and television broadcasting. *Mailing Add:* Dept Elec Eng Univ NDak Grand Forks ND 58201

THOMISON, JOEL DOUGLAS, mathematics, see previous edition

THOMMES, ROBERT CHARLES, b Chicago, Ill, Aug 31, 28. ZOOLOGY. *Educ:* De Paul Univ, BS, 50, MS, 52; Northwestern Univ, PhD, 56. *Prof Exp:* From instr to assoc prof, 56-67, chmn dept, 68-70, PROF BIOL, DE PAUL UNIV, 67- *Mem:* AAAS; Soc Zool; Soc Develop Biol; Soc Exp Biol & Med. *Res:* Developmental endocrinology. *Mailing Add:* Dept of Biol Sci 1036 Belden Ave Chicago IL 60614

THOMOPOULOS, NICK TED, b Chicago, Ill, Aug 21, 30; m 64; c 1. OPERATIONS RESEARCH, STATISTICS. *Educ:* Univ Ill, BS, 53, MA, 58; Ill Inst Technol, PhD(indust eng), 66. *Prof Exp:* Supvr opers res, Int Harvester Co, 58-66; sr scientist, IIT Res Inst, 66-68; ASSOC PROF INDUST ENG, ILL INST TECHNOL, 68- *Mem:* Inst Mgt Sci; Opers Res Soc Am. *Res:* Manufacturing and assembly methods; uncertainty in mathematical models; statistical analysis; production and inventory control. *Mailing Add:* 53 Regent Dr Oak Brook IL 60521

THOMPKINS, LEON, b Augusta, Ga, Nov 4, 36; m 62; c 2. PHARMACEUTICAL CHEMISTRY. *Educ:* Morehouse Col, BS, 61; Univ Calif, San Francisco, PhD(pharmaceut chem), 68. *Prof Exp:* Chemist, Hyman Labs, Fundamental Res Co, Inc, 62-63; sr pharmaceut chemist, 68-76, RES SCIENTIST, ELI LILLY & CO, 76- *Mem:* Am Pharmaceut Asn; Am Chem Soc; Sigma Xi; AAAS; NY Acad Sci. *Res:* Development and bioavailability of human drug dosage forms. *Mailing Add:* Lilly Res Lab Dept IC747 PO Box 618 Indianapolis IN 46206

THOMPSON, A(LEXANDER) RALPH, b Toronto, Ont, Sept 11, 14; nat US; m 37; c 2. CHEMICAL ENGINEERING. *Educ:* Univ Toronto, BASc, 36; Univ Pa, PhD(chem eng), 45. *Prof Exp:* Chem engr, Can Industs, Ltd, Ont, 36-40; asst instr chem eng, Univ Pa, 40-41, instr, 42-45, from asst prof to assoc prof, 45-52; chmn dept, 52-72, PROF CHEM ENG, UNIV RI, 52-, DIR, WATER RESOURCES CTR, 66- *Concurrent Pos:* Res adv, Gen Refractories Co, Pa, 41-43; instr supvr eng, Sci & Mgt War Training, Radio Corp Am, NJ, 45; develop engr, Sun Oil Co, Pa, 45-53; consult, Monsanto Chem Co, Mass, 55-57; mem, Univs Coun Water Resources; chmn, Nat Asn Water Inst Directors, 80- *Mem:* Am Soc Eng Educ; Am Chem Soc; fel Am Inst Chem Engrs; fel AAAS. *Res:* Water resources; desalination; refraction, dispersion and densities of binary solutions; crystallization; distillation; phase equilibria; biochemical engineering. *Mailing Add:* Dept of Chem Eng Univ of RI Kingston RI 02881

THOMPSON, ALAN MORLEY, b Omaha, Nebr, Sept 2, 25; m 50; c 2. PHYSIOLOGY. *Educ:* Iowa State Univ, BS, 49; Univ Minn, PhD(physiol), 56. *Prof Exp:* Asst physiol, Univ Minn, 52-54, teaching intern, Ford Found, 54-55, asst, Univ, 55, instr, 55-56; res fel physiol, 56-57; instr, Univ Tex Southwestern Med Sch Dallas, 58-59; asst prof zool, Iowa State Univ, 59-62; assoc prof, 62-66, assoc dean, Grad Sch, 70-80, PROF PHYSIOL, UNIV KANS MED CTR, KANSAS CITY, 66- *Mem:* Am Physiol Soc; Soc Neurosci. *Res:* Transport of materials; cerebral blood flow and permeability; tissue carbon dioxide, electrolytes and acid-base balance. *Mailing Add:* Dept Physiol Univ Kans Med Ctr Kansas City KS 66103

THOMPSON, ALLAN LLOYD, b Leeds, Que, Mar 4, 20; m 43; c 3. PHYSICAL CHEMISTRY, ENGINEERING. *Educ:* Bishop's Univ, Can, BA, 40; McGill Univ, PhD(chem), 43. *Prof Exp:* Res chemist, Nat Res Coun Can, 43-46; RES ASSOC CHEM, RADIATION LAB, MCGILL UNIV, 46-, ASSOC PROF MECH ENG, UNIV, 58- *Concurrent Pos:* From sci consult to assoc dir, Gas Dynamics Lab, McGill Univ, 53-58. *Res:* Engineering science; chemical kinetics; analytical, nuclear and high temperature chemistry; cyclotron chemical problems; ignition and corrosion studies; vacuum engineering; combustion; road safety; collision investigations; pollution control of vehicles. *Mailing Add:* Dept Mech Eng McGill Univ 817 Sherbrooke St W Montreal PQ H3A 2K6 Can

THOMPSON, ALLAN M, b Ithaca, NY, May 22, 40; m 66. PETROLOGY, SEDIMENTOLOGY. *Educ:* Carleton Col, BA, 62; Brown Univ, ScM, 64, PhD(stratig), 68. *Prof Exp:* Asst prof, 67-72, ASSOC PROF GEOL & PETROL, UNIV DEL, 72- *Concurrent Pos:* Assoc geologist, Del Geol Surv, 72- *Mem:* Geol Soc Am; Am Asn Petrol Geologists; Soc Econ Paleont & Mineral. *Res:* Sedimentology, plutonic petrology and structure; stratigraphy, structure and petrology of Appalachian orogen. *Mailing Add:* Dept of Geol Univ of Del Newark DE 19711

THOMPSON, ALONZO CRAWFORD, b Tifton, Ga, June 4, 28; m 55; c 3. ORGANIC CHEMISTRY, PHARMACEUTICAL CHEMISTRY. *Educ:* Berry Col, AB, 53; Univ Miss, MS, 55, PhD(chem), 62. *Prof Exp:* Prof chem, Miss Delta Jr Col, 55-56 & Southern State Col, 56-58; RES CHEMIST, BOLL WEEVIL RES LAB, USDA, 62- *Concurrent Pos:* Adj asst prof biochem, Miss State Univ, 74- *Mem:* Am Chem Soc; Am Inst Chemists. *Res:* Pharmaceutical synthesis; natural products; insects and plant stimulants. *Mailing Add:* Boll Weevil Res Lab USDA Box 5367 Mississippi State MS 39762

THOMPSON, ALVIN JEROME, b Washington, DC, Apr 5, 24; m 50; c 5. GASTROENTEROLOGY. *Educ:* Howard Univ, MD, 46; Am Bd Internal Med, dipl. *Prof Exp:* Intern, St Louis City Hosp, Mo, 46-47, resident, 47-51; physician & gastroenterologist, Vet Admin Hosp, Seattle, 53-57; DIR GASTROENTEROL LAB, PROVIDENCE HOSP, SEATTLE, 63-; CLIN PROF MED, SCH MED, UNIV WASH, 75- *Concurrent Pos:* Pvt med pract, Seattle, 57-; med advisor, Draft Bd, 67-; co-chmn phys health task force, King County Comprehensive Health Planning Coun, 68, vpres, 73-; mem adv bd, King County Med Serv Bur, 69-70; chief staff, Providence Hosp, Seattle, 70-71, chmn med dept, 72-74. *Mem:* Inst of Med of Nat Acad Sci; Nat Med Asn; AMA; fel Am Col Physicians. *Mailing Add:* Sch of Med Univ of Wash Seattle WA 98195

THOMPSON, ANSEL FREDERICK, JR, b Birmingham, Ala, Oct 19, 41; m 63; c 3. ENVIRONMENTAL ENGINEERING, ENGINEERING MANAGEMENT. *Educ:* Pa State Univ, BS, 63; Calif Inst Technol, MS, 65, PhD(environ health eng), 68; Environ Eng Intersoc, dipl. *Prof Exp:* Proj engr & scientist, Roy F Weston, Inc, 67-70, prin engr, Weston Europe SpA, 70-73, proj mgr, 73-75, vpres, Eng Design, 75-80, VPRES, QUALITY ASSURANCE/FINANCE, ROY F WESTON, INC, 80- *Mem:* Am Water Works Asn; Water Pollution Control Fedn; Am Soc Civil Engrs; Am Acad Environ Engrs; Prof Serv Mgt Asn. *Res:* Thermodynamics and ultrafiltration of salt-polyelectrolyte solution; automatic control of biological processes; Monte Carlo methods in analysis of biological treatment systems; systems analysis. *Mailing Add:* Roy F Weston Co Weston Way West Chester PA 19380

THOMPSON, ANSON ELLIS, b Eugene, Ore, Apr 9, 24; m 45; c 4. PLANT BREEDING, PLANT GENETICS. *Educ:* Ore State Univ, BS, 48; Cornell Univ, PhD(plant breeding), 52. *Prof Exp:* Lab instr bot, Ore State Univ, 47-48; asst plant breeding, Cornell Univ, 48-51; from instr to assoc prof veg crops, Univ Ill, Urbana, 51-63, prof plant genetics, 63-71, asst dir agr exp sta,

67-69; prof hort & head dept hort & landscape archit, Univ Ariz, 71-75, prof hort & horticulturist, Dept Plant Sci, 75-76; field staff plant scientist, Rockefeller Found, Indonesia, 76-79; prog coordr hort crops, Prog Develop & Coord Staff, Sci & Educ Admin, 79-80, NAT RES PROG LEADER, AGR RES SERV, USDA, 80- *Concurrent Pos:* Univ Ky-Int Coop Admin vis prof, Univ Indonesia, 58-60; res admin consult, Univ Ill-AID Col Contract Team, Uttar Pradesh Agr Univ, India, 67 & party chief & adv, 67-69; vis prof, Gadjah Mada Univ, Indonesia, 76-79. *Honors & Awards:* Woodbury Award, Am Soc Hort Sci, 65, Asgrow Award, 66. *Mem:* Fel AAAS; fel Am Soc Hort Sci; Am Hort Soc; Int Soc Hort Sci; Sigma Xi. *Res:* Vegetable breeding and genetics; inheritance and breeding methods for disease resistance and quality constituents; breeding; selection; native plant materials for landscaping in arid lands. *Mailing Add:* Nat Prog Staff Agr Res Serv USDA Beltsville MD 20705

THOMPSON, ANTHONY C, mathematics, see previous edition

THOMPSON, ANTHONY RICHARD, b Hull, Eng, Apr 7, 31; m 63; c 1. RADIO ASTRONOMY INSTRUMENTATION, ELECTROMAGNETIC COMPATIBILITY. *Educ:* Univ Manchester, BSc, 52, PhD, 56. *Prof Exp:* Electronic engr, Elec & Musical Instruments Ltd, Eng, 55-57; res assoc, Harvard Col Observ, 57-61, res fel, 61-62; radio astronr, Stanford Univ, 62-70, sr res assoc, 70-72; VLA proj engr, 73-74, dep mgr VLA proj, 75-78, SYSTS ENGR & FREQUENCY COORDR VLA PROJ, NAT RADIO ASTRON OBSERV, 78- *Concurrent Pos:* Vis sr res fel, Calif Inst Technol, 66-71, vis assoc, 71-72; mem, US Study Group 2, Int Radio Consult Comt, 79-; chmn radio astron subcomt, Comt on Radio Frequencies, Nat Acad Sci, 80- *Mem:* Int Astron Union; Int Union Radio Sci; Inst Elec & Electronics Engrs; Am Astron Soc. *Res:* Structure of cosmic radio sources, solar radio astronomy; electromagnetic compatibility; design of radio telescopes. *Mailing Add:* Nat Radio Astron Observ PO Box O Socorro NM 87801

THOMPSON, ANTHONY W, b Burbank, Calif, Mar 6, 40; m; c 2. METALLURGY, MATERIALS SCIENCE. *Educ:* Stanford Univ, BS, 62; Univ Wash, MS, 65; Mass Inst Technol, PhD(metall, mat sci), 70. *Prof Exp:* Res engr, Jet Propulsion Lab, 62-63; metall consult, Charles River Assocs, Mass, 67-68; mem tech staff, Sandia Labs, 70-73; mem tech staff, Rockwell Int Sci Ctr, 73-77; assoc prof, 77-80, PROF METALL, CARNEGIE-MELLON UNIV, 80- *Mem:* AAAS; Am Soc Metals; Am Inst Mech Engrs Metall Soc. *Res:* Relation between microstructure of materials and mechanical behavior, particularly strength and fracture; including environmental effects and grain size effects on polycrystal behavior; fatigue and fracture toughness of engineering materials. *Mailing Add:* 6307 Hampton St Pittsburgh PA 15206

THOMPSON, ARTHUR CARSTEN, b Detroit, Mich, Sept 21, 19; m 50; c 3. PHYSICAL CHEMISTRY. *Educ:* Wayne State Univ, BS, 46, MS, 49; Wash State Univ, 56. *Prof Exp:* From instr to asst prof phys chem, Univ Idaho, 49-57; sr res chemist, Nalco Chem Co, 57-62; assoc prof chem, Marietta Col, 62-80. *Mem:* Am Chem Soc; Sigma Xi. *Res:* Physical chemistry of polymer solutions; collodal clays; silicates; coagulation; acidic properties of bentonite. *Mailing Add:* 305 Aurora Marietta OH 45750

THOMPSON, ARTHUR HOWARD, b Duluth, Minn, June 15, 18; m 45; c 4. POMOLOGY. *Educ:* Univ Minn, BS, 41; Univ Md, PhD, 45. *Prof Exp:* Asst pomologist, USDA, Wash, 45-48, assoc horticulturist, 48-50, horticulturist, WVa, 50-52; PROF POMOL, UNIV MD, COLLEGE PARK, 52- *Mem:* Am Soc Hort Sci. *Res:* Chemical thinning of apples and peaches; chemical control of preharvest drop; fruit tree nutrition. *Mailing Add:* Dept of Hort Univ of Md College Park MD 20742

THOMPSON, ARTHUR HOWARD, b Salt Lake City, Utah, Mar 3, 42; m 65. SOLID STATE PHYSICS. *Educ:* Ohio State Univ, BSc & MSc, 66; Stanford Univ, PhD(physics), 70. *Prof Exp:* Fel, Stanford Univ, 70; group leader physics, Syva Co, Calif, 70-71; sr res physicist, Exxon Res & Eng Co, Linden, 71-76, group head, Exxon Res & Eng Co, New Princeton, 76-81, GROUP HEAD, EXXON PROD RES CO, HOUSTON, 81- *Mem:* Am Phys Soc. *Res:* Super conductivity; semiconductors; transport and magnetic properties; geophysics. *Mailing Add:* PO Box 2189 Exxon Prod Res Co Houston TX 77001

THOMPSON, ARTHUR TOTTEN, engineering education, see previous edition

THOMPSON, AYLMER HENRY, b Ill, Sept 11, 22; m 41; c 3. METEOROLOGY. *Educ:* Univ Calif, Los Angeles, MA, 48, PhD(meteorol), 60. *Prof Exp:* Lectr meteorol, Univ Calif, Los Angeles, 48-52; asst prof, Univ Utah, 52-60; PROF METEOROL, TEX A&M UNIV, 60- *Concurrent Pos:* Sci adv Found Glacier & Environ Res, Wash. *Mem:* Am Meteorol Soc; Am Geophys Union; foreign mem Royal Meteorol Soc; Int Glaciol Soc; Sigma Xi. *Res:* Synoptic meteorology of sub-tropics; satellite meteorology; inversions; meteorology of glaciated regions. *Mailing Add:* Dept of Meteorol Tex A&M Univ College Station TX 77843

THOMPSON, BARBARA, b Austin, Minn, Oct 6, 49. ORTHODONTICS. *Educ:* Univ Minn, DDC, 73; Univ NC, MPH & MS, 78. *Prof Exp:* Pvt pract dent, 74-76; ASST PROF, UNIV NC SCH DENT, 78-; PVT PRACT ORTHOD, 80- *Mem:* Am Dent Asn; Am Asn Orthod. *Res:* Craniofacial development as related to head posture and craniocervical angulation of the head. *Mailing Add:* 2721 Chapel Hill Blvd Durham NC 27707

THOMPSON, BOBBY BLACKBURN, b Lumber City, Ga, May 15, 33; m 59; c 1. MEDICINAL CHEMISTRY, ORGANIC CHEMISTRY. *Educ:* Berry Col, BA, 55; Univ Miss, MS, 56, PhD(org med chem), 63. *Prof Exp:* Asst prof, 60-70, ASSOC PROF MED CHEM, SCH PHARM, UNIV GA, 70- *Mem:* Am Chem Soc; Am Pharmaceut Asn. *Res:* Synthesis of organic and heterocyclic compounds of potential medicinal value; structural elucidation by chemical and instrumental means. *Mailing Add:* Sch of Pharm Univ of Ga Athens GA 30602

THOMPSON, BONNIE CECIL, b Baird, Tex, Dec 18, 35; m 59; c 1. SOLID STATE PHYSICS. *Educ:* NTex State Univ, BA, 57, MA, 58; Univ Tex, PhD(physics), 65. *Prof Exp:* Instr physics, NTex State Univ, 58-60; teaching asst, Univ Tex, Austin 60-61, res scientist, 61-65; asst prof, 65-74, ASSOC PROF PHYSICS, UNIV TEX, ARLINGTON, 74- *Mem:* Am Phys Soc. *Res:* Nuclear spin-lattice relaxation processes in solids; nuclear magnetic resonance of biological molecules. *Mailing Add:* Dept of Physics Univ of Tex Arlington TX 76019

THOMPSON, BRIAN J, b Glossop, Eng, June 10, 32; m 56; c 2. OPTICS. *Educ:* Univ Manchester, BScTech, 55, PhD(physics), 59. *Prof Exp:* Demonstr physics fac tech, Univ Manchester, 55-56, asst lectr, 57-59; lectr, Leeds Univ, 59-62; sr physicist, Tech Opers, Inc, 63-65, mgr phys optics dept, 65-66, dir optics dept, 66-67, mgr tech opers west & tech dir, Beckman & Whitley Div, 67-68; dir, Inst Optics, 68-75, PROF OPTICS, UNIV ROCHESTER, 68-, DEAN COL ENG & APPL SCI, 74- *Concurrent Pos:* Adj prof, Northeastern Univ, 66-67. *Honors & Awards:* Kingslake Medal & Pezuto Award, Soc Photo-Opitcal Instrumentation Engrs, 78. *Mem:* Am Phys Soc; fel Optical Soc Am; fel Brit Inst Physics & Phys Soc; fel Soc Photo-Optical Instrumentation Engrs (pres, 74-75, 75-76). *Res:* Diffraction; interference; partial coherence; holography; application to particle sizing; optical data processing. *Mailing Add:* Col of Eng & Appl Sci Univ of Rochester Rochester NY 14627

THOMPSON, BUFORD DALE, b Lake Wales, Fla, Oct 22, 22; m 44; c 3. HORTICULTURE, VEGETABLE CROPS. *Educ:* Univ Fla, BSA, 48, MSA, 49, PhD(hort), 54, JD, 76. *Prof Exp:* Asst prof veg crops & asst horticulturist, Univ Fla, 49-60, assoc prof & assoc horticulturist, 60-66, prof veg crops & horticulturist, 66-80; ATTORNEY AGR LAW, AGR LEGAL CONSULT, US ARMY, 80- *Honors & Awards:* Vaughan Award, Am Soc Hort Sci, 62. *Mem:* Am Soc Plant Physiol. *Res:* Biological and chemical changes involved in the post harvest handling, transportation and storage of horticultural crops; agricultural law. *Mailing Add:* 725 NW 40th Terr Gainesville FL 32601

THOMPSON, BYRD THOMAS, JR, b Chicago, Ill, Nov 6, 24; m 47; c 2. ENGINEERING & FLUID MECHANICS. *Educ:* Univ Ala, BS, 49; Univ Ala, Huntsville, MS, 68. *Prof Exp:* Mech engr, Tenn Valley Authority, 49-51, Monsanto Chem Corp, 51-52 & Patchen & Zimmerman Consult Engrs, 52-54; mech develop engr, Masonite Corp, 54-55; res & develop engr, Chemstrand Co Div, Monsanto Co, 55-70, sr process develop engr, 70-72; sr textile res engr, Textiles Div, 72-75, gen engr, Central Eng Dept, 75-77; mech engr, Exp Eng Dept, Oak Ridge Nat Lab, 77-81; MECH ENGR, US ARMY CORPS ENGRS, 81- *Mem:* Am Soc Mech Eng. *Res:* Mechanical engineering and engineering mechanics as applied to design, development and research of synthetic fibers-processes and machinery. *Mailing Add:* 2010 Birch St Decatur AL 35601

THOMPSON, BYRON EDWIN, b Shawano, Wis, Mar 5, 35; m 64; c 2. HYDRODYNAMICS. *Educ:* Univ Tex, BSME, 57, MSME, 61, PhD(mech eng), 65. *Prof Exp:* Engr, Pratt & Whitney Aircraft Corp, 57-59; STAFF MEM HYDRODYNAMICS,LOS ALAMOS NAT LAB,64- *Res:* Numerical hydrodynamics. *Mailing Add:* 206 Rover Blvd White Rock NM 87544

THOMPSON, CARL EUGENE, b Lucinda, Pa, June 14, 41; m 64; c 4. ANIMAL BREEDING, ANIMAL GENETICS. *Educ:* Pa State Univ, University Park, BS, 63, MS, 68; Va Polytech Inst & State Univ, PhD(animal breeding & genetics), 71. *Prof Exp:* Asst county agr agent, Agr Exten Serv, Pa State Univ, 63-66; asst prof animal sci, Ft Hays State Univ, 71-73; asst prof, 74-77, assoc prof, 77-81, PROF BEEF CATTLE BREEDING, CLEMSON UNIV, 81- *Mem:* Am Soc Animal Sci; Am Genetics Asn; Sigma Xi. *Res:* Beef cattle breeding and genetics; cross-breeding; genetic-environmental interaction; reproductive physiology. *Mailing Add:* Dept Animal Sci Clemson Univ Clemson SC 29631

THOMPSON, CHARLES ALBERT, food & medical microbiology, see previous edition

THOMPSON, CHARLES CALVIN, b Los Angeles, Calif, May 4, 35; m 60; c 2. ORAL PATHOLOGY. *Educ:* St Martin's Col, BA, 57; Univ Ore, DMD, 62; Emory Univ, MSD, 68; Am Bd Oral Path, dipl; Nat Bd Forensic Dent, dipl. *Prof Exp:* Pvt dent pract, Ore, 64-66; resident path, Dent Sch, Emory Univ, 66-68; asst prof oral diag & med, Dent Sch, Univ Calif, Los Angeles, 68-69; ASSOC PROF PATH, DENT SCH & ASST PROF DENT, MED SCH, UNIV ORE, 69- *Concurrent Pos:* Nat Inst Dent Res fel, Emory Univ, 66-68; attend consult, Wadsworth Vet Admin Hosp, Los Angeles, 68-69; oral pathologist & clin consult, 71-; instr, Mt Hood Community Col, 72-73. *Mem:* Fel Am Acad Oral Path; Int Soc Forensic Odontol-Stomatol. *Res:* Oncology, chemical, physical carcinogenesis; teratology, induction of developmental defects and explanation; forensic odontology; bone, especially effects of dimethyl sulfoxide on bone. *Mailing Add:* Dept of Path Sch of Dent Univ of Ore Health Sci Ctr Portland OR 97201

THOMPSON, CHARLES DENISON, b Niagara Falls, NY, May 4, 40. CORROSION. *Educ:* Oberlin Col, BA, 62; Am Univ, MS, 68, PhD(chem), 71. *Prof Exp:* Chemist, US Army Environ Hyg Agency, 63-65; chemist biochem, Aldridge Assocs, 69; Welch fel, Rice Univ, 71-72; CORROSION ENGR, KNOLLS ATOMIC POWER LAB, GEN ELEC CO, 73- *Mem:* Electrochem Soc. *Res:* High temperature materials corrosion and electrochemistry. *Mailing Add:* Knolls Atomic Energy Lab G2-154 Schenectady NY 12301

THOMPSON, CHARLES FREDERICK, b Dayton, Ohio, Oct 1, 43; m 67. POPULATION ECOLOGY, ORNITHOLOGY. *Educ:* Ind Univ, BA, 67, MA, 70, PhD(zool), 71. *Prof Exp:* Res fel ecol, Univ Ga, 71-72, asst prof zool, 72-73; teaching fel zool, Miami Univ, 73-75; asst prof biol, State Univ NY Col Geneseo, 75-78; ASST PROF ECOL, ILL STATE UNIV, 78- *Concurrent Pos:* Vis asst prof zool, Ind Univ, 74. *Mem:* Ecol Soc Am; Brit Ecol Soc; Am Ornithologists Union; Brit Ornithologists Union; Neth Ornithologists Union. *Res:* Regulation and dynamics of bird populations; avian breeding adaptations; structure and evolution of avian social organization. *Mailing Add:* Dept of Biol Sci Ill State Univ Normal IL 61761

THOMPSON, CHARLES WILLIAM NELSON, b Bethlehem, Pa; m 48; c 3. INDUSTRIAL ENGINEERING, MANAGEMENT SCIENCE. *Educ:* Kutztown State Col, BS, 43; Harvard Law Sch, LLB, 49; Ohio State Univ MBA, 56; Northwestern Univ, PhD(indust eng), 69. *Prof Exp:* Chief electronic reconnaissance sect, Wright Air Develop Ctr, USAF, 52-58; dir eng serv, Govt Electronics Div, Admiral Corp, 58-64; assoc prof, 68-77, PROF INDUST ENG & MGT SCI, TECHNOL INST, NORTHWESTERN UNIV, 77- *Concurrent Pos:* Consult exp technol prog, Nat Bur Standards, 75-80. *Mem:* Inst Elec & Electronic Engrs; Inst Mgt Sci; Opers Res Soc Am; Am Inst Indust Engrs; AAAS. *Res:* Theory and methodology of unstructured problems in organizations and systems, with particular emphasis on field research, including administrative experiments. *Mailing Add:* Technol Inst Northwestern Univ Evanston IL 60103

THOMPSON, CHARLEY LEWIS, JR, b Charleston, SC, Oct 12, 38; m 63; c 4. MECHANICAL ENGINEERING. *Educ:* Univ SC, BS, 64, ME, 67, PhD(energy conversion), 69. *Prof Exp:* Assoc prof thermal sci, Sch Eng, NC A&T State Univ, 70-74; CONSULT ENGR, 73- *Concurrent Pos:* Nat teaching fel, NC A&T State Univ, 70-71. *Mem:* Am Soc Mech Engrs; Am Soc Eng Educ; Nat Soc Prof Engrs. *Res:* Combustion; heat transfer; fluids; machine design; education and bio-engineering. *Mailing Add:* Box 658 Rte 2 McLeansville NC 27301

THOMPSON, CHESTER RAY, b Storrs, Utah, May 27, 15; m 40; c 4. BIOCHEMISTRY. *Educ:* Utah State Univ, BS, 38; Univ Wis, MS, 41, PhD(biochem), 43. *Prof Exp:* Chemist, Rocky Mountain Packing Corp, Utah, 36-39; biochemist, Univ Wis, 39-43, Forest Prods Lab, US Forest Serv, 43 & Purdue Univ, 44-45; plant biochemist, Univ Chicago, 45-49; head forage invest, Field Crops Lab, Western Utilization Res & Develop Div, USDA, 49-60; proj leader, 60-67, RES BIOCHEMIST, STATEWIDE AIR POLLUTION RES CTR, AGR AIR RES PROG, UNIV CALIF, RIVERSIDE, 67- *Mem:* Fel AAAS; Am Soc Plant Physiol; Am Chem Soc; Air Pollution Control Asn. *Res:* Chemical stabilization of carotene in alfalfa; occurrence of anti-oxidants in natural products; carotenoids in green plants; saponins and estrogens in forages; effects of air pollution on plants and human beings. *Mailing Add:* Statewide Air Pollution Res Ctr Univ of Calif Riverside CA 92521

THOMPSON, CLARENCE GARRISON, b Corvallis, Ore, Nov 3, 18. ENTOMOLOGY. *Educ:* Ore State Col, BS, 40; Univ Calif, MS, 47, PhD, 50. *Prof Exp:* Jr insect pathologist, Univ Calif, 50-51, asst insect pathologist, 51-53; insect pathologist, 53-70, ENTOMOLOGIST, US FOREST SERV & PROF ENTOM, AGR EXP STA, ORE STATE UNIV, USDA, 70- *Res:* Insect pathology. *Mailing Add:* US Forest Serv Ore State Univ Corvallis OR 97331

THOMPSON, CLARENCE HENRY, JR, b Perry, Kans, May 4, 18; m 42; c 3. VETERINARY MEDICINE. *Educ:* Kans State Col, DVM, 41, MS, 47. *Prof Exp:* Asst vet private vet hosp, 41; jr vet tuberc eradication, Bur Animal Indust, Agr Res Serv, USDA, 41-46, vet pathologist path div, 47-54, adminstr state exp sta div, Agr Res Serv, 54-63, asst to dir animal disease & parasite res div, 63-71, staff asst to adminr, 71-74; RETIRED. *Mem:* Am Vet Med Asn. *Res:* Animal diseases, especially virus diseases of poultry, in fields of epizoology, bacteriology, pathology and immunology. *Mailing Add:* 6203 87th Ave Hyattsville MD 20784

THOMPSON, CLIFTON C, b Franklin, Tenn, Aug 16, 39; m 59, 78; c 3. PHYSICAL CHEMISTRY. *Educ:* Middle Tenn State Univ, BS, 61; Univ Miss, PhD(phys & inorg chem), 64. *Prof Exp:* Res assoc, Univ Tex, 64-65; asst prof spectrochem, Rutgers Univ, 65; asst prof chem, Marshall Univ, 65-66; assoc prof, Mid Tenn State Univ, 66-68; from asst prof to assoc prof, Memphis State Univ, 68-74; PROF CHEM, SOUTHWEST MO STATE UNIV, 74-, DEAN, SCH SCI & TECHNOL, 74- *Concurrent Pos:* Lectr, Kanawha Valley grad ctr, WVa Univ, 66; NSF acad year exten grant, 66-68; mem, Med Technol Rev Comt, 74-80. *Mem:* Am Chem Soc; Royal Soc Chem; AAAS; Sigma Xi. *Res:* Spectral, thermodynamic and kinetic studies of molecular complexes; quantum chemistry; computer applications to physical systems. *Mailing Add:* Dept of Chem Southwest Mo State Univ Springfield MO 65802

THOMPSON, CRAYTON BEVILLE, b Paris, Tex, Dec 28, 20; m 55; c 1. ORGANIC CHEMISTRY. *Educ:* Univ Tex, BS, 42; Univ Ill, MS, 47, PhD(chem), 49. *Prof Exp:* Chem engr, Freeport Sulphur Co, 42-46; lab asst chem, Univ Ill, 47-49; RES & DEVELOP CHEMIST, EASTMAN KODAK CO, 49- *Mem:* Am Chem Soc. *Res:* Synthesis of amino acids; antihalation backings for photographic films; abrasion resistant and anitstatic applications for plastics; adhesion. *Mailing Add:* Bldg 7 Kodak Park Eastman Kodak Co Rochester NY 14650

THOMPSON, D(ONALD) W(ILLIAM), b Gosport, Eng, Mar 16, 33; m 57; c 2. CHEMICAL ENGINEERING. *Educ:* Univ Birmingham, BSc, 54, PhD(chem eng), 58. *Prof Exp:* Res fel chem eng, Univ BC, 58-60; engr, Shell Develop Co, Calif, 60-67; assoc prof, 67-77, PROF CHEM ENG, UNIV BC, 77- *Honors & Awards:* Jr Moulton Medal, Brit Inst Chem Eng, 61. *Mem:* Am Inst Chem Engrs; Chem Inst Can; Brit Inst Chem Eng. *Res:* Adsorption and chromatographic processes; cyclic separation processes; membrane separations; flow visualization; optimization methods. *Mailing Add:* Dept of Chem Eng Univ of BC Vancouver BC V6T 1W5 Can

THOMPSON, DANIEL JAMES, b Terre Haute, Ind, Feb 10, 42; m 65; c 2. TERATOLOGY, TOXICOLOGY. *Educ:* Ind State Univ, BS, 64, MA, 66; Am Bd Toxicol, dipl, 81. *Prof Exp:* Res specialist, 66-80, RES LEADER, DOW CHEM CO, 80- *Mem:* Teratology Soc; Environ Mutagen Soc; Soc Toxicol. *Res:* Reproductive physiology; perinatal toxicology. *Mailing Add:* Dept of Toxicol Dow Chem Co PO Box 68511 Indianapolis IN 46268

THOMPSON, DANIEL QUALE, b Madison, Wis, Oct 3, 18; m 53; c 4. WILDLIFE ECOLOGY, CONSERVATION. *Educ:* Univ Wis-Madison, BS, 42, MS, 50; Univ Mo, PhD(field zool), 55. *Prof Exp:* Instr field zool, Univ Mo, 50-54; from asst prof to assoc prof biol, Ripon Col, 55-62; wildlife res biologist, US Fish & Wildlife Serv & leader, NY Coop Wildlife Res Unit, Cornell Univ, 62-75; WILDLIFE ED, COLO STATE UNIV, US FISH & WILDLIFE SERV, 75- *Concurrent Pos:* Mem grad fel panel, NSF, 71-72; ed, J Wildlife Mgt, 73-74. *Mem:* Am Soc Mammal; Wildlife Soc; Ecol Soc Am. *Res:* Wildlife conservation; ecology of terrestrial vertebrates. *Mailing Add:* Ed Off Colo State Univ 270 Aylesworth SE Ft Collins CO 80523

THOMPSON, DARRELL ROBERT, b Hickory, NC, July 13, 37; m 66; c 2. BIOMATERIALS, PHYSICAL CHEMISTRY. *Educ:* Lenoir Rhyne Col, BS, 59; Univ NC, PhD(phys chem), 64. *Prof Exp:* Res chemist pigment dispersion, E I du Pont de Nemours & Co, Inc, 64-68; sr res chemist, Celanese Fibers Co, 68-70; GROUP LEADER SURG PRODS, JOHNSON & JOHNSON CORP, 70- *Mem:* Am Chem Soc; Sigma Xi; Fiber Soc. *Res:* Surgical products; surface and colloid chemistry; coatings; pigment dispersion. *Mailing Add:* 172 Windy Willow Way Somerville NJ 08876

THOMPSON, DAVID A(LFRED), b Chicago, Ill, Sept 9, 29; m 49; c 3. BIOTECHNOLOGY. *Educ:* Univ Va, BME, 51; Univ Fla, BIE, 55, MSE, 56; Stanford Univ, PhD(indust eng), 61. *Prof Exp:* Asst eng & indust, Exp Sta, Univ Fla, 55-56; actg instr indust eng, 56-58, actg asst prof, 58-61, from asst prof to assoc prof, 61-72, res assoc rehab med, 58-64, PROF INDUST ENG & ASSOC CHMN DEPT, STANFORD UNIV, 72- *Concurrent Pos:* Int consult, 58- *Mem:* Am Inst Indust Engrs; Human Factors Soc; Inst Elec & Electronics Engrs; Am Soc Eng Educ. *Res:* Analysis and design of man-machine systems, especially the physiological, neurological and psychological information processing in man. *Mailing Add:* Dept of Indust Eng Stanford Univ Stanford CA 94305

THOMPSON, DAVID ALLEN, b Gallipolis, Ohio, July 10, 50; m 72; c 1. INORGANIC CHEMISTRY, GLASS CHEMISTRY. *Educ:* Ohio State Univ, BS, 72; Univ Mich, MS, 73, PhD(chem), 77. *Prof Exp:* RES CHEMIST, CORNING GLASS WORKS, 76- *Mem:* Am Chem Soc; Am Ceramic Soc. *Res:* Glass chemistry research including composition, durability, diffusion and melting of glass as it relates to glass structure. *Mailing Add:* Corning Glass Works Sullivan Park Dr 25 Corning NY 14830

THOMPSON, DAVID DUVALL, b Ithaca, NY, June 1, 22; m 45; c 4. INTERNAL MEDICINE. *Educ:* Cornell Univ, BA, 43, MD, 46. *Prof Exp:* Intern & resident med, New York Hosp, 46-50; res fel physiol, Med Col, Cornell Univ, 50-51; instr physiol, Med Col, Cornell Univ, 51-53; resident physician, NIH, 53-55; asst prof physiol, 55-57, assoc prof med, 57-64, PROF MED, MED COL, CORNELL UNIV, 64-; ATTEND PHYSICIAN, DEPT MED, NEW YORK HOSP, 64-, DIR, 67- *Concurrent Pos:* Clin instr, Sch Med, George Washington Univ, 54-55; resident physician, NIH, 55-56; Lederle award, 55-57; from asst attend to actg physician-in-chief, Dept Med, New York Hosp, 57-67; asst vis physician, 2nd Med Div, Bellevue Hosp, 57-66, assoc vis physician, 66-; attend physician, Vet Admin Hosp, 58-; mem med adv bd, Kidney Found NY, 62-; actg chmn dept med, Cornell Univ, 65-67. *Mem:* Am Soc Clin Invest; Am Physiol Soc; Harvey Soc; Am Fedn Clin Res; Am Col Physicians. *Res:* Renal and electrolyte physiology. *Mailing Add:* New York Hosp 525 E 68th St New York NY 10021

THOMPSON, DAVID FRED, b Columbus, OHio, Mar 6, 41; m 66; c 3. TECHNICAL CERAMICS, ZIRCONIA CERAMICS. *Educ:* Ohio State Univ, BSc, 64, MSc, 64, PhD(ceramic eng), 68. *Prof Exp:* Proj engr, Edward Orton Jr Ceramic Found, 62-68; sect head, GTE Sylvania, 68-74; MGR TECH DEVELOP, ZIRCOA PROD, CORNING GLASS WORKS, 74- *Mem:* Am Ceramic Soc; Am Soc Testing & Mat. *Res:* Zirconia ceramics; solid electrolytes; processing technology; optimization of ceramic material properties; physical property measurement; test development. *Mailing Add:* 7112 Fox Hill Dr Solon OH 44139

THOMPSON, DAVID J, b Danville, Ind, Apr 17, 34; m 68; c 2. GENETICS, PLANT BREEDING. *Educ:* Univ Idaho, BS, 54, MS, 56; Cornell Univ, PhD(plant breeding), 60. *Prof Exp:* Co-geneticist, 60-63, res dir genetics & plant breeding, 63-76, VPRES, RES DIV, FERRY-MORSE SEED CO, 76- *Mem:* Int Soc Hort Sci; Am Soc Hort Sci. *Res:* Genetics, cytology and physiology of male-sterility and self-incompatibility in plants. *Mailing Add:* Ferry-Morse Seed Co San Juan Bautista CA 95045

THOMPSON, DAVID JEROME, b Sand Creek, Wis, July 21, 37; m 62; c 2. MINERAL NUTRITION. *Educ:* Univ Wis-Madison, BS, 60, MS, 61, PhD(biochem), 63; Univ Chicago, MBA, 75. *Prof Exp:* Res assoc biochem, Univ Wis-Madison, 63-64; res biochemist, 64-69, mgr tech serv, 69-78, dir tech serv, 78-79, regional sales mgr, 79-81, VPRES, SCI & TECHNOL, INT MINERALS & CHEM CORP, 81- *Concurrent Pos:* Mem, Mineral Toxic Animals Subcomt, Nat Reserve Coun, Nat Acad Sci, 76-80. *Mem:* NY Acad Sci; Am Chem Soc; AAAS; Coun Agr Sci & Technol. *Res:* Mineral nutrition of animals. *Mailing Add:* 2315 Sanders Rd Northbrook IL 60062

THOMPSON, DAVID JOHN, b Cincinnati, Ohio, Jan 11, 45; m 72; c 1. ASTROPHYSICS, GAMMA RAY ASTRONOMY. *Educ:* Johns Hopkins Univ, BA, 67; Univ Md, PhD(physics), 73. *Prof Exp:* Res assoc physics, Univ Md, 73; ASTROPHYSICIST, GODDARD SPACE FLIGHT CTR, NASA, 73- *Mem:* Am Astron Soc; Am Phys Soc. *Res:* Gamma ray astronomy and its relationship to cosmic ray physics and other aspects of astrophysics; high energy gamma ray detectors, particularly spark chambers. *Mailing Add:* Code 662 Goddard Space Flight Ctr NASA Greenbelt MD 20771

THOMPSON, DAVID RUSSELL, b Cleveland, Ohio, Apr 4, 44; m 66. ENGINEERING, FOOD SCIENCE. *Educ:* Purdue Univ, West Lafayette, BS, 66, MS, 67; Mich State Univ, PhD(agr eng), 70. *Prof Exp:* Asst prof, 70-76, assoc prof, 76-81, PROF FOOD ENG, UNIV MINN, ST PAUL, 81- *Concurrent Pos:* NSF grant, 72-73; sabbatical leave to work for Green Giant

(Pillsbury) Co, LeSueur, Minn, 78-79; mem rev team, Dept Defense Food Res Develop, Test & Eng Prog, Nat Res Coun, 80. *Mem:* Am Soc Agr Engrs; Inst Food Technol; Am Soc Eng Educ; Am Soc Heating, Refrig & Air Conditioning Engrs. *Res:* Food processing; modeling heat and mass transfer reaction kinetics of changes in nutrition; microbiological populations and organoleptic characteristics in food systems during heating and cooling processes; energy conservation in food systems. *Mailing Add:* Dept of Agr Eng Univ of Minn St Paul MN 55108

THOMPSON, DAVID WALLACE, b Chicago, Ill, Jan 27, 42; m 63; c 2. INORGANIC CHEMISTRY, ORGANOMETALLIC CHEMISTRY. *Educ:* Wheaton Col, BS, 63; Northwestern Univ, Evanston, PhD(chem), 68. *Prof Exp:* Asst prof, 67-70, ASSOC PROF CHEM, COL WILLIAM & MARY, 70- *Mem:* Am Chem Soc. *Res:* Coordination chemistry of group IV elements; use of transition elements to catalyze organic reactions. *Mailing Add:* Dept of Chem Col of William & Mary Williamsburg VA 23185

THOMPSON, DONALD LEO, b Keota, Okla, Dec 31, 43; m 65; c 3. PHYSICAL CHEMISTRY. *Educ:* Northeastern State Col, BS, 65; Univ Ark, Fayetteville, PhD(phys chem), 70. *Prof Exp:* Res assoc theoret chem, Univ Calif, Irvine, 70-71; MEM STAFF THEORET CHEM, LOS ALAMOS NAT LAB, 71- *Concurrent Pos:* Vis assoc prof physics, Univ Miss, 75-76; vis prof chem, Okla State Univ, 80-81. *Mem:* Am Chem Soc. *Res:* Theoretical molecular dynamics; reaction kinetics and intermolecular energy transfer. *Mailing Add:* Los Alamos Nat Lab PO Box 1663 Los Alamos NM 87544

THOMPSON, DONALD LEROY, b Highland Park, Mich, Nov 15, 32; m 62; c 1. HEALTH PHYSICS. *Educ:* City Col New York, BS, 61; Long Island Univ, MS, 66; St Johns Univ, PhD(phys chem), 72, cert health physics, 81. *Prof Exp:* Sr scientist med physics, Radiation Physics Lab, State Univ NY Downstate Med Ctr, 62-65, asst dir, 65-69, co-dir, 69-72; health physicist, 72-74, actg dep dir, Div Radioactive Mat Br, 75-78, DEP CHEIF NUCLEAR MED, BUR RADIOL HEALTH, 78- *Concurrent Pos:* Instr radiol, State Univ NY, 65-69, asst prof radiol sci, 69-72; instr, Found Advan Educ Sci, 73-81. *Mem:* Am Asn Physicists in Med; Health Physics Soc. *Res:* Radiation exposures related to medical and consumer products. *Mailing Add:* Bur Radiol Health 5600 Fishers Lane Rockville MD 20857

THOMPSON, DONALD LORAINE, b SDak, Feb 10, 21; m 49; c 1. AGRONOMY. *Educ:* SDak State Col, BS, 47, MS, 49; Iowa State Col, PhD(corn breeding), 53. *Prof Exp:* Asst small grain breeding, SDak State Col, 47-49; corn breeding, Iowa State Col, 49-52; PROF CROP SCI & RES AGRONOMIST, USDA, NC STATE UNIV, 52- *Mem:* Am Soc Agron. *Res:* Practical and theoretical aspects of corn breeding relating to quantitative genetics; disease resistance; relationships among economic traits; maximum production; forage evaluation. *Mailing Add:* Dept of Crop Sci & Genetics NC State Univ PO Box 5720 Raleigh NC 27607

THOMPSON, DONALD OSCAR, b Clear Lake, Iowa, Feb 27, 27; m 46; c 3. SOLID STATE PHYSICS. *Educ:* Univ Iowa, BA, 49, MS, 50, PhD, 53. *Prof Exp:* Physicist, Union Carbide Nuclear Co, 56-64; ASSOC DIR, N AM ROCKWELL SCI CTR, 64- *Mem:* Fel Am Phys Soc; Am Inst Mining, Metall & Petrol Eng. *Res:* Radiation damage in metals, particularly interaction of radiation-produced defects and dislocations; anharmonic and nonlinear effects in solids; materials research in support of nondestructive testing; nondestructive testing apparatus. *Mailing Add:* NAm Rockwell Sci Ctr 1049 Camino Dos Rios Thousand Oaks CA 91360

THOMPSON, DONOVAN JEROME, b Stoughton, Wis, Jan 30, 19; m 42; c 2. BIOSTATISTICS. *Educ:* St Olaf Col, BA, 41; Univ Minn, MA, 47; Iowa State Col, PhD(statist), 52. *Prof Exp:* Mem staff dept math, Univ Minn, 46-47 & Statist Lab, Iowa State Col, 47-53; prof biostatist, Grad Sch Pub Health, Univ Pittsburgh, 53-66; PROF BIOSTATIST, SCH PUB HEALTH & COMMUNITY MED, UNIV WASH, 66-, CHMN DEPT, 73- *Mem:* AAAS; Biomet Soc; Am Pub Health Asn; Am Statist Asn; Inst Math Statist. *Res:* Statistical theory and methodology. *Mailing Add:* Sch of Pub Health & Community Med Univ of Wash Seattle WA 98195

THOMPSON, DOUGLAS STUART, b Richmond, Calif, Dec 5, 39; m 70. PHYSICAL CHEMISTRY. *Educ:* Univ Calif, Berkeley, BS, 61; Mass Inst Technol, PhD(phys chem), 65. *Prof Exp:* NIH trainee, Univ Calif, San Diego, 66-67; res phys chemist, E I du Pont de Nemours & Co, Inc, 68-79; MEM STAFF, DEPT CHEM, HAMPDEN-SYDNEY COL, 79- *Mem:* Am Chem Soc; Sigma Xi; AAAS; Am Phys Soc. *Res:* Characterization of macromolecules; inelastic light scattering; electron spin resonance; nuclear magnetic resonance; phospholipid vesicles, micelles, spin labels and viscometry. *Mailing Add:* Dept of Chem Hampden-Sydney Col Hampden-Sydney VA 23901

THOMPSON, DUDLEY, b Kansas City, Mo, Aug 25, 29; m 51; c 2. NUCLEAR ENGINEERING. *Educ:* US Mil Acad, BS, 51; Purdue Univ, MS, 56. *Prof Exp:* Instr elec eng & nuclear physics, US Mil Acad, 56-60, asst prof, 59-60; group leader reactor opers, Brookhaven Nat Lab, 60-67, secy reactor & critical exp safety comt, 66-67; chief oper safety br, Div Reactor Licensing, USAEC, 67-72; asst dir info processing, Off Opers Eval, Directorate of Regulatory Opers, US Nuclear Regulatory Comn, 72-76, actg dir field opers, Off Inspection & Enforcement, 76-77, dep dir, Region II, 77-79, actg dep dir, Off Inspection & Enforcement, 79-80, dir, Enforcement & Investigation, 80-81; RETIRED. *Concurrent Pos:* Consult, 82- *Res:* Nuclear reactor operations; reactor safety; operator training and qualification. *Mailing Add:* 2197 Stratton Dr Potomac MD 20854

THOMPSON, EARL RYAN, b Lenoir, NC, Jan 9, 39; m 60; c 3. METALLURGICAL ENGINEERING, MATERIALS SCIENCE. *Educ:* NC State Univ, BS, 60, MS, 62; Univ VA, DSc(mat sci), 66. *Prof Exp:* Res scientist metal, Reynolds Metals Co, 61-62; sr res scientist high temp alloy res, 65-74, MGR MAT SCI, UNITED TECHNOL RES CTR, 74- *Concurrent Pos:* Newcomb fel, Univ Va, 64; mem, Solid State Sci Panel, Nat Res Coun, 76- *Honors & Awards:* Grossman's Author Award, Am Soc Metals, 70. *Mem:* Am Inst Aeronaut & Astronaut; fel Am Soc Metals; Am Inst Mining, Metall & Petrol Engrs; Am Ceramic Soc; Sigma Xi. *Res:* High temperature alloy research and development; composite materials; directional solidification; ceramics for gas turbine use; rapidly solidified alloys; processing of metals by lasers. *Mailing Add:* United Technol Res Ctr Silver Lane East Hartford CT 06108

THOMPSON, EDWARD IVINS BRADBRIDGE, b Burlington, Iowa, Dec 20, 33; m 57; c 2. MOLECULAR BIOLOGY, CELL BIOLOGY. *Educ:* Rice Inst, BA, 55; Harvard Med Sch, MD, 60. *Prof Exp:* Intern & resident med, Presby Hosp, Col Physicians & Surgeons, Columbia Univ, 60-62; res assoc neurochem, Lab Clin Sci, NIMH, 62-64, res scientist molecular biol, Lab Molecular Biol, Nat Inst Arthritis & Metab Dis, 64-69, sr res scientist molecular & cell biol, 69-73, HEAD SECT BIOCHEM GENE EXPRESSION, LAB BIOCHEM, NAT CANCER INST, 73- *Concurrent Pos:* Corresp ed, J Steroid Biochem, assoc ed, Cancer Res. *Mem:* Am Chem Soc; Endocrine Soc; Am Soc Cell Biol; Am Soc Biol Chemists; Am Asn Cancer Res. *Res:* Endocrinology; regulation of gene expression in eukaryotic cells; mechanism of steroid hormone action; effects of steroids in malignant cells. *Mailing Add:* Lab of Biochem Bldg 37 Rm 4C09 Nat Cancer Inst Bethesda MD 20014

THOMPSON, EDWARD VALENTINE, b Sharon, Conn, Feb 6, 35; m 56; c 1. PHYSICAL CHEMISTRY. *Educ:* Cornell Univ, AB, 56; Polytech Inst Brooklyn, PhD(phys chem), 62. *Prof Exp:* Chemist, Am Cyanamid Co, 56-57, res chemist, 61-66; ASSOC PROF CHEM ENG, UNIV MAINE, ORONO, 66- *Mem:* Am Chem Soc. *Res:* Polymer chemistry and physics; theory of viscoelasticity; thermodynamics. *Mailing Add:* Dept of Chem Eng Univ of Maine Orono ME 04473

THOMPSON, EMMANUEL BANDELE, b Zarla, Nigeria, Mar 15, 28. PHARMACOLOGY. *Educ:* Rockhurst Col, BS, 55; Univ Mo-Kansas City, BS, 59; Univ Nebr, Lincoln, MS, 63; Univ Wash, PhD(pharmacol), 66. *Prof Exp:* Hosp pharmacist, Univ Kans Med Ctr, 59-60; retail pharmacist, Cundiff Drug Store, 61; sr res pharmacologist, Baxter Labs Inc, Ill, 63-66; asst prof, 69-73, ASSOC PROF PHARMACOL, COL PHARM, UNIV ILL MED CTR, 73- *Concurrent Pos:* Univ Ill Grad Col grant, 69-70 & Exten, 70-71; USPHS grant, 72-74; prin res investr & consult, West Side Vet Admin Hosp, Chicago, 71- *Mem:* NY Acad Sci; Am Asn Cols Pharm; Am Pharmaceut Asn. *Res:* Cardiovascular pharmacology. *Mailing Add:* Dept of Pharmacol Univ of Ill Med Ctr Chicago IL 60612

THOMPSON, EMMETT FRANK, b El Reno, Okla, Nov 6, 36; m 61; c 3. FOREST ECONOMICS. *Educ:* Okla State Univ, BS, 58; NC State Univ, MS, 60; Ore State Univ, PhD(forest econ), 66. *Prof Exp:* From asst prof to prof forestry, Va Polytech Inst, 62-73; prof forestry & head dept, Miss State Univ, 73-77; PROF FORESTRY & HEAD DEPT, AUBURN UNIV, 77- *Mem:* Soc Am Foresters; Forest Products Res Soc. *Res:* Economics of forest resource management. *Mailing Add:* Dept of Forestry Auburn Univ Auburn AL 36830

THOMPSON, ERIC DOUGLAS, b Buffalo, NY, Mar 24, 34; m 60; c 3. SOLID STATE PHYSICS. *Educ:* Mass Inst Technol, SB & SM, 56, PhD(physics), 60. *Prof Exp:* NSF res fel, 62-63; from asst prof to assoc prof, 63-69, PROF ENG, CASE WESTERN RESERVE UNIV, 69- *Concurrent Pos:* Sr res assoc, Jet Propulsion Lab, 72-73; prog dir, NSF, 81-82. *Mem:* fel Am Phys Soc; sr mem Inst Elec & Electronics Engrs. *Res:* Theory of magnetism; collective modes in ferromagnetic metals; magnetic neutron scattering; domain wall dynamics; solid state microwave active devices; Josephson Junction devices; thermal atomic scattering. *Mailing Add:* Elec Eng & Appl Physics Case Western Reserve Univ Cleveland OH 44106

THOMPSON, ERIC FONTELLE, JR, b Montgomery, Ala, Sept 29, 32; m 60; c 4. ZOOLOGY. *Educ:* Huntingdon Col, AB, 54; Univ Ga, MS, 56, PhD(zool), 59. *Prof Exp:* Instr, 59-61, asst prof, 61-75, ASSOC PROF BIOL, UNIV SC, 75- *Concurrent Pos:* Consult, Campbell Soup Co; SC Elec & Gas. *Mem:* Ecol Soc Am; Am Soc Ichthyologists & Herpetologists; Am Soc Zoologists. *Res:* Animal behavior; physiology of behavior; biological effects of magnetic fields; ecology. *Mailing Add:* Dept of Biol Univ of SC Columbia SC 29208

THOMPSON, ERIK G(RINDE), b Dallas, Tex, May 3, 34; m 59; c 3. ENGINEERING MECHANICS. *Educ:* Southern Methodist Univ, BS, 57; Univ Tex, MS, 59, PhD(eng mech), 65. *Prof Exp:* From asst prof to assoc prof eng sci, Univ Idaho, 64-68; assoc prof, 68-76, PROF CIVIL ENG, COLO STATE UNIV, 76- *Mem:* Am Soc Eng Educ; Am Acad Mech; Sigma Xi. *Res:* Plasticity and creep in engineering materials; finite element method; metal forming analysis. *Mailing Add:* 1812 Yorktown Ft Collins CO 80526

THOMPSON, ERNEST AUBREY, JR, b Tyler, Tex, Nov 17, 45; m 67; c 1. BIOCHEMISTRY, MOLECULAR BIOLOGY. *Educ:* Southern Methodist Univ, BS, 68; Univ Tex, Dallas, PhD(biochem), 74. *Prof Exp:* Fel biochem, Med Ctr, Univ Calif, San Francisco, 74-77; ASST PROF BIOL, UNIV SC, 77- *Concurrent Pos:* Am Cancer Soc fel, 74-75; NIH fel, 76-77, grant, 78- *Res:* Hormonal control of cellular proliferation. *Mailing Add:* Dept of Biol Univ of SC Columbia SC 29208

THOMPSON, EVAN M, b Payson, Utah, Aug 7, 33; m 59; c 5. PHYSICAL ORGANIC CHEMISTRY. *Educ:* Brigham Young Univ, BA, 60, PhD(org chem), 65. *Prof Exp:* Charles F Kettering & Great Lakes Cols Asn teaching fel chem, Antioch Col, 64-65; from asst prof to assoc prof, 65-74, dean, Sch Natural Sci, 70-76, PROF CHEM, CALIF STATE COL, STANISLAUS, 74- *Mem:* AAAS; Am Chem Soc. *Res:* Organic reaction mechanisms; kinetics; chemical education. *Mailing Add:* Dept of Chem Calif State Col Stanislaus Turlock CA 95380

THOMPSON, FAY MORGEN, b St Paul, Minn, Dec 13, 35; m 55; c 2. OCCUPATIONAL HEALTH, ENVIRONMENTAL CHEMISTRY. *Educ:* Univ Minn, BA, 63, PhD(org chem), 70; Am Bd Indust Hyg, cert, 77. *Prof Exp:* Instr chem, Macalester Col, 67-68; instr occup health, Sch Pub Health, 70-78, ASST PROF ENVIRON HEALTH, SCH PUB HEALTH, UNIV MINN, 78-, OCCUP HEALTH CHEMIST, ENVIRON HEALTH & SAFETY, 74- *Concurrent Pos:* Mem adv comt hazardous waste, Minn Pollution Control Agency, 76-78; mem bd dirs, Minn Safety Coun, 78-79; mem, Comt Hazardous Substances in Lab, Nat Res Coun, 81- *Mem:* Am Indust Hyg Asn; Am Chem Soc; Am Conf Govt Indust Hygienists; Am Acad Indust Hyg; Sigma Xi. *Res:* Collection and analysis of selected air contaminants; high purity water systems; hazardous waste disposal; solid waste leachate quality; laboratory use of carcinogens. *Mailing Add:* Dept of Environ Health Univ of Minn Minneapolis MN 55455

THOMPSON, FRANCIS TRACY, b New York, NY, Nov 22, 30; m 55; c 3. ELECTRICAL ENGINEERING. *Educ:* Rensselaer Polytech Inst, BSEE, 52; Univ Pittsburgh, MS, 55, PhD(elec eng), 64. *Prof Exp:* Develop engr, Res Labs, Westinghouse Elec Corp, 53-57, fel engr, New Prod Lab, 57-61, supvry engr, Res Labs, 61-64, mgr info & control circuitry, elec systs & power conditioning, 64-69, dir instrumentation & systs res, 69-72, dir electronics & electromagnetics res, 72-76, DIR ELEC SCI RES, WESTINGHOUSE ELEC CORP, 76- *Mem:* Sr mem Inst Elec & Electronics Engrs; Instrument Soc Am. *Res:* Digital computer development; control systems; instrumentation; television systems; solid-state circuitry; magnetic and mechanical systems. *Mailing Add:* Beulah Rd Res & Develop Ctr Westinghouse Elec Corp Bldg 501 Pittsburgh PA 15235

THOMPSON, FRED C, b Snow Shoe, Pa, Feb 26, 28; m 52; c 4. ELECTRONIC ENGINEERING. *Educ:* Pa State Univ, BS, 50, MS, 58. *Prof Exp:* Engr, Martin Co, Md, 52-54; engr, HRB-Singer, Inc, 54-58, div mgr receiving systs, 58-60, staff engr, 60-63, lab dir countermeasures equip, 63-66, staff asst to tech vpres, 66-69; vpres, 68-80, PRES, LOCUS, INC, 80- *Mem:* Inst Elec & Electronics Engrs. *Res:* Very high frequency-ultra high frequency receiving systems; microwave devices. *Mailing Add:* Locus Inc PO Box 740 State College PA 16801

THOMPSON, FRED G, b Cleveland, Ohio, Nov 13, 34; m 57; c 1. MALACOLOGY. *Educ:* Univ Mich, BS, 58; Wayne State Univ, MA, 61; Univ Miami, PhD(zool), 64. *Prof Exp:* Res scientist, Univ Miami, 64-66; interim assoc cur, 66-71, assoc cur malacol, 71-81, CUR MALACOL & PROF ZOOL, FLA STATE MUS, UNIV FLA, 81- *Concurrent Pos:* NIH res grant systs Amnicolidae, 64-67. *Mem:* Am Malacol Union; Asn Syst Malacologists. *Res:* Systematics, ecology, land and freshwater mollusks. *Mailing Add:* Fla State Mus Univ of Fla Gainesville FL 32601

THOMPSON, FREDERIC CHRISTIAN, entomology, evolutionary biology, see previous edition

THOMPSON, FREDERICK NIMROD, JR, b Newport News, Va, Dec 9, 39; m 62; c 2. REPRODUCTIVE ENDOCRINOLOGY. *Educ:* Wake Forest Univ, BS, 61; Univ Ga, DVM, 65; Iowa State Univ, PhD(physiol), 73. *Prof Exp:* Instr physiol, Iowa State Univ, 67-73; ASST PROF PHYSIOL, UNIV GA, 73- *Mem:* Soc Study Reprod; Sigma Xi; Am Vet Med Asn. *Res:* Hormonal control of parturition and cardiovascular effects of adrenal corticosteroids. *Mailing Add:* Dept of Physiol & Pharmacol Univ of Ga Athens GA 30601

THOMPSON, GARY GENE, b Beach, NDak, Oct 18, 40; m 70. GEOLOGY, PALYNOLOGY. *Educ:* Univ NDak, BS, 62; Mich State Univ, PhD(geol), 69. *Prof Exp:* Geologist, Shell Develop Co, 68-69 & Shell Oil Co, 69-70; asst prof, 71-77, ASSOC PROF GEOL, SALEM STATE COL, 77- *Mem:* AAAS; Soc Econ Paleontologists & Mineralogists; Am Asn Stratig Palynologists. *Res:* Cretaceous, tertiary and quaternary palynomorph biostratigraphy and paleoecology. *Mailing Add:* Dept of Earth Sci Salem State Col Salem MA 01970

THOMPSON, GARY HAUGHTON, b Long Beach, Calif, Mar 25, 35; m 64; c 3. PHYSICAL CHEMISTRY, INORGANIC CHEMISTRY. *Educ:* Univ Colo, Boulder, BS, 60; Univ Utah, PhD(chem), 69. *Prof Exp:* Engr, Hercules Powder Co, 60-63; res chemist, Savannah River Lab, E I du Pont de Nemours & Co, Inc, 69-76; group leader, Rocky Flats Plant, 76-81, PROCESS OPER MGR, ROCKWELL INT CORP, 81- *Mem:* Am Nuclear Soc; Am Chem Soc; Am Soc Metals. *Res:* Chromatography, including gas, liquid and ion exchange; radioiodine sorption, gas-solid and gas-liquid systems; radioactive waste management and solvent extraction processes. *Mailing Add:* Rocky Flats Plant PO Box 464 Golden CO 80401

THOMPSON, GEOFFREY, b Stockton-on-Tees, Durham, Eng, Oct 18, 35; m 61; c 3. GEOCHEMISTRY, OCEANOGRAPHY. *Educ:* Univ Manchester, BSc, 61, PhD(geochem), 65. *Prof Exp:* Res chemist, Imp Chem Industs, UK, 58-59; geologist, Transvaal Gold Mines, SAfrica, 60; asst scientist, 65-70, assoc scientist, 70-78, SR SCIENTIST & CHMN DEPT CHEM, WOODS HOLE OCEANOG INST, 78- *Concurrent Pos:* Res assoc dept mineral sci, Smithsonian Inst, 70-; assoc ed, Geochimica et Cosmochmica Acta, 73- & J Marine Res, 74- *Mem:* AAAS; Geochem Soc; Am Geophys Union; Soc Appl Spectros. *Res:* Origin, evolution and geochemistry of oceanic crust; geochemistry of ocean sediments and marine organisms. *Mailing Add:* Dept Chem Woods Hole Oceanog Inst Woods Hole MA 02543

THOMPSON, GEORGE ALBERT, b Swissvale, Pa, June 5, 19; m 44; c 3. GEOPHYSICS, GEOLOGY. *Educ:* Pa State Col, BS, 41; Mass Inst Technol, MS, 42; Stanford Univ, PhD(geol), 49. *Prof Exp:* Actg instr, 47-48, lectr, 48-49, from asst prof to assoc prof, 49-60, chmn dept geol, 79-82, PROF GEOPHYS, STANFORD UNIV, 60-, CHMN, DEPT GEOPHYS, 67-, OTTO N MILLER PROF EARTH SCI, 80- *Concurrent Pos:* Geologist & geophysicist, US Geol Surv, 42-76; NSF fel, 56-57; Guggenheim fel, 63-64; G K Gilbert award seismic geol, 64; mem, Geodynamics Comt, Nat Res Coun, 75-78; consult adv comn reactor safeguards, Nuclear Res Coun, 72- *Mem:* Seismol Soc Am; Soc Explor Geophys; Soc Econ Geol; fel Geol Soc Am; Am Geophys Union. *Res:* Structure and geophysics of Basin Range Province; crust-mantle structure; lunar traverse gravity experiment; geophysics of ultramafic rocks; geology of quicksilver deposits. *Mailing Add:* Dept of Geophys Stanford Univ Stanford CA 94305

THOMPSON, GEORGE REX, b Oakley, Idaho, July 24, 43; m 63; c 4. TOXICOLOGY, PHARMACOLOGY. *Educ:* Ore State Univ, BS, 65, PhD(toxicol & pharmacol), 69. *Prof Exp:* Res asst toxicol & pharmacol, Ore State Univ, 66-69; researcher toxicol, Mason Res Inst, Mass, 69-72; supvr toxicol, Biomed Res Lab, ICI Am Inc, 72-73; head sect gen toxicol, Abbott Labs, 73-77; mgr prod safety systs, 77-80, DIR CORP SAFETY ASSURANCE, INT FLAVORS & FRAGRANCES INC, 80- *Mem:* Soc Toxicol; Am Soc Pharmacol & Exp Therapeut; Environ Mutagen Soc; Inst Food Technol. *Res:* Toxicity of marihuana or tetrahydrocannabinol, cyclamate/cyclohexylamine, new drugs, anticancer compounds and pesticides; delineation of normal physiological parameters via the utilization of toxic materials; safety criteria for flavors and fragrance; computerized safety evaluations; employee health and safety; environmental protection. *Mailing Add:* Int Flavors & Fragrances Inc 1515 Hwy 36 Union Beach NJ 07735

THOMPSON, GEORGE RICHARD, b Ann Arbor, Mich, Apr 2, 30; m 57; c 3. INTERNAL MEDICINE, RHEUMATOLOGY. *Educ:* Univ Mich, Ann Arbor, BS, 50, MD, 54. *Prof Exp:* Intern, Ohio State Univ Hosp, 54-55; resident, Hosp, 55-58, from instr to assoc prof, 62-76, PROF INTERNAL MED, MED SCH, UNIV MICH, ANN ARBOR, 76- DIR RHEUMATOL SECT, WAYNE COUNTY GEN HOSP, ELOISE, 63- *Concurrent Pos:* USPHS fel rheumatol, Rackham Arthritis Res Unit, Univ Mich Hosp, Ann Arbor, 60-62, assoc physician, 63- *Mem:* Am Rheumatism Asn; fel Am Col Physicians; Am Fedn Clin Res; Cent Soc Clin Res. *Res:* Arthritis; mucopolysaccharide metabolism; gout and urate excretion; rubella-associated arthritis. *Mailing Add:* Dept of Med Wayne County Gen Hosp 2345 Merriman Rd Westland MI 48185

THOMPSON, GERALD LEE, b Swea City, Iowa, Mar 16, 45; c 3. ORGANIC CHEMISTRY. *Educ:* Iowa State Univ, BS, 68; Ohio State Univ, PhD(chem), 72. *Prof Exp:* NIH fel, Harvard Univ, 72-74; sr org chemist, 74-79, res scientist, 80, HEAD CHEM RES DIV, ELI LILLY & CO, 80- *Mem:* Am Chem Soc. *Res:* Antitumor drug design; alkaloid synthesis; general medicinal chemistry. *Mailing Add:* Lilly Res Labs Eli Lilly & Co Indianapolis IN 46206

THOMPSON, GERALD LUTHER, b Rolfe, Iowa, Nov 25, 23; m 54; c 3. APPLIED MATHEMATICS. *Educ:* Iowa State Col, BS, 44; Mass Inst Technol, SM, 48; Univ Mich, PhD(math), 53. *Prof Exp:* Instr math, Princeton Univ, 51-53; asst prof, Dartmouth Col, 53-58; prof, Ohio Wesleyan, 58-59; PROF MATH & INDUST ADMIN, GRAD SCH INDUST ADMIN, CARNEGIE-MELLON UNIV, 59- *Concurrent Pos:* Consult, Princeton Univ, Int Bus Mach Corp, Sandia Corp, Beth Steel Corp, Timken Co, Westinghouse Elec Co & McKinsey & Co; Inst Mgt Sci rep, Math Div, Nat Res Coun, 71-73; mem, Sealift Readiness Comt, Nat Acad Sci, 74-75. *Mem:* Am Math Soc; Soc Indust & Appl Math; Inst Mgt Sci; Math Asn Am; Opers Res Soc Am. *Res:* Applications of mathematics to managerial and behavioral sciences; mathematical economics; control theory; graph theory and combinatorial problems; game theory. *Mailing Add:* Grad Sch of Indust Admin Carnegie-Mellon Univ Schenley Park Pittsburgh PA 15213

THOMPSON, GLENN MICHAEL, b Providence, RI, Sept 21, 46; m 72; c 2. HYDROGEOLOGY, ANALYTICAL CHEMISTRY. *Educ:* Univ RI, BS, 70; Memphis State Univ, MS, 73; Ind Univ, PhD(geol), 77. *Prof Exp:* ASST PROF HYDROL, UNIV ARIZ, 77- *Res:* Hydrogeochemistry, ground water dating and ground water tracing. *Mailing Add:* Dept Hydrol & Water Resources Univ of Ariz Tucson AZ 85721

THOMPSON, GORDON WILLIAM, b Vancouver, BC. EPIDEMIOLOGY. *Educ:* Univ Alta, DDS, 65; Univ Toronto, MScD, 67, PhD(epidemiol & biostatist), 71. *Prof Exp:* assoc dean & assoc prof dent, Univ Toronto, 69-77; DEAN FAC DENT, UNIV ALTA, 77- *Mem:* Biomet Soc; Int Asn Dent Res. *Res:* Biostatistical and computer applications in the fields of dental science and growth and development of humans with particular emphasis on the craniofacial complex and stomatognathic system. *Mailing Add:* Fac of Dent Univ of Alberta Edmonton AB T6G 2N8 Can

THOMPSON, GRANT, b Ogden, Utah, Feb 26, 27; m 49; c 5. ORGANIC CHEMISTRY. *Educ:* Univ Utah, BA, 50, PhD(chem), 53. *Prof Exp:* Res chemist, E I du Pont de Nemours & Co, 53-58; proj chemist, 58-59, sr chemist, 59-60, supvr new propellants sect, 60-62, mgr propellant develop dept, Wasatch Div, 63-75, MGR, RES & DEVELOP LABS, WASATCH DIV, THIOKOL CORP, 75- *Mem:* Am Chem Soc. *Res:* Mechanism of propellant cure; curing agents and catalysts for hydrocarbon propellants; mechanism of hydrocarbon propellant aging; high energy oxidizers and propellants. *Mailing Add:* Res & Develop Labs Wasatch Div Thiokol Corp PO Box 524 Brigham City UT 84302

THOMPSON, GUY A, JR, b Rosedale, Miss, May 31, 31; m 60; c 3. BIOCHEMISTRY. *Educ:* Miss State Univ, BS, 53; Calif Inst Technol, PhD(biochem), 59. *Prof Exp:* NSF res fel chem, Univ Manchester, 59-60; res assoc biochem, Univ Wash, 60-62, from instr to asst prof, 62-67; assoc prof, 67-74, PROF BOT, UNIV TEX, AUSTIN, 74- *Concurrent Pos:* NIH res career develop award, 63-67. *Mem:* AAAS; Am Soc Biol Chem; Am Oil Chem Soc; Am Chem Soc. *Res:* Lipid metabolism; biochemistry of membranes. *Mailing Add:* Dept of Bot Univ of Tex Austin TX 78712

THOMPSON, HANNIS WOODSON, JR, b Salisbury, NC, Sept 3, 28; m 51; c 2. ELECTRICAL ENGINEERING, SOLID STATE PHYSICS. *Educ:* NC State Univ, BS, 53, MS, 59; Purdue Univ, PhD(elec eng), 63. *Prof Exp:* Engr missile systs, Western Elec Co, 53-57; PROF ELEC ENG, PURDUE UNIV, 63- *Concurrent Pos:* Sr scientist, Navy Electronics Lab, 63, 64; consult, electronics & solid state, CTS Microelectronics, 62, 65- *Mem:* Inst Elec & Electronics Engrs; Am Phys Soc. *Res:* Solid state devices, oxide deposition, thin film and silicon technology. *Mailing Add:* 601 Robinson St West Lafayette IN 47906

THOMPSON, HAROLD G, organic chemistry, see previous edition

THOMPSON, HARTWELL GREENE, JR, b Hartford, Conn, Aug 30, 24; m 55; c 4. NEUROLOGY. *Educ:* Yale Univ, BA, 46; Cornell Univ, MD, 50. *Prof Exp:* From asst to assoc neurol, Col Physicians & Surgeons, Columbia Univ, 57-59; from asst prof to assoc prof, Univ Wis, 59-64; prof & chmn dept, Sch Med, WVa Univ, 64-69; prof & assoc dean student affairs, Sch Med, Univ Pa, 69-73; prof neurol & dean, Charleston Div, WVA Univ Med Ctr, 73-76; PROG DIR, DEPT OF NEUROL, HARTFORD HOSP, 76- *Concurrent Pos:* Consult, Vet Admin Hosp, Clarksburg, WVa, 64- *Mem:* AMA; Am Acad Neurol. *Res:* Neurology training programs and undergraduate education in neurology; multiple sclerosis; motor neuron disease. *Mailing Add:* Dept Neurol 80 Seymour St Hartford CT 06115

THOMPSON, HARVEY E, b Valders, Wis, Oct 30, 20; m 53; c 2. AGRONOMY. *Educ:* Univ Wis, BS, 47, MS, 48, PhD(agron, econ entom), 51. *Prof Exp:* ENTEN AGRONOMIST, IOWA STATE UNIV, 50- *Mem:* Am Soc Agron. *Res:* Forage and grain crop production. *Mailing Add:* 117 Agron Bldg Dept of Agron Iowa State Univ Ames IA 50010

THOMPSON, HAZEN SPENCER, b Frelighsburg, Que, Sept 10, 28; m 56; c 2. PLANT PATHOLOGY. *Educ:* McGill Univ, BSc, 50; Univ Toronto, MA, 52, PhD(plant path), 55. *Prof Exp:* Demonstr bot, Univ Toronto, 50-53; res off, Plant Res Inst, Res Br, Can Dept Agr, 51-65, fungicide liaison officer, Sci Info Sect, 65-73; PESTICIDE REV BIOLOGIST, ENVIRON PROTECTION SERV, ENVIRON CAN, 73- *Mem:* Can Phytopath Soc. *Res:* Chemical control of plant diseases; environmental effects of pesticides. *Mailing Add:* Environ Protection Serv Environ Can Ottawa ON K1A 1CS Can

THOMPSON, HENRY JOSEPH, b Mamaroneck, NY, Sept 5, 21; m 47; c 3. BIOLOGY. *Educ:* Whittier Col, AB, 47; Stanford Univ, MA, 48, PhD, 52. *Prof Exp:* Instr biol, Whittier Col, 48-49; actg instr, Stanford Univ, 51-52; instr bot, 52-54, from asst prof to assoc prof, 54-66, PROF BOT, UNIV CALIF, LOS ANGELES, 66- *Mem:* Am Soc Plant Taxon; Soc Study Evolution. *Res:* Systematics and evolution. *Mailing Add:* Dept of Biol Univ of Calif Los Angeles CA 90024

THOMPSON, HERBERT BRADFORD, b Detroit, Mich, Apr 22, 27; m 49. STRUCTURAL CHEMISTRY. *Educ:* Olivet Col, BS, 48; Oberlin Col, AM, 50; Mich State Col, PhD(chem), 53. *Prof Exp:* Res instr chem, Mich State Univ, 53-55; from asst prof to assoc prot, Gustavus Adolphus Col, 55-63; res assoc, Inst Atomic Res, Iowa State Univ, 63-65; res assoc, Univ Mich, 65-67; chmn dept chem, 68-69, 74-75, PROF CHEM, UNIV TOLEDO, 67- *Mem:* Am Chem Soc; Am Phys Soc. *Res:* Molecular structure and geometry; conformational analysis; data acquisition and computer applications in chemistry; electron diffraction; dipole moments. *Mailing Add:* Dept of Chem Univ of Toledo Toledo OH 43606

THOMPSON, HERBERT STANLEY, b China, June 12, 32; nat US; m 55; c 5. OPHTHALMOLOGY, NEUROLOGY. *Educ:* Univ Minn, BA, 53, MD, 61; Univ Iowa, MS, 66. *Prof Exp:* From instr to assoc prof, 67-76, PROF OPHTHAL, UNIV IOWA, 76- *Concurrent Pos:* Nat Inst Neurol Dis & Blindness spec fel clin neuro-ophthal, Univ Calif, San Francisco, 66-67; Nat Inst Neurol Dis & Blindness res career develop award, 68. *Mem:* Asn Res Vision & Ophthal; Ophthal Soc UK; Fr Soc Ophthal; Am Acad Ophthal & Otolaryngol; Am Opthal Soc. *Res:* Neuro-ophthalmology, especially of the autonomic nervous system. *Mailing Add:* Dept of Ophthal Univ of Iowa Hosps Iowa City IA 52240

THOMPSON, HOWARD DOYLE, b Cedar City, Utah, Apr 17, 34; m 56; c 5. GAS DYNAMICS, LASER VELOCIMETRY. *Educ:* Univ Utah, BS, 57; Purdue Univ, MS, 62, PhD(mech eng), 65. *Prof Exp:* Asst eng sci, 61-62, asst mech eng, 62-65, from asst prof to assoc prof, 65-74, PROF MECH ENG, PURDUE UNIV, WEST LAFAYETTE, 74- *Concurrent Pos:* Consult, Dynetics, Inc, 66-72, Detroit Diesel Allison, 74-76, Univ Dayton, 78-80, McDonnell-Douglas, 80-, Air Force Wright Aeronaut Lab, 80- & Arnold Eng Develop Ctr, 81-; assoc res scientist, Pratt & Whitney Aircraft, 69-70; sr mech engr, Arnold Eng Develop Ctr, 80-81. *Mem:* Am Inst Aeronaut & Astronaut; Am Soc Mech Engrs. *Res:* Propulsion gas dynamics; nozzle design; three-dimensional supersonic flows; optimization of aerodynamic shapes; transonic and annular flows; laser doppler velocimetry; experimental and numerical fluid mechanics; fluid mechanics in turbomachinery. *Mailing Add:* Sch of Mech Eng Purdue Univ West Lafayette IN 47907

THOMPSON, HOWARD K, JR, b Boston, Mass, May 19, 28; m 64; c 3. INTERNAL MEDICINE. *Educ:* Yale Univ, BA, 49; Columbia Univ, MD, 53. *Prof Exp:* Intern internal med, 1st Med Div, Bellevue Hosp, NY, 53-54, jr asst res, 55; clin fel, Mary I Bassett Hosp, Cooperstown, 54; cardiovasc res fel, Duke Hosp, Durham, NC, 58, sr asst res internal med, 58-59, cardiovasc res fel, 59-60, chief res, 60-61; biophys fel, Mass Inst Technol, 61-62; assoc med, Duke Univ, 62-65, asst prof biophys, 65-69, asst prof biomath, 66-69, assoc physiol, 63-69; prof med, Baylor Col Med, 71-78; PROF MED, ALBANY MED COL, 78- *Concurrent Pos:* Assoc, Am Bd Internal Med, 63- *Mem:* Fel Am Col Cardiol; NY Acad Sci. *Res:* Indicator dilution method of blood flow estimation; estimation of regional cerebral blood flow by radio-xenon inhalation; biostatistics; computers in medicine. *Mailing Add:* Dept of Med Albany Med Col Albany NY 12208

THOMPSON, HUGH ALLISON, b Chattanooga, Tenn, Mar 24, 35; m 57; c 1. MECHANICAL ENGINEERING. *Educ:* Auburn Univ, BS, 56; Tulane Univ, MSc, 62, PhD(mech eng), 64. *Prof Exp:* Process engr, Mobil Oil Corp, 56-60; from instr to assoc prof mech eng, 63-71, PROF MECH ENG, TULANE UNIV, 71-, DEAN, 76- *Mem:* Am Soc Mech Engrs. *Res:* Dynamic response of bus conductor structures to short circuit loads, of pole-mounted electric transmission lines to hurricane winds and of transformer coils to through faults. *Mailing Add:* Dept of Mech Eng Tulane Univ New Orleans LA 70118

THOMPSON, HUGH ERWIN, b Newport, RI, Aug 4, 17; m 46; c 4. ENTOMOLOGY. *Educ:* Univ RI, BS, 47; Cornell Univ, PhD(entom), 54. *Prof Exp:* Asst state entomologist, State Dept Agr & Conserv, RI, 47-48; entomologist, State Dept Agr, Pa, 53-56; asst prof, 56-63, assoc prof, 63-80, PROF ENTOM, KANS STATE UNIV, 80- *Mem:* Int Soc Arboricult; Arboricult Res & Educ Acad (pres, 78-79); Sigma Xi; Entom Soc Am; Soc Am Foresters. *Res:* Biology and control of insects attacking shade trees and ornamental plants; insect transmission of tree diseases. *Mailing Add:* Dept of Entom Kans State Univ Manhattan KS 66506

THOMPSON, HUGH WALTER, b New York, NY, Dec 7, 36; m 64. ORGANIC CHEMISTRY. *Educ:* Cornell Univ, AB, 58; Mass Inst Technol, PhD(org chem), 63. *Prof Exp:* NIH res fel, Columbia Univ, 62-64; from asst prof to assoc prof chem, 64-72, PROF CHEM, RUTGERS UNIV, NEWARK, 72- *Mem:* Am Chem Soc. *Res:* Mechanisms and stereochemical courses of organic reactions; compounds of unusual symmetry and stereochemistry; development of new synthetic methods. *Mailing Add:* Dept of Chem Rutgers Univ Newark NJ 07102

THOMPSON, IDA, b USA, Jan 21, 38. PALEOBIOLOGY, MARINE BIOLOGY. *Educ:* Univ Chicago, BA, 65, MS, 68, PhD(geol), 72. *Prof Exp:* Asst prof geol, Northern Ill Univ, 72-73; asst prof geol, Princeton Univ, 73-80; assoc res prof, Ctr Coastal & Environ Sci, Rutgers Univ, 81-82; RES ASSOC, DEPT GEOL, UNIV EDINBURGH, 82- *Mem:* Int Soc Chronobiol; Soc Vert Paleont; Anglo-Am Snail Watching Soc. *Res:* Biological rhythms of shell growth; annelid ecology and taxonomy; marine ecosystems and biogeography. *Mailing Add:* Dept Geol Univ Edinburgh Edinburgh Scotland

THOMPSON, J NEILS, b Canyon, Tex, Oct 14, 12; m 40; c 1. CIVIL ENGINEERING. *Educ:* Univ Tex, BS, 35, MS, 44. *Prof Exp:* Testing engr, Tex Hwy Dept, 35-41; from instr to assoc prof, 41-49, dir, Balcones Res Ctr, 46-77, dir, Struct Mech Res Labs, 55-78, chmn, Athletics Coun, 64-79, PROF CIVIL ENG, UNIV TEX, AUSTIN, 49- *Concurrent Pos:* Chmn, Bldg Res Adv Bd, Nat Acad Sci, 78-80; chmn tech panel to adv comt, HUD, Nat Acad Sci-Nat Acad Eng, 69-77, mem, 70-77; comnr, Tex Urban Develop Comn, State Exec Dept, 70-73; trustee, St Edwards Univ, 81- *Honors & Awards:* Wason Medal, Am Concrete Inst, 53. *Mem:* Nat Soc Prof Engrs (pres, 65-66); Am Soc Testing & Mat; Am Soc Eng Educ; Am Concrete Inst; Am Soc Civil Engrs. *Res:* Construction materials; experimental stress analysis; structural mechanics; building technology. *Mailing Add:* Dept of Civil Eng Univ of Tex Austin TX 78712

THOMPSON, JAMES ARTHUR, b Sturgeon Bay, Wis, Aug 15, 31; m 55; c 3. ENVIRONMENTAL MANAGEMENT. *Educ:* St Olaf Col, BA, 55; Iowa State Univ, MS, 58. *Prof Exp:* Anal chemist, Ames Lab, AEC, 55-59; res chemist anal div, Alcoa Res Lab, 59-61, sr chemist, Warrick Opers, Ind, 61-70, chief chemist, Wenatchee Works, 70-75, NORTHWEST ENVIRON MGR, ALUMINUM CO AM, 75- *Mem:* AAAS; Am Chem Soc; Air Pollution Control Asn; Sigma Xi; Am Indust Hyg Asn. *Res:* Instrumental analysis; industrial hygiene; air and water pollution. *Mailing Add:* Aluminum Co Am PO Box 221 Wenatchee WA 98801

THOMPSON, JAMES BURLEIGH, JR, b Calais, Maine, Nov 20, 21; m 57. PETROLOGY, GEOCHEMISTRY. *Educ:* Dartmouth Col, AB, 42; Mass Inst Technol, PhD, 50. *Hon Degrees:* DSc, Dartmouth Col, 75. *Prof Exp:* Instr geol, Dartmouth Col, 42; asst, Mass Inst Technol, 46-47, instr, 47-49; instr petrol, 49-50, asst prof petrog, 50-55, assoc prof mineral, 55-60, prof mineral, 60-77, STURGIS HOOPER PROF GEOL, HARVARD UNIV, 77- *Concurrent Pos:* Ford Found fel, 52-53; Guggenheim fel, 63. *Honors & Awards:* A L Day Medal, Geol Soc Am, 64; Roebling Medal, Mineral Soc Am, 78. *Mem:* Nat Acad Sci; AAAS; fel Geol Soc Am; fel Mineral Soc Am; fel Am Acad Arts & Sci. *Res:* Metamorphic petrology; geology of New England. *Mailing Add:* Dept Geol Sci Harvard Univ Cambridge MA 02138

THOMPSON, JAMES CHARLES, b San Antonio, Tex, Aug 16, 28; m 67; c 5. PHYSIOLOGY, SURGERY. *Educ:* Agr & Mech Col Tex, BS, 48; Univ Tex, MD, 51, MA, 52; Am Bd Surg, dipl. *Prof Exp:* Intern, Univ Tex Med Br Galveston, 51-52; asst resident surg, Hosp, Univ Pa, 52-54 & 56-58, chief resident, 58-59; from asst surgeon to assoc surgeon, Pa Hosp, 59-63; head physician, Harbor Gen Hosp, 63-67, chief surg, 67-70; PROF SURG & CHMN DEPT, UNIV TEX MED BR GALVESTON, 70-, CHIEF SURG, HOSP, 70- *Concurrent Pos:* Fel, Harrison Dept Surg Res, Sch Med, Univ Pa, 52-54 & 56-57, Albert & Mary Lasker fel, 57-59; John A Hartford Found grants, 60-; NIH grants, 60-; asst instr surg, Sch Med, Univ Pa, 53-54 & 56-58, from instr to assoc instr, 58-61, asst prof, 61-63; from assoc prof to prof, Sch Med, Univ Calif, Los Angeles, 63-70. *Mem:* AAAS; Am Surg Asn; Am Asn Surg of Trauma; Am Col Surgeons; Am Fedn Clin Res. *Res:* Gastric physiology; general surgery; organ transplantation; humoral control of gastric secretion; histamine metabolism; secretion in isolated tissue; radioimmunoassay and metabolism of gastrointestinal hormones, gastrin, cholecystokinin and secretin; molecular heterogeneity of gastrointestinal hormones. *Mailing Add:* Dept of Surg Univ of Tex Med Br Galveston TX 77550

THOMPSON, JAMES CHARLTON, b Leeds, UK, Jan 4, 41; m 65; c 2. INORGANIC CHEMISTRY. *Educ:* Cambridge Univ, BA, 62, PhD(chem), 65. *Prof Exp:* Fel, Rice Univ, 65-67; asst prof chem, 67-72, assoc chmn dept, 74-77, actg chmn, 79-80, ASSOC PROF CHEM, UNIV TORONTO, 72-,

ASSOC CHMN DEPT, 82- *Mem:* Royal Soc Chem; Chem Inst Can; Am Chem Soc. *Res:* Studies on the synthesis, structures and properties of silicon compounds, particularly those with fluorine or hydrogen bound to silicon. *Mailing Add:* 193 Roe Ave Toronto ON M5M 2J1 Can

THOMPSON, JAMES CHILTON, b Ft Worth, Tex, June 14, 30; m 55; c 3. PHYSICS. *Educ:* Tex Christian Univ, BA, 52; Rice Inst, MA, 54, PhD(physics), 56. *Prof Exp:* From asst prof to assoc prof, 56-67, PROF PHYSICS, UNIV TEX, AUSTIN, 67- *Mem:* Am Phys Soc. *Res:* Transport coefficients in solid and liquid metals; metal-ammonia solutions; metal-nonmetal transition; amorphous semiconductors. *Mailing Add:* Dept of Physics Univ of Tex Austin TX 78712

THOMPSON, JAMES EDWIN, b Maryville, Mo, Feb 2, 36; m 65; c 2. ORGANIC CHEMISTRY. *Educ:* Cent Methodist Col, AB, 56; Univ Mo, PhD(chem cyclopropanes), 61. *Prof Exp:* CHEMIST, PROCTER & GAMBLE CO, 61- *Mem:* Am Chem Soc. *Res:* Electronic effects in cyclopropanes; synthetic lipid and phospholipid, organo-phosphorus and organo-sulfur chemistry; radiochemical synthesis. *Mailing Add:* Procter & Gamble Co Miami Valley Labs Box 39175 Cincinnati OH 45247

THOMPSON, JAMES JARRARD, b Des Moines, Iowa; m 69; c 3. LIMNOLOGY. *Educ:* Univ Iowa, BA, 65, MS, 68, PhD(microbiol), 70. *Prof Exp:* Instr microbiol & immunol, Dept Microbiol, Univ Iowa, 70-71; instr, Temple Univ, 71-72, asst prof, 72-74; asst prof, 74-79, ASSOC PROF, DEPT MICROBIOL, 79-, ACTG HEAD, 81- *Concurrent Pos:* Prin investr, Nat Sci Found, 75-77, Am Heart Asn, 77-78, Arthritis Found, 78-79, NIH, 80- *Mem:* Am Asn Immmunologists; Am Soc Microbiol; AAAS; Sigma Xi; Am Asn Univ Professors. *Res:* Immmunoassay of apolipoproteins; structure and function of apolipoproteins; humoral immune responses in periodontal diseases; mechanisms of complement activation. *Mailing Add:* Dept Microbiol & Immunol, La State Univ Med Ctr 1901 Perdido St New Orleans LA 70112

THOMPSON, JAMES JOSEPH, b Waterbury, Conn, Oct 22, 40; m 63; c 3. HEALTH PHYSICS, INDUSTRIAL HYGIENE. *Educ:* Univ NMex, BA, 62; Purdue Univ, MS, 70, PhD(bionucleonics), 72; Am Bd Health Physics, cert, 76; Am Bd Indust Hyg, cert, 78; Bd Cert Safety Prof, cert, 78. *Prof Exp:* HEALTH PHYSICIST & INDUST HYGIENIST, LOVELACE INHALATION TOXICOL RES INST, 72- *Mem:* Health Physics Soc; Am Indust Hyg Asn; Am Nuclear Soc; Nat Fire Protection Asn; Internat Radiation Protection Soc. *Res:* Personnel dosimetry, thermoluminescence, applied radiation protection and industrial hygiene. *Mailing Add:* Lovelace Inhalation Toxicol Res Inst PO Box 5890 Albuquerque NM 87185

THOMPSON, JAMES LOWRY, b Syracuse, NY, Oct 5, 40; m 63; c 2. APPLIED MATHEMATICS, ENGINEERING SCIENCE. *Educ:* Brown Univ, AB, 62; Johns Hopkins Univ, PhD(mech), 68. *Prof Exp:* Asst prof math & eng sci, State Univ NY Buffalo, 68-74; MECH ENGR, US ARMY TANK AUTOMOTIVE COMMAND, 74- *Concurrent Pos:* NSF res grant, State Univ NY Buffalo, 71-73. *Mem:* AAAS; Am Math Soc; Soc Natural Philos; Soc Indust & Appl Math; Int Soc Terrain-Vehicle Systs. *Res:* Analysis and optimization of complex systems; continuum mechanics. *Mailing Add:* 1448 Anita Ave Grosse Pointe Woods MI 48236

THOMPSON, JAMES MARION, b Findlay, Ohio, July 26, 26; m 53; c 3. PLANT BREEDING, PLANT GENETICS. *Educ:* Ohio State Univ, BSc, 50, MS, 54, PhD(agron), 63. *Prof Exp:* Fel corn breeding, Agron Dept, Ohio State Univ, 54-56; corn breeder, Steckley Hybrid Corn Co, 57-62; apple breeder, Blairsville, Ga, 63-70, APPLE & PLUM BREEDER, AGR RES SERV, USDA, BYRON, GA, 70- *Mem:* Am Genetic Asn; Am Pomol Soc; Am Soc Hort Sci; Apple Breeders Coop. *Res:* Apple breeding project designed to develop new varieties adapted in the Southern Coastal Plain and in the Southern Appalachian Mountains; plum breeding project; genetic research in pears, apples and plums. *Mailing Add:* SE Fruit & Tree Nut Res Lab Agr Res Serv USDA PO Box 87 Byron GA 31008

THOMPSON, JAMES NEAL, JR, b Lubbock, Tex, May 24, 46. GENETICS. *Educ:* Univ Okla, BS, 68, BA, 68; Univ Cambridge, PhD(genetics), 73. *Prof Exp:* Fel genetics, Univ Cambridge, 73-75; asst prof, 75-79, ASSOC PROF ZOOL, UNIV OKLA, 79- *Concurrent Pos:* Marshall scholar, Univ Cambridge, 70-73. *Mem:* Genetics Soc Am; Genetical Soc Gt Brit; Sigma Xi; Soc Study Evolution. *Res:* Development and genetics of quantitative characters; genetic determination of patterns; hybrid dysgenesis and mutator genes in natural populations. *Mailing Add:* Dept Zool Univ Okla Norman OK 73069

THOMPSON, JAMES ROBERT, b Memphis, Tenn, June 18, 38; m 67. MATHEMATICS, STATISTICS. *Educ:* Vanderbilt Univ, BE, 60; Princeton Univ, MA, 63, PhD(math), 65. *Prof Exp:* Asst prof, Vanderbilt Univ, 64-67; asst prof math, Ind Univ, Bloomington, 67-70; assoc prof, 70-77, PROF MATH SCI, RICE UNIV, 77- *Concurrent Pos:* Adj clin prof, M D Anderson Hosp & Tumor Inst, 77- *Mem:* Am Math Soc; Inst Math Statist; Am Statist Asn. *Res:* Biomathematics; modelling. *Mailing Add:* Dept Math Sci Rice Univ Houston TX 77001

THOMPSON, JAMES SCOTT, b Saskatoon, Sask, July 31, 19; m 44; c 2. ANATOMY, GENETICS. *Educ:* Univ Sask, BA, 40, MA, 41; Univ Toronto, MD, 45. *Prof Exp:* Res assoc med, Univ Toronto, 46-48; lectr & asst prof anat, Univ Western Ont, 48-50; assoc prof & prof, Univ Alta, 50-62; chmn dept, 66-76, PROF ANAT, UNIV TORONTO, 63- *Concurrent Pos:* Exec secy & asst dean, Univ Alta, 53-62; vis investr, Jackson Lab, 62-63. *Mem:* Am Asn Anatomists; Genetics Soc Am; Can Asn Anatomists (vpres, 64-65 & 73-75, pres, 75-77); Genetics Soc Can. *Res:* Genetic factors in cardiovascular disease; matters related to medical education and teaching of genetics. *Mailing Add:* Dept of Anat Univ of Toronto Toronto ON M5S 1A8 Can

THOMPSON, JAMES TIPTON, animal science, animal nutrition, see previous edition

THOMPSON, JEFFERY SCOTT, b Hartford, Conn, Mar 20, 52; m 74. INORGANIC CHEMISTRY. *Educ:* Trinity Col, BS, 74; Northwestern Univ, PhD(chem), 79. *Prof Exp:* Fel biochem, Med Sch, Harvard Univ, 78-80; CHEMIST, E I DU PONT DE NUMOURS CO INC, 80- *Mem:* Am Chem Soc. *Res:* Investigation of the role of metal ions in biological processes, through the study of both native and model systems. *Mailing Add:* E I du Pont de Nemours Co Inc Exp Sta/E328-327 Wilmington DE 19898

THOMPSON, JEFFREY MICHAEL, b Eau Claire, Wis, May 10, 50. NEUROBIOLOGY, BIOCHEMISTRY. *Educ:* Mich State Univ, BS, 72; Fla State Univ, PhD(molecular biophys), 76. *Prof Exp:* Staff fel res, Nat Heart, Lung & Blood Inst, 77-78; staff fel res, 79-81, SR STAFF FEL RES, NAT INST AGING, 81- *Mem:* AAAS; Fedn Am Scientists. *Res:* Mechanisms and specificity of synapse formation and their development patterns; synapse formation of isolated cells in culture detected by electrophysiological recording; neurochemical correlates of synapse behavior. *Mailing Add:* Nat Inst Aging Baltimore City Hosp Baltimore MD 21224

THOMPSON, JERRY NELSON, b Cincinnati, Ohio, Apr 2, 39; m 65; c 2. GENETICS, BIOCHEMISTRY. *Educ:* Univ Cincinnati, BS, 64; Ind Univ, PhD(med genetics), 70. *Prof Exp:* Res asst teratology, Cincinnati Children's Hosp Res Found, 61-64; asst prof, 72-77, ASSOC PROF BIOCHEM & PEDIAT, MED CTR, UNIV ALA, BIRMINGHAM, 77- *Concurrent Pos:* USPHS fel, Univ Chicago, 70-72; Nat Found March Dimes Basil O'Connor starter res grant, Med Ctr, Univ Ala, Birmingham, 74-76. *Mem:* Am Soc Human Genetics; Tissue Cult Asn. *Res:* Biochemical and genetic studies of cell cultures of various genetic lysosomal storage diseases. *Mailing Add:* Lab of Med Genetics Univ of Ala Med Ctr Birmingham AL 35294

THOMPSON, JESSE CLAY, JR, b Hot Springs, Va, Sept 17, 26; m 50; c 3. SYSTEMATICS. *Educ:* Hampden-Sydney Col, BS, 49; Univ Va, PhD, 56. *Prof Exp:* From asst prof to assoc prof biol, Hollins Col, 55-63; prof & chmn dept, Hampden-Sydney Col, 63-67; prof, Queens Col, NC, 67-69; PROF & CHMN DEPT, ROANOKE COL, 69- *Concurrent Pos:* Mem, Va Inst Marine Sci, 61, Int Indian Ocean Exped, 63, Mt Lake Biol Sta, 65 & Eniwetok Marine Biol Lab, 66; res partic, Palmer Sta, Antarctica, 68-69. *Mem:* AAAS; Am Inst Biol Sci; Soc Protozool. *Res:* Morphology; systematics and geographical distribution of hymenostome ciliated protozoa. *Mailing Add:* Dept Biol Roanoke Col Salem VA 24153

THOMPSON, JESSE ELDON, b Laredo, Tex, Apr 7, 19; m 44; c 4. SURGERY. *Educ:* Univ Tex, BA, 39; Harvard Univ, MD, 43. *Prof Exp:* Instr surg, Boston Univ, 51-54; from asst prof to assoc prof, 54-68, CLIN PROF SURG, UNIV TEX HEALTH SCI CTR DALLAS, 68-; CHIEF CONSULT PERIPHERAL VASCULAR SURG, BAYLOR UNIV MED CTR, DALLAS, 68-, CHIEF SURG, 82- *Concurrent Pos:* Rhodes scholar physiol & Fulbright fel, Oxford Univ, 49-50. *Mem:* Int Soc Surg; Soc Vascular Surg; Am Surg Asn; Am Col Surgeons; AMA. *Res:* Vascular surgery; clinical investigation of hypertension, gastric physiology, peripheral vascular diseases and strokes; surgical management of vascular diseases. *Mailing Add:* 3600 Gaston Ave Dallas TX 75246

THOMPSON, JESSE JACKSON, speech pathology, psycholinguistics, see previous edition

THOMPSON, JOE DAVID, b Columbus, Ind, Oct 28, 47; m 67; c 2. SOLID STATE PHYSICS, LOW TEMPERATURE PHYSICS. *Educ:* Purdue Univ, BS, 69; Univ Cincinnati, MS, 71, PhD(physics), 75. *Prof Exp:* Fel superconductivity, 75-77, STAFF MEM LOW TEMPERATURE SOLID STATE PHYSICS, LOS ALAMOS NAT LAB, 77- *Mem:* Am Phys Soc; AAAS; Sigma Xi. *Res:* Type II superconductivity; superconducting and magnetic materials; high pressure physics. *Mailing Add:* MS 764 Los Alamos Nat Lab Los Alamos NM 87545

THOMPSON, JOE FLOYD, b Grenada, Miss, Apr 13, 39. COMPUTATIONAL FLUID DYNAMICS, AERODYNAMICS. *Educ:* Miss State Univ, BS, 61, MS, 63; Ga Inst Technol, PhD(aerospace eng), 71. *Prof Exp:* Aerospace engr, NASA Marshall Space Flight Ctr, 63-64; from asst prof to assoc prof, 64-75, PROF AEROSPACE ENG, MISS STATE UNIV, 75- *Concurrent Pos:* Res award, Am Soc Eng Educ, 75; consult, Argonne Nat Lab, 77- *Mem:* Am Inst Aeronaut & Astronaut. *Res:* computational fluid dynamics; numerical generation of coordinate systems. *Mailing Add:* Drawer A Dept of Aerospace Eng Miss State Univ Mississippi State MS 39762

THOMPSON, JOHN ALEC, b Newton, Mass, Nov 27, 42. MEDICINAL CHEMISTRY, PHARMACOLOGY. *Educ:* Clark Univ, BA, 64; Univ Calif, Los Angeles, PhD(org chem), 69. *Prof Exp:* Fel chem, Univ Calif, Irvine, 69-70 & Syntex Corp, Mexico City, 70-71; res chemist, pharmacol, Vet Admin Hosp, Minneapolis, 71-73; res assoc pharmacol, Univ Colo Med Ctr, 73-76; asst prof, 77-80, ASSOC PROF MED CHEM, SCH PHARM, UNIV COLO, 80- *Concurrent Pos:* Res grants, NIH, 79-82; mem, Coun for Tobacco Res, 79-82. *Mem:* Am Chem Soc; Am Soc Mass Spectrometry; Am Soc Pharmacol & Exp Therapeut. *Res:* Chemical and biochemical aspects of the metabolism of drugs and other xenobiotics; application of gaschromatographic/mass spectrometric techniques to studies in pharmacology and toxicology. *Mailing Add:* Univ of Colo Sch of Pharm Campus Box 297 Boulder CO 80309

THOMPSON, JOHN C, JR, b Thomas, WVa, Oct 4, 30; m 54; c 3. ENVIRONMENTAL HEALTH. *Educ:* Va Polytech Inst, BS, 51, MS, 58; Cornell Univ, PhD(agr econ), 62. *Prof Exp:* Res assoc phys biol, 61-65, asst prof environ radiation biol, 65-68, ASSOC PROF ENVIRON RADIATION BIOL, CORNELL UNIV, 68- *Mem:* Health Physics Soc. *Res:* Radioactive contamination of the food chain, sampling techniques, controlled human studies, radionuclide deposition and cycling, world wide evaluation of fallout; biological costs of energy production; comparative environmental analyses and energy options; animal health and veterinary economics. *Mailing Add:* Dept Prev Med Cornell Univ Ithaca NY 14853

THOMPSON, JOHN CARL, b Toronto, Ont, Nov 28, 41; m 68; c 3. CIVIL ENGINEERING, APPLIED MECHANICS. *Educ:* Univ Toronto, BSc, 63, Univ Ill, MS, 65, PhD(civil eng), 69. *Prof Exp:* Res asst prof, 69-70, asst prof, 70-76, ASSOC PROF CIVIL ENG, UNIV WATERLOO, 76- *Mem:* Soc Exp Stress Anal; Can Soc Civil Eng; Eng Inst Can. *Res:* Optimization of experimental and numerical stress analysis techniques; analysis of geotechnical instability problems. *Mailing Add:* Dept of Civil Eng Univ of Waterloo Waterloo ON N2L 3G1 Can

THOMPSON, JOHN DARRELL, b Mitchell, SDak, Sept 13, 33; m 57; c 4. PHYSICS, MOLECULAR BIOPHYSICS. *Educ:* Augustana Col, SDak, BA, 55; Iowa State Univ, MS, 62; Univ Wis, PhD(biophys), 67. *Prof Exp:* From instr to assoc prof, 57-78, PROF PHYSICS, AUGUSTANA COL, S DAK, 78- *Mem:* AAAS; Am Asn Physics Teachers. *Res:* Structure and function of Escherichia coli ribosomes; hormonal control of protein synthesis in the chick enbryo; microcomputers in the laboratory. *Mailing Add:* Dept of Physics Augustana Col Sioux Falls SD 57102

THOMPSON, JOHN EVELEIGH, b Toronto, Ont, May 30, 41; m 65. BIOCHEMISTRY, CELL BIOLOGY. *Educ:* Univ Toronto, BSA, 63; Univ Alta, PhD(plant biochem), 66. *Prof Exp:* Fel med biochem, Univ Birmingham, 66-67; asst prof biol, 68-72, assoc prof, 72-77, PROF BIOL, UNIV WATERLOO, 77- *Mem:* Can Soc Plant Physiol; Am Soc Plant Physiol. *Res:* Effects of cell differentiation on membrane structure and function in plant and animal systems; mode of membrane biosynthesis; role of membranes in cell-cell interaction. *Mailing Add:* Dept of Biol Univ of Waterloo Waterloo ON N2L 3G1 Can

THOMPSON, JOHN FANNING, b Ithaca, NY, May 24, 19; m 43; c 5. PLANT BIOCHEMISTRY. *Educ:* Oberlin Col, AB, 40; Cornell Univ, PhD(biochem), 44. *Prof Exp:* Instr biochem, Cornell Univ, 44-45; res assoc bot, Univ Chicago, 46-47; NIH fel, Univ Rochester, 47-49, res assoc, 49-50; from instr to asst prof bot, 50-55, ASSOC PROF BOT, CORNELL UNIV, 55-; PLANT PHYSIOLOGIST, PLANT, SOIL & NUTRIT LAB, USDA, 52- *Concurrent Pos:* NSF sr fel, 59-60. *Mem:* Am Soc Plant Physiol; Am Chem Soc; Am Soc Biol Chem. *Res:* Nitrogen and sulfur metabolism and mineral nutrition of plants; chromatographic techniques; control mechanisms; seed storage proteins. *Mailing Add:* US Plant Soil & Nutrit Lab USDA Tower Rd Ithaca NY 14853

THOMPSON, JOHN FREDERICK, b Los Angeles, Calif, Mar 19, 47; m 80. HEALTH SERVICES, FORENSIC PHARMACOLOGY. *Educ:* Calif State Univ, Los Angles, BSc, 69; Univ Southern Calif, PharmD, 73. *Prof Exp:* Resident clin pharmacol, Wadsworth Vet Admin Med Ctr, Los Angeles, 73-74; clin pharmacist, Los Angeles County-Univ Southern Calif Med Ctr, 74-75; ASST PROF CLIN PHARMACOL, UNIV SOUTHERN CALIF, 75-; ASST CLIN PROF, MED SCH, LOMA LINDA UNIV, 80- *Concurrent Pos:* Pres, Pharamanal Assoc, Inc, 78-; prin investr, Univ Southern Calif, 80-83; consult, Peer Standards Rev Orgn, Pasadena, 80- *Mem:* Am Col Clin Pharmacol. *Res:* Detection and analysis of adverse drug reactions and interactions; prescribing habits of physicians: analysis, and the appropriateness of drug therapy prescribing. *Mailing Add:* Sch Med Univ Southern Calif 1985 Zonal Ave Los Angles CA 90033

THOMPSON, JOHN HAROLD, JR, b Amsden, Ohio, Jan 2, 21; m 43; c 3. PARASITOLOGY. *Educ:* Heidelberg Col, AB, 43; Ohio State Univ, MS, 48; Univ Minn, PhD, 52. *Prof Exp:* From instr path to asst prof clin path, 52-70, assoc prof clin path, 70-77, ASSOC PROF LAB MED, MAYO MED SCH, UNIV MINN, 77- *Concurrent Pos:* Consult, Mayo Clin, 52- *Mem:* AAAS; Am Soc Parasitol; Wildlife Dis Asn; Am Fedn Clin Res. *Res:* Blood coagulation. *Mailing Add:* Dept of Clin Path Mayo Med Sch Univ of Minn Rochester MN 55901

THOMPSON, JOHN LESLIE, b New Castle, Pa, July 11, 17; m 42; c 2. ENVIRONMENTAL SCIENCES. *Educ:* Slippery Rock State Teachers Col, BS, 40; Univ Wis, MS, 48, PhD(geog), 56. *Prof Exp:* Teacher gen sci, Sharpsville High Sch, Pa, 40-41; from asst prof to assoc prof geog, 49-61, PROF GEOG, MIAMI UNIV, 61- *Mem:* Asn Am Geog; Am Geog Soc; Nat Coun Geog Educ; Conserv Educ Asn. *Res:* Social aspects of environmental problems. *Mailing Add:* Dept Geog Miami Univ Oxford OH 45056

THOMPSON, JOHN N, b Pittsburgh, Pa, Nov 15, 51; m 73. EVOLUTIONARY ECOLOGY. *Educ:* Wash & Jefferson Col, BA, 73; Univ Ill, Urbana, PhD(ecol), 77. *Prof Exp:* Vis asst prof entom, Univ Ill, 77-78; ASST PROF BOT & ZOOL, WASH STATE UNIV, 78- *Mem:* AAAS; Brit Ecol Soc; Ecol Soc Am; Soc Study Evolution; Am Soc Naturalists. *Res:* Coevolution of animals and plants. *Mailing Add:* Depts of Zool & Bot Wash State Univ Pullman WA 99164

THOMPSON, JOHN R, b Beltrami, Minn, Oct 6, 18; m 47; c 4. AGRONOMY. *Educ:* Univ Minn, BS, 48, MS, 52; Iowa State Univ, PhD(crop prod), 64. *Prof Exp:* From instr to assoc prof agron, Univ Minn, 52-67; SUPT, HAWAII AGR EXP STA, UNIV HAWAII, 67-, AGRONOMIST, 74- *Mem:* Am Soc Agron; Corp Sci Soc Am. *Res:* Seed and crop production; plant breeding. *Mailing Add:* 1180 Kumukoa Hilo HI 96720

THOMPSON, JOHN ROBERT, b Cleveland, Ohio, May 21, 47; m 72; c 2. ENGINEERING PHYSICS. *Educ:* Ohio State Univ, BS, 69; Univ Rochester, MS, 81. *Prof Exp:* RES PHYSICIST ELECTROPHOTOG, RES LABS, EASTMAN KODAK CO, 70- *Mem:* Inst Elec & Electronics Engrs. *Res:* Development of mathematical systems models and hardware in the field of electrophotography. *Mailing Add:* 1438 N Chigwell Lane Webster NY 14580

THOMPSON, JOHN S, b Lincoln, Nebr, Oct 29, 28; m 54, 72; c 5. INTERNAL MEDICINE, IMMUNOLOGY. *Educ:* Univ Calif, Berkeley, BA, 49; Univ Chicago, MD, 53. *Prof Exp:* Intern, Univ Chicago Hosps, 53-54; jr asst resident, Presby Hosp, New York, 54-55; sr asst resident med, Univ Chicago Hosps, 57-58, resident, 58-59; from instr to assoc prof, Sch Med, Univ Chicago, 59-69; vchmn vet affairs, Univ Iowa, 69-71, chmn dept, 71-77, prof med, 69-80; PROF & CHMN MED, UNIV KY, 80- *Concurrent Pos:* Nat Cancer Inst res fel, 58-60; Lederle med fac award, 66-68; chief med & chief sect allergy & clin immunol, Vet Admin Hosp, Iowa City. *Mem:* Fel Am Col Physicians; fel Am Acad Allergy; Transplantation Soc; Am Asn Immunologists; Am Bd Internal Med. *Res:* HLA- and B-cell typing and genetics; natural immunosupprcssivc factors in fctal prcservation. *Mailing Add:* Dept Med Univ Ky Lexington KY 40536

THOMPSON, JOHN STEWART, b Pittsburgh, Pa, Nov 19, 40. ELECTRICAL ENGINEERING. *Educ:* Lehigh Univ, BS, 62 & 63; Univ Rochester, MS, 65, PhD(elec eng), 67. *Prof Exp:* Mem tech staff signal processing res, 67-80, SUPVR SMALL BUS SYSTS DEVELOP, BELL LABS, 80- *Mem:* Inst Elec & Electronics Engrs. *Res:* Digital signal processing; digital source encoding; computer architecture and programming as applied to signal processing. *Mailing Add:* Bell Tel Labs Holmdel NJ 07733

THOMPSON, JOSEPH GARTH, b Logan, Utah, Aug 15, 35; m 60; c 7. MECHANICAL ENGINEERING, AUTOMATIC CONTROLS. *Educ:* Brigham Young Univ, BES, 60; Purdue Univ, MSME, 62, PhD(mech eng), 67. *Prof Exp:* Design engr, Space Tech Labs, Thompson, Ramo, Wooldridge, Inc, 61-62; instr mech eng, Purdue Univ, 62-63; asst prof, Univ Tex, 66-71; PROF MECH ENG, KANS STATE UNIV, 71- *Mem:* Simulation Coun; Am Soc Mech Engrs; Nat Soc Prof Engrs; Am Soc Eng Educ; Am Soc Heating, Refrig & Air Conditioning Engrs. *Res:* Modeling, design and compensation of nonlinear dynamic systems; design of regulator and feedback control systems; simulation and optimization of dynamic systems; application of microprocessors to automatic control. *Mailing Add:* Dept of Mech Eng Kans State Univ Manhattan KS 66506

THOMPSON, JOSEPH KYLE, b Columbus, Ohio, Oct 2, 20; m 56; c 3. PHYSICAL INORGANIC CHEMISTRY. *Educ:* Sterling Col, BA, 42; Univ Kans, MA, 49, PhD, 50. *Hon Degrees:* DSc, Sterling Col, 67. *Prof Exp:* Chemist, 42-46, CHEMIST, US NAVAL RES LAB, 50- *Mem:* Am Chem Soc; Sigma Xi; Am Inst Chemists. *Res:* Kinetics and mechanisms of adsorption and filtration, particularly air cleaning devices; oxides of alkali and alkaline earth metals; nuclear magnetic resonance. *Mailing Add:* US Naval Res Lab Code 6180 Washington DC 20375

THOMPSON, JOSEPH LIPPARD, b Newport News, Va, May 12, 32; m 55; c 3. RADIOCHEMISTRY, PHYSICAL CHEMISTRY. *Educ:* Va Polytech Inst, BS, 54; Pa State Univ, MS, 59, PhD(chem), 63. *Prof Exp:* Nat Res Coun res asst, Nat Bur Standards, Washington, DC, 63-64; from asst prof to assoc prof, 64-78, PROF CHEM, IDAHO STATE UNIV, 78- *Mem:* Am Chem Soc. *Res:* Chemical effects of nuclear transformations; Mössbauer effect; environmental monitoring. *Mailing Add:* Dept of Chem Idaho State Univ Pocatello ID 83201

THOMPSON, JULIA ANN, b Little Rock, Ark, Mar 13, 43. ELEMENTARY PARTICLE PHYSICS, HIGH ENERGY PHYSICS. *Educ:* Cornell Col, BA, 64; Yale Univ, MS, 66, PhD(physics), 69. *Prof Exp:* Res assoc physics, Brookhaven Nat Lab, 69-71; res assoc & assoc instr, Univ Utah, 71-72; asst prof, 72-78, ASSOC PROF PHYSICS, UNIV PITTSBURGH, 78- *Mem:* Am Phys Soc. *Res:* Application of optoelectronic techniques to high energy physics pattern recognition problems, classification of hadronic jets; glue effects via glueballs and direct photon production; strange particle interactions and decays. *Mailing Add:* Dept of Physics Univ of Pittsburgh Pittsburgh PA 15260

THOMPSON, KENNETH DAVID, b Wimbeldon, NDak, Apr 13, 40; m 65; c 2. MICROBIOLOGY, IMMUNOLOGY. *Educ:* Univ NDak, BS, 63; MS, 67, PhD(microbiol), 70. *Prof Exp:* NIH fel, Temple Univ, 70-72, instr, 72-73, asst prof microbiol & immunol, Health Sci Ctr, 73-78; ASSOC PROF PATH & MICROBIOL, MED CTR, LOYOLA UNIV, 78- *Mem:* Am Soc Microbiol; Reticuloendothelial Soc. *Res:* Tumor immunology and clinical immunology. *Mailing Add:* Clin Microbiol & Immunoserol Labs 2160 S First Ave Rm 0714-E Maywood IL 60153

THOMPSON, KENNETH LANE, b New Orleans, La, Feb 4, 43; m 67; c 1. OPERATING SYSTEMS, NETWORKS. *Educ:* Univ Calif, Berkeley, BS, 65, MS, 66. *Prof Exp:* MEM STAFF, BELL LABS, 66- *Concurrent Pos:* Lectr, Univ Calif, Berkeley, 76. *Honors & Awards:* Piorie Award, Inst Elec & Electronics Engrs, 82. *Mem:* Nat Acad Eng; Asn Comput Mach. *Mailing Add:* Bell Labs Rm 2C423 Murray Hill NJ 07974

THOMPSON, KENNETH O(RVAL), b Fielding, Sask, Sept 12, 17; US citizen; m 78; c 2. MECHANICAL ENGINEERING, AERONAUTICAL ENGINEERING. *Educ:* Univ Minn, BAeroE & BBusAdmin, 53, MSAE, 58; Univ Ala, PhD(mech eng), 67. *Prof Exp:* Prin engr, Univ Minn, 53-62; res assoc, 62-67, ASSOC PROF ENG, RES INST, UNIV ALA, HUNTSVILLE, 67-, DIR, INST & RES SUPPORT SERV, 80- *Mem:* Am Astronaut Soc; Am Inst Aeronaut & Astronaut; Am Soc Eng Sci. *Res:* Supersonic and hypersonic aerodynamics; gas dynamics; digital computers; design and operation of supersonic and hypersonic inlets, wind-tunnels and other research facilities. *Mailing Add:* Inst Servs Univ of Ala PO Box 1247 Huntsville AL 35807

THOMPSON, LANCELOT CHURCHILL ADALBERT, b Jamaica, West Indies, Mar 3, 25; US citizen; m 52; c 2. INORGANIC CHEMISTRY. *Educ:* Morgan State Col, BS, 52; Wayne State Univ, PhD(inorg chem), 56. *Prof Exp:* Instr chem, Wolmers Boys Sch, Jamaica, 55-56; Int Nickel Co fel, Pa State Univ, 57; from asst prof to assoc prof inorg chem, 58-66, asst dean col arts & sci, 64-66, PROF CHEM & DEAN STUDENT SERV, UNIV TOLEDO, 66-, VPRES STUDENT AFFAIRS, 68- *Concurrent Pos:* Consult, Owens-Ill Glass Co, Ohio, 62-64. *Mem:* AAAS; Am Chem Soc. *Res:* Determination of structure of coordination compounds; coordination polymers; solubility of hydrous oxides. *Mailing Add:* Dept of Chem Univ of Toledo Toledo OH 43606

THOMPSON, LARRY CLARK, b Hoquiam, Wash, June 13, 35; m 55; c 2. INORGANIC CHEMISTRY. *Educ:* Willamette Univ, BS, 57; Univ Ill, MS, 59, PhD(inorg chem), 60. *Prof Exp:* From asst prof to assoc prof, 60-68, PROF CHEM, UNIV MINN, DULUTH, 68-, HEAD DEPT, 72- *Concurrent Pos:* Vis prof, Univ Sao Paulo, 69. *Mem:* Am Chem Soc. *Res:* Coordination chemistry of the rare earth elements; high coordination numbers; ligands with unusual steric requirements. *Mailing Add:* Dept of Chem Univ of Minn Duluth MN 55812

THOMPSON, LARRY DEAN, b Warren, Ohio, Oct 16, 51; m 73; c 2. PHYSICAL METALLURGY, MATERIALS SCIENCE. *Educ:* Youngstown State Univ, BE, 73; Univ Calif, Berkeley, MS, 76, PhD(mat sci & eng), 78. *Prof Exp:* Res asst mat sci, Lawrence Berkeley Lab, 73-77; sr scientist mat sci, Gen Atomic Co, 77-81; PRES, PSI MET, 81- *Concurrent Pos:* Lectr, San Diego State Univ, 81- *Honors & Awards:* Achievement Award, Am Soc Metals, 77. *Mem:* Am Soc Metals; Am Inst Mining, Metal & Petrol Eng. *Res:* Structural instability of high-temperature alloys and superalloys; high-temperature gaseous corrosion of metals; phase transformations in austenitic stainless steels; alloy design of stainless steels, fracture/mechanical properties of structural materials. *Mailing Add:* PSI MET 4626 Alabama St San Diego CA 92116

THOMPSON, LARRY FLACK, b Union City, Tenn, Aug 31, 44; m 64; c 2. POLYMER CHEMISTRY. *Educ:* Tenn Technol Univ, BS, 66, MS, 68; Univ Mo-Rolla, PhD(chem), 71. *Prof Exp:* Mem tech staff chem & thin films, 70-78, HEAD ORG MAT & CHEM ENG, BELL LABS, 78- *Concurrent Pos:* Guest prof, Rutgers Univ, 72. *Mem:* Am Chem Soc. *Res:* Electron beam polymer resist studies for microfabrication of integrated electronics; thin polymer films for use in microelectronic fabrication; materials and processes for optical fiber fabrication. *Mailing Add:* 6F225 Bell Labs 600 Mountain Ave Murray Hill NJ 07974

THOMPSON, LAWRENCE HADLEY, b Tyler, Tex, July 22, 41; m 68; c 2. CELL BIOLOGY. *Educ:* Univ Tex, Austin, BS, 63, MS, 67, PhD(biophys), 69. *Prof Exp:* Fel cell biol, Ont Cancer Inst, 69-71, staff physicist, 71-73; SR SCIENTIST BIOMED SCI, LAWRENCE LIVERMORE NAT LAB, UNIV CALIF, 73- *Mem:* Am Soc Cell Biol; Environ Mutagen Soc; AAAS. *Res:* Study mechanisms of somatic cell mutation through the isolation, characterization and applications of DNA repair mutants cultured mammalian cells; develop improved in vitro test systems for mutagenesis using repair mutants. *Mailing Add:* Biomed Div L-452 Livermore Lab Univ of Calif PO Box 5507 Livermore CA 94550

THOMPSON, LEE P(RICE), b Pastura, NMex, June 29, 13; m 36; c 4. MECHANICS. *Educ:* Ind Univ, BA, 36; Agr & Mech Col, Tex, MS, 38, PhD(eng), 49. *Prof Exp:* Asst, Agr & Mech Col, Tex, 36-38, from instr to prof mech eng, 38-55; PROF ENG, DEAN COL ENG & APPL SCI & DIR SCH ENG, ARIZ STATE UNIV, 55- *Concurrent Pos:* Mgr res & testing lab, AiResearch Corp, 44-46; partic, Am Soc Eng Educ-Nat Sci Found vis engr prog. *Mem:* Am Soc Eng Educ; Am Inst Aeronaut & Astronaut. *Res:* Applied mechanics; aircraft cabin pressure systems; aircraft electronic equipment cooling research; vibrations; heat and mass transfer by electrical analogy; math studies for application of computers to solution of missile-satellite problems. *Mailing Add:* Col of Eng & Appl Sci Ariz State Univ Tempe AZ 85281

THOMPSON, LEIF HARRY, b Chadron, Nebr, Dec 6, 43; c 1. REPRODUCTIVE PHYSIOLOGY. *Educ:* Univ Nebr, BS, 67; NC State Univ, MS, 70, PhD(animal sci), 72. *Prof Exp:* Asst prof reproductive physiol, Tex Tech Univ, 72-77; EXTEN SPECIALIST ANIMAL PHYSIOL, UNIV ILL, 78- *Mem:* Am Soc Animal Sci; Soc Study Fertil; Soc Study Reprod. *Res:* Influence of environment, nutrition, development, hormonal therapy and selection on reproductive efficiency in swine, beef cattle and sheep and hormonal regulation of growth of feedlot animals. *Mailing Add:* Dept of Animal Sci Univ of Ill Urbana IL 61801

THOMPSON, LEITH STANLEY, b Morgate, PEI, Aug 22, 34; m 58; c 4. ENTOMOLOGY, PLANT PATHOLOGY. *Educ:* McGill Univ, BSc, 56; Cornell Univ, PhD(entom), 61. *Prof Exp:* RES SCIENTIST ENTOM, AGR CAN, 56-, HEAD FORAGE LIVESTOCK SECT ENTOM & ADMIN, 77- *Mem:* Entom Soc Can; Entom Soc Am. *Res:* Forage insect studies; cereal insect studies; corn insect studies; insect-transmitted viruses; biological control of insects; potato insect studies. *Mailing Add:* Res Station PO Box 1210 Charlottetown PE C1A 7M8 Can

THOMPSON, LEWIS CHISHOLM, b Brechenridge, Tex, Jan 18, 26; m 55; c 2. NUCLEAR PHYSICS. *Educ:* Rice Univ, BA, 50, MA, 52, PhD(physics), 54. *Prof Exp:* Physicist, Naval Res Lab, 54-56; sr nuclear engr, Gen Dynamics/Convair, 56-59; asst prof physics, Univ Ga, 59-63; assoc prof, La Sierra Col, 65-70; prof physics, Loma Linda Univ, 70-77; PROF PHYSICS, OAKWOOD COL, 77- *Mem:* Am Asn Physics Teachers. *Res:* Energy levels of light nuclei; nuclear instruments; nuclear shielding; low energy particle accelerators. *Mailing Add:* 322 Farmstead Rd Huntsville AL 35806

THOMPSON, LOREN EDWARD, JR, b Salem, WVa, May 8, 37; m 58, 79; c 7. GEOPHYSICS. *Educ:* Marietta Col, BS, 60; Ohio Univ, MS, 63. *Prof Exp:* Geophys interpreter explor, Phillips Petrol Co, 63-67; advan geohysicist explor res, 67-75, sr well log analyst, Appl Technol Div, Denver Res Ctr, Marathon Oil Co, 75-81; SR CONSULT, SCI SOFTWARE CORP, 81- *Concurrent Pos:* Chmn logging adv bd, Atlantic Continental Offshore Stratig Test Proj, 74-76. *Mem:* Soc Explor Geophysicists; Soc Prof Well Log Analysts. *Res:* Acoustical, electrical, nuclear and mechanical borehole geophysical devices, including electronics, data acquisition, data processing and interpretation. *Mailing Add:* 7469 S Gallup St Littleton CO 80120

THOMPSON, LORIN RAY, b Lafayette, Ind, Dec 13, 43; m 65; c 3. BIOCHEMISTRY, CELL BIOLOGY. *Educ:* Univ Calif, Riverside, BS, 65; Univ Wash, PhD(genetics), 70. *Prof Exp:* NIH fel biol, Univ Calif, San Diego, 70-71; NIH fel oncol, McArdle Lab Cancer Res, Univ Wis-Madison, 71-74; ASST PROF BIOCHEM, BAYLOR COL DENT, 74- *Mem:* Sigma Xi; Int Asn Dent Res; Am Soc Cell Biol. *Res:* Nuclear-cytoplasmic interactions; DNA replication and its control in eucarytes. *Mailing Add:* Dept of Biochem 3302 Gaston Ave Dallas TX 75246

THOMPSON, LOUIS JEAN, b Big Spring, Tex, Apr 26, 25; m 46; c 4. CIVIL ENGINEERING, SOIL MECHANICS. *Educ:* Tex A&M Univ, BSCE, 49, MSCE, 51; Univ Va, DSc(civil eng), 66. *Prof Exp:* Engr, Lockwood & Andrews, Tex, 51-52; partner, Benson-Thompson-Nash, Engrs-Architects, 52-61; asst prof civil eng, Univ NMex, 61-64; assoc prof, 66-80, PROF CIVIL ENG, TEX A&M UNIV, 80- *Concurrent Pos:* Consult, Sandia Corp, NMex, 63- *Mem:* Am Soc Civil Engrs; Am Soc Eng Educ; Int Asn Bridge & Struct Eng. *Res:* High rate of deformation of earth materials; earth penetration; wave propagation in soils and rock; earth impact; cratering; drilling; tunnelling and design of earth structures. *Mailing Add:* Dept of Civil Eng Tex A&M Univ College Station TX 77840

THOMPSON, LYELL, b Rock Island, Ill, May 10, 24; m 46; c 5. SOILS. *Educ:* Okla State Univ, BS, 48; Ohio State Univ, PhD(soils), 52. *Prof Exp:* Asst prof, Ohio State Univ, 51-53; soil scientist, Noble Found, Okla, 53-58; assoc prof agron, 58-69, PROF AGRON, UNIV ARK, FAYETTEVILLE, 69- *Mem:* Am Soc Agron; Soil Sci Soc Am. Effect of soil fertility, trace element availability and soil acidity upon crop production; increase of food production. *Mailing Add:* Dept of Agron Univ of Ark Fayetteville AR 72701

THOMPSON, LYNNE CHARLES, b St Paul, Minn, Jan 30, 44. FOREST ENTOMOLOGY, BIOLOGICAL CONTROL. *Educ:* Kans State Univ, BS, 70; Univ Minn, MS, 73, PhD(entom), 76. *Prof Exp:* Res assoc forest entom, Univ Minn, 76-77; asst prof, 77-80, PROF ENTOM, KANS STATE UNIV, 80- *Mem:* Entom Soc Am; Entom Soc Can; Sigma Xi. *Res:* Conduct research on the biology and natural control of forest and shade tree insects. *Mailing Add:* Dept of Entom Kans State Univ Manhattan KS 66506

THOMPSON, MAJOR CURT, b Cullman, Ala, May 25, 37; m 62; c 2. INORGANIC CHEMISTRY. *Educ:* Birmingham-Southern Col, BS, 59; Ohio State Univ, MS, 61, PhD(inorg chem), 63. *Prof Exp:* CHEMIST, SAVANNAH RIVER LAB, ATOMIC ENERGY DIV, E I DU PONT DE NEMOURS & CO, INC, 63- *Mem:* Am Chem Soc. *Res:* Synthesis of binary compounds of the actinide elements which are stable at high temperature; complexes of the actinides and lanthanides; solvent extraction. *Mailing Add:* Savannah River Lab E I du Pont de Nemours & Co Inc Aiken SC 29801

THOMPSON, MALCOLM J, b Baldwin, La, Feb 15, 27; m 53; c 3. ORGANIC CHEMISTRY. *Educ:* Xavier Univ, La, BS, 50, MS, 52. *Prof Exp:* Instr chem, Xavier Univ, La, 52-54; chemist, US Bur Mines, 54-55; org chemist, NIH, 55-60; res org chemist, Chem Warfare Labs, Army Chem Ctr, Md, 60-62; RES CHEMIST, INSECT PHYSIOL LAB, USDA, 62- *Mem:* Fel AAAS; Am Chem Soc. *Res:* Chemistry of steroids, sapogenins and natural products; synthesis and structural elucidations; insect hormones, isolation and structural elucidation of insect molting hormones; feeding stimulants; synthesis of compounds with gonadotropic and juvenile hormone activity. *Mailing Add:* Inst Physiol Lab Agr Res Ctr Bldg 467 BARC-E Beltsville MD 20705

THOMPSON, MARGARET A WILSON, b Northwich, Eng, Jan 7, 20; Can citizen; m 44; c 2. GENETICS. *Educ:* Univ Sask, BA, 43; Univ Toronto, PhD(human genetics), 48. *Prof Exp:* Lectr zool, Univ Toronto, 47-48 & Univ Western Ont, 48-50; lectr, Univ Alta, 50-59, asst prof human genetics, 59-62; vis investr, Jackson Lab, 62-63; res assoc pediat & lectr zool, 63-64, asst prof pediat & zool, 64, assoc prof zool, 65-70, assoc prof med cell biol, 69-72, assoc prof med genetics, 72-73, ASSOC PROF PEDIAT, UNIV TORONTO, 66-, PROF MED GENETICS, 73- *Concurrent Pos:* Muscular Dystrophy Asn Can res fel, 62-63; sr staff geneticist, Hosp for Sick Children, Toronto, 63-; mem bd dirs, Am Soc Human Genetics, 75-78; Saul Lehman vis prof, Downstate Med Ctr, State Univ NY, 81. *Mem:* Am Soc Human Genetics; Can Col Med Geneticists; Genetics Soc Can (pres, 72-73). *Res:* Human genetics. *Mailing Add:* Dept Genetics Hosp Sick Children Toronto ON M5G 1X8 Can

THOMPSON, MARGARET DOUGLAS, b Wilmington, Del, May 12, 47. GEOLOGY. *Educ:* Smith Col, BA, 69; Harvard Univ, MA, 74, PhD(geol sci), 76. *Prof Exp:* ASST PROF GEOL, WELLESLEY COL, 76- *Concurrent Pos:* Brachman-Hoffman fel, Wellesley Col, 81-83. *Mem:* Geol Soc Am; Sigma Xi. *Res:* Analysis of structure and tectonic evolution of the Boston Basin, Massachusetts. *Mailing Add:* Geol Dept Wellesley Col Wellesley MA 02181

THOMPSON, MARSHALL RAY, b Monterey, Ill, July 22, 38; m 60; c 2. CIVIL ENGINEERING. *Educ:* Univ Ill, Urbana, BS, 60, MS, 62, PhD(civil eng), 64. *Prof Exp:* Field engr, McCann & Co, Inc, 57-60; res asst, 60-63, from instr to assoc prof, 63-70, PROF CIVIL ENG, UNIV ILL, URBANA, 70- *Concurrent Pos:* Spec consult, Mil Asst Command, US Navy, Vietnam, 69-70; consult engr, Construct Eng Res Lab, US Army Corps Engrs, Caterpillar Tractor Co & var indust and govt agencies, 72-; Sect J comt rep, chmn lime stabilization comt & mem cement stabilization comt, Hwy Res Bd, Nat Acad Sci-Nat Res Coun. *Honors & Awards:* A W Johnson Mem Award, Hwy Res Bd, 70; Huber Res Prize, Am Soc Civil Engrs, 70. *Mem:* Am Soc Testing & Mat; Am Soc Eng Educ; Am Concrete Inst; Am Soc Civil Engrs. *Res:* Soil stabilization; highway materials; surficial soils; pavements. *Mailing Add:* 111 Talbot Lab Dept Civil Eng Univ of Ill Urbana IL 61801

THOMPSON, MARTIN LEROY, b Kindred, NDak, Jan 8, 35; m 63; c 3. INORGANIC CHEMISTRY. *Educ:* Concordia Col, Moorhead, Minn, BA, 56; Ind Univ, PhD(inorg chem), 64. *Prof Exp:* From instr to asst prof, 62-69, ASSOC PROF CHEM, LAKE FOREST COL, 69- *Mem:* Am Chem Soc; Sigma Xi. *Res:* Inorganic chemistry of silicon boron and phosphorus compounds. *Mailing Add:* Dept of Chem Johnson Sci Bldg Lake Forest Col Lake Forest IL 60045

THOMPSON, MARVIN P, b Troy, NY, June 22, 33; m 53; c 3. BIOCHEMISTRY. *Educ:* Kans State Univ, BS, 56, MS, 57; Mich State Univ, PhD(food sci), 60. *Prof Exp:* Biochemist, 60-71, chief, Milk Properties Lab, 71-74, res chemist, Dairy Lab, 74-80, RES LEADEER, PLANT SCI LAB, EASTERN REGIONAL RES CTR, USDA, 80- *Concurrent Pos:* Prof, Pa State Univ, 65- *Honors & Awards:* Borden Award, 70; Arthur S Flemming Award, 71; Superior Serv Award, USDA, 71. *Mem:* Am Chem Soc; Am Dairy Sci Asn; Am Soc Biol Chem. *Res:* Isolation and properties of milk proteins; genetic polymorphism of milk proteins; structure of casein micelles; accelerated curing of cheese. *Mailing Add:* USDA Eastern Regional Res Ctr Dairy Properties Lab Philadelphia PA 19118

THOMPSON, MARVIN PETE, JR, b Mackville, Ky, Sept 28, 41; m 62; c 3. WILDLIFE ECOLOGY, MAMMALOGY. *Educ:* Univ Ky, BS, 63; Kans State Univ, MS, 67; Southern Ill Univ, Carbondale, PhD(zool), 71. *Prof Exp:* From asst prof to assoc prof, 68-80, PROF BIOL, EASTERN KY UNIV, 80-, FAC RES GRANTS, 69- *Mem:* Wildlife Soc; Am Soc Mammal; Nat Wildlife Fedn. *Res:* Woodchuck ecology and physiology; ecology of pest mammals; wildlife restoration. *Mailing Add:* Dept Biol Sci Eastern Ky Univ Richmond KY 40475

THOMPSON, MARY E, b Minneapolis, Minn, Dec 21, 28. PHYSICAL INORGANIC CHEMISTRY. *Educ:* Col St Catherine, BA, 53; Univ Minn, MS, 58; Univ Calif, Berkeley, PhD(chem), 64. *Prof Exp:* Instr sci & math, Derham Hall High Sch, 53-57, 58-59; res asst chem, Lawrence Radiation Lab, Calif, Berkeley, 61-64; lab instr, 53-56, from asst prof to assoc prof, 64-78, PROF CHEM, COL ST CATHERINE, 78-, CHMN DEPT, 69- *Mem:* AAAS; Am Chem Soc; fel Am Inst Chem; The Chem Soc. *Res:* Hydrolytic polymerization in aqueous solutions; kinetics; magnetic susceptibility of solutions of transition metal polymers. *Mailing Add:* Dept of Chem Col of St Catherine 2004 Randolph Ave St Paul MN 55105

THOMPSON, MARY ELEANOR, b Cleveland, Ohio, Nov 5, 26. GEOCHEMISTRY. *Educ:* Boston Univ, BA, 48; Harvard Univ, MA, 63, PhD(geol), 64. *Prof Exp:* Mineralogist, US Geol Surv, 48-57; electrode chemist, EPSCO, Inc, Mass, 62-63; res assoc geochem, Dept Geol, Univ SC & electrode chem, Dept Geol & Sch Med, Stanford Univ, 64-67; RES SCIENTIST & MGR CHEM LIMNOL, CAN CTR INLAND WATERS, 67- *Concurrent Pos:* Co-recipient, NSF grant, Univ SC, 65-66; res assoc, Dept Geol, McMaster Univ, 68-69. *Mem:* Int Asn Hydrol Sci; Geochem Soc. *Res:* Low temperature aqueous geochemistry; specific-ion electrodes; chemical limnology. *Mailing Add:* 834 Tanager Ave Burlington ON L7T 2Y2 Can

THOMPSON, MARY ELINORE, b Winnipeg, Man, Sept 9, 44; m 68; c 3. STATISTICS. *Educ:* Univ Toronto, BSc, 65; UniY Ill, MS, 66, PhD(math), 69. *Prof Exp:* Lectr, 69-71, asst prof, 71-73, assoc prof, 73-80, PROF STATIST, UNIV WATERLOO, 80- *Mem:* Am Math Soc; Can Math Soc; Inst Math Statist; Statist Soc Can; Am Statist Asn. *Res:* Finite population sampling; probability. *Mailing Add:* Dept of Statist Univ of Waterloo Waterloo ON N2L 3G1 Can

THOMPSON, MAXINE MARIE, b Bloomington, Ill, Nov 3, 26; m 53; c 2. GENETICS, HORTICULTURE. *Educ:* Univ Calif, BS, 48, MS, 51, PhD(genetics), 60. *Prof Exp:* Jr specialist viticulture, Univ Calif, Davis, 62-63; asst prof biol, Wis State Univ, Oshkosh, 63-64; res assoc hort, 64-67, asst prof bot, 66-68, from asst prof to assoc prof hort, 68-79, PROF HORT, ORE STATE UNIV, 79- *Mem:* AAAS; Bot Soc Am; Am Soc Hort Sci. *Res:* Cytological and botanical studies related to horticultural problems, especially horticultural breeding; fruit breeding and genetics. *Mailing Add:* Dept of Hort Ore State Univ Corvallis OR 97331

THOMPSON, MAYNARD, b Michigan City, Ind, Sept 8, 36; m 55; c 2. MATHEMATICS. *Educ:* DePauw Univ, AB, 58; Univ Wis, MS, 59, PhD(math), 62. *Prof Exp:* Lectr, 62-64, from asst prof to assoc prof, 64-73, chmn dept, 74-77, PROF MATH, IND UNIV, BLOOMINGTON, 73- *Concurrent Pos:* Res assoc, Univ Md, 70-71; sr res scientist, Gen Motors Res Labs, 78. *Mem:* Am Math Soc; Math Asn Am; Soc Indust & Appl Math. *Res:* Approximation theory; complex analysis; mathematical biology. *Mailing Add:* Dept of Math Ind Univ Bloomington IN 47401

THOMPSON, MICHAEL BRUCE, b Kansas City, Mo, Aug 25, 39; c 2; c 1. EMBRYOLOGY. *Educ:* Baker Univ, BS, 63; Kans State Univ, MS, 67, PhD(biol), 69. *Prof Exp:* Head dept biol, 70-74, asst prof, 69-76, ASSOC PROF BIOL, MINOT STATE COL, 76-, CHMN DIV SCI & MATH, 74- *Mem:* Soc Study Reproduction; Am Soc Zool. *Res:* Developmental placentation. *Mailing Add:* Div of Sci & Math Minot State Col Minot ND 58701

THOMPSON, MILTON AVERY, b Salem, Ore, July 5, 29; m 57; c 3. ENVIRONMENTAL MANAGEMENT. *Educ:* San Jose State Col, BA, 51; Ore State Univ, MS, 53, PhD(phys chem), 57. *Prof Exp:* From chemist to sr chemist, Dow Chem Co, 57-61, res supvr, 62-65, sr res mgr, 66-68, dir chem res & develop, 69-70, mgr environ sci, 70-74; mgr environ sci & waste control, Rockwell Int, 75-78; environ scientist, Stearns-Roger Inc, 78-79; environ scientist, Cyprus Mines Corp, 79-80; PRIN LICENSING ENGR & DIR MINING SERV, HARDING-LAWSON ASSOC, 81- *Mem:* Am Chem Soc; Sigma Xi; Am Nuclear Soc. *Res:* Plutonium chemistry; plutonium processing, revovery and corrosion; nonaqueous plutonium chemistry. *Mailing Add:* 931 Gapter Rd Boulder CO 80303

THOMPSON, NEAL PHILIP, b Brooklyn, NY, July 18, 36; m 58; c 5. PLANT PHYSIOLOGY, PLANT ANATOMY. *Educ:* Wheaton Col, Ill, BS, 57; Miami Univ, Ohio, MA, 62; Princeton Univ, PhD(biol), 65. *Prof Exp:* Asst prof plant physiol & asst plant physiologist, 65-72, assoc prof plant physiol & assoc plant physiologist, 72-77, prof plant physiol & plant physiologist, 77-80, ASST DEAN RES, UNIV FLA, 80- *Mem:* Am Chem Soc. *Res:* Developmental structure of higher plants; translocation of materials, exogenously applied or endogenous, in higher plants, their effects on anatomical structure and their metabolism; pesticides in the environment, particularly as related to birds and fish. *Mailing Add:* 1022 McCarty Hall Univ Fla Gainesville FL 32611

THOMPSON, NOEL PAGE, b San Francisco, Calif, Oct 22, 29; m 54; c 2. BIOMEDICAL ENGINEERING. *Educ:* Stanford Univ, BA, 51, MS, 61; Univ Calif, Los Angeles, MD, 55. *Prof Exp:* Intern med, Univ Hosps, Univ Wis, 55-56; chief bioeng & physiol div, Palo Alto Med Res Found, 58-73; CHIEF MED INSTRUMENTATION LAB, PALO ALTO MED CLINIC, 64-; MEM STAFF, PHYSICIAN MED INST, 77- *Concurrent Pos:* Consult assoc prof, Stanford Univ, 61- & Univ Santa Clara, 62-68. *Mem:* AMA; Am Inst Ultrasonics in Med; Am Acad Family Physicians; Inst Elec & Electronics Engrs. *Res:* Theoretical and applied biomedical engineering; mathematics and electronic instruments as applied to research and in the practice of medicine. *Mailing Add:* Physician Med Inst 1131 Westfield Dr Menlo Park CA 94025

THOMPSON, NORMAN STORM, b Ft William, Ont, Nov 10, 23; m 51; c 4. ORGANIC CHEMISTRY. *Educ:* Univ Man, BSc, 50, MSc, 52; McGill Univ, PhD(wood chem), 54. *Prof Exp:* Res chemist, Rayonier, Inc, Wash, 53-60; res assoc, 60-69, PROF CHEM & SR RES ASSOC, INST PAPER CHEM, 69- *Mem:* AAAS; Am Chem Soc; Am Tech Asn Pulp & Paper Indust; Can Pulp & Paper Asn. *Res:* Location and composition of the constituents of wood and their behavior during pulping. *Mailing Add:* Inst of Paper Chem 913 E Glendale Appleton WI 54911

THOMPSON, OWEN EDWARD, b St Louis, Mo, Nov 20, 39; m 72; c 1. METEOROLOGY, ATMOSPHERIC PHYSICS. *Educ:* Univ Mo-Columbia, BS, 61, MS, 63, PhD(atmospheric sci), 66. *Prof Exp:* Instr physics & math, Stephens Col, 64-66; instr atmospheric sci, Univ Mo-Columbia, 66-68; asst prof, 68-72, ASSOC PROF METEOROL, UNIV MD, COLLEGE PARK, 72-, ASST PROVOST, DIV MATH & PHYS SCI & ENG, 78- *Concurrent Pos:* Wallace Eckert vis scientist, IBM Thomas J Watson Res Ctr, Yorktown Heights, NY, 75-76. *Mem:* Am Meteorol Soc; Am Geophys Union. *Res:* Dynamical and physical meteorology; atmospheric waves and oscillations; micrometeorology and boundary layer studies; forest environment; satellite meteorology; meteorological instrumentation; educational film making. *Mailing Add:* Meteorol Prog Univ of Md College Park MD 20742

THOMPSON, PATRICK HALEY, entomology, see previous edition

THOMPSON, PAUL DEVRIES, b Glen Cove, NY, Dec 6, 39; m 63; c 2. BIOMEDICAL ENGINEERING. *Educ:* Cornell Univ, BEE, 62; Univ Pa, PhD(biomed eng), 70. *Prof Exp:* Electronics engr, Mastitis Res, Agr Res Serv, USDA, 71-80; VPRES, DAIRY EQUIP CO, 80- *Mem:* Am Inst Ultrasonics in Med; Am Soc Agr Eng; Am Dairy Sci Asn; Inst Elec & Electronics Engrs. *Res:* Biological flow measurements using electromagnetic and ultrasonic techniques; applications to blood flow in all species and to milk flow in cows. *Mailing Add:* Dairy Equip Co PO Box 8050 Madison WI 53708

THOMPSON, PAUL O, b Stoughton, Wis, Feb 12, 21; m 77; c 2. PSYCHOACOUSTICS, BIOACOUSTICS. *Educ:* St Olaf Col, BA, 43; Univ Southern Calif, MA, 50. *Prof Exp:* Res psyhcologist, US Navy Electronics Lab, 48-67; res psychologist, Naval Ocean Systs Ctr, 67-82. *Mem:* Acoust Soc Am. *Res:* Speech intelligibility, intensity and pitch sensation and perception; thresholds; bioacoustics of marine mammals, particularly whales. *Mailing Add:* Naval Ocean Systs Ctr Code 4013 San Diego CA 92152

THOMPSON, PAUL WOODARD, b Manchester, NH, May 21, 09; m 36; c 2. CHEMISTRY. *Educ:* Univ Ill, BS, 30, MS, 32. *Prof Exp:* Chemist, State Water Surv, Ill, 30-32; res chemist, Sherwin Williams Paint & Varnish Co, Ill, 35-39, Acme White Lead & Color Works, Mich, 39-42 & Ethyl Corp, 42-71; RES ASSOC ECOL, CRANBROOK INST SCI, 56-, FEL, 66- *Concurrent Pos:* Mem ecol surv, Lake Mich Sand Dunes. *Honors & Awards:* Oakleaf Award, The Nature Conservancy, 75. *Mem:* AAAS; Am Chem Soc. *Res:* Oxidation reactions of tetraethyl lead; stability of halogen compounds and fuels; ecology and flora of Michigan; petroleum chemistry; conservation of natural areas; ecological survey, Sleeping Bear Dunes National Lakeshore, Huron Mountains, Michigan, and Michigan prairies. *Mailing Add:* Cranbrook Inst of Sci Bloomfield Hills MI 48013

THOMPSON, PETER ERVIN, b Urbana, Ill, Mar 20, 31; m 60; c 2. GENETICS. *Educ:* Purdue Univ, BS, 54, MS, 56; Univ Tex, PhD(genetics), 59. *Prof Exp:* NIH fel zool, Univ Calif, Berkeley, 59-60; res assoc biol, Oak Ridge Nat Lab, 60-61; from asst prof to assoc prof genetics, Iowa State Univ, 61-68; prof zool, Univ Ga, 68-72, head dept, 72-81. *Concurrent Pos:* Vis lectr, Univ Wis, 63, 64 & 66. *Mem:* Genetics Soc Am; Am Soc Nat. *Res:* Invertebrate and primate genetics; genetic control of protein synthesis; developmental regulation of gene activities; hemoglobin structures and evolution. *Mailing Add:* Dept Zool 722 Biol Sci Bldg Univ Ga Athens GA 30601

THOMPSON, PETER TRUEMAN, b Palmerton, Pa, Oct 15, 29; m 53; c 4. PHYSICAL CHEMISTRY. *Educ:* Johns Hopkins Univ, AB, 51; Univ Pittsburgh, PhD(phys chem), 57. *Prof Exp:* Res asst, Univ Pittsburgh, 51-56, res assoc & instr, 56-58; from instr to assoc prof, 58-73, chmn dept, 71-72 & 77-78, PROF CHEM, SWARTHMORE COL, 73-, CHMN DEPT, 81- *Concurrent Pos:* NSF sci fac fel, Cambridge Univ, 65-66; vis adj prof, Univ Del, 73-74 & 76-77. *Mem:* Am Chem Soc; Sigma Xi. *Res:* Physical chemistry of electolyte solutions both aqueous and non-aqueous. *Mailing Add:* Dept of Chem Swarthmore Col Swarthmore PA 19081

THOMPSON, PHEBE KIRSTEN, b Glace Bay, NS, Sept 5, 97; nat US; m 23; c 4. ENDOCRINOLOGY, GERIATRICS. *Educ:* Dalhousie Univ, MD & CM, 23. *Prof Exp:* Asst biochem, Sch Pub Health, Harvard Univ, 24-26; asst & res fel med, Metab Lab, Mass Gen Hosp, Boston, 26-29; res endocrinol, Cent Free Dispensary & Rush Med Col, 30-46; med ed & writing, 46-53; ED, J AM GERIAT SOC, 54- *Concurrent Pos:* Managing ed, J Clin Endocrinol & Metab, Endocrine Soc, 54-61, consult ed, J Clin Endocrinol & Metab & Endocrinol, 61-64. *Honors & Awards:* Thewlis Award, Am Geriat Soc, 66; Cert of Appreciation, Am Thyroid Asn, 66. *Mem:* Fel Am Med Writers' Asn; Am Pub Health Asn; fel Am Geriat Soc; fel Geront Soc Am; Am Genetic Asn. *Res:* Medical writing and editing. *Mailing Add:* 2300 Lincoln Park West Chicago IL 60614

THOMPSON, PHILIP A, b Galesburg, Ill, Sept 10, 28; m 46; c 3. FLUID MECHANICS, THERMODYNAMICS. *Educ:* Rensselaer Polytech Inst, SB, 57, SM, 58; Mass Inst Technol, ScD(mech eng), 61. *Prof Exp:* From asst prof to assoc prof, 60-74, PROF MECH ENG, RENSSELAER POLYTECH INST, 74- *Concurrent Pos:* Ford Found resident, Large Steam Turbine-Generator Dept, Gen Elec Co, 64-65; vis scientist, Max Planck Inst Stroemungsforschung, 74-78; Alexander von Humboldt sci grant, 75. *Mem:* Am Phys Soc; Am Soc Mech Engrs; Am Inst Aeronaut & Astronaut; Am Inst Mining, Metall & Petrol Engrs. *Res:* Fundamental gas dynamics; mechanics of dense fluids; acoustics; thermodynamics of real gases. *Mailing Add:* Dept of Mech Eng Rensselaer Polytech Inst Troy NY 12181

THOMPSON, PHILIP DUNCAN, b Rossville, Ind, Apr 6, 22; m 44; c 5. METEOROLOGY. *Educ:* Univ Chicago, SB, 43; Mass Inst Technol, ScD(meteorol), 53. *Prof Exp:* Proj officer meteorol, Univ Calif, Los Angeles, US Air Force, 45-46, meteorol group, Inst Advan Study, 46-48, chief atmospheric anal lab, Air Force Cambridge Res Ctr, 48-51, dir, Joint Geophys Res Directorate & Air Weather Serv Prediction Proj, 53-54, chief res & develop sect, Joint Numerical Prediction Unit, 54-58, assoc dir, Nat Ctr Atmospheric Res, 60-80. *Concurrent Pos:* Lectr, Mass Inst Technol, 53; exchange lectr, Inst Meteorol, Univ Stockholm; lectr, Univ Colo, 64-; mem subcomt meteorol probs, Nat Adv Comt Aeronaut, 49-51; mem comt atmospheric sci, Nat Acad Sci-Nat Res Coun, 61- *Honors & Awards:* Legion of Merit, 57; Meisinger Award, Am Meteorol Soc, 60. *Mem:* Sigma Xi; Royal Meteorol Soc. *Res:* Mathematical and physical basis of weather prediction; theory of large scale disturbances in atmospheric and oceanic currents; theory of turbulence. *Mailing Add:* Boulder CO

THOMPSON, PHILLIP EUGENE, b York, Pa, Nov 14, 46; m 73; c 1. SOLID STATE PHYSICS. *Educ:* Lebanon Valley Col, BS, 68; Univ Del, PhD(physics), 75. *Prof Exp:* Asst engr, York Div, Borg-Warner Corp, 69-70; asst prof physics, Lebanan Valley Col, 74-81; RES PHYSICIST, NAVAL RES LAB, 81- *Concurrent Pos:* Consult physics educ, Annville-Cleona High Sch, 80-81. *Mem:* Am Phys Soc. *Res:* Ion implantation into semiconductors for the production of solid state devices, fundamental studies of device isolation in InP by radiation damage, encapsulation/anneal studies, implantation techniques for mercury, cadmium and tellurium. *Mailing Add:* Naval Res Lab Washington DC 20375

THOMPSON, PHILLIP GERHARD, b Eagle Grove, Iowa, Jan 28, 30; m 55; c 2. ENVIRONMENTAL HEALTH, CHEMISTRY. *Educ:* St Olaf Col, BA, 54; Cornell Univ, PhD(inorg chem), 59. *Prof Exp:* Fulbright scholar & Ramsay fel, Cambridge Univ, 59; sr chemist, Cent Res Labs, 3M Co, 59-64, sr res chemist, Contract Res Lab, Cent Res, 64-68, sr res scientist, Magnetic Prod Div, 68-70; tech dir & consult, Thompson Assocs, 70-77; PATENT ADMINR, UNIV MINN, 77- *Concurrent Pos:* Mem, Metrop Coun Comprehensive Health Planning Bd, Metrop Coun, 68-70; 3M Indust lectr, 3M Co, 68-70; vis Ramsay res fel, Dept Physics & Chem, St Olaf Col, 70-71; mem & secy, St Paul Environ Qual Bd, 70-72; comprehensive environ health fel, Dept Environ Health, Sch Pub Health, Univ Minn, 72 & 73; comnr, St Paul Water Bd, 72-80, vpres, 74-80; consult, Environ Health & Safety, Univ Minn, 74, vis lectr, 74-77; dir, Minn Acad Sci, 76-80, consult, 77- *Mem:* Air Pollution Control Asn; AAAS; Am Chem Soc; Soc Univ Patent Adminr; Am Water Works Asn. *Res:* environmental chemistry; air and respirable mass sampling; water quality; trace contaminants; transformation of environmental pollutants; new synthetic techniques; unusual oxygen fluorine compounds; propellants; high performance sealants; ferrites; Mossbauer spectroscopy; university-industry technology transfer; environmental law and regulations. *Mailing Add:* 321 Morrill Hall Univ of Minn Minneapolis MN 55455

THOMPSON, QUENTIN ELWYN, b Woodstock, Ill, Oct 20, 24; m 49; c 4. INDUSTRIAL ORGANIC CHEMISTRY. *Educ:* Bradley Univ, BS, 48; Univ Wis, PhD(chem), 51. *Prof Exp:* Res chemist, 51-59, scientist, 59-67, SR FEL, MONSANTO CO, 67- *Mem:* Am Chem Soc; Sigma Xi. *Res:* Organic synthesis, analysis and structural identification; organic chemistry of sulfur, phosphorus and ozone; traction fluids and lubricants; dielectric and heat transfer fluids. *Mailing Add:* Monsanto Co Res Dept 800 N Lindbergh Blvd St Louis MO 63167

THOMPSON, RALPH J, b Greenville, Tex, Apr 11, 30; m 59; c 2. PHYSICAL CHEMISTRY. *Educ:* ETex State Col, BS & MS, 54; Univ Tex, Austin, PhD(chem), 63. *Prof Exp:* Asst prof chem, Univ Tex, Arlington, 55-59; fel, Ind Univ, 63-65; assoc prof, 65-70, PROF CHEM, EASTERN KY UNIV, 70- *Mem:* Am Chem Soc. *Res:* Nuclear magnetic resonance of boron; nucleic acid research as related to brain function. *Mailing Add:* Dept of Chem Eastern Ky Univ Richmond KY 40475

THOMPSON, RALPH J, JR, b Los Angeles, Calif, Jan 27, 28; m 48; c 3. SURGERY. *Educ:* La Sierra Col, BS, 50; Loma Linda Univ, MD, 51; Am Bd Surg, dipl, 61. *Prof Exp:* From instr to assoc prof, 64-77, PROF SURG, SCH MED, LOMA LINDA UNIV, 77- *Concurrent Pos:* Fel cancer surg, Mem Sloan-Kettering Cancer Ctr, 60-61. *Mem:* Am Soc Surg Oncol; James Ewing Soc; Am Soc Clin Oncol. *Res:* Cancer surgery. *Mailing Add:* Dept of Surg Loma Linda Univ Med Ctr Loma Linda CA 92354

THOMPSON, RALPH LUTHER, b Niangua, Mo, Feb 6, 43; m 70. PLANT TAXONOMY, PLANT GEOGRAPHY. *Educ:* Southwest Mo State Univ, BS, 71, MA, 75; Northeast La Univ, MEd, 72; Southern Ill Univ, PhD(bot), 80. *Prof Exp:* Instr bot, Dept Life Sci, Southwest Mo State Univ, 74-75; spec asst, Dept Bot, Southern Ill Univ, 76-80; ASST PROF BOT & PLANT TAXON, DEPT BIOL, BEREA COL, 80- *Concurrent Pos:* Vis asst prof, Ohio State Univ, 80. *Mem:* Sigma Xi; AAAS. *Res:* Floristic and descriptive studies of the vascular flora of Kentucky; taxonomy and distributional history of nonindigenous plants of the United States; revisionary studies in the subfamily Mimosoideae of the fabaceae (Leguminosae). *Mailing Add:* Dept Biol Berea Col Berea KY 40404

THOMPSON, RALPH NEWELL, b Boston, Mass, Mar 4, 18; m 42; c 3. CHEMICAL ENGINEERING. *Educ:* Mass Inst Technol, BS, 40. *Prof Exp:* Res engr paper mfg, Middlesex Prod, 40-42, tech dir, Falulah Paper Co, 45-48; staff engr paper chem, Calgon Corp, 48-54, res mgr water treat spec chem, 55-57, mgr res & develop, 58-63, dir res & eng, 63-67, vpres & gen mgr, Spec Chem Div, 67-70; vpres corp develop polymers, Pa Indust Chem Corp, 70-74; gen mgr, Chem Div, 74-76, GROUP V PRES SPEC CHEM, THIOKOL CORP, 76- *Honors & Awards:* Goodreau Medal, Goodreau Mem Fund, 36. *Mem:* Tech Asn Pulp & Paper Indust; Soc Chem Indust; Soc Rheology; NY Acad Sci; fel Am Inst Chemists. *Res:* Colloid chemistry; polymer chemistry; industrial water treatment; chemical engineering. *Mailing Add:* Thiokol Corp PO Box 1000 Newton PA 18940

THOMPSON, RAMIE HERBERT, b St Johnsbury, Vt, Sept 26, 33. ELECTROMAGNETICS, ELECTROEXPLOSIVES. *Educ:* Univ Pa, BSEE, 61, MSEE, 65. *Prof Exp:* PRIN SCIENTIST ELECTROMAGNETICS, FRANKLIN INST, 57- *Mem:* Inst Elec & Electronics Engrs. *Res:* Interactions of electromagnetic energy and electroexplosives. *Mailing Add:* 1518 Noble Rd Rydal PA 19046

THOMPSON, RICHARD BAXTER, b Fresno, Calif, June 1, 26; m 50; c 3. FISH BIOLOGY. *Educ:* San Jose State Col, BA, 50; Univ Wash, PhD(fisheries), 66. *Prof Exp:* Fishery res biologist, Fisheries Res Inst, Univ Wash, 50-54; fishery res biologist, Northwest Fisheries Ctr, FISHERY RES BIOLOGIST, NORTHWEST REGIONAL OFF, NAT MARINE FISHERIES SERV, NAT OCEANIC & ATMOSPHERIC ADMIN, 75- *Mem:* Am Inst Fishery Biol. *Res:* Fish ethology; orientation and navigation of anadromous fishes; sensory perception of fishes; marine game fishery resources and utilization. *Mailing Add:* 1700 Westlake Ave N Seattle WA 98109

THOMPSON, RICHARD BRUCE, b Fargo, NDak, Oct 12, 39; m 61; c 2. MATHEMATICS. *Educ:* Univ Northern Iowa, BA, 61; Univ Wis, MS, 63, PhD(topology), 67. *Prof Exp:* Asst prof, 67-70, ASSOC PROF MATH, UNIV ARIZ, 70- *Concurrent Pos:* NSF res grants, 68-71. *Mem:* Am Math Soc; Math Asn Am. *Res:* Topological fixed point theory, particularly semicomplexes, quasi-complexes and local and global fixed point indices. *Mailing Add:* Dept Math Univ Ariz Tucson AZ 85721

THOMPSON, RICHARD CLAUDE, b Kansas City, Mo, Mar 12, 39. INORGANIC CHEMISTRY. *Educ:* Univ Chicago, BS, 61; Univ Md, PhD(chem), 65. *Prof Exp:* Resident res assoc, Chem Div, Argonne Nat Lab, 65-66; asst prof chem, Ill Inst Technol, 66-67; from asst prof to assoc prof, 67-77, PROF CHEM, UNIV MO-COLUMBIA, 77- *Concurrent Pos:* Consult, Argonne Nat Lab, 66-75. *Mem:* Am Chem Soc. *Res:* Kinetics and mechanisms of inorganic reactions. *Mailing Add:* Dept of Chem Univ of Mo Columbia MO 65201

THOMPSON, RICHARD E(UGENE), b Parsons, Kans, Oct 15, 29; m 51; c 2. PROCESS DESIGN. *Educ:* Okla State Univ, BS, 51, PhD(chem eng), 63; Colo Sch Mines, MS, 59. *Prof Exp:* Reactor engr, Atomic Energy Div, Phillips Petrol Co, 51-53; process engr, Tex Div, Dow Chem Co, 53-54; from asst prof to assoc prof chem eng, 62-75, chmn dept, 77-79, PROF CHEM ENG, UNIV TULSA, 75- *Concurrent Pos:* Consult, Crest Eng, Inc, 64-; sr consult, BWT Furlow-Philbeck Assocs, Inc, 75- *Mem:* Am Inst Chem Engrs; Soc Petrol Engrs. *Res:* Equilibrium-stage processes; two-phase flow; oil and gas processing; computer simulation. *Mailing Add:* Dept of Chem Eng Univ of Tulsa 600 S College Tulsa OK 74104

THOMPSON, RICHARD EDWARD, b Wichita, Kans, Oct 17, 46; m 71; c 2. BIOCHEMISTRY. *Educ:* Wichita State Univ, BS, 68, MS, 69; Okla State Univ, PhD(biochem), 74. *Prof Exp:* Fel biochem, Univ Cincinnati, 74-77; ASST PROF BIOCHEM, N TEX STATE UNIV, 77- *Concurrent Pos:* Adj assoc prof biochem, Tex Col Osteop Med, 77-; NIH fel, Univ Cincinnati, 75-77. *Mem:* Am Chem Soc; Sigma Xi. *Res:* Physical biochemistry; enzymology; regulation of cholesterol biosynthesis. *Mailing Add:* Dept of Chem NTex State Univ Denton TX 76203

THOMPSON, RICHARD FREDERICK, b Portland, Ore, Sept 6, 30; m 60; c 3. PHYSIOLOGICAL PSYCHOLOGY. *Educ:* Reed Col, BA, 52; Univ Wis, MS, 53, PhD(physiol psychol), 56. *Prof Exp:* NIH fel physiol, Univ Wis, 56-59; from asst prof to prof med psychol, Med Sch, Univ Ore, 59-67; prof, Univ Calif, Irvine, 67-73; prof psychol, Harvard Univ, 73-75; prof psychobiol, Univ Calif, Irvine, 75-80; PROF PSYCHOL & BING PROF HUMAN BIOL, STANFORD UNIV, 80- *Concurrent Pos:* Nat Inst Ment Health res career award, 62-67, 67-73; mem adv panel psychobiol, NSF, 67-70; mem res scientist rev comt, Nat Inst Ment Health, 69-74; mem comt biol bases soc behav, Social Sci Res Coun, 72; mem US Nat Comt for the Int Brain Res Orgn, 75-78. *Honors & Awards:* Commonwealth Award, 66; Distinguished Sci Contrib Award, Am Psychol Asn, 75. *Mem:* Nat Acad Sci; Am Physiol Soc; Soc Neurosci; Am Psychol Asn; fel AAAS. *Res:* Neurophysiology; cerebral cortex and behavior; neural basis of learning. *Mailing Add:* Dept Psychobiol Stanford Univ Stanford CA 94305

THOMPSON, RICHARD JOHN, b Chapman Ranch, Tex, Aug 9, 27; div; c 2. ANALYTICAL CHEMISTRY, AIR POLLUTION. *Educ:* Univ Tex, BS, 52, MA, 56, PhD(inorg chem), 59. *Prof Exp:* Asst prof chem, Lamar State Col, 57-58 & North Tex State Univ, 59-62; from asst prof to assoc prof, Tex Tech Col, 62-68; chief metals & adv anal unit, Air Qual & Emission Data Prog & supvry res chemist, Nat Air Pollution components and sampling of large quantities of sized respirable air-borne particulate matter. serv br, Div Air Qual & Emissions Data, Bur Criteria & Standards, 69-71; chief, Air Qual Anal Lab Br, Div Atmospheric Surveillance, Environ Protection Agency, 71-73, chief, Qual Assurance & Environ Monitoring Lab, 73-75, chief, Anal Chem Br, 75-78, actg dir, Environ Monitoring Div, 78-79, chief adv, Anal Tech Br, Environ Monitoring Support Lab, Environ Res Ctr, 80 ; PROF, SCH PUB HEALTH, UNIV ALA, BIRMINGHAM, 80- *Concurrent Pos:* Res grants, Res Corp, 60-, Welch Found, 61-69 & NSF, 64-68, 74-75; adj prof, NC State

Univ, 74-; consult, Lawrence Livermore Lab, 70-72 & World Meteorol Orgn, 74-80. *Mem:* Fel AAAS; Air Pollution Control Asn; Am Chem Soc; Sigma Xi; Soc Appl Spectros. *Res:* Inorganic and analytical chemistry of rhenium; inorganic syntheses; non-aqueous solvent chemistry; development of methods for collection and analysis of atmospheric pollutants, including analysis of trace elements, organics, non-metals inorganics, and precipitation components. *Mailing Add:* Sch Pub Health Univ Ala Birmingham AL 35294

THOMPSON, RICHARD MICHAEL, b Thief River Falls, Minn, May 30, 45; m 67; c 2. BIOCHEMISTRY, ANALYTICAL CHEMISTRY. *Educ:* Univ Minn, BChem, 67; Univ Wis, PhD(biochem), 71. *Prof Exp:* asst prof pediat, Sch Med, Ind Univ, Indianapolis, 73-78; PRIN RES SCIENTIST, COLUMBUS DIV, BATTELLE MEM INST, 78- *Concurrent Pos:* NIH trainee, Baylor Col Med, 71-72, Nat Heart Inst res associateship, 72-73. *Mem:* Am Soc Mass Spectrometry. *Res:* Biochemical genetics; gas phase analytical techniques; drug metabolism; identification of natural products. *Mailing Add:* Battelle Columbus Lab 505 King Ave Columbus OH 43201

THOMPSON, RICHARD SCOTT, b Lubbock, Tex, May 24, 39; m 67; c 2. PHYSICS. *Educ:* Calif Inst Technol, BS, 61; Harvard Univ, AM, 62, PhD(physics), 65. *Prof Exp:* NSF fel, Ctr Nuclear Res, France, 66; mem, Inter-Acad Exchange Prog, Inst Theoret Physics, Moscow, 66-67 & 74-75; vis foreign scientist, Ctr Nuclear Res, France, 67-68; asst physicist, Brookhaven Nat Lab, 68-70; asst prof physics, 70-72, ASSOC PROF PHYSICS, UNIV SOUTHERN CALIF, 72- *Concurrent Pos:* Vis scientist, Univ Dortmund, Ger, 75-76. *Mem:* Am Phys Soc. *Res:* Superconductivity. *Mailing Add:* Dept Physics Univ Southern Calif Los Angeles CA 90007

THOMPSON, ROBERT ALAN, b Catskill, NY, July 16, 37; m 71; c 1. MECHANICAL ENGINEERING, PRODUCTION ENGINEERING. *Educ:* Bucknell Univ, BS, 60; Rensselaer Polytech Inst, MS, 62; Univ Rochester, PhD(mech & aerospace sci), 66. *Prof Exp:* Engr trainee truck develop, Ford Motor Co, Mich, 61-62; mech engr advan energy systs, Pratt & Whitney Aircraft Co, Conn, 62-63; mech engr appl mech unit, 66-70, MECH ENGR CORP RES & DEVELOP, PROCESS PHYSICS UNIT, GEN ELEC CO, SCHENECTADY, 70- *Concurrent Pos:* Co-prin investr, US Air Force contract, Mfg Technol Advan Metal Removal Initiatives, 80- *Honors & Awards:* Blackall Machine Tool & Gage Award, Am Soc Mech Engrs. *Mem:* Am Soc Mech Engrs; Am Acad Mechanics; Sigma Xi. *Res:* Mechanical analysis of processes for process optimization and process automation; manufacturing process conception, equipment design and development, especially machine tool dynamics, adaptive controls, in-process tool wear and part inspection sensors. *Mailing Add:* Box 44 Quaker Street NY 12141

THOMPSON, ROBERT CHARLES, b Winnipeg, Man, Apr 21, 31; m 60. MATHEMATICS. *Educ:* Univ BC, BA, 54, MA, 56; Calif Inst Technol, PhD(math), 60. *Prof Exp:* Defense sci officer, Defence Res Bd, Can, 56-57; from instr to asst prof math, Univ BC, 60-64; from asst prof to assoc prof, 64-69, PROF MATH, UNIV CALIF, SANTA BARBARA, 69- *Concurrent Pos:* Ed, J Linear & Multilinear Algebra. *Mem:* Am Math Soc; Math Asn Am; Soc Indust & Appl Math. *Res:* Algebra, especially linear algebra and number theory. *Mailing Add:* Dept of Math Univ of Calif Santa Barbara CA 93106

THOMPSON, ROBERT F(ULLEN), b Bluefield, Va, May 16, 25; m; c 2. ASTRONAUTICS, AERONAUTICAL ENGINEERING. *Educ:* Va Polytech Inst, BSAE, 44. *Prof Exp:* Mem staff, Langley Res Ctr, Nat Adv Comt Aeronaut, Va, 47-59, mem, Space Task Group, NASA, Tex, 59-62, chief, Landing & Recovery Div, 62-66, mgr Apollo Appln Prog, 66-70, mgr space shuttle prog, NASA Manned Spacecraft Ctr, 70-81, MGR SPACE SHUTTLE PROG, NASA LYNDON B JOHNSON SPACE CTR, 81- *Honors & Awards:* Space Flight Award, Am Astronaut Soc, 81; VFW Olin Teague Space Flight Award, 81. *Mem:* Fel Am Astronaut Soc; fel Am Inst Aeronaut & Astronaut. *Res:* Wind tunnel research; reusable spacecraft research & development. *Mailing Add:* 2310 Willow Pass Kingswood TX 77339

THOMPSON, ROBERT GARY, b Jewell, Iowa, Jan 20, 38; m 59; c 3. ENDOCRINOLOGY, LIPID METABOLISM. *Educ:* Univ Iowa, BA, 62, MD, 65. *Prof Exp:* Resident, Johns Hopkins Hosp, 65-68, fel, 68-71, asst prof pediat, 71-74; assoc prof, 74-80, PROF PEDIAT, UNIV IOWA, 80-, DIR PEDIAT ENDOCRINE, 74- *Mem:* Endocrine Soc; Cent Soc Clin Res; Soc Pediat Res; Am Pediat Soc; Am Diabetes Asn. *Res:* Endocrinology and diabetes with recent emphasis of nutrition on insulin secretion and lipid homeostasis. *Mailing Add:* Dept Pediat Univ Iowa Hosps Iowa City IA 52242

THOMPSON, ROBERT GENE, b Hiddenite, NC, Dec 23, 31; m 53; c 2. PHYSICAL ORGANIC CHEMISTRY. *Educ:* Univ NC, BS, 52; Univ Tenn, MS, 54, PhD(chem), 56. *Prof Exp:* Res chemist, 56-60, sr res chemist, 60-61, supvr res, 61-63, tech, 63-64, sr supvr, 64-66, tech supt, 66-71, res mgr, 71-76, bus coordr, 76-78, MFT MGR, E I DU PONT DE NEMOURS & CO, INC, 78- *Mem:* Am Chem Soc. *Res:* Vinyl and condensation polymers; synthetic textile fibers. *Mailing Add:* Textile Fibers Dept E I du Pont de Nemours & Co Inc Wilmington DE 19898

THOMPSON, ROBERT HARRY, b Columbus, Ohio, May 2, 24; m 47. MATHEMATICS, COMPUTER SCIENCE. *Educ:* Sterling Col, BS, 45, DSc, 69; Univ Kans, MA, 51. *Prof Exp:* Prof math, Sterling Col, 47-67; ASSOC PROF MATH, WASHBURN UNIV TOPEKA, 67- *Mem:* Math Asn Am. *Res:* General mathematics. *Mailing Add:* 6131 SW Smith Pl Topeka KS 66614

THOMPSON, ROBERT JAMES, b Dayton, Ohio, Sept 21, 30; m 56; c 2. MATHEMATICS. *Educ:* Ohio State Univ, BSc, 52, MSc, 54, PhD(math), 58. *Prof Exp:* Asst math, Ohio State Univ, 52-53, from asst instr to instr, 53-58; mem staff, 58-65, supvr appl math div II, 65-72, supvr numerical anal div, 72-75, SUPVR APPL MATH DIV, SANDIA NAT LAB, 75- *Mem:* Am Math Soc; Math Asn Am; Soc Indust & Appl Math. *Res:* Applied mathematics; numerical analysis. *Mailing Add:* Dept 5640 Sandia Nat Lab Albuquerque NM 87185

THOMPSON, ROBERT JOHN, JR, b San Francisco, Calif, Nov 10, 17; m 45; c 3. PHYSICAL CHEMISTRY. *Educ:* Univ Calif, Los Angeles, BS, 40; Univ Rochester, PhD(phys chem), 46. *Prof Exp:* Control chemist, Eastman Kodak Co, 37-41; res assoc, George Washington Univ, 43-46; sr res engr, M W Kellogg Co Div, Pullman, Inc, 46-53 & Bendix Aviation Corp, 53-54; vpres & dir res div, Rocketdyne Div, NAm Aviation, Inc, Calif, 54-71, vpres & gen mgr, Rocketdyne Solid Rocket Div, 71-72, sr staff scientist, Rocketdyne Div, NAm Rockwell Corp, 72-73; SPEC ASST TO DIR, APPL PHYSICS LAB, JOHNS HOPKINS UNIV, 74-, SUPVR TECH INFO, 80- *Concurrent Pos:* Mem subcomt rocket engines, NASA, 51-54 & subcomt aircraft fuels, 58, mem res adv comt energy processes, Md Gov Sci Adv Coun, 59- *Mem:* AAAS; Am Chem Soc; Am Inst Aeronaut & Astronaut; Am Inst Chem Engrs. *Res:* Guided missiles; rocket and jet propulsion; propellants and fuels; combustion; heat transfer and fluid flow; chemical processes, thermodynamics and kinetics; radiation and spectra; space science; energy processes, systems and applications. *Mailing Add:* 12912 Ruxton Rd Silver Spring MD 20904

THOMPSON, ROBERT KRUGER, b Jeffersonville, Ohio, Jan 15, 22; m 43; c 3. ENTOMOLOGY. *Educ:* Ohio State Univ, BSc, 47, MSc, 48, PhD(entom), 50. *Prof Exp:* Field aide, Bur Entom & Plant Quarantine, US Dept Agr, 46-47; field res entomologist, 50-51, field res supvr, 51-65, SUPVR BIOL RES LABS, ORTHO DIV, CHEVRON CHEM CO, 66- *Mem:* Entom Soc Am. *Res:* Chemical control of insects, weeds and plant diseases. *Mailing Add:* Ortho Div Chevron Chem Co 940 Hensley Richmond CA 94801

THOMPSON, ROBERT POOLE, b Winnipeg, Man, Feb 8, 23; m 53; c 5. DEVELOPMENTAL BIOLOGY. *Educ:* Univ Western Ont, BA, 49, MSc, 53; Univ Toronto, PhD(zool), 63. *Prof Exp:* Res officer entom, Can Dept Agr, 53-56; from instr to assoc prof biol, St Francis Xavier Univ, 56-67; assoc prof, 67-72, PROF BIOL, STATE UNIV NY COL BROCKPORT, 72- *Concurrent Pos:* Nat Res Coun Can grants, 63-68; State Univ NY Res Found fac res fel, 68-69. *Mem:* AAAS; Soc Develop Biol; Soc Study Reproduction; Am Soc Zoologists. *Res:* Homologous inhibition in the development of pattern in the embryo; time of eruption of the third molar tooth. *Mailing Add:* Dept of Biol Sci State Univ of NY Col Brockport NY 14420

THOMPSON, ROBERT RICHARD, b Springfield, Mo, Mar 30, 31; m 55; c 2. ORGANIC GEOCHEMISTRY. *Educ:* Drury Col, BS, 53; Wash Univ, St Louis, 55-56, PhD(org chem), 57. *Prof Exp:* Sr res engr, Pan Am Petrol Corp, Standard Oil Co, Ind, 57-61, tech group supvr, 61-65, staff res scientist, 65-71; res group supvr, 71-75, RES SECT DIR, AMOCO PROD CO, 75- *Mem:* Am Chem Soc; Geochem Soc. *Res:* Organic geochemistry; origin of oil; geochemical prospecting. *Mailing Add:* Res Dept Amoco Prod Co PO Box 591 Tulsa OK 74102

THOMPSON, RODGER IRWIN, b Texarkana, Tex, Aug 9, 44; div; c 2. ASTROPHYSICS. *Educ:* Mass Inst Technol, SB, 66, PhD(physics), 70. *Prof Exp:* Asst prof optical sci, 70-71, asst prof astron, 71-74, assoc prof, 74-81, PROF ASTRON, STEWARD OBSERV, UNIV ARIZ, 81- *Mem:* Am Phys Soc; Am Astron Soc. *Res:* Theoretical astrophysics including molecular physics, stellar evolution and star formation; observational infrared and visible spectroscopy with Fourier transform spectrometers. *Mailing Add:* Steward Observ Univ of Ariz Tucson AZ 85721

THOMPSON, ROGER KEVIN RUSSELL, b Eng, Dec 12, 45; m 68; c 2. ANIMAL COGNITION, COMPARATIVE PSYCHOLOGY. *Educ:* Univ Auckland, BA, 70, MA, 71; Univ Hawaii, PhD(psychol), 76. *Prof Exp:* Asst prof psychol, 76-77, ASST PROF BIOL & PSYCHOL, FRANKLIN & MARSHALL COL, 77- *Mem:* AAAS; Animal Behav Soc; Am Primatological Soc; Am Asn Univ Professors. *Res:* Comparative analysis of animal memory and related cognitive processes; animal auditory and tonic immobility. *Mailing Add:* Dept Psychol Biol Franklin Marshall Col PO Box 3003 Lancaster PA 17004

THOMPSON, RONALD HALSEY, b Brooklyn, NY, Apr 29, 26; m 51; c 2. INSTRUMENTATION, MATERIALS SCIENCE. *Educ:* Adelphi Col, BA, 50; Columbia Univ, MA, 51; Univ Pa, PhD, 59. *Prof Exp:* Technician, Cornell Univ, 51-53 & Univ Pa, 53-55; physiologist, Nat Insts Health, 55-75, Sci Dir, 68-75; teacher, 74-80, ASST PROF MAT SCI, NORTHERN VA COMMUNITY COL, 80- *Mem:* AAAS; Am Physiol Soc. *Mailing Add:* 3200 Shoreview Rd Triangle VA 22172

THOMPSON, RONALD HOBART, b Memphis, Tenn, Feb 21, 35; m 60; c 4. NUCLEAR CHEMISTRY. *Educ:* La Tech Univ, BS, 61, MS, 68; Univ Ark, PhD(chem), 72. *Prof Exp:* Chemist, Western Elec Corp, 68-70; asst prof, 72-77, ASSOC PROF CHEM, LA TECH UNIV, 77- *Mem:* Am Chem Soc; AAAS. *Res:* Cosmology; concentration of trace elements on the earth; pesticide residues in animals and man; medical applications of radioisotopes. *Mailing Add:* Dept of Chem La Tech Univ Ruston LA 71270

THOMPSON, RORY, b Seattle, Wash, May 10, 42. PHYSICAL OCEANOGRAPHY. *Educ:* San Diego State Col, AB, 62, MS, 64; Mass Inst Technol, PhD(meteorol), 68. *Prof Exp:* Res asst math statist, San Diego State Col, 62-64; fel phys oceanog, Woods Hole Oceanog Inst, 68-69; asst prof atmospheric sci, Ore State Univ, 69-70; asst scientist, Woods Hole Oceanog Inst, 70-72, assoc scientist phys oceanog, 72-75; sr res scientist, Commonwealth Sci & Indust Res Orgn, 75-79; prof oceanog, Fla State Univ, 79-80. *Mem:* Am Meteorol Soc; Am Geophys Union; Royal Meteorol Soc. *Res:* Geophysical fluid dynamics; computational mathematics; simulation. *Mailing Add:* 71 Beachcomber Ave Bundeena NSW Australia 2230

THOMPSON, ROSEMARY ANN, b San Diego, Calif, May 15, 45; m 67; c 1. MARINE BIOLOGY. *Educ:* Univ Mo-Columbia, BA, 67; Univ Calif, San Diego, PhD(marine biol), 72. *Prof Exp:* Res assoc marine biol, Univ Southern Calif, 72-73; SR BIOLOGIST, HENNINGSON, DURHAM & RICHARDSON, 74- *Concurrent Pos:* Consult environ scientist, EG&G Co, 74; consult, Hinningson, Durham & Richardson, 74. *Mem:* Sigma Xi; Am

Fisheries Soc. *Res:* Marine and aquatic biology of fish as related to pollution and modification of the environment as well as mariculture. *Mailing Add:* Henningson Durham & Richardson Sci 804 Anacapa St Santa Barbara CA 93101

THOMPSON, ROY CHARLES, JR, b Kansas City, Mo, June 19, 20; m 76; c 4. RADIATION BIOLOGY, BIOCHEMISTRY. *Educ:* Univ Tex, BA, 40, MA, 42, PhD(biochem), 44. *Prof Exp:* Tutor, Univ Tex, 40-41, instr, 41-43, res assoc biochem, 43-44, asst prof chem, 47-50; res chemist, Manhattan Dist, US Army Engrs Plutonium Proj, Metall Lab, Univ Chicago, 44-46; res chemist, Radiation Lab, Univ Calif, 46-47; res chemist, Gen Elec Co, Washington, 50-65; SR STAFF SCIENTIST, BIOL DEPT, PAC NORTHWEST LAB, BATTELLE MEM INST, 65- *Concurrent Pos:* Mem comt int exposure, Int Comn Radiol Protection; mem, Nat Coun Radiation Protection & Measurements; assoc ed, Radiation Res, 80- *Mem:* AAAS; Radiation Res Soc; Health Physics Soc. *Res:* Radiochemical study of biochemical processes; evaluation of hazards from internally deposited radioisotopes; especially plutonium and other transuranium elements. *Mailing Add:* Biol Dept Pac Northwest Lab Battelle Mem Inst Richland WA 99352

THOMPSON, ROY LLOYD, b Minn, Apr 29, 27; m 54; c 3. AGRONOMY. *Educ:* Univ Minn, BS, 51, MS, 59; Pa State Univ, PhD(agron), 67. *Prof Exp:* Field supvr, Minn Crop Improv Asn, 49-51; agronomist, Univ Minn, Morris, 56-57 & Rockefeller Found, 67-72; exten agronomist, 72-78, ASST DIR, MINN AGR EXP STA, UNIV MINN, ST PAUL 78- *Mem:* Am Soc Agron; Crop Sci Soc Am; Int Soc Tropical Root Crops. *Res:* Applied crop physiology in the management of field crops for the development and improvement of crop production systems; bean improvement cooperative. *Mailing Add:* Agr Exp Sta Univ of Minn St Paul MN 55108

THOMPSON, SAMUEL, III, b Dallas, Tex, Aug 12, 32. PETROLEUM GEOLOGY, STRATIGRAPHY. *Educ:* Southern Methodist Univ, BS, 53; Univ NMex, MS, 55. *Prof Exp:* Petrol geologist, Exxon Corp, 54-74; PETROL GEOLOGIST, NMEX BUR MINES & MINERAL RESOURCES, 74- *Mem:* Am Asn Petrol Geologists; Soc Econ Paleontologists & Mineralogists; Int Asn Sedimentologists. *Res:* Regional evaluation of the potential for petroleum exploration in southwestern New Mexico; system for analysis of sedimentary units; physico-stratigraphy, chronostratigraphy and eustatic geochronology. *Mailing Add:* NMex Bur Mines & Mineral Resources Socorro NM 87801

THOMPSON, SAMUEL LEE, b Hopkinsville, Ky, Oct 24, 41; m 59; c 2. THEORETICAL PHYSICS. *Educ:* Murray State Univ, BS, 62; Univ Ky, PhD(physics), 66. *Prof Exp:* TECH STAFF MEM, SANDIA CORP, 66- *Mem:* Am Phys Soc. *Res:* Equation of state; hydrodynamics; radiation transport; molecular relaxation. *Mailing Add:* Div 5533 Sandia Labs PO Box 5800 Albuquerque NM 87185

THOMPSON, SAMUEL STANLEY, JR, phytopathology, see previous edition

THOMPSON, SHELDON LEE, b Minneapolis, Minn, Oct 7, 38; m 62; c 3. CHEMICAL ENGINEERING. *Educ:* Univ Minn, Minneapolis, BS, 60, MS, 62. *Prof Exp:* Res engr, Sun Oil Co, 62-69, assoc engr, 69-70, chief, Eng Res Lab, 70-72, res prog mgr, Eng Res, 72-74, mgr, Venture Eng, Sun Ventures, 74-77, mgr chem, 77-80, DIR, APPL RES & DEVELOP DEPT, SUN TECH, INC, SUN CO, 80- *Mem:* Am Inst Chem Engrs; Am Petrol Inst. *Res:* Bench-scale process engineering research and appropriate computer simulation leading to the design of new petroleum and chemical plants; analytical risk-related economic studies; systems analysis and simulation of chemical projects. *Mailing Add:* Sun Tech Inc PO Box 1135 Marcus Hook PA 19061

THOMPSON, SHIRLEY WILLIAMS, b Laurens, SC, Oct 12, 41; m 69; c 3. MATHEMATICAL STATISTICS. *Educ:* Johnson C Smith Univ, BS, 63; Univ NC, MAEd, 71; Ga State Univ, PhD(career & math develop), 80. *Prof Exp:* Comput prog, Celanese Corp, Charlotte, NC, 67, Wyoming Hosp Med Serv, 68-69; instr math, C A Johnson High, Columbia, SC, 63-65; instr math, East Mechlenburg High, Charlotte, NC, 69-71, Cent Piedmont Community Col, 70, De Kalb Community Col, Ga, 75-80 & Ga State Univ, Atlanta, 76-77; ASST PROF MATH, MOREHOUSE COL, ATLANTA, 80- *Concurrent Pos:* Math consult, Proj Opportunity, Univ NC, 70, Richmond County Sch Syst, Augusta, Ga, 75-76. *Mem:* Math Asn Am; Nat Coun Teachers Math. *Res:* Testing the effects of career education awareness in mathematics on the career maturity, attitude toward mathematics and mathematics achievement of students in beginning algebra at a community college. *Mailing Add:* 3161 Weslock Circle Decatur GA 30034

THOMPSON, STEVEN RISLEY, b Hermiston, Ore, Dec 3, 38; m 68. ZOOLOGY, GENETICS. *Educ:* Portland State Col, BS, 61; Ore State Univ, MS, 64, PhD(zool), 66. *Prof Exp:* Res assoc genetics, Univ Notre Dame, 66-68; asst prof, 68-73, ASSOC PROF GENETICS, ITHACA COL, 73- *Mem:* Genetics Soc Am; Am Soc Zoologists. *Res:* Developmental genetics of Drosophila Melanogaster. *Mailing Add:* Dept of Biol Ithaca Col Ithaca NY 14850

THOMPSON, SUE ANN, b New Orleans, La, March 26, 38. REPRODUCTIVE ENDOCRINOLOGY, PROSTATIC CANCER. *Educ:* Univ Ala, BS, 59; La State Univ Med Ctr, MS, 71, PhD(physiol), 75. *Prof Exp:* Assoc biologist, Southern Res Inst, 59-65; res biologist, Med Sch, Tulane Univ, 65-82; assoc histol & anat, 75-78, ASST PROF ANAT, UNIV IOWA, 78- *Mem:* Sigma Xi; Am Asn Anatomists. *Res:* Prolactin and testosterone interaction in the initiation and maintenance of prostatic cancer using in vivo and in vitro model systems. *Mailing Add:* Dept Anat Col Med Univ Iowa Iowa City IA 52242

THOMPSON, THOMAS EATON, b San Mateo, Calif, Aug 10, 38; div; c 2. SOLID STATE PHYSICS. *Educ:* Univ Calif, Berkeley, AB, 60; Univ Pa, MS, 62, PhD(physics), 69. *Prof Exp:* Asst prof solid state electronics, Univ Pa, 70-76; SR RES PHYSICIST, SRI INT, 77- *Mem:* Am Phys Soc. *Res:* Electronic properties of metals and semiconductors; graphite intercalation compounds; photovoltaic materials; magnetic quantum effects in solids; ultrasonics; surface acoustic waves. *Mailing Add:* SRI Int 410A Menlo Park CA 94025

THOMPSON, THOMAS EDWARD, b Cincinnati, Ohio, Mar 15, 26; m 53; c 4. BIOCHEMISTRY. *Educ:* Kalamazoo Col, BA, 49; Harvard Univ, PhD(biochem), 55. *Prof Exp:* From asst prof to assoc prof physiol chem, Sch Med, Johns Hopkins Univ, 58-66; chmn dept, 66-76, PROF BIOCHEM, SCH MED, UNIV VA, 66- *Concurrent Pos:* NIH res fel biochem, Harvard Univ, 55-57; Swed-Am exchange fel, Am Cancer Soc, LKB-Produkter Fabrikasaktiebolog, Sweden, 57-58; hon res fel, Birmingham, Eng, 58. *Mem:* Am Chem Soc; Biophys Soc (pres, 76); Soc Develop Biol; Am Soc Biol Chemists; The Chem Soc. *Res:* Physical chemistry of proteins; lipid protein interactions; biological membrane structure. *Mailing Add:* Dept Biochem Univ Va Sch Med Charlottesville VA 22901

THOMPSON, THOMAS LEIGH, b Erie, Pa, Feb 18, 41; m 66; c 2. AGRICULTURAL ENGINEERING. *Educ:* Pa State Univ, BS, 62; Purdue Univ, MS, 64, PhD(agr eng), 67. *Prof Exp:* Asst elec power & processing, Dept Agr Eng, Purdue Univ, 62-63, res asst agr eng, 63-66; from asst prof to assoc prof, 66-73, PROF AGR ENG, UNIV NEBR, LINCOLN, 73- *Concurrent Pos:* Consult, Grain Drying Equip Co, Ind & tech adv, Crop Dryer's Mfrs Coun, Farm & Indust Equip Inst, 68-; consult, M & W Gear Co & Behlen Mfg Co, 78- *Mem:* Nat Soc Prof Engrs; Am Soc Agr Engrs. *Res:* Mathematical optimization methods; temporary storage of high moisture feed grains; computer simulation models for predicting the performance of grain drying and storage systems; animal growth simulators. *Mailing Add:* Dept of Agr Eng Univ of Nebr Lincoln NE 68583

THOMPSON, THOMAS LEO, b Gering, Nebr, Dec 8, 22; m 46; c 3. BACTERIAL PHYSIOLOGY. *Educ:* Univ Nebr, AB, 48, MS, 50; Univ Tex, PhD, 53. *Prof Exp:* From asst prof to assoc prof, 52-64, PROF MICROBIOL, UNIV NEBR, LINCOLN, 64-, ACTG CHMN DEPT, 70- *Mem:* Am Soc Microbiol. *Res:* Bacterial physiology, mainly resistance to antibiotics; bacterial genetics in relation to thermophily and the transformation phenomenon. *Mailing Add:* 370 Bruce Dr Lincoln NE 68510

THOMPSON, THOMAS LUMAN, b Boulder, Colo, Dec 25, 27; m 56; c 6. GEOLOGY. *Educ:* Univ Colo, BA, 50; Stanford Univ, PhD(geol), 62. *Prof Exp:* Geologist, Phillips Petrol Corp, 50-51; staff res scientist, Amoco Prod Co, 62-76; PROF GEOL & GEOPHYS, UNIV OKLA, 76- *Mem:* Geol Soc Am; Am Asn Petrol Geol; Am Geophys Union. *Res:* World tectonics; structure of continental margins; deep water petroleum and mineral exploration. *Mailing Add:* Sch of Geol Univ of Okla Norman OK 73069

THOMPSON, THOMAS LUTHER, b Houston, Tex, Feb 28, 38. GEOLOGY. *Educ:* Univ Kans, BS, 60, MS, 62; Univ Iowa, PhD(geol), 65. *Prof Exp:* GEOLOGIST, MO GEOL SURV & WATER RESOURCES, 65-, CHIEF AREAL GEOL & STRATIG, 71- *Mem:* Geol Soc Am; Paleont Soc; Soc Econ Paleont & Mineral; Int Paleont Union; Pander Soc. *Res:* Stratigraphy; biostratigraphy; micropaleontology; correlation of Paleozoic strata through the use of paleontology. *Mailing Add:* Mo Geol Surv & Water Resources PO Box 250 Rolla MO 65401

THOMPSON, THOMAS WILLIAM, b Canton, Ohio, May 25, 36; m 66; c 1. SPACE PHYSICS. *Educ:* Case Inst Technol, BS, 58; Yale Univ, ME, 59; Cornell Univ, PhD(elec eng), 66. *Prof Exp:* Engr, Sylvania Elec Prod, 59-61; res asst radar astron, Arecibo Observ, Cornell Univ, 63-64, 66-69; mem tech staff, Jet Propulsion Lab, Calif Inst Technol, 69-76; STAFF SCIENTIST, PLANETARY SCI INST, PASADENA, CA, 77- *Mem:* Am Geophys Union; Am Astron Soc; Int Astron Union; Int Union Radio Sci. *Res:* Radar astronomy; mapping of lunar radar echoes; resolution of the delay-Doppler ambiguity. *Mailing Add:* 3043 Cloudcrest Rd La Crescenta CA 91214

THOMPSON, TOMMY BURT, b Tucumcari, NMex, Apr 3, 38; m 58; c 4. ECONOMIC GEOLOGY, PETROLOGY. *Educ:* Univ NMex, BS, 61, MS, 63, PhD(geol), 66. *Prof Exp:* From asst prof to assoc prof geol, Okla State Univ, 66-73; assoc prof, 73-81, PROF GEOL, COLO STATE UNIV, 81- *Mem:* Geol Soc Am; Am Inst Mining, Metall & Petrol Engrs; Soc Econ Geologists. *Res:* Conceptual models for exploration of metallic resources; mineral resources of Colorado; igneous petrology; hydrothermal alteration of igneous rocks; exploration for uranium in sedimentary and igneous rocks. *Mailing Add:* Dept of Earth Resources Colo State Univ Ft Collins CO 80523

THOMPSON, TOMMY EARL, b Dublin, Tex, June 18, 44; m 72; c 3. PLANT GENETICS, PLANT BREEDING. *Educ:* Tex A&M Univ, BS, 66, MS, 70; Purdue Univ, West Lafayette, PhD(genetics & plant breeding), 73. *Prof Exp:* Field researcher agr econ, Tex A&M Univ, 65, res asst plant breeding, 66-67 & 69-70; res asst plant genetics, Purdue Univ, West Lafayette, 70-73, asst prof forage breeding, 73-74; res geneticist flax genetics, Agr Res Serv, NDak, 74-76, res geneticist sunflower genetics, Agr Res Ser, 76-79, RES GENETICIST PECAN GENETICS, AGR RES SERV, USDA, 79- *Concurrent Pos:* Sci adv, Flax Inst US, 74-76; nat tech adv sunflower prod, Sci & Educ Admin-Fed Res, USDA, 77-79; instr advan plant breeding, WTex State Univ, 78-79. *Mem:* Crop Sci Soc Am; Am Soc Agron; Am Genetic Asn. *Res:* Genetics; pecan research; yieldability of pecans; heritability of yield traits; heritability of dichogamy; insect resistance; disease resistance of pecans. *Mailing Add:* W R Poage Pecan Field Sta PO Box 579 Brownwood TX 76801

THOMPSON, TRUET B(RADFORD), b Noble, La, Mar 24, 17; m 41; c 3. ELECTRICAL ENGINEERING, ELECTRICAL SAFETY. *Educ:* La Polytech, BS, 47, BSEE, 48; Okla State Univ, MSEE, 50; Northwestern Univ, PhD(elec eng), 56. *Prof Exp:* From asst prof to assoc prof elec eng, Okla State Univ, 48-59; chmn dept, 60-67, PROF ENG, ARIZ STATE UNIV, 59- *Mem:* Nat Soc Prof Engrs; Inst Elec & Electronics Engrs; Asn Advan Med Instrumentation; Nat Fire Protection Asn; Am Nat Standards Inst. *Res:* Circuit theory; power systems; statistical communications theory. *Mailing Add:* 230 E Garfield St Tempe AZ 85281

THOMPSON, VICTOR CARL, b Ozawkie, Kans, May 6, 20; m 45. APICULTURE, ENTOMOLOGY. *Educ:* Kans State Univ, BS, 44; Iowa State Univ, MS, 55. *Prof Exp:* Queen breeder, Puett Co, Ga, 44; res asst apicult, Fruit & Truck Br Exp Sta, Ark, 45-51; res assoc, Iowa State Univ, 51-62; RES ASSOC, OHIO STATE UNIV, 63- *Mem:* Entom Soc Am; Am Beekeeping Fedn; Bee Res Asn. *Res:* Biology of the honey bee; disease resistance; genetics of behavior in the honey bee. *Mailing Add:* 1310 Northport Circle Columbus OH 43220

THOMPSON, VINTON NEWBOLD, b Mt Holly, NJ, July 24, 47; m 75; c 1. EVOLUTIONARY GENETICS, ECOLOGICAL GENETICS. *Educ:* Harvard Univ, AB, 69; Univ Chicago, PhD(genetics), 74. *Prof Exp:* Indust hygienist, Ill Dept Labor, 75; indust hygienist, Occup Safety & Health Admin, US Dept Labor, 75-77; ASST PROF BIOL, ROOSEVELT UNIV, 80- *Mem:* Soc Study Evolution; Genetics Soc Am. *Res:* Experimental work on the role of sex in evolution; Drosophila behavioral genetics; ecological genetics of Philanenus Spumarius, the meadow spittlebug. *Mailing Add:* 1747 W 21st Chicago IL 60608

THOMPSON, W(ILLIAM) E(DGAR), b Pittsburgh, Pa, July 25, 24; m 51; c 3. MECHANICAL ENGINEERING. *Educ:* Carnegie Inst Technol, BSME, 47; Univ Mich, MSE, 49; Ill Inst Technol, PhD(mech eng), 58. *Prof Exp:* Assoc mech engr, Cornell Aeronaut Lab, Inc, 49-50; instr mech eng, Ill Inst Technol, 50-53; res assoc, Brown Univ, 56-57; res mech engr, Cornell Aeronaut Lab, Inc, 57-61, prin mech engr, 61-63; assoc prof mech eng, Drexel Univ, 63-68; vpres, Turbo Res, Inc, Lionville, 68-74, chmn & chief officer, 74-80; WITH BORG-WARNER RES CTR, 80- *Mem:* Am Soc Mech Engrs. *Res:* Turbomachinery flows and performance optimization; three dimensional and compressible fluid mechanics; real thermodynamic properties of gas mixtures and equations of stale; vibrations in rotating systems. *Mailing Add:* Borg-Warner Res Ctr Wolf & Algonguin Rds Des Plaines IL 60016

THOMPSON, W P(AUL), b Elmira, NY, June 3, 34; m 77; c 4. PHYSICS, SYSTEMS ENGINEERING. *Educ:* Yale Univ, BS, 55; Lehigh Univ, MS, 57, PhD(physics), 63. *Prof Exp:* Mem tech staff, Aerophys Dept, 61-67, sect head, Exp Aerophys, Aerodyn & Propulsion Lab, 67-68, dir countermeasures, Reentry Systs Div, 68-74, assoc prin dir technol develop, Reentry Systs Div, 74-79, prin dir space technol planning, 79-81, DIR, AEROPHYS LAB, AEROSPACE CORP, 81- *Mem:* Am Phys Soc; assoc fel Am Inst Aeronaut & Astronaut; Sigma Xi. *Res:* Shock tube gasdynamics; gas kinetics; microwave-plasma interactions; reentry physics; electronic and optical countermeasures; system engineering. *Mailing Add:* Aerophys Lab 130/691 Aerospace Corp PO Box 92957 Los Angeles CA 90009

THOMPSON, WARREN CHARLES, b Santa Monica, Calif, May 22, 22; m 48; c 4. OCEANOGRAPHY. *Educ:* Univ Calif, Los Angeles, BA, 43; Univ Calif, San Diego, MS, 48; Agr & Mech Col Tex, PhD, 53. *Prof Exp:* Asst, Scripps Inst, Univ Calif, San Diego, 46-47, 47-48; proj dir, Tex A&M Res Found, 50-52; assoc prof aerol & oceanog, 53-59, PROF OCEANOG, NAVAL POSTGRAD SCH, 59- *Concurrent Pos:* Assoc petrol engr, Humble Oil & Ref Co, La, 47; sci liaison officer, London Br, US Off Naval Res, 60-61; vpres, Oceanog Serv Inc, Santa Barbara, 65-66; consult, 50- *Mem:* AAAS; Geol Soc Am; Soc Econ Paleont & Mineral; Am Meteorol Soc; Am Asn Petrol Geol. *Res:* Shallow water processes; ocean waves. *Mailing Add:* Dept of Oceanog Naval Postgrad Sch Monterey CA 93940

THOMPSON, WARREN ELWIN, b Joliet, Ill, June 15, 30; m 62; c 2. SCIENCE ADMINISTRATION, PHYSICAL CHEMISTRY. *Educ:* Univ Wis, BS, 51; Harvard Univ, AM, 53, PhD(chem), 56. *Prof Exp:* Fulbright scholar, Kamerlingh Onnes Lab, Univ Leiden, 55-57; instr & asst prof chem, Univ Calif, Berkeley, 57-59; asst prof, Case Western Reserve Univ, 59-65; prog mgr, Div Int Progs, 65-76, policy analyst, Div Policy Res & Anal, 76-77, PROG MGR, DIV INT PROGS, NAT SCI FOUND, 77- *Mem:* Am Chem Soc; AAAS. *Res:* Molecular spectroscopy; photochemistry; chemical studies related to astronomy. *Mailing Add:* Div Int Progs Nat Sci Found 1800 G St NW Washington DC 20550

THOMPSON, WARREN SLATER, b Utica, Miss, Aug 19, 29; m 53; c 4. WOOD SCIENCE & TECHNOLOGY. *Educ:* Auburn Univ, BS, 51, MS, 55; NC State Univ, PhD, 60. *Prof Exp:* Asst forester, Miss State Univ, 53-54; wood technologist, Masonite Corp, 57-59; asst & assoc prof forestry, La State Univ, 59-64; DIR, FOREST PROD LAB, MISS STATE UNIV, 64-, PROF WOOD SCI & TECHNOL & HEAD DEPT, 74- *Honors & Awards:* Gottschalk Award, Forest Prod Res Soc, Miss State Univ. *Mem:* Forest Prod Res Soc; Soc Wood Sci & Technol; Am Soc Testing & Mat; Tech Asn Pulp & Paper Indust; Am Wood-Preservers' Asn. *Res:* Wood pathology and preservation. *Mailing Add:* Forest Prod Lab Miss State Univ Mississippi State MS 39762

THOMPSON, WAYNE JULIUS, b Chicago, Ill, Oct 18, 52. SYNTHESIS. *Educ:* Ill Inst Technol, BS, 74; Calif Inst Technol, PhD(chem), 78. *Prof Exp:* NIH FEL, MASS INST TECHNOL, 79-80. *Mem:* Am Chem Soc. *Res:* Design and synthesis of neuroactive compounds which act specifically as neurochemical inhibitors; chemical synthesis of biologically active heterocyclic compounds using transition metal mediated processes. *Mailing Add:* Dept Chem Univ Calif Los Angeles CA 90024

THOMPSON, WESLEY JAY, b Alice, Tex, Dec 10, 47. NEUROBIOLOGY. *Educ:* NTex State Univ, BS, 70, MA, 71; Univ Calif, Berkeley, PhD(molecular biol), 75. *Prof Exp:* Fel neurobiol, Inst Physiol, Univ Oslo, 75-77; fel, Sch Med, Wash Univ, 77-78; ASST PROF ZOOL, UNIV TEX, AUSTIN, 78- *Concurrent Pos:* Muscular Dystrophy Asn fel, 75-76; NATO fel, 76-77. *Mem:* AAAS; Soc Neurosci. *Res:* Developmental neurobiology. *Mailing Add:* Dept of Zool Univ of Tex Austin TX 78712

THOMPSON, WILEY ERNEST, b Murphysboro, Ill, June 30, 41; m 62; c 2. ELECTRICAL & SYSTEMS ENGINEERING. *Educ:* Southern Ill Univ, Carbondale, BS, 63; Mich State Univ, MS, 64, PhD(elec eng), 68. *Prof Exp:* Design engr, Olin Mathieson Chem Corp, 63; asst elec eng, Mich State Univ, 63-64, res asst systs, 64-68, asst prof elec eng & systs, 68; asst prof, 68-72, assoc prof, 72-80, PROF ELEC ENG, NMEX STATE UNIV, 80- *Concurrent Pos:* Consult, White Sands Missile Range, 69-; NSF initiation grant, NMex State Univ, 70-72. *Mem:* Inst Elec & Electronics Engrs; Am Soc Eng Educ. *Res:* Systems optimization, stability; mathematical modeling; computer-aided analysis and design; systems structure; guidance and control; stochastic systems; ecological systems. *Mailing Add:* Box 3-0 Dept of Elec Eng NMex State Univ Las Cruces NM 88003

THOMPSON, WILFRED ROLAND, JR, b Indianola, Miss, Sept 30, 33; m 55; c 2. AGRONOMY. *Educ:* Miss State Univ, BS, 55, MS, 60, PhD(agron), 66. *Prof Exp:* Asst county agent, Miss Agr Exten Serv, 57-58; asst agronomist, Miss Agr Exp Sta, 60-67; asst prof turf mgt, Miss State Univ, 62-67; AGRONOMIST, POTASH & PHOSPHATE INST, 67- *Mem:* Am Soc Agron. *Res:* Soil fertility; crop and soil management; research oriented educational organization. *Mailing Add:* 621 Sherwood Rd Starkville MS 39759

THOMPSON, WILLIAM, JR, b Hyannis, Mass, Dec 4, 36; m 59; c 4. ACOUSTICS, ELECTROACOUSTIC TRANSDUCERS. *Educ:* Mass Inst Technol, BS, 58; Northeastern Univ, MS, 63; Pa State Univ, PhD(eng acoust), 71. *Prof Exp:* Jr engr, Raytheon Co, 58-60; sr engr, Cambridge Acoust Assocs, Inc, 60-66; res asst transducer studies, 66-72, asst prof, 72-78, assoc prof acoust mech, Appl Res Lab, 78-80, ASSOC PROF ENG SCI, APPL RES LAB & DEPT ENG SCI & MECH, PA STATE UNIV, 80- *Mem:* Acoust Soc Am; Inst Elec & Electronics Eng. *Res:* Electroacoustic transducer design, construction and calibration; acoustic radiation and scattering; underwater acoustics. *Mailing Add:* 601 Glenn Rd State College PA 16801

THOMPSON, WILLIAM A, b Moorestown, NJ, Oct 25, 36; m 61; c 1. SOLID STATE PHYSICS. *Educ:* Drexel Inst Tech, BS, 59; Univ Pittsburgh, PhD(physics), 64. *Prof Exp:* RES STAFF MEM PHYSICS, THOMAS J WATSON RES CTR, IBM CORP, 64- *Mem:* Am Phys Soc; Fedn Am Sci. *Res:* Electron tunneling properties of superconductors and magnetic semiconductors. *Mailing Add:* Thomas J Watson Res Ctr IBM Corp PO Box 218 Yorktown Heights NY 10598

THOMPSON, WILLIAM BALDWIN, b Meriden, Conn, Mar 28, 35; m 60; c 3. GEOPHYSICS. *Educ:* Mass Inst Technol, BS & MS, 58, PhD(geophys), 63. *Prof Exp:* Mem tech staff, Bellcomm, Inc, 63-72; head dept, Bell Labs, 72-75; dir, Am Bell Int, Inc, 75-77; MGR, AM TEL & TEL LONG LINES, 77- *Mem:* Am Geophys Union. *Res:* Electromagnetic cavity resonance phenomena in the earth's atmosphere; physical properties of lunar and planetary surfaces and atmospheres; scientific mission planning for Apollo lunar exploration and planetary missions; economic analyses of telephone network costs and investment; business economics. *Mailing Add:* Am Tel & Tel 195 Broadway Rm 30 C1175 New York NY 10007

THOMPSON, WILLIAM BELL, b Belfast, Northern Ireland, Feb 27, 22; m 52, 72; c 2. PLASMA PHYSICS. *Educ:* Univ BC, BA, 45, MA, 47; Univ Toronto, PhD(math), 50; Oxford Univ, MA, 62. *Prof Exp:* Sr fel, UK Atomic Energy Authority, Harwell, Eng, 50-53, sr scientist plasma theory, 53-60, dep chief scientist, Culham Lab, 60-62; prof, Oxford Univ, 63-65; PROF PHYSICS, UNIV CALIF, SAN DIEGO, 65- *Concurrent Pos:* Vis researcher, Plasma Physics Lab, Princeton Univ, 60; vis prof, Univ Calif, San Diego, 60-61 & Univ Colo, 72; ed, Advances in Plasma Physics; assoc ed, J Plasma Physics. *Mem:* Fel Am Phys Soc; Can Asn Physicists; fel Royal Astron Soc. *Res:* Theoretical physics; controlled thermonuclear fusion. *Mailing Add:* Dept Physics Univ Calif San Diego La Jolla CA 92037

THOMPSON, WILLIAM BENBOW, JR, b Detroit, Mich, July 26, 23; m 47, 58; c 3. OBSTETRICS & GYNECOLOGY. *Educ:* Univ Southern Calif, AB, 47, MD, 51; Am Bd Obstet & Gynec, dipl. *Prof Exp:* Intern, Harbor Gen Hosp, Los Angeles, 51-52; resident obstet & gynec, Galliinger Munic Hosp, Washington, DC, 52-53; from resident to sr resident, George Washington Univ Hosp, 53-55; asst, La State Univ, 55-56; clin instr, Univ Calif, Los Angeles, 56-62, asst clin prof, 62-64; assoc prof, Calif Col Med, 64-66; asst prof, 66-73, assoc dean med student serv, 69-73, actg chmn, 73-77, ASSOC PROF OBSTET & GYNEC & VCHMN, GYNEC DIV, COL MED, UNIV CALIF, IRVINE, 77- *Concurrent Pos:* Dir obstet & gynec, Orange County Med Ctr, Orange, 67- *Mem:* Fel Am Col Obstetricians & Gynecologists; fel Am Col Surgeons; AMA. *Res:* Techniques in tubal sterilization. *Mailing Add:* Calif Col of Med Univ of Calif Irvine CA 92664

THOMPSON, WILLIAM D, neurophysiology, see previous edition

THOMPSON, WILLIAM HORN, b Somerville, NJ, Feb 9, 37; m 60; c 3. CHEMICAL ENGINEERING. *Educ:* Pa State Univ, BS, 61, MS, 62, PhD(chem eng), 66. *Prof Exp:* Res asst, Dept Chem Eng, Pa State Univ, 62-65, instr, 65-66; engr, Petrol Processing Dept, Shell Develop Co, Calif, 66-68; group leader, Technol Dept, Wood River Refinery, Shell Oil Co, 68-69, asst mgr, Lube Oil Dept, 69-70, mgr, Refinery Lab, 70-71 & Catalytic Cracking Dept, 71-72, supt opers light oil processing, 72-73, sr staff engr, 73-74, mgr, supply & qual lube, 74-75, mfg oper, 75-77, fuels logistics, 77-78, mgr, Gasoline Bus Ctr, 78-80; SUPT, DEER PARK MFG COMPLEX, 80- *Mem:* Am Inst Chem Eng. *Res:* Physical thermodynamic and transport properties of hydrocarbons and related substances. *Mailing Add:* Shell Oil Co PO Box 2463 Houston TX 77001

THOMPSON, WILLIAM LAY, b Austin, Tex, Feb 16, 30; m 58; c 3. VERTEBRATE ZOOLOGY. *Educ:* Univ Tex, BA, 51, MA, 52; Univ Calif, Berkeley, PhD(zool), 59. *Prof Exp:* From asst prof to assoc prof, 59-71, PROF BIOL, WAYNE STATE UNIV, 71- *Mem:* Fel AAAS; Am Soc Zool; Animal Behav Soc; Am Ornith Union; Wilson Ornith Soc. *Res:* Animal behavior, especially communication and habitat selection in birds. *Mailing Add:* Dept of Biol Wayne State Univ Detroit MI 48202

THOMPSON, WILLIAM OXLEY, II, b Richmond, Va, Apr 25, 41; m 63; c 2. MATHEMATICAL STATISTICS, TECHNICAL MANAGEMENT. *Educ:* Univ Va, BA, 63; Va Polytech Inst & State Univ, PhD(statist), 68. *Prof Exp:* Teacher high sch, Va, 63-64; asst prof & adj assoc prof statist, Univ Ky, 67-75; mgr statist serv group, Tech Serv Div, Agr Mkt Serv, 74-76, dir, Tech Serv Div, 76-79, STATIST & SYSTS COORDR RES, FOREST SERV, USDA, 79- *Concurrent Pos:* Consult, Clin Res Ctr, NIMH, 68-71, consult, Addiction Res Ctr, 70-72, math statistician, 72-74; adj prof statist, Va Polytech Inst & State Univ, 78- *Mem:* Am Statist Asn; Biomet Soc; Sigma Xi. *Res:* Experimental designs and analysis for estimating linear and nonlinear models; estimation of variance components; development of statistical methodology in fields of application; biostatistics. *Mailing Add:* Forest Serv USDA 1400 Independence Ave SW Washington DC 20013

THOMPSON, WILLIAM TALIAFERRO, JR, b Petersburg, Va, May 26, 13; m 41; c 3. MEDICINE. *Educ:* Davidson Col, AB, 34; Med Col Va, MD, 38; Am Bd Internal Med, dipl, 46. *Hon Degrees:* ScD, Davidson Col, 75. *Prof Exp:* From instr to assoc prof, 46-59, chmn dept, 59-73, prof, 59-75, EMER PROF MED, MED COL VA, 75- *Concurrent Pos:* Chief med serv, McGuire Vet Admin Hosp, 55-59, consult, 59-; trustee, Mary Baldwin Col, 59-64, Union Theol Sem, 60-70 & 80- & Davidson Col, 65-73 & 78-80; mem med adv bd, Nemours Found, Del, 60-78, chmn bd mgrs, 65-78; ed, J Va Med, 76-82; med dir, Westminster Canterbury House; bd mem, Crippled Children's Hosp, St Luke's Hosp, & Med Col Va Found. *Mem:* Am Psychosom Soc; Am Fedn Clin Res; master Am Col Physicians; Am Clin & Climat Asn; NY Acad Sci. *Res:* Internal medicine, especially pulmonary pathophysiology. *Mailing Add:* 4602 Sulgrave Rd Richmond VA 23219

THOMPSON, WILMER LEIGH, JR, b Shreveport, La, June 25, 38; m 57; c 1. CLINICAL PHARMACOLOGY, MEDICINE. *Educ:* Col Charleston, BS, 58; Med Univ SC, MS, 60, PhD(pharmacol), 63; Johns Hopkins Univ, MD, 65; Am Bd Internal Med, dipl, 71. *Prof Exp:* Intern, Osler Med Serv, Johns Hopkins Hosp, 65-66, resident, 66-67 & 69-70; asst prof med & pharmacol, Sch Med, Johns Hopkins Univ, 70-74; assoc prof, 74-80, PROF MED & PHARMACOL, SCH MED, CASE WESTERN RESERVE UNIV, 80- *Concurrent Pos:* Fels med, Sch Med, Johns Hopkins Univ, 65-67 & 69-70; staff assoc, Nat Cancer Inst, 67-69; asst physician & dir med intensive care unit, Johns Hopkins Hosp, 70-74; assoc physician & dir clin pharmacol prog, Univ Hosps Cleveland, 74-; adj prof, Sch Libr Sci, Case Western Reserve Univ, 74-; adj assoc prof, Dept Pharmacol, Col Med, Ohio State Univ, 75-; Burroughs Wellcome scholar clin pharmacol, 75-80. *Mem:* Am Soc Pharmacol & Exp Therapeut; Am Med Writers Asn; Am Acad Clin Toxicol; Am Col Physicians; Am Fedn Clin Res. *Res:* Critical care medicine; human pharmacokinetics; drug interactions; clinical toxicology; cardiovascular pharmacology; clinical drug trials. *Mailing Add:* Wearn 344 Univ Hosps Cleveland OH 44106

THOMPSON, WYNELLE DOGGETT, b Birmingham, Ala, May 25, 14; m 38; c 4. BIOCHEMISTRY, ORGANIC CHEMISTRY. *Educ:* Birmingham-Southern Col, BS, 34, MS, 35; Univ Ala, MS, 56, PhD(biochem), 60. *Prof Exp:* Instr chem, Birmingham-Southern Col, 35-36; high sch instr gen sci, Ala, 36-37; jr chemist, Bur Home Econ, USDA, Washington, DC, 37-38; high sch instr gen sci, Ala, 40-41; instr chem, Birmingham-Southern Col, 41-44; instr, Exten Ctr, Univ Ala, 50-52 & 53-55; from asst prof to prof, 55-76, EMER PROF CHEM, BIRMINGHAM-SOUTHERN COL, 76- *Concurrent Pos:* Adj prof biochem, Med Col, Univ Ala, Birmingham, 76-78. *Mem:* Am Chem Soc; Sigma Xi. *Res:* Protozoa growth and culture; enzymes, structure of and assays techniques; allosteric effects; fluorescence produced; circular dichroism. *Mailing Add:* Dept of Chem Birmingham-Southern Col Birmingham AL 35254

THOMS, RICHARD EDWIN, b Olympia, Wash, June 5, 35; m 67. PALEONTOLOGY. *Educ:* Univ Wash, Seattle, BS, 57, MS, 59; Univ Calif, PhD(paleont), 65. *Prof Exp:* Teaching asst peleont, Univ Calif, 60-64; asst prof, 64-70, assoc prof, 70-80, PROF GEOL, PORTLAND STATE UNIV, 80- *Mem:* Paleont Soc. *Res:* West coast marine Tertiary biostratigraphy; ichnology. *Mailing Add:* Dept of Earth Sci Portland State Univ Portland OR 97207

THOMSEN, HARRY LUDWIG, b Boise, Idaho, June 14, 11; m 35; c 3. GEOLOGY. *Educ:* Oberlin Col, AB, 32, MA, 34. *Prof Exp:* Seismic party chief, Shell Oil Co, Calif, 35-38, seismologist, 38-41, div geophysicist, Calif & Rocky Mt area, 41-48, dist geologist, Colo, 48-51, area geologist, Okla, 51-53; spec assignment, Bataafse Petrol Maatschappij NV, Holland, 53-54; div explor mgr, Shell Oil Co, Mont, 54-60, mgr explor econ, NY, 60-66, sr staff geologist, Shell Develop Co, Tex, 66-69, spec asst to vpres explor, Shell Oil Co, 69-70; geol consult, 70-74; geophysicist, US Geol Surv, 74-76; GEOL CONSULT, 76- *Mem:* Am Asn Petrol Geol; fel Geol Soc Am; Soc Explor Geophys. *Res:* Exploration for oil and gas; development and application of methods for evaluating petroleum exploration opportunities; estimation of undiscovered oil and gas resources. *Mailing Add:* 3097 S Steele St Denver CO 80210

THOMSEN, JOHN STEARNS, b Baltimore, Md, June 10, 21; m 52; c 4. ATOMIC PHYSICS. *Educ:* Johns Hopkins Univ, BE, 43, PhD(physics), 52. *Prof Exp:* Elec engr, Gen Elec Co, 43-45; asst prof physics, Univ Md, 50-51; res staff asst, Radiation Lab, Johns Hopkins Univ, 51-52, res scientist, 52-53, 54-55; asst prof, Stevens Inst Technol, 53-54; asst prof mech eng, 55-61, res scientist, 62-70, FEL BY COURTESY PHYSICS, JOHNS HOPKINS UNIV, 70- *Concurrent Pos:* Mem comt fundamental constants, Nat Res Coun, 61-72, chmn, 69-71. *Mem:* Fel Am Phys Soc; Am Asn Physics Teachers. *Res:* Thermodynamics; irreversible processes; nonlinear electrical circuits; heat conduction with temperature dependent properties; statistical evaluation of atomic constants; x-ray wave lengths and precision experiments. *Mailing Add:* Dept of Physics Johns Hopkins Univ Baltimore MD 21218

THOMSEN, MICHELLE FLUCKEY, b Burlington, Colo, June 25, 50; m 73; c 1. SPACE PLASMA PHYSICS. *Educ:* Colo Col, BA, 71; Univ Iowa, MS, 74, PhD(physics), 77. *Prof Exp:* Res assoc, Univ Iowa, 77-80; res fel, Max Planck Inst Aeronomy, 80-81; STAFF SCIENTIST, LOS ALAMOS NAT LAB, 81- *Mem:* Am Geophys Union. *Res:* Physics of the magnetospheres of Earth, Jupiter and Saturn, particularly trapped energetic charged particles; kinetic instabilities and wave-particle interactions in space plasmas. *Mailing Add:* ESS-8 Mail Stop D438 Los Alamos Nat Lab Los Alamos NM 87545

THOMSEN, WARREN JESSEN, b Iowa, Mar 5, 22; m 43; c 3. MATHEMATICS. *Educ:* Iowa State Col, BA, 42; Univ Iowa, MS, 47, PhD(math), 52. *Prof Exp:* Instr math, Wis State Col, Whitewater, 52-53; res mathematician, Appl Physics Lab, Johns Hopkins Univ, 53-56; assoc prof math, Western Ill Univ, 56-57; prof & head dept, Mankato State Col, 57-65; head dept, 65-73, PROF MATH, MOORHEAD STATE COL, 65- *Mem:* Nat Coun Teachers Math; Math Asn Am. *Res:* Meteors; resistance of air to meteorites. *Mailing Add:* Dept of Math Moorhead State Col Moorhead MN 56560

THOMSON, ALAN, b Passaic, NJ, July 1, 28; m 53; c 6. GEOLOGY. *Educ:* WVa Univ, BS, 52, MS, 54; Rutgers Univ, PhD(geol), 57. *Prof Exp:* Asst geol, WVa Univ, 52-54; petrogr, Shell Oil Co, 57-65, sr geologist, 65, res geologist, 65-67, res assoc, 67-72, staff res geologist, 72-73, staff geologist, 73-78, SR STAFF GEOLOGIST, SHELL OIL CO, 78- *Concurrent Pos:* Instr, Odessa Col, 58-62. *Mem:* Fel Geol Soc Am; Soc Econ Paleont & Mineral; Int Asn Sedimentol. *Res:* Petrology of sedimentary rocks; determination of depositional environments. *Mailing Add:* Shell Oil Co Box 60775 New Orleans LA 70160

THOMSON, ALAN JOHN, b Nov 4, 46; Brit & Can citizen; m 67; c 2. BIOLOGICAL SYSTEMS ANALYSIS, ECOLOGY. *Educ:* Glasgow Univ, BSc, 68; McMaster Univ, PhD(ecol), 72. *Prof Exp:* Res fel physiol ecol, Inst Animal Resource Ecol, Univ BC, 72-76; RES SCIENTIST BIOL SYST ANAL, PAC FOREST RES CTR, CAN FORESTRY SERV, 76- *Concurrent Pos:* Killam res scholar, Univ BC, 74-76. *Mem:* Can Entom Soc. *Res:* Insect feeding behaviour; computer simulation of forest pest and disease dynamics and impact; effects of topography and weather on ecological processes. *Mailing Add:* Pac Forest Res Ctr 506 W Burnside Rd Victoria BC V8Z 1M5 Can

THOMSON, ASHLEY EDWIN, b Regina, Sask, June 6, 21; m 47; c 7. MEDICINE, PHARMACOLOGY. *Educ:* Univ Sask, BA, 43; Univ Man, MD, 45, MSc, 48; FRCPS(C). *Prof Exp:* Dir renal unit, Health Sci Ctr, 67-77, PROF MED, PHARMACOL & THERAPEUT, UNIV MAN, 65- *Mem:* Can Soc Nephrology; Am Soc Nephrology; Int Soc Nephrology; Am Physiol Soc; Can Soc Clin Invest. *Res:* Hemodialysis and transplantation. *Mailing Add:* Dept of Med Univ Man Sch Med 700 William Ave Winnipeg MB R3E 0Z3 Can

THOMSON, DALE S, b Cleveland, Ohio, Feb 12, 34; m 56; c 3. DEVELOPMENTAL BIOLOGY. *Educ:* Cedarville Col, AB, 56; Ohio State Univ, MS, 62, PhD(zool), 65. *Prof Exp:* Teacher, Miami Christian Sch, 56-57; from asst prof to assoc prof biol, Cedarville Col, 57-67; assoc prof, 67-74, PROF BIOL, MALONE COL, 74-, CHMN DIV SCI & MATH, 69- *Mem:* Am Sci Affil. *Res:* Developmental biology, especially cellular ultrastructure with respect to gland development in the chick; immune response in mice. *Mailing Add:* 1144 Shelley St NE North Canton OH 44721

THOMSON, DAVID JAMES, b Victoria, BC, June 25, 44; m 76. UNDERWATER ACOUSTICS. *Educ:* Univ Victoria, BS, 66, PhD(geophys), 73. *Prof Exp:* Fel physics, Univ Victoria, BC, 72-73 & Univ Alta, 73-74; DEFENCE SCIENTIST, DEFENCE RES ESTAB PAC, 74- *Mem:* Can Asn Physicists. *Res:* Geomagnetism; modelling of electric currents induced in non-uniform conductors; underwater acoustics; numerical modelling of underwater sound propagation in horizontally stratified and range dependent environments. *Mailing Add:* DREP/DND Forces Mail Off Victoria BC V0S 1B0 Can

THOMSON, DENNIS WALTER, b New York, NY, Mar 14, 41; m 65. METEOROLOGY. *Educ:* Univ Wis-Madison, BS, 63, MS, 64, PhD(meteorol), 68. *Prof Exp:* Ger Acad Exchange Serv fel, Univ Hamburg, 68-69; vis asst prof meteorol, Univ Wis-Madison, 69-70; from asst prof to assoc prof, 70-78, PROF METEOROL, COL EARTH & MINERAL SCI, PA STATE UNIV, UNIVERSITY PARK, 78- *Concurrent Pos:* Consult various industs & govt; chmn res aviation adv panel, NCAR, 73-75. *Mem:* Am Meteorol Soc. *Res:* Physical meteorology; indirect atmospheric sounding; meteorological measurements and instrumentation systems; inadvertant weather modification. *Mailing Add:* Dept of Meteorol Pa State Univ 506 Walker Bldg University Park PA 16802

THOMSON, DONALD A, b Detroit, Mich, Apr 9, 32; m 57; c 4. MARINE ECOLOGY, ICHTHYOLOGY. *Educ:* Univ Mich, BS, 55, MS, 57; Univ Hawaii, PhD(zool), 63. *Prof Exp:* From asst prof to assoc prof zool, 63-77, PROF ECOL & EVOLUTIONARY BIOL, UNIV ARIZ, 77-, CUR FISHES, 66-, CHMN MARINE SCI PROG, ECOL & EVOLUTIONARY BIOL DEPT, 73- *Concurrent Pos:* Coordr, Ariz-Sonora Marine Sci Prog, 64-66; prin investr, Off Naval Res, 65-69; chief scientist, R/V Te Vega, Stanford Exped 16, 67; assoc investr, Off Saline Water, 68. *Mem:* Am Soc Naturalists; Am Soc Ichthyol & Herpet; Asn Syst Collections; Ecol Soc Am. *Res:* Community ecology, species diversity and stability of marine shore fishes in the Gulf of California. *Mailing Add:* Dept of Ecol & Evolutionary Biol Univ of Ariz Tucson AZ 85721

THOMSON, GEORGE WILLIS, b Seward, Ill, July 10, 21; m 45; c 3. FORESTRY. *Educ:* Iowa State Univ, BS, 43, MS, 47, PhD(silvicult, soils), 56. *Prof Exp:* Instr gen forestry, 47-52, asst prof forest mgt, 52-56, assoc prof, 56-60, actg head forestry dept, 67 & 75, PROF MENSURATION & PHOTOGRAM, IOWA STATE UNIV, 60-, CHMN DEPT, 75- *Mem:* Fel Soc Am Foresters; Soc Range Mgt; Am Soc Photogram. *Res:* Forest management employing aerial photogrammetry; forest regulation; range management; case studies in land management; remote sensing from LANDSAT-1 with emphasis on forest type delineation. *Mailing Add:* Dept of Forestry Iowa State Univ Ames IA 50011

THOMSON, GERALD EDMUND, b New York, NY, June 6, 32; m 58; c 2. INTERNAL MEDICINE, NEPHROLOGY. *Educ:* Queens Col, BS, 55; Howard Univ, MD, 59. *Prof Exp:* Clin dir dialysis unit, Kings County Hosp, State Univ NY Downstate Med Ctr, 65-67; assoc dir med, Coney Island Hosp, Brooklyn, 67-70; chief div nephrology, 70-71, DIR MED, HARLEM HOSP CTR, 71-; PROF, COLUMBIA UNIV, 72- *Concurrent Pos:* NY Heart Asn fel renal dis, State Univ NY Downstate Med Ctr, 65-65; mem med adv bd, NY Kidney Found, 71-; mem, Health Res Coun City of New York, 72-75; mem, Health Res Coun State of subsurface injection; oilwell hypertension info comt & mem educ adv comt, NIH, 73; mem bd dirs, NY Heart Asn, 73-; chmn comt high blood pressure, NY Heart Asn, 75- *Mem:* Am Soc Nephrology. *Res:* Hypertension. *Mailing Add:* Harlem Hosp Ctr 506 Lenox Ave New York NY 10037

THOMSON, GORDON MERLE, b Madison, Wis, May 3, 41; m 63; c 2. BIOSTATISTICS. *Educ:* Cornell Univ, BS, 63; Iowa State Univ, MS, 66, PhD(animal breeding statist), 68. *Prof Exp:* Assoc statist & comput sci, Iowa State Univ, 68-71; STATISTICIAN, RALSTON PURINA CO, 71-, MGR BIOL SERV, RES 900, 75- *Mem:* Am Statist Asn; Am Dairy Sci Asn; Am Soc Animal Sci; Sigma Xi. *Res:* Application of statistics to biological research data; conduct of biological experiments in the areas of texicology and efficacy of feed additives. *Mailing Add:* Res Serv Ralston Purina Co Checkerboard Sq Plaza St Louis MO 63188

THOMSON, JAMES ALEX L, b Vancouver, BC, Aug 4, 28. ENGINEERING PHYSICS. *Educ:* Univ BC, BASc, 52; Calif Inst Technol, PhD(eng sci), 58. *Prof Exp:* Sr staff scientist, Space Sci Lab, Gen Dynamics-Convair, 58-67; mem tech staff, Sci & Technol Div, Inst Defense Anal, 67-68; prof eng sci, Res Inst Eng Sci & co-dir, Wayne State Univ, 68-72; VPRES ENG PHYSICS, PHYS DYNAMICS, INC, 69- *Mem:* Am Phys Soc. *Res:* Fluid dynamics; ionospheric physics; radiative transfer; oceanography. *Mailing Add:* PO Box 10367 Oakland CA 94610

THOMSON, JAMES EMSLIE, b New York, NY, Mar 23, 30; m 51; c 3. FOOD TECHNOLOGY. *Educ:* Rutgers Univ, BS, 51, MS, 54. *Prof Exp:* Food Technologist Poultry Prod Technol, Beltsville, Md, 54-71, FOOD TECHNOLOGIST POULTRY PROD TECHNOL, RUSSEL RES CTR, AGR RES SERV, USDA, ATHENS, GA, 71- *Mem:* Poultry Sci Asn; Inst Food Technologists. *Res:* Microbiology and chemistry of poultry products; food quality maintenance and improvement; efficiency of transportation and handling of live poultry. *Mailing Add:* 160 Torrey Pine Pl Athens GA 30605

THOMSON, JEFFREY JOHN, plasma physics, deceased

THOMSON, JOHN FERGUSON, b Garrett, Ind, Apr 18, 20; m 43, 73; c 2. RADIATION BIOLOGY, PHARMACOLOGY. *Educ:* Univ Chicago, SB, 41, SM, 42, PhD(pharmacol), 47. *Prof Exp:* Res assoc anat, Univ Chicago, 43-45, from res assoc to asst prof pharmacol, 46-51, mem staff, Toxicity Lab, 43-51; assoc pharmacologist, Div Biol & Med Res, Argonne Nat Lab, 51-62, actg dir, 69-70 & 74-75, assoc dir, 70-74 & 75-79, sr biologist, Div Biol & Med Res, 62-82; RETIRED. *Concurrent Pos:* Adj prof, Northern Ill Univ, 71- & Univ Ill, Chicago Circle, 71-77. *Mem:* AAAS; Soc Exp Biol & Med; Sigma Xi; Am Inst Biol Sci; Radiation Res Soc. *Res:* Radiation biology; cytoenzymology; isotope toxicity. *Mailing Add:* Rte 1 Box 105-B Scales Mound IL 61075

THOMSON, JOHN OLIVER, b Cleveland, Ohio, Feb 2, 30; m 55; c 3. PHYSICS. *Educ:* Williams Col, AB, 51; Univ Ill, MS, 53, PhD, 56. *Prof Exp:* Fulbright grant, Univ Rome, 56-57 & Univ Padua, 57-58; from asst prof to assoc prof physics, 58-72, PROF PHYSICS, UNIV TENN, KNOXVILLE, 72- *Concurrent Pos:* Consult, Physics Div, Oak Ridge Nat Lab, 58-; assoc prof, Memphis State Univ, 66-68. *Mem:* Am Phys Soc. *Res:* Solid state and low temperature physics. *Mailing Add:* Dept of Physics & Astronomy Univ of Tenn Knoxville TN 37916

THOMSON, JOHN WALTER, b Scotland, July 9, 13; nat US; m 37; c 5. BOTANY. *Educ:* Columbia Univ, AB, 35; Univ Wis, MA, 37, PhD, 39. *Prof Exp:* Dir staff, Sch Nature League, Am Mus Natural Hist, 39-41; tutor biol, Brooklyn Col, 41; instr, Wis State Teachers Col, Superior, 42-44; from asst prof to assoc prof bot, 44-62, chmn dept bot & zool, Exten, 48-67, PROF BOT, UNIV WIS-MADISON, 62- *Concurrent Pos:* Exchange prof, Helsinki Univ, 65-66. *Mem:* Am Bryol & Lichenological Soc (vpres, Am Bryol Soc, 56-57, pres, 58-59); Am Soc Plant Taxon; Torrey Bot Club (secy, 40); Int Soc Plant Taxon; British Lichen Soc. *Res:* Lichens; taxonomy and ecology of North American lichens, especially Arctic lichens; monographs, Peltigera, Physcia, Cladonia, Baeomyces. *Mailing Add:* 156 Birge Hall Univ of Wis Dept of Bot Madison WI 53706

THOMSON, JUNIUS RICHARD, b Rutherfordton, NC, Feb 24, 27; m 48; c 2. BIOLOGY. *Educ:* Emory Univ, BS, 48, MS, 49. *Prof Exp:* Asst bacteriologist, Commun Dis Ctr, US Pub Health Serv, Ga, 49-50; instr biol, Univ Chattanooga, 50-51; asst scientist, Oak Ridge Nat Lab, 51-52; res biologist, Southern Res Inst, Ala, 52-64; sr biologist, Midwest Res Inst, Mo, 64-66; res biologist, R J Reynolds Tobacco Co, 66-68; prof assoc, Adv Ctr Toxicol, Nat Acad Sci, 68-69; dir, Sci Ctr Pinellas Co, Fla, 69-70; admin analyst, Div Med Servs, Tenn Valley Auth, 70-71; CONSULT TOXICOL & BIOMED SCI, 71- *Mem:* Fel AAAS; Am Soc Zool; Soc Prof Biol; Sigma Xi; Am Pub Health Asn. *Res:* Experimental therapeutics and toxicology; mechanism of action of antimetabolites and drug resistance phenomena; combination chemotherapy; nutritional deficiencies; literature analysis; biomedical instrumentation. *Mailing Add:* 1670 E Clifton Rd NE Atlanta GA 30307

THOMSON, KEITH PATRICK BOWMER, physics, see previous edition

THOMSON, KEITH STEWART, b Heanor, Eng, July 29, 38; m 63. ZOOLOGY, PALEONTOLOGY. *Educ:* Univ Birmingham, BSc, 60; Harvard Univ, AM, 61, PhD(biol), 63. *Prof Exp:* NATO sci fel & temporary lectr zool, Univ Col, Univ London, 63-65; asst prof biol, 65-70, assoc cur vert zool, Peabody Mus Natural Hist & assoc prof biol, 70-76, dir, 77-79, PROF BIOL & CUR VERT ZOOL, PEABODY MUS NATURAL HIST, YALE UNIV, 76-, DIR, SEARS FOUND MARINE RES & OCEANOG HIST, 77-, DEAN, GRAD SCH ARTS & SCI, 79- *Concurrent Pos:* Bd mem, Woods Hole Oceanog Inst, 81- *Mem:* Am Soc Zool; Soc Nautical Res; fel Linnean Soc London; fel Zool Soc London; Soc Vert Paleont. *Res:* Vertebrate biology, especially phylogeny; paleontology and functional biology of fishes; origin of adaptations and of major groups. *Mailing Add:* Peabody Mus of Natural Hist Yale Univ New Haven CT 06520

THOMSON, KENNETH CLAIR, b Gunnison, Utah, Mar 5, 40; m 61; c 4. ECONOMIC GEOLOGY, PETROGRAPHY. *Educ:* Univ Utah, BS, 63, PhD, 70. *Prof Exp:* Illustrator-geologist, Utah Geol Surv, 59-68; from asst prof to assoc prof geol, 68-78, PROF GEOL, SOUTHWEST MO STATE UNIV, 78- *Mem:* Nat Speleol Soc; Mineral Soc Am. *Res:* Geochemistry as applied to mineral prospecting; speleology; stratigraphy of Southwestern Missouri. *Mailing Add:* Dept of Geol Southwest Mo State Univ Springfield MO 65802

THOMSON, KER CLIVE, b Toronto, Ont, Mar 2, 28; US citizen; m 55; c 2. GEOPHYSICS, SEISMOLOGY. *Educ:* Univ BC, BA, 52; Colo Sch Mines, DSc(geophys), 65. *Prof Exp:* Seismologist, Seismograph Serv Corp, Okla, 52-54; seismologist, Standard Oil Co Calif, 54-55, seismic party chief, 55-58; instr physics, Colo Sch Mines, 58-61; res physicist, 61-65, br chief seismol, 65-75, DIR TERRESTRIAL SCI LAB, AIR FORCE CAMBRIDGE RES LABS, 75- *Concurrent Pos:* Lectr, Gordon Col, 66-69 & Boston Col, 72. *Mem:* Seismol Soc Am; Am Geophys Union; Soc Explor Geophys; Europ Asn Explor Geophys; Am Sci Affil. *Res:* Earthquake focal mechanism; theoretical seismology; model seismology; wave propagation in absorptive media; seismic radiation in tectonically stressed media; nuclear test detection; structural vibration; terrestrial gravity. *Mailing Add:* Air Force Cambridge Res Labs LW Hanscom Field Bedford MA 01731

THOMSON, MICHAEL GEORGE ROBERT, b Portsmouth, Eng, Mar 7, 41; m 74; c 2. ELECTRON-OPTICS. *Educ:* Univ Cambridge, BA, 62, PhD(physics), 67. *Prof Exp:* Res assoc physics, Univ Chicago, 67-70; mem res staff physics, Res Lab Electronics, Mass Inst Technol, 70-73; MEM TECH STAFF, BELL LABS, 74- *Mem:* Electron Micros Soc Am; Am Phys Soc. *Res:* Electron optics for electron beam lithography; theory of image formation in the conventional and the scanning transmission electron microscopes; aberration theory for quadrupole and other unconventional electron lenses. *Mailing Add:* Bell Labs Murray Hill NJ 07974

THOMSON, QUENTIN ROBERT, b Lake Charles, La, Nov 14, 18; m 42; c 8. ENGINEERING. *Educ:* Ga Inst Technol, BS, 40; Univ Ariz, MS, 53; Calif Western Univ, PhD(eng econ), 75. *Prof Exp:* Exp test engr, Pratt & Whitney Aircraft Co, 40-41; engr & inspector, US Vet Admin, 51-53; from instr to assoc prof mech eng, Univ Ariz, 53-70, prof aerospace & mech eng, 70-81; CONSULT ENGR, 81- *Concurrent Pos:* Chief engr, Krueger Mfg Co, 63-67, consult, Krueger Div, Lear-Siegler, Inc, 67- & Shipley & Assoc. *Honors & Awards:* Ralph Teetor Award, Soc Automotive Engrs, 76; Am Soc Heating, Refrig & Air Conditioning Engrs Award, 76. *Mem:* Am Soc Mech Engrs; Am Soc Heating, Refrig & Air Conditioning Engrs; Am Mgt Asn; Soc Automotive Engrs. *Res:* Performance of gasoline as related to octane and distillation in automobiles. *Mailing Add:* 4730 Camino Luz Tucson AZ 85718

THOMSON, REGINALD GEORGE, veterinary pathology, see previous edition

THOMSON, RICHARD EDWARD, b Comox, BC, Apr 14, 44. PHYSICAL OCEANOGRAPHY. *Educ:* Univ BC, BS, 67, PhD(physics & oceanog), 71. *Prof Exp:* RES SCIENTIST, INST OCEAN SCI, ENVIRON CAN, 71- *Concurrent Pos:* Vis scientist, Monash Univ, Australia, 74; vis researcher, Australia, 82. *Mem:* Can Meteorol & Oceanog Soc; Am Geophys Union. *Res:* Wave propagation in random media; energetics of planetary waves and internal gravity waves; vorticity mixing and redistribution in the ocean; baroclinic tides and inertial currents; generation and propagation of shelf waves; long-term sea level fluctuations; vortex streets in the atmosphere; rectilinear leads in arctic ice. *Mailing Add:* Inst of Ocean Sci 9860 W Saanich Rd Sidney BC V8L 4B2 Can

THOMSON, RICHARD N, b Salt Lake City, Utah, Oct 11, 24; m 47; c 3. CHEMICAL ENGINEERING. *Educ:* Univ Denver, BSChE, 49, MS, 52. *Prof Exp:* Chem engr, US Bur Reclamation, 49-51; res engr, Denver Res Inst, Colo, 51-52 & E I du Pont de Nemours & Co, Inc, 52-61; res engr, 61-63, sr engr, 63-65, mgr cigaret develop, 65-69, asst dir develop, 69-72, dir develop, 72-75, dir tech serv, 75-80, DIR LAB ADMIN, RES & DEVELOP DEPT, PHILIP MORRIS, USA, 80- *Mem:* Indust Res Inst; Am Mgt Asn; Soc Res Admin. *Res:* Textile fibers research and development; tobacco processing; consumer product development; filter design and technology; research and development management. *Mailing Add:* Res & Develop Dept Philip Morris USA PO Box 26583 Richmond VA 23261

THOMSON, ROBB M(ILTON), b El Paso, Tex, Feb 4, 25; m 48; c 4. MATERIALS SCIENCE, SOLID STATE PHYSICS. *Educ:* Univ Chicago, MS, 50; Syracuse Univ, PhD(physics), 53. *Prof Exp:* Res assoc physics, Univ Ill, Urbana, 53-56, from asst prof to assoc prof metall, 56-60, prof physics & metall, 60-68; prof mat sci & chmn dept, State Univ NY Stony Brook, 68-71; SR RES SCIENTIST, NAT BUR STANDARDS, 71- *Concurrent Pos:* Dir mat sci, Adv Res Projs Agency, US Dept Defense, 65-68. *Mem:* Am Phys Soc; Am Soc Metals; Am Inst Mining, Metall & Petrol Engrs. *Res:* Theory of imperfections in solids; mechanical properties of solids. *Mailing Add:* Ctr Mat Sci Nat Bur of Standards Washington DC 20234

THOMSON, STANLEY, b Toronto, Ont, Dec 23, 23; m 46; c 5. SOIL MECHANICS, ENGINEERING. *Educ:* Univ Toronto, BASc, 50; Univ Alta, MSc, 55, PhD(soil mech, found), 63, BSc, 71. *Prof Exp:* From asst prof to assoc prof, 61-68, PROF CIVIL ENG, UNIV ALTA, 68- *Concurrent Pos:* Nat Res Coun Can oper res grants, 65-72. *Mem:* Am Soc Civil Engrs; Eng Inst Can; Can Geotech Soc; Can Soc Civil Engrs; Asn Eng Geologists. *Res:* Foundation engineering; slope stability in highly over-consolidated soils; influence of geology in soil mechanics; arctic engineering. *Mailing Add:* Dept Civil Eng Univ Alta Edmonton AB T6G 2G7 Can

THOMSON, TOM RADFORD, b Hachiman, Japan, Nov 7, 18; nat US; m 46; c 5. PHYSICAL ORGANIC CHEMISTRY. *Educ:* Univ Calif, BS, 39; Kans State Univ, MS, 40, PhD(chem), 45. *Prof Exp:* Asst chem, Kans State Univ, 39-40, instr, 42, chemist, 42-47; plant chemist, Cascade Frozen Foods, Wash, 41; from assoc prof to prof chem, Adams State Col, 47-61, head dept, 47-61; assoc prof, 61-67, dir dept, 78-81, prof, 67-81, EMER PROF, ARIZ STATE UNIV, 81- *Concurrent Pos:* Sigma Xi res grant, 54; res assoc, Univ Calif, 54; vis scholar, Utah, 59; Res Corp grant, 59-60; resident author, Addison-Wesley Publ Co, Calif, 67-68. *Mem:* Am Chem Soc. *Res:* Carbohydrates; starch chemistry; chemical education; relationship of structure to physical properties. *Mailing Add:* 4820 N Granite Reef Scottsdale AZ 85251

THOMSON, WILLIAM ALEXANDER BROWN, b London, Eng, Dec 21, 28; m 56; c 4. BIOCHEMISTRY, ANALYTICAL CHEMISTRY. *Educ:* St Andrews Univ, BSc, 51, dipl ed, 52; Univ Wis, MS, 58, PhD(biochem), 61. *Prof Exp:* Chemist, Can Packers Ltd, 53-54; from asst scientist to assoc scientist, Fisheries Res Bd Can, 54-63; sr chemist, Am Potato Co, Idaho, 63-64; asst prof food sci, NC State Univ, 64-66; sr chemist, Marine Colloids, Inc, Maine, 66-68, mgr tech opers, 68-70; sect head, 70-76, DIR, PROD RES & DEVELOP DEPT, ROSS LABS, 76- *Mem:* Am Chem Soc; Brit Biochem Soc; Royal Soc Chem. *Res:* Chemistry of polysaccharides from marine algae; biochemistry of fishery products; fluid nutritional products for pediatric and clinical use; dietary products for inborn errors of metabolism. *Mailing Add:* Prod Develop Dept Ross Labs 625 Cleveland Ave Columbus OH 43216

THOMSON, WILLIAM JOSEPH, b New York, NY, May 15, 39; m 64; c 4. CHEMICAL ENGINEERING. *Educ:* Pratt Inst, BChE, 60; Stanford Univ, MS, 62; Univ Idaho, PhD(chem eng), 69. *Prof Exp:* Asst scientist, Avco Res & Advan Develop Div, 61-62; assoc prof, 69-75, PROF CHEM ENG, UNIV IDAHO, 75- *Mem:* Am Inst Chem Engrs. *Res:* Catalytic kinetics; chemical reactor development; fluidization. *Mailing Add:* Dept of Chem Eng Univ of Idaho Moscow ID 83843

THOMSON, WILLIAM TYRRELL, b Kyoto, Japan, Mar 24, 09; US citizen; m 41; c 3. ENGINEERING. *Educ:* Univ Calif, BS, 33, MS, 34, PhD(elec eng), 38. *Prof Exp:* Asst math & physics, Univ Calif, 34-35; instr mech, Kans State Col, 37-41; res engr, Boeing Airplane Co, Wash, 41; asst prof mech, Cornell Univ, 41-44; head of vibration & flutter, Ryan Aeronaut Co, Calif, 44-46; from assoc prof to prof mech, Univ Wis, 46-51; prof eng, Univ Calif, Los Angeles, 51-66; prof mech eng & chmn dept, 66-76, EMER PROF MECH ENG, UNIV CALIF, SANTA BARBARA, 76- *Concurrent Pos:* Consult, Space Technol Labs, 55-; Fulbright res prof, Kyoto Univ, 57-58; Guggenheim fel, Ger, 61-62. *Mem:* Fel Am Soc Mech Engrs; assoc fel Am Inst Aeronaut & Astronaut. *Res:* Applied mathematics; vibrations; ultrasonic transmission and propagation; dynamics. *Mailing Add:* Dept of Mech Eng Univ of Calif Col of Eng Santa Barbara CA 93106

THOMSON, WILLIAM WALTER, b Chico, Calif, Oct 11, 30; c 2. BOTANY, CYTOLOGY. *Educ:* Sacramento State Col, BA, 53, MA, 60; Univ Calif, Davis, PhD(bot), 63. *Prof Exp:* Asst res botanist, Air Pollution Res Ctr, 63-64, from asst prof to assoc prof, 64-74, PROF BIOL, UNIV CALIF, RIVERSIDE, 74- *Mem:* AAAS; Bot Soc Am; Electron Micros Soc Am. *Res:* Ultrastructure of chloroplasts and plant membranes as related to development, physiology and stress conditions. *Mailing Add:* Dept of Bot & Plant Sci Univ of Calif Riverside CA 92502

THON, J GEORGE, b Lwow, Austria, Dec 6, 08; nat US; m 49; c 1. CIVIL & STRUCTURAL ENGINEERING. *Educ:* Univ Lwow, BS, 32; Univ London, DIC, 39, MS, 41. *Prof Exp:* Design engr, Sir William Halcrow & Partners, London, 41-48; hydraulic engr, Pioneer Serv & Eng Co, Chicago, 49-51; chief civil engr, Bechtel Corp, San Francisco, 51-58, div mgr eng, 58-74, exec consult, 74-76; CONSULT ENG, 77- *Concurrent Pos:* Vpres, Overseas Bechtel Inc, San Francisco, 58-74; consult, NSF & Nat Rec Coun; mem, US Comn Large Dams. *Honors & Awards:* Thomas Fitch Rowland Prize, Am Soc Civil Engrs, Rickey Medal, 71; Tercer Lugar Prize, Pan-Am Cong Engrs, 64. *Mem:* Nat Acad Eng; fel Am Soc Civil Engrs. *Mailing Add:* 465 Barbara Way Hillsborough CA 94010

THONNARD, NORBERT, b Berlin, Ger, Jan 22, 43; US citizen; m 64; c 4. ASTROPHYSICS, ATOMIC PHYSICS. *Educ:* Fla State Univ, BA, 64; Univ Ky, MS, 69, PhD(physics), 71. *Prof Exp:* Physicist, US Army Engr Res & Develop Labs, 64-66; consult astrophys, Battelle Pac Northwest Labs, Battelle Mem Inst, 72; fel, 70-72, STAFF MEM, DEPT TERRESTRIAL MAGNETISM, CARNEGIE INST, 72- *Mem:* Am Phys Soc; Am Astron Soc; AAAS; Int Astron Union. *Res:* Studies of systematic properties of galaxies from 21-om and optical observations; development of instrumentation for radio and optical astronomy; studies of atomic effects from interaction of charged particles with matter; observational cosmology. *Mailing Add:* Carnegie Inst 5241 Broad Branch Rd NW Washington DC 20015

THOR, DANIEL EINAR, b Davenport, Iowa, Sept 4, 38; m 71; c 1. IMMUNOLOGY, MICROBIOLOGY. *Educ:* Univ Ill Med Ctr, MD, 63, PhD(immunol, microbiol), 68. *Prof Exp:* Technologist, Blood Bank, Presby-St Luke's Hosp, Chicago, 60-63, intern surg, 63-64, resident & instr, 64-65; res investr immunol, NIH, 68-71; assoc prof immunol, microbiol & path, 71-77, PROF MICROBIOL & PATH, UNIV TEX HEALTH SCI CTR SAN ANTONIO, 77- *Concurrent Pos:* Asst prof, Univ Ill Med Ctr & lectr & asst prof, Postgrad Prog, NIH, 68-71; reviewer, Depts Med & Surg, Vet Admin Merit Rev Bd in Immunol, 72-; mem comt immunodiag, Nat Cancer Inst. *Honors & Awards:* Borden Award, Univ Ill Med Ctr, 63. *Mem:* AAAS; Fedn Am Socs Exp Biol; Am Asn Immunologists; Am Soc Microbiol; Reticuloendothelial Soc. *Res:* Cellular immunology and delayed type hypersensitivity; mechanisms of chemical mediator production, especially migration inhibition factor; chemical carcinogenesis and tumor immunity; RNA mechanisms of immunity; immune reconstruction with transfer factor. *Mailing Add:* Dept of Microbiol Univ of Tex Health Sci Ctr San Antonio TX 78284

THOR, EYVIND, b Oslo, Norway, Nov 24, 28; US citizen; m 56; c 3. FOREST GENETICS, SILVICULTURE. *Educ:* Univ Wash, Seattle, BS, 54, MS, 56; NC State Univ, PhD(forestry), 61. *Prof Exp:* Asst prof forestry res, 59-65, assoc prof forestry, 65-71, PROF FORESTRY, UNIV TENN, 71- *Concurrent Pos:* Elwood L Demmon res award, 61; US Forest Serv res grant, 66-68; grant, Inland Container Corp, 75-76. *Mem:* Soc Am Foresters. *Res:* Population genetics; breeding of trees for timber production (pines and hardwoods), Christmas trees (pine and spruce) and disease resistance (American chestnut). *Mailing Add:* Forestry Dept Univ of Tenn Knoxville TN 37916

THORBECKE, GEERTRUIDA JEANETTE, b Neth, Aug 2, 29; m 57; c 3. IMMUNOLOGY, EXPERIMENTAL PATHOLOGY. *Educ:* State Univ Groningen, MD, 50. *Prof Exp:* Asst histol, State Univ Groningen, 48-54; asst path, State Univ Leiden, 56-57; from res assoc to assoc prof, 57-70, PROF PATH, SCH MED, NY UNIV, 70- *Concurrent Pos:* Foreign Opers Mission to Neth scholar, Lobund Inst, Ind, 54-56; USPHS res grants, 59-, USPHS res career develop award, 61-71; career scientist award, Health Res Coun, City of New York, 71-72; corresp mem, Royal Dutch Acad Sci, 80. *Mem:* Am Soc Exp Path; Soc Exp Biol & Med; fel NY Acad Sci; Reticuloendothelial Soc; Brit Soc Immunol. *Res:* Antibody formation; serum proteins; lymphoid tissues; immunological tolerance; tumor immunity. *Mailing Add:* Dept of Path NY Univ Sch of Med New York NY 10016

THORBJORNSEN, ARTHUR ROBERT, b Winter, Wis, Sept 27, 36; m 62; c 2. ELECTRICAL ENGINEERING. *Educ:* Univ Wis-Madison, BSc, 62; Univ Ala, Huntsville, MSc, 68; Univ Fla, PhD(elec eng), 72. *Prof Exp:* Assoc engr elec eng, Boeing Co, Wash, 62-64, assoc res engr, Ala, 64-67; engr, Northrop Corp, 67-68; grad asst, Univ Fla, 68-72; asst prof, 72-77, ASSOC PROF ELEC ENG, UNIV TOLEDO, 77- *Concurrent Pos:* Prin investr res grant, Univ Toledo, 76 & 81; NSF grants, 74-76, 76 & 76-79. *Honors & Awards:* New Technol Award, Marshall Space Flight Ctr, NASA, 67. *Mem:* Inst of Elec & Electronics Engrs; Int Soc Hybrid Microelectronics; Sigma Xi. *Res:* Computer-aided design of electronic circuits; integrated circuit design and device modeling; electrical circuit theory. *Mailing Add:* Dept of Elec Eng Univ of Toledo Toledo OH 43606

THORESEN, ASA CLIFFORD, b Blenheim, NZ, Sept 9, 30; nat US; m 52; c 2. ORNITHOLOGY. *Educ:* Emmanuel Missionary Col, BA, 54; Walla Walla Col, MA, 58; Ore State Col, PhD, 60. *Prof Exp:* Vis prof marine inverts, Biol Sta, Walla Walla Col, 60, 70; from asst prof to assoc prof, 60-67, PROF BIOL & CHMN DEPT, ANDREWS UNIV, 67- *Concurrent Pos:* Leader biol expeds Peru, 64-65, 68 & SPac & Australia, 72; NSF grant, NZ, 66-67. *Mem:* AAAS; Cooper Ornith Soc; Am Ornith Union. *Res:* Life history and behaviorial studies of oceanic birds, particularly of the family Alcidae; ultrastructural studies of avian tissues. *Mailing Add:* Dept of Biol Andrews Univ Berrien Springs MI 49104

THORHAUG, ANITRA L, b Chicago, Ill, June 1, 40. BIOPHYSICS, MARINE BOTANY. *Educ:* Univ Miami, BS, 63, MS, 65, PhD(marine sci), 69. *Prof Exp:* Environ Sci Serv Admin assoc biophys, Atlantic Labs, Miami, Fla, 68-69; res scientist, Algology Div Fish & Appl Estuarine Ecol, 69-71, res scientist microbiol, Sch Med, Univ Miami, 71-77; PROF BIOL, FLA INT UNIV, 77- *Concurrent Pos:* Fed Water Qual Admin grant, Univ Miami, 69-70, NSF inst grant, 70-71, Nat Oceanic & Atmospheric sea grant, 70-78 & NSF grant biophysics, 70-71, AEC grant, 70; Dept Energy grant, 71-; fel, Weizmann Inst Sci, 71-; vis scientist, Donner Lab, Univ Calif, Berkeley, 71; consult various orgns & govt, 69-; mem, XII Int Bot Cong, Leningrad, 75, nat adv panel, Energy Res & Develop Admin, 77, 1st Int Symp Trop Estuarine Pollution, Djakarta, 76, environ adv panel, Ocean Thermal Energy Conversion, Energy Res & Develop Admin, 77-78, conserv comt, Am Bot Soc, 77-78; prog mgr environ studies, Nat Solar Energy Consortium, Solar Energy Res Inst, 76-77; chmn res counr comt, Biscayne Bay, Univ Miami, 75-76, symp seagrasses, 2nd Int Ecol Cong, Jerusalem, 78, ed, Thalassia. *Honors & Awards:* Diamond Award, Am Bot Soc, 75. *Mem:* AAAS; Bot Soc Am; Phycol Soc Am; Am Soc Ecol; Brit Phycol Soc. *Res:* Membrane transport biophysics; membrane transport and physiology of giant algal cells; near-shore macro-plant ecology; physiology of tropical macro-flora-temperature, salinity, light, sediment. *Mailing Add:* Dept of Biol 600 Grapetree Dr Miami FL 33149

THORINGTON, RICHARD WAINWRIGHT, JR, b Philadelphia, Pa, Dec 24, 37; m 67; c 1. BIOLOGY. *Educ:* Princeton Univ, BA, 59; Harvard Univ, MA, 63, PhD(biol), 64. *Prof Exp:* Primatologist, New Eng Regional Primate Res Ctr, 64-69, assoc mammal, Mus Comp Zool, 64-69; CUR PRIMATES, BIOL PROG, SMITHSONIAN INST, 69- *Mem:* AAAS; Am Soc Mammal; Soc Study Evolution; Int Primatol Soc. *Res:* Form and function of mammals; thermoregulation and thermal effects on development; primate ecology and taxonomy. *Mailing Add:* Primate Res Prog Smithsonian Inst Washington DC 20560

THORLACIUS, SIGURBERG ORMAR, ruminant nutrition, see previous edition

THORLAND, RODNEY HAROLD, b Lake Mills, Iowa, Feb 16, 41. SOLID STATE PHYSICS. *Educ:* Luther Col, BA, 64; Emory Univ, MSc, 69, PhD(physics), 71. *Prof Exp:* Vol, US Peace Corps, 64-67; asst prof physics, Kennesaw Jr Col, 71-72; res assoc physics, Emory Univ, 72-73; asst prof, 73-77, PROF PHYSICS, VOL STATE COMMUNITY COL, 77- *Mem:* AAAS; Am Phys Soc; Am Asn Physics Teachers; assoc Sigma Xi. *Res:* Nuclear magnetic resonance, electron paramagnetic resonance and far infrared spectroscopy. *Mailing Add:* Vol State Community Col Nashville Pike Gallatin TN 37066

THORMAN, CHARLES HADLEY, b Albany, Calif, June 14, 36; m 57; c 2. GEOLOGY. *Educ:* Univ Redlands, BS, 58; Univ Wash, MS, 60, PhD(geol), 62. *Prof Exp:* Geologist, Humble Oil & Ref Co, 62-65 & Olympic Col, Wash, 65-68; vis asst prof geol, Univ Ore, 68-71; GEOLOGIST, US GEOL SURV, 71- *Mem:* Am Asn Petrol Geol; Geol Soc Am. *Res:* Tectonics of the eastern basin and range; structure of Liberia; tectonics of southwest Arizona and southeast New Mexico. *Mailing Add:* US Geol Surv Fed Ctr Denver CO 80225

THORMAR, HALLDOR, b Iceland, Mar 9, 29; m 62; c 3. VIROLOGY. *Educ:* Copenhagen Univ, PhD(cell physiol), 56, DrPhil(virol), 66. *Prof Exp:* Res scientist, State Serum Inst, Copenhagen, Denmark, 60-62; from res scientist to assoc res scientist, Inst Exp Path, Keldur, Iceland, 62-67; CHIEF RES SCIENTIST VIROL, INST RES MENT RETARDATION, 67- *Concurrent Pos:* Investr virol, Sci Res Inst, Caracas, Venezuela, 65-66. *Mem:* Am Soc Microbiol. *Res:* Cell physiology; effect of temperature and temperature changes on cell growth and division; slow virus infections, particularly visna in sheep; isolation and study of visna virus and comparison of visna virus to other viruses; pathogenesis of slow virus infections. *Mailing Add:* Inst for Res in Ment Retardation 1050 Forest Hill Rd Staten Island NY 10314

THORN, CHARLES BEHAN, III, b Washington, Ind, Aug 14, 46; m 79; c 1. THEORETICAL PHYSICS. *Educ:* Mass Inst Technol, BS, 68; Univ Calif, Berkeley, MA, 69, PhD(particle theory), 71. *Prof Exp:* Res assoc, Europ Orgn Nuclear Res, NSF, 72; res assoc physics, Mass Inst Technol, 73, asst prof, 73-78, assoc prof, 78-80; PROF PHYSICS, UNIV FLA, 80- *Concurrent Pos:* Alfred P Sloan fel, 74; vis, Dept Appl Math & Theory Physics, Cambridge Univ, 76. *Mem:* Am Phys Soc. *Res:* Theory of elementary particles; theory of strongly interacting particles. *Mailing Add:* 215 Williamson Hall Univ Fla Gainesville FL 32611

THORN, GEORGE DENIS, b London, Eng, Feb 16, 21; m 44; c 3. AGRICULTURAL CHEMISTRY. *Educ:* Univ Alta, BSc, 43; Queen's Univ, Ont, MA, 44; McGill Univ, PhD(chem), 47. *Prof Exp:* Asst prof org chem & biochem, Mt Allison Univ, 47-51; CHEMIST, PESTICIDE RES INST, CAN DEPT AGR, 51- *Concurrent Pos:* Hon lectr, Univ Western Ont, 58. *Mem:* Am Phytopath Soc; fel Chem Inst Can. *Res:* Heterocyclic compounds; chemistry and fungicidal action of dithiocarbamates; relationship of chemical structure to biological activity; chemistry, mode of action and metabolism of systemic fungicides. *Mailing Add:* 1369 Erindale Circle London ON N5X 1V8 Can

THORN, RICHARD MARK, b New Castle, Pa, Mar 8, 47; m 69. IMMUNOBIOLOGY, VIRAL IMMUNOLOGY. *Educ:* Univ Calif, San Diego, BA, 69; Univ Pa, PhD(molecular biol), 74. *Prof Exp:* Fel immunol, Sch Med, Johns Hopkins Univ, 74-76; scientist II, Frederick Cancer Res Ctr, 76-79; ASST PROF, VET SCH, UNIV PA, 79- *Concurrent Pos:* Prin investr, 79- *Mem:* Am Asn Immunologists; NY Acad Sci. *Res:* Mechanism of target cell destruction by cytolytic T cells; mechanism of cytolytic T cell induction; role of immunity in the control of infectious disease and cancer. *Mailing Add:* Leukemia Studies Unit 382 West Street Rd Kennett Square PA 19348

THORN, ROBERT NICOL, b Coeur d'Alene, Idaho, Aug 31, 24; m 62; c 4. PHYSICS. *Educ:* Harvard Univ, PhD(physics), 53. *Prof Exp:* Div leader, 53-76, assoc dir, 76-79, actg dir, 79, DEP DIR, THEORET DESIGN DIV, LOS ALAMOS NAT LAB, 79- *Concurrent Pos:* Mem sci adv group, Space Systs Div, US Air Force, 62-63, sci adv bd, 62-, nuclear panel, 64-; mem sci adv group, Defense Nuclear Agency & Defense Intel Agency. *Honors & Awards:* E O Lawrence Award, Atomic Energy Comn, 67. *Mem:* AAAS; Am Phys Soc. *Res:* Classical theoretical physics; quantum and nuclear physics; weapons systems analysis and design. *Mailing Add:* 981 Barranca Rd Los Alamos NM 87544

THORNBER, JAMES PHILIP, b Hebden Bridge, Eng, Dec 22, 34; m 60; c 2. PLANT BIOCHEMISTRY. *Educ:* Cambridge Univ, BA, 58, MA, 61, PhD(biochem), 62. *Prof Exp:* Sci off plant biochem, Twyford Labs Ltd, Arthur Guinness, Son & Co, Ltd, 61-67; res assoc biol, Brookhaven Nat Lab, 67-69, asst scientist, 69-70; asst prof bot, 70-72, assoc prof biol, 72-75, PROF BIOL, UNIV CALIF, LOS ANGELES, 75- *Concurrent Pos:* NSF grant, Univ Calif, Los Angeles, 71-; Guggenheim Mem fel, 76-77; USDA grant, 78- *Mem:* Am Soc Biol Chem; Am Soc Photobiol; Am Soc Plant Physiol. *Res:* Photosynthesis; organization of chlorophyll in plants and bacteria; chlorophyll-protein complexes; photochemical reaction centers; membrane composition, structure and biogenesis. *Mailing Add:* Dept of Biol Univ of Calif Los Angeles CA 90024

THORNBER, KARVEL KUHN, b Portland, Ore, Apr 7, 41; m 67; c 2. SOLID STATE PHYSICS. *Educ:* Calif Inst Technol, BS, 63, MS, 64, PhD(elec eng), 66. *Prof Exp:* Res fel elec eng, Stanford Univ, 66-68; res fel physics, Univ Bristol, 68-69; MEM TECH STAFF, BELL LABS, 69- *Res:* Quantum mechanics and statistical mechanics of dissipation systems, transport properties and noise theory. *Mailing Add:* Bell Labs 600 Mountain Ave Murray Hill NJ 07974

THORNBERRY, HALBERT HOUSTON, b Corydon, Ky, Dec 28, 02; m 46; c 1. PLANT PATHOLOGY. *Educ:* Univ Ky, BS, 25, MS, 26; Univ Minn, PhD(plant path), 34. *Prof Exp:* Asst plant path, Univ Minn, 26-28 & Univ Ill, 28-31; fel, Rockefeller Inst Med Res, 31-35; jr plant pathologist, Citrus Exp Sta, Univ Calif, 35-36; asst pathologist, Univ Ky, 36-37; pathologist, Bur Plant Indust, US Dept Agr, 37-38; from asst prof to prof, 38-71, EMER PROF PLANT PATH, UNIV ILL, URBANA, 71-; CONSULT PLANT HEALTH & MGT, 72- *Concurrent Pos:* Res award, Soc Am Florists, 68. *Mem:* AAAS; Am Phytopath Soc; Am Soc Microbiol; Am Chem Soc. *Res:* Phytovirology; chemopathology; antibiotics; bacterial diseases. *Mailing Add:* 1602 S Hillcrest St PO Box 128 Urbana IL 61801

THORNBOROUGH, JOHN RANDLE, b Columbus, Ohio, Feb 2, 39. NEUROBIOLOGY, NEUROENDOCRINOLOGY. *Educ:* Ohio State Univ, BA, 60, MA, 61; NY Med Col, PhD(physiol), 72. *Prof Exp:* Instr biol, Denison Univ, 61-67; res assoc, 72-73, instr, 73-74, asst prof, 74-80, ADJ ASSOC PROF PHYSIOL, NY MED COL, 80-; ASSOC MED PROF PHYSIOL, CITY COL NY-SOPHIE DAVIS SCH BIOMED EDUC, 80-, DIR ACAD AFFAIRS, 80- *Concurrent Pos:* Adj prof physiol, Sarah Lawrence Col, 73-77. *Res:* Hypothalamic control of sodium and water metabolism. *Mailing Add:* Sophie Davis Sch Biomed Educ Rm J909 138th St & Convent Ave New York NY 10031

THORNBURG, DAVID DEVOE, b Chicago, Ill, Apr 25, 43; m 66; c 1. PHYSICAL METALLURGY. *Educ:* Northwestern Univ, BS, 67; Univ Ill, Urbana, MS, 69, PhD(metall), 71. *Prof Exp:* Mem res staff device physics, Xerox Palo Alto Res Ctr, 71-78, prin scientist & spec projs consult, 78-80; PRES, INNOVISION, 80- *Mem:* Inst Elec & Electronics Engrs; Am Phys Soc; Am Vacuum Soc; Am Inst Metall Engrs. *Res:* Advancing state of the art in two dimensional devices using circuit board technology; novel uses for conductive loaded or coated polymeric materials. *Mailing Add:* Innovision PO Box 1317 Los Altos CA 94022

THORNBURG, DONALD RICHARD, b Pittsburgh, Pa, Oct 16, 33; m 71; c 3. PHYSICAL METALLURGY, MAGNETISM. *Educ:* Rensselaer Polytech Inst, BMetE, 55; Carnegie Inst Technol, MS, 63; Carnegie-Mellon Univ, PhD(metall), 72. *Prof Exp:* Navigator, US Air Force, 55-57; sr engr magnetics, 58-73, FEL ENGR MAGNETICS, RES & DEVELOP CTR, WESTINGHOUSE ELEC CORP, 73- *Mem:* AAAS; Am Soc Metals; Am Inst Mining, Metall & Petrol Engrs; Sigma Xi. *Res:* Development of magnetic materials; calculation of texture development using crystal plasticity theory; methods for improving the properties of magnetic materials. *Mailing Add:* 387 Barclay Ave Pittsburgh PA 15221

THORNBURG, JOHN ELMER, b Syracuse, Ind, Apr 15, 42; m 70; c 2. CLINICAL PHARMACOLOGY, TOXICOLOGY. *Educ:* Purdue Univ, BS, 65, MS, 68, PhD(pharmacol), 70; Mich State Univ, DO, 76. *Prof Exp:* Fel pharmacol, 70-72, ASST PROF PHARMACOL, DEPT PHARMACOL, TOXI-FAMILY MEDICINECOL & FAMILY MED, MICH STATE UNIV, 77- *Mem:* Soc Neurosci; AAAS; Am Osteopathic Asn. *Res:* Perinatal toxicity of organophosphates; sympathetic nervous system and platelet alpha adrenergic receptors in hypertensive subjects. *Mailing Add:* Dept Pharmacol & Toxicol Mich State Univ East Lansing MI 48824

THORNBURGH, DALE A, b Tiffin, Ohio, Dec 1, 31; m 61; c 3. FOREST ECOLOGY. *Educ:* Univ Wash, BS, 59, PhD(forestry), 69; Univ Calif, Berkeley, MS, 62. *Prof Exp:* Lectr silviculture, Univ Wash, 63-64; from asst prof to assoc prof forest ecol, 64-74, chmn dept, 77-80, PROF FOREST ECOL, HUMBOLDT STATE UNIV, 74- *Mem:* Ecol Soc Am; Soc Am Foresters. *Res:* Carying capacity of subalpine meadows in wilderness areas; development of forest habitat types and successional models. *Mailing Add:* Dept of Forestry Humboldt State Univ Arcata CA 95521

THORNBURGH, GEORGE E(ARL), b Blair, Nebr, Apr 16, 23; m 43; c 4. MECHANICAL ENGINEERING. *Educ:* Univ Nebr, BS, 44; Iowa State Col, MS, 50. *Prof Exp:* Instr mech eng, Iowa State Col, 48-50; proj engr oil combustion, Lennox Furnace Co, 50-52; from asst prof to prof mech eng, 52-66, dir facilities planning, 66-67, dir planning & instnl res, 67-74, PROF MECH ENG, ORE STATE UNIV, 71- *Concurrent Pos:* Mech engr, US Bur Mines, Ore; engr, Bechtel Power Corp, 74-75. *Mem:* Am Soc Heating, Refrig & Air Conditioning Engrs; Am Soc Mech Engrs; Am Soc Eng Educ. *Res:* Heating and air conditioning engineering; energy. *Mailing Add:* Dept of Mech Eng Ore State Univ Corvallis OR 97331

THORNBURN, THOMAS H(AMPTON), b Urbana, Ill, June 29, 16; m 42; c 4. SOILS, ENGINEERING. *Educ:* Univ Ill, BS, 38; Mich State Col, PhD(soil sci), 41. *Prof Exp:* Res engr, State Hwy Dept, Mich, 41-42; res assoc civil eng, 45-48, from res asst prof to res prof, 48-57, prof civil eng, 57-75, EMER PROF, UNIV ILL, URBANA, 75- *Concurrent Pos:* Consult civil eng, 48- *Mem:* Am Soc Testing & Mat; Am Soc Civil Eng; Am Soc Photogram; Geol Soc Am; Nat Soc Prof Eng; Am Soc Eng Educ. *Res:* Construction of stabilized soil roads; highway and railroad subgrade stability; engineering properties of soils; preparation of soil maps; terrain analysis. *Mailing Add:* 1034 Tam O'Shanter Las Vegas NV 89109

THORNBURY, JOHN R, b Cleveland, Ohio, Mar 16, 29; m 55; c 2. RADIOLOGY. *Educ:* Miami Univ, AB, 50; Ohio State Univ, MD, 55. *Prof Exp:* From instr to asst prof radiol, Univ Colo, 62-63; asst prof, Univ Iowa, 63-66 & Univ Wash, 66-68; assoc prof, 68-71, PROF RADIOL, UNIV MICH, ANN ARBOR, 71- *Mem:* Asn Univ Radiologists; Radiol Soc NAm; Am Roentgen Ray Soc. *Res:* Urological radiology; application of decision theory and probability theory principles to improve radiologists diagnostic performance; applications of computer technology to diagnostic radiology; visual perception and information processing in diagnostic radiology. *Mailing Add:* Dept of Radiol E4132 Univ Hosp Univ of Mich Ann Arbor MI 48109

THORNDIKE, ALAN MOULTON, b Montrose, NY, June 27, 18; m 42; c 5. PHYSICS. *Educ:* Wesleyan Univ, BA, 39; Columbia Univ, AM, 40; Harvard Univ, PhD(chem physics), 47. *Prof Exp:* Asst physicist, Div War Res, Univ Calif, 41-42; res assoc, Div War Res, Columbia Univ, 42-43; field serv consult, Off Sci Res & Develop, 43-45; asst scientist, Brookhaven Nat Lab, 47-52, from assoc scientist to scientist, 52-58; vis prof, Johns Hopkins Univ, 58-59;

scientist, Brookhaven Nat Lab, 59-65, sr physicist, 65-70, assoc chmn physics dept, 70-73, sr physicist, 73-81; RETIRED. *Concurrent Pos:* Consult, Off Technol Assessment, 74-78. *Mem:* Am Phys Soc. *Res:* Primary cosmic radiation; meson physics; elementary particles; electronic data processing; high energy interactions; computer simulation. *Mailing Add:* Physics Dept Brookhaven Nat Lab Upton NY 11973

THORNDIKE, EDWARD HARMON, b Pasadena, Calif, Aug 2, 34; m 55; c 3. ELEMENTARY PARTICLE PHYSICS. *Educ:* Wesleyan Univ, AB, 56; Stanford Univ, MS, 57; Harvard Univ, PhD(physics), 60. *Prof Exp:* Res fel physics, Harvard Univ, 60-61; from asst prof to assoc prof, 61-72, PROF PHYSICS, UNIV ROCHESTER, 72- *Concurrent Pos:* NSF sr fel, Univ Geneva & Europ Orgn Nuclear Res, 70. *Mem:* Am Phys Soc. *Res:* Nucleon-nucleon interactions; few nucleon problems; electron-positron colliding beam phenomena; energy and environment; high energy photoproduction processes. *Mailing Add:* Dept of Physics Univ of Rochester Rochester NY 14627

THORNDIKE, EDWARD MOULTON, b New York, NY, Sept 25, 05; m 30; c 3. PHYSICS. *Educ:* Wesleyan Univ, BS, 26; Columbia Univ, MA, 27; Calif Inst Technol, PhD(physics), 30. *Prof Exp:* Fel physics, Calif Inst Technol, 30-31; instr, Polytech Inst Brooklyn, 31-38; from instr to asst prof, Queen's Col, NY, 38-43; assoc prof, Univ Southern Calif, 43-44; from asst prof to prof, 44-70, EMER PROF PHYSICS, QUEEN'S COL, NY, 70- *Concurrent Pos:* Physicist, Woods Hole Oceanog Inst, 42-43, consult, 44-45; consult, Columbia Univ, 44, 45-48, physicist, 45, res assoc, 50- *Mem:* AAAS. *Res:* Optics; oceanography. *Mailing Add:* Lamont-Doherty Geol Observ Palisades NY 10964

THORNE, BILLY JOE, b Chanute, Kans, Aug 19, 39; m 59; c 4. APPLIED MATHEMATICS. *Educ:* Phillips Unvi, AB, 59; Kans State Univ, MA, 61; Univ NMex, PhD(math), 68. *Prof Exp:* Staff mem, Sandia Nat Labs, 61-66; instr math, Smith Col, Northampton, Mass, 67-68; staff mem, Sandia Nat Labs, 68-74; div mgr, Civil Eng Res Facil, Univ NMex, 74-77; vpres, Civil Systs Inc, Subsid Sci Appl Inc, 77-80, pres, 80-81; staff mem, 81-82, DIV MGR, SANDIA NAT LABS, 82- *Concurrent Pos:* Asst vpres, Sci Appl Inc, 80-81. *Res:* The use of computational techniques for the solution of a wide range of physical and engineering problems, usually involving the numerical solution off non-linear systems of partial differential equations. *Mailing Add:* Sandia Nat Labs Div 5531 Box 5800 Albuquerque NM 87185

THORNE, CHARLES JOSEPH, b Pleasant Grove, Utah, May 28, 15; m 42; c 2. APPLIED MATHEMATICS. *Educ:* Brigham Young Univ, AB, 36; Iowa State Col, MS, 38, PhD(math physics), 41. *Prof Exp:* Asst math, Iowa State Col, 38-41; instr, Univ Mich, 41-43; asst prof, La State Univ, 43-44; develop engr, Curtiss-Wright Corp, 44-45; from asst prof to prof math, Univ Utah, 45-55; res scientist, Res Dept, US Naval Ord Test Sta, 55-60, sr res scientist & head math div, 60-61; supvry mathematician, Pac Missile Range, 61-65, sr opers res analyst, Naval Missile Ctr, 65-76, head, Assessment Div, 75-79, HEAD MGT SYSTS DIV, PAC MISSILE TEST CTR, 79- *Concurrent Pos:* Assoc prof, Univ Calif, Los Angeles, 48-49, lectr, 56-68; sr investr, US Navy Projs, 49-51; dir & prin investr, US Army Ord Projs, 51-55. *Mem:* Am Math Soc; Am Soc Mech Eng; Math Asn Am; Soc Indust & Appl Math. *Res:* Differential equations; boundary value problems; elasticity; analysis; operations research; numerical analysis. *Mailing Add:* 1447 Sunrise Ct Camarillo CA 93010

THORNE, CHARLES M(ORRIS), b Seattle, Wash, June 27, 21; m 47; c 2. ELECTRICAL ENGINEERING. *Educ:* Univ Wash, BS, 50. *Prof Exp:* Design engr, Boeing Airplane Co, 50; proj engr, 51-52, sr proof engr, 52-56, electronics div head, Weapons Qual Eng Ctr, 56-60, dir eng, 60-63, TECH DIR, WEAPONS QUAL ENG CTR, NAVAL UNDERSEA WARFARE ENG STA, 64- *Concurrent Pos:* Trustee, Oceanog Inst Wash. *Mem:* Inst Elec & Electronics Engrs; Am Soc Qual Control. *Res:* Testing and evaluation of underwater missiles; proximity fuzes, high energy batteries, pyrotechnics; environmental testing; non-destructive testing; metrology and functional testing. *Mailing Add:* Naval Undersea Warfare Eng Sta Weapons Qual Eng Ctr Keyport WA 98345

THORNE, CURTIS BLAINE, b Pine Grove, WVa, May 13, 21; m 59; c 1. MICROBIAL GENETICS. *Educ:* WVa Wesleyan Col, BS, 43; Univ Wis, MS, 44, PhD(biochem), 48. *Prof Exp:* Biochemist, US Army Biol Labs, 48-61; prof bact genetics, Ore State Univ, 61-63; biochemist, US Army Biol Labs, 63-66; PROF BACT GENETICS, UNIV MASS, AMHERST, 66- *Concurrent Pos:* Waksman hon lectr, 59. *Mem:* AAAS; Am Soc Microbiol; Am Soc Biol Chem; Brit Soc Gen Microbiol; Genetics Soc Am. *Res:* Bacterial genetics; transformation and transduction; genetics of Bacillus species. *Mailing Add:* 45 Western Lane Amherst MA 01002

THORNE, JAMES MEYERS, b Logan, Utah, June 3, 37; m 60; c 2. PHYSICAL CHEMISTRY. *Educ:* Utah State Univ, BS, 61; Univ Calif, Berkeley, PhD(chem), 66. *Prof Exp:* PROF CHEM, BRIGHAM YOUNG UNIV, 66- *Concurrent Pos:* Vis staff, Laser Div, Los Alamos Sci Lab, Univ Calif, 72- *Mem:* Am Chem Soc. *Res:* Applications of lasers to nuclear fusion, nonlinear optics; magneto and electrooptics. *Mailing Add:* 1119 E 2620 North Provo UT 84601

THORNE, JOHN CARL, b Ft Dodge, Iowa, Feb 24, 43; m 70; c 2. PLANT BREEDING, GENETICS. *Educ:* Augustana Col, Ill, BA, 65; Iowa State Univ, MS, 67, PhD(plant breeding), 69. *Prof Exp:* Res assoc soybean breeding, Iowa State Univ, 67-69; plant breeder, 69-79, SOYBEAN RES DIR, NORTHRUP, KING & CO, 79- *Mem:* Am Soc Agron; Am Soybean Asn. *Res:* Plant breeding and genetics related to soybean variety development. *Mailing Add:* Northrup King & Co PO Box 49 Washington IA 52353

THORNE, JOHN KANDELIN, b Detroit, Mich, May 7, 40. NONFERROUS METALLURGY. *Educ:* Cornell Univ, BMetE, 63, MBA, 64; Univ Mich, MS, 65, PhD(metall eng), 68. *Prof Exp:* Res assoc climax molybdenum, Amax Inc, 66-68; sr engr res & develop, Cleveland Refractory Metals, Chase Brass, 68-70; mgr prod develop, Wolverine Div, UOP Inc, 70-75, dir, Mat Sci Res Ctr, 75-76; VPRES SPEC PROD OPER, HOWMET TURBINE COMPONENTS CORP, 76- *Mem:* Am Soc Metals; Am Inst Mining, Metall & Petrol Engrs; Am Soc Testing & Mat. *Res:* Nonferrous physical metallurgy; reactive and refractory metals; nonferrous fabricating metallurgy; titanium electrowinning. *Mailing Add:* 801 Moulton Ave North Muskegon MI 49445

THORNE, KIP STEPHEN, b Logan, Utah, June 1, 40; div; c 2. ASTROPHYSICS, THEORETICAL PHYSICS. *Educ:* Calif Inst Technol, BS, 62; Princeton Univ, AM, 63, PhD(theoret physics), 65. *Hon Degrees:* DSc, Ill Col, 79; Dr, Moscow Univ, 81. *Prof Exp:* NSF vis fel physics, Princeton Univ, 65-66; Alfred P Sloan res fel, 66-70, assoc prof, 67-70, PROF THEORET PHYSICS, CALIF INST TECHNOL, 70-, WILLIAM R KENAN JR PROF, 81- *Concurrent Pos:* Lectr, Enrico Fermi Int Sch Physics, Varenna, Italy, 65, 68; Fulbright lectr, Sch Theoret Physics, Les Houches, France, 66; res fel physics, Calif Inst Technol, 66-67; Guggenheim fel, Inst Astrophys, Paris, France, 67-68; vis assoc prof, Univ Chicago, 68; vis prof, Moscow State Univ, 69, 75, 78 & 81; gov comt, Div of High Energy Astrophys, Am Astron Soc, 70-72; adj prof, Univ Utah, 71-; mem Int Comt Gen Relativity and Gravitation, 71-80; vis sr res assoc, Cornell Univ, 77; mem comt, US-USSR Coop in Physics, 78-79; mem adv bd, Inst Theoret Physics, Univ Calif, Santa Barbara, 78-80, mem, Space Sci Bd, 80- *Honors & Awards:* Sci Writing Award, Am Inst Physics-US Steel Corp, 69. *Mem:* fel AAAS; fel Am Acad Arts & Sci; fel Am Phys Soc; Sigma Xi; Nat Acad Sci. *Res:* Theoretical and relativistic astrophysics; quantum optics and quantum electronics; gravitation theory. *Mailing Add:* 130-33 Calif Inst of Technol Pasadena CA 91125

THORNE, MARLOWE DRIGGS, b Perry, Utah, Nov 4, 18; m 41; c 4. AGRONOMY. *Educ:* Utah State Agr Col, BS, 40; Iowa State Col, MS, 41; Cornell Univ, PhD, 48. *Prof Exp:* Soil physicist & head dept agron, Pineapple Res Inst, Univ Hawaii, 47-54; soil scientist & irrig work proj leader, Eastern Soil & Water Mgt Sect, Soil & Water Conserv Res Br, Agr Res Serv, US Dept Agr, 55-56; prof agron & head dept, Okla State Univ, 56-63; head dept, 63-70, PROF AGRON, UNIV ILL, URBANA, 63- *Concurrent Pos:* Water technol adv, GB Pant Univ, Pantnagar, India, 70-72. *Mem:* Soil Sci Soc Am; Am Soc Agron (pres, 77); Soil Conserv Soc Am. *Res:* Irrigation; mulching; tillage. *Mailing Add:* Dept of Agron Turner Hall Univ of Ill Urbana IL 61801

THORNE, MELVYN CHARLES, b San Francisco, Calif, Dec 27, 32; m 58; c 2. EPIDEMIOLOGY. *Educ:* Univ Calif, AB, 56; Harvard Univ, MD, 60; Johns Hopkins Univ, MPH, 68. *Prof Exp:* Epidemiologist, Field Epidemiol Res Sta, Nat Heart Inst, 61-63 & 65-66; Peace Corps physician, Morocco, 63-65; resident internal med, Mary Imogene Bassett Hosp, 66-67; rep, Pop Coun, Tunisia, 68-72; asst prof int health, 72-77, ASSOC PROF INT HEALTH, SCH HYG & PUB HEALTH, JOHNS HOPKINS UNIV, 77-, MEM STAFF HEALTH SERV ADMIN & POPULATION DYNAMICS, 78- *Concurrent Pos:* Tech adv, Urban Life-Pop Educ Inst, 73-76; health syst adv, Overseas Develop Coun Seminars, Priv Vol Orgns, 74-76; consult, Health Educ, Porter Novelli & Assocs. *Mem:* Am Pub Health Asn; Pop Asn Am. *Res:* Simple, effective methods to introduce health services into populations currently deprived of them, and to introduce population education into school systems with focus on using information in decisions. *Mailing Add:* Dept of Int Health Johns Hopkins Univ Baltimore MD 21205

THORNE, RICHARD EUGENE, b Aberdeen, Wash, Apr 12, 43; m 64; c 2. FISHERIES, HYDROACOUSTICS. *Educ:* Univ Wash, BS, 65, MS, 68, PhD(fisheries), 70. *Prof Exp:* Sr res assoc, 70-75, res assoc prof, 76-80, RES PROF FISHERIES, FISHERIES RES INST, UNIV WASH, 81- *Concurrent Pos:* Acoust expert, Food & Agr Orgn, UN, 71-; prog coordr, Div Marine Resources, Univ Wash, 73-, sr scientist, Appl Physics Lab, 78- *Mem:* Am Inst Fishery Res Biologists; Am Fisheries Soc. *Res:* Hydroacoustic techniques of fish detection and abundance estimation; ecology of fishes. *Mailing Add:* Fisheries Res Inst Univ of Wash Seattle WA 98195

THORNE, RICHARD MANSERGH, b Birmingham, Eng, July 25, 42; m 63; c 2. SPACE PHYSICS, PLASMA PHYSICS. *Educ:* Univ Birmingham, BSc, 63; Mass Inst Technol, PhD(physics), 68. *Prof Exp:* from asst prof to assoc prof meteorol, 68-75, PROF ATMOSPHERIC PHYSICS, UNIV CALIF, LOS ANGELES, 75- *Concurrent Pos:* NSF grants, 71-; mem nat comt, Int Union Radio Sci, 71-; consult, Jet Propulsion Lab, Calif Inst Technol. *Mem:* Am Geophys Union; Int Union Radio Sci. *Res:* Structure and stability of radiation belts; magnetosphere-ionosphere interactions; wave propagation in anistotropic media. *Mailing Add:* Dept of Atmospheric Sci Univ of Calif Los Angeles CA 90024

THORNE, ROBERT FOLGER, b Spring Lake, NJ, July 13, 20; m 47; c 1. SYSTEMATICS, BIOGEOGRAPHY. *Educ:* Dartmouth Col, AB, 41; Cornell Univ, MS, 42, PhD(bot), 49. *Prof Exp:* Asst bot, Cornell Univ, 45-46, instr, 48-49; from asst prof to prof, Univ Iowa, 49-62; PROF BOT, CLAREMONT GRAD SCH, 62-; CUR & TAXONOMIST, RANCHO SANTA ANA BOT GARDEN, 62- *Concurrent Pos:* Fulbright res scholar, Univ Queensland, 59-60; NSF sr fel, 60; chmn adv coun, Flora NAm Proj. *Mem:* Bot Soc Am; Am Soc Plant Taxon (secy, 57-58, pres, 68); Int Soc Plant Morphol; fel Linnean Soc London; fel Fr Soc Biogeog. *Res:* Phylogeny and geography of flowering plants; floristics; marine phanerogams and fresh-water aquatic plants. *Mailing Add:* Rancho Santa Ana Bot Garden 1500 N College Ave Claremont CA 91711

THORNER, JEREMY WILLIAM, b Quincy, Mass, Jan 18, 46. GENE REGULATION, DEVELOPMENTAL BIOLOGY. *Educ:* Harvard Col, BA, 67; Harvard Univ, PhD(biochem), 72. *Prof Exp:* Fel biochem, Sch Med, Stanford Univ, 72-74; asst prof, 74-80, ASSOC PROF MICROBIOL, UNIV

CALIF, BERKELEY, 80- *Concurrent Pos:* Prin investr res grant, Nat Inst Gen Med Sci, 75-; consult, Chron Corp, Berkeley, Calif, 82- *Mem:* Am Soc Biol Chemists; Am Soc Microbiol; Am Chem Soc; AAAS; NY Acad Sci. *Res:* Molecular and cellular basis of the interactions that control the conjugation response of the yeast Saccharomyces cerevisiae to provide information about the mechanisms of developmental gene regulation and morphogenic control in eukaryotic cells. *Mailing Add:* Dept Microbiol & Immunol Life Sci Bldg Univ Calif Berkeley CA 94720

THORNGATE, JOHN HILL, b Eau Claire, Wis, Dec 23, 35; m 56; c 3. PHYSICS. *Educ:* Ripon Col, BA, 57; Vanderbilt Univ, MS, 61, PhD, 76. *Prof Exp:* Inspector health physics, Oak Ridge Opers Off, US Atomic Energy Comn, 59; res group leader radiation dosimetry, Health Physics Div, Oak Ridge Nat Lab, 64-75, asst sect chief, 73-75, health physicist, 60-78; PHYSICIST, LAWRENCE LIVERMORE LAB, 78- *Mem:* Health Physics Soc; Am Phys Soc; Sigma Xi; Inst Elec & Electronics Engrs. *Res:* Radiation dosimetry and spectrometry. *Mailing Add:* Lawrence Livermore Lab L-386 PO Box 5505 Livermore CA 94550

THORNHILL, JAMES ARTHUR, b London, Ont, Feb 11, 51; m 76. ENDOCRINOLOGY, NEUROPHYSIOLOGY. *Educ:* Univ Western Ont, BSc, 74, MSc, 75, PhD(pharmacol), 78. *Prof Exp:* Fel, Univ Calgary, 78-80; ASST PROF ENDOCRINOL, UNIV SASK, 80- *Mem:* Am Physiol Soc; Can Physiol Soc; Can Pharmacol Soc; Soc Neurosci; AAAS. *Res:* Possible physiological role that endogenous opioid peptides (endoprhins or enkephalins) have on feeding and temperature regulation. *Mailing Add:* Dept Physiol Col Med Univ Sask Saskatoon SK S7N 0W0 Can

THORNHILL, PHILIP G, b Maidstone, England, July 7, 18; Can citizen; m 45; c 3. METALLURGY. *Educ:* Univ Toronto, BASc, 50, MASc, 51. *Prof Exp:* Res engr, 51-53, res metallurgist, 54-59, supvr metall res, 60-68, mgr process metall, 68-69, DIR METALL RES, FALCONBRIDGE NICKEL MINES LTD, 69- *Concurrent Pos:* Pres, Lakefield Res Can Ltd. *Honors & Awards:* Technol Medal, Metall Soc, 74; Airey Award, Can Inst Mining & Metall, 76. *Mem:* Am Inst Mining, Metall & Petrol Engrs; Electrochem Soc; Can Inst Mining & Metall; The Chem Soc. *Res:* Hydrometallurgical processes for extraction and refining of nickel. *Mailing Add:* 210 Arnold Ave Thornhill ON L4J 1B9 Can

THORNTON, CHARLES PERKINS, b Indianapolis, Ind, Jan 1, 27; m 54; c 2. PETROLOGY. *Educ:* Univ Va, AB, 49; Yale Univ, MS, 50, PhD(geol), 53. *Prof Exp:* Field geologist, State Geol Surv, Va, 50-52; from instr to asst prof petrog, Pa State Univ, 52-61; asst prof geol, Bucknell Univ, 61-63; assoc prof, 63-69, PROF GEOL, PA STATE UNIV, UNIVERSITY PARK, 69- *Mem:* Geol Soc Am. *Res:* Geology of central Shenandoah Valley, Virginia; petrography and petrology of volcanic rocks; volcanology. *Mailing Add:* Dept of Geosci Pa State Univ University Park PA 16802

THORNTON, DANIEL MCCARTY, III, b Richmond, Va, Jan 30, 18; m 46; c 4. TEXTILES. *Educ:* Univ Richmond, BS, 38; Univ Pa, MS, 40. *Prof Exp:* Asst instr chem, Drexel Inst Technol, 39-40; asst chemist, Wortendyke Mfg Co, Va, 40-41; res chemist, E I Du Pont de Nemours & Co, Inc, 41-43, technologist, 43-48, group leader, 48-49, field res supvr, 49, mgr orlon sales develop, 49-51, orlon customer serv, 51-52, staple fibers customer serv, 52-54, nylon tech serv, 54-60, mgr mkt, Intimate Apparel Indust, 60-64, mkt res mgr, textile fibers, 64-81; RETIRED. *Concurrent Pos:* Vchmn textile sect, NY Bd Trade; mem, Indust Sector Adv Comt on Textiles & Apparel, Dept of Com, 74-78; pres, NY Textile Anal Group, 80. *Mem:* Am Mkt Asn. *Res:* Markets and uses for fibers; consumer and trade motivational studies; psychology and sociology; textiles and clothing; marketing research. *Mailing Add:* PO Box 3923 Greenville DE 19807

THORNTON, DONALD CARLTON, b Baltimore, Md, Apr 16, 47. ANALYTICAL CHEMISTRY. *Educ:* Univ Va, BS, 69; Pa State Univ, MS & PhD(chem), 76. *Prof Exp:* Res assoc chem, Univ Fla, 76-77; ASST PROF CHEM, DREXEL UNIV, 77- *Mem:* AAAS; Am Chem Soc; Sigma Xi. *Res:* Development of electroanalytical methods; electron transfer kinetics at solid electrodes; trace analytical methods for atmospheric constitutents. *Mailing Add:* Dept of Chem 32nd & Market Sts Philadelphia PA 19104

THORNTON, EDWARD RALPH, b Syracuse, NY, July 19, 35; m 69; c 1. ORGANIC CHEMISTRY, BIOLOGICAL CHEMISTRY. *Educ:* Syracuse Univ, BA, 57; Mass Inst Technol, PhD(org chem), 59. *Hon Degrees:* MA, Univ Pa, 71. *Prof Exp:* NIH fel, Mass Inst Technol, 59-60 & Harvard Univ, 60-61; from asst prof to assoc prof, 61-69, PROF CHEM, UNIV PA, 69- *Mem:* Fedn Am Sci; Am Chem Soc; Royal Soc Chem; Am Soc Biol Chemists. *Res:* Structure and mechanism in organic and biological chemistry; glycolipid chemistry and membrane structure. *Mailing Add:* Dept of Chem D5 Univ of Pa Philadelphia PA 19104

THORNTON, ELIZABETH K, b Brooklyn, NY, June 4, 40. PHYSICAL ORGANIC CHEMISTRY. *Educ:* Mt Holyoke Col, AB, 61; Univ Pa, PhD(org chem), 66. *Prof Exp:* Teaching asst chem, Univ Pa, 61-62, NIH fel org chem, 63-66; NATO fel, Swiss Fed Inst Technol, 66-68; asst prof, 68-75, ASSOC PROF CHEM, WIDENER COL, 75- *Mem:* AAAS; Fedn Am Sci; Asn Women Sci; Am Chem Soc. *Res:* Kinetic isotope effects and reaction mechanisms; organic biochemistry. *Mailing Add:* Dept Chem Widener Col Chester PA 19013

THORNTON, GEORGE DANIEL, b Elberton, Ga, Aug 10, 10; m 39. SOILS. *Educ:* Univ Ga, BS, 36, MS, 38; Iowa State Col, PhD(soil fertility), 47. *Prof Exp:* County agr agent, Ga Exten Serv, 36; asst soil surveyor, Ga State Col, 36, instr agron, 37-40; asst agronomist, Exp Sta, Univ Ga, 40-41; asst prof soils & asst soil microbiologist, Col Agr, Univ Fla, 41-45; asst, Iowa State Col, 45-47; assoc prof soils & assoc soil microbiology, 47-51, prof soils, 51-71, soil microbiologist, 51-56, asst dean col, 56-71, EMER PROF SOILS, COL AGR, UNIV FLA, 71- *Mem:* Fel Am Soc Agron; Soil Sci Soc Am. *Res:* Soil microbiology. *Mailing Add:* PO Box 833 Venice FL 33595

THORNTON, GEORGE FRED, b Newton, Mass, Mar 8, 33; m 63; c 2. INTERNAL MEDICINE, INFECTIOUS DISEASES. *Educ:* Harvard Univ, AB, 55; Boston Univ, MD, 59. *Prof Exp:* Instr clin med, Sch Med, Yale Univ, 64-65; instr med, Johns Hopkins Univ, 65-67; from asst prof to assoc prof clin med, 72-78, CLIN PROF MED, SCH MED, YALE UNIV, 78- DIR MED SERV, WATERBURY HOSP, 72-; assoc clin prof, 75-81, CLIN PROF MED, UNIV CONN, 81- *Concurrent Pos:* Fel allergy & infectious dis, Johns Hopkins Univ, 62-64. *Mem:* AMA; Am Fedn Clin Res; fel Infectious Dis Soc Am; fel Am Col Physicians; Am Soc Microbiol. *Res:* Clinical epidemiology. *Mailing Add:* Med Serv Waterbury Hosp Waterbury CT 06720

THORNTON, HUBERT RICHARD, b Van Etten, NY, Nov 15, 32; m 59; c 2. CERAMIC ENGINEERING, METALLURGY. *Educ:* Alfred Univ, BS, 54, MS, 57; Univ Ill, PhD(ceramic eng), 63. *Prof Exp:* Res engr, Nat Bur Standards, 56-59; res assoc ceramic eng, Univ Ill, 59-63; proj standards engr, Gen Dynamics/Ft Worth, 63-67; assoc prof, 67-77, ASSOC PROF MECH ENG, TEX A&M UNIV, 77- *Mem:* Am Ceramic Soc; Am Soc Metals; Soc Aerospace Mat & Process Eng; Am Soc Mech Engrs; fel Am Inst Chem. *Res:* Explosive forming; fracture mechanics; failure modes in materials; fracture analysis; design optimization; teaching of materials and materials in design. *Mailing Add:* Dept Mech Eng Tex A&M Univ College Station TX 77840

THORNTON, JOHN ALEXANDER, b Olympia, Wash, Jan 3, 33; m 61. SOLID STATE PHYSICS, PLASMA PHYSICS. *Educ:* Univ Wash, Seattle, BS, 57, MS, 59; Northwestern Univ, PhD(plasma physics), 63. *Prof Exp:* Asst engr, Appl Physics Lab, Univ Wash, 57-58; dir diag res, Space Sci Labs, Litton Industs, Inc, Calif, 63-68; dir, 68-73, VPRES RES & DEVELOP, TELIC DIV DART & KRAFT, SANTA MONICA, 73- *Mem:* Am Phys Soc; Am Vacuum Soc; Am Inst Aeronaut & Astronaut; Am Soc Mech Eng; Sigma Xi. *Res:* Plasma discharges; thin film deposition techniques, including sputtering, evaporation and chemical vapor deposition; plasma and radiation chemistry; physics and metallurgy of metallic and non-metallic coatings; vacuum technology; photovoltaic devices; solar coatings. *Mailing Add:* 1280 Barrington Apt 22 Los Angeles CA 90025

THORNTON, JOHN IRVIN, b Sacramento, Calif, Jan 11, 41; m 75; c 3. FORENSIC CHEMISTRY. *Educ:* Univ Calif, Berkeley, BS, 62, MCriminalistics, 68, DCriminalistics, 74. *Prof Exp:* Criminologist, Contra Costa Count Sheriff's Dept, 63-72; Asst prof, 74-76, ASSOC PROF FORENSIC SCI, SCH PUB HEALTH, UNIV CALIF, BERKELEY, 76-, VCHMN, DEPT BIOMED & ENVIRON HEALTH SCI, 81- *Concurrent Pos:* Mem proj adv comt, Nationwide Crime Lab Proficiency Testing Proj, Forensic Sci Found, 74-82. *Mem:* Am Chem Soc; Am Acad Forensic Sci; Forensic Sci Soc Gt Brit; Sigma Xi. *Res:* Analysis; identification; interpretaton of physical evidence; author or coauthor of over 80 publications. *Mailing Add:* Dept Biomed & Environ Health Sci Sch Pub Health Univ Calif Berkeley CA 94720

THORNTON, JOHN WILLIAM, b Shawnee, Okla, Apr 21, 36; m 57; c 3. ZOOLOGY, CYTOLOGY. *Educ:* Okla State Univ, BS, 58; Univ Wash, PhD(zool), 64. *Prof Exp:* From asst prof to assoc prof, 60-74, PROF ZOOL, OKLA STATE UNIV, 74- *Concurrent Pos:* USPHS res grant, 65-68; staff biologist, Comn Undergrad Educ Biol Sci, 70-71; mem adv comt, Purdue Minicourse Proj. *Mem:* AAAS; Am Soc Zoologists; Am Inst Biol Sci. *Res:* Cellular ultrastructure; cell and tissue culture; undergraduate curricular improvement; investigative laboratories. *Mailing Add:* Sch of Biol Sci Okla State Univ Stillwater OK 74074

THORNTON, JOSEPH SCOTT, b Sewickley, Pa, Feb 6, 36; m 67; c 2. MATERIALS SCIENCE. *Educ:* Univ Tex, BS, 57; Carnegie Inst Technol, MS, 62; Univ Tex, Austin, PhD(mat sci), 69. *Prof Exp:* Design engr, Walworth Co, 57; res engr, Westinghouse Elec Co, 61-64; instr metall, Univ Tex, Austin, 64-66; group leader metals & composites, Tracor, Inc, 67-69; mgr mat, Horizons Inc, 67-73; dir appl sci, Tracor, Inc, 73-75; PRES & TECH DIR, TEX RES INST, INC, 75- *Mem:* Am Soc Metals; Am Soc Testing & Mat; Am Soc Mech Engrs. *Res:* Contract research administration; development and characterization of engineering materials; reliability of devices in adverse environments; failure analysis; accelerated life test development; recovery techniques for hazardous materials spills. *Mailing Add:* Tex Res Inst Inc 5902 W Bee Caves Rd Austin TX 78746

THORNTON, KENT W, b Ames, Iowa, Apr 29, 44; m 66; c 1. AQUATIC ECOLOGY, SYSTEMS SCIENCE. *Educ:* Univ Iowa, BA, 67, MS, 69; Okla State Univ, PhD(ecol), 72. *Prof Exp:* Teaching asst zool, Univ Iowa, 68-69; lectr environ systs theory, Okla State Univ, 72; asst prof biol, Bowling Green State Univ, 73-74; SYSTS ECOLOGIST, WATERWAYS EXP STA, US ARMY ENGRS, 74- *Concurrent Pos:* NSF fel, Ctr Systs Sci, Okla State Univ, 72-73; mem methods ecosyst anal, Nat Comn Water Qual, 74; actg br chief, Waterways Exp Sta, US Army Engrs, 75. *Mem:* AAAS; Am Inst Biol Sci; Ecol Soc Am; NAm Benthological Soc; Int Soc Limnol. *Res:* Systems theoretical approach to the conceptualization, analysis and application of mathematical ecosystem models for watershed-reservoir planning and management; sampling theory approach to dynamic systems. *Mailing Add:* US Army Engr Waterways Exp Sta 3909 Halls Ferry Rd Vicksburg MS 39180

THORNTON, MELVIN CHANDLER, b Sioux City, Iowa, July 2, 35; m 58; c 4. MATHEMATICS. *Educ:* Univ Nebr, BS, 57; Univ Ill, MS, 61, PhD(math), 65. *Prof Exp:* Asst prof math, Univ Wis, 65-69; asst prof, 69-73, ASSOC PROF MATH, UNIV NEBR, LINCOLN, 73- *Mem:* Am Math Soc; Math Asn Am. *Res:* General topology. *Mailing Add:* Dept of Math Univ of Nebr Lincoln NE 68588

THORNTON, MELVIN LEROY, b Billings, Mont, Nov 7, 28; m 52; c 2. BOTANY. *Educ:* Univ Denver, BA, 52; Tufts Univ, MA, 58; Univ Mont, PhD(bot), 69. *Prof Exp:* NSF fel, Birkbeck Col, Univ London, 69-70; asst prof bot, Univ Mont, 71-77, assoc prof, 77-80. *Mem:* AAAS; Brit Mycol Soc; Mycol Soc Am. *Res:* Dispersal of fungi; ecology of zoosporic fungi. *Mailing Add:* 810 First St Sultan WA 98294

THORNTON, PAUL A, b Campbell Co, Ky, June 29, 25; m 45; c 2. PHYSIOLOGY, NUTRITION. *Educ:* Univ Ky, BS, 49, MS, 53; Mich State Univ, PhD(nutrit), 56. *Prof Exp:* Asst & assoc prof nutrit, Colo State Univ, 56-62, assoc prof physiol, 63-64; vis prof, 62-63, assoc prof, 64-77, PROF PHYSIOL, UNIV KY, 77-; RES PHYSIOLOGIST, VET ADMIN HOSP, LEXINGTON, 64- *Mem:* Soc Exp Biol & Med; Am Inst Nutrit; Am Physiol Soc; Geront Soc. *Res:* Skeletal physiology and the influence of age on bone tissue change; endocrinological and other environmental factors which affect bone. *Mailing Add:* Dept of Physiol & Biophys Univ of Ky Col of Med Lexington KY 40506

THORNTON, RICHARD D(OUGLAS), b New York, NY, Sept 24, 29; m 59; c 3. ELECTRICAL ENGINEERING, COMPUTER SCIENCE. *Educ:* Princeton Univ, SB, 51; Mass Inst Technol, MS, 54, ScD(elec eng), 57. *Prof Exp:* From asst prof to assoc prof, 57-68, PROF ELEC ENG & COMPUT SCI, MASS INST TECHNOL, 68- *Concurrent Pos:* Dir, Thornton Assocs Inc. *Honors & Awards:* Baker Award, Inst Radio Eng, Inst Elec & Electronics Engrs, 59. *Mem:* AAAS; Inst Elec & Electronics Engrs. *Res:* Electronically controlled electromechanical systems; solar energy systems, electronic circuits and computer aided engineering design. *Mailing Add:* Mass Inst of Technol 36-361 Cambridge MA 02139

THORNTON, ROBERT LYSTER, b Wootton, Eng, Nov 29, 08; nat US; m 38, 77; c 3. PHYSICS. *Educ:* McGill Univ, BSc, 30, PhD(spectros), 33. *Prof Exp:* Demonstr, McGill Univ, 30-31; Moyse traveling scholar from McGill Univ, Univ Calif, 33-34, res assoc, Radiation Lab, 34-36, instr physics, Univ Mich, 36-38; res assoc, Radiation Lab, Univ Calif, 38-39; assoc prof, Wash Univ, 40-45; res physicist, Manhattan Dist Proj, 42-43, assoc dir, Lawrence Radiation Lab, 58-72, prof, 45-72, EMER PROF PHYSICS, UNIV CALIF, BERKELEY, 72- *Concurrent Pos:* Asst dir, Process Improv Div, Tenn Eastman Corp, 43-45. *Mem:* Fel Am Phys Soc. *Res:* Nuclear physics; accelerator design and construction. *Mailing Add:* 522 Cragmont Ave Berkeley CA 94708

THORNTON, ROBERT MELVIN, b Auburn, Calif, Nov 14, 37; m 57, 71; c 2. BIOLOGY, PLANT PHYSIOLOGY. *Educ:* Calif Inst Technol, BS, 59; Harvard Univ, MA, 61, PhD(biol), 66. *Prof Exp:* Sr scientist, Biol/Eng, Appl Sci Corp, Calif, 61-63; instr, Ojai Valley Sch, 63-64; instr biol, Univ Calif, Santa Cruz, 66-67, asst prof, 67-68, asst prof bot, 68-74, ASSOC PROF BOT, UNIV CALIF, DAVIS, 74- *Concurrent Pos:* NSF res grant, Univ Calif, Davis, 69-72. *Mem:* AAAS; Am Soc Plant Physiol; Bot Soc Am. *Res:* Regulatory mechanisms with particular reference to photoresponse mechanisms in the development of fungi. *Mailing Add:* Dept of Bot Univ of Calif 218 Robbins Hall Davis CA 95616

THORNTON, ROGER LEA, b Wilmington, Del, Mar 9, 35; m 58; c 3. ORGANIC CHEMISTRY. *Educ:* Univ Del, BS, 57; Mass Inst Technol, PhD(org chem), 61. *Prof Exp:* Res chemist, Del, 61-65, Va, 65-67, SR RES CHEMIST, E I DU PONT DE NEMOURS & CO, INC, DEL, 67- *Res:* Vapor-phase catalytic reactions; thermally stable condensation polymers; emulsion polymerization; flourinated compounds. *Mailing Add:* Chem & Pigments Dept E I du Pont de Nemours & Co Inc Deepwater NJ 08023

THORNTON, ROY FRED, b Upper Darby, Pa, Feb 27, 41; m 66; c 2. CHEMICAL ENGINEERING, ELECTROCHEMISTRY. *Educ:* Johns Hopkins Univ, BS, 63, PhD(chem eng), 67. *Prof Exp:* Chem engr, Battery Bus Dept, Gen Elec Co, 67-69, STAFF MEM, ELECTROCHEM, GEN ELEC CO CORP RES & DEVELOP, 69- *Mem:* Am Inst Chem Eng; Electrochem Soc. *Res:* Development of electrochemical energy storage systems. *Mailing Add:* Box 8 Corp Res & Develop Gen Elec Co Schenectady NY 12305

THORNTON, STAFFORD E, b Campbell Co, Va, July 29, 34; m 63; c 3. CIVIL ENGINEERING. *Educ:* Univ Va, BCE, 59, MCE, 62. *Prof Exp:* Instr civil eng, Univ Va, 60-61, res engr, 62-63; from asst prof to assoc prof civil eng, 63-77, head dept, 64-77, PROF CIVIL ENG & ASST DEAN, W VA INST TECHNOL, 77- *Mem:* Am Soc Civil Engrs; Am Soc Eng Educ; Nat Soc Prof Engrs. *Res:* Structural design; concrete and steel; foundations; city planning; stress analysis of rotating, shafting and cylinders. *Mailing Add:* Dept of Civil Eng WVa Inst of Technol Montgomery WV 25136

THORNTON, STEPHEN THOMAS, b Kingsport, Tenn, Oct 2, 41; m 61; c 2. EXPERIMENTAL NUCLEAR PHYSICS. *Educ:* Univ Tenn, Knoxville, BS, 63, MS, 64, PhD(physics), 67. *Prof Exp:* US Atomic Energy Comn fel, Univ Wis-Madison, 67-68; asst prof, 68-72, ASSOC PROF PHYSICS, UNIV VA, 72- *Concurrent Pos:* Consult, Physics Div, Oak Ridge Nat Lab, 72-77; Fulbright-Hays sr fel, Max Planck Inst, Heidelberg, 73-74 & 79-80. *Mem:* AAAS; Am Phys Soc. *Res:* Neutron polarization; nuclear structure studies from experimental heavy ion nuclear physics. *Mailing Add:* Dept Physics Univ Va Charlottesville VA 22903

THORNTON, WILLIAM ALOYSIUS, b New York, NY, Sept 8, 38; m 63; c 2. STRUCTURAL MECHANICS. *Educ:* Manhattan Col, BCE, 60; Case Western Reserve Univ, MSEM, 64, PhD(eng mech), 67. *Prof Exp:* Asst prof civil eng, Clarkson Col Technol, 67-72, assoc prof civil & environ eng, 72-79; CHIEF ENGR, CIVES STEEL CO, ATLANTA, GA, 79- *Concurrent Pos:* Prin investr, NSF res grant, 69-73; NASA res grant, 69-74. *Mem:* Am Soc Civil Engrs; Am Inst Aeronaut & Astronaut; Nat Soc Prof Engrs; Sigma Xi; Am Welding Soc. *Res:* Optimal design of structures; computer oriented structural analysis and design; analysis and design of structural connections. *Mailing Add:* Cives Steel Co 11 Dunwoody Park Atlanta GA 30338

THORNTON, WILLIAM ANDRUS, JR, b Buffalo, NY, June 16, 23; m 44; c 4. PHYSICS. *Educ:* Univ Buffalo, BA, 48; Yale Univ, MS, 49, PhD(physics), 51. *Prof Exp:* Res assoc labs, Gen Elec Co, 51-56; sr res engr, 56-59, fel res engr, 59-65, mgr phosphor res, 65-67, RES ENG CONSULT, WESTINGHOUSE ELEC CORP, BLOOMFIELD, 67- *Mem:* Am Phys Soc; Optical Soc Am; fel Illuminating Eng Soc. *Res:* Light and color. *Mailing Add:* Westinghouse Elec Corp Lamp Div Res Lab Bloomfield NJ 07003

THORNTON, WILLIAM EDGAR, b Faison, NC, Apr 14, 29; m; c 2. MEDICINE, ASTRONAUTICS. *Educ:* Univ NC, BS, 52, MD, 63. *Prof Exp:* Chief engr, Electronics Div, Del Mar Eng Labs, Calif, 55-59; intern, Wilford Hall Hosp, Lackland AFB, US Air Force, Tex, 64, assigned to Aerospace Med Div, Brooks AFB, 65-67; SCIENTIST-ASTRONAUT, JOHNSON SPACE CTR, NASA, 67- *Concurrent Pos:* Instr, Dept Med, Univ Tex Med Br, Galveston. *Honors & Awards:* Exceptional Serv Medal, NASA, 72; NASA Except Sci Achievement Award, 74. *Res:* Physics; biomedical instrumentation; cardiovascular; principle investigator on sky lab experiments including 1 mass measurements in space, musculo-skeletal and cardiovascular investigations. *Mailing Add:* NASA Johnson Space Ctr Houston TX 77058

THOROUGHGOOD, CAROLYN A, b Sept 1, 43; m 64; c 1. MARINE SCIENCES. *Educ:* Univ Del, BS, 65; Univ Md, MS, 66, PhD(nutrit), 68. *Prof Exp:* Asst prof food sci & nutrit, 68-72, assoc prof, 72-74, dir, Marine Adv Serv, 74-76, assoc dir, Del Sea Grant Col Prog, 76-78, ASSOC PROF MARINE STUDIES, FOOD SCI & NUTRIT, UNIV DEL, 78-, ASSOC DEAN, COL MARINE STUDIES, 80- *Concurrent Pos:* Exec dir, Del Sea Grant Col Prog, Col Marine Studies, Univ Del, 78-; Chair, Nat Coun Sea Grand Dirs, 80-81, exec comt mem, 81-; mem, Governor's Task Force Fisheries, 80-81. *Mem:* AAAS. *Res:* Nutritional biochemistry of bivalve molluscs and the sensory and nutritional evaluation and preservation of fish and shellfish; marine education and the development of policy and materials required to enhance the general public's marine literacy. *Mailing Add:* Col Marine Studies Univ Del Newark DE 19711

THORP, EDWARD O, b Chicago, Ill, Aug 14, 32; m 56; c 3. MATHEMATICS. *Educ:* Univ Calif, Los Angeles, BA, 53, MA, 55, PhD(math), 58. *Prof Exp:* Instr math, Univ Calif, Los Angeles, 58-59; C L E Moore instr, Mass Inst Technol, 59-61; from asst prof to assoc prof, NMex State Univ, 61-65; assoc prof, 65-67, PROF MATH & FINANCE, UNIV CALIF, IRVINE, 67-; PRES, OAKLEY SUTTON MGT CORP, 72-, CHMN, OAKLEY SUTTON SECURITIES CORP, 72- *Concurrent Pos:* Res grants, NSF, 62-64 & US Air Force Off Sci Res, 64-74. *Mem:* Am Stat Asn; fel Inst Math Stat; Am Finance Asn. *Res:* Functional analysis; probability theory; game theory; statistics; mathematical finance; numerical solution Stefan problems. *Mailing Add:* Dept of Math Univ of Calif Irvine CA 92664

THORP, FRANK KEDZIE, b Denver, Colo, Apr 29, 36; m 65; c 1. BIOCHEMISTRY, PEDIATRICS. *Educ:* Mich State Univ, BA, 55; Univ Chicago, MD, 60, PhD(biochem), 62. *Prof Exp:* Intern pediat, Univ Chicago, 61-62; resident, Children's Hosp Med Ctr, Boston, 62-63; instr, 65-66, asst prof, 66-72, ASSOC PROF PEDIAT, UNIV CHICAGO, 72- *Concurrent Pos:* NIH res fel biochem, Children's Hosp Med Ctr, Boston, 63-65; Joseph P Kennedy, Jr scholar, 66-; Am Acad Pediat grant, 69-; dir ment develop clin, Joseph P Kennedy, Jr Ment Retardation Res Ctr, 71-74; dir clin serv, Wyler Children's Hosp, 77- *Mem:* Am Acad Pediat; Sigma Xi; NY Acad Sci. *Res:* Teaching and clinical work in pediatrics; metabolic and nutritional diseases of children; development of nutrition training and nutrition education programs. *Mailing Add:* Dept of Pediat Univ of Chicago Chicago IL 60637

THORP, JAMES HARRISON, III, b Kansas City, Mo, July 23, 48; m 70; c 2. AQUATIC ECOLOGY, COMMUNITY ECOLOGY. *Educ:* Univ Kans, BA, 70; NC State Univ, MS, 73, PhD(zool), 75. *Prof Exp:* RES ASSOC, SAVANNAH RIVER ECOL LAB, UNIV GEORGIA, 75- *Concurrent Pos:* Vis lectr gen biol, Univ SC, 81, environ sci, 76; educ prog dir, Savannah River Ecol Lab, 77-80; assoc ed, Freshwater Invertebrate Biol, 81-; prin investr, NSF grant, 79; proj dir, Indust Fac Res Partic, NSF grant, 79. *Mem:* Ecol Soc Am; NAm Benthological Soc Am; Crustacean Soc; Estuarine Res Fedn. *Res:* Experimental field studies of factors regulating structure in benthic macroinvertebrate communities within freshwater and marine systems; functional response of communities along environmental gradients; behavioral ecology and competitive interactions among crustaceans. *Mailing Add:* Savannah River Ecol Lab PO Drawer E Aiken SC 29801

THORP, JAMES SHELBY, b Kansas City, Mo, Feb 7, 37; m 59; c 2. ELECTRICAL ENGINEERING. *Educ:* Cornell Univ, BEE, 59, MS, 61, PhD(elec eng), 62. *Prof Exp:* From asst prof to assoc prof, 62-75, PROF ELEC ENG, CORNELL UNIV, 75- *Concurrent Pos:* Consult, ADCOM, Mass, 62, Gen Elec Co, 64 & Am Elec Power Serv Corp, 77- *Mem:* Inst Elec & Electronics Engrs. *Res:* Control systems and optimal control; power systems. *Mailing Add:* 304 Phillips Hall Cornell Univ Ithaca NY 14850

THORP, ROBBIN WALKER, b Benton Harbor, Mich, Aug 26, 33; m 54, 67; c 3. INSECT TAXONOMY, ECOLOGY. *Educ:* Univ Mich, BS, 55, MS, 57; Univ Calif, Berkeley, PhD(entom), 64. *Prof Exp:* Jr specialist, Univ Calif, Berkeley, 62-63, asst specialist, 63-64, asst res entomologist, 64; asst apiculturist, 64-72, assoc prof entom & assoc apiculturist, 72-78, PROF ENTOM & APICULTURIST, UNIV CALIF, DAVIS, 78- *Mem:* AAAS; Ecol Soc Am; Soc Syst Zool; Entom Soc Am; Soc Study Evolution. *Res:* Pollination ecology, especially bee and flower relationships; ecology and systematics of bees and ecology of their biotic enemies; coevolution and coadaptation of pollinating insects and entomophilous angiosperms. *Mailing Add:* Dept of Entom Univ of Calif Davis CA 95616

THORPE, BERT DUANE, b Spanish Fork, Utah, Sept 21, 29; m 55; c 6. IMMUNOLOGY, WILDLIFE DISEASES. *Educ:* Univ Utah, BS(chem) & BS(bact), 58, PhD(microbiol), 63. *Prof Exp:* Asst chem, Univ Utah, 55-57, asst bact, 57, res bacteriologist, Epizool Lab, 58-61, res instr ecol & epizool, 61-63, from asst res prof to assoc res prof, 63-68, dir epizool lab, 61-68, clin lectr microbiol, 67-68; prof microbiol, 68-77, PROF ZOOL, UNIV NORTHERN COLO, 77- *Concurrent Pos:* Lectr, Brigham Young Univ, 65-66; consult, Dept Defense, 67-; vpres nat comt, Int Northwestern Conf Dis Man. *Mem:* Am Chem Soc; Am Asn Immunol; Am Soc Microbiol; Am Soc Trop Med & Hyg; Soc Exp Biol & Med. *Res:* Host mechanisms of resistance to infectious diseases; new methods of detection and isolation of microorganisms; zoonoses; animal infections and human diseases; natural and acquired immunity. *Mailing Add:* Dept of Zool Univ of Northern Colo Greeley CO 80639

THORPE, COLIN, b Grantham, Eng, May 1, 47; m 75; c 2. FLAVOPROTEINS, FLAVINS. *Educ:* Univ Cambridge, UK, BA, 69; Univ Kent, UK, PhD(chem), 72. *Prof Exp:* Fel biochem, Dept Biol Chem, Univ Mich, 72-78; ASST PROF BIOCHEM, DEPT CHEM, UNIV DEL, 78- *Mem:* Am Chem Soc; Biochem Soc. *Res:* Structure, function and mechanism of action of flavoproteins involved in fatty acid oxidation. *Mailing Add:* Chem Dept Univ Del Newark DE 19711

THORPE, HOWARD A(LAN), b Joplin, Mo, Nov 21, 14; m 41. PHYSICS, ENGINEERING. *Educ:* Univ Ark, BA, 37; Tulane Univ, MS, 39. *Prof Exp:* Instr physics, Pa State Univ, 40-46, res assoc, 46-47; supvry physicist, US Navy Marine Eng Lab, 47-53, physicist, Bur Ships, 53-56; res engr, Lockheed Aircraft Corp, 56-57, supvry group engr, 57-61, sr res specialist, Lockheed-Calif Co, 61-67; sr res scientist, Stanford Res Inst, 68-69; sr res engr, Aerospace Group, Rohr Industs, Inc, 69-74, eng specialist, Rohr Marine, Inc, 74-81; CONSULT ACOUST, 81- *Mem:* Acoust Soc Am; Am Inst Aeronaut & Astronaut; Marine Technol Soc; Sigma Xi. *Res:* Acoustical physics; aircraft sonar system and component research; basic environmental effects on sonar performance; submarine, ship and aircraft noise measurement, prediction and control; propagation of sound in atmosphere. *Mailing Add:* 285 Moss No 44 Chula Vista CA 92011

THORPE, JAMES F(RANKLIN), b Sandusky, Ohio, Oct 2, 26; m 49; c 3. MECHANICAL ENGINEERING. *Educ:* Univ Cincinnati, ME, 52; Univ Ky, MS, 55; Univ Pittsburgh, PhD(mech eng), 60. *Prof Exp:* Proj engr, E W Buschman Co, Ohio, 52-53; instr mech eng, Univ Ky, 53-55; engr, Bettis Atomic Power Lab, Westinghouse Elec Corp, 55-57, sr instr reactor eng, 57-59, sr engr, 60-61; assoc prof mech eng, Univ Ky, 61-67; head dept, 70-79, PROF MECH ENG, UNIV CINCINNATI, 67- *Concurrent Pos:* Consult numerous co, govt & univs, 61-; Nat Endowment for Humanities ethics fel, 78. *Mem:* Am Soc Mech Engrs; Am Soc Eng Educ; Nat Soc Prof Engrs. *Res:* Fluid mechanics; non-traditional machining; vibrations; mechanical design; product liability and product safety. *Mailing Add:* 1478 Beechgrove Dr Cincinnati OH 45238

THORPE, JOHN ALDEN, b Lewiston, Maine, Feb 29, 36; m 59; c 2. GEOMETRY. *Educ:* Mass Inst Technol, SB, 58; Columbia Univ, AM, 59, PhD(math), 63. *Prof Exp:* Instr math, Columbia Univ, 63; C L E Moore instr, Mass Inst Technol, 63-65; asst prof, Haverford Col, 65-68; assoc prof, 68-77, PROF, STATE UNIV NY STONY BROOK, 77-, DIR, GRAD PROG MATH, 80- *Concurrent Pos:* Mem, Inst Adv Study, 67-68. *Mem:* Am Math Soc; Math Asn Am. *Res:* Differential geometry; general relativity. *Mailing Add:* Dept of Math State Univ of NY Stony Brook NY 11794

THORPE, MARTHA CAMPBELL, b Tullahoma, Tenn, Apr 28, 22; m 43; c 2. PHYSICAL ORGANIC CHEMISTRY. *Educ:* Vanderbilt Univ, BA, 44; Samford Univ, MA, 68. *Prof Exp:* Anal chemist, E I du Pont de Nemours & Co, Inc, 44-45; SR CHEMIST MOLECULAR SPECTROS, SOUTHERN RES INST, 61- *Mem:* Am Chem Soc; Int Soc Magnetic Resonance. *Res:* H-1 and C-13 nuclear magnetic resonance spectroscopy of organic compounds. *Mailing Add:* Southern Res Inst 2000 Ninth Ave S Birmingham AL 35255

THORPE, MICHAEL FIELDING, b Bromley, Eng, Mar 12, 44. THEORETICAL PHYSICS. *Educ:* Univ Manchester, BSc, 65; Oxford Univ, DPhil(physics), 68. *Prof Exp:* Res assoc physics, Brookhaven Nat Lab, 68-70; from asst prof to assoc prof physics, Yale Univ, 70-77; assoc prof, 76-80, PROF PHYSICS, MICH STATE, 80- *Concurrent Pos:* Yale jr fac fel & guest scientist, Max Planck Inst Solids, Stuttgart, 72-73; sr res fel, Oxford Univ, 78. *Mem:* Am Phys Soc; Brit Inst Physics. *Res:* Theoretical solid state physics, including low temperature excitations, magnetism and amorphous solids. *Mailing Add:* Dept of Physics Mich State Univ East Lansing MI 48824

THORPE, NEAL OWEN, b Wausau, Wis, Sept 8, 38; m 60; c 3. BIOCHEMISTRY. *Educ:* Augsburg Col, BA, 60; Univ Wis, Madison, PhD(physiol chem), 64. *Prof Exp:* USPHS fel, 65-66; Am Heart Asn adv res fel, 66-67; assoc prof, 67-80, PROF BIOL, AUGSBURG COL, 80- *Concurrent Pos:* Res Corp grant & Am Heart Asn grant, 69-71; regional dir Grants, Res Corp, 73-74. *Res:* Immunochemistry and the structure of sigma virus in Drosophila. *Mailing Add:* Dept of Biol Augsburg Col 21st Ave S at 8th St Minneapolis MN 55404

THORPE, RALPH IRVING, b Halls Harbour, NS, Feb 29, 36; m 68; c 2. ECONOMIC GEOLOGY. *Educ:* Acadia Univ, BSc, 58; Queen's Univ, Ont, MSc, 63; Univ Wis-Madison, PhD(econ geol), 67. *Prof Exp:* RES SCIENTIST MINERAL DEPOSITS, GEOL SURV CAN, 65- *Mem:* Mineral Soc Am; Mineral Asn Can; Can Inst Mining & Metall; Geol Asn Can. *Res:* Genesis of metalliferous ore deposits; lead isotope interpretations; ore mineralogy. *Mailing Add:* Mineral Deposits Sect Geol Surv Can Ottawa ON K1A 0E4 Can

THORPE, RODNEY WARREN, b Boston, Mass, Sept 27, 35. APPLIED MATHEMATICS, OPERATIONS RESEARCH. *Educ:* Harvard Col, AB, 59, SM, 65, PhD(appl math), 70. *Prof Exp:* Programmer, Ling Proj, Dept Environ Syst, Harvard Univ, 59-65, comput programmer, 71-72; DIR ENVIRON SYST, APPL MATH, QEI, INC, 72- *Mem:* Sigma Xi. *Res:* Mathematical modeling of transportation problems; pollution problems; simulation operations research. *Mailing Add:* QEI Inc 119 The Great Rd Bedford MA 01730

THORPE, TREVOR ALLEYNE, b Barbados, WI, Oct 18, 36; m 63; c 2. PLANT PHYSIOLOGY. *Educ:* Allahabad Agr Inst, BScAgr, 61; Univ Calif, Riverside, MS, 64, PhD(plant sci & physiol), 68. *Prof Exp:* Nat Res Coun fel & res plant physiologist, Fruit & Vegetable Chem Lab, US Dept Agr, Calif, 68-69; from asst prof to assoc prof bot, 69-78, asst dean fac arts & sci, 74-76, PROF BOT, UNIV CALGARY, 78- *Concurrent Pos:* Chmn, Int Asn Plant Tissue Cult, 74-78. *Mem:* Can Soc Plant Physiol; Am Soc Plant Physiol; Japanese Soc Plant Physiol; Scand Soc Plant Physiol; Tissue Cult Asn. *Res:* Experimental plant morphogenesis; cytology, physiology and biochemistry of organ formation in tissue culture systems; plant propagation by tissue culture methods. *Mailing Add:* Dept of Biol Univ of Calgary Calgary AB T2N 1N4 Can

THORSELL, DAVID LINDEN, b July 6, 42; US citizen. PHYSICAL CHEMISTRY. *Educ:* Univ Minn, Duluth, BA, 60; Ohio State Univ, PhD(phys chem), 71. *Prof Exp:* Lectr & fel chem, Ohio State Univ, 72-74; ASST PROF CHEM, SEATTLE UNIV, 74-, CHMN DEPT, 76- *Mem:* AAAS; Am Chem Soc; Inter-Am Photochem Soc. *Res:* Electron paramagnetic reasonance of organic and inorganic single crystal systems; photochemistry; atmospheric chemistry. *Mailing Add:* Dept of Chem Seattle Univ Seattle WA 98122

THORSEN, ARTHUR C, b Portland, Ore, July 27, 34. EXPERIMENTAL SOLID STATE PHYSICS. *Educ:* Reed Col, BA, 56; Rice Inst, MA, 58, PhD(physics), 60; Calif Lutherna Col, MBA, 81. *Prof Exp:* Res physicist, Atomics Int Div, NAm Rockwell Corp, 60-63, mem tech staff, Sci Ctr, 63-67, mem tech staff, Autonetics Div, 67-70, mem tech staff, Res & Technol Div, Anaheim, Calif, 70-73, mem tech staff, 73-74, prog mgr independent res & develop, 74-78, DIR, CORP RES PROGS, ROCKWELL INT SCI CTR, 78- *Mem:* Am Phys Soc. *Res:* Low temperature solid state physics; electronic structure of metals; transport properties of semiconductors; thin films; superconductivity. *Mailing Add:* Rockwell Int Sci Ctr 1049 Camino dos Rios Thousand Oaks CA 91360

THORSEN, JAN, veterinary virology, see previous edition

THORSEN, RICHARD STANLEY, b New York, NY, Oct 6, 40; m 62; c 2. THERMAL SCIENCES, SOLAR ENERGY. *Educ:* City Univ New York, BS, 62; NY Univ, PhD(mech eng), 67. *Prof Exp:* PROF & HEAD DEPT MECH & AEROSPACE ENG, POLYTECH INST NY, 74-, DIR, SOLAR ENERGY APPLNS CTR, 77- *Concurrent Pos:* Consult, Grumman Aerospace Corp, 68- *Mem:* Am Soc Mech Engrs; Am Inst Aeronaut & Astronaut; Int Solar Energy Soc; Am Soc Eng Educ. *Res:* Multi-phase heat transfer; solar energy. *Mailing Add:* Polytech Inst of NY 333 Jay St Brooklyn NY 11201

THORSETT, EUGENE DELOY, b Wadena, Minn, Nov 28, 48. ORGANIC CHEMISTRY. *Educ:* Univ Minn, BA, 70; Colo State Univ, PhD(org chem), 73. *Prof Exp:* Res assoc, Rice Univ, 73-75; SR RES CHEMIST, MERCK, SHARP & DOHME RES LAB, MERCK & CO, INC, 75- *Mem:* Am Chem Soc. *Res:* Organic synthesis; organometallic chemistry; enzyme inhibitor design; organic photochemistry. *Mailing Add:* Merck & Co Inc PO Box 2000 Rahway NJ 07065

THORSETT, GRANT OREL, b Shelton, Wash, Jan 25, 40; m 63; c 3. MOLECULAR BIOLOGY. *Educ:* Wash State Univ, BS, 62; Yale Univ, MS, 65, PhD(molecular biophys), 69. *Prof Exp:* Asst prof, 67-72, assoc prof, 72-79, PROF BIOL, WILLAMETTE UNIV, 79- *Concurrent Pos:* Instr, Proj Newgate, Ore State Penitentiary, 71-72; NSF res partic, Willamette Univ, 71-73. *Mem:* AAAS. *Res:* Bacterial transformation; biochemical systematics; bacterial biochemistry; use of computers in undergraduate curricula. *Mailing Add:* Dept of Biol Willamette Univ Salem OR 97301

THORSNESS, CHARLES BENNETT, b Astoria, Ore, June 30, 46; m 68; c 2. CHEMICAL ENGINEERING. *Educ:* Ore State Univ, BS, 68; Univ Ill, MS, 73, PhD(chem eng), 75. *Prof Exp:* Res engr petrol eng, Esso Prod Res Co, 68-71; RES ENGR CHEM ENG, LAWRENCE LIVERMORE LAB, UNIV CALIF, 74- *Res:* Numerical modeling; in situ coal gasification. *Mailing Add:* Lawrence Livermore Lab PO Box 808 Livermore CA 94550

THORSON, JOHN WELLS, b Detroit, Mich, Feb 25, 33; m 64. NEUROPHYSIOLOGY, BIOPHYSICS. *Educ:* Rensselaer Polytech Inst, BS, 55, MS, 58; Univ Calif, Los Angeles, PhD(zool), 65. *Prof Exp:* Physicist, Gen Elec Co, 55-60; NIH trainee biophys, Univ Calif, Los Angeles, 60-65; NSF fel physiol, Max Planck Inst Biol, 65-66 & Oxford Univ, 66-67; asst prof neurosci, Univ Calif, San Diego, 67-68, res scientist, 68-69; vis lectr zool, Oxford Univ, 69-70; res fel, Max Planck Inst Physiol of Behav, 70-72; affil zool, Oxford Univ, 72-79; AFFIL, MAX PLANCK INST, 79- *Concurrent Pos:* Mass Inst Technol neurosci res prog fel, Univ Colo, 66; prin investr, Air Force Off Sci Res grants, 67-69 & 69-70; consult, Max Planck Inst, 75-, Univ Calif, San Diego, 80, J W Goethe Univ, Frankfurt, 80- *Mem:* AAAS; Sigma Xi; Antiquarian Horological Soc. *Res:* Experimental and theoretical analysis of the dynamics of biological systems; visual movement perception; macromolecular basis of muscle contraction; mathematics of distributed relaxation processes; computers in physiological analysis and control of experiments; methodology in behavioral experiments identifying mechanisms of sensory recognition. *Mailing Add:* The Old Marlborough Arms Combe Oxford England

THORSON, RALPH EDWARD, b Chatfield, Minn, June 25, 23; m 52; c 3. MEDICAL PARASITOLOGY, VETERINARY PARASITOLOGY. *Educ:* Univ Notre Dame, BS, 48, MS, 49; Johns Hopkins Univ, ScD(hyg), 52. *Prof Exp:* Instr parasitol, Sch Hyg & Pub Health, Johns Hopkins Univ, 52-53; assoc prof, Sch Vet Med, Ala Polytech Inst, 53-57, prof, 58-59; group leader parasitic chemother, Res Div, Am Cyanamid Co, 57-58; prof biol & head dept & Lobund Labs, Univ Notre Dame, 59-64; prof parasitol & chmn dept trop health, Am Univ Beirut, 64-66; PROF BIOL, UNIV NOTRE DAME, 66- *Concurrent Pos:* Mem awards comt, Sigma Xi, 67- *Mem:* Fel AAAS; Am Soc Parasitol (vpres, 81); Am Soc Zool; Am Soc Trop Med & Hyg; fel Am Acad Microbiol. *Res:* Immunology of parasitic infections, especially helminths; physiology of parasitic helminths. *Mailing Add:* Dept of Biol Univ of Notre Dame Notre Dame IN 46556

THORSON, THOMAS BERTEL, b Rowe, Ill, Jan 12, 17; m 41; c 2. ZOOLOGY. *Educ:* St Olaf Col, BA, 38; Univ Wash, Seattle, MS, 41, PhD(zool), 52. *Prof Exp:* Teacher high sch, Mont, 38-39 & Wash, 42-43; instr zool, Yakima Jr Col, Wash, 46-48, Univ Nebr, 48-50 & San Francisco State Univ, 52-54; asst prof, SDak State Univ, 54-56; from asst prof to assoc prof, 56-61, chmn dept, 67-71, vdir, Sch Life Sci, 75-77, PROF ZOOL, UNIV NEBR, LINCOLN, 61- *Concurrent Pos:* NSF-NIH & Off Naval Res grants, Field Expeds Cent Am, SAm & Nigeria, 60- *Mem:* Fel AAAS; Asn Trop Biol;

Sigma Xi; Am Inst Biol Sci; fel Explorers Club. *Res:* Water economy of amphibians in relation to terrestrialism; ecological and phylogenetic significance of body water partitioning in vertebrates; osmoregulation of elasmobranchs; fresh water elasmobranch biology. *Mailing Add:* Sch of Life Sci Univ of Nebr Lincoln NE 68588

THORSON, WALTER ROLLIER, b Tulsa, Okla, Sept 3, 32. THEORETICAL CHEMISTRY. *Educ:* Calif Inst Technol, BS, 53, PhD(chem), 57. *Prof Exp:* NSF fel chem, Harvard Univ, 56-57; instr, Tufts Univ, 57-58; asst prof phys chem, Mass Inst Technol, 58-64, assoc prof chem, 64-68; PROF CHEM, UNIV ALTA, 68- *Mem:* Am Phys Soc; Can Asn Physicists. *Res:* Theory of atomic collisions; electronic structure of molecules and solids; quantum mechanics. *Mailing Add:* Dept of Chem Univ of Alta Edmonton AB T6G 2G2 Can

THORSTENSEN, THOMAS CLAYTON, b Milwaukee, Wis, Nov 29, 19; m; c 3. CHEMISTRY. *Educ:* Univ Minn, BS, 42; Lehigh Univ, MS, 47, PhD, 49. *Prof Exp:* Chemist, S B Foot Tanning Co, 42-44; asst, Lehigh Univ, 46-49, res assoc, 49-51; res chemist, J S Young Co, 51-55; proj dir, Res Found, Lowell Technol Inst, 55-59; OWNER-DIR, THORSTENSEN LAB, 59- *Concurrent Pos:* Vis prof, Lowell Technol Inst, 60-; consult aid to underdeveloped nations, UN & Dept State. *Mem:* Am Chem Soc; Am Leather Chem Asn (pres, 74). *Res:* Mineral tannages chromium; iron; aluminum and zirconium; theory of mineral tannages; synthetic tanning agents. *Mailing Add:* Thorstensen Lab 66 Littleton Rd Westford MA 01886

THORSTENSON, DONALD CARL, b Chicago, Ill, Jan 4, 41; m 62; c 1. GEOCHEMISTRY. *Educ:* Monmouth Col, BA, 62; Univ Ill, Urbana, MS, 64; Northwestern Univ, PhD(geol), 69. *Prof Exp:* asst prof geol, Southern Methodist Univ, 69-78; US GEOL SURV, 78- *Res:* Low temperature aqueous geochemistry. *Mailing Add:* 11609 Foxclove Rd Reston VA 22091

THORUP, JAMES TAT, b Salt Lake City, Utah, Dec 20, 30; m 58; c 5. AGRONOMY, SOIL FERTILITY. *Educ:* Brigham Young Univ, BA, 55; NC State Col, MS, 57; Univ Calif, Davis, PhD(soils, plant nutrit), 66. *Prof Exp:* Teacher high schs & city cols, Calif, 61-66; AGRONOMIST, CHEVRON CHEM CO, 66- *Mem:* Am Soc Agron; Soil Sci Soc Am. *Res:* Factors affecting plant growth in sodic soils; registry of certified professionals in agronomy, crops and soils; pH effect on plant growth and water uptake; plant nutrition. *Mailing Add:* Suite 130 Chevron Chem Co 3001 LBJ Freeway Dallas TX 75234

THORUP, OSCAR ANDREAS, JR, b Washington, DC, Mar 12, 22; m 44; c 1. MEDICINE. *Educ:* Univ Va, BA, 44, MD, 46; Am Bd Internal Med, dipl, 55. *Prof Exp:* From asst resident to resident internal med, Hosp, Univ Va, 50-52, asst to dean, Sch Med, 53-67, dir teacher's preventorium, 53-54, from instr to assoc prof internal med, 53-66; prof & head dept, Col Med, Univ Ariz, 66-74; PROF INTERNAL MED & ASSOC DEAN, SCH MED, UNIV VA, 74- *Concurrent Pos:* Fel internal med, Hosp, Univ Va, 50; res fel, Univ NC, 52-53; AMA coun on continuing physician educ. *Mem:* AMA; Am Fedn Clin Res; fel Am Col Physicians; Am Clin & Climat Asn; Sigma Xi. *Res:* Hematology, particularly red blood cell enzymes and proteins. *Mailing Add:* Univ of Va Sch of Med Charlottesville VA 22901

THORUP, RICHARD M, b Salt Lake City, Utah, Dec 20, 30; m 57, 80; c 6. AGRONOMY, SOIL FERTILITY. *Educ:* Brigham Young Univ, BA, 55; NC State Univ, MS, 57; Univ Calif, Davis, PhD(soil sci, plant nutrit), 62. *Prof Exp:* Agronomist, 60-61, field agronomist, 61-67, regional agronomist, 67-75, NAT MGR AGRON, FERTILIZER DIV, CHEVRON CHEM CO, 75- *Mem:* Am Soc Agron; Soil Sci Soc Am; Crop Sci Soc Am. *Res:* Chemistry of phosphates in the soil, including solubility and interrelationships with soil moisture; maximum fertility studies with field and tree crops; micronutrients; effect of fertilizers on environment. *Mailing Add:* Chevron Chem Co 575 Market St San Francisco CA 94105

THOURET, WOLFGANG E(MERY), b Berlin, Ger, Aug 27, 14; US citizen; m 62. PHYSICS, ELECTRICAL ENGINEERING. *Educ:* Tech Univ, Berlin, MS, 36; Univ Karlsruhe, D Ing, 52. *Prof Exp:* Physicist, Res Dept, OSRAM Corp, Ger, 36-40, sect mgr, 40-48; lab mgr, Quarzlampen Gesellschaft, 49-52; develop engr, Lamp Div, Westinghouse Elec Corp, NJ, 52-57; assoc dir eng, 57-71, DIR ENG, DURO-TEST CORP, 71- *Mem:* Fel Am Illum Eng Soc; Am Phys Soc; NY Acad Sci; Inst Elec & Electronics Engrs; Soc Motion Picture & TV Engrs. *Res:* Gaseous discharges; spectroscopy; optical equipment, high intensity light and radiation sources; compact arc high pressure lamps; incandescent lamps; halogen quartz incandescent lamps; metal vapor additive lamps; alumina and sapphire metal vapor lamps. *Mailing Add:* Claridge House I Verona NJ 07044

THOURSON, THOMAS LAWRENCE, b Chicago, Ill, Dec 30, 25; m 47; c 3. PHYSICS. *Educ:* Ill Inst Technol, BS, 50; Northwestern Univ, MS, 52, PhD, 64. *Prof Exp:* Physicist, Int Harvester Co, 52-54, Stand Oil Co, Ind, 54-56 & Borg Warner Corp, 56-65; physicist, 65-80, MGR RES & DEVELOP, XEROX CORP, 80- *Mem:* Soc Photog Sci & Eng. *Res:* Xerography; physics of xerographic processes; xeroradiography; image processing. *Mailing Add:* Xerox Corp Pasadena CA 91107

THRAILKILL, JOHN VERNON, b San Diego, Calif, Aug 31, 30; m 52. GEOLOGY, GEOCHEMISTRY. *Educ:* Univ Colo, AB, 53, MS, 55; Princeton Univ, PhD(geol), 65. *Prof Exp:* Geologist, Continental Oil Co, 55-61; asst prof, 65-69, assoc prof, 69-77, chmn dept, 74-77, PROF GEOL, UNIV KY, 69- *Mem:* AAAS; Nat Speleol Soc; Geol Soc Am; Geochem Soc; Am Geophys Union. *Res:* Low temperature and solution geochemistry; hydrogeology of limestone terrains. *Mailing Add:* Dept of Geol Univ of Ky Lexington KY 40506

THRALL, ROBERT MCDOWELL, b Toledo, Ill, Sept 23, 14; m 36; c 3. MATHEMATICS. *Educ:* Ill Col, AB, 35; Univ Ill, AM, 35, PhD(math), 37. *Hon Degrees:* ScD, Ill Col, 60. *Prof Exp:* Instr math, Univ Mich, 37-40; mem, Inst Advan Study, 40-42; from asst prof to prof math, Univ Mich, Ann Arbor, 42-69; PROF MATH SCI & CHMN DEPT, RICE UNIV, 69- *Concurrent Pos:* Res mathematician appl math group, Nat Defense Res Comt, Columbia Univ, 44-45; mem staff radiation lab & sect chief & ed-in-chief, Mars, Mass Inst Technol, 44-46; prof opers anal, Univ Mich, Ann Arbor, 56-69, head opers res dept, 57-60, res mathematician inst sci & technol, 60-69; consult, Rand Corp, Weapon Syst Eval Group, US Dept Defense & Math Steering Comt, Army Res Off, 58-; ed-in-chief, Mgt Sci, 61-69; adj prof, Dept Comput Sci & Inst Rehab & Res, Baylor Col Med, 71- & Univ Tex Sch Pub Health, Houston, 72-; pres, Robert M Thrall & Assoc, Inc; vis prof quant methods, Univ Houston & sr scientist NSF Industs Studies, 74-75. *Mem:* AAAS; Am Math Soc; Soc Indust & Appl Math; Opers Res Soc Am; Math Asn Am; Inst Mgt Sci (pres, 69-70). *Res:* Representations of groups; rings and lie rings; operations research linear and nonlinear programming and game theory; theory of application of mathematical models. *Mailing Add:* Dept of Math Sci Rice Univ PO Box 1892 Houston TX 77001

THRASHER, DONALD MILLER, animal science, animal husbandry, deceased

THRASHER, GEORGE W, b Bloomington, Ind, July 8, 31; m 53; c 1. ANIMAL NUTRITION. *Educ:* Purdue Univ, BS, 52, MS, 54, PhD, 58. *Prof Exp:* Asst animal nutrit, Chas Pfizer & Co, 54; voc agr teacher, Morgan County Schs, Ind, 54-56; asst animal nutrit, Purdue Univ, 56-58, exten swine specialist, 58-59; res animal nutritionist, Com Solvents Corp, 59-64; asst dir animal health prod res, 64-80, DIR ANIMAL HEALTH RES, PFIZER INC, 80- *Mem:* Am Soc Animal Sci. *Res:* Antibiotics; hormones; anthelmintics; antimicrobials; chemotherapeutics; minerals; vitamins. *Mailing Add:* Animal Health Res Pfizer Inc Terre Haute IN 47808

THRASHER, L(AWRENCE) W(ILLIAM), b Gary, Ind, Dec 30, 22; m 52; c 2. MECHANICAL ENGINEERING. *Educ:* Purdue Univ, BSME, 43, MSME, 49, PhD(mech eng), 54. *Prof Exp:* Engr aircraft heating & vent systs, Martin Co, 46-47; oil field prod facilities, Arabian Am Oil Co, 49-50; res facilities nuclear res, Calif Res & Develop Corp, 52, sect supvr prod tech oil field res, Calif Res Corp, 54-65, sect supvr, Chevron Res Co, 65-68, mgr, Opers Technol Div, 68-74, VPRES PROD RES, CHEVRON OIL FIELD RES CO, 74- *Concurrent Pos:* Chmn, Coord Subcomt for Study, Enhanced Oil Recovery, Nat Petrol Coun, 75-76. *Mem:* AAAS; assoc Am Soc Mech Engrs; Soc Petrol Engrs. *Res:* Oil field production; well drilling and stimulation; fluid mechanics; ocean wave forces; dynamics of anchored vessels; enhanced oil recovery. *Mailing Add:* Prod Res Dept Chevron Oil Field Res Co La Habra CA 90631

THREADGILL, ERNEST DALE, b Tallassee, Ala, June 26, 42; m 67; c 2. AGRICULTURAL & BIOLOGICAL ENGINEERING. *Educ:* Auburn Univ, BS, 64, PhD(agr eng), 68. *Prof Exp:* From asst prof to assoc prof agr & biol eng, Miss State Univ, 68-75; ASSOC PROF & HEAD DEPT AGR ENG, COASTAL PLAIN EXP STA, UNIV GA, 75- *Mem:* Am Soc Agr Engrs. *Res:* Soil erosion and drainage; pesticide applications; air pollution; plant microclimate; fruit and vegetable mechanization; irrigation; soil tillage. *Mailing Add:* Coastal Plain Exp Sta PO Box 748 Tifton GA 31793

THREADGILL, W(ALTER) D(ENNIS), b Huron, Tenn, Mar 17, 22; m 59. CHEMICAL ENGINEERING. *Educ:* Vanderbilt Univ, BE, 50; Univ Mo, PhD(chem eng), 54. *Prof Exp:* Asst instr chem eng, Univ Mo, 50-52, asst & chem engr, Eng Exp Sta, 52-53; asst prof chem eng, 54-57, actg head dept, 56-57, head dept, 60-72, chmn dept, 75-80, PROF CHEM ENG, VANDERBILT UNIV, 57- *Mem:* Am Soc Eng Educ; Am Inst Chem Engrs. *Res:* Thermodynamics; chemical engineering unit operations. *Mailing Add:* Dept Chem Eng Box 1821 Sta B Nashville TN 37235

THREEFOOT, SAM ABRAHAM, b Meridian, Miss, Apr 10, 21; m 54; c 3. CARDIOVASCULAR DISEASES. *Educ:* Tulane Univ, BS, 43, MD, 45; Am Bd Internal Med, dipl, 53. *Prof Exp:* Intern, Michael Reese Hosp, Chicago, 45-47; from instr to prof med, Tulane Univ, 48-70; prof med & asst dean, Med Col Ga, 70-76; chief of staff, Forest Hills Div, Vet Admin Hosp, Augusta, 70-76; assoc chief of staff res, 76-79, CHIEF OF STAFF, VET ADMIN HOSP, NEW ORLEANS, 79-; PROF MED, TULANE UNIV, 76- *Concurrent Pos:* Fel med, Sch Med, Tulane Univ, 47-49; from asst vis physician to sr vis physician, Charity Hosp La, New Orleans, 47-69, consult, 69-70 & 76-; consult, Lallie Kemp Charity Hosp, Independence, 51-53; clin asst, Touro Infirmary, 53-56, dir res & med studies, 53-63, jr staff mem, 56-60, sr assoc, 60-63, sr dept med, 63-70, dir res, Touro Res Inst, 53-70; mem exec comt, Coun on Circulation, Am Heart Asn, 68-75, from vchmn to chmn, 71-75, chmn credentials comt, 72-73; mem bd consult, Int Soc Lymphology, 70-76; mem bd dirs, Am Heart Asn, 66-70 & 72-75, mem exec comt, 69-70 & 73-75. *Mem:* Soc Nuclear Med; Am Fedn Clin Res; fel Am Col Physicians; Am Heart Asn; fel Am Col Cardiol. *Res:* Electrolyte turnover in congestive heart failure; anatomy and physiology of lymphatics as a transport system and their role in pathogenesis of disease. *Mailing Add:* 1601 Perdido St Vet Admin Med Ctr New Orleans LA 70146

THREET, RICHARD LOWELL, b Browns, Ill, Nov 17, 24; m 46; c 4. GEOLOGY. *Educ:* Univ Ill, BS & AB, 47, AM, 49; Univ Wah, Seattle, PhD(geol), 52. *Prof Exp:* From instr to asst prof geol, Univ Nebr, 51-57; asst prof, Univ Utah, 57-61; from asst prof to assoc prof, Calif State Univ, San Diego, 61-68, prof, 68-80, EMER PROF GEOL, SAN DIEGO STATE UNIV, 80- *Concurrent Pos:* Vis prof, Ohio State Univ, 53, 63, 66-70 & 72-73, Col Southern Utah, 54-55 & Univ Ill, 57; chmn dept geol, San Diego State Univ, 72-73; vis prof, Western Washington State Univ, 80-82. *Mem:* Fel Geol Soc Am; Am Soc Photogram. *Res:* Colorado plateau geology; geomorphology; structural geology; photogeology. *Mailing Add:* 2803 17th St Anacortes WA 98221

THRELFALL, WILLIAM, b Preston, Eng, Oct 14, 39; m 65; c 2. PARASITOLOGY, ORNITHOLOGY. *Educ:* Univ Wales, BSc, 62, PhD(agr zool), 65. *Prof Exp:* Asst prof, 65-70, assoc prof, 70-75, PROF BIOL, MEM UNIV NFLD, 75- *Mem:* Sci fel Zool Soc London; fel Linnean Soc London; Can Soc Zool; Brit Trust Ornith; Brit Ornith Union. *Res:* Ecological and geographical aspects of parasitology; helminthology; breeding biology and migratory movements of marine birds. *Mailing Add:* Dept of Biol Mem Univ of Nfld St John's NF A1B 3X9 Can

THRELKELD, JAMES L(EROY), mechanical engineering, see previous edition

THRELKELD, STEPHEN FRANCIS H, b Watford, Eng, Dec 27, 24; m 52; c 2. BIOLOGY, GENETICS. *Educ:* Univ Alta, BSc, 57, MSc, 58; St Catharine's Col, Cambridge, PhD(bot), 61. *Prof Exp:* From asst prof to assoc prof genetics, 61-71, chmn res unit biochem, biophys & molecular biol, 64-68, assoc chmn dept biol, 66-68, PROF GENETICS, McMASTER UNIV, 71-, CHMN DEPT BIOL, 77- *Mem:* Am Soc Naturalists; Genetics Soc Am; Genetics Soc Can; Chem Inst Can; Can Soc Cell Biol. *Res:* Neurospora; recombination; Drosophila behavioral genetics. *Mailing Add:* Dept of Biol McMaster Univ Hamilton ON L8S 4K1 Can

THRIFT, FREDERICK AARON, b St George, Ga, Oct 6, 40; m 67; c 2. ANIMAL BREEDING. *Educ:* Univ Fla, BSA, 62; Univ Ga, MS, 65; Okla State Univ, PhD(animal breeding), 68. *Prof Exp:* Assoc prof, 67-78, PROF ANIMAL SCI, UNIV KY, 78- *Mem:* Biomet Soc; Am Soc Animal Sci. *Res:* Beef cattle and sheep breeding research. *Mailing Add:* Dept of Animal Sci Univ of Ky Lexington KY 40506

THRO, MARY PATRICIA, b St Charles, Mo, Mar 14, 38. PHYSICS, MATHEMATICS. *Educ:* Maryville Col, BA, 61; Fordham Univ, MS, 67; Wash Univ, PhD(educ), 76. *Prof Exp:* Teacher math, Villa Duchesne Elem & Sec Schs, St Louis, 61-64; instr physics, Maryville Col, 67-69; team mem admin, Relig of Sacred Heart, 69-73; asst prof physics, 73-77, ASSOC PROF PHYSICS & MATH, MARYVILLE COL, 77-, CHAIRPERSON DEPT, 74- *Concurrent Pos:* NSF grants, New Orleans, 69-71, Kansas City, 72-73 & Memphis, 78-79; eval chairperson, Acad Sacred Heart, 76; mem bd joint grad educ prog, Wash Univ-Maryville Col, 77-79; co-dir, Mo Jr Acad Sci, 77-; publ, J Educ Psychol, 78. *Mem:* AAAS; Sigma Xi; Am Asn Physics Teachers; Am Educ Res Asn. *Res:* Relationships between associative and content structure of physics concepts; chemical abundance of elements in the cosmos determined by analysis of ion damage recorded on meteorite crystals; spectral analysis of compounds. *Mailing Add:* Maryville Col 13550 Conway Rd St Louis MO 63141

THROCKMORTON, GAYLORD SCOTT, b Kansas City, Kans, Aug 7, 46; m 67; c 3. COMPARATIVE ANATOMY, FUNCTIONAL MORPHOLOGY. *Educ:* Univ Kans, BA, 68; Univ Chicago, PhD(evolutionary biol), 74. *Prof Exp:* Asst prof human anat, Col Dent, Univ Ill Med Ctr, 73-75; asst prof, 75-81, ASSOC PROF HUMAN ANAT, UNIV TEX HEALTH SCI CTR, 81- *Concurrent Pos:* Prin investr, NSF, 78-81; co-investr, NIH, 80-83; cur, Anat Teaching Mus, Univ Tex Health Sci Ctr, 79-; reviewer, Systs & Ecol Prog, NSF, 81- *Mem:* Am Asn Anatomists; Am Soc Zoologists; NY Acad Sci; Soc Vert Paleont; AAAS. *Res:* Form and function of the vertebrate feeding apparatus including comparison of the chewing cycle in lower vertebrates and mammals, mechanisms controlling mastication, and the effect of orthognatic surgery on function of the jaw muscles in humans. *Mailing Add:* Dept Cell Biol Univ Tex Health Sci Ctr Dallas TX 75235

THROCKMORTON, JAMES RODNEY, b St John, Wash, Sept 4, 36; m 58; c 3. PESTICIDE CHEMISTRY. *Educ:* Univ Idaho, BS, 58, MS, 60; Univ Minn, PhD(org chem), 64. *Prof Exp:* Sr chemist, Imaging Res Lab, 64-66, Contract Res Lab, 66-71, RES SPECIALIST, 3M CO, 74- *Mem:* Am Chem Soc. *Res:* Organic fluorochemicals; imaging technology. *Mailing Add:* Minn Mining & Mfg Co 230-B 3M Ctr St Paul MN 55101

THROCKMORTON, LYNN HIRAM, b Loup City, Nebr, Dec 20, 27. ZOOLOGY. *Educ:* Univ Nebr, BS, 49, MS, 56; Univ Tex, PhD(zool), 59. *Prof Exp:* Instr zool, Univ Nebr, 56; spec instr, Univ Tex, 59-60; vis asst prof, Univ Calif, 60-61; res assoc, 61-62; from instr to assoc prof, 62-71, PROF BIOL, UNIV CHICAGO, 71- *Mem:* AAAS; Am Genetics Soc; Soc Syst Zool; Am Inst Biol Sci; Sigma Xi. *Res:* Taxonomy; phylogeny and biogeography of Drosophila and other Drosophilids; biochemical evolution and speciation of Drosophila; utilization and evaluation of computer methods in taxonomy. *Mailing Add:* Dept of Biol Univ of Chicago Chicago IL 60637

THROCKMORTON, MORFORD CHURCH, b Waynesburg, Pa, July 28, 19. POLYMER CHEMISTRY. *Educ:* Grove City Col, BS, 40; Western Reserve Univ, MS, 41, PhD(phys chem), 44. *Prof Exp:* Lab asst gen chem & qual anal, Grove City Col, 38-40; chemist, Cleveland Clin Res Found, Ohio, 40-41, Res Labs, Stand Oil Co, 42 & Texaco, Inc, 43-54, group leader, 54-59; sr res chemist, Firestone Tire & Rubber Co, 60-63; sr res chemist, 64-68, RES SCIENTIST, GOODYEAR TIRE & RUBBER CO, 68- *Mem:* Am Chem Soc. *Res:* Catalysis; synthetic fuels; development of synthetic rubber; stereospecific polymerization; petrochemicals. *Mailing Add:* 967 Newport Rd Akron OH 44303

THROCKMORTON, PETER E, b St Paul, Minn, Jan 20, 27; m 48; c 3. ORGANIC CHEMISTRY. *Educ:* Univ Minn, BCHE, 48, MS, 55; Kans State Univ, PhD, 60. *Prof Exp:* Asst res engr, Tainton Co, 48-49; res engr, Glenn L Martin Aircraft Co, 49-52; chemist, Gen Mills Co, 52-56; asst, Kans State Univ, 56-59; assoc chemist, Midwest Res Inst, 59-65; sr res chemist, Ashland Oil, Inc, 65-73, SR RES CHEMIST, ASHLAND CHEM CO, 73- *Mem:* Am Chem Soc. *Res:* Heterocyclic and organometallic compounds in organic chemistry; synthesis; process research; surfactants from cornstarch; sulfur derivatives; selective oxidation of hydrocarbons. *Mailing Add:* Ashland Chem Co PO Box 2219 Columbus OH 43216

THRODAHL, MONTE C(ORDEN), b Minneapolis, Minn, Mar 25, 19; m 48; c 2. CHEMICAL ENGINEERING. *Educ:* Iowa State Col, BS, 41. *Prof Exp:* Res chemist, Org Res Dept, 41-45, group leader, 45-50, asst res dir, 50-52, mgr rubber chem sect, Org Develop Dept, 52-54, asst dir develop, 54-56, dir develop, 56-60, dir res, Org Res Dept, 60-62, dir mkt, 62-64, asst gen mgr, Int Div, 64, gen mgr, 64-66, vpres technol & dir, 66-77, GROUP VPRES & SR VPRES ENVIRON POLICY, MONSANTO CO, 77- *Mem:* Nat Acad Eng; Am Chem Soc; Com Develop Asn; fel Am Inst Chem Engrs; Soc Chem Indust. *Mailing Add:* Monsanto Co 800 N Lindbergh Blvd St Louis MO 63166

THRON, WOLFGANG JOSEPH, b Ribnitz, Ger, Aug 17, 18; US citizen; m 53; c 5. MATHEMATICS. *Educ:* Princeton, AB, 39; Rice Inst, MA, 42, PhD(math), 43. *Prof Exp:* Instr math, Harvard Univ, 43-44; from instr to assoc prof, Wash Univ, St Louis, 46-54; assoc prof, 54-57, PROF MATH, UNIV COLO, BOULDER, 57- *Concurrent Pos:* Vis prof, Free Univ Berlin, 51, Philippines, 66-67, Univ Erlangen, 70-71, Punjab Univ, India, 74-75 & Univ Trondheim, 78-79; res grant, Air Force Off Sci Res, Ger, 57-58; vis prof & Fulbright lectr, India, 62-63. *Mem:* Am Math Soc. *Res:* Complex variables, analysis of convergence and truncation errors of infinite processes in particular continued fractions; general topology, lattice of topologies, proximity, contiguity and nearness spaces, extensions of spaces. *Mailing Add:* Dept of Math Univ of Colo Boulder CO 80302

THRONE, JAMES LOUIS, b Cleveland, Ohio, July 10, 37; m 59; c 2. CHEMICAL ENGINEERING. *Educ:* Case Inst Technol, BS, 59; Univ Del, MChE, 61, PhD(chem eng), 64. *Prof Exp:* Res engr, Eng Res Labs, E I du Pont de Nemours & Co, Inc, 63-64; assoc prof chem eng, Ohio Univ, 64-68; supvr plastics processing, Am Standard, NJ, 68-71; assoc prof energetics, Univ Wis-Milwaukee, 71-72; dir plastics res, Beloit Corp, Wis, 72-74; RES ASSOC PLASTICS PROCESSING, AMOCO CHEM CORP, 74- *Concurrent Pos:* Vis prof chem eng, Univ Cincinnati, 65; adj prof plastics processing, Newark Col Eng, 68-71; prof food eng, Orgn Am States, Brazil, 72; consult, Sherwood Tech Serv, Beloit, Wis, 72-74. *Mem:* Soc Plastics Engrs; Am Inst Chem Engrs; Soc Rheology; fel Brit Plastics & Rubber Inst. *Res:* Plastics process engineering, with emphasis in thermoforming, rotational molding, structural foam molding and comparative process economics. *Mailing Add:* 109 Springwood Dr Naperville IL 60540

THRONEBERRY, GLYN OGLE, b Rule, Tex, Nov 1, 27; m 48; c 1. PLANT PHYSIOLOGY. *Educ:* NMex State Univ, BS, 50; Iowa State Col, MS, 52, PhD(plant physiol), 53. *Prof Exp:* Plant physiologist, Kans State Col, USDA, 54-55; asst prof biol, 55-57, from asst prof to assoc prof, 57-67, PROF BOT & ENTOM, NMEX STATE UNIV, 67- *Mem:* AAAS; Am Soc Plant Physiol; Am Phytopath Soc. *Res:* Plant host-pathogen relationships; intermediary metabolism; fungus physiology; plant biochemistry. *Mailing Add:* Dept of Entom & Plant Path NMex State Univ Las Cruces NM 88003

THRONER, GUY CHARLES, b Minneapolis, Minn, Sept 14, 19; m 43; c 3. TERMINAL BALLISTICS, WEAPON SYSTEMS ENGINEERING. *Educ:* Oberlin Col, AB, 43. *Prof Exp:* Mgr res & develop, Ordnance Div, Aerojet Gen, 53-63, mgr res & develop, Tactical Weapon Systs Div, Aerojet Gen Corp, 63-64; vpres & div gen mgr res & develop, FMC Corp, 64-74; dir res & develop, Vacu-Blast & Tronic Corp, 76-78; vpres prod eng, Dahlman Inc, 78-79; SECT MGR RES & DEVELOP, COLUMBUS LABS, BATTELLE MEM INST, 79- *Concurrent Pos:* Vpres & gen mgr res & develop, Steel Prod Div, FMC Corp, 64-74; exec vpres res & develop, Am Vidionetics Corp, 76-78; mem, Air Armament Bd, Bomb & Warhead Steering Comt & Underwater Weapons Steering Comt. *Mem:* Sigma Xi; Sci Res Soc Am; Am Defense Preparedness Asn. *Res:* Metal forming; high speed instrumentation; medical devices; oil field equipment; agri-machinery; weapon and space technology; author or coauthor of over 80 publications. *Mailing Add:* 2074 Nayland Rd Columbus OH 43220

THROOP, LEWIS JOHN, b Detroit, Mich, June 18, 29; m 54; c 1. ANALYTICAL CHEMISTRY. *Educ:* Wayne State Univ, BS, 54, MS, 56, PhD(anal chem), 57. *Prof Exp:* Chemist, Syntex, SA, Mex, 57-59; group leader anal chem, Mead Johnson & Co, 59-64; dept head, 64-71, asst dir anal chem, Inst Org Chem, 71-78, DIR ANAL RES, SYSTEX RES, SYNTEX CORP, 78- *Mem:* Am Chem Soc; Am Pharmaceut Asn. *Res:* Electrochemistry; organic structure characterization; laboratory automation. *Mailing Add:* Syntex Corp 3401 Hillview Ave Palo Alto CA 94304

THROW, FRANCIS EDWARD, b Ottumwa, Iowa, Oct 4, 12; m 38; c 3. RESEARCH ADMINISTRATION. *Educ:* Park Col, BA, 33; Univ Mich, MS, 36, PhD(physics), 40. *Prof Exp:* Instr physics, Milwaukee State Teachers Col, 39; instr physics & math, Polytech Inst PR, 40-41; instr physics, Altoona Undergrad Ctr, 41-42; ground sch instr math, physics & theory of flight, US Navy Pre-Flight Sch, Iowa Univ, 42-44; prof physics & head dept, Cornell Col, 44-52; chmn dept physics, Wabash Col, 52-56; asst dir physics div, Argonne Nat Lab, 56-73, asst dir radiol & environ res div, 73-77; RETIRED. *Concurrent Pos:* Consult, tech ed & writer, report on electronic control, Borg-Warner, 78, annual brochures, Argonne Univ Asn, 80, 81 & 82. *Mem:* Am Phys Soc; Am Asn Physics Teachers. *Res:* Technical editing; analytical mechanics; discharges in gases. *Mailing Add:* 719 S Gables Blvd Wheaton IL 60187

THROWER, PETER ALBERT, b Norfolk, Eng, Jan 9, 38; m 60. PHYSICS, MATERIALS SCIENCE. *Educ:* Cambridge Univ, BA, 60, MA, 63, PhD(physics), 69. *Prof Exp:* Sci officer, Atomic Energy Res Estab, Eng, 60-65, sr sci officer, 65-69; ASSOC PROF MAT SCI, PA STATE UNIV, UNIVERSITY PARK, 69- *Concurrent Pos:* Ed, Chem & Physics of Carbon, assoc ed, Carbon J. *Mem:* Am Soc Metals. *Res:* Structure and properties of carbon and graphite; irradiation damage to graphite; electron microscopy; mineral microstructures. *Mailing Add:* 302 Mineral Sci Bldg Pa State Univ University Park PA 16802

THRUPP, LAURI DAVID, b Sask, Nov 30, 30; US citizen; m 52; c 4. INFECTIOUS DISEASES, MICROBIOLOGY. *Educ:* Stanford Univ, AB, 51; Univ Wash, MD, 55. *Prof Exp:* Asst chief & chief polio surveillance, Epidemiol Br, Nat Commun Dis Ctr, 56-58; resident physician & fel, Boston City Hosp, Thorndike Serv & Harvard Med Sch, 58-63; jr asst physician, Harvard Serv, 61-63; asst prof med & med microbiol, Sch Med, Univ Southern Calif, 63-66, asst prof med, 66-68; assoc prof med & head div infectious dis, 68-77, PROF MED, DIV INFECTIOUS DIS, UNIV CALIF, IRVINE, 77- *Concurrent Pos:* Life Ins Med Res Found res fel med & bact, Boston City Hosp & Harvard Med Sch, 60-63; asst chief commun dis, Los Angeles County Gen Hosp, 63-64, attend physician, 63-, med microbiologist, 64-65; consult, Los Angeles County Health Dept, 64- & Calif State Health Dept, 66-; chief infectious dis serv, Orange County Med Ctr, 68- *Mem:* Am Fedn Clin Res; Am Soc Microbiol; Am Pub Health Asn; Infectious Dis Soc Am; NY Acad Sci. *Res:* Clinical and experimental pyelonephritis, pathogenesis and immune response, role of bacterial L-forms; gram-negative hospital-acquired infections; meningitis, clinical and immunological; bacteriology. *Mailing Add:* Infectious Dis Serv Univ of Calif Irvine Orange CA 92668

THRUSTON, ALFRED DORRAH, JR, b Greenville, SC, Nov 3, 34; m 64; c 2. ANALYTICAL CHEMISTRY. *Educ:* Ga Inst Technol, BS, 57. *Prof Exp:* Chemist, US Food & Drug Admin, 59-66; RES CHEMIST, ATHENS ENVIRON RES LAB, ENVIRON PROTECTION AGENCY, 66- *Mem:* Am Chem Soc. *Res:* Liquid chromatographic, mass spectrometric and gas chromatographic analysis of water pollutants. *Mailing Add:* Environ Res Lab College Station Rd Athens GA 30605

THUAN, TRINH XUAN, b Hanoi, Vietnam, Aug 20, 48. ASTROPHYSICS, ATRONOMY. *Educ:* Calif Inst Technol, BS, 70; Princeton Univ, PhD(astrophysics), 74. *Prof Exp:* Res fel astrophys, Calif Inst Technol, 74-76; ASST PROF ASTRON, UNIV VA, 76- *Concurrent Pos:* Vis fel, Inst d'Astrophys, Paris, 78; vis prof, Ctr d'Etudes Nucleaires de Saclay, Paris, 81. *Mem:* Am Astron Soc; Int Astron Union. *Res:* Study of the formation, clustering and evolution of galaxies; observational cosmology. *Mailing Add:* Dept of Astron PO Box 3818 Univ Sta Charlottesville VA 22903

THUENTE, DAVID JOSEPH, b Decorah, Iowa, Mar 17, 45; m 67; c 2. OPERATIONS RESEARCH, MATHEMATICAL PROGRAMMING. *Educ:* Loras Col, BS, 67; Univ Kans, MA, 69, PhD(math), 74. *Prof Exp:* Systs analyst transp, Jewel Co, Inc, 67; instr math, Univ Kans, 70-74; mem fac res staff nonlinear prog, Argonne Nat Lab, 76-77; asst prof, 74-79, ASSOC PROF APPL MATH, IND UNIV-PURDUE UNIV, FT WAYNE, 80- *Concurrent Pos:* Res grant, Purdue Univ, 75; fac res grant, Argonne Nat Lab, 76-77 & 80, consult, 80-81. *Mem:* Soc Indust & Appl Math; Opers Res Soc Am; Math Prog Soc; Sigma Xi; Asn Comput Mach. *Res:* Generalized and inexact linear programming; shortest paths in multiple criteria networks; linearly constrained nonlinear programming; mathematical modeling, inventory and queueing models, line searchers. *Mailing Add:* Dept Math Sci 2101 Coliseum Blvd Ft Wayne IN 46805

THUERING, GEORGE LEWIS, b Milwaukee, Wis, Sept 2, 19; m 45, 75; c 1. INDUSTRIAL ENGINEERING. *Educ:* Univ Wis, BS, 41, ME, 54; Pa State Univ, MS, 49. *Prof Exp:* Mfg engr, Lockheed Aircarft Corp, Calif, 41-47, supvr plant layout & space control dept, Ga Div, 51-52; from instr to assoc prof, 47-56, dir, Dept Mgt Engr, 62-77, PROF INDUST ENG, PA STATE UNIV, 56- *Concurrent Pos:* Consult. *Mem:* Am Inst Indust Engrs; Am Soc Eng Educ; Am Soc Mech Engrs (vpres, 82-84). *Res:* Manufacturing science. *Mailing Add:* Dept of Indust Eng Pa State Univ University Park PA 16802

THUESEN, GERALD JORGEN, b Oklahoma City, Okla, July 20, 38; m 60; c 2. INDUSTRIAL ENGINEERING. *Educ:* Stanford Univ, BS, 60, MS, 61, PhD(indust eng), 68. *Prof Exp:* Engr, Pac Tel Co, 61-62; mgt engr comput systs, Atlantic Refining Co, 62-63; asst prof indust eng, Arlington State Col, 63-64 & Univ Tex, Arlington, 67-68; assoc prof, 68-76, PROF INDUST ENG, GA INST TECHNOL, 76- *Honors & Awards:* Eugene L Grant Award, Am Soc Eng Educ, 77. *Mem:* Am Inst Indust Engrs; Opers Res Soc Am; Am Soc Eng Educ. *Res:* Decision analysis; engineering economy; capital budgeting; statistical decision theory. *Mailing Add:* Sch of Indust & Systs Eng Ga Inst of Technol Atlanta GA 30332

THUESON, DAVID OREL, b Twin Falls, Idaho, May 9, 47; m 69; c 5. IMMUNOPHARMACOLOGY, INFLAMMATION. *Educ:* Brigham Young Univ, BS, 71; Univ Utah, Salt Lake City, PhD(pharmacol), 76. *Prof Exp:* Fel, 75-77, res scientist immunol, 76-77, ASST PROF ALLERGY, IMMUNOL & PHARMACOL, UNIV TEX MED BR, 77- *Concurrent Pos:* Prin investr, Nat Inst Allergy & Infectious Dis, 78-81. *Mem:* Am Acad Allergy; Am Asn Immunologists. *Res:* Modification of immune and hyspersensitivity reactions by drugs and biologic products; control of lymphocyte derived elicitor and suppressor factors and the release of inflammatory mediators, especially from basophils; mechanisms of inflammation allergy. *Mailing Add:* Adult Allergy Dept Internal Med CSB 410 Univ Tex Med Br Galveston TX 77550

THUILLIER, RICHARD HOWARD, meteorology, air pollution, see previous edition

THUM, ALAN BRADLEY, b Washington, DC, May 30, 43; m 66; c 1. MARINE ECOLOGY. *Educ:* Univ Redlands, BS, 65; Univ Pac, MS, 67; Ore State Univ, PhD(marine ecol), 71. *Prof Exp:* Lectr invert zool, Univ Cape Town, 71-75; SR SCIENTIST & ENVIRON CONSULT, LOCKHEED MARINE BIOL LAB, LOCKHEED AIRCRAFT SERV, 75- *Concurrent Pos:* Consult, Bur Land Mgt, Univ Southern Calif, 76- *Mem:* Ecol Soc Am; Am Soc Limnol & Oceanog; Int Asn Meiobenthologists; Royal Soc SAfrica. *Res:* Ecology of interstitial meiofauna; ecology and systematics of turbellaria; reproductive ecology of marine benthic invertebrates. *Mailing Add:* Lockheed Marine Biol Lab 6350 Yarrow Dr Suite A Carlsbad CA 91008

THUMANN, ALBERT, b New York, NY, Mar 12, 42; m 66; c 1. ELECTRICAL & ENERGY ENGINEERING. *Educ:* City Col New York, BEE, 64; NY Univ, MSEE, 67, MSIE, 70. *Prof Exp:* Proj mgr eng construct, Bechtel Assocs, 64-77; EXEC DIR ENERGY, ASN ENERGY ENGRS, 77- *Concurrent Pos:* Adj prof, Univ Louisville & lectr, Sch Continuing Educ, NY Univ, 76- *Mem:* Nat Soc Prof Engrs; Inst Elec & Electronics Engrs; Acoust Soc Am; Asn Energy Engrs (pres, 77); Am Soc Asn Execs. *Res:* Noise control, energy and biorhythms. *Mailing Add:* Asn of Energy Engrs 464 Armoor Circle NE Atlanta GA 30324

THUMM, BYRON ASHLEY, b Malden, WVa, Jan 2, 23; m 56. ANALYTICAL CHEMISTRY. *Educ:* Morris Harvey Col, BS, 45; Duke Univ, PhD(chem), 51. *Prof Exp:* Res chemist, Am Viscose Div, FMC Corp, 51-63; ASSOC PROF CHEM, STATE UNIV NY COL, FREDONIA, 63- *Mem:* Am Chem Soc. *Res:* Solution kinetics and equilibrium; rayon spinning process; water analysis; formaldehyde complexes. *Mailing Add:* Dept of Chem State Univ of NY Col Fredonia NY 14063

THUN, RUDOLF EDUARD, b Berlin, Ger, Jan 30, 21; nat US; m 44; c 2. SOLID STATE PHYSICS. *Educ:* Univ Frankfurt, dipl, 54, PhD(physics), 55. *Prof Exp:* Physicist, Ger Gold & Silver Separation Plant, 51-55 & US Army Engrs Res & Develop Labs, Ft Belvoir, Va, 55-59; var sci & managerial positions, Int Bus Mach Corp, 59-67; mgr microelectronics, Missile Systs Div, 67-70, mgr electronic prod design lab, 70-75, mgr, Advan Electronics Lab, Missile Systs Div, 75-80, MGR, MICROELECTRONICS CTR, RAYTHEON CO, BEDFORD, 80- *Honors & Awards:* 1975 Contributions Award, Inst Elec & Electronics Engrs, 75. *Mem:* Fel Am Phys Soc; Optical Soc Am; fel Inst Elec & Electronics Engrs. *Res:* Microelectronics; physics of thin films; electron diffraction and microscopy; x-ray diffraction; physical and electron optics; solid state devices and integrated circuits. *Mailing Add:* 228 Heald Rd Carlisle MA 01741

THUNING, CLAIRE ANN, b Cincinnati, Ohio, Nov 17, 45. CANCER CHEMOTHERAPY, ONCOGENIC VIRUSES. *Educ:* St Mary-of-the-Woods Col, BA, 67; Nova Univ, MS, 77, PhD(biol), 82. *Prof Exp:* Sr res assoc, St Vincent Charity Hosp, 69-74; RES ASSOC, GOODWIN INST CANCER RES, 74- *Concurrent Pos:* Dir grad studies, Goodwin Inst Cancer Res, 81- *Mem:* AAAS; Am Soc Clin Path. *Res:* Investigating the control of cancer using combined hyperthermia and chemotherapy; the use of oxygen immunosuppression in promoting xenogeneic tumor growth and blocking autoimmune disease; properties of recombinant herpes virus strains. *Mailing Add:* Goodwin Inst Cancer Res 1850 Northwest 69th Ave Plantation FL 33313

THURBER, DAVID LAWRENCE, b Oneonta, NY, Dec 29, 34; m 64; c 1. GEOCHEMISTRY. *Educ:* Union Col, NY, BS, 56; Columbia Univ, MA, 58, PhD(geol), 63. *Prof Exp:* Res asst geochem, Lamont Geol Observ, Columbia Univ, 56-63, res scientist, 63-64, res assoc, 64-66; assoc prof geol, 66-70, PROF EARTH & ENVIRON SCI, QUEENS COL, NY, 70- *Concurrent Pos:* Am Geophys Union vis lectureship, 64; lectr, Queens Col, NY, 65-66; vis res assoc, Lamont Geol Observ, 66-70, vis sr res assoc, Lamont-Doherty Geol Observ, 70-74; vis prof, Fed Univ Bahia, 74-78. *Mem:* AAAS; Am Geophys Union; Geochem Soc. *Res:* General geochemistry; stable and radioisotope geochemistry; geochronology; hydrochemistry; soil chemistry. *Mailing Add:* Dept of Earth & Environ Sci Queens Col Flushing NY 11367

THURBER, GEORGE A, b Liscomb, Iowa, Apr 21, 07; m 30; c 2. MEDICAL ENTOMOLOGY. *Educ:* Iowa State Univ, BS, 31, MS, 32. *Prof Exp:* Flight instr, US Army Air Force, 42-45; instr biol & chem, Iowa Pub Sch, 46-58; from asst prof & exec asst to dean sch med to assoc prof, 58-70, exec asst to chancellor, Med Ctr, 64-77, prof med entom, 70-77, EMER PROF MED ENTOM, SCH MED, LA STATE UNIV MED CTR, NEW ORLEANS, 77- *Concurrent Pos:* Co-dir training prog trop med, La State Univ, 58-; consult, USPHS Hosp, Carville, La, 65- & New Orleans PsychoAnal Inst, 66-77. *Mem:* Entom Soc Am; Am Soc Trop Med & Hyg; Asn Am Med Cols. *Res:* Relative toxicity of insecticides; vectors of Chagas' disease; education in tropical medicine. *Mailing Add:* Dept of Trop Med La State Univ Med Ctr New Orleans LA 70112

THURBER, JAMES KENT, b Utica, NY, Oct 29, 33. APPLIED MATHEMATICS. *Educ:* Brooklyn Col, BS, 55; NY Univ, PhD, 61. *Prof Exp:* Asst appl math, NY Univ, 57-61; asst prof math, Adelphi Univ, 61-64; assoc math, Brookhaven Nat Lab, 64-66, mathematician, 66-69; PROF MATH, PURDUE UNIV, LAFAYETTE, 69- *Mem:* Am Math Soc; Am Nuclear Soc; Math Asn Am; Soc Indust & Appl Math; NY Acad Sci. *Res:* Neutron transport; kinetic theory of gases; asymptotic analysis; mathematical programming; applications of nonstandard analysis. *Mailing Add:* Div of Math Sci Purdue Univ Lafayette IN 47907

THURBER, ROBERT EUGENE, b Bayshore, NY, Oct 11, 32; m 53; c 4. PHYSIOLOGY, BIOPHYSICS. *Educ:* Col of the Holy Cross, BS, 54; Adelphi Univ, MS, 61; Univ Kans, PhD(physiol), 65. *Prof Exp:* Res assoc radiation biol, Brookhaven Nat Lab, Assoc Univs Inc, 56-61; from instr to assoc prof physiol, Med Col Va, Va Commonwealth Univ, 64-69; assoc prof, Jefferson Med Col, Thomas Jefferson Univ, 69-70; PROF PHYSIOL & CHMN DEPT, SCH MED, EAST CAROLINA UNIV, 70- *Concurrent Pos:* Consult, US Vet Admin, Va State Bd Med Examr & NASA, Va, 66-69, US Naval Hosp, Portsmouth, 68-69 & Psychol Consult Inc, 68-70; mem bd dirs, NC Heart Asn, 72-, pres elect, 78-79, pres, 79-80; mem, Comt Regional & Nat Res, Am Heart Asn, 81- *Mem:* AAAS; Am Physiol Soc; NY Acad Sci; Sigma Xi. *Res:* Nonequilibrium transfer and distribution of electrolytes; renal transport; radiation biology and carbohydrate metabolism. *Mailing Add:* Dept Physiol Sch Med East Carolina Univ Greenville NC 27834

THURBER, WALTER ARTHUR, b East Worcester, NY, Nov 27, 08; m 34; c 2. ORNITHOLOGY. *Educ:* Union Col NY, BS, 33; NY State Col Teachers, MS, 38; Cornell Univ, PhD(nature study), 41. *Prof Exp:* Teacher NY schs, 26-29, 33-38; asst ed, Cornell Univ, 38-39; instr physics & phys sci, State Univ

NY Teachers Col, Cortland, 40-43; asst prof physics & phys & earth sci, 43-48, prof sci, 48-58; vis prof sci educ, Syracuse Univ, 58-61, adj prof, 61-72; textbook writer, 61-80. *Concurrent Pos:* Consult, NY State Educ Dept, 43-55, NY pub schs, 47-52, Orgn Cent Am States, 66-, Ministerio de Educacion, El Salvador, 72 & Direccion General de Recursas Naturales, El Salvador, 74-; lab assoc, Lab Ornith, Cornell Univ, 70-; vis prof, Nat Univ El Salvador, 71-79. *Mem:* Fel AAAS; NY Acad Sci; Am Ornith Union; Wilson Ornith Soc; Cooper Ornith Soc. *Res:* Elementary and secondary science education; organization of syllabuses and textbooks; distribution and life histories Central American birds. *Mailing Add:* PO Box 16918 Temple Terrace FL 33687

THURBER, WILLIAM SAMUELS, b Ann Arbor, Mich, Mar 6, 22; m 43; c 4. ORGANIC CHEMISTRY. *Educ:* Mich State Univ, BS, 46, MS, 48. *Prof Exp:* Asst dir styrene polymerization lab, Dow Chem Co, 54-57, dir, Strosackers Res & Develop Group, 57-61, plant supt, 61-64, tech dir, Saginaw Bay Res Dept, 64-68, admin asst to div dir res, 68-70, sect mgr process develop & eng, 70-76, mgr, 76-81, MGR EQUAL OPPORTUNITY EMPLOY PROGS, DOW CHEM USA, 81- *Mem:* Am Chem Soc. *Res:* Styrene polymers; antioxidants; polyglycols; surface active agents. *Mailing Add:* EEO Mich Div Dow Chem USA Midland MI 48640

THURBER, WILLIS ROBERT, b Butte, Nebr, July 10, 38; m 65; c 2. SEMICONDUCTORS, MATERIALS SCIENCE. *Educ:* Nebr Wesleyan Univ, AB, 60; Univ Md, MS, 63. *Prof Exp:* Res physicist, Solid State Physics Sect, 62-66, res physicist, Electron Devices Div, 66-80, RES PHYSICIST, SEMICONDUCTORS, SEMICONDUCTOR MAT & PROCESSES DIV, NAT BUR STANDARDS, 80- *Mem:* Inst Elec & Electronic Engrs; Am Soc Testing & Mat. *Res:* Electrical and optical properties of semiconductors, particularly silicon, including Hall effect, resistivity, mobility, lifetime, infrared transmission and absorption; deep level transient spectroscopy. *Mailing Add:* Nat Bur Standards Bldg 225 Rm A331 Washington DC 20234

THURBERG, FREDERICK PETER, b Weymouth, Mass, Aug 31, 42; m 64; c 2. PHYSIOLOGY, MARINE BIOLOGY. *Educ:* Univ Mass, BA, 64, MEd, 66; Univ NH, MS, 69, PhD(zool, physiol), 72. *Prof Exp:* Teacher pub schs, Mass, 64-67; PHYSIOLOGIST, NAT MARINE FISHERIES SERV, NAT OCEANIC & ATMOSPHERIC ADMIN, 71- *Mem:* Estuarine Res Fedn; Am Soc Zoologists; Nat Shellfisheries Asn. *Res:* Physiological ecology; effects of pollutants on marine organisms; invertebrate physiology; marine biotoxins; red tides. *Mailing Add:* Northeast Fisheries Ctr Nat Marine Fisheries Serv Milford CT 06460

THURESON-KLEIN, ASA KRISTINA, b Sveg, Sweden, May 31, 34; m 61; c 2. BIOLOGY, PHARMACOLOGY. *Educ:* Univ Stockholm, MA, 58, PhD(biol), 68. *Prof Exp:* Instr bot, Univ Stockholm, 58-64; res assoc, 65-68, asst prof, 69-74, assoc prof, 74-78, PROF PHARMACOL, MED CTR, UNIV MISS, 78- *Concurrent Pos:* Pharmaceut Mfrs Asn Found fel pharmacol & morphol, Med Ctr, Univ Miss, 71-73. *Mem:* Am Soc Pharmacol & Exp Therapeut; Electron Micros Soc Am; Soc Neurosci; Sigma Xi. *Res:* Effects of pharmacological agents on uptake, storage and release of neurotransmitter from catecholamine storage vesicles, using combined biochemical and morphological methods; adrenergic innervation of brown adipose tissue; mechanisms of transmitter-release from nerve-endings at veins and arteries; morphological changes in blood-vessels after subarachnoid hemorrhage and vasospasm. *Mailing Add:* Dept of Pharmacol Univ of Miss Med Ctr Jackson MS 39216

THURLOW, JOHN FRANK, biochemistry, deceased

THURMAIER, ROLAND JOSEPH, b Chicago, Ill, June 25, 28; m 55; c 4. ORGANIC CHEMISTRY, POLYMER CHEMISTRY. *Educ:* Bradley Univ, BS, 50; Univ Iowa, MS, 58, PhD(org chem), 60. *Prof Exp:* Plant chemist, Corn Prod Ref Corp, 51-55; res chemist, E I du Pont de Nemours & Co, 60-66; ASST PROF ORG CHEM, UNIV WIS-STEVENS POINT, 66- *Concurrent Pos:* Mem, Stevens Point Transit Comn, 70; mem study comt mass transit, 72. *Mem:* AAAS; Am Chem Soc. *Res:* Polymers; stabilizers for polyurethanes. *Mailing Add:* Dept of Chem Univ of Wis Stevens Point WI 54481

THURMAN, HENRY L, JR, b Lawrenceville, Va, Jan 14, 27; m 52; c 1. ENGINEERING. *Educ:* Hampton Inst, BS, 47; Univ Ill, MS, 49. *Prof Exp:* Instr tech archit construct, 48-52, dir div indust technol, 53-56, dir technol & eng, 56-59, dean col eng, 59-72, PROF ARCHIT ENG, SOUTHERN UNIV, BATON ROUGE, 72- *Concurrent Pos:* Mem bd dirs, Comn Eng Educ, 67- *Mem:* Am Soc Eng Educ. *Res:* Structural and architectural design; shelter analysis. *Mailing Add:* Col Eng Box 9917 Baton Rouge LA 70813

THURMAN, LLOY DUANE, b Oconto, Nebr, Sept 3, 33; m 57; c 4. PLANT ECOLOGY. *Educ:* Univ Nebr, BS, 59, MS, 61; Univ Calif, Berkeley, 66. *Prof Exp:* Asst prof biol, Southern Calif Col, 65-67; from asst prof to assoc prof biol, 67-72, chmn dept natural sci, 69-73, PROF BIOL, ORAL ROBERTS UNIV, 72- *Mem:* Sigma Xi; Bot Soc Am; Ecol Soc Am; Am Sci Affil; Nat Sci Teachers Asn. *Res:* Ecology of Orthocarpus; curricula and teaching methods in biology; computers in biology and nutrition; creation versus evolution controversy. *Mailing Add:* Dept of Natural Sci 7777 S Lewis Tulsa OK 74105

THURMAN, RICHARD GARY, b Wichita, Kans, Mar 1, 40; m 70. CHEMISTRY. *Educ:* NMex State Univ, BS, 62, MS, 65; Univ Ariz, PhD(chem), 71. *Prof Exp:* Asst prof chem, Univ Ariz, 70-71; from asst prof to assoc prof chem, Univ Nebr-Omaha, 71-77; MEM STAFF, UNION CAMP, 77- *Mem:* Am Chem Soc. *Res:* Liquid and gas chromatography study of the separation processes; computer-controlled chemical instrumentation; use of computers in chemical education. *Mailing Add:* Union Camp PO Box 412 Princeton NJ 08540

THURMAN, ROBERT ELLIS, II, b Springfield, Mo, Oct 15, 39; m 62; c 4. PHYSICS. *Educ:* Mo Sch Mines, BS, 62; Univ Wis, MS, 64; Univ Mo-Rolla, PhD(physics), 77. *Prof Exp:* Res asst physics, Univ Wis, 63-66; from instr to asst prof, 66-77, ASSOC PROF PHYSICS, SOUTHWEST MO STATE UNIV, 77- *Concurrent Pos:* Physicist, US Forest Prod Lab, 63-64; NSF sci fac fel, 70-71; res asst physics, Univ Mo-Rolla, 71-72; sabbatical leave, Cloud Physics Ctr, Univ Mo-Rolla, 81-82. *Mem:* AAAS; Am Asn Physics Teachers. *Res:* Atmospheric physics; electrical mobility of water molecule cluster ions; aerosol evolution. *Mailing Add:* Dept of Physics Southwest Mo State Univ Springfield MO 65802

THURMAN, RONALD GLENN, b Carbondale, Ill, Nov 25, 41. BIOCHEMISTRY, PHARMACOLOGY. *Educ:* St Louis Col Pharm, BS, 63; Univ Ill, PhD(pharmacol), 67. *Prof Exp:* Asst prof biophys & phys biochem, Johnson Res Found, Univ Pa, 71-77; ASSOC PROF PHARMACOL, UNIV NC, CHAPEL HILL, 77- Prof Exp: Fel, Johnson Res Found, Univ Pa, 67-69; NATO fel, Inst Physiol Chem, Munich, Ger, 69-70, Alexander von Humboldt fel, 70-71; NIMH career develop award, 71-82. *Mem:* AAAS; Am Pharmaceut Soc. *Res:* Drug and alcohol metabolism. *Mailing Add:* Dept of Pharmacol Univ of NC Chapel Hill NC 19104

THURMAN, WAYNE LAVERNE, b Detroit, Mich, June 11, 23. SPEECH PATHOLOGY. *Educ:* Southeast Mo State Col, BA & BSE, 48; State Univ Iowa, MA, 49; Purdue Univ, PhD(speech path), 53. *Prof Exp:* Instr speech, Southeast Mo State Col, 49-51; PROF SPEECH PATH & CHMN DEPT, EASTERN ILL UNIV, 53- *Mem:* fel Am Speech-Lang-Hearing Asn. *Res:* Voice quality disorders severity scales; voice therapy procedures. *Mailing Add:* Dept Speech Path & Audiol Eastern Ill Univ Charleston IL 61920

THURMAN, WILLIAM GENTRY, b Jacksonville, Fla, July 1, 28; m 49; c 3. PEDIATRICS, ONCOLOGY. *Educ:* Univ NC, BS, 49; McGill Univ, MD & CM, 54. *Prof Exp:* Asst prof pediat, Tulane Univ, 60-61; assoc prof, Emory Univ, 61-62; prof, Cornell Univ, 62-64; prof & chmn dept, Sch Med, Univ Va, 64-73, dir, Ctr Delivery Health Care, 69-73; dean sch med, Tulane Univ, 73-75; prof pediat & provost, Univ Okla Health Sci Ctr, 75-79; PROF PEDIAT & PRES, OKLA MED RES FOUND, 79- *Concurrent Pos:* Fel hemat & oncol, 58-60; Markle scholar acad med, 59-64; consult, US Air Force, 59-, Comn on Cancer, 63- & Comn on Pediat Hemat, 65-; chmn dept pediat, Mem Sloan-Kettering Cancer Ctr, 62-64; prog consult, Nat Found, 64-; prog consult pediat, VI, 66-; mem, Nat Rev Comt Regional Med Prog. *Mem:* Soc Pediat Res; Am Soc Hemat; Am Soc Human Genetics; Am Asn Cancer Res; Am Pediat Soc. *Res:* Immunologic abnormalities associated with malignancy in children; clinical management of children with malignancy; evaluation of various drugs; methods and models for delivery of health care. *Mailing Add:* Okla Med Res Found 825 NE 13th St Oklahoma City OK 73104

THURMAN-SWARTZWELDER, ERNESTINE H, b Atkins, Ark, Mar 7, 20; m 64; c 2. MEDICAL ENTOMOLOGY, RESEARCH ADMINISTRATION. *Educ:* Col Ozarks, BS, 44; Univ Md, PhD(bionomics of mosquitoes), 58; Am Registry Cert Entomologists. *Prof Exp:* Asst, Tulane Univ, 44; entomologist, Commun Dis Ctr, USPHS, Fla, 45-48; entomologist in-chg ident unit, Bur Vector Control, Calif, 48-51, entomologist, Nat Microbiol Inst, Md, 51, training adv malaria control, Div Int Health, US Opers Mission, Thailand, 51-53, entomologist & spec consult, Washington, DC, 53-54, exec secy, Trop Med & Parasitol Study Sect, Div Res Grants, NIH, 54-64, res adminr collab studies, Nat Heart Inst, 64-67; asst prof, 67-70, assoc prof path, 70-76, CLIN ASSOC PROF PATH, LA STATE UNIV MED CTR, NEW ORLEANS, 76-; CONSULT, 76- *Mem:* Fel AAAS; fel Am Pub Health Asn; Entom Soc Am; Am Soc Trop Med & Hyg; Am Mosquito Control Asn (rec secy, 61-64). *Res:* Control of vectors and vector-borne diseases; taxonomy of mosquitoes; tropical medicine; science administration. *Mailing Add:* 3443 Esplanade Ave New Orleans LA 70119

THURMON, JOHN C, b Redford, Mo, Mar 4, 30; m 56; c 1. VETERINARY ANESTHESIOLOGY. *Educ:* Univ Mo, BS, 60, DVM, 62, MS, 67. *Prof Exp:* From instr to asst prof vet med, 62-70, assoc prof vet anesthesiol, 71-76, assoc prof physiol & pharmacol, 75-76, HEAD DIV, COL VET MED, UNIV ILL, URBANA, 71-, PROF VET ANESTHESIOL, VET ANAT, PHYSIOL & PHARMACOL, 76-, ASSOC PROF BIOENG, COL ENG, 72- *Concurrent Pos:* Nat Heart Inst fel, Baylor Col Med, 69; vis prof anesthesiol, Col Med, Univ Ill, Chicago, 70; consult, Bristol Labs, Syracuse, NY, 70-74, Affil Labs, Whitehall, Ill, 72-74, Bay Vet Corp, Shawnee Mission, Kans, 73-, Norden Labs, Lincoln, Nebr, 74- & Dept Med Sci, Southern Ill Univ, 75- *Mem:* Am Soc Vet Anesthesiol (pres elect, 73, pres, 74); Am Soc Anesthesiologists; Int Anesthesia Res Soc; Am Col Vet Anesthesiologists (pres, 75-77). *Res:* General anesthesia and its effects on homeostatic mechanisms of domestic and wild animals; development and design of equipment for use in veterinary anesthesia. *Mailing Add:* Dept of Vet Clin Med Univ of Ill Col of Vet Med Urbana IL 61801

THURMON, THEODORE FRANCIS, b Baton Rouge, La, Oct 20, 37; m 61; c 2. MEDICAL GENETICS. *Educ:* La State Univ, Baton Rouge, BS, 60; La State Univ, New Orleans, MD, 62. *Prof Exp:* Intern, Naval Hosp, Pensacola, Fla, 62-63, resident, Philadelphia, Pa, 63-65, pediatrician, cytogeneticist & cardiologist, St Albans, NY, 65-68; assoc prof, 69-77, PROF PEDIAT & DIR, PED GENETICS DIV, MED SCH, LA STATE UNIV, NEW ORLEANS, 77- *Concurrent Pos:* Fel med genetics, Johns Hopkins Hosp, Baltimore, 68-69; consult, La State Dept Hosps, 70- *Mem:* AAAS; Am Soc Human Genetics; Human Biol Coun; NY Acad Sci. *Res:* Genetic regulation. *Mailing Add:* Sch of Med La State Univ New Orleans LA 70112

THURMOND, JOHN TYDINGS, b Dallas, Tex, Oct 22, 41; m 69; c 3. VERTEBRATE PALEONTOLOGY, ENVIRONMENTAL GEOLOGY. *Educ:* St Louis Univ, BS, 63; Southern Methodist Univ, MS, 67, PhD(geol), 69. *Prof Exp:* Res asst to pres, Inst Study Earth & Man, Southern Methodist Univ, 70; asst prof geol, Birmingham-Southern Col, 70-77; ASSOC PROF EARTH SCI, UNIV ARK, LITTLE ROCK, 77-, CHAIRPERSON DEPT,

78- *Concurrent Pos:* Vis prof fac chem sci & pharm, San Carlos Univ, Guatemala, 71; geologist, Harbert Construct Co, Ala, 71-72; asst cordr coop univ upper-div prog, Univ Ala, Gadsden, 72. *Mem:* AAAS; Paleont Soc; Soc Vert Paleont. *Res:* Paleoecology, functional morphology, taxonomy of Mesozoic/Cenozoic fishes; Pleistocene paleoecology; Cretaceous marine reptiles; environmental geology; data retrieval in paleontology. *Mailing Add:* Dept Earth Sci Univ Ark Little Rock AR 72204

THURMOND, WILLIAM, b Lodi, Calif, Apr 11, 26; m 49; c 2. DEVELOPMENTAL PHYSIOLOGY. *Educ:* Univ Calif, Berkeley, AB, 48, MA, 50, PhD(zool), 57. *Prof Exp:* Instr zool, San Mateo Community Col, Calif, 49-50; from instr to prof zool, 76, PROF BIOL SCI, CALIF POLYTECH STATE UNIV, SAN LUIS OBISPO, 76- *Concurrent Pos:* Vis prof, Univ Frankfort, 69-70. *Mem:* Fel AAAS; Am Soc Zool; Am Inst Biol Sci. *Res:* Development of the pituitary and the developmental interdependance with other endocrine glands and the hypothalamus. *Mailing Add:* Dept of Biol Sci Calif Polytech State Univ San Luis Obispo CA 93407

THURNAUER, HANS, b Nurnberg, Ger, June 11, 08; nat US; m 35; c 3. CERAMICS. *Educ:* Tech Univ Berlin, Dipl, 31, DrEng, 58; Univ Ill, MS, 32. *Prof Exp:* Ceramic engr, Steatite-Magnesia Co, Ger, 32-33; ceramic lab asst, Steatite & Porcelain Prod, Ltd, Eng, 33-35; dir res & vpres, Am Lava Corp, Tenn, 35-55; head ceramic dept, Minn Mining & Mfg Co, 55-66; CONSULT & TECH ADV, COORS PORCELAIN CO, 67- *Concurrent Pos:* Dir, Israel Ceramic & Silicate Inst, Haifa, 64-66; consult mat comts, US Dept Defense & NASA. *Mem:* AAAS; fel Am Ceramic Soc; Electrochem Soc (pres, 57); Am Chem Soc. *Res:* Technical ceramics; solid state devices; refractory and abrasion resistant materials; nuclear ceramics. *Mailing Add:* 440 College Ave Boulder CO 80302

THURNAUER, MARION CHARLOTTE, b Chattanooga, Tenn. BIOPHYSICAL CHEMISTRY, PHYSICAL-ORGANIC CHEMISTRY. *Educ:* Univ Chicago, BA, 68, MS, 69, PhD(chem), 74. *Prof Exp:* Fel, 74-77, asst scientist, 77-81, SCIENTIST CHEM, ARGONNE NAT LAB, 81- *Mem:* Am Chem Soc; Biophys Soc; Sigma Xi; Am Soc Photobiol; Asn Women Sci. *Res:* Electron paramagnetic resonance studies (continuous wave and pulsed) of triplet state of radical pairs; magnetic resonance studies of photosynthetic systems; time resolved magnetic resonance studies; pulsed electron paramagnetic resonance studies of phtosynthetic systems. *Mailing Add:* Argonne Nat Lab 9700 S Cass Ave Argonne IL 60439

THURNER, JOSEPH JOHN, b Middletown, NY, Oct 26, 20; m 48; c 2. INORGANIC CHEMISTRY. *Educ:* Hartwick Col, BS, 49; Harvard Univ, MA, 51. *Prof Exp:* From instr to assoc prof, 51-69, chmn dept, 67-70, dir, Div Natural Sci & Math, 70-74, PROF CHEM, COLGATE UNIV, 69- *Concurrent Pos:* Consult, Indium Corp Am, 52-62. *Mem:* AAAS; Am Chem Soc. *Res:* Organometallic compounds of germanium; organometallic and inorganic compounds; alloys of indium; synthesis and analysis of indium-bearing substances. *Mailing Add:* Dept of Chem Colgate Univ Hamilton NY 13346

THUROW, GORDON RAY, b Aurora, Ill, Feb 13, 29; m 55; c 5. ZOOLOGY, ANATOMY. *Educ:* Univ Chicago, PhB, 48, BS, 50, MS, 51; Ind Univ, PhD, 55. *Prof Exp:* Asst zool & ornith, Ind Univ, 52 & 54, tech adv ed film, 55; assoc prof natural sci, Newberry Col, 57-59; fel anat, Med Col SC, 59-61; asst prof, Univ Kans, 61-66; ASSOC PROF BIOL, WESTERN ILL UNIV, 66- *Mem:* Am Soc Ichthyologists & Herpetologists; Soc Study Amphibians & Reptiles; Soc Study Evolution; Ecol Soc Am; Am Asn Anat. *Res:* Morphological, physiological and behavioral adaptations of vertebrates; transplantation; herpetology; ecology. *Mailing Add:* Dept of Biol Western Ill Univ Macomb IL 61455

THURSTON, CHARLES W(ILSON), b Biddeford, Maine, Aug 16, 22; m 51; c 4. CIVIL ENGINEERING, ENGINEERING MECHANICS. *Educ:* Union Univ, NY, BS, 43; Columbia Univ, MS, 50, PhD(appl mech), 58. *Prof Exp:* Instr civil eng, Columbia Univ, 47-50; eng draftsman & plant engr, Lone Star Cement Corp, 50-52; from instr to assoc prof civil eng, 52-66, assoc prof archit, 66-74, PROF ARCHIT, COLUMBIA UNIV, 74- *Mem:* Am Soc Eng Educ; Am Concrete Inst; Am Soc Civil Engrs; Soc Exp Stress Anal; Sigma Xi. *Res:* Reinforced concrete; materials; building research; construction systems; structural analysis and design. *Mailing Add:* Avery Hall Columbia Univ New York NY 10027

THURSTON, EARLE LAURENCE, b New York, NY, Jan 17, 43; m 62; c 3. BOTANY, CELL BIOLOGY. *Educ:* State Univ NY, Geneseo, BS, 64; Iowa State Univ, MS, 67, PhD(bot), 69. *Prof Exp:* NSF fel cell res inst, Univ Tex, Austin, 69-70; ASSOC PROF CELL BIOL & COORDR ELECTRON MICROS CTR, TEX A&M UNIV, 70- *Mem:* Bot Soc Am; Electron Micros Soc; Am Soc Cell Biol. *Res:* Developmental morphology and ultrastructure; electron microprobe analysis. *Mailing Add:* Dept of Biol Electron Micros Ctr Tex A&M Univ College Station TX 77843

THURSTON, GAYLEN AUBREY, b Garwin, Iowa, May 15, 29; m 51; c 5. ENGINEERING MECHANICS. *Educ:* Iowa State Col, BS, 50; Ohio State Univ, MS, 51; Cornell Univ, PhD(eng mech), 56. *Prof Exp:* Shell struct specialist, Jet Engine Dept, Gen Elec Co, 55-63; res scientist mech, Denver Div, Martin Marietta Corp, 63-69; prof, Univ Denver, 69-75; assoc prof mech, Univ Colo, Denver, 75-80. *Mem:* Sigma Xi; Am Soc Eng Educ. *Res:* Nonlinear mechanics; shell structures. *Mailing Add:* 506 Marlbank Dr Yorktown VA 23690

THURSTON, GEORGE BUTTE, b Austin, Tex, Oct 8, 24; m 47; c 2. BIOMEDICAL ENGINEERING, BIOPHYSICS. *Educ:* Univ Tex, BS, 44, MA, 48, PhD(physics), 52. *Prof Exp:* Res scientist, Defense Res Lab, Tex, 49-52; asst prof physics, Univ Wyo, 52-53 & Univ Ark, 53-54; from assoc prof to prof, Okla State Univ, 54-68; PROF MECH ENG & BIOMED ENG, UNIV TEX, AUSTIN, 68- *Concurrent Pos:* Consult, US Naval Ord Test Sta, 54-55; res physicist, Univ Mich, 58-59; NSF fel, Macromolecules Res Ctr, Strasbourg, 63-64; US sr scientist, Alexander von Humboldt Found, WGer, 75. *Mem:* Fel Am Phys Soc; fel Acoust Soc Am; Soc Rheol. *Res:* Acoustics; rheology; polymer science; macromolecules; optical and electrical properties of solutions. *Mailing Add:* Dept Mech Eng Univ Tex Austin TX 78712

THURSTON, HERBERT DAVID, b Sioux Falls, SDak, Mar 24, 27; m 51; c 3. PLANT PATHOLOGY. *Educ:* Univ Minn, MS, 53, PhD(plant path), 58. *Prof Exp:* Asst plant path, Univ Minn, 50-53, instr, 53-54; asst plant pathologist, Rockefeller Found, Colombia, 54-56; instr plant path, Univ Minn, 56-57; from assoc plant pathologist to plant pathologist, Rockefeller Found, Colombia, 58-67; PROF PLANT PATH, CORNELL UNIV, 67- *Mem:* Am Phytopath Soc; Potato Asn Am. *Res:* Diseases of potatoes; tropical plant pathology; nature of resistance to fungus diseases. *Mailing Add:* Dept of Plant Path Plant Sci Bldg Cornell Univ Ithaca NY 14850

THURSTON, HUGH ANSFRID, b UK, 22; m 62. ALGEBRA. *Educ:* Univ Cambridge, PhD(math), 48. *Prof Exp:* Lectr math, Bristol Univ, 46-57; asst prof, 58-59, ASSOC PROF MATH, UNIV BC, 60- *Mem:* Can Math Cong. *Res:* Abstract algebra; theory of congruences. *Mailing Add:* 4242 W King Edward Vancouver BC V6E 1N3 Can

THURSTON, JAMES N(ORTON), b Murphysboro, Ill, May 6, 15; m 40; c 4. ELECTRICAL ENGINEERING. *Educ:* Ohio State Univ, BEE, 36; Mass Inst Technol, SM, 43, ScD(elec eng), 50. *Prof Exp:* Test engr, Gen Elec Co, 36-38; geophysicist, Mott-Smith Corp, 38-40; from asst to asst prof elec eng, Mass Inst Technol, 40-49; assoc prof, Univ Fla, 49-52 & Calif Inst Technol, 52-54; prof & head dept, Clemson Univ, 54-66, alumni prof elec eng, 66-80; RETIRED. *Concurrent Pos:* Consult, Ruge-Deforest, 45-49, Firestone Tire & Rubber Co, 53- & Nat Coun Eng Examr, 73- *Mem:* Am Soc Eng Educ; sr mem Inst Elec & Electronics Engrs. *Res:* Electronic measurement and control systems; communications systems. *Mailing Add:* 322 Woodlandway Clemson SC 29631

THURSTON, JOHN ROBERT, b Maumee, Ohio, May 6, 26; m 53; c 2. BACTERIOLOGY, IMMUNOLOGY. *Educ:* Ohio State Univ, BSc, 49, MSc, 51, PhD(bact), 55. *Prof Exp:* Res microbiologist, Ohio Tuberc Hosp, Columbus, 55-57; microbiologist, Trudeau Found, Inc, NY, 57-61; RES MICROBIOLOGIST, NAT ANIMAL DIS LAB, USDA, 61- *Mem:* Soc Exp Biol & Med; Am Soc Microbiol. *Res:* Serologic investigations of mycobacteria, serologic diagnosis in tuberculosis; intradermal tuberculin testing of cattle; glycoprotein changes in tuberculous cattle; serology of nocardiosis and aspergillosis; effect of mycotoxins on the immune system. *Mailing Add:* Nat Animal Dis Lab PO Box 70 Ames IA 50010

THURSTON, M(ARLIN) O(AKES), b Denver, Colo, Sept 20, 18; m 42; c 3. ELECTRICAL ENGINEERING. *Educ:* Univ Colo, BA, 40, MS, 46; Ohio State Univ, PhD(elec eng), 55. *Prof Exp:* Assoc prof elec eng & actg head dept, Air Force Inst Technol, 46-52; res assoc, 52-55, assoc prof, 55-59, chmn dept, 65-77, PROF ELEC ENG, OHIO STATE UNIV, 59-, DIR, ELECTRON DEVICE LAB, 77- *Concurrent Pos:* Elec eng ed, Marcel Dekker, Inc, 75-; chmn bd, Nat Eng Consortium, Inc, 77-79. *Mem:* Fel Inst Elec & Electronics Engrs; Am Phys Soc; Am Soc Eng Educ. *Res:* Solid state electron devices. *Mailing Add:* Dept of Elec Eng Ohio State Univ Columbus OH 43210

THURSTON, RICHARD, b Orono, Maine, Feb 3, 22; m 48; c 2. ENTOMOLOGY. *Educ:* Univ Conn, BS, 47; Rutgers Univ, PhD(entom), 52. *Prof Exp:* Asst entom, Univ Maine, 47-48; from asst entomologist to assoc entomologist, 52-59, from asst prof to assoc prof, 57-66, PROF ENTOM, UNIV KY, 66- *Concurrent Pos:* Adv entom, Ky Team, Thailand, 73-75. *Mem:* Entom Soc Am. *Res:* Biology, ecology and control of tobacco insects; resistance to insects in Nicotiana tabacum. *Mailing Add:* Dept of Entom Univ of Ky Lexington KY 40506

THURSTON, ROBERT NORTON, b Kilbourne, Ohio, Dec 31, 24; m 49; c 4. PHYSICS. *Educ:* Ill Inst Technol, BS, 45; Ohio State Univ, MS, 48, PhD(phyiscs), 52. *Prof Exp:* Teacher high sch, Ohio, 46-47; instr aeronaut eng, Ohio State Univ, 49-50; MEM TECH STAFF, BELL TEL LABS, MURRAY HILL, 52- *Mem:* Am Phys Soc; Acoust Soc Am; Inst Elec & Electronics Eng; Soc Natural Philos; Soc Eng Sci. *Res:* Mechanics; crystal physics; communications science; liquid crystals. *Mailing Add:* Bell Labs Holmdel NJ 07733

THURSTON, RODNEY SUNDBYE, b Brooklyn, NY, Sept 17, 33; m 55; c 5. MECHANICAL ENGINEERING. *Educ:* Columbia Univ, AB, 55, BS, 56, MS, 58; Univ NMex, PhD(mech eng), 66. *Prof Exp:* Jr engr, Am Elec Power Co, NY, 56-57; teaching asst mech eng, Columbia Univ, 57-58 & Cornell Univ, 58-59; assoc group leader, 59-76, PROJ MGR, LOS ALAMOS SCI LAB, 76- *Mem:* Am Soc Mech Engrs. *Res:* Heat transfer; shock wave propagation; material damage induced by photon and neutron deposition. *Mailing Add:* Los Alamos Sci Lab PO Box 1663 Los Alamos NM 87544

THURSTON, WILLIAM R, b New York, NY, Nov 1, 15; m 37; c 1. GEOLOGY & SCIENCE ADMINISTRATION. *Educ:* Columbia Univ, AB, 38, AM, 43, PhD, 52. *Prof Exp:* Asst geologist, Cuban-Am Manganese Corp, Cuba, 38-39; asst geol, Brown Univ, 39-40; trustees asst, Columbia Univ, 40-42; geologist, US Geol Surv, 42-51, mining co, Mex, 51-52 & Nicaro Nickel Co, Cuba, 52-54; assoc prof, Sch Eng, La Polytech Inst, 54-55; exec secy div earth sci, Nat Acad Sci-Nat Res Coun, 55-59; staff geologist, US Geol Surv, 59-67; asst to sci adv, US Dept Interior, 67-70, spec asst to dir, US Geol Surv, 70-76; staff officer, Nat Acad Sci-Nat Res Coun, 76-77; CONSULT GEOLOGIST, 77- *Concurrent Pos:* Mem & nat del, Int Geol Cong, 64, 68 & 72. *Mem:* fel AAAS; Geol Soc Am; Soc Econ Geol; Am Inst Mining Metall & Petrol Engrs. *Res:* Economic geology; geology of pegmatites and fluorspar. *Mailing Add:* 2191 Cerrado Brio Tucson AZ 85718

THURSTONE, FREDRICK LOUIS, b Chicago, Ill, Feb 12, 32; m 54; c 3. BIOMEDICAL ENGINEERING, ELECTRICAL ENGINEERING. *Educ:* Univ NC, BS, 53; NC State Univ, MS, 57, PhD(elec eng), 61. *Prof Exp:* Instr elec eng, NC State Univ, 56-61, asst prof, 61-62; asst prof biomed eng, Bowman Gray Sch Med, 62-66, assoc prof, 66-67, dir dept, 62-67; assoc prof, 67-70, PROF BIOMED ENG, DUKE UNIV, 70- *Mem:* Inst Elec & Electronics Eng; Acoust Soc Am; Instrument Soc Am; Am Inst Ultrasonics in Med. *Res:* Diagnostic ultrasound; ultrasound scanning and imaging systems; ultrasound holography and visual reconstruction. *Mailing Add:* Biomed Eng Dept Duke Univ Durham NC 27706

THURSTONE, ROBERT LEON, b Chicago, Ill, July 29, 27; m 66. ELECTRICAL ENGINEERING. *Educ:* Ill Inst Technol, BS, 51; Univ Mo, MS, 53; NC State Univ, PhD(elec eng), 65. *Prof Exp:* Instr elec eng, Duke Univ, 53-57 & NC State Univ, 57-61; asst prof, 65-67, ASSOC PROF ELEC ENG, UNIV ALA, HUNTSVILLE, 67-, CHMN DEPT, 72- *Mem:* AAAS; Am Soc Eng Educ; Inst Elec & Electronics Engrs. *Res:* Energy transfer through biological tissue. *Mailing Add:* Dept of Elec Eng PO Box 1247 Huntsville AL 35807

THUT, PAUL DOUGLAS, b Exeter, NH, Feb 1, 43; m 66; c 3. PSYCHOPHARMACOLOGY. *Educ:* Hamilton Col, AB, 65; Univ RI, MS, 68; Dartmouth Col, PhD(pharmacol), 71. *Prof Exp:* Asst prof pharmacol, Col Med, Univ Ariz, 70-74; ASSOC PROF PHARM, SCH DENT, UNIV MD, 74- *Concurrent Pos:* Pharmaceut Mfrs Found grant, 72-73; consult, Vet Admin Hosp, Tucson, 72- *Mem:* Soc Neurosci; Am Soc Pharmacol & Exp Therapeut. *Res:* Psychomotor effects of l-dehydroxphenylalanine; competitive neuromuscular antagonists. *Mailing Add:* Dept Pharmacol Univ Md Sch Dent Baltimore MD 21201

THWAITE, ROBERT DAVID, b Larchmont, NY, Oct 2, 26; m 50; c 2. GEOLOGY, PHYSICAL SCIENCE. *Educ:* Dartmouth Col, BA, 49. *Prof Exp:* Res asst, Carnegie Inst Geophys Lab, 49-52; engr, Am Instrument Co, 52-54; res assoc fel, Portland Cement Asn, 54-60; ENGR RES DEPT BETHLEHEM STEEL CORP, 60- *Mem:* AAAS. *Res:* High temperature phase equilibrium studies of anhydrous silicate rock-forming systems; mineralogical and petrographic analysis of ferrous and non-ferrous raw materials. *Mailing Add:* Homer Res Lab Bethlehem Steel Corp Bethlehem PA 18016

THWAITES, THOMAS TURVILLE, b Madison, Wis, Aug 21, 31; m 53; c 2. NUCLEAR PHYSICS. *Educ:* Univ Wis, BS, 53; Univ Rochester, MA, 56, PhD(physics), 59. *Prof Exp:* Physicist, Stromberg Carlson Div, Gen Dynamics Corp, 55-56; asst prof physics, 59-66, ASSOC PROF PHYSICS, PA STATE UNIV, UNIVERSITY PARK, 66- *Mem:* Am Phys Soc. *Res:* Scattering of 200 million electron volts polarized protons; radioactive decay schemes; radiative capture of charged particles; scattering of charged particles. *Mailing Add:* Dept of Physics Pa State Univ University Park PA 16802

THWAITES, WILLIAM MUELLER, b Madison, Wis, July 10, 33; m 55; c 3. GENETICS. *Educ:* Univ Wis, BS, 55; Univ Mich, MS, 62, PhD(genetics), 65. *Prof Exp:* Asst prof, 65-70, ASSOC PROF BIOL, SAN DIEGO STATE UNIV, 70- *Concurrent Pos:* Prin investr, NSF res grant, 66-68 & 77-79; fel, Battelle Mem Inst, Richland, Washington, 72-73; vis prof, Instituto de Investigaciones Biomedicas, Mexico City, 73-74. *Mem:* Genetics Soc Am. *Res:* General, microbial and biochemical genetics; regulation of enzyme synthesis in fungi. *Mailing Add:* Dept of Biol San Diego State Univ San Diego CA 92182

THWEATT, JOHN G, b Norton, Va, Nov 21, 32; m 54; c 2. ORGANIC CHEMISTRY. *Educ:* Ga Inst Technol, BS, 54, PhD(org chem), 61. *Prof Exp:* Instr chem, Ga Inst Technol, 57-59; res chemist, 60-63, sr res chemist, res labs, 63-75, sr chemist develop dept, 75-76, TECH STAFF DYES DEPT, ORG CHEM DIV, TENN EASTMAN CO, 76- *Mem:* Sigma Xi; Am Chem Soc. *Res:* Chemistry of enamines and other electron rich olefins; process development, especially aliphatic syntheses; process improvement; hydrogenation and other high pressure reactions. *Mailing Add:* Bldg 29 Tenn Eastman Co Kingsport TN 37662

THWING, HENRY WARREN, b Orange, Va, Mar 16, 30; m 58; c 2. ALGEBRA. *Educ:* Yale Univ, BS, 51; Univ Va, MA, 55; Fla State Univ, PhD(math), 69. *Prof Exp:* Master, Woodberry Forest Sch, 55-63; asst prof math, 63-69, ASSOC PROF MATH, STETSON UNIV, 69- *Res:* Integral derivations of P-ADIC fields. *Mailing Add:* 1108 E University Ave De Land FL 32720

THYAGARAJAN, B S, b Tiruvarur, India, July 14, 29; m 56; c 3. ORGANIC CHEMISTRY. *Educ:* Loyola Col, Madras, India, MA, 51; Presidency Col, Madras, MSc, 53, PhD(chem), 56. *Prof Exp:* Fel, Northwestern Univ, 56-58; fel, Univ Wis, 58-59; reader org chem, Madras Univ, 60-68; prof, Univ Idaho, 69-74; dir earth & phys sci div, 74-77, PROF CHEM, UNIV TEX, SAN ANTONIO, 74- *Honors & Awards:* Intrasci Res Award, 66. *Mem:* Fel Am Inst Chemists; NY Acad Sci; The Chem Soc; Sigma Xi; Soc Cosmetic Chemists. *Res:* Heterocyclic chemistry; aromaticity; molecular migrations. *Mailing Add:* Earth & Phys Sci Div Univ Tex San Antonio TX 78285

THYER, NORMAN HAROLD, b Gloucester, Eng, Sept 3, 29; m 65; c 3. METEOROLOGY, MATHEMATICS. *Educ:* Univ Birmingham, BSc, 57; Univ Wash, Seattle, PhD(meteorol), 62. *Prof Exp:* Meteorol asst, Air Ministry, UK, 49-50 & Falkland Islands Dependencies Surv, 50-53; tech asst aeronaut eng, Gloster Aircraft Co, 54; micrometeorologist, Univ Wash, Seattle, 60, meteorol training expert, World Meteorol Orgn, 62-63; asst prof meteorol & physics, Univ BC, 63-66; res assoc meteorol, McGill Univ, 66-68; from asst prof to assoc prof, 68-77, CONSULT METEOROLOGIST, NOTRE DAME UNIV, NELSON, 77- *Concurrent Pos:* Climatologist, 79-80; vis prof, Univ Vercruzana, Mex, 80- *Mem:* Royal Meteorol Soc; Can Meteorol Soc. *Res:* Studies of local winds near valleys and convectional storms. *Mailing Add:* R R 2 Nelson BC V1L 5P5 Can

THYGESEN, KENNETH HELMER, b Cambridge, NY, June 30, 37; m 55; c 2. EXPERIMENTAL SOLID STATE PHYSICS. *Educ:* Washington & Lee Univ, 58; Clarkson Col Technol, MS, 60, PhD(physics), 67. *Prof Exp:* Instr physics, Clarkson Col Technol, 59-65; assoc prof, 67-77, PROF PHYSICS, STATE UNIV NY COL POTSDAM, 77-, CHMN DEPT, 76- *Mem:* Am Phys Soc; Sigma Xi; Am Asn Physics Teachers. *Res:* Solid state physics-imperfections in metal crystals; plastic deformation, electric, magnetic and thermal properties of metals and alloys; physics education. *Mailing Add:* Dept of Physics State Univ of NY Col Potsdam NY 13676

THYGESON, JOHN R(OBERT), JR, b Boston, Mass, Sept 25, 24. CHEMICAL ENGINEERING. *Educ:* Drexel Inst, BS, 47; Univ Pa, MS, 55, PhD(chem eng), 61. *Prof Exp:* Res engr, Proctor & Schwartz, Inc, 47-58; asst prof, 61-63, ASSOC PROF CHEM ENG, DREXEL UNIV, 63- *Concurrent Pos:* Consult, Proctor & Schwartz, Inc, 63- *Mem:* Am Inst Chem Engrs; Am Chem Soc. *Res:* Transport phenomena; mechanisms of the reaction of hydrogen with carbon steels; simultaneous heat and mass transfer in packed beds of particulate solids. *Mailing Add:* Dept of Chem Eng Drexel Univ Philadelphia PA 19104

THYR, BILLY DALE, b Kansas City, Kans, June 1, 32; m 58; c 3. PLANT PATHOLOGY, MYCOLOGY. *Educ:* Univ Ottawa, Kans, BA, 59; Wash State Univ, PhD(plant path), 64. *Prof Exp:* RES PLANT PATHOLOGIST, AGR RES SERV, USDA, 63-, ALFALFA RES LEADER, 80- *Mem:* AAAS; Am Phytopath Soc; Mycol Soc Am. *Res:* Bacterial diseases of tomato and other vegetables; control of bacterial diseases through host resistance; alfalfa diseases; interaction of organisms infecting alfalfa. *Mailing Add:* USDA Agr Res Serv Col Agr Univ Nev Reno NV 89557

THYSEN, BENJAMIN, b Bronx, NY, July 27, 32; m 75; c 2. LABORATORY MEDICINE, OBSTETRICS & GYNECOLOGY. *Educ:* City Col New York, BS, 54; Univ Mo, MS, 63; St Louis Univ, PhD(biochem), 67. *Prof Exp:* Res asst obstet & gynec & biochem, Albert Einstein Col Med, 59-61; asst biochem, Sch Med, Univ Mo, 61-63; instr, St Louis Univ, 67-68; sr res scientist, Technicon Corp, 68-69, group leader, 69-70; ASST PROF OBSTET, GYNEC, BIOCHEM & LAB MED & DIR ENDOCRINE LABS, ALBERT EINSTEIN COL MED, 71- *Mem:* AAAS; Endocrine Soc; Am Chem Soc; Am Asn Clin Chemists; Soc Study Reprod. *Res:* Estrogen metabolism; growth and development; laboratory medicine; mechanism of action of the steroid hormones; methodology; endocrinology. *Mailing Add:* Dept of Obstet & Gynec Albert Einstein Col of Med Bronx NY 10461

TIAB, DJEBBAR, b Ain Beida, Algeria, Sept 23, 50; m 75; c 1. PETROLEUM ENGINEERING. *Educ:* NMex Inst Mining & Technol, BSc, 74, MSc, 75; Univ Okla, PhD(petrol eng), 76. *Prof Exp:* Chief technician petrol geol, Alcore, Inc, Algeria, 69-71; res assoc petrol eng, NMex Inst Mining & Technol, 70-76, asst prof, 76-77; ASST PROF PETROL ENG, UNIV OKLA, 77- *Concurrent Pos:* NSF res scientist, 78-80. *Mem:* Assoc Soc Petrol Engrs. *Res:* Reservoir mechanics of enhanced oil recovery; well testing; natural gas technology; reservoir heterogeneities; computer applications in reservoir engineering. *Mailing Add:* 116 Mount Vernon Norman OK 73071

TIAO, GEORGE CHING-HWUAN, b London, Eng, Nov 8, 33; Chinese citizen; m 58; c 4. MATHEMATICAL STATISTICS, ECONOMIC STATISTICS. *Educ:* Nat Taiwan Univ, BA, 55; NY Univ, MBA, 58; Univ Wis-Madison, PhD(econ), 62. *Prof Exp:* Asst prof statist & bus, Univ Wis-Madison, 62-65; vis assoc prof statist, Harvard Bus Sch, 65-66; assoc prof, 66-68, prof statist & bus, 68-81, BASCOM PROF STATIST & BUS, UNIV WIS-MADISON, 81- *Concurrent Pos:* Vis lectr, Post Col Prof Educ, Carnegie Mellon Univ, 66-73; statist consult to var indust co, 66-; vis prof, Univ Essex, 70-71; chmn dept statist, Univ Wis-Madison, 73-75; vis prof, Nat Taiwan Univ, 75-76; assoc ed, J Am Statist Asn, 76-81; vis Ford Found prof, Univ Chicago, Ill, 80-81. *Mem:* Fel Royal Statist Soc; fel Am Statist Asn; fel Inst Math Statist; AAAS; Int Statist Inst. *Res:* Bayesian methods in statistics; time series analysis; statistical analysis of environmental data; economic and business forecasting. *Mailing Add:* Dept of Statist Univ of Wis Madison WI 53706

TIBBALS, HARRY FRED, III, b Jacksonville, Tex, Apr 7, 43; m 66; c 2. DATA SYSTEMS ENGINEERING, SIMULATION ANALYSIS. *Educ:* Baylor Univ, BS, 65; Univ Houston, PhD(chem), 70. *Prof Exp:* Appln consult phys sci & comput sci, Univ Glasgow, 72-74; acad staff, Comput Unit, Durham Univ, UK, 74-79; asst prof anal chem, NTex State Univ, 78-79; MEM STAFF, ADVAN ANAL DEPT, COLLINS COMMUN SYSTS DIV, ROCKWELL INT, 79- *Concurrent Pos:* Sci Res Coun fel chem, Univ Leicester, 70-72; mem commun coord group, Scottish Regional Comput Org, 72-74; systs programmer & adv nonnumerical appln, Comput Unit, Univ Durham, Eng, 74-; tutor & counr, Technol Fac, Open Univ, Eng, 76-78; analyst commun proj, NUmbrian Multi-Access Comput Org, UK, 75-78; fel & partic various advan study insts, NATO & Comn on Sci & Technol, 73-78; consult, Delta Mgt & Software Systs, 78-79. *Mem:* Am Chem Soc; Asn Comput Mach; Inst Elec & Electronics Engrs; Brit Comput Soc; Royal Soc Chem. *Res:* Applications of computer systems to problems in chemical analysis; analysis of complex systems; communications, measurement and control systems; simulation; real-time interactive man-machine systems. *Mailing Add:* PO Box 56 Wylie TX 75098

TIBBETTS, CLARK, b Hartford, Conn, Feb 18, 47; m 67, 82; c 2. VIROLOGY, MOLECULAR GENETICS. *Educ:* Amherst Col, BA, 68; Calif Inst Technol, PhD(biophysics), 72. *Prof Exp:* Fel microbiol, Wallenbery Lab, Univ Uppsala, Sweden, 72-74; asst prof, Sch Med, Univ Conn, 74-80, assoc prof, 80-82; ASSOC PROF MICROBIOL, SCH MED, VANDERBILT UNIV, 82- *Mem:* Am Soc Biol Chemists; Am Soc Virologists. *Res:* Structure and function of viral DNA sequences which regulate gene expression; viral DNA encapsidation to transfer novel genes or arrangements of genes to animal cells in culture. *Mailing Add:* Dept Microbiol Sch Med Vanderbilt Univ Nashville TN 37232

TIBBETTS, GARY GEORGE, b Omaha, Nebr, Oct 12, 39; m 64; c 3. PHYSICS. *Educ:* Calif Inst Technol, BS, 61; Univ Ill, Urbana, MS, 63, PhD(physics), 67. *Prof Exp:* Ger Res Asn grant, vis scientist, Munich Tech Univ, 67-69; SR RES PHYSICIST, GEN MOTORS RES LABS, 69- *Mem:* Am Phys Soc; Am Vacuum Soc. *Res:* Surface physics; plasma-surface interactions; adsorption of gases on surfaces; electronic and chemical properties of surfaces; carbon fibers. *Mailing Add:* Physics Dept 12 Mile & Mound Rd Gen Motors Res Labs Warren MI 48090

TIBBETTS, MERRICK SAWYER, b Keene, NH, Dec 30, 25; m 50; c 4. ORGANIC CHEMISTRY. *Educ:* Univ NH, BS, 48, MS, 51; Stevens Inst Technol, PhD(org chem), 66. *Prof Exp:* Plant chemist, Rubber Div, Eberhard Faber Pencil Co, 51-53; sr chemist, Bendix Corp, 53-62; proj leader synthetic org chem, Int Flavors & Fragrances, 66-69; sr res chemist, Florasynth, Inc, 69-70; SR RES SCIENTIST, PEPSICO INC, LONG ISLAND CITY, NY, 70- *Mem:* Am Chem Soc; Am Soc Test & Mat; Inst Food Technol; Sigma Xi. *Res:* Conformational analysis; organic synthesis; subjective-objective correlation; carbohydrate chemistry. *Mailing Add:* 16 N Cherry Lane Rumson NJ 07760

TIBBITS, DONALD FAY, b May 7, 43; US citizen. SPEECH PATHOLOGY. *Educ:* Univ Ark, BS, 64, MS, 68; Univ Mo-Columbia, PhD(speech path), 73. *Prof Exp:* Speech pathologist, Pub Schs, Ark, 63-70; teaching asst, Univ Mo-Columbia, 70-73; asst prof, Univ Ark, Fayetteville, 73-76; ASST PROF COMMUN DIS, UNIV TEX, DALLAS, 76- *Concurrent Pos:* Mem, Coun Except Children. *Mem:* Am Speech & Hearing Asn; Asn Children Learning Disabilities. *Res:* Language acquisition and development in children and adolescents; langauge disabilities in children; gestural communications. *Mailing Add:* Callier Ctr for Commun Dis 1966 Inwood Rd Dallas TX 75235

TIBBITTS, FORREST DONALD, b Tacoma, Wash, Jan 23, 29; m 51; c 1. EMBRYOLOGY. *Educ:* East Wash Col, BA, 51; Ore State Col, MA, 55, PhD, 58. *Prof Exp:* Instr sci, Ore Col Educ, 57-59; asst prof zool, 59-69, PROF BIOL, UNIV NEV, RENO, 69-, PROF ANAT, MED SCH, 71- *Mem:* AAAS; Am Asn Anat; Am Soc Zool. *Res:* Reproductive biology; placentation. *Mailing Add:* Dept of Biol Univ of Nev Reno NV 89507

TIBBITTS, THEODORE WILLIAM, b Melrose, Wis, Apr 10, 29; m 55, 75; c 4. HORTICULTURE, ENVIRONMENTAL PHYSIOLOGY. *Educ:* Univ Wis, BS, 50, MS, 52, PhD(hort, agron), 53. *Prof Exp:* From asst prof to assoc prof, 55-71, PROF HORT, UNIV WIS-MADISON, 71- *Concurrent Pos:* Res engr space biol, NAm Aviation, Inc, Calif, 65-66; bot adv, Manned Space Craft Ctr, Tex, 68-69; mem NASA rev panel, Skylab Biol Exps, 70-71 & Space Shuttle Biol Exp, 78; res leave, Lab Plant Physiol Ond, Netherlands, 74 & Climate Lab, Dept Sci & Indust Res, New Zealand, 81; vis scientist, Guelph, Can, 81. *Honors & Awards:* Marion Meadows Award, Am Soc Hort Sci, 68. *Mem:* AAAS; fel Am Soc Hort Sci; Am Soc Plant Physiol; Int Soc Hort Sci; Am Inst Biol Sci. *Res:* Environmental physiology of vegetable crops; physiological breakdowns; optimization of growth; air pollution and contaminants in enclosed environments; geophysical environment of plants; standardization in plant growth chambers. *Mailing Add:* Dept of Hort Univ of Wis 1575 Linden Dr Madison WI 53706

TIBBLES, JOHN JAMES, b Toronto, Ont, Mar 16, 24; m 51; c 2. FISHERIES. *Educ:* Ont Agr Col, BSA, 51; Univ Wis, MS, PhD(fisheries), 56. *Prof Exp:* Assoc scientist, Fisheries Res Bd Can, 56-65, DIR, SEA LAMPREY CONTROL CTR, PACIFIC & FRESHWATER FISHERIES, CAN DEPT FISHERIES & OCEANS, 66- *Mem:* Am Fisheries Soc. *Res:* Sea lamprey control. *Mailing Add:* Sea Lamprey Control Ctr Ship Canal PO Sault Ste Marie ON P6A 1P0 Can

TIBBS, JOHN FRANCISCO, b Pacific Grove, Calif, Oct 12, 38; m 66. PROTOZOOLOGY. *Educ:* Fresno State Col, BA, 60; Univ Southern Calif, MS, 64, PhD(biol), 68. *Prof Exp:* From asst prof to assoc prof zool, 68-77, DIR BIOL STA, UNIV MONT, 70-, PROF ZOOL, 77- *Mem:* AAAS; Soc Protozool. *Res:* Ecology of Arctic and Antarctic protozoans and marine invertebrates; taxonomy of the Phaeodarina; ecology of the Sarcodina. *Mailing Add:* Univ of Mont Biol Sta Bigfork MT 59911

TIBBS, NICHOLAS HOWARD, b Windsor, Eng, May 31, 45; US citizen; m 68; c 2. GEOLOGY, APPLIED GEOCHEMISTRY. *Educ:* Univ Mo-Rolla, BS, 66, MS, 69, PhD(geol), 72. *Prof Exp:* Res fel environ geol, Univ Mo-Rolla, 72-73; asst prof geol, Paducah Community Col, Univ Ky, 73-75; geologist environ geol, Nuclear Raw Mat Br, Tenn Valley Authority, 75-78; ASST PROF GEOL, SOUTHEAST MO STATE UNIV, 78- *Mem:* Sigma Xi. *Res:* Precambrian rock geochemistry in southeast Missouri. *Mailing Add:* Dept of Earth Sci Southeast Mo State Univ Cape Girardeau MO 63701

TICE, DAVID ANTHONY, b Brooklyn, NY, Dec 31, 29; m 52; c 3. THORACIC SURGERY, CARDIOVASCULAR SURGERY. *Educ:* Columbia Univ, BA, 51; NY Univ, MD, 55; Am Bd Surg, dipl, 61; Bd Thoracic Surg, dipl, 65. *Prof Exp:* Intern, Third Surg Div, Bellevue Hosp, 55-56, asst resident, 56-59; resident, Bellevue Hosp & asst surg, NY Univ, 59-60; res asst, Univ, 60-62, from instr to asst prof, 60-67, from asst attend to assoc attend, Univ Hosp, 60-68, assoc prof, Sch Med, 67-73, PROF SURG, SCH MED, NY UNIV, 73- *Concurrent Pos:* NY Heart Asn fel, Sch Med, NY Univ, 60-62; asst attend surg, Methodist Hosp Brooklyn, 60-63; from asst vis physician to assoc vis physician, Bellevue Hosp, 60-66, vis physician, 66-; consult cardiovasc surg, NY State Dept Health, 62 & Lutheran Med Ctr, 70; asst med examr, City of New York, 62-73; attend cardiovasc surg, New York Vet Admin Hosp, 63-66, attend thoracic surg, 64-66, chief surg serv, 67-74, chief thoracic & cardiovasc surg, 67-; attend surg, NY Univ Hosp, 68-; mem, Vet Admin Res & Educ Coun, Washington, DC, 72-73. *Mem:* Am Asn Thoracic Surg; fel Am Col Cardiol; fel Am Col Surgeons; Soc Univ Surgeons; Transplantation Soc. *Res:* Thoracic and cardiovascular physiology and disease. *Mailing Add:* Dept of Surg NY Univ Sch of Med New York NY 10016

TICE, LINWOOD FRANKLIN, b Salem, NJ, Feb 17, 09; m 29; c 2. PHARMACEUTICAL CHEMISTRY. *Educ:* Philadelphia Col Pharm, BS, 33, MSc, 35; St Louis Col Pharm, DSc, 54. *Prof Exp:* Res fel, Wm R Warner & Co, 31-35; res fel, Edible Mfrs Res Soc, 35-38; asst prof, 38-40, dean, 59-75, dir sch pharm, 40-71, asst dean, 41-56, assoc dean, 56-59, prof pharm, 40-75, EMER DEAN, PHILADELPHIA COL PHARM, 75-, CONSULT, 75- *Concurrent Pos:* Res fel, Sharp & Dohme, 38-40; ed, Am J Pharm, 40-77; tech ed, El Farmaceutico, 41-59 & Pharm Int, 47-59; mem revision comt, US Pharmacopoeia, 40-60, bd trustees, 60-70, 70-75; dir, Am Found Pharmaceut Ed, 54-59; mem Am Coun Pharmaceut Ed, 60-66; mem, Philadelphia Med-Pharmaceut Sci, 63- *Honors & Awards:* Remington Honor Medal, Am Pharmaceut Asn, 71. *Mem:* AAAS (vpres, 71-72); Am Chem Soc; Am Pharmaceut Asn (pres elect, 65-66, pres, 66-67); Asn Cols Pharm (pres, 55-56); fel Am Inst Chem. *Res:* Pharmaceuticals; surfactants; proteins; emulsions. *Mailing Add:* Philadelphia Col Pharm & Sci 43rd St & Kingsessing Ave Philadelphia PA 19104

TICE, RAYMOND RICHARD, b Bridgeport, Conn, Jan 22, 47. GENETIC TOXICOLOGY, HUMAN CYTOGENETICS. *Educ:* Univ Calif, San Diego, BA, 69; San Diego State Univ, MS, 72; Johns Hopkins Univ, PhD(human genetics), 76. *Prof Exp:* Res assoc, 76-78, asst scientist genetic toxicol, 78-81, ASSOC SCIENTIST, DEPT MED, BROOKHAVEN NAT LAB, 81- *Concurrent Pos:* Training grant, Dept Med, Brookhaven Nat Lab, 76-78. *Mem:* Am Soc Human Genetics; Genetic Toxicol Asn; Environ Mutagen Soc; Soc Risk Anal; Am Genetic Asn. *Res:* Examination of mechanisms of cytogenetic manifestations of genotoxic damage in vivo cytogenetic toxicological evaluation of environmental pollutants; detection of individuals at minimal risk to genotoxic agents. *Mailing Add:* Dept of Med Brookhaven Nat Lab Upton NY 11973

TICE, RUSSELL L, b Parkersburg, WVa, Dec 5, 32; m 56; c 4. PHYSICAL CHEMISTRY. *Educ:* Marshall Col, BS, 60; Univ Calif, Los Angeles, PhD(chem), 65. *Prof Exp:* Res asst chem, Univ Calif, Los Angeles, 62-65; from asst prof to assoc prof, 65-75, PROF CHEM, CALIF POLYTECH STATE UNIV, 75- *Concurrent Pos:* NSF fel, Ind Univ, 66; vis prof, Purdue Univ, 76-77. *Mem:* Am Chem Soc; Am Phys Soc. *Res:* Investigation of electron-atom and electron-molecule collision cross sections by cyclotron resonance; electron spin resonance of radicals. *Mailing Add:* Dept Chem Calif Polytech State Univ San Luis Obispo CA 93401

TICE, THOMAS E(ARL), b Florence, Ala, Jan 24, 24; m 49; c 2. ELECTRICAL ENGINEERING. *Educ:* Ohio State Univ, BEE, 47, MSc, 48, PhD(elec eng), 51. *Prof Exp:* Asst eng, Marshall Col, 43; asst math, Ohio State Univ, 47, asst elec eng, 47-48, res assoc & proj engr, Antenna Lab, 48-54, dir, 54-61, from asst prof to prof, 52-61; chief engr, Antenna & Microwave Group, Motorola, Inc, 61-67; PROF ELEC ENG & CHMN DEPT, ARIZ STATE UNIV, 67- *Mem:* Fel Inst Elec & Electronics Engrs. *Res:* Antennas; electronics; radar; microwave reflection and refraction. *Mailing Add:* Dept of Elec Eng Ariz State Univ Tempe AZ 85281

TICHAUER, ERWIN RUDOLPH, b Berlin, Ger, Apr 27, 18; m 46. OCCUPATIONAL BOIMECHANICS, OCCUPATIONAL HEALTH. *Educ:* Technische Hochschule, dipl, 38; Albertus Univ, ScD(phys sci), 40. *Prof Exp:* Dep dir area team 1065, UNRRA, 46-47; engr in-chg trainiing & res, FAMIC Ltda, Chile, 47-50; works mgr design & develop, PMS Pty Ltd, Australia, 50-53; specialist lectr eng, Univ Queensland, 53-56; expert productivity, UN Tech Assistance Admin, 56-59; sr lectr indust eng, Univ New SWales, 60-64; prof, Tex Tech Univ, 64-67; res prof, 67-68, prof biomech & dir div, Ctr Safety & Inst Rehab Med, Med Ctr, 68-77, PROF BIOMECH & DIR PROGS ERGONOMICS & BIOMECH, DEPT OCCUP HEALTH & SAFETY, NY UNIV, 77- *Concurrent Pos:* Distinguished vis prof, San Marcos Univ, Lima, 58; hon consult, Royal S Sidney Hosp, 60-64; consult, UNICEF, 61, Major Corp, 64- & Waterbury Hosp, Conn, 69-; vis assoc prof, Tex Tech Univ, 63; mem, Australian Coun Rehab of Disabled, 64-; guest lectr, USPHS, 67; chmn subcomt biomech, Comt Z-94, Am Nat Stand Inst, 68-75; Am Soc Mech Engrs rep, US Nat Comt Eng, Med & Biol, Nat Acad Eng-Nat Res Coun, 69-72; mem bd trustees comt, NJ Inst Technol, 69-; chmn biomed eng, NY Acad Med, 71-72; mem comt prosthetics res in Vet Admin, Nat Res Coun, 75-77. *Honors & Awards:* Gilbreth Medal, Soc Advan Mgt; Golden Plate Award, Acad Achievement; Outstanding Achievement Award & Distinguished Res Award, Am Inst Indust Engrs; Metrop Life Award, Nat Safety Coun. *Mem:* Fel NY Acad Sci; fel Royal Soc Health; fel Am Soc Mech Engrs; Am Inst Indust Engrs; Am Soc Eng Educ. *Res:* Occupational biomechanics, ergonomics; anatomy; medical education; medical thermography; preventive occupational medicine, safety and traumatology; functional anatomy and physiology applied to design of tasks, tools and equipment for both healthy and disabled workers; work stress on women. *Mailing Add:* 330 E 33 St Apt 12J New York NY 10016

TICHENOR, BRUCE ALAN, sanitary engineering, see previous edition

TICHO, HAROLD KLEIN, b Brno, Czech, Dec 21, 21; nat US; m. EXPERIMENTAL HIGH ENERGY PHYSICS. *Educ:* Univ Chicago, PhD(physics), 49. *Prof Exp:* Asst, Univ Chicago, 42-48; from asst prof to assoc prof, 48-58, chmn dept, 67-71, PROF PHYSICS, UNIV CALIF, LOS ANGELES, 58-, DEAN DIV PHYS SCI, 74- *Concurrent Pos:* Guggenheim fel, 66-67, 73-74. *Mem:* Am Phys Soc. *Res:* High energy nuclear physics; elementary particles. *Mailing Add:* Dept of Physics Univ of Calif Los Angeles CA 90024

TICK, PAUL A, b Margaretville, NY, Mar 9, 40; m 62; c 1. GLASS CHEMISTRY. *Educ:* Northeastern Univ, BS, 62, MS, 64; Mass Inst Technol, ScD, 67. *Prof Exp:* Res engr, Instrumentation Labs, Mass Inst Technol, 62-67; scientist crystal growth, NASA, 67-69; sr res scientist, 67-80, RES ASSOC GLASS RES, CORNING GLASS WORKS, 80- *Mem:* Sigma Xi; Am Chem Soc. *Res:* Photochromic glass research; kinetics of reactions in glass; amorphous semiconductors; electrochromics. *Mailing Add:* Corning Glass Works Sullivan Park FR-3 Painted Post NY 14870

TICKLE, ROBERT SIMPSON, b Norfolk, Va, July 31, 30; m 55; c 1. NUCLEAR PHYSICS. *Educ:* US Mil Acad, BS, 52; Univ Va, MS, 58, PhD(nuclear physics), 60. *Prof Exp:* From instr to assoc prof, 60-68, PROF PHYSICS, UNIV MICH, ANN ARBOR, 68- *Mem:* Am Phys Soc; Am Asn Physics Teachers. *Res:* Measurement of photonuclear cross sections; accelerator design and development; study of nuclear structure with charged particle experiments; study of reaction mechanisms using heavy ions. *Mailing Add:* Dept of Physics Univ of Mich Ann Arbor MI 48109

TICKNER, ALFRED WILLIAM, b Moose Jaw, Sask, Feb 3, 22; m 48; c 2. PHYSICAL CHEMISTRY, RESEARCH ADMINISTRATION. *Educ:* Univ Sask, BE, 44, MSc, 47; Univ Toronto, PhD(chem), 49. *Prof Exp:* Res fel mass spectrometry, Nat Res Coun Can, 49-51; res fel collision processes, Univ Col, London, 51-52; asst res officer, Mass Spectrometry, 52-54, assoc res officer, 55-62, sr res officer, 63-64, chief personnel adv, 64-70, actg secy, Coun, 71-72, chief personnel adv, 73-76, SR ARCHIVAL OFFICER, NAT RES COUN CAN, 76- *Mem:* Chem Inst Can. *Res:* Reactions in electric discharges; mass spectrometry as applied to chemical analysis; metal vapors; administration. *Mailing Add:* Nat Res Coun Can Ottawa ON K1A 0R6 Can

TICKNOR, LELAND BRUCE, b Centralia, Wash, May 9, 22; m 52. PHYSICAL CHEMISTRY. *Educ:* Univ Wash, BS, 44; Mass Inst Technol, PhD(phys chem), 50. *Prof Exp:* Mem staff, Dept Metall, Mass Inst Technol, 50-52; instr chem, Swarthmore Col, 52-54; phys chemist & sect leader, Res & Develop Dept, Viscose Div, FMC Corp, 54-65; sr res chemist, Appl Res Lab, US Steel Corp, 65-68; sr res chemist, 68-75, GROUP LEADER RES DEPT, DOW BADISCHE CORP, 75- *Mem:* Fiber Soc; Am Chem Soc. *Res:* Thermodynamics of solutions; retained energies of cold working in metals; cellulose chemistry; cellulose fibers; metal coatings; acrylic fibers. *Mailing Add:* Badische Corp Williamsburg VA 23185

TICKNOR, ROBERT LEWIS, b Portland, Ore, Oct 26, 26; m 50; c 3. ORNAMENTAL HORTICULTURE. *Educ:* Ore State Univ, BS, 50; Mich State Univ, MS, 51, PhD(pomol), 53. *Prof Exp:* Asst hort, Mich State Univ, 50-53; asst prof nursery culture, Univ Mass, 53-57, assoc prof, 57-59; assoc prof hort, 59-72, PROF HORT, ORE STATE UNIV, 72- *Mem:* Am Soc Hort Sci; Am Asn Bot Gardens & Arboretums; Int Plant Propagators Soc. *Res:* Chemical weed control; plant nutrition, propagation and materials. *Mailing Add:* North Willamette Exp Sta Rte 2 Box 254 Aurora OR 97002

TICKU, MAHARAJ K, b India, March 19, 48. PHARMACOLOGY. *Educ:* Birla Inst Technol & Sci, India, BS, 69; Univ Okla, MS, 72; State Univ NY, Buffalo, PhD(biochem), 76. *Prof Exp:* Teaching asst pharmacol, Univ Okla, 71-72; grad asst, State Univ NY, Buffalo, 72-75; fel, Univ Calif, Riverside, 76-78; ASST PROF PHARMACOL, UNIV HEALTH SCI CTR, SAN ANTONIO, 78-, ASST PROF PSYCHIAT, 81- *Concurrent Pos:* Res starter grant, Pharmaceut Mfg Asn, 79; career develop award, NIH, 81; travel award, Nat Sci Found, 81. *Mem:* Am Soc Pharmacol & Exp Therapeut; Soc Neurosci; Europe Brain & Behav Soc; Brit Brain Res Asn; Sigma Xi. *Res:* Molecular pharmacology of synaptic transmission; molecular mechanisms of depressant and convulsant drugs; y-aminobutyic acid synaptic pharmacology; y-aminobutyic acid pharmacology; experimental hypertension; drug receptor studies. *Mailing Add:* Dept Pharmacol Univ Tex Health Sci Ctr 7703 Floyd Curl San Antonio TX 78284

TIDBALL, CHARLES STANLEY, b Geneva, Switz, Apr 15, 28; US citizen; m 52. COMPUTER SCIENCE, PHYSIOLOGY. *Educ:* Wesleyan Univ, BA, 50; Univ Rochester, MS, 52; Univ Wis, PhD(physiol), 55; Univ Chicago, MD, 58. *Prof Exp:* Asst physiol, Univ Wis, 52-55; res asst surg, Univ Chicago, 55-56, asst physiol, 56-58, res asst, 57; intern, Madison Gen Hosp, Wis, 58-59; physician, Mendota State Hosp, 59; asst res prof, 59-63, from assoc prof from actg chmn to chmn dept, 63-71, to prof, 63-65, dir comput assisted educ, 73-78, res prof med, 72-80, HENRY D FRY PROF PHYSIOL, MED CTR, GEORGE WASHINGTON UNIV, 65-, PROF EDUC, SCH EDUC, 81- *Concurrent Pos:* USPHS fel, 60-61, USPHS res career develop award, 61-63; consult to var hosp, indust, col & govt orgn, 60- *Mem:* AAAS; Asn Am Med Cols; Am Physiol Soc; Digital Equip Comput Users Soc; Asn Develop Comput-Based Instruct Systs. *Res:* Time-sharing computer systems; computer assisted education; medical computer utilization; graduate and medical education; physiology; computer literacy; adult education; administrative computing. *Mailing Add:* Dept of Physiol George Washington Univ Med Ctr Washington DC 20037

TIDBALL, M(ARY) ELIZABETH, b Anderson, Ind, Oct 15, 29; m 52. MEDICAL PHYSIOLOGY, INSTITUTIONAL RESEARCH. *Educ:* Mt Holyoke Col, BA, 51; Univ Wis, MS, 55, PhD(physiol), 59. *Hon Degrees:* ScD, Wilson Col, 73; DSc, Trinity Col, 74, LHD, Mt Holyoke Col, 76, Cedar Crest Col, 77 & Univ of the South, 78, Goucher Col, 79; HHD, St Mary's Col, 77; LittD, Regis Col & Col St Catherine, 90. *Prof Exp:* Asst physiol, Univ Wis, 52-55, 58-59; asst histochem, Univ Chicago, 55-56, physiol, 56-58; USPHS fel, Nat Heart Inst, 59-61; staff pharmacologist, Hazelton Labs, Inc, 61-62; asst res prof pharmacol, 62-64, assoc res prof physiol, 64-70, res prof, 70-71, PROF PHYSIOL, GEORGE WASH UNIV, 71- *Concurrent Pos:* Consult, Hazelton Labs, Inc. 62-63; assoc sci coordr, Food & Drug Admin, Sci Assocs Training Prog, 66-67; consult, Food & Drug Admin, 66-68; trustee, Mt Holyoke Col, 68-73, vchmn, 72-73, Hood Col, 72-; trustee exec comn mem, 74-, chmn trustee educ comn, 74-, trustee, Hood Col, 72-; nat adv coun on NIH training progs & fels, Nat Acad Sci, 72-; exec secy, Nat Acad Sci-Nat Res Coun Comn on Human Resources in Comt on the Educ & Employment of Women in Sci & Eng, 74-75, vchmn, 77-; consult, inst res, Wellesley Col, 74-75 & Woodrow Wilson Nat Fel Found, 74-; chmn task force on women, Am Physiol Soc, 73-; consult & chmn review panels, NSF, 74-; trustee, Col Preachers, 79-; trustee, Sweet Briar Col, 78-, chmn trustee acad affairs comn, 82- *Mem:* AAAS; Am Physiol Soc; Am Asn Higher Educ; Sigma Xi. *Res:* Autacoids and neuroendocrinology; education of women; institutional research; science literacy. *Mailing Add:* 4100 Cathedral Ave NW Washington DC 20016

TIDBALL, RONALD RICHARD, b Greeley, Colo, July 13, 30; m 53, 72; c 3. SOIL SCIENCE, GEOCHEMISTRY. *Educ:* Colo State Univ, BS, 52; Univ Wash, MS, 57; Univ Calif, Berkeley, PhD(soil sci), 65. *Prof Exp:* Res Asst forestry, Univ Wash, 55-57 & Weyerhauser Co, 57; res asst soil sci, Univ Calif, 58-64; SOIL SCIENTIST, ENVIRON GEOCHEM, US GEOL SURV, 65- *Mem:* Am Quaternary Asn; Soil Sci Soc Am; Soc Environ Geochem Health. *Res:* Geochemistry of soils in relation to geologic setting; sampling designs; statistical interpretations; geochemical mapping. *Mailing Add:* US Geol Surv Box 25046 Fed Ctr Denver CO 80225

TIDD, MICHAEL JOHN, b Eng, Jan 29, 49; m 63; c 3. INDUSTRIAL DRUGS. *Educ:* Univ Col London, BSc, 61; Univ London, MB & BS, 64; MRCS & LRCP, 64; ECFMG, 69. *Prof Exp:* Dep dir spec proj, G D Searle & Co, 67-69; instr med, Vanderbilt Univ, 69-70; dir clin res, G D Searle & Co, 70-72, dir pharmacol, 72-75; dir clin res, Syntex Res Ctr, UK, 75-77; dep dir, Corp Med Off, G D Searle & Co, 77-78, spec asst to pres res & develop, 78-79, vpres med affairs, 80-81; HEAD TECHNOL ASSESSMENT, SPEC PROD GROUP, PROCTOR & GAMBLE, 81- *Concurrent Pos:* mem med comt, Asn British Pharmaceut Indust, 76-77; consult, Inveresy Res Int, 77- *Mem:* Royal Soc Med; British Med Asn. *Res:* Pharmacology; Drug metabolism and pharmacokinetics; medical devices and instruments. *Mailing Add:* 348 Grove Rd Woodlawn OH 45215

TIDD, ROBERT FREDERICK, mathematics, deceased

TIDE, RAYMOND HARRY ROY, civil engineering, see previous edition

TIDRICK, ROBERT THOMPSON, b Doleib Hill, Sudan, Aug 4, 09; US citizen; m; c 4. SURGERY. *Educ:* Tarkio Col, AB, 32; Wash Univ, MD, 36; Am Bd Surg, dipl, 43. *Prof Exp:* Intern, Univ Hosp, Univ Iowa, 36-37; intern, Am Hosp, Assiut, Egypt, 37-38; asst resident surg, Univ Hosp, Univ Iowa, 38-39, resident, 39-44, asst pathologist, 39-40, instr orthop path, 40-42, asst & instr surg, 42-44, from assoc to prof, Col Med, 44-69, head dept, 51-69; PROF SURG, MED COL OHIO, 69- *Concurrent Pos:* Honors &. *Honors & Awards:* Burdick Award, 40. *Mem:* Soc Exp Biol & Med; Am Geriat Soc; Soc Univ Surgeons; AMA; Am Surg Asn. *Res:* Diseases of the colon; cancer; traumatology. *Mailing Add:* Dept of Surg Med Col of Ohio CS 10008 Toledo OH 43699

TIDWELL, EUGENE DELBERT, b Lehi, Utah, Sept 5, 26; m 48; c 8. INSTRUMENTATION, SPECTROSCOPY. *Educ:* Brigham Young Univ, BS, 51. *Prof Exp:* Asst gas chemist copper smelt, Kennecott Copper Corp, 44-45 & 47-52; staff physicist spectros, Nat Bur Standards, 52-63; STAFF ENGR INSTRUMENTATION, ARO, INC, 63- *Res:* Theoretical spectral analysis of light gases; environmental erosion research for aeroballistics and space engineering. *Mailing Add:* 1311 Bel Aire Dr Tullahoma TN 37388

TIDWELL, THOMAS TINSLEY, b Atlanta, Ga, Feb 20, 39; m 71. ORGANIC CHEMISTRY. *Educ:* Ga Inst Technol, BS, 60; Harvard Univ, AM, 63, PhD(reaction mechanisms), 64. *Prof Exp:* NIH fel, Univ Calif, San Diego, 64-65; asst prof chem, Univ SC, 65-72; assoc prof, 72-77, assoc dean, 79-82, PROF CHEM, SCARBOROUGH COL, UNIV TORONTO, 77- *Concurrent Pos:* NIH fel, Univ EAnglia, 66-67; vis prof, Stanford Univ, 79. *Mem:* Am Chem Soc. *Res:* Steric strain; reactions of peroxides; enolate chemistry; carbonium ions; ketenes; organofluorine chemistry; oil from wood. *Mailing Add:* Dept of Chem Scarborough Col U of Toronto West Hill ON M1C 1A4 Can

TIDWELL, TROY HASKELL, JR, electrochemistry, see previous edition

TIDWELL, WILLIAM LEE, b Greenville, SC, Jan 14, 26; m 46; c 1. MICROBIOLOGY. *Educ:* Univ SC, BS, 45; Univ Hawaii, MS, 48; Univ Calif, Los Angeles, PhD(microbiol), 51. *Prof Exp:* Asst bact, Univ Hawaii, 46-48 & Univ Calif, Los Angeles, 48-51; asst prof biol, Agr & Mech Col, Tex, 51-55, asst res bact, Eng Exp Sta, 52-55; asst prof biol, 55-58, assoc prof bact, 58-62, PROF MICROBIOL, SAN JOSE STATE UNIV, 62-, CHMN MICROBIOL AREA, 78- *Concurrent Pos:* Consult, State Col Affairs, Calif State Employees Asn, 66-68. *Mem:* Am Soc Microbiol; NY Acad Sci. *Res:* General bacteriology; water and sewage bacteriology. *Mailing Add:* Dept of Biol Sci San Jose State Univ San Jose CA 95192

TIECKE, RICHARD WILLIAM, b Muscatine, Iowa, Apr 5, 17. PATHOLOGY. *Educ:* Univ Iowa, BS, 40, DDS, 42, MS, 47; Am Bd Oral Path, dipl. *Prof Exp:* Resident path, Univ Chicago, 47-49; dep dir oral path div, Armed Forces Inst Path, 49-55; assoc prof oral path, Georgetown Univ, 52-54; assoc prof path, Sch Dent, Northwestern Univ, 55-62; ASST EXEC DIR SCI AFFAIRS, AM DENT ASN, 71- *Concurrent Pos:* Consult, US Naval Hosp, Great Lakes, 55-70, Vet Admin Res Hosp, Chicago, 56-70, Vet Admin West Side Hosp & Pub Health Hosp, 56-71; prof, Col Dent, Univ Ill, Chicago, 62-; consult, Nat Cancer Inst; surgeon gen, Div Chronic Dis, USPHS; pres, Am Bd Oral Path, 67-71; prof path, Schs Dent & Med, Northwestern Univ, 74- *Mem:* Int Acad Oral Path; Am Dent Asn; fel Am Col Dent; fel Am Acad Oral Path (pres, 57); Int Asn Dent Res. *Res:* Cancer; pathologic physiology of oral disease. *Mailing Add:* 179 E Lake Shore Dr Chicago IL 60611

TIECKELMANN, HOWARD, b Chicago, Ill, Oct 29, 16; m 42; c 5. BIO-ORGANIC CHEMISTRY. *Educ:* Carthage Col, BA, 42; Univ Buffalo, PhD(org chem), 48. *Prof Exp:* Chemist, Armour Res Found, Ill, 46; from instr to prof, 46-61, chmn dept, 70-74, DISTINGUISHED TEACHING PROF CHEM, STATE UNIV NY BUFFALO, 75- *Mem:* AAAS; Royal Soc Chem; Am Inst Chemists; Am Chem Soc. *Res:* Heterocyclic compounds; pyridines; pyrimidines, alkylations and rearrangements; natural products. *Mailing Add:* Dept of Chem State Univ of NY Buffalo NY 14214

TIEDCKE, CARL HEINRICH WILHELM, b Lübeck, Ger, Mar 1, 03; nat US; m 48. CHEMISTRY, TOXICOLOGY. *Educ:* Hamburg Univ, PhD(chem), 28. *Prof Exp:* Consult, US Army, US Navy & USPHS; adv air pollution control, various industs & govts, SAm & Africa. *Concurrent Pos:* Concurrent. *Mem:* AAAS; Am Chem Soc; Am Microchem Soc; NY Acad Sci; Austrian Asn Microchem & Anal Chem. *Res:* High vacuum distillation; vegetable oils; coffee constituents; applied microchemistry; foods; pharmacology; nutrition. *Mailing Add:* 1040 Cliff Dr 2D Santa Barbara CA 93109

TIEDEMANN, ALBERT WILLIAM, JR, b Baltimore, Md, Nov 7, 24; m 53; c 4. QUALITY ASSURANCE. *Educ:* Loyola Col, Md, BS, 47; NY Univ, MS, 49; Georgetown Univ, PhD(chem), 58. *Prof Exp:* Instr chem, Mt St Agnes Col, 50-55; sr res chemist, Emerson Drug Co, 55-56, chief chemist, Emerson Drug Co Div, Warner-Lambert Pharmaceut Co, 56-60; supvr anal group, Allegany Ballistic Lab, Hercules, Inc, 61-68, supt tech serv, Radford Army Ammunition Plant, 68-72; DIR CONSOLIDATED LABS, COMMONWEALTH VA, 72- *Mem:* Am Soc Qual Control; fel Am Inst Chemists; Am Mgt Asn; Asn Food & Drug Officials; Asn Official Anal Chemists. *Res:* Development of analytical methods. *Mailing Add:* Div Consol Labs One N 14th St Richmond VA 23219

TIEDEMANN, HERMAN HENRY, b New York, NY, July 25, 17; m 44; c 3. ELECTROCHEMISTRY, PETROCHEMICALS. *Educ:* City Col New York, BChE, 39, MChE, 40. *Prof Exp:* From chem operator to group leader develop eng, Rohm & Haas Co, 40-48; sr chem engr, GAF Corp, 48-49, supv chem engr, 49-51, actg mgr chem eng, 51-52, supvr process engr, 52-57, supt ethylene chem prod, 58-60, prod mgr, heavy chems, 60-65, plant mgr, 66-70, div mgr prod control, 70-71; prod mgr, Linden Chlorine Prod, Inc, 72-74; vpres, PCF Machinery Corp, 74-75; CONSULT, 76- *Mem:* Am Inst Chem Eng. *Res:* Liquid-liquid extraction columns; use of wetting agents to improve column performance; dyes, detergent, beverages and culinary mixes; continuous anodes for chlorine cells. *Mailing Add:* 16 11th Ave N PO Box 28 Texas City TX 77590

TIEDEMANN, WILLIAM HAROLD, ELECTROCHEMICAL ENGINEERING. *Educ:* Univ Calif, Los Angeles, BS, 66, MS, 68, PhD(electro chem eng), 71. *Prof Exp:* Sr electrochemist, Globe Union, Inc, 71-76, mgr electrochem res, 76-79; ASSOC DIR RES, JOHNSON CONTROLS, INC, 79- *Mem:* Electrochem Soc. *Res:* Theoretical mathematical modeling; experimental investigations of a variety of electrochemical systems; system simulation and scale-up. *Mailing Add:* 5757 N Green Bay Ave Milwaukee WI 53201

TIEDERMAN, WILLIAM GREGG, JR, b Tulsa, Okla, Jan 29, 38; m 63; c 3. MECHANICAL ENGINEERING. *Educ:* Stanford Univ, BS, 60, MS, 61, PhD(mech eng), 65. *Prof Exp:* Engr, Shell Develop Co, 65-68; from asst prof to prof mech eng, Okla State Univ, 68-78; PROF MECH ENG, PURDUE UNIV, WEST LAFAYETTE, 78- *Mem:* Am Soc Mech Engrs; Am Inst Aeronaut & Astronaut. *Res:* Turbulence; viscous fluid mechanics; laser velocimetry; solid-liquid and liquid-liquid separation; drag reduction. *Mailing Add:* Sch of Mech Eng ME Bldg Purdue Univ West Lafayette IN 47907

TIEDJE, JAMES MICHAEL, b Newton, Iowa, Feb 9, 42; m 65; c 3. MICROBIAL ECOLOGY, SOIL MICROBIOLOGY. *Educ:* Iowa State Univ, BS, 64; Cornell Univ, MS, 66, PhD(soil microbiol), 68. *Prof Exp:* From asst prof to assoc prof, 68-78, PROF MICROBIAL ECOL, MICH STATE UNIV, 78- *Concurrent Pos:* Eli Lilly career develop grant, 74; vis assoc prof, Univ Ga, 74-75; ed, Appl Microbiol, 74-, ed in chief, 80-; consult, NSF, 74-77; vis prof, Univ Calif, Berkeley, 81-82; Sigma Xi jr res award, 81. *Mem:* Am Soc Microbiol; fel Am Soc Agron; Soil Sci Soc Am; AAAS. *Res:* Denitrification; microbial metabolism of organic pollutants; auaeroic metabolism. *Mailing Add:* Dept of Microbiol & Pub Health Mich State Univ East Lansing MI 48824

TIEFEL, RALPH MAURICE, b Brazil, Ind, Sept 3, 28; m 66. BOTANY. *Educ:* Cent Mo State Col, BS, 53; Univ Mo, MA, 55, PhD(bot), 57. *Prof Exp:* Assoc prof, 57-59, PROF BIOL, CARTHAGE COL, 60- *Mem:* Soc Econ Bot; Torrey Bot Club. *Res:* Soil and plant relationships; meristems; history of science. *Mailing Add:* Dept of Biol Carthage Col Kenosha WI 53141

TIEFENTHAL, HARLAN E, b Kalamazoo, Mich, Aug 23, 22; m 42; c 4. ORGANIC CHEMISTRY. *Educ:* Kalamazoo Col, BA, 44; Univ Ill, MS, 48; Mich State Col, PhD(chem), 50; Univ Chicago, MBA, 65. *Prof Exp:* Fel chem, Mellon Inst, 50-54, group leader, Koppers Co, Inc, 54-58, mgr fine chem group, 58-62; asst res dir, Armour Indust Chem Co, 62-65, dir spec projs, 66-68; V PRES, MDM, INC, 76-; VPRES, WESTERN SPRINGS CORP, 80- *Concurrent Pos:* Owner, Tiefenthal Assocs, 68-; exec dir, Assoc Cols Chicago Area, 69-75; lectr, George Williams Col, 72-75; pres, Deep Valley Chem Co, 73- *Mem:* Am Chem Soc; Am Oil Chemists Soc. *Res:* Grignard reactions; dehydrogenation reactions; dehydrocyclizations; polymerization; alkylation; hydrogenation; organic synthesis; amination; aliphatic amine chemistry. *Mailing Add:* 4544 Grand Ave Western Springs IL 60558

TIEH, THOMAS TA-PIN, b Peking, China, May 2, 34; US citizen; m 62; c 4. MINERALOGY. *Educ:* Univ Ill, Urbana, BS, 58; Stanford Univ, MS, 60, PhD(geol), 65. *Prof Exp:* Geologist, Bear Creek Mining Co, 60; res assoc geol, Univ Hawaii, 62-63; asst cur mining & petrol, Stanford Univ, 65-66; asst prof, 66-71, assoc prof, 71-81, PROF GEOL, TEX A&M UNIV, 81- *Concurrent Pos:* Welch Found grant, Tex A&M Univ, 69-72. *Mem:* Brit Mineral Soc; Soc Econ Paleontologists & Mineralogists. *Res:* Petrology and geochemistry. *Mailing Add:* Dept Geol Tex A&M Univ College Station TX 77843

TIELEMAN, HENRY WILLIAM, b Rotterdam, Neth, May 26, 33; Can citizen; m 62; c 2. FLUID MECHANICS. *Educ:* Ont Agr Col, BSA, 61; Univ Toronto, BAS, 62; Univ Iowa, MS, 64; Colo State Univ, PhD(civil eng), 69. *Prof Exp:* Asst prof eng mech, 69-72, assoc prof, 72-81, PROF ENG SCI & MECH, VA POLYTECH INST & STATE UNIV, 81- *Mem:* Am Soc Mech Engrs. *Res:* Fluid mechanics; turbulent boundary layers; theory of turbulence; turbulence measurements. *Mailing Add:* Dept of Eng Mech Va Polytech Inst & State Univ Blacksburg VA 24060

TIEMAN, CHARLES HENRY, JR, b Los Angeles, Calif, Sept 3, 26; div; c 2. ORGANIC CHEMISTRY. *Educ:* Univ Calif, Los Angeles, BS, 49; Univ Colo, PhD(chem), 53. *Prof Exp:* Asst, Univ Colo, 50-53; res & develop chemist, Aerojet-Gen Corp, Gen Tire & Rubber Co, 53-58; RES CHEMIST, SHELL DEVELOP CO, 58- *Mem:* Am Chem Soc. *Res:* Organic syntheses and mechanisms. *Mailing Add:* Biol Sci Res Ctr Shell Develop Co PO Box 4248 Modesto CA 95352

TIEMAN, SUZANNAH BLISS, b Washington, DC, Oct 10, 43; m 69. NEUROSCIENCES, VISION. *Educ:* Cornell Univ, AB, 65; Stanford Univ, PhD(psychol), 74. *Prof Exp:* Nat Eye Inst fel, Dept Anat, Univ Calif Med Ctr, San Francisco, 74-77; RES ASSOC, NEUROBIOL RES CTR, STATE UNIV NY ALBANY, 77- *Mem:* Am Asn Anatomists; Asn Res Vision & Ophthal; AAAS; Soc Neurosci; Asn Women in Sci. *Res:* Anatomoical and behavioral effects of restricted early visual experience. *Mailing Add:* Neurobiol Res Ctr State Univ NY 1400 Washington Ave Albany NY 12222

TIEMANN, JEROME J, b Yonkers, NY, Feb 21, 32; m 57. SOLID STATE PHYSICS. *Educ:* Mass Inst Technol, ScB, 53; Stanford Univ, PhD(physics), 60. *Prof Exp:* Asst, Stanford Univ, 53-55 & 56-57; PHYSICIST, RES & DEVELOP CTR, GEN ELEC CO, 57- *Concurrent Pos:* Consult, Radiation Lab, Univ Calif, 55-57. *Mem:* Fel Inst Elec & Electronics Engrs. *Res:* Quantum mechanics; electronics; solid state electronic device phenomena; electronic circuit and system design; signal processing circuit and system design. *Mailing Add:* Corp Res & Develop Ctr Gen Elec Co 1 River Rd Schenectady NY 12301

TIEMSTRA, PETER J, b Chicago, Ill, Oct 7, 23; m 46; c 3. FOOD CHEMISTRY. *Educ:* Northwestern Univ, BS, 44; Univ Chicago, BS, 47, MS, 48. *Prof Exp:* Anal chemist, Swift & Co, 48-49, anal res chemist, 49-53, from asst head chemist to head chemist, 53-63, head res & develop, Stabilizer Div, 63-65; res chemist, Derby Foods, Inc, Ill, 65-66, tech dir, 66-69; dir res & qual assurance, Swift Grocery Prod Co, Chicago, 69-70, dir spec serv, 70-76; dir res & qual assurance, F&F Labs, Chicago, 77-78; CORP QUAL ASSURANCE LAB MGR, WM WRIGLEY JR CO, CHICAGO, 79- *Mem:* Am Chem Soc; Am Oil Chem Soc; Am Soc Qual Control; Inst Food Technologists; Am Asn Candy Technologists. *Res:* Quality control; product research and development. *Mailing Add:* 6543 Pontiac Dr LaGrange IL 60525

TIEN, C(HANG) L(IN), b Hankow, China, July 24, 35; m 59; c 3. HEAT TRANSFER. *Educ:* Nat Taiwan Univ, BS, 55; Univ Louisville, MME, 57; Princeton Univ, MA & PhD(mech eng), 59. *Prof Exp:* Actg asst prof mech eng, 59-60, from asst prof to assoc prof, 60-68, chmn thermal systs div, 69-72, chmn dept mech eng, 74-81, PROF MECH ENG, UNIV CALIF, BERKELEY, 68- *Concurrent Pos:* Consult, Lockheed Missile & Space Co, 63-80 & Gen Elec Co, 72-80; Guggenheim fel, 65-66; res assoc prof, Miller Inst Basic Res Sci, Univ Calif, 67-68; US scientist award, Alexander von Humboldt Found, 79; Japan Soc Prom Sci fel, 80. *Honors & Awards:* Heat Transfer Mem Award, Am Soc Mech Engrs, 74, Gustus L Larson Mem Award, 75 & Max Jakob Mem Award, 81; Thermophysics Award, Am Inst Aeronaut & Astronaut, 77. *Mem:* Nat Acad Eng; Am Soc Mech Engrs; Am Inst Aeronaut & Astronaut. *Res:* Heat transfer; radiative heat transfer; thermal insulation and enclosure convection; reactor safety heat transfer. *Mailing Add:* Dept of Mech Eng Univ of Calif Col of Eng Berkeley CA 94720

TIEN, CHI, b Peking, China, Oct 8, 30; US citizen; m 60; c 2. CHEMICAL ENGINEERING. *Educ:* Nat Taiwan Univ, BSc, 52; Kans State Univ, MSc, 54; Northwestern Univ, Evanston, PhD(chem eng), 58. *Prof Exp:* Asst prof chem eng, Univ Tulsa, 57-59; from asst prof to assoc prof, Univ Windsor, 59-63; assoc prof, 63-66, PROF CHEM ENG, SYRACUSE UNIV, 66-, CHMN DEPT CHEM ENG & MAT SCI, 70- *Concurrent Pos:* Expert, US Army Cold Regions Res & Eng Lab, Hanover, NH, 59-64 & 69- *Mem:* AAAS; Am Inst Chem Engrs; Chem Inst Can. *Res:* Advanced treatment of waste water, especially by filtration and adsorption; heat transfer with phase change. *Mailing Add:* Dept of Chem Eng & Mat Sci Syracuse Univ Syracuse NY 13210

TIEN, HSIN TI, b Peking, China, Feb 1, 28; US citizen; m 53; c 4. BIOPHYSICS. *Educ:* Univ Nebr, BS, 53; Temple Univ, MA, 60, PhD(chem), 63. *Prof Exp:* Proj engr, Allied Chem Corp, 56-57; med scientist, Eastern Pa Psychiat Inst, 57-63; assoc prof chem, Northeastern Univ, 63-66; PROF BIOPHYS & CHMN DEPT, MICH STATE UNIV, 66- *Concurrent Pos:* Grants, Res Corp, 64-65, NIH, 64-, Off Saline Water, US Dept Interior, 68-71 & Dept Energy, 80-82; hon prof, Academia Sinica. *Mem:* AAAS; Am Chem Soc; Biophys Soc. *Res:* Physical chemical investigations of membranes, particularly bilayer lipid membranes; photosynthesis and vision; solar energy conversion; specific electrodes; ion-exchange equilibria; bilayer lipid membranes as models of biological membranes. *Mailing Add:* Dept of Biophys Mich State Univ East Lansing MI 48824

T'IEN, JAMES SHAW-TZUU, b China, Mar 8, 42; m 67. COMBUSTION, FLUID MECHANICS. *Educ:* Nat Taiwan Univ, BS, 63; Purdue Univ, Lafayette, MS, 66; Princeton Univ, PhD(aeronaut & mech eng), 71. *Prof Exp:* Res assoc, 70-71, asst prof, 71-75, ASSOC PROF ENG, CASE WESTERN RESERVE UNIV, 75- *Mem:* Combustion Inst; Am Inst Aeronaut & Astronaut. *Res:* Combustion and chemically-reacting flows; propulsion and fire research. *Mailing Add:* Dept of Mech & Aerospace Eng Case Western Reserve Univ Cleveland OH 44106

TIEN, JOHN KAI, b Chungking, China, June 4, 40; US citizen; m 71; c 2. HIGH TEMPERATURE ALLOYS. *Educ:* Worcester Polytech Inst, BSME, 62; Yale Univ, MEng, 64; Carnegie-Mellon Univ, MS, 68, PhD(metall & mat sci), 69. *Prof Exp:* Res supvr metall, Chase Brass & Copper Co, 64-65; sr res assoc, Pratt & Whitney Aircraft, 68-71; assoc prof, 71-76, PROF METALL & MAT SCI, COLUMBIA UNIV, 76-, DIR, CTR STRATEGIC MAT, 81- *Concurrent Pos:* Prin investr grants, NSF, NASA, Dept Energy & Air Force, 71-; consult, Industs & UN, 71-; mem, Solid State Sci Panel, Nat Acad Sci, 76- & Panel Tantalum & Niobium Supply & Availability, 80- *Mem:* Am Inst Mining, Metall & Petrol Engrs; Am Soc Metals; Metall Soc. *Res:* Physical and mechanical metallurgy of high temperature superalloys for jet engine and gas turbine applications; hydrogen embrittlement; supply and demand analysis of strategic materials. *Mailing Add:* 918 Mudd Bldg Columbia Univ New York NY 10027

TIEN, P(ING) K(ING), b China, Aug 2, 19; m; c 2. ELECTRICAL ENGINEERING. *Educ:* Nat Cent Univ, China, BS, 42; Stanford Univ, MS, 48, PhD, 51. *Prof Exp:* Res assoc, Stanford Univ, 51-52; mem tech staff, 52-59, HEAD DEPT ELECTRON PHYSICS RES, BELL TEL LABS, INC, 59- *Mem:* Nat Acad Sci; Nat Acad Eng; Am Inst Physics; fel Inst Elec & Electronics Engrs; fel Optical Soc Am. *Res:* Device physics; microwave electronics; electron dynamics; wave propagation; noise; ferrites; acoustics in solids; gas lasers; superconductivity; integrated optics. *Mailing Add:* Bell Tel Labs Inc Holmdel NJ 07733

TIEN, REX YUAN, b Hupei, China, Aug 4, 35; m; c 3. ORGANIC CHEMISTRY. *Educ:* Chung Hsing Univ, Taiwan, BS, 58; Univ RI, PhD(chem), 68. *Prof Exp:* NSF fel chem, State Univ NY Albany, 67-68; SR CHEMIST, AM HOECHST CORP, 68- *Mem:* Am Chem Soc. *Res:* Applied chemistry, dyes and pigments; photochemistry; organometallic chemistry, kinetics and instrumentation. *Mailing Add:* 129 Sturbridge Dr Warwick RI 02886

TIEN, TSENG-YING, b Hopei, China, June 28, 24; US citizen; m; c 5. CERAMICS. *Educ:* Pa State Univ, MS, 60, PhD(ceramics), 65. *Prof Exp:* Sr scientist, Westinghouse Res Labs, 60-66; assoc prof mat, 66-73, PROF MAT, UNIV MICH, ANN ARBOR, 73- *Mem:* Am Ceramic Soc; fel Am Chem Soc. *Res:* Structure and their physical properties of solid oxide materials. *Mailing Add:* 2611 Park Ridge Dr Ann Arbor MI 48103

TIEN, WEICHEN, b Anhwei, China, July 12, 38; US citizen; m 66; c 2. MICROBIAL GENETICS, INDUSTRIAL MICROBIOLOGY. *Educ:* Nat Taiwan Univ, BS, 60; Univ Ky, MS, 65, PhD(microbiol), 68. *Prof Exp:* Sr microbiologist, S B Penick & Co, CPC Int, 68-70; sr scientist antibiotics, Wyeth Labs, Inc, 70-71, supvr, 71-74; TEAM LEADER FERMENTATION, PFIZER INC, 74- *Mem:* Am Soc Microbiol; Sigma Xi. *Res:* Bacterial and fungal genetics and cultural development for new antibiotics. *Mailing Add:* Pfizer Inc Groton CT 06340

TIERCE, JOHN FORREST, b Los Angeles, Calif, Aug 17, 42; m 67; c 2. ANIMAL GENETICS, BIOSTATISTICS. *Educ:* Okla State Univ, BS, 65, MS, 67; Iowa State Univ, PhD(animal genetics), 73. *Prof Exp:* Res assoc poultry sci, Iowa State Univ, 70-73; res geneticist poultry genetics, Perdue Farms, Inc, 73-75; DIR RES POULTRY GENETICS, INDIAN RIVER INT, 75- *Mem:* Poultry Sci Asn; World Poultry Sci Asn; Biometric Soc; Am Statist Asn. *Res:* Poultry genetics. *Mailing Add:* 3407 Kings Row Nacogdoches TX 75961

TIERKEL, ERNEST SHALOM, b Philadelphia, Pa, July 2, 17; m 58; c 2. VETERINARY PUBLIC HEALTH, EPIDEMIOLOGY. *Educ:* Univ Pa, AB, 38, VMD, 42; Columbia Univ, MPH, 46; Am Bd Vet Pub Health, dipl, 54. *Prof Exp:* Vet pathologist, Bur Animal Indust, USDA, 42-45; officer-in-chg rabies res unit, Virus Lab, Commun Dis Ctr, USPHS, 46-49, asst chief vet pub health prog, 50-52, dir nat rabies control prog, 54-64; Commun Dis Ctr consult vet pub health, Va State Health Dept, 53-54; dep dir health serv, AID, 64-66; Commun Dis Ctr-AID consult zoonoses & vet epidemiol, Nat Inst Commun Dis, New Delhi, India, 66-68; asst surgeon gen & dir off sci, US Dept Health, Educ & Welfare, 68-73; CHIEF, BUR DIS CONTROL, DEL DEPT HEALTH, 73- *Concurrent Pos:* Mem, Expert Panel Rabies, WHO, 50-, Expert Comt, Rome, 53, Paris, 56 & 61, Geneva, 59 & 65, Expert Panel Zoonoses, 64-, Expert Comt, Geneva, 66; vis lectr, Univ Pa, 53, 60-66 & 73-78, Harvard Univ, 53, Univ Ga, 53-54 & 60-64, Columbia Univ, 54-55, Emory Univ, 59 & 60-63 & Johns Hopkins Univ, 64-65. *Mem:* AAAS; Sigma Xi; Asn Mil Surg US; fel Am Pub Health Asn; Conf Pub Health Vets (pres, 57-58). *Res:* Rabies; public health zoonoses; environmental and international health. *Mailing Add:* 189 S Fairfield Dr Dover DE 19901

TIERNAN, ROBERT JOSEPH, b Boston, Mass, Dec 14, 35; m 59; c 4. PHYSICS, CERAMICS. *Educ:* Boston Col, AB, 57, MS, 59; Mass Inst Technol, PhD(ceramics), 69. *Prof Exp:* Res asst accelerators, Grad Sch, Boston Col, 57-59; solid state physicist, Naval Res Lab, 59-62; atomic physicist, Nat Bur Stand, 63; develop engr, Sylvania, 63-64; AEC res asst, Grad Sch, Mass Inst Technol, 64-69; sr res scientist, Raytheon Co, Waltham, 69-74; ENGR/SCIENTIST ADVAN RES & DEVELOP, GTE/SYLVANIA, 76- *Concurrent Pos:* Res assoc, Argonne Nat Lab, 75. *Res:* Solid state physics; electronic, optical and magnetic properties of ceramics; diffusion in ceramics; mechanical properties. *Mailing Add:* 224 North St Stoneham MA 02180

TIERNAN, THOMAS ORVILLE, b Chattanooga, Tenn, July 22, 36; m 61; c 1. CHEMICAL PHYSICS, ANALYTICAL CHEMISTRY. *Educ:* Univ Windsor, BSc, 58; Carnegie Inst Technol, MS, 60, PhD(chem), 66. *Prof Exp:* Ohio State Univ Res Found res chemist, Wright-Patterson AFB, 60-61, res chemist, Off Aeronaut Space Res, Aerospace Labs, 61-67, group leader high energy chem kinetics, 67-75; PROF CHEM, WRIGHT STATE UNIV, 75-, DIR, BREHM LAB, 76- *Mem:* AAAS; Am Chem Soc; Am Phys Soc; Am Soc Lubrication Engrs; fel Am Inst Chemists. *Res:* Mass spectrometry; gas phase kinetics; ion and electron impact-phenomena; plasma characterization and diagnostics; lasers; gaseous electronics; analytical methods development; environmental monitoring, materials characterization. *Mailing Add:* 6532 Senator Lane Dayton OH 45459

TIERNEY, DONALD FRANK, b Butte, Mont, May 24, 31; m 54; c 2. PHYSIOLOGY, MEDICINE. *Educ:* Univ Calif, Berkeley, BA, 53; Univ Calif, San Francisco, MD, 56. *Prof Exp:* Intern, Philadelphia Gen Hosp, 57; asst resident, Univ Pa, 58; asst resident, Univ Calif, San Francisco, 59, asst prof physiol, 65-68; assoc prof, 68-75, PROF MED, UNIV CALIF, LOS ANGELES, 75- *Concurrent Pos:* USPHS fels, Univ Calif, San Francisco, 59-65; mem pulmonary dis adv comt, Nat Heart & Lung Inst, 73-76; chief palmonary div, Univ Calif, Los Angeles Hosp; chmn Study Sect, Pediat Specialized Ctr Res, Nat Heart Lung & Blood Inst, NIH, 80-81. *Mem:* Am Physiol Soc; Am Thoracic Soc (vpres, 76-77, pres, 78-79); Am Soc Clin Invest; Asn Am Physicians. *Res:* Pulmonary physiology, biochemistry and metabolism. *Mailing Add:* Ctr for Health Sci Univ of Calif Los Angeles CA 90024

TIERNEY, JOHN W(ILLIAM), b Oak Park, Ill, Dec 29, 23. CHEMICAL ENGINEERING, SEPARATION SYSTEMS. *Educ:* Purdue Univ, BS, 47; Univ Mich, MS, 48; Northwestern Univ, PhD(chem eng), 51. *Prof Exp:* Res engr, Pure Oil Co, 48-50, 51-54; asst prof chem eng, Purdue Univ, 54-56; dept mgr, Res Div, Univac Div, Sperry Rand Corp, 56-60; assoc prof chem eng, 60-62, PROF CHEM ENG, UNIV PITTSBURGH, 62- *Concurrent Pos:* Lectr, Univ Minn, 58-59; vis prof, Santa Maria Univ, Chile, 60-62; Fulbright lectr, Univ Barcelona, 68-69. *Res:* Application of computer techniques to chemical engineering; design and analysis of digital control systems; equilibrium and nonequilibrium staged separation calculations; distillation; extraction; tiltration; flow through porous media. *Mailing Add:* Dept Chem Eng Sch Eng Univ of Pittsburgh Pittsburgh PA 15261

TIERS, GEORGE VAN DYKE, b Chicago, Ill, Mar 23, 27; m 50; c 1. ORGANIC CHEMISTRY, PHYSICAL CHEMISTRY. *Educ:* Univ Chicago, SB, 46, SM, 50, PhD(chem), 56. *Prof Exp:* Asst pharmacol, Univ Chicago, 45-46, chemist, Ord Res Proj, 48-49; res assoc, 51-65, CORP SCIENTIST, CENT RES DEPT, 3M CO, 65- *Honors & Awards:* Carbide Award, Am Chem Soc, 59. *Mem:* Am Chem Soc. *Res:* Nuclear magnetic resonance spectroscopy; fluorine, organic, dye, polymer and physical-organic chemistry; duplicating and imaging technology. *Mailing Add:* 3M Ctr St Paul MN 55133

TIERSON, WILLIAM CORNELIUS, b Newark, NY, Dec 19, 25; m 47; c 7. FOREST ECOLOGY, WILDLIFE ECOLOGY. *Educ:* State Univ NY Col Forestry, Syracuse, BSF, 49, MF, 67. *Prof Exp:* Forester, NY State Col Environ Sci & Forestry, Syracuse, 51-68, forest mgr, 68-72, DIR WILDLIFE RES, ADIRONDACK ECOL CTR, 72- *Mem:* Soc Am Foresters; Wildlife Soc. *Res:* Northern hardwood silviculture and ecology; forest game management; wildlife population dynamics; forest fertilization and growth. *Mailing Add:* Adirondack Ecol Ctr NY State Col Environ Sci & For Newcomb NY 12852

TIERSTEN, HARRY FRANK, b Brooklyn, NY, Jan 4, 30; m 53; c 2. APPLIED MECHANICS. *Educ:* Columbia Univ, BS, 52, MS, 56, PhD(appl mech), 61. *Prof Exp:* Stress analyst, Grumman Aircraft Eng Corp, 52-53; struct designer, J G White Eng Corp, 53-56; instr civil eng, City Col New York, 56-60; res asst appl mech, Columbia Univ, 60-61; mem tech staff, Bell Tel Labs, 61-68; PROF MECH, RENSSELAER POLYTECH INST, 68- *Mem:* Am Phys Soc; Acoust Soc Am; Am Soc Mech Eng; Soc Natural Philos; Inst Elec & Electronics Engr. *Res:* Elasticity; couple stress elasticity; electromagnetism; electrostriction; piezoelectricity; magnetism; magnetoelasticity; waves; vibrations. *Mailing Add:* Dept of Mech Rensselaer Polytech Inst Troy NY 12181

TIERSTEN, MARTIN STUART, b Aug 7, 31; US citizen; m 53; c 2. PHYSICS. *Educ:* Queens Col, NY, BA, 53; Columbia Univ, AM, 58, PhD(theoret solid state physics), 62. *Prof Exp:* Tutor physics, 57-62, instr, 62-63, asst prof, 63-70, ASSOC PROF PHYSICS, CITY COL NEW YORK, 70- *Mem:* Am Phys Soc; Am Asn Physics Teachers. *Res:* Theoretical physics. *Mailing Add:* Dept of Physics City Col of New York New York NY 10031

TIESZEN, LARRY L, b Marion, SDak, Mar 2, 40; m 59; c 2. PLANT PHYSIOLOGY, PLANT ECOLOGY. *Educ:* Augustana Col, SDak, BA, 61; Univ Colo, PhD(bot), 65. *Prof Exp:* Kettering fel biol, Albion Col, 65-66; asst prof, Univ Minn, Duluth, 66; from asst prof to assoc prof, 66-75, PROF BIOL, AUGUSTANA COL, S DAK, 75-, CHMN DEPT, 77- *Concurrent Pos:* Res grants, Sigma Xi, 65-67, Arctic Inst NAm, 66-68 & NSF, 70-82; NSF vis prof, Univ Nairobi, Kenya, 75; prog assoc, NSF, 78-79; Fulbright fel, Univ Nairobi, 82; consult, Int Agencies. *Mem:* AAAS; Am Soc Plant Physiol; Ecol Soc Am; Arctic Inst NAm; Can Soc Plant Physiol. *Res:* Photosynthesis and pigments in arctic and alpine grasses; environmental influence of photosynthesis; growth under extreme conditions; physiological adaptation; United States tundra biome program; photosynthesis and water stress in finger millet and other tropical grasses; C3 and C4 photosynthesis; stable isotope ecology; tropical ecology; paleoecology; agroforestry. *Mailing Add:* Dept of Biol Augustana Col Sioux Falls SD 57102

TIETHOF, JACK ALAN, b Grand Rapids, Mich, July 23, 43; m 63; c 3. INORGANIC CHEMISTRY, SURFACE SCIENCE. *Educ:* Western Mich Univ, BS, 67, PhD(inorg chem), 71. *Prof Exp:* Res assoc inorg chem, Ohio State Univ, 71-73, lectr gen chem, 73-74; proj leader prod develop, 74-78, group leader new bus res, 78-81, GROUP LEADER CATALYST RES, ENGELHARD MINERALS & CHEM CORP, 81- *Concurrent Pos:* Nat Defense Educ Act fel, Western Mich Univ, 67-70; fel, Grad Sch, Ohio State Univ, 71-72. *Mem:* Am Chem Soc; Clay Mineral Soc. *Res:* Development of new catalysts for petroleum refining, particularly in fluidized cracking catalysts; material research include zeolites and supported precious metals. *Mailing Add:* Engelhard Minerals & Chem Menlo Park Edison NJ 08817

TIETJEN, JAMES JOSEPH, b New York, NY, Mar 29, 33; m 58; c 2. PHYSICAL CHEMISTRY. *Educ:* Iona Col, BS, 56; Pa State Univ, MS, 58, PhD(chem), 63. *Prof Exp:* Mem tech staff mat sci, 63-69, group head, 69-70, DIR MAT RES, RCA LABS, RCA CORP, 70-77, STAFF VPRES, MAT &

COMPONENTS RES, 77- *Concurrent Pos:* Assoc ed, Mat Res Bull, 71; mem Solid State Sci Adv Panel, Nat Acad Sci, 73-; mem, NASA Space Systs & Technol Adv Comt, 78- *Honors & Awards:* David Sarnoff Outstanding Achievement Awards, 67 & 70. *Mem:* Am Chem Soc; Am Inst Mining Metall & Petrol Engrs; Electrochem Soc. *Res:* Displays, semiconductor materials and devices; insulators; metallic systems; optical phenomena; electron optics; negative electron affinity effects; luminescent materials; videodisc systems. *Mailing Add:* RCA Labs 201 Washington Rd Princeton NJ 08540

TIETJEN, JOHN H, b Jamaica, NY, June 19, 40; m 68; c 2. BIOLOGICAL OCEANOGRAPHY, INVERTEBRATE ZOOLOGY. *Educ:* City Col New York, BS, 61; Univ RI, PhD(oceanog), 66. *Prof Exp:* From asst prof to assoc prof, 66-75, PROF BIOL, CITY COL NEW YORK, 75-; DIR, INST MARINE & ATMOSPHERIC SCI, CITY UNIV NY, 78-, CHMN BIOL, 81- *Concurrent Pos:* Consult, Millstone Point Co, Conn, 68- & SW Res Inst, 78; res grants, NSF, 68- & Nat Oceanic & Atmospheric Admin, 73-75. *Mem:* AAAS; Am Soc Zoologists; Am Soc Limnol & Oceanog; Am Soc Nematologists; Marine Biol Asn UK. *Res:* Estuarine ecology; physiological ecology of meiofauna; ecology and distribution of deep sea meiofauna; pollution ecology of genthos. *Mailing Add:* Dept Biol City Col New York New York NY 10031

TIETJEN, WILLIAM LEIGHTON, b Americus, Ga, Jan 3, 37; m 68; c 1. ENTOMOLOGY, ZOOLOGY. *Educ:* Univ Ga, BS, 58; Univ Tenn, PhD(radiation biol), 67. *Prof Exp:* Res asst marine biol, Marine Inst, Univ Ga, 60; from asst prof to assoc prof, 67-78, PROF BIOL, GA SOUTHWESTERN COL, 78- *Mem:* AAAS; Am Inst Biol Sci; Am Soc Limnol & Oceanog; Ecol Soc Am; Entom Soc Am. *Res:* Arthropod metabolism and energy flow; environmental effects on physiology of arthropods; wetland ecology. *Mailing Add:* Dept of Biol Ga Southwestern Col Americus GA 31709

TIETZ, NORBERT W, b Stettin, Ger, Nov 13, 26; US citizen; m 59; c 4. CLINICAL CHEMISTRY. *Educ:* Stuttgart Tech Univ, PhD(natural sci), 50. *Prof Exp:* Res fel biochem, Univ Munich, 51-54; res fel clin chem, Rockford Mem Hosp, 54-55 & Univ Chicago, 55-56; head div biochem, Reid Mem Hosp, Richmond, Ind, 56-59; assoc path, Chicago Med Sch-Univ Health Sci, 59-64, from asst prof to assoc prof clin path, 64-69, prof clin chem, 69-76; DIR CLIN CHEM, UNIV KY MED CTR & PROF PATH, COL MED, 76- *Concurrent Pos:* Dir clin chem, Mt Sinai Hosp Med Ctr, 59-76; consult, Dept Health, State of Ill, 67-76; consult, Vet Admin Hosp, Hines, Ill, 74-76 & Vet Admin Hosp, Lexington, Ky, 76- *Honors & Awards:* Chicago Clin Chem Award, 71; Award Outstanding Effort in Educ & Training, Am Asn Clin Chem, 76 & Steuben Bowl Award, 78. *Mem:* Fel AAAS; Am Asn Clin Chem; Am Chem Soc; Am Soc Clin Path; fel Am Inst Chemists. *Res:* Methodology related to clinical chemistry; enzyme chemistry. *Mailing Add:* Dept of Path Univ of Ky Med Ctr Lexington KY 40506

TIETZ, THOMAS E(DWIN), b Pittsburgh, Pa, July 22, 20; m 47; c 3. PHYSICAL METALLURGY. *Educ:* Univ Calif, BS, 44, MS, 51, PhD(phys metall), 54. *Prof Exp:* Design engr, Lane-Wells Co, 44-47; res engr, Inst Eng Res, Univ Calif, 47-50; sr metallurgist, Stanford Res Inst, 54-59; sr mem, Lockheed Palo Alto Res Lab, Lockheed Missiles & Space Co, 59-63, mgr, Metall & Composites Lab, 65-81; VIS SR STAFF ASSOC, NAT MAT ADV BD, NAT ACAD SCI, 81- *Concurrent Pos:* Vis lectr, Stanford Univ, 57-58; mem, Comt Amorphous & Metastable Mat, Nat Mat Adv Bd, Nat Acad Sci, 78-79; guest scientist, Max-Planck-Inst Metall Res, Stuttgart, WGer, 79. *Mem:* Fel Am Soc Metals; Am Inst Mining, Metall & Petrol Engrs; Am Inst Aeronaut & Astronaut; Am Powder Metall Inst. *Res:* Deformation behavior of metals; strengthening mechanisms in metals; refractory metals; powder metallurgy. *Mailing Add:* Nat Acad Sci 2101 Constitution Ave Washington DC 20418

TIETZ, WILLIAM JOHN, JR, b Chicago, Ill, Mar 6, 27; m 53; c 3. NEUROPHYSIOLOGY. *Educ:* Swarthmore Col, BA, 50; Univ Wis, MS, 52; Colo State Univ, DVM, 57; Purdue Univ, PhD(physiol), 61. *Prof Exp:* Instr vet sci, Purdue Univ, 57-59, from instr to assoc prof physiol, 59-64; sect leader, Collab Radiol Health Lab, 64-67, assoc prof physiol & biophys, Univ, 64-67, chmn dept, 67-70, vpres student-univ rels, relations, 70-71, prof physiol & biophys, Colo State Univ, 67-77; PROF VET PHYSIOL & PRES, MONT STATE UNIV, 77- DEAN COL VET MED & BIOMED SCI, 71- *Mem:* AAAS; Am Physiol Soc; Am Vet Med Asn; Conf Res Workers Animal Dis; Am Soc Vet Physiol & Pharmacol. *Res:* Radiation biology; veterinary neurophysiology and neurosurgery; effects of ionizing radiation on early embryogenesis. *Mailing Add:* Off of the Pres Mont State Univ Bozeman MT 59715

TIETZE, FRANK, b Manila, Philippines Aug 19, 24; nat US; m 54; c 4. BIOCHEMISTRY. *Educ:* Trinity Col, Conn, BS, 45; Northwestern Univ, MS, 47. 47, PhD(biochem), 49. *Prof Exp:* USPHS fel, Duke Univ, 49-50; USPHS fel, Univ Wash, 50-51, instr biochem, 51-52; instr, Univ Pa, 52-56; RES BIOCHEMIST, NAT INST ARTHRITIS & METAB DIS, 56- *Mem:* AAAS; Am Soc Biol Chem. *Res:* Mechanisms of disulfide bond reduction. *Mailing Add:* 17404 Park Mill Dr Rockville MD 20855

TIFFANY, BURRIS DWIGHT, b Kansas City, Mo, Dec 6, 20; m 54; c 3. ORGANIC CHEMISTRY. *Educ:* Univ Kansas City, BA, 42; Univ Minn, MS, 46; Univ Wis, PhD(org chem), 49. *Prof Exp:* Asst, Univ Minn, 42-44; asst antimalarials, Off Sci Res & Develop, 44-45 & Abbott Labs, 45-47; Du Pont fel. Mass Inst Technol, 49-50; instr, Univ Ky, 50-51; sr res chemist, 51-71, RES ASSOC, UPJOHN CO, 71- *Concurrent Pos:* Vis scholar, Univ Calif, Los Angeles, 66-67. *Mem:* Am Chem Soc. *Res:* Organic synthesis; antithrombotics; large scale preparation of medicinal compounds. *Mailing Add:* Dept of Chem Res Prep Upjohn Co Kalamazoo MI 49002

TIFFANY, LOIS HATTERY, b Collins, Iowa, Mar 8, 24; m 45; c 3. PLANT PATHOLOGY, MYCOLOGY. *Educ:* Iowa State Col, BS, 45, MS, 47, PhD, 50. *Prof Exp:* From instr to assoc prof, 50-65, PROF BOT & PLANT PATH, IOWA STATE UNIV, 65- *Mem:* Am Phytopath Soc; Mycol Soc Am. *Res:* Forage crop and grass diseases; ascomycetes. *Mailing Add:* Dept Bot & Plant Path Iowa State Univ Ames IA 50010

TIFFANY, MARY LOIS, biophysics, see previous edition

TIFFANY, OTHO LYLE, b Flint, Mich, Nov 26, 19; m 42; c 5. PHYSICS. *Educ:* Univ Mich, BS, 43, MS, 46, PhD(physics), 50. *Prof Exp:* Mem staff, Radiation Lab, Mass Inst Technol, 43-45; res engr, Willow Run Res Ctr, Mich, 49-58; chief scientist, Aerospace Systs Div, Bendix Corp, 58-70, dir space & earth sci, 70-80; CONSULT, 80- *Mem:* Am Phys Soc; Am Geophys Union; Inst Elec & Electronics Engrs. *Res:* Space sciences, geophysics, oceanography, environmental research. *Mailing Add:* 1828 Vinewood Blvd Ann Arbor MI 48104

TIFFANY, WILLIAM JAMES, III, b Syracuse, NY, Sept 12, 44. MARINE BIOLOGY. *Educ:* Univ Miami, BS, 66; Fla State Univ, MS, 68, PhD(physiol), 72. *Prof Exp:* Instr biol, Fla State Univ, 70-71; asst prof, New Col, Univ SFla, 71-73, res fel marine biol, 73-74; res scientist, Marine Biomed Inst, Med Br, Univ Tex, 74-75; environ scientist biol, Conservation Consults, 75-77; res scientist biomed, Mote Marine Lab, 77-80; ENVIRON SPECIALIST, HEALTH DEPT, MANATEE CO, 80- *Concurrent Pos:* Selby res fel, William G & Marie Selby Found, 73-74; mem marine adv bd, Sarasota County, Fla, 78-80; res assoc, New Col, Univ SFla, 80-; res fel, Health Res Found, Fla, 81- *Mem:* AAAS; Am Soc Zoologists. *Res:* Comparative animal physiology; renal physiology; invertebrate zoology; estuarine and intertidal ecology; benthic ecology; governmental regulation of phosphate industry. *Mailing Add:* Manatee County Health Dept 202 6th Ave E Bradenton FL 33508

TIFFIN, DONALD LLOYD, marine geophysics, geology, see previous edition

TIFFNEY, BRUCE HAYNES, b Sharon, Mass, July 3, 49. PLANT EVOLUTION, PALEOBIOLOGY. *Educ:* Boston Univ, BA, 71; Harvard Univ, PhD(biol), 77. *Prof Exp:* ASST PROF PALEOBIOL, DEPT BIOL, YALE UNIV, 77- *Concurrent Pos:* Cur, Peabody Mus Natural Hist, 77- *Mem:* Bot Soc Am; Geol Soc Am; Int Asn Plant Taxonomists; Int Asn Angiosperm Paleobot (secy-treas, 81-). *Res:* The fossil record and evolution of angiosperms with emphasis on the study of their fossilized fruiting remains; patterns and processes involved in the evolution of land plants as a group. *Mailing Add:* Dept Biol OML Yale Univ PO Box 6666 New Haven CT 06511

TIFFT, WILLIAM GRANT, b Derby, Conn, Apr 5, 32; m 65; c 6. GALAXIES, REDSHIFT. *Educ:* Harvard Univ, AB, 54; Calif Inst Technol, PhD, 58. *Prof Exp:* Hon res fel astron, Australian Nat Univ, 58-60; res assoc astron & physics, Vanderbilt Univ, 60-61; astronr, Lowell Observ, 61-64; assoc prof, 64-73, PROF ASTRON, UNIV ARIZ, 73- *Concurrent Pos:* NSF fel, 58-60. *Mem:* Am Astron Soc; Int Astron Union. *Res:* Optical stellar astronomy; galactic structure and extragalactic problems; interpretation of the redshift in galaxies, pairs of galaxies, and clusters of galaxies; large scale structures, superclusters; large scale gravitation. *Mailing Add:* Steward Observ Univ of Ariz Tucson AZ 85721

TIGCHELAAR, EDWARD CLARENCE, b Hamilton, Ont, Feb 10, 39; m 62; c 3. GENETICS, PLANT BREEDING. *Educ:* Univ Guelph, BScA, 62; Purdue Univ, MSc, 64, PhD(genetics, plant breeding), 66. *Prof Exp:* Asst prof hort, Univ Guelph, 66-67; from asst prof to assoc prof, 67-78, PROF HORT, PURDUE UNIV, WEST LAFAYETTE, 78- *Concurrent Pos:* Asst prof, Int Prog Agr, AID, Brazil, 67-69. *Mem:* Am Soc Hort Sci. *Res:* Genetics of fruit ripening; physiological genetics and breeding of vegetables. *Mailing Add:* Dept Hort Purdue Univ West Lafayette IN 47906

TIGCHELAAR, PETER VERNON, b Chicago, Ill, May 15, 41; m 63; c 2. PHYSIOLOGY. *Educ:* Calvin Col, AB, 63; Univ Ill, Urbana, MS, 66, PhD(physiol), 69. *Prof Exp:* NIH fel endocrinol, Univ Ill, 70-71; asst prof physiol, Sch Med, Ind Univ-Purdue Univ, Indianapolis, 71-75; assoc prof, 75-79, PROF BIOL, CALVIN COL, 79- *Concurrent Pos:* NIH fel endocrinol, 69-70. *Mem:* AAAS; Endocrine Soc; Am Physiol Soc. *Res:* Mammalian reproductive physiology; synthesis, control and effects of mammalian gonadotrophic hormones. *Mailing Add:* Dept of Biol Calvin Col Grand Rapids MI 49506

TIGER, LIONEL, b Montreal, Que, Feb 5, 37; m; c 1. BIOLOGICAL ANTHROPOLOGY, SOCIAL STRUCTURE. *Educ:* McGill Univ, BA, 57, MA, 59; London Sch Econ, PhD(polit sociol), 63. *Prof Exp:* Asst prof sociol, Univ BC, 63-68; assoc prof anthrop, Livingston Col, 68-70, assoc prof, Fac Grad Studies & dir grad progs, Univ, 70-72, PROF ANTHROP, GRAD SCH, RUTGERS UNIV, 72- *Concurrent Pos:* Can Coun spec award soc sci & Nat Res Coun Assoc Comt Exp Psychol, 66-67; Can Coun-Killam bequest & Guggenheim fel, 68; co-sr investr human aggress, Guggenheim Found, 72-, consult & res dir, 72- *Mem:* Am Sociol Asn; Can Sociol & Anthrop Asn; Asn Study Animal Behav; Royal Anthrop Inst Gt Brit & Ireland; Am Anthrop Asn. *Res:* Human evolution; nature and expression of sex differences; male groups; theoretical implications of biosociological research. *Mailing Add:* Guggenheim Found Res Off 17 W Ninth St New York NY 10011

TIGERTT, WILLIAM DAVID, b Wilmer, Tex, May 22, 15; m 38; c 2. PATHOLOGY. *Educ:* Baylor Univ, MD, 37, AB, 38; Am Bd Path, dipl, 42. *Prof Exp:* Intern, Baylor Hosp, 37-38, instr path, Baylor Col Med, 38-40; pathologist, Brooke Gen Hosp, Med Corps, US Army, 40-43, commanding officer, 26th Army Med Lab, Southwest Pac, 44-46 & 406th Med Gen Lab, Tokyo, 46-49, asst commandant, Army Med Serv Grad Sch, 49-54, chief spec opers br, Walter Reed Army Inst Res, 54-56, commanding officer, Army Med Unit, Ft Detrick, Md, 56-61, med officer, Field Teams, Walter Reed Army Inst Res, 61-63, dir & commandant, 63-68, commanding gen, Madigan Army Hosp, 72; assoc prof med, Sch Med, Univ Md, Baltimore City, 56-68, prof exp med, 69-71, prof path, 71-81; MEM SCI ADV BD, ARMED FORCES INST PATH, 81- *Concurrent Pos:* Fel path, Baylor Col Med, 38-40; lab consult, Far East Command, US Army, 46-49, consult, Surgeon Gen, 60-68 & 73-; consult, WHO, 61-62 & 69-71; dir comn malaria, Armed Forces Epidemiol Bd, 67-69; chmn, US Army Med Res & Develop Command Adv Panel, 73-; mem exec comt & bd dirs, Gorgas Mem Inst, 75- *Mem:* Am Asn Immunologists; fel Col Am Pathologists; fel Am Col Physicians. *Res:* Infectious diseases; immunology. *Mailing Add:* 15 Charles Plaza 2203 Baltimore MD 21201

TIGGES, JOHANNES, b Rietberg, Ger, July 7, 31; m 59; c 2. NEUROANATOMY. *Educ:* Univ Münster, PhD(zool), 61. *Prof Exp:* Res assoc neuroanat, Max Planck Inst Brain Res, 61-62; res assoc vision in primates, Yerkes Primate Labs, Fla, 62-63; res assoc neuroanat & physiol, Max Planck Inst Brain Res, 63-65; neuroanatomist, Yerkes Regional Primate Res Ctr, 66-71, sr neuroanatomist, 71-79, from asst prof to assoc prof, 67-78, PROF ANAT, EMORY UNIV, 78-, PROF, DEPT OPHTHAL, 81-, RES PROF & CHIEF, DIV NEUROBIOL, YERKES PRIMATE RES CTR, 79- *Res:* Light and electron microscopy of primate visual system. *Mailing Add:* Yerkes Regional Primate Res Ctr Emory Univ Atlanta GA 30322

TIGNER, JAMES ROBERT, b El Paso, Tex, June 17, 36; m 57; c 2. WILDLIFE BIOLOGY. *Educ:* Colo State Univ, BS, 58, MS, 60; Univ Colo, PhD(biol), 72. *Prof Exp:* Wildlife biologist, US Fish & Wildlife Serv, 60-61, proj leader, 62-70, sta leader animal damage control res, 73-81; EIS TEAM LEADER, BUR LAND MGT, DEPT INTERIOR, 81- *Mem:* Wildlife Soc; Sigma Xi. *Res:* Animal damage control, especially coyote. *Mailing Add:* 104 E Kendrick Rawlins WY 82301

TIGNER, MAURY, b Middletown, NY, Apr 22, 37; m 60; c 2. HIGH ENERGY PHYSICS. *Educ:* Rensselaer Polytech Inst, BS, 58; Cornell Univ, PhD(physics), 63. *Prof Exp:* Res assoc, 63-68, sr res assoc physics, 68-77, PROF PHYSICS & MEM STAFF, LAB ATOMIC & SOLID STATE PHYSICS, CORNELL UNIV, 77- *Mem:* Am Phys Soc; Am Vacuum Soc. *Res:* Design and development of new particle accelerators and improvement of existing designs. *Mailing Add:* Dept of Physics Cornell Univ Ithaca NY 14852

TIHEN, JOSEPH ANTON, b Harper, Kans, Nov 20, 18; m 40; c 7. ZOOLOGY. *Educ:* Univ Kans, AB, 40; Univ Rochester, PhD(zool), 45. *Prof Exp:* Asst instr zool, Univ Kans, 40-41; asst instr, Univ Rochester, 41-44, res assoc mouse genetics unit, Manhattan Proj, 44-46; asst prof zool, Tulane Univ, 46-47; asst prof, Univ Fla, 50-57, res assoc, AEC Proj, Sch Med, 57-58; asst prof zool, Univ Ill, 58-61; asst prof, 61-65, assoc prof biol, 65-70, PROF BIOL, UNIV NOTRE DAME, 70- *Mem:* Am Soc Zool; Soc Study Amphibians & Reptiles; Soc Syst Zool; Soc Study Evolution; Am Soc Ichthyologists & Herpetologists. *Res:* Systematics, Cenozoic paleontology and phylogeny of reptiles and amphibians. *Mailing Add:* Dept of Biol Univ of Notre Dame Notre Dame IN 46556

TIHON, CLAUDE, b Shanghai, China, June 12, 44; US citizen; m 69; c 1. PATHOBIOLOGY, BIOCHEMISTRY. *Educ:* Univ Colo, BA, 65; Columbia Univ, PhD(path), 71. *Prof Exp:* Res assoc virol, Inst Molecular Virol, Sch Med, St Louis Univ, 72-74; sr scientist biochem, Frederick Cancer Res Ctr, 74-76; sr investr biochem, Nat Jewish Hosp & Res Ctr, 76-80; MEM STAFF, BRISTOL LABS, DIV BRYSTOL MYERS, 80- *Concurrent Pos:* Asst prof path, Sch Med, Univ Colo, 77- *Mem:* Am Soc Cell Biol. *Res:* Eukaryotic gene regulatory mechanisms; molecular action of cyclic adenosine monophosphate in Chinese hamster ovary cells and Dictyostelium discoideum; RNA tumor virology. *Mailing Add:* Div Bristol Myers Bristol Labs PO Box 657 Syracuse NY 13201

TIKSON, MICHAEL, b Campbell, Ohio, Nov 22, 24; m 57; c 4. MATHEMATICS. *Educ:* Youngstown Univ, BS, 48; Lehigh Univ, MA, 49; Mass Inst Technol, MS, 56. *Prof Exp:* Instr math, Lehigh Univ, 49-50; guest worker, Nat Bur Standards, DC, 51-52; sr mathematician, Wright Air Develop Div, US Air Force Res & Develop Command, 52-56, chief anal sect, Digital Comput Br, 56-58, br chief, 58-60; consult & head digital comput ctr, 60-66, assoc mgr, Systs & Electronics Dept, Columbus Labs, 66-70, mgr comput systs & applns, 70-74, MGR, COMPUT & INFO SYSTS DEPT, COLUMBUS LABS, BATTELLE MEM INST, 74- *Mem:* Simulation Coun; Asn Comput Mach. *Res:* Management of research and operations in computer and information systems. *Mailing Add:* Battelle Mem Inst Columbus Labs 505 King Ave Columbus OH 43201

TILBURY, ROY SIDNEY, b Ealing, Eng, Aug 7, 32; US citizen; m 61; c 2. RADIOCHEMISTRY, BIOPHYSICS. *Educ:* Univ London, BSc, 55; McGill Univ, PhD(radiochem), 63. *Prof Exp:* Asst exp officer chem, UK Atomic Energy Res Estab, 55-59; res scientist, Union Carbide Corp, 63-67; assoc biophys, Mem Sloan-Kettering Cancer Ctr, 67-74, assoc mem biophys, 74-81; CHEMIST & PROF NUCLEAR MED, UNIV TEX SYST CANCER CTR, HOUSTON, 81- *Concurrent Pos:* Asst prof biophys, Grad Sch Med Sci, Cornell Univ, 67-74, assoc prof, 74-81; adj prof med chem, Col Pharm, Univ Ky, 78- *Mem:* Am Chem Soc; Soc Nuclear Med. *Res:* Radiochemicals and labeled compounds for use in medical research, especially cyclotron produced short-lived radionuclides. *Mailing Add:* Sect Nuclear Med Univ Tex Cancer Ctr 6723 Bertner Houston TX 77030

TILDON, J TYSON, b Baltimore, Md, Aug 7, 31; m 55; c 2. BIOCHEMISTRY. *Educ:* Morgan State Col, BS, 54; Johns Hopkins Univ, PhD(biochem), 65. *Prof Exp:* Res asst chem, Sinai Hosp, Baltimore, Md, 54-59; asst prof, Goucher Col, 67-68; res asst prof biochem & pediat, 68-71, assoc prof, 71-74, PROF PEDIAT, SCH MED, UNIV MD, BALTIMORE CITY, 74-, ASSOC PROF BIOCHEM, 72-, DIR PEDIAT RES, 70- *Concurrent Pos:* Helen Hay Whitney fel biochem, Brandeis Univ, 65-67; lectr, Antioch Col, Baltimore Campus, 72-; Josiah Macy, Jr Fac Scholar, State Univ Groningen, Neth, 75-76. *Mem:* AAAS; Am Soc Biol Chemists; Am Soc Neurochem; Am Chem Soc; Tissue Cult Asn. *Res:* Developmental biochemistry and metabolic control processes. *Mailing Add:* Dept of Pediat Univ of Md Sch of Med Baltimore MD 21201

TILFORD, SHELBY G, b Grayson Co, Ky, Jan 11, 37; m 56; c 2. ATMOSPHERIC SCIENCES, ENVIRONMENTAL SCIENCES. *Educ:* Western Ky Univ, BS, 58; Vanderbilt Univ, PhD(phys chem), 62. *Prof Exp:* Res assoc spectros, Naval Res Lab, 61-63, res chemist, 63-66, spectros consult physicist, 66-72, sect head extreme ultraviolet spectros, 72-76; space scientist solar physics, 76, discipline chief upper atmosphere, 76-78, br chief atmospheric processes, 78-81, DIV DIR ENVIRON OPERS, NASA, 81- *Concurrent Pos:* Vis prof, Univ Md, 69-76. *Res:* High resolution vacuum ultra violet spectroscopy of atoms and molecules of atmospheric, laser, and astrophysical interest; severe storms; tropospheric and stratospheric air quality; upper atmospheric research; oceanic processes; space plasma physics; solar-terrestrial theoretical studies. *Mailing Add:* 8805 Church Field Lane Laurel MD 20708

TILL, CHARLES EDGAR, b Can, June 14, 34. ENGINEERING PHYSICS. *Educ:* Univ Sask, BE, 56, MSc, 58; Univ London, PhD(reactor physics), 60. *Prof Exp:* Jr res officer physics, Nat Res Coun Can, 56-58; reactor physicist, Can Gen Elec, 61-63; asst physicist, 63-65, assoc physicist, 65-66, sect head exp develop sect, 66-68, head critical exp anal sect, 68-72, mgr zero power reactor prog, 68-72, assoc dir, Appl Physics Div, 72-73, dir appl physics, 73-80, ASSOC LAB DIR, REACTOR RES & DEVELOP, ARGONNE NAT LAB, 80- *Mem:* Am Nuclear Soc. *Res:* Fast reactor research. *Mailing Add:* Bldg 208 9700 S Cass Ave Argonne IL 60439

TILL, JAMES EDGAR, b Lloydminster, Sask, Aug 25, 31; m 59; c 3. BIOPHYSICS, MEDICAL SCIENCES. *Educ:* Univ Sask, BA, 52, MA, 54; Yale Univ, PhD(biophys), 57. *Prof Exp:* Biophysicist, Ont Cancer Inst, 57-69, head, Biores Div, 69-82; PROF BIOPHYS, UNIV TORONTO, 65-, ASSOC DEAN GRAD STUDIES, 81- *Concurrent Pos:* Res fel microbiol, Connaught Med Res Labs, 56-57. *Honors & Awards:* Gairdner Found Award, 69. *Mem:* Biophys Soc; Can Soc Cell Biol; Soc Med Decision-Making; Am Asn Cancer Res; fel Royal Soc Can. *Mailing Add:* Ont Cancer Inst Biores Div 500 Sherbourne St Toronto ON M4X 1K9 Can

TILL, MICHAEL JOHN, b Independence, Iowa, July 30, 34; m 67. PEDODONTICS. *Educ:* Univ Iowa, DDS, 61, MS, 63; Univ Pittsburgh, MEd & PhD(higher educ), 70. *Prof Exp:* Instr pedodontics, Univ Iowa, 61-63; pedodontist, Eastman Inst, Stockholm, Sweden, 63-64; asst prof, Royal Dent Col, Denmark, 64-66; asst prof, Univ Pittsburgh, 66-70; PROF PEDODONTICS, UNIV MINN, MINNEAPOLIS, 70-, CHMN DEPT, 77- *Mem:* Am Dent Asn; Int Asn Dent Res; Am Educ Res Asn; Am Soc Dent for Children; Am Acad Pedodont. *Res:* Dental educational research. *Mailing Add:* 4725 Isabel Ave Minneapolis MN 55406

TILLAY, ELDRID WAYNE, b Yerington, Nev, Feb 26, 25; m 53; c 2. INORGANIC CHEMISTRY. *Educ:* Pac Union Col, BA, 50; Stanford Univ, MS, 52; La State Univ, PhD(inorg chem), 67. *Prof Exp:* Res asst chem, Stanford Univ, 52-57; instr, Sacramento City Col, 57-60; from asst prof to assoc prof, 60-72, PROF CHEM, PAC UNION COL, 72-, HEAD DEPT, 74- *Mem:* Am Chem Soc. *Res:* Organometallic chemistry and bio-inorganic chemistry. *Mailing Add:* Dept of Chem Pacific Union College Angwin CA 94508

TILLER, CALVIN OMAH, b Richmond, Va, June 22, 25; m 52; c 2. PHYSICS. *Educ:* Col William & Mary, BS, 48; Syracuse Univ, MS, 50. *Prof Exp:* Qual engr, Eastman Kodak Co, 50-51; supvr, Optical Eng Dept, Otis Elevator Co, 51-55; physicist, Titmus Optical Co, 55-56; sr res physicist, Va Inst Sci Res, 56-68; RES SCIENTIST, RES & DEVELOP CTR, PHILIP MORRIS, INC, 68- *Honors & Awards:* J Sheldon Horsley Award, Va Acad Sci, 60; IR100 Award, Indust Res, Inc, 72. *Mem:* NAm Thermal Anal Soc; Am Phys Soc. *Res:* Solid state physics of thin metallic films; electron microscopy and diffraction; physical optics; thermal analysis of tobacco. *Mailing Add:* Phys Res Dept Philip Morris Res & Dev Ctr Richmond VA 23261

TILLER, F(RANK) M(ONTEREY), b Louisville, Ky, Feb 26, 17; m 82; c 2. CHEMICAL ENGINEERING. *Educ:* Univ Louisville, BChE, 37; Univ Cincinnati, MS, 39, PhD(chem eng), 46. *Hon Degrees:* Dr, Univ Brazil, 62 & Univ Guanabara, 67. *Prof Exp:* Technician, Charles R Long, Jr Co, 34-35; chemist, Durkee Famous Foods Div, Glidden Co, 36 & Colgate-Palmolive-Peet Co, 37; civil engr, US Corps Engrs, Ky, 39; chem engr, C M Hall Lamp Co, 40; instr chem eng, Univ Cincinnati, 40-42; from asst prof to assoc prof, Vanderbilt Univ, 42-51; dean eng, Lamar State Col, 51-55; prof chem & elec eng & dean eng, 55-63, dir, int affairs, 63-67, NSF grant, Latin Am, 66-67, dir ctr study higher educ, Latin Am, 68-73, M D ANDERSON PROF CHEM ENG, UNIV HOUSTON, 63- *Concurrent Pos:* Indust consult, 43-; dir, Gupton-Jones Col Mortuary Sci, 45-51; lectr, Humble Oil Co, 58 & Esso Res Labs, 62; AID Univ Contract dir, Univ Guayaquil, 60-64, consult, 64-67; mem, President's Sci Adv Comt, 61, Latin Am Sci Bd/Nat Acad Sci, 63-65 & Int Exchange Persons Comt, Conf Bd, Assoc Res Coun, 67; consult, Int Coop Admin Mission, Ecuador, 61; titular prof, Cath Univ Rio de Janeiro, 62; dir, univ contracts, Univ Brazil & Cath Univ Rio de Janeiro, 63-70 & Coun Rectors Brazilian Univs, 66-72; adv, Autonomous Univ Guadalajara, 64-67; consult, Union Tex Petrol contract, Univ Costa Rica, 64-68; joint prog study univ admin & finances, Off Cult Affairs, US Dept State-Gulerpe, 66-67; pres, Int Consortium Filtration Res Groups, 71-76. *Honors & Awards:* Gold Medal, Filtration Soc, 78. *Mem:* Am Inst Chem Engrs; Fine Particle Soc; Filtration Soc; Am Soc Eng Educ. *Res:* Flow through porous media; solid-liquid separation; finite differences. *Mailing Add:* Dept Chem Eng Univ Houston Houston TX 77004

TILLER, RALPH EARL, b Birmingham, Ala, Nov 16, 25; m 49; c 3. PEDIATRICS. *Educ:* Birmingham-Southern Col, BS, 47; Tulane Univ, MD, 51; Am Bd Pediat, dipl, 56. *Prof Exp:* Intern, Fitzsimmons Army Hosp, Denver, 51-52; resident pediat, Tulane Univ, 53-54, chief resident, 54-55; pvt pract, Columbus, Ga, 55-67; assoc prof, 67-71, PROF PEDIAT, SCH MED, UNIV ALA, BIRMINGHAM, 71- *Concurrent Pos:* Consult, Martin Army Hosp, US Army Med Corps, Ft Benning, Ga, 59-67; dir, State Crippled Children's Seizure Clin, Columbus, 60-67; chief pediat serv, Med Ctr, Columbus, 62-67; consult, Muscogee Health Dept, 62-67; dir outpatient clin, Children's Hosp, Birmingham, 67-69, dir inpatient teaching serv, Cystic Fibrosis Care Teaching & Res Ctr & Pediat Chest Dis Clin, 69- *Mem:* Am Acad Pediat; Am Thoracic Soc. *Res:* Tuberculosis. *Mailing Add:* Children's Hosp 1601 Sixth Ave S Birmingham AL 35233

TILLER, WILLIAM ARTHUR, b Toronto, Ont, Sept 18, 29; m 52; c 2. PHYSICS, PHYSICAL METALLURGY. *Educ:* Univ Toronto, BASc, 52, MASc, 53, PhD(phys metall), 55. *Prof Exp:* Res engr, Res Lab, Westinghouse Elec Corp, 55-57, adv physicist, 57-59, sect mgr crystallogenics, 59-64; exec head dept mat sci, 66-71, PROF MAT SCI, STANFORD UNIV, 64- *Concurrent Pos:* Guggenheim fel, Oxford Univ, 70-71. *Mem:* AAAS; Am Soc Metals; Am Soc Mining, Metall & Petrol Engrs. *Res:* Solidification and crystal growth; physics of metals; surfaces; properties of materials; solid state physics; polymers; stress corrosion cracking; biomaterials; psychoenergetics. *Mailing Add:* Dept of Mat Sci Stanford Univ Stanford CA 94305

TILLERY, BILL W, b Muskogee, Okla, Sept 15, 38; m 59, 81; c 2. SCIENCE EDUCATION. *Educ:* Northeastern Okla State Univ, BS, 60; Univ Northern Colo, MA, 65, EdD(sci educ), 67. *Prof Exp:* Teacher pub schs, Okla & Colo, 60-64; res assoc sci, Univ Northern Colo, 66-67; asst prof sci educ, Fla State Univ, 67-69; assoc prof & dir sci ctr, Univ Wyo, 69-73; assoc prof, 73-75, PROF SCI EDUC, ARIZ STATE UNIV, 75- *Mem:* Nat Sci Teachers Asn; Asn Educ Teachers Sci; Nat Asn Res Sci Teaching. *Mailing Add:* Dept of Physics Ariz State Univ Tempe AZ 85281

TILLERY, MARVIN ISHMAEL, b Idabel, Okla, Oct 10, 36; m 61; c 3. AEROSOL PHYSICS, INHALATION TOXICOLOGY. *Educ:* Univ NMex, BS, 67; Univ Rochester, MS, 71. *Prof Exp:* Tech assoc aerosol technol, Univ Rochester, 68-70; staff scientist, 71-72, SECT LEADER AEROSOL TECHNOL, LOS ALAMOS NAT LAB, 72- *Mem:* Am Indust Hyg Asn; Asn Aerosol Res. *Res:* Aerosol coagulation; generation and characterization instrumentation; aerosol filtration; development of inhalation chambers for toxicology studies. *Mailing Add:* MS 486 Los Alamos Nat Lab PO Box 1663 Los Alamos NM 87545

TILLES, ABE, b New York, NY, Mar 9, 07; m 30; c 2. ELECTRICAL ENGINEERING, FORENSIC ENGINEERING. *Educ:* Univ Calif, BS, 28, MS, 32, PhD(elec eng), 34. *Prof Exp:* Elec tester, Los Angeles Bur Power & Light, 28-30; jr testing engr, State Hwy Testing & Res Labs, Calif, 30; assoc elec eng, Univ Calif, 30-32, from instr to asst prof, 32-45, lectr, Exten Div, 31 & 38, instr defense training, 41, sr elec engr, Manhattan Proj, Radiation Lab, 44-45; asst transmission engr, Pac Gas & Elec Co, 45-54; prof elec eng, Israel Inst Technol, 54-56; consult, R W Thomas & Assocs, Calif, 56-57; sr electronic engr, Lawrence Livermore Lab, Univ Calif, 58-73; CONSULT ENGR, 73- *Concurrent Pos:* Jr elec engr, Los Angeles Bur Power & Light, 36; elec designer, Pac Gas & Elec Co, 37-38; with L S Ready, 39; assoc elec engr, Mare Island Navy Yard, 41; chief elec design engr, Southwest Eng Co, 42; develop engr, Richmond Shipyard, Kaiser Co, 42-44; ed, San Francisco Engr, 47-49; chmn, San Francisco Eng Coun, 53; consult engr, 58- *Honors & Awards:* Recipient, Founder Socs Alfred Noble Prize, 36. *Mem:* Am Soc Eng Educ; fel Inst Elec & Electronics Engrs; Sigma Xi. *Res:* Sparkover; high voltage cable; steel shaft quality; specialized electromagnetic instruments; nuclear science; electric power transmission and distribution; continuing engineering education; forensic engineering. *Mailing Add:* 2663 Pillsbury Ct Livermore CA 94550

TILLES, DAVID ALAN, entomology, ecology, see previous edition

TILLES, HARRY, b Buffalo, NY, Mar 22, 23; m 48; c 4. ORGANIC CHEMISTRY. *Educ:* Univ Buffalo, BA, 48; Univ Calif, PhD(org chem), 51. *Prof Exp:* Res chemist org synthesis, Nat Aniline Div, Allied Chem & Dye Corp, 51-53; res chemist, 53-59, group leader indust chem group, 59-62, proj officer, Nat Cancer Inst contract, 62-64, sr res chemist, 64-68, res assoc, Western Res Ctr, 68-74, SR RES ASSOC, DE GUIGNE TECH CTR, STAUFFER CHEM CO, 74- *Mem:* Sigma Xi. *Res:* Synthesis of organic chemicals for agricultural screening; optimization of chemical synthesis processes. *Mailing Add:* Stauffer Chem Co Res Ctr 1200 S 47th St Richmond CA 94804

TILLEY, BARBARA CLAIRE, b San Pafael, Calif, Apr 26, 42. BIOMETRICS, BIOSTATISTICS. *Educ:* Calif State Univ, Northridge, BA, 72; Univ Wash, MS, 75; Univ Tex, PhD(biometry), 81. *Prof Exp:* Biostatistician, Child Develop & Ment Retardation Ctr, 73-74, Mayo Clinic, 74-77; fac assoc, 78-80, ASST PROF BIOMATH, CANCER PREVENTION & BIOMETRY, SYST CANCER CTR, UNIV TEX, 80- *Concurrent Pos:* Biostatist adv, Eval & Finance Subcomt, Commun Corrections Adv Bd, 76-77, Mayo Clinic, 78-, Tex Tech, 80-, Dartmouth Breast Cancer & Diethylstibestrol Mothers Study, 80- & Spec Study Sect, NIH, 81- *Mem:* Biometrics Soc; Am Statist Asn; Am Pub Health Asn; Am Women Sci. *Res:* Developing and improving a best subset selection algorithm for categorical data analysis; carrying out epidemiologic research relating to cancer risk factors and cancer prevention as related to use of health services. *Mailing Add:* Dept Cancer Prevention Syst Cancer Ctr Univ Tex 6723 Bertner Ave Houston TX 77030

TILLEY, BRIAN JOHN, b Croydon, Eng, Apr 28, 36; m 63; c 3. ELECTRICAL ENGINEERING. *Educ:* Univ Wales, BSc, 61, PhD(elec eng), 65. *Prof Exp:* Technician, Marconis Wireless Tel Co Ltd, Eng, 54-56, jr engr, 56-58; mem sci staff, RCA Res Labs, Montreal, Que, 65-68; mem sci staff, Semiconductor Div, TRW Inc, 68-70, mem sci staff, Systs Microwave Div, 70-71; SECT HEAD, HUGHES AIRCRAFT CO, CULVER CITY, 71- *Mem:* Inst Elec & Electronics Engrs. *Res:* Process and materials; large scale integrated circuits; high-speed, low-power and low-noise transistors; high reliability passive elements. *Mailing Add:* 29026 Indian Valley Rd Palos Verdes Peninsula CA 90274

TILLEY, DAVID RONALD, b Fuquay Springs, NC, Mar 10, 30; m 65; c 1. NUCLEAR PHYSICS. *Educ:* Univ NC, BS, 52; Vanderbilt Univ, MS, 54; Johns Hopkins Univ, PhD(nuclear physics), 58. *Prof Exp:* Jr instr physics, Johns Hopkins Univ, 53-58; res assoc nuclear physics, Duke Univ, 58-61, asst prof, 61-66; assoc prof, 66-72, PROF PHYSICS, NC STATE UNIV, 72- *Concurrent Pos:* Staff physicist, Triangle Univs Nuclear Lab, 66- *Mem:* Am Phys Soc; AAAS. *Res:* Radiative captune; gamma ray spectroscopy; nuclear reactions. *Mailing Add:* Dept Physics NC State Univ Raleigh NC 27607

TILLEY, DONALD E, b Flushing, NY, July 6, 25; Can citizen; m 48; c 3. PHYSICS. *Educ:* McGill Univ, BSc, 48, PhD(physics), 51. *Prof Exp:* Res assoc physics, Radiation Lab, McGill Univ, 51-52; from asst prof to assoc prof, 52-57, head dept physics, 61-71, prof physics, Col Mil Royal, Que, 57-78, dean sci & eng, 69-78; PRIN, ROYAL MIL COL CAN, KINGSTON, 78- *Mem:* Am Phys Soc; Can Asn Physicists. *Res:* Physics of dielectrics; nuclear reactions; radioactive isotopes. *Mailing Add:* Royal Mil Col of Can Kingston ON K7L 2W3 Can

TILLEY, GEORGE LEVIS, b Doylestown, Pa, July 10, 38. PHYSICAL CHEMISTRY. *Educ:* Calif State Polytech Col, San Luis Obisop, BS, 61; Purdue Univ, PhD(chem), 67. *Prof Exp:* RES CHEMIST, UNION OIL CO, CALIF, 67- *Mem:* Sigma Xi. *Res:* Industrial catalysis. *Mailing Add:* Union Oil Res Ctr PO Box 76 Brea CA 92621

TILLEY, JEFFERSON WRIGHT, b Detroit, Mich, Dec 13, 46; m 70; c 2. ORGANIC CHEMISTRY, MEDICINAL CHEMISTRY. *Educ:* Harvey Mudd Col, BS, 68; Calif Inst Technol, PhD(chem), 72. *Prof Exp:* sr chemist, 72-80, GROUP CHIEF MED CHEM, HOFFMANN-LA ROCHE INC, 80- *Mem:* Am Chem Soc. *Res:* Heterocyclic chemistry, synthesis of novel medicinal agents with cardiovascular activity. *Mailing Add:* Hoffmann-La Roche Inc Kingsland Ave Nutley NJ 07110

TILLEY, JOHN LEONARD, b New York, NY, June 4, 28; m 51. MATHEMATICS. *Educ:* Univ Pa, BS, 50; Univ Fla, MEd, 54, PhD(math), 61. *Prof Exp:* Teacher high sch, Fla, 54-56 & St Petersburg Jr Col, 56-58; instr math, Univ Fla, 60-61; from asst prof to assoc prof, Clemson Univ, 61-64; assoc prof, 64-69, actg head dept math, 71-72, PROF MATH & DIR S D LEE HONS PROG, MISS STATE UNIV, 69- *Concurrent Pos:* Mem, Nat Collegiate Hons Coun. *Mem:* Nat Coun Teachers Math; Math Asn Am; Soc Indust & Appl Math. *Res:* Classical methods of applied mathematics. *Mailing Add:* Dept of Math Miss State Univ Mississippi State MS 39762

TILLEY, STEPHEN GEORGE, b Lima, Ohio, July 21, 43; m 65; c 2. POPULATION BIOLOGY, HERPETOLOGY. *Educ:* Ohio State Univ, BS, 65; Univ Mich, Ann Arbor, MS, 67, PhD(zool), 70. *Prof Exp:* Asst prof biol sci, 70-77, chmn dept, 77-80, ASSOC PROF BIOL SCI, SMITH COL, 77-; RES ASSOC, DEPT VERT ZOOL, SMITHSONIAN INST, 74- *Honors & Awards:* Stoye Award, Am Soc Ichthyol & Herpet, 70. *Mem:* Soc Study Evolution; Am Soc Ichthyol & Herpet; Soc Study Amphibians & Reptiles; AAAS; Ecol Soc Am. *Res:* Population biology and evolution of amphibians, especially desmognathine salamanders; genetic structures of populations. *Mailing Add:* Dept of Biol Sci Smith Col Northampton MA 01063

TILLING, ROBERT INGERSOLL, b Shanghai, China, Nov 26, 35; US citizen; m 62; c 2. GEOLOGY. *Educ:* Pomona Col, BA, 58; Yale Univ, MS, 60, PhD(geol), 63. *Prof Exp:* Geologist, US Geol Surv, Va, 62-72, Hawaiian Volcano Observ, 72-75, scientist-in-chg, Hawaiian Volcano Observ, 75-76, CHIEF OFF GEOCHEM & GEOPHYS, GEOL DIV, US GEOL SURV, 76- *Mem:* Geol Soc Am; Mineral Soc Am; Geochem Soc. *Res:* Igenous petrology and volcanology. *Mailing Add:* US Geol Surv Nat Ctr MS-906 Reston VA 22092

TILLINGHAST, JOHN AVERY, b New York, NY, Apr 30, 27; m 48; c 3. ELECTRICAL ENGINEERING. *Educ:* Columbia Univ, BS, 48, MS, 49. *Prof Exp:* Mem staff, Am Elec Power Serv Corp, 49-67, exec vpres eng & construct, 67-72, sr exec vpres, 72-75, vchmn eng & construct, 75-79; SR VPRES TECHNOL, WHEELABRATOR-FRYE INC, 79-, CHMN, WHEELABRATOR UTILITY SERV INC, 81- *Mem:* Nat Acad Eng; fel Am Soc Mech Engrs; Edison Elec Inst; Inst Elec & Electronics Engrs. *Res:* Generating unit control system. *Mailing Add:* Wheelabrator-Frye Inc Liberty Lane Hampton NH 03842

TILLITSON, EDWARD WALTER, b Charlevoix Co, Mich, Jan 13, 03; m 30; c 3. DENTAL MATERIALS, CHEMICAL ENGINEERING. *Educ:* Univ Mich, BS, 29, MS, 32. *Prof Exp:* Res & develop chem engr, Whiting Swenson Co, 29-31; chief chemist, Iodent Chem Co, 32-35; sr res chemist, Parke Davis & Co, 35-42; head develop labs, Gelatin Prod Div, R P Scherer Corp, 42-46; assoc prof chem eng, Wayne State Univ, 46-63; res assoc, Sch Dent, Univ Mich, 63-73; CONSULT ENGR, 73- *Concurrent Pos:* Consult, 46- *Mem:* Am Chem Soc; Int Asn Dent Res. *Res:* Materials science; polymers; casualty investigation; custom research instrumentation; friction and wear; stress analysis. *Mailing Add:* 255 Ridgemont Rd Grosse Pointe Farms MI 48236

TILLMAN, ALLEN DOUGLAS, b Rayville, La, June 9, 16; m 45; c 5. ANIMAL HUSBANDRY. *Educ:* Southwestern La Univ, BS, 40; La State Univ, MS, 42; Pa State Univ, PhD, 52. *Prof Exp:* Asst, La State Univ, 40-42; instr animal nutrit, Pa State Univ, 46-48; asst prof, La State Univ, 48-52; from assoc prof to prof animal husb, Okla State Univ, 52-73; VIS PROF ANIMAL HUSB, UNIV GADJAH MADA & FIELD OFFICER, ROCKEFELLER FOUND, INDONESIA, 73- *Concurrent Pos:* Gen Educ Bd fel, 51-52; res partic, Oak Ridge Inst Nuclear Studies, 56-57; consult, AEC, 57-, gen chmn, Radioisotope Conf, 59; consult, USDA exchange team, USSR, 59; consult, Estab Labs for Food & Agr Orgn, Arg, 61 & nutrit study, Libya, 62; Fulbright lectr, Univ Col, Dublin, 62-63; Nat Feed Ingredients travel fel, Europe, 66; mem, Comt Animal Nutrit, Nat Res Coun-Nat Acad Sci, 67-73; Ford Found head animal prod div, EAfrica Agr & Res Orgn, Nairobi, Kenya, 69-71. *Honors & Awards:* Am Soc Animal Sci Award, 59; Tyler Award, 67. *Mem:* AAAS; Am Soc Animal Sci; Poultry Sci Asn; Am Inst Nutrit. *Res:* Metabolism of protein; energy and minerals; vitamin and mineral deficiencies; use of radioisotopes in mineral studies. *Mailing Add:* Rockefeller Found PO Box 63 Yogyakarta Indonesia

TILLMAN, FRANK A, b Linn, Mo, July 22, 37; m 59; c 3. INDUSTRIAL ENGINEERING. *Educ:* Univ Mo, BS, 60, MS, 61; Univ Iowa, PhD(indust eng), 65. *Prof Exp:* Instr indust eng, Univ Mo, 60-61; oper res analyst, Standard Oil Ohio, 61-63; instr indust eng, Univ Iowa, 63-65; from asst prof to assoc prof, 65-69, PROF INDUST ENG, KANS STATE UNIV, 69-,

HEAD DEPT, 66-, ASSOC DIR, INST SYSTS DESIGN & OPTIMIZATION, 67- *Concurrent Pos:* Res grants, Ford Found, 63-65, NSF, 65-67; NASA fel, 66-68; pres, Systs Res Corp, 68-; dir prog control, Price Comn, Exec Off of the President & consult, 72; consult, USDA. *Mem:* Am Inst Indust Engrs; Inst Mgt Sci; Opers Res Soc Am. *Res:* Operations research; engineering statistics and quality control and the applications of quantitative techniques to the optimization of the design and control of systems. *Mailing Add:* Dept of Indust Eng Kans State Univ Manhattan KS 66506

TILLMAN, J(AMES) D(AVID), JR, b Evansville, Ind, July 4, 21; m 56; c 3. ELECTRICAL ENGINEERING. *Educ:* Univ Tenn, BS, 47, MS, 50; Auburn Univ, PhD, 68. *Prof Exp:* From instr to assoc prof, 47-60, PROF ELEC ENG, UNIV TENN, KNOXVILLE, 60-, DIR ANTENNA PROJS, 56- *Concurrent Pos:* Researcher, Eng Exp Sta, Univ Tenn, Knoxville, 50-51 & Navy & Air Force Projs, 51-64. *Mem:* Am Soc Eng Educ; Inst Elec & Electronics Engrs. *Res:* Antenna systems and arrays, especially circular symmetry; propagation studies; electronic scanning systems; scattering of pulses from long wires; transient response of antennas. *Mailing Add:* Dept of Elec Eng Univ of Tenn Knoxville TN 37916

TILLMAN, LARRY JAUBERT, b Bay St Louis, Miss, Aug 20, 48; m 70; c 1. ANATOMY. *Educ:* Univ Miss, BA, 70, MS, 72, PhD(histol, electron micros), 74. *Prof Exp:* chief electron micros, Dept Path, Brooke Army Med Ctr, 74-77; ASST PROF ANAT, MED CTR, UNIV MISS, 78- *Concurrent Pos:* Clin appointee, Dept Anat, Micros Anat Sect, Univ Tex Health Sci Ctr & Med Sch, San Antonio, 75-77. *Mem:* Soc Armed Forces Med Lab Scientists; Electron Micros Soc Am; AAAS. *Res:* Correlation of the fine structure of the cells comprising the uriniferous tubules of Gallus domesticus to their function; use of transmission and scanning electron microscopy in the diagnosis of renal and tumor disease. *Mailing Add:* Dept of Anat Univ of Miss Med Ctr Jackson MS 39216

TILLMAN, MICHAEL FRANCIS, b Seattle, Wash, Feb 10, 43; m 65; c 3. FISH BIOLOGY, POPULATION DYNAMICS. *Educ:* Univ Wash, BS, 65, MS, 68, PhD(fisheries), 72. *Prof Exp:* Fishery biologist res, Marine Fish & Shellfish Div, 72-74, leader, Cetaceans Task Unit, 74-76, leader, Cetaceans Res Unit, 76-78, dep dir, Marine Mammal Div, 78-79, DIR, NAT MARINE MAMMAL LAB, NAT MARINE FISHERIES SERV, 79- *Concurrent Pos:* Actg asst prof, Col Fisheries, Univ Wash, 72-73, affil asst prof, 73-78, affil assoc prof, 78-; sci adv to US Comnr, Int Whaling Comn, 74-, vchmn sci comt, 79-; US mem sci comt, Ad Hoc Comt Marine Mammals, Int North Pac Fisheries Comn. *Mem:* Am Fisheries Soc; Am Inst Fishery Res Biologists. *Res:* Biology, abundance, distribution, behavior, migrations and population dynamics of endangered cetacean species; assessments of exploited cetacean stocks. *Mailing Add:* Marine Mammal Div 7600 Sand Point Way Seattle WA 98115

TILLMAN, RICHARD MILTON, b Muskogee, Okla, Sept 7, 28; m 48; c 2. ORGANIC CHEMISTRY. *Educ:* Southern Methodist Univ, BS, 52, MS, 53. *Prof Exp:* From asst res chemist to sr res chemist, 53-61, res group leader, 61-63, tech asst, 63-64, supvry res scientist, 64-67, mgr, Plant Foods Res Div, 67-72, assoc mgr petrol prod div, Res & Develop, 72-75, MGR RES SERV DIV, RES & DEVELOP, CONTINENTAL OIL CO, 75- *Mem:* Sr mem Am Chem Soc; Soc Automotive Engrs. *Res:* Hydrocarbon fuels; inorganic colloids; petroleum-based specialties; plant foods; phosphate rock; phosphoric acid; sulfur; inorganic fluorides; nitrogen compounds; agricultural chemicals and specialties; environmental chemistry. *Mailing Add:* 2400 Wildwood Ponca City OK 74601

TILLMAN, ROBERT ERWIN, b Hammondsport, NY, June 29, 37; m 60; c 2. WILDLIFE ECOLOGY. *Educ:* State Univ NY, Albany, AB, 59, MA, 61; Cornell Univ, PhD(environ educ), 72. *Prof Exp:* Teacher biol, Dundee Cent Sch, NY, 59-65; asst prof biol, Dutchess Community Col, 66-69, assoc prof nat res, 71-73; coordr wildlife res, Cary Arboretum, 71-78, CHMN ENVIRON ASSESSMENT, NY BOT GARDEN, 78- *Concurrent Pos:* Mem, NY State Forest Pract Bd, 74-, chmn, 80-; mem, Comnr's Adv Comn, NY State Environ Conserv, 76-78 & NY State Forest Resources Planning Comt. *Mem:* Ecol Soc Am; Inst Ecol; Wildlife Soc. *Res:* Powerline ecology, including vegetation management on powerline rights of way; hydroelectric generation sites, including transmission line rights of way. *Mailing Add:* Cary Arboretum Box AB Millbrook NY 12545

TILLMAN, RONALD WAYNE, b Springfield, Ohio, July 21, 44; m 66; c 1. PLANT PATHOLOGY. *Educ:* Miami Univ, BA, 66; Univ Md, College Park, MS, 69, PhD(plant path), 71. *Prof Exp:* Sr instr bot, Univ Col, Univ Md, 70-71; res assoc plant path & fel, Univ Ky, 71-72; head fungicide res, Biol Res Ctr, Crop Protection Inst, 72-73; asst prof plant path, Kans State Univ, 73-77; ASST PROF PLANT PATH & PHYSIOL & MEM STAFF PLANT PROTECTION COORD COUN, VA POLYTECH INST & STATE UNIV, 77- *Mem:* Am Phytopath Soc; Nat Asn Col & Teachers Agr. *Res:* Integrated pest management and mode of action of fungicides. *Mailing Add:* Dept of Plant Path & Physiol Va Polytech Inst & State Univ Blacksburg VA 24061

TILLMAN, STEPHEN JOEL, b Springfield, Mass, Mar 31, 43; m 65; c 2. MATHEMATICS. *Educ:* Brown Univ, ScB, 65, PhD(math), 70; Lehigh Univ, MS, 78. *Prof Exp:* Instr math, Brown Univ, 69-70; asst prof, 70-75, ASSOC PROF MATH, WILKES COL, 75- *Mem:* Am Math Soc; Math Asn Am; Opers Res Soc Am. *Res:* Teaching and developing additional courses in operations research and related areas. *Mailing Add:* Dept of Math Wilkes Col Wilkes-Barre PA 18703

TILLMANNS-SKOLNIK, EMMA-JUNE H, b New York, NY, June 4, 19; m 81. INFORMATION SCIENCE. *Educ:* Hunter Col, AB, 41; NY Univ, MS, 47, PhD(org chem), 54. *Prof Exp:* Chemist, Burroughs Wellcome Co, Inc, 41-53; sr chemist, Redstone Res Div, Rohm & Haas Co, 53-56; asst ed, Org Indexing Dept, Chem Abstr, 56-60, assoc ed, 60; res chemist, Info Sect, Chem Res Dept, Atlas Chem Indust, Inc, 60-67, sr res chemist, 67-72, res info sect, ICI Am, Inc, 72-74, supvr biomed info, Res Info Sect, 74-76, INFO SCIENTIST, HEALTH & ENVIRON AFFAIRS, ICI UNITED STATES, INC, 80- *Mem:* Am Chem Soc; Drug Info Asn; Am Soc Info Sci. *Res:* Olefin-nitrile reaction; organic nomenclature. *Mailing Add:* 239 Waverly Rd Wilmington DE 19803

TILLOTSON, JAMES E, b Cambridge, Mass, Feb 9, 29; m 56; c 2. FOOD SCIENCE. *Educ:* Harvard Univ, AB, 53; Boston Univ, MA, 56; Mass Inst Technol, PhD(food sci), 64; Univ Del, MBA, 69. *Prof Exp:* Teacher, Manter Hall Sch, 57-63; res asst nutrit & food sci, Mass Inst Technol, 61-63; res chemist indust & biochem dept, E I du Pont de Nemours & Co, 64-65, develop dept, 65-66, tech rep indust & biochem dept, 66-69; dir res & develop, 69-77, V PRES TECH RES & DEVELOP, OCEAN SPRAY CRANBERRIES, INC, 77- *Mem:* Fel Am Inst Chem; Am Chem Soc; prof mem Inst Food Technol; Soc Nutrit Educ. *Res:* Commercial development of food products and agricultural chemicals; research management; technical forecasting; government regulation of agribusiness; sweeteners. *Mailing Add:* 240 Forest Ave Cohasset MA 02025

TILLOTSON, JAMES GLEN, b Brandon, Man, July 20, 23; m 48; c 3. PHYSICS. *Educ:* Univ Man, BSc, 45; Univ Western Ont, MSc, 47. *Prof Exp:* Asst prof physics, Univ NB, 47-53; dir appl physics sect, Can Armament Res & Develop Estab, 53-55; PROF PHYSICS, ACADIA UNIV, 55- *Concurrent Pos:* Consult, NB Dept Health, 51-52; Defence Res Bd Can grant, 57-59. *Mem:* Inst Elec & Electronics Engrs; Can Asn Physicists; Am Asn Physics Teachers. *Res:* Non-linear vibrations; acoustic radiation. *Mailing Add:* Dept Physics Acadia Univ Wolfville NS B0P 1X0 Can

TILLOTSON, JAMES RICHARD, b Berkeley, Calif, Oct 3, 33; m 82; c 2. INFECTIOUS DISEASES, INTERNAL MEDICINE. *Educ:* Lehigh Univ, BA, 55; Univ Calif, San Francisco, MD, 59. *Prof Exp:* Instr med, Med Sch, Harvard Univ, 67-68; asst prof, Sch Med, Univ Mich, 68-70; assoc prof, 70-80, PROF INFECTIOUS DIS & MED & HEAD DIV, ALBANY MED COL & MED CTR HOSP, 80- *Concurrent Pos:* Clin res fel, Sch Med, Wayne State Univ, 64-66 & Med Sch, Harvard Univ-Boston City Hosp, 66-68; chief, Div Infectious Dis, Wayne County Gen Hosp, 68-70; consult, Albany Vet Admin Hosp & head, Div Infectious Dis, Albany Med Ctr Hosp, 70- *Mem:* Am Fedn Clin Res; Am Soc Microbiol; fel Infectious Dis Soc Am; fel Am Col Clin Pharmacol. *Res:* Pneumonia, especially gram-negative bacillary; prostatitis; antimicrobial activity of anti-tumor drugs; antimicrobial synergy; other areas of clinical microbiology and infectious diseases. *Mailing Add:* Rm ME-424 Albany Med Col New Scotland Ave Albany NY 12208

TILLSON, HENRY CHARLES, b Philadelphia, Pa, Sept 16, 23; m 50; c 2. RUBBER CHEMISTRY, POLYMER CHARACTERIZATION. *Educ:* Mass Inst Technol, SB, 44; Pa State Univ, MS, 48, PhD(org chem), 51. *Prof Exp:* Res chemist, Res Ctr, 50-52, tech rep, 52-54, RES CHEMIST, RES CTR, HERCULES INC, 54- *Mem:* AAAS; Am Chem Soc. *Res:* Organic nitrogen compounds-nitramines; emulsion polymerization vinyl and condensation polymers, especially protective coatings; rubber compounding and crosslinking; polymer fractionation, mainly polyolifins. *Mailing Add:* Hercules Inc Research Center Wilmington DE 19899

TILMANS, ANTHONY LYNN, b New Kensington, Pa, Aug 28, 35; Div; c 3. CIVIL ENGINEERING. *Educ:* Univ Pittsburgh, BSCE, 58, MSCE, 60; Carnegie-Mellon Univ, PhD(civil eng), 68. *Prof Exp:* Design engr, Aluminum Co Am, 59-61; from instr to asst prof civil eng, Univ Pittsburgh, 61-71, assoc prof eng technol & head civil eng technol, Johnstown, 71-74; dir eng technol, Ind State Univ, Evansville, 74-81; CHAIR ENGR, TECH DEPT, CALIF STATE POLYTECH UNIV, POMONA, 81- *Concurrent Pos:* Consult, PPG Industs, Inc, 68-70. *Mem:* Am Soc Civil Engrs; Am Soc Eng Educ; Nat Soc Prof Engrs. *Res:* Engineering technology. *Mailing Add:* Eng Tech Dept Calif Polytech Pomona 3801 W Temple Ave Pomona CA 91768

TILSON, BRET RANSOM, b Yuba City, Calif, May 19, 37. MATHEMATICS, COMPUTER SCIENCE. *Educ:* Mass Inst Technol, BS, 60; Univ Calif, Berkeley, PhD(math), 69. *Prof Exp:* Asst prof math, Columbia Univ, 69-74; asst prof, 74-77, ASSOC PROF MATH, QUEEN'S COL, NY, 77- *Concurrent Pos:* Dir res & develop, Comarc Design Systs, San Francisco, 80-81. *Res:* Decomposition and complexity of finite semigroups; automata theory. *Mailing Add:* PO Box 1789 Sausalito CA 94966

TILSWORTH, TIMOTHY, b Norfolk, Nebr, Apr 6, 39; m 66; c 2. ENVIRONMENTAL HEALTH ENGINEERING. *Educ:* Univ Nebr-Lincoln, BS, 66, MS, 67; Univ Kans, PhD(environ health eng), 70. *Prof Exp:* Lab technician, Nitrogen Div, Allied Chem & Dye Corp, 60-61; civil engr technician, Scott Eng, 61-62; asst city engr, Norfolk, Nebr, 62-64; instr civil eng, Univ Nebr, 67; asst prof environ health eng, 70-74, head prog, 71-76, asst to pres, 76-77, ASSOC PROF ENVIRON QUAL ENG & CIVIL ENG, UNIV ALASKA, FAIRBANKS, 74- *Concurrent Pos:* Spec consult, Philleo Eng & Archit Serv, 71- & Hill, Ingman & Chase & Co, 71- *Mem:* Am Soc Civil Engrs; Am Asn Prof Environ Eng; Water Pollution Control Fedn; Am Water Works Asn. *Res:* Environmental health engineering; pollution control; solid waste management; biological waste water treatment; physical and chemical treatment; water quality; air pollution control. *Mailing Add:* Prog of Environ Qual Eng Univ Alaska 306 Tanana Dr Fairbanks AK 99701

TILTON, BERNARD ELLSWORTH, b Hanford, Calif, Oct 3, 23; m 46; c 3. PHARMACOLOGY. *Educ:* Pac Union Col, BA, 46; Loma Linda Univ, MD, 48; Univ Calif, Los Angeles, MS, 56, PhD, 60. *Prof Exp:* From asst prof to assoc prof, 53-75, PROF PHARMACOL, SCH MED, LOMA LINDA UNIV, 75- *Concurrent Pos:* Fel clin pharmacol, Univ Mich, 65-66. *Mem:* AAAS; Am Soc Clin Pharmacol & Therapeut. *Res:* Mode of action for neuromuscular blocking agents; clinical cardiovascular pharmacology. *Mailing Add:* Barton & Anderson Loma Linda CA 92354

TILTON, GEORGE ROBERT, b Danville, Ill, June 3, 23; m 48; c 4. GEOCHEMISTRY. *Educ:* Univ Ill, BS, 47; Univ Chicago, PhD(chem), 51. *Prof Exp:* Asst, Univ Chicago, 47-51; mem staff, Dept Terrestrial Magnetism, Carnegie Inst, 51-56, phys chemist, Geophys Lab, 56-65; PROF GEOCHEM, UNIV CALIF, SANTA BARBARA, 65- *Concurrent Pos:* Assoc ed, Geochimica Cosmochimica Acta, 74-; guest prof, Swiss Fed Inst Technol, Zurich, 71-72. *Mem:* Nat Acad Sci; Geochem Soc (pres, 80-81); fel Am Geophys Union; fel Geol Soc Am; Meteoritical Soc. *Res:* Geochemical studies applied to origin of volcanic and plutonic rocks; isotopic composition of lead in terrestrial and meteoritic materials; geologic age of minerals. *Mailing Add:* Dept of Geol Sci Univ of Calif Santa Barbara CA 93106

TILTON, JAMES EARL, b Decatur, Ill, Aug 1, 38; m 60; c 3. ANIMAL PHYSIOLOGY. *Educ:* Ill State Norm Univ, BS, 61; Okla State Univ, MS, 64, PhD(animal breeding), 66. *Prof Exp:* From asst prof to assoc prof, 65-75, PROF ANIMAL SCI, NDAK STATE UNIV, 75- *Mem:* Am Soc Animal Sci. *Res:* Embryonic mortality in adrenalectomized ewes; estrous control in the ovine; endocrine profiles of gilt estrous cycle; effect of prostaglandin E2 on CL lifespan. *Mailing Add:* Dept Animal Sci NDak State Univ Fargo ND 58102

TILTON, VARIEN RUSSELL, b Willimantic, Conn, Aug 10, 43; m 76. PLANT BIOENGINEERING. *Educ:* Northern Ariz Univ, BS, 66, MS, 75; Iowa State Univ, PhD(bot), 78. *Prof Exp:* Fel exp plant embroyol, Rockefeller Found, Univ Minn, 78-79; res assoc develop bot, Univ Ariz, 79; vis asst prof bot & electron micros, Iowa State Univ, 79-80; vis asst prof biol, cytol & electron micros, Bowling Green State Univ, 80-81; RES SCIENTIST CELL BIOL AGRIGENETICS CORP, 81- *Concurrent Pos:* Adj asst prof bot, Univ Wis, Madison, 81- & Iowa State Univ, 82- *Mem:* Am Inst Biol Sci; Am Soc Agron; Bot Soc Am; Electron Micros Soc Am; Sigma Xi. *Mailing Add:* Advan Res Lab Agrigenetics Corp E Buckeye Rd Madison WI 53716

TIMAN, HANS, b Vienna, Austria, Dec 15, 27; nat US; m 68. PHOTOMULTIPLIERS, THIN FILM PHOTOCATHODES. *Educ:* Univ Vienna, PhD, 58. *Prof Exp:* Sr engr, Allen B Dumont Labs Div, Fairchild Camera & Instrument Corp, 59-64, SR SCIENTIST, DUMONT ELECTRONICS CORP, THOMSEN-CSF, 64- *Mem:* Inst Elec & Electronics Engrs. *Res:* Turbulence theory; electron optics, including photomultipliers and image devices; photosensitive and photoemissive devices; thin film photocathodes; research on photocathodes. *Mailing Add:* Dumont Electronics Corp Thomsen-CSF 750 Bloomfield Ave Clifton NJ 07015

TIMASHEFF, SERGE NICHOLAS, b Paris, France, Apr 7, 26; nat US; m 53; c 1. PHYSICAL BIOCHEMISTRY. *Educ:* Fordham Univ, BS, 46, MS, 47, PhD(chem), 51. *Prof Exp:* Instr chem, Fordham Univ, 47-49, lectr, 49-50; res fel, Calif Inst Technol, 51 & Yale Univ, 51-55; prin phys chemist, Eastern Regional Res Lab, USDA, Pa, 55-66, head pioneering res lab, Mass, 66-73; PROF BIOCHEM, BRANDEIS UNIV, 66- *Concurrent Pos:* NSF sr res fel, Macromolecule Res Ctr, France, 59-60; adj prof, Drexel Inst Technol, 63-64; vis prof, Univ Ariz, 66; mem, Fordham Univ Coun, 68-; mem, Biophys-Phys Biochem Study Sect, NIH, 68-72; Guggenheim fel, Inst Molecular Biol, Paris, 72-73; vis prof, Univ Paris, 72-73; co-ed, Biol Macromolecules; exec ed, Archives of Biochem & Biophys; vis prof, Duke Univ, 77; distinguished lectr, Univ Maine, 79. *Honors & Awards:* Am Chem Soc Award, 63 & 66, Arthur H Flemming Award, 64. *Mem:* AAAS; Am Chem Soc; Am Soc Biol Chemists; Biophys Soc. *Res:* Structure and interactions of proteins and nucleic acids; physical methods of high polymer studies; solution thermodynamics of macromolecules. *Mailing Add:* Dept Biochem Brandeis Univ Waltham MA 02154

TIMBERLAKE, JACK W, b Middletown, Ohio, May 26, 40; m 62; c 2. ORGANIC CHEMISTRY. *Educ:* Univ Ill, MS, 65, PhD, 67. *Prof Exp:* Fel org chem, Univ Calif, Irvine, 67-68; from asst prof to assoc prof, 68-78, PROF ORG CHEM, UNIV NEW ORLEANS, 78- *Concurrent Pos:* Petrol Res Found grant, Am Chem Soc, 75-77 & 76-79; Army Res Off grant, 76-78; consult med prog, Sch Med, Tulane Univ, 76-79; Diamond Shamrock crop grant, 77-79. *Mem:* Am Chem Soc; Sigma Xi. *Res:* Physical and synthetic organic chemistry; free radical reactions; small ring heterocycles; synthesis and screening of new anti-convulsants. *Mailing Add:* Dept of Chem Univ of New Orleans New Orleans LA 70122

TIMBERLAKE, JOSEPH WILLIAM, b Kansas City, Kans, Sept 5, 40; m 67. CLINICAL BIOCHEMISTRY. *Educ:* Univ Mo-Kansas City, BA, 63, MS, 69; Univ Kans Med Ctr, Kansas City, PhD(biochem), 74. *Prof Exp:* Technologist clin chem, Res Hosp & Med Ctr, 63-65; develop chemist, Univ Kans Med Ctr, Kansas City, 66-69; lab dir, Statlabs of Kans, Inc, 73-75; CLIN BIOCHEMIST, KANSAS CITY GEN HOSP-UNIV MO MED SCH, KANSAS CITY, 75- *Mem:* Am Asn Clin Chemists. *Res:* Developmental clinical biochemistry. *Mailing Add:* Apt #101 8325 E Harry Wichita KS 67207

TIMBERLAKE, WILLIAM EDWARD, b Washington, DC, May 2, 48; m 69; c 2. MOLECULAR BIOLOGY, GENETICS. *Educ:* State Univ NY Col Forestry, BS, 70; State Univ NY Col Environ Sci & Forestry, MS, 72, PhD(biol), 74. *Prof Exp:* Assoc, Univ Geneva, 74; asst prof biol, Wayne State Univ, 74-79, assoc prof, 79-81; ASSOC PROF, PLANT GROWTH LAB, UNIV CALIF, DAVIS, 81- *Mem:* AAAS; Genetics Soc Am; Mycol Soc Am; Sigma Xi. *Res:* Regulation of gene expression in fungi and plants. *Mailing Add:* Plant Growth Lab Univ Calif Davis CA 95616

TIMBERS, GORDON ERNEST, b Regina, Sask, Sept 14, 40. FOOD SCIENCE. *Educ:* Univ BC, BSA, 62, MSA, 64; Rutgers Univ, New Brunswick, PhD(food sci), 71. *Prof Exp:* RES SCIENTIST, ENG RES SERV, CAN DEPT AGR, 64- *Mem:* Can Inst Food Sci & Technol; Inst Food Technologists. *Res:* Food engineering; development of new processes and equipment for food processing; unit operations; thermal properties of food products. *Mailing Add:* 5 Dallas Place Ottawa ON K2G 3E2 Can

TIMBLIN, LLOYD O, JR, b Denver, Colo, June 25, 27; m 50; c 1. APPLIED PHYSICS, PHYSICAL SCIENCE. *Educ:* Univ Colo, BS, 50; Univ Denver, MS, 67. *Prof Exp:* Physicist, 50-58, head Spec Invests Lab Sect, 58-63, chief Chem Eng Br, 63-70, CHIEF APPL SCI BR, DIV GEN RES, US BUR RECLAMATION, 70- *Concurrent Pos:* Mem Colo adv coun, Sem Environ Arts & Sci; chmn US team, US/USSR Joint Study Plastic Films & Soil Stabilizers, 75-; mem, Nat Sanit Found Comt on Flexible Membrane Liners, 79- *Mem:* Am Phys Soc; Am Water Works Asn; Nat Asn Corrosion Engrs; Am Soc Testing & Mat; Ecol Soc Am. *Res:* Engineering physics; corrosion engineering; corrosion mechanisms; cathodic protection; protective coatings; radioisotopes applications; water quality and pollution control; applied ecology; materials analysis and development; water treatment and desalting; weed control; remote sensing. *Mailing Add:* Div Res US Bur Reclamation Code 1520 PO Box 25007 Denver CO 80225

TIMELL, TORE ERIK, b Stockholm, Sweden, Mar 31, 21; nat US; m 47; c 3. ORGANIC CHEMISTRY. *Educ:* Royal Inst Technol, Sweden, ChemE, 46, lic, 48, DrTech(cellulose chem), 50. *Prof Exp:* Chief asst, Royal Inst Technol, Sweden, 46-50; res assoc chem, McGill Univ, 50-51; res assoc, State Univ NY Col Forestry, Syracuse, 51-52; Hibbert Mem fel, McGill Univ, 52, res assoc, 53-62; PROF FOREST CHEM, STATE UNIV NY COL ENVIRON SCI & FORESTRY, SYRACUSE, 62- *Concurrent Pos:* Chemist, Pulp & Paper Res Inst Can, 53-59, res group leader, 60-62. *Honors & Awards:* Anselme Payen Award, Am Chem Soc, 71. *Mem:* Am Chem Soc; Chem Inst Can; Int Acad Wood Sci; Int Asn Wood Anat. *Res:* Chemistry of wood and bark; ultrastructure, cytology and physiology of wood and bark; reaction wood. *Mailing Add:* State Univ of NY Col of Environ Sci & Forestry Syracuse NY 13210

TIMIAN, ROLAND GUSTAV, b Langdon, NDak, Mar 5, 20; m 49; c 5. PLANT VIROLOGY. *Educ:* NDak Agr Col, BS, 49, MS, 50; Iowa State Col, PhD(plant path), 53. *Prof Exp:* Asst bot, NDak Agr Col, 47-49, fed agent pathologist, 49-50; path res asst, Iowa State Col, 50-53; RES PLANT PATHOLOGIST, AGR RES, NDAK STATE UNIV, USDA, 53- *Concurrent Pos:* Tech adv barley, NCent Region, Agr Res Serv, USDA, 73-, mem nat barley improv comt, 78-; ed, Barley Newsletter, 76-79. *Mem:* Am Phytopath Soc; Sigma Xi. *Res:* Cereal virus diseases; diseases in barley, especially virus diseases; serology; host-virus interaction. *Mailing Add:* Dept of Plant Path NDak State Univ Fargo ND 58102

TIMIRAS, PAOLA SILVESTRI, b Rome, Italy, July 21, 23; nat US; m 46; c 2. DEVELOPMENTAL PHYSIOLOGY, NEUROENDOCRINOLOGY. *Educ:* Univ Rome, MD, 47; Univ Montreal, PhD(exp med, surg), 52. *Prof Exp:* Asst prof exp med & surg, Univ Montreal, 50-51, asst prof physiol, 51-53; asst prof pharmacol, Univ Utah, 54-55; asst physiologist, 55-58, from asst prof to assoc prof, 58-67, PROF PHYSIOL & CHMN DEPT, UNIV CALIF, BERKELEY, 67- *Mem:* AAAS; Endocrine Soc; Am Soc Pharmacol & Exp Therapeut; Am Physiol Soc; Geront Soc. *Res:* Endocrinology; environmental physiology; aging. *Mailing Add:* Dept Physiol & Anat Univ Calif Berkeley CA 94720

TIMKO, JOSEPH MICHAEL, b Danville, Ill, May 20, 49. ORGANIC CHEMISTRY. *Educ:* Univ Ill, Urbana, BS, 71; Univ Calif, Los Angeles, PhD(chem), 75. *Prof Exp:* Fel org chem, Univ Wis-Madison, 75-77; RES CHEMIST ORG CHEM, UPJOHN CO, 77- *Concurrent Pos:* NIH fel, Univ Wis-Madison, 76-77. *Mem:* AAAS; Am Chem Soc. *Res:* Development of synthesis and transformations of medicinally important compounds. *Mailing Add:* 1500-91-1 Upjohn Co Kalamazoo MI 49001

TIMKO, PATRICIA LYNN, see O'Neill, Patricia Lynn Timko

TIMKOVICH, RUSSELL, b East Chicago, Ind. BIOCHEMISTRY. *Educ:* Mich State Univ, BS, 70; Calif Inst Technol, PhD(chem), 74. *Prof Exp:* Fel, Calif Inst Technol, 74-75; asst prof, 75-80, ASSOC PROF, ILL INST TECHNOL, 80- *Mem:* Am Chem Soc; Am Soc Biol Chemists; Biophys Soc. *Res:* Biochemistry and biophysics of electron transport proteins and enzymes; bacterial electron transport systems. *Mailing Add:* Dept Chem Ill Inst Technol Chicago IL 60616

TIMM, DELMAR C, b Muscatine, Iowa, Aug 19, 40; m 62; c 2. CHEMICAL ENGINEERING. *Educ:* Iowa State Univ, BS, 62, MS, 65, PhD(chem eng), 67. *Prof Exp:* Chem engr, Esso Res & Eng Co, 62-63; from asst prof to assoc prof chem eng, 67-75, PROF CHEM ENG, UNIV NEBR, LINCOLN, 75- *Mem:* Am Chem Soc; Am Inst Chem Engrs. *Res:* Crystallization from solution; kinetics of polymerization. *Mailing Add:* Dept of Chem Eng Univ of Nebr Lincoln NE 68508

TIMM, GERALD WAYNE, b Brandon, Minn, Dec 9, 40. BIOMEDICAL ENGINEERING, ELECTRICAL ENGINEERING. *Educ:* Univ Minn, Minneapolis, BEE, 63, MS, 65, PhD(elec eng), 67. *Prof Exp:* Assoc prof neurol, Med Sch, Univ Minn, Minneapolis, 67-77, adj assoc prof mech eng, 77-80; PRES, DACOMED CORP, 80- *Concurrent Pos:* Res fel elec eng, Univ Minn, Minneapolis, 67, NIH trainee, 70-72, NIH grant, 74-; mem grad fac, Univ Minn, 71-; consult, Baylor Col Med, 72-, Am Med Systs, Inc, 73- & Purdue Univ, 74- *Mem:* AAAS; Inst Elec & Electronics Eng; sr mem Instrument Soc Am; NY Acad Sci. *Res:* Lower urinary tract and reproductive systems function; investigations of instrumentation systems to diagnose and treat impaired genito-urinary and gastrointestinal function. *Mailing Add:* Dacomed Corp 47 Southeast Bedford Minneapolis MN 55414

TIMM, HERMAN, b Kenosha, Wis, Aug 26, 26; m 49; c 7. AGRONOMY. *Educ:* Cornell Univ, BS, 51; Mich State Univ, MS, 53; Pa State Univ, PhD(agron), 56. *Prof Exp:* LECTR & SPECIALIST AGRON, UNIV CALIF, DAVIS, 56- *Mem:* Soil Sci Soc Am; Am Potato Asn; Am Soc Hort Sci. *Res:* Ecology and physiology of the potato; changes in cultural practices for high yields and better quality control of crops; agricultural recycling of waste products; effect on soil-water-plant relationships. *Mailing Add:* Dept of Veg Crops Univ of Calif Davis CA 95616

TIMM, RAYMOND STANLEY, b Bay City, Mich, Nov 28, 18; m 44; c 8. ELECTRONIC ENGINEERING, OPERATIONS RESEARCH. *Educ:* Lawrence Inst Technol, BSc, 42. *Prof Exp:* Assoc sect head electronic systs, Naval Res Lab, 42-48; sr engr naval res, Off Naval Res, 48-51; asst to pres component res, Balco Corp, 51-55; sr analyst electronic systs, Westinghouse Elec Corp, 55-57; br head systs anal, Melpar Corp, 57-58; DIV MGR SYSTS ANAL, ANAL SERV INC, 58- *Mem:* Inst Elec & Electronics Engrs; sr mem Opers Res Soc Am. *Res:* Analysis of electronic aides to navigation; research and development of antenna filter networks. *Mailing Add:* 9803 Singleton Dr Bethesda MD 20817

TIMM, ROBERT FREDERICK, b Toledo, Ohio, May 17, 31; m 53; c 2. MECHANICAL ENGINEERING. *Educ:* Univ Mich, BS, 54, MS, 60, PhD(mech eng), 67. *Prof Exp:* Engr, Johnson Serv Co, 56-58; lectr mech eng, Univ Mich-Dearborn, 60-64; asst prof, Univ Ill, 67-69; assoc prof, Mich Technol Univ, 69-76; ASST GROUP MGR, BATTELLE MEM INST, 76- *Concurrent Pos:* Consult, Univ Mich, 60-62 & 66-68; Kettering Found fel, Univ, Colo, 68; USDA grant & NSF grant, 70-72; res fel, Cranfield Inst Technol, Eng, 72. *Res:* Computerized design and simulation of mechanical systems; automatic controls; vehicle dynamics with special interests in off-highway vehicles. *Mailing Add:* Battelle Mem Inst 505 King Ave Columbus OH 43201

TIMMA, DONALD LEE, b Lebanon, Kans, Sept 1, 22; m 45; c 1. CHEMISTRY. *Educ:* Kans State Col, BS, 44; Ohio Univ, PhD(chem), 49. *Prof Exp:* Spectrographer, Tenn Eastman Co, 44-45; asst chem, Ohio Univ, 46-48; spectrographer, Monsanto Chem Co, 45-46, res physicist, Mound Lab, 49-50, res group leader, 50-51, res sect chief, 51-57; dir anal chem & methods develop, 57-67, exec dir control lab, 67, vpres qual control, 67-76, MGR CONTRACT MFG, MEAD JOHNSON & CO, 76- *Mem:* Am Chem Soc. *Res:* Analytical instrumentation; emission and absorption spectroscopy. *Mailing Add:* Qual Control Mead Johnson & Co Evansville IN 47712

TIMME, ROBERT WILLIAM, b Victoria, Tex, July 22, 40; m 62; c 2. APPLIED PHYSICS. *Educ:* Tex A&M Univ, BS, 62; Rice Univ, MA, 69, PhD(physics), 70. *Prof Exp:* Res physicist, Ames Res Lab, NASA, 62-65, aerospace engr, Manned Spacecraft Ctr, 65-66; res assoc solid state physics, Rice Univ, 66-70; prin engr electromagnetics, Lockheed Electronics Co, Inc, 70-71; head mat res sect, 73-79, RES PHYSICIST, NAVAL RES LAB, 71-, HEAD TRANSDUCER BR, 79- *Concurrent Pos:* Mem, Transducer Mat Comt, Naval Sea Systs Command, 73-; mem oceanology adv group, Naval Res Lab, 75-78; prof oceanology, Fla Inst Technol, 75-78; program manager, Sonar Transducer Reliability Improvement Program, 78- *Honors & Awards:* NASA Achievement Awards, Manned Spacecraft Ctr, 66 & Hq, 73; Res Publ Award, Naval Res Lab, 76, 79 & 80, Performance Awards, 74, 78 & 80. *Mem:* Am Phys Soc; Acoust Soc Am. *Res:* Characterization of the effects of stress, temperature and time on the piezoelectric, magnetostrictive, elastic and acoustic properties of materials applicable to sonar systems; development of long life, reliable sonar transducers. *Mailing Add:* Naval Res Labs PO Box 8337 Orlando FL 32806

TIMMER, KATHLEEN MAE, b Ellsworth, Mich, July 21, 42. ALGEBRA. *Educ:* Calvin Col, BS, 64; Purdue Univ, MS, 66; Colo State Univ, PhD(math), 72. *Prof Exp:* Instr math, Calvin Col, 66-68; ASST PROF MATH, JACKSONVILLE UNIV, 72- *Mem:* Am Math Soc. *Mailing Add:* Box 90 Jacksonville Univ Jacksonville FL 32211

TIMMER, LAVERN WAYNE, b West Olive, Mich, Aug 16, 41; m 63; c 2. PLANT PATHOLOGY. *Educ:* Mich State Univ, BS, 63; Univ Calif, Riverside, PhD(plant path), 69. *Prof Exp:* Purdue Univ-Ford Found fel plant path, Latin Am, 66-68; from asst prof to assoc prof plant path, Citrus Ctr, Tex A&I Univ, 70-78; ASSOC PROF PLANT PATH, AGR RES & EDUC CTR, UNIV FLA, LAKE ALFRED, 79- *Mem:* Am Phytopath Soc; Int Soc Citricult. *Res:* Soil-borne and virus diseases of citrus. *Mailing Add:* Univ Fla 700 Exp Sta Rd Lake Alfred FL 33850

TIMMERHAUS, K(LAUS) D(IETER), b Minneapolis, Minn, Sept 10, 24; m 52; c 1. CHEMICAL ENGINEERING. *Educ:* Univ Ill, BS, 48, MS, 49, PhD(chem eng), 51. *Prof Exp:* Process design engr, Calif Res Corp, Standard Oil Co, Calif, 52-53; from asst prof to assoc prof chem eng, 53-61, PROF CHEM ENG, UNIV COLO, BOULDER, 61-, ASSOC DEAN ENG & DIR ENG RES CTR, 63- *Concurrent Pos:* Lectr, Exten, Univ Calif, 53 & Univ Calif, Los Angeles, 61-62, 67, 70 & 78-81; ed, Advan in Cryogenic Eng, 54-; consult numerous govt & indust orgn, 55-; mem & secy-treas, Cryogenic Eng Conf Bd, 56-66, 70-; co-ed, Int Cryogenic Monogr Ser; sect head, NSF, Washington, DC, 72-73; lectr award, Am Soc Eng Educ, 80. *Honors & Awards:* S C Collins Award, 67; G Westinghouse Award, Am Soc Eng Educ, 68; Founders Award, Am Inst Chem Engrs, 78; 3-M Award, Am Soc Eng Educ, 80. *Mem:* Nat Acad Eng; fel Am Inst Chem Engrs (vpres-pres, 76-76); Am Soc Eng Educ; Am Astronaut Soc; Austrian Acad Sci. *Res:* Cryogenic processes; heat transfer; distillation; thermodynamic properties. *Mailing Add:* Eng Ctr AD 1-25 Univ of Colo Boulder CO 80309

TIMMERMANN, BARBARA NAWALANY, b Suffolk, Eng, May 30, 47; div; c 2. TERPENOID & FLAVONOID CHEMISTRY. *Educ:* Univ Nacional de Cordoba, Argentina, BA, 70; Univ Tex, Austin, MA, 77, PhD(bot), 80. *Prof Exp:* Res asst, Univ Nacional de Cordoba, 67-70; res asst, Univ Tex, Austin, 70-72, teaching asst biol, 70-72, instr, 80; RES ASSOC, UNIV ARIZ, 81- *Mem:* Phytochem Soc NAm; Am Soc Pharmcognosy; Bot Soc Am. *Res:* Detailed chemical analysis of North American desert plants, including the isolation and identification of the vast array of natural products that they produce and evaluating their potential uses as alternate sources of energy and chemical feedstocks. *Mailing Add:* Bioenergy Res Facil Univ Ariz 250 E Valencia Rd Tucson AZ 85706

TIMMERMANN, DAN, JR, b New Braunfels, Tex, Oct 8, 33; m 55; c 2. BOTANY, CROP BREEDING. *Educ:* Tex A&M Univ, BS, 55, PhD(bot), 67; Ohio State Univ, MA, 62. *Prof Exp:* Teacher high sch, Tex, 58-61 & 62-63; asst prof, 67-70, ASSOC PROF BOT, ARK STATE UNIV, 70- *Concurrent Pos:* Consult plant breeding, Plant Res Div, Bryco, Inc, 74- *Mem:* Bot Soc Am. *Res:* Electron microscopy of plant cells; effects of gaseous air pollutants on the ultrastructure of specific cell organelles; cotton and soybean breeding. *Mailing Add:* Dept of Bot Ark State Univ State University AR 72467

TIMMINS, ROBERT STONE, b Dallas, Tex, Aug 25, 33; m 55; c 3. CHEMICAL ENGINEERING. *Educ:* Univ Tex, BS, 55; Mass Inst Technol, SM, 57, ScD, 59. *Prof Exp:* Sr engr prod res, Sun Oil Co, 59-61, group leader reservoir anal, 61-62; sect chief energy transfer & nuclear effects, Avco Corp, 62-63, asst mgr mat dept, 63-64, mgr mat sci dept, 64-66; vpres res & develop, Abcor, Inc, 66-70, exec vpres, 70-71, pres, 72-77; SR V PRES, COBE LABS, INC, 77- *Mem:* Am Inst Chem Engrs; Am Chem Soc. *Res:* Separation and purification; materials; high temperature chemistry. *Mailing Add:* Cobe Labs Inc 1201 Oak St Lakewood CO 80215

TIMMONS, DARROL HOLT, b Little River, Kans, July 7, 40; m 62; c 2. NUCLEAR ENGINEERING. *Educ:* Kans State Univ, BS, 63, MS, 66, PhD(nuclear eng), 69. *Prof Exp:* Instr nuclear eng, Kans State Univ, 67-68; asst prof nuclear eng, Univ Mo-Columbia, 68-74, assoc prof, 74-79; sr engr, 79, mgr neutronics develop, 79-81, MGR INCORE MONITORING, EXXON NUCLEAR CO, 81- *Concurrent Pos:* Am Soc Eng Educ/Ford Found Eng Residency Prog partic, Commonwealth Edison Co, Ill, 71-72. *Mem:* Am Nuclear Soc. *Res:* Nuclear reactor physics, fuel management and incore monitoring. *Mailing Add:* 2101 Horn Rapids Rd Richland WA 99352

TIMMONS, RICHARD B, b Sherbrooke, Que, June 23, 38; m 63; c 3. PHYSICAL CHEMISTRY. *Educ:* St Francis Xavier Univ, BS, 58; Cath Univ Am, PhD(chem), 62. *Prof Exp:* Fel chem kinetics, Brookhaven Nat Lab, 62-64; asst prof chem, Boston Col, 64-65; from asst prof to prof chem, Cath Univ Am, 65-77; PROF CHEM & CHMN DEPT, UNIV TEX, ARLINGTON, 77- *Mem:* Am Chem Soc. *Res:* Chemical kinetics; photochemistry, particularly in the vacuum ultraviolet region; kinetic isotope effects on reaction rates; chemistry of air pollution. *Mailing Add:* Dept of Chem Univ of Tex Arlington TX 76019

TIMMS, ROBERT J, b Chicago, Ill, Jan 2, 23; m 50; c 4. MICROWAVE ENGINEERING. *Educ:* Univ Md, BS, 49; Kans State Univ, MS, 51; Northwestern Univ, PhD(appl mech), 53. *Prof Exp:* Asst appl mech, Kans State Univ, 49-51; res asst, Northwestern Univ, 52-53; res sect head, Electronic Tube Div, 53-64, RES SECT HEAD, MICROWAVE ENG DEPT, SPERRY GYROSCOPE CO, 64- *Mem:* Inst Elec & Electronics Engrs. *Res:* Microwave components and related radar and communication systems; linear beam tubes; antennas; phased arrays. *Mailing Add:* 806 Glen Cove Ave Glen Head NY 11545

TIMNICK, ANDREW, b Kremianka, Russia, Dec 29, 18; nat US; m 43; c 2. ANALYTICAL CHEMISTRY. *Educ:* Wartburg Col, BA, 40; Univ Iowa, MS, 42, PhD(phys chem), 47. *Prof Exp:* Asst, Univ Iowa, 40-42 & 46-47; control & develop chemist, Polymer Corp, Ont, 43-45; res chemist, Imp Oil, Ltd, 45-46; asst prof chem, WVa Univ, 47-49; from asst prof to assoc prof, 49-65, dir labs, 64-69, PROF CHEM, MICH STATE UNIV, 65- *Concurrent Pos:* Sr chemist, Oak Ridge Nat Lab, 52, consult, 53-62; vis prof, Univ Newcastle, 68. *Mem:* AAAS; Am Chem Soc. *Res:* Spectrophotometric, spectrofluorometric and electrometric methods of analysis. *Mailing Add:* Dept of Chem Mich State Univ East Lansing MI 48824

TIMON, WILLIAM EDWARD, JR, b Natchitoches, La, Jan 13, 24; m 46, 56; c 6. MATHEMATICAL STATISTICS. *Educ:* Northwestern State Col La, BS, 50; Tulane Univ, MS, 51; Okla State Univ, PhD, 62. *Prof Exp:* Chief comput, Western Geophys Co, 45-46; instr, Tulane Univ, 50-51; mathematician, Esso Stand Oil Co, 51-53; instr math, La State Univ, 53-54; asst prof, Northwestern State Col La, 54-56 & Southwestern La Inst, 56-57; from asst prof to prof, Northwestern State Col La, 57-65, head dept, 62-65; prof, Parsons Col, 65-74, chmn dept, 67-74; PROF MATH, GLASSBORO STATE COL, 74- *Mem:* Math Asn Am; Nat Coun Teachers Math. *Res:* Analysis of the slipped-block design. *Mailing Add:* Dept Math Glassboro State Col Glassboro NJ 08028

TIMONY, PETER EDWARD, b Orange, NJ, Dec 30, 43; m 66; c 4. ORGANIC CHEMISTRY. *Educ:* Fairleigh Dickinson Univ, BA, 67; Univ Notre Dame, PhD(org chem), 72. *Prof Exp:* Res chemistm, 71-75, sr res chemist, 75-76, supvr prod develop, 76-79, asst to dir, 79-81, MGR FUNCTIONAL FLUIDS, STAUFFER CHEM CO, 81- *Mem:* Am Chem Soc; Am Soc Lubrication Engrs. *Res:* Mechanistic organoboron chemistry; synthetic lubricants. *Mailing Add:* Eastern Res Ctr Stauffer Chem Co Dobbs Ferry NY 10522

TIMOTHY, DAVID HARRY, b Pittsburgh, Pa, June 9, 28; m 53; c 3. PLANT GENETICS, PLANT BREEDING. *Educ:* Pa State Univ, BS, 52, MS, 55; Univ Minn, PhD(plant genetics), 56. *Prof Exp:* Asst geneticist, Rockefeller Found, 56-58, assoc geneticist, 58-61; assoc prof, 61-66, PROF CROP SCI, NC STATE UNIV, 66- *Concurrent Pos:* Consult, Latin Am Sci Bd, Nat Acad Sci, 64-65; mem, Adv Comt, Orgn Trop Studies, 68-70; mem, Exec Comt, Southern Pasture & Forage Crop Improvement Conf, 68-72, chmn, 71; mem, Nat Cert Grass Variety Rev Bd, 68-74 & Nat Found Seed Proj Planning Conf, 64-68; mem germplasm task force, Nat Plant Germ Plasm Syst, US Dept Agr, 81 & Germplasm Resources Info Prog Coord Comt, 81-; assoc ed, Crop Sci, 82- *Mem:* Fel AAAS; Asn Trop Biol; Am Soc Agron; Crop Sci Soc Am; Am Inst Biol Sci. *Res:* Origin, race inter-relationships and evolution of maize; corn and forage grass breeding; germ plasm resources; evaluation and improvement methods in the Gramineae; cytotaxonomy; evolution in domesticated grasses and their wild relatives. *Mailing Add:* Dept of Crop Sci NC State Univ Raleigh NC 27650

TIMOTHY, JOHN GETHYN, b Ripley, Eng, Sept 23, 42. SPACE PHYSICS. *Educ:* Univ London, BS, 63, PhD(space physics), 67. *Prof Exp:* Res asst space physics, Mullard Space Sci Lab, Univ Col London, 67-71; physicist, Harvard Col Observ, 71-72, sr physicist, 73-78; RES ASSOC, LAB ATMOSPHERIC & SPACE PHYSICS, UNIV COLO, 78- *Mem:* Optical Soc Am; Am Geophys Union; Int Astron Union; Am Astron Soc. *Res:* Space astronomy; instrumentation for photometric measurements at extreme ultraviolet and soft x-ray wavelengths; photoelectric detector systems, imaging and nonimaging, for use at visible, ultraviolet and soft x-ray wavelengths. *Mailing Add:* Lab for Atmospheric & Space Physics Univ of Colo Boulder CO 80309

TIMOURIAN, HECTOR, b Mex, Aug 24, 33; US citizen; m 58; c 2. DEVELOPMENTAL BIOLOGY. *Educ:* Univ Calif, Los Angeles, BA, 55, PhD(zool), 60. *Prof Exp:* Commonwealth Sci & Indust Res Orgn res fel immunol, Queensland Univ, 60-61; res zoologist, Univ Calif, Los Angeles, 61-62; NIH res fel biol, Calif Inst Technol, 62-64; asst prof biol, Calif State Univ, Northridge, 64-65; BIOLOGIST, LAWRENCE LIVERMORE LAB, UNIV CALIF, 65- *Mem:* AAAS; Sigma Xi; Am Soc Cell Biol; Am Soc Zoologists. *Res:* Sperm morphology, activity and fertilization; environmental toxicology; genetic toxicology of effluents and products from energy technologies. *Mailing Add:* Lawrence Livermore Lab Univ of Calif Livermore CA 94550

TIMOURIAN, JAMES GREGORY, b New York, NY, May 5, 41. MATHEMATICS. *Educ:* Syracuse Univ, PhD(math), 67. *Prof Exp:* Asst prof math, Univ Tenn, 67-69; asst prof, 69-70, assoc prof, 70-77, PROF MATH, UNIV ALTA, 77- *Res:* Differential topology; singularities of maps on manifolds. *Mailing Add:* Dept Math Univ Alta Edmonton AB T6G 2E1 Can

TIMS, EUGENE F(RANCIS), b Madison, Wis, Oct 31, 21; m 49; c 3. ELECTRICAL ENGINEERING, NOISE CONTROL. *Educ:* La State Univ, BS, 43, MS, 49; Wash Univ, DSc(elec eng), 55. *Prof Exp:* From instr to asst prof elec eng, La State Univ, 46-50; lectr, Wash Univ, 51-55; engr sr staff, Appl Phys Lab, Johns Hopkins Univ, 55-58; sect chief engr, Martin Co, Fla, 58-59; staff engr, Fla Aero Div, Honeywell Inc, 59-60, from proj engr to prin staff engr, 60-64; PROF ELEC ENG, LA STATE UNIV, BATON ROUGE, 64- *Concurrent Pos:* Exec vpres, Nocon Corp, 70- *Mem:* AAAS; Inst Elec & Electronics Engrs; Inst Noise Control Eng; Acoust Soc Am; Midwest Noise Coun. *Res:* Noise control engineering; acoustics. *Mailing Add:* 4840 Newcomb Dr Baton Rouge LA 70808

TIMS, GEORGE B(ARTON), JR, b Purcell, Okla, June 23, 18; m 41; c 2. INDUSTRIAL ENGINEERING. *Educ:* Okla State Univ, BS, 47, MS, 49. *Prof Exp:* Asst instr mach shop, Okla State Univ, 39, instr nat defense training prog, 40, asst instr indust eng, 47, from instr to asst prof, 48-51; prof & head dept, Lamar Univ, 51-62; chief party, Western Mich Univ-AID Proj, Tech Col, Nigeria, 62-64; head dept, 64-66, assoc dean eng, 66-73, dir vet affairs, 73-74, dir coop educ, 74-79, PROF INDUST ENG, LAMAR UNIV, 64-, DIR ENG COOP EDUC, 79- *Concurrent Pos:* Agr collabr, Indust Develop Serv, Okla State Univ, 51; with Jefferson Amusement Co, 52 & Tex State Optical Co, 55-60. *Mem:* Am Soc Eng Educ; Am Inst Indust Engrs. *Res:* Management and organization. *Mailing Add:* Col of Eng Lamar Univ Univ Sta Beaumont TX 77710

TIMUSK, JOHN, b Narva, Estonia, Jan 2, 35; Can citizen; m 58; c 1. CIVIL ENGINEERING. *Educ:* Univ Toronto, BASc, 58, MASc, 61; Univ London, PhD(civil eng), 69. *Prof Exp:* Demonstr, 58-60, lectr, 60-63, from asst prof to assoc prof, 65-76, PROF CIVIL ENG, UNIV TORONTO, 76-, ASSOC, SYSTS BLDG CTR, 72- *Mem:* Am Concrete Inst. *Res:* Creep and shrinkage of portland cement concrete; development of materials for thermal insulation; plaster casts for orthopedic applications. *Mailing Add:* Dept of Civil Eng Univ of Toronto Toronto ON M5S 1A1 Can

TIMUSK, THOMAS, b Estonia, June 3, 33; Can citizen; m 57; c 2. PHYSICS. *Educ:* Univ Toronto, BA, 57; Cornell Univ, PhD(physics), 61. *Prof Exp:* Res assoc physics, Cornell Univ, 61-62; asst, Univ Frankfurt, 62-64; res asst prof, Univ Ill, Urbana, 64-65; from asst prof to assoc prof, 65-73, PROF PHYSICS, McMASTER UNIV, 74- *Concurrent Pos:* Sloan fel, 66-68. *Mem:* Am Phys Soc; Can Asn Physicist. *Res:* Solid state physics; localized vibrations; far infrared spectroscopy; excitons and electron-hole drops. *Mailing Add:* Dept of Physics McMaster Univ Hamilton ON L8S 4L8 Can

TINANOFF, NORMAN, b Baltimore, Md, Mar 10, 45; m 67; c 1. PEDIATRIC DENTISTRY. *Educ:* Gettysburg Col, BA, 63; Univ Md, DDS, 71; Univ Iowa, MS, 73. *Prof Exp:* Instr pediat dent, Univ Iowa, 73-74; asst prof, Univ Md, 74-76; ASST PROF PEDIAT DENT, HEALTH CTR, UNIV CONN, 76- *Concurrent Pos:* Fel, Vet Admin Hosp, Iowa City, 73-74; spec proj officer, US Army Inst Dent Res, 74-76; contract prin investr, US Army, 77-80. *Mem:* Int Asn Dent Res; Am Dent Asn; Int Asn Dent Children; Am Acad Pedodont. *Res:* Fluorides; preventive dentistry; bacterial attachment; enamel structure. *Mailing Add:* Dept of Pediat Dent Univ of Conn Health Ctr Farmington CT 06032

TINCHER, WAYNE COLEMAN, b Frankfort, Ky, Jan 15, 35; m 57; c 3. PHYSICAL CHEMISTRY. *Educ:* David Lipscomb Col, BA, 56; Vanderbilt Univ, PhD(chem), 60. *Prof Exp:* Res chemist, Chemstrand Res Ctr, Monsanto Co, 60-65, group leader spectros, 65-71; assoc prof textile chem, 71-77, PROF TEXTILE ENG, A FRENCH TEXTILE SCH, GA INST TECHNOL, 77- *Mem:* AAAS; Am Chem Soc; Am Asn Textile Chemists & Colorists; Sigma Xi. *Res:* Nuclear magnetic resonance spectra and structure of polymers; mechanics of polymer degradation; fiber and fabric flammability; textile process water pollution control. *Mailing Add:* Dept of Textile Eng Ga Inst of Technol Atlanta GA 30332

TINDALL, CHARLES GORDON, JR, b Trenton, NJ, Sept 3, 42; m 64; c 3. FORENSIC SCIENCE. *Educ:* Col Wooster, BA, 64; Ohio State Univ, MS, 67, PhD(org chem), 70. *Prof Exp:* Fel med chem, Nucleic Acid Res Inst, Int Chem & Nuclear Corp, 70-72; TECH SUPVR FORENSIC CHEM, NJ STATE POLICE SOUTH REGIONAL LAB, 72- *Concurrent Pos:* Adj prof, Stockton State Col, 74- & Ocean County Col, 75- *Mem:* Am Chem Soc; Royal Soc Chem; Forensic Sci Soc; Am Acad Forensic Sci. *Res:* Detection of accelerants in arson investigation; characterization of hair; toxicology and detection of drugs and poisons in blood and urine. *Mailing Add:* NJ State Police SRegional Lab Rte 30 PO Box 126 Hammonton NJ 08037

TINDALL, DONALD JAMES, b Columbia, SC, May 16, 44; m 67; c 3. ENDOCRINOLOGY, BIOCHEMISTRY. *Educ:* Univ SC, BS, 66; Clemson Univ, MS, 70; Univ NC, PhD(biochem), 73. *Prof Exp:* Instr, 76-77, ASST PROF CELL BIOL, BAYLOR COL MED, 77- *Concurrent Pos:* NIH fel cell biol, Baylor Col Med, 74-76; consult, Nat Cancer Inst, 76; NIH grant, 76-; NSF reviewer, 77-; consult, Med Res Coun; rev, J Biol Chem, Endocrinol, J Clin Endocrinol Metab, Int J Andrology, J Andrology, Anal Biochem. *Mem:* Endocrine Soc; Am Chem Soc; Am Soc Cell Biol; Tissue Cult Asn; Am Soc Andrology. *Res:* Biochemical mechanism of action of androgens in accessory sex organs of the male. *Mailing Add:* Dept of Cell Biol Baylor Col of Med Houston TX 77030

TINDALL, GEORGE TAYLOR, b Magee, Miss, Mar 13, 28; m 47; c 4. NEUROSURGERY. *Educ:* Univ Miss, AB, 48; Johns Hopkins Univ, MD, 52. *Prof Exp:* Intern gen surg, Johns Hopkins Univ, 52-53; resident neurosurg, Med Ctr, Duke Univ, 55-61, from asst prof to assoc prof, 61-68; chief neurosurg serv, Vet Admin Hosp, 61-68; prof neurosurg & chief div, Univ Tex Med Br Galveston, 68-73; PROF NEUROSURG, SCH MED, EMORY UNIV, 73- *Mem:* Cong Neurol Surgeons; Soc Neurol Surgeons; Soc Univ Neurosurgeons (pres, 65). *Res:* Hypophysectomy and neuroendocrinology; measurement of the cerebral circulation; physiologic changes induced by increases in intracranial pressure, hemorrhage and effect of various pharmacologic agents; cranial aneurysms. *Mailing Add:* Div of Neurosurg Emory Univ Clin Atlanta GA 30322

TINDALL, HOWARD WILSON, JR, b New York, NY, Feb 20, 25; m; c 4. AERONAUTICS, MECHANICAL ENGINEERING. *Prof Exp:* Mech engr, Langley Res Ctr, Nat Adv Comt Aeronaut, Va, 48-61, with Space Task Group, NASA, Tex, 61, dep asst chief mission planning, Manned Spacecraft Ctr, 62-64, dep chief mission planning & anal div, 64-70, chief of Apollo data priority coord, Apollo Spacecraft Prog, 67-70, dep dir flight opers, 70-72, DIR FLIGHT OPERS, MANNED SPACECRAFT CTR, NASA, 72- *Concurrent Pos:* Tech dir, Mass Inst Technol work on Apollo spacecraft guid & navig comput progs. *Honors & Awards:* Except Serv Medals, NASA, 69 & 70, Cert Commendation, Manned Spacecraft Ctr, 70; Norman P Hays Award, Am Inst Navig, 70. *Res:* Space flight mission planning and analysis; network and control center requirements and implementation; recovery support; computer systems used in support of space flight missions. *Mailing Add:* 16427 Brook Forest Dr Houston TX 77059

TINDELL, RALPH S, b Tampa, Fla, Jan 16, 42; div; c 2. DISTRIBUTED SYSTEMS, GRAPH THEORY. *Educ:* Univ SFla, BA, 63; Fla State Univ, MS, 65, PhD(math), 67. *Prof Exp:* Res assoc math, Univ Ga, 66; vis mem & grantee, Inst Advan Study, 66-67; asst prof, Univ Ga, 67-70; assoc prof, 70-78, PROF MATH, STEVENS INST TECHNOL, 78- *Concurrent Pos:* Res assoc, Inst Advan Study, 69-70; vis prof, Univ der Saavlandes, 76. *Mem:* Am Math Soc; Asn Mems Inst Advan Study; Europ Asn Theoret Comput Sci. *Res:* graph theory; theoretical computer science. *Mailing Add:* Dept of Pure & Appl Math Stevens Inst of Technol Hoboken NJ 07030

TINDER, RICHARD F(RANCHERE), b Long Beach, Calif, Dec 17, 30; m 69; c 4. MATERIALS SCIENCE. *Educ:* Univ Calif, Berkeley, BS, 57, MS, 58, PhD(metall), 62. *Prof Exp:* From asst prof to assoc prof metall, 61-70, assoc prof elec eng, 70-73, PROF ELEC ENG, WASH STATE UNIV, 73- *Concurrent Pos:* Vis assoc prof mech eng, Univ Calif, Davis, 72-73. *Res:* Initiation of plastic flow in crystals; mechanism of surface ionization of heated filaments; shock studies of single crystals; peizothermoelectric effects in crystals; tensor properties of solids; direct energy conversion. *Mailing Add:* Dept of Elec Eng Wash State Univ Pullman WA 99163

TING, CHIH-YUAN CHARLES, b Tsingtao, China, Feb 1, 47; m 71; c 2. ANALYTICAL CHEMISTRY, PHYSICAL ORGANIC CHEMISTRY. *Educ:* Fu-Jen Univ, Taiwan, BS, 70; Wilkes Col, MS, 73; Pa State Univ, PhD(anal chem), 78. *Prof Exp:* RES SPECIALIST, MONSANTO AGR PROD CO, 77- *Mem:* Am Chem Soc; Sigma Xi. *Res:* Electrochemistry of biological compounds; chromatographic method development for traces level of herbicide and residues; product quality control of herbicide; organic charge transfer compounds; industrial hygiene; automated analytical instrumentation development for trace level organic compounds determination. *Mailing Add:* Monsanto Agr Prod Co 800 N Lindbergh Blvd St Louis MO 63167

TING, FRANCIS TA-CHUAN, b Tsingtao, China, Apr 26, 34; US citizen; m 66. GEOLOGY. *Educ:* Nat Taiwan Univ, BS, 57; Univ Minn, MS, 62; Pa State Univ, PhD, 67. *Prof Exp:* Fel, Pa State Univ, 67-68; asst prof geol, Macalester Col, 68-69; res assoc coal petrol, Pa State Univ, 69-70; from asst prof to assoc prof geol, Univ NDak, 70-74; ASSOC PROF GEOL, WVA UNIV, 74- *Concurrent Pos:* Fel, Univ Minn, 68-69; NATO sr fel, 73. *Mem:* Sigma Xi; Geol Soc Am; Bot Soc Am; Soc Econ Paleont & Mineral; Geochem Soc. *Res:* Coal petrology and chemistry; paleobotany. *Mailing Add:* Dept of Geol & Geog WVa Univ Morgantown WV 26506

TING, IRWIN PETER, b San Francisco, Calif, Jan 13, 34; m 52; c 1. PLANT PHYSIOLOGY, METABOLISM. *Educ:* Univ Nev, BS, 60, MS, 61; Iowa State Univ, PhD(plant physiol, biochem), 64. *Prof Exp:* NSF fel, 64-65; plant physiologist, 65-66, from asst prof to assoc prof plant physiol & metab, 66-72, PROF BIOL, UNIV CALIF, RIVERSIDE, 72- *Concurrent Pos:* Vis fel, Australian Nat Univ, 72; exchange prof, Univ Paris, 74. *Mem:* AAAS; Bot Soc Am; Am Soc Plant Physiologists. *Res:* Gas transfer between plant surfaces and environment; carbon dioxide metabolism; plant isoenzymes. *Mailing Add:* Dept of Biol Univ of Calif Riverside CA 92502

TING, LU, b China, Apr 18, 25; nat US; c 3. APPLIED MATHEMATICS. *Educ:* Chiao Tung Univ, China, BS, 46; Mass Inst Technol, SM, 48; Harvard Univ, MS, 49; NY Univ, ScD(aero eng), 51. *Prof Exp:* Res assoc aerodyn, NY Univ, 51-52; spec design engr, Foster Wheeler Corp, 52-55; res prof aerodyn, Polytech Inst Brooklyn, 55-64; prof aeronaut & astronaut, 64-68, PROF MATH, NY UNIV, 68- *Concurrent Pos:* Consult, Inst Comput Appln Sci & Eng NASA Langley Res Ctr, 77- *Mem:* Soc Indust & Appl Math; Am Inst Aeronaut & Astronaut; Am Phys Soc; NY Acad Sci. *Res:* Shock deflections; boundary layer theory; supersonic wing-body interference; space mechanics; nonlinear wave propagations; perturbation methods; aeroacoustics. *Mailing Add:* Dept of Math NY Univ Washington Sq New York NY 10012

TING, ROBERT YEN-YING, b Kwei-Yang, China, March 8, 42; US citizen; m 67; c 2. RHEOLOGY, APPLIED MECHANICS. *Educ:* Nat Taiwan Univ, BS, 64; Mass Inst Technol, MS, 67; Univ Calif, San Diego, PhD(eng sci), 71. *Prof Exp:* Res staff, Aerophysics Lab, Mass Inst Technol, 67-68; mech engr surface chem, Chem Div, 71-76, sect head polymer mech, 77-80, HEAD MAT RES, UNDERWATER SOUND REFERENCE DIV, NAVAL RES LAB, 80- *Concurrent Pos:* Assoc prof lectr, George Wash Univ, 75; lectr appl rheology, Kent State Univ, 76-80; translation ed, Chinese Physics, Am Inst Physics, 81-; mem,Comt Composite Technol Transfer, Soc Plastics Indust, 77- *Mem:* Am Chem Soc; Am Inst Chem Engrs; Soc Rheology; Am Res Soc; Sigma Xi. *Res:* Research and management in underwater acoustical materials including piezoelectrics and ferroelectrics, elastomers, plastics, optical fibers, fluids and composites. *Mailing Add:* Naval Res Lab PO Box 8337 Orlando FL 32856

TING, SAMUEL C C, b Ann Arbor, Mich, Jan 27, 36; m 60; c 2. PARTICLE PHYSICS. *Educ:* Univ Mich, BSE(physics) & BSE(math), 59, MS, 60, PhD(physics), 62. *Prof Exp:* Ford Found fel, Europ Coun Nuclear Res, Switz, 63-64; instr physics, Columbia Univ, 64-65, asst prof, 65-67; assoc prof, 67-69, PROF PHYSICS, MASS INST TECHNOL, 69- *Concurrent Pos:* Ground leader, Deutches Elecktronen Synchrotronen, Hamburg, Ger, 66; assoc ed, Nuclear Physics B, 70. *Honors & Awards:* Nobel Prize in Physics, 76; Ernest Orlando Lawrence Award, 76. *Mem:* Nat Acad Sci; Europ Phys Soc; Ital Phys Soc; fel Am Phys Soc; fel AAAS; fel Am Acad Arts & Sci. *Res:* Experimental particle physics; quantum electrodynamics; interactions of photons with matter. *Mailing Add:* Lab for Nuclear Sci Mass Inst of Technol Cambridge MA 02139

TING, SHIH-FAN, b Changteh, China, Sept 27, 17; US citizen; m 47; c 1. CHEMISTRY. *Educ:* Univ Chekiang, BS, 41; Univ Ala, MS, 57, PhD(chem), 60. *Prof Exp:* Asst prof chem, Fisk Univ, 60-65; fel, Duquesne Univ, 65-66; assoc prof, 66-69, PROF CHEM, MILLERSVILLE STATE COL, 69- *Concurrent Pos:* NSF grant, 63-65. *Mem:* Am Chem Soc. *Res:* High-frequency titration; rhenium chemistry; coordination compounds; nuclear magnetic resonance studies of hydrogen bonding. *Mailing Add:* Dept of Chem Millersville State Col Millersville PA 17551

TING, SIK VUNG, b Shanghai, China, Mar 3, 18; nat US; m 46; c 3. HORTICULTURE. *Educ:* Mich State Univ, BS, 41; Ohio State Univ, MS, 43, PhD(hort), 52. *Prof Exp:* Asst, Ohio State Univ, 41-43 & 49-52, Agr Exp Sta, 43-45; assoc prof hort, Nanking Univ, 47-49; asst horticulturist, 52-60, assoc biochemist, 60-68, RES BIOCHEMIST, CITRUS EXP STA, FLA STATE CITRUS COMN & PROF BIOCHEM, Univ Fla, 68- *Mem:* Am Soc Hort Sci; Am Chem Soc; Inst Food Technologists; NY Acad Sci. *Res:* Biochemistry of horticultural plants, especially chemical components of citrus fruit. *Mailing Add:* 700 Experiment Sta Rd Lake Alfred FL 33850

TING, THOMAS C(HI) T(SAI), b Taipei, Formosa, Feb 9, 33; m 62; c 2. APPLIED MATHEMATICS, MECHANICS. *Educ:* Nat Taiwan Univ, BSc, 56; Brown Univ, PhD(appl math), 62. *Prof Exp:* Res asst appl math, Brown Univ, 59-62, res assoc eng, 62-63, asst prof, 63-65; from asst prof to assoc prof appl mech, 65-70, PROF APPL MECH, UNIV ILL, CHICAGO CIRCLE, 70- *Concurrent Pos:* Assoc mem, Ctr Advan Study, Univ Ill, 67-68; vis prof, Stanford Univ, 72-73; assoc ed, J Appl Mech, Am Soc Mech Engrs, 75- *Mem:* Math Asn Am; Am Soc Mech Engrs; Soc Indust & Appl Math; Am Acad Mech; Sigma Xi. *Res:* Continuum mechanics; viscoelasticity and viscoplasticity; wave propagations; numerical analysis; partial differential equations. *Mailing Add:* Dept of Mat Eng Univ of Ill at Chicago Circle Chicago IL 60680

TING, TSUAN WU, b Anking, Anhwei, China, Oct 10, 22; nat US; m 57; c 2. MATHEMATICS. *Educ:* Nat Cent Univ, China, BS, 47; Univ RI, MS, 56; Ind Univ, MS, 59, PhD(math), 60. *Prof Exp:* Technician, China 60th Arsenal, 47-49, assoc engr, 49-53; res asst eng, Univ RI, 54-56; math, Ind Univ, 56-59; sr mathematician, Gen Motors Res Labs, 60-61; asst prof mech, Univ Tex, 61-63; vis mem, Courant Inst Math Sci, NY Univ, 63-64; assoc prof math, NC State Univ, 64-66; PROF MATH, UNIV ILL, URBANA, 66- *Mem:* Soc Indust & Appl Math; Tensor Soc; Am Math Soc; Soc Natural Philos. *Res:* Theory of partial differential equations; mathematical physics; principles of continuum mechanics and differential geometry. *Mailing Add:* Dept of Math Univ of Ill Urbana IL 61801

TING, YU-CHEN, b Honan, China, Oct 3, 20; m 60; c 2. PLANT CYTOLOGY, PLANT GENETICS. *Educ:* Nat Honan Univ, China, BS, 44; Cornell Univ, MSA, 52; La State Univ, PhD(hort genetics), 54. *Prof Exp:* Asst bot, Nat Honan Univ, 44-47; res fel, Harvard Univ, 54-62; from asst prof to assoc prof biol, 62-67, PROF BIOL, BOSTON COL, 67- *Mem:* AAAS; Genetics Soc Am; Am Genetic Asn; Bot Soc Am; Am Soc Hort Sci. *Res:* Cytology and genetics of Ipomoea batatas and related species; flower induction and site of synthesis of pigments in sweet potato plants; cytogenetics of maize and its relatives. *Mailing Add:* Dept of Biol Boston Col Chestnut Hill MA 02167

TINGA, JACOB HINNES, b Wilmington, NC, Mar 9, 20; m 57; c 2. HORTICULTURE, PLANT PHYSIOLOGY. *Educ:* NC State Col, BS, 42; Cornell Univ, MS, 52, PhD, 56. *Prof Exp:* Assoc prof hort, Va Polytech Inst, 55-68; PROF HORT, UNIV GA, 68- *Mem:* Am Soc Hort Sci. *Res:* Effect of environment on growth of horticultural crops; ornamental and greenhouse crops; winter protection; container production; propagation of large cuttings of woody plants; nursery economics. *Mailing Add:* Dept of Hort Univ of Ga Athens GA 30602

TING-BEALL, HIE PING, b Sibu, Malaysia, Dec 15, 40; US citizen; m 70. CELL PHYSIOLOGY. *Educ:* Greensboro Col, BS, 63; Tulane Univ, MS, 65, PhD(physiol), 67. *Prof Exp:* NIH fel biophys, Mich State Univ, 67-69, res assoc biochem, 70-72; NIH trainee phys biochem, Johnson Res Found, Univ Pa, 69-70; res assoc physiol & pharm, 72-74, ASST MED RES PROF PHYSIOL & PHARM & ANAT, DUKE UNIV MED CTR, 75- *Concurrent Pos:* K E Osserman fel, Myasthenia Gravis Found, 73-74; fac res award, Duke Univ Med Ctr, 76, 77. *Mem:* Biophys Soc; Sigma Xi. *Res:* Structure and function of cell membranes; biophysics of bimolecular lipid membranes. *Mailing Add:* Dept of Anat Duke Univ Med Ctr Durham NC 27710

TINGELSTAD, JON BUNDE, b McVille, NDak, Jan 15, 35; m 60; c 3. PEDIATRICS, PEDIATRIC CARDIOLOGY. *Educ:* Univ NDak, BA, 57, BS, 58; Harvard Univ, MD, 60. *Prof Exp:* From asst prof to assoc prof pediat, Med Col Va, 67-76; PROF PEDIAT, SCH MED, ECAROLINA UNIV, 76-, CHMN DEPT, 77- *Concurrent Pos:* Intern pediat, Children's Hosp Med Ctr, Boston, 60-61, jr asst resident, 61-62; chief resident, Med Ctr, Univ Colo-Denver, 62-63; fel pediat cardiol, Children's Hosp, Buffalo, NY, 65-67. *Mem:* Am Acad Pediat; Am Col Cardiol; Am Inst Ultrasound Med; Ambulatory Pediat Asn. *Res:* Environmental contaminants of breast milk; pediatric echocardiography and education. *Mailing Add:* Dept of Pediat ECarolina Univ Sch of Med Greenville NC 27834

TINGEY, DAVID THOMAS, b Salt Lake City, Utah, Jan 30, 41; m 68; c 5. PLANT PHYSIOLOGY, AIR POLLUTION. *Educ:* Univ Utah, BA, 66, MA, 68; NC State Univ, PhD(plant physiol), 72. *Prof Exp:* Plant physiologist, Environ Protection Agency, NC State Univ, 68-73, PLANT PHYSIOLOGIST, ENVIRON PROTECTION AGENCY, NAT ECOL RES LAB, 73- *Concurrent Pos:* Asst prof bot, Ore State Univ, 74-80, assoc prof, 80- *Mem:* Am Soc Plant Physiol; Scand Soc Plant Physiol. *Res:* Studying the effects of atmospheric pollutants on plant physiology. *Mailing Add:* US Environ Protection Agency Corvallis Environ Res Lab Corvallis OR 97330

TINGEY, GARTH LEROY, b Woodruff, Utah, Apr 14, 32; m 53; c 8. NUCLEAR WASTE MANAGEMENT, COAL CHEMISTRY. *Educ:* Brigham Young Univ, BS, 54, MS, 59; Pa State Univ, PhD(phys chem), 63. *Prof Exp:* Sr scientist, Gen Elec Corp, 63-65; sr res scientist, 65-66, unit mgr mat, 66-70, RES ASSOC, PAC NORTHWEST LABS, BATTELLE MEM INST, 70- *Mem:* Am Chem Soc; Sigma Xi. *Res:* Radiation chemical studies of gaseous mixtures; inert gas sensitized radiolysis reactions; chemical kinetics; chemical studies of carbon and graphite; high temperature gas cooled nuclear reactor technology; coal chemistry; nuclear waste management. *Mailing Add:* Pac NW Lab Battelle Mem Inst Box 999 Richland WA 99352

TINGEY, WARD M, b Brigham City, Utah, Apr 9, 44; m 68; c 2. ENTOMOLOGY. *Educ:* Brigham Young Univ, BS, 66, MS, 68; Univ Ariz, PhD(entom), 72. *Prof Exp:* Asst res entomologist, Univ Calif, Davis, 72-74; asst prof entom, 74-80, ASSOC PROF ENTOM, CORNELL UNIV, 80- *Mem:* Entom Soc Am; AAAS; Potato Asn Am. *Res:* Genetic resistance of crop plants to insect pests; behavioral and developmental responses of insects to resistant host plants; host plant growth and development responses to insect injury; pest management. *Mailing Add:* Dept Entom Comstock Hall Cornell Univ Ithaca NY 14853

TINGLE, MARJORIE ANNE, b Far Rockaway, NY, Oct 5, 38. MICROBIOLOGY. *Educ:* Brown Univ, AB, 60; Univ Wis-Madison, MS, 63, PhD(bacteriol), 66. *Prof Exp:* NIH trainee bacteriol, Univ Wis, 62-66; NIH fel, Dept Biol Sci, Purdue Univ, 67-68; Am Cancer Soc fel, Lab Enzymol, Nat Ctr Sci Res, France, 68-70; res assoc, Rosenstiel Ctr, Brandeis Univ, 71-75; HEALTH SCIENTIST ADMINR, DIV RES RESOURCES, NIH, 75- *Mem:* Am Soc Microbiol; AAAS; Genetics Soc Am; NY Acad Sci. *Res:* Microbial physiology; regulation of gene expression; health administration. *Mailing Add:* Div of Res Resources NIH Bldg 31 Rm 5B23 Bethesda MD 20205

TINGLE, WILLIAM HERBERT, b Parnassus, Pa, Aug 31, 17; m 45; c 2. INSTRUMENTATION, SPECTROSCOPY. *Educ:* Univ Pittsburgh, BS, 49. *Prof Exp:* Instr eng physics, Univ Pittsburgh, 49-50; spectroscopist anal chem, 51-62, sect head anal chem, 63-72, SCI ASSOC EQUIP DEVELOP, ALCOA LABS, 73- *Concurrent Pos:* Chmn subcomt, Am Soc Testing & Mat, 62-73; adv, USA Adv Group, Int Stand Orgn Comt 79, 70-79; secretariat, Int Stand Orgn, 70-79. *Mem:* Sigma Xi; Optical Soc Am; Soc Appl Spectros; Am Chem Soc; Am Inst Physics. *Res:* Evaluating principles of measurement and control in chemical and metallurgical processes, atomic emission spectroscopy, plasma excitation, and optical instrumentation. *Mailing Add:* 3104 Leechburg Rd Lower Burrell PA 15067

TINGLEY, ARNOLD JACKSON, b Point de Bute, June 9, 20; m 46; c 2. MATHEMATICS. *Educ:* Mt Alison Univ, BA, 49; Univ Minn, PhD(math), 52. *Prof Exp:* Instr math, Univ Nebr, 52-53; from asst prof to assoc prof, 53-62, head dept, 66-73, secy senate, 75-80, PROF MATH, DALHOUSIE UNIV, 62-, REGISTR, 73-, BD GOV, 80- *Mem:* Can Math Soc. *Res:* Analysis. *Mailing Add:* Dept Math Dalhousie Univ Halifax NS B3H 4H6 Can

TINGSTAD, JAMES EDWARD, pharmacy, see previous edition

TINKER, DAVID OWEN, b Toronto, Ont, Jan 25, 40; m 62; c 4. BIOCHEMISTRY, PHYSICAL CHEMISTRY. *Educ:* Univ Toronto, BSc, 61; Univ Wash, PhD(biochem), 65. *Prof Exp:* Nat Res Coun Can fel, Univ London, 65-66; asst prof, 66-71, ASSOC PROF BIOCHEM, UNIV

TORONTO, 71- *Concurrent Pos:* Assoc ed, Can J Biochem, 74- *Mem:* Am Chem Soc; Can Biochem Soc. *Res:* Structure, occurrence, metabolism and physical chemical properties of complex lipids from biological membranes. *Mailing Add:* Dept Biochem Fac Med Univ Toronto Toronto ON M5S 1A8 Can

TINKER, EDWARD BRIAN, b Yorkton, Sask, Jan 22, 32; m 54; c 2. CHEMICAL ENGINEERING. *Educ:* Univ Sask, BE, 53, MSc, 54, PhD(chem eng), 62. *Prof Exp:* Engr, Shell Oil Co, 54-57; from asst prof to prof chem eng, Univ Regina, 57-72, vprin, 72-74, vpres, 74-81; VPRES ADMIN, UNIV SASK, 81- *Concurrent Pos:* NATO fel, Manchester Col Sci & Technol, Eng, 63-64; consult, Chemcell Ltd, 65-66; mem, Nat Adv Comt Mining & Metall Res, 75-80. *Mem:* Chem Inst Can; Can Soc Chem Eng (pres, 75-76). *Res:* Process control; dynamics and optimization; corrosion. *Mailing Add:* Univ Saskatchewan Saskatoon SK S7N 0W0 Can

TINKER, JAMES PATRICK, b Baltimore, Md, July 6, 43; m 62; c 4. RENAL PHARMACOLOGY, CARBONIC ANHYDRASE. *Educ:* Syracuse Univ, BA, 64; State Univ NY, PhD(pharmacol), 81. *Prof Exp:* Res asst, Sch Med, Johns Hopkins Univ, 61-66; res asst, 66-74, asst, 74-81, INSTR PHARMACOL, UPSTATE MED CTR, STATE UNIV NY, 81- *Concurrent Pos:* Lectr pharmacol, Col Health Related Sci, State Univ NY, 80- *Res:* Elucidation of the role of membrane bound carbonic anhydrase in the transport of bicarbonate and carbon dioxide across epithelia, primarily in the kidney. *Mailing Add:* Dept Pharmacol Upstate Med Ctr Syracuse NY 13210

TINKER, JOHN FRANK, b Wis, Mar 25, 22; m 48. CHEMISTRY, INFORMATION SCIENCE. *Educ:* Univ Va, BS, 43; Harvard Univ, PhD(chem), 51. *Prof Exp:* Instr chem, Harvard Univ, 50-52; INFO SCIENTIST, EASTMAN KODAK CO, 52- *Mem:* Am Chem Soc. *Res:* Chemical information. *Mailing Add:* Eastman Kodak Co Kodak Park B-320 Rochester NY 14650

TINKER, SPENCER WILKIE, b Anamoose, NDak, Jan 29, 09; m 38; c 1. ICHTHYOLOGY. *Educ:* Univ Wash, BS, 31; Univ Hawaii, MS, 34. *Prof Exp:* Instr zool, 33-34, ed, 35-55, from asst prof to prof, 55-72, dir, Waikiki Aquarium, 40-72, EMER RESEARCHER & DIR WAIKIKI AQUARIUM, UNIV HAWAII, 72- *Res:* Indo-Pacific fish and molluscs; whales. *Mailing Add:* 1121 Hunakai St Honolulu HI 96816

TINKHAM, MICHAEL, b Green Lake Co, Wis, Feb 23, 28; m 61; c 2. SUPERCONDUCTIVITY. *Educ:* Ripon Col, AB, 51; Mass Inst Technol, MS, 51, PhD(physics), 54. *Hon Degrees:* ScD, Ripon Col, 76. *Prof Exp:* NSF fel, Clarendon Lab, Oxford Univ, 54-55; res physicist, Univ Calif, Berkeley, 55-57, lectr, 56-57, from asst prof to prof physics, 57-66; chmn dept physics, 75-78, prof physics, 66-80, GORDON MCKAY PROF APPL PHYSICS, HARVARD UNIV, 66-, RUMFORD PROF PHYSICS, 80- *Concurrent Pos:* Guggenheim fel, 63-64; NSF sr fel, Cavendish Lab, Cambridge Univ, 71-72; Humboldt sr scientist, Univ Karlsruhe, 78-79. *Honors & Awards:* Buckley Prize, Am Phys Soc, 74. *Mem:* Nat Acad Sci; fel Am Acad Arts & Sci; fel Am Phys Soc; fel AAAS. *Res:* Superconductivity: energy gap, fluxoid quantization and macroscopic quantum interference, fluctuation effects, Josephson junctions, nonequilibrium effects including charge imbalance and energy imbalance; microwave and far-infrared magnetic resonance. *Mailing Add:* Dept Physics Harvard Univ Cambridge MA 02138

TINKLE, DONALD WARD, vertebrate zoology, evolutionary biology, deceased

TINKLEPAUGH, J(AMES) R(OOT), b Hornell, NY, July 18, 20; m 46; c 2. CERAMIC ENGINEERING. *Educ:* State Univ NY Col Ceramics, Alfred Univ, BS, 43, MS, 50. *Prof Exp:* Asst prof ceramic eng, 46-48, dir, Air Force Lab, 48-59, asst to dir res, 59-64, ASSOC PROF CERAMIC ENG, NY STATE COL CERAMICS, ALFRED UNIV, 59-, DIR TECH SERV, 64-, DIR PLACEMENT, 72- *Concurrent Pos:* Consult, Naval Ord Lab, 58- & Pratt & Whitney Aircraft Div, United Aircraft Corp, 59-65. *Mem:* Am Ceramic Soc; Nat Inst Ceramic Engrs; Am Soc Eng Educ. *Res:* Carbon bonded materials; microstructure of cermets; high temperature techniques; hot pressing; sintering; high temperature materials for aerospace; composite materials. *Mailing Add:* 22 Park St Alfred NY 14802

TINKLER, JACK D(ONALD), b Topeka, Kans, Apr 12, 36; m 60; c 2. CHEMICAL ENGINEERING. *Educ:* Univ Ill, BS, 58; Univ Del, MChE, 61, PhD(chem eng), 63. *Prof Exp:* Res engr, Res & Develop Dept, Sun Oil Co, 63-70, chief eng fundamentals, Corp Res Dept, 70-77; vpres eng, Occidental Res Corp, Occidental Petrol Corp, 77-80; WITH HOOKER CHEM CO, 80- *Mem:* Am Inst Chem Engrs; Am Chem Soc. *Res:* Kinetics; simulation; model building; process design and evaluation; technical economics. *Mailing Add:* Hooker Chem Co MPO Box 8 Niagara Falls NY 14302

TINLINE, ROBERT DAVIES, b Moose Jaw, Sask, Aug 4, 25; m 48; c 5. PLANT PATHOLOGY. *Educ:* Univ Sask, BA, 48; Univ Wis, MS, 52, PhD(plant path), 54. *Prof Exp:* Tech officer I, 48-49, tech officer II, 49-51, agr res officer, 51-67, RES SCIENTIST, AGR CAN, 67- *Mem:* Mycol Soc Am; Am Phytopath Soc; Can Phytopath Soc (pres, 77-78); Agr Inst Can. *Res:* Root and leaf diseases of cereals; variability and genetics of plant pathogenic fungi. *Mailing Add:* Agr Can Res Sta 107 Science Crescent Saskatoon SK 57H 3M5 Can

TINNEY, FRANCIS JOHN, b Brooklyn, NY, July 31, 38; m 74; c 1. MEDICINAL CHEMISTRY. *Educ:* St John's Univ, NY, BS, 59, MS, 61; Univ Md, PhD(aza steroids), 65. *Prof Exp:* Ortho Res Found fel chem, Univ Md, 65-66; assoc res chemist, 66-69, res chemist, 69-70, sr res chemist, Parke-Davis & Co, 70-78; RES ASSOC, WARNER-LAMBERT/PARKE-DAVIS & CO, 78- *Mem:* Am Chem Soc; Am Pharmaceut Asn. *Res:* Organic medicinal chemistry; steroids; heterocyclic steroids; heterocyclics; organic nitrogen containing compounds; peptides; antiallergy compounds. *Mailing Add:* Warner-Lambert/Parke-Davis & Co 2800 Plymouth Rd Ann Arbor MI 48105

TINNIN, ROBERT OWEN, b Santa Barbara, Calif, Sept 6, 43; m 65. PLANT ECOLOGY. *Educ:* Univ Calif, Santa Barbara, BA, 65, PhD(ecol), 69. *Prof Exp:* From asst prof to assoc prof, 69-80, PROF BIOL, PORTLAND STATE UNIV, 80- *Concurrent Pos:* Coordr, Environ Sci & Resources Doctoral Prog, Portland State Univ. *Mem:* Ecol Soc Am. *Res:* Host-parasite interactions and their effect on plant communities; natural systems under study are coniferous forest sites infected by arceuthobium species. *Mailing Add:* Dept Biol Portland State Univ PO Box 751 Portland OR 97207

TINOCO, IGNACIO, JR, b El Paso, Tex, Nov 22, 30; m 51; c 1. PHYSICAL CHEMISTRY. *Educ:* Univ NMex, BS, 51, DSc, 72; Univ Wis, PhD(chem), 54. *Prof Exp:* Res fel chem, Yale Univ, 54-56; from instr to assoc prof, 56-66, PROF CHEM, UNIV CALIF, BERKELEY, 66-, CHMN, 79- *Concurrent Pos:* Guggenheim fel, 64. *Honors & Awards:* Calif Sect Award, Am Chem Soc, 65. *Mem:* Am Chem Soc; Am Phys Soc; Biophys Soc; Am Soc Biol Chemists. *Res:* Biophysical chemistry. *Mailing Add:* Dept of Chem Univ of Calif Berkeley CA 94720

TINSLEY, BEATRICE MURIEL, theoretical astrophysics, cosmology, deceased

TINSLEY, BRIAN ALFRED, b Wellington, NZ, Apr 23, 37; m 61; c 2. SPACE PHYSICS. *Educ:* Univ Canterbury, BSc, 58, MSc, 61, PhD(physics), 63. *Prof Exp:* Res assoc atmospheric & space sci, 63-65, res scientist, 65-67, from asst prof to assoc prof, 67-76, PROF PHYSICS, UNIV TEX, DALLAS, 76- *Concurrent Pos:* Mem, Sci Comn Solar Physics, 76- & US Natural Comn Inst Union Geodesy & Geophysics. *Mem:* Am Geophys Union. *Res:* Optical observations of airglow and low latitude aurorae; design of optical instruments for measurement of airglow, and astronomical emissions; theoretical studies of atmospheres of earth and planets. *Mailing Add:* Dept of Physics MS F022 Univ of Tex PO Box 688 Richardson TX 75080

TINSLEY, IAN JAMES, b Sydney, Australia, Sept 23, 29; m 55; c 2. BIOCHEMISTRY. *Educ:* Univ Sydney, BSc, 50; Ore State Univ, MS, 55, PhD(food sci), 58. *Prof Exp:* Res officer, Commonwealth Sci & Indust Res Orgn, Australia, 50-53; from asst prof to assoc prof, 57-70, PROF BIOCHEM, ORE STATE UNIV, 70- *Honors & Awards:* Florasynth Award, Inst Food Technologists, 55. *Mem:* Am Inst Nutrit; Am Oil Chem Soc; Am Chem Soc. *Res:* Lipid metabolism; essential fatty acid nutrition; biochemical effects of pesticide ingestion; interactions of pesticides with lipids. *Mailing Add:* Dept of Agr Chem Ore State Univ Corvallis OR 97331

TINSLEY, RICHARD STERLING, b Richmond, Va, Mar 7, 31; m 52; c 5. CHEMICAL ENGINEERING. *Educ:* Va Polytech Inst, BS, 52, MS, 53, PhD(chem eng), 55. *Prof Exp:* Res chem engr, Nitrogen Div, Allied Chem Corp, 55-58, sr chem engr, 58-61, supvry chem engr, 61-64, mgr chem eng, 64-67, start-up chief, Grismar Complex, 67-68, mgr prod, 68-69, PROJ MGR, FIBERS DIV, ALLIED CHEM CORP, 69- *Mem:* Am Chem Soc. *Res:* Chemical engineering design and development; fiber engineering. *Mailing Add:* 2009 Surreywood Ct Richmond VA 23235

TINSLEY, SAMUEL WEAVER, b Hopkinsville, Ky, July 15, 23; m 45; c 3. ORGANIC CHEMISTRY. *Educ:* Western Ky State Col, BS, 44; Northwestern Univ, PhD(org chem), 50. *Prof Exp:* Asst prof chem, Tex Tech Col, 49-50; res chemist, 50-60, asst dir org res, 60-64, assoc dir res & develop, 64-67, mgr new chem, 67-71, mgr corp res, 71-74, dir corp res, 74-77, DIR CORP TECHNOL, UNION CARBIDE CORP, 77- *Mem:* Am Chem Soc. *Res:* Aromatic synthesis; peracids; epoxides. *Mailing Add:* Union Carbide Corp Sect F4 Old Ridgebury Rd Danbury CT 06817

TINSMAN, JAMES HERBERT, JR, b Philadelphia, Pa, Apr 22, 30; m 56; c 4. PHYSICAL ANTHROPOLOGY. *Educ:* Univ Pa, AB, 56, AM, 60; Univ Colo, MA, 66, PhD(anthrop), 71. *Prof Exp:* Instr philos & econ, 59-60, from asst to assoc prof, 60-71, chmn, Dept Soc Sci, 74-77, PROF ANTHROP, KUTZTOWN STATE COL, 71- *Concurrent Pos:* Lectr philos, Muhlenberg Col, 60-65 & anthrop, Univ Colo, 69-71; co-ed, Newsletter Pa Anthropologists; NSF fel, 64, 65-66 & 68-71. *Mem:* Fel Am Anthrop Asn; fel Soc Appl Anthrop; fel Am Soc Human Genetics; Am Asn Phys Anthrop; Soc Am Archaeol. *Res:* Contemporary human variation, anthropometric, anthroscopic and serological, as relates to human genetics, population structure and, ultimately, human evolution. *Mailing Add:* Dept of Anthrop Kutztown State Col Kutztown PA 19530

TINT, HOWARD, b Philadelphia, Pa, Jan 22, 17; m 41; c 2. BIOCHEMISTRY, BIOLOGICALS. *Educ:* Univ Pa, AB, 37, PhD(mycol, plant path), 43. *Prof Exp:* Leader scouting crews, Bur Entom & Plant Quarantine, USDA, Washington, DC, 39-40, biol tech aide, Bur Plant Indust, 41, physiologist, Bur Agr & Indust Chem, 43-45; biochemist, Wyeth, Inc, 45-50, sr res biochemist, 50-56, supvr biologics lab, Wyeth Labs, 56-60, dir, Prod Develop Div, 60-63, DIR, BIOL & CHEM DEVELOP DIV, WYETH LABS, 63- *Concurrent Pos:* Microbiologist, Off Sci Res & Develop, Johnson Found, Univ Pa, 45. *Mem:* Am Chem Soc; Sigma Xi; NY Acad Sci. *Res:* Microbiology; physiology; virology; tissue culture; cancer immunology; chemical development and pilot-plant; fine-chemicals production. *Mailing Add:* Wyeth Labs Box 8299 Philadelphia PA 19101

TINTI, DINO S, b San Bernardino, Calif, Feb 20, 41; m 62; c 3. PHYSICAL CHEMISTRY. *Educ:* Univ Calif, Riverside, BA, 62; Calif Inst Technol, PhD(chem), 68. *Prof Exp:* Res chemist, Univ Calif, Los Angeles, 67-70; from asst prof to assoc prof, 70-81, PROF CHEM, UNIV CALIF, DAVIS, 81- *Concurrent Pos:* Sloan fel, 74-78. *Mem:* Am Phys Soc. *Res:* Electronic and magnetic resonance spectroscopy of excited electronic states. *Mailing Add:* Dept of Chem Univ of Calif Davis CA 95616

TINUS, RICHARD WILLARD, b Orange, NJ, Mar 26, 36; m 58; c 2. PLANT PHYSIOLOGY. *Educ:* Wesleyan Univ, BA, 58; Duke Univ, MF, 60; Univ Calif, Berkeley, PhD(plant physiol), 65. *Prof Exp:* Plant physiologist, Agr Res Serv, 65-68, PRIN PHYSIOLOGIST & PROJ LEADER, US

FOREST SERV, USDA, 68- *Mem:* Am Soc Plant Physiologists; Soc Cryobiol; Soc Am Foresters. *Res:* Development of greenhouse container systems for tree seedling production; vegetative propagation of pine; cold and drought resistance of trees. *Mailing Add:* US Forest Serv First & Brander St Bottineau ND 58318

TINUS, W(ILLIAM) C, electrical engineering, deceased

TIO, CESARIO O, b Cebu, Philippines, Aug, 30, 32; m 62; c 2. ORGANIC SYNTHESIS, PHARMACOKINETICS. *Educ:* Univ Santo Tomas, Philippines, BS, 56; Georgetown Univ, Wash, MS, 61. *Prof Exp:* Res asst, Georgetown Univ Hosp, 61-62; res chemist II, 65-67, res chemist III, 67-78, UNIT SUPVR, WYETH LABS, INC, DIV AM HOME PROD, 78- *Res:* Drug disposition and metabolism; methods development for drug analysis; radiotracer synthesis; isolation and characterization of drug metabolites; synthesis of metabolites of drugs. *Mailing Add:* Wyeth Labs Inc PO Box 8299 Philadelphia PA 19101

TIPEI, NICOLAE, b Calarasi, Romania, Apr 6, 13; m 41; c 1. FLUID MECHANICS, AERODYNAMICS. *Educ:* Polytech Inst Bucharest, Romania, MD, 36; Romanian Acad, Dr Eng(fluid mech), 68. *Prof Exp:* From instr to emer prof aerodyn & flight mech, Polytech Inst Bucharest, 36-71; RES FEL ENGR ENG MECH, GEN MOTORS RES LABS, GEN MOTORS CORP, 72- *Concurrent Pos:* Chief engr locomotive overhaul, Romanian Railways, 37-38; chief engr airplane aerodyn, Romanian Airlines, 38-39; head dept tribology, Inst Appl Mech, Romanian Acad, 49-67. *Honors & Awards:* Mayo D Hersey Award, Am Soc Mech Engrs, 80. *Mem:* WGer Soc Appl Math & Mech; Am Inst Aeronaut & Astronaut; Am Soc Mech Engrs. *Res:* General mechanics; lubrication; tribology; flight mechanics. *Mailing Add:* Gen Motors Res Labs 12 Mile & Mound Rd Warren MI 48090

TIPLER, PAUL A, b Antigo, Wis, Apr 12, 33; m 58; c 2. NUCLEAR PHYSICS. *Educ:* Purdue Univ, BS, 55; Univ Ill, PhD(physics), 62. *Prof Exp:* Asst prof physics, Wesleyan Univ, 61-62; from asst prof to assoc prof, 62-77, PROF PHYSICS, OAKLAND UNIV, 77- *Mem:* Am Phys Soc; Am Asn Physics Teachers. *Res:* Low energy nuclear physics. *Mailing Add:* Dept of Physics Oakland Univ Rochester MI 48063

TIPPENS, DORR E(UGENE) F(ELT), b Grand Rapids, Mich, Dec 28, 23; m 43; c 3. CHEMICAL ENGINEERING. *Educ:* Purdue Univ, BS, 48. *Prof Exp:* Engr in training, Oper Dept, Am Sugar Co, 49-50, asst supt refining dept, Baltimore Refinery, 50-53, refining supt, 53-56, asst to refining mgr, 56-58, process design engr, NY, 58-59, dept head new food prod develop, Res & Develop Div, 59-64, dir process develop, 64-68, sr chem engr, 68-76, PROJ MGR, AMSTAR CORP, 76- *Mem:* Am Chem Soc; Sugar Indust Tech; Am Inst Chem Engrs. *Res:* New process development in sugar refining and new food product development, directing and administrating. *Mailing Add:* Amstar Corp 1251 Ave of the Americas New York NY 10020

TIPPER, DONALD JOHN, b Birmingham, Eng, July 21, 35; m 65; c 3. MICROBIOLOGY, MOLECULAR BIOLOGY. *Educ:* Univ Birmingham, BSc, 56, PhD(chem), 59. *Prof Exp:* Res assoc immunochem, Dept Surg Res, St Luke's Hosp, 59-60; chemist, Guinness's Brewery, Dublin, Ireland, 60-62; res asst pharmacol, Wash Univ, 62-64; res asst, Univ Wis-Madison, 64-65, from asst prof to assoc prof, 65-71; chmn dept, 71-80, PROF MICROBIOL & MOLECULAR GENETICS, MED SCH, UNIV MASS, 71- *Concurrent Pos:* USPHS career develop award, 68-71. *Mem:* Am Soc Microbiol; Brit Soc Gen Microbiol; Am Soc Biol Chemists. *Res:* Structure and biosynthesis of bacterial cell walls; mode of action of penicillins; biosynthesis of bacillus spore cortex, coats and storage proteins; yeast dsRNA-coded killer system. *Mailing Add:* Dept of Microbiol Univ of Mass Med Sch Worcester MA 01605

TIPPER, RONALD CHARLES, b Sacramento, Calif, July 17, 42; m 64; c 2. BIOLOGICAL OCEANOGRAPHY. *Educ:* Ore State Univ, BS, 64, PhD(biol oceanog), 68. *Prof Exp:* Antisubmarine warfare officer, USS Coontz DLG-9, San Diego, Calif, 68-70; res plans officer oceanog res, US Naval Oceanog Off, 70-71; sci officer environ qual div, Off Oceanographer of Navy, 71-72, aide & exec asst oceanog res & develop, 72-74, dir oceanic biol prog, Off Naval Res, 74-76 & Naval Ocean Res & Develop Activity, 76-77, cmndg officer, Oceanog Unit One, 77-78, dir, Oceanic Biol Prog, Off Naval Res, 78-81, DIR OCEAN SURV PROG, US NAVAL OCEANOG OFF, 81- *Mem:* Sigma Xi. *Res:* Oceanic biology; marine biodeterioration; distribution and abundance of Micronekton and Zooplankton; benthic ecology; geophysics; cartography; navigation. *Mailing Add:* Dir Ocean Surv Prog US Naval Oceanographic Off NSTL Station MS 39522

TIPPETT, JAMES T, b Oxford, NC, May 11, 31; m 65; c 2. COMPUTER SCIENCE, ELECTRONIC ENGINEERING. *Educ:* NC State Col, BSEE, 54, EE, 55. *Prof Exp:* ELECTRONIC ENGR, NAT SECURITY AGENCY, 55- *Mem:* AAAS; Inst Elec & Electronics Engrs; Asn Comput Mach. *Res:* Ultra high speed computer circuits; software techniques; computer languages; networks of computers; computer security; software engineering; telecommunications. *Mailing Add:* 5709 Cromwell Dr Bethesda MD 20016

TIPPIN, ROBERT BRUCE, extractive metallurgy, see previous edition

TIPPING, RICHARD H, b Abington, Pa, Aug 31, 39. MOLECULAR PHYSICS. *Educ:* Pa State Univ, BSc, 63, MSc, 66, PhD(physics), 69. *Prof Exp:* Asst prof, 69-74, assoc prof, Mem Univ Nfld, 74-77; assoc prof, 77-80, PROF PHYSICS, UNIV NEBR, OMAHA, 80- *Mem:* Am Phys Soc; Can Asn Physicists. *Res:* Molecular spectral line shapes; intensities and spectroscopic constants of diatomic molecules. *Mailing Add:* Dept of Physics Univ Nebr at Omaha Omaha NE 68182

TIPPINS, HARRY H, JR, solid state physics, optical physics, see previous edition

TIPPLES, KEITH H, b Cambridge, Eng, Feb 4, 36; m 62; c 3. CEREAL CHEMISTRY. *Educ:* Univ Birmingham, BSc, 59, PhD(appl biochem), 62. *Prof Exp:* Nat Res Coun Can res fel, 63-64, res scientist, 64-79, DIR, GRAIN RES LAB, CAN GRAIN COMN, 79- *Mem:* Am Asn Cereal Chem. *Res:* Basic and applied research on the quality of cereal grains and oilseeds aimed at understanding the chemistry and technology of end-use quality and development of improved methods for quality assessment. *Mailing Add:* Grain Res Lab Can Grain Comn 1404-303 Main St Winnipeg MB R3C 3G8 Can

TIPPO, OSWALD, b Milo, Maine, Nov 27, 11; m 34; c 2. BOTANY. *Educ:* Univ Mass, BS, 32; Harvard Univ, AM, 33, PhD(bot), 37. *Hon Degrees:* DSc, Univ Mass, 54. *Prof Exp:* Asst biol, Radcliffe Col, 35-37; instr bot, Univ Ill, 37-39, assoc, 39-41, from asst prof to prof, 41-55, actg head dept, 47-48, chmn, 48-55, dean grad col, 53-55; Eaton prof & chmn dept, dir Marsh Bot Garden & dir bot labs, Yale Univ, 55-60; provost, Univ Colo, 60-63; exec dean arts & sci, NY Univ, 63-64; provost, 64-70, chancellor, 70-71, commonwealth prof bot & higher educ, 71-76, PROF BOT, UNIV MASS, AMHERST, 76- *Concurrent Pos:* Assoc biologist, Wood Sect, Testing Lab, US Navy Yard, Philadelphia, 43-44, biologist, 44-45; ed in chief, Am J Bot, 51-53; trustee, Biol Abstr, 57-63, pres, 63-64. *Mem:* AAAS (vpres, 58); Bot Soc Am (vpres, 54, pres, 55); fel Am Acad Arts & Sci. *Res:* Plant anatomy and phylogeny; phylogeny of angiosperms. *Mailing Add:* Dept of Bot Univ of Mass Amherst MA 01003

TIPSWORD, RAY FENTON, b Beecher City, Ill, Sept 9, 31; m 52; c 2. PHYSICS. *Educ:* Eastern Ill Univ, BSEd, 53; Southern Ill Univ, MS, 57; Univ Ala, PhD(physics), 62. *Prof Exp:* Instr physics, Mo Sch Mines, 57-59; fel, Univ Ala, 62-63; asst prof, 63-68, assoc prof, 68-81, PROF PHYSICS, VA POLYTECH INST & STATE UNIV, 81- *Res:* Nuclear magnetic resonance and low temperature physics. *Mailing Add:* 11 East Ridge Dr Blacksburg VA 24060

TIPTON, ANN BAUGH, b Freeport, Tex, Sept 4, 38; m 63. PHYSICAL CHEMISTRY, FUEL SCIENCE. *Educ:* Southwestern Univ, Tex, BS, 60; Univ Tex, Austin, MA, 63, PhD(phys chem), 66. *Prof Exp:* Asst prof chem, Southwestern Univ, Tex, 64-67; Welch fel, Univ Tex, Austin, 66-69; tech specialist, Lockheed Propulsion Co, 69-75; rs res chemist, 75-78, Fuels Desulfuriation group leader, 78-80, sr res scientist, Geothermal Energy Res, 80-81, SR RES SCIENTIST PHOSPATE RES, OCCIDENTAL RES CORP, 81- *Honors & Awards:* Citation Merit Chem, Southwestern Univ, Tex, 72. *Mem:* AAAS; Am Chem Soc; Am Phys Soc; Soc Appl Spectros; Am Inst Chem Engrs. *Res:* Microwave spectroscopy and molecular structure; aging studies of solid propellants and composites; instrument automation, computer programming; synthetic fuels; coal conversion, desulfurization, combustion kinetics and liquefaction; geothermal hydrogen sulfide abatement; phosphates research. *Mailing Add:* Occidental Res Corp PO Box 19601 Irvine CA 92713

TIPTON, C(LYDE) R(AYMOND), JR, b Cincinnati, Ohio, Nov 13, 21; m 42; c 2. METALLURGICAL ENGINEERING. *Educ:* Univ Ky, BS, 46, MS, 47. *Prof Exp:* Asst, Univ Ky, 46-47; res engr, Battelle Mem Inst, 47-49; phys metallurgist, Los Alamos Sci Lab, 49-51; from asst div chief to sr tech adv, Physics Dept, Battelle Mem Inst, 51-62; dir res, Basic, Inc, 62-64; from staff mgr to asst dir, Pac Northwest Labs, 64-69, coordr corp commun, 69-73, vpres commun, 73-75, pres & trustee, Battelle Commun Co, 75-78, asst pres, 78-80, VPRES & CORP DIR COMMUN & PUB AFFAIRS, BATTELLE MEM INST, 80- *Concurrent Pos:* Consult, Atomic Energy Comn, 58-61; secy, US Deleg 2nd UN Int Conf Peaceful Uses Atomic Energy, Geneva, Switz, 58; sr fel, Otterbein Col, 78. *Mem:* AAAS; Am Soc Metals; Nat Soc Prof Engrs; Sigma Xi. *Res:* Reactor materials; technical and scientific information handling; industrial research. *Mailing Add:* Battelle Mem Inst 505 King Ave Columbus OH 43201

TIPTON, CARL LEE, b Collins, Iowa, July 26, 31; m 57; c 3. BIOCHEMISTRY. *Educ:* Univ Nebr, BS, 54, MS, 57; Univ Ill, PhD, 61. *Prof Exp:* Assoc & instr, 61-62, from asst to assoc prof, 62-78, PROF BIOCHEM, IOWA STATE UNIV, 78- *Concurrent Pos:* NIH sr fel, Univ Calif, Davis, 69-70. *Mem:* AAAS; Am Chem Soc; Phytochem Soc NAm; Am Soc Plant Physiologists; Am Soc Biol Chemists. *Res:* Biochemistry of membrane processes in plants. *Mailing Add:* Dept of Biochem & Biophys Iowa State Univ Ames IA 50010

TIPTON, CHARLES M, b Evanston, Ill, Nov 29, 27; m 53; c 4. PHYSIOLOGY. *Educ:* Springfield Col, BS, 52; Univ Ill, MS, 53, PhD(physiol), 62. *Prof Exp:* High sch teacher, Ill, 53-55; teaching asst health educ, Univ Ill, 55-57, instr, 57-58, asst physiol, 58-61; asst prof, Springfield Col, 61-63; from asst prof to assoc prof, 63-73, PROF PHYSIOL, UNIV IOWA, 73- *Concurrent Pos:* Chmn study sect appl physiol & bioeng, NIH, 73-76; ed, Med Sci Sports Exercises, 79-; mem med adv comn, Am Inst Biol Sci, 80- *Mem:* Am Physiol Soc; fel Am Heart Asn; Am Col Sports Med (pres, 74-75). *Res:* Exercise physiology, including bradycardia of training, mechanisms of cardiac hypertrophy, ligamentous strength, diabetes, endocrines and training; exercise testing; hypertension; pharmacological differences and training. *Mailing Add:* Exercise Physiol Lab Univ Iowa Iowa City IA 52240

TIPTON, DONALD LEE, mechanical engineering, see previous edition

TIPTON, GEORGE MURTHA, analytical chemistry, deceased

TIPTON, HENRY C, b Oakville, Tenn, Mar 4, 15; m 43; c 4. NUTRITION, BIOCHEMISTRY. *Educ:* Miss State Univ, BS, 39, MS, 63, PhD(animal nutrit), 65. *Prof Exp:* Asst prof biol sci, Univ SFla, 65-80; RETIRED. *Res:* Animal nutrition; relative biological value of the isomers and analogue of methionine in poultry diets. *Mailing Add:* Dept of Biol Sci Univ of S Fla Tampa FL 33620

TIPTON, ISABEL HANSON, physics, deceased

TIPTON, KENNETH WARREN, b Belleville, Ill, Nov 14, 32; m 57; c 2. PLANT GENETICS, AGRONOMY. *Educ:* La State Univ, BS, 55, MS, 59; Miss State Univ, PhD(agron, genetics), 69. *Prof Exp:* Teaching asst, 58-59, from asst prof to prof agron, Agr Exp Sta, La State Univ, Baton Rouge, 59-75; prof & supt, Red River Valley Agr Exp Sta, Bossier City, 75-79; ASSOC DIR, LA AGR EXP STA, 79- *Mem:* Am Soc Agron; Crop Sci Soc Am; Coun Agr Sci & Technol. *Res:* Varietal evaluation and adaptation of grain sorghum; varietal evaluation, breeding and genetics of small grains. *Mailing Add:* La Agr Exp Sta PO Drawer E Univ Sta Baton Rouge LA 70893

TIPTON, MERLIN J, b Watertown, SDak, Mar 23, 30; m 54; c 3. GEOLOGY. *Educ:* Univ SDak, BA, 55, MA, 58. *Prof Exp:* Geologist, 56-62, asst state geologist, 62-68, ASSOC STATE GEOLOGIST, SDAK GEOL SURV, 68-, LECTR EARTH SCI, UNIV S DAK, 76- *Mem:* Fel Geol Soc Am. *Res:* Pleistocene geology and hydrogeology. *Mailing Add:* Dept of Earth Sci & Physics Univ SDak Vermillion SD 57069

TIPTON, SAMUEL RIDLEY, physiology, deceased

TIPTON, VERNON JOHN, b Springville, Utah, July 12, 20; m 43; c 5. PARASITOLOGY, MEDICAL ENTOMOLOGY. *Educ:* Brigham Young Univ, BS, 48, MS, 49; Univ Calif, PhD, 59. *Prof Exp:* Entomologist, Walter Reed Army Inst Res, Med Serv Corps, US Army, 49-52, Calif, 52-54, commanding officer, 37th Prev Med Co, Korea, 54-55, chief entom sect, 5th Army Med Lab, St Louis, Mo, 56-59, chief environ health br, Off Surgeon, Ft Amador, CZ, 57-62, chief entom br dept prev med, Med Field Serv Sch, Ft Sam Houston, Tex, 62-66, chief dept entom, 406th Med Lab, 66-68; assoc prof zool, 68-71, PROF ZOOL, BRIGHAM YOUNG UNIV, 71-, DIR CTR HEALTH ENVIRON STUDIES, 75- *Res:* Siphonaptera; mesostigmatid mites; systematics; bionomics. *Mailing Add:* Ctr Health & Environ Studies 785 WIDB Brigham Young Univ Provo UT 84601

TIRMAN, ALVIN, b Brooklyn, NY, Nov 27, 31. PHYSICAL CHEMISTRY, MATHEMATICS. *Educ:* Hofstra Col, AB, 53; Bowling Green State Univ, MA, 65; Carnegie-Mellon Univ, PhD(chem), 70. *Prof Exp:* Asst prof math, 69-75, ASSOC PROF MATH, KINGSPORT UNIV CTR, E TENN STATE UNIV, 75- *Mem:* Math Asn Am; Am Chem Soc. *Res:* Electrode kinetics. *Mailing Add:* Dept of Math Kingsport Univ Ctr E Tenn State Univ Kingsport TN 37662

TIRRELL, MATTHEW VINCENT, b Phillipsburg, NJ, Sept 5, 50; m 76. POLYMER SCIENCE, CHEMICAL ENGINEERING. *Educ:* Northwestern Univ, BSChE, 73; Univ Mass, PhD(polymer sci), 77. *Prof Exp:* Asst prof, 77-81, ASSOC PROF CHEM ENG, UNIV MINN-MINNEAPOLIS, 81- *Concurrent Pos:* Vis prof, Univ Guadalajara. *Mem:* Am Chem Soc; Am Inst Chem Engrs; Soc Rheology; Am Phys Soc. *Res:* Engineering applications of chemistry and physics of macromolecules; polymerization reactor design; flow-induced conformational and structural changes; rheology; biopolymeric materials. *Mailing Add:* Dept Chem Eng & Mat Sci Univ Minn Minneapolis MN 55455

TISCHENDORF, JOHN ALLEN, b Lincoln City, Ind, July 22, 29; m 59; c 3. APPLIED STATISTICS, DATA ANALYSIS. *Educ:* Evansville Col, AB, 50; Purdue Univ, MS, 52, PhD(math statist), 55. *Prof Exp:* Mem tech staff, 57-59, supvr reliability & statist studies, Allentown, 59-64, supvr statist appln, 64-78, SUPVR ENG DATA ANAL, BELL TEL LABS, HOLMDEL, 78- *Concurrent Pos:* Vis lectr, Rutgers Univ, 66 & 67 & Stanford Univ, 68-69. *Mem:* Am Statist Asn; Am Soc Qual Control. *Res:* Statistics applied to engineering and management problems; data analysis; statistical consulting; mathematical modeling; reliability; sampling; order statistics; market analysis; data base management. *Mailing Add:* 53 Laurelwood Dr Colt's Neck NJ 07722

TISCHER, FREDERICK JOSEPH, b Plan, Austria, Mar 14, 13; US citizen; m 42. ELECTROPHYSICS, COMMUNICATIONS. *Educ:* Prague Tech Univ, MSc, 36, PhD(elec eng), 38. *Prof Exp:* Fel physics, Univ Berlin, 38; res assoc, Telefunken, Berlin, 38-42; owner, Tischer Phys Lab, Austria, 42-47; lectr microwaves, Royal Inst Technol, Sweden, 47-54; br chief guid lab, Ord Missile Lab, Ala, 54-56; assoc prof electromagnetics, Ohio State Univ, 56-62; asst dir res inst, Univ Ala, Huntsville, 62-64; prof electromagnetics, 64-78, EMER PROF, NC STATE UNIV, 78- *Concurrent Pos:* Vis lectr, Helsinki Inst Technol, 52; consult, Chance Vought Aircraft Co, Tex, 59-61 & Harry Diamond Labs, DC, 60-74; consult, NASA Hq, 62-63, expert consult, NASA-Goddard Space Flight Ctr, Md, 62; fel plasma physics, Princeton Univ, 62; consult, 76-; vis distinguished prof, Naval Postgrad Sch, 78-79; vis prof, Univ Bern, Switz, 80 & Swiss Fed Inst Technol, Zurich, 81. *Mem:* Fel Inst Elec & Electronics Engrs; Optical Soc Am; Am Phys Soc; Sigma Xi. *Res:* Microwaves, waveguides, plasma physics, space communications; holography; millimeter waves; satellite communications. *Mailing Add:* Dept of Elec Eng NC State Univ Raleigh NC 27650

TISCHER, RAGNAR P(ASCAL), b Berlin, Ger, Apr 30, 22; m 61; c 2. PHYSICAL CHEMISTRY, METALLURGY. *Educ:* Univ Göttingen, diplom phys, 53; Stuttgart Tech Univ, Dr rer nat(phys chem), 57. *Prof Exp:* Res assoc electrochem, Dept Chem, Univ Ill, 57-59; asst metall, Gebr Boehler A G, Edelstahlwerk Düsseldorf, Ger, 59-60; res assoc electrochem, Inst Phys Chem, Bonn, 61-63; sr res chemist, Electrochem Dept, Res Labs, Gen Motors Corp, 63-65; prin res scientist assoc, 65-66, res staff, 66-69, STAFF SCIENTIST, CHEM SCI LAB, FORD MOTOR CO, 69- *Mem:* Electrochem Soc; fel Am Inst Chem. *Res:* Electrode kinetics in aqueous solutions and in fused salts; fuel cells; corrosion of binary alloys; battery electrodes and metal deposition in organic solvents. *Mailing Add:* 1449 Suffield Ave Birmingham MI 48009

TISCHER, THOMAS NORMAN, b Milwaukee, Wis, Apr 21, 34. PHOTOGRAPHIC CHEMISTRY. *Educ:* Marquette Univ, BS, 56, MS, 58; Univ Wis, PhD(anal chem), 61. *Prof Exp:* RES ASSOC, EASTMAN KODAK CO, 61- *Mem:* Am Chem Soc; Soc Photog Scientists & Engrs. *Res:* Photographic film and process chemistry and research; analytical separations. *Mailing Add:* 115 Heritage Circle Rochester NY 14615

TISCHFIELD, JAY ARNOLD, b New York, NY, June 15, 46; m 78; c 2. SOMATIC CELL GENETICS. *Educ:* Brooklyn Col, BS, 67; Yale Univ, MPhil, 69, PhD(biol), 73. *Prof Exp:* Asst prof biol, genetics & pediat, Case Western Reserve Univ, 72-78; ASSOC PROF ANAT, CELL & MOLECULAR BIOL & PEDIAT, MED COL GA, 78- *Concurrent Pos:* Fel, Univ Calif, San Francisco, 72-73; prin investr, US Pub Health grant, 73- & NSF grant, 82- *Mem:* Genetics Soc Am; Tissue Culture Asn; Am Soc Cell Biol; Am Soc Microbiol; NY Acad Sci. *Res:* Mammalian somatic cell genetics, especially the effects of mutations on all levels of gene expression. *Mailing Add:* Dept Anat Med Col Ga Augusta GA 30912

TISCHIO, JOHN PATRICK, b Newark, NJ, Mar 17, 42; m 66; c 1. BIOCHEMISTRY. *Educ:* Fairleigh Dickinson Univ, BS, 65; Univ Rochester, PhD(biochem), 71. *Prof Exp:* asst prof biochem, Philadelphia Col Pharm & Sci, 70-77; SCIENTIST, BIOCHEM RES DIV ORTHO PHARM CORP, 77- *Concurrent Pos:* Lectr, Wagner Free Inst Sci, 71-77. *Mem:* AAAS; Am Chem Soc; Sigma Xi. *Res:* Biotransformation and disposition of drugs; methods development for drugs in biological fluids; radio immune assay technology. *Mailing Add:* Ortho Pharm Corp 43rd St & Woodland Ave Raritan NJ 19104

TISCHLER, ALLAN NEAL, b Philadelphia, Pa, Mar 12, 49; m 73. ORGANIC CHEMISTRY, BIOCHEMISTRY. *Educ:* Temple Univ, BA, 70; Univ Calif, Berkeley, PhD(chem), 74. *Prof Exp:* Asst prof chem, Univ Wis-Parkside, 74-76; asst prof chem, Univ Wis-Milwaukee, 76-80; WITH MERCK, SHARP & DOHME RES LAB, 80- *Mem:* AAAS; Am Chem Soc. *Res:* Synthetic organic chemistry; medicinal chemistry; enzymology; affinity chromatography. *Mailing Add:* Merck Sharp & Dohme Res Lab Rahway NJ 07065

TISCHLER, HERBERT, b Detroit, Mich, Apr 28, 24; m 54; c 2. INVERTEBRATE PALEONTOLOGY. *Educ:* Wayne State Univ, BS, 50; Univ Calif, Berkeley, MA, 55; Univ Mich, PhD(geol), 61. *Prof Exp:* Instr geol, Wayne State Univ, 56-58; assoc prof earth sci, Northern Ill Univ, 58-65; PROF GEOL & CHMN DEPT, UNIV NH, 65- *Concurrent Pos:* NSF sci fac fel, Columbia Univ, 64-65. *Mem:* Fel Geol Soc Am; Paleont Soc; Am Asn Petrol Geol; Soc Econ Paleont & Mineral; Nat Asn Geol Teachers. *Res:* Paleoecology of marine invertebrates; ecology of benthic foraminifera; carbonate petrology; stratigraphy. *Mailing Add:* Dept of Earth Sci James Hall Univ of NH Durham NH 03824

TISDALE, GLENN E(VAN), b Madison, Wis, July 4, 24; m 60; c 2. ELECTRICAL ENGINEERING. *Educ:* Yale Univ, BE, 44, MEng, 47, PhD(elec eng), 49. *Prof Exp:* Jr engr, Raytheon Mfg Co, 49; engr, Servo Corp Am, NY, 50 & Perkin-Elmer Corp, 51-52; sr res engr, Electro-Mech Res, Inc, 53-57, mgr systs eng dept, 57-63; pres, Sea Technol Corp, 63-64; gen mgr sea technol dept, 65, MGR INFO TECHNOL AEROSPACE DIV, WESTINGHOUSE ELEC CORP, 66- *Concurrent Pos:* Consult, Spencer-Kennedy Labs, 49-52. *Mem:* Inst Elec & Electronics Engrs. *Res:* Recognition logic; signal processing; data transmission systems; design of equipment for aerospace and underseas missions. *Mailing Add:* Westinghouse Defense & Elec Syst Ctr Box 746 Baltimore MD 21203

TISE, FRANK P, b Washington, DC, Dec 4, 51; m 81. ORGANIC PHOTOCHEMISTRY. *Educ:* Univ Md, BS, 73; Univ NC, PhD(org chem), 80. *Prof Exp:* RES CHEMIST, RES CTR, HERCULES, INC, 81- *Mem:* Am Chem Soc. *Res:* Integrated circuit photoresists. *Mailing Add:* Hercules Res Ctr Wilmington DE 19899

TISHKOFF, GARSON HAROLD, b Rochester, NY, Aug 8, 23; m 59. MEDICINE, HEMATOLOGY. *Educ:* Univ Rochester, BS, 44, PhD(pharmacol), 51, MD, 53. *Prof Exp:* AEC assoc, Univ Rochester, 46-52; instr med, Med Sch, Tufts Univ, 56-57 & Harvard Med Sch, 57-60; from asst prof to assoc prof, Sch Med, Univ Calif, Los Angeles, 60-71; PROF MED, MICH STATE UNIV & DIR, Great Lakes REGIONAL BLOOD PROG, AM RED CROSS, 71- *Concurrent Pos:* Nat Acad Sci-Nat Res Coun fel, New Eng Ctr Hosp, Tufts Univ, 55-56; assoc, Beth Israel Hosp, Boston, 57-60. *Mem:* AAAS; Am Soc Hemat; Int Soc Hemat; Int Soc Thrombosis & Haemostasis; Int Soc Blood Transfusion. *Res:* Internal medicine; hemolytic anemia; blood coagulation; blood transfusion. *Mailing Add:* 1800 E Grand River Ave Lansing MI 48912

TISHLER, MAX, b Boston, Mass, Oct 30, 06; m 34; c 2. ORGANIC CHEMISTRY. *Educ:* Tufts Col, BS, 28; Harvard Univ, AM, 33, PhD(org chem), 34. *Hon Degrees:* DSc, Tufts Col, 56, Univ Strathclyde, 69, Rider Col, 70, Fairfield Univ, 72, Upsala Col, 72, Bucknell Univ, 62, Philadelphia Col Pharm, 66 & Wesleyan Univ, 81; DEng, Stevens Inst Technol, 66 . *Prof Exp:* Asst, Tufts Col, 28; res assoc, Harvard Univ, 34-36, instr chem, 36-37; res chemist, Merck & Co, Inc, 37-41, sect head in chg process develop, 41-44, dir develop res, 44-53, process res & develop div, 53-54, vpres & exec dir sci activities, 54-56, pres, Merck Sharp & Dohme Res Labs, NJ, 57-70, mem bd dirs, Merck & Co, Inc, 62-70, sr vpres res & develop, 69-70; prof chem, 70-74, EMER PROF CHEM, WESLEYAN UNIV, 74-, UNIV PROF SCI, 72- *Concurrent Pos:* Estab Max Tishler lectr, Harvard & Max Tishler scholar, Tufts Univ, 51; ed, Org Syntheses, 60-61; life trustee, Tufts Univ & Union Jr Col; assoc trustee sci, Univ Pa, 62-66; Rennebohn lectr, Univ Wis, 63; Du Pont lectr, Dartmouth Col, 69; Welch Found lectr, Univ Tex, 69; Cecil C Brown lectr, Stevens Inst Technol, 71; Kauffman mem lectr, Ohio State Univ, 67; sci bd gov, Weizmann Inst Sci; mem, Coun Anal & Proj, Am Cancer Soc, 73-76; mem, Bd Sci Adv, Sloan Kettering Inst, 74-81. *Honors & Awards:* Indust Res Inst Medal, 61; Swedish Royal Acad Eng Sci Award, 64; Soc Chem Indust Medal, 63; Chem Pioneer Award, Am Inst Chemists, 68; Priestley Medal, Am Chem Soc, 70; Gold Medal, Am Inst Chemists, 77. *Mem:* Nat Acad Sci; Am Chem Soc (pres, 72); hon mem Am Pharm Asn; hon mem Acad Pharm Sci; hon fel Royal Soc Chem. *Res:* Development of processes; synthesis or isolation of pharmacologically active compounds; synthesis of vitamins, drugs, alkaloids and amino acids; isolation alkaloids; antibiotics; steroid synthesis. *Mailing Add:* Dept of Chem Wesleyan Univ Middletown CT 06457

TISHLER, PETER VERVEER, b Boston, Mass, July 18, 37; m 60; c 2. MEDICAL GENETICS. *Educ:* Harvard Univ, AB, 59; Yale Univ, MD, 63. *Prof Exp:* Staff assoc, Nat Inst Arthritis & Metab Dis, 66-68; house officer internal med II & IV, Harvard Med Serv, 63-66, res fel med, Thorndike Mem Lab & Channing Lab, 68-69, staff mem med & genetics, Channing Lab, Boston City Hosp & Harvard Med Sch, 69-77 & Peter Bent Hosp & Harvard Med Sch, 77-80; ASSOC CHIEF STAFF EDUC, VET ADMIN MED CTR, BROCKTON, MASS, 80- *Concurrent Pos:* Asst physician, Dept Pediat, Boston City Hosp, 69-, assoc vis physician, Dept Med, 71-77; assoc, Ctr Human Genetics, Harvard Med Sch, 71, asst prof med, 72; assoc med, Peter Bent Brigham Hosp, 76. *Mem:* AAAS; NY Acad Sci; Am Soc Human Genetics; Am Fedn Clin Res. *Res:* Genetics of chronic disease; biochemistry of diseases of porphyrin metabolism; gene mapping. *Mailing Add:* Vet Admin Med Ctr 940 Belmont St Brockton MA 02401

TISI, GENNARO MICHAEL, b New York, NY, Sept 26, 35; m 57; c 3. PULMONARY DISEASES, INTERNAL MEDICINE. *Educ:* Fordham Univ, BS, 56; Georgetown Univ, MD, 60. *Prof Exp:* From intern to resident med, Georgetown Univ Hosp, 60-65, pulmonary fel, 65-67; res fel, Cardiovasc Res Inst, Univ Calif, San Francisco, 67-68; asst prof, 68-73, ASSOC PROF MED, SCH MED, UNIV CALIF, SAN DIEGO, 73- *Concurrent Pos:* NIH fel, 65-68, spec fel, 68; pulmonary consult, US Naval Hosp, San Diego, 68- & US Naval Hosp, Camp Pendleton, 72-; chief, Pulmonary Sect, San Diego Vet Hosp, 72- *Mem:* Am Col Physicians; Am Col Chest Physicians; Am Physiol Soc; Am Fedn Clin Res. *Res:* Pulmonary mechanics. *Mailing Add:* San Diego Vet Admin Hosp La Jolla CA 92037

TISINGER, RICHARD MARTIN, JR, b Harrisonburg, Va, Oct 26, 29; m 55; c 3. DATA PROCESSING. *Educ:* Reed Col, BA, 51; Johns Hopkins Univ, PhD(nuclear physics), 63. *Prof Exp:* Staff mem weapons div, Los Alamos Sci Lab, Univ Calif, 52-56; jr instr, Johns Hopkins Univ, 57-61, res asst, 61-63; staff mem weapons div, 63-74, staff mem laser & appl photochem div, 74-77, STAFF MEM Q DIV, LOS ALAMOS NAT LAB, UNIV CALIF, 77- *Res:* Nuclear safeguards systems studies. *Mailing Add:* PO Box 1663 Univ Calif Los Alamos Nat Lab Los Alamos NM 87544

TISONE, GARY C, b Boulder, Colo, Dec 24, 37; m 59; c 4. ATMOSPHERIC PHYSICS. *Educ:* Univ Colo, BS, 59, PhD(physics), 67. *Prof Exp:* Physicist, Vallecitos Atomic Lab, Gen Elec Co, 59-61; physicist, Nat Bur Standards, 61-62; res assoc atomic physics, Univ Colo, 66-67; STAFF MEM, SANDIA CORP, 67- *Mem:* Am Phys Soc. *Res:* Electron-negative ion collisions; photodetachment of negative ions; gaseous electronics; physics of the upper atmosphere; high power gas laser research. *Mailing Add:* Sandia Labs Western Elec Co Albuquerque NM 87115

TISONE, THOMAS C, materials science, see previous edition

TISSERAT, BRENT HOWARD, b Oakland, Calif, Oct 2, 51; m 69; c 1. AGRICULTURAL SCIENCES. *Educ:* San Bernardino Jr Valley Col, AA, 71; Calif State Polytech Univ, BS, 73; Univ Calif, Berkeley, PhD(bot), 76. *Prof Exp:* Cabot fel Res, Cabot Found, Harvard Univ, 76-77; AGR RES GENETICIST, USDA, 77- *Mem:* Am Bot Soc; Crop Sci Soc Am; Palm Soc. *Res:* Palm and fruit tree crop morphogenesis; studying trees through tissue culture, protoplast, cryobiology and gene-enzyme techniques. *Mailing Add:* Fruit & Veg Chem Lab 263 S Chester Ave Pasadena CA 91106

TISUE, GEORGE THOMAS, b Carroll, Iowa, Nov 25, 40; c 2. ENVIRONMENTAL CHEMISTRY, ANALYTICAL CHEMISTRY. *Educ:* Beloit Col, BS, 61; Yale Univ, PhD(org chem), 66. *Prof Exp:* Res chemist tech ctr, Celanese Chem Co, Tex, 66 & 68; NIH fel plant biochem, Univ Freiburg, 66-67; from asst prof to assoc prof chem, Beloit Col, 68-74; chemist, Argonne Nat Lab, 74-81; RES ASSOC, CTR GREAT LAKES STUDIES, UNIV WIS-MILWAUKEE, 81- *Concurrent Pos:* Vis prof, Dept Chem, Univ Wis-Milwaukee, 81. *Mem:* AAAS; Am Chem Soc. *Res:* Biogeochemical cycling and effects of heavy metal pollutants in the Great Lakes. *Mailing Add:* 731 W 18th St Chicago IL 60616

TISZA, LASZLO, b Budapest, Hungary, July 7, 07; nat US; m 73. PHYSICS. *Educ:* Univ Budapest, PhD(physics), 32. *Prof Exp:* Res assoc, Phys Tech Inst, Kharkov, 35-37; res assoc, Col France, 37-40; instr physics, 41-45, from instr to prof physics, 41-73, EMER PROF PHYSICS, MASS INST TECHNOL, 73- *Concurrent Pos:* Guggenheim fel, 62-63; vis prof, Univ Paris, 62-63. *Mem:* Fel Am Phys Soc; fel Am Acad Arts & Sci. *Res:* Theoretical physics; statistical thermodynamics; foundations of quantum mechanics. *Mailing Add:* Dept of Physics Mass Inst of Technol Cambridge MA 02139

TITCHENER, EDWARD BRADFORD, b Cambridge, Mass, July 15, 27; m 52; c 2. BIOCHEMISTRY. *Educ:* Univ Mich, BS, 51; Ohio State Univ, MS, 54, PhD(physiol chem), 56. *Prof Exp:* Asst biochem, Ohio State Univ, 53-56; from asst prof to assoc prof, 58-74, PROF BIOCHEM, UNIV ILL COL MED, 74- *Concurrent Pos:* NIH trainee, Enzyme Inst, Univ Wis, 56-58. *Mem:* AAAS; Am Chem Soc; Am Soc Biol Chemists; NY Acad Sci. *Res:* Transfer RNA. *Mailing Add:* Dept of Biochem Univ of Ill Col of Med Chicago IL 60212

TITCHENER, JAMES LAMPTON, b Binghamton, NY, Apr 9, 22; m; c 4. PSYCHIATRY, PSYCHOANALYSIS. *Educ:* Princeton Univ, AB, 46; Duke Univ, MD, 49; Chicago Psychoanal Inst, cert psychoanal, 64. *Prof Exp:* Intern psychiat, Walter Reed Gen Hosp, 49-50; resident, Cincinnati Gen Hosp, 50-54; from instr to assoc prof, 54-68, PROF PSYCHIAT, MED CTR, UNIV CINCINNATI, 68-; MEM FAC PSYCHOANAL, CINCINNATI PSYCHOANAL INST, 74- *Concurrent Pos:* Career investr, USPHS, 55-60 & NIMH, 57-62; training & supv analyst, Cincinnati Psychoanal Inst, 74-; attend physician, Cincinnati Gen Hosp. *Mem:* Fel AAAS; fel Am Psychiat Asn; Am Psychosom Soc; Am Psychoanal Asn. *Res:* Study of the effects of physical trauma on personality functioning; family and marital dynamics and marital therapy; psychological trauma resulting from disasters such as the Buffalo Creek disaster and Beverly Hills fire. *Mailing Add:* Dept of Psychiat Univ of Cincinnati Col of Med Cincinnati OH 45267

TITELBAUM, SYDNEY, b Luck, Russia, Apr 24, 13; US citizen; m 39; c 1. ANIMAL PHYSIOLOGY, EVOLUTIONARY BIOLOGY. *Educ:* Univ Chicago, PhB, 33, PhD(physiol), 38, JD, 42. *Prof Exp:* Teaching asst physiol, Univ Chicago, 34-38; chief physiologist, Chicago Biol Res Lab, 39-59; lectr forensic med, Sch Med, Loyola Univ Chicago, 46-64; prof biol, City Cols Chicago, 60-77; PROF BIOL, FROMM INST, UNIV SAN FRANCISCO, 78- *Concurrent Pos:* Ed, Asn Off Racing Chem Jour, 56-58; consult-examr, NCent Asn Cols & Sec Schs, 66-78; dean, Bogan Col, 67-68. *Honors & Awards:* Award, Asn Off Racing Chem, 60. *Mem:* AAAS; Am Inst Biol Sci; Asn Off Racing Chem (pres, 57). *Res:* Physiology of sleep; history of science. *Mailing Add:* 3628 Fillmore St San Francisco CA 94123

TITELER, MILT, b Lakewood, NJ, Nov 8, 49. PHARMACOLOGY, BIOCHEMISTRY. *Educ:* State Univ NY, Buffalo, BS, 72, MSc, 76; Univ Toronto, PhD(pharmacol), 78. *Prof Exp:* Res asst biochem, Univ Buffalo, 73-76; from res asst to res assoc pharmacol, 76-79, ASST PROF PHARMACOL, UNIV TORONTO, 79- *Mem:* Soc Neurosci. *Res:* Neuronal receptor pharmacology; biological psychiatry; neurochemistry. *Mailing Add:* Dept Pharmacol Univ Toronto Toronto ON M5S 1A8 Can

TITKEMEYER, CHARLES WILLIAM, b Rising Sun, Ind, Jan 14, 19; m 47; c 2. ANATOMY, BACTERIOLOGY. *Educ:* Ohio State Univ, DVM, 49; Mich State Univ, MS, 51, PhD, 56. *Prof Exp:* From instr to prof anat, Mich State Univ, 49-69; PROF VET ANAT & HEAD DEPT, SCH VET MED, LA STATE UNIV, BATON ROUGE, 69- *Concurrent Pos:* Consult vet, Univ Ky Contract Team, Bogor, Indonesia, 60-62; prof & head dept vet sci, Univ Nigeria, 66-68. *Mailing Add:* 1148 Aurora Pl Baton Rouge LA 70806

TITLEBAUM, EDWARD LAWRENCE, b Boston, Mass, Mar 23, 37; m 59; c 1. ELECTRICAL ENGINEERING. *Educ:* Northeastern Univ, BSEE, 59; Cornell Univ, MS, 63, PhD(elec eng), 65. *Prof Exp:* Engr, Avco Res & Adv Develop Labs, 59-61; asst prof, 64-68, ASSOC PROF ELEC ENG, UNIV ROCHESTER, 68- *Concurrent Pos:* Consult, Gen Dynamics Corp, 64-65; vis assoc prof, Johns Hopkins Univ, 70-71. *Mem:* AAAS; Inst Elec & Electronics Engrs. *Res:* Communication systems and signals; radar; sonar; echo-location systems in nature, acoustics and hearing; bat and dolphin sonar systems. *Mailing Add:* Hopeman Eng Bldg Univ of Rochester Rochester NY 14627

TITLEY, SPENCER ROWE, b Denver, Colo, Sept 27, 28; m 51; c 3. GEOLOGY, GEOCHEMISTRY. *Educ:* Colo Sch Mines, GeolE, 51; Univ Ariz, PhD(geol), 58. *Prof Exp:* Jr geologist, NJ Zinc Co, 51, staff geologist, 53-55, res geologist, 58-60; instr geol, 57-58, from asst prof to assoc prof, 60-67, PROF GEOL, UNIV ARIZ, 67- *Mem:* Soc Econ Geol; Geol Soc Am; Soc Explor Geophys; Am Inst Mining, Metall & Petrol Eng; Am Geophys Union. *Res:* Geology of the porphyry copper deposits; mineralogy of copper-lead-zinc deposits; geology and mineral deposits of Pacific Basin. *Mailing Add:* Dept of Geosci Univ of Ariz Tucson AZ 85721

TITMAN, PAUL WILSON, b Lowell, NC, Aug 30, 20. BOTANY. *Educ:* Belmont Abbey Col, BS, 39; Univ NC, AB, 41, MA, 49; Harvard Univ, PhD(biol), 52. *Prof Exp:* Instr bot, Univ NC, 48-49; asst prof, Univ Louisville, 52-53; instr, Univ Conn, 53-55; assoc prof, 55-61, PROF BOT, CHICAGO STATE UNIV, 61- *Concurrent Pos:* Res resident, Harvard Univ, 54; chmn coun faculties, Ill State Bd Cols & Univs; consult. *Mem:* Bot Soc Am; fel Royal Hort Soc. *Res:* Morphogenesis; systematic anatomy; microbiology; paleontology. *Mailing Add:* Dept of Biol Chicago State Univ Chicago IL 60628

TITONE, LUKE VICTOR, b Marsala, Italy, Oct 25, 11; nat US; m 39; c 4. PHYSICS. *Educ:* NY Univ, MS, 40. *Prof Exp:* Instr physics, NY Univ, 40-51; PROF PHYSICS, MANHATTAN COL, 51- *Mem:* Am Phys Soc. *Res:* Atomic and nuclear physics. *Mailing Add:* 676 N Broadway Yonkers NY 10701

TITTEL, FRANK K(LAUS), b Berlin, WGer, Nov 14, 33; US citizen; m 65; c 2. PHYSICS, ELECTRICAL ENGINEERING. *Educ:* Oxford Univ, BA, 55, PhD(physics), 59. *Prof Exp:* Physicist, Gen Elec Co, 59-65; assoc prof physics, Am Univ Cairo, 65-67; assoc prof elec eng, 67-72, PROF ELEC ENG, RICE UNIV, 72- *Mem:* Am Phys Soc; Optical Soc Am; sr mem Inst Elec & Electronics Engrs. *Res:* Precision measurements of atomic constants; quantum electronics; laser development; laser spectroscopy; holography. *Mailing Add:* Dept Elec Eng Rice Univ PO Box 1892 Houston TX 77001

TITTERTON, PAUL JAMES, b Copiague, NY, Feb 23, 40; m 63; c 3. ELECTROOPTICS. *Educ:* Boston Col, BS, 61; Brandeis Univ, MS, 63, PhD(physics), 67. *Prof Exp:* SR ENG SPECIALIST, GTE SYLVANIA INC, 66- *Mem:* Optical Soc Am; Am Meteorol Soc. *Res:* Atmospheric effects on laser beams; precise optical ranging techniques; optimum optical communication methodology; sensitive optical receiver research. *Mailing Add:* GTE Sylvania Inc PO Box 188 Mountain View CA 94042

TITTIGER, FRANZ, meat science, microbiology, see previous edition

TITTLE, CHARLES WILLIAM, b Bonham, Tex, Nov 11, 17; m 43; c 7. PHYSICS. *Educ:* NTex State Univ, BS, 39, MS, 40; Mass Inst Technol, PhD(physics), 48. *Prof Exp:* Instr physics, NTex State Univ, 40-41; instr pre-radar, Southern Methodist Univ, 43; asst prof physics, NTex State Univ, 43-44; instr elec commun radar sch, Mass Inst Technol, 44-45; from assoc prof to prof physics, NTex State Univ, 48-51; head nuclear physics sect, Gulf Res & Develop Co, 51-55; dir western div, Tracerlab, Inc, 55-56, assoc tech dir, 56-57; prof nuclear eng, 57-63, chmn dept mech eng, 61-65, chmn dept physics, 65-75, PROF PHYSICS & MECH ENG, SOUTHERN METHODIST UNIV, 63- *Concurrent Pos:* Consult nuclear shielding proj, Mass Inst Technol, 48-51; consult, S W Marshall, Jr, 47, Gulf Res & Develop Co, 50, Atlantic Refining Co, 57-58, Western Co, 58-77, Well Reconnaissance, Inc, 62-64, Ling-Temco-Vought, 63-64, Mobil Oil Corp, 63-74 & 81-, Nuclear-Chicago Corp, 64-66, Core Labs, 65-81 & Gearhart Industs, 81- *Mem:* Am Phys Soc; Am Asn Physics Teachers; Am Nuclear Soc. *Res:* Neutron physics; nuclear well logging; applications of radioisotopes; boundary value problems; fundamental concepts of physics. *Mailing Add:* Dept Physics Southern Methodist Univ Dallas TX 75275

TITTMAN, JAY, nuclear science, see previous edition

TITTMANN, BERNHARD R, b Moshi, Tanzania, Sept 15, 35; US citizen; m 66; c 5. SOLID STATE PHYSICS, ACOUSTICS. *Educ:* George Washington Univ, BS, 57; Univ Calif, Los Angeles, PhD(solid state physics), 65. *Prof Exp:* Mem tech staff res & develop aerospace & systs group, Hughes Aircraft Co, 57-61; res asst solid state physics, Univ Calif, Los Angeles, 61-65, asst prof & fel, 65-66; mem tech staff, 66-79, MGR EARTH & PLANETARY SCI GROUP, SCI CTR, ROCKWELL INT, 79- *Concurrent Pos:* Vis prof physics, Univ Paris VII, Paris, France, 77-78; res grant, Ecole Normale Superior, Paris, France, 82. *Mem:* Am Phys Soc; Am Geophys Union; Inst Elec & Electronics Engrs; Sigma Xi. *Res:* Non-destructive evaluation and acoustic surface waves; acoustic properties of lunar and terrestrial rock; ultrasonic absorption of type I and type II superconductors; dislocation-electron interaction; superconductivity in high pressure polymorphs of semiconductors; ferromagnetic modes in epitaxial single crystal yttrium iron garnet; microwave conformal array antennas. *Mailing Add:* 166 Siesta Ave Thousand Oaks CA 91360

TITUS, CHARLES JOSEPH, b Mt Clemens, Mich, June 23, 23; m 49; c 2. MATHEMATICS. *Educ:* Univ Detroit, BSc, 44; Brown Univ, ScM, 45; Syracuse Univ, PhD(math), 48. *Prof Exp:* Instr math, Syracuse Univ, 48; from instr to assoc prof, 49-62, PROF MATH, UNIV MICH, ANN ARBOR, 63- *Concurrent Pos:* Vis prof, Univ Calif, 58-59; mem, Inst Defense Anal, 60-61. *Mem:* Am Math Soc. *Res:* Complex variables and generalizations; transformation semigroups; qualitative theory of differential equations; communications; geometric analysis; differential topology. *Mailing Add:* Dept of Math Univ of Mich Ann Arbor MI 48109

TITUS, CHARLES O, b Augusta, Maine, Jan 26, 27; m 54; c 7. OPHTHALMOLOGY. *Educ:* Univ Ottawa, BA & BSc, 51, MD, 55. *Prof Exp:* Chief ophthal, Travis AFB, 59-63 & US Air Force Hosp Weisbaden, 63-66; pvt pract, Chevy Chase, Md, 66-74; DIR MED AFFAIRS, SOFLENS DIV, BAUSCH & LOMB, 74-, DIR CLIN RES, 78- *Mem:* Am Acad Ophthal; Am Intraocular Implant Soc; Am Col Surgeons; Pan Am Med Asn; Asn Advan Med Instrumentation. *Mailing Add:* 19 Foxbourne Dr Penfield NY 14526

TITUS, DONALD DEAN, b Worland, Wyo, Mar 22, 44; m 66; c 2. INORGANIC CHEMISTRY. *Educ:* Univ Wyo, BS, 66; Calif Inst Technol, PhD(chem), 71. *Prof Exp:* Asst prof, 71-77, ASSOC PROF CHEM, TEMPLE UNIV, 77- *Concurrent Pos:* Am Chem Soc Petrol Res Fund grant, 71-74. *Mem:* Am Chem Soc; Am Crystallog Asn. *Res:* Transition-metal complexes, non-rigidity in hydrides, the trans-influence and selenium complexes; x-ray crystal structures. *Mailing Add:* Dept of Chem Temple Univ Philadelphia PA 19122

TITUS, DUDLEY SEYMOUR, b Ithaca, NY, Mar 18, 29; m 54. FOOD TECHNOLOGY. *Educ:* Cornell Univ, BS, 52; State Col Wash, MS, 54; Univ Ill, PhD(food tech), 57. *Prof Exp:* Asst food technol, State Col Wash, 52-54; food technologist, Merck & Co, Inc, 57-67; head food technol sect, Mallinckrodt Chem Works, 67-72, res & develop scientist, 72, mkt res specialist, Mallinckrodt, Inc, 72-77, DIR PLANNING, FOOD, FLAVOR & FRAGRANCE GROUP, MALLINCKRODT, INC, 77- *Mem:* Am Asn Cereal Chem; Int Nutrit Anemia Consultative Group; Inst Food Technol. *Res:* Food microbiology and preservation; human nutrition; cereal products canned and frozen foods; dairy products; food additives. *Mailing Add:* Mallinckrodt Inc PO Box 5840 St Louis MO 63134

TITUS, ELWOOD OWEN, b Rochester, NY, Sept 20, 19; m 51; c 2. ORGANIC CHEMISTRY. *Educ:* Williams Col, BA, 41; Columbia Univ, PhD(chem), 47. *Prof Exp:* Asst antimalarials, Div War Res, Columbia Univ, 43-46; res assoc antibiotics & metab prod, Squibb Inst Med Res, 46-50; chemist, Chem Pharmacol Lab, Nat Heart & Lung Inst, 50-77; DIR DIV DRUG BIOL, BUR DRUGS, FOOD & DRUG ADMIN, 77- *Concurrent Pos:* Mem, Nat Res Coun, 66-74. *Mem:* Am Chem Soc; Am Soc Biol Chem; Am Soc Pharmacol & Exp Therapeut; NY Acad Sci; Biophys Soc. *Res:* Organic synthesis; biochemistry; metabolism of biologically active compounds; application of counter-current distribution to metabolic studies on 4-amino-quinoline antimalarials; mechanism of action of steroids and catecholamines; lipid metabolism; biochemistry of cell membranes. *Mailing Add:* Div Drug Biol Food & Drug Admin 200 C St SW Washington DC 20204

TITUS, HAROLD, b Detroit, Mich, Jan 10, 30; m 55; c 3. SYSTEMS DESIGN, CONTROL ENGINEERING. *Educ:* Univ Kans, BS, 52; Stanford Univ, MS, 57, PhD(eng mech), 62. *Prof Exp:* PROF ELEC ENG, US NAVAL POSTGRAD SCH, 62- *Concurrent Pos:* Consult, US Naval Ord Test Sta, 65-, Stanford Res Inst & US Naval Air Develop Ctr, 66- *Mem:* Inst Elec & Electronics Engrs; Sigma Xi. *Res:* Optimum filtering, identification and control applications to naval weapons problems. *Mailing Add:* Dept Eng US Naval Postgrad Sch Monterey CA 93940

TITUS, JACK L, b South Bend, Ind, Dec 7, 26; m 49; c 5. PATHOLOGY. *Educ:* Univ Notre Dame, BS, 48; Wash Univ, MD, 52; Univ Minn, PhD(path), 62. *Prof Exp:* Physician, Rensselaer, Ind, 53-57; assoc prof path, Mayo Grad Sch Med, Univ Minn, 61-72, prof, Mayo Clin, 71-72; PROF PATH & CHMN DEPT, BAYLOR COL MED, 72- *Concurrent Pos:* Fel path, Mayo Grad Sch Med, Univ Minn, 57-61; chief path serv, Methodist Hosp, 72-; pathologist-in-chief, Harris County Hosp Dist, 72- *Honors & Awards:* Billings Gold Medal, AMA, 68, Hoektoen Gold Medal, 69. *Mem:* AMA; Am Asn Pathologists; Am Soc Clin Path; Int Acad Path; Col Am Pathologists. *Res:* Cardiac conduction system; cardiac anomalies; valvular heart disease; ischemic heart disease; atherosclerosis. *Mailing Add:* Dept Path Baylor Col Med Houston TX 77030

TITUS, JOHN ELLIOTT, b Iowa City, Iowa, July 24, 49; m 73; c 1. PLANT ECOLOGY. *Educ:* Oberlin Col, BA, 71; Univ Wis, MA, 73, PhD(bot), 77. *Prof Exp:* ASST PROF BIOL, STATE UNIV NY BINGHAMTON, 77- *Concurrent Pos:* Prin investr, NSF, 78-82, Environ Protection Agency, 81-83. *Mem:* Ecol Soc Am; Am Soc Limnol & Oceanog; AAAS; Am Inst Biol Sci; Sigma Xi. *Res:* Comparative physiological ecology of submersed macrophytes and sphagium mosses; importance of physico-chemical environmental and competition as determinants of plant distribution and abundance; community compositional change. *Mailing Add:* Dept Biol Sci State Univ NY Binghamton NY 13901

TITUS, JOHN S, b Mich, Apr 19, 23; m 46; c 4. POMOLOGY. *Educ:* Mich State Col, BS, 46, MS, 47; Cornell Univ, PhD(pomol), 51. *Prof Exp:* Instr hort, Mich State Col, 46-48; asst, Cornell Univ, 49-51; from instr to assoc prof pomol, 51-66, PROF POMOL, DEPT HORT, UNIV ILL, URBANA, 66- *Concurrent Pos:* Res assoc, Univ Calif, Davis, 62-63; Fulbright-Hays lectr, Univ Col, Dublin, 71-72. *Honors & Awards:* Gourley Award, Am Soc Hort Sci, 74. *Mem:* Fel AAAS; Am Soc Hort Sci; Am Soc Plant Physiol; Soc Exp Biol & Med. *Res:* Mineral nutrition of deciduous fruit trees; soil fertility requirements of fruit trees; soil morphology in relation to fruit tree performance; translocation in woody plants; amino acid synthesis in higher plants. *Mailing Add:* Dept of Hort Univ of Ill Urbana IL 61801

TITUS, RICHARD LEE, b Dayton, Ohio, Aug 6, 34. ORGANIC CHEMISTRY. *Educ:* DePauw Univ, BA, 56; Mich State Univ, PhD(chem), 64. *Prof Exp:* From instr to asst prof chem, Univ Toledo, 62-67; from asst prof to assoc prof, 67-73, PROF CHEM, UNIV NEV, LAS VEGAS, 73- *Mem:* AAAS; Am Chem Soc. *Res:* Synthesis of heterocyclic compounds. *Mailing Add:* Dept of Chem Univ of Nev Las Vegas NV 89154

TITUS, ROBERT CHARLES, b Paterson, NJ, Aug 9, 46. INVERTEBRATE PALEONTOLOGY. *Educ:* Rutgers Univ, BS, 68; Boston Univ, AM, 71, PhD(geol), 74. *Prof Exp:* Instr geol, Windham Col, 73-74; ASST PROF GEOL, HARTWICK COL, 74- *Mem:* Sigma Xi; Paleont Soc; Paleont Asn; Geol Soc Am; Soc Econ Paleontologists & Mineralogists. *Res:* Paleontology of Middle Ordovician fossil invertebrate benthic communities. *Mailing Add:* Dept of Geol Hartwick Col Oneonta NY 13820

TITUS, WALTER FRANKLIN, b Mamaroneck, NY, Nov 9, 25; m 52; c 4. PHYSICS. *Educ:* Amherst Col, BA, 48; Harvard Univ, PhD(physics), 54. *Prof Exp:* Physicist, Nat Bur Standards, 54-58; asst prof physics, Dartmouth Col, 58-65; assoc prof physics, Union Col, NY, 65-80. *Mem:* Am Phys Soc; Am Asn Physics Teachers. *Res:* Nuclear and high energy electron physics; particle detection. *Mailing Add:* 5 Douglas Rd Schenectady NY 12308

TITUS, WILLIAM JAMES, b Oakland, Calif, Dec 13, 41; m 67. LOW TEMPERATURE PHYSICS, STATISTICAL MECHANICS. *Educ:* Univ Calif, Davis, BS, 63; Stanford Univ, MS, 65, PhD(physics), 68. *Prof Exp:* Res assoc physics, Univ Minn, 68-70; asst prof, 70-77, ASSOC PROF PHYSICS, CARLETON COL, 77- *Mem:* Am Phys Soc; Am Asn Physics Teachers; Sigma Xi. *Mailing Add:* Dept of Physics Carleton Col Northfield MN 55057

TIUS, MARCOS A, b Izmir, Turkey, Apr 18, 53; US citizen. SYNTHETIC ORGANIC CHEMISTRY. *Educ:* Dartmouth Col, BA, 75; Harvard Univ, MS, 77, PhD(chem), 80. *Prof Exp:* ASST PROF CHEM, UNIV HAWAII, MANOA, 80- *Mem:* Am Chem Soc. *Mailing Add:* 2545 The Mall Honolulu HI 96822

TIWARI, SURENDRA NATH, b Gorakhpur, India, Jan 1, 38. AEROSPACE ENGINEERING, ENVIRONMENTAL SCIENCES. *Educ:* Univ Allahabad, BS, 59; Univ Maine, MS, 62 & 64; State Univ NY, Stony Brook, PhD(eng sci), 69. *Prof Exp:* Syst analyst, Implements Factory, India, 55-57, res engr, 57-60; res asst agr eng, Univ Maine, 60-62, instr mech eng, 62-64; instr eng, State Univ NY, Stony Brook, 64-69, res assoc radiation, 69-70, asst prof eng, 70-71; assoc prof thermal eng, 71-77, prof mech eng & mech, 77-79, EMINENT PROF MECH ENG & MECH, OLD DOMINION UNIV, 79- *Concurrent Pos:* Consult, Grumman Aerospace Corp, NY, 69-71; NASA grant, Old Dominion Univ, 71-; res consult, Langley Field, NASA, Va, 71- *Mem:* Am Inst Aeronaut & Astronaut; Am Soc Mech Engrs; AAAS; Am Soc Eng Educ; Am Asn Univ Professors. *Res:* Radiation gas dynamics; boundary layer flows; multi-phase flows; combustion processes and flow of chemically reacting and radiating gases; high temperature gas kinetics; atmospheric radiation; computational fluid mechanics; planetary entry heating. *Mailing Add:* Dept of Mech Eng Old Dominion Univ Norfolk VA 23508

TIXIER, MAURICE PIERRE, b Clermont, France, Feb 1, 13; nat US; m 39; c 2. GEOPHYSICS. *Educ:* Ecole des Arts et Metiers d'Erquelinnes, Belg, Eng, 32; Ecole Superieure d'Electricite, Paris, Eng, 33. *Prof Exp:* Field engr, Societe de Prospection Electrique, Paris, 34-35; dist engr, Schlumberger Well Surv Corp, Tex, 35-39, area mgr, Colo, 41-49, chief petrol engr, Tex, 49-52, chief field develop engr, 52-57, mgr field develop, 57-66, dir field interpretation, 66-69, dir prod logging, 69-72, tech adv, 72-77; PRES, TIXIER TECH CORP, 78- *Honors & Awards:* Gold Medal, Soc Prof Well Log Analysts, 70. *Mem:* Soc Explor Geophys; Am Asn Petrol Geol; Am Geophys Union; Am Inst Mining, Metall & Petrol Eng; Soc Petrol Eng. *Res:* Electrical logging; electrochemistry; well bore geophysics. *Mailing Add:* 2319 Bolsover Rd Houston TX 77005

TIZARD, IAN RODNEY, b Belfast, Northern Ireland, Oct 27, 42; m 69; c 2. IMMUNOLOGY. *Educ:* Univ Edinburgh, BVMS, 65, BSc, 66; Cambridge Univ, PhD(immunol), 69. *Prof Exp:* Med Res Coun Can fel, Univ Guelph, 69-71; vet res officer, Animal Dis Res Asn, 71-72; from asst prof to prof vet immunol, Univ Guelph, 72-82; PROF & HEAD, DEPT VET MICROBIOL & PARASITOL, TEX A&M UNIV, COLLEGE STATION, 82- *Mem:* Brit Soc Immunol; Royal Col Vet Surg. *Res:* Brucella serology; immunity to Protozoa; reproductive immunology; veterinary immunology. *Mailing Add:* Dept Vet Microbiol & Parasitol Tex A&M Univ College Station TX 77843

TJALMA, RICHARD ARLEN, b Holland, Mich, Sept 2, 29; m 50; c 2. VETERINARY MEDICINE. *Educ:* Mich State Univ, BS, 50, DVM, 54; Harvard Univ, MS, 65; Am Bd Vet Pub Health, dipl, 65. *Prof Exp:* Asst prof infectious dis res sect col med, Univ Iowa, 56-60; chief epizootiology sect, Nat Cancer Inst, 61-68; epidemiologist, Mayo Clin, 68-69; asst to dir, Nat Inst Environ Health Sci, 69-73; ASST DIR, NAT CANCER INST, 73- *Concurrent Pos:* Lectr col vet med, Ohio State Univ, 55-56; consult, US AID, 62; consult col vet med, Mich State Univ, 62-64, from assoc prof to prof, 64-68; consult lab infectious dis res, Col Med, Univ Iowa, 62-; consult, WHO, 65. *Mem:* Fel Am Pub Health Asn; Am Vet Med Asn. *Res:* Infectious and noninfectious disease epidemiology; comparative medicine. *Mailing Add:* Nat Cancer Inst Bethesda MD 20014

TJEPKEMA, JOHN DIRK, b Madison, Wis, June 14, 43. NITROGEN FIXATION, NITROGEN CYCLE. *Educ:* Univ Mich, BA, 65, MA, 67, PhD(bot), 71. *Prof Exp:* Res assoc, Wash Univ, 72-73, Univ Wis, 73-74 & Ore State Univ, 74-75; res fel, EMBRAPA, Rio de Janeiro, 76; ASST & ASSOC PROF SOIL BIOL, HARVARD UNIV, 76- *Mem:* Am Soc Plant Physiologists; Ecol Soc Am; Bot Soc Am; Am Soc Microbiol; Soil Sci Soc Am. *Res:* Physiology and ecology of nitrogen fixation by nodulated plants and their symbiotic bacteria; associative nitrogen fixation; nitrogen cycle of ecosystems, especially exchange of nitrogenous compounds with the atmosphere. *Mailing Add:* Harvard Forest Harvard Univ Petersham MA 01366

TJIAN, ROBERT TSE NAN, b Hong Kong, Sept 22, 49; Brit citizen; m 76. MOLECULAR BIOLOGY, BIOCHEMISTRY. *Educ:* Univ Calif, Berkeley, AB, 71; Harvard Univ, PhD(molecular biol), 76. *Prof Exp:* Staff investr molecular virol, Cold Spring Harbor Lab, 76-79; ASST PROF BIOCHEM, UNIV CALIF, BERKELEY, 79- *Concurrent Pos:* Robertson fel, Cold Spring Harbor Lab, 78. *Res:* Oncogenic viruses and their interactions with the host cell; control of gene expression; simian virus 40, a small DNA containing oncogenic virus, tumor antigen, its structure and function. *Mailing Add:* Dept of Biochem Univ of Calif Berkeley CA 94720

TJIO, JOE HIN, b Java, Indonesia, Feb 11, 19; US citizen; m 48; c 1. CYTOGENETICS. *Educ:* Univ Colo, PhD(biophys, cytogenetics), 60; Univ Zaragosa, Spain, Dr, 81. *Hon Degrees:* Dr, Univ Claude Bernard, France, 74. *Prof Exp:* Head cytogenetics, Estacion Exp de Aula Dei, 48-59; res biologist, 59-78, CHIEF CYTOGENETICS SECT LAB EXP PATH, NAT INST ARTHRITIS & METAB DIS, 74- *Concurrent Pos:* Res assoc genetics inst, Univ Lund, 59-; res collabr, Brookhaven Nat Lab, 79- *Honors & Awards:* Joseph P Kennedy Jr Found Award, 62. *Mem:* Genetics Soc Am; Am Soc Human Genetics; Am Genetic Asn; Am Soc Nat. *Res:* Plant, animal and human cytogenetics; mammalian cytogenetics. *Mailing Add:* Nat Inst of Health Bldg 10 Rm 4D-44 Bethesda MD 20014

TJIOE, DJOE TJHOO, b Medan, Indonesia, Oct 1, 37; US citizen; m 64; c 2. MAMMALIAN PHYSIOLOGY, PHARMACOLOGY. *Educ:* Sioux Falls Col, BSc, 65; Univ Wis, MSc, 67, PhD(physiol), 70. *Prof Exp:* Teaching asst physiol, Univ Wis, 65-70; ASSOC PROF PHYSIOL, CALIF STATE UNIV, LONG BEACH, 70- *Concurrent Pos:* Consult, Concept Media, 74-78. *Mem:* AAAS; Am Physiol Soc; Fedn Am Socs Exp Biol. *Res:* Cardiovascular, neuro and respiratory physiology. *Mailing Add:* Dept of Biol Calif State Univ Long Beach CA 90840

TJIOE, SARAH ARCHAMBAULT, b Philadelphia, Pa, Oct 12, 44; m 67; c 1. PHARMACOLOGY. *Educ:* Univ Pa, BA, 66, PhD(pharmacol), 71. *Prof Exp:* Instr, 72-75, ASST PROF PHARMACOL, COL MED, OHIO STATE UNIV, 75- *Concurrent Pos:* NIH training grant pharmacol, Col Med, Ohio State Univ, 71-72, Pharmaceut Mfrs Asn Found fel pharmacol-morphol, 72-74. *Mem:* Am Soc Pharmacol & Exp Therapeut; Soc Neurosci. *Res:* Neuropharmacology; neurochemistry. *Mailing Add:* Dept of Pharmacol Ohio State Univ Col of Med Columbus OH 43210

TJOSEM, THEODORE DAVID, b Paullina, Iowa, Aug 5, 18; m 43; c 4. RESEARCH ADMINISTRATION, MENTAL RETARDATION. *Educ:* Drake Univ, AB, 40; State Univ Iowa, MA, 41; Univ Wash, PhD(phychol), 59. *Prof Exp:* Actg dir, Sect Psychol Serv, Child Welfare Div, Iowa Bd Soc Welfare, 46-49; lectr psychol, Drake Univ, Iowa, 46-49; lectr, Univ Wash, 52-53, assoc, 51-53, instr, Dept Psychiat, 53-60; asst prof, Dept Psychiat & Pediat, Off Chief, US Childrens Bur Behav Sci, Ment Retardation Prog, Nat Inst Child Health & Human Develop, 65-66, DIR, MENT RETARDATION & DEVELOP DISABILITIES PROG, NAT INST CHILD HEALTH DEVELOP, NIH, 66- *Concurrent Pos:* Asst dir, Clinic Child Study, Sch Med, Univ Wash, 57-62; chief psychol & dir res, Div Child Health, Dept Pediat, Sch Med, Wash Univ, 62-64; pvt practice & consult, 53-64; Res Award, Am Asn Ment Deficiency, 82. *Mem:* fel Am Psychol Asn; Am Acad Ment Retardation; Am Asn Mental Deficiency; Ambulatory Pediat Asn. *Res:* Early diagnosis annd medical and behavioral interventions for infants and young children at high-risk for faulty development; psychophysiological aspects of early child developmment. *Mailing Add:* NIH Mental Retardation & Develop C-716 Landow Bldg 7910 Woodmont Ave Bethesda MD 20205

TJOSTEM, JOHN LEANDER, b Sisseton, SDak, June 6, 35; m 62; c 3. MICROBIOLOGY, PLANT PHYSIOLOGY. *Educ:* Concordia Col, Moorhead, Minn, BA, 59; NDak State Univ, MS, 62, PhD(bot), 68. *Prof Exp:* Instr biol, Luther Col, Iowa, 62-65; assoc prof, Concordia Col, Moorhead, Minn, 67-68; assoc prof, 68-80, PROF BIOL, LUTHER COL, IOWA, 80- *Mem:* AAAS; Am Soc Plant Physiol. *Res:* Metabolic pathways of certain carbohydrates in algae. *Mailing Add:* Dept of Biol Luther Col Decorah IA 62101

TKACHEFF, JOSEPH, JR, b Waterbury, Conn, Feb 13, 26; m 54; c 2. PHARMACY. *Educ:* RI Col Pharm, BSc, 46; Philadelphia Col Pharm, MSc, 47. *Prof Exp:* Pharmacist, E M Altman & Waterbury Drug Co, Conn, 45-46; control chemist, G F Harvey Co, 47-49, res & develop chemist, 49-50, plant chemist, 50-51, prod mgr, 51-58; SR RES PHARMACIST & GROUP LEADER PROD DEVELOP & RES, SOLID DOSAGE SECT, STERLING-WINTHROP RES INST, 58- *Mem:* Am Chem Soc; Am Pharmaceut Asn; Acad Pharmaceut Sci. *Res:* Pharmaceutical chemistry; physiological biochemistry. *Mailing Add:* Box 129 Russell Rd Greenfield Center NY 12833

TKACHUK, RUSSELL, b Redwater, Alta, Dec 25, 30; m 57; c 3. CHEMISTRY. *Educ:* Univ BC, BA, 54, MSc, 56; Univ Sask, PhD(chem), 59. *Prof Exp:* RES SCIENTIST, GRAIN RES LAB, CAN GRAIN COMN, 59- *Concurrent Pos:* Adj prof, Univ Man; fel, St Vincent's Sch Med Res, Melbourne, Australia, 68-69. *Mem:* Am Asn Cereal Chem; Am Chem Soc; Chem Inst Can; Can Inst Chem; Sigma Xi. *Res:* Chemistry of amino acids and proteins in wheat; near infrared reflectance spectroscopy. *Mailing Add:* Grain Res Lab Can Grain Comn 1404-303 Main St Winnipeg MB R3C 3G8 Can

TKACZ, JAN S, b Kittery, Maine, Oct 24, 44; m 78. ANTIFUNGAL ANTIBIOTICS. *Educ:* Univ NH, BA, 66; Rutgers Univ, PhD(microbiol), 71. *Prof Exp:* Fel biochem, Med Sch, Harvard Univ, 71-73; res assoc, M S Hershey Med Ctr, Pa State Univ, 73-74; asst res prof microbiol, Rutgers Univ, 75-78, asst prof microbiol, Waksman Inst Microbiol, 78-81; SR RES INVESTR, DEPT MICROBIOL, THE SQUIBB INST MED RES, 81- *Concurrent Pos:* NSF res fel, Dept Biol Chem, Lab Carbohydrate Res, Med Sch, Harvard Univ, 71-72; vis prof microbiol, Rutgers Univ. *Mem:* Soc Complex Carbohydrates; Am Soc Microbiol; Am Chem Soc; AAAS. *Res:* The role of glycosylation reactions in the function of eukaryotic microorganisms; antibiotics which inhibit the formation of glycoproteins and other fungal cell wall constituents. *Mailing Add:* Squibb Inst Med Res Dept Microbiol PO Box 4000 Princeton NJ 08540

TÖKES, LASZLO GYULA, b Budapest, Hungary, July 7, 37; US citizen. ORGANIC CHEMISTRY. *Educ:* Univ Southern Calif, BA, 61; Stanford Univ, PhD(chem), 65. *Prof Exp:* Nat Ctr Sci Res, France fel, Univ Strasbourg, 65-66; fel, 66-67, DEPT HEAD SPECTROS, SYNTEX RES DIV, SYNTEX CORP, 67- *Mem:* Am Chem Soc; Am Soc Mass Spectrometry. *Res:* Mass spectrometric fragmentation mechanisms; isotope labeling studies; structure elucidations by using advanced spectroscopic methods; natural product chemistry with special interest in marine chemistry. *Mailing Add:* Inst of Org Chem Syntex Res Div Syntex Corp Palo Alto CA 94304

TOALSON, WILMONT, b Clark, Mo, Feb 13, 08; m 31. APPLIED MATHEMATICS. *Educ:* William Jewell Col, 29; Univ Kans, AM, 37. *Prof Exp:* Teacher high sch, Kans, 37-41; instr math, Pratt Jr Col, 41-43; from asst prof to prof, 46-78, dept adv, 56-74, EMER PROF MATH, FT HAYS STATE UNIV, 78- *Concurrent Pos:* Consult, US Agency for Int Develop Prog, India, 66, 67. *Mem:* Math Asn Am. *Res:* Laplace transform. *Mailing Add:* Dept of Math Ft Hays State Univ Hays KS 67601

TOBA, H(ARCHIRO) HAROLD, b Puunene, Hawaii, Aug 24, 32; m 58; c 3. ENTOMOLOGY. *Educ:* Univ Hawaii, BS, 57, MS, 61; Purdue Univ, PhD(entom), 66. *Prof Exp:* RES ENTOMOLOGIST, SCI & EDUC ADMIN-AGR RES, USDA, 65- *Mem:* AAAS; Entom Soc Am; Sigma Xi. *Res:* Development of new, safe and effective methods for control of soil insect pests of vegetable and field crops. *Mailing Add:* Yakima Agr Res Lab 3706 W Nob Hill Blvd Yakima WA 98902

TOBACH, ETHEL, b Miaskovka, Russia, Nov 7, 21; nat US; m 47. ANIMAL BEHAVIOR. *Educ:* Hunter Col, BA, 49; NY Univ, MA, 52, PhD(comp psychol, physiol psychol), 57. *Hon Degrees:* DSc, Long Island Univ, 75. *Prof Exp:* Res assoc, Payne Whitney Psychiat Clin, New York, 49-53 & Pub Health Res Inst NY, Inc, 53-56; res fel comp & physiol psychol, Am Mus Natural Hist, 57-61; asst prof comp physiol & exp psychol, Sch Med, NY Univ, 61-65; assoc cur, 64-69, CUR, DEPT ANIMAL BEHAV, AM MUS NATURAL HIST, 69-; ADJ PROF, STATE UNIV NY COL PURCHASE, 81-, PRES, 69- *Mem:* AAAS; fel Am Psychol Asn; fel Animal Behav Soc; Psychonomic Soc; NY Acad Sci. *Res:* Development and evolution of behavior; emotional behavior; social behavior; neurohormonal relationships; sensory processes; autonomic phenomena. *Mailing Add:* Dept Animal Behav Am Mus Nat Hist Cent Park West at 79th St New York NY 10024

TOBACK, F(REDERICK) GARY, b Brooklyn, NY, Oct 23, 41; m 63; c 3. NEPHROLOGY, EPITHELIAL CELL GROWTH. *Educ:* Columbia Col, AB, 63; New York, Univ, MD, 67; Boston Univ, PHD(biochem), 74; Am Bd Inst Med, dipl, 74; Am Bd Nephrol, dipl, 76. *Prof Exp:* Internship internal med, Cleveland Metrop Gen Hosp, 67-68, residency, 68-69; lieutenant med, US Navy Med Corps, 69-70; res assoc med & nephrol, Sch Med, Boston Univ, 70-73; clin fel nephrol, Harvard Med Sch, Beth Israel Hosp, 74; asst prof, 74-79, ASSOC PROF MED, SCH MED, UNIV CHICAGO, 80- *Concurrent Pos:* Am Cancer Soc scholar, Salk Inst Biol Studies, 79-80; estab investr, Am Heart Asn, 80-85 & sci councils. *Mem:* Am Physiol Soc; Cent Soc Clin Res; Am & Int Soc Nephrol. *Res:* Growth of kidney cells in physiological and pathological states: regeneration after acute renal failure; potassium depletion nephropathy; compensatory renal growth; kidney phospholipid biosynthesis; role of cations in growth regulation of kidney epithelial cells in culture. *Mailing Add:* Box 83 Dept Med Univ Chicago 950 E 59th St Chicago IL 60637

TOBERMAN, RALPH OWEN, b Harrisburg, Pa, Sept 23, 23; m 46; c 3. ANALYTICAL CHEMISTRY. *Educ:* Albright Col, BS, 49. *Prof Exp:* Control chemist, Pa Ohio Steel Corp, 49-51; res asst anal chem, Sharp & Dohme, Inc, 51-52, res assoc, 52-63, unit head anal res, 63-65, specifications assoc, 65-66, HEAD CONTAINER & PROD TESTING UNIT, MERCK SHARP & DOHME RES LABS, 66- *Mem:* Am Chem Soc; Drug Info Asn. *Res:* Analysis of pharmaceutical products; methods development; specifications for new products; package research and product testing. *Mailing Add:* Hickory Hill Dr RD 1 Norristown PA 19401

TOBES, MICHAEL CHARLES, b Detroit, Mich, Oct 7, 48; m 79. BIOCHEMICAL RADIOPHARMACOLOGY, ONCOLOGY. *Educ:* Mich State Univ, BS, 70; Univ Mich, MS, 72, PhD(biol chem), 76. *Prof Exp:* Scholar, Dept Internal Med, 76-79, res investr, 79-81, DIR BIOCHEM RES UNIT, UNIV MICH, ANN ARBOR, 79-, ASST RES SCIENTIST, 81- *Mem:* AAAS; Soc Nuclear Med. *Res:* Development of gamma and positron-labeled radiopharmaceuticals for diagnostic imaging; development of radiolabeled enzyme inhibitors for the diagnosis of cancer. *Mailing Add:* R4601 Kresge I Dept Internal Med Div Nuclear Med Univ Mich Hosp Ann Arbor MI 48109

TOBEY, ARTHUR ROBERT, b Portland, Ore, Aug 4, 20; m 77; c 3. APPLIED PHYSICS. *Educ:* Yale Univ, BS, 42, MS, 46, PhD(physics), 48. *Prof Exp:* Mem staff radiation lab, Mass Inst Technol, 42-45; asst cosmic ray proj, Off Naval Res, Yale Univ, 47-48; asst prof physics, State Col Wash, 48-50; supvr physics, Armour Res Found, 50-52; sr scientist, 52-53; supvr TV res, Stanford Res Inst, 53-56, group head video systs lab, 56-59, STAFF SCIENTIST ENG DIV, SRI INT, 59- *Mem:* Am Phys Soc; Sigma Xi. *Res:* Radar and radar-type systems; neutron component of cosmic rays; electromechanical and electro-optical devices; electronic instrumentation; communication theory; man-computer systems; satellite systems modelling. *Mailing Add:* Systs Develop Dept SRI Int Menlo Park CA 94025

TOBEY, FRANK LINDLEY, JR, b Coeur d'Alene, Idaho, Aug 28, 23; m 57; c 1. VISION, PHOTOMETRY. *Educ:* Univ Mich, BSCh, 47, MSCh, 48, MS, 50, PhD(physics), 62. *Prof Exp:* Res assoc physics, Univ Mich, 50-60; res physicist, Cornell Aeronaut Lab, 62-64; fel lab astrophys, Harvard Col Observ, 64-65; fel shocktube physics, McDonnell-Douglas Corp, 66-69; res instr spectros of vision, Med Sch, Wash Univ, 70-74; ASST PROF SPECTROS OF VISION, MED SCH, UNIV FLA, 74- *Concurrent Pos:* Asst prof physics & astron, Southern Ill Univ, Edwardsville, 70. *Mem:* AAAS; Am Phys Soc; Asn Res Vision & Ophthal Sigma Xi. *Res:* Measurement of transition probabilities; atomic and molecular parameters; plasma diagnostics; optical properties of the retina and retinal receptors; spectroscopy; experimental determination of receptor waveguide properties; physics of vision. *Mailing Add:* Dept of Ophthal Box J284 JHMHC Univ of Fla Col of Med Gainesville FL 32610

TOBEY, ROBERT ALLEN, b Owosso, Mich, May 26, 37; m 60; c 2. CELL BIOLOGY, CANCER. *Educ:* Mich State Univ, BS, 59; Univ Ill, PhD, 63. *Prof Exp:* STAFF MEM, TOXICOLOGY GROUP, LOS ALAMOS NAT LAB, 64- *Mem:* AAAS; Am Soc Cell Biol; Am Soc Biol Chem; Am Soc Microbiol; Am Asn Cancer Res. *Res:* Factors controlling traverse of the life cycle; sequential biochemical markers in the mammalian cell cycle; control of mammalian cell proliferation; mechanisms of action and effects on mammalian cell growth and division of anticancer drugs; environmental pollutants and ELF electromagnetic fields. *Mailing Add:* Toxicology Group MS 880 Los Alamos Nat Lab Los Alamos NM 87545

TOBEY, STEPHEN WINTER, b Chicago, Ill, Jan 9, 36; m 53; c 4. PHARMACUETICAL CHEMISTRY. *Educ:* Ill Inst Technol, BS, 57; Univ Wis, MS, 59, PhD(inorg chem), 65. *Prof Exp:* Instr phys chem, WVa Wesleyan Col, 59-61; asst prof inorg chem, Purdue Univ, 64-65; res chemist, Eastern Res Lab, Dow Chem USA, 65-68, sr res chemist, 68-70, res dir, 70-74, dir chem lab, 73-75, mgr chem process develop, 75-76, MGR PHARMACEUT, PROCESS DEVELOP, MICH DIV, DOW USA, 76-, SR ASSOC SCIENTIST, 78- *Concurrent Pos:* Vis prof, Harvard Univ, 65. *Mem:* Am Chem Soc. *Mailing Add:* Org Chem Res Lab Bldg 438 Dow USA Midland MI 48640

TOBIA, ALFONSO JOSEPH, b Brooklyn, NY, June 19, 42. PHARMACOLOGY. *Educ:* St Louis Col Pharm, BS, 65; Purdue Univ, MS & PhD(pharmacol), 69. *Prof Exp:* Asst prof pharmacol, Univ Ga, 69-74; sr investr pharmacol, Smith Kline & French Labs, 74-77; group leader, 77-81, SECT HEAD CARDIOVASCULAR IMMUNOPHARMACOL DERMATO-PHARMACOL, ORTHO PHARMACEUT CORP, 82- *Concurrent Pos:* Ga Heart Asn res grant, Univ Ga, 71-72, Nat Heart & Lung Inst res grant hypertension, 71-74, mem coun high blood pressure coun circulation & coun basic sci, Am Heart Asn. *Mem:* Am Soc Pharmacol Exp Therapeut; Sigma Xi, Am Heart Asn; NY Acad Sci; Soc Exp Biol Med. *Res:* Renal vasodilation and hypertension; cardiovascular and biochemical pharmacology. *Mailing Add:* Cardiovasc Pharmacol Ortho Pharmaceut Corp Raritan NJ 08869

TOBIAN, LOUIS, b Dallas, Tex, Jan 26, 20; m 51. INTERNAL MEDICINE. *Educ:* Univ Tex, BA, 40; Harvard Med Sch, MD, 44. *Prof Exp:* House officer med, Peter Bent Brigham Hosp, Boston, 44; asst resident, Univ Hosp, Univ Calif, 44-45 & Parkland Hosp, Tex, 45-46; asst prof med, Univ Tex Southwestern Med Sch Dallas, 54; assoc prof, 54-64, PROF MED, SCH MED, UNIV MINN, MINNEAPOLIS, 64- *Concurrent Pos:* Res fel med, Univ Tex Southwestern Med Sch Dallas, 46-51; res fel biochem, Harvard Med Sch, 51-54; estab investr, Am Heart Asn, 51-56, mem coun arteriosclerosis, 56-, chmn, Coun High Blood Pressure Res, 72; George Brown lectureship, 69; chmn task force hypertension, Nat Heart & Lung Inst, 72-73, mem adv comt hypertension res ctrs, 72-74; chmn comt hypertension & renal vascular dis, NIH Kidney Res Surv Group, 74-75. *Mem:* Am Clin & Climat Asn; Asn Am Physicians; Am Soc Clin Invest; Am Physiol Soc; fel NY Acad Sci. *Res:* Hypertension; renal circulation; sodium excretion. *Mailing Add:* Dept of Med Univ of Minn Hosp Minneapolis MN 55455

TOBIAS, CHARLES W, b Budapest, Hungary, Nov 2, 20; nat US; m 50; c 3. ELECTROCHEMISTRY, CHEMICAL ENGINEERING. *Educ:* Univ Tech Sci, Budapest, ChemEng, 42, PhD(phys chem), 46. *Prof Exp:* Res & develop engr, United Incandescent Lamp & Elec Co, Ltd, Hungary, 42-43, 45-47; instr chem eng, 47-48, lectr, 48-50, from asst prof to assoc prof, 50-60, chmn dept chem eng, 67-72, PROF CHEM ENG, UNIV CALIF, BERKELEY, 60-, FAC SR SCIENTIST, LAWRENCE BERKELEY LAB, 54- *Concurrent Pos:* Instr phys chem, Univ Tech Sci, Budapest, 45-46; res prof, Miller Inst, 58-59; consult. *Honors & Awards:* Acheson Medal & Prize, Electrochem Soc, 72. *Mem:* Fel AAAS; Am Chem Soc; Int Soc Electrochem (pres-elect, 75-76, pres, 77-78); hon mem Electrochem Soc (pres, 72); Am Soc Eng Educ. *Res:* Current distribution in electrolytic cells; mass transfer in electrode processes; electrolytic oxidation and reduction; electrodeposition; batteries; fuel cells; nonaqueous ionizing media. *Mailing Add:* Dept Chem Eng Univ Calif Berkeley CA 94720

TOBIAS, CORNELIUS ANTHONY, b Budapest, Hungary, May 28, 18; nat US; m 43; c 2. BIOPHYSICS. *Educ:* Univ Calif, Berkeley, MA, 40, PhD(nculear physics), 42. *Prof Exp:* Physicist, 42-45, from instr to assoc prof biophys, 45-55, vchmn dept physics in-chg of med physics, 60-67, chmn, Div Med Physics, 67-71, chmn grad group biophys & med physics, 69-73, PROF MED PHYSICS, DONNER LAB, UNIV CALIF, BERKELEY, 55-, PROF ELEC ENG, 65-; PROF RADIOL, UNIV CALIF, SAN FRANCISCO, 77- *Concurrent Pos:* Fel med physics, Univ Calif, Berkeley, 45-47; Guggenheim fel, Karolinska Inst, Sweden, 56-57; vis prof, Harvard Univ, 60; mem subcomt, Nat Res Coun, mem comt radiol, Nat Acad Sci-Nat Res Coun; mem radiation study sect, NIH, 60-63; pres radiation biophys comn, Int Union Pure & Appl Physics, 69-72, coun mem, Int Union Pure & Appl Biophys, 69-75; Alexander von Humboldt US sr scientist award, 81. *Honors & Awards:* Lawrence Mem Award, 63; Annual Award, Am Nuclear Soc Aerospace Div, 72. *Mem:* Am Asn Physicists in Med; NY Acad Sci; Am Phys Soc; Radiation Res Soc (pres, 62-63); Biophys Soc. *Res:* Biological effects of radiation; cancer research; space medicine. *Mailing Add:* 103 Donner Lab Univ of Calif Berkeley CA 94720

TOBIAS, GEORGE S, b Portland, Ore, Apr 14, 16; m 53; c 5. CHEMICAL ENGINEERING. *Educ:* Ohio State Univ, BS, 38, MS, 39. *Prof Exp:* Chem engr, Eastman Kodak Co, 39-41; sr engr, Prod Res Div, Esso Res & Eng Co, 46-51, group head, 51-54, res assoc, 54-55, sect head, 55-58, asst dir prod res div, 58-61, mkt-res-tech serv coordr, Standard Oil Co, NJ, Esso Int Inc, 61-65; tech dir, Pittsburgh Activated Carbon Co, Calgon Corp, 65-70; PRES, ENVIROTROL, INC, 70- *Mem:* Am Chem Soc; Am Inst Chem Engrs; Am Inst Chemists; Soc Automotive Engrs. *Res:* Management of research, engineering and development; adsorption, activated carbon, liquid and gas phase; treatment of industrial and municipal waste and water; air pollution control and gas purification; motor and aviation fuels, lubricants and additives. *Mailing Add:* Envirotrol Inc Backbone Rd RD 5 Sewickley PA 15143

TOBIAS, JERRY VERNON, b St Louis, Mo, Oct 14, 29; c 2. PSYCHOACOUSTICS. *Educ:* Univ Mo, AB, 50; Univ Iowa, MA, 54; Western Reserve Univ, PhD(audition), 59. *Prof Exp:* Asst, Univ Iowa, 53-54; instr speech path & audiol, Ball State Teachers Col, Ind, 54-56; res assoc audition, Western Reserve Univ, 56-59; res scientist psychophys, Defense Res Lab & vis asst prof psychol, Univ Tex, 59-61; assoc prof psychol, Univ Okla, 63-71, prof, 71-80; chmn commun processes, Civil Aeromedical Inst, Fed Aviation Admin, 77-80; WITH INDUST AUDIOL, 80- *Concurrent Pos:* Mem comt hearing, bioacoust & biomech, Nat Acad Sci-Nat Res Coun; supvry psychologist, Civil Aeromed Inst, Fed Aviation Admin, 61-77. *Mem:* Fel Acoust Soc Am; Sigma Xi; fel Am Speech & Hearing Asn. *Res:* Physiological and psy- chological acoustics; audition; experimental phonetics; physiological psychology; psychophysics; sensation and perception; auditory time constants; binaural audition; noise hazards and control. *Mailing Add:* Indust Audiol PO Box 358 Norman OK 73070

TOBIAS, JOSEPH, b Olomouc, Moravia, Sept 13, 20; nat US; m 49; c 3. DAIRY SCIENCE, FOOD SCIENCE. *Educ:* Univ Ga, BS, 42; Univ Ill, PhD(dairy tech), 52. *Prof Exp:* Instr & first asst, 48-53, from asst prof to assoc prof, 53-64, prof, 64-71, EMER PROF DAIRY TECH, UNIV ILL, URBANA, 71- *Mem:* Am Dairy Sci Asn. *Res:* Bacteriological evaluation of high-temperature short-time pasteurization of milk and other dairy products; ice cream technology; electrophoresis of milk proteins; flavor chemistry; micronutrients and microconstituents in milk. *Mailing Add:* 208 E Mumford Dr Urbana IL 61801

TOBIAS, MELVIN L, b New York, NY, Apr 29, 25; m 47; c 4. NUCLEAR ENGINEERING, CHEMICAL ENGINEERING. *Educ:* City Col New York, BChE, 44; Univ Minn, PhD(chem eng), 50. *Prof Exp:* RES STAFF MEM, REACTOR DIV, OAK RIDGE NAT LAB, 50- *Concurrent Pos:* Lectr, Univ Tenn, 55-75; assoc ed, Nuclear Sci & Eng J, 75- *Mem:* Am Nuclear Soc. *Res:* Reactor theory; reactor safety; aerosol release in accidents. *Mailing Add:* Oak Ridge Nat Lab PO Box Y Oak Ridge TN 37830

TOBIAS, RUSSELL LAWRENCE, b Upper Darby, Pa, Dec 18, 48. MICROCOMPUTER DESIGN. *Educ:* Temple Univ, AB, 70; Univ Md, MS, 75, PhD(physics), 78. *Prof Exp:* Res asst physics, Dept Physics & Astron, Univ Md, 75-78; RES ANALYST, COMPUSTATICS, INC, 78- *Res:* Instrumentation design and development in graphic arts and radiology; management information system design and administration. *Mailing Add:* PO Box 2699 Warminster PA 18974

TOBIAS, RUSSELL STUART, bioinorganic chemistry, organometallic chemistry, deceased

TOBIASON, FREDERICK LEE, b Pe Ell, Wash, Sept 15, 36; m 61; c 3. PHYSICAL CHEMISTRY. *Educ:* Pac Lutheran Univ, BA, 58; Mich State Univ, PhD(phys chem), 63. *Prof Exp:* Res assoc nuclear magnetic resonance spectros, Emory Univ, 63-64; res chemist, Benger Lab, E I du Pont de Nemours & Co, Inc, 64-66; from asst prof to assoc prof, 66-73, PROF PHYS CHEM, PAC LUTHERAN UNIV, 73- *Concurrent Pos:* Consult, Reichhold Chem, Inc, 67-; chmn chem dept, Pac Lutheran Univ, 73-76 & regency prof, 75-76; consult, Bennett Lab, Inc, 80- *Mem:* Am Chem Soc. *Res:* Molecular structure; microwave spectroscopy; nuclear magnetic resonance spectroscopy; electric dipole moments; molecular characterization of polymers; wood chemistry; adhesives; polymer chain configuration calculations. *Mailing Add:* Dept of Chem Pac Lutheran Univ Tacoma WA 98447

TOBIE, JOHN EDWIN, b Collison, Ill, Dec 26, 11; m 47. IMMUNOLOGY, PARASITOLOGY. *Educ:* Univ Ill, AB, 35; La State Univ, MS, 36; Tulane Univ, PhD(parasitol), 40. *Prof Exp:* Tech asst, NIH, 37-40; instr parasitol, Tulane Univ, 41-43; parasitologist, Lab Trop Dis, NIH, 43-57, biologist, Lab Immunol, 57-61, actg chief, 61-63; chief lab germfree animal res, Nat Inst Allergy & Infectious Dis, 63-69, chief lab microbial immunity, 69-70, asst sci dir lab & clin res, 70-72; CONSULT, NAT ACAD SCI, 74- *Concurrent Pos:* Fel, La State Univ, 34-37; fel trop med, Tulane Univ, 40-41. *Honors & Awards:* Dept Health, Educ & Welfare Superior Serv Award, 63. *Mem:* Fel AAAS; Am Soc Trop Med & Hyg; Am Asn Immunologists; NY Acad Sci. *Res:* Immunological response to parasites in conventional hosts; fluorescent antibody studies on antibody production and immunoglobulin synthesis in malaria and other protozoa diseases; cellular localization of antibodies by fluorescence. *Mailing Add:* 5902 Wilson Lane Bethesda MD 20817

TOBIESSEN, PETER LAWS, b Philadelphia, Pa, Mar 30, 40; m 68. PLANT ECOLOGY. *Educ:* Wesleyan Univ, BA, 63; Pa State Univ, University Park, MS, 66; Duke Univ, PhD(bot), 71. *Prof Exp:* Asst prof, 70-77, ASSOC PROF BIOL, UNION COL, NY, 77- *Mem:* Am Soc Plant Physiol; Ecol Soc Am. *Res:* Physiological plant ecology. *Mailing Add:* Dept of Biol Union Col Schenectady NY 12308

TOBIN, ALBERT GEORGE, b Boston, Mass, June 7, 38; m 63. PHYSICAL METALLURGY. *Educ:* Mass Inst Technol, BS, 60, MS, 63; Columbia Univ, PhD(metall), 68. *Prof Exp:* Staff metallurgist, Nuclear Metals Inc, 60-62; res asst metall, Mass Inst Technol, 62-63 & Columbia Univ, 63-68; res metallurgist, Union Carbide Corp, 68-69; RES SCIENTIST, GRUMMAN AEROSPACE CORP, 69- *Mem:* Am Soc Metals. *Res:* Magnetic and dielectric materials; high temperature properties of materials; fracture and fatigue properties of titanium alloys; hydrogen embrittlement; application of materials to fusion reactors; metal matrix composites; radiation damage in ceramics; surface physics and chemistry. *Mailing Add:* Grumman Aerospace Corp 26 Bethpage NY 11787

TOBIN, ALLAN JOSHUA, b Manchester, NH, Aug 22, 42; m 81; c 2. DEVELOPMENTAL BIOLOGY, NEUROBIOLOGY. *Educ:* Mass Inst Technol, BS, 63; Harvard Univ, PhD(biophys), 69. *Prof Exp:* USPHS fels, Weizman Inst Sci, 69-70 & Mass Inst Technol, 70-71; asst prof biol, Harvard Univ, 71-74; ASST PROF BIOL, UNIV CALIF, LOS ANGELES, 74- *Concurrent Pos:* Exec dir, Hereditary Dis Found, 79- *Mem:* AAAS; Soc Develop Biol; Am Chem Soc; Soc Neurosci. *Res:* Erythroid cell development; molecular neurobiology. *Mailing Add:* Dept of Biol Univ of Calif Los Angeles CA 90024

TOBIN, ELAINE MUNSEY, b Louisville, Ky, Dec 23, 44; div; c 2. PLANT DEVELOPMENT. *Educ:* Oberlin Col, BA, 66; Harvard Univ, PhD(biol), 72. *Prof Exp:* Fel biol, Brandeis Univ, 73-75; ASST PROF BIOL, UNIV CALIF, LOS ANGELES, 75- *Mem:* Am Soc Plant Physiologists; AAAS. *Res:* Control of plant development by light. *Mailing Add:* Dept Biol Univ Calif Los Angeles CA 90024

TOBIN, JOHN ROBERT, JR, b Elgin, Ill, Dec 18, 17; m 42; c 1. INTERNAL MEDICINE, CARDIOLOGY. *Educ:* Univ Notre Dame, BS, 38; Univ Chicago, MD, 42; Univ Minn, MS, 50; Am Bd Internal Med, dipl, 52; Am Bd Cardiovasc Dis, dipl, 66. *Prof Exp:* Intern med & surg, Presby Hosp, Chicago, 42-43; resident path, Univ Chicago Clins, 46-47; asst staff, Mayo Clin, 50-51; staff, Rockwood Clin, Spokane, Wash, 51-55; dir adult cardiol, Cook County Hosp, Ill, 59-69; PROF MED, STRITCH SCH MED, LOYOLA UNIV CHICAGO, 62-, CHMN DEPT, 69- *Concurrent Pos:* Fel med, Mayo Found, 47-50, NIH spec fel physiol, 63-64; assoc & attend staff med, Cook County Hosp, 55-69; physician-in-chief, Loyola Hosp, 69- *Mem:* Fel Am Col Physicians; fel Am Col Cardiol. *Res:* Cardiovascular physiology and disease. *Mailing Add:* 2160 S First Ave Maywood IL 60153

TOBIN, MARVIN CHARLES, b St Louis, Mo, Jan 10, 23; wid; c 3. PHYSICAL CHEMISTRY, PHYSICS. *Educ:* Wash Univ, BA, 47; Ind Univ, MA, 49; Univ Conn, PhD(chem), 52. *Prof Exp:* Sr chemist, Arthur D Little, Inc, 52-53; group leader spectros, Olin Mathieson Chem Corp, 53-57; res chemist, Am Cyanamid Co, 57-60, group leader polymer physics, 60-62, solid state physics, 62-64; sr staff scientist, Perkin-Elmer Corp, 64-70; prof physics, Univ Bridgeport, 70-74; consult, 74-80; MATERIALS ENGR, NORDEN SYSTS, 80- *Mem:* AAAS; Optical Soc Am; Am Phys Soc. *Res:* Polymer physics; light scattering; molecular and laser spectroscopy; materials science. *Mailing Add:* 5 Clinton Ave Westport CT 06880

TOBIN, MICHAEL, b Russia, Jan 22, 13; nat US; m 44; c 2. INSTRUMENTATION, BIOENGINEERING. *Educ:* City Col New York, BSEE, 43; Polytech Inst Brooklyn, MSEE, 50. *Prof Exp:* Instr elec eng, Polytech Inst Brooklyn, 46-48; instr, instrumentation, Dept Neurol, Col Physicians & Surgeons, Columbia Univ, 48-50; clin asst prof biophys, State Univ NY Downstate Med Ctr, 50-65; res assoc, Dept Psychiat, Col Physicians & Surgeons, Columbia Univ, 65-77; DIR ELECTRONICS & INSTRUMENTATION, FUSION ENERGY FOUND, 77- *Mem:* AAAS; Inst Elec & Electronic Engrs. *Res:* Instrumentation; data communication, bioengineering, sensing, recording and analysis of physiologic data; logic design; interfacing to digital computers; stand-alone system design; microprocessor systems organization; history of technology and political economy. *Mailing Add:* 900 W 190th St Apt 5-H New York NY 10040

TOBIN, RICHARD BRUCE, b Buffalo, NY, Mar 6, 25; m 47; c 5. PHYSIOLOGY. *Educ:* Union Univ, NY, BS, 45; Univ Rochester, MD, 49. *Prof Exp:* Instr physiol & med, Sch Med & Dent, Univ Rochester, 54-59, asst prof & asst physician, 59-63; assoc prof med, 66-68, assoc prof physiol, 67-68, PROF MED & BIOCHEM, UNIV NEBR MED CTR, OMAHA, 68-; STAFF PHYSICIAN, VET ADMIN HOSP, OMAHA, 73- *Concurrent Pos:* USPHS fel biochem, Univ Amsterdam, 63-65. *Mem:* Am Physiol Soc; Endocrine Soc; Am Inst Nutrit; fel Am Col Physicians. *Res:* Cellular energetics; thyroid hormone regulation of intermediary metabolism. *Mailing Add:* Vet Admin Hosp 4101 Woolworth Ave Omaha NE 68105

TOBIN, ROGER LEE, b Grand Rapids, Mich, Oct 11, 40. OPERATIONS RESEARCH, TRANSPORTATION RESEARCH. *Educ:* Univ Mich, BSE, 64, MSE, 69, MA, 72, PhD(indust eng), 73. *Prof Exp:* Sr indust engr mgt, Hoover Ball & Bearing, 64-67, process engr, 67-68; assoc sr res engr transp & traffic sci, Gen Motors Res Labs, Gen Motors Corp, 73-80. *Mem:* Opers Res Soc Am. *Res:* Freight transportation, urban transportation and mathematical programming. *Mailing Add:* 440 S Catherine LaGrange IL 60525

TOBIN, SIDNEY MORRIS, b Toronto, Ont, Jan 18, 23; m 49; c 4. OBSTETRICS & GYNECOLOGY. *Educ:* Univ Toronto, MD, 46; FRCS(C), 51. *Prof Exp:* Clin lectr, 61-71, ASST PROF OBSTET & GYNEC, UNIV TORONTO, 71- *Concurrent Pos:* Chmn, Res Adv Comt, Res Dept, Mt Sinai Hosp, Toronto, 70- *Mem:* Can Med Asn; Soc Obstetricians & Gynecologists Can; Royal Col Physicians & Surgeons Can; Can Oncol Soc; Can Fel Travel Soc. *Res:* Studies to elucidate the role of herpes simplex virus type II as a carcinogen or co-carcinogen in the etiology of squamous cell carcinoma of the cervix in humans. *Mailing Add:* 69 Dunveegan Rd Toronto ON M4V 2A8 Can

TOBIN, THOMAS, b Dublin, Ireland, Aug 7, 41; US citizen; m 70. PHARMACOLOGY, VETERINARY MEDICINE. *Educ:* Univ Col Dublin, DVM, 64; Univ Guelph, MSc, 66; Univ Toronto, PhD(parmacol), 69. *Prof Exp:* Res assoc pharmacol, Univ Toronto, 66-70; asst prof, Mich State Univ, 71-75; assoc prof vet sci, 75-78, PROF VET SCI & TOXICOL, UNIV KY, 78- *Concurrent Pos:* NIH grant, 73-76; NSF grant, 74-76; Ky Equine Drug Res grant, 75-; consult equine medication & drug detection, 75- *Mem:* Am Col Vet Pharmacol & Therapeut; Am Soc Pharmacol & Exp Therapeut; Am Col Vet Toxicol; Equine Vet Asn Eng. *Res:* Equine medication; doping; drug analysis; drug disposition; pharmacokinetics; molecular pharmacology. *Mailing Add:* Dept Vet Sci Univ Ky Lexington KY 40506

TOBIN, THOMAS VINCENT, b Plymouth, Pa, Apr 8, 26; m 47; c 1. BIOLOGY. *Educ:* King's Col, BS, 51; Boston Col, MS, 53. *Prof Exp:* Asst biol, Boston Col, 51-52; from instr to asst prof, 52-62, chmn div natural sci, 71-76, ASSOC PROF BIOL, KING'S COL, 62-, DIR EDUC TV, 66- *Mem:* AAAS. *Res:* Chemoreception and proprioception in the crayfish; cold acclimitization; influence of drugs on animal behavior. *Mailing Add:* Dept Biol King's Col Wilkes-Barre PA 18711

TOBIS, JEROME SANFORD, b Syracuse, NY, July 23, 15; m 38; c 3. MEDICINE. *Educ:* City Col New York, BS, 36; Chicago Med Sch, MD, 43. *Prof Exp:* Consult phys med & rehab, Vet Admin Hosp, Bronx, NY, 48-53; prof phys med & rehab & dir, NY Med Col, 52-70; PROF PHYS MED & REHAB & CHMN DEPT, UNIV CALIF, IRVINE-CALIF COL MED, 70-, DIR DEPT, MED CTR, 77- *Concurrent Pos:* Baruch fel, Columbia Univ, 47; dir phys med & rehab, Metrop Hosp, 52-70 & Bird S Coler Hosp, 52-70; consult, City Hosp, 48 & Bur Handicapped Children, New York City Dept Health, 53-70; ed, Arch Phys Med & Rehab, 59-73; chief rehab med, Montefiore Hosp Med Ctr, 61-70; dir dept phys med & rehab, Orange County Med Ctr, 70-77. *Mem:* AAAS; AMA; Am Pub Health Asn; Am Cong Rehab Med; Am Acad Phys Med & Rehab. *Res:* Hemiplegia; cardiac rehabilitation; rehabilitation of handicapped children; geriatrics. *Mailing Add:* Dept of Phys Med & Rehab Univ of Calif Col of Med Irvine CA 92664

TOBISCH, OTHMAR TARDIN, b Berkeley, Calif, June 18, 32; m 64; c 1. STRUCTURAL GEOLOGY. *Educ:* Univ of Calif, Berkeley, BA, 58, MA, 60; Univ London, PhD(struct geol), 63. *Prof Exp:* Fulbright fel, Innsbruck, Austria, 63-64; res geologist, US Geol Surv, 64-69; from asst prof to assoc prof earth sci, 69-78, PROF EARTH SCI, UNIV CALIF, SANTA CRUZ, 78- *Mem:* Geol Soc Am; fel Geol Soc London. *Res:* Polyphase deformation in orogenic belts; quantitative strain determination of deformed rocks; genesis of orogenic belts. *Mailing Add:* Appl Sci Bldg Univ of Calif Santa Cruz CA 95064

TOBKES, MARTIN, b New York, NY, Feb 8, 28; m 52; c 2. ORGANIC CHEMISTRY. *Educ:* City Col New York, BS, 48; Polytech Inst Brooklyn, MS, 54, PhD(org chem), 63. *Prof Exp:* Res & develop chemist, Nopco Chem Co, 49-54 & Charles Bruning Co, 54-56; res org chemist, Ethicon, Inc, 56-58; res fel org chem, Polytech Inst Brooklyn, 59-63; develop chemist, 63-72, GROUP LEADER CHEM DEVELOP, LEDERLE LABS, AM CYANAMID CO, 72- *Mem:* Am Chem Soc. *Res:* Vitamin synthesis and stability; Perkin condensations; corrosion; light sensitive coatings; medicinal synthesis; polymers; antibiotics; steroids. *Mailing Add:* 98 Sutin Pl Spring Valley NY 10977

TOBOCMAN, WILLIAM, b Detroit, Mich, Mar 14, 26; m 50; c 2. THEORETICAL NUCLEAR PHYSICS. *Educ:* Mass Inst Technol, SB, 50, PhD(physics), 53. *Prof Exp:* Res assoc, Cornell Univ, 53-54; mem, Inst Adv Study, 54-56; NSF fel, Univ Birmingham, 56-57; asst prof physics, Rice Univ, 57-60; assoc prof, 60-66, PROF PHYSICS, CASE WESTERN RESERVE UNIV, 66- *Concurrent Pos:* Sloan Found fel, 61-64; res fel, Weizmann Inst, 63-64. *Mem:* Am Phys Soc. *Res:* Theory of nuclear reactions; quantum mechanical many-body problem. *Mailing Add:* Dept of Physics Case Western Reserve Univ Cleveland OH 44106

TOBUREN, LARRY HOWARD, b Clay Center, Kans, July 9, 40; m 62; c 2. ATOMIC PHYSICS, MOLECULAR PHYSICS. *Educ:* Kans State Teachers Col, BA, 62; Vanderbilt Univ, PhD(physics), 68. *Prof Exp:* sr res scientist, 67-80, MGR RADIOL PHYSICS SECT, PAC NORTHWEST LABS, BATTELLE MEM INST, 80- *Mem:* Am Phys Soc; Radiation Res Soc; AAAS. *Res:* Atomic and molecular collision processes; Auger electron studies; measurement of inner and outer shell ionization cross sections and continuum electron distributions resulting from charged particle impact. *Mailing Add:* Pac Northwest Labs Battelle Mem Inst PO Box 999 Richland WA 99352

TOBY, SIDNEY, b London, Eng, May 30, 30; m 53; c 2. PHYSICAL CHEMISTRY. *Educ:* Univ London, BSc, 52; McGill Univ, PhD, 55. *Prof Exp:* Fel photochem, Nat Res Coun, Can, 55-57; from instr to assoc prof, 57-69, PROF CHEM, RUTGERS UNIV, NEW BRUNSWICK, 69- *Mem:* AAAS; Am Chem Soc. *Res:* Kinetics of gaseous reactions; photochemistry; chemiluminescence. *Mailing Add:* Dept Chem Rutgers Univ New Brunswick NJ 08903

TOCCI, PAUL M, b Brooklyn, NY, Nov 11, 33; m 68; c 2. BIOCHEMISTRY. *Educ:* Johns Hopkins Univ, BA, 55; Univ Md, PhD(biochem), 64. *Prof Exp:* ASST PROF PEDIAT, SCH MED, UNIV MIAMI, 67- *Concurrent Pos:* Dir, Biochem Genetics Lab, 64-; mem, Int Fedn Clin Chem. *Mem:* AAAS; Am Asn Clin Chemists; fel Am Inst Chemists; Am Soc Human Genetics; Am Fedn Clin Res. *Res:* Amino acid metabolism; inborn errors of metabolism. *Mailing Add:* Dept of Pediat Univ of Miami Sch of Med Miami FL 33152

TOCCO, DOMINICK JOSEPH, b New York, NY, Jan 25, 30; m 52; c 4. BIOCHEMISTRY, PHARMACOLOGY. *Educ:* St John's Univ, BS, 51, MS, 53; Georgetown Univ, PhD(chem), 60. *Prof Exp:* Biochemist, US Army Chem Ctr, Md, 53-55, Nat Heart Inst, 55-60, Merck Inst Therapeut Res, 60-66 & Shell Develop Co, 66-70; BIOCHEMIST, MERCK SHARP & DOHME, 70- *Mem:* Am Soc Pharmacol & Exp Therapeut. *Res:* Transport of drugs and natural substances across biological membranes; drug metabolism; pharmacodynamics; experimental enzyme kinetics. *Mailing Add:* Merck Sharp & Dohme West Point PA 19486

TOCHER, RICHARD DANA, b Oakland, Calif, Oct 8, 35; m 61; c 3. PLANT PHYSIOLOGY. *Educ:* Stanford Univ, AB, 57; Univ Wash, Seattle, MS, 63, PhD(bot), 65. *Prof Exp:* Nat Res Coun Can fel marine bot, Atlantic Regional Lab, 65-66; asst prof, 66-70, ASSOC PROF BIOL, PORTLAND STATE UNIV, 70- *Mem:* Am Soc Plant Physiol. *Res:* Plant physiology and biochemistry, especially marine algae and parasitic angiosperms. *Mailing Add:* Dept of Biol Portland State Univ Portland OR 97207

TOCHER, STEWART ROSS, b Santa Rosa, Calif, May 7, 23; m 52; c 1. FORESTRY. *Educ:* Univ Calif, BS, 49, MF, 50. *Prof Exp:* Asst prof forestry, Utah State Univ, 52-56, assoc prof, 57-66; lectr, 66-70, Samuel T Dana Prof Outdoor Recreation, 70-75, PROF NATURAL RESOURCES, UNIV MICH-ANN ARBOR, 75- *Mem:* Soc Am Foresters. *Res:* Forest recreation planning and management; aerial photogrametric techniques in forest management. *Mailing Add:* 501 Huron View Dr Ann Arbor MI 48103

TOCK, RICHARD WILLIAM, b Centerville, Iowa, July 13, 40; m 65; c 3. CHEMICAL ENGINEERING, POLYMER SCIENCE. *Educ:* Univ Iowa, BS, 63, MS, 64, PhD(chem eng), 67. *Prof Exp:* From instr to asst prof chem eng, Univ Iowa, 65-67; res engr, Monsanto Co, 68-70; asst prof chem eng, Univ Iowa, 70-74; vis assoc prof, 74-75, ASSOC PROF CHEM ENG, TEX TECH UNIV, 75- *Concurrent Pos:* Consult engr, 80- *Honors & Awards:* Ralph R Teetor Award, Soc Automotive Engrs. *Mem:* Am Inst Chem Engrs; Soc Plastics Engrs; Am Soc Eng Educ; Soc Am Mil Engrs. *Res:* Membrane separation processes; polymer science, engineering materials and properties; biomass conversion; oxidations with ozone. *Mailing Add:* Dept of Chem Eng Tex Tech Univ PO Box 4679 Lubbock TX 79409

TOCKMAN, JUDITH SUSAN, cell physiology, biochemistry, see previous edition

TOCUS, EDWARD C, b Youngstown, Ohio, Apr 22, 25; m 53; c 2. PHARMACOLOGY. *Educ:* Grinnell Col, AB, 50; Univ Chicago, MS, 56, PhD(pharmacol), 59. *Prof Exp:* Res asst radiol, Wash Univ, 51-53; res assoc med, Univ Chicago, 56-60; pharmacologist, Lederle Labs, Am Cyanamid Co, NY, 60-66; pharmacologist, Bur Med, 66-70, supvry pharmacologist, Div Neuropharmacol Drugs, 70-72, CHIEF OF DRUG ABUSE STAFF, BUR DRUGS, FOOD & DRUG ADMIN, 72- *Concurrent Pos:* Mem Am del, Int Atoms for Peace Conf, Geneva, 58; consult, WHO, Geneva, Switz, 75- *Res:* Development of new drugs and regulations controlling the national and international use of drugs; develop and implement programs to control illicit use of drugs. *Mailing Add:* Food & Drug Admin Bur of Drugs 5600 Fishers Lane Rockville MD 20852

TOCZEK, DONALD RICHARD, b LaPorte, Ind, Nov 21, 38; m 72; c 3. ENTOMOLOGY, BOTANY. *Educ:* Purdue Univ, BS, 61; NDak State Univ, MS, 63, PhD(entom), 67. *Prof Exp:* Res asst entom, NDak State Univ, 61-67; PROF BIOL, HILLSDALE COL, 67- *Mem:* Entom Soc Am; Ecol Soc Am. *Res:* Basic botany; invertebrate zoology. *Mailing Add:* Dept of Biol Hillsdale Col Hillsdale MI 49242

TODARO, GEORGE JOSEPH, b New York, NY, July 1, 37; m 62; c 3. CANCER. *Educ:* Swarthmore Col, BA, 58; NY Univ, MD, 63. *Prof Exp:* Intern path, 62-63, fel, 64-65, asst prof path, NY Univ Sch Med, 65-67; from staff assoc to head molecular biol sect, Viral Carcinogenesis Br, 67-70, CHIEF, VIRAL LEUKEMIA & LYMPHOMA BR, NAT CANCER INST, NIH, 70- *Concurrent Pos:* Career develop award, USPHS, 67. *Honors & Awards:* Superior Serv Award, Dept Health Educ & Welfare, 71; Parke-Davis Award, Am Soc Exp Path, 75. *Mem:* Am Soc Microbiol; Am Asn Cancer Res; Soc Exp Biol Med. *Res:* Virus and genetic factors in cancer etiology. *Mailing Add:* Nat Cancer Inst Bldg 37 Rm 1B-22 9000 Rockville Pike Bethesda MD 20014

TODD, AARON RODWELL, b El Portal, Fla, Dec 25, 42; c 2. LINEAR TOPOLOGICAL SPACES, TOPOLOGY. *Educ:* Univ Mich, BS, 64; Univ Leeds, MSc, 68; Univ Fla, PhD(math), 72. *Prof Exp:* Asst prof math, Univ PR, 72-74; asst prof math, Brooklyn Col, 74-78; asst prof, 78-81, ASSOC PROF MATH, ST JOHN'S UNIV, NY, 78- *Mem:* Am Math Soc; NY Acad Sci; Asn Comput Sci; Asn Women Math. *Res:* Functional analysis and especially properties related to the Baire category theorem; programming languages; numerical analysis. *Mailing Add:* Dept of Math 300 Howard Ave Staten Island NY 12301

TODD, ALVA C(RESS), electrical engineering, civil engineering, deceased

TODD, CHARLES WYVIL, b Hutchinson, Minn, Feb 3, 18; m 53; c 3. BIOCHEMISTRY. *Educ:* Univ Minn, BA, 50; Univ Rochester, PhD(chem), 43. *Prof Exp:* Asst, Univ Rochester, 40-43; res chemist, Exp Sta, E I du Pont de Nemours & Co, Inc, 43-51, res supvr, 51-60; vis lectr, Biochem Div, Univ Ill, 63-66; sr res scientist, Dept Biol, 67-71, CHMN & DIR DEPT IMMUNOL, CITY OF HOPE RES INST, 71- *Concurrent Pos:* Guggenheim fel, 61; NSF fel, Pasteur Inst, 62-63. *Res:* Immunology. *Mailing Add:* Div of Immunol City of Hope Res Inst Duarte CA 91010

TODD, CLEMENT JAMESON, meteorology, see previous edition

TODD, DAVID BURTON, b Chester, Pa, Dec 21, 25; m 50; c 4. CHEMICAL ENGINEERING. *Educ:* Northwestern Univ, BS, 46, MS, 48; Princeton Univ, PhD(chem eng), 52. *Prof Exp:* Engr, Shell Develop Co, Calif, 52-62, supvr develop, 62-63; mgr eng, Podbielniak Div, Dresser Indust, Ill, 63-67; TECH DIR, BAKER PERKINS, INC, 67- *Concurrent Pos:* Mem adv comt eng & technol, Saginaw Valley State Col, 77-; mem indust adv comt, Mich Molecular Inst, 78-; lectr, Ctr Prof Advan & Plastics Inst Am, 80- *Mem:* AAAS; fel Am Inst Chem Engrs; Am Chem Soc; Am Oil Chem Soc; Soc Plastics Engrs. *Res:* Liquid-liquid extraction; fluidization; polymerization; catalysis; acid treating; equipment design. *Mailing Add:* Baker Perkins Inc 1000 Hess St Saginaw MI 48601

TODD, DAVID KEITH, b Lafayette, Ind, Dec 30, 23; m 48; c 2. CIVIL ENGINEERING, HYDROLOGY. *Educ:* Purdue Univ, BS, 48; NY Univ, MS, 49; Univ Calif, Berkeley, PhD(civil eng), 53. *Prof Exp:* Hydraul engr, US Bur Reclamation, 48-50; from instr to assoc prof civil eng, 50-62, PROF CIVIL ENG, UNIV CALIF, 62- *Concurrent Pos:* NSF fel, 57-58; NSF sr fel, 64-65; centennial prof, Am Univ Beirut, 67; Pres, David Keith Todd Consult Engrs, Inc, 78- *Honors & Awards:* Res Prize, Am Soc Civil Engrs, 60. *Mem:* Am Soc Civil Engrs; Am Geophys Union; Am Water Works Asn; Am Meteorol Soc; AAAS. *Res:* Water resources planning, development and management; surface water and groundwater hydrology; precipitation, runoff and floods; saline water intrusion underground; groundwater pollution. *Mailing Add:* 2914 Domingo Ave Berkeley CA 94705

TODD, EDWARD PAYSON, b Newburyport, Mass, Jan 26, 20; m 50; c 3. ATMOSPHERIC PHYSICS, SCIENCE ADMINISTRATION. *Educ:* Mass Inst Technol, BS, 42; Univ Colo, PhD(physics), 54. *Prof Exp:* Res physicist, United Shoe Mach Corp, Mass, 46-49; supvr appl res, Pitney-Bowes, Inc, Conn, 54-57; mem res staff physics, Univ Colo, 57-59, tech dir upper air lab, 59-63; assoc prog dir atmospheric sci sect, 60-61, prog dir aeronomy, 63-65, actg sect head atmospheric sci sect, 63-64, spec asst to assoc dir res, 65-66, dep assoc dir res, 66-70, dep asst dir res, 70-75, dep asst dir astron, atmospheric, earth & ocean sci, 75-77, actg dir, Atmospheric Sci Div, 75-76, DIR, DIV POLAR PROGS, NSF, 77- *Concurrent Pos:* Mem fed comt meteorol serv & supporting res, NSF, 70-77, chmn interdept comt atmospheric sci, 73-78, chmn, Interagency Arctic Res Coord Comt, 77-78. *Honors & Awards:* Distinguished Serv Medal, NSF, 71. *Mem:* Am Geophys Union; Am Meteorol Soc. *Mailing Add:* 312 Van Buren St Falls Church VA 22046

TODD, EDWIN HARKNESS, plant pathology, see previous edition

TODD, ERIC E(DWARD), b Marlow, Eng, Apr 27, 06; nat US; m 36; c 3. CHEMICAL ENGINEERING. *Educ:* Univ BC, BASc, 29, MASc, 30; Stanford Univ, PhD(chem, physics), 34. *Prof Exp:* Chemist, B C Cement Co, Can, 28; chemist metall assays, Consol Mining & Smelting, 29; chemist petrol, Union Oil Co, Calif, 31-32; res chemist, Mich Alkali Co, Calif, 34-35; head chemist, Calif Testing Labs, 36-39; res chemist frozen foods, Calif Consumers Corp, 39-47; tech dir packaged foods, Lady's Choice Foods, Inc, 47-48; chem engr, Ventura Farms Frozen Foods, Inc, 48-59; res chemist, Milo Harding Co, 59-80. *Concurrent Pos:* Consult chem engr, M M H Corp, 48-, Oxnard Frozen Foods Coop & H L Hunt Foods, 59-80, Gen Elec Co & Case Swayne Co, 69-81. *Mem:* AAAS; Am Chem Soc; Nat Soc Prof Engrs; Inst Food Technol. *Res:* Frozen and specialty foods; chemistry; physics. *Mailing Add:* 28730 Grayfox St Malibu CA 90265

TODD, EWEN CAMERON DAVID, b Glasgow, Scotland, Dec 25, 39; m 67; c 4. MICROBIOLOGY. *Educ:* Glasgow Univ, BSc, 63, PhD(bact taxon), 68. *Prof Exp:* Asst lectr bact, Glasgow Univ, 65-68; res scientist, 68-70, head, Methodology Sect, Food Microbiol, 71-73, HEAD, CONTAMINATED FOODS SECT, BUR MICROBIAL HAZARDS, HEALTH PROTECTION BR, DEPT NAT HEALTH & WELFARE, 74-, CHMN, FOOD-BORNE DIS REPORTING CTR, 77- *Mem:* Brit Soc Appl Bact. *Res:* Development of methods for food microbiology; public health aspects of food; microbial taxonomy; food-borne disease statistics. *Mailing Add:* Res Div Bur of Microbial Hazards Health & Welfare Can Ottawa ON K1A 0L2 Can

TODD, FRANK ARNOLD, b Merrill, Iowa, Sept 11, 11; m 36; c 2. VETERINARY MEDICINE. *Educ:* Iowa State Col, DVM, 33; Yale Univ, MPH, 35; Am Bd Vet Pub Health, dipl. *Prof Exp:* Secy res & develop bd, Off Secy Defense, US Army, 49-51; consult vet serv, Fed Civil Defense Admin, 51-54; asst to adminstr, Agr Res Serv, USDA, 54-65; WASH REP, AM VET MED ASN, 65- *Mem:* Am Vet Med Asn; Am Pub Health Asn; NY Acad Sci. *Res:* Epidemiology and epizootiology of animal diseases; exotic animal diseases; biological and chemical warfare defense; atomic energy. *Mailing Add:* 145 S Aberdeen St Arlington VA 22204

TODD, FREDERICK HENRY, naval architecture, see previous edition

TODD, GLEN CORY, b Crawfordsville, Ind, May 10, 31; m 54; c 4. PATHOLOGY. *Educ:* Ind Cent Col, BA, 54; Univ Pa, VMD, 58; Cornell Univ, PhD(path), 65; Am Col Vet Path, dipl. *Prof Exp:* Vet, Agr Res Serv, USDA, 58-62; teaching assoc path, Cornell Univ, 62-65; pathologist, Agr Res Serv, USDA, 65-66 & Vet Res Div, Food & Drug Admin, 66-67; SR PATHOLOGIST, LILLY RES LABS, ELI LILLY & CO, 67- *Mem:* Am Vet Med Asn; NY Acad Sci; Int Acad Path. *Res:* Physiopathology of vitamin E and selenium; nutritional hepatic necrosis; aflatoxicosis in animals; induced myopathies; developmental and neoplastic diseases. *Mailing Add:* 1410 Bittersweet Dr Greenfield IN 46140

TODD, GLENN WILLIAM, b Kansas City, Mo, Sept 30, 27; m 51; c 4. PLANT PHYSIOLOGY. *Educ:* Univ Mo, AB, 49, MA, 50, PhD, 52. *Prof Exp:* Res fel plant physiol, Calif Inst Technol, 52-53; jr biochemist, Citrus Exp Sta, Riverside, Calif, 53-54, asst biochemist, 54-58; from asst prof to assoc prof, 58-66, dir sch biol sci, 72-81, PROF BOT, OKLA STATE UNIV, 67-, HEAD BOT DEPT, 81- *Concurrent Pos:* Fulbright prof, Cairo Univ, 66-67 & Azerbaijan State Univ, USSR, 81; ed, Proc Okla Acad Sci, 80- *Mem:* Am Inst Biol Sci; Sigma Xi; AAAS; Am Soc Plant Physiol; Scandinavian Soc Plant Physiol. *Res:* Physiological responses of plants to environmental stress. *Mailing Add:* Botany Dept Okla State Univ Stillwater OK 74078

TODD, GORDON LIVINGSTON, b Princeton, WVa, Mar 17, 44; m 68; c 2. ANATOMY, ELECTRON MICROSCOPY. *Educ:* Kenyon Col, AB, 66; Med Col Ga, MS, 69, PhD(anat), 72. *Prof Exp:* ASST PROF ANAT, SCH MED, CREIGHTON UNIV, 72- *Concurrent Pos:* Ga Heart Asn grant, Med Col Ga, 71-72. *Mem:* AAAS; Am Asn Anat. *Res:* Lymphatics; autonomic innervation. *Mailing Add:* 822 S 120th Ave Omaha NE 68154

TODD, HAROLD DAVID, b Mt Vernon, Ill, Nov, 19, 44; m 69. CHEMISTRY. *Educ:* Univ Ill, Urbana, BS, 66; Johns Hopkins Univ, PhD(chem), 71. *Prof Exp:* ASST PROF CHEM & DIR COMPUT CTR, WESLEYAN UNIV, 71-, ADJ ASSOC PROF MATH & CHEM, COORDR ACAD COMPUT & DIR, COMPUT CTR, 80- *Mem:* Am Phys Soc. *Res:* Theoretical chemistry with emphasis upon mathematical and computational problems. *Mailing Add:* Dept of Chem Wesleyan Univ Middletown CT 06457

TODD, HARRY FLYNN, JR, b Baton Rouge, La, Apr 9, 41. ANTHROPOLOGY, MEDICAL ANTHROPOLOGY. *Educ:* La State Univ, BS, 62; George Washington Univ, JD, 65; Univ Calif, Berkeley, MA, 70, PhD(anthrop), 72. *Prof Exp:* Fel, Ctr Study Law & Soc & actg asst prof anthrop, Univ Calif, Berkeley, 72-73; lectr & fel, Med Anthrop Prog, Dept Int Health, 74-76, adj asst prof, 76-78, asst prof, 78-81, ASSOC PROF ANTHROP IN RESIDENCE, UNIV CALIF, SAN FRANCISCO, 81- *Concurrent Pos:* Ed, Med Anthrop Newsletter. *Mem:* Fel Am Anthrop Asn; fel Geront Soc; Law & Soc Asn; Soc Med Anthrop; fel Soc Appl Anthrop. *Res:* Legal problems and behavior of urban residents, with a focus on both formal and informal mechanisms and agencies used for dispute settlement and conflict management. *Mailing Add:* Med Anthrop Prog 1320 Third Ave Univ Calif San Francisco CA 94143

TODD, HOLLIS N, b Glens Falls, NY, Jan 28, 14; m 36; c 1. PHOTOGRAPHY, PHYSICS. *Educ:* Cornell Univ, BA, 34, MEd, 35. *Prof Exp:* Prof, 46-77, EMER PROF PHYSICS, ROCHESTER INST TECHNOL, 77- *Res:* Photographic physics, science and engineering. *Mailing Add:* 3213 Bay Berry Terrace Sarasota FL 33577

TODD, JAMES HOPKINS, b Greenwich, Conn, May 24, 16; m 39; c 2. GEOLOGY. *Educ:* Dartmouth Col, AB, 38; Univ Minn, PhD(geol), 42. *Prof Exp:* Instr geol, Univ Minn, 39-42; geologist & geophysicist, Calif Co, La, 42-46, dist geologist, 47, geophys supt, 48-49, div exp supt, 50-54; mgr explor dept, Stand Oil Co, Tex, 54-55, vpres & dir, 55-59, consult, Standard Oil Co, Calif, 59-60; vpres explor, prod, land & legal, Chevron Oil Co, 61-70, vpres & gen mgr explor & actg pres, Western Div, 70-76, regional vpres, Chevron USA, Inc, 77-81; RETIRED. *Mem:* Soc Explor Geophys; Am Asn Petrol Geol. *Res:* Pleistocene history of the upper Mississippi River; economic geology; petrology. *Mailing Add:* 3801 E Kentucky Ave Denver CO 80209

TODD, JAMES WYATT, b Houston Co, Ala, Dec 16, 42; m 64; c 2. ECONOMIC ENTOMOLOGY. *Educ:* Auburn Univ, BS, 66, MS, 68; Clemson Univ, PhD(entom), 73. *Prof Exp:* From field res asst to res asst entom, Auburn Univ, 64-68; asst prof, 68-77, ASSOC PROF RES ENTOM, UNIV GA, 77- *Mem:* Entom Soc Am. *Res:* Development of soybean insect pest management systems including host plant resistance; utilization of natural control agents; chemical and microbial pesticides; cultural control practices and economic injury thresholds. *Mailing Add:* Ga Coastal Plain Exp Sta PO Box 748 Tifton GA 31794

TODD, JERRY WILLIAM, b La Crosse, Wis, Jan 7, 30; m 56; c 1. ANALYTICAL CHEMISTRY. *Educ:* Wis State Univ, Platteville, BS, 51; Univ Wis, PhD(anal chem), 60. *Prof Exp:* Teacher high sch, Wis, 51-52; chemist, Liberty Powder Defense Corp, Olin Mathieson Chem Corp, 52-56; sr chemist, Cent Res Lab, 60-69, SR RES SPECIALIST, AGRICHEM ANAL LAB, 3M Co, 69- *Mem:* Am Chem Soc. *Res:* Gas and liquid chromatography, ur-vis-IR spectroscopy; titrimetry. *Mailing Add:* 3M Co 3M Ctr St Paul MN 55101

TODD, JOHN, b Carnacally, Ireland, May 16, 11; nat US; m 38. NUMERICAL ANALYSIS. *Educ:* Queen's Univ, Belfast, BSc, 31. *Prof Exp:* Lectr, Queen's Univ, Belfast, 33-37 & King's Col, London, 37-49; expert appl math, Nat Bur Stand, 47-48, chief comput lab, 49-54, numerical anal, 54-57; PROF MATH, CALIF INST TECHNOL, 57- *Concurrent Pos:* Scientist, Brit Admiralty, 39-46; Fulbright prof, Univ Vienna, 65. *Mem:* Am Math Soc; Soc Indust & Appl Math; Math Asn Am; Asn Comput Mach. *Res:* Mathematical analysis; algebra. *Mailing Add:* Dept Math 253-37 Calif Inst Technol Pasadena CA 91125

TODD, JUDSON DONALD, b Amarillo, Tex, Aug 12, 33; m 58; c 6. VIROLOGY, RESEARCH ADMINISTRATION. *Educ:* Colo State Univ, BSc, 55, DVM, 57; Univ Pa, MedSc, 66. *Prof Exp:* Instr med, Col Vet Med, Colo State Univ, 57-58; fel & asst prof med & prev med, Vet Col, Univ Pa, 64-69; head virol, Jensen Salsbery Labs, 70-72, dir biol res & develop, 72-75, DIR RES, JEN-SAL/WELLCOME RES LABS, 76- *Mem:* Am Vet Med Asn; Am Asn Indust Vet; AAAS; US Animal Health Asn. *Res:* Pathogenesis; immunology and prevention of infectious diseases of animals; respiratory diseases of horses and cattle. *Mailing Add:* 2000 S 11th St Kansas City KS 66103

TODD, KENNETH S, JR, b Three Forks, Mont, Aug, 25, 36. VETERINARY PARASITOLOGY. *Educ:* Mont State Univ, BS, 62, MS, 64; Utah State Univ, PhD(zool), 67. *Prof Exp:* Asst zool, Utah State Univ, 64-67; from asst prof to assoc prof, 67-76, PROF VET PARASITOL, UNIV ILL, URBANA, 76- *Concurrent Pos:* Actg dir ctr human ecol, Univ Ill, Urbana, 72. *Mem:* Am Soc Parasitol; Am Vet Med Asn; Am Soc Trop Med & Hyg; Am Heartworm Soc; Am Asn Vet Parasitologists. *Res:* Parasites of wildlife and domestic animals; ecology of parasitism. *Mailing Add:* Col of Vet Med Univ of Ill Urbana IL 61801

TODD, LEE JOHN, b Denver, Colo, Nov 8, 36; m 60; c 3. INORGANIC CHEMISTRY. *Educ:* Univ Notre Dame, BS, 58; Fla State Univ, MS, 60; Ind Univ, PhD(chem), 63. *Prof Exp:* Res assoc chem, Mass Inst Technol, 63-64; asst prof inorg chem, Univ Ill, Urbana, 64-68; assoc prof, 68-74, PROF CHEM, IND UNIV, BLOOMINGTON, 74- *Mem:* Am Chem Soc. *Res:* Inorganic and physical inorganic chemistry of boron and organometallic compounds. *Mailing Add:* Dept Chem A669 Chem Bldg Indiana Univ Bloomington IN 47401

TODD, LEONARD, b Glasgow, Scotland, Feb 7, 40. THEORETICAL MECHANICS. *Educ:* Strathclyde Univ, BSc, 61; Cambridge Univ, PhD(appl math), 64. *Prof Exp:* C L E Moore instr appl math, Mass Inst Technol, 64-66; lectr, Strathclyde Univ, 66-69; ASSOC PROF APPL MATH, LAURENTIAN UNIV, 69- *Concurrent Pos:* Nat Res Coun Can res grants, 69- *Res:* Theoretical fluid mechanics; asymptotic expansions with emphasis on applications. *Mailing Add:* 2348 Louisa Dr Sudbury ON P3E 4W8 Can

TODD, MARGARET EDNA, b New York, NY, Sept 14, 24; m 66. PHYSIOLOGY, MEDICAL SCIENCES. *Educ:* Mich State Univ, BS, 46; Fordham Univ, MS, 55, PhD, 58. *Prof Exp:* Med technician, Woman's Hosp & State Dept Health, Detroit, 46; med technician, 47-53, res asst blood coagulation & vascular dis, 58-72, ASST PROF BIOCHEM, DEPT SURG, MED COL, CORNELL UNIV, 72-; CONSULT HEMATOL & COAGULATION, BECTON DICKINSON CO, EAST RUTHERFORD, 77- *Concurrent Pos:* Grant, Churchill Hosp, Oxford, Eng, 62 & Mayo Clin, 63; sr scientist, Technician Instrument Corp, 73- *Mem:* AAAS; Am Soc Clin Path; Soc Study Blood; NY Acad Sci; Int Soc Hemat. *Res:* Insect physiology; blood components; separation of amino acids by paper chromatography; human blood coagulation; electrophoresis of coagulation factors; blood coagulation and anticoagulation therapy in relation to heart disease, pregnancy and kidney disease; use of the nonhuman primate as an animal model to simulate man in physiological and pharmacological studies. *Mailing Add:* 87 Roberts Rd Englewood Cliffs NJ 07632

TODD, MARY ELIZABETH, b Kingston, Ont; m 72. ANATOMY. *Educ:* Univ BC, BA, 57, MSc, 59; Univ Glasgow, PhD(zool), 62. *Prof Exp:* Lectr & head biol dept, United Col, Man, 62-63; from lectr to sr lectr anat, Univ Glasgow, 62-71; vis asst prof anat, Univ BC, 70-71; asst prof anat, Univ Western Ont, 72; sessional lectr oral biol & zool, 72-73, asst prof, 73-75, ASSOC PROF ANAT, UNIV BC, 75- *Mem:* Anat Soc Gt Brit; Can Asn Anatomists; Am Asn Anatomists; Sigma Xi. *Res:* Ultrastructure of vascular tissues; specifically developmental studies on components of the walls of vessels and on vasomotor innervation; investigation of cultured tissues. *Mailing Add:* Dept of Anat Univ of BC Vancouver BC V6T 1W5 Can

TODD, MICHAEL JEREMY, b Chelmsford, Eng, Aug 14, 47; m 71; c 1. MATHEMATICAL PROGRAMMING, NUMERICAL ANALYSIS. *Educ:* Cambridge Univ, Eng, BA, 68; Yale Univ, PhD(admin sci), 72. *Prof Exp:* Asst prof opers res, Univ Ottawa, 72-73; asst prof, 73-78, ASSOC PROF OPERS RES, CORNELL UNIV, 78- *Concurrent Pos:* Prin investr, NSF, 74-76, 77-79 & 79-82; vis res fel, Ctr Opers Res & Econometrics, Louvain, Belg, 76-77; assoc ed, Math Opers Res, 78-, co-ed, Math Prog, 80-; sr visitor, Dept Appl Math & Theoret Physics, Cambridge Univ, Eng, 80-81. *Mem:* Opers Res Soc Am; Sigma Xi; Math Programming Soc. *Res:* Computational techniques for fixed-point problems; mathematical programming; combinatorial optimization; mathematical economic. *Mailing Add:* Dept of Opers Res Cornell Univ Ithaca NY 14853

TODD, NEIL BOWMAN, b Cambridge, Mass, Jan 3, 36. EVOLUTIONARY BIOLOGY, GENETICS. *Educ:* Univ Mass, BS, 59; Harvard Univ, PhD(biol), 63. *Prof Exp:* Geneticist, Animal Res Ctr, Med Sch, Harvard Univ, 63-68; DIR & GENETICIST, CARNIVORE GENETICS RES CTR, 68- *Concurrent Pos:* Geneticist, Bio-Res, Inst, Mass, 68-69; res dir, Faunalabs, Inc, 68-72; adj prof dept biol, Boston Univ, 71-76. *Res:* Chromosomal mechanisms in the origin and evolution of mammals; population genetics and mutantallele frequencies in domestic cats. *Mailing Add:* Carnivore Genetics Res Ctr Newtonville MA 02160

TODD, PAUL WILSON, b Bangor, Maine, June 15, 36; m 57; c 4. BIOPHYSICS. *Educ:* Bowdoin Col, AB, 59; Mass Inst Technol, BS, 59; Univ Rochester, MS, 60; Univ Calif, Berkeley, PhD(biophys), 64. *Prof Exp:* Lectr med physics, Univ Calif, Berkeley, 64-66; from asst prof to assoc prof biophys, 66-77, chmn, grad prog genetics, 73-78, PROF BIOPHYS, PA STATE UNIV, 77- *Concurrent Pos:* Eleanor Roosevelt Int Cancer res fel, 67-68; mem biomed steering comt, Los Alamos Meson Physics Facility, 70-77, chmn, 73-74 & vis staff mem, Los Alamos Sci Lab, 74, mem bd dir, Los Alamos Meson Physics Facil Users Group, 76-77; vis fel, Princeton Univ, 71-72; mem biol comt, Argonne Univ Asn, 73-75 & chmn, 75; consult, Oak Ridge Nat Lab, 75-; vis prof med physics, Univ Calif, 79; assoc ed, Radiation Res, 76-79; assoc ed, Cell Biophysics, 78-; vis scientist, Univ Uppsala, 79 & Oncol Sci Ctr, Moscow, 79. *Mem:* Electrophoresis Soc; Am Soc Cell Biol; Tissue Cult Asn; Am Soc Photobiol; NY Acad Sci. *Res:* Radiation physics; cellular radiation biology; basic research related to radiation therapy; chemistry of cell surface; mammalian cell culture; cell electrophoresis; automated cytology; laser light scattering by cells. *Mailing Add:* 403 Althouse Lab PA State Univ University Park PA 16802

TODD, PETER JUSTIN, b Lackawanna, NY, June 26, 49; m 72; c 1. ION OPTICS. *Educ:* Rensselaer Polytech Inst, BS, 71; Cornell Univ, MS, 77, PhD(chem), 80. *Prof Exp:* STAFF SCIENTIST, OAK RIDGE NAT LAB, 80- *Mem:* Am Chem Soc; Am Soc Mass Spectrometry; Sigma Xi. *Res:* Organic mass spectrometry, particularly in design and construction of spectrumeters; collision and fragmentation of high energy polyatomic ions. *Mailing Add:* PO Box Y Bldg 9735 Oak Ridge TN 37830

TODD, ROBERT EMERSON, b Hartford, Conn, Dec 10, 06; m 32; c 3. ZOOLOGY, EMBRYOLOGY. *Educ:* Bowdoin Col, BS, 29; Harvard Univ, MA, 35, PhD(zool), 38. *Prof Exp:* Asst zool, Harvard Univ, 35-38; instr biol, 38-43, from asst prof to prof, 43-72, EMER PROF, ZOOL, COLGATE UNIV, 72- *Concurrent Pos:* Chmn dept zool, Colgate Univ, 55-61 & biol, 64-67. *Mem:* Am Soc Zool; AAAS. *Res:* Experimental embryology; cellular components of centrifuged frog eggs. *Mailing Add:* 58 Payne St Hamilton NY 13346

TODD, ROBIN GRENVILLE, b Devon, Eng, July 24, 48; m 78. ENTOMOLOGY. *Educ:* Univ Lancaster, BA, 71; Univ Reading, PhD(entom), 79. *Prof Exp:* Res asst entom mosquito res & control, Grand Cayman British West Duties Unit, 79-80; ENTOMOLOGIST, INSECT CONTROL & RES, INC, 80- *Mem:* Am Mosquito Control Asn; Entom Soc Am; Inst Biol. *Res:* Minnows as potential control agents of mosquitoes in Caribbean; evaluation of pesticides against household and medically important insects and arachnids. *Mailing Add:* 8420 Maymeadow Court Baltimore MD 21207

TODD, TERRENCE PATRICK, b Brantford, Ont, Aug 16, 46; m 70; c 4. GEOPHYSICS, GEOLOGY. *Educ:* Univ Toronto, BS, 69; Mass Inst Technol, PhD(geophys), 73. *Prof Exp:* Res asst geophys, Dept Earth & Planetary Sci, Mass Inst Technol, 69-73; res geophysicist, Shell Develop Co, 73-77; sr res geophysicist, Gulf Res & Develop Co, Pittsburg, Pa, 77-80, SR REGIONAL GEOPHYSICIST, GULF OIL EXP & PROD CO, BAKERSFIELD, CALIF, 80- *Res:* Elastic properties of rock and other materials. *Mailing Add:* Gulf Exp & Prod Co PO Box 1392 Bakersfield CA 93302

TODD, TERRY RAY, b De Kalb, Ill, Oct 9, 47; m 78. PHYSICS, MOLECULAR SPECTROSCOPY. *Educ:* Northern Ill Univ, BS, 69; Pa State Univ, MS, 72, PhD(physics), 76. *Prof Exp:* Nat Bur Standards-Nat Res Coun fel physics, Gaithersburg, 76-78; STAFF SCIENTIST PHYSICS, LASER ANAL INC, 78- *Mem:* Optical Soc Am; AAAS. *Res:* High resolution molecular spectroscopy in the infrared region; optics. *Mailing Add:* Laser Anal Inc 25 Wiggins Ave Bedford MA 01730

TODD, WILLIAM MCCLINTOCK, b Colon, Panama, July 17, 25; US citizen; m 47; c 2. MEDICAL MICROBIOLOGY, VIROLOGY. *Educ:* Univ Ga, BS, 50; Vanderbilt Univ, MS, 55, PhD(microbiol), 57. *Prof Exp:* Asst prof microbiol, Sch Med, Univ Miss, 57-63; ASSOC PROF MICROBIOL, MED UNITS, UNIV TENN, MEMPHIS, 63-, PROF, CTR FOR HEALTH SCI, 65- *Concurrent Pos:* USPHS fel biochem & res assoc, Vanderbilt Univ, 58-60. *Mem:* Am Soc Microbiol; Tissue Cult Asn. *Res:* Host-virus relationships. *Mailing Add:* Dept of Microbiol Univ of Tenn Ctr for Health Sci Memphis TN 38163

TODHUNTER, ELIZABETH NEIGE, b Christchurch, NZ, July 6, 01; nat US. NUTRITION. *Educ:* Univ NZ, BS, 26, MS, 28; Columbia Univ, PhD(chem), 33. *Prof Exp:* From asst prof to assoc prof nutrit, State Col Wash, 34-41; from assoc prof to prof & head dept, Univ Ala, 41-53, dean sch home econ, 53-66; NUTRIT CONSULT, 66-; VIS PROF NUTRIT, SCH MED, VANDERBILT UNIV, 67- *Concurrent Pos:* Consult to Surgeon Gen, US Air Force, 65-67; vis lectr & sci writing, 66- *Mem:* AAAS; Am Chem Soc; Am Dietetic Asn (pres, 57-58); Am Inst Nutrit. *Res:* Vitamin C in foods and body fluids; vitamin A in foods; human food consumption; dietary studies; nutritional status measurements; nutrition of elderly; history of nutrition. *Mailing Add:* Div of Nutrit Vanderbilt Univ Sch Med Nashville TN 37232

TODHUNTER, JOHN ANTHONY, b Cali, Colombia, Oct 9, 49; US citizen; m 72; c 2. BIOCHEMISTRY, MOLECULAR BIOLOGY. *Educ:* Univ Calif, Los Angeles, BS, 71; Calif State Univ, Los Angeles, MS, 73; Univ Calif, Santa Barbara, PhD(chem), 76. *Prof Exp:* Instr, Dept Chem, Calif State Univ, Los Angeles, 72-73; teaching asst, Univ Calif, Santa Barbara, 74, res asst biochem, 74-76; fel, Roche Inst Molecular Biol, Hoffman-La Roche, Nutley, 76-78; asst prof biol & chmn prog biochem, Cath Univ Am, 78-81; ASST ADMINR, PESTICIDES & TOXIC SUBSTANCES, ENVIRON PROTECTION AGENCY, 81- *Concurrent Pos:* Consult, Arral Industs, Encino, 72-; assoc, Andrulis Res Corp, Bethesda, 78-; mem, Hazardous Waste Siting Bd, State Md, 80-81. *Mem:* Am Chem Soc; AAAS; NY Acad Sci. *Res:* Mechanisms of drug and toxicant action; enzymology; dynamic behavior of biochemical systems; biochemistry of gene transcription and expression. *Mailing Add:* Dept of Biol Cath Univ of Am Washington DC 20064

TODOROVIC, PETAR N, b Belgrade, Yugoslavia, Nov 10, 32; m 64; c 3. PROBABILITY, ENGINEERING. *Educ:* Univ Belgrade, BS, 58, PhD(probability), 64. *Prof Exp:* Asst math probability & statist, Univ Belgrade, 58-64, docent, 64-66; assoc prof civil eng, Colo State Univ, 66-73; RES PROF ENG, POLYTECH SCH, UNIV MONTREAL, 73- *Mem:* Am Geophys Union; Inst Math Statist; NY Acad Sci. *Res:* Probability theory; hydrology, hydraulics and fluid mechanics. *Mailing Add:* Ecole Polytech Univ Montreal PO Box 6079-Sta A Montreal PQ H3C 3A7 Can

TODSEN, THOMAS KAMP, b Pittsfield, Mass, Oct 21, 18; m 39; c 2. SCIENCE ADMINISTRATION, BOTANY. *Educ:* Univ Fla, BS, 39, MS, 42, PhD(org chem), 50. *Prof Exp:* Asst & instr, Univ Fla, 47-50; instr, NMex Col Agr & Mech Arts, 50-51; chief chemist, White Sands Missile Range, 51-53, chief warheads engr, 53-58, sci adv off, 58-59, land combat systs eval, 59-66, dir test opers, 66-69, dir SSMPO, 69-72, tech dir army missile test & eval, 72-78; res assoc, 77-79, ASST PROF, NMEX STATE UNIV, 79- *Mem:* AAAS; Am Chem Soc; Sigma Xi. *Res:* Naturally occurring plant constituents; plant taxonomy; plant distribution. *Mailing Add:* 2000 Rose Lane Las Cruces NM 88005

TOEBES, GERRIT H, water resources, fluid mechanics, deceased

TOENISKOETTER, RICHARD HENRY, b St Louis, Mo, Mar 21, 31; m 53; c 6. ENVIRONMENTAL SCIENCES, POLYMER CHEMISTRY. *Educ:* Univ St Louis, BS, 52, MS, 56, PhD(chem), 58. *Prof Exp:* Res chemist, Union Carbide Corp, 57-67; sr res chemist, ADM Chem Co Div, Ashland Oil Co, 67-68, group leader, Ashland Chem Co, 68-70, mgr inorg chem res, 70-73, mgr foundry res, 73-78, MGR ENVIRON OCCUP SAFETY, ASHLAND CHEM CO, 78- *Mem:* Am Chem Soc; Am Ceramic Soc; Sigma Xi. *Res:* Organic and inorganic polymer chemistry; coordination and fluorine compounds; boron hydrides; materials and foundry products research; environmental science. *Mailing Add:* 6771 Masefield St Worthington OH 43085

TOENNIES, JAN PETER, b Philadelphia, Pa, May 3, 30; m 66; c 2. MOLECULAR PHYSICS. *Educ:* Brown Univ, PhD(chem), 57. *Prof Exp:* Asst, 57-67, docent, 67-71, HON PROF, INST PHYSICS, UNIV BONN, 71-; DIR, MAX PLANCK INST FLUID DYNAMICS, 69- *Concurrent Pos:* Guest docent, Gothenburg Univ, 66-75; apl prof, Univ Göttingen, 72- *Mem:* Am Phys Soc; Ger Phys Soc; Europ Phys Soc. *Res:* Molecular beam investigations of elastic, inelastic and reactive collisions; theory of inelastic scattering; chemical reactions in shock waves. *Mailing Add:* Max Planck Inst for Fluid Dynamics Böttingerstrasse 6-8 Göttingen Germany, Federal Republic of

TOENNIESSEN, GARY HERBERT, b Lockport, NY, July 9, 44; m 67. ENVIRONMENTAL SCIENCES. *Educ:* State Univ NY Buffalo, BA, 66; Univ NC, MS, 68, PhD(environ sci), 71. *Prof Exp:* Prog assoc, 71-72, asst dir natural & environ sci, 72-78, ASST DIR AGR SCI, ROCKEFELLER FOUND, 78- *Mem:* Am Soc Microbiol; Water Pollution Control Fedn. *Res:* Structure and function of aquatic ecosystems and environmental problems associated with agriculture. *Mailing Add:* Rockefeller Found 1133 Ave of the Americas New York NY 10036

TOENSING, C(LARENCE) H(ERMAN), b St Paul, Minn, Aug 23, 15; m 45; c 1. METALLURGY, PHYSICAL CHEMISTRY. *Educ:* Macalester Col, AB, 37; Mont Sch Mines, MS, 39; Carnegie Inst Technol, ScD(phys chem), 47. *Prof Exp:* Instr chem, Mont Sch Mines, 37-39; asst, Carnegie Inst Technol, 39-44, instr, 44-49; sr technologist, US Steel Corp, 44-50; asst to mgr opers, Brush Beryllium Co, Ohio, 50, res engr, Brush Electronics Co, 50-51; res & develop engr, Lamp Metals & Components Dept, Gen Elec Co, 51-59; dir res, Firth Sterling, Inc, 59-64, dir tech serv, Carmet Co, 64-69; plant mgr, Valeron Corp, 69-81; RETIRED. *Mem:* Am Chem Soc; Am Soc Metals; Am Inst Mining, Metall & Petrol Engrs. *Res:* Gas-metal reactions; chemistry and metallurgy of tungsten and molybdenum; refractory carbides and materials. *Mailing Add:* 702 Via Zapata Riverside CA 92507

TOEPFER, ALAN JAMES, b Chicago, Ill, Oct 20, 41. PULSED POWER, FUSION. *Educ:* Marquette Univ, BA, 62; Univ Southern Calif, MS, 64, PhD(physics), 68. *Prof Exp:* Res asst, Royal Inst Technol, Stockholm, 64-65; tech staff, Aerospace Corp, 65-66; tech staff, Sandia Labs, 68-75, supvr, 75-79; dir, 79-81, VPRES & DIR, RES & DEVELOP, PHYSICS INT CO, 81- *Mem:* Am Phys Soc; AAAS. *Res:* Inertial confinement fusion; pulsed power; intense relativistic electron beams; electromagnetic propulsion; radiation effects of nuclear weapons; fusion engineering. *Mailing Add:* Physics Int Co 2700 Merced St San Leandro CA 94577

TOEPFER, RICHARD E, JR, b Chicago, Ill, Oct 9, 34; m 65; c 3. DATA PROCESSING, CONTROL SYSTEMS. *Educ:* Univ Ill, BSEE, 56, MSEE, 57, PhD(elec eng), 62. *Prof Exp:* Mem tech staff, Aerospace Corp, 61-63; res specialist, Autonetics Div, N Am Aviation, Inc, 63-64; adv engr, IBM Corp, Calif, 65-69; chief systs engr, Measurex Corp, 68-69; proj mgr, Data Systs Develop Div, Hewlett Packard, 70-71, sect mgr, 71-76, prod eng mgr, Data Systs Div, 76-80; OPERS MGR, SPECTRA PHYSICS, 80- *Concurrent Pos:* Mem & subcomt chmn, Tech Adv Comt on Comput Systs, Bur East-West Trade, US Dept Commerce, 73-75. *Mem:* Inst Elec & Electronics Engrs; Soc Indust & Appl Math. *Res:* Data processing systems; process control systems; control systems theory; video systems design. *Mailing Add:* Spectra Physics 3333 N 1st St San Jose CA 95051

TOETZ, DALE W, b Milwaukee, Wis, Sept 23, 37. FISH BIOLOGY, LIMNOLOGY. *Educ:* Univ Wis, BS, 59, MS, 61; Ind Univ, PhD(zool), 65. *Prof Exp:* Actg instr zool, Univ Wis, Milwaukee, 61-62; teaching asst, Ind Univ, 62-65; asst prof, 65-69, assoc prof, 69-79, PROF ZOOL, OKLA STATE UNIV, 79- *Concurrent Pos:* Water Resources Res Inst res grant, 66-; assoc res biologist, Scripps Inst Oceanog, 74; tech consult, US Environ Protection Agency, 77. *Mem:* Am Fisheries Soc; Ecol Soc Am; Am Soc Limnol & Oceanog; Int Soc Theoret & Appl Limnol. *Res:* Limnology of nitrogen; year class formation in fish; lake restoration. *Mailing Add:* Zool Dept Okla State Univ Stillwater OK 74078

TOEWS, CORNELIUS J, b Altona, Man, Mar 22, 37; m 61; c 3. ENDOCRINOLOGY, BIOCHEMISTRY. *Educ:* Univ Man, BSc & MD, 63; Queen's Univ, Ont, PhD(biochem), 67; FRCPS(C), 69. *Prof Exp:* ASST PROF BIOCHEM & MED, MED SCH, MCMASTER UNIV, 71- *Concurrent Pos:* Med Res Coun Can Centennial res fel med, Joslin Res Lab, Harvard Univ, 68-71; jr assoc med, Peter Bent Brigham Hosp, Boston, 70-71; instr, Med Sch, Harvard Univ, 70-71. *Mem:* Can Soc Clin Invest; Can Biochem Soc; Am Diabetes Asn; Can Diabetes Asn. *Res:* Regulation of gluconeogenesis in the liver; regulation of glycolysis and intermediary metabolism in skeletal muscle. *Mailing Add:* Dept of Med McMaster Univ Med Sch Hamilton ON L8S 4L8 Can

TOEWS, DANIEL PETER, b Grande Prairie, Alta, Dec 18, 41; m 64; c 2. ANIMAL PHYSIOLOGY. *Educ:* Univ Alta, BSc, 63, MSc, 66; Univ BC, PhD(zool), 69. *Prof Exp:* Asst prof zool, Univ Alta, 69-71; assoc prof, 71-80, PROF BIOL, ACADIA UNIV, 80- *Mem:* AAAS; Can Soc Zool; Brit Soc Exp Biol. *Res:* Comparative respiration and circulation in fishes and amphibians. *Mailing Add:* Dept Biol Acadia Univ Wolfville NS B0P 1X0 Can

TOFE, ANDREW JOHN, b New York, NY, May 6, 40. NUCLEAR MEDICINE. *Educ:* Univ Dayton, BS, 63; Fla State Univ, PhD(nuclear chem), 69. *Prof Exp:* Gen mgr/sr vpres, Procter & Gamble Co, 70-72, scientist nuclear med, 72-80; MGR NUCLEAR MED, BENEDICT NUCLEAR PHARMACEUT, 81- *Mem:* Soc Nuclear Med; Am Chem Soc. *Res:* Manufacture and sales of radioisotopes for use in early detection of human disease or adnormalities. *Mailing Add:* Benedict Nuclear Pharmaceut 1313 Washington Ave Golden CO 80401

TOFFEL, GEORGE MATHIAS, b Greensburg, Pa, Jan 28, 11; m 38; c 4. CHEMISTRY. *Educ:* Vanderbilt Univ, BA, 35, MS, 36. *Prof Exp:* Instr chem, Vanderbilt Univ, 34-36; teacher high sch, Ga, 36-37; head sci dept, Marion Inst, 37-47; from asst prof to assoc prof, 47-77, EMER ASSOC PROF CHEM, UNIV ALA, TUSCALOOSA, 77- *Concurrent Pos:* Vis prof, Univ Hawaii, 64-65. *Mem:* Am Chem Soc; fel Am Inst Chem; AAAS. *Res:* Electro-organic chemistry; free radicals; resistor research; magnetic alloys of manganese; reaction mechanism studies with carbon-14 fatty acid esters; ketonization of fatty acids. *Mailing Add:* 303 Queen City Ave Tuscaloosa AL 35401

TOFT, ROBERT JENS, b Wis, Mar 2, 33; m 56; c 3. ACADEMIC ADMINISTRATION. *Educ:* Beloit Col, BA, 55; Rice Univ, MA, 57, PhD(biol), 60. *Prof Exp:* Asst biol, Rice Univ, 59-60, res asst, 60; from instr to asst prof, Bowdoin Col, 60-63; asst physiologist, Argonne Nat Lab, 63-64; from asst prof to assoc prof biol, 64-70, asst dean, 70; prog dir, NSF, 70-72; dean col IV, 72-75, prog develop officer, 75-77, DIR FED RELATIONS & PROG DEVELOP, GRAND VALLEY STATE COLS, 77- *Concurrent Pos:* Consult div biol & med res, Argonne Nat Lab, 64-; assoc dir col teacher progs NSF, 68-69; consult higher educ, 70- *Mem:* Am Asn Higher Educ. *Res:* Bone and thyroid metabolism; metabolism and toxicity of radionuclides in beagles; alternative instructional modes for undergraduate education; designed and started a totally self-paced modular college. *Mailing Add:* Grand Valley State Cols 1000 N Arl Mill Dr Arlington VA 22205

TOGASAKI, ROBERT K, b San Francisco, Calif, July 24, 32; m 59. PLANT PHYSIOLOGY, CELL BIOLOGY. *Educ:* Haverford Col, BA, 56; NIH fel & PhD(biochem), Cornell Univ, 64. *Prof Exp:* Res fel biol, Harvard Univ, 67, lectr, 67-68; asst prof, 68-73, ASSOC PROF PLANT SCI, IND UNIV, BLOOMINGTON, 73- *Concurrent Pos:* NIH fel, 65-67. *Mem:* Am Soc Plant Physiol; Am Soc Cell Biol; Genetic Soc Am; Phycol Soc Am; Japan Soc Plant Physiol. *Res:* Photosynthetic carbon metabolism and its regulation; biochemical and genetic analysis of photosynthetic mechanisms and its regulation in Chlamydomonas reinhardi, a model eukaryotic photosynthetic organism. *Mailing Add:* Dept of Biol Ind Univ Bloomington IN 47401

TOGLIA, JOSEPH U, b Pescopagano, Italy, Apr 24, 27; US citizen; c 3. NEUROLOGY. *Educ:* Liceo Scientifico, Avellino, Italy, BS, 45; Univ Rome, MD, 51. *Prof Exp:* Staff neurologist, Baylor Col Med, 60-63; prof neurol & otorhinol, 66-74, PROF NEUROL & CHMN DEPT, SCH MED, TEMPLE UNIV, 74-; CHIEF NEUROL, PHILADELPHIA GEN HOSP, 66- *Concurrent Pos:* Attend physician, Temple Univ Hosp, 66-; consult, Vet Admin Hosp, 66- & NIH, 73- *Mem:* AMA; Am Acad Neurol; Am Acad Ophthal & Otolaryngol; Pan-Am Med Asn; Ital Med Asn. *Res:* Electronystagmography; clinical vestibular physiology. *Mailing Add:* Temple Univ Hosp 3401 N Broad St Philadelphia PA 19140

TOGO, YASUSHI, b Sapporo, Japan, May 9, 20; m 48; c 1. INFECTIOUS DISEASES, VIROLOGY. *Educ:* Univ Tokyo, MD, 45, DMedSci, 52. *Prof Exp:* Asst serol, Sch Med, Univ Tokyo, 45; microbiologist, US Army Tokyo Army Hosp, 45-50; asst med, Sch Med, Univ Tokyo, 50-55; asst res, Sch Med, Univ Md, Baltimore City, 56, from instr to assoc prof med, 59-76, asoc prof internal med, 76-80. *Concurrent Pos:* Fel, Univ Md, Baltimore City, 56-59. *Mem:* Am Soc Microbiol; Infectious Dis Soc Am. *Res:* Clinical and laboratory studies of viral and other microbial vaccines and antiviral compounds. *Mailing Add:* 1227 Wine Spring Ln Baltimore MD 21204

TOGURI, JAMES M, b Vancouver, BC, Sept 22, 30; m 57; c 5. CHEMISTRY. *Educ:* Univ Toronto, BASc, 55, MASc, 56, PhD(metall), 58. *Prof Exp:* Nat Res Coun Can fel metall, Imp Col Sci & Technol, Univ London, 58-59; fel inorg chem, Tech Univ Norway, 59-61; res assoc chem, Inst Metals, Univ Chicago, 61-62; group leader, Noranda Res Ctr, Que, 62-63, head dept, 63-66; assoc prof, 66-69, PROF METALL & MAT SCI, UNIV TORONTO, 69-, CHMN DEPT, 76- *Concurrent Pos:* Royal Norweg Sci Coun fel, 60-61; grants, Nat Res Coun Can & Defence Res Bd Can, 66-; ed-in-chief, Can Metall Quart, 67- *Honors & Awards:* Estractive Metall Sci Award, Am Inst Mining, Metall & Petrol Engrs, 81. *Mem:* Am Inst Mining, Metall & Petrol Engrs; Can Inst Mining & Metall. *Res:* High temperature chemistry; thermodynamic properties; kinetics high temperature; fused salt chemistry; nonferrous pyrometallurgy. *Mailing Add:* Dept Metall & Mat Sci Univ Toronto Toronto ON M5S 1A4 Can

TOHLINE, JOEL EDWARD, b Crowley, La, July 15, 53; m 74; c 1. MULTIDIMENSIONAL HYDRODYNAMICS. *Educ:* Centenary Col La, BS, 74; Univ Calif, Santa Cruz, PhD(astron), 78. *Prof Exp:* J W Gibbs instr astron, Yale Univ, 78-80; fel astrophysics, Los Alamos Nat Lab, 80-82; ASST PROF PHYSICS & ASTRON, LA STATE UNIV, 82- *Mem:* Am Astron Soc; Int Astron Union. *Res:* Computer modeling of multidimensional, hydrodynamic flows in astrophysical phenomena; star formation and gas dynamics in galaxies. *Mailing Add:* Dept Physics & Astron La State Univ Baton Rouge LA 70803

TOHVER, HANNO TIIT, b Tartu, Estonia, Dec 18, 35; Can citizen. PHYSICS. *Educ:* Queen's Univ, Ont, BS, 57, MS, 59; Purdue Univ, PhD, 68. *Prof Exp:* Asst, Purdue Univ, 60-67; asst prof, 68-71, ASSOC PROF PHYSICS, UNIV ALA, BIRMINGHAM, 71- *Mailing Add:* Dept of Physics Univ of Ala Birmingham AL 35294

TOIDA, SHUNICHI, b Shizuoka, Japan, Jan 8, 37; m 67; c 3. ELECTRICAL ENGINEERING. *Educ:* Univ Tokyo, BS, 59; Univ Ill, Urbana, MS, 66, PhD(elec eng), 69. *Prof Exp:* Comput engr, Mitsubishi Elec Co, 59-63; asst prof, 69-76, PROF SYSTS DESIGN, UNIV WATERLOO, 76- *Concurrent Pos:* Nat Res Coun Can grant, 69-71; vis prof, Univ Dortmund, WGer, 75-76. *Mem:* Inst Elec & Electronic Engrs. *Res:* Linear graph theory and its applications. *Mailing Add:* Dept of Systs Design Univ of Waterloo Waterloo ON N2L 3G1 Can

TOIVOLA, PERTTI TOIVO KALEVI, medical physiology, neuroendocrinology, see previous edition

TOJI, LORRAINE HELLENGA, b Three Oaks, Mich, Oct 22, 38; m 65. BIOCHEMISTRY. *Educ:* Hope Col, AB, 60; Wayne State Univ, MS, 62; Univ Pa, PhD(biochem), 69. *Prof Exp:* Instr chem, Hope Col, 61-64; res assoc biochem, 69-72, ASST MEM, INST MED RES, CAMDEN, 72- *Mem:* AAAS; Am Chem Soc. *Res:* Induction and characterization of somatic cell mutants in control; virus transformed cells. *Mailing Add:* RD 2 Box 110 Sewell NJ 08080

TOKAR, MICHAEL, b Elizabeth, NJ, Apr 27, 37; m 61; c 3. CERAMICS, METALLURGY. *Educ:* Univ Mich, BS, 61; Stevens Inst Technol, MS, 64; Rutgers Univ, PhD(ceramics), 68. *Prof Exp:* Metall trainee, Nat Castings Co, Ill, 61-62; res asst res & develop high temperature mat, Am Standard Corp Res Lab, 62-65; res asst ceramic sci, Rutgers Univ, 65-67; staff mem, Los Alamos Sci Lab, Univ Calif, 67-75; sr ceramist, 75-80, SR REACTOR FUELS ENGR MAT, US NUCLEAR REGULATORY COMN, 80- *Mem:* Am Soc Metals; Am Ceramics Soc. *Res:* Analysis and evaluation of reactor fuel systems design; fabrication of ceramic nuclear fuels; measurement of physical and mechanical properties of ceramic materials; permanent magnet ferrites; high temperature oxidation-resistant coatings. *Mailing Add:* US Nuclear Regulatory Comn Washington DC 20555

TOKAY, ELBERT, b Brooklyn, NY, May 27, 16; m 40; c 2. BIOLOGY. *Educ:* City Col New York, AB, 36; Univ Chicago, PhD(physiol), 41. *Prof Exp:* Asst physiol, Univ Chicago, 39-41; instr, 41-43, from asst prof to assoc prof, 47-58, prof physiol, 58-77, PROF BIOL, VASSAR COL, 77- *Mem:* AAAS. *Res:* Drugs and other factors affecting central nervous potentials and metabolism. *Mailing Add:* Dept of Biol Vassar Col Poughkeepsie NY 12601

TOKAY, F HARRY, b St Paul, Minn, July 30, 36. AUDIOLOGY. *Educ:* St Cloud State Col, BS, 60; Mich State Univ, MA, 62, PhD(audiol), 66. *Prof Exp:* Asst prof audiol, Cent Mich Univ, 65-66 & Univ Mass, Amherst, 67-74; assoc prof audiol, 74-77, ASSOC PROF COMMUN DISORDERS, UNIV NH, 77-, CHMN COMMUN DISORDERS PROG, 74- *Mem:* Am Speech & Hearing Asn; Acoust Soc Am. *Res:* Audiology with children. *Mailing Add:* Commun Disorders Prog Univ of NH Durham NH 03824

TOKER, CYRIL, b SAfrica; US citizen. SURGICAL PATHOLOGY. *Educ:* Univ Wits, SAfrica, MBBCh, 51, MCh, 61; FRCS, 57; FRCS(E), 57. *Prof Exp:* PROF SURG PATH, HOSP & MED SCH, UNIV MD, 76- *Mailing Add:* 9417 Winterset Dr Potomac MD 20854

TOKES, ZOLTAN ANDRAS, b Budapest, Hungary, May 14, 40; m 72; c 2. BIOCHEMISTRY, DEVELOPMENTAL BIOLOGY. *Educ:* Univ Southern Calif, BSc, 64; Calif Inst Technol, PhD(biochem), 70. *Prof Exp:* Lectr biochem, Univ Malaya, 70-71; res immunol, Basel Inst Immunol, Hoffmann-LaRoche, Inc, 71-74; asst prof, 74-80, ASSOC PROF BIOCHEM, UNIV SOUTHERN CALIF & DIR CELL MEMBRANE & CELL CULTURE LABS, UNIV SOUTHERN CALIF CANCER CTR, 80- *Mem:* Am Soc Biol Chemists; Am Asn Pathologists; Am Asn Cancer Res; Int Soc Differentiation; Am Soc Cell Biologists. *Res:* Recognition of cell surface changes with differentiation; cell-cell interactions and tumor markers. *Mailing Add:* Dept Biochem Sch Med Univ Southern Calif 2025 Zonal Ave Los Angeles CA 90033

TOKITA, NOBORU, b Sapporo, Japan, Feb 20, 23; m 53. PHYSICS. *Educ:* Hokkaido Univ, BS, 47, DrSci, 56. *Prof Exp:* Res mem, Kobayashi Inst Physics, Japan, 47-52; asst prof physics, Waseda Univ, Japan, 52-57; res assoc polymer sci, Duke Univ, 57-60; sr res physicist, 60-68, RES ASSOC RES CTR, UNIROYAL INC, 68- *Mem:* Am Chem Soc; Soc Rheology. *Res:* Polymer physics; vibration and sound; rheology of elastomer and plastics; tire technology. *Mailing Add:* Oxford Mgt & Res Ctr Uniroyal Inc Middlebury CT 06749

TOKOLI, EMERY G, b Budapest, Hungary, June 6, 23, nat US; m 48; c 1. ORGANIC CHEMISTRY. *Educ:* Eötvös Lorand Univ, Budapest, MS, 47. *Prof Exp:* Res chemist, Chinoin Co Ltd, Hungary, 45-47; dir res, Fine Orgs, Inc, NJ, 48-60; sr res chemist, Minn Mining & Mfg, 60-64; res scientist, Union-Camp Paper Corp, 64-66; SCIENTIST, RES & ENG DIV, XEROX CORP, 66- *Concurrent Pos:* Instr, Fairleigh Dickinson, 58-59. *Mem:* Am Chem Soc; fel Am Inst Chem. *Res:* Nucleophilic substitution reactions; Friedel Crafts alkylations and acylations; thermally stable polymers and intermediates; fluorocarbon and silicone chemistry; lignin chemistry; organic photoconductors; redox polymers. *Mailing Add:* Res & Engr Div Xerox Corp Webster NY 14580

TOKSOZ, MEHMET NAFI, b Antakya, Turkey, Apr 18, 34. GEOPHYSICS. *Educ:* Colo Sch Mines, GpE, 58; Calif Inst Technol, MS, 60, PhD(geophys, elec eng), 63. *Prof Exp:* Res fel geophys, Calif Inst Technol, 63-65; from asst prof to assoc prof, 65-71, PROF GEOPHYSICS, MASS INST TECHNOL, 71-, DIR, GEORGE WALLACE JR GEOPHYSICS OBSERV, DEPT EARTH & PLANETARY SCI, 75- *Mem:* AAAS; Am Geophys Union; Seismol Soc Am; Soc Explor Geophys. *Res:* Seismology and structure of planetary interiors. *Mailing Add:* Dept of Earth & Planetary Sci Mass Inst of Technol Cambridge MA 02139

TOKUDA, SEI, b Ewa, Hawaii, Aug 17, 30; m 55; c 3. IMMUNOLOGY, MICROBIOLOGY. *Educ:* Univ Hawaii, BS, 53; Univ Wash, PhD(microbiol), 60. *Prof Exp:* Trainee microbiol, Univ Wash, 59-60, res instr immunol, 62-63; asst prof immunol & microbiol, Univ Vt, 63-66; from asst prof to assoc prof, 66-74, PROF IMMUNOL, SCH MED, UNIV N MEX, 74- *Concurrent Pos:* Res fel immunochem, Calif Inst Technol, 60-62; NIH fel, 61-62, NIH res grant, 64-; Am Cancer Soc res grant, 64; USPHS career develop award, 68-73; vis investr, Jackson Lab, 65 & Scripps Clin & Res Found, La Jolla, Calif, 70-71; assoc ed, J Immunol, 79-81; mem Cancer Res Manpower rev comt, Nat Cancer Inst, 76-80. *Mem:* AAAS; Am Asn Immunologists; Am Soc Microbiol; Transplantation Soc. *Res:* Immune responses of mice against syngeneic tumors; transplantation immunity; hormonal regulation of the immune response. *Mailing Add:* Dept of Microbiol Univ of N Mex Sch of Med Albuquerque NM 87131

TOKUHATA, GEORGE K, b Matsue, Japan, Aug 25, 24; US citizen; m 49. EPIDEMIOLOGY, PUBLIC HEALTH. *Educ:* Keio Univ, Japan, BA, 50; Miami Univ, MA, 53; Univ Iowa, PhD(behav sci), 56; Johns Hopkins Univ, DPH(epidemiol), 62. *Prof Exp:* Res assoc ment health, Mich State Dept Ment Health, 56-59; spec asst div chief, Div Chronic Dis, USPHS, 59-62, prin epidemiologist, 62-63; assoc prof prev med, Col Med, Univ Tenn & chief epidemiol, St Jude Children's Res Hosp, 63-67; RES DIR, DIV RES & BIOSTATIST, PA STATE DEPT HEALTH, 67- *Concurrent Pos:* USPHS fel, Med Ctr, Johns Hopkins Univ, 59-60, NIH fel, 60-61; Mary Reynold Babcock Found res grant, 59-61; Food & Drug Admin res grant; US Consumer Prod Safety Comn grant, 73-74; Maternal & Child Health Serv grant, 74-; Nat Ctr Health Statist grant, 74-; prof epidemiol & biostatist, Grad Sch Pub Health, Univ Pittsburgh; assoc prof community med, Col Med, Temple Univ. *Mem:* Fel Am Pub Health Asn; fel Am Sociol Asn. *Res:* Genetics aspects of cancer and other chronic diseases in adults and children; epidemiology of chronic diseases; evaluation of public health programs research and development. *Mailing Add:* Div Epidemiol Res Rm 1013 Pa State Dept Health PO Box 90 Harrisburg PA 17108

TOKUHIRO, TADASHI, b Yokohama, Japan, Feb 26, 30; m 56; c 2. PHYSICAL CHEMISTRY, CHEMICAL PHYSICS. *Educ:* Tokyo Col Sci, BS, 57; Tokyo Inst Technol, MS, 59, PhD(phys chem), 62. *Prof Exp:* Matsunago Sci Found grant & res assoc, Tokyo Inst Technol, 64-65; univ fel & res assoc, Ohio State Univ, 65-69; asst prof, 69-73, ASSOC PROF CHEM, UNIV DETROIT, 73- *Mem:* Am Chem Soc; Am Phys Soc; Int Soc Magnetic Resonance. *Res:* Magnetic resonance spectroscopy; nuclear quadrupole resonance spectroscopy; molecular dynamics in micellar systems; liquid structure, quantum chemistry; vibrational relaxation. *Mailing Add:* Dept of Chem Univ of Detroit Detroit MI 48221

TOKUNAGA, ALAN TAKASHI, b Puunene, Hawaii, Dec 17, 49; m 75. ASTRONOMY. *Educ:* Pomona Col, BS, 71; State Univ NY, Stony Brook, MS, 73, PhD(astron), 76. *Prof Exp:* Res assoc, Ames Res Ctr, NASA, 76-77; res assoc, Steward Observ, Univ Ariz, 77-79; ASST ASTRONOMER, UNIV HAWAII, 79- *Concurrent Pos:* Mem, Kitt Peak Nat Observ User's Comt, 78-81. *Mem:* Am Astron Soc. *Res:* Star formation; planetary atmospheres; infrared spectroscopy. *Mailing Add:* Inst Astron 2680 Woodlawn Dr Honolulu HI 96822

TOKUNAGA, CHIYOKO, b Kure, Hiroshima, Japan, Dec 7, 14. GENETICS. *Educ:* Hiroshima Univ, BA, 39; Kyoto Univ, ScD(genetics), 51. *Prof Exp:* Prof biol, Kobe Col, 51-62; biologist, Lawrence Radiation Lab, Univ Calif, 62-71; assoc res zoologist, Dept Zool, Univ Calif, Berkeley, 71-80, Dept Molecular Biol, 74-80. *Concurrent Pos:* Fulbright exchange scholar genetics, 57-59, res assoc, 61-62. *Honors & Awards:* Annual Prize, Zool Soc Japan, 59. *Mem:* Genetics Soc Am. *Res:* Pattern formation in Drosophila. *Mailing Add:* 590 Arlington Ave Berkeley CA 94707

TOLBERT, BERT MILLS, b Twin Falls, Idaho, Jan 15, 21; m 59; c 4. BIOCHEMISTRY, NUTRITION. *Educ:* Univ Calif, Berkeley, BS, 42, PhD(chem), 45. *Prof Exp:* Teaching asst, Univ Calif, Berkeley, 42-44, res chemist, Lawrence Radiation Lab, 44-57; assoc prof, 57-61, PROF CHEM, UNIV COLO, 61- *Concurrent Pos:* USPHS fel, 52-53; Int Atomic Energy Agency vis prof, Univ Buenos Aires, 62-63; biophysicist, US AEC, Washington, DC, 67-68; vis staff, Los Alamos Sci Lab, 70-; consult, Surgeon Gen Off, US Army. *Mem:* Am Chem Soc; Am Soc Biol Chem; Am Inst Nutrit; Radiation Res Soc; Soc Exp Biol Med. *Res:* Metabolism and function of ascorbic acid; radiation chemistry of proteins; catabolism of labeled compounds to 14 carbon dioxide; application of C-14 and H-3 to biochemistry; instrumentation in radiochemistry; synthesis of labeled compounds; use of stable isotopes. *Mailing Add:* Dept of Chem Univ of Colo Boulder CO 80309

TOLBERT, CHARLES RAY, b Van, WVa, Nov 14, 36; m 67; c 3. ASTRONOMY. *Educ:* Univ Richmond, BS, 58; Vanderbilt Univ, MS, 60, PhD(physics, astron), 63. *Prof Exp:* Res assoc, Kapteyn Astron Lab, Netherlands, 63-67; res assoc ctr advan studies, 67-69, asst prof, 69-70, ASSOC PROF, UNIV VA, 70- *Mem:* Am Astron Soc; Int Astron Union; Int Union Radio Sci; AAAS. *Res:* Photoelectric photometry of variable stars and binary systems; 21 centimeter radio-astronomical studies of high galactic latitudes; reduction techniques. *Mailing Add:* Leander McCormick Observ Univ Va Charlottesville VA 22903

TOLBERT, DANIEL LEE, b Fairview Heights, Ill, Oct 16, 46; m 72; c 2. NEUROSCIENCES. *Educ:* Quincy Col, BS, 68; St Louis Univ, MS, 72, PhD(anat), 75. *Prof Exp:* Fel, Dept Neurosurg, Univ Minn, 75-78; ASST PROF, DEPT ANAT, ST LOUIS UNIV, 78-, ASST PROF, DEPT SURG, 78-, DIR, MURPHY NEUROANAT RES LAB, 78- *Mem:* Am Asn Anatomists; Soc Neurosci. *Res:* Anatomical and neurophysiological study of the antogeny of corteco bulbor projection in kittens and the plasticity of connections in the adult cat tholemus; the role of the subfionical orgin in water balance. *Mailing Add:* Dept Anat St Louis Univ 1402 S Grand Blvd St Louis MO 63104

TOLBERT, GENE EDWARD, b Concordia, Kans, Sept 22, 25; m 54; c 3. ECONOMIC GEOLOGY. *Educ:* Colo Col, BA, 49; Harvard Univ, MA, 57, PhD, 62. *Prof Exp:* Geologist, US Geol Surv, Alaska, 49-52, foreign br, Brazil, 52-55; geologist, Hanna Mining Co, 57-59; prof, Univ Sao Paulo, 59-63; geologist, US Geol Surv, Pakistan, 63-65; consult, UN, 66; geologist, US Steel Corp, Brazil, 66-70; managing dir, Terraserv Projetos Geologicos Ltd, Rio de Janeiro, 71-75; consult geologist, 75-76; geologist, Off Int Geol, US Geol Surv, 76-77, chief, Br Latin Am & African Geol, 77-81; CONSULT GEOLOGIST, 81- *Mem:* Geol Soc Am; Am Soc Econ Geologists; Geochem Soc; Brazilian Geol Soc. *Res:* Economic geology; exploration geology; mineral deposits of Brazil. *Mailing Add:* Off of Int Geol PO Box 2095 Reston VA 22090

TOLBERT, LAREN MALCOLM, b New Orleans, La, Sept 30, 49; m 68; c 3. ORGANIC PHOTOCHEMISTRY, ORGANIC SYNTHESIS. *Educ:* Tulane Univ, BA, 70; Univ Wis, Madison, PhD(org chem), 75. *Prof Exp:* Res fel, Harvard Univ, 75-76; asst prof, 76-81, ASSOC PROF CHEM, UNIV KY, 81- *Mem:* Am Chem Soc; AAAS. *Res:* Organic photochemistry, particularly of anions; photodehalogenation and radicalnucleophile interactions; asymmetric induction and new synthetic methods. *Mailing Add:* Dept Chem Univ Ky Lexington KY 40506

TOLBERT, MARGARET ELLEN MAYO, b Suffolk, Va, Nov 24, 43; c 1. BIOCHEMISTRY. *Educ:* Tuskegee Inst, BS, 67; Wayne State Univ, MS, 68; Brown Univ, PhD(biochem), 74. *Prof Exp:* Instr, Opportunities Industrialization Ctr, 71-72; instr math, Tuskegee Inst, 69-70, res technician biochem, 69, asst prof chem, 73-76; assoc prof pharmaceut chem & assoc dean, Sch Pharm, Fla A&M Univ, 77-78; PROF CHEM & DIR, CARVER RES FOUND, TUSKEGEE INST, 79- *Concurrent Pos:* NIH fel, 78-79; vis res scientist, Int Inst Cellular & Molecular Path, Cath Univ Louvain, Brussels, Belg & Brown Univ, RI. *Mem:* Sigma Xi; Am Chem Soc; Orgn Black Scientists; Am Asn Cols Pharm; AAAS. *Res:* Metabolic studies involving isolated rat hepatic cells. *Mailing Add:* Carver Res Found Tuskegee Inst Tuskegee Institute AL 36088

TOLBERT, NATHAN EDWARD, b Twin Falls, Idaho, May 19, 19; m 52; c 3. BIOCHEMISTRY. *Educ:* Univ Calif, BS, 41; Univ Wis, MS, 48, PhD(biochem), 50. *Prof Exp:* Asst chem dept viticult, Col Agr, Univ Calif, 41-43, biochemist, Radiation Lab, 50; res admin, US AEC, 50-52; sr biochemist, Oak Ridge Nat Lab, 52-58; PROF BIOCHEM, MICH STATE UNIV, 58- *Mem:* Am Chem Soc; Am Soc Biol Chem; Am Soc Plant Physiol. *Res:* Plant biochemistry and plant growth substances; glycolic acid metabolism, biosynthesis and function; photosynthesis and relation to plant growth; microbodies and peroxisomes. *Mailing Add:* Dept of Biochem Mich State Univ East Lansing MI 48823

TOLBERT, ROBERT JOHN, b Pelican Rapids, Minn, Apr 16, 28; m 53; c 2. PLANT ANATOMY. *Educ:* Moorhead State Univ, BS & BA, 55; Rutgers Univ, PhD(bot), 59. *Prof Exp:* From asst prof to assoc prof biol, Univ WVa, 59-63; assoc prof, 63-65, PROF BIOL, MOORHEAD STATE UNIV, 65- *Mem:* AAAS; Bot Soc Am. *Res:* Anatomical investigation of vegetative shoot apices; comparative studies of shoot apices in the order Malvales. *Mailing Add:* Dept of Biol Moorhead State Univ Moorhead MN 56560

TOLBERT, THOMAS WARREN, b Greenwood, SC, Dec 1, 45. PHYSICAL CHEMISTRY, MOLECULAR SPECTROSCOPY. *Educ:* Wofford Col, BS, 67; State Univ NY Binghamton, PhD(chem), 74. *Prof Exp:* Asst prof chem, Wofford Col, 72-74; proj scientist, 74-75, lab supvr, Parke-Davis Med Surg Div, 75-77, proj mgr res & develop, Parke Davis Desert Div, 77-81; DIR RES & DEVELOP, FLEXIBLE TUBING DIV, AUTOMATION INDUSTS, 81- *Mem:* Am Chem Soc. *Res:* Interaction characteristics of reacting molecules. *Mailing Add:* 121 Creek Rd E Greenwood SC 29646

TOLBERT, VIRGINIA ROSE, b Scottsboro, Ala, July 16, 48. AQUATIC ECOLOGY. *Educ:* ETenn State Univ, BS, 70; Univ Tenn, Knoxville, MS, 72, PhD(ecol), 78. *Prof Exp:* Fel, Dept Zool, Univ Tenn, Knoxville, 78-79; RES ASSOC, ENVIRON SCI DIV, OAK RIDGE NAT LAB, TN, 79- *Mem:* Ecol Soc Am; NAm Benthological Soc; Cambridge Entom Soc; Sigma Xi; Asn Southeastern Biologists. *Res:* Effects of coal surface mining on aquatic communities; examination of the various aspects of pertarbation on aquatic systems; effects of energy related development on water and aquatic biota. *Mailing Add:* Oak Ridge Nat Lab PO Box X Bldg 1505 Oak Ridge TN 37830

TOLDERLUND, DOUGLAS STANLEY, b Newport, RI, Jan 14, 39; m 61; c 2. MARINE ECOLOGY, GLACIAL GEOLOGY. *Educ:* Brown Univ, BA, 60; Columbia Univ, PhD(marine geol), 69. *Prof Exp:* Sr ecologist, Raytheon Co, 69-70; assoc prof marine sci, 70-77, ASSOC PROF PHYS & OCEANIC SCI, US COAST GUARD ACAD, 77-, CHMN, MARINE SCI SECT, 78- *Mem:* Nat Asn Geol Teachers; Am Fisheries Soc; Int Oceanog Found; Glacial Geol Soc. *Res:* Estuarine ecology, especially water quality and finfish studies. *Mailing Add:* Ocean Sci Sect US Coast Guard Acad New London CT 06320

TOLE, JOHN ROY, b Washington, DC, Nov 6, 45; m 69; c 2. BIOENGINEERING. *Educ:* Drexel Inst Technol, BSEE, 68; Mass Inst Technol, SM, 70, ScD, 76. *Prof Exp:* Engr, Div Res Serv, NIH, 68; res asst, Mass Inst Technol, 68-70; lab supvr, Peter Bent Brigham Hosp, Boston, 70-72; NIH trainee, Mass Inst Technol, 72-76, res scientist, 76-81; ASSOC PROF BIOMED ENG, WORCESTER POLYTECH INST, 81- *Concurrent Pos:* Res affil, Mass Inst Technol, 81- *Mem:* Inst Elec & Electronics Engrs; Human Factors Soc. *Res:* Computer based medical instrumentation; neurological function testing; oculomotor system dynamics; man-machine interaction particularly in aviation and rehabilitation; stress physiology. *Mailing Add:* Dept Biomed Eng Salisbury Labs Rm 413 Worcester Polytech Inst Worcester MA 01609

TOLEDO, ROMEO TRANCE, b Philippines, Apr 27, 41. CHEMICAL ENGINEERING, FOOD SCIENCE. *Educ:* St Augustine Univ, Philippines, BSChE, 60; Univ Ill, MS, 65, PhD(food sci), 67. *Prof Exp:* Chem engr, Calif Packing Corp, 60-62; instr chem eng, St Augustine Univ, Philippines, 62-63; res asst, Univ Ill, 63-65, teaching asst food sci, 65-67; res chem engr, Libby McNeill & Libby, 67-68; asst prof food sci, 68-76, assoc prof, 76-79, PROF FOOD SCI, UNIV GA, 79- *Concurrent Pos:* Consult, Mead Packaging Corp, 70-76. *Mem:* Assoc mem Am Inst Chem Engrs; Inst Food Technol; Am Soc Agr Engrs. *Res:* Engineering food processing and handling systems, heat transfer in food processing systems; rheological properties of food fluids and kinetics of food degradation and microbiological inactivation. *Mailing Add:* Dept Food Sci Univ Ga Athens GA 30601

TOLER, ROBERT WILLIAM, b Norphlet, Ark, Dec 15, 28; m 50; c 4. VIROLOGY, PLANT PATHOLOGY. *Educ:* Univ Ark, BS, 50, MS, 58; NC State Univ, PhD(plant virol), 62. *Prof Exp:* Res technician rice br exp sta, Univ Ark, 51-54, specialist & plant pathologist, Agr Mission, Panama, 55-57; res plant pathologist, coastal plain exp sta, Agr Res Serv, USDA, Univ Ga, 61-65; assoc prof, 69-74, PROF PLANT PATH, TEX A&M UNIV, 74-, CEREAL VIROLOGIST, 66- *Concurrent Pos:* Consult, Foy Pittman Rice Farms, Ark, 50-51, Campos Manola Arca, SA, Manziuillo, Cuba, 54 & Ford Found, Antonia Narro Col Agr, Coahuila, Mex, 66; dir plant protection lab, Remote Sensing Ctr, Tex A&M Univ, 71- *Mem:* Am Phytopath Soc. *Res:* Physiological effects and host response in plant pathology; cereal virology identification and transmission of viruses that cause cereal diseases. *Mailing Add:* Dept of Plant Sci Tex A&M Univ College Station TX 77843

TOLGYESI, EVA, b Budapest, Hungary. ORGANIC CHEMISTRY, POLYMER CHEMISTRY. *Educ:* Budapest Technol Univ, BSc, 53; Univ Leeds, PhD(textile chem), 59. *Prof Exp:* Asst prof chem, Budapest Technol Univ, 53-56; sr chemist, Harris Res Labs, 65-69, proj supvr polymer chem, 69-74, res supvr, 74-77, GROUP LEADER, GILLETTE RES INST, 77- *Mem:* Am Chem Soc; Soc Cosmetic Chemists; AAAS. *Res:* Keratin chemistry; chemical modification of wool; moth-proofing; cationic surfactants; fluoropolymers; silicones; hair cosmetics; hair removal; controlled release polymer systems. *Mailing Add:* Gillette Res Inst 1413 Research Blvd Rockville MD 20850

TOLGYESI, WILLIAM STEVEN, organic chemistry, see previous edition

TOLIMIERI, RICHARD, b New York, NY, Nov 19, 41; m 68; c 2. PURE MATHEMATICS. *Educ:* City Col New York, BS, 63; Columbia Univ, PhD(math), 69. *Prof Exp:* Gibbs instr math, Yale Univ, 69-71; asst prof, Lehman Col, 71-72; mem, Inst Advan Studies, 72-73; asst prof, Lehman Col, 73-74; ASSOC PROF MATH, UNIV CONN, 74- *Res:* Analysis on non-Abelian groups and the application of such studies to special function and number theory. *Mailing Add:* Dept of Math Univ of Conn Storrs CT 06250

TOLIN, SUE ANN, b Montezuma, Ind, Nov 29, 38. PLANT VIROLOGY, PHYTOPATHOLOGY. *Educ:* Purdue Univ, BS, 60; Univ Nebr, MS, 62, PhD(bot), 65. *Prof Exp:* Res asst plant path, Univ Nebr, 60-65; res assoc bot & plant path, Purdue Univ, 65-66; asst prof, 66-72, ASSOC PROF PLANT PATH, VA POLYTECH INST & STATE UNIV, 72- *Mem:* Am Phytopath Soc; Am Soc Microbiol. *Res:* Identification, purification and characterization of plant pathogenic viruses; electron microscopy; mechanisms of resistance of plants to viruses. *Mailing Add:* Dept of Plant Path & Physiol Va Polytech Inst & State Univ Blacksburg VA 24061

TOLINE, FRANCIS RAYMOND, b Alliance, Nebr, Nov 3, 18; m 45; c 5. AEROSPACE ENGINEERING, NUCLEAR ENGINEERING. *Educ:* US Naval Postgrad Sch, BS, 52; Mass Inst Technol, SM, 53. *Prof Exp:* Br head air launched missile propulsion, Bur Naval Weapons, 59-60; assoc prof, 60-66, prof, 66-80, EMER PROF AEROSPACE & NUCLEAR ENG, TENN TECHNOL UNIV, 80- *Concurrent Pos:* NSF sci fac fel, 64-67. *Mem:* Am Nuclear Soc; Am Inst Aeronaut & Astronaut; Am Soc Eng Educ. *Res:* Altitude simulation for environmental testing of nuclear rocket engines; ejector-diffuser systems used in altitude simulation. *Mailing Add:* Rte 13 Box 165 Cookeville TN 38501

TOLIVER, MICHAEL EDWARD, b Albuquerque, NMex, Oct 1, 49; m 80. ENTOMOLOGY. *Educ:* Univ NMex, BS, 73; Univ Ill, MS, 77, PhD(entom), 79. *Prof Exp:* Entomologist, City Urbana, 76; res asst, Univ Ill, 77-79, asst prof entom, 80; field supvr, Macon Mosquito Abatement Dist, 81; ASST PROF BIOL, EUREKA COL, 81- *Concurrent Pos:* Mem, Lepidopter Res Found. *Mem:* Lepidopterists Soc; Am Entom Soc. *Res:* Evolution of mimetic color patterns; biogeography of southwestern lepidopter. *Mailing Add:* Div Sci & Math Eureka Col Eureka IL 61530

TOLL, JOHN SAMPSON, b Denver, Colo, Oct 25, 23; m 70; c 2. THEORETICAL PHYSICS. *Educ:* Yale Univ, BS, 44; Princeton Univ, AM, 48, PhD(physics), 52. *Hon Degrees:* DSc, Univ Md, 73 & Univ Wroclaw, 74; LLD, Adelphi Univ, 78. *Prof Exp:* Managing ed & actg chmn, Yale Sci Mag, 43-44; asst, Princeton Univ, 46-48; theoret physicist, Los Alamos Sci Lab, 50-51; staff mem & assoc dir, Proj Matterhorn, Forrestal Res Ctr, Princeton Univ, 51-53; prof physics & chmn dept physics & astron, Univ Md, 53-65; prof physics & pres, State Univ NY Stony Brook, 65-78; PRES & PROF PHYSICS, UNIV MD, COLLEGE PARK, 78- *Concurrent Pos:* Guggenheim Mem Found fel, Inst Theoret Physics, Univ Copenhagen & Univ Lund, 58-59; US deleg & head sci secretariat, Int Conf High Energy Physics, 60; mem-at-lg US nat comn, Int Union Pure & Appl Physics, 61-63; mem, Gov Adv Comt Atomic Energy, State of NY, 66-70; Nordita vis prof, Niels Bohr Inst Theoret Physics, Univ Copenhagen, 75-76. *Mem:* AAAS; Am Phys Soc; Am Asn Physics Teachers; Nat Sci Teachers Asn; Fedn Am Scientists (chmn, 61-62). *Res:* Elementary particle theory; scattering. *Mailing Add:* Off of the Pres Univ Md College Park MD 20742

TOLLE, JON WRIGHT, b Mattoon, Ill, June 26, 39; m 64. MATHEMATICS, OPERATIONS RESEARCH. *Educ:* DePauw Univ, BA, 61; Univ Minn, PhD(math), 66. *Prof Exp:* Res assoc, Argonne Nat Lab, 63; instr math, Univ Minn, 66-67; asst prof, 67-73, assoc prof math & opers res, 73-78, chmn curric opers res, 74-79, PROF MATH & OPERS RES, UNIV NC, CHAPEL HILL, 78- *Concurrent Pos:* Vis prof, Grad Sch Bus, Univ Chicago, 75 & 81-82. *Mem:* Opers Res Soc Am; Soc Indust & Appl Math; Math Asn Am. *Res:* Mathematical programming; optimization theory; numerical analysis. *Mailing Add:* Dept Math Univ NC Chapel Hill NC 27514

TOLLEFSON, CHARLES IVAR, b Moose Jaw, Sask, Oct 2, 18; m 40; c 2. BIOCHEMISTRY. *Educ:* Univ Sask, BSA, 40, MSc, 47; Univ Minn, PhD(agr biochem), 50. *Prof Exp:* Asst radioactive ruthenium, Univ Sask, 45-47; asst lactose, Univ Minn, 47-50; res biochemist, Stine Lab, E I du Pont de Nemours & Co, 50-57; res sect leader nutrit, 57-72, MGR RES & DEVELOP, R T FRENCH CO, 72- *Mem:* AAAS; Am Chem Soc; Inst Food Technologists; NY Acad Sci. *Res:* Selenium in grains; adsorption and solvent distribution of ruthenium; nutritional effects of lactose; new growth factors; nutrition of cage birds; food dehydration. *Mailing Add:* R T French Co 434 South Emerson Shelley ID 83274

TOLLEFSON, ERIC LARS, b Moose Jaw, Sask, Oct 15, 21; m 47; c 3. PHYSICAL CHEMISTRY, CHEMICAL ENGINEERING. *Educ:* Univ Sask, BA, 43, MA, 45; Univ Toronto, PhD(phys chem), 48. *Prof Exp:* Demonstr chem, Univ Sask, 41-43 & 45, asst, Directorate Chem Warfare, 43-44; jr res officer, Nat Res Coun Can, 45; lab asst, Univ Toronto, 45-47, lectr, 47-48; jr res officer, Nat Res Coun Can, 48-49, asst res officer, 50-51; chemist, Process Res Div, Stanolind Oil & Gas Co, Okla, 51-52, sr chemist, 53-56; head phys chem sect, Res Dept, Can Chem Co, Ltd, 56-66, supt chem develop dept, 65-66, tech mgr, Can Chem Co Div, Chem-Cell Ltd, Alta, 66-67; assoc prof, chem eng, 67-70, actg head dept, 71, head dept, 72-81, PROF CHEM ENG, UNIV CALGARY, 70- *Mem:* Am Chem Soc; fel Chem Inst Can. *Res:* Preparation of activated carbon from Alberta coals; recovery of hydrocarbons from aqueous wastes from oil sands; bitumen recovery operations; kinetics; atomic hydrogen with acetylene; oxidation of ethylene; Fischer-Tropsch synthesis; alcohol dehydrogenation; reduction of nitrogen oxides in stack gases; oxidation of low concentrations of hydrogen sulfide over activated carbon; biological oxidation. *Mailing Add:* Dept of Chem & Petrol Eng Univ of Calgary Calgary AB T2N 1N4 Can

TOLLEFSON, JEFFREY L, b Hampa, Idaho, July 30, 42; m 65; c 2. MATHEMATICS. *Educ:* Univ Idaho, BS, 65; Mich State Univ, MS, 66, PhD(math), 68. *Prof Exp:* NASA trainee, Mich State Univ, 65-68; asst prof math, Tulane Univ, 68-71 & Tex A&M Univ, 71-74; assoc prof, 74-77, PROF MATH, UNIV CONN, 77- *Mem:* Am Math Soc. *Res:* Topology of manifolds. *Mailing Add:* Dept of Math Univ of Conn Storrs CT 06268

TOLLEFSRUD, PHILIP BJØRN, b Fargo, NDak, June 11, 38; m 59; c 2. EXPERIMENTAL NUCLEAR PHYSICS. *Educ:* Univ NDak, BA, 64; Univ Wis, MS, 66, PhD(physics), 69. *Prof Exp:* STAFF MEM PHYSICS, SANDIA CORP, 69- *Mem:* Am Phys Soc; Sigma Xi. *Res:* Isotopic spin, fast burst reactors and simulation sciences. *Mailing Add:* 11408 Golden Gate Ave NE Albuquerque NM 87111

TOLLES, WALTER EDWIN, b Moline, Ill, Feb 1, 16; m 37; c 1. BIOPHYSICS, PHYSIOLOGY. *Educ:* Antioch Col, BS, 39; Univ Minn, MS, 41; State Univ NY Downstate Med Ctr, PhD(biophys & physiol), 69. *Prof Exp:* Asst, Kettering Found, Antioch Col, 37-39; physicist, Div War Res, Airborne Instruments Lab, Columbia Univ, 42-45; supvr, Airborne Instruments Lab, Inc, 45-54, head dept med & biol physics, 54-69; dir, Inst Oceanog & Marine Biol, 59-69; instr, 69-70, ASSOC PROF OBSTET & GYNEC, STATE UNIV NY DOWNSTATE MED CTR, 70- *Concurrent Pos:* Consult, NIH. *Mem:* AAAS; Biophys Soc; Am Soc Limnol & Oceanog; Am Phys Soc; Am Soc Cytol. *Res:* Magnetic techniques in undersea warfare; electronic countermeasures; high speed micro-scanning systems associated data handling system; physiological monitoring systems; clinical instrumentation; diagnostic computer methods. *Mailing Add:* Dept of Obstet & Gynec State Univ NY Downstate Med Ctr Brooklyn NY 11203

TOLLES, WILLIAM MARSHALL, b New Britain, Conn, June 30, 37; m 59; c 2. PHYSICAL CHEMISTRY. *Educ:* Univ Conn, BA, 58; Univ Calif, Berkeley, PhD(phys chem), 62. *Prof Exp:* Fel, Rice Univ, 61-62; from asst prof to prof, 62-78, DEAN RES & DEAN SCI & ENG, NAVAL POSTGRAD SCH, 78- *Concurrent Pos:* Consult, Naval Weapons Ctr, China Lake, summers, 66-77. *Mem:* Optical Soc Am; Am Phys Soc; Am Chem Soc; Am Soc Eng Educ. *Res:* Microwave spectroscopy; rotational spectra of molecules; electron spin resonance; microwave properties of materials; non-linear molecular spectroscopy. *Mailing Add:* Code 012/06 Naval Postgrad Sch Monterey CA 93940

TOLLESTRUP, ALVIN V, b Los Angeles, Calif, Mar 22, 24; m 44; c 2. PHYSICS. *Educ:* Calif Inst Technol, PhD(physics), 50. *Prof Exp:* Res fel physics, Calif Inst Technol, 50-53, from asst prof to prof physics, 53-77; MEM STAFF, FERMI NAT ACCELERATOR LAB, 77- *Mem:* Am Phys Soc. *Res:* Nuclear disintegration energy value determinations; interaction of 500 million electron volts; gamma rays with hydrogen and deuterium. *Mailing Add:* Fermi Nat Accelerator Lab PO Box 500 Batavia IL 60510

TOLLIN, GORDON, b New York, NY, Dec 26, 30; m 55; c 3. BIOPHYSICAL CHEMISTRY. *Educ:* Brooklyn Col, BS, 52; Iowa State Univ, PhD, 56. *Prof Exp:* Res assoc chem, Fla State Univ, 56; chemist, Lawrence Radiation Lab, Univ Calif, 56-59, NSF fel, 56-57; from asst prof to assoc prof, 59-67, PROF CHEM, UNIV ARIZ, 67-, PROF BIOCHEM, 78- *Concurrent Pos:* Sloan fel, 62-66. *Mem:* AAAS; Am Chem Soc; Biophys Soc; Am Soc Biol Chemists. *Res:* Mechanism of enzyme action; photosynthesis; free radicals in biological energy conversion; biological oxidation-reduction; phototaxis in microorganisms. *Mailing Add:* Dept of Biochem Univ of Ariz Tucson AZ 85721

TOLLMAN, JAMES PERRY, b Chadron, Nebr, Nov 6, 04; m 29; c 3. PATHOLOGY. *Educ:* Univ Nebr, BSc, 27, MD, 29; Am Bd Path, dipl, 37. *Prof Exp:* Intern & resident, Peter Bent Brigham Hosp, Boston, Mass, 29-31; from asst prof clin path to prof path, 31-74, chmn dept path & bact, 48-54, dean, 52-64, EMER PROF PATH & EMER DEAN, COL MED, UNIV NEBR, 74- *Concurrent Pos:* Vis prof, Univ Chiengmai, 64-65. *Mem:* Am Soc Clin Path; Am Asn Pathologists & Bacteriologists; fel AMA; fel Col Am Path. *Res:* Effects of dusts on tissues; effect of toxic gases; tissue changes in endocrine disturbances. *Mailing Add:* 4441 E Sixth St Tucson AZ 85711

TOLMACH, L(EONARD) J(OSEPH), b New York, NY, Apr 18, 23; m 45; c 3. CELL BIOLOGY, RADIOBIOLOGY. *Educ:* Univ Mich, BS, 43; Univ Chicago, PhD(chem), 51. *Prof Exp:* Jr chemist, Manhattan Proj, 44-46; from instr to asst prof biophys, Sch Med, Univ Colo, 51-58; assoc prof, 58-64, PROF RADIATION BIOL, SCH MED, WASHINGTON UNIV, 64-, PROF ANAT, 69- *Concurrent Pos:* Mem comt molecular biol, Washington Univ, 61-72, chmn, 64-66; NSF sr fel, 63-64; mem biophys sci training comt, Nat Inst Gen Med Sci, 66-68. *Mem:* Radiation Res Soc; Biophys Soc; Am Asn Cancer Res. *Res:* Effects of radiations and other toxic agents on cell proliferation. *Mailing Add:* Dept of Anat Washington Univ Sch of Med St Louis MO 63110

TOLMAN, CHADWICK ALMA, b Oct 11, 38; US citizen; m 62; c 3. PHYSICAL CHEMISTRY, INORGANIC CHEMISTRY. *Educ:* Mass Inst Technol, BS, 60; Univ Calif, Berkeley, PhD(phys chem), 64. *Prof Exp:* Fel & res assoc chem, Mass Inst Technol, 64-65; CHEMIST, EXP STA, E I DU PONT DE NEMOURS & CO, INC, 65- *Mem:* Am Chem Soc. *Res:* Mechanisms of homogeneous catalysis by transition metal complexes; hydrocarbon oxidations; kinetics and equilibria of organometallic reactions. *Mailing Add:* Exp Sta E I du Pont de Nemours & Co Inc Wilmington DE 19898

TOLMAN, EDWARD LAURIE, b Chelsea, Mass, Oct 9, 42; m 67; c 1. PHARMACOLOGY. *Educ:* Univ Mass, BA, 64, MA, 65; State Univ NY Upstate Med Ctr, PhD(pharmacol), 70. *Prof Exp:* NIH fel physiol, Milton S Hershey Med Ctr, Pa State Univ, 69-71, res assoc, 71-72; sr res biologist, Lederle Labs, Am Cyanamid Co, 72-77, group leader, 77-80; SECT HEAD BIOCHEM RES, ORTHO PHARMACEUTICAL CORP, 80- *Mem:* Am Soc Pharmacol & Exp Therapeut; Am Diabetes Asn; AAAS. *Res:* Disorders of carbohydrate and lipid metabolism; prostaglandins and inflammation. *Mailing Add:* Ortho Pharmaceut Corp Route 202 Raritan NJ 08869

TOLMAN, ROBERT ALEXANDER, b Springfield, Mass, Feb 28, 24; m 49; c 3. PHYSIOLOGY. *Educ:* Univ Mass, BS, 49; Ind Univ, MA, 50, PhD(zool), 54. *Prof Exp:* Asst zool, Ind Univ, 50-53, asst chem embryol, 53-54; instr physiol & pharmacol, Col Osteop Med & Surg, 54-58; cardiovasc res trainee, Dept Physiol, Med Col Ga, 58-59; from instr to asst prof physiol & biophys, Sch Med, Univ Louisville, 59-67; grants assoc, NIH, 67-68, assoc myocardial infarction br, Nat Heart & Lung Inst, 68-69, ENDOCRINOL RES PROG DIR, DIABETES, ENDOCRINOL & METABOLIC DIS PROGS, NAT INST ARTHRITIS, DIABETES & DIGESTIVE & KIDNEY DIS, 69- *Mem:* AAAS. *Res:* Thyroid, thyrotropic hormone interaction and thyroid-stimulating hormone assay; time of appearance of cardiac actin in chick embryo; ventricular pressure curves. *Mailing Add:* Rm 605 Westwood Bldg Nat Inst Arthritis Diabetes Digestive & Kidney Dis Bethesda MD 20205

TOLMSOFF, WALTER JOHN, plant pathology, biochemistry, see previous edition

TOLNAI, SUSAN, b Budapest, Hungary, Nov 29, 28; Can citizen; m 50; c 2. CELL BIOLOGY, HISTOLOGY. *Educ:* Eotvos Lorand Univ, Budapest, MD, 53. *Prof Exp:* Bacteriologist, Lab Hyg, Dept Nat Health & Welfare, Can, 57-58, biologist, 58-62; lectr, 62-63, from asst prof to assoc prof, 63-71, PROF HISTOL & EMBRYOL, FAC MED, UNIV OTTAWA, 71- *Concurrent Pos:* Nat Acad Sci Hungary fel, 53-56. *Mem:* Tissue Cult Asn; Can Soc Cell Biol; NY Acad Sci; Am Soc Cell Biol; Can Soc Immunol. *Res:* Myocardial enzymes, proteinases; lysosomal enzymes. *Mailing Add:* Dept Anat Fac of Med Univ of Ottawa Ottawa ON K1N 6N5 Can

TOLSMA, JACOB, b Passaic, NJ, Mar 4, 23; m 48; c 5. CHEMICAL ENGINEERING, POLYMER CHEMISTRY. *Educ:* Newark Col Eng, BSChE, 56, MSChE, 65. *Prof Exp:* Chem engr, Res Ctr, Uniroyal, Inc, 56-65, res engr, 65-71; res engr, Weavenit Surg Corp, 71-80; WITH MEADOX MEDICALS INC, 80. *Mem:* Am Chem Soc. *Res:* Chemical engineering development; polymers scale up; water pollution control. *Mailing Add:* Meadox Medicals Inc PO Box 530 Oakland NJ 07436

TOLSON, ROBERT HEATH, b Portsmouth, Va, July 23, 35; m 78; c 2. ATMOSPHERIC SCIENCE, PLANETARY SCIENCES. *Educ:* Va Polytech Inst & State Univ, BS, 58, MS, 63. *Prof Exp:* Aerospace scientist lunar & planetary studies, 58-72, head, Planetary Physics Br, 72-75, HEAD ATMOSPHERIC SCI BR, LANGLEY RES CTR, NASA, 75- *Honors & Awards:* H J E Reid, Langley Res Ctr, NASA, 78. *Mem:* Am Geophys Union; Am Inst Aeronaut & Astronaut. *Res:* Stratospheric minor constitutent distributions and transport; regional tropospheric pollutant photochemistry, chemistry and transport. *Mailing Add:* 804 Pelham Dr Newport News VA 23602

TOLSTEAD, WILLIAM LAWRENCE, b Howard Co, Iowa, Nov 25, 09. BOTANY. *Educ:* Luther Col, Iowa, BS, 33; Iowa State Univ, MS, 36; Univ Nebr, PhD(plant ecol), 42. *Prof Exp:* Biologist, Conserv & Surv Div, Univ Nebr, 35-42; from assoc prof to prof, 57-76, EMER PROF BIOL, DAVIS & ELKINS COL, 76-, CHMN DEPT, 72- *Mem:* Am Rhodo Soc; Am Hort Soc; Royal Hort Soc. *Res:* Plant breeding rhododendron. *Mailing Add:* Dept of Biol Davis & Elkins Col Elkins WV 26241

TOLSTED, ELMER BEAUMONT, b Philadelphia, Pa, Apr 28, 20. MATHEMATICS. *Educ:* Univ Chicago, BS, 40, MS, 41; Brown Univ, PhD(math), 46. *Prof Exp:* Instr math, Brown Univ, 42-47; from asst prof to assoc prof, 47-61, prof, 61-80, RUEBEN C & ELEANOR WINSLOW PROF MATH, POMONA COL, 80- *Concurrent Pos:* Fulbright exchange prof, Eng, 49-50; instr, Claremont Inst Music, 51- *Honors & Awards:* Ford Award, Math Asn Am, 65. *Mem:* Am Math Soc; Math Asn Am. *Res:* Subharmonic functions. *Mailing Add:* Dept of Math Pomona Col Claremont CA 91711

TOLSTOY, IVAN, b Baden-Baden, Ger, Mar 30, 23; nat US; m 47, 64; c 3. UNDERWATER SOUND, WARE THEORY. *Educ:* Univ Sorbonne, Lic es sc, 45; Columbia Univ, MA, 47, PhD(geophys), 50. *Prof Exp:* Mem sci staff, Lamont Geol Observ, Columbia Univ, 48-51; sr res engr, Stanolind Oil & Gas Co, 51-53; res scientist, Hudson Lab, Columbia Univ, 53-60, sr res assoc, 62-67, assoc dir, 64-67, prof ocean eng, 67-68; prof geol & fluid dynamics, Geophys Fluid Dynamics Inst, Fla State Univ, 68-74; distinguished vis prof acoustics, Naval Postgrad Sch, 77-78; CONSULT, 79- *Concurrent Pos:* Chief scientist, MidAtlantic Ridge Exped, Colombia, 50; consult, Gen Elec Co & Carter Oil Co, 60-62 & Schlumberger Tech Co, 62; vis prof, Univ Leeds, 71-72 & 73-76. *Mem:* AAAS; Am Phys Soc; fel Acoust Soc Am; Am Geophys Union; Sigma Xi. *Res:* Theory of acoustic and elastic wave propagation; hydrodynamics; theoretical mechanics; seismology; submarine topography and geology; applied mathematics. *Mailing Add:* Knockvennie Castle Douglas SW Scotland

TOM, BALDWIN HENG, b San Francisco, Calif, Sept 19, 40. IMMUNOLOGY. *Educ:* Univ Calif, Berkeley, BA, 63; Univ Ariz, MS, 67, PhD(microbiol), 70. *Prof Exp:* Fel, Stanford Univ Sch Med, 70-72, res assoc immunol, 72-73; instr, Sch Med, Northwestern Univ, 73-74, assoc, 74-75, asst prof surg & physiol, 75-77; ASST PROF BIOCHEM MOLECULAR BIOL & SURG, MED SCH, UNIV TEX, HOUSTON, 77- *Concurrent Pos:* Res career develop award, Nat Cancer Inst, 79-84; vis scientist, Prairie View A&M Univ, 81; Int Cancer Res exchange fel, Nottingham, Eng, 81. *Mem:* NY Acad Sci; Soc Exp Biol & Med; Tissue Cult Asn; Am Asn Immunol; Am Asn Cancer Res. *Res:* Dissection of the cellular and molecular bases for immune reactivities in tumor cell-lymphocyte interactions with liposomes and monoclonal antibodies. *Mailing Add:* Dept Surg Med Sch Univ Tex Houston TX 77030

TOM, GLENN MCPHERSON, b Honolulu, Hawaii, Sept 1, 49; m 76. INORGANIC CHEMISTRY, ANALYTICAL CHEMISTRY. *Educ:* Univ Hawaii, BS, 71; Stanford Univ, PhD(inorg chem), 75. *Prof Exp:* Fel chem, Univ Chicago, 75-77; RES CHEMIST, HERCULES RES CTR, HERCULES INC, 77- *Mem:* Am Chem Soc. *Res:* Electroanalytic chemistry; inorganic and organometallic chemistry; Zeigler-Natta polymerizations. *Mailing Add:* Hercules Res Ctr Hercules Inc Wilmington DE 19899

TOMA, RAMSES BARSOUM, b Cairo, Egypt, Nov 9, 38; US citizen; m 69; c 1. PROTEIN METABOLISM, DAIRY SCIENCE & TECHNOLOGY. *Educ:* Ain Shams Univ, Cairo, BSc, 59, MSc, 65; La State Univ, PhD(food sci & nutrit), 71, Univ Minn, MPH, 80. *Prof Exp:* Chemist, Ministry Food Supplies, Cairo, 60-68; res assoc food sci, La State Univ, 69-71; asst prof, 72-74, assoc prof & chmn, 74-79, PROF FOOD SCI & NUTRIT, UNIV NDAK, 79- *Concurrent Pos:* Dir res & develop, Food Prod Div, Evangeline Foods, La, 72; prin investr, Red River Proj, Nat Potato Coun, 75-78; mem, NDak Trade Mission to Mid East, 75-78; vis assoc prof, Mansoura Univ, Egypt, 79-80. *Mem:* Am Chem Soc; Inst Food Technol; Am Dietetic Asn; Am Public Health Asn; Am Asn Cereal Chemists. *Res:* Food analyses; protein composition; naturally occurring toxicants in foods; protein metabolism; dietary patterns of selected ethnic groups. *Mailing Add:* Univ Sta Univ NDak PO Box 8042 Grand Forks ND 58202

TOMAJA, DAVID LOUIS, b Bridggport, Conn, July 15, 46; m 69. ORGANOMETALLIC CHEMISTRY. *Educ:* Univ Conn, BA, 68; State Univ NY Albany, PhD(chem), 74. *Prof Exp:* Chemist, Gen Elec Res & Develop Ctr, 68-70; RES CHEMIST, PHILLIPS PETROL RES & DEVELOP CTR, 74- *Mem:* Am Chem Soc; Sigma Xi. *Res:* Catalytic upgrading of shale oil and coal liquids; characterization of synfuels. *Mailing Add:* Phillips Petrol Co Res & Develop Ct Bartlesville OK 74003

TOMALIA, DONALD ANDREW, b Owosso, Mich, Sept 5, 38; m 59; c 4. PHYSICAL ORGANIC CHEMISTRY. *Educ:* Univ Mich, BS, 61; Bucknell Univ, MS, 62; Mich State Univ, PhD(phys org chem), 68. *Prof Exp:* res mgr specialty prod, Chem Prod Res Lab, 62-76, assoc scientist, 76-79, SR ASSOC SCIENTIST DESIGNED POLYMERS & CHEM, DOW CHEM CO, 79- *Mem:* Am Chem Soc; Sigma Xi. *Res:* Functional monomers and polymers usually incorporating heterocyclic moieties; unusual cross linking devices; betaine surfactants and chelating agents; onium type chemistry; water borne polymer systems; polyamines; cationic polymerization. *Mailing Add:* Designed Polymers & Chem Dow Chem Co Midland MI 48640

TOMAN, FRANK R, b Ellsworth, Kans, June 6, 39; m 62; c 2. BIOCHEMISTRY, PLANT PHYSIOLOGY. *Educ:* Kans State Univ, BS, 61, MS, 63, PhD(biochem), 67. *Prof Exp:* Asst prof, 66-69, assoc prof, 69-79, PROF BIOCHEM, WESTERN KY UNIV,79- *Concurrent Pos:* Res assoc, Plant Res Lab, Mich State Univ-AEC, 73-74; sabbatical leave, Dept Plant Physiol, Univ Ky, 82. *Mem:* Am Chem Soc. *Res:* Plant proteins and enzymes; plant growth retardant chemicals; microtubules. *Mailing Add:* Dept of Biol Western Ky Univ Bowling Green KY 42101

TOMAN, KAREL, b Pilsen, Czech, Mar 19, 24; m 48; c 1. CRYSTALLOGRAPHY. *Educ:* Prague Tech Univ, Ing Chem, 48, Dr Tech(chem), 51; Czech Acad Sci, DrSc(physics), 65. *Prof Exp:* Res officer, Inst Metals, Czech, 50-56; sr res officer, Inst Solid State Physics, 56-62; head lab crystallog, Inst Macromolecular Chem, 62-68; Sci Res Coun UK sr vis res fel, Univ Birmingham, 68-69; res fel, Inst Mat Sci, Univ Conn, 69-70; PROF CRYSTALLOG, WRIGHT STATE UNIV, 70- *Concurrent Pos:* Nicolet fel, McGill Univ, 66-67. *Mem:* Am Crystallog Asn; Mineral Soc Am. *Res:* Crystal structure and imperfections. *Mailing Add:* Dept of Geol Wright State Univ Dayton OH 45431

TOMAN, KURT, b Vienna, Austria, Aug 11, 21; US citizen; m 58; c 3. IONOSPHERIC PHYSICS. *Educ:* Vienna Tech Univ, MS, 49; Univ Ill, Urbana, PhD(elec eng), 52. *Prof Exp:* Lab engr, Lecher Inst, Reichenau, Austria, 43-44 & Ctr Tube Res, Tanvald, Czech, 44-45; asst electronics, Univ Ill, Urbana, 49-52, res assoc, 52; re fel, Harvard Univ, 52-55; physicist, Air Force Cambridge Res Lab, 55-63, supvry res physicist & br chief ionospheric radio physics, 63-73, sr scientist, 73-76; PHYSICIST, IONOSPHERIC PROPAGATION, DEPT ELECTRONIC TECHNOL, ROME AIR DEVELOP CTR, 76- *Concurrent Pos:* Mem nat comn G, Int Union Radio Sci, 61-; chmn, Inst Elec & Electronics Engrs Wave Propagation Standards Comt, 72-; US mem working group, Int Electrotech Comn, 79- *Mem:* AAAS; Inst Elec & Electronics Engrs; Am Geophys Union; Sigma Xi. *Res:* Dynamics of the ionosphere; radio wave propagation; spectral analysis of internal ionospheric gravity waves; high-frequency ionospheric ducting; group and phase path studies; ionospheric Doppler analysis; method of determining ionospheric reflection height; theoretical and experimental studies of high frequency ducted propagation; propagation study for a tropospheric transhorizon radar RADC-TR-81-166. *Mailing Add:* Electromagnetic Sci Div Rome Air Develop Ctr Hanscom AFB MA 01731

TOMANEK, GERALD WAYNE, b Collyer, Kans, Sept 16, 21; m 45; c 3. BOTANY. *Educ:* Ft Hays State Univ, AB, 42, MS, 47; Univ Nebr, PhD, 51. *Prof Exp:* From asst prof to assoc prof, 47-67, actg pres univ, 75-76, PROF BIOL, FT HAYS STATE UNIV, 67-, CHMN DIV NATURAL SCI & MATH, 56-, PRES UNIV, 76- *Concurrent Pos:* Consult, Int Coop Admin Arg, 61. *Res:* Grassland ecology. *Mailing Add:* Pres Off Ft Hays State Univ 600 Park St Hays KS 67601

TOMAR, RUSSELL H, b Philadelphia, Pa, Oct 19, 37; m 65; c 2. IMMUNOLOGY, LABORATORY MEDICINE. *Educ:* George Washington Univ, BS, 59, MD, 63. *Prof Exp:* Resident, Barnes Hosp, Washington Univ, 63-65; surgeon, NIH, USPHS, 65-67; fel clin immunol, Univ Pa, 67-70, assoc, 70-71; ASST PROF MED, STATE UNIV NY UPSTATE MED CTR, 71-, DIR IMMUNOPATH LAB, 74-, ASSOC PROF PATH, 76- *Concurrent Pos:* Mem immunopath test comt, Am Bd Path, 79- *Mem:* Am Asn Immunol; Am Acad Allergy; Am Soc Clin Path; Soc Exp Med & Biol; Reticuloendotheliol Soc. *Res:* Cellular immunity; mechanisms of cellular interactions, especially transfer factor; immunodeficiency diseases; tumor immunology. *Mailing Add:* State Univ NY Upstate Med Ctr 750 E Adam St Syracuse NY 13210

TOMARELLI, RUDOLPH MICHAEL, b Pittsburgh, Pa, Jan 10, 17; m 52; c 4. BIOCHEMISTRY, NUTRITION. *Educ:* Univ Pittsburgh, BS, 38, MS, 41; Western Reserve Univ, MS, 42, PhD(biochem), 43. *Prof Exp:* Asst, Mellon Inst, 39-41; res chemist, Wyeth Inst Appl Biochem, 43-47; instr nutrit, Univ Pa, 47-50; res chemist, Wyeth Labs, Inc, 50-55, sr investr, Wyeth Inst Med Res, 55-70, mgr nutrit dept, 70-79, DIR NUTRIT SCI, WYETH LABS, INC, 79- *Concurrent Pos:* Asst prof, St Joseph's Col, Pa, 48-50. *Mem:* Am Chem Soc; Am Soc Biol Chemists; Am Inst Nutrit. *Res:* Infant nutrition. *Mailing Add:* Nutrit Dept Wyeth Labs Inc Radnor PA 19087

TOMAS, FRANCISCO, b Montreal, Que, Dec 21, 30; m 60, 81; c 2. SOFTWARE SYSTEM, SCIENCE ADMINISTRATION. *Educ:* Sir George Williams Univ, BSc, 56. *Prof Exp:* Cur physics, Lab, Sir George Williams Univ, 56-65, dir, 65-73; PLANNING OFFICER, CONCORDIA UNIV, 73- *Concurrent Pos:* Consult, Int Youth Sci Week, 66-67. *Mem:* Can Asn Physicists; Can Info Processing Soc. *Res:* Laboratory instruction and administration; programming; computerization of physics laboratory student testing; physics laboratory student testing; analytical chemistry database; instrumentation calculation aids; budget control; typesetting and telidon. *Mailing Add:* Sci Planning Off Concordia Univ 1455 Demaisonnevue Blvd W Montreal PQ H3G 1M8 Can

TOMASCH, WALTER J, b Cleveland, Ohio, July 26, 30; m 55; c 2. EXPERIMENTAL SOLID STATE PHYSICS. *Educ:* Case Western Reserve Univ, BS, 52, PhD(physics), 58; Rensselaer Polytech Inst, MS, 55. *Prof Exp:* Sr physicist, Atomics Int Div, NAm Aviation Corp, 58-68; PROF PHYSICS, UNIV NOTRE DAME, 68- *Mem:* Fel Am Phys Soc. *Res:* Superconductivity; physics of metals and alloys. *Mailing Add:* Dept of Physics Univ of Notre Dame Notre Dame IN 46556

TOMASCHKE, HARRY E, b Kendall, NY, Apr 25, 29; m 53; c 4. OPTICS. *Educ:* Mich State Univ, BS, 56; Univ Ill, MS, 58, PhD(physics), 64. *Prof Exp:* Res assoc, Coord Sci Lab, Univ Ill, Urbana, 58-64; ASSOC PROF PHYSICS, GREENVILLE COL, 64- *Mem:* Am Asn Physics Teachers; Optical Soc Am. *Res:* Electrical breakdown in vacuum; absorption of gases under ultrahigh vacuum conditions; thin film optics. *Mailing Add:* Dept of Physics Greenville Col Greenville IL 62246

TOMASELLI, VINCENT PAUL, b Weehawken, NJ, May 3, 41; m 66; c 3. PHYSICS. *Educ:* Fairleigh Dickinson Univ, BS, 62, MS, 64; NY Univ, PhD(physics), 71. *Prof Exp:* Res physicist, Uniroyal Res Ctr, 64-66; from instr to prof, 66-80, PROF PHYSICS, FAIRLEIGH DICKINSON UNIV, 74- *Concurrent Pos:* App Gov Sci Adv Comt, NJ State Panel Sci & Adv, 81-83. *Mem:* Am Phys Soc. *Res:* Infrared and far-infrared spectroscopy; infrared optical properties of materials and instrumentation. *Mailing Add:* Dept of Physics Fairleigh Dickinson Univ Teaneck NJ 07666

TOMASETTA, LOUIS RALPH, b New York, NY, Nov 1, 48; m 73. ELECTRICAL ENGINEERING, SEMICONDUCTORS. *Educ:* Mass Inst Technol, BS & MS, 71, ScD(elec eng), 74. *Prof Exp:* Mem tech staff laser syst, Lincoln Lab, Mass Inst Technol, 74-77; GROUP LEADER OPTICAL ELECTRONICS, ROCKWELL INT, 77- *Mem:* Inst Elec & Electronics Engrs; Sigma Xi. *Res:* Semiconductor devices; fiber optics; optical communication laser; laser systems; optics. *Mailing Add:* Rockwell Int 1049 Camino Dos Rios Thousand Oaks CA 91360

TOMASHEFSKI, JOSEPH FRANCIS, b Plymouth, Pa, Dec 30, 22; m 49; c 3. PHYSIOLOGY. *Educ:* Hahnemann Med Col, MD, 47; Am Bd Prev Med, dipl & cert aerospace med. *Prof Exp:* Asst biol, Temple Univ, 41-43; intern, Wilkes-Barre Gen Hosp, Pa, 47-48, resident med, 48-49; resident pulmonary dis, Jefferson Med Col & Hosp, 49-51; asst prof med & physiol, Col Med, Ohio State Univ, 53-66, assoc prof prev med & physiol, 66-72; DIR PULMONARY FUNCTION LAB & STAFF PHYSICIAN, DEPT PULMONARY DIS, CLEVELAND CLIN, 71-, HEAD DEPT, 73- *Concurrent Pos:* Dir res, Ohio Tuberc Hosp, 53-67; med res consult, Battelle Mem Inst, 59-67, med dir & med res adv, 67-17; dir pulmonary function labs, Univ Hosps, Ohio State Univ, 67; consult, US Air Force & Vet Admin; clin prof prev med, Col Med, Ohio State Univ, 72- *Mem:* Am Physiol Soc; Am Thoracic Soc; fel Am Col Chest Physicians; AMA; Aerospace Med Asn. *Res:* Pulmonary diseases; respiratory physiology; aviation medicine; pulmonary function testing; environmental medicine. *Mailing Add:* Cleveland Clin 9500 Euclid Ave Cleveland OH 44106

TOMASHEFSKY, PHILIP, b Brooklyn, NY, May 4, 24; m 48; c 2. EXPERIMENTAL PATHOLOGY. *Educ:* City Col New York, BS, 46, MS, 51; NY Univ, MS, 63, PhD(biol), 69. *Prof Exp:* Chemist, Funk Found, 48-65 & US Vitamin Corp, 65; biochemist, Dept Urol, 65-69, assoc, 69-71, asst prof path, 71-76, ASST PROF CLIN PATH, COL PHYSICIANS & SURGEONS, COLUMBIA UNIV, 76- *Mem:* Fel AAAS; NY Acad Sci; Sigma Xi; Am Inst Ultrasound Med. *Res:* Neoplastic and hyperplastic growth of the kidney and prostate and other urological tissues; chemotherapy and thermotherapy; metastasis. *Mailing Add:* Dept of Urol Col of Phys & Surg Columbia Univ New York NY 10032

TOMASI, GORDON ERNEST, b Denver, Colo, Dec 16, 30; m 54; c 3. BIOCHEMISTRY, ORGANIC CHEMISTRY. *Educ:* Colo State Col, BA, 57, MA, 58; Univ Louisville, PhD(biochem), 63. *Prof Exp:* From asst prof to assoc prof, 62-70, PROF CHEM, UNIV NORTHERN COLO, 70-, CHMN DEPT CHEM, 81- *Res:* Bioenergetics; nutritional biochemistry; mechanisms of organic reaction and enzyme catalyzed reactions. *Mailing Add:* Dept of Chem Univ of Northern Colo Greeley CO 80631

TOMASI, THOMAS B, JR, b Barre, Vt, May 24, 27; m 48; c 3. IMMUNOLOGY, BIOCHEMISTRY. *Educ:* Dartmouth Col, AB, 50; Univ Vt, MD, 54; Rockefeller Univ, PhD, 65. *Prof Exp:* Instr med, Col Physicians & Surgeons, Columbia Univ, 57-58; asst physician, Rockefeller Univ, 58-60; asst prof med, Univ Vt, 60-61, actg chmn dept, 60-62, assoc prof & chmn dept, 62-65; prof, State Univ NY Buffalo, 65-73, dir, Div Immunol & Arthritis, 64-73; WILLIAM H DONNER PROF IMMUNOL, CHMN DEPT & PROF MED, MAYO MED SCH, 73- *Concurrent Pos:* Sr investr, Arthritis & Rheumatism Found, 60-65; dir, NIH training grant arthritis & metab dis; chief med, DeGoesbriand Hosp, 61-65; asst physician, Rockefeller Univ, 64-65; mem gen med study sect, NIH. *Mem:* Arthritis & Rheumatism Asn; Asn Am Physicians; Am Asn Immunologists; Am Fedn Clin Res; Am Soc Clin Invest. *Res:* Internal medicine; immunological diseases; immunochemistry. *Mailing Add:* Dept of Immunol Mayo Med Sch Rochester MN 55901

TOMASOVIC, STEPHEN PETER, b Bend, Ore, Jan 5, 47; m 70. RADIATION BIOLOGY, CELL BIOLOGY. *Educ:* Ore State Univ, BS, 69, MS, 73; Colo State Univ, PhD(radiation biol), 77. *Prof Exp:* Fel, Dept Radiation Biol, Colo State Univ, 77; fel radiation biol, Dept Radiol, Med Ctr, Univ Utah, 78-79, asst prof, 79-80; ASST PROF, DEPT TUMOR BIOL, M D ANDERSON HOSP, 80- *Mem:* AAAS; Radiation Res Soc; Cell Kinetics Soc; Am Soc Cell Biol; Soc Anal Cytol. *Res:* Molecular biology; experimental combined modality therapy; biology of the cell cycle; tumor biology; experimental tumor metastasis. *Mailing Add:* Dept Tumor Biol M D Anderson Hosp Tumor Inst Houston TX 77030

TOMASULA, JOHN J, b Queens, NY, Feb, 17, 33; m 54; c 2. EXPERIMENTAL NEUROSURGERY, HISTOLOGY. *Educ:* Ohio Christian Col, BS, 73; Northwestern Univ, PhD(histol), 76. *Prof Exp:* ASST PROF NEUROSCI, MED CTR, NY UNIV, 59- *Concurrent Pos:* Toxicologists, K G Labs, 74-78; surgical consult, Sandoz Labs, 75. *Mem:* Soc Neurosci. *Res:* Spinal cord and brain trauma; spinal cord regeneration; physiology of spinal cord trauma and regeneration; outcome of trauma with treatment and different specific regimes. *Mailing Add:* Neurosurg Labs Old Admin Bldg Med Ctr NY Univ Bellevue 550 First Ave New York NY 10016

TOMASZ, ALEXANDER, b Budapest, Hungary, Dec 23, 30; US citizen; m 56; c 1. BIOCHEMISTRY, CELL BIOLOGY. *Educ:* Pazmany Peter Univ, Budapest, dipl, 53; Columbia Univ, PhD(biochem), 61. *Prof Exp:* Res assoc cytochem, Inst Genetics, Hungarian Nat Acad, 53-56; Am Cancer Soc fel & guest investr genetics, 61-63, from asst prof to assoc prof genetics & biochem, 63-77, PROF MICROBIOL & CHMN DEPT, ROCKEFELLER UNIV, 77- *Mem:* AAAS; Am Soc Microbiol; Am Soc Cell Biol; Harvey Soc. *Res:* Biosynthesis and functioning of cell surface structures; cell to cell interactions; control of cell division; molecular genetics. *Mailing Add:* Dept Microbiol Rockefeller Univ New York NY 10021

TOMASZ, MARIA, b Szeged, Hungary, Oct 18, 32; US citizen; m 56; c 2. ORGANIC CHEMISTRY, BIOCHEMISTRY. *Educ:* Univ Eötvös Lorand, Budapest, dipl chem, 56; Columbia Univ, MA, 59, PhD(chem), 62. *Prof Exp:* Res assoc, Rockefeller Inst, 61-62, res assoc biochem, NY Univ, 62-64, instr, 64-66; from asst prof to assoc prof chem, 66-78, PROF CHEM, HUNTER COL, 79- *Mem:* NY Acad Sci; Fedn Am Soc Exp Biol; Am Chem Soc. *Res:* Chemistry of nucleic acids; chemical basis of action of mutagens, carcinogens and antibiotics. *Mailing Add:* Dept of Chem Hunter Col New York NY 10021

TOMBACK, DIANA FRANCINE, b Los Angeles, Calif, June 9, 49. AVIAN ECOLOGY, BEHAVIORAL ECOLOGY. *Educ:* Univ Calif, Los Angeles, BA, 70, MA, 72; Univ Calif, Santa Barbara, PhD(biol sci), 77. *Prof Exp:* Teaching asst biol sci, Univ Calif, Santa Barbara, 72-73, teaching assoc, 73-76; instr biol, Dept Zool, Brigham Young Univ, 77; vis asst prof zool, Pomona

Col, 77-78; lectr biol, Univ Calif, Riverside, 78-79; NSF fel zool, Colo State Univ, 79-81; ASST PROF BIOL, DEPT BIOL, UNIV COLO, DENVER, 81- *Mem:* Ecol Soc Am; Am Ornith Union; Soc Study Evolution; Am Soc Naturalists; AAAS. *Res:* Ecological relationship between Nucifraga columbiana and Pinus albicaulis; color phase polymorphism in Buteo regalis; behavior maintaining dialect populations in Zonotrichia leucophrys nuttalli; ecology of Corvus Kubaryi. *Mailing Add:* Div Natural & Phys Sci Univ Colo 1100 Fourteenth St Denver CO 80202

TOMBALAKIAN, ARTIN S, b Jerusalem, Palestine, Nov 4, 29; Can citizen; m 59; c 3. CHEMISTRY, CHEMICAL ENGINEERING. *Educ:* Am Univ Beirut, BA, 52; Univ Toronto, MASc, 54, PhD(chem eng), 58. *Prof Exp:* Prof chem & chmn, Dept Chem & Eng, 58-70, dir, Sch Eng, 68-79, PROF CHEM & CHEM ENG, LAURENTIAN UNIV, 66- *Mem:* Fel Chem Inst Can; Am Chem Soc; Can Metall Soc. *Res:* Ion-exchange; diffusion; mass transfer; electrochemistry; sorption of crude oil derivatives on Arctic terrain; treatment of industrial waste waters; recovery of metals by hydrometallurgical techniques. *Mailing Add:* Sch Eng Laurentian Univ Sudbury ON P3E 2C6 Can

TOMBAUGH, LARRY WILLIAM, b Erie, Pa, Jan 28, 39; m 60; c 2. FOREST ECONOMICS. *Educ:* Pa State Univ, BS, 60; Colo State Univ, MS, 63; Univ Mich, PhD(resource econ), 68. *Prof Exp:* Economist, NCent Forest Exp Sta, 66-69; prin economist, Southeastern Forest Exp Sta, 69-71; prog mgr, NSF, 71-75, dir div advan environ res & technol, 75-76, dep asst dir anal & planning, 76-78; CHMN DEPT FORESTRY, MICH STATE UNIV, 78- *Concurrent Pos:* Lectr resource econ, Univ Mich, 66-69. *Mem:* Fel AAAS; Sigma Xi; Soc Am Foresters. *Res:* Economic incentives for environmental control and economics of the forest products industry. *Mailing Add:* Dept Forestry Mich State Univ East Lansing MI 48824

TOMBER, MARVIN L, b South Bend, Ind, Aug 4, 25; m 48; c 2. ALGEBRA. *Educ:* Univ Notre Dame, BS, 46; Univ Pa, PhD(math), 52. *Prof Exp:* Instr math, Amherst Col, 52-55; from asst prof to assoc prof, 55-65, PROF MATH, MICH STATE UNIV, 65- *Mem:* Am Math Soc; Math Asn Am; Inst Basic Res. *Res:* Non-associative algebras. *Mailing Add:* Dept Math Mich State Univ East Lansing MI 48823

TOMBES, AVERETT SNEAD, b Easton, Md, Sept 13, 32; m 57; c 4. INVERTEBRATE PHYSIOLOGY. *Educ:* Univ Richmond, BS, 54; Va Polytech Inst, MS, 56; Rutgers Univ, PhD, 61. *Prof Exp:* Asst prof, Clemson Univ, 61-65; NIH res fel, Univ Va, 65-66; from assoc prof to prof zool, Clemson Univ, 66-77; prof biol & chmn dept, 77-81, DEAN GRAD SCH, GEORGE MASON UNIV, 81- *Concurrent Pos:* Nat Ctr Sci Res France vis prof, Univ Lille, 71-72; fel acad admin, Am Coun Educ, Univ Del & Univ Md, 80-81. *Mem:* AAAS; Am Soc Cell Biol; Inst Soc, Ethics & Life Sci; Am Physiol Soc; Am Soc Zoologists. *Res:* Physiology and endocrinology of invertebrates; ultrastructure of invertebrate neuroendocrine tissue; physiology of adult insect diapause. *Mailing Add:* Dean Grad Sch George Mason Univ Fairfax VA 22030

TOMBLIN, FRED FITCH, b Ventura, Calif, Apr 19, 41; m 66; c 1. SPACE SCIENCE, NUCLEAR PHYSICS. *Educ:* Harvey Mudd Col, BS, 63; Univ Calif, Santa Barbara, 65, PhD(phyiscs), 67. *Prof Exp:* Mem tech staff space sci, Bellcomm, Inc, 67-72, MEM TECH STAFF, SYSTS ANAL, BELL TEL LABS, 72- *Mem:* Am Phys Soc. *Res:* Solar and stellar x-ray emission processes; atmospheric x-ray fluorescence; radiation belt phenomena. *Mailing Add:* Bell Tel Labs Bldg 5 Murray Hill NJ 07974

TOMBOULIAN, PAUL, b Rochester, NY, Oct 19, 34; m 57; c 3. TOXIC SUBSTANCE MANAGEMENT. *Educ:* Cornell Univ, AB, 53; Univ Ill, PhD(org chem), 56. *Prof Exp:* Res fel chem, Univ Minn, 56-59, instr, 57-58; from asst prof to assoc prof, 59-67, PROF CHEM, OAKLAND UNIV, 67-, CHMN DEPT, 62-, COORDR ENVIRON STUDIES, 70-, DIR ENVIRON HEALTH, 75- *Mem:* Am Chem Soc. *Res:* Water resources; instrumental analysis; water quality studies. *Mailing Add:* Dept of Chem Oakland Univ Rochester MI 48063

TOMBRELLO, THOMAS ANTHONY, JR, b Austin, Tex, Sept 20, 36; m 77; c 4. PLANETARY SCIENCE, SURFACE SCIENCE. *Educ:* Rice Univ, BA, 58, MA, 60, PhD(physics), 61. *Prof Exp:* Res fel physics, Calif Inst Technol, 61-63; from instr to asst prof, Yale Univ, 63-64; res fel, 64-65, asst prof, 65-67, assoc prof, 67-71, PROF PHYSICS, CALIF INST TECHNOL, 71- *Concurrent Pos:* NSF fel, 61-62; Alfred P Sloan Found fel, 71-73; consult, Los Alamos Sci Lab & Schlumberger; assoc ed, Nuclear Physics, 72- & Nuclear Sci Appl, 79-; chmn panel nuclear data compliations, Nat Res Coun, 80- *Mem:* Fel Am Phys Soc; AAAS; Am Geophys Union. *Res:* Nuclear structure; applications of nuclear physics; space physics; earthquake prediction research. *Mailing Add:* Kellogg Radiation Lab 106-38 Calif Inst of Technol Pasadena CA 91125

TOMCUFCIK, ANDREW STEPHEN, b Czech, Oct 26, 21; nat US; m 54; c 5. ORGANIC CHEMISTRY. *Educ:* Fenn Col, BS, 43; Western Reserve Univ, MS, 48; Yale Univ, PhD(org chem), 51. *Prof Exp:* Res chemist uranium refining, Mallinckrodt Chem Works, 46; instr chem, Fenn Col, 46-47; res chemist uranium refining, Mallinckrodt Chem Works, 49; res chemist, Am Cyanamid Co, 50-53, res chemist, Lederle Labs, 53-55, dept head, 74-76, GROUP LEADER, LEDERLE LABS, AM CYANAMID CO, 55- *Mem:* AAAS; Am Chem Soc; NY Acad Sci; Royal Soc Chem. *Res:* Chemotherapy of cancer; parasitic infections; heterocyclic chemistry; cardiovascular-renal diseases. *Mailing Add:* 48 Dearborn Dr Old Tappan Westwood NJ 07675

TOMEI, L DAVID, b Williamsport, Pa, Apr 27, 45; m 77; c 5. CELLULAR PHYSIOLOGY, CELL CYCLE REGULATION. *Educ:* Canisius Col, BS, 68, MS, 70; State Univ NY, Buffalo, PhD(biochem & pharmacol), 74. *Prof Exp:* Chemist, Plum Island Animal Dis Ctr, USDA, 73-75; res scientist, Roswell Park Mem Inst, 75-81; RES SCIENTIST, COMPREHENSIVE CANCER CTR, OHIO STATE UNIV, 81- *Mem:* Am Asn Cancer Res. *Res:* In vitro cell growth and function: cell cycle regulation during G, and the perturbation of regulation by drugs believed to be tumor promoters. *Mailing Add:* Comprehensive Cancer Ctr Ohio State Univ Columbus OH 43210

TOMER, KENNETH BEAMER, b New Kensington, Pa, Mar 13, 44; m 66; c 1. MASS SPECTROMETRY, ORGANIC CHEMISTRY. *Educ:* Ohio State Univ, BS, 66; Univ Colo, PhD(chem), 70. *Prof Exp:* Fel photochem, H C Orsted Inst, Univ Copenhagen, 70-71; fel mass spectrometry, Dept Chem, Stanford Univ, 71-73; asst prof chem, Brooklyn Col, 73-75; asst prof pediat, Med Sch, Univ Pa, 75-77; mem staff, Chem & Life Sci Div, Res Triangle Inst, 77-81; ASST DIR, MIDWEST CTR MASS SPECTROMETRY, UNIV NEBR-LINCOLN, 81- *Mem:* Am Chem Soc; Royal Soc Chem; Am Soc Mass Spectrometry. *Res:* Investigations of fragmentation mechanisms of organic compounds in a mass spectrometer; clinical and biochemical applications of mass spectrometry; environmental analysis. *Mailing Add:* Dept Chem Midwest Ctr Mass Spectrometry Univ Nebr Lincoln NE 68588

TOMES, DWIGHT TRAVIS, b Bowling Green, Ky, Sept 21, 46; m 66; c 3. PLANT GENETICS, PLANT TISSUE CULTURE. *Educ:* Western Ky Univ, BS, 68; Univ Ky, PhD(crop sci), 75. *Prof Exp:* Asst prof, 75-80, ASSOC PROF CROP SCI, UNIV GUELPH, 80- *Mem:* Am Genetics Asn; Am Soc Agron; Agr Inst Can. *Res:* Plant breeding and genetics of forage legumes with emphasis on seed yield and seedling vigor of Lotus corniculatus L; tissue culture of forage legumes including anther culture, asexual propagation and in vitro selection. *Mailing Add:* Dept Crop Sci Ont Agr Col Univ Guelph Guelph ON N1G 2W1 Can

TOMES, MARK LOUIS, b Ft Wayne, Ind, Nov 15, 17; m 44; c 2. GENETICS. *Educ:* Ind Univ, AB, 39; Agr & Mech Col, Tex, MS, 41; Purdue Univ, PhD(genetics), 52. *Prof Exp:* Chief plant res, Stokely-Van Camp, Inc, 46-48; asst geneticist, 48-53, ASSOC GENETICIST, EXP STA, PURDUE UNIV, WEST LAFAYETTE, 53-, PROF GENETICS, 59-, HEAD DEPT BOT & PLANT PATH, 69-, ASSOC DIR AGR EXP STA, 77- *Concurrent Pos:* Vis prof, Pa State Univ, 66-67. *Mem:* AAAS; Am Soc Hort Sci; Am Phytopath Soc; Genetics Soc Am; Am Genetic Asn. *Res:* Genetics and breeding of horticultural crops. *Mailing Add:* Agr Exp Sta Agr Admin Bldg Purdue Univ West Lafayette IN 47907

TOMETSKO, ANDREW M, b Mt Pleasant, Pa, Feb 13, 38; m 65; c 3. BIOCHEMISTRY, ORGANIC CHEMISTRY. *Educ:* St Vincent Col, BS, 60; Univ Pittsburgh, PhD(biochem), 64. *Prof Exp:* Res assoc biochem, Brookhaven Nat Lab, 64-65, asst scientist, 65-66; asst prof biochem, Sch Med & Dent, Univ Rochester, 66-76; PRES, LITRON LABS, LTD, 76- *Mem:* AAAS; NY Acad Sci; Sigma Xi; Am Chem Soc. *Res:* Chemical synthesis of polypeptides; protein structure and function; separation techniques in protein chemistry; photochemistry and photobiology. *Mailing Add:* Litron Labs Ltd 1351 Mt Hope Ave Rochester NY 14620

TOMEZSKO, EDWARD STEPHEN JOHN, b Philadelphia, Pa, Apr 9, 35; m 62; c 4. PHYSICAL CHEMISTRY. *Educ:* Villanova Univ, BS, 57; Pa State Univ, MS, 61, PhD(phys chem), 62. *Prof Exp:* Resident res assoc phys chem, Nat Bur Standards, 62-64; sr res chemist, Arco Chem Co Div, Atlantic Richfield Co, 64-71; asst prof chem, 71-78, assoc dir acad affairs, 81-82, ASSOC PROF CHEM, PA STATE UNIV, DELAWARE COUNTY CAMPUS, 78- *Mem:* Am Chem Soc; Catalysis Soc. *Res:* Thermodynamics; homogeneous and heterogeneous catalysis; inorganic and organic synthesis. *Mailing Add:* 4 Prince Eugene Lane Media PA 19063

TOMIC, ERNST ALOIS, b Vienna, Austria, Feb 1, 26; m 52; c 2. INORGANIC CHEMISTRY, PHYSICAL CHEMISTRY. *Educ:* Univ Vienna, PhD, 56. *Prof Exp:* Asst inorg, geochem & anal chem, Univ Vienna, 55-57; res chemist, Explosives Dept, 58-70, sr res chemist, Polymer Intermediates Dept, 70-74, staff res chemist, Polymer Intermediates Dept, 74-78, RES ASSOC PETROCHEM DEPT, EXP STA, E I DU PONT DE NEMOURS & CO, INC, 78- *Res:* Ion exchange; coordination chemistry; radiochemistry; inorganic synthesis; inorganic cements; molten salts; electrochemistry; hydrometallurgy. *Mailing Add:* 1430 Emory Rd Wilmington DE 19803

TOMICH, CHARLES EDWARD, b Gallup, NMex, Oct 23, 37; m 59; c 3. DENTISTRY, ORAL PATHOLOGY. *Educ:* Loyola Univ, La, DDS, 61; Ind Univ, Indianapolis, MSD, 68; Am Bd Oral Path, dipl. *Prof Exp:* Assoc prof, 69-78, PROF ORAL PATH, SCH DENT, IND UNIV, INDIANAPOLIS, 78- *Concurrent Pos:* USPHS training grant, Sch Dent, Ind Univ, Indianapolis, 66-69; ed, Oral Surg, Oral Med & Oral Path, Oral Path Sect, 76- *Mem:* Fel Am Acad Oral Path; Sigma Xi. *Res:* In vivo hard tissue marking agents; salivary gland histochemistry; oral neoplasms. *Mailing Add:* Dept of Oral Path Sch of Dent Ind Univ 1121 W Michigan St Indianapolis IN 46202

TOMICH, JOHN MATTHEW, b Baltimore, Md, May 29, 52; m 82. PROTEIN CHEMISTRY, ENZYMOLOGY. *Educ:* Univ Conn, BA, 74; Purdue Univ, MS, 75; Guelph-Waterloo Ctr Grad Work Chem, Waterloo, Ont, PhD(chem), 79. *Prof Exp:* FEL PROTEIN CHEM, CHEM DEPT, UNIV DEL, 79- *Mem:* Sigma Xi. *Res:* Mechanisms by which enzymes exhibit specificity for both substrates and allosteriz effects, utilizing chemical and biophysical techniques. *Mailing Add:* Chem Dept Univ Del Newark DE 19711

TOMICH, PROSPER QUENTIN, b Orange Vale, Calif, Oct 11, 20; m 46; c 5. VERTEBRATE ZOOLOGY, ANIMAL ECOLOGY. *Educ:* Univ Calif, Berkeley, AB, 43; Univ Calif, Davis, PhD(zool), 59. *Prof Exp:* Lab asst plague res, Hooper Found, Univ Calif, 43-44, res zoologist, Hastings Natural Hist Reservation, 47-52; assoc zool, Univ Calif, Davis, 56-59; ANIMAL ECOLOGIST, STATE DEPT HEALTH, HAWAII, 59- *Concurrent Pos:* Naval med res unit adv, Egyptian Govt, 46-47; arbovirus res training grant, Pa State Univ, 66-67; mem island ecosysts proj, Int Biol Prog, Univ Hawaii, 69-75; chmn, Hawaii Natural Area Reserves Syst Comn, 76- *Mem:* Fel AAAS; Ecol Soc Am; Am Soc Mammalogy; Wildlife Soc; Am Ornithologists Union. *Res:* Rodents, fleas, and plague; field ecology of mule deer, ground squirrel, mongoose, and of Arctic birds and mammals; leptospirosis in populations of small mammals; history and adaptation of mammals in Hawaiian Islands; rehabilitation of depleted subrtopical rain-forest ecosystems. *Mailing Add:* Res Unit Dept of Health Honokaa HI 96727

TOMIKEL, JOHN, b Cuddy, Pa, Apr 30, 28; m 49, 68; c 2. EARTH SCIENCE. *Educ:* Clarion State Col, BS, 51; Univ Pittsburgh, MLitt, 56, PhD(higher educ), 70; Syracuse Univ, MS, 62. *Prof Exp:* Sci teacher, Fairview High Sch, 51-63; asst prof earth sci, Edinboro State Col, 63-65; PROF GEOG & EARTH SCI, CALIFORNIA STATE COL, PA, 65- *Mem:* Nat Asn Geol Teachers. *Res:* Earth science education. *Mailing Add:* Dept of Earth Sci California State Col of Pa California PA 15419

TOMIMATSU, YOSHIO, physical chemistry, see previous edition

TOMIYASU, KIYO, b Las Vegas, Nev, Sept 25, 19; m 47. MICROWAVE ENGINEERING, ELECTRONIC ENGINEERING. *Educ:* Calif Inst Technol, BS, 40; Columbia Univ, MS, 41; Harvard Univ, MES, 47, PhD(eng sci, appl physics), 48. *Prof Exp:* Instr Lyman Lab, Harvard Univ, 48-49; proj engr, Sperry Gyroscope Co, 49-52, head eng sect, 52-55; consult engr, Microwave Lab, Calif, 55-60 & Res & Develop Ctr, NY, 60-69, CONSULT ENGR, SPACE DIV, GEN ELEC CO, 69- *Mem:* Am Phys Soc; fel Inst Elec & Electronics Engrs. *Res:* Microwave radiometry; microwave scatterometry of sea surface; communications; atmospheric propagation; radar; tropospheric propagation; ionospheric propagation; synthetic aperture radar. *Mailing Add:* Valley Forge Space Ctr Gen Elec Co PO Box 8555 Philadelphia PA 19101

TOMIZAWA, HENRY HIDEO, b San Francisco, Calif, Feb 12, 26; m; c 6. BIOCHEMISTRY. *Educ:* Iowa State Col, BS, 49; Univ Ill, PhD(chem), 52. *Prof Exp:* From res assoc med to res asst prof & lectr biochem, Univ Wash, 52-59; sr res assoc, Fels Res Inst, Ohio, 59-65; res dir, Reference Lab, Calif, 65-67; clin chem consult, 67-68; chief clin chem lab, Los Angeles Vet Admin Hosp, 68-69; head toxicol-spec chem & qual control, Reference Lab, 69-70; tech dir, 70-80, DIR RES & DEVELOP, BIO-REAGENTS & DIAG, INC, ORTHO DIAG SYSTS INC, 80- *Mem:* Am Chem Soc; Am Soc Biol Chemists; Am Asn Clin Chemists. *Res:* Research and development; clinical tests. *Mailing Add:* Ortho Diagnostic Systs Inc Irvine CA

TOMIZUKA, CARL TATSUO, b Tokyo, Japan, May 24, 23; nat US; m 56; c 4. SOLID STATE PHYSICS. *Educ:* Univ Tokyo, BS, 45; Univ Ill, MS, 51, PhD(physics), 54. *Prof Exp:* Asst physics, Univ Ill, 51-54, res assoc, 54-55, res asst prof physics & elec eng, 55-56; asst prof physics, Inst Study Metals, Univ Chicago, 56-60; head dept, 70-77, assoc dean, 77-79, PROF PHYSICS, UNIV ARIZ, 60- *Honors & Awards:* Creative Teaching Award, Univ Ariz Found, 73. *Mem:* Am Phys Soc; Phys Soc Japan. *Res:* Solid state diffusion; anelasticity; high pressure; magnetism. *Mailing Add:* Dept of Physics Univ of Ariz Tucson AZ 85721

TOMKIEWICZ, MICHA, b Warsaw, Poland, May 25, 39; Israeli citizen; c 1. PHYSICAL CHEMISTRY. *Educ:* Hebrew Univ, MS, 63, PhD(chem), 69. *Prof Exp:* Instr phys chem, Hebrew Univ, 67-69; fel, Univ Guelph, 69-71; Nat Inst Gen Med Sci fel biophys, Univ Calif, Berkeley, 71-72, Nat Inst Gen Med Sci spec fel, 72-73; fel biophys, Thomas J Watson Res Ctr, IBM Corp, 73-76; res scientist, Union Carbide Corp, Tarrytown Tech Ctr, 76-80; MEM FAC, DEPT PHYSICS, BROOKLYN COL, 80- *Res:* Using biophysical and electrochemical approaches to photolyse water with visible radiation for the purpose of converting solar energy to useful chemical energy. *Mailing Add:* Dept Physics Brooklyn Col Brooklyn NY 11210

TOMKINS, DAVID FRANCIS, analytical chemistry, see previous edition

TOMKINS, FRANK SARGENT, b Petoskey, Mich, June 24, 15; m 42, 63; c 1. ATOMIC SPECTROSCOPY. *Educ:* Kalamazoo Col, BS, 37; Mich State Col, PhD(phys chem), 42. *Prof Exp:* Physicist, Buick Motor Div, Gen Motors Corp, Ill, 41-43; physicist, 43-46, SR SCIENTIST & GROUP LEADER, ARGONNE NAT LAB, 46- *Concurrent Pos:* Guggenheim fel, Nat Ctr Sci Res, France, 60-61; consult, Bendix Corp, 63-75; Argonne Nat Lab-Argonne Univs Asn distinguished appt, 75; fel Sci Res Coun (England), 75; assoc, Harvard Col Observ, 77- *Honors & Awards:* Optical Soc Am, William F Meggers Award, 77. *Mem:* AAAS; fel Optical Soc Am; assoc Am Phys Soc; assoc Fr Phys Soc. *Res:* Physical chemistry; optical spectroscopy. *Mailing Add:* Chem Div Argonne Nat Lab Argonne IL 60439

TOMKINS, JOHN PRESTON, b Ellenton, Pa, May 5, 18; m 46; c 2. HORTICULTURE. *Educ:* Pa State Univ, BS, 40, MS, 42; Cornell Univ, PhD(pomol), 51. *Prof Exp:* Res assoc pomol, Exp Sta, State Univ NY Col Agr, Cornell Univ, 46-49; asst prof & exten specialist, Mich State Col, 50-53; horticulturist, Welch Grape Juice Co, 53; assoc prof pomol, Exp Sta, State Univ NY Col Agr, Cornell Univ, 54-62; ASSOC PROF POMOL, CORNELL UNIV, 62- *Res:* Culture of strawberries, raspberries and grapes. *Mailing Add:* Dept of Pomol Cornell Univ Ithaca NY 14850

TOMKINS, MARION LOUISE, b Pembroke, NH, Mar 28, 26. X-RAY FLUORESCENT SPECTROSCOPE. *Educ:* Univ Tampa, BS, 52; Roosevelt Univ, MS310>. *Prof Exp:* Jr res chemist, Int Minerals & Chem Corp, 52-58; chief spectrographer, Martin Marietta Corp, 58-71; DIR LABS, H KRAMER & CO, 71- *Mem:* Am Chem Soc; Soc Appl Spectros; Am Soc Testing & Mat. *Res:* Methods of analyses for high temperature alloys, geological materials and pollution control; chemical coatings for structural materials. *Mailing Add:* 1339 W 21st St Chicago IL 60608

TOMKOWIT, THADDEUS W(ALTER), b New York, NY, Sept 10, 18; m 43; c 3. CHEMICAL ENGINEERING. *Educ:* Columbia Univ, BS, 41, ChE, 42. *Prof Exp:* Semiworks supvr, 42-43, develop engr, 43-53, gen engr in charge minor construct, Chambers Works, 54-65, gen supt process dept, 65-72, mgr logistics, Org Chem Dept, Freon Prod Div, 72-74, mgr logisitcs, Org Chem Dept, 74-78, MGR LOGISTICS & WORKS SUPPLIES, DYES & PIGMENTS DEPT, E I DU PONT DE NEMOURS & CO, INC, 78- *Concurrent Pos:* Mem exec bd, Salem County Voc Inst; mem deans adv comt, Cath Univ Am, 73-76, Lehigh Univ, 75-77 & Univ Tex, Austin, 76-78; mem NSF eval comt, Worcester Polytech Inst, 76-78. *Honors & Awards:* Achievement Award, Am Polish Descent Cult Soc, 68; Founders Award, Am Inst Chem Engrs. 75. *Mem:* Am Inst Chem Engrs (pres, 72). *Res:* Fluorine and fluorocarbons; detergents; Freon products; dyestuffs and intermediates; maintenance, design, chemical construction and physical distribution. *Mailing Add:* Dyes & Pigments Dept B 6226 Wilmington DE 19898

TOMLIN, ALAN DAVID, b Woking, Eng, Jan 27, 44; Can citizen; m 66; c 4. ENTOMOLOGY, ZOOLOGY. *Educ:* Univ Western Ont, BA, 65, MSc, 67; Rutgers Univ, PhD(entom), 72. *Prof Exp:* Res asst zool, Univ Western Ont, 65-67; res officer forestry, Dept Fisheries & Forestry, Can, 67-68; res asst entom, Rutgers Univ, 68-70; res officer forestry, Environ Can, 71-72; RES SCIENTIST AGR, AGR CAN, 72- *Concurrent Pos:* Fel, Rothamsted Exp Sta, Harpenden, Eng, 74-75; sci comt mem, Biol Surv Insects Can, 76-79; hon prof, Assoc Fac, Dept Environ Biol, Univ Guelph, 77-; hon lectr, Dept Zool, Univ Western Ont, 78- *Mem:* Entom Soc Am; Entom Soc Can; fel Royal Entom Soc. *Res:* Ecology of soil arthropods; effects of pesticides on soil fauna; morphology and taxonomy of soil arthropods; biology of earthworms. *Mailing Add:* Res Inst Agr Can University Sub PO London ON N6A 5B7 Can

TOMLIN, DON C, b Meridian, Idaho, Aug 29, 32; m 58; c 1. ANIMAL NUTRITION. *Educ:* Calif State Polytech Col, BSc, 55; Univ Fla, MSc, 56, PhD(animal nutrit), 60. *Prof Exp:* Res asst, Univ Fla, 55-60; animal nutrit, Madera Milling Co, Calif, 60; fel forage eval, Ohio Agr Exp Sta, 61-62; res officer, Exp Farm, Can Dept Agr, BC, 62-65; res assoc range livestock nutrit, Utah Agr Exp Sta, 65-67; animal scientist, US Sheep Exp Sta, USDA, Idaho, 67-70; asst prof animal sci, Univ Alaska, Fairbanks, 70-75; CONSULT, AGRO-NORTH ASSOC, 75- *Mem:* Sigma Xi; Am Soc Animal Sci; Soc Range Mgt. *Res:* Ruminant nutrition; evaluation and utilization of native and domestic forages. *Mailing Add:* 1609 4th Ave Fairbanks AK 99701

TOMLINSON, EVERETT PARSONS, b Montclair, NJ, Sept 18, 14; m 80; c 3. SCIENCE EDUCATION. *Educ:* Yale Univ, BS, 36; Calif Inst Technol, PhD(physics), 42. *Prof Exp:* Asst, Calif Inst Technol, 38-41; instr physics, Princeton Univ, 46-50, lectr, 50-52; lectr, Bryn Mawr Col, 52-53; res assoc, Princeton Univ, 53-56, mem proj res staff, 56-67; MEM FAC, CAPE COD COMMUNITY COL, 67- *Mem:* AAAS; Am Phys Soc; Am Asn Physics Teachers. *Res:* Beta ray spectroscopy; high energy accelerators; electricity and magnetism. *Mailing Add:* 848 Fox Hill Rd Chatham MA 02633

TOMLINSON, GEORGE HERBERT, b Fullerton, La, May 2, 12; m; c 3. CHEMISTRY. *Educ:* Bishop's Univ, Can, BA, 31; McGill Univ, PhD(chem), 35. *Prof Exp:* Res assoc cellulose & indust chem, McGill Univ, 35-36; chief chemist, Howard Smith Chem Ltd, 36-40; res dir, Howard Smith Paper Mills Ltd, 41-60; res dir, 61-70, vpres res & environ technol, 70-77, SR SCI ADV, DOMTAR LTD, 77- *Honors & Awards:* Medal, Tech Asn Pulp & Paper Indust, 69. *Mem:* AAAS; hon life mem Can Pulp & Paper Asn; hon life mem Tech Asn Pulp & Paper Indust; Am Chem Soc. *Mailing Add:* Domtar Ltd 395 Blvd deMaisonneuve W Montreal PQ H3A 1L6 Can

TOMLINSON, GERALDINE ANN, b Vancouver, BC, Feb 5, 31; m 57. MICROBIOLOGY, BIOCHEMISTRY. *Educ:* Univ BC, BSA, 57, PhD(agr microbiol), 64; Univ Calif, Berkeley, MA, 60. *Prof Exp:* Res assoc comp biol, Kaiser Res Ctr Comp Biol, 60-61; develop pharmacol, Dept Pediat, State Univ NY Buffalo, 64-65; asst prof biol, Rosary Hill Col, 65-66; res assoc agr biochem, Stauffer Agr Ctr, Calif, 66-67; asst prof, 67-72, assoc prof, 72-82, actg chmn dept, 78-79, PROF BIOL, UNIV SANTA CLARA, 82- *Concurrent Pos:* Ames Res Ctr, NASA-Univ Santa Clara res grants, Ames Res Ctr, 68-; assoc dir summer prog planetary biol-microbiol ecol, NASA, 80 & 82. *Mem:* AAAS; Sigma Xi; Am Soc Microbiol. *Res:* Microbial physiology and biochemistry; extremely halophilic bacteria. *Mailing Add:* Dept Biol Univ Santa Clara Santa Clara CA 95053

TOMLINSON, GUS, electron microscopy, cell physiology, see previous edition

TOMLINSON, HARLEY, b Tunbridge, Vt, July 20, 32; m 58; c 2. PLANT PATHOLOGY. *Educ:* Univ Vt, BS, 59, MS, 61, PhD(bot), 65. *Prof Exp:* Asst plant pathologist, Conn Agr Exp Sta, 65-73; MEM STAFF, CHEM RES & DEVELOP, HUMPHREY CHEM CO, 73- *Mem:* Am Chem Soc; Sigma Xi. *Res:* Chemical applications and plant sciences. *Mailing Add:* 191 Knob Hill Dr Hamden CT 06518

TOMLINSON, JACK TRISH, b Bakersfield, Calif, Aug 22, 29; m 63; c 3. INVERTEBRATE ZOOLOGY. *Educ:* Univ Calif, AB, 50, MA, 52, PhD(zool), 56. *Prof Exp:* Instr biol, Oakland City Col, 54-57; from instr to assoc prof, 57-68, chmn dept, 75-76, PROF BIOL, SAN FRANCISCO STATE UNIV, 68- *Mem:* AAAS; Animal Behav Soc; Soc Syst Zool; Crustacean Soc; Ecol Soc. *Res:* Invertebrate physiology; animal behavior. *Mailing Add:* Dept of Biol San Francisco State Univ San Francisco CA 94132

TOMLINSON, JAMES EVERETT, b Petersburg, Va, July 8, 42; m 65; c 3. RUMINANT NUTRITION, DAIRY MANAGEMENT. *Educ:* Va Polytech Inst & State Univ, BS, 64, MS, 68; Univ Ky, PhD(animal nutrit), 72. *Prof Exp:* Ruminant res assoc antibiotic res, Hoechst Pharmaceut Co, 72-73; dairy nutritionist, Ralston Purina Co, 73-75; asst prof, 75-77, ASSOC PROF RES & TEACHING, MISS STATE UNIV, 77- *Concurrent Pos:* Nutrit consult. *Mem:* Am Soc Animal Sci; Am Dairy Sci Asn; Sigma Xi. *Res:* Energy sources for lactating dairy cows; supplemental concentrate feeding systems; ensiled forage utilization by dairy cows; diary heifer feeding and management; forage systems for lactating diary cows. *Mailing Add:* Dept of Dairy Sci Drawer DD Mississippi State MS 39762

TOMLINSON, JOHN LASHIER, b Salem, Ore, Sept 15, 35; m 58; c 2. PHYSICAL METALLURGY. *Educ:* Loma Linda Univ, BA, 58; Univ Ore, MA, 61; Univ Wash, PhD(metall), 67. *Prof Exp:* Physicist, Naval Ord Lab, Calif, 60-63; res engr, Boeing Co, Wash, 63-64; res assoc metall eng, Univ Wash, 64-67; res physicist, Naval Weapons Ctr, Calif, 67-69; from asst prof to assoc prof, 69-76, PROF CHEM & MAT ENG, CALIF STATE POLYTECH UNIV, POMONA, 76- *Concurrent Pos:* Eve instr, Chaffey Col, 61-63; from asst prof to assoc prof, Sch Dent, Loma Linda Univ, 70-78, prof, 78-; consult, Naval Ocean Systs Ctr, San Diego, 71-78 & RSI Assocs, La Verne, Calif, 79- *Honors & Awards:* Charles Babbage Award, Inst Electronic & Radio Engrs, London, 76. *Mem:* Metall Soc; Am Phys Soc; Sigma Xi. *Res:* Failure analysis and product liability; physical metallurgy of electronic materials; electrical properties of liquid metals and semiconductors; properties and structure of thin films; dental materials. *Mailing Add:* Dept Chem & Mat Eng Calif State Polytech Univ Pomona CA 91768

TOMLINSON, MICHAEL, b Leeds, Eng, Mar 30, 29; m 59; c 3. PHYSICAL CHEMISTRY. *Educ:* Univ Leeds, BSc, 49. *Prof Exp:* Asst exp officer radiation chem, Atomic Energy Res Estab, Harwell, Eng, 49-54; exp officer, Chalk River Nuclear Labs, Atomic Energy Can Ltd, 54-57; sr sci officer, Atomic Energy Res Estab, Harwell, Eng, 57-62; assoc res officer, Chalk River Nuclear Labs, 62-63, assoc res officer mat sci, Whiteshell Nuclear Res Estab, 63-71, head res chem br, 71-76, DIR CHEM & MAT SCI DIV, WHITESHELL NUCLEAR RES ESTAB, ATOMIC ENERGY CAN LTD, 76- *Mem:* Chem Inst Can. *Res:* Chemistry for nuclear power. *Mailing Add:* Whiteshell Nuclear Res Estab Pinawa ON R0E 1L0 Can

TOMLINSON, MICHAEL BANGS, b Miami, Fla, Oct 2, 37; m 63; c 1. MATHEMATICS. *Educ:* Reed Col, BA, 60; Univ Ore, MS, 62, PhD(math), 68. *Prof Exp:* Sci programmer, Lawrence Radiation Lab, Univ Calif, Berkeley, 63-65; asst prof math, Va Polytech Inst & State Univ, 68-69; ASST PROF MATH, UNIV MASS, BOSTON, 69- *Mem:* Am Math Soc. *Res:* Functional analysis; function algebras; Banach algebras. *Mailing Add:* Dept of Math Univ of Mass Boston MA 02116

TOMLINSON, PHILIP BARRY, b Leeds, Eng, Jan 17, 32; m 65; c 2. BOTANY. *Educ:* Univ Leeds, BSc, 53, PhD(bot), 55; Harvard Univ, AM, 71. *Prof Exp:* Fel bot, Univ Malaya, 55-56; lectr, Univ Col Ghana, 56-59 & Univ Leeds, 59-60; res scientist, Fairchild Trop Garden, Fla, 60-71; PROF BOT, HARVARD UNIV, 71- *Concurrent Pos:* Forest anatomist, Cabot Found, Harvard Univ, 65-71. *Res:* Morphology and anatomy of monocotyledons, especially palms; tropical botany. *Mailing Add:* Harvard Forest Petersham MA 01366

TOMLINSON, RAYMOND VALENTINE, b Smithers, BC, July 25, 27; m 57. BIOCHEMISTRY. *Educ:* Univ BC, BA, 54, MSc, 56; Univ Calif, Berkeley, PhD(biochem), 61. *Prof Exp:* Head technician, Children's Hosp, Vancouver, BC, 4953; res assoc, BC Neurol Inst, Vancouver, 56-57; fel, Univ BC, 61-64; asst res prof, State Univ NY Buffalo, 6466; PRIN SCIENTIST, SYNTEX CORP RES DIV, 66- *Mem:* Am Pharmaceut Asn. *Res:* Intermediary metabolism of drugs. *Mailing Add:* 4087 Orme Palo Alto CA 94306

TOMLINSON, RICHARD HOWDEN, b Montreal, Que, Aug 2, 23; m 49. PHYSICAL CHEMISTRY, INORGANIC CHEMISTRY. *Educ:* Bishop's Univ, Can, BSc, 43; McGill Univ, PhD(chem), 48. *Prof Exp:* Nat Res Coun Can fel, Cambridge Univ, 49; asst prof phys & inorg chem, 52-58, chmn dept, 67-74, PROF PHYS CHEM, MCMASTER UNIV, 58- *Mem:* The Chem Soc. *Res:* Diffusion; mass spectrometry; polymerization; radiochemistry. *Mailing Add:* Dept of Chem McMaster Univ Hamilton ON L8S 4K1 Can

TOMLINSON, WALTER JOHN, III, b Philadelphia, Pa, Apr 3, 38; m 61; c 1. OPTICS. *Educ:* Mass Inst Technol, BS, 60, PhD(physics), 63. *Prof Exp:* Consult, Edgerton, Germeshausen & Grier, Inc, 60-63, sr scientist, 63; MEM TECH STAFF, BELL LABS, 65-, SUPVR, OPTICAL RISK RECORDING GROUP, 81- *Mem:* Am Phys Soc; fel Optical Soc Am. *Res:* Optical disk memories; nonlinear optics; optical fiber components; integrated optics; photochemistry; gaseous optical masers, atomic and molecular; magnetic field effects in optical masers; isotope shifts in radioactive nuclei. *Mailing Add:* 22 Indian Creek Rd Holmdel NJ 07733

TOMLJANOVICH, NICHOLAS MATTHEW, b Susak, Yugoslavia, Mar 5, 39; US citizen; m 66; c 1. THEORETICAL PHYSICS, IONOSPHERIC PHYSICS. *Educ:* City Col New York, BS, 61; Mass Inst Technol, PhD(physics), 66. *Prof Exp:* Physicist, US Weather Bur, 62; teaching asst physics, Mass Inst Technol, 62-64; res asst elem particle physics, Lab Nuclear Sci, 64-66; MEM TECH STAFF, MITRE CORP, 66- *Concurrent Pos:* Physicist, Nat Bur Standards, 63. *Mem:* Am Phys Soc. *Res:* Radar detection theory and electromagnetic wave propagation; holography; modern optics; scattering theory; plasma physics. *Mailing Add:* 131 Nowell Farme Rd Carlisle MA 01741

TOMMERDAHL, JAMES B, b Adair, Iowa, Dec 2, 26; m 52; c 2. ELECTRICAL ENGINEERING. *Educ:* NC State Col, BS, 55, MS, 58. *Prof Exp:* Sr proj engr, Aeronaut Electronics, Inc, NC, 55-57; unit head & lead engr, Radiation Inc, Fla, 58-60; mem tech staff, 60-75, DIR, SYSTS & MEASUREMENTS DIV, RES TRIANGLE INST, 75- *Mem:* Inst Elec & Electronics Engrs. *Res:* Data acquisition systems and signal analysis; circuit and system performances modeling; design and development of very high frequency transceiver; high speed tracking systems and various instrumentation systems; design and development of airborne environmental monitoring systems. *Mailing Add:* Res Triangle Inst PO Box 12194 Research Triangle Park NC 27709

TOMOMATSU, HIDEO, b Tokyo, Japan, June 8, 29; m 68; c 1. ORGANIC CHEMISTRY, AGRICULTURAL CHEMISTRY. *Educ:* Waseda Univ, Japan, BEn, 53; Univ of the Pac, MSc, 60; Ohio State Univ, PhD(org chem), 65. *Prof Exp:* Res chemist, Hodogaya Chem Co Ltd, Japan, 53-59 & Jefferson Chem Co, Inc, Tex, 65-71; supvr, 71-80, SR MEM STAFF RES LABS, QUAKER OATS CO, 80- *Concurrent Pos:* US ed, High Polymers, Japan, 79-81. *Mem:* Am Chem Soc. *Res:* Synthesis of new elastomer of high polymer; carbohydrate chemistry, furan chemistry, new industrial chemicals and food science. *Mailing Add:* Res Labs Quaker Oats Co 617 W Main St Barrington IL 60010

TOMONTO, JAMES R, b White Plains, NY, Apr 14, 32; m 56; c 5. NUCLEAR PHYSICS. *Educ:* Villanova Univ, BS, 54; Rensselaer Polytech Inst, MS, 59. *Prof Exp:* Engr, Airborne Instruments Lab, 57; anal physicist, Nuclear Power Eng Div, Alco Prod Inc, 58-59; exp physicist, Knolls Atomic Power Lab, 59-64; mgr nuclear eng dept, Gulf United Nuclear Fuels Corp, NY, 64-74; mgr, Nuclear Anal Dept, 74-81, CONSULT, FLA POWER & LIGHT CO, 81- *Mem:* Am Nuclear Soc. *Res:* Design and analysis of water moderated power and research reactors; development of analysis methods relating to use of uranium and plutonium as a fuel in thermal power and fast breeder reactors; economic ananlysis of energy systems; development of computer analysis systems. *Mailing Add:* 14311 SW 74 Ct Miami FL 33158

TOMOZAWA, YUKIO, b Iyo-City, Japan, Sept 3, 29; nat US; m 57; c 2. THEORETICAL HIGH ENERGY PHYSICS. *Educ:* Univ Tokyo, BSc, 52, DSc(physics), 61. *Prof Exp:* Asst physics, Univ Tokyo, 56-57, Tokyo Univ Educ, 57-59, Cambridge Univ, 59-60 & Univ Col, Univ London, 60-61; res assoc, Inst Physics, Univ Pisa, 61-64; mem, Inst Advan Study, 64-66; from asst prof to assoc prof, 66-72, PROF PHYSICS, UNIV MICH, ANN ARBOR, 72- *Mem:* Am Phys Soc. *Res:* Symmetries in elementary particle physics; theories of unified gauge particle; axiomatic field theory; quantum field theory. *Mailing Add:* Randall Lab of Physics Univ of Mich Ann Arbor MI 48109

TOMPA, ALBERT S, b Trenton, NJ, Aug 26, 31; m 57; c 5. ANALYTICAL CHEMISTRY, PHYSICAL CHEMISTRY. *Educ:* St Joseph Col, BS, 54; Fordham Univ, MS, 57, PhD(anal chem), 60. *Prof Exp:* Lab instr anal chem, Fordham Univ, 54-59; res chemist, 60-74, RES CHEMIST, NAVAL SURFACE WEAPONS CTR, NAVAL ORD STA, 74- *Mem:* AAAS; Am Chem Soc. *Res:* Infrared, nuclear magnetic resonance and thermal analysis study of polymers; molecular structure of organic compounds; trace analysis of inorganic compounds; chemical degradation of propellants and recovery of ingredients; effect of additives on the thermal decomposition of polymers; kinetics of decomposition of liquid and solid propellants; toxicity and demil of propellants and explosives. *Mailing Add:* Naval Ord Sta Indian Head MD 20640

TOMPA, FRANK WILLIAM, b New York, NY, Nov 5, 48; m 72; c 3. COMPUTER SCIENCES. *Educ:* Brown Univ, ScB, 70, ScM, 70; Univ Toronto, PhD(comput sci), 74. *Prof Exp:* Lectr comput sci, Univ Toronto, 74; asst prof, 74-81, ASSOC PROF COMPUT SCI, UNIV WATERLOO, 81- *Mem:* Asn Comput Mach. *Res:* Data structures design and specification; systems design for interactive videotape; programming languages design and specification. *Mailing Add:* Dept of Comput Sci Univ of Waterloo Waterloo ON N2L 3G1 Can

TOMPKIN, GERVAISE WILLIAM, b Vinton, Iowa, July 11, 24; m 48; c 4. PHYSICAL CHEMISTRY. *Educ:* Colo State Univ, BS, 47; Univ Colo, PhD(phys chem), 51. *Prof Exp:* Chemist, Mallinckrodt Chem Works, 51-53, develop chemist, 53-55, plant mgr nuclear fuels, Mallinckrodt Nuclear, 56-59, res dir indust div, Mallinckrodt Chem, 59-61; assoc prof phys chem, Colo State Univ, 61-70; PRES, FARAD CORP, 63-; pres, Res Inst Colo, 78-80; DIR, WESTERN OPERS, SCHIERHOLZ CO, 80- *Mem:* Am Chem Soc. *Res:* Surface chemistry; development of industrial coatings and surface treatments. *Mailing Add:* 2020 Airway Ave Ft Collins CO 80521

TOMPKIN, ROBERT BRUCE, b Akron, Ohio, Apr 2, 37; m 61; c 3. FOOD MICROBIOLOGY. *Educ:* Ohio Univ, BSc, 59; Ohio State Univ, MSc, 61, PhD(microbiol), 63. *Prof Exp:* Res microbiologist, 64-65, head microbiol res div, 65-66, CHIEF MICROBIOLOGIST, RES & DEVELOP CTR, SWIFT & CO, 66- *Concurrent Pos:* Consult, Nat Acad Sci/Nat Res Coun comt nitrite & alternative curing agents in foods, 80-82 & mem study panel on microbiol criteria for foods and food ingredients, 80- *Mem:* Am Soc Microbiol; Am Meat Sci Asn; Inst Food Technologists; Int Asn Milk, Food & Environ Sanit; Am Acad Microbiol. *Res:* Prevention of food-borne diseases and food spoilage. *Mailing Add:* Res & Develop Ctr Swift & Co 1919 Swift Dr Oak Brook IL 60521

TOMPKINS, DANIEL REUBEN, b New York, NY, Oct 2, 31; m 64; c 2. HORTICULTURE, PLANT PHYSIOLOGY. *Educ:* Univ Md, BS, 59, MS, 62, PhD, 63. *Prof Exp:* Asst horticulturist, Western Wash Res & Exten Ctr, Wash State Univ, 62-68; from assoc prof to prof hort food sci, Univ Ark, Fayetteville, 69-75; PRIN HORTICULTURIST, COOP STATE SCI & EDUC RES SERV, USDA, 75- *Mem:* AAAS; Am Soc Hort Sci; Am Soc Plant Physiologists; Sigma Xi; Plant Growth Regulator Soc Am. *Res:* Growth substances; physiology of horticultural plants and administration for horticultural research. *Mailing Add:* Coop State Sci & Educ Res Serv USDA Washington DC 20250

TOMPKINS, DONALD ROY, JR, b Calif, 32; m 61; c 5. PHYSICS. *Educ:* Univ NDak, BS, 55; Univ Colo, MS, 58; Univ Ariz, PhD(physics), 64. *Prof Exp:* Asst prof physics, La State Univ, 64-67 & Univ Ga, 67-70; assoc prof, Univ Wyo, 70-76; PRES, TERRENE CORP, 76- *Mem:* AAAS. *Res:* Geophysics; mathematical physics. *Mailing Add:* Terrene Corp 604 Travis St Refugio TX 78377

TOMPKINS, E CROSBY, toxicology, pharmacology, see previous edition

TOMPKINS, EUGENE E, chemical engineering, see previous edition

TOMPKINS, GARY ALVIN, soil science, environmental chemistry, deceased

TOMPKINS, GEORGE JONATHAN, b La Plata, Md, May 6, 44. ENTOMOLOGY, IMMUNOLOGY. *Educ:* Univ Md, BS, 67, MS, 68, PhD(entom microbiol), 79. *Prof Exp:* Med entomologist, 1st Army Med Lab, US Army Ft Meade, Md, 69-70, 71-73; RES ENTOMOLOGIST, INSECT PATH LAB, USDA, 73- *Concurrent Pos:* Prev med officer, 926 Med Detachment, Vietnam, 70-71. *Mem:* Am Inst Biol Sci; Soc Invertebrate Path; Entom Soc Am. *Res:* Evaluation of effects of passaging insect viruses in alternate hosts in terms of the enhancement of the virulence and also determining if serological, biochemical or DNA changes occur; field evaluations to determine the effectiveness of these viruses for control of insect pests of cole crops. *Mailing Add:* Insect Path Lab Bldg 011A Rm 214 BARC-West Beltsville MD 20705

TOMPKINS, HARLAND GAIL, b Williamstown, Mo, Dec 7, 38; m 59; c 2. SURFACE PHYSICS, SURFACE CHEMISTRY. *Educ:* Univ Mo, BS, 60; Univ Wis-Milwaukee, MS, 68, PhD(physics), 71. *Prof Exp:* Develop engr vacuum tubes, Gen Elec Co, 62-66; MEM TECH STAFF SURFACE SCI, BELL LABS, 70- *Mem:* Am Vacuum Soc; Am Soc Testing Materials. *Res:* Diffusion in thin films; chemical reaction at surfaces; corrosion; polymer-metal surface reactions. *Mailing Add:* Bell Labs 6200 E Broad St Columbus OH 43213

TOMPKINS, HOWARD E(DWARD), b Brooklyn, NY, Apr 19, 22; m 43; c 4. COMPUTER SCIENCE. *Educ:* Swarthmore Col, BA, 42; Univ Pa, MS, 47, PhD(elec eng), 57. *Prof Exp:* Engr, Philco Corp, 42-47; instr & res asst, Moore Sch Elec Eng, Pa, 47-51, res assoc, 56-57, asst prof elec eng, 57-60; proj supvr, Burroughs Corp, 51-54, ed serv mgr, 55-56; prof elec eng, Univ NMex, 60-61; chief sect tech develop, Nat Inst Neurol Diseases & Blindness-NIMH, 61-63; prof elec eng & head dept, Univ Md, 63-67; dir info serv, Inst Elec & Electronics Engrs, NY, 67-71; chmn dept, 71-77, PROF COMPUT SCI, INDIANA UNIV PA, 71- *Mem:* Asn Comput Mach; Inst Elec & Electronics Engrs. *Res:* Curriculum development and text preparation in applied computer science, especially structured cobol, practical software engineering, and modern programming languages at undergraduate level. *Mailing Add:* Dept Comput Sci Indiana Univ Pa Indiana PA 15705

TOMPKINS, JOHN CARTER, b Los Angeles, Calif, Sept 27, 46. EXPERIMENTAL HIGH ENERGY PHYSICS. *Educ:* Univ Calif, Los Angeles, BS, 68, MS, 69, PhD(physics), 73. *Prof Exp:* Adj asst prof physics, Univ Calif, Los Angeles, 74; res assoc high energy physics, Fermi Nat Accelerator Lab, 74-76; RES ASSOC, HIGH ENERGY PHYSICS LAB, SLAC EXP STA, STANFORD UNIV, 76- *Res:* Measurement of the form factors of the pion and kaon in high energy elastic scattering experiments; the crystal ball, a large, solid angle, highly segmented sodium iodide (Ti) detector for spear. *Mailing Add:* HEPL Hansen Labs Stanford Univ Stanford CA 94305

TOMPKINS, RICHARD KELSEY, b Denver, Colo, Oct 25, 40; m 61; c 1. CLINICAL EPIDEMIOLOGY. *Educ:* Univ Colo, MD, 65. *Prof Exp:* Res assoc biochem genetics, Nat Heart & Lung Inst, 67-70; asst prof med, Dartmouth Med Sch, 70-75; assoc prof, 75-82, PROF, SCH MED, UNIV WASH, 82-, ASST DEAN, 79- *Concurrent Pos:* Dir, USPHS Hosp, 76-81; exec dir, Seattle Pub Health Hosp, 81- *Mem:* Fel Am Col Physicians; Am Fedn Clin Res. *Res:* Development of clinically validated decision rules for medical problems commonly seen in primary care practices; health services. *Mailing Add:* Seattle Pub Health Hosp PO Box 3145 Seattle WA 98114

TOMPKINS, ROBERT CHARLES, b Bucyrus, Ohio, Aug 23, 24; m 57; c 3. PHYSICAL CHEMISTRY. *Educ:* Ohio State Univ, BSc, 44. *Prof Exp:* Res engr chem, Battelle Mem Inst, 44-45; asst, Univ Chicago, 46-47; phys scientist, US Army Nuclear Defense Lab, 49071; RES CHEMIST, US ARMY BALLISTIC RES LAB, 71- *Concurrent Pos:* Mem adv comt civil defense, Nat Acad Sci-Nat Res Coun, 70-73; lectr, St Mary's Univ, Md, 75. *Mem:* Am Chem Soc; Sigma Xi; Am Phys Soc; NY Acad Sci. *Res:* Fallout from nuclear weapons; chemistry of propellants and explosives; high-pressure effects on electronic spectra; electromagnetic signatures. *Mailing Add:* 541 Valley View Rd Towson MD 21204

TOMPKINS, RONALD K, b Malta, Ohio, Oct 14, 34; m 56; c 3. SURGERY. *Educ:* Ohio Univ, BA, 56; Johns Hopkins Univ, MD, 60; Ohio State Univ, MS, 68. *Prof Exp:* NIH trainee surg & fel phys chem, Col Med, Ohio State Univ, 66-69, instr & fel phys chem, 66-69, instr surg, 68-69; asst prof, 69-73, assoc prof, 73-79, PROF SURG, SCH MED, UNIV CALIF, LOS ANGELES, 79- *Concurrent Pos:* NIH res grants, Inst Arthritis & Metab Dis, Dept Health Educ & Welfare, 68-71; res grants, John A Hartford Found, Inc, 70-78; consult, Sepulveda Vet Admin Hosp, 71-, Rand Corp Study Cholecystectomy, 76; mem, Prog Comt, Soc Univ Surgeons, 74-77, Asn Acad Surg, 75-77; hosp rep, Am Col Surgeons Southern Calif chapter, 72-76; mem, Long Range Planning Comt, Soc Surg Alimentary Tract, 74-76; pres, Int Biliary Asn, 79-81. *Honors & Awards:* Student Res Prize, Am Gastroenterol Asn, 71, Am Fedn Clin Res Western Sect, 72. *Mem:* Soc Clin Surg; Am Surg Asn; Soc Univ Surgeons; Soc Surg Alimentary Tract (secy-elect, 81); Am Gastroenterol Asn. *Res:* Biochemical and nutritional research related to diseases of the gastrointestinal tract, especially hepatobiliary and pancreatic diseases. *Mailing Add:* Dept of Surg Sch of Med Ctr for Health Sci UCLA Los Angeles CA 90024

TOMPKINS, STEPHEN STERN, b Portsmouth, Va, Nov 1, 38; m 61; c 2. MECHANICAL ENGINEERING, MATERIALS SCIENCE. *Educ:* Va Polytech Inst & State Univ, BS, 62; Univ Va, MAE, 68; Old Dominion Univ, PhD(mech eng), 78. *Prof Exp:* Res engr heat & mass transfer, 62-72, res scientist, 72-78, SR RES SCIENTIST MAT, LANGLEY RES CTR, NASA, 78- *Mem:* Am Soc Mech Engrs; Sigma Xi. *Res:* Analysis of the response of complex metallic and non-metallic materials over a wide range of environmental exposures and loading conditions; heat and mass transfer. *Mailing Add:* Mat Div Mail Stop 188B Hampton VA 23665

TOMPKINS, VICTOR NORMAN, b Milbrook, NY, May 30, 13; m 38; c 4. PATHOLOGY. *Educ:* Cornell Univ, AB, 34; Union Univ, NY, MD, 38; Am Bd Path, dipl, 46. *Prof Exp:* Resident path, New Eng Deaconess Hosp, 39-40, Albany Hosp, 40-41 & Pondville Hosp, 41-42; sr pathologist, Div Labs & Res, State Dept Health, NY, 47-49, asst dir in charge diag labs, 49-56, assoc dir, 56-58, dir, 58-68; PROF PATH, ALBANY MED COL, 60- *Concurrent Pos:* Assoc prof path, Albany Med Col, 53-60. *Mem:* AAAS; Am Soc Human Genetics; Am Soc Clin Path; Am Soc Exp Path; AMA. *Res:* Immunology. *Mailing Add:* Dept of Path Albany Med Col Albany NY 12201

TOMPKINS, WILLIS JUDSON, b Presque Isle, Maine, July 20, 41; m 67; c 2. BIOMEDICAL ENGINEERING, ELECTRICAL ENGINEERING. *Educ:* Univ Maine, BS, 63, MS, 65; Univ Pa, PhD(biomed eng), 73. *Prof Exp:* Elec engr res & develop, Sanders Assoc Inc, 65-68; assoc biomed comput, Univ Pa, 73-74; ASSOC PROF RES & TEACHING, UNIV WIS, 74- *Mem:* Sr mem Inst Elec & Electronics Engrs; Biomed Eng Soc; Asn Adv Med Instrumentation. *Res:* Computers in medicine; microcomputer-based medical instruments; electrocardiography. *Mailing Add:* Dept of Elec & Comput Eng 1425 Johnson Dr Madison WI 53706

TOMPSETT, MICHAEL F, b Eng, May 4, 39; m 67; c 3. ELECTRONICS. *Educ:* Cambridge Univ, BA, 62, MA & PhD(elec eng), 66. *Prof Exp:* Res asst mat sci, Cambridge Univ, 65-66; proj leader camera tubes, Eng Elec Valve Co, 66-69; SUPVR INTEGRATED CIRCUITS, BELL LABS, 69- *Mem:* Sr mem Inst Elec & Electronics Engrs. *Res:* Integrated circuits; charge coupled devices; imaging devices; intgrated filters; analog circuits. *Mailing Add:* Bell Labs #22 600 Mountain Ave Murray Hill NJ 07974

TOMPSETT, RALPH RAYMOND, b Tidioute, Pa, Oct 8, 13; m 42; c 4. INTERNAL MEDICINE. *Educ:* Cornell Univ, AB, 34, MD, 39. *Prof Exp:* From instr to assoc prof med, Med Col, Cornell Univ, 46-57; PROF MED, UNIV TEX HEALTH SCI CTR, DALLAS, 57- *Concurrent Pos:* Attend physician, Med Ctr, Baylor Univ, 57- & Parkland Mem Hosp, 60- *Mem:* Am Soc Clin Invest; Asn Am Physicians; master Am Col Physicians; Am Fedn Clin Res. *Res:* Infectious diseases. *Mailing Add:* Baylor Univ Med Ctr Dallas TX 75246

TOMPSON, CLIFFORD WARE, b Mexico, Mo, Dec 12, 29; m 51; c 3. PHYSICS. *Educ:* Univ Mo, BS, 51, AM, 56, PhD(physics), 59. *Prof Exp:* Physicist, US Navy Electronics Lab, San Diego, 51-55; assoc prof, 59-72, PROF PHYSICS, UNIV MO-COLUMBIA, 72- *Mem:* Am Phys Soc; Am Asn Physics Teachers. *Res:* X-ray diffraction; neutron diffraction; structure of liquids; lattice vibrations. *Mailing Add:* Dept of Physics Univ of Mo-Columbia Columbia MO 65201

TOMPSON, ROBERT NORMAN, b Adrian, Mich, Jan 7, 20; m 47; c 1. MATHEMATICAL ANALYSIS, APPLIED MATHEMATICS. *Educ:* Adrian Col, ScB, 41; Univ Nev, MS, 49; Brown Univ, PhD(math), 53. *Prof Exp:* Res inspector ord mat, US War Dept, 42-43; from asst to instr math, Univ Nev, 46-49; asst prof, Fla State Univ, 53-54; mem tech staff, Bell Tel Labs, Inc, 54-55; asst prof, Fla State Univ, 55-56; mathematician & programmer, Int Bus Mach Corp, 56; assoc prof, 56-64, PROF MATH, UNIV NEV, RENO, 64-, CHMN DEPT, 78- *Concurrent Pos:* Consult, NSF/AID Sci Asst to India Prog, 67-68. *Mem:* AAAS; Am Math Soc; Am Phys Soc. *Res:* Measure and integration theory; topology; systems theory; probability theory. *Mailing Add:* 997 Meadow St Reno NV 89502

TOMSIC, VICTOR J(OHN), b Primero, Colo, Apr 30, 24; m 52; c 5. MECHANICAL ENGINEERING. *Educ:* Univ Colo, BS, 50. *Prof Exp:* Res engr, 50-67, sr res engr & supvr permase prod, 68-75, develop technician serv & qual control, Petrol Chemicals Div, 75-80, ENG ASSOC HYDROGEN RECOVERY VEHICLE EXCHANGE CATALYSTS, E I DU PONT DE NEMOURS & CO, INC, 80- *Res:* Fuel knocking and surface ignition behavior; exhaust gas emission control; teflon heat exchanger; thermal and fluid flow coefficients; permeation. *Mailing Add:* E I du Pont de Nemours & Co Inc Wilmington DE 19898

TOMSON, MASON BUTLER, b Syracuse, Kans, Nov 18, 46; m 68. PHYSICAL CHEMISTRY, ENVIRONMENTAL SCIENCES. *Educ:* Southwestern State Univ, BS, 67; Okla State Univ, PhD(chem), 72. *Prof Exp:* Teaching asst, Okla State Univ, 67-72; instr, Dept Chem, State Univ NY, Buffalo, 72-76, res asst prof, 76-77; asst prof, 77-81, ASSOC PROF ENVIRON SCI & ENG, RICE UNIV, 81- *Concurrent Pos:* Compiler, IUPAC Solubility Data Proj, 78-79. *Mem:* Am Chem Soc. *Res:* Kinetics and thermodynamics of precipitation and dissolution of sparingly soluble salts; solution equilibria of electrolytes; trace level organics, analysis and fate in water. *Mailing Add:* Dept of Environ Sci & Eng PO Box 1892 Houston TX 77001

TOMUSIAK, EDWARD LAWRENCE, b Edmonton, Alta, Mar 3, 38; m 61; c 1. THEORETICAL NUCLEAR PHYSICS. *Educ:* Univ Alta, BSc, 60, MSc, 61; McGill Univ, PhD(theoret physics), 64. *Prof Exp:* NATO overseas fel, Oxford Univ, 64-66; from asst prof to assoc prof, 66-76, PROF PHYSICS, UNIV SASK, 76- *Mem:* Can Asn Physicists. *Res:* Nuclear structure calculations using realistic two-nucleon potentials; nuclear models and electromagnetic interactions with nuclei. *Mailing Add:* Dept Physics Univ Sask Saskatoon SK S7H 0W0 Can

TON, BUI AN, b Hanoi, Vietnam, Jan 23, 37; m 63; c 3. MATHEMATICAL ANALYSIS. *Educ:* Saigon Univ, BSc, 59; Mass Inst Technol, PhD(math), 64. *Prof Exp:* Res staff mathematician, Yale Univ, 63-64; vis asst prof, Math Res Ctr, Univ Wis, 64-65; Nat Res Coun Can fel, 65-66; asst prof math, Univ Montreal, 66-67; assoc prof, 67-71, PROF MATH, UNIV BC, 71- *Mem:* Can Math Cong. *Res:* Partial differential equations. *Mailing Add:* Dept of Math Univ of BC Vancouver BC V6T 1W5 Can

TONASCIA, JAMES A, b Los Banos, Calif, Mar 2, 44; m 65. BIOSTATISTICS. *Educ:* Univ San Francisco, BS, 65; Johns Hopkins Univ, PhD(biostatist), 70. *Prof Exp:* Asst prof, 70-77, ASSOC PROF BIOSTATIST, JOHNS HOPKINS UNIV, 77- *Mem:* Am Statist Asn; Biomet Soc; Inst Math Statist; Math Asn Am; Royal Statist Soc. *Res:* Biostatistical methods; epidemiology; statistical computing. *Mailing Add:* Dept of Biostatist Johns Hopkins Univ Baltimore MD 21205

TONDEUR, PHILIPPE, b Zurich, Switz, Dec 7, 32; m 65. MATHEMATICS. *Educ:* Univ Zurich, PhD(math), 61. *Prof Exp:* Res fel math, Univ Paris, 61-63; lectr, Univ Zurich, 63-64; res fel, Harvard Univ, 64-65; lectr, Univ Calif, Berkeley, 65-66; assoc prof, Wesleyan Univ, 66-68; PROF MATH, UNIV ILL, URBANA, 68- *Mem:* Am Math Soc; Math Soc France; Swiss Math Soc. *Res:* Geometry and topology. *Mailing Add:* Dept of Math Univ of Ill Urbana IL 61801

TONDRA, RICHARD JOHN, b Canton, Ohio, Jan 23, 43; m 66; c 2. MATHEMATICS. *Educ:* Univ Notre Dame, BS, 65; Mich State Univ, MS, 66, PhD(topology, manifold theory), 68. *Prof Exp:* Assoc prof, 68-80, PROF MATH, IOWA STATE UNIV, 80- *Mem:* Am Math Soc. *Res:* Topological and piecewise linear manifold theory. *Mailing Add:* Dept of Math Iowa State Univ Ames IA 50011

TONE, JAMES N, b Grinnell, Iowa, Feb 9, 33; m 54; c 2. ANIMAL PHYSIOLOGY. *Educ:* Coe Col, BA, 54; Drake Univ, MA, 61; Iowa State Univ, PhD(animal physiol), 63. *Prof Exp:* PROF PHYSIOL, ILL STATE UNIV, 63- *Mem:* AAAS. *Res:* Physiological effects of gossypol on mammals. *Mailing Add:* Dept of Biol Sci Ill State Univ Normal IL 61761

TONELLI, ALAN EDWARD, b Chicago, Ill, Apr 14, 42; m 74; c 2. POLYMER PHYSICS. *Educ:* Univ Kans, BS, 64; Stanford Univ, PhD(polymer chem), 68. *Prof Exp:* MEM TECH STAFF POLYMER PHYSICS, BELL LABS, 68- *Mem:* Am Chem Soc; Am Phys Soc. *Res:* Study of the conformations and physical properties of synthetic and biological macromolecules. *Mailing Add:* Bell Labs 600 Mountain Ave Murray Hill NJ 07974

TONELLI, GEORGE, b Tenafly, NJ, Feb 20, 21; m 55; c 4. VETERINARY MEDICINE. *Educ:* Parma Univ, DVM, 48. *Prof Exp:* Biologist, Peters Serum Co, Kans, 50; res vet, Animal Indust Sect, 51-55, group leader & pharmacologist, Exp Therapeut Sect, 55-60, group leader endocrinol, Endocrine Res Dept, 60-68, group leader, Toxicol Dept, 68-73, mgr toxicol/pharmacol eval, Int Div, 73-77, MGR OVERSEAS TOXICOL, MED RES DIV, LEDERLE LABS, AM CYANAMID CO, 77- *Mem:* Am Soc Pharmacol & Exp Therapeut; Endocrine Soc. *Mailing Add:* Lederle Labs Am Cyanamid Co Pearl River NY 10965

TONELLI, QUENTIN JOSEPH, b Philadelphia, Pa, Apr 6, 48; m 77. CELL BIOLOGY, BIOCHEMISTRY. *Educ:* John J Pershing Col, BA, 70; Univ Nebr, MS, 73, PhD(cell biol), 77. *Prof Exp:* Fel embryol, Marine Biol Lab, 77; assoc, 77-78, fel carcinogenesis, 78-79, RES ASSOC, INST CANCER RES, 80- *Concurrent Pos:* Consult, Cancer Info Dissemination & Anal Ctr Carcinogenesis, 80- *Mem:* AAAS; Am Soc Cell Biol; Sigma Xi. *Res:* Mechanisms of control of eukaryotic cell development and differentiation; chemical carcinogenesis, especially in mammary gland; hematopoietic cell differentiation; molecular aspects of parasitology. *Mailing Add:* Inst for Cancer Res 7701 Burholme Ave Philadelphia PA 19111

TONER, RICHARD K(ENNETH), b Terre Haute, Ind, Jan 9, 13; m 37; c 1. CHEMICAL ENGINEERING. *Educ:* Rose-Hulman Inst Technol, BS, 34; Purdue Univ, MS, 36, PhD(chem eng), 39. *Hon Degrees:* DE, Rose-Hulman Inst Technol, 72. *Prof Exp:* Instr chem eng, Purdue Univ, 37-39 & Lehigh Univ, 39-40; instr, NY Univ, 40-42, vis prof, 42-46; from asst prof to prof, 42-81, assoc chmn dept, 66-81, EMER PROF CHEM ENG, PRINCETON UNIV, 81- *Concurrent Pos:* Consult chem engr, Textile Res Inst, 44-59, ed, Textile Res Jour & dir publ, 59- *Mem:* Am Chem Soc; Am Soc Eng Educ; Am Inst Chem Engrs. *Res:* Thermodynamics. *Mailing Add:* Dept of Chem Eng A209 Eng Quad Princeton Univ Princeton NJ 08544

TONEY, FRANK MORGAN, b Nashville, Tenn, Dec 28, 25; m 54; c 2. PHYSICAL CHEMISTRY. *Educ:* Mid Tenn State Col, BS, 49; Polytech Inst Brooklyn, PhD(chem), 56. *Prof Exp:* Sr res chemist, Fibers Div, FMC Corp, 56-76; RES ASSOC, MONSEY PROD CO, 77- *Mem:* Am Chem Soc. *Res:* Physical chemistry of polymer solutions; electrode reactions; kinetics of organic reactions. *Mailing Add:* 1117 S Concord Rd West Chester PA 19380

TONEY, FRED, JR, b Mooresboro, NC, Aug 12, 37; m 77; c 5. MATHEMATICS. *Educ:* NC State Univ, BS, 59, MS, 61, PhD(math), 68. *Prof Exp:* Asst math, NC State Univ, 59-61; asst prof, Wilmington Col, NC, 61-64; asst, NC State Univ, 64-67, instr, 67-68; PROF MATH & CHMN DEPT, UNIV NC, WILMINGTON, 68- *Mem:* Math Asn Am; Am Math Soc. *Res:* Abstract algebra. *Mailing Add:* Dept of Math Univ of NC Wilmington NC 28401

TONEY, JOE DAVID, b Rosston, Ark, Aug 12, 42; m 64; c 2. INORGANIC CHEMISTRY. *Educ:* Univ Ark, Pine Bluff, BS, 64; Univ Ill, Urbana, PhD(chem), 69. *Prof Exp:* Teacher, 69-77, ASSOC PROF CHEM, CALIF STATE UNIV, FRESNO, 77- *Concurrent Pos:* Vis res assoc chem, Argonne Nat Lab, 72; lectr health manpower prog, Pacific Col, 73. *Mem:* Am Chem Soc. *Res:* Syntheses and structural characterization of transition metal chelate compounds involving amino acid ligands; visible, infrared and Raman studies of bonding in chelate complexes. *Mailing Add:* Dept of Chem Calif State Univ Fresno CA 93740

TONEY, MARCELLUS E, JR, b Baltimore, Md, Dec 25, 20; m 45; c 1. CLINICAL MICROBIOLOGY. *Educ:* Va Union Univ, BS, 42; Meharry Med Col, MT, 46; Cath Univ Am, MS, 53, PhD(zool), 56. *Prof Exp:* Assoc prof zool, 57-71, PROF BIOL, VA UNION UNIV, 71- *Concurrent Pos:* Vis prof, Va State Col, 59-; chief premed adv, Va Union Univ, 63-, coordr biol, 74-; res grants, NSF & Nat Urban League; consult, Richmond Math & Sci Ctr, NSF & Friends Adoption Asn; US Dept Health, Educ & Welfare grant pesticide res, 72-77. *Mem:* AAAS; Am Inst Biol Sci; Am Asn Biol Teachers; NY Acad Sci; Sigma Xi. *Res:* Microbiology; endocrinology. *Mailing Add:* Dept of Zool Va Union Univ Richmond VA 23220

TONG, BOK YIN, b Shanghai, China, Mar 5, 34; m 69; c 1. SOLID STATE PHYSICS, BIOPHYSICS. *Educ:* Univ Hong Kong, BSc, 57; Univ Calif, Berkeley, MA & MLS, 59; Univ Calif, San Diego, PhD(solid state physics), 67. *Prof Exp:* Asst librn, Oriental Collection, Univ Hong Kong, 59-61, asst lectr math, 61-65, lectr math, 65-67; from asst prof to assoc prof, 67-76, PROF PHYSICS, UNIV WESTERN ONT, 76- *Mem:* Am Phys Soc. *Res:* Theory of metals, surface physics and amorphous material; DNA molecules, muscle contraction and membrane activity; amorphous silicon; solar cells and devices; recrystallization of amorphous silicon. *Mailing Add:* Dept Physics Univ Western Ont London ON N6A 3K7 Can

TONG, JAMES YING-PEH, b Shanghai, China, Dec 8, 26; US citizen; m 51; c 3. PHYSICAL INORGANIC CHEMISTRY. *Educ:* Univ Calif, Berkeley, BS, 50, MS, 51; Univ Wis, PhD(chem), 54. *Prof Exp:* Res chemist, Le Roy Res Lab, Durex Plastics & Chem, Inc, 53-54; res assoc phys inorg chem, Univ Ill, 54-57; from asst prof to assoc prof, 57-68, PROF CHEM, OHIO UNIV, 68-, DIR FORENSIC CHEM, 76- *Concurrent Pos:* Chmn, policy adv comt, 208 water qual mgt, Hocking River Basin, 80- *Mem:* Am Chem Soc; fel Am Inst Chemists. *Res:* Equilibrium and kinetics studies of reaction in solution; radiochemistry; chemistry and history of photography; water chemistry. *Mailing Add:* Dept of Chem Ohio Univ Athens OH 45701

TONG, KIN NEE, b Shanghai, China, Feb 22, 22; US citizen; m 57; c 1. APPLIED MECHANICS. *Educ:* Chiao Tung Univ, BSME, 45; Syracuse Univ, MME, 49; Univ Ill, PhD(theoret & appl mech), 51. *Prof Exp:* From asst prof to assoc prof mech eng, 51-59, PROF MECH & AEROSPACE ENG, SYRACUSE UNIV, 59-, CHMN DEPT, 71- *Concurrent Pos:* Fulbright lectr, Nat Taiwan Univ, 64-65. *Mem:* Am Soc Mech Engrs; Am Soc Eng Educ. *Res:* Vibration theory. *Mailing Add:* Dept of Mech Eng Syracuse Univ Syracuse NY 13210

TONG, LONG SUN, b China, Aug 20, 15; US citizen; m 39. HEAT TRANSFER. *Educ:* Chinese Nat Inst Technol, BS, 40; Univ Fla, MS, 53; Stanford Univ, PhD(mech eng), 56. *Prof Exp:* Asst prof mech eng, Ord Eng Col, Taiwan, 47-52; sr engr, Atomic Power Dept, Westinghouse Elec Corp, 56-59, supvr thermal & hydraul design, Atomic Power Dept, 59-62, adv engr, 63-65, mgr thermal & hydraul design & develop, 65-66, mgr thermal & hydraul eng, 66-70, consult engr, PWR Syst Div, 70-72, sr consult, 72-73; asst dir, 73-81, CHIEF SCIENTIST, DIV REACTOR SAFETY RES, NUCLEAR REGULARTORY COMN, 81- *Concurrent Pos:* Lectr, Univ Pittsburgh, 57-60, adj prof, 65-72; lectr, Carnegie Inst Technol, 61-67. *Honors & Awards:* Westinghouse Order of Merit, 69; Mem Award, Heat Transfer Div, Am Soc Mech Eng, 73; Don Q Kern Award, Am Inst Chem Engrs, 81. *Mem:* Fel Am Soc Mech Eng; fel Am Nuclear Soc. *Res:* Fluid flow; thermal and hydraulic design; analysis and development of pressurized water reactors; research in water reactor safety. *Mailing Add:* 9733 Lookout Pl Gaithersburg MD 20760

TONG, MARY POWDERLY, b New York, NY, May 24, 24; m 56; c 5. MATHEMATICS. *Educ:* St Joseph's Col, NY, BA, 50; Columbia Univ, MA, 51, PhD, 69. *Prof Exp:* Instr math, St Joseph's Col, NY, 51-54, City Col New York, 54 & Columbia Univ, 54-59; asst prof, Univ Conn, 60-66; from asst prof to assoc prof, Fairfield Univ, 66-70; PROF MATH, WILLIAM PATERSON COL NJ, 70- *Concurrent Pos:* Delta Epsilon Sigma res fel, 68; NSF fac fel, 59-60. *Mem:* Am Math Soc; Math Asn Am; NY Acad Sci. *Res:* Topology; foundations of mathematics; applications of mathematics. *Mailing Add:* 725 Cooper Ave Oradell NJ 07649

TONG, PIN, b Kwang Tung, China, Dec 25, 37; m 63; c 4. STRUCTURAL MECHANICS. *Educ:* Nat Taiwan Univ, BS, 60; Calif Inst Technol, MS, 63, PhD(aeronaut, math), 66. *Prof Exp:* Sr res engr, Aeroelastic & Struct Res Lab, Mass Inst Technol, 66-67, from asst prof to assoc prof aeronaut, 67-74; adv, 74-78, CHIEF STRUCT & MECH, TRANSP SYSTS CTR, US DEPT TRANSP, 78- *Concurrent Pos:* Adj prof, Northeastern Univ, 71-73; vis prof appl mech, Univ Calif, San Diego, 73-74. *Res:* Theory of continuum mechanics and its application to structural and vehicle dynamics. *Mailing Add:* Transp Systs Ctr DTS-744 US Dept of Transp Kendal Square MA 02142

TONG, SIU WING, b Hong Kong, May 20, 50; m 79; c 1. BIOCHEMISTRY. *Educ:* Univ Calif, Berkeley, BA, 72; Harvard Univ, PhD(biophysics), 79. *Prof Exp:* RES ASSOC, BROOKHAVEN NAT LAB, 79- *Res:* Structure-function relationships of proteins from membranes and muscles by determining their amino acid sequences. *Mailing Add:* Dept Biol Brookhaven Nat Lab Upton NY 11973

TONG, STEPHEN S C, b Shanghai, China, May 3, 36; US citizen; m 67; c 2. ANALYTICAL CHEMISTRY, PHYSICAL CHEMISTRY. *Educ:* Univ Ottawa, BSc, 59; Mass Inst Technol, MS, 61; Cornell Univ, PhD(anal chem), 66. *Prof Exp:* Res chemist, Rohm and Haas Co, 61-62; fel, Argonne Nat Lab, 66-68; sr res chemist, 68-80, RES ASSOC CHEM, RES & DEVELOP LAB, CORNING GLASS WORKS, 80- *Mem:* AAAS; Am Chem Soc; Am Soc Mass Spectrometry; Sigma Xi. *Res:* Trace analysis; spark source mass spectrometry; gas chromatography; neutron activation analysis; electron microprobe; secondary ion mass spectrometry; sputler-induced photon spectrometry. *Mailing Add:* Tech Staff Div Corning Glass Works Corning NY 14830

TONG, WINTON, b Los Angeles, Calif, May 3, 27; m 51; c 3. PHYSIOLOGY, BIOCHEMISTRY. *Educ:* Univ Calif, Berkeley, BS, 47, PhD(thyroid function), 53. *Prof Exp:* Res physiologist, Univ Calif, Berkeley, 47-62; from asst prof to assoc prof, 62-71, dir grad studies, 70-72, PROF PHYSIOL, SCH MED, UNIV PITTSBURGH, 71- *Concurrent Pos:* USPHS res career develop award, 62- *Honors & Awards:* Van Meter Prize, Am Thyroid Asn, 64. *Mem:* AAAS; Am Soc Biol Chemists; Am Physiol Soc; Endocrine Soc. *Res:* Mechanisms in the biosynthesis of thyroid hormones and thyroglobulin; mechanism of action of thyrotropin; physiology of thyroid function; cultivation of thyroid cells in vitro. *Mailing Add:* Dept Physiol Sch Med Univ Pittsburgh Pittsburgh PA 15261

TONG, YULAN CHANG, b Nanking, China, Oct 21, 35. ORGANIC CHEMISTRY. *Educ:* Cheng Kung Univ, Taiwan, BS, 56; Univ Ill, MS, 58, PhD(org chem), 61. *Prof Exp:* Res assoc, Univ Mich, 61-62; org res chemist, Edgar C Britton Res Lab, Mich, 62-65, res chemist, Res Lab, Western Div, 66-70, sr res chemist, 70-72, res specialist, 72-78, sr research specialist, 78-80, RES ASSOC, RES LAB, WESTERN DIV, DOW CHEM CO, 80- *Mem:* Am Chem Soc; Int Soc Heterocyclic Chem; NY Acad Sci. *Res:* Heterocyclic chemistry. *Mailing Add:* Western Div Res Lab Dow Chem Co 2800 Mitchell Dr Walnut Creek CA 94598

TONG, YUNG LIANG, b Shantung, China, July 15, 35; m 65; c 3. STATISTICS, MATHEMATICS. *Educ:* Nat Taiwan Univ, BS, 58; Univ Minn, Minneapolis, MA, 63, PhD(statist), 67. *Prof Exp:* Asst prof statist, Univ Nebr, Lincoln, 67-69; vis asst prof, Univ Minn, 69-70; from asst prof to assoc prof, 70-76, PROF STATIST, UNIV NEBR-LINCOLN, 76- *Concurrent Pos:* Vis prof, Univ Calif, Santa Barbara, 78-79. *Mem:* Am Statist Asn; Inst Math Statist. *Res:* Mathematical and applied statistics; multivariate analysis; sequential analysis; probability inequalities. *Mailing Add:* Dept Math & Stat Univ Nebr Lincoln NE 68588

TONIK, ELLIS J, b Philadelphia, Pa, Jan 9, 21; m 48; c 3. MEDICAL MICROBIOLOGY. *Educ:* Roanoke Col, BS, 50. *Prof Exp:* Med bacteriologist diag bact, Dept Pub Welfare, Ill, Chicago State Hosp, 50-51, supvry bacteriologist, East Moline State Hosp, 51-52 & Kankakee State Hosp, 52; med bacteriologist, Process Res & Pilot Plants Div, Chem Corps Res & Develop Labs, US Dept Army, 52-60, supvry bacteriologist, Tech Eval Div, 60, actg chief animal path sect, 60-61, chief exp animal sect, Appl Aerobiol Div, 61-71, sr investr, Microbiol Res Div, 71-72; CHIEF MICROBIOL, FT HOWARD VET ADMIN HOSP, 72- *Mem:* Am Soc Microbiol; Sigma Xi. *Res:* Experimental respiratory diseases of laboratory animals; aerobiological research and technology; experimental and clinical pathology; immunology; chemotherapeutic agents; virulence of airborne particulates; laboratory diagnosis and assay methods; management of laboratory animals. *Mailing Add:* 526 Mary St Frederick MD 21701

TONKING, WILLIAM HARRY, b Newton, NJ, Apr 22, 27; m 64; c 2. MINING GEOLOGY. *Educ:* Princeton Univ, AB, 49, PhD(geol), 53. *Prof Exp:* Asst geol, Princeton Univ, 49-50 & 51-53; asst instr, Northwestern Univ, 50-51; geologist, Bear Creek Mining Co, 53-55 & Stand Oil Co, Tex, 55-62; dep mgr, Mohole Proj, 62-67, mgr spec projs, 67-75, SR MGR, MINING & GEOL & CHIEF GEOLOGIST, BROWN & ROOT INC, 75- *Honors & Awards:* Silver Medallist, Royal Soc Arts, 66. *Mem:* Geol Soc Am; Royal Soc Arts. *Res:* Petrology; volcanic rocks and ore deposits in the Southwest; petroleum geology; deep ocean engineering, geology and geophysics. *Mailing Add:* 3200 Entex Bldg 1200 Milam St Houston TX 77002

TONKS, DAVID BAYARD, b Edmonton, Alta, Aug 31, 19; m 46; c 2. BIOCHEMISTRY, CLINICAL CHEMISTRY. *Educ:* Univ BC, BA, 41; McGill Univ, PhD(org chem), 49. *Prof Exp:* Sr chemist, Clin Labs, Lab Hyg, Dept Nat Health & Welfare, Can, 48-57; asst biochemist, Biochem Dept & Res Inst, Hosp Sick Children, Toronto, 57-62; from asst prof to assoc prof, 62-75, PROF MED, MCGILL UNIV, 75-; DIR DIV CLIN CHEM, DEPT MED, MONTREAL GEN HOSP, 62- *Concurrent Pos:* tech dir, Seaforth Clin Labs, Montreal, 64-77; lab consult, Douglas Hosp, Verdun, 65-, Reddy Mem Hosp, Montreal, 66-, & Cybermedix Ltd, Toronto, 69-; mem bd dirs, Bio Res Labs, Point Claire, 65-72; Can nat rep, Int Comn Clin Chem, 66-70; secy sect clin chem, Int Union Pure & Appl Chem, 67-71, pres sect, 71-75, bur mem, 71-75, past-pres, 75-77, mem comn toxicol, 73-, mem Can nat comt, 74-; mem exec bd, Int Fedn Clin Chem, 67-75. *Honors & Awards:* Warner-Chilcott Award, Can Soc Lab Technologists, 67; Ames Award, Can Soc Clin Chem, 68; Ann Award, Que Corp Hosp Biochemists, 72. *Mem:* Am Asn Clin Chemists; Can Biochem Soc; fel Chem Inst Can; Can Soc Clin Chem (from secy to pres, 57-66, treas, 74-76); NY Acad Sci. *Res:* Development of synthetic antigens for serodiagnosis of syphilis; quality control and evaluation of laboratory precision in clinical chemistry laboratories; analytical methods in clinical chemistry. *Mailing Add:* 845 Sherbrooke St W Dept Med McGill Univ Montreal PQ H3A 2T5 Can

TONKS, DAVIS LOEL, b Pocatello, Idaho, May 6, 47; m 71; c 3. RAMAN SCATTERING, HYDROGEN DIFFUSION. *Educ:* Brigham Young Univ, BSc, 72; Univ Utah, PhD(physics), 78. *Prof Exp:* Researcher, Dept Physics, Ariz State Univ, 78-81; RESEARCHER, LOS ALAMOS NAT LAB, 81- *Concurrent Pos:* Res assoc, Ariz State Univ, 78-80. *Mem:* Am Phys Soc. *Res:* Vibronic theory of resonant Raman scattering from impurities in solids and from molecules; phonon-assisted defect tunneling in solids; theory of vibration and diffusion of hydrogen in metal hydrides. *Mailing Add:* Group T-11 Mail Stop 457 Los Alamos Nat Lab Los Alamos NM 87545

TONKS, ROBERT STANLEY, b Aberystwyth, Wales, Aug 13, 28; m 53; c 4. PATHOLOGY. *Educ:* Univ Wales, BS, 51, Med Sch, PhD(pharmacol), 54; Inst Biol, Eng, fel, 73. *Prof Exp:* Organon fel, Welsh Nat Sch Med, Cardiff, 53-54, Nat Health Serv fel, Nevill Hall Hosp, 54-56, sr fel, 56-58, univ lectr, Dept Mat Media & Pharmacol & Therapeut, 58-72, sr lectr, 72-73; prof & dir, Col Pharm, 73-77, DEAN, FAC HEALTH PROFESSORS, DALHOUSIE UNIV, 77- *Concurrent Pos:* Chmn, Pharmaceut Sci Grant Comt, Nat Res Coun Can, 76-77, Northeast Can-Am Health Coun, 80-; mem, Personel Review Comt, Nat Health & Welfare Can, 79-81; consult, NB Dept Health, 74-, Rector Riyadh Univ & Ministers Health & Educ, Saudi Arabia, 80. *Mem:* Brit Pharmacol Soc; Biochem Soc London; Physiol Soc London; Int Soc Thrombosis & Haemostasis; Can Soc Clin Invest. *Res:* Plateleb micro-emboli in circulating human blood: their role in the production of primary pulmonary thrombosis and myocardiol infarction in man and during the immune response, explaining tissue and organ transplant refection. *Mailing Add:* Dalhousie Univ 1322 Robie St Halifax NS B3H 1R8 Can

TONKYN, RICHARD GEORGE, b Portland, Ore, Mar 26, 27; m 48; c 6. ORGANIC CHEMISTRY, POLYMER CHEMISTRY. *Educ:* Reed Col, BA, 48; Univ Ore, MA, 51; Univ Wash, PhD(org chem), 60. *Prof Exp:* Instr org chem, Univ Ore, 52; supvr res, Anal Labs, Titanium Metals Corp Am, Nev, 52-54; sr res anal chemist, Allegheny Ludlum Steel Corp, Pa, 54-55; res engr, Boeing Airplane Co, Wash, 55-59; NSF fel, Univ Col, Univ London, 60-61; chemist, Union Carbide Corp, NJ, 61-67; proj scientist, 67-69; sr res chemist, Betz Labs, Inc, 69-70, group leader, 70-72, mgr org res & process develop, 72-76; dir res & develop, Mogul Corp, 76-77, V PRES RES & DEVELOP, MOGUL DIV, DEXTER CORP, 77- *Mem:* Am Chem Soc; Royal Soc Chem; Tech Asn Pulp & Paper Indust; Sigma Xi; Phys Chem Soc London. *Res:* Monomer and polymer synthesis; high pressure technology; polyelectrolyte synthesis; chemicals and processes for water treatment and water pollution control; corrosion and deposit control research; industrial cooling and boiler; microbiological control; wastewater chemistry. *Mailing Add:* Mogul Div Dexter Corp Chagrin Falls OH 44022

TONN, ROBERT J, medical entomology, see previous edition

TONNA, EDGAR ANTHONY, b Malta, May 10, 28; nat US; m 51; c 4. CELL PHYSIOLOGY, CELL CHEMISTRY. *Educ:* St John's Univ, NY, BS, 51; NY Univ, MS, 53, PhD(biol), 56. *Prof Exp:* Res collabr div exp path, Med Res Ctr, Brookhaven Nat Lab, 56-59, head histochem & cytochem res lab, 59-67; PROF HISTOL, GRAD SCH BASIC MED SCI, NY UNIV, 67-, DIR INST DENT RES, COL DENT, 71-, DIR LAB CELLULAR RES, 67- *Concurrent Pos:* Res biochemist, Hosp Spec Surg, New York, 53-56, head histochem & cytochem res lab, 56-59; adj assoc prof, Grad Sch, Long Island Univ, 56-62; consult radiobiol, Inst Dent Res, NY Univ, 64-67; ed chief, Gerodontology, 81- *Honors & Awards:* R Morton Cert & G Mendel Award, St John's Univ. *Mem:* Fel Geront Soc; fel NY Acad Sci; Histochem Soc; fel Royal Micros Soc; Sigma Xi. *Res:* Cellular contribution to skeletal and dental development, growth, repair and disease during aging; autoradiographic, cytochemical and cytological studies using optical analytical and electron microscopic techniques to determine biochemical and cell morphological changes in skeletal and dental cell parameters; cell gerontology. *Mailing Add:* Inst for Dent Res NY Univ Col of Dent 345 E 24th St New York NY 10010

TONNDORF, JUERGEN, b Göttingen, Ger, Feb 1, 14; nat US; m 40. PHYSIOLOGY. *Educ:* Univ Kiel, MD, 38; Univ Heidelberg, PhD(otolaryngol), 45. *Prof Exp:* Privat-docent otolaryngol, Univ Heidelberg, 45-47; mem res & teaching staff, Sch Aviation Med, US Air Force, Randolph Field, Tex, 47-53; from asst res prof to res prof otolaryngol, Univ Hosps, Univ Iowa, 53-62; PROF OTOLARYNGOL, COL PHYSICIANS & SURGEONS, COLUMBIA UNIV, 62- *Concurrent Pos:* USPHS res career award, 63; mem study sect commun dis, NIH, 64-68, mem proj rev comt, Commun Dis Prog, 68-71; mem sci rev comt, Deafness Res Found, 64-68; mem acoust mgt bd, Am Nat Stand Inst, 72-; chmn panel ear, nose & throat devices, Food & Drug Admin, 75- *Honors & Awards:* Von Eicken Award, 42; Ludwig Haymann Award, 70; Award of Merit, Am Otol Soc. *Mem:* Fel Acoust Soc Am; Am Otol Soc; hon mem Am Acad Ophthal & Otolaryngol; Asn Res Otolaryngol; hon mem Ger Otolaryngol Soc. *Res:* Auditory physiology, especially in reference to the ear. *Mailing Add:* Dept Otolaryngol Fowler Mem Lab Col Phys & Surg Columbia Univ New York NY 10032

TONNE, PHILIP CHARLES, b Chicago, Ill, Apr 2, 38; m 63; c 2. MATHEMATICS. *Educ:* Marquette Univ, BS, 60; Univ NC, MA, 63, PhD(math), 65. *Prof Exp:* Instr math, Univ NC, 65-66; asst prof, 66-71, ASSOC PROF MATH, EMORY UNIV, 71- *Mem:* Am Math Soc. *Res:* Classical analysis. *Mailing Add:* Dept of Math Emory Univ Atlanta GA 30322

TONNIS, JOHN A, b Scottsburg, Ind, Apr 18, 39; m 72. ORGANIC CHEMISTRY. *Educ:* Hanover Col, BA, 61; Ind Univ, MS, 64, PhD(org chem), 68. *Prof Exp:* Res chemist, Reilly Tar & Chem Co, 64-65; fel org chem, Ind Univ, 68; asst prof, 68-70, assoc prof, 70-75, PROF CHEM, UNIV WIS-LA CROSSE, 75- *Mem:* AAAS; Am Chem Soc. *Res:* Preparation and use of sulfonamides as organic chelating reagents; new synthetic methods in organic chemistry. *Mailing Add:* Dept of Chem Univ of Wis La Crosse WI 54601

TONZETICH, JOHN, b Nanaimo, BC, Oct 28, 41. GENETICS. *Educ:* Univ BC, BSc, 63; Duke Univ, MA, 67, PhD(zool), 72. *Prof Exp:* Asst prof, 70-77, ASSOC PROF BIOL, BUCKNELL UNIV, 77- *Mem:* Genetics Soc Am; Am Soc Zoologists; AAAS; Sigma Xi. *Res:* Chromosomal inversions in Drosophila species; radiation induced aberrations. *Mailing Add:* Dept of Biol Bucknell Univ Lewisburg PA 17837

TOOGOOD, JOHN ALFRED, b Chancellor, Alta, Jan 7, 15; m 41; c 4. SOILS. *Educ:* Univ Alta, BSc, 41; Univ Minn, PhD, 48. *Prof Exp:* Teacher & prin schs, Can, 34-37, teacher high sch, 41-45; from asst prof to assoc prof, 48-58, PROF SOIL SCI & CHMN DEPT, UNIV ALTA, 59- *Concurrent Pos:* Registr, Alta Inst Agrologists, 52-63, pres, 67-68. *Res:* Soil conservation. *Mailing Add:* Dept Soil Sci Univ Alta Edmonton AB T6G 2S1 Can

TOOHEY, LOREN MILTON, b Antioch, Nebr, Mar 2, 21; m 42; c 4. GEOLOGY. *Educ:* Univ Nebr, BSc, 48, MSc, 50; Princeton Univ, PhD(geol), 53. *Prof Exp:* Field & res assoc, State Mus, Univ Nebr, 36-50; res assoc, Frick Lab, Am Mus Natural Hist, 50-56; geologist, Carter Oil Co, Ill, 56-60; GEOLOGIST, EXXON CO, USA, 60- *Mem:* Geol Soc Am; Soc Vert Paleont; Am Asn Petrol Geologists; Soc Econ Paleontologists & Mineralogists. *Res:* Cenozoic vertebrate paleontology and stratigraphy; geology of petroleum; sedimentology. *Mailing Add:* Exxon Co USA Midland TX 79701

TOOHEY, RICHARD EDWARD, b Cincinnati, Ohio, Sept 2, 45; m 68. RADIOBIOLOGY, NUCLEAR PHYSICS. *Educ:* Xavier Univ, AB, 68; Univ Cincinnati, MS, 70, PhD(physics), 73. *Prof Exp:* asst physicist, 73-79, BIOPHYSICIST, CTR HUMAN RADIOBIOL, ARGONNE NAT LAB, US DEPT ENERGY, 80-, DEP GROUP LEADER, 81- *Concurrent Pos:* Consult, Ill Emergency Serv & Disaster Agency, 77-; chmn, Plutorium Intercalibration Comt, US Dept Energy, 80- *Mem:* Health Physics Soc; Am Phys Soc; AAAS; Sigma Xi; Am Asn Physicists Med. *Res:* Human radiobiology; whole-body counting; metabolism of radionuclides; radon measurements. *Mailing Add:* Div Radiol & Environ Res Agronne Nat Lab Argonne IL 60439

TOOHIG, TIMOTHY E, b Lawrence, Mass, Feb 17, 28. EXPERIMENTAL HIGH ENERGY PHYSICS. *Educ:* Boston Col, BS, 51; Univ Rochester, MS, 53; Johns Hopkins Univ, PhD(physics), 62; Woodstock Col, STB, 64, STL, 65. *Prof Exp:* Asst dir admin res, Inst Natural Sci, Woodstock Col, 63-66; assoc physicist, Brookhaven Nat Lab, 67-70; assoc head neutrino lab sect, Nat Accelerator Lab, 70-74; asst to head res div, Fermi Nat Accelerator Lab, 74-76, head, Meson Dept, 77-78; res physicist, Joint Inst Nuclear Res, Dubna, USSR, 78-79; GROUP LEADER CONSTRUCT & SCHEDULING, ACCELERATOR DIV, FERMI NAT ACCELERATOR LAB, 79- *Mem:* Am Phys Soc. *Res:* Elementary particle physics; investigation of the properties and interactions of elementary particles. *Mailing Add:* Fermi Nat Accelerator Lab PO Box 500 Batavia IL 60510

TOOKE, WILLIAM RAYMOND, JR, b Atlanta, Ga, June 18, 25; m 48; c 3. CHEMICAL ENGINEERING. *Educ:* Ga Inst Technol, BChE, 49, MSChE, 55. *Prof Exp:* Res asst, Ga Technol Exp Sta, 49-55; process engr, Am Viscose Corp, 55-58; tech dir paint res, Oliver B Cannon & Sons, 58-60; sr res engr, Eng Exp Sta, Ga Inst Technol, 60-66; head indust prod br, 66-72, PRES, TOOKE ENG ASSOCS, 72- *Concurrent Pos:* Consult, Am Viscose Corp, 60-61, Southern Mills, Inc, 62-64 & Thomas Mfg Co, 64-; NIH grant, 63-67; mem comt A2GO2, Hwy Res Bd. *Mem:* Am Chem Soc; Am Inst Chem Engrs; Am Soc Testing & Mat; Nat Asn Corrosion Engrs; Sigma Xi. *Res:* Protective coatings and plastics technology; thermoplastic films, corrosion engineering; instrumentation and testing methods for coatings and plastics. *Mailing Add:* Tooke Eng Assocs PO Box 13804 Atlanta GA 30324

TOOKER, EDWIN WILSON, b Concord, Mass, May 9, 23; m 46; c 3. ECONOMIC GEOLOGY. *Educ:* Bates Col, BS, 47; Lehigh Univ, MS, 49; Univ Ill, PhD(geol), 52. *Prof Exp:* NSF fel, Univ Ill, 52-53; geologist, Base & Ferrous Metals Br & Pac Mineral Resources Br, 53-71, chief, Pac Mineral Resources Br, 71-72, chief, Off Mineral Resources, 72-76, RES GEOLOGIST MINERAL RESOURCES, WESTERN MINERAL RESOURCE BR, US GEOL SURV, 76- *Mem:* Soc Mining Engrs; Soc Econ Geologists; Geol Soc Am. *Res:* Geology of base and precious metals ore deposits of Utah; metalogenesis and environment of ore deposition; wall rock alteration; base metal commodity resources. *Mailing Add:* 345 Middlefield Rd US Geol Surv MS 90A Menlo Park CA 94025

TOOKEY, HARVEY LLEWELLYN, b Hooper, Nebr, Dec 2, 22; m 50; c 4. BIOCHEMISTRY. *Educ:* Univ Nebr, AB, 44, MS, 50; Purdue Univ, PhD(biochem), 55. *Prof Exp:* Sr control chemist, Norden Lab, Nebr, 46-48; res chemist, 55-77, RES LEADER NATURAL TOXICANTS RES, NORTHERN REGIONAL RES CTR, USDA, 77- *Mem:* Am Chem Soc. *Res:* Enzymes of lipid metabolism; proteinases, enzymes acting on glucosinolates; chemistry of natural products; alkaloids; non-infectious diseases of cattle. *Mailing Add:* Northern Regional Res Ctr USDA Peoria IL 61604

TOOLE, BRYAN PATRICK, b Clunes, Australia, Nov 6, 40; m 63; c 2. DEVELOPMENTAL BIOLOGY, CELL BIOLOGY. *Educ:* Univ Melbourne, BSc, 62; Monash Univ, Australia, MSc, 65, PhD(biochem), 68. *Prof Exp:* Instr med, Harvard Med Sch, 70-72, asst prof biochem, 72-75; asst biochemist med, Mass Gen Hosp, 72-78, assoc biochemist, 78-80; assoc prof anat, Med Sch, Harvard Univ, 75-80; PROF ANAT & CELLULAR BIOL, SCH MED, TUFTS UNIV, 80- *Concurrent Pos:* Estab investr, Am Heart Asn, 73-78, mem, basic sci coun, 76-; prin investr, Nat Inst Dent Res, 75- *Mem:* Complex Carbohydrate Soc; Soc Develop Biol; Am Soc Cell Biol. *Res:* Role of extracellular macromolecules in embryonic development and adult tissue remodelling and their influence on normal and aberrant cell behavior. *Mailing Add:* Dept Anat & Cell Biol Sch Med Tufts Univ Boston MA 02111

TOOLE, FLOYD EDWARD, b Moncton, NB, June 19, 38; m 61. ACOUSTICS. *Educ:* Univ NB, BSc, 60; Univ London, PhD(elec eng) & DIC, 65. *Prof Exp:* Res officer, 65-80, SR RES OFFICER PHYSICS & ACOUST, NAT RES COUN CAN, 80- *Mem:* Acoust Soc Am; Audio Eng Soc; Can Acoust Asn. *Res:* Sound reproduction; loudspeaker systems; perception of sound and psychoacoustics; noise control. *Mailing Add:* Div of Physics Nat Res Coun of Can Ottawa ON K1A 0R6 Can

TOOLE, JAMES FRANCIS, b Atlanta, Ga, Mar 22, 25; m 52; c 4. STROKE, NEUROLOGY. *Educ:* Princeton Univ, BA, 47; Cornell Univ, MD, 49; LaSalle Exten Univ, LLB, 63. *Prof Exp:* Intern med, Univ Pa, 49-50, resident neurol, 53-55, instr, 57-60, assoc, 60-61, prof, 62-67, WALTER C TEAGLE PROF NEUROL, BOWMAN GRAY SCH MED, 67- *Concurrent Pos:* Fulbright fel, Nat Hosp, London, 55-56; mem res comt, Am Heart Asn, 65, chmn med ethics comt, 66-70, ed, Current Concepts Cerebrovasc Dis-Stroke, 69-72; chmn, Sixth & Seventh Princeton Conf Cerebrovasc Dis, 68 & 70; vis prof, Univ Calif, San Diego, 69-70; mem exam bd, Nat Bd Med Examr & Am Bd Psychol & Neurol; consult, WHO, Japan, 72, Moscow, 68, Abidjean, Ivory Coast, 77 & Switz, 74; mem, Stroke Long Range Planning Comt, Nat Inst Neurol & Commun Disorders & Stroke, 81. *Mem:* Asn Res Nerv & Ment Dis; fel Am Col Physicians; fel Am Acad Neurol (secy-treas, 78-82); Am Neurol Asn; Am Fedn Clin Res. *Res:* Cerebral circulation and cerebrovascular diseases; physiology and pathology of the brain. *Mailing Add:* Dept of Neurol Bowman Gray Sch of Med Winston-Salem NC 27103

TOOLES, CALVIN W(ARREN), b Burlington, Vt, June 3, 21; m 43; c 1. CIVIL ENGINEERING. *Educ:* Univ Vt, BS, 43; Iowa State Col, MS, 50. *Prof Exp:* Instr eng drawing, Univ Vt, 46-47; instr civil eng, Iowa State Col, 48-50; from asst prof to assoc prof, Va Polytech Inst, 51-60; ASSOC PROF CIVIL ENG, GA INST TECHNOL, 60- *Mem:* Am Soc Civil Engrs; Am Soc Eng Educ; Am Soc Photogram; Am Cong Surv & Mapping. *Res:* Geodetic and photogrammetric engineering. *Mailing Add:* Sch of Civil Eng Ga Inst of Technol Atlanta GA 30332

TOOLEY, F(AY) V(ANISLE), b Nokomis, Ill, May 4, 08; m 34; c 2. CERAMICS. *Educ:* Univ Ill, BS, 32, MS, 36, PhD(ceramic eng), 39. *Prof Exp:* Asst mineral wool & raw mat, State Geol Surv, Ill, 32-38; head dept glass res, Owens-Corning Fiberglas Corp, 39-46; prof glass technol, 46-72, EMER PROF GLASS TECHNOL, UNIV ILL, URBANA, 72- *Concurrent Pos:* Dir, Annual Conf Glass Probs, 46-75; mem, Int Comn Glass, 53-59; consult in glass control, prod & res & in gen res mgt. *Honors & Awards:* First Recipient, Phoenix Award, Glass Indust, 71; Toledo Glass & Ceramic Award, Am Ceramic Soc, 76. *Mem:* AAAS; fel Am Ceramic Soc; Am Soc Testing & Mat; Am Chem Soc; Soc Glass Technol Eng. *Res:* Glass research, production and control; general research management. *Mailing Add:* 2910 Silver St SW PO Box 301 Granville OH 43023

TOOLEY, RICHARD DOUGLAS, b Baltimore, Md, Apr 11, 32; div; c 3. GEOPHYSICS, SYSTEMS ENGINEERING. *Educ:* Mass Inst Technol, SB, 54, PhD(geophys), 58. *Prof Exp:* Res physicist, Calif Res Corp, 58-64; chief scientist mission & systs anal unit, Northrop Systs Labs, Hawthorne, 64-69, Palos Verdes, 69-72, PRIN SYSTS ENGR, ELECTRO-MECH DIV, NORTHROP CORP, 72- *Mem:* Sigma Xi; Am Defense Prepardness Asn. *Res:* Space science; solid body geophysics; rock physics; ultrasonic wave propagation; data processing; electrooptical systems; infrared systems; military systems analysis. *Mailing Add:* Electro-Mech Div Northrop Corp 500 E Orangethorpe Placentia CA 92801

TOOLEY, WILLIAM HENRY, b Berkeley, Calif, Nov 18, 25. PEDIATRICS. *Educ:* Univ Calif, MD, 49. *Prof Exp:* From clin instr to asst clin prof, 56-61, from asst prof to assoc prof, 61-72, chief newborn serv, hosp, 62-71, PROF PEDIAT, MED CTR, UNIV CALIF, SAN FRANCISCO, 72-, CHIEF, DIV PEDIAT PULMONARY DIS, UNIV HOSPS, 71-, SR STAFF MEM, CARDIOVASC RES INST, 63- *Concurrent Pos:* Pvt pract, Calif, 56-58. *Mem:* Am Acad Pediat; Soc Pediat Res; Am Pediat Soc. *Res:* Cardiopulmonary disease; neonatal medicine. *Mailing Add:* Dept of Pediat Univ of Calif San Francisco CA 94122

TOOM, PAUL MARVIN, b Pella, Iowa, Apr 1, 42; m 65; c 1. BIOCHEMISTRY. *Educ:* Cent Col, Iowa, BA, 64; Colo State Univ, PhD(biochem), 69. *Prof Exp:* Res asst biochem, Colo State Univ, 67-68, asst prof, 69-70; asst prof, 70-73, assoc prof, 73-78, PROF BIOCHEM, UNIV SOUTHERN MISS, 78- *Concurrent Pos:* Consult, Nat Marine Fisheries Serv, 76- *Mem:* AAAS; Am Chem Soc; Int Soc Toxinology; Inst Technologists; Sigma Xi. *Res:* Biochemistry of marine toxins; rapid methods of analysis for chemical and microbiological indicators of decomposition; analytical biochemistry. *Mailing Add:* Dept Chem Univ Southern Miss Box 8337 Hattiesburg MS 39401

TOOME, VOLDEMAR, b Estonia, Sept 10, 24; m 52. PHYSICAL CHEMISTRY. *Educ:* Univ Bonn, dipl, 48 & 52, Dr rer nat, 54. *Prof Exp:* Sci asst, Inst Phys Chem, Univ Bonn, 54; dept head control div, Merck & Co, Ger, 54-57; sr phys res chemist, 57-68, res fel, 67-70, group chief, 70-72, SR GROUP CHIEF, HOFFMANN-LA ROCHE, INC, 77- *Mem:* Am Chem Soc; NY Acad Sci. *Res:* Ultraviolet and infrared spectroscopy; optical rotatory dispersion and circular dichroism; instrumental analysis; polarography; electrochemistry; dissociation constants of organic acids and bases; physical organic chemistry; microanalysis. *Mailing Add:* Dept of Phys Chem Hoffmann-La Roche Inc Nutley NJ 07110

TOOMEY, DONALD FRANCIS, b New York, NY, Apr 15, 27; m 52; c 4. GEOLOGY, STRATIGRAPHY-SEDIMENTATION. *Educ:* Univ NMex, BS, 51, MS, 53; Rice Univ, PhD(geol), 64. *Prof Exp:* Stratigr, Shell Oil Co, 53-56, geologist, Shell Develop Co, 56-64, staff res geologist, Res Ctr, Amoco Prod Co, 64-72; prof earth sci & chmn fac earth sci, Univ Tex of the Permian Basin, 73-78; SR GEOL ASSOC, CITIES SERV CO, 78- *Concurrent Pos:* Mem bd dirs, Cushman Found Foraminiferal Res, 62-, fel, 64-, vpres, 65-68, pres, 68-69; vpres, Friends of the Algae, 77-78; ed, European Fossil Reef Models, 81. *Mem:* Paleont Soc; Soc Econ Paleontologists & Mineralogists; Am Asn Petrol Geologists. *Res:* Paleozoic algae and foraminifers; carbonate rock facies trends; development of paleoecologic criteria in relation to organic buildups through geologic time; recent environmental studies and paleoenvironmental implications. *Mailing Add:* Box 1919 Midland TX 79702

TOOMEY, JAMES MICHAEL, b Boston, Mass, Mar 2, 30; m 54; c 6. OTORHINOLARYNGOLOGY. *Educ:* Col of Holy Cross, Mass, BS, 51; Harvard Sch Dent Med, DMD, 55; Boston Univ, MD, 58. *Prof Exp:* Intern surg, Wash Univ-Barnes Hosp, Med Ctr, 58-59, asst resident surg, 61-62, asst resident otolaryngol, 62-64, chief resident, 64-65, instr, 64-65; sr instr, Med Ctr, Univ Rochester, 65-66, asst prof, 66-68; assoc prof otolaryngol & head dept, Health Ctr, Univ Conn, 68-77; MEM FAC, SCH MED, WASHINGTON UNIV, 77- *Concurrent Pos:* NIH training grant, Sch Med, Wash Univ, 63-65; consult, Newington Vet Admin Hosp, Conn, 68-; lectr, Dept Speech, Univ Conn, 69-; consult, Hartford Hosp, 69-, St Francis Hosp, Hartford, 69- & Rocky Hill Vet Admin Hosp, Conn, 71- *Mem:* Am Laryngol, Rhinol & Otol Soc; Soc Univ Otolaryngol; Am Acad Facial Plastic & Reconstruct Surg; Am Soc Maxillofacial Surg. *Res:* Skin flap physiology; laryngeal physiology; experimental laryngeal surgery. *Mailing Add:* Washington Univ Sch of Med 517 S Euclid Ave St Louis MO 63110

TOOMEY, JOSEPH EDWARD, b Somerville, NJ, Aug 8, 43; m 67; c 4. SYNTHETIC ORGANIC CHEMISTRY, STRUCTURAL CHEMISTRY. *Educ:* Rider Col, BS, 70; Purdue Univ, PhD(org chem), 76. *Prof Exp:* RES CHEMIST, REILLY LAB, REILLY TAR & CHEM CO, 75- *Mem:* Am Chem Soc. *Res:* Synthesis, isolation and structural determination of pyridine chemicals; electrochemistry of heterocyclic compounds; prediction of optical rotatory power, its relation to molecular structure and absolute configuration; unusual Diels-Adler condensation reactions; electroorganic synthesis; electroorganic synthesis. *Mailing Add:* Reilly Lab Reilly Tar & Chem Co 1500 S Tibbs Ave Indianapolis IN 46241

TOOMRE, ALAR, b Rakvere, Estonia, Feb 5, 37; US citizen; m 58; c 3. ASTRONOMY, APPLIED MATHEMATICS. *Educ:* Mass Inst Technol, BS(aeronaut eng) & BS(physics), 57; Univ Manchester, PhD(fluid mech), 60. *Prof Exp:* C L E Moore instr math, Mass Inst Technol, 60-62; fel astrophys, Inst Advan Study, 62-63; from asst prof to assoc prof, 63-70, PROF APPL MATH, MASS INST TECHNOL, 70- *Concurrent Pos:* Guggenheim fel astrophys, Calif Inst Technol, 69-70, Fairchild scholar, 75. *Mem:* AAAS; Am Acad Arts & Sci; Am Astron Soc; Int Astron Union. *Res:* Dynamical studies of galaxies; aerodynamics; rotating fluids. *Mailing Add:* Rm 2-371 Dept of Math Mass Inst of Technol Cambridge MA 02139

TOON, OWEN BRIAN, b Bethesda, Md, May 26, 47; m 68. ASTRONOMY, CLIMATOLOGY. *Educ:* Univ Calif, Berkeley, AB, 69; Cornell Univ, PhD(physics), 75. *Prof Exp:* Res assoc, Nat Res Coun, 75-77 & Cornell Univ, 77-78; RES SCIENTIST, AMES RES CTR, NASA, 78- *Mem:* Am Meterol Soc; Am Astron Soc; Am Geophys Soc. *Res:* Physics of terrestrial and planetary climates with emphasis on clouds, aerosols and radiative transfer; volcanos and climate, troposheric aerosols and climate change on Mars; clouds of Venus annd Titan. *Mailing Add:* Space Sci Div M/S 245-3 Ames Res Ctr NASA Moffett Field CA 94035

TOONEY, NANCY MARION, b Ilion, NY, Feb 19, 39. BIOCHEMISTRY, BIOPHYSICS. *Educ:* State Univ NY Albany, BS, 60, MS, 61; Brandeis Univ, PhD(biochem), 66. *Prof Exp:* Teaching intern biochem, Dept Chem & Biol, Hope Col, 66-67; fel biophys, Childrens Cancer Res Found & Sch Med, Harvard Univ, 67-73; asst prof biochem, 73-77, ASSOC PROF BIOCHEM, POLYTECH INST NY, 77- *Concurrent Pos:* NIH fel, 67-70, res career develop award, Nat Heart, Lung & Blood Inst, 75-80. *Mem:* AAAS; Am Chem Soc; Biophys Soc. *Res:* Protein chemistry, electron microscopy and optical methods of analysis; structure and function of the blood clotting proteins, fibrinogen and fibronectin; biological macromolecules. *Mailing Add:* Dept of Chem Polytech Inst NY 333 Jay St Brooklyn NY 11201

TOONG, TAU-YI, b Shanghai, China, Aug 15, 18; nat US; m 43; c 2. MECHANICAL ENGINEERING. *Educ:* Chiao-Tung Univ, BSME, 40; Mass Inst Technol, SM, 48, ScD(mech eng), 52. *Prof Exp:* Mgr, Nanyang Eng Corp, China, 42-45; plant supt, Shanghai Transit Co, 45-47; from instr to assoc prof, 51-63, PROF MECH ENG, MASS INST TECHNOL, 63- *Concurrent Pos:* Guggenheim fel, 59; consult, Joseph Kaye & Co, Stewart-Warner Corp, US Air Force, Churchill Lighting Corp, Thermo-Electron Eng Corp, Foster-Miller Assocs, Dynatech Corp, Avco-Everett Res Lab, Kenics Corp, Steam Engine Systs Corp & Factory Mutual Eng. *Mem:* Am Soc Mech Engrs; Am Soc Eng Educ; Combustion Inst; Am Inst Aeronaut & Astronaut; NY Acad Sci. *Res:* Combustion; propulsion; fluid mechanics; heat and mass transfer. *Mailing Add:* Dept of Mech Eng Rm 31-165 Mass Inst Technol Cambridge MA 02139

TOOP, EDGAR WESLEY, b Chilliwack, BC, Feb 26, 32; m 59; c 4. ORNAMENTAL HORTICULTURE. *Educ:* Univ BC, BSA, 55; Ohio State Univ, MSc, 57, PhD(plant path), 60. *Prof Exp:* Res officer, Can Dept Agr, 55-56; instr bot, Ohio State Univ, 61-62; asst prof, 62-69, ASSOC PROF HORT, UNIV ALTA, 69- *Mem:* Agr Inst Can; Can Soc Hort Sci (secy-treas, 78-81). *Res:* Greenhouse flower crops; herbaceous ornamentals. *Mailing Add:* Dept of Plant Sci Univ of Alta Edmonton AB T6G 2P5 Can

TOOPS, EDWARD CHASSELL, b Columbus, Ohio, Aug 15, 26; m 51; c 4. REACTOR PHYSICS. *Educ:* Ohio Wesleyan Univ, BA, 47; Ind Univ, MS, 49, PhD(physics), 51. *Prof Exp:* Physicist, E I du Pont de Nemours & Co, 51-55, Combustion Eng, Inc, Conn, 55-70 & Gen Elec Co, 70-71; PHYSICIST, POWER GENERATION DIV, BABCOCK & WILCOX CO, 71- *Mem:* Am Nuclear Soc. *Res:* Particle and nuclear reactions; nuclear reactor physics; mathematical analysis; alternate reactor fuel cycles. *Mailing Add:* 3135 Sedgewick Dr Lynchburg VA 24503

TOOR, ARTHUR, b Altadena, Calif, Aug 17, 38; c 4. RADIATION TRANSPORT, ASTROPHYSICS. *Educ:* Univ Calif, Berkeley, BA, 62. *Prof Exp:* Staff physicist, High Altitude Physics Group, Livermore, 63-76, leader laser appln prog, 76-78, leader, Space Appln Proj, 78-81, LEADER, EXP NON-EQUILIBRIUM RADIATION PHYSICS, LAWRENCE LIVERMORE NAT LAB, 81- *Concurrent Pos:* Consult, NASA, 78- *Mem:* Am Astron Soc; Am Phys Soc. *Res:* High-energy astrophysics; dense plasma physics; space physics. *Mailing Add:* Space Sci Applns PO Box 808 Lawrence Livermore Nat Lab Livermore CA 94550

TOOR, H(ERBERT) L(AWRENCE), b Philadelphia, Pa, June 22, 27; m 50; c 3. CHEMICAL ENGINEERING. *Educ:* Drexel Inst Technol, BS, 48; Northwestern Univ, MS, 50, PhD(chem eng), 52. *Prof Exp:* Res scientist, Monsanto Chem Ltd, 52-53; from asst prof to assoc prof chem eng, 53-61, head dept, 65-69, dean eng, 70-79, prof, 61-80, MOBAY PROF CHEM ENG, CARNEGIE-MELLON UNIV, 80- *Honors & Awards:* Colburn Award, Am Inst Chem Engrs, 64. *Mem:* AAAS; Am Inst Chem Engrs; Am Chem Soc; Am Soc Eng Educ. *Res:* Transport phenomena; heat and mass transfer; multicomponent diffusion; chemical reactions with mixing. *Mailing Add:* Schenley Park Chem Eng Dept Carnegie-Mellon Univ Pittsburgh PA 15213

TOOTHILL, RICHARD B, b Philadelphia, Pa, July 28, 36; m 59; c 2. ORGANIC CHEMISTRY. *Educ:* Lehigh Univ, BS, 58; Mass Inst Technol, MS, 60; Univ Del, PhD(org chem), 64. *Prof Exp:* Tech serv rep paper chem, Hercules Powder Co, 60-61, chemist, 61-62; res chemist, 64-67, group leader, Bound Brook Labs, 67-73, dyes res group leader, 73-78, elastomers res group leader, 78-80, TECH DIR COLOR TEXTILE, CHEM INTERMEDIATES DEPT & TEXTILE CHEM & PLASTICS ADDITIVES DEPT, AM CYANAMID CO, 81- *Mem:* Am Chem Soc. *Res:* Thiosemicarbazones; s-triazines; benzothiazoles; anthraquinone derivatives; polyurethanes; millable gum; synthetic rubber; wrinkle recovery agents; light absorbers; antioxidants; lead stabilizers; pigments. *Mailing Add:* 16 Sunrise Dr Warren NJ 07060

TOP, FRANKLIN HENRY, JR, b Detroit, Mich, Mar 1, 36; m 61; c 3. MICROBIOLOGY, VIROLOGY. *Educ:* Yale Univ, BS, 57, MD, 61. *Prof Exp:* Residency & intern pediat, Univ Minn Hosp, 61-64, res fel, Univ Minn, 64-66; investr virol, Walter Reed Army Inst Res, 66-70; chief, Dept Virol, Seato Med Res Lab, 70-73; chief, Dept Virus Dis, Walter Reed Army Inst Res, 73-76, dir, Div Commun Dis & Immunol, 76-78, dep dir, 79-81; COMNDR, US ARMY MED RES INST CHEM DEFENSE, 81- *Concurrent Pos:* Mem, Microbiol & Infectious Dis Adv Comt, Nat Inst Allergy & Infectious Dis, 76-80; prof pediat, Sch Med, Uniformed Serv Univ, 78- *Mem:* Soc Pediat Res; Am Soc Trop Med & Hyg; Am Soc Microbiol; Infectious Dis Soc Am; Am Asn Immunologists. *Res:* Epidemiology and prevention of respiratory infections caused by adenoviruses and influenza viruses; development of dengue vaccines. *Mailing Add:* US Army Med Res Inst Chem Defense Aberdeen Proving Ground MD 21010

TOPAKOGLU, H(USEYIN) C(AVIT), aerospace engineering, engineering science, see previous edition

TOPAZIAN, RICHARD G, b Greenwich, Conn, Feb 2, 30; m 58; c 4. ORAL & MAXILLOFACIAL SURGERY. *Educ:* Houghton Col, BA, 51; McGill Univ, DDS, 55; Univ Pa, cert oral surg, 57; Am Bd Oral Surg, dipl, 64. *Prof Exp:* Lectr dent & oral surg, Christian Med Col, Vellore, India, 59-61, reader, 61-63; from asst prof to assoc prof oral surg, Col Dent, Univ Ky, 63-67; prof & chmn dept, Sch Dent & Sch Med, Med Col Ga, 67-75; PROF ORAL & MAXILLOFACIAL SURG & HEAD DEPT, SCH DENT MED & PROF SURG, SCH MED, UNIV CONN, FARMINGTON, 75- *Concurrent Pos:* Consult, USPHS Hosp, Lexington, Ky, 64-67, US Army, Ft Jackson, SC, 67-75, Vet Admin Hosps, Augusta, Ga, 67-75 & Newington, Conn, 75- & Coun Dent Educ, Am Dent Asn; mem adv comt, Am Bd Oral Surg, 67-75; sect ed, J Oral & Maxillofacial Surg, 82- *Mem:* AAAS; Am Dent Asn; Am Asn Oral & Maxillofacial Surgeons; Int Asn Dent Res; fel Am Col Dent. *Res:* Dental education; research in oral surgery; bone pathology and diseases of the temporomandibular joint. *Mailing Add:* Oral & Max Surg Sch of Dent Med Univ of Conn Health Ctr Farmington CT 06032

TOPCIK, BARRY, b Passaic, NJ, Apr 7, 24; m 50. CHEMICAL ENGINEERING. *Educ:* Cooper Union, BChE, 52; Newark Col Eng, MS, 60. *Prof Exp:* Sr develop engr, Uniroyal, Inc, 44-56; chief chemist, Eberhard Faber, Inc, 56-62; proj leader butyl lab, Columbian Carbon Co, 62-64, asst mgr butyl lab, 64-67, mgr new appln lab, Cities Serv Co, Cranbury, 67-77; TECH MAT MGR, WYROUGH & LOSER, TRENTON, 77- *Mem:* Am Chem Soc; Am Inst Chem Engrs; Am Mgt Asn. *Res:* Rubber technology, including formulation, engineering, and product development associated with laboratory research and application to production. *Mailing Add:* 545 Spring Valley Dr Bridgewater NJ 08807

TOPEL, DAVID G, animal science, food science, see previous edition

TOPHAM, RICHARD WALTON, b Montgomery, WVa, May 22, 43; m 67; c 1. BIOCHEMISTRY. *Educ:* Hampden-Sydney Col, BS, 65; Cornell Univ, PhD(biochem), 70. *Prof Exp:* NIH fel, Fla State Univ, 69-71; asst prof, 71-75, ASSOC PROF CHEM, UNIV RICHMOND, 75- *Concurrent Pos:* Res scientist, Res Corp grant, 75-77. *Mem:* Am Chem Soc. Res; Role of copper-containing enzymes of blood serum in iron metabolism; characterization of enzymes and enzyme reactions of sterol biosynthesis. *Mailing Add:* Dept of Chem Univ of Richmond Richmond VA 23173

TOPICH, JOSEPH, b Steubenville, Ohio, Apr 25, 48; m 71; c 2. INORGANIC CHEMISTRY. *Educ:* Columbia Univ, BA, 70; Case Western Reserve Univ, PhD(chem), 74. *Prof Exp:* Res assoc, Univ Chicago, 74-76; ASST PROF CHEM, VA COMMONWEALTH UNIV, 76- *Mem:* Am Chem Soc; Sigma Xi. *Res:* Synthesis and characterization of new molybdenum coordination complexes; chemical properties are correlated with ligand structure and molybdenum oxidation state. *Mailing Add:* Dept Chem Va Commonwealth Univ Richmond VA 23284

TOPLISS, JOHN G, b Mansfield, Eng, June 3, 30; nat US; m 58; c 2. MEDICINAL CHEMISTRY. *Educ:* Univ Nottingham, BSc, 51, PhD(chem), 54. *Prof Exp:* Res fel chem, Royal Inst Technol, Stockholm, Sweden, 54-56 & Columbia Univ, 56-57; from res chemist to sr res chemist, Schering-Plough Corp, 57-66, sect leader, 66-68, from asst dir to assoc dir chem res, 68-73, dir chem res, 73-75, sr dir chem res, 75-79; DIR CHEM, WARNER LAMBERT/PARKE DAVIS, 79- *Mem:* Am Chem Soc; Royal Soc Chem; NY Acad Sci. *Res:* Synthesis and structure-activity relationships of drugs. *Mailing Add:* 2800 Plymouth Rd Warner Lambert/Parke Davis Pharmaceut Ann Arbor MI 48105

TOPOFF, HOWARD RONALD, b New York, NY, May 7, 41. BIOLOGY, ANIMAL BEHAVIOR. *Educ:* City Col New York, BS, 64, PhD(biol), 68. *Prof Exp:* Lectr biol, City Col New York, 67-68; res fel animal behav, Am Mus Natural Hist, 68-70; asst prof, 70-76, assoc prof, 76-79, PROF PSYCHOL, HUNTER COL, 80-; RES ASSOC ANIMAL BEHAV, AM MUS NATURAL HIST, 70- *Mem:* AAAS; Animal Behav Soc; NY Acad Sci. *Res:* Behavioral development in social insects; insect communication, behavior and physiology. *Mailing Add:* Dept Psychol Hunter Col New York NY 10021

TOPOL, LEO ELI, b Boston, Mass, Apr 15, 26; m 48; c 2. PHYSICAL CHEMISTRY. *Educ:* Northeastern Univ, BS, 46; Univ Minn, Minneapolis, PhD(phys chem), 52. *Prof Exp:* Res chemist, Oak Ridge Nat Lab, 52-57; res specialist, Atomics Int Div, NAm Aviation, Inc, 57-63, mem tech staff, Sci Ctr, 64-69 & Atomics Int Div, 69-71, mem tech staff, Sci Ctr, NAm Rockwell Corp, 71-75, MEM TECH STAFF, AIR MONITORING CTR & MEM TECH STAFF & PROG MGR, ENVIRON MONITORING & SERV CTR, ROCKWELL INT CORP, 75- *Mem:* Am Chem Soc; Sigma Xi. *Res:* Acid precipitation; air pollution; quality assurance; electrolytes; new glass compositions, electrochemistry; thermodynamics and phase studies of fused salt systems and molten metal-metal salt solutions; high-conducting solid electrolytes; solid electrochemical gas pollutant sensors. *Mailing Add:* 23435 Strathern St Canoga Park CA 91304

TOPOLESKI, LEONARD DANIEL, b Wilkes-Barre, Pa, Apr 11, 35; m 58; c 3. PLANT BREEDING, VEGETABLE CROPS. *Educ:* Pa State Univ, BS, 57, MS, 59; Purdue Univ, PhD(genetics, plant breeding), 62. *Prof Exp:* Asst prof, 62-68, assoc prof, 68-78, PROF VEG CROPS, NY STATE COL AGR & LIFE SCI, CORNELL UNIV, 78- *Mem:* Am Soc Hort Sci. *Res:* Genetics; vegetative hybridization; physiology of interspecific incompatability. *Mailing Add:* Dept of Veg Crops NY State Col of Agr & Life Sci Ithaca NY 14850

TOPOREK, MILTON, b New York, NY, Apr 18, 20; m 42; c 3. BIOCHEMISTRY, LIVER METABOLISM. *Educ:* Brooklyn Col, BA, 40; George Washington Univ, MA, 48; Univ Rochester, PhD(biochem), 52. *Prof Exp:* Res assoc org chem, George Washington Univ, 48; res assoc biochem, Univ Rochester, 48-52; res chemist, Univ Mich, 52-57; from asst prof to assoc prof, 58-72, PROF BIOCHEM, JEFFERSON MED COL, THOMAS JEFFERSON UNIV, 72- *Mem:* AAAS; Am Chem Soc; Am Inst Nutrit; Am Soc Biol Chemists. *Res:* Control of plasma protein synthesis by liver, relationship to disease states; vitamin B-12, intrinsic factor relationships. *Mailing Add:* Dept of Biochem Jefferson Med Col Thomas Jefferson Univ Philadelphia PA 19107

TOPP, G CLARKE, b Canfield, Can, Nov 12, 37. SOIL SCIENCE, PHYSICS. *Educ:* Univ Toronto, BSA, 59; Univ Wis, MSc, 62, PhD(soils), 64. *Prof Exp:* Res asst soil physics, Univ Wis-Madison, 59-64; res assoc, Univ Ill, 64-65; RES SCIENTIST SOIL PHYSICS, CAN DEPT AGR, 65- *Concurrent Pos:* Adj prof, Dept Geog, Carleton Univ, 73-81; vis lectr, Dept Soil Sci, Univ Sask, 80. *Mem:* Can Soc Soil Sci (secy, 69-72, pres, 77-78); Can Geotech Soc; Soil Sci Soc Am; Am Geophys Union. *Res:* Development of instrument to measure soil water content; soil water properties; microhydrology of soils. *Mailing Add:* Land Resource Res Inst Agr Can Ottawa ON K1A 0C6 Can

TOPP, STEPHEN V, b Longview, Tex, Oct 19, 37; m 57; c 2. REACTOR PHYSICS. *Educ:* Col William & Mary, BS, 59; Univ Va, MS, 60, PhD(physics), 62. *Prof Exp:* Res physicist, 62-67, sr physicist, 67-69, asst chief supvr, Savannah River Lab, 69-75, RES STAFF PHYSICIST, ADVAN PLANNING SECT, SAVANNAH RIVER LAB, E I DU PONT DE NEMOURS & CO, INC, 75- *Concurrent Pos:* Instr physics, Univ SC, 62- *Mem:* Am Phys Soc; Am Nuclear Soc; Opers Res Soc Am. *Res:* Neutron polarization measurements, reactor criticality measurements and lattice calculations for heavy water reactors; application of computer techniques to weapons production system modeling; decision modeling for nuclear waste management. *Mailing Add:* Savannah River Lab E I du Pont de Nemours & Co Inc Aiken SC 29801

TOPP, WILLIAM CARL, b Cleveland, Ohio, Feb 3, 48; div. CELL BIOLOGY. *Educ:* Oberlin Col, BA, 69; Princeton Univ, MA, 71, PhD(chem), 73. *Prof Exp:* Res assoc physics, Princeton Univ, 73, instr chem, 73-74, res assoc, 74; res assoc biol, 74-76, staff scientist, 76-78, SR STAFF SCIENTIST, BIOL, COLD SPRING HARBOR LAB QUANT BIOL, 78- *Mem:* Sigma Xi; Am Phys Soc. *Res:* Virus/cell interactions; cell growth control. *Mailing Add:* Cold Spring Harbor Lab Cold Spring Harbor NY 11724

TOPP, WILLIAM ROBERT, b Milwaukee, Wis, May 27, 39. MATHEMATICS. *Educ:* St Louis Univ, BA, 63, MA, 64; Univ Wash, MS, 67, PhD(math), 68. *Prof Exp:* Instr math, Univ Seattle, 67-68; asst prof, Marquette Univ, 69-70; from asst prof to assoc prof, 70-79, PROF MATH, UNIV OF THE PAC, 80- *Mem:* Math Asn Am; Asn Comput Mach; Opers Res Soc Am. *Res:* Rings; algebras. *Mailing Add:* Dept of Math Univ of the Pac Stockton CA 95204

TOPPEL, BERT JACK, b Chicago, Ill, July 2, 26; m 50; c 2. REACTOR PHYSICS. *Educ:* Ill Inst Technol, BS, 48, MS, 50, PhD(physics), 52. *Prof Exp:* Instr physics, Ill Inst Technol, 49-51; assoc physicist, Brookhaven Nat Lab, 52-56; assoc physicist, 56-66, SR PHYSICIST, APPL PHYSICS DIV, ARGONNE NAT LAB, 66- *Mem:* Am Phys Soc; Am Nuclear Soc. *Res:* Nuclear reactions initiated by charged particles and neutrons; scintillation detector studies of gamma ray events; reactor critical facility experimentation; theoretical reactor physics calculations; reactor physics computer code development. *Mailing Add:* Appl Physics Div Argonne Nat Lab Argonne IL 60439

TOPPER, LEONARD, b New York, NY, Jan 11, 29. CHEMICAL ENGINEERING, SCIENCE POLICY. *Educ:* City Col New York, BChE, 48; NY Univ, MChE, 49; Cornell Univ, PhD(chem eng), 51. *Prof Exp:* Asst prof chem eng, Johns Hopkins Univ, 53-55; prog mgr, US Atomic Energy Comn, 57-73; sr policy analyst, Off Energy Res & Develop Policy, NSF, 73-75; dir, Div Technol Evaluation, Energy Res & Develop Admin, 75-76; sr policy analyst, Off Sci & Technol Policy, Exec Off President, 76-77; dir, Div Res Assessment, Off Energy Res, US Dept Energy, 77-79; CONSULT, 79- *Mem:* Sigma Xi. *Res:* Energy technology; chemical engineering science; energy research policy. *Mailing Add:* 2126 Connecticut Ave NW Washington DC 20008

TOPPER, T(IMOTHY) H(AMILTON), b Kleinburg, Ont, May 20, 36; m 58; c 3. CIVIL ENGINEERING. *Educ:* Univ Toronto, BASc, 59; Cambridge Univ, PhD(fatigue), 62. *Prof Exp:* Lectr, 62-63, from asst prof to assoc prof, 63-69, assoc chmn dept, 66-72, chmn dept, 72-78, PROF CIVIL ENG, UNIV WATERLOO, 69- *Concurrent Pos:* Vis asst res prof, Univ Ill, 66, vis assoc prof, 68. *Mem:* Am Soc Metals; Am Soc Testing & Mat; Soc Automotive Engrs. *Res:* Mechanical behavior and fatigue of metals including applications to structures. *Mailing Add:* Dept of Civil Eng Univ of Waterloo Waterloo ON N2L 3G1 Can

TOPPER, YALE JEROME, b CHicago, Ill, Aug 11, 16; m 56; c 4. BIOCHEMISTRY. *Educ:* Northwestern Univ, BS, 42; Harvard Univ, MA, 43, PhD(chem), 47. *Prof Exp:* Assoc nutrit & physiol, Pub Health Res Inst, City of NY, Inc, 48-53; Am Heart Asn res fel, Biochem Res Lab, Mass Gen Hosp, 53-54; mem staff, 54-62, CHIEF SECT INTERMEDIARY METAB, NAT INST ARTHRITIS & METAB DIS, 62- *Mem:* Endocrine Soc; Am Soc Biol Chem. *Res:* Biochemistry of development and differentiation. *Mailing Add:* Lab of Biochem & Metab Nat Inst Arthritis Diabetes Digestive & Kidney Dis Bethesda MD 20205

TOPPETO, ALPHONSE A, b Wheeling, WVa, Jan 7, 25; m 50; c 3. ELECTRICAL ENGINEERING. *Educ:* Carnegie Inst Technol, BS, 48, MS, 49; Univ Mich, PhD(elec eng), 63. *Prof Exp:* Instr elec eng, Univ Detroit, 50-55, asst prof, 55-60, assoc prof & vchmn dept, 60-63; res physicist, Aladdin Electronics Div, Aladdin Indust, Inc, 63-68, dir res, 66-68, dir res & eng, 68-76; res prof elec eng, Vanderbilt Univ, 76-77; ngr res & develop, 77-80, MGR APPLN ENG, CORCOM, INC, 80- *Concurrent Pos:* US deleg, Int Electrotech Comn, 74- & Int Comt Radio Interference, 81- *Mem:* Inst Elec & Electronics Engrs. *Res:* Characterization and application of ferrites; theoretical and practical design of filters and delay lines; computer aided design methods; development and design of RFI filters. *Mailing Add:* 32402 N Forest Dr Grayslake IL 60030

TOPPING, ALANSON DALE, mechanics, structural engineering, see previous edition

TOPPING, JOSEPH JOHN, b Amsterdam, NY, Oct 9, 42; m 65; c 3. ANALYTICAL CHEMISTRY. *Educ:* Le Moyne Col, NY, BS, 64; Univ NH, MS, 67, PhD(chem), 69. *Prof Exp:* AEC fel anal chem, Ames Lab, Iowa State Univ, 69-70; asst prof chem, 70-75, ASSOC PROF CHEM, TOWSON STATE UNIV, 75- *Mem:* AAAS; Am Inst Chemists; Sigma Xi; NY Acad Sci; Am Chem Soc. *Res:* Instrumental analytical chemistry; development of new methods of separation and analysis of trace metals; chromatography. *Mailing Add:* Dept of Chem Towson State Univ Towson MD 21204

TOPPING, NORMAN HAWKINS, b Flat River, Mo, Jan 12, 08; m 30; c 2. INFECTIOUS DISEASES. *Educ:* Univ Southern Calif, AB, 33, MD, 36. *Prof Exp:* Intern, USPHS, Marine Hosps, San Francisco, Calif & Seattle, Wash, 36-37; mem staff med res viral & rickettsial dis, NIH, Md, 37-48, assoc dir, Insts, 48-52; vpres in-chg med affairs, Univ Pa, 52-58; pres, 58-70, chancellor, 70-80, EMER CHANCELLOR, UNIV SOUTHERN CALIF, 80- *Concurrent Pos:* Chmn res comt & mem comn virus res & epidemiol, Nat Found, 58-77. *Honors & Awards:* Ashford Award, 43; Medal, US Typhus Comn, 45. *Mem:* AAAS; Am Epidemiol Soc; Soc Exp Biol & Med; Asn Am Physicians. *Res:* Virus and rickettsial diseases. *Mailing Add:* Off Chancello Univ Southern Cal Suite 1202 3810 Wilshire Blvd Los Angeles CA 90010

TOPUZ, ERTUGRUL S, b Sumnu, Bulgaria, Dec 11, 35; Turkish citizen; m 72; c 1. MINING ENGINEERING, MINERAL ECONOMICS. *Educ:* Istanbul Tech Univ, dipl eng, 59; Univ Calif, Berkeley, MEng, 72; Columbia Univ, DEngSc, 77. *Prof Exp:* Mining engr, Mineral Res & Explor Inst, 59-65, chief planning div, 65-67, asst gen dir, 67-69, mem sci bd, 69-70; asst prof, SDak Sch Mines & Technol, 76-77; ASST PROF MINING ENG, VA POLYTECH INST & STATE UNIV, 77- *Mem:* Am Inst Mining, Metall & Petrol Engrs. *Res:* Mining evaluation and analysis; mineral economics; application of mathematical optimization techniques to problems of mining industry; mine ventilation. *Mailing Add:* Dept Mining & Minerals Eng Va Polytech Inst & State Univ Blacksburg VA 24061

TORACK, RICHARD M, b Passaic, NJ, July 23, 27; m 53; c 4. PATHOLOGY. *Educ:* Seton Hall Univ, BS, 48; Georgetown Univ, MD, 52. *Prof Exp:* Asst pathologist, Montefiore Hosp, 58-59, asst neuropathologist, 59-61; asst prof path, New York Hosp-Cornell Med Ctr, 62-65, assoc prof, 65-68, assoc attend pathologist, 62-68; assoc prof, 68-70, PROF PATH & ANAT, WASH UNIV, 70- *Concurrent Pos:* Nat Cancer Inst fel path, Montefiore Hosp, 58-59; NIH res fel, Yale Med Sch, 61-62; consult, Mem Hosp, 64-68; assoc attend, Barnes Hosp, 68- *Mem:* AAAS; Am Asn Neuropath; Am Asn Path & Bact; Histochem Soc; Am Neurol Asn. *Res:* Electron histochemistry of disease of the nervous system. *Mailing Add:* 1210 Glenvista Wash Univ St Louis MO 63122

TORALBALLA, GLORIA C, b Philippines, Jan 18, 15; nat US; m 46; c 1. CHEMISTRY, BIOCHEMISTRY. *Educ:* Univ Philippines, BS, 36, MS, 38; Univ Mich, PhD(chem), 42. *Prof Exp:* Fel, Univ Mich, 43-44; res asst org chem, Columbia Univ, 44-46; instr anal & org chem, Marquette Univ, 49-52; res assoc biochem, Columbia Univ, 54-57, asst prof chem, Barnard Col, 58-63; asst prof, Hunter Col, 64-70; assoc prof, 70-75, chmn dept, 75-78, prof, 75-80, EMER PROF CHEM, LEHMAN COL, 80- *Mem:* Am Chem Soc. *Res:* Structure and mechanism of action of porcine pancreatic amylase; analytical studies of metallo-biochemicals. *Mailing Add:* Dept of Chem Lehman Col Bronx NY 10468

TORASKAR, JAYASHREE RAVALNATH, b May 21, 38. X-RAY ASTRONOMY, MEDICAL PHYSICS. *Educ:* Bombay Univ, BSc, 59, MSc, 61; Columbia Univ, PhD(physics), 69. *Prof Exp:* Res assoc physics, Columbia Univ, 69-73 & Stanford Univ, 74-75; guest res assoc physics, Brookhaven Nat Lab, 75-81; MEM STAFF, MED PHYSICS DEPT, MEM SLOAN-KETTERING CANCER CTR, 81- *Mem:* Am Phys Soc. *Res:* Experimental x-ray astronomy; radiation physics. *Mailing Add:* 370 E 69th St New York NY 10021

TORBETT, EMERSON ARLIN, b Athens, Tenn, July 20, 39; m 61; c 3. OPERATIONS RESEARCH, MATHEMATICS. *Educ:* Ga Inst Technol, BS, 61; Univ Md, College Park, MA, 66; Stanford Univ, PhD(opers res), 72. *Prof Exp:* Instr, Ga Inst Technol, 60-61; mathematician, Nat Security Agency, 61-63; res engr, Adaptronics, Inc 63-64 & SRI Int, 64-73; prog mgr, Systs Control, Inc, 73-78; dept mgr, Western Develop Labs Div, Ford Aerospace & Commun Corp, 78-80; DIR ENG, ICOT CORP, 80- *Concurrent Pos:* Lectr, Univ Calif, Berkeley, 69-70; lectr, Stanford Univ, 69-70, res asst, 70-72; adj prof, San Jose State Univ, 73- *Mem:* Opers Res Soc Am; Inst Elec & Electronics Engrs. *Res:* System effectiveness analysis; system simulation; digital filtering and prediction; queueing theory; decision analysis under uncertainty; optimal control of stochastic systems; mathematical system reliability; design/analysis of communication networks/systems. *Mailing Add:* Icot Corp 830 Maude Ave Mountain View CA 94043

TORBIT, CHARLES ALLEN, JR, b Fountain, Colo, Nov 8, 24; m 41; c 4. DEVELOPMENTAL BIOLOGY. *Educ:* Colo State Univ, BS, 62, PhD(cell biol), 72; Colo Col, MA, 66. *Prof Exp:* Fel physiol, Sch Med, Univ Kans, 72-74; embryologist, Codding Embryol Sci Inc, 74-75; cell biologist, Stanford Res Inst, 75-80; MEM FAC, DEPT OBSTET & GYNEC, VANDERBILT UNIV, 80- *Mem:* Sigma Xi; AAAS; Electron Micros Soc Am; Soc Study

Reproduction; Int Embryo Transfer Soc. *Res:* Cell biology of ovulation, fertilization and early development of the mammalian egg and its hormonal control. *Mailing Add:* Dept Obstet/Gynec Sch Med Vanderbilt Univ Nashville TN 37235

TORCH, REUBEN, b Chicago, Ill, Dec 20, 26; m 49; c 3. PROTOZOOLOGY. *Educ:* Univ Ill, BS, 47, MS, 48, PhD(zool), 53. *Prof Exp:* Asst zool, Univ Ill, 47-53; from instr to assoc prof, Univ Vt, 53-65; from asst dean to actg dean, Col Arts & Sci, Oakland Univ, 66-73, prof biol, 65-80, dean, Col Arts & Sci, 73-80; VPRES ACAD AFFAIRS, PROF ZOOL, CALIF STATE COLLEGE, STANISLAUS, 80- *Mem:* Soc Protozoologists; Am Micros Soc; Am Soc Zoologists; Am Soc Cell Biol. *Res:* Taxonomy of marine psammophilic ciliates; nucleic acid synthesis and regeneration in ciliates. *Mailing Add:* Off Vpres Acad Affairs Calif State Col Turlock CA 95380

TORCHIA, DENNIS ANTHONY, b Reading, Pa, June 15, 39; m 67; c 3. BIOPHYSICS. *Educ:* Univ Calif, Riverside, BA, 61; Yale Univ, MS, 64, PhD(physics), 67. *Prof Exp:* NIH fel, Med Sch, Harvard Univ, 67-69; mem tech staff polymer chem, Bell Labs, 69-71; physicist, Polymers Div, Nat Bur Standards, 71-74; BIOPHYSICIST, NAT INST DENT RES, 74- *Mem:* Am Chem Soc; Am Phys Soc; Biophys Soc. *Res:* Solid state magnetic resonance studies of the molecular conformaton and motion of proteins. *Mailing Add:* Rm 106 Bldg 30 Nat Insts Health Bethesda MD 20014

TORCHIANA, MARY LOUISE, b Philadelphia, Pa, July 22, 29. PHYSIOLOGY, PHARMACOLOGY. *Educ:* Immaculata Col, Pa, BA, 51; Temple Univ, MS, 60; Boston Univ, PhD(physiol), 64. *Prof Exp:* Res assoc pharmacol, 52-58 & 63-65, sr res pharmacologist, 65, res fel pharmacol, 65-72, dir gastrointestinal res, 72-80, SR RES FEL PHARMACOL, MERCK, SHARP & DOHME RES LABS, 81- *Mem:* Am Soc Pharmacol & Exp Therapeut. *Res:* Catecholamine distribution; cardiovascular physiology and pharmacology; pharmacology of the gastrointestinal tract. *Mailing Add:* Merck Sharp & Dohme Res Labs Box 26-208 West Point PA 19486

TORCHINSKY, ALBERTO, b Buenos Aires, Arg, Mar 9, 44; m 69; c 2. MATHEMATICAL ANALYSIS. *Educ:* Univ Buenos Aires, Licenciado, 66; Univ Wis, Milwaukee, MS, 67; Univ Chicago, PhD(math), 71. *Prof Exp:* Asst prof, Cornell Univ, 71-75; asst prof, 75-77, assoc prof, 77-80, PROF MATH, IND UNIV, BLOOMINGTON, 80-, ACTG DEAN LATINO AFFAIRS, 81- *Mem:* Am Math Soc. *Res:* Problems related to singular integrals; Hp spaces and applications to differential equations. *Mailing Add:* Ind Univ Swain Hall E Bloomington IN 47405

TORDA, CLARA, b Bedapest, Hungary, Apr 1, 10; US citzen; m 42; c 1. BRAIN PHYSIOLOGY, PSYCHIATRY. *Educ:* Univ Budapest, PhD(philos), 33; Univ Milan, MD, 39. *Prof Exp:* Res assoc, Dept Biophysics, Univ Col, London, 38-39; res assoc biophysics, Univ Pa, 39-40; res assoc pharmacol, Med Col, Cornell Univ, NY, 40-42, res assoc neurol, 42-52; res psychiat, NY Stae Psychiat Inst, Columbia Univ, 52-55, sr res psychiat, 55-57; instr, Dept Psychiat, NY Med Col, NY, 60-65; PROF PSYCHIAT, NY CTR PSYCHOANAL TRAINING, 64- *Concurrent Pos:* Assoc prof, Dept Psychiat, Downstate Med Ctr, State Univ NY, Brooklyn, 64-69 & Dept Neurol, Mt Sinai Sch Med, 69-71; with Bur Child Guidance, 64-; vis prof, Univ Argentina, 67, Theoret Study Prog, NASA, Ft Collins, Colo, 71, Rockefeller Univ, 72, Stanford Univ, 74, 75 & 80, Med Col, Univ Rochester, 76; US delegate, Int congress, 69, First World Congress Biol Psychiat, 74. *Mem:* Am Med Soc; Am Psychiat Soc; Acad Psychoanal; Soc Med Psychoanalysts; Soc Child Psychiat. *Res:* Artificial intelligence; computer science; neurophysiology; biophysics; biochemistry; author or coauthor of over 300 publications. *Mailing Add:* 1409 Allsten Way Berkeley CA 94702

TORDELLA, JOHN P, b Garrett, Ind, May 24, 19; m 43; c 9. CHEMISTRY. *Educ:* Loyola Univ, Ill, BS, 41; Univ Ill, MS, 42, PhD(chem anal), 44. *Prof Exp:* Asst, Univ Ill, 41-44; res asst, Hanford Eng Works, Wash, 44-46, Ammonia Dept, 46-51, Polychem Dept, 51-60, Electrochem Dept, 60-70, RES ASSOC, POLYMER PROD DEPT, E I DU PONT DE NEMOURS & CO, INC, 70- *Mem:* AAAS; Am Chem Soc; Soc Rheol. *Res:* Rheology of molten polymers; adhesion; structure of polymer wax blends; high polymer physics; measurement of heat release rate of materials during combustion. *Mailing Add:* E I du Pont de Nemours & Co Inc Wilmington DE 19898

TORDION, GEORGES V, b Switz, June 19, 20; m. MECHANICAL ENGINEERING. *Educ:* Swiss Fed Inst Technol, Dipl, 45. *Prof Exp:* Prof mech eng, Tech State Col, Switz, 46-54; head dept 59-68, PROF MACH DESIGN, LAVAL UNIV, 54- *Mem:* Am Soc Mech Engrs; Am Gear Mfg Asn. *Res:* Applied mechanics; machine design and elements. *Mailing Add:* Dept of Mech Eng Laval Univ Quebec PQ G1K 7P4 Can

TORDOFF, HARRISON BRUCE, b Mechanicville, NY, Feb 8, 23; m 46; c 2. ZOOLOGY. *Educ:* Cornell Univ, BS, 46; Univ Mich, MA, 49, PhD(zool), 52. *Prof Exp:* Cur birds, Sci Mus, Inst Jamaica, BWI, 46-47; asst prof zool, Univ & asst cur birds, Mus, Univ Kans, 50-57, assoc prof zool & assoc cur birds, 57; from asst prof to prof zool, Univ & cur birds, Mus Zool, Univ Mich, Ann Arbor, 57-70; PROF ECOL & BEHAV BIOL & DIR, BELL MUS NATURAL HIST, UNIV MINN, MINNEAPOLIS, 70- *Concurrent Pos:* Ed, Wilson Bull, 52-54. *Mem:* Soc Vert Paleont; Am Ornithologists' Union (pres, 78-80); Cooper Ornith Soc; Wilson Ornith Soc; fel Am Ornithologists Union. *Res:* Ornithology; systematics; paleontology; morphology; behavior; breeding biology. *Mailing Add:* Bell Mus Natural Hist Univ Minn Minneapolis MN 55455

TORDOFF, WALTER, III, b Newton, Mass, Jan 2, 43; m 65; c 3. POPULATION BIOLOGY. *Educ:* Univ Mass, BA, 65; Colo State Univ, MS, 67, PhD(zool), 71. *Prof Exp:* Asst prof biol, 70-75, assoc prof, 75-81, PROF ZOOL SCI, CALIF STATE COL, STANISLAUS, 81- *Mem:* Am Soc Ichthyologists & Herpetologists; Soc Study Evolution; Soc Study Amphibians & Reptiles; Sigma Xi. *Res:* Ecology and genetics of chapparal and montane populations of reptiles and amphibians, particularly Hydromantes brunus. *Mailing Add:* Dept Biol Sci Calif State Col Stanislaus Turlock CA 95380

TORELL, DONALD THEODORE, b Mont, Oct 19, 26; m 50; c 2. ANIMAL SCIENCE. *Educ:* Mont State Col, BS, 49; Univ Calif, MS, 50. *Prof Exp:* Assoc animal husb, Univ Calif, 49-50, res asst beef cattle invest, 50-51; instr, Ariz State Col, 51; livestock specialist & lectr, Hopland Field Sta, Univ Calif, 51-81; LIVESTOCK SPECIALIST & CONSULT, 82- *Concurrent Pos:* Fulbright res sr scholar, Uganda, 61-62; specialist, Univ Chile-Univ Calif Coop Prog, 69-70. *Mem:* Am Soc Animal Sci; Soc Range Mgt. *Res:* Sheep nutrition, genetics, physiology and general sheep improvement. *Mailing Add:* 7950 Saniel Dr Ukiah CA 95482

TOREN, ERIC CLIFFORD, JR, b Chicago, Ill, Sept 16, 33; m 63; c 1. ANALYTICAL CHEMISTRY. *Educ:* Northwestern Univ, BS, 55; Univ Ill, MS, 60, PhD(chem), 61. *Prof Exp:* Instr chem, Duke Univ, 61-62, from asst prof to assoc prof, 62-70; assoc prof med & path, Med Ctr, Univ Wis-Madison, 70-75, prof, 75-77; PROF PATH, UNIV SOUTH ALA, 77- *Concurrent Pos:* Consult, Lawrence Livermore Labs, 74- *Mem:* Am Chem Soc; Am Asn Clin Chemists; NY Acad Sci; Acad Clin Lab Physicians & Scientists. *Res:* Kinetic methods of analysis; analytical instrumentation and automation laboratory computing; high performance liquid chromatography of proteins. *Mailing Add:* Dept Path Univ SAla Mobile AL 36617

TOREN, GEORGE ANTHONY, b Chicago, Ill, June 12, 24; m 49. ORGANIC CHEMISTRY. *Educ:* Hope Col, AB, 48; Purdue Univ, MS, 51, PhD(chem), 53. *Prof Exp:* PROD CONTROL SPECIALIST, MINN MINING & MFG CO, ST PAUL, 53- *Mem:* Am Chem Soc. *Res:* Boron and graphite advanced composites; pressure sensitive tapes. *Mailing Add:* 678 E Eldridge Ave Maplewood MN 55117

TOREN, PAUL EDWARD, b Lincoln, Nebr, July 18, 23; wid; c 3. ANALYTICAL CHEMISTRY. *Educ:* Univ Nebr, AB, 47, MS, 48; Univ Minn, PhD(chem), 54. *Prof Exp:* Chemist, Phillips Petrol Co, 53-59; sr chemist, 59-67, res specialist, 67-80, SR RES SPECIALIST, CENT RES LABS, 3M CO, 80- *Mem:* Am Chem Soc; Electrochem Soc. *Res:* Electroanalytical chemistry; analytical instrumentation. *Mailing Add:* Cent Res Labs 3M Co PO Box 33221 St Paul MN 55133

TORESON, WILFRED EARL, b Calif, Dec 25, 16; m 45; c 1. PATHOLOGY. *Educ:* McGill Univ, MD, 42, MSc, 48, PhD(path), 50; Am Bd Path, dipl & cert clin path, 53. *Prof Exp:* Lectr path, McGill Univ, 46-50, asst prof, 50; from instr to prof, Univ Calif, San Francisco & pathologist, Univ Hosp, 50-66; prof path, State Univ NY Downstate Med Ctr & dir labs, Univ Hosp, 66-70; PROF PATH, SCH MED, UNIV CALIF, DAVIS, 70- *Concurrent Pos:* Dir labs, South Pac Hosp, Calif, 52-58, consult, 58-66; consult, Letterman Army Hosp, 58-66; attend, Ft Miley Vet Admin Hosp, 60-66. *Mem:* Am Asn Pathologists & Bacteriologists; AMA; Col Am Pathologists; Am Soc Clin Path; Int Acad Path. *Res:* Experimental diabetes; automation and computers in clinical pathology. *Mailing Add:* 2315 Stockton Blvd Sacramento CA 95817

TORGERSON, DAVID FRANKLYN, b Winnipeg, Man, July 11, 42; m 66; c 3. MASS SPECTROMETRY. *Educ:* Univ Man, BSc, 65, MSc, 66; McMaster Univ, PhD(chem), 69. *Prof Exp:* Asst prof chem, Dept Chem, 69-70, res scientist, Cyclotron Inst, Tex A&M Univ, 70-74, sr scientist chem, 74-76; res chemist, 76-78, sect head, 78-79, HEAD CHEM, ATOMIC ENERGY CAN LTD, PINAWA, MAN, 79- *Mem:* Am Phys Soc; Am Soc Mass Spectros; Can Inst Chem. *Res:* Plasma desorption mass spectrometry of involatile solids and thin films; fission product chemistry; reactor safety research; air pollution control; new instrumentation. *Mailing Add:* Atomic Energy of Can Whiteshell Nuclear Res Estab Pinawa MB R0E 1L0 Can

TORGERSON, RONALD THOMAS, b Minneapolis, Minn, Sept 20, 36; m 63; c 2. HIGH ENERGY PHYSICS, THEORETICAL PHYSICS. *Educ:* Col St Thomas, BS, 58; Univ Chicago, MS, 62, PhD(physics), 65. *Prof Exp:* Instr physics, Univ Notre Dame, 65-68; asst prof, Ohio State Univ, 68-73; res assoc physics, 73-77, PROGRAMMER ANALYST, UNIV ALTA, 77- *Mem:* Am Phys Soc. *Res:* Quantum field theory; high energy collisions; pi pi scattering; weak and electromagnetic interactions; hadron spectroscopy. *Mailing Add:* Comput Servs Univ of Alta Edmonton AB T6G 2H7 Can

TORGESON, DEWAYNE CLINTON, b Ambrose, NDak, Oct 1, 25; m 59; c 3. PLANT PATHOLOGY. *Educ:* Iowa State Univ, BS, 49; Ore State Univ, PhD(plant path), 53. *Prof Exp:* PLANT PATHOLOGIST, BOYCE THOMPSON INST PLANT RES, INC, 52-, PROG DIR BIOREGULANT CHEM, 63-, SECY, 73- *Concurrent Pos:* Mem & chmn, Fed Insecticide, Fungicide & Rodenticide Act Sci Adv Panel, Environ Protection Agency, 76-81. *Mem:* AAAS; Am Inst Biol Sci; Am Phytopath Soc. *Res:* Fungicides; discovery and development of pesticides. *Mailing Add:* Boyce Thompson Inst Cornell Univ Ithaca NY 14853

TORIBARA, TAFT YUTAKA, b Seattle, Wash, Apr 10, 17; m 48; c 2. BIOPHYSICS, CHEMISTRY. *Educ:* Univ Wash, BS, 38, MS, 39; Univ Mich, PhD(chem), 42. *Prof Exp:* Res chemist, Dept Eng Res, Univ Mich, 42-48; scientist chem, Atomic Energy Proj, 48, from asst prof to assoc prof, 50-63, PROF RADIOBIOL & BIOPHYS, MED SCH, UNIV ROCHESTER, 63- *Concurrent Pos:* Nat Inst Gen Med Sci spec res fel, Univ Tokyo, 60-61. *Mem:* AAAS; Am Chem Soc. *Res:* Binding of ions and small molecules to serum proteins; analytical chemistry of trace materials in biological systems; measurement of environmental pollutants. *Mailing Add:* Dept of Radiobiol & Biophys Univ of Rochester Med Ctr Rochester NY 14642

TORIDIS, THEODORE GEORGE, b Istanbul, Turkey, Sept 7, 32; US citizen; m 61; c 2. STRUCTURAL DYNAMICS, APPLIED MECHANICS. *Educ:* Robert Col, Istanbul, BS, 54; Mich State Univ, MS, 61, PhD(civil eng), 64. *Prof Exp:* Design engr, EMC-RAR Contractors, 54-56; asst div engr, Raymond Concrete Pile Co, 56-57; res asst, Mich State Univ, 59-64; assoc prof eng mech, 64-77, PROF ENG & APPL SCI, GEORGE WASHINGTON UNIV, 77- *Concurrent Pos:* NSF res grants, 65-67, prin investr, 70-; co-investr, David Taylor Model Basin Res contract & prin investr, Naval Ship Res & Develop Ctr contract, 66-69; sr res scientist, Nat Biomed Res Found, 66-70. *Mem:* AAAS; Am Soc Civil Engrs. *Res:* Elastoinelastic response of beams to moving loads; improved vibration analysis of beams and plates; biomechanics, stress analysis of a bone; seismic analysis of structures; nonlinear deformations of framed structures. *Mailing Add:* Sch of Eng & Appl Sci George Washington Univ Washington DC 20006

TORIO, JOYCE CLARKE, b Biddeford, Maine, Oct 1, 34; m 55. SCIENCE ADMINISTRATION, INFORMATION SCIENCE. *Educ:* Rutgers Univ, BS, 56, MS, 61, PhD(hort, soils), 65. *Prof Exp:* Lab technician soils, Rutgers Univ, 56-61, res assoc cranberry cult, 61-65; ed biochem, hort & soils, Chem Abstr Serv, Am Chem Soc, 65-69; staff officer, Bd Agr & Renewable Resources, Nat Acad Sci, 69-74; HEAD INFO SERV, INT RICE RES INST, 74- *Mem:* Am Soc Hort Sci; Am Chem Soc; Am Inst Biol Sci. *Res:* Pomology, mineral nutrition and plants; soil fertility and analysis; plant physiology and pathology; rice culture and associated multiple cropping systems research-information management. *Mailing Add:* 10723 West Dr Fairfax VA 22030

TORKELSON, ARNOLD, b Thompson, NDak, Oct 28, 22; m 44; c 4. ORGANOMETALLIC CHEMISTRY. *Educ:* Univ NDak, BSc, 46; Purdue Univ, MS, 48, PhD, 50. *Prof Exp:* Asst, Purdue Univ, 46-48; prod develop chemist, 50-58, mgr anal chem, 58-65, mgr fluid prod develop, 65-72, mgr specialities develop, 72-76, MGR FLUIDS RESINS & SPECIALTIES PROD DEVELOP, SILICONE PROD DEPT, GEN ELEC CO, 76- *Mem:* AAAS; Am Chem Soc. *Res:* Synthesis of organosilicon compounds; rate studies on the cleavage of silicon-carbon bond; product development and research on silicone fluids, resins and specialty products. *Mailing Add:* RD 1 Burnt Hills NY 12027

TORKELSON, THEODORE RUBEN, b St James, Minn, Nov 25, 26; m 52; c 5. TOXICOLOGY. *Educ:* Gustavus Adolphus Col, BA, 51; Univ Nebr, MA, 54; Univ Pittsburgh, ScD(hyg), 66. *Prof Exp:* Toxicologist, 53-61 & 62-74, OCCUP HEALTH ASSOC, DOW CHEM CO, 74- *Mem:* Soc Toxicol; Am Indust Hyg Asn. *Res:* Industrial and solvent toxicology; industrial hygiene; industrial toxicology and occupational health. *Mailing Add:* Dow Chem Co Midland MI 48640

TORLEY, ROBERT EDWARD, b Monmouth, Ill, Jan 28, 18; m 41; c 2. CHEMISTRY. *Educ:* Monmouth Col, BS, 39; Univ Iowa, MS, 41, PhD(chem), 42. *Prof Exp:* Chemist, Am Cyanamid Co, Conn, 43-51, chemist, Chem Processing Plant, Idaho, 51-53, gen supt, 53, asst plant mgr, Bridgeville Plant, Pa, 53-56, asst plant mgr, Res Div, NY, 56-58, contract mgr govt solid rocket propellant contract, Stamford Labs, 58-62, dir, Contract Res Dept, 62-63, dir, Physics Dept, 63-71, dir, Sci Serv Dept, 71-73; vpres & dir technol, T&E Ctr, Evans Prod Co, 73-76; RETIRED. *Mem:* Fel AAAS; Am Chem Soc; Am Phys Soc. *Mailing Add:* 1820 NW Woodland Dr Corvallis OR 97330

TORMEY, DOUGLASS COLE, b Madison, Wis, Sept 2, 38. ONCOLOGY, INTERNAL MEDICINE. *Educ:* Univ Wis, BS, 60, MD, 64, PhD(oncol), 69. *Prof Exp:* Intern med, Med Ctr, Univ Calif, San Francisco, 64-65, resident, 65-66; fel oncol, Univ Wis, Madison, 66-69 & Roswell Park Mem Inst, 69-70; staff oncologist, Walter Reed Gen Hosp, 70-72; head oncol, Med Breast Cancer Serv, Nat Cancer Inst, NIH, 72-76; ASSOC PROF HUMAN ONCOL & MED, MED SCH, UNIV WIS, MADISON, 76- *Concurrent Pos:* Sr investr, Cancer & Leukemia Group B, 70-76, Nat Cancer Inst, NIH, 72-76 & Eastern Coop Oncol Group, 72-; consult, Dept Biol Sci, George Washington Univ, 74-76, William S Middleton Mem Vet Hosp, 79-, US-Japan Coop Breast Cancer Prog, 79-81. *Honors & Awards:* Borden Award, Med Sch, Univ Wis, 64. *Mem:* Am Asn Cancer Res; Am Soc Clin Oncol; Cell Kinetics Soc; Eastern Coop Oncol Group; Am Soc Hematol. *Res:* Treatment and understanding of breast cancer, and the clinical utility of the role of biomarkers in the disease. *Mailing Add:* K4/632 Clin Sci Ctr Univ Wis 600 Highland Ave Madison WI 53792

TORMEY, JOHN MCDIVIT, b Baltimore, Md, Oct 7, 34; div; c 2. PHYSIOLOGY, CELL BIOLOGY. *Educ:* Loyola Col, Md, BS, 56; Johns Hopkins Univ, MD, 61. *Prof Exp:* Fel ophthal, Johns Hopkins Univ, 61-62, instr, 62-63; res fel biol, Harvard Univ, 63-64; asst prof anat & ophthal, Johns Hopkins Univ, 64-66; staff assoc phys biol, Nat Inst Arthritis & Metab Dis, 66-68; asst prof, 68-70, assoc prof, 70-78, PROF PHYSIOL, UNIV CALIF, LOS ANGELES, 78- *Concurrent Pos:* Nat Inst Neurol Dis & Blindness fel, 61-63, spec fel, 63-66, res grants, 65-66 & 68- *Mem:* Microbeam Anal Soc; Am Physiol Soc; Am Soc Cell Biol; Am Asn Anat. *Res:* Relationship between structure and function of body tissues, especially epithelia and muscle; development of methods for localizing transport functions; electron microprobe analysis. *Mailing Add:* Dept of Physiol Univ of Calif Ctr for Health Sci Los Angeles CA 90024

TORNABENE, THOMAS GUY, b Cecil, Pa, May 6, 37; m 62; c 3. MICROBIOLOGY. *Educ:* St Edward's Univ, BS, 59; Univ Houston, MS, 62, PhD(biol chem), 67. *Prof Exp:* Instr biol, Univ Houston, 62-65; fel biochem, Nat Res Coun, Ottawa, Can, 67-68; from asst prof to assoc prof, 68-78, PROF MICROBIOL, COLO STATE UNIV, 78-, GROUP MGR MICROBIOL, SOLAR ENERGY RES INST, 80- *Mem:* Am Soc Microbiol; Am Oil Chem Soc. *Res:* Biogenesis and distribution of microbial hydrocarbons; microbial lipids and carbohydrates; metabolic pathways and mechanisms of synthesis of biochemical compounds. *Mailing Add:* Dept of Microbiol Colo State Univ Ft Collins CO 80521

TORNG, HWA-CHUNG, b Yangchow, China, Aug 12, 32; US citizen; m 60; c 2. COMPUTER ENGINEERING, ELECTRICAL ENGINEERING. *Educ:* Nat Taiwan Univ, BS, 55; Cornell Univ, MS, 58, PhD(elec eng), 60. *Prof Exp:* From asst prof to assoc prof, 60-71, PROF ELEC ENG, CORNELL UNIV, 71- *Concurrent Pos:* Mem tech staff, Switching Div, Bell Tel Labs, 66-67 & 80-81. *Mem:* Inst Elec & Electronics Engrs; Asn Comput Mach. *Res:* Very-large-scale intergration systems; computer structures and design; microprocessor systems; digital systems. *Mailing Add:* Sch Elec Eng Cornell Univ Ithaca NY 14853

TORNHEIM, LEONARD, b Chicago, Ill, Aug 21, 15; c 4. NUMERICAL ANALYSIS. *Educ:* Univ Chicago, SB, 35, SM, 36, PhD(math), 38. *Prof Exp:* Instr math, Chicago Pub Jr Cols, 38-40; instr math & statist, Antioch Col, 40-41; sect chief, Philadelphia Comput Sect, Ballistic Res Lab, Aberdeen Proving Ground, Md, 43-45; instr math, Princeton Univ, 46; from instr to asst prof, Univ Mich, 46-55; lectr, Univ Calif, 55-56; sr res assoc, Chevron Res Co, 56-80; RETIRED. *Mem:* Soc Indust & Appl Math; Math Asn Am. *Res:* Numerical analysis; industrial mathematics. *Mailing Add:* 1202 Brewster Dr El Cerrito CA 94530

TORNHEIM, PATRICIA ANNE, b Chicago, Ill, June 12, 39. ANATOMY. *Educ:* Rosary Col, BA, 61; Univ Ill, MS, 64; Univ Kans, PhD(anat), 73. *Prof Exp:* Instr anat, Univ Kans, 68-69; instr, Kansas City Col Osteop Med, 69-73; asst prof, 73-80, ASSOC PROF ANAT, UNIV CINCINNATI, 80- *Mem:* Fel AAAS; Am Asn Anatomists; Cajal Club. *Res:* Traumatic cerebral edema; metabolic cerebral edema; cerebrospinal fluid pathways. *Mailing Add:* Dept of Anat Univ of Cincinnati Col Med Cincinnati OH 45267

TORNQVIST, ERIK GUSTAV MARKUS, b Lund, Sweden, Jan 13, 24; m 69; c 1. POLYMER CHEMISTRY, BIOCHEMISTRY. *Educ:* Royal Inst Technol, Sweden, MSc, 48; Univ Wis, MS, 53, PhD(biochem), 55. *Prof Exp:* First res asst, Div Food Chem, Royal Inst Technol, Sweden, 49-51; res asst, Dept Biochem, Univ Wis, 51-55; res chemist, Chem Res Div, Esso Res & Eng Co, 55-58, res assoc, 58-66, SR RES ASSOC, ENJAY POLYMER LABS, LINDEN, EXXON RES & ENG CO, 66- *Mem:* AAAS; Am Chem Soc; NY Acad Sci; Swedish Asn Eng & Archit. *Res:* Organometallic chemistry and catalysis; polymer chemistry, especially synthesis and mechanisms of polymerization; biotechnical production of protein, fat, vitamins and antibiotics. *Mailing Add:* 38 Mareu Dr Scotch Plains NJ 07076

TORO, RICHARD FRANK, b South Amboy, NJ, Nov 11, 39; m 63; c 3. ENVIRONMENTAL ENGINEERING, CHEMICAL ENGINEERING. *Educ:* Lafayette Col, BS, 61; Univ Del, MChE, 64. *Prof Exp:* Process engr chem plants, Pullman-Kellogg, 62-65; process engr mgr eng & vpres environ eng & testing & chem res & develop, Princeton Chem Res, 65-73; V PRES & CONSULT ENVIRON ENG & TESTING, RECON SYST INC, 73- *Concurrent Pos:* Chmn, Intersoc Comt Methods Air Sampling & Anal, 76- *Mem:* Air Pollution Control Asn; Am Inst Chem Engrs; Am Chem Soc; Sigma Xi. *Res:* Chemical processing; environmental science. *Mailing Add:* Recon Syst Inc 51 Fifth St Somerville NJ 08807

TORO-GOYCO, EFRAIN, b Cabo Rojo, PR, Mar 14, 31; m 55; c 5. PHYSICAL CHEMISTRY, BIOCHEMISTRY. *Educ:* Univ PR, BS, 54, LLB, 64; Harvard Univ, MA, 56, PhD(biochem), 58. *Prof Exp:* Assoc, 58, from asst prof to assoc prof, 58-69, PROF BIOCHEM, SCH MED, UNIV PR, SAN JUAN, 69-, CHMN DEPT, 72- *Concurrent Pos:* Lederle Med Fac Award, 66-69; asst chief radioisotope serv, San Juan Vet Admin Hosp, 59-65, consult, 65-78; vis prof, Va Commonwealth Univ, 78-79; mem, NFS Grad Fel Comt & chmn, Panel Minority Grad Fel Biochem, 80-82. *Mem:* Am Chem Soc; affil AMA; Am Soc Biol Chemists. *Res:* Immunochemistry; enzymology; marine pharmacology; biochemistry of schistosomes; autoimmune diseases; biochemical pharmacology. *Mailing Add:* Dept of Biochem Univ of PR Sch of Med San Juan PR 00905

TOROK, ANDREW, JR, b Hopewell, Va, Oct 30, 25; m 51; c 2. CHEMISTRY. *Educ:* Pa State Univ, BS, 49; Stevens Inst Technol, MS, 56. *Prof Exp:* Anal chemist, William P Warner, Inc, 49-51; res chemist, Venus Pen & Pencil Co, 51-53, chief chemist, 53-57, tech dir, 57-61; prod develop mgr, Ga Kaolin Co, 61-74; DIR RES & DEVELOP, FABER-CASTELL CORP, 74- *Mem:* Am Chem Soc; Am Ceramic Soc; fel Am Inst Chemists; NY Acad Sci; Fine Particle Soc (treas, 70-73). *Res:* Clays and clay products, especially application in new fields. *Mailing Add:* 44 Long Ridge Rd Dover NJ 07801

TOROK, NICHOLAS, b Budapest, Hungary, June 13, 09; US citizen; m 39. OTOLARYNGOLOGY. *Educ:* Eötvös Lorand Univ, Budapest, 34. *Prof Exp:* From instr to asst prof otolaryngol, Eötvös Lorand Univ, Budapest, 40-47; from instr to assoc prof, 50-68, PROF OTOLARYNGOL, UNIV ILL COL MED, 68- *Concurrent Pos:* Consult, Chicago Read Hosp, Ill State Psychiat Inst, Ill Hosp Sch & Michael Reese Hosp. *Honors & Awards:* Award, Am Acad Ophthal & Otolaryngol, 69; NASA Skylab Achievement Award. *Mem:* Am Acad Ophthal & Otolaryngol; Am Laryngol, Rhinol & Otol Soc; Am Neurotol Soc (pres, 73-74); Am Acad Cerebral Palsy; affil Royal Soc Med. *Res:* Otology; neuro-ortology; vestibular studies. *Mailing Add:* Eye & Ear Infirmary Univ of Ill Col of Med Chicago IL 60612

TOROK, THEODORE ELWYN, b Pine Grove, Pa, Aug 16, 31; m 61; c 3. METALLURGICAL ENGINEERING. *Educ:* Univ Idaho, BS, 54; Lehigh Univ, MS, 62, PhD(metall eng), 65. *Prof Exp:* Metallurgist, Bendix Aviation Corp, 57-58; metallurgist, Convair/Astronaut, Gen Dynamics Corp, 58-59, group leader chem & metall, 59; metallurgist, Eng Res Ctr, Western Elec Co, NJ, 65-68; RES ENGR, HOMER RES LABS, BETHLEHEM STEEL CORP, 68- *Mem:* Am Soc Metals; Am Welding Soc. *Res:* Dilatometry; weldability; delayed cracking; hot dipped coatings; phase transformations; wire patenting and drawing. *Mailing Add:* Homer Res Labs Bethlehem Steel Corp Bethlehem PA 18016

TOROP, WILLIAM, b New York, NY, Jan 12, 38; m 60; c 2. INORGANIC CHEMISTRY, SCIENCE EDUCATION. *Educ:* Univ Pa, AB, 59, MS, 61, EdD(sci educ), 68. *Prof Exp:* Prof employee chem, Upper Darby Sr High Sch, Pa, 60-68; asst prof chem & sci educ, St Joseph's Col (Pa), 68-71; PROF CHEM, WEST CHESTER STATE COL, 71- *Concurrent Pos:* Elem sci consult, Interboro Sch Dist, Pa, 69-70; elem sci consult, Marple Newtown Sch Dist, 70-72; dir, Del Valley Inst Sci Educ, 71- *Mem:* Am Chem Soc. *Res:* Use of written laboratory reports in high school chemistry; trivalent basic polyphosphates; evaluation of elementary science programs; computer managed and computer assisted instruction. *Mailing Add:* Dept of Chem West Chester State Col West Chester PA 19380

TOROSIAN, GEORGE, b Racine, Wis, Jan 1, 36; m 64; c 2. PHARMACY, PHARMACOLOGY. *Educ:* Univ Wis-Madison, BS, 62, MS, 64, PhD(pharm), 66. *Prof Exp:* Sr pharm chemist, Menley & James Labs Div, Smith Kline & French Labs, Inc, 66-69; assoc prof pharm, Col Pharm, Univ Fla, 69-81; HEAD PREFORMULATION, ENDO LABS, E I DU PONT DE NEMOURS & CO, INC, 81- *Mem:* Am Pharmaceut Asn; Am Asn Cols Pharm; Acad Pharmaceut Sci. *Res:* Product development and design; biopharmaceutics; solution kinetics. *Mailing Add:* Endo Labs 1000 Stewart Ave Garden City NY 11530

TORP, BRUCE ALAN, b Duluth, Minn, Sept 5, 37; m 60; c 3. INORGANIC CHEMISTRY, COMPUTER SCIENCE. *Educ:* Univ Minn, BA, 59; Iowa State Univ, MS, 62, PhD(inorg chem), 64. *Prof Exp:* Sr chemist, 64-68, supvr, Inorg Chem Res Group, 68-71, lab mgr, Physics & Mat Res Lab, 71-74, dir, Mat & Electronics Res Lab, Cent Res Labs, 75-77, DIR, DATA REC PROD DIV LABS, 3M CO, 77- *Mem:* Am Chem Soc. *Res:* Coordination, transition metal and solid state chemistry; semiconductor research; magnetic materials research; magnetic media development. *Mailing Add:* Data Rec Prod Div Labs 3M Co Bldg 236-1L St Paul MN 55101

TORRANCE, DANIEL J, b Peking, China, Nov 14, 21; US citizen; m 51; c 2. RADIOLOGY. *Educ:* Univ Wash, BSc, 44; Johns Hopkins Univ, MD, 49. *Prof Exp:* Intern med, Johns Hopkins Hosp, 49-50, fel path, 50-51, asst resident radiol, 51-53, from instr to assoc prof, Sch Med, Johns Hopkins Univ, 53-63; head div, Scripps Clin & Res Found, La Jolla, Calif, 63-66; assoc prof, Sch Med, Wash Univ, 66-68; prof, Univ Calif, Los Angeles, 68-72; chief radiologist, Bay Harbor Hosp, Calif, 72-76; RADIOLOGIST & CHIEF, CHEST & GEN RADIOL SECT, HARBOR GEN HOSP, 76-; ADJ PROF RADIOL, UNIV CALIF, LOS ANGELES, 76- *Concurrent Pos:* Consult, USPHS Hosp, Baltimore, Md, 54-; radiologist, Johns Hopkins Hosp, 55-63; assoc radiologist, Mallinckrodt Inst Radiol, Barnes Hosp, St Louis, 66-; chief dept radiol, Harbor Gen Hosp, Torrance, Calif; clin prof radiol, Univ Calif, Los Angeles, 72-; consult, Vet Admin Hosp, Long Beach, Calif, 80- *Mem:* Am Col Radiol. *Res:* Chest radiograph in connection with the pulmonary circulation; problems in the radiography of pulmonary atelectasis; radiographic manifestations of pulmonary edema. *Mailing Add:* Harbor Gen Hosp 1000 W Carlson St Torrance CA 90509

TORRANCE, JERRY BADGLEY, JR, b San Diego, Calif, July 20, 41; m 64; c 2. PHYSICS. *Educ:* Stanford Univ, BS, 63; Univ Calif, Berkeley, MA, 66; Harvard Univ, PhD(appl physics), 69. *Prof Exp:* Res physicist, Thomas J Watson Res Ctr, 69-76, MGR PHYS PROPERTIES ORGANIC SOLIDS GROUP, IBM CORP, 76- *Mem:* Am Chem Soc; Am Phys Soc. *Res:* Organic solids, particularly design and synthesis of new materials and optical, transport, and magnetic properties. *Mailing Add:* IBM Corp Res Ctr K32/281 5600 Cottle Rd San Jose CA 95193

TORRANCE, KENNETH E(RIC), b Minneapolis, Minn, Aug 23, 40; m 62; c 3. MECHANICAL ENGINEERING. *Educ:* Univ Minn, Minneapolis, BS, 61, MSME, 64, PhD(mech eng), 66. *Prof Exp:* Factory Mutual Eng Co res assoc, Nat Bur Standards, 66-68; from asst prof to assoc prof, 69-81, PROF MECH & AEROSPACE ENG, CORNELL UNIV, 81- *Concurrent Pos:* Sr fel, Nat Ctr Atmospheric Res, 74-75. *Mem:* AAAS; Am Geophys Union; Am Soc Mech Engrs; Combustion Inst. *Res:* Heat transfer; fluid mechanics; numerical computations; geophysics. *Mailing Add:* Sibley Sch Mech & Aerospace Eng Grumman Hall Cornell Univ Ithaca NY 14853

TORRE, FRANK JOHN, b Newark, NJ, Oct 6, 44; m 68; c 1. PHYSICAL CHEMISTRY. *Educ:* Monmouth Col NJ, BS, 67; Rutgers Univ, PhD(phys chem), 71. *Prof Exp:* Res chem, Bell Tel Labs, 67-68; fel, Univ Rochester, 71-73; asst prof, 73-80, ASSOC PROF CHEM, SPRINGFIELD COL, 80- *Mem:* Am Chem Soc. *Mailing Add:* Dept of Chem Springfield Col Springfield MA 01109

TORRE-BUENO, JOSE ROLLIN, b Tucson, Ariz, Nov 20, 48; m 69. PHYSIOLOGY. *Educ:* State Univ NY Stony Brook, BS, 70; Rockefeller Univ, PhD(physiol), 75. Prof res assoc physiol, 75-78; MED RES ASST PROF, DEPT PHYSIOL, DUKE MED CTR, 78- *Res:* Respiratory physiology and energetics particularly during hypoxia. birds. *Mailing Add:* Dept Physiol Duke Univ Med Ctr Durham NC 27710

TORREGROSSA, ROBERT EMILE, b Bogalusa, La, Oct 24, 51; m 75; c 1. MICROBIAL PHYSIOLOGY, FERMENTATION TECHNOLOGY. *Educ:* La Tech Univ, BS, 73; Univ Ga, PhD(microbiol), 77. *Prof Exp:* res microbiologist fermentations, CPC Int Inc, 78-80; WITH CHEM DIV, ETHYL CORP, 80- *Concurrent Pos:* NSF fel, Mass Inst Technol, 77-78. *Mem:* Am Soc Microbiol; Am Chem Soc. *Res:* Biochemistry; enzyme processes; immobilized cells and enzymes; biotransformations; hydrocarbon oxidation. *Mailing Add:* PO Box 341 Ethyl Corp Chems Div Baton Rouge LA 70821

TORRENCE, PAUL FREDERICK, b New Brighton, Pa, April 22, 43; m 67; c 2. INTERFERON, NUCLEIC ACIDS. *Educ:* Geneva Col, Pa, BS, 65; State Univ NY, PhD(chem), 69. *Prof Exp:* Staff fel, Nat Inst Arthritis & Metab Dis, 69-71, sr staff fel, Nat Inst Arthritis, Metab & Digestive Dis, 71-74, RES CHEMIST, NAT INST ARTHRITIS, DIABETES & DIGESTIVE & KIDNEY DIS, NIH, 74- *Concurrent Pos:* Ad Hoc consult, Spec Proj Adv Comt, Nat Cancer Inst, 80 & Nat Inst Allergy Infectious Dis, 79- *Mem:* Am Chem Soc; Soc Exp Biol & Med; Am Soc Microbiol; AAAS. *Res:* Mechanisms of induction and action of interons; the role played by double-standard RNA and 2,5-oligoadenlates in these mechanisms and how this information may be used to design antiviral or antitumor agents. *Mailing Add:* NIH Bldg 4 Rm 126 Bethesda MD 20205

TORRENCE, ROBERT JAMES, b Pittsburgh, Pa, June 7, 37; m 59. THEORETICAL PHYSICS. *Educ:* Carnegie-Mellon Univ, BS, 59; Univ Pittsburgh, PhD(physics), 65. *Prof Exp:* Res assoc physics, Syracuse Univ, 65-67; adj prof, Ctr Advan Studies, Nat Polytech Inst, Mex, 67-68; asst prof, 68-70, chmn div appl math, 75-77, ASSOC PROF MATH, UNIV CALGARY, 70- *Res:* General relativity with emphasis on gravitational radiation. *Mailing Add:* Dept of Math Univ of Calgary Calgary AB T2N 1N4 Can

TORRES, ANDREW MARION, b Albuquerque, NMex, Jan 20, 31; m 55; c 4. BOTANY. *Educ:* Univ Albuquerque, BS, 52; Univ NMex, MS, 58; Ind Univ, PhD(bot), 61. *Prof Exp:* Instr biol, Wis State Univ, Oshkosh, 60-61; asst prof bot & genetics, Univ Wis, Milwaukee, 61-64; assoc prof, 64-70, assoc dean grad sch, 69-72, chmn dept, 79-81, PROF BOT & GENETICS, UNIV KANS, 70- *Concurrent Pos:* NSF grants, 61-; Ford Found sr adv, Univ Oriente, Venezuela, 66-67; chief of party, Aid to higher educ, Dominican Republic, 68; Calif Avocado Adv Bd, 78; vis prof, Univ Calif, Riverside, 78, Univ Nat Del Sur, 81; consult, Agr Res Orgn, Bet Dagan, Israel, 81. *Mem:* AAAS; Bot Soc Am; Soc Study Evolution; Genetics Soc Am. *Res:* Cytogenetics; chemosystematics of Compositae; alcohol dehydrogenase isozymes of sunflowers; genetics; subunit structure; activities; molecular genetics of citrus and avocado. *Mailing Add:* Dept of Bot Univ of Kans Lawrence KS 66044

TORRES, FERNANDO, b Paris, France, Nov 29, 24; m 55; c 1. NEUROLOGY, NEUROPHYSIOLOGY. *Educ:* Ger Col, Colombia, BA, 41; Nat Univ Colombia, MD, 48; Am Bd EEG, dipl, 51; Am Bd Psychiat & Neurol, dipl, 61. *Prof Exp:* Asst neurosurg, Inst Cancer, Buenos Aires, Arg, 49-50; resident neurol, Montefiore Hosp, New York, 53-55; from instr to assoc prof, 56-64, PROF NEUROL, UNIV MINN, MINNEAPOLIS, 64- *Concurrent Pos:* Fel, Johns Hopkins Hosp, 50-52, NIH res fel, 52-53; NIH spec fel, LaSalpetriere Hosp, Paris, 63-64; asst, Columbia Univ, 54-55; consult prof, Univ PR, 61- *Mem:* AAAS; fel Am Acad Neurol; Am Neurol Asn; Soc Neurosci; Am Electroencephalog Soc. *Res:* Electroencephalography; clinical neurophysiology; epilepsy; cerebrovascular physiology; developmental cerebral physiology. *Mailing Add:* Box 28 Dept of Neurol Univ of Minn Hosp Minneapolis MN 55455

TORRES-BLASINI, GLADYS, b Ponce, PR; m; c 2. MICROBIOLOGY. *Educ:* Univ PR, BS, 48; Univ Mich, Ann Arbor, MS, 52, PhD(bact), 53; Duke Univ, cert mycol, 54. *Prof Exp:* Teaching asst bact, Univ Mich, 52; assoc, 52-56, asst prof bact, 56-62, assoc prof mycol, 62-65, prof, 65-77, mem admis comt, 67-70, actg chmn, 70, PROF & HEAD, DEPT MICROBIOL & MED ZOOL, SCH MED, UNIV PR, SAN JUAN, 77-, PRES, ADMIS COMT, 71- *Concurrent Pos:* USPHS fel mycol, 54; Hoffmann-La Roche grant fungistatic drugs, 54, Trichophyton species, 56; Vet Admin Hosp grant, 56 & 57; Univ PR Sch Med & NIH grant, 58; NIH grant, 58, 60, 64 & 68-70; lectr, Hahnemann Med Sch, 62; Univ PR Med Sch Gen Res Funds grant, 64; mem, Study Sect Res, Vet Admin Hosp, San Juan, PR, 70. *Mem:* Soc Am Bacteriologists; Sigma Xi; Tissue Cult Asn. *Res:* Bacteriology; comparison of phagocytosis of various candida species. *Mailing Add:* Dept Microbiol & Med Zool Sch Med Univ PR Box 5067 San Juan PR 00936

TORRES-MEDINA, ALFONSO, b Colombia, Aug 28, 45; m 71; c 1. VETERINARY MEDICINE, VIROLOGY. *Educ:* Nat Univ Colombia, DVM, 68; Univ Nebr, Lincoln, MS, 71; Univ Nebr, Omaha, PhD(med microbiol), 73. *Prof Exp:* Asst instr vet path, Nat Univ Colombia, 69, fel, 69-71; from instr to asst prof vet sci, Univ Nebr, Lincoln, 73-75; new prod mgr diag, Miles Labs Inc, Cali, Colombia, 76-78; asst prof, 78-81, ASSOC PROF VET SCI, UNIV NEBR, 81- *Mem:* Sigma Xi. *Res:* Neonatal infectious diseases of bovine and swine, especially in regard to viral diarrheas of calves and piglets; use of gnotobiotic calves and piglets for the study of experimental infectious diseases. *Mailing Add:* Dept Vet Sci Univ Nebr Lincoln NE 68583

TORRES-PINEDO, RAMON, b Burgos, Spain, Apr 3, 29; US citizen; m 57; c 4. PEDIATRICS, GASTROENTEROLOGY. *Educ:* Univ Granada, BS, 48; Univ Madrid, MD, 56. *Prof Exp:* Intern, San Juan City Hosp, PR, 58-59; resident pediat, San Juan City Hosp & Univ Hosp, 59-61; assoc, Univ Hosp, Univ PR, 63-65, from asst prof to prof, 65-75, asst dir pediat res, Clin Res Ctr, Sch Med, 63-75, prof physiol & head dept, 66-75; PROF PEDIAT & CHIEF PEDIAT GASTROENTEROL, 75- DIR CLIN RES CTR, OKLA CHILDREN'S MEM HOSP, OKLAHOMA CITY, 78- *Concurrent Pos:* Fels pediat res, Michael Reese Hosp & Med Ctr, Univ Ill, 61-63; consult physician, San Juan City Hosp, 64-75. *Mem:* Am Fedn Clin Res; Am Inst Nutrit; Am Pediat Soc; Soc Pediat Res. *Res:* Pediatric research; electrolyte transport; intermediary metabolism; nutrition. *Mailing Add:* Clin Res Ctr Okla Children's Mem Hosp Oklahoma City OK 73126

TORRES-RODRIGUEZ, VICTOR M, b Coamo, PR, Feb 17, 26; US citizen; m 48; c 7. MEDICINE. *Educ:* Univ PR, Rio Piedras, BS, 47; Columbia Univ, MD, 51. *Prof Exp:* Dermatologist, US Army Hosp, Ft Jackson, SC, 57-59; from asst prof to assoc prof dermat, Sch Med, Univ PR, Rio Piedras, 59-67, prof, 67-74, chief, Sect Affil Hosps, 65-74; prof dermat & path, Sch Med, Univ Miami, 74-76; assoc dean acad affairs, Sch Med, Univ PR, 78-81; RETIRED. *Concurrent Pos:* Fel dermat, Columbia-Presby Med Ctr, 54-57, Lederle Int fel dermatopath, 64-65; consult, Rodriguez Army Hosp, San Juan, 62-72, various pvt hosps, 63- & Vet Admin Hosp, 70-; dir dermat residency prog, Affiliated Hosps, 66-74. *Mem:* Am Acad Dermat; Am Soc Dermatopath; Am Dermat Asn; PR Dermatol Soc. *Res:* Pathology of certain tropical dermatoses, chiefly granulomas. *Mailing Add:* 1708 Jozmin San Francisco RP Rio Piedras PR 00935

TORREY, JOHN GORDON, b Philadelphia, Pa, Feb 22, 21; m 49; c 5. PLANT PHYSIOLOGY. *Educ:* Williams Col, BA, 42; Harvard Univ, MA, 47, PhD, 50. *Prof Exp:* Harvard Univ traveling fel, Cambridge Univ, 48-49; from instr to assoc prof bot, Univ Calif, 49-60; dir, Cabot Found, 66-75, PROF BOT, HARVARD UNIV, 60- *Concurrent Pos:* Guggenheim fel, 65-66; hon sr res fel, Univ Glasgow, 73; res collabr, Div Plant Indust, Commonwealth Sci & Indust Res Orgn, Australia, 80. *Mem:* Nat Acad Sci; Am Acad Arts & Sci; Bot Soc Am; Am Soc Plant Physiol; Soc Develop Biol (pres, 63). *Res:* Physiology of root growth; physiology and biochemistry of tissue differentiation; root nodules in legumes and non-legumes. *Mailing Add:* Dept Biol Harvard Univ Petersham MA 01366

TORREY, RUBYE PRIGMORE, b Sweetwater, Tenn, Feb 18, 26; m 57; c 2. RADIATION CHEMISTRY, ANALYTICAL CHEMISTRY. *Educ:* Tenn State Univ, BS, 46, MS, 48; Syracuse Univ, PhD(chem), 68. *Prof Exp:* Res assoc & instr chem, 48-57, from asst prof to assoc prof, 57-72, PROF CHEM, TENN STATE UNIV, 72- *Concurrent Pos:* Asst lectr, Syracuse Univ, 63-68; US AEC res grant & res collabr, Brookhaven Nat Lab, 70- *Mem:* AAAS; Am Chem Soc. *Res:* Electro-analytical chemistry; gas phase reaction mechanisms using alpha radiolysis and high-pressure impact mass spectrometry; effects of various factors on polarographic diffusion coefficients using chronopotentiometric technique. *Mailing Add:* Dept of Chem Tenn State Univ Nashville TN 37203

TORREY, THEODORE WILLETT, b Woodbine, Iowa, Jan 14, 07; m 38. DEVELOPMENTAL ANATOMY. *Educ:* Univ Denver, AB, 27; Harvard Univ, AM, 29, PhD(zool), 32. *Prof Exp:* From instr to prof zool, 32-72, chmn dept, 48-66, EMER PROF ZOOL, IND UNIV, BLOOMINGTON, 72- *Mem:* AAAS; Am Soc Zool; Soc Exp Biol & Med. *Res:* Nervous system; degeneration of nerves and sense organs; embryological sense organs; embryology of urogenital system. *Mailing Add:* 421 Clover Lane Bloomington IN 47401

TORRIANI GORINI, ANNAMARIA, b Milan, Italy, Dec 19, 18; nat US; m 60; c 1. BACTERIAL PHYSIOLOGY. *Educ:* Univ Milan, PhD(natural sci), 42. *Prof Exp:* Res asst physiol & bact, Pasteur Inst, Paris, 48-55; Fulbright fel microbiol, NY Univ, 55-58; res assoc, Biol labs, Harvard Univ, 58-59; from res assoc to assoc prof, 59-75, PROF BIOL, MASS INST TECHNOL, 75- *Concurrent Pos:* NIH res career award, 63-73. *Mem:* Am Soc Biol Chemists; Am Soc Microbiol. *Res:* Control of protein synthesis; bacterial genetics; bacterial spores germination. *Mailing Add:* Dept of Biol Mass Inst of Technol Cambridge MA 02139

TORRIE, BRUCE HAROLD, b Toronto, Ont, Mar 24, 37; m 60; c 3. SOLID STATE PHYSICS. *Educ:* Univ Toronto, BASc, 59; McMaster Univ, PhD(physics), 63. *Prof Exp:* Res fel, Atomic Energy Res Estab, Harwell, Eng, 62-65; asst prof, 65-70, ASSOC PROF PHYSICS, UNIV WATERLOO, 70- *Mem:* Can Asn Physicists. *Res:* Lattice dynamics; experimental studies with raman and neutron scattering. *Mailing Add:* 140 Allen E Waterloo ON H2J 1K3 Can

TORRIE, GLENN MCGREGOR, b Orangeville, Ont, May 11, 49; m 73. THEORETICAL CHEMISTRY, PHYSICAL CHEMISTRY. *Educ:* Univ Toronto, BSc, 71, MSc, 72, PhD(theoret chem), 75. *Prof Exp:* Nat Res Coun fel theoret chem, Lab Phys Theory, Orsay, France, 75-76; ASST PROF CHEM & RES ASSOC, UNIV TORONTO, 76- *Res:* Statistical mechanics; Monte Carlo calculations on dense fluids, mixtures and electrolytes; polymer statistics and critical phenomena. *Mailing Add:* Lash Miller Chem Labs 80 St George St Toronto ON M5S 1A1 Can

TORTI, MAURICE L(EO), b Memphis, Tenn, May 31, 31; m 69. MATERIALS ENGINEERING. *Educ:* Mass Inst Technol, SB, 54, SM, 54, ScD(mech eng), 56. *Prof Exp:* Proj mgr, Nat Res Corp, 56-58, dir metall develop, 58-63, dir metall res, 63-67; chief armor prod res, 67-68, asst dir res, Protective Prod Div, 68-71, RES MGR, CERAMIC COMPONENTS, NORTON CO, 71- *Mem:* Am Soc Metals; Am Inst Mining, Metall & Petrol Engrs; Am Ceramic Soc; Am Soc Mech Engrs. *Res:* Materials engineering; refractory metals; melting; fabrication; alloy development; advanced ceramic materials; armor, hot pressing, silicon carbide and silicon nitride. *Mailing Add:* Norton Co One New Bond St Worcester MA 01606

TORTORELLO, ANTHONY JOSEPH, b Chicago, Ill, Sept 26, 45; m 71; c 3. SYNTHETIC ORGANIC CHEMISTRY, ORGANIC POLYMER CHEMISTRY. *Educ:* St Joseph's Col, BS, 67; Loyola Univ, Chicago, MS, 70, PhD(chem), 75. *Prof Exp:* res scientist chem, Am Can Co, Barrington, 74-77; SR RES CHEMIST, DE SOTO, INC, DES PLAINES, 77- *Mem:* Am Chem Soc; Fed Soc Coatings Technol. *Res:* Emulsion polymerization technology; latex coatings; specialty monomer synthesis for emulsion polymerization. initiators. *Mailing Add:* DeSoto Inc 1700 S Mount Prospect Rd Des Plaines IL 60018

TORVIK, PETER J, b Fergus Falls, Minn, Dec 6, 38; m 58; c 2. ENGINEERING MECHANICS. *Educ:* Univ Minn, BS, 60, MS, 62, PhD(eng mech), 65; Wright State Univ, BA, 80. *Prof Exp:* Asst mech & mat, Univ Minn, 60-62, res fel & instr, 62-64; from asst prof to assoc prof, 64-73, PROF MECH, AIR FORCE INST TECHNOL, 73-, HEAD, DEPT AERONAUT & ASTRONAUT, 80- *Concurrent Pos:* Vis prof, Ohio State Univ, 79. *Mem:* Am Acad Mech; Am Soc Mech Engrs; Acoust Soc Am; Am Inst Aeronaut & Astronaut; Am Soc Eng Educr. *Res:* Elasticity and wave propagation; material behavior; effects of high power lasers. *Mailing Add:* Dept of Aeronaut & Astronaut Air Force Inst of Technol Wright-Patterson AFB OH 45433

TORY, ELMER MELVIN, b Vermilion, Alta, Dec 10, 28; m 56; c 2. APPLIED MATHEMATICS, CHEMICAL ENGINEERING. *Educ:* Univ Alta, BSc, 52; Purdue Univ, PhD(chem eng), 61. *Prof Exp:* Res chemist, Aluminium Labs Ltd, 54-58; asst prof chem eng, McMaster Univ, 60-63; assoc chem engr, Brookhaven Nat Lab, 63-65; assoc prof, 65-73, PROF MATH, MT ALLISON UNIV, 73- *Mem:* Can Math Cong; Can Soc Chem Eng; NY Acad Sci; AAAS. *Res:* Theoretical and experimental studies of settling of slurries; computer simulation of random packing of spheres. *Mailing Add:* Dept of Math Mt Allison Univ Sackville NB E0A 3C0 Can

TORZA, SERGIO, b Bergamo, Italy, May 26, 39; m 70; c 3. SURFACE CHEMISTRY, HYDRODYNAMICS. *Educ:* Polytech Inst Milan, BChE & MChE, 65; McGill Univ, PhD(phys chem), 70. *Prof Exp:* Res scientist, Union Camp Corp, 70-72; mem tech staff surface chem, Bell Labs, 72-76; mgr pulp & paper res, MacMillan Bloedel Res, 76-81, ENG & TECH MGR, HARMAC DIV, MACMILLAN BLOEDEL, LTD, 81- *Mem:* Am Phys Soc; Am Chem Soc. *Res:* Newtonian, non-Newtonian and anisotropic fluids in motion; suspensions and emulsions; rheocapillarity. *Mailing Add:* Harmac Div MacMillan Bloedel Ltd Nanaimo BC V5R 5M5 Can

TOSCANO, WILLIAM MICHAEL, b Santa Barbara, Calif, June 22, 45; c 3. THERMODYNAMICS, HEAT TRANSFER. *Educ:* Univ Calif, Berkeley, BS, 67; Mass Inst Technol, SM, 69, PhD(eng), 73; Boston Univ, MBA, 80. *Prof Exp:* Res engr thermodyn, Western Elec Eng Res Ctr, 69; res assoc cryog, Mass Inst Technol, 73-74; res & develop mgr cryogenic eng, Helix Technol Inc, 74-77; DIV MGR MECH ENG & CONSULT, FOSTER-MILLER ASSOCS, 77- *Concurrent Pos:* consult, 73- *Mem:* Sigma Xi; Am Soc Mech Engrs; AAAS. *Res:* Cryogenic engineering research; heat pumps and heat engines; compressors and expanders; energy conservation; energy conversion and generation; appliances; burner technology; thermal systems; thermodynamics and heat transfer; refrigeration systems. *Mailing Add:* 82 Old Garrison Rd Sudbury MA 01776

TOSCH, WILLIAM CONRAD, b Lee's Summit, Mo, Jan 19, 34; m 57; c 3. OIL PRODUCTION. *Educ:* Univ SDak, AB, 57; Purdue Univ, MS, 60, PhD(phys chem), 62. *Prof Exp:* Teaching asst chem, Purdue Univ, 57-61, res asst, 58-62; res scientist, 62-68, RES DEPT MGR, MARATHON OIL CO-DENVER RES CTR, 68- *Concurrent Pos:* Asst prof, Arapahoe Community Col, 66-67; lectr, Casper Col. *Mem:* Soc Petrol Engrs. *Res:* Recovery of petroleum products from water-depleted reservoirs, including interfacial phenomena, rock and fluid interactions, rheology, surfactancy and polymer chemistry. *Mailing Add:* Marathon Oil Co PO Box 269 Littleton CO 80120

TOSELAND, BERNARD ALLAN, b Brooklyn, NY, Oct 25, 42; m 66; c 2. CHEMICAL ENGINEERING. *Educ:* Manhattan Col, BChE, 64; Princeton Univ, PhD(chem eng), 70. *Prof Exp:* Res scientist chem eng, Union Camp Corp, 69-77, sr process engr air prod & chem, Res & Develop Div, 77-80. *Mem:* Am Inst Chem Engrs; Sigma Xi. *Res:* Crystallization of fatty acids; turbulent mixing; scale growth; polymer chemicals; mixing and reaction kinetics. *Mailing Add:* 720 N 26 St Allentown PA 18104

TOSH, FRED EUGENE, b Bemis, Tenn, Feb 13, 30; m 55; c 3. MEDICINE, EPIDEMIOLOGY. *Educ:* Univ Tenn, MD, 54; Univ Calif, MPH, 63. *Prof Exp:* Intern, Baptist Hosp, Memphis, Tenn, 54-55; med epidemiologist, Commun Dis Ctr, USPHS, 55-57; pvt pract, Tenn, 57-58; med epidemiologist, Kansas City Field Sta, Ctr Dis Control, USPHS, 58-64, chief pulmonary mycoses unit, 64-66, dep dir ecol invests prog, 67-73, dir div qual & stand, 73-78, dir off regional health planning, USPHS Regional Off, Colo, 78-80; DIR, WICHITA-SEDGWICK COUNTY DEPT COMMUNITY HEALTH, 80- *Concurrent Pos:* Resident, Mo State Sanitorium, 60-61; instr med, Univ Kans, 64-70, asst clin prof, 70-73. *Mem:* AMA; Am Epidemiol Soc. *Res:* Public health. *Mailing Add:* Wichita-Sedgwick County Dept Community Health 1900 E 9th St Wichita KS 67214

TOSI, JOSEPH ANDREW, JR, b Worcester, Mass, July 1, 21; m 48; c 3. ECOLOGY. *Educ:* Mass State Col, BS, 43; Yale Univ, MF, 48; Clark Univ, PhD(geog), 59. *Prof Exp:* Forester & ecologist, Northern Zone, Inter-Am Inst Agr Sci, 51-52, Andean Zone, 52-63; resident staff geogr, Cent Am Field Prog, Assoc Cols Midwest, 64-67; LAND-USE ECOLOGIST & ADMINR, TROP SCI CTR, 67- *Concurrent Pos:* Consult, Forest Surv, Venezuela, 55; consult ecol surv, Colombia, 59-60; consult to comn on environ landscape planning, Int Union for Conserv Nature & Natural Resources, 73-; mem Inst Ecol. *Honors & Awards:* Order of Agr Merit, Grade of Comdr, Govt of Peru, 74. *Mem:* Soc Am Foresters; Asn Am Geog; Sigma Xi. *Res:* Tropical ecology; bioclimatology; land utilization, especially tropical rural areas; biogeography; tropical forest management; life zone ecological theory; economic botany. *Mailing Add:* Trop Sci Ctr Apt 83870 San Jose Costa Rica

TOSI, OSCAR I, b Trento, Italy, June 17, 29; US citizen. AUDIOLOGY, ACOUSTICS. *Educ:* Univ Buenos Aires, ScD; Ohio State Univ, PhD, 65. *Prof Exp:* Assoc prof physics, Univ Buenos Aires, 51-62; res assoc voice commun, Ohio State Univ, 63-65; from asst prof to assoc prof, 65-70, PROF AUDIOL & SPEECH SCI & PHYSICS, MICH STATE UNIV, 70-, DIR, INST VOICE IDENTIFICATION, 74- *Concurrent Pos:* Dept Justice-Mich State Police grant, 68-71; expert witness on voice identification, Fed & State Courts, US, Can & Europe, 68-; vpres, Int Asn Voice Identification, Inc, 72; elected staff mem voice commun tech comt, Acoust Soc Am, 74-77. *Mem:* Acoust Soc Am; Am Asn Physics Teachers; Am Speech & Hearing Asn; Int Asn Logopedics & Phoniatrics; Int Col Exp Phonology. *Res:* Voice spectrography and identification; low levels of human acoustical energy; voice identification; articulatory pauses. *Mailing Add:* 370 COM Mich State Univ East Lansing MI 48824

TOSKEY, BURNETT ROLAND, b Seattle, Wash, May 27, 29. MATHEMATICS. *Educ:* Univ Wash, BS, 52, MA, 58, PhD(algebra), 59. *Prof Exp:* From instr to assoc prof, 58-69, PROF MATH, SEATTLE UNIV, 69- *Mem:* Math Asn Am. *Res:* Abelian groups; ring theory; homological algebra; additive groups of rings. *Mailing Add:* Dept of Math Seattle Univ Seattle WA 98122

TOSTESON, DANIEL CHARLES, b Milwaukee, Wis, Feb 5, 25; m 49, 69; c 6. PHYSIOLOGY, BIOPHYSICS. *Educ:* Harvard Univ, MD, 49. *Prof Exp:* Intern med, Presby Hosp, 49-51; res fel, Dept Med, Brookhaven Nat Labs, 51-53; mem, Lab Kidney & Electrolyte Metab, Nat Heart Inst, 53-55 & 57-58; from assoc prof to prof physiol, Sch Med, Washington Univ, 58-61; James B Duke Distinguished Prof physiol & pharmacol, Sch Med, Duke Univ, 61-75, chmn dept, Lowell & Coggeshall prof med sci, Univ Chicago, 75-77, dean, Div Biol Sci & Pritzker Sch Med, 75-77; DEAN FAC MED & CAROLINE SHIELDS WALKER PROF PHYSIOL, PRES HARVARD MED CTR, HARVARD UNIV, 77- *Concurrent Pos:* NSF fel, Biol Isotope Res Lab, Univ Copenhagen, 55-56; NSF fel, Physiol Lab, Cambridge Univ, 56-57. *Mem:* AAAS; Nat Inst Med; Am Physiol Soc; Soc Gen Physiologists; Biophys Soc. *Res:* Membrane physiology. *Mailing Add:* Harvard Med Sch 25 Shattuck St Boston MA 02115

TOSTEVIN, JAMES EARLE, b Mandan, NDak, June 28, 38; m 65; c 2. PAPER CHEMISTRY. *Educ:* Carleton Col, BA, 60; Inst Paper Chem, MS, 62, PhD(paper chem), 66. *Prof Exp:* Group leader anal, Columbia Cellulose Co, Ltd, 66-69; res chemist, GROUP LEADER ANAL, ITT RAYONIER INC, 69- *Mem:* Am Soc Testing & Mat; Tech Asn Pulp & Paper Indust. *Res:* Research into application and properties of natural cellulose fibers. *Mailing Add:* 1043 Connection St Shelton WA 98584

TOTEL, GREGORY LEE, physiology, see previous edition

TOTH, BELA, b Pecs, Hungary, Oct 26, 31; US citizen; m 63; c 4. PATHOLOGY, ONCOLOGY. *Educ:* Univ Vet Sci, Budapest, DVM, 56. *Prof Exp:* From res asst to res assoc oncol, Chicago Med Sch, 59-63, asst prof, 63-66; fel exp biol, Weizmann Inst, 66-67; assoc prof path, 68-72, PROF PATH, EPPLEY INST RES CANCER, COL MED, UNIV NEBR, OMAHA, 72- *Concurrent Pos:* USPHS trainee path, 61-63, res career develop award, 69; Eleanor Roosevelt int cancer res fel, 67-68. *Mem:* AAAS; Am Asn Cancer Res; Am Soc Exp Path; NY Acad Sci; Am Asn Path & Bact. *Res:* Experimental oncology; chemical carcinogenesis; leukemogenesis. *Mailing Add:* Eppley Inst for Res in Cancer Univ of Nebr Col of Med Omaha NE 68105

TOTH, EUGENE J, b Csikvand, Hungary, Jan 27, 32; US citizen; m 55; c 2. NEUROCHEMISTRY. *Educ:* State Col Peis Hungary, BS, 54; NY Med Sch, MS, 72, PhD(biochem), 78. *Prof Exp:* Chemist, NY State Res Inst, 61-66, res scientist, 66-77; SR RES SCIENTIST, CTR NEUROCHEM, ROCKLAND RES INST, 77- *Mem:* Am Neurochem Soc; Int Neurochem Soc. *Res:* Transport and metabolism of amino acids in the central nervous system and their functional roles in health and in various neurological and mental disorders; synthesis and tumors of brain proteins; influences on protein metabolisms. *Mailing Add:* Ctr Neurochem Rockland Res Inst Ward's Island New York NY 10035

TOTH, JOZSEF, b Bekes, Hungary, June 22, 33; Can citizen; m 56; 56; c 2. HYDROGEOLOGY. *Educ:* Univ Utrecht, BSc, 58, MSc, 60, PhD(hydrogeol), 65. *Prof Exp:* From jr res officer to sr res officer hydrogeol, 60-68, HEAD GROUND WATER DIV HYDROGEOL, RES COUN ALTA, 68- *Concurrent Pos:* Mem subcomt hydrol, assoc comt geod & geophys, Nat Res Coun Can, 63-68; lectr, Univ Alta, 66-71; vis prof, Univ Calgary, 78-79. *Honors & Awards:* O E Meinzer Award, Geol Soc Am, 65. *Res:* Hydrogeology; theoretical and practical investigations of the interaction between groundwater and the geologic environment and hydrogeological applications in water resources, soil mechanics, agriculture and mineral exploration. *Mailing Add:* Alta Res Coun 11315-87th Ave Edmonton AB T6G 2C2 Can

TOTH, KENNETH STEPHEN, b Shanghai, China, Mar 17, 34; m 56; c 2. NUCLEAR PHYSICS. *Educ:* San Diego State Col, AB, 54; Univ Calif, PhD(chem), 58. *Prof Exp:* Asst chem, Univ California, 54-55, asst, Lawrence Radiation Lab, 55-58; Fulbright fel, Inst Theoret Physics, Denmark, 58-59; NUCLEAR CHEMIST, OAK RIDGE NAT LAB, 59- *Concurrent Pos:* Guggenheim fel, Niels Bohr Inst, Copenhagen, Denmark, 65-66; exchange physicist joint inst for nuclear res, Dubna, USSR, Nat Acad Sci, 75. *Mem:* Am Chem Soc; Am Phys Soc. *Res:* Nuclear properties of radioactive isotopes in rare earth region; low energy; heavy-ion nuclear reactions. *Mailing Add:* Physics Div Oak Ridge Nat Lab Oak Ridge TN 37830

TOTH, LOUIS E(DMOND), b New York, NY, Oct 18, 38; m 63. METALLURGY. *Educ:* Calif Inst Technol, BS, 60; Univ Calif, Berkeley, PhD(metall), 63. *Prof Exp:* Fel metall, Univ Calif, Berkeley, 63-64; from asst prof to assoc prof, 64-71, PROF METALL, UNIV MINN, MINNEAPOLIS, 71- *Mem:* Am Inst Mech Engrs; Electrochem Soc. *Res:* Superconducting materials; transition metal carbides and nitrides. *Mailing Add:* Dept of Chem Eng & Mat Sci Univ of Minn Minneapolis MN 55455

TOTH, LOUIS FRANCIS, JR, b Elizabeth, NJ, Nov 27, 47; m 70; c 2. EXTRACTIVE METALLURGY, CHEMICAL METALLURGY. *Educ:* Univ Mo-Rolla, BS, 70, PhD(metall eng), 75. *Prof Exp:* Res engr metall eng, Asarco Inc, 75-80; SECT HEAD REF RES SECT, ENGELHARD CORP, 80- *Mem:* Am Soc Testing & Mat; Am Inst Metall Engrs; Am Electrochem Soc; Am Soc Metals. *Res:* Pyrometallurgy, hydrometallurgy and electrometallurgy. *Mailing Add:* Engelhard Corp 113 Astor St Newark NJ 07114

TOTH, LOUIS MCKENNA, b Lexington, Ky, Aug 27, 41; m 62; c 3. PHYSICAL CHEMISTRY. *Educ:* La State Univ, Baton Rouge, BS, 63; Univ Calif, Berkeley, PhD(chem), 67. *Prof Exp:* CHEMIST, OAK RIDGE NAT LAB, 67- *Mem:* Am Chem Soc. *Res:* High temperature molten salt chemistry; infrared, Raman and Ligand-Field spectroscopy of molten salt systems; gas phase kinetics; aqueous actinide photochemistry. *Mailing Add:* Oak Ridge Nat Lab PO Box X Oak Ridge TN 37830

TOTH, PAUL EUGENE, b Welland, Ont, July 11, 20; US citizen; m 41; c 3. INDUSTRIAL HYGIENE. *Educ:* Lawrence Inst Technol, BSChE, 49. *Prof Exp:* Supvr chem, Qual Control Lab, Briggs Mfg Co, 42-49, indust hygienist, 49-54; indust hygienist, Chrysler Corp, 54-60; occup health engr indust hyg, Dept Health Mich, 60-61; MGR INDUST HYG & TOXICOL, FORD MOTOR CO, 61- *Mem:* Am Indust Hyg Asn (treas, 67-70, pres, 78-79); Acoust Soc Am; Am Soc Safety Engrs; Am Indust Hyg Found (pres, 81-82). *Mailing Add:* Ford Motor Co 900 Parlane Tower West Dearborn MI 48121

TOTH, ROBERT ALLEN, b Richmond, Ind, Aug 10, 39; div; c 3. PHYSICS. *Educ:* Earlham Col, AB, 62; Fla State Univ, MS, 66, PhD(physics), 69. *Prof Exp:* Physicist, Infrared Spectros, Nat Bur Standards, 62-66; instr Earlham Col, 66-67; assoc, Fla State Univ, 69-70; RES SCIENTIST, INFRARED SPECTROS & REMOTE SENSING, JET PROPULSION LAB, 70- *Mem:* Fel Optical Soc Am. *Res:* Infrared spectroscopy; high resolution, its application to laboratory and theoretical data and to remote sensing of the atmosphere. *Mailing Add:* Planetary Atmospheres Sect Jet Propulsion Lab Pasadena CA 91103

TOTH, ROBERT S, b Detroit, Mich, Sept 4, 31; m 53; c 3. SOLID STATE PHYSICS. *Educ:* Wayne State Univ, AB, 54, MS, 55, PhD(physics), 60. *Prof Exp:* Res assoc physics, Wayne State Univ, 55-60; sr scientist, sci lab, Ford Motor Co, 60-69; vpres, Sensors, Inc, 69-76; PRES, DEXTER RES CTR, INC, 78- *Mem:* Am Phys Soc. *Res:* Metal oxide semi-conductors; crystal structure theory of alloy phases; magnetic structure of metals and alloys; thin film physics; epitaxy; thermoelectricity; infrared physics. *Mailing Add:* Dexter Res Ctr Inc 7300 Huron River Dr Dexter MI 48130

TOTH, STEPHEN JOHN, b Elizabeth, NJ, Feb 19, 12; m 46; c 1. SOIL CHEMISTRY. *Educ:* Rutgers Univ, BS, 33, MS, 35, PhD(soil chem), 37. *Prof Exp:* Specialist forest soils, 37-39, instr agr chem, 39-42, asst soil chemist, NJ Agr Exp Sta, 39-81, from asst prof to prof soils, 46-81, assoc res specialist, 47-81, EMER PROF SOIL COLLOIDS, RUTGERS UNIV, NEW BRUNSWICK, 81- *Mem:* Fel AAAS; Am Chem Soc; Soil Sci Soc Am; fel Am Inst Chem; fel Am Geog Soc. *Res:* Soil chemistry; colloids; nutrition; radioisotopes; fertilizers; water quality; bottom sediments; wildlife crops; composts. *Mailing Add:* Dept Soils & Crops Cook Col-Rutgers Univ New Brunswick NJ 08903

TOTH, WILLIAM JAMES, b Carteret, NJ, Jan 20, 36; m 67; c 3. POLYMER CHEMISTRY. *Educ:* Rutgers Univ, New Brunswick, BA, 68; Princeton Univ, MS, 71, PhD(chem), 72. *Prof Exp:* sr res chemist, Mobil Chem Co, Mobil Oil Corp, 63-76; SR DEVELOP ASSOC, ICI AM INC, HOPEWELL, VA, 76- *Mem:* Am Chem Soc; Soc Rheology. *Res:* Chemical mechanical, dielectric, rheological and physical properties of new polymers; physical chemistry of liquid crystals; characterization of monomeric and polymeric liquid crystals. *Mailing Add:* 2651 Radstock Rd Midlothian VA 23113

TOTO, PATRICK D, b Niles, Ohio, Jan 6, 21; m 45; c 3. ORAL PATHOLOGY. *Educ:* Kent State Univ, BS, 48; Ohio State Univ, DDS, 48, MS, 50; Am Bd Oral Path, dipl, 48. *Prof Exp:* Asst prof, 50-53 & 55-57, clin dir, 55-57, assoc prof, dir res & coordr grad studies, 57-76, PROF ORAL PATH & CHMN DEPT ORAL PATH, SCH DENT, LOYOLA UNIV CHICAGO, 71- *Concurrent Pos:* Consult, Vet Admin Hosps, Hines, Ill, 53 & Chicago, 61- *Mem:* Int Asn Dent Res; Am Soc Clin Path; Am Acad Oral Path; NY Acad Sci; Am Dent Asn. *Res:* Lectin binding to premalignant and malignant oral neoplasms; induction of oral cancer; histiocyte modulation; immunopathology oral mucosa; pathogenesis of periodontitis. *Mailing Add:* Dept of Oral Path Loyola Univ of Chicago Sch Dent Maywood IL 60153

TOTON, EDWARD THOMAS, b Philadelphia, Pa, Dec 6, 42; m 70. ASTROPHYSICS. *Educ:* St Joseph's Col (Pa), BS, 64; Univ Md, College Park, PhD(physics), 69. *Prof Exp:* Air Force Off Sci Res fel, Inst Advan Study, 69-70; NSF fel, Inst Theoret Physics, Univ Vienna, 70-71; res assoc & assoc instr astrophys, Univ Utah, 71-72; res assoc physics, Univ Pa, 72-74; RES PHYSICIST, NAVAL SURFACE WEAPONS CTR, 74- *Concurrent Pos:* Vis asst prof physics, St Joseph's Col (Pa), 74-75; consult, Naval Res Lab, Washington, DC, 75- *Mem:* Am Phys Soc; AAAS. *Res:* Astrophysical studies related to structure of neutron stars, nature of radiation from galaxies, nature of universe at moment of creation; research in combustion physics, including flame propagation, ignition, quenching and noise generation; detonation physics. *Mailing Add:* R-13 Naval Surface Weapons Ctr Silver Spring MD 20910

TOTTA, PAUL ANTHONY, b Middletown, NY, May 17, 30; m 54; c 2. MATERIALS SCIENCE, METALLURGY. *Educ:* Rensselaer Polytech Inst, BMetE, 52. *Prof Exp:* Metallurgist, Gen Elec Co, 54-58; staff metallurgist, Handy & Harman, 58-59; sr engr, 59-72, mgr metal & insulator technol, 72-81, SR MEM TECH STAFF, IBM CORP, 81- *Mem:* Am Vacuum Soc; Am Soc Metals; Sigma Xi; Int Soc Hybrid Microelectronics; Electronics Components Conf. *Res:* Thin film metallurgy deposited by vacuum evaporation or sputtering for use as conductors in monolithic integrated semiconductor devices; metal and insulator technology for integrated circuit semiconductors and electronic packaging. *Mailing Add:* IBM Corp E Fishkill Facil ZIP 461 Hopewell Junction NY 12533

TOTTEN, JAMES EDWARD, b Saskatoon, Sask, Aug 9, 47; m 68; c 1. GEOMETRY. *Educ:* Univ Regina, BA, 67; Univ Waterloo, MMath, 69, PhD(geom), 74. *Prof Exp:* Nat Res Coun Can fel geom, Univ Math Inst, Tubingen, WGer, 74-76; asst prof math, St Mary's Univ, NS, 76-78; vis asst prof math, Univ Sask, 78-79; INSTR MATH & COMPUT, CARIBOO COL, KAMLOOPS, BC, 79- *Mem:* Math Asn Am; Can Math Soc. *Res:* Linear spaces, a set of elements called points and distinguished subsets of points called lines, such that two points determine a unique line and all lines have at least two points. *Mailing Add:* Dept of Math Cariboo Col Kamloops BC V2E 1H9 Can

TOTTEN, STANLEY MARTIN, b Lodi, Ohio, July 15, 36; m 58; c 5. GEOLOGY. *Educ:* Col Wooster, BA, 58; Univ Ill, MS, 60, PhD(geol), 62. *Prof Exp:* From asst prof to assoc prof, 62-71, PROF GEOL, HANOVER COL, 71- *Concurrent Pos:* NSF fel, Univ Birmingham, 68-69. *Mem:* Fel Geol Soc Am; Soc Econ Paleont & Mineral; fel Geol Soc London; Glaciol Soc; Am Quaternary Asn. *Res:* Glacial geology; Pleistocene and Paleozoic stratigraphy; sedimentary petrology. *Mailing Add:* Dept of Geol Hanover Col Hanover IN 47243

TOTTER, JOHN RANDOLPH, b Saragosa, Tex, Jan 7, 14; m 38; c 3. BIOCHEMISTRY. *Educ:* Univ Wyo, AB, 34, AM, 35; Univ Iowa, PhD(biochem), 38. *Prof Exp:* Instr chem, Univ Wyo, 35-36; asst biochem, Univ Iowa, 36-38; instr, Univ WVa, 38-39; instr, Sch Med, Univ Ark, 39-42, from asst prof to assoc prof, 42-52; biochemist, Oak Ridge Nat Lab, 52-56; biochemist, USAEC, 56-58; biochemist, Univ of the Repub, Uruguay, 58-60; prof chem & chmn div biol sci, Univ Ga, 60-62; assoc dir res, Div Biol & Med, USAEC, 63-67, dir, 67-72; assoc dir biomed & environ sci, Oak Ridge Nat Lab, 72-74, biochemist, 74-78; SCIENTIST, OAK RIDGE ASSOC UNIV, 78- *Concurrent Pos:* Nutrit biochemist, Univ Alaska, 47; prof biochem, Univ Tenn, 75- *Mem:* Am Chem Soc; Soc Exp Biol & Med; Am Soc Biol Chemists; Am Soc Nat; Am Soc Photobiol. *Res:* Amino acid and formate metabolism; synthesis and metabolism of pterins; radiation effects; luminescence. *Mailing Add:* 109 Wedgewood Dr Oak Ridge TN 37830

TOTUSEK, ROBERT, b Garber, Okla, Nov 3, 26; m 47; c 3. ANIMAL NUTRITION. *Educ:* Okla Agr & Mech Col, BS, 49; Purdue Univ, MS, 50, PhD(animal nutrit), 52. *Prof Exp:* Asst, Purdue Univ, 49-50, instr, 50-52; from asst prof to assoc prof, 52-60, PROF ANIMAL HUSB, OKLA STATE UNIV, 60- & HEAD DEPT ANIMAL SCI, 77- *Mem:* Am Soc Animal Sci. *Res:* Range cow nutrition and management. *Mailing Add:* Dept of Animal Sci Okla State Univ Stillwater OK 74074

TOU, JAMES CHIEH, b Su-yang, China, Apr 25, 36; US citizen; m 64; c 3. ANALYTICAL CHEMISTRY, PHYSICAL CHEMISTRY. *Educ:* Taiwan Norm Univ, BSc, 61; Univ Utah, PhD(chem), 66. *Prof Exp:* Teaching asst chem, Taiwan Norm Univ, 60-61; res asst, Univ Utah, 62-65; from res chemist to sr res chemist, Chem Physics Res Lab, 65-71, sr anal specialist chem, 75-78, assoc scientist, 78-81, SR ASSOC SCIENTIST, ANAL LAB, DOW CHEM CO, 81- *Honors & Awards:* V A Stenger Anal Sci Award, Dow Chem Co, 75. *Mem:* North Am Thermal Anal Soc; Am Chem Soc; Am Soc Testing & Mat; Am Soc Mass Spectrometry. *Res:* Organic mass spectrometry; chemical ionization; electron impact and field ionization; gas-chromatography-mass spectrometry; chemical property and analysis of bis-chloromethyl ether and chloromethyl methyl ether; thermal analysis; thermokinetics and high temperature chemistry; mass spectrometry; membrane permeation. *Mailing Add:* Anal Labs B-574 Mich Div Dow Chem Co Midland MI 48640

TOU, JULIUS T(SU) L(IEH), b Shanghai, China, Aug 15, 26; m 56; c 4. ELECTRICAL ENGINEERING. *Educ:* Chiao Tung Univ, BS, 47; Harvard Univ, MS, 50; Yale Univ, DEng, 52. *Prof Exp:* Proj engr, Philco Corp, 52-55; asst prof elec eng, Univ Pa, 55-57; assoc prof, Purdue Univ, 57-61, vis prof, 61-62; prof & dir comput sci lab, Northwestern Univ, 61-64; dir info sci res, Battelle Mem Inst, 64-67; GRAD RES PROF ELEC ENG, UNIV FLA, 67-, DIR CTR RES INFO, 77- *Concurrent Pos:* Consult, Philco Corp, 55-57, Barber Colman Co, 56, Int Bus Mach Corp, 60, Gen Elec Co, 61, McDonnell Douglas, 69 & Martin Marietta, 81; adj prof, Ohio State Univ, 64-67. *Mem:* Am Soc Eng Educ; fel Inst Elec & Electronics Engrs; Am Inst Mgt; Int Soc Cybernet Med. *Res:* Control and information systems; computer science; digital control; artificial intelligence; pattern recognition; computer applications; knowledge engineering. *Mailing Add:* Dept of Elec Eng Univ of Fla Gainesville FL 32601

TOUBA, ALI R, b Tabriz, Iran, Apr 25, 25; m 57; c 4. FOOD TECHNOLOGY. *Educ:* Rutgers Univ, BSc, 51, MSc, 52; Univ Ill, PhD(food technol), 56. *Prof Exp:* Asst food microbiol, Univ Ill, 53-56; assoc technologist food res, Res Ctr, Gen Foods Corp, 56-63; proj mgr food res, Tronchemics Res, Inc, 63-65; res assoc explor food res, 65-76. head explor food res, 76-81, DEPT HEAD, BETTY CROCKERS DIV, GEN MILLS, INC, 81- *Concurrent Pos:* Tech consult, Teheran, Iran, 60-63. *Mem:* Am Chem Soc; Inst Food Technologists; Am Asn Cereal Chemists; Am Soc Microbiol. *Res:* Food texture; fabricated foods; gums; space foods; freeze drying beverages; flavors; cereals and snacks; desserts; dehydrated products; fruit products; technical management. *Mailing Add:* 4609 Island View Dr Mound MN 55364

TOUBASSI, ELIAS HANNA, b Jaffa, Israel, May 28, 43; US citizen; m 67; c 2. MATHEMATICS. *Educ:* Bethel Col (Kans), AB, 66; Lehigh Univ, MS, 69, PhD(math), 70. *Prof Exp:* Sr tech aide prog design, Bell Tel Labs, 66-67; res assoc, 70-71, asst prof, 70-75, ASSOC HEAD DEPT MATH, 77- & ASSOC PROF MATH, UNIV ARIZ, 75- *Mem:* Am Math Soc; Math Asn Am. *Res:* Algebra, specifically infinite abelian groups. *Mailing Add:* Dept of Math Univ of Ariz Tucson AZ 85721

TOUCHBERRY, ROBERT WALTON, b Manning, SC, Oct 27, 21; m 48; c 4. ANIMAL BREEDING. *Educ:* Clemson Col, BS, 45; Iowa State Col, MS, 47, PhD(animal breeding, genetics), 48. *Prof Exp:* Asst dairy sci, Univ Ill, Urbana, 48-49, asst prof dairy cattle genetics, 49-55, assoc prof genetics in dairy sci, 55-59, prof, 59-70; PROF ANIMAL SCI & HEAD DEPT, UNIV MINN, ST PAUL, 70- *Concurrent Pos:* Fulbright res fel, Denmark, 56-57; geneticist, Div Biol & Med, US AEC, 67-68. *Honors & Awards:* Animal Breeding & Genetics Award, Am Soc Animal Sci, 71. *Mem:* AAAS; Am Soc Human Genetics; Genetics Soc Am; Am Diary Sci Asn; Am Genetic Asn. *Res:* Population genetics; quantitative genetics; effects of crossbreeding on the growth and milk production of dairy cattle; effects of x-irradiation on quantitative traits of mice and fruit flies; statistical studies of animal records. *Mailing Add:* Dept of Animal Sci Univ of Minn St Paul MN 55101

TOUCHETTE, NORMAN WALTER, b East St Louis, Ill, Jan 2, 25; m 48. PLASTICS CHEMISTRY. *Educ:* Ill Col, AB, 48; Inst Textile Technol, MS, 50. *Prof Exp:* From chemist to chief chemist, Fulton Bag & Cotton Mills, Ga, 50-56; res chemist, 56-63, res group leader, 63-76, MGR PLASTICIZER APPL RES & MKT TECH SERV, MONSANTO CO, 76- *Mem:* Soc Plastics Eng. *Res:* Plasticizer application and polymer modification. *Mailing Add:* Monsanto Co 800 N Lindbergh Blvd St Louis MO 63167

TOUCHSTONE, JOSEPH CARY, b Soochow, China, Nov 27, 21; US citizen; m 55; c 3. ORGANIC CHEMISTRY, BIOCHEMISTRY. *Educ:* Stephen F Austin State Univ BS, 43; Purdue Univ, MS, 46, PhD(biochem), 53. *Prof Exp:* Asst, Purdue Univ, 43-45; res assoc, Univ Tex, Southwestern Med Sch, 46-49; res assoc med, 52-56, assoc, Pepper Lab Clin Chem, Univ Hosp, 52-56, asst res prof obstet & gynec & res assoc, Harrison Dept Surg Res, Univ, 56-63, res assoc prof, 63-67, assoc prof res surg, 63-68, RES PROF OBSTET & GYNEC, SCH MED, UNIV PA, 67-, DIR STEROID LAB & PROF RES SURG, 68- *Concurrent Pos:* NIH res career award, 61-71; pres & co-founder, Chromatog Forum, 66-67, pres, 71-72, exec comt, 66- *Mem:* Am Chem Soc; Endocrine Soc; Am Soc Biol Chemists; Am Asn Clin Chemists; Am Acad Forensic Sci. *Res:* Steroid chemistry; organic synthesis; isolation and metabolism of steroid hormones; chromatography; phenol chemistry; adrenal physiology; gas chromatography of steroids; thin layer and liquid chromatography. *Mailing Add:* Univ of Pa Hosp Philadelphia PA 19104

TOUCHTON, JOSEPH TERRY, soil fertility, crop management, see previous edition

TOUGER, JEROLD STEVEN, b Brooklyn, NY, Aug 6, 45; m 69; c 2. PHYSICS. *Educ:* Cornell Univ, BA, 66; City Univ New York, PhD(physics), 74. *Prof Exp:* From asst prof to assoc prof, 74-81, PROF PHYSICS, CURRY COL, 81- *Concurrent Pos:* Proj dir, NSF grant, 80-82. *Mem:* Am Asn Physics Teachers. *Res:* Thermoelectric power; transport properties in magnetic alloys; structural linguistics applied to scientific and mathematical discourses; curriculum development in physics, calculus and integrated science. *Mailing Add:* Div of Sci & Math Curry Col Milton MA 02186

TOUGH, JAMES THOMAS, b Chicago, Ill, May 4, 38; m 60; c 2. LOW TEMPERATURE PHYSICS. *Educ:* Univ Ill, BS, 60; Univ Wash, PhD(liquid helium), 64. *Prof Exp:* Res assoc low temperature physics, 64-65, asst prof, 65-68, assoc prof physics, 68-76, PROF PHYSICS, OHIO STATE UNIV, 68- *Mem:* Am Phys Soc. *Res:* Hydrodynamics and turbulence in liquid helium II. *Mailing Add:* 174 W 18th Ave Columbus OH 43210

TOUHILL, CHARLES JOSEPH, b Newark, NJ, Aug 27, 38; m 60; c 4. ENVIRONMENTAL ENGINEERING. *Educ:* Rensselaer Polytech Inst, BCE, 60, PhD(environ eng), 64; Mass Inst Technol, SM, 61; Univ Wash, dipl, 70; Am Acad Environ Engrs, dipl, 70. *Prof Exp:* With, Gen Elec Co, 64-65 & Battelle Pac Northwest Labs, 65-71; officer in consult firms, 71-77; PRES, TOUHILL, SHUCKROW & ASSOCS, INC, 77- *Concurrent Pos:* US deleg, Int Asn Water Pollution Res, 70-71 & 79-83; mem bd trustees, Am Acad Environ Engrs, 71-78; mem ed adv bd, Environ Sci & Technol, 75-77. *Mem:* Am Inst Chem Engrs; Am Chem Soc; Am Water Works Asn; Water Pollution Control Fedn. *Res:* Management of water, wastewater, solids and toxic and hazardous materials. *Mailing Add:* 2206 Almanack Ct Pittsburgh PA 15237

TOULMIN, PRIESTLEY, III, b Birmingham, Ala, June 5, 30; m 52; c 2. GEOLOGY. *Educ:* Harvard Univ, AB, 51, PhD(geol), 59; Univ Colo, MS, 53. *Prof Exp:* Geologist, 53-56, chief br exp geochem & mineral, 66-72, GEOLOGIST, US GEOL SURV, 58- *Concurrent Pos:* Lectr vis geol scientist prog, Am Geol Inst, 64; adj assoc prof, Columbia Univ, 66; scientist, Proj Viking, NASA, 68-81, team leader inorg chem invest, 72-81; ed J Translations, Am Geochem Soc, 65-68; assoc ed Am Mineralogist, J Mineral Soc Am, 74-76; res assoc geochem, Calif Inst Technol, 76-77. *Mem:* fel Mineral Soc Am; Geochem Soc; fel Geol Soc Am; Geochem Soc; Mineral Soc Great Britain. *Res:* Igneous and sulfide petrology; phase equilibria and thermochemistry of ore minerals; mineralogy and geochemistry of Mars. *Mailing Add:* Geol Div US Geol Surv 959 Nat Ctr Reston VA 22092

TOULOUKIAN, Y(ERAM) S(ARKIS), b Istanbul, Turkey, Dec 28, 20; nat US; m 48; c 2. MECHANICAL ENGINEERING. *Educ:* Robert Col, Istanbul, BS, 39; Mass Inst Technol, MS, 41; Purdue Univ, PhD(heat transfer), 46. *Prof Exp:* Asst, Mass Inst Technol, 41-43; asst mech eng, 44-47, from asst prof to prof, 47-67, DISTINGUISHED ATKINS PROF ENG, PURDUE UNIV, 67-, DIR CTR INFO & NUMERICAL DATA ANAL & SYNTHESIS, 57- *Concurrent Pos:* Vis prof, Auburn Univ; mem bd dirs, OEA, Inc, Ill; consult; mem off critical tables, Nat Acad Sci-Nat Res Coun, 58-70; mem panel info ctrs mgrs, Engrs Joint Coun, 64-65; chmn, Gordon Res Conf on Critical Table, 66. *Honors & Awards:* Ital Soc Heat Engrs Gold Medal, Am Soc Mech Engrs. *Mem:* AAAS; assoc fel Am Inst Aeronaut & Astronaut; Am Soc Info Sci; fel Am Soc Mech Engrs. *Res:* Heat transfer; convection; conduction; radiation; thermophysics; information science. *Mailing Add:* CINDAS Purdue Univ Res Pk 2595 Yeager Rd West Lafayette IN 47906

TOUPIN, RICHARD A, b Miami, Fla, Aug 20, 26; m 50; c 3. MATHEMATICAL PHYSICS, CONTINUUM MECHANICS. *Educ:* Univ SC, BS, 46; Univ Hawaii, MS, 49; Syracuse Univ, PhD(physics), 61. *Prof Exp:* Instr physics, Univ Hawaii, 49-50; res asst theoret mech, US Naval Res Lab, 50-62; res asst appl math, res ctr, 62-74, dir math sci, 74-81, MEM STAFF SCI/ENG COMPUT, IBM SCI CTR, HEIDELBERG, 82- *Mem:* Am Math Soc; Soc Natural Philos (secy, 65-67). *Res:* Elasticity and electromagnetic theories; relativity mechanics; dielectrics; differential geometry. *Mailing Add:* IBM Res Ctr Yorktown Heights NY 10598

TOURGEE, RONALD ALAN, b Wakefield, RI, May 2, 38; c 3. MATHEMATICAL STATISTICS. *Educ:* Univ RI, BS, 60, MS, 62; Univ SFla, PhD(math), 75. *Prof Exp:* Teacher math, Keene State Col, 64-66 & Mt Holyoke Col, 66-68; TEACHER MATH, KEENE STATE COL, 68- *Mem:* Am Math Soc; Am Statist Asn. *Res:* Stochastic systems; mathematical statistics; applied probability. *Mailing Add:* Dept of Math Keene State Col Keene NH 03431

TOURIAN, ARA YERVANT, b Jerusalem, May 19, 33; US citizen; m 59; c 3. BIOCHEMICAL GENETICS. *Educ:* Am Univ Beirut, BS, 55; Iowa State Univ, MD, 58. *Prof Exp:* Intern med, Washington Hosp Ctr, DC, 58-59; resident neurol, NY Univ Med Ctr, 62-63, chief resident, 64-65; instr & fel biophys & neurol, Med Ctr, Univ Colo, 65-69; ASSOC PROF MED, MED CTR, DUKE UNIV, 69- *Concurrent Pos:* NIH res career develop award, Med Ctr, Duke Univ; vis scientist cell biol, Dept Zool, Cambridge Univ, 75-76. *Mem:* AAAS; Am Soc Neurochem; Am Acad Neurol; Cambridge Philos Soc; NY Acad Sci. *Res:* Biochemical genetics of Huntington's chorea, tissue culture/protein glycosylation and the control of hexosawine metabolism; metabolic and genetic control mechanisms of phenylalanine hydorxylase. *Mailing Add:* Duke Univ Med Ctr M3066 Durham NC 27710

TOURIGNY, GUY J, b Ponteix, Sask, Aug 22, 36; m 60; c 4. ORGANIC CHEMISTRY. *Educ:* Univ Ottawa, BA, 55; Univ Alta, BSc, 62, PhD(chem), 67. *Prof Exp:* Res assoc, Univ Ill, Urbana, 67-68; asst prof, 68-74, ASSOC PROF CHEM & CHEM ENG, UNIV SASK, 74- *Mem:* Chem Inst Can. *Res:* Mechanism of reactions; synthesis of nucleosides as antiviral agents; stereochemistry. *Mailing Add:* Dept Chem & Chem Eng Univ Sask Saskatoon SK S7N 0W0 Can

TOURIN, RICHARD HAROLD, b New York, NY, Dec 4, 22; m 48; c 2. ENERGY CONVERSION, ENERGY CONSERVATION. *Educ:* City Col New York, BS, 47; NY Univ, MS, 48. *Prof Exp:* Res physicist, Control Instrument Div, Warner & Swasey Co, 48-51, chief physicist, 51-59, mgr res lab, 59-63, div mgr, 63-71; dir mkt, Klinger Sci Apparatus Corp, 71-73; dir new prog develop, NY State Energy Res & Develop Authority, 73-78; mgr indust mktg, Stone & Webster Eng Corp, 78-81; DIR DEVELOP, SYSKA & HENNESSY, INC, 81- *Concurrent Pos:* Adj instr, Cooper Union, 55-60; US mem joint comt, Int Flame Res Found, 66-68; mem energy res adv comt, Stevens Inst Technol, 75-77. *Mem:* Fel Optical Soc Am; Am Phys Soc; Combustion Inst; AAAS; NY Acad Sci. *Res:* Energy conversion and spectroscopic gas temperature measurement; optical physics; remote sensing of environment; combined heat and power generation; rapid-scan spectroscopy; infrared spectra of hot gases. *Mailing Add:* 195-10A 67th Ave Flushing NY 11365

TOURING, ROSCOE MANVILLE, b Winnipeg, Man, June 30, 24; m 52; c 4. GEOLOGY. *Educ:* Univ Man, BS, 45; Stanford Univ, MS, 51, PhD(geol), 59. *Prof Exp:* Geologist, Int Petrol Co, Ecuador, Colombia & Peru, 46-50; geologist, Humble Oil & Ref Co, Calif & Ore, 52-64, res assoc, Esso Prod Res Co, Tex, 64-66, explor mgr, Minerals Dept, Exxon Co USA, 66-67, mgr stratig geol div, 67-69, mgr non-hydrocarbon minerals study group, Standard Oil Co NJ, NY, 69-71, sr geol scientist, Minerals Dept, 72-80. *Mem:* AAAs; Geol Soc Am; Am Asn Petrol Geol. *Res:* Adviser minerals exploration program. *Mailing Add:* 13936 Perthshire Dr Houston TX 77079

TOURNEY, GARFIELD, b Quincy, Ill, Feb 6, 27; m 50; c 3. PSYCHIATRY. *Educ:* Univ Ill, BS, 46, MD, 48; State Univ Iowa, MS, 52. *Prof Exp:* Asst prof psychiat, Sch Med, Univ Miami, 54-55; from asst prof to prof, Sch Med, Wayne State Univ, 55-67; prof, Univ Iowa, 67-71; co-chmn dept, 71-73, prof psychiat, sch med, Wayne State Univ, 71-78, chmn dept, 73-78; PROF PSYCHIAT, SCH MED, UNIV MISS, 78-, VCHMN DEPT, 81- *Concurrent Pos:* Assoc examr, Am Bd Psychiat & Neurol, 67- *Mem:* Fel Am Psychiat Asn; fel Am Col Psychiat. *Res:* Biochemical and clinical studies of schizophrenia and depressive illnesses; history of psychiatry. *Mailing Add:* Dept of Psychiat Univ of Miss Med Ctr Jackson MS 39216

TOURTELLOTTE, CHARLES DEE, b Kalamazoo, Mich, Aug 28, 31; m 55; c 4. INTERNAL MEDICINE, BIOCHEMISTRY. *Educ:* Johns Hopkins Univ, AB, 53; Temple Univ, MS & MD, 57; Am Bd Internal Med, dipl. *Prof Exp:* Intern med, Univ Mich, 57-58, resident & jr clin instr, 58-60; instr med & biochem, 63-65, from asst prof to assoc prof, 65-72, res asst prof biochem, 65-71, actg chief sect rheumatol, 66-67, PROF MED, SCH MED, TEMPLE UNIV, 72-, CHIEF SECT RHEUMATOL, SCH MED & UNIV HOSP, 67- *Concurrent Pos:* USPHS trainee rheumatol, Temple Univ, 60-61; Helen Hay Whitney Found fel biochem, Rockefeller Univ, 61-63; Arthritis Found fel, 63-66; mem, Gov Bd, Arthritis Found; consult, Vet Admin Hosp, Wilmington, Del, St Christopher's Hosp Children, Philadelphia, E I Du Pont de Nemours & Co, Inc. *Mem:* Fel Am Col Physicians; Am Rheumatism Asn; Am Fedn Clin Res. *Res:* Biochemistry and physiology of connective tissue; endochondral ossification; amino acid metabolism; histidine; heritable disorders of bone and connective tissues; rheumatic diseases; medical education. *Mailing Add:* Sect of Rheumatol Temple Univ Sch of Med Philadelphia PA 19140

TOURTELLOTTE, MARK ETON, b Worcester, Mass, Oct 25, 28; m 53; c 3. BIOCHEMISTRY. *Educ:* Dartmouth Col, BA, 50; Univ Conn, MS, 53, PhD(microbiol), 60. *Prof Exp:* From asst instr to instr bact, Univ Conn, 53-60; res assoc biophys, Yale Univ, 60-62; assoc prof, 63-67, PROF ANIMAL PATH, UNIV CONN, 67- *Mem:* AAAS; Am Soc Microbiol; Am Asn Avian Path; fel Am Inst Chem; NY Acad Sci. *Res:* Immunology; diagnostic bacteriology; lipids; chemistry and biosynthesis in mycoplasma; structure and function of biomembranes. *Mailing Add:* Dept of Pathbiol Univ of Conn Storrs CT 06268

TOURTELLOTTE, WALLACE WILLIAM, b Great Falls, Mont, Sept 13, 24; m 53; c 4. NEUROLOGY. *Educ:* Univ Chicago, PhB & BS, 45, PhD(biochem neuropharmacol), 48, MD, 51; Am Bd Psychiat & Neurol, dipl, 60. *Prof Exp:* Res assoc & instr pharmacol, Univ Chicago, 48-51; intern med, Sch Med, Univ Rochester, 51-52; resident neurol, Med Sch, Univ Mich, 54-57; from asst prof to prof, 57-71; PROF NEUROL & VCHMN DEPT, UNIV CALIF, LOS ANGELES, 71-; CHIEF NEUROL SERV & DIR, NEUROL TRAINING PROG, VET ADMIN WADSWORTH MED CTR, LOS ANGELES, 71-; DIR, NAT NEUROL RES BANK, 71- *Concurrent Pos:* Consult, Vet Admin Hosp, Ann Arbor, Mich, 58-71; chief neurol serv, Wayne County Gen Hosp, Detroit, 59-71; mem, Multiple Sclerosis Res Comt, Int Comn Correlation Neurol & Neurochem, World Fedn Neurol, 59-; vis assoc prof, Washington Univ, 63-64; asst examr, Am Bd Psychiat & Neurol, 64-; mem, Med Adv Bd, Nat Multiple Sclerosis Soc, 68-; exchange biomed investr, Vet Admin-Fr Nat Inst Health & Med Res, Paris, 72; mem, Cerebrospinal Fluid & Immunol Comns, World Fedn Neurol. *Honors & Awards:* Mitchell Award, Am Acad Neurol, 59- *Mem:* AAAS; Am Neurol Asn; Am Soc Pharmacol & Exp Therapeut; Asn Res Nerv & Ment Dis; Am Acad Neurol. *Res:* Organic neurology and neurochemical correlations in multiple sclerosis patients; cause and treatment of multiple sclerosis. *Mailing Add:* Neurol Serv Vet Admin Wadsworth Hosp Ctr Los Angeles CA 90073

TOURTELOT, HARRY ALLISON, b Lincoln, Nebr, June 15, 18; m 40, 65, 77; c 6. GEOLOGY. *Educ:* Univ Nebr, AB, 40. *Prof Exp:* Proj technician, State Geol Surv, Ala, 40-42; GEOLOGIST, US GEOL SURV, 42- *Mem:* Fel Geol Soc Am; Geochem Soc; Soc Econ Paleont & Mineral; Clay Minerals Soc; Am Asn Petrol Geol. *Res:* Stratigraphy of continental tertiary rocks; geologic structure of Central Wyoming; geochemistry of sedimentary rocks; petrology of shale; environmental geochemistry; geochemistry and health. *Mailing Add:* US Geol Surv Fed Ctr Denver CO 80225

TOURYAN, KENELL JAMES, b Beirut, Lebanon, Dec 2, 36; US citizen; m 63; c 3. SOLAR ENERGY TECHNOLOGIES. *Educ:* Univ Southern Calif, BS, 58, MS, 59; Princeton Univ, MA, 60, PhD(aerospace), 62. *Prof Exp:* Supvr reentry studies, Sandia Labs, 65-68, mgr, Aerothermodynamics Res, 68-75, mgr, Fluid & Plasmadynamics, 75-77, mgr, Fluid & Thermal Sci, 77-78; assoc dir res, Solar Energy Res Inst, 78-80, dep dir, 80-81; SR VPRES, RES & TECHNOL, FLOW INDUST, 81- *Concurrent Pos:* Adj prof, Dept Nuclear Eng, Univ NMex, 66-72; assoc ed, Am Inst Aeronaut & Astronaut J, 75-78, J Energy, 78-; high level expert, Panel UN & World Bank Renewable Energy Utilizaiton, 82- *Mem:* Am Inst Aeronaut & Astronaut; Am Phys Soc; AAAS; fel Am Sci Afflil. *Res:* Fluid dynamics; plasmadynamics; solar and renewable energy. *Mailing Add:* Flow Industries 21414 68th Ave S Kent WA 98031

TOUSEY, RICHARD, b Somerville, Mass, May 18, 08; m 32; c 1. PHYSICS. *Educ:* Tufts Univ, AB, 28; Harvard Univ, AM, 29, PhD(physics), 33. *Hon Degrees:* ScD, Tufts Univ, 62. *Prof Exp:* Instr physics, Harvard Univ, 33-36, tutor, 34-36, Cutting fel, 35-36; res instr, Tufts Univ, 36-41; head, Instrument Sect, 42-45, head, Micron Waves Br, 45-48, head, Rocket Spectros Br, 58-78, PHYSICIST, US NAVAL RES LAB, 41- *Concurrent Pos:* Darwin lectr, Royal Astron Soc, 63; Russell lectr, Am Astron Soc, 66; mem comt vision, Armed Forces-Nat Res Coun. *Honors & Awards:* Hulburt Award, 48; Medal, Photog Soc Am, 59; Ives Medal, Optical Soc Am, 60; Prix Ancel, Photog Soc France, 62; Draper Medal, Nat Acad Sci, 63; Distinguished Achievement Award, US Navy, 63; Eddington Medal, Royal Astron Soc, 64; Except Sci Achievement Medal, NASA, 74. *Mem:* Nat Acad Sci; fel Am Phys Soc; fel Optical Soc Am; Am Astron Soc (vpres,64-66); fel Am Acad Arts & Sci. *Res:* Optical properties of the atmospheres; spectroscopy from rockets; physiological optics; photographic photometry; vacuum ultraviolet. *Mailing Add:* Code 7140 US Naval Res Lab Washington DC 20375

TOUSIGNAUT, DWIGHT R, b Ironwood, Mich, Dec 4, 33; m 64; c 3. PHARMACY. *Educ:* Univ Mich, BS, 59; Univ Calif, Pharm D, 61. *Prof Exp:* Residency hosp pharm, San Francisco Med Ctr, Univ Calif, 59-61; pharmacist, Queen Elizabeth Hosp & Royal Perth Hosp, Australia, 62-63; pharmacist, Stanford Med Ctr, 63-64; Fulbright prof hosp pharm, Cairo, 64-66; dir dept prof pract, 66-72, ed int, Parmaceut Abstracts, 66-80, assoc dir bur communs & publs, 72-81, VPRES, AM SOC HOSP PHARMACISTS, 82-, DIR DIV DATA BASE SERV, 82- *Concurrent Pos:* Past mem nomenclature adv comt, Nat Libr Med. *Honors & Awards:* Bristol Award, 59. *Mem:* Am Pharmaceut Asn; Am Soc Hosp Pharmacists; Drug Info Asn (vpres, 73-74, pres, 77-80); Fedn Int Pharm. *Res:* Drug information processing and searching; pharmacy education and practice standards; drug absorption from implanted or injected routes of administration; griseofulvin solubility studies; plastic drug sorption studies. *Mailing Add:* Am Soc of Hosp Pharmacists 4630 Montgomery Ave Bethesda MD 20814

TOUSSIENG, POVL WINNING, b Nysted, Denmark, Sept 5, 18; US citizen. PSYCHIATRY. *Educ:* Copenhagen Univ, MD, 45. *Prof Exp:* Resident gen psychiat, Menninger Sch Psychiat, 50-53, John Harper Seeley fel child psychiat, Children's Div, Menninger Clin, 53-55, staff psychiatrist, 55-65; assoc prof child psychiat & pediat, 65-69, PROF CHILD PSYCHIAT, HEALTH SCI CTR, COL MED, UNIV OKLA, 69- *Concurrent Pos:* Consult, Kans Indust Sch Boys, 53-61; mem fac, Menninger Sch Psychiat, 53-65; consult, Kans Neurol Inst, 64-65, Minn Dept Ment Health, Minneapolis, 65-66 & Spec Subcomt Indian Educ, US Senate Comt Labor & Pub Welfare, 69; mem, Nat Drafting Comt Juv Studies Proj, 73-; mem bd, Psychiat Outpatients Ctr Am, 73- *Mem:* Fel Am Psychiat Asn; fel Am Orthopsychiat Asn; Soc Res Child Develop. *Res:* Childhood autism; coping devices of normal and disturbed children; various modalities of psychotherapy; adolescent experience in changing times; delinquency; adoption; delivery systems of help. *Mailing Add:* Dept of Psychiat Univ of Okla Col of Med Oklahoma City OK 73104

TOUSTER, OSCAR, b New York, NY, July 3, 21; m 44; c 1. MOLECULAR BIOLOGY, BIOCHEMISTRY. *Educ:* City Col New York, BS, 41; Oberlin Col, MA, 42; Univ Ill, Urbana, PhD(biochem), 47. *Prof Exp:* Chemist, Atlas Powder Co, 42-43; res biochemist, Abbott Labs, 44-45; from instr to assoc prof biochem, 47-58, PROF BIOCHEM, VANDERBILT UNIV, 58-, PROF MOLECULAR BIOL, 73-, CHMN DEPT MOLECULAR BIOL, 63- *Concurrent Pos:* Guggenheim fel, Oxford Univ, 57-58; H Hughes investr, Vanderbilt Univ & Oxford Univ, 57-60; consult, NIH, 61-70; mem, Subcomt Metab Intermediates, Nat Res Coun, 66-76; mem, Bd Dirs, Oak Ridge Assoc Univs, 73-, vpres, 74-76, pres, 76-; mem, Sci Adv Bd, Eunice Kennedy Shriver Ctr Ment Retardation, Waltham, Mass, 74- *Honors & Awards:* Theobald Smith Award Med Sci, AAAS, 56. *Mem:* Fel AAAS; Am Soc Biol Chemists; Biochem Soc; Am Inst Biol Sci; Am Chem Soc. *Res:* Lysosome biochemistry; membrane enzymes; carbohydrate metabolism; beta-glucuronidase chemistry and action; liver glycosidases. *Mailing Add:* Dept of Molecular Biol Vanderbilt Univ Nashville TN 37235

TOUTENHOOFD, VIM, atmospheric physics, see previous edition

TOVE, SAMUEL B, b Baltimore, Md, July 29, 21; m 45; c 3. BIOCHEMISTRY, NUTRITION. *Educ:* Cornell Univ, BS, 43; Univ Wis, MS, 48, PhD(biochem), 50. *Prof Exp:* Asst, Univ Wis, 46-50; from asst res prof to assoc res prof animal sci, 50-60, PROF BIOCHEM, NC STATE UNIV, 60-, HEAD DEPT, 75- *Concurrent Pos:* William Neal Reynolds prof biochem, NC State Univ, 75. *Mem:* AAAS; Am Chem Soc; Soc Exp Biol & Med; Am Inst Nutrit; Am Soc Biol Chemists. *Res:* Lipid and intermediary metabolism. *Mailing Add:* Dept Biochem NC State Univ Raleigh NC 27607

TOVE, SHIRLEY RUTH, b New York, NY, Jan 31, 25; m 45; c 3. BACTERIOLOGY, BIOCHEMISTRY. *Educ:* Cornell Univ, BS, 45; Univ Wis, MS, 48, PhD(bact, biochem), 50. *Prof Exp:* Instr chem, NC State Univ, 50-51, bact, 51-52; vis teacher biol, NC Col Durham, 64-65; assoc prof, Shaw Univ, 65-72, chmn dept, 65-75, consult planning, Div Natural Sci & Math, 65, prof biol, 72-77; ASSOC CHIEF, BIOL SCI PROG, CHEM & BIOL SCI DIV, US ARMY RES OFF, 76- *Mem:* Am Soc Microbiol. *Res:* Biochemistry of nitrogen fixation. *Mailing Add:* US Army Res Off PO Box 12211 Research Triangle Park NC 27709

TOVELL, WALTER MASSEY, b Toronto, Ont, June 25, 16; m 72. GEOLOGY. *Educ:* Univ Toronto, BA, 40, PhD, 54; Calif Inst Technol, MS, 42. *Prof Exp:* Geologist, Calif Standard Co, 42-46; lectr geol, Univ Toronto, 49-50, assoc prof, Univ & Col Educ, 59-64; mus asst, Royal Ont Mus, 46-48, cur geol dept, 48-72, assoc dir, 71-73, dir pro tem, 72-73, dir, 73-77; ASSOC PROF GEOL, UNIV TORONTO, 64- *Concurrent Pos:* Asst prof geol, Univ Toronto, 62-64; mem & vchmn info & educ comt, Met Toronto & Region Conserv Authority, 68-74, chmn, 75- *Mem:* Fel Geol Asn Can (secy-treas, 60-62); Mus Dirs Asn Can. *Res:* Stratigraphy and Pleistocene geology; research on geology history of Great Lakes with special emphasis on Georgian Bay. *Mailing Add:* Dept Geol Univ Toronto Toronto ON M5B 1A1 Can

TOVERUD, SVEIN UTHEIM, b Oslo, Norway, Dec 14, 29; m 54; c 3. PHARMACOLOGY, ENDOCRINOLOGY. *Educ:* Harvard Univ, DMD, 54; Norweg State Dent Sch, Cand Odont, 56; Univ Oslo, PhD, 64. *Prof Exp:* Instr physiol, Univ Oslo, 62-63, res assoc, 63-64, from asst prof to assoc prof, 65-70; assoc prof pharmacol, Sch Med, & oral biol, Sch Dent, 69-76, PROF PHARMACOL, SCH MED, UNIV NC, CHAPEL HILL, 76-, PROF ORAL BIOL, SCH DENT, 76- *Concurrent Pos:* Res fel physiol & biochem, Univ Oslo, 56-62; USPHS int fel, Sch Dent Med, Harvard Univ, 64-66. *Mem:* Fel AAAS; US Endocrine Soc; Am Soc Pharmacol & Exp Therapeut; Int Asn Dent Res; Am Soc Bone Mineral Res. *Res:* Hormonal regulation of calcium metabolism; influence of nutrition and drugs, especially vitamins and hormones on mineralizing tissues. *Mailing Add:* Dent Res Ctr Univ of NC Chapel Hill NC 27514

TOW, JAMES, b Canton, China, June 25, 36; US citizen; m 68; c 1. ELECTRICAL ENGINEERING. *Educ:* Univ Calif, Berkeley, BS, 60, MS, 62, PhD(elec eng), 66. *Prof Exp:* MEM TECH STAFF, BELL TEL LABS, 66- *Mem:* Inst Elec & Electronics Engrs. *Res:* Computer aided network and circuit analysis and design; active filter realization; digital signal processing; microprocessor applications. *Mailing Add:* Bell Tel Labs Holmdel NJ 07733

TOWBIN, EUGENE JONAS, b New York, NY, Sept 18, 18; m 49; c 4. INTERNAL MEDICINE, PHYSIOLOGY. *Educ:* NY Univ, BA, 41; Univ Colo, MS, 42; Univ Rochester, MD & PhD(physiol), 49. *Prof Exp:* Asst psychol, Univ Rochester, 42-44, asst physiol, 44-47, intern med, Duke Univ, 49-50, resident, 50-52, clin asst prof med, 55-56, from asst prof med to asst prof physiol, 56-65, from assoc prof med to assoc prof physiol, 62-69, assoc dean Sch Med, 68-78, PROF MED & PHYSIOL, SCH MED, UNIV ARK, LITTLE ROCK, 69- CHIEF OF STAFF, VET ADMIN HOSP, 68- *Concurrent Pos:* Fel cardiol, Duke Univ, 52; ward physician, Vet Admin Hosp, 55-58, exec secy & mem res comt, 56-58, asst dir prof serv for res & educ, 58-61, assoc chief of staff for res & educ, 61-72. *Mem:* Am Fedn Clin Res; Geront Soc; Am Col Physicians; Am Physiol Soc; Soc Exp Biol & Med. *Res:* Water and electrolyte metabolism; physiological regulation of thirst and hunger. *Mailing Add:* 300 E Roosevelt Rd Va Med Ctr (11) Little Rock AR 72206

TOWE, ARNOLD LESTER, b Patterson, Calif, July 25, 27; wid. PHYSIOLOGY, BIOPHYSICS. *Educ:* Pac Lutheran Col, BA, 48; Univ Wash, PhD(psychol, physiol), 53. *Prof Exp:* Res assoc, 53-54, from instr to asst prof anat & physiol, 54-58, from asst prof to assoc prof physiol & biophys, 58-65, PROF PHYSIOL & BIOPHYS, SCH MED, UNIV WASH, 65- *Concurrent Pos:* Mem, NIH Study Sect, 66-70, 78- *Res:* Neurophysiology, particularly analysis of sensory and motor systems, including gross potentials and single unit activity; cortical physiology. *Mailing Add:* Dept of Physiol & Biophys Univ of Wash Sch of Med Seattle WA 98195

TOWE, GEORGE COFFIN, b Passaic, NJ, Nov 28, 21; m 47; c 1. PHYSICS, SCIENCE EDUCATION. *Educ:* Hamilton Col (NY), BS, 43; Univ Mich, MS, 47, PhD(chem), 54. *Prof Exp:* Physicist, US Naval Ord Lab, 43-45; res assoc, Eng Res Inst, Univ Mich, 46-53; res engr, Sci Lab, Ford Motor Co, 53-55; from asst prof to assoc prof physics, Mont State Col, 55-61; prof physics, head dept & chmn div natural sci, Findlay Col, 61-62; assoc prof physics, 62-65, chmn dept, 65-72, chmn, Div Spec Progs, 74-77, PROF PHYSICS, ALFRED UNIV, 65- *Concurrent Pos:* Lectr, Univ Wyo, 59; vis scientist, Atomic Energy Res Estab, Eng, 67-68; consult, Oak Ridge Inst Nuclear Studies, 66-72 & consult educ, Australian Univs, 77-78. *Mem:* Am Asn Physics Teachers. *Res:* Radioactivity; radiation; solid state diffusion; nuclear activation analysis. *Mailing Add:* 5573 Jericho Hill Rd Alfred Station NY 14803

TOWE, KENNETH MCCARN, b Jacksonville, Fla, Jan 31, 35. GEOLOGY, ELECTRON MICROSCOPY. *Educ:* Duke Univ, AB, 56; Brown Univ, MSc, 59; Univ Ill, PhD(geol), 61. *Prof Exp:* Res assoc electron micros, Univ Ill, 61-62; Ford Found res fel geol, Calif Inst Technol, 62-64; GEOLOGIST-ELECTRON MICROSCOPIST, DEPT PALEOBIOL, SMITHSONIAN INST, 64- *Concurrent Pos:* Vis prof Geol-Paleont Inst, Univ Tubingen, 73; assoc ed Am Mineralogist, 76-81; judge, AAAS-Westinghouse Sci Jour Awards, 77-; ed, J Foraminiferal Res, 81- *Mem:* AAAS; fel Geol Soc Am; Clay Minerals Soc (treas, 81-); fel Mineral Soc Am; Int Asn Study Clays. *Res:* Biomineralogy; clay mineralogy; application of electron microscopy to geology and paleontology. *Mailing Add:* Dept of Paleobiol Smithsonian Inst Washington DC 20560

TOWELL, DAVID GARRETT, b Fillmore, NY, May 30, 37; m 60; c 2. GEOCHEMISTRY. *Educ:* Pa State Univ, BS, 59; Mass Inst Technol, PhD(geochem), 63. *Prof Exp:* Res fel geochem, Calif Inst Technol, 63-64; asst prof, 64-68, ASSOC PROF GEOCHEM, IND UNIV BLOOMINGTON, 68- *Mem:* Geochem Soc; Geol Soc Am; Mineral Soc Am. *Res:* General inorganic, rare-earth, trace element and isotope geochemistry; electron-probe microanalysis of minerals and rocks; chemical thermodynamics; phase equilibria; radiochemistry; radioactivation analysis; radiotracer studies. *Mailing Add:* Dept of Geol Ind Univ Bloomington IN 47401

TOWER, DONALD BAYLEY, b Orange, NJ, Dec 11, 19; m 47; c 1. RESEARCH ADMINISTRATION. *Educ:* Harvard Univ, AB, 41, MD, 44; McGill Univ, MSc, 48, PhD(exp neurol), 51. *Prof Exp:* Intern surg, Univ Minn Hosps, 44-45; asst resident neurosurg, Montreal Neurol Inst, McGill Univ, 48-49, assoc neurochemist, 51-53, lectr exp neurol, Fac Med, Univ, 51-52, asst prof, 52-53; chief, Sect Clin Neurochem, 53-60, chief, Lab Neurochem, 61-73, dir, 73-81, EMER DIR, NAT INST NEUROL & COMMUN DIS & STROKE, 81-; asst surgeon gen, US Pub Health Serv, 75-81; RETIRED. *Concurrent Pos:* Res fel neurochem, Montreal Neurol Inst, McGill Univ, 47-51; Markle scholar med sci, 51-53; clin clerk, Nat Hosp, London, Eng, 51; assoc prof, Sch Med & consult, Georgetown Univ, 53-81; mem, Neurol Study Sect, Div Res Grants, NIH, 54-61; mem, US Bd Civil Serv Exam, 61-67; chmn, Neurochem Deleg to USSR, US-USSR Exchange Prog Health & Med Sci, 69; mem, Basic Res Task Force, Adv Comt Epilepsies, USPHS, 69-73; chief ed, J Neurochem, 69-73; mem, Neurochem Panel, Int Brain Res Orgn, mem, Cent Coun, 74-82; temp adv neurosci, World Health Orgn, 76- *Mem:* Am Acad Neurol; Am Neurol Asn; Am Soc Biol Chemists; Int Soc Neurochem; Am Soc Neurochem (treas, 70-75). *Res:* Neurochemistry of epilepsy; cerebral amino acids and electrolytes; history of neurochemistry; neural proteins; amino acids and electrolytes; history of neurochemistry. *Mailing Add:* 7105 Brennon Lane Chevy Chase MD 20815

TOWER, MICHAEL MCKENZIE, aerospace engineering, see previous edition

TOWERS, BARRY, b Toledo, Ohio, July 20, 38; m 63. FOREST PATHOLOGY, MYCOLOGY. *Educ:* Thiel Col, BA, 61; Duke Univ, MF, 61, DF(forest path), 65. *Prof Exp:* Res asst forest path, Duke Univ & Southern Forest Dis & Insect Res Coun, 62; fel phytotoxic air pollutants, Sch Pub Health, Univ NC, Chapel Hill, 65-68; FOREST PATHOLOGIST, DIV FOREST PEST MGT, PA DEPT ENVIRON RESOURCES, 68- *Mem:* AAAS; Am Phytopath Soc; Soc Am Foresters; Sigma Xi; Int Soc Arboriculture. *Res:* Diseases of forest trees and coniferous plantations, particularly root rot diseases; phytotoxicity of air pollutants. *Mailing Add:* Div of Forest Pest Mgt 34 Airport Dr HIA Middletown PA 17057

TOWERS, BERNARD, b Preston, Eng, Aug 20, 22; c 4. PEDIATRICS, ANATOMY. *Educ:* Univ Liverpool, MB, ChB, 47; Cambridge Univ, MA, 54; Royal Col Physicians, Licentiate, 47. *Prof Exp:* House surgeon, Royal Infirmary, Liverpool, 47; asst lectr anat, Bristol Univ, 49-50; lectr anat & histol, Univ Wales, 50-54; lectr anat, Cambridge Univ, 54-70, dir med studies, 64-70; PROF PEDIAT & ANAT, SCH MED, UNIV CALIF, LOS ANGELES, 71-, CO-DIR, PROG MED, LAW & HUMAN VALUES, 77- *Concurrent Pos:* Fel med, Jesus Col, Cambridge Univ, 57-70; ed, Brit Abstr Med Sci, 54-56; chmn, Teilhard Ctr Future Man, London, 66-69; consult, Inst Human Values in Med, 71- *Mem:* Anat Soc Gt Brit & Ireland; Soc Health & Human Values (pres, 77-78); Am Asn Anatomists; fel Royal Soc Med; Brit Soc Hist Med. *Res:* Fetal and neonatal lung; development of the heart and congenital anomalies; early detection of myocardial ischemia; primate evolution, especially human; medical humanities; medical history. *Mailing Add:* Dept Pediat UCLA Ctr Health Sci Los Angeles CA 90024

TOWERS, GEORGE HUGH NEIL, b Bombay, India, Sept 28, 23; div; c 5. PHYTOCHEMISTRY, PHOTOBIOLOGY. *Educ:* McGill Univ, BSc, 50, MSc, 51; Cornell Univ, PhD, 54. *Prof Exp:* From asst prof to assoc prof bot, McGill Univ, 53-62; sr res officer, Nat Res Coun Can, 62-64; head dept, 64-70, PROF BOT, UNIV BC, 70- *Honors & Awards:* Lalor Found Award, 55. *Mem:* Fel Royal Soc Can; Can Soc Plant Physiol (pres, 65-66); Phytochem Soc NAm. *Res:* Photosensitizers and other biologically active chemicals from plants, fungi and invertebrates. *Mailing Add:* Dept of Bot Univ of BC Vancouver BC V6T 1W5 Can

TOWILL, LESLIE RUTH, b Milwaukee, Wis, Nov 19, 44. PLANT PHYSIOLOGY, PHOTOBIOLOGY. *Educ:* Univ Wis-Milwaukee, BS, 66, MS, 68; Univ Mich, Ann Arbor, PhD(bot), 73. *Prof Exp:* Sr fel biochem, Univ Wash, 73-75; ASST PROF BOT, ARIZ STATE UNIV, 75- *Concurrent Pos:* Prin investr, NSF grant, 77-79. *Mem:* Am Soc Plant Physiologists; Am Soc Photobiol; Bot Soc Am. *Res:* Mechanism of light action on initial biochemical events in plant development. *Mailing Add:* Dept of Bot & Microbiol Ariz State Univ Tempe AZ 85281

TOWLE, ALBERT, b Stockton, Calif, May 10, 25; m 46; c 3. INVERTEBRATE PHYSIOLOGY, SCIENCE EDUCATION. *Educ:* Col of Pac, AB, 46; San Jose State Col, MA, 53; Stanford Univ, PhD(biol), 62. *Prof Exp:* Chmn dept math & sci, James Lick High Sch, Calif, 50, chmn dept sci, 51, teacher biol, physiol & chem, 53-57 & 58-59, chmn dept sci, 61-64 & 65-66; asst biol, Stanford Univ, 57-58; lectr biol, 64-65, chmn dept marine biol, 72-75, PROF BIOL CALIF STATE UNIV, SAN FRANCISCO, 66- *Concurrent Pos:* Lectr, NSF partic, San Jose State Col, 60 & Purdue Univ, 65, partic, NSF Social Psychol Workshop & Conf for Dirs, DC, 68, dir, NSF-Nat Asn Sec Sch Prin Inst Sec Sch Adminr, 68; Nat Sch Teachers Asn Res Antarctica, 70; Smithsonian sponsored attendance and presentation of paper on Sipunculida, Yugoslavia, 70; res in the Galapagos, 74-75. *Mem:* AAAS; Am Inst Biol Sci; Nat Asn Biol Teachers; Nat Sci Teachers Asn. *Res:* Teaching of high school biology; behavior and ecology of terrestrial isopods; reproductive physiology of marine invertebrates; distribution of Sipunculida in the Galapagos Archepelago. *Mailing Add:* Dept Marine Biol Sch Natural Sci Calif State Univ San Francisco CA 94132

TOWLE, DAVID WALTER, b Concord, NH, May 26, 41; m 74; c 3. ESTUARINE PHYSIOLOGY, MEMBRANE BIOLOGY. *Educ:* Univ NH, BS, 65, MS, 67; Dartmouth Col, PhD(biol sci), 71. *Prof Exp:* Asst prof, 70-75, ASSOC PROF BIOL, UNIV RICHMOND, 75- *Mem:* Am Physiol Soc; Sigma Xi; Am Soc Zoologists. *Res:* Biochemistry and physiology of osmoregulation in marine and estuarine organisms; Polarity of epithelial cell function; fractionation and characterization of epithelial cell plasma membranes. *Mailing Add:* Dept of Biol Univ of Richmond Richmond VA 23173

TOWLE, HOWARD COLGATE, b Philadelphia, Pa, June 15, 47; m 76; c 2. BIOCHEMISTRY. *Educ:* Mich State Univ, BA, 69, PhD(biochem), 74. *Prof Exp:* Fel cell biol, Baylor Col Med, 74-76; asst prof med, 77-79, ASST PROF BIOCHEM, UNIV MINN, 79- *Mem:* Endocrine Soc; Am Soc Biol Chemists. *Res:* Intracellular mechanism of action of thyroid hormones; regulation of messenger RNA production by hormonal and dietary factors. *Mailing Add:* 4-225 Millard Hall Dept Biochem Univ Minn Minneapolis MN 55455

TOWLE, JACK LEWIS, b Burlington, Vt, Dec 23, 18. ORGANIC CHEMISTRY. *Educ:* Univ Vt, BS, 39, MS, 41; Iowa State Univ, PhD(org chem), 50. *Prof Exp:* Res chemist, Tech Enterprises Inc, 51-54; sr res chemist, Diamond Alkali Co, 54-56; sr res chemist, Harshaw Chem Co Div, Kewanee Oil Co, 56-58, dir org res, 58-69; dir pigment & chem res, Div Chem Prod, Chemetron Corp, 69-74, SR res assoc, 74-80. *Mem:* Am Chem Soc; The Chem Soc; Am Asn Textile Chemists & Colorists. *Res:* Sulfa drugs; new intermediates and processes; electroplating additives; organometallics; syntheses high performance dyes and pigments; phosgene chemistry. *Mailing Add:* 1219A Valley Rd Wayne NJ 07470

TOWLE, LAIRD C, b Exeter, NH, Sept 13, 33; m 56; c 4. LASER PHYSICS, SOLID STATE PHYSICS. *Educ:* Univ NH, BSc, 55, MSc, 58; Univ Va, PhD(physics), 62. *Prof Exp:* Res physicist, Avco Corp, Mass, 62-63; res physicist, Allis-Chalmers, Wis, 63-66; sect head high pressure physics, 66-77, CONSULT METAL PHYSICS BR, US NAVAL RES LAB, 77- *Mem:* Am Phys Soc. *Res:* Mechanical and electrical properties of solids under high pressure; equations of state of solids; laser and material interactions; solid-solid phase transitions; low temperature heat capacity of solids. *Mailing Add:* US Naval Res Lab Crystal Br-6430 Washington DC 20390

TOWLE, LOUIS WALLACE, b Frog Mountain, Ala, Nov 21, 08; m 31; c 2. ANALYTICAL CHEMISTRY. *Educ:* Univ Ariz, BS, 30, MS, 32. *Prof Exp:* Instr chem, Ariz State Col, 33; teacher high sch, Ariz, 33-36; res chemist, 37-44, tech serv supvr, 44-51, tech dir, 51-54, gen supt, 54-65, vpres, 69-71, gen mgr, 65-79, pres, 71-80, CHMN BD, APACHE POWDER CO, 80- *Mem:* Am Chem Soc; fel Am Inst Chem; Am Inst Mining, Metall & Petrol Eng. *Res:* Preparation and uses of acetylene di-carboxylic acid; analysis of albumen and globulin blood proteins; nitroglycerin blasting explosives; manufacturing heavy chemicals; nitric and sulphuric acids; ammonium nitrate; anhydrous ammonia; ammonium nitrate blasting agents. *Mailing Add:* Apache Powder Co PO Box M Benson AZ 85602

TOWLE, PHILIP HAMILTON, b San Francisco, Calif, Aug 11, 18. ORGANIC CHEMISTRY. *Educ:* Stanford Univ, AB, 40; Mass Inst Technol, PhD(org chem), 48. *Prof Exp:* Res chemist labs, Standard Oil Co (Ind), 48-54, group leader, 54-61, res & develop, Amoco Chem Corp, 61-64, sect leader, 64-67, div dir org chem res, 67-71, MGR RES SERV, STANDARD OIL CO (IND), 71- *Mem:* AAAS; Am Chem Soc. *Res:* Petrochemicals; aromatic oxidations; information systems. *Mailing Add:* Res Serv Dept Res Ctr Standard Oil Co (Ind) PO Box 400 Naperville IL 60540

TOWLER, MARTIN LEE, b Hockley, Tex, Sept 18, 10; m 40; c 5. NEUROLOGY, PSYCHIATRY. *Educ:* Univ Tex, MD, 35; Am Bd Psychiat & Neurol, dipl, 42. *Prof Exp:* Intern, Med Br, Univ Tex, 36, resident neurol & psychiat, 39, instr, 39-41; PROF NEUROL & PSYCHIAT, UNIV TEX MED BR GALVESTON, 46- *Concurrent Pos:* Rockefeller Found fel, Sch Med, Univ Colo, 41-42; pvt pract; consult, Surg Gen, US Army, 49; consult, Lackland AFB Hosp, 54- *Mem:* Am EEG Soc; fel Am Psychiat Asn; AMA; Asn Am Med Cols; fel Am Acad Neurol. *Res:* Effect of drugs on the electroencephalograph pattern; clinical value and limitation of antidepressant drugs. *Mailing Add:* 200 University Blvd Galveston TX 77550

TOWNE, DUDLEY HERBERT, b Schenectady, NY, Nov 7, 24. THEORETICAL PHYSICS. *Educ:* Yale Univ, BS, 47; Harvard Univ, MA, 49, PhD(physics), 54. *Prof Exp:* From instr to assoc prof, 52-63, PROF PHYSICS, AMHERST COL, 63- *Concurrent Pos:* Staff mem, Rockefeller Found, 63-64. *Mem:* AAAS; Am Phys Soc. *Res:* Scattering of electromagnetic radiation; broadening of spectral lines; wave propagation in inhomogeneous media. *Mailing Add:* Dept of Physics Amherst Col Amherst MA 01002

TOWNE, JACK C, b New York, NY, Apr 23, 27; m 50; c 2. BIOCHEMISTRY, RADIOCHEMISTRY. *Educ:* Univ Calif, Los Angeles, BS, 50; Univ Wis, MS, 52, PhD(biochem), 55. *Prof Exp:* USPHS fel, 54-56; dir biochem lab, Inst Psychosom & Psychiat Res & Training, 56-58; prin scientist biochem, Vet Admin Hosp, Tucson, Ariz, 58-70; PROF CHEM, UNIV DALLAS, 70-, CHMN DEPT, 72- *Concurrent Pos:* Asst prof, Med Sch, Northwestern Univ, 58-65; holder & co-investr, NIH grants, 59-65; lectr, Univ of the Andes, Venezuela, 64; res assoc, Col Med, Univ Ariz, 65-70. *Mem:* AAAS; Am Chem Soc; NY Acad Sci. *Res:* Enzymology; intermediary and amine metabolism; radiometric syntheses and analyses. *Mailing Add:* Dept of Chem Univ of Dallas Irving TX 75061

TOWNE, RICHARD C, engineering, see previous edition

TOWNE, RONALD ERNEST, b Biddeford, Maine, June 6, 23; m 48; c c 3. BIOLOGY, ZOOLOGY. *Educ:* Univ NH, BS, 47, MS, 51. *Prof Exp:* Fishery biologist lakes & ponds, NH Fish & Game Dept, 49-59; master navigator aircraft, Dept Defense, 59-66; POLLUTION BIOLOGIST LAKES & PONDS, NH WATER SUPPLY & POLLUTION CONTROL COMN, 67- *Concurrent Pos:* Lectr, New Eng Col, 73- *Res:* Control of algae by mixing. *Mailing Add:* 5 McKinley St Concord NH 03264

TOWNEND, ROBERT EDWARD, physical biochemistry, see previous edition

TOWNER, HARRY H, b Albany, NY, Sept 4, 49; m 72; c 1. PHYSICS, NUCLEAR ENGINEERING. *Educ:* State Univ NY Albany, BS, 72; Univ Ill, Urbana, MS, 75. *Prof Exp:* MEM PROF TECH STAFF CONTROLLED NUCLEAR FUSION, PLASMA PHYSICS LAB, PRINCETON UNIV, 75- *Mem:* Am Phys Soc; Am Nuclear Soc. *Res:* Controlled nuclear fusion and in particular the plasma physics aspects. *Mailing Add:* Plasma Physics Lab PO Box 451 Princeton NJ 08544

TOWNER, HOWARD FROST, b Los Angeles, Calif, Aug 10, 43; m 65; c 2. BIOLOGY, ECOLOGY. *Educ:* Univ Calif, Riverside, AB, 65; Stanford Univ, PhD(biol), 70. *Prof Exp:* NIH fel, Univ Calif, Los Angeles, 70-71, asst res neurologist, Ctr Health Sci, 71-72; ASST PROF BIOL, LOYOLA MARYMOUNT UNIV, 72- *Concurrent Pos:* Consult, Wadsworth Hosp, US Vet Admin, 72- *Mem:* AAAS; Ecol Soc Am; Am Soc Mammal; Am Soc Ichthyologists & Herpetologists; Sigma Xi. *Res:* Ecology of desert organisms; cytogenetics and plant evolution. *Mailing Add:* Loyola Marymount Univ Los Angeles CA 90045

TOWNER, IAN STUART, b Hastings, Eng, May 24, 40; m 66; c 3. THEORETICAL NUCLEAR PHYSICS. *Educ:* Univ London, BSc, 62, PhD(nuclear physics), 66. *Prof Exp:* Res assoc, Nuclear Physics Lab, Oxford Univ, 65-70; RES OFFICER NUCLEAR PHYSICS, CHALK RIVER NUCLEAR LABS, ATOMIC ENERGY CAN LTD, 70- *Res:* Nuclear structure; models. *Mailing Add:* Physics Div Chalk River Nuclear Labs Chalk River ON K0J 1S0 Can

TOWNER, R(AYMOND) J(AY), b Norwich, NY, Dec 23, 25; m 57; c 3. METALLURGICAL ENGINEERING. *Educ:* Rensselaer Polytech Inst, BMetE, 50, MMetE, 51; Univ Pittsburgh, PhD(metall eng), 58. *Prof Exp:* Student aide trainee metall eng, Phys Metall Div, US Naval Res Lab, 49; res asst, Rensselaer Polytech Inst, 50-51; res engr, Alcoa Res Labs, Aluminum Co Am, 51-63; fel scientist, Aerospace Elec Div, Westinghouse Elec Corp, Ohio, 63-69, FEL ENGR, BETTIS ATOMIC POWER LAB, WESTINGHOUSE ELEC CORP, 69- *Mem:* Am Soc Metals; Am Inst Mining, Metall & Petrol Engrs; Brit Inst Metals; Sigma Xi. *Res:* Physical metallurgy; development of aluminum powder metallurgy products; high strength aluminum alloys; high temperature ceramic to metal seals; dispersion strengthened magnetic materials; development and application of materials for nuclear power plants. *Mailing Add:* Bettis Atomic Power Lab PO Box 79 West Mifflin PA 15122

TOWNER, RICHARD HENRY, b Gunnison, Colo, Oct 7, 48. ANIMAL GENETICS. *Educ:* Colo State Univ, BS, 70; Univ Wis-Madison, MS, 73, PhD(genetics, meat & animal sci), 75. *Prof Exp:* GENETICIST, H&N INC, 75- *Concurrent Pos:* Affil asst prof, Col Ocean & Fisheries Sci, Univ Wash, 78- *Mem:* Am Soc Animal Sci; Am Poultry Asn. *Res:* Improvement of existing strains and development of new strains of chickens by utilizing quantative genetic principles. *Mailing Add:* 15305 NE 40th St Redmond WA 98052

TOWNES, ALEXANDER SLOAN, b Birmingham, Ala, June 19, 29; m 51; c 5. INTERNAL MEDICINE, RHEUMATOLOGY. *Educ:* Vanderbilt Univ, BA, 50, MD, 53. *Prof Exp:* From instr to assoc prof, Johns Hopkins Univ, 61-72; chief sect rheumatol, 72-75, PROF MED, COL MED, UNIV TENN, MEMPHIS, 72-; CHIEF MED SERV, MEMPHIS VET ADMIN HOSP, 75- *Concurrent Pos:* Fel med, Sch Med, Johns Hopkins Univ, 59-61; asst physician in chief, Baltimore City Hosps, 63-70. *Mem:* AAAS; Am Rheumatism Asn; Am Fedn Clin Res; fel Am Col Physicians; Am Asn Immunologists. *Res:* Clinical medicine and rheumatology; role immune reactions in pathogenesis of rheumatic diseases; correlation of clinical findings with immunologic changes and effects of therapy. *Mailing Add:* Vet Admin Hosp 1030 Jefferson Ave Memphis TN 38104

TOWNES, CHARLES HARD, b Greenville, SC, July 28, 15; m 41; c 4. PHYSICS. *Educ:* Furman Univ, BA & BS, 35; Duke Univ, MA, 37; Calif Inst Technol, PhD(physics), 39. *Hon Degrees:* Twenty-one from US & foreign univs & cols, 60-78. *Prof Exp:* Asst physics, Calif Inst Technol, 37-39; mem tech staff, Bell Tel Labs, 39-47; from assoc prof to prof physics, Columbia Univ, 48-61, chmn dept, 52-55, exec dir radiation lab, 50-52; prof physics & provost, Mass Inst Technol, 61-66, inst prof physics, 66-67; UNIV PROF PHYSICS, UNIV CALIF, BERKELEY, 67- *Concurrent Pos:* Adams fel, 50; Guggenheim fel, 55-56; Fulbright lectr, Paris, 55-56 & Tokyo, 56; lectr, Enrico Fermi Int Sch Physics, 55 & 60, dir, 63; Scott lectr, Cambridge Univ, 63; centennial lectr, Univ Toronto, 67; vpres & dir res, Inst Defense Anal, 59-61; trustee, Salk Inst Biol Studies, 63-68, Carnegie Inst, 65- & Rand Corp, 65-70; mem bd dirs, Perkin-Elmer Corp, 66-; mem corp, Woods Hole Oceanog Inst, 69-, trustee, 71-74; mem sci adv bd, US Dept Air Force, 58-61; chmn sci & tech adv comt manned space flight, NASA, 64-69, mem space prog adv coun, 71-77; mem, President's Sci Adv Comt, 66-70, vchmn, 67-69; chmn, President-Elect's Task Force on Space, 68, mem, President's Task Force Nat Sci Policy, 69; mem coun, Nat Acad Sci, 69-72, chmn space sci bd, 70-73; chmn sci adv comt, Gen Motors Corp, 71-73; mem, President's Comt Sci & Technol, 76-77; mem Bd Trustees, Gen Motors Cancer Res Found, 78-; chmn, Comt Scholarly Exchanges, Peoples' Repub China, 79-; chmn, Comt MX Basing, 81. *Honors & Awards:* Nobel Prize in Physics, 64; Res Corp Award, 58; Liebmann Mem Prize, Inst Radio Engrs, 58, Sarnoff Award, Inst Elec Engrs, 61 & Medal of Honor, Inst Elec & Electronics Engrs, 67; Comstock Award, Nat Acad Sci, 59, Carty Medal, 62; Ballantine Medal, Franklin Inst, 59 & 62; Rumford Premium, Am Acad Arts & Sci, 61; Beckman Award, Instrument Soc Am, 61; Young Medal & Prize, Brit Inst Physics & Phys Soc, 63; Priestley Award, Dickinson Col, 66; C E K Mees Medal, Optical Soc Am, 68; Michelson-Morley Award, 70; Wilhem-Exner Award, 70; Earle K Plyler Prize, Am Phys Soc; Niels Bohr Int Gold Medal. *Mem:* Nat Acad Sci; fel Am Phys Soc (pres, 67); hon mem Optical Soc Am; foreign mem Royal Soc London; Am Astron Soc. *Res:* Molecular and nuclear structure; masers; lasers; radio and infrared astronomy; microwave spectroscopy; optics; quantum electronics. *Mailing Add:* Dept of Physics Univ of Calif Berkeley CA 94720

TOWNES, GEORGE ANDERSON, b Augusta, Ga, Oct 30, 43; m 68; c 2. NUCLEAR FUEL REPROCESSING, NUCLEAR WASTE. *Educ:* Ga Inst Technol, BME, 65, MSME, 67. *Prof Exp:* Engr, USPHS, 68-70; SR ENGR & PROJ MGR, ALLIED-GEN NUCLEAR SERV, 71- *Concurrent Pos:* Chmn, Nuclear Lifting Devices, Am Nat Standards Inst, 75- *Res:* Investigations in the reprocessing and waste aspects of the nuclear fuel cycle including remote processing and handling of spent fuel; consolidation of spent fuel to enhance existing storage and transportation capacities. *Mailing Add:* 103 Sweetwater Lane Barnwell SC 29812

TOWNES, HARRY W(ARREN), b Machias, Maine, Oct 12, 37. MECHANICAL ENGINEERING. *Educ:* Brown Univ, BS, 59; Calif Inst Technol, MS, 60, PhD(mech eng), 65. *Prof Exp:* Asst prof mech eng, 65-71, assoc prof aerospace & mech eng, 71-77, prof aerospace, 77-80, PROF MECH ENG, MONT STATE UNIV, 77- *Mem:* Am Soc Mech Engrs. *Res:* Heat transfer; fluid mechanics; robotics. *Mailing Add:* Dept of Aerospace & Mech Eng Mont State Univ Bozeman MT 59715

TOWNES, HENRY KEITH, JR, b Greenville, SC, Jan 20, 13; m 37; c 2. ENTOMOLOGY. *Educ:* Furman Univ, BS & BA, 33; Cornell Univ, PhD(entom), 37. *Hon Degrees:* LLD, Furman Univ, 75. *Prof Exp:* Instr zool, Syracuse Univ, 37-38; entom, Cornell Univ, 38-40; Nat Res Coun fel, Acad Natural Sci, Pa, 40-41; jr entomologist, Bur Entom & Plant Quarantine, USDA, 41, from assoc entomologist to entomologist, 41-49; from assoc prof to prof entom, NC State Col, 49-56; ADJ PROF, UNIV MICH, ANN ARBOR, 56-; DIR, AM ENTOM INST, 61- *Concurrent Pos:* Adv, Pl Govt, 52-54; mem econ surv, US Com Co, Micronesia, 46; mem exped, Wash & Ore, 40, Ariz, 47, Colo & Calif, 48, SAm, 65-66, SAfrica, 70-71, Alaska, 73, Calif & Ariz, 74 & Nfld, 75; vis prof, Mich State Univ, 72 & Carleton Univ, 75. *Mem:* Fel Entom Soc Am; cor mem Am Entom Soc; Entom Soc Can; cor mem Netherlands Entom Soc; cor mem Chilean Entom Soc. *Res:* Insect taxonomy, especially parasitic Hymenoptera. *Mailing Add:* Am Entom Inst 5950 Warren Rd Ann Arbor MI 48105

TOWNES, MARY MCLEAN, b Southern Pines, NC, July 12, 28; m 54; c 2. CELL PHYSIOLOGY. *Educ:* NC Col Durham, BS, 49, MSPH, 50; Univ Mich, MS, 53, PhD(cell physiol), 62. *Prof Exp:* From instr to assoc prof, 50-68, PROF BIOL, NC CENT UNIV, 68-, DEAN, GRAD SCH ARTS & SCI, 79- *Concurrent Pos:* Consult biol improv prog, NSF & NC Acad Sci Prog High Sch Teachers Biol, 65-66; consult minority access to res careers, Nat Inst Gen Med Sci, NIH, 75-77. *Mem:* AAAS; Soc Gen Physiologists; NY Acad Sci; Sigma Xi; Am Soc Zoologists. *Res:* pH relations of contractility of glycerinated stalks of Vorticella convallaria; contractile properties of glycerinated stalks of Vorticella. *Mailing Add:* Grad Off NC Cent Univ Durham NC 27707

TOWNES, PHILIP LEONARD, b Salem, Mass, Feb 18, 27; m 56. GENETICS. *Educ:* Harvard Univ, AB, 48; Univ Rochester, PhD(zool), 53, MD, 59; Am Bd Pediat, dipl, 80. *Prof Exp:* Asst biol, Univ Rochester, 48-51, from instr to assoc prof anat, 52-66, asst prof pediat, 65-69, prof anat, prof genetics, Sch Med & Dent, 66-79, prof pediat, 69-79; PROF PEDIAT, SCH MED, UNIV MASS, 79- *Mem:* AAAS; Soc Pediat Res; Am Pediat Soc; Am Soc Human Genetics. *Res:* Experimental embryology; cell movements; biochemical aspects of development; enzymes; proteins; metabolic inhibitors; physiology of development; human genetics and embryology. *Mailing Add:* Dept Pediat Med Ctr Univ Mass Lake Ave North Worcester MA 01605

TOWNES, WILLIAM DAVID, b Petersburg, Va, May 15, 19; m 48; c 4. CRYSTALLOGRAPHY, MICROWAVES. *Educ:* Va State Col, BS, 40; Polytech Inst NY, MS, 55. *Prof Exp:* Elec engr radar, Signal Corps Eng Lab, 42-55, radio physicist wave propagation, Elec Command, 55-58, res physicist crystallog, 58-73, res phys scientist nuclear harding, 73-75, res phys scientist reliability, 75-78, RES PHYS SCIENTIST MICROWAVE, ELECTRONIC RES & DEVELOP, ENERGY RES & DEVELOP COMMAND, US ARMY, 78- *Mem:* Sigma Xi; Inst Elec & Electronics Engrs; Am Crystallog Asn; Am Phys Soc; Am Mineral Soc. *Res:* Physical properties of materials at microwave frequencies; crystal structure of electrical and magnetic materials. *Mailing Add:* US Army ERADCOM DELET-MJ Ft Monmouth NJ 07703

TOWNLEY, CHARLES WILLIAM, b East Liverpool, Ohio, Oct 27, 34; m 57; c 2. PHYSICAL CHEMISTRY, RESEARCH ADMINISTRATION. *Educ:* Ohio State Univ, BSc, 56, PhD(nuclear chem), 59. *Prof Exp:* Sr chemist, 59-62, fel, 62-65, chief chem physics res, 65-67, chief struct physics res, 67-70, mgr mat sci, 70-73, mgr info & commun systs, 73-74, mgr William F Clapp Labs, 74-77, sr prog mgr, Toxic Substance Res, 77-80, PROG MGR, TOXIC & HAZARDOUS MAT RES, COLUMBUS LABS, BATTELLE MEM INST, 80- *Mem:* AAAS; fel Am Inst Chem; Am Chem Soc. *Res:* Environmental monitoring, ecological effects and chemical fate of toxic chemicals; research management. *Mailing Add:* 505 King Ave Columbus OH 43201

TOWNLEY, JOHN LEWIS, III, b Fergus Falls, Minn, Jan 11, 21; m 55; c 3. PETROLEUM. *Educ:* Univ Minn, BA, 48. *Prof Exp:* Petrol geologist, Magnolia Petrol Co Div, Mobil Oil Corp, 48-50, petrol geologist, 50-59, staff geologist, 59-61, CHIEF PROD GEOLOGIST, MOBIL OIL CAN, LTD, 61- *Mem:* Am Asn Petrol Geologists; Can Soc Petrol Geologists. *Mailing Add:* Mobil Oil Can Ltd Box 800 Calgary AB T2P 2J7 Can

TOWNLEY, JUDY ANN, b San Antonio, Tex, Sept 19, 46. INFORMATION SCIENCE. *Educ:* Univ Tex, Austin, BA, 68; Harvard Univ, SM, 69, PhD(appl math), 73. *Prof Exp:* LECTR & RES FEL APPL MATH, HARVARD UNIV, 73-, DIR INFO SCI PROG, 75-; MEM STAFF, MASS COMPUT ASSOCS, INC, 73- *Mem:* Asn Comput Mach; Inst Elec & Electronics Engrs. *Mailing Add:* 8 Shady Hill Sq Cambridge MA 02138

TOWNLEY, ROBERT WILLIAM, b Lampasas, Tex, Apr 28, 07; m 29; c 2. CHEMISTRY. *Educ:* Austin Col, BA, 29; Univ Tex, MA, 35, PhD(phys chem), 38. *Prof Exp:* Anal chemist, First Tex Chem Mfg Co, 31-33; from asst to instr chem, Univ Tex, 35-37; bacteriologist, State Dept Health, Tex, 37-38, chemist, 38-39, chief chemist, 39-41; res chemist, Humble Oil & Ref Co, 41-42; indust hyg engr, USPHS, Md, 42-44; res chemist, Ciba Pharmaceut Prod, Inc, NJ, 44-50; assoc prof chem, Drew Univ, 50-54; head res dept, Personal Prod Corp, 54-57; dir Townley Res & Consult, 57-73; assoc prof Fairleigh Dickinson Univ, 58-59; CONSULT, 73- *Mem:* Am Chem Soc. *Res:* Foods; drugs; water; corrosion; air and water pollution; industrial hygiene; microbiology. *Mailing Add:* 91 Memory Lane Asheville NC 28805

TOWNLEY-SMITH, THOMAS FREDERICK, b Scott, Sask, Aug 27, 42; m 63; c 3. PLANT BREEDING. *Educ:* Univ Sask, BSA, 64, MSc, 65; Univ Guelph, PhD(plant breeding), 69. *Prof Exp:* Res asst plant breeding, Univ Guelph, 65-68: RES SCIENTIST, WHEAT BREEDING, RES STA, CAN DEPT AGR, 68- *Concurrent Pos:* Sr wheat breeder, Plant Breeding Sta, Can Int Develop Agency, Njoro, Kenya, East Africa, 72-74. *Mem:* Genetics Soc Can; Can Soc Agron. *Res:* Breeding durum wheat; genetics and cytogenetics of wheat. *Mailing Add:* Can Dept of Agr Res Sta Box 1030 Swift Current SK S9N 3X2 Can

TOWNS, CLARENCE, JR, b Little Rock, Ark, July 22, 16; m 44; c 3. PATHOLOGY, HISTOLOGY. *Educ:* Cent YMCA Col, BS, 42; Univ Ill, DDS, 45, MS, 74; Am Bd Endodontic, dipl, 57. *Prof Exp:* Instr histol, 68-69, asst instr basic sci, 70-72, ASST PROF HISTOL, COL DENT, UNIV ILL, 74- *Mem:* Sigma Xi; Am Acad Forensic Dent; Am Soc Oral Med; Am Asn Endodontics; Am Dent Asn. *Res:* Exfoliative cytology of the oral mucosa in the male Negro nonsmoker and smoker; ultra structures study of oral mucosa; comparison of normal and hyperkerototic human oral mucosa. *Mailing Add:* 200 E 75th St Chicago IL 60619

TOWNS, DONALD LIONEL, b Sioux City, Iowa, Mar 8, 35; m 60; c 2. PHYSICAL ORGANIC CHEMISTRY, CHEMICAL ENGINEERING. *Educ:* Ga Inst Technol, BChE, 57; Univ Wis, PhD(chem), 63. *Prof Exp:* Process res chemist, Agr Chem FMC Corp, 62-72, sr process res chemist, Niagara Chem Div, 72-73, process eng group leader, Indust Chem Div, 73-74, tech mgr, 74-75, Furadan prod mgr, 75-76, gen operating supt, 76-77, mgr pesticide formulation & delivery res, 77-80; PROJ MGR, HERZOG HART CORP, 80- *Mem:* Am Chem Soc; The Chem Soc; Am Inst Chem Engrs. *Res:* Technical improvement, environmental protection and production of the insecticide Furadan. *Mailing Add:* 462 Boylston St Herzog Hart Corp Boston MA 02166

TOWNS, ROBERT LEE ROY, b Bartlesville, Okla, Oct 27, 40; m 60; c 2. CHEMISTRY. *Educ:* Univ New Orleans, BS, 65; Univ Tex, Austin, PhD(phys chem), 69. *Prof Exp:* Vis asst prof chem, Univ New Orleans, 70-71; asst prof & petrol fund grant chem, Tex A&M Univ, 71-73; ASSOC PROF CHEM, CLEVELAND STATE UNIV, 73- *Concurrent Pos:* NATO grant, Advan Study Inst, Univ York, Eng, 71. *Mem:* Am Chem Soc; Am Crystallog Asn; Am Inst Physics; Am Asn Clin Chemists. *Res:* X-ray fluorescence; trace and ultratrace metal analysis in human tissues and body fluids; instrument design, development and automation; x-ray crystallography; molecular structure determination; structure/activity relationships in Treflan herbicides. *Mailing Add:* Dept of Chem Cleveland State Univ Cleveland OH 44115

TOWNSEND, ALDEN MILLER, plant genetics, tree physiology, see previous edition

TOWNSEND, CHARLEY E, b Decatur Co, Kans, July 2, 29; m 59; c 1. PLANT BREEDING, GENETICS. *Educ:* Kans State Univ, BS, 50, MS, 51; Univ Wis, PhD(agron, plant path), 56. *Prof Exp:* RES GENETICIST, AGR RES SERV, USDA & COLO STATE UNIV, 56- *Mem:* Am Soc Agron; Crop Sci Soc Am. *Res:* Breeding legumes for western ranges and pastures. *Mailing Add:* Crop Res Lab Colo State Univ Ft Collins CO 80521

TOWNSEND, CRAIG ARTHUR, b Chicago, Ill, Aug 19, 47; m 71; c 1. BIOORGANIC CHEMISTRY, ORGANIC CHEMISTRY. *Educ:* Williams Col, BA, 69; Yale Univ, PhD(org chem), 74. *Prof Exp:* Int exchange fel bio-org chem, Swiss Fed Inst Technol, 74-76; ASST PROF CHEM, JOHNS HOPKINS UNIV, 76- *Mem:* Am Chem Soc; Royal Soc Chem; AAAS. *Res:* Biosynthesis of natural products; stereochemical and mechanistic studies of enzyme action; application of spectroscopic techniques to the solution of biological problems. *Mailing Add:* Dept of Chem Johns Hopkins Univ Baltimore MD 21218

TOWNSEND, DAVID EUGENE, b Kansas City, Mo, Aug 14, 47; m 67; c 2. PHYSICAL ORGANIC CHEMISTRY, ORGANIC PHOTOCHEMISTRY. *Educ:* Univ NC, Chapel Hill, BS, 69; Fla State Univ, MS, 72, PhD(chem), 74. *Prof Exp:* Res chemist monomer process res, Rohm and Haas Co, 74-77; sr res chemist phys chem, 77-80, RES & DEVELOP MGR, FUNDAMENTAL RES & DEVELOP DIV, R J REYNOLDS TOBACCO CO, 80- *Mem:* Sigma Xi. *Res:* Mechanisms of organic photoreactions; primary photophysical processes; process development and optimization; physical aspects of tobacco research; homogeneous and heterogeneous catalysis. *Mailing Add:* 4801 Gladwyn Dr Winston-Salem NC 27103

TOWNSEND, DAVID WARREN, b Westbrook, Maine, Jan 14, 52; m 75; c 2. PLANKTON ECOLOGY, MARINE FISHES. *Educ:* Univ Maine, BA, 74, PhD(oceanog), 81; Long Island Univ, MS, 77. *Prof Exp:* RES SCIENTIST, BIGELOW LAB OCEAN SCI, DIV NORTHEASTERN RES FOUND, INC, 81- *Mem:* Am Soc Limnol & Oceanog; Estuarine Res Fedn; Sigma Xi. *Res:* Marine zooplankton and larval fish ecology; plankton ecology and trophodynamics. *Mailing Add:* Bigelow Lab Ocean Sci McKown Point West Boothbay Harbor ME 04575

TOWNSEND, DOUGLAS WAYNE, b Covington, Ky, Aug 7, 48; m 72. MATHEMATICS, STATISTICS. *Educ:* Ohio State Univ, BS, 70; Univ Ill, MSc, 75, PhD(math), 76. *Prof Exp:* ASST PROF MATH, IND-PURDUE UNIV, 76- *Mem:* Am Math Soc; Math Asn Am. *Res:* Complex analysis, primarily Nevanlinna theory for complex valued functions of a single complex variable. *Mailing Add:* Dept of Math Sci Ind-Purdue Univ Ft Wayne IN 46805

TOWNSEND, EDWIN C, b Vienna, WVa, July 7, 36; m 58; c 3. BIOMETRY. *Educ:* Univ WVa, BS, 58, MS, 64; Cornell Univ, PhD(biomet), 68. *Prof Exp:* Staff asst comput, 61-62, res assoc, 62-63, assoc prof statist, 68-74, ASSOC DIR, W VA AGR & FORESTRY EXP STA, W VA UNIV, 75- *Mem:* Biomet Soc; Am Statist Asn. *Mailing Add:* 1170 Agr Sci Bldg WVa Univ Morgantown WV 26506

TOWNSEND, FRANK MARION, b Stamford, Tex, Oct 29, 14; m 51; c 2. PATHOLOGY. *Educ:* Tulane Univ, MD, 38. *Prof Exp:* US Air Force, 40-65, pathologist, Sch Med, Washington Univ, 45-47, instr clin path, Col Med, Univ Nebr, 47-48, assoc pathologist, Scott & White Clin, Temple Univ, 49, regional consult path, Vet Admin Hosp, Tex & La, 50, chief lab serv, Lackland AFB, 50-54, dep dir, Armed Forces Inst Path, 55-59, dir, 59-63, vcommander, Aerospace Med Div, Air Force Systs Command, Brooks AFB, Tex, 63-65; pathologist, Tex State Dept Health, 65-69; clin prof path, 69-72, PROF PATH & CHMN DEPT, UNIV TEX HEALTH SCI CTR, SAN ANTONIO, 72- *Concurrent Pos:* Assoc prof, Med Br, Univ Tex, 49-58, lectr, 58-63, assoc prof, Postgrad Sch, 53-54; consult, Surgeon Gen, 54-63 & NASA, 67-74; mem, Joint Comt Aviation Path, 56-63, chmn, 60-62; mem, Armed Forces Comt Bioastronaut, Nat Res Coun, 59-60, Nat Adv Cancer Coun, 59-63, Exp Adv Panel Cancer, WHO, 58-81 & Proj Mercury Recovery Team, NASA, 60-63; regional comnr, SCent Region, Col Am Pathologist Lab Accreditation. *Honors & Awards:* Moseley Award, Aerospace Med Asn, 62; Founders Medal, Asn Mil Surgeons US, 62. *Mem:* Am Asn Pathol; fel Am Soc Clin Path; fel AMA; fel Am Col Physicians; fel Am Col Path. *Res:* Aerospace and respiratory disease pathology. *Mailing Add:* 10406 Mt Marcy Dr San Antonio TX 78213

TOWNSEND, GORDON FREDERICK, b Toronto, Ont, Mar 4, 15; m 40; c 2. APICULTURE. *Educ:* Ont Agr Col, BSA, 38; Univ Toronto, MSA, 42. *Prof Exp:* Asst med res, Banting Inst, Can, 38; from asst prof to assoc prof apicult, 39-49, head dept, 39-71, prof, 49-80, EMER PROF APICULT, ONT AGR COL, UNIV GUELPH, 81- *Concurrent Pos:* Dir, Can-Kenya & Can-Sri Lanka Apicult Prog, 71-81; consult, Can Int Develop Agency, 69-, Swed Int Develop Agency, 79-80, Univ Guelph, 80- World Bank, 81 & Chevron Res, 81. *Mem:* Bee Res Asn. *Res:* Chemistry of royal jelly; processing and packing of honey; pollination of tree fruits; apiculture in tropical rural development. *Mailing Add:* Dept of Environ Biol Ont Agr Col Univ of Guelph Guelph ON N1G 2W1 Can

TOWNSEND, HERBERT EARL, JR, b Bristol, Pa, July 1, 38; m 63; c 3. CORROSION, METALLURGICAL ENGINEERING. *Educ:* Drexel Inst Technol, BS, 63; Univ Pa, PhD(metall eng), 67. *Prof Exp:* Res engr, 67-72, RES SUPVR, HOMER RES LABS, BETHLEHEM STEEL CORP, 72- *Mem:* AAAS; Am Soc Metals; Am Soc Testing & Mat; Nat Asn Corrosion Engrs. *Res:* Transport and thermodynamic properties of molten salts; corrosion, stress corrosion cracking and hydrogen embrittlement of steel; thermodynamics of high temperature aqueous environments; corrosion protection systems; corrosion-resistant low-alloy steels; metallic coatings for protection of steel. *Mailing Add:* Homer Res Labs Bethlehem Steel Corp Bethlehem PA 18016

TOWNSEND, HOWARD GARFIELD, JR, b Rochester, NY, Sept 10, 38; m 64; c 2. ENTOMOLOGY. *Educ:* Cornell Univ, BS, 60; Va Polytech Inst, MS, 63; Pa State Univ, PhD(entom), 70. *Prof Exp:* Res asst entom, Va Polytech Inst, 60-62; experimentalist II, NY Agr Exp Sta, Geneva, 63-65; instr, Pa State Univ, 65-69; RES ENTOMOLOGST, STATE FRUIT EXP STA, SOUTHWEST MO STATE UNIV, 70- *Mem:* Entom Soc Am. *Res:* Insect and mite pests of pome and stone fruits, grapes and small fruits. *Mailing Add:* State Fruit Exp Sta Southwest Mo State Univ Mountain Grove MO 65711

TOWNSEND, J(OEL) IVES, b Greenwood, SC, Aug 20, 20. GENETICS. *Educ:* Univ SC, BS, 41; Columbia Univ, PhD(zool), 52. *Prof Exp:* Lectr, Columbia Univ, 50-51; asst prof zool, Univ Tenn, 52-60; asst prof genetics, 60-62, ASSOC PROF HUMAN GENETICS, MED COL VA, VA COMMONWEALTH UNIV, 62- *Concurrent Pos:* Prof, Univ Rio Grande do Sul, Brazil, 54. *Mem:* fel AAAS; Soc Study Evolution; Genetics Soc Am; Soc Study Social Biol; Am Genetic Asn. *Res:* Population genetics; genetics of human isolates; genetics and cytology of marginal populations of Drosophila. *Mailing Add:* Dept Human Genetics Med Col Va Va Commonwealth Univ Richmond VA 23298

TOWNSEND, JAMES SKEOCH, b Belwood, Ont, Apr 12, 34; m 60; c 4. AGRICULTURAL ENGINEERING. *Educ:* Ont Agr Col, BSA, 56; Univ Toronto, BASc, 57; Cornell Univ, MS, 65, PhD(agr eng), 69. *Prof Exp:* Teacher, St Catharines Collegiate Inst, 60-62; instr agr eng, Cornell Univ, 64-66; ASSOC PROF AGR ENG, UNIV MAN, 68- *Concurrent Pos:* Nat Res Coun & Can Dept Agr grants, Univ Man, 69-72. *Mem:* Am Soc Agr Engrs; Can Soc Agr Eng; Am Soc Eng Educ; Soc Automotive Engrs; Can Med & Biol Eng Soc. *Res:* Mechanics of machine milking; biological engineering; heat transfer problems in greenhouse operations. *Mailing Add:* Dept of Agr Eng Univ of Man Winnipeg MB R3T 2N2 Can

TOWNSEND, JAMES WILLIS, b Evansville, Ind, Sept 9, 36; m 58. ULTRASTRUCTURAL PATHOLOGY, TOXICOLOGY. *Educ:* Ball State Univ, Ind, BS, 62; Iowa State Univ, PhD(zool), 70. *Prof Exp:* Instr gen biol, anat, cell biol & physiol, Ind State Univ, Ind, 67-70, asst prof genetics, cell physiol & electron micros, 70-71; consult electron micros, Dept Path & Toxicol, Mead Johnson Res Ctr, Ind, 71-72; mgr, Dept Anat & Physiol, Lab Neurosci & Ultrastructure Res, Col Vet Med, Kans State Univ, 74-76; ASST PROF PATH, ELECTRON MICROS & CELL PATH, UNIV ARK MED SCI, 76- *Concurrent Pos:* Lectr, Am Soc Clin Path, Ill, 80-81; dir, Electron Micros Div, Path Serv Proj, Nat Ctr Toxicol Res, Food & Drug Admin, Ark, 76-81. *Mem:* Electron Micros Soc Am; Sigma Xi. *Res:* Ultrastructural pathology of humans and laboratory animals; ultrastructural effects of long-term, low dose exposure to toxins and carcinogens; applications of energy-dispersive X-ray microanalysis and stereology to problems in toxicology and pathology. *Mailing Add:* Path Dept Slot 517 Univ Ark Med Sci 4301 W Markham St Little Rock AR 72205

TOWNSEND, JOHN FORD, b Kansas City, Mo, Jan 14, 36; m 59; c 3. PATHOLOGY. *Educ:* Univ Mo-Columbia, AB, 58, MD, 61; Am Bd Path, dipl, 67. *Prof Exp:* Intern, Med Br, Univ Tex, 61-62; resident, 62-66, from asst prof to assoc prof, 68-75, vchmn dept, 75-77, interim chmn dept, 77-78, PROF PATH, SCH MED, UNIV MO-COLUMBIA, 75-, CHMN DEPT, 78- *Concurrent Pos:* Chief path serv, Vet Admin Hosp, Columbia, Mo, 72-75. *Res:* Electrical energy transport through tissue; uterine peroxidase; diabetes using animal model Mystromys albicandatus. *Mailing Add:* Dept of Path Sch of Med Univ of Mo Columbia MO 65201

TOWNSEND, JOHN MARSHALL, b Amarillo, Tex, Sept 1, 41. MEDICAL ANTHROPOLOGY. *Educ:* Univ Calif, Berkeley, BA, 63; Univ Calif, Santa Barbara, MA, 67, PhD(anthrop), 72. *Prof Exp:* Asst prof anthrop, Univ Mont, 72-73; asst prof, 73-76, ASSOC PROF ANTHROP, SYRACUSE UNIV, 76- *Mem:* Am Anthrop Asn; fel Soc Appl Anthrop; Soc Med Anthrop. *Res:* Cross-cultural mental health; labeling theory; health care delivery and human fertility. *Mailing Add:* 500 University Pl Syracuse NY 13210

TOWNSEND, JOHN ROBERT, b Brooten, Minn, Oct 26, 25; m 48; c 2. PHYSICS. *Educ:* Cornell Univ, BS, 45, PhD(physics), 51. *Prof Exp:* Physicist, Hanford Atomic Prod Opers, Gen Elec Co, Wash, 51-54; from instr to assoc prof, 54-66, PROF PHYSICS, UNIV PITTSBURGH, 66- *Mem:* Am Phys Soc; Am Asn Physics Teachers. *Res:* Radiation effects in solids; defects in metals. *Mailing Add:* Dept of Physics & Astron Univ of Pittsburgh Pittsburgh PA 15260

TOWNSEND, JOHN WILLIAM, JR, b Washington, DC, Mar 19, 24; m 48; c 4. PHYSICS. *Educ:* Williams Col, BA, 47, MA, 49. *Hon Degrees:* DSc, 61. *Prof Exp:* Asst physics, Williams Col, 47-49; physicist, US Naval Res Lab, DC, 49-50, unit head, 50-52, sect head, 52-53, asst br head, 53-55, head rocket sonde br, 55-58; chief space sci div, NASA, 58-59, asst dir, Goddard Space Flight Ctr, 59-65, dep dir, 65-68; dep adminstr, Environ Sci Serv Admin, Nat Oceanic & Atmospheric Admin, 68-70, assoc adminr, 70-77; PRES, FAIRCHILD SPACE & ELECTRONICS CO, 77- *Concurrent Pos:* Mem comt aeronomy, Int Union Geod & Geophys; mem tech panel on rocketry, US Nat Comt, Int Geophys Year; exec secy, US Rocket & Satellite Res Panel, 58-; mem Int Acad Astronaut, Int Astronaut Fedn. *Honors & Awards:* Meritorious Civilian Serv Award, US Dept Navy, 57; Outstanding Leadership Medal, NASA, 62, Distinguished Serv Medal, 71; Arthur S Fleming Award, 63. *Mem:* Nat Acad Eng; Am Phys Soc; fel Am Meteorol Soc; Sigma Xi; Am Geophys Union. *Res:* Space science and space applications; aeronomy; upper atmosphere physics; composition of the upper atmosphere; mass spectrometry; scientific, meteorological and communications satellites; design and development of sounding rockets. *Mailing Add:* Fairchild Space & Electronics Co Germantown MD 20874

TOWNSEND, JONATHAN, b Colo, July 17, 22; m 55; c 1. PHYSICS. *Educ:* Univ Denver, BS, 43; Washington Univ, MA, 48, PhD(physics), 51. *Prof Exp:* Engr, Gen Elec Co, 43-44; physicist, Carbide & Carbon Chem Co, 45-46; asst prof physics, 51-57, ASSOC PROF PHYSICS, WASHINGTON UNIV, 57- *Mem:* AAAS; Am Phys Soc. *Res:* Nuclear and paramagnetic resonance; free radicals in biology; photosynthesis; electronics. *Mailing Add:* Dept of Physics Washington Univ St Louis MO 63130

TOWNSEND, LEROY B, b Lubbock, Tex, Dec 20, 33; m 53; c 2. MEDICINAL CHEMISTRY. *Educ:* NMex Highlands Univ, BA, 55, MS, 57; Ariz State Univ, PhD(chem), 65. *Prof Exp:* Res assoc chem, Ariz State Univ, 60-65; res assoc, Univ Utah, 65-67, asst res prof, 67-69; asst prof, 69-71, asst res prof chem, 67-79, from assoc prof med chem to prof, 71-79; PROF CHEM & MED CHEM, UNIV MICH, ANN ARBOR, 79- *Concurrent Pos:* Consult, Heterocyclic Chem Corp, 69- *Mem:* Am Chem Soc; Royal Soc Chem; Int Soc Heterocyclic Chem (treas, 73-77, pres-elect, 78-79, pres, 80-81). *Res:* Nitrogen heterocycles, for example pyrrole, pyrimidine, imidazo(4,5-c) pyridine, pyrazole, pyrazolo(3,4-d)pyrimidine, purine, pyrrolo(2,3-d) pyrimidine, pyrazolo(4,3-d)pyrimidine imidazole and the nucleosides arabinofuranosides, ribopyranosides, 2'-deoxyribofuranosides and ribofuranosides of these systems with biological and chemotherapeutic interest as well as structure elucidation and chemical synthesis of certain antibiotics. *Mailing Add:* Col of Pharm Univ of Mich Ann Arbor MI 48109

TOWNSEND, MARJORIE RHODES, b Washington, DC, Mar 12, 30; m 48; c 4. ENGINEERING. *Educ:* George Washington Univ, BEE, 51. *Prof Exp:* Electronics engr basic & appl sonar res, Naval Res Lab, 51-59; sect head design & develop elec instruments, Goddard Space Flight Ctr, NASA, 59-65, tech asst to chief syst div, 65-66, proj mgr small astron satellites, 66-75, proj mgr appl explorer mission, 75-76, mgr preliminary syst design group advan syst design, 76-80; CONSULT, 80- *Honors & Awards:* Knight, Italian Repub Order, 72; Fed Women's Award, 73. *Mem:* fel Inst Elec & Electronics Engrs; assoc fel Am Inst Aeronaut & Astronaut; AAAS; Am Geophys Union. *Res:* Advanced space and ground systems design for a large variety of missions in space and terrestrial applications and in space sciences; new applications for use of the space shuttle. *Mailing Add:* 3529 Tilden St NW Washington DC 20008

TOWNSEND, MILES AVERILL, b Buffalo, NY, Apr 16, 35; m 57; c 5. MECHANICAL ENGINEERING, BIOMECHANICS. *Educ:* Univ Mich, BS, 58; Univ Ill, Urbana, advan cert, 63, MS, 67; Univ Wis-Madison, PhD(mech eng), 71. *Prof Exp:* Res engr, Sundstrand Corp, Ill, 59-63; design engr, Twin Disc, Inc, 63-64; sr engr, Westinghouse Elec Corp, Calif, 64-66; proj engr, Twin Disc, Inc, Ill, 66-68; lectr mech eng, Univ Wis-Madison, 68-69; assoc prof, Univ Toronto, 71-74; prof mech eng, Vanderbilt Univ, 74-81; WILSON PROF & CHMN MECH & AERO ENG, UNIV VA, 82- *Concurrent Pos:* US rep educ, Int Fedn Theory of Mach & Mech, 77. *Honors & Awards:* Am Soc Eng Educ Outstanding Award, 78. *Mem:* Am Soc Mech Engrs; AAAS; Sigma Xi. *Res:* Optimal design, optimal and adaptive control; biomechanics; modeling, dynamics. *Mailing Add:* Dept Mech & Aero Eng Univ Va Charlottesville VA 22901

TOWNSEND, PALMER W, b New York, NY, Aug 1, 26; m 49; c 5. CHEMICAL ENGINEERING. *Educ:* Dartmouth Col, AB, 47; Columbia Univ, BS, 47, MS, 48, PhD(chem eng), 56. *Prof Exp:* Instr chem eng, Columbia Univ, 48-53; sr engr, Pilot Plant Div, Cent Res Labs, Air Reduction Co, Inc, 53-56, sect head, Chem Eng Div, 57-61, asst dir, 61-64, mgr exp eng, Cent Eng Dept, 64-66, asst to group vpres, 66-67, dir commercial develop, Airco Chem & Plastics Div, 67-70; dir commercial develop, Plastics Div, Allied Chem Corp, 70-72; CONSULT, 72- *Mem:* Am Chem Soc; Am Inst Chem Engrs; Soc Plastics Engrs; Soc Plastics Indust; Commercial Develop Asn. *Res:* Plastics research and development in products and processes; chemicals and monomers; applications and market research; materials selection; energy development. *Mailing Add:* 9 Bristol Ct Berkeley Heights NJ 07922

TOWNSEND, RALPH N, b Normal, Ill, May 20, 31; m 58; c 2. MATHEMATICS. *Educ:* Ill Wesleyan Univ, BS, 53; Univ Ill, MS, 55, PhD(math), 58. *Prof Exp:* Asst math, Univ Ill, 54-58; asst prof math, San Jose State Col, 58-60; from asst prof to assoc prof, 60-71, asst dean, Col Arts & Sci, 69-75, PROF MATH, BOWLING GREEN STATE UNIV, 71-, ASSOC DEAN, COL ARTS & SCI, 75- *Mem:* Am Math Soc; Math Asn Am. *Res:* Analysis, including Schwartz distributions; complex analysis. *Mailing Add:* Dept of Math Bowling Green State Univ Bowling Green OH 43402

TOWNSEND, SAMUEL FRANKLIN, b Montague, Mich, Mar 22, 35; m 58; c 2. BIOLOGY, ANATOMY. *Educ:* Kalamazoo Col, AB, 57; Univ Mich, MS, 59, PhD(anat), 61. *Prof Exp:* From asst prof to assoc prof biol, Kalamazoo Col, 61-69, chmn dept, 66-69; assoc prof anat, Col Med, Univ Cincinnati, 69-81; PROF BIOL & CHMN, DIV NATURAL SCI & MATH, HILLSDALE COL, MICH, 81- *Concurrent Pos:* Partic, NSF Res Participation Prog Col Teachers, 64-66. *Mem:* Am Asn Anatomists. *Res:* Cellular differentiation in the adult rat; healing and control of experimental ulcers. *Mailing Add:* Hillsdale Col Hillsdale MI 49242

TOWNSEND, STANLEY JAMES, air pollution, electrical engineering, see previous edition

TOWNSEND, WESLEY PETER, b Farmingdale, NY, May 21, 43; m 65; c 2. METALLIZATION TECHNIQUES, POLYMERIC MATERIALS. *Educ:* Dartmouth Col, AB, 65; Univ Fla, PhD(chem), 70. *Prof Exp:* Res staff surface chem, 70-77, RES LEADER CHEM TECHNOL, WESTERN ELEC CO, INC, 77- *Mem:* Electrochem Soc. *Res:* Development of materials and fabrication technologies for use in electronics; interconnection of integrated circuits with hybrids and printed wiring boards; polymers; surface chemistry; physics; metallization. *Mailing Add:* Eng Res Ctr Western Elec Co Inc PO Box 900 Princeton NJ 08540

TOWNSHEND, JOHN LINDEN, b Hamilton, Ont, Feb 6, 26; m 53; c 2. PLANT PATHOLOGY. *Educ:* Univ Western Ont, BSc, 51, MSc, 52; Imp Col, Univ London, dipl, 63. *Prof Exp:* Tech officer, Forest Path Unit, Forest Prod Lab, Dept Northern Affairs & Nat Resources, Can, 52; RES SCIENTIST, RES BR, CAN DEPT AGR, 52- *Mem:* Soc Nematol; Can Phytopath Soc; Europ Soc Nematol. *Res:* Ecology of plant parasitic nematodes; forage nematodes; host-parasite relationships-ultrastructures. *Mailing Add:* Res Sta Box 185 Can Dept Agr Vineland Station ON L0R 2E0 Can

TOWNSLEY, PHILIP MCNAIR, b Vancouver, BC, Nov 21, 25; m 52; c 3. INDUSTRIAL MICROBIOLOGY. *Educ:* Univ BC, BSA, 49; Univ Calif, Berkeley, MS, 50, PhD(comp biochem), 56. *Prof Exp:* Biochemist, Dept Agr, Govt Can, 56-61, group leader, Process & Prod Group, Fishery Res Bd, 61-63; group leader biochem, BC Res Coun, 63-67; PROF INDUST MICROBIOL, UNIV BC, 67- *Concurrent Pos:* Mem bd dirs, John Dunn Agencies Ltd & Pac Micro-Bio Cult Ltd. *Mem:* Inst Food Technol; Can Inst Food Sci & Technol; Int Asn Plant Tissue Cult; Can Soc Microbiol. *Res:* Practical application of basic research. *Mailing Add:* Dept Food Sci Fac of Agr Sci Univ of BC Vancouver BC V6T 1W5 Can

TOWNSLEY, SIDNEY JOSEPH, b Colorado Springs, Colo, Aug 6, 24; m 50; c 5. RADIOBIOLOGY. *Educ:* Univ Calif, AB, 47; Univ Hawaii, MS, 50; Yale Univ, PhD(zool), 54. *Prof Exp:* Asst prof marine zool & asst, Marine Lab, 54-60, assoc prof marine biol, 60-66, prof, 66-70, PROF MARINE ZOOL, UNIV HAWAII, 70- *Mem:* Am Soc Zoologists; Am Soc Limnol & Oceanog; Ecol Soc Am. *Res:* Ecology of radioisotopes in marine organisms; systematics; stomatopod Crustacea and cephalopod mollusks; histochemistry and physiology of heavy metals. *Mailing Add:* Dept of Zool Univ of Hawaii Honolulu HI 96822

TOWSE, DONALD FREDERICK, b Somerville, Mass, Dec 5, 24; m 45; c 6. GEOLOGY. *Educ:* Mass Inst Technol, BS, 48, PhD(geol), 51; Am Inst Prof Geologists, cert. *Prof Exp:* Geologist, Amerada Petrol Corp, 48-49, 50-51; asst prof geol, Univ NDak, 51-54; geologist, State Geol Surv, NDak, 51-54; consult geologist, 54-56; vis assoc prof, Univ Calif, Los Angeles, 56-57; proj geologist, Kaiser Aluminum & Chem Corp, 57-60, sr proj geologist, Kaiser Cement & Gypsum Corp, 60-71, sr geologist, Kaiser Explor & Mining Co, 71-73; geologist, 74-80, SECT LEADER GEOL, LAWRENCE LIVERMORE NAT LAB, UNIV CALIF, 80- *Concurrent Pos:* Managing dir, Delta Res Inst, 79- *Honors & Awards:* Pres Award, Am Asn Petrol Geologists, 52. *Mem:* Am Asn Petrol Geologists; Am Inst Mining, Metall & Petrol Engrs. *Res:* Stratigraphy and petroleum resources; carbonate oil reservoirs; cement raw materials; laterites; uranium ores; geothermal resources; geology and economics of geothermal energy deposits; geologic disposal of nuclear and hazardous waste. *Mailing Add:* Lawrence Livermore Nat Lab Box 3011 San Jose CA 95116

TOY, ARTHUR DOCK FON, b Canton, China, Sept 13, 15; nat US; m 42; c 3. INDUSTRIAL CHEMISTRY. *Educ:* Univ Ill, BS, 39, MS, 40, PhD(chem), 42. *Prof Exp:* Res chemist, Victor Chem Works Div, Stauffer Chem Co, 42-53, dir org res, 53-59, assoc dir res, 59-63, dir res, 63-65; vis scientist, Cambridge Univ, 65-66; sr scientist, Stauffer Chem Co, Westport, Conn, 66-68, sr scientist & actg mgr, Chem Res Dept, 68-70, sr scientist & actg mgr, Specialities Dept, 70-72, chief scientist, 72-74, dir, Eastern Res Ctr, 75-81, dir res, 79-80; CONSULT, STANFORD, CONN, 80- *Mem:* Am Chem Soc; Royal Soc Chem; AAAS. *Res:* Organic phosphorus compounds for plastic applications and insecticides; allyl aryl-phosphonate flame resistant plastic; economic process for synthesis of phosphorus insecticides; aquo ammono phosphoric acids; organic reaction mechanisms. *Mailing Add:* 14 Katydid Lane Stanford CT 06903

TOY, ARTHUR JOHN, JR, b Pasadena, Calif. RADIATION BIOPHYSICS, HEALTH PHYSICS. *Educ:* Calif State Univ, Hayward, BS, 69; Univ Kans, MS, 71, PhD(radiation biophys), 73. *Prof Exp:* RES & DEVELOP SCIENTIST ENVIRON SCI & HEALTH PHYSICIST, LAWRENCE LIVERMORE LAB, 69- *Mem:* Sigma Xi; Health Physics Soc. *Res:* Radiation accidents. *Mailing Add:* Lawrence Livermore Lab Box 5505 Livermore CA 94550

TOY, HAROLD DWIGHT, b Kittanning, Pa, Oct 3, 17; m 41; c 1. ENVIRONMENTAL SCIENCE. *Educ:* US Air Force Inst Technol, BS, 42. *Hon Degrees:* Dr, Nathaniel Hawthorne Col, 69. *Prof Exp:* Mgr reliability eng, Kollsman Instrument Corp, NY, 58-60; mgr natural resources & chief flight res, Manned Spacecraft Ctr, NASA, Tex, 60-69; pres, Earth Resources Assoc, Inc, 69-70; vpres res & develop, Motivation Res Ctr, 71-72; asst to dir parks div, 72-76, ADMINR TECH PROGS, TEX PARKS & WILDLIFE DEPT, 76- *Concurrent Pos:* Mem bd adv, Gulf Univs Res Corp, 69-70; consult to exec secy, Nat Comn Outer Space, Mex, 69-; mem, Comt for Study Land Use & Environ Control, Tex, 71-72 & Gov Youth Secretariat Adv Comt, 72- *Mem:* AAAS; Am Geophys Union; Inst Elec & Electronics Engrs; Am Inst Aeronaut & Astronaut; Am Fedn Scientists. *Res:* Human engineering and environmental control of biological communities; human factors research in space-oriented sub-systems design; aerospace electronic subsystem research and development and data intelligence systems. *Mailing Add:* Tex Parks & Wildlife Dept 4200 Smith School Rd Austin TX 78744

TOY, MADELINE SHEN, b Shanghai, China, Nov 6, 28; US citizen; m 51; c 1. FLUORINE CHEMISTRY, POLYMER CHEMISTRY. *Educ:* Col St Teresa (Minn), BS, 49; Univ Wis, MS, 51; Ohio State Univ, MS, 57; Univ Pa, PhD(org chem), 59. *Prof Exp:* Mgr org lab, Freelander Res & Develop Div, Dayco Corp, Calif, 59-60; asst prof, Calif State Univ, Northridge, 60-61; staff mem, Int Tel & Tel Corp, Fed Labs, 61-63; res scientist & sect chief, Astropower Lab, McDonnell Douglas Corp, 64-69, head polymer sci, Douglas Adv Res Labs, 69-70; sr polymer chemist, Stanford Res Inst, Menlo Park, 71-75; sr scientist, 75-80, HEAD CHEM LAB, SCI APPLN, INC, 80- *Mem:* AAAS; Am Chem Soc; fel Am Inst Chemists; NY Acad Sci; fel Royal Soc Chem. *Res:* Optically active polymers; fire retardant polyurethanes; high temperature plastics; thermoplastic films; high energy perfluorinated salts; surface polymerizations on metal substrates; fluoroelastomers; multifunctional fluoropolymers; perfluoropolymer-forming reactions; flame resistant surface treatments; organic chemistry; fuel cell electrolytes. *Mailing Add:* Sci Appln Inc 1257 Tasman Dr Sunnyvale CA 94086

TOY, STEPHEN THOMAS, immunology, virology, see previous edition

TOY, WILLIAM W, b Chicago, Ill, Mar 11, 50. COMMUNICATIONS, MICROWAVE RADIO. *Educ:* Mass Inst Technol, SB, 73, SMEE, 73, PhD(physics), 78. *Prof Exp:* MEM TECH STAFF, BELL LABS, INC, 78- *Mem:* Am Phys Soc; Inst Elec & Electronics Engrs; Sigma Xi. *Res:* Microwave propagation effects and their influence on digital transmission facilities; alternative communications schemes. *Mailing Add:* Rm WB1C201 Bell Labs Inc Holmdel NJ 07733

TOYAMA, THOMAS KAZUO, b Minot, NDak, Feb 25, 24. HORTICULTURE. *Educ:* Univ Minn, BS, 53, PhD(plant breeding), 61. *Prof Exp:* Res officer, Can Dept Agr, 61-63; horticulturist, 63-70, res horticulturist, 70-75, supvry res horticulturist, Sci & Educ Admin-Agr Res, USDA, 75-77; HORTICULTURIST, WASH STATE UNIV, 77- *Concurrent Pos:* Horticulturist, Wash State Univ, 63-70. *Mem:* AAAS; Am Soc Hort Sci; Am Pomol Soc. *Res:* Plant breeding; breeding, genetics and cytology of stone fruits. *Mailing Add:* Irrigated Agr Res & Ext Ctr Prosser WA 99350

TOZER, THOMAS NELSON, b San Diego, Calif, July 4, 36. PHARMACEUTICAL CHEMISTRY, PHARMACY. *Educ:* Univ Calif, San Francisco, BS & PharmD, 59, PhD(pharmaceut chem), 63. *Prof Exp:* Lectr chem & pharmaceut chem, Univ Calif, San Francisco, 63; NIMH fel, 63-65; asst prof, 65-74, assoc prof, 74-81, PROF PHARM & PHARMACEUT CHEM, UNIV CALIF, SAN FRANCISCO, 81- *Concurrent Pos:* Pharmacist, 59-; fel, Lab Chem Pharmacol, Nat Heart Inst, 63-65. *Mem:* AAAS; Am Pharmaceut Asn; Acad Pharmaceut Sci; Am Chem Soc; NY Acad Sci. *Res:* Catecholamine and indole metabolism; biological transport systems, especially the brain; drug metabolism; biopharmaceutics; pharmacokinetics. *Mailing Add:* Sch of Pharm Univ of Calif San Francisco CA 94143

TOZLOSKI, ALBERT HENRY, b Sunderland, Mass, Apr 20, 26; m 52. ECONOMIC ENTOMOLOGY, INVERTEBRATE ZOOLOGY. *Educ:* Univ Mass, BS, 50, MS, 52, PhD(entom, bot), 54. *Prof Exp:* Instr biol, Teachers Col, Conn, 55-59, asst prof biol, 59-65, chmn dept, 65-74, PROF BIOL, CENT CONN STATE COL, 74- *Mem:* AAAS; Ecol Soc Am; Entom Soc Am. *Res:* Ecology; invertebrate zoology. *Mailing Add:* Dept of Biol Cent Conn State Col New Britain CT 06050

TRABANT, EDWARD ARTHUR, b Los Angeles, Calif, Feb 28, 20; m 43; c 3. APPLIED MATHEMATICS. *Educ:* Occidental Col, AB, 41; Calif Inst Technol, PhD(appl math), 47. *Prof Exp:* From instr to prof math & eng sci, Purdue Univ, 47-60; dean sch eng, State Univ NY Buffalo, 60-66; vpres acad affairs, Ga Inst Technol, 66-68; PRES, UNIV DEL & PROF ENG SCI, COL ENG, 68- *Concurrent Pos:* Consult, Allison Div, Gen Motors, Ind, 50-55, Argonne Nat Lab, Ill, 55-61; Carborundum Corp, NY, 64-68 & Army Sci Adv Panel, 66-71. *Mem:* Am Soc Eng Educ; Am Soc Mech Eng; Am Math Soc; Am Nuclear Soc. *Mailing Add:* Off of the Pres Univ of Del Newark DE 19711

TRABER, DANIEL LEE, b Victoria, Tex, Apr 28, 38; m 59. PHYSIOLOGY, PHARMACOLOGY. *Educ:* St Mary's Univ, Tex, BA, 59; Univ Tex, MA, 62, PhD(physiol), 65. *Prof Exp:* Asst physiol, Med Br, Univ Tex, 60-65; fel pharmacol, Col Med, Ohio State Univ, 65-66; asst prof physiol & res asst prof anesthesiol, 66-70, dir, Interdisciplinary Labs, 70-72, assoc prof, 70-74, PROF ANESTHESIOL & PHYSIOL, UNIV TEX MED BR GALVESTON, 74-, DIR, INTEGRATED FUNCTIONAL LAB, 72- *Concurrent Pos:* Chief, Div Anesthesia Res, Shriners Burn Inst, Galveston, 71-78. *Mem:* AAAS; Am Physiol Soc; Am Burn Asn; Soc Exp Biol & Med; Am Soc Pharmacol & Exp Therapeut. *Res:* Shock, endotoxemia and sepsis. *Mailing Add:* Dept Anesthesiol & Physiol Univ Tex Med Br Galveston TX 77550

TRACE, ROBERT DENNY, b Zanesville, Ohio, Oct 27, 17; m 50; c 2. GEOLOGY. *Educ:* Southern Methodist Univ, BS, 40; Univ Calif, Los Angeles, MA, 47. *Prof Exp:* geologist, US Geol Surv, 42-77; sr geologist, Ky Geol Surv, 77-81; RETIRED. *Concurrent Pos:* Instr, Hopkinsville Community Col, Ky, 66-70. *Mem:* Fel Geol Soc Am; Soc Econ Geol. *Res:* Stratigraphic and structural geology of fluorspar-zinc-lead deposits. *Mailing Add:* 412 Eagle St Princeton KY 42445

TRACEY, JOSHUA IRVING, JR, b New Haven, Conn, May 2, 15; m 46; c 2. GEOLOGY. *Educ:* Yale Univ, BA, 37, MS, 43, PhD(geol), 50. *Prof Exp:* GEOLOGIST, US GEOL SURV, 42- *Mem:* AAAS; Soc Econ Paleont & Mineral; Geol Soc Am; Am Asn Petrol Geol; Am Geophys Union. *Res:* Bauxite; geology and ecology of coral reefs; geology and resources of the Pacific Islands; tertiary stratigraphy of the fossil basing southwestern Wyoming. *Mailing Add:* Nat Ctr Stop 930 US Geol Surv Reston VA 22092

TRACEY, MARTIN LOUIS, JR, b Boston, Mass, Mar 3, 43; m 66; c 2. GENETICS. *Educ:* Providence Col, AB, 65; Brown Univ, PhD(biol), 71. *Prof Exp:* Fel genetics, Univ Calif, Davis, 71-73; dir genetics, Bodega Marine Lab, Calif, 73-74; asst prof biol, Brock Univ, 74-77; asst prof biol, 77-78, ASSOC PROF BIOL & CHMN, FLA INT UNIV, 79- *Mem:* AAAS; Genetics Soc Am; Am Soc Naturalists; Can Genetics Soc; Soc Study Evolution. *Res:* Speciation and genetic differentiation; recombination; polymorphism; genetic organization; genetic control of behavior; aquaculture. *Mailing Add:* Dept of Biol Sci Fla Int Univ Miami FL 33199

TRACHEWSKY, DANIEL, b Montreal, Que, Nov 4, 40; m 67; c 2. ENDOCRINOLOGY, MOLECULAR BIOLOGY. *Educ:* McGill Univ, BSc, 61, MSc, 63, PhD(biochem), 66. *Prof Exp:* Res assoc biochem of reproduction, Biomed Div Pop Coun, Rockefeller Univ, 65-67; dir molecular biol, Montreal Clin Res Inst, 68-75; asst prof med, McGill Univ, 69-75; from asst prof to assoc prof med, Univ Montreal, 69-75; assoc prof med, biochem & molecular biol, 75-81, PROF MED, HEALTH SCI CTR, UNIV OKLA, 81- *Concurrent Pos:* Grants, Can Med Res Coun, Que Med Res Coun & Que Heart Found, Montreal Clin Res Inst, 68-; off referee, reviewing grant applns, Can Med Res Coun, 69- *Mem:* NY Acad Sci; Endocrine Soc; Am Fedn Clin Res; Int Platform Asn; Soc Exp Biol & Med. *Res:* Mechanism of action of steroid and peptide hormones at the molecular level; pathophysiology of hypertension. *Mailing Add:* Health Sci Ctr Univ of Okla PO Box 26901 Oklahoma City OK 73190

TRACHMAN, EDWARD GRANT, b New York, NY, Apr 10, 46; m 68. MECHANICAL ENGINEERING, TRIBOLOGY. *Educ:* Cooper Union, BE, 66; Calif Inst Technol, MS, 67; Northwestern Univ, Evanston, PhD(mech eng), 71. *Prof Exp:* Assoc sr res engr, Res Labs, Gen Motors Corp, 71-75; mem tech staff, RCA Labs, 75-77; head eng anal dept, Vadetec Corp, 77-81; CHIEF ENGR, APPL RES AUTOMOTIVE OPERS, ROCKWELL INT CORP, 81- *Concurrent Pos:* Fac asst, Lawrence Inst Technol, 71-75. *Mem:* Am Soc Mech Engrs; Sigma Xi; Am Soc Lubrication Engrs; Soc Automotive Engrs. *Res:* Traction drives; elastohydrodynamics; lubrication; rheological effects on the lubrication process; mechanical design; solid and fluid mechanics. *Mailing Add:* 2135 W Maple Rd Rockwell Int Corp Troy MI 48084

TRACHT, MYRON EDWARD, b New York, NY, June 8, 28; m 56; c 3. PATHOLOGY. *Educ:* Princeton Univ, AB, 48, Univ Chicago, MS, 54, PhD(physiol) & MD, 55. *Prof Exp:* Pathologist, US Naval Med Res Inst, 56-58; asst prof, 61-69, ASSOC PROF PATH, COL PHYSICIANS & SURGEONS, COLUMBIA UNIV, 69-; DIR LABS, HOLY NAME HOSP, 65- *Concurrent Pos:* USPHS res fel path, Mt Sinai Hosp, 58-61; res assoc, Sch Med, Georgetown Univ, 56-58; asst attend pathologist, Presby Hosp, New York, 61-63; assoc pathologist, Beth Israel Hosp, 63-65. *Res:* Fat transport and metabolism; liver injury; endocrine influences on metabolism. *Mailing Add:* United Hospitals 15 S 9th St Newark NJ 07107

TRACHTENBERG, EDWARD NORMAN, b New York, NY, Dec 8, 27; m 54; c 3. ORGANIC CHEMISTRY. *Educ:* NY Univ, AB, 49; Harvard Univ, AM, 51, PhD(org chem), 53. *Prof Exp:* Instr chem, Columbia Univ, 53-58; from asst prof to assoc prof, 58-70, PROF CHEM, CLARK UNIV, 70- *Concurrent Pos:* NSF fel, Univ London, 67-68. *Mem:* Am Chem Soc; Am Inst Chem; Royal Soc Chem. *Res:* Mechanism of organic reactions; organic synthesis; selenium dioxide oxidation of organic compounds; 1, 3-dipolar cycloadditions. *Mailing Add:* Dept of Chem Clark Univ Worcester MA 01610

TRACHTENBERG, ISAAC, b New Orleans, La, Aug 20, 29; div; c 2. ELECTROCHEMISTRY. *Educ:* Rice Inst, BA, 50; La State Univ, MS, 52, PhD(chem), 57. *Prof Exp:* Assoc chemist, Am Oil Co, Tex, 57-59, chemist, 59-60, sr chemist & group leader, 60-; mem tech staff, 60-63, br head basic electrochem, 63-66, chem kinetics, 66-68, systs anal process control, 69-70, br head environ monitoring, 71-72, br head sensors res & develop, 72-74, mgr process control, Semiconductor Group, 74-75, mgr qual & reliability assurance, Semiconductor Group, 74-80, SOLAR ENERGY PROJ, TEX INST, 80- *Concurrent Pos:* VChmn & chmn, Gordon Res Con Electrochem, 68-69; ed j battery div, Electrochem Soc, 69-72. *Mem:* Am Chem Soc; Electrochem Soc; Nat Asn Corrosion engrs. *Res:* Semiconductors; ion-selective electrochemical sensors; environmental sciences and monitoring; semiconductor device quality and reliability; energy conversion; electrochemistry. *Mailing Add:* Tex Instruments MS 158 PO Box 225303 Dallas TX 75222

TRACHTENBERG, MICHAEL CARL, b New York, NY, June 22, 41; m 64; c 4. NEUROPHYSIOLOGY, CELL BIOLOGY. *Educ:* City Col New York, BA, 62; Univ Calif, Los Angeles, PhD(anat neurosci), 67. *Prof Exp:* Res biologist, Boston Vet Admin Hosp, 69-70; instr neurol, Sch Med, Boston Univ, 69-73, asst prof, 73-78; ASSOC PROF NEUROSURG, PHYSIOL & BIOPHYS, MED BR, UNIV TEX, GALVESTON, 78- *Concurrent Pos:* Nat Inst Neurol Dis & Stroke res fel surg, Med Sch, Harvard Univ, 67-69; Eric Slack-Gyr Found vis researcher neuroanat & neurophysiol, Univ Zurich, 70-71; instr anat, Med Sch, Harvard Univ, 71-72; asst neurophysiologist, McLean Hosp, 71-73; instr anat & psychiat, Med Sch, Harvard Univ, 71-73; res biologist, Boston Vet Med Hosp, 73-74, res physiologist, 74-78. *Mem:* Am Soc Neurochem; AAAS; Soc Neurosci; Am Epilepsy Soc; NY Acad Sci. *Res:* glial cell physiology and biochemistry in the normal and diseased retina and brain; concentration on ion transport and concomitant metabolic alterations. *Mailing Add:* Div of Neurol Surg Univ Tex Med Br Galveston TX 77550

TRACHTMAN, MENDEL, b May 6, 29; US citizen; m 50; c 3. RADIATION CHEMISTRY, PHOTOCHEMISTRY. *Educ:* Temple Univ, AB, 51; Drexel Inst Technol, MS, 56; Univ Pa, PhD(chem), 61. *Prof Exp:* Res chemist, Frankford Arsenal, Philadelphia, Pa, 51-67; PROF CHEM, PHILADELPHIA COL TEXTILES & SCI, 67- *Concurrent Pos:* Res Corp res grant, Philadelphia Col Textiles & Sci, 72-74. *Mem:* Am Chem Soc. *Res:* Determination of quenching cross sections of aromatic molecules; fading properties of various dye molecules. *Mailing Add:* Dept of Chem Philadelphia Col of Textiles & Sci Philadelphia PA 19144

TRACTON, MARTIN STEVEN, b Brockton, Mass, Feb 9, 45; m 66; c 1. METEOROLOGY. *Educ:* Univ Mass, Amherst, BS, 66; Mass Inst Technol, MS, 69, PhD(meteorol), 72. *Prof Exp:* Asst prof meteorol, Naval Postgrad Sch, 72-75; RES METEOROLOGIST, NAT METEOROL CTR, NAT OCEANIC & ATMOSPHERIC ADMIN, 75- *Mem:* Am Meteorol Soc. *Res:* Synoptic-dynamic aspects of the role of cumulus convection in the development of extratropical cyclones; test and evaluation of numerical prediction models. *Mailing Add:* 13011 Rhame Dr Oxon Hill MD 20022

TRACY, C RICHARD, b Glendale, Calif, May 24, 43; m 67; c 1. ECOLOGY. *Educ:* Calif State Univ, Northridge, BA, 66, MS, 68; Univ Wis, PhD(zool), 72. *Prof Exp:* Res assoc environ studies, Univ Wis, 72-73, lectr, 73-74, asst scientist, 73-74; asst prof, Natural Resource Ecol Lab, 75-77, asst prof, 74-79, ASSOC PROF ZOOL, COLO STATE UNIV, 79- *Concurrent Pos:* Asst prof biol, Univ Mich Biol Sta, 74-; nat adv comt person, Univ Wis, Biotron, 74-; ed, Ecol & Ecological Monogr, 78-; Guggenhein fel, 80-81. *Mem:* AAAS; Am Soc Naturalists; Ecol Soc Am; Sigma Xi; Am Soc Ichthyologists & Herpetologists. *Res:* Biophysical ecological techniques to study evolutionary ecological questions of adaptations to physical environments; dispersal; dispersion; habitat selection and space utilization in animals. *Mailing Add:* Dept of Zool-Entom Colo State Univ Ft Collins CO 80523

TRACY, DAVID J, b Covington, Ky, Jan 22, 37. ORGANIC CHEMISTRY. *Educ:* Villa Madonna Col, AB, 59; Univ Ill, MS, 61, PhD(chem), 64. *Prof Exp:* Res specialist, 64-69, TECH ASSOC, GAF CORP, 69- *Mem:* Am Chem Soc. *Res:* Acetylenics; photographic couplers; surfactants. *Mailing Add:* 209 Comly Rd Apt M-24 Lincoln Park NJ 07035

TRACY, DERRICK SHANNON, b Mirzapur, India, July 1, 33; m 69. MATHEMATICAL STATISTICS. *Educ:* Univ Lucknow, BSc, 51, MSc, 53; Univ Mich, MS, 60, ScD(math), 63. *Prof Exp:* Lectr math, Ewing Col, Allahabad, 53-55; sr lectr math statist, Govt Col Bhopal, 56-59; res asst math, Univ Mich, 61-63; asst prof statist, Univ Conn, 63-65; assoc prof, 65-70, PROF MATH, UNIV WINDSOR, 70- *Concurrent Pos:* Nat Res Coun Can res grants, 66-; Defence Res Bd Can res grants, 68-; consult, Bell Tel Co Can & Ont Inst Studies Educ, 67-; consult, Walter Reed Army Res Inst, 68; vis prof, Univ Calif, Riverside, 72-73 & Univ Waterloo, 74; assoc ed Can J Statist, 73-77; Can Coun travel grant to Poland, 75 & India, 77; vis prof, Univ Fed do Rio de Janeiro, 76 & 78; Ministry External Affairs travel grant, Brazil & India, 76; Nat Res Coun exchange scientist, Brazil, 78; vis prof, Indian Statist Inst, 80. *Mem:* Am Statist Asn; Inst Math Statist; Am Math Soc; Math Asn Am; Indian Statist Inst. *Res:* Products of generalized k-statistics; finite moment formulae; symmetric functions; finite sampling; matrix derivatives in multivariate analysis. *Mailing Add:* Dept of Math Univ of Windsor Windsor ON N9B 3P4 Can

TRACY, HUBERT J(EROME), b Little Rock, Ark, Feb 18, 18; m 63. CIVIL ENGINEERING. *Educ:* Univ Ark, BS, 39; La State Univ, MS, 51; Ga Inst Technol, PhD(civil eng), 65. *Prof Exp:* HYDRAUL ENGR, US GEOL SURV, 46- *Mem:* Am Soc Civil Engrs. *Res:* Open channel flow. *Mailing Add:* US Geol Surv Rm 301 900 Peachtree St Atlanta GA 30309

TRACY, JAMES FRUEH, b Isle of Pines, July 29, 16; US citizen; m 57; c 2. NUCLEAR PHYSICS. *Educ:* Univ Ill, BS, 40; Univ Calif, MS, 49, PhD(physics), 53. *Prof Exp:* Elec engr, Gen Elec Co, NY, 40-46; opers analyst, Broadview Res & Develop, Calif, 53; PHYSICIST, LAWRENCE LIVERMORE LAB, UNIV CALIF, 53- *Mem:* Am Phys Soc. *Res:* Physics design of nuclear weapons; application of nuclear explosives to industry and science. *Mailing Add:* 1262 Madison Ave Livermore CA 94550

TRACY, JOSEPH CHARLES, JR, b Wilkes Barre, Pa, Jan 15, 43; m 66; c 3. SOLID STATE PHYSICS, SURFACE PHYSICS. *Educ:* Rensselaer Polytech Inst, BEE, 64; Cornell Univ, PhD(appl physics), 68. *Prof Exp:* Fel surface physics, NAm Rockwell Sci Ctr, Calif, 68-69, mem tech staff, 69-70; mem tech staff, Bell Tel Labs, Murray Hill, 70-73; group leader, 73-75, ASST DEPT HEAD, DEPT PHYSICS, GEN MOTORS RES LAB, 75- *Concurrent Pos:* Chmn, Nat Acad Sci Eval Panel Nat Bur Standards Ctr Thermodyn & Molecular Sci, 79-80, Eval Panel Ctr Chem Physics, Nat Bur Standards, 80-82; panel mem, Nat Acad Sci Eval Panel, Nat Bur Standards Nat Measurement Lab, 79-82. *Mem:* AAAS; Soc Automotive Engrs; Am Phys Soc; Am Vacuum Soc. *Res:* Surface physics; electron spectroscopy; semiconductor physics; management of research. *Mailing Add:* Dept Physics Gen Motors Res Lab Warren MI 48090

TRACY, JOSEPH WALTER, b Seattle, Wash, June 22, 24; m 50; c 5. INORGANIC CHEMISTRY, MEAT SCIENCE. *Educ:* Univ Wash, BS, 51, MS, 54, PhD(chem), 60. *Prof Exp:* Assoc res engr, Boeing Airplane Co, 54-58; prof chem, Northwest Nazarene Col, 60-70; chemist, CHG Meat Inspection Lab, Idaho State Dept Agr, 70-81. *Mem:* Am Chem Soc. *Res:* Meat analysis; x-ray crystallography; crystal structures of simple inorganic compounds. *Mailing Add:* 823 Ninth Ave S Nampa ID 83651

TRACY, M JOANNA, b Newark, NJ, Oct 22, 00. EXPERIMENTAL MEDICINE. *Educ:* Fordham Univ, BS, 28; Catholic Univ Am, MS, 38; Inst Divi Thomae, PhD, 60. *Prof Exp:* Prof biol & chem, Caldwell Col Women, 41-80, chmn, Nat Sci Div, 46-72; RETIRED. *Concurrent Pos:* Researcher, Inst Divi Thomae. *Mem:* AAAS; Am Chem Soc; Am Asn Biol Teachers; Nat Sci Teachers Asn. *Res:* Testing efficacy of a beef brain extract on staphlococcus aureus infections in mice; testing extent of immunity from infection following injections of beef brain extract; immunity in C3H mice to transplantable lymphosarcoma 6C3HED following injections of viable tumor cells. *Mailing Add:* Natural Sci Div Caldwell Col for Women Caldwell NJ 07006

TRACY, PHILIP T, b Chester, Pa, Jan 14, 30; m 50; c 2. PLASMA PHYSICS, ELECTROMAGNETICS. *Educ:* San Diego State Col, BS, 58. *Prof Exp:* Physicist, Gen Dynamics Corp, 58-61; sr physicist, Geophys Corp Am, 61-62; res scientist, Kaman Nuclear, 62-69, sr scientist, KMS Technol Ctr, 69-73, SR RES SCIENTIST, KAMAN SCI CORP, 73- *Mem:* Am Phys Soc. *Res:* Electromagnetic theory. *Mailing Add:* Kaman Sci Corp PO Box 7463 Colorado Springs CO 80933

TRACY, RICHARD E, b Klamath Falls, Ore, Apr 30, 34; m 62; c 2. PATHOLOGY. *Educ:* Univ Chicago, BA, 55, MD & PhD(path), 61. *Prof Exp:* Intern, Presby Hosp, Denver, Colo, 61-62; res assoc path, Univ Chicago, 62-64, instr, 64-65; asst prof, Med Sch, Univ Ore, 65-67; asst prof, 67-73, assoc prof, 73-81, PROF PATH, SCH MED, LA STATE UNIV,, NEW ORLEANS, 81- *Concurrent Pos:* USPHS trainee, 62-65. *Honors & Awards:* Bausch & Lomb Medal, 61; Joseph A Capps Prize, 65. *Mem:* AAAS; Am Heart Asn; Am Soc Exp Path. *Res:* Arteriosclerotic and hypertensive cardiovascular and renal disease; biostatistics. *Mailing Add:* Dept of Path La State Univ Sch of Med New Orleans LA 70112

TRACY, WILLIAM E, b Memphis, Tenn, Aug 16, 34; m 56; c 3. PEDODONTICS. *Educ:* Univ Tenn, DDS, 61; Am Bd Pedodont, dipl, 71. *Prof Exp:* Res asst dent mat, Dent Sch, 60-61, instr pediat, Med Sch & instr dent, Dent Sch, 61-62, asst prof dent, 62-68, ASSOC PROF DENT, DENT SCH, UNIV ORE, 68-, INSTR PEDIAT & DENT MED, MED SCH, 67-, MEM STAFF, CHILD STUDY CLIN, 71- *Concurrent Pos:* Nat Inst Dent Res fel growth & develop, Dent Sch, Univ Ore, 61-62, spec fel, 65-; Nat Inst Child Health & Human Develop career develop award, 66-67, res grant, 66-71. *Mem:* AAAS; Am Acad Pedodont; Am Soc Dent Children; Am Dent Asn; Int Asn Dent Res. *Res:* Growth and development of children; dentofacial growth. *Mailing Add:* 12555 SW Third Beaverton OR 97005

TRADER, MARY WARREN, b New Orleans, La, Jan 27, 22; m 46; c 3. CANCER CHEMOTHERAPY. *Educ:* St Mary's Dominican Col, New Orleans, BS, 42. *Prof Exp:* Sci aide, Southern Reg Res Lab, USDA, 42; jr chemist, US Food & Drug Admin, New Orleans, 42-46; RES BIOLOGIST & HEAD, EXP LEUKEMIA SECT, SOUTHERN RES INST, 56- *Mem:* AAAS. *Mailing Add:* Southern Res Inst 2000 9th Ave S PO Box 3307-A Birmingham AL 35255

TRAEXLER, JOHN F, b Brooklyn, NY, Feb 21, 30; m 55; c 4. MECHANICAL ENGINEERING, ELECTRICAL ENGINEERING. *Educ:* Pratt Inst Technol, BME, 51; Univ Pa, MSME, 54, PhD(eng mech), 65. *Prof Exp:* Design engr, 51-57, sr engr, 57-62, fel engr, 62-67, mgr mech develop, 67-70, mgr technol develop, 70-77, adv engr, 77-78, mgr turbine develop, 78-80, MGR STEAM TURBINE GENERATOR ENG, WESTINGHOUSE ELEC CORP, 80- *Concurrent Pos:* Mem, Pressure Vessel Res Comt, 59-79. *Mem:* Am Soc Mech Engrs. *Res:* Application of plasticity and creep to turbomachinery mechanical design; dynamics and vibrations problems in turbomachinery. *Mailing Add:* 45 Brennan Dr Bryn Mawr PA 19010

TRAFICANTE, DANIEL DOMINICK, b Jersey City, NJ, Nov 20, 33; m 55; c 4. STRUCTURAL CHEMISTRY. *Educ:* Syracuse Univ, BS, 55; Mass Inst Technol, PhD(org chem), 62. *Prof Exp:* Instr gen chem, US Air Force Acad, 62-63, res assoc, org chem, Frank J Seiler Res Lab, 63-66, chief anal & prog br, 544th aerospace reconnaissance tech wing, 66-67; res assoc chem, Univ Calif, Davis, 67-68; lectr chem & dir, Undergrad Labs, Mass Inst Technol, 68-71, dir chem spectrometry, 70-80. *Concurrent Pos:* Prof chem & head dept, Bellevue Col, 66-67; consult, Nuclear Advan Corp, 75- *Mem:* Am Chem Soc. *Res:* Nuclear magnetic resonance spectroscopy. *Mailing Add:* 153 Washington Ave Secaucus NJ 07094

TRAGER, WILLIAM, b Newark, NJ, Mar 20, 10; m 35; c 3. PARASITOLOGY. *Educ:* Rutgers Univ, BS, 30; Harvard Univ, AM, 31; PhD(biol), 33. *Hon Degrees:* ScD, Rutgers Univ, 65. *Prof Exp:* Nat Res Coun fel med, 33-34; fel, Rockefeller Inst, 34-35, asst, 35-40, assoc 40-50, assoc mem, 50-59, assoc prof, 59-64, PROF PARASITOL, ROCKEFELLER UNIV, 64- *Concurrent Pos:* Ed J, Soc Protozool, 53-65; mem study sect parasitol & trop med, Nat Inst Allergy & Infectious Dis, 54-58 & 66-70; mem training grant comt, 61-64; mem malaria comn, Armed Forces Epidemiol Bd, 65-70; guest investr, W African Inst Trypanosomiasis Res, 58-59; vis prof, Fla State Univ, 62, Med Sch, Puerto Rico, 63 & Med Sch, Nat Univ Mex, 65; Guggenheim found fel, 73; mem malaria immunol steering comt, WHO, 76-; mem microbiol & infectious dis adv comt, Nat Inst Allergy & Infectious Dis, 78-80. *Honors & Awards:* S T Darling Medal & Prize, World Health Orgn, 80; First Triannual Int Award, Rameshwardas Birla Kosh, Bombay, 82. *Mem:* Nat Acad Sci; Am Soc Parasitol (pres, 74); Soc Protozool (pres, 60-61); Am Soc Trop Med & Hyg (vpres, 64-65, pres, 78-79); NY Acad Sci. *Res:* Insect physiology; physiology of parasitisms; cultivation of intracellular parasites; malaria. *Mailing Add:* Rockefeller Univ York Ave & 66th St New York NY 10021

TRAGER, WILLIAM FRANK, b Winnipeg, Man, Oct 17, 37; m 60; c 3. PHARMACEUTICAL CHEMISTRY, ORGANIC CHEMISTRY. *Educ:* Univ San Francisco, BSc, 60; Univ Wash, PhD(pharmaceut chem), 65. *Prof Exp:* NIH fel pharm, Chelsea Col Sci & Technol, London, 65-67; fel, Univ Wash, 67; asst prof chem & pharmaceut chem, Sch Pharm, Univ San Francisco, 67-72; assoc prof, 72-77, PROF PHARMACEUT CHEM, SCH PHARM, UNIV WASH, 77- *Mem:* Am Chem Soc. *Res:* Drug metabolism studies and mass spectroscopy. *Mailing Add:* Sch of Pharm Univ of Wash Seattle WA 98195

TRAHAN, DONALD HERBERT, b North Adams, Mass, Mar 14, 30; m 61, 76; c 1. MATHEMATICS. *Educ:* Univ Vt, BS, 52; Univ Nebr, MA, 54; Univ Pittsburgh, PhD, 61. *Prof Exp:* Instr math, Univ Mass, 56-59; asst prof, Univ Pittsburgh, 61-65; asst prof & chmn dept, Chatham Col, 65-66; ASSOC PROF MATH, NAVAL POSTGRAD SCH, 66- *Concurrent Pos:* Hays-Fulbright lectr, Nat Univ Ireland, 63-64. *Mem:* Am Math Soc; Math Asn Am. *Res:* Complex variables; univalent function theory; real analysis. *Mailing Add:* 19514 Creekside Ct Salinas CA 93908

TRAHANOVSKY, WALTER SAMUEL, b Conemaugh, Pa, June 15, 38; m 67; c 3. ORGANIC CHEMISTRY. *Educ:* Franklin & Marshall Col, BS, 60; Mass Inst Technol, PhD(chem), 63. *Prof Exp:* NSF fel chem, Harvard Univ, 63-64; from instr to assoc prof, 64-74, PROF CHEM, IOWA STATE UNIV, 74- *Concurrent Pos:* A P Sloan fel, 70-72. *Mem:* AAAS; Am Chem Soc; Royal Soc Chem. *Res:* Physical-organic chemistry, including the study of oxidations and reductions of organic compounds; oxidative cleavages; cyclization reactions; free radicals; carbocations; arene tricarbonylchromium complexes; flash vacuum pyrolysis; methylenecyclobutenones; tropolone derivatives. *Mailing Add:* Dept of Chem Iowa State Univ Ames IA 50011

TRAIL, CARROLL C, b Forney, Tex, Dec 25, 27; m 51; c 3. NUCLEAR PHYSICS. *Educ:* Agr & Mech Col Tex, BS, 49, MS, 51, PhD, 56. *Prof Exp:* Asst physics, Argonne Nat Lab, 56-60, assoc physicist, 60-64; assoc prof, 64-68, chmn dept, 69-76, PROF PHYSICS, BROOKLYN COL, 68- *Concurrent Pos:* Vis prof, Linear Accelerator Lab, Orsay, France, 70-71; vis scientist, Mass Inst Technol, 77-78; fel, Sci Fac Imp Prog, NSF, 77-78. *Mem:* Fel Am Phys Soc. *Res:* Low energy; nuclear experimentation. *Mailing Add:* Dept of Physics Brooklyn Col Brooklyn NY 11210

TRAIL, STANLEY M, statistics, see previous edition

TRAIN, CARL T, b Lindsborg, Kans, Jan 19, 39; m 60; c 3. PARASITOLOGY, INVERTEBRATE ZOOLOGY. *Educ:* Bethany Col (Kans), BS, 61; Kans State Univ, MS, 63, PhD(parasitol), 67. *Prof Exp:* Asst zool, Kans State Univ, 61-64, instr, 66-67; asst prof, 67-73, assoc prof, 73-79, PROF BIOL, SOUTHEAST MO STATE UNIV, 79- *Mem:* Am Soc Parasitol; Am Micros Soc. *Res:* General parasitology, biology and reproduction of nematodes; life cycles of parasites; anthelmintic studies and testing; application of statistical measurements to parasitological studies; parasites of aquatic birds. *Mailing Add:* Dept Biol Southeast Mo State Univ Cape Girardeau MO 63701

TRAINA, PAUL J(OSEPH), b New York, NY, Mar 8, 34; m 55; c 5. CIVIL ENGINEERING. *Educ:* Manhattan Col, BCE, 55; Univ Mich, MS, 60. *Prof Exp:* Chief water resources, Southeast Region, USPHS, 60-64; asst dir comprehensive planning, Fed Water Pollution Control Admin, 64-67, dir tech progs, Southeast Region, 67-71, dir off water progs, 71-73, dir enforcement, 73-79, DIR WATER DIV, REGION IV, ENVIRON PROTECTION AGENCY, 79- *Mem:* Am Soc Civil Engrs; Water Pollution Control Fedn; NY Acad Sci; Air Pollution Control Asn. *Res:* Implementation of all federal water supply and water quality control environmental laws in southeast United States; plan, direct, implement and evaluate regional water programs. *Mailing Add:* Environ Protection Agency 345 Courtland St Atlanta GA 30308

TRAINA, VINCENT MICHAEL, b Oceanside, NY, May 8, 43. TOXICOLOGY. *Educ:* Rutgers Univ, BA, 65, MS, 70, PhD(physiol), 73; Am Bd Toxicol, dipl, 81. *Prof Exp:* Res investr toxicol, Squibb Inst Med Res, 66-74; mgr toxicol, 74-79, ASSOC DIR TOXICOL & PATH, CIBA-GEIGY CORP, 79- *Honors & Awards:* Supvry Develop Prog Award, Squibb Inst, 74. *Mem:* Sigma Xi; Environ Mutagen Soc; Am Soc Zoologists; Am Inst Biol Sci; Am Col Toxicol. *Res:* Body fluid volumes and concentrations and electrolyte changes during periods of prolonged starvation; all phases of toxicology. *Mailing Add:* Ciba-Geigy Corp Morris Ave Summit NJ 07901

TRAINER, DANIEL OLNEY, b Chicago, Ill, July 13, 26; m 55; c 2. WILDLIFE DISEASES. *Educ:* Ripon Col, BS, 50; Univ Wis-Madison, MS, 55, PhD(bact), 61. *Prof Exp:* Res virologist, Fromm Labs, 55-56; pathologist, Wis Conserv Dept, 56-62; from asst prof to prof vet sci, Univ Wis-Madison, 62-71; dean, Col Natural Resources, 71-80, VCHANCELLOR, UNIV WIS-STEVENS POINT, 80- *Honors & Awards:* Distinguished Serv Award, Wildlife Dis Asn, 73. *Mem:* AAAS; Wildlife Dis Asn (vpres, 66-68, pres, 68-70); Wildlife Soc; Am Inst Biol Sci; Soc Am Foresters. *Res:* Ecology of disease, especially diseases of wild or natural populations. *Mailing Add:* Col of Natural Resources Univ of Wis Stevens Point WI 54481

TRAINER, DAVID GIBSON, b Allentown, Pa, Mar 11, 45; m 74. PHYSIOLOGY. *Educ:* Washington & Jefferson Col, AB, 67; Univ Maine, MSc, 69; Univ NH, PhD(zool), 75. *Prof Exp:* Asst prof, 75-78, ASSOC PROF BIOL, EAST STROUDSBURG STATE COL, 78- *Mem:* AAAS; Am Soc Zoologists. *Res:* Physiology of invertebrates; immune response. *Mailing Add:* Dept of Biol East Stroudsburg State Col East Stroudsburg PA 18301

TRAINER, JOHN EZRA, JR, b Allentown, Pa, Aug 31, 43; m 67; c 3. HELMINTHOLOGY, BIOLOGICAL CHEMISTRY. *Educ:* Muhlenburg Col, BS, 65; Wake Forest Univ, MA, 67; Univ Okla, PhD(zool), 71. *Prof Exp:* Teaching asst, Wake Forest Univ, 65-67; teaching asst, Univ Okla, 67-69; asst prof, 71-78, ASSOC PROF BIOL, JACKSONVILLE UNIV, 78-, VPRES & DEAN FAC, 81- *Concurrent Pos:* Teaching asst biol sta, Mich State Univ, 66 & Univ Okla, 67; consult, Environ Ctr. *Mem:* Am Soc Parasitol; Am Soc Zool; Am Inst Biol Sci; AAAS. *Res:* Ecology, biochemistry and ultrastructure of the Pentastomida and other parasitic helminths. *Mailing Add:* Dept of Biol Jacksonville Univ Jacksonville FL 32211

TRAINER, JOHN EZRA, SR, b Allentown, Pa, Feb 8, 14; m 39; c 2. ORNITHOLOGY. *Educ:* Muhlenberg Col, BS, 35; MS, Cornell Univ, 38, PhD(ornith), 46. *Prof Exp:* Teacher biol, Tenn State Teachers Col, 38-39; from instr to prof, 39-65, sr prof, 65-80, EMER PROF BIOL, MUHLENBERG COL, 80- *Mem:* Wilson Ornith Soc; Am Ornith Union. *Res:* Hearing ability of birds; auditory acuity of certain birds; respiration of birds; vertebrate morphology. *Mailing Add:* Dept of Biol Muhlenberg Col Allentown PA 18104

TRAINOR, FRANCIS RICE, b Pawtucket, RI, Feb 11, 29; m 56. PHYCOLOGY. *Educ:* Providence Col, BS, 50; Vanderbilt Univ, MA, 53, PhD(biol), 57. *Prof Exp:* From instr to assoc prof, 57-67, PROF BOT, UNIV CONN, 67- *Concurrent Pos:* Consult, Elec Boat Div, Gen Dynamics Corp, Conn, 58-61; Fulbright res scholar, Stockholm, 70; Fulbright lectr, Greece & Yugoslavia, 71. *Honors & Awards:* Distinguished Fac Award, Univ Conn, 62; Darbaker Award, Bot Soc Am, 65. *Mem:* AAAS; Phycol Soc Am (vpres, 68, pres, 69); Brit Phycol Soc; Int Phycol Soc; Am Inst Biol Sci. *Res:* Sexual reproduction in unicellular algae; algal nutrition and morphogenesis; eutrophication. *Mailing Add:* Biol Sci Group Bot Sect Univ Conn Storrs CT 06268

TRAINOR, GEORGE L, b Staten Island, NY, Aug 19, 52; m 75. BIO-ORGANIC CHEMISTRY. *Educ:* Stevens Inst Technol, BS, 74; Harvard Univ, MA & PhD(chem), 79. *Prof Exp:* Res asst org chem, Stevens Inst Technol, 71-74, Harvard Univ, 75-79; res assoc, Columbia Uni, 79-81; CHEMIST ORG CHEM, CENT RES & DEVELOP, E I DU PONT DE NEMOURS & CO, INC, 81- *Concurrent Pos:* Teaching asst org chem, Stevens Inst Technol, 73-74, Harvard Univ, 74-77. *Mem:* Sigma Xi; Am Chem Soc. *Res:* Organic chemistry of biologically relevant processes. *Mailing Add:* Exp Sta E I Du Pont de Nemours & Co Inc Bldg 328-203 Wilmington DE 19898

TRAINOR, LYNNE E H, b Chamberlain, Sask, Dec 4, 21; div; c 3. THEORETICAL PHYSICS. *Educ:* Univ Sask, BA, 46, MA, 47; Univ Minn, PhD(physics), 51. *Prof Exp:* Fel, Nat Res Coun Can, 51-52; asst prof physics, Queen's Univ, Ont, 52-55; vis prof, Univ BC, 55-56; from asst prof to prof, Univ Alta, 56-63; PROF PHYSICS, UNIV TORONTO, 63- *Concurrent Pos:* Chmn, North York Bd Educ, 70-72. *Mem:* Am Phys Soc; Can Asn Physicists (secy, 66-68, hon secy-treas, 68-70); Biophys Soc. *Res:* properties of nuclear matter; statistical mechanics of Bose-Einstein systems; properties of thin helium films; field approach to structuralism in theoretical biology; theoretical biology and biophysics; pattern formation and morphology of developmental systems; structure and function of DNA; transmembrane transport. *Mailing Add:* Dept Physics Univ Toronto Toronto ON M5S 1A7 Can

TRAINOR, ROBERT JAMES, b Bell, Calif, June 15, 44; m. PHYSICS. *Educ:* Calif State Polytech Univ, BS, 66; Univ Calif, Riverside, MS, 69, PhD(physics), 74. *Prof Exp:* Res assoc physics, Argonne Nat Lab, 74-76; PHYSICIST, LAWRENCE LIVERMORE NAT LAB, 76- *Mem:* Am Phys Soc. *Res:* Experimental condensed matter physics; properties of matter at extreme high pressures and temperatures; laser-matter interactions. *Mailing Add:* Lawrence Livermore Nat Lab Mail Stop L-355 Livermore CA 94550

TRAISMAN, HOWARD SEVIN, b Chicago, Ill, Mar 18, 23; m 56; c 3. PEDIATRICS. *Educ:* Northwestern Univ, BS, 43, BM, 46, MD, 47. *Prof Exp:* Intern, Cook County Hosp, Chicago, 46-47; resident, Children's Mem Hosp, 49-51; from instr to assoc, 52-57, from asst prof to assoc prof, 62-73, PROF PEDIAT, MED SCH, NORTHWESTERN UNIV, CHICAGO, 73- *Concurrent Pos:* Attend pediatrician, Children's Mem Hosp, 52- & Northwestern Mem Hosp, 67- *Mem:* Am Acad Pediat; Am Pediat Soc; Endocrine Soc; Lawson Wilkins Pediat Endocrine Soc; Am Diabetes Asn. *Res:* Juvenile Diabetes Mellitus. *Mailing Add:* 1325 W Howard St Evanston IL 60202

TRAITOR, CHARLES EUGENE, b West Frankfort, Ill, Jan 28, 34; m 57; c 2. PHARMACOLOGY, TOXICOLOGY. *Educ:* St Louis Col Pharm, BS, 60; Purdue Univ, MS, 63, PhD(pharmacol), 65. *Prof Exp:* RES PHARMACOLOGIST & RES GROUP LEADER, TOXICOL EVAL DEPT, LEDERLE LABS DIV, AM CYANAMID CO, 65- *Res:* Toxicology of drugs on various organ systems; biochemical and other methods of detection of toxicological changes. *Mailing Add:* 187 Highview Ave Pearl River NY 10965

TRAJMAR, SANDOR, b Bogacs, Hungary, Sept 7, 31; US citizen; m 57; c 1. MOLECULAR PHYSICS. *Educ:* Debrecen Univ, dipl, 55; Univ Calif, Berkeley, PhD(phys chem), 61. *Prof Exp:* Chemist, N Hungarian Chem Works, 55-57; chemist, Stauffer Chem Co, 57-58; teaching asst phys chem, Univ Calif, Berkeley, 58-59, res asst, Lawrence Radiation Lab, 59-61; SR SCIENTIST, JET PROPULSION LAB, CALIF INST TECHNOL, 61-, HEAD MOLECULAR SPECTROS GROUP, 70- *Concurrent Pos:* Res fel, Calif Inst Technol, 64-66, sr res fel, 69- *Honors & Awards:* NASA Medal Except Sci Achievement, 73. *Mem:* Am Chem Soc; fel Am Phys Soc. *Res:* High temperature chemistry; molecular spectroscopy; low-energy electron scattering; atomic physics. *Mailing Add:* 4800 Oak Grove Dr Pasadena CA 91103

TRALLI, NUNZIO, physics, deceased

TRAMA, FRANCESCO BIAGIO, b Philadelphia, Pa, Dec 13, 27; m 54. LIMNOLOGY. *Educ:* Temple Univ, AB, 48, MA, 50; Univ Mich, PhD(zool), 57. *Prof Exp:* Asst limnol, Acad Natural Sci Philadelphia, 50-53; asst prof zool, Chicago Teachers Col, 57-60; asst prof, 60-63, ASSOC PROF ZOOL, RUTGERS COL, RUTGERS UNIV, NEW BRUNSWICK, 63-, ASSOC DEAN, 73- *Concurrent Pos:* Res assoc, Great Lakes Res Inst, Univ Mich, 57-61. *Mem:* Fel AAAS; Am Soc Limnol & Oceanog; Ecol Soc Am. *Res:* Trophic dynamics and energy transfer in aquatic ecosystem; primary productivity in fresh water. *Mailing Add:* Dept of Zool Rutgers Col of Rutgers Univ New Brunswick NJ 08903

TRAMBARULO, RALPH, b East Longmeadow, Mass, Jan 24, 25; m 55; c 4. PHYSICS, PHYSICAL CHEMISTRY. *Educ:* Yale Univ, BS, 44, PhD(phys chem), 49. *Prof Exp:* Res assoc, Duke Univ, 49-52; asst prof physics, Pa State Col, 52-53 & Univ Del, 53-56; MEM TECH STAFF, BELL TEL LABS, 56- *Mem:* Inst Elec & Electronics Engrs. *Res:* Microwave physics and spectroscopy; microwave integrated circuits. *Mailing Add:* Bell Tel Labs Box 400 Holmdel NJ 07733

TRAMELL, PAUL RICHARD, b El Centro, Calif, Mar 10, 43; m 67; c 1. PHARMACOLOGY, BIOCHEMISTRY. *Educ:* Fresno State Col, BA, 65, MA, 67; Rice Univ, PhD(biochem), 70. *Prof Exp:* Dir instrumentation, Cent Calif Med Labs, 65-67; biochemist, Abbott Labs, 71-72; SR PHARMACOLOGIST, ALZA CORP, 72- *Concurrent Pos:* Nat Inst Dent Res fel, Rice Univ, 70-; NIH fel pharmacol, Med Sch, Stanford Univ, 70-71. *Mem:* AAAS. *Res:* Enzymology; drug metabolism; pharmacokinetics. *Mailing Add:* Dept of Pharmacol Alza Corp Palo Alto CA 94304

TRAMMEL, KENNETH, b Skipperville, Ala, Oct 30, 37; m 58; c 4. ENTOMOLOGY. *Educ:* Univ Fla, BS, 60, PhD(entom), 65. *Prof Exp:* Res assoc citrus pest control, Citrus Exp Sta, Univ Fla, 64-65, asst entomologist, 65-67; entomologist, CIBA Agrochem Co, Fla, 67-69; assoc prof entom, NY State Agr Exp Sta, Cornell Univ, 69-75; OWNER & PRES, AGR CHEM DEVELOP SERV, INC, 75- *Mem:* Entom Soc Am; Weed Sci Soc Am. *Res:* Apple and pear pest management; field application of sex pheromones for monitoring and control of pests; contract field research with pesticides on fruit, vegetables and field crops. *Mailing Add:* Agr Chem Develop Serv Inc RD 1 Lester Rd Phelps NY 14532

TRAMMELL, GEORGE THOMAS, b Marshall, Tex, Feb 5, 23; m 45; c 4. THEORETICAL PHYSICS. *Educ:* Rice Inst, BA, 44; Cornell Univ, PhD, 50. *Prof Exp:* Physicist, Oak Ridge Nat Lab, 50-61; PROF PHYSICS, RICE UNIV, 61- *Mem:* Am Phys Soc. *Res:* Particle theory; solid state theory. *Mailing Add:* Dept of Physics Rice Univ Houston TX 77001

TRAMMELL, GROVER J(ACKSON), JR, b Attalla, Ala, July 17, 19; m 45; c 5. MECHANICAL ENGINEERING. *Educ:* Tulane Univ, BS, 49, MS, 50. *Prof Exp:* Instr math, La State Univ, 50-52, asst prof eng mech, 52-57; PROF MECH ENG, LA TECH UNIV, 57-, DIR CONTINUING EDUC, 67- *Mem:* Am Soc Eng Educ; Am Soc Mech Engrs; Nat Soc Prof Engrs. *Res:* Vibrations; solid mechanics; thermodynamics. *Mailing Add:* Dept of Mech Eng La Tech Univ Ruston LA 71270

TRAMMELL, JACK HARMAN, JR, poultry nutrition, see previous edition

TRAMMELL, REX COSTO, b Sevier County, Tenn, Nov 9, 38. NUCLEAR SCIENCE, SEMICONDUCTOR MATERIALS. *Educ:* Univ Tenn, BS, 65, MS, 69. *Prof Exp:* Staff physicist radiation detectors, 65-71, staff physicist semiconductor mat, 71-78, SR SCIENTIST, EG&G ORTEC INC, 78- *Honors & Awards:* EG&G Germeshausen Award, 78. *Mem:* Sr mem Inst Elec & Electronics Engrs. *Res:* Germanium crystal growth technology as applied to germanium gamma-ray spectrometers. *Mailing Add:* EG&G ORTEC Inc 100 Midland Lane Oak Ridge TN 37831

TRAMONDOZZI, JOHN EDMUND, b Malden, Mass, Aug 28, 42. ORGANIC CHEMISTRY. *Educ:* Boston Col, BS, 64, PhD(chem), 72. *Prof Exp:* Asst prof chem, 69-75, ASSOC PROF CHEM, CURRY COL, 75- *Mem:* Am Chem Soc; AAAS. *Res:* Reactions and syntheses of organic sulfur compounds, especially sufinates and sulfones; organic reactions in fused salt media. *Mailing Add:* Dept of Chem Sci Div Curry Col Milton MA 02186

TRAMPUS, ANTHONY, b Cleveland, Ohio, July 22, 27. MATHEMATICS. *Educ:* Case Inst Technol, BS, 51, PhD(math), 57; George Washington Univ, MS, 53. *Prof Exp:* Mathematician, Nat Bur Stand, DC, 51-53, Firestone Tire & Rubber Co, 53-56 & Gen Elec Co, 57-63; staff mathematician, Interstate Electronics Corp, Calif, 63-70; res mathematician, Univ Dayton Res Inst, 70-72; mathematician consult, Nat Space Technol Labs, Sperry Corp, 72-77; mathematical statistician, 77-80, OPER RES ANALYST, FED ENERGY REGULATORY COMN, DEPT ENERGY, 80- *Mem:* Am Math Soc; Soc Indust & Appl Math; Math Asn Am. *Res:* Function theory in linear algebra; mathematical analysis in science and engineering. *Mailing Add:* 2001 Columbia Pike Apt 214 Arlington VA 22204

TRAMS, EBERHARD GEORG, b Berlin, Ger, Jan 30, 26; nat US; m 50; c 3. BIOCHEMISTRY, PHARMACOLOGY. *Educ:* Andreas Gym, Berlin, BS, 46; George Washington Univ, PhD, 54. *Prof Exp:* Res assoc chemother, Cancer Clin, George Washington Univ, 51-55, asst prof pharmacol, Sch Med, 55-58; biochemist, Sect Lipid Chem, 58-60, actg chief, 60-64, CHIEF SECT PHYSIOL & METAB, DEVELOP & METAB NEUROL BR, NAT INST NEUROL & COMMUN DIS & STROKE, 64- *Mem:* Soc Exp Biol & Med; Am Soc Pharmacol & Exp Therapeut; Am Soc Biol Chemists; Soc Gen Physiologists; Am Soc Neurochem. *Res:* Neurochemistry; structure and function of complex lipids and plasma membrane; marine biology; chemical pharmacology. *Mailing Add:* Develop & Metab Neurol Br Nat Inst of Neurol & Commun Dis Bethesda MD 20205

TRAN, NANG TRI, b Binh Dinh, Viet Nam, Jan 2, 48. THIN FILM TECHNOLOGY. *Educ:* Kyushu Inst Technol, BEE, 73, MEE, 75; Univ Japan, PhD(elec eng), 79. *Prof Exp:* Res scientist, Sharp Electronic Inc, 79-80; RES SCIENTIST, ARCO SOLAR INDUST, 80- *Mem:* Japan Soc Appl Physics; Phys Soc Japan; Am Vacuum Soc; Inst Elec & Electronics Engrs. *Res:* Electrical and optical properties of zinc and sulfur; amorphous semiconductors and the devices based on these materials. *Mailing Add:* 1536 Earl Ave Simi Valley CA 93065

TRANIELLO, JAMES FRANCIS ANTHONY, b Somerville, Mass, Aug 24, 52; m 78. BEHAVIORAL ECOLOGY, SOCIOBIOLOGY. *Educ:* Boston Univ, AB, 74; Univ Mass, MS, 76; Harvard Univ, PhD(biol), 80. *Prof Exp:* Lectr biol & ethol, 80-81, RES ASSOC ENTOM, HARVARD UNIV, 81-; ASST PROF INSECT BIOL & SOCIOBIOL, BOSTON UNIV, 81- *Mem:* Int Union Study Social Insects; AAAS; Animal Behav Soc. *Res:* Behavioral ecology and sociobiology of insects, including communication, foraging behavior, defensive behavior and caste evolution. *Mailing Add:* Dept Biol Boston Univ 2 Cummington St Boston MA 02215

TRANK, JOHN W, b Minneapolis, Minn, July 24, 28; m 52; c 3. PHYSIOLOGY, ELECTRICAL ENGINEERING. *Educ:* Univ Minn, BEE, 51, MS, 56, PhD(physiol), 61. *Prof Exp:* From instr biophys to instr physiol, Univ Minn, 54-61; lectr, McGill Univ, 61-63, asst prof, 63-64; asst prof, 64-70, ASSOC PROF PHYSIOL, MED CTR, UNIV KANS, 70- *Concurrent Pos:* Dep dir univ surg clin, Montreal Gen Hosp, 61-64. *Mem:* AAAS; Am Physiol Soc; Inst Elec & Electronics Engrs; Biophys Soc. *Res:* Engineering analysis of cardiovascular control and instrumentation for biological research; bioengineering; mechanics of muscle contraction. *Mailing Add:* Dept Physiol Univ Kans Med Ctr Kansas City KS 66103

TRAN-MANH, NGO, nuclear medicine, medical physics, see previous edition

TRANNER, FRANK, b Chelsea, Mass, May 22, 22; m 49; c 4. PHARMACY, CHEMISTRY. *Educ:* Mass Col Pharm, BS, 43. *Prof Exp:* Develop & control chemist, Hat Corp Am, 44-46; develop chemist, Remington Rand Inc, 47-54 & Rilling-Dermetics Inc, 54-56; asst chief chemist, Germaine Monteil Cosmetiques, 57-59; develop chemist & sect head, 60-69, res mgr, 69-72, dir tech serv, 72-76, DIR APPL TECHNOL, CHESEBROUGH-POND'S INC, 76- *Mem:* Fel Am Inst Chemists; Am Chem Soc; Am Pharmaceut Asn; Soc Cosmetic Chem. *Res:* Research and development of cosmetic, food, toiletry and pharmaceutical products and processes. *Mailing Add:* 23 Beech Tree Circle Trumbull CT 06611

TRANQUADA, ROBERT ERNEST, internal medicine, see previous edition

TRANSUE, LAURENCE FREDERICK, b Summerfield, Kans, Apr 2, 14; m 58. PHYSICAL CHEMISTRY. *Educ:* Tarkio Col, AB, 36; Univ Nebr, AM, 39, PhD(phys chem), 41. *Prof Exp:* Asst, Univ Nebr, 37-41; res chemist, E I du Pont de Nemours & Co, Inc, 41-50, supvr, 50-52, supt & res mgr, Photo-prod Dept, 52-78; RETIRED. *Mem:* Am Chem Soc; Soc Photog Sci & Eng. *Res:* Surface films; chemistry and physics of photography. *Mailing Add:* 110 Wendover Rd Rochester NY 14610

TRANSUE, WILLIAM REAGLE, b Pen Argyl, Pa, Nov 30, 14; m 36; c 3. MATHEMATICAL ANALYSIS. *Educ:* Lafayette Col, BS, 35; Lehigh Univ, MA, 39, PhD(math), 41. *Prof Exp:* Asst, Inst Advan Study, 42-43; assoc physicist, Ord Dept, US Dept Army, 43-44, physicist, 44-45; assoc prof math, Kenyon Col, 45-48; asst, Inst Advan Study, 48-49; prof math, Kenyon Col, 49-66; prof math, State Univ NY Binghamton, 66-81. *Concurrent Pos:* Fulbright scholar, Italy, 51-52; NSF fac fel, Paris, 60-61. *Mem:* Am Math Soc; Math Asn Am. *Res:* Functional analysis; theory of measure and integration. *Mailing Add:* RD 1 Box 322 Mt Bethel PA 18343

TRANTHAM, J(OSEPH) C(OLLIER), b Waco, Tex, Aug 28, 18; m 44; c 4. PETROLEUM ENGINEERING, CHEMISTRY. *Educ:* Baylor Univ, AB, 39; Brown Univ, PhD(chem), 42. *Prof Exp:* Res chemist, Tex Co, 42-46; from assoc prof to prof chem, Baylor Univ, 46-53; res chemist, Phillips Petrol Co, 53-60, mgr pilot projs sect prod res, 60-69, sr secondary recovery engr, Explor & Prod Dept, 69-74, reservoir eng consult, Natural Resources Group, 74-79, staff dir enhanced oil recovery, Explor & Prod Group, 79-81; SR ENGR, KEPLINGER ASSOC INC, 82- *Mem:* Soc Petrol Engrs. *Res:* Physical and analytical chemistry; molecular association in nonpolar solvents; analytical research; behavior of associating molecules in electromagnetic fields; petroleum well stimulation; oil recovery by thermal methods; secondary and tertiary oil recovery engineering. *Mailing Add:* 4733 Dartmouth Dr Bartlesville OK 74003

TRAPANI, IGNATIUS LOUIS, b San Francisco, Calif, Nov 19, 25; m 52; c 2. PHYSIOLOGY, IMMUNOLOGY. *Educ:* Univ San Francisco, BS, 48, MS, 50; Stanford Univ, PhD(physiol), 56. *Prof Exp:* Asst physiol, Stanford Univ, 51-54, jr res assoc, 54-56; USPHS fel, Calif Inst Technol, 56-58, res fel immunochem, 56-60; asst chief dept exp immunol, Nat Jewish Hosp, 60-69, actg chief, 63-69; asst prof microbiol, Univ Colo Med Ctr, Denver, 65-69; PROF CHEM, COLO MOUNTAIN COL, 69-, CHMN DEPT SCI & MATH, 75- *Mem:* AAAS; Am Physiol Soc; Am Asn Immunol; Soc Exp Biol & Med; NY Acad Sci. *Res:* Physiological and physico-chemical properties of plasma substitutes; physiology and immunology of animals at high altitude and low temperatures; antigen-antibody complexes, immunophysiological parameters of antibody formation; appropriate technology; science and man; energy and its societal implications. *Mailing Add:* Div Sci & Math 3000 Co Rd 114 Glenwood Springs CO 81601

TRAPANI, ROBERT-JOHN, b New York, NY, Sept 8, 29; m 54; c 2. IMMUNOLOGY. *Educ:* NY Univ, AB, 49; Cath Univ Am, PhD, 60. *Prof Exp:* Med bacteriologist, Walter Reed Army Inst Res, 53-55; med bacteriologist, Nat Cancer Inst, 55-61; DIR DEPT IMMUNOL, MICROBIOL ASSOCS, INC, 61- *Res:* Natural resistance, immunity and influencing factors; Gram-negative endotoxins; human histocompatability; transplantation immunity. *Mailing Add:* Microbiol Assocs Inc 4846 Bethesda Ave Bethesda MD 20014

TRAPIDO, HAROLD, b Newark, NJ, Dec 10, 16; m 53; c 1. MEDICAL ENTOMOLOGY. *Educ:* Cornell Univ, BS, 38, AM, 39, PhD(zool), 43. *Prof Exp:* Asst zool, Cornell Univ, 38-42; biologist, Gorgas Mem Lab, 46-56; dep dir, Virus Res Ctr, India, 56-62; mem staff, Rockefeller Found & vis prof, Univ Del Valle, Colombia, 64-70; PROF TROP MED & MED PARASITOL, SCH MED, LA STATE UNIV, NEW ORLEANS, 70-, ACTG HEAD, 79- *Concurrent Pos:* Consult, USPHS, 47-49; consult, Div Med & Pub Health, Rockefeller Found, 50 & 52; mem, Expert Panel Malaria, WHO, 52-58, Expert Panel Virus Dis, 58-; mem, Sci Adv Bd, Indian Coun Med Res, 57-60 & Gorgas Mem Inst Tropical & Prev Med, 74-; mem, Inst Int Med, La State Univ Med Ctr. *Mem:* Fel AAAS; Royal Soc Trop Med & Hyg; Am Soc Parasitol; Am Soc Trop Med & Hyg; Soc Study Evolution. *Res:* Biology of arthropods and ecology of arthropod borne virus diseases. *Mailing Add:* Dept of Trop Med La State Univ Sch of Med New Orleans LA 70112

TRAPP, ALLAN LAVERNE, b Stockbridge, Mich, July 20, 32; m 55; c 4. VETERINARY PATHOLOGY. *Educ:* Mich State Univ, BS, 54, DVM, 56; Iowa State Univ, PhD(vet path), 60. *Prof Exp:* Vet livestock investr, Animal Dis Eradication Br, USDA, 56-57; res assoc animal dis res, Iowa State Univ, 57-60; asst prof, Ohio Agr Exp Sta, Ohio State Univ, 60-65, assoc prof, Ohio Agr Res & Develop Ctr, 65-66; assoc prof animal dis res, 66-70, PROF ANIMAL DIS DIAG WORK & TEACHING, MICH STATE UNIV, 70- *Concurrent Pos:* Mem, Med Adv Coun, Detroit Zoo, 69- *Mem:* Wildlife Dis Asn; Am Vet Med Asn. *Res:* Respiratory diseases of cattle; gastrointestinal diseases of cattle and swine; naturally occuring diseases in wild fishes. *Mailing Add:* Animal Health Diag Lab Mich State Univ Dept of Path East Lansing MI 48823

TRAPP, CHARLES ANTHONY, b Chicago, Ill, July 9, 36; m 58; c 2. PHYSICAL CHEMISTRY. *Educ:* Loyola Univ, Ill, BS, 58; Univ Chicago, MS, 60, PhD(chem), 63. *Prof Exp:* NSF fel physics, Oxford Univ, 62-63; asst prof chem, Ill Inst Technol, 63-69; assoc prof, 69-74, assoc prof chem, 74-81, PROF CHEM, UNIV LOUISVILLE, 81- *Concurrent Pos:* Petrol Res Fund starter grant, 63-64, type A res grant, 65-68; NSF res grant, 64-67; consult, Argonne Nat Lab, 69-; Res Corp grant, 70-72. *Mem:* Am Phys Soc. *Res:* Magnetic properties of matter; electron spin resonance in transition metal compounds, organic free radicals and biologically important compounds; electrical conductivity studies of nonmetals. *Mailing Add:* Dept of Chem Univ of Louisville Louisville KY 40208

TRAPP, GENE ROBERT, b Hammond, Wis, June 16, 38; m 60. MAMMALOGY. *Educ:* Wash State Univ, BS, 60; Univ Alaska, MS, 62; Univ Wis, PhD(zool), 72. *Prof Exp:* Res asst, Coop Wildlife Res Unit, Univ Alaska, 60-62; teaching asst, Dept Biol, Univ NMex, 62-63; wildlife biologist, US Soil Conserv, Honesdale, Pa, 63-64 & Br River Basin Studies, US Fish & Wildlife Serv, Tex, 64-65; teaching asst, Dept Zool, Univ Wis-Madison, 65-70; collabr carnivore res, US Nat Park Serv, Zion Nat Park, 67-69; asst prof, 70-76, ASSOC PROF BIOL, CALIF STATE UNIV, SACRAMENTO, 76- *Mem:* Am Soc Mammalogists; Ecol Soc Am; Animal Behav Soc; Wildlife Soc; AAAS. *Res:* The behavioral ecology of mammals, especially carnivores. *Mailing Add:* Dept of Biol Sci Calif State Univ Sacramento CA 95819

TRAPP, GEORGE E, JR, b Pittsburgh, Pa, June 30, 44; m 68; c 2. APPLIED MATHEMATICS. *Educ:* Carnegie-Mellon Univ, BS, 66, MS, 67, PhD(math), 70. *Prof Exp:* assoc prof 70-76, PROF COMPUT SCI, W VA UNIV, 76-; CONSULT, WESTINGHOUSE ELEC CORP, 70- *Mem:* Soc Indust & Appl Math; Sigma Xi; Am Math Soc; Asn Comput Mach. *Res:* Algebraic analysis of electrical networks and numerical analysis. *Mailing Add:* Dept of Statist & Comput Sci WVa Univ Morgantown WV 26506

TRAPP, ROBERT F(RANK), b Taylorville, Ill, Nov 4, 32; m 53; c 3. ENGINEERING PHYSICS, NUCLEAR ENGINEERING. *Educ:* Univ Ill, BS, 54. *Prof Exp:* Asst, Cyclotron Lab, Univ Ill, 54; assoc engr, Douglas Aircraft Co, Inc, 56-57, adv design coordr, 57-60, supvr adv propulsion, 60-61, chief proj engr, 61-62; br chief life sci, NASA, 62-68; chief res div, Weapons Eval & Control Bur, Arms Control & Disarmament Agency, Va, 68-72; mfrs rep, TDM, Inc, Fairfax, 72-76; dir tech res, Panasonic Co, 76-77; PRES, MICROELECTRONICS TECHNOL CORP, 77- *Mem:* Inst Elec & Electronic Engrs; Soc Automotive Engrs; Am Phys Soc; Am Mgt Asn; Int Soc Hybrid Microelectronics. *Res:* High temperature and thermal properties of materials for reactor cores and missile nosecones; engineering design and supervision of all aspects of nuclear rockets and aerospace life sciences; electronic components and subsystems applicable to consumer and industrial products; areas include hybrid circuits, monolytic IC's, sensors, displays, controllers, etc. *Mailing Add:* Microelectronics Technol Corp 2446 Watson Ct Palo Alto CA 94303

TRAPPE, JAMES MARTIN, b Spokane, Wash, Aug 16, 31; m 63; c 4. MYCOLOGY, FOREST PATHOLOGY. *Educ:* Univ Wash, BS, 53, PhD(forest bot), 62; State Univ NY, MS, 55. *Prof Exp:* Forester, Colville Nat Forest, 53-56, res forester, Pac Northwest Forest & Range Exp Sta, 56-65,

PROJ LEADER & PRIN MYCOLOGIST, PAC NORTHWEST FOREST & RANGE EXP STA, US FOREST SERV, 65-; assoc prof bot, 65-76, PROF BOT & FORESTRY, ORE STATE UNIV, 76- *Concurrent Pos:* NSF grants, 66-67, 68-69, 70-71, 74, 76 & 78; Am Philos Soc grants for mycol res, Univ Torino, Italy, 67-68, Nat Polytech Inst, Mex, 72; Japan Soc Prom Sci res fel, 75; mem, Joint Comn on Rural Reconstruct, Repub China, 77, Kuwait Inst Sci Res, 79. *Mem:* Fel AAAS; Brit Mycol Soc; Mex Soc Mycol; Mycol Soc Am; Japanese Mycol Soc. *Res:* Taxonomy of fungi, especially hypogeous species, Mycorrhizae; biological control of root diseases. *Mailing Add:* Pac NW Forest & Range Exp Sta 3200 Jefferson Way Corvallis OR 97331

TRAQUAIR, JAMES ALVIN, b London, Ont, Aug 1, 47. MYCOLOGY, PLANT PATHOLOGY. *Educ:* Univ Western Ont, BSc, 70; Univ Alta, PhD(mycol), 74. *Prof Exp:* Nat Res Coun Can fel plant path, Univ Western Ont, London, 74-77; res assoc mycol, Erindale Col, Univ Toronto, 77-78; plant pathologist forage path, Lethbridge, Alta, 78-81, TREE FRUIT PATHOLOGIST, RES STA, AGR CAN, HARROW, ONT, 81- *Mem:* Can Phytopath Soc; Can Bot Asn; Brit Mycol Soc; Mycol Soc Am; Can Soc Microbiol. *Res:* Biosystematics of polyporaceous basidiomycetes; microbial ecology; hyperparasitism of fungi; ultrastructure of fungi; host-parasite relations and epidemiology of snowmold diseases of winter cereals, forage legumes and grasses; biocontrol of canker, powdery mildew and replant disorders; tree fruit mycorrhizae. *Mailing Add:* Res Sta Agr Can Harrow ON N0R 1G0 Can

TRASK, CHARLES BRIAN, b Bar Harbor, Maine, June 13, 44; m 69; c 2. SEDIMENTOLOGY, COAL GEOLOGY. *Educ:* Amherst Col, BA, 66; Univ Tex, Austin, MA, 72; Syracuse Univ, PhD(geol), 76. *Prof Exp:* Res geologist, Gulf Sci & Technol Co, Gulf Oil Corp, 76-77; asst geologist, 77-81, ASSOC GEOLOGIST COAL, ILL STATE GEOL SURV, 81- *Mem:* Geol Soc Am; Int Asn Sedimentologists; Soc Econ Paleontologists & Mineralogists; Sigma Xi. *Res:* Sedimentary petrology; depositional environments of Pennsylvanian strata; coastal geology; coal geology. *Mailing Add:* 615 E Peabody Dr Champaign IL 61820

TRASK, NEWELL JEFFERSON, JR, geology, see previous edition

TRASKOS, RICHARD THOMAS, b New Britain, Conn, Jan 3, 40; m 64; c 2. POLYMER SCIENCE, CHEMICAL ENGINEERING. *Educ:* Univ Notre Dame, BS, 61; Mass Inst Technol, DSc(chem eng), 66. *Prof Exp:* RES ENGR, ROGERS CORP, 69- *Mem:* Am Chem Soc; Soc Photog Sci & Eng. *Res:* Development of polymer-based printing plates; study of lithography. *Mailing Add:* Herrick Rd Brooklyn CT 06234

TRASLER, DAPHNE GAY, b Iquique, Chile, July 2, 26; Can citizen; m 51; c 2. GENETICS. *Educ:* McGill Univ, BSc, 48, MSc, 54, PhD, 58. *Prof Exp:* Demonstr genetics, McGill Univ, 47; chief asst plant genetics, Inst Cotton Genetics, Peru, 49-51; demonstr genetics, 52-53, res assoc develop genetics & teratol, 58-70, ASSOC PROF BIOL, McGILL UNIV, 70- *Concurrent Pos:* Grants, NSF, 59-62, Asn Aid Crippled Children, 65-66, NIH, 66-69 & Nat Res Coun Can, 70-76 & Med Res Coun, 76; mem study sect, Div Res Grants, NIH, 80-82. *Mem:* Genetics Soc Can; Teratology Soc (pres, 72-73). *Res:* Gene-teratogen interaction and embryonic mechanisms in mouse neural tube defects; mouse teratology. *Mailing Add:* McGill Univ Dept of Biol 1205 Ave Docteur Penfield Montreal PQ H3A 1B1 Can

TRASS, O(LEV), b Estonia, Oct 9, 31; m 61; c 2. CHEMICAL ENGINEERING. *Educ:* Princeton Univ, BSE, 55; Mass Inst Technol, ScD(chem eng), 58. *Prof Exp:* From asst prof to assoc prof, 58-68, PROF CHEM ENG & APPL CHEM, UNIV TORONTO, 68- *Concurrent Pos:* Vis prof, Swiss Fed Inst Technol, 68-69; dir & consult, Chem Eng Res Consults, Ltd Can; mem, Grants Comt on Chem & Metall Eng, Nat Res Coun Can, 72-73, co-chmn, 73-74, chmn, 74-75; assoc chmn, Div Eng Sci, Univ Toronto, 74-77; vpres, Gen Comminution, Inc, 75-; vis prof, Ecole Nat Superieur Indust Chiniques, Nancy, France, 78. *Mem:* Am Chem Soc; Am Inst Chem Engrs; fel Chem Inst Can; Can Soc Chem Eng; Asn Advan Baltic Studies. *Res:* Fluid flow and mass transfer; solid-fluid interface phenomena; high temperature chemical reactions in shock tubes; comminution and particle dynamics; coal slurry fuels technology. *Mailing Add:* Dept of Chem Eng & Appl Chem Univ of Toronto Toronto ON M5S 1A4 Can

TRATHEN, ROLAND H(ENRY), b Rosendale, NY, Jan 11, 08; m 34; c 1. MECHANICS. *Educ:* Rensselaer Polytech Inst, CE, 30, MCE, 34. *Prof Exp:* Instr civil eng, 30-37, instr mech, 37-39, from asst prof to prof appl mech, 39-76, EMER PROF APPL MECH, RENSSELAER POLYTECH INST, 76- *Concurrent Pos:* Consult. *Mem:* Am Soc Metals; Soc Exp Stress Anal. *Res:* Experimental stress analysis; stress corrosion of magnesium alloys; damping capacity of metals; applied mechanics. *Mailing Add:* Box 214 RD 5 Troy NY 12180

TRAUB, ALAN CUTLER, b Hartford, Conn, Jan 20, 23; m 51; c 3. ELECTRO-OPTICS. *Educ:* Trinity Col, Conn, BS, 47; Univ Cincinnati, MS, 49, PhD(physics), 52. *Prof Exp:* Res physicist, Am Optical Co, 52-56; res physicist, Fenwal, Inc, 56-61, chief res engr, 61-63; mem tech staff, Mitre Corp, Mass, 63-70; chief scientist, Foto-Mem, Inc, 70-71; consult, 71-73; prod develop engr, Identicon Corp, 73-74; advan develop mgr, Vanzetti Infrared & Comput Systs, Inc, 74-80, ADVAN DEVELOP MGR, VANZETTI SYSTS, INC, 80- *Concurrent Pos:* Res fel, Tufts Univ, 72-73. *Honors & Awards:* Soc Tech Writers & Publ Award of Excellence, 70. *Mem:* Optical Soc Am. *Res:* Spectrophotometry; colorimetry; thin optical films; optical and thermal sensors; visual perception; three-dimensional displays; fiber optics; aerospace electro-optical instrumentation; atmospheric optical propagation; optical communications systems; laser applications; optical memories. *Mailing Add:* 56 Donna Rd Framingham MA 01701

TRAUB, JOSEPH FREDERICK, b WGer, June 24, 32; nat US; m 69; c 2. COMPUTER SCIENCE. *Educ:* City Col New York, BS, 54; Columbia Univ, PhD(appl math), 59. *Prof Exp:* Mem tech staff, Bell Tel Labs, Inc, NJ, 59-70; prof comput sci & math & head, Dept Comput Sci, Carnegie-Mellon Univ, 71-79; EDWIN HOWARD ARMSTRONG PROF COMPUT SCI, CHMN, DEPT COMPUT SCI & PROF MATH, COLUMBIA UNIV, 79- *Concurrent Pos:* Vis Mackay prof, Univ Calif, Berkeley, 78-79; mem staff, Int Math & Statist Libr, Houston, 70-81; mem adv comt fed judicial ctr; mem sci coun, Inst de Res d'Info et d'Automatique, Paris, 76-80, cent steering comt, Comput Sci & Eng Res Study, NSF & liaison to panel on theoret comput sci & panel on numerical complexity, 74-80; mem adv comt, Carnegie-Mellon Inst Res, 78-79, Inst Defense Anal, 76-79 & math & comput sci, NSF, 78-; mem, Conf Bd Math Sci & spec interest group numerical math; ed, J Comput & Syst Sci, 73- & Int J Comput & Math Appln, 74- *Mem:* Fel AAAS; Asn Comput Mach; Soc Indust & Appl Math; Am Math Soc. *Res:* Computational complexity; parallel computation; algorithmic analysis; numerical mathematics; large scientific problems. *Mailing Add:* Columbia Univ 406 Southwest Mudd New York NY 10027

TRAUB, RICHARD KIMBERLEY, b Bessemer, Mich, Mar 13, 34; m 56; c 2. MEDICAL RESEARCH. *Educ:* Johns Hopkins Univ, BES, 56; Towson State Col, MA, 71; Univ Del, MS, 75. *Prof Exp:* Res engr, Plastics Dept, Du Pont Co, 59-62; chief of group, Defense Develop & Eng Lab, 62-72, Human Factors Eng, 72-74, prog dir prophylaxis & ther, Biomed Lab, 74-80, PRIN INVESTR, NEUROTOX & EXP THERMAL BR, US MED RES INST DEFENSE, 80- *Concurrent Pos:* Mem, Pyrotech Comt, Am Ordnance Asn, 62-72; clin psychologist, Harford County, State Md, 71-; intel specialist, Surgeon Gen, US Army & mem, Acad Coun, Edgewood Arsenal, 73- *Mem:* Am Psychol Asn; Soc for Neurosci. *Res:* Therapy and prophylaxis against chemical warfare agents including basic mechanisms. *Mailing Add:* Edgewood Arsenal Biomed Lab Gunpowder MD 21010

TRAUB, ROBERT, b New York, NY, Oct 26, 16; m 39; c 2. MEDICAL ENTOMOLOGY. *Educ:* City Col New York, BS, 38; Cornell Univ, MS, 39; Univ Ill, PhD(med entom), 47. *Prof Exp:* Asst entom, Univ Ill, 39-41; chief dept parasitol, Med Ctr, US Army, 47-55, commanding officer, Med Res Unit, Malaya, 55-59, chief, Prev Med & Entom Res Br, Med Res & Develop Command, 59-62; PROF MICROBIOL, SCH MED, UNIV MD, 62- *Concurrent Pos:* Parasitologist, 4th Hoogstraal Exped, Mex, 41; field dir, Army Med Res Units, Malaya, NBorneo & Labrador, 47-55; Comn Hemorrhagic Fever, Korea, 52 & 53; Univ Md Sch Med Res Units, Pakistan, Ethiopia, Burma, Australia, Thailand & New Guinea; hon assoc, Field Mus, Ill, Smithsonian Inst, DC & Bishop Mus, Honolulu; consult ectoparasite-borne dis, WHO, US Army & US Navy; mem, Comn Rickettsial Dis, Armed Forces Epidemiol Bd, 64-73. *Mem:* AAAS; Entom Soc Am; fel Am Soc Parasitol; fel Am Soc Trop Med & Hyg; Soc Syst Zool. *Res:* Ecology and control of vectors and reservoirs of disease; systematics of Siphonaptera and trombiculid mites. *Mailing Add:* Dept of Microbiol Univ of Md Sch of Med Baltimore MD 21201

TRAUB, WESLEY ARTHUR, b Milwaukee, Wis, Sept 25, 40; m 63; c 1. INFRARED ASTRONOMY, STRATOSPHERIC COMPOSITION. *Educ:* Univ Wis-Milwaukee, BS, 62; Univ Wis, MS, 64, PhD(physics), 68. *Prof Exp:* PHYSICIST, CTR ASTROPHYS, SMITHSONIAN & HARVARD COL OBSERVS, 68-; LECTR ASTRON, HARVARD UNIV, 76- *Concurrent Pos:* Res assoc eng & appl physics, Harvard Univ, 68-74. *Mem:* AAAS; Am Astron Soc; Am Phys Soc; Optical Soc Am; Sigma Xi. *Res:* Far-infrared spectroscopy of astronomical objects and the terrestrial atmosphere to determine molecular abundances; infrared astronomical all-sky photometry with helium-cooled telescope on Spacelab-2; far-infrared laboratory spectroscopy of molecules of stratospheric interest; coherent arrays of optical telescopes for astronomy from space, design studies; Fourier-transform infrared spectrometers. *Mailing Add:* Smithsonian & Harvard Col Observs 60 Garden St Cambridge MA 02138

TRAUGER, DAVID LEE, b Ft Dodge, Iowa, June 16, 42; div; c 2. ZOOLOGY, ECOLOGY. *Educ:* Iowa State Univ, BS, 64, MS, 67, PhD(animal ecol), 71. *Prof Exp:* Instr zool & entom, Iowa State Univ, 67-70, asst prof zool & entom & exec secy environ coun, 70-72; wildlife res biologist, Northern Prairie Wildlife Res Ctr, Jamestown, NDak, 72-75, asst dir, 75-79, CHIEF, DIV WILDLIFE ECOL RES, FISH & WILDLIFE SERV, US DEPT INTERIOR, WASHINGTON, DC, 79- *Concurrent Pos:* Wildlife technician, Northern Prairie Wildlife Res Ctr, 66-70. *Mem:* Wildlife Soc; Am Ornith Union; Cooper Ornith Union; Wilson Ornith Soc. *Res:* Breeding biology, population dynamics, habitat requirements of waterfowl, particularly diving ducks in prairie parklands and subarctic taiga. *Mailing Add:* Div Wildlife Ecol Res US Fish & Wildlife Serv Washington DC 20240

TRAUGER, DONALD BYRON, b Exeter, Nebr, June 29, 20; m 45; c 2. PHYSICS. *Educ:* Nebr Wesleyan Univ, AB, 42. *Prof Exp:* Physicist, Manhattan Proj, Columbia Univ, 42-44; engr, Union Carbide Corp, 44-54; head irradiation eng dept, 54-64, dir gas-cooled reactor prog, 64-70, ASSOC DIR NUCLEAR & ENG TECHNOL, OAK RIDGE NAT LAB, 70- *Mem:* AAAS; fel Am Nuclear Soc; Am Phys Soc; Sigma Xi. *Res:* Reactor technology; gas cooled reactor fuels; nuclear irradiation tests of fuels and materials; liquid metals; behavior of gases; isotope separation. *Mailing Add:* Oak Ridge Nat Lab Oak Ridge TN 37830

TRAUGH, JOLINDA ANN, b Detroit, Mich. BIOCHEMISTRY, MOLECULAR BIOLOGY. *Educ:* Univ Calif, Davis, BS, 60; Univ Calif, Los Angeles, PhD(microbiol), 70. *Prof Exp:* Res asst, Gerbers Baby Foods, 60-62 & Univ Calif, Berkeley, 62-64; USPHS res fel molecular biol, Univ Calif, Davis, 71-73; asst prof, 73-78, ASSOC PROF BIOCHEM, UNIV CALIF, RIVERSIDE, 78-, CHMN DEPT, 81- *Concurrent Pos:* Resident scholar, Study & Conf Ctr, Rockefeller Found, Belliago, Italy, 79. *Res:* Regulation of protein synthesis; protein kinases. *Mailing Add:* Dept Biochem Univ Calif Riverside CA 92521

TRAUGOTT, STEPHEN C(HARLES), b Frankfurt, Ger, Dec 10, 27; nat US; m 55; c 2. FLUID DYNAMICS, HEAT TRANSFER. *Educ:* Johns Hopkins Univ, BES, 49, MSE, 51, DEng, 56. *Prof Exp:* Sr scientist, Res Dept, Martin Co, 57-66, chief aerophys res staff, 60-62, PRIN RES SCIENTIST, RES INST ADVAN STUDY, MARTIN MARIETTA LABS, 66- *Concurrent Pos:* Adj prof, Drexel Inst Technol, 59; vis lectr, Johns Hopkins Univ, 62-66; adj prof, Univ Md, 66-67; vis assoc prof, Cornell Univ, 67-68. *Mem:* Am Inst Aeronaut & Astronaut; Am Phys Soc; Soc Natural Philos. *Res:* High speed flow; radiation gas dynamics; dynamics of atmospheres; aluminum smelting. *Mailing Add:* Martin Marietta Labs 1450 S Rolling Rd Baltimore MD 21227

TRAUL, KARL ARTHUR, immunology, virology, see previous edition

TRAUMANN, KLAUS FRIEDRICH, b Schweinfurt, Ger, Mar 23, 24; nat US; m 58. ORGANIC CHEMISTRY. *Educ:* Univ Heidelberg, PhD(org chem), 54. *Prof Exp:* Res chemist, Carothers Lab, 54-66, sr res chemist, Textile Res Lab, 67-73, DEVELOP ASSOC, TEXTILE RES LAB, E I DU PONT DE NEMOURS & CO, INC, 73- *Mem:* Am Chem Soc. *Res:* Synthetic organic fibers. *Mailing Add:* Textile Res Lab E I du Pont de Nemours & Co Inc Wilmington DE 19898

TRAURIG, HAROLD HENRY, b Chicago, Ill, July 28, 36; m 59; c 3. ANATOMY, ENDOCRINOLOGY. *Educ:* Mankato State Col, BS, 58; Univ Minn, PhD(anat), 63. *Prof Exp:* From instr to asst prof, 63-69, ASSOC PROF ANAT, MED CTR, UNIV KY, 69- *Concurrent Pos:* NIH res grants, 64-67 & 68-72; res fel neurochem, Ohio State Univ, 70-71. *Mem:* Am Asn Anatomists; Soc Exp Biol & Med; Soc Study Reproduction. *Res:* Cytology; neurobiology; radioautography; cell proliferation. *Mailing Add:* Dept of Anat Univ of Ky Med Ctr Lexington KY 40506

TRAURING, MITCHELL, b Brooklyn, NY, Mar 8, 22; m 43; c 2. OPERATIONS RESEARCH. *Educ:* Brooklyn Col, BA, 41; Johns Hopkins Univ, MA, 47; Univ Calif, Los Angeles, MS, 76. *Prof Exp:* Physicist, Nat Adv Comt Aeronaut, 41-46; optical engr, Bur Ships, US Dept Navy, 49; ballistician & sect head, Ballistics Res Labs, Ord Corps, US Dept Army, 49-53; sect head, Guided Missiles Div, Repub Aviation Corp, 53-57; asst sect head, Ground Systs Group, Hughes Aircraft Co, 57-59, sr staff physicist, Res Labs, 59-63, sr staff engr, Aerospace Corp, Calif, 63-68; sr mem tech staff, Data Systs Div, Litton Industs, Inc, 68-72; consult opers anal, 72-78; SR STAFF PHYSICIST, HUGHES AIRCRAFT CO, 78- *Mem:* Sigma Xi; Opers Res Soc Am. *Res:* Weapon, electronic and space systems; automatic recognition; business and international economics. *Mailing Add:* 1645 Comstock Ave Los Angeles CA 90024

TRAUT, ROBERT RUSH, b Utica, NY, Oct 21, 34; m 62; c 1. BIOCHEMISTRY, MOLECULAR BIOLOGY. *Educ:* Haverford Col, AB, 56; Rockefeller Univ, PhD(biochem), 62. *Prof Exp:* Res asst, Inst Molecular Biol, Univ Geneva, 64-68, Am Heart Asn estab investr, 68-70; assoc prof, 70-76, PROF BIOL CHEM, SCH MED, UNIV CALIF, DAVIS, 76- *Concurrent Pos:* Jane Coffin Childs Mem Fund fel molecular biol, Med Res Coun Lab Molecular Biol, Cambridge Univ, 62-64; Am Heart Asn estab investr, Univ Calif, Davis, 70-73. *Mem:* AAAS; Am Soc Microbiol; NY Acad Sci; Am Soc Biol Chem. *Res:* Mechanism and regulation of protein synthesis; structure and function of ribosomes. *Mailing Add:* Dept of Biol Chem Sch of Med Univ of Calif Davis CA 95616

TRAUTH, CHARLES ARTHUR, JR, mathematics, see previous edition

TRAUTMAN, JACK CARL, b Cushing, Okla, Dec 7, 29; m 57; c 1. DAIRY SCIENCE, BIOCHEMISTRY. *Educ:* Univ Idaho, BS, 51; Univ Calif, MS, 53; Univ Wis, PhD(dairy tech), 58. *Prof Exp:* Asst dairy indust, Univ Calif, 51-53; asst dairy & food indust, Univ Wis, 56-58, from instr to asst prof dairy indust, 58-59; asst prof dairy technol, Ohio State Univ, 59-60; supvr indust prod & processes, 60-72, MGR BIOL RES, OSCAR MAYER & CO, 72- *Concurrent Pos:* Mem sci adv comt, Fats & Protein Res Found. *Mem:* Am Chem Soc; Am Meat Sci Asn; Inst Food Technol. *Res:* Process development of animal biologicals; professional activity as a scientific entrepreneur developing processes for biologicals needed in human disease states; engineering scale-ups, new plant construction and their business management; products include enzymes, anti-coagulants and blood fractions. *Mailing Add:* Oscar Mayer & Co Res Div 910 Mayer Ave Madison WI 53701

TRAUTMAN, MILTON BERNHARD, b Columbus, Ohio, Sept 7, 99; m 40; c 1. ZOOLOGY. *Hon Degrees:* DSc, Col Wooster, 51 & Ohio State Univ, 78. *Prof Exp:* Asst, Bur Sci Res, Ohio Div COnserv, 30-34; asst cur, Mus Zool, Univ Mich, 34-39; res biologist, Stone Lab, 39-40, res assoc, Stone Inst Hydrobiol, 40-55, lectr zool & cur vert collections, Dept Zool & Entom, 55-69, prof fac biol, Col Biol Sci, 69-72, EMER PROF ZOOL & EMER CUR BIRDS, OHIO STATE UNIV, 72- *Concurrent Pos:* Asst dir inst fisheries res, State Conserv Dept, Mich, 34-35, res assoc, 35-36; mem, Univ Mich Zool Exped, Yucatan, 36; consult, US Bur Comm Fish, 59 & 61; mem, Ohio State Univ Exped, Inst Polar Studies, Alaska, 65; res assoc biol, John Carroll Univ, 72-74. *Honors & Awards:* Wildlife Soc Award, 58. *Mem:* AAAS; Wilson Ornith Soc (treas, 43-45); Am Soc Ichthyol & Herpet (vpres, 46-49); Am Ornith Union. *Res:* Factors affecting animal distribution and abundance; animal behavior; changes in animal and plant distribution and abundance in Ohio since 1750; endangered vertebrates; Great Lakes wetlands; author of over 140 publications. *Mailing Add:* Mus of Zool 1813 N High St Ohio State Univ Columbus OH 43210

TRAUTMAN, RODES, b Portsmouth, NH, Apr 7, 23; m 46; c 3. BIOPHYSICS. *Educ:* Yale Univ, BE, 44; Univ Calif, PhD(biophys), 50. *Prof Exp:* Res asst phys biochem, Donner Lab, Univ Calif, 50-54; asst phys chem, Med Lab, Rockefeller Univ, 54-57; CHIEF RES PHYSICIST, PLUM ISLAND ANIMAL DIS CTR, USDA, 57- *Concurrent Pos:* Res collabr, Brookhaven Nat Lab, 56- *Mem:* Biophys Soc; Sigma Xi. *Res:* Application of physics and mathematics to virus research; analytical and preparative ultracentrifugation; programming and utilization of digital computers; simulation of immunochemical reactions; information retrieval. *Mailing Add:* USDA Plum Island Animal Dis Ctr PO Box 848 Greenport NY 11944

TRAVELLI, ARMANDO, b Rome, Italy, Feb 6, 34; m 70. NUCLEAR ENGINEERING & SCIENCE. *Educ:* Univ Rome, Dr Ing, 58; Rensselaer Polytech Inst, PhD(nuclear eng, sci), 63. *Prof Exp:* Res asst nuclear eng & sci, Rensselaer Polytech Inst, 61-63; asst prof nuclear eng, Mass Inst Technol, 63-65; asst nuclear engr, 65-68, nuclear engr, 68-69, head, Fast Flux Test Facil Sect, 69-74, head, Physics Reactor Safety Sect, 74-76, assoc dir, Safety Test Facil Proj, 76-78, MGR, REACTOR PROG, APPL PHYSICS DIV, ARGONNE NAT LAB, 78- *Concurrent Pos:* Ford Found res fel eng, 63-65. *Mem:* Am Nuclear Soc; AAAS; Sigma Xi. *Res:* Analysis and design of research reactors, safety test facilities, critical experiments and fast breeder reactors; neutron transport and high-order perturbation theories; analysis of neutron waves and pulses. *Mailing Add:* Appl Physics Div 9700 S Cass Ave Argonne IL 60439

TRAVER, ALFRED ELLIS, b New York, NY, Dec 17, 39; m 66; c 1. MECHANICAL ENGINEERING, SYSTEMS ENGINEERING. *Educ:* Mass Inst Technol, BS, 61; Iowa State MS, 62; Univ Tex, Austin, PhD(mech eng), 68. *Prof Exp:* Researcher, Mass Inst Technol-Harvard Joint Ctr Urban Studies, 60-61; aerosysts engr, Gen Dynamics Corp, 63-64; engr-scientist, Tracor, Inc, 66-70; PROF MECH ENG & ACTG CHMN DEPT SYSTS ENG, TENN TECHNOL UNIV, 70- *Concurrent Pos:* Vis prof mech eng, Univ Tex, Austin. *Mem:* Am Soc Mech Engrs; Opers Res Soc Am; Inst Elec & Electronics Engrs; Am Soc Eng Educ; Nat Soc Prof Engrs. *Res:* Simulation and modeling of dynamic systems; control systems; design studies; interface of technology and the law. *Mailing Add:* Dept of Mech Eng Tenn Technol Univ Cookeville TN 38501

TRAVER, JANET HOPE, b Boston, Mass, Apr 18, 26. BIOCHEMISTRY. *Educ:* Cornell Univ, BS, 47; Mich State Univ, MS, 49. *Prof Exp:* Asst nutrit, Mich State Univ, 47-49; res assoc biochem, 50-65, res biochemist, 65-77, SR RES BIOCHEMIST, STERLING-WINTHROP RES INST, 77- *Res:* Isolation of natural products. *Mailing Add:* 11 Brilan Ave East Greenbush NY 12061

TRAVERS, JOHN JOSEPH, b Philadelphia, Pa, May 20, 18; m 42; c 4. BIOCHEMISTRY. *Educ:* St Joseph's Col, Pa, BS, 39; Univ Detroit, MS, 41; Fordham Univ, PhD(biochem), 51. *Prof Exp:* Res chemist, Arlington Chem Co, 46-48; asst, Fordham Univ, 48-51, res assoc, 51, head org chemist sect, Eastern Res Div, Stauffer Chem Co, 53-55; sr res assoc, Res & Develop Div, Lever Bros Co, 55-62; mgr semibasic res dept, 62-64, dir res, 64-70, SR RES & DEVELOP ASSOC, AVON PROD, INC, 70- *Mem:* Am Chem Soc. *Res:* Biometrics; biocidal agents; toxicology; skin structure and function. *Mailing Add:* 38 Johnson's Lane New City NY 10956

TRAVERS, WILLIAM BRAILSFORD, b Long Beach, Calif, June 13, 34; m 58; c 3. GEOLOGY. *Educ:* Stanford Univ, BS, 56, MS, 59; Princeton Univ, PhD(geol), 72. *Prof Exp:* Geologist, Stand Oil Co, Calif, 59-61; geologist, Sante Fe Drilling Co, 61-63; chief geologist, Santa Fe Int, Inc, 63-67; asst instr geol, Princeton Univ, 67-71; asst prof, 72-78, ASSOC PROF GEOL SCI, CORNELL UNIV, 78- *Concurrent Pos:* Consult petrol geologist; vpres, Anacapa Oil Co, 67-; vis prof, Stanford Univ, 79; res vis, Oxford Univ, 80. *Mem:* AAAS; fel Geol Soc Am; Am Asn Petrol Geol; Am Geophys Union; fel Geol Asn Can. *Res:* Problems of mountain building; deformation of continental margins; structural geology and sedimentology; continental rifting; tectonism in Italy, western United States and western Canada. *Mailing Add:* Dept of Geol Sci Cornell Univ Ithaca NY 14853

TRAVERSE, ALFRED, b Port Hill, Prince Edward Island, Sept 7, 25; nat US; m 51; c 4. PALYNOLOGY, PALEOBOTANY. *Educ:* Harvard Univ, SB, 46, AM, 48, PhD(paleobot), 51; Episcopal Theol Sem Southwest, MDiv, 65. *Prof Exp:* Coal technologist, Lignite Res Lab, US Bur Mines, NDak, 51-55, head fuels micros lab, Colo, 55; geologist, Shell Develop Co, 55-62; palynological consult, Tex, 62-65; asst prof geol, Univ Tex, 65-66; assoc prof, 66-70, PROF PALYNOLOGY, PA STATE UNIV, UNIVERSITY PARK, 70- *Concurrent Pos:* Mem, Int Comn Palynology, 73-76, pres, 77-80; vis prof, Swiss Fed Tech Inst, Zürich, 80-81. *Mem:* Am Asn Stratig Palynologists (pres, 70-71); AAAS; Paleont Soc; Geol Soc Am; Bot Soc Am; Int Asn Plant Taxon. *Res:* Palynology of Cenozoic and older rocks; theory of palynology. *Mailing Add:* Dept of Geosci Deike 435 Pa State Univ University Park PA 16802

TRAVIS, DAVID M, b Nashville, Tenn, June 6, 26; m 53; c 3. INTERNAL MEDICINE, PHARMACOLOGY. *Educ:* Vanderbilt Univ, BA, 47, MD, 51; Am Bd Internal Med, dipl, 60, recert, 77. *Prof Exp:* Intern & resident med, Boston City Hosp, Harvard Univ, 51-54; from asst prof to assoc prof pharmacol & med, Col Med, Univ Fla, 58-70, prof, 70-80; PROF MED & PHARMACOL, UNIV NDAK, 80- *Concurrent Pos:* Teaching fel, Harvard Med Sch, 52-54; Nat Heart Inst res fel, Peter Bent Brigham Hosp, Boston, 56-58; Nat Heart & Lung Inst sr res fel, Harvard Univ, 71-72; mem corp, Marine Biol Lab, Woods Hole, 62- *Honors & Awards:* Borden Res Award, 51. *Mem:* Am Fedn Clin Res; Am Col Physicians; Am Physiol Soc; Soc Gen Physiol; Am Soc Pharmacol & Exp Therapeut. *Res:* Respiratory physiology and pharmacology; biological role of respiratory gases in health and disease. *Mailing Add:* Dept Med & Pharmacol NDak Sch Med 1919 Elm St N Fargo ND 58102

TRAVIS, DENNIS MICHAEL, biology, genetics, see previous edition

TRAVIS, HUGH FARRANT, b Grand Rapids, Mich, Sept 5, 22; m 48; c 2. ANIMAL NUTRITION, PHYSIOLOGY. *Educ:* Mich State Univ, BS, 47, MS, 52, PhD(poultry nutrit), 61. *Prof Exp:* Biologist, 48-60, physiologist, 61-62, res animal husbandman, 62-65, LEADER FUR ANIMAL INVESTS, SCI & EDUC ADMIN-AGR RES, USDA, 65- *Concurrent Pos:* Assoc prof, Cornell Univ, 62- *Mem:* AAAS; Am Soc Animal Sci; Am Inst Nutrit. *Res:* Nutrition, physiology and husbandry of fur-bearing animals. *Mailing Add:* US Fur Animal Exp Sta Cornell Univ 321 Morrison Hall Ithaca NY 14850

TRAVIS, IRVEN, b McConnelsville, Ohio, Mar 30, 04; m 35; c 3. ELECTRICAL ENGINEERING, MATHEMATICS. *Educ:* Drexel Inst Technol, BS, 26; Univ Pa, MS, 28, DSc(elec eng), 38. *Hon Degrees:* DEng, Drexel Inst Technol, 62. *Prof Exp:* Prof elec eng, Univ Pa, 28-49, supvr res, Moore Sch Elec Eng, 46-48; dir res, Burroughs Corp, 49-52, vpres, 52-69, mem bd dirs, 50-71; MGT CONSULT, 69- *Concurrent Pos:* Consult, Gen Elec Co, 38-40, Reeves Instrument Corp, 46-48 & Burroughs Corp, 48-49; chmn bd eng educ & vpres, IPAC, Pa State Univ; trustee, Detroit Inst Technol. *Mem:* Fel AAAS; Am Soc Eng Educ; Am Soc Naval Engrs; Am Ord Asn; fel Inst Elec & Electronics Engrs. *Res:* Applied mathematics; weapons systems, especially antiaircraft fire control and missiles; information processing systems; communications. *Mailing Add:* 121 S Valley Rd Paoli PA 19301

TRAVIS, J(OHN) C(HARLES), b Cheboygan, Mich, Aug 6, 27; m 51; c 2. ELECTRICAL ENGINEERING. *Educ:* Purdue Univ, BSEE, 47, MSEE, 50, PhD(elec eng), 55. *Prof Exp:* From instr to asst prof, Purdue Univ, 47-56; mem tech staff, Hughes Aircraft Co, 56-60 & Aerospace Corp, 60-66; sr staff engr, TRW Systs, Calif, 66-69; assoc group dir, Off of Systs Requirements, 69-70, MEM TECH STAFF, OFF FOR DEVELOP, AEROSPACE CORP, 70- *Concurrent Pos:* Lectr, Univ Calif, Los Angeles, 57 & 60- *Mem:* Inst Elec & Electronics Engrs. *Res:* Automatic control; circuit theory; systems engineering. *Mailing Add:* 13910 Fiji Way Marina Del Rey CA 90291

TRAVIS, JAMES, b Winnipeg, Can, Nov 11, 35; m 60; c 4. BIOCHEMISTRY. *Educ:* Univ Man, BSc, 58, MSc, 60; Univ Minn, PhD(biochem), 64. *Prof Exp:* Fel biochem, Johns Hopkins Univ, 64-66; asst prof, Univ Md, 66-67; asst prof, 67-72, assoc prof, 72-76, PROF BIOCHEM, UNIV GA, 78- *Concurrent Pos:* USPHS career develop award, 72-77. *Mem:* Am Soc Biol Chem. *Res:* Protein structure and function. *Mailing Add:* Dept of Biochem Univ of Ga Athens GA 30601

TRAVIS, JAMES ROLAND, b Iowa City, Iowa, Dec 20, 25; m 50. PHYSICS, EXPLOSIVES. *Educ:* Tufts Univ, BS, 49; Johns Hopkins Univ, PhD(physics), 56. *Prof Exp:* Res assoc spectros, Johns Hopkins Univ, 56-57; MEM STAFF, LOS ALAMOS NAT LAB, 57- *Mem:* Am Phys Soc; Sigma Xi; Combustion Inst. *Res:* Physics of detonation and shock waves; atomic and molecular spectroscopy. *Mailing Add:* Los Alamos Nat Lab PO Box 1663 Los Alamos NM 87545

TRAVIS, JOHN RICHARD, b Billings, Mont, Sept 3, 42; div; c 2. COMPUTATIONAL FLUID DYNAMICS. *Educ:* Univ Wyo, BS, 65; Purdue Univ, MS, 69, PhD(nuclear eng), 71. *Prof Exp:* Asst scientist reactor anal & safety, Argonne Nat Lab, 71-73; STAFF MEM NUMERICAL FLUID DYNAMICS, LOS ALAMOS NAT LAB, 73- *Mem:* Am Soc Mech Engr; Am Nuclear Soc; Sigma Xi. *Res:* Develop computational fluid dynamics and transport phenomena models for analyzing safety issues involving nuclear reactors. *Mailing Add:* Theoret Div T-3 MS 216 Los Alamos Nat Lab Los Alamos NM 87545

TRAVIS, LARRY DEAN, b Burlington, Iowa, July 29, 43. SPACE PHYSICS. *Educ:* Univ Iowa, BA, 65, MS, 67; Pa State Univ, University Park, PhD(astron), 71. *Prof Exp:* Asst prof physics, Pa State Univ, Worthington Scranton Campus, 71-73; MEM STAFF, INST SPACE STUDIES, 73- *Mem:* AAAS; Am Astron Soc; Am Geophys Union. *Res:* Planetary atmospheres. *Mailing Add:* Inst for Space Studies 2880 Broadway New York NY 10025

TRAVIS, LUTHER BRISENDINE, b Atlanta, Ga, May 25, 31; m 80; c 6. PEDIATRIC NEPHROLOGY, PEDIATRIC DIABETES. *Educ:* NGa Col, BS, 51; Med Col Ga, MD, 55. *Prof Exp:* Intern, Med Col Va, 55-56; resident pediat, Wyeth Labs, Col Med, Baylor Univ, 58-60; from asst prof to assoc prof pediat, 62-73, co-dir pediat nephrology, 64-71, PROF PEDIAT, UNIV TEX MED BR, GALVESTON, 73-, DIR PEDIAT NEPHROLOGY & DIABETES, 71- *Concurrent Pos:* Nat Inst Arthritis & Metab Dis fel pediat nephrology, Univ Tex Med Br, Galveston, 60-62; vis prof, William Beaumont Army Hosp, El Paso, Tex, 66-80; consult, NIH, 78-80 & Food & Drug Asn, 80-82. *Mem:* Am Soc Nephrology; Am Soc Pediat Nephrology; Am Acad Pediat; Am Fedn Clin Res; Soc Pediat Res. *Res:* Medical diseases of the kidney in children, particularly glomerulonephritis, nephrosis and pyelonephritis; juvenile Diabetes Mellitus; author or coauthor of over 150 publications. *Mailing Add:* Dept Pediat Univ Tex Med Br Galveston TX 77550

TRAVIS, RANDALL HOWARD, b Curdsville, Ky, July 11, 24; div; c 2. PHYSIOLOGY. *Educ:* Univ Chicago, BS, 47; Case Western Reserve Univ, MD, 52. *Prof Exp:* Intern, Univ Hosps, Cleveland, 52-53, jr asst resident, 53-54, asst resident, 54-55; sr instr physiol & med, 59-63, asst prof physiol, 63-68, ASSOC PROF PHYSIOL, CASE WESTERN RESERVE UNIV, 68-, ASST PROF MED, 63-; DIR ENDOCRINOL, CLEVELAND METROP GEN HOSP, 74- *Concurrent Pos:* Nat Heart Inst res fel, 55-57; Am Heart Asn res fel, 57-59; estab investr, Am Heart Asn, 59-64; asst physician, Univ Hosps, Cleveland, 59-; attend physician, Wade Park Vet Admin Hosp, 59-; assoc dir employees clin & consult endocrinol, Univ Hosps, Cleveland, 67-; asst phys, Cuyahoga County Hosp, 73-75, assoc, 75- *Mem:* Endocrine Soc; Cent Soc Clin Res. *Res:* Experimental endocrinology, adrenal and renal hormones relating to cardiovascular system and to nervous system. *Mailing Add:* 3395 Scranton Rd Cleveland OH 44109

TRAVIS, ROBERT LEROY, b Oakland, Calif, Oct 7, 40; m 63; c 2. PLANT PHYSIOLOGY, AGRONOMY. *Educ:* Univ Calif, Davis, BS, 64, MS, 66, PhD(plant physiol), 69. *Prof Exp:* Fel plant physiol, Univ Ga, 69-73, asst prof bot, 73-74; res agronomist herbicides, US Borax Res Corp, 74-76; asst prof, 76-79, ASSOC PROF AGRON, UNIV CALIF, DAVIS, 79- *Mem:* Am Soc Plant Physiologists. *Res:* Development of plasma membrane in higher plants; protein synthesis; photosynthetic efficiency. *Mailing Add:* Dept of Agron Univ of Calif Davis CA 95616

TRAVIS, ROBERT VICTOR, b Ames, Iowa, Aug 6, 33; m 55; c 5. ENTOMOLOGY. *Educ:* Cornell Univ, BS, 55; Univ Md, MS, 57, PhD(entom), 61. *Prof Exp:* Horticulturist, Agr Res Serv, USDA, 55-60; teacher sci & chmn dept, Gwynn Park High Sch, Md, 60-63; assoc prof biol, Mansfield State Col, 63-66; ASSOC PROF BIOL, WESTMINSTER COL, PA, 66- *Concurrent Pos:* Owner, Garden Pest Control Co, 58-61. *Mem:* Nat Asn Biol Teachers; Entom Soc Am. *Res:* Mechanism of plant virus transmission; insect physiology and behavior; new methods of illustrating general biological principles using microorganisms and insects; biological clocks; insect diapause. *Mailing Add:* 620 S Market St New Wilmington PA 16142

TRAVIS, RUSSELL BURTON, b San Francisco, Calif, June 18, 18; m 40, 60; c 6. STRUCTURAL GEOLOGY. *Educ:* Colo Sch Mines, GeolE, 43; Univ Calif, PhD(geol), 51. *Prof Exp:* Geologist, Stand Oil Co Calif, 46; teaching asst, Univ Calif, 47-50; asst prof geol, Univ Idaho, 51; sr geologist, Int Petrol Co, Ltd, 51-53; asst prof geol, Colo Sch Mines, 53-56; sr geologist, Int Petrol Co, Ltd, Peru, 56-62, 67-68, Fla, 62-63 & Colombia, 63-67 & 69-73; consult petrol geol, 77-80; TECH ADV, GEOL/COMPUT APPL, PETROLEOS DEL PERU, 73-77 & 80- *Mem:* Am Inst Prof Geologists; fel Geol Soc Am; Am Asn Petrol Geologists. *Res:* Computer science in petrology, petrography and petroleum geology; stratigraphy-sedimentation. *Mailing Add:* Yungay 425 San Miguel Lima Peru

TRAVNICEK, EDWARD ADOLPH, b Morse Bluff, Nebr, Mar 19, 36; m 66; c 2. ORGANIC CHEMISTRY, CHEMICAL ENGINEERING. *Educ:* Univ Nebr, Lincoln, BS, 58, MS, 60; Kans State Univ, PhD(chem eng), 68. *Prof Exp:* Testing engr chem eng, Atomic Energy Div, Phillips Petrol Co, 59-61; mgr chem lab, TRW Capacitor, Nebr, 61-63, consult, 63-68; sr res chem engr, Monsanto Co, Mo, 68-70 & Mass, 70-72; SR RES ENGR, RES DEPT, AM OPTICAL CORP, SOUTHBRIDGE, 72- *Concurrent Pos:* Lab asst, Kans State Univ, 66. *Mem:* Am Inst Chem Engrs; Am Chem Soc; Sigma Xi. *Res:* Polymer processing and formulation; dye and monomer synthesis, purification and analysis; gas chrom analytical techniques; mechanical, electrical and thermoelectric devices; liquid diffusion. *Mailing Add:* 74 Hillside Rd Southbridge MA 01550

TRAWICK, WILLIAM GEORGE, b Sandersville, Ga, Aug 16, 24; m 48; c 2. CLINICAL CHEMISTRY, PHYSICAL CHEMISTRY. *Educ:* Ga Inst Technol, BS, 48; PhD(phys chem), 55; Am Bd Clin Chem, dipl, 76. *Prof Exp:* Chemist, Union Carbide Nuclear Co, Tenn, 54-58; assoc prof phys chem, La Polytech Inst, 58-61; chmn dept chem, 62-74, PROF CHEM, GA STATE UNIV, 61- *Concurrent Pos:* Bd dirs, Nat Registry Clin Chem, 80- *Mem:* Am Chem Soc; Sigma Xi; Am Asn Clin Chemists. *Res:* Elemental analysis of human tissues and clinical correlations; instrument development for clinical chemistry. *Mailing Add:* Dept Chem Ga State Univ Atlanta GA 30303

TRAWINSKI, BENON JOHN, b Poland, Oct 20, 24; m; c 1. MATHEMATICAL STATISTICS. *Educ:* McMaster Univ, BSc, 58; Va Polytech Inst & State Univ, PhD(math statist), 61. *Prof Exp:* Asst prof statist, Va Polytech Inst & State Univ, 60-61; from asst prof to assoc prof biostatist, Tulane Univ, 61-65; assoc prof statist, Univ Ky, 65-66; ASSOC PROF BIOSTATIST, MED CTR, UNIV ALA, BIRMINGHAM, 66-, DIR GRAD PROG, 69- *Concurrent Pos:* NIH fel, 62; Nat Res Coun Can grant, 63; vis lectr, NSF, 71-; univ statist & math sci curric consult. *Mem:* AAAS; Inst Math Statist; Am Statist Asn; Am Math Soc; NY Acad Sci. *Res:* Theoretical and applied research in statistics, especially order and nonparametric statistics and decision theory. *Mailing Add:* Dept of Biostatist Univ of Ala Med Ctr Birmingham AL 35233

TRAWINSKI, IRENE PATRICIA MONAHAN, b Bayonne, NJ, Mar 17, 29; m 63; c 1. MATHEMATICAL STATISTICS. *Educ:* Rutgers Univ, BSc, 50; Univ Ill, MS, 51; Va Polytech Inst, PhD(math statist), 61. *Prof Exp:* From instr to prof math, Keuka Col, 51-63, head dept, 57-63; assoc prof, La State Univ, New Orleans, 64-66; ASSOC PROF BIOSTATIST, UNIV ALA, BIRMINGHAM, 66- *Mem:* Math Asn Am; Am Statist Asn; Biomet Soc; Sigma Xi. *Res:* Multivariate analysis. *Mailing Add:* Dept of Biostat Univ of Ala Birmingham AL 35294

TRAXLER, JAMES THEODORE, b Le Center, Minn, Oct 17, 29; m 56; c 5. SYNTHETIC ORGANIC CHEMISTRY, PESTICIDE CHEMISTRY. *Educ:* St John's Univ, Minn, BA, 51; Univ Notre Dame, PhD(org chem, biochem), 56. *Prof Exp:* Res chemist, Cent Res Labs, Armour & Co, Ill, 55-60 & Am Cyanamid Co, Conn, 60-62; head org lab, Durkee Foods Div, Glidden Co, Ill, 62-66; sr res chemist, Peter Hand Found, Ill, 66-69; org res specialist, Growth Sci Ctr, Int Minerals & Chem Corp, Libertyville, 69-74; RES SCIENTIST, VELSICOL CHEM CORP, CHICAGO, 74- *Mem:* AAAS; Am Chem Soc. *Res:* Amino acids and alcohols; pesticides; heterocycles; natural products; polycyclic aromatics; antimalarials. *Mailing Add:* 1630 Ashland Ave Evanston IL 60201

TRAXLER, RICHARD WARWICK, b New Orleans, La, July 25, 28; m 52; c 3. BACTERIAL PHYSIOLOGY. *Educ:* Univ Tex, BA, 51, MA, 55, PhD(bact), 58. *Prof Exp:* Asst serologist, Port Arthur Health Dept, 49-52; asst, Univ Tex, 54-58; asst prof bact, Univ Southwestern La, 58-62, from assoc prof to prof microbiol, 62-71; PROF PLANT PATH & ENTOM & MICROBIOL & CHMN DEPT, UNIV RI, 71- *Mem:* Am Soc Microbiol; Soc Indust Microbiol; Biodeterioration Soc. *Res:* Microbial physiology, especially degradation; aliphatic hydrocarbons and related molecules. *Mailing Add:* Dept of Plant Path & Entom Univ of RI Kingston RI 02881

TRAYLOR, MELVIN ALVAH, b Chicago, Ill, Dec 16, 15; m 41, 70; c 2. ORNITHOLOGY. *Educ:* Harvard Univ, AB, 37. *Prof Exp:* Assoc, Div Birds, 40-48, res assoc, 48-55, assoc cur, 55-62, cur birds, 72-77, chmn dept zool, 77-80, EMER CUR, FIELD MUS NATURAL HIST, 81- *Concurrent Pos:* Mem expeds, Yucatan, Mex, 39-40, Galapagos Island, 41, US, 41, Mex, 48 & Africa, 61-62; pelagic fishing surv, Oper Crossroads, Bikini Atoll, 46. *Mem:* Wilson Ornith Soc; fel Am Ornith Union; hon mem, Soc Orinthol France; Brit Ornith Union. *Res:* Taxonomy of Neotropical and African birds; biogeography of South America. *Mailing Add:* Field Mus Natural Hist Chicago IL 60605

TRAYLOR, PATRICIA SHIZUKO, b San Francisco, Calif, Jan 21, 30; m 59; c 2. CHEMISTRY, BIOCHEMISTRY. *Educ:* Univ Calif, Berkeley, AB, 51; Univ Wis, MS, 53; Harvard Univ, PhD(chem), 63. *Prof Exp:* Res biochemist, Univ Calif, Berkeley, 53-55; chemist, Dow Chem Co, 55-59; NIH res fel, 63-66; from asst prof to assoc prof, 66-77, PROF CHEM, UNIV SAN DIEGO, 77- *Mem:* AAAS; Am Chem Soc; NY Acad Sci. *Res:* Mechanisms of reactions. *Mailing Add:* Dept of Chem Univ of San Diego San Diego CA 92110

TRAYLOR, TEDDY G, b Sulphur, Okla, May 21, 25; m 59; c 6. ORGANIC CHEMISTRY. *Educ:* Univ Calif, Los Angeles, AB, 49, PhD(chem), 52. *Prof Exp:* Sr res chemist, Dow Chem Co, Calif, 52-59; fel, Harvard Univ, 59-61, instr chem, 61; from asst prof to assoc prof, 61-68, PROF CHEM, UNIV CALIF, SAN DIEGO, 68- *Concurrent Pos:* Consult, Rohm and Haas Res Labs, Pa, 63-74; Guggenheim fel, 76. *Mem:* Am Chem Soc. *Res:* Organometallic chemistry; autoxidation; oxygen transport; bioorganic chemistry. *Mailing Add:* Dept of Chem D-006 Univ of Calif San Diego La Jolla CA 92093

TRAYNHAM, JAMES GIBSON, b Broxton, Ga, Aug 5, 25; m 80; c 2. ORGANIC CHEMISTRY. *Educ:* Univ NC, BS, 46; Northwestern Univ, PhD(chem), 50. *Prof Exp:* Instr chem, Northwestern, 49-50; asst prof, Denison Univ, 50-53; from asst prof to assoc prof, 53-63, chmn dept, 68-73, vchancellor advan studies & res & dean, Grad Sch, 73-81, PROF CHEM, LA STATE UNIV, BATON ROUGE, 63- *Concurrent Pos:* Res assoc, Ohio State Univ, 51-53; Am Chem Soc Petrol Res Fund int award, Swiss Fed Inst Technol, 59-60; NATO sr fel sci, Univ Saarland, 72. *Mem:* Am Chem Soc; Sigma Xi. *Res:* mechanisms of reactions; alicyclic systems; halogenations. *Mailing Add:* Off of Advan Studies & Res La State Univ Baton Rouge LA 70803

TRAYNOR, LEE, b Flint, Mich, July 9, 38; m 60; c 2. ORGANIC CHEMISTRY, POLYMER CHEMISTRY. *Educ:* Mich State Univ, BS, 60; Univ Mich, PhD(org chem), 64. *Prof Exp:* Res chemist, 64-67, sr res chemist, 67-72, RES ASSOC, B F GOODRICH CO, 72- *Mem:* Am Chem Soc. *Res:* Organic reaction mechanisms; heterogeneous catalysis; new methods in vinyl polymerization. *Mailing Add:* 2824 Yellow Creek Rd Akron OH 44313

TRAYSTMAN, RICHARD J, b Brooklyn, NY, April 5, 42; m 71. CARDIOVASCULAR & PULMONARY PHYSIOLOGY. *Educ:* Long Island Univ, BS, 63, MA, 66; Johns Hopkins Univ, PhD(cardiopulmonary physiol), 71. *Prof Exp:* Teaching & res fel physiol, Brooklyn Col Med, 63-66; instr, Bowman Gray Sch Med, 71-72; asst prof, 73-77, ASSOC PROF ENVIRON PHYSIOL, SCH HYG, JOHNS HOPKINS UNIV, 78-, DIR RES LABS, ANESTHESIOL & CRITICAL CARE MED, 80-, ASSOC PROF ANESTHESIOL, 80- *Concurrent Pos:* Fel, Bowman Gray Sch Med, 71-72. *Mem:* Am Physiol Soc; Microcirculatory Soc; Am Soc Anesthesiol; Am Thoracic Soc. *Res:* Control of cerebral circulation in fetal, neonatal and adult animals; physiological interrelationships between the circulatory system. *Mailing Add:* Dept Anesthesiol Critical Care Med Johns Hopkins Hosp 600 N Wolfe St Baltimore MD 21205

TREADO, PAUL A, b Ironwood, Mich, Mar 6, 36; m 59; c 6. NUCLEAR PHYSICS. *Educ:* Univ Mich, BSE(math) & BSE(physics), 58, MS, 59, PhD(physics), 61. *Prof Exp:* Assoc prof, 62-73, PROF PHYSICS, GEORGETOWN UNIV, 73-, CHMN DEPT, 76- *Concurrent Pos:* Consult, US Dept Navy, 62- *Mem:* Am Phys Soc; Sigma Xi. *Res:* Few nucleon physics and multiparticle breakup reactions; radiation damage; elemental analysis; pollution from coal power plant. *Mailing Add:* Dept of Physics Georgetown Univ Washington DC 20057

TREADWAY, ROBERT HOLLAND, physical chemistry, deceased

TREADWAY, WILLIAM JACK, JR, b Johnson City, Tenn, Feb 22, 49; m 71. CHEMISTRY. *Educ:* Univ Ill, Urbana-Champaign, BS, 72; Loyola Univ Chicago, PhD(biochem), 76. *Prof Exp:* Teaching asst biochem, Loyola Univ Chicago Med Ctr, 71-73, res asst, 73-75; res assoc immunochem, Jefferson Med Col, 75-77; res assoc immunol, Sch Med, Temple Univ, 77-78; res instr med, Bowman Gray Sch Med, 78-81; INSTR CHEM & BIOCHEM, PARKLAND COL, 81- *Mem:* Am Chem Soc; AAAS; Am Rheumatism Asn. *Res:* Immunology; immunochemistry; biochemistry. *Mailing Add:* 2400 W Bradley Ave Parkland Col Champaign IL 61820

TREADWELL, CARLETON RAYMOND, b Burlington, Mich, Dec 28, 11; m 41; c 2. BIOCHEMISTRY. *Educ:* Battle Creek Col, AB, 34; Univ Mich, MS, 35, PhD(biochem), 39. *Prof Exp:* Asst biochem, Univ Mich, 35-39; from instr to assoc prof, Col Med, Baylor Univ, 39-43, assoc prof, Southwestern Med Found, 43-45; from asst prof to assoc prof, 45-52, prof, 52-78, chmn dept, 59-78, EMER PROF BIOCHEM, SCH MED, GEORGE WASHINGTON UNIV, 78- *Mem:* AAAS; Am Soc Biol Chemists; Soc Exp Biol & Med; Am Inst Nutrit. *Res:* Cholesterol metabolism; composition of tissue lipids; fat metabolism; interrelationships of carbohydrate and fat metabolism; amino acids; lipotropism. *Mailing Add:* Dept of Biochem George Washington Univ Sch of Med Washington DC 20037

TREADWELL, ELLIOTT ALLEN, b Rockford, Ill, May 14, 47; m 80. COMPUTER SCIENCE, PHYSICAL CHEMISTRY. *Educ:* Cent State Univ Ohio, BS, 69; State Univ NY Stony Brook, MA, 71; Cornell Univ, MS, 73, PhD(exp high energy physics), 78. *Prof Exp:* Res asst high energy physics, Wilson Synchrotron, Cornell Univ, 73-78; res assoc, 78-81, ASSOC SCIENTIST ACCELERATOR & HIGH ENERGY PHYSICS, FERMI NAT ACCELERATOR LAB, 81- *Mem:* Am Phys Soc; Nat Soc Black Physicists. *Res:* Neutrino-nucleon scattering at 400 billion electron volts, utilizing a 15 foot neon-hydrogen bubble chamber. *Mailing Add:* Fermi Nat Accelerator Lab PO Box 500 Batavia IL 60505

TREADWELL, GEORGE EDWARD, JR, b Selma, Ala, Dec 22, 41. BOTANY, BIOCHEMISTRY. *Educ:* King Col, BA, 64; Iowa State Univ, MS, 67, PhD(biochem, plant physiol), 70. *Prof Exp:* Asst prof, 70-77, ASSOC PROF BIOL, EMORY & HENRY COL, 77- *Mem:* Am Chem Soc; Bot Soc Am. *Res:* Plant physiology; vitamin B-2; chromatography. *Mailing Add:* PO Drawer DDD Emory VA 24327

TREADWELL, KENNETH MYRON, b Cleveland, Ohio, May 5, 23; m 51; c 1. MECHANICAL ENGINEERING, NUCLEAR ENGINEERING. *Educ:* US Naval Acad, BS, 48; US Naval Postgrad Sch, BS, 54; Mass Inst Technol, SM, 55. *Prof Exp:* Engr thermal design, 55-59, supvr, 59-64, mgr thermal & fuel design, 64-68, mgr reactor anal, 68-70, mgr reactor eng, 70-72, mgr naval fuel element develop, 72-77, MGR FUEL ELEMENT DEVELOP & STATIST, BETTIS ATOMIC POWER LAB, WESTINGHOUSE ELEC CORP, 77- *Mem:* Am Soc Mech Engrs; Am Soc Naval Engrs; Sigma Xi. *Res:* Analysis, engineering design and operation of naval and power nuclear reactors; engineering and materials science. *Mailing Add:* 4983 Parkvue Dr Pittsburgh PA 15236

TREADWELL, PERRY EDWARD, b Chicago, Ill, June 18, 32; m 52; c 4. MICROBIOLOGY. *Educ:* Univ Calif, Los Angeles, AB, 55, PhD(microbiol), 58. *Prof Exp:* Fel ment health, Univ Calif, Los Angeles, 58-60; instr bact, Univ Minn, 60-62; from asst prof to assoc prof, Emory Univ, 62-74; DIR, EXP ENERGY ENVIRON, 74- *Mem:* Am Asn Immunol; Am Soc Microbiol. *Res:* Effect of physical and psychological stress on mice; cytology of mammalian cells in culture; immunology, pathology and enzymology of shock in mice, including role of lysosomes of the reticuloendothelial system; antigen-antibody complexes in human disease; alternative energy systems. *Mailing Add:* 2813 Hwy 212 Covington GA 30209

TREAGAN, LUCY, b Novosibirsk, Russia, July 20, 24; US citizen; m 42; c 2. MICROBIOLOGY. *Educ:* Univ Calif, Berkeley, AB, 45, PhD(bact), 60. *Prof Exp:* Lectr, Col Holy Names, Calif, 61-66; asst prof biol, 66-73, assoc prof, 73-78, PROF BIOL, UNIV SAN FRANCISCO, 78- *Concurrent Pos:* Lectr, Univ San Francisco, 62-66. *Res:* Viral inhibitors; immunological study of interferons; effect of metals on the immune response. *Mailing Add:* Dept of Biol Univ of San Francisco San Francisco CA 94117

TREANOR, CHARLES EDWARD, b Buffalo, NY, Oct 22, 24; m 50; c 5. PHYSICS, AERODYNAMICS. *Educ:* Univ Minn, BA, 47; Univ Buffalo, PhD(physics), 55. *Prof Exp:* Instr physics, Univ Buffalo, 53; physicist, Cornell Aeronaut Lab, Inc, 54-68, head aerodyn res dept, 68-78, VPRES PHYS SCI GROUP, CALSPAN CORP, 78- *Mem:* Fel Am Phys Soc; assoc fel Am Inst Aeronaut & Astronaut; Combustion Inst. *Res:* High temperature gases; spectroscopy; hypersonic flows; molecular interactions. *Mailing Add:* Phys Sci Group Calspan Corp Buffalo NY 14225

TREANOR, KATHERINE P, b Buffalo, NY, Apr 23, 27. GENETICS. *Educ:* D'Youville Col, AB, 48; Univ Buffalo, PhD(genetics), 62. *Prof Exp:* Lab asst biol, Canisius Col, 48-52; instr, D'Youville Col, 52-53; from instr to asst prof, 53-66, ASSOC PROF BIOL, CANISIUS COL, 66- *Mem:* Genetics Soc Am; Genetics Soc Can. *Res:* Enzyme deficiencies associated with genetic mutations. *Mailing Add:* Dept of Biol Canisius Col Buffalo NY 14208

TREAT, CHARLES HERBERT, b Cambridge, Mass, Dec 9, 31; m 56; c 3. NUMERICAL ANALYSIS, HEAT TRANSFER. *Educ:* Purdue Univ, BSCE, 53, MSE, 59; Univ NMex, PhD(mech eng), 68. *Prof Exp:* Instr eng graphics, Purdue Univ, 56-59; staff mem heat transfer, Sandia Corp, 59-61; instr mech eng, Univ NMex, 61-68; asst prof eng sci, 68-72, asst prof comput & info sci, 72-75, assoc prof comput & info sci, 75-78, assoc prof, 78-81, PROF & CHMN ENG SCI DEPT, TRINITY UNIV, TEX, 81- *Concurrent Pos:* Res assoc, United Nuclear Corp, 63 & Los Alamos Sci Lab, 64; consult, Sch Aerospace Med, Brooks AFB, Tex, 68, Q-Dot Corp, NMex, 69, Southwest Res Inst, 81-82 & small comput systs, 81-; dir instrumentation, Solar Heating & Cool Proj, Trinity Univ, 75-78. *Mem:* Am Soc Mech Eng. *Res:* Solar Energy. *Mailing Add:* Dept of Eng Sci Trinity Univ San Antonio TX 78284

TREAT, DONALD FACKLER, b Hartford, Conn, Feb 14, 25; m 49; c 4. MEDICAL EDUCATION. *Educ:* Univ Mich, Ann Arbor, BA, 46, MD, 49; Am Bd Family Pract, dipl. *Prof Exp:* Intern gen pract, Univ Hosp, Ann Arbor, Mich, 49-50, resident, 50-52; pvt pract, Springfield, Vt, 54-69; actg dir, Family Med Prog & dir Grad Educ Family Med, 78-81, ASSOC PROF FAMILY MED, SCH MED & DENT, UNIV ROHESTER, 69-, CHMN DEPT, 81- *Concurrent Pos:* Vis prof, Univ Vt & Univ Colo, 80. *Mem:* Soc Teachers Family Med; Am Acad Family Practioners. *Res:* Family medicine; medical audit and peer review; measurement of attitudinal change in residents; defining patterns of medical care. *Mailing Add:* 885 South Ave Rochester NY 14620

TREAT, JAY EMERY, JR, b Trinidad, Colo, Nov 16, 20; m 45; c 4. PHYSICS. *Educ:* Univ Ariz, BS, 42; Cornell Univ, PhD, 54. *Prof Exp:* Mem staff magnetrons, Radiation Lab, Mass Inst Technol, 42-45; asst gen physics, Cornell Univ, 45-48, cosmic rays and nuclear physics, 48-51; asst prof nuclear physics, 51-58, ASSOC PROF PHYSICS, UNIV ARIZ, 58- *Mem:* Am Phys Soc; Am Asn Physics Teachers. *Res:* Cosmic rays; electromagnetic theory; elementary particles. *Mailing Add:* Dept of Physics Univ of Ariz Tucson AZ 85721

TREAT-CLEMONS, LYNDA GEORGE, b Wooster, Ohio, May 23, 46; m 79; c 1. GENETICS, BIOLOGY. *Educ:* Ohio State Univ, BS, 73, MS, 74, PhD(genetics), 78. *Prof Exp:* Assoc genetics, Ohio State Univ, 73-78; ASSOC GENETICS & ZOOL, ARIZ STATE UNIV, 78- *Mem:* Genetics Soc Am; AAAS; Soc Develop Biol; Sigma Xi. *Res:* Eukaryotic gene regulation through development. *Mailing Add:* Dept Zool Ariz State Univ Tempe AZ 85281

TREBLE, DONALD HAROLD, b Liverpool, Eng, Apr 14, 34; m 59; c 2. BIOCHEMISTRY. *Educ:* Bristol Univ, BSc, 55; Univ Liverpool, PhD(biochem), 59. *Prof Exp:* From asst prof to assoc prof, 63-75, PROF BIOCHEM, ALBANY MED COL, 75- *Concurrent Pos:* Res fel biochem, Inst Animal Physiol, Babraham, Eng, 58-59, Cambridge Univ, 59-61 & Harvard Med Sch, 61-63. *Mem:* Am Soc Biol Chemists. *Res:* Lipid metabolism. *Mailing Add:* Dept of Biochem Albany Med Col Albany NY 12208

TREE, DAVID R, b Wanship, Utah, July 18, 36; m 58; c 5. ENERGY USAGE, ACOUSTICS. *Educ:* Brigham Young Univ, BES, 62, MS, 63; Purdue Univ, PhD(mech eng), 66. *Prof Exp:* Assoc prof, 66-74, PROF MECH ENG, PURDUE UNIV, 74- *Concurrent Pos:* US Dept Health, Educ & Welfare fel, Univ Southampton, 70-71. *Mem:* Am Soc Heating, Refrig & Air-Conditioning; Am Soc Eng Educ. *Res:* Two-phase flow in small diameter tubes; acoustic and machine noise reduction; air-conditioners and heat pumps; internal combustion engine noise control; energy usage in residential buildings. *Mailing Add:* Sch Mech Eng Purdue Univ Lafayette IN 47907

TREECE, JACK MILAN, b Findlay, Ohio, Dec 19, 32; m 54; c 3. BIOCHEMISTRY. *Educ:* Ohio State Univ, BS, 54, MSc, 55, PhD(biochem genetics), 60. *Prof Exp:* Res asst biol res, Ohio Agr Exp Sta, 54-60; tech mgr genetics, Cent Ohio Breeding Asn, 60-62; Nat Acad Sci-Nat Res Coun res fel biochem, Animal Protein Pioneering Lab, Eastern Regional Res Utilization Lab, Agr Res Serv, USDA, 62-63; asst prof, Sch Vet Med, Univ Pa, 63-66; asst prof biochem, Univ Del, 66-70; dir, Blood Plasma & Components, Inc, 70-77; sr res biochemist, E I du Pont de Nemours & Co, Inc, 77-80. *Mem:* Sigma Xi; Am Chem Soc; Am Asn Clin Chemists; NY Acad Sci. *Res:* Clinical biochemistry and related product development. *Mailing Add:* 501 S W 80th Dr Gainsville FL 32607

TREECE, ROBERT EUGENE, b Bluffton, Ohio, Oct 1, 27; m 55; c 3. ECONOMIC ENTOMOLOGY. *Educ:* Ohio State Univ, BS, 51, MS, 53; Cornell Univ, PhD(econ entom), 57. *Prof Exp:* Asst exten specialist entom, Rutgers Univ, 56-58; asst prof entom & asst entomologist, Agr Exp Sta, Ohio State Univ, 58-64, from assoc prof to prof, Ohio Agr Res & Develop Ctr, 64-73, ASSOC CHMN ENTOM DEPT, OHIO AGR RES & DEVELOP CTR, OHIO STATE UNIV, 73- *Mem:* Entom Soc Am; AAAS; Coun Agr Sci & Technol. *Res:* Bionomics and control of insect pests of livestock and forage crops. *Mailing Add:* Dept Entom Ohio Agr Res & Develop Ctr Wooster OH 44691

TREFETHEN, JOSEPH MUZZY, b Kent's Hill, Maine, May 27, 06; m 31; c 3. GEOLOGY. *Educ:* Colby Col, AB, 31; Univ Ill, MS, 32; Univ Wis, PhD(geol), 35. *Prof Exp:* Instr geol, Univ Mo, 35-38; from asst prof to prof, 38-71, EMER PROF, UNIV MAINE, 71-; CONSULT GEOLOGIST, 71- *Concurrent Pos:* Field geologist, State Geol Surv, Maine, 29-32, dir, 42-55; dir, State Geol Surv, Wis, 35; vis lectr, Stephens Col, 35-36. *Mem:* Fel Geol Soc Am; Sigma Xi. *Res:* Structural and applied geology; economic geology of the non-metallics; engineering geology. *Mailing Add:* Friendship ME 04547

TREFETHEN, LLOYD MACGREGOR, b Boston, Mass, Mar 5, 19; m 44; c 2. FLUID MECHANICS. *Educ:* Webb Inst Naval Archit, BS, 40; Mass Inst Technol, MS, 42; Cambridge Univ, PhD, 50. *Prof Exp:* Appln engr, Gen Elec Co, 40-44; sci consult, US Off Naval Res, Eng, 47-50; physicist, tech aide to chief scientist & exec secy, US Naval Res Adv Comt, Washington, DC, 50-51; exec secy, Nat Sci Bd & tech aide to dir, NSF, 51-54; asst prof mech eng, Harvard Univ, 54-58; chmn dept, 58-69, PROF MECH ENG, TUFTS UNIV, 58- *Concurrent Pos:* NSF fel, Cambridge Univ, 56; vis prof, Univ Sydney, 65 & 72 & Stanford Univ, 79; vis fel, Seattle Res Ctr, Battelle Mem Inst, 71; hon res assoc, Harvard Univ, 78. *Honors & Awards:* Golden Eagle Award, Comn Int Nontheatrical Events, 67; Prix de Physique, Inst Sci Film Festival, 68. *Mem:* Soc Naval Archit & Marine Engrs; Am Soc Mech Engrs. *Res:* Heat transfer. *Mailing Add:* Dept of Mech Eng Tufts Univ Medford MA 02155

TREFFERS, HENRY PETER, microbiology, see previous edition

TREFFERS, RICHARD ROWE, b Bethany, Conn, Nov 7, 47; m 72; c 2. ASTRONOMY. *Educ:* Yale Univ, BA, 69; Univ Calif, Berkeley, PhD(astron), 73. *Prof Exp:* Asst res astronomer, Univ Ariz, 74-76; asst res astronomer, Ames Res Ctr, NASA, 76; ASST RES ASTRONOMER, UNIV CALIF, 76- *Mem:* Am Astron Soc. *Res:* Infrared astronomy and spectroscopy as applied to planets and interstellar matter. *Mailing Add:* Dept Astron Univ Calif Berkeley CA 94720

TREFFERT, DAROLD ALLEN, b Fond du Lac, Wis, Mar 12, 33; m 55; c 4. MEDICINE, PSYCHIATRY. *Educ:* Univ Wis, BA, 55, MD, 58. *Prof Exp:* Intern, Sacred Heart Gen Hosp, Eugene, Ore, 58-59; resident psychiat, Univ Wis Hosp, Madison, 59-62; dir, Child-Adolescent Unit, Winnebago Ment Health Inst, 62-64, dir, 64-79; EXEC DIR, FOND DU LAC COUNTY HEALTH CARE CTR, 79- *Concurrent Pos:* Chmn, Controlled Substances Bd Wis, 70-; mem, Adv Coun Health Probs Educ, Dept Pub Instr Wis, 73- *Mem:* Am Asn Psychiat Adminr; Am Psychiat Asn; Am Col Psychiat. *Res:* Epidemiology of infantile autism; alcoholism and drug abuse; rights of the mentally ill. *Mailing Add:* 459 E First St Fond du Lac WI 54935

TREFFNER, WALTER SEBASTIAN, inorganic chemistry, physical chemistry, deceased

TREFIL, JAMES S, b Chicago, Ill, Sept 10, 38; m 60; c 4. PARTICLE PHYSICS. *Educ:* Univ Ill, BS, 60; Oxford Univ, BA & MA, 62; Stanford Univ, MS & PhD(physics), 66. *Prof Exp:* Res assoc physics, Stanford Linear Accelerator Ctr, 66; Air Force Off Sci Res fel, Europ Ctr Nuclear Res, 66-67; res assoc, Mass Inst Technol, 67-68; asst prof, Univ Ill, Urbana, 68-70; assoc prof & fel, Ctr Advan Studies, 70-75, PROF PHYSICS, UNIV VA, 75- *Res:* Theoretical fluid mechanics; magnetic monopoles; medical physics. *Mailing Add:* Dept Physics Univ Va Charlottesville VA 22901

TREFNY, JOHN ULRIC, b Greenwich, Conn, Jan 28, 42; m 67. PHYSICS. *Educ:* Fordham Univ, BS, 63, Rutgers Univ, New Brunswick, PhD(physics), 68. *Prof Exp:* Res assoc physics, Cornell Univ, 67-69; asst prof physics, Wesleyan Univ, 69-77; asst prof, 77-79, ASSOC PROF PHYSICS, COLO SCH MINES, 77- *Concurrent Pos:* Consult, Inst for Future, 70, Solar Energy Res Inst, 78-81. *Mem:* Am Phys Soc; Sigma Xi; Am Asn Physics Teachers. *Res:* Low temperature experimental studies of liquid and solid helium and amorphous semiconductors; certain areas in superconductivity including the surface sheath and the Josephson effect and general topics in low temperature physics; thermoelectric materials. *Mailing Add:* Dept of Physics Colo Sch of Mines Golden CO 80401

TREFONAS, LOUIS MARCO, b Chicago, Ill, June 21, 31; m 57; c 6. STRUCTURAL CHEMISTRY, PHYSICAL BIOCHEMISTRY. *Educ:* Univ Chicago, BA, 51, MS, 54; Univ Minn, PhD, 59. *Prof Exp:* From asst prof to assoc prof, 59-66, PROF CHEM, UNIV NEW ORLEANS, 66-, CHMN DEPT, 64- *Concurrent Pos:* NIH spec fel, 72-73; hon res assoc, Harvard Univ, 72-73. *Res:* Molecular structure studies by x-ray diffraction; small ring nitrogen compounds; structures of biologically interesting compounds by x-ray diffraction techniques. *Mailing Add:* Dept of Chem Univ of New Orleans New Orleans LA 70122

TREGILLUS, LEONARD WARREN, b Toronto, Ont, Sept 28, 21; nat US; m 45; c 3. PHYSICAL CHEMISTRY. *Educ:* Antioch Col, BS, 44; Univ Calif, PhD(chem), 50. *Prof Exp:* RES ASSOC PHOTOCHEM, EASTMAN KODAK CO, 50- *Mem:* Am Chem Soc; Soc Photog Sci & Eng; Soc Motion Picture & TV Engrs. *Res:* Photographic film preparation and processing. *Mailing Add:* 297 Pinecrest Dr Rochester NY 14617

TREGLIA, THOMAS A(NTHONY), b Stamford, Conn, Oct 3, 24; m 49; c 2. ENGINEERING. *Educ:* Fordham Univ, AB, 46. *Prof Exp:* Res chemist, US Indust Chem, Inc, 46-50; asst chief mat develop br, US Dept Army, 52-56, chief mat res br, 56-63, chief eng anal br, 63-65, chief weapons eng div, 65-72, dir prod assurance, Edgewood Arsenal, 72-76, assoc tech dir, 76-80; VPRES ENG, WINDSTAR AVIATION INC, 80- *Mem:* Am Chem Soc. *Res:* Management of quality assurance and reliability assessment programs for chemical systems and items during research and development, production and stockpile phases; product and materials engineering; chemical processes. *Mailing Add:* 7 E Ring Factory Rd Bel Air MD 21014

TREHU, ANNE MARTINE, b Princeton, NJ, Jan 7, 55. SEISMOLOGY, MARINE GEOPHYSICS. *Educ:* Princeton Univ, BA, 75; Mass Inst Technol, PhD(marine seismol), 82. *Prof Exp:* ASSOC, US GEOL SURV, 82- *Mem:* Am Geophys Union. *Res:* Interpretation of data recorded by ocean bottom seismometers to study offshore crystal structure and earthquake activity. *Mailing Add:* Quissett Campus US Geol Surv Woods Hole MA 02543

TREHUB, ARNOLD, b Malden, Mass, Oct 19, 23; m 50; c 3. PSYCHOPHYSIOLOGY. *Educ:* Northeastern Univ, AB, 49; Boston Univ, MA, 51, PhD(clin psychol), 54. *Prof Exp:* Clin psychologist, 54-59, DIR PSYCHOL RES LAB, NORTHAMPTON VET ADMIN MED CTR, 59- *Concurrent Pos:* Vis lectr, Univ Mass, 59-66; lectr, Clark Univ, 60-62; mem grad fac, Univ Mass, Amherst, 70-, adj prof, 71- *Mem:* AAAS; Am Psychol Asn; NY Acad Sci; Soc Neurosci. *Res:* Electrophysiology of brain; biomathematics; artificial intelligence; neurophysiology. *Mailing Add:* 145 Farview Way Amherst MA 01002

TREHUB, SANDRA E, b Montreal, Que, May 21, 38; c 3. DEVELOPMENT PSYCHOLOGY, PERCEPTION. *Educ:* McGill Univ, BCom, 59, MA, 71, PhD(psychol), 73. *Prof Exp:* Asst prof, 73-78, ASSOC PROF PSYCHOL, UNIV TORONTO, 78- *Concurrent Pos:* Consult, Res Inst, Hosp Sick Children, 75- *Res:* Documentation of the development of auditory abilities in infancy and early childhood including simple detection and discrimination of acoustic signals in quiet and noisy backgrounds and the extraction of pattern or structure from complex auditory events. *Mailing Add:* Ctr Res Human Develop Erindale Col Univ Toronto Mississauga ON L5L 1C6 Can

TREI, JOHN EARL, b Freeport, Ill, Sept 19, 39; m 66; c 2. RUMINANT NUTRITION, PHYSIOLOGY. *Educ:* Univ Ill, BS, 61; Univ Ariz, MS, 63, PhD(agr biochem, nutrit), 66. *Prof Exp:* Res & teaching assoc animal sci, Univ Ariz, 63-66; sr scientist animal nutrit, Smith Kline & French Labs, 66-71, sr investr, Smith Kline Corp, 71-73, asst mgr develop animal health prod, 73-74; assoc prof, 74-80, PROF ANIMAL SCI, CALIF STATE POLYTECH UNIV, 80-, SUPVR, BEEF UNIT & FEEDMILL, 75- *Mem:* Am Soc Animal Soc; Am Inst Biol Sci; NY Acad Sci; Am Dairy Sci Asn; Sigma Xi. *Res:* Energy metabolism; feed additive evaluations. *Mailing Add:* Dept of Animal Sci 3801 W Temple Ave Pomona CA 91768

TREICHEL, PAUL MORGAN, JR, b Madison, Wis, Dec 4, 36; m 61; c 2. INORGANIC CHEMISTRY. *Educ:* Univ Wis, BS, 58; Harvard Univ, AM, 60, PhD(chem), 62. *Prof Exp:* Teaching asst chem, Harvard Univ, 61-62; NSF fel, Queen Mary Col, London, 62-63; from asst prof to assoc prof, 63-72, PROF CHEM, UNIV WIS-MADISON, 72- *Mem:* Am Chem Soc; Royal Soc Chem. *Res:* Organometallic chemistry, including metal carbonyls, cyclopentadienyls, alkyls and related compounds; organophosphorus and organoboron chemistry. *Mailing Add:* Dept of Chem Univ of Wis Madison WI 53706

TREICHLER, RAY, b Rock Island, Ill, Sept 10, 07; m 42. AGRICULTURAL CHEMISTRY, BIOLOGICAL CHEMISTRY. *Educ:* Pa State Col, BS & MS, 29; Univ Ill, PhD, 39. *Prof Exp:* Chemist, Exp Sta, Agr & Mech Col, Tex, 29-37; spec asst animal nutrit, Univ Ill, 37-38; chemist, Exp Sta, Agr & Mech Col, Tex, 39-40; vis scientist, Univ Ill, 40-41; chemist, US Fish & Wildlife Serv, 41-42, technologist, 42-43, chemist, 43-44; res & develop div & head biol activities sect, Off Qm Gen, US Dept Army, 45-52, head chem & biol br, 53; chief agts br, Res & Eng Command, US Army Chem Corps, 53-55, asst to dir med res, 55-58; scientist, US Air Force, 58-68; TECH SERV MGR, H

D HUDSON MFG CO, 68- *Mem:* NY Acad Sci; Am Soc Trop Med & Hyg; Entom Soc Am; Am Mosquito Control Asn; Am Soc Agr Engrs; application equipment for pesticides. *Res:* Biology of natural products; environmental pollution; research and development of pesticides; application equipment. *Mailing Add:* H D Hudson Mfg Co Suite 819 1625 I St NW Washington DC 20006

TREICK, RONALD WALTER, b Scotland, SDak, June 8, 34; m 55; c 2. MICROBIAL PHYSIOLOGY. *Educ:* Univ SDak, BA, 56, MA, 57; Ind Univ, PhD(bact), 65. *Prof Exp:* Med technician, Univ SDak, 57-58; res asst infectious dis, Upjohn Co, 58-62; from asst prof to assoc prof, 65-77, PROF MICROBIOL, MIAMI UNIV, 77- *Concurrent Pos:* Res grants, Miami Univ, 65-66, 68-69, 70-71 & 72- *Mem:* AAAS; Am Soc Microbiol. *Res:* Antimicrobial agents; effect of metabolic inhibitors on bacterial macromolecular synthesis; inhibition of bacterial luminescence; bacteria lipid metabolism. *Mailing Add:* Dept of Microbiol Miami Univ Oxford OH 45056

TREIMAN, SAM BARD, b Chicago, Ill, May 27, 25; m 52; c 3. PHYSICS. *Educ:* Univ Chicago, PhD(physics), 52. *Prof Exp:* Res assoc physics, Univ Chicago, 52; from instr to assoc prof, 52-63, PROF PHYSICS, PRINCETON UNIV, 63- *Mem:* Nat Acad Sci; Am Phys Soc; Am Acad Arts & Sci. *Res:* Cosmic ray physics; fundamental particles; field theory. *Mailing Add:* Joseph Henry Labs Princeton Univ Princeton NJ 08540

TREISTMAN, STEVEN NEAL, b New York, NY, May 3, 45; m 67; c 2. NEUROBIOLOGY. *Educ:* State Univ NY, Binghamton, BA, 67; Univ NC, Chapel Hill, PhD(neurobiol), 72. *Prof Exp:* Teacher biol, Heuvelton Cent Sch, 67-69; neurobiol trainee, Sch Med, Univ NC, 69-72; fel, Sch Med, NY Univ, 72-75; res assoc, Friedrich Miescher Inst, Basel, 75-76; asst prof biol, Bryn Mawr Col, 76-80; STAFF SCIENTIST EXP BIOL, WORCESTER FOUND, 80- *Concurrent Pos:* Scottish Rite Found Schizophrenia res grant, 73-75; NSF grant, 77-80; NIH res grant, 79-82, NSF res grant, 81-; corp mem, Marine Biol Lab, Woods Hole, Mass; adj assoc prof pharmacol, Univ Mass Med Ctr. *Mem:* Soc Neurosci; AAAS. *Res:* Neurobiology of simple systems; biochemical correlates of long-term changes in electrical membrane characteristics. *Mailing Add:* Worcester Found 222 Maple Ave Shrewsbury MA 01545

TREITEL, SVEN, b Freiburg, Ger, Mar 5, 29; US citizen; m 58; c 4. GEOPHYSICS. *Educ:* Mass Inst Technol, BS, 53, MS, 55, PhD(geophys), 58. *Prof Exp:* Geophysicist, Stand Oil Co Calif, 58-60; res assoc commun theory, Pan Am Petrol Corp, 60-65, group supvr, 66-71, mgr res sect, 71-74, sr res assoc, 74-77, RES CONSULT, AMOCO PROD CO, 77- *Honors & Awards:* Fessenden Medal, Soc Explor Geophys, 69. *Mem:* Inst Elec & Electronic Engrs; Soc Explor Geophys; Sigma Xi; Europ Asn Explor Geophys; Seismol Soc Am. *Res:* Application of statistical communication theory to seismic analysis. *Mailing Add:* Amoco Prod Co Res Ctr PO Box 591 Tulsa OK 74102

TREITERER, JOSEPH, b Grafrath, Ger, Dec 7, 18; m 53; c 2. TRANSPORTATION ENGINEERING. *Educ:* Munich Tech Univ, Dipl Ing, 49, DSc(traffic eng), 58. *Prof Exp:* Sci asst civil engr & lectr munic eng & city traffic, Munich Tech Univ, 48-55; chief res officer, Nat Inst Rd Res Coun Sci & Indust Res, SAfrica, 56-63; from asst prof to assoc prof civil eng, 63-72, PROF CIVIL ENG, OHIO STATE UNIV, 72- *Concurrent Pos:* Consult, Water Supply, Sewage & Traffic, Munich, 50-55; mem, Ger Res Coun Hwy Pract, 55; lectr, Pretoria Univ, 60-63; mem tech comt, Inter-Provincial Adv Bd Rd Traffic Legis, Repub SAfrica, 60-63; chmn steering comt transp planning, Natural Resources Develop Coun, 61-63; mem, Hwy Res Bd, Nat Acad Sci-Nat Res Coun, 64. *Res:* Automatic control and guidance of motor vehicles; theory of traffic flow; aerial photogrammetry techniques for traffic surveys; transportation systems. *Mailing Add:* Dept of Civil Eng 2070 Neil Ave Columbus OH 43210

TREITLER, THEODORE LEO, b New York, NY, Apr 18, 20; m 47; c 2. PHYSICAL CHEMISTRY. *Educ:* City Col New York, BS, 47; Stevens Inst Technol, MS, 50; Rutgers Univ, PhD(phys chem), 56. *Prof Exp:* Res chemist, Corning Glass Works, NY, 55-57, Colgate-Palmolive Co, 57-61 & Thomas A Edison Labs, 61-63; chemist, Inorg Res & Develop Dept, FMC Corp, 64-70; assoc dir res, 70-80, MGR PROD EVAL, RES & DEVELOP DEPT, BLOCK DRUG CO, INC, JERSEY CITY, 80- *Concurrent Pos:* Instr, Rutgers Univ, 54 & 62, Fairleigh Dickinson Univ, 59-67 & Stevens Inst, 79-80. *Mem:* Am Chem Soc. *Res:* Electrochemistry; ion exchange; surface chemistry; fuel cells; inorganic chemical purification; inorganic synthesis; glass and ceramics; detergency; gas measurement; phosphate chemistry; barium chemistry; phase compatibility; nonprescription drugs, analgesics, dental products and medicated shampoos; denture adhesive systems, synthetic, natural and mixtures. *Mailing Add:* 744 Ridgewood Rd Millburn NJ 07041

TRELA, EDWARD, b Cleveland, Ohio, May 4, 12; m 44; c 4. PHYSICAL METALLURGY. *Educ:* Fenn Col, BS, 39; Case Inst Technol, MS, 48. *Prof Exp:* Metallurgist, Nat Smelting Co, 39-48; res metallurgist, Apex Smelting Co, 48-65; from asst prof to assoc prof, 65-77, EMER ASSOC PROF PHYS METALL, CLEVELAND STATE UNIV, 77-, EMER PROF CHEM ENG, 80- *Mem:* Am Soc Metals; Am Foundrymen's Soc; Am Inst Mining, Metall & Petrol Engrs; Soc Die Casting Engrs. *Res:* Metal and foundry physics; x-ray metallography; corrosion and protection; liquid metals technology-nonferrous; heat treatment; failure analysis; non destructive testing. *Mailing Add:* 4215 W 58th St Cleveland OH 44144

TRELA, JOHN MICHAEL, b Greenfield, Mass, Nov 15, 42; m 68; c 3. BIOCHEMISTRY, MICROBIOLOGY. *Educ:* Tufts Univ, BS, 65; Univ Mass, Amherst, MS, 67; State Univ NY, Stony Brook, PhD(biochem), 71. *Prof Exp:* Instr biol sci, State Univ NY, Stony Brook, 70-72; asst prof, 72-78, ASSOC PROF BIOL SCI, UNIV CINCINNATI, 78- *Mem:* Am Soc Microbiol; Am Asn Univ Prof. *Res:* Microbial physiology, with special emphasis on micromolecular synthesis in thermophilic bacteria. *Mailing Add:* Dept of Biol Sci Univ of Cincinnati Cincinnati OH 45221

TRELA, WALTER JOSEPH, b Pawtucket, RI, May 31, 36; m 62; c 2. LOW TEMPERATURE PHYSICS. *Educ:* Brown Univ, BS, 58; Stanford Univ, PhD(physics), 67. *Prof Exp:* Asst prof physics, Haverford Col, 67-72; staff mem, 73-80, ASST DIV LEADER, LOS ALAMOS NAT LAB, 80- *Mem:* Am Phys Soc; AAAS. *Res:* Low temperature physics with primary emphasis on liquid helium and superconductivity; quantum fluids and solids. *Mailing Add:* Physics Div Los Alamos Nat Lab Los Alamos NM 87544

TRELAWNY, GILBERT STERLING, b Cincinnati, Ohio, Nov 12, 29; m 50; c 3. MICROBIAL PHYSIOLOGY. *Educ:* Delaware Valley Col, BS, 57; Lehigh Univ, MS, 60, PhD(biol), 66. *Prof Exp:* From instr to asst prof microbiol, Delaware Valley Col, 57-66; PROF BIOL, JAMES MADISON UNIV, VA, 66-, HEAD DEPT, 71- *Concurrent Pos:* NSF res grant, 67-69. *Mem:* Mycol Soc Am. *Res:* Microbial metabolism and nutrition. *Mailing Add:* Dept of Biol James Madison Univ Harrisonburg VA 22801

TRELEASE, RICHARD DAVIS, b Chicago, Ill, Sept 23, 17; m 42; c 6. FOOD CHEMISTRY. *Educ:* Univ Ill, BS, 40. *Prof Exp:* Chemist, Swift & Co, 40-42, res chemist poultry, 43-44; food technician, Qm Food & Container Inst, 44-45; asst to vpres res, 48-50, head frozen food res, 50-63, mgr processed meats res, 63-71, mgr meat res, 71-72, gen mgr, Processed Meats Res, 72-73, mgr contract res, 73-80, MGR PROCESSED MEAT RES, SWIFT & CO, 80- *Mem:* Am Chem Soc; Inst Food Technol. *Res:* Food processing and preservation; poultry products; frozen foods; cured meats. *Mailing Add:* Swift & Co Res & Develop Ctr 1919 Swift Dr Oak Brook IL 60521

TRELEASE, RICHARD NORMAN, b Las Vegas, Nev, Nov 6, 41; m 65; c 2. PLANT CELL BIOLOGY, PLANT PHYSIOLOGY. *Educ:* Univ Nev, Reno, BS, 63, MS, 65; Univ Tex, Austin, PhD(cell biol), 69. *Prof Exp:* NIH fel, Univ Wis-Madison, 69-71; asst prof, 71-76, assoc prof, 76-81, PROF BIOL, ARIZ STATE UNIV, 81- *Concurrent Pos:* Adv panel mem, NSF Cell Biol Prog, 78-80. *Mem:* AAAS; Am Soc Cell Biol; Am Soc Plant Physiol; Sigma Xi. *Res:* Oilseed metabolism, especially cottonseeds, aspects of maturation and germination; application of enzyme and immunocytochemistry; enzymology; cell fractionation. *Mailing Add:* Dept of Bot & Microbiol Ariz State Univ Tempe AZ 85281

TRELFORD, JOHN D, b Toronto, Ont, Feb 7, 31; US citizen; c 3. OBSTETRICS & GYNECOLOGY, ONCOLOGY. *Educ:* Univ Toronto, MD, 56; FRCS(C), 64; FRCOG. *Prof Exp:* Asst prof obstet & gynec, Med Sch, Ohio State Univ, 65-70; assoc prof, 70-75, PROF OBSTET & GYNEC, SCH MED, UNIV CALIF, DAVIS, 75- *Concurrent Pos:* Grants, Univ Calif, Davis, 71-72; dir, Oncol Serv, Sacramento Med Ctr, 72-; consult, Vet Admin Hosp, Martinez, Calif, 72-; dir, Am Cancer Soc, Yolo County. *Mem:* Fel Am Col Surgeons; Soc Obstet & Gynaec Can; fel Am Col Obstet & Gynec. *Res:* Antigenicity of the trophoblastic cell and its relationship to cancer. *Mailing Add:* Dept of Obstet & Gynec 4301 X St Rm 207 Sacramento CA 95817

TRELKA, DENNIS GEORGE, b Lorain, Ohio, June 11, 40; m 66; c 2. ANIMAL PHYSIOLOGY. *Educ:* Kent State Univ, BA, 67, MA, 68; Cornell Univ, PhD(animal physiol), 72. *Prof Exp:* Res asst invert zool, Kent State Univ, 67-68; res asst animal physiol, Cornell Univ, 68-72; asst prof, 72-77, ASSOC PROF ANIMAL PHYSIOL, WASHINGTON & JEFFERSON COL, 77- *Mem:* Zool Soc Am; AAAS; Sigma Xi. *Res:* Influence of biogenic amines on blood glucose levels in crayfish; hemorrhagic shock studies on pigs; the effect of carotid ligation on changes in cerebral spinal fluid in rats. *Mailing Add:* Dept of Biol Washington & Jefferson Col Washington PA 15301

TRELOAR, ALAN EDWARD, b Melbourne, Australia, Sept 27, 02; nat US; m 29, 49; c 3. MEDICAL ANTHROPOLOGY, BIOMETRICS. *Educ:* Univ Sydney, BSc, 26; Univ Minn, MS, 29, PhD(agr biochem), 30. *Prof Exp:* Demonstr geol, Univ Sydney, 24-25; from instr to assoc prof biomet, Univ Minn, 29-47, prof biostatist, Sch Pub Health, 47-56; asst dir res, Am Hosp Asn, 56-59; chief statist & anal br, Div Res Grants, NIH, 59-61, spec asst to dir for biomet, Nat Inst Neurol Dis & Blindness, 61-66, chief reproduction anthropometry sect, Nat Inst Child Health & Human Develop, 66-74; dir mensuration & reproduction hist res prog, Ruth E Boynton Health Serv, Univ Minn, Minneapolis, 74-77; from assoc dir to dir to consult, menstrual & reproductive health res prog, Dept Obstet & Gynec, Univ NC, 77-81; VPRES CTR ADVAN REPRODUCTIVE HEALTH, CHAPEL HILL, NC, 81- *Concurrent Pos:* Consult, USPHS, 53-58; dir, Hosp Res & Educ Trust, 57-59. *Mem:* Human Biol Coun; fel AAAS; fel Am Statist Asn; Pop Asn Am; Am Fertil Soc. *Res:* Biometry of the menstrual cycle and gestation period; relationship of menstrual history to illness; effects of oral contraceptives. *Mailing Add:* 9714 Campana Dr Sun City AZ 85351

TRELSTAD, ROBERT LAURENCE, b Redding, Calif, June 16, 40; m 61; c 4. EMBRYOLOGY, PATHOLOGY. *Educ:* Columbia Univ, BA, 61; Harvard Univ, MD, 66. *Prof Exp:* Intern path, Mass Gen Hosp, 66-67; NIH res assoc embryol, 67-69; ASST PATHOLOGIST, MASS GEN HOSP, 72-, CHIEF PATH, SHRINERS BURNS INST, 75- *Concurrent Pos:* Helen Hay Whitney Found res fel path, Mass Gen Hosp, 69-72; Am Cancer Soc fac res award, 72-77; asst prof path, Harvard Med Sch, 72-77; assoc prof path, Harvard Med Sch, 77-; mem cell biol study sect, NIH, 77-; assoc ed, Develop Biol, 78- *Mem:* Soc Develop Biol; Am Soc Cell Biol; Am Soc Zoologists; Int Soc Develop Biol. *Res:* Biological function of connective tissues in normal growth and development and in disease. *Mailing Add:* Dept of Path Shriners Burns Inst MGH Boston MA 02114

TREMAINE, JACK H, b Galt, Ont, June 15, 28; m 56; c 3. PLANT VIROLOGY. *Educ:* McMaster Univ, BSc, 51, MSc, 53; Univ Pittsburgh, PhD(virol), 57. *Prof Exp:* Plant pathologist, 52-64, PLANT VIROLOGIST, CAN DEPT AGR, 64- *Mem:* Am Phytopath Soc. *Mailing Add:* 3936 W 22nd Vancouver BC V6S 1K1 Can

TREMAINE, PETER RICHARD, b Toronto, Ont, Dec 20, 47; m 72. PHYSICAL CHEMISTRY. *Educ:* Univ Waterloo, Ont, BSc, 69; Univ Alta, PhD(phys chem), 74. *Prof Exp:* Nat Res Coun Can fel surface chem, Pulp & Paper Res Inst Can, Montreal, 74-75; asst res officer phys chem, Whiteshell Nuclear Res Estab, Atomic Energy Can, 75-80; ASSOC RES OFFICER PHYS CHEM, OIL SANDS RES DEPT, ALBERTA RES COUN, 80- *Mem:* Chem Inst Can. *Res:* Thermodynamics of high temperature, high pressure aqueous systems. *Mailing Add:* Alberta Res Coun Oil Sands Dept 11315-87 Ave Edmonton AB T6G 2C2 Can

TREMAINE, SCOTT DUNCAN, b Toronto, Ont, May 25, 50. ASTROPHYSICS. *Educ:* McMaster Univ, BSc, 71; Princeton Univ, MA, 73, PhD(physics), 75. *Prof Exp:* Res fel, Calif Inst Technol, 75-77 & Cambridge Univ, 77-78; res fel, Inst Advan Study, 78-81; ASSOC PROF, MASS INST TECHNOL, 81- *Mem:* Am Astron Soc. *Res:* Theoretical studies in dynamics; galactic structure; cosmology; planetary rings. *Mailing Add:* Rm 6-211 Mass Inst Technol Cambridge MA 02139

TREMBA, EDWARD LOUIS, b Highland Park, Mich, Feb 26, 43; m 79; c 4. CRATERING, GEOTECHNICAL ENGINEERING. *Educ:* Univ Mich, BSc, 65; Ohio State Univ, MSc, 67, PhD(geol), 73. *Prof Exp:* Geologist, Air Forces Weapons Lab, US Air Force, 73-74; asst prof geol, Grand Valley State Cols, 74-78; RES ENGR APPL GEOL, NMEX ENG RES INST, UNIV NMEX, 78- *Concurrent Pos:* Lectr geol, Univ NMex, 79- *Res:* Explosive cratering studies; atoll geologic; geophysical studies; geotechnical site evaluations. *Mailing Add:* NMex Eng Res Inst Univ NMex PO Box 25 Albuquerque NM 87131

TREMBLAY, GEORGE CHARLES, b Pittsfield, Mass, Oct 13, 38; c 4. BIOCHEMISTRY. *Educ:* Mass Col Pharm, BS, 60; St Louis Univ, PhD(biochem), 65. *Prof Exp:* Am Cancer Soc fel biol chem, Harvard Univ, 65-66; from asst prof to assoc prof, 66-75, PROF BIOCHEM, UNIV RI, 75- *Concurrent Pos:* Res grants, Nat Inst Child Health & Human Develop, 67-70, Nat Inst Arthritis & Metab Dis, 71-74, Nat Cancer Inst, 74-77, NSF, 76-79 & Nat Inst Arthritis Metab & Diag Dis, 79-82. *Mem:* AAAS. *Res:* Regulatory mechanisms involved in the control of cellular metabolism. *Mailing Add:* Dept of Biochem Univ of RI Kingston RI 02881

TREMBLAY, GILLES, b Montreal, Que, Apr 18, 28; m 75; c 3. PATHOLOGY. *Educ:* Univ Montreal, BA, 48, MD, 53. *Prof Exp:* Resident path, Hotel-Dieu Hosp, 54-55; resident path, New Eng Deaconess Hosp, Boston, Mass, 55-57; pathologist, Hotel-Dieu Hosp, Montreal, 59-61; pathologist, Notre-Dame Hosp, 61-64; prof path & chmn dept, Fac Med, Univ Montreal, 64-70; PROF PATH, McGILL UNIV, 70-, SR PATHOLOGIST, ROYAL VICTORIA HOSP, 77- *Concurrent Pos:* Nat Res Coun Can med res fel, Hotel-Dieu Hosp, Montreal, 53-54; Can Cancer Soc Allan Blair Mem res fel histochem, Postgrad Med Sch, Univ London, 57-59. *Mem:* Am Asn Cancer Res; Am Asn Pathologists; Can Asn Path; Int Acad Path. *Res:* Experimental studies on tumor cell-host cell interaction; ultrastructural and cytochemical studies on breast carcinoma. *Mailing Add:* Dept of Path 3775 University St Montreal PQ H3A 2B4 Can

TREMBLAY, JEAN-PAUL, computer science, see previous edition

TREMBLY, LYNN DALE, b Parma, Idaho, July 26, 39; m 68; c 2. EXPLORATION GEOPHYSICS. *Educ:* Eastern Ore Col, BS, 62; Ore State Univ, MS, 65, PhD(geophysics), 68. *Prof Exp:* From res asst to res assoc geophysics, Ore State Univ, 62-67; res scientist, 67-70, advan scientist geophys, 70-76, SR RES GEOPHYSICIST, MARATHON OIL CO, 76- *Mem:* Soc Explor Geophysicists; Sigma Xi; Am Geophys Union. *Res:* Origination and conducting of original and reative research through the application of both theoretical and experimental techniques in seismology. *Mailing Add:* Marathon Oil Co Denver Res Ctr Box 269 Littleton CO 80121

TREMELLING, MICHAEL, JR, b Rigby, Idaho, Oct 14, 45; m 66; c 2. PHYSICAL ORGANIC CHEMISTRY. *Educ:* Idaho State Univ, BA, 68; Yale Univ, MPhil, 70, PhD(chem), 72. *Prof Exp:* Res assoc, Calif Inst Technol, 72-73; asst prof, 74-80, ASSOC PROF CHEM, VASSAR COL, 80- *Mem:* Am Chem Soc; AAAS. *Res:* Solution dynamics of free radicals; high temperature heterogenous reactions. *Mailing Add:* Dept of Chem Vassar Col Poughkeepsie NY 12601

TREMMEL, CARL GEORGE, b Lakewood, Ohio, June 25, 33; m 54; c 3. ANALYTICAL CHEMISTRY. *Educ:* Kent State Univ, BS, 55; Iowa State Univ, MS, 58. *Prof Exp:* RES CHEMIST, EASTMAN KODAK CO, 58- *Mem:* Am Chem Soc. *Res:* Photographic chemistry; physical chemistry of color photography; electrochemistry. *Mailing Add:* 349 Colebrook Dr Rochester NY 14617

TREMOR, JOHN W, b East Aurora, NY, Jan 24, 32; m 59; c 2. COMPARATIVE PHYSIOLOGY, ENVIRONMENTAL BIOLOGY. *Educ:* Univ Buffalo, BA, 53, MA, 57; Univ Ariz, PhD(zool), 62. *Prof Exp:* Res asst biochem, Vet Admin Hosp, Buffalo, NY, 58; teaching asst radiation biol, NSF Inst Biol Sta, Mont State Univ, 59; instr biol & bot, Phoenix Col, 62; asst prof physiol & embryol, Humboldt State Col, 62-63; group leader gen biol, Biosatellite Proj, 63-72, dep chief earth sci applns off, Ames Res Ctr, NASA, 72-74; proj scientist, biomed exp sci satellite & joint USSR/US biol satellite prog, 74-76; MGR SPACE SHUTTLE PLANT EXP & DEP PROJ SCIENTIST, AMES LIFE SCI PAYLOAD SPACELAB III & PRIN INVESTR, SPACELAB IV, AMES RES CTR, NASA, 77- *Mem:* AAAS. *Res:* Development and implementation of biological experiments for space flight; developmental biology of amphibians. *Mailing Add:* Biosysts Div Code LB NASA Ames Res Ctr Moffett Field CA 94035

TREMPER, RANDOLPH TILDEN, b Kingsburg, Calif, June 6, 44; m 65; c 2. CERAMICS ENGINEERING, MATERIALS SCIENCE. *Educ:* Univ Calif, Berkeley, BS, 66, MS, 67; Univ Utah, PhD(mat sci), 71. *Prof Exp:* Res ceramist, Lamp Envelope Mat Res Lab, 71-75, mgr, 75-78, MGR ENG, DEPT LAMP GLASS & COMPONENTS DEPT, GEN ELEC LIGHTING BUS GROUP, GEN ELEC CO, 78- *Mem:* Am Ceramic Soc. *Res:* Processing and characterization of ceramic materials; synthesis of ultra-pure materials; mechanical, optical, heat transfer properties of ceramics and glass; glass melting technology; properites design and processing of metal and plastic components. *Mailing Add:* Dept of Lamp Glass Prod 24400 Highland Rd Richmond Heights OH 44143

TRENBERTH, KEVIN EDWARD, b Christchurch, NZ, Nov 8, 44; m 70; c 1. METEOROLOGY. *Educ:* Univ Canterbury, BSc, 66; Mass Inst Technol, ScD, 72. *Prof Exp:* Meteorologist res, NZ Meteorol Serv, 66-77, supt dynamic meteorol, 77; ASSOC PROF METEOROL, UNIV ILL, 77- *Concurrent Pos:* Mem, NZ Working Group Global Data Processing Syst, Comn Basic Syst, World Meteorol Orgn, 75-77; NSF grant, 78-; consult, Nat Oceanic & Atmospheric Admin, 80-; ed, Monthly Weather Review, Am Meteorol Soc, 81- *Mem:* Am Meteorol Soc; AAAS. *Res:* Dynamics of climate and climate change; meteorology of the southern hemisphere; numerical weather prediction; dynamics of the stratosphere. *Mailing Add:* 6-105 CSL Univ Ill Urbana IL 61801

TRENCH, ROBERT KENT, b Belize City, Brit Honduras, Aug 3, 40; nat US; m 68. MARINE BIOLOGY, BIOCHEMISTRY. *Educ:* Univ West Indies, BSc, 65; Univ Calif, Los Angeles, MA, 67, PhD(invert zool), 69. *Prof Exp:* UK Sci Res Coun fel, Oxford Univ, 69-71; instr, Yale Univ, 71-72, asst prof, 72-76; assoc prof biol, 76-80, PROF BIOL & GEOL, UNIV CALIF, SANTA BARBARA, 80- *Mem:* AAAS; Am Soc Limnol & Oceanog; Am Soc Cell Biol; Soc Exp Biol UK. *Res:* Coral reef biology and ecology; biochemical integration of plasmids in autotroph-heterotroph endosymbioses; intercellular recognition phenomena. *Mailing Add:* Dept Biol Sci Univ Calif Santa Barbara CA 93106

TRENCH, WILLIAM FREDERICK, b Trenton, NJ, July 31, 31; m 54; c 4. MATHEMATICS. *Educ:* Lehigh Univ, BA, 53; Univ Pa, MA, 55, PhD(math), 58. *Prof Exp:* Instr, Moore Sch Elec Eng, Univ Pa, 53-56; mathematician, Gen Elec Co, Pa, 56-57; eng specialist, Philco Corp, Pa, 57-59; engr, Radio Corp Am, NJ, 59-64; assoc prof math, 64-67, PROF MATH, DREXEL UNIV, 67- *Mem:* Math Asn Am; Am Math Soc; Soc Indust & Appl Math. *Res:* Applied mathematics; differential equations; numerical analysis. *Mailing Add:* Dept of Math Drexel Univ Philadelphia PA 19104

TRENHAILE, ALAN STUART, b Ebbw Vale, SWales, Apr 14, 45; m 66. GEOMORPHOLOGY. *Educ:* Univ Wales, BS, 66, PhD(geog), 69. *Prof Exp:* Asst prof, 69-73, assoc prof, 73-78, PROF GEOG, UNIV WINDSOR, 78- *Concurrent Pos:* Mem, Brit Geomorphol Res Group. *Mem:* Inst Brit Geog; Can Asn Geogr; Asn Am Geogr. *Res:* Shore platforms and Pleistocene raised platforms; morphometry and spatial variation of glacial features, with particular reference to drumlins, eskers and cirques; beach processes and cliff erosion; air photography; shore platforms in Eastern Canada; glacial morphometry. *Mailing Add:* Dept of Geog Univ of Windsor Windsor ON N9B 3P4 Can

TRENHOLM, ANDREW RUTLEDGE, b Charleston, SC, May 1, 42; m 66; c 2. CHEMICAL CHEMISTRY. *Educ:* Clemson Univ, BS, 64; Ga Inst Technol, MS, 68. *Prof Exp:* Sanitary engr, Health Dept, Dade County, Fla, 64-67; chem engr, Union Carbide Corp, 68-70; environ engr, US Environ Protection Agency, 70-79; SECT HEAD, MIDWEST RES INST, 79- *Res:* Multimedia environmental research in air pollution, water pollution, solid waste and hazardous waste. *Mailing Add:* 425 Volker Blvd Kansas City MO 64110

TRENHOLM, HAROLD LOCKSLEY, b Amherst, NS, July 24, 41; m 68. TOXICOLOGY, AGRICULTURE. *Educ:* McGill Univ, BSc, 63; Cornell Univ, PhD(physiol), 68. *Prof Exp:* Asst physiol, State Univ NY Vet Col, Cornell, 63-67; res scientist, Res Labs, Health Protection Br, 67-73, dir res bur, nonmed use drugs directorate, Can Dept Health & Welfare, 73-77; AGR TOXICOLOGIST, AGR CAN, 77- *Mem:* Am Chem Soc; Can Asn Res Toxicol; NY Acad Sci. *Res:* Drug abuse; toxicology. *Mailing Add:* Animal Res Ctr Agr Can Ottawa ON K1A 0C6 Can

TRENHOLME, JOHN BURGESS, b Portland, Ore, Feb 4, 39; m 69; c 1. LASER ENGINEERING, NUMERICAL ANALYSIS. *Educ:* Calif Inst Technol, BS, 61, MS, 62, PhD(mat sci), 69. *Prof Exp:* Scientist lasers & light sources, Naval Res Lab, Washington, DC, 69-72; physicist laser fusion, 72-78, SR SCIENTIST SOLID STATE LASER PROG, LAWRENCE LIVERMORE LAB, 78- *Mem:* AAAS. *Res:* Laser fusion; laser design and engineering; numerical simulation of laser pumping and propagation; nonlinear optics; optical design. *Mailing Add:* 120 Montclair Ct Danville CA 94526

TRENKLE, ALLEN H, b Alliance, Nebr, July 23, 34; m 56; c 3. NUTRITION, BIOCHEMISTRY. *Educ:* Univ Nebr, BSc, 56; Iowa State Univ, MSc, 58, PhD(nutrit), 60. *Prof Exp:* NIH res fel, Univ Calif, Berkeley, 61-62; from asst prof to assoc prof animal sci, 62-71, PROF ANIMAL SCI, IOWA STATE UNIV, 71- *Mem:* Am Soc Animal Sci; Am Chem Soc; Soc Exp Biol & Med; NY Acad Sci; Am Inst Nutrit. *Res:* Physiology of growth hormone and insulin secretion; endocrinology studies with ruminants; influence of hormones on growth and development of mammals; protein metabolism in ruminants. *Mailing Add:* 301 Kildee Hall Iowa State Univ Ames IA 50011

TRENT, DENNIS W, b Bend, Ore, Oct 17, 35; m 55; c 6. MICROBIOLOGY, BIOCHEMISTRY. *Educ:* Brigham Young Univ, BS, 59, MS, 61; Univ Okla, PhD(med sci), 64. *Prof Exp:* From asst prof to assoc prof bact, Brigham Young Univ, 67-69; from asst prof to assoc prof microbiol, Univ Tex Med Sch, San Antonio, 69-74; CHIEF IMMUNOCHEM BR, VECTOR-BORNE DIS DIV, CTR DIS CONTROL, USPHS, 74- *Concurrent Pos:* NIH res grants, 66-72. *Mem:* Am Soc Microbiol. *Res:* Biochemistry of togavirus replication; immunology; vival nucleic acids. *Mailing Add:* Vector-Borne Dis Div Ctr for Dis Control PO Box 2037 Ft Collins CO 80522

TRENT, DONALD STEPHEN, b Cloverdale, Ore, Mar 29, 35; m 58; c 3. MECHANICAL ENGINEERING, APPLIED MATHEMATICS. *Educ:* Ore State Univ, BS, 62, MS, 64, PhD(mech eng), 72. *Prof Exp:* Develop engr, Battelle Mem Inst, 64-67; lectr, Ore State Univ, 67-68, res asst, 68-70; sr res engr, 70-73, res assoc, 73-75, RES & DEVELOP MGR, PAC NORTHWEST LAB, BATTELLE MEM INST, 76- *Concurrent Pos:* Mech engr, Environ Protection Agency, Ore, 68-70; instr, Columbia Basin Col, 70-72; standard chmn, Am Nat Standard Inst, 75-; consult, Am Chem Res Soc, 82- *Mem:* Am Soc Mech Engrs; Am Nuclear Soc; Sigma Xi; NY Acad Sci. *Res:* Computational heat transfer and fluid flow in natural convecting systems; numerical modeling of free turbulence, thermal plumes and air-sea interactions; reactor heat transfer; thermal hydraulics of advanced energy systems. *Mailing Add:* Pac Northwest Lab Battelle Blvd Battelle Mem Inst Richland WA 99352

TRENT, HAROLD FRANCIS, b Roanoke, Va, Feb 5, 18; m 65; c 2. MECHANICAL ENGINEERING, PHYSICS. *Educ:* Roanoke Col, BS, 41; Va Polytech Inst, MS, 58. *Prof Exp:* Shop inspector, Norfolk & Western Railway, 38-47; serv engr, Nathan Mfg Co, 47-48; asst prof eng graphics, Va Polytech Inst, 48-51; proj engr, Western Elec Co, 51-53; asst prof eng graphics, 53-58, assoc prof mech eng, 58-59, assoc prof eng graphics, 59-63, assoc prof indust eng, 63-68, ASSOC PROF ENG FUNDAMENTALS, VA POLYTECH INST & STATE UNIV, 68- *Concurrent Pos:* Resident consult, Poly Sci Corp, 60-63. *Res:* Electro-mechanical instrumentation; telemetry of earth satellites and planetary reconnaissance vehicles. *Mailing Add:* Dept of Eng Fundamentals Va Polytech Inst & State Univ Blacksburg VA 24060

TRENT, JOHN ELLSWORTH, b Wabash, Ind, Sept 22, 42; m 68; c 2. ANALYTICAL CHEMISTRY. *Educ:* Manchester Col, BA, 64; Ohio State Univ, PhD(org chem), 70. *Prof Exp:* RES CHEMIST, STANDARD OIL CO, IND, 71- *Mem:* Am Chem Soc. *Res:* Analytical instrumentation. *Mailing Add:* Standard Oil Co Ind PO Box 400 Naperville IL 60566

TRENT, WALTER RUSSELL, b Charleston, Mo, Sept 27, 08; m 31; c 6. CHEMISTRY. *Educ:* Drury Col, BS, 29. *Prof Exp:* Jr res chemist, Monsanto Chem Co, WVa, 29-30; asst org chem, Pa State Col, 30-34; sr org res chemist, Colgate-Palmolive-Peet Co, NJ, 34-46; dir res, Nat Home Prod Co, NY, 46-47; sr proj chemist, Colgate-Palmolive Co, 47-50, chief chemist, 50-62; chem dir, John T Stanley Co, 62-65; sr res chemist, Stauffer Chem Co, 65-67; dir appl res, J H Baxter Co, 67-70; INDUST CONSULT, 70- *Mem:* Am Chem Soc. *Res:* Organic chemical synthesis; synthetic detergents; soap processes; applications research. *Mailing Add:* Rte 2 Box 100C Monroe OR 97456

TRENTELMAN, GEORGE FREDERICK, b Amsterdam, NY, Apr 27, 44. PHYSICS. *Educ:* Clarkson Col Technol, BS, 66; Mich State Univ, MS, 68, PhD(physics), 70. *Prof Exp:* Res assoc nuclear physics, Mich State Univ, 70-71; asst prof, 71-76, ASSOC PROF PHYSICS, NORTHERN MICH UNIV, 76- *Concurrent Pos:* Vis physicist, Inst Nuclear Sci, Univ Tokyo, 72-73. *Mem:* Am Phys Soc. *Res:* Nuclear physics. *Mailing Add:* Dept of Physics Northern Mich Univ Marquette MI 49855

TRENTHAM, JIMMY N, b Dresden, Tenn, Jan 7, 36; m 65; c 2. MICROBIOLOGY. *Educ:* Univ Tenn, Martin, BS, 58; Vanderbilt Univ, PhD(microbiol), 65. *Prof Exp:* From asst prof to assoc prof microbiol, 65-73, chmn dept biol, 69-73, provost, 73-79, vchancellor, 76-79, PROF, UNIV TENN, MARTIN, 73- *Concurrent Pos:* NSF res fel, 67-69. *Mem:* AAAS; Am Soc Microbiologists; Am Inst Biol Sci. *Res:* Microbial ecology, including qualitative and quantitative fluctuations of bacterial populations in freshwater and effects of temperature and nutritional factors on the structure of bacterial communities in freshwater. *Mailing Add:* Univ Tenn Martin TN 38237

TRENTIN, JOHN JOSEPH, b Newark, NJ, Dec 15, 18; m 46; c 2. EXPERIMENTAL BIOLOGY. *Educ:* Pa State Univ, BS, 40; Univ Mo, AM, 41, PhD(endocrinol), 47. *Prof Exp:* Res asst, Univ Mo, 47-48; Childs fel anat, Sch Med, Yale Univ, 48-51, from instr to asst prof, 51-54; from assoc prof to prof, 54-60, actg chmn dept, 58-60, PROF EXP BIOL & HEAD DIV, BAYLOR COL MED, 60- *Concurrent Pos:* Assoc prof anat, Univ Tex Dent Br, 54-60; mem, Adv Comt Pathogenesis Cancer, Am Cancer Soc, 58-60, Comt Tissue Transplantation, Nat Res Coun, 60-70 & Comt Med Res & Educ, Vet Admin Hosp, Houston, 60-65; consult, Univ Tex M D Anderson Hosp & Tumor Inst, 59-62; mem, Bd Sci Counrs, Nat Cancer Inst, 63-65, chmn, 65-67; mem, Spec Animal Leukemia Ecol Studies Comt, NIH, 64-67. *Honors & Awards:* Esther Langer-Bertha Teplitz Mem Award, Ann Langer Res Found, Chicago, 63; Golden Plate Award, Am Acad Achievement, 65. *Mem:* AAAS; Soc Exp Biol & Med; NY Acad Sci; Am Asn Exp Path; Am Asn Cancer Res. *Res:* Cancer research; human cancer viruses; genetics; immunology; tissue and organ transplantation; hematology; cancer immunity; radiobiology; graft-versus-host diseases; immunological tolerance. *Mailing Add:* Div Exp Biol Baylor Col Med Tex Med Ctr Houston TX 77030

TREPKA, ROBERT DALE, b Crete, Nebr, Dec 16, 38; m 61; c 3. ORGANIC CHEMISTRY. *Educ:* Grinnell Col, BA, 61; Univ Calif, Los Angeles, PhD(org chem), 65. *Prof Exp:* NATO fel org chem, Munich, 65-66; MGR, PHOTOG PROD DIV, 3M CO, 66- *Mem:* Am Chem Soc; Soc Photog Sci & Eng. *Res:* Physical organic chemistry; organic stereochemistry; photographic chemistry; synthetic organic chemistry. *Mailing Add:* 6381 Birchwood Rd Woodbury MN 55125

TREPKA, WILLIAM JAMES, b Crete, Nebr, Apr 17, 33; m 55; c 3. POLYMER CHEMISTRY, RUBBER CHEMISTRY. *Educ:* Doane Col, BA, 55; Iowa State Univ, PhD(chem), 60. *Prof Exp:* RES CHEMIST, PHILLIPS PETROL CO, 60- *Mem:* Am Chem Soc; Soc Automotive Engrs. *Res:* Polymer and rubber synthesis. *Mailing Add:* 115 Ramblewood Rd Bartlesville OK 74003

TREPTOW, RICHARD S, b Chicago, Ill, Feb 8, 41; m 68; c 2. INORGANIC CHEMISTRY. *Educ:* Blackburn Col, BA, 62; Univ Ill, Urbana, MS, 64, PhD(chem), 66. *Prof Exp:* Staff chemist, Procter & Gamble Co, 66-72; asst prof chem, 72-75, ASSOC PROF CHEM, CHICAGO STATE UNIV, 75- *Mem:* Am Chem Soc. *Res:* Transition metal compounds; forensic chemistry; physical biochemistry. *Mailing Add:* Dept of Phys Sci Chicago State Univ Chicago IL 60628

TRESCOTT, PETER CHAPIN, b Evanston, Ill, Dec 12, 39; m 63; c 3. HYDROGEOLOGY. *Educ:* Williams Col, BA, 62; Univ Ill, Urbana, MS, 64, PhD(geol), 67. *Prof Exp:* Geologist, NS Dept Mines, Halifax, 67-70; RES HYDROLOGIST, US GEOL SURV, 70- *Mem:* Am Asn Petrol Geologists; Am Geophys Union. *Res:* Areal variation in properties of porous media; digital simulation of flow through porous media; coupled flow in porous media. *Mailing Add:* 2510 Foxcraft Way Reston VA 22091

TRESHOW, MICHAEL, b Copenhagen, Denmark, July 14, 26; nat US; m 51; c 1. PLANT PATHOLOGY. *Educ:* Univ Calif, Los Angeles, BS, 50; Univ Calif, Davis, PhD(plant path), 54. *Prof Exp:* Sr lab technician, Univ Calif, 52-53; plant pathologist, Columbia-Geneva Steel Div, US Steel Corp, 53-61; from asst prof to assoc prof bot, 61-67, assoc prof biol, 67-70, PROF BIOL, UNIV UTAH, 70- *Mem:* Air Pollution Control Asn; Am Phytopath Soc; Mycol Soc Am; Bot Soc Am. *Res:* Environmental pathology, particularly diseases caused by air pollutants; diseases of fruit crops; environmental stress. *Mailing Add:* Dept of Biol Univ of Utah Salt Lake City UT 84112

TRESSLER, DONALD KITELEY, food chemistry, deceased

TRESSLER, RICHARD ERNEST, b Bellefonte, Pa, June 14, 42; m 65; c 3. CERAMICS, MATERIALS SCIENCE. *Educ:* Pa State Univ, BS, 63, PhD(ceramic sci), 67; Mass Inst Technol, SM, 64. *Prof Exp:* Sr scientist mat res, Tem Pres Res, Inc, Pa, 67; nuclear res officer, US Air Force, McClellan AFB, 67-68, mat scientist, Mat Lab, Wright-Patterson AFB, 68-70, tech area mgr, 70-71; NSF fel, Univ Essex, 71-72; asst prof, 72-76, ASSOC PROF CERAMIC SCI, PA STATE UNIV, UNIVERSITY PARK, 76- *Concurrent Pos:* Adj asst prof, Univ Cincinnati, 69-71. *Honors & Awards:* Sci Achievement Medal, Systs Command, US Air Force, 70. *Mem:* Am Ceramic Soc; Metall Soc; Nat Inst Ceramic Engrs; Electrochem Soc. *Res:* Fabrication and mechanical behavior of structural ceramic and composite materials; fracture and strengthening mechanisms; IC processing and properties. *Mailing Add:* Dept of Mat Sci Pa State Univ University Park PA 16802

TRETIAK, OLEH JOHN, b Podkamen, Ukraine, Jan 18, 39; US citizen; m 65. ELECTRICAL ENGINEERING, BIOMEDICAL ENGINEERING. *Educ:* Cooper Union, BS, 58; Mass Inst Technol, SM, 60, ScD, 63. *Prof Exp:* Asst prof elec eng, Mass Inst Technol, 63-66, res assoc biomed, 66-73; pfoj engr storage tubes, Image Instruments, 66; ASSOC PROF ELEC ENG, DREXEL UNIV, 73- *Concurrent Pos:* Consult, Raytheon Corp, 64-65, Cognos Corp, 70-71 & E G & G Inc, 71-72; Soviet Union exchange scholar, Nat Acad Sci, 72. *Mem:* Inst Elec & Electronic Engrs; Asn Comput Mach; Soc Nuclear Med; AAAS. *Res:* Medical imaging systems; fundamental limitations of computed tomography and the design and optimization of computer algorithms; pictorial pattern recognition; mathematical modeling of images with the view of developing robust feature extraction methods; evaluation of the utility of images. *Mailing Add:* Drexel Univ 32nd & Chestnut Sts Philadelphia PA 19104

TRETTER, JAMES RAY, organic chemistry, see previous edition

TRETTER, STEVEN ALAN, b Greenbelt, Md, May 28, 40; m 68; c 1. ELECTRICAL ENGINEERING. *Educ:* Univ Md, College Park, BSEE, 62; Princeton Univ, MA, 64, PhD(elec eng), 66. *Prof Exp:* Mem tech staff elec eng, Hughes Aircraft Co, 65-66; ASSOC PROF ELEC ENG, UNIV MD, COLLEGE PARK, 66- *Concurrent Pos:* Suppl engr, Ctr Explor Studies, IBM Corp, 68; consult, Vitro Corp Am, 69-70, Rixon Electronics, Inc, 70- & US Naval Res Lab, 74- *Mem:* Inst Elec & Electronics Engrs. *Res:* Statistical communication theory; error correcting codes; digital filtering and communications. *Mailing Add:* 601 Hawkesbury Terr Silver Spring MD 20904

TREU, JESSE ISAIAH, b New York, NY, Apr 10, 47; m 70; c 1. BIOPHYSICS, OPTICS. *Educ:* Rensselaer Polytech Inst, BS, 68; Princeton Univ, MA, 71, PhD(physics), 73. *Prof Exp:* Physicist optics & immunol, 73-75, liaison scientist components & mat group, Gen Elec Res & Develop Ctr, 75-77; PROG MGR ADV DEVELOP, AUTOMATED EQUIP FOR HEMAT & HISTOL, TECHNICON CORP, 77- *Mem:* Am Phys Soc; Am Asn Physicists Med; Biphys Soc. *Mailing Add:* Technicon Corp Tarrytown NY 10591

TREUMANN, WILLIAM BORGEN, b Grafton, NDak, Feb 26, 16; m 45, 48; c 3. PHYSICAL CHEMISTRY. *Educ:* Univ NDak, BS, 42; Univ Ill, MS, 44, PhD(phys chem), 47. *Prof Exp:* Asst chem, Univ Ill, 42-46, asst math, 46; from asst prof to prof phys chem, NDak State Univ, 46-55; assoc prof, 60-62, assoc dean acad affairs, 68-70, prof, 62-80, dean, 70-80, EMER PROF PHYS CHEM & DEAN FAC MATH & SCI, MOORHEAD STATE UNIV,80- *Mem:* AAAS; Am Chem Soc; Am Inst Chemists. *Res:* Complex ion formation. *Mailing Add:* Off of Acad Affairs Moorhead State Univ Moorhead MN 56560

TREVATHAN, LARRY EUGENE, b Phoenix, Ariz, Apr 13, 47; m 70; c 2. PLANT PATHOLOGY, PLANT PHYSIOLOGY. *Educ:* Univ Tenn, BS, 69; Va Polytech Inst & State Univ, PhD(plant path), 78. *Prof Exp:* ASST PROF & ASST PLANT PATHOLOGIST, MISS STATE UNIV, 78- *Mem:* Sigma Xi. *Res:* Physiology of pathogenesis of diseases of forage crops; genetic basis and inheritance of resistance in forage grasses. *Mailing Add:* Dept of Plant Path & Weed Sci PO Drawer PG Mississippi State MS 39762

TREVELYAN, BENJAMIN JOHN, b Beamsville, Ont, Nov 8, 22; m 53; c 4. PHYSICAL CHEMISTRY. *Educ:* McMaster Univ, BA, 44; McGill Univ, PhD(chem), 51. *Prof Exp:* Chemist, Aluminum Co Can, Ltd, Que, 44-47; asst res dir, Fraser Co, Ltd, NB, 51-53, res dir, 53-60; res scientist, WVa Pulp & Paper Co, 60-62; dir res, Celfibe Div, Johnson & Johnson, 62-65; mgr pulp res & eng, Kimberly-Clark Corp, 65-69, dir pulp & wood prep, Res & Eng, 69-73; indust liaison officer, Pulp & Paper Res Inst Can, 73-77; consult, Sync-Rust Ltd, Montreal, 77-78; ASSOC DIR DEVELOP, ITT RAYONIER, 78- *Mem:* Tech Asn Pulp & Paper Indust; Am Chem Soc; Can Pulp & Paper Asn. *Res:* Pulp and paper technology. *Mailing Add:* 1 Strawberry Hill Apt 6B Stamford CT 06902

TREVES, JEAN FRANCOIS, b Brussels, Belg, Apr 23, 30; m 62; c 2. PURE MATHEMATICS. *Educ:* Univ Sorbonne, Lic, 53, Dr(math), 58. *Prof Exp:* Asst prof math, Univ Calif, Berkeley, 58-60; assoc prof, Yeshiva Univ, 61-64; prof, Purdue Univ, 64-71; PROF MATH, RUTGERS UNIV, NEW BRUNSWICK, 71- *Concurrent Pos:* Sloan fel, 60-64; vis prof, Univ Sorbonne, 65-67, Univ Paris, 74-75; mem, Mission Orgn Am States In Brazil, 61; Guggenheim fel, 77-78. *Honors & Awards:* Chauvenet Prize, Am Math Soc, 71. *Mem:* Am Math Soc; Math Soc France. *Res:* Partial differential equations; functional analysis. *Mailing Add:* Dept of Math Rutgers Univ New Brunswick NJ 08903

TREVES, SALVADOR, b Ramallo, Arg, Aug 3, 40; US citizen; m 66; c 2. NUCLEAR MEDICINE, PEDIATRICS. *Educ:* Nat Col Ill, Buenos Aires, BA, 59; Univ Buenos Aires, MD, 66. *Prof Exp:* Asst physician, Ctr Nuclear Med, Hosp Clin, Univ Buenos Aires, 66; res fel, Inst Med & Exp Surg, Univ Montreal, 67; resident nuclear med, Royal Victoria Hosp, McGill Univ, 67-68; clin fel & res assoc nuclear med & clin fel med, Yale-New Haven Hosp, Sch Med, Yale Univ, 68-70; instr, 70-73, ASST PROF RADIOL, HARVARD MED SCH, 73- *Concurrent Pos:* Head nuclear med, Childrens Hosp Med Ctr, 70-73, chief pediat nuclear med, 75-, nuclear radiologist, 76- *Mem:* Soc Nuclear Med; Sigma Xi; Am Heart Asn; Soc Pediat Radiol. *Res:* Development of ultrashort lived radionuclide generators for angiocardiography in children; development of magnifying collimators for children; development of computer software for nuclear medicine functional studies. *Mailing Add:* Div of Nuclear Med 300 Longwood Ave Boston MA 02115

TREVES, SAMUEL BLAIN, b Detroit, Mich, Sept 11, 25; m 60; c 2. VOLCANOLOGY, PETROLOGY. *Educ:* Mich Col Mining & Technol, BS, 51; Univ Idaho, MS, 53; Ohio State Univ, PhD(geol), 58. *Prof Exp:* Geologist, Ford Motor Co, 51, State Bur Mines & Geol, Idaho, 52 & Otago Catchment Bd, NZ, 53-54; from instr to assoc prof geol, 59-55; chmn dept, 64-70, PROF GEOL, UNIV NEBR, LINCOLN, 66-, CHMN DEPT, 75- *Concurrent Pos:* Chief scientist, Antarctica Expeds, 60-75 & Greenland Exped, 62-64. *Honors & Awards:* Antarctic Serv Medal, 68. *Mem:* AAAS; fel Geol Soc Am; Nat Asn Geol Teachers; Royal Soc NZ. *Res:* Petrography; economic geology; antarctic geology. *Mailing Add:* 1710 B St Lincoln NE 68502

TREVILLYAN, ALVIN EARL, b Moline, Ill, Apr 12, 36; m 58; c 4. ORGANIC CHEMISTRY. *Educ:* Augustana Col, BA, 57; Purdue Univ, MS, 59, PhD(organometallics), 62. *Prof Exp:* Res chemist, Sinclair Res Inc, 62-69; RES CHEMIST, AMOCO CHEM, 69- *Mem:* Am Chem Soc. *Res:* Organometallics; petrochemicals. *Mailing Add:* 504 E Bauer Rd Naperville IL 60540

TREVINO, DANIEL LOUIS, b Edinburg, Tex, May 15, 43; m 65; c 2. NEUROPHYSIOLOGY. *Educ:* Univ Tex, Austin, BA, 65, PhD(physiol), 70. *Prof Exp:* Instr physiol, Sch Med Univ NC, Chapel Hill, 72-73, asst prof, 73-79; assoc dir student affairs & res asst prof anat, Sch Med, Univ NMex, Albuquerque, 79-81; RES ASSOC PROF ANAT & ASST DEAN STUDENT AFFAIRS, SCH MED,UNIV TEX MED BR, GALVESTON, 81- *Concurrent Pos:* USPHS fel, Univ Tex Southwest Med Sch Dallas, 70 & Marine Biomed Inst, Galveston, 70-72; fel neurobiol, Sch Med, Univ NC, Chapel Hill, 72- *Mem:* AAAS; Sigma Xi; Soc Neurosci. *Res:* Sensory neurophysiology; pain. *Mailing Add:* 165 Gail Borden Bldg Univ Tex Med Br Galveston TX 77550

TREVINO, GILBERTO STEPHENSON, b Laredo, Tex, Jan 11, 25; m 60; c 2. INFECTIOUS DISEASES, RESEARCH ADMINISTRATION. *Educ:* Tex A&M Univ, DVM, 52, MS, 59; Mich State Univ, PhD(path), 68. *Prof Exp:* Gen vet pract, Ventura Animal Hosp, 52; asst base vet, Ft Sam Houston, US Army, 53-54; gen vet pract, El Paso Vet Hosp, 54; instr vet med & surg, Tex A&M Univ, 54-59; path trainee, Armed Forces Inst Path, 59-60; chief, Dept Vet Lab, US Army Med Command, 406th MGL, 60-63, asst chief path, Med Res Lab, Ft Knox, 63-65; chief path, US Army Med Res Inst Infectious Dis, 68-70, Med Res Second Nutrit Lab, 70-73; mem, Dept Defense Liaison Off, US Army, 73-76; dir, Inst Trop Vet Med, 76-79, PROF VET PATH, TEX A&M UNIV, 76- *Concurrent Pos:* Preceptor, US Army Vet Path Preceptorship Prog, 68-73; consult foreign animal dis, US Army Surg Gen, 74-76. *Mem:* Sigma Xi; Am Vet Med Asn; US Animal Health Asn; Am Col Vet Pathologists; Am Asn Vet Lab Diagnosticians. *Res:* Tick cell line of Boophilus ticks to laboratory cultivation; babesiosis and anaplasmosis. *Mailing Add:* Rt 5 Box 1372 College Station TX 77840

TREVINO, SAMUEL FRANCISCO, b San Antonio, Tex, Apr 2, 36; m 58; c 5. SOLID STATE PHYSICS. *Educ:* St Mary's Univ, Tex, BS, 58; Univ Notre Dame, PhD(physics), 63. *Prof Exp:* RES PHYSICIST, ARRADCOM, DOVER, NJ, 64- *Concurrent Pos:* Guest physicist, Reactor Radiation Div, Nat Bur Stand, 71- *Honors & Awards:* Paul A Siple Award, Dept Army, 70. *Res:* Molecular spectroscopy using inelastic scattering of low energy neutrons, particularly vibrational properties of polymers and molecular crystals; low energy nuclear physics involving reactions producing polarized neutrons. *Mailing Add:* Reactor Radiation Div Nat Bur Standards Washington DC 20234

TREVITHICK, JOHN RICHARD, b St Thomas, Ont, Nov 30, 38; c 1. BIOCHEMISTRY. *Educ:* Queen's Univ, Ont, BSc, 61; Univ Wis-Madison, PhD(physiol chem), 65. *Prof Exp:* Nat Res Coun fel, Univ BC, 65-67; asst prof, 67-72, assoc prof, 73-80, PROF BIOCHEM, UNIV WESTERN ONT, 80- *Concurrent Pos:* Ed, J Can Fedn Biol Socs, 71-72 & 77-80. *Mem:* Can Biochem Soc; Can Fedn Biol Socs; Am Chem Soc. *Res:* Biochemistry of development and differentiation, mechanism of cortical cataract formation, especially diabetic and microwave cataracts; extracellular enzymes of microorganisms; histones and nuclear proteins; the lens. *Mailing Add:* Dept of Biochem Univ of Western Ont London ON N6A 5C1 Can

TREVOR, ANTHONY JOHN, b London, Eng, Dec 27, 34; m 63; c 4. BIOCHEMICAL PHARMACOLOGY, NEUROCHEMISTRY. *Educ:* Univ Southampton, BSc, 60; Univ London, PhD(biochem), 63. *Prof Exp:* Lectr, 64-65, from asst prof to assoc prof, 65-77, PROF PHARMACOL, SCH MED, UNIV CALIF, SAN FRANCISCO, 77-, ACTG CHMN, 78- *Concurrent Pos:* NSF res grants, 72-74 & 75-; USPHS fel neuropharmacol, Sch Med, Univ Calif, San Francisco, 63-64, NIH res grants, 66-75. *Mem:* AAAS; Am Soc Pharmacol & Exp Therapeut; Am Soc Neurochem; Int Soc Neurochem; Soc Toxicol. *Res:* Brain enzymes purification, acetylcholinesterase, mechanisms of action and biodisposition of anesthetics. *Mailing Add:* Dept of Pharmacol Univ of Calif Sch of Med San Francisco CA 94143

TREVORROW, LAVERNE EVERETT, b Moline, Ill, Nov 1, 28; m 50; c 2. INORGANIC CHEMISTRY, PHYSICAL CHEMISTRY. *Educ:* Augustana Col, Ill, AB, 50; Okla State Univ, MS, 52; Univ Wis, PhD(chem), 55. *Prof Exp:* Asst, Okla State Univ, 50-52; asst, Univ Wis, 52-55; asst chemist, 55-59, ASSOC CHEMIST, ARGONNE NAT LAB, 59- *Mem:* Am Chem Soc. *Res:* Chemistry of fluorine and metal fluorides; uranium, neptunium, plutonium and fission elements; molten salt batteries; analysis of radioactive waste disposal systems and nuclear fuel cycle systems; technological economics. *Mailing Add:* Argonne Nat Lab 9700 S Cass Ave Argonne IL 60439

TREVOY, DONALD JAMES, b Saskatoon, Sask, Jan 27, 22; m 46; c 4. SOLID STATE CHEMISTRY, ENERGY CONVERSION. *Educ:* Univ Sask, BE, 44, MSc, 46; Univ Ill, PhD(chem eng), 49. *Prof Exp:* Chem engr, Nat Res Coun Can, 44-46; SR LAB HEAD, EASTMAN KODAK CO, 49- *Mem:* Am Chem Soc; AAAS; NY Acad Sci; Electrochem Soc. *Res:* Liquid-liquid extraction; thermal diffusion; high vacuum evaporation of liquids; physical chemistry of lithography; antistatic agents; photochemistry; organic semiconductors; conducting coatings; batteries; solar energy conversion. *Mailing Add:* Bldg 82 Kodak Park Eastman Kodak Co Rochester NY 14650

TREW, JOHN ALLAN, b Lemsford, Sask, Sept 6, 23; m 49; c 4. BIOCHEMISTRY. *Educ:* Univ Sask, BSA, 50, MSc, 51; Univ Western Ont, PhD(biochem), 57. *Prof Exp:* Biochemist, Regina Gen Hosp, 51-54 & 57-63; assoc prof, 65-73, PROF PATH, UNIV HOSP, UNIV SASK, 73- *Mem:* Can Soc Clin Chemists; Chem Inst Can; Asn Clin Scientists; Can Biochem Soc. *Res:* Identification of fungal enzymes; protein electrophoresis; cancer; lactic dehydrogenase; computer applications in clinical pathology; cancer research. *Mailing Add:* Path Dept Univ Hosp of Sask Saskatoon SK S7N OXO Can

TREWELLA, JEFFREY CHARLES, NUCLEAR MAGNETIC RESONANCE SPECTROSCOPY, MASS SPECTROMETRY. *Educ:* Lock Haven State Col, Pa, BS, 75; Pa State Univ, PhD(chem), 79. *Prof Exp:* Res chemist, 79-81, SR RES CHEMIST, MOBIL RES DEVELOP CORP, 81- *Mem:* Am Chem Soc; Soc Appl Spectrosc. *Res:* Hydrogen bonding in liquids by nuclear magnetic resonance techniques; developed liquid chromatographic and high resolution mass spectrometric methods for the characterization of shale oils; developed inductively coupled plasma methods for multielemental analysis of both agreous and organic samples. *Mailing Add:* 121 Franklin Dr Mullica Hill NJ 08062

TREWILER, CARL EDWARD, b Sheridan, NY, Sept 17, 34; m 54; c 4. POLYMER CHEMISTRY. *Educ:* Alfred Univ, BA, 56; Univ Akron, PhD(polymer sci), 66. *Prof Exp:* Resin chemist, Durez Plastics Div, Hooker Chem Co, 56-58; develop engr, Laminated Prod Bus Dept, Gen Elec Co, Ohio, 58-64; staff chemist polymerization, Akron Univ, 64-66; polymer chemist, 66-78, MGR PAPER & COMPOSITE PROD DEVELOP, LAMINATED PROD BUS DEPT, GEN ELEC CO, 78- *Mem:* Am Chem Soc. *Res:* Thermosetting resins and polymers in laminate applications. *Mailing Add:* Coshocton OH

TREWYN, RONALD WILLIAM, b Edgerton, Wis, Aug 24, 43; m 70; c 1. CARCINOGENESIS, CELL BIOLOGY. *Educ:* Wis State Univ, BS, 70; Ore State Univ, PhD(microbiol), 74. *Prof Exp:* Res assoc biochem, Univ Colo Health Sci Ctr, 74-77, instr, 77-78; ASST PROF PHYSIOL CHEM, OHIO STATE UNIV, 78- *Concurrent Pos:* Res scientist, Comp Cancer Ctr, Ohio State Univ, 78-, dir, Tumor Procurement Serv, 81- *Mem:* Am Asn Cancer Res. *Res:* Cellular changes in the transfer RNA metabolism associated with carcinogenesis in an effort to elucidate the role of these changes in the neoplastic process. *Mailing Add:* Physiol Chem Ohio State Univ 1645 Neil Ave Columbus OH 43210

TREXLER, BRYSON DOUGLAS, JR, hydrogeology, see previous edition

TREXLER, DAVID WILLIAM, b Walla Walla, Wash, Apr 22, 20; m 44; c 3. GEOLOGY, PALEONTOLOGY. *Educ:* Southern Methodist Univ, BS, 41; Johns Hopkins Univ, PhD(geol), 55. *Prof Exp:* Instr geol, Southern Methodist Univ, 49; asst, Southwestern La Inst, 50-53; photogeologist, Geophoto Servs, Colo, 53-56; asst prof, 56-71, ASSOC PROF GEOL, COLO SCH MINES, 71- *Mem:* Geol Soc Am; Paleont Soc; Am Asn Petrol Geologists. *Res:* Mesozoic mollusks; coccoliths; photogeology. *Mailing Add:* Dept of Geol Colo Sch of Mines Golden CO 80401

TREXLER, DENNIS THOMAS, b Compton, Calif, Aug 6, 40; m 66. REMOTE SENSING, GEOTHERMAL. *Educ:* Univ Southern Calif, BS, 65, MS, 68. *Prof Exp:* Eng geologist, State Calif Dept Water Resources, 66-67, Geolabs, Inc, 67-68; staff geologist, Space Div, Aerojet-Gen Corp, 68-70; mgr, Microwave Sensor Systs Div, Spectran Inc, 70-71; res assoc, Mackay Sch Mines, Univ Nev, 71-74 & Nev Bur Mines & Geol, 74-81; DIR & PRIN INVESTR, DIV EARTH SCI, ENVIRON RES CTR, 81- *Concurrent Pos:* Consult, Am Mus Natural Hist, 74- *Mem:* Am Asn Petrol Geologists; Geothermal Resources Coun; Sigma Xi. *Res:* Assessment and application of geothermal resources; interpretation and application of remote sensing techniques; earthquake hazards assessment; geoarcheology to determine holocene climatic conditions. *Mailing Add:* Suite 200 255 Bell St Reno NV 89503

TREXLER, FREDERICK DAVID, b Rahway, NJ, Feb 24, 42; m 64; c 2. PHYSICS. *Educ:* Houghton Col, BS, 64; Pa State Univ, University Park, PhD(solid state sci), 71. *Prof Exp:* Asst prof, 69-71, assoc prof, 71-78, PROF PHYSICS, HOUGHTON COL, 78- *Mem:* Am Asn Physics Teachers. *Res:* Teaching physics, computer applications thereof; solid state electronics. *Mailing Add:* Dept of Physics Houghton Col Houghton NY 14744

TREXLER, JOHN PETER, b Allentown, Pa, Nov 8, 26; m 50; c 2. GEOLOGY, STRATIGRAPHY. *Educ:* Lehigh Univ, BA, 50, MS, 53; Univ Mich, PhD(geol), 64. *Prof Exp:* Asst geologist, Lehigh Portland Cement Co, 50-52; geologist, Fuels Br, US Geol Surv, 53-59; assoc prof geol, 62-69, chmn dept, 62-69, chmn sci div, 67-70, PROF GEOL, JUNIATA COL, 69-, CHMN DEPT, 74- *Concurrent Pos:* NSF fel, Princeton Univ, 70-71. *Mem:* Fel Geol Soc Am; Am Asn Petrol Geologists. *Res:* Field geology; stratigraphy and structural geology of sedimentary rocks of central and eastern Pennsylvania, particularly in the anthracite region. *Mailing Add:* Dept of Geol Juniata Col Huntingdon PA 16652

TREYBAL, ROBERT E(WALD), b New York, NY, Mar 31, 15; m 41; c 1. CHEMICAL ENGINEERING. *Educ:* NY Univ, BS, 35, MS, 36; Columbia Univ, PhD(chem eng), 42. *Prof Exp:* Chem engr, Atlantic Refining Co, 36-37; from instr to asst prof chem eng, NY Univ, 37-44; chem engr, M W Kellogg Co Div, Pullman, Inc, 44-46; from assoc prof to prof chem eng, NY Univ, 46-73; prof chem eng & chmn dept, Univ RI, 73-80. *Concurrent Pos:* Lectr, Humble Oil & Refining Co, 61 & 66; consult, Union Carbide Metals Co, Jones & Laughlin Steel Corp, Res Ctr, Gen Foods Corp, Nat Distillers Prods Corp, Esso Res & Eng Co, US Stoneware, Inc, Tenn Eastman Co & FMC Corp. *Honors & Awards:* Tyler Award, Am Inst Chem Engrs, 56, William H Walker Award, 63; Westinghouse Award, Am Soc Eng Educ, 57. *Mem:* Am Chem Soc; Am Soc Eng Educ; fel Am Inst Chemists; Am Inst Chem Engrs; fel NY Acad Sci. *Res:* Liquid extraction; mass transfer operations; diffusional separations. *Mailing Add:* 34 Birchwood Dr Colchester VT 05446

TREYBIG, LEON BRUCE, b Yoakum, Tex, Aug 29, 31; m 57; c 3. MATHEMATICS. *Educ:* Univ Tex, BA, 53, PhD(math), 58. *Prof Exp:* Spec instr math, Univ Tex, 54-58; instr, Tulane Univ, 58-59, res assoc, 59-60, from asst prof to prof, 60-70; PROF MATH, TEX A&M UNIV, 70- *Mem:* Am Math Soc. *Res:* Point set topology; separability in metric spaces; continuous images of ordered compacta; knot theory. *Mailing Add:* Dept of Math Tex A&M Univ College Station TX 77843

TREZEK, GEORGE J, b Chicago, Ill, July 10, 37; m 62; c 2. MECHANICAL ENGINEERING. *Educ:* Gen Motors Inst, BME, 61; Univ Ill, MS, 62, PhD(mech eng), 65. *Prof Exp:* Asst prof mech eng, Northwestern Univ, 65-66; from asst prof to assoc prof, 66-74, PROF MECH ENG, UNIV CALIF, BERKELEY, 74- *Concurrent Pos:* Res consult, Cal Recovery Systs, Inc & WHO. *Mem:* Am Soc Mech Engrs; Am Soc Testing & Mat. *Res:* Solid waste management; size reduction, material and energy recovery from wastes; direct energy conversion; power plant waste heat dispersal and utilization problems; energy agro waste systems. *Mailing Add:* Dept of Mech Eng Univ Calif 6171 Etcheverry Berkeley CA 94720

TRIA, JOHN JOSEPH, JR, b Shelby, NC, May 26, 46; m 76. PHYSICAL CHEMISTRY. *Educ:* Duke Univ, BS, 68; Fla State Univ, PhD(phys chem), 77. *Prof Exp:* Res fel phys chem dept chem, Fla State Univ, 77-78; res fel phys chem dept chem, Ohio State Univ, 78-79; SR RES CHEMIST, MONSANTO CO, 79- *Mem:* Am Chem Soc; Sigma Xi. *Res:* Chemical kinetics; radiation chemistry; chemical instrumentation. *Mailing Add:* Monsanto Co 800 N Lindberth T3E St Louis MO 63166

TRIANDAFILIDIS, GEORGE EMMANUEL, b Istanbul, Turkey, Nov 6, 22; US citizen; m 56; c 2. CIVIL ENGINEERING, SOIL MECHANICS. *Educ:* Robert Col, Istanbul, BS, 45; Univ Ill, Urbana, MS, 47, PhD, 60. *Prof Exp:* From instr to asst prof civil eng, Univ Ill, Urbana, 57-61; asst prof, Rice Univ, 61-64; assoc prof, 64-68, PROF CIVIL ENG, UNIV NMEX, 68- *Concurrent Pos:* Consult, 57- & Eric H Wang Civil Eng Res Facility, 61-64; mem, Hwy Res Bd, Nat Acad Sci-Nat Res Coun. *Mem:* Am Soc Civil Engrs; Am Soc Testing & Mat; Int Soc Soil Mech & Found Engrs. *Res:* Soil mechanics and foundations, especially dynamic properties of earth materials and soil-structure interaction phenomena; soil and rock mechanics; foundations and pavements. *Mailing Add:* Dept of Civil Eng Univ of NMex Albuquerque NM 87131

TRIANTAPHYLLOPOULOS, DEMETRIOS, b Athens, Greece, July 8, 20; m 54. PHYSIOLOGY, INTERNAL MEDICINE. *Educ:* Athens Sch Med, MD, 46. *Prof Exp:* From asst prof to assoc prof physiol, Univ Alta, 60-65; assoc prof, Wayne State Univ, 65-69; SR RES SCIENTIST & HEAD COAGULATION DEPT, AM NAT RED CROSS BLOOD RES LAB, 69- *Concurrent Pos:* Res assoc, Med Res Coun Can, 60-66. *Mem:* Am Physiol Soc; Can Physiol Soc; Am Soc Hemat; Int Soc Hemat; Am Heart Asn. *Res:* Blood coagulation; immunohematology. *Mailing Add:* Coagulation Dept Am Nat Red Cross Blood Res Lab Bethesda MD 20014

TRIANTAPHYLLOPOULOS, EUGENIE, b Astros, Greece, Nov 27, 21; US citizen; m 54. MEDICINE, BIOCHEMISTRY. *Educ:* Nat Univ Athens, MD, 47; Univ Alta, PhD(biochem), 57. *Prof Exp:* Nat Cancer Inst Can res fel, Univ Alta, 57-60, res assoc blood coagulation, 60-62; Can Heart Found res fel, Univ Alta & Wayne State Univ, 62-67; res scientist, Mt Carmel Mercy Hosp, Detroit, Mich, 68-69; NIH grant & chief coagulation res, Washington Hosp Ctr, 69-74; MED OFFICER, BUR DRUGS, FOOD & DRUG ADMIN, 74- *Concurrent Pos:* Asst prof, Univ Alta, 65-66. *Mem:* AAAS; Am Physiol Soc; Can Biochem Soc; Am Soc Clin Pharmacol & Therapeut; NY Acad Sci. *Res:* Blood coagulation; fibrinolysis; hemolysis. *Mailing Add:* Bur of Drugs Food & Drug Admin Rockville MD 20857

TRIANTAPHYLLOU, ANASTASIOS CHRISTOS, b Amaliapolis-Volou, Greece, Nov 30, 26; m 60; c 1. CYTOGENETICS, NEMATODES. *Educ:* Athens Superior Sch Agr, Greece, BS, 49, MS, 50; NC State Col, PhD(plant path, bot), 59. *Prof Exp:* Nematologist, Benaki Phytopath Inst, Greece, 50-60; asst geneticist, 60-62, from asst prof to assoc prof genetics, 62-68, PROF GENETICS, NC STATE UNIV, 68- *Mem:* AAAS; Genetics Soc Am; Soc Nematol; Am Inst Biol Sci. *Res:* Cytogenetics, evolution mode of reproduction and sexuality of nematodes; genetics and cytology of plant parasitic nematodes. *Mailing Add:* Dept of Genetics NC State Univ Raleigh NC 27607

TRIANTAPHYLLOU, HEDWIG HIRSCHMAN, b Fuerth, Bavaria, Ger, Jan 16, 27; nat US; m 60; c 1. PLANT NEMATOLOGY. *Educ:* Univ Erlangen, PhD(zool), 51. *Prof Exp:* Tech asst, 54-55, res instr, 55-57, from asst prof to assoc prof, 57-67, PROF PLANT PATH, NC STATE UNIV, 67- *Concurrent Pos:* Ed, J , Soc Nematol, 69-73; ed, Nematologica, Soc Europ Nematologists, 75- *Honors & Awards:* Res Award, Sigma Xi, 62. *Mem:* Soc Europ Nematologists; Soc Nematol. *Res:* Taxonomy and biology of free-living and plant-parasitic nematodes; ultrastructure of plant parasitic nematodes. *Mailing Add:* Dept of Plant Path NC State Univ PO Box 5397 Raleigh NC 27607

TRIBBEY, BERT ALLEN, b Moorpark, Calif, Aug 8, 38; m 61; c 2. ZOOLOGY, ECOLOGY. *Educ:* Univ Calif, Santa Barbara, AB, 61; Univ Tex, PhD(zool), 65. *Prof Exp:* Asst prof, 65-69, assoc prof, 69-81, PROF BIOL, CALIF STATE UNIV, FRESNO, 81-, CHMN DEPT, 72- *Mem:* AAAS; Ecol Soc Am; Am Soc Limnol & Oceanog. *Res:* Structure and succession of aquatic communities; ecology of temporary ponds; physiological ecology of freshwater invertebrates. *Mailing Add:* Dept of Biol Calif State Univ Fresno CA 93710

TRIBBLE, LELAND FLOYD, b Oxnard, Calif, July 12, 23; m 52; c 4. ANIMAL SCIENCE. *Educ:* Univ Mo, BS, 49, MS, 50, PhD(agr), 56. *Prof Exp:* Instr animal husb, Univ Mo, 49-56, assoc prof, 56-67; PROF ANIMAL HUSB, TEX TECH UNIV, 67- *Concurrent Pos:* Vis prof, Kans State Univ, 65-66; nonruminant nutritionist, USDA, Washington, DC, 74-75. *Mem:* AAAS; Am Soc Animal Soc; Sigma Xi. *Res:* Animal nutrition; swine production and management. *Mailing Add:* Dept of Animal Sci Tex Tech Univ Lubbock TX 79409

TRIBBLE, ROBERT EDMOND, b Mexico, Mo, Jan 7, 47; m 69. NUCLEAR PHYSICS. *Educ:* Univ Mo, Columbia, BS, 69; Princeton Univ, PhD(nuclear physics), 73. *Prof Exp:* Instr physics, Princeton Univ, 73-75; asst prof, 75-78, ASSOC PROF PHYSICS, TEX A&M UNIV, 78- *Mem:* Am Phys Soc. *Res:* Experimental research to determine isospin mixing in light nuclei; nuclear weak interaction experiments that will determine the role of nuclear induced weak currents. *Mailing Add:* Cyclotron Inst Tex A&M Univ College Station TX 77843

TRIBUS, MYRON, b San Francisco, Calif, Oct 30, 21; m 45; c 2. ENGINEERING. *Educ:* Univ Calif, Berkeley, BS, 42, Los Angeles, PhD(eng), 49. *Prof Exp:* From lectr to assoc prof eng, Univ Calif, Los Angeles, 46-58, prof, 58-61; dean, Thayer Sch Eng, Dartmouth Col, 61-69; asst secy commerce for sci & technol, 69-71; sr vpres res & eng, Info Technol Group, Xerox Corp, 71-75; DIR, CTR ADVAN ENG STUDY, MASS INST TECHNOL, 75- *Concurrent Pos:* Consult, Gen Elec Co, 50- & NATO, 53; dir icing res, Univ Mich, 51-54; Presidential appointee, Nat Adv Comn Oceans & Atmosphere, 72- *Honors & Awards:* Wright Bros Medal, Soc Automotive Engrs, 45; Bane Award, Inst Aerospace Sci, Am Inst Aeronaut & Astronaut, 46; Alfred Noble Prize, 52. *Mem:* Soc Automotive Engrs; Am Soc Mech Engrs; Am Inst Aeronaut & Astronaut. *Res:* Heat transfer; thermodynamics; decision theory. *Mailing Add:* 90 Carlton St Brookline MA 02146

TRICE, VIRGIL GARNETT, JR, b Indianapolis, Ind, Feb 3, 26; m 58; c 3. CHEMICAL ENGINEERING, INDUSTRIAL ENGINEERING. *Educ:* Purdue Univ, BS & MS, 45; Ill Inst Technol, MS, 70. *Prof Exp:* Chem engr, Argonne Nat Lab, 49-71; nuclear waste mgt engr, Energy Res & Develop Admin, 71-77; sr prog analyst, 77-81, PROG MGR, US DEPT ENERGY, 81- *Mem:* Sigma Xi; Am Nuclear Soc. *Res:* Radioactive waste management. *Mailing Add:* 8112 Exodus Dr Gaithersburg MD 20879

TRICE, WILLIAM HENRY, b Geneva, NY, Apr 4, 33; m 55; c 2. RESEARCH ADMINISTRATION. *Educ:* State Univ NY Col Forestry, BS, 55; Inst Paper Chem, MS, 60, PhD(phys chem), 63. *Prof Exp:* Res scientist, 63-66, group leader res & develop, 66-68, sect leader, 68-72, tech dir bleached div, 72-74, VPRES RES & DEVELOP & CORP TECH DIR, UNION CAMP CORP, 74- *Concurrent Pos:* Chmn res comt, Univ Maine Pulp & Paper Found, 76-77. *Mem:* Tech Asn Pulp & Paper Indust. *Res:* Fatty acid and terpene chemistry; pulp and paper chemistry; engineering in fields related to pulp and paper. *Mailing Add:* Union Camp Corp 1600 Valley Rd Wayne NJ 07470

TRICHE, TIMOTHY JUNIUS, b San Angelo, Tex, June 4, 44; m 71. PATHOLOGY. *Educ:* Cornell Univ, AB, 66; Tulane Univ, MD & PhD(path), 71. *Prof Exp:* Resident path, Barnes Hosp, St Louis, Mo, 71-74; sr staff fel, 74-77, CHIEF ULTRASTRUCT PATH SECT, LAB PATH, NAT CANCER INST, 77- *Res:* Membrane receptor sites; tumor cell membrane proteins; tumor cell secretory products; diagnostic and investigative electron microscopy of tumors. *Mailing Add:* 7607 Exeter Rd Bethesda MD 20014

TRICK, GORDON STAPLES, b Winnipeg, Man, May 6, 27; m 52; c 4. PHYSICAL CHEMISTRY. *Educ:* McGill Univ, BS, 49, PhD(chem), 52; Univ Western Ont, MS, 50. *Prof Exp:* Ramsay Mem fel, London, 53; sci serv officer, Defence Res Bd Can, 53-56; sr res chemist & res scientist, Goodyear Tire & Rubber Co, 56-71; EXEC DIR MANITOBA RES COUN & DIR RES & TECHNOL BR, DEPT OF ECON DEVELOP & TOURISM, GOVT MANITOBA, 71- *Concurrent Pos:* Adj prof, Univ Manitoba, 72-; mem adv bd sci & tech info, Nat Res Coun Can, 72-78, Standards Coun Can, 78- *Mem:* Am Chem Soc; Chem Inst Can. *Res:* Gas and liquid phase kinetics; molecular weights of polymers; phase transitions in polymers; stress-strain properties; technology transfer; innovation development; science policy. *Mailing Add:* Manitoba Res Coun Govt of Manitoba Winnipeg MB R3C 3H8 Can

TRICK, TIMOTHY NOEL, b Dayton, Ohio, July 14, 39. ELECTRICAL ENGINEERING. *Educ:* Univ Dayton, BEE, 61; Purdue Univ, MSEE, 62, PhD(elec eng), 66. *Prof Exp:* From asst prof to assoc prof, 65-75, PROF ELEC ENG, UNIV ILL, 75- *Concurrent Pos:* Consult, Intersci Res Inst, 69; summer fac fel, Am Soc Eng Educ-NASA, 70 & 71; consult, Rome Air Develop Ctr, 73-75; vis assoc prof, Univ Calif, Berkeley, 73-74; vis lectr, Nat Inst Astrophysics, Optics & Electronics, Mex, 75. *Honors & Awards:* Guillemin-Cauer Award, Inst Elec & Electronics Engrs, 76. *Mem:* Fel Inst Elec & Electronics Engrs; Sigma Xi. *Res:* Numerical methods and computer algorithms for the analysis and desing of electrical circuits; analysis and design of large-scale integrated circuits and of analog and digital filters. *Mailing Add:* Dept of Elec Eng Univ of Ill Urbana IL 61801

TRICKEY, SAMUEL BALDWIN, b Detroit, Mich, Nov 28, 40; div; c 2. THEORETICAL PHYSICS, SOLID STATE PHYSICS. *Educ:* Rice Univ, BA, 62; Tex A&M Univ, MS, 66, PhD(physics), 68. *Prof Exp:* Physicist, Mason & Hanger, Silas Mason Corp, Tex, 62-64; vis asst prof, Univ Fla, 68-70, asst prof, 70-73, assoc prof, 73-77; prof & chmn dept physics, Tex Tech Univ, 77-79; PROF PHYSICS & CHEM, UNIV FLA, 79- *Concurrent Pos:* Vis staff mem, Los Alamos Sci Lab, 71; consult, Quantum Physics Group, Redstone Arsenal, Ala, 72-76; consult phys sci, IBM Res Labs, San Jose, Calif, 75-76; dir comput quantum theory proj, Univ Fla, 82- *Mem:* Fel Am Phys Soc; Am Asn Physics Teachers. *Res:* Theory of quantum crystals, rare gas solids, computational methods in solid state physics, energy band theory; lattice dynamics; quantum chemistry. *Mailing Add:* Dept Physics Univ Fla Gainesville FL 32611

TRICOLES, GUS P, b San Francisco, Calif, Oct 18, 31; m 53; c 2. OPTICS, ELECTRICAL ENGINEERING. *Educ:* Univ Calif, BA, 55, MS, 62, PhD, 71; San Diego State Col, MS, 58. *Prof Exp:* Asst res engr, Gen Dynamics/Convair, 55, res engr, 55-59, sr res engr, 59; physicist, Smyth Res Assocs, 59-61 & Univ Calif, 62; PHYSICIST, ELECTRONICS DIV, GEN DYNAMICS CORP, 62- *Mem:* Inst Elec & Electronics Engrs; Optical Soc Am. *Res:* Microwave optics; diffraction; physical optics; holograms; antennas; waves. *Mailing Add:* PO Box 81127 Gen Dynamics Electronics Div San Diego CA 92138

TRICOMI, VINCENT, b New York, NY, Sept 16, 21; m 49; c 6. OBSTETRICS & GYNECOLOGY. *Educ:* Syracuse Univ, AB, 42; State Univ NY Downstate Med Ctr, MD, 50. *Prof Exp:* From instr to assoc prof, 55-69, clin prof, 69-74, asst dean, 70-74, PROF OBSTET & GYNEC, STATE UNIV NY DOWNSTATE MED CTR, 74-, ASSOC DEAN, 70-; DIR MED AFFAIRS, BROOKLYN-CUMBERLAND MED CTR, 74- *Concurrent Pos:* Brooks scholar, 54-55; consult, Lutheran Med Ctr, 69- & Kings County Med Ctr, 71- *Mem:* Soc Gynec Invest; Sigma Xi. *Res:* Human cytogenetics. *Mailing Add:* Brooklyn Hosp 121 DeKalb Ave Brooklyn NY 11201

TRIEBWASSER, JOHN, b Emery, SDak, Feb 16, 36; m 57; c 2. INTERNAL MEDICINE, CARDIOLOGY. *Educ:* Univ Mo, MD, 61; Am Bd Internal Med, dipl, 68. *Prof Exp:* Residency internal med, Wilferd Hall, US Air Force Med Ctr, Lackland AFB, Tex, 65; chief internal med sect, Wright Patterson US Air Force Med Ctr, 65-67; chief metab sect, Clin Sci Div, Sch Aerospace Med, Brooks AFB, Tex, 67-71, chmn dept med cardiovasc res, 73-78; fel cardiol, Univ Tex Southwestern Med Ctr, Dallas, 71-73; chmn dept med, Wright Patterson US Air Force Med Ctr, 78-80; DIR MED SURVEILLANCE, HEALTH & ENVIRON SCI, DOW CHEM USA, 80- *Concurrent Pos:* Clin asst prof med, Univ Tex Med Sch, San Antonio, 69-71; clin assoc prof, Wright State Univ, Dayton, Ohio, 78- *Honors & Awards:* Paul Dudley White Award, Asn Mil Surgeons US, 78. *Mem:* Fel Am Col Physicians; fel Am Col Preventive Med; fel Aerospace Med Asn; Soc Physicians (pres, 77); AMA. *Res:* Exercise stress testing and the use of radionuclide imaging techniques for the detection of subclinical coronary artery disease; automated electrocardiogram analysis using mathematical approaches to signal analysis. *Mailing Add:* 4922 Sturgeon Creek Pkwy Midland MI 48640

TRIEBWASSER, SOL, b New York, NY, Aug 16, 21; m 41; c 2. PHYSICS. *Educ:* Brooklyn Col, AB, 41; Columbia Univ, MA, 48, PhD, 52. *Prof Exp:* Instr physics, Brooklyn Col, 47-50; asst, Radiation Lab, Columbia, 51; mem tech staff, 52-69, ASST DIR APPL RES, RES CTR, IBM CORP, 69- *Mem:* Fel Am Phys Soc; Sigma Xi; fel Inst Elec & Electronics Engrs. *Res:* Atomic structure; microwave spectroscopy; solid state physics; ferroelectricity; photoconductivity; semiconductors. *Mailing Add:* IBM Corp Res Ctr PO Box 218 Yorktown NY 10598

TRIEFF, NORMAN MARTIN, b Brooklyn, NY, May 11, 29; div; c 4. ENVIRONMENTAL CHEMISTRY, TOXICOLOGY. *Educ:* Polytech Inst Brooklyn, BS, 50; Univ Iowa, MS, 55; NY Univ, PhD(chem), 63. *Prof Exp:* Res asst biochem, Atran Labs, Mt Sinai Hosp, New York, 54-55; instr chem, Cooper Union, 55-58; res assoc biochem, Isaac Albert Res Ctr, Jewish Chronic Dis Hosp, Brooklyn, NY, 61-62; supvr blood res, Blood derivatives Sect, Mich Dept Pub Health, 63-65; asst prof chem, Drexel Inst, 65-68; asst prof toxicol & phys chem, 68-70, from asst prof to assoc prof, 70-72, PROF PREV MED & COMMUNITY HEALTH, UNIV TEX MED BR GALVESTON, 77- *Concurrent Pos:* Nat Ctr for Air Pollution Control grant, 66-68; consult, US Army Corps Engr, 67-68 & US Coast Guard, 70-71; Robert A Welch Found res grant, 70-; consult, La Conroe, Tex Pac Co, & Heat Systs Ultrasonics, Inc, Plainview, NY, 75- *Mem:* Fel Am Inst Chemists; Am Chem Soc; Air Pollution Control Asn; Am Indust Hyg Asn; Am Acad Indust Hyg; NY Acad Sci. *Res:* Environmental chemistry; development of analytic methods of drugs, toxins and environmental pollutants; odor analysis and olfaction; structure-activity relations. *Mailing Add:* Dept Prev Med & Commun Hlth Univ of Tex Med Br Galveston TX 77550

TRIER, JERRY STEVEN, b Frankfurt, Ger, Apr 12, 33; US citizen; m 57; c 3. INTERNAL MEDICINE, GASTROENTEROLOGY. *Educ:* Univ Wash, MD, 57. *Hon Degrees:* AM, Harvard Univ, 73. *Prof Exp:* Intern med, Univ Rochester, 57-58, asst resident, 58-59; clin assoc, Nat Cancer Inst, 59-61; trainee gastroenterol, Univ Wash, 61-63; asst prof med, Univ Wis, 63-67; assoc prof, Univ NMex, 67-69; assoc prof med & anat, Sch Med, Boston Univ, 69-73; assoc prof, 73-76, PROF MED, HARVARD MED SCH, 76- *Concurrent Pos:* USPHS grant, 64-67; USPHS grant, Univ NMex, 67-69; USPHS grants, Sch Med, Boston Univ, 69-; assoc physician, Univ Hosp, Boston & Boston City Hosp, 69-73; consult, Vet Admin Hosp, Boston, 69-, Chelsea Naval Hosp, 71-74 & US Vet Admin Cent Off, Washington, DC, 71-; physician & dir div gastroenterol, Brigham & Women's Hosp, Boston, 73-; NIH gen med & study sect, 74-78. *Mem:* Asn Am Physicians; Am Soc Clin Invest; Am Gastroenterol Asn; Am Fedn Clin Res; Am Soc Cell Biol. *Res:* Functional morphology of the gastrointestinal tract of humans in health and disease; developmental morphology of the intestine; cell renewal in the alimentary tract. *Mailing Add:* Dept Med Brigham & Women's Hosp Boston MA 02115

TRIFAN, DANIEL SIEGFRIED, b Cleveland, Ohio, Dec 23, 18; m 48; c 3. PHYSICAL CHEMISTRY, ORGANIC CHEMISTRY. *Educ:* Baldwin-Wallace Col, BS, 40; Western Reserve Univ, MS, 41; Harvard Univ, MA, 46, PhD(chem), 48. *Prof Exp:* Res fel phys & org chem, Univ Calif, Los Angeles, 48-49, instr org chem, 49-50; asst prof, Bowling Green State Univ, 50-51; asst prof phys, org & polymer chem & head chem sect, Plastics Lab, Princeton Univ, 51-64; PROF CHEM, FAIRLEIGH DICKINSON UNIV, 64- *Mem:* Am Chem Soc. *Res:* Organic reaction mechanisms; polymer chemistry. *Mailing Add:* Dept of Chem Fairleigh Dickinson Univ Rutherford NJ 07070

TRIFAN, DEONISIE, b Cleveland, Ohio, July 27, 15; m 48; c 1. APPLIED MATHEMATICS. *Educ:* Baldwin-Wallace Col, AB, 37; Univ Toledo, MA, 40; Brown Univ, PhD(appl math), 48. *Prof Exp:* Instr math, Bluffton Col, 40-41; res assoc appl math, Brown Univ, 47-48; instr math, Case Inst Technol, 48-49; from asst prof to assoc prof, 49-67, PROF MATH, UNIV ARIZ, 67- *Concurrent Pos:* Consult, Radio Corp Am, 57-58. *Mem:* Am Math Soc; Math Asn Am. *Res:* Elasticity and plasticity. *Mailing Add:* Dept of Math Univ of Ariz Tucson AZ 85721

TRIFARO, JOSE MARIA, b Mercedes, Arg, Nov 29, 36; m 64; c 2. PHARMACOLOGY. *Educ:* Liceo Militar Gen San Martin, BA, 54; Univ Buenos Aires, MD, 61. *Prof Exp:* Demonstr anat, Univ Buenos Aires, 57-58, instr pharmacol, 61-62, lectr physiol, 62-64; lectr, 67-68, asst prof, 68-72, assoc prof, 72-78, PROF PHARMACOL, MCGILL UNIV, 78- *Concurrent Pos:* A Thyssen Found res fel, Arg, 62-63; res fel, Nat Res Coun, Arg, 63-64; Rockefeller Found res fel, US, 64-66; NIH res fel, 66-67; Med Res Coun Can scholar, 68. *Mem:* Am Soc Pharmacol & Exp Therapeut; Pharmacol Soc Can. *Res:* Cellular and molecular mechanism of hormone and neurotransmitter release; role of contractile proteins in secretory cell functions. *Mailing Add:* Dept of Pharmacol & Therapeut McGill Univ Montreal PQ H3G 1Y6 Can

TRIFFET, TERRY, b Enid, Okla, June 10, 22; m 46; c 3. MATHEMATICAL MODELING & MECHANICS. *Educ:* Univ Okla, BA, 45; Univ Colo, BS, 48, MS, 50; Stanford Univ, PhD(struct mech), 57. *Prof Exp:* Instr eng, Univ Colo, 47-50; gen engr rocket & guided missile res, US Naval Ord Test Sta, 50-55; gen engr radiol res & head radiol effects br, US Naval Radiol Defense Lab, 55-59; assoc prof appl mech, Mich State Univ, 59-63, prof mech & mat sci, 63-76; ASSOC DEAN RES, COL ENG, UNIV ARIZ, 76- *Concurrent Pos:* Mem apex comt, US Naval Res Labs, 59-65; consult, US Dept Defense, 59-65, Battelle Mem Inst, 65-68 & Lear-Siegler, Inc, 65-; Australian Res Grants Comt res fel math physics, Univ Adelaide, 66-67 & 72-73. *Mem:* Am Phys Soc; Am Math Soc; Soc Eng Sci; Soc Indust & Appl Math; Inst Elec & Electronics Engrs. *Mailing Add:* Col Eng Univ Ariz Tucson AZ 85721

TRIFUNAC, ALEXANDER DIMITRIJE, b Yugoslavia, July 29, 44; US citizen; m 67. PHYSICAL CHEMISTRY, MAGNETIC RESONANCE. *Educ:* Columbia Univ, BA, 66; Univ Chicago, PhD(chem), 71. *Prof Exp:* Res asst chem, Univ Chicago, 66-71; res assoc chem, Univ Notre Dame, 71-72 & Univ Chicago, 72; asst scientist, 74-77, SCIENTIST, CHEM DIV, ARGONNE NAT LAB, 77- *Concurrent Pos:* Presidential intern, Argonne Nat Lab, 72-73. *Mem:* Am Chem Soc; Sigma Xi. *Res:* Chemistry and physics of transient reactive intermediates in radiation and photochemistry; development of novel time resolved magnetic resonance methods for study of transient radicals in liquids. *Mailing Add:* Chem Div Argonne Nat Lab 9700 S Cass Argonne IL 60439

TRIFUNAC, NATALIA PISKER, b Budapest, Hungary, June 26, 42; US citizen; m 66; c 1. BIOCHEMISTRY. *Educ:* Univ Belgrade, BS, 65; Calif Inst Technol, PhD(chem), 69. *Prof Exp:* Res assoc dept chem, Calif Inst Technol, 69-70; res assoc, Columbia Univ, 70-71, res assoc dept biochem, Col Physicians & Surgeons, 71-72; instr biochem, 72-75, asst prof, Dept Obstet & Gynec, Sect Reprod Biol, 75-78, ASST PROF RES BIOCHEM DEPT PATH, SCH MED, UNIV SOUTHERN CALIF, 78- *Concurrent Pos:* Consult, Jet Propulsion Lab, Calif Inst Technol, 78- *Res:* Cell surface changes during lymphocyte transformation; reproductive biology; human spermatozoa metabolism and survival. *Mailing Add:* Dept of Path 2025 Zonal Ave Los Angeles CA 90033

TRIGG, GEORGE LOCKWOOD, b Washington, DC, Sept 30, 25; wid; c 2. THEORETICAL PHYSICS. *Educ:* Washington Univ, AB, 47, AM, 50, PhD(physics), 51. *Prof Exp:* Asst physics, Washington Univ, 47-50; asst prof, Knox Col, 51-54, actg chmn dept, 51-52; from asst prof to assoc prof, Ore State Univ, 54-62; asst ed, 62-65, ED, PHYS REV LETTERS, AM PHYS SOC, 65- *Concurrent Pos:* NSF fel, 57-58; asst ed, Phys Rev & Phys Rev Letters, 58; consult, Funk & Wagnalls Dictionary, 66-71 & Am Heritage Dictionary, 67-70; mem comt symbols, units & terminology, Nat Res Coun, 71-; consult, Wiley Int Dictonary Med & Biol, 81- *Mem:* Fel AAAS; fel Am Phys Soc; Fedn Am Sci; Am Asn Physics Teachers; Soc Scholarly Publ. *Res:* Elementary particle theory; fundamentals of quantum theory; history of physics. *Mailing Add:* Phys Rev Letters Brookhaven Nat Lab Upton NY 11973

TRIGG, WILLIAM WALKER, b Little Rock, Ark, Dec 4, 31; m 57; c 2. INORGANIC CHEMISTRY. *Educ:* Univ Ark, BSChE, 56, MS, 60; La State Univ, PhD(inorg chem), 66. *Prof Exp:* Control chemist, Niagara Chem Div, Food Mach & Chem Corp, 56-57; from instr to assoc prof, 59-75, PROF CHEM, ARK POLYTECH COL, 75-, HEAD DEPT, 66- *Mem:* Am Chem Soc; Am Inst Chem Engrs. *Res:* Precipitation from homogeneous solution and studies of ion solvent effects in solvents of low dielectric constant. *Mailing Add:* Dept of Chem Ark Polytech Col Russellville AR 72801

TRIGGER, KENNETH JAMES, b Carsonville, Mich, Sept 6, 10; m 39; c 3. MECHANICAL ENGINEERING. *Educ:* Mich State Univ, BS, 33, MS, 35, ME, 43. *Prof Exp:* Asst, Mich State Col, 33-34, instr mech eng, 35-36; instr mech eng, Swarthmore Col, 37-38 & Lehigh Univ, 38-39; assoc, 39-40, from asst prof to prof, 40-77, EMER PROF MECH ENG, UNIV ILL, URBANA, 77- *Concurrent Pos:* Consult, Nuclear Div, Union Carbide Corp, Continental Can Co, Aeroprojects Inc & Atlantic Richfield Co. *Honors & Awards:* Blackall Award, Am Soc Mech Engrs, 57; Medal, Soc Mfg Eng, 59. *Mem:* Fel Am Soc Mech Engrs; Am Soc Metals; Am Soc Eng Educ; Soc Mfg Engrs. *Res:* Metal cutting and machinability; physical metallurgy; cutting temperatures and temperature distribution in cutting of metals; mechanism of tool wear. *Mailing Add:* Dept of Mech Eng Univ of Ill Urbana IL 61801

TRIGGER, KENNETH ROY, b Chicago, Ill, Mar 7, 24; m 46; c 4. COMPUTER SIMULATIONS, SHOCK HYDRODYNAMICS. *Educ:* Stanford Univ, BS, 49, MS, 50, PhD(physics), 56. *Prof Exp:* Staff scientist, Los Alamos Sci Lab, 55-56, Hughes Res & Develop Labs, 56-58, Lawrence Livermore Lab, 58-62, Stanford Linear Accelerator Ctr, 62-64, Lawrence Livermore Lab, 64-65 & Appl Theory, Inc, 65-67; STAFF SCIENTIST, LAWRENCE LIVERMORE NAT LAB, 68- *Mem:* Am Phys Soc. *Res:* Chemical and nuclear explosive devices. *Mailing Add:* Lawrence Livermore Nat Lab PO Box 808 L-389 Livermore CA 94550

TRIGGLE, DAVID J, b London, Eng, May 4, 35; m 59; c 1. PHARMACOLOGY, MEDICINAL CHEMISTRY. *Educ:* Univ Southampton, BSc, 56; Univ Hull, PhD(org chem), 59. *Prof Exp:* Fel org chem, Univ Ottawa, 59-61; res fel, Bedford Col, London, 61-62; asst prof biochem pharmacol, 62-65, assoc prof biochem pharmacol & theoret biol, 65-69, PROF BIOCHEM PHARMACOL & THEORET BIOL, SCH PHARM, STATE UNIV NY BUFFALO, 69-, CHMN DEPT BIOCHEM PHARMACOL, 71- *Concurrent Pos:* NIH res grants, 61- *Mem:* Am Chem Soc; Royal Soc Chem; Am Soc Pharmacol & Exp Therapeut. *Res:* Molecular pharmacology of adrenergic and cholinergic systems; organic reaction mechanisms; synthesis of organic heterocyclic systems; ion translocation and cell membranes; molecular basis of neurotransmitter action. *Mailing Add:* Dept Biochem Pharmacol Sch Pharm State Univ NY Buffalo NY 14260

TRIGLIA, EMIL J, b Lucca, Italy, Aug 26, 21; US citizen; m 48; c 5. ANALYTICAL CHEMISTRY. *Educ:* City Col New York, BS, 43. *Prof Exp:* Chemist, Ledoux & Co, Inc, 46-51; group leader anal chem, Chem Construct Corp & Am Cyanamid Co, 51-56; sr res chemist, Minerals & Chem, Philipp Corp, 56-61, res group supvr, 61-68; group leader anal & phys testing, Engelhard Minerals & Chem Corp, Menlo Park, 68-74, mgr anal & phys measurements, 74-81; LAB SUPVR, SPEX INDUST INC, METUCHEN, NJ, 81- *Mem:* Am Chem Soc; Tech Asn Pulp & Paper Indust; Am Soc Testing & Mat. *Res:* Analyses of minerals, ores and rocks by chemical and instrumental methods. *Mailing Add:* 12 Sharon Ct Metuchen NJ 08840

TRILLING, CHARLES A(LEXANDER), b Wiesbaden, Ger, Apr 13, 23; nat US; m 49; c 3. CHEMICAL ENGINEERING, NUCLEAR ENGINEERING. *Educ:* Calif Inst Technol, BS, 44; Mass Inst Technol, ScD(chem eng), 49. *Prof Exp:* Res assoc, Chem Warfare Serv Develop Lab, Mass Inst Technol, 44-45, res assoc chem eng, 47-49; chem engr, Dennison Mfg Co, 49-50; sr res engr, Atomic Energy Res Dept, N Am Aviation, Inc, 50-52; process engr, United Engrs & Constructors, Inc, 52-54; sr res engr, Atomics Int Div, NAm Aviation, Inc, 54-55, proj engr, 55-59, group leader org reactors develop, 56-59, chief proj engr, 59-61, assoc dir, Org Reactors Dept, 61-62, proj mgr org cooled reactors, 62-65, mgr heavy water org cooled reactors prog off, 65-67, mem tech staff, Fast Breeder Prof Off, Atomic Int Div, NAm Rockwell Corp, 67-69, pollution control technol, 69-72, proj mgr coal gasification, Rockwell Int, 73-78, PROG MGR, ADVAN TECHNOL PROCESS DESIGN, ENVIRON & ENERGY SYSTS DIV, ROCKWELL INT, CANAGO PARK, 78- *Mem:* AAAS; Am Chem Soc; Am Nuclear Soc; Am Inst Chem Engrs. *Res:* Nuclear power reactor development and engineering; organic cooled reactor concept for economic generation of electric power; air pollution control; coal gasification and liquefaction. *Mailing Add:* 5254 Melvin Ave Tarzana CA 91356

TRILLING, GEORGE HENRY, b Bialystok, Poland, Sept 18, 30; nat US; m 55; c 3. ELEMENTARY PARTICLE PHYSICS. *Educ:* Calif Inst Technol, BS, 51, PhD(physics), 55. *Prof Exp:* Res fel physics, Calif Inst Technol, 55-56; Fulbright res fel, Polytech Sch, Paris, 56-57; from asst prof to assoc prof, Univ Mich, 57-60; assoc prof, 60-64, chmn dept, 68-72, PROF PHYSICS, UNIV CALIF, BERKELEY, 64- *Concurrent Pos:* NSF sr fel, Europ Orgn Nuclear Res, 66-67, Guggenheim fel, 73-74. *Mem:* Fel Am Phys Soc. *Res:* Properties of elementary particle produced by high energy accelerators. *Mailing Add:* Dept Physics Univ Calif Berkeley CA 94720

TRILLING, LEON, b Poland, July 15, 24; nat US; m 46; c 2. AERONAUTICS, ASTRONAUTICS. *Educ:* Calif Inst Technol, BS, 44, MS, 46, AeroEng, 47, PhD, 48. *Prof Exp:* Physicist, US Naval Ord Test Sta, 44-46; asst, Calif Inst Technol, 46-48, res fel, 48-49, instr, 49-50; Fulbright scholar, Univ Paris, 50-51; res assoc, 51-54, from asst prof to assoc prof, 54-62, PROF AERONAUT ENG, MASS INST TECHNOL, 62-, MEM FAC, COL SCI, TECHNOL & SOC, 78- *Concurrent Pos:* Guggenheim fel & vis prof, Sorbonne Univ, 63-64; vis prof, Aeronaut Dept, Delft Tech Univ, Neth, 74-75; consult. *Res:* Aerodynamics; gas dynamics; kinetic theory of gases; gas surface interactions. *Mailing Add:* 180 Beacon St Boston MA 02116

TRIMBERGER, GEORGE WILLIAM, b Neilsville, Wis, Dec 8, 09; m 38; c 3. DAIRY SCIENCE. *Educ:* Univ Wis, BS, 33; Univ Nebr, MS, 42, PhD(zool), 48. *Prof Exp:* Herd supt, Univ Nebr, 34-40, instr dairy prod, 40-44; from asst prof to assoc prof, 44-50, PROF DAIRY HUSB, CORNELL UNIV, 50- *Concurrent Pos:* Vis prof & proj leader, Univ Philippines, 55-57 & 66-67 & Ahmadu Bello Univ, Nigeria, 75-77. *Mem:* AAAS; Am Soc Animal Sci; Am Diary Sci Asn; Am Genetic Asn. *Res:* Artificial insemination; reproduction and nutrition in dairy cattle. *Mailing Add:* Morrison Hall Cornell Univ Ithaca NY 14850

TRIMBLE, JOHN LEONARD, b Detroit, Mich, Feb 27, 44. BIOLOGICAL ENGINEERING, REHABILITATION SCIENCE. *Educ:* Univ Ill, Chicago, BS, 68; Med Ctr, Univ Ill, PhD(physiol, bioeng), 72. *Prof Exp:* res assoc & asst prof, Eye Res Labs, Univ Chicago, 72-79; ENG DIR, REHAB ENG RES & DEVELOP CTR, HINES VET ADMIN HOSP, 79- *Concurrent Pos:* Vis assoc biol, Calif Inst Technol, 77-79; consult, Rehab Eng Res & Develop Ctr, Hines Vet Admin Hosp, 78-79 & Nat Ctr Health Care Technol, NIH, 80- *Mem:* Inst Elec & Electronics Engrs; Sigma Xi; Soc Neurosci. *Res:* Sensory neurophysiology; neural modelling; biological signal processing; communication aids for disabled. *Mailing Add:* Box 20 Rehab Eng Res & Develop Ctr Hines IL 60141

TRIMBLE, MARY ELLEN, b Englewood, NJ, Nov 1, 36. PHYSIOLOGY, BIOLOGY. *Educ:* Wellesley Col, AB, 58; Syracuse Univ, MA, 59; Case Western Reserve Univ, PhD(biol), 69. *Prof Exp:* Res assoc develop biol, Brown Univ, 68-70; res assoc physiol, 70-71, ASST PROF PHYSIOL, STATE UNIV NY UPSTATE MED CTR, 72-; RES BIOLOGIST, VET ADMIN HOSP, SYRACUSE, 71- *Mem:* AAAS; Am Soc Nephrology; Am Physiol Soc; Int Soc Nephrology. *Res:* Renal physiology, particularly countercurrent mechanism, metabolic aspects of sodium transport and lipid metabolism. *Mailing Add:* Dept of Physiol State Univ NY Upstate Med Ctr Syracuse NY 13210

TRIMBLE, ROBERT BOGUE, b Baltimore, Md, July 2, 43; m 69. BIOCHEMISTRY, MOLECULAR BIOLOGY. *Educ:* Rensselaer Polytech Inst, BS, 65, MS, 67, PhD(microbiol), 69. *Prof Exp:* Health Res Inc fel, 69-70, res scientist, 70-72, assoc res scientist, 73-80, SR RES SCIENTIST, LAB MED INST, DIV LABS & RES, NY STATE DEPT HEALTH, 70- *Mem:* AAAS; Am Soc Microbiol; Am Soc Biol Chemists. *Res:* Regulation of enzyme synthesis and activity; bacteriophage biochemistry; viral genetic expression; glycoprotein biosynthesis; pyrimidine nucleotide interconversions; geomicrobiology. *Mailing Add:* NY State Dept Health Empire State Plaza-E524 Albany NY 12201

TRIMBLE, RUSSELL FAY, b Montclair, NJ, Feb 23, 27; m 50; c 3. INORGANIC CHEMISTRY. *Educ:* Mass Inst Technol, BS, 48, PhD(chem), 51. *Prof Exp:* Instr chem, Univ Rochester, 51-54; from asst prof to assoc prof, 54-70, PROF CHEM, SOUTHERN ILL UNIV, CARBONDALE, 70- *Concurrent Pos:* Abstractor, Chem Abstr, 54-, tech translator, 59-; vis lectr, Univ Ill, 63-64. *Mem:* AAAS; Am Chem Soc; Am Inst Chemists; Am Translators Asn. *Res:* Coordination compounds; inorganic synthesis. *Mailing Add:* Dept of Chem & Biochem Southern Ill Univ Carbondale IL 62901

TRIMBLE, RUSSELL HAROLD, chemical physics, see previous edition

TRIMBLE, VIRGINIA LOUISE, b Los Angeles, Calif, Nov 15, 43; m 72. ASTRONOMY, ASTROPHYSICS. *Educ:* Univ Calif, Los Angeles, BA, 64; Calif Inst Technol, MS, 65, PhD(astron), 68; Cambridge Univ, MA, 69. *Prof Exp:* Res fel astrophys, Inst Theoret Astron, Cambridge Univ, 68; asst prof astron, Smith Col & Four Cols Observ, 68-69; NATO sr fel, Inst Theoret Astron, Cambridge Univ, 69-70, vis fel, 70-71; from asst prof to assoc prof, 71-80, PROF PHYSICS, UNIV CALIF, IRVINE, 80- *Concurrent Pos:* Vis asst prof astron, Univ Md, College Park, 72-74, vis assoc prof, 74-80, vis prof, 80-; Sloan fel, 72-74; nat lectr, Sigma Xi, 74-77. *Mem:* Am Astron Soc; Royal Astron Soc; Europ Phys Soc; Int Astron Union; Int Soc Gen Relativity & Gravitation. *Res:* Late phases of stellar evolution; supernovae; white dwarfs; neutron stars; collapsed configurations; binary stars. *Mailing Add:* Dept of Physics Univ of Calif Irvine CA 92717

TRIMITSIS, GEORGE B, b Assiut, Egypt, Nov 28, 39; m 64; c 1. ORGANIC CHEMISTRY. *Educ:* Am Univ Cairo, BSc, 64; Va Polytech Inst & State Univ, PhD(org chem), 68. *Prof Exp:* Res assoc org res, Ohio State Univ, 68-69; asst prof org chem, Western Mich Univ, 69-76; MEM FAC, DIV NAT SCI, UNIV PITTSBURGH, 76- *Mem:* Am Chem Soc. *Res:* Formation, study and synthetic applications of carbanions. *Mailing Add:* Div of Nat Sci Univ of Pittsburgh Johnstown PA 15904

TRIMMER, JOHN DEZENDORF, b Washington, DC, Sept 19, 07; m 30; c 2. PHYSICS. *Educ:* Elizabethtown Col, AB, 26; Pa State Univ, MS, 33; Univ Mich, PhD(physics), 36. *Hon Degrees:* DSc, Elizabethtown Col, 53. *Prof Exp:* Asst prof aeronaut eng, Mass Inst Technol, 37-41, res assoc underwater sound, 41-43; physicist, Tenn Eastman Co, 43-46; prof physics, Univ Tenn, 46-57; prof, Univ Mass, 57-66, head dept, 57-63; prof & head dept, 66-73, EMER PROF PHYSICS, WASHINGTON COL, 73- *Mem:* AAAS; Am Phys Soc; Acoust Soc Am; Soc Gen Systs Res. *Res:* Instrumentation; principles of measurement; communication; physics of ionized fluids; cybernetics; general systems theory; optical physics. *Mailing Add:* 159A Pelham Lane Jamesburg NJ 08831

TRIMMER, ROBERT WHITFIELD, b Binghamton, NY, Dec 13, 37; m 65; c 2. INDUSTRIAL ORGANIC CHEMISTRY. *Educ:* Hope Col, Mich, AB, 60; Rensselaer Polytech Inst, PhD(org chem), 73. *Prof Exp:* Asst res polymer chem, Schenectady Chem Co, 60; asst res med chemist, Sterling Winthrop Res Inst, Sterling Drug, Inc, 64-69; SUPVR LAB PROD DEVELOP & ORG CHEMIST, SUMNER DIV, MILES LABS, INC, 73- *Mem:* Am Chem Soc; Royal Soc Chem; AAAS; Org Reactions Catalysis Soc; Am Sci Affil. *Res:* Hydrogenation technology; specialty products; pharmaceuticals; aryl and alkyl amines as intermediates and polymer catalysts; quaternary ammonium compounds, citric acid derivatives; heterocycles; organic photochemistry; development of new synthetic methods. *Mailing Add:* Miles Lab Inc Corp Res Elkhart IN 46514

TRINDLE, CARL OTIS, b Des Moines, Iowa, Aug 26, 41; m 62; c 1. THEORETICAL CHEMISTRY. *Educ:* Grinnell Col, BA, 63; Tufts Univ, PhD(phys chem), 67. *Prof Exp:* NSF fel theoret chem, Yale Univ, 67-68; res assoc, Argonne Nat Lab, 68-69; asst prof, 69-73, ASSOC PROF THEORET CHEM, UNIV VA, 73- *Concurrent Pos:* Consult, Argonne Nat Lab, 69-; vis asst prof, Mideast Tech Univ, 71; Sloan Found fel, 71-73; vis assoc prof, Mideast Tech Univ, 73; vis scientist, Israel Inst Technol, 76; Nat Acad Sci exchange fel, Yugoslavia, 79. *Mem:* AAAS; Am Chem Soc. *Res:* Impact of orbital topology on organic stereo-chemistry; localized description of charge distributions; group theory of easily rearranged systems. *Mailing Add:* Dept of Chem Univ of Va Charlottesville VA 22901

TRINE, FRANKLIN DAWSON, b Cincinnati, Ohio, July 12, 30; m 48; c 4. MATHEMATICS. *Educ:* Wis State Univ, Platteville, BS, 53; Univ Wis, MS, 57, PhD(math educ), 65. *Prof Exp:* Instr high sch, Ill, 53-56 & 57-58; from instr to assoc prof, 58-66, PROF MATH, UNIV WIS-PLATTEVILLE, 66-, CHMN DEPT, 76- *Mem:* Math Asn Am. *Res:* Foundations of mathematics; mathematics education, particularly at junior college and college level. *Mailing Add:* Dept of Math Univ of Wis Platteville WI 53818

TRINKAUS, ERIK, b New Haven, Conn, Dec 24, 48. PHYSICAL ANTHROPOLOGY. *Educ:* Univ Wis, BA, 70; Univ Pa, MA, 73, PhD(anthrop), 75. *Prof Exp:* Asst prof, 75-77, ASSOC PROF ANTHROP, HARVARD UNIV, 77- *Mem:* Am Asn Phys Anthropologists. *Res:* Paleontological study of Middle and Upper Pleistocene hominids emphasizing the behavioral interpretation of fossil remains; reconstructing human evolutionary history using complex evolutionary models as well as comparative anatomy. *Mailing Add:* Dept Anthrop Peabody Mus Harvard Univ Cambridge MA 02138

TRINKAUS, JOHN PHILIP, b Rockville Center, NY, May 23, 18; m 63; c 3. CELL BIOLOGY, DEVELOPMENTAL BIOLOGY. *Educ:* Wesleyan Univ, BA, 40; Columbia Univ, MA, 41; Johns Hopkins Univ, PhD(embryol), 48. *Prof Exp:* From instr to assoc prof, 48-64, PROF BIOL, YALE UNIV, 64- *Concurrent Pos:* Mem staff embryol, Marine Biol Lab, Woods Hole, 53-57, 70 & 78; master, Branford Col, Yale Univ, 66-73, dir grad studies biol, 65-66; Guggenheim fel, Lab Exp Embryol, Col France, 59-60; chmn, Gordon Conf Cell Contract & Movement, 79. *Mem:* Soc Develop Biol; Am Soc Zoologists; Tissue Cult Asn; Am Soc Cell Biol; Int Inst Embryol. *Res:* Cytodifferentiation; mechanism of morphogenetic cell movements; teleost development; contact behavior and locomotion of normal and transformed cells; fine structure. *Mailing Add:* Dept of Biol Yale Univ New Haven CT 06520

TRINKAUS-RANDALL, VICKERY E, b Albuquerque, NMex, Jan 11, 53. OPTHALMOLOGY. *Educ:* Kenyon Col, AB, 74; Univ Wis-Madison, PhD(zool), 81. *Prof Exp:* Fel, Marine Biol Lab, 81; RES FEL, EYE RES INST RETINA FOUND, 81- *Mem:* Sigma Xi; Am Res Vision & Ophthal. *Res:* Trabecular meshwork of the eye for the presence of non-muscle contractile filaments to examine their role in the aqueous outflow; the role of divalent cations on hemidesmosome formation in the cornea. *Mailing Add:* Eye Res Inst Retina Found 20 Staniford St Boston MA 02114

TRINKLEIN, DAVID HERBERT, b Jefferson City, Mo, July 3, 47. FLORICULTURE, PLANT GENETICS. *Educ:* Lincoln Univ, BS, 69; Univ Mo, Ms, 71, PhD(hort), 74. *Prof Exp:* Res asst hort, Univ Mo, 70-75; res scientist plant sci, Farmland Industs, 75-76; exten horticulturist, Lincoln Univ, 76-77; ASST PROF HORT, UNIV MO, 77- *Mem:* Sigma Xi. *Res:* Physiology and genetics of flower crops with allied interest in energy conservation in the greenhouse. *Mailing Add:* 1-43 Agr Bldg Univ of Mo Columbia MO 65211

TRINKO, JOSEPH RICHARD, JR, b Washington DC, Dec 20, 39; m 65; c 2. NUCLEAR ENGINEERING, ELECTRICAL ENGINEERING. *Educ:* Univ Tenn, BS, 63, MS, 65, PhD(nuclear eng), 67. *Prof Exp:* Asst nuclear engr breeder, Ebasco Serv, 70-73; SR NUCLEAR ENGR REACTOR ANAL, MIDDLE SOUTH SERV, 73- *Mem:* Elec Power Res Inst. *Res:* Advanced methods of reactor core analysis; stress corrosion mechanisms in nuclear systems. *Mailing Add:* Middle South Serv PO Box 61000 New Orleans LA 70161

TRINLER, WILLIAM A, b Louisville, Ky, Dec 24, 29; m 62; c 1. ORGANIC CHEMISTRY. *Educ:* Univ Louisville, BS, 55, PhD(org chem), 59. *Prof Exp:* Chemist, E I du Pont de Nemours & Co, 59-60; from asst prof to assoc prof, 60-74, PROF ORG CHEM, IND STATE UNIV, TERRE HAUTE, 74- *Mem:* Am Chem Soc; Am Inst Chemists. *Res:* Synthesis and polymerization of vinyl monomers; liquid chromatography. *Mailing Add:* Dept of Chem Ind State Univ Terre Haute IN 47809

TRIOLO, ANTHONY J, b Philadelphia, Pa, Aug 8, 32; m 59; c 3. PHARMACOLOGY. *Educ:* Philadelphia Col Pharm, BS, 59; Jefferson Med Col, MS, 62, PhD(pharmacol), 64. *Prof Exp:* From instr to asst prof, 67-72, assoc prof, 72-81, PROF PHARMACOL, JEFFERSON MED COL, 81- *Res:* Neuropharmacological effects of tremorine on motor reflex activity; toxicological interactions between organochlorine or organophosphate insecticides and Benzo-(a)-pyrene carcinogenesis. *Mailing Add:* Dept of Pharmacol Jefferson Med Col Philadelphia PA 19107

TRIONE, EDWARD JOHN, b Ill, Mar 10, 26; m 49; c 3. BIOCHEMISTRY. *Educ:* Chico State Col, BA, 50; Ore State Col, PhD(bot), 57. *Prof Exp:* Chem technician, Ore State Col, 53-54, asst, 54-57; res plant pathologist, Univ Calif, 57-59; PLANT BIOCHEMIST, ORE STATE UNIV, 59-, PROF BOT & PLANT PATH, 76- *Mem:* Am Soc Plant Physiologists; Bot Soc Am; Am Phytopath Soc; Can Soc Plant Physiologists; Japanese Soc Plant Physiologists. *Res:* Biochemistry and physiology of reproduction in higher plants and fungi; biochemistry of host-pathogen interactions. *Mailing Add:* Dept of Bot & Plant Path Ore State Univ Corvallis OR 97331

TRIPARD, GERALD EDWARD, b Saskatoon, Sask, Apr 18, 40; m 63; c 2. NUCLEAR PHYSICS. *Educ:* Univ BC, BSc, 62, MSc, 64, PhD(physics), 67. *Prof Exp:* Nat Res Coun Can fel, Swiss Fed Inst Technol, 67-69; asst prof physics, 69-76, ASSOC PROF PHYSICS, WASH STATE UNIV, 76- *Res:* Neutron scattering; final state interactions; stopped pions. *Mailing Add:* Dept of Physics Wash State Univ Pullman WA 99163

TRIPATHI, BRENDA JENNIFER, b Rochford, Eng, July 5, 46; m 69; c 2. OPHTHALMOLOGY, CELL BIOLOGY. *Educ:* Univ London, BSc, 67, PhD(med), 71. *Prof Exp:* Res asst path, Univ Col Hosp, London, 67-69; res asst, Inst Ophthal, Univ London, 69-72, lectr, 72-77; res assoc & asst prof ophthal, Univ Chicago, 77-80. *Mem:* Royal Soc Med, London; Asn Res Vision & Ophthal; Sigma Xi; AAAS; Royal Microscopical Soc, London. *Res:* Visual science; anatomy; physiology; surgical pathology; experimental pathology; clinical research; cell biology; electron microscopy; tissue culture; biochemistry; immunology; microbiology; cerebrospinal fluid physiology and pathology. *Mailing Add:* 5545 S Harper Chicago IL 60637

TRIPATHI, G N R, b Gorakhpur, India, Jan 1, 44; m 62; c 3. CHEMICAL PHYSICS, SOLID STATE PHYSICS. *Educ:* Univ Gorakhpur, India, BSc, 60, MSc, 62, PhD(physics), 68. *Prof Exp:* Fel physics, Univ Gorakhpur, India, 62-65, sr lectr, 65-76; vis sr lectr & acad staff fel, Dept Physics, Univ Manchester & Manchester Inst Sci & Technol, 76-77; SCIENTIST RADIATION RES, RADIATION LAB, UNIV NOTRE DAME, 78- *Res:* Time resolved raman scattering of molecular transients and excited states; low temperature spectroscopy of oriented crystal films; molecular photophysics; gas phase spectroscopy. *Mailing Add:* Radiation Lab Univ Notre Dame Notre Dame IN 46556

TRIPATHI, KAMALA KANT, b Varanasi, India, July 10, 34; m 51; c 4. BIOCHEMISTRY, ANALYTICAL CHEMISTRY. *Educ:* Banaras Hindu Univ, BS, 54; Univ Bihar, DVM, 59; Univ Mo-Columbia, 64, PhD(biochem), 68. *Prof Exp:* Vet surgeon & exten officer, Govt Bihar, 59-63; res asst, Univ Nebr, Lincoln, 64-65; res asst bioanal chem, Univ Mo-Columbia, 65-68, NIH fel, 68-70; RES SCIENTIST CANCER CHEMOTHER, AM MED CTR DENVER, 70- *Res:* Cancer biochemistry, proteins, fatty acids, amino acids and steroids; analytical, immunochemical, ion-exchange, electrophoretic, gas-liquid and thin-layer chromatographic methods and their applications. *Mailing Add:* Am Med Ctr at Denver 6401 W Colfax Ave Spivak CO 80214

TRIPATHI, RAMESH CHANDRA, b Jamira, India, July 1, 36; Brit citizen; m 69; c 2. CLINICAL OPHTHALMOLOGY, OCULAR PATHOLOGY. *Educ:* Univ Agra, MD, BS, 59; Univ Lucknow, MS, 63; DORCS&P, 65; Univ London, PhD(med), 70; Royal Col Pathologists, MRCPath, 74. *Prof Exp:* Resident ophthal, Med Col Kanpur, Lucknow Univ, 59-64; res fel, Univ Ghent, 64-65; registrar, S W Middlesex Hosp, London, 65-67; lectr, Inst Ophthal, London Univ, 67-70, sr lectr, 70-77; PROF OPHTHAL, UNIV CHICAGO, 77- *Concurrent Pos:* Attend opthalmologist & asst surgeon, Div Railway Hosp, Govt India, 63-64; hon registrar, Charing Cross Hosp, 65-67; Hayward res fel, Inst Ophthal, Univ London, 67-68; sr registrar, Moorfields Eye Hosp, London, 67-68, chief clin asst, 68-72, consult ophthal & pathologist, 72-77; electron microscopist, Univ Chicago, 77-; ocular pathologist, 77- & NIH grant, 77-80; exec ed, Exp Eye Res. *Honors & Awards:* Ophthalmologic Prize, Royal Soc Med, 71; Royal Eye Hosp Prize, Ophthal Soc, UK, 76. *Mem:* Asn Res Vision & Ophthal; Am Acad Ophthal; Royal Soc Med; Royal Col Pathologists. *Res:* Ophthalmology; visual science; anatomy; physiology; surgical pathology; experimental pathology; clinical research; cell biology; electron microscopy; tissue culture; biochemistry; immunology; microbiology; micrography; ophthalmic microsurgery; laser surgery; physiology and pathology of cerebrospinal fluid. *Mailing Add:* Dept of Ophthal Box 437 950 E 59th St Chicago IL 60637

TRIPATHI, UMA PRASAD, b Lumbini, Nepal, Apr 29, 45; c 2. INORGANIC CHEMISTRY, COSMETIC CHEMISTRY. *Educ:* Univ Gorakhpur, India, BSc, 63; Univ Allahabad, India, MSc, 65; Mont State Univ, PhD(inorg chem), 72. *Prof Exp:* Anal chemist, Nepal Bur Mines, Kathmandu, 65; asst prof chem, Trichandra Col, Kathmandu, 65-67; sr res chemist, Cosmetics, Chesebrough-Pond's Inc, 72-75; sr chemist, Gillette Co, 75-76; group leader, 76-78, sect mgr, 78-81, ASSOC DIR, AM CYANAMID CO, 82- *Mem:* Soc Cosmetic Chemists; Am Chem Soc. *Res:* Elucidation of molecular and crystal structures of organometallics; inorganic synthesis; inorganic reaction mechanisms; emulsion technology; surface active agents; hair science; insecticides; household products. *Mailing Add:* Cyanamid Consumer Prod Div 697 Rte 46 Clifton NY 07015

TRIPATHI, VIJAI KUMAR, b Kanpur, India, Dec 23, 42; m 68. ELECTRICAL ENGINEERING. *Educ:* Agra Univ, BSc, 58; Univ Allahabad, MScTech, 61; Univ Mich, Ann Arbor, MS, 64, PhD(elec eng), 68. *Prof Exp:* Sr res asst elec eng, Indian Inst Technol, Bombay, 61-63; res asst, Electron Physics Lab, Univ Mich, Ann Arbor, 63-65, res assoc, 65-67; asst prof elec eng, Univ Okla, 68-74; asst prof, 74-77, ASSOC PROF, ORE STATE UNIV, 77- *Mem:* Inst Elec & Electronics Engrs. *Res:* Microwave circuits and devices; solid state devices; electromagnetic fields. *Mailing Add:* Dept of Elec & Comput Eng Ore State Univ Corvallis OR 97331

TRIPATHY, DEOKI NANDAN, b Dwarahat, India, July 1, 33; m 69; c 2. VETERINARY MICROBIOLOGY. *Educ:* Utter Pradesh Agr Univ, India, BVS & AH, 64; Univ Ill, Urbana, MS, 67, PhD(vet microbiol), 70; Am Col Vet Microbiologists, dipl, 72. *Prof Exp:* Fel, 64-65, res asst, 65-70, assoc, 70-73, asst prof, 73-77, ASSOC PROF VET MICROBIOL, UNIV ILL, URBANA, 77- *Mem:* Am Vet Med Asn; Am Asn Avian Pathologists; Am Soc Microbiol; Am Col Vet Microbiologists; US Animal Health Asn. *Res:* Pathogenesis, epidemiology and characterization of avian pox viruses; immune response of ducks to Pasteurella anatipestifer and duck hepatitis virus; immunization and evaluation of immune response to leptospirosis. *Mailing Add:* Dept of Vet Path & Hyg Univ of Ill Urbana IL 61801

TRIPATHY, SUKANT K, b Chakradharput, India, Aug 4, 52; m 81. STRUCTURE PROPERTY, POLYMER THEORY. *Educ:* Indian Inst Technol, India, BSc, 72, MSc, 74; Case Western Reserve Univ, PhD(macromolecular sci), 81. *Prof Exp:* MEM TECH STAFF, GTE LABS INC, 81- *Concurrent Pos:* Consult & lectr, Case Western Reserve Univ, 77-81. *Mem:* Am Phys Soc; Am Chem Soc. *Res:* Characterization and understanding of polymer microstructure using physical methods and theoretical modelling, establishing structure property relationships; new organic materials and novel polymeric applications. *Mailing Add:* GTE Labs Inc 40 Sylvan Rd Waltham MA 02254

TRIPLEHORN, CHARLES A, b Bluffton, Ohio, Oct 27, 27; m 49; c 2. ENTOMOLOGY. *Educ:* Ohio State Univ, BS, 49, MS, 52; Cornell Univ, PhD(entom), 57. *Prof Exp:* Asst prof entom, Univ Del, 52-54, Ohio Agr Exp Sta, 57-62 & Ohio State Univ, 62-64; entomologist, US AID, Brazil, 64-66; assoc prof, 66-67, PROF ENTOM, OHIO STATE UNIV, 67- *Mem:* Entom Soc Am; Soc Syst Zool; Coleopterists Soc (pres, 76). *Res:* Taxonomy of Coleoptera; animal ecology; herpetology. *Mailing Add:* Dept of Entom Ohio State Univ Columbus OH 43210

TRIPLEHORN, DON MURRAY, b Bluffton, Ohio, July 24, 34; m 57; c 4. GEOLOGY. *Educ:* Ohio Wesleyan Univ, BA, 56; Ind Univ, MA, 57; Univ Ill, PhD(geol), 61. *Prof Exp:* Instr geol, Col Wooster, 60-61; res geologist, Tulsa Res Ctr, Sinclair Oil & Gas Co, 61-69; assoc prof, 69-76, PROF GEOL, UNIV ALASKA, FAIRBANKS, 76- *Mem:* Geol Soc Am; Int Asn Sedimentologists; Am Asn Petrol Geologists; Soc Econ Paleontologists & Mineralogists; Am Asn Geol Teachers. *Res:* Glauconite; coal geology; clay mineralogy; shale petrology; diagenesis. *Mailing Add:* Dept of Geol Univ of Alaska Fairbanks AK 99701

TRIPLETT, EDWARD LEE, b Denver, Colo, July 14, 30; m 51; c 3. ZOOLOGY. *Educ:* Stanford Univ, BS, 51, PhD, 56. *Prof Exp:* Actg instr biol, Stanford Univ, 54-55; from instr to assoc prof, 55-73, PROF BIOL, UNIV CALIF, SANTA BARBARA, 73- *Mem:* AAAS; Soc Develop Biol. *Res:* Development of the nervous system; cell differentiation of neural plate cells; control of protein synthesis in developing systems. *Mailing Add:* Dept of Biol Sci Univ of Calif Santa Barbara CA 93106

TRIPLETT, GLOVER BROWN, JR, b Miss, June 2, 30; m 51; c 1. AGRONOMY. *Educ:* Miss State Univ, BS, 51, MS, 55; Mich State Univ, PhD(farm crops), 59. *Prof Exp:* From asst prof to assoc prof, 59-67, PROF AGRON, OHIO AGR RES & DEVELOP CTR, 67-, AGRONOMIST, 59- *Mem:* Am Soc Agron; Weed Sci Soc Am. *Res:* Crop production and management; no-tillage cropping systems. *Mailing Add:* Ohio Agr Res & Dev Ctr Wooster OH 44691

TRIPODI, DANIEL, b Cliffside Park, NJ, May 13, 39; m 63. IMMUNOCHEMISTRY, MICROBIOLOGY. *Educ:* Univ Del, BS, 61, MS, 63; Temple Univ, PhD(microbiol, immunol), 66. *Prof Exp:* Asst microbiol, Univ Del, 63; sr scientist, Ortho Res Found, 66-69, dir div immunol & diag res, 69-74; res asst prof, Sch Med, Temple Univ, 69-74, res assoc prof microbiol microbiol, 73-77; gen mgr, biomed div, New Eng Nuclear Corp, 74-77; dir, tech planning group, Becton, Dickinson & Co, 77-80; DIR TECH SERV, ORTHO DIAGNOSTICS, 80- *Mem:* Am Soc Microbiol; Am Asn Immunol. *Res:* Physical and chemical aspects of structures which display serological reactivity. *Mailing Add:* Ortho Diagnostics Raritan NJ 08869

TRIPP, JOHN RATHBONE, b Barberton, Ohio, Oct 18, 39; m 71. INVERTEBRATE ZOOLOGY, EMBRYOLOGY. *Educ:* Ore State Univ, BSc, 62; Ohio State Univ, MSc, 65, PhD(zool), 70. *Prof Exp:* Res specialist, Introductory Biol Prog, Ohio State Univ 69-70; ASST PROF DEPT BIOL, FLA SOUTHERN COL, 71- *Concurrent Pos:* Prin investr, Cottrell Found Col Sci grant, 75. *Mem:* Am Soc Zoologists; Am Inst Biol Sci; AAAS; Am Arachnological Soc. *Res:* Spider embryology and marine invertebrate zoology. *Mailing Add:* Dept of Biol Fla Southern Col Lakeland FL 33802

TRIPP, JOHN STEPHEN, b Salina, Kans, Aug 3, 38. ELECTRONIC ENGINEERING, COMPUTER SCIENCE. *Educ:* Kans State Univ, BS, 61, MS, 62; Univ Mich, Ann Arbor, MS, 67, PhD(comput sci), 71. *Prof Exp:* AEROSPACE TECHNOLOGIST, LANGLEY RES CTR-NASA, 62- *Concurrent Pos:* Lectr geol, Washington Univ, 81- *Mem:* Inst Elec & Electronic Engrs. *Res:* Analysis and simulation of physical systems; synthesis of control techniques for automation of aerospace test facilities; application of digital computers to automatic control. *Mailing Add:* Langley Res Ctr-NASA Mail Stop 238 Hampton VA 23665

TRIPP, MARENES ROBERT, b Poughkeepsie, NY, Aug 20, 31; m 55; c 4. INVERTEBRATE PATHOLOGY. *Educ:* Colgate Univ, AB, 53; Univ Rochester, MS, 56; Rutgers Univ, PhD(zool), 58. *Prof Exp:* Res fel trop pub health, Harvard Univ, 58-60; from asst prof to assoc prof, 60-71, PROF BIOL SCI, UNIV DEL, 71-, INTERIM DIR, SCH LIFE & HEALTH SCI, 81- *Mem:* AAAS; Am Soc Parasitol; Soc Invert Path; Am Soc Zoologists; Int Soc Develop Comp Immunol. *Res:* Invertebrate defense mechanisms. *Mailing Add:* Sch Life & Health Sci Univ Del Newark DE 19711

TRIPP, ROBERT D, b Oakland, Calif, Jan 9, 27; m 64; c 3. PHYSICS. *Educ:* Mass Inst Technol, BS, 49; Univ Calif, PhD, 55. *Prof Exp:* From asst prof to assoc prof, 60-66, PHYSICIST, LAWRENCE BERKELEY LAB, UNIV CALIF, 55-, PROF PHYSICS, UNIV CALIF, BERKELEY, 66- *Concurrent Pos:* Physicist, AEC, France, 59-60; NSF sr fel, Europ Orgn Nuclear Res, Switz, 64-65, vis scientist, 71-72. *Res:* Elementary particle physics. *Mailing Add:* Dept of Physics Univ of Calif Berkeley CA 94720

TRIPP, RUSSELL MAURICE, b Holton, Kans, July 12, 16; m 37; c 7. RADIOLOGY, GEOPHYSICS. *Educ:* Colo Sch Mines, GeolE, 39, MGeophysEng, 43; Mass Inst Technol, ScD(geol), 48. *Prof Exp:* Geophysicist, Geotech Corp, Tex, 36-41, asst to pres in-chg res, 43-46; instr geol & geophys, Colo Sch Mines, 41-43; sr scientist, Bur Ships, US Dept Navy, 46; consult geologist & geophysicist, 47-49; vpres & dir res, Res Inc, 49-53; pres, Explor, Inc, 52-58; PRES, TRIPP RES CORP, 55- *Concurrent Pos:* Managing partner, Tripp Lead & Zinc Co, 52-, pres, Tripp Prod, Inc, 62-; dir, Sonic Res Corp, 56-; consult, Bostwick Propecting Co, 56- & Archilithic Corp, 58-; pres, Skia Corp, 72-; managing partner, Saratoga Develop Co. *Mem:* Soc Info Display; Soc Photog Scientists & Engrs; Soc Photo Optical Instrumentation Engrs; AAAS; Sigma Xi. *Res:* Geophysical and geochemical exploration for minerals; relation between clay minerals, organic matter and radioelements in sediments; genesis of uranium ore bodies; mineral benefication; free viewing depth-perception radiography; nuclear medicine instrumentation; animal genetics; ophthalmic surgical instrumentation. *Mailing Add:* Tripp Res Corp 15231 Quito Rd Saratoga CA 95070

TRIPPE, ANTHONY PHILIP, b Buffalo, NY, Aug 30, 43; m 65; c 3. NUCLEAR ENGINEERING, COMPUTER SCIENCE. *Educ:* Rochester Inst Technol, BS, 66; Fairleigh Dickinson Univ, MS, 72. *Prof Exp:* Lab tech anal chem, Eastman Kodak Co, 63-66; chemist polymers, Smith Kline & French Labs, 66-67; reliability engr quality assurance, US Army Picatinny Arsenal, 67-72; prin engr, Calspan Corp, 72-76; MGR PROG DEVELOP, IRT CORP, 77- *Concurrent Pos:* Fire protection engr, Allstate Insurance Co, 74-75. *Mem:* AAAS; Am Chem Soc; Am Soc Test & Mat; Combustion Inst. *Res:* Nondestructive testing using nuclear techniques; study of systems using computerized analytical models; application of pattern recognition to automated control. *Mailing Add:* IRT Corp 7650 Convoy Ct San Diego CA 92111

TRIPPE, THOMAS GORDON, b Los Angeles, Calif, Nov 17, 39; div; c 3. EXPERIMENTAL HIGH ENERGY PHYSICS. *Educ:* Univ Calif, Los Angeles, PhD(physics), 68. *Prof Exp:* Physicist, Univ Calif, Los Angeles, 68-69; physicist, Europ Orgn Nuclear Res, 69-70; PHYSICIST, LAWRENCE BERKELEY LAB, 71- *Concurrent Pos:* NSF fel, 69-70. *Mem:* Am Phys Soc. *Res:* Experimental weak interactions; particle properties. *Mailing Add:* Lawrence Berkeley Lab Berkeley CA 94720

TRISCARI, JOSEPH, b Italy, Apr 17, 45; US citizen; m 66; c 3. OBESITY, LIPID METABOLISM. *Educ:* Cornell Univ, BS, 71; Fairleigh Dickinson Univ, MS, 75; Columbia Univ, PhD(nutrit), 80. *Prof Exp:* Lab asst, Dept Biochem, Cornell Univ, 68-71; ASST RES GROUP CHIEF, DEPT PHARMACOL II, HOFFMANN LA ROCHE, 71- *Mem:* Am Inst Nutrit; Soc Exp Biol & Med; AAAS; NY Acad Sci. *Res:* Lipid and carbohydrate regulation and metabolism; appetite regulation and energy balance; pharmacologic agents for the treatment of obesity and hyperlipidemia. *Mailing Add:* Dept Pharmacol II Hoffman La Roche Nutley NJ 07110

TRISCHKA, JOHN WILSON, b Bisbee, Ariz, Dec 30, 16; m 46; c 2. PHYSICS. *Educ:* Univ Ariz, BS, 37; Cornell Univ, PhD(physics), 43. *Prof Exp:* Test engr, Gen Elec Co, 37-38; asst physics, Cornell Univ, 39-42, instr, 42-45; res physicist, Los Alamos Sci Lab, Univ Calif, 45; assoc physics, Columbia Univ, 46-48; from asst prof to assoc prof, 48-56, PROF PHYSICS, SYRACUSE UNIV, 56- *Mem:* AAAS; Am Phys Soc; Am Asn Physics Teachers; Am Meteorol Soc. *Res:* Radio frequency spectroscopy of molecules; molecular beams; surface physics; atmospheric physics. *Mailing Add:* Dept of Physics Syracuse Univ Syracuse NY 13210

TRISCHLER, FLOYD D, b Pittsburgh, Pa, Aug 31, 29; m 51; c 6. ORGANIC CHEMISTRY, POLYMER CHEMISTRY. *Educ:* Univ Pittsburgh, BS, 51. Res chemist, Pa Indust Chem Corp, 53-55, asst lab mgr, 55-56; develop & tech chemist, Tar Prod Div, Koppers Co, 56-58, asst group leader, Res Dept, 58-63; sr res chemist, Narmco Res & Develop, Whittaker Corp, Calif, 63-65, prog mgr, 65-69; mgr mkt & admin asst to pres, Mat Systs Corp, Calif, 69-72; exec vpres, Taylor Bldg Corp, Ind, 72-73; PRES GUADALUPE BUILDERS, IND, 73- *Mem:* Am Chem Soc. *Res:* Polymer applications and research; pulp and paper; organic coatings; fluorine compounds; elastomers; adhesives; high performance polymers. *Mailing Add:* 8249 Filly Lane Plainfield IN 46168

TRISKA, FRANK JOHN, aquatic ecology, microbial ecology, see previous edition

TRISLER, JOHN CHARLES, b Eva, La, Dec 24, 33; m 53; c 2. ORGANIC CHEMISTRY. *Educ:* La Polytech Inst, BS, 56; Tex Tech Univ, PhD(org chem), 59. *Prof Exp:* From asst prof to assoc prof, 59-66, PROF CHEM, LA TECH UNIV, 66-, HEAD DEPT, 78- *Mem:* Am Chem Soc. *Res:* Organic reaction mechanisms. *Mailing Add:* Dept of Chem La Tech Univ Ruston LA 71270

TRISTAN, THEODORE A, b Mexico City, Mex, Oct 5, 24; US citizen; m 48; c 4. RADIOLOGY. *Educ:* Univ Nebr, BS, 47, MD & MSc, 50; Univ Pa, MS, 58; Am Bd Radiol, dipl, 57. *Prof Exp:* Intern, Hosp, Univ Pa, 50-51; instr radiol, Med Ctr, Univ Rochester, 56-59, sr instr, 59; from asst prof to assoc prof, Univ Pa, 59-65, lectr, 65-70; CLIN PROF RADIOL & ANAT, HERSHEY MED CTR, PA STATE UNIV, 70- *Concurrent Pos:* Fel radiol, Univ Pa Hosp, 53-56; Am Cancer Soc fel, 53-54; NIH grants, Univ Rochester, 58-59 & Univ Pa, 59-63; Nat Res Coun Picker Found grant, Univ Pa, 58-65; mem & task group chmn, Int Comn Radiation Units & Measurements, 64-67; assoc prof radiol, Hahnemann Med Col, 70-73. *Mem:* Radiol Soc NAm (secy, 75-79, pres elect, 81 & pres, 82); Am Roentgen Ray Soc; AMA; fel Am Col Radiol. *Res:* Image intensification, image quality and information development, storage and retrieval; analysis of the function of motion in cinefluorography with regard to its value in development of diagnostic criteria in clinical radiology. *Mailing Add:* Dept of Radiol Polyclin Med Ctr Harrisburg PA 17105

TRITCHLER, DAVID LYNN, b Portage, Wis, Dec 17, 44; m 75. BIOMETRICS, BIOSTATISTICS. *Educ:* Univ Nebr, BA, 70, MS, 75; Harvard Sch Pub Health, ScD, 80. *Prof Exp:* Asst prof, Cornell Univ, 81; ASST PROF BIOSTATIST, HARVARD SCH PUB HEALTH, 81- *Concurrent Pos:* Assoc, Mem Sloan Kettering Cancer Ctr, 80-81; asst prof, Sidney Farber Cancer Inst, 81- *Mem:* Am Statist Asn; Biometric Soc; Soc Indust & Appl Math. *Res:* Computational algorithms for nonparametric statistics; survival analysis; discrete data analysis. *Mailing Add:* Div Biostatist Sidney Farber Cancer Inst 44 Binney St Boston MA 02115

TRITES, RONALD WILMOT, b Moncton, NB, July 17, 29; m 56; c 5. PHYSICAL OCEANOGRAPHY. *Educ:* Univ NB, BSc, 50; Univ BC, MA, 52, PhD(physics), 55. *Prof Exp:* Phys oceanogr, Fisheries Res Bd Can, 50-55 & 56-66 & Defence Res Bd Can, 55-56; head appl oceanog, Bedford Inst Oceanog, 66-70; adv Atlantic, Fisheries Res Bd Can, 70-71; head coastal oceaonog div, Bedford Inst Oceanog, 71-75, SR OCEANOGR, MARINE ECOL LAB, BEDFORD INST OCEANOG, 75- *Honors & Awards:* Hon Lectr, Dalhousie Univ, 60-77. *Res:* Coastal and estuarine circulation, mixing and dispersion processes; role of physical processes in production of fish stocks. *Mailing Add:* 2 Eljay Dr Dartmouth NS B2W 2C1 Can

TRITSCH, GEORGE LEOPOLD, b Vienna, Austria, Apr 8, 29; nat US; m 51; c 3. BIOCHEMISTRY. *Educ:* NY Univ, BS, 48; Univ Md, MS, 51; Purdue Univ, PhD(biochem), 54. *Prof Exp:* Res assoc, Med Col, Cornell Univ, 54-56, res assoc, Rockefeller Inst, 56-59; assoc cancer res scientist, 59-77, CANCER RES SCIENTIST, ROSWELL PARK MEM INST, 77- ASSOC PROF BIOCHEM, STATE UNIV NY BUFFALO, 68- *Concurrent Pos:* Asst res prof, State Univ NY Buffalo, 63-68; res prof, Niagara Univ, 71- *Mem:* Am Soc Pharmacol & Exp Therapeut; Soc Exp Biol & Med; Am Soc Biol Chemists; Am Inst Nutrit; Am Asn Cancer Res. *Res:* Cancer chemotherapy; control of enzyme activity; role of purine metabolism in the control of the immune response. *Mailing Add:* Roswell Park Mem Inst 666 Elm St Buffalo NY 14206

TRITSCHLER, LOUIS GEORGE, b St Louis, Mo, Jan 24, 27; m 47; c 2. VETERINARY MEDICINE, VETERINARY SURGERY. *Educ:* Univ Mo, BSAgr, 49, DVM, 60, MS, 62. *Prof Exp:* From instr to asst prof, 60-72, assoc prof, 72-77, PROF VET MED & SURG, UNIV MO-COLUMBIA, 77-, DIR, EQUINE CTR, 79- *Mem:* Am Vet Med Asn; Am Asn Equine Practrs; Am Asn Vet Clinicians. *Res:* Use of estrone in the treatment of anestrus in cattle; evaluation of bulls for breeding soundness; wound treatment and fracture repair in equine. *Mailing Add:* Vet Hosp & Clin Univ of Mo-Columbia Columbia MO 65201

TRITTON, THOMAS RICHARD, b Lakewood, Ohio, Dec 20, 47; m 77; c 1. BIOPHYSICAL CHEMISTRY, MOLECULAR PHARMACOLOGY. *Educ:* Ohio Wesleyan Univ, BA, 69; Boston Univ, PhD(chem), 73. *Prof Exp:* Fel biophys chem, 73-75, asst prof, 75-80, ASSOC PROF PHARMACOL, SCH MED, YALE UNIV, 80- *Concurrent Pos:* NIH fel, Yale Univ, 74-75; NIH res career develop award, 80. *Mem:* Am Chem Soc; Sigma Xi; Am Soc Biol Chemists. *Res:* Biophysical approaches to macromolecular interactions; the role of the ribosome as a receptor for drug action; membrane dynamics and the cell surface as a target for antineoplastic agents. *Mailing Add:* Dept Pharmacol 333 Cedar St New Haven CT 06510

TRITZ, GERALD JOSEPH, b Sioux City, Iowa, Apr 12, 37; m 66; c 2. MICROBIOLOGY, GENETICS. *Educ:* Utah State Univ, BS, 62; Colo State Univ, MS, 65; Univ Tex Med Sch Houston, PhD(biomed res), 70. *Prof Exp:* Res microbiologist, USPHS, 65-67; NIH fel microbiol, Univ Tex MD Anderson Hosp & Tumor Inst, Houston, 70; asst prof microbiol, Univ Ga, 70-76; assoc prof & chmn dept, 76-81, PROF MICROBIOL & IMMUNOL, KIRKSVILLE COL OSTEOP MED, 81- *Concurrent Pos:* NSF grant, 71- *Mem:* Am Soc Microbiol. *Res:* Pyridine nucleotide metabolism and its control. *Mailing Add:* Dept of Microbiol & Immunol Kirksville Col of Osteop Med Kirksville MO 63501

TRIVEDI, KISHOR SHRIDHARBHAI, b Bhavnagar, India, Aug 20, 46; m 73; c 2. COMPUTER SCIENCES. *Educ:* Indian Inst Technol, Bombay, BTech, 68; Univ Ill, Urbana-Champaign, MS, 72, PhD(comput sci), 74. *Prof Exp:* Assoc customer engr, Int Bus Mach World Trade Corp, Bombay, 68-70; res asst comput sci, Univ Ill, Urbana-Champaign, 70-74, res assoc, 74-75; asst prof, 75-79, ASSOC PROF COMPUT SCI, DUKE UNIV, 79- *Concurrent Pos:* Consult, various Res Inst & Indust Labs, 79-; nat lectr, 81-82. *Mem:* Comput Soc India; Am Asn Comput Mach; Inst Elec & Electronics Engrs Comput Soc. *Res:* Algorithms for construction and performance evaluation of computer operating systems; different methods of computer system organization and techniques to exploit the systems; new organizations of arithmetic units. *Mailing Add:* Dept of Comput Sci Duke Univ Durham NC 27706

TRIVEDI, ROHIT K, b Bhavnagar, India, Mar 8, 39. METALLURGY, MATERIALS SCIENCE. *Educ:* Indian Inst Technol, Kharagpur, BS, 60; Carnegie Inst Technol, MS, 64, PhD(metall, mat sci), 66. *Prof Exp:* Res scientist, Sci Lab, Ford Motor Co, 63-64; res assoc metall, Inst Atomic Res, 65-66, assoc metallurgist, 67-70; from asst prof to assoc prof metall, 67-76, PROF MAT SCI & ENG, IOWA STATE UNIV, 76-; METALLURGIST, AMES LAB, US ATOMIC ENERGY COMN, 70- *Concurrent Pos:* Vis assoc prof, Stanford Univ, 69-70. *Mem:* Am Soc Metals; Am Inst Mining, Metall & Petrol Engrs. *Res:* Structure, energetics and kinetics of surfaces and interfaces; stability of interphase boundaries. *Mailing Add:* Dept of Metall Iowa State Univ Ames IA 50011

TRIVELPIECE, ALVIN WILLIAM, b Stockton, Calif, Mar 15, 31; m 53; c 3. PLASMA PHYSICS. *Educ:* Calif Polytech State Col, BS, 53; Calif Inst Technol, MS, 55, PhD(elec eng), 58. *Prof Exp:* From asst prof to assoc prof elec eng, Univ Calif, Berkeley, 59-66; prof physics, Univ Md, College Park, 66-76; vpres eng & res, Maxwell Labs, San Diego, 76-78; corp vpres, Sci Applications Inc, La Jolla, Calif, 78-81; DIR, OFF ENERGY RES, US DEPT ENERGY, DC, 81- *Concurrent Pos:* Fulbright scholar, Delft Technol Univ, 58-59; consult to govt & indust, 61-; Guggenheim fel, 67-68; asst dir res, Div Controlled Thermonuclear Res, AEC, 73-75. *Mem:* Fel AAAS; Am Nuclear Soc; Sigma Xi; fel Am Phys Soc; fel Inst Elec & Electronics Engrs. *Res:* Plasma physics and controlled thermonuclear fusion research; particle accelerators; microwave devices; electromagnetic waves. *Mailing Add:* 3001 Veazey Terr Northwest #1410 Washington DC 20008

TRIVETT, TERRENCE LYNN, b Madison, Tenn, Oct 3, 40; m 65. BACTERIOLOGY. *Educ:* Southern Missionary Col, BS, 64; Univ Ore, PhD(microbiol), 69. *Prof Exp:* From asst prof to assoc prof, 69-77, PROF BIOL, PAC UNION COL, 77- *Mem:* Am Soc Microbiol; AAAS. *Res:* Carbohydrate metabolism of Listeria monocytogenes; pathogenesis of Neisseria meningitidis. *Mailing Add:* Dept of Biol Pac Union Col Angwin CA 94508

TRIVICH, DAN, b Jenkins, Ky, May 20, 16; m 43; c 3. PHYSICAL CHEMISTRY. *Educ:* Ohio State Univ, BA, 38, PhD(chem), 42. *Prof Exp:* Asst, Ohio State Univ, 38-42; res chemist, United Chromium, Inc, 42-48; from asst prof to assoc prof, 48-57, PROF CHEM, WAYNE STATE UNIV, 57- *Concurrent Pos:* Vis prof, Karlsruhe Tech Univ, 58-59; vis prof & Fulbright-Hays advan res scholar, Lab Physics, Ecole Normale Superieure, Paris, 65-66; vis prof & Fulbright lectr, Lab Physics Solids, Univ Paris, 72-73. *Mem:* Am Chem Soc; Int Solar Energy Soc; Electrochem Soc. *Res:* Chemistry of the solid state; chemical aspects of semiconductors; photovoltaic cells; solar energy conversion; electrochemistry. *Mailing Add:* Dept of Chem Wayne State Univ Detroit MI 48202

TRIVISONNO, CHARLES F(RANCIS), b Cleveland, Ohio, Dec 30, 24; m 58; c 3. ANALYTICAL CHEMISTRY, ORGANIC CHEMISTRY. *Educ:* Case Inst Technol, BS, 45, MS, 49. *Prof Exp:* Squad trainee, Goodyear Tire & Rubber Co, 48, res chemist, 48-53, group leader uranium chem, Goodyear Atomic Corp, 53-65, supvr chem anal, 65-70, supvr, Chem Dept, 70-73, SUPVR, CHEM ANAL DEPT, GOODYEAR ATOMIC CORP, 73- *Mem:* Am Chem Soc; Sigma Xi. *Res:* Preparation characterization and study of physical properties of condensation polymers; chemical development and chemical analyses, uranium, trace constituents, environmental, and industrial hygiene, related to operation of uranium isotope enrichment plant. *Mailing Add:* Chem Anal Dept PO Box 628 Piketon OH 45661

TRIVISONNO, JOSEPH, JR, b Cleveland, Ohio, Feb 28, 33; m 57; c 4. SOLID STATE PHYSICS. *Educ:* John Carroll Univ, BS, 55, MS, 56; Case Western Reserve Univ, PhD(physics), 61. *Prof Exp:* Instr physics & math, John Carroll Univ, 55-58 & physics, Case Western Reserve Univ, 58-61; asst prof, 61-62, from asst prof to assoc prof, 63-69, PROF PHYSICS, JOHN CARROLL UNIV, 69-, CHMN DEPT, 79- *Concurrent Pos:* Vis prof, Univ Ariz, 74. *Mem:* Am Asn Physics Teachers; Am Phys Soc. *Res:* Elastic constants of metals; magnetoacoustic studies; ultrasonics; low temperature physics; superconductivity. *Mailing Add:* Dept of Physics John Carroll Univ Cleveland OH 44118

TRIX, PHELPS, b Detroit, Mich, Apr 29, 21; m 46; c 3. ORGANIC CHEMISTRY, WASTE DISPOSAL. *Educ:* Olivet Col, BS, 43; Ind Univ, MA, 44; Pa State Col, PhD(chem), 49. *Prof Exp:* Jr res chemist, Parke, Davis & Co, 44-46; sect head org lab, Wyandotte Chem Corp, 49-53, mgr mkt develop, 53-59, dir prod develop, 59-69; assoc prof chem, 69-74, vpres acad affairs, 71-74, PROF CHEM, DETROIT INST TECHNOL, 74- *Mem:* Am Chem Soc; Am Inst Chemists; AAAS. *Res:* Polyurethanes; nutritional biochemistry. *Mailing Add:* Dept of Chem Detroit Inst of Technol Detroit MI 48201

TRIZNA, DENNIS BENEDICT, b Joilet, Ill, Oct 25, 41; m 63; c 3. RADAR, PHYSICS. *Educ:* Ill Benedictine Col, BS, 63; Iowa State Univ, MS, 66, PhD(physics), 70. *Prof Exp:* RES PHYSICIST RADAR, NAVAL RES LAB, 70- *Honors & Awards:* Res Publication Award, Naval Res Lab, 72 & 77. *Mem:* Am Phys Soc; Inst Elec & Electronic Engrs; Am Geophys Union; Int Union Radio Scientists. *Res:* Remote sensing of geophysical phenomena with radar; remote sensing of ocean waves using high frequency radar; air-sea interaction and the marine boundary layer; general wave propagation. *Mailing Add:* US Naval Res Lab Code 5325 4555 Overlook Ave Washington DC 20375

TRKULA, DAVID, b Patton Twp, Pa, Aug 19, 27; m 54; c 3. BIOPHYSICS, VIROLOGY. *Educ:* Univ Pittsburgh, BS, 49, MS, 55, PhD(biophys), 59. *Prof Exp:* Instr physics, Johnstown Col, Univ Pittsburgh, 57-59; asst biophysicist, M D Anderson Hosp & Tumor Inst, 59-61; physicist, US Army Biol Labs, Ft Detrick, 61-68; ASST PROF BIOPHYS, BAYLOR COL MED, 68- *Res:* Introduction of genes into mammalian cells and their identification; study of expression in transformed cells of nucleic acids and enzymes. *Mailing Add:* Div of Biochem Virol Baylor Col of Med Tex Med Ctr Houston TX 77030

TROBAUGH, FRANK EDWIN, JR, b West Frankfort, Ill, Oct 20, 20; m 51; c 4. MEDICINE. *Educ:* Univ Ill, AB, 40; Harvard Med Sch, MD, 43; Am Bd Internal Med, dipl, 55. *Prof Exp:* Asst physician, Barnes Hosp, St Louis, Mo, 52-54; DIR SECT HEMAT & ASSOC CHMN DEPT MED FOR LAB & RES, RUSH-PRESBY-ST LUKE'S MED CTR, 74- ATTEND PHYSICIAN, 60-, DIR, OFF CONSOL LAB SERV, 81-; PROF MED, RUSH COL MED, 71- *Concurrent Pos:* Assoc attend physician med, Presby-St Luke's Hosp, 59-60, dir blood bank, 54-69, consult, 69-; assoc prof, Univ Ill, 59-64, prof, 64-72. *Mem:* Fel Am Soc Hemat; fel Am Col Physicians; Am Fedn Clin Res; fel Int Soc Hemat; AMA. *Res:* Hematology. *Mailing Add:* Presby-St Luke's Hosp 1753 W Congress Pkwy Chicago IL 60612

TROEH, FREDERICK ROY, b Grangeville, Idaho, Jan 23, 30; m 51; c 3. SOIL SCIENCE. *Educ:* Univ Idaho, BSAgr, 51, MSAgr, 52; Cornell Univ, PhD(soil sci), 63. *Prof Exp:* Soil scientist, Soil Conserv Serv, 52-59; from asst prof to assoc prof, 63-76, PROF AGRON, IOWA STATE UNIV, 76- *Mem:* Am Soc Agron; Soil Sci Soc Am; Soil Conserv Soc Am. *Res:* Soil formation and classification; measuring the rate of soil creep; soil permeability relationships with microbial activity. *Mailing Add:* Dept of Agron Iowa State Univ Ames IA 50011

TROELSTRA, ARNE, b Zelhem, Neth, Mar 30, 35; m 59; c 1. PHYSICS, BIOENGINEERING. *Educ:* State Univ Utrecht, BS, 55, MS, 58, PhD(med physics), 64. *Prof Exp:* Res assoc vision res, Inst Perception, Nat Defense Res Orgn, Neth, 60-65; assoc prof bioeng, Univ Ill, Chicago, 65-69; assoc prof elec eng, Rice Univ, 69-76, prof, 76-80. *Concurrent Pos:* Assoc biomed eng, Presby-St Luke's Hosp, Chicago, 66-69; consult, Biosysts Div, Whittaker Corp, 66-69; lectr ophthalmol, Univ Tex Med Sch, Houston, 74- *Mem:* Inst Elec & Electronic Engrs. *Res:* Vision research; biological control systems; systems analysis of biological systems; electroretinography; biomedical instrumentation. *Mailing Add:* Rte 6 Box 45 Franklin NC 28734

TROEN, PHILIP, b Portland, Maine, Nov 24, 25; m 53; c 3. MEDICINE. *Educ:* Harvard Univ, AB, 44, MD, 48; Am Bd Internal Med, dipl. *Prof Exp:* Intern, Boston City Hosp, 48-49, asst resident med, 49-50; chief med serv, US Army Hosp, Kobe, Japan, 50-52; asst, Harvard Univ, 53-54, instr, 56-59, assoc, 59-60, asst prof, 60-64; assoc chmn dept, 69-79, PROF MED, SCH MED, UNIV PITTSBURGH, 64-, VCHMN DEPT, 79-; PHYSICIAN-IN-CHIEF, MONTEFIORE HOSP, 64- *Concurrent Pos:* Teaching fel, Harvard Univ, 52-53, res fel, 55-56; Ziskind teaching fel, Beth Israel Hosp, 55-60; fel endocrinol & metab, Mayo Clin, 54-55, Kendall-Hench res fel, 55; teaching fel med, Tufts Univ, 53-54; Guggenheim fel, Stockholm, Sweden, 60-61; asst resident, Beth Israel Hosp, 50 & 52-53, resident, 53-54, asst, 55-56, assoc, 56-64, asst vis physician, 59-64; sr instr, Tufts Univ, 57-60; mem, Contract Rev Comt, Nat Inst Child Health & Human Develop, Contraceptive Develop Br. *Mem:* Am Soc Clin Invest; Am Fedn Clin Res; Endocrine Soc; Am Soc Biol Chemists; Am Soc Andrology (vpres-pres, 79-81). *Res:* Endocrinology; internal medicine. *Mailing Add:* Montefiore Hosp 3459 Fifth Ave Pittsburgh PA 15213

TROESCH, BEAT ANDREAS, b Bern, Switz, Mar 2, 20; nat US; m 48; c 4. APPLIED MATHEMATICS. *Educ:* Swiss Fed Inst Technol, Zurich, dipl, 47, PhD(math), 52. *Prof Exp:* Asst mech & physics, Swiss Fed Inst Technol, Zurich, 47-52; res assoc appl math, Inst Math, NY Univ, 52-56; head appl math sect, Comput Ctr, Ramo-Wooldridge Corp, 56-58 & Space Tech Labs, 58-61; mgr comput sci dept, Aerospace Corp, 61-66; PROF AEROSPACE ENG & MATH, UNIV SOUTHERN CALIF, 66- *Concurrent Pos:* Consult, Aerospace Corp, 66- *Mem:* Math Asn Am; Soc Indust & Appl Math; Am Math Soc; Sigma Xi. *Res:* Applied mathematics and numerical analysis in hydrodynamics and gas dynamics; elliptic and hyperbolic partial differential equations. *Mailing Add:* 523 N Elm Dr Beverly Hills CA 90210

TROFIMENKO, SWIATOSLAW, organic chemistry, see previous edition

TROFIMENKOFF, FREDERICK N(ICHOLAS), b Veregin, Sask, Aug 10, 34; m 57; c 3. ELECTRICAL ENGINEERING, PHYSICS. *Educ:* Univ Sask, BSc, 57, MSc, 59; Univ London, PhD(elec eng) & DIC, 62. *Prof Exp:* Jr res off, Div Bldg Res, Nat Res Coun Can, 57-59; asst prof elec eng, Univ Sask, 62-66; assoc prof, 66-68, head dept, 68-78, PROF ELEC ENG, UNIV CALGARY, 68- *Honors & Awards:* Publ Award, Brit Inst Elec Engrs, 66. *Mem:* Inst Elec & Electronics Engrs; Can Asn Physicists; Am Soc Eng Educ; Eng Inst Can. *Res:* Electronics and instrumentation. *Mailing Add:* 20 Varcourt Pl NW Calgary AB T3A 0G8 Can

TROGDON, WILLIAM OREN, b Anadarko, Okla, Nov 1, 20; m 42; c 2. SOILS. *Educ:* Okla State Univ, BS, 42; Ohio State Univ, PhD(soil fertility), 49. *Prof Exp:* Asst agronomist, Agr Exp Sta, Univ Tex, 48; soil scientist, Res Div, Soil Conserv Serv, USDA, 49; chmn dept agr & dir soils lab, Midwestern Univ, 49-53; agronomist, Olin Mathieson Chem Corp, 53-58; prof agron & head dept, Tex A&M Univ, 58-63; exec vpres, Best Fertilizers Co, Tex, 63-65; dir agron & mkt develop, Occidental Agr Chem Corp, 65-66; PRES, TARLETON STATE UNIV, 66- *Mem:* Am Soc Agron; Crop Sci Soc Am; Soil Sci Soc Am; Am Chem Soc; Soil Conserv Soc Am. *Res:* Soil fertility and management, especially fertilizer usage; fertilizer technology; salinity control and water quality; polyphosphate fertilizers; academic administration. *Mailing Add:* Off of Pres Tarleton State Univ Stephenville TX 76402

TROIANO, A(LEXANDER) R(OBERT), b Boston, Mass, Sept 5, 08; m 38; c 2. PHYSICAL METALLURGY. *Educ:* Harvard Univ, AB, 31, ScD(metall), 39; Mass Inst Technol, MS, 37. *Prof Exp:* Instr physics, Middlesex Col, 31-35; asst instr phys metall, Harvard Univ, 37-39; from assoc prof to prof, Univ Notre Dame, 39-49; assoc prof, 49-53, prof & head dept, 53-67, repub steel distinguished prof phys metall, 67-78, SR RES SCIENTIST, CASE WESTERN RESERVE UNIV, 78- *Concurrent Pos:* Keynote lectr, Brit Iron & Steel Res Inst, Harrogate, Eng, 62 & Int Conf Heat Treatment, Bremen, Ger, 66; distinguished vis prof, NY Univ, 65-66; keynote lectr, Int Conf Hydrogen in Metals, Paris, France, 72. *Honors & Awards:* Hunt Award, Am Inst Mining, Metall & Petrol Engrs, 40; Howe Medal, Am Soc Metals, 57, Sauveur Achievement Medal, 68; Le Chatlier Gold Medal, 80. *Mem:* Am Soc Metals; Am Soc Testing & Mat; Am Foundrymen's Soc; Am Inst Mining, Metall & Petrol Engrs. *Res:* Heat treatment of steels; phase transformations in solid state; gases in metals; stress corrosion; materials for geothermal energy. *Mailing Add:* Dept Metall Case Western Reserve Univ Cleveland OH 44106

TROITSKY, MICHAEL S(ERGE), b St Petersburgh, Russia, Sept 20, 17; Can citizen; m 52; c 1. CIVIL ENGINEERING. *Educ:* Univ Belgrade, Dipl eng, 40, DSc(struct eng), 43. *Prof Exp:* Asst prof civil eng, Univ Belgrade, 43-47; proj br engr, Ministry Transp, Belg, 48-50; bridge engr & group leader, Found Co, Can, 51-62; vis asst prof & Ford Found grant, Univ Calif, Los Angeles, 62-63; asst prof civil eng & appl mech, McGill Univ, 64-68; assoc prof, 68-77, PROF ENG, SIR GEORGE WILLIAMS CAMPUS, CONCORDIA UNIV, 77- *Concurrent Pos:* Prof, Univ Montreal, 60-62. *Mem:* Am Soc Civil Engrs; Int Asn Bridge & Struct Engrs; Eng Inst Can; Am Soc Eng Educ. *Res:* Structures; bridges; stiffness of plates and shells; applied elasticity; structural dynamics. *Mailing Add:* Sir George Williams Campus 1455 de Maisonneuve Montreal PQ H3G 1M8 Can

TROJAN, PAUL K, b Chicago, Ill, Sept 8, 31; m 53; c 3. METALLURGICAL ENGINEERING. *Educ:* Univ Mich, BS, 55, MS, 56, PhD(metall eng), 61. *Prof Exp:* Engr-trainee, Engine & Foundry Div, Ford Motor Co, 52-53; instr metall eng, Univ Mich, 58-61, from asst prof to assoc prof, 61-70, chmn, Div Eng, 62-64, PROF METALL ENG, UNIV MICH-DEARBORN, 70-, ACTG DEAN, SCH ENG, 80- *Concurrent Pos:* Mich Mem Phoenix res grant, 64-67. *Honors & Awards:* Howe Medal, Am Soc Metals, 63; Thomas Pangborn Gold Medal, Am Foundrymen's Soc, 78. *Mem:* Am Foundrymen's Soc; Am Soc Metals; Am Soc Eng Educ. *Res:* Cast metals; liquid metal processing solidification; relationship of processing and service performance; structure of engineering materials. *Mailing Add:* Eng Sch Admin Univ Mich 4901 Evergreen Dearborn MI 48128

TROLAN, J KENNETH, b Madras, Ore, Jan 17, 17; m 41, 66; c 5. SURFACE PHYSICS. *Educ:* Linfield Col, BA, 39; Ore State Univ, MA, 48, PhD(physics), 50. *Prof Exp:* Instr physics, Univ Alaska, 41-42; mem staff, Radiation Lab, Mass Inst Technol, 42-45; instr & res asst, Ore State Univ, 45-48; from asst to assoc prof, Linfield Col, 48-57, asst dir res, Res Inst, 51-62; asst dir res & develop physics & eng, Field Emission Corp, 62-64; PROF PHYSICS, UNIV REDLANDS, 64- *Concurrent Pos:* Consult, NSF-AID Sci Educ Improv Prog, India, 66. *Mem:* Am Phys Soc; Am Asn Physics Teachers. *Res:* Basic field emission research and use of the pulsed field emission microscope to observe surface migration and dislocation in metals. *Mailing Add:* Dept of Physics Univ of Redlands Redlands CA 92373

TROLL, JOSEPH, b Paterson, NJ, May 5, 20; m 43; c 2. SOIL SCIENCE, AGROSTOLOGY. *Educ:* Univ RI, BS, 54, MS, 57; Univ Mass, PhD(nematol), 65. *Prof Exp:* Asst, Univ RI, 54-57; asst prof agron, 57-65, assoc prof plant & soil sci, 65-71, PROF PLANT & SOIL SCI, UNIV MASS, AMHERST, 71- *Res:* Turf management; plant pathology and nematology. *Mailing Add:* Dept of Plant & Soil Sci Univ of Mass Amherst MA 01003

TROLL, RALPH, b Reinheim, Ger, Oct 8, 32; US citizen; m 58; c 3. ZOOLOGY, BOTANY. *Educ:* Univ Ill, BS, 57, MS, 58; Univ Minn, PhD(parasitol), 65. *Prof Exp:* From instr to assoc prof, 59-72, chmn dept, 68-77, PROF BIOL, AUGUSTANA COL, ILL, 72- *Mem:* Am Inst Biol Sci; Hist Sci Soc; Soc Study Evolution; Am Soc Naturalists. *Res:* Ecology of myxomycetes; abnormal development in vertebrates; Johann Wolfgang Von Goethe's contribution to science. *Mailing Add:* Dept Biol Augustana Col Rock Island IL 61201

TROLL, WALTER, b Vienna, Austria, Oct 25, 22; nat US; m 44; c 2. BIOCHEMISTRY, ORGANIC CHEMISTRY. *Educ:* Univ Ill, BS, 44; Pa State Univ, MS, 46; NY Univ, PhD(biochem), 51. *Prof Exp:* Instr biochem, Univ Cincinnati, 51-52, asst prof, 52-54; assoc, Cancer Res Inst, New Eng Deaconess Hosp, 54-56; from asst prof to prof indust med, 56-76, PROF ENVIRON MED, SCH MED, NY UNIV, 76- *Concurrent Pos:* Asst dir, May Inst Med Res, Cincinnati, Ohio, 51-54. *Mem:* Am Soc Biol Chem; Am Chem Soc; NY Acad Sci. *Res:* Assay of amino acids; synthetic substrates for enzymes involved in blood clotting; metabolism of aromatic amines and its relation to carcinogenesis; role of free oxygen radicals in tumor promotion. *Mailing Add:* Dept Environ Med NY Univ Sch Med New York NY 10016

TROLLER, JOHN ARTHUR, b Hartford, Wis, Apr 17, 33; m 56; c 4. MICROBIOLOGY. *Educ:* Univ Wis, BS, 55, MS, 56, PhD(bact), 62. *Prof Exp:* GROUP LEADER MICROBIOL, WINTON HILL TECH CTR, PROCTER & GAMBLE CO, 62-, SR RES SCIENTIST, 78- *Mem:* AAAS; Am Soc Microbiol; Inst Food Technologists; Soc Indust Microbiol; Brit Soc Appl Bact. *Res:* Food technology and microbiology; water relations of microorganisms; mechanism of action of food preservatives; staphylococcal food poisoning and other food-borne diseases; food hygiene and snitation. *Mailing Add:* Procter & Gamble Co Winton Hill Tech Ctr Cincinnati OH 45224

TROMANS, D(ESMOND), b Birmingham, Eng, Mar 7, 38; m 61; c 2. PHYSICAL METALLURGY. *Educ:* Leeds Univ, BSc, 60, PhD(metall), 63. *Prof Exp:* Res assoc, 63-66, asst prof, 66-71, ASSOC PROF METALL ENG, UNIV BC, 71- *Concurrent Pos:* Sr indust fel, Nat Res Coun, MacMillan Bloedel Res Ltd, Vancouver, 76. *Honors & Awards:* Campbell Award, Nat Asn Corrosion Engrs, 65. *Mem:* Am Soc Metals; Nat Asn Corrosion Engrs; Brit Inst Metals; Electrochem Soc. *Res:* Stress corrosion; fracture of metals; electron diffraction and microscopy; corrosion. *Mailing Add:* 8585 145 A St Surrey BC V3S 2Z3 Can

TROMBA, ANTHONY JOSEPH, b Brooklyn, NY, Aug 10, 43. PURE MATHEMATICS. *Educ:* Cornell Univ, BA, 65; Princeton Univ, MA, 67, PhD(math), 68. *Prof Exp:* Asst prof math, Stanford Univ, 68-69; vis prof, Univ Pisa, Italy, 70; assoc prof, 70-77, PROF MATH, UNIV CALIF, SANTA CRUZ, 77- *Concurrent Pos:* Woodrow Wilson & NSF fels; vis prof, Univ Calif, Stony Brook, 74; mem, Inst Advan Study, 75. *Res:* Topological methods in non-linear analysis. *Mailing Add:* Dept of Math Univ of Calif Santa Cruz CA 95064

TROMBA, FRANCIS GABRIEL, b New York, NY, Oct 19, 20; m 43; c 4. PARASITOLOGY. *Educ:* Univ Md, PhD(zool), 53. *Prof Exp:* Parasitologist, USDA, Md, 53-55, parasitologist in-chg field sta, Ga, 55-56, actg proj leader helminths & dis swine, 56-58, proj leader, 58-61, prin res parasitologist & proj leader immunol res, Animal Dis & Parasite Res Div, 61-71, leader anti-parasitic invests, Nat Animal Parasite Lab, 71-72, chief, Nonruminant Helminthic Dis Lab, 72-78, ZOOLOGIST, NONRUMINANT PARASITE DIS LAB, ANIMAL PARASITOL INST, 78- *Concurrent Pos:* Ed, Proceedings, Helminth Soc Wash, 66-71. *Mem:* Am Soc Parasitol. *Res:* Life histories, morphology, and host-parasite relationships of parasitic helminths; diagnosis, pathology, immunology, and biological control of helminthic diseases. *Mailing Add:* Animal Parasitol Inst Agr Res Ctr Beltsville MD 20705

TROMBETTA, LOUIS DAVID, b New York, NY, Sept 8, 46; m 73. CELL BIOLOGY, PATHOLOGY. *Educ:* Fordham Univ, BS, 68, MS, 69, PhD(biol), 74. *Prof Exp:* Res assoc path, Issac Albert Res Inst, 73-80; ASST PROF, ST JOHN 'S UNIV, 80- *Concurrent Pos:* Adj res assoc path, Kingsbrook Jewish Med Ctr. *Mem:* NY Acad Sci; Electron Micros Soc Am; Sigma Xi. *Res:* Insect development and endocrinology by electron microscopy and histochemistry, cell pathology, neuropathology and histogenesis. *Mailing Add:* 471 Wolf's Lane Pelham Manor NY 10803

TROMBKA, JACOB ISRAEL, b Detroit, Mich, Jan 7, 30; m 52; c 3. RADIATION PHYSICS, SPACE PHYSICS. *Educ:* Wayne State Univ, BS, 52, MS, 54; Univ Mich, PhD(nuclear sci), 62. *Prof Exp:* Res physicist, Oak Ridge Inst Nuclear Studies, 54-56; res assoc nuclear eng & fel gamma ray spectros, Univ Mich, 56-62; sr scientist, Jet Propulsion Lab, Calif Inst Technol, 62-64; prog scientist, Hq, NASA, 64-65, STAFF SCIENTIST, GODDARD SPACE FLIGHT CTR, NASA, 65- *Concurrent Pos:* Mem panel in-flight exp, NASA, 63-66, mem working group, Manned Space Flight Exp Bd, 64-66, secy & mem, Geochem Working Group Planetology Subcomt, 65, mem, Terrestrial Bodies Sci Working Group, 77-; adj prof, Law Sch, Georgetown Univ, 67-; co-investr, Apollo 15 & 16 x-ray, gamma ray & alpha particle spectrometer exp, 68-; mem Apollo sci working panel, 71-; prin investr, Apollo 17 & Apollo-Soyuz Crystal Activation Exp, 71 & 75-; vis prof, Dept Chem, Univ Md, 76- *Honors & Awards:* John Lindsay Mem Award, Goddard Space Flight Ctr, 72. *Mem:* Am Phys Soc; Am Nuclear Soc; Sigma Xi; NY Acad Sci. *Res:* Gamma ray spectroscopy; techniques in activation analysis, dosimetry and tracer techniques; planetary physics; gamma ray astrophysics; gamma-ray, x-ray and neutron-gamma ray in situ and remote sensing methods; gamma and x-ray imaging. *Mailing Add:* Goddard Space Flight Ctr NASA Greenbelt MD 20770

TROMBLE, JOHN M, b Lincoln, Kans, Jan 26, 32; m 52; c 2. HYDROLOGY, SOIL SCIENCE. *Educ:* Utah State Univ, BS, 61; Univ Ariz, MS, 64, PhD(watershed hydrol), 73. *Prof Exp:* Res assoc watershed hydrol, Univ Ariz, 64-67; asst dir, Southwest Watershed Res Ctr, 67-74, RES HYDROLOGIST, JORNADA EXP RANGE, AGR RES SERV, USDA, 74- *Mem:* Crop Sci Soc Am; Soc Range Mgt; Am Soc Agron; Soil Sci Soc Am; Int Soil Sci Soc. *Res:* Watershed hydrological studies; runoff, erosion, infiltration, simultaneous transfer of heat and water in soils; evaluation of consumptive use of water by native vegetation. *Mailing Add:* Jornada Exp Range PO Box 698 Las Cruces NM 88004

TROMMEL, JAN, b Rotterdam, Netherlands, July 16, 26; m 54; c 2. PHYSICAL CHEMISTRY. *Educ:* Univ Utrecht, BSc, 47, MA, 51, PhD(phys chem), 54. *Prof Exp:* Mgr res, Royal Dutch Explosive Co, Amsterdam, 54-64, vpres res, 64-67; MGR MAT CHARACTERIZATION, XEROX CORP, 67- *Concurrent Pos:* Mem, Adv Group Rockets, Dutch Govt, 57-67; Netherlands govt rep, AC 60 Group Experts Explosives & Propellants, NATO, 63-67. *Mem:* Am Chem Soc; NY Acad Sci; Royal Netherlands Chem Soc. *Res:* X-ray diffraction; scanning and transmission electron microscopy; electron microprobe; propellants; explosives; rocket propellants; secondary ion mass spectroscopy; image processing. *Mailing Add:* 3333 Elmwood Ave Rochester NY 14610

TROMMERSHAUSEN-SMITH, ANN T, see Bowling, Ann T

TROPF, CHERYL GRIFFITHS, b Newark, NJ, Oct 15, 46; m 68; c 1. APPLIED MATHEMATICS. *Educ:* Col William & Mary, BS, 68; Univ Va, MAM, 72, PhD(appl math), 73. *Prof Exp:* Sr mathematician, Appl Physics Lab, Johns Hopkins Univ, 73-80; cong sci fel, US Senate Subcomt Sci, Technol & Space, 80-81; PROJ MGR OPERATING REACTORS, US NUCLEAR REGULATORY COMN, 81- *Concurrent Pos:* Instr, Johns Hopkins Evening Col, 74- *Mem:* Soc Indust & Appl Math. *Res:* Application of analytical mathematical techniques to the modelling of physical systems; scientific/technological management and policy. *Mailing Add:* 13060 St Patricks Ct Highland MD 20777

TROPF, WILLIAM JACOB, b Chicago, Ill, Jan 14, 47; m 68. OPTICS, MILITARY SYSTEMS. *Educ:* Col William & Mary, BS, 68; Univ Va, PhD(physics), 73. *Prof Exp:* Proj dir, B-K Dynamics, Inc, Rockville, 73-76; PRIN PHYSICIST, ASST SUPVR, DYNAMICS ANAL GROUP, APPL PHYSICS LAB, JOHNS HOPKINS UNIV, LAUREL, 77- *Mem:* Am Phys Soc; Optical Soc Am; Sigma Xi. *Res:* Analysis and modelling of missile guidance and control systems; determination of guidance and control requirements for advance weapon systems. *Mailing Add:* 13060 St Patricks Ct Highland MD 20777

TROPP, BURTON E, b New York, NY, Aug 8, 40; m 65; c 3. BIOCHEMISTRY. *Educ:* Brooklyn Col, BS, 61; Harvard Univ, PhD(biochem), 66. *Prof Exp:* NIH fel bacteriol, Harvard Med Sch, 65-67; asst prof biochem, Richmond Col, NY, 67-70; from asst prof to assoc prof, 70-76, PROF BIOCHEM, QUEEN'S COL, CITY UNIV NEW YORK, 76- *Concurrent Pos:* Vis scientist, Weizmann Inst, 78-79. *Mem:* AAAS; Am Chem Soc; NY Acad Sci; Am Soc Microbiol; Am Soc Biol Chemists. *Res:* Effect of drugs upon lipid metabolism. *Mailing Add:* Dept of Chem Queen's Col Flushing NY 11367

TROPP, HENRY S, b Chicago, Ill, July 15, 27; m 54; c 3. MATHEMATICS. *Educ:* Purdue Univ, BS, 49; Ind Univ, MS, 53. *Prof Exp:* Instr math, Mont Sch Mines, 55-57; from asst prof to assoc prof, Humboldt State Col, 57-72; prin investr, Comput Hist Proj, Smithsonian Inst, 71-74; PROF MATH, HUMBOLDT STATE UNIV, 74- *Concurrent Pos:* Vis lectr, Asn Comput Mach, 73-; mem, Prog Comt, Int Res Conf Hist Comput. *Mem:* Math Asn Am; Hist Sci Soc; Can Soc Hist & Philos Math; Asn Comput Mach. *Res:* History of mathematics; history of computers. *Mailing Add:* Dept of Math Humboldt State Univ Arcata CA 95521

TROREY, A(LAN) W(ILSON), b London, Eng, May 8, 26; m 50; c 2. ENGINEERING, PHYSICS. *Educ:* Univ BC, BASc, 49; Stanford Univ, MS, 51, PhD(electronic eng), 54. *Prof Exp:* SR RES ASSOC, CHEVRON OIL FIELD RES CO, STANDARD OIL CO CALIF, 54- *Concurrent Pos:* Founding ed, Trans Geosci Electronics, Inst Elec & Electronics Engrs, 65-67; designed & installed seismic data process syst, Standard Oil Co, Calif, 67. *Mem:* Soc Explor Geophys. *Res:* Exploration seismology; elastic wave propagation; classical physics; mathematics of linear systems; digital computer systems. *Mailing Add:* Chevron Oil Field Res Co Box 446 La Habra CA 90631

TROSCINSKI, EDWIN S, b Chicago, Ill, May 8, 28; m 52; c 7. CHEMICAL ENGINEERING. *Educ:* Univ Ill, BS, 51. *Prof Exp:* Chem engr, Gen Labs, US Rubber Co, 51-53; process engr, Corn Prods Refining Co, 53-56; res engr, Standard Oil Co, Inc, 56-57, proj engr, 57-59, proj supvr, 59-62; sr res chemist, 62-67, group leader, 67-69, tech dir, 69-72, mgr mkt & res, 72-74, mgr corp mkt servs, 74-76, mgr admin & planning servs, 76-81, PROJ MGR SNYFUELS, NALCO CHEM CO, 81- *Mem:* Am Inst Chem Engrs; Nat Asn Corrosion Engrs; Soc Petrol Engrs. *Res:* Corrosion phenomena with respect to metal and alloys and of special environments; water technology, particularly stabilization and corrosion phenomena; oil field emulsion breaking. *Mailing Add:* Nalco Chem Co 2901 Butterfield Rd Oak Brook IL 60521

TROSKO, JAMES EDWARD, b Muskegon, Mich, Apr 2, 38; m 60; c 1. GENETICS, ONCOLOGY. *Educ:* Cent Mich Univ, BA, 60; Mich State Univ, MS, 62, PhD(radiation genetics), 63. *Prof Exp:* Fel, Oak Ridge Nat Lab, 63-64, Am Cancer Soc fel, 64-65; res scientist radiation biophys, Biol Div, Oak Ridge Nat Lab, 65-66; asst prof sci & philos, Dept Natural Sci, 66-70, assoc prof carcinogenesis & med ethics, 70-77, PROF CARCINOGENESIS & MED ETHICS, DEPT HUMAN DEVELOP, MICH STATE UNIV, 77- *Concurrent Pos:* Nat Cancer Inst career develop award, 72; consult, Oak Ridge Nat Lab, 70-72; vis prof oncol, McArdle Lab Cancer Res, Univ Wis-Madison, 72-73; consult, Wis Res & Develop Ctr Cognitive Learning, 73-74; mem biol comt, Argonne Nat Lab, 76-79. *Honors & Awards:* Searle Award, UK Environ Mutagen Soc Award, 79. *Mem:* AAAS; Genetics Soc Am; Am Asn Cancer Res; Tissue Cult Asn; Soc Toxicol. *Res:* Molecular basis for genetic and environmental influences on carcinogenesis and aging; integration of science and human values. *Mailing Add:* Dept Human Develop Col Human Med Mich State Univ East Lansing MI 48824

TROSMAN, HARRY, b Toronto, Ont, Dec 9, 24; nat US; m 52; c 3. PSYCHIATRY, PSYCHOANALYSIS. *Educ:* Univ Toronto, MD, 48. *Prof Exp:* Intern, Grace Hosp, Detroit, Mich, 48-49; resident, Psychopath Hosp, Iowa City, Iowa, 49-51; resident, Cincinnati Gen Hosp, Ohio, 51-52; from asst prof to assoc prof, 54-74, PROF PSYCHIAT, PRITZKER SCH MED, UNIV CHICAGO, 75- *Concurrent Pos:* Psychoanal training, Chicago Inst Psychoanal, 54-62, fac mem, 65-, training & supv analyst, 74-; consult, Chicago Police Dept, 61-, Ill State Psychiat Inst, 60- *Honors & Awards:* Franz Alexander Prize, Chicago Inst Psychoanal, 65. *Mem:* Am Psychiat Asn; Int Psychoanal Asn; fel Am Col Psychoanalysts; Am Psychoanal Asn. *Res:* Psychoanalysis and the arts; applied psychoanalysis; creativity. *Mailing Add:* Dept of Psychiat Univ of Chicago Sch of Med Chicago IL 60637

TROSPER, JAMES HAMILTON, b Indianapolis, Ind, May 26, 44; m 68. MEDICAL ENTOMOLOGY. *Educ:* Ind Univ, AB, 67; Univ Ga, MS, 71, PhD(entom), 74. *Prof Exp:* Entomologist, Dis Vector Ecol Control Ctr, US Navy, 74-76; entomologist, US Naval Med Res Unit 2, 76-79; MEM STAFF, DEFENSE POST MGT INFO ANAL CTR, 81- *Mem:* Entom Soc Am; Sigma Xi. *Res:* Factors which control susceptibility of mosquitoes to malaria parasites; isolation of arboviruses and determination of their primary vectors; control of medically important insects. *Mailing Add:* 220 Delbrick Lane Indianapolis IN 46229

TROSPER, TERRY LOUISE, biophysics, see previous edition

TROSS, CARL HENRY, physics, mathematics, see previous edition

TROSS, RALPH G, b Bad Kreuznach, Ger, Jan 17, 23; US citizen; m 47; c 2. MATHEMATICAL PHYSICS. *Educ:* Sophia Univ, Japan, BS, 52; Mo Sch Mines, BS, 59; Univ Mo-Rolla, MS, 66, PhD(physics), 68. *Prof Exp:* NASA fel physics, Univ Mo-Rolla, 64-67, instr math, 67-68, res assoc physics, 68; asst prof, 68-69, actg chmn dept math, 70-71, chmn comput comt, 71-75, ASSOC PROF MATH, UNIV OTTAWA, 69-, DIR CONTINUING EDUC, 78- *Concurrent Pos:* Nat Res Coun grant, 68-; mem adv comt, Algonquin Col, Ottawa, 71-75 & Univ Ottawa, St Lawrence, 78-81; educ develop grant, Comt Ont Univs, 74; chmn, Comn Continuing Educ, Univ Ottawa. *Mem:* Am Phys Soc; Can Asn Physicists; Am Math Soc; Soc Indust & Appl Math; Sigma Xi. *Res:* Statistical mechanics; Ising model; cooperative phenomena. *Mailing Add:* Dept Math & Continuing Educ Serv Univ Ottawa Ottawa ON K1N 6N5 Can

TROST, BARRY M, b Philadelphia, Pa, June 13, 41. ORGANIC CHEMISTRY. *Educ:* Univ Pa, BA, 62; Mass Inst Technol, PhD(org chem), 65. *Prof Exp:* From asst prof to prof, 65-76, HELFAER PROF CHEM, UNIV WIS-MADISON, 76-, CHMN, DEPT CHEM, 80- *Concurrent Pos:* Assoc ed, J Am Chem Soc & adv, NSF Chem Sect, 73-; Sloan fel; Dreyfuss Found teacher-scholar grant; consult, E I du Pont de Nemours & Co; Am-Swiss Found fel; consult, Merck Co & E I du Pont de Nemours & Co; mem comt chem sci, Nat Acad Sci, 80-; centenary lectr, Chem Soc London, 82. *Honors & Awards:* Award, Am Chem Soc, 77; Baekland Medal, 81. *Mem:* Nat Acad Sci; Royal Soc Chem; Am Chem Soc; fel AAAS. *Res:* Development of new synthetic methods; synthesis of natural products and theoretically important systems; investigations of model biogenetic systems. *Mailing Add:* Dept of Chem Univ of Wis Madison WI 53706

TROST, CHARLES HENRY, b Erie, Pa, Apr 4, 34; m 60; c 1. VERTEBRATE ZOOLOGY, PHYSIOLOGICAL ECOLOGY. *Educ:* Pa State Univ, BS, 60; Univ Fla, MS, 64; Univ Calif, Los Angeles, PhD(zool), 68. *Prof Exp:* Grad fac grant, 69-70, asst prof biol, 68-81, ASSOC PROF BIOL, IDAHO STATE UNIV, 81- *Mem:* Am Ornithologists Union; Cooper Ornith Soc; Wilson Ornith Soc; Am Soc Zoologists; Am Soc Mammalogists. *Res:* Water balance and energetics of birds and mammals; relation of behavior to the adaptations of animals to their environment. *Mailing Add:* Dept of Biol Idaho State Univ Pocatello ID 83201

TROST, HENRY BIGGS, b Lancaster, Pa, Aug 18, 20; m 43; c 3. ORGANIC CHEMISTRY. *Educ:* Franklin & Marshall Col, BS, 42. *Prof Exp:* Anal chemist, Org Anal Group, 42-44, shift supvr, Acid Lab, Badger Ord Works, 44-45, Org Anal Lab, 45-46, Size & Solvents Anal Lab, Naval Stores Res Div, 55-61, MEM STAFF INDUST LABS DIV, HERCULES INC, 61- *Mem:* Am Chem Soc. *Res:* Product application, development, formulation and sales service type work on water soluble polymers and surface active agents. *Mailing Add:* Res Ctr Hercules Inc Wilmington DE 19899

TROSTEL, LOUIS J(ACOB), JR, b Baltimore, Md, May 21, 27; m 53; c 3. CERAMICS ENGINEERING. *Educ:* Ohio State Univ, BCerE & MS, 51, PhD(ceramic eng), 55. *Prof Exp:* Res assoc ceramic eng, Res Found, Ohio State Univ, 50-51 & 52-55; ceramic res engr, 55-65, sr res engr, 65-69, res assoc, 68-78, RES MGR COM PROD, RES & DEVELOP DEPT, INDUST CERAMICS DIV, NORTON CO, WORCESTER, 78- *Honors & Awards:* Award of Merit, Am Soc Testing & Mat, 76. *Mem:* Fel Am Ceramic Soc; Am Inst Ceramic Engrs; fel Am Soc Testing & Mat. *Res:* Ceramic applications and development of cermets; refractory coatings; special refractories. *Mailing Add:* Mirick Rd Princeton MA 01541

TROTT, GENE F, b Louisville, Ky, May 27, 29; m 55; c 4. RUBBER CHEMISTRY. *Educ:* Univ Louisville, BA, 54, MS, 68, PhD, 71. *Prof Exp:* Chemist, Pillsbury Co, 54-56; res chemist & group leader, Am Synthetic Rubber Corp, 56-66; chemist, Gen Elec Co, Louisville, Ky, 66-73; mgr res & develop, Burton Rubber Processing Co, 73-77; TECH DIR, AM SYNTHETIC RUBBER CORP, LOUISVILLE, 77- *Mem:* Am Chem Soc. *Res:* Polymer chemistry; polymer characterization; biopolymeric interactions; polymerization kinetics. *Mailing Add:* 2301 St Andrews Rd Jeffersonville IN 47130

TROTT, LAMARR BRICE, marine ecology, ichthyology, see previous edition

TROTT, S M, b Barros, PR, Jan 22, 15; m 41; c 3. MATHEMATICS. *Educ:* US Naval Acad, SB, 36; Univ Tasmania, BSc, 52, PhD(math), 67; Univ Toronto, MA, 62. *Prof Exp:* Head dept math & physics, Hobart Tech Col, 52-55; sr lectr mech eng, Univ Tasmania, 55-63; assoc prof math, Univ Sask, Regina Campus, 63-65; ASSOC PROF MATH, UNIV TORONTO, 65- *Res:* Geometric algebra. *Mailing Add:* 45 Dunfield Toronto ON M4S 2H3 Can

TROTT, WINFIELD JAMES, b Lockport, NY, Mar 11, 15; m 41; c 3. UNDERWATER ACOUSTICS. *Educ:* Hillsdale Col, BS, 38. *Prof Exp:* Lab instr physics, Columbia Univ, 39-40; res physicist, Res Div, Gen Motors Corp, 40-46; res physicist, Res Lab, Ford Motor Co, 46-47; head res dept, Underwater Sound Ref Div, Naval Res Lab, Fla, 48-67; prin scientist, Sci-Atlanta, Inc, Ga, 67-70; supvry res physicist, Acoust Div, 70-78, CONSULT, 5100 NAVAL RES LAB, 78- *Concurrent Pos:* Liaison scientist, London Br Off, Off Naval Res, 66-67; chmn, Writing Subcomt Underwater Transducers, Am Nat Standards Inst; control agent, Working Group 7 Ultrasonics, Int Round-Robin Hydrophone Calibration Tech Comt, 29, Int Electrotech Comn. *Mem:* AAAS; fel Acoust Soc Am; Sigma Xi. *Res:* Instrument development; acoustics; underwater sound. *Mailing Add:* Acoust Div Naval Res Lab Code 5100 Washington DC 20375

TROTTA, PAUL P, b Brooklyn, NY, Sept 10, 42. BIOCHEMISTRY. *Educ:* Columbia Col, BA, 64, Downstate Med Ctr, State Univ NY, PhD(biochem), 68. *Prof Exp:* Res fel, 68-70, instr biochem, Med Col, 70-74, assoc cancer res, Sloan-Kettering Inst, 74-81, ASST PROF BIOCHEM, MED COL, CORNELL UNIV, 81-, CONSULT, SLOAN-KETTERING INST, 82- *Concurrent Pos:* Fac res award, Am Cancer Soc, 79. *Mem:* Am Soc Biol Chemists; Am Chem Soc; NY Acad Sci; Am Asn Cancer Res; AAAS. *Res:* Structure-function relations and regulatory properties of enzymes and other proteins; physico-chemical characterization of macromolecules in general and especially proteins; use of anti-metabolites for determining the biological consequences of inhibiting specific points in metabolism. *Mailing Add:* Dept Biochem Med Col Cornell Univ 1300 York Ave New York NY 10021

TROTTER, GORDON TRUMBULL, b Washington, DC, Aug 27, 34; m 65; c 2. COMPUTER SCIENCES. *Educ:* Univ Md, BS, 56; Johns Hopkins Univ, MS, 72. *Prof Exp:* Mathematician, Nat Bur Stand, 56-58; from assoc mathematician to mathematician appl physics lab, Johns Hopkins Univ, 58-66; res mathematician & supvr comput opers, IIT Res Inst, 66-67; MATHEMATICIAN & SUPVR INFO PROCESSING PROG PROJ, APPL PHYSICS LAB, JOHNS HOPKINS UNIV, 67- *Concurrent Pos:* Asst, Grad Sch, Univ Md, 56-58. *Mem:* Asn Comput Mach. *Res:* Information storage and retrieval systems; text processing; software management; programming theory. *Mailing Add:* 10626 Fable Row Columbia MD 21044

TROTTER, HALE FREEMAN, b Kingston, Ont, May 30, 31. MATHEMATICS. *Educ:* Queen's Univ, Ont, BA, 52, MA, 53; Princeton Univ, PhD(math), 56. *Prof Exp:* Fine instr math, Princeton Univ, 56-58; asst prof, Queen's Univ, Ont, 58-60; vis assoc prof, 60-62, assoc prof, 63-69, PROF MATH, PRINCETON UNIV, 69-, ASSOC DIR COMPUT CTR, 62- *Mem:* Am Math Soc; Can Math Cong; Math Asn Am; Asn Comput Mach. *Res:* Knot theory; computing. *Mailing Add:* Dept of Math Princeton Univ Princeton NJ 08540

TROTTER, JAMES, b Dumfries, Scotland, July 15, 33; m 57; c 2. PHYSICAL CHEMISTRY. *Educ:* Univ Glasgow, BSc, 54, PhD(chem), 57, DSc(chem), 63. *Prof Exp:* Asst lectr chem, Univ Glasgow, 54-57, Nat Res Coun Can fel physics, 57-59, Imp Chem Indust fel chem, 59-60; from asst prof to assoc prof, 60-65, PROF CHEM, UNIV BC, 65- *Mem:* AAAS; Am Crystallog Asn; Chem Inst Can; The Chem Soc; Royal Inst Chemists. *Res:* Chemistry; crystallography. *Mailing Add:* Dept Chem Univ BC Vancouver BC V6T 1W5 Can

TROTTER, JOHN ALLEN, b Robstown, Tex, May 26, 45; m 78; c 1. ULTRASTRUCTURE, CYTOCHEMISTRY. *Educ:* Johns Hopkins Univ, BA, 69; Univ Wash, PhD(biol structure), 76. *Prof Exp:* Guest worker, NIH, 77-78; ASST PROF ANAT, MED SCH, UNIV NMEX, 78- *Concurrent Pos:* Assoc ed, Anatomical Record. *Mem:* Am Soc Cell Biol; Am Asn Anatomists; Biophys Soc; Electron Micros Soc Am; NY Acad Sci. *Res:* Organization and function of the cytoskeleton; structure, function, development and pathology of the muscle-enden junction; regulation of actomyosin contractility in non-muscle cells. *Mailing Add:* Dept Anat Univ NMex Sch Med Albuquerque NM 87131

TROTTER, JOHN WAYNE, b Clifton, Tex, Jan 8, 48. ORGANIC CHEMISTRY. *Educ:* Tex Lutheran Col, BS, 70; Tex A&M Univ, PhD(chem), 75. *Prof Exp:* sr chemist, 76-80, PROD SUPVR, MOBAY CHEM CORP, 80- *Mem:* Am Chem Soc; AAAS. *Mailing Add:* 904 Westcott 183 Houston TX 77007

TROTTER, MILDRED, b Monaca, Pa, Feb 3, 99. ANATOMY. *Educ:* Mt Holyoke Col, AB, 20; Wash Univ, ScM, 21, PhD(anat), 24. *Hon Degrees:* DSc, Western Col, 56 & Mt Holyoke Col, 60 & Wash Univ, 80. *Prof Exp:* Asst anat, 20-24, from instr to assoc prof, 24-46, prof gross anat, 46-58, prof anat, 58-67, EMER PROF ANAT & LECTR, DEPT ANAT & NEUROBIOL & CONSULT ANAT, DEPT RADIOL, WASH UNIV, 67- *Concurrent Pos:* Nat Res Coun fel, Oxford Univ, 25-26; vis prof, Makerere Univ Col, Uganda, 63; anthropologist, US Dept Army, Hawaii, 48-49 & Manila, Philippines, 51; consult, USPHS, 43-63, Mallinckrodt Inst Radiol, 48- & Rockefeller Found Med & Natural Sci, 63; assoc ed, Am J Phys Anthrop, 68-72. *Mem:* AAAS; Am Asn Anatomists; Asn Phys Anthrop (vpres, 52-54, pres, 55-57); Anthrop Asn; Anat Soc Gt Brit & Ireland. *Res:* Hair; skeleton; articulations; physical anthropology; human anatomy. *Mailing Add:* Dept of Anat & Neurobiol Wash Univ Sch of Med St Louis MO 63110

TROTTER, NANCY LOUISA, b Monaca, Pa, July 26, 34. CYTOLOGY, ELECTRON MICROSCOPY. *Educ:* Oberlin Col, AB, 56; Brown Univ, ScM, 58, PhD(cytol), 60. *Prof Exp:* From instr to asst prof histol, Col Physicians & Surgeons, Columbia Univ, 61-68; ASSOC PROF ANAT, JEFFERSON COL MED, THOMAS JEFFERSON UNIV, 68- *Concurrent Pos:* USPHS trainee, 60, fel, 61, res grant, 62-68. *Mem:* Am Asn Anatomists. *Res:* Hepatomas; liver cytology; partial hepatectomy. *Mailing Add:* Box 95 RD 1 Enon Valley PA 16120

TROTTER, PATRICK CASEY, b Longview, Wash, Jan 26, 35; div; c 2. PULP & PAPER CHEMISTRY. *Educ:* Ore State Univ, BS, 57; Inst Paper Chem, MS, 59, PhD(chem), 61. *Prof Exp:* Sect leader, Paperboard & Coatings Group, Pulp & Paperboard Res Dept, 61-68, DEPT MGR, FIBER PROD RES & DEVELOP DIV, WEYERHAEUSER CO, 68- *Mem:* Tech Asn Pulp & Paper Indust. *Res:* Long range and basic research on pulping, bleaching, papermaking and properties of paper and paperboard. *Mailing Add:* Weyerhaeuser Co Tacoma WA 98401

TROTTER, PHILIP JAMES, b Jackson, Mich, Jan 31, 41. PHYSICAL CHEMISTRY. *Educ:* Ill Inst Technol, BS, 64; Univ Colo, PhD(phys chem), 67. *Prof Exp:* Fel molecular complexes, New Eng Inst & Univ Conn, 67-69; res chemist Raman spectra & surface studies, Shell Res, Holland, 69-72; SR RES CHEMIST RAMAN & INFRARED SPECTRA, EASTMAN KODAK CO, 73- *Mem:* Am Chem Soc; Soc Appl Spectros. *Res:* Reaction systems and dye structures; laser-Raman and infrared spectroscopic applications; surface reactions; instrument development. *Mailing Add:* Eastman Kodak Co 343 State St Rochester NY 14650

TROTTER, ROBERT RUSSELL, b Morgantown, WVa, Apr 23, 15; m 56. OPHTHALMOLOGY. *Educ:* WVa Univ, AB & BS, 40; Temple Univ, MD, 42. *Prof Exp:* Asst ophthal res, Howe Lab, Harvard Med Sch, 47, instr, 52-55, instr ophthal, 56-60; clin assoc prof surg, 61-63, assoc prof, 63-65, PROF SURG, MED CTR, WVA UNIV, 65-, CHHMN, DIV OPHTHAL, 61-, CLIN PROF OPHTHAL, 80- *Concurrent Pos:* Fel, Harvard Med Sch, 48-49; resident ophthal, Mass Eye & Ear Infirmary, 49-51, dir glaucoma consult serv & asst to chief ophthal, 55-60. *Mem:* AMA; Am Acad Ophthal & Otolaryngol; Am Col Surgeons; Asn Res Vision & Ophthal. *Res:* Glaucoma; testing vision of pre-school children. *Mailing Add:* Div of Ophthal WVa Univ Med Ctr Morgantown WV 26506

TROTZ, SAMUEL ISAAC, b Chattanooga, Tenn, Nov 6, 27; m 55; c 2. CHEMISTRY. *Educ:* Univ Chattanooga, BS, 48; Univ Tenn, MS, 51; St Louis Univ, PhD, 56. *Prof Exp:* Asst chem, Univ Tenn, 48-50 & Univ St Louis, 52-55; res chemist, Olin Mathieson Chem Corp, 55, sr res chemist & group leader, 55-59, proj supvr org div, 59-66, sect mgr, 66-70, tech mgr chem group, 70-74, MGR RES & DEVELOP, OLIN CORP, 74- *Mem:* AAAS; Am Chem Soc; Sigma Xi. *Res:* Synthesis; product development; custom chemicals process chemistry; oxyhalogens; water chemistry; antimicrobial agents; organic chemistry; organometallics; boranes; light metal hydrides; heterocyclics; high energy fuels; polymers. *Mailing Add:* Chem Group Res Olin Corp 275 Winchester Ave New Haven CT 06511

TROUBETZKOY, EUGENE SERGE, b Clamart, Seine, France, Apr 7, 31; US citizen; m 58; c 3. THEORETICAL PHYSICS. *Educ:* Univ Paris, B es Sc, 49, lic es SC, 53; Columbia Univ, PhD(physics), 58. *Prof Exp:* Res asst physics, Columbia Univ, 53-58; sr scientist, United Nuclear Corp, NY, 58-64, adv scientist, 64-69; sr res assoc, Div Nuclear Sci & Eng, Columbia Univ, 69-70; MEM STAFF, MAGI CORP, 70- *Mem:* Am Phys Soc. *Res:* Neutrons; radiation transport theory and calculations applied to shielding and reactor calculations. *Mailing Add:* Magi Corp 3 Westchester Plaza Elmsford NY 10523

TROUP, STANLEY BURTON, b Minneapolis, Minn, Feb 9, 25; m 49; c 2. INTERNAL MEDICINE, HEMATOLOGY. *Educ:* Univ Minn, Minneapolis, BS, 48, BM, 49, MD, 50; Mass Inst Technol, MS, 72; Am Bd Internal Med, dipl, 57. *Prof Exp:* Intern med, Strong Mem Hosp, Univ Rochester, 49-50, intern path, 50-51, asst resident med, 51-52; resident, Beth Israel Hosp, Harvard Univ, 52-53; from instr to prof med, Strong Mem Hosp, Univ Rochester, 58-74; prof med, dir med ctr & vpres, 74-82, PROF MED, HEALTH CARE & HUMAN VALUES, UNIV CINCINNATI, 82- *Concurrent Pos:* Fel path, Strong Mem Hosp, Univ Rochester, 50-51, fel hemat, 55-58; NIH spec fel, Kocher Inst, Univ Bern, 61-62; Alfred P Sloan fel mgt, Mass Inst Technol, 71-72; chief med, Rochester Gen Hosp, 65-74; consult, Genesee, St Mary's & Highland Hosps, Rochester & Vet Admin Hosp, Bath, NY, 65-; consult spec ctrs res, NIH, 71-72; vis prof health mgt, Mass Inst Technol, 80. *Mem:* Fel Am Col Physicians; Am Fedn Clin Res; Am Soc Hemat. *Res:* Bleeding disorders; hemolytic anemia; medical education and management. *Mailing Add:* Rm 6452 Eden & Bethesda Avenues College Med Cincinnati OH 45267

TROUPE, RALPH A(NDERSON), b Darby, Pa, Apr 21, 16; m 51; c 4. CHEMICAL ENGINEERING. *Educ:* Drexel Inst Technol, BS, 39; Va Polytech Inst, MS, 40; Univ Tex, PhD(chem eng), 49. *Prof Exp:* Instr chem eng, Northeastern Univ, 40-43, assoc prof, 46-47; prod supvr & engr, Gen Tire & Rubber Co, 43-46; asst prof chem eng, Univ Tex, 49; assoc prof, Univ Louisville, 49-50; tech supt, Goodyear Synthetic Rubber Corp, 50-54; res prof, 54-62, prof, 62-81, EMER PROF CHEM, NORTHEASTERN UNIV, 81-, CHMN DEPT, 62- *Mem:* Am Chem Soc; Nat Asn Corrosion Engrs; Am Inst Chem Engrs. *Res:* Organic process development; corrosion; unit operations. *Mailing Add:* 4 Parker Rd Wakefield MA 01880

TROUSDALE, WILLIAM LATIMER, b Littleton, NH, Nov 10, 28; m 55; c 4. PHYSICS. *Educ:* Trinity Col, Conn, BS, 50; Rutgers Univ, PhD, 56. *Prof Exp:* Asst prof physics, Trinity Col, Conn, 55-61; res assoc, Univ Pa, 61-62; asst prof, 62-66, ASSOC PROF PHYSICS, WESLEYAN UNIV, 66- *Concurrent Pos:* Consult, United Aircraft Corp, 56-61; vis scientist, Brookhaven Nat Lab, 66-67. *Mem:* Am Phys Soc. *Res:* Mössbauer effect; magnetism; low temperature physics; physical electronics; holography. *Mailing Add:* Dept of Physics Wesleyan Univ Middletown CT 06457

TROUSE, ALBERT CHARLES, b Hanford, Calif, May 19, 21; m 47; c 4. AGRONOMY. *Educ:* Univ Calif, BS, 43, MS, 48; Univ Hawaii, PhD(soil physics), 64. *Prof Exp:* Soil scientist, USDA, Nev, Calif & Hawaii, 46-51; assoc agronomist, Exp Sta, Hawaiian Sugar Planters Asn, 51-57, sr agronomist, 58-63; SOIL SCIENTIST, NAT TILLAGE MACH LAB, AGR RES SERV, SOUTHERN REGION, USDA, 64- *Mem:* Soil Conserv Soc Am; Am Soc Agron; Am Soc Agr Eng; AAAS; Int Soil Tillage Orgn. *Res:* Soil physical properties; requirements for plant root bed and seed bed with respect to various crops and climatic situations, soil strength and aeration; interactions of roots of various species to each other. *Mailing Add:* PO Box 792 Auburn AL 36830

TROUT, DAVID LYNN, b Ann Arbor, Mich, Aug 2, 27; m 59; c 3. PHYSIOLOGY. *Educ:* Swarthmore Col, AB, 51; Duke Univ, MA, 54, PhD(physiol, pharmacol), 58. *Prof Exp:* Lab technician, Baxter Labs, 51-52; asst physiol & pharmacol, Duke Univ, 54-58; sr biochemist, Cent Ref Lab, Vet Admin Hosp, Durham, NC, 58-61; res physiologist, US Air Force Sch Aerospace Med, Brooks AFB, Tex, 61-66; res physiologist, Human Nutrit Res Div, Agr Res Serv, 66-71, RES PHYSIOLOGIST, NUTRIT INST, SCI & EDUC ADMIN-AGR RES, USDA, 71- *Mem:* Fel AAAS; Am Physiol Soc; Am Inst Nutrit; Soc Exp Biol & Med. *Res:* Carbohydrate nutrition; physiological adaptation to diet; lipid transport and metabolism; gastric emptying. *Mailing Add:* 8905 Royal Ridge Lane Laurel MD 20811

TROUT, DENNIS ALAN, b Washington, DC, July 26, 47; m 75. AIR POLLUTION, METEOROLOGY. *Educ:* Pa State Univ, BS, 68, MS, 69, PhD(meteorol, air pollution), 73. *Prof Exp:* Res asst, Dept Meteorol, Pa State Univ, 68-70, res asst, Ctr Air Environ Studies, 70-71; environ/syst analyst, Environ Tech Appl Ctr, US Air Force, 71-73; STAFF METEOROLOGIST, BATTELLE-COLUMBUS LABS, BATTELLE MEM INST, 73- *Concurrent Pos:* Lectr air pollution & meteorol, Ohio State Univ, 75. *Mem:* Am Meteorol Soc; Air Pollution Control Asn; Am Geophys Union; AAAS; Sigma Xi. *Res:* Ambient air quality measurements and analysis; computer modeling of atmospheric dispersion of air pollutants; development of dynamic emission control strategies; assessment of trace contaminant emissions and resulting ambient concentrations. *Mailing Add:* 531 N Addison Rd Villa Park IL 60181

TROUT, PAUL EUGENE, b Baker, Mont, Sept 17, 21; m 48; c 3. CHEMISTRY. *Educ:* Mont State Col, BS, 43; Lawrence Col, MS, 48, PhD(chem), 51. *Prof Exp:* Res asst, Am Box Bd Co, 50-54; vpres & tech dir, Waldorf Paper Prod Co, 54-61; mgr container bd res, 62-69, CORP MGR ENVIRON CONTROL, CONTAINER CORP AM, 69- *Mem:* AAAS; Am Chem Soc; Tech Asn Pulp & Paper Indust. *Res:* Wet strength of paper; neutral sulfite pulping of hardwood; lignin investigations; air and water pollution abatement; paper and cellulose chemistry. *Mailing Add:* Container Corp Am 500 E North Ave Carol Stream IL 60187

TROUT, WILLIAM EDGAR, JR, chemistry, deceased

TROUT, WILLIAM EDGAR, III, b Staunton, Va, Apr 21, 37. GENETICS. *Educ:* Univ Richmond, BS, 59; Ind Univ, AM, 64, PhD(genetics), 65. *Prof Exp:* USPHS res fel radiation genetics, Biol Div, Oak Ridge Nat Lab, 65-66; RES SCIENTIST, BIOL DEPT, CITY OF HOPE MED CTR, 66- *Mem:* AAAS; Genetics Soc Am; Nat Speleol Soc. *Res:* Behavior genetics of Drosophila melanogaster. *Mailing Add:* Dept of Biol City of Hope Med Ctr Duarte CA 91010

TROUTMAN, JAMES SCOTT, b Hannibal, Mo, Mar 7, 30; m 52; c 2. ENGINEERING, OPERATIONS RESEARCH. *Educ:* US Naval Acad, BS, 52. *Prof Exp:* Sr engr, Corvey Div, Melpar, Inc, 56-58; weapon syst analyst, 58-60, corp secy, 60-76, VPRES, ANSER, ARLINGTON, VA, 76- *Mem:* AAAS; fel Am Astronaut Soc (past treas & dir); Opers Res Soc Am; Sigma Xi. *Res:* Electronics and communications systems; seismology; electronic parts for extreme environments; weapon systems analysis and operations research; intelligence systems; research and development management. *Mailing Add:* 5624 Newington Ct Bethesda MD 20016

TROUTMAN, JOSEPH LAWRENCE, b Concordia, Ky, June 21, 21; m 45; c 4. PLANT PATHOLOGY. *Educ:* Univ Ky, BS, 50; Univ Wis, PhD(plant path), 57. *Prof Exp:* Asst agron, Univ Ky, 50-53; from asst prof to assoc prof plant path & physiol, Res Div, Va Polytech Inst, 57-68; assoc prof, 68-74, ASSOC PLANT PATHOLOGIST, AGR EXP STA, UNIV ARIZ, 74- *Mem:* AAAS. Am Phytopath Soc. *Res:* Diseases of vegetables and citrus. *Mailing Add:* Univ of Ariz Agr Exp Sta Rte 1 Box 587 Yuma AZ 85364

TROUTMAN, RICHARD CHARLES, b Columbus, Ohio, May 16, 22; m; c 3. OPHTHALMOLOGY. *Educ:* Ohio State Univ, BA, 42, MD, 45; Am Bd Ophthal, dipl, 51. *Prof Exp:* Intern ophthal, New York Hosp, 45-46; resident, Cornell Med Ctr, 48-50, from instr to asst prof, Med Col, Cornell Univ, 52-55; PROF OPHTHAL & CHMN DIV, STATE UNIV NY DOWNSTATE MED CTR, 55- *Concurrent Pos:* Instr, Manhattan Eye, Ear & Throat Hosp, 51-55, mem courtesy staff, 55-, surgeon dir, 61-; consult hosps, 54-; vis surgeon, Kings County Hosp, 55-; mem courtesy staff, Cornell Med Ctr, New York Hosp, 55-, attend surgeon, 71-; mem courtesy staff, New York Eye & Ear Infirmary, 55-; mem ophthal postgrad training comt, Nat Inst Neurol Dis & Blindness, 59-63; consult neurol & blindness div, Bur State Serv, Dept Health, Educ & Welfare, 63-67; mem, Bd Dirs, Baraquer Inst, 63-73. *Mem:* Am Asn Res Vision & Ophthal; fel Am Col Surgeons; fel Am Acad Ophthal & Otolaryngol; fel NY Acad Med; Am Ophthal Soc. *Res:* Orbital surgery and surgery of the anterior segment of the eye; microsurgery and stereotaxic ophthalmic surgery. *Mailing Add:* 755 Park Ave New York NY 10021

TROUTNER, DAVID ELLIOTT, b Eolia, Mo, Oct 11, 29; m 55; c 3. NUCLEAR CHEMISTRY. *Educ:* Washington Univ, AB, 52, PhD(chem), 59; Univ Mo-Rolla, MS, 56. *Prof Exp:* From asst prof to assoc prof, Univ Mo-Rolla, 59-61; assoc prof, 61-69, chmn dept, 71-78, PROF CHEM, UNIV MO-COLUMBIA, 69- *Concurrent Pos:* Vis scientist, Oak Ridge Nat Lab, 67-68. *Mem:* Am Chem Soc; Soc Nuclear Med. *Res:* Radioisotopes in medicine; radiochemical studies of nuclear fission. *Mailing Add:* Dept of Chem Univ of Mo-Columbia Columbia MO 65211

TROW, JAMES, b Chicago, Ill, Apr 21, 22; m 47. GEOLOGY. *Educ:* Univ Chicago, SB, 43, SM, 45, PhD(geol), 48. *Prof Exp:* From asst prof to assoc prof geol, 47-59, PROF GEOL, MICH STATE UNIV, 59- *Concurrent Pos:* Consult, indust & govt, 58-60, Chevron Resources, 71-76 & Mich Geol Surv, 77-79. *Mem:* Soc Mining Engrs; Can Inst Mining & Metall; Geol Soc Am; Am Geophys Union. *Res:* Chemical thermodynamics, structural geology and Pleistocene sedimentology applied to mining exploration for uranium, gold, diamonds, copper and iron. *Mailing Add:* Dept of Geol Mich State Univ East Lansing MI 48824

TROWBRIDGE, DALE BRIAN, b Glendale, Calif, May 17, 40; m 66; c 1. ORGANIC CHEMISTRY. *Educ:* Whittier Col, AB, 61; Univ Calif, Berkeley, MS, 64, PhD(org chem), 70. *Prof Exp:* Chemist, Aerojet Gen Corp, 61-62; teacher chem high sch, Calif, 64-66; from asst prof to assoc prof, 69-77, PROF CHEM, CALIF STATE COL, SONOMA, 77- *Mem:* Sigma Xi; Am Chem Soc. *Res:* Preparation and study of organo-phosphorus compounds of biological interest. *Mailing Add:* Dept Chem Sonoma State Univ Rohnert Park CA 94928

TROWBRIDGE, FREDERICK LINDSLEY, b Newark, NJ, June 8, 42; m 70; c 2. NUTRITION, EPIDEMIOLOGY. *Educ:* Princeton Univ, BA, 64; Harvard Univ, MD, 68; London Sch Hyg & Trop Med, MSc, 74. *Prof Exp:* Med epidemiologist nutrit epidemiol, Ctr Dis Control, USPHS, 71-77; ASST PROF INT HEALTH EPIDEMIOL, SCH HYG & PUB HEALTH, JOHNS HOPKINS UNIV, 77- *Mem:* Int Health Soc; Am Pub Health Asn. *Res:* Field assessment of nutrition status; epidemiologic studies in nutrition; methods of nutriontal surveillance. *Mailing Add:* Sch of Hyg & Pub Health 615 N Wolfe St Baltimore MD 21205

TROWBRIDGE, GEORGE CECIL, b Delta, Colo, May 6, 38; m 58; c 2. COMPUTER SCIENCE, MATHEMATICS. *Educ:* Western State Col, Colo, BA, 60; Univ Ill, MS, 64. *Prof Exp:* Teacher math, Lamar High Sch, 60-61; teacher, Delta County Jct Sch Dist number 50, 61-63 & 64-65; teacher, Western State Col, Colo, 65-67; res mathematician electro-magnetic pulse, 67-68, sr res mathematician & proj leader, 68-71, dep prog mgr, Dikewood Industs Inc, 71-79, DIR COMPUT SERV, HANCOCK/DIKEWOOD SERV INC, 79- *Res:* Application of computers to health care information; computer and mathematical applications in the physical sciences. *Mailing Add:* Hancock/Dikewood Serv 1009 Bradbury Dr SE Albuquerque NM 87106

TROWBRIDGE, JAMES RUTHERFORD, b Glen Ridge, NJ, Sept 19, 20; m 49; c 3. SURFACE CHEMISTRY. *Educ:* Yale Univ, BS, 42, MS, 48, PhD(org chem), 50. *Prof Exp:* Group leader, Explor Org Div, 51-57, sr proj chemist, 57-62, RES ASSOC, CHEM RES SECT, COLGATE-PALMOLIVE RES CTR, 62- *Mem:* Am Chem Soc; Am Oil Chem Soc. *Res:* Surface active agents. *Mailing Add:* Colgate-Palmolive Res Ctr 909 River Rd Piscataway NJ 08854

TROWBRIDGE, LEE DOUGLAS, b Akron, Ohio, Oct 25, 49; m 70; c 3. PHYSICAL CHEMISTRY. *Educ:* Mich State Univ, BS, 70; Harvard Univ, MA, 71, PhD(chem physics), 78. *Prof Exp:* Develop assoc, 78-81, DEVELOP STAFF MEM, NUCLEAR DIV, OAK RIDGE GASEOUS DIFFUSION PLANT, UNION CARBIDE, 81- *Mem:* Am Phys Soc; Am Vacuum Soc; Am Chem Soc. *Res:* Gas phase and surface reactions of uranium tetrafluoride; materials studies for the uranium tetrafluoride gas centrifuge enrichment program. *Mailing Add:* Nuclear Div MS 271 Union Carbide PO Box P Oak Ridge TN 37830

TROWBRIDGE, LESLIE WALTER, b Curtiss, Wis, May 21, 20; m 46; c 4. SCIENCE EDUCATION. *Educ:* Wis State Univ, Stevens Point, BS, 40; Univ Chicago, MS, 48; Univ Wis, MS, 53; Univ Mich, PhD(sci educ), 61. *Prof Exp:* Teacher jr high sch, Wis, 41 & 46, instr high sch, 46-54; univ scholar, Univ Mich, 54-62; from asst prof to assoc prof, 62-70, chmn dept sci educ, 66-72, PROF SCI EDUC, UNIV NORTHERN COLO, 70-, CHAIRPERSON DEPT SCI EDUC, 81- *Concurrent Pos:* Fel, NY Univ, 69-70. *Mem:* Nat Sci Teachers Asn (pres, 73-74); Nat Asn Res Sci Teaching. *Mailing Add:* Dept of Sci Educ Univ of Northern Colo Greeley CO 80631

TROWER, W(ILLIAM) PETER, b Rapid City, SDak, May 25, 35; m 57, 63; c 3. EXPERIMENTAL PHYSICS. *Educ:* Univ Calif, Berkeley, AB, 57; Univ Ill, Urbana, MS, 63, PhD(physics), 66. *Prof Exp:* Physicist, Lawrence Radiation Lab, Univ Calif, Berkeley, 60-62; res asst, Digital Comput Lab & Dept Physics, Univ Ill, Urbana, 62-66; asst prof, 66-70, assoc prof, Col Archit, 73-75, ASSOC PROF PHYSICS, VA POLYTECH INST & STATE UNIV, 70- *Concurrent Pos:* Chmn, Gordon Res Conf Multiparticle Prod Processes, 73; dir, Coun Munic Performance, NY, 73-75; co-chmn, Physics in Collision Res Conf, 81. *Honors & Awards:* Bronze Medal, Int Film & TV Festival NY, 73. *Mem:* Fel Am Phys Soc; fel AAAS; European Physical Soc. *Res:* Experimental nuclear and particle physics; scientific computer applications. *Mailing Add:* 1105 Highland Circle SE Blacksburg VA 24060

TROXEL, BENNIE WYATT, b Osawatomie, Kans, Aug 9, 20; m 46; c 2. GEOLOGY. *Educ:* Univ Calif, Los Angeles, BA, 51, MA, 58. Prof geologist, Calif Div Mines & Geol, Div Mines & Geol, 52-71; sci ed, Geol Soc Am, 71-75; MEM STAFF, DIV MINES 75-77; mem fac, Calif State Univ, Sacramento, 75-77; MEM FAC, UNIV CALIF, DAVIS, 77-; CONSULT GEOLOGIST, 77- *Mem:* Soc Econ Geologists; AAAS; Geol Soc Am; Asn Earth Sci Eds; Am Inst Mining, Metall & Petrol Engrs. *Res:* Geology of Death Valley region; geologic factors that influence slope stability in urban areas of California; mineral resources; Precambrian stratigraphy and faults in California. *Mailing Add:* 2961 Redwood Rd Napa CA 94558

TROXEL, DONALD EUGENE, b Trenton, NJ, Mar 11, 34; m 63; c 1. ELECTRICAL ENGINEERING. *Educ:* Rutgers Univ, BS, 56; Mass Inst Technol, SM, 60, PhD(elec eng), 62. *Prof Exp:* From instr to asst prof, 61-67, ASSOC PROF ELEC ENG, MASS INST TECHNOL, 67- *Concurrent Pos:* Ford Found fel, 62-64. *Mem:* Inst Elec & Electronics Engrs. *Res:* Digital systems applications; communications; electronics; computers; image processing. *Mailing Add:* Dept of Elec Eng Mass Inst of Technol Cambridge MA 02139

TROXELL, HARRY EMERSON, JR, b Northumberland, Pa, Sept 19, 21; m 78; c 4. WOOD SCIENCE & TECHNOLOGY. *Educ:* Duke Univ, BS, 43, MF, 47, DF, 61. *Prof Exp:* Instr forest mgt, 47-49, from asst prof to assoc prof wood technol, 49-62, head, Dept Wood Sci, 74-79, PROF WOOD SCI, COLO STATE UNIV, 62-, ASSOC DEAN, COL FORESTRY & NATURAL RESOURCES, 79- *Mem:* Soc Am Foresters; Forest Prods Res Soc; Soc Wood Sci & Technol; Sigma Xi. *Res:* Wood products. *Mailing Add:* 624 Armstrong Ave Ft Collins CO 80521

TROXELL, TERRY CHARLES, b Allentown, Pa, Jan 1, 44; m 64; c 2. PHYSICAL CHEMISTRY. *Educ:* Muhlenberg Col, BS, 65; Cornell Univ, PhD(biophys chem), 71. *Prof Exp:* Res assoc phys chem, Univ Ore, 71-74; sr phys chemist, Eli Lilly & Co, 74-77; SCI ADMINR, FOOD & DRUG ADMIN, 77- *Mem:* Am Chem Soc; AAAS. *Res:* Scientific policy and administration; food safety, especially regulation of food additives and food packaging. *Mailing Add:* Food & Drug Admin 200 C St Washington DC 20204

TROXLER, RAYMOND GEORGE, b New Orleans, La, Sept 21, 39; m 63; c 2. PATHOLOGY. *Educ:* Univ Southwestern La, BS, 64; La State Univ, MD, 64. *Prof Exp:* CHIEF CLIN PATH, CLIN SCI DIV, US AIR FORCE SCH AEROSPACE MED, 71- *Concurrent Pos:* Clin asst prof, Univ Tex Health Sci Ctr, San Antonio, 72-82; consult clin path, US Air Force Surg Gen. *Res:* Early detection of latent coronary artery disease by laboratory screening of blood and serum. *Mailing Add:* 10318 Willowick San Antonio TX 78217

TROXLER, ROBERT FULTON, b Santa Monica, Calif, July 11, 38; m 64. BIOCHEMISTRY. *Educ:* Grinnell Col, BS, 60; Pa State Univ, MS, 62; Univ Chicago, PhD(bot), 65. *Prof Exp:* Res assoc bot, Univ Chicago, 65-66; res assoc med, 66-68, from asst prof to assoc prof, 68-80, PROF BIOCHEM, SCH MED, BOSTON UNIV, 80- *Mem:* Am Fedn Clin Res; Am Soc Biol Chemists; AAAS; Am Soc Plant Physiologists; AAAS. *Res:* Porphyrin and bile pigment chemistry and biochemistry; protein sequence. *Mailing Add:* Dept of Biochem 80 E Concord St Boston MA 02118

TROY, DANIEL JOSEPH, b St Louis Co, Mo, Feb 2, 32; m 55; c 6. MATHEMATICS. *Educ:* St Louis Univ, BS, 53, MS, 58, PhD(math), 61. *Prof Exp:* Instr math, St Louis Univ, 58-61; asst prof, Ohio State Univ, 61-67; ASSOC PROF MATH, PURDUE UNIV, 67- *Mem:* Am Math Soc; Math Asn Am. *Res:* Complex variable. *Mailing Add:* Dept Math Calumet Campus Purdue Univ Hammond IN 46323

TROY, FREDERIC ARTHUR, b Evanston, Ill, Feb 16, 37; m 59; c 2. BIOCHEMISTRY, ONCOLOGY. *Educ:* Washington Univ, BS, 61; Purdue Univ, West Lafayette, PhD(biochem), 66. *Prof Exp:* Am Cancer Soc res fel physiol chem, Sch Med, Johns Hopkins Univ, 66-68; from asst prof to assoc prof biol chem, 68-79, PROF BIOL CHEM, SCH MED, UNIV CALIF, DAVIS, 80- *Concurrent Pos:* USPHS res grant, Sch Med, Univ Calif, Davis, Nat Cancer Inst res grant, 71-83; Nat Cancer Inst career res develop award, 75-80; co-dir tumor biol training grant, Nat Cancer Inst, 72-; Am Cancer Soc-Eleanor Roosevelt-Int Cancer fel, Int Union Against Cancer, Stockholm, 76-77. *Mem:* Am Soc Microbiol; Am Inst Chemists; Am Soc Biol Chemists; Am Chem Soc; Brit Biochem Soc. *Res:* Role of tumor-associated surface antigens in immune surveillance; chemistry and biosynthesis of bacterial capsular polymers; nuclear magnetic resonnance studies of lipid structure on protein function; conformation and dynamics of glycosyl carrier polyisoprenoids; the role of bacterial membranes in the synthesis of macromolecules; Epstein-Barr Virus induced membrane changes in human lymphoma cells. *Mailing Add:* Dept of Biol Chem Univ of Calif Sch of Med Davis CA 95616

TROY, WILLIAM CHRISTOPHER, b Rochester, NY, July 7, 47. APPLIED MATHEMATICS. *Educ:* St John Fisher Col, BS, 69; State Univ NY Buffalo, MA, 70, PhD(math), 74. *Prof Exp:* Asst prof math, 74-80, ASSOC PROF MATH, UNIV PITTSBURGH, 80- *Concurrent Pos:* NIH res grant, 75-77. *Mem:* Am Math Soc. *Res:* Application of the theory of differential equations to mathematical problems arising in biology, neurophysiology and chemistry which includes nerve conduction and the Belousov-Zhabotinskii chemical reaction. *Mailing Add:* Dept of Math Univ fo Pittsburgh Pittsburgh PA 15260

TROYER, ALVAH FORREST, b LaFontaine, Ind, May 30, 29; m 50; c 4. PLANT BREEDING, CORN BREEDING. *Educ:* Purdue Univ, BS, 54; Univ Ill, MS, 56; Univ Minn, PhD(plant breeding & genetics), 64. *Prof Exp:* Res assoc, Univ Ill, Urbana, 55-56; res fel, Univ Minn, St Paul, 56-58; sta mgr, Pioneer Corn Co, Mankato, 58-65; res coordr, Northern Res, Pioneer Hi-Bred Int, Inc, 65-67, Eastern Res, 71-77; dir, 77-81, VPRES, RES & DEVELOP, PFIZER GENETICS, INC, ST LOUIS, 81- *Mem:* Sigma Xi; AAAS; Am Soc Agron; Crop Sci Am; NY Acad Sci. *Res:* Increasing the effectiveness and efficiency of corn breeding in all possible ways so that superior products for agriculture will be developed. *Mailing Add:* 248 Glen Hollow Chesterfield MO 63017

TROYER, JAMES RICHARD, b Goshen, Ind, Feb 26, 29; m 51; c 3. PLANT PHYSIOLOGY, HISTORY OF BOTANY. *Educ:* DePauw Univ, BA, 50; Ohio State Univ, MS, 51; Columbia Univ, PhD(bot), 54. *Prof Exp:* Vis asst prof biol, Univ Ala, 54-55; instr plant physiol, Sch Forestry, Yale Univ, 55-57; asst prof bot, 57, assoc prof, 61-69, PROF BOT, NC STATE UNIV, 69- *Concurrent Pos:* Fel, Biomath Training Prog, NC State Univ, 64-66. *Mem:* AAAS; Am Soc Plant Physiol; Bot Soc Am. *Res:* Mathematical plant physiology; flavonoid substances of plants. *Mailing Add:* Dept Bot NC State Univ Raleigh NC 27607

TROYER, JOHN ROBERT, b Princeton, Ill, Feb 5, 28; m 56; c 4. ANATOMY. *Educ:* Syracuse Univ, AB, 49; Cornell Univ, PhD(histol, embryol), 55. *Prof Exp:* Asst histol & embryol, Cornell Univ, 49-54; from instr to assoc prof anat, 54-69, actg chmn dept, 71-72, vchmn dept in chg teaching, 73-79, PROF ANAT, SCH MED, TEMPLE UNIV, 69-, CHMN, ANAT DEPT, 79- *Mem:* AAAS; Am Asn Anat; Am Soc Mammal; NY Acad Sci; Sigma Xi. *Res:* Liver glycogen, porphyrin synthesis and neurosecretion in the hibernating bat; gross anatomy, normal development and abnormal development of the human heart; medical education. *Mailing Add:* Dept Anat Temple Univ Sch Med Philadelphia PA 19122

TROYER, ROBERT JAMES, b Sturgis, Mich, Sept 21, 28; m 54; c 3. MATHEMATICS. *Educ:* Ball State Univ, BS, 50; Ind Univ, MAT, 56, PhD(math), 60. *Prof Exp:* Instr math, Ind Univ, 60-62, asst prof, 62-65; vis fel, Dartmouth Col, 65-66; from asst prof to assoc prof, Univ NC, Chapel Hill, 66-68; vis assoc prof, 68-69, assoc prof, 69-70, PROF MATH, LAKE FOREST COL, 70- *Concurrent Pos:* Vis scholar, Northwestern Univ, 74-75. *Mem:* Math Asn Am. *Res:* Topology; geometry. *Mailing Add:* Dept of Math Lake Forest Col Lake Forest IL 60045

TROYER, STEPHANIE FANTL, b Jan 30, 44; US citizen; m 65; c 1. DIFFERENTIAL TOPOLOGY. *Educ:* Swarthmore Col, BA, 65; Northeastern Univ, MS, 67, PhD(math), 73. *Prof Exp:* Instr, 70-74, ASST PROF MATH, UNIV HARTFORD, 74- *Concurrent Pos:* Vis assoc prof math, Brown Univ, 82; consult, Computopia Corp, Set Logic Assocs & AAAS consult prog for minority insts; NSF working sci grants. *Mem:* Am Math Soc; Math Asn Am; Asn Women Math. *Res:* Extension problems in low codimension, particularly for curves and surfaces. *Mailing Add:* Univ of Hartford West Hartford CT 06117

TROZZOLO, ANTHONY MARION, b Chicago, Ill, Jan 11, 30; m 55; c 6. ORGANIC CHEMISTRY, PHOTOCHEMISTRY. *Educ:* Ill Inst Technol, SB, 50; Univ Chicago, SM, 57, PhD(chem), 60. *Prof Exp:* Asst chemist, Chicago Midway Labs, 52-53; assoc chemist, Armour Res Found, 53-56; mem tech staff, Bell Tel Labs, 59-75; HUISKING PROF CHEM, UNIV NOTRE DAME, IND, 75- *Concurrent Pos:* Adj prof, Columbia Univ, 71; Phillips Lectr, Univ Okla, 71; Reilly Lectr, Univ Notre Dame, 72; Brown Lectr, Rutgers Univ, 75; assoc ed, J Am Chem Soc, 75-77; Faraday lectr, Northern Ill Univ, 76; ed, Chem Rev, 77-; Butler lectr, SDak State Univ, 78; mem, Gordon Res Conf Coun; vis prof, Univ Colo, 81. *Honors & Awards:* Am Inst Chemists Award, 50; Halpern Award, NY Acad Sci, 80. *Mem:* Fel AAAS; Am Chem Soc; fel Am Inst Chemists; Int Solar Energy Soc; fel NY Acad Sci. *Res:* Free radicals; carbenes; charge transfer complexes; electron spin resonance; organic solid state; singlet molecular oxygen; polymer stabilization; chemically-induced dynamic nuclear polarization; laser spectroscopy. *Mailing Add:* Dept Chem Univ Notre Dame Notre Dame IN 46556

TRPIS, MILAN, b Mojsova Lucka, Czechoslovakia, Dec 20, 30; US citizen; m 56; c 3. MEDICAL ENTOMOLOGY. *Educ:* Comenius Univ, Bratislava, Prom Biol, 56; Charles Univ, Prague, Dr rer nat(zool, med entom), 60. *Prof Exp:* Res asst entom, Faunistic Lab, Slovak Acad Sci, 53-56, sci asst, Dept Biol, 56-60, scientist, 60-62, independent scientist & head, Dept Ecol Physiol Insects, Inst Landscape Biol, 62-65; res assoc med entom, Univ Ill, Urbana, 66-67; res assoc, Can Dept Agr, Alta, 67-68; independent scientist & head, Dept Ecol Physiol Insects, Slovak Acad Sci, 68-69; entomologist-ecologist, EAfrica Aedes Res Unit, WHO, UN, Tanzania, 69-71; from asst fac fel to assoc fac fel, Vector Biol Labs, Dept Biol, Univ Notre Dame, Ind, 71-74; assoc prof, 74-78, PROF MED ENTOM, LABS MED ENTOM, DEPT PATHOBIOL, JOHNS HOPKINS UNIV, 78- *Concurrent Pos:* Dir, Biol Res Inst Am, 72-77; proj dir epidemiol river blindness (onchocerciasis), Liberia & Sierra Leone, 81-84. *Honors & Awards:* First Prize Award, Slovak Acad Sci, Bratislava, 61. *Mem:* AAAS; Am Soc Trop Med & Hyg; Am Soc Parasitologists; Entom Soc Am; Am Mosquito Control Asn. *Res:* Parasitic insects, particularly their population dynamics, ecological genetics of populations, behavior and behavioral genetics; embryonic development of insects; biological and genetic control of vectors; ecology of vector-borne diseases. *Mailing Add:* Dept of Pathobiol Labs Med Entom Johns Hopkins Sch Hyg & Pub Hlth Baltimore MD 21205

TRUANT, JOSEPH PAUL, microbiology, immunology, see previous edition

TRUAX, DONALD R, b Minneapolis, Minn, Aug 29, 27; m 50; c 3. MATHEMATICAL STATISTICS. *Educ:* Univ Wash, BS, 51, MS, 53; Stanford Univ, PhD(statist), 55. *Prof Exp:* Res fel math, Calif Inst Technol, 55-56; asst prof, Univ Kans, 56-59; from asst prof to assoc prof, 59-69, PROF MATH, UNIV ORE, 69- *Concurrent Pos:* Managing ed, Inst Math Statist, 75-81. *Mem:* Am Math Soc; Math Asn Am; Am Statist Asn; fel Inst Math Statist. *Res:* Testing statistical hypotheses; multiple decision problems. *Mailing Add:* Dept of Math Univ of Ore Eugene OR 97403

TRUAX, ROBERT LLOYD, b Gillett, Ark, May 8, 28; m 52; c 2. MATHEMATICS. *Educ:* Ark State Teachers Col, BSE, 50; Univ Miss, MA, 58; Okla State Univ, EdD(math educ), 64. *Prof Exp:* Coordr math, Pub Schs, Ark, 50-62; assoc prof math, Southern State Col, 63-65; assoc prof, Northeast La State Col, 65-67; ASSOC PROF MATH, UNIV MISS, 67- *Mem:* Math Asn Am. *Res:* Multivariable function approximations; statistical analysis of research related to paper industry. *Mailing Add:* Dept of Math Univ of Miss University MS 38677

TRUBATCH, JANETT, b New York, NY, Oct 13, 42; m 62; c 2. NEUROSCIENCE. *Educ:* Polytech Inst Brooklyn, BSc, 62; Brandeis Univ, MA, 64, PhD(physics), 68. *Prof Exp:* Asst prof physics, Calif State Univ, Los Angeles, 67-68; res fel biol, Calif Inst Technol, 68-74; asst prof physiol, NY Med Col, 74-77; PROG DIR NEUROBIOL, NSF, 77- *Res:* Mechanisms of synaptic transmission; neural basis of memory and learning; synapse formation; mathematical modeling of biological systems. *Mailing Add:* Div of Neurobiol NSF Washington DC 20550

TRUBATCH, SHELDON L, b Brooklyn, NY, Mar 12, 42; m 62; c 2. THEORETICAL PHYSICS, BIOPHYSICS. *Educ:* Polytech Inst Brooklyn, BS, 62; Brandeis Univ, MA, 64, PhD(physics), 68, JD, 77. *Prof Exp:* Assoc prof physics, Calif State Univ, Long Beach, 67-77; mem staff, 77-80, SR ATTORNEY, OFF GEN COUNSEL, US NUCLEAR REGULATORY COMN, 80- *Res:* Non-relativistic field theory; sensory physiology. *Mailing Add:* 3838 Garrison St Northwest Washington DC 20016

TRUBEK, MAX, b New York, NY, Nov 28, 98; m 37; c 1. MEDICINE. *Educ:* Johns Hopkins Univ, AB, 22; Univ Md, MD, 26. *Prof Exp:* House physician, Bellevue Hosp, 27-29; asst pathologist, Newark City Hosp, 29-31; assoc prof med, NY Univ-Bellevue Med Ctr, 44-56, PROF CLIN MED, MED SCH, NY UNIV, 56- *Concurrent Pos:* Vis physician, Bellevue Hosp, 46-; attend physician, Univ Hosp, 52- *Res:* Clinical medicine. *Mailing Add:* 121 E 60th St New York NY 10022

TRUBERT, MARC, b Soissons, France, Feb 7, 27; US citizen; m 56; c 2. APPLIED MECHANICS, ELECTRONICS. *Educ:* Univ Paris, BS, 50; Spec Sch Pub Works, Paris, BS, 51; Univ Fla, MS, 60, PhD(eng mech), 62. *Prof Exp:* Res engr, Nat Off Aeronaut Study & Res, Paris, 53-57; develop engr, Compagnie Generale de TSF, Paris, 57-58; asst in res eng mech, Univ Fla, 58-62, asst prof, 62-63; asst prof, Univ Calif, Berkeley, 63-65; res engr, 65-66, mem tech staff, 66-70, GROUP SUPVR, JET PROPULSION LAB, 70- *Concurrent Pos:* Instr, Exten Sch, Univ Calif, Los Angeles, 65- *Mem:* Acoust Soc Am; Am Inst Aeronaut & Astronaut. *Res:* Structural dynamics; flutter, vibration, random vibration, frequency domain method and analog methods; attitude control of spacecraft; furlable antennas. *Mailing Add:* 1205 N Reeder Ave Covina CA 91722

TRUBEY, DAVID KEITH, b Coldwater, Mich, Apr 23, 28; m 50; c 2. RADIATION PHYSICS, RADIATION PROTECTION. *Educ:* Mich State Univ, BS, 53. *Prof Exp:* Physicist, 53-54 & 55-56, mgr radiation shielding info ctr, 66-70, MEM STAFF, OAK RIDGE NAT LAB, 72- *Concurrent Pos:* Lectr, Oak Ridge Sch Reactor Technol, 60-62. *Mem:* AAAS; fel Am Nuclear Soc; Health Physics Soc. *Res:* Radiation shielding, transport and dosimetry. *Mailing Add:* Oak Ridge Nat Lab PO Box X Oak Ridge TN 37830

TRUBOWITZ, SIDNEY, b Brooklyn, NY, Aug 25, 11; m 49; c 2. HEMATOLOGY, CELL PHYSIOLOGY. *Educ:* Columbia Univ, AB, 31; Univ Chicago, MD, 36. *Prof Exp:* Chief hemat, Vet Admin Hosp, Staten Island, NY, 47-51, chief hemat & hamat res, Vet Admin Hosp, East Orange, NJ, 52-80; CHIEF, HEMAT & ONCOL SECT, ST ELIZABETH HOSP, ELIZABETH, NJ, 80- *Concurrent Pos:* Fel, Nat Transfusion Ctr, France, 51-52; prof, Col Med, NJ, 65- *Mem:* Am Soc Hemat. *Res:* Structure and function of the marrow matrix and its role in marrow regeneration. *Mailing Add:* St Elizabeth Hosp 225 Williamson St Elizabeth NJ 07207

TRUCE, WILLIAM EVERETT, b Chicago, Ill, Sept 30, 17; m 40; c 2. CHEMISTRY. *Educ:* Univ Ill, BS, 39; Northwestern Univ, PhD(chem), 43. *Prof Exp:* Instr chem, Wabash Col, 43-44; res chemist, Swift & Co, Ill, 44-46; from asst prof to assoc prof, 46-56, PROF CHEM, PURDUE UNIV, WEST LAFAYETTE, 56- *Concurrent Pos:* Guggenheim fel, Oxford Univ, 57. *Mem:* Am Chem Soc; Royal Soc Chem. *Res:* Organic sulfur chemistry; acetylenes; vinylic halides; organic theory and its relationship to synthetic organic chemistry. *Mailing Add:* Dept of Chem Purdue Univ West Lafayette IN 47907

TRUCHARD, JAMES JOSEPH, b Sealy, Tex, June 25, 43; m 66; c 4. ACOUSTICS, ELECTRONIC ENGINEERING. *Educ:* Univ Tex, BS, 64, MA, 67, PhD(elec eng), 74. *Prof Exp:* Lab res asst, Appl Res Labs, Univ Tex, Austin, 63-65, res scientist acoust electronics, 65-80; WITH NAT INSTRUMENTS, 80- *Mem:* Acoust Soc Am. *Res:* Transducer measurement systems; digital signal processing of acoustic signals; nonlinear acoustics; parametric receiving arrays for acoustic signals. *Mailing Add:* 8900 Shoal Creek Nat Instruments Austin TX 78758

TRUCKER, DONALD EDWARD, b Jamaica, NY, Jan 20, 26; m 49; c 3. PHOTOGRAPHIC SCIENCE, ORGANIC CHEMISTRY. *Educ:* Polytech Inst Brooklyn, BS, 47, PhD(chem), 51; Purdue Univ, MS, 48. *Prof Exp:* Asst chem, Purdue Univ, 47-48; res chemist, Wyandotte Chem Corp, Mich, 51-57; chem specialist, GAF Corp, 57-63, group leader electrophotog, 63-68, tech assoc, 68-74, group leader, Photobinders/Coating Develop, 74-78, mgr, Chem/Base Develop, 78-80, mgr mfg tech, 80-81; MGR TESTING TECHNOL, ANITEC IMAGE CORP, 81- *Honors & Awards:* Serv Award, Soc Photog Scientists & Engrs, 73. *Mem:* Am Chem Soc; Soc Photog Scientists & Engrs; Royal Soc Chem. *Res:* Photographic science; electrophotography; chlorination of hydrocarbons; alkylene oxides. *Mailing Add:* 115 Morgan Rd Binghamton NY 13903

TRUDEL, GERALD JOSEPH, radiation chemistry, polymer chemistry, see previous edition

TRUDEL, MICHEL D, b Montreal, Que, Feb 5, 44; Can citizen; m 67; c 2. VIROLOGY. *Educ:* Univ Montreal, BA, 65, BSc, 68, MSc, 70; Univ Sherbrooke, PhD(cell biol), 73. *Prof Exp:* Fel cell membranes, Nat Cancer Inst, 73-74; asst prof, 74-75, PROF VIROL INST ARMAND-FRAPPIER, 75- *Concurrent Pos:* Grants, Formation Researcher, Ministry of Educ, Que, 76-78, Health & Welfare, Can, 76-78, Nat Res Coun Can, 78-81 & Can Med Res Coun, 79-83. *Mem:* NY Acad Sci; Am Soc Microbiol; Can Soc Microbiologists. *Res:* Viral subunit vaccines and the implication of the physical form of the viral proteins that induce the immune response. *Mailing Add:* Inst Armand-Frappier 531 Boul des Prairies CP 100 Laval-des-Rapides PQ H7N 4Z3 Can

TRUDEN, JUDITH LUCILLE, b Duluth, Minn, Sept 29, 31. VIROLOGY. *Educ:* Wayne State Univ, BA, 53, MS, 55; Univ Miami, PhD(microbiol), 67. *Prof Exp:* Technician virol, Henry Ford Hosp, Detroit, Mich, 55-59; USPHS res fel, Pub Health Res Inst, New York, NY, 68-71; res instr, Med Col Wis, 71-74, res assoc, 74; scholar molecular biol, Univ Mich, Ann Arbor, 75-78; RES ASSOC, WAYNE STATE UNIV, DETROIT, 78- *Mem:* Am Soc Microbiol. *Res:* RNA synthesis in respiratory syncytial virus-infected cells. *Mailing Add:* Dept of Immunol & Microbiol Wayne State Univ Detroit MI 48201

TRUE, NANCY S, b Waterbury, Conn, Sept 30, 51. PHYSICAL CHEMISTRY. *Educ:* Univ Conn, PhD(phys chem), 77. *Prof Exp:* Assoc chem, Univ Conn, 77-78, Univ Col London, 78-79 & Cornell Univ, 79-80; ASST PROF CHEM, UNIV CALIF, DAVIS, 80- *Mem:* Am Phys Soc; Am Chem Soc; Sigma Xi. *Mailing Add:* Dept Chem Univ Calif Davis CA 95616

TRUE, RENATE (SCHLENZ), biological oceanography, see previous edition

TRUE, WILLIAM WADSWORTH, b Rockland, Maine, Dec 27, 25; m 54; c 4. PHYSICS, NUCLEAR STRUCTURE. *Educ:* Univ Maine, BS, 50; Univ RI, MS, 52; Ind Univ, PhD(physics), 57. *Prof Exp:* Instr physics, Princeton Univ, 57-60; from asst prof to assoc prof, 60-69, PROF PHYSICS, UNIV CALIF, DAVIS, 69- *Mem:* Am Phys Soc. *Res:* Theoretical nuclear physics. *Mailing Add:* Dept of Physics Univ of Calif Davis CA 95616

TRUEBLOOD, EMILY WALCOTT EMMART, cytology, see previous edition

TRUEBLOOD, KENNETH NYITRAY, b Dobbs Ferry, NY, Apr 24, 20; m 70. CHEMISTRY. *Educ:* Harvard Univ, AB, 41; Calif Inst Technol, PhD(chem), 47. *Prof Exp:* Asst chem, Calif Inst Technol, 43-46, res fel, 47-49; from instr to assoc prof, 49-60, dean, Col Lett & Sci, 71-74, chmn dept chem, 65-70, PROF CHEM, UNIV CALIF, LOS ANGELES, 60- *Concurrent Pos:* Fulbright award, 56-57; mem, US Nat Comt Crystallog, 60-65; vis prof, Ibadan, 64-65; vis scientist, Inst Elemento-Org Compounds, Moscow, 65; Guggenheim fel, 76. *Mem:* Am Chem Soc; Am Crystallog Asn (pres, 61). *Res:* X-ray studies of molecular and crystal structure. *Mailing Add:* Dept of Chem Univ of Calif Los Angeles CA 90024

TRUELOVE, BRYAN, b Bradford, Eng. WEED SCIENCE. *Educ:* Sheffield Univ, BSc, 55, PhD(plant physiol), 61. *Prof Exp:* Asst lectr bot, Manchester Univ, 60-62, lectr, 62-67; assoc prof bot, 68-75, PROF BOT & MICROBIOL, AUBURN UNIV, 75- *Concurrent Pos:* Vis asst prof, Univ Ill, 65. *Mem:* Soc Exp Biol & Med; Am Soc Plant Physiologists; Weed Sci Soc Am. *Res:* Mitochondrial metabolism, particularly in relation to their energy linked functions and the effects of aging in mitochondria; mode of action of herbicides and effects on plant physiological processes and metabolism. *Mailing Add:* Dept Bot Plant Path & Microbiol Auburn Univ Auburn AL 36849

TRUEMAN, RICHARD E(LIAS), b Chicago, Ill, Oct 7, 25; m 53; c 4. OPERATIONS RESEARCH. *Educ:* Northwestern Univ, BSEE, 48; Stanford Univ, MSEE, 49; Univ Southern Calif, PhD(eng), 68. *Prof Exp:* Instr elec eng, Univ Nev, 49-50; design engr, Westinghouse Elec Corp, Pa, 50-51; elec engr, City Pub Serv Dept, Glendale, Calif, 51-53; engr, Jet Propulsion Lab, Calif Inst Technol, 53-55; sr res engr, Gen Dynamics/Convair, 55-57; appl sci rep, Int Bus Mach Corp, 57-59; sr consult, Touche, Ross, Bailey & Smart, 59-61; sr staff mathematician, Hughes Aircraft Co, Calif, 61-68; PROF MGT SCI, CALIF STATE UNIV, NORTHRIDGE, 68- *Concurrent Pos:* Lectr, Univ Southern Calif & Univ Calif, Los Angeles, 68; vis assoc prof, Naval Postgrad Sch, 69; vis prof mgt, San Diego State Univ, 74-75; vis prof opers res, Univ Canterbury, Christchurch, NZ, 79. *Mem:* Inst Mgt Sci; Am Inst Decision Sci. *Res:* Formulation, evaluation and utilization of mathematical models; computer Monte Carlo simulation. *Mailing Add:* 4919 Dunman Ave Woodland Hills CA 91364

TRUEMAN, THOMAS LAURENCE, b Media, Pa, Sept 24, 35; m 61; c 2. PHYSICS. *Educ:* Dartmouth Col, AB, 57; Univ Chicago, MS, 58, PhD(physics), 62. *Prof Exp:* Res assoc physics, 62-64, from asst physicist to physicist, 65-74, SR PHYSICIST & GROUP LEADER, BROOKHAVEN NAT LAB, 74-, DEP CHMN, PHYSICS DEPT, 80- *Concurrent Pos:* Guggenheim fel, Oxford Univ, 72-73; vis prof, Univ D'Aix-Marseille, 78-79. *Mem:* Fel Am Phys Soc. *Res:* High energy theory; scattering theory; strong interactions. *Mailing Add:* Brookhaven Nat Lab Upton NY 11973

TRUESDALE, LARRY KENNETH, b San Mateo, Calif, Jan 3, 47. CHEMICAL SYNTHESIS. *Educ:* Univ Calif, San Diego, AB, 69; Univ Calif, Los Angeles, PhD(chem), 74. *Prof Exp:* Res fel chem, Mass Inst Technol, 74-75; res chemist, Allied Chem Corp, 75-78; SR SCIENTIST CHEM, HOFFMANN-LAROCHE INC, 79- *Concurrent Pos:* Adj prof organometall chem, Rutgers Univ, Newark, 81. *Mem:* Am Chem Soc. *Res:* Chemical synthesis; synthetic methods; oxidations; and organometallics. *Mailing Add:* Hoffmann-LaRoche Inc 340 Kingsland Nutley NJ 07110

TRUESDELL, ALFRED HEMINGWAY, b Washington, DC, Sept 10, 33; m 64. GEOLOGY, CHEMISTRY. *Educ:* Oberlin Col, AB, 57; Harvard Univ, AM, 61, PhD(geol), 62. *Prof Exp:* GEOCHEMIST, US GEOL SURV, 55- *Concurrent Pos:* Res assoc, Stanford Univ, 64- *Mem:* AAAS; Am Mineral Soc; Geochem Soc. *Res:* Application of physical chemistry to the study of geologic processes; electrochemistry of membranes; ion exchange equilibria and energetics; solution geochemistry; chemistry and physics of geothermal systems. *Mailing Add:* US Geol Surv 345 Middlefield Rd Menlo Park CA 94025

TRUESDELL, CLIFFORD AMBROSE, III, b Los Angeles, Calif, Feb 18, 19; m 39, 51; c 1. MATHEMATICS. *Educ:* Calif Inst Technol, BS, 41, MS, 42; Brown Univ, cert, 42; Princeton Univ, PhD(math), 43. *Hon Degrees:* Dr Eng, Milan Polytech Inst, 64; DSc, Tulane Univ, 76; Fil Dr, Uppsala Univ, 79; Dr Phil, Basel Univ, 79. *Prof Exp:* Asst math & hist, Calif Inst Technol, 41-42; asst mech, Brown Univ, 42; instr math, Princeton Univ, 42-43 & Univ Mich, 43-44; mem staff, Radiation Lab, Mass Inst Technol, 44-46; chief theoret mech subdiv, Naval Ord Lab, 46-48, head theoret mech sect, Naval Res Lab, 48-51; prof math, Ind Univ, 50-61; PROF RATIONAL MECH, JOHNS HOPKINS UNIV, 61- *Concurrent Pos:* From lectr to assoc prof, Univ Md, 46-50; consult, Naval Res Lab, 51-55, Nat Bur Standards, 59-62, Sandia Corp, 66, Ga Inst Technol, 73-74 & US Nuclear Regulatory Comn, 75-; ed, J Rational Mech & Anal, 52-56 & Arch Hist Exact Sci, 60-; Guggenheim fel, 57; ed, Arch Rational Mech & Anal, 57-66, co-ed, 67-; co-ed, Ergebnisse der Angewandten Math, 57-62; NSF sr res fel, Univ Bologna & Univ Basel, 60-61; ed, Springer Tracts Natural Philos, 62-66 & 79-, co-ed, 67-78; Walker-Ames prof, Univ Wash, 64; distinguished vis prof, Syracuse Univ, 65; 75th Anniversary lectr, Drexel Inst Technol, 66-67; Lincean prof, Ital Acad Lincei, Rome, 70, 73 & 74; lectr, Fed Univ Rio de Janeiro, 72. *Honors & Awards:* Bingham Medal, Soc Rheol, 63; Panetti Int Medal & Prize, Acad Sci Turin, 67; Birkhoff Prize, Am Math Soc & Soc Indust & Appl Math, 78; Ordine del Cherubino, Univ Pisa, 78. *Mem:* Soc Natural Philos (secy, 63-65 & 70-71, chmn, 67-68); Int Acad Hist Sci; hon mem, Ital Acad Sci; Int Acad Philos Sci; foreign mem Lincean Acad Sci. *Res:* Rational mechanics. *Mailing Add:* 119 Latrobe Johns Hopkins Univ Baltimore MD 21218

TRUESDELL, SUSAN JANE, b Oak Park, Ill, Mar 22, 45. MOLECULAR BIOLOGY, MICROBIOLOGY. *Educ:* Mich State Univ, BS, 67; Univ Calif, Los Angeles, PhD(molecular biol), 71. *Prof Exp:* Am Cancer Soc fel, Univ Mich, 71-73; MICROBIOLOGIST MOLECULAR BIOL, PFIZER, INC, 73- *Concurrent Pos:* Instr introductory microbiol, Conn Col, 77 & 78. *Mem:* Am Soc Microbiol; AAAS. *Res:* Genetics and physiology of penicillin production; viruses that infect penicillium chrysogenum; microbiol enzyme production. *Mailing Add:* Fermentation Res & Develop Pfizer Inc Groton CT 06340

TRUESWELL, RICHARD W(ILLIAM), b Newark, NJ, Oct 12, 29; m 53; c 4. INFORMATION SCIENCE, COMPUTER SYSTEMS. *Educ:* Stevens Inst Technol, ME, 52, MSc, 58; Northwestern Univ, PhD(indust eng & mgt sci), 64. *Prof Exp:* Mfg engr, Westinghouse Elec Corp, Pa & NY, 54-56; instr indust eng, Stevens Inst Technol, 57-58; from instr to assoc prof, 58-65, chmn dept, 65-66, head dept indust eng & opers res, 66-76, PROF INDUST ENG & OPERS RES, UNIV MASS, AMHERST, 76- *Concurrent Pos:* Consult, Savage Arms Corp, SHadley Elec Light Dept, Prophylactic Brush Co & Nonotuck Mfg Co, 59-; consult, Assoc Data Processing Co, NJ, 59-64, dir res, 64-66; Joseph Lucas vis prof, Univ Birmingham, 71-72; pres, R W Trueswell, Inc, 68-; vpres, Inst Info Studies, Inc & Info Servs, Inc, 77-; pres, Trulim, Inc. *Mem:* Am Soc Mech Engrs; Am Inst Indust Engrs; Am Soc Eng Educ; Sigma Xi; Am Soc Info Sci. *Res:* Systems engineering; library systems, systems research and automation design; information searching behavior of scientists. *Mailing Add:* Dept Indust Eng & Oper Res Univ Mass Amherst MA 01002

TRUEX, RAYMOND CARL, b Norfolk, Nebr, Dec 11, 11; m 38; c 2. ANATOMY. *Educ:* Nebr Wesleyan Univ, AB, 34; St Louis Univ, MS, 36; Univ Minn, PhD(anat), 39. *Prof Exp:* From instr to assoc prof anat, Col Physicians & Surgeons, Columbia Univ, 38-48; prof & head div, Hahnemann Med Col, 48-61; PROF ANAT, SCH MED, TEMPLE UNIV, 61- *Concurrent Pos:* USPHS award prof, 61-; consult, NIH, 62-66 & Nat Bd Med Examrs, 67-71 & 75-79. *Honors & Awards:* AMA Awards, 52 & 58. *Mem:* AAAS; Geront Soc; Am Asn Anatomists (pres, 71); Harvey Soc; Am Vet Med Asn. *Res:* Histological changes with age and pathology of the human nervous system; histology and physiology of the conduction system and circulation of the heart. *Mailing Add:* Dept of Anat Temple Univ Sch of Med Philadelphia PA 19140

TRUEX, TIMOTHY JAY, b Goshen, Ind, June 11, 45. INORGANIC CHEMISTRY. *Educ:* Hanover Col, BS, 67; Mass Inst Technol, PhD(inorg chem), 72. *Prof Exp:* Res scientist inorg chem, Ford Motor Co, 72-80. *Mem:* Am Chem Soc. *Res:* Atmospheric environmental chemistry; catalysis chemistry; chemistry of surface coatings. *Mailing Add:* 1141 Thomas Rd Wayne PA 19087

TRUFANT, SAMUEL ADAMS, b New Orleans, La, May 24, 19; m 45; c 4. MEDICINE, NEUROLOGY. *Educ:* Tulane Univ, BS, 40, MD, 43; Am Bd Psychiat & Neurol, dipl, 51. *Prof Exp:* Asst gross anat, Tulane Univ, 40-41; Rockefeller fel neurol, Washington Univ, 47-49, USPHS res fel, 49-50; from asst prof to assoc prof, 50-62, from asst dean to assoc dean, Col Med, 51-62, prof, 62-70, EMER PROF NEUROL, COL MED, UNIV CINCINNATI, 70-; PROF NEUROL, TULANE UNIV, 79- *Concurrent Pos:* Consult, Wright-Patterson AFB, Ohio, 52-; dir pediat neurol, Children's Hosp, 59-71; dir, Am Bd Psychiat & Neurol, 66-73, vpres, 71, pres, 72-; proj officer, India Neurol & Sensory Dis Serv Prog, USPHS, 66-; mem, Residency Rev Comt Psychiat & Neurol, 67-72, chmn, 70-72; ed, Trans, Am Neurol Asn, 68-73. *Mem:* Am Neurol Asn (vpres, 65, secy-treas, 68-73, pres, 75); Asn Res Nerv & Ment Dis; Asn Am Med Cols (asst secy, 59-64); Am Acad Neurol. *Res:* Clinical neurology; electroencephalography. *Mailing Add:* Dept Psychiat & Neurol Sch Med Tulane Univ 1430 Tulane Ave New Orleans LA 70112

TRUHLAR, DONALD GENE, b Chicago, Ill, Feb 27, 44; m 65. PHYSICAL CHEMISTRY, MOLECULAR PHYSICS. *Educ:* St Mary's Col, Minn, BA, 65; Calif Inst Technol, PhD(chem), 70. *Prof Exp:* Student aide chem, Argonne Nat Lab, 65; from asst prof to assoc prof chem, 69-76, PROF CHEM & CHEM PHYSICS, UNIV MINN, MINNEAPOLIS, 76- *Concurrent Pos:* Sr vis fel, Battelle Mem Inst, Columbus, 73; & Sloan res fel, 73-77; vis fel, Joint Inst Lab Astrophysics, Boulder, Colo, 75-76. *Mem:* Am Phys Soc; Am Chem Soc. *Res:* Theory and computations for collision processes involving atoms, molecules and electrons; potential energy surfaces for triatomic systems; theory of molecular spectroscopy. *Mailing Add:* Dept of Chem Univ of Minn Minneapolis MN 55455

TRUITT, EDWARD BYRD, JR, b Norfolk, Va, Aug 23, 22; m 49; c 2. PHARMACOLOGY. *Educ:* Med Col Va, BS, 43; Univ Md, PhD(pharmacol), 50. *Prof Exp:* Asst prof pharmacol, Bowman Gray Sch Med, Wake Forest Col, 50-55; from assoc prof to prof, Sch Med, Univ Md, Baltimore City, 55-67; sr res fel, Columbus Labs, Battelle Mem Inst & prof pharmacol, Col Med, Ohio State Univ, 67-72; res prof pharmacol, Sch Med, George Washington Univ, 73-76; PROG CHIEF & PROF PHARMACOL, COL MED, NORTHEASTERN OHIO UNIV, 76- *Concurrent Pos:* Robins Co fel, Bowman Gray Sch Med, Wake Forest Col, 50-55. *Mem:* Res Soc Alcoholism; Am Chem Soc; Am Soc Pharmacol & Exp Therapeut; Soc Exp Biol & Med; NY Acad Sci. *Res:* Neuropharmacology; psychopharmacology; drug metabolism; alcoholism; marijuana and drug abuse research. *Mailing Add:* Prog Pharmacol Northeastern Ohio Univ Col Med Rootstown OH 44272

TRUITT, MARCUS M(CCAFFERTY), b Enid, Okla, Oct 10, 21; m 42; c 2. CIVIL ENGINEERING. *Educ:* Okla State Univ, BS, 47; Harvard Univ, MS, 48; Stanford Univ, Engr, 51; Johns Hopkins Univ, PhD, 68. *Prof Exp:* Soil mechanic, United Fruit Co, Cent Am, 48-49; asst prof civil eng, Univ Ala, 49-50; from asst prof to prof eng, 51-77, chmn dept civil & mech eng, 68-77, PROF CIVIL & MECH ENG, TEX A&I UNIV, 77- *Concurrent Pos:* Consult, 53-; city engr, Kingsville, Tex, 53-; res assoc, Johns Hopkins Univ, 66- *Mem:* Am Soc Civil Engrs; Am Soc Eng Educ. *Res:* Municipal engineering; environmental engineering; application of computer simulation techniques to hurricane track predictions. *Mailing Add:* Dept of Civil & Mech Eng Tex A&I Univ Kingsville TX 78363

TRUITT, ROBERT LINDELL, b Carbondale, Ill, July 26, 46; m 67; c 5. MICROBIOLOGY, TRANSPLANTATION IMMUNOLOGY. *Educ:* Southern Ill Univ, Carbondale, BA, 68, PhD(microbiol), 73. *Prof Exp:* Fel germfree syst, Lobund Lab, Univ Notre Dame, 72-74; res assoc, 74-77, SR SCIENTIST TUMOR IMMUNOL, WINTER RES LAB, MT SINAI MED CTR, 77- *Concurrent Pos:* Fel, United Cancer Coun, 72-73 & Damon Runyon Mem Fund Cancer Res, 73-75; NIH/Nat Cancer Inst res grants, 75, 77 & 79; spec fel, Leukemia Soc Am, 76-78, scholar, 78- *Mem:* Am Asn Immunologists; Fedn Am Soc Exp Biol; Sigma Xi; Am Soc Microbiol; Int Soc Exp Hemat. *Res:* Germfree animal systems; tumor immunology; bone marrow transplantation; virology. *Mailing Add:* Winter Res Lab Mt Sinai Med Ctr PO Box 342 Milwaukee WI 53201

TRUJILLO, EDUARDO E, b Horconcitos, Panama, Apr 22, 30. PLANT PATHOLOGY. *Educ:* Univ Ark, BSA, 56, MS, 57; Univ Calif, PhD(plant path), 62. *Prof Exp:* Res asst plant path, Univ Calif, 57-62; asst plant pathologist, 62-65, asst prof plant path & asst specialist, 65-67, assoc prof, 67-74, prof plant path, 74-80, PROF BOT SCI, UNIV HAWAII, 80-, ASSOC PLANT PATHOLOGIST, 67- *Concurrent Pos:* Consult, Pac Southwest Forest & Range Exp Sta, US Forest Serv, 63- *Mem:* AAAS; Am Phys Soc; Am Soc Hort Sci. *Res:* Aspects of research dealing with soil borne pathogens, mainly ecology and epidemiology of Pythium and Phytophthoras in tropical environments; biology of Fusarium species. *Mailing Add:* Dept of Plant Path Univ of Hawaii at Manoa Honolulu HI 96822

TRUJILLO, PATRICIO EDUARDO, b Santa Fe, NMex, Jan 21, 37; m 62; c 4. ANALYTICAL CHEMISTRY, GEOCHEMISTRY. *Educ:* Univ NMex, BS, 60. *Prof Exp:* Chemist, NMex Bur Revenue, 59-60; lieutenant missile tech, USAF, 61-64; chief chemist, Eberline Instrument Corp, 64-67; STAFF MEM CHEM, LOS ALAMOS NAT LAB, 67- *Mem:* Health Physics Soc; Am Indust Hygiene Asn; Am Chem Soc. *Res:* Analytical chemistry related to geothermal energy. *Mailing Add:* 1069 Calle Largo Santa Fe NM 87501

TRUJILLO, PHILLIP M, b Chimayo, NMex, Feb 5, 21; m 45; c 3. AGRONOMY. *Educ:* NMex State Univ, BS, 47; Univ Md, MS, 51. *Prof Exp:* County exten agent, NMex State Univ, 47-48; instr farm training prog, State Dept Voc Agr, NMex, 48-49; asst supvr, Farmers Home Admin, USDA, 51-52; assoc prof & supt, 52-80, EMER ASSOC PROF AGRON, ESPANOLA VALLEY BR STA, NMEX STATE UNIV, 80- *Mem:* Am Soc Agron. *Res:* Improvement of agronomic crops. *Mailing Add:* Espanola Valley Br Sta NMex State Univ Dept Agron Alcalde NM 87511

TRUJILLO, RALPH EUSEBIO, b Embudo, NMex, Sept 22, 40; m 70. BIOCHEMISTRY. *Educ:* Univ NMex, BS, 62; Ind Univ, PhD(biochem), 67. *Prof Exp:* Mem Peace Corps, Ecuador, 62-64; USPHS fel biochem, Univ Tex M D Anderson Hosp & Tumor Inst, 67-69; MEM TECH STAFF, SANDIA LABS, 69- *Res:* Response of macromolecular systems to thermal, chemical and radiation environments. *Mailing Add:* Div 4445 Sandia Labs Albuquerque NM 87115

TRUJILLO, STEPHEN MICHAEL, b Culver City, Calif, Mar 5, 32; m 59. ATOMIC PHYSICS, ELECTRICAL ENGINEERING. *Educ:* Univ Kans, BSc, 58; Univ London, DPHil(physics), 75. *Prof Exp:* Staff scientist physics, Convair Div, Gulf Oil Corp, 69-72; prin physicist, IRT Corp, 72-80; SR SCIENTIST, INESCO INC, 80- *Concurrent Pos:* Vis res fel physics, Univ London, 70-75. *Mem:* Am Phys Soc; Inst Physics, Eng; Inst Elec & Electronics Engrs; Am Vacuum Soc. *Res:* Molecular physics; scientific instrumentation; electro optics. *Mailing Add:* INESCO Inc 11077 N Torrey Pines Rd La Jolla CA 92037

TRULSON, OLOF CONRAD, b Concord, NH, Jan 2, 33; m 53; c 3. PHYSICS, PHYSICAL CHEMISTRY. *Educ:* Univ NH, BS, 54; Iowa State Univ, MS, 56, PhD(physics), 59. *Prof Exp:* Staff scientist phys chem, Union Carbide Res Inst, 60-66, develop scientist physics, Space Sci & Eng Lab, Union Carbide Corp, 66-69; dep dir mat sci admin, Advan Res Projs Agency, Off Secy Defense, 69-71; prod mgr, 71-73, dir sales, 73-74, dir tech serv, 74-75, dir carbon fiber develop admin, 75-79, BUS CONTROLLER, CARBON PROD DIV, UNION CARBIDE CORP, 79- *Res:* Commercial process for manufacturing carbon fibers from a pitch precursor; applications for carbon fibers in high performance composites. *Mailing Add:* Carbon Prod Div 12900 Snow Rd Parma OH 44130

TRUM, BERNARD FRANCIS, b Natick, Mass, Dec 10, 09; m 36; c 4. VETERINARY MEDICINE. *Educ:* Boston Col, AB, 31; Cornell Univ, DVM, 35. *Prof Exp:* Prof zootechnol, Univ Mayor de San Simon, Bolivia, 49-50 & Univ Tenn, 51-56; vet, US AEC, 56-58; lectr & dir, Animal Res Ctr, Harvard Med Sch, 58-78; dir, New Eng Regional Primate Res Ctr, 62-78; RETIRED. *Concurrent Pos:* Mem, Nat Coun Radiation Protection & Measurement; vpres, Pathobiology, Inc, 78- *Mem:* Am Asn Lab Animal Sci (pres, 65); Radiation Res Soc; Soc Exp Biol & Med; NY Acad Sci. *Res:* Effects of total body radiation; zootechnics of domestic and laboratory animals. *Mailing Add:* 247 Washington St Sherborn MA 01770

TRUMAN, JAMES WILLIAM, b Akron, Ohio, Feb 5, 45; m 70. NEUROBIOLOGY. *Educ:* Univ Notre Dame, BS, 67; Harvard Univ, MA, 69, PhD(biol), 70. *Prof Exp:* Harvard Soc Fels jr fel, Harvard Univ, 70-73; from asst prof to assoc prof, 73-78, PROF ZOOL, UNIV WASH, 78- *Honors & Awards:* Newcomb Cleveland Prize, AAAS, 70; NIH Res Career Develop Award, 76-81. *Mem:* Entom Soc Am; Soc Neurosci; Western Soc Naturalists; Am Soc Zoologists; Soc Gen Physiol. *Res:* Physiological aspects of circadian rhythms; interaction of hormones with the nervous system. *Mailing Add:* Dept of Zool Univ of Wash Seattle WA 98195

TRUMBO, BRUCE EDWARD, b Springfield, Ill, Dec 12, 37. STATISTICS. *Educ:* Knox Col, Ill, AB, 59; Univ Chicago, SM, 61, PhD(statist), 65. *Prof Exp:* Asst prof math, San Jose State Col, 63-64; from asst prof to assoc prof, 65-72, chmn dept, 70-75, PROF STATIST, CALIF STATE UNIV, HAYWARD, 72- *Concurrent Pos:* Consult, 64-70; vis assoc prof, Stanford Univ, 67-69 & 71; coun fel, Acad Admin Internship Prog, Am Coun Educ, 68-69; prog dir statist res, NSF, 74-75 & 78-79. *Mem:* Am Statist Asn; Inst Math Statist. *Res:* Application of statistical methods to social, behavioral and biological sciences; probability. *Mailing Add:* Dept of Statist Calif State Univ Hayward CA 94542

TRUMBORE, CONRAD NOBLE, b Denver, Colo, Feb 17, 31; m 55; c 2. PHYSICAL CHEMISTRY. *Educ:* Dickinson Col, BS, 52; Pa State Univ, PhD(chem), 55. *Prof Exp:* Fulbright grant, Inst Nuclear Res, Netherlands, 55-56; asst scientist, Argonne Nat Lab, 56-57; instr chem, Univ Rochester, 57-60; asst prof, 60-66, ASSOC PROF CHEM, UNIV DEL, 66- *Concurrent Pos:* USPHS spec fel, Inst Cancer Res, Sutton, Eng, 67-68. *Mem:* AAAS; Radiation Res Soc; Am Chem Soc. *Res:* Primary chemical processes in radiation chemistry of aqueous solutions; correlations between photochemistry and radiation chemistry; biological radiation chemistry; pulse radiolysis and flash photolysis. *Mailing Add:* 113 Dallas Ave Newark DE 19711

TRUMBORE, FORREST ALLEN, b Denver, Colo, Dec 28, 27; m 51; c 2. PHYSICAL CHEMISTRY. *Educ:* Dickinson Col, BS, 46; Univ Pittsburgh, PhD(chem), 50. *Prof Exp:* Aeronaut res scientist thermodyn alloys, Lewis Flight Propulsion Lab, Nat Adv Comt Aeronaut, 50-52; MEM TECH STAFF, BELL LABS, INC, 52- *Mem:* AAAS; Electrochem Soc. *Res:* Solubilities and electrical properties of impurities in semiconductors; crystal growth; photoluminescence and electroluminescence in semiconductors; battery materials. *Mailing Add:* 30 Glen Oaks Ave Summit NJ 07901

TRUMBULL, ELMER ROY, JR, b Lawrence, Mass, Apr 5, 24; m 54; c 3. ORGANIC CHEMISTRY. *Educ:* Dartmouth Col, AB, 44; Univ Ill, PhD(org chem), 47. *Prof Exp:* Asst chem, Univ Ill, 44-46; res assoc, Mass Inst Technol, 47-48, Du Pont fel, 51-52; instr, Tufts Col, 48-51; asst prof chem, Brown Univ, 52-58; from asst prof to assoc prof, 58-63, dir div natural sci & math, 64-70, PROF CHEM, COLGATE UNIV, 63-, CHMN DEPT, 70- *Concurrent Pos:* NSF fac fel, Univ Ariz, 66-67; res assoc, Eidgenoessische Technische Hochschule, Zurich, 71-72; vis prof, Ore State Univ, 78-79. *Mem:* Am Chem Soc; Royal Soc Chem. *Res:* Elimination reactions; natural products. *Mailing Add:* Dept of Chem Colgate Univ Hamilton NY 13346

TRUMMEL, J(OHN) MERLE, b Maroa, Ill, Dec 28, 16; m 42; c 4. MECHANICAL ENGINEERING. *Educ:* Univ Ill, BS, 39; Iowa State Univ, MS, 40; Univ Iowa, PhD(mech eng), 60. *Prof Exp:* Instr mech eng, 41-44, asst prof, 44-58, instr, 58-59, assoc prof, 60-61, actg chmn dept, 65-66, PROF MECH ENG, UNIV IOWA, 61- *Concurrent Pos:* Consult, Oak Ridge Nat Lab, 54-58, Hawkeye Prod Corp, Iowa, 60-61 & Pioneer-Cent Div Bendix Corp, 61-63. *Mem:* Am Soc Mech Engrs; Am Soc Eng Educ. *Res:* Heat transport by unsteady flows; design and analysis of mechanical systems; mechanical engineering measurement and instrumentation. *Mailing Add:* Div of Mat Eng Univ of Iowa Iowa City IA 52242

TRUMMER, MAX JOSEPH, b Bogota, Colombia, Aug 12, 24; US citizen; m 45; c 1. THORACIC SURGERY. *Educ:* Univ Ill, MD, 48; Univ Pa, MS, 65; Am Bd Surg, dipl, 58; Bd Thoracic Surg, dipl, 61. *Prof Exp:* Resident thoracic surg, US Naval Hosp, Med Corps, US Navy, 58-60, chief thoracic surgeon, San Diego, 67-70; chief thoracic and cardiac surg, Los Angeles County-Olive View Med Ctr, 70-71; DIR SURG TEACHING PROG, MERCY HOSP & MED CTR, SAN DIEGO, 71- *Concurrent Pos:* Assoc clin prof thoracic surg, Univ Southern Calif, 69- & Univ Calif, San Diego, 70- *Mem:* Fel Am Col Surgeons; fel Am Col Chest Physicians; Soc Thoracic Surg; Am Asn Thoracic Surg; fel Am Col Cardiology. *Res:* Lung transplantation; open-heart surgery; cardiopulmonary physiology. *Mailing Add:* Mercy Hosp & Med Ctr 4077 Fifth Ave San Diego CA 92103

TRUMMER, STEVEN, b Banska-Bystrica, Czech, Aug 20, 25; US citizen; m 61; c 2. ANALYTICAL CHEMISTRY. *Educ:* Budapest Polytech Inst, MS, 47; Hungarian Acad Sci, PhD(spectros), 56. *Prof Exp:* Teaching asst soil chem, Univ Agr Sci, Hungary, 47-48; chemist anal of metals, Csepel Iron Works, Hungary, 48-52; scientist spectros, Cent Res Inst Physics, Budapest, 52-56; scientist polymer develop, Bell Tel Labs, 57-66; RES GROUP LEADER ANAL CHEM, POLAROID CORP, 66- *Mem:* Am Chem Soc. *Mailing Add:* Dept of Anal Chem Polaroid Corp Cambridge MA 02139

TRUMP, BENJAMIN FRANKLIN, b Kansas City, Mo, July 23, 32; m 61; c 2. PATHOLOGY, CELL BIOLOGY. *Educ:* Univ Mo-Kansas City, BA, 53; Univ Kans, MD, 57. *Prof Exp:* Intern path, Med Ctr, Univ Kans, 57-58, resident, 58-59; resident anat, Sch Med, Univ Wash, 59-60, resident-trainee, 60-61, investr exp path, Armed Forces Inst Path, 61-63; asst prof path, Sch Med, Univ Wash, 63-65; from assoc prof to prof, Med Ctr, Duke Univ, 65-70; PROF PATH & CHMN DEPT, SCH MED, UNIV MD, BALTIMORE CITY, 70- *Concurrent Pos:* Fel, Med Ctr, Univ Kans, 58-59; US Food & Drug Admin fel, Univ Assoc for Res & Educ in Path; NIH fel & training grant, Univ Md; mem bd dirs, Univ Assoc for Res & Educ in Path, 70-; mem, Md Post Mortem Exam Comn, 70-; consult, US Food & Drug Admin, 71- & Vet Admin Hosp, Baltimore, Md, 72-; docent, Dept Cell Biol, Univ Jyvaskyla, Finland, 73-; Am Cancer Soc prof oncol, & dir, Md Cancer Prog, 77- *Mem:* AAAS; Am Asn Path & Bact; Am Soc Exp Path; Am Soc Cell Biol; Am Soc Microbiol. *Res:* Cellular and subcellular pathology; membrane structure and functions; lysosome structure and function; chemical carcinogenesis; kidney pathophysiology; fish physiology and pathology; environmental pathology. *Mailing Add:* Dept of Path Sch of Med Baltimore MD 21201

TRUMP, JOHN G(EORGE), b New York, NY, Aug 21, 07; m 35; c 3. ELECTRICAL ENGINEERING. *Educ:* Polytech Inst Brooklyn, EE, 29; Columbia Univ, MA, 31; Mass Inst Technol, DSc(elec eng), 33. *Prof Exp:* Instr elec eng, Polytech Inst Brooklyn, 29-31; res assoc, Mass Inst Technol, 33-36, from asst prof to prof elec eng, 36-73, dir, High Voltage Res Lab, 46-80. *Concurrent Pos:* Tech aide & secy, Microwave Comt, Nat Defense Res Comt & Off Sci Res & Develop, 40-44; dir, Brit Br Radiation Lab, Eng & France, 44-45; chmn bd, High Voltage Eng Corp, 47-70, tech dir, 47-80; chmn bd trustees, Lahey Clin Found, 74- *Honors & Awards:* Lamme Medal, Inst Elec & Electronics Engrs, 60. *Mem:* Nat Acad Eng; Inst Elec & Electronics Engrs; Am Phys Soc. *Res:* Insulating properties of high vacuum and compressed gases; acceleration of charged particles to high energies by Van de Graaff accelerators and study of physical and biological properties of such radiation; application of energized electrons to sterilization of surgical materials, cross-linking of polymeric materials and the disinfection of municipal waste water and sludge. *Mailing Add:* High Voltage Res Lab Mass Inst of Technol Cambridge MA 02139

TRUMP, ROBERT PAUL, b Kimmerlings, Pa, Feb 12, 31; m 52; c 3. MINING & PETROLEUM ENGINEERING. *Educ:* Pa State Univ, BS, 54, MS, 55. *Prof Exp:* Res geologist, 55-66, res engr, 66-69, SR RES ENGR, GULF RES & DEVELOP CO, 69- *Mem:* Am Inst Mining, Metall & Petrol Engrs. *Res:* Rock mechanics; buckling; strain and pressure measurements; structural geology; clay permeability. *Mailing Add:* Gulf Res & Develop Co PO Drawer 2038 Pittsburgh PA 15230

TRUMPLER, PAUL R(OBERT), b Rahway, NJ, Nov 3, 14; m 38; c 3. MECHANICAL ENGINEERING, APPLIED MECHANICS. *Educ:* Lafayette Col, BS, 36; Yale Univ, PhD(mech eng), 40. *Prof Exp:* Instr heat power eng, Ill Inst Technol, 39-41; mech engr, Western Elec Co, NJ, 41-42; heat transfer develop engr, Nat Defense Res Comt, M W Kellogg Co Div, Pullman, Inc, NY, 42-47; engr, Centrifugal Eng Dept, Clark Bros Co, Inc, 47-49; prof mech eng, Ill Inst Technol, 49-57; prof, Univ Pa, 57-69, dir sch mech eng, 57-60; founder & pres, Turbo Res, Inc, 61-74; PRES, TURBO RES FOUND, 66-; FOUNDER & PRES, TRUMPLER ASSOCS, INC & TURBOTHERM CORP, 74- *Concurrent Pos:* Indust consult. *Mem:* Fel Am Soc Mech Engrs; fel Am Soc Eng Educ. *Res:* Hydrodynamic bearings; dynamics of turbomachines; balancing; disk stresses; vibrations; gas turbines. *Mailing Add:* Trumpler Assocs Inc 1442 Phoenixville Pike Westchester PA 19380

TRUMPOWER, BERNARD LEE, b Chambersburg, Pa, July 20, 43; m 64. BIOCHEMISTRY. *Educ:* Univ Pittsburgh, BS, 65; St Louis Univ, PhD(biochem), 69. *Prof Exp:* Asst prof, 72-77, ASSOC PROF BIOCHEM, DARTMOUTH MED SCH, 77- *Concurrent Pos:* NIH fel, Cornell Univ, 69-71. *Mem:* Fed Am Socs Exp Biol. *Res:* Bioenergetics; membrane structure. *Mailing Add:* Dept of Biochem Dartmouth Med Sch Hanover NH 03755

TRUNK, GERARD VERNON, b Baltimore, Md, May 9, 42. ELECTRICAL ENGINEERING. *Educ:* Johns Hopkins Univ, BES, 63, PhD(elec eng), 67. *Prof Exp:* Elec engr radar, Naval Res Lab, 67-74; vis fel elec eng, Johns Hopkins Univ, 74-75; head radar anal staff, 75-79, HEAD, RADAR ANAL BR, NAVAL RES LAB, 79- *Concurrent Pos:* Sabatical lectr, Johns Hopkins Univ, 74- *Mem:* Inst Elec & Electronics Engrs; Sci Res Soc Am. *Res:* Radar systems; detection and estimation theory; simulation; and pattern recognition. *Mailing Add:* Code 5308 Naval Res Lab Washington DC 20375

TRUNNELL, JACK B, b Milledgeville, Ill, Oct 21, 18; m 42; c 6. MEDICINE. *Educ:* Brigham Young Univ, BA, 42; Univ Utah, MD, 45. *Prof Exp:* Asst, Sloan-Kettering Inst, 48-50; from asst prof to assoc prof med, Post-Grad Sch Med, Univ Tex, 50-58, head exp med, M D Anderson Hosp & Tumor Clin, 50-58; prof develop biol, Brigham Young Univ, 58-68, dean col family living, 58-61, dir ctr cell res, 61-68; CHIEF MED, GULF COAST HOSP & CLIN, 72- *Concurrent Pos:* Fel med, Sloan-Kettering Inst, 46-48; fel, Mem Hosp, New York, 47-50; asst res, Mem Hosp, New York, 46-47; lectr, US Naval Med Ctr, 46-50; consult, Brookhaven Nat Labs, 48-50; instr, Med Sch, Cornell Univ, 49-50; mem med staff, New York Hosp, 49-50; pvt pract, 69-; chief med, Baytown Med Ctr Hosp, 72. *Mem:* Soc Nuclear Med; Endocrine Soc; AMA; Am Thyroid Asn; Acad Psychosom Med. *Res:* Cancer; endocrinology; radioisotopes; psychosomatics; nutrition. *Mailing Add:* Gulf Coast Clin 2800 Garth Rd Baytown TX 77520

TRUNZO, FLOYD F(RANK), b Apollo, Pa, Dec 3, 17; m 46; c 3. CHEMICAL ENGINEERING. *Educ:* Univ Ala, BS, 41, MS, 47. *Prof Exp:* Observer, Process Control, Carnegie Ill Steel Corp, 41; jr engr pilot resin develop, Westinghouse Res Labs, 47-48, assoc engr wire insulation develop, 48-53, res engr, 53-62, sr res engr, 62-76, sr res scientist, 76-77, fel engr, 77-81; RETIRED. *Mem:* Am Chem Soc. *Res:* Wire insulation for motors, transformers and magnet wires; composite insulating materials for electrical power and generating equipment. *Mailing Add:* 106 Jamison Ln Monroeville PA 15146

TRUONG, XUAN THOAI, b French Cochin-China, Nov 17, 30; US citizen. PHYSICAL MEDICINE, PHYSIOLOGY. *Educ:* West Liberty State Col, BS, 52; Columbia Univ, MD, 56; Univ Louisville, PhD(physiol), 64; Am Bd Phys Med & Rehab, dipl, 65. *Prof Exp:* Intern surg, Ind Univ Med Ctr, 56-57; resident phys med & rehab, Univ Louisville Hosps, 58-61, instr, Sch Med, Univ, 62-64; clin & res consult, Inst Phys Med & Rehab, 64-68; asst prof, Baylor Col Med, 68-71; DIR RES & EDUC, INST PHYS MED & REHAB, 72- *Concurrent Pos:* Clin investr, Vet Admin Hosp, Houston, 69-71; asst prof, Peoria Sch Med, Univ Ill, 72- *Mem:* Am Physiol Soc; Am Acad Phys Med & Rehab; Inst Elec & Electronics Engrs; Am Asn Electromyog & Electrodiag; Am Med Asn. *Res:* Mechanical properties of muscle tissue; electrophysiology of neuro-muscular system; engineering devices for neuro-muscular disabilities. *Mailing Add:* Inst of Phys Med & Rehab 619 NE Glen Oak Ave Peoria IL 61603

TRUPIN, GENE LOUIS, b New York, NY, Sept 5, 40. ANATOMY, BIOLOGY. *Educ:* Cornell Univ, BS, 61; Univ Mich, MS, 68, PhD(anat), 73. *Prof Exp:* ASST PROF ANAT, MED SCH, RUTGERS UNIV, 72- *Mem:* Am Asn Anatomists; NY Acad Sci. *Res:* Regeneration of injured muscle and nerve; regeneration of amputated limbs. *Mailing Add:* Dept of Anat Rutgers Univ Med Sch Piscataway NJ 08854

TRUPIN, JOEL SUNRISE, b Brooklyn, NY, Mar 15, 34; m 57; c 1. BIOCHEMISTRY, NUTRITION. *Educ:* Cornell Univ, BS, 54, MNS, 56; Univ Ill, PhD(biochem), 63. *Prof Exp:* Asst prof microbiol, Sch Med, St Louis Univ, 66-71; ASSOC PROF GENETICS & MOLECULAR MED, MEHARRY MED COL, 71- *Concurrent Pos:* Am Cancer Soc res fel biochem genetics, Nat Heart Inst, 63-66. *Mem:* AAAS; Am Chem Soc; Am Soc Microbiol. *Res:* Biochemistry and regulation of amino acid biosynthesis; transfer RNA; protein and amino acid nutrition. *Mailing Add:* Grad Studies Meharry Med Col Nashville TN 37208

TRUPP, CLYDE RULON, b St Anthony, Idaho, May 14, 41; m 64; c 2. PLANT BREEDING. *Educ:* Univ Idaho, BS, 63, MS, 65; Iowa State Univ, PhD(plant breeding), 69. *Prof Exp:* Asst prof hybrid wheat breeding, Mich State Univ, 69-75; PLANT BREEDER SUGAR BEETS, AMALGAMATED SUGAR CO, 75- *Mem:* Am Soc Agron; Crop Sci Soc Am; Sigma Xi. *Res:* Breeding improved hybrid varieties of sugar beets for commercial culture and processing. *Mailing Add:* Beet Seed Develop Amalgamated Sugar Co Nyssa OR 97913

TRURAN, JAMES WELLINGTON, JR, b Brewster, NY, July 12, 40; m 65; c 3. ASTROPHYSICS. *Educ:* Cornell Univ, BA, 61; Yale Univ, MS, 63, PhD(physics), 66. *Prof Exp:* Resident res assoc, Goddard Inst Space Studies, NASA, NY, 65-67; res fel physics, Calif Inst Technol, 68-69; from assoc prof to prof physics, Belfer Grad Sch Sci, 70-73; PROF ASTRON, UNIV ILL, URBANA-CHAMPAIGN, 73- *Concurrent Pos:* Mem bd contribr, Comments Astrophys & Space Physics, 73-74; ed, Contributions Nuclear & High-energy Astrophys, Physics Letters B, 74-80; trustee, Aspen Ctr Physics, 79-; assoc, Ctr Advan Sci, Univ Ill; sr vis fel, Inst Astron, Univ Cambridge, England & Guggenheim Mem Found fel, 79-80. *Honors & Awards:* Yale Sci & Eng Asn Annual Award, Advan Basic or Appl Sci, 80. *Mem:* Am Phys Soc; Am Astron Soc; Int Astron Union. *Res:* Nucleosynthesis; nuclear reactions in stars; mechanisms of nova and supernova explosions; stellar evolution; galactic evolution; origin of cosmic rays; white dwarfs; binary evolution. *Mailing Add:* Dept of Astron Univ of Ill Urbana IL 61801

TRUS, BENES L, b Tyler, Tex, May 9, 46; m 72; c 2. IMAGE PROCESSING. *Educ:* Tulane Univ, BS, 68; Calif Inst Technol, PhD(phys chem), 72. *Prof Exp:* Jane Coffin Childs fel, Calif Inst Technol, 72-75; staff fel, Lab Biochem, Nat Inst Dent Res, 75-77, sr staff fel, 77-80, RES CHEMIST, COMPUT SYST LAB, DIV COMPUT RES & TECHNOL, NIH, 80- *Mem:* Am Crystallog Asn; Inst Elec & Electronic Engrs; Sigma Xi. *Res:* Computer analysis of chemical problems, biochemical problems, and electron microscopy; image processing and morphological analysis; molecular graphics and computer modeling; collagen structure analysis. *Mailing Add:* Rm 2055 Bldg 12A Nat Inst Health Bethesda MD 20205

TRUSCOTT, BASIL LIONEL, b Chambers, Nebr, Aug 4, 16; m 48. BIOLOGY, ANATOMY. *Educ:* Drew Univ, BA, 39; Syracuse Univ, MA, 40; Yale Univ, MS, 42, PhD(exp embryol), 43, MD, 50; Am Bd Neurol, dipl, 59. *Prof Exp:* Instr anat, Georgetown Univ, 43-45; instr biol, Yale Univ, 46, instr anat, 47-51; asst prof, Sch Med, Univ NC, 51-54; from assoc prof to prof neurol, Albany Med Col, 60-68; asst dean student admis, 73-77, assoc dean, 77-78, PROF NEUROL, BOWMAN GRAY SCH MED, 68- *Concurrent Pos:* Chief neurol sect, Vet Admin Hosp, Albany, NY, 60-68; dir comprehensive stroke prog, NC Regional Med Prog, 68-73. *Mem:* Am Asn Anat; Am Acad Neurol; fel Am Col Physicians. *Res:* Hypophysial-gonadal interaction; vitamin A physiology and steroid interrelationships; epidemiology of stroke; physiology; pathology; zoology; chemistry; neurology. *Mailing Add:* 460 Briarlea Rd Winston-Salem NC 27104

TRUSCOTT, FREDERICK HERBERT, b Meredith, NY, Mar 16, 26; m 54; c 2. PLANT PHYSIOLOGY. *Educ:* State Univ NY Albany, AB, 50; Rutgers Univ, PhD(bot), 55. *Prof Exp:* Asst bot, Rutgers Univ, 52-55; res fel, Jackson Mem Lab, Bar Harbor, Maine, 55-56; instr bot, Univ RI, 56-58; from asst prof to assoc prof, 58-65, chmn dept, 72-75, PROF BIOL, STATE UNIV NY ALBANY, 65- *Mem:* Bot Soc Am; Am Soc Plant Physiologists; Am Inst Biol Sci. *Res:* Morphogenesis; photophysiology. *Mailing Add:* Dept of Biol State Univ of NY Albany NY 12222

TRUSCOTT, ROBERT BRUCE, b Winnipeg, Man, July 9, 28; m 53; c 5. VETERINARY MICROBIOLOGY. *Educ:* Univ Toronto, BSA, 50, MSA, 53, DVM, 62; Univ Waterloo, PhD(microbiol physiol), 66. *Prof Exp:* Supvr, Animal House, Univ Western Ont, 50; fermentation supvr, Merck & Co Ltd, Que, 50-51; res asst microbiol, Ont Agr Col, Guelph, 51-53; lectr poultry path, Ont Vet Col, Univ Guelph, 53-76, assoc prof vet microbiol, 69-76; RES SCIENTIST, HEALTH ANIMALS BR, CAN DEPT AGR, ANIMAL PATH LAB, SACKVILLE, NB, 77- *Mem:* Int Orgn Mycoplasmologists; Microbiol; Am Soc Microbiol; Poultry Sci Asn; Am Asn Avian Pathologists; Can Vet Med Asn. *Res:* Avian salmonella; bovine mycoplasmas, detection, pathology and control. *Mailing Add:* Animal Path Lab PO Box 1410 Sackville NB E0A 3C0 Can

TRUSELL, FRED CHARLES, b Kansas City, Mo, May 12, 31; m 57; c 2. ANALYTICAL CHEMISTRY. *Educ:* Univ Mo, Kansas City, BA, 52, BS, 56; Iowa State Univ, MS, 59, PhD(chem), 61. *Prof Exp:* Asst prof chem, Tex Tech Col, 61-64; res chemist, 64-76, SR RES CHEMIST, DENVER RES CTR, MARATHON OIL CO, 76- *Mem:* Am Chem Soc. *Res:* Composition and analysis of crude oils; organic geochemistry. *Mailing Add:* Denver Res Ctr Marathon Oil Co PO Box 269 Littleton CO 80160

TRUSHENSKI, SCOTT PAUL, b St Cloud, Minn, Sept 19, 45; m 64; c 2. CHEMICAL ENGINEERING. *Educ:* Univ Minn, Minneapolis, BCE, 67; Carnegie-Mellon Univ, MS, 69, PhD(chem eng), 72. *Prof Exp:* SR RES ENGR, AMOCO PROD CO, 71- *Mem:* Am Inst Mining, Metall & Petrol Engrs. *Res:* Porous media, especially high temperature kinetics, iron oxide reduction and mass transport; reservoir engineering, particularly improved oil recovery methods. *Mailing Add:* Amoco Prod Co 4502 E 41st St Tulsa OK 74115

TRUSK, AMBROSE, b DePue, Ill, Sept 16, 21. ANALYTICAL CHEMISTRY. *Educ:* St Mary's Col, Minn, BS, 43; Univ Minn, MA, 51; Univ Notre Dame, MS, 62, PhD(chem), 66. *Prof Exp:* Instr physics, St Mary's Col, Minn, 43-45; teacher high sch, Minn, 45-47 & Mo, 47-49; from instr to assoc prof, 49-67, PROF CHEM & CHMN DEPT, ST MARY'S COL, MINN, 67- *Mem:* Am Chem Soc; Sigma Xi; Nat Asn Adv Health Prof. *Res:* Fluorometric methods of analysis; structure of inorganic compounds. *Mailing Add:* Dept of Chem St Mary's Col Winona MN 55987

TRUSSELL, HENRY JOEL, b Atlanta, Ga, Feb 3, 45; m 68; c 2. COMPUTER SCIENCE, ELECTRICAL ENGINEERING. *Educ:* Ga Inst Technol, BS, 67; Fla State Univ, MS, 68; Univ NMex, PhD(elec eng & comput sci), 76. *Prof Exp:* mem staff, Los Alamos Sci Lab, 69-80; ASSOC PROF, NC STATE UNIV, 80- *Concurrent Pos:* Adj prof, Univ NMex, 77; vis prof, Heriot-Watt Univ, Edinburgh, Scotland, 78-79. *Mem:* Inst Elec & Electronics Engrs. *Res:* Image processing; restoration, enhancement and pattern recognition. *Mailing Add:* NC State Univ PO Box 5275 Raleigh NC 27650

TRUSSELL, PAUL CHANDOS, b Vancouver, BC, July 4, 16; m 43; c 2. BACTERIOLOGY. *Educ:* Univ BC, BSA, 38; Univ Wis, MS, 42, PhD(agr bact), 43. *Prof Exp:* Chief res microbiologist, Ayerst, McKenna & Harrison, Ltd, Que, 44-47; head div appl biol, 47-61, DIR, BC RES COUN, 61- *Concurrent Pos:* Consult interferon, Pac Isotopes & Pharm Ltd; mem, Sci Coun BC, chmn, Forest Res Coun BC; partner, Trustwood China Corp. *Mem:* Am Soc Microbiol; Inst Food Technologists. *Res:* Agricultural bacteriology; industrial fermentations; antibiotics; marine borer control; industrial coatings; food spoilage; water pollution; bacteriological leaching of ores; forestry; research administration. *Mailing Add:* 5968 Collingwood St Vancouver BC V6N 1T3 Can

TRUST, TREVOR JOHN, b Melbourne, Australia, June 24, 42. MICROBIOLOGY. *Educ:* Univ Melbourne, BSc, 64, MSc, 66, PhD(microbiol), 69. *Prof Exp:* Lectr microbiol, Royal Melbourne Inst Technol, 69; asst prof, 69-73, assoc prof, 73-80, PROF BACT, UNIV VICTORIA, BC, 81- *Concurrent Pos:* Vis res fel, Southampton Fac Med, 77-78. *Mem:* Can Soc Microbiol; Am Soc Microbiol; Brit Soc Gen Microbiol. *Res:* Microbiology of fish; fish diseases; molecular basis for bacterial virulence. *Mailing Add:* Dept of Biochem & Microbiol Univ of Victoria Victoria BC V8W 2Y2 Can

TRUTT, DAVID, mathematics, see previous edition

TRUXAL, FRED STONE, b Great Bend, Kans, Feb 20, 22; m 43; c 2. ENTOMOLOGY. *Educ:* Univ Kans, AB, 47, MA, 49, PhD(entom), 52. *Prof Exp:* Agent, Bur Entom & Plant Quarantine, USDA, 42; asst instr biol & entom, Univ Kans, 47-52; cur entom, 52-61, CHIEF CUR LIFE SCI DIV, LOS ANGELES COUNTY MUS NATURAL HIST, 61- *Concurrent Pos:* Asst to state entomologist, Kans, 48-51; asst prof, Ottawa Univ, Kans, 51-52; adj prof, Univ Southern Calif, 57-; biol consult, Pac Horizons; mem expeds, Mex, Cent Am, Brazil & Peru. *Mem:* Fel AAAS; Entom Soc Am; Soc Study Evolution; Soc Syst Zool. *Res:* Biology, ecology and taxonomy of aquatic and semiaquatic Hemiptera. *Mailing Add:* Life Sci Div Los Angeles Co Mus of Natural Hist Los Angeles CA 90007

TRUXAL, JOHN G(ROFF), b Lancaster, Pa, Feb 19, 24; m 49; c 2. ELECTRICAL ENGINEERING. *Educ:* Dartmouth Col, AB, 44; Mass Inst Technol, BS, 47, DSc, 50. *Hon Degrees:* DE, Purdue Univ, 64 & Ind Inst Technol, 71. *Prof Exp:* Asst elec eng, Mass Inst Technol, 47-48 & 49-50; from asst prof to assoc prof, Purdue Univ, 50-54; assoc prof, Polytech Inst Brooklyn, 54-57, prof & head dept, 57-61, vpres ed develop, 61-64, dean eng, 64-66, provost, 66-71; dean col eng, 71-75, DISTINGUISHED TEACHING PROF, DEPT TECHNOL & SOCIETY, STATE UNIV NY STONY BROOK, 75- *Concurrent Pos:* Mem, President's Sci Adv Comt, 70-72; mem vis comt, Nat Bur Stand, 71-75. *Mem:* Nat Acad Engrs; AAAS; Am Soc Eng Educ; fel Inst Elec & Electronics Engrs; Instrument Soc Am (pres, 65-66). *Res:* Network theory; feedback control systems. *Mailing Add:* Col of Eng State Univ of NY Stony Brook NY 11794

TRUXILLO, STANTON GEORGE, b New Orleans, La, June 23, 41; m 65; c 2. GEOPHYSICS. *Educ:* Loyola Univ, La, BS, 63; La State Univ, Baton Rouge, PhD(physics), 69. *Prof Exp:* Fel, Coastal Studies Inst, La State Univ, Baton Rouge, 68-70; asst prof physics, Univ Tampa, 70-73, assoc prof, 73-79, prof, 79-81; PETROL GEOPHYSICIST, AMOCO PROD CO, 81- *Concurrent Pos:* Am Coun Educ Fel, 77-78. *Mem:* Am Phys Soc; Soc Explor Geophysicists; Southeastern Geophys Soc. *Res:* Time-dependent rotating fluid dynamics; fluid dynamics of circulatory system; acoustics. *Mailing Add:* Amoco Prod Co 0340 Poydras St New Orleans LA 70150

TRYBUL, THEODORE, b Chicago, Ill Apr 12, 35; m 59; c 6. MECHANICAL ENGINEERING, OPERATIONS RESEARCH. *Educ:* Univ Ill, BS, 57; Univ NMex, MS, 63; George Washington Univ, DSc, 76. *Prof Exp:* Staff mem nuclear energy, Sandia Labs, 57-64; eng sect head missiles, Gen Dynamics Corp, 64-65; tech dir space syst, Aerospace Corp, 65-67; dept mgr oper res, Raytheon Co, 67-68; div chief syst anal, US Army Advan Mat Concepts Agency, 68-74; chief estimates & studies, Mat Develop & Readiness Command, 74-80, DIR, TESTING & EVAL COMMAND, US ARMY, 80- *Concurrent Pos:* Prof, Calif State Polytech Col, 64-67; prof, Univ Northern Colo, 68-74; lectr, Nat Comn Fluidics & Fluerics, 68-; lectr, Dept Army Res grant, 71-72; prof, George Washington Univ, 71-; prof, Am Univ, 76-78. *Mem:* Am Defense Preparedness Asn; Am Soc Mech Engrs; Oper Res Soc Am; Int Soc Technol Assessment. *Res:* Thermodynamics; heat transfer; nuclear energy; statistics; transportation; space; solar energy; systems analysis; gas dynamics; communications-electronics. *Mailing Add:* Bldg 314 Rm 219 Aberdeen Proving Ground MD 21005

TRYFIATES, GEORGE P, b Mesolongi, Greece, Feb 26, 35; US citizen; m 59; c 4. BIOCHEMISTRY, CANCER. *Educ:* Univ Toledo, BS, 58; Bowling Green State Univ, MA, 59; Rutgers Univ, PhD(biochem), 63. *Prof Exp:* Teaching & res asst biol, Bowling Green State Univ, 58-59; res asst biochem, Rutgers Univ, 59-62; res assoc, Grad Sch Med, Univ Pa & Sch Med, Temple Univ, 62-64; res biochemist, P Lorillard Co, NC, 64-66; instr pharmacol, Sch Med, Duke Univ, 66-67, assoc, 67; asst prof biochem, 67-72, ASSOC PROF BIOCHEM, SCH MED, W VA UNIV, 72- *Concurrent Pos:* USPHS trainee, Grad Sch Med, Univ Pa & Sch Med, Temple Univ, 62-64, USPHS grants, Nat Cancer Inst. *Mem:* AAAS; Am Chem Soc; Soc Exp Biol & Med; Am Inst Nutrit; Am Soc Biol Chemists. *Res:* Enzyme regulation in vivo and in vitro; hormone action; molecular aspects of control of neoplasia; nutritional control of tumor growth and of expression of enzyme activity. *Mailing Add:* Dept of Biochem WVa Univ Med Ctr Morgantown WV 26506

TRYON, EDWARD POLK, b Terre Haute, Ind, Sept 4, 40. THEORETICAL HIGH ENERGY PHYSICS, COSMOLOGY. *Educ:* Cornell Univ, AB, 62; Univ Calif, Berkeley, PhD(physics), 67. *Prof Exp:* Res assoc physics, Columbia Univ, 67-68, asst prof, 68-71; asst prof, 71-74, ASSOC PROF PHYSICS, HUNTER COL, CITY UNIV NEW YORK, 74- *Mem:* Am Phys Soc; NY Acad Sci; Sigma Xi. *Res:* Gravitational interactions; high energy theory; pion-pion interaction. *Mailing Add:* Dept of Physics 695 Park Ave New York NY 10021

TRYON, JOHN G(RIGGS), b Washington, DC, Dec 18, 20; m 48; c 2. ENGINEERING PHYSICS. *Educ:* Univ Minn, BS, 41; Cornell Univ, PhD(eng physics), 52. *Prof Exp:* Mem tech staff, Bell Tel Labs, Inc, 51-58; prof elec eng & head dept, Univ Alaska, 58-69; prof, Tuskegee Inst, 69-75; PROF ENG, UNIV NEV, LAS VEGAS, 75-, CHMN DEPT, 80- *Mem:* Am Phys Soc; Inst Elec & Electronics Engrs; Int Solar Energy Soc; Sigma Xi; Am Soc Eng Educ. *Res:* Solar and natural heating and cooling. *Mailing Add:* Dept of Eng Univ of Nev Las Vegas NV 89154

TRYON, ROLLA MILTON, JR, b Chicago, Ill, Aug 26, 16; m 45. BOTANY. *Educ:* Univ Chicago, BS, 37; Univ Wis, PhM, 38; Harvard Univ, MS, 40, PhD(bot), 41. *Prof Exp:* Lab technician, Chem Warfare Serv, Mass Inst Technol, 42; instr bot, Dartmouth Col, 42, lab technician, 43-44; instr bot, Univ Wis, 44-45; asst prof plant taxon, Univ Minn, 45-48; assoc prof, Wash Univ, St Louis, 48-57; CUR, HERBARIUM & CUR FERNS, GRAY HERBARIUM, HARVARD UNIV, 58-, PROF BIOL, 72- *Concurrent Pos:* Cur, Herbarium, Minneapolis, Minn, 46-48; asst cur herbarium, Mo Bot Garden, 48-57. *Mem:* Am Soc Plant Taxon; Am Fern Soc; Bot Soc Am. *Res:* Taxonomy of pteridophytes; Doryopteris; Pteridium; ferns and fern allies of Wisconsin, Minnesota and Peru. *Mailing Add:* Gray Herbarium Harvard Univ 22 Divinity Ave Cambridge MA 02138

TRYPHONAS, HELEN, b Greece, June 21, 39; m 62; c 2. IMMUNOTOXICOLOGY, FOOD ALLERGY. *Educ:* Univ Sask, BSc, 68, MSc, 72. *Prof Exp:* Dept asst microbiol, West Col Vet Med, Univ Sask, 72-74; supvr microbiol, 74-77, biologist II immunol, 77-82, SCIENTIST II IMMUNOTOXICOL, HEALTH & WELFARE CAN, 82- *Res:* Immunotoxicity studies of food additives and environmental contaminants in man and experimental animals; the casual relationship of food allergies to behavioral abnormalities in children. *Mailing Add:* Toxicol Res Div Bur Food Chem Health Protection Br Health & Welfare Tunney's Pasture Ottawa ON K1A 0L2 Can

TRYPHONAS, LEANDER, veterinary pathology, toxicology, see previous edition

TRYTTEN, GEORGE NORMAN, b Pittsburgh, Pa, Apr 21, 28; m 52; c 5. MATHEMATICS. *Educ:* Luther Col, Iowa, AB, 51; Univ Wis, MS, 53; Univ Md, PhD(math), 62. *Prof Exp:* Asst math, Univ Wis, 51-53; asst, Inst Fluid Dynamics & Appl Math, Univ Md, 53-57; mathematician, US Naval Ord Lab, 57-62; res assoc math, Inst Fluid Dynamics & Appl Math, Univ Md, College Park, 62-63, from res asst prof to res assoc prof, 63-69, assoc dean sponsored res & fels, Grad Sch, 67-69; vpres, Math Sci Group, Inc, 69-70; free-lance filmstrip producer, 70-71; prof math & chmn dept, Hood Col, 71-72; assoc prof, 72-75, PROF MATH, LUTHER COL, IOWA, 75- *Mem:* AAAS; Am Math Soc; Math Asn Am. *Res:* Partial differential equations; fluid dynamics; numerical solution of partial differential equations; celestial mechanics. *Mailing Add:* Dept of Math Luther Col Decorah IA 52101

TRYTTEN, ROLAND AAKER, b Tower City, NDak, Oct 15, 13; m 42; c 6. CHEMISTRY. *Educ:* St Olaf Col, AB, 35; Univ Wis, PhD(chem), 41. *Prof Exp:* Control chemist, Kimberly-Clark Corp, 41-42; instr chem, Ripon Col, 42-45; instr, Cent State Teachers Col, 45-51, chmn dept, 49-51; chmn dept, 51-72, PROF CHEM, UNIV WIS-STEVENS POINT, 51- *Mem:* Am Chem Soc. *Res:* Foams; foaming tendency of aqueous aliphatic alcohol solutions; sulfur dioxide determination in polluted air. *Mailing Add:* Dept of Chem Univ of Wis Stevens Point WI 54481

TRZASKOMA, PATRICIA POVILITIS, US citizen; m 61; c 2. ELECTROCHEMISTRY, CORROSION. *Educ:* Barnard Col, BA, 61; Am Univ, MS, 72, PhD(chem), 76. *Prof Exp:* Chemist anal chem, Gen Dynamics, 61-62; res chemist fuel cell res, Apollo Prog, Pratt & Whitney Aircraft Corp, 62-65; ASST PROF CHEM, GEORGE MASON UNIV, 77- *Mem:* Electrochem Soc; Am Chem Soc. *Res:* Electrochemistry with emphasis on the kinetics of electrode surface reactions; application of this work to the technological problems of metals corrosion; passivation and inhibition; fast reaction kinetics; corrosion behavior of novel materials; ion implanted materials; metal matrix composites. *Mailing Add:* 6443 Sienna Ct Falls Church VA 22043

TRZCIENSKI, WALTER EDWARD, JR, b Montague City, Mass, Sept 19, 42; m 65. GEOLOGY. *Educ:* Bowdoin Col, AB, 65; McGill Univ, PhD(geol), 71. *Prof Exp:* NASA fel, Princeton Univ, 71; asst prof geol, Brooklyn Col, 71-72; asst prof, 72-76, ASSOC PROF GEOL, ECOLE POLYTECH,

MONTREAL, 76- *Mem:* AAAS; Geol Soc Am; Mineral Soc Am; Mineral Asn Can; Geol Asn Can. *Res:* Metamorphic and igneous petrology and mineralogy-geochemistry, especially in the northern Appalachians. *Mailing Add:* Dept of Geol Eng Ecole Polytech Montreal PQ H3A 3C7 Can

TSAGARIS, THEOFILOS JOHN, b Fernandina, Fla, June 27, 29; m 54; c 3. INTERNAL MEDICINE, CARDIOLOGY. *Educ:* Univ Fla, BS, 50; Emory Univ, MD, 54. *Prof Exp:* Chief cardiol, Vet Admin Hosp, Wood, Wis, 62-65; from asst prof to assoc prof, 65-75, PROF INTERNAL MED, UNIV UTAH, 75-, RES ASST PROF PHYSIOL, 76-; CHIEF CARDIOL, VET ADMIN HOSP, SALT LAKE CITY, 65- *Concurrent Pos:* Fel cardiol, Emory Univ, 59-60 & Univ Utah, 60-62; asst prof, Marquette Univ, 62-65. *Mem:* Am Fedn Clin Res. *Res:* Hemodynamics; coronary blood flow. *Mailing Add:* Vet Admin Hosp Salt Lake City UT 84112

TSAHALIS, DEMOSTHENES THEODOROS, b Anavriti, Greece, Mar 20, 48; m 71; c 2. FLUID MECHANICS, FLUID-STRUCTURE INTERACTION. *Educ:* Nat Tech Univ Greece, dipl mech & elec eng, 71; Va Polytech Inst & State Univ, MSc, 72, PhD(eng mech), 74. *Prof Exp:* Res engr, 74-80, SR RES ENGR RES & DEVELOP, SHELL DEVELOP CO, 80- *Mem:* Am Inst Aeronaut & Astronaut; Tech Chamber Greece; Sigma Xi; Am Soc Mech Engrs; AAAS. *Res:* Unsteady laminar and turbulent boundary layers and separation; skin friction reduction with compliant walls; stability and entrainment of stratified flows; vortex-induced vibrations; modeling of oil spill trajectories. *Mailing Add:* 16223 Paso Dobble Houston TX 77083

TSAI, ALAN CHUNG-HONG, b Chang-hua Hsien, Taiwan, June 18, 43; m 69; c 2. NUTRITION. *Educ:* Taiwan Prov Chung Hsing Univ, BS, 66; Wash State Univ, MS, 69, PhD(nutrit), 72. *Prof Exp:* Res assoc nutrit, Mich State Univ, 72-73; asst prof, 73-76, ASSOC PROF NUTRIT, UNIV MICH, ANN ARBOR, 76- *Mem:* Am Inst Nutrit; NY Acad Sci. *Res:* Cholestdrol feeding associated metabolic alterations including enzyme activities; microsomal activities; tissue lipid peroxidation and insulin metabolism; nutrition of dietary fiber, its effect on cholesterol metabolism and gastrointestinal functions; interaction of Vitamin E and the function of thyroid hormones; metabolic effects of exercise training and detraining. *Mailing Add:* Human Nutrit Prog Univ Mich Ann Arbor MI 48109

TSAI, BILIN PAULA, b Seattle, Wash, May 23, 49. CHEMICAL PHYSICS. *Educ:* Univ Chicago, BS, 71; Univ NC, Chapel Hill, PhD(chem physics), 75. *Prof Exp:* Res assoc chem physics, Univ Nebr, Lincoln, 75-76; ASST PROF CHEM, UNIV MINN, DULUTH, 76- *Mem:* Sigma Xi; Am Chem Soc; Am Soc Mass Spectrometry; Am Phys Soc. *Mailing Add:* Dept of Chem Univ of Minn Duluth MN 55812

TSAI, BOH CHANG, b Taiwan, China, Jan 2, 44; US citizen; m 69; c 2. POLYMER SCIENCE, CHEMICAL ENGINEERING. *Educ:* Nat Taiwan Univ, BS, 67; Univ Akron, MS, 70, PhD(polymer sci), 73. *Prof Exp:* Staff mat engr polymer processing, Acushnet Co, 73-78; SR RES SCIENTIST POLYMER SCI & ENG, AM CAN CO, 78- *Concurrent Pos:* Fel, Inst Polymer Sci, Univ Akron, 73-78; vis lectr polymer sci, Southeastern Mass Univ, 75-76. *Mem:* Am Chem Soc; Rheology Soc. *Res:* Interaction of structure-property-processing of polymeric materials. *Mailing Add:* Tech Ctr Am Can Co Barrington IL 60010

TSAI, CHESTER E, b Amoy, China, Mar 7, 35; m 62; c 2. ALGEBRA. *Educ:* Nat Taiwan Univ, BA, 57; Marquette Univ, MS, 61; Ill Inst Technol, PhD(math), 64. *Prof Exp:* Instr math, Ill Inst Technol, 62-64; from asst prof to assoc prof, 64-78, PROF MATH, MICH STATE UNIV, 78- *Mem:* Am Math Soc; Math Asn Am. *Res:* Non-associative algebra. *Mailing Add:* Dept of Math Mich State Univ East Lansing MI 48823

TSAI, CHIA-YIN, b Taichung, Taiwan, Dec 15, 37; m 67; c 2. GENETICS, BIOCHEMISTRY. *Educ:* Nat Taiwan Univ, BS, 60; Purdue Univ, Lafayette, PhD(genetics), 67. *Prof Exp:* Res asst genetics, 63-67, res assoc, 67-69, asst prof, 69-74, assoc prof, 74-80, PROF GENETICS, PURDUE UNIV, WEST LAFAYETTE, 80- *Mem:* Am Soc Plant Physiologists; Crop Sci Soc Am. *Res:* Carbohydrate metabolism and storage protein synthesis in maize; nutritional quality of protein and grain yield potential of maize. *Mailing Add:* Dept of Bot & Plant Path Purdue Univ West Lafayette IN 47907

TSAI, CHING-LONG, b Kaohsiung, Taiwan, May 25, 45; m 73; c 2. SOLID STATE PHYSICS. *Educ:* La State Univ, PhD(physics), 76. *Prof Exp:* Res & teaching asst physics, La State Univ, 71-76; res assoc, Ill Inst Technol, 76-78; physicist, Nat Standards Co, 78-80. *Mem:* Am Phys Soc. *Res:* Low temperature solid state physics. *Mailing Add:* 71 Bridge St Medfield MA 02052

TSAI, CHISHIUN S, b Chia-yi, Taiwan, Dec 19, 33; m 65. BIOCHEMISTRY, ENZYMOLOGY. *Educ:* Nat Taiwan Univ, BS, 56; Purdue Univ, MS, 61, PhD(biochem), 63. *Prof Exp:* Fel chem, Cornell Univ, 63; fel biosci, Nat Res Coun Can, 63-64, asst res officer, 64-65; from asst prof to assoc prof, 65-76, PROF CHEM & BIOCHEM, CARLETON UNIV, 76- *Concurrent Pos:* Res assoc, Univ Tex, 72; vis sci, Foxchase Cancer Res Inst, 73. *Mem:* Am Chem Soc; Can Biochem Soc; Am Soc Biol Chemists. *Res:* Function and reactivity of enzymes in relation with the structures of enzymes; substrates and inhibitors. *Mailing Add:* Dept of Chem Carleton Univ Ottawa ON K1S 5B6 Can

TSAI, CHUN-CHE, b Chiayi, Taiwan, China, Sept 17, 37; US citizen; m 63; c 3. PHYSICAL CHEMISTRY, BIOCHEMISTRY. *Educ:* Cheng-Kung Univ, Taiwan, BS, 60; Ind Univ, Bloomington, PhD(chem), 68. *Prof Exp:* Fel crystallog, Univ Pa, 68-69; fel bio-crystallog, Cornell Univ, 69-71; res chemist phys chem, Univ Colo, Boulder, 71-72; sr res assoc biophys chem & molecular biol, Univ Rochester, 72-76; asst prof biochem, 76-80, ASSOC PROF CHEM, KENT STATE UNIV, 80- *Concurrent Pos:* Res asst prof, Dept Microbiol & Immunol, Col Med, Northeastern Ohio Univ, 78- *Mem:* Am Chem Soc; Am Biophys Soc; Am Crystallog Asn; AAAS; Sigma Xi. *Res:* Biological crystallography; drug-nucleic acid interactions; structure and function of nucleic acids; molecular associations and interactions in biological systems. *Mailing Add:* Dept Chem Kent State Univ Kent OH 44242

TSAI, CHUNG-CHIEH, b Taiwan, Oct 1, 48; c 3. REACTION INJECTION MOLDING. *Educ:* Nat Cheng Kung Univ, Taiwan, BS, 71; Univ Lowell, MS, 77, PhD(chem), 80. *Prof Exp:* Lab instr chem, Nat Cheng Kung Univ, 73-74; res asst polymer, Univ Lowell, 75-79; RES CHEMIST POLYMER, STAUFFER CHEM CO, 79- *Mem:* Am Chem Soc; Soc Plastic Engrs. *Res:* Polyelectrolytes; ionomers; epoxy adhesives; polyurethane; thermosets; synthesis of polymers for electronic application. *Mailing Add:* 144 Grandview Rd South Salem NY 10590

TSAI, FRANK Y, b Tsing Tao, China, Feb 6, 34; m 64; c 2. FLUID MECHANICS, HYDRAULICS. *Educ:* Nat Taiwan Univ, BS, 55; Univ Minn, MS, 60, PhD, 68. *Prof Exp:* Teaching asst civil eng, Univ Minn, 58-60, res fel, St Anthony Falls Hydraul Lab, 60-68; asst prof eng mech & sub-head, Dept Eng Sci & Mech, Iowa State Univ, 68-73; sr engr, Ebasco Serv, Inc, 73-75; tech adv, Off Flood Ins, Fed Ins Admin, 75-79, SR TECH ADV, FED EMERGENCY MGT AGENCY, US DEPT HOUSING & URBAN DEVELOP, 79- *Mem:* Am Soc Civil Engrs; Sigma Xi; Am Water Res Asn; Coastal Soc. *Res:* Storm surge; coastal engineering; hydraulics and hydrology; models; supercavitating flow; polymer flow; bioengineering. *Mailing Add:* 4800 Jennichelle Ct Fairfax VA 22032

TSAI, JOSEPH CHO CHUAN, b Tokyo, Japan, Aug 14, 30, US citizen. ELECTRICAL ENGINEERING. *Educ:* Nat Taiwan Univ, BS, 54; Ohio State Univ, MS, 58, PhD(elec eng), 62. *Prof Exp:* Sr scientist silicon device processing, Molecular Electronics Div, Westinghouse Elec Corp, 62-66; MEM TECH STAFF SILICON INTEGRATED CIRCUIT, BELL LABS, AM TELEPHONE & TELEGRAPH CO, 66- *Mem:* Inst Elec & Electronics Engrs. *Res:* Solid state diffusion; ion implantation; applications of secondary ion mass spectrometry; silicon integrated circuit process developments. *Mailing Add:* Rm 128 Bell Labs Am Telephone & Telegraph Co Reading PA 19604

TSAI, KUEI-WU, b Taiwan, Jan 22, 41; m 69; c 2. SOILS, FOUNDATION ENGINEERING. *Educ:* Nat Taiwan Univ, BSCE, 62; Princeton Univ, MSCE & MA, 65, PhD(soils eng), 67. *Prof Exp:* From asst prof to assoc prof, 67-76, PROF CIVIL ENG, SAN JOSE STATE UNIV, 76-, CHMN DEPT, 81- *Concurrent Pos:* Proj engr, Dames & Moore, 69-74, sr engr, 74-75, consult, 75- *Mem:* Am Soc Civil Engrs. *Res:* Shear strength of clays; slope stability; settlement; land reclamation and development; penetrometer method; difficult foundation problems; design of dams; soils investigation and foundation recommendation; site improvement. *Mailing Add:* Dept Civil Eng San Jose State Univ San Jose CA 95192

TSAI, KUO-CHUN, b Tou-Nan, Taiwan, Aug 16, 37; nat US; m 67; c 2. SANITARY & ENVIRONMENTAL ENGINEERING. *Educ:* Cheng Kung Univ, BS, 60; Univ Fla, MS, 69; Univ Mo-Rolla, PhD(civil), 77. *Prof Exp:* Teaching asst, Cheng Kung Univ, 63-64, instr, 64-70, assoc prof, 70-73; proj engr, Harwood Beebe Co, C E Maguire, Inc, 76-79; proj leader, AWARE, Inc, 79-80; ASST PROF ENVIRON ENG, UNIV LOUISVILLE, 80- *Concurrent Pos:* Environ consult, Miller, Wihry & Lee, Inc, 81- *Mem:* Am Soc Prof Engrs; Am Soc Civil Engrs; Water Pollution Control Fedn; Asn Environ Eng Professors; Int Asn Water Pollution Res. *Res:* Biological wastewater treatment, particularly activated sludge process for both biochemical oxygen demand and nitrogen removal; steam stripping of wastewater for ammonia and sulfide removal; chemical coagulation of water and wastewater. *Mailing Add:* Dept Chem & Environ Eng Univ Louisville Louisville KY 40292

TSAI, LIN, b Hong Kong, May 30, 22; US citizen. ORGANIC CHEMISTRY. *Educ:* Chinese Nat Southwest Assoc Univ, BSc, 46; Univ Ore, MA, 49; Fla State Univ, PhD(org chem), 54. *Prof Exp:* Res assoc chem, Ohio State Univ, 54-57; res scientist, Worcester Found Exp Biol, 57-59; vis scientist, 59-62, ORG CHEMIST, NAT HEART INST, 62- *Mem:* Am Chem Soc; Royal Soc Chem. *Res:* Syntheses, reactions and microbial degradations of heterocyclic compounds; stereochemistry of enzymic reactions. *Mailing Add:* NIH Bldg 3 Room 110 Bethesda MD 20205

TSAI, LUNG-WEN, b Taipei, Taiwan, Feb 20, 45; US citizen; m 71; c 2. MACHINE DESIGN, MECHANICAL ENGINEERING. *Educ:* Nat Taiwan Univ, BS, 67; State Univ NY, MS, 70; Stanford Univ, PhD(mech eng), 73. *Prof Exp:* Develop engr, Hewlett-Packard Corp, 73-78; RES ENGR MECH ENG, GEN MOTORS CORP, 78- *Mem:* Assoc mem Am Soc Mech Engrs. *Res:* Mechanism and machine design; control system analysis and design; vibration and stress analysis. *Mailing Add:* Mech Res Dept Gen Motors Res Labs Warren MI 48090

TSAI, MING-JER, b Taichung, Taiwan, Nov 3, 43; m 71; c 2. BIOCHEMISTRY, MOLECULAR BIOLOGY. *Educ:* Nat Taiwan Univ, BS, 66; Univ Calif, Davis, PhD(biochem), 71. *Prof Exp:* Damon Runyon fel, Univ Tex M D Anderson Hosp & Tumor Inst Houston, 71-73; instr, 73-79, ASSOC PROF CELL BIOL, BAYLOR COL MED, 79- *Mem:* Am Soc Cell Biol; Sigma Xi. *Res:* Hormonal regulation of gene expression; chromatin structure; precursors of mRNA and their processing; initiation of RNA synthesis by DNA-dependent RNA polymerases. *Mailing Add:* Dept of Cell Biol Baylor Col of Med Houston TX 77030

TSAI, MIN-SHEN CHEN, carbohydrate biochemistry, see previous edition

TSAI, STEPHEN W, b Peiping, China, July 6, 29; US citizen; m 54; c 2. MECHANICS. *Educ:* Yale Univ, BE, 52, DEng(mech), 61. *Prof Exp:* Proj engr, Foster Wheeler Corp, 52-58; dept mgr mat res, Aeronutronic Div, Philco Corp, 61-66; prof eng, Washington Univ, 66-68; chief scientist, 68-76, SCIENTIST, AIR FORCE MAT LAB, WRIGHT-PATTERSON AFB, 76- *Concurrent Pos:* Lectr, Univ Calif, Los Angeles, 65-66; ed-in-chief, J Composite Mat, 66-; ed, Int J Fibre Sci & Technol, 68-; affil prof, Washington Univ, 68-; Battelle vis prof, Ohio State Univ, 69. *Mem:* Am Inst Aeronaut & Astronaut; Sigma Xi; Am Phys Soc; Soc Rheol. *Res:* Mechanics of composite materials for structural applications. *Mailing Add:* Air Force Mat Lab AFML/CA Wright-Patterson AFB OH 45433

TSAI, TOM CHUNG HSIUNG, polymer chemistry, colloid chemistry, see previous edition

TSAI, TSUI HSIEN, b Taichung, Formosa, Nov 19, 35; m 63; c 1. PHARMACOLOGY. *Educ:* Nat Taiwan Univ, BS, 58; WVa Univ, MS, 63, PhD(pharmacol), 65. *Prof Exp:* Sect head autonomic pharmacol, Merrell-Nat Labs, Ohio, 65-71; sr res pharmacologist, Wellcome Res Labs, 71-77; asst dir res support & biomet, Merrell Nat Labs, 77-80; ASSOC DIR CLIN INVEST, MERRELL DOW PHARMACEUT, INC, 80- *Concurrent Pos:* Fel, Harvard Med Sch, 64-66. *Mem:* Am Soc Pharmacol & Exp Therapeut. *Res:* Autonomic and cardiovascular pharmacology. *Mailing Add:* Merrell Dow Pharmaceut Inc 2110 E Galraith Rd Cincinnati OH 45215

TSAI, WU-YANG, b Taiwan, Nov 16, 42; US citizen; m 69; c 1. PLASMA PHYSICS. *Educ:* Nat Taiwan Univ, BS, 65; Harvard Univ, MA, 67, PhD(physics), 71. *Prof Exp:* Asst res physicist, Univ Calif, Los Angeles, 71-72, adj asst prof, 72-77; asst prof physics, Univ Miami, 77-79; SR SCIENTIST, R & D ASSOCS, 79- *Concurrent Pos:* Res physicist, Source Theory Prog, A P Sloan Found grant, 75-78; prin investr, NSF grant, 78-80. *Mem:* Am Phys Soc; Sigma Xi. *Res:* Magnetohydrodynamics equations and code; acceleration of high density plasma by coaxial gun; pulsed power systems; radiative heat transport; electromagnetic radiation theory. *Mailing Add:* R & D Assocs PO Box 9695 Marina Del Ray CA 90291

TSAI, Y(U)-M(IN), b Taiwan, Formosa, Mar 31, 37; m 63; c 1. ENGINEERING MECHANICS. *Educ:* Taipei Inst Technol, Taiwan, dipl civil eng, 57; Univ Tenn, ScM, 62; Brown Univ, ScM, 64, PhD(eng), 67. *Prof Exp:* Res assoc eng, Brown Univ, 66-67; from asst prof to assoc prof eng mech, 67-77, PROF ENG MECH, IOWA STATE UNIV, 77- *Concurrent Pos:* Nat Sci Found res initiation grants, 69-70. *Res:* Elasticity; stress waves; fracture mechanics. *Mailing Add:* Dept of Eng Sci & Mech Iowa State Univ Ames IA 50010

TSAI, YUAN-HWANG, b Ping-Tung, Taiwan, Jan 28, 36; US citizen; m 64; c 3. MICROBIOLOGY. *Educ:* Nat Taiwan Univ, BS, 59; Univ Utah, MS, 64, PhD(parasitol), 67. *Prof Exp:* Lab instr clin parasitol, Med Sch, Nat Taiwan Univ, 61-62; asst biol, parasitol & med entom, Univ Utah, 62-66; parasitologist, Trop Dis Ctr, St Clare's Hosp, New York, 66-67; SR MICROBIOLOGIST, BRISTOL LABS, 68- *Mem:* Am Soc Microbiol. *Res:* Antimicrobial agents and chemotherapy; experimental bacterial meningitis and therapy; pharmacokinetics of antibiotics. *Mailing Add:* Dept of Microbiol Bristol Labs Thompson Rd Syracuse NY 13201

TSAI, YUNG SU, b Yuli, Taiwan, Feb 1, 30, US citizen; m 61; c 2. THEORETICAL PHYSICS, ELEMENTARY PARTICLE PHYSICS. *Educ:* Nat Taiwan Univ, BS, 54; Univ Minn, MS, 56, PhD(physics), 58. *Prof Exp:* Res assoc theoret physics, Stanford Univ, 59-61, asst prof, 61-63, SR STAFF MEM THEORET PHYSICS, STANFORD LINEAR ACCELERATOR CTR, STANFORD UNIV, 63- *Mem:* Am Phys Soc; Sigma Xi. *Res:* Passage of particles through matter; production of particles; energy loss and straggling due to ionization; bremsstrahlung and pair productions; radiative corrections to scatterings; properties of tay leptons; physics of electron-positron collision. *Mailing Add:* Stanford Linear Accelerator Ctr Stanford Univ Stanford CA 94305

TSAKONAS, STAVROS, b Resht, Iran, July 11, 20; nat US; m 54; c 1. ENGINEERING MECHANICS. *Educ:* Nat Univ Greece, BS, 44; Columbia Univ, MS, 52, PhD(eng, eng mech), 56. *Prof Exp:* Design engr, Defense Dept, Greece, 45-50; asst hydraul, Sch Eng, Columbia Univ, 52-56; lectr math & staff scientist, Davidson Lab, 56-60, chief fluid dynamics sect, 60-72, assoc prof appl math, 60-77, RES ASSOC PROF OCEAN ENG, STEVENS INST TECHNOL, 77- *Mem:* Am Soc Civil Engrs. *Res:* Applied mechanics; fluid dynamics; applied mathematics. *Mailing Add:* Davidson Lab Castle Point Hoboken NJ 07030

TSAKUMIS, THEODORE GEORGE, polymer chemistry, see previous edition

TSAN, ALICE TUNG-HUA, b Taiwan, Rep China, Dec 3, 49; m 73. NUMERICAL ANALYSIS, APPLIED MATHEMATICS. *Educ:* Nat Taiwan Univ, BS, 71; State Univ NY Stony Brook, MS, 73, PhD(numerical anal), 75. *Prof Exp:* Vis fel res math, NIH, 75-77; systs engr, Gen Elec Info Serv Co, 77-81; SR RES MATH, EXXON PROD RES CO, 81- *Mem:* Am Math Soc; Soc Indust & Appl Math; Inst Elec & Electronics Engrs. *Res:* Development of a multinephron model of the kidney that is adequate for the interpretation of experimental data; engineering analysis and function specifications for new hardware and software of a computer system; mathematical models for computer system analysis; interactive graphic packages for velocity analysis to assist seismic exploration and processing. *Mailing Add:* #2 Sleepy Oaks Circle Houston TX 77024

TSAN, MIN-FU, b Taiwan, Jan 27, 42; m 75. HEMATOLOGY, NUCLEAR MEDICINE. *Educ:* Nat Taiwan Univ, MB, 67; Harvard Univ, PhD(physiol), 71; Am Bd Internal Med, dipl, 75, 78; Am Bd Nuclear Med, dipl, 76. *Prof Exp:* Intern med, Nat Taiwan Univ Hosp, 66-67; med officer, Chinese Navy, 67-68; med intern, Boston Vet Admin Hosp, 71-72; med resident, 72-73, fel hematol, Johns Hopkins Hosp, 73-75; asst prof med, Radiol & Radiol Sci, Mech Sch & asst prof environ health, Sch Pub Health & Hyg, 75-79, ASSOC PROF MED, RADIOL & RADIOL SCI, MED SCH & ASSOC PROF, ENVIRON HEALTH, SCH PUB HEALTH & HYG, JOHNS HOPKINS UNIV, 79- *Mem:* AAAS; Am Fedn Clin Res; Am Soc Hematol; Am Soc Nuclear Med. *Res:* Metabolism and function of neutrophils. *Mailing Add:* Johns Hopkins Med Inst 615 N Wolfe St Baltimore MD 21205

TSANDOULAS, GERASIMOS NICHOLAS, b Preveza, Greece, Aug 14, 39; m 64, 74. ELECTRICAL ENGINEERING. *Educ:* Harvard Univ, BA, 61, BS, 63; Univ Pa, PhD(elec eng), 67. *Prof Exp:* Engr, Kel Corp, Mass, 63-64; staff mem antenna res, Mass Inst Technol, 67-74, staff scientist, EM Techniques Group, 74-77, syst engr, Airborne Radar Group, Lincoln Lab, 77-79; asst leader & leader, Lincoln C-Band Observable Radar, US Army, Krems, Austria & Kwajalein, Marshall Islands, 79-81. *Mem:* AAAS; Inst Elec & Electronics Engrs; Sigma Xi. *Res:* Electromagnetic scattering and diffraction; antennas and arrays; wave propagation; radar systems; airborne moving target indicator radar. *Mailing Add:* Lincoln Lab Mass Inst Technol Lexington MA 02173

TSANG, CHARLES PAK WAI, Can citizen. ENDOCRINOLOGY. *Educ:* McGill Univ, BSc, 61, MSc, 65, PhD(steroid biochem), 68. *Prof Exp:* Staff scientist, Worcester Found Exp Biol, 68-70; fel steroid & cyclic necleotide protein-binding assays, Queen Mary Hosp, Montreal, 70-71; RES SCIENTIST REPRODUCTIVE PHYSIOL, ANIMAL RES INST, 71- *Res:* Metabolism of steroid hormones in relation to pregnancy and control of parturition in the sheep; hormonal control of egg production and shell quality in the hen. *Mailing Add:* Animal Res Ctr Ottawa ON K1A 0C6 Can

TSANG, GEE, b Macao, Mar 29, 38; Can citizen; m 70; c 2. FLUID MECHANICS, ICE ENGINEERING. *Educ:* Univ New South Wales, BE, 63, MEngSc, 65; Univ Waterloo, PhD(fluid mech), 68. *Prof Exp:* Asst engr, New South Wales Water Conserv & Irrig Comn, 63-64; tech officer, Water Res Lab, Univ New South Wales, 64-65; instr fluid mech, Univ Guelph, 68-69; res assoc air pollution, Mass Inst Technol, 69-70; asst prof fluid mech & dynamics, Univ Guelph, 70-72; RES SCIENTIST, CAN CTR INLAND WATERS, 72- *Mem:* Int Asn Hydraul Res; NY Acad Sci. *Res:* Air and water pollution; atmospheric diffusion; hydraulics of cold regions; ice mechanics; micrometeorology; oil spill containment and recovery; ice and hydraulics; cold weather hydraulic instrument development. *Mailing Add:* Hydraul Res Div Nat Water Res PO Box 5050 Burlington ON L7R 4A6 Can

TSANG, JAMES CHEN-HSIANG, b New York, NY, June 1, 46. SOLID STATE PHYSICS. *Educ:* Mass Inst Technol, BS & MS, 68, PhD(elec eng), 73. *Prof Exp:* RES STAFF MEM SEMICONDUCTOR PHYSICS, IBM RES CTR, IBM CORP, 73- *Mem:* Am Phys Soc. *Res:* Raman spectroscopy of solids and surfaces; optical spectroscopy of solids. *Mailing Add:* IBM Res Ctr PO Box 218 Yorktown Heights NY 10598

TSANG, JOSEPH CHIAO-LIANG, b Hong Kong, Oct 11, 36; US citizen; m 69. MICROBIAL BIOCHEMISTRY. *Educ:* Grantham Teachers Col, Hong Kong, dipl, 58; Univ Okla, BS, 62, MS, 65, PhD(biochem), 68. *Prof Exp:* Res asst, Okla Med Res Found, 64-68; asst prof, 68-72, assoc prof, 72-78, PROF CHEM & BIOCHEM, ILL STATE UNIV, 78- *Concurrent Pos:* Adj prof, Peoria Sch Med, Univ Ill, 73-; prof biochem, Med Sch, Jinan Univ, China, 80- *Mem:* Am Chem Soc; Roayl Soc Chem; Am Soc Microbiol. *Res:* Biochemical and pharmacological studies of Serratia marcescens as a bacterium causing nosocomial diseases: role of the pigment, prodigiosin, in the stability of the cell envelope and transfer of R-plasmids; interactions of antibiotics and surfactants with the outer membrane components such as lipopolysaccharides and phospholipids. *Mailing Add:* Dept Chem Ill State Univ Normal IL 61761

TSANG, KANG TOO, b Hong Kong. PLASMA PHYSICS. *Educ:* Chinese Univ Hong Kong, BSc, 70; State Univ NY Stony Brook, MA, 71; Princeton Univ, PhD(plasma physics), 74. *Prof Exp:* res staff plasma physics, Oak Ridge Nat Lab, 74-81; SR RES PHYSICIST, SCI APPLICATIONS, INC, 81- *Concurrent Pos:* adj prof, Nuclear Eng Dept, NC State Univ, Raleigh, 78. *Mem:* Am Phys Soc. *Res:* Theoretical investigation of equilibrium, stability and transports in thermonuclear plasma. *Mailing Add:* Sci Applications Inc 934 Pearl St Boulder CO 80302

TSANG, REGINALD C, b Hong Kong, Sept 20, 40; UK citizen; m 66; c 2. NEONATOLOGY, NUTRITION. *Educ:* Univ Hong Kong, MBBS, 66. *Prof Exp:* Intern med & surg, Queen Mary Hosp, Hong Kong Univ, 64-65, resident pediat, 65-66; resident psychiat, Hong Kong Psychiat Hosp, 65; intern pediat & med, Michael Reese Hosp, Chicago, 66-67, resident pediat, 67-68, fel neonatology, 68-69; fel, Cincinnati Gen Hosp & Childrens Hosp, 69-71; asst prof pediat & obstet & gynec, 71-75, dir, fels div pediat res, 74-76, assoc prof, 75-79, PROF PEDIAT & OBSTET & GYNEC, UNIV CINCINNATI, 79- *Concurrent Pos:* Attend pediatrician, Childrens Hosp, Cincinnati & NIH grant neonatal mineral metab, Nat Inst Child Health & Human Develop, 71-; attend pediat, Cincinnati Gen Hosp, 71- *Mem:* Am Fedn Clin Res; Am Pediat Soc; Soc Pediat Res; Endocrine Soc; Am Col Nutrit. *Res:* Pathophysiology of disturbances in calcium-phosphate-magnesium homeostasis in the neonate; examination of parathyroid hormone, vitamin D, glucagon and calcitonin; diabetic pregnancy; pediatric hyperlipoproteinemia; identification and prevention of premature atherosclerosis. *Mailing Add:* Dept Pediat Col Med Univ Cincinnati Cincinnati OH 45267

TSANG, SIEN MOO, b Shanghai, China, Apr 12, 12; nat US; m 46; c 1. PHOTOCHEMISTRY. *Educ:* St John's Univ, China, BS, 36; Cornell Univ, MS, 40, PhD(org chem), 44. *Prof Exp:* Chemist, H Z Synthetic Chem Industs, Ltd, China, 36-37; instr, St John's Univ, China, 38-39; asst, Nat Defense Res Comt Proj, Cornell Univ, 42-44, res assoc, B F Goodrich Co Proj, 44-45; res chemist, Am Cyanamid Co, 45-46; chemist, Wahca Chem Corp, 47-48; from res chemist to sr res chemist, Am Cyanamid Co, 49-63; Am Cyanamid Co sr res award, Univ Sheffield, 63-64; res assoc, 65-74, PRIN RES SCIENTIST, AM CYANAMID CO, 74- *Honors & Awards:* Naval Ord Develop Award, Bur Ord, Navy Dept, 46. *Mem:* Am Chem Soc. *Res:* Aromatic substitution reactions; organic photochemistry; photostabilizations of polymers. *Mailing Add:* 303 Susan Ct North Plainfield NJ 07060

TSANG, TUNG, b Shanghai, China, Aug 17, 32; US citizen; m 57; c 1. PHYSICAL CHEMISTRY. *Educ:* Ta-Tung Univ, China, BS, 49; Univ Minn, MS, 52; Univ Chicago, PhD(chem), 60. *Prof Exp:* Chemist, Minneapolis-Honeywell Regulator Co, 52-55 & 56; asst chemist, Argonne Nat Lab, 60-64, assoc chemist, 64-67; phys chemist, Nat Bur Standards, 67-69; assoc prof, 69-75, PROF PHYSICS, HOWARD UNIV, 75- *Concurrent Pos:* NAS-NRC sr res fel, NASA Goddard Space Flight Ctr, 75-76. *Mem:* Am Phys Soc. *Res:* Magnetic resonance and susceptibility; statistical physics; photoelectron spectroscopy. *Mailing Add:* Dept of Physics Howard Univ Washington DC 20059

TSAO, CHEN-HSIANG, b Shanghai, China, Jan 21, 29; US citizen; m 57; c 2. PHYSICS. *Educ:* Univ Wash, Seattle, BS, 53, MS, 56, PhD(physics), 61. *Prof Exp:* Res assoc particle physics, Univ Wash, Seattle, 56-60, res instr, 60-61; res assoc high energy physics, Enrico Fermi Inst Nuclear Studies, Univ Chicago, 61-65; Nat Acad Sci-Nat Res Coun resident res assoc fel, 65-66, RES PHYSICIST LAB COSMIC RAY PHYSICS, US NAVAL RES LAB, 66- *Mem:* Am Phys Soc; Sigma Xi. *Res:* Elementary particle physics; high energy interactions; astrophysics. *Mailing Add:* Lab for Cosmic Ray Physics Code 7023 US Naval Res Lab Washington DC 20375

TSAO, CHIA KUEI, b China, Jan 14, 22; m 52; c 4. MATHEMATICAL STATISTICS. *Educ:* Univ Ore, MA, 50, PhD(math statist), 52. *Prof Exp:* Asst math, Univ Ore, 48-52; from instr to assoc prof, 52-63, PROF MATH, WAYNE STATE UNIV, 63- *Mem:* Am Math Soc; Math Asn Am; Inst Math Statist. *Res:* Nonparametric statistics. *Mailing Add:* Dept of Math Wayne State Univ Detroit MI 48202

TSAO, CHING H, b China, Nov 16, 20; US citizen; m 52; c 2. MECHANICAL ENGINEERING. *Educ:* Chiao Tung Univ, BS, 41; Mich State Univ, MS, 48; Ill Inst Technol, PhD(eng mech), 52. *Prof Exp:* Asst prof civil eng, Univ Southern Calif, 53-55; res engr, Hughes Aircraft Co, 55-61; head stress anal sect, Aerospace Corp, 61-65; assoc prof mech eng, 65-69, PROF MECH ENG, CALIF STATE UNIV, LONG BEACH, 69- *Mem:* Am Soc Eng Educ; Soc Exp Stress Anal; Am Inst Aeronaut & Astronaut; Sigma Xi. *Res:* Theoretical and experimental stress. *Mailing Add:* Dept of Mech Eng Calif State Univ Long Beach CA 90840

TSAO, CHING HSI, b Hopei, China, Jan 24, 18; nat US; m 53; c 3. ENTOMOLOGY. *Educ:* Chekiang Univ, BS, 40; Univ Minn, MS, 48, PhD(entom), 51. *Prof Exp:* Asst entomologist, Ministry Agr & Forestry, China, 40-41; asst entom, Tsing Hwa, China, 41-43; sr asst entomologist, Inst Zool, China Acad Sci, 44-46; asst entom, Univ Minn, 49-52; US State Dept scholar, Entom Res Sect, USDA, Md, 52-54; entomologist, USDA, 54-61; asst prof entom, 61-67, ASSOC PROF ENTOM, UNIV GA, 67- *Mem:* AAAS; Entom Soc Am. *Res:* Behavior of insects; laboratory and field ecology of insects; insect physiology. *Mailing Add:* Dept of Entom Univ of Ga Athens GA 30602

TS'AO, CHUNG-HSIN, b Nanking, China, 33; m 62; c 3. PHYSIOLOGY, EXPERIMENTAL PATHOLOGY. *Educ:* Tunghai Univ, Taiwan, BS, 60; Ind Univ, Bloomington, MA, 61; Yale Univ, PhD(physiol), 66. *Prof Exp:* Res assoc hemat, Montefiore Hosp & Med Ctr, 66-67; res assoc physiol, Sch Med, Univ Chicago, 67-72, asst prof path, 68-72; asst prof, 73-75, assoc prof, 75-80, PROF PATH, MED SCH, NORTHWESTERN UNIV, CHICAGO, 80- *Concurrent Pos:* Dir path, Coagulation Lab, Chicago Northwestern Mem Hosp, 73- *Mem:* AAAS; Am Soc Hemat; NY Acad Sci; Int Soc Thrombosis & Haemostasis; Am Soc Exp Path. *Res:* Experimental thrombosis; vascular morphology and function. *Mailing Add:* 201 Riverside Dr Northfield IL 60093

TSAO, FRANCIS HSIANG-CHIAN, b China, July 22, 36. BIOCHEMISTRY, ORGANIC CHEMISTRY. *Educ:* Taiwan Chung Hsing Univ, BS, 61; Dalhousie Univ, MS, 66; Iowa State Univ, PhD(biochem), 72. *Prof Exp:* Anal chemist qual control, Biotech Indust, London, Ont, 67-68; fel lipolytic enzymes, Univ Chicago, 72-74; fel pulmonary dis, 74-76, ASST SCIENTIST RES LUNG SURFACTANT, UNIV WIS-MADISON, 76- *Concurrent Pos:* Pediat award, Spec Ctr Res, NIH, 81-86. *Mem:* Sigma Xi; Am Chem Soc. *Res:* Metabolism of lung surfactant phospholipids. *Mailing Add:* Dept Pediat Madison Gen Hosp Madison WI 53715

TSAO, GEORGE T, b Nanking, China, Dec 4, 31; m 60; c 3. CHEMICAL ENGINEERING, MICROBIOLOGY. *Educ:* Nat Taiwan Univ, BSc, 53; Univ Fla, MSc, 56; Univ Mich, PhD(chem eng), 60. *Prof Exp:* Asst prof physics, Olivet Col, 59-60; chem engr, Merck & Co, Inc, 60-61; res chemist, Tenn Valley Authority, 61-62; sect leader hydrolysis & fermentation, Res Dept, Union Starch & Refining Co, Inc Div, Miles Labs, Inc, 62-65, asst res dir, 65-66; from assoc prof to prof chem eng, Iowa State Univ, 66-77; PROF CHEM ENG, PURDUE UNIV, 77- *Mem:* Am Chem Soc; Am Inst Chem Engrs; Am Soc Eng Educ. *Res:* Biological technology; fermentation; agricultural and natural products utilization; waste disposal; organic synthesis; industrial carbohydrates; process development; enzyme engineering. *Mailing Add:* Dept of Chem Eng Purdue Univ West Lafayette IN 47907

TSAO, KEH CHENG, b Kiangsu, China, Apr 20, 23; m 57; c 2. MECHANICAL ENGINEERING. *Educ:* Nat Chung Cheng Univ, BS, 46; Ill Inst Technol, MS, 56; Univ Wis, PhD(mech eng), 61. *Prof Exp:* Assoc prof mech eng, SDak Sch Mines & Technol, 61-67; assoc prof, 67-74, PROF MECH ENG, UNIV WIS-MILWAUKEE, 74- *Mem:* AAAS; Am Soc Eng Educ; Am Soc Mech Engrs. *Res:* High temperative measurement in combustion and arc heated gases; diesel combustion and ignition delays; energy recovery; air quality and modeling; coal combustion and hot gas cleaning. *Mailing Add:* Dept Energetics Univ Wis Milwaukee WI 53221

TSAO, MAKEPEACE UHO, b Shanghai, China, Aug 28, 18; nat US; m 47; c 4. CHEMISTRY. *Educ:* Univ Tatung, BS, 37; Univ Mich, MS, 41, PhD(pharmaceut chem), 44. *Prof Exp:* Wm S Merrill Co fel, Univ Mich, 44-45, sr biochemist, 46-48, head biochemist, 48-52, from asst prof to assoc prof biochem, 52-67; PROF SURG, UNIV CALIF, DAVIS, 67- *Mem:* AAAS; Am Chem Soc; Am Soc Biol Chemists; Biomet Soc; NY Acad Sci. *Res:* Synthetic medicinals; physiological chemistry of premature and newborn infants; biochemical analytical methods; multiple molecular forms of enzymes; carbohydrate metabolism; experimental diabetes; Neurospora crassa. *Mailing Add:* Dept of Surg Univ of Calif Davis CA 95616

TSAO, PETER, b Kiangsu, China, June 9, 26. PHYSICS, GEOPHYSICS. *Educ:* John Carroll Univ, BS, 51, MS, 52; Tex A&M Univ, PhD, 70. *Prof Exp:* Instr physics, Undergrad Div, Univ Ill, 56-58; asst prof, 58-72, ASSOC PROF PHYSICS, NORTHERN ILL UNIV, 72- *Mem:* Am Phys Soc; Am Asn Physics Teachers; Inst Elec & Electronics Engrs; Seismol Soc Am. *Res:* Ultraviolet-visible and Raman spectroscopy of small molecules. *Mailing Add:* 2801 Willow Run Dr De Kalb IL 60115

TSAO, PETER HSING-TSUEN, b Shanghai, China, Mar 22, 29; nat US; m 56; c 1. PLANT PATHOLOGY. *Educ:* Univ Wis, BA, 52, PhD(plant path), 56. *Prof Exp:* Jr plant pathologist, 56-58, asst plant pathologist, 58-64, assoc prof plant path, 64-70, PROF PLANT PATH, UNIV CALIF, RIVERSIDE, 70- *Concurrent Pos:* Guggenheim fel, 66-67; consult Thailand dept agr, UN Food & Agr Orgn, 73-74; res consult, Nat Sci Coun, Taiwan, 74-80. *Mem:* Am Phytopath Soc; Mycol Soc Am; Brit Mycol Soc; Am Inst Biol Sci. *Res:* Ecology of soil fungi; citrus root diseases; antagonism and antibiotics. *Mailing Add:* Dept of Plant Path Univ of Calif Riverside CA 92521

TSAO, SAI HOI, b Hong Kong, Oct 19, 36; Can citizen; m 61; c 3. ELECTRICAL METROLOGY, ELECTRONIC INSTRUMENT DESIGN. *Educ:* Univ BC, BASc, 59, MASc, 61; Univ Birmingham, UK, PhD, 65. *Prof Exp:* Assoc res off, 61-79, SR RES OFFICER, NAT RES COUN CAN, 79- *Mem:* Inst Elec & Electronics Engrs. *Res:* High precision electrical standards, measurements and instrumentation. *Mailing Add:* Div of Physics Nat Res Coun Ottawa ON K1A 0R6 Can

TSAO, UTAH, b Shanghai, China, June 6, 13; nat US; m 40; c 2. CHEMICAL ENGINEERING. *Educ:* Tatung Univ, China, BSc, 33; Univ Mich, MSc, 37, DSc(chem eng), 40. *Prof Exp:* Plant engr, Audubon Sugar Factory, La, 39-40; res engr, Eng Res Dept, Univ Mich, 40-41; petrol engr, Nat Resources Comn, China, 41-42; process engr, 42-53, staff process engr, 53-64, mgr chem plant design, 64-78, CONSULT, LUMMUS CO, 78- *Mem:* Am Inst Chem Engrs; Chinese Inst Engrs (vpres, Am Sect, 48, pres, 67). *Res:* Design of ethylene oxide and glycol, vinyl acetate, polyvinyl alcohol, vinyl chloride, chloroform, carbon tetrachloride, urea, acetylene from hydrocarbons, polyvinyl pyrolidone, phenol and acetone plants, ethylene cracking heaters, caprolactum, chlorine-caustic, formaldehyde, styrene, aluminum chloride, aromatic nitriles; process improvements. *Mailing Add:* 1887 Kennedy Blvd Jersey City NJ 07305

TSAO-WU, NELSON TSIN, b Tientsin, China, Sept 9, 34; US citizen; m 59; c 3. ELECTRONIC ENGINEERING. *Educ:* Loughborough Col Technol, DLC, 57; Univ London, BSc, 57; Northeastern Univ, MSEE, 65, PhD(elec eng), 68. *Prof Exp:* Engr, Rediffusion Ltd, Hong Kong, 57-59; audio engr, Far East Broadcasting Co, Hong Kong, 59-60; asst educ officer, Hong Kong Govt, 61-63; biomed engr, Harvard Med Sch & Peter Bent Brigham Hosp, 65-67; MEM TECH STAFF, BELL TEL LABS, 68- *Mem:* Inst Elec & Electronics Engrs. *Res:* Switching networks; coding theory; mathematical modeling; signal theory; software engineering and development. *Mailing Add:* Syst Anal Dept 11900 N Pecos St Denver CO 80234

TSAROS, C(ONSTANTINE) L(OUIS), b East Chicago, Ind, Sept 6, 21; m 50; c 4. CHEMICAL ENGINEERING, ENGINEERING ECONOMICS. *Educ:* Purdue Univ, BS, 43; Univ Mich, MS, 48. *Prof Exp:* Chem engr, Armour & Co, Ill, 43-46; assoc chem engr, Inst Gas Technol, Ill Inst Technol, 48-51; chem engr, Standard Oil Co, Ind, 51-57; chem engr, 57-64, supvr process econ, 64-70, MGR, PROCESS ECON, INST GAS TECHNOL, ILL INST TECHNOL, 70- *Mem:* Am Gas Asn; Am Inst Chem Engrs; Am Asn Cost Engrs; Sigma Xi. *Res:* Chemical engineering design and process development; process economics in petroleum processing, hydrocarbon conversion, energy studies and synthetic fuels. *Mailing Add:* Inst of Gas Technol 3424 S State St Chicago IL 60616

TSAUR, BOR-YEU, b Taiwan, June 8, 55. ELECTRONIC ENGINEERING. *Educ:* Nat Taiwan Univ, BS, 77; Calif Inst Technol, MS, 78, PhD(elec eng), 80. *Prof Exp:* Vis scientist, IBM Res Ctr, 79; RES STAFF MEM, LINCOLN LAB, MASS INST TECHNOL, 80- *Mem:* Am Phys Soc; Inst Elec & Electronics Engrs; Mat Res Soc; Metall Soc-Am Inst Metal Engrs. *Res:* Development of novel crystal growth technique for preparing large-area single-crystal semiconductor sheets on insulting substrates for integrated electronic devices; novel electronic devices or circuits; processing technologies; device physics based on the semiconductor on insulator structures. *Mailing Add:* Lincoln Lab Mass Inst Technol Lexington MA 02173

TSAY, JIA-YEONG, biostatistics, mathematical statistics, see previous edition

TSCHABOLD, EDWARD EVERTT, b Wichita Falls, Tex, Dec 7, 34; div; c 2. PLANT PHYSIOLOGY. *Educ:* Midwestern Univ, BS, 57; Miami Univ, MA, 62; Colo State Univ, PhD(plant physiol), 67. *Prof Exp:* RES PLANT PHYSIOLOGIST, LILLY RES LABS, 67- *Mem:* Am Soc Agron; Am Soc Plant Physiologists. *Res:* Basic and applied aspects of agricultural plant growth regulators; genetic modifications. *Mailing Add:* Lilly Res Labs Greenfield Res Labs G785 Greenfield IN 46140

TSCHANG, PIN-SENG, b Penang, Malaysia, May 14, 34; m 62; c 2. ELECTRICAL ENGINEERING. *Educ:* Ore State Univ, BS, 58, MS, 59; Newark Col Eng, DEngSci(elec eng), 67. *Prof Exp:* Instr elec eng, Newark Col Eng, 59-62; res engr, Electronics Res Labs, Columbia Univ, 62-65, sr res engr, 65-67; RES ASSOC, RES LABS, EASTMAN KODAK CO, 67- *Mem:* Inst Elec & Electronics Engrs; Brit Inst Elec Engrs. *Res:* Electronics and scientific instrumentation; television; digital signal processing; electronic memories. *Mailing Add:* Eastman Kodak Co Res Labs 343 State St Rochester NY 14650

TSCHANTZ, BRUCE A, b Akron, Ohio, Sept 15, 38; m 62; c 2. CIVIL ENGINEERING, WATER RESOURCES. *Educ:* Ohio Northern Univ, BSCE, 60; NMex State Univ, MSCE, 62, ScD(civil eng), 65. *Prof Exp:* Civil engr, Facilities Div, White Sands Missile Range, 65; from asst prof to assoc prof civil eng, 69-76, PROF CIVIL ENG, UNIV TENN, KNOXVILLE, 76- *Concurrent Pos:* Consult, Exec Off Pres, Off Sci & Technol Policy, Washington, DC, 77-79; chief, Fed Dam Safety, Fed Emergency Mgt Agency, Washington, DC, 80. *Honors & Awards:* Dow Chem Co Award, Am Soc Eng Educ, 69. *Mem:* Am Soc Eng Educ; Am Soc Civil Engrs. *Res:* Remote sensing of the environment, particularly water resources; analysis of the safety of dams; unsteady open channel flow; hydrologic impact of coal strip mining. *Mailing Add:* Dept of Civil Eng Univ of Tenn Knoxville TN 37916

TSCHANZ, CHARLES MCFARLAND, b Mackay, Idaho, July 9, 26; m 58; c 3. GEOLOGY. *Educ:* Univ Idaho, BS, 49; Stanford Univ, MS, 51. *Prof Exp:* Geologist, Colo, US Geol Surv, 49-50, Pioche, Nev, 51-53, chief uranium-copper proj, NMex, 53-55, geochem researcher, 55-56, chief mapping proj, Lincoln County, Nev, 56-60, advisor, Bolivian Mineral Resources, US Opers Mission, USAID, 60-65, geol consult, Nat Mineral Inventory, Colombia, 65-69, proj chief, Boulder Mountains Mapping Proj, Idaho, 69-70, proj chief mineral eval, Sawtooth Nat Recreation Area, Idaho, 71-74, proj chief, Boulder Mountains, Idaho, 74-82. *Mem:* Geol Soc Am; Geochem Soc; Soc Econ Geol. *Res:* Regional mapping and economic evaluation as an integrated project; geochemistry, especially distribution of minor elements in igneous rocks; geology of eastern Nevada, Colorado Plateau, Bolivian Altiplano and Sierra Nevada of Santa Marta, Colombia. *Mailing Add:* 876 S Moore Denver CO 80226

TSCHANZ, CHRISTIAN, b Heimberg, Switz, Dec 22, 42. PHARMACOLOGY, CLINICAL CHEMISTRY. *Educ:* Univ Berne, Switz, MD, 72. *Prof Exp:* Asst clin chem, Univ Berne, Switz, 71-72, fel clin pharmacol, 73-75; fel, Univ Kans, 75-77; resident internal med & fel pharmacol, Med Ctr, Univ Kans, 78-79; ASST PROF MED & PHARMACOL, DUKE UNIV MED CTR, 79- *Mem:* AMA. *Res:* Drug metabolism; pharmacokinetics; drug toxicity. *Mailing Add:* Duke Univ Med Ctr Durham NC 27710

TSCHARNER, CHRISTOPHER J, organic chemistry, physical chemistry, see previous edition

TSCHIEGG, CARL EMERSON, b Bluffton, Ohio, Apr 14, 24; m 50; c 2. PHYSICS. *Educ:* Bowling Green State Univ, BS, 49. *Prof Exp:* Physicist, Sound Sect, Nat Bur Standards, 50-82; RETIRED. *Honors & Awards:* Meritorious Serv Award, US Dept Com, 61. *Mem:* Am Phys Soc; sr mem Inst Elec & Electronics Eng. *Res:* Ultrasonics; underwater sound. *Mailing Add:* Bldg 233 Room A 147 Nat Bur Standards Washington DC 20234

TSCHINKEL, WALTER RHEINHARDT, b Lobositz, Czech, Sept 15, 40; US citizen; m 68. BIOLOGY, INSECT BEHAVIOR. *Educ:* Wesleyan Univ, BA, 62; Univ Calif, Berkeley, MA, 65, PhD(comp biochem), 68. *Prof Exp:* Fel biol, Dept Neurobiol & Behav, Cornell Univ, 68-70; lectr entom, Rhodes Univ, 70; asst prof, 70-75, ASSOC PROF BIOL SCI, FLA STATE UNIV, 75- *Concurrent Pos:* NSF grants, 71-; consult, Environ Protection Agency, 73-75; vis assoc prof, Entom Dept, Univ Calif, Berkeley, 77; mem panel regulatory biol, NSF, 77- & consult integrated basic res, 78- *Mem:* AAAS; Entom Soc Am. *Res:* Insect behavior and chemical communication; biology of ants; biology of tenebrionid beetles. *Mailing Add:* Dept of Biol Sci Fla State Univ Tallahassee FL 32306

TSCHIRGI, ROBERT DONALD, b Sheridan, Wyo, Oct 9, 24. PHYSIOLOGY. *Educ:* Univ Chicago, BS, 45, MS, 47, PhD, 49, MD, 50. *Prof Exp:* Asst physiol, Univ Chicago, 45-48, from instr to asst prof, 48-53; from assoc prof to prof, Sch Med, Univ Calif, Los Angeles, 53-66; vchancellor acad planning, 66-67, vchancellor acad affairs, 67-68, PROF NEUROSCI, UNIV CALIF, SAN DIEGO, 66- *Concurrent Pos:* Dir med educ study, Univ Hawaii, 63-64; univ dean planning, Univ Calif, 64-66; consult, NSF. *Mem:* Int Brain Res Orgn; fel AAAS; Am Physiol Soc; Biophys Soc. *Res:* Intracranial fluids and barriers; direct current potentials in central nervous system; neurophysiology of perception. *Mailing Add:* Dept of Neurosci Sch of Med Univ of Calif at San Diego La Jolla CA 92093

TSCHIRLEY, FRED HAROLD, b Ethan, SDak, Dec 19, 25; m 48; c 5. ECOLOGY. *Educ:* Univ Colo, BA, 51, MA, 54; Univ Ariz, PhD, 63. *Prof Exp:* Res asst, Univ Ariz, 52-53, instr, 53-54; range scientist, Crops Res Div, Agr Res Serv, USDA, 54-68, asst br chief, Crops Protection Res Br, 68-71, asst coordr environ qual activ sci & educ, 71-73, coordr environ qual activ, Off Secy, 73-74; chmn dept, 74-80, PROF BOT & PLANT PATH, MICH STATE UNIV, 74- *Mem:* AAAS; Weed Sci Soc Am; Soc Range Mgt; Ecol Soc Am. *Res:* Woody plant control; physiological ecology. *Mailing Add:* Dept of Bot & Plant Path Mich State Univ East Lansing MI 48224

TSCHOEGL, NICHOLAS WILLIAM, b Zidlochovice, Czech, June 4, 18; m 46; c 2. PHYSICAL CHEMISTRY. *Educ:* New South Wales, BSc, 54, PhD(chem), 58. *Prof Exp:* Sr res officer, Bread Res Inst, Australia, 58-61; proj assoc dept chem, Univ Wis, 61-63; sr phys chemist, Stanford Res Inst, 63-65; assoc prof mat sci, 65-67, PROF CHEM ENG, CALIF INST TECHNOL, 67- *Concurrent Pos:* Consult, Phillips Petrol Co, 67-; Alexander von Humboldt Found award, 70. *Mem:* Am Phys Soc; Am Chem Soc; Soc Rheol; Brit Soc Rheol; Royal Australian Chem Inst. *Res:* Polymer rheology; physical chemistry of macromolecules; mechanical properties of polymeric materials. *Mailing Add:* Dept of Chem Eng Calif Inst of Technol Pasadena CA 91125

TSCHUDY, DONALD P, b Palmerton, Pa, Nov 8, 26; m 51; c 2. INTERNAL MEDICINE, BIOCHEMISTRY. *Educ:* Princeton Univ, AB, 46; Columbia Univ, MD, 50; Am Bd Internal Med, dipl, 61. *Prof Exp:* Intern med, Presby Hosp, New York, 51-52, asst resident, 52-53; asst resident, Francis Delafield Hosp, 53-54; clin assoc, Clin Ctr, NIH, 54-55, SR INVESTR, METAB SERV, CLIN CTR, NAT CANCER INST, 55- *Mem:* Am Soc Clin Invest; Am Fedn Clin Res; Am Soc Biol Chemists; AMA. *Res:* Clinical and biochemical research on porphyrin metabolism and the porphyrias; research on tumor-host relationships. *Mailing Add:* NIH Clin Ctr Nat Cancer Inst Bethesda MD 20014

TSCHUDY, ROBERT HAYDN, b Pocatello, Idaho, May 7, 08; m 34. PALEOBOTANY. *Educ:* Univ Wash, Seattle, BS, 32, MS, 34, PhD, 37. *Prof Exp:* Instr bot, Univ Wyo, 37-38; res biologist, Scripps Inst, Univ Calif, 39-41; assoc prof bot, Willamette Univ, 41-45; res biologist, Creole Petrol Corp, 45-49, asst res coordr, 49-50; dir, Palynological Res Lab, 50-61; mem res staff, Paleont & Stratig Br, US Geol Surv, 61-78; RETIRED. *Concurrent Pos:* Lectr, Univ Colo, 55-56 & 64-66 & Univ Minn, 58; annuitant, US Geol Surv, 78- *Mem:* Bot Soc Am; Geol Soc Am. *Res:* Palynology. *Mailing Add:* US Geol Surv Denver Fed Ctr Bldg 25 Denver CO 80225

TSCHUIKOW-ROUX, EUGENE, b Kharkov, USSR, Jan 16, 36; US citizen; m 59. PHYSICAL CHEMISTRY. *Educ:* Univ Calif, Berkeley, BS, 57, PhD(chem), 61; Univ Wash, Seattle, MS, 58. *Prof Exp:* Sr scientist, Jet Propulsion Lab, Calif Inst Technol, 60-65; Nat Acad Sci-Nat Res Coun res assoc chem, Nat Bur Standards, 65-66; assoc prof, 66-71, PROF CHEM, UNIV CALGARY, 71-, CHMN DEPT, 73- *Concurrent Pos:* Vis scholar, Univ Calif, Santa Barbara, 72; consult, Jet Propulsion Lab, Calif Inst Technol, 73. *Mem:* Am Chem Soc; Am Phys Soc; Can Inst Chem. *Res:* Gas phase reaction kinetics; high temperature shock tube studies; kinetic isotope effects; photochemistry; reaction dynamics; unimolecular reactions; gas phase ion-molecule reactions. *Mailing Add:* Dept Chem Univ Calgary Calgary AB T2N 1N4 Can

TSCHUNKO, HUBERT F A, b Weidenau, Austria, Sept 9, 12; US citizen; m 46; c 2. PHYSICS, OPTICS. *Educ:* Darmstadt Tech Univ, Diplom-Ing, 35. *Prof Exp:* Develop engr aeronaut indust, Europe, 36-45; res assoc astron, Astron Observ, Heidelberg, 45-50; engr pvt indust, WGer, 51-57; physicist, US Air Force, Wright-Patterson AFB, 57-65; opticist electronics res ctr, 65-70, OPTICIST, NASA GODDARD SPACE FLIGHT CTR, 70- *Honors & Awards:* Apollo Achievement Award, NASA, 69. *Mem:* AAAS; Optical Soc Am; Ger Soc Aeronaut & Astronaut. *Res:* wave optics; performances of large and space optical systems, as space telescopes, space cameras, space energy collectors and space energy transmitters. *Mailing Add:* NASA Goddard Space Flight Ctr Code 717 Greenbelt MD 20771

TSE, FRANCIS LAI-SING, b Hong Kong, Jan 20, 52; Brit citizen; m 79. PHARMACOKINETICS, DRUG METABOLISM. *Educ:* Univ Wis-Madison, BS, 74, MS, 75, PhD(pharmaceut), 78. *Prof Exp:* Asst prof pharmacokinetics, Rutgers Univ, 78-80; SR SCIENTIST & UNIT HEAD, DRUG METAB, SANDOZ, INC, 81- *Concurrent Pos:* Prin investr, Nat Inst Drug Abuse, 80-81; vis asst prof pharmaceut, Rutgers Univ, 81-, mem grad fac, 80- *Mem:* Am Pharmaceut Asn; NY Acad Sci; Sigma Xi; Int Soc Study Xenobiotics; Am Pharmaceut Asn-Acad Pharmaceut Sci. *Res:* Absorption, distribution, metabolism and excretion of therapeutic agents in laboratory animals and humans; influence of various environmental and physiological factors on drug pharmacokinetics. *Mailing Add:* Drug Metab Sect Sandoz Inc East Hanover NJ 07936

TSE, FRANCIS S, b Canton, China, Dec 15, 19; US citizen; m 52; c 2. MECHANICAL ENGINEERING. *Educ:* Univ Hong Kong, BSc, 41; Purdue Univ, Lafayette, MSME, 42; Univ Pa, MBA, 49; Ohio State Univ, PhD(mech eng), 57. *Prof Exp:* Jr engr, Baldwin Locomotive Works, Pa, 42-45; engr, Fairbanks Morse, Wis, 46-47; instr & res assoc mech eng, Ohio State Univ, 47-57; from asst prof to assoc prof, Mich State Univ, 57-62; NSF fel, Purdue Univ, Lafayette, 62-63; PROF MECH ENG, UNIV CINCINNATI, 63- *Concurrent Pos:* NSF grants undergrad educ, Univ Cincinnati, 64-66. *Mem:* Am Soc Eng Educ; Am Soc Mech Engrs; Instrument Soc Am. *Res:* Vibrations; control theory; measurement and instrumentation; machine dynamics. *Mailing Add:* 10167 Lochcrest Dr Cincinnati OH 45231

TSE, HAROLD F, b China, Jan 24, 22; m 53. CHEMICAL ENGINEERING, PETROLEUM CHEMISTRY. *Educ:* St John's Univ, China, BS, 49; Ohio State Univ, MS, 51, PhD(chem eng), 59. *Prof Exp:* Sr researcher chem eng, Sun Oil Co, 60-77; MEM STAFF, ENGLEHARD INDUST DIV, 77- *Mem:* Am Inst Chem Engrs; Am Chem Soc. *Res:* Synthesis; separation and purification; product evaluation. *Mailing Add:* Englehard Indust Div 429 Delanay St Newark NJ 07105

TSE, ROSE (LOU), b Shanghai, China, July 27, 27; US citizen; m 53. ORGANIC CHEMISTRY, MEDICINE. *Educ:* St John's Univ, China, BS, 49; Mt Holyoke Col, MA, 50; Yale Univ, PhD(org chem), 53; Med Col Pa, MD, 60; Am Bd Internal Med, dipl & cert rheumatology. *Prof Exp:* Instr, Ohio State Univ, 53-55; res assoc, Univ Pa, 55-56; intern, Philadelphia Gen Hosp, 60-61, resident internal med, 61-64; assoc in med, 68-71, asst prof clin med, 71-75, ASSOC PROF MED, SCH MED, UNIV PA, 75- *Concurrent Pos:* Attend physician, Philadelphia Gen Hosp, 64-68, sr attend physician, 68-, assoc chief spec ward cardiol, 68-71, chief rheumatology sect, 71-; clin instr internal med, Med Col Pa, 64-68. *Mem:* Fel Am Col Physicians; fel Am Inst Chemists; fel Am Col Angiol; Am Heart Asn; Am Rheumatism Asn. *Res:* Reaction mechanisms; organic synthesis; electrocardiology; inflammatory mediators; non-steroidal inflammatory agents; cardiology; rheumatology; catecholamines; cyclic adenosine monophosphate; prostaglandin; crystal-induced synovitis. *Mailing Add:* 130 E Levering Mill Rd Bala-Cynwyd PA 19004

TSE, WARREN W, b Hong Kong, Mar 13, 39; m 68; c 2. HUMAN PHYSIOLOGY. *Educ:* Univ Cincinnati, BS, 65; Univ Wis, MS, 67, PhD(physiol), 70. *Prof Exp:* Lectr physiol, Univ Wis, 69-70, fel physiol, 70-72; res assoc cardiol, Albany Med Col, 72-75; ASST PROF PHYSIOL, DEPT PHYSIOL & BIOPHYS, CHICAGO MED SCH, UNIV HEALTH SCI, 75- *Mem:* Am Physiol Soc. *Res:* Electrophysiological properties of single fibers of atrioventricular node and purkinje fibers of dog hearts. *Mailing Add:* Dept of Physiol & Biophys Chicago Med Sch North Chicago IL 60064

TSEN, CHO CHING, b Chekiang, China, Oct 12, 22; nat US; m 52, 78; c 5. BIOCHEMISTRY, NUTRITION. *Educ:* Nat Chekiang Univ, China, BS, 44, MS, 46; Univ Calif, PhD(biochem), 58. *Prof Exp:* Res chemist, Taiwan Sugar Exp Sta, 46-50; from instr to assoc prof biochem, Taiwan Prov Col Agr, 51-54; fel, Nat Res Coun Can, 58-59; chemist, Grain Res Lab, Bd Grain Comnrs Can, 59-65, scientist, 65-67; res group leader, Am Inst Baking, Ill, 67-69; PROF CEREAL CHEM & BAKING SCI, KANS STATE UNIV, 69- *Concurrent Pos:* Consult, Lauhoff Grain Co, 76-78, Fortified Biscuits Proj, US Agency Int Develop, Sri Lanka, 78 & Soy Fortification Prog, UN, Food & Agr Orgn & Develop Prog, Sri Lanka, 80; vis scientist, Cereal Chem & Baking Technol, People's Repub China, 80; mem adv comt, Taiwan Food Indust, Econ Affairs, Repub China, 77- *Mem:* AAAS; Am Chem Soc; Am Asn Cereal Chemists; Inst Food Technologists; Int Union Food Sci & Technol. *Res:* Cereal and food chemistry; baking technology; enrichment and fortification of cereal products and nutrition of cereal products. *Mailing Add:* Dept Grain Sci & Indust Kans State Univ Manhattan KS 66506

TSENG, CHARLES C, b Fuchow, Fukien, China, Dec 20, 32; m 65; c 2. PLANT ANATOMY, MORPHOLOGY. *Educ:* Taiwan Norm Univ, BS, 55; Taiwan Univ, MS, 57; Univ Calif, Los Angeles, PhD(plant sci), 65. *Prof Exp:* From asst prof to assoc prof bot, Windham Col, 65-75; assoc prof, 75-80, PROF BIOL, PURDUE UNIV, CALUMET CAMPUS, 80- *Mem:* AAAS; Bot Soc Am; Am Inst Biol Sci; Am Soc Plant Taxon. *Res:* Floral anatomy of Umbelliferae and Araliaceae; palynology of angiosperms and gymnosperms; taxonomy of Umbelliferae; biochemistry. *Mailing Add:* Dept of Biol Purdue Univ Hammond IN 46323

TSENG, CHEN HOWARD, b Miaoli, Taiwan, Dec 11, 38; m 65; c 3. NUCLEAR MEDICINE, RADIOISOTOPIC PATHOLOGY. *Educ:* Kaohsiung Med Col, MD, 64; Ohio State Univ, MS, 68; Univ Okla, PhD(med sci), 72. *Prof Exp:* Chief path & transfusion serv, Hosp, Sidney, NY, 74-76; chief, Vet Admin Med Ctr, Ohio, 76-78, Vet Admin West Side Med Ctr, Chicago, 78-79, CHIEF LAB SERV, VET ADMIN MED CTR, FARGO, NDAK, 80- *Concurrent Pos:* Instr path, Col Med, Univ Okla, 71-72; asst prof, Med Sch, Univ Pittsburgh, 72-73; assoc prof, Sch Med, Wright State Univ, 76-78, Col Med, Univ Ill, 78-79; prof path, Sch Med, Univ NDak, 80- *Mem:* fel Am Col Pathologists; fel Am Soc Clin Pathologists; Int Acad Path; Am Soc Nephrology; Electron Micros Soc Am. *Res:* Development of new staining techniques for histopathology in various tissues; ultrastructural features of pathology. *Mailing Add:* Vet Admin Med Ctr Elm St & 21st Ave N Fargo ND 58102

TSENG, CHIEN KUEI, b Tao Yuan, Taiwan, Feb 21, 34; m 66; c 2. ORGANIC CHEMISTRY. *Educ:* Cheng Kung Univ, Taiwan, BS, 57; WVa Univ, MS, 64; Ill Inst Technol, PhD(chem), 68. *Prof Exp:* USPHS fels, Ill Inst Technol, 67-68; from res chemist to sr res chemist, 68-71, SUPVR ANAL CHEM, STAUFFER CHEM CO, 71- *Mem:* Am Chem Soc. *Res:* Nuclear magnetic resonance; structure determination; stereochemistry; phosphorus chemistry; infrared and mass spectroscopy. *Mailing Add:* Stauffer Chem Co 1200 S 47th St Richmond CA 94804

TSENG, FUNG-I, b Pingtung, Taiwan, Jan 12, 36; m 65; c 3. ELECTRICAL ENGINEERING, ELECTROMAGNETICS. *Educ:* Nat Taiwan Univ, BS, 58; Chiao Tung Univ, MS, 60; Syracuse Univ, PhD(elec eng), 66. *Prof Exp:* Res engr antennas, Syracuse Univ, 66-69; ASST PROF ELEC ENG, ROCHESTER INST TECHNOL, 69- *Mem:* Inst Elec & Electronics Engrs; Optical Soc Am. *Res:* Optimization of antenna arrays in noisy environments subject to random fluctuations. *Mailing Add:* Dept of Elec Eng Rochester Inst of Technol Rochester NY 14623

TSENG, HSIANG LEN, b Wukingfu via Swatow, China, Apr 24, 13; US citizen; m 52; c 4. PATHOLOGY. *Educ:* Hsiang Ya Sch Med, MD, 37; Univ Basel, MD, 48; Am Bd Path, cert anat path, 55, cert clin path, 66. *Prof Exp:* Vol asst, Inst Anat Path, Univ Basel, 47-48; vol asst internal med, Bürgerspital, Basel, 48; vol asst, Postgrad Med Sch, Univ London, 48; resident internal med, St Catherine Hosp, Brooklyn, NY, 49-51; resident path, Univ Hosp, New York, 51-52; asst pathologist, Ill Masonic Hosp, 52-55; chief pathologist, St Elizabeth Hosp, Washington, DC, 55-57; chief pathologist, Provident Hosp, Baltimore, 57-69; pathologist, 69-70, CHIEF ANAT PATH, ST ELIZABETH HOSP, WASHINGTON, DC, 70- *Concurrent Pos:* Fel, Malaria Inst India, Delhi, 42; clin instr, Col Med, Univ Ill, 54-55. *Mem:* Fel Am Col Path; Am Soc Cytol; Int Acad Path. *Res:* Anatomical and clinical pathology; myocarditis, both idiopathic and tuberculous type; acute sicklemia. *Mailing Add:* 1211 LaGrande Rd Silver Spring MD 20903

TSENG, LINDA, b China, Sept 29, 36; US citizen; m 63; c 1. PHYSICAL CHEMISTRY, BIOCHEMISTRY. *Educ:* Cheng Kung Univ, Taiwan, BS, 55; Univ NDak, PhD(chem), 68. *Prof Exp:* assoc prof biochem, 76-80, ASSOC PROF OBSTET & GYNEC, HEALTH SCI CTR, STATE UNIV NY STONY BROOK, 80- *Honors & Awards:* Irma Hirsh Res Award, Irma Hirsh Inc, 76. *Mem:* AAAS; Endocrine Soc. *Res:* Steroid biochemistry; hormone action. *Mailing Add:* Dept of Obstet & Gynec State Univ NY Stony Brook NY 11794

TSENG, MICHAEL TSUNG, b Chungking, China, Jan 25, 44; US citizen; m 70; c 1. ENDOCRINOLOGY, PATHOLOGY. *Educ:* Iowa State Univ, BS, 67; State Univ NY, Buffalo, PhD(exp path), 73. *Prof Exp:* Res assoc biochem, Ore Regional Primate Res Ctr, 73-74; asst prof anat, Upstate Med Ctr, State Univ NY, 74-78; ASSOC PROF ANAT & ONCOL ASSOC CANCER CTR, HELATH SCI CTR, UNIV LOUISVILLE, 78- *Concurrent Pos:* Instr anat, Sch Med, Univ Ore, 73-74; prin investr, Univ Award, State Univ NY, 73-76; prin investr, Am Cancer Soc, 78-82. *Mem:* Am Asn Anatomists; Am Soc Cell Biol; Am Asn Pathologists; Sigma Xi; Endocrine Soc. *Res:* Characterization of mammary epithelium in physioligical and pathological states; endocrine control of vitellogenesis in amphibians; in vitro screening test for anticancer agents. *Mailing Add:* Dept of Anat Univ of Louisville Louisville KY 40292

TSENG, SAMUEL CHIN-CHONG, b Tainan, Taiwan, Mar 6, 33; m 57. SOLID STATE ELECTRONICS. *Educ:* Ching-Kung Univ, Taiwan, BS, 56; Chiao Tung Univ, MS, 60; Yale Univ, ME, 61; Univ Calif, Berkeley, PhD(solid state electronics), 66. *Prof Exp:* Res engr, Electron Tube Div, Litton Industs, Inc, Calif, 66-68; staff engr, 68-69, MEM RES STAFF, T J WATSON RES CTR, IBM CORP, 69- *Mem:* Am Phys Soc; Inst Elec & Electronics Engrs. *Res:* Excitation, propagation and amplification of surface elastic waves in piezoelectric crystals and ceramics; application of surface waves to delay lines, matched filters, binary sequence recognitions and signal processing in general. *Mailing Add:* T J Watson Res Ctr IBM Corp Yorktown Heights NY 10598

TSENG, SHIN-SHYONG, b Tainan, Taiwan, Nov 24, 38; US citizen; m 67; c 2. ORGANIC CHEMISTRY. *Educ:* Nat Taiwan Univ, BS, 61; Kent State Univ, MA, 64; Univ Chicago, PhD(org chem), 69. *Prof Exp:* Fel natural prod synthesis, Univ Chicago, 69-70; fel photochem, Syva Res Inst, 70-72; res assoc gas-solid photochem, Ames Res Ctr, NASA, 72-73; assoc res scientist chem carcinogenesis, Inst Environ Med, Med Ctr, NY Univ, 73-77; SR RES CHEMIST CHEM LIGHT, AM CYANAMID CO, 77- *Mem:* Am Chem Soc. *Res:* Chemiluminescence; photochemistry; chemical carcinogenesis; chemistry of electron-rich olefins; organic synthesis; charge-transfer complexes. *Mailing Add:* Chem Res Div Am Cyanamid Co Bound Brook NJ 08805

TSERNOGLOU, DEMETRIUS, b Mytilene, Greece, Feb 10, 35. BIOPHYSICS, CRYSTALLOGRAPHY. *Educ:* Univ London, BSc, 60; Dalhousie Univ, MSc, 62; Yale Univ, MS, 64, PhD(molecular biophys), 66. *Prof Exp:* Fel molecular biophys, Yale Univ, 67-69; res asst prof biochem, Sch Med, Wash Univ, 69-71; from asst prof to assoc prof, 71-78, PROF DEPT BIOCHEM, SCH MED, WAYNE STATE UNIV, 78- *Concurrent Pos:* Lectr biochem, Yale Univ, 68-69; vis prof, Univ Athens, 75-76 & Biozentrum Basel, 80; vis fel, All Souls Col, Oxford, 80-81. *Res:* Crystallographic study of structure and function of proteins; blood clotting; neurotoxins. *Mailing Add:* Dept Biochem 540 E Canfield Detroit MI 48201

TSERPES, NICOLAS A, b Messene, Greece, 1936; US citizen; m 68. MATHEMATICS, PROBABILITY. *Educ:* Wayne State Univ, BS, 61, MA, 64, PhD(math), 68. *Prof Exp:* Res phys scientist statist, Corps Eng, US Lake Surv, Detroit Dist, 63-64 & 66-67; assoc prof, 68-76, PROF MATH, UNIV SOUTH FLA, 76- *Concurrent Pos:* Univ res coun grant, Univ SFla, 71-73; prof & chmn gen math, Univ Patras, Greece, 75-77. *Mem:* Am Math Soc; Math Asn Am. *Res:* Theory and measure on topological semigroups; probability structures and random walks on semigroups; mathematical statistics; stochastic differential-integral equations. *Mailing Add:* Dept Math Univ South Fla Tampa FL 33620

TSIAPALIS, CHRIS MILTON, biochemistry, see previous edition

TSIATIS, ANASTASIOS A, b New York, NY, July 12, 48; m 70; c 1. BIOMETRICS, BIOSTATISTICS. *Educ:* Mass Inst Technol, BS, 70; Univ Calif, Berkeley, PhD(statist), 74. *Prof Exp:* Asst prof statist, Univ Wis-Madison, 74-79; assoc mem biostatist, St Jude Children's Res Hosp, 79-81; ASSOC PROF BIOSTATIST, SCH PUB HEALTH, HARVARD UNIV & SIDNEY FARBER CANCER INST, 81- *Mem:* Am Statist Asn; Biometrics Soc; Inst Math Statist. *Res:* Application of survival analysis in clinical trials with specific emphasis on sequential rules for stopping a trial early if large treatment differences occur. *Mailing Add:* Sidney Farber Cancer Inst 44 Binney St Dept Biostatist Boston MA 02115

TSIBRIS, JOHN-CONSTANTINE MICHAEL, b Jannina, Greece, Dec 22, 36; m 69; c 2. BIOCHEMISTRY, ENDOCRINOLOGY. *Educ:* Nat Univ Athens, BSc, 59; Cornell Univ PhD(biochem), 65. *Prof Exp:* Vis scientist, Univ Fla, 69-71, asst prof biochem, 71-77, assoc prof, Dept Obstet & Gynec, 77-79; ASSOC PROF, DEPT OBSTET/GYNEC & PHYSIOL/BIOPHYSICS, MED CTR, UNIV ILL, CHICAGO, 79- *Concurrent Pos:* NIH trainee biophys chem, 67-68, grant, 69-78, career develop award, 69-77; Am Diabetes Asn, 80-81. *Mem:* AAAS; NY Acad Sci; Am Soc Biol Chem; Am Chem Soc; Soc Gynecologic Invest. *Res:* Chemical carcinogenesis; steroid and peptide hormone receptors; diabetes; fertility control. *Mailing Add:* Col Med Univ Ill Chicago IL 60612

TSICHRITZIS, DENNIS, b May 29, 43; Greek citizen; m 65. COMPUTER SCIENCE. *Educ:* Athens Tech Univ, Dipl elec eng, 65; Princeton Univ, MA, 67, PhD(elec eng), 68. *Prof Exp:* Asst prof, 68-71, assoc prof, 71-76, PROF COMPUT SCI, UNIV TORONTO, 76- *Concurrent Pos:* Consult, Elec Eng Consociates, 72- & DBMS Inc, 72- *Mem:* Asn Comput Mach; Inst Elec & Electronics Engrs; Can Info Processing Soc; Can Comput Sci Asn. *Res:* Office information systems; data base management systems; small business systems; computational complexity. *Mailing Add:* Dept Comput Sci Univ Toronto Toronto ON M5S 1A1 Can

TSIEN, HSIENCHYANG, b Nanking, China, July 26, 39; m 66; c 2. MICROBIOLOGY. *Educ:* Nat Taiwan Univ, BS, 61; Cath Univ Louvain, Belg, DrS(microbiol & biochem), 67. *Prof Exp:* Asst, Cath Univ Louvain, 67-68 & 70-72; res instr microbiol, Temple Univ, 72-75; res fel, 68-70, ASST PROF MICROBIOL, UNIV MINN, 75- *Mem:* Am Soc Microbiol; AAAS. *Res:* Soil microbiology; microorganism-plant symbiotic nitrogen fixation; microbial ecology; microbial physiology; structure and function of bacterial cell membranes and cell walls. *Mailing Add:* Dept of Microbiol Univ of Minn Minneapolis MN 55455

TSIGDINOS, GEORGE ANDREW, b Trikkala, Greece, May 30, 29; nat US; m 52; c 3. INORGANIC CHEMISTRY. *Educ:* Univ Boston, AB, 53, AM, 55, PhD(inorg chem), 61. *Prof Exp:* Res chemist res & eng div spec projs dept, Monsanto Chem Co, 59-61, res chemist, Boston Labs, Monsanto Res Corp, 61-65; sr res chemist, 65-74, RES SUPVR, CLIMAX MOLYBDENUM CO, 74- *Mem:* Am Chem Soc. *Res:* Heteropoly compounds; synthesis and characterization of molybdenum, tungsten and vanadium compounds and their application to catalysis; inorganic fluorine chemistry; inorganic polymers; electrochemistry of molybdenum; molybdenum flame retardants; molybdenum flame retardants and smoke suppressants; molybdenum coatings. *Mailing Add:* 1810 Traver Rd Ann Arbor MI 48105

TSIN, ANDREW TSANG CHEUNG, b Hong Kong, July 19, 50; UK & Can citizen; m 79. VISUAL PHYSIOLOGY. *Educ:* Dalhousie Univ, BSc, 73; Univ Alta, MSC, 76, PhD(zool), 79. *Prof Exp:* Teaching asst zool, Univ Alta, 73-75, sr lab demonstrator, 75-76, res asst physiol, 78-79; mem staff, Dept Opthal, Baylor Col Med, Tex Med Ctr, 79-81; ASST PROF, DIV ALLIED HEALTH & LIFE SCI, UNIV TEX, SAN ANTONIO, 81- *Mem:* Am Soc Zoologists; NY Acad Sci; AAAS; Asn Researchers Vision & Opthal; Soc Neurosci. *Res:* Visual pigments and vitamin A in animals. *Mailing Add:* Dept Opthal Tex Med Ctr Houston TX 77030

TSIPIS, KOSTA M, b Athens, Greece, Feb, 12, 34; US citizen; m 70; c 3. NUCLEAR PHYSICS. *Educ:* Rutgers Univ, BSc, 58, MSc, 60; Columbia Univ, PhD(nuclear physics), 66. *Prof Exp:* Res assoc particle physics, 66-68, asst prof, 68-71, SR RES PHYSICIST, MASS INST TECHNOL, 71- *Concurrent Pos:* Sr consult, Stockholm Int Peace Res Inst, 73-77; sr res fel, Ctr Int Studies, Mass Inst Technol, 73-77. *Mem:* Am Phys Soc. *Res:* Particle physics; technical and scientific aspects of national defense policy. *Mailing Add:* Dept of Physics 77 Massachusetts Ave Cambridge MA 02135

TSIVIDIS, YANNIS P, b Piraeus, Greece, 1946. ELECTRICAL ENGINEERING, ELECTRONICS. *Educ:* Univ Minn, Minneapolis, BEE, 72; Univ Calif, Berkeley, MS, 73, PhD(eng), 76. *Prof Exp:* Engr electronics, Motorola Semiconductor, Phoenix, Ariz, 74; lectr elec eng, Univ Calif, Berkeley, 76; asst prof, 76-81, ASSOC PROF ELEC ENG, COLUMBIA UNIV, 81- *Concurrent Pos:* Mem tech staff, Bell Labs, Am Telephone & Telegraph Co, 77, resident vis, 77-; vis assoc prof, Mass Inst Technol, 80. *Mem:* Sr mem Inst Elec & Electronics Engrs; Sigma Xi. *Res:* Design, analysis and simulation of integrated circuits; electronics; semiconductor device modellng; signal processing; circuit theory. *Mailing Add:* Dept Elec Eng Columbia Univ New York NY 10027

TSO, MARK ON-MAN, b Hong Kong, China, Oct 19, 36; US citizen; m 64; c 2. OPHTHALMOLOGY, PATHOLOGY. *Educ:* Univ Hong Kong, MB, BS, 61. *Prof Exp:* Res assoc, Armed Forces Inst Path, 71-76; PROF OPHTHAL, DIR GEORGIANA THEOBALD OPHTHALMIC PATH LAB & DIR MACULAR CLIN, EYE & EAR INFIRMARY, UNIV ILL, 76- *Concurrent Pos:* Fel ophthal path, Armed Forces Inst Path, 67-68, res fel, 68-69; assoc res prof ophthal, Med Ctr, George Washington Univ, 73-76; William Friedkin scholar, 76; mem, Vis Disorder Study Sect, NIH, 78- *Honors & Awards:* Distinguished Serv Award, Armed Forces Inst Path, 71; Army Commendation Medal, 71. *Mem:* Fel Am Acad Ophthal & Otolayrngol; Asn Res Vision & Ophthal. *Res:* Experimental pathology; clinical ophthalmology, especially diseases of retina and macula; electron microscopy; tissue culture; ocular oncology. *Mailing Add:* Eye & Ear Infirmary 1855 W Taylor St Chicago IL 60612

TS'O, PAUL ON PONG, b Hong Kong, July 17, 29; m 55; c 3. BIOPHYSICAL CHEMISTRY. *Educ:* Lingnan Univ, China, BS, 49; Mich State Univ, MS, 51; Calif Inst Technol, PhD, 55. *Prof Exp:* Res fel biol, Calif Inst Technol, 55-61, sr res fel, 61-62; assoc prof biophys chem, 62-67, PROF BIOPHYS CHEM, JOHNS HOPKINS UNIV, 67-, DIR DIV BIOPHYSICS SCH HYGIENE & PUB HEALTH, 73- *Concurrent Pos:* Consult, Nat Cancer Inst; assoc ed, Molecular Pharmacol, 64-, Biochem, 66-74, Biophys J, 69-72, Biochem Biophys Acta, 71-81, Cancer Review, 73-, Cancer Res, 75-, J Environ Health Sci, 76-; mem, Biophysics Study Sect, NIH, 76-80. *Mem:* Am Chem Soc; Am Soc Biol Chemists; Biophys Soc; Am Asn Cancer Res; Am Soc Microbiol. *Res:* Physical, organic and biochemistry and biology of nucleic acids and nuclear magnetic resonance on biological systems; basic mechanisms of carcinogenesis and in vitro neoplastic transformation, tissue culture differentiation, aging and anti-viral substances (interferon). *Mailing Add:* Sch of Hygiene & Pub Health Johns Hopkins Univ 615 N Wolfe St Baltimore MD 21205

TSO, TIEN CHIOH, b Hupeh, China, July 25, 17; nat US; m 49; c 2. PHYTOCHEMISTRY. *Educ:* Nanking Univ, China, BS, 41, MS, 44; Pa State Univ, PhD(agr biochem), 50. *Prof Exp:* Supt exp farm, Ministry Social Affairs, China, 44-46; secy, Tobacco Improv Bur, 46-47; chemist res lab, Gen Cigar Co, 50-51; chemist div tobacco & spec crops, USDA, 52; asst prof & res assoc agron, Univ Md, 53-59; res plant physiologist, Tobacco & Sugar Crops Res Br, 59-62, sr plant physiologist, 62-64, prin plant physiologist, 64-66, leader tobacco qual invests, Tobacco & Sugar Crops Res Br, 66-72, CHIEF TOBACCO LAB, BELTSVILLE AGR RES CTR, AGR RES SERV, USDA, 72-, SR EXEC SERV, 79- *Concurrent Pos:* Mem, Tobacco Chem Res Conf, Tobacco Workers Conf, World Conf Tobacco & Health, Tobacco Working Group, Lung Cancer Task Force & Int Tobacco Working Group. *Honors & Awards:* Coresta Prize, 78. *Mem:* Fel AAAS; fel Am Agron Soc; Am Chem Soc; fel Am Inst Chem; Am Soc Plant Physiol. *Res:* Plant physiology; tobacco alkaloids; biochemistry; culture; radio elements; health related components; tobacco production research relating to smoking and health. *Mailing Add:* Agr Res Ctr W USDA Beltsville MD 20705

TS'O, TIMOTHY ON-TO, b Hong Kong, Nov 9, 34; US citizen; m 63; c 2. NEUROPHARMACOLOGY, BEHAVIORAL TOXICOLOGY. *Educ:* Univ Hong Kong, MB & BS, 59; Stanford Univ, PhD(neuropharmacol & psychopharmacol), 68; Am Bd Psychiat & Neurol, dipl, 79. *Prof Exp:* Demonstr, Dept Path, Fac Med, Univ Hong Kong, 60-62; sr res specialist pharmacol, Dow Chem Co, Mich, 68-74; res prof human biol, Saginaw Valley State Col, Mich, 74-75; lab chief neuropharmacol, Long Island Res Inst, 75-79; psychiatrist, Vet Admin Med Ctr, Northport, NY, 77-79; PSYCHIATRIST, VET ADMIN MED CTR, NORTH CHICAGO, 79-; ASSOC PROF PSYCHIAT & BEHAV SCI, UNIV HEALTH SCI, CHICAGO MED SCH, 79- *Concurrent Pos:* House physician & surgeon, Govt Surg Unit & Univ Med Unit, Queen Mary Hosp, Hong Kong, 59-60; resident, Dept Psychiat, State Univ NY Stony Brook, 75-7, res asst prof, 77-79. *Mem:* NY Acad Sci; AAAS; Biophys Soc; Am Psychiat Asn. *Res:* Effects of central nervous system drugs and toxicants on performance, memory and learning; computer system applications in behavioral pharmacology and toxicology, psychiatry and in electroencephalogram analysis; biomathematics; broncho-genic carcinoma; congenital tumors. *Mailing Add:* PO Box 147 Libertyville IL 60048

TSOKOS, CHRIS PETER, b Greece, Mar 25, 37; US citizen; c 3. APPLIED MATHEMATICS. *Educ:* Univ RI, BS & MS, 61; Univ Conn, PhD(math statist & probability), 67. *Prof Exp:* Consult opers res anal bur naval weapons, US Naval Air Sta, 64; proj engr elec boat div, Gen Dynamics Corp, 61-63; asst prof math, Univ RI, 63-69; assoc prof statist, Va Polytech Inst, 69-71; prof math & statist, 71-76, DIR GRAD PROG STATIST & STOCHASTIC SYSTS, UNIV S FLA, 71- *Concurrent Pos:* RI Res Coun res grants 65-66 & 67-68; NSF lectr, Univ RI, 65-68; consult, US Army Electronics Command Ctr, Ft Monmouth, NJ; dir contracts, AFSOR, 74-79, NASA, 75-79 & Bur Land Mgt, 74-77; vpres, Robert M Thrall & Assocs, Houston. *Mem:* AAAS; Am Math Soc; fel Am Statist Asn; Opers Res Soc Am. *Res:* Statistical theory and applications; stochastic integral equations; stochastic systems theory; biomathematics; stochastic modeling; time series; stochastic differential games; Bayesian reliability theory and simulation. *Mailing Add:* Dept of Math Univ of SFla Tampa FL 33620

TSOKOS, JANICE OSETH, b Canacao, Philippines, June 29, 40; US citizen; m; c 3. BIOCHEMISTRY. *Educ:* Univ RI, BS, 62, PhD(biochem), 70. *Prof Exp:* Asst prof biol sci, Va Polytech Inst & State Univ, 69-72; res assoc biochem, 72-73, asst prof, 73-79, ASSOC PROF CHEM, UNIV SOUTH FLA, 79- *Mem:* Am Chem Soc; AAAS; NY Acad Sci; Sigma Xi. *Res:* Investigations in cardiac muscle and liver mitochondrial physiology; role of intracellular calcium in cell injury and metabolic regulation. *Mailing Add:* Dept of Chem Univ South Fla Tampa FL 33620

TSOLAS, ORESTES, b Istanbul, Turkey; US citizen. MICROBIOLOGY, IMMUNOLOGY. *Educ:* Robert Col, Istanbul, BSc, 54; Cambridge Univ, MA, 57; Albert Einstein Col Med, PhD(molecular biol), 67. *Prof Exp:* Asst prof molecular biol, Albert Einstein Col Med, 70-80; ASST MEM, ROCHE INST MOLECULAR BIOL, 72- *Concurrent Pos:* Prof, Univ Sao Paulo, 69-; adj prof, Rutgers Univ, 74-; vis lectr, Rotterdam Med Fac, Neth, 72; vis asst prof microbiol & immunol, Albert Einstein Col Med, 80- *Res:* Structure, function, biology and technology of enzymes. *Mailing Add:* Roche Inst of Molecular Biol Hoffman-La Roche Inc Nutley NJ 07110

TSONG, IGNATIUS SIU TUNG, b Hong Kong, Jan 4, 43; Australian citizen; m 70; c 1. PHYSICS, MATERIALS SCIENCE. *Educ:* Univ Leeds, BSc, 66, MSc, 67; Univ London, PhD(physics), 70. *Prof Exp:* Fel physics, Univ Essex, 70-73; sr tutor, Monash Univ, 73-76; res assoc, 76-78, ASST PROF MAT RES, PA STATE UNIV, 78-, RES ASSOC, MAT RES LAB, 80- *Mem:* Am Phys Soc; Mineral Soc Am; Am Ceramic Soc; Am Vacuum Soc; AAAS. *Res:* Sputter-induced optical emission; surface characterization using ion beam techniques; analysis of hydrogen in solids; physics of particle-solid interactions. *Mailing Add:* Mat Res Lab Pa State Univ University Park PA 16802

TSONG, TIAN YOW, b Taiwan, Sept 6, 34; m 71; c 2. BIOPHYSICAL CHEMISTRY, BIOCHEMISTRY. *Educ:* Chung Hsing Univ, Taiwan, BS, 64; Yale Univ, MS, 67, MPh, 68, PhD(phys biochem), 69. *Prof Exp:* Asst prof, 72-75, ASSOC PROF PHYSIOL CHEM, SCH MED, JOHNS HOPKINS UNIV, 75- *Concurrent Pos:* Fel, Stanford Univ, 70-72; NSF res grant, Sch Med, Johns Hopkins Univ, 73-; NIH res grant, 75- *Mem:* Am Chem Soc; Biophys Soc; Am Soc Biol Chemists; AAAS. *Res:* Physical chemistry of proteins, nucleic acids and membrane lipids and its correlation to biological functions. *Mailing Add:* Dept of Physiol Chem Johns Hopkins Univ Sch of Med Baltimore MD 21205

TSONG, TIEN TZOU, b Taiwan, China, Sept 6, 34; m 64; c 3. SOLID STATE PHYSICS. *Educ:* Taiwan Norm Univ, BSc, 59; Pa State Univ, MS, 64, PhD(physics), 66. *Prof Exp:* Res assoc physics, 67-69, from asst prof to assoc prof, 69-74, PROF PHYSICS, PA STATE UNIV, 75- *Concurrent Pos:* Fel, Japan Soc Prom Sci. *Mem:* Fel Am Phys Soc; Am Vacuum Soc; fel Japan Soc Promotion Sci; Mat Res Soc. *Res:* Surface physics; field effect on metal surface; field ionization; field desorption and field ion microscopy; atomic processes on solid surfaces. *Mailing Add:* 201 Davey Lab Pa State Univ University Park PA 16802

TSONG, YUN YEN, b Taiwan, China, Jan 15, 37; m 67; c 2. BIOCHEMISTRY, ORGANIC CHEMISTRY. *Educ:* Nat Taiwan Univ, BS, 60; Univ Wis-Madison, PhD(biochem), 68. *Prof Exp:* Sr med chemist, Smith Kline & French Labs, 68-70; res assoc biochem, 70-72, STAFF SCIENTIST BIOCHEM, POP COUN, ROCKEFELLER UNIV, 72- *Mem:* AAAS; Am Chem Soc; Endocrine Soc. *Res:* Mechanism of action of steroid and peptide hormones; metabolism and microbial transformation of steroids. *Mailing Add:* Pop Coun Rockefeller Univ 66th & York Ave New York NY 10021

TSONOPOULOS, CONSTANTINE, b Megalopolis, Greece, Sept 5, 41; US citizen; m 69; c 1. CHEMICAL ENGINEERING, THERMODYNAMICS. *Educ:* Ga Inst Technol, BChemEng, 64, MS, 65; Univ Calif, Berkeley, PhD(chem eng), 70. *Prof Exp:* Engr appl thermodynamics, 70-71, res engr, 71-74, sr res engr, 74-78, sr staff engr, 78-80, eng assoc, 80-82, SR ENG ASSOC, EXXON RES & ENG CO, SUBSID EXXON CORP, 82- *Concurrent Pos:* Adj prof, NJ Inst Technol, 76 & 78. *Mem:* Am Inst Chem Engrs; Am Chem Soc; Am Petrol Inst. *Res:* Thermodynamics of fluid-phase equilibria; properties of polar systems and electrolyte solutions (hydrocarbon/water/weak electrolytes); synthetic liquids (from coal or shale). *Mailing Add:* Exxon Res & Eng Co PO Box 101 Florham Park NJ 07432

TSOU, F(U) K(ANG), b Kiangsu, China, May 25, 22; m 50. HEAT TRANSFER, FLUID MECHANICS. *Educ:* Nat Cent Univ, China, BS, 43; Univ Toronto, MS, 58; Univ Minn, PhD(mech eng), 65. *Prof Exp:* Engr, Taiwan Mach Mfg Co, 51-57; res asst & fel mech eng, Univ Minn, 58-62; from asst prof to assoc prof, 65-75, PROF MECH ENG, DREXEL UNIV, 75- *Mem:* Am Soc Mech Engrs; Am Acad Mech. *Res:* Technique of coaling; numerical heat transfer. *Mailing Add:* Dept of Mech Eng Drexel Univ Philadelphia PA 19104

TSOU, KWAN CHUNG, b Shanghai, China, Apr 5, 22; m 49; c 3. ORGANIC CHEMISTRY, BIOCHEMISTRY. *Educ:* Nat Cent Univ, China, BS, 44; Univ Nebr, PhD(chem), 50. *Prof Exp:* Res assoc chem, Harvard Univ, 50-55; dir res, Monomer-Polymer & Dajac Labs, Borden Chem Co, 55-56, develop mgr, 56-69, head cent res lab, 60-63; ASSOC PROF CHEM, HARRISON DEPT SURG RES, SCH MED, UNIV PA, 63-, ASSOC PROF PHARMACOL, DEPT PHARMACOL, 75- *Concurrent Pos:* Assoc, Beth Israel Hosp, Boston, Mass, 53-55. *Mem:* AAAS; Am Chem Soc. *Res:* Enzyme, polymer, synthetic and structural organic chemistry; histochemistry, cancer chemotherapy and cancer diagnosis. *Mailing Add:* Harrison Dept of Surg Res Univ of Pa Sch of Med Philadelphia PA 19104

TSOULFANIDIS, NICHOLAS, b Ioannina, Greece, May 6, 38; m 64; c 2. NUCLEAR ENGINEERING, PHYSICS. *Educ:* Nat Univ Athens, BS, 60; Univ Ill, Urbana, MS, 65, PhD(nuclear eng), 68. *Prof Exp:* Res asst physics, Nuclear Res Ctr, Democritus, Athens, Greece, 61-63; from instr to assoc prof, 68-80, PROF NUCLEAR ENG, UNIV MO-ROLLA, 80- *Mem:* Nat Soc Prof Engrs; Am Soc Eng Educ; Am Nuclear Soc. *Res:* Neutron and gamma transport; reactor physics; nuclear fuel cycle. *Mailing Add:* Dept of Nuclear Eng Univ of Mo Rolla MO 65401

TSU, T(SUNG) C(HI), b Haining, China, Aug 27, 15; nat US; m 48; c 1. MECHANICAL ENGINEERING. *Educ:* Chiao Tung Univ, BSc, 37; Univ Toronto, MASc, 41; Mass Inst Technol, ScD(aeronaut eng), 44. *Prof Exp:* Asst engr, Bur Aeronaut Res, China, 39-40; engr, Div Indust Coop, Mass Inst Technol, 44-45; consult engr, Gen Mach Corp, Ohio, 45-47; res assoc, Pa State Col, 47-49, assoc prof, 50-52; sr engr, Aviation Gas Turbine Div, 52-55, res engr, Res Labs, 55-57, ADV ENGR, RES LABS, WESTINGHOUSE ELEC CORP, 57- *Concurrent Pos:* Adj prof, Drexel Inst Technol, 53-54. *Mem:* AAAS; Am Soc Mech Engrs. *Res:* Space vehicles propulsion; magnetohydrodynamics; fluid mechanics; thermodynamics; energy conversion; design optimization. *Mailing Add:* Westinghouse Res & Develop Ctr Pittsburgh PA 15235

TSUANG, MING TSO, b Tainan, Taiwan, Nov 16, 31; m 58; c 3. PSYCHIATRY. *Educ:* Nat Taiwan Univ, MD, 57; Univ London, PhD(psychiat), 65. *Hon Degrees:* DSc, Univ London, 81. *Prof Exp:* Lectr psychiat & sr psychiatrist, Dept Neurol & Psychiat, Nat Taiwan Univ Hosp, 61-63; vis res worker psychiat, Med Res Coun Psychiat Genetics Res Unit, Maudsley Hosp & Inst Psychiat, Univ London, 63-65; lectr psychiat & sr psychiatrist, Dept Neurol & Psychiat, Nat Taiwan Univ Hosp, 65-68, assoc prof psychiat & sr psychiatrist, 68-71; vis assoc prof psychiat & staff psychiatrist, Barnes & Renard Hosp, Sch Med, Wash Univ, 71-72; assoc prof psychiat & staff psychiatrist, 72-75, PROF PSYCHIAT & PREV MED, IOWA PSYCHIAT HOSP, COL MED, UNIV IOWA, 75- *Concurrent Pos:* Res fel, Nat Coun Sci Develop, Repub China, 60-70; fel, Sino-Brit Fel Trust, UK, 63-65; collab investr, Int Pilot Study Schizophrenia, WHO, Geneva, Switz, 66-71; consult psychiatrist, Vet Admin Hosp, Iowa City, Iowa, 72-; chief staff psychiatrist, EWard, Psychiat Hosp, Univ Iowa, 73-; vis prof, Dept Psychiat, Univ Oxford, Eng, 79-80; Josiah Macy fac scholar award, 79-80. *Mem:* Psychiat Res Soc; AAAS; Am Psychopath Asn; Behav Genetics Asn; Am Psychiat Asn. *Res:* Long-term follow-up and family studies of schizophrenia, mania, depression and atypical psychoses; diagnostic classification of mental disorder; psychiatric genetics; clinical psychopharmological research. *Mailing Add:* Dept Psychiat Col Med Univ Iowa Iowa City IA 52242

TSUBOI, KENNETH KAZ, b Seno, Japan, Feb 7, 22; nat US; m 47; c 2. BIOCHEMISTRY. *Educ:* St Thomas Col, BS, 44; Univ Minn, MS, 46, PhD(biochem), 48. *Prof Exp:* Asst physiol chem, Univ Minn, 44-47; res assoc path, Washington Univ, 48; res assoc oncol, Univ Kans Med Ctr, Kansas City, 48-51; res assoc biochem, Columbia Univ, 51-55; asst prof, Med Col, Cornell Univ, 55-60; assoc prof pediat, 60-66, sr res assoc, 66-73, ADJ PROF PEDIAT, SCH MED, STANFORD UNIV, 73- *Concurrent Pos:* Estab investr, Am Heart Asn, 59-64; vis prof, Univ Tokyo, 67. *Mem:* Am Soc Biol Chemists; Biophys Soc; Am Asn Cancer Res. *Res:* Cellular and muscle biochemistry; enzymology. *Mailing Add:* Dept of Pediat Stanford Univ Stanford CA 94305

TSUCHIYA, HENRY MITSUMASA, b Seattle, Wash, Dec 9, 14; m 41; c 2. BACTERIOLOGY. *Educ:* Univ Wash, Seattle, BS, 36, MS, 38; Univ Minn, PlhD(bact), 42. *Prof Exp:* Asst bact, Univ Minn, 40-42, res fel, 42-44, res assoc, 44-47; microbiologist, USDA, 47-56; assoc prof chem eng, 56-63, PROF CHEM ENG, UNIV MINN, MINNEAPOLIS, 63-, PROF MICROBIOL, 66- *Concurrent Pos:* Off Sci Res & Develop, 42-45. *Mem:* AAAS; Am Chem Soc; Ecol Soc Am; Am Soc Limnol & Oceanog; Am Inst Biol. *Res:* Industrial fermentations; sulfonamide chemotherapy; treatment of industrial wastes; physiology of microorganisms; biological polymerization and depolymerization; bioengineering; dynamics of microbial populations; ecology. *Mailing Add:* Dept of Chem Eng Univ of Minn Minneapolis MN 55455

TSUCHIYA, MIZUKI, b Matsuyama, Japan, May 2, 29; m 56; c 2. PHYSICAL OCEANOGRAPHY. *Educ:* Univ Tokyo, BS, 53, ScD(oceanog), 62. *Prof Exp:* Res asst geophys, Univ Tokyo, 55-60; instr oceanog, Meteorol Col, Japan Meteorol Agency, 60-64; res assoc, Johns Hopkins Univ, 64-67; lectr, Univ Tokyo, 67-69; asst res oceanographer, 69-73, assoc res oceanographer, 73-79, RES OCEANOGRAPHER, INST MARINE RESOURCES, SCRIPPS INST OCEANOG, 79- *Honors & Awards:* Okada Takematsu Prize, Oceanog Soc Japan, 67. *Mem:* Am Geophys Union. *Res:* Circulation and distributions of water characteristics in the ocean. *Mailing Add:* Scripps Inst Oceanog La Jolla CA 92093

TSUCHIYA, TAKUMI, b Oita-Ken, Japan, Mar 10, 23; m 53; c 2. PLANT CYTOLOGY, PLANT GENETICS. *Educ:* Gifu Univ, BAgr, 43; Kyoto Univ, BAgr, 47, DAgr(genetics), 60. *Prof Exp:* Asst prof biol, Beppu Univ, 50-57; cytogeneticist, Kihara Inst Biol Res, 57-63; Nat Res Coun Can fel plant cytogenetics, Univ Man, 63-64; cytogeneticist, Children's Hosp, Winnipeg, 64-65; res assoc plant cytogenetics, Univ Man, 65-68; assoc prof plant cytogenetics, 68-73, PROF GENETICS, COLO STATE UNIV, 73- *Concurrent Pos:* Rockefeller Found travel grant insts & univs, US & Can, 61; coordr genetic & linkage studies barley, Int Barley Genetics Symp, 70-; chmn, Int Comt Nomenclature & Symbolization Barley Genes, 70-; chmn barley genetics comt, Am Barley Res Workers' Conf, 71- *Mem:* Genetics Soc Am; Am Soc Agron; Crop Sci Soc Am; Am Genetics Asn; Genetics Soc Can. *Res:* breeding of barley, sugar beet, triticale, rye; cytogenetic and evolutionary studies of species of Gramineae; cytotaxonomy of tree species in Taxodiaceae. *Mailing Add:* Dept of Agron Colo State Univ Ft Collins CO 80523

TSUDA, ROY TOSHIO, b Honolulu, Hawaii, Dec 25, 39; m 59; c 3. PHYCOLOGY. *Educ:* Univ Hawaii, BA, 63, MS, 66; Univ Wis-Milwaukee, PhD(bot), 70. *Prof Exp:* Instr biol, 67-68, asst prof dept biol & marine lab, 68-70, assoc prof marine sci, Marine Lab, 70-74, assoc dir marine sci, 69-71, prof marine sci & dir Marine Lab, 74-78, DEAN GRAD SCH & RES, UNIV GUAM, 78- *Concurrent Pos:* gen ed, Micronesica, Univ Guam, 72-76, chmn, Coral Reef Comt, Pac Sci Asn, 75-81; chmn coral reef comt, Int Asn Biol Oceanog, 79-81; mem comt ecology, Int Union Conserv Nature & Natural Resources, 81-, Survival Serv comt, 77- *Mem:* Am Soc Limnol & Oceanog; Asn Trop Biol; Phycol Soc Am. *Res:* Taxonomy and ecology of tropical marine algae; primary productivity. *Mailing Add:* Grad Sch & Res Univ of Guam PO EK Agana GU 96910

TSUEI, YEONG GING, b China, Feb 25, 32; m 62; c 4. APPLIED MECHANICS. *Educ:* Cheng Kung Univ, Taiwan, BSCE, 56; Colo State Univ, MCE, 60, PhD(fluid mech), 63. *Prof Exp:* Asst, Cheng Kung Univ, Taiwan, 56-58; from instr to assoc prof, 61-76, PROF MECH, UNIV CINCINNATI, 76- *Mem:* Am Inst Aeronaut & Astronaut; Am Soc Civil Engrs; Am Soc Eng Educ. *Res:* Fluid and engineering mechanics. *Mailing Add:* Dept of Mech Eng Univ of Cincinnati Cincinnati OH 45221

TSUI, BENJAMIN MING WAH, b Hong Kong, June 1, 48; m 75. MEDICAL PHYSICS. *Educ:* Chung Chi Col, BSc, 70; Dartmouth Col, AM, 72; Univ Chicago, PhD(med physics), 77. *Prof Exp:* Res assoc med physics, 77-79, ASST PROF, DEPT RADIOL & FRANKLIN MCLEAN RES INST, UNIV CHICAGO, 79- *Honors & Awards:* Sci Res Award, Eastman Kodak Co, 77. *Mem:* Am Asn Physicists Med; Soc Nuclear Med. *Res:* Theory and instrumentation in radiation detection; image formation and recording in nuclear medicine; biokinetic study of radiopharmaceuticals. *Mailing Add:* Franklin McLean Res Inst 950 E 59th St Chicago IL 60637

TSUI, DANIEL CHEE, b Honan, China, Feb 28, 39; US citizen; m 64; c 2. SOLID STATE PHYSICS. *Educ:* Augustana Col, BA, 61; Univ Chicago, MS & PhD(physics), 67. *Prof Exp:* MEM TECH STAFF SOLID STATE PHYSICS, BELL LABS, 68- *Mem:* Am Phys Soc. *Res:* Electronic properties of metals, surface properties of semiconductors; low temperature physics. *Mailing Add:* Bell Labs 600 Mountain Ave Murray Hill NJ 07974

TSUI, JAMES BAO-YEN, b Shantung, China; US citizen. ELECTRICAL ENGINEERING. *Educ:* Nat Taiwan Univ, BS, 57; Marquette Univ, MS, 61; Univ Ill, PhD(elec eng), 65. *Prof Exp:* From asst prof to assoc prof elec eng, Univ Dayton, 65-73; ELECTRONICS ENGR, AVIONICS LAB, WRIGHT-PATTERSON AFB, 73- *Concurrent Pos:* Scientist, Labtron Corp Am, 68-69. *Mem:* Am Soc Eng Educ; Inst Elec & Electronics Engrs. *Res:* Rare earth cobalt permanent magnets and their applications; microwave receivers. *Mailing Add:* AFAL/WRP-1 Wright-Patterson AFB OH 45433

TSUI, TIEN-FUNG, b Oct 13, 47; Repub of China citizen; m 75. GEOCHEMISTRY. *Educ:* Nat Taiwan Univ, BS, 69; Harvard Univ, MS, 72, PhD(geochem), 76. *Prof Exp:* Nat Res Coun fel geochem, Ames Res Ctr, NASA, 76-78; ASST GEOLOGIST COAL GEOCHEM, ILL STATE GEOL SURV, 78- *Res:* Trace elements and mineral matters in coal; trace element geochemistry of terrestrial and extraterrestrial rocks; geochemistry of hydrothermal ore solutions; emission spectroscopy. *Mailing Add:* Natural Resources Bldg Ill State Geol Surv Urbana IL 61801

TSUI, Y(AW) T(ZONG), b Wuhu, China, Oct 7, 21; US citizen; m 53; c 1. PHYSICS, ENGINEERING SCIENCE. *Educ:* Nat Cent Univ, China, BS, 43; Univ Colo, MS, 49; Ohio State Univ, PhD(fluid mech, heat transfer), 53. *Prof Exp:* Sr engr, Clevite Res Ctr, Clevite Corp, 53-55; proj engr, Stewart-Warner Corp, 55-57; sr res engr, Aero Div, Minneapolis- Honeywell Regulator Co, 57; res assoc aeronaut eng & lectr mech eng, Inst Technol, Univ Minn, 58-60; res physicist, Cent Res Labs, 3M Co, 60-70; SR RESEARCHER, HYDRO-QUEBEC INST RES, 70- *Mem:* Am Soc Mech Engrs; Acoust Soc Am. *Res:* Continuum mechanics; acoustics; heat and thermodynamics; applied mathematics. *Mailing Add:* Hydro-Quebec Inst of Res Varennes PQ S0L 2P0 Can

TSUJI, FREDERICK ICHIRO, b Honolulu, Hawaii, Aug 23, 23. BIOCHEMISTRY. *Educ:* Cornell Univ, AB, 46, MS, 48, PhD(biochem), 50. *Prof Exp:* Asst biochem & nutrit, Cornell Univ, 48-49; res biochemist, Children's Fund Mich, 49-50; asst prof biochem & pharmacol, Duquesne Univ, 50-52; res asst biol, Princeton Univ, 52-55; tech dir res lab, Vet Admin Hosp, Pittsburgh, Pa, 55-72; Hancock fel, Univ Southern Calif, 72-76; prog dir biochem, NSF, 76-78; VIS RES PROF BIOL, UNIV SOUTHERN CALIF, 78-; BIOCHEMIST, BRENTWOOD VET ADMIN HOSP, LOS ANGELES, 72-76 & 78-; ASSOC RES BIOCHEMIST, SCRIPPS INST OCEANOG, UNIV CALIF, SAN DIEGO, 79- *Concurrent Pos:* Res assoc, Mercy Hosp, 51-52; Anathan fel inst res, Montefiore Hosp, 52; investr, Marine Biol Lab, Woods Hole, 53-54; lectr, Univ Pittsburgh, 56-65, from adj assoc prof to adj prof, 65-72; sr scientist, Te Vega Exped Pac Ocean, Hopkins Marine Sta, Stanford Univ, 66; mem, Alpha Helix Biol Exped to New Guinea, Scripps Inst Oceanog, Univ Calif, San Diego, 69; vis prof dept med chem, Fac Med, Kyoto Univ, Japan, 74. *Mem:* Am Soc Biol Chem; Am Chem Soc; Biophys Soc; Am Asn Immunol; Soc Gen Physiol. *Res:* Bioluminescence; chemistry of antigen-antibody reactions. *Mailing Add:* Dept of Biol Sci Univ of Southern Calif Los Angeles CA 90007

TSUJI, GORDON YUKIO, b Honolulu, Hawaii, July 31, 42; m 67; c 3. SOIL PHYSICS. *Educ:* Univ Hawaii, BS, 65, MS, 67; Purdue Univ, Lafayette, PhD(soil physics), 71. *Prof Exp:* Asst soil scientist dept agron & soil sci, 71-74, PROJ MGR, UNIV HAWAII/US AID BENCHMARK SOILS PROJ, UNIV HAWAII, 74- *Concurrent Pos:* AID fel, Univ Hawaii. 71- *Mem:* Am Soc Agron; Sigma Xi; Int Soc Soil Sci. *Res:* Water movement in soils; infiltration of water into soils; water distribution under drip irrigation; tropical meteorology; United States soil taxonomy and agricultural development; agrotechnology transference. *Mailing Add:* Dept Agron & Soil Sci Univ Hawaii 3190 Maile Way Honolulu HI 96822

TSUJI, KIYOSHI, b Kyoto, Japan, May 31, 31; m 58; c 3. MICROBIOLOGY, ANALYTICAL CHEMISTRY. *Educ:* Kyoto Univ, BS, 54; Univ Mass, MS, 56, PhD(food technol), 60. *Prof Exp:* Fel food sci, Rutgers Univ, 59-60; staff microbiol, Nat Canners Asn, Calif, 60-63; res assoc food sci, Mass Inst Technol, 63-64; res assoc anal res & develop, 64-71, sr res scientist, 71-74, SR SCIENTIST, CONTROL ANAL RES & DEVELOP, UPJOHN CO, 74- *Honors & Awards:* William E Upjohn Prize, Upjohn Co, 71; ed, GLC & HPLC Determination of Therapeut Agents, 78. *Mem:* Am Chem Soc; Am Soc Microbiol; Inst Food Technologists. *Res:* Analytical microbiology; microbioassay automation; analysis of antibiotics by gas-liquid chromatography and high-performance liquid chromatography; sterility test; analysis of vitamins; endotoxin detection by Limulus amebocyte lysate; environmental control. *Mailing Add:* Upjohn Co 7831-41-1 Kalamazoo MI 49001

TSUK, ANDREW GEORGE, b Budapest, Hungary, July 11, 32; US citizen; m 63; c 2. PHYSICAL CHEMISTRY, POLYMER CHEMISTRY. *Educ:* Budapest Polytech Inst, dipl chem eng, 54; Polytech Inst Brooklyn, PhD(chem), 64. *Prof Exp:* Engr, Indust Fermentations, Hungary, 54-56; res chemist, Schwarz Bioresearch, Inc, 58-62, tech asst to pres, 64-65, dir radiochem div, 65-66; sr res chemist, W R Grace & Co, Md, 66-72; group leader pharmaceut develop, 72-74, RES ASSOC, AYERST LABS, INC, 74- *Mem:* Am Chem Soc. *Res:* Polymers in pharmaceutical dosage forms; physical chemistry of polymers; polyelectrolytes; biomedical materials; biological macromolecules; ion-exchange and radioactive tracers. *Mailing Add:* Pharmaceut Sci Ayerst Labs Inc Rouses Point NY 12979

TSUKADA, MATSUO, b Nagano, Japan, Jan 4, 30; m 56; c 2. ECOLOGY, PALEOECOLOGY. *Educ:* Shinshu Univ, Japan, BS, 53; Osaka City Univ, MA, 58, PhD(biol), 61. *Prof Exp:* Japan Acad Sci fel, Osaka City Univ, 61; Seessel fel, Yale Univ, 61-62, res assoc palynology, 62-66, lectr & res assoc biol, 66-68; assoc prof, 69-71, PROF BOT, UNIV WASH, 71-, DIR LAB PALEOECOL, 69-, ADJ PROF GEOL & QUATERNARY STUDIES, 76- *Concurrent Pos:* Sigma Xi res grant, Yale Univ, 63-64, Am Philos Soc res grant, 64-65; prin investr NSF res grants, Univ Wash, 70- *Mem:* Ecol Soc Am; Am Soc Limnol & Oceanog; Am Quaternary Asn; Am Asn Stratig Palynologists; Bot Soc Japan. *Res:* Present and past environmental changes on a global scale, mainly by means of modern and fossil plants, including pollen and also animals, chemicals and heavy metals, such as lead and cadmium. *Mailing Add:* Dept Bot Quaternary Res Ctr Univ of Wash Seattle WA 98195

TSUNG, YEAN-KAI, b Taiwan, July 30, 43; US citizen; m 72; c 2. SOMATIC CELL GENETICS, TUMOR BIOLOGY. *Educ:* Nat Taiwan Univ, BS, 67; Univ Ill, MS, 71, PhD(plant path), 74. *Prof Exp:* Asst prof genetics, Univ Mich, 75-76; trainee immunol, Div Immunol, Duke Univ Med Ctr, 76-77; asst geneticist, E K Shriver Ctr Ment Retardation, 77-81; ASST PROF HUMAN GENETICS, SCH MED, BOSTON UNIV, 82- *Concurrent Pos:* Consult, Brain Res, Inc, 80- *Mem:* AAAS. *Res:* Immunological identification of human cell membrane components by the development of cross membrane transport, defective mutants and monoclonal antibodies distinguishing the mutants from wild type population. *Mailing Add:* Ctr Human Genetics Sch Med Boston Univ 80 E Concord St Boston MA 02118

TSURUTANI, BRUCE TADASHI, b Los Angeles, Calif, Jan 29, 41. SPACE PLASMA PHYSICS. *Educ:* Univ Calif, Berkeley, BA, 63, PhD(physics), 72. *Prof Exp:* RES SCIENTIST & MEM TECH STAFF PHYSICS, JET PROPULSION LAB, CALIF INST TECHNOL, 72- *Mem:* AAAS; Am Geophys Union; Int Union Radio Sci; Sigma Xi. *Res:* Plasma instabilities; wave-particle interactions; interplanetary and planetary magnetic fields; particle acceleration processes; magnetospheric and heliospheric physics; x-ray sources. *Mailing Add:* Jet Propulsion Lab 4800 Oak Grove Dr Pasadena CA 91103

TSUTAKAWA, ROBERT K, b Seattle, Wash, Mar 28, 30; m 61; c 3. STATISTICS. *Educ:* Univ Chicago, BS, 56, MS, 57, PhD(statist), 63. *Prof Exp:* Res specialist, Boeing Co, 58-60 & 63-65; res assoc statist, Univ Chicago, 65-68; assoc prof, 68-78, PROF STATIST, UNIV MO-COLUMBIA, 78- *Mem:* Am Statist Asn; Inst Math Statist. *Res:* Statistical inference. *Mailing Add:* Dept Statist Univ Mo Columbia MO 65201

TSUTSUI, ETHEL ASHWORTH, b Geneva, NY, May 31, 27; m 56; c 1. BIOCHEMISTRY. *Educ:* Keuka Col, BA, 48; Univ Rochester, PhD(biochem), 54. *Prof Exp:* Res assoc med sch med & dent, Univ Rochester, 53-55; Nat Cancer Inst fel, Sloan-Kettering Inst Cancer Res, 55-56; lectr, Tokyo Med & Dent Univ, Japan, 56-57; asst prof biol & res biochemist, C F Kettering Found, Antioch Col, 57-60; res assoc Inst Cancer Res, Col Physicians & Surgeons, Columbia Univ, 60-63, res assoc dept biochem, 63-65; asst prof biol sci, Hunter Col, 65-69; assoc prof biol, 69-71, prof biol, 71-80, PROF BIOCHEM & BIOPHYS, TEX A&M UNIV, 80- *Mem:* AAAS; Am Asn Cancer Res; Am Chem Soc; fel NY Acad Sci; Harvey Soc. *Res:* Enzymatic methylation of nucleic acids; biochemistry of cancer cells; tRNA metabolism during insect development. *Mailing Add:* Dept of Biochem & Biophysics Tex A&M Univ College Station TX 77843

TSUTSUI, MINORU, b Wakayama, Japan, Mar 31, 18; nat US; m 56; c 1. ORGANOMETALLIC CHEMISTRY. *Educ:* Gifu Univ, Japan, BA, 38; Univ Tokyo, MS, 41; Yale Univ, MS, 53, PhD(chem), 54; Nagoya Univ, DSc(chem), 60. *Prof Exp:* Asst prof chem, Univ Tokyo, 50-53, assoc pharmaceut inst, 56-57; vis res fel, Sloan-Kettering Inst Cancer Res, NY, 54-56; res chemist cent res lab, Monsanto Chem Co, 57-60; res scientist res div, NY Univ, 60-68, assoc prof chem, 66-68, lectr, 65; PROF CHEM, TEX A&M UNIV, 69- *Concurrent Pos:* Mem spec proj, Mass Inst Technol, 51; vis res fel, Brookhaven Nat Lab, 55; consult, Union Carbide Co, 63-73, Maruzen Oil Co, 63, Glidden Co, 64 & 65, Toyo Rayon Corp, 65, Kurashiki Rayon Co, 66, Tokuyama Soda Co, 67 & Celanese Co, 73-; mem bd, Southwest Catalysis Soc, 72-74; partic, US-Russia Cultural Exchange Prog; mem bd, Nard Inst, Japan. *Honors & Awards:* Morrison Award, NY Acad Sci, 60. *Mem:* AAAS; Am Chem Soc; NY Acad Sci (vpres, 65-66, pres-elect, 67, pres, 68); Royal Soc Chem; Chem Soc Japan. *Res:* Organotransition-metal chemistry; catalysis, conductors and biological aspects; diagnostic and chemotherapeutic tumor localizers. *Mailing Add:* Dept of Chem Tex A&M Univ College Station TX 77843

TSUZUKI, TOSHIO, physical chemistry, see previous edition

TTERLIKKIS, LAMBROS, b Beirut, Lebanon, Oct 17, 34; US citizen; m 60; c 2. PHYSICS. *Educ:* Walla Walla Col, BSc, 59; Univ Denver, MSc, 62; Univ Calif, Riverside, PhD(physics), 68. *Prof Exp:* Res asst solid state physics, Denver Res Inst, Univ Denver, 59-62; assoc physicist, IBM Corp, 62-63; NIH res assoc biophys, Inst Molecular Biophys, Fla State Univ, 68-70; asst prof, 70-74, ASSOC PROF PHYS PHARMACEUT, FLA A&M UNIV, 74- *Mem:* AAAS; Soc Nuclear Med; Am Pharmaceut Asn. *Res:* Pharmacokinetics of drug metabolism; physicochemical properties of drugs; solid state physics; optical properties of biopolymers. *Mailing Add:* Sch of Pharm Fla A&M Univ Tallahassee FL 32307

TU, ANTHONY T, b Taipei, Formosa, Apr 12, 30; US citizen; m 57; c 5. BIOCHEMISTRY. *Educ:* Nat Taiwan Univ, BS, 53; Univ Notre Dame, MS, 56; Stanford Univ, PhD(biochem), 60. *Prof Exp:* Res assoc biochem, Yale Univ, 61-62; asst prof, Utah State Univ, 62-67; assoc prof, 67-70, PROF BIOCHEM, COLO STATE UNIV, 70- *Concurrent Pos:* NIH career develop award, 69-73; vis prof, Ain Shan Univ, Cairo, Egypt, 81. *Mem:* Am Chem Soc; Am Soc Biol Chem. *Res:* Snake venom toxins and enzymes; metal-nucleotide interaction; raman spectroscopy. *Mailing Add:* Dept of Biochem Colo State Univ Ft Collins CO 80523

TU, CHEN CHUAN, b Husin, Oct 5, 18; nat US; m 47; c 2. CHEMISTRY. *Educ:* Chinese Nat Col Pharm, dipl, 42; Purdue Univ, MS, 49, PhD, 51. *Prof Exp:* Asst, Chinese Nat Chekiang Univ, 42-47; asst, Purdue Univ, 47-51, res fel, 51-52; res asst, Inst Paper Chem, 52-56; res assoc, 56-57, SR SCIENTIST, EXP STA, HAWAIIAN SUGAR PLANTERS' ASN, 57- *Mem:* Am Chem Soc; Int Soc Sugarcane Technol. *Res:* Biochemistry; natural products; sugar technology; food science. *Mailing Add:* 1644 Ulueo St Kailula HI 96734

TU, CHEN-PEI DAVID, b Taipei, China, Nov 23, 48; US citizen. GENE EXPRESSION, TRANSPOSABLE ELEMENTS. *Educ:* Nat Taiwan Univ, Taipei, BS, 70; Cornell Univ, PhD(biochem & molecular biol), 76. *Prof Exp:* Fel biochem genetics, Med Sch, Stanford Univ, 76-80; ASST PROF BIOCHEM & MOLECULAR BIOL, PA STATE UNIV, 80- *Concurrent Pos:* Fel, Am Cancer Soc, 76-78. *Mailing Add:* Biochem Prog 108 Althouse Lab Pa State Univ University Park PA 16802

TU, CHIN MING, b Hsinchu, Taiwan, Dec 14, 32; Can citizen; m 62; c 3. MICROBIOLOGY, BIOCHEMISTRY. *Educ:* Chung Hsing Univ, Taiwan, BSc, 56; Univ Sask, MSc, 63; Ore State Univ, PhD(microbiol), 66. *Prof Exp:* Asst org chem & soil fertil dept agr chem, Chung Hsing Univ, Taiwan, 58-60; asst soil sci, Univ Sask, 60-62; asst microbiol, Ore State Univ, 63-66; RES SCIENTIST RES INST, CAN DEPT AGR, 66- *Mem:* Am Soc Microbiol; Can Soc Microbiol. *Res:* Interaction between pesticides and soil microorganisms; soil science. *Mailing Add:* Res Ctr Can Dept Agr London ON N6A 5B7 Can

TU, CHINGKUANG, b Keichou, China, Feb 1, 44; m 72; c 2. BIOCHEMISTRY, PHARMACOLOGY. *Educ:* Chunghsin Univ, Taiwan, BS, 68; Univ Miami, PhD(chem), 72. *Prof Exp:* Fel chem, Univ Fla, 72-73, fel biochem & pharmacol, 73-75, assoc instr, 75-80. *Mem:* Am Chem Soc. *Res:* Study enzyme carbonic anhydrase, mechanism, kinetics and inhibition, by stable isotope technique; GC-MS-Data system application to medical science. *Mailing Add:* 427 NW 98th St Gainesville FL 32610

TU, JUI-CHANG, b Tainan, Taiwan, Aug 14, 36; Can citizen; m 64; c 2. PHYTOPATHOLOGY. *Educ:* Nat Taiwan Univ, BSc, 59, MSc, 61; Wash State Univ, PhD(plant path), 66. *Prof Exp:* Res assoc, Iowa State Univ, 67-69; res scientist, Univ Alta, 69-70, from asst prof to assoc prof & asst dir biol & electron micros, 70-78; RES SCIENTIST, HARROW RES STA, AGR CAN, 78- *Mem:* Am Phytopath Soc; Can Phytopath Soc; Sigma Xi; Can Seed Growers Asn. *Res:* Diseases of legume crops and their control. *Mailing Add:* Harrow Res Sta Harrow ON N0R 1G0 Can

TU, KING-NING, b Canton, China, Dec 30, 37; m 65; c 2. MATERIALS SCIENCE. *Educ:* Nat Taiwan Univ, BS, 60; Brown Univ, MS, 64; Harvard Univ, PhD(appl physics), 68. *Prof Exp:* Res asst mat sci, Brown Univ, 63-64; res asst appl physics, Harvard Univ, 66-68, res fel, 68; mgr diffusion & kinetics group, 72-78, MEM RES STAFF PHYS SCI, IBM WATSON RES CTR, 68-, SR MGR THIN FILM SCI, 78- *Concurrent Pos:* Sci Res Coun sr vis fel, Cavendish Lab, Cambridge Univ, Eng, 75-76. *Mem:* Am Soc Metals; Am Vacuum Soc; fel Am Phys Soc; Mat Res Soc (pres, 81). *Res:* Phase transformations in alloys; kinetics in thin solid films; electrical properties of metal-silicon interfaces and compounds; device metallurgy. *Mailing Add:* IBM Watson Res Ctr IBM Corp Yorktown Heights NY 10598

TU, SHIAO-CHUN, b Honan, China, Dec 29, 43; US citizen; m 70; c 1. BIOCHEMISTRY, BIOPHYSICS. *Educ:* Nat Taiwan Univ, BS, 66; Cornell Univ, MNS, 69, PhD(biochem), 73. *Prof Exp:* Res assoc biochem, Grad Sch Nutrit, Cornell Univ, 73; res fel biol, Biol Labs, Harvard Univ, 73-77; ASST PROF BIOCHEM & BIOPHYS, DEPT BICHEM & BIOPHYS SCI, UNIV HOUSTON, 77- *Concurrent Pos:* Tutor biol, Harvard Univ, 74-75; NIH fel, 75-77; res career develop award, 81-86. *Mem:* Sigma Xi; AAAS; Biophys Soc; Am Soc Photobiol; Am Chem Soc. *Res:* Mechanisms of biological oxidation; structure-function relationships of flavin and pyridine nucleotide-dependent enzymes; optical spectroscopy in biochemical studies. *Mailing Add:* Dept Bichem & Biophys Sci Univ Houston Houston TX 77004

TU, SHU-I, b Chungking, China, Jan 3, 43; m 69; c 1. BIOPHYSICAL CHEMISTRY. *Educ:* Nat Taiwan Univ, BS, 65; Yale Univ, MPhil, 68, PhD(chem), 69. *Prof Exp:* Res assoc biochem, Yale Univ, 69-72; res asst prof, State Univ NY Buffalo, 72-74; asst prof chem, State Univ NY Stony Brook, 74-81; RES CHEMIST, EASTERN REGIONAL RES CTR, AGR RES SERV, USDA, PHILADELPHIA, 81- *Mem:* Am Chem Soc; Biophys Soc; Sigma Xi. *Res:* Structure of inner mitochondrial membrane, mechanism of oxidative phosphorylation and photophosphorylation and conversion of light into electrochemical potential in reconstituted bacteriorhodopsin systems. *Mailing Add:* US Dept Agr Res Ctr 600 E Mermaid Lane Philadelphia PA 19118

TU, YIH-O, b Kiangsi, China, Jan 8, 20; m 60; c 1. APPLIED MATHEMATICS. *Educ:* Col Ord Eng, Chungking, China, BS, 46; Carnegie Inst Technol, MS, 54; Rensselaer Polytech Inst, PhD(math), 59. *Prof Exp:* Designer mech eng, Rockwell Mfg Co, Pa, 53-55; STAFF MATHEMATICIAN, IBM CORP, 59- *Mem:* Am Math Soc; Am Phys Soc; Am Soc Mech Eng; Soc Eng Sci; Soc Indust & Appl Math. *Res:* Fluid mechanics; elasticity; vibration and elastic stability; continuum mechanics. *Mailing Add:* IBM Res Lab 5600 Cottle Rd San Jose CA 95193

TUAN, DEBBIE FU-TAI, b Kiangsu, China, Feb 2, 30. PHYSICAL CHEMISTRY, CHEMICAL PHYSICS. *Educ:* Taiwan Univ, BS, 54, MS, 58; Yale Univ, MS, 60, PhD(chem), 61. *Prof Exp:* Teaching asst chem, Taiwan Univ, 54-55; NSF res fel, Yale Univ, 61-64; NASA res grant & proj assoc theoret chem inst, Univ Wis, 64-65; from asst prof to assoc prof, 65-73, summer res fels, 66, 68 & 71, PROF CHEM, KENT STATE UNIV, 73- *Concurrent Pos:* Res fel, Harvard Univ, 70; res fel, Harvard Univ, 70; vis scientist, SRI Int, 81. *Mem:* Am Phys Soc; Am Chem Soc; Sigma Xi. *Res:* Many electron theory of atoms and molecules; perturbation theory; other applications of quantum mechanics to chemical problems. *Mailing Add:* Dept of Chem Kent State Univ Kent OH 44242

TUAN, HANG-SHENG, b Hankow, Hupei, China, Oct 23, 35; m 65. ELECTRICAL ENGINEERING. *Educ:* Nat Taiwan Univ, BS, 58; Univ Wash, MS, 61; Harvard Univ, PhD(appl physics), 65. *Prof Exp:* Res fel electronics, Harvard Univ, 65; asst prof elec sci, 65-69, assoc prof, 69-80, PROF ELEC ENG, STATE UNIV NY, STONY BROOK, 80- *Res:* Electromagnetic theory; antenna and wave propagation; plasma physics, microwave acoustics. *Mailing Add:* Dept of Elec Sci State Univ of NY Stony Brook NY 11794

TUAN, SAN FU, b Tientsin, China, May 14, 32; m 63; c 4. THEORETICAL PHYSICS, APPLIED MATHEMATICS. *Educ:* Oxford Univ, BA, 54, MA, 58; Univ Calif, PhD(appl math), 58. *Prof Exp:* Res assoc, Univ Chicago, 58-60; asst prof, Brown Univ, 60-62; assoc prof, Purdue Univ, 62-65; vis prof, Univ Hawaii, 65-66; mem inst adv study, Princeton Univ, 66-72; PROF THEORET PHYSICS, UNIV HAWAII, 66- *Concurrent Pos:* Mackinnon scholar, Magdalen Col, Oxford Univ, 51-54; consult, Argonne Nat Lab, 63-70; John S Guggenheim fel, 65-66; dir & co-ed proc, Second, Third, Fifth, Sixth & Seventh Hawaii Topical Conf Particle Physics, 67, 69, 73, 75 & 77; vis lectr, Bariloche Atomic Ctr, Argentina & Univ Buenos Aires, 69-70; vis lectr, US-China Sci Coop Prog, 70-71; vis prof, Peking Univ & Inst Theoret Physics, 79-80. *Mem:* Am Math Soc; fel Am Phys Soc. *Res:* Mathematical physics; theory of elementary particles; superconductivity; political science. *Mailing Add:* Dept of Physics & Astron Univ of Hawaii Honolulu HI 96822

TUAN, TAI-FU, b Tientsin, China, Sept 7, 29; US citizen; m 68. THEORETICAL PHYSICS. *Educ:* Cambridge Univ, BA, 51; La State Univ, MS, 53; Univ Pittsburgh, PhD(physics), 59. *Prof Exp:* Instr physics, Northwestern Univ, 59-60; univ res fel, Univ Birmingham, 61-64, Dept Sci & Indust Res res fel, 64-65; from asst prof to assoc prof, 65-71, PROF PHYSICS, UNIV CINCINNATI, 71- *Concurrent Pos:* US Air Force res grant, 70- *Mem:* Am Phys Soc; Am Geophys Union. *Res:* Scattering theory; atmospheric physics; research in airglow, gravity waves and magnetohydrodynamics models for magnetosphere. *Mailing Add:* Dept of Physics Univ of Cincinnati Cincinnati OH 45221

TUBB, RICHARD ARNOLD, b Weatherford, Okla, Dec 18, 31; m 57; c 2. LIMNOLOGY, FISHERIES. *Educ:* Okla State Univ, BS, 58, MS, 60, PhD(zool), 63. *Prof Exp:* Res asst aquatic biol lab, Okla State Univ, 60-62; asst prof biol, Univ NDak, 63-66; asst leader fisheries, SDak Coop Fishery Unit, 66-67; leader, Ohio Coop Fishery Unit, 67-75; PROF & HEAD DEPT FISHERIES & WILDLIFE MGT, ORE STATE UNIV, , 75- *Mem:* Am Soc Limnol & Oceanog; Am Fisheries Soc; Am Inst Fishery Res Biol. *Res:* Herbivorous insect population in oil refinery effluent holding pond series; investigations of whirling disease of trout; freshwater bivalves as stream monitors for pesticides; environmental impact of nuclear power plants on fresh water fish; colonization of artificial reefs by fish. *Mailing Add:* Dept Fisheries & Wildlife Mgt O-e State Univ Corvallis OR 97331

TUBBS, ELDRED FRANK, b Buffalo, NY, Mar 31, 24; m 49; c 3. OPTICS, ATOMIC SPECTROSCOPY. *Educ:* Carnegie Inst Technol, BS, 49; Johns Hopkins Univ, PhD(physics), 56. *Prof Exp:* Sr physicist res ctr, Am Optical Co, 55-58; res physicist microwave physics lab, Sylvania Elec Prod Inc, 58-60; res physicist, WCoast Br, Gen Tel & Electronics Labs, Inc, 60-63; from asst prof to assoc prof physics, Harvey Mudd Col, 63-72, prof, 72-79; MEM TECH STAFF, JET PROPULSION LAB, 79- *Honors & Awards:* Prize, Am Asn Physics Teachers, 67. *Mem:* Optical Soc Am; Soc Photo-Optical Instrumentation Engrs. *Res:* Optical instruments; interferometry; absolute f-values; teaching apparatus. *Mailing Add:* Jet Propulsion Lab Pasadena CA 91125

TUBBS, ROBERT KENNETH, b Gary, Ind, Nov 25, 36; m 56; c 3. COLLOID CHEMISTRY, SURFACE CHEMISTRY. *Educ:* Ohio State Univ, BS, 58, PhD(colloid chem), 62. *Prof Exp:* Res chemist electrochem dept, Del, 62-67, staff scientist, 67-68, res supvr, 68-70, gen tech supt indust chem dept, NY, 70-73, sr res supvr, Plastics Dept, 73-74, prod mgr, 74-75, develop mgr plastics dept, 75-76, com develop mgr pharmaceut, 76-77, PROD MGR, E I DU PONT DE NEMOURS & CO, INC, 78- *Res:* Structure and interactions of macromolecules; kinetics of polymerization; molecular biology; emulsion polymerization; coatings; adhesives. *Mailing Add:* Plastics Dept E I du Pont de Nemours & Co Inc Wilmington DE 19809

TUBIS, ARNOLD, b Pottstown, Pa, Mar 28, 32; m 59; c 2. PHYSIOLOGICAL ACOUSTICS, MUSICAL ACOUSTICS. *Educ:* Mass Inst Technol, BS, 54, PhD(theoret physics), 59. *Prof Exp:* Res asst, Mass Inst Technol, 54-57; asst prof physics, Worcester Polytech Inst, 58-60; res assoc, 60-62, from asst prof to assoc prof, 62-69, asst head dept, 66-73, PROF PHYSICS, PURDUE UNIV, 69- *Concurrent Pos:* Asst physicist, Brookhaven Nat Lab, 59; res assoc, Argonne Nat Lab, 61; vis physicist, Lawrence Radiation Lab, 63, Stanford Linear Accelerator Ctr, 71 & Los Alamos Sci Lab, 72. *Mem:* AAAS; Sigma Xi; Acoustical Soc America; fel Am Phys Soc; Am Asn Physics Teachers. *Res:* Physiological and musical acoustics; theory of atomic structure; theory of interactions of nuclei and elementary particles. *Mailing Add:* Dept of Physics Purdue Univ West Lafayette IN 47906

TUBIS, MANUEL, b Philadelphia, Pa, July 14, 09; m 36; c 1. NUCLEAR MEDICINE. *Educ:* Philadelphia Col Pharm, BSc, 31; Univ Pa, MSc, 32; Univ Tokyo, PhD(pharmaceut sci), 66. *Prof Exp:* Chemist, US Food & Drug Admin, 35-44; pharmaceut res chemist, Wyeth, Inc, 44-46; res chemist, Dartell Labs, 46-47; tech dir, Am Biochem Corp, 47-48; biochemist, 48-70, chief biochemist, Nuclear Med Serv, 70-79, CONSULT RES CHEMIST, VET ADMIN HOSP, WADSWORTH MED CTR, 79- *Concurrent Pos:* Asst prof sch med, Univ Calif, Los Angeles, 53-68; consult nuclear med & radiopharm, Int Atomic Energy Agency, Vienna; adj prof biomed chem & co-dir radiopharm prog, Sch Pharm, Univ Southern Calif, 74-, consult radiopharmaceut & nuclear med, 74- *Honors & Awards:* Super Performance Award, US Vet Admin, 75. *Mem:* Fel & hon mem, Am Inst Chem; Am Chem Soc; Soc Nuclear Med. *Res:* Application of radioisotopes to biochemistry, medicine and pharmacy; research and development of new labeled radiopharmaceuticals; supervision of preparation, production and quality control. *Mailing Add:* Nuclear Med Serv Vet Admin Wadsworth Med Ctr Los Angeles CA 90073

TUCCI, JAMES VINCENT, b Hollis, NY, Feb 13, 39; m 62; c 1. CHEMICAL PHYSICS. *Educ:* Hofstra Univ, BA, 62; Univ Mass, MS, 66, PhD(chem), 67. *Prof Exp:* Instr physics, 66-67, from asst prof to assoc prof, 67-73, actg chmn dept, 67-71, PROF PHYSICS, UNIV BRIDGEPORT, 73-, CHMN DEPT, 72- *Concurrent Pos:* NSF grant, 67-70; Conn Res Comn res grant, 68-70. *Mem:* Optical Soc Am; Am Phys Soc. *Res:* Laser Raman spectroscopy; vibrational spectroscopy. *Mailing Add:* Dept Physics Univ Bridgeport Bridgeport CT 06602

TUCCIARONE, JOHN PETER, b New York, NY, Apr 9, 40; m 63; c 3. MATHEMATICS. *Educ:* Fordham Univ, BS, 61; St John's Univ, NY, MA, 63, JD, 66; NY Univ, PhD(math), 69. *Prof Exp:* Asst prof math, St John's Univ, NY, 62-74; assoc prof, 74-80, PROF MATH, MERCY COL, 80-; DIR, PROB ANAL CORP, 71- *Concurrent Pos:* Attorney pvt practice, NY, 70- *Mem:* Math Asn Am. *Res:* Numerical analysis; computer science; application of computers to instruction. *Mailing Add:* 390 Bedford Rd Pleasantville NY 10570

TUCCIO, SAM ANTHONY, lasers, see previous edition

TUCHINSKY, PHILIP MARTIN, b Philadelphia, Pa, June 17, 45. COMPUTER SCIENCE. *Educ:* Queens Col, BA, 66; Courant Inst, NY Univ, MS, 68, PhD(math), 71. *Prof Exp:* Instr math, NY Univ, 69-70; adj instr, Cooper Union Advan Sci & Art, 70-71; asst prof, Kalamazoo Col, 71-72; asst prof math, Ohio Wesleyan Univ, 72-78; RES ENGR COMPUT SCI DEPT, FORD RES & ENG CTR, 78- *Concurrent Pos:* Great Lakes Col Asn teaching fel, Lilly Found Grant, 75; vis lectr, Math Asn Am, 76- *Mem:* Am Math Soc; Math Asn Am. *Res:* Information systems development for car design and engineering applications. *Mailing Add:* 7623 Charlesworth Dearborn Heights MI 48127

TUCHMAN, ALBERT, b Brooklyn, NY, July 1, 35; m 57; c 4. PHYSICS. *Educ:* Yeshiva Univ, BA, 56; Mass Inst Technol, PhD(physics), 63. *Prof Exp:* Staff scientist res & develop div, 63-64, group leader propulsion, 64-66, sect chief plasma physics space systs div, 66-70, sr consult scientist systs div, 70-73, PRIN STAFF SCIENTIST PHYSICS, AVCO CORP, 73- *Mem:* Asn Orthodox Jewish Scientists; *Res:* Plasma, quantum and elementary particle physics; optical and infrared sources; infrared optical design; missile countermeasures; optical, infrared and laser countermeasures; infrared target signatures; electrode phenomena; re-entry simulation and ablation measurement; satellite detection; high energy lasers. *Mailing Add:* Avco Corp Systs Div 201 Lowell St Wilmington MA 01887

TUCHOLKE, BRIAN EDWARD, b Hot Springs, SDak, Mar 19, 46; m 68; c 1. MARINE GEOLOGY, OCEANOGRAPHY. *Educ:* SDak Sch Mines & Technol, BS, 68; Mass Inst Technol, PhD(oceanog), 73. *Prof Exp:* Teaching asst sedimentology, Mass Inst Technol, 68-70; teaching asst marine geol, Woods Hole Oceanog Inst, 70-72, res asst, 72-73; fel, Lamont-Doherty Geol Observ, Columbia Univ, 73-74, res assoc, 74-78, sr res assoc, 78-79; ASSOC SCIENTIST MARINE GEOL, WOODS HOLE OCEANOG INST, 79- *Concurrent Pos:* Corp mem, Woods Hole Oceanog Inst, 76-79; vis sr res assoc, Lamont-Doherty Geol Observ, Columbia Univ, 79-; proj co-leader, Decade NAm Geol, Geol Soc Am, 80- *Mem:* Am Asn Petrol Geologists; Am Geophys Union; fel Geol Soc Am; Sigma Xi. *Res:* Seismic stratigraphy; oceanic rock stratigraphy; paleo-oceanography; benthic boundary layer processes; physical properties of sediments; sedimentology. *Mailing Add:* Woods Hole Oceanog Inst Woods Hole MA 02543

TUCK, DENNIS GEORGE, b UK, Apr 8, 29; m 56; c 3. INORGANIC CHEMISTRY, ORGANOMETALLIC CHEMISTRY. *Educ:* Univ Durham, BSc, 49, PhD(chem), 56, DSc, 71. *Prof Exp:* Brit Coun fel, Inst du Radium, Paris, France, 52-53; sci officer chem, Windscale Works, UK Atomic Energy Auth, Eng, 53-56; lectr inorg chem, Univ Nottingham, 59-65; from assoc prof to prof chem, Simon Fraser Univ, 66-72; PROF CHEM & HEAD DEPT, UNIV WINDSOR, 72- *Concurrent Pos:* Res fel chem, Univ Manchester, 56-59; res fel lab nuclear sci, Cornell Univ, 57-58; vis expert, Concepcion Univ, Chile, 64; mem chem grant selection comt, Nat Res Coun Can, 72-74; dir, Can Patents & Develop Ltd, 81- *Mem:* Royal Soc Chem; fel Chem Inst Can. *Res:* Coordination chemistry of non-transition metals, especially indium; complexes in aqueous solution; use of electrochemical methods in inorganic and organometallic chemistry. *Mailing Add:* Dept of Chem Univ of Windsor Windsor ON N9B 3P4 Can

TUCK, LEO DALLAS, b San Francisco, Calif, Oct 12, 16; m 53; c 2. PHYSICAL CHEMISTRY. *Educ:* Univ Calif, AB, 39, PhD(chem), 48. *Prof Exp:* Res assoc radiation lab, Univ Calif, 42; res assoc chem dept, Univ Chicago, 42-43; res assoc radio res lab, Harvard Univ, 43-45; lectr & res asst chem, 48-50, instr, 50-51, from asst prof to assoc prof, 51-63, vchancellor acad affairs, 71-73, PROF CHEM & PHARMACEUT CHEM, SCH PHARM, UNIV CALIF, SAN FRANCISCO, 63-, ASSOC DEAN, 80- *Mem:* Fel AAAS; Am Chem Soc; Am Phys Soc; Am Pharmaceut Asn. *Res:* Thermodynamics and electrochemistry; thermodynamics of nonisothermal systems; chemistry of boron and uranium compounds; electrolytes in aqueous and nonaqueous solutions; microwave electronics; chemistry of free radicals; magnetic resonance spectroscopy. *Mailing Add:* Univ of Calif Sch of Pharm San Francisco Med Ctr San Francisco CA 94143

TUCKER, ALAN, b Worthing, Eng, Sept 17, 47; US citizen; m 68; c 2. CARDIOPULMONARY PHYSIOLOGY, HIGH ALTITUDE PHYSIOLOGY. *Educ:* Univ Calif, Santa Barbara, BA, 68, PhD(biol), 72. *Prof Exp:* Res assoc physiol, Cardiovasc Pulmonary Res Lab, Med Ctr, Univ Colo, 73-74, fel, 74-76; asst prof physiol, Sch Med, Wright State Univ, 76-79; ASSOC PROF PHYSIOL, COLO STATE UNIV, 79- *Concurrent Pos:* Coun Circulation mem, Am Heart Asn. *Honors & Awards:* Res Serv Award, Nat Heart & Lung Inst, 74. *Mem:* Am Physiol Soc; Am Thoracic Soc; Soc Exp Biol & Med. *Res:* Control of the pulmonary circulation; hypoxia and high altitude physiology; pharmacology of pulmonary and systemic vasculature; respiratory physiology; environmental physiology. *Mailing Add:* Dept Physiol & Biophysics Colo State Univ Ft Collins CO 80523

TUCKER, ALAN CURTISS, b Princeton, NJ, July 6, 43; m 68. MATHEMATICS. *Educ:* Harvard Univ, BA, 65; Stanford Univ, MS, 67, PhD(math), 69. *Prof Exp:* Vis asst prof math, Math Res Ctr, Univ Wis-Madison, 69-70; asst prof, 70-77, PROF APPL MATH & STATIST, STATE UNIV NY STONY BROOK, 77-, CHMN, 78- *Concurrent Pos:* Res consult, Rand Corp, 64-71; vis assoc prof comput sci, Univ Calif, San Diego, 76-77; chmn panel gen math sci prog, Math Asn Am, 77-, mem var comt. *Mem:* Am Math Soc; Soc Indust & Appl Math; AAAS; Am Statist Asn; Math Asn Am. *Res:* Extremal characterization problems in graph theory; zero-one matrices; combinatorial algorithms. *Mailing Add:* Dept Appl Math & Statist State Univ of NY Stony Brook NY 11794

TUCKER, ALLEN BRINK, b Highland, Ind, Oct 12, 36; m 63; c 2. NUCLEAR PHYSICS. *Educ:* Mass Inst Technol, BS, 58; Stanford Univ, PhD(physics), 65. *Prof Exp:* Asst prof physics, San Jose State Col, 63-65 & Iowa State Univ, 65-70; assoc prof, 70-77, PROF PHYSICS, SAN JOSE STATE UNIV, 77- *Mem:* Am Phys Soc; Am Asn Physics Teachers. *Res:* Neutron scattering; nuclear spectroscopy; delayed neutrons. *Mailing Add:* Dept of Physics San Jose State Univ San Jose CA 95192

TUCKER, ALLEN BROWN, b Worcester, Mass, Feb 19, 42; m 65; c 1. MATHEMATICS. *Educ:* Wesleyan Univ, BA, 63; Northwestern Univ, MS, 69, PhD(appl math), 70. *Prof Exp:* Systs analyst, Norton Co, 63-67; asst prof comput sci, Univ Mo-Rolla, 70-71; asst prof, 71-76, ASSOC PROF COMPUT SCI, GEORGETOWN UNIV, 76-, DIR ACAD COMPUT CTR, 76-, DIR COMPUT SCI PROG, 79- *Concurrent Pos:* Vpres, Tabor, Inc-Systs Consult, 74-79; assoc ed, J Comput Lang, 75- *Mem:* Asn Comput Mach; Sigma Xi. *Res:* Formal languages; automata theory; programming languages; computer applications. *Mailing Add:* Dept Math Georgetown Univ 37th & O St NW Washington DC 20007

TUCKER, ANNE NICHOLS, b Ashland, Ky, Oct 16, 42; m 65; c 1. TOXICOLOGY, MICROBIOLOGY. *Educ:* Univ Ky, BS, 64, PhD(toxicol), 76. *Prof Exp:* Res assoc biochem, Univ Ky, 65-74; fel toxicol, 76-78, ASST PROF, MED COL VA, 78- *Concurrent Pos:* Nat Cancer Inst-Nat Res Serv Award fel, 76; spec consult, Food & Drug Admin, 78-; consult, Indust Health Found, 78-79. *Mem:* Am Col Toxicol. *Res:* Metabolic activation of carcinogens; immunotoxicology. *Mailing Add:* 2824 London Park Dr Midlothian VA 23113

TUCKER, ARTHUR SMITH, b Hopei, China, May 2, 13; m 45, 81; c 2. MEDICINE, RADIOLOGY. *Educ:* Oberlin Col, AB, 35; Yale Univ, MD, 39. *Prof Exp:* Radiologist, Atomic Bomb Casualty Comn, Japan, 48-50; instr radiol, Univ Calif, 50-51; radiologist, Cleveland Clin, Ohio, 51-56; from asst prof to assoc prof, 56-72, prof radiol, Sch Med, Case Western Reserve Univ, 72-78; PROF RADIOL, UNIV MICH, 78- *Mem:* Roentgen Ray Soc; Radiol Soc NAm; AMA. *Res:* Pediatric radiology. *Mailing Add:* Mott Hosp Radiol Univ Mich Ann Arbor MI 48109

TUCKER, BILLY BOB, b Cheyenne, Okla, Jan 13, 28; m 49; c 3. AGRONOMY. *Educ:* Okla State Univ, BS, 52, MS, 53; Univ Ill, PhD, 55. *Prof Exp:* Soil scientist, Agr Res Serv, USDA, 55-56; from asst prof to assoc prof agron, 56-67, prof, 67-79, REGENTS PROF AGRON, OKLA STATE UNIV, 79- *Mem:* Am Soc Agron; Soil Sci Soc Am; Soil Conserv Soc Am. *Res:* Soil management, especially improvment and maintenance of soil productivity; soil chemistry, plant nutrition and fertilizer technology. *Mailing Add:* Dept of Agron Okla State Univ Stillwater OK 74074

TUCKER, CHARLES EUGENE, b Montgomery, Ala, July 2, 33; m 58; c 2. BIOLOGY. *Educ:* Huntingdon Col, BA, 59; Univ Ala, MS, 65, PhD(biol), 67. *Prof Exp:* Assoc prof biol, 67-80, PROF BIOL, LIVINGSTON UNIV, 80-, CHMN, DIV NATURAL SCI & MATH, 70-, ASSOC DEAN, GEN STUDIES HEALTH-RELATED PROG, 75- *Mem:* Am Soc Ichthyologists & Herpetologists; Sigma Xi. *Res:* Vertebrate field zoology; ichthyology; survey of fishes. *Mailing Add:* Sta 7 Livingston Univ Livingston AL 35470

TUCKER, CHARLES LEROY, JR, b Winston-Salem, NC, May 19, 21; m 49; c 2. PLANT CHEMISTRY. *Educ:* The Citadel, BS, 43; NC State Col, MS, 52. *Prof Exp:* Jr anal chemist div tests & mat, NC State Hwy Comn, 47-48, anal chemist dept conserv & develop water resources div, 48-50; chemist anal res, Liggett & Myers Tobacco Co, 52-58; res chemist, 58-67, mgr leaf & flavor res, 67-68, mgr prod develop, 68-80, DIR PROD DEVELOP, LORILLARD RES CTR, 80- *Mem:* Am Chem Soc. *Res:* Chemical and physical constitution of tobacco, especially as related to final tobacco product characteristics; analytical methods peculiar to tobacco and tobacco smoke. *Mailing Add:* 903 Caswell Dr Greensboro NC 27408

TUCKER, CHARLES THOMAS, b Laredo, Tex, Aug 6, 36; m 64. MATHEMATICS. *Educ:* Tex A&M Univ, BS & BA, 58; Univ Tex, MA, 62, PhD(math), 66. *Prof Exp:* Chem engr, Tracor, Inc, Tex, 60-62, engr & scientist, 63-66; asst prof math, 66-73, ASSOC PROF MATH, UNIV HOUSTON, 73- *Mem:* Am Math Soc; Math Asn Am. *Res:* Sonar signal processing; pure mathematics. *Mailing Add:* Dept of Math Univ of Houston Houston TX 77004

TUCKER, CHARLES WINFRED, JR, physical chemistry, see previous edition

TUCKER, DAVID PATRICK HISLOP, b Trinidad, West Indies, Oct 26, 34; m 66; c 1. HORTICULTURE. *Educ:* Univ Birmingham, BSc, 58; Univ Calif, PhD(plant sci), 66. *Prof Exp:* Agronomist, Dept Agr, Brit Honduras, 60-63; agronomist, 66-74, assoc prof & assoc horticulturist, 74-80, PROF FRUIT CROPS & HORTICULTURIST, AGR RES & EDUC CTR, UNIV FLA, 80- *Mem:* Am Soc Hort Sci. *Res:* All aspects of citrus production. *Mailing Add:* Agr Res & Educ Ctr Univ of Fla PO Box 1088 Lake Alfred FL 32611

TUCKER, DON, b Seligman, Mo, May 19, 24; m 54; c 3. BIOPHYSICS. *Educ:* Univ Ill, BS, 51; Fla State Univ, PhD(physiol), 61. *Prof Exp:* Res asst, Univ Ill, 51-54; jr elec engr, Raytheon Tel & Radio, 54; res assoc, 54-57, USPHS trainee, 61-64, res investr biol sci, 64-72, ASSOC RESEARCHER BIOL SCI, FLA STATE UNIV, 72- *Mem:* AAAS; Am Phys Soc. *Res:* Biophysics of chemical senses; biological effects of high intensity ultrasound; response characteristics of olfactory, vomeronasal and trigeminal receptor responses to odorants; chemoreceptor mechanisms, including taste; neural coding in chemical senses. *Mailing Add:* 2704 Keator Tallahassee FL 32304

TUCKER, DON HARRELL, b Brown County, Tex, Jan 21, 30; m 51; c 5. MATHEMATICS. *Educ:* West Tex State Univ, BA, 51; Univ Tex, MA, 55, PhD(math), 58. *Prof Exp:* Res scientist mil physics res lab, Balcones Res Ctr, Univ Tex, 52-53, instr math, Univ, 53-58; from asst prof to assoc prof, 58-67, PROF MATH, UNIV UTAH, 67- *Concurrent Pos:* Vis prof, Cath Univ Am, 68-69; guest prof, Univ Marburg, 66 & 69, vis lectr, Math Asn Am, 71- *Mem:* Am Math Soc; Math Asn Am. *Res:* Functional analysis; abstract summability theory; differential equations. *Mailing Add:* Dept Math Univ Utah Salt Lake City UT 84112

TUCKER, EDMUND BELFORD, b NS, Can, May 6, 22; m 46; c 3. PHYSICS. *Educ:* Mt Allison Univ, BSc, 43; Oxford Univ, BA, 48; Yale Univ, MS, 49, PhD(physics), 51. *Prof Exp:* Res assoc physics, Univ Minn, 50-52, asst prof, 53, res assoc, 53-55; physicist res & develop ctr, 55-66, mgr personnel & admin info sci lab, 66-69, consult educ rels, NY, 69-71, consult, Conn, 71-75, MGR SCI & TECHNOL SUPPORT PROG, GEN ELEC CO, CONN, 75- *Mem:* AAAS; Am Soc Eng Educ; Sigma Xi; Am Phys Soc. *Res:* Linear accelerators; magnetic resonance; microwave ultrasonics; crystal fields; energy related problems. *Mailing Add:* Gen Elec Co 3135 Easton Turnpike Fairfield CT 06431

TUCKER, GABRIEL FREDERICK, JR, b Bryn Mawr, Pa, June 18, 24; m 47; c 6. LARYNGOLOGY. *Educ:* Princeton Univ, AB, 47; Johns Hopkins Univ, MD, 51; Am Bd Otolaryngol, dipl, 58. *Prof Exp:* Asst prof pharmacol, Sch Med, Univ NC, 52-53; instr otolaryngol, Sch Med, Johns Hopkins Univ, 56; instr surg, Sch Med, Univ NC, 57-58; asst prof laryngol & otol, Sch Med, Johns Hopkins Univ & otolaryngologist, Johns Hopkins Hosp, 58-62; clin prof laryngol & bronchoespophagol, Chevalier Jackson Clin, Sch Med, Temple Univ, 62-75; PROF OTOLARYNGOL & MAXILLOFACIAL SURG, NORTHWESTERN UNIV, CHICAGO, 75-; HEAD DIV OTOLARYNGOL, DIV BRONCHOLOGY & DEPT COMMUN DIS, CHILDREN'S MEM HOSP, 79- *Concurrent Pos:* Fel bronchoesophagol & laryngol surg, Grad Sch Med, Univ Pa, 53-54; fel laryngol & otol, Sch Med, Johns Hopkins Univ, 54-56; vis otolaryngologist, Baltimore City Hosp, 59-62; consult, Clin Ctr, NIH, 60-62; chief bronchoesophagology, St Christopher's Hosp, 66-; consult-lectr laryngol, US Naval Hosp, Philadelphia, 67-; consult, Episcopal Hosp & Shriner's Hosp Crippled Children, Philadelphia; mem, Am Joint Comt Cancer Staging & End Results Reporting, Task Force on Larynx; lectr div grad med, Univ Pa, 68-, lectr grad bronchol, esophagol & laryngol surg, 71-; vis res prof laryngol bronchoesophagol, Hahnemann Med Col, 72-; consult otolaryngol, Lankenau Hosp, 74- *Honors & Awards:* Honor Award, Am Acad Ophthal & Otolaryngol, 69. *Mem:* AAAS; AMA; fel Am Col Chest Physicians; fel Am Acad Ophthal & Otolaryngol; fel Am Laryngol Asn. *Res:* Bronchoesophagology; laryngeal pathology; prevention of foreign bodies accidents. *Mailing Add:* Children's Mem Hosp 2300 Children's Plaza Chicago IL 60614

TUCKER, GAIL SUSAN, b New York, NY, Aug 30, 45. DEVELOPMENTAL BIOLOGY. *Educ:* Mercy Col, BA, 67; Univ Kans, Lawrence, PhD(cell biol/develop biol), 73. *Prof Exp:* Res asst develop biol, 68-72, res asst mycology, Univ Kans, Lawrence, 72-73; instr, Mercy Col, 73-75; res assoc, 76-79, RES ASST PROF, BASCOM PALMER EYE INST, SCH MED, UNIV MIAMI, 79- *Concurrent Pos:* Fel, Eye Inst, Col Physicians & Surgeons, Columbia Univ, 73-75; vis fel, Biol Labs, Harvard Univ, 80; consult, Pub Sch Syst, Dade County, Fla, 77- *Mem:* Am Asn Res Vision & Ophthal; Soc Neurosci; AAAS; Women in Cell Biol; Am Soc Cell Biol. *Res:* Light and electron microscopy of retinal development and cytoarchitecture of the normal and visually deprived amphibian and cat retina; retinal aging in the cat, rat and human; corneal dystrophy in the cat. *Mailing Add:* Bascom Palmer Eye Inst Sch Med Univ Miami 1638 NW 10th Ave Miami FL 33136

TUCKER, GARY EDWARD, b Michigan Valley, Kans, Aug 17, 41; m 60; c 2. BOTANY. *Educ:* Kans State Teachers Col, BA, 64; Univ NC, Chapel Hill, MA, 67; Univ Ark, PhD(bot), 76. *Prof Exp:* Asst prof, 66-77, PROF BIOL & CUR HERBARIUM, ARK TECH UNIV, 77- *Concurrent Pos:* Consult, var state & fed agencies. *Mem:* Int Asn Plant Taxonomists. *Res:* Endangered and threatened plant species of Southeastern states; endangered and threatened plant species of Arkansas; woody flora of Arkansas; vascular plant family lauraceae of Southeastern US; wetlands of US. *Mailing Add:* PO Box 1385 Ark Tech Univ Russellville AR 72801

TUCKER, GARY JAY, b Cleveland, Ohio, May 6, 34; m 56; c 2. PSYCHIATRY. *Educ:* Oberlin Col, AB, 56; Western Reserve Univ, MD, 60. *Prof Exp:* Asst med dir, Acute Psychiat Inpatient Div, Yale-New Haven Hosp, Yale Univ, 67-68, from asst prof to assoc prof psychiat, Sch Med, 67-71, med dir, Psychiat Inpatient Div, Med Ctr, 68-71, attend psychiatrist, 69-71, asst chief psychiat, 70-71; assoc prof psychiat, 71-74, dir residency training, 71-78, PROF PSYCHIAT, DARTMOUTH MED SCH, 74-, CHMN DEPT, 78- *Concurrent Pos:* Fel psychiat, Sch Med, Yale Univ, 61-64; consult, Norwich State Hosp, Conn, 67-68, Univ Conn, 68-70, Off Aviation Med, Fed Aviation Admin, Dept Transp, 68-70, Vet Admin Hosp, West Haven, Conn, 70-71 & White River Junction, Vt, 71- *Mem:* Fel Am Psychiat Asn. *Res:* Behavioral implications of neurologic functions; psychopathology and hospital psychiatry. *Mailing Add:* Dept of Psychiat Dartmouth Med Sch Hanover NH 03755

TUCKER, HARVEY MICHAEL, b New Brunswick, NJ, Nov 27, 38; m 60; c 3. OTOLARYNGOLOGY, SURGERY. *Educ:* Bucknell Univ, BS, 60; Jefferson Med Col, MD, 64. *Prof Exp:* Resident, Jefferson Med Col, 69; asst otolaryngol, Barnes Hosp, Washington Univ, 69-70; assoc prof otolaryngol, State Univ NY Upstate Med Ctr, 70-75; CHMN, DEPT OTOLARYNGOL & COMMUN DIS, CLEVELAND CLIN FOUND, 75- *Concurrent Pos:* Fel head & neck surg, Barnes Hosp, Washington Univ, 69-70. *Honors & Awards:* S Macuen Smith Award, Jefferson Med Col, 64; Benjamin Shuster Award, Am Acad Plastic & Reconstruct Surg, 70. *Mem:* Fel Am Col Surgeons; fel Am Acad Facial Plastic & Reconstruct Surg; Am Soc Surg; fel Am Acad Head & Neck Surg; fel Am Acad Ophthal & Otolaryngol. *Res:* Laryngeal reinnervation and transplantation; cancer surgery of the head and neck. *Mailing Add:* 9500 Euclid Ave Cleveland OH 44106

TUCKER, HERBERT ALLEN, b Milford, Mass, Oct 25, 36; m 59; c 3. ANIMAL PHYSIOLOGY. *Educ:* Univ Mass, BS, 58; Rutgers Univ, MS, 60, PhD(animal physiol), 63. *Prof Exp:* From asst prof to assoc prof mammary physiol, 62-75, PROF MAMMARY PHYSIOL, MICH STATE UNIV, 75- *Concurrent Pos:* NIH spec fel, Univ Ill, 69. *Honors & Awards:* Borden Award, Am Dairy Sci Asn, 79. *Mem:* AAAS; Am Soc Animal Sci; Am Dairy Sci Asn; Soc Exp Biol & Med; Am Physiol Soc. *Res:* Endocrinology of mammary development and lactation; environmental control hormones, growth, lactation; radioimmunoassay of hormones; endocrinology of reproduction; hormone binding to mammary cells. *Mailing Add:* Dept Sci Mich State Univ East Lansing MI 48824

TUCKER, HOWARD GREGORY, b Lawrence, Kans, Oct 3, 22; m 46; c 4. MATHEMATICS. *Educ:* Univ Calif, AB, 48, MA, 49, PhD(math), 55. *Prof Exp:* Instr math, Rutgers Univ, 52-53; asst prof, Univ Ore, 55-56; from asst prof to prof, Univ Calif, Riverside, 56-68; PROF MATH, UNIV CALIF, IRVINE, 68- *Mem:* Am Math Soc; Math Asn Am; Inst Math Statist; Am Statist Asn; Biometric Soc. *Res:* Probability theory; mathematical statistics. *Mailing Add:* Dept of Math Univ of Calif Irvine CA 92664

TUCKER, HUEL CLIVE, electrical engineering, see previous edition

TUCKER, IRWIN WILLIAM, b New York, NY, Oct 30, 14; m 73; c 1. ORGANIC CHEMISTRY, ENVIRONMENTAL ENGINEERING. *Educ:* George Washington Univ, BS, 39; Univ Md, PhD(org chem), 48. *Prof Exp:* Chemist, USDA, Washington, DC, 36-45; asst, Univ Md, 45-48; res chemist, Ligget & Meyers Tobacco Co, NC, 48-51; indust specialist, Indust Eval Bd, US Dept Com, 51-53; dir res, Brown & Williamson Tobacco Corp, 53-59, mem, Bd Dirs, 56-59; prof eng res, 66-81, prof environ eng, 77-81, EMER PROF ENG RES & ENVIRON ENG, UNIV LOUISVILLE, 81- *Concurrent Pos:* Dir, Inst Indust Res, 66-72; pres, Coun Environ Balance, 73- *Mem:* Am Chem Soc; Air Pollution Control Asn; Inst Food Technologists. *Res:* Synthetic and determination of structure; fermentation chemistry; enzyme chemistry; chemistry of natural products; air pollution and solid wastes. *Mailing Add:* 1810 Crossgate Lane Louisville KY 40222

TUCKER, JAMES, b Shamrock, Okla, July 17, 22; m 46; c 4. VETERINARY SCIENCE. *Educ:* Okla State Univ, BS, 47, MS, 48, DVM, 51. *Prof Exp:* Asst prof vet path, Univ Ga, 51-53; PROF VET SCI & HEAD DIV VET MED & MICROBIOL, UNIV WYO, 53- *Mem:* AAAS; Am Vet Radiol Soc; Am Vet Med Asn; Am Asn Vet Nutritionists; Am Col Vet Toxicol. *Res:* Diseases and toxicology of cattle and sheep. *Mailing Add:* Div of Vet Med & Microbiol Univ Wyo PO Box 3354 Univ Sta Laramie WY 82070

TUCKER, JOHN MAURICE, b Yamhill Co, Ore, Jan 7, 16; m 42; c 3. BOTANY. *Educ:* Univ Calif, Berkeley, AB, 40, PhD(bot), 50. *Prof Exp:* Botanist, Univ Calif Exped, El Salvador, Cent Am, 41-42; asst bot, Univ Calif, Berkeley, 46-47; assoc, 47-49, instr & jr botanist, Exp Sta, 49-51, from asst prof & asst botanist to assoc prof & assoc botanist, 51-63, assoc, Exp Sta, 47-49, PROF BOT & BOTANIST, UNIV CALIF, DAVIS, 63-, DIR, ARBORETUM, 72- *Concurrent Pos:* Guggenheim fel, 55-56. *Mem:* Int Asn Plant Taxon; Bot Soc Am; Soc Study Evolution; Am Soc Plant Taxon. *Res:* Systematics and evolution of oaks of North America; classification of Fagaccae of the New World. *Mailing Add:* Dept Bot Univ Calif Davis CA 95616

TUCKER, JOHN SHEPARD, comparative physiology, aquatic biology, see previous edition

TUCKER, KENNETH WILBURN, b Santa Barbara, Calif, Aug 8, 24; m 53. APICULTURE. *Educ:* Univ Calif, BS, 50, PhD(entom), 57. *Prof Exp:* Res fel, Univ Minn, 54-60; instr biol, Lake Forest Col, 60-63; asst res apiculturist, Univ Calif, Davis, 63-66; RES ENTOMOLOGIST, USDA, 66- *Mem:* AAAS; Entom Soc Am; Int Bee Res Asn; Genetics Soc Am; Am Genetic Asn. *Res:* Genetics of honey bees. *Mailing Add:* Bee Breeding & Stock Ctr Lab Rt 3 Box 82-B Ben Hur Rd Baton Rouge LA 70808

TUCKER, PAUL ARTHUR, b Albemarle, NC, May 14, 41; m 65. TEXTILES, MICROSCOPY. *Educ:* NC State Univ, BS, 63, MS, 66, PhD(fiber & polymer sci), 73. *Prof Exp:* Instr textiles, NC State Univ, 64-71, asst prof, 73; NATO vis fel, Dept Textile Indust, Univ Leeds, 74; asst prof textiles, 75-80, ASSOC PROF TEXTILE MAT & MGT, SCH TEXTILES, NC STATE UNIV, 80- *Mem:* Royal Micros Soc. *Res:* Seeking the basic materials science underlying fibrous materials and relating applied technology to this science; polymer fine structure; microscopy; yarn processing; particulate analyses. *Mailing Add:* Sch of Textiles NC State Univ Raleigh NC 27607

TUCKER, RAY EDWIN, b Somerset, Ky, Dec 31, 29; m 53; c 3. ANIMAL SCIENCE. *Educ:* Univ Ky, BS, 51, MS, 66, PhD(animal nutrit), 68. *Prof Exp:* Asst prof animal sci, Va Polytech Inst & State Univ, 68-69; asst prof, 69-80, ASSOC PROF ANIMAL SCI, UNIV KY, 80- *Mem:* Am Soc Animal Sci. *Res:* Ruminant nutrition; starch utilization; urea utilization; magnesium deficiency; vitamin A antagonists; poultry litter as a feedstuff for ruminants. *Mailing Add:* Dept of Animal Sci Univ of Ky Lexington KY 40506

TUCKER, RICHARD LEE, b Wichita Falls, Tex, July 19, 35; m 56; c 2. CIVIL ENGINEERING, MECHANICS. *Educ:* Univ Tex, BS, 58, MS, 60, PhD(civil eng), 63. *Prof Exp:* Proj engr, Eng-Sci Consult, 58-60; instr civil eng, Univ Tex, 60-62; from asst prof to prof, Univ Tex, Arlington, 62-74, assoc dean eng, 67-74; vpres, Luther Hill & Assoc, Inc, Dallas, 74-76; PROF CIVIL ENG, UNIV TEX, AUSTIN, 76- *Mem:* Am Soc Eng Educ; Am Soc Civil Engrs; Nat Soc Prof Engrs; Am Soc Testing & Mat; Soc Exp Stress Anal. *Res:* Construction engineering; project management. *Mailing Add:* Dept of Civil Eng Univ of Tex Austin TX 78712

TUCKER, ROBERT H, b Clovis, NMex, Aug 3, 44; m; c 3. THEORETICAL PHYSICS. *Educ:* Univ Ariz, BS, 65; Iowa State Univ, PhD(physics), 70. *Prof Exp:* Asst ed physics, Phys Rev Lett, 71-74; ed physics, Phys Rev A, 74-78; Tech writer, Sandia Labs, Livermore, Calif, 78- *Mailing Add:* 110 Diamond Dr Livermore CA 94550

TUCKER, ROY WILBUR, b Exeter, Calif, Jan 25, 27; m 54; c 2. MATHEMATICS. *Educ:* Stanford Univ, BS, 51, MA, 53, MS, 54. *Prof Exp:* Instr math, Colo Col, 54-55; instr, Modesto Jr Col, 55-59; from asst prof to assoc prof, 59-71, coordr comput ctr, 64-65 & consult, 65-66, PROF MATH, HUMBOLDT STATE UNIV, 71- *Mem:* Math Asn Am; Soc Indust & Appl Math; Asn Comput Mach. *Res:* Numerical analysis; linear algebra. *Mailing Add:* Dept of Math Humboldt State Univ Arcata CA 95221

TUCKER, RUTH EMMA, b Warrensburg, Ill, Feb 17, 01. NUTRITION. *Educ:* Univ Ill, AB, 23, MS, 25; Univ Chicago, PhD(nutrit, food chem), 48. *Prof Exp:* Asst, Univ Ill, 23-25; instr food & nutrit, Kans State Col, 25-37; prof home econ, Univ Alaska, 37-42; prof & res prof food & nutrit, 44-72, EMER PROF FOOD & NUTRIT, UNIV RI, 72- *Mem:* AAAS; fel Am Pub Health Asn; Am Dietetic Asn; Am Home Econ Asn. *Res:* Food chemistry. *Mailing Add:* 64 Linden Dr Kingston RI 02881

TUCKER, SHIRLEY COTTER, b St Paul, Minn, Apr 4, 27; m 53. BOTANY. *Educ:* Univ Minn, Minneapolis, BA, 49, MS, 51; Univ Calif, Davis, PhD, 56. *Prof Exp:* Scientist plant path, Univ Minn, 55-56, res fel bot, 57-60, instr, 60; res fel biol, Northwestern Univ, 61-63; res fel bot, Univ Calif, 63-66; from asst prof to assoc prof, 68-77, PROF BOT, LA STATE UNIV, BATON ROUGE, 77- *Mem:* Bot Soc Am; Am Bryol & Lichenological Soc; Brit Lichen Soc; Sigma Xi. *Res:* Developmental anatomy of flower and vegetative shoots; determinate growth; plant anatomy; morphology; lichenology. *Mailing Add:* Dept of Bot La State Univ Baton Rouge LA 70803

TUCKER, THOMAS CURTIS, b Hanson, Ky, Nov 1, 26; m 47; c 3. SOILS, PLANT NUTRITION. *Educ:* Univ Ky, BS, 49; Kans State Univ, MS, 51; Univ Ill, PhD, 55. *Prof Exp:* Asst soils, Kans State Univ, 49-51, instr, 51; asst soil fertility, Univ Ill, 51-55; asst prof soils, Miss State Univ, 55-56; from assoc prof to prof agr chem & soils, 56-74, PROF SOILS, WATER & ENG & SOIL SCIENTIST, AGR EXP STA, UNIV ARIZ, 74- *Concurrent Pos:* Vis prof, NC State Univ, 66-67; vis scientist, Univ Ariz, Tuscon, 77-78. *Mem:* Soil Sci Soc Am; Am Soc Agron; Am Chem Soc. *Res:* Agronomy; soil fertility and chemistry; analytical chemistry; soil-plant relationships; soil nitrogen transformations, fixation, fertilizer use efficiency using 15-nitrogen labelled materials. *Mailing Add:* Dept of Soils Univ of Ariz Tucson AZ 85721

TUCKER, THOMAS WILLIAM, b Princeton, NJ, July 15, 45; m 68; c 2. MATHEMATICS. *Educ:* Harvard Univ, AB, 67; Dartmouth Univ, PhD(math), 71. *Prof Exp:* Instr math, Princeton Univ, 71-73; ASSOC PROF MATH, COLGATE UNIV, 73- *Concurrent Pos:* Consult, Inst Defense Anal, 74, 75 & 78; vis lectr, Vis Lectr Prog, Math Asn Am, 74-; NSF res grant, 76-77; vis assoc prof, Darmouth Col, 78-79; consult, Col Bds & Educ Testing Serv. *Mem:* Math Asn Am; Am Math Soc. *Res:* Three-dimensional topology and combinatorics, especially topological graph theory. *Mailing Add:* Dept of Math Colgate Univ Hamilton NY 13346

TUCKER, VANCE ALAN, b Niagara Falls, NY, Apr 4, 36. COMPARATIVE PHYSIOLOGY. *Educ:* Univ Calif, Los Angeles, BA, 58, PhD(zool), 63; Univ Wis, MS, 60. *Prof Exp:* NSF fel zool, Univ Mich, 63-64; from asst prof to assoc prof zool, 64-73, PROF ZOOL, DUKE UNIV, 73- *Concurrent Pos:* NSF res grants & Duke Univ Coun Res grants, 65-75. *Mem:* AAAS. *Res:* Vertebrate locomotion, respiration, circulation, energy metabolism; avian aerodynamics. *Mailing Add:* Dept of Zool Duke Univ Durham NC 27706

TUCKER, W(ILLIAM) HENRY, b Seaford, Del, July 7, 20; wid; c 2. CHEMICAL ENGINEERING. *Educ:* Univ Va, BS, 42; Mass Inst Technol, MS, 46, ScD(chem eng), 47. *Prof Exp:* Res assoc, Manhattan Proj, 44-45; res engr & supvr eng res, Servel, Inc, 47-53; assoc prof chem eng, Purdue Univ, Lafayette, 53-69; PROF CHEM ENG & HEAD DEPT, TRI-STATE UNIV, 69- *Concurrent Pos:* Adv, Cheng Kung Univ, Taiwan, 58-59; vis teacher, Swiss Fed Inst Technol, 59; consult, Whirlpool Res, 62-69; Am Inst Chem Eng traveling fel study co-op educ, Gt Brit, 69; mid-career fel, Lilly Endowment, Inc, 78-79; mem, Theol Dialogue Sci & Technol, United Ministries Educ, 79- *Mem:* Sigma Xi; Am Soc Eng Educ; Am Inst Chem Engrs. *Res:* Absorption refrigeration and chemical heat pump; process design and economics; energy conservation; solar refrigeration. *Mailing Add:* Dept of Chem Eng Tri-State Univ Angola IN 46703

TUCKER, WALTER EUGENE, JR, b Atlanta, Ga, Aug 7, 31; m 56; c 3. VETERINARY PATHOLOGY. *Educ:* Univ Ga, DVM, 56; Am Col Vet Pathologists, dipl, 62. *Prof Exp:* From resident to staff mem, Vet Path Div, Armed Forces Inst Path, 58-62; sr pathologist, Dow Chem Co, 62-68; mgr path sect, Wyeth Labs Inc, 68-74; HEAD DEPT TOXICOL & EXP PATH, BURROUGHS WELLCOME CO, 74- *Mem:* Int Acad Pathologists; Soc Toxicol Pathologists; Am Col Vet Pathologists. *Res:* Research and development of pharmaceutical and agricultural chemicals with emphasis on characterization and safety evaluation of toxicopathologic responses in laboratory and domestic animals following administration of candidate human and veterinary chemotherapeutic agents. *Mailing Add:* Burroughs Wellcome Co 3030 Cornwallis Rd Research Triangle Park NC 27709

TUCKER, WILLIAM PRESTON, b Louisville, Ky, Sept 23, 32; m 59; c 3. ORGANIC CHEMISTRY. *Educ:* Wake Forest Col, BS, 57; Univ NC, MA, 60, PhD(chem), 62. *Prof Exp:* NIH fel, Univ Ill, 62-63; from asst prof to assoc prof chem, 63-72, PROF CHEM, NC STATE UNIV, 72- *Mem:* Am Chem Soc. *Res:* Chemistry of organic compounds of divalent sulfur; natural products. *Mailing Add:* Dept of Chem NC State Univ Raleigh NC 27650

TUCKER, WILLIE GEORGE, b Tampa, Fla, Nov 26, 34. ORGANIC CHEMISTRY. *Educ:* Tuskegee Inst, BS, 56, MS, 58; Univ Okla, PhD(org chem), 62. *Prof Exp:* PROF CHEM, SAVANNAH STATE COL, 62-, HEAD DEPT, 69- *Mem:* AAAS; Am Chem Soc; Sigma Xi. *Res:* Chlorination with cupric chloride; halogenation of pyridine. *Mailing Add:* Dept of Chem Box 20395 Savannah State Col Savannah GA 31404

TUCKER, WOODSON COLEMAN, JR, b Halsey, Ky, Sept 17, 08; m 32, 73; c 2. ACADEMIC ADMINISTRATION, PHYSICAL CHEMISTRY. *Educ:* Univ Fla, BS, 29, MS, 30, PhD(chem), 53. *Prof Exp:* Chemist, Superior Earth Co, 31-36; asst gen mgr in chg prod, United Prod Co, 36-38; chemist & tech adv to supt, Edgar Plastic Kaolin Co, 40-41; interim instr chem, Univ Fla, 46-51; instr, 51-52, from asst prof to prof, 52-78, asst vchancellor acad affairs, 69-78, EMER PROF CHEM, UNIV NEW ORLEANS, 78- *Mem:* Am Chem Soc; Sigma Xi. *Res:* Physical and thermodynamic properties of terpenes; chemical education. *Mailing Add:* 53 Tomino Way Hot Springs Village AR 71909

TUCKERMAN, MURRAY MOSES, b Boston, Mass, July 19, 28; m 48; c 4. PHARMACEUTICAL CHEMISTRY. *Educ:* Yale Univ, BS, 48; Temple Univ, BS, 53; Rensselaer Polytech Inst, PhD(chem), 58. *Prof Exp:* Asst anal chem, Sterling-Winthrop Res Inst, 53-55, res assoc, 55-58; assoc prof chem, 58-62, proj dir & radiol health specialist training prog, 63-69, head dept, 61-72, PROF CHEM, SCH PHARM, TEMPLE UNIV, 62- *Concurrent Pos:* Resident res assoc, Argonne Nat Lab, 59; mem bd revision, US Pharmacopeia, 60-; consult clin ctr, NIH, 59-65; sci adv, Food & Drug Admin, 67-71, comn labs & servs for control of drugs, 64-; temp hon mem secretariat Europ pharmacopeia, Coun Europe, 74. *Mem:* Fel Am Inst Chem; Am Chem Soc; Am Acad Pharmaceut Sci; Int Pharmaceut Fedn; Soc Qual Control. *Res:* Pharmaceutical analysis; drug standards; reference standards; pharmaceutical quality assurance. *Mailing Add:* Temple Univ Sch of Pharm 3307 N Broad St Philadelphia PA 19140

TUCKETT, ROBERT P, b Salt Lake City, Utah, March 11, 43; m 69; c 1. NEUROPHYSIOLOGY, SOMATOSENSORY PHYSIOLOGY. *Educ:* Univ Utah, BS, 65, PhD(biophysics & bioeng), 72. *Prof Exp:* Biophysicist, Artificial Heart Test Ctr, 71-72; fel neurophysiol, 72-77, res assoc, 77-79, res instr, 79-81, ASST RES PROF, UNIV UTAH, 81- *Concurrent Pos:* Prin investr, NIH grant, 79- *Mem:* Am Physiol Soc; Soc Neurosci. *Res:* Study of cutaneous receptor behavior and transfer of information in somatosensory pathways; mechanism by which the sensation of itch is transmitted to central nervous system. *Mailing Add:* Physiol Dept Rm 156 Univ Utah 410 Chipeta Way Salt Lake City UT 84108

TUCKEY, STEWART LAWRENCE, b Browns Valley, Minn, Aug 24, 05; m 36; c 1. DAIRY TECHNOLOGY. *Educ:* Univ Ill, Urbana, BS, 28, MS, 30, PhD(dairy tech), 37. *Prof Exp:* Asst dairy mfg, 28-30, instr, 30-32, assoc, 32-37, from asst prof to assoc prof, 37-57, prof dairy technol, 57-72, EMER PROF DAIRY TECHNOL, UNIV ILL, URBANA, 72- *Concurrent Pos:* Sabbatical, Neth Inst Dairy Res, Ede, 67. *Honors & Awards:* Borden Award, 39; Charles E Pfizer Award, Am Dairy Sci Asn, 69. *Mem:* Am Chem Soc; Am Dairy Sci Asn. *Res:* Biochemical and microbiological changes in cheese; microbiol clotting enzyme for cheese. *Mailing Add:* 919 W Charles St Champaign IL 61820

TUCKSON, COLEMAN REED, JR, b Washington, DC, Sept 2, 23; m 49; c 2. DENTISTRY. *Educ:* Howard Univ, DDS, 47; Univ Pa, MScD, 53. *Prof Exp:* From instr to assoc prof, 48-64, PROF DENT RADIOL, COL DENT, HOWARD UNIV, 64-, CHMN DEPT ORAL DIAG & RADIOL, 68-, ASSOC DEAN COL, 74- *Mem:* AAAS; Am Acad Dent Radiol (pres, 71-72); Int Asn Dent Res. *Res:* Oral surgery, dental radiology. *Mailing Add:* Howard Univ Col of Dent 600 W St NW Washington DC 20059

TUDDENHAM, W(ILLIAM) MARVIN, b Salt Lake City, Utah, July 8, 24; m 45; c 4. PHYSICAL CHEMISTRY, FUEL TECHNOLOGY. *Educ:* Univ Utah, BA, 47, MS, 48, PhD(fuel technol), 54. *Prof Exp:* Res anal chemist, Eastman Kodak Co, 48-50; res lab technician, 53-55, sr scientist, 55-59, head chem, Phys Methods & Spec Studies Sect, 59-72, mgr anal tech dept, Metal Mining Div Res, 72-78, dir anal serv, Utah Copper Div, 78-80, MGR PROD QUAL PROJS & PROCESS TECHNICIAN, KENNECOTT MINERALS CO, 80- *Mem:* Am Chem Soc; Am Inst Mining, Metall & Petrol Engrs; Sigma Xi. *Res:* Application of infrared and x-ray in process control; application of solar energy for high temperature research; role of catalysis in the oxidation of carbon; quality control in copper production. *Mailing Add:* Kennecott Res Ctr Box 11248 1515 Mineral Square Salt Lake City UT 84147

TUDDENHAM, WILLIAM J, b Salt Lake City, Utah, Nov 15, 22; m 47; c 3. RADIOLOGY, ROENTGENOLOGY. *Educ:* Univ Utah, BA, 43; Univ Pa, MD, 50, MSc, 56; Am Bd Radiol, dipl, 55. *Prof Exp:* Asst biochem, Calif Inst Technol, 43-44; intern, Univ Hosp, 50-51, asst instr, Sch Med, 51-54, instr, 54-56, assoc, 56-57, from asst prof to assoc prof, 57-61, PROF RADIOL, SCH MED, UNIV PA, 61-, DIR DEPT RADIOL, PA HOSP, 62- *Concurrent Pos:* Resident, Univ Hosp, Univ Pa, 51-54, mem staff, 54-67, chief diag sect, 59-61; mem fund lectr, Radiol Soc North Am, 61. *Honors & Awards:* Bronze Medal, Roentgen Ray Soc, 56, Cert Merit, 58; Lindback Award, Univ Pa, 64. *Mem:* Roentgen Ray Soc; Radiol Soc NAm; AMA; Am Col Radiol. *Res:* Visual physiology of roentgen interpretation. *Mailing Add:* Pa Hosp Dept of Radiol Eighth & Spruce Sts Philadelphia PA 19107

TUDOR, DAVID CYRUS, b Wildwood, NJ, May 10, 18; m 41; c 1. POULTRY PATHOLOGY. *Educ:* Rutgers Univ, BS, 40; Univ Pa, VMD, 51. *Prof Exp:* Instr high sch, NJ, 40-44; res asst poultry path, Rutgers Univ, 51-59, assoc res specialist, 59-66, res prof poultry path, 66-78; RETIRED. *Concurrent Pos:* Assoc ed, Poultry Sci, Poultry Sci Asn, 73-75. *Mem:* Am Vet Med Asn; Am Asn Avian Path; US Animal Health Asn; NY Acad Sci; World Poultry Sci. *Res:* Poultry science; infectious nephrosis; Salmonella and chronic respiratory disease; mycoplasma; pox; pet bird diseases; pigeon diseases. *Mailing Add:* 29 Station Rd Cranbury NJ 08512

TUDOR, JAMES R, b Ft Smith, Ark, Mar 26, 22; m 72; c 1. ELECTRICAL ENGINEERING. *Educ:* Univ Mo, BS, 48, MS, 50; Ill Inst Technol, PhD(elec eng), 60. *Prof Exp:* Sr asst engr, Union Elec Co, 50-52; from asst prof to assoc prof elec eng, 52-65, PROF ELEC ENG, UNIV MO-COLUMBIA, 65-, MO ELEC UTILITIES PROF POWER SYSTS ENG, 69- *Concurrent Pos:* Proj dir, Signal Corps, US Army, 56-57 & 58. *Mem:* Inst Elec & Electronics Engrs. *Res:* Transmission lines; energy conversion; electric circuits; power systems; computer control of electric power systems. *Mailing Add:* RD 1 Hallsville MO 65255

TUEL, WILLIAM GOLE, JR, b Indianapolis, Ind, Apr 16, 41. COMPUTER GRAPHICS, DATA BASES. *Educ:* Rensselaer Polytech Inst, BEE, 62, MEE, 64, PhD(elec eng), 65. *Prof Exp:* Mem res staff, 65-76, mgr power syst studies group, 70-72, mgr exp comput studies, 73-76, MEM SCI STAFF, IBM SCI CTR, 76- *Mem:* Inst Elec & Electronics Engrs; Asn Comput Mach. *Res:* Interactive computer graphics for mapping; geographic data bases; electric power system computations and simulation. *Mailing Add:* 6042 Monteverde Dr San Jose CA 95120

TUELLER, PAUL T, b Paris, Idaho, July 30, 34; m 63; c 4. PLANT ECOLOGY, RANGE MANAGEMENT. *Educ:* Idaho State Univ, BS, 57; Univ Nev, MS, 59; Ore State Univ, PhD, 62. *Prof Exp:* From asst prof to assoc prof range sci, 62-73, head, Div Renewable Natural Resources, 80, PROF RANGE SCI, UNIV NEV, RENO, 73- *Mem:* Soc Range Mgt; Soc Am Foresters; Am Soc Photogram. *Res:* Range ecology, especially vegetation-soil relationships; management of big game populations; remote sensing pf renewable natural resources. *Mailing Add:* Div Renewable Natural Resources Univ Nev Reno NV 89512

TUERPE, DIETER ROLF, b Chemnitz, Ger, Dec 29, 40; US citizen; m 79; c 1. ATMOSPHERIC PHYSICS, NUCLEAR PHYSICS. *Educ:* Polytech Inst Brooklyn, BS, 62; Univ Calif, Berkeley, MA, 66; Univ Calif, Davis, PhD(appl sci), 73. *Prof Exp:* Physicist, Lawrence Livermore Lab, 67-80; WITH PHYSICS INT CO, 80- *Mem:* Am Phys Soc. *Res:* Nuclear Hartree-Fock calculation; atmospheric boundary layer models; equations of state; social and economic systems modelling. *Mailing Add:* Physics Int Co 2700 Merced St San Leandro CA 94577

TUESDAY, CHARLES SHEFFIELD, b Trenton, NJ, Sept 7, 27; m 52; c 3. RESEARCH ADMINISTRATION. *Educ:* Hamilton Col, NY, AB, 51; Princeton Univ, MA & PhD(phys chem), 55. *Prof Exp:* Res chemist panelyte div, St Regis Paper Corp, 50-51; res asst, Princeton Univ, 51-55; sr res chemist fuels & lubricants dept, 55-64, supvry res chemist, 64-67, from asst head to head, 67-72, head environ sci dept & actg head phys chem dept, 72-74, TECH DIR, RES LABS, GEN MOTORS CORP, 74- *Concurrent Pos:* Consult vapor-phase org air pollutants panel, Nat Res Coun, 72-76; mem, Air Pollution Res Adv Comt, Coord Res Coun, 70-, chmn, 78-80; mem comt mat substitution methodology, Nat Res Coun, 79-81. *Mem:* AAAS; Am Chem Soc; Soc Automotive Eng. *Res:* Catalysis; corrosion; molecular energy exchange; air pollution control; atmospheric chemistry; polymers; metallurgy; analytical chemistry. *Mailing Add:* Gen Motors Res Labs Warren MI 48090

TUFARIELLO, JOSEPH JAMES, b Brooklyn, NY, Oct 3, 35; m 60; c 4. ORGANIC CHEMISTRY. *Educ:* Queens Col, NY, BS, 57; Univ Wis-Madison, PhD(chem), 62. *Prof Exp:* Assoc org chem, Purdue Univ, Lafayette, 62; NIH fel, Cornell Univ, 62-63; assoc prof, 63-80, PROF ORG CHEM, STATE UNIV NY, BUFFALO, 80- *Mem:* AAAS; Am Chem Soc; The Chem Soc. *Res:* Organic synthesis; synthesis and reactivity of strained or otherwise unique carbocyclic systems; synthesis of natural products; organometallic chemistry; chemistry of 1,3-dipolar compounds. *Mailing Add:* Dept of Chem State Univ of NY Buffalo NY 14214

TUFF, DONALD WRAY, b San Francisco, Calif, May 4, 35; m 55; c 3. PARASITOLOGY, TAXONOMY. *Educ:* San Jose State Col, BA, 57; Wash State Univ, MS, 59; Tex A&M Univ, PhD(entomol), 63. *Prof Exp:* From asst prof to assoc prof biol, 63-73, PROF BIOL, SOUTHWEST TEX STATE UNIV, 73- *Mem:* Entom Soc Am; Soc Syst Zool. *Res:* Taxonomy of avian Mallophaga; parasites of wildlife; medical entomology. *Mailing Add:* Dept of Biol Southwest Tex State Univ San Marcos TX 78666

TUFFEY, THOMAS J, US citizen. ENVIRONMENTAL SCIENCES. *Educ:* Rutgers Univ BS, 68, MS, 72, PhD(environ sci), 73. *Prof Exp:* VPRES RESOURCES ENG, ROY F WESTON, INC, 76- *Concurrent Pos:* Mem fac, Col Eng, Rutgers Univ, 76, vis asst prof, 77. *Res:* Surface water monitoring systems and water quality modeling simulations; nitrogen cycle-nitrication-dentrification; siting, restoration and environmental assessments of lakes and reservoirs; watershed management; land management of waste sludges. *Mailing Add:* Roy F Weston Inc Weston Way West Chester PA 19380

TUFFLY, BARTHOLOMEW LOUIS, b Houston, Tex, Apr 9, 28; m 58; c 3. PHYSICAL CHEMISTRY, ANALYTICAL CHEMISTRY. *Educ:* Univ Tex, BA, 48, MA, 50, PhD(chem), 52. *Prof Exp:* Chemist, Carbide & Carbon Chem Co, 52-60; chemist, Rocketdyne Div, NAm Rockwell Corp, 60-73, CHEMIST, ROCKETDYNE DIV, ROCKWELL INT CORP, 73- *Mem:* Water Pollution Control Fedn. *Res:* Mass spectrometry; pollution; water management; environmental control systems; rocket propellants. *Mailing Add:* 4709 Dunman Ave Woodland Hills CA 91364

TUFT, RICHARD ALLAN, b Newark, NJ, Oct 9, 40; m 63; c 3. QUANTUM OPTICS. *Educ:* Pa State Univ, BS, 63; Mass Inst Technol, MS, 66; Worcester Polytech Inst, PhD(physics), 71. *Prof Exp:* Engr optical physics, Aerospace Syst Div, RCA Corp, 63-68 & 70-71; ASST PROF PHYSICS, WORCESTER POLYTECH INST, 71- *Concurrent Pos:* Consult, Govt & Com Syst Div, RCA Corp, 71- *Mem:* Optical Soc Am; Sigma Xi. *Res:* Experimental investigations in light scattering spectroscopy using photon correlation spectrometer; development of holographic displays and information storage devices. *Mailing Add:* Burnham Rd Bolton MA 01740

TUFTE, MARILYN JEAN, b Iron Mountain, Mich, Nov 20, 39; m 72. BACTERIOLOGY. *Educ:* Northern Mich Univ, AB, 61; Univ Wis, Madison, MS, 65, PhD(bact), 68. *Prof Exp:* Trainee & fel, Univ Wis, Madison, 68; asst prof biol, 68-71, ASSOC PROF BIOL, UNIV WIS-PLATTEVILLE, 71- *Mem:* Am Soc Microbiol. *Res:* Electron microscopic analysis of guinea pig peritoneal phagocytes infected with strains of Brucella abortus of different degrees of virulence. *Mailing Add:* Dept of Biol Univ of Wis Platteville WI 53818

TUFTE, OBERT NORMAN, b Northfield, Minn, May 30, 32; m 56; c 4. SOLID STATE PHYSICS. *Educ:* St Olaf Col, BA, 54; Northwestern Univ, PhD(physics), 60. *Prof Exp:* Asst physics, Northwestern Univ, 54-59; DEPT MGR TECHNOL CTR, HONEYWELL CORP, 60- *Mem:* Am Phys Soc; Inst Elec & Electronics Engrs. *Res:* Semiconductors; electrical and optical properties of solids; solid state devices; integrated circuit technology. *Mailing Add:* Honeywell Corp Technol Ctr 10701 Lyndale Ave Bloomington MN 55420

TUFTS, DONALD WINSTON, b Yonkers, NY, Mar 5, 33; m 56; c 3. ELECTRICAL ENGINEERING. *Educ:* Williams Col, BA, 55; Mass Inst Technol, BS & MS, 58, ScD(elec eng), 60. *Prof Exp:* Asst prof appl math, Harvard Univ, 62-67; PROF ELEC ENG & COMPUT SCI, UNIV RI, 67- *Mem:* AAAS; Inst Elec & Electronics Engrs. *Res:* Information theory; communication theory; computer science; signal processing; underwater sound; data transmission. *Mailing Add:* Dept of Elec Eng Univ of RI Kingston RI 02881

TUGWELL, PETER, b Mar 30, 44; Brit citizen; m 71; c 2. CLINICAL EPIDEMIOLOGY, INTERNAL MEDICINE. *Educ:* Univ London, MBBS, 69, MD, 76; FRCP(C), 76; McMaster Univ, MSc, 77. *Prof Exp:* House officer med, Royal Free & WMiddlesex Hosps, London, 69-70; sr house officer, Whittington Hosp, London, 70-71; res fel & registr, Ahmadu Bello Univ, Nigeria, 71-74; chief resident internal med, 75-76, CLIN EPIDEMIOLOGIST & ATTENDING PHYSICIAN, MCMASTER UNIV, 77-, CHMN, DEPT EPIDEMIOL & BIOSTATISTICS, 79- *Mem:* Royal Col Physicians & Surgeons Can; Soc Epidemiologic Res; Am Rheumatology Asn; Am Asn Clin Res. *Res:* Rheumatology; effectiveness studies; educational evaluation; evaluation of quality of care. *Mailing Add:* McMaster Univ 1200 Main St W Hamilton ON L8S 4J9 Can

TUINSTRA, KENNETH EUGENE, b Des Moines, Iowa, Dec 22, 40; m 63; c 2. ECOLOGY, LIMNOLOGY. *Educ:* Univ Wyo, BS, 62; Mont State Univ, PhD(bot), 67. *Prof Exp:* Res assoc plant ecol, Mont State Univ, 67, Fed Water Pollution Control Admin fel & res assoc limnol, 67-68; asst prof biol, Westmont Col, 68-80; MEM FAC, DEPT BIOL, CENTRAL COL, 80- *Mem:* AAAS; Am Soc Limnol & Oceanog; Ecol Soc Am. *Res:* Ecology of freshwater phytoplankton and zooplankton; population ecology; systems ecology. *Mailing Add:* Dept Biol Central Col Pella IA 50219

TUITE, JOHN F, b New York, NY, Nov 23, 27; m 54; c 6. PHYTOPATHOLOGY. *Educ:* Hunter Col, BA, 51; Univ Minn, MS, 53, PhD(plant path), 56. *Prof Exp:* From asst prof to assoc prof plant path, 56-69, PROF PLANT PATH, PURDUE UNIV, 69- *Mem:* Am Phytopath Soc; Bot Soc Am; Soc Indust Microbiol; Am Asn Cereal Chem; Sigma Xi. *Res:* Identification; ecology of fungi growing on stored grain; production and detection of mycotoxins. *Mailing Add:* Dept Bot & Plant Path Lilly Hall Purdue Univ West Lafayette IN 47907

TUITE, ROBERT JOSEPH, b Rochester, NY, Aug 28, 34; m 58; c 3. RESEARCH MANAGEMENT, PHOTOGRAPHIC CHEMISTRY. *Educ:* St John Fisher Col, BS, 56; Univ Ill, PhD(org chem), 60. *Prof Exp:* Asst chem, Univ Ill, 56-57, asst pub health serv, 59; from res chemist to sr research chemist, 59-67, res assoc res labs, 67-70, head color photo chem lab, 70-73, from head to sr head, Color Reversal Systs Lab, 73-74, asst dir, 74-76, dir Color Photog Div, 76-78, dir Color Instant Photog Div, 78-81, ASST TO THE DIR, RES LABS, EASTMAN KODAK CO, 81- *Mem:* Am Chem Soc; Soc Photog Scientists & Engrs; Soc Motion Picture & TV Engrs. *Res:* Applied photochemistry; color photographic imaging chemistry; color photographic systems design; parametrization of color photographic system response and correlation with molecular structure and other systems variables. *Mailing Add:* Res Labs Eastman Kodak Co Rochester NY 14650

TUITES, DONALD EDGAR, b Saginaw, Mich, Dec 27, 25; m 50; c 4. POLYMER CHEMISTRY. *Educ:* Univ Rochester, BS, 49; Clarkson Tech Univ, MS, 52; Cornell Univ, PhD(org chem), 56. *Prof Exp:* Chemist, NY, 55-63, chemist electrochem dept, Del, 63-71, CHEMIST PLASTICS PROD & RESINS DEPT, E I DU PONT DE NEMOURS & CO, INC, DEL, 72- *Mailing Add:* E I du Pont de Nemours & Co Inc Chestnut Run Wilmington DE 19898

TUITES, RICHARD CLARENCE, b Rochester, NY, Oct 31, 33; m 54; c 4. ORGANIC CHEMISTRY, POLYMER CHEMISTRY. *Educ:* Univ Rochester, BS, 55; Univ Ill, PhD(org chem), 59. *Prof Exp:* Res chemist, E I du Pont de Nemours & Co, Inc, 58-62; from chemist to sr chemist, 62-72, RES ASSOC, EASTMAN KODAK CO, 72- *Mem:* Am Chem Soc; Soc Photog Scientists & Engrs. *Res:* Photographic chemistry. *Mailing Add:* Eastman Kodak Co 1669 Lake Ave Rochester NY 14650

TUKEY, HAROLD BRADFORD, JR, horticulture, see previous edition

TUKEY, JOHN WILDER, b New Bedford, Mass, June 16, 15; m 50. STATISTICS, STATISTICAL ANALYSIS. *Educ:* Brown Univ, ScB, 36, ScM, 37; Prineton Univ, MA, 38, PhD(math), 39. *Hon Degrees:* ScD, Case Inst Technol, 62, Brown Univ, 65, Yale Univ, 68 & Univ Chicago, 69. *Prof Exp:* Instr math, Princeton Univ, 39-41, res assoc, Fire Control Res Off, 41-45; mem tech staff, 45-58, asst dir res commun prin, 58-61, ASSOC EXEC DIR RES COMMUN PRIN DIV, BELL LABS, 61-; PROF STATIST, PRINCETON UNIV, 65-, DONNER PROF SCI, 76- *Concurrent Pos:* From asst prof to prof math, Princeton Univ, 41-65, chmn dept statist, 65-70; Guggenheim fel, 49-50; fel, Ctr Advan Study Behav Sci, 57-58; visitor, Commonwealth Sci & Indust Res Orgn, Canberra, Australia, 71 & Stanford Linear Accelerator Ctr, Calif, 72. Mem, US deleg, Tech Working Group 2 of Conf on Discontinuance of Nuclear Weapon Tests, Geneva, Switz, 59 & UN Conf on Human Environ, Stockholm, Sweden, 72; mem, President's Sci Adv Comt, Off Sci & Technol, 60-63, chmn, Panel on Environ Pollution, 64-65 & Panel on Chem & Health, 71-72; mem, President's Air Qual Adv Bd, 68-71 & President's Comn on Fed Statist, 70-71; mem, Sci Info Coun, NSF, 62-64; chmn anal adv comt, Nat Assessment Educ Progress, 63-73 & chmn sci panel of anal adv comt, 73-; mem coun, Nat Acad Sci, 69-71, chmn class III, 69-72 & chmn climatic impact comt, 75-; mem, Nat Adv Comt for Oceans & Atmosphere, 75- *Honors & Awards:* S S Wilks Medal, Am Statist Asn, 65; Nat Medal of Sci, 73; Hitchcock Prof, Univ Calif, Berkeley, 75. *Mem:* Nat Acad Sci; Am Philos Soc; Am Acad Arts & Sci; Int Statist Inst; hon mem Royal Statist Soc. *Res:* Theoretical, applied and mathematical statistics; point set topology; fire control equipment; military analysis. *Mailing Add:* Dept Statist Princeton Univ Princeton NJ 08544

TUKEY, LOREN DAVENPORT, b Geneva, NY, Dec 4, 21; m 52; c 2. HORTICULTURE. *Educ:* Mich State Univ, BS, 43, MS, 47; Ohio State Univ, PhD(hort), 52. *Prof Exp:* Asst hort, Ohio State Univ, 47-50; asst prof & assoc prof pomol, 50-66, PROF POMOL, PA STATE UNIV, 66- *Concurrent Pos:* Mem coop fruit res prog, Inst Nat Tech Agr, Argentina, 65-70; assoc ed, J Hort Sci, Eng; ed, Pa State Hort Reviews. *Mem:* Fel AAAS; fel Am Soc Hort Sci; Bot Soc Am; Am Soc Plant Physiol; fel Royal Hort Soc. *Res:* Pomology; growth and development-plant growth regulators; plant-environmental relationships; phyto-engineering. *Mailing Add:* 103 Tyson Bldg Dept Hort Pa State Univ University Park PA 16802

TUKEY, RONALD BRADFORD, b Hudson, NY, July 19, 24; m 51; c 6. POMOLOGY. *Educ:* Mich State Col, BS, 47, MS, 48; Cornell Univ, PhD(pomol), 52. *Prof Exp:* Asst pomol, NY State Agr Exp Sta, Geneva, 48-50; from asst prof to assoc prof hort, Purdue Univ, 50-65; EXTEN HORTICULTURIST, WASH STATE UNIV, 65- *Concurrent Pos:* Vis lectr, Guerrero, Mex, 78; orchard consult, 57- *Mem:* Am Pomol Soc; Am Soc Hort Sci; Int Soc Hort Sci. *Res:* Tree fruit physiology, especially dwarfing, nutrition, performance, soil management and irrigation, tree adaptation, appraisal, orchard management and economics. *Mailing Add:* Dept of Hort Wash State Univ Pullman WA 99163

TULAGIN, VSEVOLOD, b Leningrad, Russia, June 16, 14; US citizen; m 38. CHEMISTRY. *Educ:* Calif Inst Technol, BS, 37; Univ Calif, Los Angeles, MA, 41, PhD(chem), 43. *Prof Exp:* Chemist, Wesco Water Paints, Inc, Calif, 37-39; Nat Defense Res Comt asst, Univ Calif, Los Angeles, 42-43; res chemist, Gen Aniline & Film Corp, Pa, 43-47, group leader, 47-52, res specialist & group leader, Ansco Div, 52-57; res supvr, Minn Mining & Mfg Co, 57-60, mgr res photo prod, 60-66; res mgr, Xerox Corp, 66-69, chief scientist, 69-77; RETIRED. *Honors & Awards:* Kosar Mem Award, Soc Photog Sci & Eng. *Mem:* Am Chem Soc; Soc Photog Sci & Eng. *Res:* Paint technology; chemical synthesis; color photography; polychrome photoelectrophoresis. *Mailing Add:* 106 E Olive CT Rte 3 Pine Knoll Shores Morehead City NC 28557

TULCZYJEW, WLODZIMIERZ MAREK, b Wlodawa, Poland, June 18, 31; m 75. MATHEMATICAL PHYSICS. *Educ:* Univ Warsaw, MS, 56, PhD(physics), 59, DSc, 65. *Prof Exp:* From instr to assoc prof physics, Univ Warsaw, 56-68; assoc prof, 69-77, PROF MATH, UNIV CALGARY, 78- *Concurrent Pos:* Brit Coun fel, Imp Col, Univ London, 59-60; vis asst prof, Lehigh Univ, 60-61; US NSF sr foreign scientist fel, Boston Univ, 66; vis prof, Univ Paris, 74-75, Max Planck Inst, Munich, 76-78, Max Plank Inst, Starnberg, 76; Heinrich-Hertz-Stifting fel, Univ Bonn, 77, NATO & Consiglio Nazionale Delle Richerche Professorships, Univ Torino, 77-81. *Mem:* Int Soc Gen Relativity & Gravitation; Am Math Soc; NY Acad Sci; Italian Math Union. *Res:* Differential geometry applied to physics and the calculus of variations. *Mailing Add:* Dept Math & Statist Univ Calgary Calgary AB T2N 1N4 Can

TULECKE, WALTER, b Detroit, Mich, Feb 10, 24; m 78; c 4. BOTANY. *Educ:* Univ Mich, BA, 46, MS, 50, PhD(bot, 53. *Prof Exp:* Asst prof bot, Ariz State Col, 53-55; res assoc, Brooklyn Bot Garden, 55-57; res botanist, Chas Pfizer & Co, 57-59; assoc plant physiologist, Boyce Thompson Inst, 59-67; PROF BIOL, ANTIOCH COL, 67- *Mem:* AAAS; Bot Soc Am; Am Inst Biol Sci; Soc Econ Bot. *Res:* Plant science and nutrition. *Mailing Add:* Dept of Biol Antioch Col Yellow Springs OH 45387

TULEEN, DAVID L, b Oak Park, Ill, Sept 19, 36; m 60; c 4. ORGANIC CHEMISTRY. *Educ:* Wittenberg Univ, BS, 58; Univ Ill, PhD(org chem), 62. *Prof Exp:* Fel, Pa State Univ, 62-63; asst prof, 63-68, ASSOC PROF ORG CHEM, VANDERBILT UNIV, 68- *Mem:* Am Chem Soc; Royal Soc Chem. *Res:* Sulfur chemistry. *Mailing Add:* Dept Chem Vanderbilt Univ Box 1613 Sta B Nashville TN 37203

TULENKO, JAMES STANLEY, b Holyoke, Mass, June 1, 36; m 65; c 3. NUCLEAR PHYSICS, APPLIED MATHEMATICS. *Educ:* Harvard Univ, BA, 58, MA, 60; Mass Inst Technol, MS, 63; George Washington Univ, MBA, 80. *Prof Exp:* Mgr nuclear develop, United Nuclear Corp, NY, 63-70; mgr physics, Nuclear Mat & Equip Corp, 70-71; mgr physics, Nuclear Power Generation Div, 71-74, MGR NUCLEAR FUEL ENG, BABCOCK & WILCOX, 74- *Concurrent Pos:* Adj prof systs anal, George Washington Univ. *Mem:* Fel Am Nuclear Soc. *Res:* Mechanical and material design nuclear fuel; thermal hydraulic behavior of nuclear cores; reactor physics; fuel management of nuclear reactors; fuel cycle economics of nuclear power plants; plutonium recycle in thermal water reactors. *Mailing Add:* Babcock & Wilcox PO Box 1260 Lynchburg VA 24505

TULENKO, THOMAS NORMAN, b Pittsburgh, Pa, Dec 2, 42; m 73; c 1. VASCULAR DISEASE, HYPERTENISON RESEARCH. *Educ:* Grove City Col, BS, 66; Duquesne Univ, MS, 68; Botson Univ, 72. *Prof Exp:* Lectr biol, Gwynedd Mercy Col, 74-76; instr physiol, Sch Med, Temple Univ, 75-77; ASST PROF OBSTET & GYNEC, MED COL PA, 81-, ASSOC PROF PHYSIOL, 82- *Concurrent Pos:* Dir, City-Wide Bd Rev, 81-; consult, McGraw-Hill Pub, 81- *Mem:* Am Physiol Soc; AAAS. *Res:* Regulation of arterial activity in human blood vessels and the nature of their involvement in various disease states; atherosclerosis, certain forms of hypertension intrauterine growth retardation; utilizes physiological, pharmacological and biochemical techniques; author or coauthor of 25 publications. *Mailing Add:* Dept Physiol & Biochem Med Col Pa Philadelphia PA 19129

TULER, FLOYD ROBERT, b Chicago, Ill, May 24, 39; m 61; c 2. MATERIALS SCIENCE. *Educ:* Univ Ill, Urbana, BS, 60, MS, 62; Cornell Univ, PhD(mat sci & eng), 67. *Prof Exp:* Tech staff mem stress wave response-solids, Sandia Labs, 66-69; vpres tech dynamic response mat, Effects Technol Inc, 69-74; ASSOC PROF MAT SCI, HEBREW UNIV, ISRAEL, 74- *Concurrent Pos:* Panel mem nat mat adv bd ad hoc comt, Nat Acad Sci, 68-69. *Mem:* Am Soc Testing & Mat; Sigma Xi. *Res:* Mechanical properties of metals and reinforced composite materials; fracture; fatigue initiation and propagation; impact and impulsive loading; mechanical testing and nondestructive testing techniques; failure prediction and analysis. *Mailing Add:* Sch Appl Sci & Technol Mat Sci Div Hebrew Univ Jerusalem Israel

TULI, JAGDISH KUMAR, b India, Aug 7, 41; US citizen; m 75; c 2. NUCLEAR SPECTROSCOPY. *Educ:* Delhi Univ, MS, 65; Ind Univ, MS, 69, PhD(physics), 71. *Prof Exp:* Res assoc, Nat Acad Sci, Ind Univ, 71-73; physicist, Dept Atomic Energy, India, 73-75, Lawrence Berkeley Lab, 76-77; PHYSICIST, BROOKHAVEN NAT LAB, 77- *Concurrent Pos:* Ed, Nuclear Data Sheets, 81- *Mem:* Am Phys Soc. *Mailing Add:* Brookhaven Nat Lab Bldg 197D Upton NY 11973

TULIN, LEONARD GEORGE, b Mozyr, Russia, May 20, 20; US citizen; m 48; c 1. STRUCTURAL MECHANICS. *Educ:* Univ Colo, BSCE, 50, MSCE, 52; Iowa State Univ, PhD(theoret & appl mech), 65. *Prof Exp:* From instr to assoc prof, 50-61, chmn dept, 72-77, PROF CIVIL ENG, UNIV COLO, BOULDER, 61- *Honors & Awards:* Wason Award, Am Concrete Inst, 64. *Mem:* Am Soc Civil Engrs; Am Concrete Inst; Am Soc Testing & Mat; Soc Exp Stress Anal. *Res:* Mechanics and materials; cyclic loading of concrete; creep of concrete and rock; triaxial response of concrete, coal and coal measure rock. *Mailing Add:* Dept of Civil & Environ Eng Univ of Colo Eng Ctr Boulder CO 80309

TULIN, MARSHALL P(ETER), b Hartford, Conn, Mar 14, 26; m 55; c 2. HYDRODYNAMICS. *Educ:* Mass Inst Technol, BS, 46, MS, 59. *Prof Exp:* Aeronaut res scientist, Nat Adv Comt Aeronaut, 46-50; physicist & head turbulence & frictional sect, David W Taylor Model Basin, US Dept Navy, 50-54, aeronaut res engr, Mech Br, Off Naval Res, 54-57, sci liaison officer, London Br Off, 57-59; vpres & dir, 59-71, CHIEF EXEC OFFICER & BD CHMN, HYDRONAUTICS, INC, 71- *Concurrent Pos:* Bd chmn, Hydronautics-Israel, Ltd. *Honors & Awards:* Meritorious Civilian Serv Award, US Dept Navy, 57. *Mem:* Am Geophys Union; NY Acad Sci. *Res:* Supercavitating, turbulent, stratified and polymer flows; hydrofoil and propeller theory; wakes. *Mailing Add:* Hydronautics Inc Pindell School Rd Laurel MD 20810

TULINSKY, ALEXANDER, b Philadelphia, Pa, Sept 25, 28; m 55; c 4. STRUCTURAL CHEMISTRY. *Educ:* Temple Univ, AB, 52; Princeton Univ, PhD(chem), 56. *Prof Exp:* Res assoc, Protein Struct Proj, Polytech Inst Brooklyn, 55-59; asst prof chem, Yale Univ, 59-65; assoc prof chem, 65-67, assoc prof biochem, 67, prof biochem, 68-73, PROF CHEM, MICH STATE UNIV, 68- *Concurrent Pos:* Alberta Heritage Found vis scientist award, Univ Calgary, 81; vis prof chem, Univ SC, Columbia, 82. *Mem:* Am Crystallog Asn; Am Chem Soc. *Res:* X-ray crystallographic structure determination of biological molecules; structure and function of enzymes; chymotrypsiu, aldolases, blood clotting proteins, ribonuclease T1, progesterone receptor. *Mailing Add:* Dept of Chem Mich State Univ East Lansing MI 48824

TULIP, THOMAS HUNT, b Anchorage, Alaska, Nov 16, 52; m 78. ORGANOTRANSITION METAL CHEMISTRY. *Educ:* Univ Vt, BS, 74; Northwestern Univ, MS, 75, PhD(chem), 78. *Prof Exp:* RES CHEMIST, CENT RES & DEVELOP, E I DU PONT DE NEMOURS & CO, INC, 78- *Mem:* Am Chem Soc. *Res:* Interactions of small organic molecules with transition metal centers; synthesis and characterization of novel complexes and the examination of their reactivity patterns; homogeneous catalysis. *Mailing Add:* Cent Res & Develop Dept E I Du Pont de Nemours & Co Inc Wilmington DE 19898

TULIS, JERRY JOHN, microbiology, immunology, see previous edition

TULK, ALEXANDER STUART, b Hamilton, Ont, Feb 25, 18; m 46; c 4. APPLIED CHEMISTRY. *Educ:* McMaster Univ, BSc, 44, MSc, 45; Pa State Univ, PhD(inorg chem), 51. *Prof Exp:* Lectr, McMaster Univ, 45-47; asst, Pa State Univ, 47-50; sr engr, 50-52, engr in-chg, 52-55, adv develop engr, 55-56, eng specialist, 56-57, eng mgr, 57-67, eng mgr inorg mat, 67-71, sr eng specialist, Electronic Mat, 71-73, SR ENG SPECIALIST, SPEC PROJ, GTE PRODS CORP, 73- *Honors & Awards:* Sullivan Award, Am Chem Soc, 74. *Mem:* Am Chem Soc; Electrochem Soc; Chem Inst Can. *Res:* Chemical warfare; photosensitive materials; liquid bright gold; fluorocarbon chemistry; electroplating of precious metals; germanium; silicon and gallium arsenide preparation; semiconductor measurements; chemistry of tungsten, molybdenum, rare earths, tantalum and niobium. *Mailing Add:* 510 Poplar St Towanda PA 18848

TULL, JACK PHILLIP, b Jackson, Mich, Dec 2, 30; m 52; c 3. MATHEMATICS. *Educ:* Univ Ill, PhD(math), 57. *Prof Exp:* From instr to asst prof, 56-61, ASSOC PROF MATH, OHIO STATE UNIV, 61- *Concurrent Pos:* Vis sr lectr, Univ Adelaide, 63-64; prof & head dept, Univ Zambia, 70-71, dean humanities & social sci, 71. *Mem:* Am Math Soc; Math Asn Am; London Math Soc. *Res:* Analytic theory of numbers. *Mailing Add:* Dept of Math Ohio State Univ Columbus OH 43210

TULL, JAMES FRANKLIN, b New York, NY, May 26, 47; m 67; c 2. STRUCTURAL GEOLOGY, GEOTECTONICS. *Educ:* Univ NC, BS, 69; Rice Univ, PhD(geol), 73. *Prof Exp:* Asst prof geol, Univ Ala, 73-78, assoc prof, 78-81; ASSOC PROF GEOL, FLA STATE UNIV, 81- *Concurrent Pos:* Consult, Geol Survey Ala, 75-76, E I du Pont de Nemours & Co, Inc, 78-, Amoco Petrol Co, 81 & Champlin Petrol Co, 81. *Mem:* Geol Soc Am; Geol Soc Norway. *Res:* Structural evolution of mountain systems, particularly the development of metamorphic and igneous terraines; studying metamorphism associated with orogenesis and relationships between structural and metamorphic events. *Mailing Add:* Dept Geol Fla State Univ Tallahassee FL 32306

TULL, ROBERT GORDON, b Jackson, Mich, May 1, 29; m 52; c 4. ASTRONOMY. *Educ:* Univ Ill, BS, 52, MS, 57; Univ Mich, PhD(astron), 63. *Prof Exp:* Res scientist, 61, from instr to asst prof, 62-70, RES SCIENTIST ASTRON, UNIV TEX, AUSTIN, 70- *Concurrent Pos:* NSF grants, 63-66, 74-78 & 78-82; mem high resolution spectrograph instrument definition team, NASA Large Space Telescope, 73-76; consult, Electronic Vision Co Div of Sci Appln Inc, 74-; consult Europ Southern Observ, 78-; consult, Asiago Observ, Italy & Wise Observ, Israel, 75-; vis scientist, Chinese Acad Sci, 81; mem, Steering Comt, Nat New Technol Telescope, 81- *Mem:* AAAS; Am Astron Soc; Int Astron Union; Optical Soc Am. *Res:* photoelectric spectrophotometry of astronomical sources; astronomical instrumentation; development and application of multi-channel image detectors for astronomical spectrophotometry; design of large telescopes. *Mailing Add:* Dept of Astron Univ of Tex Austin TX 78712

TULLER, ANNITA, b New York, NY, Dec 30, 10; m 38; c 2. MATHEMATICS. *Educ:* Hunter Col, BA, 29; Bryn Mawr Col, MA, 30, PhD(math), 37. *Prof Exp:* Substitute math, Hunter Col, 30-31; teacher high sch, NY, 31-35; from tutor to assoc prof math, Hunter Col, 37-68; prof, 68-71, EMER PROF MATH, LEHMAN COL, 71- *Mem:* AAAS; Am Math Soc; Hist Sci Soc; Math Asn Am. *Res:* Differential geometry; ergodic theory. *Mailing Add:* 139-62 Pershing Crescent Jamaica NY 11435

TULLIER, PETER MARSHALL, JR, b New Orleans, La, Aug 15, 16; m 43; c 9. OPERATIONS RESEARCH, SYSTEMS ANALYSIS. *Educ:* Loyola Univ, New Orleans, BS, 38; La State Univ, Baton Rouge, MS, 40. *Prof Exp:* Instr high sch, La, 40-41; from instr to asst prof math, Loyola Univ, 45-52;

mathematician, Dept Geophys, Calif Co, 52-53; assoc prof math, Southwestern La Inst, 53-60; opers anal, Naval Sci Dept, US Naval Acad, 60-67; opers analyst, Pac Tech Analysts, Inc, 67-71; dir opers res, Southeast Asia Comput Assocs, 71-74; PRIN ANALYST, OPERS RES, INC, 74- *Concurrent Pos:* Consult, Electronic Compatibility Anal Ctr, res analyst, Mathematica, 76, logistics res analyst, Ketron, 79; lectr math, Univ Md Far East Div, Saigon; lectr systs anal for Vietnamese analysts, Comput Ctr, Govt Vietnam; sr staff analyst, Innovation Resources, 81. *Mem:* Opers Res Soc Am. *Res:* Computer software marketing; management information systems and design; data processing in developing countries. *Mailing Add:* 39 Murray Ave Annapolis MD 21401

TULLIO, VICTOR, b Philadelphia, Pa, May 29, 27; m 51; c 2. CHEMISTRY. *Educ:* Univ Pa, BS, 48; Univ Ill, PhD(org chem), 51. *Prof Exp:* Asst, Univ Ill, 48-49; res chemist, 51-61, supvr new dye eval, 64-69, tech asst textile dyes, 69-71, supvr new dye eval, 71-72, SR RES CHEMIST, E I DU PONT DE NEMOURS & CO, INC, 72- *Mem:* Am Asn Textile Chemists & Colorists; Am Chem Soc. *Res:* Organic chemistry; dyes; dyeing of synthetic fibers. *Mailing Add:* 1304 Chadwick Rd Wilmington DE 19803

TULLIS, J PAUL, b Ogden, Utah, July 24, 38; m 58; c 4. CIVIL ENGINEERING. *Educ:* Utah State Univ, BS, 61, PhD(civil eng), 66. *Prof Exp:* Gen contractor commercial construct, Paul & Milo Tullis Gen Contractors, 61-63; asst prof civil eng, Colo State Univ, 66-70, assoc prof, 70-80; PROF CIVIL ENG, UTAH WATER RES LAB, UTAH STATE UNIV, 80- *Res:* Cavitation research, viscous drag reduction and hydraulic modeling. *Mailing Add:* Utah Water Res Lab UMC 82 Utah State Univ Logan UT 84322

TULLIS, JAMES EARL, b Cincinnati, Ohio. GENETICS. *Educ:* Miami Univ, BS, 51; Ohio State Univ, MS, 54, PhD(genetics), 61. *Prof Exp:* Instr zool, Ohio Univ, 56-59; asst prof, Wash State Univ, 61-65; asst prof, 65-71, ASSOC PROF, IDAHO STATE UNIV, 71- *Mem:* AAAS; Genetics Soc Am. *Mailing Add:* Dept of Biol Idaho State Univ Pocatello ID 83209

TULLIS, JAMES LYMAN, b Newark, Ohio, June 22, 14; m 37; c 4. BIOCHEMISTRY. *Educ:* Duke Univ, MD, 40; Am Bd Internal Med, dipl, 48. *Prof Exp:* Intern med, Roosevelt Hosp, New York, 40-41, sr intern & resident physician, 41-42; from assoc dir to dir blood characterization & preservation lab, 51-55, RES ASSOC BIOCHEM, HARVARD MED SCH, 54-, SR INVESTR, PROTEIN FOUND, 56-, DIR CYTOL LABS, 60-, PROF MED, 75- *Concurrent Pos:* Donner Found res fel, Harvard Med Sch, 45-48; asst, Peter Bent Brigham Hosp, Boston, 46-50, assoc, 55-58, sr assoc, 58-; attend physician, West Roxbury Vet Admin Hosp, 48-; attend physician & hematologist, New Eng Deaconess Hosp, 49-, chief hemat & chemother clin, 57-, chmn gen med div, 60-, chmn dept med, 64-; consult, Panel Mil & Field Med, Div Med Sci, Res & Develop Bd, US Secy Defense, 52-54; consult, Cambridge City Hosp, 54-60; vpres & treas, Int Cong Hemat, 55-56; assoc clin prof med, Harvard Med Sch, 70-75. *Honors & Awards:* Glycerol Producers Award, 57; Hektoen Medal, AMA, 58; Katsunuma Award, Int Soc Hemat, 59. *Mem:* Fel Am Soc Hemat (pres, 58-59); fel AMA; fel Am Col Physicians; fel NY Acad Sci; Int Soc Hemat (vpres, 56-58, secy gen, western hemisphere, 58-). *Res:* Chemical interactions between blood cells and plasma proteins. *Mailing Add:* 110 Francis St Boston MA 02215

TULLIS, JULIA ANN, b Swedesboro, NJ, Feb 21, 43; m 65. GEOLOGY. *Educ:* Carleton Col, AB, 65; Univ Calif, Los Angeles, PhD(geol), 71. *Prof Exp:* Res asst geol, Inst Geophys, Univ Calif, Los Angeles, 69-70; asst res prof, 71-77, assoc res prof, 77-79, PROF, DEPT GEOL SCI, BROWN UNIV, 79- *Mem:* Am Geophys Union; Mineral Soc Am. *Res:* Experimental rock deformation; deformation mechanisms of crustal rocks and minerals. *Mailing Add:* Dept of Geol Sci Brown Univ Providence RI 02912

TULLIS, RICHARD EUGENE, b Long Beach, Calif, Apr 26, 36; m 62; c 3. COMPARATIVE PHYSIOLOGY, COMPARATIVE ENDOCRINOLOGY. *Educ:* Univ Wash, BS, 63; Univ Hawaii, MS, 68, PhD(zool), 72. *Prof Exp:* Res asst, Univ Hawaii, 70-71; asst prof, 72-76, assoc prof, 76-81, PROF PHYSIOL, CALIF STATE UNIV, HAYWARD, 81- *Concurrent Pos:* Partic guest, Biomed Div, Lawrence Livermore Lab, 73-; NSF sci equip grant, 74. *Mem:* Sigma Xi; Am Soc Zoologists; AAAS. *Res:* Neuroendocrine control of hydromineral regulation in crustaceans including isolation of neuroendocrine substances, enzyme regulation mechanisms and target organ identification; basic physiological invertebrate functions affected by environmental and man-made substances. *Mailing Add:* Dept of Biol Sci Calif State Univ Hayward CA 94542

TULLIS, TERRY EDSON, b Rapid City, SDak, July 21, 42; m 65. STRUCTURAL GEOLOGY, GEOPHYSICS. *Educ:* Carleton Col, AB, 64; Univ Calif, Los Angeles, MS, 67, PhD(struct geol), 71. *Prof Exp:* Actg instr geol, Univ Calif, Los Angeles, 69-70; asst prof, 70-76, ASSOC PROF GEOL, BROWN UNIV, 76- *Concurrent Pos:* Sloan res fel, Brown Univ, 73-75; vis fel res, Sch Earth Sci, Australian Nat Univ, 76; geologist, US Geol Surv, 77. *Mem:* Am Geophys Union; Geol Soc Am; AAAS. *Res:* Experimental rock deformation; tectonophysics; plate tectonics; origin of slaty cleavage and schistosity; thermodynamic systems under nonhydrostatic stress; rheology of rocks at high temperature and pressure; study of in situ stress; rock friction. *Mailing Add:* Dept of Geol Sci Brown Univ Providence RI 02912

TULLOCH, ALEXANDER PATRICK, b Garelochhead, Scotland, Nov 27, 27; m 57; c 4. ORGANIC CHEMISTRY. *Educ:* Univ Glasgow, BSc, 49, PhD(chem), 55, DSc, 72. *Prof Exp:* Tech off org chem, Imp Chem Industs, Ltd, 54-58; fel, 56-57, asst res off, 58-62, assoc res off, 62-69, SR RES OFF, FATS & OILS LAB, PRAIRIE REGIONAL LAB, NAT RES COUN CAN, 69- *Mem:* Am Oil Chemists Soc. *Res:* Organic chemistry of lipids; gas chromatography of fats and waxes; nuclear magnetic resonance spectroscopy; synthesis of specifically dentrated fatty acids. *Mailing Add:* Prairie Regional Lab Nat Res Coun Can Saskatoon SK S7N 0W9 Can

TULLOCH, GEORGE SHERLOCK, b Bridgewater, Mass, Aug 3, 06; m 31; c 2. PARASITOLOGY. *Educ:* Mass Col, BS, 28; Harvard Univ, MS, 29, PhD(entom), 31. *Prof Exp:* Asst biol, Harvard Univ, 28-31; from instr to prof, 32-65, EMER PROF BIOL, BROOKLYN COL, 65-; RES DIR, GEORGE S TULLOCH & ASSOCS, 70- *Concurrent Pos:* Asst, Radcliffe Col, 29-30; assoc entomologist, PR Insect Pest Surv, 35-36; chief entomologist, State Mosquito Surv, Mass, 39; Rockefeller Found fel, Brazil, 40-41; consult, Arctic Aeromed Lab, US Air Force, 54-55, res scientist, 65-67; vis prof, Univ Queensland, 61; res scientist, US Air Force Sch Aerospace Med, 67-69; vis investr, Southwest Found Res & Educ, Tex, 70-; consult, Dept Path & Labs, Nassau County Med Ctr, NY, 71- *Mem:* AAAS; Am Soc Parasitol; Entom Soc Am. *Res:* Arthropod carried and parasitic diseases of man and animals; life cycle and therapy of canine dirofilariasis; collection of parasitic antigens for skin tests. *Mailing Add:* 6146 Sunset Haven San Antonio TX 78249

TULLOCK, ROBERT JOHNS, b Atascadero, Calif, Oct 3, 40; m 62; c 3. SOIL CHEMISTRY. *Educ:* Calif State Polytech Col, San Luis Obispo, BS, 67; Purdue Univ, West Lafayette, MS, 70, PhD(soil chem), 72. *Prof Exp:* Asst prof soil sci, Univ Calif, Riverside, 72-73; asst prof soil sci, Ore State Univ, 74-76; ASST PROF SOIL SCI, CALIF STATE POLYTECH UNIV, POMONA, 76- *Mem:* Am Soc Agron; Soil Sci Soc Am; Clay Minerals Soc. *Res:* Physicochemical properties of colloidal surfaces. *Mailing Add:* Dept of Soil Sci Calif State Polytech Univ Pomona CA 91768

TULLY, EDWARD JOSEPH, JR, b Brooklyn, NY, Jan 22, 30. MATHEMATICS. *Educ:* Fordham Univ, AB, 51, MS, 52; Tulane Univ, PhD(math), 60. *Prof Exp:* Instr math, St John's Univ, Minn, 56-57; asst, Tulane Univ, 57-60; NSF fel, Calif Inst Technol, 60-61; lectr, Univ Calif, Los Angeles, 61-63; lectr, 63-64, asst prof, 64-68, ASSOC PROF MATH, UNIV CALIF, DAVIS, 68- *Mem:* Am Math Soc; Math Asn Am. *Res:* Algebraic theory of semigroups; ordered algebraic systems; application of algebra to linguistics. *Mailing Add:* Dept of Math Univ of Calif Davis CA 95616

TULLY, FRANK PAUL, b Hartford, Conn, Apr 27, 46; m 74, 81. PHYSICAL CHEMISTRY. *Educ:* Clark Univ, BA, 68; Univ Chicago, MS, 69, PhD(chem), 73. *Prof Exp:* Res asst chem, Clark Univ, 65-68; res asst, Univ Chicago, 68-73; fel, Univ Toronto, 73-74; NSF fel chem, Mich State Univ, East Lansing, 74-76; mem fac eng exp sta, Appl Sci Div, Ga Inst Technol, 76-80; MEM TECH STAFF, SANDIA NAT LABS, LIVERMORE, CALIF, 80- *Concurrent Pos:* NSF energy related fel, 75. *Mem:* Am Phys Soc. *Res:* Use of the crossed molecular beam method in studies of elastic, inelastic and reactive scattering; photoconization; gas-phase reaction kinetics; laser photochemistry. *Mailing Add:* Sandia Nat Labs Livermore CA 94550

TULLY, JOHN CHARLES, b New York, NY, May 17, 42; m 71. CHEMICAL PHYSICS. *Educ:* Yale Univ, BS, 64; Univ Chicago, PhD(chem), 68. *Prof Exp:* NSF fel chem, Univ Colo, 68-69 & Yale Univ, 69-70; MEM TECH STAFF, BELL LABS, 70- *Concurrent Pos:* Vis prof chem, Princeton Univ, 81-82. *Mem:* Am Chem Soc; Am Phys Soc. *Res:* Theory of chemical rate processes, molecular collisions and gas-surface interactions. *Mailing Add:* Bell Labs Murray Hill NJ 07974

TULLY, JOHN PATRICK, b Brandon, Man, Nov 29, 06; m 38; c 3. OCEANOGRAPHY. *Educ:* Univ Man, BSc, 31; Univ Wash, Seattle, PhD(oceanog chem), 48. *Prof Exp:* Sci asst chem, Fisheries Res Bd Can, 31-36, hydrog, 36-46, oceanogr-in-chg, Pac Oceanog Group, 46-65, oceanog consult, 66-69; consult, 69-75; RETIRED. *Concurrent Pos:* Hon lectr, Univ BC, 50-53. *Honors & Awards:* Mem, Order of Brit Empire, 46; Commemorative Medal, Albert I of Monaco, 67, 70. *Mem:* AAAS (pres western div, 63); Am Soc Limnol & Oceanog; Am Geophys Union; Royal Soc Can. *Res:* Oceanographic chemistry; seawater structure; estuarine mechanisms; physical and chemical processes and submarine acoustics. *Mailing Add:* 2740 Fandell Ave Nanaimo BC V9S 393 Can

TULLY, JOSEPH GEORGE, JR, b Sterling, Colo, July 14, 25; m 57; c 1. MEDICAL MICROBIOLOGY. *Educ:* Portland Univ, BS, 49; Brigham Young Univ, MS, 51; Cincinnati Univ, PhD(microbiol), 55. *Hon Degrees:* Dr, Univ Bordeaux, France, 80. *Prof Exp:* Asst prof microbiol, Col Med, Cincinnati Univ, 55-57; microbiologist, Walter Reed Army Inst Res, 57-61, chief, Dept Microbiol, 61-62; res microbiologist, 62-68, HEAD MYCOPLASMA SECT, NAT INST ALLERGY & INFECTIOUS DIS, 68- *Concurrent Pos:* China med bd fel, Cent Am, 56; attend microbiologist, Cincinnati Gen Hosp, Ohio, 56-57; mem bd, Food & Agr Orgn/WHO Prog on Comp Mycoplasmology, 69-78, chmn bd, 72-77; mem, Int Subcomt Taxon of Mycoplasmatales, 70-; chmn, Int Org Mycoplasmology, 75-78; mem adv bd, Bergey's Mgt Syst Bacteriol, 80-81. *Mem:* Fel AAAS; Am Asn Immunol; fel Am Acad Microbiol; Am Soc Microbiol; Soc Exp Biol & Med. *Res:* Bacillary dysentery; immunology and pathogenesis of enteric diseases; typhoid infection in primates; basic biology of the mycoplasmas; murine mycoplasmas; spiroplasmas. *Mailing Add:* Mycoplasma Sec Nat Inst Allergy & Infectious Dis Bldg 550 Frederick Cancer Res Ctr Frederick MD 21701

TULLY, PHILIP C(OCHRAN), b Grand Island, Nebr, Jan 11, 23; m 45; c 4. CHEMICAL & NUCLEAR ENGINEERING. *Educ:* Iowa State Univ, BS, 47; Univ Pittsburgh, MS, 55; Okla State Univ, PhD(chem eng), 65. *Prof Exp:* Process engr, Plastics Div, Koppers Co, Inc, 47-54, mgr training, 54-56, asst prod supt polyethylene, 56-59, chief plant engr, 59-61; asst chem eng, Okla State Univ, 61-64; proj leader, Phase Equilibrium, Helium Res Ctr, 64-71, chem engr, Tech Servs Unit, Helium Opers, 71-76, HELIUM TECHNOLOGIST, HELIUM OPERS, US BUR MINES, 76- *Mem:* Am Chem Soc; Am Inst Chem Engrs. *Res:* Cryogenic, high pressure phase equilibria research and physical properties determinations on helium bearing systems. *Mailing Add:* Rte 4 Box 10 Amarillo TX 79119

TULSKY, EMANUEL GOODEL, b Philadelphia, Pa, Dec 6, 23; m 50; c 2. RADIOLOGY. *Educ:* Jefferson Med Col, MD, 48. *Prof Exp:* Attend radiologist, Delafield Hosp, New York, 52-53; assoc radiologist, Sch Med & Univ Hosp, Temple Univ, 53-55; assoc radiol, Div Grad Med & asst prof radiol, Univ Pa, 55-65; RADIOLOGIST & DIR DIV RADIATION THER & NUCLEAR MED, ABINGTON MEM HOSP, PA, 65- *Concurrent Pos:* Assoc radiologist & dir, Tumor Clin, Hosp Univ Pa, 55-67; asst prof radiol, Med Col Pa, 62- *Mem:* Radiol Soc NAm; AMA; Am Col Radiol. *Res:* Intracavitary radiation dosimetry; isotopic studies of gastrointestinal absorption; cancer therapy; synergistic action of radiation and cytotoxics. *Mailing Add:* Dept of Radiol Abington Mem Hosp Abington PA 19001

TULUNAY-KEESEY, ULKER, b Ankara, Turkey, Oct 18, 32. OPHTHALMOLOGY. *Educ:* Mt Holyoke Univ, BA, 55; Brown Univ, MA, 57, PhD(physiol), 59. *Prof Exp:* Instr, 62-65, asst prof, 65-70, assoc prof, 70-75, PROF, DEPT OPHTHAL, UNIV WIS-MADISON, 75- *Concurrent Pos:* Prin investr, NIH & Nat Eye Inst, 62- *Mem:* Fel Optical Soc Am; Asn Res Vision & Ophthal. *Res:* Influence of eye measurements in vision, specifically contrast sensitivity, acuity and motion dedection; description of channels serving visual perception. *Mailing Add:* Dept Ophthal Univ Wis Madison WI 37062

TUMA, DAVID TOUFIC, b Beirut, Lebanon, Jan 1, 40; US citizen; m 69. ELECTRICAL ENGINEERING. *Educ:* Am Univ Beirut, BEng, 61; Univ Calif, Berkeley, MS, 63, PhD(elec eng), 66. *Prof Exp:* Actg asst prof elec eng, Univ Calif, Berkeley, 66; sr elec engr, Aerojet-Gen Nucleonics, 66-67; asst prof elec eng, Univ Calif, Irvine, 67-71; asst prof, 71-78, assoc prof, 78-81, PROF ELEC ENG, CARNEGIE-MELLON UNIV, 81- *Concurrent Pos:* Consult, Westinghouse Elec Corp, 74-, Pullman-Swindell, 76-80 & Brown-Boveri, 79- *Honors & Awards:* Excellence in Eng Educ Award, Am Soc Elec Engrs, 80. *Mem:* Am Phys Soc; Inst Elec & Electronics Engrs. *Res:* Electric arcs; electrical breakdown; electromagnetics; plasma physics. *Mailing Add:* Dept of Elec Eng Carnegie-Mellon Univ Pittsburgh PA 15213

TUMA, DEAN J, b Howells, Nebr, Oct 20, 41; m 64; c 3. BIOLOGICAL CHEMISTRY. *Educ:* Creighton Univ, BS, 64, MS, 68; Univ Nebr, PhD(biochem), 73. *Prof Exp:* Instr, 73-75, ASST PROF INTERNAL MED & BIOCHEM, COL MED, UNIV NEBR, 75-; RES CHEMIST BIOCHEM, VET ADMIN HOSP, OMAHA, 64- *Mem:* Am Asn Study Liver Dis; Am Fedn Clin Res. *Res:* Investigation of the role of ethanol, drugs and nutrition in liver metabolism and liver disease. *Mailing Add:* 2223 S 161 Circle Omaha NE 68130

TUMA, GERALD, b Oklahoma City, Okla, July 19, 14; m 38; c 2. ELECTRICAL ENGINEERING. *Educ:* Univ Okla, BS, 39, MEE, 41. *Prof Exp:* From instr to prof elec eng, 40-66, chmn dept, 58-62, dir sch, 66-77, DAVID ROSS BOYD PROF ELEC ENG, UNIV OKLA, 66- *Mem:* Am Soc Eng Educ; Inst Elec & Electronics Engrs. *Res:* Communications; feedback control systems; analog simulation; digital computers. *Mailing Add:* Sch of Elec Eng 202 W Boyd St Norman OK 73019

TUMA, HAROLD J, b Belleville, Kans, Feb 28, 33; m 56; c 3. MEAT SCIENCE, FOOD SCIENCE. *Educ:* Kans State Univ, BS, 55, MS, 58; Okla State Univ, PhD(food sci), 61. *Prof Exp:* Asst food sci, Okla State Univ, 58-61; asst prof animal sci, SDak State Univ, 61-65; assoc prof animal sci, Kans State Univ, 65-73, prof, 73-80; MEM FAC ANIMAL SCI, UNIV WYO, 80- *Mem:* Am Meat Sci Asn. *Res:* Histological and physiological characteristics of muscle associated with meat quality. *Mailing Add:* 128 Knight Hall Univ Wyo Laramie WY 82070

TUMA, JAN J, b Prague, Czech, Dec 21, 19; nat US; m 45; c 1. CIVIL ENGINEERING. *Educ:* Prague Tech Univ, BS, 47; Okla State Univ, MS, 51; Univ Colo, PhD, 67. *Prof Exp:* From assoc prof to prof civil eng, Okla State Univ, 52-68, head dept, 58-68; eng consult res & writing, 68-77; PROF CIVIL ENG, ARIZ STATE UNIV, 77- *Concurrent Pos:* NSF fac fel, Univ Colo, 65 & Swiss Fed Inst Technol, 66-67. *Mem:* Am Soc Civil Engrs; Am Soc Eng Educ; Nat Soc Prof Engrs. *Res:* Windstress analysis; analysis of rigid frames by infinite series; theory of structures; thin plates and shells; structural analysis and design; space structures. *Mailing Add:* 1951 E Hermosa Dr Tempe AZ 85282

TUMAN, VLADIMIR SHLIMON, b Kermanshah, Iran, May 21, 23; US citizen; m 51; c 3. PHYSICS, GEOPHYSICS. *Educ:* Univ Birmingham, BSc, 48; Univ London, DIC, 49; Stanford Univ, PhD(geophys), 64. *Prof Exp:* Geophysicist, Anglo Iranian Oil Co, SW Iran, 50-52; actg chief petrol, Nat Iranian Oil Co, 52-55, engr trainee, Europe & USA, 55-56; sr petrol physicist, Nat Iranian Consortium, 56-57; res physicist, Atlantic Refining Oil Co, Dallas, Tex, 57-59; assoc prof petrol eng, Univ Ill, Urbana, 59-62; res assoc geophys, Stanford Univ, 62-65, res physicist, Res Inst, 65-66; assoc prof physics, 66-67, chmn dept phys sci, 66-71, PROF PHYSICS, CALIF STATE COL, STANISLAUS, 67- *Concurrent Pos:* Calif Res Corp grant, 60-61; consult, Esso Res Lab, 61, Schlumberger Well Logging Co, 61 & Sinclair Oil Co, 61; Am Petrol Inst grants, 61-63; consult, Comput Symp, Stanford Univ, 63-64, res assoc, Physics Dept, 65-; lectr, Varian Assoc, Palo Alto, Calif, 66. *Mem:* fel Royal Astron Soc; Am Phys Soc; Am Asn Physics Teachers; Am Geophys Union; Soc Explor Geophys. *Res:* Development of cryogenic gravity meter to study earth eigen vibrations and look for gravitational radiation. *Mailing Add:* Dept of Physics Calif State Col at Stanislaus Turlock CA 95380

TUMBLESON, MYRON EUGENE, b Mountain Lake, Minn, Mar 13, 37; m 58; c 3. BIOCHEMISTRY, NUTRITION. *Educ:* Univ Minn, BS, 58, MS, 61, PhD(nutrit), 64. *Prof Exp:* From res assoc to asst prof animal sci, Univ Minn, 64-66; asst prof vet physiol & pharmacol, Univ Mo-Columbia & res assoc med biochem, Sinclair Comp Med Res, 66-69; assoc prof, 66-69, res assoc, Sinclair Comp Med Res, 64-80, PROF VET ANAT & PHYSIOL, UNIV MO-COLUMBIA & RES PROF, SINCLAIR COMP MED RES, 80-; res assoc, 69-80, RES PROF SINCLAIR COMP MED RES, 80- *Mem:* Am Inst Nutrit; Soc Exp Biol & Med; Am Soc Neurochem; Am Soc Biol Chemists; Sigma Xi. *Res:* Protein-calorie malnutrition; alcoholism and aging, using miniature swine as biomedical research subjects. *Mailing Add:* Dept of Vet Anat-Physiol Univ of Mo Columbia MO 65201

TUMELTY, PAUL FRANCIS, b Boston, Mass, May 9, 41. SOLID STATE PHYSICS. *Educ:* Boston Col, BS, 62; Univ Iowa, MS, 64, PhD(physics), 70. *Prof Exp:* Prin res engr, Honeywell, Inc, 70-73; physicist, 73-80, SR RES PHYSICIST, ALLIED CORP, 80- *Mem:* Am Phys Soc; Inst Elec & Electronics Engrs; Sigma Xi. *Res:* Magnetic properties of epitaxially-grown garnet films; liquid-phase expitaxy of garnet films; transport properties of semiconductors, Kondo effect; low-temperature physics. *Mailing Add:* Mat Lab Allied Corp PO Box 1021R Morristown NJ 07960

TUMEN, HENRY JOSEPH, b Philadelphia, Pa, Apr 7, 02; m 26; c 1. MEDICINE. *Educ:* Univ Pa, AB, 22, MD, 25; Am Bd Internal Med, dipl, 52. *Prof Exp:* Prof clin gastroenterol, 54-60, prof med & chmn dept, 60-71, EMER PROF MED, GRAD SCH MED, UNIV PA, 71- *Concurrent Pos:* Consult, Walter Reed Army Med Ctr, DC, 58- & Albert Einstein Med Ctr, 60-; chmn, Am Bd Internal Med, 58-60. *Mem:* Am Soc Gastrointestinal Endoscopy; Am Gastroenterol Asn; Am Col Physicians. *Res:* Gastroenterology. *Mailing Add:* 1830 Rittenhouse Square Philadelphia PA 19103

TUMILOWICZ, JOSEPH J, virology, immunology, see previous edition

TUMOSA, NINA JEAN, b Dover-Foxcroft, Maine, Oct 12, 51. IMMUNOHISTOCHEMISTRY, NEUROSCIENCE. *Educ:* Rensslear Polytech Inst, BS, 73, MS, 74; State Univ NY, Albany, PhD(biol sci), 82. *Prof Exp:* FEL, ALTA HERTIAGE RES FOUND, UNIV CALGARY, 82- *Mem:* Asn Res Vison & Opthal; AAAS; Am Women Sci; Women Eye Res. *Res:* Behavioral anatomical and immunohistochemical changes that occur in the brain following altered visual experience. *Mailing Add:* Dept Anat Health Sci Ctr B134 3300 Hosp Dr NW Univ Calgary Calgary AB T2N 4N1 Can

TUMULTY, PHILIP A, b Jersey City, NJ, Nov 4, 12; m 42; c 5. MEDICINE. *Educ:* Georgetown Univ, AB, 35; Johns Hopkins Univ, MD, 40; Am Bd Internal Med, dipl, 48. *Prof Exp:* Intern med, Johns Hopkins Hosp, 40-41, asst resident, 41-42 & 45-46, resident, 46-47, from instr to assoc prof, Johns Hopkins Univ, 46-53, from asst dir to dir, Med Clin, Johns Hopkins Hosp, 48-53, physician-in-chg, Med Surg Group Clin, 48-53; prof med & dir dept, Sch Med, St Louis Univ, 53-54; from assoc prof to prof, 55-76, DAVID J CARVER PROF MED, SCH MED, JOHNS HOPKINS UNIV, 76- CHMN PVT MED SERV, JOHNS HOPKINS HOSP, 55-, PHYSICIAN-IN-CHG, PVT PATIENT CLIN, 56- *Concurrent Pos:* Am Col Physicians clin fel, Johns Hopkins Hosp, 46-47; regional consult, Vet Admin, 54-55; consult, Baltimore City Hosp, 55-; spec consult, NIH, 59-; consult, Vet Admin & USPHS Hosps, 60- & Walter Reed Hosp, 61- *Mem:* Asn Am Physicians; Am Soc Internal Med; Am Clin & Climat Asn. *Res:* Bacterial endocarditis; collagen diseases. *Mailing Add:* Johns Hopkins Hosp 601 N Broadway Baltimore MD 21205

TUNA, NAIP, b Constanta, Romania, Aug 18, 21; m 49; c 2. INTERNAL MEDICINE, CARDIOVASCULAR DISEASES. *Educ:* Istanbul Univ, MD, 47; Univ Minn, PhD(med), 58. *Prof Exp:* Asst med, Therapeut Clin, Istanbul Univ, 49-52; resident med, St Joseph's Hosp, Lexington, Ky, 52-53; from instr to asst prof, 57-64, assoc prof, 64-80, PROF MED, MED SCH, UNIV MINN, MINNEAPOLIS, 80- *Concurrent Pos:* Am Heart Asn res fel, Univ Minn, Minneapolis, 58-59, advan res fel, 59-61. *Mem:* Fel Am Col Physicians; fel Am Col Cardiol; fel Am Heart Asn; Am Fedn Clin Res. *Res:* Electro and vector cardiography; cardiology. *Mailing Add:* Dept of Med Univ of Minn Minneapolis MN 55455

TUNC, DEGER CETIN, b Izmir, Turkey, Apr 2, 36; m 63; c 2. PHYSICAL CHEMISTRY, BIOPOLYMERS. *Educ:* Columbia Univ, BS, 63; Fairleigh Dickinson Univ, MA, 66; Rutgers Univ, PhD(phys chem), 72. *Prof Exp:* Res chemist cellulose, Eastern Res, ITT Rayonier, 63-66; res scientist surg dressings, 66-74, sr res scientist bioeng & biochem, Cent Res, 74-81, RES ASSOC, ORTHOP RES, JOHNSON & JOHNSON, 81- *Concurrent Pos:* UN guest lectr, Dept Bioeng, Ege Univ, Izmir, Turkey, 79 & Dept Chem, Tubitak, Izmit, Turkey, 81. *Mem:* Am Chem Soc; Soc Biomat; Soc Turkish Architects Engrs & Scientists Am (pres, 72-74); Orthop Res Soc. *Res:* Polyelectrolytes; body absorbable polymers; health care products in general; wound healing; orthopedics; gastrointestinal problems and drugs; controlled release membranes; biomedical devices; absorbable internal bone fixation devices. *Mailing Add:* Cent Res 501 George St New Brunswick NJ 08903

TUNG, CHI CHAO, b Shanghai, China, Mar 24, 32; US citizen; m 64; c 2. STRUCTURAL MECHANICS. *Educ:* Tung-Chi Univ, China, BS, 53; Univ Calif, Berkeley, MS, 61, PhD(struct eng & struct mech), 64. *Prof Exp:* Asst prof struct eng, Univ Ill, Urbana, 64-69; assoc prof, 69-76, PROF STRUCT ENG, NC STATE UNIV, 76- *Mem:* Am Soc Civil Engrs; Am Soc Eng Educ. *Res:* Application of probability and statistics to civil engineering problems; ocean engineering. *Mailing Add:* Dept of Civil Eng NC State Univ Raleigh NC 27650

TUNG, CHI FANG, b Shanghai, China, Apr 16, 21; US citizen; m 53; c 2. CERAMICS ENGINEERING, GLASS TECHNOLOGY. *Educ:* Nat Chao Tung Univ, China, BS, 47; Univ Ill, Urbana, MS, 51, PhD(ceramic eng), 53. *Prof Exp:* Ceramic engr, I-Feng Enameling Co, 47-48; res engr, O Hommel Co, 53-54; Glascote Prod Inc, 54-55; sr ceramic engr, 55-56, supvr glass res & develop, 56-68, sr ceramic eng specialist, 68-69, mgr inorg res & develop, Reflective Prod Div, 69-80, CORP SCIENTIST, TCM DIV, 3M CO, 81- *Mem:* Am Ceramic Soc; Nat Inst Ceramic Engrs. *Res:* Ceramic-metal system; glass of high index of refraction; reflex reflective material; optics; nucleation of glass. *Mailing Add:* 3M Co Bldg 209BW 3M Ctr St Paul MN 55144

TUNG, CHIN (FRANK), b China, Oct 22, 39; m 65; c 1. COMPUTER SCIENCE & ENGINEERING. *Educ:* Nat Taiwan Univ, BS, 61; Rice Univ, MS, 64; Univ Calif, Los Angeles, PhD(eng), 68. *Prof Exp:* RES STAFF MEM, IBM RES LAB, 68- *Concurrent Pos:* Lectr, Univ Santa Clara, 69- *Mem:* Inst Elec & Electronics Engrs. *Res:* Language-oriented computing; computer arithmetic. *Mailing Add:* IBM Res Labs IBM Corp San Jose CA 95114

TUNG, FRED FU, b Manchouli, Heilungkiang. BIOCHEMISTRY. *Educ:* Taiwan Prov Col Agr, BS, 56; Univ Vt, MS, 63; Univ Mich, MS, 66; Univ Mo, PhD(biochem), 70. *Prof Exp:* Res asst agr chem, Taiwan Prov Col Agr, 58-59; fel biochem, State Univ NY Albany, 70-73; biochemist, 74-78, CLIN HEALTH SCIENTIST, MICH DEPT PUB HEALTH, 78- *Mem:* Am Chem Soc; AAAS; NY Acad Sci. *Res:* Use of plasmin to modify immune serum globulin for intravenous administration; isolation and purification of anticancer drugs; research and development of bacterial vaccine. *Mailing Add:* Mich Dept Pub Health PO Box 30035 Lansing MI 48909

TUNG, HSI-TANG, b Taiwan, Oct 20, 39; US citizen; m 69; c 1. MICROBIOLOGY, VETERINARY MEDICINE. *Educ:* Nat Taiwan Univ, DVM, 66; NDak State Univ, MS, 69; NC State Univ, PhD(microbiol), 72. *Prof Exp:* Vet microbiologist poultry biol, Maag & Easterbrooks Inc, 72-73; mgr prod develop, Vineland Labs Inc, Damon Corp, 73-75, tech dir res qual control & tech serv, 75-77; sr microbiologist poultry biol, Abbott Labs, 77-80; WITH BEECHAM LAB, 80- *Mem:* Am Vet Med Asn; Am Soc Microbiologists; Am Asn Avian Pathologists; World Vet Poultry Asn; Am Asn Indust Vet. *Res:* Poultry biologics research; fermentations; bacterial physiology; mycotoxins. *Mailing Add:* Beecham Lab E Lincoln Rd White Hall IL 62092

TUNG, JOHN SHIH-HSIUNG, b Keelung, Taiwan, July 19, 28; m 54; c 4. MATHEMATICS. *Educ:* Taiwan Norm Univ, BA, 50; Pa State Univ, MA, 60, PhD(math), 62. *Prof Exp:* Asst civil eng, Taihoku Imp Univ, Taiwan, 44-45; asst instr math, Taipei Inst Technol, 50-53; asst math & indust educ, Taiwan Norm Univ, 53-56, instr, 56-58; asst math, Pa State Univ, 58-60 & 61-62; asst prof, 62-66, assoc prof, 66-76, PROF MATH, MIAMI UNIV, OHIO, 76- PROF STATIST, 78- *Mem:* Math Asn Am; Am Math Soc. *Res:* Theory of functions of a complex variable; infinite and orthogonal series; matrix algebra. *Mailing Add:* Dept of Math Miami Univ Oxford OH 45056

TUNG, KA-KIT, b Canton, China, Dec 6, 48; US citizen; m 76. DYNAMIC METEOROLOGY, FLUID MECHANICS. *Educ:* Calif Inst Technol, BSc & Msc, 72; Harvard Univ, PhD(appl math), 77. *Prof Exp:* Res scientist fluid mech, Dynamimcs Technol Inc, 77-80; ASST PROF APPL MATH, MASS INST TECHNOL, 79- *Concurrent Pos:* Res fel, Harvard Univ, 77-79; consult, Dynamics Technol Inc, 80- *Res:* Large scale wave motions in the earth's atmosphere; internal waves in the ocean. *Mailing Add:* 6 Locke Lane Lexington MA 02173

TUNG, LU HO, b Tientsin, China, Dec 7, 23; US citizen; m 67; c 3. POLYMER CHEMISTRY. *Educ:* Tsing Hua Univ, China, BS, 48; Univ Ill, MS, 50, PhD(chem eng), 51. *Prof Exp:* Phys chemist, 53-59, assoc scientist, 59-70, RES SCIENTIST, DOW CHEM CO, 70- *Mem:* AAAS; Sigma Xi; Am Chem Soc. *Res:* Polymer physical chemistry. *Mailing Add:* 1702 Bldg Dow Chem Co Midland MI 48640

TUNG, MARVIN ARTHUR, b Sask, Can, Nov 9, 37; c 3. FOOD SCIENCE. *Educ:* Univ BC, BSA, 60, teaching cert, 61, MSA, 67, PhD(food sci), 70. *Prof Exp:* Teacher sch bd, 61-70; assoc prof, 70-80, PROF FOOD SCI, UNIV BC, 80- *Mem:* Can Inst Food Sci & Technol; Inst Food Technologists; Brit Inst Food Sci & Technol; Can Soc Agr Eng; Micros Soc Can. *Res:* Food rheology; microstructure of food systems; food processing and packaging. *Mailing Add:* Dept Food Sci Univ BC Vancouver BC V6T 2A2 Can

TUNG, MING SUNG, b Taiwan, Feb 25, 42; US citizen; m 70; c 2. DENTAL CHEMISTRY. *Educ:* Cheng-Kung Univ, Taiwan, BS, 64; Brown Univ, PhD(chem), 73. *Prof Exp:* Fel, Univ Md, 72-74, vis prof chem, 74; PROJ LEADER, DENT CHEM, AM DENT ASN HEALTH FOUND, RES UNIT, 74- *Honors & Awards:* E H Hatton Award, Int Asn Dent Res, 76. *Mem:* Am Chem Soc; Am Asn Dent Res; Int Asn Dent Res; Sigma Xi. *Res:* Calcium phosphate and fluoride chemistry as applied to dental and bone sciences; physical chemistry of biological systems; study of physical properties of biopolymers such as DNA, polypeptides, proteins and enzymes. *Mailing Add:* 12112 Suffolk Terrace Gaithersburg MD 20878

TUNG, S(HAO) E, chemical engineering, see previous edition

TUNG, SHYH-SHYAN, b Peking, China, May 15, 47; m 76; c 1. HEAT TRANSFER, FLUID MECHANICS. *Educ:* Cheng Kung Univ, BS, 69; State Univ NY, Stony Brook, MS, 73, PhD(mech eng), 78. *Prof Exp:* RES ENGR, HEAT TRANSFER RES INC, 78- *Mem:* Am Soc Mech Engrs. *Res:* Industrial research on heat exchangers. *Mailing Add:* Heat Transfer Res Inc 1000 S Fremont Ave Alhambra CA 91802

TUNG, WU-KI, b Kunming, China, Oct 16, 39; m 63; c 2. THEORETICAL PHYSICS, ELEMENTARY PARTICLE PHYSICS. *Educ:* Univ Taiwan, BS, 60; Yale Univ, PhD(physics), 66. *Prof Exp:* Res assoc theoret physics, Inst Theoret Physics, State Univ NY Stony Brook, 66-68; mem staff, Inst Adv Study, 68-70; asst prof physics & mem staff, Dept Physics, Enrico Fermi Inst, Univ Chicago, 70-75; assoc prof, 75-79, PROF PHYSICS, ILL INST TECHNOL, 79-, CHMN DEPT, 81- *Mem:* Am Phys Soc. *Res:* High energy theoretical physics. *Mailing Add:* Dept Physics Ill Inst Technol Chicago IL 60616

TUNHEIM, JERALD ARDEN, b Claremont, SDak, Sept 3, 40; m 63; c 1. SOLID STATE PHYSICS. *Educ:* SDak State Univ, BS, 62, MS, 64; Okla State Univ, PhD(physics), 68. *Prof Exp:* Asst prof, 68-72, assoc prof, 72-78, PROF PHYSICS, SDAK STATE UNIV, 78-, HEAD DEPT, 80-82. *Mem:* Am Phys Soc; Am Asn Physics Teachers. *Res:* Alpha particle model of sulphur nucleus; electron spin resonance measurements of transition metal ions in stannic oxide; surface effects on conductivity of stannic oxide; application and development of models for remote sensing application. *Mailing Add:* Dept of Physics SDak State Univ Brookings SD 57006

TUNICK, ALLEN A, b Chicago, Ill, Nov 14, 41; m 71. PHYSICAL ORGANIC CHEMISTRY. *Educ:* Mass Inst Technol, BS, 63; Univ Calif, Berkeley, PhD(chem), 69. *Prof Exp:* Res chemist, 69-78, SR RES CHEMIST, ALLIED CHEM CORP, 78- *Mem:* Am Chem Soc; AAAS. *Res:* Synthesis and mechanism in organic chemistry, ion exchange, metal complexation and membrane phenomena. *Mailing Add:* Allied Corp Box 1021R-CRL Morristown NJ 07960

TUNIK, BERNARD D, b New York, NY, Dec 22, 21; m 49; c 3. PHYSIOLOGY. *Educ:* Univ Wis, BA, 42; Columbia Univ, MA, 51, PhD(zool), 59. *Prof Exp:* Asst cytol, Sloan-Kettering Inst, 50-52; asst zool, Columbia Univ, 52-55; instr anat, Sch Med, Univ Pa, 58-60; dep chmn dept, 62-63 & 64-65, ASSOC PROF BIOL SCI, STATE UNIV NY STONY BROOK, 60- *Concurrent Pos:* Nat Inst Arthritis & Metab Dis spec fel, Dept Polymer Sci, Weizmann Inst, 66-67; vis scholar, Dept Zool, Univ Calif, Berkeley, 75. *Mem:* AAAS; Am Soc Cell Biol. *Res:* Cellular physiology; mechanochemical aspects of muscle contraction; triggers of muscle hypertrophy. *Mailing Add:* Dept Neurobiol & Behav State Univ NY Stony Brook NY 11790

TUNIS, C(YRIL) J(AMES), b Montreal, Que, July 31, 32; m 51; c 3. ELECTRICAL ENGINEERING. *Educ:* McGill Univ, BEng, 54, MSc, 56; Univ Manchester, PhD(elec eng), 58. *Prof Exp:* Staff engr, 58-65, SR ENGR, COMPUT DESIGN, IBM CORP, ENDICOTT, 65- *Concurrent Pos:* Lectr, Harpur Col, State Univ NY, 59-60 & Lehigh Univ, 61-62; vis prof, Stanford Univ, 66-67. *Honors & Awards:* Babbage Award, Brit Inst Elec Engrs. *Mem:* Fel Inst Elec & Electronics Engrs. *Res:* Design of advanced digital computer systems. *Mailing Add:* 624 Valleyview Dr Endwell NY 13760

TUNIS, MARVIN, b New York, NY, Apr 18, 25; m 52; c 4. BIOCHEMISTRY. *Educ:* Hunter Col, AB, 50; Univ Ill, MS, 51, PhD(biochem), 54. *Prof Exp:* Res assoc, Univ Ill, 54-55; USPHS fel, Col Physicians & Surgeons, Columbia Univ, 55-56; sr cancer res scientist, Roswell Park Mem Inst, 57-68; assoc prof, 68-77, PROF CHEM, STATE UNIV NY COL BUFFALO, 77- *Mem:* Am Chem Soc; Am Soc Biol Chemists; Am Asn Cancer Res. *Res:* Biochemistry and metabolism of nucleic acids, proteins, glycoproteins and mucopolysaccharides; enzymology. *Mailing Add:* Dept of Chem State Univ of NY Col Buffalo NY 14222

TUNKEL, STEVEN JOSEPH, b New York, NY, Jan 15, 29; m 52; c 3. CHEMICAL ENGINEERING, PHYSICAL CHEMISTRY. *Educ:* Polytech Inst Brooklyn, BS, 51; Newark Col Eng, MS, 56. *Prof Exp:* Res engr pilot plants, Allied Chem Corp, 51-56; mgr res eng aerospace, Thiokol Chem Corp, 56-68; mgr mkt res jet engines, Austenal Div, Howmet Corp, 68-70; mgr process res new plant start-up, Celanese Chem Corp, 70-72; CHIEF CHEM ENGR FIRE & EXPLOSION, HAZARDS RES CORP, 72- *Mem:* Am Chem Soc; Am Inst Chem Engrs; Combustion Inst; Nat Soc Prof Engrs. *Res:* Fire and explosion hazard evaluation of chemicals and chemical processes. *Mailing Add:* Hazards Res Crop Denville NJ 07834

TUNNELL, WILLIAM C(LOTWORTHY), b Knoxville, Tenn, May 19, 15; m 42; c 2. MECHANICAL ENGINEERING. *Educ:* Univ Tenn, BS, 40. *Prof Exp:* Engr, Blue Ridge Glass Corp, 40-43, Tenn Eastman Co, 43-47, Oak Ridge Nat Lab, 47-68 & Nuclear Div, Union Carbide Corp, 68-79; RETIRED. *Concurrent Pos:* Consult engr, 79- *Mem:* Nat Soc Prof Engrs. *Res:* Electromagnetic separation of isotopes; high temperature components of atomic power reactors; critical assemblies; nuclear reactions; liquid metals; pulse reactors; environmental statements for nuclear power plants. *Mailing Add:* 104 Ditman Ln Oak Ridge TN 37830

TUNNICLIFF, GODFREY, b Malvern, Eng, Jan 6, 41; m 71; c 2. NEUROCHEMISTRY. *Educ:* Univ Col Wales, BSc, 64; Univ Southampton, MSc, 67, PhD(biochem), 69. *Prof Exp:* Res biochemist, Liebig's Extract Meat Co Ltd, London, 64-66; fel, City of Hope Nat Med Ctr, Duarte, Calif, 69-71; fel, Univ Sask, 71-72, asst prof biochem, 72-74; dir, Lab Neurochem, Clin Res Inst Montreal, Que, 74-77; asst prof, 78-81, ASSOC PROF BIOCHEM, SCH MED, IND UNIV, 81- *Mem:* Can Biochem Soc; Int Soc Neurochem. *Res:* Role of gamma-aminobutyric acid in the functioning of the central nervous system. *Mailing Add:* Evansville Ctr for Med Educ 8600 University Blvd Evansville IN 47712

TUNNICLIFFE, PHILIP ROBERT, b Derby, Eng, May 3, 22; Can citizen; m 46; c 2. PHYSICS. *Educ:* Univ London, BSc, 42. *Prof Exp:* Res staff, Telecommun Res Estab, Malvern, Eng, 42-46, UK Atomic Energy Auth, Ont, Can, 46-49 & Atomic Energy Res Estab, Harwell, Eng, 49-51; res staff, Atomic Energy Can Ltd, 51-61, br head electronics, 61-63, br head appl physics, 63-67, br head accelerator physics, 67-78; RETIRED. *Concurrent Pos:* Consult, Los Alamos Sci Lab, 79-80. *Mem:* Am Phys Soc. *Res:* Microwave tubes; neutron, low energy nuclear, reactor and accelerator physics; reactor control and instrumentation. *Mailing Add:* 6 Beach Ave Deep River ON K0S 1P0 Can

TUNSTALL, LUCILLE HAWKINS, b Thurber, Tex, Jan 17, 22; m 44; c 2. MICROBIOLOGY, IMMUNOLOGY. *Educ:* Univ Colo, BS, 43; Wayne State Univ, MS, 59, PhD(biol, microbiol), 63. *Prof Exp:* Med technologist, Med Sch, Univ Colo, 43-45, Presby Hosp Colo, 45-47, Evangel Deaconess Hosp, 50-52, Sinai Hosp Detroit, 52-55 & Brent Gen Hosp, 55-58; res & tech asst biol, Wayne State Univ, 58-62; asst prof, Delta Col, 62-65; assoc prof, Saginaw Valley Col, 65-67; prof & chmn dept, Bishop Col, 67-71; assoc dir, United Bd Col Develop, 71-72; prof biol & dir, Allied Health Prog, Clark Col, 72-75; PROF BIOL, ATLANTA UNIV, 72-; CHMN, ALLIED HEALTH PROFESSIONS DEPT, CALIF STATE UNIV, 75-, CLIN PROF, ALLIED HEALTH SCH, 78- *Concurrent Pos:* Consult, United Bd Col Develop, 72-; consult, Nat Urban League, Moton Consortium Admis & Financial Aid & Univ Assocs, 72-74; spec consult, Nat Inst Gen Med Sci, 75- *Mem:* AAAS; Am Soc Clin Path; Am Soc Microbiol; Am Soc Cell Biol; NY Acad Sci. *Res:* L-variation; frequency of occurrence and pathogenicity of organisms; immunological studies of blood and pleural fluid in patients with coronary thrombosis; cell wall-deficient bacteria in microbial ecology. *Mailing Add:* 620 Peachtree St NE Atlanta GA 30308

TUNTURI, ARCHIE ROBERT, b Portland, Ore, July 28, 17; m 48. ANATOMY. *Educ:* Reed Col, AB, 39; Univ Ore, MS, 43, MD & PhD(anat), 44. *Prof Exp:* Asst, 40-44, from instr to asst prof, 43-59, ASSOC PROF ANAT, SCH MED, ORE HEALTH SCI UNIV, 59- *Concurrent Pos:* Dir contract, US Off Naval Res, 47-69. *Mem:* Int Brain Res Orgn; Am Asn Anatomists; Am Physiol Soc; sr mem Inst Elec & Electronics Engrs; Acoust Soc Am. *Res:* Physiology, biophysics and communication aspects of the auditory cortex in the brain; neuroanatomy; hearing and acoustics; use of computer techniques for the study of the nervous system; spinal cord injury, anatomy and physiology. *Mailing Add:* Dept of Anat Sch Med Ore Health Sci Univ Portland OR 97201

TUOMI, DONALD, b Willoughby, Ohio, Sept 12, 20; m 45; c 2. PHYSICAL CHEMISTRY. *Educ:* Ohio State Univ, BS, 43, PhD(phys chem), 52. *Prof Exp:* Res scientist, SAM Lab, Columbia Univ, 43-45 & Carbide & Carbon Chem Corp, 45-46; res assoc photoemissive surfaces, Res Found, Ohio State Univ, 50-53; mem staff semiconductor devices, Lincoln Lab, Mass Inst Technol, 53-54; res chemist, Baird Assocs, Inc, 54-55 & Res Lab, McGraw-Edison Co, 55-61; mgr solid state physics, 61-78, SR SCIENTIST, RES LAB, BORG-WARNER CORP, 78- *Mem:* AAAS; Electrochem Soc; Am Phys Soc; Am Chem Soc; Am Crystallog Asn. *Res:* Structural chemistry; semiconductors; photoemissive surfaces; electrochemistry; charge transfer phenomena; thermoelectric cooling devices and semiconductor alloys; polymer solid state structural chemistry. *Mailing Add:* R C Ingersoll Res Ctr Borg-Warner Corp Des Plaines IL 60018

TUOMINEN, FRANCIS WILLIAM, b Floodwood, Minn, Mar 1, 43; m 64; c 4. BIOCHEMISTRY. *Educ:* Univ Minn, Duluth, BS, 65; Univ Minn, Minneapolis, MS, 68, PhD(biochem), 70. *Prof Exp:* NSF fel carcinogenesis, Oak Ridge Nat Lab, 70-71; sect leader, Gen Mills Chem Inc, 71-76, mgr res & develop, 76-78; DIR RES & DEVELOP CHEM, HENKEL CORP, 78- *Concurrent Pos:* Consult, Sch Pub Health, Univ Minn, 65-66 & Oak Ridge Nat Lab, 71-72. *Mem:* Am Chem Soc; Am Soc Microbiol; Indust Res Inst; AAAS. *Res:* New products, processes and applications for specialty chemicals. *Mailing Add:* Res & Develop 2010 E Hennepin Ave Minneapolis MN 55413

TUOMY, JUSTIN M(ATTHEW), b Bemidji, Minn, Mar 7, 14; m 48; c 1. FOOD TECHNOLOGY, CHEMICAL ENGINEERING. *Educ:* Univ Minn, BChE, 38. *Prof Exp:* Chem engr, Northern Regional Res Lab, USDA, 40-48; food technologist, Oscar Mayer & Co, 48-49, head qual control, 49-55, plant mgr, 55-56; tech sales mgr equip, L C Spiehs Co, 56-57; plant mgr, Horton Fruit Co, 57-58; food technologist, Qm Food & Container Inst, 58-59, supvr food technol, 59-63, supvr food technol, US Army Natick Labs, 63-77, chief, Animal Prod Group, US Army Res & Develop Command, 77-80, CHIEF, FOOD TECHNOL DIV, US ARMY RES & DEVELOP LABS, 80- *Mem:* Am Chem Soc; Am Soc Qual Control; Inst Food Technol; Sigma Xi. *Res:* Dairy, poultry, fish, meat and combination products for military and stress subsistence; development of food and food systems for use in space; program management for central food preparation systems. *Mailing Add:* US Army Res & Develop Command Kansas St Natick MA 01760

TUOVINEN, OLLI HEIKKI, b Helsinki, Finland, April 8, 44; m 72; c 3. GEOMICROBIOLOGY, ENVIRONMENTAL MICROBIOLOGY. *Educ:* Univ Helsinki, Finland, MSc, 69, LicSc, 70; London, Eng, PhD(microbiol), 73. *Prof Exp:* Fel agr biochem, Waite Agr Res Inst, SAustralia, 73-76; assoc prof microbiol, Univ Helsinki, 76; res assoc biotechnol, Univ Minn, 78; vis assoc prof microbiol, 78-80, asst prof, 80-82, ASSOC PROF MICROBIOL, OHIO STATE UNIV, 82- *Concurrent Pos:* Chief investr, Int Atomic Energy Agency, Austria, 73-78; sr res fel, Acad Sci & Univ Helsinki, 76; prin investr, Ministry Trade & Indust, Finland, 78-; adj fac, Univ Helsinki, 78- *Mem:* Soc Int Limnol; Soc Microbiol; Am Soc Microbiol. *Res:* Chemolithotrophic bacteria; microbiological methods in the recovery of metals; microbiological corrosion; microbiological aspects of drinking water and well water quality; acid mine drainage pollution; environmental cycling of sulfur and iron. *Mailing Add:* Dept Microbiol Ohio State Univ 484 W 12th Ave Columbus OH 43210

TUPAC, JAMES DANIEL, b Chisholm, Minn, May 4, 27; m 47; c 2. MATHEMATICS, PHYSICS. *Educ:* Univ Minn, BS, 50, MS, 51. *Prof Exp:* Mathematician, US Naval Missile Test Ctr, Calif, 51-53; mathematician, Rand Corp, Calif, 53-59, head comput serv, 59-68; PRES, PRC COMPUT CTR INC, 68- *Concurrent Pos:* Lectr, Exten Div, Univ Calif, Los Angeles, 60-62; mem comput adv coun, Nat Ctr Atmospheric Res, 66-69. *Mem:* Asn Comput Mach. *Res:* Applied mathematical, numerical and computer systems analyses; computer programming; computer center management. *Mailing Add:* PRC Comput Ctr Inc 1500 Planning Res Dr McLean VA 22102

TUPIN, JOE PAUL, b Comanche, Tex, Feb 17, 34; m 55; c 3. PSYCHIATRY. *Educ:* Univ Tex, Austin, BS, 55; Univ Tex Med Br, Galveston, MD, 59. *Prof Exp:* Resident psychiatrist, Univ Tex Med Br, Galveston, 60-62; resident, NIMH, 63-64; NIMH career teaching award, Group Advan Psychiat, 64-66; assoc prof psychiat & assoc dean, Univ Tex Med Br, Galveston, 68-69; assoc prof, 69-71, vchmn dept, 70-76, PROF PSYCHIAT, SCH MED, UNIV CALIF, DAVIS, 71-, CHMN DEPT, 76- *Concurrent Pos:* Fel, Group Advan Psychiat, 60-62; dir, Psychiat Consult Serv, Sacramento Med Ctr, 69-; consult, Calif Med Facil, Vacaville, 69- & Twin & Sibling Study, NIMH, 69-; consult, Dept Corrections, State of Calif, 71; chmn, NIMH Clin Psychopharmacol Rev Comt, 75-77. *Mem:* Fel Am Psychiat Asn; Soc Biol Psychiat; Am Col Psychiat; Soc Health & Human Values; Am Psychosomatic Soc. *Res:* Teaching of medical education; psychopharmacology; identification and treatment of violent behavior. *Mailing Add:* Dept Psychiat Univ Calif 2233 Stockton Blvd Sacramento CA 95817

TUPPER, CHARLES JOHN, b Miami, Ariz, Mar 7, 20; m 42; c 2. INTERNAL MEDICINE. *Educ:* San Diego State Col, BS, 43; Univ Nebr, MD, 48. *Prof Exp:* Asst prof internal med, Med Sch, Univ Mich, 56-59, secy med sch, 57, assoc prof & asst dean, 59-66; prof med & dean, Sch Med, 66-80, PROF INTERNAL MED, COMMUNITY HEALTH & FAMILY PRACTICE, SCH MED, UNIV CALIF, DAVIS, 80- *Concurrent Pos:* Consult, St Joseph Mercy Hosp, 56- *Honors & Awards:* Billings Bronze Medal, AMA, 55. *Mem:* Am Soc Internal Med; AMA; Am Col Health Asn; Asn Am Med Cols; fel Am Col Physicians. *Res:* Medical education; application of principles of preventive medicine to care of the individual patient through periodic health examination; evaluation of diagnostic procedures for effectiveness and reliability. *Mailing Add:* Dept Community Health Univ Calif Sch Med Davis CA 95616

TUPPER, W R CARL, b New Glasgow, NS, Feb 15, 15; m 43; c 3. OBSTETRICS & GYNECOLOGY. *Educ:* Dalhousie Univ, BSc, 39, MD, CM, 43; FRCOG; FRCS(C). *Prof Exp:* Head dept, 59-77, prof obstet & gynec, 59-81, MEM FAC, DALHOUSIE UNIV, 81- *Mem:* Am Col Surgeons; Am Col Obstet & Gynec; Can Soc Obstet & Gynec; Int Col Surgeons. *Mailing Add:* Dept Obstet & Gynec Fac Med Dalhousie Univ Halifax NS B3H 1W3 Can

TURBAK, ALBIN FRANK, b New Bedford, Mass, Sept 23, 29; m 52; c 2. TEXTILES. *Educ:* Southeastern Mass Technol Inst, BS, 51; Inst Textile Tech, MS, 53; Ga Inst Technol, PhD, 57. *Prof Exp:* Res chemist, Esso Res Co, 57-63; corp res dir, Teepak Inc, 63-72; mgr basic res, ITT Rayonier Co, 72-82; PROF & DIR, SCH TEXTILES, GA INST TECHNOL, 82- *Mem:* AAAS; Am Chem Soc; Am Asn Textile Chem & Colorists; NY Acad Sci; fel Royal Soc Dyers & Colorists. *Res:* Cellulose, protein and synthetic polymer research; polymer modification; new process and methods research; phosphorus chemistry; dyeing and finishing of textiles; food products research; paper products and wood research. *Mailing Add:* Textile Eng Ga Inst Technol Atlanta GA 30332

TURBYFILL, CHARLES LEWIS, b Newland, NC, Feb 27, 33; m 55; c 2. RESEARCH ADMINISTRATION. *Educ:* Univ Ore, BA, 55, MS, 57; Univ Ga, PhD(zool), 64. *Prof Exp:* Prin investr, Worcester Found Exp Biol, 64-66 & Armed Forces Radiobiol Res Inst, 66-72; health sci adminr, Nat Heart Blood & Lung Inst, NIH, 72-76, head instl training, Nat Cancer Inst, NIH, 75-76, CHIEF, CTR & SPECIAL PROJ SECT, REV BD, NAT HEART BLOOD & LUNG INST, NIH, 76- *Mem:* Am Soc Zool; Brit Soc Endocrinol; NY Acad Sci. *Res:* Primate cardiovascular physiology, atherosclerosis. *Mailing Add:* 5333 Westbard Ave Bethesda MD 20014

TURCHAN, OTTO CHARLES, b Ostrava, Czech, Dec 30, 25; nat US; m 52; c 2. PHYSICS, ENGINEERING. *Educ:* Tech Univ Brunn, Ger, Dipl Ing, 45; Charles Univ, Prague, RNDr(physics), 47; Detroit Univ, BS, 50, MS, 53. *Prof Exp:* Res engr, Junkers Airplane Works, Ger, 43; dir res & develop, Turchan Follower Mach Co, Mich, 46-55; mem tech staff & group head inertial systs develop, Res & Develop Labs, Hughes Aircraft Co, Calif, 55-61; mem tech staff & sect head spec projs, Systs Res Labs, Space Technol Labs, Inc, 61-62; mem tech staff, Spec Studies Directorate, Satellite Systs Div, Aerospace Corp, 62-65; sr staff engr & tech consult spacecraft eng, Space Systs Div, Lockheed Missiles & Space Co, 65-66; sr tech specialist, Space & Info Systs Div, NAm Aviation, Inc, 66-67; prog develop engr advan systs, Autonetics Div, NAm Rockwell Corp, 67-70 & Bechtel Corp, 70-71; prin engr, Bedford Labs, Raytheon Co, 71-72; proj engr, Bechtel Power Corp, 72-77; PRIN SCIENTIST, NUCLEAR ENERGY SYSTS, 77- *Mem:* AAAS; Am Phys Soc; Am Nuclear Soc; Am Geophys Union; Am Inst Aeronaut & Astronaut. *Res:* Mathematics; astrophysics; celestial dynamics; space physics; space vehicle systems; aeronautical-astronautical navigation and guidance; astrionics systems; automatic control systems in nuclear power and propulsion; advanced nuclear and thermonuclear power systems; plasma systems; nuclear physics; radiology and nuclear medicine. *Mailing Add:* Nuclear Energy Systs PO Box 3373 Beverly Hills CA 90212

TURCHECK, JOSEPH EDWARD, b Brownville, Pa, Nov 26, 42; m 71. APPLIED MATHEMATICS. *Educ:* Pa State Univ, BS, 64; Columbia Univ, MA, 65, PhD(math), 72. *Prof Exp:* Instr math, Clarkson Col Technol, 69-71; asst prof, Va Polytech Inst, 72-73; asst prof math, St Lawrence Univ, 73-77; MEM STAFF, CTR FOR NAVAL ANAL, 77- *Mem:* Am Math Soc; Math Asn Am. *Res:* Abstract theory of asymptotic expansions for solutions of algebraic differential equations; application of the theory of abstract differential fields with order relations to problems in asymptotic expansions. *Mailing Add:* 2273 Chestnut Burr Ct Reston VA 22091

TURCHI, IGNATIUS JOSEPH, b Philadelphia, Pa, Dec 6, 48; m 71. ORGANIC CHEMISTRY. *Educ:* Drexel Univ, BSc, 71; Univ Tex, Austin, PhD(org chem), 75. *Prof Exp:* ASSOC SR INVESTR ORG CHEM, SMITH KLINE & FRENCH LABS, 78- *Concurrent Pos:* Alexander von Humboldt fel, Univ Munich, 75-76; fel, Princeton Univ, 76-78. *Mem:* Am Chem Soc; AAAS. *Res:* Heterocyclic chemistry; cycloaddition reactions; qualitative molecular orbital theory and its use in elucidating reaction mechanisms and predicting the course of organic reactions; synthetic methods. *Mailing Add:* Org Chem F-50 1500 Spring Garden Sts Philadelphia PA 19101

TURCHI, JOSEPH J, b Philadelphia, Pa, Feb 16, 33; m 59; c 3. INTERNAL MEDICINE, ONCOLOGY. *Educ:* Univ Pa, BA, 54; Jefferson Med Col, MD, 58. *Prof Exp:* Head clin hemat & cancer chemother, US Naval Hosp, Bethesda, Md, 62-54; sr investr med, Hahnemann Med Col, 64-69; clin asst prof med, 69-80, CLIN ASSOC PROF MED, THOMAS JEFFERSON UNIV, 80- *Concurrent Pos:* Nat Cancer Inst grant, Misericordia Hosp, 66-; assoc dept path, Hemat Sect & attend physician dept med, Misericordia Hosp, 64-, Nat Cancer Inst prin investr hemat res, 66- *Mem:* Am Col Physicians. *Mailing Add:* Township & Belfield Ave Havertown PA 19083

TURCHI, PETER JOHN, b New York, NY, Dec 30, 46. INDUCTIVE ENERGY SYSTEMS, PLASMA DYNAMICS. *Educ:* Princeton Univ, BSE, 67, MA, 69, PhD(aero & mech sci), 70. *Prof Exp:* Res asst, Guggenheim Propulsion Labs, Princeton Univ, 63-70; plasma physicist, Air Force Weapons Lab, 70-72; res physicist, Naval Res Lab, 72-77, chief, Plasma Technol Br, 77-80; staff scientist, 80-81, DIR, WASHINGTON RES LAB, RES &

DEVELOP ASSOCS, INC, 81- *Concurrent Pos:* Lectr, 4th Sch Plasma Physics, Novosibirsk, USSR, 74, Christophilos Mem Sch Plasma Physics, Greece, 77 & Air Force Pulsed Power Lectr Series, 80; chmn, 2nd Int Conf Megagauss Magnetic Field Generation, 79, Conf Prime-Power High Energy Space Systs, 82; mem, Tech Comt, Int Pulsed Power Conf, Inst Elec & Electron Engrs, 79; ed, Megagauss Physics & Technol, Plenum Press, 80. *Mem:* Am Phys Soc; Sigma Xi. *Res:* Electromagnetic energy and matter to create high energy density systems for rocket propulsion; controlled nuclear fusion; nuclear weapons simulation. *Mailing Add:* Res & Develop Assocs Inc Suite 500 1401 Wilson Blvd Arlington VA 22209

TURCHINETZ, WILLIAM ERNEST, b Winnipeg, Man, Nov 18, 28; m 54; c 2. PHYSICS. *Educ:* Univ Man, BSc, 52, MSc, 53, PhD(physics), 55. *Prof Exp:* Asst prof physics, Univ Man, 55-56; res fel, Australian Nat Univ, 56-59; Sloan Found fel, 59-69, mem res staff, 60-65, lectr, 65-68, head opers, Bates Linear Accelerator, 73-80, SR RES SCIENTIST, MASS INST TECHNOL, 68-, ASSOC DIR, BATES LINEAR ACCELERATOR, 80- *Concurrent Pos:* Chmn, Gordon Conf Photonuclear Reactions, 69-71. *Res:* Nuclear physics; particle accelerators; radiation therapy; science education. *Mailing Add:* Mass Inst Technol Bates Lab PO Box 95 Middleton MA 01949

TURCK, MARVIN, b Chicago, Ill, June 13, 34; m 56; c 4. INTERNAL MEDICINE, INFECTIOUS DISEASE. *Educ:* Univ Ill, BS, 57, MD, 59; Am Bd Internal Med, dipl. *Prof Exp:* Intern med, Res & Educ Hosp, Ill, 59-60; fel, Univ Wash, 60-62; resident & asst, Res & Educ Hosp, Ill, 62-63, chief resident, Cook County Hosp Serv, 63-64; head, Div Infectious Dis & prog dir, Res Infectious Dis Lab, King County Hosp, 64-68; chief med, USPHS Hosp, 68-72; PROF MED, UNIV WASH, 72-, PHYSICIAN-IN-CHIEF DEPT MED, HARBORVIEW MED CTR, 72- *Concurrent Pos:* Instr, Univ Ill, 63-64; from asst prof to assoc prof, Univ Wash, 64-72; attend physician, King County Hosp, Wash, 64-; attend physician & consult, Univ Wash Hosp, 66; attend physician, USPHS Hosp, 66. *Mem:* Am Fedn Clin Res; Infectious Dis Soc Am; fel Am Col Physicians. *Res:* Laboratory and clinical aspects of pyelonephritis; investigation of new antibiotics. *Mailing Add:* Harborview Med Ctr 325 Ninth Ave Seattle WA 98104

TURCO, CHARLES PAUL, b Brooklyn, NY, Sept 23, 34; m 55; c 4. PARASITOLOGY, NEMATOLOGY. *Educ:* St John's Univ, NY, BS, 56, MS, 58, MS, 60; Tex A&M Univ, PhD(biol), 69. *Prof Exp:* Teacher, High Sch, NY, 56-64; dir univ develop, 71-74, assoc prof, 65-81, dir develop, 74-81, PROF BIOL, LAMAR UNIV, 81-, DIR RES & PROGS, 81- *Concurrent Pos:* Sigma Xi res award, 68. *Mem:* Am Soc Parasitol; Am Inst Biol Sci; Am Soc Nematol. *Res:* Nematodes of rice and associated insect pests; nematode parasites associated with man's domestic animals. *Mailing Add:* Off of Res & Progs Lamar Univ Beaumont TX 77710

TURCO, RICHARD PETER, b New York, NY, Mar 9, 43; m 67; c 1. AERONOMY. *Educ:* Rutgers Univ, New Brunswick, BS, 65; Univ Ill, Urbana, MS, 67, PhD(elec eng), 71. *Prof Exp:* NSF res grant, Space Sci Div, Ames Res Ctr, NASA, Moffett Field, Calif, 71; SCIENTIST AERONOMY, R&D ASSOCS, 71- *Mem:* Am Inst Aeronaut & Astronaut; Am Geophys Union. *Res:* Dynamics and photochemistry of the ambient and disturbed atmosphere; effects of pollutants on the and mesosphere; characteristics of charged species in the lower ionosphere; phenomena related to atmospheric nuclear explosions; properties of terrestrial and space radiation. *Mailing Add:* R&D Assocs PO Box 9695 Marina Del Rey CA 90291

TURCO, SALVATORE J, b Philadelphia, Pa, Mar 4, 32; m 57; c 2. PHARMACY. *Educ:* Philadelphia Col Pharm & Sci, BSc, 59, MSc, 66, PharmD, 67. *Prof Exp:* Instr sterile prod, Philadelphia Col Pharm & Sci, 66-67; from instr to asst prof, 67-73, assoc prof, 73-78, PROF PHARM, SCH PHARM, TEMPLE UNIV, 78- *Concurrent Pos:* Indust res grants, Temple Univ, 69, Roche award, 72, univ grant, 72-73. *Mem:* Am Pharmaceut Asn; Am Soc Hosp Pharmacists. *Res:* Parenteral products; particulate matter in parenterals; hospital pharmacy. *Mailing Add:* Dept Pharm Temple Univ Sch Pharm Philadelphia PA 19140

TURCOTTE, DONALD LAWSON, b Bellingham, Wash, Apr 22, 32; m 57; c 2. GEOPHYSICS, FLUIDS. *Educ:* Calif Inst Technol, BS, 54, DPh(aeronaut eng), 58; Cornell Univ, MAeroE, 55. *Prof Exp:* Asst prof aeronaut eng, US Naval Postgrad Sch, 58-59; from asst prof to prof aeronaut eng, 59-72, PROF GEOL SCI, CORNELL UNIV, 72-, CHMN GEOL SCI, 80- *Concurrent Pos:* NSF fel, Oxford Univ, 65-66, Guggenheim fel, 72-73. *Honors & Awards:* Day Medal, Geol Soc Am, 81. *Mem:* Am Phys Soc; Geol Soc Am; Am Geophys Union; Seismol Soc Am. *Res:* Mantle convection; geophysical heat transfer; behavior of faults; distribution of stress; evolution of sedimentary basins. *Mailing Add:* Kimble Hall Cornell Univ Ithaca NY 14850

TURCOTTE, EDGAR LEWIS, b Duluth, Minn, June 7, 29. PLANT GENETICS. *Educ:* Univ Minn, BA, 51, MS, 57, PhD(genetics), 58. *Prof Exp:* PLANT GENETICIST, USDA, 58- *Mem:* AAAS; Am Genetic Asn; Am Soc Agron; Genetics Soc Can. *Res:* Genetics and speciation of Gossypium barbadense. *Mailing Add:* Univ of Ariz Cotton Res Ctr 4207 E Broadway Phoenix AZ 85040

TURCOTTE, JEREMIAH G, b Detroit, Mich, Jan 20, 33; m 58; c 4. SURGERY. *Educ:* Univ Mich, BS, 55, MD, 57; Am Bd Surg, dipl, 64. *Prof Exp:* Resident, 58-63, from instr to assoc prof, 63-71, PROF SURG, MED SCH, UNIV MICH, ANN ARBOR, 71-, CHMN DEPT, 74- *Concurrent Pos:* Co-investr, USPHS Res Grant, 64-; consult, Ann Arbor Vet Admin Hosp & Wayne County Gen Hosp. *Mem:* Fel Am Col Surg; Transplantation Soc; Soc Univ Surgeons; Soc Surg Alimentary Tract; Asn Acad Surg. *Res:* Portal hypertension; organ transplantation. *Mailing Add:* Dept of Surg Univ of Mich Med Ctr Ann Arbor MI 48109

TURCOTTE, JOSEPH GEORGE, b Boston, Mass, Dec 25, 36; m 62; c 5. ORGANIC CHEMISTRY, MEDICINAL CHEMISTRY. *Educ:* Mass Col Pharm, BS, 58, MS, 60; Univ Minn, PhD(med chem), 67. *Prof Exp:* Sr biochemist, Spec Lab Cancer Res & Radioisotope Serv, Vet Admin Hosp, Minneapolis, 65-67; from asst prof to assoc prof med chem, 67-77, PROF MED CHEM, COL PHARM, UNIV RI, 77- *Concurrent Pos:* Res comt grants, Univ RI, 67-69; res grants, Nat Cancer Inst, 67-70, RI Water Resources Ctr, 68-69, RI Heart Asn, 70-72 & Nat Heart & Lung Inst, 71- *Mem:* AAAS; NY Acad Sci; Am Chem Soc; Am Pharmaceut Asn. *Res:* Synthesis of potential medicinal agents, including phospholipids, anticancer agents, antihypertensives, molluscicides, parasympathomimetic and parasympatholytic agents. *Mailing Add:* Dept of Med Chem Univ of RI Col of Pharm Kingston RI 02881

TUREK, ANDREW, b Lemberg, Poland, Nov 11, 35; Can citizen; m 58; c 2. GEOCHEMISTRY. *Educ:* Univ Edinburgh, BSc, 57; Univ Alta, MSc, 62; Australian Nat Univ, PhD(geophys), 66. *Prof Exp:* Chemist, Scottish Agr Industs, 57-58; mine geologist, Lake Cinch Mines Ltd, Can, 58-60 & Sherritt-Gordon Mines, 62-63; res coordr geol, Can Dept Mines & Natural Resources, Man, 66-69; assoc prof, Northern Ill Univ, 69-71; assoc prof geol & chem, 71-77, PROF GEOL, UNIV WINDSOR, 77- *Concurrent Pos:* Vis scientist, US Geol Survey, Denver, 78-79. *Mem:* Geol Asn Can; AAAS; Geochem Soc. *Res:* Economic geology; geochronology; analytical geochemistry. geostatistics. *Mailing Add:* Dept of Geol Univ of Windsor Windsor ON N9B 3P4 Can

TUREK, FRED WILLIAM, b Detroit, Mich, July 31, 47; m 70. REPRODUCTIVE ENDOCRINOLOGY, CIRCADIAN RHYTHMS. *Educ:* Mich State Univ, BS, 69; Stanford Univ, PhD(biol sci), 73. *Prof Exp:* Fel reproductive biol, Univ Tex, Austin, 73-75; asst prof reproductive endocrinol, 75-80, ASSOC PROF, DEPT NEUROBIOL & PHYSIOL, NORTHWESTERN UNIV, 80- *Concurrent Pos:* NIH fel, 73; res career develop award, 78-83; vis asst prof, Dept Anat, Univ Calif, Los Angeles, 79; vis scientist, Dept Zool, Univ Bristol, Eng, 81. *Mem:* Am Soc Zoologists; Soc Neurosci; Soc Study of Reproduction; Am Physiol Soc; Endocrine Soc. *Res:* Role of the photoperiod in regulating the hypothalamo-pituitary-gonadal axis in birds and mammals; neural basis for the generation of circadian rhythms. *Mailing Add:* Dept Neurobiol & Physiol Northwestern Univ Evanston IL 60201

TUREK, WILLIAM NORBERT, b St Paul, Minn, June 30, 31; m 66. SYNTHETIC ORGANIC CHEMISTRY. *Educ:* Col St Thomas, BS, 53; Univ Md, PhD(org chem), 58. *Prof Exp:* From asst prof to assoc prof, 63-75, PROF CHEM, ST BONAVENTURE UNIV, 75-, CHMN DEPT, 77- *Mem:* Am Chem Soc. *Res:* Pyrrolines; substituted furans; vinyl heterocycles. *Mailing Add:* Dept of Chem St Bonaventure Univ St Bonaventure NY 14778

TUREKIAN, KARL KAREKIN, b New York, NY, Oct 25, 27; m 62; c 2. GEOCHEMISTRY. *Educ:* Wheaton Col, Ill, AB, 49; Columbia Univ, MA, 51, PhD, 55. *Prof Exp:* Lectr geol, Columbia Univ, 53-54, res assoc geochem, Lamont Geol Observ, 54-56; from asst prof to prof, 56-72, HENRY BARNARD DORIS PROF GEOL & GEOPHYS, YALE UNIV, 72- *Concurrent Pos:* Guggenheim fel, 62-63; consult, President's Comn Marine Sci Eng & Resources, 67-68 & Oceanog Panel, NSF, 68-71; ed, J Geophys Res, 69-75 & Earth & Planetary Sci Letters, 75-; mem, US Nat Comn Geochem, Nat Acad Sci, 70-73, Climate Res Bd, 77-80 & Ocean Sci Bd, 79-82; group experts Sci Aspects Marine Pollution, UN; co-ed, Earth & Planetary Sci Lett, 75- *Mem:* Fel AAAS; fel Geol Soc Am; Geochem Soc (pres, 75-76); Am Chem Soc; fel Meteoritical Soc. *Res:* Marine geochemistry; geochemistry of trace elements; planetary evolution. *Mailing Add:* Dept of Geol & Geophys Yale Univ Box 6666 New Haven CT 06511

TUREL, FRANZISKA LILI MARGARETE, b Berlin, Ger, Jan 10, 24; nat Can. PLANT PHYSIOLOGY. *Educ:* Swiss Fed Inst Tech, dipl, 47, Dr sc nat, 52. *Prof Exp:* Asst to prof, Inst Appl Bot, Swiss Fed Inst Tech, 47-50; asst to dir, Swiss Fed Exp Sta, Waedenswil, 50-53; fel, Prairie Regional Lab, Nat Res Coun Can, 53-55, asst res officer, 55-58; res assoc bact, 58-59, lectr, 65-69, asst prof, 69-75, ASSOC PROF PLANT PHYSIOL, UNIV SASK, 75-, RES ASSOC PLANT PHYSIOL, 60- *Mem:* AAAS; Can Bot Asn. *Res:* Plant pathology; physiology of host-parasite relationships. *Mailing Add:* 844 Univ Dr Saskatoon SK S7N 0J7 Can

TURER, JACK, b New York, NY, Mar 18, 12; m 38; c 1. ORGANIC CHEMISTRY, PHYSICAL CHEMISTRY. *Educ:* City Col New York, BS, 34; Fairleigh Dickinson Univ, MAS, 69. *Prof Exp:* Res chemist, US Pub Rds Admin, 36-39; res chemist, USDA, 39-41, Eastern Regional Res Labs, 41-45; chief chemist, Va-Carolina Chem Corp, 45-52; tech dir, Textile Chem, Witco Chem Corp, 52-66, tech mgr automotive lubricants & petrol prod, 66-72, corp dir labeling govt regulations & chem adv, 72-77; CHEM INDUST SPECIALIST TOXIC SUBSTANCES CONTROL ACT & FED REGULATIONS EXPERT, OFF TOXIC SUBSTANCES, ENVIRON PROTECTION AGENCY, 77- *Concurrent Pos:* Abstr, Chem Abstracts, 53-; consult. *Mem:* Am Chem Soc; Am Soc Test & Mat; Am Asn Textile Chem & Colorists; Am Inst Chem; Am Soc Lubrication Eng. *Res:* Soils; chemurgy; electrochemistry; oils and fats; proteins for synthetic textile fibers; textile chemicals and finishes; automotive lubricants and petrochemicals; pollution control; labeling; government regulations. *Mailing Add:* Apt 434N 1600 S Eads St Arlington VA 22202

TURESKY, SAMUEL SAUL, b Portland, Maine, Feb 22, 16; m 52; c 5. DENTISTRY. *Educ:* Harvard Univ, AB, 37; Tufts Col, DMD, 41. *Prof Exp:* Res assoc oral path & periodont, 47-55, from asst prof to assoc prof, 55-71, PROF PERIDONT, SCH DENT MED, TUFTS UNIV, 71- *Mem:* Int Asn Dent Res. *Res:* Histochemistry of gingiva; calculus and plaque formation and prevention. *Mailing Add:* 1758 Beacon St Brookline MA 02146

TURGEON, ALFRED J, b White Plains, NY, Sept 13, 43; m 66; c 1. WEED SCIENCE, ECOLOGY. *Educ:* Rutgers Univ, New Brunswick, BS, 65; Mich State Univ, MS, 70, PhD(weed sci), 71. *Prof Exp:* Asst prof, 71-77, ASSOC PROF HORT, UNIV ILL, URBANA, 77- *Concurrent Pos:* Mem, NCent Weed Control Conf. *Mem:* Weed Sci Soc Am; Am Soc Agron. *Res:* Turfgrass ecology and cultural systems; life history and control of weeds in turf; fate of herbicides in turf ecosystems. *Mailing Add:* 10 Hort Field Lab Univ of Ill Urbana IL 61801

TURGEON, JEAN, b Montreal, Que, May 8, 36. MATHEMATICS. *Educ:* Univ Toronto, MA, 65, PhD, 68. *Prof Exp:* Asst prof math, Univ Montreal, 69-73; ASSOC PROF MATH, CONCORDIA UNIV, 73- *Mem:* AAAS; Am Math Soc; Math Asn Am; Can Math Cong. *Res:* Geometry. *Mailing Add:* Dept of Math Concordia Univ Montreal PQ H3C 3J7 Can

TURGEON, JUDITH LEE, b Topeka, Kans, Mar 19, 42. NEUROENDOCRINOLOGY, REPRODUCTIVE PHYSIOLOGY. *Educ:* Washburn Univ, BA, 65; Univ Kans, PhD(anat), 69. *Prof Exp:* Res assoc physiol, Sch Med, Univ Md, 69-71, asst prof, 71-75; asst prof, 75-80, ASSOC PROF HUMAN PHYSIOL, SCH MED, UNIV CALIF, DAVIS, 80- *Mem:* Soc Study Reproduction; Endocrine Soc; Am Physiol Soc. *Res:* Hypothalamic control of gonadotrophin secretion by the anterior pituitary; mechanisms in hormone secretion. *Mailing Add:* Dept Human Physiol Sch Med Univ Calif Davis CA 95616

TURI, PAUL GEORGE, b Battonya, Hungary, Apr 16, 17; US citizen; m 41; c 1. INDUSTRIAL PHARMACY, ANALYTICAL CHEMISTRY. *Educ:* Pazmany Peter Univ, Budapest, MS, 40, PhD(pharm), 46. *Prof Exp:* Mgr, Szanto Pharm Labs, Budapest, 46-48; res coord, Pharmaceut Indust Ctr, 48-49; dep dir, Pharm Res Inst, 50-53, head pharm res & develop, 55-56; dep mgr qual control dept, Chinoin Chem Works, 53-55; anal chemist, Chase Chem Co, NJ, 57-59; sr scientist, 59-60, group leader anal res, 60-63, head anal labs, 63-70, mgr pharm res, 70-74, ASSOC SECT HEAD, SANDOZ PHARMACEUT, SANDOZ INC, 75- *Concurrent Pos:* Hon asst prof, Pazmany Peter Univ, Budapest, 46-48, hon adj prof, 48-56; lectr, Budapest Tech Univ, 52-55. *Mem:* Am Pharmaceut Asn; Acad Pharmaceut Sci; Int Pharmaceut Fedn; Am Chem Soc. *Res:* Pharmaceutical analysis; pharmacy research and development. *Mailing Add:* Pharm Res Dept Sandoz Inc Rte 10 East Hanover NJ 07936

TURINO, GERARD MICHAEL, b New York, NY, May 16, 24; m 51; c 3. MEDICINE. *Educ:* Princeton Univ, AB, 45; Columbia Univ, MD, 48. *Prof Exp:* Mem staff, Div Med Sci, Nat Res Coun, 51-53; resident med, Bellevue Hosp, New York, 53-54; assoc, 56-60, from asst prof to assoc prof, 60-72, PROF MED, COL PHYSICIANS & SURGEONS, COLUMBIA UNIV, 72- *Concurrent Pos:* Nat Found Infantile Paralysis fel, Col Physicians & Surgeons, Columbia Univ, 54-56, NY Heart Asn sr fel, 56-60; asst physician, Presby Hosp, New York, 56-61, from asst attend physician to assoc attend physician, 61-72, dir, Cardiovasc Lab, 66-, attend physician, 72-; consult, Vet Admin Hosp, East Orange, NJ; mem, Career Invest Health Res Coun, New York, 61; vpres coun, Am Heart Asn, 78-81. *Mem:* AAAS; Harvey Soc; Asn Am Physicians; Am Soc Clin Invest; Am Physiol Soc. *Res:* Internal medicine; cardio-pulmonary physiology. *Mailing Add:* Col Physicians & Surgeons Columbia Univ 630 W 168th St New York NY 10032

TURINSKY, JIRI, b Prague, Czech, Apr 9, 35; m 64; c 2. PHYSIOLOGY, BIOCHEMISTRY. *Educ:* Charles Univ, Prague, MD, 59, PhD(physiol), 62. *Prof Exp:* Instr & res assoc physiol, Med Sch, Charles Univ, Prague, 59-66, asst prof, 68-69; asst prof, 70-71, assoc prof, 71-79, PROF PHYSIOL, ALBANY MED COL, 79- *Concurrent Pos:* Res fel surg res, Med Sch, Univ Pa, 66-68. *Mem:* Am Physiol Soc; Am Diabetes Asn; Am Burn Asn. *Res:* Regulation of hormone secretion; endocrine control of metabolism; control of metabolism after trauma. *Mailing Add:* Dept of Physiol Albany Med Col Albany NY 12208

TURITTO, VINCENT THOMAS, b New York, NY, June 4, 44; m 70; c 3. BIOMATERIALS, HEMOSTASIS. *Educ:* Manhattan Col, BChemE, 65; Columbia Univ, DEngSc, 72. *Prof Exp:* Prof bioeng, Univ Rio de Janeiro, 72-73; res asst, F Hoffmann La Roche & Co, Ltd, 73-74; RES ASSOC, ST LUKES-ROOSEVELT HOSP & COLUMBIA UNIV, 74- *Concurrent Pos:* Prin investr, Am Heart Asn, 77-80 & NIH, 82-85; established investr, Am Heart Asn, 77-82. *Mem:* NY Acad Sci; AAAS; Sigma Xi; Soc Rheology; Int Soc Thrombosis & Nemostasis. *Res:* Application of engineering principles for understanding blood and surface interactions as they pertain in hemostasis and thrombosis. *Mailing Add:* Dept Med St Lukes-Roosevelt Hosp 478 W 59th St New York NY 10019

TURK, AMOS, b New York, NY, Feb 28, 18; m 41; c 3. ORGANIC CHEMISTRY. *Educ:* City Col New York, BS, 37; Ohio State Univ, MA, 38, PhD(chem), 40. *Prof Exp:* Res assoc, Explosives Res Lab, Pa, 42-44 & Allegany Ballistics Lab, Md, 44-46; instr org chem, City Col New York, 46-49; dir res & develop, Connor Eng Corp, 49-54; from asst prof to assoc prof, 56-66, PROF CHEM, CITY COL NEW YORK, 67-; CONSULT CHEMIST, 54- *Mem:* Am Chem Soc; Am Soc Test & Mat; Am Indust Hyg Asn; Air Pollution Control Asn; NY Acad Sci. *Res:* Organic synthesis; activated carbon; air analysis and purification; odors. *Mailing Add:* 7 Tarrywile Lake Dr Danbury CT 06810

TURK, DONALD EARLE, b Dryden, NY, Sept 4, 31. NUTRITION, BIOCHEMISTRY. *Educ:* Cornell Univ, BS, 53, MNS, 57; Univ Wis, PhD(biochem, nutrit), 60. *Prof Exp:* Asst prof, 60-67, assoc prof poultry sci, 67-74, assoc prof food sci, 74-78, PROF FOOD SCI, CLEMSON UNIV, 78- *Concurrent Pos:* From vchmn to chmn, SC Nutrit Comt, 75-77. *Mem:* AAAS; Poultry Sci Asn; Am Chem Soc; Am Inst Nutrit; Sigma Xi. *Res:* Protein and energy relationships in the fowl; mineral metabolism in obese humans; trace mineral metabolism; digestive tract disease and nutrient absorption; trace mineral deficiency and nucleic acid metabolism. *Mailing Add:* Food Sci Dept Clemson Univ Clemson SC 29631

TURK, FATEH(FRANK) M, b June 11, 24; Can citizen; m 60; c 2. AGRICULTURE, BIOLOGY. *Educ:* Univ Bombay, BSc, 47; Univ Sind Pakistan, MSc, 52; Univ Minn, PhD(plant path), 56. *Prof Exp:* Res scientist & lectr, Govt Res Sta & Sci Col, 47-52; res asst, Univ Minn, 53-55; tech adv, A M Lotia Chem Co, Pakistan, 56-57; microbiologist, Gallowhur Chem Can, Montreal, 60-78; SR EVAL OFFICER PESTICIDES, AGR CAN, 61- *Concurrent Pos:* Adv, Western Comt Plant Dis Control, 77-81. *Mem:* Can Phytopath Soc; Can Pest Mgt Soc. *Res:* Fungicides and nematicides. *Mailing Add:* K W Neatby Bldg Pesticide Div Ottawa ON K1A 0C6 Can

TURK, GREGORY CHESTER, b Elizabeth, NJ, Nov 16, 51; m 74; c 3. LASER SPECTROSCOPY, ATOMIC SPECTROMETRY. *Educ:* Rutgers Col, BA, 73; Univ Md, PhD(anal chem), 78. *Prof Exp:* RES CHEMIST, NAT BUR STANDARDS, 76- *Mem:* Am Chem Soc; Soc Applied Spectros. *Res:* Application of lasers for spectroscopic chemical analysis, in particular the development of laser-enhanced ionization spectrometry in flames. *Mailing Add:* Bldg 222/Rm-A223 Ctr Anal Chem Nat Bur Standards Washington DC 20234

TURK, KENNETH LEROY, b Mt Vernon, Mo, July 14, 08; m 34. DAIRY HUSBANDRY. *Educ:* Univ Mo, BS, 30; Cornell Univ, MS, 31, PhD(animal husb), 34. *Prof Exp:* Asst animal husb, Cornell Univ, 31-34, from exten instr to exten asst prof, 34-38; prof dairy husb, Univ Md, 38-44, head dept, 40-44; prof animal husb, 44-74, dir int agr develop, 63-74, head dept, 45-63, EMER PROF ANIMAL SCI, CORNELL UNIV, 74- *Concurrent Pos:* Vis prof, Univ Philippines, 54-55; consult, Rockefeller Found, 58-62; mem, Expert Panel Dairy Educ, Food & Agr Orgn, 65-71, Expert Panel Animal Husb Educ, 69-71; tech adv comt, Inst Nutrit Cent Am & Panama, 67-69; mem, Working Group Agr Res, US-USSR Joint Comn Sci & Tech Coop, 72. *Mem:* AAAS; Am Soc Animal Sci; Am Dairy Sci Asn (pres, 59-60); Asn US Univ Dir Int Agr Progs (pres, 71-72). *Res:* Nutrition of dairy calves and cows; nutritive value of hay and pasture crops; dairy cattle breeding; international agricultural development; animal science. *Mailing Add:* 803 Hanshaw Rd Ithaca NY 14850

TURK, LELAND JAN, b Tulare, Calif, July 18, 38; m 56; c 3. GEOLOGY, HYDROLOGY. *Educ:* Fresno State Col, BA, 61; Stanford Univ, MS, 63 & 67, PhD(geol), 69. *Prof Exp:* Jr geologist, Mobil Oil Libya Ltd, Tripoli, Libya, 63-65, geologist, 65-66; asst prof, 68-72, ASSOC PROF GEOL, UNIV TEX, AUSTIN, 72- *Concurrent Pos:* Prof engr, Tex; ed-in-chief, Environ Geol, 74-; partner, Turke-Kehle & Assocs, Consult Geologists. *Mem:* Geol Soc Am; Asn Eng Geol; Am Geophys Union; Am Inst Prof Geologists; Am Water Res Asn. *Res:* Hydrogeology; environmental geology; petroleum geology. *Mailing Add:* Dept of Geol Sci Univ of Tex Austin TX 78712

TURKANIS, STUART ALLEN, b Everett, Mass, Dec 15, 36; m 64; c 2. PHARMACOLOGY. *Educ:* Mass Col Pharm, BS, 58, MS, 60; Univ Utah, PhD(pharmacol), 67. *Prof Exp:* Asst prof, 67-76, ASSOC PROF PHARMACOL, COL MED, UNIV UTAH, 76- *Concurrent Pos:* USPHS fel, Univ Col, Univ London, 67-69. *Mem:* AAAS; Am Soc Pharmacol & Exp Therapeut; Soc Neurosci. *Res:* Pharmacology and physiology of synaptic transmission; mechanisms of action of antiepileptic drugs; pharmacology of marijuana and its surrogates. *Mailing Add:* Dept of Pharmacol Univ of Utah Med Ctr Salt Lake City UT 84112

TURKDOGAN, ETHEM TUGRUL, b Istanbul, Sept 12, 23; m 50; c 2. METALLURGY. *Educ:* Univ Sheffield, BMet, 47, MMet, 49, PhD, 51. *Prof Exp:* Res metallurgist, Res & Develop, Brit Oxygen Co, Eng, 50-51; head phys chem sect, Brit Iron & Steel Res Asn, 51-59; staff scientist, 59-64, mgr chem metall, 64-72, SR RES CONSULT, US STEEL FUNDAMENTAL RES LAB, 72- *Concurrent Pos:* Mem Adv Off Critical Tables Comt, Nat Acad Sci, 66-69; mem high temperature chem panel, Nat Res Coun; A Frank Golick lectr, Univ Mo-Rolla; Howe Mem lectr, Iron & Steel Soc, 78. *Honors & Awards:* Brunton Medal, Univ Sheffield, 51; Andrew Carnegie Silver Medal, Brit Iron & Steel Inst, 53; Robert W Hunt Medal, Am Inst Mining, Metall & Petrol Engrs, 67; Mathewson Gold Medal, Metall Soc, 75; Chipman Award, Iron & Steel Soc, 78; Kroll Medal, Metals Soc, 78. *Mem:* Am Inst Mining, Metall & Petrol Engrs; Brit Iron & Steel Inst; Can Inst Mining & Metall; Am Iron & Steel Inst. *Res:* Chemical metallurgy; physical chemistry of high temperature reactions of interest to metallurgical processes and related subjects. *Mailing Add:* Res Lab US Steel Corp Monroeville PA 15146

TURKEL, RICKEY MARTIN, b New York, NY, Apr 12, 43; m 65; c 2. ORGANIC CHEMISTRY. *Educ:* Hofstra Univ, BA, 63; Mass Inst Technol, PhD(org chem), 68; Ohio State Univ, MA, 76. *Prof Exp:* Fel org chem, Hebrew Univ, Jerusalem, 68-69 & Tulane Univ, 69-70; assoc abstractor, 70-71, assoc ed, 71-76, SR ASSOC ED, CHEM ABSTR SERV, 77- *Concurrent Pos:* Consult, translator Russian, Serbocroation & Hebrew Tech Literature. *Honors & Awards:* Award, Am Chem Soc, 63. *Mem:* Am Chem Soc. *Res:* Synthetic organic chemistry; organometallic chemistry; literature chemistry; Hebrew and Slavic linguistics. *Mailing Add:* 2980 Fair Ave Columbus OH 43209

TURKELTAUB, PAUL CHARLES, b Brooklyn, NY, Jan 10, 44; m 67; c 2. ALLERGY, CLINICAL IMMUNOLOGY. *Educ:* Brooklyn Col, BS, 65; Univ Pittsburgh, MD, 69. *Prof Exp:* RES INVESTR ALLERGENIC PROD BR, BUR BIOLOGICS, 77- *Concurrent Pos:* Consult, Nat Ctr Health Statist, 78- *Mem:* Am Acad Allergy. *Res:* Investigating the safety and efficacy of allergenic products used for the diagnosis and treatment of allergic diseases. *Mailing Add:* Rm 214 Bldg 29 8800 Rockville Pike Bethesda MD 20014

TURKEVICH, ANTHONY, b New York, NY, July 23, 16; m 48; c 2. NUCLEAR CHEMISTRY, SPACE CHEMISTRY. *Educ:* Dartmouth Col, BA, 37; Princeton Univ, PhD(phys chem), 40. *Hon Degrees:* DSc, Dartmouth Col, 71. *Prof Exp:* Res assoc molecular spectra, Dept Physics, Univ Chicago, 40-41, res chemist, Metall Lab, 43-45; res chemist, SAM Labs, Columbia Univ, 42-43; res physicist, Los Alamos Sci Lab, 45-46; from asst prof to assoc prof, 46-50, James Franck prof, 65-71, PROF CHEM, ENRICO FERMI

INST & CHEM DEPT, UNIV CHICAGO, 50-, JAMES FRANCK DISTINGUISHED SERV PROF, 71- *Concurrent Pos:* NSF fel, Europ Orgn Nuclear Res, Switz, 61-62; J W Kennedy Mem lectr, Univ Wash, St Louis, 64; NSF fel, Orsay, France, 70; consult, Labs, US AEC. *Honors & Awards:* E O Lawrence Award, US AEC, 62; Atoms for Peace Award, 69; Nuclear Applns Award, Am Chem Soc, 72. *Mem:* Nat Acad Sci; AAAS; Am Chem Soc; Am Acad Arts & Sci; Royal Soc Arts. *Res:* Reactions of energetic particles with complex nuclei; radioactivity in meteorites; chemical composition of the moon and meteorites. *Mailing Add:* Enrico Fermi Inst Univ of Chicago 5640 S Ellis Ave Chicago IL 60637

TURKEVICH, JOHN, b Minneapolis, Minn, Jan 20, 07; m 36; c 2. PHYSICAL CHEMISTRY. *Educ:* Dartmouth Col, BS, 28, MA, 30; Princeton Univ, AM, 32, PhD(chem), 34. *Prof Exp:* Instr, Dartmouth Col, 28-31; from instr to prof, Princeton Univ, 36-55, Eugene Higgins prof chem, 55-77; MEM STAFF, FRICK CHEM LABS, 77- *Concurrent Pos:* Consult, M W Kellogg Co Div, Pullman, Inc, NY, 36-, Radio Corp Am Labs, 43-, Brookhaven Nat Lab, 47, US Energy Res & Develop Admin, 50- & US Dept State; chmn, US Deleg Educators, USSR, 58; rep, US Sci Am Nat Exhib, Moscow, 59; actg sci attache, US Embassy, Moscow, 60, sci attache, 61; lectr, US Army War Col & US Air War Col; Phi Beta Kappa vis scholar, 61. *Honors & Awards:* Award, Mfg Chemists Asn, 56. *Mem:* Am Chem Soc; Am Phys Soc. *Res:* Catalysis; molecular structure; synthesis and characterization of mondisperse noble metals, sulica, alumina nd zeolites for heterogeneous and homogeneous catalysis; synthesis of drugs for cancer and study of biochemistry of drug action and cancer. *Mailing Add:* Frick Chem Labs Princeton NJ 08544

TURKINGTON, ROBERT (ROY) ALBERT, b Portadown, Northern Ireland, Apr 8, 51; Brit citizen; m 75; c 2. PLANT ECOLOGY. *Educ:* New Univ Ulster, BSc, 72; Univ Col North Wales, dipl ecol, 74, PhD(plant ecol), 75. *Prof Exp:* Fel plant ecol, Univ Western Ont, 76-77; ASST PROF BOT, UNIV BC, 77- *Mem:* Brit Ecol Soc; Can Bot Asn; Ecol Soc Am. *Res:* Plant population biology, with special reference to neighbor relationships among grasses and legumes. *Mailing Add:* Dept of Bot Univ of BC Vancouver BC V6T 2B1 Can

TURKINGTON, ROGER W, b Manchester, Conn, Jan 13, 36; m 60; c 1. MEDICINE, BIOCHEMISTRY. *Educ:* Wesleyan Univ, AB, 58; Harvard Med Sch, MD, 63; Am Bd Internal Med, dipl. *Prof Exp:* Intern med, Duke Univ Hosp, 63-64, resident, 64-65; res assoc, NIH, 65-67; res assoc, Sch Med, Duke Univ, 67-68, asst prof med, 68-69, asst prof med & biochem, 69-71; assoc prof med, Univ Wis-Madison, 71-73; CHIEF ENDOCRINOL, ST LUKES HOSP, 73- *Concurrent Pos:* Chief endocrinol, Vet Admin Hosp, Durham, NC, 67-71. *Mem:* Am Soc Clin Invest; Am Soc Cancer Res; Endocrine Soc; Am Soc Biol Chem; Am Fedn Clin Res. *Res:* Biochemistry of development and cancer; mechanisms of hormone action. *Mailing Add:* St Luke's Hosp 2900 W Oklahoma Ave Milwaukee WI 53215

TURKKI, PIRKKO REETTA, b Laitila, Finland, Aug 27, 34; m 57; c 2. NUTRITION, FOOD SCIENCE. *Educ:* Helsinki Home Econ Teacher's Col, dipl, 57; Univ Mass, Amherst, MS, 62; Univ Tenn, Knoxville, PhD(nutrit, food sci), 65. *Prof Exp:* Res assoc biochem, Univ Tenn, 65-66; NIH res fel, Albany Med Col, 66-68; asst prof, 68-72, assoc prof, 72-78, asst dean, Col Human Develop, 75-79, PROF NUTRIT, SYRACUSE UNIV, 78- *Mem:* Am Dietetic Asn; Soc Nutrit Educ; Nutrit Today Soc. *Res:* Phospholipid metabolism in choline deficiency; role of diet in hyperlipemia; riboflavin status in protein/energy deprivation. *Mailing Add:* 200 Slocum Hall Col Human Develop Syracuse Univ Syracuse NY 13210

TURKOT, FRANK, b Woodlynne, NJ, Sept 29, 29; m 59; c 4. PHYSICS. *Educ:* Univ Pa, BA, 51; Cornell Univ, PhD(physics), 59. *Prof Exp:* Res assoc particle physics, Lab Nuclear Studies, Cornell Univ, 59-60; from asst physicist to sr physicist, Brookhaven Nat Lab, NY, 60-74; PHYSICIST, FERMILAB, 74- *Mem:* Fel Am Phys Soc. *Res:* Experiments in elementary particle physics to study photoproduction processes and high energy collisions of strongly-interacting particles; particle accelerator research. *Mailing Add:* Fermilab PO Box 500 Batavia IL 60510

TURKOWSKI, FRANK JOSEPH, b Syracuse, NY, Aug 20, 35; m 73; c 3. ECOLOGY, WILDLIFE BIOLOGY. *Educ:* Ariz State Uniiv, BS, 60, PhD(zool), 69. *Prof Exp:* Mammal control agent, US Fish & Wildlife Serv, Bur Sports Fisheries & Wildlife, 60-63; lab tech asst & jr scientist, Mus Natural Hist, Univ Minn, 65-66; dir, Natural H Hist & Arts Prog & Educ & Res, Ariz Zool Soc, 66-72; wildlife res biologist, Wildlife Res Br, US Forest Serv, 72-74; WILDLIFE RES BIOLOGIST, WILDLIFE RES BR, US FISH & WILDLIFE SERV, 75- *Concurrent Pos:* NSF wildlife res biologist, US Forest Serv; dir educ, Phoenix Zoo Auxiliary & Fauna Preserv Soc. *Mem:* Am Soc Mammalogists; Wildlife Soc. *Res:* Mammalian ecology and wildlife biology, especially Carnivora; predator-prey relationships; mammalian depredations control research. *Mailing Add:* US Fish & Wildlife Serv PO Drawer 1051 Uvalde TX 78801

TURKSTRA, CARL J, b Hamilton, Ont, Oct 29, 36; m 64; c 2. CIVIL ENGINEERING, STRUCTURAL ENGINEERING. *Educ:* Queen's Univ, Ont, BSc, 58; Univ Ill, MS, 60; Univ Waterloo, PhD(struct safety), 63. *Prof Exp:* Engr, F R Harris, Consult Engrs, 62-63; lectr civil eng, Univ Col, Univ London, 63-65; asst prof, 65-71, assoc prof, 71-77, PROF CIVIL ENG, MCGILL UNIV, 77- *Concurrent Pos:* Res grants, Nat Res Coun Can, 65-; mem, Int Joint Comt on Struct Safety, 76-; chmn, Comt on Limit States Design in Masonry, Nat Bldg Code of Can, 77-; consult struct engr, 68- *Honors & Awards:* State of the Art Award, Am Soc Civil Engrs, 73. *Mem:* Am Soc Civil Engrs; Am Acad Mech; Can Soc Civil Eng. *Res:* Choice of structural safety levels based on probabilistic and decision theory concepts; structural masonry; optimum structural design. *Mailing Add:* Dept Civil Eng 817 Sherbrooke St W McGill Univ Montreal PQ H3A 2T5 Can

TURLAPATY, PRASAD, b Vijayawada, India, June 1, 42; m 72; c 1. HYPERTENSION. *Educ:* Andhra Univ, India, BSc, 60, BPharm, 64, MPharm 65; Univ Hawaii, PhD(pharmacol), 71. *Prof Exp:* Fel pharmacol, Univ Tex Health Sci Ctr, San Antonio, 72-74; scientist pharamacol, Postgrad Med Inst, Pondicherry, India, 75-77; instr physiol, Downstate Med Ctr, State Univ NY, Brooklyn, 77-78, asst prof, 78-80; clin invest assoc, 80-81, SR CLIN INVEST ASSOC MED, IVES LABS INC, NEW YORK, 82- *Mem:* Am Physiol Soc; NY Acad Sci; AAAS. *Res:* Physiology and pharmacology of vascular smooth muscle in various disease states such as hypertension and diabetes; role of magnesium and calcium in the control of vascular smooth muscle tone. *Mailing Add:* Ives Labs Inc 685 Third Ave New York NY 10017

TURLEY, HUGH PATRICK, cell physiology, biology, see previous edition

TURLEY, JUNE WILLIAMS, b Boston, Mass, Apr 12, 29; m 50; c 3. X-RAY CRYSTALLOGRAPHY, ECONOMIC STATISTICS. *Educ:* Wilkes Col, BS, 50; Pa State Univ, MS, 51, PhD(biochem), 57. *Prof Exp:* Asst x-ray crystal struct anal, Pa State Univ, 53-56, res assoc, 56-57; from res chemist to sr res chemist, Dow Chem Co, 57-71, res mgr, Anal Labs, 71-74, ECON PLANNER, ECON PLANNING & DEVELOP, DOW CHEM CO, 74- *Mem:* Am Chem Soc; World Future Soc; Sigma Xi; Women's Nat Sci Fraternity. *Res:* Crystal and molecular structure analysis; identification and analysis of compounds using x-ray methods; computing analysis; industrial projects correlating chemical process and business data for long range economic planning. *Mailing Add:* Econ Planning & Develop Bldg 2030 The Dow Chem Co Midland MI 48640

TURLEY, KEVIN, b New York, NY, May 21, 46. CARDIAC SURGERY, PHYSIOLOGY. *Educ:* Fordham Univ, BA, 68; Med Col Wis, MD, 72. *Prof Exp:* Intern surgery, Ohio State Univ, 72-73; gen surgery resident, Univ SFla, 73-75, chief resident, 75-76; chief resident, 76-78, INSTR CARDIAC SURGERY, UNIV CALIF, SAN FRANCISCO, 78- *Concurrent Pos:* Fel, Cardiovascular Res Inst, 78- *Res:* Cardiovascular research; right ventricular function pulmonary hypertension both chronic and acute; aortic insufficency and deep hypothermia and total circulatory arrest. *Mailing Add:* Dept of Surgery Univ of Calif San Francisco CA 94121

TURLEY, RICHARD EYRING, b El Paso, Tex, Dec 29, 30; m 54; c 7. OPERATIONS RESEARCH, NUCLEAR & SYSTEMS ENGINEERING. *Educ:* Univ Utah, BS, 55, MS, 58; Iowa State Univ, PhD(nuclear eng), 66. *Prof Exp:* Engr, Convair Div, Gen Dynamics Corp, Tex, 55-56 & El Paso Natural Gas Co, 56-57; asst prof mech & nuclear eng, Univ Utah, 57-62; asst prof eng sci & nuclear eng, Iowa State Univ, 63-67; sect mgr systs anal, Battelle-Northwest, 67-71, res assoc systs eng, 71-72; assoc prof, 72-81, PROF MECH & INDUST ENG, UNIV UTAH, 81- *Concurrent Pos:* Mem adv bd, Wash/Alaska Regional Med Prog, 70-72; alt state rep, Western Interstate Nuclear Bd, 72-78; exec dir, Utah Nuclear Energy Comn, 72-73; sci adv, State of Utah, 73-77; consult to indust. *Mem:* Am Inst Indust Engrs. *Res:* Waste management policy; operations research; technology assessment; energy conservation; engineering economics; energy; management and systems engineering; simulation and modeling. *Mailing Add:* 3791 Viking Rd Salt Lake City UT 84109

TURLEY, SHELDON GAMAGE, b Pa, June 13, 22; m 50; c 3. PHYSICS. *Educ:* Pa State Univ, BS, 50, MS, 51, PhD(physics), 57. *Prof Exp:* Res assoc physics of aerosols, Pa State Univ, 52-53; res physicist, 57-62, SR RES PHYSICIST, DOW CHEM CO, 62- *Mem:* Sigma Xi; Am Phys Soc. *Res:* High polymer physics, especially with dynamic mechanical and electrical properties of polymers and their relationship to molecular structure. *Mailing Add:* Bldg 438 Dow Chem Co Midland MI 48640

TURMAN, ELBERT JEROME, b Granite, Okla, Jan 26, 24; m 49; c 2. ANIMAL SCIENCE. *Educ:* Okla State Univ, BS, 49; Purdue Univ, MS, 50, PhD(physiol), 53. *Prof Exp:* From instr to asst prof animal husb, Purdue Univ, 50-55; from asst prof to assoc prof, 55-63, PROF ANIMAL SCI, OKLA STATE UNIV, 63- *Mem:* Soc Study Reproduction; Am Soc Animal Sci. *Res:* Physiology of reproduction of beef cattle, sheep and swine. *Mailing Add:* Dept of Animal Sci Okla State Univ Stillwater OK 74078

TURNACLIFF, R(OBERT) D(ALE), b Minneapolis, Minn, Mar 27, 24; m 52. MECHANICAL ENGINEERING. *Educ:* Univ Minn, BSME, 45, MSME, 47, PhD(mech eng), 57. *Prof Exp:* Res engr, Minn & Ont Paper Co, 47-49; res assoc mech eng, Univ Minn, 49-51, instr, 53-57; mem sr staff, Space Technol Lab, 57-60; lab dir, Aerospace Corp, 60-81. *Mem:* Am Inst Aeronaut & Astronaut; Am Soc Mech Engrs. *Res:* Heat transfer and gas dynamics research in aerodynamics and rocket propulsion systems. *Mailing Add:* 2445 Via Somoma Palos Verdes CA 90274

TURNBLOM, ERNEST WAYNE, b Boston, Mass, Nov 1, 46; m 73; c 1. ORGANIC CHEMISTRY. *Educ:* Worcester Polytech Inst, BS, 68; Columbia Univ, PhD(chem), 72. *Prof Exp:* Instr org chem, Princeton Univ, 72-74; res chemist, 74-77, RES LAB HEAD, EASTMAN KODAK CO, 77- *Mem:* Am Chem Soc. *Res:* Organophosphorus chemistry; pentaalkylphosphoranes and related compounds; chemistry of other main group elements; electrophotographic processes and materials; novel imaging systems. *Mailing Add:* Eastman Kodak Co Res Labs 1669 Lake Ave Rochester NY 14650

TURNBULL, BRUCE FELTON, b Cleveland, Ohio, Mar 2, 28; m 51; c 3. PHYSICAL CHEMISTRY. *Educ:* Case Inst Technol, BS, 50; Faith Theol Sem, BD, 54; Western Reserve Univ, MS, 55, PhD(phys chem), 63. *Prof Exp:* Chemist, Gen Motors Corp, Ohio, 50-51; asst prof chem, Cedarville Col, 55-63; from asst prof to assoc prof, 63-70, PROF CHEM, CLEVELAND STATE UNIV, 70-, OMBUDSMAN, 71- *Mem:* AAAS; Am Chem Soc; Am Asn Physics Teachers. *Res:* Thermodynamics; molecular structure studies with infrared spectroscopy. *Mailing Add:* Dept of Chem Cleveland State Univ Cleveland OH 44115

TURNBULL, BRUCE WILLIAM, b Purley, Eng, Oct 8, 46; m 72; c 2. BIOMETRICS, BIOSTATISTICS. *Educ:* Cambridge Univ, BA, 67; Cornell Univ, MS, 70, PhD(statist), 71. *Prof Exp:* Asst prof statist, Stanford Univ, 71-72; lectr math, Oxford Univ, 72-76; ASSOC PROF OPER RES STATIST, CORNELL UNIV, 76- *Honors & Awards:* Snedecor Award, Am Statist Asn, 79. *Mem:* Biomet Soc; Am Statist Asn; Oper Res Soc Am; Royal Statist Soc; Statist Soc Can. *Res:* Statistical design and analysis of long-term animal studies; general biomedical statistics; survival analysis; relaibility and life testing; quality control. *Mailing Add:* 356 Upson Hall Cornell Univ Ithaca NY 14853

TURNBULL, CRAIG DAVID, b Reading, Pa, Aug 28, 40; m 61; c 4. BIOSTATISTICS, PUBLIC HEALTH. *Educ:* Albright Col, BA, 62; Univ NC, Chapel Hill, MPH, 65, PhD(biostatist), 71. *Prof Exp:* Statistician pub health, Pa State Health Dept, 62-64; biostatistician & clin instr, Health Res Found, State Univ NY, Buffalo, 65-68; from instr to asst prof, 71-77, ASSOC PROF BIOSTATIST, UNIV NC, 78- *Concurrent Pos:* Statist consult, Dept Pub Health, NC, 70-76, Am Col Obstet & Gynec, 71-74 & Sch Nursing, Univ NC, Chapel Hill, 72-75; statist consult & adv bd mem, Asn Schs Pub Health, 74-79; prin investr, Doctoral & Postdoctoral Res Training, 76-; prof dir, BSPH Biostatist, 76-; co-dir, Health Admin Postdoctoral Training, 78-80. *Mem:* Am Statist Asn; Am Pub Health Asn; Sigma Xi; Biomet Soc. *Res:* Public health statistics; perinatal mortality; mental health problems; complications of pregnancy; cogenital malformations. *Mailing Add:* Dept Biostatist Univ NC Chapel Hill NC 27514

TURNBULL, DAVID, b Stark Co, Ill, Feb 18, 15; m 46; c 3. PHYSICAL CHEMISTRY. *Educ:* Monmouth Col, BS, 36; Univ Ill, PhD(phys chem), 39. *Hon Degrees:* ScD, Monmouth Col, 58. *Prof Exp:* Instr phys chem, Case Inst Technol, 39-43, asst prof, 43-46, res proj leader, 45-46; res assoc, Res Lab, Gen Elec Co, 46-51, mgr chem metall sect, 51-58, phys chemist, 58-62; GORDON McKAY PROF APPL PHYSICS, HARVARD UNIV, 62- *Honors & Awards:* Acta Metallurgica Gold Medal, 79; Von Hipple Prize, Mat Res Soc, 79. *Mem:* Nat Acad Sci; AAAS; fel Am Acad Arts & Sci; Am Chem Soc; fel Am Phys Soc. *Res:* Thermionic emission; thermodynamic properties of gases at high pressures; corrosion in non-aqueous media; diffusion in metals; kinetics of nucleation in solid state transformation; solidification; theory of liquids; glass. *Mailing Add:* Div Eng & Appl Physics Pierce Hall Harvard Univ Cambridge MA 02138

TURNBULL, G(ORDON) KEITH, b Cleveland, Ohio, Nov 10, 35; m 57; c 5. METALLURGY. *Educ:* Case Inst Technol, BS, 57, MS, 59, PhD, 62. *Prof Exp:* Res engr, 62-65, sr res engr, 65-69, group leader, 69-71, sect head, Pa, 71-77, div mgr, Alcoa Res Labs, 77-79, asst dir, 79-80, MGR BUS PLANNING SERVS, CORP PLANNING, ALUMINUM CO AM, PA, 80- *Mem:* Am Soc Metals; Am Foundrymen's Soc; Am Inst Mining, Metall & Petrol Engrs; Sigma Xi; Am Soc Eng Educ. *Res:* Solidification of metals; grain refinement of solidifying metals; aluminum alloy development; control of residual stresses in metals; aluminum and titanium forging research; ingot casting, melting, energy and fabricating. *Mailing Add:* Alcoa Res Labs Alcoa Tech Ctr Alcoa Center PA 15069

TURNBULL, KENNETH, b Edinburgh, Scotland, July 12, 51. MESOIONIC CHEMISTRY, ORGANOSULFUR CHEMISTRY. *Educ:* Heriot Watt Univ, Scotland, BSc, 73, PhD(org chem), 76. *Prof Exp:* Res assoc, Erindale Col, Univ Toronto, 76-78; asst prof chem, Grinnell Col, 78-80; ASST PROF ORG CHEM, WRIGHT STATE UNIV, 80- *Mem:* Am Chem Soc. *Res:* Preparation of novel, fused ring and mesoionic compounds; photochromic sydnones; sulfur analogues of n-nitrosamines; unusual compounds containing the Sequals-S linkage in stable configuration. *Mailing Add:* Chem Dept Wright State Univ Dayton OH 45435

TURNBULL, LENNOX BIRCKHEAD, b Richmond, Va, Mar 18, 25; m 63; c 2. ORGANIC CHEMISTRY. *Educ:* Davidson Col, BS, 47; Univ Va, PhD(org chem), 51. *Prof Exp:* Sr res chemist, Merck & Co, Inc, 51-55; res assoc pharmacol, Med Col Va, 56-63; sr res chemist, 63-72, ASSOC DIR DRUG METAB, A H ROBINS CO, 72- *Mem:* AAAS; Am Chem Soc; Toxicol Soc. *Res:* Synthetic medicinal chemistry; steroid hormones; tobacco chemistry; isolation of natural products; tissue residue; drug metabolism. *Mailing Add:* A H Robins Co 1211 Sherwood Ave Richmond VA 23220

TURNBULL, ROBERT JAMES, b Washington, DC, July 26, 41; m 65; c 2. ELECTRICAL ENGINEERING, NUCLEAR ENGINEERING. *Educ:* Mass Inst Technol, BS & MS, 64, PhD(elec eng), 67. *Prof Exp:* From asst prof to assoc prof, 67-77, PROF ELEC ENG, UNIV ILL, URBANA, 77- *Mem:* Inst Elec & Electronics Engrs; Am Phys Soc. *Res:* Electromechanics; electrohydrodynamics; heat transfer; fluid mechanics; controlled thermonuclear fusion; ion sources. *Mailing Add:* Dept of Elec Eng Univ of Ill Urbana IL 61801

TURNDORF, HERMAN, b Paterson, NJ, Dec 22, 30; m 59; c 2. ANESTHESIOLOGY. *Educ:* Oberlin Col, AB, 52; Univ Pa, MD, 56; Am Bd Anesthesiol, dipl, 62. *Prof Exp:* Asst dir, US Naval Hosp, Portsmouth, Va, 59-61; asst anesthetist, Mass Gen Hosp, 61-63; coordr clin affairs, Mt Sinai Hosp, New York, 63-70; prof anesthesiol & chmn dept, Sch Med, WVa Univ, 70-74; PROF ANESTHESIOL & CHMN DEPT, SCH MED, NY UNIV, 74- *Concurrent Pos:* From asst attend anesthetist to assoc attend anesthetist, Mt Sinai Hosp, 63-66; dir anesthesiol, NY Univ Hosp & Bellevue Hosp Med Ctr, 74-; consult anesthesiol, US Naval Hosp, Portsmouth Va & Manhattan Va Hosp, 74- *Mem:* Fel Am Col Anesthesiol; fel Am Soc Anesthesiol; Am Thoracic Soc; AMA; fel Am Col Chest Physicians. *Mailing Add:* New York NY 10016

TURNEAURE, JOHN PAUL, b Yakima, Wash, Jan 16, 39; m 68; c 2. LOW TEMPERATURE PHYSICS. *Educ:* Univ Wash, BS, 61; Stanford Univ, PhD(physics), 67. *Prof Exp:* Res assoc, 66-69, res physicist, 69-75, actg asst prof, 70-73, SR RES ASSOC PHYSICS, STANFORD UNIV, 75- *Mem:* Am Phys Soc. *Res:* Study of radio frequency properties of superconductors, time variations of the fundamental physical constants and general relativistic time effects; development of ultra-stable superconducting cavity oscillators and superconducting microwave structures for particle accelerators. *Mailing Add:* 845 Garland Dr Palo Alto CA 94303

TURNER, ALMON GEORGE, JR, b Detroit, Mich, June 9, 32; m 64; c 3. THEORETICAL CHEMISTRY, INORGANIC CHEMISTRY. *Educ:* Univ Mich, BS, 55; Purdue Univ, MS, 56, PhD(inorg chem), 58. *Prof Exp:* Assoc prof inorg chem, NDak Agr Col, 58-59; instr & fel chem, Carnegie Inst Technol, 59-61; asst prof inorg chem, Polytech Inst Brooklyn, 61-66; assoc prof, 66-74, PROF CHEM, UNIV DETROIT, 74- *Mem:* Am Chem Soc; Am Phys Soc. *Res:* Chemical bonding; electronic structure of molecules; polyhedral molecules; nitrogen-sulfur chemistry; prebiotic chemistry of sulfur. *Mailing Add:* Dept of Chem Univ of Detroit 4001 W McNichols Rd Detroit MI 48221

TURNER, ALVIS GREELY, b Manheim, Pa, Feb 26, 29; m 56; c 2. ENVIRONMENTAL SCIENCES, ENVIRONMENTAL TOXICOLOGY. *Educ:* Univ NC, BA, 52, MSPH, 58, PhD(environ sci), 70; Am Intersoc Acad Cert Sanit, Dipl, 70. *Prof Exp:* Sr sanitarian, Caswell County Health Dept, 54-58; supvr prev med, Arabian Am Oil Co, 58-66; asst prof, 66-80, ASSOC PROF ENVIRON SCI, UNIV NC, CHAPEL HILL, 80- *Mem:* Nat Environ Health Asn; Am Pub Health Asn. *Res:* Hazardous waste management; environmental risk assessment. *Mailing Add:* Dept Environ Sci & Eng Univ NC Chapel Hill NC 27514

TURNER, ANDREW, b Glasgow, Scotland, Dec 24, 22; nat US; m 50; c 2. CHEMICAL ENGINEERING. *Educ:* Univ Mich, BS, 49, MS, 50, PhD(chem eng), 58. *Prof Exp:* Chem engr, Union Carbide Corp, 53-71; sect chief, 72-78, ASST OFF CHIEF, OHIO ENVIRON PROTECTION AGENCY, 78- *Mem:* Am Chem Soc; Am Inst Chem Engrs; Water Pollution Control Conf. *Res:* Synthetic resins and plastics. *Mailing Add:* 417 Montreal Pl Westerville OH 43081

TURNER, ANDREW B, b Lock Haven, Pa, Dec 23, 40. ORGANIC CHEMISTRY. *Educ:* Franklin & Marshall Col, AB, 62; Bucknell Univ, MS, 65; Univ Va, PhD(chem), 68. *Prof Exp:* Interim asst prof chem, Univ Fla, 68-69; asst prof chem, Lycoming Col, 69-74; asst prof chem, St John Fisher Col, 74-80; MEM FAC, CHEM DEPT, ST VINCENT COL, 80- *Mem:* Am Chem Soc. *Res:* Aziridines; synthetic tropane alkaloid analogs; nuclear magnetic resonance spectroscopy. *Mailing Add:* Chem Dept St Vincent Col Latrobe PA 15650

TURNER, ANNE HALLIGAN, b Columbus, Ohio, Feb 3, 41; m 66; c 2. ORGANIC CHEMISTRY. *Educ:* Middlebury Col, AB, 63; Univ Rochester, PhD(chem), 69. *Prof Exp:* Lectr chem, Prince George's Commun Col, 69-79; RES ASSOC, DEPT CHEM, HOWARD UNIV, 79- *Concurrent Pos:* Instr chem, Grad Sch, US Dept Agr, 70-75. *Mem:* Am Chem Soc; AAAS. *Res:* Application of hydrogen, carbon 13 and phosphorus 31 nuclear magnetic resonance problems of structure, kinetics and/or conformation in chemisty or biochemistry. *Mailing Add:* Dept Chem Howard Univ Washington DC 20059

TURNER, ARTHUR FRANCIS, b Detroit, Mich, Aug 8, 06; m 34; c 2. OPTICS, PHYSICS. *Educ:* Mass Inst Technol, BS, 29; Univ Berlin, PhD(physics), 35. *Prof Exp:* From asst to instr physics, Mass Inst Technol, 35-39; from physicist to head optical physics dept, Bausch & Lomb, Inc, 39-71; prof, 71-78, PROF EMER OPTICAL SCI, UNIV ARIZ, 71- *Concurrent Pos:* Mem US Nat Comt, Int Comn Optics, 60-65. *Honors & Awards:* Frederic Ives Medalist, Optical Soc Am, 71. *Mem:* Fel Am Phys Soc; fel Optical Soc Am (pres, 68); Brit Inst Physics & Phys Soc. *Res:* Optical physics; evaporated thin films; infrared. *Mailing Add:* Optical Sci Ctr Univ of Ariz Tucson AZ 85721

TURNER, BARBARA BUSH, b Los Angeles, Calif; m 72; c 2. NEUROENDOCRINOLOGY, NEUROCHEMISTRY. *Educ:* Immaculate Heart Col, BA, 67, MA, 70; Univ Calif, Los Angeles, PhD(neurosci), 74. *Prof Exp:* Fel B S McEwen Lab, Rockefeller Univ, 74-76; res assoc, Ment Health Res Inst, Univ Mich, 76-78; VIS ASST PROF BIOL, VA POLYTECH INST & STATE UNIV, 79- *Concurrent Pos:* Res fel, NIH & Nat Inst Neurol & Commun Dis & Stroke, 74-76; NIMH fel res training biol sci, 76-77; vis asst prof psychol, Va Polytech Inst & State Univ, 78-81. *Mem:* Soc Neurosci; Am Soc Zoologists; Int Soc Psychoneuroendocrinol; NY Acad Sci; Int Soc Develop Neurosci. *Res:* Brain-hormone interactions; glucocorticoid binding in the brain; corticoid receptor regulation; regulation of neuronal activity by glucocorticoids. *Mailing Add:* Dept Biol & Psychol Va Polytech Inst & State Univ Blacksburg VA 24061

TURNER, BARBARA HOLMAN, b Evergreen, Ala, Aug 31, 26; m 50; c 2. ECOLOGY. *Educ:* Miss State Col for Women, BS, 47; Univ Kans, MT, 48; Vanderbilt Univ, MA, 66, PhD(ecol), 72. *Prof Exp:* Asst prof biol, George Peabody Col, 66-72; asst prof, 73-76, ASSOC PROF MICRO-MED TECHNOL, MISS STATE UNIV, 76- *Mem:* Am Inst Biol Sci; Ecol Soc; Bot Soc; Sigma Xi; Am Soc Med Technologists. *Res:* Interactions between microorganisms and higher plants. *Mailing Add:* Dept of Biol Sci Drawer Y Mississippi State MS 39762

TURNER, BARRY EARL, b Victoria, BC, Sept 8, 36; m 62. RADIO ASTRONOMY. *Educ:* Univ BC, BSc, 59, MSc, 62; Univ Calif, Berkeley, PhD(astron), 67. *Prof Exp:* Res off elec eng, Nat Res Coun Can, 62-64; from res assoc radio astron to assoc scientist, 67-74, SCIENTIST, NAT RADIO ASTRON OBSERV, 74- *Concurrent Pos:* mem site rev team, Space Telescope, Assoc Univ, Inc, 80 & NSF, 81; titulaire & chmn vis comt, Observ Paris, 81. *Mem:* Int Astron Union; Am Astron Soc; Union Radio Sci Int. *Res:* Theoretical and observational studies of interstellar molecules, interstellar chemistry, physics of the interstellar medium. *Mailing Add:* Nat Radio Astron Observ Edgemont Rd Charlottesville VA 22901

TURNER, BILLIE LEE, b Yoakum, Tex, Feb 22, 25; div; c 2. SYSTEMATIC BOTANY. *Educ:* Sul Ross State Col, BS, 49; Southern Methodist Univ, MS, 50; Wash State Univ, PhD(bot), 53. *Prof Exp:* From instr to assoc prof, 53-58, chmn dept, 67-74, PROF BOT & DIR PLANT RESOURCES CTR, UNIV TEX, AUSTIN, 59- *Concurrent Pos:* Vis prof & NSF sr fel, Univ Liverpool, 65-66; assoc investr ecol study African veg, 56-57. *Honors & Awards:* NY Bot Garden Award, 65. *Mem:* AAAS; Bot Soc Am (secy, 58-59 & 60-64, vpres, 65); Am Soc Plant Taxon; Soc Study Evolution; Int Asn Plant Taxon. *Res:* Plant geography; chromosomal studies of higher plants; flora of Texas and Mexico; biochemical systematics. *Mailing Add:* Dept of Bot Univ of Tex Austin TX 78712

TURNER, BRUCE JAY, b Brooklyn, NY, Sept 19, 45; m 72; c 2. EVOLUTIONARY BIOLOGY, ICHTHYOLOGY. *Educ:* City Univ New York, Brooklyn, BS, 66; Univ Calif, Los Angeles, MA, 67, PhD(biol), 71. *Prof Exp:* Fel biochem genetics, Ment Health Res Unit, Neuropsychiat Inst, Univ Calif, 72-74; res assoc, Rockefeller Univ, 74-76; vis res scientist evolutionary biol, Mus Zool, Univ Mich, 76-78; ASST PROF BIOL, VA POLYTECH INST & STATE UNIV, 78- *Mem:* Soc Study Evolution; Am Soc Naturalists; Am Soc Ichthyologists & Herpetologists; Soc Syst Zool; Am Fisheries Soc. *Res:* Evolutionary and ecological genetics of fish populations (polymorphism and differentiation); emphasis on biochemical genetic (allozymic) and chromosomal studies; general ichthyology and systematics. *Mailing Add:* Dept of Biol Va Polytech Inst & State Univ Blacksburg VA 24061

TURNER, CARLTON EDGAR, b Choctaw Co, Ala, Sept 13, 40. CHEMISTRY, PHARMACOGNOSY. *Educ:* Univ Southern Miss, BS, 66, MS, 69, PhD(org chem), 70. *Prof Exp:* Fel pharmacog res, Inst Pharmaceut Sci, Sch Pharm, Univ Miss, 70-71, proj supvr & coord marihuana proj, dept pharmacog, 71-72, dir Cannabis Proj, 72, assoc dir res, 72-80. *Mem:* AAAS; Am Soc Pharmacog; Soc Econ Bot; Am Chem Soc. *Res:* Organo-silicone compounds hypotensive agents; chemistry of cannabinoids; gas chromatographic and thin layer chromatographic techniques for separation of natural products; phyto chemistry. *Mailing Add:* 8218 Clifton Farm Ct Alexandria VA 22306

TURNER, CHARLIE DANIEL, JR, b Birmingham, Ala, Feb 24, 46; m 67; c 2. AEROELASTICITY, STRUCTURAL DYNAMICS. *Educ:* Univ Ala, BS, 71; Va Polytech Inst & State Univ, MS, 76, PhD(aerospace eng), 80. *Prof Exp:* Aerospace engr structural dynamics, Air Force Armament Technol Lab, 71-78; group leader dynamics, Cessna Aircraft, 78-79; dynamics engr structural dynamics, Beech Aircraft, 79-81; ASST PROF AEROELASTICITY, NC STATE UNIV, 81- *Concurrent Pos:* Adj prof, Wichita State Univ, 80-81; consult, Accident Reconstruction Analysis Corp, 81 & Lewis, Wilson, Lewis & Jones, 81-82. *Mem:* Am Inst Aeronaut & Astronaut. *Res:* Analytical and experimental subcritical flutter analysis; feedback system approach for subcritical flight flutter testing; wing and control surface; tab aeroelastic analysis; wing and store aeroelastic analysis. *Mailing Add:* 6940 Three Bridges Circle Raleigh NC 27612

TURNER, CHRISTY GENTRY, II, b Columbia, Mo, Nov 28, 33; m 57; c 3. PHYSICAL ANTHROPOLOGY, DENTAL ANTHROPOLOGY. *Educ:* Univ Ariz, BA, 57, MA, 58; Univ Wis, Madison, PhD(phys anthrop), 67. *Prof Exp:* Actg asst prof phys anthrop, Univ Calif, Berkeley, 63-66; from asst prof to assoc prof, 66-75, asst dean, Grad Col, 72-76, PROF PHYS ANTHROP, ARIZ STATE UNIV, 75- *Concurrent Pos:* Am Dent Asn & NIH dent epidemiol & biomet trainee; collabr phys anthrop, US Nat Park Serv, 69-; fel, Ctr Advan Study Behav Sci, Stanford Univ, 70-71; Nat Geog Soc grants, 72, 73 & 79-81. *Mem:* Am Asn Phys Anthropologists; Sigma Xi; Soc Am Archaeol; AAAS. *Res:* Co-evolution of human biology and culture; dental morphology, genetics and related behavior; biology and culture of New World peoples, especially southwestern United States Indians and Alaskan Aleuts; origins of peoples of Pacific and New World. *Mailing Add:* Dept of Anthrop Ariz State Univ Tempe AZ 85281

TURNER, DANIEL STOUGHTON, b Madison, Wis, Feb 8, 17; m 44; c 4. PETROLEUM, GEOLOGY. *Educ:* Univ Wis, PhB, 40, PhM, 42, PhD(geol), 48. *Prof Exp:* Field geologist, Buchans Mining Co, Nfld, 47; geologist, US AEC, Colo, 48; asst prof geol, Univ Wyo, 49-50; geologist, Carter Oil Co, Okla, 51 & Petrol Res Co, Colo, 52-53; div geologist, Wm R Whittaker Co, Ltd, 53; geol consult, 54-63; consult, Earth Sci Curric Proj, Boulder, 63-65; PROF GEOL, EASTERN MICH UNIV, 65- *Mem:* Geol Soc Am; Soc Econ Geol; Am Asn Petrol Geol. *Res:* Arctic geology and glaciation; permafrost; thermal activity of Yellowstone National Park; hydrodynamics of oil; Rocky Mountain petroleum exploration; earth science education. *Mailing Add:* Dept of Geog & Geol Eastern Mich Univ Ypsilanti MI 48197

TURNER, DANNY WILLIAM, b Shelby, NC, Oct 8, 47; m 70; c 1. CLUSTER ANALYSIS, MULTIVARIATE GRAPHICS. *Educ:* Clemson Univ, BS, 69, PhD(math), 73. *Prof Exp:* Asst prof math, Baylor Univ, 73-76; software analyst, Tex Instruments, 76; asst prof, 76-79, ASSOC PROF MATH, BAYLOR UNIV, 79- *Mem:* Classification Soc; Math Asn Am; Am Statist Asn. *Res:* Cluster analysis and in particular multivariate graphics. *Mailing Add:* 405 Georgia Waco TX 76706

TURNER, DAVID GERALD, b Toronto, Ont, Dec 13, 45. OBSERVATIONAL ASTRONOMY. *Educ:* Univ Waterloo, BSc, 68; Univ Western Ont, MSc, 70, PhD(astron), 74. *Prof Exp:* Fel astron, David Dunlap Observ, 74-76; asst prof, Laurentian Univ, 76-78; asst prof astron, Univ Toronto, 78-80; ASST PROF, DEPT PHYSICS & ASTRON, LAURENTIAN UNIV, 80- *Concurrent Pos:* Connaught fel, Univ Toronto, 75; Nat Sci & Eng Res Coun res fel, Laurentian Univ, 80- *Mem:* Can Astron Soc; Am Astron Soc; Royal Astron Soc Can; Int Astron Union; Planetarium Asn Can. *Res:* Interstellar extinction; star clusters and associations; variable stars and galactic structure; the distance scale in the universe; stellar spectroscopy. *Mailing Add:* Dept Physics & Astron Laurentian Univ Sudbury ON P3E 2C6 Can

TURNER, DAVID LEE, b Afton, Wyo, Nov 20, 49; m 69; c 4. STATISTICAL ANALYSIS. *Educ:* Colo State Univ, BS, 71, MS, 73, PhD(statist), 75. *Prof Exp:* From res asst to instr statist, Colo State Univ, 71-75; asst prof, 75-81, ASSOC PROF STATIST, UTAH STATE UNIV, 81- *Mem:* Sigma Xi; Am Statist Soc; Biomet Soc. *Res:* Tolerance intervals and bands for regression; analysis of unbalanced data; analysis of categorical data. *Mailing Add:* Dept Appl Statist/Comput Sci Utah State Univ Logan UT 84322

TURNER, DENNIS ROBERT, b London, Eng, Jan 13, 20; US citizen; m 50; c 2. PHYSICAL CHEMISTRY. *Educ:* Lake Forest Col, BS, 42; Univ Mich, MSCh, 47, PhD(chem), 50. *Prof Exp:* Res chemist, Westinghouse Res Labs, 42-45 & 49-52; supvr, 61, MEM TECH STAFF CHEM, BELL LABS, 52- *Mem:* Am Electroplaters' Soc; hon mem Electrochem Soc (secy, 69-75, vpres, 75-78, pres, 78-79); AAAS. *Res:* Semiconductor electrochemistry; lead-acid and nickel cadmium batteries; electroplating process research and development; automatic plating bath analyzer controllers; continuous strip plating systems with computer monitoring and control. *Mailing Add:* Bell Labs 600 Mountain Ave Murray Hill NJ 07974

TURNER, DEREK T, b London, Eng, Dec 19, 26; m 55; c 2. PHYSICAL CHEMISTRY, POLYMER CHEMISTRY. *Educ:* Northern Polytech Eng, BSc, 51; Nat Col Rubber Technol, Eng, AIRI, 52; Univ London, PhD(chem), 57. *Prof Exp:* Res chemist, Brit Insulated Callenders Cables, Ltd, Eng, 52-55; sr chemist, Brit Rubber Producers Res Asn, 55-63; res fel, Camille Dreyfus Lab, Res Triangle Inst, 62-63, sr chemist, 62-68; from assoc prof to prof metall eng, Drexel Univ, 68-70; prof oral biol, 70-74, PROF OPER DENT, UNIV NC, CHAPEL HILL, 74- *Mem:* Am Chem Soc; Am Phys Soc; Soc Rheol; Int Asn Dent Res; Soc Biomat. *Res:* Radiation chemistry and photochemistry of polymers; solution properties of polymers; biomaterials. *Mailing Add:* Dent Res Ctr Univ of NC Chapel Hill NC 27514

TURNER, DONALD LLOYD, b Richmond, Calif, Dec 21, 37; c 3. GEOLOGY, GEOCHRONOLOGY. *Educ:* Univ Calif, Berkeley, AB, 60, PhD(geol), 68. *Prof Exp:* Nat Res Coun res assoc, Isotope Geol Br, US Geol Surv, Colo, 68-69, Calif, 69-70; assoc prof, 70-80, PROF GEOL, GEOPHYS INST & DEPT GEOL, UNIV ALASKA, FAIRBANKS, 80- *Mem:* Am Geophys Union. *Res:* Geochronology, K-Ar and fission track dating applied to problems of regional tectonics; radiometric calibration of paleontological time scales and geothermal systems; geological and geophysical exploration for geothermal resources. *Mailing Add:* Geophys Inst Univ Alaska Fairbanks AK 99701

TURNER, DONALD W, b St Louis, Mo, Jan 24, 32; m 57; c 6. INFLAMMATION, IMMUNE RESPONSES. *Educ:* Washington Univ, St Louis, BS, 57, DDS, 60; Md Univ, College Park, PhD(microbiol), 74. *Prof Exp:* Dentist, 60-64; US Navy, 64-, dentist, 64-70, dental researcher immunol, 74-81, COMMANDING OFFICER, NAVAL DENT RES INST, US NAVY, 81- *Concurrent Pos:* Asst prof microbiol, Univ Md, 75-; mem, Oral Med & Biol Study Sect, Nat Inst Dent Res, 76-81; lectr, Sch Dent, Northwestern Univ, 81-; vis prof, Sch Dent, Univ Ill & Chicago Med Sch, Univ Health Sci, 81- *Mem:* Am Dent Asn; Am Asn Dent Res; Int Asn Dent Res; Am Soc Microbiol; Int Asn Dentists. *Res:* The immunologic basis for dental diseases, especially in periodontal disease; transplantation immunology; inflammatory process in periodontal lesions. *Mailing Add:* Naval Dent Res Inst Bldg 1-H Naval Base Great Lakes IL 60088

TURNER, DOUGLAS HUGH, b Staten Island, NY, July 24, 46. BIOPHYSICAL CHEMISTRY. *Educ:* Harvard Col, AB, 67; Columbia Univ, PhD(phys chem), 72. *Prof Exp:* Fel biophys chem, Univ Calif, Berkeley, 73-74; asst prof, 74-81, ASSOC PROF CHEM, UNIV ROCHESTER, 81- *Concurrent Pos:* Tech collabr, Brookhaven Nat Lab, 70-; Alfred P Sloan fel, 79- *Mem:* Am Chem Soc; Am Phys Soc. *Res:* Structure and function of nucleic acids; laser temperature jump kinetics; florescence detected circular dichroism. *Mailing Add:* Dept of Chem Univ of Rochester Rochester NY 14627

TURNER, EARL WILBERT, b Bozeman, Mont, Feb 6, 18; m 39; c 5. BIOCHEMISTRY, PROTEIN CHEMISTRY. *Educ:* Mont State Univ, BS, 46, MS, 47; Univ Minn, PhD(biochem), 50. *Prof Exp:* Instr biochem & food chem, Univ Minn, 47-50; biochemist, Protein & Food Res, Oscar Mayer & Co, Wis, 50-51, chief chemist & head res lab, 51-55; chief animal prod br, Qm Food & Container Inst Armed Forces, Ill, 55-56; dir res, Int Packers, Ltd, Ill, 56-66; DIR APPL RES, ITT CONTINENTAL BAKING CO, INC, 67- *Mem:* AAAS; Am Chem Soc; Inst Food Technol; Am Asn Cereal Chemists. *Res:* Meat science, cereal chemistry, lipid chemistry, microbiology, food chemistry; product and process development, meat products, frozen prepared foods, bakery products, food safety and microbiology; immunochemistry; food systems; edible fats and oils; special rations for armed forces. *Mailing Add:* 53 Hobart Ave Port Chester NY 10573

TURNER, EDWARD FELIX, JR, b Newport News, Va, Apr 21, 20; m 45; c 3. PHYSICS. *Educ:* Washington & Lee Univ, BS & BA, 50; Mass Inst Technol, MS, 52; Univ Va, PhD(physics), 54. *Prof Exp:* Asst prof physics, George Washington Univ, 54-57; assoc prof, 57-59, PROF PHYSICS, WASHINGTON & LEE UNIV, 59-, CHMN DEPT, 61- *Concurrent Pos:* Consult & physicist, Diamond Ord Fuze Lab, 57-58; consult, US Off Educ, 65- *Mem:* AAAS; Am Phys Soc; Am Asn Physics Teachers. *Res:* Solid state physics; electrical properties of solids; electronics; astronomy. *Mailing Add:* 23 Sellers Ave Lexington VA 24450

TURNER, EDWARD HARRISON, b Cleveland, Ohio, Dec 21, 20; m 45; c 4. MAGNETISM. *Educ:* Harvard Univ, SB, 42, AM, 47, PhD, 50. *Prof Exp:* Mem staff, Radiation Lab, Mass Inst Technol, 42-45; MEM TECH STAFF UNDERSEA OPTICAL CABLE, BELL TEL LABS, INC, 49- *Mem:* Am Phys Soc; sr mem Inst Elec & Electronics Eng. *Res:* Optical wave guide propagation; electro-magnetic theory in gyrotropic media; spin waves in ferrimagnetic materials. *Mailing Add:* Rm 3D 329A Bell Tel Labs PO Box 400 Holmdel NJ 07733

TURNER, EDWARD V, b Belmont, Ohio, May 19, 13; m 39; c 1. PEDIATRICS. *Educ:* Ohio Univ, AB, 34; Harvard Med Sch, MD, 38. *Prof Exp:* From asst prof to assoc prof, 48-68, PROF PEDIAT, COL MED, OHIO STATE UNIV, 68- *Mem:* Fel Am Acad Pediat. *Res:* Clinical pediatrics; medical education. *Mailing Add:* 345 Walnut Cliffs Dr Columbus OH 43213

TURNER, EDWIN LEWIS, b Knoxville, Tenn, May 3, 49; m 71; c 1. EXTRAGALACTIC ASTRONOMY, COSMOLOGY. *Educ:* Mass Inst Technol, SB, 71; Calif Inst Technol, PhD(astron), 75. *Prof Exp:* Res fel physics & astron, Inst Advan Study, 75-77; asst prof astron, Harvard Col Observ, Harvard Univ, 77-78; asst prof, 78-81, ASSOC PROF ASTROPHYS SCI, PRINCETON UNIV OBSERV, 81- *Concurrent Pos:* User's comt mem, Kitt Peak Nat Observ, 75-77; Alfred P Sloan res fel, 80; mem bd dir, Asn Univ Res Astron, 80- *Mem:* Am Astron Soc; Int Astron Union. *Res:* Dynamics of galaxies and clusters of galaxies; quasars and active galactic nuclei; the cosmic x-ray background; image processing; gravitational lenses. *Mailing Add:* Peyton Hall Princeton Univ Observ Princeton NJ 08544

TURNER, EDWIN MORRIS, b Steele, Mo, Nov 28, 44; m 71. PHYSICAL CHEMISTRY. *Educ:* Mich State Univ, BS, 66; Univ Wis, Madison, PhD(phys chem), 70. *Prof Exp:* Lectr & grant chem, Univ Wis, Madison, 70-71; grant, Univ Ky, 71-72; DIR PHYS CHEM LAB, UNIV WIS, MADISON, 72- *Res:* Dielectric properties of highly polar liquids. *Mailing Add:* Dept of Chem Univ of Wis Madison WI 53706

TURNER, ELLA VICTORIA, b Columbia, Mo, Jan 23, 46; m 66; c 2. IMMUNOLOGY. *Educ:* Univ Ark, BA, 67; Univ Louisville, PhD(microbiol), 73. *Prof Exp:* Res asst, Univ Louisville, 73-74, res assoc, Dept Microbiol & Immunol, 74-78, adj asst prof, 78-80. *Concurrent Pos:* Consult, Tissue Typing Lab, Jewish Hosp, Louisville, 77-80. *Mem:* Am Asn Clin Histocompatability Testing; Am Soc Microbiol. *Res:* Immunologic parameters of tumor growth and rejection; effects of mediators of inflammation and of specific immunological responses on tumor growth; regulation of immune responses. *Mailing Add:* 6380 Candlewood Memphis TN 33119

TURNER, ERNEST CRAIG, JR, b West Jefferson, NC, June 15, 27; m 53; c 3. ENTOMOLOGY. *Educ:* Clemson Col, BS, 48; Cornell Univ, PhD(entom), 53. *Prof Exp:* Asst econ entom, Cornell Univ, 48-53; assoc prof entom, 53-65, PROF ENTOM, VA POLYTECH INST & STATE UNIV, 65-, ASSOC ENTOMOLOGIST, AGR EXP STA, 53- *Mem:* Am Mosquito Control Asn; Entom Soc Am. *Res:* Medical and veterinary entomology. *Mailing Add:* 1413 Locust Ave Blacksburg VA 24060

TURNER, EUGENE BONNER, b Wolf Point, Mont, Oct 6, 22; m 46; c 3. PHYSICS. *Educ:* Mont State Col, BS, 44; Univ Mich, MS, 50, PhD(physics), 56. *Prof Exp:* Mem tech staff, Ramo-Wooldridge Corp, Calif, 56-58 & Space Tech Labs, Inc, 58-60; mem tech staff, 60-68, head lasers & optics dept, Electronics Res Lab, 68-69, sr staff engr, Develop Planning Div, 69-73, staff engr, 73-75, STAFF SCIENTIST, LABS DIV, AEROSPACE CORP, 75- *Mem:* Am Phys Soc; Optical Soc Am; Soc Photo-Optical Instrument Eng (pres, 70); Sigma Xi; Am Inst Aeronaut & Astronaut. *Res:* Plasma physics; spectroscopy; optical and photographic instrumentation; lasers; optical systems; strategic space systems. *Mailing Add:* Labs Div Aerospace Corp PO Box 92957 Los Angeles CA 90009

TURNER, FRANCIS JOHN, b Auckland, NZ, Apr 10, 04; nat US; m 30; c 1. PETROLOGY. *Educ:* Univ NZ, MSc, 26, DSc(geol), 34. *Hon Degrees:* DSc, Univ Auckland, 65. *Prof Exp:* From lectr to sr lectr geol, Otago Univ, 26-46; from assoc prof to prof, 46-72, EMER PROF GEOL, UNIV CALIF, BERKELEY, 72- *Concurrent Pos:* Sterling fel, Yale Univ, 38-39; Guggenheim fel, 51 & 59-60; Fulbright fel, 56. *Honors & Awards:* Hector Medal, Royal Soc NZ, 56; Lyell Medal, Geol Soc London, 70. *Mem:* Nat Acad Sci; fel Geol Soc Am; fel Mineral Soc Am; hon fel Geol Soc London; fel Royal Soc NZ. *Res:* Petrology of ultrabasic rocks in New Zealand; metamorphic and igneous petrology; fabric of deformed rocks and artificially deformed rocks and minerals; deformation of mineral crystals; metamorphic paragenesis and facies. *Mailing Add:* 2525 Hill Ct Berkeley CA 94708

TURNER, FRANK JOSEPH, b New York, NY, Nov 23, 25; m 51; c 3. MICROBIOLOGY, IMMUNOLOGY. *Educ:* St John's Univ, NY, BS, 50; Rutgers Univ, MS, 58, PhD, 71. *Prof Exp:* Bacteriologist, Nepera Chem Co, Inc, 51-52; asst scientist, Warner Inst Therapeut Res & Warner-Chilcott Labs Div, 52-53, assoc scientist, Warner-Chilcott Labs Div, 53-56, scientist, 56-60, sr scientist, Warner-Lambert Res Inst, 61-64, sr res assoc, 64-72, dir, 72-77, DIR RES, DEPT MICROBIOL & IMMUNOL, GEN DIAG DIV, WARNER-LAMBERT CO, 77- *Mem:* AAAS; Am Soc Microbiol; NY Acad Sci. *Res:* Chemotherapy of bacterial, fungal and viral diseases; investigation of host defense mechanisms; immunology of delayed hypersensitivity; disinfecting properties of hydrogen peroxide; diagnostic reagents. *Mailing Add:* Dept Microbiol & Immunol Gen Diag Warner-Lambert Co Morris Plains NJ 07950

TURNER, FRED, JR, b Paris Crossing, Ind, Jan 13, 20; m 42, 76; c 1. AGRICULTURAL CHEMISTRY, SOILS. *Educ:* Univ Ariz, BS, 48; State Col Wash, MS, 51; Mich State Univ, PhD(soil sci), 57. *Prof Exp:* Asst soils, State Col Wash, 48-50; soil scientist, Irrig Exp Sta, Agr Res Serv, USDA, Prosser, Wash, 50-51 & Northern Great Plains Exp Sta, NDak, 54; asst soils, Mich State Univ, 54-57; asst prof agr chem & soils & agr chemist, Univ Ariz, Safford, 57-61, supt & agr chemist, Safford Exp Sta, 61-66, adv soils, US AID-Univ Ariz Contract, Sch Agron, Univ Ceara, Brazil, 66-68, supt, Safford Exp Sta, 68-80, area exten soil specialist, 75-80; SOIL SCIENTIST & EXTEN SOIL SPECIALIST, UNIV ARIZ, TUCSON, 80- *Concurrent Pos:* Soils specialist, USAID-Univ Ariz contract, Saana, Yemen, 78; consult soils & water, North Yemen, 81. *Mem:* Sigma Xi; Soil Sci Soc Am; Am Soc Agron; Coun Agr Sci & Technol. *Res:* Various salinity aspects of irrigation waters and soils; fertility and management of salt load in irrigation agriculture to minimize water pollution; fertility and management of tropical soils. *Mailing Add:* Dept Soils Water & Eng Agr Sci Bldg 417 Univ Ariz Tucson AZ 85721

TURNER, FRED ALLEN, b Chicago, Ill, Mar 16, 33; m 64; c 2. ORGANIC CHEMISTRY. *Educ:* Univ Ill, BS, 55, MS, 58, PhD(pharmaceut chem), 63. *Prof Exp:* Instr, Univ Ill, Chicago, 58-59 & 61-62; from instr to assoc prof, 62-74, PROF CHEM, ROOSEVELT UNIV, 74- *Concurrent Pos:* NSF fel, 59-61. *Mem:* Am Chem Soc; Sigma Xi. *Res:* Synthesis of medicinal compounds; study of organic halogenating agents; synthesis of heterocyclic systems. *Mailing Add:* Dept of Chem Roosevelt Univ 430 S Michigan Ave Chicago IL 60605

TURNER, FREDERICK BROWN, b Carlinville, Ill, Feb 4, 27; div. VERTEBRATE ZOOLOGY. *Educ:* Univ Calif, AB, 49, MA, 50, PhD(zool), 57. *Prof Exp:* Asst zool, Univ Calif, 50-52 & 55-56; instr, Ill Col, 52-53; seasonal park naturalist, Death Valley Nat Monument, Calif, 53-55; instr biol, Wayne State Univ, 56-60, univ res coun res fel, 60; vis asst prof zool, 60-61, MEM STAFF, LAB BIOMED & ENVIRON SCI, UNIV CALIF, LOS ANGELES, 61- *Concurrent Pos:* NSF partic, Inst Desert Biol, Ariz State Univ, 59. *Mem:* AAAS; Ecol Soc Am. *Res:* Population ecology of reptiles; ecosystem analysis; environmental effects of energy development in arid environments. *Mailing Add:* Lab Nuclear Med & Radiation Biol Univ Calif Los Angeles CA 90024

TURNER, GEORGE CLEVELAND, b Spokane, Wash, Jan 26, 25; m 52; c 1. ECOLOGY, SCIENCE EDUCATION. *Educ:* Stanford Univ, BA, 47; Utah State Univ, MS, 50; East Wash State Col, MEd, 52; Ariz State Univ, EdD(sci ed), 64. *Prof Exp:* Teacher high schs, Wash, 52-53 & Calif, 53-60; assoc prof, 60-67, chmn dept sci educ, 64-77, PROF BIOL & SCI EDUC, CALIF STATE UNIV, FULLERTON, 67-, ASSOC VPRES UNIV RES, 77- *Concurrent Pos:* Lectr, Claremont Grad Sch, 57-60; dir, NSF grants for adv topics inst for high sch biol teachers, 65-67, intern-master's degree prog for sci teachers, 67-, Human Ecol Inst, 69- & Urban Sci Intern Teaching Proj, 72-; dir, Off Educ grant for biol sci curriculum study test eval team, 66-67; pres, Calif Intersci Coun, 73-75; dir, Energy and the Environ Inst, & Calif Statewide Energy Consortium, 75- *Mem:* Nat Sci Teachers Asn; Nat Asn Biol Teachers. *Res:* Ecology of rodents, Wasatch Mountains, Utah; scientific enquiry. *Mailing Add:* Univ Res Calif State Univ Fullerton CA 92634

TURNER, GODFREY ALAN, b Cardiff, UK, Feb 8, 20; m 55; c 2. CHEMICAL ENGINEERING. *Educ:* Univ London, BSc, 49, Univ Col, dipl, 50; Univ Manchester, PhD(chem eng), 58. *Prof Exp:* Chem engr, Brit Oxygen Co, Ltd, 50-51; Postans Paints Ltd, 51-53; Petrochem Ltd, 53-54; lectr chem eng, Manchester Col Sci & Eng, 54-60; chief chem engr, Fisons Fertilizers Ltd, 60-64; PROF CHEM ENG, UNIV WATERLOO, 64- *Mem:* Chem Inst Can. *Res:* Physical and engineering properties of small solids; thermal and flow properties; determination of parameters by travelling waves; processing particulate materials by mechanical vibrations. *Mailing Add:* Dept of Chem Eng Univ of Waterloo Waterloo ON N2L 3G1 Can

TURNER, HAL RUSSELL, b Des Moines, Iowa, Sept 4, 46; m 66; c 2. MICROBIAL PHYSIOLOGY. *Educ:* Iowa State Univ, BS, 69, MS, 73, PhD(bact), 75. *Prof Exp:* SR RESEARCHER FUNDAMENTAL BIOCHEM, CPC INT INC, 75- *Mem:* Am Soc Microbiol; AAAS; Soc Indust Microbiol; Sigma Xi. *Res:* All areas of microbial physiology with special interests in the areas of enzymology; natural product isolation and metabolic regulation. *Mailing Add:* CPC Int Inc Moffett Tech Ctr Argo IL 60501

TURNER, HOWARD S(INCLAIR), b Jenkintown, Pa, Nov 27, 11; m 36; c 3. CHEMICAL ENGINEERING. *Educ:* Swarthmore Col, AB, 33; Mass Inst Technol, PhD(org chem, chem eng), 36. *Prof Exp:* Res chemist & supvr, E I Du Pont De Nemours Co, Del, 36-47; dir res & develop div, Pittsburgh Consol Coal Co, 47-54; vpres res & develop, Jones & Laughlin Steel Corp, 54-65; pres & dir, 65-70, chmn, 71-78, chmn exec comt, 78-82, DIR, TURNER CONSTRUCT CO, 52- *Concurrent Pos:* Dir, Ingersoll-Rand Co & Dime Savings Bank of NY. *Mem:* Nat Acad Eng; Am Chem Soc. *Res:* Processes of iron ore beneficiation, reduction and steelmaking. *Mailing Add:* Turner Construct Co 633 Third Ave New York NY 10017

TURNER, J HOWARD, b San Diego, Calif, Oct 16, 27; m 49; c 4. HUMAN GENETICS. *Educ:* Utah State Univ, BS, 57, MS, 59; Univ Pittsburgh, ScD(human genetics), 62. *Prof Exp:* Instr zool & res asst genetics, Utah State Univ, 57-59; res assoc cytogenetics, 61-62, asst prof human genetics, 62-66, assoc prof, 66-71, PROF BIOSTATIST, UNIV PITTSBURGH, 71- *Concurrent Pos:* Res assoc, Magee Womens Hosp, 64- *Mem:* AAAS; Soc Human Genetics; Am Genetic Asn; Genetics Soc Am; Am Pub Health Asn. *Res:* Developmental cytogenetics; somatic cell genetics; statistical genetics. *Mailing Add:* Rm 316 Grad Sch Pub Health Univ of Pittsburgh Pittsburgh PA 15213

TURNER, JACK ALLEN, b Milner, Colo, Feb 2, 42; m 66; c 2. ECOLOGY. *Educ:* Colo State Univ, BS, 68; SDak State Univ, MS, 71; Univ Okla, PhD(ecol), 74. *Prof Exp:* Asst bact, SDak State Univ, 69-72; asst prof, 74-77, ASSOC PROF BIOL, UNIV SC, SPARTANBURG, 77- *Mem:* Am Soc Microbiol; Ecol Soc Am. *Res:* The antimicrobial activity of various types of textile finishes. *Mailing Add:* 121 Greengate Lane Spartanburg SC 29302

TURNER, JAMES A, b Anna, Ill, Jan 9, 48. ORGANIC CHEMISTRY, PESTICIDE CHEMISTRY. *Educ:* Murray State Univ, BS, 71; Fla State Univ, PhD(org chem), 76. *Prof Exp:* Sr res chemist energy res, Hydrocarbons & Energy Lab, 76-78, SR RES CHEMIST AGR CHEM SYNTHESIS, AGR PROD RES, DOW CHEM CO, 78- *Mem:* Am Chem Soc. *Res:* Synthesis of new agricultural chemicals. *Mailing Add:* Agr Prod Res 2800 Mitchell Dr Walnut Creek CA 94598

TURNER, JAMES DAVID, b Bristol, Va, Aug 23, 52. NUCLEAR PHYSICS. *Educ:* Wake Forest Univ, BS(physics) & BA(phil), 73; Duke Univ, PhD(physics), 78. *Prof Exp:* Asst prof physics, Eastern Ky Univ, 78-79; ASST PROF PHYSICS, FURMAN UNIV, 79- *Mem:* Am Phys Soc. *Res:* Studies of giant dipole resonances via polarized and unpolarized proton capture reactions. *Mailing Add:* Dept of Physics Furman Univ Greenville SC 29613

TURNER, JAMES E, b Roann, Ind, Oct 11, 26. BIOCHEMISTRY. *Educ:* Manchester Col, BS, 50; Univ Ind, MA, 53, PhD(chem), 58. *Prof Exp:* Nat Res Coun fel & resident res assoc, Argonne Nat Lab, 58-60; chemist, Northern Regional Lab, USDA, 60-61; sr scientist, 61-68, res assoc, 68-75, assoc dir diag res & develop, 75-77, DIR CHEM & HEMAT RES, GEN DIAG DIV, WARNER-LAMBERT CO, 77- *Mem:* AAAS. *Res:* Protein structure studies; isolation and characterization of cereal proteins; optical rotation of proteins; transmethylation in plants; peptide hormone structure and synthesis; development of clinical chemistry assays and controls. *Mailing Add:* Warner-Lambert Res Inst 170 Tabor Rd Morris Plains NJ 07950

TURNER, JAMES ELDRIDGE, b Richmond, Va, Oct 1, 42; m 67; c 3. NEUROBIOLOGY, ELECTRON MICROSCOPY. *Educ:* Va Mil Inst, BA, 65; Univ Richmond, MS, 67; Univ Tenn, PhD(zool), 70. *Prof Exp:* Teaching asst zool, Univ Tenn, 67-69; NIH res trainee neurobiol & electron micros, Dept Anat, Sch Med, Case Western Reserve Univ, 71; asst prof biol, Va Mil Inst, 71-72; NIH res fel neurobiol & electron micros, Dept Anat, Sch Med, Case Western Reserve Univ, 72-74; asst prof, 74-78, ASSOC PROF ANAT, BOWMAN GRAY SCH MED, 78- *Concurrent Pos:* Vis prof, psychiat, dept neurochem, Max Planck Inst, Munich, WGer, 80-81; Basil Oconnor Starter res fel, March Dimes, 75-78. *Mem:* AAAS; Soc Neurosci; Am Soc Zool; Am Asn Anatomists; Sigma Xi. *Res:* Nerve injury, repair and regeneration; neurotrophic phenomenia. *Mailing Add:* Dept of Anat Bowman Gray Sch of Med Winston-Salem NC 27103

TURNER, JAMES HENRY, b Stuart, Va, June 13, 22. PARASITOLOGY. *Educ:* Univ Md, BS, 47, MS, 52, PhD(zool), 57. *Prof Exp:* Entomologist, Div Insects, Dept Zool, US Nat Mus, 48; from jr parasitologist to sr res parasitologist, Animal Dis Parasite Res Div, Agr Res Serv, USDA, 48-62; prin res parasitologist, Beltsville Parasitol Lab & McMaster Health Lab, Commonwealth Sci & Indust Res Orgn, Australia, 62-64; HEALTH SCIENTIST ADMINSTR, IMMUNOBIOL STUDY SECT, DIV RES GRANTS, NIH, 64- *Concurrent Pos:* Tutorial lectr, Univ Md, 58-61; Fulbright res fel, Australia, 62-63. *Honors & Awards:* Ransom Mem Award, 60. *Mem:* Am Soc Parasitol; Am Soc Trop Med & Hyg; Transplantation Soc. *Res:* Pathogenesis and immunological aspects of parasitic infections. *Mailing Add:* 2600 Brinkley Rd Oxon Hill MD 20021

TURNER, JAMES HENRY, solid state physics, see previous edition

TURNER, JAMES HOWARD, b Colorado Springs, Colo, July 18, 12. ANALYTICAL CHEMISTRY. *Educ:* Colo Col, AB, 33; Univ Iowa, MS, 36. *Prof Exp:* Asst chem, Colo Col, 31-33 & Calif Inst Technol, 33-34; anal chemist, SW Shattuck Chem Corp, Colo, 41-44; asst chem, Univ Iowa, 45; chemist, Colo Fuel & Iron Corp, 47-48; res chemist, Holly Sugar Corp, 48-54; anal chemist, Holloman Air Force Base, NMex, 55-59 & US Bur Mines, 59-61; anal chemist, US Geol Surv, 61-78; RETIRED. *Mem:* emer mem Am Chem Soc; assoc Cooper Ornith Soc; Am Ornith Union. *Res:* Spectrophotometric methods of analysis; sugar analysis; sugar beet by-products; rarer metal analysis; infrared analysis. *Mailing Add:* 807 N Wahsatch Ave Colorado Springs CO 80903

TURNER, JAMES MARSHALL, b Washington, DC, Aug 20, 44; m 67; c 3. PLASMA PHYSICS. *Educ:* Johns Hopkins Univ, BA, 66; Mass Inst Technol, PhD(physics), 71. *Prof Exp:* Lectr physics, Lesley Col, 70-71; res staff mem, Mass Inst Technol, 66-71; asst prof, Southern Univ, 71-73; assoc prof physics, Morehouse Col, 73-76, prof, 76-80; MEM FAC, COMPUT CTR, UNIV MO, ROLLA, 80- *Mem:* Am Phys Soc; Am Geophys Union; Inst Elec & Electronics Engrs; AAAS. *Res:* Instabilities in weakly ionized plasmas; MHD structures and plasma properties in the solar wind; structure of hemoglobin S. *Mailing Add:* Morehouse Col Comput Ctr Univ Mo Rolla MO 65401

TURNER, JAMES WILLIAM, animal breeding, statistics, see previous edition

TURNER, JAN ROSS, b Okla, Sept 25, 37; m 62; c 2. MICROBIOLOGY. *Educ:* Ore State Univ, BS, 61, MS, 63, PhD(microbial physiol), 65. *Prof Exp:* Res asst microbial physiol, Ore State Univ, 61-65; AEC fel microbiol, Biol Div, Pac Northwest Labs, Battelle Mem Inst, 65-67, sr res scientist, 67-73; SR MICROBIOLOGIST, LILLY RES LABS, 73- *Mem:* AAAS; Am Chem Soc; Am Soc Microbiol. *Res:* Microbial physiology; sterol biosynthesis; biochemical genetics; aromatic amino acid metabolism; medical mycology; clinical microbiology; antibiotic mechanisms. *Mailing Add:* Lilly Res Labs Indianapolis IN 46206

TURNER, JANICE BUTLER, b Lincolnton, Ga, Dec 1, 36; m 58; c 1. MOLECULAR SPECTROSCOPY. *Educ:* Ga State Col for Women, AB, 58; Emory Univ, MS, 59; Univ SC, PhD(chem), 70. *Prof Exp:* From instr to asst prof chem, 59-70, assoc prof, 70-77, PROF CHEM, AUGUSTA COL, 77-, CHMN, 76- *Mem:* Sigma Xi; Coblentz Soc; Am Chem Soc. *Res:* Preparation and strucutre determination of organogermanes-microwave studies. *Mailing Add:* Dept of Chem & Physics Augusta Col 2500 Walton Way Augusta GA 30910

TURNER, JOHN CHARLES, b Houston, Tex, Sept 28, 49; m 71; c 2. STATISTICS. *Educ:* Rice Univ, BA, 72; Princeton Univ, MA, 74, PhD(statist), 76. *Prof Exp:* Asst prof math, Univ SFla, 76-78; ASST PROF MATH, US NAVAL ACAD, 78- *Mem:* Am Statist Asn; Sigma Xi. *Res:* Applied statistics. *Mailing Add:* Dept Math US Naval Acad Annapolis MD 21401

TURNER, JOHN DEAN, b Pasadena, Calif, Oct 2, 30. MEDICINE. *Educ:* Univ Calif, Berkeley, BA, 52; McGill Univ, MD, CM, 56. *Prof Exp:* Intern med, Mass Gen Hosp, 56-57, asst resident, 57-58; attend physician, Nat Heart Inst, 61-65; asst prof med, Baylor Col Med, 65-71; ASSOC PROF MED, SCH MED, UNIV CALIF, SAN DIEGO, 71- *Concurrent Pos:* Paul Dudley White fel cardiol, Mass Gen Hosp, 59-60, teaching fels, 59-61; res fel med, Peter Bent Brigham Hosp, Harvard Univ, 58-59; staff assoc, President's Comn Heart Dis, Cancer & Stroke, 64; fel coun epidemiol, Am Heart Asn, 65-; mem staff, Vet Admin Hosp, La Jolla, 77- *Mem:* Am Heart Asn; fel Am Col Physicians; Am Oil Chem Soc; Am Pub Health Asn. *Res:* Cardiovascular hemodynamics and epidemiology; angiocardiography in the diagnosis of valvular and congenital heart disease; external scintillation counting in detection of intracardiac shunts; lipid composition in human erythrocytes and plasma; lipid and lipoprotein metabolism in human plasma. *Mailing Add:* 209 Westbourne La Jolla CA 92037

TURNER, JOHN K, b Fairfield, Ill, May 7, 23; m 46; c 5. ANIMAL PHYSIOLOGY. *Educ:* Millikin Univ, AB, 47; Univ Ill, MA, 49; Univ Wis, PhD(physiol), 60. *Prof Exp:* Physiologist, Army Med Res Lab, Ft Knox, Ky, 59-61 & Vet Admin Hosp, Long Beach, Calif, 61-64; ASSOC PROF BIOL SCI, WESTERN ILL UNIV, 65- *Concurrent Pos:* Lectr, Sch Med, Univ Calif, Los Angeles, 62-65. *Res:* Reflex regulation of respiration and circulation. *Mailing Add:* Dept of Biol Sci Western Ill Univ Macomb IL 61455

TURNER, JOHN LINDSEY, b Birmingham, Ala, Sept 9, 49; m 70; c 2. ENGINEERING MECHANICS. *Educ:* Auburn Univ, BSME, 71, MS, 72; Univ Ill, PhD(mech), 75. *Prof Exp:* Res scientist, Firestone Res Labs, 75-77; asst prof mech eng, 77-81, ASSOC PROF AGR ENG, AUBURN UNIV, 81- *Mem:* Soc Exp Stress Anal; Am Soc Agr Eng; Sigma Xi. *Res:* Experimental and numerical methods of stress analysis and structural mechanics; combined applications of experimental and computer based techniques for improved methods of analysis and design. *Mailing Add:* Dept Agr Eng Auburn Univ Auburn AL 36849

TURNER, KENNETH CLYDE, b Mt Vernon, Wash, Apr 6, 34; m 55; c 3. RADIO ASTRONOMY, RADIO INTERFEROMETRY. *Educ:* Portland Univ, BS, 57; Princeton Univ, PhD(physics), 62. *Prof Exp:* Instr physics, Princeton Univ, 62; Carnegie fel, 62-64; res staff assoc, 64-66, Carnegie Inst Washington Dept Terrestrial Magnetism, res staff mem, 66-78; SR RES ASSOC, NAT ASTRON & IONSPHERE CTR, ARECIBO, PUERTO RICO, 78- *Concurrent Pos:* Dir, Arg Inst Radio Astron, 70-73; vis prof, Nat Univ La Plata, 72-73. *Mem:* AAAS; Am Phys Soc; Am Astron Soc; Int Union Radio Sci; Int Astron Union. *Res:* Experimental foundations of relativity; hydrogen line and galactic continuum radio astronomy; observational cosmology; radio instrumentation. *Mailing Add:* Arecibo Observ PO Box 995 Arecibo PR 00612

TURNER, LEAF, b Brooklyn, NY, Mar 23, 43; m 66; c 3. THEORETICAL PHYSICS. *Educ:* Cornell Univ, AB, 63; Univ Wis, Madison, MS, 64, PhD(theoret physics), 69. *Prof Exp:* Fel, Weizmann Inst Sci, Rehovot, Israel, 69; fel physics, Univ Toronto, 69-71; asst scientist, Space Sci & Eng Ctr, Univ Wis, Madison, 71-72, proj assoc, 72-74; STAFF MEM, LOS ALAMOS NAT LAB, UNIV CALIF, 74- *Concurrent Pos:* Instr physics, Scarborough Col, Univ Toronto, 70-71; NSF fel, Inst Theoret Physics, Brandeis Univ, 70. *Mem:* Am Phys Soc; Sigma Xi. *Res:* Current algebra; phenomenological lagrangians; interactions of mesons and baryons; quantum field theory; symmetries in high energy physics; high energy phenomenology; scattering theory; plasma kinetic theory; magnetohydrodynamics; optics. *Mailing Add:* Los Alamos Nat Lab PO Box 1663 Los Alamos NM 87545

TURNER, LINCOLN HULLEY, b Chicago, Ill, June 30, 28. MATHEMATICS. *Educ:* Univ Chicago, MS, 48; Purdue Univ, PhD(math), 57. *Prof Exp:* Mathematician, Space Tech Labs, Inc, 58-60; prof math, Univ Minn, 60-63; PROF MATH, UNIV TENN, KNOXVILLE, 63- *Mem:* Am Math Soc; Math Asn Am; Soc Indust & Appl Math. *Res:* Real variables; calculus of variations; applied mathematics. *Mailing Add:* 5709 Lyons View Pk 2308 Knoxville TN 37919

TURNER, MALCOLM ELIJAH, JR, b Atlanta, Ga, May 27, 29; m 48, 68; c 8. MATHEMATICAL BIOLOGY, STATISTICS. *Educ:* Duke Univ, BA, 52; NC State Univ, MES, 55, PhD(statist), 59. *Prof Exp:* Asst biostatist, Univ NC, 53-54; sr res assoc biomet, Med Sch, Univ Cincinnati, 55, asst prof, 56-58; assoc prof & Williams res fel, Va Commonwealth Univ, 58-63, chmn div biomet, Dept Biophys & Biomet, 59-63; prof statist & biomet & chmn dept, Emory Univ, 63-69, prof math, 66-69; prof biostatist & biomath & assoc prof physiol & biophys, 70, PROF MATH, UNIV ALA, BIRMINGHAM, 72-, CHMN DEPT BIOMATH, 75- *Concurrent Pos:* Asst statistician, NC State Univ, 57-58; managing ed, Biometrics, 62-69; vis prof & chmn, Dept Biomet, Med Ctr, Univ Kans, 68-69; consult, Southern Res Inst, 74- *Honors & Awards:* Smith Kline & French lectr, Med Ctr, Univ Kans, 65. *Mem:* Fel AAAS; Soc Indust & Appl Math; hon fel Am Statist Asn; Soc Math Biol; Biometric Soc. *Res:* Application of mathematics and statistics to biological research. *Mailing Add:* Dept Biomath Univ Ala Birmingham AL 35294

TURNER, MANSON DON, b Pleasanton, Tex, Nov 15, 28; m 53; c 3. PHYSIOLOGY. *Educ:* Baylor Univ, BS, 50, MS, 51; Univ Tenn, PhD(physiol), 55. *Prof Exp:* Lab instr, Baylor Univ, 50-51; res asst, Univ Tenn, 51-54, instr clin physiol, 54-55; res asst prof surg, Sch Med, Univ Miss, 55-57, asst prof biochem, 58-61, assoc prof res surg & asst prof physiol & biophys, 61-65; supvry res physiologist, US Air Force Sch Aerospace Med, 65; assoc prof surg & physiol, 65-69, ASSOC PROF PHYSIOL & BIOPHYS & RES PROF SURG, SCH MED, UNIV MISS, 69- *Concurrent Pos:* Attend in physiol, Vet Admin Hosp, Jackson, 58-; consult, Oak Ridge Inst Nuclear Studies, 62-65. *Mem:* Transplantation Soc; Cryobiol Soc; Am Heart Asn; Am Physiol Soc. *Res:* Organ preservation; cardiovascular physiology. *Mailing Add:* Dept of Surg Univ of Miss Sch of Med Jackson MS 39216

TURNER, MATTHEW X, b Rockaway, NY, July 27, 28; m 58; c 5. CYTOLOGY, IMMUNOLOGY. *Educ:* Fordham Univ, BS, 56, MS, 62, PhD(cytol), 68. *Prof Exp:* Jr bacteriologist, NY State Conserv Dept, 56-58; jr isotope officer, State Univ NY Downstate Med Ctr, 58-60, radiation officer, 60-62, res asst anat & cytol, 62-66, NIH fel cytol & immunol, 67-68; microbiologist, US Naval Appl Sci Lab, NY, 66-67; asst prof, 68-72, ASSOC PROF BIOL, JERSEY CITY STATE COL, 72-, CHMN BIOL DEPT, 75- *Mem:* Reticuloendothelial Soc; Am Soc Microbiol. *Res:* Effect of antigen upon the cellular and humoral responses in normal and immunized animals; determination of x-ray and drugs upon antigenic stimulation in normal and immunized mice. *Mailing Add:* 22 Hillery Dr Flanders NJ 07836

TURNER, MICHAEL D, b Weston, Eng, Oct 26, 27; m 57; c 4. MEDICINE, BIOCHEMISTRY. *Educ:* Bristol Univ, MB, ChB, 50, MD, 59; Univ Rochester, PhD(biochem), 64. *Prof Exp:* Tutor med, Postgrad Med Sch, Univ London, 54-57; lectr, Royal Free Hosp Med Sch, 60-63; consult med, 63-64, from assoc prof to prof, 64-72, SEGAL-WATSON PROF GASTROENTEROL, SCH MED & DENT, UNIV ROCHESTER, 72- *Concurrent Pos:* Lederle med fac fel, 63-66. *Mem:* Am Fedn Clin Res; Am Gasteroenterol Asn; Brit Soc Gastroenterol. *Res:* Liver diseases and portal hypertension; chemistry and immunology of gastric macromolecules. *Mailing Add:* Sch Med & Dent 601 Elmwood Ave Rochester NY 14642

TURNER, MICHAEL STANLEY, b Los Angeles, Calif, July 29, 49; m 78. ASTROPHYSICS, RELATIVITY. *Educ:* Calif Inst Technol, BS, 71; Stanford Univ, MS, 73, PhD(physics), 78. *Prof Exp:* Instr physics, Stanford Univ, 78; ENRICO FERMI FEL, ENRICO FERMI INST, UNIV CHICAGO, 78- *Mem:* Sigma Xi. *Res:* General relativity, particularly the generation and detection of gravitational waves; astrophysics, especially supernovae and cosmology. *Mailing Add:* Enrico Fermi Inst 5630 Ellis Ave Chicago IL 60637

TURNER, MORTIMER DARLING, b Greeley, Colo, Oct 24, 20; m 45, 65; c 4. ECONOMIC GEOLOGY, ENGINEERING GEOLOGY. *Educ:* Univ Calif, Berkeley, BS, 43, MS, 54; Univ Kans, PhD, 72. *Prof Exp:* Mech & elec engr, Aberdeen Proving Grounds, US Dept Army, 46; asst geol sci, Univ Calif, Berkeley, 48; from jr mining geologist to asst mining geologist, Calif State Div Mines, 48-54; state geologist, Econ Develop Admin, PR, 54-58; phys sci administr & asst to dir, Antarctic Res Prog, NSF, 59-61; res assoc geol, Univ Kans, 62-65; prog dir, Antarctic Earth Sci, Off Antarctic Progs, 65-70, PROG MGR, POLAR EARTH SCI, DIV POLAR PROGS, NSF, 70-; ASSOC PROF LECTR GEOL, GEORGE WASHINGTON UNIV, 72- *Concurrent Pos:* Consult, 55-59; mem, Orgn Comt, 1st Conf Clays & Clay Technol, 52 & Caribbean Geol Conf, 59; mem, US Planning Comt, 2nd Int Conf Permafrost, Nat Acad Sci; mem, 19th, 20th (vpres), 21st, 22nd, 24th (US Govt deleg), and 25th Int Geol Congs. *Mem:* Geol Soc Am; Am Geog Soc; Geol Asn London; Geol Asn PR; Am Polar Soc. *Res:* Tectonics, economic geology and engineering geology of California, Puerto Rico, Caribbean area and Antarctica; geology of early man in North America; engineering geology of costal zones. *Mailing Add:* 3920 Rickover Rd Silver Spring MD 20902

TURNER, NOEL HINTON, b Redlands, Calif, Dec 24, 40; m 66; c 2. PHYSICAL CHEMISTRY. *Educ:* Univ Calif, Berkeley, BS, 62; Univ Rochester, PhD(phys chem), 68. *Prof Exp:* RES CHEMIST, US NAVAL RES LAB, 68- *Mem:* AAAS; Am Chem Soc; Sigma Xi. *Res:* Surface chemistry; gas-solid interactions with reinforcement fibers; electron spectroscopy for chemical analysis and auger electron spectroscopy; kinetics of gas phase reactions and gas-solid adsorption. *Mailing Add:* Chem Div Code 6170 Naval Res Lab Washington DC 20375

TURNER, PAUL JESSE, b Culver City, Calif, Jan 15, 48; m 69; c 2. SPECTROSCOPY, COMPUTER SOFTWARE. *Educ:* Univ Calif, Riverside, BSc, 70, MSc, 74; Univ Calif, Santa Barbara, PhD(chem), 81. *Prof Exp:* Res asst chem, Univ Calif, 73-79; fel chem, Univ Conn, Storrs, 79-81; ASST PROF CHEM, BUCKNELL UNIV, 81- *Mem:* Am Chem Soc. *Res:* Physical chemistry; statistical mechanics; quantum mechanics; spectroscopy specifically statistical mechanical models for aqueous solutions of peptides, organic molecules, Rauan & ultraviolet spectroscopy of biological molecules. *Mailing Add:* Dept Chem Bucknell Univ Lewisburg PA 17837

TURNER, RALPH B, b Lynchburg, Va, Mar 1, 31; m 53; c 2. BIOCHEMISTRY. *Educ:* Va Polytech Inst, BS, 52; Univ Tex, PhD(chem), 63. *Prof Exp:* Res biochemist, Entom Res Div, USDA, 63-68; RES BIOCHEMIST, DEPT BOT & ENTOM, N MEX STATE UNIV, 68- *Mem:* Fel AAAS; fel Am Inst Chem; Am Chem Soc; Sigma Xi; NY Acad Sci. *Res:* Insect nutrition and development; insect embryogenesis; proteolytic enzymes. *Mailing Add:* Box 3BE NMex State Univ Las Cruces NM 88003

TURNER, RALPH WALDO, b Blakely, Ga, Nov 9, 38. PHYSICAL CHEMISTRY, MATHEMATICS. *Educ:* J C Smith Univ, BS, 59; Univ Pittsburgh, PhD(phys chem), 65. *Prof Exp:* Res asst chem, Univ Pittsburgh, 60-64; res engr, Gen Tel & Electronics, 65-66, advan res engr, 66-67; prof sci educ, 67-68, prof chem & physics, 68-69, dir div basic studies, 69-77, PROF CHEM, FLA A&M UNIV, 69- *Concurrent Pos:* US Off Educ grant, Fla A&M Univ, 62-; dir 13 col prog, Fla A&M Univ, 68-69; consult, Inst Servs Educ, 68-72. *Mem:* AAAS; Am Chem Soc; Am Crystallog Asn; Sigma Xi. *Res:* Structure of metal ion aromatic complexes using x-ray crystallography. *Mailing Add:* Dept of Chem Fla A&M Univ Tallahassee FL 32307

TURNER, RAYMOND MARRINER, b Salt Lake City, Utah, Feb 25, 27; m 49; c 3. ECOLOGY. *Educ:* Univ Utah, BS, 48; State Col Wash, PhD(plant ecol), 54. *Prof Exp:* Instr range mgt, Univ Ariz, 54-56, asst prof, 56, instr bot, 56-57, asst prof, 57-62; RES BOTANIST, US GEOL SURV, 62- *Concurrent Pos:* NSF res grant, 57-60. *Mem:* AAAS; Ecol Soc Am; Bot Soc Mex. *Res:* Ecology of arid and semi-arid regions. *Mailing Add:* US Geol Surv 301 W Congress Tucson AZ 85701

TURNER, REX HOWELL, b Birmingham, Ala, Aug 22, 41; m 60; c 2. CELLULOSE CHEMISTRY. *Educ:* Univ S Ala, BS, 68; Univ Ga, PhD(chem), 73. *Prof Exp:* Res asst org chem, Univ Ga, 68-73; develop chemist, Millmaster Onyx Corp, 73-74; SR RES ASSOC INT PAPER CO, 74- *Mem:* Am Chem Soc; Am Asn Textile Chemists & Colorists. *Res:* Isolation and enrichinhomogeneities; macrocyclic synthesis via thermochemical and photochemical decomposition of ketone peroxides; ozonolysis mechanism non-chlorine bleaching of wood pulp; acetylation of wood pulp. *Mailing Add:* Int Paper Co PO Box 2787 Mobile AL 36652

TURNER, ROBERT, b Boston, Mass, Jan 23, 25; m 56; c 3. ELECTRICAL ENGINEERING. *Educ:* Mass Inst Technol, SB, 45; Harvard Univ, SM, 48. *Prof Exp:* Proj engr, Sperry Gyroscope Co, NY, 48-53; analyst, Opers Eval Group, Mass Inst Technol, Washington, DC, 53-55; sr engr, 55-80, PRIN STAFF ENGR, APPL PHYSICS LAB, JOHNS HOPKINS UNIV, 80- *Mem:* Am Phys Soc. *Res:* Servomechanism design; systems analysis; plasma physics; gas lasers. *Mailing Add:* Appl Physics Lab Johns Hopkins Rd Laurel MD 20707

TURNER, ROBERT DAVISON, b Goose Creek, Tex, Oct 16, 29; m 50; c 4. COMMAND & CONTROL SYSTEMS, ENGINEERING PHYSICS. *Educ:* St Lawrence Univ, SB, 49; Harvard Univ, AM, 51, PhD(appl math), 54. *Prof Exp:* Commun theory analyst & consult anal & synthesis, Advan Electronics Ctr, Gen Elec Co, 54-63; staff mem, Inst Defense Anal, 63-68, asst to pres, 68-69, staff mem, Sci & Technol Div, 69-74; staff specialist, Net Tech Assessment, Off Dir Defense Res & Eng, Off Secy Defense, 74-77, spec asst tech plans & res, Off Asst Secy Defense, Commun, Command, Control & Intel, 77-81, DIR STRATEGIC & THEATER NUCLEAR FORCES COMMAND, CONTROL & COMMUN, OFF SECY DEFENSE, US DEPT DEFENSE, 81- *Concurrent Pos:* Vis asst prof, Cornell Univ, 55; mem sci adv bd, US Air Force, 67-71, consult, 71-; consult, Defense Sci Bd, Off Secy Defense, 71-78; mem, Naval Res Adv Comt Lab, Adv Bd Undersea Warfare, 71-74. *Res:* Synthesis and evaluation of sensor information handling systems. *Mailing Add:* 9200 Quintana Dr Bethesda MD 20817

TURNER, ROBERT E L, b Montclair, NJ, Nov 15, 36; m 60; c 3. MATHEMATICS. *Educ:* Cornell Univ, BEngPhys, 59; NY Univ, PhD(math), 63. *Prof Exp:* From asst prof to assoc prof, 63-71, PROF MATH, UNIV WIS-MADISON, 71- *Mem:* Am Math Soc. *Res:* Functional analysis; differential equations. *Mailing Add:* Dept of Math Univ of Wis Madison WI 53706

TURNER, ROBERT JAMES, b Loda, Ill, Nov 15, 21; m 47; c 2. ORGANIC CHEMISTRY. *Educ:* Univ Ill, BS, 47; Univ Wis, MS, 49, PhD(org chem), 50. *Prof Exp:* Asst, Alumni Res Found, Univ Wis, 47-49; res chemist, Mallinckrodt Chem Works, 50-55, group leader, 55; group leader, 56-58, res supvr, 58-64, asst dir res, 64-68, dir res, 68-78, TECH DIR, RES, MORTON CHEM CO, MORTON-NORWICH PROD, INC, 78- *Mem:* Am Chem Soc. *Res:* Synthetic organic chemistry; hydrogenation; hydroformylation; polymers; surface coatings; adhesives; emulsions and dispersions. *Mailing Add:* Morton Chem Co Res Dept 1275 Lake Ave Woodstock IL 60098

TURNER, ROBERT LAWRENCE, b Chicago, Ill, Nov 4, 45; m 66; c 2. ORGANIC POLYMER CHEMISTRY. *Educ:* Albion Col, BA, 67; Mich State Univ, PhD(org chem), 72. *Prof Exp:* Teaching asst org chem, Mich State Univ, 67-69, res asst, 71-72; res chemist, 72-74, staff chemist, 74-76, RES SUPVR, E I DU PONT DE NEMOURS & CO INC, 76- *Res:* Development of new polymer-catalyst systems for use in low energy and nonpolluting protective organic coatings for industrial use. *Mailing Add:* 200 Ridgecote Lane 945 Stephenson Hwy Troy MI 48084

TURNER, ROBERT SCOTT, JR, b Seattle, Wash, May 18, 42; m 72; c 3. DEVELOPMENTAL BIOLOGY. *Educ:* Seattle Univ, BS, 64; Univ Ore, PhD(develop biol), 71. *Prof Exp:* Fel, Dept Biol Chem, Princeton Univ, 71-72, Dept Biochem, Univ Basel, Switz, 72-74; res fel, Dept Biol Chem, Harvard Med Sch, 74-75; ASST PROF BIOL, WESLEYAN UNIV, 75- *Mem:* Am Soc Cell Biol; Soc Develop Biol. *Res:* Genetic control of the synthesis and structure of cell membrane components involved in cell interactions during development and neoplasia; the nature and control of the interactions between these surface components. *Mailing Add:* Dept of Biol Wesleyan Univ Middletown CT 06457

TURNER, ROBERT STUART, b Red Oak, Iowa, June 25, 12; m 42; c 2. NEUROANATOMY. *Educ:* Dartmouth Col, AB, 33; Yale Univ, PhD(anat), 38. *Prof Exp:* Instr biol, Dartmouth Col, 33-35; asst resident in neuroanat, Med Sch, Yale Univ, 37-38; from instr to prof anat, 38-77, EMER PROF ANAT, STANFORD UNIV, 77- *Concurrent Pos:* NIH spec fel, 48-49; consult, Agnews State Hosp & Vet Admin Hosp, 59-69. *Mem:* AAAS; Am Asn Anat; corresp mem Mex Soc Anat; Pan Am Soc Anat. *Res:* Functional anatomy of nervous system; comparative neurology and neurophysiology. *Mailing Add:* 345 Iris Way Palo Alto CA 94303

TURNER, RUTH DIXON, b Melrose, Mass, Dec 7, 14. MALACOLOGY. *Educ:* Bridgewater Teachers Col, BS, 36; Cornell Univ, MA, 43; Radcliffe Col, PhD, 54. *Hon Degrees:* DSC, New Eng Col, 79. *Prof Exp:* Teacher high sch, Vt, 36-37 & jr high sch, Mass, 37-40; asst ed, Boston Soc Natural Hist, 40-42, asst cur birds, 41-42; instr ornith, Vassar Col, 43-44; biologist, William F Clapp Labs, Mass, 44-45; res mollusks, Mus Comp Zool, 45-55, res assoc malacol & Agassiz fel oceanog & zool, 55-75, PROF BIOL, HARVARD UNIV & CUR MALACOL, MUS COMP ZOOL, 75- *Concurrent Pos:* Res assoc, Inst Marine Biol, PR, 56-; consult, William F Clapp Labs, 57- *Mem:* AAAS; Soc Syst Zool; Am Malacol Union. *Res:* Marine boring and fouling mollusks; taxonomy and biology of mollusks, particularly Western Atlantic marine and North American freshwater. *Mailing Add:* Mollusk Dept Mus Comp Zool Harvard Univ Cambridge MA 02138

TURNER, STANLEY EUGENE, nuclear chemistry, see previous edition

TURNER, TERRY EARLE, b NS, Can, Jan 18, 21; nat US; m 42; c 2. PHYSICS. *Educ:* Acadia Univ, BSc, 43, BA, 44; McGill Univ, PhD(physics), 48. *Prof Exp:* Jr res physicist optics, Nat Res Coun Can, 44-45; head physics lab, Sprague Elec Co, 48-51; chief combustion br, Ballistic Res Labs, Aberdeen Proving Ground, Md, 51-56; group leader, Spark Heated Wind Tunnel, Missiles & Space Div, Lockheed Aircraft Corp, 56-59; develop prog mgr, Boeing Co, 59-72; CONSULT PHYSICIST, 72- *Mem:* Am Inst Aeronaut & Astronaut; Am Phys Soc; Combustion Inst. *Res:* High temperature physics; spectroscopy; combustion. *Mailing Add:* 18161 Brittany Dr SW Seattle WA 98166

TURNER, THOMAS BOURNE, b Prince Frederick, Md, Jan 28, 02; m 27; c 2. MICROBIOLOGY. *Educ:* St John's Col, Md, BS, 21; Univ Md, MD, 25. *Hon Degrees:* ScD, Univ Md, 66. *Prof Exp:* Intern, Hosp for Women of Md, 25-26; resident, Mercy Hosp, 26-27; Loeb fel, Sch Med, Johns Hopkins Univ, 27-28, instr med, 28-31, assoc, 31-32; mem staff, Int Health Div, Rockefeller Found, 32-39, clin dir, Jamaica Yaws Comn, 32-34, labs, 34-36; lectr med & pub health admin, Sch Hyg & Pub Health, 36-39, prof microbiol, Sch Med, 39-68, dean, 57-68, EMER DEAN, SCH MED, JOHNS HOPKINS UNIV, 68- *Concurrent Pos:* Consult, Surgeon Gen, US Army; vchmn comt virus res & epidemiol, Nat Found, 49-67; coord, Regional Med Prog for Md, 67-68; physician, out-patient dept, Johns Hopkins Hosp; mem bd visitors, St John's Col, Md; pres, Alcoholic Beverage Med Res Found, 82- *Mem:* Am Soc Clin Invest; Asn Am Physicians; Asn Am Med Cols (past pres); Am medicine, and alcoholism. Dis Asn (past pres). *Res:* Spirochetal diseases; poliomyelitis; tetanus; internal medicine. *Mailing Add:* Johns Hopkins Univ Sch Med 720 Rutland Ave Baltimore MD 21205

TURNER, THOMAS JENKINS, b Albany, Ga, Sept 11, 26; m 48; c 4. SOLID STATE PHYSICS. *Educ:* Univ NC, BS, 47; Clemson Col, MS, 49; Univ Va, PhD(physics), 51. *Prof Exp:* Instr physics, Clemson Col, 47-49; asst prof, Univ NH, 52; from asst prof to prof, Wake Forest Univ, 53-78, chmn dept, 56-74, vpres & dean, 78-81, PROVOST, STETSON UNIV, 81- *Mem:* Fel Am Phys Soc; Am Asn Physics Teachers. *Res:* Defects in crystalline materials; color centers; internal friction. *Mailing Add:* Stetson Univ De Land FL 32720

TURNER, VERAS D, b Tompkinsville, Ky, Oct 19, 25; m 50; c 2. MATHEMATICS. *Educ:* Northwestern Univ, BS, 46; Univ Ill, MA, 49; Univ Okla, PhD, 68. *Prof Exp:* Teacher math, Moark Col, 49-51 & high sch, Ill, 53-56; chmn dept math, Astron & Statist, 73-78, actg dean, 77-78, PROF MATH, MANKATO STATE UNIV, 56-, DEAN, COL NAT SCI, MATH & HOME ECON, 78- *Mem:* Math Asn Am. *Mailing Add:* Col Natural Sci Math & Home Econ Mankato State Univ Mankato MN 56001

TURNER, VERNON LEE, JR, b New Orleans, La, Apr 17, 24; m 47; c 4. CHEMISTRY. *Educ:* Clemson Col, BS, 47; Canisius Col, MS, 52. *Prof Exp:* Res chemist, Spencer Kellogg & Sons, 47-48; res chemist, Textile Fibers Dept, Pioneering Res Div, 48-52, Indust & Biochem Dept, Res Div, 52-62, res chemist, Film Dept, 62-76, RES CHEMIST, POLYMER PROD DEPT, E I DU PONT DE NEMOURS & CO, INC, 76- *Mem:* Sigma Xi; Am Soc Testing & Mat. *Res:* Catalytic hydrogenation and deodorization of vegetable oils; instrumentation and application of radioisotopes in analytical chemistry; general physical and chemical development in the analytical field; thin film deposition; high vacuum technology. *Mailing Add:* E I Du Pont de Nemours & Co Inc PPD-TSL Chestnut Run North Hills DE 19809

TURNER, WALTER W(EEKS), b Augusta, Maine, Aug 3, 22; m 49; c 4. ELECTRICAL ENGINEERING. *Educ:* Mass Inst Technol, BS & MS, 47. *Prof Exp:* From instr to assoc prof, 47-65, PROF ELEC ENG, UNIV MAINE, ORONO, 65- *Mem:* Am Soc Eng Educ; Inst Elec & Electronics Engrs; Nat Soc Prof Engrs. *Res:* Instrumentation, communications and control. *Mailing Add:* Dept of Elec Eng Univ of Maine Orono ME 04469

TURNER, WILLIAM, JR, b Bell, Calif, June 27, 40; m 62; c 2. ENTOMOLOGY. *Educ:* Univ Calif, Berkeley, AB, 63, MS, 66, PhD(entom), 71. *Prof Exp:* Lab technician entom, Univ Calif, Berkeley, 63-64, from asst to assoc entomologist, 64-67, NIH trainee, 67-70; asst prof & asst entomologist, 70-76, ASSOC PROF ENTOM & ZOOL & ASSOC ENTOMOLOGIST, WASH STATE UNIV, 76- *Mem:* Entom Soc Am; Entom Soc Can; Soc Syst Zool. *Res:* Insect biosystematics; zoogeography, phylogeny and biology of Diptera; swarming behavior in insects; medical entomology, especially biting flies as vectors of pathogens. *Mailing Add:* Dept of Entom Wash State Univ Pullman WA 99164

TURNER, WILLIAM JOSEPH, b Canandaigua, NY, Mar 7, 27; m 51; c 4. SOLID STATE PHYSICS. *Educ:* Villanova Univ, BS, 49; Cath Univ, PhD(physics), 55. *Prof Exp:* Physicist, Naval Res Lab, Washington, DC, 51-52 & Nat Bur Standards, 52-56; assoc physicist, Phys Res Dept, 56-57, staff physicist, Res Lab, 57-58, proj physicist, 58-59, develop physicist & res staff mem semiconductor physics, 59-61, res staff mem optical properties of semiconductors, 61-64, MGR RES STAFF OPERS, THOMAS J WATSON RES CTR, IBM CORP, 64- *Mem:* Fel Am Phys Soc. *Res:* Use of optical absorption, reflection and luminescence measurements to study the intrinsic, lattice and extrinsic properties of semiconductors. *Mailing Add:* Thomas J Watson Res Ctr PO Box 218 IBM Yorktown Heights NY 10598

TURNER, WILLIAM RICHARD, b Drexel Hill, Pa, June 26, 36; m 60; c 3. ANALYTICAL CHEMISTRY. *Educ:* Philadelphia Col Pharm, BS, 58; Univ Conn, MS, 61, PhD(anal chem), 64. *Prof Exp:* Chemist, Borden Chem Co, 58-59; fel, Univ Mich, 64; SR RES CHEMIST, ICI AM, 65- *Mem:* Am Chem Soc; Sigma Xi. *Res:* Liquid chromatography; electroanalytical chemistry, especially organic polarography, votammetry at solid electrodes, coulometric titrimetry and amperometric titrimetry. *Mailing Add:* Corp Res Dept ICI Am Wilmington DE 19897

TURNER, WILLIE, b Suffolk, Va, Feb 1, 35; m 64; c 2. VIROLOGY, IMMUNOLOGY. *Educ:* Md State Col, BS, 57; Ohio State Univ, MS, 59, PhD(microbiol), 61. *Prof Exp:* NIH fel, Naval Med Res Inst, 61-62, Nat Inst Allergy & Infectious Dis grant, 62-64; asst prof microbiol, Meharry Med Col, 62-66; head microbiol sect, Viral Biol Br, Nat Cancer Inst, 70-71; PROF MICROBIOL & CHMN DEPT, COL MED, HOWARD UNIV, 71- *Concurrent Pos:* NIH staff fel oncol virol, Nat Cancer Inst, 66-69, sr fel, 69-70. *Mem:* AAAS; Am Soc Microbiol; Am Asn Immunologists; Am Asn Cancer Res; Soc Exp Biol & Med. *Res:* Oncogenic virology, especially interaction of oncogenic and nononcogenic viruses in vitro and in vivo; immunology of murine oncogenic virus as well as the immunology involved with tumors induced by these agents in vivo. *Mailing Add:* Dept of Microbiol Howard Univ Col of Med Washington DC 20001

TURNEY, TULLY HUBERT, b Lakewood, Ohio, Sept 7, 36; m 62; c 1. ZOOLOGY. *Educ:* Oberlin Col, AB, 58; Univ NC, PhD(zool), 63. *Prof Exp:* Fel, Oak Ridge Nat Labs, 63-64; instr zool, Univ NC, 64-65; assoc prof biol, 65-74, chmn dept, 67-76, PROF BIOL, HAMPDEN-SYDNEY COL, 74- *Mem:* AAAS; Am Inst Biol Sci. *Res:* Cell control mechanisms; molecular biochemistry; physiology. *Mailing Add:* Dept of Biol Hampden-Sydney Col Hampden-Sydney VA 23943

TURNIPSEED, GLYN D, b Hazlehurst, Miss, Dec 19, 42; m 67; c 1. PLANT PHYSIOLOGY. *Educ:* Delta State Univ, BS, 66; Miss State Univ, PhD(bot), 73. *Prof Exp:* Sci teacher biol chem, Jackson Pub Schs at Wingfield High Sch, 66-70; asst bot, Miss State Univ, 70-73; asst prof, 73-80, ASSOC PROF BIOL, ARK POLYTECH COL, 80- *Concurrent Pos:* Ark Nat Heritage Comn. *Mem:* Soc Study of Amphibians & Reptiles; Am Mus Nat Hist; Audubon Soc. *Res:* Nitrogen source preference of Oophila ambystomatis; feeding efficiency of larval anurans; population density of larval anurans; Arkansas amphibian and reptillian distributions. *Mailing Add:* Dept of Biol Ark Tech Univ Russellville AR 72801

TURNIPSEED, MARVIN ROY, b Carrollton, Miss, Nov 11, 34; m 57; c 2. REPRODUCTIVE PHYSIOLOGY, BIOCHEMISTRY. *Educ:* Miss State Univ, BS, 56, MEd, 63; Univ Ga, PhD(zool), 69. *Prof Exp:* NIH fel steroid biochem, Med Sch, Univ Minn, Minneapolis, 69-71, res assoc steroid biochem, 71-78; asst prof, 78-80, ASSOC PROF, DEPT BIOL, QUINNIPIAC COL, HAMDEN, 80- *Concurrent Pos:* Res affil, Dept Obstet & Gynec, Yale Univ, 80- *Mem:* Endocrine Soc; AAAS. *Res:* Placental aromatase action upon testosterone stearate and testosterone linolenate; anatomy and physiology and radiation biology; receptors involved in reproduction of female mammals; ovarian production of steroid hormones in response to trophic hormones; plasma and urinary estrogens and adrenal metabolism in newborn babies; endocrinology. *Mailing Add:* Box 92 Quinnipiac Col Hamden CT 06518

TURNIPSEED, SAMUEL GUY, entomology, see previous edition

TURNOCK, WILLIAM JAMES, b Winnipeg, Man, May 17, 29; m 58; c 3. POPULATION ECOLOGY, BIOLOGICAL CONTROL. *Educ:* Univ Man, BSA, 49; Univ Minn, MS, 51, PhD(entom), 59. *Prof Exp:* Res scientist, Div Forest Biol, Can Dept Agr, 49-61 & Forest Entom & Path Br, Can Dept Forestry, Man, 61-70; sci adv, Can Ministry State for Sci & Technol, 70-72; SECT HEAD INTEGRATED PEST CONTROL, RES BR, CAN DEPT AGR, 72- *Concurrent Pos:* Hon prof, Grad Sch, Univ Man, 65-70; Can del, Int Coord Coun Man & Biosphere, UNESCO, 71. *Mem:* Ecol Soc Am; Entom Soc Can (pres, 79-80). *Res:* Integrated and biological control of agriculture pests. *Mailing Add:* Agr Res Sta 195 Dafoe Rd Winnipeg MB R3T 2M9 Can

TURNQUEST, BYRON W, b Chicago, Ill, Dec 16, 24; m 51; c 4. ORGANIC CHEMISTRY. *Educ:* DePaul Univ, BS, 49, MS, 51; Ill Inst Technol, PhD(phys org chem), 57. *Prof Exp:* Res chemist, Sinclair Res Inc, Harvey, 56-60, sr res chemist, 60-66, mgr prod res & develop, 73-78, nat mgr, Quality Admin, 75-78, SR RES CHEMIST & SECT LEADER, ARCO, 66-, MGR RES & DEVELOP, PROD DIV, 78- *Res:* Physical and synthetic organic chemistry; engine oils; engine oil additives; greases; catalysis. *Mailing Add:* Harvey Res Ctr ARCO 400 E Sibley Blvd Harvey IL 60426

TURNQUIST, CARL RICHARD, b Midland, Mich, May 12, 44; m 69; c 2. POLYMER CHEMISTRY. *Educ:* Westminister Col, BA, 66; Univ Wis-Madison, PhD(chem), 72. *Prof Exp:* Res chemist textile fibers, E I du Pont de Nemours, Co, Inc, 72-75; sr chemist, 75-78, res prog supvr, 78, chem & polymer supvr, Cardiol & Radiol Prods, 78-82, STAFF ENGR, USCI CARDIOL & RADIOL DIV, C R BARD, INC, 82- *Mem:* Am Chem Soc; Soc Plastics Engrs; AAAS; Sigma Xi. *Res:* Development of medical devices (implantable artificial arteries and heart catheters); analysis; material and process development; biotesting; physician interactions. *Mailing Add:* 106 Kenney Lane Concord MA 01742

TURNQUIST, MARK ALAN, b July 26, 49; US citizen; m 71; c 2. TRANSPORTATION ENGINEERING. *Educ:* Mich State Univ, BS, 71; Mass Inst Technol, SM, 72, PhD(transp systs anal), 75. *Prof Exp:* Res asst, Dept Elec Eng & Systs Sci, Mich State Univ, 70-71; teaching & res asst, Dept Civil Eng, Mass Inst Technol, 71-75; asst prof transp eng, Dept Civil Eng & transp Ctr, Northwestern Univ, 75-79; ASSOC PROF TRANSP ENG, SCH CIVIL/ENVIRON ENG, CORNELL UNIV, 79- *Concurrent Pos:* Consult, Inst Gas Technol, Chicago, Ill, 75-76, John Hamburg & Assocs, Inc, Chicago, Ill, 77-78 & City of Chicago, 79-81. *Mem:* Opers Res Soc Am; Soc Comput Simulation. *Res:* Transportation systems design, operations and control, including questions of vehicle routing and scheduling, service reliability, and cost of operations. *Mailing Add:* Sch Civil/Environ Eng Cornell Univ Ithaca NY 14853

TURNQUIST, PAUL KENNETH, b Lindsborg, Kans, Jan 3, 35; m 62; c 2. AGRICULTURAL ENGINEERING. *Educ:* Kans State Univ, BS, 57; Okla State Univ, MS, 61, PhD(agr eng), 65. *Prof Exp:* Res engr, Caterpillar Tractor Co, 57; from instr to asst prof agr eng, Okla State Univ, 58-62; assoc prof, SDak State Univ, 64-70; engr in residence, Caterpillar Tractor Co, 70-71; prof agr eng, SDak State Univ, 71-76; PROF AGR ENG & HEAD DEPT, AUBURN UNIV, 77- *Mem:* Am Soc Agr Engrs; Am Soc Eng Educ; Sigma Xi; Natural Soc Professional Engrs. *Res:* Agricultural power and machinery for tillage and harvesting; operator safety; environmental control. *Mailing Add:* Dept of Agr Eng Auburn Univ Auburn AL 36849

TURNQUIST, RALPH OTTO, b Lindsborg, Kans, Aug 10, 28; m 65; c 2. MECHANICAL ENGINEERING, INSTRUMENTATION. *Educ:* Kans State Univ, BS, 52, MS, 61; Case Inst Technol, PhD(fluid controls), 65. *Prof Exp:* Engr, Aircraft Gas Turbine Div, Westinghouse Elec Co, Mo, 54-59; instr mech eng, Kans State Univ, 59-62; res asst fluid control systs, Case Inst Technol, 62-65; from asst prof to assoc prof mech eng, 65-77, PROF MECH ENG, KANS STATE UNIV, 77- *Mem:* Am Soc Mech Engrs; Am Soc Eng Educ; Int Standards Asn. *Res:* Turbojet engine fuel distribution and atomization; automatic control theory; fluid control systems; fluidics. *Mailing Add:* Dept of Mech Eng Kans State Univ Manhattan KS 66502

TURNQUIST, RICHARD LEE, b Rugby, NDak, Aug 12, 44; m 66. PHYSIOLOGY, BIOCHEMISTRY. *Educ:* Concordia Col, BA, 66; Utah State Univ, PhD(physiol), 71. *Prof Exp:* Fel biochem, Utah State Univ, 71-74; ASST PROF BIOL, AUGUSTANA COL, 74- *Mem:* AAAS; Sigma Xi. *Res:* Ultrastructural changes and responses during detoxication of xenobiotics in mammals and insects. *Mailing Add:* Dept of Biol Augustana Col Rock Island IL 61201

TURNQUIST, TRUMAN DALE, b Kipling, Sask, Apr 8, 40; m 64; c 2. ANALYTICAL CHEMISTRY. *Educ:* Bethel Col, Minn, BA, 61; Univ Minn, PhD(anal chem), 65. *Prof Exp:* assoc prof, 65-76, PROF CHEM, MT UNION COL, 76- *Mem:* Am Chem Soc. *Res:* Metal complex formation; solvent extraction of metal complexes; spectrophotometry. *Mailing Add:* Dept of Chem Mt Union Col Alliance OH 44601

TURNROSE, BARRY EDMUND, b New Britain, Conn, June 3, 47; m 70; c 2. SPACE ASTRONOMY, DIGITAL IMAGE PROCESSING. *Educ:* Wesleyan Univ, BA, 69; Calif Inst Technol, PhD(astron), 76. *Prof Exp:* Resident res assoc astron, NASA-Johnson Space Ctr, Houston, 75-77; resident astronomer image processing, 77-80, SECT MGR, INT ULTRAVIOLET EXPLORER, COMPUT SCI CORP, GODDARD SPACE FLIGHT CTR, 80- *Mem:* Am Astron Soc. *Res:* Extragalactic astronomy; spectrophotometry of galaxies; stellar content of galaxies; surface photometry of extragalactic objects; astronomical image processing; ultraviolet astronomy. *Mailing Add:* Comput Sci Corp Syst Sci Div 8728 Colesville Rd Silver Spring MD 20910

TUROFF, MURRAY, b San Francisco, Calif, Feb 13, 36; m 61; c 1. COMPUTER SCIENCE, OPERATIONS RESEARCH. *Educ:* Univ Calif, Berkeley, BA, 58; Brandeis Univ, PhD(physics), 65. *Prof Exp:* Syst engr, IBM Corp, 61-64; mem prof staff syst anal, Inst Defense Anal, 64-68; opers res & info systs, Off Emergency Preparedness, 68-73; PROF COMPUT & INFO SCI, NJ INST TECHNOL, 73- *Concurrent Pos:* Lectr, Am Univ, 70-73. *Mem:* AAAS; Inst Mgt Sci; Opers Res Soc Am; Asn Comput Mach; Am Soc Cybernet. *Res:* Delphi design; computerized conferencing systems; information systems design; technology assessment and forecasting; gaming, simulation and modeling; policy analyses. *Mailing Add:* NJ Inst of Technol 323 High St Newark NJ 07102

TUROFF, ROBERT DAVID, b New York, NY, May 29, 35; m 58; c 2. SOLID STATE PHYSICS. *Educ:* Queens Col, NY, BS, 57; Rutgers Univ, MS, 60, PhD(physics), 64. *Prof Exp:* Asst prof, San Francisco State Col, 64-65; asst prof, 65-76, ASSOC PROF PHYSICS, ANTIOCH COL, 76- *Mem:* Am Phys Soc; Am Asn Physics Teachers. *Res:* Magnetic resonance; low temperature magnetism. *Mailing Add:* Dept of Physics Antioch Col Yellow Springs OH 45387

TURPEN, JAMES BAXTER, b Sheridan, Wyo, Sept 27, 45; div; c 2. DEVELOPMENTAL BIOLOGY, IMMUNOLOGY. *Educ:* Univ Denver, BS, 67, MS, 69; Tulane Univ, PhD(biol), 73. *Prof Exp:* USPHS fel immunol, Med Ctr, Univ Rochester, 74-76; ASST PROF BIOL, PA STATE UNIV, 76- *Concurrent Pos:* Prin investr, USPHS-NIH grant, 77-85; USPHS res career develop award, 80-85. *Mem:* Am Soc Zoologists; Am Asn Anatomists; AAAS; Int Soc Study Differentiation. *Res:* Development of hematopoietic cells; comparative immunology. *Mailing Add:* 208 Mueller Lab Pa State Univ University Park PA 16802

TURPENING, ROGER MUNSON, seismology, see previous edition

TURPIN, FRANK THOMAS, b Troy, Kans, June 4, 43; m 70; c 2. ECONOMIC ENTOMOLOGY. *Educ:* Washburn Univ, BS, 65; Iowa State Univ, PhD(entom), 71. *Prof Exp:* Asst prof, 71-77, ASSOC PROF ENTOM, PURDUE UNIV, 77- *Concurrent Pos:* Consult, US Environ Protection Agency, 73-, Pesticide Industs, 75- & USAID, Tanzania, 81. *Mem:* Entom Soc Am. *Res:* Biology; ecology; population dynamcis and control of insects attacking corn. *Mailing Add:* Entom Hall Purdue Univ West Lafayette IN 47907

TURPIN, ROBERT D(AVIS), b Amarillo, Tex, Dec 16, 21; m 48; c 3. CIVIL ENGINEERING. *Educ:* Univ Tex, BS, 48, MS, 49; Ohio State Univ, PhD(photogram), 57. *Prof Exp:* From instr to asst prof civil eng, Univ Tex, 49-55; instr, Ohio State Univ, 54-55; from asst prof to assoc prof, Univ Tex, 55-60; Ford Found vis assoc prof, Univ Wis, 60-61; assoc prof, Univ Tex, 61-66; PROF CIVIL ENG, TEX A&M UNIV, 66- *Concurrent Pos:* Mem photogram sect, Hwy Res Bd, Nat Acad Sci-Nat Res Coun, 67- *Mem:* Am Soc Photogram; Am Soc Eng Educ; Nat Soc Prof Engrs; Am Soc Civil Engrs. *Res:* Applications of photogrammetry to engineering, the sciences and medicine. *Mailing Add:* Dept of Civil Eng Tex A&M Univ College Station TX 77843

TURRELL, BRIAN GEORGE, b Shoreham-by-Sea, Eng, May 6, 38; m 62; c 3. PHYSICS. *Educ:* Oxford Univ, BA, 59, MA & DPhil(nuclear orientation), 63. *Prof Exp:* Asst lectr physics, Univ Sussex, 63-64; from asst prof to assoc prof, 64-70, PROF PHYSICS, UNIV BC, 76- *Res:* Nuclear orientation; nuclear magnetic resonance; use of these techniques to study hyperfine interactions in magnetic materials. *Mailing Add:* Dept of Physics Univ of BC Vancouver BC V6T 1W5 Can

TURRELL, EUGENE SNOW, b Hyattsville, Md, Feb 27, 19; div; c 1. PSYCHIATRY. *Educ:* Ind Univ, BS, 39, MD, 47; Am Bd Psychiat & Neurol, dipl, 53. *Prof Exp:* Asst physiol, Ind Univ, 39-42; res assoc, Fatigue Lab, Harvard Univ, 42-43; res assoc physiol, Ind Univ, 43-44, asst biochem, Sch Med, 45-47; med house officer, Peter Bent Brigham Hosp, Boston, 47-48; resident psychiat, Kankakee State Hosp, Ill, 48-49; clin asst, Sch Med, Univ Calif, 49-52; asst prof, Sch Med, Ind Univ, 52-53; assoc prof, Sch Med, Univ Colo, 53-58, asst dean sch, 57; prof & chmn dept, Sch Med, Marquette Univ, 58-63, clin prof, 63-69; sr psychiatrist, 69-72, dir, Ctr Spec Probs, Community Ment Health Serv, City & County of San Francisco, 72-75; STAFF PSYCHIATRIST, MIDTOWN COMMUNITY MENT HEALTH CTR, WISHARD MEM HOSP, 75-; ASSOC PROF, DEPT PSYCHIAT, IND UNIV SCH MED, 75- *Concurrent Pos:* Resident, Langley Porter Clin, 49-50; chief psychiat consult serv, Robert W Long Hosp, Indianapolis, Ind, 52-53; med dir, Colo Psychopath Hosp, 53-54; assoc attend, Denver Gen Hosp, 53-57, dir psychiat serv, 57-58; attend, Vet Admin Hosp, Denver, 53-58; mem staff psychosom div, Colo Gen Hosp, 54-57; dir psychiat serv, Milwaukee Sanitarium Found, 58-65; consult, Hosp Ment Dis, Milwaukee, 58-69, Vet Admin Hosp, Wood, Wis, 58-69, Columbia Hosp, 59-69 & Milwaukee Children's Hosp, 60-69. *Honors & Awards:* Sigma Xi. *Mem:* AAAS; Am Psychiat Asn; AMA. *Res:* Psychosomatic medicine; psychotherapy. *Mailing Add:* 1001 W Tenth St Indianapolis IN 46202

TURRELL, GEORGE CHARLES, b Portland, Ore, June 19, 31; m 54; c 4. PHYSICAL CHEMISTRY. *Educ:* Lewis & Clark Col, BA, 50; Ore State Univ, MS, 52, PhD(phys chem), 54. *Prof Exp:* Asst, Ore State Univ, 50-52; mem tech staff, Electron Device Dept, Bell Tel Labs, Inc, 54-56; res assoc, Metcalf Res Lab, Brown Univ, 56-57, instr chem, 57-58; Guggenheim fel, Bellevue Labs, Nat Ctr Sci Res, France, 58-59; asst prof chem, Howard Univ, 59-62, assoc prof, 62-67; exchange prof & Fulbright fel, Infrared Spectros Lab, Univ Bordeaux, 66-67, vis prof, 67-70; prof, Nat Univ Zaire, Kisangani, 70-71 & Kinshasa, 71-72; actg ed, Can Jour Spectroscopy, 72; vis prof chem, Univ Montreal, 72-74 & McGill Univ, 73-75; res prof chem, Univ Laval, Que, 75-79; engr, Bomem, Inc, 79-80; vis prof, Molecular Physics Lab, Univ Limoges, 80-81; PROF, INFRARED & RAMAN SPECTROSCOPY LAB, UNIV SCI TECH LILLE, FRANCE, 81- *Mem:* Am Phys Soc; Coblentz Soc; Can Spectroscopy Soc. *Res:* Molecular spectroscopy; studies of molecular interactions in solids and liquids using infrared and Raman spectroscopy. *Mailing Add:* Univ Sci Tech Lille LASIR Bat C5 59655 Villeneuve d'Ascq France

TURRELL, SYLVIA JONES, physical chemistry, see previous edition

TURRO, NICHOLAS JOHN, b Middletown, Conn, May 18, 38; m 60; c 2. ORGANIC CHEMISTRY. *Educ:* Wesleyan Univ, BA, 60; Calif Inst Technol, PhD(chem), 63. *Prof Exp:* Instr, 64-65, from asst prof to assoc prof, 65-69, PROF ORG CHEM, COLUMBIA UNIV, 69-, CHMN, CHEM DEPT, 81. *Concurrent Pos:* NSF fel, Harvard Univ, 63-64; consult, E I du Pont de Nemours & Co, 64-; vis prof, Pa State Univ, 66; Sloan Found fel, 66-68; mem ed bd, J Org Chem, J Molecular Photochem, 75- *Honors & Awards:* Pure Chem Award, Am Chem Soc, Halpern Award Photochem, NY Acad Sci, 77. *Mem:* Nat Acad Sci; AAAS; Am Chem Soc; Royal Soc Chem; fel NY Acad Sci. *Res:* Photochemistry; electronic energy transfer in fluid solution. cycloaddition reactions; thermal rearrangements; dioxetane chemistry; chemiluminescence; micellar chemistry; application of laser techniques to organic photochemistry; emulsion polymerization; magnetic field effects. *Mailing Add:* 125 Downey Dr Tenafly NJ 07670

TURSE, RICHARD S, b Jersey City, NJ, Mar 24, 35; m 64; c 3. ANALYTICAL CHEMISTRY, SPECTROCHEMISTRY. *Educ:* Rutgers Univ, BS, 56, MS, 58, PhD(anal chem), 60. *Prof Exp:* Instr anal chem, Rutgers Univ, 56-58; SR RES CHEMIST, COLGATE-PALMOLIVE CO, 60- *Mem:* Soc Appl Spectros; Am Pharm Asn. *Res:* Development of atomic absorption methods for determination of trace metals in consumer products for safety and environmental reasons; development of X-ray diffraction and fluorescence techniques for sample identification. *Mailing Add:* Colgate-Palmolive Co 909 River Rd Piscataway NJ 08854

TUSING, THOMAS WILLIAM, b New Market, Va, Feb 2, 20; m 49; c 5. PHARMACOLOGY. *Educ:* George Washington Univ, BS, 42; Med Col Va, MD, 50. *Prof Exp:* Med dir, Hazleton Labs, Inc, 51-58, dir res & vpres, 58-69; MED DIR PHARMACEUT RES & DEVELOP DIV, MALLINCKRODT INC, 69- *Mem:* AMA; Indust Med Asn; Soc Toxicol. *Mailing Add:* 13561 Featherstone Dr St Louis MO 63131

TUSTANOFF, EUGENE RENO, b Windsor, Ont, Jan 30, 29; m 54; c 4. BIOCHEMISTRY. *Educ:* Assumption Col, BA, 52; Detroit Univ, MS, 54; Western Ont Univ, PhD(biochem), 59. *Prof Exp:* Res assoc biochem, Western Ont Univ, 55-59; fel, Western Reserve Univ, 59-61; Life Ins Med Res fel, Oxford Univ, 61-62; asst scientist, Hosp for Sick Children, Univ Toronto, 62-64; assoc biochem, Univ Toronto, 63-65, asst prof pharmacol, 64-65; assoc prof biochem, McMaster Univ, 65-67; assoc prof path chem, 67-72, assoc prof clin biochem, 72-75, PROF CLIN BIOCHEM, UNIV WESTERN ONT, 75- *Mem:* Can Biochem Soc; Brit Biochem Soc; Am Soc Biol Chem; Am Asn Clin Chem. *Res:* Biogenesis and control of mitochondria; biogenesis of membranes; biochemistry of tumour model systems; biochemistry of middle molecules in uremia. *Mailing Add:* Dept of Biochem Victoria Hosp Univ of Western Ont London ON N6A 4G5 Can

TUSZYNSKI, ALFONS ALFRED, b Poland, Apr 30, 21; US citizen; m 45; c 2. ELECTRONICS, MICROELECTRONICS. *Educ:* Univ London, BSc, 52; Newark Col Eng, MSc, 62, DEngSc(integrated circuits), 69. *Prof Exp:* Mem staff various co, Gt Brit & Can, 52-59; creative specialist, Am Optical Co, 60-63; proj engr, Singer Gen Precision, 63-66; mgr applns, Sprague Elec Co, 66-67; consult, Sylvania & Singer Gen Precision, 67-69; mgr res & develop, Solitron Devices Inc, 69-70; ASSOC PROF ELEC ENG, UNIV MINN, MINNEAPOLIS, 70- *Concurrent Pos:* Consult, Solitron Devices Inc, 70- *Mem:* Sr mem Inst Elec & Electronics Engrs. *Res:* Large scale integration and micropower techniques pertaining to linear and digital systems; microcircuits. *Mailing Add:* Dept of Elec Eng Univ of Minn Minneapolis MN 55455

TUTAS, DANIEL JOSEPH, chemistry, biochemistry, see previous edition

TUTEUR, FRANZ BENJAMIN, b Frankfurt, Ger, Mar 6, 23; nat US; m 52; c 2. ELECTRICAL ENGINEERING. *Educ:* Univ Colo, BS, 44; Yale Univ, MEng, 49, PhD(elec eng), 54. *Prof Exp:* From instr to assoc prof elec eng, 50-66, PROF ENG & APPL SCI, YALE UNIV, 66- *Concurrent Pos:* Guest lectr & consult, Israel Inst Technol, 57; consult, Tech Res Group, NY, 57-58,

Sikorsky Aircraft Co, Conn, 58, Melpar, Inc, Mass, 59-61, Rand Corp, Calif, 62-77, Anal Sci Corp, Mass, 70- & Perkin-Elmer Corp, 72-77; vis prof, Univ Calif, Berkeley, 65-66; vis res marine physicist, Scripps Inst Oceanog, San Diego, Calif, 78. *Mem:* Inst Elec & Electronics Engrs. *Res:* Communications theory; sonar; control systems; adaptive systems; automatic electroencephalography. *Mailing Add:* Elec Eng Dept Yale Univ New Haven CT 06520

TUTHILL, ARTHUR F(REDERICK), b Cutchogue, NY, Dec 18, 16; m 41; c 5. MECHANICAL ENGINEERING, THERMODYNAMICS. *Educ:* Carnegie Inst Technol, BS, 38; Univ Wis, MS, 39. *Prof Exp:* Instr mech eng, Cooper Union, 39-42; instr, 46-56, PROF MECH ENG, UNIV VT, 56- *Mem:* Am Soc Mech Engrs; Am Soc Eng Educ. *Res:* Air distribution, environmental engineering. *Mailing Add:* Dept of Mech Eng Univ of Vt Burlington VT 05401

TUTHILL, HARLAN LLOYD, b Fillmore, NY, Nov 24, 17; m 41, 71; c 2. RESEARCH MANAGEMENT. *Educ:* Houghton Col, BS, 39; coornell Univ, PhD(phys chem), 43. *Prof Exp:* Res chemist, Rohm & Haas Co, 43-46; head phys chem sect, Smith Kline & French Labs, 46-48, tech dir, 48-54, sci dir int div, 54-57, asst dir res & develop labs, 57-62, vpres, SmithKline Instruments, Inc, 62-65; dir prod develop & assoc dir, Squibb Inst Med Res, E R Squibb & Sons, Inc, 65-70; dir health & med res, 70-77, ASSOC DIR SCI & TECHNOL LABS, INT PAPER CO, 77- *Mem:* AAAS; Am Chem Soc; Sigma Xi. *Res:* Health and environmental sciences; analytical and materials sciences. *Mailing Add:* Int Paper Co Box 797 Tuxedo Park NY 10987

TUTHILL, SAMUEL JAMES, b San Diego, Calif, Sept 6, 25; m 52; c 3. GEOLOGY, PALEOECOLOGY. *Educ:* Drew Univ, AB, 51; Syracuse Univ, MS, 60; Univ NDak, MA, 63, PhD(geol), 69. *Prof Exp:* Geologist, NDak Geol Surv, 63-64; asst prof geol, Muskingum Col, 64-68; asst state geologist, Iowa Geol Surv, 68-69, dir & state geologist, 69-75; vpres energy resources/ utilization, Environ & Res, 77-78, SR VPRES, IOWA ELEC LIGHT & POWER CO, 78- *Concurrent Pos:* NSF grants, Muskingum Col expeds Alaska, 65-66, 67-69; adj prof, Univ Iowa, 69-; adminr, Iowa Oil & Gas Admin, 69-; mem, Iowa Natural Resources Coun, 70-; mem, Iowa Land Rehab Coun, 70-; secy, Iowa State Map Adv Coun, 72; sci adv to US Secy Interior, 75-; spec asst energy policy to chmn Presidents Energy Resources Coun, 75-76; dir Off Indust Energy Conserv, US Dept Com, 75-76; adv, US Fed Energy Admin, 75-76, asst adminr conserv & environ, 76-77; COMNR, Upper Miss River Basin Comn, Iowa, 80-82. *Mem:* AAAS; fel Geol Soc Am; Asn Am State Geol; fel Explorers Club. *Res:* Research management; water; minerals; environmental protection; landuse planning; remote sensing; resources managemental development. *Mailing Add:* Exec Off Iowa Elec Light & Power Co PO Box 351 Cedar Rapids IA 52406

TUTHILL, SAMUEL MILLER, b Rocky Point, NY, Jan 7, 19; m 41; c 3. ANALYTICAL CHEMISTRY. *Educ:* Wesleyan Univ, BA, 39, MA, 41; Ohio State Univ, PhD(chem), 48. *Prof Exp:* Lab asst chem, Wesleyan Univ, 39-41; anal chemist, Mallinckrodt Chem Works, 41-45; lab asst chem, Ohio State Univ, 45-46, from asst instr to instr, 47-48; anal chemist, Mallinckrodt, Inc, 48-56, dir qual control, 56-70, corp dir qual control, 70-72, corp dir qual assurance, 72-76, dir corp anal serv, 76-81, MEM TECH COMT & QUAL CONTROL CONSULT, MALLINCKRODT, INC, 81- *Concurrent Pos:* Mem comt revision, US Pharmacopeia; comt reagent specif, Am Chem Soc. *Mem:* Am Chem Soc; Am Soc Qual Control; Pharmaceut Mfrs Asn; Acad Pharmaceut Sci; Parenteral Drug Asn. *Res:* Methods of analysis of pharmaceutical and reagents chemicals; separation by electrodeposition; instrumental methods of analysis; separation of rhodium from iridium by electrolysis with control of the cathode potential; determination of rare earths in steels; analysis of opium and narcotics; good manufacturing practice in manufacture of drugs. *Mailing Add:* Mallinckrodt Inc Mallinckrodt & Second St PO Box 5439 St Louis MO 63147

TUTIHASI, SIMPEI, b Tokyo, Japan, Mar 2, 22; US citizen; m 47; c 2. SOLID STATE PHYSICS. *Educ:* Kyoto Univ, BSc, 46, DSc(physics), 56. *Prof Exp:* Res assoc solid state physics, Inst Optics, Univ Rochester, 56-59; sr engr, Sylvania Elec Prods, Inc, 59-64; SCIENTIST, RES LABS, XEROX CORP, 64- *Mem:* Am Phys Soc; Optical Soc Am. *Res:* Solid state spectroscopy; spectroscopy of ordered crystals, photoconductivity, luminescence. *Mailing Add:* 1217 Majestic Way Webster NY 14580

TUTTE, WILLIAM THOMAS, b Newmarket, Eng, May 14, 17; m 49. MATHEMATICS. *Educ:* Cambridge Univ, PhD(math), 48. *Prof Exp:* Lectr, Univ Toronto, 48-52, from asst prof to assoc prof, 52-62; PROF MATH, UNIV WATERLOO, 62- *Honors & Awards:* Henry Marshall Tory Medal, Royal Soc Can, 75. *Mem:* Am Math Soc; Math Asn Am; fel Royal Soc Can; Can Math Soc; London Math Soc. *Res:* Graph theory; matroid theory. *Mailing Add:* Dept Math Univ Waterloo Waterloo ON N2L 3G1 Can

TUTTLE, DAVID F(EARS), b Briarcliff Manor, NY, July 5, 14; m 44; c 2. ELECTRICAL ENGINEERING. *Educ:* Amherst Col, AB, 34; Mass Inst Technol, SB & SM, 38, ScD(elec eng), 48. *Prof Exp:* Mem tech staff, Bell Tel Labs, NY, 38-42; prof, 48-79, EMER PROF ELEC ENG, STANFORD UNIV, 79- *Concurrent Pos:* Fulbright lectr, France, 54-55 & Spain, 61-62; assoc prof, Univ Aix-Marseille, 68-69; vis prof math, Ga Inst Tech, 81-82. *Mem:* Fel AAAS; fel Inst Elec & Electronics Engrs. *Res:* Network theory. *Mailing Add:* Dept of Elec Eng Stanford Univ Stanford CA 94305

TUTTLE, DONALD MONROE, b Bay City, Mich, Feb 1, 17; m 47; c 3. ENTOMOLOGY. *Educ:* Mich State Univ, BS, 40, MS, 47; Univ Ill, PhD(entom), 52. *Prof Exp:* Lab asst entom, Mich State Col, 40; instr, Univ Maine, 47-49; asst, Univ Ill, 49-52; PROF & RES ENTOMOLOGIST, UNIV ARIZ, 52- *Mem:* Entom Soc Am; Acarological Soc Am. *Res:* Citrus, alfalfa, melon and turf insects; systematics and biology of Tetranychoidea. *Mailing Add:* Univ Ariz Farm 6425 W Eighth St Yuma AZ 85364

TUTTLE, ELBERT P, JR, b Ithaca, NY, Sept 1, 21; m 52; c 5. PHYSIOLOGY, INTERNAL MEDICINE. *Educ:* Princeton Univ, AB, 42; Harvard Univ, MD, 51. *Prof Exp:* Asst med, Harvard Med Sch & Mass Gen Hosp, 54-56; from asst prof to assoc prof, 57-66, PROF MED, SCH MED, EMORY UNIV, 66- *Concurrent Pos:* Nat Heart Inst res fel, 53-56; Am Heart Asn res fel, 57; chair cardiovasc res, Ga Heart Asn, 58-72. *Mem:* Am Fedn Clin Res. *Res:* Inorganic metabolism; renal and circulatory physiology; hypertension; nephrology. *Mailing Add:* Dept of Med Emory Univ Sch of Med Atlanta GA 30303

TUTTLE, ELIZABETH R, b Boston, Mass, Dec 5, 38. THEORETICAL PHYSICS. *Educ:* Univ NH, BS, 60; Univ Colo, MS, 61, PhD(physics), 64. *Prof Exp:* From asst prof to assoc prof, 64-78, PROF PHYSICS, UNIV DENVER, 76- *Mem:* Am Phys Soc; Am Asn Physics Teachers; Nat Soc Prof Engrs. *Res:* Theory of quantum fluids at very low temperatures with applications to liquid He4, liquid He3 and He3-He4 mixtures. History of science and technology. *Mailing Add:* Dept of Physics Univ of Denver Denver CO 80208

TUTTLE, MERLIN DEVERE, b Honolulu, Hawaii, Aug 26, 41. POPULATION ECOLOGY, MAMMALOGY. *Educ:* Andrews Univ, BA, 65; Univ Kans, MA, 69, PhD(pop ecol), 74. *Prof Exp:* Co-dir, Smithsonian Venezuelan Res Proj, Smithsonian Inst, 65-67; res assoc pop ecol, Univ Minn, 72; CUR MAMMALS, MILWAUKEE PUB MUS, 75- *Concurrent Pos:* Consult endangered bats, Tenn Valley Authority, 76- *Mem:* Am Soc Mammalogists; Am Soc Naturalists; Ecol Soc Am; Soc Study Evolution; Nat Speleol Soc. *Res:* Niche breadth, intra- and inter-specific competition, reproductive and survival strategies; foraging behavior in refuging species and the energetics of thermoregulation, hibernation and migration. *Mailing Add:* Milwaukee Pub Mus Vert Div 800 W Wells St Milwaukee WI 53233

TUTTLE, O FRANK, b Olean, NY, June 25, 16; m 41; c 2. GEOLOGY. *Educ:* Pa State Col, BS, 39, MS, 40; Mass Inst Technol, PhD(petrol), 48. *Prof Exp:* Asst, Off Sci Res & Develop, Mass Inst Technol, 42, phys chemist, Geophys Lab, 42-45; phys chemist, US Naval Res Lab, Washington, DC, 45-47, petrologist, Geophys Lab, 47-53; prof geochem & chmn div earth sci, Pa State Univ, 53-65, dean col mineral industs, 59-60; prof geochem, Stanford Univ, 65-70. *Honors & Awards:* Mineral Soc Award, Mineral Soc, 49; Day Medal, Geol Soc Am, 67; Roebling Medal, Mineral Soc, 75. *Mem:* Nat Acad Sci; fel Geol Soc Am; fel Mineral Soc Am; Brit Mineral Soc. *Res:* Application of phase equilibria in silicate systems to petrology; mineralogy of rock forming minerals; structural petrology; high temperature and high pressure syntheses of minerals and rocks; growth of large single crystals. *Mailing Add:* 4850 W Lazy C Dr Tucson AZ 85705

TUTTLE, RICHARD SUNESON, b Pottsville, Pa, Aug 18, 30; m 60; c 1. PHYSIOLOGY, PHARMACOLOGY. *Educ:* State Univ NY, PhD(pharm), 60. *Prof Exp:* Res fel, 60-64, RES ASSOC NEUROPHYSIOL, MASONIC MED RES FOUND, 64- *Concurrent Pos:* USPHS fel, 60-61; NIH grants, 63-; Fogarty fel, Sweden, 78. *Mem:* Am Physiol Soc; Am Soc Pharmacol Exp Therapeut. *Res:* Pharmacology of cardiac glycosides and electrolytes; neurophysiology of vasomotor regulation; centrally evoked histamine release; role of histamine in control of cardiovascular tone; cardiovascular effects of imidazoles and mesenteric Pacinian baroreceptors. *Mailing Add:* Masonic Med Res Found Bleeker St Utica NY 15301

TUTTLE, ROBERT LEWIS, b Boston, Mass, July 26, 22; m 42; c 2. MICROBIOLOGY. *Educ:* Univ NH, BS, 43; Univ Rochester, MD, 47. *Prof Exp:* Asst trop med, Bowman Gray Sch Med, 48-50, from instr to assoc prof microbiol, 50-70, chmn dept, 55-62, assoc dean, 62-69, acad dean, 69-70; prof microbiol, Univ Tex Med Sch Houston, 70-80, assoc dean acad affairs, 70-75, dean, 75-80. *Mailing Add:* PO Box 20708 Houston TX 77025

TUTTLE, RONALD RALPH, b Colorado Springs, Colo, July 10, 36; m 63; c 1. PHARMACOLOGY, PHYSIOLOGY. *Educ:* Colo Col, BA, 60; Univ Man, MS, 64, PhD(pharmacol), 66. *Prof Exp:* Fel pharmacol, Emory Univ, 66-67; sr pharmacologist, 67-71, res scientist, 71-74, res assoc pharmacol, 74-78, RES ADV, LILLY RES LABS, 78- *Concurrent Pos:* Mem coun circulation fel, Am Heart Asn. *Mem:* Am Soc Pharmacol & Exp Therapeut. *Res:* Cardiovascular pharmacology. *Mailing Add:* Lilly Res Labs Indianapolis IN 46206

TUTTLE, RUSSELL HOWARD, b Marion, Ohio, Aug 18, 39; m 68; c 2. PRIMATOLOGY, PALEOANTHROPOLOGY. *Educ:* Ohio State Univ, BSc, 61, MA, 62; Univ Calif, Berkeley, PhD(anthrop), 65. *Prof Exp:* PROF ANTHROP, UNIV CHICAGO, 64-, ASSOC SCIENTIST PRIMATOLOGY, YERKES PRIMATE RES CTR, 70- *Concurrent Pos:* Wenner-Gren res grants, Univ Chicago, 65, 66 & 69, NSF res grants, 66-67, USPHS res career develop award, 68-73; vis res prof, Japan Soc Promotion Sci, 74 & 80. *Mem:* AAAS; Am Anthrop Asn; Am Asn Phys Anthropologists; Int Primatological Soc; Sigma Xi. *Res:* Behavior and comparative functional morphology of anthropoid primates and available fossils in order to elucidate the evolution of human bipedalism, tool use and other subsistence behaviors. *Mailing Add:* Dept Anthrop Univ Chicago 1126 E 59th St Chicago IL 60637

TUTTLE, SHERWOOD DODGE, b Medford, Mass, June 8, 18; m 41; c 3. GEOMORPHOLOGY. *Educ:* Univ NH, BS, 39; Wash State Univ, MS, 41; Harvard Univ, MA & PhD(geol), 53. *Prof Exp:* Instr geol, Wash State Univ, 41, 46-48; from asst prof to assoc prof, 52-62, chmn dept geol, 63-68, PROF GEOL, UNIV IOWA, 62-, ASSOC DEAN COL LIB ARTS, 70- *Concurrent Pos:* Res assoc, Woods Hole Oceanog Inst, 59-66; Fulbright lectr, Chinese Univ Hong Kong, 68-69. *Mem:* Col Fel Geol Soc Am; Nat Asn Geol Teachers. *Res:* Glacial geology; shorelines. *Mailing Add:* Dept of Geol Univ of Iowa Iowa City IA 52242

TUTTLE, THOMAS R, JR, b Somerville, Mass, Mar 28, 28; m 54; c 3. PHYSICAL CHEMISTRY. *Educ:* Northeastern Univ, BS, 53, MS, 55; Wash Univ, St Louis, PhD, 57. *Prof Exp:* Actg asst prof chem, Stanford Univ, 57-60; asst prof, 60-64, ASSOC PROF CHEM, BRANDEIS UNIV, 64- *Mem:* Am Chem Soc; Am Phys Soc. *Res:* Electron distribution in ion radicals by electron spin-resonance; molecular motions in solutions; properties of metal solutions in ammonia and other solvents. *Mailing Add:* Dept of Chem Brandeis Univ Waltham MA 02154

TUTTLE, WARREN WILSON, b Fulton, Mo, Aug 2, 30; m 52; c 4. NEUROPHARMACOLOGY. *Educ:* Univ Mo, BA, 52; Univ Kans City, BS, 58, MS, 60; Univ Calif, San Francisco, PhD(pharmacol), 66. *Prof Exp:* Asst prof pharmacol, Univ Mo-Kans City, 65-68; asst prof med pharmacol & therapeut, Sch Med, Univ Calif, Irvine, 68-69; asst prof pharmacol, Univ Mo-Kans City, 69-72; actg chmn dept, Kansas City Col Osteop Med, 72-73, assoc prof pharmacol, 72-80, chmn dept, 72-80, ASSOC PROF & CHMN DEPT, COL OSTEOP MED, UNIV HEALTH SCI, 80- *Res:* Drug metabolism; electroencephalographic investigation into the sites of action of various drugs in the central nervous system. *Mailing Add:* Dept Pharmacol Col Osteop Med Univ Health Sci Kansas City MO 64124

TUTUPALLI, LOHIT VENKATESWARA, b Guntur, Andhra Pradesh, India, Aug 10, 45; m 74. PHARMACOGNOSY, PHYTOCHEMISTRY. *Educ:* Andhra Univ, BS, 63; Bombay Univ, BS, 66, MS, 68; Univ of the Pac, PhD(pharmacog), 74. *Prof Exp:* Res pharmacist product develop, M/S Pfizer (India), Ltd, Bombay, 68-69; from teaching asst to instr pharmacog, Univ of the Pac, 69-74; RES SCIENTIST, CALIF CEDAR PROD RES LAB, 74- *Mem:* Am Pharmaceut Asn; Am Chem Soc; NY Acad Sci; Am Soc Pharmacog; Forest Prod Res Soc. *Res:* Investigating the medicinal and economic uses of natural products. *Mailing Add:* Calif Cedar Prod Res Lab PO Box 8449 Stockton CA 95208

TUTWILER, FRANK BRYAN, physical chemistry, organic chemistry, see previous edition

TUTWILER, GENE FLOYD, b Peoria, Ill, Sept 19, 45; m 68; c 2. BIOCHEMISTRY, ENDOCRINOLOGY. *Educ:* Western Ill Univ, BS, 67; Univ Mich, Ann Arbor, PhD(biochem), 70. *Prof Exp:* Lab asst quant anal, Western Ill Univ, 66-67; sr scientist, 70-74, group leader, 74-77, res fel, 77-80, SECT HEAD ENDOCRINOL & METAB, DEPT BIOL RES, MCNEIL PHARMACEUT, INC, 80- *Concurrent Pos:* Teaching fel biochem, Univ Mich, Ann Arbor, 67-70; vis asst prof, Temple Univ, 73-74 & Bucks County Community Col, 74- & Univ Pa, 77-78; Adj asst prof, Temple Univ, 79- & Univ Pa, 80- *Mem:* NY Acad Sci; Am Endocrine Soc; AAAS; Am Diabetes Asn; Soc Exp Biol & Med. *Res:* Diabetes; obesity; protein purification; isolation pituitary proteins; free fatty acid metabolism; carbohydrate metabolism; atherosclerosis. *Mailing Add:* Biol Res Dept McNeil Pharmaceut Inc Springhouse PA 19477

TUUL, JOHANNES, b Tarvastu, Estonia, May 23, 22; US citizen; m 57; c 2. PHYSICS. *Educ:* Stockholm Univ, BS, 55, MA, 56; Brown Univ, ScM, 57, PhD(physics), 60. *Prof Exp:* Instr elec eng, Stockholm Tech Inst, 47-49; res engr, Elec Prospecting Co, Sweden, 49-53; elec engr, L M Ericsson Tel Co, 54-55; res asst physics, Brown Univ, 55-57, 58-60, res assoc, 60; res physicist, Stamford Res Labs, Am Cyanamid Co, Conn, 60-62; sr res physicist, Bell & Howell Res Ctr, Calif, 62-65; asst prof, 65-68, assoc prof, 68-74, chmn dept physics & earth sci, 71-75, PROF PHYSICS, CALIF STATE POLYTECH UNIV, 74- *Concurrent Pos:* Consult, Bell & Howell Res Ctr, 65 & Teledyne Inc, 68; vis assoc prof, Pahlavi Univ, Iran, 68-70; resident dir, Calif State Univ & Col Int Prog, Sweden & Denmark, 77-78. *Mem:* AAAS; Am Phys Soc; Am Chem Soc; Am Vacuum Soc; Am Asn Physics Teachers. *Res:* Adsorption of gases on solids; low-energy electron diffraction studies of effects of adsorption and ion bombardment on initially clean surfaces; ultra-high vacuum technology; mass spectrometry. *Mailing Add:* Dept Physics Calif State Polytech Univ Pomona CA 91768

TUVE, MERLE ANTONY, b Canton, SDak, June 27, 01; m 27; c 2. PHYSICS. *Educ:* Univ Minn, BS, 22, AM, 23; Johns Hopkins Univ, PhD(physics), 26. *Hon Degrees:* DSc, Case Western Reserve Univ, 48, Kenyon Col, 49, Williams Col, 49, Johns Hopkins Univ, 50, Augustana Col, 52, Alaska, 53; LLD, Carleton Col, 61. *Prof Exp:* Instr physics, Princeton Univ, 23-24 & Johns Hopkins Univ, 24-26; assoc physicist, Carnegie Inst Dept Terrestrial Magnetism, 26-28, physicist, 28-38, chief physicist, 38-46, dir, 46-66, DISTINGUISHED SERV MEM, CARNEGIE INST WASHINGTON, 66- *Concurrent Pos:* Dir appl physics lab, Johns Hopkins Univ, 42-46; ed, J Geophys Res, 49-53; mem nat comt, Int Geophys Year, 54-59; chmn geophys res bd, Nat Acad Sci-Nat Res Coun, 60-70. *Honors & Awards:* Presidential Medal for Merit, 46; Award, Res Corp, 47; Scott Award, 48; Comstock Prize, Nat Acad Sci, 49; Potts Medal, Franklin Inst, 50; Barnard Medal, Columbia, 55; Bowie Medal, Am Geophys Union, 63; Award, Cosmos Club, 66. *Mem:* Nat Acad Sci (home secy, 66-71); AAAS (vpres, 47); fel Am Phys Soc; Am Philos Soc; Am Acad Arts & Sci. *Res:* Nuclear physics; geophysics; echo investigations of Kennelly-Heaviside layer; high voltage vacuum tubes; high-speed protons; transmutations of atomic nuclei; nuclear forces; deep seismic shots; earth's crust; radio astronomy. *Mailing Add:* 135 Hesketh St Chevy Chase MD 20015

TUVE, RICHARD LARSEN, b Canton, SDak, Feb 1, 12; m 36; c 2. PHYSICAL CHEMISTRY, INORGANIC CHEMISTRY. *Educ:* Am Univ, BA, 35. *Hon Degrees:* DSc, Carleton Col, 61. *Prof Exp:* Asst chemist, Res Assocs, Inc, 35-38; asst chemist, US Naval Res Lab, 38-40, assoc phys chemist, 40-41, head, Eng Res Br, 41-70; CONSULT, APPL PHYSICS LAB, JOHNS HOPKINS UNIV, SILVER SPRING, 70- *Concurrent Pos:* Mem comt fire res conf, Nat Acad Sci-Nat Res Coun, 55-68. *Mem:* Fel AAAS; Am Chem Soc; Am Inst Chem Eng; fel Am Inst Chem; Inst Chem Eng. *Res:* Chemistry of fire extinguishment; foam extinguishment methods and materials; flame propagation; surface chemistry; special explosives; fire fighting equipment design; combustion inhibition. *Mailing Add:* 9211 Crosby Rd Silver Spring MD 20910

TUVESON, ROBERT WILLIAMS, b Chicago, Ill, Aug 30, 31. GENETICS, BOTANY. *Educ:* Univ Ill, BS, 54, MS, 56; Univ Chicago, PhD(bot), 59. *Prof Exp:* Asst prof biol, Wayne State Univ, 59-61; asst prof bot, Univ Chicago, 61-68; assoc prof, 68-77, PROF BOT, UNIV ILL, URBANA-CHAMPAIGN, 77- *Concurrent Pos:* NIH spec fel, Dartmouth Col, 65-66. *Mem:* AAAS; Mycol Soc Am; Bot Soc Am; Genetics Soc Am. *Res:* Fungal genetics; viruses of fungi; radiation sensitivity. *Mailing Add:* Dept of Bot Univ of Ill Urbana IL 61801

TUZAR, JAROSLAV, b Czech, Mar 25, 15; nat US; m 48; c 1. MATHEMATICS. *Educ:* Charles Univ, Prague, MA, 39 & 45, ScD(math), 48. *Prof Exp:* Asst prof, State Tech Col, Prague, 45-48; Rockefeller Found fel, Univ Chicago, 48-50; dir control & res lab, Salerno-Megowen Biscuit Co, 50-70; assoc prof, 70-80, PROF MATH, NORTHEASTERN ILL UNIV, 80- *Concurrent Pos:* Lectr, Northwestern Univ, 60-70. *Mem:* AAAS; Math Asn Am; Am Statist Asn. *Res:* Mathematical probability and statistics; pedagogy of mathematics. *Mailing Add:* Dept of Math Northeastern Ill Univ Chicago IL 60625

TUZSON, JOHN J(ANOS), b Budapest, Hungary, Apr 29, 29; US citizen; m 60; c 3. FLUID MECHANICS. *Educ:* Conserv Nat Arts et Metiers, France, MMech Eng, 55; Mass Inst Technol, ScD(mech eng), 59. *Prof Exp:* Res asst mech eng, Mass Inst Technol, 56-58; res engr fluid dynamics, Whirlpool Corp, Mich, 58-61; assoc prof, Mich State Univ, 61; res engr fluid mech, IIT Res Inst, 62-63; asst dir, Res Ctr, Borg-Warner Corp, Des Plaines, 63-79; MGR FLUID TECHNOL, ALLIS-CHALMERS, MILWAUKEE, 79- *Concurrent Pos:* Teaching asst, Ill Inst Technol, 62-72; ed, Proc Nat Conf Fluid Power, 62-72. *Mem:* AAAS; Sigma Xi; Am Soc Mech Engrs. *Res:* Swirling flow; two phase flow; turbomachinery; hydraulic, pneumatic and fluidic controls; process equipment; slurry. *Mailing Add:* 1220 Maple Ave Evanston IL 60202

TUZZOLINO, ANTHONY J, b Chicago, Ill, July 1, 31; m 54; c 2. PHYSICS, SOLID STATE PHYSICS. *Educ:* Univ Chicago, MS, 55, PhD(physics), 58. *Prof Exp:* PHYSICIST, UNIV CHICAGO, 58- *Res:* Semiconductor nuclear particle and photon detectors. *Mailing Add:* 6615 N Knox Lincolnwood IL 60646

TWARDOCK, ARTHUR ROBERT, b Normal, Ill, July 20, 31; m 54; c 4. VETERINARY PHYSIOLOGY, NUCLEAR MEDICINE. *Educ:* Univ Ill, BS, 54, DVM, 56; Cornell Univ, PhD(animal physiol), 61. *Prof Exp:* Vet practioner, Hillcrest Animal Hosp, 56-57; res asst radiobiol, Cornell Univ, 57-60, res assoc phys biol, 60-62; from asst prof to assoc prof, 62-70, actg head, Dept Vet Physiol & Pharm, 74-77, PROF, VET PHYS, UNIV ILL, URBANA, 70-, ASSOC DEAN ACAD AFFAIRS, 73- *Mem:* AAAS; Am Physiol Soc; Am Soc Vet Physiol & Pharmacol; Am Vet Med Asn; Conf Res Workers Animal Diseases. *Res:* Mineral metabolism; placental transfer of mineral elements; applications of radioisotope techniques in veterinary nuclear medicine. *Mailing Add:* Col of Vet Med Univ of Ill Urbana IL 61801

TWAROG, BETTY MACK, b New York, NY, Aug 28, 27; m 47; c 1. PHYSIOLOGY. *Educ:* Swarthmore Col, AB, 48; Tufts Col, MS, 49; Radcliffe Col, PhD(biol), 52. *Prof Exp:* Asst, Harvard Univ, 52 & Res Div, Cleveland Clin, 52-53; res assoc & instr, Tufts Col, 53-55; res fel, Harvard Univ, 55-58; instr, 58-60; USPHS trainee, Oxford Univ, 60-61; asst prof physiol & biophys, Sch Med, NY Univ, 61-65; res fel, Harvard Univ, 65-66; from asst prof to assoc prof, 66-70, prof biol, Tufts Univ, 70-75; prof anat sci, State Univ NY, Stony Brook, 75-81; PROF & CHMN BIOL, BRYN MAWR COL, 82- *Concurrent Pos:* John Simon Guggenheim Mem fel, 72-73; prog dir, NSF, 77-78. *Mem:* Soc Gen Physiologists (pres, 78-79); Soc Neurosci; Am Physiol Soc; fel AAAS; Am Soc Zoologists. *Res:* Physiology and pharmacology of smooth muscle; neurophysiology; neuropharmacology. *Mailing Add:* Dept Biol Bryn Mawr Col Bryn Mawr PA 19010

TWAROG, ROBERT, b Lowell, Mass, Mar 17, 35; m 58; c 2. MICROBIAL BIOCHEMISTRY. *Educ:* Univ Conn, BS, 56, MS, 58; Univ Ill, PhD(microbiol), 62. *Prof Exp:* Lab officer, US Air Force Epidemiol Lab, San Antonio, Tex, 62-65; asst prof, 65-74, ASSOC PROF BACT, SCH MED, UNIV NC, CHAPEL HILL, 74- *Mem:* AAAS; Am Soc Microbiol. *Res:* Control mechanisms of microbial processes; molecular biology; microbiology. *Mailing Add:* Dept Bact & Immunol Univ NC Sch Med Chapel Hill NC 27514

TWEDT, ROBERT MADSEN, b Rochester, Minn, July 4, 24; m 72. MICROBIOLOGY. *Educ:* Univ Minn, BS, 45; Univ Colo, MS, 49, PhD(microbiol), 52. *Prof Exp:* Res fel microbiol, Western Reserve Univ, 52-54; asst scientist, Univ Minn, 54-56, res fel physiol chem, 56-59; from asst prof to assoc prof biol, Univ Detroit, 59-67; res microbiologist, Nat Ctr Urban & Indust Health, 67-69, from microbiologist to asst chief, Food Microbiol Br, 69-77, actg chief, 78-79, CHIEF, BACTERIAL PHYSIOL BR, FOOD & DRUG ADMIN, 80- *Concurrent Pos:* Am Cancer Soc fel, 52-53; microbiologist, Fed Water Pollution Control Admin, 66; adj prof, Univ Detroit, 68-70. *Mem:* Am Soc Microbiol; fel Am Acad Microbiol; AAAS; Int Asn Milk, Food & Environ Sanitarians; Sigma Xi. *Res:* Research and field investigations to identify, evaluate and resolve microbiological problems of public health significance associated with foods. *Mailing Add:* Food Microbiol Br Food & Drug Adm 1090 Tusculum Ave Cincinnati OH 45226

TWEED, JOHN, b Greenock, Scotland, Mar 29, 42; m 66; c 2. APPLIED MATHEMATICS. *Educ:* Univ Strathclyde, MSc, 65; Univ Glasgow, PhD(appl math), 68, DSc, 81. *Prof Exp:* From asst lectr to lecr math, Univ Glasgow, 65-69, vis asst prof, NO State Univ, 69-70; Univ Glasgow, 70-73; vis prof, NC State Univ, 73-74; assoc prof math, 74-77, PROF MATH & COMPUT SCI, OLD DOMINION UNIV, 77- *Mem:* Soc Indust & Appl Math; fel Brit Inst Math & Appln; Am Acad Mech. *Res:* Applications of transform techniques and integral equations to the solution of mixed boundary value problems in fracture mechanics. *Mailing Add:* Dept of Math & Comput Sci Old Dominion Univ Norfolk VA 23508

TWEEDDALE, MARTIN GEORGE, b Bristol, Eng, Aug 22, 40. CLINICAL PHARMACOLOGY. *Educ:* King's Col, Univ London, BSc, 62, PhD(pharmacol), 65; Westminister Med Sch, Univ London, MB, BS, 67; FRCPS(C), 72. *Prof Exp:* Asst prof, 73-78, ASSOC PROF MED CLIN PHARMACOL, FAC MED, MEM UNIV NFLD, 78-; ASSOC PHYSICIAN INTERNAL MED, GEN HOSP, ST JOHN'S, NFLD, 73-, CHMN INTENSIVE CARE UNIT, 80- *Concurrent Pos:* Develop grant, Can Found Advan Clin Pharmacol, 73-77. *Mem:* Can Soc Clin Invest; Can Crit Care Soc; Can Pharmacol Soc; Am Soc Clin Pharmacol & Therapeut; Can Hypertension Soc (secy-treas, 79-81). *Res:* In vivo and in vitro study of drug interactions and pharmacokinetics of diuretics; clinical trials in hypertension therapy; the development of hydraulic pharmacokinetic models. *Mailing Add:* Fac of Med Mem Univ of Nfld St John's NF A1B 3V6 Can

TWEEDELL, KENYON STANLEY, b Sterling, Ill, Mar 28, 24; m 56; c 5. DEVELOPMENTAL BIOLOGY, ONCOLOGY. *Educ:* Univ Ill, BS, 47, MS, 49, PhD(zool,physiol), 53. *Prof Exp:* Res assoc biol, Control Systs Lab, Univ Ill, 51-54; instr zool, Univ Maine, 54-56, asst prof, 56-58; from asst prof to assoc prof, 58-68, PROF BIOL, UNIV NOTRE DAME, 68- *Concurrent Pos:* Corp mem, Marine Biol Lab, Woods Hole. *Mem:* AAAS; Int Soc Develop Biol; Am Soc Zool; Sigma Xi; Soc Develop Biol. *Res:* Experimental pathology; transmissable tumors of Amphibia; developmental biology, especially oogenesis, ovulation, regeneration in invertebrates, cytodifferentiation in normal and malignant cells. *Mailing Add:* Dept Biol Box 369 Univ Notre Dame Notre Dame IN 46556

TWEEDIE, ADELBERT THOMAS, b Saginaw, Mich, Jan 5, 31; m 53; c 3. POLYMER CHEMISTRY. *Educ:* Univ Mich, BSCh, 53; Univ Ill, PhD(org chem), 56. *Prof Exp:* Res chemist, Dow Chem Co, Mich, 56-58 & Aerojet-Gen Corp, Calif, 58-62; tech supvr rocket propellants, Union Carbide Corp, WVa, 62-64; MGR MAT ENG, SPACE DIV, GEN ELEC CO, KING OF PRUSSIA, 64- *Concurrent Pos:* Mem Mat Adv Comt, NASA. *Mem:* Am Inst Aeronaut & Astronaut; Am Chem Soc. *Res:* Behavior of materials in the space environment; vibration damping; application of materials to spacecraft; polymers; solar energy; fracture mechanics of viscoelastic materials. *Mailing Add:* 24 Harvey Lane Malvern PA 19355

TWEEDIE, VIRGIL LEE, b Norborne, Mo, Feb 18, 18; m 43; c 3. ORGANIC CHEMISTRY. *Educ:* Univ Mo, AB, 41, MA, 43; Univ Tex, PhD(chem), 51. *Prof Exp:* Res chemist, Commercial Solvents Corp, 42-46; asst prof, 46-48, assoc prof, 50-53, PROF CHEM, BAYLOR UNIV, 53- *Mem:* AAAS; Am Chem Soc. *Res:* Allylic compounds; organometallics; complex metal hydrides and alkides; hydrogenolysis. *Mailing Add:* 7720 Tallahassee Rd Waco TX 76710

TWEEDLE, CHARLES DAVID, b Astoria, Ore, Jan 22, 44. NEUROBIOLOGY. *Educ:* Univ Ore, BA, 66, MA, 67; Mich State Univ, PhD(zool), 70. *Prof Exp:* NIH fel, Yale Univ, 70-72; NIH Res Grant & Res Assoc, 72-73; asst prof, Dept Biomech & Zool, 73-78, ASSOC PROF ANAT & ZOOL, MICH STATE UNIV, 78- *Mem:* AAAS; Soc Neurosci; Am Soc Zool; Am Asn Anatomists. *Res:* Developmental neurobiology; trophic effects of nerves; neuromuscular development; nerve regeneration; dendritic stability and development; neurophysiology of simple nervous systems. *Mailing Add:* Dept of Anat Mich State Univ East Lansing MI 48824

TWEEDY, BILLY GENE, b Cobden, Ill, Dec 31, 34; m 57; c 3. PLANT PATHOLOGY. *Educ:* Univ Southern Ill, BS, 56; Univ Ill, MS, 59, PhD(plant path), 61. *Prof Exp:* Asst plant pathologist, Boyce Thompson Inst Plant Res, 61-65; asst prof plant path, Univ Mo-Columbia, 65-69, from assoc prof to prof, 69-73; mgr residue invest, 73-78, DIR, BIOCHEM DEPT, CIBA-GEIGY CORP, 78- *Mem:* AAAS; Am Phytopath Soc; Am Chem Soc; Weed Sci Soc Am; Sigma Xi. *Res:* Degradation of pesticides; integrated pest control; fungus physiology; fruit pathology. *Mailing Add:* 111 Cresthill Dr Jamestown NC 27282

TWEEDY, JAMES ARTHUR, b Cobden, Ill, Nov 29, 39; m 64; c 2. HORTICULTURE. *Educ:* Southern Ill Univ, BS, 62; Mich State Univ, MS, 64, PhD(hort), 66. *Prof Exp:* From asst prof to assoc prof, 66-74, asst dean, Sch of Agr, 74-75, asst vpres acad affairs & res, 76-78, PROF PLANT INDUST, PLANT & SOIL SCI DEPT, SOUTHERN ILL UNIV, 74- *Mem:* Weed Sci Soc Am. *Res:* Influence of herbicides on plant physiological processes; evaluation of herbicides for weed control in agronomic and horticultural crops. *Mailing Add:* Dept of Plant & Soil Sci Southern Ill Univ Carbondale IL 62901

TWEET, ARTHUR GLENN, b Aberdeen, SDak, Sept 20, 27; m 50; c 3. SOLID STATE PHYSICS. *Educ:* Harvard Univ, AB, 48; Univ Wis, MS, 49, PhD(physics), 53. *Prof Exp:* Physicist, Semiconductor Sect, Res Labs, Gen Elec Corp, 53-59, liaison scientist, 59-61, physicist, Biol Studies Sect, 61-64; mgr phys imaging br, Advan Imaging Technol Lab, 64-68, mgr, Imaging Res Lab, 68-72, mgr technol planning, Info Technol Group, 72-75, MGR, TECH STRATEGIC PLANNING, XEROX CORP, 75- *Concurrent Pos:* Adj prof, Rensselaer Polytech Inst, 62. *Mem:* Fel Am Phys Soc. *Res:* Energy transfer in excited molecules; unconventional photographic systems; dye sensitized reactions; electrical and surface properties of polymers; surface chemistry of chromophores; optical properties of large molecules; imperfections in semiconductors and insulators; nonaqueous electrochemistry; decision analysis; technological forecasting; operations analysis and modelling. *Mailing Add:* Xerox Corp Xerox Sq 280 Weymouth Dr Rochester NY 14625

TWELVES, ROBERT RALPH, b Chicago, Ill, Nov 4, 27; m 53; c 3. ORGANIC CHEMISTRY. *Educ:* Univ Utah, BS, 50, MA, 52; Univ Minn, PhD(org chem), 57. *Prof Exp:* Asst, Univ Utah, 50-51; process develop chemist, Merck & Co, 52-53; asst, Univ Minn, 53-55; RES CHEMIST, E I DU PONT DE NEMOURS & CO, INC, 57- *Mem:* Am Chem Soc; Sigma Xi. *Res:* Fluorochemicals; dyes and intermediates; synthetic organic chemistry. *Mailing Add:* Exp Sta 353/141A E I du Pont de Nemours & Co Inc Wilmington DE 19898

TWENHOFEL, WILLIAM STEPHENS, b Madison, Wis, Aug 30, 18; m 51; c 5. GEOLOGY. *Educ:* Univ Wis, BA, 40, PhD(geol), 52. *Prof Exp:* Geologist, US Geol Surv, Washington, DC, 42-45; physicist, US Naval Res Lab, 45-46; geologist, US Geol Surv, 47-64, chief, Br Spec Projs, 64-81; CONSULT, 81- *Honors & Awards:* Meritorious Serv Award, US Dept Interior, 73- *Mem:* AAAS; Geol Soc Am; Asn Eng Geol. *Res:* Geology of Alaska; growth of artificial crystals; geologic disposal of radioactive waste; structural and uranium geology; engineering geology of underground nuclear explosions. *Mailing Add:* 820 Estes St Lakewood CO 80215

TWENTE, JANET, physiology, zoology, see previous edition

TWENTE, JOHN W, b Lawrence, Kans, Dec 18, 26; m 53; c 1. ZOOLOGY. *Educ:* Univ Kans, AB, 50; Univ Mich, MS, 52, PhD(zool), 54. *Prof Exp:* Interim instr biol, Univ Fla, 54-55; instr zool, Col Pharm, Univ Ill, 55-56; instr, Univ Utah, 57-58, asst prof, 58-62, res biologist, 62-66; ASSOC PROF BIOL & INVESTR, DALTON RES CTR, UNIV MO-COLUMBIA, 66- *Mem:* Am Soc Zool; Ecol Soc Am; Am Soc Mammal. *Res:* Physiological ecology and behavior; hibernation physiology. *Mailing Add:* Dalton Res Ctr Univ of Mo Columbia MO 65211

TWERSKY, VICTOR, b Poland, Aug 10, 23; nat US; m 50; c 3. MATHEMATICAL PHYSICS, MULTIPLE SCATTERING THEORY. *Educ:* City Col New York, BS, 47; Columbia Univ, AM, 48; NY Univ, PhD(physics), 50. *Prof Exp:* Assoc, Guid Device Proj, Biol Dept, City Col New York, 46-49; asst physics, NY Univ, 49, res assoc electromagnetic theory, Inst Math Sci, 50-53; assoc, Nuclear Develop Assocs, 51-53; specialist theoret physics, Electronic Defense Labs, Sylvania Electronic Systs-West, Sylvania Elec Prod, Inc Div, Gen Tel & Electronics Corp, 53-58, sr specialist & lab consult, 58-60, sr scientist, 60-66, head res, Electronics Defense Labs, 58-66 & Sylvania Electronic Systs-West, 64-66; PROF MATH, UNIV ILL, CHICAGO CIRCLE, 66- *Concurrent Pos:* Mem tech res comt, Am Found Blind, 47-49; lectr math, Stanford Univ, 56-58; vis prof, Technion-Israel Inst Technol, 62-63, Courant Inst Math Sci, 63, Stanford Univ, 67-78, Hebrew Univ Jerusalem, 72 & Weizmann Inst Sci, Rehovoth & Ben-Gurion Univ Negev, Beer Sheva, 79; consult, Sylvania Elec Prod Inc Div, Gen Tel & Electronics Corp, 66; mem ctr advan study, Univ Ill, 69-70; Guggenehim fel, 72-73 & 79-80; mem at large, Conf Bd Math Sci, 75-77; mem US Comn B, Int Union Radio Sci. *Mem:* Fel AAAS; fel Am Phys Soc; fel Acoust Soc Am; fel Optical Soc Am; fel Inst Elec & Electronics Engrs. *Res:* Multiple scattering of electromagnetic and acoustic waves; rough surfaces; gratings; scattering and propagation in random distributions; radiative diagnostics of biological cells; relativistic scattering; applied mathematics; obstacle perception by the blind. *Mailing Add:* Dept Math Univ Ill Box 4348 Chicago IL 60680

TWETO, OGDEN, b Abercrombie, NDak, June 10, 12; m 40; c 2. ECONOMIC GEOLOGY. *Educ:* Univ Mont, AB, 34, MA, 37; Univ Mich, PhD(geol), 47. *Prof Exp:* Instr, Univ NC, 39-40; geologist, 40-61, chief, South Rockies Br, 61-65, asst chief geologist & chief off econ geol, 65-68, RES GEOLOGIST, US GEOL SURV, 68- *Mem:* AAAS; Geol Soc Am; Soc Econ Geol; Mineral Soc Am; Am Inst Mining, Metall & Petrol Eng. *Res:* Geology and mineral deposits of Southern Rocky Mountains. *Mailing Add:* US Geol Surv MS 912 Box 25046 Denver CO 80225

TWIDWELL, LARRY G, b Jackson, Mo, July 5, 39; m 61; c 3. EXTRACTIVE & CHEMICAL METALLURGY. *Educ:* Mo Sch Mines, BS, 61, MS, 62; Colo Sch Mines, DSc, 66. *Prof Exp:* Develop engr, Rocky Flats Div, Dow Chem Co, 62-63; assoc metallurgist, Monsanto Res Corp, 65-67; staff mem nuclear reactors, Reactor Develop Div, Sandia Corp, 67-69; assoc prof, 69-76, PROF METALL ENG & HEAD DEPT, MONT COL MINERAL SCI & TECHNOL, 76- *Concurrent Pos:* Proj officer, Environ Protection Agency, 78-80. *Mem:* Am Inst Mining, Metall & Petrol Engrs; Am Soc Eng Educ; Am Inst Mining & Metall Engrs. *Res:* Containment of radioisotopes at elevated temperatures; reactor development; thermodynamics of metallic solutions; nonferrous and ferrous process metallurgy; environmental and thermodynamics of metallic solutions; self-paced instruction. *Mailing Add:* Dept Metall & Mineral Processing Mont Col Mineral Sci & Technol Butte MT 59701

TWIEG, DONALD BAKER, b Port Arthur, Tex, Dec 8, 44; m 69; c 1. BIOMEDICAL NUCLEAR MAGNETIC RESONANCE IMAGING. *Educ:* Rice Univ, BA, 68, MS, 71; Southern Methodist Univ, PhD(biomed eng), 77. *Prof Exp:* Engr, Boeing Co, 72-73; ASST PROF, DEPT RADIOL, UNIV TEX HEALTH SCI CTR, DALLAS, 77- *Concurrent Pos:* Fac mem, Biomed Eng Grad Prog, Univ Tex Health Sci Ctr, Dallas, 77-, Radiol Sci Grad Prog, 82- *Mem:* Inst Elec & Electronics Engrs; AAAS. *Res:* Theoretical investigations of nuclear magnetic resonance imaging processes; modeling of nuclear magnetic resonance imaging performance in biomedical applications; applications of optimal estimation and sampling theory in nuclear magnetic resonance imaging. *Mailing Add:* Dept Radiol Univ Tex Health Sci Ctr 5323 Harry Hines Blvd Dallas TX 75235

TWIEST, GILBERT LEE, b Grand Rapids, Mich, Apr 23, 37; m 58; c 3. ORNITHOLOGY, SCIENCE EDUCATION. *Educ:* Mich State Univ, BS, 61, MS, 63; Univ Toledo, PhD(sci educ), 68. *Prof Exp:* Instr biol, Kellogg Community assoc prof, 68-76, PROF SCI EDUC, CLARION STATE COL, 76- *Concurrent Pos:* Ed, Newsletter, Coun Elementary Sci Int. *Mem:* Nat Asn Res Sci Teaching; Nat Sci Teachers Asn; Coun Elem Sci Int; Wilson Ornith Soc. *Res:* Methods of teaching students the processes needed to solve problems. *Mailing Add:* Dept of Biol Clarion State Col Clarion PA 16214

TWIGG, BERNARD ALVIN, b Cumberland, Md, Oct 15, 28; m 51; c 4. HORTICULTURE, FOOD SCIENCE. *Educ:* Univ Md, BS, 52, MS, 54, PhD, 59. *Prof Exp:* Asst hort, 52-54, from instr to assoc prof, 54-69, PROF HORT, UNIV MD, COLLEGE PARK, 69-, CHMN DEPT, 75- *Mem:* Am Soc Hort Sci; Inst Food Technologists. *Res:* Objective evaluation of food products; statistical quality control; food chemistry and physics; horticultural food processing. *Mailing Add:* Dept of Hort Univ of Md College Park MD 20740

TWIGG, HOMER LEE, b Westminster, Md, Apr 10, 26; m 55; c 6. MEDICINE, RADIOLOGY. *Educ:* Univ Md, MD, 51; Am Bd Radiol, dipl, 56. *Prof Exp:* Intern med, USPHS Hosp, Boston, 51-52, intern surg serv outpatient clin, 52, resident radiol, Baltimore, 55-56, chief radiol, Detroit, 56-57; actg chmn & dir dept, 67-69, from asst prof to assoc prof, 57-70, chmn dept, 69-79, PROF RADIOL, GEORGETOWN UNIV HOSP, 70- *Concurrent Pos:* Spec assignment, US Dept Interior, 52; consult, Vet Admin Hosp, DC, 60-, St Elizabeth's Hosp, 65- & NIH, 65- *Mem:* AMA; fel Am Col Radiol; Am Roentgen Ray Soc; Radiol Soc NAm. *Mailing Add:* Dept Radiol Georgetown Univ Hosp Washington DC 20007

TWILLEY, IAN CHARLES, b London, Eng, Apr 4, 27; m 54; c 4. CHEMISTRY. *Educ:* Univ London, BSc, 53, FRIC, Royal Inst Chem, 62. *Prof Exp:* Sr chemist, Nelsons Silk Ltd, Eng, 53-56 & Micanite & Insulators, Ltd, 56-57; sr develop chemist, Textile Fibers Div, Du Pont of Can, 57-59; sect leader moulding polymers, Nat Aniline Div, 59-60, group leader polymer res, 60-61, res supvr, 61-65, process develop supvr, 65-66, mgr systs eng, 66-68, mgr eng res, Fibers Div, 68-69, asst chief engr, 69, tech dir polyester, 69-72, tech dir home furnishings, 72-76, mgr govt & indust affairs & liaison, 76-77, mgr advan technol, Fibers Div, Allied Chem Corp, 77-81, DIR ADVAN TECHNOL, FIBERS & PLASTICS CO, ALLIED CORP, PETERSBURG, 81- *Mem:* Am Chem Soc; Am Inst Chem Eng; Can Soc Chem Eng; fel Chem Inst Can; Royal Inst Chem. *Res:* Polymeric and textile processes and products; production and design problems; polymer and textile chemistry; polyamide and polyester technology. *Mailing Add:* 12625 Merry Dr Chester VA 23831

TWINING, LINDA CAROL, b Paterson, NJ, July 8, 52; m 80. IMMUNOPARASITOLOGY. *Educ:* William Paterson Col NJ, BA, 72; Rutgers Univ, MS, 75; Univ Ill Urbana-Champaign, PhD(zool), 82. *Prof Exp:* Teaching asst biol zool, Rutgers Univ, 72-74, immunol & parasitol, Univ Ill, 74-81; ASST PROF IMMUNOL & PARASITOL, NORTHEAST MO STATE UNIV, 81- *Mem:* Am Soc Microbiol. *Res:* Immunoparasitology, particularly the immune response to Plasmodium, both the in vivo and in vitro response are of interest, especially the role of the macrophage; phenomenon of immunosuppression in protozoal and helminth infections. *Mailing Add:* Div Sci Northeast Mo State Univ Kirksville MO 63501

TWINING, SALLY SHINEW, b Bowling Green, Ohio, July 28, 47; m 71; c 1. PROTEASES, PROTEASE INHIBITORS. *Educ:* Bowling Green State Univ, BS, 69, MA, 71; Ohio State Univ, PhD(physiol chem), 76. *Prof Exp:* Instr chem, Bowling Green State Univ, 71-73; Mayo fel, immunol, Mayo Clin, 76-78; res assoc, 79-80, INSTR BIOCHEM, MED COL WIS, 80- *Mem:* Sigma Xi; Am Chem Soc; AAAS. *Res:* Role of proteases and protease inhibitors in coeneal degredation; activation of pepsinogen; properties of pepsinogens; pepsin from dogs and fish. *Mailing Add:* Dept Biochem Med Col Wis 8701 Watertown Plank Rd Milwaukee WI 53226

TWISS, PAGE CHARLES, b Columbus, Ohio, Jan 2, 29; m 54; c 3. GEOLOGY. *Educ:* Kans State Univ, BS, 50, MS, 55; Univ Tex, PhD(geol), 59. *Prof Exp:* Instr, 53-55, from asst prof to assoc prof, 59-69, head dept, 68-77, PROF GEOL, KANS STATE UNIV, 69- *Concurrent Pos:* Co-investr, NSF grants, 60-62, 66, 67-68; res scientist, Univ Tex, 66-67. *Mem:* AAAS; fel Geol Soc Am; Am Asn Petrol Geol; Soc Econ Paleont & Mineral; Clay Minerals Soc. *Res:* Sedimentary and igneous petrology; clay mineralogy; stratigraphy, tectonics, petrology and geochemistry of Mesozoic and Cenozoic rocks of Trans-Pecos Texas and Chihuahua, Mexico; grass phytoliths; petrology of recent dust deposits. *Mailing Add:* 2327 Bailey Dr Manhattan KS 66502

TWISS, ROBERT JOHN, b Baltimore, Md, May 12, 42; m 68; c 2. GEOLOGY. *Educ:* Yale Univ, BS, 64; Princeton Univ, MA, 68, PhD(geol), 70. *Prof Exp:* NATO fel geol, Australian Nat Univ, 70-71; asst prof, 71-78, ASSOC PROF GEOL, UNIV CALIF, DAVIS, 78- *Mem:* Am Geophys Union; Geol Soc Am; Sigma Xi. *Res:* Continuum mechanics theory applied to understanding the behavior of geologic materials; deformation mechanisms in silicates; structural analysis of tectonites. *Mailing Add:* Dept of Geol Univ of Calif Davis CA 95616

TWITCHELL, PAUL F, b Somerville, Mass, Mar 7, 32; m 56; c 4. METEOROLOGY. *Educ:* Boston Col, BS, 53, MS, 62; Pa State Univ, BS, 54; Univ Wis-Madison, PhD, 76. *Prof Exp:* Weather officer, US Air Force, 53-57; res engr, Res Dept, Melpar, Inc, Mass, 57-60; sr res engr, Appl Sci Div, 60-62; phys sci coordr, 62-72, PHYS SCI ADMINR, BOSTON BR, OFF NAVAL RES, 72- *Mem:* Am Meteorol Soc; Am Geophys Union. *Res:* Physical processes in the terrestrial atmosphere. *Mailing Add:* 36 Laurel Ave Wellesley Hills MA 02181

TWITCHELL, THOMAS EVANS, b Springfield, Ohio, Sept 4, 23; m 56; c 4. NEUROLOGY. *Educ:* Univ Mich, MD, 46. *Prof Exp:* Res fel physiol, Med Sch, Yale Univ, 47; intern neurol, Boston City Hosp, 47-48, res fel, Harvard Med Sch & Boston City Hosp, 48-49; asst resident med, New Eng Ctr Hosp, 54, chief resident neurol, 54-55; from instr to asst prof, 55-63, ASSOC PROF NEUROL, SCH MED, TUFTS UNIV, 63- *Concurrent Pos:* USPHS res fel, Yale Univ, 49-51; res assoc, Mass Inst Technol, 63-; neurologist, New Eng Med Ctr Hosps, 63- *Mem:* AAAS; Asn Res Nerv & Ment Dis; Am Neurol Asn; AMA; Am Fedn Clin Res. *Res:* Neurophysiology of primate motor function; physiologic nature of development of behavior in infants; sensory mechanisms in movement; clinical neurology; applied neurophysiology; neuropsychology. *Mailing Add:* Dept Neurol Sch Med Tufts Univ Boston MA 02111

TWOHY, DONALD WILFRED, b Clackamas, Ore, Sept 9, 24; m 55; c 1. PARASITOLOGY. *Educ:* Ore State Col, BS, 48, MS, 51; Johns Hopkins Univ, ScD, 55. *Prof Exp:* Aquatic biologist, Ore State Game Comn, 49-51; res asst, Sch Hyg & Pub Health, Johns Hopkins Univ, 55-56; asst prof zool, Okla State Univ, 56-60; instr, 60-62, asst prof microbiol, 62-77, ASSOC PROF MICROBIOL & PUB HEALTH, MICH STATE UNIV, 77- *Mem:* Am Soc Parasitologists; Am Soc Trop Med & Hyg; Soc Protozool. *Res:* Parasitic protozoa; cellular immunity. *Mailing Add:* Dept of Microbiol & Pub Health Mich State Univ East Lansing MI 48824

TWOMBLY, GRAY HUNTINGTON, b Newton, Mass, Apr 27, 05; m 34; c 3. OBSTETRICS & GYNECOLOGY. *Educ:* Franklin & Marshall Col, AB, 25; Harvard Univ, MD, 29; Am Bd Surg, dipl, 40; Am Bd Obstet & Gynec, dipl, 54. *Hon Degrees:* DSC, Franklin & Marshall Col, 49. *Prof Exp:* Intern surg, Mass Gen Hosp, 30-32; asst resident, Free Hosp Women, 32; intern, Mem Hosp, 33-37; asst prof cancer res, Columbia Univ, 42-48, asst prof clin obstet & gynec, Col Physicians & Surgeons, 48-52; PROF GYNEC, SCH MED, NY UNIV & ASSOC DIR GYNEC, UNIV HOSP, 52- assoc dir gynec, Univ Hosp, 52-73; RETIRED. *Concurrent Pos:* Fel, Mem Hosp, New York, 33-37, from clin asst to asst surgeon, 37-48; asst attend gynecologist, Sloane Hosp Women, 48-52 & Delafield Hosp, 50-52; consult, Yonkers Gen Hosp, 59-72, Holy Name Hosp, Teaneck, NJ, 59-72, Queen's Gen Hosp, 62-69 & St Luke's Hosp, 66- *Mem:* Am Gynec Soc; Am Radium Soc (vpres, 59); Am Asn Cancer Res; Am Cancer Soc; Soc Pelvic Surg (pres, 71-72). *Res:* Cancer and steroid research. *Mailing Add:* 450 Riverside Dr New York NY 10027

TWOMBLY, JOHN C, b Denver, Colo, Nov 26, 21. ELECTRICAL ENGINEERING. *Educ:* Univ Colo, BS, 44, PhD(elec eng), 59; Stanford Univ, MS, 50. *Prof Exp:* Engr, Manhattan Dist, Los Alamos Sci Labs, 45-46; instr elec eng, 46-49, res assoc electronics, 51-58, assoc prof elec eng, 59-62, PROF ELEC ENG, UNIV COLO, BOULDER, 62- *Concurrent Pos:* Fac study & res fel from Univ Colo, Swiss Fed Inst Technol, 65-66. *Mem:* Inst Elec & Electronics Engrs. *Res:* Electron devices; space-charge dynamics; network theory. *Mailing Add:* Dept of Elec Eng Univ of Colo Boulder CO 80302

TWOMEY, ARTHUR CORNELIUS, b Midland, Ont, Oct 15, 08; nat US; m 34; c 1. ZOOLOGY. *Educ:* Univ Alta, BS, 33; Univ Ill, MSc, 35, PhD(zool), 37. *Prof Exp:* Asst zool, Univ Ill, 33-37; asst cur & field collector, Dept Ornith, Carnegie Mus, Carnegie Inst, 37-44, lectr, 43-44, dir field expeds & cur ornith, Carnegie Mus, 44-74, dir dept educ, Inst, 48-74; RETIRED. *Concurrent Pos:* Asst paleot exped, 27; conductor expeds, Can, 28-34, 46-47, 54, Arctic Regions & Hudson Bay, 31-34, 36, 38, Pac Coast, 33, Utah, 37, NMex, 39, Ariz, 40, Ore, 41, Peru, Chile, Tierra del Fuego & Galapagos Islands, 39, Bahama Islands, 42, Delta of Mackenzie River, 42-43, 55, 66, Isles of Bahia, Honduras, 47, Repub of Honduras, 48-51, EAfrica, Kenya, Uganda, Tansania, 60, 63, 64, 65, Mozambique, Batswana, 65, Pamir Mt, Afghanistan, 69, Gobi Desert & Alti Mt, Outer Mongolia, 70, Caucasus Mt, USSR, 71. *Mem:* AAAS; Soc Syst Zool; Ecol Soc Am; Wilson Ornith Soc; Am Ornith Union. *Res:* Animal ecology; general, economic, life history systematics and physiological ornithology; climatology relating to ornithology. *Mailing Add:* 555 North Ave Ft Lee NJ 07024

TWOMEY, JEREMIAH JOHN, b Co Cork, Ireland, July 30, 34; m 77; c 3. CELLULAR IMMUNOLOGY. *Educ:* Nat Univ Ireland, MB, BCh, BAO, 58. *Prof Exp:* From asst prof to assoc prof, 67-79, PROF MED, BAYLOR COL MED, 79- *Mem:* Fel Am Col Physicians; Am Fedn Clin Res; fel Royal Irish Acad Med; Am Soc Hemat; Am Asn Immunologists. *Res:* Immune regulation-physiology and pathophysiology; lymphomas-immune responses; thymic hormone; immunobiology of aging. *Mailing Add:* Vet Admin Hosp 2002 Holcombe Blvd Houston TX 77211

TYAN, MARVIN L, b Los Angeles, Calif, Nov 29, 26; m 50; c 2. INTERNAL MEDICINE, EXPERIMENTAL BIOLOGY. *Educ:* Univ Calif, Berkeley, BA, 49; Univ San Francisco, MD, 52. *Prof Exp:* Intern med, Boston City Hosp, Mass, 52-53; resident, Boston Vet Admin Hosp, 53-54; sr asst resident, San Francisco County Hosp, Calif, 54-55; pvt pract, 56-61; sr investr exp path, US Naval Radiol Defense Lab, 61-68 & Stanford Res Inst, Calif, 68-71; prof bact, Immunol & Oral Biol, Dent Res Ctr, Univ NC, Chapel Hill, 71-77; PROF MED, UNIV CALIF, LOS ANGELES, 77- *Concurrent Pos:* Fel hemat, Stanford Lane Hosp, San Francisco, 55-56; fel, Tumor Biol Inst, Karolinska Inst, Sweden, 63-64. *Honors & Awards:* Gold Medal Sci Achievement, US Naval Radiol Defense Lab, 64; Superior Civil Serv Award, Bur Ships, US Navy. *Mem:* AAAS; NY Acad Sci. *Res:* Ontogeny of immune system of the mouse; processes involved in transplantation immunity. *Mailing Add:* Vet Admin Wadsworth Hosp Ctr Wilshire & Sawtelle Blvds Los Angeles CA 90073

TYBERG, JOHN VICTOR, b Grantsburg, Wis, May 4, 38; m 60; c 1. CARDIOVASCULAR PHYSIOLOGY. *Educ:* Bethel Col, Minn, BA, 60; Univ Minn, PhD(physiol), 67, MD, 72. *Prof Exp:* Res assoc med, Harvard Med Sch, 69; res physiologist, Riverside Res Inst, 69-71; res scientist cardiol, Cedars-Sinai Med Ctr, 71-73; ASST PROF MED & PHYSIOL & STAFF MEM, CARDIOVASC RES INST, MED CTR, UNIV CALIF, SAN FRANCISCO, 74- *Concurrent Pos:* Lectr, Med Ctr, Univ Calif, San Francisco, 69-71; mem, Basic Sci Coun, Am Heart Asn, 74- *Mem:* Am Heart Asn; Am Physiol Soc. *Res:* Mechanics and metabolism of ischemic myocardium; diastolic dynamics. *Mailing Add:* Dept of Med Div of Cardiol Univ of Calif Med Ctr San Francisco CA 94143

TYBOR, PHILIP THOMAS, b Fredericksburg, Tex, Oct 3, 48; m 69; c 4. FOOD SCIENCE. *Educ:* Tex A&M Univ, BS, 70, PhD(food sci), 73. *Prof Exp:* dir protein res, 73-80, FOOD PROD DEVELOP DIR, CENT SOYA CO, INC, 80- *Mem:* Inst Food Technologists; Am Asn Cereal Chemists; Am Chem Soc. *Res:* Administration of research programs pertaining to the development of food products for food service, protein applications development and the exploration of new food technologies. *Mailing Add:* Cent Soya Co Inc Ft Wayne Nat Bank Bldg Ft Wayne IN 46802

TYCE, FRANCIS ANTHONY, b South Wales, Eng, Oct 31, 17; US citizen; m 52; c 1. PSYCHIATRY. *Educ:* Univ Durham, BS & MD, 52; Univ Minn, MS, 64; Am Bd Psychiat & Neurol, dipl, 64. *Prof Exp:* House surgeon, Teaching Hosp, Durham, Eng, 52-53; rotating intern, St Vincents Hosp, Erie, Pa, 53-54; gen pract, Seaham Harbor, 54-56; actg supt, Rochester State Hosp, 60-61; asst prof psychiat, Mayo Grad Sch Med, Univ Minn, 69-73, assoc prof, 73-77, PROF PSYCHIAT, MAYO MED SCH, ROCHESTER, MINN, 77-; SUPT, ROCHESTER STATE HOSP, 71- *Concurrent Pos:* Fel psychiat, Mayo Clin,

56-60; lectr, Mayo Found, 65-; consult, WHO, 67-; vpres, Zumbro Valley Med Soc, Rochester, Minn, 71-72, pres, 72-73; task force comt, Psychiat Rehab in Correctional Systs, 73-; Field Rep Accreditation Coun for Psychiat Facil-Jt Comn on Accreditation of Hosps, 73-; mem, Juvenile Delinquency-Nat Adv Comt on Criminal Justice Stand & Goals, 75- *Mem:* Fel Psychiat Soc; Asn Med Supt Ment Hosp (pres elect, 67-68 & pres, 68-); chmn, Am Psychiat Asn. *Res:* Neurophysiology, especially electrical stimulation of the brain in rats; psychiatric program design in mental hospitals. *Mailing Add:* Am Asn Psychiat 2110 E Center Rochester MN 55901

TYCE, GERTRUDE MARY, b Wark, Eng, Mar 26, 27; m 52; c 1. BIOCHEMISTRY. *Educ:* Univ Durham, BSc, 48, PhD(plant physiol & biochem), 52. *Prof Exp:* Instr chem, Villa Maria Col, Pa, 52-53; instr biol & chem, Nottingham & Dist Tech Col Eng, 54-56; res asst biochem, Mayo Clin, 58-63, res assoc, 63-71, ASSOC CONSULT BIOCHEM, MAYO CLIN & MAYO FOUND, 71- *Mem:* AAAS; Am Chem Soc; Am Soc Exp Path. *Res:* Metabolism of glucose, amino acids and biogenic amines in brain and liver. *Mailing Add:* Dept of Microbiol Mayo Med Sch Rochester MN 55901

TYCE, ROBERT CHARLES, b San Diego, Calif, July 9, 47. MARINE PHYSICS, OCEAN ENGINEERING. *Educ:* Univ Calif, San Diego, BA, 69, PhD(appl ocean sci), 77. *Prof Exp:* Asst programmer ocean instrumentation, Scripps Inst Oceanog, 69-70, res asst marine physics, Marine Phys Lab, 70-76; sr acoustics engr ocean vehicle instrumentation, Hydro Prod, 77-78; ASST RES ENGR MARINE PHYSICS, MARINE PHYS LAB, SCRIPPS INST OCEANOG, 78- *Concurrent Pos:* Physicist, Scripps Inst Oceanog, 76-77, res fel, 77-78; consult, Hydro Prod, 78- *Mem:* Acoust Soc Am; assoc mem Soc Explor Geophysicists; Marine Technol Soc; Am Geophys Union; Inst Elec & Electronics Engrs. *Res:* Underwater acoustics and geophysics; deep ocean engineering and instrumentation; vehicle technology; computer science; digital signal processing. *Mailing Add:* Marine Phys Lab Univ of Calif San Diego CA 92152

TYCHSEN, PAUL C, b Chicago, Ill, Nov 1, 16; m 43; c 2. GEOLOGY. *Educ:* Carleton Col, BA, 41; Univ Nebr, MSc, 49, PhD(geol), 54. *Prof Exp:* Geolgist, US Geol Surv, 46-49; Proj rep Australia, Earth Sci Curric Proj, Am Geol Inst, 72-73; CHMN DEPT GEOL, UNIV WIS-SUPERIOR, 52- *Honors & Awards:* Johnson Wax Found teaching award, 65. *Mem:* AAAS; fel Geol Soc Am; Nat Asn Geol Teachers. *Res:* Stratigraphy; field-mapping; geomorphology. *Mailing Add:* Dept of Geosci Univ of Wis Superior WI 54880

TYCKO, DANIEL H, b Los Angeles, Calif, Nov 14, 27; m 52; c 3. BIOPHYSICS, BIOMEDICAL ENGINEERING. *Educ:* Univ Calif, Los Angeles, BA, 50; Columbia Univ, PhD(physics), 57. *Prof Exp:* Sr res assoc, Nevis Labs, Columbia Univ, 57-66; assoc prof physics, Rutgers Univ, 66-67; eng comput sci, State Univ NY, Stony Brook, 67-70, prof, 70-79, prof, State Univ NY, New Paltz, 79-80; PRIN SCIENTIST, TECHNICON INSTRUMENTS CORP, 80- *Concurrent Pos:* Res collab, Saclay Nuclear Res Ctr, France, 61-62; consult, Technicon Instruments Corp, 70-80. *Mem:* Am Phys Soc; Asn Comput Mach; Inst Elec Electronic Engrs; AAAS. *Res:* Image processing by computers; pattern recognition; applications to cytology and hematology; flow cytometry instrumentation; application of light scattering to the measurement of the properties of cells. *Mailing Add:* Technicon Instruments Corp 511 Benedict Ave Tarrytown NY 10591

TYCZKOWSKI, EDWARD ALBERT, b Providence, RI, May 15, 24; m 50. ORGANIC CHEMISTRY. *Educ:* Brown Univ, ScB, 49; Duke Univ, PhD(chem), 53. *Prof Exp:* Res assoc, US Army Off Ord Res, Duke Univ, 52-53; res chemist, Gen Chem Div, Allied Chem & Dye Corp, 53-56 & Pennsalt Chem Corp, 56-62; process chemist, Air Prod & Chem Corp, 62-63; vpres, Hynes Chem Res Corp, 63-66; sr res chemist, Fibers Div, Beaunit Corp, 66-67, res assoc, 67-72; PRES, ARMAGEDDON CHEM CO, 72- *Mem:* AAAS; Am Chem Soc. *Res:* Organic fluorine chemistry; reactions of elementary fluorine with organic compounds; flame reactions; explosions; reactor design; organic synthesis; polymer chemistry; fiber structure. *Mailing Add:* 824 E Forest Hills Blvd Durham NC 27707

TYE, ARTHUR, b Rutherglen, Australia, Sept 13, 09; nat US; m 41, 65. PHARMACOLOGY. *Educ:* Ohio State Univ, PhD(pharm), 50. *Prof Exp:* Asst & lectr pharm, Peiping Union Med Col, China, 32-38, head dept, 39-41; head pharmaceut prods div, Oriental Corp, China, 42-47; from asst prof to assoc prof, 50-60, prof, 60-70, EMER PROF PHARM, COL PHARM, OHIO STATE UNIV, 70- *Concurrent Pos:* Adminr, Redwood Health Consortium, 72- *Mem:* AAAS; Am Pharmaceut Asn; Am Soc Pharmacol & Exp Therapeut. *Res:* Autonomic nervous system; steric aspects of adrenergic drugs; structure-action relationships; chemical pharmacology; modular systems approach to allied health education. *Mailing Add:* 219 Mocking Bird Circle Santa Rosa CA 95405

TYE, BIK-KWOON, b Hong Kong, Jan 7, 47; m 71. MOLECULAR BIOLOGY, MOLECULAR GENETICS. *Educ:* Wellesley Col, BA, 69; Univ Calif, San Francisco, MSc, 71; Mass Inst Technol, PhD(microbiol), 74. *Prof Exp:* Helen Hay Whitney Found fel biochem, Sch Med, Stanford Univ, 74-77; ASST PROF BIOCHEM, CORNELL UNIV, 77- *Res:* DNA replication and repair; DNA packaging in Bacteriophage. *Mailing Add:* Wing Hall Cornell Univ Ithaca NY 14853

TYE, SZE-HOI HENRY, b Shanghai, China, Jan 15, 47; m 71; c 1. THEORETICAL PHYSICS, ELEMENTARY PARTICLE PHYSICS. *Educ:* Calif Inst Technol, BS, 70; Mass Inst Technol, PhD(physics), 74. *Prof Exp:* Res assoc physics, Stanford Linear Accelerator Ctr, Stanford Univ, 74-77, Fermi Nat Accelerator Lab, 77-78; SR RES ASSOC PHYSICS, NEWMAN LAB NUCLEAR STUDIES, CORNELL UNIV, 78- *Mem:* Am Phys Soc. *Mailing Add:* Newman Lab Nuclear Studies Cornell Univ Ithaca NY 14853

TYERYAR, FRANKLIN JOSEPH, JR, b Frederick, Md, Apr 29, 35; m 59; c 3. MEDICAL MICROBIOLOGY. *Educ:* Univ Md, BS, 60, MS, 62, PhD(microbiol), 68. *Prof Exp:* Microbiologist, US Bur Mines, US Dept Interior, 62-63, US Dept Army, Ft Detrick, 63-71 & Dept Microbiol, Naval Med Res Inst, 71-73; MICROBIOLOGIST, NAT INST ALLERGY & INFECTIOUS DIS, 73- *Mem:* Am Soc Microbiol; Sigma Xi; Infectious Dis Soc Am. *Res:* Microbial genetics and physiology, specifically gene exchange mechanisms by transformation and transduction; development and testing of viral vaccines for clinical use; clinical evaluation of viral vaccines for efficacy; persistent viral infections; prevention and control of virus caused respiratory disease. *Mailing Add:* Nat Inst of Allergy & Infectious Dis Nat Insts of Health Bethesda MD 20205

TYHACH, RICHARD JOSEPH, b New York, NY, Aug 14, 49; m 73; c 1. BIOCHEMISTRY. *Educ:* Queens Col, BA, 70, MA, 73; City Univ New York, PhD(biochem), 76. *Prof Exp:* Lectr chem, Queens Col, City Univ New York, 71-76; Damon Runyon-Walter Winchell Cancer Fund fel biol chem, Harvard Med Sch, 76-78; res scientist biochem, 78-81, SR RES SCIENTIST BIOCHEM, AMES CO, LABS, INC, 81- *Mem:* Am Chem Soc; Am Asn Clin Chemists; Sigma Xi. *Res:* Lipid metabolism and enzymology; biomembranes; clinical biochemistry and immunoassay technology. *Mailing Add:* Ames Co 1127 Myrtle St Elkhart IN 46515

TYHURST, JAMES STEWART, b Victoria, BC, Feb 24, 22; m 49; c 2. PSYCHIATRY. *Educ:* McGill Univ, BSc, 41, MD, CM, 44. *Prof Exp:* Res asst & demonstr psychiat, McGill Univ, 48-49, sr res psychiatrist & demonstr, 49-50; asst prof, Col Med & asst, Cornell Univ, 50-53; asst prof, McGill Univ, 53-60; head dept, 60-70, PROF PSYCHIAT, UNIV BC, 60- *Concurrent Pos:* Lectr psychiat, Dalhousie Univ, 50-51; dir, Psychiat Clin, Digby, NS, 51-53; assoc psychiatrist, Royal Victoria Hosp, Montreal, Que, 53-60; consult, Can Dept Vet Affiars, 53-; mem, Adv Bd, Nat Lab Group Develop, 54- *Mem:* AAAS; fel Am Psychiat Asn; Can Psychiat Asn; Can Med Asn. *Res:* Psychopharmacology; social, clinical, community and industrial psychiatry; behavior of individuals and groups in emergencies; ageing and retirement; displacement and migration. *Mailing Add:* Dept of Psychiat Univ of BC Vancouver BC V6T 1W5 Can

TYKODI, RALPH JOHN, b Cleveland, Ohio, Apr 18, 25; m 55; c 3. PHYSICAL CHEMISTRY. *Educ:* Northwestern Univ, BS, 49; Pa State Univ, PhD, 54. *Prof Exp:* Instr, Ill Inst Technol, 55-57, from asst prof to assoc prof, 57-65; assoc prof chem, 65-68, assoc dean, Col Arts & Sci, 69-72, PROF, SOUTHEASTERN MASS UNIV, 68- *Mem:* Am Chem Soc; Am Phys Soc. *Res:* Equilibrium and non-equilibrium thermodynamics. *Mailing Add:* Dept Chem Southeastern Mass Univ North Dartmouth MA 02747

TYLER, ALBERT VINCENT, b Philadelphia, Pa, June 25, 38; m 60; c 2. FISHERIES. *Educ:* Univ Pa, BA, 60; Univ Toronto, MA, 64, PhD(synecol), 68. *Prof Exp:* Scientist, Fisheries Res Bd Can, 64-74, assoc prof, 74-81, PROF FISHERIES, ORE STATE UNIV, 81- *Mem:* Am Fisheries Soc; Can Soc Zool; Sigma Xi. *Res:* Physiological and ecological energetics; competitive and predatory relationships among fishes; population dynamics. *Mailing Add:* Dept Fisheries & Wildlife Ore State Univ Corvallis OR 97331

TYLER, AUSTIN LAMONT, b Provo, Utah, July 21, 36; m 60; c 5. CHEMICAL ENGINEERING. *Educ:* Univ Utah, BS, 61, PhD(chem eng), 65. *Prof Exp:* Supvr & mem staff, Semiconductor Processing, Bell Tel Labs, 65-70; ASSOC PROF CHEM ENG, UNIV UTAH, 70- *Mem:* Am Inst Chem Engrs. *Res:* Particle behavior in acceleration gas streams; fabrication processes for silicon semiconductors; kinetics of oil shale retorting processes. *Mailing Add:* Dept of Chem Eng Univ of Utah Salt Lake City UT 84112

TYLER, BONNIE MORELAND, b New York, NY, Jan 5, 41; m 63; c 3. MICROBIAL PHYSIOLOGY, MOLECULAR BIOLOGY. *Educ:* Wheaton Col, BA, 62; Mass Inst Technol, PhD(biol), 68. *Prof Exp:* Res assoc bact, Univ Calif, Davis, 68-70; instr microbiol, Mass Inst Technol, 70-73, asst prof, 73-77, assoc prof, 77-80. *Mem:* Sigma Xi; Am Soc Microbiol; Am Soc Biol Chemists. *Res:* Regulation of transcription and translation in bacteria; studies with whole cells and with purified transcription systems on factors regulating transcription. *Mailing Add:* 1114 Caddington Rd Ithaca NY 14850

TYLER, DAVID BERNARD, physiology, pharmacology, deceased

TYLER, DAVID E, b Carlisle, Iowa, July 12, 28; m 52; c 2. VETERINARY PATHOLOGY. *Educ:* Iowa State Univ, BS, 53, DVM, 57, PhD(vet path), 63; Purdue Univ, MS, 60. *Prof Exp:* Instr, Purdue Univ, 57-60; asst prof, Iowa State Univ, 60-64, assoc prof, 64-66; PROF VET PATH & HEAD DEPT, COL VET MED, UNIV GA, 66- *Mem:* Am Vet Med Asn; Am Col Vet Path; Am Asn Vet Med Educr; Conf Res Workers Animal Diseases. *Res:* Epidemiology, pathology and immunology of the bovine mucosal disease-virus diarrhea complex; respiratory complex of calves epidemiology and pathology. *Mailing Add:* Dept of Path Col of Vet Med Univ of Ga Athens GA 30602

TYLER, FRANK HILL, b Villisca, Iowa, Jan 5, 16; m 41; c 3. MEDICINE. *Educ:* Willamette Univ, BA, 38; Johns Hopkins Univ, MD, 42. *Prof Exp:* Intern med, Johns Hopkins Hosp, 42-43; from asst resident to resident, Peter Bent Brigham Hosp, Boston, 43-47; research instr, 47-54, from asst prof to assoc prof, 50-59, PROF MED, MED SCH, UNIV UTAH, 59- *Mem:* Am Soc Clin Invest; Endocrine Soc; Am Fedn Clin Res; Asn Am Physicians; Master, Am Col Physicians, 81. *Res:* Disease of the muscle; human inheritance; metabolism of steroids and metabolic disorders. *Mailing Add:* 50 N Medical Dr Salt Lake City UT 84132

TYLER, GEORGE LEONARD, b Bartow, Fla, Oct 18, 40; c 2. PLANETARY EXPLORATION, RADAR ASTRONOMY. *Educ:* Ga Inst Technol, BS, 63; Stanford Univ, MS, 64, PhD(elec eng), 67. *Prof Exp:* Res assoc, 67-79, res engr, 69-71, sr res assoc, Ctr Radar Astron, 71-74, ADJ PROF, DEPT ELEC ENG, STANFORD UNIV, 74-; TEAM LEADER, VOYAGER RADIO

SCI TEAM, NASA, 79- *Mem:* Inst Elec & Electronics Engrs; Am Astron Soc; Am Geophys Union; Int Astron Union; Int Union Radio Sci. *Res:* Radio propagation experiments in space including theory and experiment; radio occultation measurements of planetary rings and atmospheres; radar astronomy including observation and interpretation of radiowave scatter from planetary surfaces using both spacecraft and ground based techniques; terrestrial applications of remote sensing. *Mailing Add:* Standard Electronic Lab Ctr Radar Astron Stanford Univ Stanford CA 94305

TYLER, GEORGE WILLIAM, b Smyth Co, Va, Oct 16, 08; m 33; c 3. MATHEMATICS. *Educ:* Emory & Henry Col, BS, 30; Duke Univ, MA, 35; Va Polytech Inst, PhD(statist), 49. *Prof Exp:* Teacher schs, Va, 30-40; from instr to asst prof math, Va Polytech Inst, 40-44, assoc prof, 46-48; assoc physicist, Div War Res, Univ Calif, 44-46; consult, Navy Electronics Lab, 48-51; opers analyst & team chief, Hqs, US Air Force, 51-61; scientist, Inst Defense Anal, 61-63 & Ctr Naval Anal, 63-66; sr scientist, Tech Ctr, Supreme Hqs, Allied Powers, Europe, 66-69; SCI CONSULT, 69- *Honors & Awards:* Meritorious civilian serv award, US Air Force, 58. *Mem:* Opers Res Soc Am; Math Asn Am; Am Statist Asn; Inst Math Statist. *Res:* Experimental design; sampling; variance analysis; error control; systems simulation and analysis; weapons effects and arms control. *Mailing Add:* 3331 Bayshore Blvd NE St Petersburg FL 33703

TYLER, JACK D, b Snyder, Okla, July 18, 40; m 69. ORNITHOLOGY, ECOLOGY. *Educ:* Southwestern State Col, BS, 62; Okla State Univ, MS, 65; Univ Okla, PhD(zool), 68. *Prof Exp:* Teaching asst gen zool, Univ Okla, 64-66; from instr to assoc prof biol, 67-78, PROF BIOL, CAMERON UNIV, 78- *Concurrent Pos:* Ed, Bull Okla Orinth Soc, 72- *Mem:* Am Soc Mammal; Wilson Ornith Soc; Am Orinth Union. *Res:* Ecological relationships between certain birds in southwest Oklahoma and among vertebrates in prairie dog towns. *Mailing Add:* Dept of Biol Cameron Univ Lawton OK 73501

TYLER, JAMES CHASE, b Shanghai, China, Mar 31, 35; US citizen; m 58; c 2. ICHTHYOLOGY. *Educ:* George Washington Univ, BS, 57; Stanford Univ, PhD(biol), 62. *Prof Exp:* Actg instr gen biol, Stanford Univ, 61; asst curator ichthyol, Acad Natural Sci Philadelphia, 62-66, assoc curator, 67-72; asst dir, Lerner Marine Lab, Am Mus Natural Hist, 72-73, dir, 73-75; prog dir biol res resources, Div Environ Biol, NSF, Washington, DC, 75-80; RES ASSOC, AM MUS NATURAL HIST, 76-; RES ASSOC, NAT MUS NATURAL HIST, 80- *Concurrent Pos:* NSF grants, 63-72. *Mem:* Am Soc Ichthyol & Herpet. *Res:* Ichthyology, especially the anatomy and phylogeny of plectognath fishes and their classification; behavior and ecology of coral reef fishes; sea turtle biology. *Mailing Add:* Office of Endangered Species F6 Nat Marine Fisheries Serv Washington DC 20235

TYLER, JEAN MARY, b Sheffield, Eng, Apr 7, 28. ENDOCRINOLOGY, IMMUNOCHEMISTRY. *Educ:* Univ London, BSc, 49, PhD(org chem), 55. *Prof Exp:* Asst lectr org chem, Univ London, 51-55; Imp Chem Industs fel, Univ Edinburgh, 55-59; res fel, Univ West Indies, 59-60; res assoc immunochem, Inst Microbiol, Rutgers Univ, 60-64; NATO res fel org chem, Univ Newcastle, 64-65; sr hosp biochemist, Dept Med, Royal Free Hosp, London, Eng, 65-66; res fel chem, Imp Col Sci & Technol, Univ London, 66-68; asst res prof med, 68-74, ASSOC RES PROF MED, MED COL GA, 74- *Honors & Awards:* Commonwealth Award, Royal Soc & Nuffield Found, 59; NATO Award, 64. *Mem:* Royal Soc Chem; Endocrine Soc; Am Diabetes Asn; NY Acad Sci. *Res:* Carbohydrate chemistry; immunochemistry of microbial polysaccharide antigens; radioimmunoassay of peptide hormones; diabetes. *Mailing Add:* Div Metabolic & Endocrine Dis Dept Med Med Col Ga Augusta GA 30912

TYLER, JOHN HOWARD, b Madison, Wis, Aug 29, 35; m 75. GEOLOGY. *Educ:* Univ Wis, BS, 58; Va Polytech Inst, MS, 60; Univ Mich, PhD(geol), 63. *Prof Exp:* Res asst geol, Va Polytech Inst, 58-60; res asst geol & paleont, Univ Mich, 60-63; tech asst, US Geol Surv, Calif, 63-64; fel, Univ of Wales, Swansea, 64-65; air photo interpreter, Itek Corp, Calif, 65-66 & Mark Systs Inc, 66; PROF GEOL, SAN FRANCISCO STATE UNIV, 66- *Mem:* Geol Soc Am; Soc Econ Paleont & Mineral. *Res:* Structural geology; remote sensing; stratigraphy; sedimentology; photogeology. *Mailing Add:* Dept Geosci San Francisco State Univ San Francisco CA 94132

TYLER, LESLIE J, b Salamanca, NY, Nov 2, 19; m 47; c 7. ORGANIC CHEMISTRY. *Educ:* Univ Scranton, BS, 42; Pa State Univ, MS, 47, PhD(org chem), 48. *Prof Exp:* Res chemist silicon chem, 48-51, lab supvr resin res, 51-62, dir develop, 62-68, bus mgr fluids, 68-73, dir res, 73-75, V PRES RES & DEVELOP, DOW CORNING CORP, 75- *Mem:* Am Chem Soc; Res Soc Am. *Res:* Silicon research; silica research; organosilicon research. *Mailing Add:* Dow Corning Corp PO Box 1767 Midland MI 48640

TYLER, MARY STOTT, b Princeton, NJ, Apr 1, 49. DEVELOPMENTAL BIOLOGY. *Educ:* Swarthmore Col, BA, 71; Univ NC, Chapel Hill, MS, 73, PhD(zool), 75. *Prof Exp:* NSF-NATO fel develop biol, Dalhousie Univ, 75-76; asst prof, 76-80, ASSOC PROF ZOOL, UNIV MAINE, ORONO, 80- *Concurrent Pos:* Fac res grant, Univ Maine, 77-78; NIH res grant, 78-81. *Mem:* Soc Develop Biol; AAAS; Int Asn Dent Res. *Res:* Interacting systems in the developing vertebrate embryo; light-microscopic and ultrastructural aspects of tissue interactions; developmental capabilities of epithelial and mesenchymal tissues in experimental in vitro systems. *Mailing Add:* Dept of Zool Univ of Maine Orono ME 04469

TYLER, MAX EZRA, b Groveland, NY, June 1, 16; m 45; c 2. MICROBIAL ECOLOGY. *Educ:* Cornell Univ, BS, 38; Ohio State Univ, MS, 40, PhD(bact), 48. *Prof Exp:* Asst bacteriologist, Ohio State Univ, 38-41; instr, Colo State Col, asst, Exp Sta, 41-42; bacteriologist, US War Dept, 46-53; head dept, 53-71, PROF BACT, UNIV FLA, 53- *Mem:* Fel AAAS; Am Soc Microbiol; fel Am Pub Health Asn; Brit Soc Gen Microbiol. *Res:* Ecology; grass-associated N fixation; physiology; taxonomy marine, estuarine bacteria; water pollution; bacterial sampling from air. *Mailing Add:* Dept of Microbiol 1053 McCarty Univ Fla Gainesville FL 32611

TYLER, R(ONALD) A(NTHONY), b Burnham, Eng, June 4, 20; nat Can; m 42; c 1. THERMODYNAMICS, AERODYNAMICS. *Educ:* Univ London, BSc, 40. *Prof Exp:* Asst, Univ London, 40-42; engr, Bristol Aeroplane Co, Eng, 42-46; mathematician, Valve Res Labs, Standard Tel & Cables, Ltd, 46-47; asst res officer, 47-51, assoc res officer, 51-55, sr res officer, 55-61, PRIN RES OFFICER, DIV MECH ENG, NAT RES COUN CAN, 61-, HEAD, GAS DYNAMICS LAB, 77- *Mem:* Assoc fel Am Inst Aeronaut & Astronaut; assoc fel Can Aeronaut & Space Inst. *Res:* Turbomachinery, particularly aircraft turbines; locomotive gas turbine power plants; vertical take off and landing lift-propulsion systems. *Mailing Add:* 728 Lonsdale Rd Ottawa ON K1K 0K2 Can

TYLER, SETH, b Chicago, Ill, Feb 26, 49; m 70. INVERTEBRATE ZOOLOGY, ELECTRON MICROSCOPY. *Educ:* Swarthmore Col, BA, 70; Univ NC, Chapel Hill, PhD(zool), 75. *Prof Exp:* Killam fel anat, Dalhousie Univ, 75-76; asst prof, 76-82, ASSOC PROF ZOOL, UNIV MAINE, 82- *Concurrent Pos:* Prin investr, NSF grant, Univ Maine, 77-85; mem bd reviewers, Trans Am Micros Soc, 79-82; assoc prof zool & dir, Electron Micros Ctr, Wash State Univ, 80. *Mem:* Am Soc Zoologists; Am Microscopical Soc; Sigma Xi; Electron Micros Soc Am; Int Asn Meiobenthologists. *Res:* Comparative ultrastructure of lower metazoans; phylogeny of invertebrates; meiobenthology. *Mailing Add:* Dept Zool Univ Maine Orono ME 04469

TYLER, TIPTON RANSOM, b Milwaukee, Wis, Jan 3, 41; m 62; c 3. BIOCHEMISTRY, PHARMACOLOGY. *Educ:* Colo State Univ, BS, 63, PhD(nutrit), 68; NC State Univ, MS, 65; Am Bd Toxicol, dipl, 80. *Prof Exp:* Sr res chemist, Merck Sharp & Dohme Res Labs, 68-74; asst prof animal sci, Univ Ill, Urbana-Champaign, 74-75; sr scientist chem hyg fel, Carnegie-Mellon Univ, 76-81; ASST COORD DIR APPL TOXICOL, UNION CARBIDE CORP, 81- *Concurrent Pos:* Adj assoc prof toxicol, Univ Pa, 79- *Mem:* AAAS; Am Chem Soc; Soc Toxicol; Am Soc Pharmacol & Exp Therapeut. *Res:* Toxicology; drug metabolism; residues in tissues; disposition and clearance from animals; toxicology. *Mailing Add:* Union Carbide Corp PO Box 8361 South Charleston WV 25303

TYLER, VARRO EUGENE, b Auburn, Nebr, Dec 19, 26; m 47; c 2. PHARMACOGNOSY. *Educ:* Univ Nebr, BS, 49; Univ Conn, MS, 51, PhD(pharmacog), 53. *Prof Exp:* Assoc prof pharmacog, Univ Nebr, 53-57; assoc prof pharmacog, Univ Wash, 57-61, prof, 61-66, chmn dept pharmacog & dir drug plant gardens, 57-66; DEAN, SCH PHARM & PHARMACOL SCI, PURDUE UNIV, 66-, DEAN, SCH PHARM, NURSING & HEALTH SCI, 79- *Honors & Awards:* Found res achievement award, Am Pharmaceut Asn, 66. *Mem:* Am Asn Cols Pharm (pres, 70-71); Am Soc Pharmacog (pres, 59-61); Am Pharmaceut Asn; Am Coun Pharmaceut Educ (pres, 74-78); fel Acad Pharmaceut Sci. *Res:* Alkaloid biosynthesis; drug plant cultivation; phytochemical analysis; medicinal and toxic constituents of higher fungi; herbal medicine. *Mailing Add:* Sch Pharm and Pharmacol Sci Purdue Univ West Lafayette IN 47907

TYLER, WALTER STEELE, b Caspian, Mich, Nov 2, 25; m 49; c 2. ANATOMY. *Educ:* Mich State Col, DVM, 51; Univ Calif, Davis, PhD(comp path), 56. *Prof Exp:* Lectr vet sci, 52-57, from asst prof to assoc prof vet med, 57-67, actg chmn dept, 65-67, chmn dept, 67-70, jr vet, Exp Sta, 52-56, asst vet, 56-62, prof vet med, 67-76, PROF ANAT, UNIV CALIF, DAVIS, 76-, ANATOMIST, 62-, DIR, CALIF PRIMATE RES CTR, 72- *Concurrent Pos:* Fel, Postgrad Med Sch, Univ London, 63-64. *Mem:* Am Asn Anatomists; Am Asn Vet Anat (secy-treas, 66-67); Am Physiol Soc; Am Soc Zool; Am Vet Med Asn. *Res:* Relationship of structure to function in health and disease; pulmonary anatomy; emphysema; air pollution; histochemistry; scanning and transmission; electron microscopy; comparative anatomy; primate morphology. *Mailing Add:* Dept of Anat Univ of Calif Sch of Vet Med Davis CA 95616

TYLER, WILLARD PHILIP, b Newton, Mass, Nov 8, 09; m 35, 55; c 3. ANALYTICAL CHEMISTRY. *Educ:* Ore State Col, BS, 31, MS, 33; Univ Ill, PhD(anal chem), 38. *Prof Exp:* Instr, Clark Jr Col, 34-36; res analyst, BF Goodrich Co, 36-38, sect leader, Res Ctr, 38-74; RETIRED. *Mem:* Am Chem Soc. *Res:* Classical and instrumental chemical analysis; absorption spectroscopy; x-ray diffraction; gas chromatography; electroanalytical methods; high polymers. *Mailing Add:* 8471 Whitewood Rd Brecksville OH 44141

TYLER, WINFIELD WARREN, solid state physics, see previous edition

TYLUTKI, EDMUND EUGENE, b Chicago, Ill, Nov 6, 26; m 56; c 6. MYCOLOGY. *Educ:* Univ Ill, BS, 51, MS, 52; Mich State Univ, PhD(mycol), 55. *Prof Exp:* Asst bot, Univ Ill, 51-52; bot & plant path, Mich State Univ, 52-55; actg asst prof plant path & actg asst plant pathologist, Wash State Univ, 56; asst prof, 56-65, ASSOC PROF BOT, UNIV IDAHO, 65- *Concurrent Pos:* Ed-in-chief, Jour Idaho Acad Sci, 65-, pres, 70-71; actg chmn, Dept Biol Sci, Univ Idaho, 75-76. *Mem:* Mycol Soc Am; Classifaction Soc; Int Asn Plant Taxonomists. *Res:* Computer applications to fungal taxonomy; taxonomy of fleshy fungi of the Pacific northwest. *Mailing Add:* Dept of Biol Sci Univ of Idaho Moscow ID 83843

TYMCHATYN, EDWARD DMYTRO, b Leoville, Sask, Nov 11, 42. MATHEMATICS, TOPOLOGY. *Educ:* Univ Sask, BA, 63, Hons, 64; Univ Ore, MA, 65, PhD(math), 68. *Prof Exp:* Asst prof, 68-71, assoc prof, 71-76, PROF MATH, UNIV SASK, 76- *Concurrent Pos:* Natural Sci & Eng Res Coun res grant, Univ Sask, 69-; vis assoc prof, Univ Ore, 75; vis prof, Ctr de Invest del Inst Politec Nac, Mexico City, 79 & Univ Ala, Birmingham, 81-82; mem fel comt, Natural Sci & Eng Res Coun, 79-82. *Mem:* Am Math Soc. *Res:* General topology and point set topology; continua; low dimensional spaces; partially ordered spaces and topological semigroups. *Mailing Add:* Dept of Math Univ of Sask Saskatoon SK S7N 0W0 Can

TYNAN, EUGENE JOSEPH, b Middletown, Conn, Sept 15, 24. PALYNOLOGY. *Educ:* Univ Conn, BA, 53; Univ Mass, MS, 56; Univ Okla, PhD, 62. *Prof Exp:* Instr, 59-62, asst prof, 62-70, actg chmn dept, 66-70, ASSOC PROF GEOL, UNIV RI, 70- *Mem:* Sigma Xi; Am Asn Stratig Palynologists. *Res:* Taxonomy, ecology and stratigraphic application of spores, pollen and other lesser known groups of microfossils. *Mailing Add:* Dept of Geol Univ of RI Kingston RI 02881

TYNDALL, JESSE PARKER, b Jones Co, NC, Jan 9, 25; m 65; c 1. BIOLOGY, SCIENCE EDUCATION. *Educ:* Atlantic Christian Col, AB, 45; Univ NC, Chapel Hill, MA, 49; Univ Fla, EdD, 56. *Prof Exp:* Teacher, Jones County Bd Educ, NC, 45-47; from instr to assoc prof biol & sci educ, 49-52, prof sci educ, 52-73, PROF BIOL, ATLANTIC CHRISTIAN COL, 52-, CHMN DEPT SCI, 54- *Concurrent Pos:* Mem bd dirs, Joint Comn Nursing Educ, NC Bd Educ & Bd Gov, 69-72, chmn, 72-73. *Mem:* Fel AAAS. *Res:* Genetics; nursing education. *Mailing Add:* Dept of Sci Atlantic Christian Col Wilson NC 27893

TYNER, DAVID ANSON, b Berrien Co, Mich, Feb 19, 22; m 49; c 4. ORGANIC CHEMISTRY. *Educ:* Univ Mich, BS, 44, MS, 49, PhD(org chem), 52. *Prof Exp:* RES CHEMIST, G D SEARLE & CO, 52- *Concurrent Pos:* Civilian res chemist, Manhattan Proj, 44-45. *Mem:* Am Chem Soc. *Res:* Total and partial synthesis of steroids; peptides. *Mailing Add:* 909 Glendale Rd Glenview IL 60025

TYNER, GEORGE S, b Omaha, Nebr, Oct 9, 16; m; c 2. SURGERY, OPHTHALMOLOGY. *Educ:* Univ Nebr, BS, 40, MD, 42; Univ Pa, MS, 52; Am Bd Ophthal, dipl, 50. *Prof Exp:* Intern, Philadelphia Gen Hosp, 42-43, resident ophthal, 47-48; resident, Hosp Univ Pa, 48-51, asst instr ophthal, Sch Med, Univ Pa, 48-52; from asst instr to asst clin prof, Sch Med, Univ Colo, 52-61, assoc dean & asst to vpres med affairs, 63-71, chief glaucoma clin & assoc prof ophthal, 64-71; dean, 74-81, PROF OPHTHAL, SCH MED, TEX TECH UNIV, 71-, EMER DEAN, 81- *Concurrent Pos:* Res fel, Univ Pa, 48-51; asst abstr ed, Am J Ophthal, 52-57; pvt pract, Colo, 52-61; mem, Colo State Bd Basic Sci Exam, 62-67; mem consult staff, Children's Hosp & Denver Gen Hosp; mem courtesy staff, St Luke's Hosp; mem assoc staff, St Mary's Hosp, 73. *Mem:* Fel Am Col Surg; Am Acad Ophthal & Otolaryngol; AMA. *Mailing Add:* Deans Off Tex Tech Univ Sch Med Lubbock TX 79430

TYNER, MACK, b Laurel Hill, Fla, Feb 1, 17; m 46. CHEMICAL ENGINEERING. *Educ:* Univ Fla, BSChE, 38; Univ Cincinnati, MS, 40, PhD(phys chem), 41. *Prof Exp:* Tech control engr, Kimberly Clark Corp, NY, 41-42; res engr, Univ Wis, 42-43; asst chem engr, Armour Res Found, Ill, 42-45; PROF CHEM ENG, UNIV FLA, 45- *Mem:* Instrument Soc Am; Am Inst Chem Engrs. *Res:* Process dynamics and control; systems engineering; instrumentation; chemical reaction engineering. *Mailing Add:* Dept of Chem Eng Univ of Fla Gainesville FL 32611

TYNES, ARTHUR RICHARD, b Great Falls, Mont, Oct 1, 26; m 46; c 5. OPTICS. *Educ:* Mont State Univ, BS, 50; Ore State Univ, MS, 53, PhD(physics), 63. *Prof Exp:* Physicist, US Bur Mines, 51-54; instr physics, Ore State Univ, 54-61; MEM TECH STAFF, BELL LABS, 61- *Mem:* Optical Soc Am. *Res:* Spectroscopy; plasma diagnositics; physical optics; applications of lasers to optical measurements; light scattering and light transmission; fiber optics. *Mailing Add:* 120 Bruce Rd Red Bank NJ 07701

TYOR, MALCOLM PAUL, b New York, NY, Apr 20, 23; m 47; c 4. MEDICINE. *Educ:* Univ Wis, AB, 44; Duke Univ, MD, 46; Am Bd Internal Med, dipl, 57. *Prof Exp:* Intern, Madison Gen Hosp, Univ Wis-Madison, 46-47; resident med, Bowman Gray Sch Med, Wake Forest Col, 49-51, fel gastroenterol, 51-52; clinician, Med Div, Oak Ridge Inst Nuclear Studies, 52-54; physician, pvt pract, 54-55; assoc, 55-57, from asst prof to assoc prof, 57-62, PROF MED, MED SCH, DUKE UNIV, 62-, CHIEF DIV GASTROENTEROL, MED CTR, 65- *Concurrent Pos:* Asst chief med serv & chief radioisotope serv & gastroenterol, Vet Admin Hosp, Durham, 55- *Mem:* AAAS; AMA; Am Gastroenterol Asn; Am Fedn Clin Res; Am Soc Clin Invest. *Res:* Gastroenterology. *Mailing Add:* Div of Gastroenterol Duke Univ Med Ctr Durham NC 27710

TYRAS, GEORGE, b Czestochowa, Poland, Nov 26, 20; US citizen; m 52; c 2. APPLIED PHYSICS, ELECTRICAL ENGINEERING. *Educ:* Newark Col Eng, BS, 54; Univ Wash, MS, 57, PhD(elec eng, physics, math), 62. *Prof Exp:* Res specialist electromagnetic wave propagation, Aerospace Div, Boeing Co, 54-62; assoc prof elec eng, Univ Ariz, 62-67; PROF ELEC ENG, UNIV HOUSTON, 67- *Mem:* Inst Elec & Electronics Engrs. *Res:* Electromagnetic wave propagation and diffraction; physical optics; partial coherence; optics of anisotropic crystals; thin films. *Mailing Add:* 10827 Briar Forrest Houston TX 77042

TYREE, SHEPPARD YOUNG, JR, b Richmond, Va, July 4, 20; m 43; c 5. INORGANIC CHEMISTRY. *Educ:* Mass Inst Technol, BS, 42, PhD(inorg chem), 46. *Prof Exp:* From asst to instr chem, Off Sci Res & Develop, Mass Inst Technol, 42-46; from asst prof to assoc prof, 46-57, prof, Univ NC, 57-66; chmn dept, 68-73, PROF CHEM, COL WILLIAM & MARY, 66- *Concurrent Pos:* Lectr, Morehead Planetarium, 51-52; vis prof, NC Col Durham, 52 & Puerto Rico, 63; sci off, US Off Naval Res, 54-55, liaison scientist, London, 65-66; chmn, Gordon Res Conf Inorg Chem, 57. *Honors & Awards:* Herty Medal, Am Chem Soc, 64- *Mem:* Fel AAAS; Am Chem Soc; Royal Soc Chem. *Res:* Metal halides; solution chemistry of inorganic ions. *Mailing Add:* Dept of Chem Col of William & Mary Williamsburg VA 23185

TYRER, HARRY WAKELEY, b Palmira, Colombia, Sept 20, 42; US citizen; m 68; c 3. ELECTRICAL ENGINEERING, BIOLOGY. *Educ:* Univ Miami, BSEE, 65; Duke Univ, MS, 69, PhD(elec eng), 72. *Prof Exp:* Asst prof elec eng, NC A&T Univ, 71-72; res & teaching assoc, Duke Univ, 67-72; instrumentation engr, Becton Dickinson Res Ctr, 73-76, prin investr automated cytol, 76-79; DIR, BIOMED ENG & BIOPHYS, CANCER RES CTR, 79-; ASSOC PROF, DEPT ELEC ENG, UNIV MO, COLUMBIA, 79- *Concurrent Pos:* Adj lectr, Sch Med, Johns Hopkins Univ, 78- *Mem:* Inst Elec & Electronics Engrs; Am Soc Cytol; Soc Anal Cytol; NY Acad Sci. *Res:* Flow systems, applications and development; high resolution image analysis and processing; acoustic imaging. *Mailing Add:* PO Box 1268 Columbia MO 65205

TYREY, LEE, b Chicago, Ill, Oct 26, 37; m 61; c 3. NEUROENDOCRINOLOGY, PHYSIOLOGY. *Educ:* Univ Ill, Urbana, BSc, 63, MSc, 64, PhD(physiol), 69. *Prof Exp:* Assoc, 70-72, ASST PROF ANAT & ASSOC PROF OBSTET & GYNEC, MED CTR, DUKE UNIV, 76-, DIR OBSTET-GYNEC ENDOCRINE LAB, 70- *Concurrent Pos:* NIH res fel, Med Ctr, Duke Univ, 69-70, Duke Endowment res grant, 71-73, Pop Coun res grant, 74-76; NC United Community Serv grant, 75-76. *Res:* Neural control of gonadotropin secretion; effects of drugs of abuse on reproductive function; radioimmunoassay of protein hormones. *Mailing Add:* Dept of Obstet-Gynec Duke Univ Med Ctr Box 3244 Durham NC 27710

TYRL, RONALD JAY, b Lawton, Okla, June 16, 43; m 65; c 3. PLANT TAXONOMY. *Educ:* Park Col, BA, 64; Ore State Univ, MS, 67, PhD(syst bot), 69. *Prof Exp:* Herbarium asst taxon, Ore State Univ, 65-69; asst prof biol, Park Col, 70-72; asst prof, 72-77, ASSOC PROF BOT & CURATOR HERBARIUM, OKLA STATE UNIV, 77- *Mem:* Am Soc Plant Taxon. *Res:* Plant biosystematics; evolutionary mechanisms; cytogenetic patterns. *Mailing Add:* Sch Biol Sci Okla State Univ Stillwater OK 74074

TYRRELL, DAVID, b Doncaster, Gt Brit, Aug 4, 40; m 65. BIOCHEMISTRY. *Educ:* Univ Birmingham, BSc, 61; Imp Col, dipl & Univ London, PhD(biochem), 64. *Prof Exp:* Demonstr biochem, Imp Col, Univ London, 61-64; RES SCIENTIST, FOREST PEST MGT INST, 64- *Mem:* Soc Invertebrate Path; Am Soc Microbiol. *Res:* Fungal biochemistry and physiology; fungal pathogens of insects. *Mailing Add:* Forest Pest Mgr Inst PO Box 490 Sault Ste Marie ON P6A 5M7 Can

TYRRELL, ELIZABETH ANN, b Pittsfield, Mass, Oct 16, 31. MICROBIOLOGY. *Educ:* Simmons Col, BS, 53; Univ Mich, MS, 56, PhD(bact), 62. *Prof Exp:* Res asst virol, Parke, Davis & Co, Mich, 53-55; from inst to asst prof, 60-71, assoc prof microbiol, 71-79, PROF BIOL SCI, SMITH COL, 79- *Mem:* AAAS; Am Soc Microbiol. *Res:* Concentrated culture of microorganisms; autolysis in bacteria. *Mailing Add:* Clark Sci Ctr Smith Col Northampton MA 01063

TYRRELL, HENRY FLANSBURG, b Gloversville, NY, Aug 4, 37; m 69. NUTRITION, BIOMETRY. *Educ:* Iowa State Univ, BS, 59; Cornell Univ, MS, 64, PhD(nutrit), 66. *Prof Exp:* Asst prof animal sci, Cornell Univ, 66-69; res dairy husbandman, Energy Metab Lab, Animal Husb Res Div, Agr Res Serv, USDA, 69-72, RES ANIMAL SCIENTIST, RUMINANT NUTRIT LAB, NUTRIT INST, 72- *Mem:* Am Dairy Sci Asn; Am Soc Animal Sci. *Res:* Utilization of energy by domestic animals; nitrogen utilization by ruminant animals; energy requirements for growthl lactation in cattle. *Mailing Add:* Ruminant Nutrit Lab Nutrit Inst Agr Res Ctr Beltsville MD 20705

TYRRELL, JAMES, b Kilsyth, Scotland, Apr 19, 38; m 80; c 1. THEORETICAL CHEMISTRY. *Educ:* Univ Glasgow, BS, 60, PhD(chem), 63. *Prof Exp:* Teaching fel chem, McMaster Univ, 63-65; fel, Div Pure Physics, Nat Res Coun, 65-67; from asst prof to assoc prof, 67-80, actg chmn, 80-81, PROF CHEM, SOUTHERN ILL UNIV, 80- *Mem:* Am Chem Soc. *Res:* Theoretical calculations on atoms and molecules with particular application to transition metal systems and to the study of internal rotation. *Mailing Add:* Dept of Chem Southern Ill Univ Carbondale IL 62901

TYRRELL, WARREN AYRES, b St Louis, Mo, Oct 2, 14; m 38; c 2. PHYSICS, ENGINEERING. *Educ:* Yale Univ, BS, 35, PhD(physics), 39. *Prof Exp:* Mem tech staff, Bell Tel Labs, 39-52, tel instrument engr, 52-56, head underwater acoustics res dept, 56-65, tech rels mgr, 65-70, exec mgr, 70-72, exec dir tech rels div, 72-76, exec dir tech rels & info systs div, 76-79; RETIRED. *Concurrent Pos:* Consult & lectr, 79- *Mem:* AAAS; Accoustical Soc Am; Inst Elec & Electronics Engrs. *Res:* Acoustics and underwater sound; optics; microwave radio; systems engineering; research and development administration in communications; training of research and development management personnel. *Mailing Add:* Young's Rd New Vernon NJ 07976

TYRRELL, WILLIS W, JR, b Mobile, Ala, Feb 12, 30; m 52; c 4. GEOLOGY. *Educ:* Fla State Univ, BS, 52; Yale Univ, MS, 54, PhD(geol), 57. *Prof Exp:* Asst, Fla State Univ, 52-53; field asst, Texaco, 54; geologist, Pan Am Petrol Corp, 55-64, res group supvr, 64-68, sr staff geologist, Amoco Prod Co, New Orleans, La, 68-73, geol assoc, 73-77, STAFF GEOL ASSOC, INT AMOCO PROD CO, HOUSTON, TEX, 77- *Mem:* Geol Soc Am; Am Asn Petrol Geol; Soc Econ Paleont & Mineral. *Res:* Stratigraphy; petroleum exploration; sedimentary petrology; carbonate petrology. *Mailing Add:* Box 4381 Int Amoco Prod Co Chicago IL 60680

TYSON, BRUCE CARROLL, JR, b Greenville, NC, Aug 17, 36. ANALYTICAL CHEMISTRY. *Educ:* Duke Univ, BS, 58; Princeton Univ, MA, 60; Univ Del, PhD(anal chem), 69. *Prof Exp:* Res chemist, US Army Edgewood Arsenal, Md, 63-67; res assoc anal chem, 68-75, DIR ANAL RES, A H ROBINS CO, 75- *Mem:* Am Chem Soc. *Res:* Drug purity evaluation; identification of trace impurities; polarography; thermometric titrations. *Mailing Add:* A H Robins Co 1211 Sherwood Ave Richmond VA 23220

TYSON, GRETA E, b Medford, Mass, Nov 2, 33. ZOOLOGY. *Educ:* State Teachers Col Bridgewater, BS, 55; Univ NH, MS, 57; Univ Calif, Berkeley, PhD(zool), 67. *Prof Exp:* NIH fel biol struct, Univ Wash, 67-69, NIH fel path, 69-70, instr, 70-72; asst prof, Univ Md, Baltimore, 72-76; assoc prof, 76-80, PROF, MISS STATE UNIV, 80-, HEAD, ELECTRON MICROSCOPE CTR, 76- *Mem:* Am Asn Anat; Am Soc Cell Biol; Am Soc Zool; Am Micros Soc; Electron Micros Soc Am. *Res:* Comparative renal morphology; structure and function of microtubules and microfilaments; ultrastructure of crustacean sense organs. *Mailing Add:* Electron Microscope Ctr Miss State Univ Mississippi State MS 39762

TYSON, J ANTHONY, b Pasadena, Calif, Apr 5, 40. ASTRONOMY. *Educ:* Stanford Univ, BS, 62; Univ Wis, MS, 64, PhD(physics), 67. *Prof Exp:* Nat Res Coun-Air Force Off Sci Res fel, Univ Chicago, 67-68; vis lectr physics, Sussex Univ & Hebrew Univ, Jerusalem, 68-69; MEM TECH STAFF, BELL LABS, 69- *Mem:* Am Astron Soc; Am Phys Soc; AAAS; fel Royal Astron Soc. *Res:* Optical astronomy; astrophysics; experimental gravitation and relativity; gravitational radiation; radio astronomy. *Mailing Add:* Bell Labs Murray Hill NJ 07974

TYSON, JOHN EDWARD ALFRED, b Hamilton, Ont, May 27, 35; c 3. REPRODUCTIVE ENDOCRINOLOGY. *Educ:* Univ Western Ont, MD, 56 & 60; Am Bd Obstet & Gynec, dipl, 72 & 79. *Prof Exp:* Fel gynec & obstet, Sch Med, Johns Hopkins Univ, 66-68, instr, 68-69, asst prof, 69-71, assoc prof, 71-78; PROF & CHMN, UNIV MANITOBA, 78-, OBSTET & GYNEC CHIEF, 78-, PROF PHYSIOL, 79- *Concurrent Pos:* Mem med adv bd, Planned Parenthood Md, 70-78; chmn, Comt Int Reference Prep Placental Lactogen 69; ed-in-chief, Current Topics Obstet & Gynec, 72-78; mem, Adv Bd Educ TV, Md State Bd Educ, 67-69, Am Asn Planned Parenthood Physicians, 69-71, Nat Primate Cent Comt, Ottawa, 78-, Fertil & Maternal Clin Trials, Med Res Coun, Can, 80-; consult, Planned Parenthood Md, 67-78, reprod, Nat Zoo, Smithsonian Inst, 74-78, res, Agency Int Develop, US Dept State, 74-78, Prog Pub Health Educ, Can Broadcasting Corp, 76-79, field consult, Inst Nutrit Cent Am & Panama, 77-78, Nat Heart, Lung & Blood Inst, NIH, 78- *Mem:* Fel Am Col Obstetricians & Gynecologists; Am Diabetes Asn; Soc Gynec Invest; Endocrin Soc; Perinatal Res Soc. *Res:* Reproductive endocrinology, principally in those areas having to do with gestational diabetes, infertility, endocrinology of breastfeeding and neuroendocrinology of reproduction and prolactin physiology. *Mailing Add:* Dept Obstet Gynec Reprod Sci Univ Manitoba 59 Emily St Winnipeg MB R3E 0W3 Can

TYSON, JOHN JEANES, b Abington, Pa, Dec 12, 47; m 69; c 3. THEORETICAL BIOLOGY, CELL BIOLOGY. *Educ:* Wheaton Col, BS, 69; Univ Chicago, PhD(chem physics), 73. *Prof Exp:* NATO fel theoret biol, Max Planck Inst Biophys Chem, 73-74; asst prof math, State Univ NY, Buffalo, 74-75; Nat Cancer Inst fel cell biol, Inst Biochem & Cancer Res, Univ Innsbruck, 76-77; ASST PROF BIOL, VA POLYTECH INST & STATE UNIV, 78- *Concurrent Pos:* Co-investr, NSF grant, 75-77, prin investr, 80-83; prin investr, NIH grant, 80- *Res:* Control of cell cycle events; chemical oscillations and traveling waves. *Mailing Add:* Dept of Biol Va Polytech Inst & State Univ Blacksburg VA 24061

TYSON, RALPH ROBERT, b Philadelphia, Pa, Dec 14, 20; m 45; c 3. SURGERY. *Educ:* Dartmouth Col, AB, 41; Univ Pa, MD, 44; Am Bd Surg, dipl, 52; Pan-Am Med Asn, dipl. *Prof Exp:* From instr to assoc prof surg, 52-62, chief sect vascular surg, 62-73, PROF SURG, SCH MED, TEMPLE UNIV, 62-, CHMN DEPT & DIV, 73- *Concurrent Pos:* Assoc surgeon, St Christopher's Hosp, Philadelphia; consult surg, Chestnut Hill Hosp, Philadelphia & Wilkes Barre Vet Admin Hosp; mem Nat Bd Med Exam. *Mem:* AMA; fel Am Col Surg; NY Acad Sci; Am Fedn Clin Res; Int Cardiovasc Soc. *Mailing Add:* Dept of Surg Temple Univ Sch of Med Philadelphia PA 19140

TYSON, WILLIAM RUSSELL, b Bourlamaque, Que, Sept 5, 39; m 73; c 3. MATERIALS SCIENCE. *Educ:* Univ Toronto, BASc, 61; Cambridge Univ, PhD(metall), 65. *Prof Exp:* Fel metall, Univ Toronto, 66-67; fac mem physics, Trent Univ, 67-73; res scientist mat sci, 73-80, HEAD ENG METAL PHYS SECT, PMRL CANMET, 80- *Mem:* Am Inst Mining & Metall; Am Soc Metals; Can Inst Mining & Metall. *Res:* Hydrogen in metals; fracture mechanics. *Mailing Add:* PMRL Canmet 568 Booth St Ottawa ON K1A 0G1 Can

TYSVER, JOSEPH BRYCE, b Hazen, NDak, Mar 2, 18; m 45; c 1. APPLIED STATISTICS, OPERATIONS RESEARCH. *Educ:* Wash State Univ, BA, 42, MA, 48; Univ Mich, PhD(statist), 57. *Prof Exp:* Assoc res engr, Eng Res Inst, Univ Mich, 51-57; res specialist, Boeing Airplane Co, 57-63; statistician, Stanford Res Inst, 63-67; ASSOC PROF STATIST, NAVAL POSTGRAD SCH, 67-, ASSOC PROF OPER RES, 73- *Concurrent Pos:* Statistician, Litton Sci Support Lab, 68. *Mem:* Inst Math Statist; Am Math Soc; Math Asn Am; Inst Indust & Appl Math. *Res:* Statistical applications for engineering and military systems; sensitivity testing. *Mailing Add:* Dept Opers Res & Admin Sci Naval Postgrad Sch Monterey CA 93940

TYZNIK, WILLIAM JOHN, b Milwaukee, Wis, Apr 26, 27; m 50; c 5. ANIMAL NUTRITION. *Educ:* Univ Wis, BS, 48, MS, 49, PhD(nutrit), 51. *Prof Exp:* Asst nutrit, Univ Wis, 48-51; from asst prof to assoc prof animal nutrit, 51-59, PROF ANIMAL SCI & VET PREV MED, OHIO STATE UNIV, 59- *Mem:* Am Soc Animal Sci; Am Dairy Sci Asn. *Res:* Ruminant and monogastric nutrition; digestive physiology of equines and nutrition of zoological animals. *Mailing Add:* Dept of Animal Sci Ohio State Univ Columbus OH 43210

TZAGOURNIS, MANUEL, b Youngstown, Ohio, Oct 20, 34; m 58; c 5. MEDICINE, ENDOCRINOLOGY. *Educ:* Ohio State Univ, BS, 56, MD, 60, MMS, 65. *Prof Exp:* Intern med, Philadelphia Gen Hosp, Pa, 60-61; resident internal med, Univ Hosp, 61-62 & 64-65, chief resident internal med, 66-67, asst prof med, Col Med, 67-70, assoc prof med, 70-74, assoc dean, 75-76, PROF MED, COL MED, OHIO STATE UNIV, 74-, ASST DEAN RES & CONTINUING MED EDUC, 76- *Concurrent Pos:* USPHS fel endocrinol & metab, Ohio State Univ Hosp, 65-66. *Mem:* Am Fedn Clin Res; Am Diabetes Asn; AMA. *Res:* Diabetes, glucose metabolism and insulin secretion, especially as they relate to lipid disorders and coronary atherosclerosis. *Mailing Add:* Ohio State Univ Hosp Columbus OH 43210

TZANAKOU, M EVANGELIA, b Athens, Greece. NEUROPHYSIOLOGY, CYBERNETICS. *Educ:* Univ Athens, BS, 68; Syracuse Univ, MS, 74, PhD(physics), 77. *Prof Exp:* Fel biophysics, Physics Dept, Syracuse Univ, 77-80; ASST PROF BIOMED ENG, DEPT ELEC ENG, RUTGERS UNIV, 81- *Concurrent Pos:* Consult, Eye Defect & Vision Res Found, 78-80, biophysics, Syracuse Univ, 80-81. *Mem:* Soc Neurosci; Asn Res Vision & Opthalmol; Biophys Soc; Sigma Xi; Inst Elec & Electronic Engrs. *Res:* Information processing in the visual system is examined in the computer controlled techniques; recordings are done both in animals and in humans with a response feedback method where the information flow is reversed and a feature extractor becomes a feature generator. *Mailing Add:* Dept Elec Eng Rutgers Univ PO Box 909 Piscataway NJ 08854

TZENG, CHU, b Tainan, Taiwan, Sept 19, 40; US citizen; m 69; c 2. FOOD SCIENCE & TECHNOLOGY, BIOCHEMICAL ENGINEERING. *Educ:* Nat Taiwan Univ, BS, 63, MS, 66; Mass Inst Technol, ScD(food sci & technol), 72. *Prof Exp:* Res assoc biochem eng, Mass Inst Technol, 73-74; dir res & develop food indust, Milbrew Inc, 74-80; DIR FERMENTATION TECHNOL, ABCOR INC, 80- *Mem:* Inst Food Technologists; Am Chem Soc; Am Soc Microbiol; Am Inst Chem Engrs; Soc Indust Microbiol. *Res:* Fermentation engineering and fermentor design; recovery processes of yeast and alcohol fermentation technology; functional properties of food ingredients. *Mailing Add:* Abcor Inc 850 Main St Wilmington MA 01887

TZENG, KENNETH KAI-MING, b Kaifeng, China, Aug 6, 37; m 61; c 2. ELECTRICAL ENGINEERING, COMPUTER SCIENCES. *Educ:* Nat Taiwan Univ, BS, 59; Univ Ill, MS, 62, PhD(elec eng), 69. *Prof Exp:* Jr engr, IBM Corp, 62-63; elec res engr, Nat Cash Register Co, 63-65; from asst prof to assoc prof elec eng, 69-77, PROF ELEC ENG, LEHIGH UNIV, 77- *Concurrent Pos:* NSF res initiation grant, 70-71, res grants, 73-79; instr, In-Hour Continuing Educ Prog, Bell Labs, 72-80, consult, 80-81. *Mem:* Inst Elec & Electronics Engrs. *Res:* Error control in digital computing and communication systems; computer networks. *Mailing Add:* Dept Elec & Comput Eng Lehigh Univ Packard Lab Bldg 19 Bethlehem PA 18015

TZENG, WEN-SHIAN VINCENT, b Taipei, Taiwan, May 7, 43; m 72; c 2. METALLURGICAL ENGINEERING. *Educ:* Cheng Kung Univ, Taiwan, BSE, 66; Univ Conn, PhD(metall), 75. *Prof Exp:* Sr res scientist, Firestone Tire & Rubber Co, 75-80; METALLURGIST RES & DEVELOP, CHOMERICS, INC, 80- *Mem:* Am Soc Metals; Am Vacuum Soc; Electron Micros Am; Am Powder Metall Inst; Microbeam Anal Soc. *Res:* Metal powder surface chemistry and physics for electrical conductive behavior and their industrial application; electron microscopy; surface analysis; elastomer compounding and testing. *Mailing Add:* 54 Eastway Reading MA 01867

TZIANABOS, THEODORE, b Manchester, NH, Feb 12, 33. VIROLOGY. *Educ:* Univ NH, BA, 55, MS, 59; Univ Mass, PhD(microbiol), 65; Am Bd Med Microbiol, dipl. *Prof Exp:* Res instr microbiol, Dept Poultry Dis, Univ NH, 55-57; microbiologist, Diagnostic Virol, State Mass, 59-60; res instr microbiol, Dept Vet Sci, Univ Mass, 60-65; resident, Ctr Dis Control, 65-67; res microbiologist, Med Sci Div, Ft Detrick, 67-70; microbiologist, Beckman Instruments, 70-71; RES MICROBIOLOGIST VIROL, CTR DIS CONTROL, 71- *Concurrent Pos:* Mem bd trustees, Am Type Cult Collection, Rockville, Md, 78-82. *Mem:* Am Soc Microbiologists; Am Soc Trop Med & Hyg; Res Soc Am; Am Soc Rickettsiology. *Res:* Development and research on rickettsial products involving serologic tests, including fluorescent microscopy; purification and protein composition of rickettsiae. *Mailing Add:* 6959 Lockridge Dr Doraville GA 30360

TZODIKOV, NATHAN ROBERT, b Brooklyn, NY, Feb 28, 52. BIORGANIC CHEMISTRY, RADIOCHEMISTRY. *Educ:* State Univ NY, Stony Brook, BS, 73; Mass Inst Technol, PhD(org chem), 77. *Prof Exp:* Sr chemist lubricants, Texaco Inc, 77-78; chemist radiochem res, 78-80, GROUP LEADER RADIOCHEM RES, NEW ENGLAND NUCLEAR, 80- *Mem:* AAAS; Am Chem Soc. *Res:* Organic synthesis; radiochemical research; radiochemical synthesis. *Mailing Add:* New England Nuclear 549 Albany St Boston MA 02118

U

U, RAYMOND, genetics, radiobiology, see previous edition

UBELAKER, DOUGLAS HENRY, b Horton, Kans, Aug 23, 46; m 75. PHYSICAL ANTHROPOLOGY. *Educ:* Univ Kans, Lawrence, BA, 68, PhD(anthrop), 73. *Prof Exp:* CUR PHYS ANTHROP & CHMN, DEPT ANTHROP, SMITHSONIAN INST, 73- *Mem:* AAAS; Am Asn Phys Anthrop; Am Anthrop Asn; Am Acad Forensic Sci; Soc Am Archaeol. *Res:* Physical anthropology of North America, Latin America; skeletal biology; prehistoric demography; forensic anthropology. *Mailing Add:* Nat Mus of Natural Hist Smithsonian Inst Washington DC 20560

UBELAKER, JOHN E, b Everest, Kans, Mar 21, 40. PARASITOLOGY. *Educ:* Univ Kans, BA, 62, MA, 65, PhD(zool), 67. *Prof Exp:* Fel parasitol, Emory Univ, 67-68; asst prof biol, 68-71, assoc prof, 71-74, PROF BIOL, SOUTHERN METHODIST UNIV, 74- *Mem:* Am Soc Parasitol; Am Soc Zool; Am Micros Soc; Wildlife Dis Asn. *Res:* Helminthology; transmission, scanning electron microscopy; helminth reproduction; pathophysiology of lungworm infections. *Mailing Add:* Dept of Biol Southern Methodist Univ Dallas TX 75275

UBEROI, M(AHINDER) S(INGH), b Delhi, India, Mar 13, 24; nat US. AERONAUTICAL ENGINEERING, ASTRONAUTICS. *Educ:* Punjab Univ, India, BSc, 44; Calif Inst Technol, MS, 46; Johns Hopkins Univ, DEng, 52. *Prof Exp:* Res asst aeronaut eng, Johns Hopkins Univ, 52-53; res assoc aerospace eng, Univ Mich, 53-56, from assoc prof to prof, 56-63; chmn dept aerospace eng sci, 63-77, PROF AEROSPACE ENG SCI & FEL, JOINT INST LAB ASTROPHYS, UNIV COLO, BOULDER, 63- *Concurrent Pos:* Guggenheim fel, 58-59. *Mem:* Am Inst Aeronaut & Astronaut; Am Phys Soc; Am Soc Eng Educ. *Res:* Turbulent flows; statistical analysis of random functions; magnetohydrodynamics; aerothermodynamics. *Mailing Add:* Dept of Aerospace Eng Sci Univ of Colo Boulder CO 80309

UCCI, POMPELIO ANGELO, b Warwick, RI, Jan 15, 22; m 49; c 4. PHYSICAL CHEMISTRY, MATHEMATICS. *Educ:* Univ RI, BS, 43. *Prof Exp:* Res chemist, Celanese Corp Am, 43-44; 46-52; sr res chemist, 52-54, group leader synthetic fibers, 54-58, sect head, 58-69, site mgr, New Enterprise Div, 69-71, sr res specialist, 71-75, ENG FEL, TEXTILES DIV, MONSANTO CO, 75- *Mem:* AAAS; Am Chem Soc. *Res:* Solution and melt properties of natural and synthetic fiber forming polymers; fundamental mechanical and engineering properties; statistics and quality control; paper making from synthetic fibers; testing equipment and procedures. *Mailing Add:* 4070 Aiken Rd Pensacola FL 32503

UCHIDA, IRENE AYAKO, b Vancouver, BC, Apr 8, 17. CYTOGENETICS. *Educ:* Univ Toronto, PhD(human genetics), 51. *Prof Exp:* Res assoc, Hosp Sick Children, Toronto, Ont, 51-59; proj assoc, Univ Wis, 59-60; lectr pediat, Univ Man, 60-62, from asst prof to assoc prof, 63-69, asst prof anat, 67-69; PROF PEDIAT & PATH & DIR REGIONAL CYTOGENETICS LAB, MED CTR, MCMASTER UNIV, 69- *Concurrent Pos:* Mem, Sci Coun Can & grants comt, Med Res Coun, 70-73; Med Res Coun vis prof, Univ Western Ont, 73; consult, Int Prog Radiation Genetics, Nuclear Energy Agency, Orgn Econ Coop & Develop, Paris, 73 & Am Bd Med Genetics, 80-; mem adv comt genetic serv, Ont Ministry Health, 79- & mem task force high technol diag procedures & equip, Ont Coun Health, 80-; mem, Mental Retardation Comt, Nat Inst Child Health & Human Develop, 80- *Mem:* AAAS; Am Soc Human Genetics (pres, 68); Can Col Med Geneticists; Genetics Soc Can. *Res:* Human genetics; cytogenetics. *Mailing Add:* Dept of Pediat McMaster Univ Hamilton ON L8N 3Z5 Can

UCHIDA, RICHARD NOBORU, b Honolulu, Hawaii, Sept 4, 29; m 55; c 3. MARINE SCIENCES. *Educ:* Univ Wash, Seattle, BS, 51. *Prof Exp:* Fishery res biologist, 54-76, SUPVRY BIOLOGIST, US DEPT OF COM, NOAA, NAT MARINE FISHERIES SERV, SOUTHWEST FISHERIES CTR, HONOLULU LAB, 76- *Concurrent Pos:* Counr, Hawaiian Acad Sci, 75-76. *Mem:* AAAS; Am Fisheries Soc; Am Inst Fishery Res Biol; Smithsonian Inst; Int Oceanog Found. *Res:* Distribution, life history and relative abundance of demersal and pelgic fishes, mollusks, and crustaceans in waters surrounding central and western Pacific islands and overlying seamounts. *Mailing Add:* Nat Marine Fisheries Serv Honolulu Lab PO Box 3830 Honolulu HI 96812

UCHTMAN, VERNON ALBERT, b Cincinnati, Ohio, Oct 18, 41; m 68; c 3. PHYSICAL INORGANIC CHEMISTRY. *Educ:* Univ Cincinnati, BS, 63; Univ Wis-Madison, PhD(inorg chem), 68. *Prof Exp:* RES CHEMIST & SECT HEAD, WINTON HILL TECH CTR, PROCTER & GAMBLE CO, 68- *Mem:* AAAS; Am Chem Soc; Sigma Xi. *Res:* Molecular structure determination; x-ray crystallography; detergency; metal ion binding and control in aqueous solutions; dental research. *Mailing Add:* Winton Hill Tech Ctr Procter & Gamble Co Cincinnati OH 05224

UCHUPI, ELAZAR, b New York, NY, Oct 31, 28. GEOLOGY. *Educ:* City Col New York, BS, 52; Univ Southern Calif, MS, 54, PhD(geol), 62. *Prof Exp:* Res asst geol, Univ Southern Calif, 55-62; res asst 62-64, assoc scientist, 64-79, SR SCIENTIST, WOODS HOLE OCEANOG INST, 79- *Mem:* Geol Soc Am; Am Asn Petrol Geol; Soc Econ Paleont & Mineral; Am Geophys Union. *Res:* Sedimentation; submarine geomorphology; tectonics; geologic development of continental margins. *Mailing Add:* Dept of Geol & Geophys Woods Hole Oceanog Inst Woods Hole MA 02543

UCKO, DAVID A, b New York, NY, July 9, 48; m 72; c 1. INORGANIC CHEMISTRY, BIOINORGANIC CHEMISTRY. *Educ:* Columbia Col, BA, 69; Mass Inst Technol, PhD(chem), 72. *Prof Exp:* Asst prof chem, Hostos Community Col, 72-76; asst prof chem, Antioch Col, 76-79, assoc prof, 79; res coordr, 79-80, SCI DIR, MUS SCI & INDUST, CHICAGO, 81- *Concurrent Pos:* NIH fel, Columbia Univ, 72; fac res fel, Res Found, State Univ NY, 75; adj staff scientist, C F Kettering Res Lab, 78. *Mem:* Am Chem Soc; Sigma Xi; Royal Soc Chem; Am Asn Mus. *Mailing Add:* Mus Sci & Indust 57th St & Lake Shore Dr Chicago IL 60637

UDALL, JOHN ALFRED, b Holbrook, Ariz, Sept 11, 29; m 50; c 3. INTERNAL MEDICINE, CARDIOLOGY. *Educ:* Brigham Young Univ, BS, 51; Temple Univ, MD, 58. *Prof Exp:* Resident internal med & cardiol, Med Ctr, Univ Calif, San Francisco, 59-62; dir med educ, Maricopa County Gen Hosp, Phoenix, Ariz, 62-66; asst prof, 66-69, ASSOC PROF MED & CARDIOL, COL MED, UNIV CALIF, IRVINE, 69- *Concurrent Pos:* Consult cardiovasc dis, Long Beach Vet Admin Hosp, Calif, 66- & Fairview State Hosp Retarded Children, Costa Mesa, 69-; dir med serv, Orange County Med Cyr, Calif, 71- *Mem:* AAAS; fel Am Col Cardiol; fel Am Col Physicians; Am Fedn Clin Res; Asn Hosp Med Educ. *Res:* Pervenous pacemaker electrode endocardial implantation; clinical research in all aspects of oral anticoagulant therapy, especially the problem of the lack of stability of long-term therapy. *Mailing Add:* Dept of Med Univ of Calif Col of Med Irvine CA 92664

UDALL, JOHN NICHOLAS, JR, b Washington, DC, Dec 30, 40; m 67; c 2. MEDICINE, NUTRITIONAL BIOCHEMISTRY. *Educ:* Brigham Young Univ, BSc, 65; Temple Univ, MD, 69; Am Bd Pediat, dipl. *Prof Exp:* Intern med & pediat, Los Angeles County/Univ Southern Calif Med Ctr, 69-70; general med officer, Indian Health Serv, USPHS, 70-72; resident pediat, Los Angeles County/Univ Southern Calif Med Ctr, 72-74; fel pediat nutrit & gastroenterol, Baylor Col Med, 74-76; fel clin nutrit, Mass Inst Technol, Mass Gen Hosp & Children's Hosp Med Ctr, 77-80; ASST DIR, CLIN RES CTR, MASS INST TECHNOL, 80-; ASST PROF PEDIAT, HARVARD MED SCH, 81- *Concurrent Pos:* Nutrit consult eval acceptability & tolerance to purified single cell protein for adult human feeding, Dir, Nevin S Scrinshaw, 77-78; co-pirin investr, NIH grant, 78-80. *Mem:* Fel Am Acad Pediat; fel Am Bd Nutrit; NAM Soc Pediat Gastroenterol. *Res:* Effect of early nutrition on gastrointestinal development; obesity in infancy and childhood; pathophysiology of cholera. *Mailing Add:* 92 Munroe St Belmont MA 02178

UDANI, KANAKKUMAR HARILAL, b Rajkot, India, Dec 4, 36; US citizen; m 66; c 2. FOOD SCIENCE, CHEMICAL ENGINEERING. *Educ:* Gujarat Univ, India, BSc, 57; Univ Bombay, BSc, 59; Univ Ill, Urbana, MS, 61, PhD(food sci), 65. *Prof Exp:* Res fel chem eng, Univ Bombay, 59; supvr qual control, Accent Int, Div Int Minerals & Chem Corp, 61-62; sr food technologist, H J Heinz Co, 65-68; SR SCIENTIST II OIL PROD, RES & DEVELOP DIV, KRAFICO CORP, GLENVIEW, 68- *Mem:* Inst Food Technologists. *Res:* Dehydration of foods; oils, fats and starch technology; aseptic systems; emulsifiers and stabilizers; processed food rheology; flavor science; product, process and market development. *Mailing Add:* Krafico Corp 801 Waukegan Rd Glenview IL 60025

UDANI, LALIT KUMAR HARILAL, b Rajkot, India, Aug 19, 27; US citizen; m 70; c 1. CHEMICAL ENGINEERING. *Educ:* Univ Bombay, BSc, 49; Univ Nagpur, BSc, 52; Univ Mich, Ann Arbor, MSE, 56, DSc(chem eng), 62. *Prof Exp:* Develop engr, Kordite Co, NY, 61-63; specialist process develop, Chem Div, Gen Elec Co, Mass, 63-67; res engr, Org Chem Div, FMC Corp, Md, 67-69; supvry process engr, 69-80, SR PROCESS SPECIALIST, CATALYTIC INC, PHILADELPHIA, 80- *Mem:* Am Chem Soc; Sigma Xi. *Res:* Organic chemicals and polymer process research; water pollution abatement for industrial systems; processes for clean fuels and electrode coke from coal, flue gas desulfurization; corporate planning and business development for synthetic fuels projects. *Mailing Add:* 11 Elbow Lane Cherry Hill NJ 08034

UDD, JOHN EAMAN, b Rochester, NY, June 18, 37; Can citizen; m 70; c 2. ROCK MECHANICS, MINING ENGINEERING. *Educ:* McGill Univ, BEng, 59, MEng, 60, PhD(mining eng), 70. *Prof Exp:* Lectr, 61-64, asst prof, 64-70, ASSOC PROF MINING ENG, MCGILL UNIV, 70-, DIR, MINING PROG, 78- *Mem:* Eng Inst Can; Can Geotech Soc; Can Inst Mining & Metall. *Res:* Applications of methods of stress analysis to mining engineering; studies of stresses in the earth's crust; engineering properties of geological materials; ground control and mine stability. *Mailing Add:* Dept of Mining and Metall Eng McGill Univ 3450 University St Montreal PQ H3A 2A7 Can

UDELHOFEN, JOHN HENRY, petroleum chemistry, see previous edition

UDELSON, DANIEL G(ERALD), b New York, NY, Mar 7, 29; m 67; c 2. AEROSPACE & MECHANICAL ENGINEERING. *Educ:* George Washington Univ, AB, 53; Harvard Univ, AM, 54, PhD, 61. *Prof Exp:* Asst prof aero & mech eng, Col Indust Tech, 60-64, assoc prof, Col Eng, 64-70, PROF, COL ENG, BOSTON UNIV, 70-, CHMN AERODYN MECH ENG, 81- *Concurrent Pos:* Consult, Avco Missile Systs Div, Ctr Nuclear Studies, French Atomic Energy Comn, Urology Dept, Boston Univ Med Sch & Cambridge Air Force Res Labs. *Mem:* Assoc fel Am Inst Aeronaut & Astronaut; Am Soc Eng Educ; Am Soc Mech Engrs. *Res:* Fluid and applied mechanics. *Mailing Add:* 237 Marlborough St Boston MA 02116

UDEM, STEPHEN ALEXANDER, b New York, NY, Apr 4, 44. VIROLOGY, INFECTIOUS DISEASES. *Educ:* City Col New York, BS, 64; Albert Einstein Col Med, PhD(genetics), 71, MD, 72. *Prof Exp:* Intern internal med, Bronx Munic Hosp Complex, 72-73, resident, 73-74; NIH fel infectious dis, Montefiore/Albert Einstein/Jacobi Hosps & Albert Einstein Col Med, 74-76; ASST PROF MED & DEPT CELL BIOL, ALBERT EINSTEIN COL MED, 76- *Concurrent Pos:* Rita Allen Found scholar. *Mem:* Am Soc Microbiol; Infectious Dis Soc. *Res:* Investigation of persistent viral infections and their relationship to the production of chronic disease, particularly chronic neurological and rheumatic diseases. *Mailing Add:* Dept Cell Biol & Dept Med Albert Einstein Col of Med New York NY 10461

UDEN, PETER CHRISTOPHER, b Southampton, Eng, May 19, 39; m 67; c 3. CHROMATOGRAPHY. *Educ:* Bristol Univ, BSc, 61, PhD(chem), 64. *Prof Exp:* Instr chem, Univ Ill, Urbana, 65-66; ICI fel, Univ Birmingham, 66-67, lectr, 67-70; asst prof, 70-72, assoc prof, 79-79, PROF ANAL CHEM, UNIV MASS, AMHERST, 72- *Concurrent Pos:* Mallinckrodt Chem Corp res assoc, Univ Ill, Urbana, 64-66. *Mem:* Am Chem Soc; Royal Soc Chem; Brit Inst Petrol. *Res:* Analytical and inorganic chemistry; separation and thermal methods; gas and liquid chromatography; mass spectrometry; metal complexes. *Mailing Add:* GRC Towers Dept Chem Univ Mass Amherst MA 01003

UDENFRIEND, SIDNEY, b New York, NY, Apr 5, 18; m 43; c 2. BIOCHEMISTRY. *Educ:* City Col New York, BS, 39; NY Univ, MS, 42, PhD(biochem), 48. *Hon Degrees:* DSc, New York Med Col, 74. *Prof Exp:* Lab asst bact, City Dept Health, New York, 40-42; asst chemist, Res Div, NY Univ, 42-45, asst biochem, Col Med, 45-48; instr, Sch Med, Wash Univ, 48-50; chief sect cellular pharmacol, Chem Pharmacol Lab, Nat Heart Inst, 50-56, chief lab clin-biochem, 56-58; DIR, ROCHE INST MOLECULAR BIOL, 68- *Concurrent Pos:* NIH spec fel, St Mary's Hosp Med Sch, Univ London, 57; mem bd trustees, Wistar Inst, 68-71; adj prof dept biochem, City Univ New York, 68-; adj prof dept human genetics & develop, Columbia Univ Col Physicians & Surgeons, 69-; mem panel narcotics, Off Sci & Technol, 72-73; mem sci adv bd, Scripps Clin & Res Found, 74-78 & Inst Cellular & Molecular Path, 74-; mem adv comt to dir, NIH, 76-78; mem adv bd, Weizmann Inst Sci, 78-; mem bd trustees, NY Acad Sci, 78- *Honors & Awards:* Cert merit, Am Med Asn, 56; Flemming Award, 58; superior serv award, Dept Health, Educ & Welfare, 65, distinguished serv award, 66; Van Slyke Award, 67; Gairdner Award, 67; Hillebrand Award, Am Chem Soc, 62; Ames Award, Am Asn Clin Chem, 69; Torald Sollman Award, Am Soc Pharmacol & Exp Therapeut, 75; City of Hope Res Award, 75. *Mem:* Nat Acad Sci; AAAS; Am Chem Soc; Am Soc Biol Chemists; Am Soc Pharmacol & Exp Therapeut(secy, 62-64); Soc Exp Biol & Med. *Res:* Peptide and protein biochemistry; neurochemistry. *Mailing Add:* Roche Inst of Molecular Biol Nutley NJ 07110

UDIN, SUSAN BOYMEL, b Philadelphia, Pa, Aug 11, 47; m 67. DEVELOPMENT NEUROBIOLOGY. *Educ:* Mass Inst Technol, BS, 69, PhD(life sci), 75. *Prof Exp:* Sr staff mem, Nat Inst Med Res, Mill Hill, 78-79; ASST PROF NEUROBIOL, STATE UNIV NY BUFFALO, 79- *Concurrent Pos:* Fel, Psychol Dept, Mass Inst Technol, 75-77, Nat Inst Med Res, Mill Hill, 77-78. *Mem:* AAAS; Soc Neurosci; Sigma Xi; Asn Women Sci. *Res:* Effects of early visual experience on formation of connections in the brain. *Mailing Add:* Div Neurobiol 327 Cary Hall State Univ NY Buffalo NY 14214

UDIPI, KISHORE, b Udipi, SIndia, May 19, 40; m 73; c 1. POLYMER CHEMISTRY. *Educ:* Univ Bombay, BSc Hons, 59, MSc, 63; Univ Akron, PhD(polymer chem), 72. *Prof Exp:* Works mgr paints & polymers, Bombay Paints, India, 63-68; fel, Princeton Univ, 72-73; res chemist polymer chem, Phillips Petrol Co, 73-80; WITH MONSANTO PLASTICS & RESINS, 80- *Mem:* Am Chem Soc; Soc Plastics Engrs. *Res:* Polymer synthesis; study of polymer microstructure and chemical modifications of polymers. *Mailing Add:* Monsanto Plastics & Resins 730 Worchester St Indian Orchard MA 01151

UDOLF, ROY, b New York, NY, Aug 7, 26; m 50; c 4. PSYCHOLOGY, ENGINEERING. *Educ:* NY Univ, BEE, 50, Brooklyn Law Sch JD, 54; Hofstra Univ, MA, 63; Adelphi Univ, PhD(psychol), 71; Am Bd Forensic Psycol, dipl. *Prof Exp:* Test engr, Am Bosch Arma Corp, 56-63; asst dept head eng, Gyrodyne Co Am, 63-67; assoc prof, 67-80, PROF PSYCHOL, HOFSTRA UNIV, 80- *Concurrent Pos:* Human factors consult, Litcom Div, Litton Industs, 71-73. *Mem:* Am Psychol Asn; Am Psychol-Law Soc. *Res:* Human engineering; hypnosis; forensic psychology. *Mailing Add:* Dept of Psychol Hofstra Univ Hempstead NY 11550

UDOVIC, DANIEL, b Cleveland, Ohio, July 9, 47; m 68; c 2. POPULATION BIOLOGY. *Educ:* Univ Tex, Austin, BA, 70; Cornell Univ, PhD(entom), 74. *Prof Exp:* asst prof, 73-81, ASSOC PROF BIOL, UNIV ORE, 81- *Mem:* AAAS; Ecol Soc Am; Soc Study Evolution; Am Soc Naturalists. *Res:* Population biology, with emphasis on mathematical models of coevolution and speciation, plant-insect interactions and evolution of flowering strategies in plants. *Mailing Add:* Dept of Biol Univ of Ore Eugene OR 97403

UDVARDY, MIKLOS DEZSO FERENC, b Debrecen, Hungary, Mar 23, 19; nat US; m 51; c 3. ZOOLOGY. *Educ:* Debrecen Univ, PhD, 42. *Prof Exp:* Asst biologist, Hungarian Inst Ornith, 42-45; res assoc, Biol Res Inst, Hungarian Acad Sci, 45-48; res fel zool, Univ Helsinki, 48-49 & Univ Uppsala, 49-50; asst cur, Swedish Mus Natural Hist, 51; vis lectr ecol, Univ Toronto, 51-52; lectr zool, Univ BC, 52-53, from asst prof to assoc prof, 53-66; PROF BIOL SCI, CALIF STATE UNIV, SACRAMENTO, 66- *Concurrent Pos:* Asst scientist, Fisheries Res Bd Can, 52-55; vis prof, Univ Hawaii, 58-59; vis spec lectr, Univ Calif, Los Angeles, 63-64; vis prof, Univ Bonn, 70-71; Fulbright lectr, Honduras, 71-72; mem, Int Protecting Bd, Biol Sta Wilhelmiberg, Austria & Point Reyes Bird Observ; consult, Int Union Conserv Nature, 80- *Mem:* Am Ornith Union; Ecol Soc Am; Cooper Ornith Soc; Nat Audubon Soc; Wilson Ornith Soc. *Res:* biogeography, especially distributional and ornithology. animal ecology and behavior; ornithology; biology and distribution of. *Mailing Add:* Dept of Biol Sci Calif State Univ Sacramento CA 95819

UDVARHELYI, GEORGE BELA, b Budapest, Hungary, May 14, 20; US citizen; m 56; c 3. NEUROSURGERY. *Educ:* St Stephan Col, Hungary, BA, 38; Pazmany Peter Univ, MD, 44; Univ Buenos Aires, MD, 52. *Prof Exp:* Resident neurol, Univ Budapest Hosp, 44-46; fel, Univ Vienna, 46-47; fel neuropath & psychiat, Univ Berne, 47-48; resident neurosurg, Hosp Espanol, Cordoba, 48-50; resident & surgeon, Univ Buenos Aires, 50-52; registr, Univ Edinburgh, 53-55; from instr neurosurg to asst prof neurosurg & radiol, 56-63, ASSOC PROF RADIOL, SCH MED, JOHNS HOPKINS UNIV, 63-, PROF NEUROSURG, 69- *Concurrent Pos:* WGer fel neurosurg, Univ Cologne, 52-53; Brit Coun scholar, Univ Edinburgh, 53-55; NIH fel neurosurg, Sch Med, Johns Hopkins Univ, 55-56; NIH res fel, 57-58; consult, Baltimore City Hosp, 58-, Danville Hosp, 58-71 & Harrisburg State Hosp, 59-71. *Mem:* AMA; Am Asn Neuropath; Am Asn Neurol Surg; Cong Neurol Surg; Soc Fr Speaking Neurosurgeons. *Res:* Clinical neurosurgery; neuroradiology; cerebral circulation; pediatric neurosurgery; pituitary surgery. *Mailing Add:* Dept of Neurosurg & Radiol Johns Hopkins Hosp Baltimore MD 21205

UEBBING, JOHN JULIAN, b Chicago, Ill, July 7, 37; m 66; c 2. ELECTRICAL ENGINEERING, ELECTRONICS. *Educ:* Univ Notre Dame, BS, 60; Mass Inst Technol, MS, 62; Stanford Univ, PhD(elec eng), 67. *Prof Exp:* Staff engr, Gen Motors Defense Res Labs, 62-63; staff engr surface sci & electron spectros, Varian Assocs, 66-72; staff engr electronics, Electromagnetic Systs Lab, 72-73; develop engr, 73-75, SECT MGR OPTOELECTRONICS, HEWLETT-PACKARD, 75- *Concurrent Pos:* Consult, Stanford Univ, 74-77 & Radio Sci Inc, 75-77. *Mem:* Int Soc Hybrid Microelectronics. *Res:* Light emitting diode products; plastic optics; electron spectroscopy; surface science. *Mailing Add:* 665 Towle Way Palo Alto CA 94306

UEBEL, JACOB JOHN, b Chicago, Ill, Dec 25, 37; m 58; c 3. ORGANIC CHEMISTRY. *Educ:* Carthage Col, BA, 59; Univ Ill, MA, 62, PhD(chem), 64. *Prof Exp:* Res assoc, Univ Mich, 64; from asst prof to assoc prof, Univ NH, 64-73, prof org chem, 73-80; RES SCIENTIST, EASTMAN KODAK CO, ROCHESTER, NY, 80- *Concurrent Pos:* Vis prof, Univ Calif-Riverside, 71-72; vis scientist, Eastman Kodak Co, Rochester, NY & NSF sci fac fel, 78-79. *Mem:* Am Chem Soc; Sigma Xi. *Res:* Organic magnetic resonance and conformational analysis. *Mailing Add:* 5 Landmark Lane Pittsford NY 14534

UEBELE, CURTIS EUGENE, b Kenosha Co, Wis, Dec 3, 35; m 58; c 6. POLYMER CHEMISTRY. *Educ:* Carroll Col, Wis, BS, 58; Univ Kans, PhD(chem), 65. *Prof Exp:* Proj leader, 65-75, res assoc, 75, SUPVR POLYMER RES, STANDARD OIL CO OHIO, CLEVELAND, 78- *Mem:* Am Chem Soc. *Res:* Formulation and evaluation of polyvinyl and polyolefin resins. *Mailing Add:* 128 Eldred Ave Bedford OH 44146

UEBERSAX, MARK ALAN, b Baltimore, Md, Feb 13, 48; m 74. AGRICULTURE, FOOD SCIENCE. *Educ:* Delaware Valley Col, BS, 70; Mich State Univ, MS, 72, PhD(food sci), 77. *Prof Exp:* Food scientist prod develop, R T French Co, 73; MEM FAC, DEPT FOOD SCI & HUMAN NUTRIT, MICH STATE UNIV, 77- *Mem:* Inst Food Technologists; Am Soc Hort Sci; Am Asn Cereal Chemists; Sigma Xi. *Res:* Chemical and physical evaluation of processed fruits and vegetables; evaluation of processing techniques on nutrient retention, yield and overall quality of processed foods. *Mailing Add:* Dept of Food Sci & Human Nutrit Mich State Univ East Lansing MI 48824

UECKER, FRANCIS AUGUST, b Ft Wayne, Ind, Dec 18, 30; m 61; c 4. MYCOLOGY. *Educ:* Quincy Col, BS, 56; Univ Ill, Urbana, MS, 59, PhD(bot), 62. *Prof Exp:* Asst prof bot, Univ Ill, Urbana, 62-63, biologist, 63; asst prof, Winona State Col, 63-65; RES MYCOLOGIST, AGR RES CTR, PLANT PROTECTION INST, USDA, 65- *Mem:* AAAS; Mycol Soc Am. *Res:* Cytology and cytotaxonomy of fungi, especially Tuberales and pyrenomycetes. *Mailing Add:* 4611 Barbara Dr Beltsville MD 20705

UECKERT, DARRELL NEAL, range ecology, insect ecology, see previous edition

UEDA, CLARENCE TAD, b Kansas City, Mo, July 6, 42; m 71; c 2. PHARMACOKINETICS, BIOPHARMACEUTICS. *Educ:* Contra Costa Col, AA, 63; Univ Calif, San Francisco, PharmD, 67, PhD(bipharmaceut), 74. *Prof Exp:* Asst prof biopharmaceut & pharmacokinetics, 74-77, CHMN DEPT PHARMACEUT & DIR CLIN PHARMACOKINETICS, CARDIOVASC CTR, UNIV NEBR, 76-, ASSOC PROF PHARMACEUT, 77- *Concurrent Pos:* Consult, Sandoz Ltd, 82- *Mem:* Am Pharmaceut Asn; Acad Pharmaceut Sci; Am Soc Clin Pharmacol & Therapeut; Am Col Clin Pharmacol; AAAS. *Res:* Intestinal lymphatic drug absorption; pharmacokinetics of cardiovascular drugs; placental drug transfer pharmacokinetics; in vitro and in vivo forcasting of drug pharmacokinetics. *Mailing Add:* Dept Pharmaceut Med Ctr Univ Nebr 42nd & Dewey Ave Omaha NE 68105

UEHARA, HIROSHI, b Kobe City, Japan, Mar 7, 23; m 47; c 2. MATHEMATICS. *Educ:* Univ Tokyo, MS, 49; Osaka Univ, DSc, 54. *Prof Exp:* Instr math, Nagoya Univ, 49-51; asst prof, Math Inst, Kyushu Univ, 53-56; prof, Univ of the Andes & Nat Univ Colombia, 56-58; asst prof, Univ Southern Calif, 58-60; assoc prof, Univ Iowa, 60-64; PROF MATH, OKLA STATE UNIV, 64- *Concurrent Pos:* Lectr, Nat Univ Mex, 58. *Mem:* Am Math Soc; Math Soc France; Math Soc Japan. *Res:* Algebraic topology. *Mailing Add:* Dept of Math Okla State Univ Stillwater OK 74074

UELAND, KENT, b Chicago, Ill, May 27, 31; m 54; c 4. OBSTETRICS & GYNECOLOGY. *Educ:* Carleton Col, BA, 53; Univ Ill, BS & MD, 57; Am Bd Obstet & Gynec, dipl, 67. *Prof Exp:* Intern, Med Sch, Univ Ore, 57-58; asst resident obstet & gynec, King County & Univ Hosps, 60-61; from asst instr to prof obstet & gynec, Univ Wash, 61-77, dir obstet, Univ Hosp, 68-77; PROF OBSTET & GYNEC & CHIEF MATERNAL FETAL MED, STANFORD UNIV, 77- *Concurrent Pos:* Res fel cardiovasc res, Univ Wash, 63; res fel med, Univ Ore, 63-64; resident, King County & Univ Hosps, 61-62, chief resident, 63; consult, Santa Clara Valley Med Ctr, San Jose, Calif, Naval Regional Med Ctr, Oakland, Calif, Childbirth Educ Asn & Nat Found March of Dimes. *Mem:* Perinatal Res Soc; Soc Obstet, Anesthesia & Perinatal; Am Col Obstet & Gynec; Soc Gynec Invest. *Res:* Pregnancy and cardiovascular dynamics; toxemia of pregnancy; control of labor; pregnancy and heart disease. *Mailing Add:* Dept of Gynec & Obstet Stanford Univ Stanford CA 94305

UELTZ, HERBERT FRANK, b Morristown, NJ, Dec 14, 20. HIGH TEMPERATURE CHEMISTRY. *Educ:* Rutgers Univ, BS, 42, MS, 43, PhD(ceramics), 49. *Prof Exp:* Res assoc ceramics, Rutgers Univ, 46-49; res assoc, Norton Co, 49-62; dir res, Gen Abrasive Co, 62-71, vpres res & develop, 71-79; CONSULT, 79- *Honors & Awards:* Dresser Award for Innovation. *Mem:* Fel Am Inst Chem; NY Acad Sci; AAAS. *Res:* Abrasive and refractory substances. *Mailing Add:* 140 William St Youngstown NY 14174

UENG, CHARLES E(N) S(HIUH), b Kiangtu, Kiangsu, China, Sept 8, 30; m 62; c 2. SOLID MECHANICS. *Educ:* Cheng Kung Univ, BS, 53; Kans State Univ, MS, 60, PhD(appl mech), 63. *Prof Exp:* Struct engr, Taiwan Power Co, China, 53-58; res assoc appl mech, Kans State Univ, 62-63, asst prof, 63-64; asst prof & assoc prof, 64-77, PROF ENG MECH, GA INST TECHNOL, 77- *Concurrent Pos:* Consult, Reliance Elec Co, Westinghouse Elec Corp, Combustion Eng, Inc, Electro-Mech Co, Victoreen Instruments & Wolfe & Mann Mfg Co; res grants, NASA & NSF. *Mem:* Am Soc Civil Engrs; Am Acad Mech; Soc Eng Sci; Am Soc Eng Educ. *Res:* Composite structures; vibration; elastic stability; variational principles; earthquake engineering. *Mailing Add:* Sch of Eng Sci & Mech Ga Inst of Technol Atlanta GA 30332

UETZ, GEORGE WILLIAM, b Philadelphia, Pa, Dec 8, 46. ZOOLOGY, ECOLOGY. *Educ:* Albion Col, BA, 68; Univ Del, MS, 70; Univ Ill, PhD(ecol), 76. *Prof Exp:* Res asst entom, Univ Del, 68-70; teacher biol, Sanford Sch, 70-72; res asst zool, Univ Ill, 72-75, teaching asst ecol, 75-76; asst prof, 76-80, ASSOC PROF BIOL SCI, UNIV CINCINNATI, 80- *Concurrent Pos:* Assoc cur, Cincinnati Mus Natural Hist, 76-; Sigma Xi grant, 76-77; Nat Geog Soc grant, 78-79; Elec Power Res Inst grant, 78-80. *Mem:* Am Arachnological Soc; Brit Arachnological Soc; Ecol Soc Am; Entom Soc Am; Animal Behavior Soc. *Res:* Ecology and behavior of arthropords, especially spiders; ecology and behavior of communal spiders; resource partitioning in wandering spiders and orb-weavers; behavioral reproductive isolation in wolf spiders; spider community structure; behavior ethology and entomology. *Mailing Add:* Dept of Biol Sci Univ of Cincinnati Cincinnati OH 45221

UFFEN, ROBERT JAMES, b Toronto, Ont, Sept 21, 23; m 49; c 2. GEOPHYSICS. *Educ:* Univ Toronto, BASc, 49, MA, 50; Univ Western Ont, PhD(physics), 52. *Hon Degrees:* DSc, Univ Western Ont, 70, Queen's Univ, Ont, 67 & Royal Mil Col Can, 78. *Prof Exp:* Lectr physics & geol, Univ Western Ont, 51-53, from asst prof to assoc prof geophys, 53-58, prof & head dept, 58-61, actg head dept physics, 60-61, asst prin, Univ Col Arts & Sci, 60-61, prin, 61-65, dean col sci, 65-66; mem, Defence Res Bd Can, 63-66, vchmn, 66-67, chmn, 67-69; chief sci adv to cabinet, Can Govt, 69-71; dean faculty appl sci, 71-80, PROF GEOPHYSICS, QUEEN'S UNIV, ONT, 71- *Concurrent Pos:* Consult, Kennco Explor Ltd, 52-59; res fel, Inst Geophys Univ Calif, Los Angeles, 53; Can deleg, Int Union Geod & Geophys, Rome, 54, Toronto, 57, Helsinki, 60, Tokyo, 62 & Int Union Geol Sci, New Delhi, 64; consult, Utah Construct Co, 55-58; mem Nat Adv Comt Res Geol Sci, 58-61; mem, Nat Res Coun Can, 63-66; mem, Nat Feasibility Comt Proj Oilsand, 59; chmn, Can Sci Comt, Int Upper Mantle Proj, 60-65; consult, Stanford Res Inst, 61-62; ed, Earth & Planetary Sci Letters, 65-69 & Tectonophysics, 67-; mem, Coun Regents for Cols Appl Arts & Technol, Prov Ont, 66-69 & 72-75; mem Sci Coun Can, 67-71; mem, Can Eng Manpower Coun, 72-; mem, Ctr Resource Studies, 73-; counr, Assoc Prof Engrs Ont, 75-79; mem, Fisheries Res Bd Can, 75-78; vchmn bd, Ont Hydro, 74-79. *Mem:* AAAS; fel Royal Soc Can; Am Geophys Union; fel Geol Soc Am; Am Inst Mining, Metall & Petrol Eng. *Res:* Geothermometry; internal constitution of the earth; paleomagnetism; science policy; radioactive waste management. *Mailing Add:* Fac of Appl Sci Queen's Univ Kingston ON K7L 3N6 Can

UFFEN, ROBERT L, b Oxnard, Calif, Dec 2, 37. MICROBIOLOGY. *Educ:* Stanford Univ, BA, 62; Univ Mass, Amherst, MA, 64, PhD(microbiol), 68. *Prof Exp:* NIH fel, Univ Ill, Urbana, 68-70; asst prof, 70-77, ASSOC PROF MICROBIOL, MICH STATE UNIV, 77- *Mem:* AAAS; Am Soc Microbiol; Am Chem Soc; NY Acad Sci. *Res:* General microbiology and microbial physiology; regulation during cell differentiation; bacterial photosynthesis; ecology. *Mailing Add:* Dept of Microbiol Mich State Univ East Lansing MI 48824

UGARTE, EDUARDO, b Santa Ana, El Salvador, Oct 22, 35; m 63; c 4. BIOCHEMISTRY, MICROBIOLOGY. *Educ:* Nat Univ Mex, lic biochem, 62; Univ El Salvador, Dr(biochem), 65; Univ Rio de Janeiro, dipl oral microbiol, 66; Inter-Am Inst Agr Sci, El Salvador, dipl agr sci educ, 69. *Prof Exp:* Assoc prof biochem, Sch Dent, Univ El Salvador, 65-67, secy dept basic sci, 66, secy curriculum comn, 66-67, prof chem, Sch Agron Sci, 67-68, chief prof biochem, 68-70; researcher biochem, United Med Labs, 70-74; dir, Analytico Lab, 75; vpres, Page Biochem Labs, Inc, 75-76; tech dir, Nat Health Labs, Ft Lauderdale, 76-77; MEM STAFF RES CANCER TISSUE, ONCORNOVAIRUS, LIFE SCI RES INC, ST PETERSBURG FLA, 78- *Concurrent Pos:* Fel bact & virol, Life Labs, Ecuador, 63-64; fel oral microbiol, Pan-Am Health Orgn, Brazil, 66; lab clin supvr, Tampa Gen Hosp, Fla, 79-80; lab dir, St Petersburg Gen Hosp, Fla, 80-81; pres, Hemato Control Prod, Intersci Inc, Portland, Ore, 81-82. *Mem:* Am Chem Soc; Microbiol Soc El Salvador. *Res:* Relation of the mechanism of different hormones between pituitary and thyroid glands; development of the radioimmunoassays for these hormones; radiolabeling materials for different fractions. *Mailing Add:* 5216 Denver St NE St Petersburg FL 83703

UGENT, DONALD, b Chicago, Ill, Dec 20, 33; m 62; c 3. PLANT TAXONOMY, ECONOMIC BOTANY. *Educ:* Univ Wis, Madison, BS, 56, MS, 61, PhD(bot), 66. *Prof Exp:* Asst prof bot, 68-71, ASSOC PROF BOT, SOUTHERN ILL UNIV, CARBONDALE, 72- *Concurrent Pos:* NSF Proj assoc, 66-67; cur, Herbarium, Southern Ill Univ, 68-; mem trop studies comt, Assoc Univs Int Educ, 70-76; reviewer grants, NSF, 70- *Mem:* Soc Econ Bot; Sigma Xi. *Res:* Biosystematics of the wild and cultivated species of Solanum, section tuberarium, potatoes; ethnobotany; phytogeography. *Mailing Add:* Dept of Bot Southern Ill Univ Carbondale IL 62901

UGINCIUS, PETER, b Geniai, Lithuania, Feb 23, 36; US citizen; m 62; c 4. GEODESY. *Educ:* Kalamazoo Col, BA, 58; Ind Univ, MS, 61; Cath Univ Am, PhD(physics), 68. SUPVRY GEODESIST, NAVAL SURFACE WEAPONS CTR, 72- *Concurrent Pos:* Adj prof, Va Polytech Inst & State Univ, 72- *Mem:* Am Phys Soc; Am Geophys Union. *Res:* Physical geodesy; earth gravitational field. *Mailing Add:* Naval Surf Weapons Ctr Ocean Geodesy Br K-12 Dahlgren VA 22448

UGLEM, GARY LEE, b Grand Forks, NDak, Sept 19, 41; m 64; c 2. PARASITOLOGY, ZOOLOGY. *Educ:* Univ NDak, BS, 66, MS, 68; Univ Idaho, PhD(zool), 72. *Prof Exp:* Instr parasitol, Univ Idaho, 71; NIH fel, Rice Univ, 72-74; asst prof, 74-78, ASSOC PROF BIOL SCI, UNIV KY, 78- *Mem:* Am Micros Soc; Am Soc Parasitologists; Am Inst Biol Sci. *Res:* Physiology of host-parasite relations; membrane transport in parasitic helminths; Acanthocephalan life histories. *Mailing Add:* Sch of Biol Sci Univ of Ky Lexington KY 40506

UGOLINI, FIORENZO CESARE, b Florence, Italy, Jan 16, 29; m 63; c 2. SOILS. *Educ:* Rutgers Univ, BS, 57, PhD(soils), 60. *Prof Exp:* Arctic Inst NAm fel, Rutgers Univ, 60-61, asst prof soils, 61-64; asst prof & res assoc, Ohio State Univ, 64-66; assoc prof, 66-73, PROF SOILS, UNIV WASH, 73- *Concurrent Pos:* NATO prof, Univ Milan. *Mem:* AAAS; Am Polar Soc; Am Soc Agron; Int Soc Soil Sci; Arctic Inst NAm; Int Union Quaternary Res. *Res:* Soil formation and weathering in the cold regions, including Arctic, Antarctica and Alpine environments; soil development and the impact of time on glacial deposits, chronologically different; forest soils; paleosoils. *Mailing Add:* Col of Forest Resources AR-10 Univ of Wash Seattle WA 98195

UGURBIL, KAMIL, b Tire, Turkey, July 11, 49. NUCLEAR MAGNETIC RESONANCE SPECTROSCOPY. *Educ:* Columbia Univ, NY, AB, 71, PhD(chem), 77. *Prof Exp:* Fel res biophysics, Bell Labs, 76-79; ASST PROF BIOCHEM, COLUMBIA UNIV, 79- *Concurrent Pos:* Consult, Bell Labs, 80- *Mem:* Am Chem Soc; Biophys Soc; AAAS. *Res:* Applications of nuclear magnetic resonance spectroscopy to biological problems, primarily to studies of intact cells and organs. *Mailing Add:* Dept Biochem Columbia Univ 630 W 168th St New York NY 10032

UHERKA, DAVID JEROME, b Wagner, SDak, June 2, 38; m 65; c 2. NUMERICAL ANALYSIS. *Educ:* SDak Sch Mines & Technol, BS, 60; Univ Utah, MA, 63, PhD(math), 64. *Prof Exp:* Mathematician, US Naval Radiol Defense Lab, Calif, 62; mathematician & programmer, US Army Natick Labs, Mass, 64-66; asst prof, Ariz State Univ, 66-68; assoc prof, 68-76, PROF MATH, UNIV NDAK, 76- *Concurrent Pos:* Consult, US Army Natick Labs, 66-68; sabbatical leave, scientist in residence, Argonne Nat Lab, 81-82. *Mem:* Math Asn Am; Am Math Soc; Am Soc Eng Educ; Soc Indust & Appl Math. *Res:* Functional and numerical analysis; computer applications; stirling engines. *Mailing Add:* Dept of Math Univ of ND Grand Forks ND 58202

UHERKA, KENNETH LEROY, b Wagner, SDak, May 30, 37; m 67; c 4. ENERGY CONSERVATION, ENVIRONMENTAL ENGINEERING. *Educ:* SDak Sch Mines & Technol, BS, 59; Univ Ariz, MS, 61; Purdue Univ, Lafayette, PhD(aeronaut & eng sci), 71. *Prof Exp:* Instr aerospace eng, Purdue Univ, Lafayette, 61-67; assoc scientist, Res Inst, Ill Inst Technol, 67-68; asst prof air & water resources, Univ Ill, Chicago Circle, 68-76; PROJ MGR, ARGONNE NAT LAB, 76- *Mem:* Am Soc Mech Engrs; Am Inst Aeronaut & Astronaut; Int Solar Energy Soc. *Res:* Stirling engines and other advanced power systems, new energy conservation technologies and laboratory tests for critical component research and development; atmospheric and plasma physics; urban meteorology; environmental pollution control. *Mailing Add:* Argonne Nat Lab Bldg 308 Argonne IL 60439

UHL, ARTHUR E(DWARD), b Chicago, Ill, Nov 11, 29; div; c 3. PETROLEUM ENGINEERING. *Educ:* Univ Southwestern La, BS, 50; Univ Tulsa, BS, 52, MPE, 53. *Prof Exp:* Asst prof petrol eng, Univ Southwestern La, 58-60; assoc petrol engr, Inst Gas Technol, Ill Inst Technol, 60-62, res assoc prod-pipeline-reservoir eng, 62-65, asst prof, 60-65, asst chmn dept gas technol, 63-65; supvry engr, 65-66, sr supvry engr, 66-68, asst chief engr, 68-69, chief gas/liquified natural gas engr, 69-71, prin engr, Gas & Liquified Natural Gas Systs, 71-72, asst mgr, Asia-Pac Opers, 72-74, mgr projs, 75-77, mgr resource develop progs, 78-79, eng mgr, Planning & Develop, 79-80, MGR SPEC PROJ OPERS, BECHTEL INC, 81- *Concurrent Pos:* Consult, McGraw-Hill Pub Co, Inc, 58-60, Layne & Bowler, 59, Tenn Gas Transmission Co, 59, Natural Gas Pipeline Co Am & Columbia Gas Syst; mem liquified natural gas task group, Nat Energy Surv, Fed Power Comn, 71-72; mem tech adv subcomt, Comt Conserv Energy, 72-73. *Mem:* Am Inst Mining, Metall & Petrol Engrs. *Res:* Oil and gas production, processing and transmission; fuel energy logistics systems, energy resources development. *Mailing Add:* 130 Harvard Ave Mill Valley CA 94941

UHL, CHARLES HARRISON, b Schenectady, NY, May 28, 18; m 45; c 4. BOTANY. *Educ:* Emory Univ, BA, 39, MS, 41; Cornell Univ, PhD(bot), 47. *Prof Exp:* Asst, 41-42, 45-46, from instr to asst prof, 46-52, ASSOC PROF BOT, CORNELL UNIV, 52- *Mem:* AAAS; Bot Soc Am; Genetics Soc Am; Soc Study Evolution; Int Asn Plant Taxon. *Res:* Chromosomes and evolution, especially of Crassulaceae. *Mailing Add:* Dept of Bot Cornell Univ Ithaca NY 14583

UHL, DALE LYNDEN, nuclear chemistry, see previous edition

UHL, EDWARD GEORGE, b Elizabeth, NJ, Mar 24, 18; m 42, 66; c 4. APPLIED PHYSICS. *Educ:* Lehigh Univ, BS, 40. *Hon Degrees:* DSc, Lehigh Univ, 75. *Prof Exp:* Mem staff, Glenn L Martin Co, Md & Fla, 46-59; vpres, Teledyne Ryan Aeronaut Co, Calif, 59-61; pres, 61-76, CHMN & CHIEF EXEC OFFICER, FAIRCHILD INDUSTS, INC, 76- *Concurrent Pos:* Directorships, Am Satellite Corp, Fairchild Industs, Inc, Md Nat Corp & Md Nat Bank; chmn vis comt, Ctr Energy Res, Lehigh Univ; bd nominations, Aviation Hall Fame; bd trustees, Nat Security Indust Asn; bd gov, Nat Space Club; trustee, Lehigh Univ & Johns Hopkins Univ. *Honors & Awards:* John C Jones Award, Am Defense Preparedness Asn, 75. *Mem:* Fel Am Inst Aeronaut & Astronaut; Am Defense Preparedness Asn; Soc Automotive Eng. *Res:* Aircraft and spacecraft design. *Mailing Add:* Fairchild Industs Inc Germantown MD 20767

UHL, JOHN JERRY, JR, b Pittsburgh, Pa, June 27, 40. MATHEMATICS. *Educ:* Col William & Mary, BS, 62; Carnegie Inst Technol, MS, 64, PhD(math), 66. *Prof Exp:* Asst prof, 68-72, assoc prof, 72-75, PROF MATH, UNIV ILL, URBANA-CHAMPAIGN, 75- *Mem:* Am Math Soc; Math Asn Am. *Res:* Functional analysis and integration theory. *Mailing Add:* 273 Altgeld Hall Univ of Ill Dept of Math Urbana IL 61801

UHL, V(INCENT) W(ILLIAM), b Philadelphia, Pa, May 16, 17. CHEMICAL ENGINEERING. *Educ:* Drexel Inst Technol, BS, 40; Lehigh Univ, MS, 49, PhD(chem eng), 52. *Prof Exp:* Develop engr, Sun Oil Co, 40-44; asst mgr heat transfer div, Downingtown Iron Works, 44-46; instr chem eng, Lehigh Univ, 47-51; mgr process equip div, Bethlehem Foundry & Mach Co, 51-54; assoc prof chem eng, Villanova Univ, 54-57; from assoc prof to prof, Drexel Inst Technol, 57-63; Union-Camp Prof & chmn dept, 63-74, PROF CHEM ENG, UNIV VA, 74- *Concurrent Pos:* Consult, Bethlehem Corp, 54-70, R M Armstrong Co, 58-61, Atlantic Res Corp, 66-68, Joy Mfg Co, 70-73 & Philadelphia Gear Corp, 73-; NSF fac fel, Mass Inst Technol, 62-63; sr chem eng adv, US Environ Protection Agency, NC, 76-78. *Mem:* Am Chem Soc; Am Soc Eng Educ; fel Am Inst Chem Engrs. *Res:* Heat transfer, mixing, especially viscous fluids; technical economics; cost-benefit analysis; uncertainty analysis. *Mailing Add:* Dept of Chem Eng Univ of Va Charlottesville VA 22901

UHLENBECK, GEORGE EUGENE, b Batavia, Java, Dec 6, 00; nat US; m 27; c 1. PHYSICS. *Educ:* State Univ Leiden, PhD, 27. *Hon Degrees:* ScD, Univ Notre Dame, 55, Case Inst Technol, 59, Univ Colo, 68, Yeshiva Univ, 69. *Prof Exp:* Asst theoret physics, State Univ Leiden, 25-27; from instr to assoc prof, Univ Mich, 27-35; prof, State Univ Utrecht, 35-39; Henry S Carhart prof, Univ Mich, 39-60; prof physics & physicist, 60-74, EMER PROF PHYSICS, ROCKEFELLER UNIV, 74- *Concurrent Pos:* Mem staff, Radiation Lab, Mass Inst Technol, 43-45; Lorentz prof, State Univ Leiden, 54-55; Van der Waals prof, Univ Amsterdam, 63-64. *Honors & Awards:* Max

Planck Medal, 64; Lorentz Medal, 70. *Mem:* Nat Acad Sci; fel Am Phys Soc (pres, 59); Am Philos Soc; Netherlands Phys Soc; Nat Acad Lincei. *Res:* Theory of atomic structure and quantum mechanics; statistical mechanics and the kinetic theory of matter; nuclear physics. *Mailing Add:* Rockefeller Univ York Ave & E 66th St New York NY 10021

UHLENBECK, KAREN K, b Cleveland, Ohio, Aug 24, 42; m 65. MATHEMATICS. *Educ:* Univ Mich, BA, 64; Brandeis Univ, PhD(math), 68. *Prof Exp:* Instr math, Mass Inst Technol, 68-69; lectr, Univ Calif, Berkeley, 69-71; asst prof math, Univ Ill, Urbana, 71-76; assoc prof, 76-78, PROF MATH, UNIV ILL, CHICAGO CIRCLE, 78- *Concurrent Pos:* Sloan fel, 74-76. *Mem:* Am Math Soc; Asn Women Math. *Res:* Calculus of variations; global analysis. *Mailing Add:* Dept Math Univ Ill Chicago Circle Box 4348 Chicago IL 60680

UHLENBECK, OLKE CORNELIS, b Ann Arbor, Mich, Apr 20, 42. BIOPHYSICAL CHEMISTRY. *Educ:* Univ Mich, Ann Arbor, BS, 64; Harvard Univ, PhD(biophys), 69. *Prof Exp:* Miller fel, Univ Calif, Berkeley, 69-71; asst prof, 71-75, assoc prof, 76-79, PROF BIOCHEM & CHEM, UNIV ILL, URBANA, 79- *Concurrent Pos:* NIH res grant, Univ Ill, Urbana, 71- *Res:* Nucleic acid interactions; structure and function of RNA. *Mailing Add:* Dept of Biochem Univ Ill at Urbana-Champaign Urbana IL 61801

UHLENBROCK, DIETRICH A, b Schweinfurt, Ger, Oct 13, 37. APPLIED MATHEMATICS, MATHEMATICAL PHYSICS. *Educ:* Univ Cologne, Vordiplom, 59; NY Univ, MS, 62, PhD(physics), 63. *Prof Exp:* Adj asst prof theoret physics, Univ & res assoc, Courant Inst, NY Univ, 63-64; vis mem, Inst Adv Study, NJ, 64-66; asst prof, 66-68, assoc prof, 68-76, PROF MATH & PHYSICS, UNIV WIS-MADISON, 76- *Concurrent Pos:* Prof math, Free Univ Berlin, 73-78; vis prof math, Nat Autonomous Univ Mex, 81. *Res:* Classical and quantum statistical physics; quantum field theory; mathematical physics. *Mailing Add:* Dept Math Univ Wis Madison WI 53706

UHLENHOPP, ELLIOTT LEE, b Hampton, Iowa, Dec 8, 42; m 67; c 2. BIOCHEMISTRY. *Educ:* Carleton Col, BA, 65; Columbia Univ, PhD(biochem), 71. *Prof Exp:* Res chemist, Univ Calif, San Diego, 73-74; asst prof chem, Whitman Col, 75-78; asst prof, 78-80, ASSOC PROF CHEM, GRINNELL COL, 80- *Concurrent Pos:* Fel, Damon Runyon Mem Fund, Cancer Res Inc, 71-73. *Mem:* Sigma Xi; Biophys Soc; Am Chem Soc; AAAS. *Res:* Viscoelastic characterization of high molecular weight native and denatured DNA from bacterial and eukaryotic cells; chromosome structure; DNA damage and repair. *Mailing Add:* Dept of Chem Grinnell Col Grinnell IA 50112

UHLENHUTH, EBERHARD HENRY, b Baltimore, Md, Sept 15, 27; m 52; c 3. PSYCHIATRY, PSYCHOPHARMACOLOGY. *Educ:* Yale Univ, BS, 47; Johns Hopkins Univ, MD, 51. *Prof Exp:* USPHS fel psychiat, Johns Hopkins Univ, 52-56, from instr to assoc prof, 56-68; chief, Adult Psychiat Clin, 68-76, assoc prof psychiat, 68-73, PROF PSYCHIAT, UNIV CHICAGO, 73-, PROF CLIN PHARMACOL, 75- *Concurrent Pos:* Consult, Patuxent Inst, 56-57; asst psychiatrist chg, Outpatient Dept, Johns Hopkins Hosp, 56-61, consult, Div Plastic Surg, 59-60, psychiatrist chg, Outpatient Dept, 61-62; USPHS career teacher trainee, Johns Hopkins Univ, 57-59, USPHS career res develop awards, 62-68; consult, Ill State Psychiat Inst, 68-75; Clin Psychopharmacol Res Rev Comt, Psychopharmacol Br, NIMH, 68-72, consult, Ment Health Task Force, Mid-Southside Planning Orgn, 70-75, Woodlawn Ment Health Ctr, 71-73, & US Food & Drug Admin, 71-74; mem psychopharmacol adv comt, 74-78. *Honors & Awards:* Assoc Clin Psychiatrists' Award, 58; USPHS Res Sci Award, 76-81. *Mem:* Fel Am Col Neuropsychopharmacol; fel Am Psychiat Asn; Col Int Neuro-Psychopharmacol; AAAS; Psychiat Res Soc. *Res:* Clinical psychopharmacology; anxiety and depression; life stress; evaluation of treatments; consumption of psychotherapeutic drugs. *Mailing Add:* Pritzker Sch Med Univ Chicago Chicago IL 60637

UHLHORN, KENNETH W, b Mankato, Minn, Sept 24, 33; m 54; c 3. SCIENCE EDUCATION. *Educ:* Mankato State Col, BS, 54; Univ Minn, MA, 60; Univ Iowa, PhD(biol, sci ed), 63. *Prof Exp:* Teacher pub sch, Minn, 56-60; instr biol & physics, Univ Iowa, 60-63, asst prof biol, 63; assoc prof, 63-68, PROF SCI EDUC, IND STATE UNIV, TERRE HAUTE, 68-, DIR SCI TEACHING CTR, 66- *Mem:* Nat Asn Res Sci Teaching; Nat Sci Teachers Asn. *Res:* Preparation, use and application of science experience inventories and their role in teaching science; science for elementary education majors; children's concept of science and scientists based on their drawings of scientists; the physics and perception of photography to undergraduate and graduate students. *Mailing Add:* Sci Teaching Ctr Ind State Univ Terre Haute IN 47809

UHLIG, HERBERT H(ENRY), b Haledon, NJ, Mar 3, 07; m 41; c 3. MATERIAL SCIENCE, ELECTROCHEMISTRY. *Educ:* Brown Univ, ScB, 29; Mass Inst Technol, PhD(phys chem), 32. *Prof Exp:* Phys chemist, Rockefeller Inst, 32-33; res chemist, Lever Bros Co, 34-36, asst chief chemist, 36-37; res assoc, Corrosion Lab, Mass Inst Technol, 37-40; res assoc, Gen Elec Co, 40-46; from assoc prof to prof metall, 46-72, In Charge Corrosion Lab, 46-75, EMER PROF METALL, MASS INST TECHNOL, 72- *Concurrent Pos:* Guggenheim fel, Max Planck Inst Phys Chem, 61; chmn, Int Corrosion Coun, 75-78. *Honors & Awards:* Whitney Award, Nat Asn Corrosion Engrs, 51; Palladium Medal, Electrochem Soc, 61; U R Evans Award, Inst Corrosion Sci & Technol, Gt Brit, 80. *Mem:* Hon mem Electrochem Soc (pres, 55-56); Am Chem Soc; Am Soc Metals; Nat Asn Corrosion Engrs; Am Acad Arts & Sci. *Res:* Corrosion and passivity; stainless steels; meteorites. *Mailing Add:* Dept of Mat Sci & Eng Mass Inst of Technol Cambridge MA 02139

UHLIR, ARTHUR, JR, b Chicago, Ill, Feb 2, 26; m 54; c 3. ELECTRICAL ENGINEERING, PHYSICS. *Educ:* Ill Inst Technol, BS, 45, MS, 48; Univ Chicago, PhD(physics), 52. *Prof Exp:* Asst engr mech, Armour Res Found, 45-48; mem tech staff transistors, Bell Labs, 51-58; vpres & dir semiconductors, Microwave Assocs, Inc, 58-69; dir res, Comput Metrics Inc, 69-73; chm elec eng, 70-75, dean eng, 75-80, PROF ELEC ENG, COL ENG, TUFTS UNIV, 70- *Concurrent Pos:* Dir, Harvard Apparatus Corp, 75-79. *Mem:* Fel Inst Elec & Electronics Engrs; Am Phys Soc; Sigma Xi; AAAS. *Res:* Microwave devices and measurements. *Mailing Add:* Col of Eng Tufts Univ Medford MA 02155

UHLMANN, DONALD ROBERT, b Chicago, Ill, Sept 22, 36; m 58; c 6. GLASS TECHNOLOGY, POLYMER SCIENCE. *Educ:* Yale Univ, BS, 58; Harvard Univ, PhD(appl physics), 63. *Prof Exp:* Res fel appl physics, Harvard Univ, 63-65; from asst prof to assoc prof ceramics, 65-75, PROF CERAMICS & POLYMERS, MASS INST TECHNOL, 75- *Concurrent Pos:* Convenor sci coun mat processing, Univ Space Res Asn, 77-78, mem sci coun, 78-80; Guggenheim fel, 81-82. *Honors & Awards:* F H Norton Award, 79; George W Murey Award, Am Ceramic Soc, 81. *Mem:* Am Phys Soc; Am Inst Mining, Metall & Petrol Engrs; fel Am Ceramic Soc; Brit Soc Glass Technol; Ceramic Educ Coun. *Res:* Structure and properties of glasses; crystallization phenomena; structure and properties of polymers. *Mailing Add:* Dept Mat Sci & Eng Mass Inst Technol Cambridge MA 02139

UHR, JONATHAN WILLIAM, b New York, NY, Sept 8, 27; m 54; c 2. MEDICINE. *Educ:* Am Bd Internal Med, dipl, 60. *Prof Exp:* PROF MED & MICROBIOL & CHMN DEPT MICROBIOL, UNIV TEX HEALTH SCI CTR DALLAS, 69- *Mem:* Am Asn Immunol; Am Soc Clin Invest; Am Rheumatism Asn; Am Soc Exp Path; Asn Am Physicians. *Res:* Immunology. *Mailing Add:* Dept of Microbiol Univ of Tex Southwestern Med Sch Dallas TX 75235

UHR, LEONARD MERRICK, b Philadelphia, Pa, June 26, 27; m 49; c 2. COMPUTER SCIENCE, PSYCHOLOGY. *Educ:* Princeton Univ, BA, 49; Johns Hopkins Univ, MA, 51; Univ Mich, PhD(psychol), 57. *Prof Exp:* Assoc prof psychol, Univ Mich & res psychologist & coordr psychol sci, Ment Health Res Inst, 57-65; PROF COMPUT SCI, UNIV WIS-MADISON, 65- *Mem:* Am Psychol Asn; Asn Comput Mach; Inst Elec & Electronics Eng. *Res:* Dynamic computer models of perceptual and cognitive processes; perception; learning; computers and education; intelligent systems. *Mailing Add:* Dept Comput Sci Univ Wis Madison WI 53706

UHRAN, JOHN JOSEPH, JR, ELECTRICAL ENGINEERING, COMPUTER SCIENCES. *Educ:* Manhattan Col, BEE, 57; Purdue Univ, MSEE, 63, PhD(elec eng), 67. *Prof Exp:* Sr engr, Hazeltine Res Corp, 57-61; instr, Purdue Univ, 63-66; asst prof, 66-69, assoc prof, 69-79, PROF ELEC ENG, UNIV NOTRE DAME, 79- *Concurrent Pos:* Mem staff, Lincoln Lab, Mass Inst Technol, 78-79; consult indust; assoc ed, Transactions on Commun. *Mem:* Inst Elec & Electronics Engrs. *Res:* Hardware/software development; microcomputer applications; modelling and simulation techniques; communication theory; digital signal processing. *Mailing Add:* Dept Elec Eng Univ Notre Dame Notre Dame IN 46556

UHRICH, DAVID LEE, b Buffalo, NY, Jan 5, 39; m 61; c 3. PHYSICS. *Educ:* Canisius Col, BS, 60; Univ Pittsburgh, PhD(physics), 65. *Prof Exp:* Fels, Univ Pittsburgh, 66 & Iowa State Univ, 66-67; asst prof, 67-71, assoc prof, 71-77, PROF PHYSICS, KENT STATE UNIV, 77-, MEM LIQUID & CRYSTAL INST, 77- *Mem:* Am Phys Soc. *Res:* Mössbauer effect studies of liquid crystals and solids. *Mailing Add:* Dept of Physics Kent State Univ Kent OH 44242

UICKER, JOHN J(OSEPH), b Lawrence, Mass, Apr 12, 05; m 34; c 8. MECHANICAL ENGINEERING. *Educ:* Univ NH, BS, 31, ME, 35; Pa State Col, MS, 43. *Prof Exp:* coop engr, Amoskeag Mfg Co, 29 & Martin Construct Co, 30; instr mech eng, Univ NH, 31-37 & Pa State Col, 37-40; instr, 40-43, from asst prof to prof, 43-58, actg dir dept, 43-47, dir dept, 47-52, chmn, 52-58 & 60-62, actg dean col eng & archit, 58-60, dean col eng, 62-65, prof mech eng, 65-70, EMER PROF MECH ENG, UNIV DETROIT, 70- *Concurrent Pos:* Mech eng mem, Bd Rules & Appeals, Dept Bldg & Safety Eng, Detroit, Mich, 53-73; consult, State Bd Registr Prof Engrs, Mich, 49-73; consult struct bur, Bldg Off Conf Am, 55-73. *Mem:* Fel Am Soc Mech Engrs; Am Soc Heating, Refrig & Air-Conditioning Engrs; Am Soc Eng Educ (secy, 44). *Res:* Refrigeration; thermodynamics; heat transfer; fan performance. *Mailing Add:* Box 119 RFD 3 Harbor Beach MI 48441

UICKER, JOHN JOSEPH, JR, b Derry, NH, July 11, 38; m 61; c 6. MECHANICAL ENGINEERING. *Educ:* Univ Detroit, BME, 61; Northwestern Univ, Evanston, MS, 63, PhD(mech eng), 65. *Prof Exp:* From asst prof to assoc prof, 67-75, PROF MECH ENG, UNIV WIS-MADISON, 75-, DIR, COMPUT-AIDED ENG CTR, 81- *Concurrent Pos:* Mem, US Coun Int Fedn for Theory of Mach & Mechanisms, 69-, ed-in-chief, Mechanism & Mach Theory, 73-78; grants, Ford Motor Co, 70- & NSF, 70-73; prin res engr assoc & Am Soc Eng Educ resident fel, Advan Anal Technol Dept, Ford Motor Co, Mich, 72-73; Sr Fulbright lectr, Cranfield, England, 78-79. *Honors & Awards:* Ralph R Teeter Award, Soc Automotive Engrs, 68. *Mem:* Am Soc Mech Engrs; Am Soc Eng Educ; Asn Comput Mach. *Res:* Kinematic and dynamic analysis of mechanical systems; spatial linkage analysis; computer-aided design; computer graphics. *Mailing Add:* Dept of Mech Eng 1513 University Ave Madison WI 53706

UITTO, JOUNI JORMA, b Helsinki, Finland, Sept 15, 43; m 65; c 1. DERMATOLOGY, BIOCHEMISTRY. *Educ:* Univ Helsinki, BM, 65, MD & PhD(med biochem), 70. *Prof Exp:* Intern med, surg, med biochem, Univ Helsinki Cent Hosp, 69; instr med biochem, Univ Helsinki, 70-71; clin asst dermat, Univ Cent Hosp, Univ Copenhagen, 71; from instr to asst prof biochem, Rutgers Med Sch, Col Med & Dent NJ, 73-75; instr med & resident fel dermat, Sch Med, Washington Univ, 75-78, asst prof med & biochem, 78-80; ASSOC PROF MED, SCH MED, & ASSOC CHIEF & DIR, DIV DERMAT, MED CTR, UNIV CALIF, LOS ANGELES, 80- *Concurrent Pos:* Fel, Gen Clin Res Ctr, Philadelphia Gen Hosp & Dept Dermat, Univ Pa, 71-72. *Mem:* Soc Invest Dermat; Am Soc Clin Invest; Am Soc Biol Chem; Am Acad Dermat; Am Chem Soc. *Res:* Biochemistry of connective tissues; collagen metabolism; investigative dermatology. *Mailing Add:* Dept Dermat Harbor-Univ Calif Los Angeles Med Ctr Torrance CA 90509

UITTO, VELI-JUKKA V, b Helsinki, Finland, Sept 15, 46; m 72; c 2. BIOCHEMISTRY, PERIODONTICS. *Educ:* Univ Helsinki, DDS, 72, PhD(biochem), 76. *Prof Exp:* Instr, Dept Med Chem, Univ Helsinki, 72-73, instr, Dept Peridont, 73-75; fel, Dept Biochem, Med Sch, Rutgers Univ, 75-76; asst prof, Dept Peridont, Univ Helsinki, 76-78; instr, Dept Oral Biol, 78-79, asst prof, 79-81, ASSOC PROF, DEPT PERIODONT, NORTHWESTERN UNIV, 81- *Concurrent Pos:* Scientist, Finnish Acad, 76; New Investr Award, NIH, 80. *Mem:* Finnish Dent Soc; Scandinavian Soc Periodont; Int Asn Dent Res. *Res:* Proteolytic enzymes in gingiva and lenkocytes; biochemistry of basement membrane collagen. *Mailing Add:* Dept Oral Biol Dent Sch Northwestern Univ 303 E Chicago Ave Chicago IL 60611

UKELES, RAVENNA, b New York, NY, Aug 1, 29. MICROBIOLOGY. *Educ:* Hunter Col, BS, 49; NY Univ, MSc, 56, PhD(biol), 60. *Prof Exp:* RES MICROBIOLOGIST, LAB EXP BIOL, NAT MARINE FISHERIES SERV, 59- *Mem:* Soc Protozool; Phycol Soc Am; Am Soc Microbiol; NY Acad Sci. *Res:* Nutrition of protozoa and algae; growth of organisms in mass culture; algae as potential food sources for invertebrates. *Mailing Add:* Lab for Exp Biol Nat Marine Fisheries Serv Milford CT 06460

UKLEJA, PAUL LEONARD MATTHEW, b Chicago, Ill, Nov 22, 46; m 67; c 1. PHYSICS, LIQUID CRYSTAL PHYSICS. *Educ:* New Col, Fla, BA, 67; Univ Chicago, MS, 69; Kent State Univ, PhD(physics), 76. *Prof Exp:* Peace Corps vol sci & math, Govt Malta, 70-73; res assoc & fel, Kent State Univ, 76-78; asst prof physics, Southeastern Mass Univ, 78-80. *Res:* Liquid crystal physics, orientational ordering, fluctuations, and self diffusion in partially ordered systems including those having biological relevance. *Mailing Add:* 204 Maple St New Bedford MA 02740

UKRAINETZ, PAUL RUVIM, b Erwood, Sask, Dec 28, 35; m 63; c 3. MECHANICAL ENGINEERING. *Educ:* Univ Sask, BS, 57; Univ BC, MASc, 60; Purdue Univ, PhD(mech eng), 62. *Prof Exp:* Eng trainee, Bristol Aeroplane Co Ltd, 57-59; from asst prof to assoc prof mech eng, 62-71, PROF MECH ENG, UNIV SASK, 71-, HEAD DEPT, 74- *Honors & Awards:* Ralph R Teetor Award, Soc Automotive Engrs, 74. *Mem:* Soc Automotive Engrs; Am Soc Eng Educ; Can Soc Mech Engrs; Eng Inst Can. *Res:* Investigations into problems associated with fluid power control systems; study of the dynamics of cables with particular reference to power transmission line vibration; experimental stress analysis. *Mailing Add:* Dept of Mech Eng Univ of Sask Saskatoon SK S7N 0W0 Can

ULABY, FAWWAZ TAYSSIR, b Damascus, Syria, Feb 4, 43; US citizen; m 68; c 3. ELECTRICAL ENGINEERING. *Educ:* Am Univ Beirut, BS, 64; Univ Tex, Austin, MSEE, 66, PhD(elec eng), 68. *Prof Exp:* From asst prof to prof elec eng, 68-80, DIR REMOTE SENSING LAB, CTR RES, UNIV KANS, 76-, J L CONSTANT DISTINGUISHED PROF, 80- *Concurrent Pos:* Res grants, US Army, Univ Kans, 68-, NSF, 72- & 76-, Sandia Labs & Eglin AFB, 78- & NASA, 70-; assoc dir remote sensing lab, Ctr Res, Inc, Kans, 69-71; consult, govt & univ. *Mem:* Fel Inst Elec & Electronics Engrs; Int Soc Photogram; Int Union Radio Sci. *Res:* Millimeter wave propagation; remote sensing; microwave radiometry; radar systems; optical data processing. *Mailing Add:* Remote Sensing Lab Ctr Res 2291 Irving Hill Dr Campus W Lawrence KS 66045

ULAGARAJ, MUNIYANDY SEYDUNGANALLUR, b Tuticorin, India; Can Citizen; Mar 6, 44; m 70. ENTOMOLOGY, AGRICULTURE. *Educ:* Madras Univ, India, BScAg, 64; Indian Agr Res Inst, MSc, 70; Univ Fla, Gainesville, PhD(entom), 74. *Prof Exp:* Res asst entom, Dept Agr, Coimbatore, India, 64-68; res & teaching asst entom, Univ Fla, Gainesville, 71-74, assoc entom, 74-75; res assoc, McGill Univ, MacDonald Campus, Montreal, 75-80; lectr, Comput Sci Dept, Concordia Univ, Montreal, 80-81; AGT, SYSTS & METHODS, EDMONTON, 81- *Concurrent Pos:* Assoc entom, Univ Fla, Gainesville, 74; res assoc, Purdue Univ, WLafayette, Ind, 75. *Mem:* AAAS; Can Info Processing Soc. *Res:* System analysis: research and planning of current and future systems, system evaluation. *Mailing Add:* Systs & Methods Floor 27D 10020 100 St Edmonton ON T5J 0N5 Can

ULAM, STANISLAW MARCIN, b Lwow, Poland, Apr 3, 09; m 41; c 1. MATHEMATICS, MATHEMATICAL PHYSICS. *Educ:* Polytech Inst, Poland, MA, 32, Dr Math Sc, 33. *Hon Degrees:* Univ NMex, 65, Pittsburgh Univ, 78, Univ Wis, 78. *Prof Exp:* Mem, Inst Adv Study, 36; lectr math, Harvard Univ, 39-40; asst prof, Univ Wis, 41-43; from mem staff to res adv, Los Alamos Sci Lab, 43-65; prof math, Univ Colo, Boulder, 65-76; GRAD RES PROF, UNIV FLA, 74- *Concurrent Pos:* Assoc prof, Univ Southern Calif, 45-46; vis lectr, Harvard Univ, 51; vis prof, Mass Inst Technol, 56-57; chmn math sect, AAAS & mem bd govs, Weizmann Inst Sci Rehovot, Israel, 75- *Honors & Awards:* Polish Millenium Prize, Jurzykowski Found. *Mem:* Nat Acad Sci; Am Math Soc; AAAS; Am Phys Soc; Math Asn Am. *Res:* Set theory; functions of real variable; mathematical logic; thermonuclear reactions; topology; Monte Carlo method. *Mailing Add:* 1122 Old Santa Fe Trail Santa Fe NM 87501

ULANOWICZ, ROBERT EDWARD, b Baltimore, Md, Sept 17, 43; m 67. THEORETICAL BIOLOGY. *Educ:* Johns Hopkins Univ, BES, 64, PhD(chem eng), 68. *Prof Exp:* Res asst phys chem, Univ Göttingen, 64; res asst chem eng, Johns Hopkins Univ, 64-68; asst prof, Cath Univ Am, 68-70; res asst prof, Natural Resources Inst, 70-75, ASSOC PROF, CTR ENVIRON & ESTUARINE STUDIES, UNIV MD, 75- *Concurrent Pos:* Sci comt oceanic res, Int Coun Sci Unions, working group No 59, Biol Models in Oceanog. *Mem:* Atlantic Estuarine Res Soc; Estuarine Res Fedn. *Res:* Mass and energy transfer in ecosystems; ecosystem structure analysis; thermodynamics of ecosystems; hydrographical modeling. *Mailing Add:* Ctr Environ & Estuarine Studies Univ of Md PO Box 38 Solomons MD 20688

ULBERG, LESTER CURTISS, b Wis, Dec 2, 17; m 45; c 1. REPRODUCTIVE PHYSIOLOGY. *Educ:* Univ Wis, BS, 48, MS, 49, PhD(reprod physiol), 52. *Prof Exp:* Asst reprod physiol, Univ Wis, 47-50, instr, 50-52; instr animal husb, Miss State Col, 52-55, assoc prof, 55-57; assoc prof, 57-60, PROF ANIMAL HUSB, NC STATE UNIV, 60- *Concurrent Pos:* Agent, USDA, 50-52. *Mem:* AAAS; Am Soc Animal Sci; Am Dairy Sci Asn; Brit Soc Study Fertil. *Res:* Early embryonic development; hormone control of ovarian activity. *Mailing Add:* Dept of Animal Sci NC State Univ Raleigh NC 27607

ULBRECHT, JAROMIR (JOSEF), b Ostrava, Czech, Dec 16, 28; Brit citizen; m 52; c 2. CHEMICAL ENGINEERING, RHEOLOGY. *Educ:* Czech Inst Technol, Prague, Ing, 52; Inst Chem Technol, Prague, PhD(chem eng), 58. *Prof Exp:* Assoc dir chem eng, Rubber Res Inst, 57-62; head eng rheology, Czech Acad Sci, 62-68; prof chem eng, Univ of Salford, 68-78; PROF & CHMN DEPT CHEM ENG, STATE UNIV NY, BUFFALO, 78- *Concurrent Pos:* Res prof, Inst Chem Technol, Prague, 66-68; vis prof Univ Technol, Aachen, 67; ed-in-chief, Chem Eng Commun, 77- *Mem:* Am Inst Chem Eng; Brit Inst Chem Eng; Soc Rheology; Brit Soc Rheology; Sigma Xi. *Res:* Momentum and mass transfer in rheologically complex and multiphase systems; mixing and gas-liquid and liquid-liquid contacting. *Mailing Add:* Dept of Chem Eng Furnas Hall Amherst NY 14260

ULBRICH, CARLTON WILBUR, b Meriden, Conn, Oct 1, 32; m 62; c 2. ATMOSPHERIC PHYSICS. *Educ:* Univ Conn, BSME, 60, MS, 62, PhD(physics), 65. *Prof Exp:* Res asst physics, Univ Conn, 61-65; asst prof, Wittenberg Univ, 65-66; asst prof, 66-74, assoc prof, 74-79, PROF PHYSICS, CLEMSON UNIV, 79- *Mem:* Am Meteorol Soc. *Res:* Radar motorology. *Mailing Add:* Dept of Physics Clemson Univ Clemson SC 29631

ULDRICK, JOHN PAUL, b Donalds, SC, Apr 11, 29; m 54; c 1. MECHANICAL ENGINEERING, THEORETICAL MECHANICS. *Educ:* Clemson Univ, BCE, 50, BME, 56, MS, 58; Univ Fla, PhD(eng mech), 63. *Prof Exp:* Bridge inspector, SC Hwy Dept, 50-51; res engr, J E Sirrine Co, Engrs, 53-54; instr eng, Clemson Univ, 55-58, asst prof eng mech, 58-60; instr, Univ Fla, 60-61; assoc prof, Clemson Univ, 63-66; from assoc prof to prof eng, 66-70, prof mech eng & chmn dept, 70-73, PROF & DIR ENG MECH, MAT & DESIGN, US NAVAL ACAD, 73- *Concurrent Pos:* Fac assoc, Lockheed Aircraft Corp, Ga, 57; NSF initiation eng res grant, 64-66; NASA res grant, 68-69; consult, D W Taylor Naval Ship Res & Develop Ctr, Annapolis, 76- *Mem:* Am Soc Mech Engrs; Am Soc Eng Educ; Sigma Xi. *Res:* Hydrodynamics of fish locomotion; optical data processing and information storage; flow noise, structural vibrations and time series analysis. *Mailing Add:* Dept of Mech Eng US Naval Acad Annapolis MD 21402

ULERY, DANA LYNN, b East St Louis, Mo, Jan 2, 38; c 2. SYSTEMS ANALYSIS, SOFTWARE ENGINEERING. *Educ:* Grinnell Col, BA, 59; Univ Del, MS, 72, PhD(comput sci), 75. *Prof Exp:* Res engr, Jet Propulsion Lab, NASA, 60-63; programmer, Getty Oil Co, 63-64; lectr comput sci, Dept Comput Sci, Univ Del, 70-75, fel, 75-76, lectr, 76-77; sr software engr, 77-82, SUPVR STATIST SOFTWARE, E I DU PONT DE NEMOURS & CO, INC, 82- *Concurrent Pos:* Vis lectr, Inst Statist & Comput Sci, Cairo Univ, 76; consult, Am Univ, Cairo, 76. *Mem:* Sigma Xi; Inst Elec & Electronics Engrs; Asn Comput Mach; Am Soc Qual Control. *Res:* Language standards and compiler-compiler development for applications software in an industrial environment; role of software engineering in industrial quality programs; symbolic and numeric algorithms for partial differential equations. *Mailing Add:* Eng Dept E I du Pont de Nemours & Co Inc Wilmington DE 19898

ULEVITCH, RICHARD JOEL, b Cleveland, Ohio, Apr 4, 44; m 74; c 1. BIOCHEMISTRY, IMMUNOPATHOLOGY. *Educ:* Washington & Jefferson Col, BA, 66; Univ Pa, PhD(biochem), 71. *Prof Exp:* Fel, Univ Minn, 71-72, 72-75, MEM STAFF, SCRIPPS CLIN & RES FOUND, 75- *Concurrent Pos:* NIH fel, 78-81, 75-77. *Mem:* Am Asn Immunologists; Am Asn Path. *Res:* Biochemical mechanisms of inflammatory disease processes. *Mailing Add:* Scripps Clin & Res Found 10666 N Torrey Pines Rd La Jolla CA 92037

ULFELDER, HOWARD, b Mexico City, Mex, Aug, 15, 11; US citizen; m 32; c 4. OBSTETRICS & GYNECOLOGY, SURGERY. *Educ:* Harvard Univ, BA, 32, MD, 36. *Prof Exp:* Intern surg, Mass Gen Hosp, 37-39; asst, 40-46, instr, 46-48, clin assoc, 48-49, clin assoc gynec, 49-53, from asst clin prof to clin prof, 53-62, Joe V Meigs Prof Gynec, Harvard Med Sch, 62-76. *Concurrent Pos:* Resident surg, Mass Gen Hosp, 39-41, asst, 41-46, asst surgeon, 46-55, vis surgeon & chief gynec serv, 55-; physician, Pondville Hosp, 48-; consult surgeon, Mass Eye & Ear Infirmary, 48-; chief of staff, Vincent Mem Hosp, 55-76. *Mem:* AAAS; Am Gynec Soc; Soc Univ Surg; Soc Pelvic Surg (secy-treas, 54, pres, 59); fel AMA. *Res:* Carcinoma of the cervix; biological mechanics of pelvic support; stilbestrol, adenosis carcinoma syndrome. *Mailing Add:* Mass Gen Hosp 275 Charles St Boston MA 02114

ULICH, BOBBY LEE, b Bryan, Tex, Aug 13, 47; m 65; c 1. LARGE TELESCOPE TECHNOLOGY, RADIO ASTRONOMY. *Educ:* Tex A&M Univ, BS, 69; Calif Inst Technol, MS, 70; Univ Tex, Austin, PhD(elec eng), 73. *Prof Exp:* Head telescope oper, Tucson Div, Nat Radio Astron Observ, Assoc Univs Inc, 73-79; ASST DIR, MULTIPLE MIRROR TELESCOPE OBSERV, UNIV ARIZ, 79- *Concurrent Pos:* Mem, US Nat Comt Int Union Radio Sci, Comn J. *Mem:* Inst Elec & Electronic Engrs; Am Astron Soc; Int Astron Union. *Res:* Millimeter wavelength instrumentation and calibration techniques; solar system astronomy; interstellar molecules. *Mailing Add:* Multiple Mirror Telescope Observ Univ Ariz Tucson AZ 85721

ULICH, WILLIE LEE, b Somerville, Tex, Nov 10, 20; m 39; c 2. AGRICULTURAL ENGINEERING. *Educ:* Tex A&M Univ, BS, 43, MS, 47; Harvard Univ, PhD(pub admin), 51. *Prof Exp:* Res asst, Tex A&M Univ, 46-47, exten engr, 48-61; farm labor supvr, Fed Exten Serv, 47-48; PROF AGR ENG & CHMN DEPT, TEX TECH UNIV, 61- *Concurrent Pos:* Mem, Tex Air Control Bd, 69, 71- *Honors & Awards:* James F Lincoln Found

Award, 49-50. *Mem:* Am Soc Agr Engrs; Am Soc Eng Educ. *Res:* Covance systems and particulate control in cotton gins; efficiency studies of irrigation well pumping plants; confined animal odor and waste disposal systems; soil surface modification for soil and water conservation; farm machinery design; brush harvesting. *Mailing Add:* Dept of Agr Eng Tex Tech Univ Lubbock TX 79409

ULINSKI, PHILIP STEVEN, b Detroit, Mich, Feb 17, 43. NEUROANATOMY. *Educ:* Mich State Univ, BS, 64, MS, 67, PhD(zool), 69. *Prof Exp:* Asst prof biol, Oberlin Col, 69-70; asst prof anat, Sch Dent, Loyola Univ Chicago, 70-74; asst prof, 75-78, ASSOC PROF ANAT, UNIV CHICAGO, 79- *Concurrent Pos:* NIH fel, Univ Chicago, 75-81. *Mem:* AAAS; Am Soc Zool; Soc Neurosci; Am Asn Anat. *Res:* Comparative anatomy of reptilian nervous systems. *Mailing Add:* Dept of Anat Univ of Chicago Chicago IL 60637

ULLMAN, ARTHUR WILLIAM JAMES, b New York, NY, Dec 30, 36. MATHEMATICS. *Educ:* Univ Miami, BS, 57; Rice Univ, MS, 64, PhD(math), 66. *Prof Exp:* Instr math, Rice Univ, 61-62; asst prof, Tex Christian Univ, 64-66; asst prof philos, Tex A&M Univ, 66-67; prof & chmn dept, State Univ NY Col New Paltz, 68-71, resident dir, State Univ NY prog, Int Documentation Ctr, Cuernavaca, Mex, 71-72, PROF MATH, STATE UNIV NY COL NEW PALTZ, 72- *Concurrent Pos:* Founder & pres, MH Hedging Analysts, Inc, 74; contract to produce educ modules on health, Empire State Col, State Univ NY, 75. *Mem:* Am Math Soc; Asn Symbolic Logic. *Res:* Logic applying algebraic and analytic techniques to the study of logical theories; mathematical analysis of various commodity markets; potential conflict of interest between the medical profession and the public interest. *Mailing Add:* Dept of Math Col of New Paltz New Paltz NY 12561

ULLMAN, EDWIN FISHER, b Chicago, Ill, July 19, 30; m 54; c 2. BIOCHEMISTRY. *Educ:* Reed Col, AB, 52; Harvard Univ, AM, 53, PhD(org chem), 56. *Prof Exp:* Res chemist, Lederle Labs, Am Cyanamid Co, 55-60, group leader, Cent Res Div, 60-66; sci dir, Synvar Assocs, 66-70, VPRES & DIR RES, SYVA CORP, 70- *Concurrent Pos:* Adv bd, J Org Chem, 70-75 & J Immunoassay, 80- *Honors & Awards:* Mallinckrodt Award, Clin Ligand Assay Soc, 81. *Mem:* AAAS; Am Chem Soc; Royal Soc Chem; Am Asn Clin Chemists. *Res:* Reaction mechanisms; chemistry of stable radicals; photochemistry; enzyme chemistry; immunochemical assay methods. *Mailing Add:* Syva Co PO Box 10058 900 Arastradero Rd Palo Alto CA 94303

ULLMAN, FRANK GORDON, b New York, NY, Dec 14, 26; m 51; c 3. SOLID STATE PHYSICS. *Educ:* NY Univ, BA, 49; Polytech Inst Brooklyn, PhD(physics), 58. *Prof Exp:* Jr engr, Sylvania Elec Prod, Inc, 51-54; asst physics, Polytech Inst Brooklyn, 54-57, res assoc, 57-58; sr physicist, Nat Cash Register Co, 58-66; PROF ELEC ENG, UNIV NEBR, LINCOLN, 66- *Mem:* Am Phys Soc. *Res:* Light scattering; ferroelectricity; photoconduction; luminescence. *Mailing Add:* Dept Elec Eng Univ Nebr Lincoln NE 68588

ULLMAN, JACK DONALD, b Chicago, Ill, Sept 5, 29; m 54. NUCLEAR PHYSICS. *Educ:* Univ Ill, BS, 51, MS, 56, PhD(physics), 60. *Prof Exp:* Physicist, Bur Ships, Dept Navy, 51-53 & US Bur Stand, 60-61; res assoc, Dept Nuclear Physics, Univ Strasbourg, 61-62; res assoc physics, Columbia Univ, 62-70; ASSOC PROF PHYSICS, LEHMAN COL, 70- *Mem:* Am Phys Soc. *Res:* Nuclear structure physics; weak interactions. *Mailing Add:* Dept of Physics & Astron Lehman Col Bedford Park Blvd Bronx NY 10468

ULLMAN, JEFFREY D(AVID), b New York, NY, Nov 22, 42. COMPUTER SCIENCE. *Educ:* Columbia Univ, BS, 63; Princeton Univ, PhD(elec eng), 66. *Prof Exp:* Mem tech staff, Bell Tel Labs, NJ, 66-69; assoc prof elec eng, Princeton Univ, 69-74, prof elec eng & comput sci, 74-79; PROF COMPUT SCI, STANFORD UNIV, 79- *Mem:* Asn Comput Mach. *Res:* Compilers; data bases; theory of algorithms. *Mailing Add:* Dept of Elec Eng & Comput Sci Stanford Univ Stanford CA 94305

ULLMAN, JOSEPH LEONARD, b Buffalo, NY, Jan 30, 23. MATHEMATICS. *Educ:* Univ Buffalo, BA, 42; Stanford Univ, PhD(math), 49. *Prof Exp:* From instr to assoc prof, 49-66, PROF MATH, UNIV MICH, ANN ARBOR, 66- *Mem:* Am Math Soc; Math Asn Am. *Res:* Complex variable theory; potential theory; approximation theory in the complex plane. *Mailing Add:* Dept of Math Univ of Mich Ann Arbor MI 48104

ULLMAN, NELLY SZABO, b Vienna, Austria, Aug 11, 25; US citizen; m 47; c 4. APPLIED MATHEMATICS, BIOSTATISTICS. *Educ:* Hunter Col, BA, 45; Columbia Univ, MA, 48; Univ Mich, Ann Arbor, PhD(biostatist), 69. *Prof Exp:* Res assoc, Radiation Lab, Mass Inst Technol, 45; res assoc, Microwave Res Inst, Polytech Inst Brooklyn, 45-46, instr math, 45-63; instr, 63-64, asst prof, 64-66, 68-71, assoc prof, 71-78, FULL PROF MATH, EASTERN MICH UNIV, 78- *Mem:* Am Asn Univ Prof (treas, 71-); Am Math Asn; Am Statist Soc; Biomet Soc. *Res:* Integral equations; mathematical models in biological data; nonlinear parameter estimation; mathematical statistics. *Mailing Add:* 1430 Granger Ave Ann Arbor MI 48104

ULLMAN, ROBERT, b New York, NY, Nov 21, 20; m 47; c 4. POLYMER CHEMISTRY, PHYSICAL CHEMISTRY. *Educ:* City Col New York, BS, 41; Polytech Inst Brooklyn, MS, 46, PhD(chem), 50. *Prof Exp:* Res chemist, Ridbo Lab, 41-42, Columbia Univ, 42-45 & Carbide & Chem Co, 45-46; asst & instr chem, Polytech Inst Brooklyn, 46-47, from instr to assoc prof math, 47-59, assoc prof chem, 59-63; STAFF SCIENTIST, FORD MOTOR CO, 63- *Concurrent Pos:* Fulbright fel, Univ Groningen, 52; assoc prof, Univ Strasbourg, 61-62, Guggenheim fel, Ctr Res on Macromolecules, Strasbourg, France, 61-62; Fulbright fel, 77-78; adj lectr nuclear eng, Univ Mich, 74-, adj prof chem, 75 & 80- *Mem:* AAAS; Am Chem Soc; fel Am Phys Soc; Sigma Xi. *Res:* Macromolecules viscosity; chain statistics; surface chemistry; light scattering; magnetic resonance and relaxation; rheology; molecular motion in liquids and solutions; neutron scattering from macromolecules; rubber elasticity. *Mailing Add:* Sci Res Staff Ford Motor Co Dearborn MI 48121

ULLOM, STEPHEN VIRGIL, b Washington, DC, Nov 9, 38; m 66; c 2. MATHEMATICS. *Educ:* Am Univ, BA, 62; Harvard Univ, MA, 64; Univ Md, PhD(math), 68. *Prof Exp:* Asst prof math, 70-74, assoc prof, 74-78, PROF MATH, UNIV ILL, URBANA, 78- *Concurrent Pos:* NSF fel, Math Inst, Karlsrube, WGer & King's Col, Univ London, 68-69; mem, Inst Advan Study, 69-70. *Mem:* Am Math Soc. *Res:* Algebraic number theory; class groups of integral group rings; K-theory of groups and orders. *Mailing Add:* Dept of Math Univ Ill Urbana IL 61801

ULLREY, DUANE EARL, b Niles, Mich, May 27, 28; m 61, 76. ANIMAL NUTRITION. *Educ:* Mich State Univ, BS, 50, MS, 51; Univ Ill, PhD(animal nutrit), 54. *Prof Exp:* Asst animal sci, Univ Ill, 51-54; instr physiol & pharmacol, Okla State Univ, 54-55; from asst prof to assoc prof, 56-68, PROF ANIMAL HUSB, MICH STATE UNIV, 68-, PROF FISH & WILDLIFE, 73- *Concurrent Pos:* Moorman fel nutrit res, 70; mem comt animal nutrit, Nat Res Coun; adv comt life sci, Coun Int Exchange Scholars Nat Acad Sci-Nat Res Coun, 74-77; dir Mich State Univ Inst Nutrit, 74-76; res assoc, San Diego Zoo, 78- *Honors & Awards:* Am Feed Mfrs Asn Nutrit Res Award, 67; G Bohstedt Mineral Res Award, 69. *Mem:* Am Am Soc Animal Sci; Am Inst Nutrit; Am Asn Zoo Veterinarians. *Res:* Nutrient requirements of swine; normal development of the swine fetus; hematology of domestic animals; nutrition of wild animals; mineral and vitamin metabolism. *Mailing Add:* Dept of Animal Husb Mich State Univ East Lansing MI 48824

ULLRICH, DAVID FREDERICK, b Waterbury, Conn, Sept 10, 37. MATHEMATICS. *Educ:* Rensselaer Polytech Inst, BS, 59; Case Western Reserve Univ, MS, 62; Carnegie-Mellon Univ, PhD(differential equations), 67. *Prof Exp:* ASST PROF MATH, NC STATE UNIV, 66- *Mem:* Am Math Soc; Math Asn Am. *Res:* Non-linear ordinary differential equations. *Mailing Add:* Dept of Math NC State Univ Raleigh NC 27607

ULLRICH, FELIX THOMAS, b Elizabeth, NJ, June 1, 39; m 68. PHYSICS, ELECTRICAL ENGINEERING. *Educ:* Rutgers Col, BA, 61; Univ Pittsburgh, PhD(physics), 70. *Prof Exp:* Mem tech staff physics, Riverside Res Inst, 70 & GTE Labs, 70-72; advan res & develop engr, GTE Sylvania, 72-75; PROF TECH STAFF MEM ELEC ENG, PLASMA PHYSICS LAB, PRINCETON UNIV, 75- *Mem:* Inst Elec & Electronics Engrs; Am Phys Soc. *Mailing Add:* Plasma Physics Lab Princeton Univ PO Box 451 Princeton NJ 08544

ULLRICH, ROBERT LEO, b Ottumwa, Iowa, Sept 8, 47. PATHOLOGY, RADIATION CARCINOGENESIS. *Educ:* Creighton Univ, BS, 69, MS, 71; Univ Rochester, PhD(radiation biol), 75. *Prof Exp:* Res assoc, 74-76, HEAD RADIATION CARCINOGENESIS UNIT, BIOL DIV, OAK RIDGE NAT LAB, 76- *Concurrent Pos:* Mem, biol basis radiation protection criteria, Nat Coun Radiat Protection & Measurements Sci Comt, 77-; consult, Comt Fed Res Biol & Health Effects Ionizing Radiation, Nat Acad Sci, 80-81. *Mem:* Am Asn Cancer Res; Radiation Res Soc; AAAS; NAm Late Effects Group. *Res:* Mechanisms of radiation carcinogenesis and cocarcinogenesis. *Mailing Add:* Biol Div Oak Ridge Nat Lab PO Box Y Oak Ridge TN 37830

ULLRICK, WILLIAM CHARLES, b Evanston, Ill, June 6, 24; m 48; c 3. PHYSIOLOGY. *Educ:* Northwestern Univ, BS, 49; Univ Ill, MS, 51, PhD(physiol), 55. *Prof Exp:* Lab asst zool, comp anat & embryol, Northwestern Univ, 48-49; asst physiol, Col Med, Univ Ill, 50-54; from instr to assoc prof, 54-63, PROF PHYSIOL, SCH MED, BOSTON UNIV, 63- *Concurrent Pos:* USPHS career res develop awards, 59-; mem bd dirs, Harvard Apparatus Co, Mass, 58-61. *Mem:* AAAS; Biophys Soc; Am Physiol Soc; NY Acad Sci. *Res:* Muscle physiology and biochemistry. *Mailing Add:* Dept of Physiol Boston Univ Sch of Med Boston MA 02118

ULLYOT, GLENN EDGAR, b Clark Co, SDak, Mar 11, 10; m 35. ORGANIC CHEMISTRY. *Educ:* Univ Minn, BChem, 33; Univ Ill, MS, 35, PhD(org chem), 38. *Prof Exp:* Res chemist, Smith Kline & French Labs, 37-45, head org chem sect, 45-50, dir chem labs, 50-57, assoc dir res, 57-67, dir sci liaison res & develop div, 67-75; CONSULT, 75- *Concurrent Pos:* Mem ad hoc comt anticonvulsants, Nat Inst Neurol & Commun Dis & Stroke, 69-72, epilepsy adv comt, 72-76 & 81-84; consult, Epilepsy Br, Neurol Dis Progs, 75, Franklin Inst Res Lab, Sci Liaison, 76-80 & Biosearch Inc, 81- *Mem:* AAAS; Am Chem Soc; fel Am Inst Chem; Am Soc Pharmacol & Exp Therapeut; Acad Pharmaceut Sci. *Res:* Research and development administration; synthetic medicinal agents; central nervous system active agents; diuretics; structure-biological activity relation. *Mailing Add:* Box 205 Kimberton PA 19442

ULM, EDGAR H, b McKeesport, Pa, July 23, 42; m 65; c 1. BIOCHEMISTRY. *Educ:* Ind Univ Pa, BA, 65; Ohio Univ, MS, 67; Purdue Univ, PhD(biochem), 72. *Prof Exp:* Res assoc biochem, St Louis Univ Med Sch, 71-73; sr res biochemist, 73-76, RES FEL, MERCK INST, 76- *Concurrent Pos:* NIH res fel, 72-73. *Mem:* Am Chem Soc; AAAS. *Res:* Biochemistry renin angiotensin; biochemistry of hypertension; rational drug design based on specific alterations of enzymatic activities; metabolism and disposition of enalaprilmaleate. *Mailing Add:* Merck Inst Therapeut Res West Point PA 19486

ULM, LESTER, JR, b Palm Harbor, Fla, Aug 5, 22; m 45; c 2. ELECTRICAL ENGINEERING. *Educ:* Ga Inst Technol, BEE, 49. *Prof Exp:* Test engr, Gen Elec Co, 49-50; student engr, 50, sr inspector, 50-51, from jr engr to sr engr, 51-57, from assoc engr to engr, 57-58, gen engr, 58-62, dir eng, 62-74, dir methods & procedures, 74-80, VPRES SERV, TAMPA ELEC CO, 80- *Mem:* Am Soc Eng Educ; Inst Elec & Electronics Engrs. *Res:* Electrical utility engineering. *Mailing Add:* Tampa Elec Co PO Box 111 Tampa FL 33601

ULMER, DAVID D, b McCall, Idaho, Nov 10, 29; m 54; c 2. INTERNAL MEDICINE, PHYSICAL CHEMISTRY. *Educ:* Univ Idaho, BS, 50; Wash Univ, MD, 54. *Prof Exp:* Intern, Peter Bent Brigham Hosp, 54-55, asst resident physician, 55-56; res fel med, Harvard Med Sch, 58-61, from instr to assoc prof, 61-72; prof, Univ Southern Calif, 72-79; PROF MED & CHMN DEPT, CHARLES R DREW POSTGRAD MED SCH, 72-; PROF IN

RESIDENCE, MED SCH, UNIV CALIF, LOS ANGELES, 79- *Concurrent Pos:* Nat Found fel, 58-60; Nat Inst Arthritis & Metab Dis fel, 60-61; NIH res career develop award, 61-71; asst med, Peter Bent Brigham Hosp, 58-61, jr assoc, 61-63, chief resident physician, 63-64, assoc med, 64-67, sr assoc, 67-71, physician, 71-72; chief internal med, Martin Luther King Hosp, Los Angeles, 72- *Mem:* Am Chem Soc; Am Soc Biol Chem. *Res:* Role of metals in biological systems; abnormal metal metabolism in disease; metal toxicology. *Mailing Add:* Los Angeles County-King Hosp 12021 S Wilmington Ave Los Angeles CA 90059

ULMER, GENE CARLETON, b Cincinnati, Ohio, Jan 28, 37; m 60; c 4. THERMODYNAMICS, ORE DEPOSITS. *Educ:* Univ Cincinnati, BS, 58; Pa State Univ, PhD(geochem), 64. *Prof Exp:* Asst geochem, Pa State Univ, 59-62, staff res asst, Col Mineral Industs, 62-64; engr, Homer Res Labs, Bethlehem Steel Corp, Pa, 64-69; assoc prof, 69-74, PROF GEOL, TEMPLE UNIV, 74- *Mem:* AAAS; Mineral Soc Am; Am Ceramic Soc; Am Geophys Union. *Res:* High temperature phase equilibria; oxide systems; oxidation reduction reactions, equilibria and kinetics; experimental petrology; materials research, especially spinels, diamonds and silicates, ultramafics in Africa and basalts in Idaho-Oregon; high pressure-high temperature research. *Mailing Add:* Rm 307 Buery Hall Temple Univ Dept of Geol Philadelphia PA 19122

ULMER, MARTIN JOHN, b US, June 4, 20; m 46; c 4. HELMINTHOLOGY. *Educ:* Univ Mich, BS, 42, MS, 43, PhD(zool), 50. *Prof Exp:* From asst prof to assoc prof, 50-59, PROF ZOOL, IOWA STATE UNIV, 59-, GRAD FAC, 53-, ASSOC DEAN GRAD COL, 71-, DISTINGUISHED PROF, 81- *Concurrent Pos:* Univ Va-Mt Lake Biol Sta, 60, 63. *Honors & Awards:* Ward Medal, Am Soc Parasitol, 66. *Mem:* Am Soc Parasitol (treas, 59-62, pres, 77); Am Micros Soc (pres, 82); Am Soc Zool; Wildlife Dis Asn. *Res:* Life cycles and host-parasite relationships of helminths. *Mailing Add:* Dept Zool Iowa State Univ Ames IA 50010

ULMER, MELVILLE PAUL, b Washington, DC, Mar 12, 43; m 68; c 1. X-RAY ASTRONOMY. *Educ:* Johns Hopkins Univ, BA, 65; Univ Wis, PhD(physics), 70. *Prof Exp:* Res assoc physics, Univ Calif, San Diego, 70-74; astrophysicist, Smithsonian Astrophys Observ, 74-76; ASST PROF PHYSICS & ASTRON, NORTHWESTERN UNIV, 76- *Mem:* Am Astron Soc; Int Astron Union; Am Phys Soc; Royal Astron Soc. *Res:* Measurement of spectra and positions of galactic and extragalactic x-ray sources; application of x-ray astronomy to studies in cosmology, galactic structure and the interstellar medium. *Mailing Add:* Dept of Physics & Astron Northwestern Univ Evanston IL 60201

ULMER, RICHARD CLYDE, b Lancaster, Ohio, July 4, 09; m 36; c 1. PHYSICAL CHEMISTRY. *Educ:* Ohio State Univ, AB, 30, PhD(chem), 36. *Prof Exp:* Chief chemist, Columbus and Southern Ohio Elec Co, 30-33; asst head chem div, Res Dept, Detroit Edison Co, 36-45; tech dir, E F Drew & Co, Inc, 45-53; mgr res, Combustion Eng, Inc, Windsor, 53-66, exec engr, 66-74; RETIRED. *Mem:* Am Chem Soc; Am Soc Mech Eng. *Res:* Water treatment and corrosion in the power boiler and electric utility fields. *Mailing Add:* 3000 S Course Dr 610 Pompano Beach FL 33060

ULOTH, ROBERT HENRY, b Valley City, NDak, Mar 17, 27; m 50; c 2. ORGANIC CHEMISTRY. *Educ:* Valley City State Col, BS, 49; Univ NDak, MSc, 54. *Prof Exp:* Assoc chemist, 54-58, chemist, 59-60, sr scientist, 60-68, res assoc, 68-69, patent coordr, 69-70, PATENT AGENT, MEAD JOHNSON & CO, 70- *Mem:* Am Chem Soc. *Res:* Synthetic pharmaceutical drugs. *Mailing Add:* Mead Johnson Res Ctr Evansville IN 47721

ULREY, STEPHEN SCOTT, b Wilmington, Del, July 29, 46; m 69; c 2. INDUSTRIAL ORGANIC CHEMISTRY, PROCESS DEVELOPMENT. *Educ:* WVa Univ, BS, 68; Ohio State Univ, PhD(org chem), 73. *Prof Exp:* DEVELOP CHEMIST, AM CYANAMID CO, 74- *Mem:* Am Chem Soc. *Res:* Catalysis in organic chemistry, especially enzyme model compounds; industrial process development. *Mailing Add:* 1400 Sheridan Rd Dept 453 Abbott Labs North Chicago IL 60064

ULRICH, AARON JACK, b Benton, Ill, Feb 27, 21; m; c 2. REACTOR PHYSICS. *Educ:* Univ Chicago, BS, 43, MS, 50. *Prof Exp:* Instr physics, Univ Chicago, 43-44; jr physicist, Oak Ridge Nat Lab, 44-46; asst physicist, 50-51, assoc physicist, 51-72, PHYSICIST, ARGONNE NAT LAB, 72- *Mem:* Am Phys Soc; Am Nuclear Soc; Sigma Xi. *Res:* Nuclear fission power reactors, safety test reactor design, planning and analysis of critical experiments and reactor safety tests; energy conversion; plasma physics and thermonuclear power reactors. *Mailing Add:* Appl Physics Div Argonne Nat Lab 9700 Cass Ave Argonne IL 60439

ULRICH, ARLENE LOUISE, microbiology, see previous edition

ULRICH, BENJAMIN H(ARRISON), JR, b Olean, NY, Nov 5, 22; m 45; c 3. AERONAUTICAL ENGINEERING. *Educ:* Pa State Univ, BS, 44, MS, 49. *Prof Exp:* Aeronaut res scientist, Nat Adv Comt Aeronaut, 44 & 46-47; asst prof mech, Pa State Univ, 49-50; educ specialist, US Marine Corps Inst, 50-51; asst prof aeronaut eng, Univ WVa, 51-55, assoc prof aerospace eng, 56-66; PROF AEROSPACE ENG & ENG SCI & CHMN DEPT, PARKS COL AERONAUT TECHNOL, ST LOUIS UNIV, 66- *Concurrent Pos:* Stress analyst, N Am Aviation, Inc, 53; flight test engr, Boeing Aircraft Co, 55; ed, Aero Div J, Am Soc Eng Educ, 59-62. *Mem:* Am Soc Eng Educ; Soc Exp Stress Anal; Am Inst Aeronaut & Astronaut. *Res:* Theories of failure and structural loading. *Mailing Add:* Dept of Aerospace Eng & Eng Sci St Louis Univ Cahokia IL 62206

ULRICH, DALE V, b Wenatchee, Wash, Mar 1, 32; m 53; c 3. PHYSICS. *Educ:* La Verne Col, BA, 54; Univ Ore, MS, 56; Univ Va, PhD(physics), 64. *Prof Exp:* Instr, 58-61, from asst prof to assoc prof, 64-67, PROF PHYSICS & DEAN COL, BRIDGEWATER COL, 67- *Concurrent Pos:* NSF res grant, 64-68. *Mem:* Am Asn Physics Teachers; Am Phys Soc. *Res:* Partial specific volume studies on biological macromolecules; density studies in the critical region of single component systems. *Mailing Add:* Bridgewater Col Bridgewater VA 22812

ULRICH, FLOYD SEYMOUR, b Huron, SDak, Feb 22, 15; m 41; c 4. MEDICINAL CHEMISTRY, ANALYTICAL CHEMISTRY. *Educ:* Huron Col, SDak, BA, 40; Kans State Univ, MS, 51; Okla State Univ, PhD, 56. *Prof Exp:* Asst prof chem, Huron Col, SDak, 46-52; tech asst to chief chemist, Celanese Chem Co, 55-65; instr pharm, Sch Pharm, Southwestern Okla State Univ, 65-67, assoc prof med chem, 67-80; RETIRED. *Mem:* Am Chem Soc; Acad Pharmaceut Sci; Sigma Xi. *Res:* Nonaqueous high resistance, organic, polarographic analysis. *Mailing Add:* Dept Pharm Southwestern Okla State Univ Weatherford OK 73096

ULRICH, FRANK, b Frankfurt-am-Main, Ger, Aug 30, 26; nat US; m 57; c 3. CELL PHYSIOLOGY. *Educ:* Univ Calif, BA, 48, PhD, 52. *Prof Exp:* Jr res endocrinologist, Univ Calif, 52-53; estab investr, Am Heart Asn, 57-62; asst prof, Yale Univ, 62-67; sr res assoc, Grad Sch Nutrit, Cornell Univ, 67-69; ASSOC PROF PHYSIOL, DEPT SURG, SCH MED, TUFTS UNIV, 69- *Concurrent Pos:* Brown Mem fel physiol, Sch Med, Yale Univ, 53-54; Nat Cancer Inst fel, 54-56; Arthritis & Rheumatism Found fel, 56-57. *Mem:* Am Soc Cell Biol; Am Physiol Soc; Brit Biochem Soc; Soc Exp Biol Med. *Res:* Ion transport in mitochondria, ions and cell respiration; enzyme kinetics; macrophage physiology. *Mailing Add:* Surg Unit Vet Admin Hosp 150 S Huntington Ave Boston MA 02130

ULRICH, GAIL DENNIS, b Devils Slide, Utah, Oct 29, 35; m 58; c 5. CHEMICAL ENGINEERING. *Educ:* Univ Utah, BS, 59, MS, 62; Mass Inst Technol, DSc(chem eng), 64. *Prof Exp:* Sr researcher chem eng, Atomics Int Div, NAm Aviation, 64-65; res engr, Billerica Res Ctr, Cabot Corp, 65-70; asst prof, 70-76, ASSOC PROF CHEM ENG, UNIV NH, 77- *Mem:* Combustion Inst. *Res:* Particle formation in flames; furnace combustion and incineration; chemical engineering process design. *Mailing Add:* Dept Chem Eng Kingsbury Hall Univ NH Durham NH 03824

ULRICH, GEORGE ERWIN, geology, see previous edition

ULRICH, HENRI, b Rheinsberg, Ger, May 4, 25; nat US; m 54; c 4. ORGANIC POLYMER CHEMISTRY. *Educ:* Univ Berlin, dipl, 52, Dr rer nat, 54. *Prof Exp:* Instr org chem, Univ Berlin, 53-54; res assoc, Res Found, Ohio State Univ, 55-56; res chemist, Olin Mathieson Chem Corp, Ohio, 56-59; group leader org res, Carwin Co, 59-62, head org res, Donald S Gilmore Res Lab, 62-65, mgr chem res & develop, 65-76, dir, 76-81, VPRES, DONALD S GILMORE RES LABS, UPJOHN CO, 82- *Mem:* AAAS; Am Chem Soc; Soc Ger Chem. *Res:* Isocyanates; polyurethanes; agricultural chemicals; light sensitive chemicals. *Mailing Add:* Upjohn Co 410 Sackett Pt Rd North Haven CT 06473

ULRICH, JOHN AUGUST, b St Paul, Minn, May 15, 15; m 40; c 6. MICROBIOLOGY, BACTERIOLOGY. *Educ:* St Thomas Col, BS, 38; Univ Minn, PhD(bact), 47; Am Bd Microbiol, dipl, 63. *Prof Exp:* Teacher, High Sch, Minn, 38-41; asst bact, 41-45 & Hormel Inst, 45-46; first asst, Mayo Clin, 49-50, consult, 50-65, assoc prof bact, Mayo Grad Sch Med, Univ Minn, 65-69, assoc prof microbiol, Univ, 66-69; PROF MICROBIOL, MED SCH, UNIV N MEX, 69- *Concurrent Pos:* Res fel, Hormel Inst, Univ Minn, 46-49; consult, Econ Labs, Mo, 45, Hormel Packing Plant, Minn, 47-, NIH, 56-, Nat Commun Dis Ctr, 63-, NASA, 65-, Vet Admin, 69-, Sandia Labs, 70- & Midwest Res Inst, 71- *Mem:* AAAS; Am Soc Microbiol; Mycol Soc Am; Am Chem Soc; Am Acad Microbiol. *Res:* Skin bacteriology; hospital epidemiology; surgery air recirculation; infected wounds; chemotherapy; food preservation; low temperature; bacterial metabolism; medical mycology and bacteriology. *Mailing Add:* Dept Microbiol Sch Med Univ NMex Albuquerque NM 87131

ULRICH, MERWYN GENE, b Norfolk, Nebr, July 14, 36; m 58. ZOOLOGY. *Educ:* Westmar Col, BA, 58; Univ SDak, MA, 62; Univ Southern Ill, PhD(zool), 66. *Prof Exp:* asst prof, Westmar Col, 66-68, assoc prof, 68-74. *Concurrent Pos:* Vis prof biol, Silliman Univ, Phillippines, 72-73; aquacult specialist, World Bank Bangkok, Thailand, 74-75; adj prof biol, Westmar Col, 74- *Mem:* Am Fisheries Soc; Sigma Xi. *Res:* Fisheries management and culture. *Mailing Add:* 1600 Hiawatha Trail Sioux City IA 51104

ULRICH, PETER B, optical physics, see previous edition

ULRICH, RENEE SANDRA, neuroendocrinology, see previous edition

ULRICH, STEPHEN EDGAR, chemistry, see previous edition

ULRICH, VALENTIN, b Palmerton, Pa, Aug 5, 26. GENETICS. *Educ:* Rutgers Univ, AB, 53, PhD, 61. *Prof Exp:* From asst prof to assoc prof, 57-68, chmn develop biol fac, 74-77, PROF GENETICS, W VA UNIV, 68-, GENETICIST, 77- *Concurrent Pos:* Consult, Nat Tech Adv Comt Pesticides in Water Environ, 70 & Environ Protection Agency, 70-75. *Mem:* AAAS; Genetic Soc Am. *Res:* Biochemistry and genetics of heterosis. *Mailing Add:* Plant Sci Div WVa Univ Morgantown WV 26506

ULRICH, WERNER, b Munich, Ger, Mar 12, 31; US citizen; m 59; c 2. ELECTRICAL ENGINEERING. *Educ:* Columbia Univ, BS, 52, MS, 53, EngScD(elec eng), 57; Univ Chicago, Grad Sch Bus, MBA, 75. *Prof Exp:* Mem tech staff, 53-58, supvr, Switching Syst Develop, 58-64, dept head, 64-68, dir advan switching technol, 68-77, head, Systs Reliability Design Dept, 77-81, MEM LEGAL & PATENT STAFF, BELL LABS, 81- *Concurrent Pos:* Vis lectr, Univ Calif, Berkeley, 66-67. *Mem:* Asn Comput Mach; fel Inst Elec & Electronics Engrs. *Res:* System design and development of automatic fault recovery facilities for program controlled electronic telephone switching systems. *Mailing Add:* Bell Tel Labs Naperville IL 60540

ULRICH, WILLIAM FREDERICK, b Pinckneyville, Ill, Nov 4, 26; m 51; c 3. INORGANIC CHEMISTRY, ANALYTICAL CHEMISTRY. *Educ:* Southern Ill Univ, BS, 49; Univ Ill, PhD, 52. *Prof Exp:* Supvr spectrochem group, Shell Develop Co, 52-56; supvr appln eng, 55-66, mgr appl res, Sci

Instruments Dir, 66-74, MGR CLIN MKT DEVELOP, BECKMAN INSTRUMENTS, INC, 74- *Mem:* Am Chem Soc; Soc Appl Spectros (treas, 67-69); Spectros Soc Can; Am Asn Clin Chemists. *Res:* Analytical instrumentation, ultraviolet and infrared spectrophotometry; atomic absorption; gas chromatography; electrochemistry; radioimmunoassay. *Mailing Add:* Sci Instruments Div PO Box C19600 Irvine CA 92713

ULRICHSON, DEAN LEROY, b Alma, Nebr, Mar 6, 37; m 61; c 3. CHEMICAL ENGINEERING. *Educ:* Univ Nebr, Lincoln, BSc, 62; Univ Ill, Urbana, MSc, 63; Iowa State Univ, PhD(chem eng), 70. *Prof Exp:* Res engr, E I du Pont de Nemours & Co, Inc, 63-68; res asst chem eng, 69-70, asst prof, 70-74, assoc prof, 74-81, PROF CHEM ENG, IOWA STATE UNIV, 81- *Mem:* Am Inst Chem Engrs; Am Soc Eng Educ; Nat Soc Prof Engrs. *Res:* Thermodynamics; solid-gas reaction kinetics; modelling and simulation of chemical processes. *Mailing Add:* 231 Sweeney Hall Iowa State Univ Ames IA 50011

ULRYCH, TADEUSZ JAN, b Warsaw, Poland, Aug 9, 35; Can citizen; m 58; c 2. GEOPHYSICS. *Educ:* Univ London, BSc, 57; Univ BC, MSc, 61, PhD(geophys), 63. *Prof Exp:* Asst prof geophys, Univ Western Ont, 61-64; Nat Res Coun fel, Oxford Univ, 64-65 & Bernard Price Inst Geophys, 65; asst prof, Univ BC, 65-67; vis prof, Petrobras, Salvador, Brazil, 67-68; assoc prof, 68-74, PROF GEOPHYS, UNIV BC, 74- *Concurrent Pos:* Vis lectr, B A Oil, Alta, Can, 66. *Mem:* Am Geophys Union. *Res:* Applications of communication theory to geophysics and astronomy; isotope geophysics. *Mailing Add:* Dept Geophys & Astron Univ BC Vancouver BC B6T 1W5 Can

ULSAMER, ANDREW GEORGE, JR, b Yonkers, NY, Nov 13, 41; m 65; c 3. BIOCHEMISTRY, TOXICOLOGY. *Educ:* Siena Col, BS, 63; Albany Med Col, PhD(biochem), 67. *Prof Exp:* USPHS fel, Nat Heart Inst, Md, 67-68, staff fel, 68-70; res biochemist, Div Toxicol, US Food & Drug Admin, 70-73; res biochemsist, 73-75, chief Biochem Br, 75-80, DIR DIV HEALTH EFFECTS, CONSUMER PROD SAFETY COMN, 80- *Concurrent Pos:* Proj adv group, Food & Drug Admin, Dept Housing & Urban Develop & Nat Inst Drug Abuse. *Mem:* AAAS; Soc Toxicol; NY Acad Sci; Sigma Xi. *Res:* Evaluation of the hazards posed by toxic substances found in consumer products, with particular emphasis on indoor air pollutants. *Mailing Add:* Consumer Prod Safety Comn 5401 Westbard Ave Bethesda MD 20014

ULSTROM, ROBERT, b Minneapolis, Minn, Feb 23, 23; m 46; c 3. MEDICINE. *Educ:* Univ Minn, BS, 44, MD, 46. *Prof Exp:* Intern & resident, Strong Mem Hosp, Rochester, NY, 46-48; from instr to asst prof pediat, Univ Minn, 50-53; asst prof, Univ Calif, Los Angeles, 53-56; from assoc prof to prof, Sch Med, Univ Minn, 56-64; prof & chmn dept, Sch Med, Univ Calif, Los Angeles, 64-67; assoc dean med sch, 67-70, PROF PEDIAT, MED SCH, UNIV MINN, MINNEAPOLIS, 67- *Concurrent Pos:* Markle scholar, 54-59; consult, Hennepin County Gen Hosp, 56-; mem study sect, NIH, 64-68; examr, Am Bd Pediat, 71-, mem bd, 80- *Mem:* AAAS; Soc Pediat Res; Endocrine Soc; Lawson Wilkins Pediat Endocrine Soc; Am Pediat Soc. *Res:* Metabolism of children, particularly the endocrine aspects of the neo-natal period; developmental endocrinology. *Mailing Add:* Dept of Pediat Univ of Minn Med Sch Minneapolis MN 55455

ULTEE, CASPER JAN, b Noordwyk, Netherlands, Apr 5, 28; nat US; m 50; c 4. MOLECULAR SPECTROSCOPY, PHYSICAL CHEMISTRY. *Educ:* Hope Col, BA, 50; Purdue Univ, PhD(chem), 54. *Prof Exp:* Res chemist, Linde Co Div, Union Carbide Corp, 54-60; chemist, Res & Adv Develop Div, Avco Corp, 60-61; sr res scientist, 61-67, prin scientist, Res Lab, United Aircraft Corp, 67-76, mgr chem physics, 76-81, MGR CHEM PHYSICS & COMBUSTION SCI, UNITED TECHNOL RES CTR, 81- *Mem:* Am phys Soc; Am Chem Soc. *Res:* Infrared, Raman and electron spin resonance spectroscopy; molecular structure; chemical kinetics; spectroscopy of high temperature arcs; gas phase and chemical lasers. *Mailing Add:* 55 Harvest Lane Glastonbury CT 06033

ULTMAN, JAMES STUART, b Chicago, Ill, Oct 24, 43; m 67; c 3. CHEMICAL ENGINEERING, BIOENGINEERING. *Educ:* Ill Inst Technol, BS, 65; Univ Del, MChE, 67, PhD(chem eng), 69. *Prof Exp:* Asst prof, 70-76, assoc prof, 76-81, PROF CHEM ENG, PA STATE UNIV, UNIVERSITY PARK, 81- *Concurrent Pos:* Instr, Univ Del, 69, NIH fel, 69-70; Fulbright-Hays lectr, Technion-Israel Inst Technol, 77-78. *Mem:* Am Inst Chem Engrs; Am Asn Med Instrumentation. *Res:* Mass transfer; electrochemistry. *Mailing Add:* 106 Fenske Lab Pa State Univ University Park PA 16802

ULTMANN, JOHN ERNEST, b Vienna, Austria, Jan 6, 25; US citizen; m 52; c 3. HEMATOLOGY, ONCOLOGY. *Educ:* Columbia Univ, MD, 52; Am Bd Internal Med, dipl. *Prof Exp:* Intern, NY Hosp-Cornell Med Ctr, 52-53, asst resident med, 53-54, asst med & resident hemat, 54-55; instr med, Col Physicians & Surgeons, Columbia Univ, 56-61, assoc, 61-62, asst prof, 62-68; assoc prof, 68-70, PROF MED, SCH MED, UNIV CHICAGO, 70-, DIR CANCER RES CTR, 73-; DIR CLIN ONCOL, FRANKLIN McLEAN MEM RES INST, 68- *Concurrent Pos:* Nat Cancer Inst trainee, NY Hosp-Cornell Med Ctr, 53-55; Am Cancer Inst Soc fel hemat, Col Physicians & Surgeons, Columbia Univ, 55-56; from asst vis physician to vis physician, Francis Delafield Hosp, 56-68; career scientist, Health Res Coun City New York, 59-68; asst physician, Presby Hosp, 59-65, asst attend physician, 65-68; clin asst vis physician, 1st Med Div, Bellevue Hosp, 61-62, asst vis physician, 63-68; consult, Harlem Hosp, 66-68; assoc dean res prog sch med Univ Chicago, 78- *Mem:* Fel Am Col Physicians; Am Asn Cancer Res; Am Soc Hemat; Am Soc Clin Oncol; Int Soc Hemat. *Res:* Chemotherapy cancer, lymphoma and leukemia; pathophysiology of anemia of cancer; immune defects of patients with lymphoma. *Mailing Add:* 950 E 59th St Chicago IL 60637

ULUG, ESIN M, Can citizen. COMMUNICATIONS SYSTEMS, INFORMATION SYSTEMS. *Educ:* Univ Durham, BSc, 53, MSc, 64; Carleton Univ, PhD(elec eng), 73. *Prof Exp:* Engr switching equip, Bell Can, 54-56; mgr eng, Can Gen Elec, 56-70; mgr tech develop, subsyst technol, Microsyst Int, 70-72; staff engr spec proj, Bell Can, 72-74; prof syst eng & comput sci, Carleton Univ, 74-78; mgr commun syst, Tex Instruments, 78-80; MGR COMMUN SYST, GEN ELEC CORP, 80- *Concurrent Pos:* Consult, Bell Can, Telesat Can & Govt Can, 74-78, Tex Instruments, 77-78. *Mem:* Inst Elec & Electronic Engrs; Inst Elec Eng UK. *Res:* Data communication systems; satellite communications; encoded voice; communication protocols; local area computer networks; real time systems; information theory; algebraic topological methods; queueing theory. *Mailing Add:* 1506 Wheatly Ct Schenectady NY 12309

ULVEDAL, FRODE, b Oslo, Norway, Nov 20, 32; US citizen; m 57; c 1. PHYSIOLOGY, ENDOCRINOLOGY. *Educ:* St Svithun's Col, Norway, BS, 51; Drew Univ, BA, 55; Emory Univ, PhD(physiol), 59. *Prof Exp:* Chief physiol support div, Laughlin AFB, Tex, 59-60, aviation physiologist, US Air Force Sch Aerospace Med, 60-62, chief adv res unit, SMBE, 62-65, chief chem sect, 65-66, chief sealed environ sect & task scientist, 66-68, chief sealed environ br, 68-72; chief pulmonary scor br, Nat Heart & Lung Inst, 72-74; actg dir, 74-77, SUPVRY TOXICOLOGIST, WASTES & TOXIC SUBSTANCES, HEALTH EFFECTS DIV, ENVIRON PROTECTION AGENCY, 77- *Concurrent Pos:* Fel, Emory Univ, 66. *Mem:* Am Physiol Soc; Endocrine Soc; Am Col Toxicol. *Res:* Effects of altered atmospheric conditions like altitude and gaseous composition on man and other animals during prolonged exposures in space cabin environments; oxygen toxicity at decreased pressure, especially in regard to endocrinology, hematology and biochemistry; toxicology of environmental pollutants. *Mailing Add:* Wastes & Toxics Substances Health Effects Div 401 M St SW Washington DC 20460

UMAN, MARTIN A(LLAN), b Tampa, Fla, July 3, 36; m 62; c 3. ELECTRICAL ENGINEERING. *Educ:* Princeton Univ, BSE, 57, MA, 59, PhD(elec eng), 61. *Prof Exp:* Assoc prof elec eng, Univ Ariz, 61-65; fel scientist, Westinghouse Res Labs, Pa, 65-71; PROF ELEC ENG, UNIV FLA, 71- *Concurrent Pos:* Pres, Lightning Location & Protection, Inc, 75- *Mem:* Inst Elec & Electronics Engrs; Am Geophys Union; Am Meteorol Soc; Int Union Geophys & Geod. *Res:* Gaseous electronics and breakdown phenomena; electromagnetic field theory. *Mailing Add:* Dept of Elec Eng Univ of Fla Gainesville FL 32611

UMAN, MYRON F, b Tampa, Fla, Oct 13, 39; m 63; c 1. ELECTRICAL ENGINEERING, PLASMA PHYSICS. *Educ:* Princeton Univ, BSEE, 61, MA, 66, PhD(elec eng), 68; Univ Ill, Urbana, MS, 62. *Prof Exp:* Res asst, Plasma Physics Lab, Princeton Univ, 64-68; asst prof elec eng, Univ Calif, Davis, 68-74; prog mgr, NSF, 74-75; SR STAFF OFFICER, NAT ACAD SCI, 75-, ASSOC EXEC SECY, ENVIRON STUDIES BD, 80- *Concurrent Pos:* Chmn fac, Col Eng, Univ Calif, Davis, 70-71; Am Soc Eng Educ-Ford Found resident fel, East Fishkill Facility, IBM Systs Prods Div, NY, 72-73; Sloan resident fel, Nat Acad Sci, 73-74. *Mem:* AAAS; Am Phys Soc; NY Acad Sci; Sigma Xi. *Res:* Plasma waves and heating; applications of science and technology to public policy decision making; environmental, energy and mineral resource policy. *Mailing Add:* 2101 Constitution Ave NW Washington DC 20418

UMANS, ROBERT SCOTT, b New York, NY, Dec 17, 41. BIOPHYSICAL CHEMISTRY, CELLULAR PHYSIOLOGY. *Educ:* Columbia Univ, AB, 62; Yale Univ, MS, 63, PhD(chem), 66. *Prof Exp:* Res assoc biophys chem, Johns Hopkins Univ, 66-68, NIH fel, 67-68; res assoc, Inst Biophys & Biochem, Paris, 68-69; Mass Div, Am Cancer Soc res grant, Boston Univ, 71-72, asst prof chem, 69-75; asst prof chem, Boston Col, 76-77; asst prof chem, Wellesley Col, 77-80; RES FEL PHYSIOL, SCH PUB HEALTH, HARVARD UNIV, 80- *Mem:* Am Chem Soc. *Res:* Biochemical studies of the role in cancer causation and treatment of steroid hormones and chemicals. *Mailing Add:* Dept Chem Sch Pub Health Harvard Univ Cambridge MA 02138

UMANZIO, CARL BEEMAN, b Thompsonville, Conn, Apr 9, 07; m 29; c 1. MICROBIOLOGY. *Educ:* Univ Boston, AM, 35; Wash Univ, St Louis, PhD, 50. *Prof Exp:* Asst med mycol, Sch Med, Univ Boston, 34-35; educ adv, Civilian Conserv Corps, 35-37; teacher, High Sch, Mass, 37-39; mem staff pharm, Franklin Tech Inst, 39-47; prof bact & parasitol & chmn dept microbiol, 47-74, EMER PROF MICROBIOL, KIRKSVILLE COL OSTEOP MED, 74- *Concurrent Pos:* Mem staff pharm, Cambridge Jr Col, 42-47; consult, 47- *Mem:* Am Soc Microbiol; Mycol Soc Am; Sigma Xi; Am Soc Trop Med & Hyg; Nat Asn Biol Teachers. *Res:* Medical mycology; parasitology; hypersensitivity; antibiotics. *Mailing Add:* Dept Microbiol Kirksville Col Osteop Med Kirksville MO 63501

UMBERGER, ERNEST JOY, b Burke, SDak, Aug 5, 09; m 32; c 3. PHARMACOLOGY, ENDOCRINOLOGY. *Educ:* George Washington Univ, BS, 37, MA, 41; Georgetown Univ, PhD(biochem), 48. *Prof Exp:* Asst sci aide fermentation sect, Bur Agr Chem & Eng, USDA, 37-39, jr chemist, Div Allergen Invests, 39-42, asst chemist, Naval Stores Res Div, 42-43; asst chemist, Div Pharmacol, US Food & Drug Admin, 43-44, pharmacologist, 44-47, chief endocrine sect, Drug Pharmacol Br, 57-67, chief drug anal br, Div Pharmaceut Sci, Bus Sci Consumer Protection & Environ Health Serv, 67-70, dir div drug biol, Off Pharmaceut Res & Testing, Bur Drugs, 70-71; RES CONSULT ENDOCRINE PHYSIOL, GRAD SCH ARTS & SCI, GEORGE WASHINGTON UNIV, 71-, CONSULT ENDOCRINOL & PHARMACOL, 71- *Mem:* Am Chem Soc; Soc Exp Biol & Med; Endocrine Soc. *Res:* Fermentation; chemistry of allergenic proteins; rosin esters; absorption of calomel from ointments; bioassay of estrogens; androgens, gonadotropins and adrenocorticotropic hormone; metabolism of steroid hormones; central nervous systems endocrine relationships. *Mailing Add:* 4811 Flanders Ave Kensington MD 20895

UMBREIT, GERALD ROSS, b Minneapolis, Minn, June 17, 30; m 53; c 3. ANALYTICAL CHEMISTRY. *Educ:* Augustana Col, SDak, BA, 54; Iowa State Univ, PhD(anal chem), 57. *Prof Exp:* Res asst, Ames Lab, AEC, Iowa, 54-57; res assoc, Upjohn Co, Mich, 58-63; res scientist, Lockheed Missiles & Space Co, Calif, 63-64; appln lab mgr, F & M Sci Div, Hewlett-Packard Co, Pa, 64-66; PRES, GREENWOOD LABS, 66- *Mem:* Am Chem Soc. *Res:* Chromatography; ion exchange. *Mailing Add:* Greenwood Labs 903 E Baltimore Pike Kennett Square PA 19348

UMBREIT, WAYNE WILLIAM, b Marksan, Wis, May 1, 13; m 37; c 3. BACTERIOLOGY, BIOCHEMISTRY. *Educ:* Univ Wis, BA, 34, MS, 36, PhD(bact, biochem), 39. *Prof Exp:* Asst bact & biochem, Univ Wis, 34-37, instr bact & chem, 38-41, asst prof bact, 41-44; instr soil microbiol, Rutgers Univ, 37-38; assoc prof bact, Cornell Univ, 44-46, prof, 46-47; head enzyme chem dept, Merck Inst Therapeut Res, 47-56, assoc dir, 56-58; prof bact & head dept, Rutgers Univ, 58-75. *Honors & Awards:* Lilly Award, 47; Waksman Award, 57; Carski Award, 68. *Mem:* AAAS; Am Soc Microbiol; Am Chem Soc; Am Soc Biol Chem; fel Am Acad Microbiol (vpres, 60). *Res:* Mode of action of antibiotics; nature of autotrophic bacteria; transformations of morphine by microorganisms. *Mailing Add:* Dept of Microbiol Nelson Biol Labs Rutgers Univ New Brunswick NJ 08903

UMEN, MICHAEL JAY, b Jamaica, NY, Feb 10, 48; m 69; c 1. REGULATORY AFFAIRS. *Educ:* Queens Col, BA, 69; Mass Inst Technol, PhD(org chem), 73. *Prof Exp:* Res scientist, sr scientist org med chem, Johnson & Johnson, 74-77, mgr res info serv dept, McNeil Pharmaceut, 77-80, dir, 80-81; INDEPENDENT CONSULT, 81- *Mem:* Am Chem Soc; Proprietary Asn; Am Med Writers Asn. *Res:* Pharmaceutical and medical device development; preparation of regulatory documents, literature reviews, publication manuscripts and technology assessments; evaluation of new product and licensing opportunities; coordination of preclinical and clinical trials; management consulting. *Mailing Add:* 544 Custis Rd Glenside PA 19038

UMEZAWA, HIROOMI, b Saitama-Ken, Japan, Sept 20, 24; m 58; c 2. THEORETICAL PHYSICS, SOLID STATE PHYSICS. *Educ:* Nagoya Univ, BS, 46, PhD(physics), 51. *Prof Exp:* Assoc prof physics, Nagoya Univ, 52-56; from assoc prof to prof, Univ Tokyo, 56-65; prof, Univ Naples, 65-66; prof, Univ Wis-Milwaukee, 66-67, distinguished prof, 67-75; KILLAM MEM PROF PHYSICS, UNIV ALTA, 75- *Concurrent Pos:* Imp Chem Indust fel, Univ Manchester, 53-55; vis prof, Univ Wash, 56, Univ Md, 57, Univ Iowa, 57 & Univ Aix Marseille, 59-60; leading mem Naples group of struct of matter, Ctr Nat Res, Italy, 65-66. *Mem:* Am Phys Soc; Phys Soc Japan; Italian Phys Soc. *Res:* Theoretical research on quantum field theory, high energy particle physics and many-body-problems. *Mailing Add:* Dept of Physics Univ of Alta Edmonton AB T6G 2S1 Can

UMHOLTZ, CLYDE ALLAN, b Du Quoin, Ill, Dec 20, 47. PROCESS DESIGN. *Educ:* Univ Ill, BS, 69, MBA, 71; Univ Melbourne, DSc, 75. *Prof Exp:* Eng planning analyst, Chem Mfg Group, W R Grace & Co & Subsidiaries; MGR, RES SERV, CTR INDUST CONSULT, MEMPHIS STATE UNIV, 78- *Concurrent Pos:* Consult, var energy, chemical & nuclear industs, 78-; vis lectr, Eng Sch, var univs, 79-; adj prof, Memphis State Univ, 80- *Mem:* Am Inst Chem Engrs; Am Chem Soc. *Res:* Angle trisector; energy considerations of Haber cycle; comprehensive engineering and economic studies of the sulfur, sulfuric acid and phosphate manufacturing industries; cost and materials science studies for the nuclear industry. *Mailing Add:* 3580 Hanna Dr Memphis TN 38128

UMMINGER, BRUCE LYNN, b Dayton, Ohio, Apr 10, 41; m 66; c 2. COMPARATIVE PHYSIOLOGY, ENVIRONMENTAL PHYSIOLOGY. *Educ:* Yale Univ, BS, 63, MS, 66, MPhil, 68, PhD(biol), 69. *Prof Exp:* From asst prof to assoc prof biol sci, Univ Cincinnati, 69-75, prof, 75-80, actg head dept, 73-75, admin intern, Off Develop, 74-75, fel, Grad Sch, 77-80, dir grad affairs biol sci, 78-80; DIR, REGULATORY BIOL PROG, NSF, 80- *Concurrent Pos:* NSF grant, Univ Cincinnati, 71-79; trainee, Nat Aeronaut & Space Admin, 64-67; trainee, NSF, 67-79; mem adv screening comt life sci, Coun Int Exchange Scholars, (Fulbright-Hays), 78-81; mem Space Shuttle Life Sci Proposal Rev Panel, Am Inst Biol Sci- NASA, 78; assoc ed, J Exp Zool, 77-; mem adv bd, Campbell Com Col, 77- *Honors & Awards:* Sigma Xi Distinguished Res Award, 73. *Mem:* Fel AAAS; Am Soc Zoologists; Am Inst Biol Sci; Am Soc Ichthyologists & Herpetologists; Ecol Soc Am. *Res:* Comparative physiology, biochemistry and endocrinology of fish acclimated to environmental extremes of temperature and salinity; carbohydrate metabolism and osmoregulation in fish; stress physiology of fish; low temperature biology. *Mailing Add:* Regulatory Biol Prog NSF 1800 G St NW Washington DC 20550

UMPHLETT, CLYDE JEFFERSON, botany, see previous edition

UN, HOWARD HO-WEI, b Hong Kong, June 8, 38; m 67; c 2. ORGANIC POLYMER CHEMISTRY. *Educ:* Beloit Col, BS, 60; Univ Mich, MSCh, 63, PhD(org chem), 65. *Prof Exp:* Res chemist, Exp Sta Lab, 65-69, tech rep, Chestnut Run Lab, 69-71, tech rep, Fluorocarbons Mkt, 71-74, mkt rep, fluorocarbons sales, 74-76, sr mkt rep, 76-77, supvr & prod coord, Bus Servs Div, Plastic Prods & Resins Dept, 77-79, EXPORT MKT MGR, INT MKT, POLYMER PROD DEPT, E I DU PONT DE NEMOURS, & CO, INC, 79- *Mem:* Am Chem Soc. *Res:* Fluorocarbon chemistry and polymers; thermally stable polymers. *Mailing Add:* Polymer Prod Dept Du Pont Bldg E I Du Pont de Nemours & Co Inc Wilmington DE 19898

UNAKAR, NALIN J, b Karachi, Pakistan, Mar 26, 35; m 62; c 2. CELL BIOLOGY. *Educ:* Gujarat Univ, India, BSc, 55; Univ Bombay, MSc, 61; Brown Univ, PhD(biol), 65. *Prof Exp:* Res asst biol, Indian Cancer Res Ctr, 55-61; res assoc path, Univ Toronto, 65-66; asst prof biol, 66-69, assoc prof biol sci, 69-74, PROF & CHMN DEPT BIOL SCI, OAKLAND UNIV, 74- *Concurrent Pos:* Nat Cancer Inst Can fel, 65-66; NIH res grant, 71- *Mem:* AAAS; Am Soc Cell Biol; Asn Res Vision & Opthal. *Res:* Cell ultrastructure and function; control of cell division; human and experimental cataracts; wound healing. *Mailing Add:* Dept of Biol Sci Oakland Univ Rochester MI 48063

UNANGST, PAUL CHARLES, b Fountain Hill, Pa, Apr 19, 44; m 69. MEDICINAL CHEMISTRY. *Educ:* Lehigh Univ, BS, 65; Carnegie-Mellon Univ, MS, 68, PhD(org chem), 70. *Prof Exp:* Res chemist, Ozone Systs Div, Welsbach Corp, 70-72; assoc chem, Lehigh Univ, 72-73; asst prof, East Stroudsburg State Col, 72-73; SR SCIENTIST WARNER-LAMBERT CO, 73- *Mem:* Am Chem Soc. *Res:* Imidates; conjugated nucleophilic addition; 1, 5-benzo-diazepenes; quinaldines; antimalarials; anti-allergy agents; CNS agents. *Mailing Add:* Warner-Lambert/Parke-Davis 2800 Plymouth Rd Ann Arbor MI 48106

UNANUE, EMIL R, b Havana, Cuba, Sept 13, 34; m 65; c 3. IMMUNOLOGY. *Educ:* Inst Sec Educ, BSc, 52; Univ Havana Sch Med, MD, 60; Harvard Univ, MA, 74. *Prof Exp:* Assoc exp path, Scripps Clin & Res Found, 60-70; intern path, Presby Univ Hosp, Pittsburgh, Pa, 61-62; res fel exp path, Scripps Clin & Res Found, 62-65; res fel immunol, Nat Inst Med Res London, 66-68; from asst prof to assoc prof path, 71-74, prof, 74-77, EDWARD MALLIOCKRODT JR PROF IMMUNOPATH, HARVARD MED SCH, 77- *Concurrent Pos:* Prof path, Harvard Med Sch. *Honors & Awards:* T Duckett Jones Award, Helen Hay Whitney Found, 68; Parke-Davis Award, Am Soc Exp Path, 73. *Mem:* Am Soc Exp Path; Am Soc Immunologists; Brit Soc Immunol; Reticuloendothelial Soc. *Res:* The cellular basis of the immune response; regulatory mechanisms in immunity. *Mailing Add:* Dept of Path Harvard Med Sch Boston MA 02115

UNBEHAUN, LARAINE MARIE, b Kearney, Nebr, May 4, 40; m 65. PLANT PATHOLOGY. *Educ:* Kearney State Col, BAEd, 61; Univ Northern Colo, MA, 64; Va Polytech Inst & State Univ, PhD(plant path), 69. *Prof Exp:* Teaching assoc biol, Univ Colo, Boulder, 64-65; asst prof, 69-71, assoc prof, 71-80, PROF BIOL, UNIV WIS-LA CROSSE, 80- *Mem:* Am Phytopath Soc; Sigma Xi. *Res:* Pectic enzyme production by Thielaviopsis basicola grown on synthetic and natural media; enzyme purification; characterization of pectic enzymes produced in black root rot diseased tobacco. *Mailing Add:* Dept Biol Univ Wis La Crosse WI 54601

UNDEEN, ALBERT HAROLD, parasitology, see previous edition

UNDERBRINK, ALAN GEORGE, plant cytology, radiobiology, see previous edition

UNDERDAHL, NORMAN RUSSELL, b Minn, June 5, 18; m 48; c 1. BACTERIOLOGY, VIROLOGY. *Educ:* St Olaf Col, BA, 41; Univ Minn, MS, 48. *Prof Exp:* Asst scientist, Hormel Inst, Univ Minn, 46-55; from asst prof to assoc prof, 55-68, PROF VET SCI, UNIV NEBR, LINCOLN, 68- *Concurrent Pos:* Mem, Conf Res Workers Animal Dis. *Honors & Awards:* Serv Award, Nat SPF Swine Accrediting Agency, 74. *Mem:* Assoc Am Vet Med Asn; Asn Gnotobiotics; Am Soc Microbiol. *Res:* Elimination of swine diseases by repopulation with disease-free pigs; isolation of causative agents of swine diseases using antibody-devoid, disease-free pig, obtained by surgery, as the host animal. *Mailing Add:* Dept of Vet Sci Univ of Nebr Lincoln NE 68583

UNDERDOWN, BRIAN JAMES, b Montreal, Que, Mar 23, 41; m 65; c 1. IMMUNOLOGY. *Educ:* McGill Univ, BSc, 64, PhD(immunol), 68. *Prof Exp:* Med Res Coun Can fel, Sch Med, Washington Univ, 68-70; ASST PROF MED & GRAD SECY INST OF IMMUNOL, UNIV TORONTO, 70- *Mem:* Can Soc Immunol. *Res:* Studies of the IgA immune response; studies of the structure of antibody molecules. *Mailing Add:* Dept of Med Univ of Toronto Toronto ON M5S 2R8 Can

UNDERHILL, ANNE BARBARA, b Vancouver, BC, June 12, 20. ASTROPHYSICS. *Educ:* Univ BC, BA, 42, MA, 44; Univ Chicago, PhD(astrophys), 48. *Hon Degrees:* DSc, York Univ, 69. *Prof Exp:* Nat Res Coun Can fel, Copenhagen Observ, 48-49; astrophysicist, Dom Astrophys Observ, 49-62; prof astrophys, State Univ Utrecht, 62-70; chief lab optical astron, 70-77, SR SCIENTIST, ASTRON & SOLAR PHYSICS LAB, GODDARD SPACE FLIGHT CTR, NASA, 77- *Concurrent Pos:* Vis lectr, Harvard Univ, 55-56; vis prof, Univ Colo, 67; Inst Astrophysics, Paris, 78-79. *Mem:* Am Astron Soc; Astron Soc Pac; Royal Astron Soc Can; Royal Astron Soc; Int Astron Union. *Res:* Atmospheres of hot stars; shell stars; model atmospheres; ultraviolet spectra of stars. *Mailing Add:* Code 680 Goddard Space Flight Ctr Greenbelt MD 20771

UNDERHILL, EDWARD WESLEY, b Regina, Sask, Jan 28, 31; m 54; c 3. PLANT BIOCHEMISTRY. *Educ:* Univ Sask, BScP, 54, MSc, 56; Univ RI, PhD(pharmacog), 60. *Prof Exp:* Lectr pharm, Univ Sask, 54-55, asst prof, 60-61; from asst res off to assoc res off, 61-74, SR RES OFF, NAT RES COUN CAN, 74- *Mem:* Am Emtomol Soc; Can Entomol Soc. *Res:* Isolation and characterization of insect sex pheromones and attractants, paricularly of Lepidoptera; application of sex pheromones for monitoring and controling insect populations. *Mailing Add:* Nat Res Coun 110 Gymnasium Rd Saskatoon SK S7N 0W9 Can

UNDERHILL, GLENN, b Trenton, Nebr, Oct 30, 25; m 58; c 5. THEORETICAL PHYSICS, ASTRONOMY. *Educ:* Nebr State Col, BS, 55; Univ Nebr, MA, 57, PhD(physics), 63. *Prof Exp:* Instr physics, Univ Nebr, 59-61; assoc prof, 63-68, PROF PHYSICS, KEARNEY STATE COL, 68-, HEAD DEPT PHYSICS & PHYS SCI, 71- *Mem:* Am Phys Soc; Am Asn Physics Teachers; Am Sci Affiliation. *Res:* Structure of beryllium-9 nucleus; interaction of radiation with matter. *Mailing Add:* Dept of Physics & Phys Sci Kearney State Col Kearney NE 68847

UNDERHILL, JAMES CAMPBELL, b Duluth, Minn, June 8, 23; m 43; c 3. ZOOLOGY. *Educ:* Univ Minn, BA, 49, MA, 52, PhD(zool), 55. *Prof Exp:* From asst prof to assoc prof zool, Univ SDak, 55-59; from asst prof to assoc prof, 59-69, coordr gen zool prog, 70-77, PROF ZOOL & BEHAV BIOL, UNIV MINN, MINNEAPOLIS, 69- *Mem:* Am Soc Ichthyol & Herpet; Ecol Soc Am; Soc Study Evolution; Am Fisheries Soc; Am Soc Limnol & Oceanog. *Res:* Ecology of minnows and darters; variation in fishes; aquatic ecology. *Mailing Add:* Dept of Ecol Univ of Minn Minneapolis MN 55455

UNDERKOFLER, WILLIAM LELAND, b Ames, Iowa, Nov 10, 36; m 61; c 3. ANALYTICAL CHEMISTRY. *Educ:* Iowa State Univ, BS, 58; Univ Wis, PhD(anal chem), 64. *Prof Exp:* Staff chemist, 63-71, ADV CHEMIST, IBM CORP, 71- *Mem:* Am Chem Soc. *Res:* Electrochemistry; electrochemical analysis; electroplating; general chemical analysis. *Mailing Add:* 340 Rayelene Dr Box 339 RD 2 Vestal NY 13850

UNDERWOOD, ARTHUR LOUIS, JR, b Rochester, NY, May 18, 24; m 48; c 3. BIOCHEMISTRY. *Educ:* Univ Rochester, BS, 44, PhD(biochem), 51. *Prof Exp:* Res assoc, Atomic Energy Proj, Univ Rochester, 46-51; res assoc anal chem, Mass Inst Technol, 51-52; from asst prof to assoc prof, 52-62, PROF CHEM, EMORY UNIV, 62- *Concurrent Pos:* Res fel biochem, Univ Rochester, 48-51; res assoc, Cornell Univ, 59-60. *Mem:* Fel AAAS; Am Chem Soc. *Res:* Ionic micelles with organic counterions; effects of counterion structure upon charge, critical micelle concentration and aggregation number; role of counterion in micellar solubilization; aqueous micellar systems as solvents in analytical chemistry. *Mailing Add:* Dept of Chem Emory Univ Atlanta GA 30322

UNDERWOOD, BARBARA ANN, b Santa Ana, Calif, Aug 24, 34. NUTRITION, BIOCHEMISTRY. *Educ:* Univ Calif, Santa Barbara, BA, 56; Cornell Univ, MS, 58; Columbia Univ, PhD(nutrit biochem), 62. *Prof Exp:* Res asst nutrit, Cornell Univ, 58-59; res asst nutrit biochem, Columbia Univ & St Luke's Hosp, 59-61; res assoc, Inst Int Med, Univ Md, 62-64, asst prof, 64-66; res assoc, Columbia Univ, 66-68, asst prof nutrit sci, 68-72; assoc prof nutrit, Pa State Univ, 72-77, dir div biol health, 74-76; ASSOC PROF NUTRIT, MASS INST TECHNOL, 78- *Concurrent Pos:* Nutrit Found future leaders grant, 67-69; adv comt mem, Am Found Overseas Blind, 73-; mem malnutrit panel, US-Japan Med Res Comt, 74; mem Nat Acad Sci-Int Nutrit Progs Comt, 74-79; Int Vitamin A consult group, 75-; US deleg, World Health Assembly, 75-; mem adv comt, Off Sci & Technol Policy, 78-79. *Mem:* Am Inst Nutrit; Am Pub Health Asn; NY Acad Sci; Am Soc Clin Nutrit. *Res:* Malnutrition children; lipid metabolism; absorption and metabolism fat soluble vitamins in cystic fibrosis; vitamin A; breast feeding and child development; nutrition and nation development in developing countries. *Mailing Add:* Nutrit & Food Sci Mass Inst Technol Cambridge MA 02139

UNDERWOOD, DONALD LEE, b Grand Rapids, Mich, Apr 20, 28; m 56; c 2. PHYSICAL CHEMISTRY. *Educ:* Wheaton Col, BS, 50; Princeton Univ, MA, 53. *Prof Exp:* Res chemist, Personal Care Div, Gillette Co, 54-55, from res supvr to sr res supvr, 55-73, prin engr, 73-80, ASST DIR RES, GILLETTE ADVAN TECHNOL LAB, 80- *Mem:* Am Chem Soc; Soc Cosmetic Chemists; Am Inst Chemists. *Res:* Sorption and diffusion of salt, acid and water in human hair; hair cosmetics; physics; appliance engineering and development. *Mailing Add:* Gillette Advan Technol Lab 83 Rogers St Cambridge MA 02142

UNDERWOOD, DOUGLAS HAINES, b Ravenna, Ohio, Nov 29, 34; m 58; c 2. MATHEMATICS. *Educ:* Case Inst Technol, BS, 56; Univ Calif, Berkeley, MA, 58; Univ Wis-Madison, PhD, 68. *Prof Exp:* Assoc prof, 58-74, PROF MATH, WHITMAN COL, 74- *Mem:* Am Math Soc; Math Asn Am. *Res:* Commutative rings. *Mailing Add:* 1134 Alyarade Terrace Walla Walla WA 99362

UNDERWOOD, ERVIN E(DGAR), b Gary, Ind, Jan 30, 18; m; c 3. PHYSICAL METALLURGY. *Educ:* Purdue Univ, BS, 49; Mass Inst Technol, SM, 51, ScD(metall), 54. *Prof Exp:* Metall observer, Open Hearth Dept, US Steel Corp, Inc, 40-41; res asst metall res, Mass Inst Technol, 49-54; metall consult, Battelle Mem Inst, 54-62; staff scientist, Lockhead Missles & Space Co, 62-65, res dir mat, 65-71; Alcoa prof mech eng, 71-74, mem res staff, 74-80, PROF METALL, FRACTURE & FATIGUE RES LAB, SCH CHEM ENG, GA INST TECHNOL, 80- *Concurrent Pos:* Vis scientist, Max Planck Inst Metal Res, Stuttgart, 74-75; consult legal, sci & indust mat. *Mem:* Am Inst Mining, Metall & Petrol Engrs; Am Soc Metals; Int Soc Stereol (pres, 71-75). *Res:* High temperature deformation of metals and alloys; fracture and fatigue; superplasticity; stereology. *Mailing Add:* Rm 122 Sch Chem Eng & Metall Ga Inst Technol Atlanta GA 30332

UNDERWOOD, HERBERT ARTHUR, JR, b Austin, Tex, Sept 4, 45; m 81. BIOLOGICAL RHYTHMS. *Educ:* Univ Tex, Austin, BA, 67, MA, 68, PhD(zool), 72. *Prof Exp:* Fel zool, Max-Planck Inst, 72-73; fel, Univ Tex, Austin, 73-75; asst prof, 75-80, ASSOC PROF ZOOL, NC STATE UNIV, 80- *Mem:* Am Soc Zoologists; AAAS; Sigma Xi. *Res:* Role of the eyes and extraretinal photoreceptors in the control of the biological clock of lizards; vertebrate photoperiodism; behavioral thermoregulation in poikilotherms; involvement of the pineal system in vertebrate circadian rhythms. *Mailing Add:* Dept of Zool NC State Univ Raleigh NC 27650

UNDERWOOD, JAMES HENRY, b Minster, Eng, Apr 18, 38; m 65. SOLAR PHYSICS, X-RAY ASTRONOMY. *Educ:* Univ Leicester, BSc, 59, PhD(physics), 63. *Prof Exp:* Res assoc space res, Nat Acad Sci, NSF, 63-66; aerospace scientist, NASA Goddard Space Flight Ctr, 66-72; staff scientist space res, Aerospace Corp, 72-77; mem staff, Inst Plasma Res, Stanford Univ, 77-80; WITH JET PROPULSION LAB, 80- *Mem:* Int Astron Union; Am Astron Soc; Optical Soc Am. *Res:* Application of x-ray techniques, in particular x-ray optics and crystal spectroscopy, to the study of the solar coronal plasma and other celestial x-ray sources. *Mailing Add:* Jet Propulsion Lab Mail Code 169-506 4800 Oak Grove Dr Pasadena CA 91103

UNDERWOOD, JAMES ROSS, JR, b Austin, Tex, May 15, 27; m 61; c 3. STRUCTURAL GEOLOGY, PETROLEUM ENGINEERING. *Educ:* Univ Tex, Austin, BS, 48, BS, 49, MA, 56, PhD(geol), 62. *Prof Exp:* Petrol eng trainee, Sohio Petrol Co, 49-50, jr petrol engr, 50-51, petrol engr, 53-54; instr geol, Univ Tex, 56-57, Univ Tex-Agency Int Develop asst prof, Univ Baghdad, 62-65; asst prof, Univ Fla, 65-67; from assoc prof to prof geol, WTex State Univ, 67-77; PROF GEOL & HEAD DEPT, KANS STATE UNIV, 77- *Concurrent Pos:* On leave as Exxon-sponsored prof, Univ Libya, 69-71. *Mem:* Geol Soc Am; Am Asn Petrol Geol; Soc Econ Paleontologists & Mineralogists; Am Geophys Union; Am Inst Mining, Metall & Petrol Engrs. *Res:* Structural geology; geomorphology; planetology, especially Mercury and Mars and Terrestrial impact structures; geology of Trans-Pecos Texas, northern Chihuahua and the Middle East; petroleum engineering, especially drilling and production; planetary geology. *Mailing Add:* Dept of Geol Kans State Univ Manhattan KS 66506

UNDERWOOD, LAWRENCE STATTON, b Kansas City, Kans, July 29, 36; m 64; c 2. PHYSIOLOGICAL ECOLOGY. *Educ:* Univ Kans, BA, 59; Syracuse Univ, MS, 68; Pa State Univ, University Park, PhD(zool), 71. *Prof Exp:* Teacher pub schs, Kans, Mo & Alaska, 57-67; asst biol, Pa State Univ, University Park, 68-71; asst prof zool, Univ Conn, West Hartford Br, 71-73; asst dir sci, Naval Arctic Res Lab, 73-76; res analyst, 76-80, SUPVR INFO SCI SERV, ARCTIC ENVIRON INFO & DATA CTR, 80- *Concurrent Pos:* Int Biol Prog, NSF & Arctic Inst NAm grants, Naval Arctic Res Lab, 71-72. *Mem:* AAAS; Am Inst Biol Sci; Ecol Soc Am; fel Arctic Inst NAm; Int Soc Biometeorol. *Res:* Physiological and behavioral adjustments in cold acclimatized mammals to varying environmental conditions; environmental and information transfer; establishing a system of ecological reserves in Alaska. *Mailing Add:* Arctic Environ Info & Data Ctr 707 A St Anchorage AK 99501

UNDERWOOD, LOUIS EDWIN, b Danville, Ky, Feb 20, 37; m 60; c 3. PEDIATRICS, ENDOCRINOLOGY. *Educ:* Univ Ky, AB, 58; Vanderbilt Univ, MD, 61. *Prof Exp:* From intern to asst resident pediat, Vanderbilt Univ, 61-63; asst resident, Univ NC, 63-64; instr, Vanderbilt Univ, 64-65; attend pediat, US Naval Hosp, Chelsea, Mass, 65-67; instr, 69-70, asst prof, 70-75, assoc prof, 75-80, PROF PEDIAT, SCH MED, UNIV NC, CHAPEL HILL, 80- *Concurrent Pos:* USPHS fel endocrinol, 67-70. *Mem:* AAAS; Am Fedn Clin Res; Endocrine Soc; Soc Pediat Res; Lawson Wilkins Pediat Endocrine Soc. *Res:* Pediatric endocrine diseases; growth problems and hormonal control of growth. *Mailing Add:* Dept of Pediat Univ of NC Sch of Med Chapel Hill NC 27514

UNDERWOOD, REX J, b Eugene, Ore, Nov 13, 26; m 50; c 2. MEDICINE. *Educ:* Stanford Univ, AB, 50; Univ Ore, MS & MD, 55. *Prof Exp:* From instr to assoc prof anesthesiol, Med Sch, Univ Ore, 58-67; asst dir anesthesiol, 67-68, DIR ANESTHESIOL, BESS KAISER HOSP, 68- *Mem:* AMA; Am Soc Anesthesiol. *Res:* Anesthesiology, particularly related to cardiovascular physiology. *Mailing Add:* Bess Kaiser Hosp 5055 Greeley Ave Portland OR 97217

UNDERWOOD, ROBERT GORDON, b Nashville, Tenn, Feb 3, 45; m 68; c 2. APPLIED MATHEMATICS, OPERATIONS RESEARCH. *Educ:* Univ NC, Chapel Hill, BS, 67; Univ Va, PhD(appl math), 74. *Prof Exp:* Health Serv Officer, US Pub Health Serv, 68-70; asst prof, Univ SC, 74-78; ASST PROF MATH, COLO SCH MINES, 78- *Mem:* Soc Indust & Appl Math; Am Math Asn. *Res:* Applied mathematics; optimization, game theory and control theory. *Mailing Add:* Dept of Math Colo Sch Mines Golden CO 80401

UNDEUTSCH, WILLIAM CHARLES, b Hamilton, Ohio, Oct 6, 25; m 54; c 4. ORGANIC CHEMISTRY. *Educ:* Univ Cincinnati, BS, 48, MS, 50; Univ Del, PhD(chem), 53. *Prof Exp:* Lab technician, Children's Hosp Res Found, 48, 50; res chemist, Photo Prods Dept, E I du Pont de Nemours & Co, Inc, 53-58; SR ED CHEM ABSTR SERV, OHIO STATE UNIV, 58- *Res:* Chemical literature. *Mailing Add:* Chem Abstr Serv PO Box 3012 Columbus OH 43210

UNELL, PHILIP MYLES, mathematical analysis, see previous edition

UNG, MAN T, b South Vietnam, Apr 1, 38; US citizen; m 60; c 2. COMPUTER SCIENCE, MATHEMATICS. *Educ:* Univ Wis, BS, 59; Ill Inst Technol, MS, 62; Univ Southern Calif, PhD(elec eng), 70. *Prof Exp:* Asst res engr, IIT Res Inst, 61-63; mgr educ & training, Electronic Assocs, Inc, 63-70; mgr comput & math serv, Dillingham Environ Co, 70-71; asst prof elec eng, 72-76, adj asst prof, 76-79, ADJ ASSOC PROF ELEC ENG, UNIV SOUTHERN CALIF, 79- *Concurrent Pos:* Ed, Analog/Hybrid Comput Educ Soc, 65-68. *Mem:* Simulation Coun; Marine Technol Soc; Sr mem Soc Comput Simulation. *Res:* Modeling of ecological systems; hybrid computer applications in engineering. *Mailing Add:* Dept of Elec Eng Univ of Southern Calif Los Angeles CA 90007

UNGAR, ANDREW, b Romania, Oct 17, 22; nat US; m 50; c 2. APPLIED STATISTICS. *Educ:* City Col, BChE, 47; Univ Chicago, MS, 55. *Prof Exp:* Statistician, IIT Res Inst, 48-59, asst supvr comput appln & opers res, 59-62, mgr opers res, 62-64, sr scientist, 64-66; sr analyst, Matson Res Corp, Calif, 66-68, assoc tech dir, 68-70; prog dir, Manalytics, Inc, 70-73; SR QUANTITATIVE ANALYST, METROP TRANSP COMN, 73- *Mem:* Am Statist Asn; Opers Res Soc Am; Sigma Xi. *Res:* Combinatorial analysis; digital computer applications; probability; operations research. *Mailing Add:* 20 Oak Vale Ave Berkeley CA 94705

UNGAR, EDWARD WILLIAM, b New York, NY, Feb 6, 36; m 78; c 3. TECHNICAL MANAGEMENT, RESEARCH ADMINISTRATION. *Educ:* City Col New York, BME, 57; Ohio State Univ, MSc, 59, PhD(mech eng), 66. *Prof Exp:* Res engr, 57-63, prog dir, Fluid & Thermal Mech Div, 63-66, assoc div chief, 66, chief fluid & gas dynamics div, 66-70, mgr eng physics sect, 70-71, mgr eng physics dept, 71-74, mgr energy & environ processes res dept, 74-76, assoc dir, 76-78, DIR, COLUMBUS DIV, BATTELLE MEM INST, 78- *Mem:* Am Soc Mech Engrs; AAAS. *Res:* Physical, life and social sciences. *Mailing Add:* Battelle Mem Inst Columbus Div 505 King Ave Columbus OH 43201

UNGAR, ERIC E(DWARD), b Vienna, Austria, Nov 12, 26; nat US; m 51; c 4. MECHANICAL ENGINEERING. *Educ:* Wash Univ, BSME, 51; Univ NMex, MS, 54; NY Univ, DEngSc(mech eng), 57. *Prof Exp:* Aero-ord engr, Sandia Corp, 51-53; instr mech eng, NY Univ, 53-57, asst prof, 57-58, res scientist, 58; sr eng scientist & mgr appl physics dept, 58-68, assoc div dir, 68-

76, PRIN ENGR, BOLT BERANEK & NEWMAN, INC, 76- *Mem:* fel Am Soc Mech Engrs; assoc fel Am Inst Aeronaut & Astronaut; fel Acoust Soc Am; Inst Noise Control Eng. *Res:* Structural and machinery dynamics; vibrations and noise; stress analysis; machine design. *Mailing Add:* Bolt Beranek & Newman Inc 50 Moulton St Cambridge MA 02238

UNGAR, FRANK, b Cleveland, Ohio, Apr 30, 22; m 48; c 4. BIOCHEMISTRY, ENDOCRINOLOGY. *Educ:* Ohio State Univ, BA, 43; Western Reserve Univ, MSc, 48; Tufts Univ, PhD(biochem, physiol), 52. *Prof Exp:* Res staff mem, Cleveland Clin, 47-48; res staff mem, Worcester Found Exp Biol, 51-58; assoc prof, 58-67, PROF BIOCHEM, MED SCH, UNIV MINN, MINNEAPOLIS, 68- *Concurrent Pos:* Fulbright sr scholar, Univ Col, Cork, 74-75; asst vis prof chem, Clark Univ, 56-58; consult cancer chemother group, NIH, 65-72. *Mem:* AAAS; Am Chem Soc; Endocrine Soc; Am Soc Biol Chem. *Res:* Regulation of hormone action; metabolism of steroid hormones. *Mailing Add:* Dept of Biochem Univ of Minn Med Sch Minneapolis MN 55455

UNGAR, GERALD S, b Wilkes-Barre, Pa, Jan 27, 41; m 59; c 3. MATHEMATICS. *Educ:* Franklin & Marshall Col, BA, 61; Rutgers Univ, MS, 63, PhD(topol), 66. *Prof Exp:* Asst prof math, La State Univ, Baton Rouge, 66-68 & Case Western Reserve Univ, 68-70; ASSOC PROF MATH, UNIV CINCINNATI, 70- *Mem:* Am Math Soc. *Res:* Fiber maps; local homogeneity. *Mailing Add:* 2488 E Galbraith Rd Cincinnati OH 45237

UNGAR, IRWIN A, b New York, NY, Jan 21, 34; m 59; c 3. PLANT ECOLOGY. *Educ:* City Col New York, BS, 55; Univ Kans, MA, 57, PhD(bot), 61. *Prof Exp:* Instr bot, Univ RI, 61-62; asst prof, Quincy Col, 62-66; from asst prof to assoc prof, 66-73, PROF BOT, OHIO UNIV, 74- *Concurrent Pos:* Sigma Xi res awards, 59 & 66; NSF grants, 63-65, 67-69, 74-75, 76-78 & 80-83, panelist, 66; res grant, Ohio Univ, 66-68, 74-75 & 78-79, John C Baker res grant, 72-73; res grant, Ohio Biol Surv, 70-71 & 74-75; res assoc, Ctr Nat Res Sci grant, France, 72-73; Res Inst fel, Ohio Univ, 74. *Mem:* AAAS; Ecol Soc Am; Bot Soc Am; Sigma Xi. *Res:* Vegetation-soil relations on acid and saline soils; ecology of halophytes; studies in salt tolerance and behavior of species under field conditions. *Mailing Add:* Dept of Bot Ohio Univ Athens OH 45701

UNGER, ISRAEL, b Tarnow, Poland, Mar 30, 38; Can citizen; m 64. CHEMISTRY. *Educ:* Sir George Williams Univ, BSc, 58; Univ NB, MSc, 60, PhD(chem), 63. *Prof Exp:* Fel, Univ Tex, 63-65; from asst prof to assoc prof, 65-74, PROF CHEM, UNIV NB, FREDERICTON, 74- *Mem:* Chem Inst Can. *Res:* Kinetics and photochemistry of small organic molecules; photochemistry of pesticides. *Mailing Add:* Dept of Chem Univ of NB Fredericton NB E3B 5A3 Can

UNGER, JAMES WILLIAM, b Marshfield, Wis, Apr 1, 21; m 47; c 1. PLANT MORPHOLOGY. *Educ:* Wis State Col, Stevens Point, BS, 42; Univ Wis, MS, 47, PhD(bot), 53. *Prof Exp:* Asst prof bot, Hope Col, 47-51; prof bot & chmn dept biol, 53-67, PROF BIOL, UNIV WIS-OSHKOSH, 67- *Mem:* Am Inst Biol Sci; Bot Soc Am. *Res:* Anatomical considerations of gymnosperm tissue cultures; anatomical studies of stem apices and stem to root vascular transitions; membrane permeability studies; tissue culture of orange. *Mailing Add:* Dept Biol Univ Wis Oshkosh WI 54901

UNGER, JOHN DUEY, b Harrisburg, Pa, Mar 2, 43; m 66; c 3. GEOPHYSICS, SEISMOLOGY. *Educ:* Mass Inst Technol, BS & MS, 67; Dartmouth Col, PhD(geol), 69. *Prof Exp:* Geophysicist, Hawaiian Volcano Observ, US Geol Surv, Hawaii Nat Park, 69-74, geophysicist, Nat Ctr for Earthquake Res, 74-76, GEOPHYSICIST, LAND INFO & ANAL OFF, US GEOL SURV NAT CTR, RESTON VA, 76- *Mem:* AAAS; Geol Soc Am; Am Geophys Union; Seismol Soc Am. *Res:* Volcanic seismology; deformation studies of active volcanoes; general microearthquake seismology; environmental geology. *Mailing Add:* US Geol Surv Nat Ctr 12201 Sunrise Valley Dr Reston VA 22092

UNGER, LLOYD GEORGE, b Stickney, SDak, Feb 24, 18; m 47; c 4. PHYSICAL CHEMISTRY. *Educ:* Yankton Col, BA, 39; Pa State Univ, MS, 41, PhD(phys chem), 45. *Prof Exp:* Lab asst, Pa State Univ, 39-44; res chemist, CPC Int Inc, Ill, 44-68; assoc prof, 68-80 PROF PHYS SCI & CHEM, WRIGHT COL, 80- *Mem:* Fel AAAS; Am Chem Soc. *Res:* Cereal proteins; textile chemicals. *Mailing Add:* 99 Lawton Rd Riverside IL 60546

UNGER, MICHAEL, b Haifa, Israel, Feb 11, 44; m 69; c 2. PULMONARY DISEASES, PULMONARY PHYSIOLOGY. *Prof Exp:* Intern internal med, Wayne State Univ Gen Hosp, 71-72; resident, Mt Sinai Hosp Med Ctr, 72-74, chief resident internal med, 73; res fel pulmonary dis, Cornell Univ Med Ctr, 74-76; ASST PROF PULMONARY MED, UNIV PA, 76- *Concurrent Pos:* Asst chief pulmonary sect & med dir respiratory ther, Presby Univ Pa Med Ctr, 76-; Office Naval Res grant, 78-; consult, Am Col Physicians, 77-78. *Mem:* Am Thoracic Soc; Am Col Physicians; Am Fedn Clin Res. *Res:* Pulmonary physiology; pulmonary hypertension induced by intermittent hypoxemia; effects on right ventricular functions; oxygen exchange mechanisms in the shock lung syndrome. *Mailing Add:* Pulmonary Sect Med Ctr 51 N 39th St Philadephia PA 19104

UNGER, PAUL WALTER, b Winchester, Tex, Sept 10, 31; m 60; c 6. SOIL SCIENCE. *Educ:* Tex A&M Univ, BS, 61; Colo State Univ, MS, 63, PhD(soil sci), 66. *Prof Exp:* SOIL SCIENTIST, AGR RES SERV, USDA, 65- *Concurrent Pos:* Assoc ed, Soil Sci Soc, Am J, 77-; assoc ed, Iowa State J Res, 80- *Mem:* Am Soc Agron; Soil Sci Soc Am; Soil Conserv Soc Am; Coun Agr Sci & Technol. *Res:* Soil management and moisture conservation, especially tillage and crop residue management as they relate to soil structure, water movement and water storage in the soil. *Mailing Add:* Conserv & Prod Res Lab PO Drawer 10 Bushland TX 79012

UNGER, ROGER HAROLD, b New York, NY, Mar 7, 24; m 46; c 3. INTERNAL MEDICINE. *Educ:* Yale Univ, BS, 44; Columbia Univ, MD, 47; Am Bd Internal Med, dipl, 56. *Hon Degrees:* Dr, Univ Geneva, 76. *Prof Exp:* From intern to resident med, Bellevue Hosp, New York, 47-51; dir, Dallas Diabetes Unit, Tex, 51-52; clin instr, 52-59, from asst prof to assoc prof, 59-70, PROF MED, UNIV TEX HEALTH SCI CTR DALLAS, 71- *Concurrent Pos:* Clin instr, Postgrad Med Sch, NY Univ, 51-56; chief gastroenterol sect, Vet Admin Hosp, Dallas, 58-64, chief metab sect, 64-74, dir res, 65-75; vis prof, Univ Geneva, 72-73. *Honors & Awards:* Lilly Award, Am Diabetes Asn, 64; Tinsley Harrison Award, 67; Middleton Award, Vet Admin, 69; David Rumbaugh Award, Juvenile Diabetes Fedn; 75; Banting Medal, Am Diabetes Asn, 75. *Mem:* Am Diabetes Asn; Am Fedn Clin Res; Am Soc Clin Invest; Endocrine Soc; Asn Am Physicians. *Res:* Diabetes. *Mailing Add:* 4500 S Lancaster Rd Dallas TX 75216

UNGER, S(TEPHEN) H(ERBERT), b New York, NY, July 7, 31; m 60; c 2. ELECTRICAL ENGINEERING, COMPUTER SCIENCE. *Educ:* Polytech Inst Brooklyn, BEE, 52; Mass Inst Technol, SM, 53, ScD, 57. *Prof Exp:* Asst elec eng, Res Lab Electronics, Mass Inst Technol, 54-57; mem tech staff, Bell Tel Labs, Inc, 57-61; assoc prof elec eng, 61-68, prof elec eng, 68-79, PROF COMPUT SCI, COLUMBIA UNIV, 79- *Concurrent Pos:* Adj asst prof, Columbia Univ, 60-61; consult, Res Labs, RCA Corp, 64-69; Guggenheim fel, 67; consult, Western Elec Eng Res Ctr, 71; vis prof comput sci, Danish Tech Univ, 74-75. *Mem:* AAAS; Am Asn Univ Professors; fel Inst Elec & Electronics Engrs; Asn Comput Mach. *Res:* Switching circuit theory; digital computer systems; programming theory; pattern recognition; technological aids to the democratic process; programming languages; computer conferencing; engineering ethics. *Mailing Add:* Dept Comput Sci Columbia Univ New York NY 10027

UNGER, VERNON EDWIN, JR, b Easton, Md, Dec 14, 35; m 58; c 2. INDUSTRIAL ENGINEERING, OPERATIONS RESEARCH. *Educ:* Johns Hopkins Univ, BES, 57, MS, 64, PhD(opers res), 68. *Prof Exp:* Staff asst, AAI, Inc, 57-65; prof indust eng, Ga Inst Technol, 68-79, assoc dir res, 74-79; PROF INDUST ENG & HEAD DEPT, AUBURN UNIV, 79- *Mem:* Opers Res Soc Am; Am Inst Indust Eng. *Res:* Operations research and engineering economics. *Mailing Add:* Dept Indust Eng Auburn Univ Auburn AL 36830

UNGLAUBE, JAMES M, b Milwaukee, Wis, Apr 13, 42; m 64; c 1. ORGANIC CHEMISTRY. *Educ:* Carthage Col, BA, 63; Univ Iowa, MS, 66, PhD(org chem), 68. *Prof Exp:* Teaching asst org chem, Univ Iowa, 63-64; asst prof chem, 67-70, assoc prof chem & acad dean, Lenoir Rhyne Col, 70-77; ASST DIR DEPT HIGHER EDUC, LUTHERAN CHURCH AM, 77- *Mem:* Am Asn Higher Educ; Am Chem Soc. *Res:* Chemical education; organic chemistry syntheses, including heterocyclic nitrogen compounds. *Mailing Add:* Lutheran Church in Am 231 Madison Ave New York NY 10016

UNGRIN, JAMES, nuclear physics, see previous edition

UNGVICHIAN, VICHATE, b Bangkok, Thailand, May 22, 49. ANTENNA DESIGNS, COMPUTER MODELLING. *Educ:* Khon-Kaen Univ, Thailand, BSEE, 67; Ohio State univ, MS, 74; Ohio Univ, PhD(elec eng), 81. *Prof Exp:* FEL ELECTROMAGNETICS, ELEC ENG DEPT, OHIO UNIV, 81- *Mem:* Inst Elec & Electronics Engrs; Sigma Xi. *Res:* Electromagnetic fields as applied to instrument landing systems; computer models to calculate the ground scattering by using the uniform theory of diffraction, including all rays up to the second and most of the third order types of rays. *Mailing Add:* Elec Eng Dept Ohio Univ Athens OH 45701

UNIK, JOHN PETER, b Chicago, Ill, May 18, 34; m 57; c 2. NUCLEAR CHEMISTRY. *Educ:* Ill Inst Technol, BS, 56; Univ Calif, Berkeley, PhD(chem), 60. *Prof Exp:* From asst chemist to assoc chemist, 60-74, sect head, 73-74, SR CHEMIST & ASSOC DIR CHEM DIV, ARGONNE NAT LAB, 74- *Concurrent Pos:* Consult, Oak Ridge Nat Lab, 74-, US Nuclear Data Comt, 78- & Lawrence Berkeley Lab, 79- *Mem:* Am Phys Soc; Am Chem Soc. *Res:* Nuclear fission and heavy ion reactions. *Mailing Add:* Argonne Nat Lab Bldg 200 9700 S Cass Ave Argonne IL 60439

UNKLESBAY, NAN F, b North Vancouver, BC, May 28, 44; m 74. FOOD SCIENCE, NUTRITION. *Educ:* Univ BC, BHE, 66; Univ Wis, Madison, MS, 71, PhD(food sci), 73. *Prof Exp:* Dietary consult, Dept Health, Govt Nfld & Labrador, 67-70; asst prof food systs mgt, 73-76, asst prof 76-80, ASSOC PROF FOOD SCI & NUTRIT, UNIV MO, COLUMBIA, 81- *Concurrent Pos:* Consult, NSF, 75-76. *Mem:* Inst Food Technologists; Am Dietetic Asn; Can Dietetic Asn. *Res:* Major amounts of energy utilization within the food industry; optimization of resource utilization in food services while maintaining microbial safety, quality and nutritional value. *Mailing Add:* 1504 W Lexington Circle Columbia MO 65201

UNLAND, MARK LEROY, b Jacksonville, Ill, Mar 17, 40; m 62; c 2. PHYSICAL CHEMISTRY. *Educ:* MacMurray Col, AB, 62; Univ Ill, Urbana, MS, 64, PhD(chem), 66. *Prof Exp:* RES CHEMIST, MONSANTO CO, 66- *Mem:* Am Chem Soc; Sigma Xi; Sci Res Soc NAm. *Res:* Molecular structure; catalyst development, fundamental studies of heterogeneous catalysts and catalysis mechanisms. *Mailing Add:* Monsanto Enviro-Chem Systs Inc PO Box 14547 St Louis MO 63178

UNNAM, JALAIAH, b Tangutur, India, Dec 1, 47; m 73; c 2. MATERIALS SCIENCE. *Educ:* Indian Inst Technol, BTech, 70; Va Polytech Inst & State Univ, MS, 72, PhD(mat sci), 75. *Prof Exp:* Instr metall, Va Polytech Inst & State Univ, 74 & 75, res assoc mat sci, 75-77; res fel, George Washington Univ, 77-78; VIS PROF MAT SCI, VA POLYTECH INST & STATE UNIV, 78- *Mem:* Am Soc Metals; Digital Equip Comput Users Soc; Sigma Xi. *Res:* Solid state diffusion; x-ray diffraction; composite materials; numerical analysis and computer programming; electron microprobe; scanning electron microscope; quantitative metallography; mechanical testing; electroplating; oxidation. *Mailing Add:* MS 188B NASA Hampton VA 23665

UNOWSKY, JOEL, b St Paul, Minn, Dec 11, 38; m 75; c 4. INDUSTRIAL MICROBIOLOGY, MICROBIAL GENETICS. *Educ:* Univ Minn, Minneapolis, BA, 61; Northwestern Univ, Evanston, PhD(bact), 66. *Prof Exp:* Res fel, E I du Pont de Nemours & Co, Inc, 65-66; sr microbiologist, 66-79, asst res grouup, 79, RES GROUP CHIEF, HOFFMANN-LA ROCHE INC, 79- *Concurrent Pos:* adj assoc prof, Seton Hall Univ, 76. *Mem:* AAAS; Am Soc Microbiol; Sigma Xi. *Res:* Resistance transfer factor; antibiotic strain development; antibiotic screening; mutation and genetics; chemotherapy. *Mailing Add:* Hoffmann-La Roche Inc Nutley NJ 07110

UNRATH, CLAUDE RICHARD, b Benton Harbor, Mich, Nov 29, 41; m 76; c 2. HORTICULTURE. *Educ:* Mich State Univ, BS, 63, MS, 66, PhD(hort), 68. *Prof Exp:* Asst prof, 68-73, ASSOC PROF TREE FRUIT PHYSIOL, N C STATE UNIV, 73- *Mem:* Am Soc Hort Sci; Am Pomol Soc. *Res:* Applied tree fruit physiology, apple research, growth regulator physiology, environmental control and modification and cultural improvement and efficiency. *Mailing Add:* Dept Hort Sci NC State Univ Box 249 Rte 2 Fletcher NC 28732

UNRAU, ABRAHAM MARTIN, b Orenbourg, Can, Feb 16, 26; m 52; c 3. BIOCHEMISTRY, PLANT PHYSIOLOGY. *Educ:* Univ BC, BSA, 52, MSA, 53; Univ Minn, PhD(hort sci), 56, PhD(biochem), 60. *Prof Exp:* Asst hort, Exp Farms, Can Dept Agr, 50; asst & instr biol, genetics & hort, Univ BC, 51-53, fel chem, 61; asst hort, Univ Minn, 53-56, res asst & res fel, 56-59; asst chemist, Univ Hawaii, 59-61; assoc prof plant chem, Univ Man, 61-66; PROF ORG CHEM, SIMON FRASER UNIV, 66- *Mem:* Am Chem Soc; Agr Inst Can. *Res:* Carbohydrate chemistry; plant biochemistry; synthesis of biologically important organic compounds. *Mailing Add:* Dept of Chem Simon Fraser Univ Burnaby BC V5A 1S6 Can

UNRAU, DAVID GEORGE, b Leamington, Ont, July 21, 38; m 62; c 4. BIOCHEMISTRY. *Educ:* Univ Toronto, BSA, 62; Purdue Univ, MS, 65, PhD(biochem), 67. *Prof Exp:* Res scientist, Union Camp Corp, NJ, 67-71; RES CHEMIST, ITT RAYONIER INC, WHIPPANY, 71-, RES GROUP LEADER, 74- *Mem:* Am Chem Soc. *Res:* Carbohydrate modification for industrial uses; flame retardants for cellulosics; viscose; new rayon fiber development. *Mailing Add:* ITT Rayonier Inc S Jefferson & Cedar Knoll Dr Whippany NJ 07981

UNRUH, HENRY, JR, b Greensburg, Kans, Dec 31, 26; m 50; c 2. PHYSICS. *Educ:* Wichita State Univ, AB, 50; Kans State Univ, MS, 52; Case Inst Technol, PhD(physics), 60. *Prof Exp:* Instr physics, Fenn Col, 54-57; asst prof, Colo State Univ, 59-61; assoc prof, 61-72, PROF PHYSICS, WICHITA STATE UNIV, 72- *Mem:* Am Phys Soc. *Res:* Magnetic properties of solids. *Mailing Add:* Dept of Physics Wichita State Univ Wichita KS 67208

UNRUH, JERRY DEAN, b Colorado Springs, Colo, Nov 4, 44; m 66; c 2. INDUSTRIAL ORGANIC CHEMISTRY. *Educ:* Colo State Univ, BS, 66; Ore State Univ, PhD(org chem), 70. *Prof Exp:* Res chemist, 70-73, sr res chemist, 73-78, staff chemist, 78-81, RES ASSOC, CORPUS CHRISTI TECH CTR, CELANESE CHEM CO, 81- *Mem:* Sigma Xi; AAAS; Am Chem Soc. *Res:* Organic free radicals; linear free energy relationships; molecular orbital theory; organometallic chemistry; homogeneous catalysis. *Mailing Add:* Box 9077 Corpus Christi TX 78408

UNRUH, WILLIAM GEORGE, b Winnipeg, Man, Aug 28, 45; m 74. THEORETICAL PHYSICS. *Educ:* Univ Man, BSc, 67; Princeton Univ, MA, 69, PhD(physics), 71. *Prof Exp:* Nat Res Coun Can fel physics, Birkbeck Col, Univ London, 71-72; Miller fel physics, Miller Inst Basic Res & Univ Calif, Berkeley, 73-74; asst prof appl math, McMaster Univ, 74-76; asst prof, 76-80, ASSOC PROF PHYSICS, UNIV BC, 80- *Res:* Relation between quantum mechanics and gravitation; quantum gravity wave detectors. *Mailing Add:* Dept Physics Univ BC Vancouver BC V6T 1W5 Can

UNSWORTH, BRIAN RUSSELL, b London, Eng, July 30, 37; m 66; c 2. BIOCHEMISTRY. *Educ:* Univ London, BSc, 61, PhD(biochem), 65. *Prof Exp:* Proj assoc biochem, Univ Wis-Madison, 65-67; USPHS fel biol, Univ Calif, San Diego, 67-69; asst prof, 69-76, ASSOC PROF BIOL, MARQUETTE UNIV, 76- *Mem:* Am Col Sports Med. *Res:* Biochemical alterations in muscle with use and disuse; myogenesis in the rat; structural analysis of myosin light and heavy chains in various animal model systems; changes in sarcoplasmic reticulum structure and function during development. *Mailing Add:* Dept of Biol Marquette Univ Milwaukee WI 53233

UNT, HILLAR, b Tallinn, Estonia, Mar 17, 35; US citizen; m 61. MECHANICAL ENGINEERING. *Educ:* Univ Southern Calif, BS, 58, MS, 60, PhD, 69. *Prof Exp:* Lectr mech eng, Univ Southern Calif, 58-60; asst prof, 60-65, assoc prof & chmn dept, 65-67, PROF MECH ENG, CALIF STATE UNIV, LONG BEACH, 70-, CHMN DEPT, 74- *Mem:* Am Soc Mech Engrs; Am Soc Metals; Am Inst Aeronaut & Astronaut; Acoust Soc Am; Soc Exp Stress Anal. *Res:* Mechanical vibration; bio-engineering; engineering education. *Mailing Add:* Dept of Mech Eng Calif State Univ Long Beach CA 90840

UNTCH, KARL GEORGE, b Cleveland, Ohio, Apr 24, 31; m 53; c 2. ORGANIC CHEMISTRY. *Educ:* Oberlin Col, BA, 53; Univ NDak, MS, 55; Columbia Univ, MA, 57, PhD(org chem), 59. *Prof Exp:* Du Pont teaching fel, Columbia Univ, 57-58; fel org chem, Univ Wis, 58-60; Fundamental Res staff fel, Mellon Inst, 60-66; assoc prof chem, Belfer Grad Sch Sci, Yeshiva Univ, 66-68; dept head, Syntex Res, 68-80, prin scientist, 80-81; CONSULT CHEM, HANA BIOL INC, 81-; INSTR, EVERGREEN VALLEY COL, 82- *Concurrent Pos:* Alfred P Sloan fel, 67-69. *Mem:* Am Chem Soc. *Res:* Aromaticity; chemistry of unsaturated medium sized ring compounds; synthesis and structure of natural products; synthesis of heterocyclic systems; total synthesis of prostaglandins; synthesis of anti-infammatory and cardiovascular agents. *Mailing Add:* 7203 Via Carrizo San Jose CA 95135

UNTERBERG, WALTER, b Vienna, Austria, May 22, 25; US citizen; m 48; c 2. MECHANICAL & CHEMICAL ENGINEERING. *Educ:* Univ Manchester, BSc, 45, MSc, 46; Univ Calif, Los Angeles, PhD(chem eng), 64. *Prof Exp:* Demonstr eng, Univ Manchester, 45-46; layout draftsman, Redmond Co Inc, Mich, 46-47; instr mech eng, Gen Motors Inst, 47-50; develop engr, Marquardt Corp, Calif, 50-52, sr engr, 52-54, group engr, 54-59; mgr thermal power sect, Turbo Div, Sundstrand Corp, Calif, 59-60; sr tech specialist energy conversion, Rocketdyne Div, NAm Aviation, Inc, 60-66, prin scientist, 66-77; PROJ DEVELOP ENGR, ROCKETDYNE, ROCKWELL INT CORP, 77- *Concurrent Pos:* Mem gas bearing adv group, Off Naval Res, 61-62; lectr, Univ Southern Calif, 64-68; res fel eng, Univ Calif, Los Angeles, 64-68. *Mem:* Am Soc Mech Engrs; Am Inst Chem Engrs; assoc fel Am Inst Aeronaut & Astronaut; Combustion Inst; fel Brit Inst Mech Eng. *Res:* Fluid mechanics; heat and mass transfer; combustion and ignition; thermodynamics; lubrication; weightlessness; thermal stress; liquid propellants; chemical processing; desalination; water pollution. *Mailing Add:* 1454 S Saltair Ave West Los Angeles CA 90025

UNTERBERGER, ROBERT RUPPE, b New York, NY, Apr 27, 21; m 44; c 3. PHYSICS. *Educ:* State Univ NY Col Forestry, Syracuse, BS, 43; Syracuse Univ, BS, 43; Duke Univ, PhD(physics), 50. *Prof Exp:* Lab instr physics, Syracuse Univ, 43; electronics engr, Watson Labs, NJ, 46; res physicist, Chevron Res Co, Standard Oil Co, Calif, 50-52, sr res physicist, 52-54, tech asst mgr, 54-56, res assoc, 56-59, supvr res physicist, 59-65, sr res assoc, 65-68; PROF GEOPHYS, TEX A&M UNIV, 68- *Concurrent Pos:* Electronic engr, White Sands Proving Ground, 46; consult to many salt and potash companies in US, Can & Europe. *Mem:* Am Phys Soc; Inst Elec & Electronics Eng; Soc Explor Geophysists; Asn Explor Geophysists. *Res:* Geophysics; acoustics; electronic instrumentation; microwave spectroscopy; structure of molecules; secondary frequency standards for K-band and higher frequencies; electron spin resonance; optical pumping; high sensitivity magnetometry; electromagnetic wave and acoustic wave propagation in rocks. *Mailing Add:* Dept Geophys Tex A&M Univ College Station TX 77843

UNTERHARNSCHEIDT, FRIEDRICH J, b Essen, Ger, July 17, 26. NEUROPATHOLOGY, NEUROLOGY. *Educ:* Univ Münster, MD, 53, Venia Legendi, 61; Ger Bd Neurol & Psychiat, cert, 57. *Prof Exp:* Asst neurol & psychiat, Univ Hosp Neurol & Psychiat, Bonn, 52-57; assoc, Neuropath Inst, Univ Bonn, 57-61; res assoc, Ger Res Inst Psychiat, Max Planck Inst, Munich, 61-66; res prof neuropath & chief div neuropath & exp neurol, Univ Tex Med Br Galveston, 66-72; mem staff, Naval Aerospace Med Res Lab, 72-80, MEM STAFF, NAVAL BIODYNAMICS LAB, DETACHMENT, NEW ORLEANS, 70- *Mem:* Ger Neurol Soc; Ger Asn Neuropath; Japanese Soc Neurol & Psychiat; Ger Soc Scientists & Physicians; Am Asn Neuropath. *Res:* Psychiatry; mechanics and pathomorphology of the central nervous system traumas; virus-induced tumors; neurovirology, especially safety tests of polio and measle vaccines; general and special neuropathology; malformations of the nervous system; diseases of the spinal cord. *Mailing Add:* Naval Biodynamics Lab Box 29407 Michoud Sta New Orleans LA 70189

UNTERMAN, RONALD DAVID, b Brooklyn, NY, March 6, 46; m 79; c 1. RECOMBINANT DNA TECHNOLOGY, ENVIRONMENTAL MICROBIOLOGY. *Educ:* Haverford Univ, BA, 68; Columbia Univ, PhD(biochem), 82. *Prof Exp:* Res worker biochem, Dept Surg, 76-77, res asst, Dept Biochem, 77-81; STAFF SCIENTIST MOLECULAR BIOL, CORP RES & DEVELOP, GEN ELEC CO, 81- *Mem:* AAAS. *Res:* Applications for recombinant DNA technology, biodegradation of environmental pollutants, biosynthesis of aromatic amino acids and cancer diagnosis; possible biological molecules for microelectronic uses. *Mailing Add:* Gen Elec Co Corp Res & Develop PO Box 8 Schenectady NY 12301

UNTERMYER, S(AMUEL), II, nuclear engineering, see previous edition

UNTERSTEINER, NORBERT, b Merano, Italy, Feb 24, 26. GLACIOLOGY. *Educ:* Innsbruck Univ, PhD(geophys), 50. *Prof Exp:* Asst prof meteorol, Univ Vienna, 51-56, res meteorologist, Cent Estab Meteorol & Geodyn, Vienna, Austria, 57-62; res assoc prof, 63-67, PROF ATMOSPHERIC SCI & GEOPHYS, UNIV WASH, 67- *Concurrent Pos:* Docent, Univ Vienna, 61; consult, Rand Corp, Calif, 65-72; mem, Int Comn Polar Meteorol, World Meteorol Orgn, 66-74; mem comt Polar res, Nat Acad Sci, 70-77; vpres, Int Comn Snow & Ice, Asn Sci Hydrol, Int Union Geod & Geophys, 61-76; proj dir, Div Marine Resources, 70-78; sci adv polar affairs, Off Naval Res, Washington, DC, 78-80; dir res & develop, Off Ocean Prog, Nat Oceanic & Atmospheric Admin, Washington, DC, 80-81. *Honors & Awards:* Austrian Hon Cross Arts & Sci, 60. *Mem:* AAAS; Am Geophys Union; Ger Polar Soc; Norweg Polar Soc. *Res:* Heat and mass budget of glaciers; physical properties of sea ice; sea-air interactions in polar regions; polar climatology. *Mailing Add:* Dept of Atmospheric Sci Univ of Wash Seattle WA 98105

UNTI, THEODORE WAYNE JOSEPH, b Kenosha, Wis, Mar 11, 31. COMPUTER SCIENCE, PLASMA PHYSICS. *Educ:* Marquette Univ, BS, 54; Univ Pittsburgh, MS, 60, PhD(gen relativity physics), 64. *Prof Exp:* Sr physicist, Am Optical Co, Pa, 64-66; SR PHYSICIST, JET PROPULSION LABS, 66- *Concurrent Pos:* Physicist & consult optics, Fairchild Space-Sci Div, Calif, 66; vis prof physics, Nat Univ, Costa Rica, 77. *Res:* Computer science; solar wind; shape of magnetosphere; diffraction theory; lens design; statistical and spectral analysis; mathematics peripheral to lens design. *Mailing Add:* PO Box 8624 La Crescenta CA 91214

UNTRAUER, RAYMOND E(RNEST), b Nevada, Iowa, Feb 9, 26; m 49; c 7. STRUCTURAL ENGINEERING. *Educ:* Iowa State Col, BS, 48; Univ Colo, MS, 51; Univ Ill, PhD(civil eng), 61. *Prof Exp:* Surveyor eng dept, Mo Pac RR, Co, 48-49; instr civil eng, Univ Colo, 49-51; struct designer, C F Braun & Co, Calif, 51-52; from asst prof to assoc prof civil eng, Univ Ark, 52-57; res assoc, Univ Ill, 57-61; assoc prof, Iowa State Univ, 61-65, prof civil eng & dir struct res lab, Eng Res Inst, 65-72; head dept, 72-79, PROF CIVIL

ENG, PA STATE UNIV, 72- *Mem:* Am Soc Civil Engrs; Am Soc Eng Educ; Am Concrete Inst. *Res:* Reinforced and prestressed concrete; structural dynamics; analysis by numerical methods. *Mailing Add:* Dept of Civil Eng 212 Sackett Pa State Univ University Park PA 16802

UNWIN, STEPHEN CHARLES, b Bromley, Eng, Sept 8, 53. RADIO ASTRONOMY. *Educ:* Univ Cambridge, BA, 76, PhD(radio astron), 79. *Hon Degrees:* MA, Univ Cambridge, 80. *Prof Exp:* Researcher, Dept Physics, Univ Cambridge, 76-79; RES FEL RADIO ASTRON, OWENS VALLEY RADIO OBSERV, CALIF INST TECHNOL, 79- *Mem:* Fel Royal Astron Soc; Am Astron Soc. *Res:* Radio astronomy using interfero metric techniques; mapping of compact radio sources using very long baseline interferometric methods; kinematics and spectra of variable sources. *Mailing Add:* Owens Valley Radio Observ Calif Inst Technol Mail Code 105-24 Pasadena CA 91125

UNZ, HILLEL, b Darmstadt, Ger, Aug 15, 29; nat US; m 60; c 3. WAVE PROPAGATION, QUANTUM WAVE MECHANICS. *Educ:* Israel Inst Technol, BS, 53, dipl, 61; Univ Calif, Berkeley, MS, 54, PhD(elec eng), 57. *Prof Exp:* Res asst, Microwave Antenna Lab, Univ Calif, Berkeley, 53-57; from asst prof to assoc prof elec eng, 57-62, PROF ELEC ENG, UNIV KANS, 62- *Concurrent Pos:* Consult, 58-; NSF fel, Cavendish Lab, Univ Cambridge, 63-64; vis prof, Israel Inst Technol, 64. *Mem:* Sr mem Inst Elec & Electronics Engrs. *Res:* Electromagnetic theory; antenna arrays; propagation in the ionosphere; plasma dynamics; drifting plasmas; theory of plates; quantum wave mechanics. *Mailing Add:* Dept of Elec Eng Univ of Kans Lawrence KS 66045

UNZ, RICHARD F(REDERICK), b Syracuse, NY, Sept 15, 35; m 65; c 1. ENVIRONMENTAL MICROBIOLOGY, ENVIRONMENTAL SCIENCES. *Educ:* Syracuse Univ, BS, 57, MS, 60; Rutgers Univ, PhD(environ sci), 65. *Prof Exp:* Res chemist, Metrop Sanit Dist Greater Chicago, 65-66; asst prof, 66-71, assoc prof sanit microbiol, 71-81, PROF ENVIRON MICROBIOL, PA STATE UNIV, 81- *Mem:* Am Soc Microbiol; Water Pollution Control Fedn; Am Acad Microbiol. *Res:* Physiology of iron and sulfur-oxidizing bacteria; biology of acid mine drainage; ecology and physiology of microorganisms in polluted waters; disinfection of water and wastewater; algae inhibitors. *Mailing Add:* Dept of Civil Eng Pa State Univ 116 Sackett Bldg University Park PA 16802

UNZICKER, JOHN DUANE, b Harvey, Ill, May 8, 38; m 71; c 1. ENTOMOLOGY. *Educ:* Univ Ill, BS, 62, MS, 63, PhD(entom), 66. *Prof Exp:* Res assoc Trichoptera, Ill Nat Hist Surv, 66-67, asst taxonomist, 67-76; asst prof zool, 72-75, ASST PROF AGR ENTOMOL, UNIV ILL, URBANA, 78-; ASSOC TAXONOMIST, ILL NATURAL HIST SURV, 76- *Concurrent Pos:* NSF grant reviewer, 68-; consult, St John's Hosp Regional Poison Resource Ctr, Springfield, 78- *Mem:* Am Arachnol Soc: Entom Soc Am; Sigma Xi. *Res:* Biosystematics of aquatic insects. *Mailing Add:* Faunistic Surv & Insect Identification Sect 93 Nat Resources Bldg 607 E Peabody St Champaign IL 61820

UOTILA, URHO A(NTTI KALEVI), b Pöytyä, Finland, Feb 22, 23; nat US; m 49; c 6. GEODESY. *Educ:* Finland Inst Tech, BS, 46, MS, 49; Ohio State Univ, PhD(geod), 59. *Prof Exp:* Surveyor & geodesist, Finnish Govt, 44-46 & 46-51; from res asst to res assoc, 52-58, from lectr to assoc prof geol, 55-65, PROF GEOL, OHIO STATE UNIV, 65-, CHMN DEPT, 64-, RES SUPVR, 59- *Concurrent Pos:* Geodesist, Swedish Govt, 46; mem, Solar Eclipse Exped Greenland, 54; gravity comt mem, Int Asn Geod, 60-, pres spec study group 5.30, 67-71, sect V, 71-; mem geod adv panel, Nat Acad Sci to US Coast & Geod Surv, 64-66; mem geod & cartog working group, Space Sci Steering Comt, NASA, 65-67, geod & cartog adv subcomt, 67-72; vis prof, Tech Univ Berlin, 67 & Univ Fed Parana, Brasil, 73-75 & 77; mem bd dirs, Int Gravity Bur, France, 75-; mem bd trust, Univ Space Res Asn, 73-75. Nat Acad Sci-Nat Acad Eng ad hoc comt NAm datum, Div Earth Sci, Nat Res Coun, 68-70 & mem comt Geod, 75-78. *Honors & Awards:* Kaarina & W A Heiskanen Award, 62; Apollo Achievement Award, NASA, 69. *Mem:* Fel Am Geophys Union (vpres geod sect, 64-68, pres, 68-70); Am Cong Surv & Mapping (vpres, 77-78, pres-elect, 78-); Am Soc Photogram; Can Inst Surv; foreign mem Finnish Nat Acad Sci. *Res:* Geometric and physical geodesy and statistical analysis of data. *Mailing Add:* Dept of Geodetic Sci Ohio State Univ 1958 Neil Ave Columbus OH 43210

UPADHYAY, JAGDISH M, b Jambusar, Gujerat, India, July 2, 31; m 63; c 1. MICROBIOLOGY, BIOCHEMISTRY. *Educ:* Gujerat Univ, India, BPharm, 51; Univ Mich, MS, 57; Wash State Univ, PhD(bact), 63. *Prof Exp:* Chemist, Sarabhai Chem, India, 51-55; grant, Univ Tex, 63-65; asst prof microbiol, 65-67, ASSOC PROF MICROBIOL, LOYOLA UNIV, LA, 68- *Concurrent Pos:* NIH grants, Schlieder Found, 70-72. *Mem:* Am Soc Microbiol; Brit Soc Gen Microbiol. *Res:* Growth and metabolism of psychrophilic microorganisms and soil amebas; lytic enzymes; cell-wall composition; thermophilic microorganisms; carotenoid pigments. *Mailing Add:* Dept of Biol Sci Loyola Univ New Orleans LA 70118

UPATNIEKS, JURIS, b Riga, Latvia, May 7, 36; US citizen; m 68; c 2. COHERENT OPTICS. *Educ:* Univ Akron, BS, 60; Univ Mich, MS, 65. *Prof Exp:* Instr microwaves, Ordnance Sch, US Army, 61-62; from res asst to res engr holography, Willow Run Labs, Univ Mich, 60-72; RES ENGR COHERENT OPTICS, ENVIRON RES INST OF MICH, 73- *Concurrent Pos:* Consult to various pvt & govt orgn, 66-; adj assoc prof, Dept Elec & Comput Design, Univ Mich, 74- *Honors & Awards:* Robert Gordown Mem Award, Soc Photographic Instr Eng, 65; R W Wood Prize, Optical Soc Am, 75; Holley Medal Am Soc Mech Engrs, 76. *Mem:* Optical Soc Am; Inst Elec & Electronics Engrs; Soc Photo-Optical Instrumentation Engrs. *Res:* Holography; optical data processing; holographic optical elements. *Mailing Add:* Environ Res Inst of Mich PO Box 8618 Ann Arbor MI 48107

UPCHURCH, JONATHAN EVERETT, b Chicago, Ill, Jan 2, 51; m 71; c 1. TRANSPORTATION ENGINEERING. *Educ:* Univ Ill, BS, 71, MS, 75; Univ Md, PhD(civil eng), 82. *Prof Exp:* Transp engr, Harland Bartholomew & Assocs, 72-76; dir tech affairs, Inst Transp Engrs, Washington, DC, 76-80; res engr, Off Res, Fed Hwy Admin, Washington, DC, 81-82; ASST PROF CIVIL ENG, COL ENG & APPL SCI, ARIZ STATE UNIV, 82- *Concurrent Pos:* Consult, Am Asn State Hwy & Transp Officials, 80-; secy, Nat Comt Uniform Traffic Control Devices, 79- *Mem:* Transp Res Bd; Inst Transp Engrs; Am Soc Civil Engrs. *Res:* Traffic engineering; traffic operations; development of standards for traffic control devices which result in the most economical operation for the motoring public. *Mailing Add:* Dept Civil Eng Col Eng & Appl Sci Ariz State Univ Tempe AZ 85287

UPCHURCH, ROBERT PHILLIP, b Raleigh, NC, Feb 9, 28; m 48; c 3. PLANT PHYSIOLOGY, WEED SCIENCE. *Educ:* BS & MS, NC State Univ, 49; Univ Calif, PhD(plant physiol), 53. *Prof Exp:* Instr crop sci, NC State Univ, 49-51, from asst prof to prof, 53-65; sr res group leader, Monsanto Co, 65-70, res mgr, 70-73, mgr res, 73-75; head, Dept Plant Sci, 75-81, DIR AGR DEVELOP & ASSOC DIR, AGR EXP STA, UNIV ARIZ, 81- *Concurrent Pos:* Consult, Shell Develop Co, 62-65 & Eli Lilly & Co, 79-; Sigma Xi res award, NC State Univ, 63; mem, Weeds Subcomt, Nat Acad Sci, 64-68; ed, Southern Weed Conf, 66-69. *Mem:* Am Soc Plant Physiol; Am Soc Agron; Crop Sci Soc Am; fel Weed Sci Soc Am (pres, 72-). *Res:* Response of plants to phytoactive chemicals and the influence of soil and climate factors on the expression of such responses. *Mailing Add:* Dept Plant Sci Col Agr Univ Ariz Tucson AZ 85721

UPCHURCH, SAM BAYLISS, b Murfreesboro, Tenn, June 30, 41; m 64. ENVIRONMENTAL GEOLOGY, SEDIMENTOLOGY. *Educ:* Vanderbilt Univ, AB, 63; Northwestern Univ, Evanston, MS, 66, PhD(geol), 70. *Prof Exp:* Resident in res marine geol, Northwestern Univ, Evanston, 67-68; res phys scientist chem limnol, Lake Surv Ctr, Nat Oceanic & Atmospheric Admin, 68-71; asst prof geol, Mich State Univ, 71-74; ASSOC PROF GEOL, UNIV SOUTH FLA, 74- *Concurrent Pos:* Mem limnol work group, Great Lakes Basin Comn, 68-75, mem bd tech adv, 69-75; consult hydrol & geoarcheol, 73- *Mem:* Soc Econ Paleont & Mineral; Geol Soc Am; Am Water Resources Asn; Am Asn Petrol Geologists; Southeastern Geol Soc (vpres, 79-80). *Res:* Trace element-sediment interaction; ground-water chemistry; carbonate sediment genesis and diagenesis; chert petrology; mathematical geology; geohydrology; land-use planning. *Mailing Add:* Dept Geol Univ South Fla Tampa FL 33620

UPDEGRAFF, DAVID MAULE, b Woodstock, NY, Dec 19, 17; m 43; c 3. MICROBIOLOGY. *Educ:* Univ Calif, Los Angeles, AB, 41; Univ Calif, PhD(microbiol), 47. *Prof Exp:* Res assoc & actg dir, Am Petrol Inst Res Proj, Scripps Inst, Univ Calif, 46; sr res chemist, Field Res Labs, Magnolia Petrol Co, 47-50, sr res technologist, 50-55; res microbiologist, Cent Res Dept, Minn Mining & Mfg Co, Minn, 55-68; head microbiol sect, Chem Div, Denver Res Inst, Univ Denver, 68-72; head basic res dept, Cawthron Inst, 72-75; vpres, Resource Industs Int, Ltd, 75-77; PROF CHEM & GEOCHEM, COLO SCH MINES, 77- *Mem:* AAAS; Am Soc Microbiol; Soc Indust Microbiol. *Res:* Biochemistry of carotenoid pigments; bacterial physiology; marine and petroleum microbiology; applied microbiology; fermentations; ecology of water pollution and waste treatment. *Mailing Add:* Dept of Chem & Geochem Colo Sch of Mines Golden CO 80401

UPDEGRAFF, WILLIAM EDWARD, b Williamsport, Pa, Sept 8, 37; m 63; c 3. NUCLEAR PHYSICS, COMPUTER SCIENCE. *Educ:* Dickinson Col, BA, 59; Pa State Univ, University Park, MS, 62; Ohio Univ, PhD(physics), 69. *Prof Exp:* From instr to asst prof physics, Lycoming Col, 62-65; assoc prof & head dept, Simpson Col, 69-74; assoc dean, fac natural sci, 74-76, DIR ACAD COMPUT CTR, STATE UNIV COL AT BUFFALO, 76- *Concurrent Pos:* Instr, Iowa Methodist Hosp, Des Moines, Iowa, 70-72; dir comput ctr, Simpson Col, 72-74. *Mem:* Am Asn Physics Teachers; Am Asn Higher Educ. *Res:* Computer oriented physics development at the undergraduate level; dynamic collective model of nuclear photofission. *Mailing Add:* State Univ NY 1300 Elmwood Ave Buffalo NY 14222

UPDEGROVE, LOUIS B, b Kingsville, Tex, Sept 10, 28; m 52; c 2. CHEMICAL ENGINEERING. *Educ:* Mass Inst Technol, SB, 53. *Prof Exp:* Chem engr, Chemstrand Corp, Fla, 53-56; res engr, Sci Labs, Ford Motor Co, 56-57; lab develop supvr, Kordite Corp, NY, 57-62; tech dir, Standard Packaging Corp, 62-65; process develop mgr, Alcolac Chem Corp, 65; vpres & mgr res & develop, Vogt Mfg Corp, NY, 65-69; vpres eng, J H Day Co, Cincinnati, 69-77; PRES, TYLER SCOTT INC, TERRACE PARK, 77- *Mem:* Am Chem Soc; Soc Plastics Engrs. *Res:* Applied plastics research and development; packaging; coatings; emulsion polymers; polymer processing; solids drying; pigment dispersion; research management. *Mailing Add:* 313 Rugby Ave Terrace Park OH 45174

UPDIKE, OTIS L(EE), JR, b Roanoke, Va, Feb 12, 20; m 45; c 4. BIOMEDICAL & CHEMICAL ENGINEERING. *Educ:* Univ Va, BChE, 41; Univ Ill, PhD(chem eng), 44. *Prof Exp:* Asst, Eng Exp Sta, Univ Ill, 41-44; chem engr res dept, Westvaco Chlorine Prod Corp, 44-46; assoc prof chem eng, 46-60, res engr, Eng Exp Sta, 51-59, PROF CHEM ENG & MEM PARTIC FAC, RES LABS, ENG SCI, UNIV VA, 60-, PROF CHEM & BIOMED ENG, 67- *Concurrent Pos:* Consult, Philip Morris & Co, 52-59; tech consult, US Naval Air Missile Test Ctr, 54-55; vpres, Jefferson Res Labs, 55-58; NSF sci fac fel & vis assoc, Calif Inst Technol, 59-60; chmn, Joint Automatic Control Conf, 69. *Mem:* AAAS; Am Inst Chem Engrs; Biomed Eng Soc; Inst Elec & Electronics Engrs; Instrument Soc Am. *Res:* Instrumentation and automatic control; computer applications in process and biomedical engineering; dynamics of process, physiological and instrumentation systems; data acquisition and interpretation. *Mailing Add:* Sch of Eng & Appl Sci Thornton Hall Univ of Va Charlottesville VA 22903

UPESLACIS, JANIS, b Bad-Rothenfelde, Ger, Jan 12, 46; US citizen; m 68; c 2. PHARMACEUTICAL CHEMISTRY. *Educ:* Univ Nebr-Lincoln, BS, 67; Harvard Univ, MA, 69, PhD(org chem), 75. *Prof Exp:* Asst nuclear physics, Walter Reed Army Med Ctr, US Army, 69-71; res chemist, 75-80, GROUP LEADER, LEDERLE LABS, AM CYANAMID CO, 75- *Mem:* Am Chem Soc. *Res:* Synthetic applications of carbohydrates; antiatherogenic agents; prostaglandins; antidiabetes agents; inhibitors of complement-mediated diseases; antineoplastic agents. *Mailing Add:* Lederle Labs Pearl River NY 10965

UPGREN, ARTHUR REINHOLD, JR, b Minneapolis, Minn, Feb 21, 33; m 67; c 1. ASTRONOMY. *Educ:* Univ Minn, BA, 55; Univ Mich, MS, 58; Case Inst Technol, PhD(astron), 61. *Prof Exp:* Res assoc astron, Swarthmore Col, 61-63; astronr, US Naval Observ, 63-66; asst prof astron, 66-73, actg chmn dept, 68-77, adj assoc prof, 73-77, actg dir, Van Vleck Observ, 68-77, assoc prof astron, 77-81, VAN VLECK PROF ASTRON, WESLEYAN UNIV, 81-, CHMN DEPT & DIR, VAN VLECK OBSERV, 77- *Concurrent Pos:* Vis lectr, Univ Md, 64-66; vpres & exec officer, Fund Astrophys Res, Inc, 72- *Mem:* Am Astron Soc; Royal Astron Soc; Int Astron Union. *Res:* Galactic structure; photographic astrometry. *Mailing Add:* Dept Astron Van Vleck Observ Wesleyan Univ Middletown CT 06457

UPHAM, ROY HERBERT, b Boston, Mass, Feb 9, 20; m 45; c 8. ORGANIC CHEMISTRY. *Educ:* Boston Col, BS, 41, MS, 48. *Prof Exp:* Chemist, Howe & French, Inc, 41-42, Cities Serv Oil Co, 42, Rock Island Arsenal, 44-45 & E I du Pont de Nemours & Co, Inc, 47-49; PROF CHEM, ST ANSELM COL, 49- *Mem:* Am Chem Soc. *Res:* Reaction mechanisms; teaching methods; computer applications. *Mailing Add:* Dept Chem St Anselm Col Manchester NH 03102

UPHAM, ROY WALTER, b Ogden, Kans, Apr 11, 20; m 69. VETERINARY MEDICINE, FOOD TECHNOLOGY. *Educ:* Kans State Univ, DVM, 43; Mass Inst Technol, MS, 60; Am Bd Vet Pub Health, dipl. *Prof Exp:* Instr food technol, US Army Med Serv Sch, 54-56, proj off radiation of foods prog, US Army, 56-58, mil adv, Food Prog for Vietnam, 62-63, chief lab br food testing, Defense Personnel Supply Command, 63-65, chief standardization br, Mil Specifications, Natick Army Lab, 65-66; CHIEF DIV FOOD, DRUGS & DAIRIES, REGULATORY AGENCY, ILL DEPT PUB HEALTH, SPRINGFIELD, 66- *Mem:* Inst Food Technologists; Asn Food & Drug Officials (pres, 81-82). *Res:* Application of controlled food processing to safeguard and protect public health. *Mailing Add:* Dept Pub Health 535 W Jefferson Springfield IL 62706

UPHOFF, DELTA EMMA, b Brooklyn, NY, Jan 23, 22. GENETICS. *Educ:* Russell Sage Col, AB, 44; Univ Rochester, MS, 47. *Prof Exp:* Asst radiation genetics, Manhattan Proj, Rochester, 46-47; zoologist, Radiation Lab, Univ Calif, 47-48; geneticist, Mound Lab, Monsanto Chem Co, Ohio, 48-49; biologist, Lab Pathophysiol, 49-80, RES BIOLOGIST, NAT CANCER INST, 80- *Mem:* Fel AAAS; Genetics Soc Am; Radiation Res Soc; Am Genetic Asn; Am Asn Cancer Res. *Res:* Immunogenetics of bone marrow transplantations. *Mailing Add:* Nat Cancer Inst Bethesda MD 20205

UPHOLT, WILLIAM BOYCE, b Orlando, Fla, Sept 14, 43; m 80; c 1. MOLECULAR BIOLOGY. *Educ:* Pomona Col, BA, 65; Calif Inst Technol, PhD(chem), 71. *Prof Exp:* Res fel molecular biol, Damon Runyon Mem Fund Cancer Res, Biochem Lab, Univ Amsterdam, 71-73; res fel, Dept Embryol, Carnegie Inst Wash, Baltimore, 73-75; RES ASSOC MOLECULAR BIOL, DEPT PEDIAT & BIOCHEM, UNIV CHICAGO, 75- *Res:* Physical chemistry of nucleic acids, mitochondrial biogenesis, DNA replication, organization of genetic material, developmental biology, control of gene expression during cartilage differentiation. *Mailing Add:* Univ Chicago Hosp Box 413 5825 S Maryland Ave Chicago IL 60637

UPLEDGER, JOHN EDWIN, b Detroit, Mich, Feb 10, 32; c 4. OSTEOPATHIC MEDICINE, BIOMECHANICS. *Educ:* Wayne State Univ, BA, 53; Kirksville Col Osteop Med, DO(osteop), 63. *Prof Exp:* Physician pvt pract family med, 64-75; assoc prof, 75-80, PROF BIOMECH, MICH STATE UNIV, 80- *Mem:* AAAS; Int Asn Study Pain; fel Am Acad Osteop; Am Osteop Asn. *Res:* Cranial mechanics and brain development; neuromusculoskeletal physiology, function and structure; childhood brain injuries and dysfunctions. *Mailing Add:* 414 E Fee Hall Mich State Univ East Lansing MI 48824

UPPULURI, V R RAO, b Machilipattanam, India, Feb 22, 31; m 60; c 1. MATHEMATICAL STATISTICS. *Educ:* Andhra Univ, India, MA, 54; Ind Univ, Bloomington, PhD(math), 63. *Prof Exp:* Res asst math & statist, Tata Inst Fundamental Res, 54-57; res asst math, Ind Univ, Bloomington, 57-61; res assoc statist, Mich State Univ, 61-62, biophys & statist, 62-63; sr math statistician, Oak Ridge Nat Lab, 63-74; mem staff, Nuclear Div, Union Carbide Corp, 74-77, SR RES STAFF MEM, UNION CARBIDE NUCLEAR DIV, 77- *Concurrent Pos:* Lectr, Oak Ridge Traveling Lect Prog, Oak Ridge Assoc Univs & Oak Ridge Nat Lab, 64-; sr engr & scientist, Douglas Aircraft Co, 66; vis lectr prog, Comt Statist Southern Regional Educ Bd, 67-; adj prof, Univ Tenn, 67-; consult, Syst Develop Corp, 67- & med div, Oak Ridge Assoc Univ, 67-; vis prof, Univ Sao Paulo, 70 & Univ Minn, 71. *Mem:* Fel AAAS; fel Am Statist Asn; Am Math Soc. *Res:* Probability; statistics; stochastic approach for a better understanding of the structure of physical and natural phenomena; limit theorems in random difference equations and applications of probability. *Mailing Add:* Math & Statist Res Dept Union Carbide Corp Oak Ridge TN 37830

U'PRICHARD, DAVID C, b Rothesay, Scotland, May 27, 48; m 71; c 2. NEUROPHARMACOLOGY, NEUROCHEMISTRY. *Educ:* Univ Glasgow, BSc, 70; Univ Kans, MS, 74, PhD(pharmacol), 75. *Prof Exp:* Res scientist biochem, UK Ministry of Technol Lab, Torry, Scotland, 68; res scientist pharmacol, Ethicon, Gmbh, Hamburg, Ger, 70; res assoc, Johns Hopkins Univ, 75-78; asst prof pharmacol, 78-80, ASSOC PROF PHARMACOL, NEUROBIOL & PHYSIOL, NORTHWESTERN UNIV, 81- *Concurrent Pos:* NIH fel, USPHS, 75-77. *Mem:* AAAS; Brit Asn Advan Sci; Soc Neurosci; Europ Neurosci Asn; Brit Pharmacol Soc. *Res:* Sympathetic nervous system and central catecholaminergic neurotransmission mechanisms; identification, characterization and isolation of catecholaminergic receptors; cellular mechanism of action of psychoactive drugs and antihypertensive agents; endogenous opioid peptides in cultured cells. *Mailing Add:* Dept of Pharmacol 303 E Chicago Ave Chicago IL 60611

UPSON, DAN W, b Hutchinson, Kans, July 30, 29; m 59; c 3. PHARMACOLOGY, PHYSIOLOGY. *Educ:* Kans State Univ, DVM, 52, MS, 62, PhD(physiol), 69. *Prof Exp:* Vet, Pvt Pract, 52-59; instr pharmacol & physiol, 59-69, assoc prof pharmacol, 69-73, asst dean, 72-73, PROF PHARMACOL, COL VET MED, KANS STATE UNIV, 73-, DIR TEACHING RESOURCES, 75- *Concurrent Pos:* Consult, Tevcon Ind Inc, 70- *Mem:* Am Vet Med Asn; Am Acad Vet Pharmacol & Therapeut; Am Acad Vet Consult. *Res:* Veterinary pharmacology and clinical pharmacology. *Mailing Add:* Vet Teaching Bldg Col Vet Med Kans State Univ Manhattan KS 66506

UPSON, LAWRENCE L(EWIS), chemical engineering, see previous edition

UPTHEGROVE, W(ILLIAM) R(EID), b Ann Arbor, Mich, Nov 10, 28; m 53; c 5. METALLURGICAL ENGINEERING, ENGINEERING EDUCATION. *Educ:* Univ Mich, BSE, 50, MSE, 54, PhD(metall eng), 57. *Prof Exp:* From asst prof to assoc prof metall eng, Univ Okla, 56-62, chmn sch, 56-62; sect leader powder metall res & develop, Res Labs, Int Nickel Co, Inc, NJ, 62-64; prof mech eng & chmn dept, Univ Tex, Austin, 64-70; prof metall & mech eng & dean, Col Eng, 70-81, REGENTS PROF ENG, UNIV OKLA, 81- *Concurrent Pos:* Indust consult, 64-; consult educ planning, US Overseas Inst, 70- *Mem:* Am Inst Mining, Metall & Petrol Engrs; Am Soc Metals; Am Soc Mech Engrs; Nat Soc Prof Engrs; Am Soc Eng Educ. *Res:* Powder metallurgy; diffusion; cryogenic behavior of materials; design and materials properties. *Mailing Add:* 202 W Boyd Rm 108 Univ Okla Norman OK 73019

UPTON, ARTHUR CANFIELD, b Ann Arbor, Mich, Feb 27, 23; m 46; c 3. EXPERIMENTAL PATHOLOGY. *Educ:* Univ Mich, BA, 44, MD, 46. *Prof Exp:* Intern, Univ Hosp, Univ Mich, 47, resident path, Med Sch, 48-50, instr, 50-51; pathologist, Biol Div, Oak Ridge Nat Lab, 51-54, chief, Path-Physiol Sect, 54-69; chmn dept path, Health Sci Ctr, 69-70, dean, Sch Basic Health Sci, 70-75, prof path, State Univ NY Stony Brook, 69-77, attend pathologist, Med Dept, Brookhaven Nat Lab, 69-77, DIR, NAT CANCER INST, NIH, 77- *Concurrent Pos:* Mem subcomts biol effectiveness of radiation & long term effects of radiation, Nat Acad Sci-Nat Res Coun, 57-; Ciba Found lectr, Univ London, 59; rep, USA Nat Comt on the Int Union against Cancer, 72-; mem, Int Comn Radiol Protection, 74-; chmn, Int Comn Radiol Protection, 73-; mem, Nat Coun Radiation Protection & Measurements, 65-, adv comt, Ctr on Human Radiobiol, Argonne Nat Lab, 72-, sci adv group, US-Japan Coop Cancer Res Prog, 74-, sci adv bd, Nat Ctr for Toxological Res, 74-, sci coun, Int Agency for Res on Cancer, WHO, 75- *Honors & Awards:* Lawrence Award, 65. *Mem:* AAAS; Sigma Xi; Radiation Res Soc (pres, 65-66); Am Soc Exp Path (pres, 67-68); Am Asn Cancer Res (pres, 63-64). *Res:* Pathology of radiation injury and endocrine glands; cancer; carcinogenesis; experimental leukemia; aging. *Mailing Add:* Nat Cancer Inst NIH 9000 Rockville Pike Bethesda MD 20014

UPTON, G VIRGINIA, b New Haven, Conn, Oct 17, 29; wid; c 3. PHYSIOLOGY, BIOCHEMISTRY. *Educ:* Albertus Magnus Col, BA, 51; Yale Univ, MS, 61, PhD(physiol), 64. *Prof Exp:* NIH fel peptide chem, Yale Univ, 63-66, chief endocrine & polypeptide lab, Vet Admin Hosp, Yale Univ, 66-74, sr res assoc med, Sch Med, 71-74; assoc dir clin res, 74-78, ASSOC MED DIR, WYETH INT LTD, 78- *Concurrent Pos:* Asst prof comp endocrinol, Eve Div, South Conn State Col, 66-67. *Mem:* Am Asn Cancer Res; Endocrine Soc; NY Acad Sci; Int Soc Neuroendocrinol; Am Physiol Soc. *Res:* Neuroendocrinology; hypothalamic-pituitary-adrenal relationships; isolation of pituitary peptides and tumor peptides with hormonal activity; relationship between endocrine disorders and hypothalamic dysfunction. *Mailing Add:* Wyeth Int Ltd PO Box 8616 Philadelphia PA 19101

UPTON, RONALD P, b Boston, Mass, May 6, 41; m 65; c 2. ANALYTICAL CHEMISTRY. *Educ:* New Bedford Inst Tech, BS, 63; Univ Del, PhD(anal chem), 68. *Prof Exp:* Staff chemist, Res Lab, 67-70, MGR QUAL CONTROL, PFIZER INC, 70- *Mem:* Am Chem Soc. *Res:* Quality control; instrumental analysis; infrared, ultraviolet, atomic absorption and nuclear magnetic spectroscopies; gas and high pressure liquid chromatography, in vitro diagnostics and pharmaceutical analysis. *Mailing Add:* 28 Babcock Rd North Stonington CT 06359

UPTON, THOMAS HALLWORTH, b Dallas, Tex, Apr 14, 52; m 78. CATALYSIS, SURFACE SCIENCE. *Educ:* Stanford Univ, BS, 74; Calif Inst Technol, PhD(theoret), 80. *Prof Exp:* RES CHEMIST, EXXON RES & ENG CORP, 80- *Mem:* Am Chem Soc; Am Phys Soc. *Res:* Theoretical investigations of mechanisms in homogeneous, heterogeneous catalysis and surface science. *Mailing Add:* Exxon Res & Eng PO Box 45 Linden NJ 07036

URBACH, FREDERICK, b Vienna, Austria, Sept 6, 22; nat US; m 52; c 3. DERMATOLOGY. *Educ:* Univ Pa, BS, 43; Jefferson Med Col, MD, 46; Am Bd Dermat, dipl, 53. *Prof Exp:* Asst instr dermat, Med Sch, Univ Pa, 49-50, instr, 50-52, assoc, 52-54; chief dermat serv, Roswell Park Mem Inst, 54-58; assoc prof dermat, 58-60, prof res dermat, 60-67, PROF DERMAT & CHMN DEPT, SCH MED, TEMPLE UNIV, 67-, MED DIR, SKIN & CANCER HOSP, 67- *Concurrent Pos:* Fel, Hosp Univ Pa, 49-52; Damon Runyon res fel clin cancer, Univ Pa, 51-53; asst vis physician, Philadelphia Gen Hosp, 51-54; mem, Int Cong Dermat, London, 52; from asst med dir to assoc med dir, Skin & Cancer Hosp, Temple Univ, 58-67; mem, US Nat Comt Photobiol, Nat Res Coun, 73-80; dir, Ctr Photobiol, 77- *Honors & Awards:* Hellerstrom Medal, Swed Derm Soc, 78; Ritter Medal, Germ Derm Soc, 80. *Mem:* Fel

AAAS; Soc Invest Dermat; Soc Exp Biol & Med; Am Asn Cancer Res; Am Acad Dermat. *Res:* Blood supply of cancer; biologic effects of ultraviolet radiation; photobiology; epidemiology of cancer. *Mailing Add:* Skin & Cancer Hosp 3322 N Broad St Philadelphia PA 19140

URBACH, FREDERICK LEWIS, b New Castle, Pa, Nov 21, 38; m 60; c 2. INORGANIC CHEMISTRY. *Educ:* Pa State Univ, University Park, BS, 60; Mich State Univ, PhD(chem), 64. *Prof Exp:* Res assoc & fel, Ohio State Univ, 64-66; asst prof, 66-74, assoc prof, 74-80, PROF CHEM, CASE WESTERN RESERVE UNIV, 80- *Mem:* Am Chem Soc. *Res:* Chemistry of metal chelates containing multidentate ligands; stereochemistry and optical activity; role of transition metal ions in biological processes. *Mailing Add:* Dept Chem Case Western Reserve Univ Cleveland OH 44106

URBACH, HERMAN B, b New York, NY, Jan 19, 23; m 56; c 2. ELECTROCHEMISTRY, MECHANICAL ENGINEERING. *Educ:* Univ Ind, AB, 48; Columbia Univ, MA, 50; Case Western Reserve Univ, PhD, 54; George Washington Univ, MS, 76. *Prof Exp:* Group leader, Olin Mathieson Chem Corp, 53-59; res scientist, Res Lab, United Aircraft Corp, 59-65, consult electrochem, Pratt & Whitney Aircraft Div, 60-63; SCI STAFF ASST POWER & PROPULSION, POWER SYSTS DIV, US NAVAL RES & DEVELOP CTR, ANNAPOLIS, 65- *Concurrent Pos:* Guest prof mech eng, US Naval Acad, 81- *Mem:* Am Inst Aeronaut & Astronaut; Am Soc Mech Engrs; NY Acad Sci; Sigma Xi; Am Chem Soc. *Res:* Kinetics of the oxygen electrode; fuel cells; theory of porous electrodes; ozone and plasma kinetics; atomic reactions; boranes; magnetohydrodynamics; biphase turbines; gas and steam turbines. *Mailing Add:* Power Systs Div Code 272T David Taylor Naval Ship Systs Annapolis MD 21402

URBACH, JOHN C, b Vienna, Austria, Feb 18, 34; US citizen; m 56; c 3. OPTICS. *Educ:* Univ Rochester, BS, 55, PhD(optics), 62; Mass Inst Technol, MS, 57. *Prof Exp:* Assoc physicist, Int Bus Mach Corp, 57-58; NATO fel sci, Royal Inst Tech, Sweden, 61-62; scientist, NY, 63-66, sr scientist, 66-67, mgr optical & imaging anal br, 67-68, mgr optical sci br, 68-70, mgr optical sci area, 70-75, MGR OPTICAL SCI LAB, PALO ALTO RES CTR, XEROX CORP, 75- *Concurrent Pos:* Chmn tech group info processing & holography, Optical Soc Am, 76-77; mem, US Nat Comt, Int Comn Optics, 75-77. *Mem:* Fel Optical Soc Am; Soc Photog Sci & Eng; Soc Photo-Optical Instrument Eng. *Res:* Optical techniques for information storage and retrieval; effects of recording materials upon holographic imaging; unconventional photography, especially electrophotography; evaluation of optical and photographic image quality; laser scanning. *Mailing Add:* Xerox Palo Alto Res Ctr 3333 Coyote Hill Rd Palo Alto CA 94304

URBACH, JOHN ROBERT, b Vienna, Austria, Aug 2, 24; US citizen; m 55; c 2. MEDICINE. *Educ:* Univ Pa, MD, 47; Am Bd Internal Med, dipl, 54. *Prof Exp:* Intern, Philadelphia Gen Hosp, Pa, 47-48, resident med & cardiol, 48-50; asst prof physiol & biophys & assoc prof med, 65-72, CLIN PROF MED & ASST PROF PHYSIOL & BIOPHYS, MED COL PA, 72- *Mem:* Am Heart Asn. *Res:* Cardiology; physiology. *Mailing Add:* Med Col of Pa 3300 Henry Ave Philadelphia PA 19129

URBACH, KARL FREDERIC, b Vienna, Austria, Nov 9, 17; nat US; m 52; c 2. HOSPITAL ADMINISTRATION. *Educ:* Reed Col, BA, 42; Northwestern Univ, PhD(chem), 46, MD, 51. *Prof Exp:* Asst, Eve Sch, Northwestern Univ, 42-46, asst chem, Dent Sch, 43-45, asst pharmacol, Med Sch, 45-47, lectr chem, Univ, 46-47, instr chem & pharmacol, Univ & Med Sch, 47-50; resident anesthesiol, USPHS Hosp, Staten Island, NY, 52-54; actg chief, USPHS Hosp, San Francisco, 54-55; chief anesthesiol, USPHS Hosp, Staten Island, 55-69; chief med educ & res, USPHS Hosp, San Francisco, 69-70, dir, 70-79; RETIRED. *Concurrent Pos:* NIH res fel, USPHS, 51-52. *Mem:* AAAS; Soc Exp Biol & Med; AMA; Am Soc Anesthesiol; Asn Mil Surg US. *Res:* Synthesis of vasopressors and testing, local anesthetics and testing; histamine methods for identification; actions; metabolism; pharmacology; evaluation of coronary dilators; anesthesia; hypnotics. *Mailing Add:* 2 Atalaya Terr San Francisco CA 94117

URBAIN, WALTER MATHIAS, b Chicago, Ill, Apr 8, 10; m 39; c 2. PHYSICAL CHEMISTRY, FOOD SCIENCE. *Educ:* Univ Chicago, SB, 31, PhD(chem), 34. *Prof Exp:* Phys chemist, Swift & Co, 33-50, assoc dir res, 50-59, dir eng res & develop dept, 59-65; prof, 65-75, EMER PROF FOOD SCI, MICH STATE UNIV, 75- *Concurrent Pos:* Mem comn radiation preservation of foods, Nat Res Coun, 56-62, chmn, 59-62, mem adv bd mil personnel supplies, 62-; mem adv comt isotopes & radiation develop, AEC, 64-66, chmn adv comt radiation pasteurization of foods, Am Inst Biol Sci, 71-; sci ed, Food Technol & J Food Sci, Inst Food Technologists, 66-70; consult, US Food & Drug Admin, 74-80; vis prof food science & technol, Univ Calif, Davis, 82. *Honors & Awards:* Outstanding Civilian Serv Medal, US Army, 62; Indust Achievement Award, Inst Food Technologists, 63; Food Eng Award, Dairy & Food Industs Supply Assoc/Am Soc Agr Engrs. *Mem:* Am Chem Soc; Am Inst Chem Eng; Inst Food Technologists; Optical Soc Am; AAAS. *Res:* Activity coefficients; detergent action of soaps; meat pigments; color standards; egg processing; meat packaging and processing; spectrochemical analysis of foods; x-ray diffraction; instrumentation; microwave heating; treatment of foods with ionizing radiation; spun protein foods. *Mailing Add:* 10645 Welk Dr Sun City AZ 85373

URBAN, EMIL KARL, b Milwaukee, Wis, May 27, 34; m 63; c 1. ORNITHOLOGY, VERTEBRATE ZOOLOGY. *Educ:* Univ Wis, BS, 56, PhD(zool), 64; Univ Kans, MA, 58. *Prof Exp:* Asst prof biol, Haile Sellassie I Univ, 64-67, assoc prof, 67-75; assoc prof zool, Univ Ark, 75-76; PROF & CHMN BIOL, AUGUSTA COL, 76- *Mem:* AAAS; Am Ornith Union; Brit Ornith Union; Cooper Ornith Soc; Wilson Ornith Soc. *Res:* Birds of Africa; biology of African pelicans, cormorants, and ibises; monitoring of ciconiid colonies in Southeast United States. *Mailing Add:* Dept of Biol August Col Augusta GA 30904

URBAN, EUGENE WILLARD, b Omaha, Nebr, Apr 20, 35; m 60; c 8. PHYSICS. *Educ:* Harvard Univ, BS, 57; Univ Ala, MS, 63, PhD(physics), 70. *Prof Exp:* Physicist space res, US Army Ballistic Missile Agency, 59-60; physicist, 60-70, SUPVRY PHYSICIST SPACE RES, GEORGE C MARSHALL SPACE FLIGHT CTR, NASA, 70- *Honors & Awards:* NASA Medal Except Sci Achievement, 75. *Mem:* Am Phys Soc; Sigma Xi. *Res:* Low temperature physics; superconducting instruments for space experiments; properties and applications of superfluid liquid helium in space; superfluid helium systems for space experiment cooling. *Mailing Add:* Marshall Space Flight Ctr NASA Marshall Space Flight Ctr AL 35812

URBAN, JAMES BARTEL, geology, palynology, deceased

URBAN, JAMES EDWARD, b Dime Box, Tex, Jan 5, 42; m 63; c 2. MICROBIAL PHYSIOLOGY. *Educ:* Univ Tex, Austin, BA, 65, PhD(microbiol), 68. *Prof Exp:* NSF fel, 68-70, asst prof, 70-77, ASSOC PROF BIOL, KANS STATE UNIV, 77- *Mem:* Am Soc Microbiol. *Res:* Regulation of cell division; medium and growth rate influences on the bacterial cell cycle; bacteroid morphogenesis in the Rhizobium clover symbiosis. *Mailing Add:* Div Biol Ackert Hall Kans State Univ Manhattan KS 66506

URBAN, JOSEPH, b Brooklyn, NY, Mar 6, 21; m 47; c 4. CHEMISTRY, METALLURGY. *Educ:* Cooper Union, BChE, 43; Polytech Inst Brooklyn, MChE, 47, DrChE, 50. *Prof Exp:* Res chemist, Manhattan Proj, Columbia Univ, 43-44; res engr, Kellex Corp, 44-45; petrol res, M W Kellogg Co Div, Pullman, Inc, 45-47; instr chem, Adelphi Col, 47-50; PROF SCI, WEBB INST NAVAL ARCHIT, 48-, DEAN, 69- *Concurrent Pos:* Consult, Gen Elec Co, 50-52, A Pollak, 51-53 & J L Finck Labs, 53-56. *Res:* Catalysis; petroleum. *Mailing Add:* 69-64 64th St Glendale NY 11385

URBAN, MICHAEL K, developmental biology, molecular biology, see previous edition

URBAN, PAUL, b Philadelphia, Pa, June 11, 38. CELL BIOLOGY. *Educ:* Washington Univ, AB, 62; Tufts Univ, PhD(biol), 67. *Prof Exp:* Instr biol, Yale Univ, 67-68; asst prof biol sci, Union Col, NY, 68-74; MEM, ELECTRON MICROS UNIT, VET ADMIN HOSP, 74- *Mem:* Bot Soc Am; Phycol Soc Am; Am Soc Cell Biol. *Res:* Fine structure of reproduction in plants; gametogenesis; sporogenesis; gamete fusion; pronuclear fusion and early development. *Mailing Add:* Electron Micros Unit 113A Vet Admin Hosp Albany NY 11208

URBAN, RICHARD WILLIAM, b Newark, NY, July 30, 45; m 67; c 2. MICROBIOLOGY, MOLECULAR BIOLOGY. *Educ:* Ariz State Univ, BS, 70; Univ Hartford, MA, 73; Univ Colo, PhD(biol), 78. *Prof Exp:* vis asst prof biol, microbiol & immunol, Metrop State Col, 78-79; res fel immunol, Dept Surg, Univ Colo Med Ctr, 78-79; RES ASST PROF TUMOR IMMUNOL, UTAH STATE UNIV, 79- *Concurrent Pos:* Researcher, Oncol Unit, Univ Colo Med Ctr & Dept of EPO Biol, Boulder Campus, 75-; res assoc, Dept Surg, Univ Calif Med Ctr, 80-; prin investr tumor immunother, New Agent Develop, 80-; independent investr tumor immunol, Dept Surg/EPO biol, Univ Colo, 80- *Mem:* Am Soc Microbiol; Sigma Xi; AAAS; NY Acad Sci. *Res:* Development and clinical evaluation of new tumor immunotherapeutic agents. *Mailing Add:* Denison Lab Rm 108 Univ Colo Boulder CO 80309

URBAN, THEODORE JOSEPH, b Chicago, Ill, May 29, 26; m 56; c 1. PHYSIOLOGY. *Educ:* Northwestern Univ, BS, 49, MS, 50; Purdue Univ, PhD(biol), 54. *Prof Exp:* Instr biol, Berea Col, 53-54; assoc prof, 54-68, PROF BIOL, CREIGHTON UNIV, 68-, ASST DEAN DENT SCH, 69- *Mem:* AAAS; Am Soc Zoologists; Int Asn Dent Res. *Res:* Minor element metabolism; salivary gland hormones and factors; cleft palate research. *Mailing Add:* Dept of Oral Biol Creighton Univ Dent Sch Omaha NE 68131

URBAN, WILLARD EDWARD, JR, b Chicago, Ill, Sept 16, 36; m 57; c 3. BIOMETRICS, ANIMAL BREEDING. *Educ:* Va Polytech Inst & State Univ, BS, 58; Iowa State Univ, MS, 60, PhD(animal breeding), 63. *Prof Exp:* Animal husbandman, Animal Husb Res Div, Agr Res Serv, USDA, 58-63; asst prof, 63-68, statistician, Agr Exp Sta, 63-72, asst dir, 72-80, ASSOC PROF BIOMET, UNIV NH, 68-, ASSOC DIR, AGR EXP STA, 80- *Mem:* Biomet Soc; Am Soc Animal Sci. *Res:* Role of heredity and environment in economic traits of livestock; statistical methods for analyzing non-orthogonal data. *Mailing Add:* Agr Exp Sta Univ NH Durham NH 03824

URBANEK, VINCENT EDWARD, b Chicago, Ill, Jan 2, 27; m 49; c 2. PROSTHODONTICS, DENTISTRY. *Educ:* Northwestern Univ, Evanston, BS, 51, MA, 52; Univ Ill, Chicago, DDS, 57. *Prof Exp:* Instr removable prosthodontics, Col Dent, Univ Ill Med Ctr, 57-63, asst prof, 63-67, assoc prof oral diag & oral med, 67-70; PROF REMOVABLE PROSTHODONTICS, SCH DENT, MED COL GA, 70- *Concurrent Pos:* Mem attend staff, Eugene Talmadge Mem Hosp, 70- *Mem:* Fel Am Col Dent; Am Dent Asn; Am Prosthodont Soc; Am Acad Oral Med. *Res:* Removable prosthodontics; oral diagnosis; mandibular dysfunction as related to the temporomandibular joints, neuromuscular components and dental occlusion; effects of corticosteroids on vesiculobullous lesions of the oral mucosa. *Mailing Add:* Dept of Prosthodontics Med Col of Ga Sch of Dent Augusta GA 30902

URBANIK, ARTHUR RONALD, b Union City, NJ, Apr 17, 39; m 66; c 2. ORGANIC CHEMISTRY, TEXTILE CHEMISTRY. *Educ:* St Vincent Col, BS, 61; WVa Univ, MS, 63, PhD(org chem), 67. *Prof Exp:* Sr res chemist, Bjorksten Res Labs, 67; SR RES CHEMIST, DAN RIVER, INC, 67- *Concurrent Pos:* Lectr chem, Stratford Col, 72-73. *Mem:* Am Chem Soc; assoc Sigma Xi; Am Asn Textile Chem & Colorists. *Res:* Textile chemicals and finishes; organic chemical process development; dyeing auxiliaries; applied dyeing theory. *Mailing Add:* 709 Brightwell Dr Danville VA 24540

URBAS, BRANKO, b Zagreb, Yugoslavia, July 24, 29; m 56; c 1. ORGANIC CHEMISTRY, BIOCHEMISTRY. *Educ:* Univ Zagreb, Diplom Chem, 53, DSc(org chem), 60. *Prof Exp:* Group leader, Synthetic Org Chem, Pliva Chem & Pharmaceut Works, Zagreb, Yugoslavia, 52-60; sect leader polymer chem, Org Chem Indust, 60-61; Nat Res Coun Can fel carbohydrates, Ottawa Univ, Ont, 61-63; asst prof & NIH grant dept biochem, Purdue Univ, Lafayette, 63-65; res scientist, Res Br, Can Dept Agr, 65-68; SR RES CHEMIST, MOFFETT TECH CTR, CPC INT, INC, ARGO, 68- *Mem:* Am Chem Soc; Croatian Chem Soc. *Res:* Synthetic organic and carbohydrate chemistry. *Mailing Add:* 813 Belair Dr Darien IL 60559

URBATSCH, LOWELL EDWARD, b Osage, Iowa, July 5, 42; m 65; c 2. SYSTEMATIC BOTANY. *Educ:* Univ Northern Iowa, BA, 64; Univ Ga, PhD(bot), 70. *Prof Exp:* Asst prof bot, Chadron State Col, 70-71; asst prof plant syst & biol, Univ Tex, Austin, 71-75; ASST PROF PLANT SYSTS, LA STATE UNIV, BATON ROUGE, 75- *Mem:* Int Asn Plant Taxon; Am Soc Plant Taxon. *Res:* Cytological and biochemical systematics of genera in the Compositae. *Mailing Add:* Dept of Bot La State Univ Baton Rouge LA 70803

URBSCHEIT, NANCY LEE, b Viroqua, Wis, Sept 7, 46. RESPIRATORY PHYSIOLOGY, PHYSICAL MEDICINE. *Educ:* State Univ NY Buffalo, BS, 68, MA, 70, PhD(physiol), 73. *Prof Exp:* From instr to asst prof physiol, State Univ NY Buffalo, 73-76, asst to the vpres health sci, 73-76; asst prof phys therapy educ, Univ Iowa, Iowa City, 76-79; staff physical therapist, St Lawrence Hosp, Lansing, Mich, 79; chief physical therapist, Palo Alto County Hosp, 80-81; ASSOC PROF PHYS THERAPY, EAST CAROLINA UNIV, 81- *Res:* Motor unit discharge patterns in elderly man reciprocal inhibition in hemiparetic man; mapping the activity of intercostal muscles in anesthetized cats during mechanical loading, in particular, positive and negative pressure breathing, threshold loading and elastic loading and chemical loading of respiration. *Mailing Add:* East Carolina Univ Greenville NC 27834

URDANG, ARNOLD, b Brooklyn, NY, Feb 10, 28; m 52; c 2. PHARMACEUTICAL CHEMISTRY, PHARMACY. *Educ:* Long Island Univ, BS, 49; Columbia Univ, MS, 52; Univ Conn, PhD(pharmaceut chem), 55. *Prof Exp:* Asst prof phys pharm, Long Island Univ, 55-58; res dir pharm, E Fougera & Co, NY, 58-64; asst dir clin res, Winthrop Prod Inc, Div, Sterling Drug Inc, 64-67, asst dir new prod, 67-69, dir tech coord, Winthrop Labs, 69-77, MGR SCI AFFAIRS, PHARMACEUT GROUP, STERLING DRUG, INC, 77- *Concurrent Pos:* Res Corp grant, 56-58. *Mem:* AAAS; Am Pharmaceut Asn; Am Chem Soc. *Res:* Development of new pharmaceuticals both from the aspect of new product development as well as the investigation of potential new chemical compounds. *Mailing Add:* Sterling Drug Inc 90 Park Ave New York NY 10016

URDY, CHARLES EUGENE, b Georgetown, Tex, Dec 27, 33; m 62; c 1. X-RAY CRYSTALLOGRAPHY, INORGANIC CHEMISTRY. *Educ:* Huston-Tillotson Col, BS, 54; Univ Tex, Austin, PhD(chem), 62. *Prof Exp:* Prof chem, Huston-Tillotson Col, 61-62; assoc prof, NC Col, Durham, 62-63; prof, Prairie View Agr & Mech Col, 63-72; PROF CHEM, HUSTON-TILLOTSON COL, 72- *Concurrent Pos:* Robert A Welch Found fel, Univ Tex, Austin, 62. *Mem:* Fel Am Inst Chem; Am Crystallog Asn; Am Chem Soc; Sigma Xi. *Res:* Determination of the crystal structures of coordination compounds of the transition metals by x-ray diffraction methods. *Mailing Add:* 7311 Hartnell Dr Austin TX 78723

URE, ROLAND WALTER, JR, b New York, NY, June 22, 25; m 49; c 4. SEMICONDUCTORS. *Educ:* Univ Mich, BSE, 47; Calif Inst Technol, MS, 48; Univ Chicago, PhD(physics), 57. *Prof Exp:* Eng aide underwater acoustics, US Naval Ord Lab, 43-45; jr engr, Res Lab, Westinghouse Elec Corp, 48-50, res physicist, 55-63, fel physicist, 63-69; PROF MAT SCI & ELEC ENG, COL ENG, UNIV UTAH, 69- *Mem:* AAAS; Am Phys Soc; sr mem Inst Elec & Electronics Eng. *Res:* Solid state physics; ionic crystals; transport properties of semiconductors; thermoelectric and microwave semiconductor devices; quantum effects in semiconductors; electrical engineering; positron annihilation; chemically sensitive field effect transistors; silicon integrated circuits; photodiodes; materials for energy conversion. *Mailing Add:* Col of Eng Univ of Utah Salt Lake City UT 84112

URELES, ALVIN L, b Rochester, NY, Aug 8, 21; m 53; c 3. MEDICINE. *Educ:* Univ Rochester, MD, 45; Am Bd Internal Med, dipl; Am Bd Nuclear Med, dipl. *Prof Exp:* Intern, Beth Israel Hosp, Boston, 45-46, from resident to chief resident med, 48-51; from clin instr radiol & med to clin asst prof med, 51-64, assoc prof med, 64-67, clin assoc radiol, 61-67, PROF MED, SCH MED & DENT, UNIV ROCHESTER, 69-; ASSOC HEAD ENDOCRINOL & METAB DIV & CHIEF MED, GENESEE HOSP, 67- *Concurrent Pos:* Asst physician, Strong Mem Hosp, Rochester, NY, 51-58, sr assoc physician, 64- *Mem:* Fel Am Col Physicians; Int Soc Internal Med; Am Soc Internal Med; Endocrine Soc; AMA. *Res:* Thyroid disease. *Mailing Add:* Genesee Hosp 224 Alexander St Rochester NY 14607

URESK, DANIEL WILLIAM, b Price, Utah, July 18, 43; m 71; c 2. RANGE SCIENCE, WILDLIFE MANAGEMENT. *Educ:* Univ Utah, BS, 65, MS, 67; Colo State Univ, PhD(range sci), 72. *Prof Exp:* Res scientist, Battelle Pac Northwest Labs, 73-77; pres intern, 72-73, RES BIOLOGIST RANGE-WILDLIFE, ROCKY MT FOREST & RANGE EXP STA, FOREST SERV, USDA, 77- *Concurrent Pos:* Fac affil, SDak Sch Mines, SDak State Univ, Brigham Young Univ & Colo State Univ, 78; referee, J Wildlife Mgt, 78; proposal referee, NSF, 78. *Mem:* Sigma Xi; Soc Range Mgt. *Res:* Basic range ecology; plant production; livestock grazing; dietary analyses; plant-animal wildlife relationships; nutrition studies. *Mailing Add:* Rocky Mt Forest & Range Exp Sta Sch of Mines Campus Rapid City SD 57701

URETSKY, MYRON, b New York, NY, May 28, 40; m 81; c 4. COMPUTER SCIENCE, DATA PROCESSING. *Educ:* City Col NY, BBA, 61; Ohio State Univ, MBA, 62, PhD(acct), 62. *Prof Exp:* Asst prof acct, Univ Ill, 64-67; assoc prof bus, Columbia Univ, 67-70; PROF INFO SYST, NY UNIV, 70- *Concurrent Pos:* Fulbright scholar, 79; consult, 80- *Mem:* Inst Mgt Sci; Am Inst Cert Pub Acct; Asn Comput Mach. *Res:* Impact of computers on society; management fraud; simulation and gaming; East-West trade; technology assessment. *Mailing Add:* Grad Sch of Bus Admin NY Univ 100 Trinity Pl New York NY 10006

URETZ, ROBERT BENJAMIN, b Chicago, Ill, June 27, 24; m 55; c 2. BIOPHYSICS. *Educ:* Univ Chicago, BS, 47, PhD(biophys), 54. *Prof Exp:* Asst cosmic rays, 48-50, from instr to assoc prof biophys, 54-64, chmn dept biophys, 66-69; asst cosmic rays, 48-50, from instr to assoc prof biophys, 54-64, prof, 64-73, chmn, Dept Biophys, 66-69, assoc dean, 69-70, dep dean basic sci, 70-76, assoc vpres, Med Ctr & dep dean acad affairs, 76, actg vpres, Med Ctr & actg dean, Div Biol Sci & Pritzker Sch Med, 76-77, RALPH W GERARD PROF BIOPHYS & THEORET BIOL, DIV BIOL SCI & PRITZKER SCH MED, UNIV CHICAGO, 73-, VPRES, MED CTR & DEAN, DIV BIOL SCI & PRITZKER SCH MED, 77- *Mem:* Radiation Res Soc; Biophys Soc; Am Soc Cell Biol; Am Asn Med Cols; AMA. *Res:* Mechanism of biological effects of various radiations; optical analysis of biological structure. *Mailing Add:* Dept Biol Sci & Pritzker Sch Med Univ Chicago 950 E 59th Box 417 Chicago IL 60637

UREY, HAROLD CLAYTON, chemistry, deceased

URIBE, ERNEST GILBERT, b Sanger, Calif, Nov 25, 35; m 57; c 3. PLANT BIOCHEMISTRY. *Educ:* Fresno State Col, AB, 57; Univ Calif, Davis, MS, 62, PhD(plant physiol), 65. *Prof Exp:* Res asst bot & biochem, Univ Calif, Davis, 58-65; res assoc biochem, Johns Hopkins Univ, 65-66 & Cornell Univ, 66-67; asst prof biol, Yale Univ, 67-74; ASSOC PROF BOT, WASH STATE UNIV, 74- *Concurrent Pos:* Res fels, NSF, 65-66 & NIH, 66-67. *Mem:* AAAS; Am Soc Plant Physiologists; Biophys Soc; Am Soc Biol Chemists. *Res:* Membrane transport in higher plants; energy conversion in photosynthesis mechanism of photosynthetic phosphorylation. *Mailing Add:* Dept Bot Wash State Univ Pullman WA 99163

URICCHIO, WILLIAM ANDREW, b Hartford, Conn, Apr 21, 24; m 50; c 5. BIOLOGY, HELMINTHOLOGY. *Educ:* Catholic Univ, BA, 49, MS, 51, PhD(zool), 53. *Prof Exp:* Asst prof, 53, PROF BIOL & CHMN DEPT, CARLOW COL, 53- *Concurrent Pos:* Guest prof, Carnegie-Mellon Univ, 63-68, NSF vis prof, 67-68; vchmn, bd dirs, Human Life & Natural Family Planning Found; mem bd dirs, Duquesne Univ; pres, Int Fedn Family Life Promotion. *Honors & Awards:* Bishop-Wright Award, 62; Knight of St Gregory the Great. *Mem:* Fel AAAS; Am Soc Zool; Nat Asn Biol Teachers; Sigma Xi; Nat Asn Sci Teachers. *Res:* Sexuality; science education; natural family planning. *Mailing Add:* 1402 Murray Ave Pittsburgh PA 15217

URICK, ROBERT JOSEPH, b Brooklyn, NY, Apr 1, 15; m 55; c 3. UNDERWATER ACOUSTICS. *Educ:* Brooklyn Col, BS, 35; Calif Inst Technol, MS, 39. *Prof Exp:* Asst seismologist, Shell Oil Co, Tex, 36-38; chief computer, Tex Co, 39-42; physicist, Radio & Sound Lab, US Dept Navy, Calif, 42-45, Naval Res Lab, Wash, DC, 45-55; physicist, Ord Res Lab, Pa State Univ, 55-57, Mine Defense Lab, Fla, 57-60, US Naval Ord Res Lab, 60-74 & Naval Surface Weapons Ctr, 74-75; ACOUSTIC CONSULT, 75-; ADJ PROF, CATH UNIV AM, 77- *Honors & Awards:* Distinguished Civilian Serv Award, Navy Dept, 75. *Mem:* Fel Acoust Soc Am. *Res:* Underwater sound; sonar; sound propagation. *Mailing Add:* 11701 Berwick Rd Silver Spring MD 20904

URITAM, REIN AARNE, b Tartu, Estonia, Apr 11, 39; US citizen; m 70. ELEMENTARY PARTICLE PHYSICS. *Educ:* Concordia Col, Moorhead, Minn, BA, 61; Oxford Univ, BA, 63; Princeton Univ, MA, 65, PhD(physics), 68. *Prof Exp:* Res assoc physics, Princeton Univ, 67-68; asst prof, 68-74, ASSOC PROF PHYSICS, BOSTON COL, 74- *Mem:* Am Phys Soc; Philos Sci Asn; Hist Sci Soc. *Res:* Theory of elementary particles; weak interactions; current algebra; high-energy hadron collisions; history and philosophy of science. *Mailing Add:* Dept of Physics Boston Col Chestnut Hill MA 02167

URIU, KIYOTO, b Berryessa, Calif, May 25, 17; m 49; c 4. POMOLOGY, PLANT PHYSIOLOGY. *Educ:* Univ Calif, BS, 48, MS, 50, PhD(plant physiol), 53. *Prof Exp:* Prin lab technol, 53-55, jr pomologist, 55-56, asst pomologist, 56-63, assoc specialist, 63-64, assoc pomologist, 64-70, POMOLOGIST, UNIV CALIF, DAVIS, 70-, LECTR, 62- *Mem:* Am Soc Hort Sci; Am Soc Plant Physiol. *Res:* Mineral nutrition, especially microelements of deciduous fruit trees; water relations of deciduous fruit trees. *Mailing Add:* Dept of Pomology Univ of Calif Davis CA 95616

URKOWITZ, HARRY, b Philadelphia, Pa, Oct 1, 21; m 46; c 2. ELECTRICAL ENGINEERING. *Educ:* Drexel Inst Technol, BS, 48; Univ Pa, MS, 54, PhD, 72. *Prof Exp:* From jr engr to sr engr, Res Div, Philco Corp, 48-53, proj engr, 53-56, sect engr, 56-58, sr res specialist, 58-64; sr eng specialist, Gen Atronics Corp, 64-70; PRIN MEM ENG STAFF, MISSILE & SURFACE RADAR DIV, RCA CORP, 70- *Concurrent Pos:* Adj prof, Drexel Inst Technol, 52- *Mem:* Fel Inst Elec & Electronics Engrs. *Res:* Signal detection theory; signal processing; radar. *Mailing Add:* 9242 Darlington Rd Philadelphia PA 19115

URONE, PAUL, b Pueblo, Colo, Nov 29, 15; m 43; c 2. CHEMISTRY, AIR POLLUTION CONTROL. *Educ:* Western State Col Colo, AB, 38; Ohio State Univ, MS, 47, PhD, 54. *Prof Exp:* Teacher, High Sch, Colo, 38-42; chemist, Colo Fuel & Iron Corp, 42-45; chief chemist, Div Indust Hyg, State Dept Health, Ohio, 47-55; from asst prof to prof chem, Univ Colo, Boulder, 55-70; prof atmospheric chem, 71-81, EMER PROF, CHEM & ENVIRON ENG SCI, UNIV FLA, 81- *Concurrent Pos:* Consult, Martin Co, 60-61; Univ Colo fac fel, Univ Calif, Los Angeles, 61-62; sci adv, Food & Drug Admin, 66-; Dept Health, Educ & Welfare air pollution fel, Univ Fla, 67; mem, Air Pollution Nat Manpower Adv Comt; sulfur oxides subcomt, Intersoc Comt of Methods of Sampling & Anal; Inter Govt Personnel Act Fel, Denver Fed Ctr, 77-78 & Air Pollution Control, Repub Korea, 81. *Mem:* Am Chem Soc; Am Indust Hyg Asn; Am Conf Govt Indust Hygienists; Air Pollution Control

Asn. *Res:* Polarography of hydrocarbon combustion products; chemical analysis of air contaminants in industrial hygiene and air pollution; theoretical and applied gas chromatography; thermal and photochemical reactions of sulfur dioxide in air; air pollution control. *Mailing Add:* Dept of Environ Eng Univ of Fla Gainesville FL 32611

URONE, PAUL PETER, b Pueblo, Colo, Feb 11, 44; m 65. NUCLEAR PHYSICS, MEDICAL PHYSICS. *Educ:* Univ Colo, BA, 65, PhD(physics), 70. *Prof Exp:* Teaching asst, Dept Physics, Univ Wash, 65-66; res asst nuclear physics, Univ Colo, 66-70; staff physicist, Kernfysisch Versneller Inst, Univ Groningen, Neth, 70-71; nuclear info res assoc, State Univ NY Stony Brook, 71-73; asst prof, 73-77, ASSOC PROF PHYSICS, CALIF STATE UNIV, SACRAMENTO, 77- *Concurrent Pos:* Consult, Calif State Univ & Cols, 74-78 & Crocker Nuclear Lab, Univ Calif, Davis, 74-78. *Mem:* Am Phys Soc; Sigma Xi. *Res:* Optical model of nucleus, nuclear data compilations, basic and applied neutron physics research. *Mailing Add:* Dept of Physics Calif State Univ Sacramento CA 95819

URQUHART, ANDREW WILLARD, b Burlington, Vt, Aug 24, 39; m 64; c 2. MATERIALS SCIENCE, METALLURGY. *Educ:* Dartmouth Col, BA, 61, MS, 64, PhD(metall), 71. *Prof Exp:* Engr, Div Naval Reactors, USAEC, 62-67, CREARE, Inc, 67-68; metallurgist corrosion, 71-75, BR MGR INORG MAT, GEN ELEC CORP RES & DEVELOP, 75- *Mem:* Am Soc Metals; Electrochem Soc. *Res:* Corrosion of materials for power generation systems, especially the corrosion of nuclear reactor materials; high pressure materials, high temperature chemistry, and materials removal. *Mailing Add:* Bldg K-1 Rm 4A45 PO Box 8 Schenectady NY 12301

URQUHART, JOHN, III, b Pittsburgh, Pa, Apr 24, 34; m 57; c 3. PHYSIOLOGY, ENDOCRINOLOGY. *Educ:* Rice Univ, BA, 55; Harvard Univ, MD, 59. *Prof Exp:* Intern surg, Mass Gen Hosp, 59-60, asst resident, 60-61; investr exp cardiovasc dis, NIH, 61-63; from asst prof to prof physiol, Sch Med, Univ Pittsburgh, 63-70; prof biomed eng, Univ Southern Calif, 70-71; prin scientist & dir biol res, 71-74, pres, Alza Res, 74-78, CHIEF SCIENTIST & SR V PRES, ALZA CORP, 78- *Concurrent Pos:* Josiah Macy, Jr fel obstet, Harvard Med Sch, 59-61; USPHS res career develop award, Nat Heart Inst, 63-70; NIH grants, 63-71 & 66-71; consult, Physiol Training Comt, NIH, 70-73. *Honors & Awards:* Borden Prize, Harvard Univ, 59; Upjohn Award, Endocrine Soc, 62; Bowditch lectr, Am Physiol Soc, 69. *Mem:* Am Physiol Soc; Endocrine Soc; Biomed Eng Soc (pres, 76-77). *Res:* Dynamics of drug and hormone action; pharmacology. *Mailing Add:* Alza Corp 950 Page Mill Rd Palo Alto CA 94304

URQUHART, N SCOTT, b Columbia, SC, Mar 15, 40; m 59; c 7. STATISTICS. *Educ:* Colo State Univ, BS, 61, MS, 63, PhD(statist), 65. *Prof Exp:* From asst prof to assoc prof biol statist, Cornell Univ, 65-70; assoc prof, 70-75, PROF EXP STATIST, N MEX STATE UNIV, 75- *Mem:* Am Statist Asn; Inst Math Statist; Biomet Soc. *Res:* Development and dissemination of statistical methods used in biological research; teaching and development of teaching techniques for statistical methods. *Mailing Add:* Dept of Exp Statist NMex State Univ Las Cruces NM 88003

URQUILLA, PEDRO RAMON, b San Miguel, El Salvador, July 28, 39; m 64; c 2. CLINICAL PHARMACOLOGY. *Educ:* Cath Inst of the East, BA, 57; Univ El Salvador, MD, 65. *Prof Exp:* Instr pharmacol, Univ El Salvador, 64-65, Pan Am Health Orgn fel, 66-68, NIH fel, 68-69, assoc prof, 69-72, asst dean, Sch Med, 71-72; assoc prof pharmacol, Univ Madrid, 72-73; asst prof pharmacol, WVa Univ, 73-75, assoc prof, 75-79; assoc dir med res, Miles Lab, 79-81; ASSOC DIR CLIN RES, PFIZER INC, 81- *Mem:* Am Soc Pharmacol & Exp Therapeut; Am Soc Clin Pharmacol Therapuet; AMA. *Res:* Analysis of the pharmacological receptors of cerebral arteries; pharmacological studies on cerebral vasospasm. *Mailing Add:* Dept Clin Res Pfizer Cent Res Groton CT 06340

URRY, DAN WESLEY, b Salt Lake City, Utah, Sept 14, 35; m; c 3. MOLECULAR BIOPHYSICS, BIOCHEMISTRY. *Educ:* Univ Utah, BA, 60, PhD(phys chem), 64. *Prof Exp:* Fel, Univ Utah, 64; Harvard Corp Fel, 64-65; vis investr, Chem Biodynamics Lab, Univ Calif, 65-66; prof lectr, Dept Biochem, Univ Chicago, 67-70; dir div molecular biophys, Lab Molecular Biol, 70-72, PROF BIOCHEM, UNIV ALA, BIRMINGHAM, 70-, DIR LAB MOLECULAR BIOPHYS, 72- *Concurrent Pos:* Assoc mem, Inst Biomed Res, AMA, 65-69, mem, 69-70; vis prof, Univ di Padova, Centro di Studi sui Biopolimeri, 77; vchmn, Southern Region Res Review & Cert Subcomt, Am Heart Asn, 79-80, chmn, 81-82; Alexander von Humboldt Found award, Ger, 79-80; mem biophysics & biophys chem B study sect, Div Res Grants, NIH, 80-84. *Mem:* AAAS; Am Soc Biol Chem; Am Chem Soc; Biophys Soc; Am Inst Biol Chem. *Res:* Methods of absorption, optical rotation and nuclear magnetic resonance spectroscopies to study polypeptide conformation and its relation to biological function; emphasis on membrane structure, mechanism of ion transport, membrane active polypeptides, elastin, and atherosclerosis. *Mailing Add:* Lab of Molecular Biophys Univ of Ala Birmingham AL 35294

URRY, GRANT WAYNE, b Salt Lake City, Utah, Mar 12, 26; m 46; c 4. INORGANIC CHEMISTRY. *Educ:* Univ Chicago, SB, 47, PhD(chem), 53. *Prof Exp:* Asst bot, Univ Chicago, 46-47, res assoc, 47-48, asst chem, 49-52, res assoc, 53-55; asst prof, Wash Univ, 55-58; from assoc prof to prof, Purdue Univ, 58-68; prof, 68-70, chmn dept, 68-73, ROBINSON PROF CHEM, TUFTS UNIV, 70- *Concurrent Pos:* Sloan fel, 56-58; consult, E I du Pont de Nemours & Co, Inc. *Mem:* AAAS; Am Chem Soc; Fedn Am Sci. *Res:* Chemistry of convalently bonded inorganic compounds and electron spin resonance. *Mailing Add:* Dept Chem Tufts Univ Medford MA 02155

URRY, RONALD LEE, b Ogden, Utah, June 5, 45; m 71; c 1. REPRODUCTIVE PHYSIOLOGY, UROLOGY. *Educ:* Weber State Col, BS, 70; Utah State Univ, MS, 72, PhD(physiol), 73. *Prof Exp:* Teaching & res asst physiol, Dept Biol, Utah State Univ, 70-72, NDEA fel, 72-73; dir urol res lab & asst prof urol surg, Sch Med & Dent, Univ Rochester, 73-76; ASSOC PROF ZOOL, BRIGHAM YOUNG UNIV & RES ASSOC PROF SURG, DIV UROL, UNIV UTAH MED CTR, 76- *Mem:* Soc Study Reprod; AAAS; Am Fertil Soc; Endocrine Soc; Am Andrology Soc. *Res:* Relationship of stress and biogenic amines to male reproduction; testicular tissue culture, testicular perfusion, male infertility studies, vasectomy and vasovasostomy, and testicular physiology and endocrinology. *Mailing Add:* Dept of Zool Brigham Young Univ Provo UT 84602

URRY, WILBERT HERBERT, b Salt Lake City, Utah, Nov 5, 14; m 36; c 4. CHEMISTRY. *Educ:* Univ Chicago, BS, 38, PhD(chem), 46. *Prof Exp:* Lectr sci, Mus Sci & Indust, Chicago, 37-40, cur & consult chem, 40-44; instr, 44-48, from asst prof to assoc prof, 48-58, prof, 58-80, EMER PROF CHEM, UNIV CHICAGO, 80- *Concurrent Pos:* Daines Mem lectr, Univ Kans, 54; Carbide & Carbon Prof fel, 56; vis prof, Univ Calif, 58-59; consult, Monsanto Co, Commercial Solvents Corp, Wyandotte Chem Corp & US Naval Weapons Ctr, Calif, 51- *Mem:* AAAS; Am Chem Soc. *Res:* Reaction of free radicals in solution; rearrangements of free radicals and anions; organic photochemistry; homogeneous catalysis via complex ions; chemistry of hydrazines; structure and synthesis of natural products. *Mailing Add:* Dept of Chem Univ of Chicago Chicago IL 60637

URSELL, JOHN HENRY, b Leeds, Eng, June 9, 38. MATHEMATICS. *Educ:* Oxford Univ, BA, 59, MA & DPhil(math), 63. *Prof Exp:* Asst prof math, Pa State Univ, 62-63; assoc prof, State Univ NY Col Fredonia, 63-64; ASST PROF MATH, QUEEN'S UNIV, ONT, 64- *Mem:* Am Math Soc; Can Math Cong; Math Asn Am; fel Royal Asiatic Soc Gt Brit & Ireland. *Res:* Topological semigroups; algebra; graph theory; comparative religions; mathematical sociology; statistics. *Mailing Add:* 34 Main Kingston ON K7K 3Y4 Can

URSENBACH, WAYNE OCTAVE, b Lethbridge, Alta, Dec 4, 23; m 44; c 7. CHEMISTRY. *Educ:* Brigham Young Univ, BSc, 47, MSc, 48. *Prof Exp:* Asst chemist, Dept Agr Res, Am Smelting & Refining Co, 42-43 & 46-51; lab supvr health physics, Dow Chem Co, Colo, 51-52; asst, Explosives Res Group, Univ Utah, 52-55, res assoc, 55-59, asst res prof, Inst Metals & Explosives, 59-61; mgr prod & res develop, Inter-Mountain Res & Eng Co, 61-65, asst res dir, 65-66; prod mgr, Ireco Chem, 66-69, mgr planning, 69-70, dir res, 70-71; asst gen mgr, Res Inst, 74-75, RES ASSOC, UTAH ENG EXP STA, UNIV UTAH, 71-, V PRES & DIR, APPL TECHNOL DIV, RES INST, 75- *Concurrent Pos:* Consult, 71- *Mem:* Am Chem Soc; AAAS; Am Petrol Credit Asn. *Res:* Air pollution; agricultural chemistry; health physics; theory of detonation; explosion and long range blast effects; terminal ballistics; seismology. *Mailing Add:* 4635 S 1175 East Salt Lake City UT 84117

URSIC, STANLEY JOHN, b Milwaukee, Wis, Apr 2, 24; m 50; c 3. WATERSHED MANAGEMENT, FOREST HYDROLOGY. *Educ:* Univ Minn, BS, 49; Yale Univ, MF, 50. *Prof Exp:* Res forester, Univ Ill, 50-51; PROJ LEADER, SOUTHERN FOREST EXP STA, USDA FOREST SERV, 51- *Concurrent Pos:* Mem, Int Union Forestry Res Orgn; assoc ed, Southern J Appl Forestry. *Mem:* Soc Am Foresters. *Res:* Effects of forestry practices, including rehabilitation of eroding lands, on water quality, yields and distribution; flow processes on forested lands. *Mailing Add:* USDA Forest Serv PO Box 947 Oxford MS 38655

URSILLO, RICHARD CARMEN, b Lawrence, Mass, Oct 26, 26; m 66. PHARMACOLOGY. *Educ:* Tufts Univ, BS, 49, PhD(pharmacol), 54; Univ Calif, MS, 52. *Prof Exp:* From instr to asst prof pharmacol, Univ Calif, Los Angeles, 54-62; sect head pharmacol, Lakeside Labs, 62-66, dir pharmacol dept, 66-75; HEAD DEPT PHARMACOL, MERRELL RES CTR, 75- *Concurrent Pos:* USPHS spec fel, Inst Sanita, Italy, 60-61. *Mem:* Am Soc Pharmacol & Exp Therapeut. *Res:* Pharmacology of autonomic and central nervous systems. *Mailing Add:* Dept of Pharmacol 2110 E Galbraith Rd Cincinnati OH 45215

URSINO, DONALD JOSEPH, b Toronto, Ont, Nov 11, 35; m 60; c 3. PLANT PHYSIOLOGY, RADIATION BOTANY. *Educ:* Pomona Col, BA, 56; Queen's Univ, Ont, MSc, 64, PhD(biol), 67. *Prof Exp:* Teacher sci, High Sch, 57-63; Nat Res Coun Can fel, Milan, 67-69; asst prof biol, 69-72, chmn dept biol sci, 74-77, ASSOC PROF BIOL, BROCK UNIV, 72- *Mem:* Am Soc Plant Physiol; Can Soc Plant Physiol. *Res:* Effects of ionizing radiation on plant metabolism; translocation of photosynthate; nitrogen metabolism. *Mailing Add:* Dept of Biol Sci Brock Univ St Catherines ON L2M 3B1 Can

URSINO, JOSEPH ANTHONY, b Brooklyn, NY, Feb 28, 39. ORGANIC CHEMISTRY. *Educ:* St John's Univ, NY, BS, 60, MS, 62, PhD(chem), 67. *Prof Exp:* From asst prof to assoc prof, 66-71, PROF CHEM, STATE UNIV NY AGR & TECH COL FARMINGDALE, 71- *Mem:* Am Chem Soc; NY Acad Sci; Am Soc Eng Educ. *Res:* Synthesis and properties of heterocyclic organotin compounds. *Mailing Add:* 2299 Narwood Ct Merrick NY 11566

URSO, PAUL, b Sicily, Italy, Aug 3, 25; US citizen; m 52; c 2. IMMUNOLOGY, ZOOLOGY. *Educ:* St Francis Col, NY, BS, 50; Marquette Univ, MS, 52; Univ Tenn, PhD(zool), 61. *Prof Exp:* Asst zool, Marquette Univ, 50-52; instr biol, Cardinal Stritch Col, 52-53; biologist, Nat Cancer Inst, 53-55; jr biologist, Oak Ridge Nat Lab, 55-57, assoc biologist, 58-59; from asst prof to assoc prof biol, Seton Hall Univ, 61-71; sr scientist, Med Div, Oak Ridge Assoc Univs, 71-81; ASST PROF, DEPT MICROBIOL & IMMUNOL, MOREHOUSE SCH MED, 81- *Concurrent Pos:* Consult, Biol Div, Oak Ridge Nat Lab, 61-63; res partic, Oak Ridge Inst Nuclear Studies, 63- *Mem:* Transplantation Soc; Radiation Res Soc; Am Asn Immunologists; Reticuloendothelial Soc; Soc Exp Hemat. *Res:* Antibody formation; immune cell interactions; immunologic recovery of chimeras; transplantation in chimeras; immunocarcinogenesis. *Mailing Add:* Dept Microbiol & Immunol Morehouse Sch Med Atlanta GA 30314

URSPRUNG, JOSEPH JOHN, b Godre, Hungary, Mar 19, 24; Can citizen; m 55; c 2. ORGANIC CHEMISTRY, MEDICINAL CHEMISTRY. *Educ:* Queen's Univ, Ont, BA, 51, MA, 52; Univ Ill, Urbana, PhD(org chem), 55. *Prof Exp:* Res chemist, Chas Pfizer & Co, 55-59; res assoc med chem, 59-63, HEAD DEPT CARDIOVASC DIS RES, UPJOHN CO, 63- *Mem:* Am Chem Soc. *Res:* Organic synthesis; heterocyclic chemistry; cardiovascular diseases. *Mailing Add:* Dept of Cardiovasc Dis Res Upjohn Co Kalamazoo MI 49001

URTASUN, RAUL C, Can citizen. ONCOLOGY, EXPERIMENTAL RADIOBIOLOGY. *Educ:* Univ Buenos Aires, MD, 60; FRCP(C), 67; Am Bd Radiol, dipl radiother, 67. *Prof Exp:* Res fel oncol, Harvard Med Sch, 63-64; instr radiation oncol, Johns Hopkins Univ, 66-68; asst prof, McGill Univ, 68-70; PROF RADIATION ONCOL, UNIV ALTA, 70- *Mem:* Am Soc Therapeut Radiologists; Am Soc Clin Oncologists; Am Soc Cancer Res; Am Soc Nuclear Res; Royal Col Physicians & Surgeons Can. *Res:* Clinical radiobiology; radiosensitizers; combined modalities in the treatment of cancer; high linear energy transfer particle radiation. *Mailing Add:* 26 Wellington Crescent Edmonton AB T5N 3V2 Can

URTIEW, PAUL ANDREW, b Nish, Yugoslavia, Feb 23, 31; US citizen; m 61; c 2. THERMODYNAMICS, AERONAUTICAL ENGINEERING. *Educ:* Univ Calif, Berkeley, BS, 55, MS, 59, PhD(mech eng), 64. *Prof Exp:* Res engr, Detonation Lab, 59-64, asst res engr, Propulsion Dynamics Lab, 64-67, engr, Physics Dept, 67-73, ENGR, CHEM & MAT SCI DEPT, LAWRENCE LIVERMORE LAB, UNIV CALIF, 73- *Concurrent Pos:* Consult, Hiller Aircraft Corp, Calif, 63-64 & MB Assocs, 66. *Mem:* Combustion Inst; Am Inst Aeronaut & Astronaut. *Res:* High pressure physics of shocked solid materials; nonsteady wave dynamics; wave interaction processes in reactive and nonreactive media; graphical and experimental techniques applicable in research. *Mailing Add:* Chem Dept L324 PO Box 808 Livermore CA 94550

URY, HANS KONRAD, b Berlin, Ger, Nov 4, 24; US citizen; m 55. BIOSTATISTICS, MATHEMATICAL STATISTICS. *Educ:* Univ Calif, Berkeley, AB, 45 & 55, MA, 64, PhD(statist), 71. *Prof Exp:* Res asst statist, Inst Eng Res, Univ Calif, Richmond, 61-62; res assoc, Stanford Univ, 62-63; biostatistician, Calif State Dept Pub Health, 63-66; statist consult, Comput Ctr, San Francisco Med Ctr, Univ Calif, 67; spec consult, Calif State Dept Pub Health, 67-68; res specialist biostatist, 68-71; biostatistician & consult statist, 71-75, SR STATISTICIAN, MED METHODS RES DEPT, PERMANENTE MED GROUP, OAKLAND, 75- *Concurrent Pos:* Instr, Exten Div, Univ Calif, Berkeley, 67-80; statist consult, Environ Resources, Inc, Calif, 68-70; chmn, San Francisco Bay Area Biostatist Colloquium, 74-75; statist consult, Grad Training Prog Orthop Phys Therapy, Kaiser-Permanente, Hayward, 79- *Mem:* Am Statist Asn; Biomet Soc; Inst Math Statist; fel Royal Statist Soc. *Res:* Nonparametric statistics; statistical techniques for evaluating adverse drug reactions; chronic disease epidemiology; application of computers to biostatistics; multiple comparison methods; statistical efficiency comparisons; sample size determination for comparing rates or proportions. *Mailing Add:* 2050 Drake Dr Oakland CA 94611

USBORNE, WILLIAM RONALD, b Rochester, NY, Nov 22, 37; m 62; c 2. MEAT & FOOD SCIENCE. *Educ:* Cornell Univ, BS, 59; Univ Ill, Urbana, MS, 61; Univ Ky, PhD(meat & animal sci), 67. *Prof Exp:* Res asst meat sci, Univ Ill, 59-61; res assoc, Cornell Univ, 61-62; res asst, Univ Ky, 63-64, instr, 64-65, res asst, 65-66; fel meat chem, Tex A&M Univ, 66-67; asst prof meat sci, Univ Minn, St Paul, 68-69; assoc prof meat sci, 69-79, PROF & CHMN FOOD SCI, UNIV GUELPH, 79- *Concurrent Pos:* Welch Found fel, 67-68; fel, Tex A&M Univ, 68. *Mem:* Am Soc Animal Sci; Am Meat Sci Asn; Am Inst Food Technologists; Can Inst Food Sci & Technol; Agr Inst Can. *Res:* Meat chemistry and technology; meat animal evaluation techniques; meat processing and quality. *Mailing Add:* Dept Food Sci Univ Guelph Guelph ON N1G 2N9 Can

USCAVAGE, JOSEPH PETER, b Middleport, Pa, Nov 12, 25. BACTERIOLOGY, MYCOLOGY. *Educ:* Pa State Univ, BS, 49; Univ Ill, MS, 50, PhD, 53. *Prof Exp:* Asst bact, Univ Ill, 50-53; technician parasitol & bact, Hektoen Inst Med Res, Cook County Hosp, Chicago, 51; instr bact, NY Med Col, 54-58; assoc microbiol, Sch Vet Med, Univ Pa, 58-61; MEM STAFF, RES DIV, WILLIAM H RORER, INC, 61- *Mem:* AAAS; Am Soc Microbiol; Am Chem Soc; NY Acad Sci. *Res:* Medical bacteriology and mycology; bacterial physiology. *Mailing Add:* William H Rorer Inc 500 Virginia Dr Ft Washington PA 19034

USCHOLD, RICHARD L, b Buffalo, NY, Sept 10, 28; m 51; c 9. MATHEMATICS. *Educ:* Canisius Col, BS, 53; Univ Notre Dame, MS, 55; State Univ NY Buffalo, PhD(math), 63. *Prof Exp:* Instr math, Nazareth Col, NY, 55-56; from instr to asst prof, 56-64, chmn dept, 66-72, ASSOC PROF MATH, CANISIUS COL, 64- *Mem:* Am Math Soc; Math Asn Am; Hist Sci Soc. *Mailing Add:* Dept of Math Canisius Col Buffalo NY 14208

USDIN, EARL, b Brooklyn, NY, Mar 6, 24; m 49; c 4. PSYCHOPHARMACOLOGY, PHARMACOLOGY. *Educ:* Johns Hopkins Univ, AB, 43; Ohio State Univ, PhD(org chem), 51. *Prof Exp:* Res assoc, Inst Cancer Res, Philadelphia, 51-59; from assoc res prof to res prof, NMex Highlands Univ, 59-62; head biochem res dept, Inst Psychosom & Psychiat Res, Michael Reese Hosp, 62; head biochem & immunochem br, Melpar, Inc, 62-66; sr res biochemist, Life Systs Div, Hazelton Lab, 66; sr scientist, Atlantic Res Corp, Va, 66-68; exec secy, Preclin Psychopharmacol Res Rev Comt, 68-74, CHIEF PHARMACOL SECT, PSYCHOPHARMACOL BR, NIMH, 72- *Concurrent Pos:* Res fel, Univ Pa, 51; Am Cancer Soc fel, Univ Uppsala & Royal Inst Technol, Sweden, 55-56; dir joint ment health res proj, NMex State Hosp-NMex Highlands Univ, 59-62; lectr, Nobel Found & Univ Göttingen, 61; ed, Commun Psychopharmacol. *Mem:* AAAS; Am Asn Cancer Res; Am Chem Soc; Am Soc Biol Chemists; Biophys Soc. *Res:* Drug metabolism; drug assay methodology; natural products; enzymology and purification techniques; mechanism of drug action; cholinesterases and cholinesterase inhibitors; folic acid-active substances. *Mailing Add:* Psychopharmacol Res Br Nat Inst of Ment Health Rockville MD 20857

USDIN, VERA RUDIN, b Vienna, Austria, May 31, 25; nat US; m 49; c 4. BIOCHEMISTRY. *Educ:* Sterling Col, BS, 45; Duke Univ, MA, 47; Ohio State Univ, PhD(biochem), 51. *Prof Exp:* Res assoc physiol chem, Grad Sch Med, Univ Pa, 51-56; chemist, Res Labs, Rohm and Haas Co, 56-59; assoc res prof physiol chem, NMex Highlands Univ, 59-62; head physiol chem br, Melpar, Inc, Va, 62-67; proj supvr, 67-69, res supvr, 69-73, GROUP LEADER, GILLETTE RES INST, INC, 73- *Mem:* Am Chem Soc; Am Soc Cell Biol; Int Asn Dent Res. *Res:* Biochemistry of skin; enzyme inhibition; salivary proteins; dental plaque. *Mailing Add:* Gillette Res Inst Inc 1413 Research Blvd Rockville MD 20850

USENIK, EDWARD A, b Eveleth, Minn, Jan 16, 27; m 55; c 2. VETERINARY MEDICINE. *Educ:* Univ Minn, BS, 50, DVM, 52, PhD(vet med, path), 57. *Prof Exp:* Instr vet surg & radiol, Col Vet Med, Univ Minn, 52-57, asst prof, 57-59; med assoc exp path, Med Dept, Brookhaven Nat Lab, 59-60; assoc prof vet surg & radiol, 60-64, PROF VET SURG & RADIOL, COL VET MED, UNIV MINN, ST PAUL, 64- *Concurrent Pos:* Collabr med dept, Brookhaven Nat Lab, 60-; Rockefeller consult, Col Vet Med, Lima, 65-66; mem adv coun, Inst Lab Animal Resources, Nat Res Coun-Nat Acad Sci; on leave to fac vet sci, Nat Univ, Neirobi, Kenya, 72-74. *Res:* Gastrointestinal diseases; anesthesia in veterinary medicine. *Mailing Add:* Col of Vet Med Univ of Minn St Paul MN 55101

USHER, DAVID ANTHONY, b Harrow, Eng, Nov 1, 36; m 74. BIO-ORGANIC CHEMISTRY. *Educ:* Victoria Univ, NZ, BSc, 58, MSc, 60; Univ Cambridge, PhD(chem), 63. *Prof Exp:* Res fel chem, Harvard Univ, 63-65; asst prof, 65-70, ASSOC PROF CHEM, CORNELL UNIV, 70- *Concurrent Pos:* NIH career develop award, 68-73; vis prof, Oxford Univ, 71-72. *Honors & Awards:* NZ Inst Chem Prize, 58. *Mem:* Am Chem Soc; AAAS. *Res:* Chemical evolution; chemical reactions of nucleic acids; enzyme action. *Mailing Add:* Dept of Chem Cornell Univ Ithaca NY 14853

USHER, PETER DENIS, b Bloemfontein, SAfrica, Oct 27, 35; US citizen; m 61; c 1. ASTRONOMY. *Educ:* Univ of the Orange Free State, BS, 56, MS, 59; Harvard Univ, PhD(astron), 66. *Prof Exp:* Fel, Harvard Col Observ, 66-67; sr scientist, Am Sci & Eng, Inc, Mass, 67-68; asst prof, 68-73, ASSOC PROF ASTRON, PA STATE UNIV, UNIVERSITY PARK, 73- *Concurrent Pos:* Sabbatical leave, Hale Observ, 75-76. *Mem:* Int Astron Union; Am Astron Soc; Royal Astron Soc. *Res:* Perturbation theory; variable galaxies; stellar structure. *Mailing Add:* Dept of Astron 507 Davey Lab Pa State Univ University Park PA 16802

USHER, THERON, JR, electrical engineering, see previous edition

USHER, W(ILLIA)M MACK, b Devol, Okla, Nov 10, 27; m 52. MATHEMATICAL STATISTICS, EDUCATIONAL ADMINISTRATION. *Educ:* Okla State Univ, BS, 52, MS, 58. *Prof Exp:* Asst registr, Okla State Univ, 54-58; statistician, Tex Instruments, Inc, 58-59, opers res analyst, 59-61, mgr, 61-63, corp systs develop mgr, 63-67; dir instnl res, 67-69, DIR COMPUT & INFO SYST, OKLA STATE UNIV, 69- *Mem:* Am Statist Asn; Asn Comput Mach; Asn Instnl Res; Col & Univ Mach Rec; Col & Univ Systs Exchange. *Res:* Development of management information systems. *Mailing Add:* Dept Comput & Info Syst Okla State Univ Stillwater OK 74074

USHERWOOD, NOBLE RANSOM, b Atlanta, Ill, Jan 13, 38; m 63; c 1. SOIL FERTILITY, PLANT NUTRITION. *Educ:* Southern Ill Univ, BS, 59, MS, 60; Univ Md, PhD(soils, plant physiol), 66. *Prof Exp:* Res asst soil fertil & test correlation, Univ Md, 60-66; asst prof soil fertil & plant nutrit, Univ Del, 66-67; midwest agronomist, Ill, 67-69, dir, Potash Res Asn Northern Latin Am, Guatemala, 69-71, dir Fla & Latin Am, Potash Inst, 71-77, V PRES, POTASH & PHOSPHATE INST, 77- *Concurrent Pos:* Assoc ed, J Agron Educ. *Honors & Awards:* Award of Merit, Ministry Agr, Guatemala. *Mem:* Am Soc Agron; Soil Sci Soc Am; Brazilian Soc Sci. *Res:* Nitrogen, phosphorus, potassium, magnesium and manganese soil fertility and plant nutrition; sub-surface irrigation feasability studies. *Mailing Add:* Potash & Phosphate Inst 2801 Buford Hwy Northeast Atlanta GA 30329

USHIJIMA, RICHARD N, microbiology, virology, see previous edition

USHIODA, SUKEKATSU, b Tokyo, Japan, Sept 18, 41; m 68. PHYSICS. *Educ:* Dartmouth Col, AB, 64; Univ Pa, MS, 65, PhD(physics), 69. *Prof Exp:* Asst prof, 69-74, assoc prof, 74-78, PROF PHYSICS, UNIV CALIF, IRVINE, 78- *Mem:* Optical Soc Am; Am Phys Soc; Phys Soc Japan. *Res:* Solid state physics; optical properties of solids. *Mailing Add:* Dept of Physics Univ of Calif Irvine CA 92717

USLENGHI, PIERGIORGIO L, b Turin, Italy, Aug 31, 37; m 78; c 3. THEORETICAL PHYSICS, ELECTRICAL ENGINEERING. *Educ:* Turin Polytech Inst, Laurea, 60; Univ Mich, MS, 64, PhD(physics), 67. *Prof Exp:* Asst prof elec eng, Turin Polytech Inst, 61; assoc res engr, Conductron Corp, 62-63; res physicist, Univ Mich, Ann Arbor, 63-70; assoc prof info eng, 70-74, PROF INFO ENG, UNIV ILL, CHICAGO CIRCLE, 74- *Concurrent Pos:* NASA, NSF & Dept Defense grants. *Mem:* Inst Elec & Electronics Engrs; Int Union Radio Sci; Sigma Xi. *Res:* Antennas; radars; quantum electronics; nonlinear phenomena. *Mailing Add:* Dept Info Eng Box 4348 Chicago IL 60680

USMANI, RIAZ AHMAD, b Farrukhabad, India, Nov 1, 34; m 54; c 3. NUMERICAL ANALYSIS. *Educ:* Aligarh Muslim Univ, India, BSc, 56, MSc, 57; Univ BC, PhD(numerical anal), 67. *Prof Exp:* Lectr math, Col Eng & Technol, Aligarh Muslim Univ, Indian, 57-61; teaching asst, Univ BC, 61-65; sessional lectr, Univ Calgary, 65-66; asst prof, 66-75, assoc prof comput sci, 75-76, assoc prof, 76-79, PROF APPL MATH, UNIV MAN, 79- *Res:* Numerical integration of differential equations; initial and boundary value problems in ordinary differential equations. *Mailing Add:* Dept Appl Math Univ Man Winnipeg MB R3T 2N2 Can

USSELMAN, MELVYN CHARLES, b Ottawa, Ont, Jan 5, 46; m 79; c 1. ORGANIC CHEMISTRY, HISTORY OF CHEMISTRY. *Educ:* Univ Western Ont, BSc, 68, PhD(chem), 72, MA, 75. *Prof Exp:* asst prof chem, 75-81, asst prof, Dept Hist Med & Sci, 76-81, ASSOC PROF CHEM & DEPT HIST MED & SCI, UNIV WESTERN ONT, 81- *Mem:* Hist Sci Soc; Am Chem Soc; Soc Hist Technol; Brit Soc Hist Alchemy & Chem; Can Soc Hist & Philos Sci. *Res:* History of chemistry, 18th-20th centuries; the work of W H Wollaston; platinum metallurgy. *Mailing Add:* Dept Chem Univ Western Ont London ON N6A 5B7 Can

USSELMAN, THOMAS MICHAEL, b Bismarck, ND, Aug 9, 47; m 73. GEOPHYSICS, GEOCHEMISTRY. *Educ:* Franklin & Marshall Col, BA, 69; Lehigh Univ, MS, 71, PhD(geol), 73. *Prof Exp:* Nat Res Coun res assoc geochem, Johnson Space Ctr, NASA, 73-75, fel, Lunar Sci Inst, 75-76; vis prof geol, State Univ NY Buffalo, 76-78; STAFF OFFICER, NAT ACAD SCI, 78- *Concurrent Pos:* Co-editor, 7th Lunar Sci Conf Proc, 76. *Mem:* Am Geophys Union; Geol Soc Am; Meteoritical Soc. *Res:* Experimental geochemistry and geophysics including study of planetary interiors, crystallization of igneous melts, and effect of volatiles. *Mailing Add:* Geophysics Res Bd Nat Acad Sci 2101 Constitution Ave NW Washington DC 20418

UTECH, FREDERICK HERBERT, b Merrill, Wis, Apr 19, 43. SYSTEMATIC BOTANY, *Educ:* Univ Wis-Madison, BS, 66, MS, 68; Wash Univ, PhD(biol), 73. *Prof Exp:* Lectr bot, Univ Wis, Marshfield, 70; vis scientist, US-Jap Coop Sci Prog, 74-75; fel bot, Jap Soc Prom Sci, 75-76; ASSOC CUR BOT, CARNEGIE MUS NATURAL HIST, 76- *Concurrent Pos:* NSF fel, Washington Univ, 71-72 & 72-73; fel, Univ Wis-Madison & res assoc, Washington Univ, 74-76; adj res scientist, Hunt Inst Bot Doc, 77-; M Graham Netting Res Fund grant, Carnegie Mus, 77-78, 78- *Mem:* Bot Soc Am; Int Asn Plant Taxon; AAAS. *Res:* Biosystematic investigations of the living elements of the Arcto-Tertiary geoflora in the Northern hemisphere; floral vascular anatomy of the Liliaceae; cytotaxonomy and systematics of the Liliaceae. *Mailing Add:* Sect Bot Carnegie Mus Natural Hist 4400 Forbes Ave Pittsburgh PA 15213

UTERMOHLEN, VIRGINIA, b New York, NY, June 17, 43; m 72; c 1. IMMUNOLOGY. *Educ:* Wash Univ, BS, 64; Columbia Univ, MD, 68; Am Bd Pediat, dipl. *Prof Exp:* Intern, resident & chief resident pediat, St Luke's Hosp, New York, 68-71; fel immunol, Rockefeller Univ, 71-74; asst prof biochem, 74-77, ASST PROF NUTRIT SCI, CORNELL UNIV, & ASST PROF, NY STATE COL VET MED, 77- *Concurrent Pos:* NIH fel, 71-72; NY Heart Asn fel, 72-74; guest investr immunol, Rockefeller Univ, 74- *Mem:* Harvey Soc; Am Asn Immunologists; Am Med Women's Asn. *Res:* Nutrition and cell-mediated immunity. *Mailing Add:* N204B MVR Cornell Univ Ithaca NY 14853

UTGAARD, JOHN EDWARD, b Anamoose, NDak, Jan 22, 36; m 61; c 4. GEOLOGY, PALEOZOOLOGY. *Educ:* Univ NDak, BS, 58; Ind Univ, AM, 61, PhD(geol), 63. *Prof Exp:* Res assoc paleont, US Nat Mus, Smithsonian Inst, 63-65; from asst prof to assoc prof geol, 65-73, PROF GEOL, SOUTHERN ILL UNIV, CARBONDALE, 73- *Concurrent Pos:* Smithsonian fel evolutionary & syst biol, Smithsonian Inst, 72. *Mem:* Geol Soc Am; Am Asn Petrol Geologists; Paleont Soc; Brit Palaeont Asn; Soc Econ Paleont & Mineral. *Res:* Fossil bryozoans; carboniferous paleoecology and depositional environments; paleobiology of Paleozoic bryozoans; paleoecology of Late Paleozoic fossil communities. *Mailing Add:* Dept of Geol Southern Ill Univ Carbondale IL 62901

UTGARD, RUSSELL OLIVER, b Star Prairie, Wis, July 30, 33; m 56; c 3. GEOLOGY, SCIENCE EDUCATION. *Educ:* Wis State Col, River Falls, BS, 57; Univ Wis, MS, 58; Ind Univ, Bloomington, MAT, 66, EdD(sci), 69. *Prof Exp:* Instr geol, Joliet Jr Col, Ill, 58-67; asst prof, 69-72, ASSOC PROF GEOL, OHIO STATE UNIV, 72- *Concurrent Pos:* Teaching asst, Ind Univ, Bloomington, 65-66. *Mem:* Am Asn Petrol Geologists; Nat Asn Geol Teachers; Nat Sci Teachers Asn; Geol Soc Am. *Res:* Environmental geology. *Mailing Add:* Dept of Geol Ohio State Univ Columbus OH 43210

UTGOFF, VADYM V, b Sevastopol, Russia, Aug 3, 17; m 46; c 3. AEROSPACE ENGINEERING. *Educ:* US Naval Acad, BS, 39; US Naval Postgrad Sch, BS, 48; Mass Inst Technol, MS, 49. *Prof Exp:* ASSOC PROF AEROSPACE ENG, US NAVAL ACAD, 64- *Mem:* AAAS; Am Inst Aeronaut & Astronaut; Am Helicopter Soc. *Res:* Flight dynamics; rotary wing aerodynamics. *Mailing Add:* Dept of Aerospace Eng US Naval Acad Annapolis MD 21402

UTHE, JOHN FREDERICK, b Saskatoon, Sask, Feb 27, 38; m 63; c 3. FISHERIES. *Educ:* Univ Sask, BA, 59, Hons, 60, MA, 61; Univ Western Ont, PhD(biochem), 68. *Prof Exp:* Res scientist, Fresh Water Inst, Fisheries Res Bd, Can, 63-72, RES MGR, TECHNOL BR, FISHERIES & OCEANS CAN, 72- *Res:* Analytical chemistry applied to toxic residues and the biochemical effects of such residues on fish. *Mailing Add:* 32 Simcoe Pl Halifax NS B3M 1H3 Can

UTHE, P(AUL) M(ICHAEL), JR, b Watertown, SDak, May 12, 30; m 52; c 3. NUCLEAR ENGINEERING. *Educ:* SDak State Univ, BS, 52; Air Univ, MS, 57. *Prof Exp:* Nuclear planning officer, Wright Air Develop Ctr, US Air Force, 52-53, nuclear res officer, 54-55; physicist, Oak Ridge Nat Lab, 53-54; physicist, Propulsion Div, Lawrence Radiation Lab, Univ Calif, 57-58, directing physicist, 58-62; res engr, Stanford Res Inst, 62-63; prin engr, Electronics Assocs, Inc, 63-65; PRES, UTHE TECHNOL, INT, 66- *Concurrent Pos:* Systs Engr, 65-66. *Mem:* Am Nuclear Soc; sr mem Inst Elec & Electronics Engrs; sr mem Instrument Soc Am. *Res:* Neutron spectroscopy; propulsion systems analysis; heat transfer; gas dynamics; ultrasonics; mass spectroscopy. *Mailing Add:* Uthe Technol Int 325 N Mathilda Sunnyvale CA 94086

UTKE, ALLEN R, b Moline, Ill, Feb 5, 36; m 57; c 3. INORGANIC CHEMISTRY. *Educ:* Augustana Col, Ill, BS, 58; Univ Iowa, MS, 61, PhD(inorg chem), 63. *Prof Exp:* Sr res chemist, Chem Div, Pittsburgh Plate Glass Co, Tex, 62-64; assoc prof, 64-78, PROF CHEM, UNIV WIS-OSHKOSH, 78- *Mem:* Am Chem Soc. *Res:* Chemistry of the alkali and alkaline earth metals and their reactions in liquid ammonia. *Mailing Add:* Dept of Chem Univ of Wis Oshkosh WI 54902

UTKHEDE, RAJESHWAR SHAMRAO, b Kalmeshwar, India, Apr 18, 39; m; c 2. GENETICS, PLANT BREEDING. *Educ:* Nagpur Univ, BSc, 61; Indian Agr Res Inst, PhD(genetics), 68. *Prof Exp:* Res assoc genetics, Rockefeller Found, 67-70; millet breeder, Haryana Agr Univ, 71-72; corn breeder, Ministry Agr, Tanzania, 72-75; fel plant path, Simon Fraser Univ, 75-77, res assoc, 77-80; PLANT PATHOLOGIST, AGR CAN, 80- *Concurrent Pos:* Res assoc, Can Ministry Manpower & Immigration, 75-76. *Mem:* Genetics Soc Can; Indian Soc Genetics; Can Soc Phytopath; Am Phytopath Soc. *Res:* Breeding for disease resistance; control of soilborne diseases by integrated use of resistance, microbial antagonist and chemical treatment. *Mailing Add:* Res Sta Agr Can Summerland BC V0H 1Z0 Can

UTKU, SENOL, b Suruc, Turkey, Nov 23, 31; m 64; c 2. ENGINEERING. *Educ:* Istanbul Tech Univ, MS, 54; Mass Inst Technol, MS, 59, ScD(struct eng), 60. *Prof Exp:* Res engr, Math & Appln Dept, Int Bus Mach Corp, 59-60; asst prof struct, Mass Inst Technol, 60-62; assoc prof, Mid East Tech Univ, Ankara, 62-63; exec chief, Comput Ctr, Istanbul Tech Univ, 63-65; sr res engr, Jet Propulsion Lab, Calif Inst Technol, 65-68, mem tech staff, 68-70; from assoc prof to prof civil eng, 70-78, PROF CIVIL ENG & COMPUT SCI, DUKE UNIV, 78- *Concurrent Pos:* Consult, Math & Appln Dept, Int Bus Mach Corp & Lincoln Lab, Mass Inst Technol, 60-61, Mitre Corp, 61-62, Westinghouse Res & Develop Ctr, 70, Langley Res Ctr, NASA, 71 & Jet Propulsion Lab, Calif Inst Technol, 71-; lectr, Istanbul Tech Univ, 62-63, Univ Southern Calif, 66-70, Univ Wash, 68 & Univ Mo-Rolla, 70-; mem, NATO Study Group Comput Sci, Brussels, 68-70. *Mem:* Am Soc Civil Engrs; Am Soc Eng Educ. *Res:* Engineering and structural mechanics; applied mathematics. *Mailing Add:* Dept of Civil Eng Duke Univ Durham NC 27706

UTLAUT, WILLIAM FREDERICK, b Sterling, Colo, July 26, 22; m 46; c 3. TELECOMMUNICATIONS. *Educ:* Univ Colo, BSEE, 44, MSEE, 50, PhD(elec eng), 66. *Prof Exp:* Engr large motor design, Gen Elec Co, 46-48; instr elec eng, Univ Colo, 48-54; electronic engr radio propagation, Dept Commun, Nat Bur Standards, 54-64; dir ionospheric telecommun lab, Environ Sci & Services Admin, Dept Com, 64-67; DIR TELECOMMUN RES & ENG, INST TELECOMMUN SCI, NAT TELECOMMUN & INFO ADMIN, DEPT COM, 67- *Concurrent Pos:* Chmn, Spectrum Utilization & Monitoring, US Study Group I, Int Radio Consult Comt, 72- *Honors & Awards:* Gold Medal, US Dept Com, 71. *Mem:* Int Union Radio Sci; fel Inst Elec & Electronics Engrs. *Res:* Radiowave propagation and ionospheric modification by high-powered ground-based radio frequency transmitters; radio spectrum utilization studies. *Mailing Add:* Inst for Telecommun Sci Nat Telecommun & Info Admin Boulder CO 80303

UTLEY, JOHN FOSTER, III, b Detroit, Mich, June 23, 44; m 71. PLANT SYSTEMATICS, BIOLOGY. *Educ:* Univ SFla, BA, 68; Duke Univ, PhD(bot), 77. *Prof Exp:* Cur bot, Div Natural Hist, Mus Nac de Costa Rica, 73-76; fel, US Nat Herbarium, Smithsonian Inst, 76-77; ASST PROF BIOL, UNIV NEW ORLEANS, 78- *Mem:* Sigma Xi; Soc Study Evolution; Int Asn Plant Taxonomists. *Res:* Systematics; evolution and ecology of epiphytic angiosperms. *Mailing Add:* Dept of Biol Sci Univ of New Orleans New Orleans LA 70122

UTLEY, PHILIP RAY, b Ill, Dec 18, 41; m 63; c 3. ANIMAL SCIENCE. *Educ:* Southern Ill Univ, Carbondale, BS, 64; Univ Mo-Columbia, MS, 67; Univ Ky, PhD(animal sci), 69. *Prof Exp:* Asst instr animal sci, Southern Ill Univ, Carbondale, 63-65; assoc prof, 70-78, PROF ANIMAL SCI, UNIV GA, COASTAL PLAINS EXP STA, TIFTON, 78- *Mem:* Am Soc Animal Sci. *Res:* Beef cattle nutrition and management. *Mailing Add:* Univ of Ga Coastal Plain Exp Sta Tifton GA 31794

UTTER, FRED MADISON, b Seattle, Wash, Nov 25, 31; m 58; c 3. BIOCHEMICAL GENETICS. *Educ:* Univ Puget Sound, BSc, 54; Univ Wash, MSc, 64; Univ Calif, Davis, PhD(genetics), 69. *Prof Exp:* Serologist, 59-60, CHEMIST, BIOL LAB, US BUR COM FISHERIES, 60- *Concurrent Pos:* Affiliate asst prof, Univ Wash, 71, affil assoc prof, 76, affil prof, 82. *Mem:* AAAS; Genetics Soc Am; Am Genetic Asn; Am Inst Fishery Res Biol; Europ Soc Animal Blood Group Res. *Res:* Use of biochemical methods for the detection of genetic variations in fish for use in studies of fish populations; induced gynogenesis and polyploidy in salmon. *Mailing Add:* 2725 Montlake Blvd Seattle WA 98112

UTTER, MERTON FRANKLIN, biochemistry, deceased

UTTERBACK, NYLE GENE, b Oskaloosa, Iowa, Jan 19, 31; m 58; c 3. EXPERIMENTAL PHYSICS. *Educ:* Iowa State Univ, BS, 53, PhD(physics), 57. *Prof Exp:* Res asst, Ames Lab, AEC, 51-57; Fulbright scholar, Ger, 57-58; sr physicist, Ord Res Lab, Univ Va, 58-59; asst prof & res physicist, Denver Res Inst, 59-63; staff scientist, Gen Motors Corp, Calif, 63-72; staff scientist, Mission Res Corp, Santa Barbara, 72-75; consult, TRW, Redondo Beach, Calif, 76-81, CONSULT, SANSUM MED RES FOUND, SANTA BARBARA, 81- *Mem:* Am Phys Soc. *Res:* Laser technology; atomic and molecular reaction kinetics; diabetic microangiopathy. *Mailing Add:* 718 Willowglen Rd Santa Barbara CA 93105

UTZ, JOHN PHILIP, b Rochester, Minn, June 9, 22; m 47; c 5. MEDICINE. *Educ:* Northwestern Univ, BS, 43, MD, 47; Georgetown Univ, MS, 49. *Prof Exp:* Researcher, Lab for Infectious Dis, Nat Inst Allergy & Infectious Dis, 47-49, chief infectious dis serv, 52-65; prof med & chmn div immunol & infectious dis, Med Col Va, 65-73; dean fac, 73-78, PROF MED, GEORGETOWN UNIV, 73- *Concurrent Pos:* Fel, Mayo Found, 49-52;

intern, Evans Mem Hosp, Boston, 46-47; consult, Clin Ctr, NIH, US Vet Admin & Hoffmann-La Roche Pharmaceut Co; pres, Nat Found Infectious Dis, 72-75. *Mem:* Am Fedn Clin Res; Am Col Physicians; Am Col Chest Physicians; Soc Exp Biol & Med; Am Thoracic Soc. *Res:* Clinical investigations in infectious diseases. *Mailing Add:* Georgetown Univ Hosp Washington DC 20007

UTZ, WINFIELD ROY, JR, b Boonville, Mo, Nov 17, 19; m 41; c 3. MATHEMATICAL ANALYSIS. *Educ:* Cent Col, Mo, AB, 41; Univ Mo, MA, 42; Univ Va, PhD(math), 48. *Prof Exp:* Asst instr math, Univ Mo, 42; instr, Univ Notre Dame, 42-43; instr, Univ Va, 44-48; instr, Univ Mich, 48-49; from asst prof to assoc prof, 49-69, PROF MATH, UNIV MO-COLUMBIA, 69-, CHMN DEPT, 70- *Concurrent Pos:* Mem, Inst Advan Study, Princeton Univ, 55-56; vis scholar, Univ Calif, Berkeley, 62-63; vis prof, Brown Univ, 69. *Mem:* Am Math Soc; Math Asn Am; London Math Soc. *Res:* Surface dynamics; topological dynamics; differential equations. *Mailing Add:* Dept of Math Univ of Mo Columbia MO 65201

UVELLI, DAVID ALBERT, b Sonora, Calif, July 12, 47; m 73. CHEMICAL ENGINEERING. *Educ:* Stanford Univ, BS, 69; Univ Wash, MS, 71, PhD(chem eng), 76. *Prof Exp:* Res engr, 71-73, RES ASST PROF CHEM ENG, UNIV WASH, 76- *Mem:* Am Inst Chem Eng; AAAS. *Res:* Bioengineering; development of equipment to treat diseases of blood; process development for the recovery of valuable chemicals. *Mailing Add:* Benson Hall BF-10 Univ of Wash Seattle WA 98195

UWAYDAH, IBRAHIM MUSA, b Qualqiliya, Jordan, Sept 18, 43; US citizen; m 68; c 2. ANTI-INFLAMMATORY, ANTIALLERGY. *Educ:* Am Univ Beirut, BSc, 67; Univ Kans, Lawrence, PhD(med chem), 74. *Prof Exp:* Fel res assoc pharmacol, Med Col Va, 74-77; SR RES ORG CHEM & MED CHEM, A H ROBINS CO, 77- *Concurrent Pos:* Adj assoc prof pharmacol, Med Col Va, 78- *Mem:* Am Chem Soc; Chem Soc London; NY Acad Sci; Sigma Xi; Int Soc Heterocyclic Chem. *Res:* Design and synthesis of potentially active bioactive agents; inflammation area; H2-antagonists (gastrointestinal); central nervous system area (analgesics); B-blockers. *Mailing Add:* A H Robins Res Labs 1211 Sherwood Ave Box 26609 Richmond VA 23261

UY, WILLIAM CHENG, b Manila, Philippines, Feb 11, 40; US citizen; m 69; c 4. ENGINEERING, CHEMICAL ENGINEERING. *Educ:* De La Salle Col, Philippines, BSChE, 65; Northwestern Univ, MS, 67, PhD(chem eng), 70. *Prof Exp:* Res engr, 70-74, SR RES ENGR, E I DU PONT DE NEMOURS & CO, INC, 74- *Mem:* Soc Rheol; Am Chem Soc. *Res:* Polymer characterization; fiber fatigue resistance; fiber finishes; melt and wet fiber spinning; rheology; polymerization. *Mailing Add:* Pioneering Res Lab Du Pont Exp Sta Wilmington DE 19898

UYEDA, CARL KAORU, b San Bernardino, Calif, July 11, 22; m 76; c 2. ANATOMY, CYTOPATHOLOGY. *Educ:* Syracuse Univ, BA, 47, MS, 49; Univ Md, PhD(anat), 66. *Prof Exp:* Div head cancer cytol dept, Md State Dept Health, 50-58; instr cytopath, Sch Med, Univ Md, 58-64, instr anat, 62-67; asst prof path & anat, Univ Ark, Little Rock, 67-73, assoc dir sch cytotechnol & dir cytopath Lab, Med Sci, 67-77, assoc prof path, 73-77; CYTOPATHOLOGIST, PATH LAB, LOS GATOS, CALIF, 77- *Concurrent Pos:* Res assoc, Sch Med, Johns Hopkins Univ, 56-65, sr cytologist, 65-67; sr cytologist, Ark State Dept Health, 65-67; contractor, Nat Ctr Toxicol Res, Food & Drug Admin, Ark, 71-77; consult, Vet Admin Hosp, Little Rock, 72-77. *Mem:* Am Soc Cytol; Int Acad Cytol; Pan-Am Cancer Cytol Soc; Am Asn Anat; NY Acad Sci. *Res:* Cytogenetics; abnormal cytogenetic changes; clinical carcinoma and congenital anomalies; spontaneous leukemic C3H and C57 mice; cytopathology, refinement of interpretation in structural change of cancer; neoplasm of mice bladder; circadian rhythmicity in bronchogenic carcinoma and mice tissue. *Mailing Add:* 102 Los Patios Los Gatos CA 95030

UYEDA, CHARLES TSUNEO, b Penryn, Calif, Feb 20, 29; m 56; c 2. MEDICAL MICROBIOLOGY. *Educ:* San Jose State Col, BA, 51; Miami Univ, MA, 52; Stanford Univ, PhD(med microbiol), 56. *Prof Exp:* Officer-in-charge diag microbiol, 406th Med Gen Lab, US Army, Japan, 56-57; bacteriologist microbiol, 6th US Army Area Lab, Ft Baker, 57-58, lab serv, Vet Admin Hosp, Oakland, 58-63; MICROBIOLOGIST, LAB SERV, VET ADMIN MED CTR, PALO ALTO, 63- *Concurrent Pos:* Clin lab officer, US Army Med Serv Corps, 58-; res assoc, Sch Med, Stanford Univ, 63-78, clin asst prof path, 78-; instr, San Francisco State Univ, 79- *Mem:* Am Soc Microbiol; Sigma Xi. *Res:* Rapid and automated methods in the diagnosis and treatment of infectious diseases as well as in the immunology of multiple sclerosis; serology and immunology. *Mailing Add:* Vet Admin Med Ctr 3801 Miranda Ave Palo Alto CA 94304

UYEDA, KOSAKU, b Kokawa Naga-gun, Japan, Mar 15, 32; US citizen; m 57; c 2. BIOCHEMISTRY. *Educ:* Ore State Univ, BS, 55, MS, 57; Univ Calif, Berkeley, PhD(biochem), 62. *Prof Exp:* Asst prof, 67-72, assoc prof, 72-81, PROF BIOCHEM, UNIV TEX HEALTH SCI CTR, DALLAS, 82-; RES CHEMIST, VET ADMIN HOSP, 67-, CHIEF CELLULAR REGULATION, 71- *Concurrent Pos:* Fel, Univ Calif, Berkeley, 62; NIH fel, Pub Health Res Inst NY, 62-64; scholar, Univ Calif, Berkeley, 64-67. *Mem:* Am Chem Soc; Am Soc Biol Chem. *Res:* Elucidation of the mechanism of action of enzymes and allosteric enzymes and their roles in regulation of carbohydrate metabolism. *Mailing Add:* Gen Med Res Vet Admin Hosp 4500 S Lancaster Dallas TX 75216

UYEHARA, OTTA A(RTHUR), b Hanford, Calif, Sept 9, 16; m 45; c 3. MECHANICAL ENGINEERING. *Educ:* Univ Wis, BS, 42, MS, 43, PhD(chem eng), 45. *Prof Exp:* Alumni Res Found fel, 45-46, res assoc, 46-47, from asst prof to assoc prof mech eng, 47-57, PROF MECH ENG, UNIV WIS-MADISON, 57- *Concurrent Pos:* Invited lectr, India, 68, Prof of Japan, Internal Combustion Engines, 76 & Norway Technol Inst, 77. *Honors & Awards:* Arch T Colwell Merit Award, Am Soc Automotive Engrs, 66 & 79, Horning Mem Award, 67; Benjamin Smith Reynolds Award, 67; Dugold Clerk Award, Brit Inst Mech Engrs, 71. *Mem:* Fel Soc Automotive Engrs; Am Soc Mech Engrs; Am Soc Automotive Engrs; Am Soc Eng Educ. *Res:* Emission and combustion in internal combustion engines; instantaneous flame temperature indicators; influence of operating variables; fuel droplet vaporization in transient state; compression temperature measurement in internal combustion engines. *Mailing Add:* Dept Mech Eng 1513 University Ave Madison WI 53706

UYEKI, EDWIN M, b Seattle, Wash, Mar 12, 28; m 51; c 3. PHARMACOLOGY, RADIOBIOLOGY. *Educ:* Kenyon Col, AB, 49; Univ Chicago, PhD(pharmacol), 53. *Prof Exp:* Instr pharmacol, Univ Chicago, 53-54; instr, Sch Med, Western Reserve Univ, 54-60, sect assoc radiation biol, 54-60; sr scientist, Hanford Labs Gen Elec Co, 60-65; assoc prof, 65-70, PROF PHARMACOL, MED CTR, UNIV KANS, 70- *Mem:* AAAS; Am Soc Pharmacol & Exp Therapuet; Am Soc Cell Biol; Radiation Res Soc. *Res:* Immunopharmacology; immunosuppressants on antibody formation; bone marrow transplantation in radiation chimeras; radiation effects; short term tissue culture. *Mailing Add:* Dept of Pharmacol Univ of Kans Med Ctr Kansas City KS 66103

UYEMOTO, JERRY KAZUMITSU, b Fresno, Calif, May 27, 39; m 65; c 1. PLANT PATHOLOGY, PLANT VIROLOGY. *Educ:* Univ Calif, Davis, BS, 62, MS, 64, PhD(plant path), 68. *Prof Exp:* Lab technician, Univ Calif, Davis, 63-67; from asst prof to assoc prof virol, Cornell Univ, 68-77; assoc prof, 77-80, PROF, KANS STATE UNIV, 80- *Mem:* Asn Appl Biologists; British Soc Gen Microbiol; Am Phytopath Soc. *Res:* Epidemiology and control of plant virus diseases. *Mailing Add:* Dept of Plant Path Kans State Univ Manhattan KS 66506

UYEMURA, DENNIS GEORGE, biochemistry, molecular biology, see previous edition

UYENO, EDWARD TEISO, b Vancouver, BC, Apr 5, 21; m 69. PHARMACOLOGY. *Educ:* Univ Toronto, BA, 47, MA, 52, PhD(psychol), 58. *Prof Exp:* Res assoc psychol, Stanford Univ, 58-61, RES PSYCHOLOGIST & PHARMACOLOGIST, STANFORD RES INST, 61- *Concurrent Pos:* NIH grants, 63-66, 68-70, 71-73 & 75-78. *Mem:* Am Soc Pharmacol & Exp Therapeut; Am Psychol Asn; Psychonomic Soc; Behav Genetics Asn; Int Primatological Soc. *Res:* Behavioral psychopharmacology; effects of drugs on learning, retention, and reproduction of animals; interaction effects of drugs; self-administration of alcohol and narcotics by rats; analgesics and narcotic antagonists; behavioral toxicology. *Mailing Add:* Life Sci Div Stanford Res Inst Menlo Park CA 94025

UZES, CHARLES ALPHONSE, b Downey, Calif, Dec 14, 39; m 67; c 1. THEORETICAL PHYSICS. *Educ:* Calif State Univ, Long Beach, BS, 62; Univ Calif, Riverside, MA, 64, PhD(physics), 67. *Prof Exp:* Asst prof, 67-73, ASSOC PROF PHYSICS, UNIV GA, 73- *Mem:* Am Phys Soc. *Res:* The use of non-perturbative calculational methods in the nonlinear classical and quantum mechanical problems of field and many body theory, and in solid state physics. *Mailing Add:* Dept of Physics Univ of Ga Athens GA 30602

UZGIRIS, EGIDIJUS E, b Lithuania, Jan 11, 41; m 67. PHYSICS. *Educ:* Univ Ill, BS, 62; Harvard Univ, MS, 64, PhD(physics), 68. *Prof Exp:* Res assoc, Harvard Univ, 68-69; res assoc, Joint Inst Lab Astrophys, Univ Colo, 69-70; PHYSICIST, GEN ELEC RES & DEVELOP CTR, 70- *Concurrent Pos:* Vis scientist, Sch Med, Stanford Univ, 81-82. *Honors & Awards:* Indust Res-100 Award, Indust Res Mag, 81. *Mem:* Am Phys Soc; Biophys Soc; NY Acad Sci; AAAS. *Res:* Biophysics; light scattering; frequency and wavelength standards; nonlinear absorption spectroscopy. *Mailing Add:* Gen Elec Res & Develop Ctr PO Box 8 Schenectady NY 12301

UZIEL, MAYO, b Seattle, Wash, May 3, 30; m 67; c 2. BIOLOGICAL CHEMISTRY. *Educ:* Univ Wash, BSc, 52, PhD(biochem), 55. *Prof Exp:* Nat Found Infantile Paralysis fel, Rockefeller Inst, 55-57; asst prof biochem, Sch Med, Tufts Univ, 57-62; biochemist, Mass Eye & Ear Infirmary, 62-64; biochemist, Biol Div, 64-81, BIOCHEMIST, HEALTH & SAFETY RES DIV, OAK RIDGE NAT LAB, 81- *Concurrent Pos:* Mem subcomt specification & criteria nucleotides & related compounds, Nat Sci Found-Nat Res Coun, 68-75; prof, Univ Tenn, 71- *Mem:* AAAS; Am Soc Biol Chem; Am Chem Soc. *Res:* Structure and function of biological macromolecules; risk assessment. *Mailing Add:* Oak Ridge Nat Lab Box X Health & Safety Res Div Oak Ridge TN 37830

UZMAN, BETTY GEREN, neurobiology, pathology, see previous edition

UZNANSKI-BOTTEI, RITA MARLENE, b Chicago, Ill, Aug 13, 33; m 60; c 4. ANALYTICAL CHEMISTRY. *Educ:* Rosary Col, BA, 54; Univ Ill, Urbana, PhD(anal chem), 58. *Prof Exp:* Teaching asst chem & chem eng, Univ Ill, Urbana, 54-58; from instr to asst prof chem, St Ambrose Col, 58-60; vis lectr, St Mary's Col, Ind, 60-61; ASSOC LECTR CHEM, IND UNIV, SOUTH BEND, 71- *Concurrent Pos:* Consult, Ultrasonic Lab, Pioneer Cent Div, Bendix Aviation Corp, Iowa, 58-60. *Mem:* Am Chem Soc. *Res:* X-ray analysis; radiochemical analysis. *Mailing Add:* 19341 Wedgewood Dr South Bend IN 46637

UZODINMA, JOHN E, b Onitsha, Nigeria, July 26, 29; m 57; c 4. PREVENTIVE MEDICINE, MICROBIOLOGY. *Educ:* Grinnell Col, BA, 54; Univ Iowa, MS, 56, PhD(prev med, microbiol), 65. *Prof Exp:* Bacteriologist, State Hyg Labs, Iowa, 57-58; microbiologist, Broadlawns County Hosp, Des Moines, 58-61; PROF BIOL, JACKSON STATE UNIV, 64-, CHMN DEPT, 67- *Mem:* AAAS; Am Soc Clin Path; Am Inst Biol Sci; Am Soc Microbiol; Royal Soc Trop Med & Hyg. *Res:* Host-parasite relationships; effect of insulin, serotonin and thyroxine on the penetration of tissue culture cells by Toxoplasma gondii; effect of certain drugs on Trypanosoma equiperdum infections in mice. *Mailing Add:* Dept of Biol Box 17111 Jackson MS 39209

UZZELL, THOMAS, b Charleston, SC, Apr 6, 32. SYSTEMATIC BIOLOGY, VERTEBRATE BIOLOGY. *Educ:* Univ Mich, BA, 53, MS, 58, PhD(zool), 62. *Prof Exp:* From instr to asst prof biol, Univ Chicago, 62-67; asst prof & asst curator herpet, Peabody Mus, Yale Univ, 67-72, fel, Berkeley Col, 70-72; assoc curator, 72-77, CURATOR HERPET, ACAD NATURAL SCI, 77- *Concurrent Pos:* Adj assoc prof, Univ Pa, 74- *Mem:* Am Soc Naturalists; AAAS; Am Soc Ichthyol & Herpet; Soc Study Evolution; Soc Syst Zool. *Res:* Origin and evolution of hybrid species of vertebrates; determination of the generic and specific limits of South American lizards of the family Teiidae. *Mailing Add:* 2424 Golf Rd Philadelphia PA 19131

V

VAALA, ALLEN RICHARD, b Wilmington, Del, Jan 2, 44; m 67, 78; c 3. EXPERIMENTAL PHYSICS. *Educ:* Col Wooster, BA, 65; Pa State Univ, PhD(physics), 71. *Prof Exp:* SR RES PHYSICIST, RES LABS, EASTMAN KODAK EASTMAN KODAK CO, 71- *Res:* Thermally stimulated current and conductivity techniques; thermoluminescent studies; ultra-low current measurement; crystal growth. *Mailing Add:* 1669 Lake Ave Eastman Kodak Co Rochester NY 14650

VAALA, GORDON THEODORE, b Madison, Minn, Sept 11, 08; m 40; c 4. CHEMISTRY. *Educ:* St Olaf Col, AB, 30; Mass Inst Technol, PhD(org chem), 36. *Prof Exp:* Asst, Mass Inst Technol, 30-31; res chemist, Exp Sta, E I Du Pont de Nemours & Co, Inc, 36-39, group leader, 39-45, asst dir, Fairfield Lab, 45-49 & Newburgh Lab, 49-52, mgr trade prod sales, NY, 52-53, dir sales, Fabrics Div, 53-59, mgr, Planning Div, 59-72; RETIRED. *Res:* High polymers; plasticizers; amino acids; coated fabrics; synthetic rubbers. *Mailing Add:* 1609 Shipley Rd Wilmington DE 19803

VACCA, LINDA LEE, b Paterson, NJ, Mar 10, 47. NEUROSCIENCE, HISTOCHEMISTRY. *Educ:* Col William & Mary, BS, 68; Tulane Univ, MS, 71, PhD(biol), 73. *Prof Exp:* Res asst ecol, Marine Biol Lab, 69, teaching asst, comp physiol, 69-70, biol, Tulane Univ, 70-71; res assoc histochem, La State Univ Med Sch, 71-73; vis fel psychiat res, Dept of Path, Col Physicians & Surgeons NY State Psychiat Inst, 73-74; instr neuroanat, Dept of Physiol, NY Univ Med Ctr, 74-76; asst prof, dept physiol, 76-80, ASST PROF NEUROSCI RES, DEPT OF PATH & ANAT, MED COL OF GA, 76- *Concurrent Pos:* Mem Biol Stain Comn, 72-; NIMH fel, NY State Psychiat Inst, 73-74; dir histopath, Dept of Path, Med Col Ga, 76-, biomed res grant, Med Col Ga, 78-79 & 79-80; mem, Comt Combat Huntingtons Dis, 80-81 & 81-82; NSF travel fel, VI Int Cong Histochem & Cytochem, England, 80; invited speaker, Winter Conf Brain Res, 82. *Mem:* Sigma Xi; Histochem Soc; Soc Neurosci; Am Asn Anat. *Res:* Histochemical identification of neurotransmitters; ultrastructural evaluation of neural circuits in central nervous system; immunocytochemical tracing of pain pathways in spinal cord which contain substance P, methionine enkephalin, and other peptides; peptides in basal ganglia and Huntington's disease. *Mailing Add:* Dept of Path Med Col of Ga Augusta GA 30912

VACCARO, F(RANK) E(MELIO), b Memphis, Tenn, Mar 18, 24; m 55; c 6. ELECTRICAL ENGINEERING. *Educ:* Univ Tenn, BS, 48; Stevens Inst Technol, ME, 53. *Prof Exp:* Engr microwaves devices opers, Dept Electronic Components & Devices, Radio Corp Am, 49-56, eng leader, 56-59, mgr, 59-64, eng leader, Microwave Dept, RCA Corp, 64-76; MEM STAFF, MTS RES LAB, 76- *Mem:* Inst Elec & Electronics Engrs. *Res:* Microwave tubes; microwave and solid state devices. *Mailing Add:* Mts Res Lab 10 Hamlin Rd East Brunswick NJ 08902

VACHON, RAYMOND NORMAND, b Lawrence, Mass, Jan 14, 40; m 70; c 4. ORGANIC CHEMISTRY, POLYMER CHEMISTRY. *Educ:* Lowell Technol Inst, BS, 63; Princeton Univ, PhD(chem), 67. *Prof Exp:* Res grant, Inst Sci & Technol, Univ Manchester, 67-69; sr res chemist, Burlington Industs, Inc, 69-72; res chemist, 72-74, SR RES CHEMIST, TENN EASTMAN CO, 74- *Mem:* Am Asn Textile Chemists & Colorists; Am Chem Soc. *Res:* Water dispersible condensation polyesters for use as textile warp sizes; binders for nonwoven fabrics and adhesives. *Mailing Add:* 440 Forest Hills Rd Kingsport TN 37663

VACHON, REGINALD IRENEE, b Norfolk, Va, Jan 29, 37; m 60; c 2. MECHANICAL ENGINEERING. *Educ:* Auburn Univ, BME, 58, MSNS, 60; Okla State Univ, PhD(mech eng), 63; Jones Law Sch, LLB, 69. *Prof Exp:* Instr physics, Auburn Univ, 58-59, assoc prof mech eng, 63-67, alumni prof, 67-78, prof, 78-80, assoc researcher heat transfer, Res Found, 60-61; PRES, VACHON NIX & ASSOCS, 80- *Concurrent Pos:* Mem, Southern Interstate Nuclear Bd. *Mem:* Am Soc Mech Engrs; Am Inst Aeronaut & Astronaut; Am Soc Eng Educ; Nat Soc Prof Engrs; Am Bar Asn. *Res:* Thermoscience; conduction in solids; gas dynamics; boiling and convection heat transfer; power systems; systems approach management. *Mailing Add:* Vachon Nix & Assocs PO Box 1182 Atlanta GA 30301

VACHTSEVANOS, GEORGE JOHN, b Kozani, Greece, Nov 6, 38; US citizen; m 69; c 1. ENVIRONMENTAL SCIENCES, SYSTEMS ANALYSIS. *Educ:* City Col New York, BEE, 62; NY Univ, MEE, 63; City Univ New York, PhD(systs), 70. *Prof Exp:* Lectr elec eng, City Col New York, 63-69; asst prof environ sci, 69-76, ASST PROF PURE & APPL SCI, RICHMOND COL, NY, 76- *Mem:* Inst Elec & Electronics Engrs; Soc Eng Sci. *Res:* Environmental systems; analog and digital simulation of environmental systems; mathematical modeling and computational algorithms. *Mailing Add:* Div of Pure & Appl Sci 130 Stuyvesant Pl Staten Island NY 10301

VACIK, DOROTHY NOBLES, b Memphis, Tenn, Dec 16, 38; m 67; c 3. ORGANIC CHEMISTRY, PHARMACEUTICAL CHEMISTRY. *Educ:* Memphis State Univ, BS, 60; Univ Miss, PhD(pharmaceut chem), 65. *Prof Exp:* Asst prof pharmaceut chem & bionucleonics, Univ, 65-68, lab supvr & gen analyst, Dept Animal Sci, 71-72, lab dir, Drug Control Lab, Dept Pharm & Vet Admin Hosp, NDak State Univ, 72-73; CONSULT CHEMIST, UNIV S ALA COL MED, 73- *Mem:* Am Chem Soc; Am Pharmaceut Asn. *Res:* Development of analytical techniques for drug determination in human therapy. *Mailing Add:* 1220 Vendome Dr W Mobile AL 36609

VACIK, JAMES P, b North Judson, Ind, Nov 30, 31; m 67; c 6. PHARMACEUTICAL CHEMISTRY, BIONUCLEONICS. *Educ:* Purdue Univ, BS, 55, MS, 57, PhD(bionucleonics), 59. *Prof Exp:* Asst prof & res fel bionucleonics, Purdue Univ, 59-60; assoc prof pharmaceut chem & chmn dept, NDak State Univ, 60-63, prof pharmaceut chem & bionucleonics & chmn dept, 63-76; ASSOC PROF PHARMACOL & DIR ENVIRON SAFETY, UNIV S ALA, 76- *Mem:* AAAS; Health Physics Soc; Am Pharmaceut Asn; Am Conf Gov & Ind Hyg. *Res:* Bionucleonics including metabolism, uptake and distribution of radioisotope tracers and large animal biosynthesis; synthesis of benzodioxans; antiviral agents. *Mailing Add:* Col Med Univ SAla Mobile AL 36688

VACIRCA, SALVATORE JOHN, b Bronx, NY, July 20, 22; c 2. RADIATION PHYSICS, HEALTH PHYSICS. *Educ:* City Col New York, BS, 48; NY Univ, MS, 54, PhD(radiation physics), 70; Am Bd Health Physics, dipl, 60. *Prof Exp:* Res asst nuclear electronics instrumentation, Sloan Kettering Inst Cancer Res, 48-54, asst physicist, Mem-Sloan Kettering Ctr Cancer & Allied Dis, 54-56, asst attend physicist, 56-61; co-dir nuclear med lab, State Univ NY Downstate Med Ctr, 65-70, chmn radiation technol prog, 69-71, from asst prof to assoc prof radiol, 73-78, dir radiation physics lab & radiation safety off, 61-78; DIR MED PHYSICS DIV, DEPT RADIOL, NORTH SHORE UNIV HOSP, 78-; PROF CLIN RADIOL, CORNELL MED SCH, 78- *Concurrent Pos:* Instr & res assoc, Sloan Kettering Div, Med Col, Cornell Univ, 55-61; dir radiol physics & radiation safety off, Kings County Hosp Ctr, 61-78, sr med physicist, Prof Staff, 72; consult physicist, Col Health Related Professions, State Univ NY, 71-; consult physicist, Coney Island Hosp, 72; adj assoc prof, York Col, NY, 72 & City Col New York, 74. *Mem:* Am Asn Physicists in Med; Health Physics Soc. *Res:* Radiation dosimetry as applied to therapy; film and thermoluminescent synergistic dosimetry system used as a method of mapping dose distribution; health physics problems as applied to hospital environment. *Mailing Add:* North Shore Univ Hosp 300 Community Dr Manhasset NY 11030

VACQUIER, VICTOR, b Leningrad, Russia, Oct 13, 07; nat US; m 31; c 2. GEOPHYSICS. *Educ:* Univ Wis, BS, 27, MA, 28. *Prof Exp:* Asst instr physics, Univ Wis, 27-30; geophysicist, Gulf Res & Develop Co, Pa, 30-42; mem staff airborne instruments lab, Columbia Univ, 42-44; marine instruments engr, Sperry Gyroscope Co, 44-53; prof geophys & prin geophysicist, NMex Inst Mining & Technol, 53-57; prof geophys, Scripps Inst Oceanog, 57-74, EMER PROF GEOPHYS, UNIV CALIF, SAN DIEGO, 74- *Mem:* Soc Explor Geophys; Geol Soc Am; Am Geophys Union; Franklin Inst. *Res:* Geomagnetism; airborne magnetometry; terrestrial heat flow. *Mailing Add:* Scripps Inst of Oceanog Univ of Calif San Diego La Jolla CA 92093

VACQUIER, VICTOR DIMITRI, b Pittsburgh, Pa, July 20, 40; m 73. DEVELOPMENTAL & CELL BIOLOGY. *Educ:* San Diego State Univ, BA, 63; Univ Calif, Berkeley, PhD(zool), 68. *Prof Exp:* Researcher, Intern Lab, Genetics & Biophysics, Naples, Italy, 68-69; mem staff, Hopkins Marine Sta, Stanford Univ, 70-71 & Scripps Inst Oceanog, Univ Calif, San Diego, 71-73; from asst prof to assoc prof zool, Univ Calif, Davis, 73-78; assoc prof, 78-80, PROF MARINE BIOL, SCRIPPS INST OCEANOG, UNIV CALIF, SAN DIEGO, 80- *Mem:* AAAS; Am Soc Cell Biol; Soc Develop Biol; Int Soc Develop Biol. *Res:* Biochemistry of fertilization. *Mailing Add:* A-002 Marine Biol Res Div Univ of Calif La Jolla CA 92093

VADAS, ROBERT LOUIS, b New Brunswick, NJ, Aug 5, 36; m 61; c 3. MARINE ECOLOGY, PHYCOLOGY. *Educ:* Utah State Univ, BS, 62; Univ Wash, PhD(bot), 68. *Prof Exp:* Asst prof bot, 67-72, asst prof zool, 68-72, assoc prof, 72-77, PROF BOT, OCEANOG & ZOOL, UNIV MAINE, ORONO, 77- *Concurrent Pos:* Maine Yankee Nuclear Atomic Power Co study grant, 69-74; Off Water Resources grants, 70-72 & 72-75. *Mem:* Ecol Soc Am; Am Soc Naturalists; Phycol Soc Am; Brit Phycol Soc; Int Phycol Soc. *Res:* Ecology of kelp communities; marine plant-herbivore interactions; algal distributions; culture and physiology of algae; thermal enrichment in marine communities; influence of pesticides on marine microalgae. *Mailing Add:* Dept of Bot Univ of Maine Orono ME 04473

VADHWA, OM PARKASH, b Mandi Maklot Ganj, India, May 10, 41; m 67; c 1. AGRONOMY. *Educ:* Rajasthan Univ, India, BS, 61; Punjab Agr Univ, MS, 63; Utah State Univ, PhD(agron), 71. *Prof Exp:* Lectr agron, Punjab Agr Univ, Hissar Campus, 63-65; fel agron & plant sci, Utah State Univ, 70-71; assoc prof natural resources, Ala A&M Univ, 71-72; ASST PROF AGRON, ALCORN STATE UNIV, 72- *Mem:* Am Soc Agron; Am Asn Univ Prof. *Res:* Forage crops; crop production; soil fertility and plant nutrition; vegetable crops. *Mailing Add:* Dept of Agron Alcorn State Univ Lorman MS 39096

VADLAMUDI, SRI KRISHNA, b Moparru, Tenali, AP, India, Aug 15, 27; US citizen; m 54; c 4. MICROBIOLOGY, IMMUNOLOGY. *Educ:* Madras Univ, DVM, 52; Univ Wis, Madison, MS, 59, PhD(microbiol), 63. *Prof Exp:* Head cancer chemother res, Microbiol Asn, Inc, 66-74; sci expert cancer, Smithsonian Sci Info Exch, 75; EXEC SECY, PANELS OF IMMUNOL & CLIN TOXICOL, BUR MED DEVICES, FOOD & DRUG ADMIN, HHS, 75-, ACTG IMMUNOL BR CHIEF, 77- *Concurrent Pos:* Vet surgeon, Animal Husbandry Dept, Govt AP, India, 52-55; res vet, Govt NVD Lab, Guntur, India, actg supt, Govt Livestock Res Sta, 57; proj asst Dept of Vet Sci, Univ of Wis-Madison, 57-62; sr microbiologist, Dept of Infectious Dis, Abbott Lab, 62-65; chief, viral chemother div, Microbiol Asn, Inc, 65-66.

Mem: Am Soc Microbiol; Am Asn Cancer Res; Am Asn Path; Am Vet Med Asn; Sigma Xi. *Res:* Cancer chemotherapy and immunotherapy; tumor biology and metastasis; immunotoxicology; epizootiology and epidemiology of viral diseases, particularly arbor viruses; infection and immunity; pharmacology. *Mailing Add:* Bur of Med Devices 8757 Georgia Ave Silver Spring MD 20910

VAFAKOS, WILLIAM P(AUL), b Brooklyn, NY, Oct 12, 27; m 62; c 3. MECHANICAL ENGINEERING, APPLIED MECHANICS. *Educ:* Polytech Inst Brooklyn, BME, 51, MME, 55, PhD(appl mech), 60; Brooklyn Law Sch, JD, 76. *Prof Exp:* Engr, Westinghouse Elec Corp, 51-53; sr engr, Ford Instrument Co, 53-57; res assoc, 57-60, from asst prof to assoc prof, 60-68, PROF MECH & AEROSPACE ENG, POLYTECH INST NEW YORK, 76- *Mem:* Am Soc Mech Engrs; assoc fel Am Inst Aeronaut & Astronaut. *Res:* Thin-walled structures. *Mailing Add:* 967 E 17th St Brooklyn NY 11230

VAFOPOULOU-MANDALOS, XANTHE, b Thessaloniki, Greece, Aug 22, 49; US citizen; m 72. MOLECULAR DEVELOPMENTAL BIOLOGY, INSECT ENDOCRINOLOGY. *Educ:* Aristotelian Univ, BA, 72; Bridgewater State Col, MA, 78; Univ Conn, PhD(develop biol), 80. *Prof Exp:* Teaching asst, 76-80, ASST PROF IN RESIDENCE BIOL, UNIV CONN, 81- *Concurrent Pos:* Lectr-instr, W Alton Jones Cell Sci Ctr & Tissue Culture Asn, Inc, 80-; res assoc, Univ Conn, 81- *Mem:* AAAS; Soc Develop Biol; Am Soc Zoologists. *Res:* Regulation of gene activity by insect hormones; molecular interactions between hormones and tissues in vivo and in vitro; synthesis of tissue-specific RNA's and proteins during development. *Mailing Add:* Biol Sci Group U-42 Univ Conn Storrs CT 06268

VAGELATOS, NICHOLAS, b Kefallinia, Greece, Mar 8, 45; m 79; c 1. PROGRAM DEVELOPMENT MANAGEMENT, NUCLEAR TECHNOLOGY. *Educ:* Univ Mich, BSE, 67, MSE, 69, PhD(nuclear eng), 73. *Prof Exp:* Res assoc, Neutron spectros, Nat Bur Stand, US Dept of Com, 73-75; sr scientist, 76-78, prin scientist, 78-80, MGR PROG DEVELOP, NUCLEAR SYSTS DIV, IRT CORP, 80- *Concurrent Pos:* Nat Res Coun fel, Nat Bur Stand, US Dept of Com, 73-75. *Mem:* Am Phys Soc. *Res:* Interaction of radiation with matter; radiation detection and measurement; nuclear technology applications in natural resources evaluation. *Mailing Add:* IRT Corp PO Box 80817 San Diego CA 92138

VAGELOS, P ROY, b Westfield, NJ, Oct 8, 29; m 55; c 4. BIOCHEMISTRY. *Educ:* Univ Pa, AB, 50; Columbia Univ, MD, 54. *Prof Exp:* Intern med, Mass Gen Hosp, Boston, 54-55, asst resident, 55-56; sr asst surgeon, Lab Cellular Physiol, Nat Heart Inst, 56-59, surgeon, 59-61, actg chief sect enzymes, 59-60, sr surgeon, Lab Biochem, 61-62; sr surgeon, Pasteur Inst, Paris, 62-63; sr surgeon & res chemist, Lab Biochem, Nat Heart Inst, 63-64, head sect comp biochem, 64-66; chmn dept biol chem, Sch Med, Wash Univ, 66-75, dir div biol & biomed sci, 74-75; sr vpres, 75-76, corp sr vpres, 81, PRES, MERCK SHARP & DOHME RES LABS, MERCK & CO, INC, 76- *Concurrent Pos:* NIH & NSF grants. *Mem:* Nat Acad Sci; Nat Inst Med; AAAS; Am Chem Soc; Am Soc Biol Chem. *Res:* Mechanism of lipid biosynthesis; involvement of acyl carrier protein in fatty acid biosynthesis. *Mailing Add:* Merck Sharp & Dohme Res Labs Merck & Co Inc Rahway NJ 07065

VAGLIO-LAURIN, ROBERTO, b Milano, Italy, Aug 7, 29; nat US; m 58; c 2. FLUID MECHANICS. *Educ:* Univ Rome, DrEng(civil eng), 50, DrEng(aeronaut eng), 52; Polytech Inst Brooklyn, PhD(appl mech), 54. *Prof Exp:* Prof engr, Univ Rome, 50-52; from res assoc to prof aero- aerospace eng, Polytech Inst Brooklyn, 52-64, asst dir aerospace res, 62-64, dir aerospace inst, 64; mem staff, Inst Defense Anal, 64-65; PROF AERONAUT & ASTRONAUT, NY UNIV, 65- *Concurrent Pos:* Consult, Curtiss-Wright Corp, 55-56, Gen Appl Sci Labs, 56-57, Grumman Aerospace Corp, 61-, Inst Defense Anal, 65-, Lincoln Lab, Mass Inst Technol, 65- & Advan Technol Labs, 67-; libero docente, Univ Rome, 59- *Mem:* Assoc fel Am Inst Aeronaut & Astronaut; Am Phys Soc. *Res:* Theoretical physics of fluids; aerodynamics; propulsion; systems analysis. *Mailing Add:* 333 Hempstead Ave Rockville Center NY 11570

VAGNINI, LIVIO L, b North Bergen, NJ, Apr 26, 17; m 49; c 3. CHEMISTRY. *Educ:* Fordham Col, BS, 38. *Prof Exp:* Chemist, H A Wilson Co Div, Englehard Industs, Inc, NJ, 40-42; chief forensic chemist, US Army Criminal Invest Lab, France, 44-46, chief chemist, US Army Graves Regist Lab, Belg, 46-48, chief forensic chemist, Ger, 48-60; microanalyst, US Food & Drug Admin, Washington, DC, 60-63; sr chemist, Cent Intel Agency, 63-73; tech staff mem, Mitre Corp, Va, 73-75; consult criminalist, 75; tech staff, Planning Res Corp, Va, 75-77; PROG DIR, L MIRANDA & ASSOC, 78-81. *Mem:* Fel Am Inst Chem; Am Chem Soc; Asn Off Anal Chem; fel Am Acad Forensic Sci; Int Soc Forensic Toxicol. *Res:* Forensic chemistry; microchemistry; serology of dried blood factors; analysis of narcotics; optical crystallography of drugs; microanalysis of foods and drugs; x-ray spectrometry. *Mailing Add:* 26360 Mission Fields Rd Carmel CA 93923

VAGNUCCI, ANTHONY HILLARY, b Terni, Italy, July 9, 28; US citizen; m 62; c 3. MEDICINE, PHYSIOLOGY. *Educ:* Univ Genoa, MD, 54. *Prof Exp:* Intern med, Wesson Mem Hosp, Springfield, Mass, 57-58; resident, NY Univ-Bellevue Med Ctr, 58-60; Am Heart Asn res fel renal physiol, Med Sch, NY Univ, 60-62; advan res fel, Hypertension Unit, Dept Med, Peter Bent Brigham Hosp, Boston, 62-63 & advan res fel endocrinol, 63-64; jr assoc med & assoc dir endocrinol metab unit, Peter Bent Brigham Hosp, 64-65; asst prof, 65-70, ASSOC PROF MED, SCH MED, UNIV PITTSBURGH, 70-; HEAD ADRENAL UNIT, MONTEFIORE HOSP, 65- *Concurrent Pos:* Res assoc, Harvard Med Sch, 64-65. *Mem:* Am Fedn Clin Res; Endocrine Soc; NY Acad Sci. *Res:* Diurnal aspect of electrolyte homeostasis; adrenal physiopathology; hypertensive disease. *Mailing Add:* Dept of Med 3459 Fifth Ave Pittsburgh PA 15213

VAHALA, GEORGE MARTIN, b Tabor, Czech, Mar 26, 46; Australian citizen; m 70. MAGNETOHYDRODYNAMICS, PLASMA PHYSICS. *Educ:* Univ Western Australia, BSc Hons, 67; Univ Iowa, MS, 69, PhD(physics), 72. *Prof Exp:* Res assoc plasma physics, Univ Tenn, Knoxville, 72; res scientist magnetohydrodynamics, Courant Inst Math Sci, NY Univ, 72-74; asst prof, 74-80, PROF PHYSICS, COL WILLIAM & MARY, 80- *Res:* Magnetohydrodynamics and guiding-center stability of containment devices; spectral theory and its interpretation in plasma physics as well as in magnetohydrodynamics; transport effects in plasmas; nonlinear dynamics. *Mailing Add:* Dept of Physics Col of William & Mary Williamsburg VA 23185

VAHEY, DAVID WILLIAM, b Youngstown, Ohio, Nov 21, 44. OPTICAL PHYSICS, ELECTROOPTICS. *Educ:* Mass Inst Technol, BS, 66; Calif Inst Technol, MS, 67, PhD(elec eng), 73. *Prof Exp:* Fel physics, Columbus Labs, Battelle Mem Inst, 73-74, res scientist, 74-75, res scientist physics, 75-81; SR STAFF PHYSICIST, ACCU RAY CORP, 81- *Mem:* Optical Soc Am; Sigma Xi. *Res:* Optical inspection and measurement techniques; optical sensors. *Mailing Add:* Accu Ray Corp 650 Ackerman Rd Columbus OH 43202

VAHLDIEK, FRED W(ILLIAM), b Eilsleben, Ger, Feb 5, 33; US citizen; m 59; c 1. CHEMICAL ENGINEERING, CHEMISTRY. *Educ:* Univ Halle, BSc, 53, MSc, 54. *Prof Exp:* Anal chemist, Iron & Steel Co, Ger, 54-55 & E F Drew Co, NJ, 55-56; RES MAT ENGR & GROUP LEADER, AIR FORCE MAT LAB, WRIGHT-PATTERSON AFB, 59- *Honors & Awards:* Sustained Superior Performance Award, US Air Force, 64, Outstanding Performance Award, 66. *Mem:* AAAS; Am Chem Soc; Sigma Xi; fel Am Inst Chemists. *Res:* High pressure-high temperature research on refractory, monmetallic materials; electron microscopy studies on metallic and nonmetallic high temperature materials; oxidation on metallic and refractory solids; high temperature x-ray of solids. *Mailing Add:* 5851 Barrett Dr Dayton OH 45431

VAHOUNY, GEORGE V, b New York, NY, Feb 22, 32; m 55; c 3. CARDIOVASCULAR DISEASES. *Educ:* George Washington Univ, BS, 53, MS, 55, PhD, 58. *Prof Exp:* From instr to assoc prof, 56-69, PROF BIOCHEM, GEORGE WASHINGTON UNIV, 69- *Concurrent Pos:* Lectr, Univ Tex Southwestern Med Sch Dallas, 57. *Honors & Awards:* William B Peck Sci Res Award, Interstate Postgrad Med Asn, 66. *Mem:* Soc Exp Biol & Med; Am Soc Biol Chem; Am Inst Nutrit. *Res:* Absorption and metabolism of lipids, especially cholesterol; cholesterol esterase systems; effects of hormones on fat absorption from the small intestine. *Mailing Add:* Dept of Biochem George Washington Univ Washington DC 20052

VAICAITIS, RIMAS, b Sakei, Lithuania, Apr 30, 41; US citizen; m 65; c 2. AERONAUTICAL ENGINEERING. *Educ:* Univ Ill, Urbana, BS, 67, MS, 68, PhD(aero eng), 70. *Prof Exp:* Res asst eng, Univ Ill, 67-70; from asst prof to assoc prof, 70-78, DIR INST OF FLIGHT STRUCT, COLUMBIA UNIV, 77- *Concurrent Pos:* Res engr NASA, Langley Res Ctr, 76-77; consult, US Air Force, 75-, US Army, 76-, Rockwell Int, 78-, Modern Anal, Inc, 74- *Mem:* Am Inst Aeronaut & Astronaut; Am Soc Civil Eng. *Res:* Fluid-solid interactions; random vibrations; structural acoustics. *Mailing Add:* Dept of Civil Eng Columbia Univ New York NY 10027

VAIDHYANATHAN, V S, b Madras, India, Dec 15, 33; m 65; c 1. BIOPHYSICS. *Educ:* Annamalai Univ, Madras, BSC, 53, MA, 54; Ill Inst Technol, PhD(chem), 61. *Prof Exp:* Res assoc chem, Univ Kans, 60-62; chief math & statist sect, Southern Res Support Ctr, 62-63, chief theoret sci sect, 63-66; assoc prof theoret biol, State Univ NY, Buffalo, 66-70, assoc prof biophyics, 67-72, assoc prof pharmaceut & biophysics, 72-80. *Concurrent Pos:* Consult, Vet Admin Hosp, New Orleans; vis prof theoret biol, State Univ NY Buffalo, 65; Europ Molecular Biol Orgn fel, 69. *Mem:* AAAS; Am Chem Soc; Biophys Soc. *Res:* Statistical mechanics; active transport; nerve potentials; biophysics of membranes. *Mailing Add:* 114 Caryhall Buffalo NY 14214

VAIDYA, AKHIL BABUBHAI, b Gonda, India, Oct 24, 47; m 73. MOLECULAR VIROLOGY, CELL BIOLOGY. *Educ:* Univ Bombay, BSc, 67, PhD(appl biol), 72. *Prof Exp:* Res asst ultrastruct, Cancer Res Inst, Bombay, 70-72; res assoc molecular biol, Inst Med Res, 72-75, assoc, 75-77; ASST PROF MICROBIOL, HAHNEMANN MED COL, 77- *Mem:* Am Soc Microbiol. *Res:* Characteristics and mechanisms of malignant transformation of epithelial cells, especially by mouse mammary tumor viruses; control of eukaryotic gene expression; molecular biology of tumor viruses; molecular biology of malarial parasites. *Mailing Add:* Dept of Microbiol 230 N Broad St Philadelphia PA 19102

VAIL, CHARLES BROOKS, b Bessemer, Ala, Apr 29, 23; m 44; c 2. PHYSICAL CHEMISTRY. *Educ:* Birmingham-Southern Col, BS, 45; Emory Univ, MS, 47, PhD(chem), 51. *Prof Exp:* Instr chem, Armstrong Col, 48-49; chemist, Southern Res Inst, 51-53; prof phys sci, Coker Col, 53-56; assoc prof chem, Agnes Scott Col, 56-57; prof chem & acad dean, Hampden-Sydney Col, 57-65; assoc exec secy, Comn on Cols, 65-68; dean, Sch Arts & Sci, Ga State Univ, 68-73; PRES, WINTHROP COL, 73- *Mem:* Am Chem Soc. *Res:* Thermal diffusion in liquids; heats of vaporization; photochemistry. *Mailing Add:* Winthrop Col Rock Hill SC 29733

VAIL, CHARLES R(OWE), b Glens Falls, NY, Oct 16, 15; m 39; c 3. ELECTRICAL ENGINEERING, ACADEMIC ADMINISTRATION. *Educ:* Duke Univ, BSEE, 37; Univ Mich, MS, 46, PhD(elec eng), 56. *Prof Exp:* Engr, Gen Elec Co, 37-39; from instr to prof elec eng, Duke Univ, 39-67, exec officer dept, 53-56, chmn dept, 56-64, assoc dean grad study & res, Sch Eng, 64-67, actg dean, 65; prof elec eng & electronic sci, Southern Methodist Univ, 67-73, assoc dean eng, 67-70, vpres, Univ, 70-73; assoc dean, Col Eng, 73-79, PROF ELEC ENG, GA INST TECHNOL, 73-, DIR, DEPT CONTINUING EDUC, 79- *Concurrent Pos:* Consult, Chem War Res Proj, Duke Univ, 45, Solid State Div, US Naval Res Lab, 52-58, Gen Elec Co, 56-58 & NC Res Triangle Inst, 60-63; mem, Gov's Sci Adv Comt, NC, 61-64; mem tech utilization adv bd, NC Bd Sci & Technol, 65-67; agent & mem corp sect, Asn Media-Based Continuing Educ for Engrs, Inc, 76- *Mem:* AAAS; fel Inst Elec & Electronics Engrs; Nat Soc Prof Engrs; Soc Hist Technol. *Res:* High voltage phenomena; dielectric materials; superconducting circuitry; thin-film properties. *Mailing Add:* Dept Continuing Educ Ga Inst of Technol Atlanta GA 30332

VAIL, EDWIN GEORGE, b Toledo, Ohio, July 25, 21; m 46; c 5. MEDICAL PHYSIOLOGY, BIOENGINEERING. *Educ:* Univ Toledo, BSc, 47; Ohio State Univ, MSc, 48, PhD(aviation physiol), 53. *Prof Exp:* Proj engr, Aerospace Med Lab, Wright Air Develop Ctr, Ohio, 51-53, chief respiration sect, 53-54, proj scientist, 54-60, chief personnel protection equip & crew escape group X-20 syst prog officer, 60-62, asst chief, Bioastronaut Div, 63-64; chief human eng & space suit res & develop, Hamilton Standard, United Aircraft Corp, Conn, 64-69; mem staff physiol, Naval Coastal Systs Lab, Panama City, 70-78; PRES, VAIL APPL RES CO, INC, 73- *Mem:* Aerospace Med Asn; Undersea Med Soc; Sigma Xi. *Res:* Aerospace and oceanographic physiology, including respiratory, cardiovascular, environmental stress tolerance; space-pressure suits, diving equipment and life support system research and development of medical devices. *Mailing Add:* 4502 Vista Ln Lynn Haven FL 32444

VAIL, JOHN MONCRIEFF, b Winnipeg, Man, Oct 17, 31; m 54; c 1. SOLID STATE PHYSICS. *Educ:* Univ Man, BSc, 55, MSc, 56; Brandeis Univ, PhD(physics), 60. *Prof Exp:* IBM res asst, Brandeis Univ, 57-59; Nat Res Coun Can fel, McGill Univ, 60-61; Leverhulme fel, Univ Liverpool, 61-62; from asst prof math physics to assoc prof physics, 62-72, PROF PHYSICS, UNIV MAN, 72- *Concurrent Pos:* Vis lectr, St Andrews Univ, 68-69; vis res assoc, AERE Harwell, 75-76. *Mem:* Can Asn Physicists; Am Phys Soc; Brit Inst Physics. *Res:* Solid state theory, applied to properties of localized defects in crystalline materials. *Mailing Add:* Dept of Physics Univ of Man Winnipeg MB R3T 2N2 Can

VAIL, SIDNEY LEE, b New Orleans, La, Aug 10, 28; m 53; c 4. ORGANIC CHEMISTRY, TEXTILES. *Educ:* Tulane Univ, BS, 49, PhD(org chem), 65; La State Univ, MS, 51. *Prof Exp:* Org chemist, Dow Chem Co, 51-53; sr chemist, Am Cyanamid Co, 55-59; proj leader, 59-72, RES LEADER COTTON TEXTILE CHEM LAB, SOUTHERN REGIONAL RES CTR, USDA, 72-, CHIEF, 76- *Concurrent Pos:* Exchange scientist, Shirley Inst, Eng, 65-66; adj prof textile chem, Sch Textiles, NC State Univ, Raleigh, 79- *Mem:* Am Chem Soc; Am Asn Textile Chemists & Colorists; Fiber Soc; Sigma Xi. *Res:* Petrochemicals, synthesis and process chemistry; organic synthesis and mechanisms of textiles; nuclear magnetic resonance; plant chemistry; chemical modification of cotton. *Mailing Add:* Southern Regional Res Ctr 1100 Robert E Lee Blvd New Orleans LA 70119

VAILLANCOURT, DE GUISE, b Montreal, Que, Dec 11, 20; m 52; c 5. INTERNAL MEDICINE, RHEUMATOLOGY. *Educ:* Univ Montreal, BA, 41, MD, 47; Columbia Univ, DSc(med), 53; FRCP(C), 55, FACP, 62. *Prof Exp:* PROF MED, FAC MED, UNIV MONTREAL, 55-, DIR CONTINUING MED EDUC, 56-, VDEAN FAC MED, 68- *Concurrent Pos:* Attend physician, Hotel-Dieu Hosp, 52- *Mem:* Fel Am Col Physicians; Am Rheumatism Asn; Can Med Asn; Can Rheumatism Asn (pres, 67); Can Asn Continuing Med Educ. *Res:* Continuing medical education; clinical medicine. *Mailing Add:* Fac Med Univ Montreal PO Box 6207 Sta A Montreal PQ H3C 3T7 Can

VAILLANCOURT, REMI ETIENNE, b Maniwaki, Que, June 16, 34. MATHEMATICS. *Educ:* Univ Ottawa, BA, 57, BSc, 61, BTh, 63, MSc, 64, MTh, 65; NY Univ, PhD(math), 69. *Prof Exp:* Instr, NY Univ, 68-69; Off Naval Res res assoc, Univ Chicago, 69-70; chmn dept, 72-76, ASSOC PROF MATH, UNIV OTTAWA, 70- *Mem:* Am Math Soc; Math Asn Am; Can Math Soc; Fr-Can Asn Advan Sci. *Res:* Partial differential equations; pseudo-differential operators; finite difference and finite element methods. *Mailing Add:* Dept of Math Univ of Ottawa Ottawa ON K1N 9B4 Can

VAILLANT, GEORGE EMAN, b New York, NY, June 16, 34; m 71; c 5. PSYCHIATRY. *Educ:* Harvard Univ, AB, 55, MD, 59. *Prof Exp:* Resident, Mass Ment Health Ctr, 60-63; staff psychiatrist, USPHS, Lexington, Ky, 63-65; from asst prof to assoc prof psychiat, Sch Med, Tufts Univ, 66-71; assoc prof, 71-76, PROF PSYCHIAT, HARVARD MED SCH, 76- *Concurrent Pos:* Dir study adult develop, Harvard Univ, 72-; dir training, Dept Psychiat, Mass Ment Health Ctr, 81-; consult, Div Manpower & Training, NIMH, 76-79; fel, Ctr Advan Study Behav Sci, 78-79; NIH res sci award, 81- *Mem:* Fel Am Psychiat Asn; Soc Life Hist Res in Psychopath; Int Soc Study Behav Develop. *Res:* Long term follow up in adult development and in psychopathology. *Mailing Add:* Dept of Psychiat 1493 Cambridge St Cambridge MA 02139

VAILLANT, HENRY WINCHESTER, b New York, NY, Dec 17, 36; m 58; c 3. POPULATION BIOLOGY. *Educ:* Harvard Univ, AB, 58, MD, 62, SMHyg, 69. *Prof Exp:* Intern med, Boston City Hosp, 62-63, resident, 63-64; res assoc, Nat Inst Child Health & Human Develop, 64-66; resident, Boston City Hosp, 66-67; res fel obstet & gynec, Harvard Med Sch, 67-68, ASST PROF POP STUDIES, SCH PUB HEALTH, HARVARD UNIV, 68- *Concurrent Pos:* Consult cancer control prog, USPHS, 68. *Mem:* Am Pub Health Asn. *Res:* Clinical human reproductive physiology. *Mailing Add:* 321 Main Acton MA 01720

VAIRAVAN, KASIVISVANATHAN, b Madras, India, July 9, 39; m 67; c 2. ELECTRICAL ENGINEERING, COMPUTER SCIENCE. *Educ:* Univ Madras, BE, 62; George Washington Univ, MS, 65; Univ Notre Dame, PhD(elec eng), 68. *Prof Exp:* Jr elec engr, Madras State Elec Bd, 62-63; asst prof elec eng, 68-71, assoc prof elec eng & comput sci, 71-77, PROF ELEC ENG & COMPUT SCI, UNIV WIS-MILWAUKEE, 77- *Concurrent Pos:* Mem tech staff, Bell Tel Labs, 70; vis researcher, Hiroshima Univ, 80; vis lectr, var res ctrs in Japan. *Mem:* Inst Elec & Electronics Engrs. *Res:* Parallel computation; distributed processing; software science; computer organizations. *Mailing Add:* Dept Elec Eng & Comput Sci Univ Wis Milwaukee WI 53201

VAISEY-GENSER, FLORENCE MARION, b Winnipeg, Man, Apr 3, 29; m 53, 76; c 2. FOOD SCIENCE & TECHNOLOGY. *Educ:* Univ Man, BSc, 49; McGill Univ, MSc, 51. *Prof Exp:* Head food acceptance, Defense Res Med Labs, 51-53; metab dietician, Victoria Gen Hosp, 53-54; lectr, foods & Nutrit, Ore State Col, Corvallis, 56-60; asst prof, Univ Guelph, 62-65; from asst prof to assoc prof, 65-73, head dept, 78-80, PROF FOOD & NUTRIT, UNIV MAN, 73-, ASSOC DEAN, FAC GRAD STUDIES, 81- *Concurrent Pos:* Adv Bd, Can Food Prod Develop Ctr, 75-; res grant, Agr Can, 75-77 & 80-, Alberta Agr, 79-, Man Res Coun, 71-77, Canola Coun Can, 70- & Fisheries Res Bd, 66-69; guest prof, Swiss Fed Inst Technol, 71-72. *Honors & Awards:* Queen Elizabeth Silver Jubilee Medal, 77. *Mem:* Can Inst Food Sci & Technol (vpres, 78-79, pres, 80-81); Can Dietetic Asn; Can Home Econ Asn; Am Asn Cereal Chem; Inst Food Technol. *Res:* Sensory evaluation of foods and their components; rapeseed oil; plant proteins; amino acids; energy in cookery. *Mailing Add:* Dept of Foods & Nutrit Univ of Man Winnipeg MB R3T 2N2 Can

VAISHNAV, RAMESH, b Jamnagar, India, Apr 2, 34; US citizen; m 64. SOFT TISSUE BIOMECHANICS, FRACTURE MECHANICS. *Educ:* Gujarat Univ, BSc, 52, BS, 55; Univ Mich, Ann Arbor, MSE, 58; Univ Ill, Urbana, PhD(theoret & appl mech), 61. *Prof Exp:* Div overseer, Irrig Proj Div, Pub Works Dept, India, 55-56; res asst soil mech, Univ Mich, Ann Arbor, 57-58; struct engr bridge design, Vogt, Ivers, Seaman & Assoc, Cincinnati, 58-59; from res asst to res assoc concrete res, Univ Ill, Urbana, 59-61; asst prof, 61-65, assoc prof, 65-70, PROF, CATHOLIC UNIV AM, 70- *Concurrent Pos:* Consult, Fairchild-Hiller Corp, & Goddard Space Flight Ctr, 65-68, Singer-Link Info Sci Co, 68-72; vis scientist, NIH, 67, guest worker, 67-80, consult & prin investr res grants, 71-; prin investr res grants, Nat Sci Found, 71- *Mem:* Am Acad Mech; Am Soc Mech Engrs; Soc Rheology; Cardiovasc Syst Dynamics Soc; Soc Biorheology. *Res:* Rheology of concrete; continuum mechanics: linear and nonlinear elasticity and viscoelasticity; theories of plates and shells; finite element methods; creep, fracture and fatigue of materials; biomechanics of soft tissue. *Mailing Add:* Dept Civil Eng Catholic Univ Am Washington DC 20064

VAISNYS, JUOZAS RIMVYDAS, b Kaunas, Lithuania, Mar 12, 37; US citizen. PHYSICAL CHEMISTRY. *Educ:* Yale Univ, BS, 56; Univ Calif, Berkeley, PhD(chem), 60. *Prof Exp:* ASSOC PROF APPL SCI, YALE UNIV, 67- *Mem:* Am Phys Soc; Sigma Xi; Asn Advan Baltic Studies; Am Chem Soc. *Res:* Evolution; ecology; biological dynamics. *Mailing Add:* Kline Geol Lab Yale Univ New Haven CT 06520

VAITKEVICIUS, VAINUTIS K, b Kaunas, Lithuania, Jan 12, 27; US citizen; m 51; c 6. ONCOLOGY. *Educ:* Univ Frankfurt, MD, 51. *Prof Exp:* Intern med, Grace Hosp, Detroit, 51-52, resident, 55-56; resident internal med, Detroit Gen Hosp, 56-58; assoc physician, Henry Ford Hosp, Detroit, 59-62; clin dir oncol, Detroit Inst Cancer Res, 62-66; from assoc prof to prof med & dir oncol, 66-73, PROF ONCOL & CHMN DEPT, SCH MED, WAYNE STATE UNIV, 73- *Concurrent Pos:* Fel cancer res, Detroit Inst Cancer Res, Mich, 58-59; consult, Detroit-Macomb Hosps Asn, Harper Hosp, Mt Carmel Mercy Hosp, Sinai Hosp & Vet Admin Hosp; clin dir, Comprehensive Cancer Ctr Detroit, 78- *Mem:* AAAS; Am Col Physicians; Am Asn Cancer Res; Am Asn Cancer Educ; Am Soc Hemat. *Res:* Mechanism of metastases; pharmacology of cytostatic drugs. *Mailing Add:* Dept of Oncol Wayne State Univ Sch of Med Detroit MI 48201

VAITUZIS, ZIGFRIDAS, medical microbiology, see previous edition

VAJK, J(OSEPH) PETER, b Budapest, Hungary, Aug 3, 42; US citizen; m 70; c 4. PHYSICS, SPACE INDUSTRIALIZATION. *Educ:* Cornell Univ, AB, 63; Princeton Univ, MA, 65, PhD(physics), 68. *Prof Exp:* Sr physicist, Lawrence Livermore Lab, Univ Calif, 68-76; consult, 76-79, SR SCIENTIST, SCI APPLNS INC, CALIF, 77- *Mem:* Am Phys Soc; Sigma Xi; Am Inst Aeronaut & Astronaut. *Res:* Relativistic astrophysics and cosmology; general relativity theory; evolution of relativistic cosmological models; theory of electromagnetic pulses from nuclear explosions; world dynamics; socioeconomic implications of space industrialization and colonization; space technology assessment; atmospheric photochemistry and dynamics modeling; alternative futures research. *Mailing Add:* Sci Appl Inc Suite 104 1811 Santa Rita Rd Pleasanton CA 94566

VAKILI, NADER GHOLI, b Bushir, Iran, Jan 14, 27; nat US; m 53; c 6. PLANT PATHOLOGY, PLANT GENETICS. *Educ:* Northwestern Univ, BS, 52; Univ Chicago, MS, 53; Purdue Univ, PhD, 58. *Prof Exp:* Pathologist, United Fruit Co, 58-65; asst plant pathologist, Everglades Exp Sta, Univ Fla, 65-67; area agron adv, US Agency Int Develop, US Dept Agr, 67-69; mem staff, 69-79, RRES PLANT PATHOLOGIST, IOWA STATE UNIV, USDA, 79- *Mem:* Am Phytopath Soc; Am Soc Agron; Am Inst Biol Sci; Sigma Xi. *Res:* Genetics of pathogenicity; taxonomy and genetics of disease resistance in musa; vegetable diseases. *Mailing Add:* Iowa State Univ 411 Bessey Hall Ames IA 50011

VAKILZADEH, JAVAD, b Esfahan, Iran, June 26, 27. PUBLIC HEALTH, EPIDEMIOLOGY. *Educ:* Sharaf Col, Iran, BS, 48; Univ Teheran, DVM, 52; Univ Pittsburgh, CPH, 58; Univ NC, MPH, 59. *Prof Exp:* Epidemiologist, Int Coop Admin, Iran, 53-57; res scientist, NC Sanitorium Syst, 59-63, from asst to actg dir res respiratory dis, 63-68; mem fac, Med Ctr, Duke Univ, 68-72; epidemiologist, Int Fertility Res Prog, Pop Ctr, Univ NC, Chapel Hill, 72-80. *Concurrent Pos:* Consult epidemiologist, Haitian-Am Tuberc Inst, 63- *Mem:* Fel Am Pub Health Asn; Am Vet Med Asn; Am Vet Epidemiol Soc. *Res:* Research and teaching of epidemiology; environmental health; communicable disease control. *Mailing Add:* 634 Kensington Dr Chapel Hill NC 27514

VALA, MARTIN THORVALD, JR, b Brooklyn, NY, Mar 28, 38; m 66; c 3. PHYSICAL CHEMISTRY, SPECTROCHEMISTRY. *Educ:* St Olaf Col, BA, 60; Univ Chicago, SM, 62, PhD(chem), 64. *Prof Exp:* NSF fel chem, Copenhagen Univ, 65-66; US-Japan Coop Sci Prog fel, Univ Nagoya, 66-67; asst prof, 68-72, assoc prof, 72-78, PROF CHEM, UNIV FLA, 78-

Concurrent Pos: Merck Found fel, 70-71; vis prof, Advan Sch Physics & Chem, 73-74; NATO fel, 73-74; Fulbright sr fel, Franco-Am Scholar Exchange Comn, 73-74; vis scientist, US-India Exchange Scientists Prog, India, 77; vis scientist, Univ Poznan, Poland, 81. *Mem:* Am Phys Soc; Am Chem Soc; Am Inst Chem; InterAm Photochem Soc. *Res:* Optical and magnetic properties of organic molecules and transition metal atoms, dimers and complexes. *Mailing Add:* Dept of Chem Univ of Fla Gainesville FL 32601

VALACH, MIROSLAV, b Hnusta, Czech, Sept 12, 26; US citizen; m 52; c 1. INFORMATION & COMPUTER SCIENCE. *Educ:* Prague Tech Univ, ME, 51; Czech Acad Sci, PhD(math & physics), 58. *Prof Exp:* Mgr peripheral equip, Res Inst Mach Mach, Czech, 51-64; consult engr, Gen Elec Co, Ariz, 65-69; prof into & computer sci, Ga Inst Technol, 69-74; res dir, Karsten Mfg Corp, 74-80; WITH FRIDAY COMPUT INC, 80- *Mem:* Asn Comput Mach; Inst Elec & Electronics Engrs. *Res:* Switching theory; cybernetics; artifical intelligence; computer hardware; linguistics. *Mailing Add:* Friday Comput Inc 2218 Old Middlefield Way No 2 Mountain View CA 94043

VALADARES, JOSEPH R E, pharmacology, biochemistry, see previous edition

VALANIS, BARBARA MAYLEAS, b Harrisburg, Pa, Oct 4, 42; m 78; c 1. EPIDEMIOLOGY. *Educ:* Cornell Univ, BS, 65; Columbia Univ, MEd, 71, DrPH(epidemiol), 75. *Prof Exp:* Dist nurse, Vis Nurse Serv of NY, 65-69; instr pub health nursing, Columbia Univ Sch of Nursing, 69-71; asst prof, Fairleigh Dickinson Univ, 72-73; res worker, Columbia Univ, 73-75, staff assoc, 75-77, res assoc epidemiol, 77-78; assoc prof, 78-80, PROF, COL NURSING & HEALTH, UNIV CINCINNATI, 80-, ASST PROF EPIDEMIOL, COL MED, 78- *Concurrent Pos:* Columbia Univ Cancer Res Ctr fel, 75-78; vpres & prog evaluation consult, Eval Assoc, Inc, 76-78. *Mem:* Am Pub Health Asn; Soc Epidemiol Res; Sigma Xi; Nat League Nursing. *Res:* Social epidemiology; cancer epidemiology; reproductive epidemiology; health services evaluation; stress; occupational exposures. *Mailing Add:* Col of Nursing & Health Univ of Concinnati Cincinnati OH 45221

VALASSI, KYRIAKE V, b Salonika, Greece, May 15, 17; US citizen. HYPERALIMENTATION NUTRITION ASSESSMENT. *Educ:* Syracuse Univ, BS, 50; Cornell Univ, MS, 51; Ore State Univ, PhD(nutrit & biochem), 56. *Prof Exp:* PROF NUTRIT, CATH UNIV AM, 56- *Concurrent Pos:* Consult, Off Int Res, 61-67, Pan Am Health Orgn, 72-74, Food & Drug Admin, 78, Nat Coun Dis Control, 67-74, Nutrit Cancer NIH, 79; lectr, Corner Univ, 68, Ore State Univ, 69. *Mem:* Am Dietetic Asn; Soc Nutrit Educ; Am Inst Nutrit; Am Soc Parental & Enteral Nutrit. *Res:* Assessment of nutritional status of population groups; dietary survey methodology and training in foreign countries; nutritional management of cancer patients in a variety of therapeutic regiments; enteral hyperalimentation to patients undergoing treatment for burns. *Mailing Add:* 2700 Virginia Ave NW 605 Washington DC 20037

VALBERG, LESLIE S, b Churchbridge, Sask, June 3, 30; m 54; c 3. MEDICINE. *Educ:* Queen's Univ, Ont, MD, 54, MSc, 58; FRCPS(C), 60. *Prof Exp:* Lectr med, Queen's Univ, Ont, 60-61; res assoc, Med Res Coun, Can, 61-65; from asst prof to prof med, Queen's Univ, Ont, 61-75; PROF MED & CHMN DEPT, UNIV WESTERN ONT, 75- *Concurrent Pos:* Consult, Univ Hosp, London, 75- *Mem:* Am Gastroenterol Asn; Am Fedn Clin Res; fel Am Col Physicians; fel Royal Col Physicians & Surgeons Can; Can Soc Clin Invest. *Res:* Iron metabolism; absorption of metals. *Mailing Add:* Dept of Med Univ Hosp Univ of Western Ont London ON N6A 5B8 Can

VALCARCE, ARLAND CASIANO, b Brigham City, Utah, Mar 11, 23; m 47; c 5. ENTOMOLOGY. *Educ:* Univ Utah, BS, 49; Utah State Univ, MS, 53. *Prof Exp:* Entomologist & supvr grasshopper control proj, USDA, 50-51, inspector, Plant Quarantine Div, 52-54, res entomologist, Entom Res Div, 54-62; entomologist, US Forest Serv, 62-80; CONSULT ENTOMOLOGIST, 80- *Res:* Insect and disease pest management on agricultural crops, forest and shade trees and ornamentals contracting. *Mailing Add:* 3473 Manchester St Boise ID 83704

VALDES-DAPENA, MARIE A, b Pottsville, Pa, July 14, 21; m 45; c 11. PEDIATRICS, PATHOLOGY. *Educ:* Immaculate Col, Pa, BS, 41; Temple Univ, MD, 44. *Prof Exp:* St Christopher's Hosp Children grant, 58-; instr, Grad Sch Med, Univ Pa, 48-55, vis lectr, 60-; consult pediat path, Div Med Exam, Dept Pub Health, Philadelphia, 67-70; mem, Perinatal Biol & Infant Mortality Res & Training Comt Nat Inst Child Health & Human Develop, 71-75; consult, Lankenau Hosp, Philadelphia, 71-76; consult & lectr, US Naval Hosp, Philadelphia, 72. *Concurrent Pos:* St Concurrent. *Mem:* Pediat Path Club; Int Acad Path; Path Soc Gt Brit & Ireland. *Res:* Causes of neonatal mortality; sudden unexpected death in infancy; gynecologic pathology in infancy and childhood; iatrogenic diseases in the perinatal period. *Mailing Add:* Dept Path (D-33) Univ Miami PO Box 016960 Miami FL 33101

VALDIVIESO, DARIO, b Fusagasuga, Colombia, Dec 12, 36; US citizen. MEDICAL MICROBIOLOGY, PARASITOLOGY. *Educ:* Univ Andes, Colombia, BS, 60, MS, 62; Univ PR Sch Med, PhD(med zool), 67. *Prof Exp:* Coordr biochem, Seneca Col, Toronto, 68-70; resident med microbiol, US Nat Ctr Dis Control, Atlanta, 70-72; instr microbiol, Univ Tex Sch Med, San Antonio, 72-73; RES ASSOC MAMMAL, ROYAL ONT MUS, 73-; INT TECH REP, GIBCO DIV, DEXTER CORP, OHIO, 81- *Concurrent Pos:* Specialist microbiologist pub health & med lab microbiol, Am Acad Microbiol, 74-; vis prof microbiol, Pontificia Univ Javeriana, Colombia, & Fulbright-Hays Latin Am teaching fel, 75-77. *Mem:* Am Soc Microbiologists; Am Soc Trop Med & Hyg. *Res:* Comparative biochemistry of proteins; microbiology of human pathogens; immunochemistry of human parasitic and mycotic diseases. *Mailing Add:* Gibco Div Dexter Corp PO Box 200 Chagrin Falls OH 44022

VALDSAAR, HERBERT, b Tallinn, Estonia, Dec 6, 25; nat US; m 59; c 2. HIGH TEMPERATURE CHEMISTRY. *Educ:* Aachen Tech Univ, Dipl, 50; Univ Maine, MS, 52; Univ Fla, PhD(chem), 56. *Prof Exp:* Res chemist, 56-71, SR RES CHEMIST, CHEMS & PIGMENTS DEPT, E I DU PONT DE NEMOURS & CO, INC, 71- *Mem:* Am Ceramic Soc. *Res:* High temperature inorganic reactions; preparation of high purity silicon; synthetic abrasives; new pigments; high temperature refractories; pigment coatings. *Mailing Add:* Exp Sta E I du Pont de Nemours & Co Inc Wilmington DE 19898

VALEGA, THOMAS MICHAEL, b Linden, NJ, May 23, 37; m 58; c 4. ORGANIC CHEMISTRY, DENTISTRY. *Educ:* Rutgers Univ, BS, 59, PhD(org chem), 63. *Prof Exp:* Chemist, Pesticide Chem Res Br, Entom Res Div, Agr Res Serv, USDA, 63-67; grants assoc, NIH, 67-68, health scientist adminr, Nat Inst Environ Health Sci, 68-69, coordr contracts artificial kidney-chronic uremia prog, Nat Inst Arthritis & Metab Dis, 69-72; prog analyst, Off Categorical Progs, Prog Planning & Eval, Environ Protection Agency, DC, 72; health scientist adminr, periodontal dis prog, 72-74, CHIEF RESTORATIVE MATERIALS PROG, EXTRAMURAL PROGS, NAT INST DENT RES, NIH, 74- *Mem:* Int Asn Dent Res; AAAS; Am Chem Soc; Nat Audubon Soc; Soc Biomaterials. *Res:* Peroxide and carbamate chemistry; insecticide and insecticide synergist chemistry; insect attractant and insect pheromone chemistry; medicinal chemistry; bioengineering; biomaterials; health sciences administration; oral biology; dental chemistry. *Mailing Add:* 19005 Willow Grove Rd Olney MD 20832

VALENCICH, TRINA J, b Long Beach, Calif, Feb 3, 43; c 1. PHYSICAL CHEMISTRY. *Educ:* Univ Calif, Irvine, BA, 68, PhD(chem), 74. *Prof Exp:* Adj asst prof chem, Univ Calif, Los Angeles, 73-76; asst prof, Tex A&M Univ, 76; ASST PROF CHEM, CALIF STATE UNIV, LOS ANGELES, 77- *Mem:* Am Chem Soc; Am Physics Soc. *Res:* Classical trajectory simulation of microscopic physical and chemical processes. *Mailing Add:* Dept of Chem Univ of Calif Los Angeles CA 90032

VALENSTEIN, ELLIOT SPIRO, b New York, NY, Dec 9, 23; m 47; c 2. NEUROSCIENCES, PSYCHOLOGY. *Educ:* City Col New York, BS, 49; Univ Kans, MA, 53, PhD(psychol), 54. *Prof Exp:* Asst anat & psychol, Univ Kans, 51, asst, Endocrinol Lab, 53-54, USPHS res fel anat, 54-55; chief lab neuropsychol, Walter Reed Army Inst Res, Walter Reed Army Med Ctr, 59-61; from assoc to prof psychol & sr res assoc, Fels Res Inst, Antioch Col, 61-70; PROF PSYCHOL, NEUROSCI LAB, UNIV MICH, ANN ARBOR, 70- *Concurrent Pos:* Mem, Exp Psychol Study Sect, Nat Sci Adv Bd, 64-66; vis prof, Univ Calif, Berkeley, 69-70; mem, Neurobiol Rev Panel, NSF, 71-72; mem, Exp Psychol Study Sect, NIH, 75-79; mem, Maternal & Child Health Res Comn, Nat Inst Child Health Develop, 80-; Kenneth Craik res award, Cambrige Univ, 80-81. *Mem:* Fel AAAS; fel Am Psychol Asn (pres, Div Comp & Physiol Psychol, 75-76); Int Brain Res Orgn; NY Acad Sci; Soc Exp Psychol. *Res:* Hormones and behavior; development of behavioral capacities; physiological and comparative psychology; nervous system and motivation. *Mailing Add:* Neurosci Lab Univ Mich Ann Arbor MI 48104

VALENTA, LUBOMIR JAN-VACLAV, b Czech, Feb 29, 32; m 70; c 1. MEDICINE, ENDOCRINOLOGY. *Educ:* Col Podebrady, BS, 50; Charles Univ, Prague, MD, 56, PhD(biochem), 66. *Prof Exp:* Instr surg, Univ Kosica, Czech, 56-57; family pract, Health Ctr Revuca & Kladno, 57-62; investr endocrinol, Res Inst Endocrinol, Prague, 62-68; assoc prof med, Sch Med, Mich State Univ, 72-74; assoc prof med, 75-78, PROF PHYSIOL & BIOL SCI, UNIV CALIF, IRVINE, 78-, HEAD DIV ENDOCRINOL, DEPT MED, 75- *Concurrent Pos:* Fels, Hosp Nestle & Univ Lausanne, 68-69, Univ Marseille, 69-71 & Mass Gen Hosp & Harvard Med Sch, 71-72; adv, Great Soviet Encycl, 73-; reviewer, J Clin Endocrinol & Metab, 73-; mem adv bd, J Cancer, 73- *Mem:* Am Dermat Asn; AMA; Am Thyroid Asn; Endocrine Soc. *Res:* Mechanism of hormone action; structure-function relationship of protein hormones. *Mailing Add:* Dept of Med Div of Endocrinol Univ of Calif Irvine CA 92668

VALENTA, ZDENEK, b Havlickuv Brod, Czech, June 14, 27; Can citizen; m 57; c 3. ORGANIC CHEMISTRY. *Educ:* Swiss Fed Inst Technol, Dipl Ing Chem, 50; Univ NB, MSc, 52, PhD(chem), 53. *Prof Exp:* Spec lectr chem, Univ NB, 53-54, lectr, 54-56; Univ NB fel & res assoc, Harvard Univ, 56-57; from asst prof to assoc prof chem, 57-63, chmn dept, 63-72, PROF CHEM, UNIV NB, 63- *Honors & Awards:* Merck, Sharp & Dohme Lect Award, Chem Inst Can, 67. *Mem:* Chem Inst Can; fel Royal Soc Can. *Res:* Total synthesis of organic molecules of biological and pharmaceutical interest; study of organic reactions and stereochemistry. *Mailing Add:* Dept of Chem Univ of NB Fredericton NB E3B 6E2 Can

VALENTE, FRANK ANTHONY, b Padula, Italy, Jan 22, 99; nat US; m 26. REACTOR PHYSICS, NUCLEAR PHYSICS. *Educ:* NY Univ, BS, 22, MS, 24, PhD(nuclear physics), 39. *Prof Exp:* Instr physics, NY Univ, 24-25; instr, High Sch, NY, 25-26; asst physicist, Picatinny Arsenal, US Dept War, 26-28 & Nat Bur Standards, 28-30; physicist, Devoe & Raynolds Co, 30; res physicist, Westinghouse Elec & Mfg Co, 30-31; physicist, Socony-Vacuum Oil Co, Inc, 31-42; asst officer in charge crystal br, Signal Lab, US Army, NJ, 42-43, asst opers officer, Manhattan Dist, Chicago, 43 & Clinton Lab, Tenn, 43-44, chief prod units, Manhattan Dist, Hanford Eng Works, 44-47; chief nuclear energy div, Cent Intel Agency, 54-56; prof physics, Rensselaer Polytech Inst, 56-60, prof nuclear eng & sci, 60-65, dir sub-critical reactor lab, 57-66; prof physics, 66-72, EMER PROF PHYSICS, SEATTLE UNIV, 72-, DIR NUCLEAR FACILITY, 74-; EMER PROF NUCLEAR ENG & SCI, RENSSELAER POLYTECH INST, 65- *Concurrent Pos:* Mem staff tech dir, Oper Sandstone, 48, Oper Greenhouse, Eniwetok Atoll & Oper Ranger, Nev, 51; lectr, Georgetown Univ, 47-56; mem vis comt, NY Univ Col Eng, 54-57; consult, US Govt, 56-66. *Mem:* Fel AAAS; fel Am Phys Soc; Am Nuclear Soc; NY Acad Sci. *Res:* Formation of long range detection system of nuclear explosion; calorimetry of propellants; spectroscopy; electricity and magnetism; rheology; x-rays; heat transfer; nuclear reactors of both the fusion and fission types. *Mailing Add:* 10240 SE 13th Pl Bellevue WA 98004

VALENTEKOVICH, MARIJA NIKOLETIC, b Dubrovnik, Yugoslavia, Feb 5, 32; m 62; c 2. CHEMISTRY. *Educ:* Univ Zagreb, MSChE, 57, PhD(chem), 63. *Prof Exp:* Res assoc, Rudjer Boskovic Inst, Zagreb, Yugoslavia, 57-65; fel & res assoc, Radiocarbon Lab, Univ Ill, Urbana, 65-67 & Univ Southern Calif, 67-68; sr chemist, Cyclo Chem Co, 68-69, dir qual control, 69-73; head dept radioisotopes, Curtis Nuclear Co, 73-74; dir qual control, Nichols Inst, 74-76, dir radiochem, 76-79; PRIN DEVELOP CHEMIST, BECKMAN INSTRUMENT INC, 79- *Mem:* Am Chem Soc; Am Soc Clin Chem; Clin Radioassay Soc. *Res:* Clinical diagnostics, particularly radioimmunoassays; radiolabelling of peptides and hormones; development and evaluation of new immunoassay techniques. *Mailing Add:* 33 Silver Spring Dr Rolling Hills Estates CA 90274

VALENTINE, BARRY DEAN, b New York, NY, June 6, 24; m 53; c 2. ENTOMOLOGY, HERPETOLOGY. *Educ:* Univ Ala, BS, 51, MS, 54; Cornell Univ, PhD(entom), 60. *Prof Exp:* Asst prof biol, Miss Southern Col, 55-57, actg head dept, 57; from asst prof to assoc prof zool & entom, 60-74, PROF ZOOL, OHIO STATE UNIV, 74- *Concurrent Pos:* Consult, Standard Fruit Co, 56, Lerner Marine Lab, Am Mus Natural Hist, 65, Dames & Moore Inc, 72 & US Army Corps Engr, 72 & Rockefeller Brothers Fund, 78; entomologist zool expeds, Haiti & Jamaica, 56, Cent Am, 56, Mexico, 59, Bahama Islands, 65 & 72, Kenya & Tanzania, 71, 74 & 75; Entom Soc Am travel grant, London, Eng, 64; Ohio State Univ develop fund travel grant, London, Copenhagen, Stockholm & Paris, 70. *Mem:* Entom Soc Am; Am Soc Ichthyologists & Herpetologists; Soc Study Amphibians & Reptiles. *Res:* Theory and practice of systematics and zoogeography, especially the weevil family Anthribidae of the world and salamanders of Eastern United States; comparative grooming behavior of arthropods. *Mailing Add:* Dept of Zool Ohio State Univ Columbus OH 43210

VALENTINE, BOB LEON, b Dry Prong, La, Feb 5, 29; m 55; c 2. MEDICAL MICROBIOLOGY, BIOCHEMISTRY. *Educ:* La Col, BA, 54; La State Univ, MS, 56; Purdue Univ, PhD(microbiol), 63. *Prof Exp:* Clin lab technologist, Baptist Hosp, 46-47 & Murrells Clin Hosp, 51-53; res asst microbiol, La State Univ, 53-56; microbiologist, US Govt, 56-57 & Miles Labs, Inc, 57-61; Instr microbiol, Purdue Univ, 61-63; assoc prof, Miss State Univ, 63-67; DIR BIOL SAFETY, SHERWOOD MED INDUSTS, INC, 67- *Concurrent Pos:* Consult poultry & cattle indust, Miss State Univ, 64-67. *Mem:* AAAS; Am Soc Microbiol. *Res:* Diseases of animals and humans; safety of medical devices. *Mailing Add:* Sherwood Med Industs Inc 11802 Westline Industrial Dr St Louis MO 63141

VALENTINE, DONALD H, JR, b Orange, NJ, Nov 7, 40; m 66. ORGANOMETALLIC CHEMISTRY, PHOTOCHEMISTRY. *Educ:* Wesleyan Univ, BA, 62; Calif Inst Technol, PhD(photochem), 66. *Prof Exp:* NSF fel, Stanford Univ, 65-66; asst prof chem, Princeton Univ, 66-71; sr chemist, Hoffmann-La Roche Inc, 71-74, res fel, 74, group chief, 75-80; WITH CATALYTICA ASSOC, 80- *Concurrent Pos:* Lectr, Bell Tel Labs, 70-71; lectr, Exten Div, Rutgers Univ, 72 & 76; ed, Molecular Photochem, 72-77. *Res:* Redox reactions; spectroscopy; homogeneous catalysis; asymmetric synthesis. *Mailing Add:* Catalytica Assoc 3255 Scott Blvd Suite 7E Santa Clara CA 95051

VALENTINE, FORREST THERRILL, b Laurel, Miss, Dec 4, 36; m 58; c 4. ELECTRICAL ENGINEERING, COMPUTER SCIENCE. *Educ:* Miss State Univ, BS, 57; Univ Miss, MS, 62; Tex A&M Univ, PhD(elec eng), 65. *Prof Exp:* Engr, Chance Vought Aircraft, Tex, 57-60; asst prof elec eng, Univ Miss, 60-63; mem tech staff & mgr comput systs, Serv Group, 66-76, MEM TECH STAFF, EQUIP GROUP, TEX INSTRUMENTS, 76- *Mem:* Inst Elec & Electronics Engrs; Soc Explor Geophysicists. *Res:* Large scale computer systems including interactive computer graphics and their use in geophysics; computer systems including microprocessor based and distributed systems. *Mailing Add:* Tex Instruments Inc 13500 N Central Exp PO Box 6015 Dallas TX 75222

VALENTINE, FRANK ROSSITER, b Woodbridge, NJ, Dec 6, 15; m 40; c 2. ORGANIC CHEMISTRY. *Educ:* Yale Univ, BS, 37, PhD(org chem), 41. *Prof Exp:* Asst chem, Rutgers Univ, 37-38 & Yale Univ, 38-41; res chemist, Naugatuck Chem Div, US Rubber Co, 41-48; chemist, Homosote Co, Trenton, 79-60, tech dir, 60-81; RETIRED. *Concurrent Pos:* Consult, 81- *Mem:* Am Chem Soc; Tech Asn Pulp & Paper Indust. *Res:* Sterols of sponges; agricultural and rubber chemicals; process research in resins; diarylamine carbonates as rubber antioxidants. *Mailing Add:* Fiddlers Creek Rd Titusville NJ 08560

VALENTINE, FRED TOWNSEND, b Detroit, Mich, Sept 1, 34; m 64; c 2. IMMUNOLOGY, INFECTIOUS DISEASES. *Educ:* Harvard Univ, AB, 56, MD, 60. *Prof Exp:* Asst prof, 69-75, ASSOC PROF MED, SCH MED, NY UNIV, 75- *Concurrent Pos:* Attend med, Manhattan Vet Admin Hosp, 70-; assoc attend med, Univ Hosp & assoc attend physician, Bellevue Hosp, New York, 76- *Mem:* Am Asn Immunologists; Infectious Dis Soc Am; Transplant Soc; Harvey Soc. *Res:* Cellular immunology, immunological defenses against infectious agents and against neoplasia. *Mailing Add:* Dept of Med Sch of Med NY Univ 550 First Ave New York NY 10016

VALENTINE, FREDRICK ARTHUR, b Detroit Lakes, Minn, June 26, 26; m 66; c 3. FOREST GENETICS. *Educ:* St Cloud State Teachers Col, BS, 49; Univ Wis, MS, 53, PhD(genetics), 57. *Prof Exp:* Instr genetics, Univ Wis, 54-56; from asst prof to assoc prof forest bot, 56-69, PROF ENVIRON & FOREST BIOL, STATE UNIV NY COL ENVIRON SCI & FORESTRY, 69- *Mem:* Genetics Soc Am; Am Genetic Asn. *Res:* Genetic control of growth and wood properties in Populus tremuloides, the genetics of Hypoxylon mammatum susceptibility to canker in Populus spp; genetics of resistance to verticillium wilt in urban maple trees. *Mailing Add:* Dept Environ & Forest Biol State Univ NY Col Env Sci & For Syracuse NY 13210

VALENTINE, JAMES WILLIAM, b Los Angeles, Calif, Nov 10, 26; m 57; c 2. GEOLOGY. *Educ:* Phillips Univ, BA, 51; Univ Calif, Los Angeles, MA, 54, PhD(geol), 58. *Prof Exp:* Asst geol, Univ Calif, Los Angeles, 52-55, asst geophys, 57-58; from asst prof to assoc prof geol, Univ Mo, 58-64; assoc prof, Univ Calif, Davis, 64-68, prof geol, 68-77; PROF GEOL SCI, UNIV CALIF, SANTA BARBARA, 77- *Concurrent Pos:* Fulbright res scholar, Australia, 62-63; Guggenheim fel. *Mem:* AAAS; Geol Soc Am; Ecol Soc Am; Paleont Soc (pres, 73-74); Soc Econ Paleont & Mineral. *Res:* Evolutionary paleoecology. *Mailing Add:* Dept of Geol Sci Univ of Calif Santa Barbara CA 93106

VALENTINE, JIMMIE LLOYD, b Shreveport, La, Oct 18, 40; m 63; c 3. PHARMACOLOGY. *Educ:* Centenary Col La, BS, 62 & 64; Univ Miss, MS, 66, PhD(med chem), 68. *Prof Exp:* Sr scientist med chem, Mallinckrodt Pharmaceut, 68-73; asst prof, Univ Mo, Kansas City, 73-78; ASSOC PROF PHARMACOL, ORAL ROBERTS UNIV, 78- *Concurrent Pos:* Consult to various pvt & pub orgn, 73-; adj prof, Univ Mo, 78- *Mem:* Am Chem Soc; Am Pharmaceut Asn; Am Soc Mass Spectrometry; AAAS; Am Soc Pharmacol & Exp Therapeut. *Res:* Analysis of physiological specimens; human breath analysis; drug effects on endocrine function; laser analysis of drugs and physiological fluids; gas liquid chromatography and high pressure liquid chromatography-mass spectrometry of physiological fluids; alcoholism. *Mailing Add:* Dept of Pharmacol Oral Roberts Univ Tulsa OK 74171

VALENTINE, JOAN SELVERSTONE, b Auburn, Calif, Mar 15, 45. BIOINORGANIC CHEMISTRY, INORGANIC CHEMISTRY. *Educ:* Smith Col, AB, 67; Princeton Univ, PhD(chem), 71. *Prof Exp:* Instr chem, Princeton Univ, 71-72; from asst prof to assoc prof chem, Douglass Col, Rutgers Univ, New Brunswick, 72-80; assoc prof, 80-81, PROF CHEM, UNIV CALIF, LOS ANGELES, 81- *Mem:* Am Chem Soc; Biophys Soc; Royal Soc Chem; AAAS. *Res:* Synthesis of models for metal-containing biological materials; bioinorganic chemistry of oxygen and superoxide. *Mailing Add:* Univ Calif 405 Hilgard Ave Los Angeles CA 90024

VALENTINE, JOSEPH EARL, b Kansas City, Kans, Apr 6, 33; m 55; c 2. MATHEMATICS. *Educ:* Southwest Mo State Col, BSEd, 58; Univ Ill, Urbana, MS, 60; Univ Mo-Columbia, PhD(distance geom), 67. *Prof Exp:* Teacher high sch, Ill, 58-59; teacher & prin high sch, Mo, 60-61; from instr to asst prof math, Southwest Mo State Col, 61-68; asst prof, 68-70, assoc prof math, Utah State Univ, 70-77, PROF MATH, UNIV TEX, SAN ANTONIO, 77- *Concurrent Pos:* Fulbright fel, Univ Jordan, 71-72. *Mem:* Am Math Soc; Math Asn Am. *Res:* Distance geometry; non-euclidean geometry. *Mailing Add:* Dept of Math, Comput Sci & Univ of Tex San Antonio TX 78282

VALENTINE, MARTIN DOUGLAS, b Greenwich, Conn, Apr 13, 35; m 57; c 4. ALLERGY, CLINICAL IMMUNOLOGY. *Educ:* Union Col, BS, 56; Tufts Univ, MD, 60; Am Bd Internal Med, cert, 72; Am Bd Allergy & Immunol, cert, 74. *Prof Exp:* Instr, Sch Med, Harvard Univ, 68-70; asst prof, 70-76, ASSOC PROF, SCH MED, JOHNS HOPKINS UNIV, 76- *Concurrent Pos:* Staff physician allergy, Lahey Clin Found, Boston, 68-70; physician allergy, Lahey Clin Found, Boston, 68-70; physician allergy, Johns Hopkins Hosp & Good Samaritan Hosp, Baltimore, 70-; chmn comt insects, Am Acad Allergy, 75-77, chmn res coun, 77-80; chmn study group hymenotera venoms, Nat Inst Allergy & Infectious Dis, 77- *Mem:* Am Acad Allergy; Am Asn Immunologists; Am Soc Internal Med; Am Thoracic Soc. *Res:* Mechanisms of immediate hypersensitivity reactions; allergy to hymeroptera venoms. *Mailing Add:* 5601 Loch Raven Blvd Baltimore MD 21239

VALENTINE, RAYMOND CARLYLE, b Piatt Co, Ill, Sept 20, 36; m 58; c 1. BIOCHEMISTRY. *Educ:* Univ Ill, Urbana, BS, 58, MS, 60, PhD(microbiol), 62. *Prof Exp:* Asst microbiol, Univ Ill, Urbana, 58-62; fel, Rockefeller Inst, 62-64; asst prof biochem, Univ Calif, Berkeley, 64-70; asst prof in residence microbial biochem, Univ Calif, San Diego, 72-74; mem staff, 74-77, ASSOC PROF PLANT GROWTH LAB, UNIV CALIF, DAVIS, 77- *Mem:* Am Soc Microbiol; fel Am Soc Biol Chemists. *Res:* Nitrogen fixation; ferredoxin; microbial biochemistry and genetics. *Mailing Add:* Plant Growth Lab Univ of Calif Davis CA 95616

VALENTINE, WILLIAM NEWTON, b Kans City, Mo, Sept 29, 17; m 40; c 3. MEDICINE. *Educ:* Tulane Univ, MD, 42; Am Bd Internal Med, dipl, 49. *Prof Exp:* Intern med, Strong Mem Hosp, Rochester, NY, 42-43, asst resident, 43, chief resident, 43-44; instr, Sch Med, Univ Rochester, 47-48, head sect hemat, AEC Proj, 47-53; asst clin prof, 49-50, from asst prof to assoc prof, 50-57, chmn dept, 63-71, PROF MED, SCH MED, UNIV CALIF, LOS ANGELES, 57- *Concurrent Pos:* Assoc, St John's Hosp, Santa Monica, Calif, 47, hon consult, 52; sr attend, Harbor Hosp, Torrance, 50; consult, AEC Proj, 53; consult, Hemat Study Sect, NIH, 55-58, mem coun, Inst Arthritis & Metab Dis, 66-70; mem, Am Bd Internal Med, 64-67. *Mem:* Nat Acad Sci; AAAS; Am Soc Clin Invest; Asn Am Physicians; master Am Col Physicians. *Res:* Hematology. *Mailing Add:* Dept of Med Univ of Calif Ctr for Health Sci Los Angeles CA 90024

VALENTINI, JAMES JOSEPH, b Martins Ferry, Ohio, Mar 20, 50; m 81. CHEMICAL DYNAMICS, ATOMIC & MOLECULAR PHYSICS. *Educ:* Univ Pittsburgh, BS, 72; Univ Chicago, MS, 73; Univ Calif, Berkeley, PhD(chem), 76. *Prof Exp:* Chaim Weizmann fel, Harvard Univ, 77-78; J Robert Oppenheimer fel, 78-80, STAFF MEM, LOS ALAMOS NAT LAB, 80- *Mem:* Am Phys Soc; Sigma Xi; Am Chem Soc; AAAS. *Res:* Chemical dynamics; experimental studies employing molecular beam and laser spectroscopic methods. *Mailing Add:* CNC-2 MS-732 Los Alamos Sci Lab Los Alamos NM 87545

VALENTY, STEVEN JEFFREY, b Minneapolis, Minn, May 28, 44; m 69; c 2. POLYMER SURFACE CHEMISTRY, PHOTOCHEMISTRY. *Educ:* Lewis Col, BA, 66; Pa State Univ, PhD(org chem), 71. *Prof Exp:* Fel, Royal Inst London, 71-72; STAFF SCIENTIST, CORP RES & DEVELOP CTR, GEN ELEC CO, NY, 72- *Mem:* Am Chem Soc; AAAS. *Res:* Design and develop new materials and processes using the theory and tools of polymer surface science. *Mailing Add:* Corp Res & Develop Ctr Gen Elec Co PO Box 8 Schenectady NY 12301

VALENTY, VIVIAN BRIONES, b Tarlac, Philippines, Dec 15, 44; US citizen; m 69; c 2. ORGANIC CHEMISTRY. *Educ:* Mapua Inst Technol, BS, 64; Pa State Univ, PhD(chem), 71. *Prof Exp:* Res asst cereal chem, Int Rice Res Inst, 64-66; asst prof chem, Skidmore Col, 75-77; res assoc, Div Labs & Res, NY State Dept Health, 77-81; RES CHEMIST, A E STALEY MFG CO, 81- *Mem:* Am Chem Soc; Sigma Xi; AAAS. *Res:* Organic chemistry applied to biomolecules; chemicals from carbohydrates. *Mailing Add:* Res & Develop Div A E Staley Mfg Co Decatur IL 62525

VALENZENO, DENNIS PAUL, b Cleveland, Ohio, June 15, 49; m 72; c 2. MEMBRANE BIOPHYSICS, PHOTOSENSITIZATION. *Educ:* Case Western Reserve Univ, BS, 71, MS, 75, PhD(physiol), 76. *Prof Exp:* NIH fel, Emory Univ, 76-80; ASST PROF PHYSIOL, UNIV KANS MED CTR, 80- *Concurrent Pos:* Porter vis lectr, Spelman Col, 78-79; instr, Emory Univ, 79-80; prin investr, Am Heart Asn, 80. *Mem:* Am Soc Photobiol; Biophys Soc. *Res:* Membrane biophysics in nerve axons and red blood cells, particularly sensitization of membrane functions to visible light by photosensitizing dyes. *Mailing Add:* Dept Physiol Univ Kans Med Ctr 39th Rainbow Blvd Kansas City KS 66103

VALENZUELA, GASPAR RODOLFO, b Coelemu, Chile, Jan 6, 33; US citizen; m 58; c 2. THEORETICAL PHYSICS, ENGINEERING. *Educ:* Univ Fla, BSEE, 54, MSE, 55; Johns Hopkins Univ, DrEng, 65. *Prof Exp:* Assoc eng, Westinghouse Elec Corp, Md, 55-57; sr staff assoc, Appl Physics Lab, Johns Hopkins Univ, 57-59, res staff asst, Carlyle Barton, 59-64, mem sr res staff, Appl Physics Lab, 64-68; RES ELECTRONIC ENGR, NAVAL RES LAB, WASHINGTON, DC, 68- *Concurrent Pos:* Mem, Inter-Union Comn Radio Meteorol, 78- *Mem:* Sr mem Inst Elec & Electronics Engrs; Am Geophys Union; Am Meteorol Soc; Int Union Radio Sci. *Res:* Electromagnetic theory; rough surface scattering; interaction of electromagnetic waves with ocean; oceanography; nonlinear interactions in geophysics; hydrodynamics; wave dynamics; radio-oceanography; remote sensing. *Mailing Add:* 10132 Spring Pools Lane Columbia MD 21044

VALEO, ERNEST JOHN, b New London, Conn, Aug 6, 45; m 70; c 3. PLASMA PHYSICS. *Educ:* Rensselaer Polytech Inst, BS, 67; Princeton Univ, MA, 69, PhD(astrophys sci), 71. *Prof Exp:* Res asst plasma physics lab, Princeton Univ, 72-73; physicist, Lawrence Livermore Lab 73-76; RES PHYSICIST, PLASMA PHYSICS LAB, PRINCETON UNIV, 77- *Concurrent Pos:* Consult, Lab Laser Energetics, Univ Rochester, 77- & Lawrence Livermore Lab, Univ Calif, 77- *Mem:* Am Phys Soc. *Res:* Theoretical plasma physics, especially as related to controlled thermonuclear fusion research. *Mailing Add:* Plasma Physics Lab PO 451 Princeton NJ 08544

VALERINO, DONALD MATTHEW, b Syracuse, NY, June 23, 41; m 63; c 2. PHARMACOLOGY, TOXICOLOGY. *Educ:* Rensselaer Polytech Inst, BS, 63; Univ Vt, PhD(pharmacol), 70. *Prof Exp:* Res asst pharmacol, Hazelton Labs, 63-65; asst prof pharmacol, Hershey Med Sch, Pa State Univ, 72-75; criteria mgr & pharmacologist, Nat Inst Occup Safety & Health, 75-79; pres, Vale-Am Corp, 79-80; SR INDUST HYG-TOXICOLOGIST, NY STATE DEPT LABOR, 81- *Concurrent Pos:* Staff fel, Nat Cancer Inst, 70-72; consult, Paul deHaen Co, 71-72. *Res:* Biochemical pharmacology-metabolism of antitumor drugs, pargyline and nitrogen heterocycles, studies of microsomal enzyme induction, toxicology of drug metabolites, criteria document preparation and development of health standards. *Mailing Add:* Bldg 12 Rm 213 State Campus NY State Dept Labor Albany NY 12240

VALERIOTE, FREDERICK AUGUSTUS, b Montreal, Que, May 19, 41; m 66; c 3. BIOPHYSICS. *Educ:* Univ Toronto, BSc, 62, MA, 64, PhD(med biophys), 66. *Prof Exp:* Can Cancer Soc fel, Ont Cancer Inst, 66-67; Med Res Coun Can fel, NIH, 67-68, USPHS vis fel, 68-69; assoc prof, 69-76, PROF RADIOL, EDWARD MALLINCKRODT INST RADIOL, MED SCH, WASHINGTON UNIV, 69-, ASSOC DIR, DEPT RADIATION ONCOL, 76- *Concurrent Pos:* Mem ed bd, Cell & Tissue Kinetics. *Mem:* Am Asn Cancer Res; Cell Kinetics Soc (pres); Am Asn Cancer Educ. *Res:* Cancer research; experimental cancer chemotherapy; cell population kinetics. *Mailing Add:* 3621 Juniata St Louis MO 63116

VALERO, FRANCISCO PEDRO JORGE, b Cordoba, Arg, Mar 12, 36; US citizen; m 62; c 3. ATOMIC SPECTROSCOPY, MOLECULAR SPECTROSCOPY. *Educ:* Univ La Plata, Arg, Licenciado, 60, PhD(physics), 65. *Prof Exp:* Instr physics, Univ La Plata, Arg, 60-66, assoc prof, 66-67; resident res assoc, Nat Acad Sci, 68-69; SR SCIENTIST PHYSICS, AMES RES CTR, NASA, 69- *Concurrent Pos:* Res assoc, Nat Acad Sci-Nat Res Coun, 68-69; mem comt on line spectra elements, Nat Acad Sci, 71-76. *Mem:* Optical Soc Am. *Res:* Spectra of neutral and highly ionized elements; spectra of laser generated plasmas; molecular spectroscopy of astrophysical interest; atmospheric radiometry and physics. *Mailing Add:* Ames Res Ctr NASA Moffett Field CA 94035

VALI, GABOR, b Budapest, Hungary, Oct 22, 36; US citizen; m 56; c 3. ATMOSPHERIC PHYSICS. *Educ:* Sir George Williams Univ, BSc, 61; McGill Univ, MSc, 64, PhD(physics), 68. *Prof Exp:* Lectr agr physics, Macdonald Col, McGill Univ, 65-68, asst prof, 68-69; asst prof atmospheric sci, 69-72, assoc prof, 72-76, PROF ATMOSPHERIC SCI, UNIV WYO, 76- *Mem:* Am Meteorol Soc; Am Asn Physics Teachers. *Res:* Mechanisms and the role of ice nucleation in the atmosphere; development of ice elements in clouds; physics of precipitation; weather modification; atmospheric aerosols; human impact; weather modification. *Mailing Add:* Univ Wyo Dept Atmospheric Sci PO Box 3038 University Sta Laramie WY 82070

VALIAVEEDAN, GEORGE DEVASIA, b Erattupetta, India, Mar 29, 32; m 65; c 2. ORGANIC CHEMISTRY. *Educ:* Univ Madras, BSc, 52; Georgetown Univ, MS, 60, PhD(org chem), 62. *Prof Exp:* Lab instr chem, St Joseph's Col, India, 52-53; high sch teacher, Ceylon, 54-55; instr, St Sylvester's Jr Col, 56-57; res asst steroid & carbohydrate chem, Georgetown Univ, 60-62; res fel, Sch Chem, Univ Minn, Minneapolis, 62-65; res chemist, 65-74, SR RES CHEMIST, PHOTO PROD DEPT, E I DU PONT DE NEMOURS & CO, INC, PARLIN, 74- *Mem:* Am Chem Soc. *Res:* Steroids; carbohydrates; microbial metabolites; aromatic hydrocarbons; polymer chemistry; dyes and pigments; photochemistry; photographic processes. *Mailing Add:* 9 Coventry Dr Freehold NJ 07728

VALISALO, PAAVO EMIL, b Viipuri, Finland, May 20, 16; US citizen; m 40; c 3. COMPUTER SCIENCE, INDUSTRIAL ENGINEERING. *Educ:* Finnish Inst Technol, dipl eng, 44, Techn lic, 69; Helsinki Tech Univ, Finland, PhD(hybrid simulation), 73. *Prof Exp:* Tech mgr & plant indust engr, Finland, 43-47; managing dir knitwear factory, 46-57; consult engr, 57-59; rep, European exporters, Fla, 59-61; asst prof indust & systs eng, 61-70, ASSOC PROF INDUST & SYSTS ENG, UNIV FLA, 70- *Concurrent Pos:* Independent mach designer & consult, Finland, 47-51; mgt consult, Rastor Oy, 57-59. *Mem:* Sr mem Am Inst Indust Engrs; sr mem Simulation Coun; sr mem Eng Soc Finland; sr mem Int Asn Analogue Comput. *Res:* Hybrid computer simulation of stochastic processes; generation of random time series; adaptive optimization techniques of power systems in a hybrid computer. *Mailing Add:* Dept of Indust & Systs Eng Univ of Fla Gainesville FL 32611

VALK, HENRY SNOWDEN, b Washington, DC, Jan 26, 29. THEORETICAL NUCLEAR PHYSICS. *Educ:* George Washington Univ, BS, 53, MS, 54; Wash Univ, PhD(physics), 57. *Prof Exp:* Asst, Wash Univ, 54-56; asst prof physics, Univ Ore, 57-59; asst prog dir physics, NSF, 59-60; from asst prof to prof physics, Univ Nebr, Lincoln, 60-70, chmn dept, 66-70; DEAN, COL SCI & LIBERAL STUDIES, GA INST TECHNOL, 70- *Concurrent Pos:* Prog dir theoret physics, NSF, 65-66; vis prof, Univ Frankfurt, 70. *Mem:* Fel Am Phys Soc; Am Math Soc; Am Asn Physics Teachers; Math Asn Am. *Res:* College administration. *Mailing Add:* Col Sci & Liberal Studies Ga Inst Technol Atlanta GA 30332

VALK, WILLIAM LOWELL, b Muskegon, Mich, Aug 23, 09; m 37; c 2. SURGERY. *Educ:* Univ Mich, AB, 34, MD, 37. *Prof Exp:* Instr surg, Med Sch, Univ Mich, 40-43; assoc prof, 46-47, PROF SURG, UNIV KANS MED CTR, 47- *Mem:* Soc Univ Surg; Clin Soc Genito-Urinary Surg; Am Surg Asn; Am Urol Asn; AMA. *Res:* Urological surgery; physiology of kidney. *Mailing Add:* 5401 W 81st Prairie Village KS 66208

VALLABHAN, C V GIRIJA, b Trichur, India, May 24, 35; m 61; c 3. CIVIL ENGINEERING, ENGINEERING MECHANICS. *Educ:* Univ Kerala, BSc, 57; Univ Mo-Rolla, MS, 60; Univ Tex, Austin, PhD(civil eng), 67. *Prof Exp:* Jr engr, Kerala Pub Works Dept, India, 57; lectr civil eng, Eng Col, Trichur, India, 58-59, asst prof, 60-64; asst prof, 66-76, assoc prof, 76-80, PROF CIVIL ENG, TEX TECH UNIV, 80- *Mem:* Am Soc Civil Engrs. *Res:* Finite element technique for solving elasticity and plasticity problems in structural and soil mechanics; deterministic and probabilistic analysis of soil-structure interaction problems. *Mailing Add:* Dept of Civil Eng Tex Tech Univ Lubbock TX 79409

VALLBONA, CARLOS, b Barcelona, Spain, July 29, 27; m 56; c 4. PEDIATRICS, COMMUNITY MEDICINE. *Educ:* Univ Barcelona, BA & BS, 44, MD, 50. *Prof Exp:* Physician, Sch Child Health, Spain, 51-52; intern & resident, Sch Med, Univ Louisville, 53-55; from instr to assoc prof pediat & physiol, 56-67, from instr to assoc prof rehab, 57-67, PROF REHAB, BAYLOR COL MED, 67-, PROF & CHMN DEPT COMMUNITY MED, 69-; CHIEF COMMUN MED SERV, HARRIS COUNTY HOSP DIST, 69- *Concurrent Pos:* Fel, Children's Int Ctr, Univ Paris, 52-53; consult, Nat Heart, Lung & Blood Inst, Nat Ctr Health Servs Res, Nat Ctr Health Care Technol, Nat Ctr Health Statist & Off Health Resources Opportunity. *Mem:* AAAS; Soc Pediat Res; Am Col Chest Physicians; Am Cong Rehab Med; AMA. *Res:* Pediatric rehabilitation; cardiorespiratory physiology in disabled persons and the newborn; application of electronic data processing techniques in health care; rehabilitation community medicine; community medicine; prevention of hypertension. *Mailing Add:* Dept of Community Med Baylor Col of Med Houston TX 77030

VALLEAU, JOHN PHILIP, b Toronto, Ont, Jan 17, 32; m 57; c 2. STATISTICAL MECHANICS, CHEMICAL PHYSICS. *Educ:* Univ Toronto, BA, 54, MA, 55; Cambridge Univ, PhD(theoret chem), 58. *Prof Exp:* Nat Res Coun Can fel, 58-60; from asst prof to assoc prof, 61-74, PROF CHEM, UNIV TORONTO, 74- *Concurrent Pos:* Res visitor, Faculty Sci, Orsay, France, 68-69, Norweg Inst Technol, Trondheim, 78-79. *Res:* Theory of liquids and phase changes and of solutions; Monte Carlo and molecular dynamic computations; theory of surface phenomena. *Mailing Add:* Lash Miller Lab Univ of Toronto Toronto ON M5S 1A1 Can

VALLEE, BERT L, b Hemer, WGer, June 1, 19; nat US; m 47. BIOCHEMISTRY, BIOPHYSICS. *Educ:* Univ Bern, BS, 38; NY Univ, MD, 43. *Hon Degrees:* MA, Harvard Univ, 60. *Prof Exp:* Res fel med, 45-49, from res assoc to assoc, 49-55, from asst prof to prof, 55-65, Paul C Cabot prof biol chem, 65-80, PAUL C CABOT PROF BIOCHEM SCI, HARVARD MED SCH, 80- *Concurrent Pos:* Nat Res Coun sr fel, Mass Inst Technol, 48-51; Hughes fel, Harvard Med Sch, 51-64; mem staff, Div Indust Coop, Mass Inst Technol, 45-48, res assoc biol, 48-; Merck Sharpe & Dohme prof, Univ Wash, 62; Arthur Kelley lectr, Purdue Univ, 63; mem adv bd, La Trinidad Health Care Facil, Caracas, Venezuela, 70- & Metrop Univ, Caracas, 70-; DuPont lectr, Univ SC, 71; Venable lectr, Univ NC, 72; mem bd gov, Tel Aviv Univ, 72-; Tracy & Ruth Storer vis prof life sci, Univ Davis, Calif, 79, vis prof, Oberlin Col, Ohio, 79; chmn, Sect Biochem, Nat Acad Sci, 81; Bauchman lectr, Calif Inst Technol, 76; chmn, US Nat Comt Int Union Biochem, 76; Arthur K Watkins vis prof chem & life sci, Wichita State Univ, 78; vis prof, Univ Zurich & Fed Inst Technol, Zurich, 78. *Honors & Awards:* Warner-Chilcott Award, Am Asn Clin Chem, 69; Linderstrom-Lang Medal & Award, 80; Willard Gibbs Medal & Award, Am Chem Soc, 81. *Mem:* Nat Acad Sci; Biochem Soc; Am Soc Clin Invest; Am Chem Soc; Optical Soc Am. *Res:* Composition, conformation, structure, function and mechanism of action of metalloenzymes; local conformation of enzymes; enzyme kinetics; physical chemistry; emission; atomic absorption; absorption spectroscopy; circular dichroism; magnetic circular dichroism; physics of spectrographic sources. *Mailing Add:* Biophys Res Lab Peter Bent Brigham Hosp Boston MA 02115

VALLEE, JACQUES P, b Verdun, Que, Sept 5, 45. ASTROPHYSICS, RADIO ASTRONOMY. *Educ:* Univ Montreal, BA, 65, BSc, 68, MSc, 69; Univ Toronto, PhD(astron), 73. *Prof Exp:* Res fel astrophysics, Sterrewacht te Leiden, Holland, 73-75; res asst, Herzberg Inst, 75-76; res assoc astrophysics, Queen's Univ, Kingston, 76-80; RES OFFICER, HERZBERG INST, 80- *Concurrent Pos:* Exec mem, comt scientist observ astron, Mont Megantic, 79-80. *Mem:* Can Astron Soc; Can Asn Phys; Am Astron Soc; Royal Astron Soc Can; Int Astron Union. *Res:* Galactic studies of spiral arm magnetic fields, emission regions, molecular clouds and B-type stars; extragalactic studies of nearby galaxies, head-tail galaxies and Abell clusters; computer modeling of astronomical processes. *Mailing Add:* 100 Sussex Dr Inst Herzberg Ottawa ON K1A 0R6 Can

VALLEE, RICHARD BERT, b New York, NY, Aug 27, 45. BIOCHEMISTRY. *Educ:* Swarthmore Col, BA, 67; Yale Univ MPh & PhD(biol), 74. *Prof Exp:* Fel molecular biol, Lab Molecular Biol, Univ Wis-Madison, 74-78; MEM STAFF, WORCESTER FOUND EXP BIOL, SHREWSBURY, 78- *Mem:* Biophys Soc; AAAS. *Res:* Proteins associated with cytoplasmic microtubles. *Mailing Add:* Worcester Found for Exp Biol Shrewsbury MA 01545

VALLEE, RICHARD EARL, b Cincinnati, Ohio, June 21, 28; m 51. PHYSICAL CHEMISTRY, INORGANIC CHEMISTRY. *Educ:* Univ Cincinnati, BS, 51, MS, 52, PhD(chem), 62. *Prof Exp:* Chemist, Procter & Gamble Co, 47-48; asst, Univ Cincinnati, 51; chemist, Monsanto Chem Co, 52-59, group leader, 59-60, ASF fel, 61-62, group leader, Monsanto Res Corp, 62-63, sect mgr, 63-67, mgr nuclear technol, 67-69, mgr non-weapons progs, 69-72, MGR TECHNOL APPLN & DEVELOP, MONSANTO RES CORP, 72- *Mem:* AAAS; Am Chem Soc. *Res:* Preparation, evaluation and handling of radioactive compounds; high temperature compounds; vacuum technology; isotope separation. *Mailing Add:* 619 S Bourbon St Blanchester OH 45107

VALLENTINE, JOHN FRANKLIN, b Ashland, Kans, Aug 1, 31; m 50; c 3. RANCH MANAGEMENT, RANGE IMPROVEMENTS. *Educ:* Kans State Univ, BS, 52; Utah State Univ, MS, 53; Tex A&M Univ, PhD(range mgt, animal nutrit), 59. *Prof Exp:* Res aide, Rocky Mountain Forest & Range Exp Sta, US Forest Serv, 52; range conservationist, US Bur Land Mgt, 55-56; res asst range mgt, Exp Sta, Tex A&M Univ, 56-58; exten range specialist, Utah State Univ, 58-62; assoc prof range exten & res, Univ Nebr, 62-68; PROF RANGE SCI, BRIGHAM YOUNG UNIV, 68- *Mem:* Soc Range Mgt; Am Soc Animal Sci. *Res:* Range science and agricultural bibliography. *Mailing Add:* 114 Range Sci Lab Brigham Young Univ Provo UT 84602

VALLE-RIESTRA, J(OSEPH) FRANK, b Oakland, Calif, Nov 12, 24; m 48; c 2. CHEMICAL ENGINEERING. *Educ:* Univ Calif, BAS, 45; Calif Inst Technol, BS, 48, MS, 49. *Prof Exp:* Air pollution chemist, Los Angeles County Air Pollution Control Dist, Calif, 46-47; air pollution chemist, Truesdail Labs, 48; res asst chem eng, Calif Inst Technol, 48-49; res & develop engr, 49-62, sr res engr, 62-75, res specialist, Western Div, 70-75, sr res specialist, 75-78, assoc scientist, 78-81, SR ASSOC SCIENTIST, WESTERN DIV, DOW CHEM CO, 81- *Concurrent Pos:* Lectr chem eng, Univ Calif, Berkeley, 74- *Mem:* Fel Am Inst Chem; fel Am Inst Chem Engrs; Inst Food Technologists. *Res:* Transport phenomena in electrochemical and high temperature gaseous systems; high temperature kinetics; physical chemistry of graphite; solvent extraction; secondary fiber technology; food process engineering. *Mailing Add:* Western Div Labs Dow Chem Co PO Box 1398 Pittsburg CA 94565

VALLEROY, VINCENT V, chemical & petroleum engineering, see previous edition

VALLERSCHAMP, ROBERT EVAN, chemical engineering, see previous edition

VALLESE, LUCIO M(ARIO), b Naples, Italy, Sept 27, 15; nat US; m 54; c 2. ELECTRICAL ENGINEERING, PHYSICS. *Educ:* Univ Naples, Dott Elec Eng, 37; Carnegie Inst Technol, DSc(elec eng), 48. *Prof Exp:* Res assoc, Navy Inst Elec Commun, Leghorn, Italy, 37-39; from instr to asst prof elec eng, Univ Rome, 39-47; from asst prof to assoc prof physics, Duquesne Univ, 48-51; from asst prof to assoc prof elec eng, Polytech Inst Brooklyn, 51-59; sr scientist, Labs, Int Tel & Tel Corp, 59-68; pres, Electrophys Corp, Nutley, 69-80. *Concurrent Pos:* Adj prof, Polytech Inst Brooklyn, 59-65. *Mem:* Am Phys Soc; Optical Soc Am; Inst Elec & Electronics Engrs. *Res:* Electromagnetic theory; circuit theory; solid state devices; quantum electronics. *Mailing Add:* 340 Ridgewood Ave Glen Ridge NJ 07028

VALLETTA, ROBERT M, b Waterbury, Conn, Nov 10, 31; m 55; c 4. PHYSICAL CHEMISTRY. *Educ:* Univ Conn, BA, 53, MS, 56; Iowa State Univ, PhD(phys chem), 59. *Prof Exp:* Res physicist, Cent Res Lab, Am Mach & Foundry Co, 59-63; staff chemist, Components Div, Vt, 63-68, develop engr, 68-69, sr engr, 69-75, SR ENGR, GEN PROD DIV, IBM CORP, CALIF, 75- *Mem:* Am Chem Soc. *Res:* Solid state chemistry and physics. *Mailing Add:* IBM Gen Prod Div Monterey & Cottle Rds San Jose CA 95138

VALLEY, KARL ROY, b Canton, Ohio, Aug 20, 43; m 72. INSECT TAXONOMY. *Educ:* Kent State Univ, BS, 65, MS, 68; Cornell Univ, PhD(entom), 74. *Prof Exp:* ENTOMOLOGIST, PA DEPT AGR, 72- *Mem:* Entomol Soc Am. *Res:* Biology and taxonomy of adults and immature stages of various families of acalyptrate Diptera. *Mailing Add:* Bur Plant Indust Pa Dept Agr Harrisburg PA 17120

VALLEY, LEONARD MAURICE, b Little Falls, Minn, July 3, 33; m 58; c 3. MOLECULAR PHYSICS. *Educ:* St John's Univ, Minn, BA(physics) & BA(math), 55; Iowa State Univ, PhD(physics), 60. *Prof Exp:* From asst prof to assoc prof physics, 60-72, PROF PHYSICS, ST JOHN'S UNIV, MINN, 72-, CHMN DEPT, 70- *Concurrent Pos:* Vis assoc prof, Univ Denver, 67-68. *Mem:* Am Phys Soc. *Res:* Vibrational, rotational and translational relaxation in gas molecules undergoing collisions; relaxation time. *Mailing Add:* Dept of Physics St John's Univ Collegeville MN 56321

VALLEY, SHARON LOUISE, b Bay City, Mich, Oct 18, 41; m 75. PHARMACOLOGY, INFORMATION SCIENCE. *Educ:* Univ Mich, BS, 63, PhD(pharmacol), 67. *Prof Exp:* Intern pharm, Schulz Pharm, 60-62 & Health Serv Pharm, Univ Mich, 62-63; PHARMACOLOGIST SCI INFO, NAT LIBR MED, NIH, 67- *Concurrent Pos:* Mem comt user educ, Nat Fedn Abstracting & Indexing, 78-79; bd gov, Col Pharm Alumni Soc, Univ Mich, 78- *Honors & Awards:* Plaque and Gavel Award, Am Pharmaceut Asn, 62, Cert of Recognition, 63; Lundsford Richardson Award, Richardson Merrill Inc, 63; Qual Performance Awards, Nat Libr of Med, 70 & 73, Bd of Regents Award, 74. *Mem:* Drug Info Asn; NY Acad Sci; Am Med Writers Asn; Am Pharmaceut Asn; Soc Exp Biol & Med. *Res:* Cardiovascular pharmacology; toxicology. *Mailing Add:* Lister Hill Nat Ctr Biomed Commun 8600 Rockville Pike 38A 75-715 Bethesda MD 20209

VALLIER, TRACY L, b Oakland, Iowa, Sept 19, 36; m 57; c 4. MARINE GEOLOGY. *Educ:* Iowa State Univ, BS, 62; Ore State Univ, PhD(geol), 67. *Prof Exp:* Assoc prof geol, Ind State Univ, 66-72; geologist, Deep Sea Drilling Proj, Scripps Inst Oceanog, 72-75; MARINE GEOLOGIST, US GEOL SURV, 75- *Mem:* Geol Soc Am; Soc Econ Paleont & Mineral; Am Geophys Union. *Res:* Geology of the Aleutian Island Arc; deep sea sedimentation; igneous petrology; geology of northeastern Oregon and western Idaho. *Mailing Add:* US Geol Surv 345 Middlefield Rd Menlo Park CA 94025

VALLOTTON, WILLIAM WISE, b Valdosta, Ga, Nov 26, 27; m 50; c 4. MEDICINE. *Educ:* Duke Univ, AB, 47; Med Col Ga, MD, 52. *Prof Exp:* Intern, Univ Wis Hosp, 52; resident ophthal, Duke Univ Hosp, 53-56; instr, Duke Univ, 54-55, assoc, 55-56; chief, Eye, Ear, Nose & Throat Dept, US Naval Hosp, Beaufort, SC, 56-58; assoc prof, 58-65, PROF OPHTHAL, MED UNIV SC, 65-, CHMN DEPT, 67- *Concurrent Pos:* Consult, Vet Admin Hosp, Durham, NC, 55-56; consult, Vet Admin Hosp, Charleston, US Naval Hosp, SC State Hosp, Charleston Mem Hosp, St Francis Xavier Hosp & Williamsburg County Mem Hosp; mem, Res Prev Blindness, Inc & SC Eye Bank, Inc; counr, Southern Med Asn, 75-80. *Honors & Awards:* Honors Award, Am Acad Ophthal & Otolaryngol, 68. *Mem:* Am Acad Ophthal; Am Intra-Ocular Implant Soc; Asn Res Vision & Ophthal; AMA. *Res:* Ophthalmology. *Mailing Add:* Dept of Ophthal Med Univ of SC Charleston SC 29403

VALLOWE, HENRY HOWARD, b Pittsburgh, Pa, Nov 18, 24; m 48. ENDOCRINOLOGY. *Educ:* Pa State Teachers Col, BS, 49; Univ Chicago, MS, 50, PhD(zool), 54. *Prof Exp:* Instr biol, Wright Jr Col, Ill, 52-56; assoc prof zool, Ohio Univ, 56-67; PROF BIOL, INDIANA UNIV, PA, 67- *Mem:* AAAS; Am Soc Zoologists. *Res:* Endocrines of poikilotherms; sexual physiology; phylogeny of endocrines; circadian rhythms. *Mailing Add:* Dept of Biol Indiana Univ of Pa Indiana PA 15701

VALLS, ORIOL TOMAS, b Barcelona, Spain, Oct 15, 47; US citizen; m 74; c 2. CONDENSED MATTER PHYSICS. *Educ:* Univ Barcelona, BSc, 69; Brown Univ, MSc, 72, PhD(physics), 75. *Prof Exp:* Res assoc physics, James Franck Inst, Univ Chicago, 75-77; Miller fel, Univ Calif, Berkeley, 77-78; ASST PROF PHYSICS, UNIV MINN, 78- *Mem:* Am Phys Soc; Sigma Xi. *Res:* Dynamics of phase transitions; properties of quantum fluids. *Mailing Add:* Tate Lab of Physics 116 Church St SE Minneapolis MN 55455

VALSAMAKIS, EMMANUEL, b Istanbul, Turkey, May 11, 33; US citizen; m 60; c 2. SOLID STATE ELCTRONICS. *Educ:* Robert Col, Istanbul, BSEE, 55; Rensselaer Polytech Inst, MEE, 58, PhD(plasma physics), 63. *Prof Exp:* Instr elec eng, Rensselaer Polytech Inst, 56-61, res asst, 61-62; res scientist, Grumman Aircraft Eng Corp, 62-67; adv physicist, 67-76, MEM RES STAFF, IBM CORP, 76- *Mem:* Inst Elec & Electronics Engrs; Am Phys Soc. *Res:* Cryogenic tunneling device design and circuit analysis; experimental investigation of plasmas from pulsed plasma sources; bipolar, field effect transistor and cryogenic tunneling device design and circuit analysis for memory and logic applications. *Mailing Add:* IBM Corp B/300-45A E Fishkill Facility Hopewell Junction NY 12533

VALTIN, HEINZ, b Hamburg, Ger, Sept 23, 26; nat US; m 53; c 2. PHYSIOLOGY, INTERNAL MEDICINE. *Educ:* Swarthmore Col, AB, 49; Cornell Univ, MD, 53. *Prof Exp:* From instr to prof, 57-73, ANDREW C VAIL PROF PHYSIOL, DARTMOUTH MED SCH, 73-, CHMN DEPT, 77- *Concurrent Pos:* Consult, Hitchcock Clin, 61- *Mem:* Am Physiol Soc; Am Fedn Clin Res; Am Soc Clin Invest; Am Soc Nephrology; Int Soc Nephrology. *Res:* Kidney, electrolyte and water metabolism; neuroendocrinology. *Mailing Add:* Dept of Physiol Dartmouth Med Sch Hanover NH 03755

VALVANI, SHRI CHAND, b Mar 20, 40; Indian citizen. PHARMACEUTICAL CHEMISTRY, PHARMACEUTICS. *Educ:* Univ Saugar, BPharm, 65; Univ Mich, Ann Arbor, MS, 69, PhD(pharmaceut chem), 71. *Prof Exp:* Res scientist, 70-77, SR RES SCIENTIST, UPJOHN CO, PHARM RES, 77- *Mem:* Acad Pharmaceut Sci; Am Chem Soc; Am Pharmaceut Asn. *Res:* Thermodynamics of solution process and its effect on drug design, physico-chemical parameters influencing performance of various drug dosage forms, computer applications in a typical pharmacy research laboratory or environment. *Mailing Add:* Upjohn Co Pharm Res Kalamazoo MI 49001

VALVASSORI, GALDINO E, b Milan, Italy, July 16, 26; US citizen; m 55; c 4. MEDICINE, RADIOLOGY. *Educ:* Univ Milan, MD, 50; Am Bd Radiol, dipl, 59. *Prof Exp:* Resident radiol, Univ Milan, 51-53; resident, Mem Hosp, New York, 54-56; asst prof, Univ Chicago, 60-65; assoc prof, 65-67, PROF RADIOL, UNIV ILL MED CTR, 67- *Concurrent Pos:* Dir dept radiol, Ill Eye & Ear Infirmary, Chicago, 65-; consult, Grant Hosp, Chicago, 66, Henrotin Hosp, Chicago, 68 & Mercy Hosp, Chicago, 71; pres, Int Collegium Radiol in Otolaryngol, 79-82. *Mem:* AMA; Am Col Radiol; Am Roentgen Ray Soc; Radiol Soc NAm; Am Acad Ophthal & Otolaryngol. *Res:* Radiology of the head and neck; development and refinement of new radiographic techniques for study of temporal bone in pathological conditions of the ear. *Mailing Add:* 55 E Washington Chicago IL 60602

VALYI, EMERY I, b Murska Sobota, Yugoslavia, July 14, 11; nat US; m 39; c 2. APPLIED MECHANICS, MATERIAL SCIENCE. *Educ:* Fed Inst Technol, Zurich, ME, 33, DSc(phys metall, appl mech), 37. *Prof Exp:* Res engr, Swiss Fed Inst Testing Mat, 34-37; metall engr, Injecta Ltd, 37-40; mgr die casting mach div, Hydraul Press Mfg Co, 40-42; vpres, Sam Tour & Co, 43-45; pres, ARD Corp, 45-62; consult, Ford Motor Co, Int Harvester Co, Continental Can Co, Owens-Ill, Inc, Olin Corp & Molins Mach Co, 62-71; CONSULT, NAT CAN CORP, 71-; PRES, TPT MACH CORP, 75- *Mem:* Am Soc Metals; Am Inst Mining, Metall & Petrol Engrs; Soc Plastics Engrs; fel Am Inst Chemists; Soc Petrol Indust. *Res:* Materials technology; rheology; metal casting; plastic molding; container technology. *Mailing Add:* 3 Eversley Ave Norwalk CT 06851

VAMPOLA, ALFRED LUDVIK, b Dwight, Nebr, July 10, 34; m 56; c 8. SPACE PHYSICS. *Educ:* Creighton Univ, BS, 56; St Louis Univ, MS, 58, PhD(physics), 61. *Prof Exp:* Sr physicist, Convair Div, Gen Dynamics Corp, 61-62; staff scientist, 62-80, SR SCIENTIST SPACE PHYSICS, AEROSPACE CORP, 80- *Mem:* Am Geophys Union. *Res:* Magnetospheric physics; solar particles; spacecraft environment interactions. *Mailing Add:* Aerospace Corp PO Box 92957 El Segundo CA 90245

VANABLE, JOSEPH WILLIAM, JR, b Providence, RI, May 29, 36; m 62; c 2. DEVELOPMENTAL BIOLOGY. *Educ:* Brown Univ, AB, 58; Rockefeller Inst, PhD(biol), 62. *Prof Exp:* Asst prof, 61-72, ASSOC PROF BIOL, PURDUE UNIV, WEST LAFAYETTE, 71- *Concurrent Pos:* NIH spec fels, Univ Ore, 69 & Yale Univ, 69-70. *Mem:* Soc Develop Biol; Am Soc Zool. *Res:* Regeneration; the role of endogenous electrical fields in reduced ipislateral projections; visual mutants; neurogenesis; the specification of neural pathways during development. *Mailing Add:* Dept Biol Sci Purdue Univ West Lafayette IN 47906

VAN ALLEN, JAMES ALFRED, b Mt Pleasant, Iowa, Sept 7, 14; m 45; c 5. PHYSICS. *Educ:* Iowa Wesleyan Col, BS, 35; Univ Iowa, MS, 36, PhD(physics), 39. *Hon Degrees:* ScD, Iowa Wesleyan Col, 51, Grinnell Col, 57, Coe Col, 58, Cornell Col, 59, Univ Dubuque, 60, Univ Mich, 61, Northwestern Univ, 61, Ill Col, 63, Butler Col, 66, Boston Col, 66, Southampton Col, 67 & Augustana Col, 69. *Prof Exp:* Carnegie res fel nuclear physics, Dept Terrestrial Magnetism, Carnegie Inst, 39-41, physicist, 41-42; physicist appl physics lab, Johns Hopkins Univ, 42 & 46-50; prof physics, 51-72, CARVER PROF PHYSICS, UNIV IOWA, 72-, HEAD DEPT PHYSICS & ASTRON, 51- *Concurrent Pos:* Mem, Int Sci Radio Union; mem, Rocket & Satellite Res Panel, 46-, chmn, 47-48, mem exec comt, 58-; mem subcomt upper atmosphere, Nat Adv Comt Aeronaut, 48-52; leader sci exped, Cent Pac, 49, Gulf Alaska, 50, Arctic, 52, Int Geophys Year, Arctic, Atlantic, Cent Pac, SPac & Antarctic, 57; Guggenheim Mem Found fel, Brookhaven Nat Lab, 51; res assoc, Princeton Univ, 53-54; mem tech panel earth satellite prog, Int Geophys Year, 55-58, chmn working group internal instrumentation, 56-58, tech panel rocketry, 55-58, tech panel cosmic rays, 56-58, tech panel aurora & airglow, 57-58; adv comt nuclear physics, Off Naval Res, 57-; adv comt physics, Nat Sci Found, 57-60; mem space sci bd, Nat Acad Sci, 58-70, chmn Ad Hoc Panel Small Planetary Probes, 66; mem panel sci & technol, Comt Sci & Astronaut, US House Rep, 61-; consult, President's Sci Adv Comt; consult particles & fields subcomt, Nat Aeronaut & Space Admin, 61-, mem ad hoc sci adv comt, 66; chmn, Iowa's Int Coop Year Comt Sci & Advan Technol, 65; lectr, NATO Conf, Bergen, Norway, 65; mem, Planetary Missions Bd, 67; foreign mem, Royal Swedish Acad Sci, 81. *Honors & Awards:* Hickman Medal, Rocket Soc, 49, First Annual Res Award, 61, Hill Award, Inst Aerospace Sci, 60, Am Inst Aeronaut & Astronaut; Physics Award, Wash Acad Sci, 49; Space Flight Award, Am Astronaut Soc, 58; Distinguished Civilian Serv Medal, US Army, 59; Space Flight Award, Int Acad Astronaut, 61; First Iowa Award Sci, 61; Elliot Cresson Medal, Franklin Inst, 61; Golden Omega Award, Elec Insulation Conf, 63; John A Fleming Awards, 63 & 64, Am Geophys Union; Comdr Order du Merite pour la Recherche et L'Invention, 64; Iowa Broadcasters Asn Award, 64; Space Sci Award, Am Inst Aeronaut & Astronaut, 82. *Mem:* Nat Acad Sci; fel Am Phys Soc; fel Am Geophys Union; fel Inst Elec & Electronics Engrs; fel Am Astronaut Soc. *Res:* Nuclear physics; cosmic rays; use of rockets in physical research; satellites and space probes in planetary and solar physics. *Mailing Add:* Dept of Physics & Astron Univ of Iowa Iowa City IA 52242

VAN ALLEN, MAURICE WRIGHT, b Mt Pleasant, Iowa, Apr 3, 18; m 49; c 4. NEUROLOGY. *Educ:* Iowa Wesleyan Col, BA, 39; Univ Iowa, MD, 42; Am Bd Neurol Surg, dipl, 54; Am Bd Psychiat & Neurol, dipl, 63. *Prof Exp:* Chief neurol serv, Vet Admin Hosp, Iowa City, 54-59, asst dir prof serv for res, 57-59; assoc prof, 59-65, PROF NEUROL, COL MED, UNIV IOWA, 65-, HEAD DEPT, 74- *Concurrent Pos:* Attend physician & consult physician, Vet Admin Hosp; prog dir, Neurosensory Ctr, Nat Inst Neurol Dis & Stroke, 61; mem, Nat Adv Dent Res Coun, 75; chief ed, Arch of Neurol, 76- *Mem:* Fel Am Acad Neurol; Am Neurol Asn; Harvey Cushing Soc; AMA; Asn Res Nerv & Ment Dis. *Res:* Disorders of ocular movement and muscles; reaction time in cerebral disease; visual perceptive disorders. *Mailing Add:* Dept Neurol Univ Hosp Iowa City IA 52240

VAN ALLER, ROBERT THOMAS, b Mobile, Ala, June 18, 33; m 59; c 2. ORGANIC CHEMISTRY, BIOCHEMISTRY. *Educ:* Univ Ala, BS, 60, MS, 62, PhD(sulfonyl halides), 65. *Prof Exp:* Res assoc chem, Univ Miss, 65-67; aerospace technologist, Marshall Space Flight Ctr, NASA, 67-68; chmn dept chem, 68-70, dean, Col Sci, 70-71, DEAN, GRAD SCH, UNIV SOUTHERN MISS, 71- *Mem:* Am Chem Soc. *Res:* Reactions of aliphatic sulfonyl halides; biosynthesis of phytosterols and monocyclic monoterpenes. *Mailing Add:* Grad Sch Box 5024 Univ of Southern Miss Hattiesburg MS 39401

VAN ALSTINE, JAMES BRUCE, b Whitefish Bay, Wis, July 30, 49; m 70; c 2. PALEOECOLOGY. *Educ:* Winona State Univ, BA, 70; Univ NDak, MS, 74, PhD(geol), 80. *Prof Exp:* Instr, 74-80, ASST PROF GEOL, UNIV MINN, MORRIS, 80- *Mem:* Soc Econ Paleontologists & Mineralogists; Sigma Xi. *Res:* Paleoecology of nonmarine and brackish water faunas of Cretaceous and Paleocene ages. *Mailing Add:* Dept Geol Univ Minn Morris MN 56267

VAN ALSTINE, RALPH ERSKINE, economic geology, deceased

VAN ALSTYNE, JOHN PRUYN, b Albany, NY, Sept 12, 21; m 44; c 3. MATHEMATICS. *Educ:* Hamilton Col, BS, 44; Columbia Univ, MA, 52. *Prof Exp:* Vis instr math, Hamilton Col, 43-44, from instr to assoc prof, 48-61; assoc prof, 61-66, actg head dept, 68-71, PROF MATH, WORCESTER POLYTECH INST, 66-, DEAN ACAD ADVISING, 71- *Mem:* Am Math Soc; Math Asn Am. *Res:* Functional equations; linear algebra. *Mailing Add:* Boynton Hall Worcester Polytech Inst Worcester MA 01609

VAN ALTEN, LLOYD, b East Grand Rapids, Mich, Jan 2, 24; m 51; c 2. INORGANIC CHEMISTRY. *Educ:* Calvin Col, AB, 45; Purdue Univ, West Lafayette, MS, 48; Univ Wash, PhD(chem), 54. *Prof Exp:* Teacher, Lynden Christian High Sch, 48-50; Olin-Mathieson fel, Univ Wash-Boron Chem, 54-55; from asst prof to assoc prof, 55-68, PROF CHEM, SAN JOSE STATE UNIV, 68- *Mem:* Am Chem Soc; Sigma Xi. *Res:* Boranes; carboranes; absolute intensities in infrared spectroscopy; environmental mercury. *Mailing Add:* 2991 Fireside Dr San Jose CA 95128

VAN ALTEN, PIERSON JAY, b Grand Rapids, Mich, Feb 21, 28; m 53; c 2. EMBRYOLOGY, IMMUNOLOGY. *Educ:* Calvin Col, AB, 50; Mich State Univ, MS, 55, PhD(zool, physiol), 58. *Prof Exp:* From asst prof to assoc prof, 60-73, PROF ANAT, UNIV ILL MED CTR, 73- *Concurrent Pos:* NIH fel exp embryol & immunobiol, Univ Calif, Los Angeles, 58-60; Am Cancer Soc scholar, Univ Bern, 73-74; vis assoc prof pediat, Univ Minn, 66-67; guest prof immunobiol, Univ Bern, 73-74; mem, Res Comt, Ill Div Am Cancer Soc, 75-78. *Mem:* AAAS; Reticuloendothelial Soc (treas, 78-80); Am Asn Immunol; Am Asn Anat; Soc Develop Biol. *Res:* Immunological ability of gut-associated lymphoid tissue; experimental embryology and immunobiology; phagocytosis-promoting activity of plasma and cell surface fibronectins; graft-versus-host disease and immunological competence of chicken embryo; development of brain antigens in hamsters; culture of lymphocytes and human myeloma cells. *Mailing Add:* Dept of Anat Univ of Ill at the Med Ctr Chicago IL 60680

VAN ALTENA, WILLIAM F, b Hayward, Calif, Aug 15, 39; c 2. ASTRONOMY. *Educ:* Univ Calif, Berkeley, BA, 62, PhD(astron), 66. *Prof Exp:* From asst prof to assoc prof astron, Yerkes Observ, Univ Chicago, 66-74, dir observ, 72-74; chmn dept, 75-81, PROF ASTRON, YALE UNIV, 74- *Concurrent Pos:* Mem comt photographic plates & films, Am Nat Standards Inst. *Mem:* Am Astron Soc; Int Astron Union. *Res:* Trigonometric parallaxes and proper motions. *Mailing Add:* Yale Univ Observ PO Box 2023 Yale Sta New Haven CT 06437

VANAMAN, SHERMAN BENTON, b Lexington, Ky, July 25, 28; m 55; c 2. MATHEMATICS. *Educ:* Univ Louisville, BA, 49; Univ Ky, MS, 51; Univ Md, PhD(math educ), 67. *Prof Exp:* Instr math, Univ Ky, 51-55; assoc prof & actg head dept, 56-66, PROF MATH & CHMN DEPT, CARSON-NEWMAN COL, 66- *Mem:* Math Asn Am; Nat Coun Teachers Math. *Res:* Learning theory, especially mathematics-education. *Mailing Add:* Dept of Math Carson-Newman Col Jefferson City TN 37760

VANAMAN, THOMAS CLARK, b Louisville, Ky, Aug 12, 41; m 62; c 2. BIOCHEMISTRY, MICROBIOLOGY. *Educ:* Univ Ky, BS, 64; Duke Univ, PhD(biochem), 68. *Prof Exp:* From asst prof to assoc prof, 70-79, PROF MICROBIOL & IMMUNOL, MED CTR, DUKE UNIV, 79-, DIR CANCER CTR BASIC RES, 81- *Concurrent Pos:* Am Chem Soc fel, Med Ctr, Stanford Univ, 69-70, NSF res grant, 71-73 & NIH res grant, 71-85; Josiah Macy, Jr Found fac scholar, 77-78. *Mem:* NY Acad Sci; Am Soc Biol Chemists; Am Soc Microbiologists. *Res:* Study of the structure, function and evolution of proteins; evolution, structure and function of calcium dependent regulatory proteins; mechanisms of stimulus-response coupling; viral proteins and their roles in viral infection, replication and transformation. *Mailing Add:* Dept of Microbiol & Immunol Duke Univ Med Ctr Durham NC 27710

VANAMBURG, GERALD LEROY, b Hunter, Kans, Dec 17, 41; m 63; c 2. PLANT ECOLOGY, BOTANY. *Educ:* Ft Hays Kans State Col, BS, 64, MS, 65; Tex A&M Univ, PhD(plant ecol), 69. *Prof Exp:* Asst prof, 69-76, ASSOC PROF BIOL, CONCORDIA COL, MOORHEAD, MINN, 76- *Concurrent Pos:* Expert, Int Atomic Energy Agency, 70-71. *Mem:* Ecol Soc Am; Am Inst Biol Sci; Soc Range Mgt. *Res:* Soil-vegetation relationships; biogeochemical cycling. *Mailing Add:* Dept of Biol Concordia Col Moorhead MN 56560

VANAMEE, PARKER, b Portland, Maine, Aug 9, 19; m 53; c 6. PHYSIOLOGY. *Educ:* Yale Univ, BS, 42; Cornell Univ, MD, 45. *Prof Exp:* Intern, RI Hosp, Providence, 45-46; res fel, Sloan-Kettering Inst Cancer Res, 51-54, res assoc, 55-58, assoc, 58-60; asst prof, 56-61, ASSOC PROF MED, MED COL, CORNELL UNIV, 61-; ASSOC MEM, SLOAN-KETTERING INST CANCER RES, 60- *Concurrent Pos:* From asst resident to chief resident med, Mem Hosp Cancer & Allied Dis, 51-54, clin asst, 54-57, from asst attend physician to assoc attend physician, 57-69, attend physician, 69-, chief clin physiol & renal serv, Dept Med, 70-; asst vis physician, James Ewing Hosp, New York, 57-61, assoc vis physician, 61-; consult, Urol Dept, USPHS Hosp, Staten Island, NY; adj assoc prof clin pharm, Brooklyn Col Pharm, 77- *Mem:* AAAS; fel Am Col Physicians; Am Fedn Clin Res; AMA; Am Soc Clin Nutrit. *Res:* Medicine; clinical physiology. *Mailing Add:* Mem Sloan-Kettering Cancer Ctr 1275 York Ave New York NY 10021

VAN ANDEL, TJEERD HENDRIK, b Rotterdam, Netherlands, Feb 15, 23; US citizen; m 62; c 6. MARINE GEOLOGY. *Educ:* State Univ Groningen, BSc, 46, MSc, 48, PhD(geol), 50. *Prof Exp:* Asst prof geol, State Agr Univ, Wageningen, 48-50; sedimentologist, Royal Dutch Shell Res Lab, 50-53; sr sedimentologist, Cia Shell de Venezuela, 53-56; assoc res geologist, Scripps Inst Oceanog, Univ Calif, 57-64, res geologist, 64-68, lectr geol, 57-68; prof geol, Sch Oceanog, Ore State Univ, 68-76; PROF OCEANOG, DEPT GEOL, STANFORD UNIV, 76- *Concurrent Pos:* Vis prof, Univ Calif, Berkeley, 63; sr fel, Woods Hole Oceanog Inst, 63; sci adv, Deep Sea Drilling Proj, 64-68; res assoc geol, Scripps Inst Oceanog, Univ Calif, 68-72; mem geodynamics comt, Nat Acad Sci, 70-75; managing consult, Int Ocean Explor, NSF, 71-72; vis prof geophys, Stanford Univ, 74-75; group chmn, Sci

Comt Ocean Res, UNESCO, 75-78; co-ed, UNESCO World Ocean Atlas Comn. *Honors & Awards:* F P Shepard Medal, 78; N B Watkins Award, 80. *Mem:* AAAS; Am Asn Petrol Geol; Soc Econ Paleont & Mineral; Geol Soc Am; Am Geophys Union. *Res:* Recent sediments of continents and oceans; origin and nature of the continental shelf; geology and geophysics of mid-ocean ridges; paleoceanography; deep-diving research submersibles; geo-archeology. *Mailing Add:* Dept of Geol Stanford Univ Stanford CA 94305

VANANTWERP, CRAIG LEWIS, b Binghampton, NY, Feb 24, 50; m 72; c 1. NUCLEAR MAGNETIC RESONANCE SPECTROSCOPY. *Educ:* Juniata Col, BS, 72; Stanford Univ, PhD(org chem), 77. *Prof Exp:* Asst prof chem, Rochester Inst Technol, 77-80; SOFTWARE DEVELOP ENGR, NICOLET MAGNETICS CORP, DIV NICOLET INSTRUMENTS, 80- *Mem:* Am Chem Soc. *Res:* Develop and implement state of the art research capabilities into nuclear magnetic resonance spectrometer products. *Mailing Add:* Nicolet Magnetics Corp 255 Fourier Ave Fremont CA 94536

VAN ANTWERP, WALTER ROBERT, b Franklin, Ind, Aug 16, 25; m 46; c 2. SOLID STATE PHYSICS. *Educ:* Ind Univ, AB, 49; Univ Md, MS, 58. *Prof Exp:* Res physicist, Chem Res & Develop Lab, US Dept Army, 50-58 & Nuclear Defense Lab, Edgewood Arsenal, 58-60, chief solid state physics br, 60-64, chief nuclear physics div, 64-69; chief, Exp Physics Br, Ballistics Res Labs, Aberdeen Proving Ground, 69-81; CONSULT, 81- *Mem:* AAAS; Am Phys Soc; Electron Micros Soc Am; Am Nuclear Soc. *Res:* Solid state and nuclear physics; radiation damage and detection; gamma-ray spectroscopy; thin films. *Mailing Add:* 110 Woodland Dr Bel Air MD 21014

VAN ARMAN, CLARENCE GORDON, b Detroit, Mich, Dec 29, 17; m 43, 69; c 3. PHARMACOLOGY. *Educ:* Univ Chicago, SB, 39; Northwestern Univ, MS, 48, PhD(pharmacol), 49. *Prof Exp:* Chemist, Price Extract Co, 39-40; chemist, G D Searle & Co, Ill, 40-41, pharmacologist, 50-60; res assoc pharmacol, Med Sch Northwestern Univ, 49-50; chief pharmacologist, Chem Therapeut Res Labs, Miles Labs, Inc, 60-61; mgr pharmacol eval sect, Wyeth Labs, Inc, 61-63; dir pharmacol res dept, Chas Pfizer & Co, 63-65; sr res fel, 65-75; sr investr, Merck Inst Therapeut Res, 75-77, DIR OF BIOL RES, WYETH LABS, 77- *Concurrent Pos:* Lectr, Med Sch, Northwestern Univ, 54-61. *Mem:* AAAS; Am Soc Pharmacol & Exp Therapeut; Soc Exp Biol & Med; Am Soc Clin Pharmacol & Therapeut; Am Rheumatism Asn. *Res:* Inflammation; polypeptides; analgesics; diuretics; cardiac drugs; glomerulomephritis. *Mailing Add:* Dept of Biol Res Wyeth Labs Radnor PA 19087

VAN ARSDEL, JOHN HEDDE, b Chicago, Ill, Nov 22, 21; m 63; c 5. ENGINEERING PSYCHOLOGY. *Educ:* Purdue Univ, BS, 50; Commonwealth Univ, MA, 55, PhD(psychol), 56; Denver Univ, MA, 58. *Prof Exp:* Human factors engr, US Army Electronic Proving Ground, Ariz, 58-63; sr develop engr advan syst, Goodyear Aerospace Corp, Litchfield Park, Ariz, 63-66; sr human factors engr Minute Man III, Bell Aerosyst Corp, Niagara Falls, NY, 66-68; supvr comput lab, Col Bus Admin, Denver Univ, 68-73; human factors scientist syst eng, Syst Develop Corp, Colo Springs, Colo, 73-75; teacher & supvr acad & sci, Northrop, 76-80; writer med training manuals, Acad Health Sci, US Army, Fort Sam Houston, Tex, 81, OPERS RES ANALYST, US ARMY, FT HUACHUCA, ARIZ, 81- *Concurrent Pos:* Statistician & oper res anal, State Hwy Info Off, Denver, Colo, 72. *Res:* Hypno-therapy in clinical treatment of demorol addiction; effectiveness and survival in hostile environments; launching system accessibility requirements; maintenance program human factors analysis. *Mailing Add:* PO Box 2894 Sierra Vista AZ 85635

VAN ARSDEL, PAUL PARR, JR, b Indianapolis, Ind, Nov 4, 26; m 50; c 2. MEDICINE. *Educ:* Yale Univ, BS, 48; Columbia Univ, MD, 51. *Prof Exp:* Intern med, Presby Hosp, New York, 51-52, asst resident, 52-53; asst, Sch Med, Univ Wash, 53-55; asst, Presby Hosp, New York, 55-56; from instr to assoc prof, 56-69, PROF MED, SCH MED, UNIV WASH, 69-, HEAD SECT ALLERGY, 56- *Concurrent Pos:* Res fel med, Sch Med, Univ Wash, 53-55, Mass Mem Hosp & Sch Med, Boston Univ, 55 & Presby Hosp, New York, 55-56; mem, Growth & Develop Training Comt, Nat Inst Child Health & Human Develop, 70-74; consult, Vet Admin Hosp, USPHS Hosp, King County Hosp, Children's Hosp & Univ Hosp. *Mem:* AAAS; fel Am Col Physicians; Am Asn Immunol; Asn Am Med Cols; Am Acad Allergy (secy, 64-68, pres, 71-72). *Res:* Hypersensitivity; human immunology; histamine release and metabolism; drug sensitivity; autoantibodies. *Mailing Add:* BB 1333 Rm 13 Dept of Med Univ Hosp Seattle WA 98195

VAN ARSDEL, WILLIAM CAMPBELL, III, b Indianapolis, Ind, June 27, 20; div. PHARMACOLOGY. *Educ:* Ore State Col, BS, 49, MS, 51, PhD(physiol, zool), 59; Univ Ore, MS, 54. *Prof Exp:* Mem staff, Prod Control Lab, US Rubber Co, Ind, 41-45; lab asst pharmacol, Ore State Univ, 51-54, teaching fel zool & res asst animal husb, 54-59, jr animal physiologist, 59-60, asst in animal physiol, 60-63; PHARMACOLOGIST, BUR DRUGS, US FOOD & DRUG ADMIN, 63- *Mem:* AAAS; NY Acad Sci; Sigma Xi; Soc Exp Biol & Med. *Res:* Toxicology; teratology; electrocardiology; physiology; marine biology; anthropometry. *Mailing Add:* Cardio-Renal Drug Prod HFD-110 Bur Drugs US Food & Drug Admin Rockville MD 20852

VAN ARTSDALEN, ERVIN ROBERT, b Doylestown, Pa, Nov 13, 13; m 45. PHYSICAL CHEMISTRY, INORGANIC CHEMISTRY. *Educ:* Lafayette Col, BS, 35; Harvard Univ, AB, 39, PhD(phys chem), 41. *Prof Exp:* Asst chem, Harvard Univ, 36-40; from instr to asst prof, Lafayette Col, 41-45; res scientist, Los Alamos Sci Lab, 45-46; asst prof chem, Cornell Univ, 46-51; prin chemist, Oak Ridge Nat Lab, 51-56; asst dir res, Parma Res Ctr, Union Carbide Corp, 56-63; John W Mallet Prof chem & chmn dept, Univ Va, 63-68; chmn dept, 68-72, PROF CHEM, UNIV ALA, 68- *Concurrent Pos:* Res assoc, Nat Defense Res Comt, Sch Med, Johns Hopkins Univ, 43-44; res assoc, Carnegie Inst Technol, 45; lectr, Western Reserve Univ, 59; mem coun, Oak Ridge Assoc Univs, 63-69, mem bd dir, 69-75, staff mem, Inst Energy Anal, 75-76. *Mem:* AAAS; Am Chem Soc; Am Phys Soc; fel Am Inst Chemists. *Res:* Energy analysis; adsorption indicators; photochemistry; bond strengths; reaction kinetics; thermodynamics and structure of inorganic systems; high temperature chemistry; fused salts; atomic energy; Mössbauer spectroscopy; radiochemistry; nuclear chemistry. *Mailing Add:* Dept of Chem Univ of Ala University AL 35486

VANAS, DON WOODRUFF, b Rochester, NY, June 11, 20; m 45. PHYSICAL CHEMISTRY. *Educ:* State Univ NY, BA, 43; Univ Rochester, PhD(phys chem), 46. *Prof Exp:* Res chemist rayon dept, E I du Pont de Nemours & Co, 46-52; res chemist biochem dept, Bristol Labs, Inc, 52-53; sr chemist, 53-55, res assoc, 55-71, asst dir chem div, 71-77, asst dir, 77-79, DIR ANAL SCI DIV, EASTMAN KODAK CO, 79- *Mem:* Am Chem Soc. *Res:* Physics and physical chemistry of polymeric melts, solutions and solids. *Mailing Add:* Research Labs Eastman Kodak Co 1669Lake Ave Rochester NY 14650

VAN ASDALL, WILLARD, b Knox, Ind, Apr 29, 34. PLANT ECOLOGY. *Educ:* Valparaiso Univ, AB, 56; Purdue Univ, SM, 58; Univ Chicago, PhD(bot), 61. *Prof Exp:* Instr biol, Knox Col, Ill, 61; asst prof, Duquesne Univ, 62-63; from asst prof to assoc prof bot, 62-76, ASSOC PROF GEN BIOL, UNIV ARIZ, 76- *Mem:* Ecol Soc Am; Bot Soc Am. *Res:* Physiological ecology of desert plant species, especially winter-spring desert ephemerals. *Mailing Add:* Dept of Biol Sci Univ of Ariz Tucson AZ 85721

VANASSE, GEORGE ALFRED, b Woonsocket, RI, Oct 8, 24; m 61; c 3. OPTICS, SPECTROSCOPY. *Educ:* Univ RI, BS, 50; Boston Col, MS, 52; Johns Hopkins Univ, PhD(physics), 58. *Prof Exp:* Physicist spectros, Air Force Cambridge Res Lab, 52; teaching asst physics, Johns Hopkins Univ, 52-55, res asst, 55-58, res staff asst, 58-59; vis lectr, Goucher Col, 59; RES PHYSICIST, AIR FORCE GEOPHYS LAB, BEDFORD, 59- *Concurrent Pos:* Vis lectr, Lowell Technol Inst, 64-65. *Honors & Awards:* Guenter Loeser Award, Air Force Geophys Lab, 78. *Mem:* Am Phys Soc; fel Optical Soc Am. *Res:* Spectrometric techniques. *Mailing Add:* 71 Old Stage Rd Chelmsford MA 01824

VAN ATTA, CHARLES W, b New London, Conn, Feb 24, 34; m 58; c 1. FLUID MECHANICS. *Educ:* Univ Mich, BS, 58, MS, 59; Calif Inst Technol, PhD(aeronaut), 65. *Prof Exp:* Scientist, Jet Propulsion Lab, Calif Inst Technol, 64-65; from asst prof to assoc prof eng sci & oceanog, 65-75, PROF ENG SCI & OCEANOG, UNIV CALIF, SAN DIEGO, 75- *Res:* Transition and turbulence in fluid flow; geophysical fluid mechanics. *Mailing Add:* 5226 Urey Hall Univ of Calif PO Box 109 San Diego CA 92093

VANATTA, JOHN CROTHERS, III, b Lafayette, Ind, Apr 22, 19; m 44; c 2. PHYSIOLOGY. *Educ:* Ind Univ, AB, 41, MD, 44; Am Bd Internal Med, dipl, 53. *Prof Exp:* Intern, Wayne County Gen Hosp, 44-45, asst resident med, 46-47; instr physiol & pharmacol, 49-50, from asst prof to assoc prof physiol, 50-57, PROF PHYSIOL, UNIV TEX HEALTH SCI CTR DALLAS, 57- *Concurrent Pos:* Fel physiol & pharmacol, Univ Tex Southwestern Med Sch Dallas, 47-48 & fel exp med, 48-49; consult, Div Nuclear Educ & Training, USAEC, 64-67; adj prof physiol, Inst Technol, Southern Methodist Univ, 69-81. *Mem:* Am Physiol Soc; Soc Exp Biol & Med; AMA. *Res:* Sodium metabolism; transport functions of urinary bladder of toad; epithelial transport, toad urinary bladder and frog skin. *Mailing Add:* Dept of Physiol Univ of Tex Health Sci Ctr 5323 Harry Hines Blvd Dallas TX 75235

VAN ATTA, JOHN R, b Boston, Mass, May 16, 39; m 60; c 2. BIOPHYSICS. *Educ:* Univ Calif, Santa Barbara, BA, 62; Univ Mich, PhD(biophys), 68. *Prof Exp:* Res scientist, 68-72, dir basic res, 72-74, dir prod develop, 74-82, GEN MGR, CARNATION RES LABS, 82- *Mem:* Inst Food Technologists; Am Chem Soc. *Res:* Protein chemistry, especially protein structure. *Mailing Add:* 601 Toyopa Dr Pacific Palisades CA 90272

VAN ATTA, LESTER CLARE, b Portland, Ore, Apr 18, 05; m 29; c 3. PHYSICS, ELECTRICAL ENGINEERING. *Educ:* Reed Col, BA, 27; Wash Univ, MS, 29, PhD(physics, math), 31. *Prof Exp:* Res asst physics, Princeton Univ, 31-32; res assoc & asst prof, Mass Inst Technol, 32-40, sr staff mem radar, Radiation Lab, 40-45; br leader, Naval Res Lab, Washington, DC, 45-50; dir microwave lab & dir res labs physics & electronics, Hughes Aircraft Co, Culver City, Calif, 50-62; chief scientist, Lockheed Missiles & Space, Sunnyvale, Calif, 62-64; asst dir, Res Ctr NASA, Cambridge, MA, 64-70; assoc dean & prof elec eng, Univ Mass, 70-73, adj prof, 73-76. *Mem:* Fel Am Phys Soc; fel Inst Elec & Electronics Engrs; assoc fel Inst Aeronaut & Astronaut. *Res:* High voltage generation; high energy bombardment; radar; microwave antennas and systems. *Mailing Add:* PO Box 5 Laytonville CA 95454

VAN ATTA, ROBERT ERNEST, b Ada, Ohio, Feb 29, 24; m 46; c 2. ANALYTICAL CHEMISTRY. *Educ:* Ohio Northern Univ, BA, 48; Purdue Univ, MS, 50; Pa State Col, PhD(chem), 52. *Prof Exp:* Instr chem, Ohio Northern Univ, 47-48; instr, Pa State Col, 51-52; assoc prof & head dept, Ohio Northern Univ, 52-54, dir, Div Natural Sci, 53-54; from asst prof to prof chem, Southern Ill Univ, 54-69; prof & head dept, 69-79, PROF CHEM, BALL STATE UNIV, 79- *Mem:* Fel Am Inst Chem; Am Chem Soc; Am Soc Testing & Mat. *Res:* Polarography of organic compounds; electrochemical measurements; flame photometry; kinetics; gas chromatography; organic reaction mechanisms; infrared spectroscopy; natural waters analysis; inexpensive instrumentation. *Mailing Add:* Dept of Chem Ball State Univ Muncie IN 47306

VAN AUKEN, OSCAR WILLIAM, b Morristown, NJ, Dec 7, 39; m 61; c 3. PHYSIOLOGICAL ECOLOGY, PLANT ECOLOGY. *Educ:* High Point Col, BS, 62; Univ Utah, MS, 65, PhD(biol), 69. *Prof Exp:* Asst prof biol, Southwest Tex State Univ, 69-71; sr res scientist, Southwest Res Inst, 71-73, mgr environ biol, 75-76; assoc found scientist, Southwest Found Res & Educ, 73-75; ASSOC PROF DIV ALLIED HEALTH & LIFE SCI, UNIV TEX, 76- *Mem:* Ecol Soc Am; Scand Soc Plant Physiol; AAAS; Bot Soc Am. *Res:* Plant, animal and environmental interaction; effects, metabolism and degradation of xenobiotics. *Mailing Add:* Div of Allied Health & Life Sci Univ of Tex San Antonio TX 78285

VAN AUSDAL, RAY GARRISON, b Cincinnati, Ohio, Sept 16, 43. ATOMIC PHYSICS, MUSICAL ACOUSTICS. *Educ:* Miami Univ, AB, 64, MA, 66; Univ Mich, Ann Arbor, PhD(physics), 72. *Prof Exp:* Asst prof physics, Northern Mich Univ, 72-73 & Kalamazoo Col, 73-74; ASST PROF PHYSICS, UNIV PITTSBURGH, JOHNSTOWN, 74- *Res:* Development of effective teaching methods and materials in physics. *Mailing Add:* Dept of Physics Univ of Pittsburgh Johnstown PA 15905

VAN BAAK, DAVID ALAN, b Tokyo, Japan, July 13, 52; m 80. MICROWAVE SPECTROSCOPY, ATOMIC BEAM SPECTROSCOPY. *Educ:* Calvin Col, BS, 73; Harvard Univ, MA, 75, PhD(physics), 79. *Prof Exp:* Nat Res Coun & Nat Bur Standards fel physics, Joint Inst Lab Astrophysics, 79-80; ASST PROF PHYSICS, CALVIN COL, 80- *Mem:* Am Phys Soc. *Res:* Fine and hyperfine structure in simple atoms; quantum-electrodynamical effects. *Mailing Add:* Dept Physics Calvin Col Grand Rapids MI 49506

VAN BAVEL, CORNELIUS H M, b Breda, Neth, Sept 15, 21; nat US; m 47; c 8. AGRONOMY, BIOLOGY. *Educ:* State Agr Univ, Wageningen, MS, 45; Iowa State Univ, MSc, 46, PhD(soil physics), 49. *Prof Exp:* Instr physics, State Agr Univ, Wageningen, 41-43; soil surveyor, Neth Govt, 44; consult, Bolivia, SAm, 47; res assoc, Agr Exp Sta, Iowa State Univ, 48-50; assoc prof agron, NC State Univ, 50-54; soil scientist, Agr Res Serv, USDA, 54-61, chief physicist, Water Conserv Lab, 61-67; prof agron & biol, 67-77, PROF SOIL & CROP SCI, TEX A&M UNIV, 67- *Concurrent Pos:* Consult, Int Atomic Energy Agency, 62 & 64. *Honors & Awards:* Superior Serv Award, USDA, 63; Horton Award, Am Geophys Union, 67. *Mem:* Soil Sci Soc Am; fel Am Soc Agron; Am Geophys Union; Int Soil Sci Soc (Am secy, 59-60); Int Asn Sci Hydrol. *Res:* Hydraulics of soils; gaseous diffusion in soils; micrometeorology; nuclear radiation methods in soil-plant systems; water resources; arid land problems; evaporation; environmental biology; irrigation; plant water balance. *Mailing Add:* Dept of Soil & Crop Sci Tex A&M Univ College Station TX 77843

VAN BEAUMONT, KAREL WILLIAM, b Amsterdam, Netherlands, Sept 26, 30; US citizen; m 59; c 2. PHYSIOLOGY. *Educ:* Acad Phys Educ, The Hague, BS, 55; Cath Univ Louvain, MS, 57; Univ Ill, MS, 62; Ind Univ, PhD(physiol), 65. *Prof Exp:* Instr physiol, Univ Ind, 64-66; res physiologist, Miami Valley Labs, Proctor & Gamble Co, Ohio, 66-68; asst prof, 68-73, ASSOC PROF PHYSIOL, SCH MED, ST LOUIS UNIV, 73- *Res:* Temperature regulation; neural control systems; high altitude physiology; physiology of exercise; acceleration stress; biometeorology; body fluids and electrolytes; hematology. *Mailing Add:* Dept of Physiol St Louis Univ Sch of Med St Louis MO 63104

VAN BELLE, GERALD, b Enschede, Netherlands, July 23, 36; Can citizen; m 63; c 2. STATISTICS. *Educ:* Univ Toronto, BA, 62, MA, 64, PhD(math), 67. *Prof Exp:* Statistician, Connaught Med Res Labs, Univ Toronto, 57-62; from asst prof to assoc prof statist, Fla State Univ, 67-74, dir statist consult ctr, 71-74; vis assoc prof biostatist, 74-75, assoc prof, 75-76, PROF BIOSTATIST, UNIV WASH, 76- *Mem:* Am Statist Asn; Biomet Soc. *Res:* Application of statistics to biological and health-related problems. *Mailing Add:* Dept of Biostatist Univ of Wash Seattle WA 98195

VAN BERGEN, FREDERICK HALL, b Minneapolis, Minn, Sept 21, 14; c 4. ANESTHESIOLOGY. *Educ:* Univ Minn, MB, 41, MD, 42, MS, 52. *Prof Exp:* From instr to assoc prof, 48-57, assoc dir, 53-54, actg dir, 54-55, head dept, 55-77, prof 57-77, EMER PROF ANESTHESIOL, MED SCH, UNIV MINN, MINNEAPOLIS, 77- *Mem:* Am Soc Anesthesiol; Int Anesthesia Res Soc; AMA; Acad Anesthesiol. *Res:* Development and testing of respirators and respiratory assistors; evaluation of effects of respiratory patterns upon cardiovascular function; evaluation of pulmonary compliance under conditions of anesthesia; gas mass spectrometer. *Mailing Add:* 2005 Argonne Dr Minneapolis MN 55421

VAN BREDERODE, ROBERT ADRIAN, b Hackensack, NJ, Aug 1, 43; m 66. CHEMICAL ENGINEERING. *Educ:* Cornell Univ, BS, 66, PhD(chem eng), 69. *Prof Exp:* res chem engr, Plastics Res Lab, Exxon Res & Eng Co, 69-80. *Mem:* Am Chem Soc; Soc Plastics Engrs. *Res:* Response of polymers in high speed testing; glass reinforced polymers; polymer powder. *Mailing Add:* 11 W Burr Oak Dr Arlington Heights IL 60004

VAN BRUGGEN, JOHN TIMOTHY, b Chicago, Ill, Aug 12, 13; m 36; c 3. BIOCHEMISTRY. *Educ:* Linfield Col, BA, 37; Univ Ore, MA, 39; St Louis Univ, PhD(biochem), 44. *Prof Exp:* Instr biochem, Sch Med & biochemist, St Mary's Hosp, St Louis Univ, 43-45; res assoc, 45-47, from asst prof to assoc prof, 47-62, coord first yr med educ, 71-76, dir teaching labs, 72-81, prof, 72-81, EMER PROF BIOCHEM, MED SCH, ORE HEALTH SCI UNIV, 81- *Concurrent Pos:* USPHS sr fel, Univ Copenhagen, 59-60, actg chmn dept biochem; biochemist-biophysicist, Med Br, Div Biol & Med, USAEC, 67-68. *Mem:* AAAS; Am Chem Soc; Am Soc Biol Chem. *Res:* Metabolism of estrogens; isolation of penicillin B; clinical procedures; biochemistry of Vitamin A; lipid metabolism; metabolism of the diabetic; membrane transport and metabolism. *Mailing Add:* 3749 SW Chehalem Ave Portland OR 97201

VAN BRUGGEN, THEODORE, b Hawarden, Iowa, Jan 26, 26; m 48; c 2. BOTANY. *Educ:* Buena Vista Col, BS, 48; Univ SDak, MA, 50; Univ Iowa, PhD(bot), 58. *Prof Exp:* Instr biol, Northwestern Col, 50-55; from asst prof to prof bot & chmn dept, 58-59, ASSOC DEAN COL ARTS & SCI, UNIV SDAK, VERMILLION, 69- *Concurrent Pos:* Asst prog dir, NSF, 65-66. *Mem:* AAAS; Bot Soc Am; Mycol Soc Am; Am Soc Plant Taxon. *Res:* Plant systematics; flora of South Dakota, especially identification of vascular plants. *Mailing Add:* Col Arts & Sci Univ of SDak Vermillion SD 57069

VAN BRUNT, RICHARD JOSEPH, b Jersey City, NJ, May 11, 39; m 72; c 1. ATOMIC PHYSICS, MOLECULAR PHYSICS. *Educ:* Univ Fla, BS, 61, MS, 64; Univ Colo, Boulder, PhD(physics), 69. *Prof Exp:* Res asst atomic & molecular physics, Univ Fla, 64 & Joint Inst Lab Astrophys, Univ Colo, Boulder, 64-69; res assoc, 69-71, asst prof atomic & molecular physics, Univ Va, 71-76; physicist & res assoc basic atomic physics, Joint Inst Lab Astrophysics, Univ Colo, Boulder, 75-78; PHYSICIST GAS DISCHARGES, NAT BUR STANDARDS, WASHINGTON, DC, 78- *Concurrent Pos:* Univ grant, Univ Va, 72-73; vis mem, Joint Inst Lab Astrophys, Univ Colo, Boulder, 75-77. *Mem:* AAAS; Am Phys Soc; Inst Elec & Electronics Engrs; Am Asn Physics Teachers. *Res:* Experimental and theoretical studies of ionization and excitation by electron impact and photon absorption; measurement of electron-atom scattering; fundamental studies of high voltage gas discharge phenomena and corona. *Mailing Add:* Dept Com Nat Bur Standards Washington DC 20234

VAN BUIJTENEN, JOHANNES PETRUS, b Netherlands, May 8, 28; nat US; m 63; c 3. FOREST GENETICS. *Educ:* State Agr Univ, Wageningen, BS, 52; Univ Calif, Berkeley, MS, 55; Tex A&M Univ, PhD(genetics), 56. *Prof Exp:* Forest geneticist, Inst Paper Chem, 56-60, Tex Forest Serv, 60-66 & Northeastern Forest Exp Sta, NH, 66-68; assoc prof, 68-71, PROF FOREST GENETICS, TEX A&M UNIV, 71-, PRIN GENETICIST, TEX FOREST SERV, TEX A&M UNIV, 68- *Concurrent Pos:* NSF travel grant, 63; consult, Tex Forest Serv, 66-68. *Mem:* AAAS; Tech Asn Pulp & Paper Indust; Soc Am Foresters. *Res:* Genetic improvement of forest trees for growth rate, drought resistance, wood quality, disease resistance; physiology of forest trees as related to forest tree improvement. *Mailing Add:* Forest Genetics Lab Tex Forest Serv College Station TX 77843

VAN BUREN, ARNIE LEE, b Reynoldsburg, Ohio, Nov 28, 39; m 69; c 2. ACOUSTICS. *Educ:* Birmingham-Southern Col, BS, 61; Univ Tenn, PhD(physics), 67. *Prof Exp:* Res assoc acoustics, Univ Tenn, 67-68; res physicist, Naval Res Lab, Washington, DC, 68-76; res physicist, Underwater Sound Ref Detail, 76-79, HEAD METHOD SECT, NAVAL RES LAB, ORLANDO, FLA, 79- *Mem:* Fel Acoustical Soc Am. *Res:* Underwater acoustic measurements; acoustic radiation; nonlinear acoustics. *Mailing Add:* Code 8283 PO Box 8337 Orlando FL 32806

VAN BUREN, JEROME PAUL, b Brooklyn, NY, Oct 17, 26; m 53; c 3. BIOCHEMISTRY. *Educ:* Cornell Univ, BS, 50, MNS, 51, PhD, 54. *Prof Exp:* Proj leader cereal chem, Gen Mills, Inc, 54-57; from asst prof to assoc prof biochem, 57-69, PROF BIOCHEM, CORNELL UNIV, 69- *Concurrent Pos:* Consult food & agr, USPHS, 62-65; vis prof, Swiss Fed Inst Technol, 64-65; vis prof, Agr Univ, Holland, 71-72, Imperial Col, London, 80. *Mem:* Am Chem Soc; Inst Food Technologists. *Res:* Protein interactions in food; anthocyanins and polyphenols; wine chemistry; effects of salts on vegetable texture; pectic substances; food color and pigments. *Mailing Add:* Dept of Food Sci & Technol Cornell Univ Geneva NY 14456

VAN BUREN, JOHN MILLER, neurophysiology, neuroanatomy, see previous edition

VAN CAMP, HARLAN LARUE, biophysics, see previous edition

VAN CAMP, W(ILLIAM) M(ORRIS), b Lafayette, Ind, Feb 2, 21; m 56; c 2. HEAT TRANSFER, THERMODYNAMICS. *Educ:* Purdue Univ, BS, 47, MS, 50, PhD(mech eng), 52. *Prof Exp:* From asst instr eng to asst prof mech eng, Purdue Univ, 46-55; chief prod develop engr, Olin Mathieson Chem Corp, 55-56; scientist, 56-67, head plasma physics res lab, 56-70, sr scientist, 68-70, AIRCRAFT DESIGN SPECIALIST, McDONNELL AIRCRAFT CO, 70- *Concurrent Pos:* Consult, Kimberly-Clark Paper Co, 53, Ord Corps, US Army, 53-55 & Babcock & Wilcox Co, 54; vis lectr, Washington Univ, 57-58, vis assoc prof, 58-59. *Mem:* Inst Environ Sci. *Res:* Heat transfer; fuel systems; aerothermodynamics; plasma physics. *Mailing Add:* 1050 White Rd St Louis MO 63144

VAN CAMPEN, DARRELL R, b Two Buttes, Colo, July 15, 35; m 58; c 2. NUTRITION, BIOCHEMISTRY. *Educ:* Colo State Univ, BS, 57; NC State Univ, MS, 60, PhD(nutrit), 62. *Prof Exp:* NIH fel biochem, Cornell Univ, 62-63; res chemist, US Plant, Soil & Nutrit Lab, USDA, 63-80; asst prof animal nutrit, Cornell Univ, 72-80; LAB DIR, US PLANT, SOIL & NUTRIT LAB, USDA, 80-; ASSOC PROF ANIMAL NUTRIT, CORNELL UNIV, 80- *Mem:* AAAS; Am Inst Nutrit; Soc Exp Biol & Med; NY Acad Sci. *Res:* Mineral metabolism; absorption and utilization of trace minerals. *Mailing Add:* Plant Soil & Nutrit Lab USDA Tower Rd Ithaca NY 14853

VANCE, BENJAMIN DWAIN, b Cave City, Ark, May 7, 32; m 52; c 4. PLANT PHYSIOLOGY. *Educ:* Tex Tech Col, BS, 58; Univ Mo, AM, 59, PhD(bot), 62. *Prof Exp:* Asst prof biol, Tex Tech Col, 62-63; asst prof, 63-70, ASSOC PROF BIOL, NORTH TEX STATE UNIV, 70- *Concurrent Pos:* Res grants, NTex Fac Res-Tex Col & Coord Bd, 66-67 & Nat Commun Dis Ctr, 66-68. *Mem:* AAAS; Bot Soc Am; Am Soc Plant Physiol; Phycol Soc Am. *Res:* Physiology of blue-green algae; phytohormones; action of phytochrome. *Mailing Add:* Dept of Biol NTex State Univ Denton TX 76203

VANCE, DENNIS WILLIAM, b Quincy, Ill, Nov 20, 38; m 61; c 1. ELECTROOPTICS. *Educ:* St Lawrence Univ, BS, 60; Univ Fla, MS, 62, PhD(physics), 65. *Prof Exp:* SCIENTIST, XEROX RES LABS, 65-, MGR DISPLAY TECHNOL AREA, 75- *Mem:* Am Phys Soc. *Res:* Surface physics; display systems engineering and technology. *Mailing Add:* Xerox Corp Palo Alto Res Ctr 3333 Coyote Hill Rd Palo Alto CA 94304

VANCE, EDWARD F(LAVUS), b Mansfield, Tex, Sept 1, 29; m 56; c 4. ELECTRICAL ENGINEERING. *Educ:* Univ Calif, Los Angeles, BS, 54; Univ Denver, MSEE, 58. *Prof Exp:* Design engr, NAm Aviation, Inc, 54-56; from instr to asst prof elec eng, Univ Denver, 56-59; res engr, Stanford Res Inst, 59-67, sr res engr, 67-76, prog mgr, 76-80, STAFF SCIENTIST, SRI INT, 80- *Mem:* Inst Elec & Electronics Engrs. *Res:* Electromagnetic coupling; cable shields and transmission lines; high voltage phenomena; electrical discharges; aircraft and rocket electrification. *Mailing Add:* SRI Int 333 Ravenswood Ave Menlo Park CA 94025

VANCE, ELBRIDGE PUTNAM, b Cincinnati, Ohio, Feb 7, 15; m 75; c 4. MATHEMATICS. *Educ:* Col Wooster, AB, 36; Univ Mich, MA, 37, PhD(math), 39. *Prof Exp:* Dir statist lab, Univ Mich, 38; from instr to asst prof math, Univ Nev, 39-43; lectr, 43-46, from asst prof to assoc prof, 46-54, actg dean faculty, 66-70, PROF MATH, OBERLIN COL, 54-, CHMN DEPT, 48- *Concurrent Pos:* NSF fel, Stanford Univ, 60-61; Columbia Univ & US AID consult, Ranchi Univ, India, 65; math assoc, Univ Auckland, 67; instr, Glenville High Sch & Phillips Acad, 73; ed, Am Math Monthly. *Mem:* AAAS; assoc Am Math Soc; assoc Math Asn Am. *Res:* Continuous transformations; foundations of mathematics; topology. *Mailing Add:* Dept of Math Oberlin Col Oberlin OH 44074

VANCE, HUGH GORDON, b Forest, Ont, Sept 18, 24; m 53; c 1. ANALYTICAL CHEMISTRY, BIOCHEMISTRY. *Educ:* Univ Western Ont, BSc, 50, PhD(path chem), 56. *Prof Exp:* Nat Res Coun Can fel, Dept Anat, McGill Univ, 55-57; res assoc biochem, Sinai Hosp of Baltimore, Ind, Md, 57-61, Nat Cancer Inst fel dept med, 60-61; asst prof chem, 61-65, ASSOC PROF CHEM, MORGAN STATE COL, 65- *Mem:* Am Chem Soc. *Res:* Investigations of the nature and content of mucopolysaccharides in skin; structural determination of the carbohydrate moiety of glycoporteins. *Mailing Add:* 2908 Mayfield Rd Baltimore MD 21207

VANCE, IRVIN ELMER, b Mexico, Mo, Apr 8, 28; m 58; c 3. MATHEMATICS EDUCATION. *Educ:* Wayne State Univ, BS, 57; Washington Univ, MA, 59; Univ Mich, Ann Arbor, DEduc(math), 67. *Prof Exp:* From asst prof to assoc prof math, Mich State Univ, 66-71; ASSOC PROF MATH, NMEX STATE UNIV, 71- *Concurrent Pos:* Consult, Morel Lab Math Proj, 67; asst dir, Grand Rapids Math Lab Proj, 68-69; dir inner city math proj, Mich State Univ, 69-72, dir, sch-community outreach proj one, 73-75 & elementary teachers math proj, NMex State Univ, 77-80. *Mem:* AAAS; Nat Coun Teachers Math; Am Math Soc; Math Asn Am. *Res:* Finite projective planes; inductive learning and teaching of mathematics; laboratory techniques at school level and individualized instruction at the college level. *Mailing Add:* 207 Walden Hall Dept Math Sci NMex State Univ Las Cruces NM 88001

VANCE, JOHN MILTON, b Houston, Tex, Oct 5, 37; m 58; c 4. MECHANICAL ENGINEERING. *Educ:* Univ Tex, Austin, BS, 60, MS, 63, PhD(mech eng), 67. *Prof Exp:* Mech engr, Houston Div, Armco Steel Corp, 60-62; res engr, Res & Tech Dept, Texaco Inc, 63-64; group leader missile decoy anal, Tracor, Inc, 67-69; asst prof mech eng, Univ Fla, 69-77; PROF, TEX A&M UNIV, 77- *Concurrent Pos:* Consult, Harris Mineral Prod, 70-; sci adv, Air Mobility Res & Develop, US Army, 71-72; US Army res grant, Univ Fla, 72-73. *Mem:* Am Soc Mech Engrs; Am Soc Eng Educ. *Res:* Dynamics of rotating machinery; dynamic stability of mechanical systems; bearings; mechanical design synthesis; turobmachinery; helicopters. *Mailing Add:* Dept Mech Eng Tex A&M Univ College Station TX 77843

VANCE, JOSEPH ALAN, b Aberdeen, Wash, Mar 15, 30; m 49; c 3. GEOLOGY. *Educ:* Univ Wash, BSc, 51, PhD, 57. *Prof Exp:* Asst prof geol, 57-68, ASSOC PROF GEOL, UNIV WASH, 68- *Mem:* Geol Soc Am; Mineral Soc Am. *Res:* Igneous and metamorphic petrology; structure and stratigraphy; geology of the Pacific Northwest. *Mailing Add:* Dept of Geol Univ of Wash Seattle WA 98195

VANCE, JOSEPH FRANCIS, b Kansas City, Mo, July 24, 37. MATHEMATICS, STATISTICS. *Educ:* Southwest Tex State Col, BS, 59; Univ Tex, Austin, MA, 62, PhD(math), 67. *Prof Exp:* Teacher high sch, Tex, 60-61; spec instr math, Univ Tex, Austin, 66-67, asst prof, 67-68; from asst prof to assoc prof, 68-74, PROF MATH, ST MARY'S UNIV, TEX, 74- *Mem:* Am Math Soc. *Res:* Analysis; specialty, integration theory. *Mailing Add:* Dept of Math St Mary's Univ San Antonio TX 78284

VANCE, MILES ELLIOTT, b Findlay, Ohio, Jan 2, 32; m 55; c 3. PHYSICAL OPTICS, GEOMETRICAL OPTICS. *Educ:* Bowling Green State Univ, BA, 53; Ohio State Univ, PhD(physics), 62. *Prof Exp:* Instr physics, Ohio State Univ, 61-62; res physicist, Res & Develop Lab, NY, 62-68, sr res physicist, Electronics Res Lab, NC, 68-73, sr res physicist, Biomed Tech Ctr, 73-76, SR RES PHYSICIST, RES & DEVELOP LAB, CORNING GLASS WORKS, 76- *Mem:* Optical Soc Am; Inst Elec & Electronics Engrs. *Res:* Applied optics; gradient-index optics; clinical instruments; microscopy; spectroscopy. *Mailing Add:* Corning Glass Works Res & Develop Lab Corning NY 14830

VANCE, OLLIE LAWRENCE, b Birmingham, Ala, Feb 5, 37; m 56; c 2. ENGINEERING. *Educ:* Auburn Univ, BSME, 59, MSME, 61; Univ Tex, Austin, PhD(mech eng), 67. *Prof Exp:* Instr mech eng, Auburn Univ, 59-61; eng design analyst, Pratt & Whitney Inc, 61-62; asst prof mech eng, Auburn Univ, 62-64; ASSOC PROF ENG, UNIV ALA, BIRMINGHAM, 67- *Res:* Vibrations; linear elasticity. *Mailing Add:* 3401 Norwich Dr Birmingham AL 35294

VANCE, PAUL A(NDREW), JR, b Ft Wayne, Ind, Feb 17, 30; m 53; c 3. ELECTRICAL ENGINEERING. *Educ:* Univ Ill, BS, 51, MS, 52, PhD(elec eng), 54. *Prof Exp:* Res engr, Eng Res Lab, Exp Sta, 54-58, res proj engr, 58-61, sr res engr, Mech Res, Eng Res & Develop Labs, 61-65, sr res engr, Orchem Dept, Jackson Lab, 65-77, sr engr, Photo Prod Dept, Instrument Prod Div, 77-79, SR ENGR, PHOTO PROD DEPT, CLIN SYST DIV, E I DU PONT DE NEMOURS & CO, INC, 79- *Mem:* Instrument Soc Am. *Res:* Optics; electronics; electromechanics. *Mailing Add:* Glasgow Site E I du Pont de Nemours & Co Inc Wilmington DE 19898

VANCE, ROBERT FLOYD, b Columbus, Ohio, May 12, 26; m 53; c 3. INORGANIC CHEMISTRY. *Educ:* Otterbein Col, BS, 49; Univ Ill, MS, 50, PhD(chem), 52. *Prof Exp:* Res chemist, Battelle Mem Inst, 52-58; develop supvr, Girdler Catalysts Div, Chemetron Corp, 58-60; sr chemist, Gen Elec Co, 60-80; MGR ENVIRON LAB, STATE OF KY, 81- *Mem:* Am Chem Soc. *Res:* Gas chromatography; mass spectrometry; thermal analysis. *Mailing Add:* 7502 Tudor Ct Louisville KY 40222

VANCE, ROBERT W(ILLARD), b Boise, Idaho, Aug 10, 09; m 35, 50; c 4. CHEMICAL ENGINEERING. *Educ:* Univ Idaho, BS, 34. *Prof Exp:* Res chem engr, Swift & Co, Ill, 36-40; tech rep adhesives, Flintkote Co, NY, 46-47; res chem engr, Utah Power & Light Co, 47-50; chief tech serv, Chem Corps, US Army, 51-56; tech staff engr, Ramo-Wooldridge Corp, Calif, 56-58, Space Technol Labs, 58-60 & Aerospace Corp, 60-74; CONSULT, 74- *Concurrent Pos:* Mem adv bd, Col Eng, Univ Idaho, 69-72; co-chmn biotechnol panel, President's Space Task Group, 68; mem, Nat Res Coun, 69-73. *Honors & Awards:* Nat Helium Centennial Comt Meritorious Serv Award, Cryogenic Eng Conf, 66. *Mem:* Sigma Xi; assoc fel Am Inst Aeronaut & Astronaut; Nat Asn Corrosion Engrs; Cryogenic Soc Am (pres, 71); Soc Cryobiol. *Res:* Cryogenic energy systems; space power systems; contamination and corrosion control. *Mailing Add:* 3 Rockinghorse Rd W Rancho Palos Verdes CA 90274

VANCE, VELMA JOYCE, b Wilder, Idaho, May 13, 29. VERTEBRATE ZOOLOGY. *Educ:* Col Idaho, BS, 51; Univ Ariz, MS, 53; Univ Calif, Los Angeles, PhD(zool), 59. *Prof Exp:* Asst, Crookham Co, 52-54 & Univ Calif, Los Angeles, 54-58; instr biol, Occidental Col, 59; from asst prof to assoc prof zool, 59-71, PROF ZOOL, CALIF STATE UNIV, LOS ANGELES, 71- *Concurrent Pos:* Animal behavior; vertebrate biology. *Mailing Add:* Dept of Biol Calif State Univ Los Angeles CA 90032

VANCE, WILLIAM HARRISON, b Phoenix, Ariz, Nov 6, 34; m 73; c 2. FLUID DYNAMICS, HEAT TRANSFER. *Educ:* Univ NMex, BS, 56; Univ Wash, PhD(chem eng), 62. *Prof Exp:* NSF fel, Swiss Fed Inst Technol, 62-63; sr engr, 64-76, FEL ENGR, BETTIS ATOMIC POWER LAB, WESTINGHOUSE ELEC CORP, 77- *Mem:* Am Inst Chem Engrs. *Res:* Experimentation and analysis in fluid dynamics and heat transfer. *Mailing Add:* Bettis Atomic Power Lab PO Box 79 West Mifflin PA 15122

VAN CITTERS, GORDON WAYNE, JR, b Minneapolis, Minn, April 5, 47; m 70; c 3. INSTRUMENTATION. *Educ:* Princeton Univ, AB, 69; Univ Tex, Austin, PhD(astron), 76. *Prof Exp:* Res assoc, Univ Tex, Austin, 74-78, res scientist, 78-79; PROG DIR, ASTRON, INSTRUMENTATION & DEVELOP, NAT SCI FOUND, 79- *Concurrent Pos:* Co-investr, Space Telescope High Speed Photometer Team, 77-; consult, Dresser Indust, 74-79 & NAPP, Inc, Austin, 76-, Sci Appln, Inc, 79- *Mem:* Int Astron Union. *Res:* Astronomical instrumentation; high speed photometry of compact objects (cataclysmic variables, pulsars), occultations by moon and planets, high precision photometry and radial velocity measurement. *Mailing Add:* Div Astron Sci Nat Sci Found Washington DC 20550

VAN CITTERS, ROBERT L, b Alton, Iowa, Jan 20, 26; m 49; c 4. CARDIOVASCULAR PHYSIOLOGY. *Educ:* Univ Kans, AB, 49, MD, 53. *Prof Exp:* Intern, Med Ctr, Univ Kans, 53-54, resident internal med, 55-58; res assoc, Scripps Clin Res Found, Univ Calif, 61-62; asst prof cardiovasc physiol, 63-64, assoc prof physiol & biophys 63-68, Robert L King chair cardiovasc res, 63-68, mem staff, Regional Primate Res Ctr, 64-68, assoc dean, Sch Med, 68-70, PROF PHYSIOL, BIOPHYS & MED, & DEAN, SCH MED, UNIV WASH, 70- *Concurrent Pos:* Nat Heart Inst res fel, Univ Kans, 55-56 & trainee, 56-57, spec res fel, 58-59; res fel, Sch Med, Univ Wash, 59-62; NIH career res award, 62; res grants, Nat Heart Inst, 62-67, Am Heart Asn, 62-67, US Air Force res grant, 67; exchange scientist, Joint US-USSR Sci Exchange, 62; mem, Myocardial Infarction Comt, Nat Heart & Lung Inst, 71-73; mem, Bd Trustees, Wash State Heart Asn; mem exec coun, Asn Am Med Col, 72-; mem Admin Bd, Coun Deans, 72-; mem spec med adv group, Vet Admin, 74-78, chmn, 77-78; mem, Gen Res Support Prog Adv Comt, NIH, 75-78; mem, Inst Med, Nat Acad Sci, 78. *Mem:* AAAS; Am Physiol Soc; Am Heart Asn; Am Fedn Clin Res; NY Acad Sci. *Res:* Cardiovascular physiology, left ventricular function and control, regional flow distribution, exercise and diving; development of instrumentation and techniques for studying cardiovascular dynacmis in healthy subjects during spontaneous activity. *Mailing Add:* Off of the Dean Univ of Wash Sch of Med Seattle WA 98195

VANCKO, ROBERT MICHAEL, b Johnson City, NY, Sept 15, 42; m 66; c 2. MATHEMATICS. *Educ:* Pa State Univ, BA, 64, MA, 65, PhD(math), 69. *Prof Exp:* Lectr math, Univ Man, 67-69; ASST PROF MATH, OHIO UNIV, 69- *Mem:* Am Math Soc. *Res:* Universal algebra; general algebraic systems; topological algebraic systems. *Mailing Add:* Dept of Math Ohio Univ Athens OH 45701

VANCLEAVE, ALLAN BISHOP, b Medicine Hat, Alta, Aug 19, 10; m 34; c 4. PHYSICAL CHEMISTRY. *Educ:* Univ Sask, BSc, 31, MSc, 33; McGill Univ, PhD, 35; Cambridge Univ, PhD, 37. *Prof Exp:* 1851 Exhib scholar, Cambridge Univ, 35-37; from asst prof to prof chem, Univ Sask, 37-62; chmn div natural sci, 62-69, dir sch grad studies, 65-69, dean grad studies & res, Univ Regina, 69-76; RETIRED. *Mem:* Fel Chem Inst Can; Royal Soc Can. *Res:* Active hydrogen; viscosity of gases; catalysis; accomodation coefficient method of measuring gas adsorption; reactions of cyanogen halides; radiation chemistry; properties of Saskatchewan volcanic ashes; beneficiation of low grade uranium ores; flotation characteristics of minerals; x-ray fluorescence analysis. *Mailing Add:* 1001 McNiven Ave Regina SK S4S 3X4 Can

VAN CLEAVE, HORACE WILLIAM, b Cherryvale, Kans, July 9, 31; m 56; c 2. ENTOMOLOGY. *Educ:* Tex A&M Univ, BS, 52, MS, 58; Okla State Univ, PhD(entom), 69; Am Registry Prof Entom, cert. *Prof Exp:* Teacher high sch, Tex, 54-56; surv entomologist, Okla State Univ, 58-61, instr, 62-64; from asst prof to assoc prof, 64-75, PROF ENTOM, TEX A&M UNIV, 75- *Mem:* Entom Soc Am. *Res:* Insect pests of pecans; taxonomy of aphids; economic entomology. *Mailing Add:* Dept of Entom Tex A&M Univ College Station TX 77843

VAN CLEVE, JOHN WOODBRIDGE, b Kansas City, Mo, Nov 22, 14; m 47; c 3. CARBOHYDRATE CHEMISTRY. *Educ:* Antioch Col, BS, 37; Univ Minn, PhD(biochem), 51. *Prof Exp:* Jr res chemist, Aluminum Co Am, 43-45, assoc res chemist, 45-48; RES CHEMIST, CEREAL CROPS LAB,

NORTHERN REGIONAL RES LAB, USDA, 51- *Mem:* AAAS; Am Chem Soc; Sigma Xi; NY Acad Sci. *Res:* Carbohydrate chemistry; coorelation of anomeric configuration of glycosides; methylation analysis of dextrans; synthesis of derivitives of erythrose and glucose. *Mailing Add:* USDA Northern Regional Res Lab 1815 N University St Peoria IL 61604

VAN COTT, HAROLD PORTER, b Schenectady, NY, Nov 16, 25; m 53; c 3. ENGINEERING SCIENCE, ERGONOMICS. *Educ:* Univ Rochester, BA, 48; Univ NC, MA, 52, PhD(psychol), 53. *Prof Exp:* Prog dir, Am Inst Res, 55-58, dir, Inst Human Performance, 64-68, dir human ecol, 74-75; develop engr, IBM Corp, 58-64; dir, Off Commun, Am Psychol Asn, 68-74; chief human factors, Nat Bur Standards, 75-78, chief consumer sci, 78-81; CHIEF SCIENTIST, BIOTECHNOL, INC, 81- *Concurrent Pos:* Consult to various pvt & govt orgn, 64- *Mem:* Fel Am Psychol Asn; fel Human Factors Soc; fel AAAS; Sigma Xi; Am Soc Biomech. *Res:* Ergonomics as it is applied to the design and evaluation of products and process control systems. *Mailing Add:* BioTechnol Inc 3027 Rosemary Lane Falls Church VA 22042

VAN COTT, HARRISON CORBIN, b Schenectady, NY, Mar 13, 20; m 43; c 2. MINERALOGY, MICROSCOPY. *Educ:* Univ Rochester, AB, 42; Columbia Univ, MA, 63. *Prof Exp:* Petrographer, US Bur Mines, 43-45; mineralogist, Corning Glass Works, 46-78; mem fac, Dept Mat Eng, Va Polytech Inst & State Univ, 78-79. *Mem:* Mineral Soc Am; Am Ceramic Soc; Brit Soc Glass Technol; Mineral Asn Can; Brit Ceramic Soc. *Res:* Composition and crystallization of ceramics and glasses; microscopy. *Mailing Add:* Dept Mat Eng Va Polytech Inst & State Univ Blacksburg VA 24061

VAN COUVERING, JUDITH ANNE HARRIS, b Tulsa, Okla, Feb 20, 38; div; c 4. PALEONTOLOGY. *Educ:* Univ Calif, Berkeley, BA, 60; Univ Cambridge, PhD(geol), 72. *Prof Exp:* CUR FOSSIL VERTEBRATES & ASSOC PROF NATURAL HIST, UNIV COLO MUS, 77-, ASSOC PROF GEOL, UNIV COLO, BOULDER, 77- *Mem:* Soc Vertebrate Paleont; fel Linnean Soc. *Res:* African tertiary faunas and paleoenvironments; origin of modern terrestrial communities; biogeography; evolutionary problems. cichlid fish evolution; science and philosophy. *Mailing Add:* Univ of Colo Mus Boulder CO 80309

VANDAM, LEROY DAVID, b New York, NY, Jan 19, 14. ANESTHESIOLOGY. *Educ:* Brown Univ, PhB, 34; NY Univ, MD, 38. *Hon Degrees:* MA, Harvard Univ, 68. *Prof Exp:* Fel surg, Sch Med, Johns Hopkins Univ, 45-47; asst prof anesthesia, Sch Med, Univ Pa, 52-54; from assoc clin prof to clin prof, 54-67, prof, 67-79, EMER PROF ANESTHESIA, HARVARD MED SCH, 79- *Concurrent Pos:* Consult, Valley Forge Army Hosp & Philadelphia Naval Hosp, 52-54, Children's Boston Lying In, Chelsea Naval, West Roxbury Vet Admin, Rutland Vet Admin, Winchester, Burbank & Nantucket Cottage Hosps, 54-; chmn adv panel anesthesiol, US Pharmacopoeia, 54-60; ed-in-chief, J Anesthesiol, 64; chmn comn anesthesia, Nat Acad Sci-Nat Res Coun, 65; pres, Boston Med Libr, 79- *Mem:* Am Soc Anesthesiol; AMA; Sigma Xi. *Res:* Pharmacology, physiology and biochemistry of surgery and anesthesia. *Mailing Add:* 11 Holly Rd Waban MA 02115

VANDE BERG, JERRY STANLEY, b Sheldon, Iowa, June 1, 40; m 79; c 3. ELECTRON MICROSCOPY, TISSUE CULTURE. *Educ:* Univ Nebr, BSc, 64, MSc, 65; Va Polytech Inst & State Univ, PhD(physiol), 69. *Prof Exp:* Instr entom, Va Polytech Inst & State Univ, 67-69; asst prof neurophysiol, Wayne State Univ, 69-74; res assoc, Univ Wis-Madison, 74-79; asst prof electron microscopy, Old Dominion Univ, 75-79; dir core res, 79-82, CHIEF CLIN & RES, ELECTRON MICROSOPY LAB, VET ADMIN MED CTR, 82- *Concurrent Pos:* Lectr, Univ Calif, San Diego Med Sch, 79-80, Eastern Va Med Sch, 78-79. *Mem:* Electron Microscopy Soc Am. *Res:* Cellular mechanisms of contraction in wound healing. *Mailing Add:* Vet Admin Med Ctr 151 3350 La Jolla Village Dr San Diego CA 92161

VANDEBERG, JOHN LEE, b Appleton, Wis, June 14, 47; m 75; c 2. GENETICS. *Educ:* Univ Wis-Madison, BS, 69; La Trobe Univ, Melbourne, BS, 70; Macquarie Univ, PhD(genetics), 75. *Prof Exp:* Tutor genetics, Macquarie Univ, Sydney, 73-75; res assoc genetics, Univ Wis-Madison, 75-79; ASST PROF, DEPT ANAT, UNIV TEX HEALTH SCI CTR, SAN ANTONIO, 80-, ASST PROF, DEPT PATH, 81- *Concurrent Pos:* Fel, Pop Coun, 76-77; NIH trainee, 77-78; assoc found scientist genetics prog, Southwest Found Res & Educ, 80-81, dir, Dept Genetics, 82- *Mem:* AAAS; Genetics Soc Am; Sigma Xi. *Res:* Biochemical genetics, isozymes of marsupials and non-human primates, sex chromosome evolution and dosage compensation. *Mailing Add:* Dept Genetics Southwest Found Res & Educ PO Box 28147 San Antonio TX 78284

VANDE BERG, WARREN JAMES, b Orange City, Iowa, Sept 28, 43; m 62; c 3. PHYCOLOGY. *Educ:* Iowa State Univ, BS, 66; Ind Univ Univ, Bloomington, PhD(phycol), 70. *Prof Exp:* Asst prof, 70-75, ASSOC PROF BIOL, NORTHERN MICH UNIV, 75- *Mem:* Phycol Soc Am. *Res:* Control of cellular development in Volvox. *Mailing Add:* Dept of Biol Northern Mich Univ Marquette MI 49855

VAN DE CASTLE, JOHN F, b New York, NY, Sept 30, 33; m 57; c 4. POLYMER CHEMISTRY, PETROLEUM CHEMISTRY. *Educ:* St John's Col, BS, 55; Univ Md, PhD(org chem), 60. *Prof Exp:* Chemist, Hoffmann-La Roche, Inc, 55, Nat Bur Standards, 56 & Am Cyanamid Co, 57; group leader elastomers, Esso Res & Eng Co, NJ, 59-65, investment planning & mkt adv, Esso Chem Co, Inc, NY, 65-71; asst to vpres, Englehard Minerals & Chem Co, 71-72, mgr com develop, 72-77; mgr technol acquision, 77-81, VPRES ARCO TECHNOL, ARCO CHEM CO, 81- *Res:* Synthesis and characterization of ethylene propylene copolymers and terpolymers, polybutadienes; chemical modification of polymers; Ziegler and organometallic catalytic studies; technology licensing for petroleum and petrochemical industries; petroleum and petrochemical processing; hydrogenation processes; oxidation processes. *Mailing Add:* 20 Fox Chase Dr Watchung NJ 07060

VANDEGAER, JAN EDMOND, b Tienen, Belg, July 28, 27; nat US; m 51; c 4. BIOMEDICAL CHEMISTRY, ENVIRON COAGULANTS. *Educ:* Cath Univ Louvain, BS, 48, MS, 50, PhD(phys chem), 52. *Prof Exp:* Asst res proteins, Cath Univ Louvain, 52-54; fel, Nat Res Coun Can, 54-55; res chemist, Dow Chem Co, 55-59; sr chemist & proj leader, J T Baker Chem Co, 59-60, sr chemist & group leader, 60-62; mgr polymer res, Wallace & Tiernan, Inc, 62-65, dir cent res, 65-70; dir lab res, Chem Group, Dart Industs Inc, 70-74; dir res, 74-77, vpres, 75-77, CONSULT, CHEM PROD DEVELOP, ALCOLAC INC, 77- *Concurrent Pos:* Scholar, Biochem Inst, Finland, 53 & Cambridge, 54. *Mem:* Asn Res Dirs; Soc Plastics Engrs; Am Chem Soc. *Res:* Physical chemistry of proteins; polymer chemistry; correlation of physical properties of high polymers and molecular structure; biomedical applications; plastics engineering; microencapsulation; polyolefins, surfactants, cosmetics and emulsion polymerization; research administration; technical planning. *Mailing Add:* 427 Auds Lane Pasadena MD 21122

VAN DE GRAAFF, KENT MARSHALL, b Ogden, Utah, May 21, 42; m 62; c 4. GROSS ANATOMY, MAMMALOGY. *Educ:* Weber State Col, BS, 65; Univ Utah, MS, 69; Northern Ariz Univ, PhD(zool), 73. *Prof Exp:* Asst prof vet sci, Univ Minn, St Paul, 73-75; ASST PROF HUMAN ANAT, BRIGHAM YOUNG UNIV, 75- *Honors & Awards:* A Brazier Howell Honoriarum, Am Soc Mammalogists, 72. *Mem:* Am Soc Mammalogists; Am Soc Zoologists; Am Soc Vet Anatomists. *Res:* Functional morphological aspects of mammalian posture and locomotion. *Mailing Add:* Dept of Zool 575 Widtsoe Bldg Brigham Young Univ Provo UT 84602

VANDEGRIFT, ALFRED EUGENE, b Chanute, Kans, Nov 10, 37; m 59; c 4. RESEARCH ADMINISTRATION. *Educ:* Univ Kans, BS, 59; Univ Calif, Berkeley, PhD(chem eng), 63. *Prof Exp:* Assoc chem engr, 63-65, sr chem engr, 65-69, head, Environ Sci Sect, 69-73, asst dir, Phys Sci Div, 73-74, dir, NStar Div, Minneapolis, 74-77, dir, Econ & Mgt Sci Div, 77-80, VPRES, SOCIAL & ENG SYSTS, MIDWEST RES INST, 80- *Concurrent Pos:* Lectr gen eng, Univ Mo-Kansas City, 67-72; adj prof indust eng, Univ Mo-Columbia, 78- *Mem:* AAAS; Sigma Xi. *Res:* Pollution control and environmental assessment; mathematical modeling of physical and social phenomena; energy studies-alternative fuels; surface chemistry-oscillating jet studies of surface and interfacial tension; management science. *Mailing Add:* Midwest Res Inst 425 Volker Blvd Kansas City MO 64110

VANDEGRIFT, VAUGHN, b Jersey City, NJ, Dec 7, 46; m 69; c 3. BIOCHEMISTRY. *Educ:* Montclair State Col, BA, 68, MA, 70; Ohio Univ, PhD(biochem), 74. *Prof Exp:* Teacher chem, River Dell Regional High Sch, Oradell, NJ, 68-70; asst prof chem & biol, Ill State Univ, 74-76; assoc prof med biochem, Southern Ill Univ, 80-81; asst prof, 76-79, ASSOC PROF CHEM, MURRAY STATE UNIV, 79- *Mem:* Sigma Xi; Am Chem Soc; Biophys Soc. *Res:* Role of DNA associated histone proteins in chromosomal structure and function; use of circular dichroism in the study of nucleoprotein complexes. *Mailing Add:* Dept Chem Murray State Univ Murray KY 42071

VANDEHEY, ROBERT C, b Hollandtown, Wis, July 19, 24. ENTOMOLOGY. *Educ:* Univ Notre Dame, MS, 57, PhD(biol), 61. *Prof Exp:* Instr high sch, Pa, 49-55; from instr to asst prof, 55-69, ASSOC PROF BIOL, ST NORBERT COL, 69- *Concurrent Pos:* NIH res fel, Inst Genetics, Johannes Gutenberg Univ, Mainz, 63-64; res assoc, Mt St Mary's Col, Calif, 71-72. *Mem:* AAAS; Entom Soc Am; Am Mosquito Control Asn; Sigma Xi. *Res:* Genetic variability and control of the mosquitoes, especially Aedes aegypti and Culex pipiens. *Mailing Add:* St Norbert Col De Pere WI 54115

VAN DE KAMP, PETER CORNELIS, b Plainfield, NJ, Aug 25, 40; m 64; c 2. GEOLOGY, GEOCHEMISTRY. *Educ:* Lehigh Univ, BA, 62; McMaster Univ, MSc, 64; Univ Bristol, PhD(geochem), 67. *Prof Exp:* Geologist, Shell Develop Co, Tex & Calif, 67-71 & Shell Oil Co, Colo, 71-73; res prof, Univ Man, 73-74; vpres, Geo-Logic, Inc, 74-77; independent petrol explor consult, 77-79; PARTNER, GEORESOURCES ASSOC, 79- *Mem:* Soc Econ Paleont & Mineral; Geol Soc Am; Am Asn Petrol Geol; Geol Soc London. *Res:* Stratigraphy; sedimentary, metamorphic and igneous petrology and geochemistry. *Mailing Add:* 1750 Cabernet Lane St Helena CA 94574

VAN DE KAR, LOUIS DAVID, b Amsterdam, Nethelands, Apr 15, 47; m 78. NEUROPHARMACOLOGY, NEUROENDOCRINOLOGY. *Educ:* Univ Amsterdam, BS, 71, MS, 74; Univ Iowa PhD(pharmacol), 78. *Prof Exp:* Rea assoc pharmacol, Netherlands Cent Inst Brain Res, 74-75; fel physiol, Univ Calif, San Francisco, 79-81; ASST PROF PHARMACOL, STRITCH SCH MED, LOYOLA UNIV, 81- *Concurrent Pos:* Fel, Fulbright-Hays Found, 75. *Mem:* Int Soc Neuroendocrinol. *Res:* Role of serotonergic and catecholamineroic neurons in the regulation of luteinizing homrone carticosterone and prolactin secretion; neuroanatomy and physiology of brain serotonin; role of brain serotonin in cardiovascular homeostasis. *Mailing Add:* Dept Pharmacol Stritch Sch Med Loyola Univ 2160 S First Ave Maywood IL 60153

VANDE KIEFT, LAURENCE JOHN, b Grand Rapids, Mich, May 14, 32; m 62; c 2. SOLID STATE PHYSICS, OPTICAL PHYSICS. *Educ:* Calvin Col, BA, 53; Univ Conn, MS, 55, PhD(physics), 68. *Prof Exp:* Sr physicist, Bendix Res Labs, 58-62; teaching & res asst, Univ Conn, 62-63 & 64-68; res physicist, Signature & Propagation Lab, 68-72, chief, Optical & Microwave Systs Br, Concepts Anal Lab, 72-75, dep proj mgr, 75-79, EXPLOSIVES FORMULATION TEAM LEADER, TERMINAL BALLISTICS DIV, BALLISTIC RES LAB, US ARMY ABERDEEN PROVING GROUND, MD, 79- *Mem:* Am Phys Soc. *Res:* Electron paramagnetic resonance investigations of radiation effects in single crystals; laser interactions with the atmosphere; laser semiactive terminal homing; computer simulation. *Mailing Add:* US Army Ballistic Res Labs Attn DRDAR-BLT-E Aberdeen Proving Ground MD 21005

VAN DEMARK, DUANE R, b Elida, Ohio, Feb 26, 36; div; c 2. SPEECH PATHOLOGY. *Educ:* Hiram Col, BA, 58; Univ Iowa, MA & PhD(speech path, audiol), 62. *Prof Exp:* Instr speech path, Ind Univ, 62-65; asst prof, 65-68, assoc prof speech path & otolaryngol, 68-75, PROF SPEECH PATH & OTOLARYNGOL & MAXILLOFACIAL SURG, UNIV IOWA, 75- *Concurrent Pos:* Ind Univ Found res grant, 65; Am-Scand Found George Marshall fel, 70; Nat Inst Dent Res spec fel, 70; partic, Int Cong Cleft Palate, 67-69 & 73, mem prog comt, 68, secy & asst to secy gen, 69; sect ed, Cleft Palate J. *Mem:* Am Cleft Palate Educ Found; Am Speech & Hearing Asn; Am Cleft Palate Asn (vpres, 80, pres, 82). *Res:* Cleft palate research. *Mailing Add:* Dept of Otolaryngol Univ of Iowa Iowa City IA 52242

VANDEMARK, J S, b Fairgrove, Mich, Mar 24, 19; m 45; c 1. HORTICULTURE, VEGETABLE CROPS. *Educ:* Mich State Univ, BS, 41, MS, 46; Univ Ill, PhD(hort), 60. *Prof Exp:* From asst prof to assoc prof hort, Purdue Univ, 47-57; commodity dir, Am Farm Fedn, 57-58; dir res, Cent Aquirre Sugar Co, 58-60; assoc prof, 60-63, prof, 63-79, EMER PROF HORT, UNIV ILL, URBANA, 79- *Mem:* Am Soc Hort Sci. *Res:* Commercial production and fertility of sugar cane and vegetable crops. *Mailing Add:* 1103 Dorner Dr Urbana IL 61801

VANDEMARK, NOLAND LEROY, b Columbus Grove, Ohio, July 6, 19; m 40; c 3. PHYSIOLOGY, NURTURING CREATIVITY. *Educ:* Ohio State Univ, BS, 41, MS, 42; Cornell Univ, PhD, 48. *Prof Exp:* Asst animal husb, Ohio State Univ, 41-42; vitamin chemist, State Dept Agr, Ohio, 42; asst animal husb, Cornell Univ, 42-44, 48; livestock specialist, US Dept Army, Austria, 46-47; from asst prof to prof physiol, Univ Ill, Urbana, 48-64; prof dairy sci & chmn dept, Col Agr & Home Econ, Ohio State Univ & Ohio Agr Res & Develop Ctr, 64-73, mem fac, Coop Exten Serv, Univ, 64-73; dir, Agr Exp Sta, 74-81, PROF ANIMAL SCI, CORNELL UNIV, 74-; DIR RES, NY STATE COL AGR & LIFE SCI, 74- *Honors & Awards:* Borden Award, 59; Gold Medal, Ital Govt, 64; Citation, Ital Soc Animal Sci, 72. *Mem:* AAAS; Am Soc Animal Sci; Am Dairy Sci Asn; Am Physiol Soc; Brit Soc Study Fertil. *Res:* Physiology and biochemistry of reproductive processes in cattle, especially semen production; sperm metabolism; female reproductive processes; artificial insemination and fertility-sterility problems; research management. *Mailing Add:* 292 Roberts Hall Cornell Univ Ithaca NY 14853

VAN DEN AKKER, JOHANNES ARCHIBALD, b Los Angeles, Calif, Dec 5, 04; m 30, 58; c 1. THERMODYNAMICS, OPTICS. *Educ:* Calif Inst Technol, BS, 26, PhD(physics), 31. *Prof Exp:* Instr physics, Wash Univ, 30-35; res assoc & chmn dept, 35-56, sr res assoc physics & chmn dept physics & math, 56-70, res counsr, 65-70, EMER PROF PHYSICS, INST PAPER CHEM, LAWRENCE UNIV, 70-; CONSULT RES & DEVELOP, AM CAN CO, NEENAH, 71- *Concurrent Pos:* Sr Fulbright lectr, Univ Manchester Inst Sci & Technol, 61-62. *Honors & Awards:* Res & Develop Award, Tech Asn Pulp & Paper Indust, 67, Gold Medal, 68. *Mem:* Fel AAAS; fel Am Phys Soc; fel Optical Soc Am; Am Asn Physics Teachers; fel Tech Asn Pulp & Paper Indust. *Res:* Spatial distribution of x-ray photoelectrons; optical properties of paper; spectrophotometry and color measurement; instrumentation of all properties of paper; paper and fiber physics. *Mailing Add:* One Brokaw Pl Appleton WI 54911

VAN DEN AVYLE, JAMES ALBERT, b South Bend, Ind, Sept 13, 46; m 68. METALLURGY. *Educ:* Purdue Univ, BS, 68; Mass Inst Technol, SM, 69, PhD(metall), 75. *Prof Exp:* STAFF MEM, SANDIA LABS, 68- *Mem:* Am Soc Metals, Am Soc Testing & Mat. *Res:* Fracture of metals, mechanical properties of metals. *Mailing Add:* Org 5822 Sandia Nat Labs Albuquerque NM 87185

VANDENBELT, JOHN MELVIN, physical chemistry, see previous edition

VANDENBERG, EDWIN JAMES, b Hawthorne, NJ, Sept 13, 18; m 50; c 2. POLYMER CHEMISTRY. *Educ:* Stevens Inst Technol, ME, 39. *Hon Degrees:* DrEng, Stevens Inst Technol, 65. *Prof Exp:* Res chemist, 39-44, asst shift supvr, Sunflower Ord Works, Kans, 44-45, from res chemist to sr res chemist, 45-65, res assoc, 65-78, SR RES ASSOC, 78- RES ASSOC, RES CTR, HERCULES INC, 78- *Concurrent Pos:* Mem adv bd, J Polymer Sci, 66- & Marcamolecules, 77-80. *Honors & Awards:* Indust Res 100 Award, 65. *Mem:* Am Chem Soc. *Res:* Paper sizing; soil stabilization; emulsion polymerization; peroxide reactions; polymers; Ziegler, viny ether, epoxide and graft polymerizations; polypropyiene, epichlorohydrin elastomers; mechanism of polymerization; water soluble polymers and elastomers. *Mailing Add:* Hercules Inc Res Ctr Wilmington DE 19899

VANDENBERG, JOANNA MARIA, b Heemstede, Netherlands, Jan 24, 38; div; c 2. X-RAY DIFFRACTION, THIN FILM PREPARATION. *Educ:* Leiden State Univ, BS, 59, MS, 62, PhD(structural chem), 64. *Prof Exp:* Teaching asst, Lab Crystallog, Univ Amsterdam, 62-64; res chemist, Royal Dutch & Shell Lab, 64-68; fel, 68-69, MEM TECH STAFF, BELL LABS, MURRAY HILL, 72- *Concurrent Pos:* Consult, Bell Labs, 72. *Mem:* Am Phys Soc. *Res:* In site x-ray analysis of thin film interface reactions in metal semiconductor and metal-metal interfaces; polycrystalline and single crystal films; superconductivity of bulk and thin film materials. *Mailing Add:* Bell Labs 600 Mountain Ave Murray Hill NJ 07974

VAN DEN BERG, L, b Hattem, Neth, Mar 14, 29; Can citizen; m 53; c 4. BIOCHEMICAL ENGINEERING, FOOD SCIENCE. *Educ:* State Agr Univ, Wageningen, MSc, 53; Univ Man, MSc, 55. *Prof Exp:* sr res officer food technol, 56-80, PRIN RES OFFICER, BIOL PROD FUELS, DIV BIOL SCI, NAT RES COUN CAN, 80- *Mem:* Am Soc Microbiol; Am Asn Adv Sci; Inst Food Technologists; Can Inst Food Sci & Technol. *Res:* Application of refrigeration to food preservation, including freezing and frozen storage of meat and vegetables and storage of fresh vegetables; anaerobic digestion of food plant waste; methanogenesis from biomass; jermemter design. *Mailing Add:* Div Biol Sci Nat Res Coun Can Ottawa ON K1A 0R6 Can

VANDENBERG, STEVEN GERRITJAN, b Den Helder, Netherlands, July 7, 15; nat US; m 48. BEHAVIORAL GENETICS, PSYCHOLOGY. *Educ:* Univ Groningen, DrsJur, 46; Univ Mich, PhD, 55. *Prof Exp:* Psychologist, Ionia State Hosp for Criminally Insane, 47-48; asst psychol, Univ Mich, 48-50, psychologist, Inst Human Biol, 51-57, assoc dir schizophrenia study, Ment Health Res Inst, 57-60; psychologist, Sch Med, Univ Louisville, 60-67; PROF PSYCHOL, UNIV COLO, BOULDER, 67- *Concurrent Pos:* Psychologist, State Child Guid Clin, Mich, 49-50; lab schs, Eastern Mich Univ & pub schs, Mich, 51; exec ed, Behav Genetics, 70-77; Nat Inst Ment Health res career develop award, 62-67; vis prof genetics, Univ Hawaii, 74-75 & Univ Amsterdam, 80-81. *Mem:* Am Soc Human Genetics; Soc Res Child Develop; Soc Personality Assessment; Am Psychol Asn; Brit Psychol Soc. *Res:* Objective measures of personality; behavior genetics; factor analysis and test theory; computer applications in the behavior sciences. *Mailing Add:* Dept Psychol Univ Colo Boulder CO 80309

VANDENBERG, STUART R, metallurgical engineering, see previous edition

VANDENBERGH, JOHN GARRY, b Paterson, NJ, May 5, 35; m 58; c 2. ANIMAL BEHAVIOR, ENDOCRINOLOGY. *Educ:* Montclair State Col, AB, 57; Ohio Univ, MA, 59; Pa State Univ, PhD(zool), 62. *Prof Exp:* Res biologist, Nat Inst Neurol Dis & Blindness, 62-65; res scientist, NC Dept Ment Health, 65-76; PROF & HEAD DEPT ZOOL, NC STATE UNIV, 76- *Concurrent Pos:* NIMH grant, 67-; mem, Nat Primate Adv Comt, NIH; mem psychobiol panel, NSF; mem comt conserv non-human primates, Nat Res Coun-Nat Acad Sci; mem rev comt basic behav processes, NIMH; mem adv comt, Calif Primate Res Ctr & Caribbean Primate Ctr. *Mem:* Am Soc Zoologists; Animal Behav Soc (pres, 82-83); Am Soc Mammal; Soc Study Reproduction; Int Primatol Soc. *Res:* Environmental control of reproduction; endocrine basis of behavior; pheromones and reproduction; rodent and primate social behavior. *Mailing Add:* Dept of Zool NC State Univ Raleigh NC 27650

VAN DEN BERGH, SIDNEY, b Wassenaar, Holland, May 20, 29; c 3. ASTRONOMY. *Educ:* Princeton Univ, AB, 50; Ohio State Univ, MSc, 52; Univ Göttingen, Dr rer nat(astron), 56. *Prof Exp:* Asst prof astron, Ohio State Univ, 56-58; from lectr to prof astron, Univ Toronto, 58-77; DIR, DOMINION ASTROPHYS OBSERV, 77- *Concurrent Pos:* Pres & chmn bd, Can, France & Hawaii Telescope Corp, 82. *Mem:* Am Astron Soc; Royal Soc Can; Royal Astron Soc; Int Astron Union (vpres, 76-82). *Res:* Extragalactic nebulae; star clusters; variable stars; supernovas. *Mailing Add:* Dominion Astrophys Observ 5071 W Saanics Rd Victoria BC V8X 4M6 Can

VAN DEN BERGHE, JOHN, b Rotterdam, Netherlands, Jan 30, 23; m 50; c 9. ORGANIC CHEMISTRY, POLYMER CHEMISTRY. *Educ:* Univ Utah, BA, 47, MS, 48; Univ Wis, PhD(org chem), 52. *Prof Exp:* SR RES CHEMIST, EASTMAN KODAK CO, 52- *Mem:* Am Chem Soc. *Res:* Polyesters; polycarbonates; polyesteramides; substituted polystyrenes and other polyolefins; Diels-Alder reaction; pyrolysis reactions; emulsion polymerization; identification of copolymer and terpolymer compositions; non-aqueous titrimetry; molecular weight distribution of polymers. *Mailing Add:* 34 Tanglewood Dr Rochester NY 14616

VAN DEN BOLD, WILLEM AALDERT, b Amsterdam, Neth, Mar 30, 21; m 50; c 5. GEOLOGY, PALEONTOLOGY. *Educ:* State Univ Utrecht, PhD, 46. *Prof Exp:* Micropaleontologist, Royal Dutch Shell Group, 46-58; assoc prof geol, 58-59, PROF GEOL, LA STATE UNIV, BATON ROUGE, 59- *Mem:* Paleont Res Inst; Soc Econ Paleontologists & Mineralogists. *Res:* Post-Paleozoic ostracoda; planktonic Foraminifera. *Mailing Add:* Dept of Geol La State Univ Baton Rouge LA 70803

VANDEN BORN, WILLIAM HENRY, b Rhenen, Netherlands, Nov 17, 32; Can citizen; m 58; c 5. WEED SCIENCE, PLANT PHYSIOLOGY. *Educ:* Univ Alta, BSc, 56, MSc, 58; Univ Toronto, PhD(plant physiol), 61. *Prof Exp:* Fel, Dept Plant Sci, 60-61, from asst prof to assoc prof, 61-72, chmn dept, 70-75, PROF WEED SCI & CROP ECOL, UNIV ALTA, 72- *Concurrent Pos:* Assoc ed, Weed Sci, 81-84 & Can J Plant Sci, 81-84. *Mem:* Weed Sci Soc Am; Can Soc Plant Physiol; Can Soc Agron; Am Sci Affil. *Res:* Weed biology; weed control; herbicide physiology. *Mailing Add:* Dept of Plant Sci Univ of Alta Edmonton AB T6G 2P5 Can

VAN DEN BOSCH, ROBERT, entomology, deceased

VANDENBOSCH, ROBERT, b Lexington, Ky, Dec 12, 32; m 56; c 2. NUCLEAR CHEMISTRY. *Educ:* Calvin Col, AB, 54; Univ Calif, PhD(chem), 57. *Prof Exp:* From asst chemist to assoc chemist, Agronne Nat Lab, 57-63; PROF CHEM, UNIV WASH, 63- *Mem:* Fel Am Phys Soc. *Res:* Heavy ion nuclear reactions and nuclear fission. *Mailing Add:* Dept of Chem Univ of Wash Seattle WA 98195

VANDEN EYNDEN, CHARLES LAWRENCE, b Cincinnati, Ohio, June 25, 36. NUMBER THEORY. *Educ:* Univ Cincinnati, BS, 58; Univ Ore, MA, 60, PhD(math), 62. *Prof Exp:* NSF fel, Univ Mich, 62-63; asst prof math, Univ Ariz, 63-65 & Miami Univ, 65-67; vis asst prof, Pa State Univ, 67-68; asst prof, Ohio Univ, 68-69; assoc prof, 69-74, PROF MATH, ILL STATE UNIV, 74- *Concurrent Pos:* Vis prof, Portland State Univ, 77-78. *Mem:* Am Math Soc; Math Asn Am. *Res:* Diophantine approximation; elementary number theory; combinatorial theory; sequences of integers. *Mailing Add:* Dept of Math Ill State Univ Normal IL 61761

VANDEN HEUVEL, WILLIAM JOHN ADRIAN, III, b Brooklyn, NY, Mar 7, 35; m 60; c 3. DRUG METABOLISM, ANALYTICAL BIOCHEMISTRY. *Educ:* Princeton Univ, AB, 56, AM, 58, PhD(org chem), 60. *Prof Exp:* Instr chem, Lipid Res Ctr, Col Med, Baylor Univ, 62, asst prof, Dept Biochem, 62-64; sr res biochemist, 64-67, res fel, Dept Biochem, 67-72, sr res fel, Dept Drug Metab, 72-76, sect dir, Animal Drug Metab & Radiochem, 76-79, SR INVESTR, MERCK SHARP & DOHME RES

LABS, 79- *Concurrent Pos:* Sr asst scientist, Nat Heart Inst, 60-62; vis scientist, Bucknell Univ, 79-84. *Mem:* AAAS; Am Chem Soc; Am Soc Mass Spectrometry; Am Soc Pharm Exp Therapeut. *Res:* Development of gas chromatographic and mass spectrometric methods for the identification and quantification of drugs, metabolites and natural products; derivatization techniques; drug residue studies; organic mass spectrometry; use of radioactive and stable isotopes. *Mailing Add:* Merck Sharp & Dohme Res Labs Rahway NJ 07065

VAN DEN NOORT, STANLEY, b Lynn, Mass, Sept 8, 30; m 54; c 5. NEUROLOGY. *Educ:* Dartmouth Col, AB, 51; Harvard Univ, MD, 54. *Prof Exp:* Asst prof neurol, Sch Med, Case Western Reserve Univ, 65-71; PROF MED (NEUROL) & DEAN, COL MED, UNIV CALIF, IRVINE, 71- *Mailing Add:* 101 City Dr S Orange CA 92668

VANDE NOORD, EDWIN LEE, b Pella, Iowa, Sept 10, 38; m 62; c 2. SPACE PHYSICS. *Educ:* Grinnell Col, BA, 60; Univ NMex, MS, 63, PhD(physics), 68. *Prof Exp:* Res asst physics, Grinnel Col, 60-61; asst, Univ NMex, 61-68, res assoc, 68-69; res scientist, Douglas Advan Res Labs, Calif, 69-70; staff scientist, 70-75, mgr advan progs, 75-78, asst dir, 78-80, DIR, BALL AEROSPACE SYSTS DIV, 80- *Mem:* Optical Soc Am; Am Inst Aeronaut & Astronaut; Sigma Xi. *Res:* Photometry of zodiacal light; interplanetary dust; infrared Fourier transform spectroscopy; space instrumentation; remote sensing; earth radiation budget instrumentation. *Mailing Add:* Ball Aerospace Systs Div PO Box 1062 Boulder CO 80306

VAN DEN SYPE, JAAK STEFAAN, b Dendermonde, Belg, July 15, 35. METALLURGICAL ENGINEERING, MATERIALS SCIENCE. *Educ:* Univ Louvain, MetEng, 59; Univ Pa, MSc, 61, PhD(metall eng), 65. *Prof Exp:* Instr metall, Sch Metall Eng, Univ Pa, 66-67, asst prof, 67-70; SR RES METALLURGIST, TARRYTOWN TECH CTR, LINDE DIV, UNION CARBIDE CORP, 70- *Mem:* Am Phys Soc; Am Inst Mech Engrs; Am Soc Metals. *Res:* Surface physics; phase transformations; mechanical properties. *Mailing Add:* Tarrytown Tech Ctr Linde Div Union Carbide Corp Tarrytown NY 10591

VAN DE POEL, JOSEPHUS, b Groenlo, Holland, Sept 15, 25; m 62; c 1. ORGANIC CHEMISTRY, ANALYTICAL CHEMISTRY. *Educ:* Univ Leiden, BS, 47, MS, 52, PhD(org chem), 56. *Prof Exp:* Instr anal chem, Univ Leiden, 53-56; res chemist, E I du Pont de Nemours & Co, 56-58; from asst prof to assoc prof, 58-68, PROF ANAL CHEM, WELLS COL, 68- *Concurrent Pos:* NSF res grant, 63-65; fel, Ga Inst Technol, 67. *Mem:* Am Chem Soc. *Res:* Radiochemistry; stability and radiocyanide exchange of eight-coordinate molybdenum and tungsten cyanide complexes; tetracyano complexes of molybdenum; synthesis of potassium octacyanomolybdate (IV). *Mailing Add:* Dept of Chem Wells Col Aurora NY 13026

VANDEPOPULIERE, JOSEPH MARCEL, b Parkville, Mo, June 21, 29; m 53; c 4. NUTRITION, BIOCHEMISTRY. *Educ:* Cent Mo State Univ, AB, 51; Univ Mo, Columbia, MS, 54; Univ Fla, PhD(animal husb), 60. *Prof Exp:* Res asst agr chem, Univ Mo, Columbia, 51-54; asst mgr, Biol Lab, Ralston Purina, 54-57; res asst animal husb, Univ Fla, 57-60; asst mgr boiler res, Ralston Purina, 60-62, mgr broiler res, 62-69, mgr field res & tech serv US, Can & Mex, 69-72; ASSOC PROF DEPT POULTRY HUSB, UNIV MO, COLUMBIA, 72- *Concurrent Pos:* Travel grant, World Poultry Sci Asn, 78. *Mem:* Poultry Sci Asn (secy-treas, 77-); World Poultry Sci Asn; Can Feed Mfg Nutrit Coun. *Res:* Efficient conversion of agriculture and industrial residuals to human food through the use of a monogastric-polygastric biological team; insect and ectoparasite control in the avian species. *Mailing Add:* Dept of Poultry Husb Univ of Mo Columbia MO 65211

VANDEPUTTE, JOHN, b Catasauqua, Pa, May 3, 18; m 41; c 3. ORGANIC CHEMISTRY. *Educ:* Albright Col, BS, 43; Rutgers Univ, MS, 45, PhD(chem), 51. *Prof Exp:* Instr org chem, Rutgers Univ, 48-51; res assoc, 51-68, mgr res proj planning & coordr, 68-75, MGR PRECLIN RES ADMIN, SQUIBB INST MED RES, 75- *Concurrent Pos:* Mem, Proj Mgt Inst. *Mem:* Am Chem Soc. *Res:* Isolation, purification and identification of natural products and development of processes for their production. *Mailing Add:* Preclin Res Admin PO Box 4000 Princeton NJ 08540

VANDER, ARTHUR J, b Detroit, Mich, Dec 28, 33; m 55; c 3. PHYSIOLOGY. *Educ:* Univ Mich, BA, 55, MD, 59. *Prof Exp:* Intern med, New York Hosp-Cornell Med Ctr, 59-60; from instr to assoc prof, 60-69, PROF PHYSIOL, UNIV MICH, ANN ARBOR, 69- *Mem:* AAAS; Am Physiol Soc; Am Soc Nephrol; Soc Exp Biol & Med. *Res:* Renal physiology. *Mailing Add:* Dept of Physiol Univ of Mich Ann Arbor MI 48104

VAN DER BECK, ROLAND REED, b Newark, NJ, Dec 14, 25; m 49; c 3. CERAMICS. *Educ:* Rutgers Univ, BSc, 49; Ohio State Univ, MSc, 50; PhD(ceramic eng), 52. *Prof Exp:* Res asst ceramic res, Res Found, Ohio State Univ, 49-52; sr engr, Carborundum Co, NY, 52-56, sr coordr, 56-57, mgr prod eng, Pa, 57-59; mgr ceramic res, Foote Mineral Co, Pa, 60-63 & M&T Chem, Inc, 63-70; vpres res, Pfaudler, Sybron Corp, Rochester, 70-80; VPRES RES, AM OLEAN TILE CO, LANSDALE, PA, 70- *Mem:* Am Ceramic Soc. *Mailing Add:* 59 Reitz Pkwy Pittsford NY 14534

VANDER BEEK, LEO CORNELIS, b The Hague, Netherlands, Aug 28, 18; nat US; m 44; c 4. PLANT PHYSIOLOGY. *Educ:* Western Mich Univ, AB, 52; Univ Mich, MS, 53, PhD(bot), 57. *Prof Exp:* Asst, Univ Mich, 52-53, 54-55; from asst prof to assoc prof, 56-62, PROF BIOL, WESTERN MICH UNIV, 62- *Mem:* AAAS; Am Soc Plant Physiol; Am Inst Biol Sci. *Res:* Plant growth regulators; effect of audible sound on plant development. *Mailing Add:* Dept of Biol Western Mich Univ Kalamazoo MI 49008

VANDERBERG, JEROME PHILIP, b New York, NY, Feb 5, 35; m 67; c 2. PARASITOLOGY, CELL PHYSIOLOGY. *Educ:* City Col New York, BS, 55; Pa State Univ, MS, 57; Cornell Univ, PhD(med entom), 61. *Prof Exp:* Fel biol, Johns Hopkins Univ, 62-63; from asst prof to assoc prof, 63-74, PROF PARASITOL SCH MED, NY UNIV, 74- *Mem:* Am Soc Trop Med & Hyg; Am Soc Parasitol; Soc Protozool. *Res:* Cellular physiology of insects and of host-parasite complex; biology of mosquitoes; malariology; invasion of host cells by malaria parasite. *Mailing Add:* Div Parasitol Med Sch NY Univ New York NY 10016

VAN DER BIJL, WILLEM, b Alphen aan den Rijn, Netherlands, Aug 15, 20; nat US; m 46; c 2. METEOROLOGY. *Educ:* Vrije Univ, Netherlands, BSc, 41, MSc, 43; Univ Utrecht, PhD(meteorol), 52. *Prof Exp:* Res assoc climat, Royal Netherlands Meteorol Inst, 46-56; assoc prof physics & meteorol, Kans State Univ, 56-61; ASSOC PROF METEOROL, NAVAL POSTGRAD SCH, 61- *Concurrent Pos:* Fel statist & meteorol, Univ Chicago, 54-55. *Mem:* Am Meteorol Soc; Am Geophys Union; Sigma Xi. *Res:* Physics of the atmosphere; statistical treatment of data; statistical analysis of geophysical data. *Mailing Add:* Dept Meteorol Naval Post-Grad Sch Monterey CA 93940

VANDERBILT, DAVID HAMILTON, b Huntington, NY, Aug 20, 54; m 81. AMORPHOUS SEMICONDUCTORS, THEORY OF DEFECTS. *Educ:* Swarthmore Col, Ba, 76; Mass Inst Technol, PhD(physics), 81. *Prof Exp:* FEL, UNIV CALIF, BERKELEY, 81- *Mem:* Am Phys Soc; Sigma Xi. *Res:* Theoretical solid state physics; electronic structure of amorphous or other non-periodic systems, particularly semiconductors; chalcogenide glasses. *Mailing Add:* Dept Physics Univ Calif Berkeley CA 94720

VANDERBILT, JEFFREY JAMES, b Sheboygan, Wis, July 18, 51; m. ORGANIC CHEMISTRY. *Educ:* Calvin Col, BS, 73; Univ Mich, MS, 76, PhD(org chem), 78. *Prof Exp:* Res chemist, 78-80, SR CHEMIST ORG CHEM, TENN EASTMAN CO, 80- *Mem:* Am Chem Soc. *Res:* Process research and development. *Mailing Add:* Res Lab Bldg 150-B Tenn Eastman Co Kingsport TN 37660

VANDERBILT, VERN C, JR, b Indianapolis, Ind, Mar 29, 20; m 42; c 3. ENGINEERING. *Educ:* Purdue Univ, BS, 42, MS, 47, PhD(electronic instrumentation, servo control), 54. *Prof Exp:* Asst prof aeronaut, Purdue Univ, 46-52; private pract, 52-54; res engr, Gen Elec Co, 54-55; chief res engr in charge, Gen Res & Road Testing Depts, Dynamometer Lab & Electronics Div, Perfect Circle Corp, 56-62, mgr electronics div, 62-64; pres, Dynamic Precision Controls Corp, 64-74; PRES, VANDERBILT ASSOCS, 74- *Mem:* Inst Elec & Electronics Engrs; Soc Automotive Engrs; Am Soc Metals; Nat Soc Prof Engrs. *Res:* Electronic instrumentation and servo control as applied to internal combustion engines and automotive equipment. *Mailing Add:* Vanderbilt Assocs PO Box 31 Hagerstown IN 47346

VANDERBORGH, NICHOLAS ERNEST, b Bay Shore, NY, June 24, 38; c 3. ANALYTICAL CHEMISTRY. *Educ:* Hope Col, AB, 60; Southern Ill Univ, MS, 62, PhD(chem), 64. *Prof Exp:* Asst prof chem, Univ Minn, 64-66; from asst prof to assoc prof, Univ NMex, 66-75; staff mem, 75-77, ALT GROUP LEADER, LOS ALAMOS SCI LAB, 77- *Concurrent Pos:* Staff mem, Sandia Labs, 66-69; guest staff mem, Univ New Castle Upon Tyne, 73; res fels, Mead John & Assoc Western Univs. *Mem:* Am Chem Soc; Brit Chem Soc; AAAS. *Res:* The use of pyrolosis-chromatography for characterization of geomaterials; underground processing and monitoring. *Mailing Add:* In-Situ Sci MS 329 Los Alamos Sci Lab Los Alamos NM 87545

VAN DER BURG, SJIRK, b Makkum, Netherlands, Mar 23, 26; nat US; m; c 3. ORGANIC CHEMISTRY. *Educ:* Univ Groningen, Drs, 55. *Prof Exp:* Asst, Univ Groningen, 52-55; res chemist, Rubber Found, Delft Univ Technol, 55-56 & Res Ctr, US Rubber Co, NJ, 56-61; mgr mat res, US Rubber Tire Co, 61-66, develop mgr, Uniroyal Europ Tire Develop Ctr, Ger, 66-67, dir, 67-80; DIR, TYRE TECH DIV, DUNLOP LTD, 80- *Mem:* Am Chem Soc; Royal Netherlands Chem Soc; Plastics & Rubber Inst; NY Acad Sci. *Res:* Rubber chemistry and technology; plastics. *Mailing Add:* Tyre Tech Div Dunlop Ltd Fort Dunlop Erdington Birmingham B24 9QT England

VANDERBURG, VANCE DILKS, b Grand Rapids, Mich, July 22, 37; m 66. NUCLEAR ENGINEERING. *Educ:* Syracuse Univ, BS, 60; Purdue Univ, MS, 63, PhD(high energy physics), 65. *Prof Exp:* Physicist, US AEC, 65-67; asst physicist, Brookhaven Nat Lab, 67-69, assoc physicist, 69-73, physicist, 73; nuclear engr, Am Elec Power Serv Corp, 74-75; plant nuclear engr, 75-80, TECH DEPT PROD SUPVR, DONALD C COOK NUCLEAR PLANT, 80- *Mem:* Am Phys Soc; Am Nuclear Soc; Sigma Xi. *Res:* Experimental particle physics. *Mailing Add:* 1619 Forres Ave St Joseph MI 49085

VANDER BURGH, LEONARD F, b Chandler, Minn, Oct 10, 31; m 70; c 1. PHYSICAL ORGANIC CHEMISTRY. *Educ:* Hamline Univ, BS, 53; Univ Wash, PhD(org chem), 58. *Prof Exp:* Res chemist rubber, Shell Oil Co, 57-61; res chemist, polymers, 62-63, sr chemist paper, 63-66, group leader, 66-71, SR SCIENTIST, STARCH, A E STALEY MFG CO, 71- *Mem:* Am Chem Soc. *Res:* New starch derivatives, new processes for modifying starch and starch-synthetic polymer combinations. *Mailing Add:* RR 2 Box 22 Bethany IL 61914

VAN DEREN, JOHN MEDEARIS, JR, b Cynthiana, Ky, July 12, 29; m 53; c 4. ANALYTICAL CHEMISTRY. *Educ:* Univ Cincinnati, BS, 50; La State Univ, MS, 53, PhD(biochem), 59. *Prof Exp:* Asst, La State Univ, 58-59; asst food technologist & biochemist, Clemson Col, 59-61; res biochemist, Monsanto Co, Mo, 61-68; ANAL RES CHEMIST, RES DEPT, BUCKMAN LABS, INC, 68- *Res:* Pesticide residue analysis; methods development; food additives analysis; herbicide metabolism. *Mailing Add:* Res Dept Buckman Labs Inc 1256 N McLean Blvd Memphis TN 38108

VANDERGRAAF, TJALLE T, b Gravemoer, Netherlands, Sept 3, 36; Can citizen; m 66; c 4. ANALYTICAL CHEMISTRY, RADIOCHEMISTRY. *Educ:* Calvin Col, BS, 63; Pa State Univ, PhD(chem), 69. *Prof Exp:* RES SCIENTIST GEOCHEM & APPL CHEM BR, WHITESHELL NUCLEAR RES ESTAB, ATOMIC ENERGY CAN LTD, 69- *Mem:* Chem Inst Can; Can Nuclear Soc. *Res:* Radionuclide interaction with on geological materials; redox reactions of multivalent radionuclides in geological environments;

migration of radionuclides through crystalline rock formations; low temperature rock/water reactions; autoradiography of sorbeo radionuclide distributions. *Mailing Add:* Geochem & Appl Chem Br Atomic Energy Can Whiteshell Nuclear Res Estab Pinawa MB R0E 1L0 Can

VANDERGRAFT, JAMES SAUL, b Gooding, Idaho, Apr 29, 37. NUMERICAL ANALYSIS, NUMERICAL SOFTWARE. *Educ:* Stanford Univ, BS, 59, MS, 63; Univ Md, PhD(math), 66. *Prof Exp:* Programmer, Lawrence Radiation Lab, 59-60; num analyst, Bellcomm Inc, Washington, DC, 63-64; asst prof comput sci, Univ Md, 66-73, assoc prof, 73-79; ASST DIR, AUTOMATED SCI GROUP INC, SILVER SPRING, MD, 79- *Concurrent Pos:* Tech consult, Apollo Proj, Bellcomm Inc, 69-70; guest prof math, Swiss Fed Inst Zurich, 74. *Mem:* Soc Indust & Appl Math; Math Asn Am; Asn Comput Mach. *Res:* Numerical solution of linear and nonlinear systems of equations; numerical algorithms and numerical software; modeling and simulation. *Mailing Add:* 772 11th St SE Washington DC 20003

VANDER HAAR, ROY WILLIAM, b Sioux City, Iowa, Apr 26, 24; m 44; c 4. ANALYTICAL CHEMISTRY. *Educ:* Wesleyan Univ, AB, 47; Iowa State Col, PhD(anal chem), 52. *Prof Exp:* Res chemist, Am Oil Co, Ind, 52-70; res chemist, 70-75, SR RES CHEMIST, AMOCO RES CTR, STANDARD OIL CO, IND, 75- *Mem:* Am Chem Soc; Am Soc Mass Spectrometry. *Res:* Mass spectrometry; instrumental analytical chemistry. *Mailing Add:* Standard Oil Co Ind Amoco Res Ctr PO Box 400 Naperville IL 06056

VANDER HART, DAVID LLOYD, b Rehoboth, NMex, May 20, 41; m 64; c 2. PHYSICAL CHEMISTRY, POLYMER CHEMISTRY. *Educ:* Calvin Col, AB, 63; Univ Ill, Urbana, PhD(phys chem), 68. *Prof Exp:* Fel microwave spectros, Univ Ill, 68-69; RES CHEMIST, NAT BUR STANDARDS, 69- *Mem:* Am Phys Soc. *Res:* Nuclear magnetic resonance, particularly carbon-13, application to the characterization of polymer solids. *Mailing Add:* Div 563.00 Nat Bur Standards Washington DC 20234

VAN DER HEEM, PETER, physical chemistry, chemical engineering, see previous edition

VANDERHEIDEN, BERNARDO S, biochemistry, see previous edition

VAN DER HELM, DICK, b Velsen, Netherlands, Mar 16, 33; m 60; c 6. PHYSICAL CHEMISTRY. *Educ:* Univ Amsterdam, Drs, 56, DSc(x-ray diffraction), 60. *Prof Exp:* Res assoc x-ray diffraction, Ind Univ, 57-59 & Inst Cancer Res, Philadelphia, 59-62; from asst prof to prof, 62-77, GEORGE LYMAN CROSS RES PROF PHYS CHEM, UNIV OKLA, 77- *Concurrent Pos:* NIH Develop Award, 69-74. *Mem:* Am Chem Soc; Am Crystallog Asn; Royal Netherlands Chem Soc. *Res:* Molecular structure determination by means of x-ray diffraction of natural products, siderochromes and peptides. *Mailing Add:* Dept of Chem 620 Parrington Oval Univ of Okla Norman OK 73019

VANDERHOEF, LARRY NEIL, b Frazee, Minn, Mar 20, 41; m 63; c 2. HORMONE PHYSIOLOGY, DEVELOPMENT. *Educ:* Univ Wis-Milwaukee, BS, 64, MS, 65; Purdue Univ, Lafayette, PhD(plant physiol), 69. *Prof Exp:* Nat Res Coun fel, Univ Wis-Madison, 69-70; assoc prof, Univ Ill, Urbana, 70-76, head biol progs, 74-76, prof plant develop, 76-80, head bot dept, 77-80; PROVOST, DIV AGR & LIFE SCI, UNIV MD, COLLEGE PARK, 80- *Mem:* AAAS; Am Soc Plant Physiol. *Res:* Plant hormones and nucleic acid metabolism; nitrogen fixation. *Mailing Add:* 1104 Symons Hall Div Agr & Life Sci Univ Md College Park MD 20742

VANDERHOEK, JACK YEHUDI, b Hilversum, Neth, Jan 1, 41; US citizen; m 66. BIOCHEMISTRY, ORGANIC CHEMISTRY. *Educ:* City Col New York, BS, 60; Mass Inst Technol, PhD(org chem), 66. *Prof Exp:* Sr res chemist, Gen Mills, Inc, 66-68, group leader vitamin E and sterol synthesis, 68-69; NIH spec fel, Princeton Univ, 69-70 & Univ Fla, 71; res assoc biochem, Univ Mich, Ann Arbor, 71-72, instr, 72-74; lectr, Hadassah Univ Hosp, Hebrew Univ Med Sch, Jerusalem, Israel, 74-76; res assoc med & pharmacol, Univ Conn Health Ctr, Farmington, 77-78; ASST RES PROF BIOCHEM, GEORGE WASHINGTON UNIV, WASHINGTON, DC, 78- *Mem:* Am Chem Soc; NY Acad Sci; AAAS. *Res:* Lipid metabolism including leukotrienes, prostaglandins and thrombosanes; lipid mediators in allergic and inflammatory disease. *Mailing Add:* Dept of Biochem George Washington Univ Washington DC 20006

VAN DER HOEVEN, THEO A, b Indonesia, Feb 13, 33; US citizen; m 60; c 3. PHARMACOLOGY. *Educ:* Brooklyn Col, BS, 65; Columbia Univ, PhD(biochem), 71. *Prof Exp:* Instr biochem, Univ Mich, 71-74; asst prof med chem, Univ Md, Baltimore, 74-77; assoc prof pharmacol & exp therapeut, 77-80, ASSOC PROF BIOCHEM, ALBANY MED COL, 80- *Mem:* Am Chem Soc; Am Soc Pharmacol Exp Therapeut. *Res:* Hormonal regulation of drug metabolism; membrane bound enzymes. *Mailing Add:* Dept Biochem Albany Med Col Albany NY 12208

VAN DER HOFF, BERNARD MARIA EUPHEMIUS, b Utrecht, Netherlands, Aug 19, 19; Can citizen; m 49; c 4. POLYMER CHEMISTRY, POLYMER PHYSICS. *Educ:* Tech Inst Amsterdam, Ing, 41; Delft Univ Technol, Ir, 50. *Prof Exp:* Sci officer electrochem anal, Delft Univ Technol, 50-51; fel surface energy, Nat Res Coun Can, 51-53; sr chemist, Polymer Corp, Ltd, 53-57, res assoc, 57-66; PROF POLYMER CHEM & PHYSICS, UNIV WATERLOO, 67- *Concurrent Pos:* Consult, Dunlop Res Ctr, 69- *Mem:* Am Chem Soc; Chem Inst Can. *Res:* Emulsion polymerization; rheology; viscoelasticity; structural characterization of elastomers; degradation of polymers; mechanical properties of elastomer vulcanizates. *Mailing Add:* Dept of Chem Eng Univ of Waterloo Waterloo ON N2L 3G1 Can

VANDERHOFF, JOHN W, b Niagara Falls, NY, Aug 2, 25; m 50; c 2. POLYMER CHEMISTRY, COLLOID CHEMISTRY. *Educ:* Niagara Univ, BS, 47; Univ Buffalo, PhD(phys chem), 51. *Prof Exp:* Chemist, Phys Res Lab, Dow Chem Co, 50-56, proj leader, 56-58, assoc scientist, 58-70, Plastics Dept Res Lab, 63-70; assoc prof, 70-74, DIR, NAT PRINTING INK RES INST, ASSOC DIR COATINGS, CTR SURFACE & COATINGS RES, LEHIGH UNIV, 70-, PROF CHEM, 74-, CO-DIR EMULSION POLYMERS INST, 75- *Concurrent Pos:* Participant, Dow Career Scientist Assignment Prog, van't Hoff Lab, Utrecht, 65-66. *Honors & Awards:* Res award, Union Carbide Chem, 64-65. *Mem:* AAAS; fel Am Inst Chem; Am Chem Soc. *Res:* Polymerization kinetics; solution properties of polymers; mechanism of emulsion polymerization; latex properties; foamed plastics; mechanism of latex film formation; colloidal properties of latexes; monodisperse latexes; printing inks; deinking of wastepaper. *Mailing Add:* Ctr for Surface & Coatings Res Lehigh Univ Bethlehem PA 18015

VANDERHOLM, DALE HENRY, b Villisca, Iowa, Mar 28, 40; m 67; c 2. AGRICULTURAL ENGINEERING. *Educ:* Iowa State Univ, BS, 62, MS, 69; Colo State Univ, PhD(agr eng), 72. *Prof Exp:* Watershed planning engr, Iowa Soil Conserv Serv, USDA, 62-63; instr, Iowa State Univ, 67-68, asst prof agr eng water supply & waste treat, 72-73; asst prof, 73-77, ASSSOC PROF AGR ENG WATER, SUPPLY & WASTE TREAT, UNIV ILL, URBANA-CHAMPAIGN, 77-, ASST DIR, ILL AGR EXP STA, 81- *Concurrent Pos:* Res award, Great Plains Livestock Comt, 77; vis res fel, NZ Agr Inst, Lincoln Col, Cantebury, 79-80. *Mem:* Am Soc Agr Engrs; Soil Conserv Soc Am. *Res:* Treatment and handling of livestock wastes, particularly land application systems and feedlot runoff control systems; treatment of domestic sewage by recirculating sand filters and aerobic package systems. *Mailing Add:* 212 Mumford Hall Ill Agr Exp Sta Univ Ill 1301 W Gregory Urbana IL 61801

VAN DER HOVEN, ISAAC, b Rotterdam, Netherlands, July 13, 23; US citizen; m 56; c 4. METEOROLOGY. *Educ:* Pa State Univ, BS, 51, PhD(meteorol), 56; Mass Inst Technol, MS, 52. *Prof Exp:* Res assoc meteorol, Pa State Univ, 52-55; res meteorologist, Brookhaven Nat Lab, US Weather Bur, 55-57, Nev Test Site, 57-61, Off Meteorol Res, DC, 61-65; CHIEF AIR RESOURCES ENVIRON LAB, NAT OCEANIC & ATMOSPHERIC ADMIN, 65- *Mem:* Am Meteorol Soc. *Res:* Atmospheric turbulence and diffusion; micrometeorology; meteorology as related to use of atomic energy. *Mailing Add:* Air Resources Environ Lab Nat Oceanic & Atmospheric Admin Silver Spring MD 20910

VAN DER HULST, JAN MATHIJS, b 's-Gravenhage, Neth, Jan 26, 48; m 70; c 3. ASTRONOMY. *Educ:* Univ Groningen, Drs, 73, PhD(astron), 77. *Prof Exp:* Res assoc astron, Nat Radio Astron Observ, 77-78; ASST PROF ASTRON, UNIV MINN, 79- *Mem:* Am Astron Soc; Nederlandse Astron Club. *Mailing Add:* Dept of Astron 116 Church St SE Minneapolis MN 55455

VAN DERIPE, DONALD R, pharmacology, see previous edition

VANDER JAGT, DAVID LEE, b Grand Rapids, Mich, Jan 13, 42; m 67. BIOCHEMISTRY. *Educ:* Calvin Col, AB, 63; Purdue Univ, Lafayette, PhD(chem), 67. *Prof Exp:* NIH fel biochem, Northwestern Univ, 67-69; asst prof, 69-74, ASSOC PROF BIOCHEM, UNIV NMEX, 74- *Concurrent Pos:* Res career develop award, Nat Cancer Inst, 74- *Mem:* AAAS; Am Chem Soc; Am Soc Biol Chemists. *Res:* Enzyme, coenzyme reaction mechanisms of glutathione requiring enzymes, especially glyoxalase; metabolic role of methylglyoxal; biomedical applications of 13-C; metabolism of chemical carcinogens. *Mailing Add:* Dept of Biochem Univ of N Mex Sch of Med Albuquerque NM 87131

VANDERJAGT, DONALD W, b Muskegon, Mich, Feb 25, 38; m 58; c 4. COMBINATORICS. *Educ:* Hope Col, AB, 59; Fla State Univ, MS, 61; Western Mich Univ, PhD(math), 73. *Prof Exp:* Instr math, Cent Univ Iowa, 62-64; from asst prof to assoc prof, 64-75, PROF MATH, GRAND VALLEY STATE COLS, 75- *Mem:* Am Math Soc; Math Asn Am; Asn Comput Mach; Nat Coun Teachers Math. *Res:* Graph theory, local properties, degree sets, Hamiltonian properties, generalized Ramsey theory. *Mailing Add:* Dept of Math & Comput Sci Grand Valley State Cols Allendale MI 49401

VANDER KLOET, SAM PETER, b Heidenschap, Frisia, Feb 18, 42; Can citizen; m 70; c 1. PLANT TAXONOMY, PLANT ECOLOGY. *Educ:* Queen's Univ, BA, 68, PhD(biol), 72. *Prof Exp:* Asst prof, 72-80, PROF BIOL, ACADIA UNIV, 80-, CUR E C SMITH HERBARIUM, 72- *Mem:* Bot Soc Am; Can Bot Asn; Int Asn Plant Taxon. *Res:* Biosystematics of Vaccinium & Cyanococcus. *Mailing Add:* Dept Biol Acadia Univ Wolfville NS B0P 1X0 Can

VAN DER KLOOT, ALBERT PETER, b Chicago, Ill, Jan 22, 21; m 48; c 2. FOOD CHEMISTRY. *Educ:* Mass Inst Technol, SB, 42. *Prof Exp:* Chemist flower preserv, Flower Foods, Inc, 46-47; chemist biscuits & crackers, Independent Biscuit Mfg Tech Inst, 47-52; chief chemist brewing & foods, 52-57, PRES, WAHL-HENIUS INST, INC, 57- *Mem:* Am Soc Brewing Chem; Am Chem Soc; Inst Food Technol; AAAS. *Res:* Commercial application of plant tissue culture; soda cracker fermentation; freeze drying of microorganisms; vapor pressure-moisture relationships; statistical analysis of brewing process; gas chromatography; alcoholic beverages; trace components of food. *Mailing Add:* Wahl-Henius Inst Inc 4206 N Broadway Chicago IL 60613

VAN DER KLOOT, WILLIAM GEORGE, b Chicago, Ill, Feb 18, 27; m 63; c 2. PHYSIOLOGY. *Educ:* Harvard Univ, SB, 48, PhD(biol), 52. *Prof Exp:* Nat Res Coun fel, Cambridge Univ, 52-53; instr biol, Harvard Univ, 53-56; from asst prof to assoc prof zool, Cornell Univ, 56-58; prof pharmacol & chmn dept, Sch Med, NY Univ, 58-61, prof physiol & chmn dept physiol & biophys, 61-71; PROF PHYSIOL & BIOPHYS & CHMN DEPT, STATE UNIV NY STONY BROOK, 71- *Concurrent Pos:* Consult, NSF, 59-65 & NIH, 68-; ed, Biosci, 81- *Mem:* AAAS; Sigma Xi; Am Physiol Soc. *Res:* Comparative physiology and pharmacology. *Mailing Add:* Dept Physiol & Biophys Health Sci Ctr State Univ NY Stony Brook NY 11794

VANDERKOOI, JANE M, b Rochester, NY, Feb 28, 44. BIOCHEMISTRY, BIOPHYSICS. *Educ:* Cent Univ Iowa, BA, 67; St Louis Univ, PhD(biochem), 71. *Prof Exp:* Fel biophys, 71-73, res assoc, Johnson Found, 73-75, asst prof, 75-81, ASSOC PROF BIOCHEM, DEPT BIOCHEM & BIOPHYS, UNIV PA, 81- *Concurrent Pos:* NIH fel, 75. *Mem:* Biophys Soc; Am Soc Biol Chem. *Res:* Membrane structure and function. *Mailing Add:* Dept of Biochem & Biophys Univ of Pa Philadelphia PA 19104

VANDER KOOI, LAMBERT RAY, b Lynden, Wash, Jan 8, 35; m 65; c 1. ELECTRICAL ENGINEERING. *Educ:* Univ Mich, BSE, 58, MSE, 61, PhD(elec eng), 68; Calvin Col, BS, 59. *Prof Exp:* Engr, Systs Div, Bendix Corp, 58-61; assoc res engr, Radar & Optics Lab, Inst Sci & Technol, Univ Mich, 61-68; engr, Res & Develop Div, Kelsh Instrument Co, 68; radar systs engr, Polhemus Assocs, Inc, Mich, 69-70; ASSOC PROF ELEC ENG & TECHNOL, WESTERN MICH UNIV, 70- *Mem:* Inst Elec & Electronics Engrs. *Res:* Stochastic control systems; synthetic aperture radar systems; digital circuits and systems; active networks. *Mailing Add:* Dept of Elec Eng Western Mich Univ Kalamazoo MI 49008

VANDERKOOI, NICHOLAS, JR, physical chemistry, see previous edition

VANDERKOOI, WILLIAM NICHOLAS, b Paterson, NJ, Dec 19, 29; m 54; c 3. INDUSTRIAL CHEMISTRY. *Educ:* Calvin Col, AB, 51; Purdue Univ, MS, 53, PhD(phys chem), 55. *Prof Exp:* Lab asst chem & physics, Calvin Col, 48-51, asst, Off Naval Res, 50-51; chem, Purdue Univ, 51-52, US Air Force contract, 52, instruments, 52-53; res chemist, C C Kennedy Res Lab, 55-64, group leader, Polymer & Chem Res Lab, 64-69, assoc scientist, Hydrocarbon & Monomers Res Lab, 69-81, ASSOC SCIENTIST, DESIGNED POLYMERS & CHEM RES LAB, DOW CHEM CO, 81- *Mem:* Sigma Xi; Am Chem Soc. *Res:* Polymerization kinetics; radiation grafting; polymer synthesis and properties; metal chelation and purification; hydrocarbon analyses; high temperature reactions; hydrocarbon pyrolysis; petrochemical acrylamide process and polymerization; processes; catalysis; alkylation processes. *Mailing Add:* Dow Chemical Co 677 Bldg Midland MI 48640

VANDERKOOY, JOHN, b Neth, Jan 1, 41; Can citizen; m 65; c 1. SOLID STATE PHYSICS, ELECTRO-ACOUSTICS. *Educ:* McMaster Univ, BEng, 63, PhD(physics), 67. *Prof Exp:* Nat Res Coun Can fel physics, Cambridge Univ, 67-69; res assoc, 69-70, asst prof, 70-79, ASSOC PROF PHYSICS, UNIV WATERLOO, 79- *Concurrent Pos:* Nat Res Coun Can grants, 69-81. *Mem:* Can Asn Physicists; Audio Eng Soc. *Res:* Low temperature solid state physics of metals; audio, transducer design and measurement. *Mailing Add:* Dept of Physics Univ of Waterloo Waterloo ON N2L 3G1 Can

VANDERLAAN, MARTIN, b San Francisco, Calif, Nov 6, 48. CYTOLOGY, ONCOLOGY. *Educ:* Univ Calif, Santa Barbara, BA, 70; NY Univ, MS, 72, PhD(environ health), 75. *Prof Exp:* Assoc res scientist oncol, Inst Environ Med, NY Univ, 72-76; BIOMED SCIENTIST CELL BIOL, LAWRENCE LIVERMORE LAB, 76- *Mem:* Am Asn Cancer Res; AAAS. *Res:* Cancer cytology; enzyme and immuno-cytochemistry; carcinogenesis; hybridomas. *Mailing Add:* Biomed Div Lawrence Livermore Lab PO Box 5507 Livermore CA 94550

VANDERLAAN, WILLARD PARKER, b Muskegon, Mich, June 5, 17; m 44; c 3. ENDOCRINOLOGY. *Educ:* Harvard Med Sch, MD, 42. *Prof Exp:* Intern med, Boston City Hosp, 42-43, asst resident path, 43; instr pharmacother, Harvard Med Sch, 44-45; fel endocrinol, J H Pratt Diag Hosp, Boston, 45-47; from asst prof to assoc prof med, Med Sch, Tufts Univ, 47-56; HEAD LUTCHER BROWN CTR FOR DIABETES & ENDOCRINOL, SCRIPPS CLIN & RES FOUND, 56-; PROF MED, UNIV CALIF, SAN DIEGO, 68- *Concurrent Pos:* Fel med, Thorndike Mem Lab, Boston City Hosp, 44; consult, Boston Vet Admin Hosp, 54-56; mem endocrinol study sect, NIH, 71-75, chmn, 74-75. *Mem:* Am Thyroid Asn; Endocrine Soc; Am Soc Clin Invest. *Res:* Growth hormone; prolactin; thyroid physiology. *Mailing Add:* Scripps Clin & Res Found 10666 N Torrey Pines Rd La Jolla CA 92037

VANDERLASKE, DENNIS P, b Mineola, NY, Jan 15, 48; m 78. ELECTROOPTICS. *Educ:* State Univ NY Stony Brook, BE, 69; George Washington Univ, MS, 75; Cent Mich Univ, MA, 81. *Prof Exp:* Jr engr, 69-73, proj engr, 73-79, PROG MGR, NIGHT VISION & ELECTRO-OPTICS LAB, US ARMY ELECTRONICS RES & DEVELOP COMMAND, 79- *Mem:* Inst Elec & Electronics Engrs. *Res:* Infrared imaging, primarily for military applications and relation with other electro-optical technologies and field evaluation of this technology; solid state electronics as applied to future generation thermal imaging system technology. *Mailing Add:* Night Vision & Electro-optics Labs DELNV-IT Ft Belvoir VA 22060

VANDERLIN, CARL JOSEPH, JR, b Williamsport, Pa, Apr 28, 26; m 50; c 6. MATHEMATICS. *Educ:* Univ Chicago, PhB, 48, SB, 50; Univ Wis, MS, 52. *Prof Exp:* Asst math, Univ Wis, 51-54, instr, 54-55; from instr to assoc prof, Wis State Col, Whitewater, 55-61, actg chmn dept, 59-60; lectr math, 61-77, assoc prof human develop, 77-79, PROF MATH, UNIV WIS-EXTEN, 79- *Concurrent Pos:* Univ Wis-US Agency Int Develop consult, Inst Adult Studies, Univ Nairobi, 67, vis lectr, 68-71, chief of party, 70-71. *Mem:* Math Asn Am; Nat Coun Teachers Math; Nat Univ Exten Asn; US Metric Asn. *Mailing Add:* 629 Lowell Hall 610 Langdon St Madison WI 53706

VANDERLIND, MERWYN RAY, b Grand Rapids, Mich. PHYSICS, POLYMER CHEMISTRY. *Educ:* Hope Col, BA, 58; Ohio Univ, MS, 60, PhD(physics), 64. *Prof Exp:* Nuclear eng reactors, Atomics Int, 60-61; res physicist, polymers, Rohm & Haas Chem, 64-66; mgr phys sci, 66-78, mgr venture develop, 78-81, ASSOC DIR, CORP TECH DEVELOP, BATTELLE MEM INST, 81- *Concurrent Pos:* Consult, Nat Acad Sci & Nat Acad Eng, 68-72; mem alumni grad coun res, Ohio Univ, 76- *Mem:* Am Phys Soc; Sigma Xi. *Res:* Radiation transport; nuclear weapons effects; polymer physics; laser applications; reactor engineering. *Mailing Add:* Battelle Mem Inst 505 King Ave Columbus OH 43201

VANDERLINDE, RAYMOND E, b Newark, NY, Feb 28, 24; m 48; c 3. BIOCHEMISTRY. *Educ:* Syracuse Univ, AB, 44, MS(educ), 45, MS(chem), 47, PhD(biochem), 50; Am Bd Clin Chem, dipl, 60. *Prof Exp:* Teacher high sch, NY, 45-46; from asst prof to assoc prof biochem, Sch Med, Univ Md, 50-57; asst prof, Col Med, State Univ NY Upstate Med Ctr, 57-62; assoc lab dir & clin chemist, Mem Hosp Cumberland, Md, 62-65; dir labs clin chem, Div Labs & Res, NY State Dept Health, 65-77; PROF & DIR, DIV CLIN CHEM, DEPT PATH & MED & DIV CLIN BIOCHEM, DEPT BIOL CHEM, HAHNEMANN MED COL, 77- *Concurrent Pos:* Lab admin dir & clin biochemist, Syracuse Mem Hosp, 57-62; consult, Madison County Lab, NY, 59-62, Rome City Lab, 61-62 & Meyersdale Community Hosp Lab, Pa, 64-65; clin asst prof, Med Ctr, Univ WVa, 64-65; adj assoc prof, Albany Med Col, 70-; mem diag prods adv comt, Food & Drug Admin, 72-75. *Mem:* Am Chem Soc; fel Am Asn Clin Chemists (treas, 82); Asn Clin Sci; assoc Am Soc Clin Path; Acad Clin Lab Physicians & Scientists. *Res:* Clinical chemistry; clinical enzymology and diabetes. *Mailing Add:* Dept of Path & Lab Med 230 N Broad St Philadelphia PA 19102

VAN DER LINDE, REINHOUD H, b Amsterdam, Holland, July 14, 29; US citizen; m 58; c 5. MATHEMATICS. *Educ:* NY Univ, BA, 53, MS, 56; Rensselaer Polytech Inst, PhD(math), 68. *Prof Exp:* Res asst, NY Univ, 54-56; PROF MATH, BENNINGTON COL, 56- *Mem:* Math Asn Am. *Res:* Random Eigenvalue problems; differential equations; functional analysis. *Mailing Add:* Dept of Math Bennington Col Bennington VT 05201

VANDERLINDEN, CARL R, b Pella, Iowa, Sept 26, 23; m 45; c 2. CHEMICAL ENGINEERING. *Educ:* Univ Wash, BS, 44; Iowa State Univ, PhD(chem eng), 50. *Prof Exp:* Instr chem eng, Iowa State Univ, 46-50; dir res & develop shelter prod, 69-73, dir res & develop govt contracts, 73-75, vpres dir, 75-79, vpres dir res & develop contracts & appl tech, Johns-Manville Sales Corp, 79-81, DIR RES & DEVELOP, CONTRACTS & APPL TECH, MANVILLE SERV CORP, 81- *Concurrent Pos:* Chmn tech comt, Perlite Inst, 64-70, dir, 70-72, vpres, 72-; mem bldg indust mfg res coun, Nat Acad Sci; mem thermal insulations comt, Nat Inst Bldg Sci. *Mem:* Am Inst Chem Engrs; Am Chem Soc; Am Soc Indust Chemists. *Res:* Minerals including diatomite and perlite; synthetic silicates; filtration; water treatment; building materials and construction systems. *Mailing Add:* Manville Res & Develop Ctr Ken-Caryl Ranch Denver CO 80217

VANDERLIP, RICHARD L, b Woodston, Kans, May 6, 38; m 60; c 3. AGRONOMY. *Educ:* Kans State Univ, BS, 60; Iowa State Univ, MS, 62, PhD(agron), 65. *Prof Exp:* From asst prof to assoc prof, 64-76, PROF AGRON, KANS STATE UNIV, 76- *Mem:* Am Soc Agron; Soil Sci Soc Am; Crop Sci Soc Am. *Res:* Ecology of crop plants, especially climatic interrelationships. *Mailing Add:* Dept of Agron Throckmorton Hall Kans State Univ Manhattan KS 66506

VANDER LUGT, ANTHONY, b Dorr, Mich, Mar 7, 37; m 59; c 2. ELECTROOPTICS & ELECTRICAL ENGINEERING. *Educ:* Calvin Col, BS, 59; Univ Mich, BSEE, 59, MSEE, 62; Univ Reading, PhD, 69. *Prof Exp:* Res asst, Radar & Optics Lab, Willow Run Labs, Inst Sci & Technol, Univ Mich, 59-63, res assoc, 63-64, assoc res engr, 64-65, res engr & asst head optics group, 65-69; mgr res & develop, Electro-Optics Ctr, Radiation Inc, 69-73; dir, Electro-Optics Dept, 73-79, SR SCIENTIST, ADVAN TECHNOL DEPT, GOVT COMMUN SYSTS DIV, HARRIS CORP, 79- *Concurrent Pos:* Consult, Gen Elec Co, 64-66, Tex Instruments, Inc, 65-66 & Bendix Res Lab, 66; Am ed, Optica Acta, 69-75; assoc ed, Wave Electronics, 81- *Mem:* Fel Optical Soc Am; Inst Elec & Electronics Engrs; Soc Photog Instrumentation Engrs. *Res:* Optical data-processing; complex spatial filtering and optical matched filtering; modulation transfer functions of recording media; holography; acousto-optic devices; optical storage and retrieval; distributed microprocessors. *Mailing Add:* 232 Cocoa Ave Indialantic FL 32903

VANDER LUGT, KAREL L, b Pella, Iowa, Apr 25, 40; m 64; c 1. SOLID STATE PHYSICS. *Educ:* Hope Col, BA, 62; Wayne State Univ, PhD(exp solid state physics), 67. *Prof Exp:* Nat Res Coun assoc physics, Naval Res Lab, Washington, DC, 67-68; ASST PROF PHYSICS, AUGUSTANA COL, SDAK, 69- *Mem:* AAAS; Am Asn Physics Teachers; Hist Sci Soc. *Res:* Radiation damage in crystals; experimental solid state physics. *Mailing Add:* Dept of Physics Augustana Col Sioux Falls SD 57102

VAN DER MAATEN, MARTIN JUNIOR, b Alton, Iowa, Aug 6, 32; m 56; c 2. VETERINARY VIROLOGY. *Educ:* Iowa State Univ, DVM, 56, PhD(vet bact), 64. *Prof Exp:* Vet practice, 58-60; res asst vet virol, Iowa State Univ, 60-61, Nat Inst Allergy & Infectious Dis fel, 61-64, asst prof, 64-67; VET LAB OFFICER, NAT ANIMAL DIS CTR, US DEPT AGR, 67- *Mem:* Am Vet Med Asn; Am Soc Microbiol; Vet Cancer Soc. *Res:* Virological and serological studies of bovine lymphosarcoma and bovine leukemia virus; bovine viral reproductive disease. *Mailing Add:* Nat Animal Dis Ctr US Dept of Agr PO Box 70 Ames IA 50010

VANDERMEER, JOHN H, b Chicago, Ill, July 21, 40; m 69; c 1. POPULATION BIOLOGY. *Educ:* Univ Ill, Urbana, BS, 61; Univ Kans, MA, 64; Univ Mich, Ann Arbor, PhD(ecol), 69. *Prof Exp:* Sloan Found fel, Univ Chicago, 69-70; asst prof ecol, State Univ NY Stony Brook, 70-71; asst prof, 71-74, ASSOC PROF ZOOL, UNIV MICH, ANN ARBOR, 74- *Mem:* Am Soc Ichthyologists & Herpetologists; Am Soc Naturalists; Ecol Soc Am. *Res:* Role of population processes as determiners of the structure of biological communities. *Mailing Add:* Dept of Zool Univ of Mich Ann Arbor MI 48104

VAN DER MEER, JOHN PETER, b Netherlands, June 25, 43; Can citizen; m 66; c 2. GENETICS, PHYCOLOGY. *Educ:* Univ Western Ont, BSc, 66; Cornell Univ, PhD(genetics), 71. *Prof Exp:* Fel biochem, Charles H Best Inst, Univ Toronto, 71-74; RES OFFICER GENETICS, NAT RES COUN CAN, 74- *Mem:* Genetics Soc Can; Genetics Soc Am; Int Phycol Soc. *Res:* Genetics of marine red algae. *Mailing Add:* Atlantic Res Lab NRC 1411 Oxford St Halifax NS B3H 3Z1 Can

VANDERMEER, R(OY) A, b Chicago, Ill, Sept 7, 34; m 56; c 2. PHYSICAL METALLURGY. *Educ:* Ill Inst Technol, BS, 56, PhD(phys metall), 61. *Prof Exp:* Res assoc metall, Ill Inst Technol, 58-60; metallurgist, Oak Ridge Nat Lab, 60-80; METALLURGIST, NUCLEAR DIV, Y-12 PLANT, UNION CARBIDE CORP, 80; PROF METALL ENG, UNIV TENN, 81- *Concurrent Pos:* Lectr, Univ Tenn, 63-66 & Ford Found grant prof, 66-80; vis prof mat sci, Univ Rochester, 74-75, vis prof metall eng, Ill Inst Tech, 80. *Mem:* Am Inst Mining, Metall & Petrol Engrs; Am Soc Metals. *Res:* Grain boundary migration in metals; recovery and recrystallization of metals and alloys; uranium alloy; phase transformations. *Mailing Add:* Metal & Ceramics Div Oak Ridge Nat Lab PO Box X Oak Ridge TN 37831

VANDER MEER, ROBERT KENNETH, b Chicago, Ill, Nov 29, 42; m 64; c 2. CHEMICAL ECOLOGY, ORGANIC CHEMISTRY. *Educ:* Blackburn Col, BA, 64; John Carroll Univ, MS, 66; Pa State Univ, PhD(org chem), 72. *Prof Exp:* Lectr chem, Univ South Pac, Fiji Islands, 72-76; RES CHEMIST CHEM ECOL, SCI & EDUC ADMIN, USDA, 77- *Concurrent Pos:* Am Cancer Soc fel, Cornell Univ, 76-77. *Mem:* Fel Am Chem Soc; Royal Soc Chem; Entom Soc Am. *Res:* Isolation and identification of insect pheromones and defensive secretions; analytical organic chemistry; insect biochemistry; the interaction of plants and insects; insect and animal behavior and physiology. *Mailing Add:* Sci & Educ Admin USDA PO Box 14565 Gainesville FL 32604

VAN DER MEULEN, JOSEPH PIERRE, b Boston, Mass, Aug 22, 29; m 60; c 3. NEUROLOGY, NEUROPHYSIOLOGY. *Educ:* Boston Col, AB, 50; Boston Univ, MD, 54. *Prof Exp:* Intern med, Cornell Med Div, Bellevue Hosp, New York, 54-55, asst resident, 55-56; asst resident neurol, Harvard Neurol Unit, Boston City Hosp, 58-59, resident, 59-60; Nat Inst Neurol Dis & Blindness fel, Nobel Inst Neurophysiol, Karolinska Inst, Sweden, 60-62; instr, Harvard Neurol Unit, Boston City Hosp, 62-66, assoc, 66-67; asst prof, Sch Med, Case Western Reserve Univ, 67-69, assoc prof neurol & biomed eng, 69-71; prof neurol & chmn dept, 71-79, dir dept neurol, 71-79, VPRES HEALTH AFFAIRS, LOS ANGELES COUNTY-UNIV SOUTHERN CALIF MED CTR, 77- *Concurrent Pos:* Fel, Harvard Neurol Unit, Boston City Hosp, Mass, 62-66; ed, Arch of Neurol, 76- *Mem:* Am Acad Neurol; Am Neurol Asn. *Res:* Neurophysiology of abnormalities of posture and movement; computer assisted image analysis muscle biopsies; motor control systems in humans. *Mailing Add:* Dept of Neurol LAC-USC Med Ctr Los Angeles CA 90033

VANDERPLAATS, GARRET NIEL, b Modesto, Calif, Feb 14, 44; m 79. AUTOMATED DESIGN OPTIMIZATION. *Educ:* Ariz State Univ, BS, 69, MS, 68; Case Western Reserve Univ, PhD(eng mech), 71. *Prof Exp:* Res scientist aero eng, Ames Res Ctr, NASA, 71-79; ASSOC PROF MECH ENG, NAVAL POSTGRAD SCH, 79- *Mem:* Am Soc Mech Engrs; fel Am Inst Aeronaut & Astronaut; Am Soc Civil Engrs. *Res:* Development of automated optimization techniques for engineering design, with application to structural, aeronautical and mechanical systems. *Mailing Add:* 676 Van Buren Circle Monterey CA 93940

VANDERPLOEG, HENRY ALFRED, b Chicago, Ill, Aug 23, 44; m 68. AQUATIC ECOLOGY. *Educ:* Mich Technol Univ, BS, 66; Univ Wis-Madison, MS, 68; Ore State Univ, PhD(biol oceanog), 72. *Prof Exp:* Aquatic ecologist modelling radionuclide cycling in aquatic systs, Environ Sci Div, Oak Ridge Nat Lab, 72-74; BIOL OCEANOGR PLANKTON ECOL GREAT LAKES, GREAT LAKES ENVIRON RES LAB, NAT OCEANIC & ATMOSPHERIC ADMIN, 74- *Mem:* AAAS; Am Soc Limnol & Oceanog; Ecol Soc Am; Sigma Xi. *Res:* Ecology of selective feeding of zooplankton; dynamics of seasonal succession of Great Lakes plankton. *Mailing Add:* Great Lakes Environ Res Lab 2300 Washtenaw Ave Ann Arbor MI 48104

VAN DER PUIJE, PATRICK DAVID, b Accra, Ghana, Aug 24, 37. ELECTRONICS. *Educ:* Univ London, BSc, 62, Imp Col, DIC & PhD(eng), 66. *Prof Exp:* Mem sci staff circuit theory, Bell-Northern Res Ltd, 67-70; ASSOC PROF ENG, CARLETON UNIV, 70- *Res:* Characterization of active 2-ports. *Mailing Add:* Dept of Electronics Carleton Univ Ottawa ON M1S 5S6 Can

VANDERRYN, JACK, b Groningen, Netherlands, Apr 14, 30; nat US; m 56; c 4. PHYSICAL CHEMISTRY, RESEARCH ADMINISTRATION. *Educ:* Lehigh Univ, BA, 51, MS, 52, PhD(chem), 55. *Prof Exp:* Asst, Lehigh Univ, 51-55; asst prof chem, Va Polytech Inst, 55-58; chemist, Res & Develop Div, US Atomic Energy Comn, Tenn, 58-62, tech adv to asst gen mgr res & develop, Washington, DC, 62-67; US Dept State sr sci adv to US Mission, Int Atomic Energy Agency, 67-71; tech asst, Off Gen Mgr, US Atomic Energy Comn, Washington, DC, 71-72, tech asst to dir, Div Appl Technol, 72-74, chief, Energy Technol Br, Div Appl Technol, 74-75, actg dir div energy storage, 75, dir, Off Int Res & Develop Progs, US Energy Res & Develop Admin, 75-77, DIR, OFF INT RES & DEVELOP PROGS, US DEPT ENERGY, 77- *Mem:* AAAS. *Res:* Science policy development; energy technology development; research and development administration; international cooperation in energy research and development; science policy. *Mailing Add:* 8112 Whittier Blvd Bethesda MD 20034

VANDERSALL, JOHN HENRY, b Helena, Ohio, July 20, 28; m 63; c 2. ANIMAL NUTRITION. *Educ:* Ohio State Univ, BS, 50, MS, 54, PhD(dairy sci), 59. *Prof Exp:* Instr dairy sci, Agr Exp Sta, Ohio State Univ, 57-59; from asst prof to assoc prof, 59-71, PROF DAIRY SCI, UNIV MD, COLLEGE PARK, 71- *Mem:* Fel AAAS; Am Soc Animal Sci; Am Dairy Sci Asn; Sigma Xi. *Res:* Effects of forages on milk production and growth and physiological bases for differences; effects of feeds upon the composition of milk. *Mailing Add:* Dept of Dairy Sci Univ of Md College Park MD 20740

VANDER SANDE, JOHN BRUCE, b Baltimore, Md, Mar 27, 44; m 72. MATERIALS SCIENCE. *Educ:* Stevens Inst Technol, BE, 66; Northwestern Univ, Evanston, PhD(mat sci), 70. *Prof Exp:* Fulbright scholar metall, Oxford Univ, 70-71; asst prof, 71-75, ASSOC PROF METALL, MASS INST TECHNOL, 75- *Mem:* Am Inst Mining, Metall & Petrol Engrs; Electron Microscopy Soc Am; New Eng Soc Electron Microscopy (vpres, 78, pres, 79). *Res:* Physical and mechanical behavior of crystalline solids; electron microscopy and electron diffraction. *Mailing Add:* Dept of Metall & Mat Sci Mass Inst of Technol Rm 13-5017 Cambridge MA 02139

VANDERSLICE, JOSEPH THOMAS, b Philadelphia, Pa, Dec 21, 27; m 54; c 7. PHYSICAL CHEMISTRY. *Educ:* Boston Col, BS, 49; Mass Inst Technol, PhD(phys chem), 53. *Prof Exp:* From instr to asst prof chem, Catholic Univ, 52-56; from asst prof to prof chem, Univ Md, College Park, 56-78, dir, Inst Molecular Physics, 67-68, prof molecular physics, 62-76, head, Dept Chem, 68-76; PROF CHEM, NUTRIT INST, US DEPT AGR, 78-, RES CHEMIST, 78- *Mem:* Inst Food Technol; Am Chem Soc; fel Am Phys Soc. *Res:* Intermolecular forces; thermodynamic temperature scale; interpretations of molecular beam experiments; transport properties of high temperature gases; franck-condon factors and interpretation of spectroscopic data on diatomic molecules; auroral spectroscopy; vitamin B6 composition in biological materials. *Mailing Add:* Nutrit Inst Beltsville Agr Res Ctr Beltsville MD 20705

VANDERSLICE, THOMAS AQUINAS, b Philadelphia, Pa, Jan 8, 32; m 56; c 4. PHYSICAL CHEMISTRY. *Educ:* Boston Col, BA, 53; Catholic Univ, PhD(phys chem), 56. *Prof Exp:* Asst, Catholic Univ, 53-54, Fulbright fel, 56; res assoc, Res & Develop Ctr, 56-62, mgr eng, Vacuum Prod Oper, 62-64, mgr, Vacuum Prod Bus Sect, 64-66, gen mgr, Info Devices Dept, Okla, 66-68, dep div gen mgr, Info Systs Progs Dep Div, Ariz, 68-70, vpres & div gen mgr, Electronic Components Bus Div, 70-72, vpres & group exec, Spec Systs & Prod Group, Gen Elec Co, 72-77, V PRES & SECT EXEC, POWER SYSTS SECT, GEN ELEC CO, 78- *Concurrent Pos:* Trustee, Comt Econ Develop; mem, Aspen Inst Humanistic Studies; mem bd trustees, Boston Col, Fairfield Univ & Clarkson Col. *Mem:* Am Chem Soc; Am Phys Soc; Am Vacuum Soc. *Res:* Surface chemistry; mass spectrometry; high vacuum technology; gaseous discharges. *Mailing Add:* Gen Elec Co Fairfield CT 06431

VANDER SLUIS, KENNETH LEROY, b Holland, Mich, Dec 19, 25; m 52; c 3. PHYSICS. *Educ:* Baldwin-Wallace Col, BS, 47; Pa State Univ, MS, 50, PhD(physics), 52. *Prof Exp:* PHYSICIST, OAK RIDGE NAT LAB, 52- *Concurrent Pos:* Res guest, Spectros Lab, Mass Inst Technol, 60-61; mem comt line spectra of the elements, Nat Res Coun, 61-72. *Mem:* Am Phys Soc; Optical Soc Am; Sigma Xi. *Res:* Experimental atomic spectroscopy, echelle gratings, interferometry, gas laser systems. *Mailing Add:* PO Box X Oak Ridge Nat Lab Oak Ridge TN 37830

VAN DER SLUYS, WILLIAM, b Paterson, NJ, Aug 15, 12; m 34; c 2. MECHANICAL ENGINEERING. *Educ:* Stevens Inst Technol, ME, 33. *Prof Exp:* Develop engr, Chrysler Corp, 34-51; from asst mgr to mgr eng design, Pullman-Standard Div, Pullman, Inc, Ill, 51-59, assoc dir res, 59-64, dir res & develop, 64-66, gen mgr passenger car eng, 66-72, dir mkt-transit, 72-73, vpres mkt, 73-74, vpres & gen mgr, 74-76, vpres opers, 76-77; RETIRED. *Mem:* Fel Am Soc Mech Engrs. *Res:* Railroad freight and passenger cars. *Mailing Add:* 2426 Lakeshore Ct Lakes of Four Seasons Crown Point IN 46307

VANDERSPURT, THOMAS HENRY, b Lawrence, Mass, Apr 1, 46; m 71; c 2. PHYSICAL INORGANIC CHEMISTRY. *Educ:* Lowell Technol Inst, BS, 67; Princeton Univ, MA & PhD(chem), 72. *Prof Exp:* Fel catalysis chem, Princeton Univ, 72-73; res chemist, 73-77, SR RES CHEMIST CATALYSIS CHEM, CELANESE RES CO, CELANESE INC, 77- *Mem:* NY Acad Sci; Sigma Xi; Am Chem Soc; NAm Catalysis Soc. *Res:* Supported metal alloy catalysts; metal/metal oxide selective oxidation catalysts; homogenous selective dimerization carbonylation catalysis; homogeneous selective aromatic acetoxylation; catalysis; supported hydroformylation catalysis. *Mailing Add:* Celanese Res Co Box 1000 Summit NJ 07901

VANDER STOUW, GERALD GORDON, b Rochester, NY, May 15, 37; m 60; c 2. ORGANIC CHEMISTRY, INFORMATION SCIENCE. *Educ:* Calvin Col, AB, 58; Ohio State Univ, PhD(org chem), 64. *Prof Exp:* Res asst chem, 64-70, group leader, Chem Info Sci Dept, 70-74, RES & DEVELOP PROJ MGR, CHEM ABSTR SERV, 74- *Mem:* AAAS; Am Chem Soc; Am Soc Info Sci. *Res:* Mechanized indexing and retrieval of chemical information; computer-based processing and searching of chemical information, especially chemical structures and nomenclature. *Mailing Add:* Chem Abstr Serv PO Box 3012 Columbus OH 43210

VAN DER VAART, HUBERTUS ROBERT, b Makassar, Celebes, Indonesia, Mar 2, 22; m 50; c 3. MATHEMATICS, STATISTICS. *Educ:* Univ Leiden, Drs, 50, PhD(theoret biol), 53. *Prof Exp:* Sci officer, Univ Leiden, 50-57; vis assoc prof exp statist, NC State Col, 57-58 & statist, Univ Chicago, 58; extraordinary prof theoret biol, Univ Leiden, 58-60, prof, 60-62, dir inst theoret biol, 58-62, dir cent comput inst, 61-62; assoc prof, 62-63, PROF STATIST & MATH, N C STATE UNIV, 63-, DREXEL PROF BIOMATH, 74- *Concurrent Pos:* Co-ed, Acta Biotheoretica, 53-75; Netherlands Orgn Pure Res fel, 57-58; co-ed, Statistica Neerlandica, 60-74; mem, Panel Life Sci, Comt Undergrad Prog Math, 67-70; mem, Panel Instructional Mats Appl Math, Comt Undergrad Prog Math, Math Asn Am, 74-76. *Mem:* Biomet Soc; Am Math Soc; Math Asn Am; Inst Math Statist; Soc Indust & Appl Math. *Res:* Mathematical statistics; probability; stochastic processes; theoretical biology; principles of scientific method; mathematical models for biosystems. *Mailing Add:* Inst of Statist NC State Univ PO Box 5457 Raleigh NC 27650

VANDER VALK, PAUL DAVID, b Passaic, NJ, Jan 15, 47; m 70. ORGANIC CHEMISTRY. *Educ:* Iowa Wesleyan BS, 69; Univ Iowa, MS, 71, PhD(org chem), 74. *Prof Exp:* RES CHEMIST ORG SYNTHESIS, EASTMAN KODAK CO, 74- *Mailing Add:* 92 Lake Lea Rd Rochester NY 14617

VAN DER VEEN, JAMES MORRIS, b Chicago, Ill, Sept 19, 31; m 59; c 3. ORGANIC CHEMISTRY, X-RAY CRYSTALLOGRAPHY. *Educ:* Swarthmore Col, BA, 53; Harvard Univ, AM, 56, PhD(org chem), 59. *Hon Degrees:* MEng, Stevens Inst Technol, 80. *Prof Exp:* Fels, Ga Inst Technol, 58-59 & Argonne Nat Lab, 59-60; res assoc nuclear magnetic resonance spectros, Retina Found, 60-61; from asst prof to assoc prof, 61-76, PROF ORG CHEM, STEVENS INST TECHNOL, 76- *Concurrent Pos:* Consult, Picatinny Arsenal, NJ, 63-68 & Exxon Corp, 74-78. *Mem:* AAAS; Am Crystallog Asn; Am Chem Soc; Sigma Xi; The Chem Soc. *Res:* Physical organic chemistry; x-ray crystallography; computer methods in chemistry. *Mailing Add:* Dept of Chem & Chem Eng Stevens Inst of Technol Hoboken NJ 07030

VANDERVEEN, JOHN EDWARD, b Prospect Park, NJ, May 13, 34; m 67; c 2. NUTRITION, CHEMISTRY. *Educ:* Rutgers Univ, BS, 56; Univ NH, PhD(chem, nutrit), 61. *Prof Exp:* Res chemist, US Air Force Sch Aerospace Med, 64-75; DIR DIV NUTRIT, BUR FOODS, FOOD & DRUG ADMIN, DEPT HEALTH, EDUC & WELFARE, 75- *Mem:* Am Inst Nutrit; Am Chem Soc; Am Inst Clin Nutrit; Inst Food Technologists; Am Dairy Sci Asn. *Res:* Nutritional requirements of the American population; assessment of the nutritional quality of the national food supply; energy and mineral requirements and effects of excess nutrient intakes. *Mailing Add:* HFF 260 FDA 200 C St SW Washington DC 20204

VANDERVEEN, JOHN WARREN, b Mount Vernon, NY, Dec 2, 33; m 59; c 2. CHEMICAL ENGINEERING. *Educ:* Univ Nebr, BS, 60, MS, 61; Univ Minn, PhD(chem eng), 65. *Prof Exp:* SUPVR CHEM PROCESSES SECT, PHILLIPS RES CTR, 65- *Res:* Reactor analysis; combustion; process simulation and optimization; chemical kinetics; fluid mechanics; process control; fermentation; economics; design. *Mailing Add:* 207 PTC Phillips Res Ctr Phillips Petrol Co Bartlesville OK 74004

VANDER VELDE, GEORGE, b Chicago, Ill, June 24, 43; m 66; c 3. ANALYTICAL CHEMISTRY, MASS SPECTROMETRY. *Educ:* Hope Col, BA, 65; Univ Houston, PhD(biophysics), 71. *Prof Exp:* Res scientist assoc, natural prod, Dept Bot, Univ Tex, Austin, 70-73, instr biol, Exten Serv, 72-73; res chemist anal chem, Nat Ctr Toxicol Res, Jefferson, 73-74; appl support chemist/prod mgr mass spectrometry, Finnigan Corp, Sunnyvale, Calif, 74-77; assoc dir, Finigan Inst, 77-79; dir tech serv, O H Mat Co, Findlay, Ohio, 79-81; VPRES DEVELOP, ENVIRON TESTING & CERT CORP, EDISON, NJ, 81- *Mem:* Am Chem Soc; Am Soc Mass Spectrometry; Am Soc Testing & Mat; Sigma Xi; Phytochem Soc NAm. *Res:* Applications of mass spectrometry to various analyses, environmental, biomedical, toxicological; analytical chemistry methodology, development; hazardous materials characterization and analysis. *Mailing Add:* Environ Testing & Cert Corp 284 Raritan Ctr Parkway Edison NJ 08817

VANDER VELDE, JOHN CHRISTIAN, b Mich, Sept 25, 30; m 53; c 3. PHYSICS. *Educ:* Hope Col, AB, 52; Univ Mich, MA, 53, PhD(physics), 58. *Prof Exp:* From instr to assoc prof physics, 58-67, PROF PHYSICS, UNIV MICH, ANN ARBOR, 67- *Concurrent Pos:* Assoc in res, LePrince-Ringuet Lab, Polytech Sch, Paris, 66-67; mem prog comt, Argonne Nat Lab, 71-74; mem users exec comt, Nat Accelerator Lab, 72-74; vis scientist, Saclay Nuclear Res Ctr, France, 74. *Mem:* Fel Am Phys Soc. *Res:* Elementary particle physics. *Mailing Add:* Dept of Physics Univ of Mich Ann Arbor MI 48109

VANDER VELDE, W(ALLACE) E(ARL), b Jamestown, Mich, June 4, 29; m 54; c 2. AERONAUTICAL ENGINEERING. *Educ:* Purdue Univ, BSAE, 51; Mass Inst Technol, ScD(instrumentation), 56. *Prof Exp:* Staff engr, Instrumentation Lab, Mass Inst Technol, 53-56; dir applns eng, GPS Instrument Co, Inc, 56-57; asst prof aeronaut eng, 57-61, assoc prof aeronaut & astronaut, 61-65, PROF AERONAUT & ASTRONAUT, MASS INST TECHNOL, 65- *Concurrent Pos:* Consult, various indust co, 58- *Mem:* Fel Am Inst Aeronaut & Astronaut; Inst Elec & Electronics Engrs. *Res:* Automatic control systems; navigation and guidance of aerospace vehicles; instrumentation systems. *Mailing Add:* Dept Aeronaut & Astronaut Rm 33-107 Mass Inst of Technol Cambridge MA 02139

VANDERVEN, NED STUART, b Ann Arbor, Mich, July 15, 32; m 61; c 2. PHYSICS. *Educ:* Harvard Col, AB, 55; Princeton Univ, PhD(physics), 62. *Prof Exp:* Instr physics, Princeton Univ, 59-61; from instr to assoc prof, 61-79, PROF PHYSICS, CARNEGIE-MELLON UNIV, 79- *Mem:* Am Phys Soc. *Res:* Magnetic resonance; solid state physics; biophysics. *Mailing Add:* Dept of Physics Carnegie-Mellon Univ Pittsburgh PA 15213

VAN DER VOO, ROB, b Zeist, Netherlands, Aug 4, 40; m 66; c 2. GEOLOGY, GEOPHYSICS. *Educ:* State Univ Utrecht, BSc, 61, Drs, 65 & 69, PhD(geol, geophys), 69. *Prof Exp:* Res assoc paleomagnetism, State Univ Utrecht, 65-70; vis asst prof, 70-72, asst prof, 72-75, assoc prof, 75-79, PROF GEOPHYS, UNIV MICH, ANN ARBOR, 79-, CHMN, DEPT GEOL SCI, 81- *Mem:* Am Geophys Union; Geol Soc Am; Ger Geol Asn; Royal Netherlands Geol & Mining Soc; Royal Acad Sci Neth. *Res:* Paleomagnetism, plate tectonics of the Atlantic Ocean and Mediterranean Sea; stratigraphy and tectonics of Pyrenean-Alpine Mountain belt; surface waves of earthquakes and nuclear explosions. *Mailing Add:* Dept Geol Sci Univ of Mich Ann Arbor MI 48104

VAN DER VOORN, PETER C, b Haarlem, Netherlands, Feb 25, 40; US citizen; m 65. ELECTROPHOTOGRAPHY. *Educ:* Wichita Univ, BS, 61; Univ Ill, PhD(inorg chem), 65. *Prof Exp:* TECH ASSOC, EASTMAN KODAK CO, 65- *Mem:* Am Chem Soc. *Res:* Electrophotographic developers; inorganic photoconductors; solid state chemistry. *Mailing Add:* Eastman Kodak Co Kodak Park Rochester NY 14617

VANDERVOORT, PETER OLIVER, b Detroit, Mich, Apr 25, 35; m 56; c 2. ASTRONOMY. *Educ:* Univ Chicago, AB, 54, SB, 55, SM, 56, PhD(physics), 60. *Prof Exp:* Vis res assoc, Nat Radio Astron Observ, Assoc Univs, Inc, WVa, 60; NSF fel, Princeton Univ Observ, 60-61; asst prof, 61-65, assoc prof astron, 65-80, PROF ASTRON & ASTROPHYS, UNIV CHICAGO, 80- *Concurrent Pos:* NSF sr fel, Leiden Observ, Netherlands, 67-68. *Mem:* Int Astron Union; Am Astron Soc; Am Phys Soc; Royal Astron Soc. *Res:* Hydrodynamic stability; gas dynamics; interstellar matter; stellar dynamics; galactic structure. *Mailing Add:* Dept of Astron & Astrophys Univ of Chicago 1100 E 58th St Chicago IL 60637

VANDER WALL, EUGENE, b Munster, Ind, Feb 8, 31; m 53; c 4. PHYSICAL INORGANIC CHEMISTRY. *Educ:* Calvin Col, BS, 52; Univ Colo, PhD(chem), 57. *Prof Exp:* Res chemist, Atomic Energy Div, Phillips Petrol Corp, Idaho, 56-60, supvr chemist, 60-63; mem sci staff, Aerojet-Gen Corp, Sacramento, 63-64, supvr liquid propellant res, 64-67, tech supvr liquid propellant res & develop, 67-71, supvr chem res lab, 71-74, MGR CHEM PROCESSES, AEROJET LIQUID ROCKET CO, 74- *Concurrent Pos:* Nat Reactor Testing Sta prof, Univ Idaho, 57-58 & 60-61; mem bd trustees, Bethesda Hosp, Denver, Colo. *Mem:* Fel Am Inst Chem; Am Chem Soc. *Res:* Gelation of liquids; characterization of hazardous chemicals; material-fluid compatibility evaluation; liquid propellant research; development of chemical processes for disposal of hazardous wastes. *Mailing Add:* 5552 Wildwood Way Citrus Heights CA 95610

VANDER WENDE, CHRISTINA, b Paterson, NJ, June 12, 30. BIOCHEMISTRY, PHARMACOLOGY. *Educ:* Upsala Col, BS, 52; Rutgers Univ, MS, 56, PhD(biochem), 59. *Prof Exp:* Jr pharmacologist, Wallace & Tiernan, Inc, 52-53 & Schering Corp, 53-55; pharmacologist, Maltbie Labs, 55-56; asst physiol & biochem, Rutgers Univ, 56-59; sr res scientist, E R Squibb & Sons, 59-60; sr res scientist, Vet Admin Hosp, 60-64; assoc prof pharmacol & biochem, 64-69, PROF PHARMACOL, RUTGERS UNIV, NEW BRUNSWICK, 69- *Concurrent Pos:* Nat Cancer Inst res grant, 61-67; Eastern Leukemia Asn Inc res scholar, 67-69; Epilepsy Found grants, 69-70 & 72-73; Pharmaceut Mfrs Asn grant, 70-72; Nat Drug Abuse Inst grant, 73-76; lectr, Exten Serv, Rutgers Univ, 61-63; dir undergrad res, Upsala Col, 61-64; lectr, All Souls Hosp, Morristown, NJ, 62. *Honors & Awards:* Sci Achievement Award, Upsala Col, 68; Apothecary Awards, Rutgers Univ, 69 & 71. *Mem:* AAAS; Am Soc Pharmacol & Exp Theraput; Soc Neurosci; Acad Pharmaceut Sci; NY Acad Sci. *Res:* Biochemical pharmacology of central nervous system metabolism and enzymology; toxicology. *Mailing Add:* Col of Pharm Rutgers Univ New Brunswick NJ 08903

VANDERWERF, CALVIN ANTHONY, b Friesland, Wis, Jan 2, 17; m 42; c 6. ORGANIC CHEMISTRY. *Educ:* Hope Col, AB, 37; Ohio State Univ, PhD, 41; Hope Col, ScD, 63; St Benedict's Col, LLD, 66. *Prof Exp:* From instr to prof chem, Univ Kans, 41-63; prof chem & pres, Hope Col, 63-71; PROF CHEM & DEAN COL ARTS & SCI, UNIV FLA, 71- *Concurrent Pos:* Consult, Smith, Kline & French Co, 47-63 & Pan Am Oil Co, 58-63; dir, Kativo Chem Co, Ltd, Costa Rica, 63-; trustee, Res Corp, 65-; consult ed, Burgess Publ Corp, 72- *Mem:* Am Chem Soc; fel NY Acad Sci; Royal Soc Chem. *Res:* Aromatic fluorine compounds; phase diagrams; unsaturated lactones; epoxides; synthesis of medicinals; mechanisms of organic reactions; nitrogen containing constituents of petroleum; organo-boron and organo-phosphorous compounds. *Mailing Add:* Col of Arts & Sci Univ of Fla Gainesville FL 32601

VAN DER WERFF, TERRY JAY, b Hammond, Ind, May 16, 44; m 68; c 5. BIOMEDICAL & MECHANICAL ENGINEERING. *Educ:* Mass Inst Technol, SB & SM, 68; Oxford Univ, DPhil(eng sci), 72. *Prof Exp:* Staff engr, Aro Inc, 67-68; asst prof mech eng, physiol & biophys & clin sci, Colo State Univ, 70-73, NSF grant, 72-73; vis asst prof med, Univ Colo Med Ctr, 73-74; head, Dept Biomed Eng, Univ Cape Town & Groote Schuur Hosp, SAfrica, 74-80; DEAN SCI & ENG, SEATTLE UNIV, 81- *Concurrent Pos:* Consult, Rand Corp, 67 & 69-70 & Los Alamos Sci Lab, 72. *Honors & Awards:* Teetor Award, Soc Automotive Engrs, 72. *Mem:* AAAS; Am Phys Soc; Am Soc Mech Engrs; Biomed Eng Soc; Am Soc Eng Educ. *Res:* Nonlinear oscillations; reaction-diffusion systems; cardiovascular fluid dynamics; dynamics of the eye; fluid mechanics; similarity transformations; applied mathematics. *Mailing Add:* Sch Sci & Eng Seattle Univ Seattle WA 98122

VANDERWERFF, WILLIAM D, b Philadelphia, Pa, Dec 31, 29; m 58; c 4. ORGANIC CHEMISTRY. *Educ:* Univ Pa, BS, 51, PhD(org chem), 60. *Prof Exp:* Prod supvr explosives, E I du Pont de Nemours & Co, 51-53; res chemist, 59-70, chief new prods res, 70-77, staff scientist, 77-82, STRATEGIC PLANNING SPECIALIST, SUNTECH, INC, 82- *Mem:* Am Chem Soc. *Res:* Auto-oxidation; hydrocarbon chemistry; petrochemicals; polymer technology. *Mailing Add:* Suntech Inc PO Box 1135 Marcus Hook PA 19061

VANDER WEYDEN, ALLEN JOSEPH, chemistry, see previous edition

VANDERWIEL, CAROLE JEAN, b Cleveland, Ohio, May 6, 50; m 76. MICROSCOPIC ANATOMY, PHYSIOLOGY. *Educ:* Univ Tex, BS, 72; Baylor Univ Med Ctr, PhD(anat), 76. *Prof Exp:* Technician biochem, Univ Tex Health Sci Ctr, 68-70; technician serol, Harris Hosp, Ft Worth, 70-72; grad asst anat, Baylor Col Dent, Dallas, 73-76; res assoc endocrinol, Dent Res Ctr, 77-78, fel orthop, 78-80, ASST PROF, DEPT SURG, SCH MED, UNIV NC, 80- *Concurrent Pos:* Grant, Baylor Col Dent, 74-76 & NSF, 80-83; nat res serv award, NIH, 78-80. *Honors & Awards:* Award, Pfizer Pharmaceut Found, 81. *Mem:* AAAS; Am Soc Bone & Mineral Res. *Res:* Role of hormones, especially parathyroid hormone and calcitonin, on calcium fluxes between bone fluid and blood utilizing histological and physiological techniques; diagnosis of metabolic bone disease by quantitative histomorphometric analysis of human bone biopsies. *Mailing Add:* Dept of Surg Div of Orthop Univ NC Sch of Med Chapel Hill NC 27514

VANDERWIELEN, ADRIANUS JOHANNES, b Germany, Mar 28, 44; US citizen; m 68; c 2. ANALYTICAL CHEMISTRY, PHYSICAL CHEMISTRY. *Educ:* San Diego State Univ, BSc, 70; Univ Calif, PhD(chem), 74. *Prof Exp:* Res fel phys chem, Univ Alta, 74-75; res scientist anal chem, 75-80, HEAD, PROD CONTROL DIV, UPJOHN CO, 80- *Mem:* Am Chem Soc. *Res:* Analytical research and development in particle sizing methods; physical characterization of pharmaceutical powders; thermal analyses; chromatography and methods validation. *Mailing Add:* Prod Control Div Upjohn Co Kalamazoo MI 49001

VANDERWOLF, CORNELIUS HENDRIK, b Edmonton, Alta, Dec 13, 35; m 62. NEUROSCIENCES. *Educ:* Univ Alta, BSc, 58; McGill Univ, MSc, 59, PhD(psychol), 62. *Prof Exp:* Res fel biol, Calif Inst Technol, 62-63; Nat Res Coun fel, Brain Res Inst, Switzerland, 63-64; from asst prof to assoc prof psychol, McMaster Univ, 64-68; assoc prof, 68-73, PROF PSYCHOL, UNIV WESTERN ONT, 73- *Concurrent Pos:* Nat Res Coun res grants, 64- *Mem:* AAAS; Animal Behav Soc; Can Psychol Asn; Can Physiol Soc; Soc Neurosci; Psychonomic Soc. *Res:* Role of forebrain structures in patterning and control of motor activity. *Mailing Add:* Dept Psychol Univ Western Ont London ON N6A 5C2 Can

VANDER WYK, JAMES COLBY, research administration, see previous edition

VANDER WYK, RAYMOND WINSTON, b Waltham, Mass, June 26, 16; m 43; c 3. MICROBIOLOGY. *Educ:* Mass Col Pharm, BS, 37, PhC, 39, MS, 42; Boston Univ, AM, 42; Harvard Univ, PhD, 50. *Prof Exp:* Asst pharmacog & biol, 39-45, from instr pharmacog, plant anat & microtech to assoc prof biol, 45-55, PROF MICROBIOL, MASS COL PHARM, 55- *Concurrent Pos:* Bacteriologist, 7th Gen Hosp, 42-46; pres & treas, Pharmaceut Res Assocs, Inc, 68-; consult, Purdue-Frederick Res Ctr & Pent-Cal, Inc. *Mem:* Soc Cosmetic Chem; Am Pharmaceut Asn; Am Soc Microbiol. *Res:* Microbiological flora of the human scalp; dandruff causes; cosmetic chemistry; antibiotics; dermatology. *Mailing Add:* Dept Biol Sci & Allied Health Sci Mass Col Pharm 179 Longwood Ave Boston MA 02115

VANDERZANT, CARL, b Nymegen, Neth, Sept 7, 25; nat US; m 52; c 2. FOOD MICROBIOLOGY. *Educ:* State Agr Univ, Wageningen, BS, 47, MS, 49; Iowa State Univ, MS, 50, PhD(dairy bact), 53. *Prof Exp:* From asst prof to assoc prof dairy sci, 53-62, PROF FOOD MICROBIOL, TEX A&M UNIV, 62- *Mem:* Am Soc Microbiol; Inst Food Technologists. *Res:* Bacteriological problems of foods. *Mailing Add:* Dept of Animal Sci Tex A&M Univ College Station TX 77843

VANDERZANT, ERMA SCHUMACHER, b Elwood, Ill, Jan 30, 20; m 52; c 2. BIOCHEMISTRY. *Educ:* Iowa State Univ, BS, 42, PhD(biochem), 53. *Prof Exp:* BIOCHEMIST, COTTON INSECTS BR, ENTOM RES DIV, SCI & EDUC ADMIN-AGR RES, USDA, TEX A&M UNIV, 54- *Honors & Awards:* Super Serv Award, USDA, 59; J Everett Bussart Mem Award, Entom Soc Am, 71. *Mem:* Am Chem Soc; Entom Soc Am; Am Inst Nutrit. *Res:* Chemically defined diets for insects; nutrition and metabolism of growth factors, lipides and amino acids. *Mailing Add:* 1303 Broadmoor Bryan TX 77801

VANDERZEE, CECIL EDWARD, b Wetonka, SDak, Apr 26, 12; m 44. PHYSICAL CHEMISTRY. *Educ:* Jamestown Col, BS, 38; Univ Iowa, PhD(chem), 49. *Prof Exp:* Instr, Jamestown Col, 39 & high sch, SDak, 39-42; from instr to assoc prof, 49-58, vchmn dept, 65-70, PROF CHEM, UNIV NEBR, LINCOLN, 58- *Concurrent Pos:* Mem bd dirs, Calorimetry Conf, 64-66, chmn elec, 67-68, chmn, 68-69, counsellor, 73-76; assoc mem, Comn Thermodyn, Int Union Pure & Appl Chem, 76-83. *Honors & Awards:* Huffman Mem Award, Calorimetry Conf, 75. *Mem:* Am Chem Soc. *Res:* Thermodynamics; calorimetry. *Mailing Add:* Dept of Chem Univ of Nebr Lincoln NE 65888

VAN DER ZIEL, ALDERT, b Zandeweer, Netherlands, Dec 12, 10; nat US; m 35; c 3. PHYSICS. *Educ:* Univ Groningen, BA, 30, MA, 33, PhD(physics), 34. *Prof Exp:* Electronics physicist, N V Philips' Incandescent Lamp Works, Netherlands, 34-47; assoc prof physics, Univ BC, 47-50; PROF ELEC ENG, UNIV MINN, MINNEAPOLIS, 50- *Concurrent Pos:* Grad res prof, Univ Fla, 68. *Honors & Awards:* Vincent Bendix Award, Am Soc Eng Educ, 75. *Mem:* Nat Acad Eng; Am Phys Soc; fel Inst Elec & Electronics Engrs. *Res:* Noise in a wide variety of solid state devices, such as transistors, field effect transistors, cryogenic devices and radiation detectors; theory of such devices. *Mailing Add:* Dept of Elec Eng Univ of Minn Minneapolis MN 55455

VAN DER ZIEL, JAN PETER, b Eindhoven, Netherlands, Aug 17, 37; US citizen; m 65; c 2. SOLID STATE PHYSICS. *Educ:* Univ Minn, BS, 59; Harvard Univ, MS, 61, PhD(appl physics), 64. *Prof Exp:* Res fel appl physics, Harvard Univ, 64-65; MEM TECH STAFF, BELL LABS, 65- *Mem:* Am Phys Soc. *Res:* Lasers and nonlinear optics; optical spectroscopy. *Mailing Add:* 1D-465 Bell Labs Murray Hill NJ 07974

VANDER ZWAAG, ROGER, b Holland, Mich, Dec 27, 38; m 64; c 3. BIOSTATISTICS. *Educ:* Hope Col, AB, 60; Purdue Univ, MS, 62; Johns Hopkins Univ, PhD(biostat), 68. *Prof Exp:* Asst prof biostat, Sch Med, Vanderbilt Univ, 68-77; ASSOC PROF BIOSTAT, UNIV TENN, 77- *Mem:* Am Statist Asn. *Res:* Epidemiology. *Mailing Add:* Dept of Community Med Univ of Tenn Memphis TN 38163

VAN DER ZWET, TOM, b Borneo, Indonesia, Apr 7, 32; nat US; m 55, 80; c 3. PLANT PATHOLOGY. *Educ:* Col Trop Agr, Deventer, Netherlands, BS, 52; La State Univ, BS, 55, MS, 57, PhD(plant path), 59. *Prof Exp:* Plant pathologist, Tung Res Lab, Bogalusa, La, 59-65, Fruit Lab, Plant Genetics & Germplasm Inst, Agr Res Ctr, Beltsville, Md, 65-79, PLANT PATHOLOGIST, APPALACIAN FRUIT RES STA, KEARNEYSVILLE, WVA, USDA, 79- *Concurrent Pos:* Adj prof, WVa Univ, Morgantown, 79. *Honors & Awards:* Stark Award, Am Soc Hort Sci, 78. *Mem:* Am Phytopath Soc; Int Soc Hort Sci; Int Soc Plant Path. *Res:* Diseases of tropical and subtropical crops; soil and leaf spot fungi; fire blight of pome fruit. *Mailing Add:* US Dept Agr Appalachian Fruit Res Sta Kearneysville WV 25430

VAN DE STEEG, GARET EDWARD, b Minneapolis, Minn, Feb 8, 40; m 65; c 2. RADIOCHEMISTRY, PHYSICAL CHEMISTRY. *Educ:* Marquette Univ, BS, 62; Univ NMex, PhD(chem), 68. *Prof Exp:* Sr res chemist, 68-75, proj res chemist, 75-78, SR PROJ ANAL CHEMIST, KERR-McGEE CORP, 78- *Mem:* Sigma Xi (secy, 81); Am Chem Soc. *Res:* Dilute solution chemistry of actinides, lanthanides and fission products; solvent extraction of boron, actinides, lanthanides and transition metals; health physics; analytical methods development; radiochemical tracer studies; selenium chemistry. *Mailing Add:* 2312 NW 113th Pl Oklahoma City OK 73120

VAN DEUSEN, JAMES LOWELL, b Champaign, Ill, Sept 12, 28; m 81; c 1. TREE IMPROVEMENT, SILVICULTURE. *Educ:* Iowa State Univ, BS, 55, MS, 57. *Prof Exp:* RES FORESTER, ROCKY MT FOREST & RANGE EXP STA, US FOREST SERV, 57- *Res:* Improvement of tree species for the northern Great Plains. *Mailing Add:* USFS Shelterbelt Lab First and Brander Bottineau ND 58318

VAN DEUSEN, RICHARD L, b Norwich, NY, Jan 31, 26; m 52; c 3. POLYMER CHEMISTRY. *Educ:* Muhlenberg Col, BS, 50; Univ Miami, MS, 55; Univ Buffalo, PhD(chem), 60. *Prof Exp:* Cytotechnologist, Cancer Inst Miami, 51-54; chemist, Olin-Mathieson Chem Corp, 56; instr chem, Univ Buffalo, 56-59; res chemist, Ansco Div, Gen Aniline & Film Co, 59-60; res chemist, 60-70, CHIEF POLYMER BR, US AIR FORCE MAT LAB, 70- *Mem:* Am Chem Soc; AAAS; Sigma Xi; Am Inst Chem; Int Soc Heterocyclic Chem. *Res:* Photopolymerization; cyclopolymerization kinetics; solid state polymerization; polycondensation; thermally stable plastics, elastomers and fibrous materials. *Mailing Add:* 2902 Stauffer Dr Xenia OH 45385

VAN DE VAART, HERMAN, b Arnhem, Netherlands, Apr 11, 34; m 60; c 2. SOLID STATE ELECTRONICS. *Educ:* Delft Univ Technol, Ing, 58, PhD(tech sci), 69. *Prof Exp:* Res asst elec eng, Delft Univ Technol, 56-58; res engr, Transitron Electronic Corp, Mass, 60-62; res asst, 62-65, res staff mem, 65-73, mgr solid state devices dept, 73-80, mgr signal processing dept, 80-81, DIR APPL PHYSICS LAB, SPERRY RES CTR, SPERRY RAND CORP, 81- *Mem:* Am Phys Soc; sr mem Inst Elec & Electronics Eng. *Res:* Semiconductor technology; quadrupole and ferro magnetic resonance; microwave magnetics; solid state delay lines; ultrasonics; ferrites. *Mailing Add:* Sperry Res Ctr 100 North Rd Sudbury MA 01776

VAN DE VEN, THEODORUS GERTRUDUS MARIA, b s-Hertogenbosch, Holland, Feb 22, 46. PHYSICAL CHEMISTRY. *Educ:* State Univ Utrecht, BSc, 69, MSc, 71; McGill Univ, PhD(phys chem), 76. *Prof Exp:* Res fel rheology, Univ Sydney, 76-77; ASSOC SCIENTIST PHYS CHEM, PULP & PAPER RES INST CAN, MCGILL UNIV, 78- *Mem:* Can Pulp & Paper Asn. *Res:* Fundamental research in the areas of microrheology and wetting and spreading. *Mailing Add:* Pulp & Paper Bldg McGill Univ 3420 University St Montreal PQ H3A 2T5 Can

VAN DEVENTER, WILLIAM CARLSTEAD, b Salisbury, Mo, Oct 22, 08; m 34; c 1. BIOLOGY. *Educ:* Cent Methodist Col, AB, 30; Univ Ill, AM, 32, PhD(field biol), 35. *Prof Exp:* Asst biol, Cent Methodist Col, 28-30; asst zool, Univ Ill, 30-34; biologist, Monroe County Parks, NY, 34-35; prof biol, St Viator Col, 35-38; instr zool, Stephens Col, 38-43, prof biol, 43-53; head dept, 53-63, prof, 53-79, EMER PROF BIOL, WESTERN MICH UNIV, 79- *Mem:* AAAS; Ecol Soc Am; Nat Sci Teachers Asn; Nat Asn Res Sci Teaching (vpres, 54, pres, 55). *Res:* Biology of Crustacea; ecology of birds; field biology; human ecology; science education. *Mailing Add:* Dept of Biol Western Mich Univ Kalamazoo MI 49008

VANDEVOORDE, JACQUES PIERRE, b Tourcoing, France, Apr 19, 30; US citizen; m 60; c 2. BIOCHEMISTRY. *Educ:* Loyola Univ, La, BA, 51; Tulane Univ, MS, 61, PhD(biochem), 68. *Prof Exp:* Asst biochemist, Touro Infirmary, 61-68; sr biochemist, Hoffmann-LaRoche Inc, 68-74, group chief, 74-77, asst dir immunol dept, 77-81. *Mem:* Clin Radio Assay Soc; Reticuloendothelial Soc; Tissue Cult Asn; Am Asn Clin Chem. *Res:* Biochemical immunology; chemotherapy; clinical research; cancer detection; immunopharmacology. *Mailing Add:* Immunol Dept Hoffmann-La Roche Inc Nutley NJ 07110

VANDE VUSSE, FREDERICK JOHN, b Holland, Mich, Sept 26, 39; m 61; c 3. PARASITOLOGY. *Educ:* Hope Col, BA, 61; Iowa State Univ, MS, 64, PhD(zool), 67. *Prof Exp:* ASSOC PROF BIOL, GUSTAVUS ADOLPHUS COL, 67- *Concurrent Pos:* Vis prof, Silliman Univ, Philippines, 70-71. *Mem:* Am Micros Soc; Am Soc Parasitol; Wildlife Dis Asn. *Res:* Parasites of wildlife; systematics of Trematoda and Hirudinea. *Mailing Add:* Dept of Biol Gustavus Adolphus Col St Peter MN 56082

VANDEWATER, STUART LESLIE, b Campbellford, Ont, Nov 16, 24; m 50; c 2. ANESTHESIOLOGY. *Educ:* Univ Toronto, MD, 47; FRCPS(C), 53; Am Bd Anesthesiol, dipl, 64. *Prof Exp:* R S McLaughlin fel, Toronto Gen Hosp, Univ Toronto, 52-53, clin teacher anesthesia, Fac Med, 53-59; head dept, 60-71, PROF ANESTHESIA, FAC MED, QUEEN'S UNIV, ONT, 60-, ASSOC DEAN & SECY, 71- *Concurrent Pos:* Sr anesthetist, Kingston Gen Hosp, 60-71; consult, Can Armed Med Servs, Ongwanada Sanatorium & Ont Hosp, Rockwood, 60- & Can Armed Forces Med Comt, 64-69; examr, Royal Col Physicians & Surgeons Can, 63-70. *Mem:* Am Soc Anesthesiol; Acad Anesthesiol; Can Anesthetists Soc (vpres, 65-67, pres, 67-68, hon secy, 72-); Royal Soc Med; NY Acad Sci. *Res:* Clinical and laboratory anesthesia. *Mailing Add:* Fac of Med Queen's Univ Kingston ON K7L 3N6 Can

VAN DE WETERING, RICHARD LEE, b Bellingham, Wash, Aug 2, 28; m 60; c 2. MATHEMATICS. *Educ:* Univ Wash, Seattle, BS, 50; Western Wash State Col, EdM, 55; Stanford Univ, PhD(math), 60. *Prof Exp:* From asst prof to assoc prof, 60-67, PROF MATH, SAN DIEGO STATE UNIV, 67-, DEPT CHAIR, 79- *Concurrent Pos:* Res grant, Delft Univ Technol, 66-67; res assoc, Math Inst, Univ Groningen, 73-74. *Mem:* Am Math Soc; Math Asn Am. *Res:* Ordinary differential equations and integral transforms. *Mailing Add:* Dept of Math San Diego State Univ San Diego CA 92182

VANDEWIELE, RAYMOND LAURENT, b Kortryk, Belg, Oct 2, 22; m 54; c 3. OBSTETRICS & GYNECOLOGY. *Educ:* Cath Univ Louvain, MD, 47. *Prof Exp:* Fel, Col Physicians & Surgeons, Columbia Univ, 52-54 & Yale Univ, 54-55; from instr to prof gynec, 55-68, WILLARD C RAPPLEYE PROF OBSTET & GYNEC & CHMN DEPT, COL PHYSICIANS & SURGEONS, COLUMBIA UNIV, 71-; DIR OBSTET & GYNEC SERV, COLUMBIA-PRESBY MED CTR, 71- *Concurrent Pos:* From asst to attend, Columbia-Presby Med Ctr, 58-68; dir, Int Inst Study Human Reproduction, 70-; consult, Clin Ctr, NIH, 71- *Mem:* Soc Gynec Invest; Endocrine Soc. *Res:* Reproductive physiology; biochemistry of endocrine organs, especially adrenal, testis and ovary. *Mailing Add:* Dept of Obstet & Gynec Columbia-Presby Med Ctr New York NY 10032

VANDE WOUDE, GEORGE, b Brooklyn, NY, Dec 25, 35; m 59; c 4. BIOCHEMISTRY, VIROLOGY. *Educ:* Hofstra Col, BA, 59; Rutgers Univ, MS, 62, PhD(biochem), 64. *Prof Exp:* Agr Res Serv-Nat Acad Sci res assoc, 64-65; res chemist, Plum Island Animal Dis Lab, USDA, 65-72; head, Human Tumor Studies Sect, Viral Biol Br, 72-77, head, Virus Tumor biochem Sect, 77-81, CHIEF, LAB MOLECULAR BIOL, NAT CANCER INST, 81- *Mem:* AAAS; Am Chem Soc. *Res:* Chemical and physical properties of viruses; virus-host cell interactions. *Mailing Add:* Lab Molecular Oncol Nat Cancer Inst Bethesda MD 20014

VAN DIJK, CHRISTIAAN PIETER, b Amsterdam, Neth, Nov 10, 15; US citizen; m 63; c 3. PHYSICAL ORGANIC CHEMISTRY, CHEMICAL ENGINEERING. *Educ:* Amsterdam Munic Univ, BS, 36, MS, 40; Delft Univ Technol, PhD(org chem), 46. *Prof Exp:* Lab mgr org chem, Delft Univ Technol, 40-48; asst dept head, Shell Lab Amsterdam, Royal Dutch Shell Co, Neth, 48-57; sr chemist, Dow Chem Co, 57-60; sr scientist, M W Kellogg Co, NJ, 60-75, SR SCIENTIST, PULLMAN KELLOGG RES & DEVELOP CTR, 75- *Concurrent Pos:* Chmn, Nat Exam Comt towards Qual Sci Coworkers, 43-56; consult, Chemische Fabriek Rotterdam, Neth, 46-48. *Honors & Awards:* Chem Pioneer Award, Am Inst Chemists, 76. *Mem:* Am Chem Soc; Royal Neth Chem Soc; Sigma Xi. *Res:* Inventing new process forms for conversions in the petroleum, petrochemical and polymer field; combined information from the fields of organic and physical chemistry with design-engineering calculations. *Mailing Add:* 10722 Glenway Houston TX 77070

VAN DILLA, MARVIN ALBERT, b New York, NY, June 18, 19; div; c 4. BIOPHYSICS. *Educ:* Mass Inst Technol, PhD(physics), 51. *Prof Exp:* Res asst, Mass Inst Technol, 46-51; asst res prof physics, Radiobiol Lab, Univ Utah, 51-57; mem staff, Biomed Res Group, Los Alamos Sci Lab, 57-72; CYTOPHYSICS SECT LEADER, BIOMED & ENVIRON RES DIV, LAWRENCE LIVERMORE LAB, 72- *Mem:* AAAS; Soc Anal Cytol. *Res:* Radiation detection and measurement; biological effects of radiation; cell analysis and sorting by high speed flow methods; flow cytometry; cell cycle analysis; flow cytogenetics; cancer diagnosis; mutagenesis; carcinogenesis; sperm cell analysis. *Mailing Add:* Lawrence Livermore Lab Livermore CA 94550

VANDIVER, BRADFORD B, b Orlando, Fla, Mar 7, 27; m 58; c 2. GEOLOGY. *Educ:* Univ Colo, BA, 57, MS, 58; Univ Wash, Seattle, PhD(geol), 64. *Prof Exp:* Explor geologist, Tenn Gas Transmission Co, Bolivia, 58-60; asst prof geol, Univ Ore, 64-65; PROF GEOL, STATE UNIV NY COL POTSDAM, 65- *Concurrent Pos:* Prof, Univ Munich, Ger, 72. *Mem:* Fel Geol Soc Am; Sigma Xi. *Res:* Metamorphic petrology and structural geology, Cascades, Rocky Mountains, Alps, Adirondacks, Odenwald, (Germany); environmental geology. *Mailing Add:* Dept Geol State Univ of NY Potsdam NY 13676

VANDIVIERE, H MAC, b Dawsonville, Ga, Mar 26, 21; m 41; c 2; m 68. PREVENTIVE PEDIATRICS, CHEST DISEASE. *Educ:* Mercer Univ, AB, 43, MA, 44; Univ NC, MD, 60. *Prof Exp:* From instr to asst prof biol, Mercer Univ, 42-48; chief spec serv, Res Lab, State Dept Pub Health, Ga, 48-51; res bacteriologist, NC Sanatorium Syst, 51-53, dir dept res, 53-67; assoc prof community med, 67-72, prof, 72-80, PROF PEDIAT & DIR, DIV PREV & COMMUNITY PEDIAT, COL MED, UNIV KY, 80- *Concurrent Pos:* Am Pub Health Asn fel epidemiol; instr bact, Univ Mich, 44-46; dir labs & res, Gravely Sanatorium, 53-62; med dir, Haitian Am Tuberc Inst, Jeremie, Haiti, 62-; asst prof community health sci, Sch Med, Duke Univ, 65-67; consult, Dept Pub Health & adv, President's Comt Control Tuberc, Repub Haiti, 65-; clin assoc prof, Sch Pub Health, Univ NC, 69-; dir div tuberc & fungal dis, State Health Dept, Ky, 72-73, dir div remedial health servs, 73-76. *Mem:* Am Thoracic Soc; Am Pub Health Asn; AMA; Am Teachers Prev Med; Soc Epidemiol Res. *Res:* Antituberculosis vaccination; purification of tuberculoproteins, diagnostic skin-testing methods; epidemiology. *Mailing Add:* Dept Community Med Col Med Univ Ky Lexington KY 40506

VANDLEN, RICHARD LEE, b Battle Creek, Mich, Oct 22, 47. BIOCHEMISTRY, NEUROCHEMISTRY. *Educ:* Mich State Univ, BS, 69, PhD(phys chem), 72. *Prof Exp:* Fel neurochem, Calif Inst Technol, 72-75, res fel, 75-76; SR RES BIOCHEMIST, MERCK SHARP & DOHME RES LABS, 76- *Concurrent Pos:* NIH fel, Calif Inst Technol, 74-75. *Mem:* Sigma Xi; Am Crystallog Asn; NY Acad Sci; AAAS. *Res:* Regulation of hormone synthesis and release; hormone and neurotransmitter receptors; protein structure and function; cell culture. *Mailing Add:* Merck Sharpe & Dohme Res Labs PO Box 2000 Rahway NJ 07065

VAN DOEREN, RICHARD EDGERLY, b Tulsa, Okla, Mar 31, 37; m 60; c 3. ACOUSTICS, ELECTRONICS. *Educ:* Colo Sch Mines, BSc, 60; Ohio State Univ, MSc, 64, PhD(elec eng), 68. *Prof Exp:* Physicist, US Naval Air Develop Ctr, Pa, 60-64; res assoc electromagnetic theory, Electro Sci Lab, Ohio State Univ, 64-69; sr engr, N Star Res & Develop Inst, 69-74; PRES, MIDWEST ACOUST & ELECTRONICS, INC, 74- *Mem:* Inst Elec & Electronics Engrs; Acoust Soc Am; Inst Noise Control Eng; Am Consult Engrs Coun. *Res:* Acoustical noise reduction techniques, acoustical response of rooms; acoustic measurement techniques and systems; human response to sound; electroacoustic systems; computer methods in acoustics. *Mailing Add:* 6617 Limerick Lane Minneapolis MN 55435

VAN DOLAH, ROBERT FREDERICK, b Portland, Ore, Nov 4, 49. MARINE ECOLOGY, INVERTEBRATE ZOOLOGY. *Educ:* Marietta Col, BS, 71; Univ Md, MS, 75, PhD(zool), 77. *Prof Exp:* ASST MARINE SCIENTIST MARINE ECOL, SC WILDLIFE & MARINE RESOURCES DEPT, 78- *Mem:* Ecol Soc Am; AAAS; Estuarine Res Fedn. *Res:* Population and community ecology with particular emphasis on the regulatory processes operating in marine and estuarine systems. *Mailing Add:* SC Marine Resources Res Inst PO Box 12559 Charleston SC 29412

VAN DOLAH, ROBERT WAYNE, b Cheyenne, Wyo, Feb 1, 19; m 42; c 3. CHEMISTRY. *Educ:* Whitman Col, AB, 40; Ohio State Univ, PhD(org chem), 43. *Prof Exp:* Asst chem, Ohio State Univ, 40-42; asst to sci dir, William S Merrell Co, Ohio, 43-44, res chemist & group leader, 44-46; actg head org chem br, US Naval Ord Test Sta, Calif, 46-48, head, 48-53, head chem div, 53-54; chief, Explosives Res Lab, Pittsburgh Mining & Safety Res Ctr, US Bur Mines, 54-71, res dir, 71-78; CONSULT, 78- *Honors & Awards:* Nitro Nobel Medal, 67. *Mem:* Fel AAAS; fel Am Inst Chem; Am Chem Soc; Sigma Xi. *Res:* Propellants and explosives; combustion; mine safety; industrial safety. *Mailing Add:* 202 Cherokee Rd Pittsburgh PA 15241

VAN DOMELEN, BRUCE HAROLD, b Shelby, Mich, May 27, 33; m 57; c 4. PHYSICS. *Educ:* Kalamazoo Col, BA, 55; Univ Wis, MA, 57, PhD(physics), 60. *Prof Exp:* Staff mem, 60-62, sect supvr phys metall, 62-65, div supvr anal physics, 65, tech adv syst res, 65-69, div supvr explor power sources, 69-78, DIV SUPVR EXPLOSIVES PROJS & TESTS DIV, SANDIA LABS, 78- *Concurrent Pos:* Actg chmn, Govenor's Sci Adv Comt, NMex, 66-70, Governor's sci adv, 66-75; NMex mem, Western Interstate Nuclear Bd, 67-77, chmn, 71-73; mem Nat Governors' Coun Sci & Technol, 70-75. *Mem:* Am Phys Soc. *Res:* Explosives; physical chemistry. *Mailing Add:* 8204 La Sala Cuadra NE Albuquerque NM 87111

VAN DONGEN, CORNELIS GODEFRIDUS, b Geertruidenberg, Netherlands, Mar 20, 34; m 69. ANIMAL HUSBANDRY, REPRODUCTIVE PHYSIOLOGY. *Educ:* Wageningen State Agr Univ, BS, 57, MS, 59; Univ Ill, Urbana, MS, 62, PhD(dairy sci), 64. *Prof Exp:* Res fel pharmacol, Harvard Univ, 64-65; res assoc physiol, Brown Univ, 66; asst prof pharmacol, NY Med Col, 66-67; res assoc, 67-76, V PRES, BIO-RES INST, INC, 76- *Concurrent Pos:* Grants, NIH; investr, US Dept Agr Contract; consult, Bio Res Consults. *Mem:* Am Dairy Sci Asn; Am Soc Animal Sci; Brit Soc Study Fertil; Soc Study Reproduction; Am Asn Lab Animal Sci. *Res:* Husbandry, nutrition and reproductive physiology of inbred and hybrid hamsters; sex ratio shifts; pharmacological and toxicological effects on mammalian systems in vivo; sperm cell physiology; carcinogenicity testing. *Mailing Add:* Bio-Res Inst 9 Commercial Ave Cambridge MA 02141

VAN DOORNE, WILLIAM, b Utrecht, Neth, Dec 12, 37; US citizen; m 61; c 3. INORGANIC CHEMISTRY. *Educ:* Calvin Col, BS, 60; Univ Mich, MS, 62, PhD, 65. *Prof Exp:* From asst prof to assoc prof chem, 66-74, PROF CHEM, CALVIN COL, 74-, CHMN DEPT, 77- *Concurrent Pos:* Vis assoc prof, Univ Hawaii, 72-73. *Mem:* Am Chem Soc. *Res:* Phophorus-nitrogen compounds; synthetic inorganic chemistry; crystallography. *Mailing Add:* Calvin Col 1801 E Beltline Ave SE Grand Rapids MI 49506

VANDOR, SANDOR LASZLO, biochemical pharmacology, see previous edition

VAN DOREN, DAVID MILLER, JR, agronomy, soil physics, see previous edition

VAN DREAL, PAUL ARTHUR, b Chicago, Ill, Feb 15, 32; m 57; c 2. BIOCHEMISTRY, CYTOLOGY. *Educ:* Calvin Col, BS, 57; Mich State Univ, PhD(bot, biochem, cytol), 61. *Prof Exp:* Clin biochemist, St Lawrence Hosp, 61-63; NIH fel, Biol Div, Oak Ridge Nat Lab, 63-64; asst prof biochem, Med Sch, Univ Ore, 64-66; from asst prof to assoc prof clin chem, Med Sch, Univ Wash, 66-71, dir lab computer div, 69-71; vpres & dir res, Hycel Inc, 71-72; tech mgr radioimmunoassay develop, Corning Glass Works, Inc, 72-73; assoc prof path & clin chem, Med Sch, Univ Ky, 73-74; lab dir & tech dir, Nat Health Labs, Inc, 74-75; vpres & lab dir, Herner Analytics, 75-77; lab dir, Clin Lab Med Serv, 77-80; WITH DIAG DIV, ABBOT LABS, 80- *Concurrent Pos:* Lectr biochem, Mich State Univ, 62-63; Nat Cancer Inst fel carcinogenesis, Med Sch, Univ Ore, 64-66; consult, Ortec Div, EG & G, 67-71, Clin Instruments Div, Beckman Instruments, 67-, Pesticide Res Lab, Dept of Health, State of Wash, 68-69, Bausch & Lomb Inc, 69- & Corning Glass Inc, 74-; Bausch & Lomb Grant electrophoresis, Med Sch, Univ Wash, 69-70. *Mem:* AAAS; Am Chem Soc; fel Am Asn Clin Chemists; Am Soc Clin Path; Asn Clin Scientists. *Res:* New clinical laboratory diagnostic techniques; aging; patient normals as a function of age and disease onset; biochemistry of the cell cycle. *Mailing Add:* Diag Div Abbott Labs MS 2172 PO Box 2020 Irving TX 75061

VAN DRESER, MERTON LAWRENCE, b Des Moines, Iowa, June 5, 29; m 52; c 2. CERAMIC ENGINEERING, MATERIALS SCIENCE. *Educ:* Iowa State Univ, BS, 51. *Prof Exp:* Tech supvr fiberglass mfg, Owens-Corning Fiberglas Corp, 54-57; res engr, 57-60, res sect head basic refractory res, 60-63, lab mgr, 63-65, assoc dir res, 65-69, dir refractories res, 69-72, DIR, NON-METALL MAT RES, KAISER ALUMINUM & CHEM CORP, 72- *Concurrent Pos:* Mem tech adv comn, Refractories Inst, 74-, chmn, 80-; mem adv bd, Dept Ceramic Eng, Univ Ill, 75-78. *Mem:* Fel Am Ceramic Soc (vpres, 73-74); Brit Ceramic Soc; Nat Inst Ceramic Eng; Am Inst Mining, Metall & Petrol Eng; hon mem Am Soc Testing & Mat. *Res:* Refractories, sintering of refractory oxides and silicates; chemical and ceramic bonding of refractory powders; development of refractory products for application in iron, steel, glass, non-ferrous metal and petro-chemical industries. *Mailing Add:* 40 Castledown Rd Pleasanton CA 94566

VANDRUFF, LARRY WAYNE, b Elmira, NY, Apr 28, 42; m 66; c 2. WILDLIFE BIOLOGY, URBAN ECOLOGY. *Educ:* Mansfield State Col, BS, 64; Cornell Univ, MS, 66, PhD(wildlife ecol), 71. *Prof Exp:* Res asst vert ecol & genetics, Cornell Univ, 64-66, res asst wildlife ecol, NY Wildlife Res Unit, 66-70; asst prof vert biol, 70-77, ASSOC PROF WILDLIFE BIOL, STATE UNIV NEW YORK COL ENVIRON SCI & FORESTRY, 77- *Mem:* Am Soc Mammal; Wildlife Soc; Ecol Soc Am; Am Nature Study Soc. *Res:* Field studies in the ecology of urban wildlife species; waterfowl biology and wetland ecology; dynamics of homeotherm populations and wildlife; habitat relationships. *Mailing Add:* Dept Biol SUNY Col Environ Sci & Forestry Syracuse NY 13210

VAN DUSER, ARTHUR L, b Appleton, Wis, Dec 6, 11; m 39; c 2. PREVENTIVE MEDICINE, PUBLIC HEALTH. *Educ:* Univ Wis, BS, 36, MD, 38; Univ Mich, MS, 47; Am Bd Prev Med, cert pub health & gen prev med, 50. *Prof Exp:* Dist health officer, Wis State Bd Health, 41-46, dir, Cancer Control Div, 47-72, dir, Veneral Dis Control Div, 49-69, dir, Lab Eval Div, 60-80, dep dir, Bur Prev Dis, 69-80; RETIRED. *Mem:* Am Pub Health Asn; AMA; Pub Health Cancer Asn Am; Am Social Health Asn. *Res:* Application of social-medical knowledge to the prevention and detection of cancer; improvement in qualitative and quantitative medical laboratory services, including methods, evaluations, standards and approving systems. *Mailing Add:* 524 Clifden Dr Madison WI 53711

VAN DUUREN, BENJAMIN LOUIS, b SAfrica, May 5, 27; nat US; div; c 2. ORGANIC CHEMISTRY. *Educ:* Univ SAfrica, BS, 46 & 48, MS, 49; Univ Orange Free State, ScD, 51. *Prof Exp:* Res assoc, Univ Ill, 51-53 & Univ Calif, Los Angeles, 53-54; res chemist, E I du Pont de Nemours & Co, NY, 54-55; from instr chem to assoc prof, 55-69, PROF ENVIRON MED, NY UNIV MED CTR, 69- *Concurrent Pos:* Consult, Environ Protection Agency, 75- & NSF, 79- *Mem:* Am Chem Soc; Am Asn Cancer Res. *Res:* Chemistry of pyrrolizidine alkaloids and benzofuran fish toxic compounds; infrared spectroscopy; fluorescence spectroscopy of aromatic compounds; environmental carcinogens; carcinogenesis and metabolism of carcinogens; tobacco and cancer. *Mailing Add:* Dept Environ Med NY Univ Med Ctr 550 First Ave New York NY 10016

VAN DUYNE, RICHARD PALMER, b Orange, NJ, Oct 28, 45. ANALYTICAL CHEMISTRY, CHEMICAL PHYSICS. *Educ:* Rensselaer Polytech Inst, BS, 67; Univ NC, PhD(anal chem), 71. *Prof Exp:* Asst prof, 71-76, assoc prof anal chem, 76-79, PROF ANAL/PHYS CHEM, NORTHWESTERN UNIV, EVANSTON, 79- *Concurrent Pos:* Fel, Alfred P Sloan Found, 74- *Honors & Awards:* Coblentz Mem Prize, 80. *Mem:* Am Chem Soc; Electrochem Soc; AAAS; Am Phys Soc. *Res:* Radical ion chemistry; surface Raman spectroscopy; chemical applications of lasers; time-resolved fluorescence spectroscopy; tunable dye laser resonance Raman spectroscopy; laboratory computer systems. *Mailing Add:* Dept of Chem Northwestern Univ Evanston IL 60201

VAN DYK, JOHN WILLIAM, b Paterson, NJ, May 2, 28; m 51; c 3. PHYSICAL CHEMISTRY. *Educ:* Rutgers Univ, AB, 50; Columbia, AM, 51, PhD(chem), 54. *Prof Exp:* Asst chem, Columbia Univ, 50-52; res chemist, Polychems Dept, 54-64, STAFF CHEMIST, FABRICS & FINISHES DEPT, E I DU PONT DE NEMOURS & CO, INC, 64- *Mem:* Am Chem Soc. *Res:* Polymerization kinetics; surface chemistry; polymer chemistry; paint chemistry; color science; visual perception; computer science. *Mailing Add:* 106 Cambridge Dr Windshills Wilmington DE 19803

VAN DYKE, CECIL GERALD, b Effingham, Ill, Feb 4, 41; m 69; c 4. PLANT PATHOLOGY, FUNGUS-HOST ULTRASTRUCTURE. *Educ:* East Ill Univ, BSEd, 63; Univ Ill, Urbana, MS, 66, PhD(plant path), 68. *Prof Exp:* NIH res assoc, Univ Ill, Urbana, 68; res assoc, 68-69, instr bot, 69, asst prof, 69-76, ASSOC PROF BOT & PLANT PATH, NC STATE UNIV, 76- *Concurrent Pos:* Tech comt biol control weeds/fungal plant pathogens, Southern Regional Prog. *Mem:* Am Phytopath Soc; Mycol Soc Am; Bot Soc Am; Sigma Xi; Creation Res Soc. *Res:* Ultrastructure of fungi and fungus-host pathological interactions and biological control. *Mailing Add:* Dept of Bot NC State Univ Raleigh NC 27650

VAN DYKE, CHARLES H, b Rochester, Pa, Sept 19, 37; m 66; c 1. INORGANIC CHEMISTRY, ORGANOMETALLIC CHEMISTRY. *Educ:* Geneva Col, BS, 59; Univ Pa, PhD(inorg chem), 64. *Prof Exp:* Asst prof chem, 63-70, ASSOC PROF CHEM, CARNEGIE-MELLON UNIV, 70- *Mem:* Am Chem Soc; Royal Soc Chem. *Res:* Synthesis and study of volatile hydride derivatives of the Group IV elements. *Mailing Add:* Dept Chem Carnegie-Mellon Univ 4400 Fifth Ave Pittsburgh PA 15213

VAN DYKE, CRAIG, b Detroit, Mich, Oct 4, 41; m 69; c 1. PSYCHIATRY, PSYCHOPHARMACOLOGY. *Educ:* Univ Wash, BS, 63, MD, 67. *Prof Exp:* Asst prof psychiat, Yale Univ, 74-78; ASSOC PROF PSYCHIAT, UNIV CALIF, SAN FRANCISCO, 79- *Concurrent Pos:* Mem staff, Vet Admin Med Ctr, 79- *Mem:* Am Psychiat Asn; Am Psychosomatic Soc; Int Col Psychosomatic Med. *Res:* Psychopharmacology of drugs of abuse. *Mailing Add:* Vet Admin Med Ctr 4150 Clement San Francisco CA 94121

VAN DYKE, HENRY, b Pittsburgh, Pa, Oct 1, 21; m 43; c 4. MICROBIOLOGY. *Educ:* Western Reserve Univ, BS, 47; Univ Mich, MA, 49, PhD(zool), 55. *Prof Exp:* Malariologist, US Pub Health Serv, 52; instr zool, Univ Mich, 52-53; asst prof biol, Carleton Col, 53-60 & Ore Col Educ, 60-63; ASSOC PROF BIOL, ORE STATE UNIV, 63- *Mem:* AAAS; Soc Protozool; Am Soc Microbiol; Marine Biol Asn UK, Am Soc Limnol & Oceanog. *Res:* Ecology, physiology, culture and photobiology of marine communities. *Mailing Add:* 3300 NW Van Buren Corvallis OR 97331

VAN DYKE, JOHN WILLIAM, JR, b Holland, Mich, Nov 15, 35; m 59; c 3. ORGANIC CHEMISTRY. *Educ:* Hope Col, AB, 58; Univ Ill, PhD(org chem), 62. *Prof Exp:* SR RES CHEMIST, THERAPEUT RES LAB, MILES LABS, INC, 62- *Mem:* Am Chem Soc. *Res:* Organic synthesis of pharmacologically active compounds. *Mailing Add:* Miles Labs Inc 1127 Myrtle St Elkhart IN 46515

VAN DYKE, KNOX, b Chicago, Ill, June 23, 39; m 78; c 5. PHARMACOLOGY, BIOCHEMISTRY. *Educ:* Knox Col, AB, 61; St Louis Univ, PhD(biochem), 66. *Prof Exp:* Res assoc pharmacol, 66-68, sr res pharmacologist, 68-69, from asst prof to assoc prof pharmacol, 69-77, PROF PHARMACOL & TOXICOL, MED CTR, WVA UNIV, 77- *Concurrent Pos:* WHO grant, 70-, training grant malaria; WVa Heart Asn grant, 70-; NIH instnl cancer & gen res WVa rep, Oak Ridge Assoc Univs, 72-75 & Merck, Sharp & Dohme. *Mem:* AAAS; Am Chem Soc; Am Soc Pharmacol & Exp Therapeut; Int Soc Biochem Pharmacol. *Res:* malariology and mechanism of drug resistance; automated analysis of enzyme and nucleic acid systems; radioimmunoassay; mechanisms of antimalarial drugs; adrenergic transmitter-energy complexes; adenosine utilization and syntheses; measurement of bioluminescent and chemiluminescent reaction; inflammatory drugs and free radicals. *Mailing Add:* Dept Pharmacol WVa Univ Med Ctr Morgantown WV 26506

VAN DYKE, MILTON D(ENMAN), b Chicago, Ill, Aug 1, 22; m 46, 62; c 6. FLUID MECHANICS. *Educ:* Harvard Univ, BS, 43; Calif Inst Technol, MS, 47, PhD(aeronaut), 49. *Prof Exp:* Aeronaut res scientist, Nat Adv Comt Aeronaut, 43-46 & 50-58; aeronaut engr, Douglas Aircraft Co, 48; consult aerodynamicist, Rand Corp, 49-50; vis prof, Univ Paris, 58-59; prof aeronaut eng, 59-75, PROF APPL MECH, STANFORD UNIV, 75- *Concurrent Pos:* Lectr, Stanford Univ, 50-58; Guggenheim fel, 54-55; Nat Acad Sci exchange vis, USSR, 65. *Mem:* Nat Acad Eng; Am Phys Soc. *Res:* Compressible flow theory; viscous flow theory. *Mailing Add:* Div of Appl Mech Stanford Univ Stanford CA 94305

VAN DYKE, RUSSELL AUSTIN, b Rochester, NY, Feb 8, 30; m 56; c 2. BIOCHEMISTRY, MICROBIOLOGY. *Educ:* Hope Col, BS, 51; Univ Mich, MS, 53; Univ Ill, PhD(animal biochem), 60. *Prof Exp:* Asst animal biochem, Univ Ill, 56-60; res assoc radio biochem, Univ Colo, 60-61; sr res biochemist, Dow Human Health Res, Dow Chem Co, Mich, 61-68; asst prof biochem, Mayo Grad Sch Med, 69-73, asst prof biochem, Mayo Med Sch, 73, assoc prof biochem, Mayo Med Sch, 73-79, assoc prof anesthesiol, Mayo Med Sch, 74-79, CONSULT, DEPT ANESTHESIOL, MAYO CLIN, ROCHESTER, MINN, 68-, ASSOC PROF PHARMACOL, MAYO MED SCH, 73-, PROF ANESTHESIOL & BIOCHEM, MAYO MED SCH, 79-, CONSULT, DEPT CELL BIOL, MAYO CLIN, 80- *Mem:* AAAS; Am Chem Soc; Am Soc Pharmacol & Exp Therapeut; Soc Toxicol; Am Soc Anesthesiol. *Res:* Biochemical pharmacology; drug metabolism; cell membrane and transport; enzymatic dechlorination in mammals. *Mailing Add:* Dept of Anesthesiol Mayo Clin Rochester MN 55901

VAN DYNE, GEORGE M, ecology, nutrition, deceased

VANE, ARTHUR B(AYARD), b Portland, Maine, June 1, 15; m 42; c 3. PHYSICAL CHEMISTRY, ELECTRICAL ENGINEERING. *Educ:* Univ Wash, Seattle, BS, 37; Ore State Col, MS, 41; Stanford Univ, EE, 49. *Prof Exp:* Staff mem, Radiation Lab, Mass Inst Technol, 42-45; physicist, US Naval Ord Test Sta, 45-47; res assoc, Microwave Lab, Stanford Univ, 47-49; sr engr, Varian Assocs, 49-55, mgr systs develop, 55-58, mgr systs dept, Radiation Div, 58-62; mgr microwave dept, Melabs, Inc, 62-65; sr scientist, Cent Res Labs, Varian Assocs, 65-71; vpres, Sonoma Eng & Res, Santa Rosa, 71-75; sr scientist, Addington Labs, Sunnyvale, 75-77; VPRES, WESTMONT LABS, PALO ALTO, 77- *Concurrent Pos:* Consult, Varian Assocs, Solid State West Div, 78-; comptroller, Cult Systs Res, 79- *Mem:* AAAS; fel Am Inst Chemists; Am Chem Soc; Inst Elec & Electronics Engrs. *Res:* Microwave techniques; solid state microwave devices. *Mailing Add:* 823 Valparaiso Ave Menlo Park CA 94025

VANE, FLOIE MARIE, b Dawson, Minn, Nov 25, 37. DRUG METABOLISM. *Educ:* Gustavus Adolphus Col, BS, 59; Mich State Univ, PhD(org chem), 63. *Prof Exp:* Sr chemist, 64-72, group chief, 73-78, SECT HEAD, HOFFMANN-LA ROCHE, INC, 79- *Concurrent Pos:* NIH fel, Mass Inst Technol, 63-64; vis asst prof, Baylor Col Med, 68-69. *Mem:* Am Chem Soc; Royal Soc Chem; Am Soc Mass Spectrometry; Am Soc Pharmacol & Exp Therapeut. *Res:* Structure determination of organic compounds by spectroscopic methods such as nuclear magnetic resonance and mass spectroscopy; structure identification of drug metabolites. *Mailing Add:* Hoffmann-La Roche Inc Nutley NJ 07110

VAN ECHO, ANDREW, b Barton, Ohio, Jan 27, 18; m 45; c 1. ENGINEERING & MATERIALS SCIENCE. *Educ:* Ohio State Univ, BS, 42. *Prof Exp:* Res asst, Manhattan Proj, Univ Chicago, 43-45; chief inspector, Joslyn Mfg & Supply Co, 45-47, asst works mgr, Wm E Pratt Mfg Co Div, 47-49, asst supt wire mill, 49-54, supvr prod control, 54-56, chief metallurgist & mgr processing & qual control, 56-63; asst chief fuels & mat br, US Atomic Energy Comn, 63-73; metall engr, US Energy Res & Develop Admin, 73-77; metall engr, 77-80, SR MAT ENGR, US DEPT ENERGY, 80- *Concurrent Pos:* Mem, World Metall Cong, 57; Govt liaison rep of DOE, Nat Acad Sci adv bd, comt on fatigue crack initiation at elevated temperatures, 77-78; mem joint US-USSR working group metall, Joint US-USSR Comn Sci & Tech Coop, 73-78 & 78- *Honors & Awards:* Award of Merit, Am Soc Testing & Mat, 73, Hon Award, 75. *Mem:* Am Soc Metals; fel Am Soc Testing & Mat. *Res:* Uranium processing and fabrication; stainless steel melting, processing and fabrication; refractory alloy consolidation, processing and fabrication; silicon plating of steels; V-alloy development; engineering properties of structural materials for high temperature design. *Mailing Add:* US Dept of Energy NE-50/RRT/GTN Washington DC 20545

VAN ECHO, DAVID ANDREW, b Ft Wayne, Ind, July 19, 47; m 71; c 2. ONCOLOGY, INTERNAL MEDICINE. *Educ:* Xavier Univ, BS, 69; Univ Md, MD, 73. *Prof Exp:* Intern & resident internal med, Univ Hosp, Baltimore, Md, 73-75; fel med oncol, Baltimore Cancer Res Ctr, 75-77; ASSOC PROF MED, UNIV MD SCH MED, 78- *Concurrent Pos:* Investr, Nat Cancer Inst, NIH, 77-78, sr investr, 78- *Mem:* Am Col Physicians. *Res:* Phase I and II studies in solid tumors and acute leukemia; whole-body hyperthermia. *Mailing Add:* Baltimore Cancer Res Ctr 22 S Greene St Baltimore MD 21201

VAN ECK, EDWARD ARTHUR, b Grand Rapids, Mich, May 26, 16; m 46; c 2. MICROBIOLOGY. *Educ:* Hope Col, BA, 38; Univ Mich, MSc, 41, PhD(bact), 50. *Prof Exp:* Instr bact, Univ Mich, 48-50; asst prof, Univ Kans, 50-53; purchasing agent, Stand Grocer Co, Mich, 53-58; lectr & reader microbiol, Christian Med Col, Vellore, India, 58-63, assoc prof, 62-63; prof, 63-80, EMER PROF BIOL, NORTHWESTERN COL, IOWA, 80- *Concurrent Pos:* Vis prof Univ Kans, 72-73. *Mem:* AAAS; Am Soc Microbiol; Sigma Xi. *Res:* Antigenic constitution of the Salmonellae; serological survey for presence of leptospirosis in South India; tumor immunology. *Mailing Add:* Dept of Biol Northwestern Col Orange City IA 51041

VAN ECK, WILLEM ADOLPH, b Wageningen, Netherlands, July 27, 28; nat US; m 56; c 3. SOIL SCIENCE, HYDROLOGY. *Educ:* Wageningen State Agr Univ, BSc, 51; Mich State Univ, MSc, 54, PhD(soil sci), 58. *Prof Exp:* Asst plant ecol, Wageningen State Agr Univ, 50, soil surv, 51; forester, Gold Coast Govt Surv Team, 52; asst soil fertil, Mich State Univ, 52-53, soil surv & forest soils, 52-56; from asst prof to assoc prof, 57-66, PROF SOIL SCI & STATE EXTEN SPECIALIST, W VA UNIV, 66- *Concurrent Pos:* Vis sr lectr, Makerere Univ, Uganda, 66-72; pres, Acad Assocs, Econ-Environ Consults. *Mem:* AAAS; Soil Sci Soc Am; Ecol Soc Am; Soc Am Foresters; Soil Conserv Soc Am. *Res:* Effect of environment on soil and vegetation development, especially as applied to forest and watershed management; relation of soil morphology and pedology to soil and water conservation and to physical land use planning; assessment of soil fertility in agronomy and forestry. *Mailing Add:* Div of Plant Sci W Va Univ Morgantown WV 26506

VAN EEDEN, CONSTANCE, b Delft, Netherlands, Apr 6, 27; m 60; c 1. STATISTICS. *Educ:* Univ Amsterdam, BSc, 49, MA, 54, PhD, 58. *Prof Exp:* Res assoc, Math Ctr, Univ Amsterdam, 54-60; vis assoc prof, Mich State Univ, 60-61; res assoc, Univ Minn, Minneapolis, 61-64; assoc prof, 65-68, PROF MATH, UNIV MONTREAL, 68- *Concurrent Pos:* Assoc prof & actg dir statist ctr, Univ Minn, Minneapolis, 64-65; res mem, Math Res Ctr, Univ Wis-Madison, 69. *Mem:* Can Statist Soc; Int Statist Inst; Inst Math Statist; Am Statist Asn; Can Math Soc. *Res:* Mathematical statistics. *Mailing Add:* Dept Math & Statist Univ of Montreal PO Box 6128 Montreal PQ H3C 3S7 Can

VANEFFEN, RICHARD MICHAEL, b Milwaukee, Wis, June 24, 53. ELECTROCHEMICAL METHODS. *Educ:* Univ Notre Dame, BS, 75; Univ Wis, Madison, PhD(anal chem), 79. *Prof Exp:* SR RES CHEMIST, DOW CHEM USA, 79- *Mem:* Am Chem Soc. *Res:* Electrochemical analysis and fundamental electrochemical research; application of electrochemical techniques to the solution of industrial process problems. *Mailing Add:* Anal Labs Dow Chem Co 1602 Bldg Midland MI 48640

VANELLI, RONALD EDWARD, b Quincy, Mass, July 5, 19; m 53; c 2. ORGANIC CHEMISTRY. *Educ:* Harvard Univ, AB, 41, MA & PhD(chem), 50. *Prof Exp:* Sr res chemist, Photo Prods Dept, E I du Pont de Nemours & Co, 50-51; DIR, CHEM LABS & LECTR CHEM, HARVARD UNIV, 51-, DIR SCI CTR, 72- *Mem:* Am Chem Soc. *Res:* Isonorcamphor; color and constitution. *Mailing Add:* Harvard Univ Chem Lab 12 Oxford St Cambridge MA 02138

VAN ELSWYK, MARINUS, JR, b Madera, Calif, July 30, 29; m 50; c 3. PLANT BREEDING, GENETICS. *Educ:* Fresno State Col, BS, 56; Univ Calif, Davis, MEd, 57; Univ Ariz, PhD(plant sci, agron), 67. *Prof Exp:* From instr to assoc prof plant sci & agron, 57-70, PROF PLANT BREEDING, STATIST & AGRON, CALIF STATE UNIV, FRESNO, 70-, ASST DEAN SCH AGR & HOME ECON, 77- *Concurrent Pos:* Consult, agr develop, 80- *Mem:* Am Soc Agron; Crop Sci Soc Am; Am Genetics Asn; Am Asn Univ Professors. *Res:* Agronomy; field plot techniques; plant breeding and appropriate technology. *Mailing Add:* Sch of Agr & Home Econ Calif State Univ Fresno CA 93740

VAN EMDEN, MAARTEN HERMAN, b Rheden, Netherlands. COMPUTER SCIENCE. *Educ:* Delft Univ Technol, MEng, 66; Univ Amsterdam, DSc(math & natural sci), 71. *Prof Exp:* Res assoc comput, Math Ctr, Amsterdam, 66-71; fel, IBM Thomas J Watson Res Ctr, 71-72; res fel artificial intel, Univ Edinbrugh, 72-75; ASST PROF COMPUT SCI, UNIV WATERLOO, 75- *Mem:* Inst Elec & Electron Engrs; Asn Comput Mach. *Res:* Methods of programming and of problem solving in general; development of program languages; theory of computation; applications of firts-order predicate logic. *Mailing Add:* 229 Dick Waterloo ON N2L 1N3 Can

VAN ENKEVORT, RONALD LEE, b Escanaba, Mich, Dec 20, 39; m 62; c 1. MATHEMATICS. *Educ:* Univ Wash, BS, 62; Ore State Univ, MS, 66, PhD(math), 72. *Prof Exp:* High sch teacher, 62-67; asst prof, 71-77, ASSOC PROF MATH, UNIV PUGET SOUND, 77- *Mem:* Am Math Soc. *Res:* Additive number theory. *Mailing Add:* Dept of Math Univ of Puget Sound Tacoma WA 98416

VAN EPPS, DENNIS EUGENE, b Rock Island, Ill, Nov 26, 46; m 73; c 2. IMMUNOLOGY. *Educ:* Western Ill Univ, BS, 68; Univ Ill, PhD(microbiol), 72. *Prof Exp:* NIH fel immunol, 72-74, ASST PROF MED & MICROBIOL, UNIV NMEX, 74- *Concurrent Pos:* Arthritis Found fel, 74-; prin investr, Nat Heart Lung, & Blood Inst, 79-82. *Honors & Awards:* Young Investr Pulmonary Res Award, Nat Heart & Lung Inst, 74. *Mem:* Am Soc Microbiol; Am Asn Immunologists; Am Fedn Clin Res; Sigma Xi. *Res:* Normal and abnormal phagocytic cell function and humoral factors which may alter this function; basic mechanisms of leukocyte locomotion; neutrophyl activation; cell surface receptor modulation. *Mailing Add:* Dept Med & Microbiol NMex Sch Med Albuquerque NM 87131

VAN EPPS, GORDON ALMON, b Salt Lake City, Utah, Apr 1, 20; m 45; c 4. FIELD CROPS. *Educ:* Utah State Univ, BS, 42, MS, 48. *Prof Exp:* Asst prof field crops, Calif State Polytech Col, 48-51; asst prof agron, Snow Col, 52-54; asst prof, 54-64, assoc prof agron, 64-77, ASSOC PROF PLANT & RANGE SCI, UTAH STATE UNIV, 77- *Concurrent Pos:* Adv under contract with Utah State, Iran, 61-64 & Bolivia, 66-68. *Mem:* Soc Range Mgt. *Res:* Rehabilitate with vegetation disturbed sites in the northern desert; seed production of indigenous browse shrubs and forbs on crop land; shrub/grass/plant mixtures for livestock grazing. *Mailing Add:* Snow Field Sta Utah State Univ Ephraim UT 84627

VAN ERT, MARK DEWAYNE, b Los Angeles, Calif, June 14, 47; m 68; c 3. INDUSTRIAL HYGIENE. *Educ:* Calif State Univ, Chico, BA, 69; Univ NC, Chapel Hill, MS, 71, PhD(indust hyg & toxicol), 74. *Prof Exp:* INDUST HYGIENIST & LAB DIR, OCCUP HEALTH STUDIES GROUP, DEPT ENVIRON SCI & ENG, UNIV NC, CHAPEL HILL, 74- *Res:* Assessment of work environments for potentially hazardous exposures, relating such exposures to health status; development of methodology for environmental assessment; determining the toxicological properties of environmental insults. *Mailing Add:* Occup Health Studies Group Suite 32 NCNB Plaza Chapel Hill NC 27514

VAN ESELTINE, WILLIAM PARKER, b Syracuse, NY, Aug 21, 24; m 48; c 2. BACTERIOLOGY. *Educ:* Oberlin Col, AB, 44; Cornell Univ, MS, 47, PhD(bact), 49. *Prof Exp:* Asst bact, NY State Agr Exp Sta, 44-45 & Cornell Univ, 46-48; assoc prof, Clemson Col, 48-52; asst prof vet hyg, 52-59, assoc prof vet microbiol & prev med, 59-67, PROF MED MICROBIOL, COL VET MED, UNIV GA, 67- *Mem:* AAAS; Am Soc Microbiol; Am Inst Biol Sci. *Res:* Microbiology of foods; bactericidal and bacteriostatic agents; physiology and taxonomy of bacteria, especially animal pathogens. *Mailing Add:* Dept of Med Microbiol Col of Vet Med Univ of Ga Athens GA 30602

VAN ESSEN, DAVID CLINTON, b Glendale, Calif, Sept 14, 45; m 69; c 2. BIOLOGY, NEUROSCIENCE. *Educ:* Calif Inst Technol, BS, 67; Harvard Univ, PhD(neurobiol), 71. *Prof Exp:* Res fel neurobiol, Harvard Med Sch, 71-73, neurophysiol, Inst Physiol, Univ Oslo, 73-75 & anat, Univ Col London, 75-76; asst prof, 76-79, ASSOC PROF BIOL, CALIF INST TECHNOL, 79- *Concurrent Pos:* Fel NIH, 71-73, Helen Hay Whitney Found, 73-76; mem adv panel, Sensory Physiol & Perception Prog, NSF, 78-81. *Mem:* AAAS; Soc Neurosci; Asn Res Vision & Ophthal. *Res:* Visual cortex; functional organization of extrastriate areas in primates; neuromuscular development; control of synapse formation and elimination. *Mailing Add:* Div of Biol Calif Inst of Technol Pasadena CA 91125

VAN ETTEN, HANS D, b Peoria, Ill, Sept 16, 41; m 63; c 2. PLANT PATHOLOGY. *Educ:* Wabash Col, BA, 63; Cornell Univ, MS, 66, PhD(plant path), 70. *Prof Exp:* Asst prof, 70-77, ASSOC PROF PLANT PATH, CORNELL UNIV, 77- *Concurrent Pos:* Vis prof, Univ Munster, WGer, 78-79. *Mem:* AAAS; Am Phytopath Soc; NAm Photochem Soc; Am Soc Microbiol. *Res:* Physiology of disease. *Mailing Add:* Dept of Plant Path Cornell Univ Ithaca NY 14853

VAN ETTEN, JAMES L, b Cherrydale, Va, Jan 7, 38; m 60; c 1. MICROBIAL PHYSIOLOGY. *Educ:* Carleton Col, BA, 60; Univ Ill, MS, 63, PhD(path), 65. *Prof Exp:* NSF fel microbiol, Univ Pavia, 65-66; from asst prof to assoc prof, 66-74, PROF PLANT PATH, UNIV NEBR, LINCOLN, 74- *Mem:* AAAS; Am Phytopath Soc; Soc Gen Microbiol; Am Soc Microbiol. *Res:* Biochemistry of fungal spore germination and bacteriophage; biochemistry. *Mailing Add:* Dept of Plant Path Univ of Nebr Lincoln NE 68583

VAN ETTEN, JAMES P(AUL), b Perry, NY, Mar 27, 22; m 47; c 7. ELECTRONIC ENGINEERING. *Educ:* US Coast Guard Acad, BS, 43; Mass Inst Technol, EE, 50. *Prof Exp:* Sr proj engr, 58-59, exec engr, 59-60, assoc lab dir, 60-62, lab dir, 62-66, dir navig systs, 66-69, chief scientist avionics, 69-70, DIR COMMUN, NAVIG & IDENTIFICATION SYSTS, LABS, ITT CORP, 70- *Mem:* Am Inst Navig; sr mem Inst Elec & Electronics Engrs. *Res:* Hyperbolic, rho-rho and rho-theta radio navigation systems and equipment; integrated airborne navigation systems and equipment; ground transmitting equipment for LORAN and TACAN; radio navigation systems. *Mailing Add:* 18 Prospect South Orange NJ 07079

VAN ETTEN, ROBERT LEE, b Evergreen Park, Ill, June 11, 37; c 3. CHEMISTRY. *Educ:* Univ Chicago, BS, 59; Univ Calif, Davis, MS 64, PhD(chem), 65. *Prof Exp:* Technician, Ben May Labs, Cancer Res, Univ Chicago, 57-59; teaching asst, Univ Calif, Davis, 60-63; NIH fel Northwestern Univ, 65-66; asst prof, 66-70, assoc prof, 70-81, PROF CHEM, PURDUE UNIV, WEST LAFAYETTE, 80- *Concurrent Pos:* Res career develop award, NIH, 69-73; Alexander von Humboldt fel, Marburg, Germany, 75-76. *Mem:* Am Chem Soc; Am Soc Biol Chemists; Am Asn Univ Prof; NY Acad Sci; Am Asn Clin Chem. *Res:* Mechanisms of enzymatic catalysis; kinetics and mechanisms of solution reactions; enzyme models; clinical chemistry of phosphatases and sulfatases; oxygen-18 isotope effects on carbon-13 and nitrogen-15 normal mode rejection. *Mailing Add:* Dept Chem Purdue Univ West Lafayette IN 47907

VAN EYS, JAN, b Hilversum, Neth, Jan 25, 29; nat US; m 55; c 2. BIOCHEMISTRY. *Educ:* Vanderbilt Univ, PhD, 55; Univ Wash, MD, 66. *Prof Exp:* Fel biochem, McCollum-Pratt Inst, Johns Hopkins Univ, 55-57; from asst prof to prof biochem, Sch Med, Vanderbilt Univ, 57-73, from asst prof to prof pediat, 68-73; prof pediat, 73-79, MOSBACHER PROF PEDIAT, UNIV TEX SYST CANCER CTR, M D ANDERSON HOSP & TUMOR INST, 79-, HEAD DEPT PEDIAT, 73- *Concurrent Pos:* Investr, Howard Hughes Med Inst, 57-66. *Mem:* Am Soc Biol Chemists; Am Inst Nutrit; NY Acad Sci. *Res:* Metabolism and enzymology in glycolysis; pediatric hematology, oncology and nutrition in cancer. *Mailing Add:* Dept of Pediat M D Anderson Hosp & Tumor Inst Houston TX 77025

VAN FAASEN, PAUL, b Holland, Mich, June 6, 34; m 58; c 2. PLANT TAXONOMY. *Educ:* Hope Col, BA, 56; Mich State Univ, MS, 62, PhD(bot), 71. *Prof Exp:* Chemist, Parke-Davis Co, 56-57; instr biol warfare, US Army, 57-58, technician comp physiol sect, 58-59; instr biol, Lake rest Col, 62-63; from instr to asst prof, 63-72, ASSOC PROF BIOL, HOPE COL, 72- *Mem:*

Bot Soc Am; Am Soc Plant Taxonomists; Int Asn Plant Taxonomists; Am Inst Biol Sci; Sigma Xi. *Res:* Biosystematics of Aster, especially those of northeast United States; biology of weeds. *Mailing Add:* Dept of Biol Hope Col Holland MI 49423

VAN FLANDERN, THOMAS CHARLES, b Cleveland, Ohio, June 26, 40; m 63; c 4. CELESTIAL MECHANICS. *Educ:* Xavier Univ, Ohio, BS, 62; Yale Univ, PhD(astron), 69. *Prof Exp:* Astronomer, 63-75, CHIEF, CELESTIAL MECH BR, US NAVAL OBSERV, 75- *Concurrent Pos:* Consult, Jet Propulsion Lab, 71. *Mem:* Am Astron Soc; Am Geophys Union; Int Astron Union; AAAS; Am Phys Soc. *Res:* Lunar motion; asteroids; comets; occulations; cosmology; gravitation; solar system astronomy. *Mailing Add:* US Naval Observ Washington DC 20390

VANFLEET, HOWARD BAY, b Salt Lake City, Utah, June 5, 31; m 54; c 7. SOLID STATE PHYSICS. *Educ:* Brigham Young Univ, BS, 55; Univ Utah, PhD(physics), 61. *Prof Exp:* Asst physics, Univ Utah, 56-60; from asst prof to assoc prof, 60-69, PROF PHYSICS, BRIGHAM YOUNG UNIV, 69- *Concurrent Pos:* Res grants, US Air Force Off Sci Res, Brigham Young Univ, 62-66, NSF, 69-77; phys scientist, US Army Electronics Command, 66-67; vis prof physics, Am Univ, Cairo, 73-74; consult, Codevintec Pac, Inc, 75-76. *Mem:* Am Phys Soc. *Res:* Ultra high pressure solid state physics; particular phenomena, such as solid state diffusion, Mössbauer effects, melting and high pressure calibration. *Mailing Add:* Dept of Physics Brigham Young Univ Provo UT 84602

VAN FOSSAN, DONALD DUANE, b El Paso, Tex, Jan 5, 29; m 49; c 3. BIOCHEMISTRY. *Educ:* Sul Ross State Col, BS, 49; Univ Tex, MA, 52, PhD(biochem), 54, MD, 61. *Prof Exp:* Asst, Univ Tex, 52-54; res biochemist, Air Force Sch Aviation Med, 54-57, head lab sect, Dept Phyiol-Biophys, 56-57; instr clin path & consult clin labs, Hosp, Univ Tex Med Br, 57-61; intern, St Joseph Hosp, Ft Worth, Tex, 61-62, resident path, Univ Tex, 62-66; dir clin path, Med Ctr, Baylor Univ, 66-69; assoc dir chem, St John's Hosp, 74-76; asst chmn dept, 73-76, CLIN PROF PATH, SOUTHERN ILL UNIV, 69- *Concurrent Pos:* Instr anal chem, Trinity Univ, 56; dir clin path, St John's Hosp, 68-; dir clin chem, St John Hosp, 76- *Mem:* Col Am Pathologists; AMA; Am Soc Clin Pathologists. *Res:* Analytic biochemistry; pathology; endocrinology. *Mailing Add:* Southern Ill Univ Sch Med PO Box 3926 Springfield IL 62708

VAN FOSSEN, DON B, b Des Moines, Iowa, Apr 15, 42; m 62; c 1. APPLIED MECHANICS, AEROSPACE ENGINEERING. *Educ:* Iowa State Univ, BS, 64; Univ Mo-Rolla, BS, 68. *Prof Exp:* Test engr struct, McDonnell Aircraft, 64-69; sr res engr, 69-72, GROUP SUPVR APPL MECH, BABCOCK & WILCOX CO, 72- *Concurrent Pos:* mem subcomt shells, Pressure Vessel Res Comt, Welding Res Coun, 77-; tech adv, Struct Anal Prog, User's Group, 77- *Mem:* Am Soc Mech Engrs. *Res:* Applied research in the application of the finite element method to structural analysis and heat transfer for general structures. *Mailing Add:* Babcock & Wilcox Co PO Box 835 Alliance OH 44601

VAN FOSSEN, PAUL, b Mansfield, Ohio, Aug 21, 23; m 47; c 2. ORGANIC CHEMISTRY. *Educ:* Univ Cincinnati, AB, 45; Princeton Univ, MA, 47, PhD(chem), 49. *Prof Exp:* Res chemist cellulose derivatives & org nitrogen compounds, E I du Pont de Nemours & Co, Inc, 49-52, tech rep cellulose derivatives & org chem, 52-56, supt chem prod, Sales Develop Lab, 56-60, asst dir, Carney's Point Develop Lab, 60-61, mgr mkt serv, Chem Prod Sales Div, 61-65, mgr admin serv, 65-69, mgr indust prod, 69-72, prod mgr, 72-75, new prod mgr, 75-77; RETIRED. *Res:* Electric blasting caps; blasting supplies and accessories. *Mailing Add:* 2007 Marsh Rd Wilmington DE 19810

VAN FRANK, RICHARD MARK, b Lansing, Mich, Oct 11, 30; m 54; c 2. CELL BIOLOGY, ANALYTICAL BIOCHEMISTRY. *Educ:* Mich State Univ, BS, 52, MS, 56. *Prof Exp:* Officer in-chg biol lab, US Naval Damage Control Training Ctr, Philadelphia, 52-54; SR SCIENTIST, DIV MOLECULAR & CELL BIOL, LILLY RES LABS, ELI LILLY & CO, 57- *Mem:* AAAS; NY Acad Sci; Electrophoresis Soc. *Res:* Development of methodology for fractionation of cells and isolation and analysis of subcellular particles and substances. *Mailing Add:* Div Molecular & Cell Biol Lilly Res Labs Eli Lilly & Co Indianapolis IN 46285

VAN GEET, ANTHONY LEENDERT, b Rotterdam, Neth, July 24, 29; US citizen; m 56; c 3. PHYSICAL CHEMISTRY, ANALYTICAL CHEMISTRY. *Educ:* Delft Univ Technol, ChemEng, 55; Univ Southern Calif, PhD(phys chem), 61. *Prof Exp:* Res assoc chem, Mass Inst Technol, 61-63; asst prof, State Univ NY Buffalo, 63-69; assoc prof, Oakland Univ, 69-70; ASSOC PROF CHEM, STATE UNIV NY COL OSWEGO, 70- *Mem:* AAAS; Am Chem Soc; Royal Neth Chem Soc. *Res:* Nuclear magnetic resonance of protons, lithium, sodium and fluorine in solution; hydration, complexation and ion-pairing of monovalent ions; determination of trace amounts of heavy metals in lake water; instrumentation. *Mailing Add:* Dept of Chem State Univ of NY Oswego NY 13126

VAN GELDER, ARTHUR, JR, b Paterson, NJ, Jan 13, 38; m 60; c 2. ELECTRICAL ENGINEERING. *Educ:* Univ Pa, BSEE, 59; City Col New York, MEE, 64, PhD(elec eng), 68. *Prof Exp:* Asst proj engr, Kearfott Div, Gen Precision, Inc, 60-61; lectr elec eng, City Col New York, 61-68; asst prof, Univ Del, 68-75; asst prof elec eng, Miami Univ, 75-80; ASST PROF ELEC ENG, LAFAYETTE COL, 80- *Mem:* Inst Elec & Electronics Engrs; Am Soc Eng Educ. *Res:* Electronic circuits; microprocessors; digital systems. *Mailing Add:* Elec Eng Dept Lafayette Col Easton PA 18042

VAN GELDER, NICO MICHEL, b Sumatra, Netherlands E Indies, Dec 24, 33; Can citizen; m 59; c 3. BIOCHEMISTRY, PHYSIOLOGY. *Educ:* McGill Univ, BSc, 55, PhD(biochem), 59. *Prof Exp:* Life Ins Med Res Fund fel, Cambridge Univ, Eng, 59-60; res fel neurophysiol & neuropharmacol, Harvard Med Sch, 60-62; asst prof pharmacol, Sch Med, Tufts Univ, 62-67; assoc prof, 67-77, PROF PHYSIOL & EXEC NEUROL SCI RES CTR, UNIV MONTREAL, 77-, BD ADV, NEUROCHEM RES, 75- & RES & DEVELOP, 81- *Concurrent Pos:* Res grants, Nat Inst Neurol Dis & Blindness, 62-66, Nat Multiple Sclerosis Soc, 66- & Med Res Coun Can Neurol Sci Group, 67-; assoc ed, Can J Biochem, 76-78; med adv, Savoy Found Epilepsy, 80-; assoc, Montreal Neurol Inst, 80- *Mem:* Am Soc Neurochem; Int Soc Neurochem; NY Acad Sci; Int Brain Res Orgn; Can Epilepsy Soc. *Res:* Biochemistry of epilepsy; structure-activity relationships; biochemistry of brain damage; malnutrition; genetic contribution to epilepsy; function of taurine. *Mailing Add:* Dept Physiol Univ Montreal C P 6208 Succursale A Montreal PQ H3C 3T8 Can

VAN GELDER, RICHARD GEORGE, b New York, NY, Dec 17, 28; m 62; c 3. MAMMALOGY. *Educ:* Colo Agr & Mech Col, BS, 50; Univ Ill, MS, 52, PhD(zool), 58. *Prof Exp:* Asst zool, Colo Agr & Mech Col, 47-50 & Univ Ill, 50-53; from asst to instr mammal, Univ Kans, 54-56; from asst cur to assoc cur mammals, 56-69, chmn dept, 59-74, CUR MAMMALS, AM MUS NATURAL HIST, 69- *Concurrent Pos:* Lectr, Columbia Univ, 58-59, asst prof, 59-63; mem bd dirs, Archbold Exped, Inc, 64-75 & Quincy Bog Natural Area, 76-; prof lectr, State Univ NY Downstate Med Ctr, 70-73. *Mem:* AAAS; Am Soc Mammalogists (vpres, 67-68, pres, 68-70); Wildlife Soc; Soc Syst Zool. *Res:* Mammalian taxonomy, evolution, behavior and ecology. *Mailing Add:* Am Mus of Natural Hist Central Park W at 79th St New York NY 10024

VAN GELUWE, JOHN DAVID, b Rochester, NY, Sept 18, 16; m 53; c 2. ENTOMOLOGY. *Educ:* State Univ NY, BS, 39. *Prof Exp:* Asst, Exten Serv, State Univ NY Col Agr, Cornell Univ, 39-44; dir res & develop, Soil Bldg Div, Coop GLF Exchange, Inc, 44-64; mgr prod develop, Agr Chem Div, 64-67, tech dir, 67-70, ASST DIR FIELD & FARM RES, CIBA-GEIGY CORP, 70- *Mem:* Fel Am Soc Hort Sci; fel Entom Soc Am; fel Am Phytopath Soc; Weed Sci Soc Am. *Res:* Formulations, basic laboratory evaluation and field testing of insecticides, fungicides and herbicides. *Mailing Add:* Ciba-Geigy Corp Agr Div 8823 Boylston Rd Colfax NC 27235

VAN GEMERT, BARRY, b Attleboro, Mass, Feb 17, 46; m 69; c 2. ORGANIC CHEMISTRY. *Educ:* Univ Mass, BS, 68; Univ RI, MS, 72; Purdue Univ, PhD(org chem), 76. *Prof Exp:* SR RES CHEMIST, PPG INDUSTS, 76- *Mem:* Am Cher Soc. *Res:* Organo sulfur chemistry, chlorinated solvent stabilization. *iling Add:* 7331 Shadyview Ave NW Massillon OH 44646

VAN GINNEKEN, ANDREAS J M, b Wynegem, Belg, Jan 1, 35. PHYSICS. *Educ:* Univ Chicago, MSc, 59, PhD(chem), 66. *Prof Exp:* Res assoc physics, McGill Univ, 66-70; PHYSICIST, FERMI NAT LAB, 70- *Mem:* Am Phys Soc; Am Asn Physics Teachers. *Res:* nuclear and particle physics; radiation physics; nyclear chemistry. *Mailing Add:* Fermi Nat Lab Batavia IL 60510

VAN GROENEWOUD, HERMAN, b Breda, Netherlands, May 27, 26; Can citizen; m 50; c 2. FOREST ECOLOGY. *Educ:* Univ Sask, BA, 56, MA, 60; Swiss Fed Inst Technol, ScD(geobot), 65. *Prof Exp:* Res scientist forest path, Lab Saskatoon, 54-65, RES SCIENTIST FOREST ECOL, MARITIMES FOREST RES CTR, GOVT CAN, 65- *Mem:* Can Bot Asn; Brit Ecol Soc; Ecol Soc Am; Can Inst Forestry. *Res:* Forest site studies; multivariate analysis; watershed studies. *Mailing Add:* Maritimes Forest Res Ctr Box 4000 Fredericton NB E3B 5P7 Can

VAN GULICK, NORMAN MARTIN, b Los Angeles, Calif, July 1, 26; m 48; c 2. ORGANIC CHEMISTRY. *Educ:* Univ Colo, AB, 48; Univ Southern Calif, PhD, 54. *Prof Exp:* Asst prof chem, Univ Ore, 56-60; res chemist, 60-80, RES ASSOC, ELASTOMER CHEM DEPT, E I DU PONT DE NEMOURS & CO, INC, 80- *Mem:* Am Chem Soc; Sigma Xi. *Res:* Organic polymer chemistry; organometallic and organic fluorine chemistry; reaction mechanisms. *Mailing Add:* Exp Sta E I du Pont de Nemours & Co Inc Wilmington DE 19898

VAN GUNDY, DONALD A(USTIN), b Sterling, Colo, June 2, 26; m 53; c 2. CRYOGENIC ENGINEERING. *Educ:* Univ Colo, BS, 51, MS, 57. *Prof Exp:* Engr, Mallinckrodt Chem Works, Mo, 51-53; proj leader, Nat Bur Standards, Colo, 53-60; proj engr, Beech Aircraft Corp, Colo, 60-67; assoc cryogenic engr, Argonne Nat Lab, 67-77; SR MEM TECH STAFF, BALL AEROSPACE SYSTS DIV, 77- *Mem:* Am Soc Mech Engrs. *Res:* Analysis and design of superfluid helium ground support equipment. *Mailing Add:* PO Box 1062 Boulder CO 80306

VAN GUNDY, SEYMOUR DEAN, b Whitehouse, Ohio, Feb 24, 31; m 54; c 2. PLANT PATHOLOGY, NEMATOLOGY. *Educ:* Bowling Green State Univ, BA, 53; Univ Wis, PhD, 57. *Prof Exp:* Res assoc, Univ Wis, 53-57; from asst nematologist to assoc nematologist, 57-68, assoc dean res, 68-71, asst vchancellor res, 71-72, PROF NEMATOL, UNIV CALIF, RIVERSIDE, 68-, CHMN DEPT, 72- *Concurrent Pos:* NSF sr fel, Australia, 65-66; ed-in-chief, J Nematol, 67-71. *Mem:* Fel AAAS; fel Am Phytopath Soc; Soc Nematol (vpres, 72-73, pres, 73-74); Soc Europ Nematol; Am Inst Biol Sci. *Res:* Biology and control of nematodes. *Mailing Add:* Dept Nematol Univ Calif Riverside CA 92521

VAN HALL, CLAYTON EDWARD, b Grand Rapids, Mich, Apr 24, 24; m 51; c 2. ANALYTICAL CHEMISTRY. *Educ:* Hope Col, AB, 49; Mich State Univ, MSc, 54, PhD(anal chem), 56. *Prof Exp:* Asst, Mich State Univ, 52-56; chemist, 56-58, anal chemist, 58-61, anal specialist, 61-65, anal res specialist, 65-72, ASSOC SCIENTIST, DOW CHEM CO, 72- *Mem:* Am Chem Soc. *Res:* Instrumental methods; trace gas methods; trace element methods; purity of inorganic compounds; primary standards; water analysis. *Mailing Add:* 3712 Wintergreen Dr Midland MI 48640

VAN HANDEL, EMILE, b Rotterdam, Holland, Mar 29, 18; nat US; m 46; c 2. ORGANIC CHEMISTRY. *Educ:* State Univ Leiden, BS, 38, MS, 41; State Inst Technol, Delft, MS, 41; Univ Amsterdam, PhD(biochem), 54. *Prof Exp:* Indust chemist, 45-54; res biochemist, St Anthon's Hosp, Voorburg, Holland,

54-55, asst prof physiol, Univ Tenn, 55-58; BIOCHEMIST, FLA MED ENTOM LAB, UNIV FLA, VERO BEACH, 58- *Concurrent Pos:* Consult study sect trop med & parasitol, NIH, 78-82. *Mem:* Am Heart Asn; Am Soc Biol Chemists. *Res:* Lipid and carbohydrate chemistry and metabolism; insect biochemistry; atherosclerosis. *Mailing Add:* Fla Med Entom Lab Univ Fla Vero Beach FL 32960

VAN HARN, GORDON L, b Grand Rapids, Mich, Dec 30, 35; m 58; c 3. PHYSIOLOGY. *Educ:* Calvin Col, AB, 57; Univ Ill, MS, 59, PhD(physiol), 61. *Prof Exp:* Assoc prof biol, Calvin Col, 61-68 & Oberlin Col, 68-70; PROF BIOL, CALVIN COL, 70- *Concurrent Pos:* Res assoc, Blodgett Mem Hosp, 70-76. *Mem:* AAAS; Am Sci Affil. *Res:* Smooth muscle contractile and electrical activity; intestinal smooth muscle; cardiac muscle. *Mailing Add:* Dept of Biol Calvin Col Grand Rapids MI 49506

VAN HARREVELD, ANTHONIE, b Haarlem, Neth, Feb 16, 04; nat US; m 28; c 2. PHYSIOLOGY. *Educ:* Univ Amsterdam, BA, 25, MA, 28, PhD(animal physiol), 29, MD, 30. *Prof Exp:* Asst physiol, Univ Amsterdam, 27-31; chief asst, State Univ Utrecht, 31-34; asst, 34-35, from instr to prof, 35-74, EMER PROF PHYSIOL, CALIF INST TECHNOL, 74- *Concurrent Pos:* Consult, Los Angeles County Gen Hosp, 43-55; res assoc, Univ Calif, 44; corresp mem, Royal Neth Acad Sci. *Mem:* AAAS; Am Physiol Soc; Soc Neurosci. *Res:* Electrophysiology of nerve muscle and central nervous system; nerve regeneration; metabolism; segmental physiology; water and electrolyte distribution in central nervous system. *Mailing Add:* Div Biol Calif Inst of Technol 1201 E California Blvd Pasadena CA 91125

VAN HASSEL, HENRY JOHN, b Paterson, NJ, May 2, 33; m 60. DENTISTRY, PHYSIOLOGY. *Educ:* Maryville Col, BA, 54; Univ Md, DDS, 63; Univ Wash, MSD, 64, PhD(physiol), 69. *Prof Exp:* Asst prof endodont & physiol, 69-71, res assoc physiol, Regional Primate Res Ctr, 69-76, ASSOC PROF PHYSIOL, MED SCH, UNIV WASH, 71-, ASSOC PROF ENDODONT, DENT SCH, 71-, ASSOC PROF BIOPHYS, 76-; DEP CHIEF DENT SERV & DIR ENDODONT RESIDENCY, USPHS HOSP, SEATTLE, 71- *Concurrent Pos:* Consult, US Army, Ft Lewis, Wash, 69-; chmn, Nat Workshop Pulp Biol, 71-; vchmn, Sect Physiol, Am Asn Dent Schs, 72- *Honors & Awards:* First recipient Carl A Schlack Award, Asn Mil Surgeons US, 71. *Mem:* Am Dent Asn; Am Asn Endodont; Int Asn Dent Res. *Res:* Oral physiology; psychophysiology; neurophysiology of pain. *Mailing Add:* Dept of Physiol Univ of Wash Seattle WA 98195

VAN HATTUM, ROLLAND JAMES, b Grand Rapids, Mich, July 14, 24; m 49; c 5. SPEECH PATHOLOGY, AUDIOLOGY. *Educ:* Western Mich Univ, BS, 50; Pa State Univ, MS, 52, PhD(speech path-audiology), 54. *Prof Exp:* Instr speech path, Pa State Univ, 50-54; dir spec educ, Kent County, Mich, 58-63; chmn dept, 63-80, PROF COMMUN DIS, STATE UNIV NY COL BUFFALO, 63- *Concurrent Pos:* Consult speech & hearing, Children's Hosp, Grand Rapids, Mich, 57-63, speech, hearing & lang, Buffalo Children's Hosp, 65-76; lectr spec educ, Univ Mich & Mich State Univ, 58-63; res assoc, Eastman Dent Ctr, 63-68; audiologist, Joel Bernstein, MD, 71-; fac exchange scholar, State Univ NY, 78- *Honors & Awards:* Citation, Mich Asn Retarded Children, 63; Honors, NY State Speech & Hearing Asn, 74. *Mem:* Fel Am Speech & Hearing Asn (vpres, 71-74, pres, 77). *Res:* Communication programs for mildly, moderately and severely retarded; automated programs. *Mailing Add:* Dept Commun Dis State Univ NY Col Buffalo NY 14222

VAN HAVERBEKE, DAVID F, b Eureka, Kans, July 15, 28. TAXONOMY, SILVICULTURE. *Educ:* Kans State Univ, BS, 50; Colo State Univ, MS, 59; Univ Nebr, PhD(bot), 67. *Prof Exp:* Res forester, Rocky Mountain Forest & Range Exp Sta, 58 & Southeastern Forest Exp Sta, 59-62, RES FORESTER, ROCKY MOUNTAIN FOREST & RANGE EXP STA, USDA, 62- *Concurrent Pos:* Assoc prof forestry, Univ Nebr-Lincoln. *Mem:* Soc Am Foresters. *Res:* Forest botany and genetics; forest tree improvement; noise abatement; shelterbelt management. *Mailing Add:* Forestry Sci Lab Rocky Mountain Range Exp Sta Univ of Nebr Lincoln NE 68583

VAN HECKE, GERALD RAYMOND, b Evanston, Ill, Nov 1, 39. PHYSICAL CHEMISTRY. *Educ:* Harvey Mudd Col, BS, 61; Princeton Univ, AM, 63, PhD(phys chem), 66. *Prof Exp:* Chemist, Shell Develop Co, 66-70; asst prof, 70-74, assoc prof, 74-80, PROF CHEM, HARVEY MUDD COL, 80- *Concurrent Pos:* Vis res assoc fundamental physics, Univ Lille, France, 77; vis res assoc biophys, Boston Univ, 77; Nat Acad Sci exchange scientist, Inst Phys Chem, Polish Acad Sci, Warsaw, 80. *Mem:* AAAS; Am Chem Soc; Royal Soc Chem; fel Am Inst Chemists; Sigma Xi. *Res:* Nuclear magnetic resonance studies of paramagnetic transition metal complexes; thermodynamics and physical properties of liquid crystals. *Mailing Add:* Dept of Chem Harvey Mudd Col Claremont CA 91711

VAN HEERDEN, PIETER JACOBUS, b Utrecht, Neth, Apr 14, 15; nat US; m 49; c 2. PHYSICS. *Educ:* Univ Utrecht, PhD(physics), 45. *Prof Exp:* Res physicist, Bataafse Petrol Co, Neth, 44-45; vis lectr, Harvard Univ, 48-49, res fel nuclear physics, 49-53; res assoc, Gen Elec Res Lab, NY, 53-62; physicist, Polaroid Res Labs, 62-81; LECTR & CONSULT, FOUND PHYSICS, MATH THEORY INTELLIGENCE & ARTIFICIAL INTELLIGENCE, 82- *Mem:* Am Phys Soc; Neth Phys Soc. *Res:* Experimental nuclear and solid state physics; foundation of physics; foundation of scientific knowledge and intelligence. *Mailing Add:* 308 Holden Wood Rd Concord MA 01742

VAN HEUVELEN, ALAN, b Buffalo, Wyo, Dec 15, 38; m 62; c 1. PHYSICS. *Educ:* Rutgers Univ, BA, 60; Univ Colo, PhD(physics), 64. *Prof Exp:* Assoc prof physics, 64-74, PROF PHYSICS, NMEX STATE UNIV, 74- *Mem:* Am Phys Soc. *Res:* Biophysics using electron spin resonance to study enzymes. *Mailing Add:* Dept of Physics NMex State Univ Las Cruces NM 88003

VAN HEYNINGEN, EARLE MARVIN, b Chicago, Ill, Oct 15, 21; m 51; c 4. ORGANIC CHEMISTRY. *Educ:* Calvin Col, AB, 43; Univ Ill, PhD(org chem), 46. *Prof Exp:* Res chemist, 46-65, res scientist, 65-66, res assoc, 66-69, dir agr chem, Greenfield Labs, 69-72, DIR CHEM, LILLY RES LABS, ELI LILLY & CO, 72- *Mem:* Am Chem Soc. *Res:* Synthesis of barbituric acids; antimalarials, anti-arthritics; cholesterol lowering agents; cephalosporin antibiotics. *Mailing Add:* Lilly Res Labs Chem Res Indianapolis IN 46206

VAN HEYNINGEN, ROGER, b Chicago, Ill, Oct 2, 27; m 51; c 3. SOLID STATE PHYSICS. *Educ:* Calvin Col, AB, 51; Univ Ill, MS, 55, PhD, 58. *Prof Exp:* Sr physicist, 58-62, res assoc, 62-66, asst div head, 66-67, PHYSICS DIV DIR, EASTMAN KODAK CO, 67- *Mem:* Am Phys Soc; Optical Soc Am. *Res:* Electronic and optical properties of insulating and semiconducting solids. *Mailing Add:* Res Labs Eastman Kodak Co Rochester NY 14650

VAN HISE, JAMES R, b Tracy, Calif, Aug 11, 37; m 64; c 2. NUCLEAR CHEMISTRY, PHYSICAL CHEMISTRY. *Educ:* Walla Walla Col, BS, 59; Univ Ill, PhD(phys chem), 63. *Prof Exp:* Res assoc nuclear chem, Oak Ridge Nat Lab, 63-65; from asst prof to assoc prof chem & physics, Andrews Univ, 65-69; prof physics & chmn dept, Tri-State Col, 69-72; PROF CHEM, PAC UNION COL, 72- *Concurrent Pos:* Consult radiol phys & nuclear chem, Lawrence Livermore Nat Lab, 74- *Mem:* Am Chem Soc; Am Phys Soc. *Res:* Nuclear photodisintegration; alpha, beta and gamma ray spectroscopy; positron annihilation in organic media. *Mailing Add:* 566 Sunset Dr Angwin CA 94508

VAN HOLDE, KENSAL EDWARD, b Eau Claire, Wis, May 14, 28; m 50; c 4. PHYSICAL CHEMISTRY. *Educ:* Univ Wis, BS, 49, PhD(chem), 52. *Prof Exp:* Res chemist textile fibers dept, E I du Pont de Nemours & Co, 52-55; res assoc, Univ Wis, 55-56, asst prof chem, Univ Wis-Milwaukee, 56-57; from asst prof to prof, Univ Ill, Urbana, 57-67; PROF BIOPHYS, ORE STATE UNIV, 67- *Concurrent Pos:* Guggenheim fel, 73-74; Am Cancer Soc res professorship, 76- *Mem:* Am Soc Biol Chem. *Res:* Physical chemistry of macromolecules; biophysical chemistry. *Mailing Add:* Dept of Biochem & Biophys Ore State Univ Corvallis OR 97331

VAN HOOK, ANDREW, b Paterson, NJ, June 3, 07; m 34; c 5. PHYSICAL CHEMISTRY. *Educ:* Polytech Inst Brooklyn, BS, 31; NY Univ, PhD(phys chem), 34. *Prof Exp:* Indust & consult chem, 26-28; metall engr, Westinghouse Lamp Co, 28-29; instr, NY Univ, 31-34; res chemist, Autoxygen Co, 34-36; instr phys chem, Lafayette Col, 36-38; asst prof, Univ Idaho, 38-42 & Lafayette Col, 42-44; assoc prof, Univ Wyo, 44-46; PROF PHYS CHEM, COL OF THE HOLY CROSS, 46- *Mem:* AAAS; Am Chem Soc; assoc Am Inst Chem Engrs. *Res:* Kinetics; crystallization; sugar technology; theory of liquids and concentrated solutions. *Mailing Add:* Dept of Chem Col of the Holy Cross Worcester MA 01610

VAN HOOK, JAMES PAUL, b Paterson, NJ, Oct 16, 31; m 57; c 5. PHYSICAL CHEMISTRY, ENGINEERING MANAGEMENT. *Educ:* Col of the Holy Cross, BS, 53; Princeton Univ, PhD(chem), 58. *Prof Exp:* Res chemist, M W Kellogg Co Div, Pullman, Inc, 57-62, supvr, 62-65, sect head process res, 65-74; process develop mgr, Corp Eng Dept, Allied Chem Corp, 74-76; process technol mgr & lab coordr, Foster Wheeler Energy Corp, 77-81, TECHNOL MGR, FOSTER WHEELER SYNFUELS CORP, 81- *Mem:* AAAS; Am Chem Soc; Am Inst Chem Engrs. *Res:* Catalytic oxidation for chlorine production; steam-hydrocarbon reactions for production of synthesis gas, hydrogen or synthetic natural gas; coal gasification; air pollution control; delayed coking and solvent deasphalting; shale oil processing. *Mailing Add:* 102 Harrison Brook Dr Basking Ridge NJ 07920

VAN HOOK, ROBERT IRVING, JR, b Rome, Ga, Jan 21, 42; m 64; c 2. ENVIRONMENTAL SCIENCE, ECOLOGY. *Educ:* Clemson Univ, BS, 66, PhD(entom), 69. *Prof Exp:* Assoc res ecologist radiation effects, Ecol Sci Div, 70-72, res ecologist animal ecol, Environ Sci Div, 73-76, tech asst life sci, Dir Staff, 76-77, prog mgr, ecosyst studies, 77-80, SECT HEAD, TERRESTRIAL ECOL SECT, ENVIRON SCI DIV, OAK RIDGE NAT LAB, 80- *Concurrent Pos:* Adj asst prof, Ecol Prog, Univ Tenn, 77- *Mem:* Ecol Soc Am; Sigma Xi; AAAS. *Res:* Management of and participation in basic and applied ecological research concerning productivity, biogeochemical cycling, and pollutant effects associated with fossil and non-fossil energy systems; current emphasis on glorac carbon cycling, acid rain and biomass production. *Mailing Add:* Environ Sci Div Oak Ridge Nat Lab Oak Ridge TN 37830

VAN HOOK, WILLIAM ALEXANDER, b Paterson, NJ, Jan 14, 36; m 62; c 3. PHYSICAL CHEMISTRY. *Educ:* Col of the Holy Cross, BS, 57; Johns Hopkins Univ, MA, 59, PhD(chem), 61. *Prof Exp:* Res assoc phys chem, Brookhaven Nat Lab, 61-62; from asst prof to assoc prof, 62-72, PROF CHEM, UNIV TENN, KNOXVILLE, 72- *Concurrent Pos:* Fulbright res fel, Belg, 67-68; Nat Acad Sci exchange fel, Yugoslavia, 71. *Mem:* AAAS; Am Chem Soc. *Res:* Isotope effects on chemical and physical properties of molecular systems; solutions. *Mailing Add:* Dept of Chem Univ of Tenn Knoxville TN 37916

VAN HOOSIER, GERALD L, JR, b Weatherford, Tex, June 4, 34; m 59; c 2. LABORATORY ANIMAL SCIENCE, ANIMAL VIROLOGY. *Educ:* Agr & Mech Col Tex, DVM, 57. *Prof Exp:* Head animal test sect, Div Biol Standards, NIH, 57-59, in serv training, Viral & Rickettsial Dis Lab, Calif State Dept Health, 59-60, head appl virol sect, Div Biol Standards, 60-62; from instr to assoc prof exp biol, Baylor Col Med, 62-69; from asst prof to assoc prof vet path & dir lab animal resources, Wash State Univ, 69-75; DIR DIV ANIMAL MED & PROF PATH, UNIV WASH, 75- *Concurrent Pos:* Resident path, Baylor Col Med, 69-70 & Wash State Univ, 70-71; mem animal resources adv comt, Animal Res Bd, NIH, 74-78. *Mem:* AAAS; Am Asn Lab Animal Sci; Am Soc Exp Path; Am Vet Med Asn. *Res:* Laboratory animal disease and medicine; comparative pathology; animal virology. *Mailing Add:* Div of Animal Med SE-20 Univ of Wash Seattle WA 98195

VAN HORN, D(AVID) A(LAN), b Des Moines, Iowa, Apr 4, 30; m 60; c 2. CIVIL ENGINEERING. *Educ:* Iowa State Univ, BS, 51, MS, 56, PhD(struct eng), 59. *Prof Exp:* Hwy engr, Fed Hwy Admin, 51-54; asst, Iowa State Univ, 54-55, instr civil eng, 55 & 56-58, instr theoret & appl mech, 55-56, from asst prof to assoc prof civil eng, 58-62; res assoc prof, 62-66, PROF CIVIL ENG, LEHIGH UNIV, 66-, CHMN DEPT, 67- *Mem:* Am Soc Civil Engrs; Am Concrete Inst; Am Soc Eng Educ. *Res:* Structural engineering; behavior of prestressed and reinforced concrete members and structures; behavior of structural materials; structural analysis. *Mailing Add:* Dept of Civil Eng Lehigh Univ Bethlehem PA 18015

VAN HORN, DAVID DOWNING, b Rochester, NY, Apr 23, 21; m 45. METAL PHYSICS, MATHEMATICS. *Educ:* Univ Rochester, BA, 42; Case Inst Technol, PhD(physics), 49. *Prof Exp:* Instr physics, Univ Rochester, 43-44; jr physicist, Clinton Eng Works, 44-46; instr physics, Case Inst Technol, 46-49; res assoc metall, Knolls Atomic Power Lab, 49-57, GROUP LEADER CHEM & METALL ENG, INCANDESCENT LAMP DEPT, GEN ELEC CO, 57- *Mem:* Am Phys Soc; Am Soc Metals; Am Asn Physics Teachers; Math Asn Am; Am Inst Mining, Metall & Petrol Engrs. *Res:* Solid state diffusion; mechanical properties; heat transfer; tungsten; incandescent lamps; radiation measurements. *Mailing Add:* Incandescent Lamp Dept 3437 Gen Elec Co Cleveland OH 44112

VAN HORN, DIANE LILLIAN, b Waukesha, Wis, Aug 21, 39; m 72; c 3. PHYSIOLOGY, ELECTRON MICROSCOPY. *Educ:* Univ Wis-Madison, BS, 61; Marquette Univ, MS, 66, PhD(physiol), 68. *Prof Exp:* Res assoc, Wood Vet Admin Ctr, 66-67, supvry scientist, Electron Micros Lab, 69-75; from instr to assoc prof, 68-77, PROF PHYSIOL & OPHTHAL, MED COL WIS, 77-; CHIEF ELECTRON MICROS SECT, WOOD VET ADMIN CTR, 75- *Concurrent Pos:* Seeing Eye Inc res grant, Med Col Wis, 69-72, Nat Eye Inst res grant, 72-79; Nat Eye Inst Ctr grant, 77-81. *Honors & Awards:* Willaim & Mary Greve Int Res Scholar Award, Res Prevent Blindness, Inc, 81. *Mem:* Am Asn Univ Prof; Am Physiol Soc; Asn Res Vision & Ophthal; Electron Micros Soc Am. *Res:* Corneal physiology and ultrastructure; electron microscopy of ocular and other tissues. *Mailing Add:* Electron Micros Lab Wood Vet Admin Ctr Wood WI 53193

VAN HORN, DONALD H, b Hinsdale, Ill, Oct 9, 28; m 59; c 2. ECOLOGY. *Educ:* Kalamazoo Col, BA, 50; Univ Ill, MS, 52; Univ Colo, PhD(zool), 61. *Prof Exp:* Asst prof biol, Lake Forest Col, 61-62 & Utica Col, 62-65; vis asst prof, 65-71, assoc prof, 71-74, chmn dept, 74-77, PROF BIOL, UNIV COLO, COLORADO SPRINGS CTR, 74- *Mem:* AAAS; Am Ornith Union; Ecol Soc Am; Am Soc Zoologists. *Res:* Terrestrial ecology, especially community and population analysis of mountain animals. *Mailing Add:* Dept of Biol Univ of Colo Colorado Springs CO 80907

VAN HORN, GENE STANLEY, b Oakland, Calif, June 26, 40; m 62; c 3. SYSTEMATIC BOTANY. *Educ:* Humboldt State Univ, AB, 63; Univ Calif, Berkeley, PhD(bot), 70. *Prof Exp:* Vis asst prof biol, Tex Tech Univ, 70-71; asst prof, 71-78, assoc prof, 78-80, PROF BIOL, UNIV TENN, CHATTANOOGA, 80- *Concurrent Pos:* Tex State Inst Funds grant, Tex Tech Univ, 71; Univ Chattanooga Found grant, Univ Tenn, Chattanooga, 72-73. *Mem:* Bot Soc Am; Inst Asn Plant Taxonomists; Am Soc Plant Taxonomists; Torrey Bot Club. *Res:* Biosystematics and evolution of angiosperms, especially asteraceae; floristics; biogeography. *Mailing Add:* Dept of Biol Univ of Tenn Chattanooga TN 37401

VAN HORN, HAROLD H, JR, b Pomona, Kans, Jan 13, 37; m 58; c 3. DAIRY SCIENCE. *Educ:* Kans State Univ, BS, 58, MS, 59; Iowa State Univ, PhD(dairy nutrit), 62. *Prof Exp:* Assoc prof dairy nutrit & mgt & exten dairyman, Iowa State Univ, 61-70; PROF DAIRY SCI & CHMN DEPT, UNIV FLA, 70-, ANIMAL NUTRITIONIST, 74- *Mem:* Am Dairy Sci Asn; Am Soc Animal Sci. *Res:* Improved dairy feeding and management practices; nutrition research in the use of urea in dairy rations. *Mailing Add:* Dept of Dairy Sci Univ of Fla Gainesville FL 32611

VAN HORN, HUGH MOODY, b Williamsport, Pa, Mar 5, 38; m 60; c 3. ASTROPHYSICS. *Educ:* Case Inst Technol, BS, 60; Cornell Univ, PhD(astrophys), 66. *Prof Exp:* Res assoc, 65-67, asst prof, 67-72, assoc prof astrophys, 72-77, PROF PHYSICS & ASTRON, UNIV ROCHESTER, 77-, CHMN, DEPT PHYSICS & ASTRON, 80- *Concurrent Pos:* Vis fel, Joint Inst Lab Astrophys, Univ Colo, Boulder, 73-74; invited speaker, Am Astron Soc, 80. *Mem:* Int Astron Union; Am Astron Soc; AAAS. *Res:* Degenerate dwarfs and neutron stars; structure, evolution, oscillations and atmospheres; nuclear reactions and equation of state in stars; accretion disk structure and oscillations. *Mailing Add:* Dept of Physics & Astron Univ of Rochester Rochester NY 14627

VAN HORN, JOHN R(OBERT), b Lakewood, Ohio, July 3, 21; m 50; c 5. PHYSICS, NUCLEAR ENGINEERING. *Educ:* Oberlin Col, AB, 43; Univ Ill, MS, 48. *Prof Exp:* Jr scientist, Metall Lab, Univ Chicago, 43-45 & Los Alamos Sci Lab, 45-46; asst physics, Univ Ill, 46-49; asst to dir res physics & nuclear eng, Bettis Atomic Power Lab, 50-55, mgr educ & training, 55-61, mgr prof develop lab, 61-68, mgr corp, 68-69, adminr, 69-76, ASST DIR CORP TECH EDUC, WESTINGHOUSE ELEC CORP, PITTSBURGH, 76- *Mem:* Am Phys Soc; Am Nuclear Soc; Am Soc Eng Educ. *Res:* Mass spectroscopy; nuclear cross-section measurements; isotope abundances in rare earths; design of nuclear reactors. *Mailing Add:* 1081 Clifton Rd Bethel Park PA 15102

VAN HORN, KENT R(OBERTSON), b Cleveland, Ohio, July 05; m 32; c 2. METALLURGY. *Educ:* Case Inst Technol, BS, 26; Yale Univ, MS, 28, PhD(metall), 29. *Hon Degrees:* DSc, Case Inst Technol, 55. *Prof Exp:* Res metallurgist, Alcoa Res Labs, 29-44, asst chief, 44-45, chief, 45-48, from asst dir res to dir, 48-62, V PRES RES & DEVELOP, ALUMINUM CO AM, 62- *Concurrent Pos:* Lectr, Case Inst Technol, 31-48. *Honors & Awards:* Ste Claire-Deville Medal, Fr Soc Metall, 65; Gold Medal, Am Soc Metals, 70; Platinum Medal, Brit Inst Metals, 73. *Mem:* Hon mem & fel Am Soc Metals (treas, 39-41, vpres, 44, pres, 45); hon mem Am Soc Nondestructive Testing (pres, 46); fel Am Inst Mining, Metall & Petrol Engrs; Fr Soc Metall. *Res:* Metallurgy of aluminum alloys. *Mailing Add:* 373 Fox Chapel Rd Pittsburgh PA 15238

VAN HORN, LLOYD DIXON, b Bartlesville, Okla, Mar 25, 38; m 59; c 2. CHEMICAL ENGINEERING. *Educ:* Rice Univ, BA, 59, PhD(chem eng), 66. *Prof Exp:* Res engr, Shell Oil Co, Tex, 66-68, supvr chem eng res & develop, 68-69, asst to mgr mfg res & develop, head off, NY, 69-70, sr engr, head off, Houston, 70-72; CONSULT ENGR, BILES & ASSOCS, HOUSTON, 72- *Mem:* Am Chem Soc. *Res:* Chemical reactor analysis and simulation; multiphase fluid flow in packed beds; applications of advanced process computer control; thermodynamics of hydrocarbon-hydrogen systems. *Mailing Add:* 14838 LaQuinta Lane Houston TX 77079

VAN HORN, RUTH WARNER, b Waterloo, Iowa, Mar 24, 18; m 45. ORGANIC CHEMISTRY. *Educ:* Univ Calif, Los Angeles, BA, 39, MA, 40; Pa State Univ, PhD(org chem), 44. *Prof Exp:* Org chemist, Am Cyanamid Co, 44-48; instr chem, Hunter Col, 48-49; from asst prof to assoc prof, 49-64, PROF CHEM, FRANKLIN & MARSHALL COL, 64- *Mem:* AAAS; Am Chem Soc. *Res:* Synthesis. *Mailing Add:* Dept of Chem Franklin & Marshall Col Lancaster PA 17604

VAN HORN, WENDELL EARL, b Cantril, Iowa, Feb 8, 29; m 59; c 4. CHEMICAL ENGINEERING. *Educ:* Iowa State Col, BS, 52; Univ Chicago, MBA, 74. *Prof Exp:* Develop engr, Minn Mining & Mfg Co, 53-56; process develop engr, 56-70, mgr chem eng res & develop, 70-77, sr res assoc, 77-81, SR PROCESS ASSOC, QUAKER OATS CO, TEX, 81- *Mem:* Am Inst Chem Engrs. *Res:* Pollution control; development of waste acetic acid recovery methods; process development of furfural manufacturing methods; liquid phase and vapor phase catalytic processes; fluized bed combustion. *Mailing Add:* Quaker Oats Co 12901 Bay Park Rd Pasadena TX 77507

VAN HORNE, ROBERT LOREN, b Malvern, Iowa, Dec 26, 15; m 41, 63; c 5. PHARMACOGNOSY, PHARMACY. *Educ:* Univ Iowa, BS, 41, MS, 47, PhD, 49. *Prof Exp:* Instr pharm, Univ Iowa, 49-51, from asst prof to assoc prof pharmacog, 51-56; dean, Sch Pharm, 56-75, dir continuing educ, Sch Pharm, 75-80, PROF PHARM, UNIV MONT, 56- *Concurrent Pos:* Mem fac adv coun, Gov of Mont; dir, Western Area Alcohol Educ & Training Prog, Nev, 74-; chmn, Mont Adv Coun Alcohol & Drug Dependence, 76- *Mem:* Am Asn Cols Pharm; Am Pharmaceut Asn. *Res:* Water soluble embedding materials for microtechnique; polyethylene glycols as substitutes for glycerin and ethanol in pharmaceutical preparations; surfactants in the preparation of coal tar lotions; anionic exchange resins for alkaloid separation; phytochemistry of mistletoe species. *Mailing Add:* Sch of Pharm Univ of Mont Missoula MT 59801

VAN HOUTEN, FRANKLYN BOSWORTH, b New York, NY, July 14, 14; m 43; c 3. GEOLOGY. *Educ:* Rutgers Univ, BS, 36; Princeton Univ, PhD(geol), 41. *Prof Exp:* Instr geol, Williams Col, 39-42; from asst prof to assoc prof, 47-55, PROF GEOL, PRINCETON UNIV, 55- *Concurrent Pos:* Consult, 41-; geologist, US Geol Surv, 48- & Geol Surv Can, 53; vis prof, Univ Calif, Los Angeles, 63, State Univ NY Binghamton, 71 & Univ Basel, 71. *Mem:* Fel Geol Soc Am; hon mem Soc Econ Paleontologists & Mineralogists; Am Asn Petrol Geologists; Int Asn Sedimentol; hon mem Colombian Geol Soc. *Res:* Sedimentology; clay minerals; zeolites; iron oxides; red beds; Triassic rocks, eastern North America and northwestern Africa, continental drift reconstructions; Cenozoic nonmarine deposits, western United States and northern South America; modern marine sediments; molasse facies in orogenic belts; phanerozoic oolctic ironstones; Nubian soundstone of northern Africa. *Mailing Add:* Dept of Geol & Geophys Sci Princeton Univ Princeton NJ 08540

VAN HOUTEN, MARK STEVEN, b Brooklyn, NY, Oct 13, 49; m 76. NEUROENDOCRINOLOGY. *Educ:* State Univ NY, BA, 71; Tufts Univ, Boston, PhD(anat), 78. *Prof Exp:* Fel, 77-79, RES ASSOC NEUROENDOCRINOL, MCGILL UNIV, 79- *Concurrent Pos:* Co-prin investr, Can Diabetic Asn, 78-80 & Juvenile Diabetes Asn, 80-82. *Res:* Central nervous system receptors for blood-borne peptide hormones, localization and characterization. *Mailing Add:* 3550 Jeanne Mance Apt 620 Montreal PQ H2X 3P7 Can

VAN HOUTEN, ROBERT, b Peoria, Ill, Oct 2, 23; m 47; c 4. MATERIALS ENGINEERING, NUCLEAR ENGINEERING. *Educ:* Washington Univ, St Louis, BS, 47, PhD(chem eng), 50; Oak Ridge Sch Reactor Technol, cert, 56. *Prof Exp:* Res engr, Victor Div, Radio Corp Am, 50-52; sect head res eng, Metals & Ceramics Div, P R Mallory & Co, 52-56, assoc lab dir chem & metall res, 57-58; prin & lead engr, Aircraft Nuclear Propulsion Dept, Gen Elec Co, Ohio, 58-64, mgr reactor mat develop, Nuclear Mat & Propulsion Oper, 64-70; mem staff, Atomics Int, Canoga Park, 70-73; REACTOR SAFETY ENGR, US NUCLEAR REGULATORY COMN, 74- *Concurrent Pos:* Consult, Oak Ridge Nat Lab, 56-59; lectr, Univ Cincinnati, 61-66, adj assoc prof, 66-70. *Mem:* Am Nuclear Soc; Res Soc Am. *Res:* Chemical, metallurgical, electrochemical and nuclear materials and processes for high temperature extreme duty; metal hydrides fabrication; light water reactor nuclear fuels testing and evaluation under accident conditions. *Mailing Add:* US Nuclear Regulatory Comn Mail Stop 1130 SS Washington DC 20555

VANHOUTTE, JEAN JACQUES, b Courtrai, Belg, Aug 27, 32; US citizen; m 60; c 4. PEDIATRIC RADIOLOGY. *Educ:* Catholic Univ London, MD, 59. *Prof Exp:* Instr radiol, Johns Hopkins Univ, 63-65; asst prof, Univ Colo, 65-71; assoc prof, 71-74, PROF & VCHMN, DEPT RADIOL, UNIV OKLA HEALTH SCI CTR, 74- *Concurrent Pos:* Chief radiologist, Okla Childrens Mem Hosp, 71- *Mem:* Fel Am Col Radiol; Am Roentgen Ray Soc; Radiol Soc NAm; Soc Pediat Radiol; Asn Univ Radiologists. *Res:* Application of radiological sciences and imaging sciences to pediatrics. *Mailing Add:* State Okla Teaching Hosp PO Box 26307 Oklahoma City OK 73126

VAN HOUWELING, CORNELIUS DONALD, b Mahaska County, Iowa, July 19, 18; m 42; c 5. VETERINARY MEDICINE. *Educ:* Iowa State Univ, DVM, 42, MS, 66. *Prof Exp:* Vet, Springfield, Ill, 42-43; dir vet med rels, Ill Agr Asn, 46-48; dir prof rels & asst exec secy, Am Vet Med Asn, 48-53; instr, Col Vet Med, Univ Ill, 53-54; dir livestock regulatory progs, Agr Res Serv, USDA, 54-56, asst adminr, 56-61, asst dir regulatory labs, Nat Animal Dis Lab, Iowa, 61-66; dir bur vet med, 67-78, SPEC ASST TO COMNR FOR AGR MATTERS, US FOOD & DRUG ADMIN, ROCKVILLE, MD, 78- *Concurrent Pos:* Mem comn vet educ, Southern Regional Educ Bd; mem subcomt laws, rules & regulations animal health, Nat Res Coun; chmn adv comt humane slaughter, US Secy Agr; mem & chmn, Coun Pub Health & Regulatory Vet Med & organizing comt, Am Col Vet Preventive Med; chmn, Food & Drug Admin task force on antibiotics in animal feeds, 70-71. *Honors & Awards:* Award, Am Mgt Asn, 57; Cert Merit Outstanding Work Performance, 60 & Outstanding Leadership, 64; Equal Employment

Opportunity Award, Food & Drug Admin, 74; Karl F Meyer Gold Headed Cane Award, Am Vet Epidemiol Soc, 78. *Mem:* Fel AAAS; Am Asn Food Hyg Veterinarians (pres, 78); US Animal Health Asn; Nat Asn Fed Veterinarians; World Asn Vet Food Hyg. *Res:* Regulatory veterinary medicine. *Mailing Add:* 4303 Ballard Ct Fairfax VA 22039

VAN HOVEN, GERARD, b Los Angeles, Calif, Nov 23, 32; m 56; c 2. PLASMA PHYSICS, SOLAR PHYSICS. *Educ:* Calif Inst Technol, BS, 54; Stanford Univ, PhD(physics), 63. *Prof Exp:* Mem tech staff, Bell Tel Labs, 54-56; electron physicist, Gen Elec Co, 56-63; res assoc, W W Hansen Labs Physics, Stanford Univ, 63-65, res physicist, Inst Plasma Res, 65-68; from asst prof to assoc prof, 68-79, PROF PHYSICS, UNIV CALIF, IRVINE, 79- *Concurrent Pos:* Fulbright fel, Vienna Tech Univ, 63-64; consult, Gen Elec Co, 63-65, Varian Assocs, 65-68, Smithsonian Astrophys Observ, 75, Aerospace Corp, 75-77 & Nat Acron & Space Admin, 79-81; Langley-Abbot vis scientist, Ctr Astrophys, Harvard Univ, 75; vis astrophysicist, Oss Astrofisico Arcetri, 76, vis prof, 81-82. *Mem:* Am Phys Soc; Am Astron Soc. *Res:* Solar-terrestrial activity magnetohydrodynamics, especially magnetic field reconnection instabilities and coronal structure; nonlinear plasma wave interactions. *Mailing Add:* Dept of Physics Univ of Calif Irvine CA 92717

VAN HUFF, NORMAN E(DGAR), chemical engineering, heat transfer, see previous edition

VAN HULLE, GLENN JOSEPH, b Oconto, Wis, Dec 20, 37; m 63; c 3. FOOD SCIENCE. *Educ:* Univ Wis-Madison, BS, 64, MS, 65, PhD(food sci), 69. *Prof Exp:* DEPT HEAD APPL RES & DEVELOP, GEN MILLS INC, 69- *Mem:* Inst Food Technologists. *Res:* New product and process development in meat, dairy and soy based products. *Mailing Add:* Gen Mills Inc 9200 Wayzata Blvd Minneapolis MN 55426

VAN HUYSTEE, ROBERT BERNARD, b Amsterdam, Holland, Sept 29, 31; Can citizen; m 58; c 1. BIOCHEMISTRY, BOTANY. *Educ:* Univ Sask, BA, 59, MA, 61; Univ Minn, St Paul, PhD(hort), 64. *Prof Exp:* Fel physiol, Purdue Univ, 64-66; asst prof radiobiol, 66-69, assoc prof plant sci, 69-79, PROF PLANT SCI, UNIV WESTERN ONT, 79- *Mem:* Am Soc Plant Physiol; Radiation Res Soc; Can Soc Plant Physiol. *Res:* Process of cold acclimation and its metabolism in plants; metabolism in cultured plant cells; nucleic acid metabolism in photo induction and as related to ionizing radiation effects. *Mailing Add:* Dept of Plant Sci Univ of Western Ont London ON N6A 5B7 Can

VANICEK, C DAVID, b Waterloo, Iowa, Oct 12, 39. FISHERIES MANAGEMENT. *Educ:* Iowa State Univ, BS, 61, MS, 63; Utah State Univ, PhD(fishery biol), 67. *Prof Exp:* Fishery biologist, US Fish & Wildlife Serv, 63-67; from asst prof to assoc prof, 67-79, PROF BIOL, CALIF STATE UNIV, SACRAMENTO, 79- *Mem:* Am Fisheries Soc; Am Inst Biol Sci; Am Inst Fishery Res Biol; Pac Fishery Biologists; Desert Fishes Coun. *Res:* Freshwater fishery biology and management. *Mailing Add:* Dept of Biol Sci Calif State Univ Sacramento CA 95819

VANICEK, PETR, b Susice, Czech, July 18, 35; m 60; c 3. GEODESY, GEOPHYSICS. *Educ:* Prague Tech Univ, Dipl Ing, 59; Czech Acad Sci, PhD(math physics), 68. *Prof Exp:* Div head land surv, Prague Inst Surv & Cartog, 59-63; consult numerical anal & comput prog, Fac Tech & Nuclear Physics, Prague Tech Univ, 63-67; sr res fel & sr sci officer, Inst Coastal Oceanog & Tides, Nat Environ Res Coun Gt Brit, 68-69; Nat Res Coun Can fel, Dept Energy, Mines & Resources, 69-71; dir grad studies, Dept Surv Eng, Univ NB, 75-76, assoc prof, 71-76, prof geod, 76-81; PROF SURV SCI, UNIV TORONTO, 81- *Concurrent Pos:* Can rep, Comn Recent Crustal Movements, Int Union Geod & Geophys, 77-; secy subcomt geod, Nat Res Coun Can, 72-74; mem, Can Subcomt Geodynamics, 75-80; vis prof, Nat Res Coun Can, Univ Parana, Brazil, 75, 76 & 79, Univ San Paolo, 81 & Univ Stuttgart, WGer, 81; vis scientist, Nat Oceanic & Atmospheric Admin, Nat Acad Sci, 78. *Mem:* NY Acad Sci; Am Geophys Union; Can Inst Surv; fel Geol Asn Can; fel NY Acad Sci. *Res:* Physical and dynamical geodesy; earth tides, crustal movements and mean sea level; applied mathematics, especially spectral analysis and mechanics. *Mailing Add:* Surv Sci Univ Toronto 3359 Mississauga Rd Mississauga ON L5L 1C6 Can

VANIER, JACQUES, b Dorion, Que, Jan 4, 34; m 61; c 2. QUANTUM ELECTRONICS. *Educ:* Univ Montreal, BA, 55, BSc, 58; McGill Univ, MSc, 60, PhD(physics), 63. *Prof Exp:* Lectr physics, McGill Univ, 61-63; physicist, Quantum Electronics Div, Varian Assocs, Mass, 63-67 & Hewlett-Packard Co, 67; assoc prof, 68-71, PROF ELEC ENG, LAVAL UNIV, 71- *Concurrent Pos:* Lectr, Univ Montreal, 62. *Mem:* Can Asn Physicists; sr mem Inst Elec & Electronics Engrs; Am Phys Soc. *Res:* Electron paramagnetic resonance; nuclear magnetic resonance; optical pumping; masers; frequency standards; atomic clocks; atomic and molecular physics; electromagnetism; solid state physics; thermal physics. *Mailing Add:* Quantum Electronics Lab Dept Elec Eng Laval Univ Quebec PQ G1K 7P4 Can

VANIER, PETER EUGENE, b St Kitts, Leeward Islands, Feb 26, 46; Brit citizen; m 71. SOLID STATE PHYSICS. *Educ:* Cambridge Univ, BA, 67; Syracuse Univ, MS, 69, PhD(physics), 76. *Prof Exp:* Res assoc physics, Yeshiva Univ, 76-78; ASST SCIENTIST MAT SCI, BROOKHAVEN NAT LAB, 78- *Mem:* Am Phys Soc. *Res:* Electronic, magnetic and optical properties of semiconductors; properties of amorphous semiconductors related to solar cell applications. *Mailing Add:* Bldg 480 Brookhaven Nat Lab Upton NY 11973

VAN INWEGEN, RICHARD GLEN, b Brooklyn, NY, Nov 24, 44; m 67; c 3. BIOCHEMISTRY, PHYSIOLOGY. *Educ:* State Univ NY, Binghamton, BA, 66, MA, 69; Univ Ill, Urbana-Champaign, PhD(physiol), 72. *Prof Exp:* Res assoc pharmacol, Univ Tex Med Sch, Houston, 72-76; sr res scientist biochem, USV Pharmaceut Corp, 76-79; GROUP LEADER BIOCHEM, REVLON HEALTH CARE GROUP, 79- *Mem:* Sigma Xi; NY Acad Sci. *Res:* Cyclic nucleotides in asthma and hypertension; cyclic nucleotide associated enzymes-cyclases, kinases and phosphodiesterases; receptor biochemistry. *Mailing Add:* Revlon Health Care Group One Scarsdale Rd Tuckahoe NY 10707

VAN ITALLIE, THEODORE BERTUS, b Hackensack, NJ, Nov 8, 19; m 48; c 5. MEDICINE. *Educ:* Harvard Univ, SB, 41; Columbia Univ, MD, 45; Am Bd Internal Med, dipl, 54. *Prof Exp:* Intern med, St Luke's Hosp, New York, 45-46, from asst resident to resident, 48-50; res fellow nutrit, Sch Pub Health, Harvard Univ, 50-51, res assoc, 51-52, asst prof clin nutrit, Schs Med & Pub Health, 55-57; instr, 52-55, from assoc clin prof to clin prof, 57-71, PROF MED, COL PHYSICIANS & SURGEONS, COLUMBIA UNIV, 71-, ASSOC DIR INST HUMAN NUTRIT, 67- *Concurrent Pos:* From asst to assoc, Peter Bent Brigham Hosp, Boston, 50-57; dir lab nutrit res, St Luke's Hosp, 52-55, asst attend physician, 53-55, attend physician, 57-, dir med, 57-75; vis lectr, Sch Pub Health, Harvard Univ, 57-60; mem gastroenterol & nutrit training comt, NIH, 69-73; mem food & nutrit bd, Nat Acad Sci, 70-74; Nat Inst Arthritis, Metab & Digestive Dis Adv Coun, 78-81; ed-in-chief, Am J Clin Nutrit, 79-81; special adv, Surgeon Gen Human Nutrit, 80-81. *Mem:* Soc Exp Biol & Med; Am Clin & Climat Asn; Am Fedn Clin Res; fel Am Col Physicians; Am Soc Clin Nutrit (pres, 75-76). *Res:* Carbohydrate and lipid physiology and biochemistry; clinical nutrition; metabolism; control of food intake and regulation of body fat; body composition. *Mailing Add:* St Luke's Hosp Ctr 421 W 113th St New York NY 10025

VAN KAMMEN, DANIEL PAUL, b Dordrecht, Netherlands, Aug 26, 43; US citizen; m 70; c 1. PSYCHOPHARMACOLOGY. *Educ:* Univ Utrecht Med Sch, MD, 66, PhD(pharmacol), 78. *Prof Exp:* UNIT CHIEF & STAFF PSYCHIATRIST, NAT INST MENTAL HEALTH, 73- *Concurrent Pos:* Comn mem, Behav & Clin Res Rev Comt, 75-78; fac mem, Wash Sch Psychiat, 75-; bd mem, Minsana Res Found, 78-; vis prof, Dept Psychiat, Univ Ala, Birmingham, 78; consult, Vet Admin & Nat Heart, Lung & Blood Inst, 79. *Mem:* Am Col Neuropsychopharmacol; AAAS; Int Psychoneuroendocrinol; Soc Neurosci; Collegium Int Neuropsychopharmacol. *Res:* Biochemical and pharmacological exploitation of schizophrenia and manic-depressive illness; spiral fluid studies; endocrinology. *Mailing Add:* Rm 4N214 Bldg 10 Nat Inst Mental Health Bethesda MD 20205

VAN KAMPEN, KENT RIGBY, b Brigham City, Utah, July 30, 36; m 59; c 3. VETERINARY PATHOLOGY. *Educ:* Utah State Univ, BS, 61; Colo State Univ, DVM, 67; Univ Calif, Davis, PhD(comp path), 67. *Prof Exp:* Vet pathologist, Poisonous Plant Res Lab, Agr Res Serv, USDA, Utah, 67-70; assoc prof vet sci, Utah State Univ, 68-70; dir res, Intermountain Labs, Inc, 69-77; prof & head, Dept Animal, Dairy & Vet Sci, Utah State Univ, Logan, 77-80. *Concurrent Pos:* Adj assoc prof, Col Med, Univ Utah, 69- *Mem:* AAAS; Am Col Vet Path; Am Vet Med Asn; fel Am Col Vet Toxicol. *Res:* Pathogenesis of animal diseases related to similar disorders in man; pathology of natural and man made toxicants in animals; mechanisms of carcinogenesis. *Mailing Add:* 3300 Saratoga Lane Plymouth MN 55441

VANKERKHOVE, ALAN PAUL, b Rochester, NY, Mar 18, 33; m 56; c 8. OPTICAL PHYSICS. *Educ:* Univ Rochester, BS, 64, MS, 71. *Prof Exp:* RES ASSOC OPTICAL PHYSICS, EASTMAN KODAK CO, 64- *Mem:* Optical Soc Am; Soc Photograph Scientists & Engrs; Soc Mfg Engrs. *Res:* Optical studies related to other disciplines such as organic chemistry and materials science; application of geometric and physical optics to consumer products; laser technology; holography; microscopy. *Mailing Add:* Eastman Kodak Co Kodak Park Bldg Rochester NY 14650

VAN KEUREN, ROBERT W, b Virginia, Minn, Jan 2, 22; m 49; c 3. AGRONOMY. *Educ:* Wis State Univ, BS, 43; Univ Wis, MS, 52, PhD, 54. *Prof Exp:* Instr, Wis Pub Schs, 46-50; res asst, Univ Wis, 51-54; asst & assoc agronomist, Wash State Univ, 54-62; assoc prof, 62-70, PROF AGRON, OHIO STATE UNIV & OHIO AGR RES & DEVELOP CTR, 70- *Mem:* Am Soc Agron; Crop Sci Soc Am; Am Soc Animal Sci. *Res:* Ecological and physiological factors associated with adaptation and utilization of forage plants; production, management and utilization of forage crops and pastures. *Mailing Add:* Dept of Agron Ohio Agr Res & Develop Ctr Wooster OH 44691

VANKIN, GEORGE LAWRENCE, b Baltimore, Md, Apr 22, 31; m 56; c 2. CELL BIOLOGY. *Educ:* NY Univ, BS, 54, PhD(zool), 62; Wesleyan Univ, MA, 56. *Prof Exp:* Res asst genetics, Wesleyan Univ, 56; teaching fel biol, NY Univ, 56-59, res asst embryol, 59-62, lectr biol, 61-62; from asst prof to assoc prof, 62-75, PROF BIOL, WILLIAMS COL, 75- *Concurrent Pos:* Vis asst prof, Med Col, Cornell Univ, 68. *Mem:* Soc Syst Zool; Am Soc Zoologists; Soc Develop Biol. *Res:* Ultrastructure of differentiating amphibian red blood cells; electron microscopy of post-implantation mouse embryos. *Mailing Add:* Dept of Biol Williams Col Williamstown MA 01267

VAN KLAVEREN, NICOLAAS, b Amersfoort, Neth, Feb 2, 34; m 59; c 3. CHEMICAL ENGINEERING, COMPUTER SCIENCE. *Educ:* Delft Univ Technol, MSc, 59, DSc(chem eng), 66; Pepperdine Univ, MBA, 78. *Prof Exp:* Vis prof, Steven's Inst Technol, 64. *Concurrent Pos:* Asst prof chem eng, Delft Univ Technol, 61-66; SR ENG ASSOC, CHEVRON RES CO, 66- Concurrent. *Mem:* Am Inst Chem Engrs; Neth Royal Inst Eng. *Res:* Chemical engineering science; process design; user oriented software for process engineering and business and strategic planning; modeling of technical, economical and social processes; management of complex organizations; organizational development. *Mailing Add:* 2635 Mira Vista Dr El Cerrito CA 94530

VAN KLEY, HAROLD, b Chicago, Ill, Mar 7, 32; m 59; c 2. BIOCHEMISTRY, PROTEIN CHEMISTRY. *Educ:* Calvin Col, AB, 53; Univ Wis, MS, 55, PhD(biochem), 58. *Prof Exp:* From instr to sr instr, 58-61, ASST PROF BIOCHEM, SCH MED, ST LOUIS UNIV, 61-; DIR BIOCHEM RES, ST MARY'S HEALTH CTR, 67- *Mem:* Am Pancreatic Asn; AAAS; Am Chem Soc; Sigma Xi; Am Soc Biol Chemists. *Res:* Protein structure, especially as related to biological function and regulatory mechanisms in metabolism; protein changes in neoplasia; pancreatic enzymes. *Mailing Add:* Lab for Biochem Res St Mary's Health Ctr St Louis MO 63117

VAN KRANENDONK, JAN, b Delft, Neth, Feb 8, 24; m 52; c 3. THEORETICAL PHYSICS. *Educ:* Univ Amsterdam, PhD(physics), 52. *Prof Exp:* Res asst, Univ Amsterdam, 50-54; lectr, State Univ Leiden, 55-58; assoc prof, 58-60, PROF PHYSICS, UNIV TORONTO, 60- *Concurrent Pos:* Neth Orgn for Pure Res fel, Harvard Univ, 53-54. *Honors & Awards:* Steacie Prize, 64. *Mem:* Am Phys Soc; fel Royal Soc Can; Can Asn Physicists; corresp mem Neth Acad Sci. *Res:* Molecular and solid-state physics. *Mailing Add:* Dept Physics Univ Toronto Toronto ON M5S 1A7 Can

VAN KREY, HARRY P, b Combined Locks, Wis, Oct 2, 31; m 52; c 2. PHYSIOLOGY, AGRICULTURE. *Educ:* Univ Calif, Davis, BS, 60, PhD(animal physiol), 64. *Prof Exp:* Fel, Univ Wis, 64-65; assoc prof, 65-80, PROF AVIAN PHYSIOL, VA POLYTECH INST & STATE UNIV, 80- *Mem:* AAAS; Sigma Xi; Poultry Sci Asn; World Poultry Sci Asn; Soc Study Reproduction. *Res:* Avian reproductive physiology; poultry science. *Mailing Add:* Dept of Poultry Sci Va Polytech Inst & State Univ Blacksburg VA 24061

VAN LAAN, GORDON JAMES, b Bay City, Mich, Aug 6, 22. ORNAMENTAL HORTICULTURE. *Educ:* Mich State Univ, BS, 48, MS, 49; Wash State Univ, PhD(hort), 53. *Prof Exp:* Agr missionary, Am Bd Comnrs For Missions, Angola, Port W Africa, 53-59; park foreman, City Walnut Creek, Calif, 60; nurseryman, Navlet's Nursery, 61; from asst prof to assoc prof, 61-73, PROF ORNAMENTAL HORT, CALIF STATE UNIV, CHICO, 73- *Mem:* Am Soc Hort Sci; Am Hort Soc. *Res:* Management practices in California nurseries with special attention to employee relations, merchandising and management problems; propagation of difficult to propagate ornamental shrubs and trees. *Mailing Add:* Dept of Plant & Soil Sci Calif State Univ Chico CA 95929

VAN LANCKER, JULIEN L, b Auderghem, Belg, Aug 14, 24; m 49; c 3. PATHOLOGY. *Educ:* Cath Univ Louvain, MD, 50. *Prof Exp:* Asst path, Cath Univ Louvain, 50-53; vis instr, Univ Kans, 53-54; Runyon fel oncol, Univ Wis, 54-55; asst path, Cath Univ Louvain, 55-56; asst prof path, Univ Utah, 56-60; assoc prof path & chief path sect, Primate Res Ctr, Univ Wis, 60-66; prof med sci, Brown Univ, 66-70; PROF PATH & CHMN DEPT, UNIV CALIF, LOS ANGELES, 70- *Mem:* Radiation Res Soc; Am Soc Exp Path; Am Soc Biol Chemists; NY Acad Sci; Int Acad Path. *Res:* Cell biology; chemical pathology; molecular mechanisms in disease. *Mailing Add:* Dept Path Ctr for Health Sci Univ of Calif Los Angeles CA 90024

VAN LANDINGHAM, HUGH F(OCH), b Greensboro, NC, Apr 12, 35; m 64; c 1. ELECTRICAL ENGINEERING. *Educ:* NC State Univ, BS, 57; NY Univ, MEE, 59; Cornell Univ, PhD(elec eng), 67. *Prof Exp:* Mem tech staff, Bell Tel Labs, NJ, 57-62; asst prof elec eng, 66-70, assoc prof, 70-80, PROF ELEC ENG, VA POLYTECH INST & STATE UNIV, 80- *Mem:* Inst Elec & Electronics Engrs. *Res:* Communication and control systems. *Mailing Add:* Dept of Elec Eng Va Polytech Inst & State Univ Blacksburg VA 24061

VAN LANDINGHAM, JOHN W, environmental chemistry, see previous edition

VAN LANEN, ROBERT JEROME, b Green Bay, Wis, July 30, 43. BIO-ORGANIC CHEMISTRY, PHYSICAL ORGANIC CHEMISTRY. *Educ:* St Norbert Col, BS, 65; Univ Colo, Boulder, PhD(org chem), 71. *Prof Exp:* NIH fel chem, Univ Wis-Madison, 71-73; ASSOC PROF CHEM, ST XAVIER COL, 73- *Mem:* AAAS; Am Chem Soc; NY Acad Sci. *Res:* Mechanisms of enzyme-catalyzed reactions; model systems; chemistry of small ring compounds. *Mailing Add:* St Xavier Col 103rd & Central Park Ave Chicago IL 60655

VAN LEAR, DAVID HYDE, b Clifton Forge, Va, Dec 1, 40. FORESTRY, SOILS. *Educ:* Va Polytech Inst, BS, 63, MS, 65; Univ Idaho, PhD(forest sci), 69. *Prof Exp:* Fel sch forestry, Univ Fla, 68-69; soil scientist, US Forest Serv, 69-71; assoc prof, 71-77, PROF SILVICULT, CLEMSON UNIV, 77- *Mem:* Soc Am Foresters; Soil Sci Soc Am. *Res:* Hardwood silviculture; environmental forestry; forest fertilization; soil-site relationships; strip mining. *Mailing Add:* Dept of Forestry Clemson Univ Clemson SC 29631

VAN LEER, JOHN CLOUD, b Washington, DC, Feb 14, 40; m 62; c 3. PHYSICAL OCEANOGRAPHY, OCEAN ENGINEERING. *Educ:* Case Inst Technol, BSME, 62; Mass Inst Technol, ScD(phys oceanog), 71. *Prof Exp:* Engr, Draper Lab, Mass Inst Technol, 62-65, from res asst to res assoc phys oceanog, Mass Inst Technol, 65-71; asst prof, 71-75, ASSOC PROF PHYS OCEANOG, ROSENSTIEL SCH MARINE & ATMOSPHERIC SCI, UNIV MIAMI, 76- *Mem:* Sigma Xi; Am Geophys Union; Marine Technol Soc. *Res:* Physical oceanographic research on continental shelves and deep ocean; response to wind forcing, surface and bottom boundary layers; development of ocean instruments, notably the Cyclesonde, an automatic oceanographic radiosonde. *Mailing Add:* Univ Miami 4600 Rickenbacker Causeway Miami FL 33149

VAN LEEUWEN, GERARD, b Hull, Iowa, July 4, 29; m 52; c 2. PEDIATRICS. *Educ:* Calvin Col, BA, 50; Univ Iowa, MD, 54. *Prof Exp:* Intern, Butterworth Hosp, Mich, 54-55; resident pediat, Univ Mo-Columbia, 57-59, from instr to asst prof, 62-69; prof pediat & chmn dept, Univ Nebr Med Ctr, Omaha, 69-78; assoc med dir, Sect Med Care, Mo Div Health, 78-80; PROF & ACTG CHMN, PEDIAT DEPT, MED SCH, UNIV KANS, WICHITA, 80- *Concurrent Pos:* NIH trainee, 62-64; Am Thoracic Soc fel, 64-66; Nat Found Birth Defects grant, 66; proj consult, Head Start, 65; dir, Nat Found Treatment Ctr, 66; dir, Emergency Med, Univ Nebr, 76-78. *Mem:* Am Acad Pediat; Am Pediat Soc. *Res:* Neonatal physiology and hypogylcemia; hyaline membrane syndrome; teratology. *Mailing Add:* Pediat Dept Univ Kans Lawrence KS 66045

VAN LENTE, KENNETH ANTHONY, b Holland, Mich, Mar 29, 03; m 29; c 4. PHYSICAL CHEMISTRY. *Educ:* Hope Col, AB, 25, MS, 26; Univ Mich, PhD, 31. *Prof Exp:* Asst, Univ Mich, 27-31; from asst prof to prof, 31-71, EMER PROF PHYS CHEM, SOUTHERN ILL UNIV, CARBONDALE, 71- *Mem:* Am Chem Soc. *Res:* Liquid junction potentials; constant temperature baths; composition of plating baths; chemical education. *Mailing Add:* 1209 W Chautauqua Carbondale IL 62901

VAN LIER, JAN ANTONIUS, b Ginneken, Neth, Nov 17, 24; m 54; c 4. PHYSICAL CHEMISTRY. *Educ:* Univ Utrecht, BS, 51, MS, 54, PhD(phys chem), 59; Cleveland State Univ, JD, 77. *Prof Exp:* Res assoc mineral eng, Mass Inst Technol, 55-58; instr colloid chem, Univ Utrecht, 58-59; res chemist, Philips Electronics, Holland, 59-60; sr res chemist, 60-74, STAFF RES CHEMIST, PARMA TECH CTR, UNION CARBIDE CORP, 74- *Mem:* Am Chem Soc; Royal Neth Chem Soc. *Res:* Microbalance techniques; solubility of quartz; battery materials; differential and thermogravimetric analysis; solid electrolytes; basic electrochemistry; ternary phase diagrams; surface chemistry; wetting phenomena. *Mailing Add:* Parma Tech Ctr Union Carbide Corp Parma OH 44130

VAN LIER, JOHANNES ERNESTINUS, b Amsterdam, Neth, May 26, 42; m 66. BIOCHEMISTRY. *Educ:* Delft Univ Technol, Ir, 66; Univ Tex Med Br Galveston, PhD(biochem), 69. *Prof Exp:* Res assoc, Univ Tex Med Br Galveston, 66-69, instr, 69-70; asst prof, 70-75, assoc prof, 75-81, PROF NUCLEAR MED RADIOBIOL, MED CTR, UNIV SHERBROOKE, 81- *Concurrent Pos:* Med Res Coun Can res grant, 70- *Mem:* AAAS; Fedn Am Socs Exp Biol; Am Chem Soc; Can Fedn Biol Socs; Soc Nuclear Med. *Res:* radiopharmaceuticals for nuclear med; radiosensitisens and anticancer agents. *Mailing Add:* Dept of Nuclear Med Univ of Sherbrooke Med Ctr Sherbrooke PQ J1H 5N4 Can

VAN LIEW, HUGH DAVENPORT, b Spokane, Wash, Jan 28, 30; m 59; c 3. MEDICAL PHYSIOLOGY. *Educ:* State Col Wash, BS, 51; Univ Rochester, MS, 53, PhD(physiol), 56. *Prof Exp:* Res fel, Sch Pub Health, Harvard Univ, 59-61; asst prof physiol, Stanford Univ, 61-63; from asst prof to assoc prof, 63-74, PROF PHYSIOL, STATE UNIV NY BUFFALO, 74- *Mem:* AAAS; Am Physiol Soc; Undersea Med Soc. *Res:* Diffusion of gases through tissues; gas tensions in the tissues; subcutaneous gas pockets as models of decompression sickness bubbles; diffusion and convection in the lung. *Mailing Add:* Dept of Physiol State Univ of NY Buffalo NY 14214

VAN LIEW, JUDITH BRADFORD, b Boston, Mass, Jan 22, 30; m 59; c 3. PHYSIOLOGY. *Educ:* Bates Col, BS, 51; Univ Wash, MS, 54; Univ Rochester, PhD(physiol), 58. *Prof Exp:* Res assoc biochem, Woman's Med Col Pa, 58-60; res assoc med, 64-70, res asst prof, 70-74, ASST PROF PHYSIOL, SCH MED, STATE UNIV NY BUFFALO, 74-; ASSOC PROF PHYSIOL & RES PHYSIOLOGIST, VET ADMIN HOSP, BUFFALO, 73- *Mem:* Am Physiol Soc; Am Soc Nephrology. *Res:* Physiology of normal and abnormal proteinuria. *Mailing Add:* Vet Admin Hosp 3495 Bailey Ave Buffalo NY 14215

VAN LINT, VICTOR ANTON JACOBUS, b Samarinda, Indonesia, May 10, 28; US citizen; m 50; c 4. PHYSICS. *Educ:* Calif Inst Technol, BS & PhD(physics), 54. *Prof Exp:* Instr physics, Princeton Univ, 54-55; physicist, Gen Atomic Div, Gen Dynamics Corp, 57-65, assoc dir spec nuclear effects lab, 65-69, mgr defense sci dept, Gulf Radiation Technol, 69-70, vpres, Gulf Energy & Environ Systs & mgr, Gulf Radiation Technol Div, 70-73; pres, Intelcom Radiation Technol, 73-74, consult, 74-75; MGR, ELEC APPLN DIV, MISSION RES CORP, 75- *Mem:* Am Phys Soc; fel Inst Elec & Electronics Engrs. *Res:* Radiation effects, including solid state physics, atomic physics, and electronic systems analysis. *Mailing Add:* 1032 Skylark Dr La Jolla CA 92037

VAN LOON, EDWARD JOHN, b Danville, Ill, Dec 3, 11; m 54; c 1. BIOCHEMISTRY. *Educ:* Univ Ill, AB, 36; Rensselaer Polytech Inst, MS, 37, PhD(chem), 39. *Prof Exp:* Res assoc & instr physiol & pharmacol, Albany Med Col, Union NY, 39-43; instr & asst prof biochem, Mich State Univ, 46; asst & assoc prof, Sch Med, Univ Louisville, 46-49; chief, Med Res Lab, Vet Admin Hosp, 49-55; group leader & head biochem sect, Smith Kline & French Labs, 55-67; chief, Spec Pharmacol Animal Lab, Food & Drug Admin, 67-75; RETIRED. *Concurrent Pos:* Mem, Am Bd Clin Chemists. *Mem:* Am Soc Clin Invest; Am Inst Nutrit; Am Soc Pharmacol & Exp Therapeut; Am Chem Soc; Am Soc Biol Chem. *Res:* Clinical biochemistry; intermediary metabolism; biochemical pharmacology and drug metabolism; clinical biochemistry. *Mailing Add:* 1412 Kent St Durham NC 27707

VAN LOON, JON CLEMENT, b Hamilton, Ont, Jan 9, 37; m 61; c 1. GEOLOGY, CHEMISTRY. *Educ:* McMaster Univ, BSc, 59; Univ Toronto, PhD(anal chem), 64. *Prof Exp:* From asst prof to assoc prof anal geochem, 64-77, PROF GEOL, UNIV TORONTO, 77- *Res:* Application of modern analytical methods to the analysis of natural products, with particular emphasis on environmental samples. *Mailing Add:* 38 Paultiel Dr Willowdale ON M2M 3P3 Can

VAN LOPIK, JACK RICHARD, b Holland, Mich, Feb 25, 29; div; c 1. RESEARCH ADMINISTRATION, MARINE SCIENCES. *Educ:* Mich State Univ, BS, 50; La State Univ, MS, 53, PhD(geol), 55. *Prof Exp:* Field investr, Coastal Studies Inst, La State Univ, 51-54, instr geol, 54; geologist, Waterways Exp Sta, Corps Engrs, US Army, 54-57, asst chief & chief geol br, 57-61; res scientist, chief area eval sect & mgr space & environ sci prog, Geosci Opers, Tex Instruments Inc, 61-66, tech requirements dir, 66-68; chmn dept marine sci, 68-74, PROF MARINE SCI & DIR SEA GRANT DEVELOP, LA STATE UNIV, BATON ROUGE, 68-, DEAN, CTR WETLAND RESOURCES, 70- *Concurrent Pos:* Mem, Nat Res Coun Earth Sci Div, Nat Acad Sci-Nat Res Coun, 67-72, chmn panel geog & human & cult resources, Comt Remote Sensing Progs for Earth Resources Surv, 69-; mem, La Adv Comn Coastal & Marine Resources, 71-73, Nat Adv Comt on Oceans & Atmosphere, 78-; mem bd dirs, Gulf South Res Inst, 74-; chmn, Coastal Resources Directorate, US Nat Comt for Man & the Biosphere, US Nat Comn for UN Educ, Sci & Cult Orgn, 75- *Mem:* Fel Geol Soc Am; Am Mgt Asn; Soc Res Adminr; fel AAAS; sr mem Am Astronaut Soc. *Res:* Photogeology and remote sensing; deltaic and arid zone geomorphology and sedimentation; military and engineering geology; terrain analysis and quantification; lunar and earth-orbiting-satellite exploration; coastal zone management. *Mailing Add:* Ctr for Wetland Resources La State Univ Baton Rouge LA 70803

VAN MAANEN, EVERT FLORUS, b Harderwyk, Neth, Sept 17, 18. PHARMACOLOGY. *Educ:* State Univ Utrecht, BS, 38, Phil Drs, 45; Harvard Univ, PhD(pharmacol), 49. *Prof Exp:* From instr to assoc prof, 49-66, PROF PHARMACOL, COL MED, UNIV CINCINNATI, 66- *Concurrent Pos:* Dir biol sci, Wm S Merrell Co Div, Richardson-Merrell, Inc, 55-62. *Mem:* AAAS; Am Soc Pharmacol & Exp Therapeut; Soc Exp Biol & Med. *Res:* Neuromuscular transmission; cholinesterase inhibitors; cardiovascular agents; autonomic drugs; theories of drug action. *Mailing Add:* Dept of Pharmacol Univ Cincinnati Col of Med Cincinnati OH 45267

VANMARCKE, ERIK HECTOR, b Menen, Belg, Aug 6, 41; m 65; c 3. CIVIL ENGINEERING. *Educ:* Cath Univ Louvain, Engr, 65; Univ Del, MS, 67; Mass Inst Technol, PhD(eng), 70. *Prof Exp:* Instr civil eng, 68-69, NSF res grants, 70-81, PROF CIVIL ENG, MASS INST TECHNOL, 69- *Concurrent Pos:* Consult eng. *Honors & Awards:* Raymond C Reese Award, Am Soc Civil Engrs, 75. *Mem:* Am Soc Civil Engrs; Earthquake Eng Res Inst; Am Geophys Union. *Res:* Structural engineering; vibrations induced by wind, earthquakes and water waves; dam safety. *Mailing Add:* Dept of Civil Eng Mass Inst of Technol Cambridge MA 02139

VAN MARTHENS, EDITH, b Vienna, Austria, Nov 17, 40; US citizen. VETERINARY MEDICINE, NUTRITION. *Educ:* Vet Univ, Vienna, DVM, 61. *Prof Exp:* Res assoc physiol & microcirculation, NY Univ, 62-65; SR VET, NUTRIT, UNIV CALIF, LOS ANGELES, 65-, ASST RES VET, NUTRIT & PRENATAL BRAIN DEVELOP, 73- *Mem:* Am Asn Zool Vets; Am Asn Zool Parks & Aquariums. *Res:* Effects on prenatal malnutrition and brain development. *Mailing Add:* Univ of Calif NPI/MR Rm 48-149 760 Westwood Plaza Los Angeles CA 90024

VAN METER, CLARENCE TAYLOR, medicinal chemistry, pharmaceutical chemistry, deceased

VAN METER, DAVID, b Southampton, NY, Mar 27, 19; m 50. APPLIED PHYSICS, INFORMATION SCIENCES. *Educ:* Mass Inst Technol, BS & SM, 43; Harvard Univ, MA, 53, PhD, 55. *Prof Exp:* Mem tech staff, Bell Tel Labs, 43-46; asst prof elec eng, Pa State Univ, 46-52; lab mgr, Melpar, Inc, 55-60 & Litton Systs, Inc, 60-66; chief comput res lab, Electronics Res Ctr, NASA, 66-70; chief, Info Sci Div, 70-77, chief, Systs Develop Div, 78-80, SR TECH STAFF MEM, TRANSP SYSTS CTR, US DEPT TRANSP, 80- *Concurrent Pos:* Lectr, Harvard Univ, 55 & 59; ed, Trans Info Theory, 64-67. *Res:* Computer science; information theory. *Mailing Add:* 10 Byron Boston MA 02108

VAN METER, DONALD EUGENE, b Ashtabula, Ohio, Aug 30, 42; m 64; c 1. SOIL CONSERVATION. *Educ:* Purdue Univ, Lafayette, BS, 64; Mich State Univ, MS, 65; Ind Univ, Bloomington, DEduc, 71. *Prof Exp:* County agt agr, Coop Exten Serv, Purdue Univ, 65-68; PROF NATURAL RESOURCES, BALL STATE UNIV, 69-, CHMN DEPT, 79- *Mem:* Soil Conserv Soc Am; Am Soc Agron. *Res:* Natural resource management; agriculture extension education in developing nations. *Mailing Add:* Dept of Natural Resources Ball State Univ Muncie IN 47306

VAN METER, JAMES P, b Tiffin, Ohio, Dec 8, 36; m 61; c 1. ORGANIC CHEMISTRY. *Educ:* Ohio State Univ, BSc, 58, PhD(chem), 64. *Prof Exp:* RES CHEMIST, EASTMAN KODAK CO, 64- *Res:* Organic synthesis in small ring compounds; heterocyclic chemistry; photochemistry; photographic research; synthesis of liquid crystals. *Mailing Add:* Eastman Kodak Co Res Lab 343 State St Rochester NY 14650

VAN METER, JAMES T(UTTLE), b Northampton, Mass, Mar 27, 25; m 57; c 3. AERONAUTICAL ENGINEERING. *Educ:* Mass Inst Technol, SB, 47, SM, 48, AeroE, 54. *Prof Exp:* Res engr, Cornell Aeronaut Lab, 47, United Aircraft Corp, Conn, 48-52 & Mass Inst Technol, 52-55; sr res engr, 55-57, prin res engr, 57-59, res staff engr, 59-60, res supvr, 60-64, res planning staff engr, 64-65, planning staff engr, 65-68, mgr, US Air Force civil aviation systs & technol requirements, 68-77, mgr avionics planning, 77-79, SR STAFF ENGR, COMMERCIAL AVIATION OPER, AVIONICS DIV, HONEYWELL, INC, 79- *Concurrent Pos:* Lectr, Dept Aeronaut Eng, Univ Minn, 57-58. *Mem:* Inst Navig; Inst Elec & Electronics Engrs; Am Inst Aeronaut & Astronaut; Sigma Xi. *Res:* Business and product planning, including aircraft control, guidance and navigation systems and instrumentation. *Mailing Add:* 4800 Gaywood Dr Minnetonka MN 55343

VAN METER, WAYNE PAUL, b Fresno, Calif, Feb 16, 26; m 48; c 4. INORGANIC CHEMISTRY. *Educ:* Ore State Col, BS, 50, MS, 52; Univ Wash, PhD(inorg chem), 59. *Prof Exp:* Chemist, Hanford Atomic Prod Oper, Gen Elec Co, Wash, 51-56; from asst prof to assoc prof, 59-71, PROF CHEM, UNIV MONT, 71- *Mem:* Am Chem Soc. *Res:* Measurement of trace concentrations of metals in biological systems; development of sample processing techniques and instrumentation for atomic absorption spectrometry. *Mailing Add:* Dept of Chem Univ of Mont Missoula MT 59812

VAN METRE, THOMAS EARLE, JR, b Newport, RI, Jan 11, 23; m 47; c 5. MEDICINE. *Educ:* Harvard Univ, BS, 43, MD, 46; Am Bd Internal Med, dipl, 55. *Prof Exp:* Intern med, Johns Hopkins Hosp, 46-47, asst resident, 47-48, 50 & 51-52, Am Cancer Soc fel, 52-53; asst prof internal med, Sch Med, St Louis Univ, 53-54; from instr to asst prof, 56-70, ASSOC PROF MED, MED SCH, JOHNS HOPKINS UNIV, 70-, PHYSICIAN, JOHNS HOPKINS HOSP, 56-, PHYSICIAN-IN-CHG ADULT ALLERGY CLIN, 66- *Concurrent Pos:* Pvt pract, 54-; mem attend staff, Baltimore City Hosp, 54- & Union Mem Hosp, 59- *Mem:* AMA; Am Fedn Clin Res; Am Col Physicians; Am Acad Allergy (pres, 78); Am Clin & Climat Asn. *Res:* Allergy; effect of corticosteroids on growth; uveitis; asthma. *Mailing Add:* 11 E Chase St Baltimore MD 21202

VAN METTER, RICHARD LAWRENCE, b Yonkers, NY, Mar 8, 49; m 69; c 4. BIOPHYSICS. *Educ:* Manhattan Col, BS, 71; Univ Rochester, PhD(physics), 77. *Prof Exp:* RES PHYSICIST, EASTMAN KODAK RES LAB, 77- *Mem:* Am Phys Soc; Am Soc Photobiol; Soc Photog Sci & Eng; Sigma Xi; Am Asn Physics Teachers. *Res:* Excitation energy transfer in photosynthetic and other biological systems; signal-to-noise propagation in imaging systems particularly related to photographic image structure; molecular spectroscopy. *Mailing Add:* Eastman Kodak Res Lab 2000 Lake Ave Rochester NY 14650

VAN MIDDELEM, CHARLES HENRY, biochemistry, see previous edition

VAN MIDDLESWORTH, LESTER, b Washington, DC, Jan 13, 19; m 48; c 4. PHYSIOLOGY, MEDICINE. *Educ:* Univ Va, BS, 40, MS, 42 & 44; Univ Calif, Berkeley, PhD(physiol), 47; Univ Tenn, MD, 51. *Prof Exp:* Chief chemist, Piedmont Apple Prod Corp, Va, 39-44; res assoc, Radiation Lab & teaching asst physiol, Univ Calif, 44-46; from instr to assoc prof, 46-59, PROF PHYSIOL & BIOPHYS, CTR HEALTH SCI, UNIV TENN, MEMPHIS, 59-, PROF MED, 74- *Concurrent Pos:* Res asst physiol, Univ Va, 42-44; intern, John Gaston Hosp, 51-52; USPHS career res award, 61- *Mem:* Am Chem Soc; Am Physiol Soc; Endocrine Soc; Am Thyroid Asn. *Res:* Vapor phase catalysis; hormone synthesis; carbohydrate metabolism; aviation medicine; anoxia; metabolism of plutonium, radium, iodide, thiocyanate and thyroxine; thyroid physiology; goiter; audiogenic seizures; radioactive fallout. *Mailing Add:* Dept of Physiol & Biophys Univ Tenn Ctr for Health Sci Memphis TN 38163

VAN MIEROP, LODEWYK H S, b Surabaya, Java, Mar 31, 27; US citizen; m 54; c 5. MEDICINE. *Educ:* State Univ Leiden, MD, 52; Am Bd Pediat, cert pediat cardiol. *Prof Exp:* Lectr anat, McGill Univ, 61-62; from asst prof to assoc prof pediat, Albany Med Col, 62-66; assoc prof, 66-68, PROF PEDIAT & PATH, COL MED, UNIV FLA, 68-, GRAD RES PROF, 78- *Concurrent Pos:* NIH res career develop award, 64-73; res assoc, Mt Sinai Hosp, New York, 63-66; mem comt nomenclature of heart, NIH, 67-68; mem southern regional res rev comt, Am Heart Asn, 68-72. *Mem:* Am Pediat Soc; Am Heart Asn; Am Asn Anat; fel Am Acad Pediat; fel Am Col Cardiol. *Res:* Pediatric cardiology; pathology and pathogenesis of congenital heart disease; cardiac embryology. *Mailing Add:* Dept of Pediat Univ of Fla Col of Med Gainesville FL 32601

VANN, DOUGLAS CARROLL, b Coronado, Calif, May 3, 39; m 61; c 1. IMMUNOBIOLOGY. *Educ:* Univ Calif, Berkeley, AB, 60; Univ Calif, Santa Barbara, PhD(biol), 66. *Prof Exp:* Jr scientist, Inter-Am Trop Tuna Comn, 60-62; res assoc immunol, Biol Div, Oak Ridge Nat Lab, 66-68; USPHS training grant, Scripps Clin & Res Found, 68-70; asst prof, 70-73, ASSOC PROF GENETICS, UNIV HAWAII, HONOLULU, 73- *Concurrent Pos:* Prin investr, USPHS res grant, 71-77. *Mem:* AAAS. *Res:* Cellular basis of immune responses. *Mailing Add:* Dept of Genetics Univ of Hawaii Honolulu HI 96822

VANN, ROBERT LEE, b Wake Forest, NC, Mar 17, 22; m 46; c 3. PEDIATRICS, PHARMACEUTICS. *Educ:* Wake Forest Univ, BS, 42; Bowman Gray Sch Med, MD, 45. *Prof Exp:* Intern, Barnes Hosp, St Louis, Mo, 45-46; pvt pract, 48-51; resident pediat, NC Baptist Hosp, 51-53; mem staff, Pvt Diag Clin, Bowman Gray Sch Med, 53-61; pvt pract, 61-68; assoc med develop dir, E R Squibb & Sons, 68-73; clin res dir, 73-79, med dir, 79-81, SR DIR CLIN RES, BEECHAM LABS, 81- *Concurrent Pos:* Assoc clin prof pediat, Col Med, East Tenn State Univ, 77- *Mem:* AMA; Am Acad Pediat; Am Soc Microbiol; Am Soc Clin Pharmacol & Therapeut. *Mailing Add:* Beecham Labs 501 Fifth St Bristol TN 37620

VANN, W(ILLIAM) PENNINGTON, b Belton, Tex, Sept 9, 35; m 62; c 3. CIVIL ENGINEERING. *Educ:* Columbia Univ, BA, 58, BS, 59, MS, 60; Rice Univ, PhD(civil eng), 66. *Prof Exp:* Struct designer civil eng, Walter P Moore, Consult Engr, Tex, 60; asst prof, Rice Univ, 66-72; ASSOC PROF CIVIL ENG, TEX TECH UNIV, 72- *Concurrent Pos:* Mem, Earthquake Eng Res Inst, 67- *Mem:* Am Soc Civil Engrs; Am Concrete Inst; Seismol Soc Am. *Res:* Dynamic response of inelastic structural systems; static and dynamic behavior of inelastic structure, including buckling, energy absorption and failure; mobile homes; wind engineering. *Mailing Add:* Dept of Civil Eng Tex Tech Univ Lubbock TX 79409

VANN, WILLIAM L(ONNIE), b McAlpin, Fla, Sept 21, 23; m 46; c 1. ELECTRICAL ENGINEERING. *Educ:* Univ Fla, BEE, 50. *Prof Exp:* Test engr, Gen Elec Co, 50; assoc engr, 50-55, proj supvr, 58-62, asst group supvr, 62-69, group supvr, 69-72, SR ENGR, APPL PHYSICS LAB, JOHNS HOPKINS UNIV, 55-, STAFF ENGR, 72-, PROJ ENGR, 81- *Mem:* Inst Elec & Electtronics Engrs. *Res:* Microwave and radar development; data acquisition and tracking radars; systems engineering; engineering management. *Mailing Add:* Appl Phys Lab Johns Hopkins Rd Laurel MD 20810

VAN NESS, HENDRICK C(HARLES), b New York, NY, Jan 18, 24; m 50; c 1. CHEMICAL ENGINEERING. *Educ:* Univ Rochester, BS, 44, MS, 46; Yale Univ, DEng, 53. *Prof Exp:* Instr eng, Univ Rochester, 45-47; chem engr, M W Kellogg Co, Pullman, Inc, 47-49; asst prof chem eng, Purdue Univ, 52-56; from asst prof to assoc prof, 56-63, chmn div fluid, chem & thermal processes, 69-74, PROF CHEM ENG, RENSSELAER POLYTECH INST, 63- *Concurrent Pos:* Fulbright lectr, King's Col, Univ Durham, 58-59; vis prof, Univ Calif, Berkeley, 66. *Mem:* Am Chem Soc; Am Inst Chem Engrs. *Res:* Thermodynamics; phase equilibria. *Mailing Add:* Dept of Chem & Environ Eng Rensselaer Polytech Inst Troy NY 12181

VAN NESS, JAMES E(DWARD), b Omaha, Nebr, June 24, 26; m 48; c 4. ELECTRICAL ENGINEERING. *Educ:* Iowa State Col, BS, 49; Northwestern Univ, MS, 51, PhD(elec eng), 54. *Prof Exp:* Asst & res engr, 49-51, lectr elec eng, 52-53, from asst prof to assoc prof, 54-60, dir, Univ

Comput Ctr, 62-65, chmn dept elec eng, 69-72, PROF ELEC ENG & COMPUT SCI, NORTHWESTERN UNIV, EVANSTON, 60- *Concurrent Pos:* Vis assoc prof, Univ Calif, 58-59; vis prof, Mass Inst Technol, 73-74. *Mem:* Fel Inst Elec & Electronics Engrs; Asn Comput Mach. *Res:* Use of digital computers in power system problems; numerical analysis; control systems. *Mailing Add:* Dept of Elec Eng & Comput Sci Northwestern Univ Evanston IL 60201

VAN NESS, JOHN WINSLOW, b McLean Co, Ill, Aug 16, 36; m 64; c 2. STATISTICS. *Educ:* Northwestern Univ, BS, 59; Brown Univ, PhD(appl math), 64. *Prof Exp:* Vis asst prof statist, Stanford Univ, 64-65, actg asst prof, 65-66; asst prof math, Univ Wash, 66-71; assoc prof statist, Carnegie-Mellon Univ, 71-73; assoc prof, 73-75, head, Prog Math Sci, 73-78, PROF, UNIV TEX, DALLAS, 75-, ASSOC DEAN, SCH NATURAL SCI & MATH, 78-, HEAD, PROG MATH SCI, 80- *Mem:* Inst Math Statist; fel Am Statist Asn; Classification Soc. *Res:* Theoretical and applied statistics; biostatistics; multivariate and time series analysis; classification and discriminant analysis; stochastic processes and their applications. *Mailing Add:* Prog in Math Sci Univ of Tex at Dallas PO Box 688 Richardson TX 75080

VAN NESTE, ANDRE, b Brussels, Belg, July 15, 38; Can citizen; m 67; c 3. MATERIALS SCIENCE, METALLURGY. *Educ:* Laval Univ, BSc, 60, DSc(metall), 63. *Prof Exp:* Researcher electron micros, Chem Metall Div, Nat Ctr Sci Res, Paris, 63-65; assoc prof metall, 65-77, PROF METALL, DEPT METALL & VDEAN EDUC, FAC SCI & ENG, LAVAL UNIV, 77- *Concurrent Pos:* Asn Foreign Tech Trainees in France fel, 63-64; Nat Res Coun Can fel, 64-65. *Mem:* Am Soc Metals; Can Inst Mining & Metall; Am Soc Eng Educ. *Res:* Mechanical properties of materials, fatigue, fracture, wear; service failure analysis. *Mailing Add:* Departement Metallurgie Univ Laval Quebec PQ G1K 7P4 Can

VANNICE, MERLIN ALBERT, b Broken Bow, Nebr, Jan 11, 43; m 71. CHEMICAL ENGINEERING, CATALYSIS. *Educ:* Mich State Univ, BS, 64; Stanford Univ, MS, 66, PhD(chem eng), 70. *Prof Exp:* Engr, Dow Chem Co, 66; res engr, Corp Res Labs, Exxon Res & Eng Co, 71-75, sr res engr, 75-76; assoc prof, 76-80, PROF CHEM ENG, PA STATE UNIV, 80- *Concurrent Pos:* Indust fel, Sun Oil Co, Pa, 69-71. *Mem:* Am Chem Soc; Am Inst Chem Engrs; Catalysis Soc NAm; Sigma Xi; Nat Res Soc. *Res:* Adsorption and heterogeneous catalysis, including CO hydrogenation reactions, kinetics, catalyst preparation and characterization, surface diffusion and metal-support interations. *Mailing Add:* Dept Chem Eng Pa State Univ University Park PA 16802

VAN NIEL, CORNELIS BERNARDUS, b Haarlem, Netherlands, Nov 4, 1897; nat US; m 25; c 3. BIOCHEMISTRY. *Educ:* Delft Univ Technol, Chem E, 23, DSc, 28. *Hon Degrees:* DSc, Princeton Univ, 46, Rutgers Univ, 54; LLD, Univ Calif, 68. *Prof Exp:* Conservator, Microbiol Lab, Delft Univ Technol, 24-28; assoc prof microbiol, 28-35, prof, 35-46, Herstein prof biol, 46-63, EMER HERSTEIN PROF BIOL, HOPKINS MARINE STA, STANFORD UNIV, 63- *Concurrent Pos:* Rockefeller fel, 35-36; Guggenheim fel, 46 & 55-56; chmn adv comt biochem, Off Naval Res, 50-53; vis prof, Univ Calif, Santa Cruz, 64-68. *Honors & Awards:* Nat Medal Sci, 64; Emil Christian Hansen Medal, Denmark, 64; Rumford Medal, Am Acad Arts & Sci, 67; Antonie Van Leeuwenhoek Medal, Royal Netherlands Acad Sci, 70. *Mem:* Nat Acad Sci; AAAS; hon mem Am Soc Microbiol (pres, 54); Am Acad Arts & Sci; Fr Soc Microbiol. *Res:* General microbiology; biochemistry of microorganisms; photosynthesis. *Mailing Add:* Camino Del Monte & Santa Fe Carmel CA 93921

VANNIER, WILTON EMILE, b Pasadena, Calif, June 6, 24; m 53; c 2. IMMUNOCHEMISTRY, BIOCHEMISTRY. *Educ:* Univ Calif, San Francisco, MD, 48; Calif Inst Technol, PhD(immunochem), 58. *Prof Exp:* Instr exp med, Sch Pub Health, Univ NC, 51-54; immunochemist, Lab Immunol, Nat Inst Allergy & Infectious Dis, Md, 58-64, head, Immunochem Sect, 64-68; assoc prof biochem, Sch Med, Univ Southern Calif, 68-70; RES MED OFFICER, NAVAL MED RES INST, NAT NAVAL MED CTR, 70- *Concurrent Pos:* Res fel, Calif Inst Technol, 57-60. *Mem:* Fel AAAS; Am Chem Soc; Am Asn Immunol; Am Acad Allergy. *Res:* Parasite immunology; chemistry of antibodies and antigen-antibody reactions. *Mailing Add:* Naval Med Res Inst Nat Naval Med Ctr Bethesda MD 20814

VAN NORMAN, GILDEN RAMON, b Jamestown, NY, Dec 11, 32; m 58. PHOTOGRAPHIC CHEMISTRY, POLYMER CHEMISTRY. *Educ:* Univ Rochester, BS, 54; Mass Inst Technol, PhD(org chem), 57. *Prof Exp:* TECH ASSOC, EASTMAN KODAK CO, 57- *Mem:* AAAS; Am Chem Soc. *Mailing Add:* 520 Churchill Dr Rochester NY 14616

VAN NORMAN, JOHN DONALD, b Jamestown, NY, Sept 11, 34; m 58; c 1. ANALYTICAL CHEMISTRY, CLINICAL CHEMISTRY. *Educ:* Univ Rochester, BS, 55; Rensselaer Polytech Inst, PhD(anal chem), 59. *Prof Exp:* Res assoc chem, Brookhaven Nat Lab, 59-61, from asst chemist to chemist, 61-69; assoc prof, 69-77, PROF CHEM, YOUNGSTOWN STATE UNIV, 77- *Mem:* AAAS; Am Chem Soc; Am Asn Clin Chemists; NY Acad Sci. *Res:* Spectrophotometry and electroanalytical chemistry of bile pigments; radioimmunoassay; atomic absorption. *Mailing Add:* Dept of Chem Youngstown State Univ Youngstown OH 44555

VAN NORMAN, RICHARD WAYNE, b Spencer, Iowa, Mar 12, 23; m 46. PLANT PHYSIOLOGY. *Educ:* Iowa State Teachers Col, BA, 46; Univ Minn, PhD(bot), 50. *Prof Exp:* Asst bot, Univ Minn, 46-49; asst prof, Pa State Univ, 50-55; asst prof exp biol, 55-58, actg head dept, 58-60, assoc prof, 58-65, PROF BIOL, UNIV UTAH, 65- *Concurrent Pos:* Writer, Biol Sci Curriculum Study, 61-63; asst prog dir, Course Content Improv Sect, NSF, 63-64; AID-NSF consult, Gujarat Univ, India, 68 & Ravishankar Univ, India, 69; mem comt examr, Grad Rec Exam Biol Test, 72-82, chmn, 76-82. *Mem:* Fel AAAS; Am Soc Plant Physiologists; Am Inst Biol Sci. *Res:* Photosynthetic pigments; cellular metabolism; biological education. *Mailing Add:* Dept of Biol Univ of Utah Salt Lake City UT 84112

VANNOTE, ROBIN L, b Summit, NJ, Aug 12, 34; m 59; c 4. AQUATIC ECOLOGY. *Educ:* Univ Maine, BS, 57; Mich State Univ, MS, 62, PhD(limnol), 63. *Prof Exp:* Biologist, Water Qual Br, Tenn Valley Authority, 63-65, chief biol sect, 65-66; DIR, STROUD WATER RES CTR, ACAD NATURAL SCI PHILADELPHIA, 66- *Concurrent Pos:* Mem pesticide monitoring subcomt, Fed Comt Pest Control, 64-66; adj prof entom & appl ecol, Univ Del, 74- *Mem:* AAAS; Am Fisheries Soc; Am Soc Limnol & Oceanog; Ecol Soc Am. *Res:* Ecology of streams and rivers; interactions with terrestrial landscapes, production ecology; detrital systems, energy flow and nutrient budgets, geomorphology of streams; effects of channel modifications, drainage, and rural runoff on biotic productivity and system stability; ecology of regulated river systems. *Mailing Add:* Stroud Water Res Ctr Acad Natural Sci RD 1 Box 512 Avondale PA 19311

VAN OERS, WILLEM THEODORUS HENDRICUS, b Amsterdam, Neth, Mar 17, 34; m 60; c 2. NUCLEAR PHYSICS. *Educ:* Univ Amsterdam, PhD(math, physics), 63. *Prof Exp:* From res asst to res assoc, Inst Nuclear Physics Res, Amsterdam, Neth, 57-64; asst res physicist, Cyclotron Lab, Univ Calif, Los Angeles, 64-66, asst prof physics, 66-67; assoc prof, 67-74, PROF PHYSICS, UNIV MAN, 67- *Concurrent Pos:* Vis assoc prof, Univ Calif, Los Angeles, 71-72; vis scientist, Ctr Nuclear Studies, Saclay, 75-76; vis scientist, Tri-Univ-Meson-Facil, Vancouver, 81-82. *Mem:* Am Phys Soc; Can Asn Physicists; NY Acad Sci; Sigma Xi. *Res:* Nuclear reactions induced by various types of particle beams at low and intermediate energies; phenomenological and theoretical analyses of few-nucleon problems; nuclear optical model; symmetries. *Mailing Add:* Dept Physics Univ Man Winnipeg MB R3T 2N2 Can

VANONI, VITO A(UGUST), b Camarillo, Calif, Aug 30, 04; m 34. HYDRAULICS. *Educ:* Calif Inst Technol, BS, 26, MSc, 32, PhD(civil eng, hydraul), 40. *Prof Exp:* Jr struct engr, Bethlehem Steel Corp, 26-28 & 30-31; draftsman, Am Bridge Co, 28-30; from proj supvr to hydraul eng & supvr lab, USDA, 35-47, assoc dir, Hydrodyn Lab, Nat Defense Res Comt, 41-46, from asst prof to prof hydraul, 42-74, EMER PROF HYDRAUL, CALIF INST TECHNOL, 74- *Concurrent Pos:* Consult river probs. *Mem:* Nat Acad Eng; hon mem Am Soc Civil Engrs. *Res:* Sediment transportation; hydraulics of open channels; harbor and coastal engineering. *Mailing Add:* Div Eng & Appl Sci Calif Inst Technol Pasadena CA 91125

VAN ORDEN, HARRIS O, b Smithfield, Utah, Oct 6, 17; m 48; c 1. ORGANIC CHEMISTRY. *Educ:* Utah State Agr Col, BS, 38; Wash State Univ, MS, 42; Mass Inst Technol, PhD(org chem), 51. *Prof Exp:* From asst prof to assoc prof chem, Utah State Agr Col, 46-52; NIH spec fel, Univ Utah, 53; assoc prof, 54-59, actg head dept, 58-59, PROF CHEM, UTAH STATE UNIV, 60- *Mem:* Fel AAAS; Am Chem Soc; Sigma Xi. *Res:* Synthetic organic and bio-organic chemistry; protein sequence studies; synthesis of peptides; enzyme specificity studies. *Mailing Add:* Dept of Chem Utah State Univ Logan UT 84321

VAN ORDEN, LUCAS SCHUYLER, III, b Chicago, Ill, Nov 3, 28; m 53; c 4. NEUROBIOLOGY, PSYCHOPHARMACOLOGY. *Educ:* Northwestern Univ, BS, 50, MS, 52, MD, 56; Yale Univ, PhD(pharmacol), 66. *Prof Exp:* Intern, Harper Hosp, Detroit, 56-57; asst resident surg, Med Ctr, Yale Univ, 61-62; Nat Inst Neurol Dis & Blindness spec fel neuroanat, Dept Anat, Harvard Med Sch, 66-67; from asst prof to assoc prof, 67-73, PROF PHARMACOL, COL MED, UNIV IOWA, 73- *Concurrent Pos:* Resident psychiat, Univ of Iowa, 75-76; dir, Chem Dependency Unit, Ment Health Inst, Mt Pleasant & adj prof pharmacol & psychiat, Univ Iowa Col Med, 78- *Mem:* AMA; Am Med Soc Alcoholism; Am Soc Pharmacol & Exp Therapeut. *Res:* Neuropharmacology; autonomic nervous system fine structure and histochemistry of adrenergic transmitter; quantitative cytochemistry, immunocytochemistry; alcohol and drug abuse. *Mailing Add:* Depts Pharmacol & Psychiat Univ of Iowa Col of Med Iowa City IA 52242

VAN ORDER, ROBERT BRUCE, b Glenvale, Ont, Mar 19, 15; nat US; m 42; c 3. ORGANIC CHEMISTRY. *Educ:* Queen's Univ, Can, BA, 38, MA, 39; NY Univ, PhD(org chem), 42. *Prof Exp:* Asst, NY Univ, 39-42; res org chemist, Stamford Res Labs, Am Cyanamid Co, 42-46, plant chemist, Calco Chem Div, 46-53, asst chief chemist, Org Chem Div, Bound Brook Lab, 53-55 & Mkt Develop Dept, 55-62; tech dir, Pearsall Chem Co, 62-63; mgr sales develop, Am Cyanamid Co, Bound Brook, 63-69, mgr org chem res & develop, Wayne, 69-77 & Bound Brook, 77-80; RETIRED. *Mem:* Fel Am Inst Chemists; Am Chem Soc. *Res:* Structure and synthesis of antibiotics; inorganic pigments and chemicals; dyestuffs and pigment dispersions; market development and sales development of new chemical products. *Mailing Add:* 58 Sycamore Ave Berkeley Heights NJ 07922

VAN OSDALL, THOMAS CLARK, b Ashland, Ohio, July 19, 11; m 39; c 1. INORGANIC CHEMISTRY. *Educ:* Ashland Col, BS, 32; Ohio State Univ, MS, 39. *Hon Degrees:* DSc, Ashland Col, 80. *Prof Exp:* Prin, Hayesville High Sch, 32-36; instr chem & chmn dept sci, Santa Ana Col, 39-41; res chemist, Goodyear Tire & Rubber Co, 43-47; assoc prof chem, Ashland Col, 47-48; instr chem & chmn dept sci, Santa Ana Col, 48-57; chmn dept, 67-77, prof, 57-80, EMER PROF CHEM, ASHLAND COL, 81- *Concurrent Pos:* Guest lectr, Orange Coast Col, 58; lectr art-sci prog, Sussex Univ, 66 & interdisciplinary arts-sci prog, Ashland Col, 66- *Mem:* Am Chem Soc. *Res:* Separation of rare elements; polymerization of synthetic rubber; organosols and plastisols; high vacuum techniques; industrial waste problems; water chemistry and water pollution problems. *Mailing Add:* Dept Chem Ashland Col Ashland OH 44805

VAN OSS, CAREL J, b Amsterdam, Neth, Sept 7, 23; m 51; c 3. IMMUNOCHEMISTRY, PHYSICAL BIOCHEMISTRY. *Educ:* Univ Paris, PhD(phys biochem), 55. *Prof Exp:* Fel colloid chem, Van't Hoff Lab, Univ Utrecht, 55-56; fel phys chem, Ctr Electrophoresis, Sorbonne, 56-57; dir lab phys biochem, Nat Vet Col Alfort, 57-63; asst head dept microbiol, Montefiore Hosp, NY, 63-65; assoc prof biol, Marquette Univ, 66-68; assoc prof, 68-72, PROF MICROBIOL, SCH MED, STATE UNIV NY

BUFFALO, 72-, HEAD IMMUNOCHEM LAB, 68-, ADJ PROF CHEM ENG, 79- *Concurrent Pos:* French Ministry Agr res fel, 55-57; master of res, French Nat Agron Inst, 62-63; consult, Amicon Corp, 64-67; dir serum & plasma depts, Milwaukee Blood Ctr, 65-68; prin investr, USPHS res grant, 66-75; consult, Gen Elec Co, 67; mem consult comt electrophoresis & other chem separation processes in outer space, NASA, 71-; exec ed, Preparative Biochem, 71-, Separation & Purification Methods, 72-, ed, Immunol Commun, 82-; consult mem immunol panel, Diag Prod Adv Comt, Food & Drug Admin, 75- *Mem:* Am Chem Soc; fel Am Inst Chemists; Am Asn Immunologists; Am Soc Microbiol; Reticuloendothelial Soc. *Res:* Membrane separation methods; precipitation in immunochemical, organic and inorganic systems; diffusion; sedimentation; physical surface properties of cells; mechanism of phagocytic engulfment; cell separation methods; van der Waals interactions between cells and/or polymers in liquids; opsonins. *Mailing Add:* Immunochem Lab Dept of Microbiol State Univ of NY Sch of Med Buffalo NY 14214

VAN OSTENBURG, DONALD ORA, b East Grand Rapids, Mich, July 19, 29; m 51; c 2. SOLID STATE PHYSICS. *Educ:* Calvin Col, BS, 51; Mich State Univ, MS, 53, PhD(physics), 56. *Prof Exp:* Assoc physicist, Armour Res Found, Ill Inst Technol, 56-59; from asst physicist to assoc physicist, Argonne Nat Lab, 59-70; PROF PHYSICS, DE PAUL UNIV, 70- *Concurrent Pos:* Pres, Cent States Univ Inc, 81-82. *Mem:* Am Phys Soc; Am Sci Affiliation. *Res:* Static electrification; electron paramagnetic resonance; lattice dynamics; magnetism; nuclear magnetic resonance; electronic structure of metals and alloys; semiconductor devices; biophysics. *Mailing Add:* Dept Physics De Paul Univ 2219 N Kenmore Chicago IL 60614

VAN OVERBEEK, JOHANNES, b Schiedam, Holland, Jan 2, 08; nat US; m 32, 48; c 6. PLANT PHYSIOLOGY, BIOLOGY. *Educ:* State Univ Leiden, BS, 28; Univ Utrecht, MS, 32, PhD(bot), 33. *Hon Degrees:* Dr, Univ Belg, 60. *Prof Exp:* Asst bot, Univ Utrecht, 33-34; asst plant hormones, Calif Inst Technol, 34-37, instr, 37-39, asst prof plant physiol, 39-43; plant physiologist, Inst Trop Agr, PR, 43-44, head dept, 44-46, asst dir, 46-47; chief plant physiologist & head dept plant physiol, Agr Lab, Shell Develop Co, 47-67; head dept, 67-73, prof biol, 67-78, EMER PROF BIOL, TEX A&M UNIV, 78- *Concurrent Pos:* Hon prof, Col Agr, Univ PR, 44-47; ed, Plant Physiol, 67-78; mem, Gov Adv Panel Use of Agr Chem, Tex, 70. *Honors & Awards:* Award, Am Soc Agr Sci, PR, 48. *Mem:* AAAS; Charles Reed Barnes hon mem Am Soc Plant Physiologists; Bot Soc Am; Soc Gen Physiol; Am Inst Biol Sci. *Res:* Plant hormones; physiology of growth; applied plant physiology. *Mailing Add:* Dept of Biol Tex A&M Univ Col of Sci College Station TX 77843

VAN PATTER, DOUGLAS MACPHERSON, b Montreal, Que, July 4, 23; m 50; c 4. NUCLEAR PHYSICS. *Educ:* Queen's Univ, Can, BSc, 45; Mass Inst Technol, PhD(physics), 49. *Prof Exp:* Jr physicist, Nat Res Coun Can, 45-46; asst physics, Mass Inst Technol, 46-49, res assoc, 49-52; res assoc, Univ Minn, 52, asst prof, 52-54; physicist, Bartol Res Found, Franklin Inst, 54-76; BARTOL PROF PHYSICS & BARTOL RES FOUND, UNIV DEL, 76- *Concurrent Pos:* Chmn subcomt nuclear constants, Nat Acad Sci-Nat Res Coun, 59-64; vis prof, Inst Nuclear Physics, Univ Frankfurt, 72. *Mem:* Fel Am Phys Soc; AAAS; Meteoritical Soc. *Res:* Nuclear reactions using electrostatic accelerators; proton microprobe; elemental compositions using induced x-rays of tektites and meteorites. *Mailing Add:* Bartol Res Found Univ Del Newark DE 19711

VANPEE, MARCEL, b Hasselt, Belg, Dec 4, 16; US citizen; m 48; c 3. PHYSICAL CHEMISTRY. *Educ:* Cath Univ Louvain, BS, MS & PhD(phys chem), 40, Agrege de l'Enseignement Superieur, 56. *Prof Exp:* Nat Res fel radio & photochem, Nat Found Sci Res, Belg, 40-45; head lab sci res, Nat Inst Mines, Belg, 46-56; prof physics, Univ Leopoldville, Congo, 56-57; supvry chemist, US Bur Mines, Pa, 57-60; sr scientist, Reaction Motor Div, Thiokol Chem Corp, 60-68; prof chem eng, Univ Mass, Amherst, 68-80. *Concurrent Pos:* Lectr & researcher, Cath Univ Louvain, 40-45; mem, Nat Found Sci Res, Belg, 40-; res fel, Univ Minn, Minneapolis, 48; staff physicist, Edsel B Ford Inst, Mich, 50. *Honors & Awards:* Awards, Prix Jean Stass, 40, Prix Louis Empain, Belg Acad Sci, 43 & Prix Frederic Swartz, 54. *Mem:* Combustion Inst; Am Inst Aeronaut & Astronaut. *Res:* Radiochemistry; photochemistry; kinetics of combustion reactions; cool flames; ignition; flame spectroscopy and structure; high energy fuel and oxidizers; rocket exhaust radiation; hypergolic ignition; atomic and chemiluminescent reactions; reentry observables. *Mailing Add:* 151 Rolling Ridge Rd Amherst MA 01002

VAN PELT, ARNOLD FRANCIS, JR, b Orange, NJ, Sept 24, 24; m 47; c 2. ECOLOGY. *Educ:* Swarthmore Col, BA, 45; Univ Fla, MS, 47, PhD(biol), 50. *Prof Exp:* Assoc prof biol, Appalachian State Teachers Col, 50-54; prof, Tusculum Col, 54-57, prof biol & chem, 57-63; prof biol, 63-80, chmn, Dept Sci & Math, 64-71, MOORE PROF BIOL, GREENSBORO COL, 81-, DIR, ALLIED HEALTH PROGS, 75- *Concurrent Pos:* Sewell grant, Highlands Biol Sta, 53-54; res grants, 53-78; NSF grants, 55-56 & 62; consult, Univ Ga ecol team, Savannah River Plant, AEC, 60, Oak Ridge Nat Lab, Biol Div, 69-70, 73; mem conf plant biochem, Inst Paper Chem, 61; Piedmont Univ Ctr grants, 64-67, 71 & 72; Res Corp Brown-Hazen Fund grant, 65-67; mem radiation biol conf, Oak Ridge Inst Nuclear Studies, 65; mem conf molecular genetics, S W Ctr Advan Studies, 68; Savannah River Ecol Lab, Ecol of Ants, 74, 76-78; Burroughs-Wellcome grant, 79. *Mem:* AAAS; Sigma Xi; Entom Soc Am; Asn Southwestern Naturalists. *Res:* Ecology of mountain ants; mouse genetics; guinea pig leukemia; nest relocation in harvester ants. *Mailing Add:* Dept Biol Greensboro Col Greensboro NC 27420

VAN PELT, RICHARD W(ARREN), b Chicago, Ill, Dec 22, 33; c 3. MECHANICAL ENGINEERING, SERVO SYSTEMS. *Educ:* Stanford Univ, BS, 55; Univ Ill, MS, 60; Case Inst Technol, PhD(mech eng), 65. *Prof Exp:* Sr engr, Systs Develop Div, IBM Corp, 65-78; ADV ENGR, TAPE DIV, STORAGE TECHNOL CORP, 78- *Mem:* Instrument Soc Am; Inst Elec & Electronics Engrs. *Res:* Numerical control, development of special purpose computers for process control and for real time control of fluid and electric servo systems; simulation and analysis of dynamics of electromechanical systems. *Mailing Add:* 1315 Meadow Ave Boulder CO 80302

VAN PELT, ROLLO WINSLOW, JR, b Chicago, Ill, Dec 14, 29; m 54; c 2. PATHOLOGY. *Educ:* Wash State Univ, BA, 54, DVM, 56; Mich State Univ, MS, 61, PhD(path), 65; Am Col Vet Pathologists, dipl, 65. *Prof Exp:* Vet, Rose City Vet Hosp, Ore, 56-57, Tigard Vet Hosp, 57 & Willamette Vet Hosp, 57-59; res asst arthrology, Mich State Univ, 59-60, res assoc, 60-62, Nat Inst Arthritis & Metab Dis fel, 62-64, spec fel, 64-65, from asst prof to assoc prof path, 65-70; vis assoc prof zoophysiol & path, Inst Arctic Biol, Univ Alaska, Fairbanks, 70-71, assoc prof zoophysiol & path, 71-78; CHIEF OF STAFF & PATHOLOGIST, ALASKA VET MED & SURG CLINIC, 78- *Concurrent Pos:* Upjohn Co grant-in-aid, 62-64; All Univ res grant, Mich State Univ, 63-65. *Mem:* Am Vet Med Asn; Am Col Vet Pathologists; Am Vet Radiol Soc; Am Soc Vet Clin Path; Sigma Xi. *Mailing Add:* Alaska Vet Med & Surg Clinic Star Rte Box 31095 Fairbanks AK 99701

VAN PELT, WESLEY RICHARD, b Passaic, NJ, Oct 17, 43; m 65; c 1. HEALTH PHYSICS, INDUSTRIAL HYGIENE. *Educ:* Rutgers Univ, New Brunswick, BA, 65, MS, 66; NY Univ, PhD(nuclear eng), 71; Am Bd Health Physics, cert, 73, Am Bd Indust Hygiene, 76. *Prof Exp:* Asst res scientist aerosol physics, Med Ctr, NY Univ, 67-71; environ scientist, Environ Analysts, Inc, NY, 71-72; industrial hygienist, Radiation Safety Off, 72-77, asst mgr safety & indust hygiene, 77-80, MGR SAFETY & INDUST HYGIENE, HOFFMANN-LA ROCHE INC, 80- *Concurrent Pos:* Consult, NJ Comn Radiation Protection, 76-77 & mem, NJ X-ray Technician Bd Examnrs, 78- & NJ Panel Sci Adv, 81- *Mem:* Sigma Xi; Health Physics Soc; Am Indust Hyg Asn; NY Acad Sci; AAAS. *Res:* Applied health physics; radiation protection program development; interaction of airborne radioactivity with natural aerosols; measurement and study of the natural ionizing radiation background. *Mailing Add:* 340 Kingsland St Hoffmann-La Roche Inc Nutley NJ 07110

VAN PERNIS, PAUL ANTON, b Owyhee, Nev, Sept 7, 14; m 39; c 8. MEDICINE. *Educ:* Hope Col, AB, 35; Rush Med Col, MD, 39; Am Bd Path, dipl, 46. *Prof Exp:* Intern, St Mary's Hosp, Grand Rapids, Mich, 39-40; resident, St Luke's Hosp, Chicago, Ill, 40-42; dir labs, Butterworth Hosp, Grand Rapids, 46-51; instr path, Sch Med, Univ Ill, 51-53, clin asst prof, 53-64; dir labs, Swedish-Am Hosp, Ill, 59-72; asst dir, Dept Grad Med Educ, Am Med Asn, 72-78; JOINT COMT, ACCREDITED HOSPS, 78- *Concurrent Pos:* Instr, Univ Chicago, 40-41; Borland fel, St Luke's Hosp, Chicago, Ill, 40-42; mem, Governor's Adv Comt Blood Banks & Clin Labs, Ill State Health Dept. *Honors & Awards:* Foster Welfare Found Prize, 53-64. *Mem:* AMA; fel Am Col Physicians. *Res:* health care hospitals; blood banking; diagnostic radioisotopes. *Mailing Add:* 240 Longfellow Dr Wheaton IL 60187

VAN PILSUM, JOHN FRANKLIN, b Prairie City, Iowa, Jan 28, 22; m 58; c 6. BIOCHEMISTRY. *Educ:* Univ Iowa, BS, 43, PhD, 49. *Prof Exp:* Instr biochem, Long Island Col Med, 49-51; asst prof, Univ Utah, 51-54; from asst prof to assoc prof, 54-63, PROF BIOCHEM, MED SCH, UNIV MINN, MINNEAPOLIS, 71- *Mem:* Am Soc Biol Chemists; Am Inst Nutrit. *Res:* Guanidinium compound metabolism. *Mailing Add:* Dept Biochem 227 Millard Hall Univ Minn Col of Med Sci Minneapolis MN 55455

VAN POOLEN, LAMBERT JOHN, b Detroit, Mich, Apr 20, 39; m 62; c 2. MECHANICAL ENGINEERING. *Educ:* Calvin Col, BS, 64; Ill Inst Technol, BSME, 64, MSME, 65, PhD(mech & aerospace eng), 69. *Prof Exp:* PROF ENG, CALVIN COL, 69- *Mem:* AAAS; Am Soc Eng Educ. *Res:* Thermodynamics; heat transfer; management; decision making; environmental studies; general engineering; thermodynamic properties of coexistence data. *Mailing Add:* Dept Eng Calvin Col Grand Rapids MI 49506

VAN POOLLEN, H(ENDRIK) K(AREL), b Hague, Neth, May 10, 27; m 51; c 5. MINING ENGINEERING. *Educ:* Delft Univ, BSc, 48; Colo Sch Mines, MSc, 50, DSc, 55. *Prof Exp:* Reservoir engr, Standard Vacuum Petrol Co, Indonesia, 51-54; reservoir supvr, Halliburton Oil Well Cementing Co, Okla, 55-58; res engr, Ohio Oil Co, 58-66, sr res engr, Marathon Oil Co, 66-69; PRES, H K VAN POOLLEN & ASSOCS, 69- *Concurrent Pos:* Lectr, Colo Sch Mines; consult groundwater, Colo State Univ; consult earthquakes, US Corps Engrs. *Mem:* Am Inst Mining, Metall & Petrol Engrs; Neth Royal Inst Eng. *Res:* Petroleum production; reservoir problems. *Mailing Add:* H K Van Poollen & Assocs 1100 W Littleton Rd Littleton CO 80120

VANPRAAGH, RICHARD, b Ont, Can, Apr 11, 30; m 62; c 3. PEDIATRIC CARDIOLOGY, PEDIATRIC CARDIAC PATHOLOGY. *Educ:* Univ Toronto, MD, 54. *Prof Exp:* Asst prof pediat, Sch Med, Northwestern Univ, 65; Clin assoc path, 65-67, asst clin prof, 67-70, assoc prof, 70-73, PROF PATH & EMBRYOL, HARVARD MED SCH, 74- *Concurrent Pos:* Asst dir, Congenital Heart Dis Res & Training Ctr, Hektoem Inst Med Res, Chicago, 63-65; dir cardiac path & embryol & res assoc, Med Ctr, Children's Hosp, 65- *Honors & Awards:* Morgani lectr, Univ Padova, Italy, 73; Haile Selassie lectr, Nat Heart Hosp, London, 73. *Mem:* Fel Am Col Cardiol. *Res:* Correlation of clinical, pathologic, embryologic and etiologic findings concerning congenital heart disease, in order to improve diagnostic accuracy and surgical success; description of newly recognized forms of congenital heart disease; new surgical operations; causes of heart disease in infants and children. *Mailing Add:* Harvard Med Sch 300 Longwood Ave Boston MA 02115

VAN PUTTEN, JAMES D, JR, b Grand Rapids, Mich, Apr 14, 34; m 59; c 2. NUCLEAR PHYSICS. *Educ:* Hope Col, AB, 55; Univ Mich, AM, 57, PhD(physics), 60. *Prof Exp:* Instr physics, Univ Mich, 60-61; NATO fel, Europ Orgn Nuclear Res, Geneva, 61-62; asst prof, Calif Inst Technol, 62-67; assoc prof, 67-70, PROF PHYSICS, HOPE COL, 70-, CHMN DEPT, 75- *Concurrent Pos:* Consult, Electro-Optical Systs, 63-67, Teledyne Corp, 67-70, Donnelly Mirrors, 67- & Maes, Inc, 68- *Mem:* AAAS; Am Phys Soc. *Res:* Bubble chambers; counter and spark chamber techniques; satellite bourn space physics experiments; nuclear charge structure; use of microcomputers in process control. *Mailing Add:* Dept of Physics Hope Col Holland MI 49423

VAN RAALTE, CHARLENE D, b Springfield, Mass, Oct 29, 47; m 71. BIOLOGY, ECOLOGY. *Educ:* Skidmore Col, BA, 69; Boston Univ, PhD(marine biol), 75. *Prof Exp:* Fel estuarine ecol, Dalhousie Univ, 75-77; ASST PROF ECOL, HAMPSHIRE COL, 77- *Mem:* Am Soc Limnol & Oceanog; Am Women Sci; Ecol Soc Am; AAAS. *Res:* Salt marsh ecology, riverine marsh ecology, nitrogen fixation, aquaculture. *Mailing Add:* Sch of Natural Sci Hampshire Col Amherst MA 01102

VAN RAALTE, JOHN A, b Copenhagen, Denmark, Apr 10, 38; US Citizen; m 63; c 2. RESEARCH ADMINISTRATION. *Educ:* Mass Inst Technol, SB & SM, 60, EE, 62, PhD(solid state physics, elec eng), 64. *Prof Exp:* Res asst lab insulation res, Mass Inst Technol, 60-64; mem tech staff, 64-70, head displays & device concepts, 70-79, HEAD VIDEO DISC REC & PLAYBACK RES, RCA RES LABS, 79- *Mem:* Sr mem Inst Elec & Electronics Engrs; Am Phys Soc; fel Soc Info Display (secy, 81-82, treas, 81-). *Res:* Materials; dielectrics; electro-optic materials; lasers; displays; video disc. *Mailing Add:* RCA Res Labs Princeton NJ 08540

VAN REEN, ROBERT, b Paterson, NJ, June 12, 21. BIOCHEMISTRY. *Educ:* NJ State Teachers Col, Montclair, AB, 43; Rutgers Univ, PhD(biochem), 49. *Prof Exp:* Assoc biochemist, Brookhaven Nat Lab, 49-51; res assoc, McCollum-Pratt Inst, Johns Hopkins Univ, 51-53, asst prof biol, 53-56; supv chemist & assoc head dent div, Naval Med Res Inst, 56-61, head nutrit biochem div, 61-70; chmn dept, 70-80, PROF FOOD SCI & HUMAN NUTRIT, UNIV HAWAII, HONOLULU, 70- *Honors & Awards:* McLester Award, Asn Mil Surgeons of US, 59. *Mem:* Am Dietetic Asn; Soc Nutrit Educ; Am Soc Biol Chemists; Inst Food Technologists; Am Inst Nutrit. *Res:* Mammalian and avian nutrition; requirements and functions of vitamins and trace elements; interrelationships between trace elements and enzyme systems; experimental dental caries; metabolism in calcified tissues; nutrition and urolithiasis. *Mailing Add:* Dept of Food & Nutrit Sci Univ of Hawaii Honolulu HI 96822

VAN REMOORTERE, EMILE C, b Herstal, Belg, July 5, 21; m 48; c 3. CARDIOVASCULAR PHYSIOLOGY, PHARMACOLOGY. *Educ:* State Univ Liege, BNatural & MedSci, 41, DrMed, 45. *Prof Exp:* Asst physiopath, State Univ Liege, 48-54, assoc, 54-57; prof physiol, State Univ Belg Congo, 57-63, dean Med Sch, 59-60; head dept cardiovasc pharmacol, Belg Chem Union, Brussels, 63-69; PROF PHARMACOL, SCH MED, UNIV NEV, RENO, 70- *Concurrent Pos:* Belg-Am Educ Found fel, Cardiovasc Dept, Michael Reese Hosp, Chicago, 46-48. *Res:* Cardiac electrophysiology; general electrocardiography. *Mailing Add:* Sch Med Univ of Nev Reno NV 89557

VAN RENSBURG, WILLEM CORNELIUS JAMSE, b SAfrica, Nov 28, 38; m 62; c 3. APPLIED GEOLOGY. *Educ:* Univ Pretoria, BSc, 61, MSc, 63; Univ Wis, PhD(geol), 65. *Prof Exp:* Sr geologist, SAfrica Geol Surv, 60-67; dep dir, SAfrica Nat Dept Planning, 67-73; head, Econ & Corting Div, Nat Inst Metall, 73-75; tech dir, SAfrica Minerals Bur, 79-81; assoc dir, Bur Econ Geol, 79-81, PROF GEOL & PETROL ENG, UNIV TEX, 81- *Concurrent Pos:* Commissioner, Pres Comn Conserv SAfrica's Coal Resources, 70-75; B P Prof, Rand Afrikaans Univ, 76-78; dir, Tex Mining & Mineral Resources Res Inst & Coal Res Consortium, Tex Univ, 79-81. *Mem:* Soc Econ Geologists; SAfrican Coal Processing Soc. *Res:* Strategic minerals; evaluation of coal resources; international coal trade. *Mailing Add:* 7619 Rockpoint Dr Austin TX 78731

VAN REUTH, E(DWARD) C(HARLES), metal physics, materials engineering, see previous edition

VAN RHEENEN, VERLAN H, b Oskaloosa, Iowa, Feb 15, 39; m 62; c 2. ORGANIC CHEMISTRY. *Educ:* Cent Col, Iowa, BA, 61; Univ Wis, PhD(org chem), 66. *Prof Exp:* SR SCIENTIST, UPJOHN CO, 66- *Mem:* Am Chem Soc. *Res:* Total synthesis of natural products; new synthetic methods; steroid chemistry; prostaglandin synthesis. *Mailing Add:* 2112 Vanderbilt Rd Kalamazoo MI 49002

VAN RIJ, WILLEM IDANIEL, b Brielle, Neth, Apr 19, 42; US citizen; m 68; c 2. COMPUTER SCIENCES, PLASMA PHYSICS. *Educ:* Univ Auckland, BS, 64, MS, 66; Fla State Univ, PhD(physics), 70. *Prof Exp:* Res assoc theoret nuclear physics, Brookhaven Nat Lab, 70-72 & Univ Wash, 72-74; COMPUT PHYSICIST, OAK RIDGE NAT LAB, 74- *Mem:* Am Phys Soc. *Res:* Computer simulations of plasmas for controlled thermonuclear research. *Mailing Add:* 7820 Castlecomb Rd Powell TN 37849

VAN RIPER, CHARLES, III, b New York, NY, Sept 24, 43; m 77; c 2. ORNITHOLOGY. *Educ:* Colo State Univ, BS, 66, MEd, 67; Univ Hawaii, PhD(zool), 78. *Prof Exp:* Teacher sci, Hawaii Prep Acad, 69-72; res & teaching asst zool, Univ Hawaii, 72-75; wildlife biologist avian censuses, US Fish & Wildlife Serv, 75-76; res biologist avian dis, Avian Dis Lab, Univ Hawaii, 77-79; UNIT LEADER, CALIF POLYTECH STATE UNIV/UNIV CALIF, 79- *Concurrent Pos:* Mem, Endangered Species Recovery Team, US Fish & Wildlife Serv, 74-; res grants, Ctr Field Res & Earthwatch, 78-80 & Nat Geog, 80-81; adj asst prof, Dept Zool, Univ Calif, Davis, 80- *Mem:* Assoc mem Sigma Xi; Am Ornithologists Union; Wilson Ornith Soc; Am Soc Parasitologists; Soc Am Naturalists. *Res:* Population biology and life history of bird species; avian diseases; endangered bird species. *Mailing Add:* Univ Calif Davis CA 96716

VAN RIPER, GORDON EVERETT, b Flat Rock, Mich, Dec 7, 17; m 43; c 1. AGRONOMY. *Educ:* Mich State Univ, BS, 55; Univ Wis, MS, 57, PhD(agron), 58. *Prof Exp:* From asst prof to assoc prof agron, Univ Nebr, 58-64; mgr, Dept Agron, Deere & Co, 64-69, mgr, Dept Res Coord, 69-73; pres, Jay Dee Equip, Inc, 73-81; CONSULT, 81- *Concurrent Pos:* Vpres, Agr Res Inst, 71-72; pres, Am Forage & Grassland Coun, 72. *Mem:* Am Soc Agron; Crop Sci Soc Am. *Res:* Crop physiology. *Mailing Add:* Jay Dee Equip Inc Rte 2 Kewanee IL 61443

VAN RIPER, KENNETH ALAN, b New Brunswick, NJ, Feb 7, 49. ASTROPHYSICS, PHYSICS. *Educ:* Cornell Univ, AB, 70; Univ Pa, PhD(physics), 76. *Prof Exp:* Res assoc, Enrico Fermi Inst, Univ Chicago, 76-78; res assoc astrophys, dept physics, Univ Ill, Urbana, 78-80; WITH LOS ALAMOS NAT LAB, 80- *Mem:* Am Phys Soc; Am Astron Soc; Sigma Xi. *Res:* Stellar collapse and explosion; supernovae; neutrino astrophysics; neutron star formation and evolution; dense, hot matter. *Mailing Add:* Los Alamos Nat Lab PO Box 1663 Los Alamos NM 87545

VAN ROGGEN, AREND, b Nijmegen, Neth, Jan 2, 28; m 52; c 1. ELECTRODYNAMICS, COMPUTER SCIENCE. *Educ:* State Univ Leiden, Drs(phys chem), 53; Duke Univ, PhD(physics), 56. *Prof Exp:* Asst, Lab Phys Chem, State Univ Leiden, 48-54, sci clerk, 56; asst physics, Duke Univ, 54-56; from res physicist to sr res physicist, E I Du Pont De Nemours & Co, Inc, 56-72, sr res specialist, 72-75, res assoc, 75-81; CONSULT, 82- *Concurrent Pos:* Mem conf elec insulation and dielectric phenomena, Nat Acad Sci-Nat Res Coun; ed, Inst Elec & Electronic Engrs Elec Insulation Soc Transactions on Elec Insulation, 77-; secy, Conf Elec INsulation & Diaelec Phenomena, 80-81, vchmn/treas, 82-83. *Mem:* Am Phys Soc; Am Soc Testing & Mat; Inst Elec & Electronic Engrs; Elec Insulation Soc; NY Acad Sci. *Res:* Electronic and magnetic structure of matter; paramagnetic resonance; dielectrics; physics instrumentation; interaction of electric fields and materials; computational aspects of above. *Mailing Add:* RD2 Kennett Square Wilmington PA 19348

VAN ROOSBROECK, WILLY WERNER, b Antwerp, Belg, Aug 10, 13; nat US; m 45. SEMICONDUCTORS. *Educ:* Columbia Univ, AB, 34, MA, 37. *Prof Exp:* Res physicist, 37-78, CONSULT, BELL LABS, 78- *Mem:* AAAS; fel Am Phys Soc; NY Acad Sci. *Res:* Mathematical physics of semiconductors; theory of current-carrier injection and transport and of amorphous and relaxation semiconductors; rectification, trapping, recombination, radiation, high-field, space-charge and switching effects. *Mailing Add:* 19 Whittredge Rd Summit NJ 07901

VAN ROSSUM, GEORGE DONALD VICTOR, b London, Eng, Dec 13, 31; m 59; c 4. CELL PHYSIOLOGY, BIOCHEMICAL PHARMACOLOGY. *Educ:* Oxford Univ, MA, 59, DPhil(biochem), 60. *Prof Exp:* NATO fel physiol chem, Univ Amsterdam, 60-62; NIH fel, Johnson Res Found, Univ Pa, 62-63, res assoc phys biochem, Sch Med, 63-64; reader biochem, Christian Med Col, Vellore, India, 65-67; vis asst prof phys biochem, Johnson Res Found, Sch Med, Univ Pa, 67-69; actg chmn dept, 73-75, PROF PHARMACOL, SCH MED, TEMPLE UNIV, 69- *Concurrent Pos:* NATO vis prof, Inst Gen Path, Cath Univ, Rome, 71. *Mem:* Brit Biochem Soc; Am Soc Biol Chemists; Am Soc Pharmacol & Exp Therapeut. *Res:* Ion and water transport; tissue electrolytes in cancer; control of energy metabolism. *Mailing Add:* Dept of Pharmacol Temple Univ Sch of Med Philadelphia PA 19140

VAN RYSWYK, ALBERT LEONARD, b Castor, Alta, May 10, 28; m 58; c 2. SOIL FERTILITY, SOIL MORPHOLOGY. *Educ:* Univ BC, BS, 50, MSc, 55; Wash State Univ, PhD(soils), 69. *Prof Exp:* Soil surveyor, Doukhobor Lands, Univ BC, 50-54 & Soil Surv Br, BC Dept Agr, 54-58; SOILS RES RANGELANDS, RES BR, CAN DEPT AGR, 58- *Concurrent Pos:* Mem, Can Comt Soil Fertility, 75-77. *Mem:* Can Soc Soil Sci; Int Soc Soil Sci; Soil Sci Soc Am; Agr Inst Can; Soc Range Mgt. *Res:* Soil-test calibration for yield response of forage crops grown on grasslands, wetlands and forested lands; and under irrigation; soil moisture and vegetation relationships affecting yield of rangeland grasses; soil genesis. *Mailing Add:* Res Sta Agr Can 3015 Ord Rd Kamloops BC V2B 8A7 Can

VAN RYZIN, JOHN R, b Milwaukee, Wis, May 5, 35; div; c 4. MATHEMATICAL STATISTICS, BIOSTATISTICS. *Educ:* Marquette Univ, BS, 57, MS, 59; Mich State Univ, PhD(statist), 64. *Prof Exp:* Instr statist, Mich State Univ, 62-63; asst mathematician, Argonne Nat Lab, 63-66; res assoc statist, Stanford Univ, 66-67; assoc prof math, Univ Wis-Milwaukee, 67-69; assoc prof statist, Univ Wis-Madison, 69-73, prof, 73-79; PROF MATH STATIST & BIOSTATIST, COLUMBIA UNIV, 80- *Concurrent Pos:* NSF grant, Stanford Univ, 66-67. *Mem:* Fel Inst Math Statist; fel Am Statist Asn; fel Royal Statist Soc; Int Asn Statist in Phys Sci; Biometric Soc. *Res:* Inference procedures in statistics; empirical Bayes theory; decision theory; classification and pattern recognition procedures; survival analysis; risk assessment methodology. *Mailing Add:* Dept Math Statist Columbia Univ New York NY 10027

VAN RYZIN, MARTINA, b Appleton, Wis, June 10, 23. HISTORY OF SCIENCE, MATHEMATICS. *Educ:* Silver Lake Col, Wis, BA, 46; Marquette Univ, MS, 56; Univ Wis, PhD(hist of sci), 60. *Prof Exp:* Head dept math, 57-70, from instr to assoc prof math, 60-69, PROF MATH, SILVER LAKE COL, 69-, ACAD DEAN, 70- *Mem:* Math Asn Am; Hist Sci Soc. *Res:* History of mathematics, especially Medieval period; Arabic-Latin tradition of Euclid's elements in the 12th century. *Mailing Add:* Off of the Acad Dean Silver Lake Col Manitowoc WI 54220

VAN SAMBEEK, JEROME WILLIAM, b Milbank, SDak, Aug 1, 47; m 72; c 3. PLANT PHYSIOLOGY. *Educ:* SDak State Univ, BS, 69; Washington Univ, PhD(plant physiol), 75. *Prof Exp:* Fel plant path, Univ Mo, 75; res plant physiologist, Southern Forest Exp Sta, La, 75-79, RES PLANT PHYSIOLOGIST, NORTH CENT FOREST EXP STA, ILL, 79- *Mem:* Am Soc Plant Physiologists; Plant Growth Regulator Soc Am. *Res:* Stress physiology of higher plants in relationship to wounding; host-pathogen and host-insect interactions. *Mailing Add:* NCent Forest Exp Sta Southern Ill Univ Carbondale IL 62901

VAN SANT, JAMES HURLEY, JR, b Ashland, Ohio, Jan 16, 33; m 60; c 2. MECHANICAL ENGINEERING. *Educ:* Univ Idaho, BS, 56, MS, 60; Ore State Univ, PhD(mech eng), 64. *Prof Exp:* Asst flight test engr, Test Div, Douglas Aircraft Co, Calif, 56-57; instr mech eng, Univ Idaho, 57-59; res staff assoc heat transfer & fluid mech res, Gen Atomic Div, Gen Dynamics Corp, Calif, 59-61; res asst, Eng Exp Sta, Ore State Univ, 62-64; mech engr, Heat

Transfer Res, Lawrence Livermore Lab, Univ Calif, 64-71; sr researcher, Hydro Que Inst Res, Can, 71-78; RES & DEVELOP ENGR, LAWRENCE LIVERMORE NAT LAB, UNIV CALIF, 78- *Concurrent Pos:* Guest prof, Univ Que. *Mem:* Am Soc Mech Engrs. *Res:* Heat transfer and fluid mechanics; free and forced flow; conduction; evaporation; thermal properties; high temperature and cryogenic systems. *Mailing Add:* Lawrence Livermore Nat Lab Magnetic Fusion Eng Div Livermore CA 94550

VAN SAUN, WILLIAM ARTHUR, b Ashland, Pa, Dec 23, 46; m 69; c 3. ORGANIC CHEMISTRY, PESTICIDE CHEMISTRY. *Educ:* Ursinus Col, BS, 68; Villanova Univ, PhD(chem), 75. *Prof Exp:* Chemist med chem, Merck, Sharp & Dohme Res Labs, 68-72; res chemist pesticide chem, 75-79, res chemist, 79-80, MGR ORG SYNTHESIS, AGR CHEM GROUP, FMC CORP, 80- *Concurrent Pos:* Adj asst prof, Mercer Co Community Col, 78-; vis lectr org chem, Rider Col, 79. *Mem:* Am Chem Soc. *Res:* Organic synthesis, pesticides, quantitative structure-activity relationships, organosulfur chemistry; plant regulator chemistry. *Mailing Add:* FMC Corp PO Box 8 Princeton NJ 08540

VAN SCHAACK, EVA BLANCHE, botany, deceased

VAN SCHAIK, PETER HENDRIK, b Arnhem, Neth, Apr 18, 27; US citizen; m 54; c 5. PLANT BREEDING. *Educ:* Ont Agr Col, Univ Guelph, BSA, 52; Univ Toronto, MSA, 54; Purdue Univ, PhD(plant breeding), 56. *Prof Exp:* Res agronomist cotton, Agr Res Serv, USDA, Brawley, Calif, 57-64, coord res agronomist food legumes, Tehran, Iran & New Delhi, India, 64-70, res agronomist peanut res, Holland, Va, 70-72, asst area dir, 72-80, ASSOC AREA DIR, AGR RES SERV, USDA, FRESNO, CALIF, 80- *Concurrent Pos:* Consult, Ford Found, 70, Rockefeller Found, 70 & Experience Inc, 71, 76. *Mem:* Am Soc Agron. *Res:* Crop breeding; agronomy; foreign development; tropical agriculture. *Mailing Add:* Agr Res Serv USDA PO Box 8143 Fresno CA 93747

VAN SCHILFGAARDE, JAN, b The Hague, Netherlands, Feb 7, 29; nat US; m 51; c 3. AGRICULTURAL ENGINEERING. *Educ:* Iowa State Col, BS, 49, MS, 50, PhD(agr eng, soil physics), 54. *Prof Exp:* Instr & assoc agr eng, Iowa State Col, 49-54; from asst prof to prof agr eng, NC State Col, 54-64; chief water mgt engr, Soil & Water Conserv Div, Agr Res Serv, 64-67, assoc dir, 67-71, dir, 71-72, DIR, US SALINITY LAB, USDA, 72- *Concurrent Pos:* Vis prof, Ohio State Univ, 62; adj prof soils, Univ Calif, Riverside, 74- *Honors & Awards:* John Deere Medal, Am Soc Agr Engrs, 77. *Mem:* Am Soc Agr Engrs; Am Soc Civil Engrs; Soil Sci Soc Am; Soil Conserv Soc Am. *Res:* Management of water for crop production, especially by agricultural drainage. *Mailing Add:* US Salinity Lab 4500 Glenwood Riverside CA 92501

VAN SCHMUS, WILLIAM RANDALL, b Aurora, Ill, Oct 4, 38; m 61; c 3. GEOLOGY, METEORITICS. *Educ:* Calif Inst Technol, BS, 60; Univ Calif, Los Angeles, PhD(geol), 64. *Prof Exp:* From asst prof to assoc prof, 67-75, PROF GEOL, UNIV KANS, 75- *Concurrent Pos:* Mem adv panels, NASA, NSF & Nat Acad Sci. *Mem:* Am Geophys Union; Geochem Soc; Meteoritical Soc; Geol Soc Am. *Res:* Geochronology and geochemistry of Precambrian rocks in North America; mineralogy and petrology of meteorites. *Mailing Add:* Dept of Geol Univ of Kans Lawrence KS 66045

VAN SCIVER, STEVEN W, b Philadelphia, Pa, Mar 13, 48; m 69; c 2. CRYOGENICS, HEAT TRANSFER. *Educ:* Lehigh Univ, BS, 70; Univ Wash, MS, 72, PhD(physics), 76. *Prof Exp:* Proj assoc superconductivity, 76-77, asst scientist, 77-79, ASST PROF NUCLEAR ENG, UNIV WIS-MADISON, 79- *Concurrent Pos:* Consult, Gen Atomic, San Diego & Lawrence Livermore Nat Lab, 80- *Mem:* Am Phys Soc; Inst Elec & Electronics Engrs. *Res:* Cryogenics; heat transfer and transport in superfluid helium; low temperature properties of materials; design of superconducting magnets for fusion and energy storage. *Mailing Add:* 529 Eng Res Bldg 1500 Johnson Dr Madison WI 53706

VAN SCIVER, WESLEY J, b Philadelphia, Pa, Sept 6, 17; m 59; c 3. PHYSICS, OCEANOGRAPHY. *Educ:* Mass Inst Technol, BS, 40; Stanford Univ, PhD(physics), 55. *Prof Exp:* Dir res, scintillation crystals, Radiation at Stanford, Inc, 54-60; vis prof physics, Univ PR, 61-62; assoc prof, 62-65, PROF PHYSICS, LEHIGH UNIV, 65- *Mem:* Am Phys Soc; Optical Soc Am. *Res:* Electronic processes in insulating solids; time resolved optical spectroscopy of solids; physical and optical spectroscopy of solids; scintillation and ultraviolet luminescence; physical and optical oceanography. *Mailing Add:* Dept of Physics Lehigh Univ Bethlehem PA 18015

VAN SCOTT, EUGENE JOSEPH, b Macedon, NY, May 27, 22; m 48; c 3. DERMATOLOGY. *Educ:* Univ Chicago, BS, 45, MD, 48. *Prof Exp:* Intern, Millard Fillmore Hosp, Buffalo, NY, 48-49; resident physician dermat, Univ Chicago, 49-52; assoc, Univ Pa, 52-53; chief dermat br, Nat Cancer Inst, 53-68, sci dir gen labs & clins, 66-68; PROF DERMAT, HEALTH SCI CTR, TEMPLE UNIV, 68-; ASSOC DIR SKIN & CANCER HOSP PHILADELPHIA, 68- *Honors & Awards:* Taub Int Mem Award, 64; Clarke White Award, 65; Albert Lasker Award, 72; Stephen Rothman Award, Soc Invest Dermat, 75; Lila Gruber Cancer Res Award, Am Acad Dermat, 80; Howard Fox lectr, NY Acad Med, 81. *Mem:* Hon mem Can Dermat Asn; Soc Invest Dermat; Am Dermat Asn; Am Asn Cancer Res; Am Acad Dermat. *Res:* Biology and physiology of epithelial growth; differentiation and neoplasia; pathogenesis of psoriasis; biology; immunologic aspects and clinical management of cutaneous lymphomas. *Mailing Add:* Skin & Cancer Hosp 3322 N Broad St Philadelphia PA 19140

VANSELOW, CLARENCE HUGO, b Syracuse, NY, Sept 30, 28; m 51; c 7. PHYSICAL CHEMISTRY. *Educ:* Syracuse Univ, BS, 50, MS, 51, PhD, 58. *Prof Exp:* Instr chem, Colgate Univ, 55-56; prof, Thiel Col, 56-64; ASSOC PROF CHEM, UNIV NC, GREENSBORO, 64- *Mem:* Am Chem Soc. *Res:* Gas phase radiation chemistry; kinetic theory of precipitation processes. *Mailing Add:* Dept of Chem Univ of NC Greensboro NC 27412

VANSELOW, NEAL A, b Milwaukee, Wis, Mar 18, 32; m 58; c 2. MEDICAL ADMINISTRATION, ALLERGY. *Educ:* Univ Mich, AB, 54, MD, 58, MS, 63. *Prof Exp:* From instr to assoc prof internal med, Univ Mich, Ann Arbor, 63-74, from assoc prof to prof postgrad med & chmn dept, 67-74; prof internal med & dean, Col Med, Univ Ariz, 74-77; PROF INTERNAL MED, VPRES & CHANCELLOR, UNIV NEBR, 77- *Concurrent Pos:* Consult, Ann Arbor Vet Admin Hosp, 64-74. *Mem:* Fel Am Acad Allergy; Am Col Physicians. *Res:* Mechanisms of aspirin sensitivity; immunosuppression and immunologic adjuvants. *Mailing Add:* Univ of Nebr Med Ctr Omaha NE 68105

VANSELOW, RALF W, b Berlin, Ger, July 12, 31; m 61. PHYSICAL CHEMISTRY, SURFACE CHEMISTRY. *Educ:* Tech Univ Berlin, BS, 57, Dipl Ing, 62, Dr Ing, 66. *Prof Exp:* Res asst field emission micros, Fritz Haber Inst, Max Planck Soc, 52-66, res assoc, 66-68; asst prof, 68-74, dir, Lab Surface Studies, 76-78, assoc prof chem, 74-80, chmn dept, 78-81, PROF, UNIV WIS-MILWAUKEE, 80- *Mem:* Ger Chem Soc; Am Chem Soc; Ger Vacuum Soc; Am Vacuum Soc. *Res:* Studies of metal surfaces by means of field electron and field ion microscopy; adsorption; surface migration; epitaxial growth. *Mailing Add:* Dept of Chem Univ of Wis Milwaukee WI 53201

VAN SICKLE, DALE ELBERT, b Ft Collins, Colo, Oct 8, 32; m 62; c 2. PHYSICAL ORGANIC CHEMISTRY. *Educ:* Colo State Univ, BS, 54; Univ Utah, MS, 56; Univ Calif, PhD, 59. *Prof Exp:* Asst chem, Univ Utah, 54-55 & Univ Calif, 56-59; org chemist, Stanford Res Inst, 59-69; SR RES CHEMIST, TENN EASTMAN CO, 69- *Mem:* AAAS; Am Chem Soc; Sigma Xi. *Res:* Mechanisms and kinetics of reactions; oxidation of hydrocarbons; thermodynamics of fluid phase equilibria. *Mailing Add:* Res Labs Eastman Chem Div Kingsport TN 37662

VAN SICKLE, DAVID C, b Des Moines, Iowa, Jan 9, 34; m 56. HISTOLOGY, PATHOBIOLOGY. *Educ:* Iowa State Univ, DVM, 57; Purdue Univ, PhD(develop anat), 66. *Prof Exp:* Gen pract, Ill, 57-58 & 60-61; from instr to assoc prof, 61-75, PROF HISTOL & EMBRYOL, PURDUE UNIV, WEST LAFAYETTE, 75- *Concurrent Pos:* Morris Animal Found fel, 64-66; adj prof anat, Sch Med, Ind Univ, 75-; pres, Confr Res Workers Animal Dis, 81; adj prof, Col US Air Force Reserve, 77-; adj prof grad studies, Wright State Univ, Ohio, 81- *Mem:* Sigma Xi; Am Asn Anat; NY Acad Sci. *Res:* Osteogenesis and abnormalities associated with errors in osteogenesis; orthopedic pathobiology in arthritis, hip dysplasia, and osteochondritis. *Mailing Add:* Dept Vet Anat Purdue Univ West Lafayette IN 47906

VAN SICLEN, DEWITT CLINTON, b Carlisle, Pa, Oct 25, 18; m 49; c 4. GEOLOGY. *Educ:* Princeton Univ, AB, 40, MA, 47, PhD(geol), 51; Univ Ill, MS, 41. *Prof Exp:* Jr geologist, Peoples Natural Gas Co, Pa, 41-42 & 46; field geologist, Drilling & Explor Co, Inc, 47-50; consult, 50-51; exec officer, Off Sci Res, US Dept Air Force, 51-52; res geologist, Pan-Am Prod Co, 52-56; sr geologist, Pan-Am Petrol Corp, 56-59; assoc prof, 59-65, chmn dept, 60-67, PROF GEOL, UNIV HOUSTON, 65- *Mem:* Am Asn Petrol Geologists; Nat Asn Geol Teachers; Am Inst Prof Geologists; Soc Petrol Engrs. *Res:* Deposition, deformation and alteration of sedimentary rocks; behavior of subsurface fluids; petroleum geology; surficial geology and active faults of Texas-Louisiana coastal plain; tectonics of Gulf of Mexico Region. *Mailing Add:* Dept Geol Univ Houston Houston TX 77004

VAN SLUYTERS, RICHARD CHARLES, b Chicago, Ill, June 12, 45; m 68. PHYSIOLOGICAL OPTICS, NEUROPHYSIOLOGY. *Educ:* Ill Col Optom, BS, 67, OD, 68; Ind Univ, Bloomington, PhD(physiol optics), 72. *Prof Exp:* ASSOC PROF OPTOM-PHYSIOL OPTICS & NEUROBIOL, SCH OPTOM, UNIV CALIF, BERKELEY, 75- *Concurrent Pos:* Am Optom Found Res fel, 68-69; Nat Eye Inst fel, 69-71 & spec res fel, 72-74; NSF fel, 71-72; Miller Inst Basic Res Sci fel, Univ Calif, Berkeley, 74-76; Sloan fel, 78-80. *Mem:* Soc Neurosci; AAAS; Asn Res Vision & Ophthal; fel Am Acad Optom. *Res:* Neurophysiology of developing mammalian visual systems. *Mailing Add:* Sch of Optom Univ of Calif Berkeley CA 94720

VAN SLYKE, ARTHUR LAWTON, b Perth, Ont, June 13, 25; m 50; c 2. FORESTRY, FOREST BIOMETRY. *Educ:* Univ NB, BSc, 49; Univ Mich, MF, 52. *Prof Exp:* Jr forester, NB Int Paper Co Div, Can Int Paper Co, 49-50, res forester, Causapscal Forest Res Sta, 50-56, supt, 56 & 57; PROF FORESTRY, UNIV NB, FREDERICTON, 57- *Res:* Tree crown measures to evaluate growth rates and to assist in management planning; inventory for stand management; stand area estimates. *Mailing Add:* Fac Forestry Univ NB Bag Serv #44555 Fredericton NB E3B 6C2 Can

VAN SLYKE, RICHARD M, b Manila, Philippines, Aug 17, 37; U S citizen; m 69. OPERATIONS RESEARCH. *Educ:* Stanford Univ, BS, 59; Univ Calif, Berkeley, PhD(opers res), 65. *Prof Exp:* Asst prof elec & indust eng, Univ Calif, Berkeley, 65-69; vpres, Network Anal Corp, 69-80; PROF ELEC ENG & COMPUT SCI, STEVENS INST TECHNOL, 80- *Concurrent Pos:* Consult, Rand Corp, 62-66 & Crown Zellerbach Corp, 63-65. *Mem:* Soc Indust & Appl Math; Opers Res Soc Am; Am Math Soc; Inst Elec & Electronics Engrs. *Res:* Mathematical techniques for optimization, especially for information network design and analysis. *Mailing Add:* Elec Eng Comput Sci Dept Stevens Inst Technol Hoboken NJ 07030

VANSOEST, PETER JOHN, b Seattle, Wash, June 30, 29; m 59; c 3. ANIMAL NUTRITION. *Educ:* Wash State Univ, BS, 51, MS, 52; Univ Wis, PhD(nutrit), 55. *Prof Exp:* Biochemist, Agr Res Serv, USDA, 57-68; assoc prof animal nutrit, 68-73, PROF ANIMAL NUTRIT, CORNELL UNIV, 73- *Honors & Awards:* Am Feed Mfrs Award, 67; Hoblitzelle Nat Award Agr, 68; Am Grassland Coun Merit Cert, 68. *Mem:* AAAS; Am Dairy Sci Asn; Am Soc Animal Sci; Asn Off Anal Chem. *Res:* Ruminant digestion and metabolism; chemistry of fibrous feedstuffs and methods of analysis; forage chemistry. *Mailing Add:* 120 Homestead Circle Ithaca NY 14850

VANSPEYBROECK, LEON PAUL, b Wichita, Kans, Aug 27, 35; m 59; c 3. X-RAY ASTRONOMY. *Educ:* Mass Inst Technol, BS, 57, PhD, 65. *Prof Exp:* Res assoc high energy physics, Mass Inst Technol, 65-67; staff scientist x-ray astron, Am Sci & Eng, Inc, Mass, 67-74; STAFF SCIENTIST, CTR FOR ASTROPHYS, 74- *Res:* Solar and stellar astronomy; physics of the solar corona. *Mailing Add:* Ctr for Astrophys 60 Garden St Cambridge MA 02138

VAN STEE, ETHARD WENDEL, b Traverse City, Mich, July 17, 36; m 60; c 2. PHARMACOLOGY, TOXICOLOGY. *Educ:* Mich State Univ, BS, 58, DVM, 60; Ohio State Univ, MS, 66, PhD(vet physiol, pharmacol), 70. *Prof Exp:* Res pharmacologist, 6570 Aerospace Med Res Lab, Wright-Patterson AFB, Ohio, 67-75; HEAD, INHALATION TOXICOL SECT, NAT INST ENVIRON HEALTH SCI, 75- *Concurrent Pos:* Adj assoc prof pharmacol, Univ NC, 75- *Mem:* Soc Toxicol; Am Soc Pharmacol & Exp Therapeut; Am Vet Med Asn; AAAS; Am Soc Vet Physiologists & Pharmacologists. *Res:* Inhalation toxicology; halogenated alkanes, anesthetics; cardiovascular pharmacology. *Mailing Add:* Nat Inst Environ Health Sci PO Box 12233 Research Triangle Park NC 27709

VAN STEENBERGEN, ARIE, b Vlaardingen, Neth, Feb 26, 28; m 53; c 4. PHYSICS. *Educ:* Delft Univ Technol, MSc, 52; McGill Univ, PhD(physics, math), 57. *Prof Exp:* Res asst electron beam optics, Delft Univ Technol, 50-53; res physicist, Nat Defense Res Lab, The Hague, Neth, 53-54; res assoc nuclear magnetic resonance, McGill Univ, 54-57; head alternating gradient synchrotron div, 65-74, sr physicist, 75-77, HEAD NAT SYNCHROTRON LIGHT SOURCE, BROOKHAVEN NAT LAB, 77- *Concurrent Pos:* Consult, Radiation Dynamics, Inc, 60- *Mem:* Am Phys Soc; Europ Phys Soc. *Res:* High energy particle accelerators and storage rings; particle beam dynamics; synchrotron radiation sources. *Mailing Add:* Brookhaven Nat Lab Upton NY 11973

VANSTONE, J R, b Owen Sound, Ont, Aug 12, 33; m 56; c 3. MATHEMATICS. *Educ:* Univ Toronto, BA, 55, MA, 56; Univ Natal, PhD(math), 59. *Prof Exp:* Lectr math, 59-61, from asst prof to assoc prof, 61-76, PROF MATH, UNIV TORONTO, 76- *Mem:* Can Math Cong; Math Asn Am; Am Math Soc; Soc Indust & Appl Math. *Res:* Differential geometry. *Mailing Add:* Dept of Math Univ of Toronto Toronto ON M5S 1A1 Can

VAN STONE, JAMES MORRIL, b Bridgeport, Conn, Jan 19, 24; m 49; c 2. ZOOLOGY. *Educ:* Princeton Univ, PhD, 54. *Prof Exp:* From asst prof to assoc prof biol, 54-65, PROF BIOL, TRINITY COL, CONN, 65- *Mem:* Am Soc Zoologists; Am Asn Anatomists. *Res:* Amphibian regeneration; experimental zoology. *Mailing Add:* Dept of Biol Trinity Col Hartford CT 06106

VANSTONE, SCOTT ALEXANDER, b Chatham, Ont, Sept 14, 47; m 70; c 1. MATHEMATICS. *Educ:* Univ Waterloo, BMath, 70, MMath, 71, PhD(math), 74. *Prof Exp:* Asst prof, 74-80, ASSOC PROF MATH, UNIV ST JEROME'S COL, 80- *Res:* The existence and construction of balanced incomplete block designs and regular pairwise balanced designs which are closely related to finite linear spaces and balanced equidistant codes; coding theory. *Mailing Add:* Univ St Jerome's Col Waterloo ON N2L 3G1 Can

VAN STRIEN, RICHARD EDWARD, b Battle Creek, Mich, Sept 17, 20; m 42; c 3. ORGANIC CHEMISTRY. *Educ:* Hope Col, AB, 42; Univ Pa, MS, 44, PhD(org chem), 48. *Prof Exp:* Res chemist, Standard Oil Co, Ind, 47-60, sect leader, Res & Develop Dept, 60-61, sect leader in-chg prod appln new chem, Amoco Chem Corp, 61-67, asst dir polymers & plastics div, Ind, 67-69, div dir, Condensation Polymer Div, 69-76, DIV DIR, EXPLOR RES DIV, AMOCO CHEM CORP, 76- *Mem:* Am Chem Soc. *Res:* Synthetic detergents; gelling agents; surface coatings; high-performance plastics; adhesives. *Mailing Add:* Res & Develop Dept Amoco Chem Corp PO Box 400 Naperville IL 60566

VAN STRYLAND, ERIC WILLIAM, b South Bend, Ind, June 3, 47; m 78. LASER PHYSICS. *Educ:* Humboldt State Univ, BS, 70; Univ Ariz, MS, 75, PhD(physics), 76. *Prof Exp:* Res assoc laser physics, Optical Sci Ctr, Univ Ariz, 72-76; res scientist, Ctr Laser Studies, Univ Southern Calif, 76-78; ASST PROF LASER PHYSICS, DEPT PHYSICS, NORTH TEX STATE UNIV, 78- *Mem:* Am Phys Soc; Optical Soc Am; Laser Inst Am. *Res:* Ultrashort light pulses and their generation measurement and uses; optical coherent transient effects; lifetime measurements; nonlinear absorption; laser induced damage; laser material interactions. *Mailing Add:* Dept of Physics N Tex State Univ Denton TX 76203

VAN SWAAY, MAARTEN, b The Hague, Neth, Aug 1, 30; m 54; c 4. ANALYTICAL CHEMISTRY. *Educ:* State Univ Leiden, BS, 53, Drs(chem), 56; Princeton Univ, PhD(chem), 56. *Prof Exp:* Sr res asst phys chem, State Univ Leiden, 56-59; res assoc instr anal, Eindhoven Technol Univ, 59-63; asst prof, 63-69, ASSOC PROF ANAL CHEM, KANS STATE UNIV, 69- *Concurrent Pos:* Consult, Am Inst Prof Educ. *Mem:* Am Chem Soc. *Res:* Chemical instrumentation; computer interfacing and control. *Mailing Add:* Dept of Chem Kans State Univ Manhattan KS 66506

VAN TAMELEN, EUGENE EARL, b Zeeland, Mich, July 20, 25; m 51; c 3. CHEMISTRY. *Educ:* Hope Col, AB, 47; Harvard Univ, MA, 49, PhD(chem), 50. *Hon Degrees:* DSc, Hope Col & Bucknell Univ, 71. *Prof Exp:* From instr to prof org chem, Univ Wis, 50-61, Adkins prof chem, 61-62; chmn dept, 74-78, PROF CHEM, STANFORD UNIV, 62- *Concurrent Pos:* Guggenheim fels, 65 & 73; prof extraordinarius, Neth, 67-74; mem adv bd, Chem & Eng News, 68-70, Synthesis, 69- & Accounts of Chem Res, 70-73; ed, Bioorg Chem, 71-82. *Honors & Awards:* Award in Pure Chem, Am Chem Soc, 61 & Award for Creative Work in Synthetic Org Chem, 70; Baekeland Award, 65. *Mem:* Nat Acad Sci; Am Acad Arts & Sci; Am Chem Soc. *Res:* Chemistry of natural products including structure, synthesis and biosynthesis; new reactions. *Mailing Add:* Dept of Chem Stanford Univ Stanford CA 94305

VAN TASSEL, ROGER A, b Orange, NJ, Oct 19, 36. AERONOMY. *Educ:* Wesleyan Univ, AB, 58; Northeastern Univ, MS, 68, PhD, 72. *Prof Exp:* Chemist, Lunar-Planetary Lab, 61-67, RES CHEMIST, AERONOMY LAB, AIR FORCE GEOPHYS LAB, 67- *Mem:* AAAS; Sigma Xi; Am Geophys Union; Optical Soc Am. *Res:* Atomic spectra in the vacuum ultraviolet; oscillator strengths of atomic transitions; ultraviolet airglow originating in the upper atmosphere. *Mailing Add:* Air Force Geophys Lab Aeronomy Div Hanscom AFB MA 01731

VAN TASSELL, MORGAN HOWARD, b Johnson City, NY, Oct 31, 23; m 53; c 1. MICROBIOLOGY. *Educ:* Univ Wis, BS, 50. *Prof Exp:* Plant bacteriologist, Commercial Solvents Corp, Ill, 50-52; res microbiologist, Cent Res Dept, Anheuser-Busch, Inc, 53-57, supvr microbiologist, Fermentation Pilot Lab, 57-60; asst plant mgr, Sheffield Chem Div, Nat Dairy Prod Corp, 60-62, plant mgr, Kraftco Corp, 62-75; DIR WATER SERV, CITY OF ONEONTA, NY, 75- *Mem:* Am Soc Microbiol. *Res:* Industrial microbiology; applied and developmental research of fermentations; mutational development and selection of cultures; pilot scale equipment; automated continuous fermentations; enzymatic hydrolysis of proteins. *Mailing Add:* City of Oneonta Dept of Water 110 East St Oneonta NY 13820

VAN TASSELL, WILLIAM FRED, b St Charles, Mich, Nov 22, 27; m 66; c 2. AERODYNAMICS, FLUID MECHANICS. *Educ:* Mass Inst Technol, BS, 59, MS, 61, PhD(aerospace eng), 70. *Prof Exp:* Aerodyn engr, Res & Advan Develop Div, Avco Corp, 59-61; asst aerodyn, Mass Inst Technol, 61; sr staff scientist re-entry vehicle design, Res & Advan Develop Div, Avco Corp, 61-63; instr mech, State Univ NY, Buffalo, 63-67; sr aeronaut engr, Cornell Aeronaut Lab, Inc, 67-69; asst prof aeronaut & astronaut eng, Univ Ill, Urbana, 69-77; PROF MECH ENG, UNIV NEV, RENO, 77- *Mem:* Soc Indust & Appl Math; Am Soc Eng Educ. *Res:* Second order boundary layer theory; numerical fluid, reentry vehicle and flight dynamics; vehicle stability and control. *Mailing Add:* Dept of Mech Eng Univ of Nev Reno NV 89557

VAN THIEL, DAVID H, b Cut Bank, Mont, Sept 5, 41. GASTROENTEROLOGY, ENDOCRINOLOGY. *Educ:* Univ Calif, Los Angeles, MD, 67. *Prof Exp:* From instr to asst prof, 73-78, ASSOC PROF MED, UNIV PITTSBURGH SCH MED, 78- *Concurrent Pos:* Res fel, Univ Calif Med Ctr, Los Angeles, 64; intern, NY Hosp, 67-68, asst resident, 68-69; clin assoc, Endocrinol Br Nat Cancer Inst, 69-70 & Reprod Res Br, NIH, 70-71; sr asst resident, Univ Hosp, Boston, 71-72, res fel, 72-73; USPHS Career Develop Award, NIH, 77. *Mem:* Am Fedn Clin Res; Am Asn Study Liver Dis; Am Gastroenterol Asn; fel Am Col Physicians. *Res:* Endocrine alterations associated with liver disease with special interest in alcoholic liver disease. *Mailing Add:* Univ of Pittsburgh Sch of Med Pittsburgh PA 15261

VAN THIEL, MATHIAS, b Sitobonda, Java, Sept 18, 30; US citizen; m 59; c 3. PHYSICAL CHEMISTRY, PHYSICS. *Educ:* Cornell Univ, BA, 54, Univ Calif, Berkeley, PhD(phys chem), 58. *Prof Exp:* Fel phys chem & shock tube kinetics, Univ Minn, Minneapolis, 58-59; RES PHYSICIST HIGH PRESSURE EQUATION OF STATE, LAWRENCE LIVERMORE LAB, 59- *Mem:* Am Chem Soc; AAAS; Sigma Xi; Am Physics Soc. *Res:* Infrared spectroscopy-matrix isolation; high temperature gas phase kinetics-shock tube; shock waves and high pressure equations of state; hydrodynamic code calculations; shaped charge design and penetration modeling. *Mailing Add:* Lawrence Livermore Nat Lab PO Box 808 Livermore CA 94550

VAN'T HOF, JACK, b Grand Rapids, Mich, Apr 11, 32; m 52; c 2. CELL BIOLOGY, RADIOBIOLOGY. *Educ:* Calvin Col, AB, 57; Mich State Univ, PhD(bot), 61. *Prof Exp:* Biologist, Hanford Labs, Gen Elec Corp, 61-62; res assoc radiobiol & fel, Biol Dept, Brookhaven Nat Lab, 62-64, asst cytologist, 64-65; asst prof cytol, Dept Bot, Univ Minn, 65-66; CYTOLOGIST, BIOL DEPT, BROOKHAVEN NAT LAB, 66- *Mem:* Am Soc Cell Biol; Bot Soc Am; Am Soc Plant Physiol; Radiation Res Soc. *Res:* Study of cell population kinetics in complex plant tissue emphasizing physiological, cytochemical and radiological events that occur in and govern the duration of the mitotic cycle of proliferating cells. *Mailing Add:* Biol Dept Brookhaven Nat Lab Upton NY 11973

VANT-HULL, LORIN LEE, b Sioux Co, Iowa, June 26, 32; m 55; c 3. PHYSICS. *Educ:* Univ Minn, Minneapolis, BS, 54; Univ Calif, Los Angeles, MS, 55; Calif Inst Technol, PhD(physics), 67. *Prof Exp:* Res engr, Res Lab, Hughes Aircraft Co, 54-58; sr res scientist cryogenic devices, Sci Lab, Ford Motor Co, 66-69; assoc prof, 69-77, PROF PHYSICS, UNIV HOUSTON, 77- *Concurrent Pos:* Consult, Lawrence Berkeley Lab, Univ Calif, 70-71 & Manned Spacecraft Ctr, NASA, 71-72; prog mgr, Solar Energy Lab, Univ Houston, 74-; consult, Battelle Pac Northwest Lab, 78-80; assoc ed, J of Solar Energy; prin investr, numerous solar cent receiver grants & contracts, Dept Enegry & various indust firm, 73- *Mem:* Am Inst Physics; Solar Energy Soc; Sigma Xi. *Res:* Superconductivity; quantum interference and its use in instrumentation; solar energy; large scale efficient generation of solar electricity; solar tower central receiver systems optimization and performance. *Mailing Add:* Dept of Physics Univ of Houston Houston TX 77004

VAN TIENHOVEN, ARI, b The Hague, Neth, Apr 22, 22; nat US; m 50; c 3. ANIMAL PHYSIOLOGY. *Educ:* Univ Ill, MS & PhD(animal sci), 53. *Prof Exp:* Asst prof poultry husb, Miss State Col, 53-55; from asst prof to assoc prof avian physiol, 55-69, PROF ANIMAL PHYSIOL, COL AGR & LIFE SCI, CORNELL UNIV, 69- *Concurrent Pos:* NATO fel, 61-62; assoc ed, Biol of Reproduction, 74- *Honors & Awards:* Am Soc Agr Engrs Paper Award, 71. *Mem:* AAAS; Am Soc Zoologists; Poultry Sci Asn; Am Asn Anat; Soc Study Reproduction. *Res:* Neuroendocrinology; reproductive physiology; temperature regulation of birds. *Mailing Add:* Dept of Poultry Sci Cornell Univ Ithaca NY 14853

VAN TILL, HOWARD JAY, b Ripon, Calif, Nov 28, 38; m 58; c 4. ASTRONOMY. *Educ:* Calvin Col, BS, 60; Mich State Univ, PhD(physics), 65. *Prof Exp:* Res scientist physics, Univ Calif, Riverside, 65-66; asst prof, Univ Redlands, 66-67; PROF PHYSICS, CALVIN COL, 67- *Concurrent Pos:* Res scientist, Dept Astron, Univ Tex, Austin, 74. *Mem:* Am Astron Soc; Am Phys Soc; Am Asn Physics Teachers. *Res:* Study of interstellar molecular clouds using millimeter-wave techniques. *Mailing Add:* Dept of Physics Calvin Col Grand Rapids MI 49506

VAN'T RIET, BARTHOLOMEUS, b Arnhem, Neth, June 25, 22; nat US; m 55; c 3. ANALYTICAL CHEMISTRY. *Educ:* Vrye Univ, Neth, BSc, 50; Univ Minn, PhD(anal chem), 57. *Prof Exp:* Asst anal chem, Vrye Univ, Neth, 48-51; from asst to instr, Univ Minn, 51-57; instr chem, Univ Va, 58-64; ASSOC PROF CHEM, MED COL VA, 64- *Honors & Awards:* Chem Pioneer Award, Am Inst Chemists, 73. *Mem:* Am Chem Soc. *Res:* Application of complexing agents in mammals; dispersion of calculi by surface reactions; drug analysis. *Mailing Add:* Dept of Pharmaceut Chem Med Col of Va Box 581 Richmond VA 23298

VAN TUYL, ANDREW HEUER, b Fresno, Calif, July 6, 22; m 55; c 4. MATHEMATICS. *Educ:* Fresno State Col, AB, 43; Stanford Univ, MA, 46, PhD(math), 47. *Prof Exp:* Asst chem, Stanford Univ, 43-44, asst elec eng, 44-45, asst physics, 46, asst math, 46-47; MATHEMATICIAN, NAVAL SURFACE WEAPONS CTR, 47- *Concurrent Pos:* Res assoc, Ind Univ, 53. *Mem:* Fel AAAS; Am Inst Aeronaut & Astronaut; Am Math Soc; Soc Indust & Appl Math; NY Acad Sci. *Res:* Potential theory; special functions; hydrodynamics; gas dynamics. *Mailing Add:* Naval Surface Weapons Ctr White Oak Silver Spring MD 20910

VAN TUYL, HAROLD HUTCHISON, b Ft Worth, Tex, Oct 13, 27; m 52; c 4. RADIOCHEMISTRY. *Educ:* Agr & Mech Col, Tex, BS, 48. *Prof Exp:* Res chemist, Gen Elec Co, 48-65; res chemist, 65-70, MGR NUCLEAR FUEL CYCLE, PAC NORTHWEST LABS, BATTELLE MEM INST, 70- *Mem:* Am Nuclear Soc; Am Chem Soc. *Res:* Fission product recovery; dose rate and shielding calculations; fission product and transuranics generation calculations; transuranic element separations; nuclear chemistry. *Mailing Add:* 2158 Hudson Ave Richland WA 99352

VAN TUYLE, GLENN CHARLES, b Wilkes-Barre, Pa, May 28, 43. BIOCHEMISTRY. *Educ:* Lafayette Col, AB, 65; Thomas Jefferson Univ, PhD(biochem), 71. *Prof Exp:* Chemist org chem, Rohm & Haas Chem Co, 66-68; teaching & res asst biochem, Thomas Jefferson Univ, 68-71; assoc, State Univ NY, Stony Brook, 71-74; ASSOC PROF BIOCHEM, MED COL VA, VA COMMONWEALTH UNIV, 74- *Concurrent Pos:* Assoc prof res grant, Nat Inst Gen Med Sci, 76-82. *Honors & Awards:* Paul S Pinchuck Award, Thomas Jefferson Univ, 72. *Mem:* Am Soc Cell Biol; Am Soc Biol Chemists. *Res:* Mitochondrial biogenesis; DNA structure, packaging and replications. *Mailing Add:* Dept of Biochem Med Col Va Va Commonwealth Univ Richmond VA 23298

VAN TYLE, WILLIAM KENT, b Frankfort, Ind, Feb 10, 44. PHARMACOLOGY. *Educ:* Butler Univ, BS, 67; Ohio State Univ, MSc, 69, PhD(pharmacol), 72. *Prof Exp:* Asst prof, 72-75, ASSOC PROF PHARMACOL, BUTLER UNIV, 75- *Concurrent Pos:* Secy-treas, Dist 4, Am Asn Cols Pharm-Nat Asn Bds Pharm, 75- *Mem:* Am Asn Col Pharm; Am Diabites Asn. *Res:* Bioavailability of drugs to central nervous system and drug effects on central neurotransmitters. *Mailing Add:* Butler Univ 4600 Sunset Ave Indianapolis IN 46208

VAN UITERT, LEGRAND G(ERARD), b Salt Lake City, Utah, May 6, 22; m 45; c 3. MATERIALS SCIENCE, INORGANIC CHEMISTRY. *Educ:* George Washington Univ, BS, 49; Pa State Univ, MS, 51, PhD(chem), 52. *Prof Exp:* MEM TECH STAFF, BELL TEL LABS, INC, 52- *Honors & Awards:* W R G Baker Award, Inst Elec & Electronics Engrs, 71; H N Potts Award, Franklin Inst, 75; IRI Award, Indust Res Inst, 76; Creative Invention Award, Am Chem Soc, 78; Am Phys Soc Int Prize, 81. *Mem:* Nat Acad Eng; Am Chem Soc. *Res:* Magnetic oxides; luminesence; lasers, electro-optic and non-linear devices; magnetic bubble domain materials, fiber optics, passive displays and dielectric films. *Mailing Add:* Bell Tel Labs Inc 600 Mountain Ave Murray Hill NJ 07974

VAN UMMERSEN, CLAIRE ANN, b Chelsea, Mass, July 28, 35; m 58; c 2. DEVELOPMENTAL BIOLOGY, ANIMAL PHYSIOLOGY. *Educ:* Tufts Univ, BS, 57, MS, 60, PhD(biol), 63. *Prof Exp:* Res asst radiobiol, Tufts Univ, 57-60, res assoc, 60-67, lectr biol, 67-68; asst prof, 68-74, assoc dean acad affairs, Liberal Arts Col, 75-76, assoc vice chancellor acad affairs, 76-77, interim chancellor, 78-79, ASSOC PROF BIOL, UNIV MASS, BOSTON, 74-, DIR, ENVIRON SCI CTR & DIR BIOL GRAD PROG, 79- *Concurrent Pos:* Fel, Tufts Univ, 63-67; mem teaching fac, Lancaster Courses in Ophthal, Colby Col, 62- *Mem:* AAAS; Am Soc Zoologists; Soc Develop Biol; Sigma Xi. *Res:* Biological effects of microwave radiation on the eye and the developing embryo. *Mailing Add:* Dept of Biol Univ of Mass Harbor Campus Boston MA 02125

VAN VALEN, LEIGH MAIORANA, b Albany, NY, Aug 12, 35; m 59; c 2. EVOLUTIONARY BIOLOGY. *Educ:* Miami Univ, BA, 56; Columbia Univ, MA, 57, PhD(zool), 61. *Prof Exp:* Boese fel, Columbia Univ, 61-62; NATO fel, Univ Col, London, 62-63; res fel vert paleont, Am Mus Natural Hist, 63-66; asst prof anat, 67-68, from asst prof to assoc prof evolutionary biol, 68-73, assoc prof biol, 73-76, PROF BIOL, UNIV CHICAGO, 76- *Concurrent Pos:* Managing ed, Evolutionary Theory, 73-; ed, Evolutionary Monographs, 77- *Mem:* Soc Study Evolution (vpres, 73); Soc Vert Paleont; Ecol Soc Am; Philos Sci Asn; Am Soc Naturalists (treas, 69-72, vpres, 74-75). *Res:* Energy in ecology and evolution; extinction; ecological control of large-scale evolutionary patterns; analytical paleoecology; energy and evolution; the phenotype; competition; natural selection of plants and animals; evolutionary theory; biological variation; evolution of development; basal radiation of placental mammals. *Mailing Add:* Dept of Biol Univ of Chicago 1103 E 57th St Chicago IL 60637

VAN VALIN, CHARLES CARROLL, b Wakefield, Nebr, Aug 10, 29; m 54. ATMOSPHERIC CHEMISTRY, ATMOSPHERIC PHYSICS. *Educ:* Nebr State Teachers Col, BA, 51; Univ Colo, Boulder, MS, 58. *Prof Exp:* Teacher sci, Ralston High Sch, Nebr, 53-54; chemist pesticide mfg, Shell Chem Co, Denver, 57-58; res chemist sugar chem, Great Western Sugar Co, Denver, 58-60; res chemist pesticide res, Fish-Pesticide Res Lab, Bur Sport Fisheries & Wildlife, Dept Interior, 61-66; RES CHEMIST ATMOSPHERIC RES, ENVIRON RES LABS, NAT OCEANIC & ATMOSPHERIC ADMIN, DEPT COM, 66- *Concurrent Pos:* Abstractor, Chem Abstracts Serv, Am Chem Soc, 62-64. *Mem:* Am Chem Soc; AAAS; Am Geophys Union; Sigma Xi. *Res:* Chemical and physical processes of precipitation formation, as related to inadvertent weather modification from energy production; reactions in polluted atmospheres, especially gas-to-particle mechanisms in powerplant plumes. *Mailing Add:* Nat Oceanic & Atmospheric Admin RX8 US Dept Com 325 Broadway Boulder CO 80303

VAN VALKENBURG, ERNEST SCOFIELD, b Tecumseh, Mich, Aug 16, 23; m 46; c 6. APPLIED PHYSICS, ELECTRICAL ENGINEERING. *Educ:* Univ Mich, BS, 45. *Prof Exp:* Physicist instrumentation, US Naval Res Lab, 45-51; res engr comput, Univ Mich, 51-57; mgr info systs, Bendix Corp, 57-69, dir eng electronics, 69-74; MGR RES & DEVELOP CONTRACTS, LEEDS & NORTHRUP CO, 74- *Concurrent Pos:* Eng mgr, Apollo Lunar Surface Exp Package Bendix/NASA, 67-69. *Mem:* Inst Elec & Electronics Engrs; Comput Soc. *Res:* Sensors and data processing techniques for process measurements and/or control in industrial, defense or space applications. *Mailing Add:* Leeds & Northrup Co Dickerson Rd North Wales PA 19454

VAN VALKENBURG, JEPTHA WADE, JR, b Ann Arbor, Mich, Mar 26, 25; m 49; c 3. PHYSICAL CHEMISTRY, SURFACE CHEMISTRY. *Educ:* Kalamazoo Col, BS, 49; Univ Wis, MS, 51; Univ Mich, PhD(phys chem), 55; William Mitchell Col Law, JD, 79. *Prof Exp:* Chemist, Dow Chem Co, Mich, 54-58, proj leader pesticidal formulations res, 58-60, group leader, 60-66, mgr patent admin, 66-68; supvr phys chem res, 68-71, info scientist specialist, 71-73, mem patent liaison staff, 73-80, MGR REGULATORY AFFAIRS & INT RES & DEVELOP, DATA REC PROD LAB, 3M CO, 81- *Mem:* Am Chem Soc. *Res:* Patents; pesticidal formulations; surfactants; emulsions; diffusion; kinetics; encapsulation and surface coatings; biological correlations; computer media; federal and state regulations. *Mailing Add:* Data Rec Prod Div 3M Bldg 236-1C-18 St Paul MN 55144

VAN VALKENBURG, M(AC) E(LWYN), b Union, Utah, Oct 5, 21; m 43; c 6. ELECTRICAL ENGINEERING, SYSTEM THEORY. *Educ:* Univ Utah, BS, 43; Mass Inst Technol, SM, 46; Stanford Univ, PhD(elec eng), 52. *Prof Exp:* Mem staff, Radiation Lab, Mass Inst Technol, 43-45, asst, Electronics Lab, 45-46; from instr to assoc prof elec eng, Univ Utah, 46-55; acting instr, Stanford Univ, 49-51; from assoc prof to prof, Univ Ill, Urbana, 55-66, assoc dir, Coord Sci Lab, 59-66; prof & chmn dept, Princeton Univ, 66-74; PROF ELEC ENG, UNIV ILL, 74- *Concurrent Pos:* Ed, Trans Circuit Theory, Inst Elec & Electronics Engrs, 60-63, ed Proc, 65-68; vis prof, Univ Calif, Berkeley, 62-63 & Univ Hawaii, 78-79; Thompson vis prof, Univ Ill, 72-73; Guillemin Prize, Guillemin Found, 78. *Honors & Awards:* Westinghouse Award, Am Soc Eng Educ, 63, Lamme Award, 78; Educ Medal, Inst Elec & Electronics Engrs, 72. *Mem:* Nat Acad Eng; fel Inst Elec & Electronics Engrs (vpres, 69-71); Am Soc Eng Educ; Sigma Xi. *Res:* Circuit theory; analog filter theory; systems theory; energy systems. *Mailing Add:* Dept of Elec Eng Univ of Ill Urbana IL 61801

VAN VECHTEN, DEBORAH, b Washington, DC, Oct 24, 47; m 70. LOW TEMPERATURE PHYSICS, THEORETICAL SOLID STATE PHYSICS. *Educ:* Brown Univ, ScB, 69; Univ Md, College Park, MS, 75, PhD(physics), 79. *Prof Exp:* Vis asst prof physics, Ga Inst Technol, 78-79; assoc, Nat Res Coun, 79-81; ASST PROF PHYSICS, HOWARD UNIV, 81- *Concurrent Pos:* Guest scientist, Nat Bur Standards, 81. *Mem:* Am Phys Soc; Am Asn Physics Teachers. *Res:* Role of fluctuations in phase transitions; percolation theory; properties and applications of superconductors; non-equilibrium superconductivity; gold compound superconductors; noise thermometers; thermal fluctuations impact on two dimensional resistive transition; measurement theory in quantum mechanics. *Mailing Add:* Dept Physics Howard Univ Washington DC 20059

VAN VECHTEN, JAMES ALDEN, b Washington, DC, July 29, 42. THEORETICAL SOLID STATE PHYSICS, SEMICONDUCTORS. *Educ:* Univ Calif, Berkeley, AB, 65; Univ Chicago, PhD(physics), 69. *Prof Exp:* Infrared res officer semiconductors, US Naval Res Lab, Wash, 69-71; mem tech staff electro optic res, Bell Tel Lab, Murray Hill, 71-74; RES STAFF MEM SEMICONDUCTOR PHYSICS, THOMAS J WATSON RES CTR, IBM, 74- *Mem:* Fel Am Phys Soc; Electrochem Soc. *Res:* Theoretical study of covalently bonded solids, their electronic, optical, mechanical and thermochemical properties; co-developer of the dielectric scale of electronegativity. *Mailing Add:* Thomas J Watson Res Ctr IBM PO Box 218 Yorktown Heights NY 10598

VAN VELD, ROBERT DALE, b Killduff, Iowa, Jan 31, 24; m 46; c 3. TEXTILE PHYSICS. *Educ:* Purdue Univ, BS, 49, MS, 51, PhD(physics), 55. *Prof Exp:* Asst, Purdue Univ, 55; res engr, 56-60, res proj engr, Eng Res Lab, Exp Sta, 60-61, sr res physicist, Kinston Plant, 61-65, res assoc, 65-66, tech supvr, 66-68, supvr res & develop, 68-77, RES FEL, E I DU PONT DE NEMOURS & CO INC, 77- *Mem:* Fiber Soc. *Res:* Microscopy. *Mailing Add:* E I du Pont de Nemours & Co Inc Kinston NC 28501

VAN VELDHUIZEN, PHILIP ANDROCLES, b Hospers, Iowa, Nov 6, 30; m 52; c 3. MATHEMATICS, STATISTICS. *Educ:* Cent Col, BA, 52; Univ Iowa, MS, 60. *Prof Exp:* Teacher jr high sch, 54; instr, Exten Ctr, Univ Ga, 54-56; instr math, Cent Col, 56-59; asst prof, Sacramento State Col, 60-63; assoc prof, 63-74, PROF MATH, UNIV ALASKA, FAIRBANKS, 74- *Concurrent Pos:* Spec lectr & resource personnel, Mod Math Prog, Fairbanks, Anchorage & Kodiak, Alaska, 64-67; mem adv bd every pupil eval prog, Northwest Regional Lab, State Dept of Educ, 75-81; mem, Fairbanks North

Star Borough Sch Bd, 78-81, clerk, 78-80, treas, 80-81. *Mem:* Math Asn Am; Am Statist Asn. *Res:* Social basis of mathematics teaching and learning; effect of the social setting has on the learning and teaching atmosphere in a secondary classroom. *Mailing Add:* Dept Math Univ Alaska Fairbanks AK 99701

VAN VERTH, JAMES EDWARD, b Huntington, WVa, Jan 26, 28; m 65; c 2. ORGANIC SYNTHESIS, ORGANIC MECHANISMS. *Educ:* Xavier Univ, Ohio, BS, 50; Univ Detroit, MS, 52; Ind Univ, PhD(org chem), 57. *Prof Exp:* Sr res chemist, Monsanto Chem Co, 56-61; asst, Yale Univ, 61-63; from asst prof to assoc prof, 63-75, PROF CHEM, CANISIUS COL, 75- *Mem:* Am Chem Soc. *Res:* Reactions of singlet oxygen. *Mailing Add:* Dept of Chem Canisius Col Buffalo NY 14208

VAN VLACK, LAWRENCE H(ALL), b Atlantic, Iowa, July 21, 20; m 43; c 2. MATERIALS SCIENCE & ENGINEERING. *Educ:* Iowa State Col, BS, 42; Univ Chicago, PhD(geol), 50. *Prof Exp:* Ceramist, US Steel Corp, 42-43, petrogr, 43-52, process metallurgist, 52-53; assoc prof mat & metall eng, 53-58, chmn dept, 67-73, PROF MAT & METALL ENG, UNIV MICH, ANN ARBOR, 58- *Concurrent Pos:* Vis prof, Univ Calif, Berkeley, 61, Univ Melbourne, 67, Univ Kanpur, 69 & Monash Univ, 73. *Honors & Awards:* A Sauveur Award, Am Soc Metals, 79. *Mem:* Fel AAAS; fel Am Ceramic Soc; fel Am Soc Metals; Am Soc Eng Educ; Am Inst Mining, Metall & Petrol Engrs. *Res:* Refractories; slags; nonmetallic inclusions; ceramic materials; process metallurgy; materials science instruction; nickel oxide. *Mailing Add:* 1510 Glen Leven Ann Arbor MI 48103

VAN VLECK, FRED SCOTT, b Clearwater, Nebr, Dec 12, 34; m 60; c 5. MATHEMATICS. *Educ:* Univ Nebr, BSc, 56, MA, 57; Univ Minn, PhD(math), 60. *Prof Exp:* Instr math, Mass Inst Technol, 60-62; from asst prof to assoc prof, 62-68, PROF MATH, UNIV KANS, 68- *Concurrent Pos:* Vis prof, Univ Colo, 71-72. *Mem:* Math Asn Am; Am Math Soc; Soc Indust & Appl Math. *Res:* Optimal control theory; measurable multiplevalued functions; ordinary differential equations; optimization. *Mailing Add:* Dept of Math Univ of Kans Lawrence KS 66045

VAN VLECK, LLOYD DALE, b Clearwater, Nebr, June 11, 33; m 58; c 2. GENETICS, ANIMAL SCIENCE. *Educ:* Univ Nebr, BS, 54, MS, 55; Cornell Univ, PhD(animal breeding), 60. *Prof Exp:* Res assoc animal breeding, 59-60, res geneticist, 60-62, from asst prof to assoc prof animal genetics, 62-73, PROF ANIMAL GENETICS, CORNELL UNIV, 73- *Concurrent Pos:* Vis prof, Univ Nebr, Lincoln, 73 & Scandinavian Grad Prog Animal Breeding, Uppsala, 75. *Honors & Awards:* Am Soc Animal Sci Award, 72; Nat Asn Animal Breeders Award, Am Dairy Sci Asn, 74. *Mem:* Biomet Soc; Am Dairy Sci Asn; Am Soc Animal Sci. *Res:* Methods of improving genetic value of large animals using genetic theory, statistical technique for unbalanced data, and computer processing of large numbers of records. *Mailing Add:* Dept Animal Sci Cornell Univ Ithaca NY 14853

VAN VLEET, JOHN F, b Lodi, NY, Mar 23, 38; m 61; c 2. VETERINARY PATHOLOGY. *Educ:* Cornell Univ, DVM, 62; Univ Ill, MS, 65, PhD(vitamin E deficiency), 67. *Prof Exp:* Asst vet, 62-63; USPHS trainee vet path, Univ Ill, 63-66, instr, 66-67; from asst prof to assoc prof, 67-76, PROF VET PATH, PURDUE UNIV, WEST LAFAYETTE, 76- *Mem:* Vet Med Asn; Int Acad Path; Am Col Vet Path. *Res:* Ultrastructural and nutritional pathology. *Mailing Add:* Dept of Vet Microbiol & Path Purdue Univ West Lafayette IN 47907

VAN VLIET, ANTONE CORNELIS, b San Francisco, Calif, Jan 11, 30; m 53; c 4. WOOD SCIENCE, COMMUNICATIONS. *Educ:* Ore State Univ, BS, 53, MS, 58; Mich State Univ, PhD, 70. *Prof Exp:* Instr forest prod, Ore State Univ, 55-59; asst to plant mgr plywood prod, Bohemia Lumber Co, 59-60; asst prof forest prod, 63-65, asst prof wood prod, Exten, 63-71, ASSOC PROF FOREST PROD, ORE STATE UNIV, 65-, DIR, OFF CAREERS, PLANNING & PLACEMENT, 71- *Concurrent Pos:* State rep, District 35, Ore Legislature, 75. *Mem:* Forest Prod Res Soc. *Res:* Plywood production; wood anatomy and utilization; company educational programs; behavioral aspect of communications; management science. *Mailing Add:* Forest Prods Dept Ore State Univ Corvallis OR 97331

VAN VLIET, CAREL M, b Dordrecht, Neth, Dec 27, 29; US citizen; m 53; c 4. THEORETICAL PHYSICS, ELECTRICAL ENGINEERING. *Educ:* Free Univ, Amsterdam, BS, 49, MA, 53, PhD(physics), 56. *Prof Exp:* Fel elec eng, Univ Minn, Minneapolis, 56-57, asst prof, 57-58; asst dir physics lab, Free Univ, Amsterdam, 58-60; from assoc prof to prof elec eng, Univ Minn, Minneapolis, 60-66, prof elec eng & physics, 66-69; PROF ELEC ENG & PHYSICS, MATH RES CTR, UNIV MONTREAL, 69- *Concurrent Pos:* Vis prof, Univ Fla, 74 & 78- *Mem:* Am Phys Soc; Am Sci Affil; Europ Phys Soc; Neth Phys Soc; sr mem Inst Elec & Electronics Engrs. *Res:* Statistical mechanics; solid state physics; solid state electronics; noise and fluctuation phenomena. *Mailing Add:* 30 Normandy Dr Montreal PQ H3R 3H8 Can

VAN VORIS, PETER, b Bethlehem, Pa, Mar 10, 48; m 71; c 1. ECOLOGY, ECOSYSTEM ANALYSIS. *Educ:* Kenyon Col, BA, 70; State Univ NY Buffalo, MS, 73; Univ Tenn, PhD(ecol), 77. *Prof Exp:* Instr biol & ecol, Trocaire Col, 72-74; res asst, Oak Ridge Nat Lab, 74-76; RES SCIENTIST ECOL, COLUMBUS DIV, BATTELLE MEM INST, 77- *Concurrent Pos:* Fed fel, State Univ NY Buffalo, 71-72; consult, Chem-Trol Pollution Serv Inc, Model City, NY, 71-73; Dept Energy/Oak Ridge Assoc Univs fel, Oak Ridge Nat Lab, 76-77. *Honors & Awards:* Outstanding Col & Univ Educator Award, Asn Am Cols & Univs, 74. *Mem:* Ecol Soc Am; Am Inst Biol Sci; AAAS; Am Soc Naturalists; Audubon Soc. *Res:* The phenomena of Stability in ecosystems; the relationship of the measure of complexity with ecosystem stability; terrestrial microcosm development; environmental assessment. *Mailing Add:* Ecol & Ecosysts Anal Sect 505 King Ave Columbus OH 43201

VAN VOROUS, TED, b Billings, Mont, Jan 6, 29; m 51; c 5. ANALYTICAL CHEMISTRY. *Educ:* Mont State Col, BS, 53, MS, 54. *Prof Exp:* Anal chemist, Dow Chem Co, 54-56, scientist-chemist, 56-59, sr chemist, 59-60, group supvr, 60-62, res group mgr, 62-69; pres, VTA Inc, 69-75; pres, Vac-Tac Systs, 76-81; PRES, VAN VOROUS CONSULTS & E-LINE/USA, 81- *Mem:* Am Vacuum Soc; Geochem Soc; Sigma Xi. *Res:* High vacuum research; evaporation processes; ionphenomena; electron microsopy-metallurgy; electron microprobe analysis; instrumentation development; x-ray and emission spectroscopy; high temperature materials; epitaxial structures; planar magnetron sputtering. *Mailing Add:* Van Vorous Consults 5547 Central Ave Boulder CO 80301

VAN VORST, WILLIAM D, b Cuthbert, Ga, Aug 20, 19; m 49; c 3. CHEMICAL & SYSTEMS ENGINEERING. *Educ:* Rice Inst Technol, BS, 41, ChE, 42; Mass Inst Technol, SM, 43; Univ Calif, Los Angeles, PhD, 53. *Prof Exp:* Res engr, Northrop Aircraft, Inc, 43-46 & N Am Aviation, Inc, 46; from lectr to assoc prof eng, 46-73, chmn eng systs dept, 75-78, PROF ENG, UNIV CALIF, LOS ANGELES, 73- *Concurrent Pos:* Consult, Aerospace Industs, Inc, 49-59; overseas exp & consult int develop, 59-; vpres acad affairs, Robert Col, Istanbul, 69-71, adv foreign fac, Bogazici Univ. *Mem:* AAAS; Am Soc Eng Educ; Am Inst Chem Engrs; fel Inst Advan Eng; Int Asn Hydrogen Energy. *Res:* Engineering systems; industrial development and role of technology in developing countries; environmental engineering-pollution abatement; hydrogen and alcohols as alternative vehicular fuels; energy conversion-alternative sources. *Mailing Add:* 7629 Boelter Hall SEAS/ESD Univ of Calif Los Angeles CA 90024

VAN VUNAKIS, HELEN, b New York, NY, June 15, 24; m 58; c 2. BIOCHEMISTRY. *Educ:* Hunter Col, BA, 46; Columbia Univ, PhD(biochem), 51. *Prof Exp:* USPHS fel & res assoc, Johns Hopkins Univ, 51-54; sr res scientist, State Dept Health, NY, 54-58; from asst prof to assoc prof, 58-74, PROF BIOCHEM, BRANDEIS UNIV, 74- *Concurrent Pos:* NIH career res award. *Res:* Structure of proteins and nucleic acids; interaction of pharmacologically active compounds with specific antibodies and cellular receptor sites. *Mailing Add:* Dept of Biochem Brandeis Univ Waltham MA 02154

VAN WAGNER, CHARLES EDWARD, b Montreal, Que, Dec 9, 24; m 55; c 3. FORESTRY, CHEMICAL ENGINEERING. *Educ:* McGill Univ, BEng, 46; Univ Toronto, BScF, 61. *Prof Exp:* Chief chemist, Can Pittsburg Industs, 46-58; RES SCIENTIST, CAN DEPT ENVIRON, 60- *Mem:* Can Inst Forestry. *Res:* Forest fire; measurement and theory of fire behavior; variation in moisture content of forest fuel with weather; use of prescribed fire in forest management; ecological effects of forest fire. *Mailing Add:* Petawawa Nat Forestry Inst Chalk River ON K0S 1S0 Can

VAN WAGNER, EDWARD M, b Highland Falls, NY, Nov 3, 24; m 52; c 3. ELECTRICAL ENGINEERING. *Educ:* Univ Rochester, BS, 51. *Prof Exp:* Lab technician, Distillation Prod Div, Eastman Kodak Co, 51-53; elec engr, Consol Vacuum Corp, 53-55, physicist, Haloid Co, 55-58 & Haloid Xerox Corp, 58-65, scientist, 65-67, mgt photoreceptor process design, 67-69, SYSTS ANALYST, RES LAB DIV, XEROX CORP, ROCHESTER, 69- *Res:* Vacuum gauges; electrical instrumentation and control of vacuum production systems; graphic arts applications for xerography; design of chemical process equipment; vacuum equipment; welding and forming equipment and electrooptical test equipment. *Mailing Add:* 89 Anytrell Dr Webster NY 14580

VAN WAGTENDONK, JAN WILLEM, b Palo Alto, Calif, Feb 21, 40; m 68; c 2. FOREST ECOLOGY. *Educ:* Ore State Univ, BS, 63; Univ Calif, Berkeley, MS, 68, PhD(wildland res sci), 72. *Prof Exp:* RES SCIENTIST FIRE ECOL, YOSEMITE NAT PARK, NAT PARK SERV, 72- *Mem:* Soc Am Foresters; Ecol Soc Am; Soc Comput Simulation. *Res:* Ecological role of fire in the Sierra Nevada ecosystems; recreational carrying capacities for wilderness areas. *Mailing Add:* Nat Park Serv Yosemite Nat Park El Portal CA 95318

VAN WAGTENDONK, WILLEM JOHAN, b Jakarta, Indonesia, Apr 10, 10; nat US; m 37; c 3. BIOCHEMISTRY. *Educ:* State Univ Utrecht, AB, 31, MA, 34, PhD(biochem), 37. *Prof Exp:* Instr org chem, State Univ Utrecht, 35-37; res chemist, N V Polaks, Frutal Works, Neth, 37-39; res assoc biol, Stanford Univ, 39-41; from asst prof to assoc prof biochem, Ore State Col, 41-46; assoc prof zool, Ind Univ, 46-60; prof biochem, Sch Med, Univ Miami, 60-71; prof biochem, Talladega Col, 71-74; DISTINGUISHED PROF CHEM, BREVARD COL, NC, 79- *Concurrent Pos:* NSF & NIH grants, 48-; scientist, Vet Admin Hosp, Coral Gables, Fla, 60-62, chief basic res, 62-71; liaison off, Study Sect, NIH, 64-67, mem, 67-71; chmn basic sci prog comt, Vet Admin, 66-71; Nat Acad Sci-Polish Acad Sci exchange prof, M Nencki Inst Exp Biol, Warsaw, Poland, 72-73. *Mem:* Fel AAAS; Am Soc Biol Chem; Soc Protozool; fel NY Acad Sci. *Res:* Biochemistry and nutrition of Paramecium aurelia and its endosymbiotes. *Mailing Add:* PO Box 206 Cedar Mountain NC 28718

VAN WART, HAROLD EDGAR, b Bay Shore, NY, Oct 29, 47; m 74; c 2. BIOCHEMISTRY, PHYSICAL CHEMISTRY. *Educ:* State Univ NY, Binghamton, BA, 69; Cornell Univ, MS, 71, PhD(biophys chem), 74. *Prof Exp:* Temp asst prof chem, Cornell Univ, 74-75; NIH fel biochem, Harvard Med Sch, 75-78; ASST PROF BIOCHEM, FLA STATE UNIV, 78- *Mem:* Am Chem Soc; AAAS. *Res:* Structure-function relationships in enzymes, enzyme mechanism, Raman and resonance Raman studies of biomolecules; enzymology, proteolytic enzymes, role of proteolysis in biological control, metalloenzymes. *Mailing Add:* Dept Chem Fla State Univ Tallahassee FL 32306

VAN WAZER, JOHN ROBERT, b Chicago, Ill, Apr 11, 18; m 40; c 1. CHEMISTRY. *Educ:* Northwestern Univ, BS, 40; Harvard Univ, AM, 41, PhD(phys chem), 42. *Prof Exp:* Phys chemist, Eastman Kodak Co, 42-44; res group leader, Clinton Eng Works, Tenn, 44-46; phys chemist, Rumford Chem Works, RI, 46-49; head physics res, Great Lakes Carbon Corp, 49-50; sr scientist, Monsanto Co, 50-68; PROF CHEM, VANDERBILT UNIV, 68- *Concurrent Pos:* Asst res dir, Monsanto Co, 51-60, dir chem dynamics res, 64-67. *Mem:* AAAS; Am Chem Soc; Soc Rheol; NY Acad Sci; Ger Chem Soc. *Res:* Chemistry of phosphorus compounds; substituent-exchange or redistribution reactions; inorganic chemistry; rheology; applied nuclear-magnetic resonance; photoelectron spectroscopy; applied quantum mechanics; nuclear-medical chemistry; nutrition. *Mailing Add:* Dept of Chem Vanderbilt Univ Box 1521 Sta B Nashville TN 37235

VAN WEERT, GEZINUS, b Rotterdam, Neth, Aug 24, 33; Can citizen; m 58; c 2. EXTRACTIVE METALLURGY, IRON FOUNDRY METALLURGY. *Educ:* Technol Univ Delft, BSc, 56, MSc, 58; Univ Toronto, MASc, 59. *Prof Exp:* Test engr metall, Inco, Copper Cliff, Ont, 59-61; res & develop investr, NJ Zinc, Pa, 61-63; mgr process metall, Falconbridge Nickel Mines, Toronto, 63-78; DIR METALL, TECH & ECON SERV, QUI-FER ET TITANE INC, 78- *Concurrent Pos:* Proc ed, Hydrometall Sect, Can Inst Mining & Metall, 72-77. *Honors & Awards:* Technol Award, Metall Soc, 73. *Mem:* Can Inst Mining & Metall; Am Inst Mining, Metall & Petrol Engrs; Am Inst Chem Engrs; Am Foundrymen Soc; Ductile Iron Soc. *Res:* Non-ferrous extractive metallurgy, both hydro and pyro, and operational aspects of the ductile iron foundry industry. *Mailing Add:* Qit-Fer et Titane Inc Suite 700 Montreal PQ H3A 2V2 Can

VAN WIJNGAARDEN, ARIE, b Holland, Apr 8, 33; Can citizen; m 57; c 3. PHYSICS. *Educ:* McMaster Univ, PhD(physics), 62. *Prof Exp:* Teacher physics, 62-70, assoc prof, 70-73, PROF PHYSICS, UNIV WINDSOR, 73- *Concurrent Pos:* Nat Res Coun-Ont Res Found res grants, 62- *Res:* Radiative processes and lamb shift. *Mailing Add:* Dept of Physics Univ of Windsor Windsor ON N9B 3P4 Can

VAN WINGEN, N(ICO), b Amsterdam, Netherlands, Apr 17, 11; nat US; m 49; c 1. PETROLEUM ENGINEERING. *Educ:* Calif Inst Technol, BS, 34; Univ Calif, MS, 38. *Hon Degrees:* DSc, Adamson Univ, Manila, 63. *Prof Exp:* Prod engr, Richfield Oil Corp, 38-40, sr prod engr, 40-42, asst chief engr, 42-44, chief eval engr, 44-47; prof petrol eng, Univ Okla, 47-49 & Univ Southern Calif, 50-76; CONSULT, 47- *Mem:* Am Inst Mining, Metall & Petrol Engrs; Sigma Xi; Soc Petrol Eval Engrs. *Res:* Appraisal of oil and gas properties; reservoir analysis; enhanced recovery of oil. *Mailing Add:* 1197 San Marino Ave San Marino CA 91108

VAN WINKLE, MICHAEL GEORGE, b Newark, Ohio, July 25, 39; c 3. IMMUNOLOGY, IMMUNOCHEMISTRY. *Educ:* Ohio State Univ, BSc, 62, MSc, 64, PhD(immunol), 66. *Prof Exp:* Group leader res atopic allergy, Riker Lab, 3M Co, 66-71; head, Dept Immunol, Nucleic Acid Res Inst, Int Chem & Nuclear Corp, 71-73; mgr, Dept Hepatitis, Curtis Labs, Inc, 73-76; mgr hepatitis opers, Nuclear Med Labs, Inc, 76-78; SR RES IMMUNOCHEMIST, CLIN IMMUNOASSAY RES & DEVELOP, BECKMAN INSTRUMENTS, INC, 78- *Mem:* Am Asn Immunol; Am Soc Microbiol; AAAS. *Res:* Research and development on clinical immunoassays. *Mailing Add:* RIA Develop Beckman Instrument Inc Irvine CA 92714

VAN WINKLE, QUENTIN, b Grand Forks, NDak, Mar 10, 19; m 41; c 4. CHEMISTRY. *Educ:* SDak Sch Mines & Technol, BS, 40; Ohio State Univ, PhD(chem), 47. *Prof Exp:* Asst chem, Ohio State Univ, 40-43, res assoc eng, Exp Sta, 44; asst chemist metall lab, Univ Chicago, 44-46; res assoc chem, Ohio State Univ, 46-48, from asst prof to assoc prof, 48-59, prof, 59-80; RETIRED. *Concurrent Pos:* Consult, E I du Pont de Nemours & Co, 57-75. *Mem:* AAAS; Am Chem Soc. *Res:* Physico-chemical properties of proteins, high polymers; nucleic acids; surface chemistry. *Mailing Add:* 280 Dixon Ct Columbus OH 43214

VAN WINKLE, THOMAS LEO, b New Haven, Conn, May 18, 22. CHEMICAL ENGINEERING. *Educ:* Yale Univ, BE, 42, ME, 44, DEng(chem eng), 49. *Prof Exp:* Jr scientist nuclear eng, Los Alamos Sci Lab, 45-46; engr, Brookhaven Nat Lab, 48-49; teacher math, chem & physics, Portsmouth Abbey Sch, 52-73, headmaster, 57-73; vis fel & lectr chem eng, Yale Univ, 73-75; ASSOC PROF CHEM ENG, CATH UNIV AM, 75-, DEPT CHMN, 81- *Concurrent Pos:* Prin engr, Tetra Tech, Inc, 75-79; environ systs scientist, Mitre Corp, 79-80; chem eng, Naval Res Lab, 80- *Mem:* Am Inst Chem Engrs; AAAS; Sigma Xi. *Res:* Energy conservation, especially the comparative study of energy requirements of natural and synthetic fibers; quantitative determination of chemicals required for sewage treatment; effect of compostion on freezing point of Navy fuels. *Mailing Add:* Cath Univ of Am Washington DC 20064

VAN WINKLE, WEBSTER, JR, b Plainfield, NJ, Nov 18, 38; m 61; c 3. ENVIRONMENTAL SCIENCES. *Educ:* Oberlin Col, BA, 61; Rutgers Univ, New Brunswick, PhD(zool), 67. *Prof Exp:* Res assoc, Shellfish Res Lab, Rutgers Univ, 66-67; asst prof biol, Col William Mary, 67-70; USPHS fels, NC State Univ, 70 & 72; res assoc, 72-75, res staff mem, Environ Sci Div, 75-78, HEAD, AQUATIC ECOL SECT, OAK RIDGE NAT LAB, 79- *Concurrent Pos:* NSF fel, Marine Lab, Duke Univ, 69; NSF sci fac fel, NC State Univ, 71-72. *Mem:* AAAS; Ecol Soc Am; Am Fisheries Soc. *Res:* Assessment of environmental impacts on aquatic ecosystems; fish population modeling; spectral analysis of environmental time series; data analysis. *Mailing Add:* Aquatic Ecol Sect Oak Ridge Nat Lab Oak Ridge TN 37830

VAN WINTER, CLASINE, b Amsterdam, Netherlands, Apr 8, 29. MATHEMATICAL PHYSICS. *Educ:* Univ Groningen, BSc, 50, MSc, 54, PhD(physics), 57. *Prof Exp:* Res asst physics, Univ Groningen, 51-58, sci officer, 58-68; PROF MATH & PHYSICS, UNIV KY, 68- *Concurrent Pos:* Fel physics, Univ Birmingham, 57 & Niels Bohr Inst Theoret Physics, Univ Copenhagen, 63; vis assoc prof physics, Ind Univ, Bloomington, 67-68. *Mem:* Am Math Soc; Am Phys Soc. *Res:* Three-and more-body problem in quantum mechanics; quantum scattering theory; functional analysis; complex variables. *Mailing Add:* Dept of Math Univ of Ky Lexington KY 40506

VAN WOERT, MELVIN H, b Brooklyn, NY, Nov 3, 29; m 55. INTERNAL MEDICINE. *Educ:* Columbia Univ, BA, 51; NY Med Col, MD, 56. *Prof Exp:* From intern to resident internal med, Univ Chicago, 56-60, res asst gastroenterol, 62-63; from asst scientist to assoc scientist, Brookhaven Nat Lab, 63-67; from asst prof to assoc prof med & pharmacol, Sch Med, Yale Univ, 67-74; prof internal med & head, Sect Clin Pharmacol, 74-78, PROF PHARMACOL, MT SINAI SCH MED, 74-, PROF NEUROL, 78- *Mem:* AAAS; fel Am Col Physicians; Soc Neurosci; Soc Neurochem; Am Soc Pharmacol & Exp Therapeut. *Res:* Neuropharmacological approaches to extrapyramidal disease; serotonin metabolism and myoclonus. *Mailing Add:* Dept of Neurol Mt Sinai Sch of Med New York NY 10029

VAN WORMER, KENNETH A(UGUSTUS), JR, b Mannsville, NY, Oct 4, 30; m 57; c 4. CHEMICAL ENGINEERING. *Educ:* Clarkson Col Technol, BS, 52, MS, 54; Mass Inst Technol, ScD(chem eng), 61. *Prof Exp:* Engr chem eng, Gen Elec Co, 52-53; from instr to assoc prof, 54-79, chmn dept, 71-78, PROF CHEM ENG, TUFTS UNIV, 79- *Mem:* Am Soc Eng Educ; Am Inst Chem Engrs. *Res:* Solar engineering; energy conservation; waste water treatment; liquid-liquid extraction; heterogeneous catalysis in the direct reduction of iron ore; applied thermodynamics; applications of digital computers to chemical engineering; reaction kinetics; contribution of nucleation to phase transformations; applied mathematics; optimization. *Mailing Add:* Dept of Chem Eng Tufts Univ Medford MA 02155

VAN WYK, JUDSON JOHN, b Maurice, Iowa, June 10, 21; m 44; c 4. PEDIATRICS, ENDOCRINOLOGY. *Educ:* Hope Col, AB, 43; Johns Hopkins Univ, MD, 48; Am Bd Pediat, dipl. *Prof Exp:* Intern & asst resident pediat, Johns Hopkins Hosp, 48-50; resident, Cincinnati Children's Hosp, Ohio, 50-51; investr metab, Nat Heart Inst, 51-53; fel pediat endocrinol, Johns Hopkins Univ, 53-55; from asst prof to assoc prof pediat, 55-62, prof, 62-75, KENAN PROF PEDIAT, SCH MED, UNIV NC, CHAPEL HILL, 75- *Concurrent Pos:* Attend physician, NC Mem Hosp, 55-; Markle scholar med sci, 56-61; USPHS res career award, 62-; mem training grants comt in diabetes & metab, NIH, 67-71 & endocrine study sect, 71-75; vis scientist, Karolinska Inst, Sweden, 68-69; consult, Womack Army Hosp, Ft Bragg. *Mem:* Endocrine Soc; Soc Pediat Res; fel Am Acad Pediat; Am Pediat Soc; Lawson Wilkins Pediat Endocrine Soc (pres, 76-77). *Res:* Human sex differentiation; pituitary function and hormonal control of growth and sexual maturation; isolation and physiologic role of somatomedin. *Mailing Add:* Dept of Pediat Univ of NC Sch of Med Chapel Hill NC 27514

VAN WYLEN, GORDON J(OHN), b Grant, Mich, Feb 6, 20; m 51; c 5. MECHANICAL ENGINEERING. *Educ:* Calvin Col, AB, 42; Univ Mich, BSE, 42, MSE, 47; Mass Inst Technol, ScD(mech eng), 51. *Prof Exp:* Indust engr, E I du Pont de Nemours & Co, 42-43; instr mech eng, Pa State Univ, 46-48; asst, Mass Inst Technol, 49-51; from asst prof to prof, Univ Mich, Ann Arbor, 51-72, chmn dept, 58-65, dean col eng, 65-72; PRES, HOPE COL, 72- *Mem:* Fel AAAS; Nat Soc Prof Engrs; Am Soc Mech Engrs. *Res:* Thermodynamics and cryogenics. *Mailing Add:* Hope Col Holland MI 49423

VANYO, JAMES PATRICK, b Wheeling, WVa, Jan 29, 28. APPLIED MECHANICS, LAW. *Educ:* WVa Univ, BSME, 52; Salmon P Chase Col, JD, 59; Univ Calif, Los Angeles, MA, 66, PhD(eng), 69. *Prof Exp:* Asst supvr commun, Am Tel & Tel Co, NY, 52-53; pres, Van Industs, Inc, Ohio, 54-59; asst to pres, Remanco, Inc, Calif, 59-61; proposal specialist, Marquardt Corp, 61-63; planning analyst, Litton Industs, 69-70; asst prof, 71-80, ASSOC PROF ENG & LAW, UNIV CALIF, SANTA BARBARA, 80- *Concurrent Pos:* Lectr, Sinclair Col, Ohio, 56-57; consult rotating fluids. *Mem:* Am Phys Soc. *Res:* Dynamics of rotating nonrigid bodies and fluids; interaction between law and technology in large scale systems. *Mailing Add:* Dept Mech Eng Univ Calif Santa Barbara CA 93106

VAN ZANDT, GERTRUDE, chemistry, deceased

VAN ZANDT, LONNIE L, b Bound Brook, NJ, Sept 29, 37; m 61; c 3. SOLID STATE PHYSICS. *Educ:* Lafayette Col, BS, 58; Harvard Univ, AM, 59, PhD(physics), 64. *Prof Exp:* Mem staff, Sci Lab, Ford Motor Co, 62-64 & Lincoln Lab, Mass Inst Technol, 64-67; asst prof, 67-70, ASSOC PROF PHYSICS, PURDUE UNIV, WEST LAFAYETTE, 70- *Res:* Physics of biological molecules; transition metal oxides. *Mailing Add:* Dept of Physics Purdue Univ West Lafayette IN 47907

VAN ZANDT, PAUL DOYLE, b Vandalia, Ill, Dec 29, 27; m 54; c 1. PARASITOLOGY. *Educ:* Greenville Col, AB, 52; Univ Ill, MS, 53; Univ NC, MSPH, 55, PhD(parasitol), 60. *Prof Exp:* Asst pub health, Univ NC, 58-61; from asst prof to assoc prof biol, 61-69, PROF BIOL, YOUNGSTOWN STATE UNIV, 69- *Mem:* Fel AAAS; Am Soc Parasitol; Am Soc Trop Med & Hyg; Royal Soc Trop Med & Hyg. *Res:* Immunology of animal parasites; medical parasitology and microbiology. *Mailing Add:* Dept of Biol Youngstown State Univ Youngstown OH 44503

VAN ZANDT, THOMAS EDWARD, b Highland Park, Mich, July 10, 29; m 61; c 2. RADAR METEOROLOGY. *Educ:* Duke Univ, BS, 50; Yale Univ, PhD, 55. *Prof Exp:* Physicist, Sandia Corp, 54-57; PHYSICIST, AERONOMY LAB, NAT OCEANIC & ATMOSPHERIC ADMIN, 57- *Concurrent Pos:* Vis lectr, Univ Colo, 61-70, adj prof, 70- *Mem:* Am Geophys Union; Am Meteorol Soc; Int Union Radio Sci. *Mailing Add:* Aeronomy Lab Nat Oceanic & Atmospheric Admin Boulder CO 80302

VAN ZANT, KENT LEE, b Humboldt, Nebr, July 5, 47; m 71. GEOLOGY, PALYNOLOGY. *Educ:* Earlham Col, AB, 69; Univ Iowa, MS, 73, PhD(geol), 76. *Prof Exp:* Asst prof geol, Beloit Col, 76-78; ASST PROF GEOL, EARLHAM COL, 78- *Concurrent Pos:* Nat Acad Sci res grant, USSR, 76-77; Res Corp grant, 77. *Mem:* Geol Soc Am; Am Quaternary Asn; Am Asn Stratig Palynologists; Int Order Palaeobotanists. *Res:* Quaternary paleobotany in the midwestern United States and in the southern USSR. *Mailing Add:* Dept of Geol Earlham Col Richmond IN 47374

VAN ZWALENBERG, GEORGE, b Neth, Sept 7, 30; US citizen; m 53, 76; c 3. MATHEMATICS. *Educ:* Calvin Col, BS, 53; Univ Fla, MA, 55; Univ Calif, Berkeley, PhD(math), 68. *Prof Exp:* Instr math, Bowling Green State Univ, 59-60; vis lectr, Calvin Col, 60-61, asst prof, 61-63; asst prof, Calif State Univ, Fresno, 63-67; chmn dept, 74-77, PROF MATH, CALVIN COL, 68- *Concurrent Pos:* Math Asn Am vis lectr, High Schs, 65-66. *Mem:* Am Math Soc; Math Asn Am. *Res:* Complex variables. *Mailing Add:* Dept of Math Calvin Col Grand Rapids MI 49506

VAN ZWIETEN, MATTHEW JACOBUS, b Zeist, Netherlands, Apr 6, 45; US citizen; m 66; c 2. VETERINARY PATHOLOGY. *Educ:* Univ Calif, Davis, BS, 67, DVM, 69; Am Col Vet Pathologists, dipl, 74. *Prof Exp:* Sci investr cell biol & path, Med Res Inst Infectious Dis, US Army, 69-71; res fel, New Eng Regional Primate Res Ctr & Animal Res Ctr, Harvard Med Sch, 71-75, assoc path, 75-76; MEM STAFF, INST EXP GERONTOL, 76- *Concurrent Pos:* Res assoc path, Angell Mem Animal Hosp, 71-74, consult, 75-76; res assoc path, Children's Hosp Med Ctr, 73-75; head diag procedures, New Eng Regional Primate Res Ctr & Animal Res Ctr, Harvard Med Sch, 75-76. *Mem:* Am Col Vet Pathologists; Int Acad Path; Am Asn Lab Animal Sci; Am Vet Med Asn. *Res:* Diseases of aging in laboratory animals; mechanisms of radiation induced mammary carcinogenesis in rats; identification and development of spontaneous animal diseases as models for their human counterparts. *Mailing Add:* Inst Exp Gerontol TNO PO Box 5815 2280HV Rijswijk Netherlands

VAN ZYTVELD, JOHN BOS, b Hammond, Ind, Nov 12, 40; m 61; c 3. SOLID STATE PHYSICS. *Educ:* Calvin Col, AB, 62; Mich State Univ, MS, 64, PhD(physics), 67. *Prof Exp:* Fel physics, Univ Sheffield, 67-68; from asst prof to assoc prof, 68-76, PROF PHYSICS, CALVIN COL, 76- *Concurrent Pos:* Res physicist, Battelle Mem Inst, Ohio, 69; sr fel, Dept Physics, Univ Leicester, Eng, 74-75; sr Fulbright-Hays lectr physics, Yarmouk Univ, Irbid, Jordan, 80-81. *Mem:* AAAS; Am Phys Soc; Am Asn Physics Teachers; Am Sci Affiliation. *Res:* Electron transport properties of solid and liquid metals, alloys and semiconductors. *Mailing Add:* Dept of Physics Calvin Col Grand Rapids MI 49506

VARADAN, VASUNDARA VENKATRAMAN, b Guntur, India, June 10, 48; m 73. MECHANICS, PHYSICS. *Educ:* Kerala Univ, India, BSc, 67, MSc, 69; Univ Ill, Chicago Circle, PhD(physics), 74. *Prof Exp:* Res assoc mech, Cornell Univ, 74-77; asst prof, 77-81, ASSOC PROF MECH, OHIO STATE UNIV, 81- *Concurrent Pos:* Prin investr, Rockwell Int, 77-81; co-prin investr, Off Naval Res, 78-; Nat Oceanic & Atmospheric Asn grant, 78-80, Naval Res Lab, 79 & Ames Lab, Army Res Off & Naval Coastal Systs Ctr, 81- *Mem:* Acoust Soc Am; Soc Eng Sci. *Res:* Wave propagation; scattering; statistical mechanics; classical field theory. *Mailing Add:* Dept Eng Mech 155 W Woodruff Ave Columbus OH 43210

VARADARAJAN, KALATHOOR, b Bezwada, India, Apr 13, 35; m 61; c 2. MATHEMATICS, TOPOLOGY. *Educ:* Loyola Col, Madras, India, BA, 55; Columbia Univ, PhD(topology), 60. *Prof Exp:* Res fel math, Tata Inst Fundamental Res, India, 60-61, fel, 61-67; vis assoc prof, Univ Ill, Urbana, 67-69; reader, Tata Inst Fundamental Res, India, 69-71; vis prof, Ramanujan Inst, Madras, 71; assoc prof, 71-73, PROF MATH, UNIV CALGARY, 73- *Mem:* Am Math Soc; Can Math Cong. *Res:* Algebraic and differential topology; homological algebra. *Mailing Add:* Dept Math Statist & Comput Sci Univ of Calgary 2920 24th Ave NW Calgary AB T2N 1N4 Can

VARADY, JOHN CARL, b Niagara Falls, NY, Feb 26, 35; m 66. BIOSTATISTICS. *Educ:* Calif Inst Technol, BS, 56; Univ Wash, MA, 58; Univ Calif, Los Angeles, PhD(biostatist), 65. *Prof Exp:* Opers res analyst, Radioplane Div, Northrop Corp, 57-58; sr mathematician, Systs Develop Corp, 58-65; chief biostatist, Calif Dept Ment Hyg, 65-66; dir comput servs, Univ Cincinnati, 66-70; DIR BIOSTATIST, SYNTEX LABS, 70- *Mem:* Am Statist Asn; Asn Comput Mach. *Mailing Add:* Biostatistics Syntex Labs Res 3401 Hillview Palo Alto CA 94304

VARAIYA, PRAVIN PRATAP, b Bombay, India, Oct 29, 40; m 63. ELECTRICAL ENGINEERING, ECONOMICS. *Educ:* Univ Bombay, India, BS, 60; Univ Calif, Berkeley, MS, 62, PhD(elec eng), 66. *Prof Exp:* Mem tech staff commun, Bell Tel Labs, 62-63; from asst prof to assoc prof, 66-70, PROF ELEC ENG, UNIV CALIF, BERKELEY, 70-, PROF ECON, 77- *Concurrent Pos:* Fel Guggenheim Found, 71-72; vis prof elec eng, Mass Inst Technol, 74-75; res prof, Miller Found, 78-79. *Mem:* Inst Elec & Electronics Engrs. *Res:* System theory; urban economics; computer communications. *Mailing Add:* Dept of Elec Eng Univ of Calif Berkeley CA 94720

VARAN, CYRUS O, b Hamadan, Iran, Mar 26, 34; m; c 1. CIVIL ENGINEERING. *Educ:* SDak State Univ, BS, 58; Univ Kans, MS, 60; Univ Del, PhD(appl sci), 64. *Prof Exp:* Struct engr, Howard, Needles, Tammen & Bergendoff, Consult Engrs, 58-60; asst prof civil eng, Univ NMex, 64-71, assoc prof, 71-80. *Concurrent Pos:* Res assoc, Univ Del Res Found res grant, 63-64; prin investr, grants, Univ NMex, 65, NSF, 65-67 & Sandia Labs, 70-71 & 71-72; investr, US Corps Engrs grant, 70. *Mem:* Am Soc Civil Engrs; Am Soc Eng Educ. *Res:* Dynamics of structures; discrete and macro mechanics; design of guyed towers and articulated lattice shell structures; dynamics of grid-stiffened and ribbed plates; seismic design of building structures. *Mailing Add:* 1624 Sagebrush Tr SE Albuquerque NM 87123

VARANASI, PRASAD, b Vijayavada, India, Dec 20, 38; m 72. PLANETARY ATMOSPHERES, SPECTROSCOPY. *Educ:* Andhra Univ, India, BSc, 57; Indian Inst Sci, Bangalore, MSc, 61; Mass Inst Technol, SM, 62; Univ Calif, San Diego, PhD(eng physics), 67. *Prof Exp:* Asst prof, 67-71, ASSOC PROF ENG PHYSICS, STATE UNIV NY STONY BROOK, 71- *Concurrent Pos:* NASA grant; assoc ed, J Quant Spectros & Radiative Transfer, 73-78. *Mem:* Am Inst Aeronaut & Astronaut. *Res:* Infrared spectroscopy as applied to planetary atmospheres; experimental work on collision broadening of spectral lines and molecular structure. *Mailing Add:* Dept of Mech Eng State Univ of NY Stony Brook NY 11790

VARANASI, SURYANARAYANA RAO, b Narsapur, India, Oct 4, 39; US citizen; m 65. ENGINEERING MECHANICS. *Educ:* Andhra Univ, BE, 60; Calif Inst Technol, MS, 61; Univ Wash, PhD(aerospace eng), 68. *Prof Exp:* Res engr appl mech, Gas Turbine Div, Boeing Co, 65-66; res engr, Dept Comput, 66-69, SPECIALIST ENGR FATIGUE & FRACTURE RES, STRUCT TECHNOL, BOEING COM AIRPLANE CO, 69- *Concurrent Pos:* Consult, Math Sci Corp, 63. *Mem:* Am Soc Testing & Mat. *Res:* Fracture mechanics; fatigue; structural integrity; damage tolerance; stress analysis; finite element methods; plasticity; viscoelasticity; wave propagation; applied mathematics; computer applications. *Mailing Add:* Struct Technol Boeing Com Airplane Co Seattle WA 98124

VARANASI, USHA SURYAM, b Bassien, Burma. BIOCHEMISTRY, CHEMISTRY. *Educ:* Univ Bombay, BSc, 61; Calif Inst Technol, MS, 64; Univ Wash, PhD(chem), 68. *Prof Exp:* Res assoc lipid biochem, Oceanic Inst, Oahu, Hawaii, 69-71; assoc res prof, 71-75, RES PROF CHEM, SEATTLE UNIV, 75-; SUPVR RES CHEMIST & TASK MGR, NORTHWEST FISHERIES CTR, NAT MARINE FISHERIES SERV, NAT OCEANIC & ATMOSPHERIC ADMIN, 75- *Concurrent Pos:* Vis scientist, Pioneer Res Unit, Northwest Fisheries Ctr, Nat Marine Fisheries Serv, Nat Oceanic & Atmospheric Admin, Wash, 69-72, res chemist, 75-80; affil assoc prof chem, Univ Wash, 80- *Mem:* Am Soc Biol Chemists; Am Chem Soc; Soc Exp Biol & Med. *Res:* Biochemical effects of xenobiotics in fish; interactions of carcinogens with cellular macromolecules such as DNA and protein; lipid structure and metabolism; chemistry of bioacoustics; reaction kinetics in binary solvent systems; adaptive mechanisms in marine organisms; environmental conservation research in biochemistry. *Mailing Add:* 2725 Montlake Blvd E Nat Oceanic & Atmospheric Admin Seattle WA 98112

VARANDANI, PARTAB T, b Karachi, India, Sept 5, 29; US citizen; m 62; c 3. BIOCHEMISTRY, ENDOCRINOLOGY. *Educ:* Agra Univ, BSc, 50, MSc, 52; Univ Ill, PhD(biochem, animal nutrit), 59. *Prof Exp:* Res asst biochem, Indian Vet Res Inst, 52-56; res assoc, Radiocarbon Lab, Univ Ill, 59-61 & Roswell Park Mem Inst, 61-63; sr investr, 63-72, SR SCIENTIST & CHIEF, SECT ENDOCRINOL, FELS RES INST, 72-, FELS PROF BIOL CHEM, SCH MED, WRIGHT STATE UNIV, 77- *Concurrent Pos:* NIH rev panel, Diabetes Res & Training Ctr Appln, 77, NIH Metab Study Sect, 77-80. *Mem:* Am Chem Soc; Am Soc Biol Chemists; Endocrine Soc; Am Diabetes Asn; Am Asn Immunol. *Res:* Carbohydrate and fat metabolism; metabolism and function of vitamin A; immunochemistry, structure, metabolism and regulation of enzymes and hormones; pepsin, glutathione-insulin-transhydrogenase, insulin, growth hormone and glucagon; discovery of the sequentail degradative pathway of insulin. *Mailing Add:* Sect of Endocrinol Fels Res Inst Yellow Springs OH 45387

VARBERG, DALE ELTHON, b Forest City, Iowa, Sept 9, 30; m 55; c 3. MATHEMATICS. *Educ:* Univ Minn, BA, 54, MA, 57, PhD(math), 59. *Prof Exp:* From asst prof to assoc prof, 58-65, PROF MATH, HAMLINE UNIV, 65- *Concurrent Pos:* NSF fel, Inst Advan Study, 64-65; sci fac fel, Univ Wash, 71-72. *Mem:* Am Math Soc; Math Asn Am. *Res:* Stochastic and Gaussian processes; measure theory; convexity theory. *Mailing Add:* Dept of Math Hamline Univ St Paul MN 55104

VARDANIS, ALEXANDER, b Athens, Greece, Mar 13, 33; Can citizen; m 59; c 3. BIOCHEMISTRY. *Educ:* Univ Leeds, BSc, 55; McGill Univ, MSc, 58, PhD(biochem), 60. *Prof Exp:* RES OFF BIOCHEM, RES INST, CAN DEPT AGR, UNIV WESTERN ONT, 61- *Concurrent Pos:* Nat Res Coun Can fel, 59-61. *Mem:* Chem Inst Can. *Res:* Intermediary metabolism of carbohydrates, particularly glycogen metabolism; chitin biosynthesis; protein kinases. *Mailing Add:* Res Inst Can Dept Agr University Sub PO London ON N6A 5B7 Can

VARDARIS, RICHARD MILES, b Lakewood, Ohio, Nov 28, 34; m 70; c 2. NEUROENDOCRINOLOGY, NEUROPSYCHOPHARMACOLOGY. *Educ:* Case Western Reserve Univ, BA, 62; Univ Ore, MS, 67, PhD(med psychol), 68. *Prof Exp:* From asst prof to assoc prof, 67-77, PROF PSYCHOL, KENT STATE UNIV, 78- *Concurrent Pos:* NIH res grants, 72-82; chmn, Biopsychol Prog, Kent State Univ, 76-, dir, Div Biomed Sci, 76-79; res prof neurobiol, Northeastern Col Med, Ohio Univ, 77-; co-prin investr, NSF res grant, 78-80. *Mem:* Soc Neurosci; NY Acad Sci; AAAS; Sigma Xi. *Res:* Effects of steroid hormones and related compounds on excitability of brain tissue; behavioral effects of gonadal steroids and drugs of abuse; neurobiological analysis of linguistic phenomena. *Mailing Add:* Dept Psychol Kent State Univ Kent OH 44242

VARDEMAN, STEPHEN BRUCE, b Louisville, Ky, Aug 27, 49; m 70. MATHEMATICAL STATISTICS, ENGINEERING STATISTICS. *Educ:* Iowa State Univ, BS, 71, MS, 73; Mich State Univ, PhD(statist), 75. *Prof Exp:* asst prof statist, Purdue Univ, West Lafayette, 75-81; ASST PROF STATIST, IOWA STATE UNIV, AMES, 81- *Mem:* Am Statist Asn; Inst Math Statist. *Res:* Compound and empirical Bayes decision problems, pattern recognition problems; admissibility in finite population sampling problems. *Mailing Add:* Snedecor Hall Dept Statist Iowa State Univ Ames IA 50011

VARDI, JOSEPH, US citizen. CHEMICAL ENGINEERING. *Educ:* Univ Cincinnati, PhD(chem eng), 64. *Prof Exp:* Engr, 64-67, SR RES ENGR, EXXON RES & ENG CO, 67- *Mem:* Am Inst Chem Engrs; Am Chem Soc. *Res:* Air pollution and fuels research; impact of fuels and their combustion products on the environment; application of catalysis and adsorption to new processes to control automotive air pollution; conduction and radiation heat transfer. *Mailing Add:* 1344 Taft Rd Teaneck NJ 07666

VARDIMAN, RONALD G, b Louisville, Ky, Sept 17, 32; m 69; c 1. PHYSICAL METALLURGY, PHYSICS. *Educ:* Univ Notre Dame, BS, 54, MS, 56, PhD(metall), 61. *Prof Exp:* METALLURGIST, METALL DIV, US NAVAL RES LAB, WASHINGTON, DC, 61- *Mem:* AAAS; Sigma Xi; Am Inst Mining, Metall & Petrol Engrs; Am Soc Metals. *Res:* Effects of defect structure on properties, including work on ion implantation, superconducting materials, diffusion, dislocation observation, sintering and crystal growth. *Mailing Add:* 12618 Prestwick Dr Ft Washington MD 20022

VARGA, CHARLES E, b Philadelphia, Pa, Sept 13, 45; c 2. PHYSICAL ORGANIC CHEMISTRY. *Educ:* St Joseph's Col, Pa, BS, 67, MS, 69. *Prof Exp:* Develop chemist packaging, Single Serv Div Lab, Int Paper Co, 69-73; res mgr cold rolling lubricants, Metals Div Lab, 73-80, PROD MGR, NON-FERROUS ROLLING LUBRICANTS, PRIMARY METALS PROD DIV, QUAKER CHEM CORP, 81- *Mem:* Am Chem Soc; Am Soc Lubricant Eng. *Res:* Lubrication theory; metal organic bonding and chemisorption; surface activity; bidentate molecules. *Mailing Add:* Quaker Chem Corp Elm & Lime Sts Conshohocken PA 19428

VARGA, GABRIELLA ANNE, b Budapest, Hungary, Aug 8, 51; US citizen; m 77. ANIMAL NUTRITION, NUTRITION. *Educ:* Duquesne Univ, BS, 73; Univ RI, MS, 75; Univ Md, PhD(animal sci), 78. *Prof Exp:* Res asst ruminant nutrit, Univ RI, 73-75; res asst, Univ Md, 75-78; FEL RUMINANT NUTRIT, W VA UNIV, 79- *Mem:* Am Soc Animal Sci; AAAS; Appl Environ Micros; Am Soc Dairy Soc. *Res:* Specializing in utilization of non-protein nitrogen compounds by ruminants; feeding of animal waste to ruminants; utilization and microbiological aspects are also of interest; effect of feed intake in dairy cows in early lactation; utilization of dietary fiber by dairy cows. *Mailing Add:* Dept of Animal & Vet Sci W Va Univ Morgantown WV 26505

VARGA, GIDEON MICHAEL, JR, b Brooklyn, NY, Feb 13, 41. INORGANIC CHEMISTRY. *Educ:* Manhattan Col, BS, 62; Georgetown Univ, PhD(inorg chem), 67; New York Univ, MBA, 75. *Prof Exp:* STAFF CHEMIST, EXXON RES & ENG CO, 67- *Mem:* Am Chem Soc; Sigma Xi. *Res:* Characterization of inorganic and organic compounds; properties of distillate fuels; nox emission control; pollution monitoring instrumentation; energy conservation; electrochemistry; heteropoly electrolytes and blues; polarography; heterogeneous catalysis; fuel cells. *Mailing Add:* Apt 20 1196 Lake Ave Clark NJ 07066

VARGA, LOUIS P, b Portland, Ore, Mar 25, 22; m 48; c 4. ANALYTICAL CHEMISTRY, RADIOCHEMISTRY. *Educ:* Reed Col, BA, 48; Univ Chicago, MS, 50; Ore State Univ, PhD(anal chem), 60. *Prof Exp:* Chemist, Hanford Labs, 50-53; instr & res assoc, Reed Col, 53-57; res assoc anal chem, Mass Inst Technol, 60-61; asst prof chem, 61-67, ASSOC PROF CHEM, OKLA STATE UNIV, 67- *Concurrent Pos:* Vis staff mem, Los Alamos Sci Lab, 68-78. *Mem:* Am Chem Soc; Sigma Xi. *Res:* Analytical instrumentation; water analysis; rare earth spectra. *Mailing Add:* Dept of Chem Okla State Univ Stillwater OK 74078

VARGA, RICHARD S, b US, Oct 9, 28; m 51; c 1. MATHEMATICS. *Educ:* Case Inst Technol, BS, 50; Harvard Univ, AM, 51, PhD(math), 54. *Prof Exp:* Adv mathematician, Bettis Atomic Power Lab, Westinghouse Elec Co, 54-60; prof math, Case Western Reserve Univ, 60-69; UNIV PROF MATH, KENT STATE UNIV, 69- *Concurrent Pos:* Consult, Gulf Res & Develop Co, 60, Argonne Nat Lab, 61 & Los Alamos Sci Lab, 68-; Guggenheim fel, Harvard Univ & Calif Inst Technol, 63; Sherman Fairchild scholar, Calif Inst Technol, 74; Gast prof, Munich Tech Univ, 76. *Mem:* Am Math Soc; Soc Indust & Appl Math; Math Asn Am. *Res:* Numerical analysis; approximation theory. *Mailing Add:* Dept of Math Kent State Univ Kent OH 44242

VARGAS, JOSEPH MARTIN, JR, b Fall River, Mass, Mar 11, 42; m 63; c 2. PLANT PATHOLOGY. *Educ:* Univ RI, BS, 63; Okla State Univ, MS, 65; Univ Minn, Minneapolis, PhD(plant path), 68. *Prof Exp:* Asst prof, 68-74, ASSOC PROF BOT & PLANT PATH, MICH STATE UNIV, 74- *Mem:* Am Phytopath Soc. *Res:* Turfgrass pathology; resistance to fungicides; pesticide degradation. *Mailing Add:* Dept of Bot & Plant Path Mich State Univ East Lansing MI 48823

VARGAS, LESTER LAMBERT, b Providence, RI, May 20, 21; m 48. CARDIOVASCULAR SURGERY. *Educ:* Brown Univ, AB, 43; George Washington Univ, MD, 45. *Prof Exp:* Asst surg, Col Physicians & Surgeons, Columbia Univ, 52-55; asst clin prof, Sch Med, Tufts Univ, 59-62; prof surg, 63-70, PROF MED SCI, DIV BIOL & MED SCI, BROWN UNIV, 70- *Concurrent Pos:* Lectr, Sch Nursing, Brown Univ, 42; dir cardiac surg & Cardiovasc Surg Res Lab, RI Hosp, 56-70, surgeon-in-chief, 63-69, assoc surgeon-in-chief, 69-; lectr, Sch Med, Tufts Univ, 63- *Mem:* Am Col Cardiol; Am Col Chest Physicians; Am Col Surgeons; Am Thoracic Soc; Int Cardiovasc Soc. *Mailing Add:* 110 Lockwood St Providence RI 02903

VARGHESE, SANKOORIKAL LONAPPAN, b Narakal, Kerala, Mar 13, 43; Indian citizen; m 71; c 2. EXPERIMENTAL ATOMIC PHYSICS. *Educ:* Kerala Univ, BSc, 63, MSc, 65; Univ Louisville, MS, 67; Yale Univ, PhD(physics), 74. *Prof Exp:* Res asst physics, Yale Univ, 68-74, res staff physicist, 74; res assoc physics, Kans State Univ, 74-77; vis asst prof, ECarolina Univ, 77-80; MEM FAC, DEPT PHYSICS, UNIV SOUTHERN ALA, 80- *Mem:* Am Phys Soc; Sigma Xi. *Res:* Positron and positronium research, first observation of the n 2 state of positronium; accelerator based atomic physics, first direct lifetime measurement of x-ray emitters in the pico-second range; Mössbauer studies. *Mailing Add:* Dept of Physics Univ Southern Ala Mobile AL 36688

VARGO, ROBERT ALLEN, b Cleveland, Ohio, Jan 29, 40; m 65; c 2. PHYSIOLOGY. *Educ:* Augusta Col, BS, 67; Med Col Ga, PhD(physiol), 72. *Prof Exp:* Instr, 72-74, asst prof, 74-80, ASSOC PROF PHYSIOL, MED COL GA, 80- *Mailing Add:* Dept of Physiol Med Col of Ga Augusta GA 30902

VARGO, STEVEN WILLIAM, b Whiting, Ind, Sept 9, 31; m 56; c 3. AUDIOLOGY. *Educ:* Ind State Univ, BS, 54; Purdue Univ, MS, 57; Ind Univ, PhD(audiol), 65. *Prof Exp:* Assoc prof audiol, Ill State Univ, 65-71; Nat Inst Neurol Dis & Stroke spec res fel, Auditory Res Lab, Northwestern Univ, Evanston, 71-73; ASSOC PROF SURG, HERSHEY MED CTR, PA STATE UNIV, 73- *Mem:* Am Speech & Hearing Asn; Acoust Soc Am. *Res:* Scientific study of communication behavior with primary emphasis on the auditory mechanism of both normal and abnormal systems. *Mailing Add:* 102 W Chocolate Ave Hershey PA 17033

VARIN, ROGER ROBERT, b Bern, Switz, Feb 15, 25; nat US; m 51; c 3. PHYSICAL CHEMISTRY. *Educ:* Univ Bern, PhD(chem), 51. *Prof Exp:* Fel phys chem, Harvard Univ, 51-52; res chemist, E I du Pont de Nemours & Co, 52-57, res assoc, 57-62; dir res, Riegel Textile Corp, 62-71; PRES, VARINIT CORP, 71- *Concurrent Pos:* Pres, Technol Assocs, Greenville, SC, 71- & Varinit S A, Fribourg, Switz, 74- *Mem:* AAAS; Am Chem Soc; Am Asn Textile Chem; Fiber Soc; Am Asn Textile Chem & Colorists. *Res:* Fiber physics and chemistry; textile technology; polymer physics and chemistry; rheology. *Mailing Add:* 4 Barksdale Rd Greenville SC 29607

VARINEAU, VERNE JOHN, b Escanaba, Mich, Mar 11, 15; m 45; c 4. MATHEMATICS. *Educ:* Col St Thomas, BS, 36; Univ Wis, AM, 38, PhD(math), 40. *Prof Exp:* Asst, Univ Wis, 36-39; from instr to assoc prof, 40-72, PROF MATH, UNIV WYO, 72- *Concurrent Pos:* NSF sci fac fel, Stanford Univ, 63-64. *Mem:* Am Math Soc; Math Asn Am. *Res:* Matrices with elements in a principal ideal ring. *Mailing Add:* Dept of Math Univ of Wyo Laramie WY 82070

VARKEY, THANKAMMA EAPEN, b Palai, India, Oct 31, 36; m 64; c 1. ORGANIC CHEMISTRY. *Educ:* Kerala Univ, BSc, 56, MSc, 57; Temple Univ, PhD(chem), 74. *Prof Exp:* Lectr chem, Kerala Univ, 57-64; prof, Alphonsa Col, India, 64-68; fel, Drexel Univ, 74-76 & Tex Christian Univ, 76-77; fel chem, Lamar Univ, 77-79; fel chem, Lehigh Univ, 79-80; ASST PROF, WILSON COL, CHAMBERSBURG, PA, 80- *Mem:* Am Chem Soc; Sigma Xi. *Res:* Synthesis and conformational analysis of steroids; synthesis, structure and stereochemistry of nitrogen-sulfur ylides (iminosulfuranes). *Mailing Add:* Dept Chem Wilson Col Chambersburg PA 17201

VARLASHKIN, PAUL, b San Antonio, Tex, Aug 28, 31; m 54; c 4. SOLID STATE PHYSICS. *Educ:* Univ Tex, BS, 52, MA, 54, PhD(physics), 63. *Prof Exp:* Asst, Defense Res Lab, Univ Tex, 51-52, physicist, 52-53; from res scientist to chief res & develop, Electro-Mech Co, 53-63; fel & res assoc, Univ NC, 64-66; asst prof physics, La State Univ, Baton Rouge, 66-72; ASSOC PROF PHYSICS, ECAROLINA UNIV, 72- *Concurrent Pos:* Res physicist, White Sands Proving Grounds, 52. *Mem:* Am Phys Soc; Sigma Xi; Am Asn Physics Teachers. *Res:* Positron annihilation; liquid metals; positronium formation; solid state physics; chemical physics; metal-ammonia solutions. *Mailing Add:* Dept Physics ECarolina Univ Greenville NC 27834

VARMA, ANDRE A O, b Paramaribo, Surinam, June 10, 27; Dutch citizen; m 52; c 3. MEDICINE, BIOSTATISTICS. *Educ:* Sch Med Surinam, Med Doct, 50; Columbia Univ, MSc, 60. *Prof Exp:* Dist health officer med, Govt Surinam, 58-60, head biostatist pub health, 60-67; from asst prof to assoc prof biostatist, Pub Health, Columbia Univ, 67-74; assoc prof, 74-81, PROF COMMUNITY & PREV MED, STATE UNIV NY, STONY BROOK, 81- *Concurrent Pos:* Consult, Netherlands Govt, 65-66, Pan Am Health Orgn, 66 & WHO, 78; fel, Surinam Govt, 62-64 & US & Surinam Govts, 68-70; chmn, Dept Community Med, State Univ NY Stony Brook, 78- *Mem:* Am Statist Asn; Biomet Soc; Am Pub Health Asn; NY Acad Sci; Harvey Soc. *Res:* Design and analysis of clinical trials; epidemiology of cancer; emergency medical services; complications in post-abortion pregnancies; public health. *Mailing Add:* Sch of Med Health Sci Ctr State Univ of NY Stony Brook NY 11794

VARMA, ARUN KUMAR, b Faizabad, India. MATHEMATICS. *Educ:* Banaras Hindu Univ, BSc, 55; Univ Lucknow, MSc, 58; Univ Alta, PhD(math), 64. *Prof Exp:* Lectr math, Univ Rajasthan, 64-66; fel, Univ Alta, 66-67; from asst prof to assoc prof, 67-77, PROF MATH, UNIV FLA, 77- *Mem:* Am Math Soc. *Res:* Interpolation theory; approximation theory; numerical analysis. *Mailing Add:* Dept of Math Univ of Fla Gainesville FL 32611

VARMA, ASHA, b Bareilly, India, Mar 19, 42; US citizen; m 67; c 2. ANALYTICAL CHEMISTRY. *Educ:* Agra Univ, India, BSc, 58, MSc, 60; Banaras Hindu Univ, India, PhD(chem), 63. *Prof Exp:* Sr res fel chem, Banaras Hindu Univ, India, 63-64, Nat Chem Lab, 64-66; asst dir res chem, Forensic Sci Lab, Sugar, India, 66-68; sci pool officer chem, H B Technol Inst, Kanpur, India, 69-70; res assoc anal chem, Inst Mat Sci, Univ Conn, Storrs, 73-75; RES SCIENTIST ANAL CHEM, LAB RES STRUCTURE MATTER, UNIV PA, 77- *Concurrent Pos:* Res fel, Banaras Hindu Univ, Varanasi, India, 60-63; fel chem, Univ Conn, Storrs, 66-67. *Mem:* Am Chem Soc; fel Am Inst Chemists. *Res:* Atomic absorption; emission ultraviolet and infrared spectroscopy; electroanalytical techniques; author or coauthor of 28 publications. *Mailing Add:* Lab Res Structure Matter Univ Pa 3231 Walnut St Philadelphia PA 19104

VARMA, MAN MOHAN, b Patiala, India, July 5, 32; m 66. ENVIRONMENTAL ENGINEERING. *Educ:* Ala Polytech Inst, BS, 57; Iowa State Col, MS, 58; Okla State Univ, MS, 60; Univ Okla, PhD(eng sci), 63. *Prof Exp:* Instr eng sci, Univ Okla, 60-61, res assoc, 61-62, asst prof, 62-63; asst prof, Tufts Univ, 63-65; dir sanit eng, Morgeroth & Assocs, Mass, 65-66; assoc prof, 66-71, PROF BIO-ENVIRON ENG, HOWARD UNIV, 71-, DIR BIO-ENVIRON ENG & SCI, 66- *Concurrent Pos:* Consult, Morgeroth & Assocs, 66-; WHO consult, 72-; environ eng consult, Ministry Pub Health, Kuwait, 75-; vis prof, Harvard Univ, 75-76. *Mem:* Water Pollution Control Fedn; Am Water Works Asn; Nat Environ Health Asn; NY Acad Sci; Am Soc Testing & Mat. *Res:* Health effects caused by certain environmental contaminants; formation of trihalomethanes in water, enumeration of bacteria by ATP and Luciferase; kinetics of removal of halogenoted compounds by adsorption and biokinetics. *Mailing Add:* 704 Chichester Lane Silver Spring MD 20904

VARMA, MATESH NARAYAN, b Saugor, India, Sept 9, 43; m 67; c 3. PHYSICS, RADIATION PHYSICS. *Educ:* Univ Jabalpur, India, BSc, 61, MSc, 63; Case Western Reserve Univ, MS, 69, PhD(physics), 71. *Prof Exp:* Sci officer reactor eng, Bhabha Atomic Res Ctr, India, 63-67; univ fel physics, Case Western Reserve Univ, 67-71, res assoc solid state physics, 71-72; scientist radiation physics, Safety & Environ Protection Div, Brookhaven Nat

Lab, 72-80. *Mem:* Health Physics Soc; Bevalac Users Asn. *Res:* Micro dosimetry; surface physics; thin films; Mössbauer spectroscopy; ultrahigh vacuum technology; reactor physics; health physics. *Mailing Add:* 9 Chelsea Dr Mt Sinai NY 11766

VARMA, RAJENDRA, b India, Dec 26, 42; US citizen; m 69. MEDICAL RESEARCH, BIOCHEMISTRY. *Educ:* Univ Delhi, BS, 58, MS, 60; Univ NSW, Australia, PhD(biochem), 66. *Prof Exp:* Lectr & res worker chem, Univ Delhi, 60-62; lectr, Sydney Tech Col, Australia, 63-66; fel biochem, Iowa State Univ, 67 & Purdue Univ, Lafayette, 68; asst prof chem, Alliance Col, 68-69; assoc prof, Edinboro State Col, 69-71; DIR, BIOCHEM DEPT, WARREN STATE HOSP, 71- *Mem:* Fel Am Inst Chemists; Am Chem Soc; Sigma Xi; NY Acad Sci. *Res:* Carbohydrate chemistry; biochemistry of glycoproteins and glycosaminoglycans from eye, brain and biological fluids. *Mailing Add:* Dept Biochem Warren State Hosp Warren PA 16365

VARMA, RANBIR S, b India, July 18, 38; US citizen; m 69; c 2. CLINICAL BIOCHEMISTRY, MEDICAL RESEARCH. *Educ:* Glancy Med Col, BS, 65; Panjab Univ, BS Hons, 66, MS Hons, 68; State Univ NY Buffalo, MA, 71; Am Bd Bioanalysis, cert, 75. *Prof Exp:* Res asst pharmacol, All India Inst Med Sci, New Delhi, 61-62, asst res officer anesthesiol, 68; res scholar radiation biol, Univ Jaipur, India, 69; clin chem trainee, Sch Med, State Univ NY Buffalo, 69-71; CLIN BIOCHEMIST, WARREN STATE HOSP, PA, 71- *Mem:* Fel Am Inst Chemists; Biochem Soc UK; Asn Clin Biochem UK; Sigma Xi. *Res:* Glycoproteins and glycosaminoglycans of tissues and biological fluids; biological psychiatry. *Mailing Add:* Biochem Dept Warren State Hosp Warren PA 16365

VARMA, RAVI KANNADIKOVILAKOM, b Tripunithura, India, Dec 23, 37; m 65; c 2. MEDICINAL CHEMISTRY. *Educ:* Maharaja's Col, Ernakulam, India, BSc, 57, MSc, 59; Univ Poona, PhD(org chem), 65. *Prof Exp:* Sci asst chem, Nat Chem Labs, Poona, India, 59-65; res fel org chem, Purdue Univ, Lafayette, 65-66; staff scientist bio-org chem, Worcester Found, Mass, 66-69; res fel org chem, Harvard Univ, 70-72; SR RES INVESTR, E R SQUIBB & SONS, INC, 72- *Mem:* Am Chem Soc; Royal Soc Chem. *Res:* Organic synthesis; chemistry of biologically active molecules; mechanism of action of drugs. *Mailing Add:* Dept of Org Chem E R Squibb & Sons Inc Princeton NJ 08540

VARMA, SHAMBHU D, b Ghazipur, India; US citizen. BIOCHEMISTRY. *Educ:* Univ Allahabad, India, BSc, 55, MSc, 57; Univ Rajasthan, PhD(biochem), 64. *Prof Exp:* Chmn biochem, Chem Dept, Punjab Agne Univ, India, 65-69; univ scientist, Nat Eye Inst, NIH, Bethesda, Md, 72-76; PROF & DIR RES EYE BIOCHEM, DEPT OPTHALMOL, MED SCH, UNIV MD, 76- *Concurrent Pos:* Consult, Pres Comt Diabetes, Ophthalmol Sect, Nat Eye Inst; William Friedkin Res Award, Prevent Blindness, Inc, 77. *Mem:* AAAS; Asn Res Vision & Ophthalmol. *Res:* Intermediary metabolism, diabetes; sorbitol pathway in lens; aldose reductase; mechanism of action of flavonoids and other drugs in lens; superoxide, its implications in ocular diseases, particularly cataracts; nutrients and ocular manifestations; transport mechanisms. *Mailing Add:* Ophthalmol Dept Sch Med Univ Md 655 W Baltimore St Baltimore MD 21201

VARMA, SURENDRA K, b Lucknow, India, Dec 10, 39; m 67; c 2. PEDIATRICS, ENDOCRINOLOGY. *Educ:* King George Med Col, MBBS, 62, MD, 68; SN Med Col, Agra, DCH, 64; Am Bd Pediat, dipl, 76, dipl & cert endocrinol, 78. *Prof Exp:* Res assoc endocrinol, Dept Nutrit & Food Sci, Mass Inst Technol, 72-74; instr pediat, Harvard Med Sch, 73-74; asst prof, 74-78, actg assoc chmn, 77-79, ASSOC CHMN PEDIAT, SCH MED, TEX TECH UNIV, 79-, ASSOC PROF PEDIAT, 78- *Concurrent Pos:* Res fel, K G Med Col, 65-66; res fel, Harvard Med Sch, Peter Bent Brigham Hosp, 68-69 & Children's Hosp Med Ctr, 69-71; clin res fel, Mass Gen Hosp, 72-73, clin assoc, 73-74; dir, Endocrine Div, Tex Tech Univ Sch Med, 78-; pres, Am Diabetes Asn, NTex Affil, Inc, 81- *Mem:* Endocrine Soc; Am Thyroid Asn; Lawson Wilkins Pediat Endocrine Soc; Am Diabetes Asn; Am Acad Pediat. *Res:* Perinatal thyroid pathophysiology; growth hormone and factors; carbohydrate metabolism. *Mailing Add:* Dept of Pediat Sch of Med Lubbock TX 79430

VARMUS, HAROLD ELLIOT, b Freeport, NY, Dec 18, 39; m 69; c 2. MOLECULAR VIROLOGY, ONCOGENESIS. *Educ:* Amherst Col, BA, 61; Harvard Univ, MA, 62; Columbia Univ, MD, 66. *Prof Exp:* Lectr, 70-72, from asst prof to assoc prof, 72-79, PROF MICROBIOL, UNIV CALIF, SAN FRANCISCO, 79- *Concurrent Pos:* Assoc ed, Cell & Virol, 74- *Mem:* AAAS; Am Soc Microbiol; Am Soc Virol. *Res:* Mechanisms of viral replication and oncogenesis, using retroviruses and hepatits B viruses. *Mailing Add:* Dept Microbiol & Immunol HSE465 Univ Calif San Francisco CA 94143

VARNELL, THOMAS RAYMOND, b Whiteriver, Ariz, Jan 27, 31; m 57; c 3. BIOCHEMISTRY, PHYSIOLOGY. *Educ:* Univ Ariz, BS, 57, MS, 58, PhD(agr biochem), 60. *Prof Exp:* Instr animal nutrit, Univ Wyo, 60-62; res biochemist, Dept Health, Educ & Welfare, Food & Drug Admin, 62-63; asst prof animal nutrit, 63-65, from asst prof to assoc prof animal physiol, 65-73, PROF ANIMAL PHYSIOL, UNIV WYO, 73- *Concurrent Pos:* Stanford Res Inst grant, 61-64. *Mem:* Animal Nutrit Res Coun. *Res:* Metabolism of vitamin A and carotene; lipid metabolism; intestinal transport and metabolism of amino acids; potassium requirements and availability. *Mailing Add:* Div of Animal Sci Univ of Wyo Laramie WY 82070

VARNER, JOSEPH ELMER, b Nashport, Ohio, Oct 7, 21; c 4. PLANT PHYSIOLOGY. *Educ:* Ohio State Univ, BSc, 42, MSc, 43, PhD(biochem), 49. *Hon Degrees:* Dr, L'Universite DeNancy, 77. *Prof Exp:* Chemist, Owens-Corning Fiberglas Corp, 43-44; res engr, Battelle Mem Inst, 46-47; res assoc, Res Found, Ohio State Univ, 49-50, asst prof agr biochem, 50-53; res fel, Calif Inst Technol, 53-54; from assoc prof to prof biochem, Ohio State Univ, 54-61; prof, Res Inst Advan Study, 61-65 & Mich State Univ, 65-73; PROF BIOCHEM, WASHINGTON UNIV, 73- *Concurrent Pos:* NSF fel, Cambridge Univ, 59-60 & Univ Wash, 71-72. *Mem:* AAAS; Am Soc Biol Chem; Am Soc Plant Physiol. *Res:* Plant biochemistry; biochemistry of aging cells; action mechanism of plant hormones; glycoproteins. *Mailing Add:* Dept of Biol Washington Univ St Louis MO 63130

VARNER, LARRY WELDON, b San Antonio, Tex, June 25, 44; m 67; c 1. ANIMAL NUTRITION, WILDLIFE RESEARCH. *Educ:* Abilene Christian Col, BS, 66; Univ Nebr, Lincoln, MS, 68, PhD(nutrit), 70. *Prof Exp:* Asst animal sci, Univ Nebr, Lincoln, 66-69, res assoc animal nutrit, 69-70, asst prof, 70-71; res scientist, USDA, 71-74, ASSOC PROF ANIMAL NUTRIT, TEX A&M UNIV, 74- *Mem:* Wildlife Soc; Am Soc Animal Sci; Soc Range Mgt. *Res:* Ruminant nutrition; nitrogen and energy metabolism; wildlife nutrition. *Mailing Add:* PO Drawer 1051 Uvalde TX 78801

VARNERIN, LAWRENCE J(OHN), JR, b Boston, Mass, July 10, 23; m 52; c 8. SOLID STATE PHYSICS, MATERIALS SCIENCE. *Educ:* Mass Inst Technol, PhD(physics), 49. *Prof Exp:* Res engr, Electronics Div, Sylvania Elec Prod, Inc, 49-52; res physicist, Res Labs, Westinghouse Elec Corp, 52-57; mem tech staff solid state devices, 57-66, head, Magnetic & Microwave Mat & Device Dept, 66-80, HEAD, MICROWAVE DEVICE DEPT, BELL LABS, 80- *Mem:* Fel Am Phys Soc; Inst Elec & Electronics Engrs. *Res:* Microwave gallium arsenide field effect transistors. *Mailing Add:* Bell Labs Murray Hill NJ 07974

VARNES, DAVID JOSEPH, b Howe, Ind, Apr 5, 19; m 43, 66; c 2. ENGINEERING GEOLOGY. *Educ:* Calif Inst Technol, BS, 40. *Prof Exp:* Lab instr geol, Northwestern Univ, 40-41; recorder & jr geologist, 41, asst geologist, 43-45, assoc geologist, 45-48, chief br eng geol, 61-64, GEOLOGIST, US GEOL SURV, 48- *Concurrent Pos:* Mem comts, Transp Res Bd, Nat Acad Sci-Nat Res Coun. *Honors & Awards:* E B Burwell Jr Award, Geol Soc Am, 70 & 76. Distinguished Serv Award, US Dept Interior, 75. *Mem:* Asn Eng Geologists; Geol Soc Am; Int Asn Eng Geol; Am Soc Test & Mat. *Res:* Geologic studies of Lake Bonneville; landslides; mechanics of soil and rock deformation; logic of mapping. *Mailing Add:* US Geol Surv Denver Fed Ctr Denver CO 80225

VARNES, MARIE ELIZABETH, b Cleveland, Ohio, Dec 20, 42; m 68; c 2. BIOCHEMISTRY, RADIATION BIOLOGY. *Educ:* Notre Dame Col, BS, 65; Ind Univ, PhD(biochem), 73. *Prof Exp:* Res asst, 76-77, res assoc, 77-79, instr, 79-81, ASST PROF, DEPT RADIOL, DIV RADIATION BIOL, CASE WESTERN RESERVE UNIV, 81- *Concurrent Pos:* Co-investr, Am Cancer Soc grant, 77-78 & Nat Cancer Inst grant, 78- *Mem:* AAAS; Radiation Res Soc; Sigma Xi. *Res:* Metabolism of nitro drugs used as radiosensitizers; influence of hormones and thiols on radiation response. *Mailing Add:* Dept of Radiol Case Western Reserve Univ Cleveland OH 44106

VARNEY, EUGENE HARVEY, b South Egremont, Mass, Dec 25, 23; m 56; c 3. PLANT PATHOLOGY. *Educ:* Univ Mass, BS, 49; Univ Wis, PhD, 53. *Prof Exp:* Plant pathologist, USDA, 53-56; asst res specialist, 56-59, assoc prof plant path, 59-64, PROF PLANT PATH, RUTGERS UNIV, NEW BRUNSWICK, 64- *Mem:* AAAS; Am Phytopath Soc; Mycol Soc Am. *Res:* Diseases of small fruits; plant virology; mycology. *Mailing Add:* Dept of Plant Path Cook Col Rutgers Univ New Brunswick NJ 08903

VARNEY, ROBERT NATHAN, b San Francisco, Calif, Nov 7, 10; m 48; c 2. MOLECULAR PHYSICS. *Educ:* Univ Calif, AB, 31, MA, 32, PhD(physics), 35. *Prof Exp:* Instr physics, Univ Calif, 35-36 & NY Univ, 36-38; asst prof, Washington Univ, 38-41, from assoc prof to prof, 46-64; sr mem & sr consult scientist, Lockheed Palo Alto Res Lab, 64-75; NSF sr fel, US Army Ballistic Res Labs, 75-76. *Concurrent Pos:* Vis mem tech staff, Bell Tel Labs, NJ, 51-52; mem exec comt, Gaseous Electronics Conf, 51-53, 60-62 & 65-, secy, 67; NSF sr fel, Royal Inst Technol, Sweden, 58-59; mem, Gov Sci Adv Comt, Mo, 61-64; Fulbright lectr, Inst Atomic Physics, Innsbruck Univ, 71-72, 76-77, guest prof atomic physics, 77-78. *Honors & Awards:* Austrian Cross Honor for Sci & Art, 81. *Mem:* Fel AAAS; fel Am Phys Soc; Am Asn Physics Teachers. *Res:* Ion-molecule reactions; collisions of positive ions in gases; spark breakdown; secondary electron emission. *Mailing Add:* 4156 Maybell Way Palo Alto CA 94306

VARNEY, WILLIAM YORK, b Forest Hills, Ky, Apr 1, 17; m 40; c 2. ANIMAL HUSBANDRY. *Educ:* Univ Ky, BS, 51, MS, 52; Mich State Univ, PhD, 60. *Prof Exp:* Prin pub schs, Ky, 39-43; dist mgr, Southern States Coop, Va, 52-53; sales promoter, Swift & Co, Ill, 53-54; from instr to prof animal husb, 54-77, EXTEN PROF ANIMAL SCI, UNIV KY, 77- *Mem:* Am Soc Animal Sci; Inst Food Technologists. *Res:* Carcass studies of beef, pork and lamb. *Mailing Add:* Div of Animal Sci Univ of Ky Col of Agr Lexington KY 40506

VARNHORN, MARY CATHERINE, b Baltimore, Md, July 8, 14. MATHEMATICS. *Educ:* Col Notre Dame, Md, AB, 36; Cath Univ Am, AM, 37, PhD(math), 39. *Prof Exp:* Instr math, Col Notre Dame, Md, 39-40; from instr to assoc prof, 40-72, prof & chmn dept, 72-80, EMER PROF, TRINITY COL, DC, 80- *Mem:* Math Asn Am; Am Math Soc. *Res:* Modern algebra; properties of quartic functions of one variable. *Mailing Add:* 6111 Northdale Rd Baltimore MD 21228

VARNUM, WILLIAM SLOAN, b St Louis, Mo, Jan 23, 41. PHYSICS. *Educ:* Wash Univ, BS, 63; Fla State Univ, PhD(physics), 67. *Prof Exp:* Instr physics, Fla State Univ, 67-68; assoc scientist missile physics, Radiation Serv Co, 68-69; guest res scientist, Max-Planck-Institut Plasmaphysik, 69-70; res fel ionospheric physics, Max Planck Institut Ionosphären-Physik, 70-72; asst prof physics, New Col Sarasota, 72-73; NIH fel med physics, Univ Calif, Los Angeles, 73-74; STAFF MEM PHYSICS, LOS ALAMOS SCI LAB, 74- *Concurrent Pos:* Consult, Rand Corp, 73-75. *Mem:* Am Phys Soc. *Res:* Plasma physics; laser fusion; nuclear weapons design. *Mailing Add:* Los Alamos Sci Lab PO Box 1667 Los Alamos NM 87545

VARON, ALBERT, b New York, NY, July 14, 36. ANALYTICAL CHEMISTRY. *Educ:* City Col New York, BS, 58; Rutgers Univ, PhD(anal chem), 64. *Prof Exp:* CHEMIST, E I DU PONT DE NEMOURS & CO, INC, 63- *Mem:* Am Chem Soc. *Res:* Liquid and gas chromatography; analytical methods development. *Mailing Add:* E I Du Pont de Nemours & Co Inc PO Box 2000 Deer Park TX 77536

VARON, MYRON IZAK, b Chicago, Ill, Aug 20, 30; m 59; c 3. RADIOBIOLOGY, MEDICINE. *Educ:* Univ Chicago, PHB, 50; Northwestern Univ, BSM, 52, MD, 55; Univ Rochester, MS, 63, PhD(radiation biol), 65. *Prof Exp:* Intern, Cook County Hosp, Chicago, 55-56; Med Corps, US Navy, 56-79, med officer, USS Lenawee, 56-58 & Armed Forces Spec Weapons Proj, 58-59, asst to mgr naval reactor br, Idaho Br Off, AEC, 59-60, sr med officer & radiation safety officer, USS Long Beach, 60-62, assoc surg, Univ Rochester, 62-65, med dir radiation biol, Naval Radiol Defense Lab, 65-67, from asst dep sci dir to dir, Armed Forces Radiobiol Res Inst, 67-75, dep comndg officer, Nav Med Res & Develop command, Med Corps, US Navy, 75-79; VPRES & SCI DIR, AMYOTROPHIC LATERAL SCLEROSIS SOC AM, 79- *Concurrent Pos:* Lectr, US Naval Hosp, Oakland, Calif, 66-67. *Mem:* Health Physics Soc; Radiation Res Soc; Asn Mil Surg US; NY Acad Sci; Soc Nuclear Med. *Res:* Health cells; molecular mechanism of action of nerve growth factor; tropic factors directed to neurons and glial cell; radiation safety of nuclear reactors; labeled antibody localization for cancer therapy; nuclear weapons effects; radiation behavioral effects; radiation recovery and residual injury; experimental pathology. *Mailing Add:* 15300 Ventura Blvd Suite 315 Amyotrophic Lateral Sclerosis Soc Am Sherman Oaks CA 91403

VARON, SILVIO SALOMONE, b Milan, Italy, July 25, 24; m 60 & 67; c 2. NEUROCHEMISTRY, NEUROBIOLOGY. *Educ:* Univ Lausanne, EngD, 45; Univ Milan, MD, 59. *Prof Exp:* Resident asst prof neurochem, Inst Psychiat, Univ Milan, 60-63; res assoc, Dept Biochem, City of Hope Med Ctr, Duarte, Calif, 61-63; res assoc neurobiol, Dept Biol, Wash Univ, 63-64, assoc prof, 64-65; vis assoc prof, Dept Genetics, Sch Med, Stanford Univ, 65-67; assoc prof, 67-72, PROF NEUROBIOL, DEPT BIOL, MED SCH, UNIV CALIF, SAN DIEGO, 72- *Concurrent Pos:* App mem, Pres Coun Spinal Cord Injury. *Mem:* Int Soc Neurochem; Am Soc Neurochem; Soc Neurosci; Am Soc Cell Biol; Int Soc Develop Neurosci. *Res:* Structure and properties of the nerve growth factor protein; dissociation fractionation and culture of cells from nervous tissues; in vitro study of neuroglial cells; molecular mechanism of action of nerve growth factor; search for trophic factors directed to neurons and glial cells; in vivo models for neural regeneration. *Mailing Add:* Dept of Biol Univ Calif San Diego Med Sch La Jolla CA 92037

VARRICCHIO, FREDERICK, b Brooklyn, NY, May 18, 38; m 62; c 2. BIOCHEMISTRY, DEVELOPMENTAL BIOLOGY. *Educ:* Univ Maine, Orono, BS, 60; Univ NDak, MS, 64; Univ Md, Baltimore, PhD(biochem), 66. *Prof Exp:* Asst biochem, Univ Freiburg, WGer, 66-67; researcher molecular biol, Nat Ctr Sci Res, France, 67-69; fel internal med, Yale Univ, 69-72; asst prof, Mem Sloan-Kettering Inst Cancer Res, 72-77; prof exp oncol, Nova Univ, 77-79; PROF CHEM & CHMN DEPT, NAT COL CHIROPRACTIC, LOMBARD, ILL, 80- *Concurrent Pos:* Vis prof, Max Planck Inst Nutrit, Dortmund, Ger, 79; fac res assoc, Oak Ridge Nat Lab, 79-; res assoc, Argonne Nat Lab, 80-; adj prof chem, Col DuPage, 80- *Mem:* Am Soc Biol Chemists; Am Chem Soc; Am Soc Microbiol; Am Asn Pathologists; Ger Soc Biol Chemists. *Res:* Nuclear proteins; transfer ribonucleic in growth, differentiation and tumors. *Mailing Add:* Dept Chem Nat Col Chiropractic 200 E Roosevelt Rd Lombard IL 60187

VARS, HARRY MORTON, b Edelstein, Ill, July 2, 03; m; c 3. PHYSIOLOGICAL CHEMISTRY. *Educ:* Univ Colo, AB, 24; Yale Univ, PhD(physiol chem), 29. *Prof Exp:* Asst chem, Cornell Univ, 24-25; asst physiol chem, Yale Univ, 26-28, instr, 28-31; res assoc biol, Princeton Univ, 31-34; Merck fel physiol, 34-36, assoc, Harrison Dept Surg Res, 36-40, from asst prof to prof biochem in surg res, 40-73, EMER PROF BIOCHEM IN SURG RES, HARRISON DEPT SURG RES, SCH MED, UNIV PA, 73- *Concurrent Pos:* Responsible investr, Comt Med Res, Off Emergency Mgt, 42-44; res chemist, Bryn Mawr Hosp, 44-46. *Mem:* Am Chem Soc; Am Soc Biol Chemists; Soc Exp Biol & Med; fel Am Inst Nutrit; Am Soc Parenteral & Enteral Nutrit. *Res:* Protein, amino acid and liver metabolism; adrenal cortical hormones; hepatotoxic agents; liver regeneration; enzymes; dietary factors; parenteral nutrition. *Mailing Add:* Harrison Dept of Surg Res Univ of Pa Sch of Med Philadelphia PA 19104

VARSA, EDWARD CHARLES, b Marissa, Ill, Oct 18, 38; m 65; c 2. SOIL FERTILITY. *Educ:* Southern Ill Univ, Carbondale, BS, 61; Univ Ill, Urbana, MS, 65; Mich State Univ, PhD(soil sci), 70. *Prof Exp:* Asst agron, Univ Ill, 64-65; asst soil sci, Mich State Univ, 65-66, instr, 66-68, teaching asst, 68-70; ASST PROF SOILS, SOUTHERN ILL UNIV, CARBONDALE, 70- *Mem:* Am Soc Agron; Soil Sci Soc Am. *Res:* Soil fertility research on, and the fate of, applied fertilizer nitrogen in soils. *Mailing Add:* Dept of Plant & Soil Sci Southern Ill Univ Carbondale IL 62901

VARSAMIS, IOANNIS, b Alexandria, UAR, July 24, 32; Can citizen; m 58. PSYCHIATRY. *Educ:* Univ Alexandria, MB, ChB, 57; Conjoint Bd, London, Eng, dipl psychol med, 61; Univ Man, dipl psychiat, 64; FRCP(C), 65. *Prof Exp:* Psychiatrist, Winnipeg Psychiat Inst, 64-68, med supt, 68-73; PSYCHIATRIST, GRACE GEN HOSP, 74-; ASSOC PROF PSYCHIAT, UNIV MAN, 67- *Mem:* Can Med Asn; Can Psychiat Asn. *Res:* Phenomenology of schizophrenia; geriatric psychiatry. *Mailing Add:* Dept of Psychiat Grace Gen Hosp Winnipeg MB R3J 3A7 Can

VARSEL, CHARLES JOHN, b Fayette City, Pa, Jan 11, 30; m 50; c 6. FOOD CHEMISTRY, FOOD BIOCHEMISTRY. *Educ:* St Vincent Col, BA, 54; Univ Richmond, MS, 58; Med Col Va, PhD, 70. *Prof Exp:* Chemist, Linde Air Prod Co, Union Carbide & Carbon Corp, 54-55 & Res & Develop Dept, Philip Morris, Inc, 55-59; res assoc fuel technol, Pa State Univ, 59-60; from res chemist to sr res chemist, Res & Develop Dept, Philip Morris, Inc, Va, 60-69; prin chemist, Food Div, Citrus Res & Develop, 69-70, mgr chem, 70-73, dir citrus res & develop, 73, DIR RES & DEVELOP, FOODS DIV, COCA-COLA CO, 73- *Mem:* AAAS; Am Chem Soc; Inst Food Technol. *Res:* Instrumental analysis; citrus chemistry; essential oils; mass spectroscopy; chemistry of natural products. *Mailing Add:* Coca Cola Co Foods Div Dept Res & Develop PO Box 2079 Houston TX 77001

VARSHNEYA, ARUN KUMAR, b Agra, India, May 25, 44; m 73; c 2. GLASS TECHNOLOGY, CERAMICS. *Educ:* Agra Univ, BSc, 62; Univ Sheffield, BScTech, 65; Case Western Reserve Univ, MS, 68, PhD(glass, ceramics), 70. *Prof Exp:* Sr scientist glass res, Sci Labs, Ford Motor Co, 70-73; res scientist, 73-80, CONSULT CERAMIST, LIGHTING BUS GROUP, GEN ELEC CO, 80- *Mem:* Am Ceramic Soc; assoc Nat Inst Ceramic Engrs. *Res:* Diffusion and other physical properties of glass; radiotracer methodology; glass strengthening; stresses in glass; glass-to-metal seals; heat transfer in glass; finite element analysis; author of over 50 pulications. *Mailing Add:* Gen Elec Co Nela Park Cleveland OH 44112

VARSHNI, YATENDRA PAL, b Allahabad, India, May 21, 32. ASTROPHYSICS, SOLID STATE PHYSICS. *Educ:* Univ Allahabad, BSc, 50, MSc, 52, PhD(physics), 56. *Prof Exp:* Asst prof physics, Univ Allahabad, 55-60, fel, Nat Res Coun Can, 60-62; from asst prof to assoc prof, 62-69, PROF PHYSICS, UNIV OTTAWA, 69- *Mem:* Am Phys Soc; Can Asn Physicists; Brit Inst Physics; Royal Astron Soc UK; Am Astron Soc. *Res:* Molecular and nuclear structure; quasi-stellar objects; lattice dynamics; energy levels of nuclei. *Mailing Add:* Dept of Physics Univ of Ottawa Ottawa ON K1N 6N5 Can

VARTANIAN, PERRY H(ATCH), JR, b Rochester, NY, June 14, 31; m 58; c 3. ELECTRICAL ENGINEERING. *Educ:* Calif Inst Technol, BS, 53; Stanford Univ, PhD(elec eng), 56. *Prof Exp:* Sect head, Sylvania Elec Prod, Inc, 54-57, vpres & dir, Melabs, Calif, 57-69; dir res & develop, Bus Equip Div, SCM Corp, 69-80; CONSULT, 80- *Mem:* Inst Elec & Electronics Engrs. *Mailing Add:* 199 Brookwood Dr Woodside CA 94061

VARTERESSIAN, K(EGHAM) A(RSHAVIR), b Bahcecik, Izmit, Turkey, Jan 25, 08; nat US; m 46; c 2. NUCLEAR CHEMISTRY. *Educ:* Pa State Col, BS, 30, MS, 31, PhD(chem eng), 35. *Prof Exp:* Res asst chem, Pa State Col, 35-37, instr chem eng, 37-38 & 42-43, res assoc, 39-42 & 44-45, instr physics, Army Specialized Training Prog, 43-44; chem engr, Standard Oil Develop Co, 38-39; instr chem & head dept, Am Univ Cairo, 45-49; assoc chem engr, Argonne Nat Lab, 49-50, sr chem engr, Chem Eng Div, 50-55 & 65-68, sr chem engr, Reactor Anal & Safety Div, 68-73; RETIRED. *Concurrent Pos:* Instr & chmn Chem Eng Dept, Int Sch Nuclear Sci & Eng, Argonne Nat Lab, 55-65. *Mem:* Emer mem Am Chem Soc; emer assoc mem Am Inst Chem Engrs; emer fel Am Inst Chemists. *Res:* Phase distribution of radioactive decay heat sources in spent nuclear fuel; unit operations in the reprocessing and waste treatment in nuclear fuel cycles; fission spectra. *Mailing Add:* 130 Paseo Farallon Aptos CA 95003

VARTSKY, DAVID, b Bielawa, Poland, July 2, 46; Israel citizen; m 71; c 2. MEDICAL PHYSICS. *Educ:* Technion, Israel, BSc, 71; Birmingham Univ, MSc, 74, PhD(physics), 76. *Prof Exp:* Res assoc, 76-77, asst scientist, 77-80, ASSOC SCIENTIST MED PHYSICS, BROOKHAVEN NAT LAB, 80- *Mem:* Inst Elec & Electronics Engrs. *Res:* Medical applications of nuclear physics; determination of body composition by neutron activation analysis in-vivo; in-vivo determination of toxic metals in the body. *Mailing Add:* Brookhaven Nat Lab Med Res Ctr Upton NY 11973

VARTY, ISAAC WILLIAM, b Consett, Eng, Feb 9, 24; m 52; c 3. FOREST ENTOMOLOGY. *Educ:* Aberdeen Univ, BSc, 50, PhD(entom), 54. *Prof Exp:* Asst forest zool, Aberdeen Univ, 50-54; dist forest officer, Forestry Comn, Scotland, 54-58; FOREST RES SCIENTIST, MARITIMES FOREST RES CTR, CAN FORESTRY SERV, 58- *Mem:* Entom Soc Can; Can Inst Forestry. *Res:* Environmental impact of forest spraying; introduction of exotic parasites for control of forest pests; insecticide drift. *Mailing Add:* Maritimes Forest Res Ctr Can Forestry Serv Environ Can Box 4000 Fredericton NB E3B 5P7 Can

VAS, STEPHEN ISTVAN, b Budapest, Hungary, June 4, 26; Can citizen; m 53. MEDICAL MICROBIOLOGY, IMMUNOLOGY. *Educ:* Pazmany Peter Univ, Budapest, MD, 50, PhD(microbiol), 56. *Prof Exp:* Lectr microbiol, Pazmany Peter Univ, 48-49, asst prof, 49-50; Rockefeller res fel microbiol, McGill Univ, 57-59, asst virologist, 59-60, from asst prof to prof immunol, 60-77, chmn dept, 72-77; assoc prof med, 77-80, PROF MED MICROBIOL, UNIV TORONTO, 77-, PROF MED, 80- *Concurrent Pos:* Microbiologist-in-chief & sr physician, Royal Victoria Hosp, 72-77; microbiologist-in-chief & physician, Toronto Western Hosp, 77- *Mem:* Am Soc Microbiol; Can Soc Microbiol; Can Soc Immunol; Can Med Asn; Can Asn Med Microbiol. *Res:* Antibody synthesis; synthesis of complement; effect of antibodies on bacteria and on tissue cells; peritoneal dialysis. *Mailing Add:* Dept of Microbiol Toronto Western Hosp Toronto ON L5P 1B3 Can

VASAK, OTTO R(OBERT), b Chicago, Ill, May 22, 17; m 41; c 4. CHEMICAL ENGINEERING. *Educ:* Univ Wis, BS, 39. *Prof Exp:* Chem engr, Soya Prod Div, Glidden Co, 39-41, Sherwin-Williams Co, 45-47 & Western Regional Res Lab, Bur Agr & Indust Chem, USDA, 47-51; staff engr, 51-54, res engr, 54-55, lead res engr, 55-57, supvr process eng, 57-58, plant mgr, Ortho Div, 58-61, plant supt, 61-63, MGR PROCESS RES & ENG, ORTHO DIV, CHEVRON CHEM CO, 63- *Mem:* Am Inst Chem Engrs. *Res:* Sulfonations; chlorinations; nitrations; condensations; Diels-Adler reactions; food dehydration and processing wastes; fertilizer manufacture. *Mailing Add:* Chevron Chem Co Ortho Div 940 Hensley St Richmond CA 94804

VASARHELYI, DESI D, b Hungary, Sept 27, 10; nat US; m 57. CIVIL ENGINEERING. *Educ:* Univ Cluj, BA, 28; Budapest Tech Univ, Dipl, 33, DSc(eng), 44. *Prof Exp:* Asst bridge struct & concrete, Budapest Tech Univ, 32; design & field engr, Palatinus Co, 36; lectr, Inst Higher Tech Educ,

Budapest, 44; engr, Brit Army, Austria, 46; res engr, 50-52, from instr to assoc prof, 52-61, prof, 61-80, EMER PROF CIVIL ENG, UNIV WASH, 80- *Mem:* Am Soc Civil Engrs; Am Welding Soc; Soc Exp Stress Anal; Int Asn Bridge & Struct Engrs. *Res:* Stress analysis; structural theory; engineering materials; steel structures. *Mailing Add:* 4055 NE 57th St Seattle WA 98105

VASAVADA, KASHYAP V, b Ahmedabad, India, July 25, 38; m 69; c 2. THEORETICAL PHYSICS. *Educ:* Univ Baroda, BS, 58; Univ Delhi, MS, 60; Univ Md, PhD(physics), 64. *Prof Exp:* Nat Acad Sci fel physics, Goddard Space Flight Ctr, NASA, 64-66; asst prof, Univ Conn, 66-70; assoc prof, 70-74, PROF PHYSICS, IND UNIV-PURDUE UNIV, INDIANAPOLIS, 74- *Mem:* Am Phys Soc. *Res:* High energy physics; scattering theory; atomic physics; theoretical physics. *Mailing Add:* 4026 Steinmetz Dr Indianapolis IN 46254

VASCONCELOS, AUREA C, b Caquas, Puerto Rico, Dec 25, 35; US citizen; m 68. PLANT PHYSIOLOGY. *Educ:* Univ Puerto Rico, BS, 57; George Washington Univ, MA, 61; Univ Chicago, PhD(biol), 69. *Prof Exp:* Asst prof biol, Univ Puerto Rico, 61-65; vis asst prof plant physiol, 70-72, ASSOC PROF BOT, RUTGERS UNIV, 72- *Mem:* AAAS; Am Soc Plant Physiol; NY Acad Sci; Am Soc Cell Biol. *Res:* Chloroplast development; golgi function. *Mailing Add:* Dept Biol Sci-Bot Nelson Biol Labs PO Box 1059 Piscataway NJ 08854

VASEK, FRANK CHARLES, b Maple Heights, Ohio, May 9, 27; m 54; c 2. BOTANY. *Educ:* Ohio Univ, BS, 50; Univ Calif, Los Angeles, PhD(bot), 55. *Prof Exp:* Asst bot, Univ Calif, Los Angeles, 50-54; from instr to assoc prof, 54-68, PROF BOT, UNIV CALIF, RIVERSIDE, 68- *Mem:* Bot Soc Am; Ecol Soc Am; Soc Study Evolution; Am Soc Plant Taxon. *Res:* Plant taxonomy; evolution; population dynamics. *Mailing Add:* Dept of Bot & Plant Sci Univ of Calif Riverside CA 92521

VASERSTEIN, LEONID, IV, b Kuibyshev, USSR, Sept 15, 44; m 68; c 2. ALGEBRAIC K-THEORY, ARITHMETIC GROUPS. *Educ:* Moscow State Univ, MS, 66, PhD(math), 69. *Prof Exp:* Sr researcher & head, Sect Oper Res Prog, All-Union Inst Info & Tech Econ Res Elec Indust, 69-78; PROF MATH, PA STATE UNIV, 79- *Concurrent Pos:* Mem jury, All-Union Math Olimpiads, USSR, 62-77; Vis prof, Univ Bielefeld, Inst des Hautes Etuudes Sci, France, 78, Univ Chicago, 79 & Cornell Univ, 79-80. *Mem:* Am Math Soc. *Res:* Operations research, dynamical systems. *Mailing Add:* 1152 Smithfield Circle State College PA 16801

VASEY, CAREY EDWARD, b Bristol, Pa, Feb 12, 27; m 49; c 2. INSECT MORPHOLOGY, INSECT TAXONOMY. *Educ:* Lycoming Col, BA, 53; Syracuse Univ, MS, 59; State Univ NY Col Environ Sci & Forestry, PhD(forensic entom), 75. *Prof Exp:* Indust microbiologist vitamin assay, Publicker Indust, Philadelphia, Pa, 51-53; lab technician histol technol, Med Ctr, Univ Kans, 53-55; teacher biol, James Buchanan Sch, Mercersburg, Pa, 55-58, Coatesville Area Schs, Coatesville, Pa, 59-60; instr, Philadelphia Col Pharm & Sci, 60-64; asst prof, 64-74, ASSOC PROF BIOL, COL ARTS & SCI, STATE UNIV NY, GENESEO, 74- *Mem:* AAAS; Am Entom Soc. *Res:* Morphology and ultrastructure of selected families of diptera in an attempt to establish taxonomic affinities between them. *Mailing Add:* Biol Dept Col Arts & Sci State Univ NY Geneseo NY 14454

VASEY, EDFRED H, b Mott, NDak, Aug 29, 33; m 55; c 4. SOIL FERTILITY, SOIL CONSERVATION. *Educ:* NDak State Univ, BS, 55, MS, 57; Purdue Univ, PhD(plant nutrit), 62. *Prof Exp:* From asst prof to assoc prof, 61-67, EXTEN SOILS SPECIALIST, EXTEN SERV, NDAK STATE UNIV, 67-, PROF SOILS, 69-, HEAD, PLANT SCI SECT, NDAK COOP EXTEN SERV, 71- *Mem:* Soil Sci Soc Am; Coun Agr Sci & Technol; Sigma Xi; Soil Conservation Soc Am. *Res:* Fertility needs of crops grown on North Dakota soils. *Mailing Add:* Rm 203E Waldron Hall NDak State Univ Sta Fargo ND 58105

VASEY, FRANK BARNETT, b Webster City, Iowa, Feb 6, 42; m 68; c 1. RHEUMATOLOGY, INTERNAL MEDICINE. *Educ:* Cornell Col, BA, 64; Univ NDak, BS, 66; Univ Pa, MD, 68. *Prof Exp:* Asst prof internal med, McGill Univ & Royal Victoria Hosp, Montreal, 76-77; ASST PROF MED, RHEUMATOLOGY, UNIV S FLA, 77- *Concurrent Pos:* Rheumatology fel, Royal Victoria Hosp, McGill Univ, 74; dir, Rheumatology & Immunol Clin Lab, Univ SFla, 77-78 & Rheumatology & Immunol Res Lab, Vet Admin Hosp, Tampa, 78- *Mem:* Fel Am Col Physicians. *Res:* Immunogenetics basis of psoriatic arthritis. *Mailing Add:* Dept Internal Med 12901 N 30th St Box 19 Tampa FL 33612

VASHISHTA, PRIYA DARSHAN, b Aligarh, India, Aug 24, 44; m 70; c 1. SOLID STATE PHYSICS, MATERIALS SCIENCE. *Educ:* Agra Univ, BS, 60; Aligarh Univ, MS, 62; Indian Inst Technol, PhD(physics), 67. *Prof Exp:* Fel, St Andrews Univ, UK, 66-68; res assoc, McMaster Univ, 68-70; asst prof physics, Northwestern Univ, 70-71; asst prof, Western Mich Univ, 71-72; RES PHYSICIST, ARGONNE NAT LAB, 72-, DIR SOLID STATE SCI DIV, 79- *Concurrent Pos:* Vis scientist, Theoret Physics Div, Atomic Energy Res Estab, UK, 68, Inst Theoret Physics, Sweden, 71; fel appl comput, Thomas J Watson Res Ctr, IBM, 72; mem tech staff, Bell Labs, 76; vis assoc prof, Univ Calif, San Diego, 76-77; co-ed, J Solid State Ionics, Amsterdam, 79-; mem, Solid State Sci Panel, NSF, 79-82. *Mem:* Am Phys Soc; AAAS; Sigma Xi. *Res:* Theoretical physics of condensed matter; electron-phonon interaction and superconductivity in metals and alloys; many-body interactions in metals and semiconductors; molecular dynamics studies of condensed matter; phase transitions on surfaces. *Mailing Add:* Solid State Sci Div Bldg 223 Argonne Nat Lab Argonne IL 60439

VASICKA, ALOIS, b Czech, Sept 23, 17; US citizen. OBSTETRICS & GYNECOLOGY. *Educ:* Masaryk Univ, MD, 45; Am Bd Obstet & Gynec, dipl, 60. *Prof Exp:* Resident obstet & gynec, Univ Hosp, Brno, Czech, 45-50; intern, Beverly Hosp, Mass, 52; asst resident obstet & gynec, Boston Lying-in Hosp, 52-53; resident gynec path, Free Hosp Women, Brookline, 53-54; asst gynec, Peter Bent Brigham Hosp, Boston, 54-55; resident obstet & gynec, Cleveland Metrop Gen Hosp, Ohio, 55-56, asst, 56-57, asst vis obstetrician & gynecologist, 57-61; obstetrician & gynecologist, John Sealy Hosp, Galveston, Tex, 61-65; CHIEF OBSTET & GYNEC, CONEY ISLAND HOSP, MAIMONIDES MED CTR, 65-; PROF OBSTET & GYNEC, STATE UNIV NY DOWNSTATE MED CTR, 65- *Concurrent Pos:* Res fels, Peter Bent Brigham Hosp, Boston & Harvard Med Sch, 54-55; demonstr, Sch Med, Western Reserve Univ, 56-57, from instr to asst prof, 57-61; prof, Univ Tex, 61-65. *Mem:* Soc Gynec Invest; Am Col Obstet & Gynec; AMA; Am Fertil Soc. *Res:* Physiology of human obstetrics; uterine and fetal physiology; uterine contractility and myometrial function at its cellular level. *Mailing Add:* Dept of Obstet & Gynec 4802 Tenth Ave Brooklyn NY 11219

VASIL, INDRA KUMAR, b Basti, India, Aug 31, 32; m 59; c 2. BOTANY. *Educ:* Banaras Hindu Univ, BSc, 52; Univ Delhi, MSc, 54, PhD(bot), 58. *Prof Exp:* Res asst bot, Univ Delhi, 54-58, asst prof, 59-63; res assoc, Univ Wis, 63-65; scientist, Indian Agr Res Inst, 65-67; assoc prof bot, 67-74, prof, 74-79, GRAD RES PROF, UNIV FLA, 79- *Concurrent Pos:* Res assoc, Univ Ill, 62-63. *Honors & Awards:* Sr US Scientist Award for Res, Fed Repub Ger, 74. *Mem:* AAAS; Int Asn Plant Tissue Cult; Bot Soc Am; Int Soc Plant Morphol. *Res:* Developmental morphology; physiology of reproduction in flowering plants; morphogenesis and differentiation in higher plants; plant tissue and organ culture, especially of cereals and grasses. *Mailing Add:* Dept Bot Univ Fla Gainesville FL 32611

VASIL, MICHAEL LAWRENCE, b San Diego, Calif, Sept 6, 45; m 71; c 1. PARASITOLOGY, BIOCHEMISTRY. *Educ:* Univ Tex, El Paso, BS, 71, Med Sch Dallas, PhD(microbiol), 75. *Prof Exp:* Chief bacteriologist, Providence Hosp, 67-71; res asst, Univ Tex, 71-75; instr, Univ Ore Med Sch, 75-77; asst prof, Univ Calif Los Angeles Sch Med, 77-78; ASST PROF MICROBIOL, UNIV COLO MED SCH, 78- *Concurrent Pos:* Prin investr res grants, Proctor & Gamble, 80-, Cystic Fibrosis Found, 79-81. *Mem:* Am Soc Microbiol; Am Soc Clin Pathologists; Sigma Xi. *Res:* Mechanism of bacterial pathogenesis and the development of bacterial vaccines; rational approach classical microbial genetics as well as recombinants DNA technology including psendomonas aeruginosa esclerichia coli, staphutococcns anreas and legionella pnenmphila. *Mailing Add:* Dept Microbiol & Immunol Univ Colo Med Sch Box B175 Denver CO 80262

VASILAKOS, NICHOLAS PETROU, b Athens, Greece, Jan 1, 54. CHEMICAL ENGINEERING. *Educ:* Nat Tech Univ Athens, BS, 76; Calif Inst Technol, MS, 78, PhD(coal desulfurization), 81. *Prof Exp:* ASST PROF CHEM ENG, UNIV TEX, AUSTIN, 81- *Mem:* Am Inst Chem Engrs; Am Chem Soc; Sigma Xi. *Res:* Coal desulfurization by chemical treatment; coal liquefaction by super critical solvent extraction; production of liquid hydrocarbon fuels from urban, industrial and agricultural wastes by catalytic hydrogenolysis. *Mailing Add:* Dept Chem Eng Univ Tex Austin TX 78712

VASILE, MICHAEL JOSEPH, b Newton, NJ, May 11, 40. PHYSICAL CHEMISTRY. *Educ:* Rutgers Univ, BS, 62; Princeton Univ, MA, 64, PhD(chem), 66. *Prof Exp:* Res fel chem, Nat Res Coun Can, 66-68; MEM TECH STAFF, BELL LABS, 68- *Mem:* Electrochem Soc; Am Soc Mass Spectrometry; Am Vacuum Soc. *Res:* Mass spectrometry of inorganic fluorides; plasma chemistry; secondary ion mass spectrometry; surface chemistry. *Mailing Add:* Bell Labs 1A259 Mountain Ave Murray Hill NJ 07974

VASILEVSKIS, STANISLAUS, b Latvia, July 20, 07; nat US; m 29; c 2. ASTRONOMY. *Educ:* Univ Latvia, PhD(math), 39. *Prof Exp:* Asst astron, Univ Latvia, 28-32, from instr to asst prof, 33-44; res assoc, Leipzig Observ, 45; assoc prof, UNRRA Univ, Munich, 46-47; asst, 49-54, lectr, 54, from asst astronr to assoc astron, 54-64, prof astron, Univ, 66-74, EMER PROF ASTRON, UNIV CALIF, SANTA CRUZ, 74-, ASTRONR, LICK OBSERV, 64- *Concurrent Pos:* Vis prof astron, Leiden Univ, Neth, 75-76. *Mem:* Am Astron Soc. *Res:* Astrometry, particularly stellar proper motions and trigonometric parallexes. *Mailing Add:* Lick Observ Univ of Calif Santa Cruz CA 95064

VASILIAUSKAS, EDMUND, b Lithuania, June 18, 38; US citizen; m 70; c 4. ORGANIC CHEMISTRY. *Educ:* Rochester Inst Technol, BS, 63; Loyola Univ Chicago, PhD(org chem), 70. *Prof Exp:* Chemist, Olin Corp, 63-65 & Witco Chem Corp, 70-71; instr, 71-74, assoc prof, 74-80, PROF CHEM, MORAINE VALLEY COMMUNITY COL, 80- *Mem:* Am Chem Soc. *Res:* Study of the derivatives of benzonorbornene. *Mailing Add:* Dept of Chem Moraine Valley Community Col Palos Hills IL 60465

VASILOS, THOMAS, b New York, NY, Oct 18, 29; m 54; c 2. CERAMICS, CHEMISTRY. *Educ:* Brooklyn Col, BS, 50; Mass Inst Technol, DSc(ceramics), 54. *Prof Exp:* Asst ceramics, Mass Inst Technol, 50-53; res engr, Ford Motor Co, 53; mgr, Ceramics Res Dept, Corning Glass Works, 55-57; sect chief metals & ceramics, Res & Adv Develop Div, 57-66, mgr mat sci dept, Avco Systs Div, 66-77, MGR, ELECTRO CHEM FACIL, AVCO CORP, 77- *Concurrent Pos:* Consult, Mat Adv Bd, Nat Acad Sci, 61- *Honors & Awards:* Ross Coffin Purdy Award, Am Ceramic Soc, 67. *Mem:* Am Ceramic Soc. *Res:* Thermal and mechanical properties of ceramics; crystal growing; ferroelectric ceramics and crystals; nuclear fuel ceramics; ceramic coatings; metal reinforced ceramics; diffusion in crystals; plastic-ceramic composites; composite formulation and properties; refractory metals. *Mailing Add:* Avco Corp Electro Chem Facil 201 Towell St Wilmington MA 01887

VASINGTON, FRANK D, b Norwich, Conn, Nov 3, 28; m 52; c 4. BIOCHEMISTRY. *Educ:* Univ Conn, AB, 50, MS, 52; Univ Md, PhD(biochem), 55. *Prof Exp:* Asst prof biochem, Sch Med, Univ Md, 55-57; Nat Found res fel, McCollum-Pratt Inst, Johns Hopkins Univ, 57-59, asst prof physiol chem, Sch Med, 59-64; assoc prof, 64-68, exec officer biol sci group, 67-71, head biochem & biophys sect, 67-77, assoc dean, Col Lib Arts & Sci, 76-78, PROF BIOCHEM, UNIV CONN, 68-, ASSOC V PRES ACAD AFFAIRS, 78- *Mem:* AAAS; Am Chem Soc; Am Soc Biol Chem. *Res:* Mitochondrial metabolism; active transport processes in mitochondria and bacteria. *Mailing Add:* Gulley Hall Box U-86 Univ of Conn Storrs CT 06268

VASKA, LAURI, b Rakvere, Estonia, May 7, 25; nat US; m 54; c 5. INORGANIC CHEMISTRY. *Educ:* Univ Göttingen, BS, 49; Univ Tex, PhD(chem), 56. *Prof Exp:* Fel Magnetism & chemisorption, Northwestern Univ, 56-57; res fel inorg chem, Mellon Inst, 57-64; assoc prof, 64-67, PROF INORG CHEM, CLARKSON COL TECHNOL, 67- *Concurrent Pos:* Fulbright-Hays fel, Univ Helsinki, 72. *Honors & Awards:* Boris Pregel Award, NY Acad Sci, 71. *Mem:* AAAS; Am Chem Soc; Catalysis Soc; fel NY Acad Sci; Royal Soc Chem. *Res:* Coordination chemistry; homogeneous catalysis; oxygen-carrying complexes; noble metal chemistry. *Mailing Add:* Dept of Chem Clarkson Col of Technol Potsdam NY 13676

VASKO, JOHN STEPHEN, b Cleveland, Ohio, Mar 17, 29; m 52; c 6. CARDIOVASCULAR & THORACIC SURGERY. *Educ:* Ohio State Univ, DDS, 54, MD, 58. *Prof Exp:* Instr anat & physiol, Cols Med & Dent, Ohio State Univ, 54-55, instr oper dent & consult prosthetic dent, Col Dent, 54-58; intern surg, Johns Hopkins Univ Hosp, 58-59, asst instr cardiac surg, Sch Med, Johns Hopkins Univ, 59-60; asst resident surgeon, Vanderbilt Univ Hosp, chief resident surgeon & chief labs exp surg, Nat Heart Inst, 64-66; assoc prof, 66-73, PROF THORACIC & CARDIOVASC SURG, COL MED, OHIO STATE UNIV, 73- *Concurrent Pos:* Halsted res fel cardiac surg, Sch Med, Johns Hopkins Univ, 59-60; asst resident surgeon cardiac surg, Johns Hopkins Hosp, 59-61; mem, Tech Rev Comt, Artificial Heart Prog, NIH & mem, Adv Comt, Coun Cardiovasc Surg, Am Heart Asn, 65-; partic, NIH Grad Prog, 65. *Mem:* AAAS; Asn Acad Surg; Soc Thoracic Surg; AMA; Am Col Surgeons. *Res:* Cardiovascular physiology. *Mailing Add:* Dept of Surg Ohio State Univ Col of Med Columbus OH 43210

VASKO, MICHAEL RICHARD, b Detroit, Mich, Mar 29, 48; m 80. NEUROCHEMISTRY, NEUROPHARMACOLOGY. *Educ:* Univ Mich, Ann Arbor, BS, 70, PhD(pharmacol), 76. *Prof Exp:* Res fel, Dept Pharmacol, Med Sch, Univ Mich, Ann Arbor, 71-75; instr pharmacol & neurol, Univ Tex Health Sci Ctr Dallas, 75-77, asst prof, 77-80; vis res fel, Dept Pharmacol, Inst Animal Physiol, Eng, 80-81; CHIEF, PHARMACOL SECT, VET ADMIN CTR, DALLAS, 81-; ASST PROF, DEPT PHARMACOL, UNIV TEX HEALTH SCI CTR DALLAS, 81-, MEM GRAD FAC BIOMED SCI, 81- *Concurrent Pos:* Chief, Neuropharmacol Lab & staff pharmacologist, Vet Admin Med Ctr, Dallas, 75-80. *Mem:* Soc Neurosci; Int Soc Neurochem. *Res:* Involvement of neurotransmitters in the antinociceptive effects of narcotic analgesics; characterization of the interactions between neurotransmitters in the central nervous system. *Mailing Add:* Pharmacol Sect 11E Vet Admin Med Ctr 4500 S Lancaster Rd Dallas TX 75216

VASLOW, DALE FRANKLIN, b Chicago, Ill, Aug 27, 45. PLASMA PHYSICS. *Educ:* Univ Wis, BS, 67, MS, 69, PhD(elec engr), 73. *Prof Exp:* STAFF SCIENTIST PLASMA PHYSICS, GEN ATOMIC CO, 74- *Mem:* Inst Elec & Electronics Engrs; Sigma Xi. *Res:* Solid state laser design; low light level image detection system; optical design; laser Thomson Scattering experiment; solid ablation in a plasma; fast neutron induced chemistry. *Mailing Add:* Box 81608 San Diego CA 92138

VASOFSKY, RICHARD WILLIAM, b Waukegan, Ill, May 14, 46. PHYSICAL CHEMISTRY, SURFACE SCIENCE. *Educ:* Univ Denver, BS, 68; Ore State Univ, MS, 71, PhD(phys chem), 75. *Prof Exp:* Res asst phys chem, Ore State Univ, 69-74; res assoc physics, Clarkson Col Technol, 75-77, res asst prof, 78; consult surface sci, Rome Air Develop Ctr, 78-80. *Mem:* Am Chem Soc; Am Vacuum Soc; Clay Mineral Soc; Int Soc Hybrid Microelectron; AAAS. *Res:* Adsorption by clays; gas-solid interactions; chemisorption; thin films; desorption; vacuum and ultramicrobalance techniques and applications. *Mailing Add:* PO Box 425 Loudon TN 37774

VASQUEZ, ALPHONSE THOMAS, b Boston, Mass, Apr 19, 38; m 65. MATHEMATICS. *Educ:* Mass Inst Technol, BS, 59; Univ Calif, Berkeley, PhD(math), 62. *Prof Exp:* Mem, Inst Advan Study, 62-64; res assoc math, Brandeis Univ, 64-65, asst prof, 65-67; assoc prof, 67-77, PROF MATH, GRAD DIV, CITY UNIV NEW YORK, 77- *Concurrent Pos:* NSF fel, 62-63. *Mem:* Am Math Soc. *Res:* Algebraic and differential topology; homological algebra. *Mailing Add:* Grad Div City Univ of NY 33 W 42nd St New York NY 10036

VASSALLE, MARIO, b Viareggio, Italy, May 26, 28; m 59; c 4. PHYSIOLOGY. *Educ:* Univ Pisa, MD, 53. *Prof Exp:* Fulbright travel grant, 58-62; NIH trainee, Med Col Ga, 59-60; NY Heart Asn fel, State Univ NY Downstate Med Ctr, 60-62; NIH fel, Physiol Inst, Bern, Switz, 62-64; from asst prof to assoc prof, 65-71, PROF PHYSIOL, STATE UNIV NY DOWNSTATE MED CTR, 71- *Concurrent Pos:* Mem coun basic sci, Am Heart Asn, 69- & Nat Conf Cardiovasc Dis, 69; assoc ed, Am J Physiol. *Mem:* AAAS; Am Physiol Soc; Harvey Soc; NY Acad Sci. *Res:* Cardiac electrophysiology, particularly cardiac automaticity and its control. *Mailing Add:* Dept of Physiol State Univ NY Downstate Med Ctr Brooklyn NY 11203

VASSALLO, DONALD ARTHUR, b Waterbury, Conn, June 7, 32; m 60; c 4. POLYMER CHEMISTRY. *Educ:* Univ Conn, BA, 54; Univ Ill, MS, 56, PhD(anal chem), 58. *Prof Exp:* RES ASSOC, PLASTICS DEPT, E I DU PONT DE NEMOURS & CO, INC, 58- *Mem:* AAAS; Am Chem Soc; Soc Plastics Eng. *Res:* Automatic nonaqueous titrations; thermogravimetry; differential thermal analysis, especially polymers; polymer melt rheology; polymer structure-property correlations; polyolefins; polyvinyl alcohol. *Mailing Add:* Plastics Dept Exp Sta E I du Pont de Nemours & Co Inc Wilmington DE 19898

VASSALLO, FRANKLIN A(LLEN), b Waterbury, Conn, Feb 22, 34; m 66. MECHANICAL ENGINEERING. *Educ:* Univ Conn, BS, 56; Univ Ill, MS, 57. *Prof Exp:* Asst mech engr, Cornell Aeronaut Lab, 57-59, assoc mech engr, 59-62, res engr, 62-67, prin res engr, 67-70, sect head, 70-78; SECT HEAD, CALSPAN CORP, 78- *Res:* Heat transfer and erosion in rapid fire weapons; determination of gas enthalpy; heat transfer and flow processes in high heat flux environments; hazardous materials transport. *Mailing Add:* Calspan Corp 4455 Genesee St Buffalo NY 14221

VASSAMILLET, LAWRENCE FRANCOIS, b Elizabethville, Congo, Sept 14, 24; nat US; m 54; c 2. SOLID STATE ANALYSIS. *Educ:* Mass Inst Technol, BSc, 46, MS, 50; Univ Liege, DSc(phys sci), 52; Carnegie Inst Technol, PhD(physics), 57. *Prof Exp:* Jr physicist, Monsanto Chem Co, Ohio, 47-48; physicist, Nat Carbon Co Div, Union Carbide Corp, 53; fel, Carnegie-Mellon Univ, 57-63, sr fel, Inst Sci, 63-67, assoc prof metall & mat sci, 67-80; PRIN RES SCIENTIST, COLUMBUS LABS, BATTELLE MEM INST, 80- *Mem:* Am Phys Soc; Electron Micros Soc Am; Microprobe Anal Soc; Metall Soc. *Res:* X-ray diffraction; inperfections in crystals; electron probe microanalysis; electron microscopy. *Mailing Add:* Columbus Labs Battelle Mem Inst 505 King Ave Columbus OH 43201

VASSEL, BRUNO, b Allahabath, Brit India, Oct 17, 08; nat US; m 36; c 3. BIOCHEMISTRY. *Educ:* Yale Univ, BS, 36; Univ Mich, MS, 37, PhD(biochem), 39. *Prof Exp:* Lab asst biochem, Univ Mich, 37-39; res biochemist, Am Cyanamid Co, 39-43; assoc prof biochem & res agr chemist exp sta, NDak Col, 43-46; supvr org & biochem res, Int Minerals & Chem Corp, 46-55; DIR RES, JOHNSON & JOHNSON OF BRAZIL, 55-, MEM EXEC COMT, 59- *Honors & Awards:* Robert W Johnson Medal Res & Develop, 64. *Mem:* AAAS; Am Chem Soc; Am Oil Chem Soc; Am Soc Sugar Beet Technol. *Res:* Protein isolations; monosodium glutamate processes; amino acid analyses and syntheses; pharmaceuticals; polarograph; flotation reagents; detergents; starch derivatives; surgical and pharmaceutical products. *Mailing Add:* Apt 613 2525 E First St Ft Myers FL 33901

VASSELL, GREGORY S, b Moscow, Russia, Dec 24, 21; m 57; c 2. ELECTRICAL ENGINEERING. *Educ:* Tech Univ, Berlin, Ger, Dipl Eng, 51; NY Univ, MBA, 54. *Prof Exp:* From asst engr to sr engr elec eng, 51-61, sect head high voltage planning, 62-66, assoc chief syst planning engr,, 66-67, chief syst planning engr, 67-68, asst vpres bulk power supply planning, 68-73, vpres & dir, 73-76, SR VPRES & DIR SYST PLANNING, AM ELEC POWER SERV CORP, 76- *Concurrent Pos:* Chmn, Syst Reliability Adv Panel, East Cent Reliability Group, 67-69; mem, Tech Adv Comt Transmission, Fed Power Comn, 68-70, NCent Reg Task Force, Fed Energy Regulatory Comn, 79-81, US Nat Comt, World Energy Conf. *Mem:* Nat Acad Eng; fel Inst Elec & Electronics Engrs. *Res:* Electric power supply planning; energy resource planning. *Mailing Add:* 2247 Pinebrook Rd Upper Arlington OH 43220

VASSELL, MILTON O, b Jamaica, West Indies, May 8, 31; m 58; c 2. THEORETICAL PHYSICS. *Educ:* NY Univ, BA, 58, PhD(physics), 64. *Prof Exp:* RES SCIENTIST, GTE LABS, INC, 64- *Mem:* Am Phys Soc; Sigma Xi. *Res:* Many particle physics; transport theory in semiconductors and metals; nonlinear optics; physics of lasers; acoustic surface wave propagation; acousto-electric effects; electron optics; integrated optics; optical guided wave propagation; holography. *Mailing Add:* GTE Labs Inc 40 Sylvan Rd Waltham MA 02154

VASSILIADES, ANTHONY E, b Chios, Greece, Nov 26, 33; US citizen; m 57; c 2. PHYSICAL CHEMISTRY, POLYMER CHEMISTRY. *Educ:* Wagner Col, BS, 56; Syracuse Univ, MS, 58; Polytech Inst Brooklyn, PhD(phys chem), 62. *Prof Exp:* From asst prof to assoc prof chem, Wagner Col, 61-66; assoc dir res, Champion Papers, Inc, 66-68, dir res, Champion Papers Group, US Plywood-Champion Papers, Inc, 68-70, vpres & dir res & develop, 70-76, V PRES & DIR SCI, CHAMPION INT CORP, 76- *Concurrent Pos:* Consult, Champion Papers, Inc, 64-66. *Mem:* Am Chem Soc; NY Acad Sci. *Res:* Coacervation of charged colloidal systems; transport phenomena in liquids; physical chemistry of high polymers; surface phenomena. *Mailing Add:* Champion Int Corp Knightsbridge Dr Hamilton OH 45020

VASSILIOU, ANDREAS H, b Ora, Larnaca, Cyprus, Nov 30, 36; m 65; c 1. MINERALOGY. *Educ:* Columbia Univ, BS, 63, MA, 65, PhD(mineral), 69. *Prof Exp:* Asst prof, 69-75, ASSOC PROF GEOL, RUTGERS UNIV, 75- *Mem:* Geol Soc Am; Mineral Soc Am. *Res:* Mineralogy of uranium, particularly the nature of urano-organic deposits in the Colorado Plateau and elsewhere. *Mailing Add:* 15 Neptune Ct Somerset NJ 08873

VASSILIOU, EUSTATHIOS, b Athens, Greece, Aug 22, 34; m 60; c 3. COATINGS CHEMISTRY. *Educ:* Nat Tech Univ Athens, BScChE, 58; Univ Manchester, PhD(chem), 64. *Prof Exp:* Res chemist, Nuclear Res Ctr, Democritus, Greece, 64-66; res fel solid state physics, Harvard Univ, 66-67; res chemist, 67-73, staff chemist, 73-78, res assoc, Marshall Lab, 78-79, res supvr, 79-80, RES ASSOC, EXP STA, E I DU PONT DE NEMOURS & CO, INC, 80- *Mem:* Am Chem Soc. *Res:* Inorganic physical chemistry; physics and chemistry of glasses; vanadium; thermistors; anodic films; luminescence; ozone physics; semiconductor surface phenomena; magnetic phenomena; lubrication; structural plastics; fluorocarbon and other high temperature resistant coatings; corrosion resistant coatings; electrodeposition of coatings. *Mailing Add:* 12 S Townview Lane Newark DE 19711

VASSOS, BASIL HARILAOS, chemical instrumentation, analytical chemistry, see previous edition

VASTANO, ANDREW CHARLES, b New York, NY, Feb 26, 36; m 58; c 4. PHYSICAL OCEANOGRAPHY, NUMERICAL ANALYSIS. *Educ:* NC State Univ, BS, 56; Univ NC, MS, 60; Tex A&M Univ, PhD(phys oceanog), 67. *Prof Exp:* Anal engr, Pratt & Whitney Aircraft Corp, 56-57; sonar engr, Western Elec Co, Bell Tel Co, 60-62; instr physics, Tex A&M Univ, 62-63, res scientist, 63-66; assoc prof phys oceanog, Univ Fla, 66-67; asst scientist, Woods Hole Oceanog Inst, 67-69; instr, 64, ASSOC PROF OCEANOG, TEX A&M UNIV, 69- *Mem:* Am Geophys Union. *Res:* Numerical studies of tsunami and storm surges; theory of gravity waves; mesoscale ocean dynamics; topographic interaction of current systems. *Mailing Add:* Dept of Oceanog Tex A&M Univ College Station TX 77843

VASTOLA, EDWARD FRANCIS, b Waterbury, Conn, June 1, 24; m 49; c 2. MEDICINE, NEUROLOGY. *Educ:* Yale Univ, BS, 45; Columbia Univ, MD, 47; Am Bd Psychiat & Neurol, dipl. *Prof Exp:* Instr neurol, Sch Med, Washington Univ, 53-55; from asst prof to prof neurol, Col Med, State Univ NY Downstate Med Ctr, 55-74, head dept, 59-73; PROF NEUROL, SCH MED, WASH UNIV, 74-; CHIEF NEUROL, ST LOUIS CITY HOSP, 74- *Concurrent Pos:* Dir dept neurol, Kings County Hosp, 59-73; consult, Vet Admin Hosp, Brooklyn; vis neurologist, Ft Hamilton Vet Admin Hosp; mem neurol staff, Huntington Hosp, NY. Res; Neurophysiology; clinical neurology. *Mailing Add:* Neurol Sect 1515 Lafayette Ave St Louis MO 63104

VASTOLA, FRANCIS J, b Buffalo, NY, Feb 22, 28; m 69. LABORATORY INSTRUMENTATION & CONTROL. *Educ:* Univ Buffalo, BA, 50; Pa State Univ, PhD(fuel technol), 59. *Prof Exp:* Chemist, Nat Bur Standards, Washington, DC, 50-52; asst & res assoc, 56-59, from asst prof to assoc prof fuel sci, 59-72, PROF FUEL SCI, PA STATE UNIV, 72- *Mem:* Am Chem Soc. *Res:* Mass spectrometry; solid and gaseous combustion; kinetics and instrumentation. *Mailing Add:* Dept of Mat Sci Pa State Univ University Park PA 16802

VASU, BANGALORE SESHACHALAM, b Bangalore, India, May 20, 29; Indian citizen; m 65; c 1. BIOLOGY. *Educ:* Univ Madras, BSc, 49, MSc, 62; Stanford Univ, PhD(biol), 65. *Prof Exp:* Asst prof zool, Pachaiyappa's Col, Madras Univ, 50-59, lectr, Zool Res Lab, 59-62; Fulbright res fel biol, Stanford Univ, 62-65; AEC fel, Univ Notre Dame, 65-67; asst prof zool, Ohio Wesleyan Univ, 67-68; UNESCO specialist biol, Univ Zambia, 68-73; asst prof biol, Calif State Univ, Chico, 74-78; PROF BIOL, MENLO COL, 78- *Concurrent Pos:* Fulbright grant, US Educ Found India, 62. *Mem:* Sigma Xi; Am Inst Biol Sci; AAAS; Radiation Res Soc; Marine Biol Asn UK. *Res:* Age-related changes at the cellular and moleuclar level. *Mailing Add:* Dept of Biol Sci Menlo Col Menlo Park CA 94025

VASUDEVA, BACHALLI R, b Hospet, India, July 27, 34; US citizen; m 64. AEROSPACE ENGINEERING, FLUID MECHANICS. *Educ:* Univ Mysore, BE, 54; Indian Inst Sci, Bangalore, ME, 56, MS, 58; Johns Hopkins Univ, PhD(mech), 65. *Prof Exp:* Res asst aeronaut, Johns Hopkins Univ, 60-65; res assoc aerospace eng, Pa State Univ, 65-67; assoc consult, Aeronaut Res Asn, Princeton Univ, 67-69; res scientist, Aero Chem Res Labs, Princeton Univ, 69-72; tech mgr, Techne Inc, 72-81; SR SYSTS ENGR, TECHNICON INSTRUMENTS, 81- *Res:* Boundary layer and laminar instability theories; experimental fluid mechanics; instrumentation; hot wire anemometry; design and development of scientific instrumentation; development of automated medical instrumentation. *Mailing Add:* 9 Jacob Dr PO Box 163 Princeton Junction NJ 08550

VATNE, ROBERT DAHLMEIER, b Pipestone, Minn, Oct 21, 34; m 63; c 1. PARASITOLOGY. *Educ:* Augustana Col, SDak, BA, 56; Kans State Univ, MS, 58, PhD(parasitol), 63. *Prof Exp:* Asst prof biol, St Cloud State Col, 63-64; assoc scientist, Salsbury Labs, Iowa, 65-66, scientist, 67-69; res specialist, 70-73, regist specialist, 74-81, PROD REGIST MGR, DOW CHEM CO, USA, 81- *Mem:* Am Soc Parasitol. *Res:* Etiology and chemotherapy of histomoniasis, coccidiosis and helminthiasis. *Mailing Add:* Agr Prod Dept Dow Chem Co PO Box 1706 Midland MI 48640

VATSIS, KOSTAS PETROS, b Patras, Greece, May 6, 45. ENZYMOLOGY. *Educ:* Calif State Univ, Long Beach, BS, 67, MS, 69; Univ Ill Med Ctr, PhD(pharmacol), 75. *Prof Exp:* Res asst pharmacol, Col Med, Univ Ill, 69-75; scholar biol chem, Med Sch, Univ Mich, 75-76, lectr, 76-78; ASST PROF PHARMACOL, MED SCH, NORTHWESTERN UNIV, 78- *Concurrent Pos:* Consult, Dept Pharmacol, Col Med, Univ Ill, 77-; prin investr, starter grant, Pharamaceut Mfg Asn Fedn, Inc, 80-81, res grant NIH, 80-83. *Res:* Physiochemical studies on the mechanism of interaction of components of the nicotinamide-adenine dinucleotide phosphate and nicotinamide dinucleotide linked electron transport chains in mammalian hepatic microsomes: modulation of the cytochrome phosphorous 450 containing monooxygenase system by cytochrome b5 and related membrane-bound proteins. *Mailing Add:* Dept Pharmacol Med & Dent Sch Northwestern Univ 303 E Chicago Ave Chicago IL 60611

VAUCHER, JEAN G, b Can, 42. COMPUTER SCIENCE. *Educ:* Univ Ottawa, BSc, 62; Univ Manchester, MSc, 64, PhD, 68. *Prof Exp:* Researcher, IBM, Can, 68-70; from asst prof to assoc prof, 70-79, chmn, 81-85, PSSOC PROF COMPUT SYSTS, UNIV MONTREAL, 79- *Mem:* Asn Comput Mach. *Res:* Simulation; real-time control; parallelism; structured programming. *Mailing Add:* Dept of Info Sci PO 6128 Sta A Montreal PQ H3C 3J7 Can

VAUDO, ANTHONY FRANK, b Brooklyn, NY, Jan 21, 46; m 67; c 1. PHYSICAL CHEMISTRY. *Educ:* City Col New York, BS, 66; Mass Inst Technol, PhD(phys chem), 70. *Prof Exp:* NSF fel, Boston Univ, 70-71; sr develop chemist, St Regis Paper Co, 71-74, tech dir, Laminated & Coated Prods Div, 74-80. *Mem:* Am Chem Soc; Soc Photog Sci & Eng; Tech Asn Pulp & Paper Indust. *Res:* Photochemistry and its applications to imaging materials. *Mailing Add:* 6534 Wickerwood Dr Dallas TX 75248

VAUGHAN, ARTHUR HARRIS, JR, b Salem, Ohio, July 19, 34; m 59, 76; c 4. ASTRONOMY, TECHNICAL MANAGEMENT. *Educ:* Cornell Univ, BEngPhys, 58; Univ Rochester, PhD(physics, astron), 65. *Prof Exp:* Jr res scientist, Avco-Everett Res Lab, Mass, 58-59; fel, 64-65, asst astronr, 65-66, staff assoc, 66-67, mem staff, Hale Observ, 67-81, RES ASSOC, MT WILSON & LAS CAMPANAS OBSERV, CARNEGIE INST WASHINGTON, 81-; MGR PROGS, ASTRON SYSTS, APPL OPTICS DIV, PERKIN-ELMER CORP, 81- *Honors & Awards:* James Arthur Prize, Smithsonian Inst, 81. *Mem:* Am Astron Soc; Int Astron Union. *Res:* Development and application of astronomical instrumentation; Synoptic measurements of stellar chromospheric activity and its variation with time, revealing rates of stellar rotation and long-term changes, in some cases analogous to the solar cycle. *Mailing Add:* Carnegie Inst Wash 813 Santa Barbara St Pasadena CA 91106

VAUGHAN, BURTON EUGENE, b Santa Rosa, Calif, May 31, 26; m 49; c 2. PHYSIOLOGY, BIOPHYSICS. *Educ:* Univ Calif, Berkeley, AB, 49, PhD, 55. *Prof Exp:* Vis scientist, White Mountain High Altitude Res Sta, Calif, 53-54; proj leader, Oper Deepfreeze I, US Exped to Antarctic, 55; staff scientist biophys br, US Naval Radiol Defense Lab, 56-61, br head, 62-69; MGR ECOSYSTS DEPT, PAC NORTHWEST LABS, BATTELLE MEM INST, 69- *Concurrent Pos:* Actg instr, Sch Med, Stanford Univ, 57, Lectr, 60-63, res assoc, 63-70; consult, Clin Invest Ctr, Oakland Naval Hosp, 60-61 & US Naval Med Res Unit 2, Taipei, Taiwan, 61, 64 & 65; trustee, Independent Sch Dist, 63, presiding off, 64-65; rep, County Comt Sch Dist Orgn, 65; mem bd educ, Castro Valley Unified Sch Dist, 65, pres, 66-67; consult, Govt Health Facil, Manila, Philippines; sci coun chmn, Pac Sci Ctr Found, Seattle, 75-78, mem exec comn & trustee, 78- *Mem:* Am Soc Plant Physiol; Am Physiol Soc; Biophys Soc; NY Acad Sci; Radiation Res Soc. *Res:* Electrolyte and other absorption processes, including permeability, metabolically coupled transport; gastro-intestinal irradiation injury in the mammal; ionic uptake, discrimination and fixation by terrestrial plant and marine algal tissues; radiocontamination processes in organisms and ecological systems; pollution biology and pathways; plant and animal physiology. *Mailing Add:* Eco-Systs Dept Pac Northwest Labs Box 999 Richland WA 99352

VAUGHAN, CHARLES EDWIN, b Mathiston, Miss, Jan 18, 33; m 57; c 1. AGRONOMY. *Educ:* Miss State Univ, BS, 55, MS, 62; NC State Univ, PhD(agron), 69. *Prof Exp:* Asst agronomist & asst prof agron, 59-69, assoc prof, 69-77, ASSOC AGRONOMIST, 69-, PROF AGRON, MISS STATE UNIV, 77- *Mem:* Am Soc Agron; Asn Off Seed Anal. *Res:* Seed physiology; seed deterioration; quality control in seed programs. *Mailing Add:* Dept of Agron Miss State Univ Mississippi State MS 39762

VAUGHAN, DAVID ARTHUR, b Mattoon, Wis, Mar 5, 23; m 51; c 1. NUTRITION. *Educ:* Univ Calif, BA, 49; Univ Ill, MA, 54, PhD(animal nutrit), 55. *Prof Exp:* Res physiologist, Arctic Aeromed Lab, US Dept Air Force, 55-59, supvry chemist, 59-68, res biochemist, US Air Force Sch Aerospace Med, 68-69; res biochemist, Nutrit Inst, Sci & Educ Admin-Agr Res, USDA, 69-79; RETIRED. *Mem:* Am Physiol Soc; Am Inst Nutrit. *Res:* Survival nutrition in the Arctic; vitamin B requirements and intermediary metabolism during stress; biochemistry of hibernation; protein nutrition. *Mailing Add:* 8533 Pineway Dr Laurel MD 20707

VAUGHAN, DAVID SHERWOOD, b Attleboro, Mass Jan 2, 23; m 46; c 2. MECHANICAL ENGINEERING. *Educ:* Yale Univ, BE, 47; Case Inst Technol, MS, 53. *Prof Exp:* Eng draftsman, Fairbanks Morse & Co, 47-48; eng technician, White Motor Co, 48-51; sr engr, Goodyear Aircraft Corp, 51-54; proj engr, Paragon Gear Works, 54-55; sr engr, 55-70, PROJ ENGR, FACET ENTERPRISES, ELMIRA, 70- *Mem:* Am Soc Mech Engrs; Soc Automotive Engrs. *Res:* Machine design; stress analysis; magnetic circuits; fluid mechanics; materials. *Mailing Add:* Box 253 RD 1 Erin NY 14838

VAUGHAN, DEBORAH WHITTAKER, b Concord, NH, Nov 30, 43; m 66. NEUROANATOMY. *Educ:* Univ Vt, BA, 66; Boston Univ, PhD(biol), 71. *Prof Exp:* USPHS fel, 71-72, res asst prof, 72-78, ASST PROF NEUROANAT, SCH MED, BOSTON UNIV, 78- *Res:* Electron microscopic analysis of neocortex, primarily of rat, in regards to the effects of aging on the brain. *Mailing Add:* Dept of Anat Boston Univ Sch of Med Boston MA 02118

VAUGHAN, DOUGLAS STANWOOD, b Biddeford, Maine, July 12, 46; m 76. POPULATION DYNAMICS, RISK ASSESSMENT. *Educ:* Univ NH, BS, 68; Pa State Univ, MA, 70; Univ RI, PhD(oceanog), 77. *Prof Exp:* Statistician, Environ Protection Agency, 71-73; RES ASSOC, OAK RIDGE NAT LAB, 77- *Mem:* Biomet Soc; Am Fisheries Soc; Ecol Soc Am; Int Oceanog Found; AAAS. *Res:* Application of statistical methods and population and community modeling approaches to assessing the effects of one or more stresses on fish populations, and the development of approaches for environmental risk assessment; incorporation of density dependence into modelling of fish populations; use of matrix models for describing population dynamics. *Mailing Add:* Environ Sci Div PO Box X Oak Ridge TN 37830

VAUGHAN, E(DWIN) MARVIN, b Matoka, WVa, Dec 2, 21; m 42; c 4. ENGINEERING PHYSICS. *Educ:* Va Polytech Inst, BS, 43, MS, 49. *Prof Exp:* Instr physics, Va Polytech Inst, 46-47; electronic engr, Appl Physics Lab, Johns Hopkins Univ, 48-49; prof physics & chmn dept, St Ambrose Col, 49-63; phys sci adminstr res off, Res & Develop Directorate, US Army Weapons/Armament Command, 63-76, chief sci info div, 68-71; ELECTRONIC ENGR, LARGE CALIBER MAINTENANCE ENG DIV, MAINTENANCE DIRECTORATE, US ARMY ARMAMENT MAT READINESS COMMAND, 77- *Concurrent Pos:* Instr, NATO Spec Weapons Sch, Ger, 52-53; consult & ed adv, Instrument & Life Support Div, Bendix Corp, 55-63; chmn, Sci Div, Eve Col, Palmer Jr Col, Iowa, 65-77. *Res:* Automatic testing; biophysics; energy conversion; quantum electronics; thermal imaging; nuclear radiation. *Mailing Add:* DRSAR-MAL-F Large Caliber Eng Armament Mat Readiness Command Rock Island IL 61299

VAUGHAN, FRIZELL LOUIS, medical microbiology, cell biology, see previous edition

VAUGHAN, HERBERT EDWARD, b Ogdensburg, NY, Feb 18, 11; m 47. MATHEMATICS. *Educ:* Univ Mich, BS, 32, AM, 33, PhD(math), 35. *Prof Exp:* Instr math, Brown Univ, 35-36; Lloyd fel, Univ Mich, 36-37; instr, 37-41, assoc, 41-45, from asst prof to assoc prof, 45-60, PROF MATH, UNIV ILL, URBANA, 60-, MEM UNIV COMT ON SCH MATH PROJ EDUC, 56- *Mem:* Am Math Soc; Math Asn Am; Asn Symbolic Logic. *Res:* Topology; abstract spaces. *Mailing Add:* Dept of Math Univ of Ill Urbana IL 61801

VAUGHAN, J RODNEY M, b Margate, Eng, May 2, 21; US citizen; m 48; c 3. MICROWAVE ENGINEERING, COMPUTER AIDED DESIGN. *Educ:* Cambridge Univ, BA, 48, MA, 57, PhD, 72. *Prof Exp:* Engr, Res Labs, Elec & Musical Indust, Eng, 48-57; sr engr & proj mgr, Tube Dept, Gen Elec

Co, NY, 57-68; CHIEF SCIENTIST, TUBE DIV, LITTON INDUSTS, INC, SAN CARLOS, 68- *Concurrent Pos:* Chmn, MIL-E-I, Microwave Rev Comt, 66-68; lectr math, Col of Notre Dame, Calif, 69-70; chmn adv bd, Air Force Thermionic Eng Res Prog, 79-80. *Mem:* Sr mem Inst Elec & Electronics Engrs; Electron Devices Soc (secy, 81). *Res:* Research and advanced development of high power microwave tubes, using advanced computer methods. *Mailing Add:* 2 Sequoia Way Redwood City CA 94061

VAUGHAN, JAMES ROLAND, b Allentown, Pa, June 7, 28; m 50; c 3. MICROBIOLOGY, BIOCHEMISTRY. *Educ:* Muhlenberg Col, BS, 52; Lehigh Univ, MS, 54, PhD(biol), 61. *Prof Exp:* From instr to assoc prof microbiol, 56-67, PROF MICROBIOL, MUHLENBERG COL, 67-, HEAD DEPT, 65- *Mem:* AAAS; Am Soc Microbiol; Am Chem Soc; Am Soc Cell Biol. *Res:* Microbial physiology, aerobiology and biochemistry of mucopolysaccharides and bacterial pigments. *Mailing Add:* Dept of Biol Muhlenberg Col Allentown PA 18104

VAUGHAN, JERRY EUGENE, b Gastonia, NC, Oct 30, 39; m 69. MATHEMATICS, TOPOLOGY. *Educ:* Davidson Col, BS, 61; Duke Univ, PhD(math), 65. *Prof Exp:* Teaching asst math, Duke Univ, 62-63; assoc prof, Eve Div, Univ Md, 66-67; asst prof, Univ NC, Chapel Hill, 67-73; assoc prof, 73-76, PROF MATH, UNIV NC, GREENSBORO, 76- *Mem:* Am Math Soc; Math Asn Am. *Res:* General topology; generalized metric spaces; product spaces; cardinal invariant properties. *Mailing Add:* Dept of Math Univ of NC Greensboro NC 27412

VAUGHAN, JOHN DIXON, b Clarksville, Va, Mar 3, 25; m 62. PHYSICAL CHEMISTRY. *Educ:* Col William & Mary, BS, 50; Univ Ill, PhD(chem), 54. *Prof Exp:* Asst phys chem, Univ Ill, 50-51, AEC, 51-54; res chemist, Chem Dept, Exp Sta, E I du Pont de Nemours & Co, 54-58; asst prof phys chem, Va Polytech Inst, 59-62 & Univ Hawaii, 62-64; assoc prof, 64-71, PROF PHYS CHEM, COLO STATE UNIV, 71- *Mem:* Am Chem Soc. *Res:* Molecular mechanics; homogeneous catalysis; reactivities of heterocycles. *Mailing Add:* Dept of Chem Colo State Univ Ft Collins CO 80523

VAUGHAN, JOHN HEATH, b Richmond, Va, Nov 11, 21; m 46; c 4. IMMUNOLOGY, MEDICINE. *Educ:* Harvard Univ, AB, 42, MD, 45. *Prof Exp:* Intern med, Peter Bent Brigham Hosp, 45-56, resident, 48-51; Nat Res Coun fel med sci, Col Physicians & Surgeons, Columbia Univ, 51-53; asst prof, Med Col Va, 53-58; assoc prof med & asst prof bact, Sch Med & Dent, Univ Rochester, 58-63, prof med & head div immunol & infectious dis, 63-70; chmn clin div, 70-74, chmn dept clin res, 74-77, HEAD DIV CLIN IMMUNOL, SCRIPPS CLIN & RES FOUND, 77- *Concurrent Pos:* Fel, Peter Bent Brigham Hosp, Boston, 48-51; consult, NIH, 56-63, mem bd sci counr, Nat Inst Allergy & Infectious Dis, 68-72; mem allergy clin immunol res comt, NIH, 80- *Mem:* Am Soc Clin Invest; Asn Am Physicians; Am Asn Immunol; Am Rheumatism Asn (pres, 70-71); Am Acad Allergy (pres, 66-67). *Res:* Immunological phenomena in internal medicine; allergy; arthritis; hemolytic disease. *Mailing Add:* Scripps Clin & Res Found 10666 N Torrey Pines Rd La Jolla CA 92037

VAUGHAN, JOHN THOMAS, b Tuskegee, Ala, Feb 6, 32; m 56; c 3. VETERINARY MEDICINE. *Educ:* Auburn Univ, DVM, 55, MS, 63. *Prof Exp:* From instr to assoc prof large animal surg & med, Auburn Univ, 55-70; prof vet surg & dir large animal hosp, NY State Vet Col, Cornell Univ, 70-74; chmn dept Large Animal Surg & Med, 74-77, DEAN, SCH VET MED, AUBURN UNIV, 77- *Mem:* Am Vet Med Asn; Am Asn Equine Practitioners (pres, 81); Am Asn Vet Clinicians; Am Col Vet Surg (pres, 80). *Res:* Large animal and equine surgery and medicine; general surgery of the equine system with emphasis on urogenital and gastrointestinal surgery. *Mailing Add:* Dept of Large Animal Surg & Med Auburn Univ Auburn AL 36820

VAUGHAN, LINDA ANN, b Brooklyn, NY, July 26, 50; m 74; c 1. HUMAN NUTRITION. *Educ:* Univ Calif, Davis, BS, 72; Cornell Univ, MNS, 74; Univ Ariz, PhD(agr biochem, nutrit), 77. *Prof Exp:* Nutritionist II pub health nutrit, Maricopa Co Health Dept, 74-75; nutrit consult cardiac rehab, Dr A E Smith, Tempe, Ariz, 77; asst prof, Dept Food & Nutrit, Univ Nebr, 77-79; ASST PROF, DEPT HOME ECON, ARIZ STATE UNIV, 79- *Mem:* Am Dietetic Asn; Inst Food Technologists; Soc Nutrit Educ; Am Inst Nutrit; Am Sch Health Asn. *Res:* Maternal and infant nutrition; composition of human milk. *Mailing Add:* Dept Home Econ Ariz State Univ Tempe AZ 85281

VAUGHAN, LOY OTTIS, JR, b Birmingham, Ala, June 30, 45; m 66; c 1. MATHEMATICS. *Educ:* Fla State Univ, BA, 66; Univ Ala, MA, 67, PhD(math), 70. *Prof Exp:* Asst prof, 69-80, ASSOC PROF MATH, UNIV ALA, BIRMINGHAM, 80- *Mem:* Am Math Soc; Math Asn Am. *Res:* General topology, fixed and almost fixed point theory of continua. *Mailing Add:* Dept of Math Univ of Ala Birmingham AL 35294

VAUGHAN, MARTHA, b Dodgeville, Wis, Aug 4, 26; m 51; c 3. BIOCHEMISTRY. *Educ:* Univ Chicago, PhB, 44; Yale Univ, MD, 49. *Prof Exp:* Asst instr res med, Univ Pa, 51-52; Nat Res Coun fel, 52-54, from sr asst surgeon to sr surgeon, 54-62, MED DIR, NAT HEART INST, 62- *Concurrent Pos:* mem metab study sect, Div Res Grants, USPHS, 65-68, head sect metab, 68-74, chief, Lab Cellular Metab, 74-; int fel rev comt, Fogarty Int Ctr, 73-74, 77-78; bd dir, Found Adv Educ Sci, Inc, 79-; vchmn, Gordon Conf Cyclei Nucleotides, 81, chmn, 82. *Mem:* Am Soc Biol Chemists; Am Soc Clin Invest; Asn Am Physicians. *Res:* Mechanism of hormone action. *Mailing Add:* Rm 5N-307 Bldg 10 NIH Bethesda MD 20014

VAUGHAN, MICHAEL RAY, b Newport News, Va, Aug 11, 44; m 71; c 3. POPULATION DYNAMICS, HABITAT ECOLOGY. *Educ:* NC State Univ, BS, 71; Ore State Univ, MS, 74; Univ Wis,Madison, PhD(wildlife ecol), 79. *Prof Exp:* Res asst wildlife ecol, Ore State Univ, 71-74, Univ Wis-Madison, 74-79; actg asst leader, Wis Coop Wildlife Res Univ, 79-80, ASST LEADER VA COOP WILDLIFE RES UNIT POP DYNAMICS, VA POLYTECH INST & STATE UNIV, US FISH & WILDLIFE SERV, 80- *Mem:* Wildlife Soc. *Res:* Population dynamics and cyclic phenomena especially snowshoe hares, mountain goats, black bears, wild turkeys and white-tailed deer. *Mailing Add:* Va Coop Wildlife Res Unit 148 Cheatham Hall Va Polytech & State Univ Blacksburg VA 24061

VAUGHAN, MICHAEL THOMAS, b Washington, DC, Sept 29, 40; m 78; c 2. MINERALS ELASTICITY, MANTLE MINERALOGY. *Educ:* Shimer Col, BS, 60; Univ Cincinnati, MS, 65; State Univ, NY, MS, 76, PhD(geophysics), 79. *Prof Exp:* Instr physics, Thomas More Col, 68-70; asst prof, WVa State Col, 71-74; teaching asst geol, State Univ NY, 75-76, fel res asst geophysics, 76-79; asst geophysicist, Hawaii Inst Geophysics, 79-81; ASST PROF GEOL, UNIV ILL, CHICAGO, 81- *Mem:* Am Geophys Union; Geol Soc Am; Mineral Soc Am. *Res:* Relations between crystal structure and elasticity, especially in high-pressure phases of oxides and silicates, by measuring the single-crystal elastic constants of suitable well-characterized crystals with known crystal structures. *Mailing Add:* Dept Geol Sci Univ Ill Box 4348 Chicago IL 60680

VAUGHAN, NANCY DONOVAN, b Lexington, Mass, July 21, 51; m 76. RADIOACTIVE WASTE DISPOSAL. *Educ:* Colo Sch Mines, BSGE, 73; Univ RI, MS, 77. *Prof Exp:* Consult, Coastal Resources Ctr, 70-77; info analyst, 77-79, dir, Info Ctr, 79-80, RES ASSOC, UNION CARBIDE, OAK RIDGE NAT LAB, 80- *Concurrent Pos:* Reservoir eng aide, Getty Oil Co, 73; res asst, Univ RI, 73-75; NSF adv, Oceanog Prog High Sch Students, Univ RI, 75 & 76. *Mem:* Am Asn Petrol Geologists; Geol Soc Am; Soc Women Engrs; Am Nuclear Soc. *Res:* Determining the effect of geologic and hydrologic regimes on advanced shallow land burial methods of low-level radioactive waste. *Mailing Add:* 1018 Lovell View Circle Knoxville TN 37922

VAUGHAN, NICK HAMPTON, b Graham, Tex, Feb 11, 23; m 60; c 2. MATHEMATICS. *Educ:* NTex State Univ, BS, 47, MS, 48; La State Univ, PhD(math), 68. *Prof Exp:* Mathematician, US Naval Ord Plant, Ind, 51-53; res assoc math, Statist Lab, Purdue Univ, Lafayette, 53-55; sr aerophysics engr, Gen Dynamics, Tex, 55; instr math, La State Univ, 55-58; asst prof, NTex State Univ, 58-65; instr, La State Univ, 65-68; assoc prof, 68-78, PROF MATH, NTEX STATE UNIV, 78- *Mem:* Am Math Soc; Math Asn Am. *Res:* Commutative rings; ideal theory; algebraic number theory. *Mailing Add:* Dept of Math NTex State Univ Denton TX 76203

VAUGHAN, PHILIP ALFRED, b Palo Alto, Calif, Sept 21, 23; m 45; c 2. PHYSICAL CHEMISTRY. *Educ:* Pomona Col, BA, 43; Calif Inst Technol, PhD(chem), 49. *Prof Exp:* Chemist, Union Oil Co Calif, 43-46; Hale fel, Calif Inst Technol, 49-50; from asst prof to prof chem, Rutgers Univ, 50-68; vpres, V&E Mfg Co, Calif, 68, exec vpres, 68-80, PRES, VEMCO CORP, 80- *Res:* Crystal and molecular structure; x-ray crystallography; structure and properties of solutions. *Mailing Add:* Vemco Corp 766 SFair Oaks Pasadena CA 91105

VAUGHAN, ROBERT WALTON, b McAlester, Okla, Sept 9, 41; m 62; c 1. CHEMICAL ENGINEERING, SOLID STATE CHEMISTRY. *Educ:* Univ Okla, BS, 63; Univ Ill, Urbana, MS, 65, PhD(chem eng), 67. *Prof Exp:* From asst prof to assoc prof, 69-77, PROF CHEM ENG & CHEM PHYSICS, CALIF INST TECHNOL, 77- *Mem:* AAAS; Am Phys Soc; Am Chem Soc. *Res:* Chemistry and physics of solids; surface chemistry. *Mailing Add:* 227 Spalding Calif Inst of Technol Pasadena CA 91125

VAUGHAN, TERRY ALFRED, b Los Angeles, Calif, May 5, 28; m 50; c 2. VERTEBRATE ZOOLOGY. *Educ:* Pomona Col, BA, 50; Claremont Cols, MA, 52; Univ Kans, PhD, 58. *Prof Exp:* Asst zool, Univ Kans, 52-54 & 56-58; asst biologist, Colo State Univ, 58-64, assoc biologist, 64-70; PROF ZOOL, NORTHERN ARIZ UNIV, 70- *Mem:* Am Soc Mammalogists; Cooper Ornith Soc. *Res:* Chiropteran and rodent ecology; functional morphology. *Mailing Add:* Dept of Zool Northern Ariz Univ Flagstaff AZ 86011

VAUGHAN, THERESA PHILLIPS, b Kearney, Nebr, Oct 13, 41; m 69. ALGEBRA. *Educ:* Antioch Col, BA, 64; Am Univ, MA, 68; Duke Univ, PhD(math), 72. *Prof Exp:* Math programmer, Naval Ship Res & Develop Ctr, 64-69; asst prof math, NC Wesleyan Col, Rocky Mt, 72-73; LECTR MATH, UNIV NC, GREENSBORO, 74- *Mem:* Am Math Soc. *Res:* Polynomials and linear structure of finite fields; enumeration of sequences of integers by patterns; 2x2 matrices with positive integer entries; computation of discriminants. *Mailing Add:* Dept of Math Univ of NC Greensboro NC 27412

VAUGHAN, VICTOR CLARENCE, III, b Toledo, Ohio, July 19, 19; m 41; c 3. PEDIATRICS. *Educ:* Harvard Univ, AB, 39, MD, 43; Am Bd Pediat, dipl, 51, cert pediat allergy, 60. *Prof Exp:* Instr pediat, Sch Med, Yale Univ, 45-47 & 49-50, asst prof, 50-52; assoc prof, Sch Med, Temple Univ, 52-57; prof & chmn dept, Med Col Ga, 57-64; chmn dept, 64-76, PROF PEDIAT, SCH MED, TEMPLE UNIV, 64-; nat bd med examr, sr fel med eval, 77-81, SR MED EVAL OFFICER, 81- *Concurrent Pos:* Res fel, Harvard Med Sch, 47-49; mem bd, Am Bd Pediat, 60-65 & 68-73, secy, 63-65, pres, 73; med dir, St Christopher's Hosp Children, 64-76. *Mem:* Fel Am Acad Allergy; Soc Pediat Res (vpres, 64-65); Am Acad Pediat; Am Fedn Clin Res; Am Pediat Soc. *Res:* Hemolytic disease of newborn; human genetics; allergic disorders of children; human growth and development; medical education and evaluation. *Mailing Add:* Nat Bd Med Examiners 3930 Chestnut St Philadelphia PA 19104

VAUGHAN, WILLIAM MACE, b Mt Vernon, NY, Aug 26, 42; m 65; c 2. ENVIRONMENTAL SCIENCE, SOFTWARE SYSTEMS. *Educ:* Wittenberg Univ, BS, 64; Univ Ill, Urbana-Champaign, MS, 66, PhD(biophys), 69. *Prof Exp:* Res assoc radiation sensitivity environ & monitoring, Ctr Biol Natural Systs, Wash Univ, St Louis, 69-71, coordr nitrogen proj, fertilizers-environ impact, 71-74; VPRES SERV, AIR QUAL MEASUREMENTS, ENVIRON MEASUREMENTS INC, 74-; PRES SOFTWARE SERV, ENG MGT INFO CORP, 81- *Concurrent Pos:* Lectr dept technol & human affairs, Wash Univ, 73-77. *Mem:* Air Pollution Control Asn; AAAS. *Res:* Development of field determination of important processes in the transformation of sulfur dioxide to sulfate through ambient measurements; document progress in environment cleanup; development of user friendly computer software for the general aviation, business and technical markets. *Mailing Add:* Environ Measurements Inc 8505 Delmar Blvd University City MO 63124

VAUGHAN, WILLIAM WALTON, b Clearwater, Fla, Sept 7, 30; m 51; c 4. METEOROLOGY, AEROSPACE SCIENCES. *Educ:* Univ Fla, BS, 51; Fla State Univ, cert meteorol, 52; Univ Tenn, PhD, 76. *Prof Exp:* Meteorologist, US Air Force, 52-55, res & develop meteorologist, Air Force Armament Ctr, 55-57, tech asst meteorol, Army Ballistic Missile Agency, 58-60; chief, Aerospace Environ Off, 60-65, chief, Aerospace Environ Div, 65-76, CHIEF, ATMOSPHERIC SCI DIV, MARSHALL SPACE FLIGHT CTR, NASA, 76- *Honors & Awards:* Exceptional Serv Medal, NASA, 69; Losey Atmospheric Sci Medal, Am Inst Aeronaut & Astronaut, 80. *Mem:* Am Meteorol Soc; Am Inst Aeronaut & Astronaut; Am Geophys Soc; AAAS; Sigma Xi. *Res:* Applied research in aerospace sciences and especially meteorology relative to space system and spacecraft experiment development. *Mailing Add:* 5606 Alta Dena Dr Huntsville AL 35802

VAUGHAN, WORTH E, b New York, NY, Feb 1, 36; m 69; c 4. PHYSICAL CHEMISTRY. *Educ:* Oberlin Col, AB, 57; Princeton Univ, AM, 59, PhD(phys chem), 60. *Prof Exp:* Res assoc phys chem, Princeton Univ, 60-61; from asst prof to assoc prof, 61-78, PROF CHEM, UNIV WIS, MADISON, 78- *Mem:* AAAS; Am Phys Soc; Am Chem Soc. *Res:* Dielectric and nuclear magnetic relaxation in liquids; irreversible statistical mechanics. *Mailing Add:* Dept Chem Univ Wis Madison WI 53706

VAUGHAN, WYMAN RISTINE, b Minneapolis, Minn, Oct 28, 16; m 43; c 2. CHEMISTRY. *Educ:* Dartmouth Col, AB, 39, AM, 41; Harvard Univ, AM, 42, PhD(org chem), 44. *Prof Exp:* Instr chem, Dartmouth Col, 39-41; res assoc, Harvard Univ, 42-44; res assoc, Dartmouth Col, 44-46; res assoc, Univ Mich, 46-47, from instr to prof, 47-66; prof chem & head dept, 66-76, EMER PROF, UNIV CONN, 81- *Mem:* Am Chem Soc; NY Acad Sci. *Res:* Synthetic organic chemistry; Diels-Alder reaction; sterochemistry; reaction mechanisms; potential anticancer agents; molecular rearrangements. *Mailing Add:* Dept Chem Univ Conn Storrs CT 06268

VAUGHEN, VICTOR C(ORNELIUS) A(DOLPH), b Wilmington, Del, Oct 8, 33; m 59; c 3. CHEMICAL ENGINEERING, CHEMISTRY. *Educ:* Stetson Univ, BS, 57; Mass Inst Technol, SB, 56, SM, 57, PhD(chem eng), 60. *Prof Exp:* Group leader, 63-76, mgr hot cell opers, 76-80, mgr fossil energy assessments, 80-81, prog mgr fossil energy eval, 81, SECT HEAD, ENG COORD & ANAL SECT, CHEM TECHNOL DIV, OAK RIDGE NAT LAB, NUCLEAR DIV, UNION CARBIDE CORP, 81- *Mem:* Am Nuclear Soc; Am Inst Chem Engrs; Nat Soc Prof Engrs; AAAS. *Res:* Nuclear fuel reprocessing; high radioactivity level chemical development; special isotope purification and production by solvent extraction and ion exchange; safety and radiation control and operation and maintenance of hot cells; coal liquefaction technology assessements. *Mailing Add:* Oak Ridge Nat Lab PO Box X Oak Ridge TN 37830

VAUGHN, CHARLES MELVIN, b Deadwood, SDak, Nov 23, 15; m 41; c 2. PARASITOLOGY, PROTOZOOLOGY. *Educ:* Univ Ill, BA, 39, MA, 40; Univ Wis, PhD(invert zool), 43. *Prof Exp:* Asst zool, Univ Ill, 39-40 & Univ Wis, 40-43; from asst prof to assoc prof, Miami Univ, 46-51; assoc dir, Field Serv Unit, Am Found Trop Med, 52-53; prof zool & chmn dept, Univ SDak, 53-65; prof zool & physiol & chmn dept, 65-71, actg dean res, 69-71, chmn dept, 71-78, PROF ZOOL, MIAMI UNIV, 71- *Concurrent Pos:* Asst prof parasitol & sr parasitologist, Inst Trop Med, Bowman Gray Sch Med, Wake Forest Col, 50-52, assoc dir, 51-52; dir, NSF Acad Year Inst, Univ SDak, 58-64, prog dir, NSF Col & Elem Prog, Res Training & Acad Year Study Prog, 64-65; consult, NSF, 65-69; biologist, Ohio State Univ-US AID Indian Educ Proj, 66 & NSF-US AID India Educ Proj, 67. *Honors & Awards:* Benjamin Harrison Medal, Miami Univ, 79. *Mem:* AAAS; Am Soc Parasitol; Am Micros Soc (pres, 73); Soc Protozool; Am Soc Trop Med & Hyg. *Res:* Human and animal parasitology; malaria parasite and vector surveys; intestinal parasite surveys; schistosomiasis survey and control; physiology and ecology of gastropoda; life history and culture methods in protozoa, other invertebrates. *Mailing Add:* Dept of Zool 282 Upham Hall Miami Univ Oxford OH 45056

VAUGHN, CLARENCE BENJAMIN, b Philadelphia, Pa, Dec 14, 28; m 53; c 4. ONCOLOGY, PHYSIOLOGICAL CHEMISTRY. *Educ:* Benedict Col, BS, 51; Howard Univ, MS, 55, MD, 57; Wayne State Univ, PhD(physiol chem), 65. *Prof Exp:* Res fel oncol, Detroit Inst Cancer Res, 65-67; ASSOC BIOCHEM & ASST PROF ONCOL, WAYNE STATE UNIV, 67-; DIR ONCOL, PROVIDENCE HOSP, 73- *Concurrent Pos:* Mem consult staff, Depts Med, Blvd Gen Hosp & Kirwood Gen Hosp, 67-, Oakwood Hosp, 68-, Detroit Mem Hosp, 70- & Crittenton Hosp, Rochester, Mich, 72-; clin dir, Milton A Darling Mem Ctr, Mich Cancer Found, 70-72; mem, Coop Breast Cancer Study Group. *Mem:* AMA; Am Col Physicians; NY Acad Sci. *Res:* Organic acid metabolism; prophyria metabolism; estrogen metabolism. *Mailing Add:* Wayne State Univ Detroit MI 48202

VAUGHN, GWENYTH RUTH, b Lander, Wyo, June 8, 17; c 1. SPEECH PATHOLOGY, AUDIOLOGY. *Educ:* Univ Denver, BA, 39, MA, 42, PhD(speech path, audiol), 59. *Prof Exp:* Dean of personnel & head dept speech, Colo Womens Col, 41-44; dean of women & head dept speech, Univ of the Americas, 46-49; dir & founder, Johnson Sch Handicapped Children & Sch Spec Educ, Mexico City, 44-57; assoc prof speech path & audiol, head dept & dir speech & hearing clin, Idaho State Univ, 60-65; dir med ctr speech lang clin, head sect speech pathophysiol & dir clin communicology & asst dir training, Res & Training Ctr, 66, PROF SPEECH PATH & AUDIOL & DIR VET ADMIN DIV, DEPT BIOCOMMUN, SCHS MED & DENT, UNIV ALA, BIRMINGHAM, 66-, ASST PROF PHYSIOL & BIOPHYS, 76-; VET ADMIN MED DIST COORDR AUDIOL & SPEECH PATH, BIRMINGHAM VET ADMIN HOSP, 67- *Concurrent Pos:* Dir, Voc Rehab Admin Proj, Idaho, 62-65, Title III Proj, Birmingham Pub Schs, 69-72, Univ Ala Sch Med & Vet Admin Proj, Birmingham, 72-73 & Vet Admin Exchange Med Info Proj, Birmingham, 73-76. *Honors & Awards:* Adminr Commendation, Vet Admin, 73, Outstanding Hamdicapped Fed Employee of the Yr, Vet Admin, President of US, 73. *Mem:* Fel Am Speech & Hearing Asn; Acad Rehab Audiol; fel Am Asn Ment Deficiency. *Res:* Health care delivery systems to persons with communicative disorders; programs for the hearing impaired. *Mailing Add:* Dept of Biocommun Univ Ala Sch Med Birmingham AL 35294

VAUGHN, JACK C, b Burbank, Calif, July 4, 37; m 63; c 3. CELL BIOLOGY. *Educ:* Univ Calif, Los Angeles, BA, 60; Univ Tex, PhD(bot), 64. *Prof Exp:* Asst zool, Univ Calif, Los Angeles, 60-61; USPHS fel, Univ Wis, 64-66; from asst prof to assoc prof, 66-75, PROF ZOOL, MIAMI UNIV, 75- *Concurrent Pos:* NSF res grant, 67-69 & 70-71; investr, Marine Biol Lab, Woods Hole, 70 & 71. *Mem:* AAAS; Am Inst Biol Scientists; Am Soc Cell Biol; Int Fedn Cell Biol; Am Soc Zoologists. *Res:* Cell biology; chromosome structure and function. *Mailing Add:* Dept of Zool Miami Univ Oxford OH 45056

VAUGHN, JAMES E, JR, b Kansas City, Mo, Sept 17, 39; m 61; c 2. NEUROSCIENCE. *Educ:* Westminster Col, BA, 61; Univ Calif, Los Angeles, PhD(anat), 65. *Prof Exp:* Fel brain res, Univ Edinburgh, 65-66; asst prof anat, Boston Univ, 66-70; HEAD SECT NEUROANAT & ULTRASTRUCT, DIV NEUROSCI, CITY OF HOPE RES INST, 70- *Mem:* Am Asn Anat; Am Soc Cell Biol; Soc Neurosci. *Res:* Fine structure of central nervous tissue. *Mailing Add:* City of Hope Res Inst 1500 E Duarte Rd Duarte CA 91010

VAUGHN, JAMES L, b Marshfield, Wis, Mar 2, 34; m 55; c 4. INSECT PATHOLOGY. *Educ:* Univ Wis, BS, 57, MS, 59, PhD(bact), 62. *Prof Exp:* Res officer tissue cult virol, Insect Path Res Inst, Can Dept Forestry, 61-65; SUPVRY MICROBIOLOGIST, INSECT PATH LAB, USDA, 65-, CHIEF, INSECT PATH LAB, 79- *Mem:* Am Soc Microbiol; Soc Invert Path; Tissue Cult Asn. *Res:* Methods for growth of insect tissue in vitro; study of processes of virial infection and development in in vitro insect systems. *Mailing Add:* Insect Path Lab Rm 214 Bldg 011A Agr Res Ctr-W USDA Beltsville MD 20705

VAUGHN, JOE WARREN, b Otterbein, Ind, Oct 8, 33; m 55; c 4. INORGANIC CHEMISTRY, PHYSICAL CHEMISTRY. *Educ:* DePauw Univ, BA, 55; Univ Ky, MS, 57, PhD(phys chem), 59. *Prof Exp:* Welch Found fel, Univ Tex, 59-61; from asst prof to assoc prof chem, 61-70, PROF CHEM, NORTHERN ILL UNIV, 70- *Mem:* Am Chem Soc. *Res:* Nonaqueous solvent; fluoro complexes of trivalent chromium; stereochemistry of coordination compounds; synthesis of cis-trans isomers. *Mailing Add:* Dept of Chem Northern Ill Univ De Kalb IL 60115

VAUGHN, JOHN B, b Birmingham, Ala, Mar 3, 24; m 45; c 6. EPIDEMIOLOGY. *Educ:* Auburn Univ, DVM, 49; Tulane Univ, MPH, 56. *Prof Exp:* From instr to asst prof, 57-60, assoc prof, 70-79, assoc dean, 77-79, PROF EPIDEMIOL & ACTG CHMN, DEPT APPL HEALTH SCI, SCH PUB HEALTH & TROP MED, TULANE UNIV, 79- *Concurrent Pos:* Consult, Epidemiol Sect, La State Dept Health, New Orleans, 57-; epidemic aid coordr, Sch Pub Health & Trop Med with Asn Schs Pub Health & Ctr Dis Control, 80-; liaison person, Sch Pub Health & Trop Med with Asn Schs Pub Health & Ctr Dis Control, 80-; mem contrib fac, Prev Med Residency Training Prog, Sch Pub Health & Trop Med, 80- *Mem:* Am Pub Health Asn; Soc Epidemiol Res. *Res:* Zoonotic epidemiology; author of numerous publications. *Mailing Add:* 1430 Tulane Ave New Orleans LA 70112

VAUGHN, MICHAEL THAYER, b Chicago, Ill, Aug 6, 36. PHYSICS. *Educ:* Columbia Univ, AB, 55; Purdue Univ, PhD(physics), 60. *Prof Exp:* Res assoc physics, Univ Pa, 59-62; asst prof, Ind Univ, 62-64; assoc prof, 64-73, PROF PHYSICS, NORTHEASTERN UNIV, 73- *Concurrent Pos:* Vis scientist, Argonne Nat Lab, 67, Deutsches Elektronen Synchrotron, Hamburg, 70, Univ Vienna, 70 & Int Ctr Theoret Physics, Trieste, 71; vis prof, Tex A&M Univ, 75 & Southampton Univ, 79; Sci Res Coun, sr vis fel. *Mem:* Am Phys Soc. *Res:* Elementary particle physics; theoretical physics. *Mailing Add:* Dept of Physics Northeastern Univ Boston MA 02115

VAUGHN, MOSES WILLIAM, b Rock Hill, SC, Nov 2, 13; m 42; c 3. FOOD TECHNOLOGY. *Educ:* WVa State Col, BS, 38; Mich State Univ, MS, 42 & 49; Univ Mass, PhD(food technol), 51. *Prof Exp:* Prof food technol, 46-69, prof agr, 69-76, PROF ANIMAL NUTRIT & FOOD TECHNOL, UNIV MD, EASTERN SHORE, 76- *Mem:* AAAS; Inst Food Technologists. *Res:* Combination jellies and jams; chemical methods for detecting meat spoilage; nitrogen partitions in fish meal; bacteriological effects of ionizing radiations in fishery products; bacterial flora of bottom muds; effects of washing shellstock and shucked oysters to bacterial quality, microwave opening of oysters; nutritive value of selected pork products. *Mailing Add:* Dept of Agr Univ of Md Eastern Shore Princess Anne MD 21853

VAUGHN, PETER PAUL, b Altoona, Pa, Aug 22, 28; m 48; c 3. VERTEBRATE PALEONTOLOGY. *Educ:* Brooklyn Col, BA, 50; Harvard Univ, MA, 52, PhD(biol), 54. *Prof Exp:* Instr anat, Univ NC, 54-56; asst prof zool & asst cur fossil vert, Univ Kans, 56-57; assoc cur vert paleont, US Nat Mus, 57-58; from asst prof to assoc prof, 59-67, PROF ZOOL, UNIV CALIF, LOS ANGELES, 67- *Concurrent Pos:* Res assoc, Los Angeles County Mus, 61- *Mem:* Soc Vert Paleont; Paleont Soc. *Res:* Comparative vertebrate anatomy and paleontology; Paleozoic tetrapods; late Paleozoic vertebrate faunas and paleobiogeography. *Mailing Add:* Dept of Biol Univ of Calif Los Angeles CA 90024

VAUGHN, REESE HASKELL, b Farragut, Iowa, Oct 1, 08; m 35; c 5. FOOD MICROBIOLOGY. *Educ:* Simpson Col, AB, 30; Iowa State Col, MS, 32, PhD(bact), 35. *Prof Exp:* Lab asst biol, Simpson Col, 28-30; asst bact, Iowa State Col, 35-36; from instr to assoc prof food technol, Univ Calif, Berkeley, 36-52; from jr bacteriologist to assoc bacteriologist, 36-52, prof, 52-76, food technologist, 56-76, EMER PROF FOOD TECHNOL, UNIV CALIF, DAVIS, 76-, EMER FOOD TECHNOLOGIST, 76- *Concurrent Pos:* Rockefeller Found fel, 57; Fulbright lectr, 67; consult, 76- *Mem:* Am Soc Microbiol; Am Soc Enol; Am Pub Health Asn; Inst Food Technol; Royal Soc Health. *Res:* Food fermentations and bacteria causing them; spoilage of foods; bacterial indices of sanitation; food plant waste disposal; pectolytic activity of microbes. *Mailing Add:* Dept of Food Sci & Technol Univ of Calif Davis CA 95616

VAUGHN, RICHARD CLEMENTS, b Ionia, Mich, Jan 17, 25; m 47; c 5. INDUSTRIAL ENGINEERING. *Educ:* Mich State Univ, BA, 48; Toledo Univ, MIE, 55. *Prof Exp:* Res & indust engr, various Ohio Co, 51-57; asst prof indust eng, Univ Fla, 57-62; assoc prof, 62-68, PROF INDUST ENG, IOWA STATE UNIV, 68- *Concurrent Pos:* Consult, Liberty Bell Mfg Co, 59-61; instr math, Univ Toledo, 51-57; sabbatical. *Res:* Quality control, product liability, operations research. *Mailing Add:* 212 Marston Hall Iowa State Univ Ames IA 50011

VAUGHN, ROBERT DONALD, b Cincinnati, Ohio, Mar 3, 30. CHEMICAL ENGINEERING. *Educ:* Purdue Univ, BSChE, 51; Univ Del, MChE, 53, PhD(chem eng), 56. *Prof Exp:* Engr, Shell Develop Co, 55-60; from asst prof to assoc prof chem eng, Purdue Univ, 60-64; supvr process develop, Res Div, W R Grace & Co, MD, 64-65, mgr, 65-67; dir process develop & inorg res, Wyandotte Chem Corp, 67-71, mgr eng qual & pollution control, Mich, 71-73, dir planning, 73-77, dir technol, BASF Wyandotte Corp, 77-79; MGR DEVELOP, EXXON CHEM CO, 79- *Honors & Awards:* Alan P Colburn Award, Am Inst Chem Engrs, 58. *Mem:* Am Inst Chem Engrs; Am Chem Soc; Com Develop Asn. *Res:* Non-Newtonian fluid behavior; chemical and engineering systems analysis and synthesis; development of chemical and polymer processes; commercial and business development. *Mailing Add:* Exxon Chem Co PO Box 271 Florham Park NJ 07932

VAUGHN, THOMAS HUNT, b Clay, Ky, Nov 11, 09; m 30; c 3. ORGANIC CHEMISTRY. *Educ:* Univ Notre Dame, BS, 31, MS, 32, PhD(org chem), 34. *Prof Exp:* Vpres, Vitox Labs, Ind, 33-34; head dept org res, Union Carbide & Carbon Res Labs, Inc, NY, 34-39; dir org res, Mich Alkali Co, 39-41, asst dir res, 41-43; asst dir, Wyandotte Chem Corp, 43-45, dir, 45-48, vpres, 48-53; vpres res & develop, Colgate-Palmolive Co, 53-57; exec vpres, Pabst Brewing Co, 57-60; PRES, THOMAS H VAUGHN & CO, WARETOWN, 60- *Concurrent Pos:* Consult to Secy Navy & Qm Gen, US Army, 43-53; mem Scand Res & Indust Tour, 46; lectr, Prog Bus Admin for Top Level Ger Indust Leaders, Mutual Security Agency Sem, 52; pres, Tech Sect, World Conf Surface Active Agents, Paris, 54; dir, Indust Res Inst, 54-58, from vpres to pres, 57-58; chmn, Conf Admin Res, 55; mem adv bd, Off Critical Tables, Nat Acad Sci, 56; mem adv bd, Col Sci, Univ Notre Dame, 56-; ed, Res Mgt, 58-69; pres, Myzon Labs, Chicago, Ill, 60-62; tech consult, UN, 70- *Mem:* AAAS; fel Am Inst Chem; Am Inst Chem Eng; Am Chem Soc; Soc Indust Chem. *Res:* Unsaturated compounds and their derivatives; polyols; detergents; polymers; research and business administration. *Mailing Add:* Box 577 Waretown NJ 08758

VAUGHN, WILLIAM ALBERT, b Joplin, Mo, July 15, 26; m 51; c 3. CHEMICAL ENGINEERING. *Educ:* Univ Cincinnati, BSChE, 52. *Prof Exp:* Res engr, 52-64, res group leader, 64-70, RES SECT MGR, MONSANTO CO, 70- *Mem:* Am Inst Chem Engrs. *Res:* Process development; pilot planting. *Mailing Add:* 2513 St Francis St Akron OH 44313

VAUGHN, WILLIAM KING, b Denison, Tex, July 28, 38; m 60; c 2. BIOSTATISTICS. *Educ:* Tex Wesleyan Col, BS, 60; Southern Methodist Univ, MS, 65; Tex A&M Univ, PhD(statist), 70. *Prof Exp:* Med technologist, St Joseph Hosp, Ft Worth, Tex, 61-63; res analyst biostatist, Univ Tex MD Anderson Hosp & Tumor Inst, 65-67; asst prof, 70-77, ASSOC PROF BIOSTATIST, SCH MED, VANDERBILT UNIV, 77- *Mem:* Am Statist Asn; Sigma Xi. *Res:* Clinical trials; simulation and Monte Carlo studies; design of experiments; statistical methodology in toxicology; biometrics. *Mailing Add:* Dept of Prev Med Sch of Med Vanderbilt Univ Nashville TN 37232

VAUGHT, ROBERT L, b Alhambra, Calif, Apr 4, 26; m 55; c 2. MATHEMATICS. *Educ:* Univ Calif, AB, 45, PhD(math), 54. *Prof Exp:* From instr to asst prof math, Univ Wash, 54-58; from asst prof to assoc prof, 58-63, PROF MATH, UNIV CALIF, BERKELEY, 63- *Concurrent Pos:* Fulbright scholar, Univ Amsterdam, 56-57; NSF fel, Univ Calif, Los Angeles, 63-64; Guggenheim fel, 67. *Mem:* Am Math Soc; Asn Symbolic Logic. *Res:* Foundations of mathematics. *Mailing Add:* Dept of Math Univ of Calif Berkeley CA 94720

VAUN, WILLIAM STRATIN, b Hartford, Conn, Oct 10, 29; m 61; c 1. MEDICINE. *Educ:* Trinity Col, Conn, BS, 51; Univ Pa, MD, 55. *Prof Exp:* Resident internal med, Hartford Hosp, Conn, 55-57 & 59-61; asst dir med, St Luke's Hosp, Cleveland, Ohio, 62-65; assoc prof med, 69-72, actg dean, Sch Continuing Educ, 72-73, PROF MED, HAHNEMANN MED COL, 72-; DIR MED EDUC, MONMOUTH MED CTR, 65- *Concurrent Pos:* Consult, Am Bd Internal Med, 73-77 & Nat Acad Sci, 75-76; chmn adv coun, Off Consumer Health Educ, Rutgers Med Sch, 73-75; trustee, Monmouth Col, West Long Branch, NJ, 79-, Hosp Res & Educ Trust NJ, 80- *Mem:* Asn Hosp Med Educ (vpres, 72-73). *Mailing Add:* Monmouth Med Ctr Long Branch NJ 07740

VAUPEL, DONALD BRUCE, b Hackensack, NJ, Aug 30, 42; m 67; c 2. PHARMACOLOGY. *Educ:* Wittenberg Univ, BA, 64; Univ Ky, MS, 70, PhD(pharmacol), 74. *Prof Exp:* Chemist qual control, Lederle Labs, Am Cyanamid Co, 64-66; PHARMACOLOGIST, ADDICTION RES CTR, NAT INST DRUG ABUSE, 72- *Concurrent Pos:* Asst adj prof pharmacol, Col Med, Univ Ky, 78- *Mem:* Sigma Xi; Am Soc Pharmacol & Exp Therapeut. *Res:* Various classes of hallucinogens; determining the degree of pharmacologic equivalence between test drugs and selected prototypes in the dog using pharmacodynamic, behavioral, tolerance and appetite suppressant measures. *Mailing Add:* Pharmacol Dept Addiction Res Ctr PO Box 12390 Lexington KY 40583

VAUPEL, MARTIN ROBERT, b Evansville, Ind, July 24, 28. ANATOMY, EMBRYOLOGY. *Educ:* Ind Univ, AB, 49; Tulane Univ, PhD(anat), 54. *Prof Exp:* Res asst, 49-50, grad asst, 50-54, from instr to asst prof, 54-71, ASSOC PROF ANAT, TULANE UNIV, 71- *Mem:* Teratology Soc. *Res:* Congenital anomalies of nervous system; teratology. *Mailing Add:* Dept of Anat Tulane Univ Sch of Med New Orleans LA 70112

VAURIO, JUSSI KALERVO, b Finland, Mar 4, 40; m 63; c 3. NUCLEAR ENGINEERING. *Educ:* Helsinki Univ Technol, dipl, 67, Lic Technol, 70, Dr Sci, 72. *Prof Exp:* Operating Engr reactor operations, Helsinki Univ Technol, 66-67; researcher reactor kinetics, Tech Res Ctr, Finland, 68-71; nuclear engr reactor safety, Imatra Power Co, 72-75; nuclear engr probalistic risk, 75-80, RES PROG MGR, RELIABILITY & RISK ASSESSMENT, ARGONNE NAT LAB, ILL, 80- *Concurrent Pos:* Lectr & prof, Helsinki Univ Technol, 65-71; alternate mem, Finnish Radiation Protection Comn, 67-69. *Mem:* Am Nuclear Soc; Soc Risk Analysis; Soc Reliability Engrs; Finnish Nuclear Soc. *Res:* Nuclear reactor kinetics; noise analysis; stochastic processes; information and estimation theory; reliability analysis of systems and structures; probabilistic risk assesment of complex systems relevant to nuclear power plants. *Mailing Add:* Bldg 107 Argonne Nat Lab 9700 S Cass Ave Argonne IL 60439

VAUSE, EDWIN H(AMILTON), b Chicago, Ill, Mar 30, 23; m 51; c 5. CHEMICAL ENGINEERING, CHEMISTRY. *Educ:* Univ Ill, BS, 47, MS, 48; Univ Chicago, MBA, 52. *Hon Degrees:* DSc, Univ Evansville, 77. *Prof Exp:* Chem engr, Standard Oil Co, 48-49, sr chem engr, 49-50, res projs engr, 50-51, asst gen foreman, Mfg Projs Div, 51-52, Light Oils Div, 52-53 & Hwy Oils Div, 53-57; dir lab admin, Mead Johnson & Co, 57-60; VPRES, CHARLES F KETTERING FOUND, 60- *Mem:* Am Inst Chem Engrs; NY Acad Sci; Agr Res Inst. *Res:* Management of chemical and biological sciences and engineering; chemical engineering research on nitrogen fixation and fertilizer production. *Mailing Add:* Charles F Kettering Found 5335 Far Hills Ave Dayton OH 45429

VAUX, HENRY JAMES, b Bryn Mawr, Pa, Nov 6, 12; m 37; c 2. FORESTRY. *Educ:* Haverford Col, BS, 33; Univ Calif, MS, 35, PhD(agr econ), 48. *Prof Exp:* Instr forestry, Ore State Col, 37-42; asst economist, La Agr Exp Sta, 42-43; assoc economist, US Army, 43; assoc economist, US Forest Serv, 46-48; from lectr to assoc prof forestry, Sch Forestry, 48-53, dean, Sch Forestry & assoc dir, Agr Exp Sta, 55-65, prof, 53-78, EMER PROF FORESTRY, SCH FORESTRY, UNIV CALIF, BERKELEY, 78- *Concurrent Pos:* Consult ed, McGraw-Hill Bk Co, 74-76; chmn, Calif Bd Forestry, 76- *Mem:* AAAS; fel Soc Am Foresters; Forest Hist Soc; hon mem Soc Foresters Finland. *Res:* Long term timber supply; price behavior and market structures for forest products. *Mailing Add:* 622 San Luis Rd Berkeley CA 94707

VAUX, JAMES EDWARD, JR, b Pittsburgh, Pa, June 13, 32; m 54; c 3. CHEMISTRY, STATISTICS. *Educ:* Carnegie Inst, BS, 52, MS, 64, PhD(chem), 67. *Prof Exp:* Chemist, E I du Pont de Nemours & Co, Inc, 53-57; teacher, Shady Side Acad, 57-64; asst dir, 64-67, EXEC DIR, FOUND STUDY CYCLES, 67-; LECTR CHEM, UNIV PITTSBURGH, 65- *Mem:* Am Chem Soc; Am Statist Asn. *Res:* Organic and analytical chemistry; statistics. *Mailing Add:* Dept of Chem Univ of Pittsburgh Pittsburgh PA 15260

VAVICH, MITCHELL GEORGE, b Miami, Ariz, Aug 24, 16; m 37; c 1. NUTRITION. *Educ:* Univ Ariz, BS, 38, MS, 40; Pa State Univ, PhD(biochem), 43. *Prof Exp:* Asst physiol chem, Pa State Univ, 40-42, instr biochem, 43-46; from assoc prof to prof agr biochem, 46-75, head dept, 69-75, prof food sci, 75-81, EMER PROF, UNIV ARIZ, 81- *Concurrent Pos:* Spec field staff mem, Rockefeller Found, 65-67; chmn, Comt Agr Biochem & Nutrit, 69- *Mem:* AAAS; Am Chem Soc; Am Inst Nutrit. *Res:* Fluorides, ascorbic acid; vitamins in canned foods; interrelationships of vitamins and other food components; carotenes and vitamin A; nutritional status; biochemistry of cyclopropenoid fatty acids; nutrient value of dietary proteins. *Mailing Add:* 25 Calle de Amistad Tucson AZ 85716

VAVRA, JAMES JOSEPH, b Boulder, Colo, Aug 30, 29; m 51; c 5. INFECTIOUS DISEASES. *Educ:* Univ Colo, BA, 51; Univ Wis, MS, 53, PhD, 55. *Prof Exp:* Res assoc, Dept Biochem, 55-57, res assoc & proj leader, Dept Microbiol, 57-62, sr res scientist, Dept Clin Res, 62-64 & Dept Microbiol, 64-68, HEAD DEPT INFECTIOUS DIS RES, UPJOHN CO, 68- *Mem:* AAAS; Am Soc Microbiol; NY Acad Sci. *Res:* Fermentation biochemistry, especially metabolism; antibiotic-pathogen relationships, especially resistance development. *Mailing Add:* Dept of Infectious Dis Upjohn Co Kalamazoo MI 49001

VAVRA, JOSEPH PETER, soil fertility, agronomy, see previous edition

VAWTER, ALFRED THOMAS, b Los Angeles, Calif, Mar 30, 43; m 66; c 2. ECOLOGY, EVOLUTIONARY BIOLOGY. *Educ:* Univ Calif, Irvine, BS, 70; Cornell Univ, PhD(biol), 77. *Prof Exp:* Lectr ecol, Cornell Univ, 76-77; scholar evolution, Univ Calif, Los Angeles, 77-78; ASST PROF BIOL, WELLS COL, 78- *Concurrent Pos:* Consult, Resource Planning Assocs, 78-80. *Mem:* Am Soc Naturalists; Soc Study Evolution; Cooper Ornith Soc; Lepidop Soc; AAAS. *Res:* Population biology, especially ecological genetics of Lepidoptera; molecular evolution. *Mailing Add:* Dept of Biol Wells Col Aurora NY 13026

VAWTER, SPENCER MAX, b Morgan Co, Ind, Feb 18, 37; m 72; c 3. PHYSICS. *Educ:* Franklin Col, BA, 59; DePaul Univ, MS, 67; Univ Mich, Ann Arbor, cert physiol, 68; Univ Southern Calif, cert comput systs, 70. *Prof Exp:* Student, Defense Projs Div, Western Elec Co at Lincoln Lab, Mass Inst Technol, 59-60; systs planning & develop engr, Western Elec Co, 60-63; dir ionizing radiation sect, AMA, Chicago, 63-66 & med physics sect, 66-70, assoc dir dept med instrumentation, 70-73; asst to pres, 73-74, VPRES, BIO-DYNAMICS, INC, 74- *Mem:* Am Phys Soc; Instrument Soc Am; Asn Advan Med Instrumentation. *Res:* Interaction of electromagnetic energy with human tissue, especially the effect of laser energy on the human eye; application of physical principles to medical practice; application of physical sciences to health care. *Mailing Add:* 8021 Knue Rd Boehringer Mannheim Corp Indianapolis IN 46250

VAYO, HARRIS WESTCOTT, b Chicago, Ill, Nov 15, 35; m 62; c 3. APPLIED MATHEMATICS. *Educ:* Culver-Stockton Col, BA, 57; Univ Ill, MS, 59, PhD(math), 63. *Prof Exp:* Asst math, Univ Ill, 57-62; res fel biomath, Harvard Univ, 63-65; from asst prof to assoc prof, 65-74, PROF MATH, UNIV TOLEDO, 74- *Concurrent Pos:* Mem coun basic sci, Am Heart Asn, 67-; vis prof, McGill Univ, 76. *Mem:* Math Asn Am; Am Math Soc; Am Acad Mech. *Res:* Applications of mathematics to biological and medical problems, particularly cardiovascular work and muscular electrical conduction theory. *Mailing Add:* Dept of Math Univ of Toledo Toledo OH 43606

VAZAKAS, ARISTOTLE JOHN, b Haverhill, Mass, July 9, 22; m 56; c 2. MEDICINAL CHEMISTRY. *Educ:* Mass Col Pharm, BS, 43, MS, 49; Purdue Univ, PhD(pharmaceut chem), 52. *Prof Exp:* From asst prof to assoc prof chem, Sch Pharm, Temple Univ, 52-58; sr res chemist, Nat Drug Co, 58-64; chemist, Div New Drugs, Bur Med, US Food & Drug Admin, 64-66; asst mgr regulatory affairs, 66-69, MGR REGULATORY COMPLIANCE, JOHNSON & JOHNSON, 69- *Mem:* Am Chem Soc; Am Pharmaceut Asn. *Res:* Synthetic organic medicinal chemistry. *Mailing Add:* Cairns Pl & Marian Dr RD 2 Belle Mead NJ 08502

VAZQUEZ, ALFREDO JORGE, b Buenos Aires, Arg, Jan 21, 37; m 62; c 1. NEUROPHARMACOLOGY, ELECTROPHYSIOLOGY. *Educ:* Bernadino Rivadavia Col, Arg, BS, 54; Univ Buenos Aires, MD, 62. *Prof Exp:* From intern to resident med, Tigre Hosp, Arg, 59-61; instr pharmacol, Chicago Med Sch, 62-65, assoc, 65-67; asst prof, Fac Med, Univ Man, 67-71; ASSOC PROF PHARMACOL, CHICAGO MED SCH, 71-, V PRES DEPT, 77- *Concurrent Pos:* Res assoc, Lab Psychopharmacol, Nat Neuropsychiat Inst, Buenos Aires, 60-62. *Mem:* Pharmacol Soc Can; Soc Biol Psychiat; Soc Neurosci; Am Soc Pharmacol & Exp Therapeut. *Res:* Physiology and pharmacology of the cerebral cortex; epilepsy; drug abuse and hallucinogenic drugs. *Mailing Add:* Dept of Pharmacol 3333 N Greenbay Rd North Chicago IL 60064

VAZQUEZ, JACINTO JOSEPH, b Havana, Cuba, Aug 17, 23; nat US; m 48; c 2. PATHOLOGY. *Educ:* Inst Havana, BAS, 40; Univ Havana, MD, 48; Ohio State Univ, MS, 54. *Prof Exp:* Instr & chief resident path, Ohio State Univ, 52-55; from instr to assoc prof, Sch Med, Univ Pittsburgh, 55-61; assoc mem, Scripps Clin & Res Found, 61-63; from assoc prof to prof path, Med Ctr, Duke Univ, 63-70; prof path & chmn dept, Med Ctr, Univ Ky, 70-74; mem & asst dir, 74-77, MEM & ASSOC DIR, SCRIPPS CLIN & RES FOUND, 77- *Mem:* Am Soc Exp Path; Am Asn Path & Bact; Am Asn Immunologists; NY Acad Sci; Int Acad Path. *Res:* Experimental pathology; immunology; immunopathology; antibody formation; immunopathology antigen-antibody reactions; immunohematology. *Mailing Add:* Scripps Clin & Res Found 10666 N Torrey Pines Rd La Jolla CA 92037

VEACH, ALLEN MARSHALL, b Lancaster, SC, Sept 21, 33. ACCELERATOR PHYSICS. *Educ:* Univ Ala, BS, 56; Univ Akron, MS, 59. *Prof Exp:* Physicist phys testing, B F Goodrich Co, 56-57, microscopist chem micros, 57-59; develop specialist isotope separation, 59-60, physicist plasma physics, 60-70, RES PHYSICIST ION SOURCES & ACCELERATORS, OAK RIDGE NAT LAB, 70- *Mem:* Am Phys Soc. *Res:* Plasma physics; accelerators; ion sources; high vacuum; isotope separation; electron and ion emission; electrical and gas discharges; ion and electron optics; ionization phenomena; mass spectroscopy. *Mailing Add:* PO Box 323 Oak Ridge TN 37830

VEAL, BOYD WILLIAM, JR, b Chance, SDak, May 21, 37; m 62; c 2. SOLID STATE PHYSICS. *Educ:* SDak State Univ, BS, 59; Univ Pittsburgh, MS, 62; Univ Wis, PhD(physics), 69. *Prof Exp:* Engr, Westinghouse Res Labs, 59-63; asst physicist, 69-73, PHYSICIST, ARGONNE NAT LAB, 73- *Mem:* Am Phys Soc. *Res:* Electronic properties of solids. *Mailing Add:* Argonne Nat Lab Argonne IL 60439

VEAL, DONALD L, b Chance, SDak, Apr 17, 31; m 53; c 2. METEOROLOGY. *Educ:* SDak State Univ, BS, 53; Univ Wyo, MS, 60, PhD, 64. *Prof Exp:* Instr civil eng, SDak State Univ, 57-58; from instr to assoc prof, 58-67, asst dir natural resources res inst, 67-70, PROF ATMOSPHERIC SCI, UNIV WYO, 67-, HEAD DEPT, 70- *Mem:* Am Meteorol Soc; Royal Meteorol Soc; Sigma Xi; Am Soc Eng Educ; Am Soc Civil Engrs. *Mailing Add:* Univ of Wyo Laramie WY 82071

VEALE, WARREN LORNE, b Antler, Sask, Mar 13, 43; m 66; c 1. PHYSIOLOGY, NEUROPSYCHOLOGY. *Educ:* Univ Man, BSc, 64; Purdue Univ, West Lafayette, MSc, 68, PhD(neuropsychol), 71. *Prof Exp:* Instr psychol, Brandon Univ, 64-66, lectr, 66-67; from asst prof to assoc prof, 70-76, PROF MED PHYSIOL, FAC MED, UNIV CALGARY, 76-, ASSOC DEAN RES & ADMINR GRAD STUDIES PROG, 74- *Concurrent Pos:* Vis scientist, Nat Inst Med Res, London, Eng, 69; mem sci adv comt non-med use of drugs, Nat Health & Welfare-Med Res Coun, 73-74, chmn comt, 74-77; mem, Med Res Coun, 77-, mem, Studentship Comt, 77-, chmn, 78-, mem, Prog Grants Comt, 78-; consult, Health & Welfare, Health Prevention & Promotion Directorate, 78-; mem res comt, Alta Provincial Cancer Hosps Bd, 78-; regional ed, Pharmacol, Biochem & Behav. *Mem:* Can Psychol Soc; Soc Neurosci; Can Biochem Soc; NY Acad Sci; Am Physiol Soc. *Res:* Central nervous systems' involvement in temperature regulation, fever and action of antipyretics; neurohumoral changes in brain related to alcoholism. *Mailing Add:* Div of Med Physiol Univ of Calgary Calgary AB T2N 1N4 Can

VEATCH, RALPH WILSON, b Ringwood, Okla, May 1, 00; m 32; c 2. MATHEMATICS. *Educ:* Univ Tulsa, AB, 25; Northwestern Univ, MA, 27. *Prof Exp:* From instr to asst prof math, Ursinus Col, 27-30; from asst prof to prof, 30-70, head dept, 47-65, EMER PROF MATH, UNIV TULSA, 70- *Mem:* Math Asn Am; Sigma Xi. *Res:* Physics; applied mathematics; tensor analysis; astronomy; rotation of a rigid body passing through a swarm of meteors. *Mailing Add:* 332 NSanta Fe Tulsa OK 74127

VEAZEY, SIDNEY EDWIN, b Wilmington, NC, Sept 18, 37; m 62; c 4. PHYSICS. *Educ:* US Naval Acad, BS, 59; Duke Univ, PhD(physics), 65. *Prof Exp:* US Navy, 55-, electronics mat officer & main propulsion asst, USS Pollack, 66-68, navigator-opers off, USS Ulysses S Grant, 68-71 & USS James Madison, 71-72, dep dir trident submarine design develop proj, Naval Ship Eng Ctr, 72, chief Naval mat, Combat Systs Adv Group, Naval Mat Command, 72-73, exec asst to chief Naval develop, 73-74, design mgr nuclear attack submarines, Naval Ship Eng Ctr, 74-76, dep div head, Combat Systs Dept, Naval Surface Weapons Ctr, 76-77, dep dept head, Strategic Systs Dept, 77-78, dept comndr eval & officer-in-chg, Naval Surface Weapons Ctr, White Oak Lab, Silver Spring, Md, 78-80, MEM FAC, NAVAL SYST ENG DEPT, US NAVAL ACAD, US NAVY, 80- *Mem:* Am Soc Naval Engrs. *Res:* Microwave spectroscopy of the alkali fluorides; application of lasers to communication from ships; SEAMOD weapons systems for advanced platforms; nuclear power; submarines. *Mailing Add:* Naval Syst Eng Dept US Naval Acad Annapolis MD 21402

VEAZEY, THOMAS MABRY, b Paris, Tenn, Jan 13, 20; m 38; c 3. ORGANIC CHEMISTRY. *Educ:* Murray State Univ, BS, 40; Univ Ill, PhD(org chem), 53. *Prof Exp:* Chemist & job instr supvr, E I du Pont de Nemours & Co, Inc, 41-45; res chemist, Devoe & Raynolds Co, 45-50; res chemist, Chemstrand Corp, 53-55, develop group leader synthetic fibers, 55-58, supvr develop, 58-63; mgr patent liaison, Monsanto Textiles Div, 63-70, SR DEVELOP ASSOC, MONSANTO TEXTILES CO, 71- *Mem:* Am Chem Soc. *Res:* Chemical and spinning process development of synthetic textile fibers. *Mailing Add:* 2026 Woodland St SE Decatur AL 35601

VEBER, DANIEL FRANK, b New Brunswick, NJ, Sept 9, 39; m 59; c 2. MEDICINAL CHEMISTRY, PEPTIDE CHEMISTRY. *Educ:* Yale Univ, BA, 61, MS, 62, PhD(org chem), 64. *Prof Exp:* Sr chemist, 64-66, res fel, 66-72, sr res fel, 72-75, assoc dir med chem, 75-79, dir, 79-80, SR DIR MED CHEM, MERCK SHARP & DOHME RES LABS, 80- *Concurrent Pos:* Mem planning comt, Am Peptide Symp, 79- *Mem:* Sigma Xi; NY Acad Sci; AAAS; Am Chem Soc. *Res:* Protein and peptide synthesis; new methods and protecting groups in peptide synthesis; chemical and biological properties of enzymes and peptide hormones; chemistry of heterocyclic compounds; conformational analysis. *Mailing Add:* Merck Sharp & Dohme Res Labs West Point PA 19486

VEBLEN, DAVID RODLI, b Minneapolis, Minn, Apr 27, 47; m 76. MINERALOGY, PETROLOGY. *Educ:* Harvard Univ, BA, 69, MA, 74, PhD(geol), 76. *Prof Exp:* fac res assoc geol, Ariz State Univ, 76-79, asst prof geol, 79-81; ASST PROF GEOL, JOHNS HOPKINS UNIV, 81- *Concurrent Pos:* Fel, Ariz State Univ, 76- *Mem:* Mineral Soc Am; Am Geophys Union; Mineral Asn Can; AAAS. *Res:* Crystal chemistry and defect structures of silicate minerals, especially chain and sheet silicates; asbestos minerals; x-ray diffraction and electron microscopy; applications of mineralogy to igneous and metamorphic petrology. *Mailing Add:* Dept Earth & Planetary Sci Johns Hopkins Univ Baltimore MD 21218

VEDAM, KUPPUSWAMY, b Vedharanyam, India, Jan 15, 26; m 56; c 2. PHYSICS, MATERIALS SCIENCE. *Educ:* Univ Nagpur, BSc, 46, MSc, 47; Univ Saugor, PhD(physics), 51. *Prof Exp:* Lectr physics, Indian Govt Educ Serv, 46-47; lectr, Univ Saugor, 47-48 & 51-53; sr res asst, Indian Inst Sci, 53-56; res assoc, Pa State Univ, 56-57, asst prof, 57-59; sr res officer, Atomic Energy Estab, Bombay, India, 60-62; sr res assoc, 62-64, assoc prof, 63-70, PROF PHYSICS, PA STATE UNIV, 70- *Concurrent Pos:* Mem panel piezoelec transducers, Indian Stand Inst, 61-62. *Mem:* Am Phys Soc; Optical Soc Am; Phys Soc Japan. *Res:* Crystal physics; optics; ferroelectricity; x-ray and neutron diffraction; high pressure physics, physics of surfaces and materials characterization. *Mailing Add:* Dept of Physics Pa State Univ University Park PA 16802

VEDAMUTHU, EBENEZER RAJKUMAR, b Tamilnadu, India, June 23, 32; m 63; c 2. FOOD SCIENCE, FOOD TECHNOLOGY. *Educ:* Univ Madras, BSc, 53; Nat Dairy Res Inst, India, dipl, 56; Univ Ky, MS, 61; Ore State Univ, PhD(microbiol), 65. *Prof Exp:* Dairy asst, Govt Madras, Animal Husb Serv India, 57-59; assoc microbiol, Ore State Univ, 65-66; Dept Health, Educ & Welfare trainee dairy microbiol, Iowa State Univ, 66-67, asst prof food technol, 67-71; asst prof microbiol, Ore State Univ, 71-72; sr microbiologist, 72-75, CHIEF RES MICROBIOLOGIST, MICROLIFE TECHNICS, SARASOTA, 75- *Concurrent Pos:* Cheese technol consult, 67-; mem chapter revision comt stand methods examination dairy prod, Am Pub Health Asn, 75- *Mem:* AAAS; Int Asn Milk, Food & Environ Sanit; Inst Food Technologists; Am Dairy Sci Asn; Am Soc Microbiol. *Res:* Microbiology of dairy and food products, especially starter and spoilage flora. *Mailing Add:* 3505-27th Ave W Bradenton FL 33505

VEDBRAT, SHARANJIT S, b Panjab, India, Dec 22, 46; m 73; c 1. CELL BIOLOGY. *Educ:* Panjab Univ, BS, 67, MS, 69; Univ Ill, Urbana, MS, 73, PhD(biol), 75. *Prof Exp:* Fel, cell biol, Univ Ky Med Ctr, 75-77; VIS INVESTR CANCER GENETICS & VIROL, SLOAN-KETTERING INST, 78- *Mem:* Am Soc Cell Biol; Am Genetics Soc. *Res:* Genetics, somatic cell genetics, especially in tumor specific antigens and their gene localization. *Mailing Add:* 309 E 87th St Apt 6-N New York NY 10028

VEDDER, JAMES FORREST, b Pomona, Calif, June 3, 28; m 70; c 2. PLANETARY SCIENCES, MICROPARTICLE ACCELERATORS. *Educ:* Pomona Col, BA, 49; Univ Calif, PhD(nuclear physics), 58. *Prof Exp:* Asst nuclear physics, Radiation Lab, Univ Calif, 51-58; res scientist, Missiles & Space Co, Lockheed Aircraft Corp, 58-63; RES SCIENTIST, AMES RES CTR, NASA, 63- *Mem:* Am Phys Soc; Am Geophys Union; Sigma Xi. *Res:* Nuclear physics; beta decay; space physics; meteoroids; microparticle accelerators; remote sensing of soil moisture; measurement of stratospheric halocarbons. *Mailing Add:* NASA Ames Res Ctr Moffett Field CA 94035

VEDDER, WILLEM, b Ouder-Amstel, Neth, July 17, 24; nat US; m 55. CHEMISTRY. *Educ:* Univ Amsterdam, PhD, 58. *Prof Exp:* Mem sci staff, Dept Chem, Univ Amsterdam, 55-58; res assoc, Princeton Univ, 58-60; phys chemist, Metall & Ceramics Lab, 60-68, mgr phys chem lab, 68-72, mgr technol eval oper, 74-78, MGR RES & DEVELOP PLANNING, CORP RES & DEVELOP, GEN ELEC CO, 78- *Mem:* Am Phys Soc. *Res:* Solid state chemistry; energy science and technology; technology assessment; research and development planning. *Mailing Add:* Gen Elec Corp Res & Develop PO Box 8 Schenectady NY 12301

VEDEJS, EDWIN, b Riga, Latvia, Jan 31, 41; US citizen. ORGANIC CHEMISTRY. *Educ:* Univ Mich, Ann Arbor, BS, 62; Univ Wis-Madison, PhD(chem), 66. *Prof Exp:* Nat Acad Sci-Air Force Off Sci Res fel chem, Harvard Univ, 66-67; assoc prof, 67-77, PROF CHEM, UNIV WIS-MADISON, 77- *Concurrent Pos:* A P Sloan fel, 71-73. *Mem:* Am Chem Soc. *Res:* Synthetic organic and organophosphorus chemistry; thermal rearrangements. *Mailing Add:* Dept of Chem Univ of Wis Madison WI 53706

VEDERAS, JOHN CHRISTOPHER, b Detmold, Ger, 47; US citizen. BIOORGANIC CHEMISTRY. *Educ:* Stanford Univ, BSc, 69; Mass Inst Technol, PhD(chem), 73. *Prof Exp:* Res assoc chem, Univ Basel, Switz, 73-76 & Purdue Univ, 76-77; ASST PROF CHEM, UNIV ALTA, 77- *Mem:* Am Chem Soc; Brit Chem Soc; Chem Inst Can; Sigma Xi. *Res:* Mechanism and stereochemistry of enzymes in amino acid metabolism; radiochemical synthesis; biosynthesis of secondary metabolites. *Mailing Add:* Dept of Chem Univ of Alta Edmonton AB T6G 2G2 Can

VEDROS, NEYLAN ANTHONY, b New Orleans, La, Oct 6, 29; m 55; c 2. MICROBIOLOGY, IMMUNOLOGY. *Educ:* La State Univ, BSc, 51, MSc, 57; Univ Colo, PhD(microbiol), 60. *Prof Exp:* Nat Inst Allergy & Infectious Dis fel, Med Sch, Univ Ore, 60-62; chief bact div, Naval Med Res Inst, Bethesda, Md, 62-66; res microbiologist, Biol Lab, 66-68, DIR NAVAL BIOMED RES LAB & PROF MED MICROBIOL & IMMUNOL, UNIV CALIF, BERKELEY, 68- *Honors & Awards:* Lab Sect Award, Am Pub Health Asn, 66. *Mem:* Int Asn Aquatic Animal Med; Am Soc Microbiol; Am Asn Immunol; Soc Exp Biol & Med; Asn Mil Surg US. *Res:* Immunochemistry of Neisseria Meningitidis; host-parasite studies in marine pinnipeds; ecology of terrestrial and marine fungi. *Mailing Add:* Naval Biosci Lab Naval Supply Ctr Oakland CA 94625

VEDVICK, THOMAS SCOTT, b Tacoma, Wash, June 23, 44; m 67; c 2. HEMOGLOBINOPATHIES, PROTEINS. *Educ:* Univ Puget Sound, BS, 66; Western Wash State Col, MS, 68; Univ Ore, PhD(biochem), 72. *Prof Exp:* Lectr, biol, 76-77, ASST RES BIOCHEMIST, UNIV CALIF, SAN DIEGO, 72- *Concurrent Pos:* Prin investr, NIH, 78-80; lectr, chem dept, Univ Calif, San Diego, 81- *Res:* Thalassemia syndromes; regulational control of the switches of globin chain synthesis from the fetal form of hemoglobin to the adult type of hemoglobin at or about the time of birth; determination of the microheterogeneity of human fetal hemoglobin gamma chains; mechanism of drug induced hemolytic anemias. *Mailing Add:* Dept Path Mail Stop D-006 Univ Calif San Diego La Jolla CA 92093

VEECH, JOSEPH A, plant pathology, plant physiology, see previous edition

VEECH, RICHARD L, b Decatur, Ill, Sept 19, 35; m 65; c 3. BIOCHEMISTRY, MEDICINE. *Educ:* Harvard Univ, BA, 57, MD, 62; Oxford Univ, PhD(biochem), 69. *Prof Exp:* CHIEF, LAB METAB, NAT INST ALCOHOL ABUSE & ALCOHOLISM, 78- *Mem:* Brit Biochem Soc; Am Soc Biol Chemists; Am Inst Nutrit; Neurochem Soc. *Res:* Control of metabolic processes. *Mailing Add:* Nat Inst of Alcohol Abuse & Alcoholism 1250 Washington Ave Rockville MD 20852

VEECH, WILLIAM AUSTIN, b Detroit, Mich, Dec 24, 38; m 65; c 1. MATHEMATICS. *Educ:* Dartmouth Col, AB, 60; Princeton Univ, PhD(math), 63. *Prof Exp:* H B Fine instr math, Princeton Univ, 63-64, Higgins lectr, 64-66; asst prof, Univ Calif, Berkeley, 66-69; assoc prof, 69-72, PROF MATH, RICE UNIV, 72- *Concurrent Pos:* Mem math, Inst Advan Study, Princeton Univ, 68-69, 72 & 76-77; NSF grant, Rice Univ, 69-, Alfred P Sloan fel, 71-73; mem adv comt math & comput sci, NSF, 79- *Mem:* Am Math Soc. *Res:* Topological dynamics; ergodic theory; probability theory; functional analysis; almost periodic functions; number theory. *Mailing Add:* Dept of Math Rice Univ Houston TX 77001

VEEN-BAIGENT, MARGARET JOAN, b Toronto, Ont, Dec 23, 33; m 69; c 2. NUTRITION. *Educ:* Univ Toronto, BA, 55, MA, 56, PhD(nutrit), 64. *Prof Exp:* From lectr to asst prof, 56-71, ASSOC PROF NUTRIT, SCH HYG, UNIV TORONTO, 71- *Mem:* Nutrit Soc Can; Brit Nutrit Soc; Am Inst Nutrit; NY Acad Sci. *Res:* Cholesterol metabolism; ascorbic acid requirements. *Mailing Add:* Dept Nutrit Sci Fac Med Univ Toronto Toronto ON M5S 1A8 Can

VEENEMA, RALPH J, b Prospect Park, NJ, Dec 13, 21; m 44; c 4. UROLOGY. *Educ:* Calvin Col, AB, 42; Jefferson Med Col, MD, 45; Am Bd Urol, dipl, 57. *Prof Exp:* Asst resident, Vet Admin Hosps, Alexandria, La, 46 & Jackson, Miss, 47; asst resident path, Paterson Gen Hosp, 48 & surg path, Col Physicians & Surgeons, Columbia Univ, 49; asst resident urol, Vet Admin Hosp, Bronx, 49; asst resident & resident, Columbia-Presby Med Ctr, 50-52, from asst to assoc, 53-58, asst clin prof, 58-60, from asst prof to assoc prof clin urol, 60-68, PROF CLIN UROL, COL PHYSICIANS & SURGEONS, COLUMBIA UNIV, 68- *Concurrent Pos:* Assoc urologist, St Joseph Hosp, Paterson, NJ, 53-56; chief, Urol Outpatient Clin, Columbia-Presby Med Ctr, 55-60, from asst attend urologist to assoc attend urologist, 55-68, attend urologist, 68-, chief urol, Francis Delafield Hosp, Cancer Res Inst, 60-75; attend urologist & chief urol serv, Valley Hosp, Ridgewood, NJ, 56-60, consult, 60-; consult, USPHS Hosp, Staten Island, NY, 61- & Harlem Hosp, New York, 62- *Honors & Awards:* Am Urol Asn 2nd Prize, 62, 1st Prize, 64. *Mem:* Am Asn Genito-Urinary Surg; Am Urol Asn; fel Am Col Surgeons; fel AMA; NY Acad Med (secy, 60-61). *Res:* Pathophysiology of genitourinary neoplasms. *Mailing Add:* 161 Fort Washington Ave New York NY 10032

VEENING, HANS, b Neth, May 7, 31; nat US; m 57. ANALYTICAL CHEMISTRY. *Educ:* Hope Col, AB, 53; Purdue Univ, MS, 55, PhD, 59. *Prof Exp:* From instr to assoc prof, 58-72, PROF CHEM, BUCKNELL UNIV, 72- *Concurrent Pos:* NSF fac fel with Dr J F K Huber, Univ Amsterdam, 66-67; NIH spec res fel, Biochem Separations Sect, Oak Ridge Nat Lab, 72-73; NSF grants, 68-72 & 76-78; Petrol Res Fund grants, 68-83; prof in charge short course on automated anal, Am Chem Soc, 76-; NIH grant, 78-81. *Mem:* AAAS; Sigma Xi; Am Chem Soc. *Res:* High performance liquid chromatography of phsiological fluids; mass spectrometry of biochemically active compounds; automated methods of analysis; gas chromatography. *Mailing Add:* Dept of Chem Bucknell Univ Lewisburg PA 17837

VEESER, LYNN RAYMOND, b Sturgeon Bay, Wis, Sept 18, 42; m 65. NUCLEAR PHYSICS. *Educ:* Univ Wis-Madison, BS, 64, MS, 65, PhD(physics), 68. *Prof Exp:* STAFF MEM PHYSICS, LOS ALAMOS SCI LAB, 67- *Mem:* Am Phys Soc. *Res:* Low energy nuclear physics. *Mailing Add:* Los Alamos Sci Lab PO Box 1663 Los Alamos NM 87545

VEGH, EMANUEL, b New York, NY, Nov 20, 36; m 60; c 3. MATHEMATICS. *Educ:* Univ Del, BA, 58, MA, 60; Univ NC, PhD(math), 65. *Prof Exp:* Lectr math, Univ Del, 58-60 & Univ NC, 60-63; RES MATHEMATICIAN, US NAVAL RES LAB, 63- *Concurrent Pos:* Assoc prof lectr, George Washington Univ, 65-67 & Univ Md, 67- *Honors & Awards:* Res Publ Award, US Naval Res Lab, 69. *Mem:* Math Asn Am; Am Math Soc; London Math Soc; Sigma Xi. *Res:* Number theory; algebra; combinatories. *Mailing Add:* US Naval Res Lab 4555 Overlook Ave SW Washington DC 20390

VEGORS, STANLEY H, JR, b Detroit, Mich, Jan 5, 29; m 51; c 3. NUCLEAR PHYSICS. *Educ:* Middlebury Col, BA, 51; Mass Inst Technol, BS, 51; Univ Ill, MS, 52, PhD(physics), 55. *Prof Exp:* Res assoc physics, Univ Ill, 55-56; physicist, Phillips Petrol Co, 56-58; assoc prof physics, 58-61, head dept, 58-65, PROF PHYSICS, IDAHO STATE UNIV, 61- *Mem:* Am Phys Soc; Int Solar Energy Soc. *Res:* Radioactivity, solar energy, nuclear safeguards; nuclear waste disposal. *Mailing Add:* Dept of Physics Idaho State Univ Pocatello ID 83201

VEGOTSKY, ALLEN, b New York, NY, Mar 2, 31; m 67; c 1. BIOLOGICAL CHEMISTRY. *Educ:* City Col New York, BS, 52; Fla State Univ, MS, 57, PhD(chem), 61. *Prof Exp:* Asst biochem, NY Univ, 52 & Fla State Univ, 55-60; NIH fel, Purdue Univ, 60-63; asst prof biol & chem, Wheaton Col, Mass, 63-69; assoc prof, Wells Col, 69-74; biosci coordr, Biomed Interdisciplinary Curric Proj, 74-77; asst med dir, Cystic Fibrosis Found, 77-78; RES ADMINR, AM CANCER SOC, 78- *Mem:* AAAS; Sigma Xi. *Res:* Research administration; mutagenesis; curriculum development. *Mailing Add:* 25 Scenic Circle Croton NY 10520

VEHRENCAMP, SANDRA LEE, b Glendale, Calif, Feb 11, 48; m 73; c 2. ANIMAL BEHAVIOR, ORNITHOLOGY. *Educ:* Univ Calif, Berkeley, BA, 70; Cornell Univ, PhD(animal behav), 76. *Prof Exp:* lectr, 76-79, ASST PROF BIOL, UNIV CALIF, SAN DIEGO, 79- *Concurrent Pos:* Exped leader, grant, Nat Geog Soc, 78- *Mem:* Brit Ornith Union; Am Ornith Union. *Res:* Evolution of avian social organization, including field studies of ecology and behavior; sociobiology. *Mailing Add:* Dept of Biol C-016 Univ of Calif San Diego La Jolla CA 92093

VEHSE, ROBERT CHASE, b Morgantown, WVa, Sept 9, 36; m 61; c 2. SOLID STATE PHYSICS. *Educ:* WVa Univ, BA, 58; Univ Tenn, Knoxville, PhD(physics), 64. *Prof Exp:* Mem tech staff compound semiconductor mat, Bell Tel Labs, 68-72, SUPVR COMPOUND SEMICONDUCTOR MAT GROUP, BELL LABS, 73- *Mem:* Am Phys Soc; Electrochem Soc. *Res:* Development of processes useful for production of epitaxial layers of semiconductor materials. *Mailing Add:* Dept 2354 Bell Labs 2525 N 11th St Reading PA 19604

VEHSE, WILLIAM E, b Morgantown, WVa, Apr 28, 32; m 56; c 4. PHYSICS. *Educ:* WVa Univ, BA, 55; Carnegie Inst, MS, 59, PhD(physics), 62. *Prof Exp:* From asst prof to assoc prof physics, 61-72, PROF PHYSICS, WVA UNIV, 72-, CHMN DEPT, 75- *Mem:* Am Phys Soc; Am Asn Physics Teachers. *Res:* Nuclear and electron resonance in metals; optics. *Mailing Add:* Dept of Physics WVa Univ Morgantown WV 26506

VEIDIS, MIKELIS VALDIS, b Riga, Latvia, Jan 25, 39; m 63; c 3. CHEMISTRY. *Educ:* Univ Queensland, BSc, 63, MSc, 67; Univ Waterloo, PhD(chem), 69. *Prof Exp:* Chemist, Queensland Govt Chem Lab, 63-67; res fel chem, Harvard Univ, 69-71; metallurgist, 71-75, VPRES RES & DEVELOP, WAKEFIELD CORP, 75- *Concurrent Pos:* Vis res scientist, Chem Dept, Northeastern Univ, 78- *Mem:* Am Chem Soc; Royal Australian Chem Inst. *Res:* Chemistry of metal surfaces as related to sintering phenomena; crystallographic studies of structures of inorganic complexes and compounds of biological interest. *Mailing Add:* Wakefield Corp Wakefield MA 01880

VEIGEL, JON MICHAEL, b Mankato, Minn, Nov 10, 38; m 62. ENERGY POLICY, ALTERNATIVE ENERGY. *Educ:* Univ Wash, BS, 60; Univ Calif, Los Angeles, PhD(phys inorg chem), 65. *Prof Exp:* Res chemist, Jackson Lab, E I du Pont de Nemours & Co, Inc, Del, 65; asst prof phys inorg chem & res chemist, F J Seiler Res Lab, US Air Force Acad, 65-68; asst prof, Joint Sci Dept, Claremont Cols, 68-73; assoc prof energy & environ, Calif State Col, Dominguez Hills, Calif, 73-74; dir energy prog & cong sci fel, Off Technol Assessment, US Cong, 74-75; adminr alternatives div, Energy Comn, Sacramento, Calif, 75-78; chief mkt develop, Solar Energy Res Inst, Golden, Colo, 78-79, asst dir technol commercialization, 79, div mgr planning applications & impacts, 79-81; EXEC DIR, ALTERNATIVE ENERGY CORP, RESEARCH TRIANGLE PARK, NC, 81- *Concurrent Pos:* Mem sci & pub policies comt, AAAS, 75-79; mem synthesis panel, Nat Acad Study Nuclear Power & Alternative Systs, 75-76. *Mem:* AAAS. *Res:* National energy policy; commercialization of alternative energy technologies; technology assessment. *Mailing Add:* Alternative Energy Corp Research Triangle Park NC 27709

VEILLON, CLAUDE, b Church Point, La, Jan 11, 40. ANALYTICAL CHEMISTRY, SPECTROSCOPY. *Educ:* Univ Southwestern La, BS, 62; Univ Fla, MS, 63, PhD(anal chem), 65. *Prof Exp:* Res chemist, Nat Bur Standards, 65-67; from asst prof to assoc prof anal chem, Univ Houston, 67-74; vis scientist, Harvard Med Sch, 74-76; RES CHEMIST, HUMAN NUTRIT RES CTR, 76- *Concurrent Pos:* Nat Acad Sci-Nat Res Coun res assoc, 65-67; res fel, NIH/Nat Cancer Inst, 74-76. *Mem:* Am Chem Soc; Soc Appl Spectros; Optical Soc Am; Am Inst Physics. *Res:* Isotopic analysis; trace metal analysis; analytical instrumentation; trace metal metabolism. *Mailing Add:* Human Nutrit Res Ctr USDA Bldg 307 Rm 215 Beltsville MD 20705

VEINOTT, ARTHUR FALES, JR, b Boston, Mass, Oct 12, 34; m 60; c 2. OPERATIONS RESEARCH. *Educ:* Lehigh Univ, BS & BA, 56; Columbia Univ, EngScD(indust eng), 60. *Prof Exp:* Asst prof indust eng, 62-64, assoc prof, 64-67, PROF OPERS RES, STANFORD UNIV, 67-, CHMN DEPT, 75- *Concurrent Pos:* Western Mgt Sci Inst grant, 64-65; Off Naval Res contract, 64-80; consult, Rand Corp, 65- & IBM Res Ctr, 68-69; NSF grant, 67-, mem res initiation grant panel, 71; vis prof, Yale Univ, 72-73; ed, J Math Opers Res, 74-80; Guggenheim fel, 78-79. *Mem:* Inst Mgt Sci; Am Math Soc; Math Prog Soc; Oper Res Soc Am; fel Inst Math Statist. *Res:* Development of lattice programming, a qualitative theory of optimization for predicting the direction of change of optimal decisions resulting from alteration of problem parameters; structure and computation of optimal policies for inventory systems and dynamic programs. *Mailing Add:* Dept Opers Res Stanford Univ Stanford CA 94305

VEIRS, VAL RHODES, b Allegan, Mich, Sept 20, 42; m 64; c 1. ATMOSPHERIC PHYSICS. *Educ:* Case Inst Technol, BS, 64; Ill Inst Technol, PhD(physics), 69. *Prof Exp:* Res physicist, Zenith Radio Corp, 64-65; asst prof physics, Ill Inst Technol, 69-71; asst prof, 71-80, ASSOC PROF PHYSICS, COLO COL, 80- *Mem:* AAAS; Am Asn Physics Teachers. *Res:* Numerical and urban diffusion modeling. *Mailing Add:* Dept of Physics Colo Col Colorado Springs CO 80903

VEIS, ARTHUR, b Pittsburgh, Pa, Dec 23, 25; m 51; c 3. BIOCHEMISTRY, PHYSICAL CHEMISTRY. *Educ:* Univ Okla, BS, 47; Northwestern Univ, PhD(phys chem), 51. *Prof Exp:* Instr phys chem, Univ Okla, 51-52; res chemist, Dept Phys Chem, Armour & Co, 52-60, head dept, 59-60; assoc prof biochem, 60-65, asst dean grad affairs, 68-70, assoc dean med & grad schs, 70-76, PROF BIOCHEM, SCH MED, NORTHWESTERN UNIV, CHICAGO, 65-, CHMN DEPT ORAL BIOL, SCH DENT, 77- *Concurrent Pos:* Spec instr, Crane Jr Col, 55-56 & Loyola Univ, 57-58; Guggenheim fel, 67; fel NIH Fogarty Sr Int Scholar Award, European Molecular Biol Lab, Grenoble & Weizmann Inst Sci, Rehovot, Israel, 77; chmn & mem spec prog adv comt, Nat Inst Dent Res, Dent Res Inst, 74-78. *Honors & Awards:* Biol Mineralization Award, Int Asn Dental Res, 81. *Mem:* Am Chem Soc; Am Soc Biol Chemists; Biophys Soc; NY Acad Sci; Int Asn Dent Res. *Res:* Physical chemistry and biology of the connective tissue systems; colloid chemistry; biological mineralization. *Mailing Add:* Dept of Oral Biol Northwestern Univ Dent Sch Chicago IL 60611

VEIT, JIRI JOSEPH, b Prague, Czech, Apr 15, 34; m 61. ATOMIC PHYSICS, NUCLEAR PHYSICS. *Educ:* Univ London, BSc, 55, PhD(nuclear physics), 59; Univ Birmingham, MSc, 56. *Prof Exp:* Instr physics, Univ BC, 59-62; lectr, Univ London, 62-63; from asst prof to assoc prof, 63-71, PROF PHYSICS, WESTERN WASH STATE UNIV, 71- *Mem:* Am Phys Soc; Am Asn Physics Teachers. *Res:* Positronium; stripping and pickup reactions; nuclear reaction mechanisms; nuclear structure. *Mailing Add:* Dept of Physics Western Wash State Univ Bellingham WA 98225

VEITH, DANIEL A, b Metairie, La, Apr 18, 36; m 56; c 2. SOLID STATE PHYSICS. *Educ:* Tulane Univ, BS, 56, PhD(physics), 63; Univ Calif, Los Angeles, MS, 58. *Prof Exp:* Mem tech staff, Hughes Aircraft Co, 56-59; sci specialist space div, Chrysler Corp, 63-67; PROF PHYSICS & DEPT HEAD, NICHOLLS STATE UNIV, 67- *Res:* Nucleation and growth of thin crystalline films. *Mailing Add:* Dept of Physics Nicholls State Univ Thibodaux LA 70301

VEITH, FRANK JAMES, b New York, NY, Aug 29, 31; m 54; c 4. SURGERY, TRANSPLANTATION BIOLOGY. *Educ:* Cornell Univ, AB, 52, MD, 55. *Prof Exp:* NIH fel, Harvard Med Sch, 63-64; asst prof surg, Cornell Univ, 64-67; assoc prof, 67-71, PROF SURG, ALBERT EINSTEIN COL MED, 71-; CO-DIR KIDNEY TRANSPLANT UNIT, MONTEFIORE HOSP, 67-, ATTEND SURG & CHIEF VASCULAR SURG, 72- *Concurrent Pos:* Markle scholar acad med, Cornell Univ, Albert Einstein Col Med & Montefiore Hosp, 64-69; career scientist award, Health Res Coun, City New York & Montefiore Hosp, 65-72; assoc attend surgeon, Montefiore Hosp, 67-71; consult, Heart-Lung Proj Comt, 71- *Mem:* Soc Univ Surgeons; Soc Vascular Surg; Am Asn Thoracic Surg; Am Surg Asn; Transplantation Soc. *Res:* Lung transplantation, pulmonary physiology, kidney transplantation and vascular surgery. *Mailing Add:* Dept of Surg Montefiore Hosp & Med Ctr New York NY 10467

VEITH, ILZA, b Ludwigshafen, Ger, May 13, 15; nat US; m 35. HISTORY OF MEDICINE. *Educ:* Johns Hopkins Univ, MA, 44, PhD(hist of med), 47; Juntendo Univ, Tokyo, Dr Med Sci, 75. *Prof Exp:* Am Asn Learned Soc grant, 48; lectr hist of med, Univ Chicago, 49-51, from asst prof to assoc prof, 51-64; prof hist of health sci & vchmn dept, 64-67, prof hist of psychiat, 67-79, EMER PROF PSYCHIAT & HIST OF HEALTH SCI, SCH MED, UNIV CALIF, SAN FRANCISCO, 79- *Concurrent Pos:* NSF res grant, 53-56; consult, Armed Forced Med Libr, 47-56 & NIH, 59-62; D J Davis mem lectr, Col Med, Univ Ill, 58; vis prof, Univ Calif, Los Angeles, 58; Kuntz mem lectr, Sch Med, St Louis Univ, 61; Alfred P Sloan vis prof, Menninger Sch Psychiat, Topeka, Kans, 63, 64 & 66; vis prof, Med Sch, Univ Chicago, 68-; chmn hist res comt, World Fedn Neurol, 68-; Logan Clendening lectr, Sch Med, Univ Kans, 71; All-Univ Lectr, Univ Calif, Santa Barbara, 72; hon mem Inst Hist of Med & Med Res, India & Ger Soc Hist Med, Sci & Technol. *Mem:* Hist Sci Soc; Am Asn Hist Med (secy-treas, 55); hon fel Am Psychiat Asn; Int Soc Hist Med; fel Royal Soc Med. *Res:* History of Chinese and Japanese medicine; history of psychiatry, particularly hysteria. *Mailing Add:* Dept Hist Health Sci Univ Calif Med Ctr San Francisco CA 94143

VEITH, KARL FREDERICK, b St Peter, Minn, Oct 7, 39; m 62; c 1. SEISMOLOGY, GEOPHYSICS. *Educ:* Univ Minn, BS, 61, MS, 66; Southern Methodist Univ, PhD(geophys), 74. *Prof Exp:* Res geophysicist thermal res, US Bur Mines, 62-66; sr res geophysicist seismol res, Teledyne Geotech, 66-81; RES GEOPHYSICIST, SOHIO PETROL CO, 81- *Mem:* Am Geophys Union; Seismol Soc Am; Soc Explor Geophysicists. *Res:* Development of high resolution vibraeis and sign bit analysis techniques; development of techniques for high precision seismic event location and location reliability estimates; automatic event detection, phase association, and earthquake parameterization; resolution of designated, simple arrivals from complex multipathed waveforms. *Mailing Add:* Sohio Petrol Co Geophys Data Ctr Suite 1200 LB 25 5400 LBS Freeway Dallas TX 75228

VEJVODA, EDWARD, b New York, NY, Apr 18, 24; m 49; c 3. INDUSTRIAL CHEMISTRY. *Educ:* Univ Northern Colo, BA, 49, MA, 51. *Prof Exp:* Anal chemist, Anal Labs, Dow Chem Co, 52-56, res chemist, 56-60, sr res chemist res & develop labs, 60-62, anal supvr, 62-64, anal proj supvr, Dow Chem Int, Ger, 64-65, res staff asst, Chem-Physics Res & Develop Labs, 65-68, res mgr, Chem Res & Develop, 68-72, sr res mgr, 72-75; chem opers dir, 75-80, PLUTONIAN OPERS DIR, ROCKWELL INT, 81- *Mem:* Am Chem Soc; Nat Mgt Asn; Sigma Xi; Am Electroplaters Soc; Inst Nuclear Mat Mgt. *Res:* Actinide chemistry; development of analytical methods for the assay and impurity analysis of the actinide elements, especially optical emission spectroscopy for the impurity analysis of plutonium and americium compounds; process development for the separation and purification of plutonium compounds; waste management and processing; plutonian fabrication. *Mailing Add:* Rockwell Int Rocky Flats Plant Golden CO 80401

VELA, ADAN RICHARD, b Laredo, Tex, Oct 28, 30; m 55; c 4. PHYSIOLOGY. *Educ:* Baylor Univ, BS, 52; Univ Tenn, PhD(physiol) 62. *Prof Exp:* Res assoc data anal, Comput Ctr, Univ Tenn, 63; asst prof surg, 63-71, ASSOC PROF SURG, SCH MED, LA STATE UNIV MED CTR, 71- *Res:* Gastrointestinal physiology; esophageal motility; spinal fluid pressure and production; Escherichia coli endotoxin. *Mailing Add:* Dept of Surg La State Univ Sch of Med New Orleans LA 70112

VELA, GERARD ROLAND, b Eagle Pass, Tex, Sept 18, 27; m 53; c 4. MICROBIOLOGY. *Educ:* Univ Tex, BA, 50, MA, 51, PhD(microbiol), 64. *Prof Exp:* Res asst, Univ Tex, 50-51; res asst biochem, Southwest Found Res, 52-54; res asst immunol, Sch Med, Harvard Univ, 54-57; head clin chemist, Santa Rosa Hosp, San Antonio, Tex, 57-59; res microbiologist, US Air Force Sch Aerospace Med, 59-65; from asst prof to assoc prof microbiol, 65-72, PROF MICROBIOL, N TEX STATE UNIV, 72- *Concurrent Pos:* Fulbright lectr, Bogota, Colombia, 72; ed, Tex J Sci, 75- *Mem:* Am Acad Microbiol. *Res:* Nature of microorganisms in their natural habitat; biochemical interrelationships in mixed cultures of microorganisms; physiology of azotobacter; microbiology of industrial waste-waters. *Mailing Add:* Dept of Biol NTex State Univ Denton TX 76203

VELARDO, JOSEPH THOMAS, b Newark, NJ, Jan 27, 23; m 48. BIOLOGY, ANATOMY. *Educ:* Northern Colo Univ, AB, 48; Miami Univ, SM, 49; Harvard Univ, PhD(biol, physiol, endocrinol), 52. *Prof Exp:* Asst org & inorg chem, Northern Colo Univ, 47-48; asst & instr zool & human heredity, Miami Univ, 48-49; res fel biol & endocrinol, Harvard Univ, 52-53, res assoc path, Sch Med, 53-54, res assoc surg, 54-55; asst prof anat, Sch Med, Yale Univ, 55-61; prof & chmn dept, NY Med Col, 61-62; dir, Inst Study Human Reproduction & dir educ prog, 62-67; chmn dept, 67-73, PROF ANAT, STRITCH SCH MED, LOYOLA UNIV, CHICAGO, 67- *Concurrent Pos:* Asst surg, Peter Bent Brigham Hosp, Boston, 54-55; Lederle med fac award, 55-58; prof biol, John Carroll Univ, 62-67; US del, Int Cong Reproduction, Vatican, 64; head dept res, St Ann Hosp, Cleveland, 64-67; ed, Endocrinol Reprod, Essentials Human Reprod, Biol Reprod & Uterus & Enzymes Female Gen Syst. *Honors & Awards:* Rubin Award, Am Soc Study Sterility, 55. *Mem:* Brit Soc Endocrinol; Endocrine Soc; fel Geront Soc; Am Physiol Soc; fel NY Acad Sci. *Res:* Endocrinology of reproduction; anatomy, physiology, biochemistry, histochemistry and cytochemistry of reproductive organs. *Mailing Add:* 607 E Wilson Rd Old Grove East Lombard IL 60148

VELECKIS, EWALD, b Kybartai, Lithuania, Aug 1, 26; US citizen; m 55; c 1. CHEMISTRY. *Educ:* Univ Ill, BS, 53; Ill Inst Technol, MS, 57, PhD(chem), 60. *Prof Exp:* CHEMIST, ARGONNE NAT LAB, 59- *Mem:* Am Chem Soc. *Res:* Phase equilibria in inorganic systems; molecular beams; alloy thermodynamics; metallic solutions and liquid state; fusion reactors; metal hydrides; hydrogen storage. *Mailing Add:* Argonne Nat Lab 9700 S Cass Ave Argonne IL 60439

VELENYI, LOUIS JOSEPH, b Budapest, Hungary, June 17, 34; US citizen; m 57; m 3. INORGANIC CHEMISTRY, CATALYSIS. *Educ:* Case Western Reserve Univ, BA, 70, PhD(chem), 75. *Prof Exp:* Res asst clin chemist, Case Western Reserve Univ, Highland View Hosp, 62-72; PROJ LEADER, CHEMIST, STANDARD OIL CO, OHIO, 75- *Mem:* Am Chem Soc. *Res:* Synthesis and nmr study of porphyrins and phthalocyanines; catalysis of various reactions. *Mailing Add:* 4440 Warrensville Ctr Rd Warrensville Heights OH 44128

VELETSOS, A(NESTIS), b Istanbul, Turkey, Apr 28, 27; nat US; m 66. CIVIL ENGINEERING. *Educ:* Robert Col, Istanbul, BS, 48; Univ Ill, Urbana, MS, 50, PhD(civil eng), 53. *Prof Exp:* From asst prof to prof civil eng, Univ Ill, Urbana, 53-64, assoc mem, Ctr Advan Study, 61-62; prof, 64-68, chmn dept, 64-72, BROWN & ROOT PROF ENG, RICE UNIV, 66- *Concurrent Pos:* Struct designer, F L Ehasz, NY, 50 & Skidmore, Owings & Merrill, Ill, 53; consult, 53-; NSF consult, Indian Inst Technol, Bombay, 69; vis prof, Cath Univ Rio de Janeiro, vis 70 & Univ Calif, Berkeley, 77; mem, Earthquake Eng Res Inst, vpres, 74-77; chmn, US Joint Comt Earthquake Eng, 77- *Honors & Awards:* Norman Medal, Am Soc Civil Engrs, 59, Res Prize, 61, Newmark Medal, 78. *Mem:* Am Soc Civil Engrs; Seismol Soc Am; Int Asn Bridge & Struct Engrs. *Res:* Structural engineering and mechanics, particularly dynamics of structures and earthquake engineering; offshore structures. *Mailing Add:* Dept of Civil Eng Rice Univ Houston TX 77001

VELEZ, SAMUEL JOSE, b San Juan, PR, July 19, 45; m 67; c 3. NEUROPHYSIOLOGY. *Educ:* Univ PR, BS, 66, MS, 69; Yale Univ, PhD(neurophysiol), 74. *Prof Exp:* Instr biol, Univ PR, 66; biologist, US Naval Sta, San Juan, PR, 66 & 67-68; res asst pharmacol, Sch Med, Univ PR, 67-68; teaching asst neurophysiol, Yale Univ, 70 & 71; NIH fel zool, Univ Tex, Austin, 74-76; ASST PROF BIOL SCI, DARTMOUTH COL, NH, 76- *Mem:* AAAS; Soc Neurosci; Sigma Xi. *Res:* Patterns of neuronal connections; rules of connectivity in neuromuscular connections; nerve-muscle trophic interactions; facilitation at the neuromuscular junction; regeneration of neuromuscular connections; developmental neurobiology. *Mailing Add:* Dept of Biol Sci Dartmouth Col Hanover NH 03755

VELEZ, WILLIAM YSLAS, b Tucson, Ariz, Jan 15, 47; m 68; c 2. NUMBER THEORY, ALGEBRA. *Educ:* Univ Ariz, BS, 68, MS, 72, PhD(math), 75. *Prof Exp:* Mem tech staff math, Sandia Labs, 75-77; asst prof, 77-80, ASSOC PROF MATH, UNIV ARIZ, 81- *Mem:* Math Asn Am. *Res:* Elementary and algebraic number theory; field theory. *Mailing Add:* Dept of Math Univ of Ariz Tucson AZ 85721

VELICK, SIDNEY FREDERICK, b Detroit, Mich, May 3, 13; m 41; c 2. BIOCHEMISTRY. *Educ:* Wayne State Univ, BS, 35; Univ Mich, MS, 36, PhD(biol chem), 38. *Prof Exp:* Rockefeller Found fel, Johns Hopkins Univ, 39-40; Int Cancer Res Found fel, Yale Univ, 41-45; from asst prof to prof biol chem, Sch Med, Wash Univ, 45-64; PROF BIOL CHEM & HEAD DEPT, COL MED, UNIV UTAH, 64- *Concurrent Pos:* Mem biochem study sect, NIH, 65-69. *Mem:* Nat Acad Sci; Am Soc Biol Chemists; Am Chem Soc. *Res:* Bacterial lipids; protein chemistry and metabolism; mechanism of enzyme action. *Mailing Add:* Dept of Biochem Univ of Utah Col of Med Salt Lake City UT 84112

VELIKY, IVAN ALOIS, b Zilina, Czech, Mar 23, 29; m 52; c 2. BIOLOGICAL CHEMISTRY. *Educ:* Slovak Tech Univ, Bratislava, EngC, 50, DiplEng, 52; Slovak Acad Sci, PhD, 60. *Prof Exp:* From asst prof to assoc prof biochem, Slovak Tech Univ, Bratislava, 52-65; fel, Prairie Regional Lab, 65-67, assoc res officer, 67-75, SR RES OFFICER, DIV BIOL SCI, NAT RES COUN CAN, 75- *Mem:* Chem Inst Can; Can Biochem Soc; Int Asn Plant Tissue Cult; Can Soc Microbiologists. *Res:* Physiology and biochemistry of microorganisms; physiology of cell growth in suspension cultures (fermentors); biosynthesis of secondary metabolites and biotransformation of biologically active compounds by cell cultures; immobilized cells and proteins. *Mailing Add:* Div of Biol Sci Nat Res Coun Ottawa ON K1A 0R6 Can

VELKOFF, HENRY RENE, b Cleveland, Ohio, May 14, 21; m 50; c 3. MECHANICAL & AERONAUTICAL ENGINEERING. *Educ:* Purdue Univ, BSME, 42; Ohio State Univ, MSME, 52, PhD, 62. *Prof Exp:* Analyst, Lockheed Aircraft Corp, 42-44; res engr, Aerotor Assocs, 44 & Nat Adv Comt Aeronaut, 44; develop engr, Wright-Patterson AFB, 44-46, sect head rotary wing helicopter rotor res, 47-56, br chief, 56-57, br chief vertical takeoff landing turbine res, 57-59, consult elec propulsion, 59-63; prof mech eng, Ohio State Univ, 63-72; chief scientist, US Army Aviation Res & Develop Lab, 72-74; PROF MECH ENG, OHIO STATE UNIV, 74- *Concurrent Pos:* Consult, Air Br, Off Naval Res, 63-64, Wright-Patterson AFB, 64-66, Aviation Labs, US Army, 66-72, Vertol Div, Boeing Co, 65-67 & Battelle Mem Inst, 68-70; US Army Res Off grant electrofluidmech, 64-72; mem spec subcomt vertical takeoff landing aircraft, NASA, 65, beyond the horizon study comt, US Air Force, 66, aviation sci adv group, US Army, 70-72, sci adv bd, United Aircraft Corp, 71-72 & 74- & adv bd NASA helicopters, Nat Res Coun, 78. *Honors & Awards:* Distinguished res award, US Air Force, 62. *Mem:* Am Soc Mech Engrs; hon fel Am Helicopter Soc; Am Inst Aeronaut & Astronaut; Electrostatic Soc Am. *Res:* Electrofluidmechanics; interactions of electro-static fields with gaseous boundary layers, heat transfer, condensation, freezing and flames; helicopter non-steady boundary layers; helicopter water flow fields. *Mailing Add:* Dept of Mech Eng Robinson Lab Ohio State Univ Columbus OH 43210

VELLA, FRANCIS, b Malta, July 24, 29; m 56; c 5. BIOCHEMISTRY, GENETICS. *Educ:* Royal Univ Malta, BSc, 49, MD, 52; Oxford Univ, BA, 54, MA, 58; Univ Singapore, PhD(biochem), 62. *Prof Exp:* Asst lectr biochem, Univ Singapore, 56-57, lectr, 57-60; sr lectr, Univ Khartoum, 60-64, reader biochem genetics, 64-65; vis assoc prof biochem, 65-66, assoc prof, 66-71, PROF BIOCHEM, UNIV SASK, 71- *Concurrent Pos:* Tutor, WHO Lab Course in Abnormal Hemoglobins, Ibadan, Nigeria, 63; lectr, NATO Advan Course in Pop Genetics, Rome, Italy, 64; vis prof biochem, Univ Cambridge, 73-74; mem, Comt Educ, Int Union Biochem, 79-; external examr & vis prof, El Fateh Univ, Libya, 80; vis prof, Kuwait Univ, 81. *Honors & Awards:* Chevalier, Order of St Sylvester, Vatican City, Italy, 65. *Mem:* fel Chem Inst Can; fel Royal Soc Chem; fel Royal Col Path. *Res:* Molecular genetics; abnormal human hemoglobins; hereditary enzyme deficiencies in man; teaching methods in biochemistry. *Mailing Add:* Dept of Biochem Univ of Sask Saskatoon SK S7N 0W0 Can

VELLA, PHILIP PETER, b Syracuse, NY, Aug 18, 37. MEDICAL BACTERIOLOGY, IMMUNOLOGY. *Educ:* Univ Notre Dame, BS, 59, PhD(biol), 65. *Prof Exp:* Res asst microbiol, Bristol Labs, 59-61; sr res virologist, 64-68, res fel, 68-71, sr res fel, 71-75, sr investr, 75-80, DIR BACT VACCINES, MERCK & CO, INC, 80- *Mem:* Am Soc Microbiol. *Res:* Research and development of vaccines against human, bacterial diseases. *Mailing Add:* Dept Virus & Cell Biol Merck & Co Inc West Point PA 19486

VELLACCIO, FRANK, b New Haven, Conn, Sept 24, 48; m 70; c 1. BIO-ORGANIC CHEMISTRY. *Educ:* Fordham Univ, BS, 70; Mass Inst Technol, PhD(org chem), 74. *Prof Exp:* ASST PROF CHEM, COL HOLY CROSS, 74- *Mem:* Sigma Xi; Am Chem Soc. *Res:* Synthetic methods for peptide synthesis; intromolecular acyl transfers. *Mailing Add:* Dept of Chem Col of the Holy Cross Worcester MA 01610

VELLA-COLEIRO, GEORGE, b Malta, Mar 15, 41. PHYSICS. *Educ:* Royal Univ Malta, BSc, 61; Oxford Univ, MA, 63, DPhil(physics), 67. *Prof Exp:* MEM TECH STAFF PHYSICS, BELL TEL LABS, 67- *Mem:* Am Phys Soc. *Res:* Magnetism; semiconductors; Josephson devices. *Mailing Add:* Bell Tel Labs Rm 2D313 Murray Hill NJ 07974

VELLIOS, FRANK, b St Louis, Mo, Sept 8, 22; m 50. PATHOLOGY. *Educ:* Wash Univ, MD, 46; Am Bd Path, dipl. *Prof Exp:* Instr path, Wash Univ, 51-52; from asst prof to prof, Sch Med, Ind Univ, Indianapolis, 52-68, chmn dept, 65-68; prof, Case Western Reserve Univ, 68-69; prof path, Southwestern Med Sch, Univ Tex Health Sci Ctr, Dallas, 69-78; prof path, Univ Ore Health Sci Ctr, 78-80; MEM FAC, DEPT PATH, EMORY UNIV HOSP, 80- *Concurrent Pos:* Ed, Jour, Am Soc Clin Path, 65- *Mem:* Am Soc Clin Path; Am Asn Path; Am Med Asn; Am Soc Cytol; Int Acad Path. *Res:* Surgical pathology, especially human neoplasms. *Mailing Add:* Dept Path Emory Univ Hosp 1364 Clifton Rd NE Atlanta GA 30322

VELLTURO, ANTHONY FRANCIS, b Ansonia, Conn, Dec 3, 36. APPLIED CHEMISTRY, ORGANIC CHEMISTRY. *Educ:* Yale Univ, BS, 58, MS, 59, PhD(org chem), 62. *Prof Exp:* NIH fel, Tulane Univ, La, 64-65; sr res chemist, Techni-Chem Co, Conn, 65-70; sr develop chemist, 70-73, group leader, 73-77, MGR TECH DEPT, CIBA-GEIGY CHEM CO, 77- *Mem:* Am Chem Soc. *Res:* Reaction mechanisms; synthetic organic chemistry. *Mailing Add:* Ciba-Geigy Corp PO Box 71 Toms River NJ 08753

VELTRI, ROBERT WILLIAM, b McKeesport, Pa, Dec 1, 41; m 62; c 2. MICROBIOLOGY. *Educ:* Youngstown Univ, BA, 63; WVa Univ, MS, 65, PhD(microbiol), 68. *Prof Exp:* Asst prof microbiol, Med Ctr, WVa Univ, 68-72, assoc prof, 72-75, prof microbiol & otolaryngol, 76-81, dir otolaryngic res, Div Otolaryngol, 68-81; DIR RES & DEVELOP, BIOL CORP AM, 81- *Concurrent Pos:* Immunol consult, Dent Sci Inst, Univ Tex, Houston, 72-74; vis prof microbiol, Univ Chile, Santiago, 81; regional dir, Cancer Res Lab, Nat Found Cancer Res, 79- *Mem:* AAAS; assoc fel Am Acad Ophthal & Otolaryngol; Soc Gen Microbiol; Am Soc Microbiol, Am Asn Cancer Res. *Res:* Role of tonsils in immunobiology; virology and immunology of herpesvirus infections; microbiology and immunology of otolaryngic infections; isolation and identification of human tumor-associated antigens; Epstein-Barr virus-host relationships. *Mailing Add:* Biol Corp Am 1230 Wilson Dr West Chester PA 19380

VEMULA, SUBBA RAO, b Pradesh, India, Dec 30, 24; m 56; c 2. FRICTION, DESIGNS. *Educ:* Rensselaer Polytech Inst, MS, 68, PhD(mech), 74. *Prof Exp:* Jr civil engr design bridges, 77-79, asst civil engr, 79-81, SR CIVIL ENGR, DESIGN & CONSTR DIV, BUR STRUCTURES, NY STATE DEPT TRANSP, 81- *Mem:* Am Soc Mech Engrs. *Res:* Friction. *Mailing Add:* 27 Pinehurst Ave Albany NY 12205

VEMURI, SURYANARAYANA, b Dec 23, 43; m 68; c 2. ELECTRICAL ENGINEERING. *Educ:* Osmania Univ, BE, 65; Indian Inst Sci, ME, 68; Univ NB, MScE, 70, PhD(elec eng), 75. *Prof Exp:* res assoc, Univ NB, 73-75; asst prof, Univ Alaska, Fairbanks, 75-76; asst prof elec eng, Univ Nebr, 77-79; ASSOC PRIN ENGR, HARRIS CONTROLS DIV, 79- *Concurrent Pos:* Consult, Lincoln Elec Syst, 78; adj prof, Fla Inst Technol, 79- *Mem:* Inst Elec & Electronics Engrs. *Res:* Computer modeling and analysis of electric power systems; load forecasting and planning, load modeling, optimum operation, load flow, fault and stability analysis. *Mailing Add:* Harris Controls Div Harris Corp PO Box 430 Melbourne FL 32901

VEMURI, VENKATESWARARAO, b Chodavaram, India, Jan 17, 38; m 65; c 3. DISTRIBUTED PROCESSING, SOFTWARE SYSTEMS. *Educ:* Andhra Univ, India, BE, 58; Univ Detroit, MS, 63; Univ Calif, PhD(eng), 68. *Prof Exp:* Tech asst elec testing, Bhilai Steel Works, India, 58-61; jr engr, Radio Corp Am, 63-64; systs analyst, Environ Dynamics, Inc, 68-69; asst res engr, Univ Calif, Los Angeles, 69-70; asst prof aeronaut, astronaut & eng sci, Purdue Univ, 70-73; assoc prof comput sci, State Univ NY, Binghamton, 73-81; MEM TECH STAFF, TRW, REDONDO BEACH, CALIF, 81- *Concurrent Pos:* Res engr, Univ Southern Calif, 68-69; consult, Environ Dynamics, Inc, 69-70. *Mem:* Inst Elec & Electronics Engrs. *Res:* Computational methods and computer architecture; distributed processing; modeling and simulation. *Mailing Add:* TRW/DSSG Bldg R-2 Redondo Beach CA 90278

VENA, JOSEPH AUGUSTUS, b Jersey City, NJ, Apr 18, 31; m 56; c 2. CYTOLOGY. *Educ:* St Peter's Col, BS, 52; Fordham Univ, MS, 55, PhD(cytol), 63. *Prof Exp:* Teacher high sch, 53-57; from instr to asst prof biol, Fordham Univ, 57-63; assoc prof, 63-66, PROF BIOL, TRENTON STATE COL, 66- *Concurrent Pos:* Sigma Xi res grant, 66-67; res consult, Univ Calif, Berkeley; consult, USPHS, 73-; NSF grant, 74. *Mem:* AAAS; Sigma Xi; Am Soc Cell Biol. *Res:* Coordinated studies of ultrastructural changes and electrophysiological properties in conduction system of canine heart during pharmacohogically induced alterations. *Mailing Add:* Dept of Biol Trenton State Col Trenton NJ 08625

VENABLE, DOUGLAS, b Charleston, WVa, Aug 17, 20; m 43; c 1. PHYSICS. *Educ:* Hampden-Sydney Col, BS, 42; Univ Va, MS, 47, PhD(physics), 50. *Prof Exp:* Design engr indust electronics div, Westinghouse Elec Corp, 42-46; mem staff, 50-57, alt group leader, 57-65, group leader, 65-72, alt div leader, 72-76, dep asst dir, 76-79, prog mgr, 79-80, DEP ASSOC DIR, LOS ALAMOS NAT LAB, UNIV CALIF, 80- *Concurrent Pos:* Adj prof, Los Alamos Grad Ctr, Univ NMex, 57, 58 & 61. *Mem:* Fel AAAS; fel Am Phys Soc. *Res:* Crystal physics; electron beam dynamics; electron linear accelerators, gaseous discharges; flash radiography; detonation phenomena; hydrodynamics and shock wave phenomena. *Mailing Add:* 118 Aztec Ave Los Alamos NM 87544

VENABLE, JOHN HEINZ, JR, b Atlanta, Ga, June 9, 38; m 62. MOLECULAR BIOPHYSICS. *Educ:* Duke Univ, BS, 60; Yale Univ, MS, 63, PhD(biophys), 65. *Prof Exp:* Vis scientist, King's Col, Univ London, 65-67; asst prof molecular biol, 67-72, ASSOC PROF MOLECULAR BIOL, VANDERBILT UNIV, 72-, ASSOC DEAN, 81- *Concurrent Pos:* NSF fel, 65-66; USPHS fel, 66-67. *Mem:* AAAS; Biophys Soc; Sigma Xi. *Res:* Macromolecular structure; biophysical chemistry; transition-metal complexes; x-ray diffraction; electron paramagnetic resonance. *Mailing Add:* Dept of Molecular Biol Vanderbilt Univ Nashville TN 37235

VENABLE, JOHN HOWARD, b Oklahoma City, Okla, Oct 16, 29; m 50; c 2. VETERINARY ANATOMY, HISTOLOGY. *Educ:* Okla State Univ, DVM, 53, MS, 56; Harvard Univ, PhD(anat), 65. *Prof Exp:* Instr vet anat, Okla State Univ, 54-56; from asst prof to prof, 56-71, prof physiol sci & head dept, 71-75; PROF ANAT & CHMN DEPT, COL VET MED & BIOMED SCI, COLO STATE UNIV, 76- *Concurrent Pos:* NSF sci fac fel, Harvard Med Sch, 61-62, univ res fel anat, 62-64; NIH res grant, 64-72. *Mem:* Am Vet Med Asn; Am Asn Anat; Am Asn Vet Anat. *Res:* Electron microscopy; autoradiography; anatomy and cytology of skeletal muscles. *Mailing Add:* Col of Vet Med & Biomed Sci Colo State Univ Ft Collins CO 80521

VENABLE, PATRICIA LENGEL, b Elyria, Ohio, Aug 6, 30; m 65; c 2. BOTANY. *Educ:* Col Wooster, BA, 52; Ohio State Univ, MSc, 54, PhD(bot), 63. *Prof Exp:* Instr bot, Hanover Col, 54-55; instr biol, Muskingum Col, 55-56 & Col Wooster, 56-60; vis instr bot & zool, Ohio State Univ, Lakewood Br, 62; assoc prof biol, State Univ NY Col Buffalo, 63-65 & Rider Col, 66-70; master biol, Lawrenceville Sch, 74-79; co-adj biol, Trenton State Col, 79-80; prog dir, Stony Brook-Millstone Watersheds Asn, 80-81; BIOL COORDR & TEACHER, PRINCETON DAY SCH, 81- *Mem:* AAAS; Bot Soc Am; Fern Soc. *Res:* Morphological and biosystematic work with vascular plants, especially ferns and the Compositae. *Mailing Add:* 10 Monroe Ave Lawrenceville NJ 08648

VENABLE, WALLACE STARR, b Wilkensburg, Pa, Apr 19, 40; m 62. ENGINEERING EDUCATION, ENGINEERING MECHANICS. *Educ:* Cornell Univ, BA, 62; Univ Toledo, MSES, 64; WVa Univ, EdD(eng educ), 72. *Prof Exp:* Instr, 66-72, lectr, 72-74, asst prof mech, 74-80, ASSOC PROF MECH & AEROSPACE ENG, WVA UNIV, 80- *Concurrent Pos:* Eng analyst, Hedenburg & Venable, 62- *Mem:* Am Soc Eng Educ; Am Soc Mech Engrs; Am Educ Res Asn; Nat Soc Prof Engrs. *Res:* Development and evaluation of educational methods and materials in engineering; accident analysis. *Mailing Add:* Box 125 Rte 13 Morgantown WV 26505

VENABLE, WILLIAM HOWELL, JR, optical physics, see previous edition

VENABLES, JOHN DUXBURY, b Cleveland, Ohio, Feb 6, 27; m 48; c 3. PHYSICS. *Educ:* Case Inst Technol, BS, 54; Univ Warwick, PhD, 71. *Prof Exp:* Physicist, Parma Res Ctr, Union Carbide Corp, 54-64; MGR, MAT & SURFACE SCI DEPT & PRIN SCIENTIST, MARTIN MARIETTA LABS, MARTIN MARIETTA CORP, 64- *Mem:* AAAS; Am Phys Soc; Electron Micros Soc Am; Am Inst Mining, Metall & Petrol Engrs. *Res:* Defect structure of solids; radiation effects in solids; ordering effects in transition metal carbides; high temperature ceramics; adhesive bonding; electron microscopy. *Mailing Add:* Martin Marietta Labs 1450 S Rolling Rd Baltimore MD 21227

VENARD, CARL ERNEST, b Marion, Ohio, Jan 10, 09; m 34; c 2. ZOOLOGY. *Educ:* Ohio State Univ, BA, 31, MSc, 32; NY Univ, PhD(helminth), 36. *Prof Exp:* Asst zool, Ohio State Univ, 32-34; asst biol, NY Univ, 34-36; from instr to prof zool & entom, 36-73, EMER PROF ZOOL & ENTOM, OHIO STATE UNIV, 73- *Mem:* Am Soc Parasitol; Entom Soc Am; Am Soc Zoologists. *Res:* Parasites of game birds and fishes; taxonomy and distribution of helminths; morphology of linguatulida; biology of fleas and mosquitoes. *Mailing Add:* 35 Indian Springs Dr Columbus OH 43214

VENDITTI, JOHN M, b Baltimore, Md, Feb 19, 27; m 51; c 3. PHARMACOLOGY, BIOCHEMISTRY. *Educ:* Univ Md, BS, 49, MS, 57; George Washington Univ, PhD(pharmacol), 65. *Prof Exp:* Biologist, 51-58, head screening sect, 63-66, CHIEF DRUG EVAL BR, NAT CANCER INST, 66-, PHARMACOLOGIST, 58- *Mem:* AAAS; Am Asn Cancer Res; Soc Exp Biol & Med; Am Soc Pharmacol & Exp Therapeut; NY Acad Sci. *Res:* Experimental cancer chemotherapy; biochemical and pharmacological actions of potential antitumor agents. *Mailing Add:* Drug Eval Br Nat Cancer Inst Bethesda MD 20014

VENEMA, GERARD ALAN, b Grand Rapids, Mich, Jan 26, 49; m 69; c 3. TOPOLOGY. *Educ:* Calvin Col, AB, 71; Univ Utah, PhD(math), 75. *Prof Exp:* instr math, Univ Tex, Austin, 75-77; mem, Inst Advan Study, Princeton, NJ, 77-79; asst prof, 79-81, ASSOC PROF MATH, CALVIN COL, 81- *Mem:* Am Math Soc; Math Asn Am. *Res:* Geometric topology and applications to shape theory. *Mailing Add:* Dept of Math Calvin Col Grand Rapids MI 49506

VENEMA, HARRY J(AMES), b Grand Rapids, Mich, July 28, 22; m 45; c 5. ELECTRICAL ENGINEERING. *Educ:* Univ Ill, BS, 44, MS, 47, PhD(elec eng), 50. *Prof Exp:* Asst, Elec Eng Lab, Univ Ill, 47-50; elec engr, Missile Guid Sect, Gen Elec Co, 50-53, elec engr, Magnetic Appln Sect, 53-56; mgr mil eng, Electronics Div, Stewart-Warner Corp, 56-59, ELECTRONIC RES, ROY C INGERSOLL RES CTR, BORG-WARNER CORP, 59- *Mem:* Sigma Xi; Inst Elec & Electronics Engrs. *Mailing Add:* Roy C Ingersoll Res Ctr Wolf & Algonquin Rds Des Plaines IL 60018

VENEMAN, PETER LOURENS MARINUS, b Oudenrijn, The Netherlands, Nov 27, 47; m 73. SOIL GENESIS, SOIL PHYSICS. *Educ:* State Agr Univ, Wageningen, BS, 72; Univ Wis, Madison, MS, 75, PhD(soils), 77. *Prof Exp:* Res asst soils, Univ Wis-Madison, 72-77; ASST PROF SOILS, UNIV MASS, AMHERST, 77- *Mem:* Am Soc Agron; Soil Sci Soc Am. *Res:* Formation, morphology and classification of spodosol soils, suitability rating of soils for the disposal of liquid wastes; suitability of soil for fruit production; lead and arsenic pesticide residues in soils. *Mailing Add:* Dept of Plant & Soil Sci Univ of Mass Amherst MA 01003

VENERABLE, JAMES THOMAS, b Cobden, Ill, Aug 24, 23; m 49; c 4. ORGANIC CHEMISTRY. *Educ:* Univ Ill, AB, 44; Univ Wis, PhD(org chem), 49. *Prof Exp:* Res & develop chemist, Mallinckrodt Chem Works, 49-53, mgt res, 53-56, proj leader prod develop, 56-59; res supvr org chem, Morton Chem Co, 59-65, supvr org, photog & anal res & develop, Info Servs & Tech Personnel, Morton Int, Inc, 65-71; assoc prof chem, Wilbur Wright Col, 71; PRES, RIVERVIEW ENTERPRISES, 71- *Concurrent Pos:* Partner, Thon's Garden Mums, Propagation Crysanthemums & Poinsettias. *Mem:* AAAS; Am Chem Soc; Sigma Xi. *Res:* Ketene acetals; pharmaceuticals; photographic chemicals; agricultural chemicals; thiocyanates and isothiocyanates; acridanes and polyphenols; plant tissue culture; water-proof writing materials. *Mailing Add:* 10425 Woodbine Lane Huntley IL 60142

VENETSANOPOULOS, ANASTASIOS NICOLAOS, b Athens, Greece, June 19, 41. ELECTRICAL ENGINEERING, COMMUNICATIONS. *Educ:* Nat Tech Univ, Athens, dipl elec & mech eng, 65; Yale Univ, MS, 66, MPh, 68, PhD(commun), 69. *Prof Exp:* Res asst, N V Phillips, Neth, 64; asst in instr, Yale Univ, 66-68, res asst, 68-69; lectr elec eng, 68-70, asst prof, 70-73, assoc prof, 73-81, chmn commun group, 74-78, assoc chmn dept, 78-79, PROF ELEC ENG & CHMN COMMUN GROUP, UNIV TORONTO, 81- *Concurrent Pos:* Consult, Elec Eng Consociates Ltd, 69-; Nat Res Coun Can fel, Univ Toronto, 69-; Defense Res Bd Can fel, 72-75. *Mem:* Inst Elec & Electronics Engrs; fel Eng Inst Can; Sigma Xi; AAAS; Can Soc Elec Engrs. *Res:* Digital signal processing; communication networks; channel modeling; signal design. *Mailing Add:* Dept Elec Eng Univ Toronto Toronto ON M5S 1A4 Can

VENEZIALE, CARLO MARCELLO, b Philadelphia, Pa, Oct 2, 32; m 59; c 2. BIOCHEMISTRY, ENDOCRINOLOGY. *Educ:* Haverford Col, BA, 54; Univ Pa, MD, 58; Univ Minn, MS, 64; Univ Wis, PhD(biochem), 69. *Prof Exp:* Intern, Grad Hosp, Univ Pa, 58-59; resident internal med, Mayo Clin, 61-64, staff asst metab & endocrinol, 64-65; instr biochem, 70-71, asst prof biochem & med, 71-74, assoc prof biochem & med, Mayo Grad Sch Med, Univ Minn, 74-78; PROF BIOCHEM & MED, MAYO MED SCH, 78- *Concurrent Pos:* Consult, Mayo Clin, 65 & 69-; vis prof, Dept Biochem, Univ Wis, 81-82. *Mem:* Am Diabetes Asn; Endocrine Soc; Am Soc Biol Chemists; Am Soc Andrology. *Res:* Regulation of carbohydrate metabolism; mechanisms of action of androgens. *Mailing Add:* Dept Cell Biol Mayo Med Sch Rochester MN 55905

VENEZIAN, GIULIO, b Torino, Italy, Dec 9, 38; m 68; c 2. HYDRODYNAMICS, APPLIED MECHANICS. *Educ:* McGill Univ, BEng, 60; Calif Inst Technol, PhD(eng sci), 65. *Prof Exp:* Res fel eng sci, Calif Inst Technol, 65-68; asst prof ocean eng, 68-72, ASSOC PROF OCEAN ENG, UNIV HAWAII, 72- *Res:* Rotating fluid dynamics; magnetohydrodynamics; classical physics; applications to geophysics; water waves; geophysical fluid dynamics. *Mailing Add:* 6370 Hawaii Kai Dr 29 Honolulu HI 96825

VENEZKY, DAVID LESTER, b Washington, DC, Sept 12, 24; m 50; c 2. INORGANIC CHEMISTRY. *Educ:* George Washington Univ, BS, 48; Univ NC, PhD(chem), 62. *Prof Exp:* Phys sci aide trace elements unit, US Geol Surv, 48-49; chemist, US Naval Res Lab, 49-55; instr chem, Univ NC, 58-60; asst prof inorg chem, Auburn Univ, 60-62; res chemist, 62-69, head reaction mechanism sect, Inorg Chem Div, 69-75, head solution chem sect, 75-81, HEAD INORG & ELECTROCHEM BR, US NAVAL RES LAB & ASSOC SUPT, CHEM DIV, 81- *Mem:* Am Chem Soc; Sigma Xi. *Res:* Coordination compounds and aggregation of inorganic substances in solutions; studies to elucidate the methods of preparation, structure and properties of inorganic polymers. *Mailing Add:* Code 6130 US Naval Res Lab Washington DC 20375

VENGRIS, JONAS, b Daglienai, Lithuania, Mar 26, 09; nat US; m 38; c 2. AGRONOMY. *Educ:* Dotnuva Agr Col, Lithuania, BS, 34, MS, 36; Univ Bonn, Dr agr sci, 39. *Prof Exp:* Asst field crops, Agr Col, Lithuania, 34-37, sr asst, 39-41, docent, 41-44; assoc prof, Baltic Univ, Ger, 46-49; from asst prof agron to assoc prof agron, 50-64, assoc prof plant & soil sci, 64-70, prof, 70-81, EMER PROF PLANT & SOIL SCI, UNIV MASS, AMHERST, 81- *Mem:* Weed Sci Soc Am; Int Weed Sci Soc. *Res:* Weed biology and control. *Mailing Add:* 29 Valley Lane Amherst MA 01002

VENHAM, LARRY LEE, b Akron, Ohio, June 24, 41; m 63; c 1. PEDODONTICS, PSYCHOLOGY. *Educ:* Ohio State Univ, DDS, 65, MS, 67, PhD(psychol), 72. *Prof Exp:* NIH fel, 67-69; asst prof, 70-78, ASSOC PROF DENT EDUC, HEALTH CTR SCH DENT MED, UNIV CONN, 78- *Concurrent Pos:* Am Inst Res Creative Talent Award, 72; Nat Inst Dent Res spec dent award, 75- *Mem:* Am Psychol Asn; Int Asn Dent Res; Soc Res Child Develop; Am Soc Dent Children. *Res:* Child development; situational stress, anxiety and coping behavior in response to dental stress; developmental factors in developing stress tolerance. *Mailing Add:* 390 Broad St Windsor CT 06095

VENIER, CLIFFORD GEORGE, b Trenton, Mich, June 17, 39; m 65; c 3. ORGANIC SULFUR CHEMISTRY, COAL CHEMISTRY. *Educ:* Univ Mich, BS, 62; Ore State Univ, PhD(org chem), 66. *Prof Exp:* Res assoc chem, Univ Tex, 66-67; asst prof chem, Tex Christian Univ, 67-74, assoc prof, 74-80; SR CHEMIST, AMES LAB, IOWA STATE UNIV, 80- *Concurrent Pos:* Vis assoc prof, Univ Nijmegen, Neth, 75. *Mem:* AAAS; Am Chem Soc; Royal Soc Chem; Sigma Xi. *Res:* Organic sulfur chemistry; reaction mechanisms; quantum organic chemistry. *Mailing Add:* Ames Lab Iowa State Univ Ames IA 50011

VENIT, STEWART MARK, b New York, NY, Apr 4, 46; m 72. MATHEMATICS. *Educ:* Queens Col, NY, BA, 66; Univ Calif, Berkeley, MA, 69, PhD(math), 71. *Prof Exp:* Asst prof, 71-77, assoc prof, 77-80, PROF MATH, CALIF STATE UNIV, LOS ANGELES, 80- *Mem:* Am Math Soc. *Res:* Numerical solution of partial differential equations. *Mailing Add:* Dept of Math Calif State Univ Los Angeles CA 90032

VENKATA, SUBRAHMANYAM SARASWATI, b Nellore, India, June 28, 42; Indian & US citizen; m 71; c 2. ELECTRICAL ENGINEERING. *Educ:* Andhra Univ, BSEE, 63; Indian Inst Technol, MSEE, 65; Univ SC, PhD(eng), 71. *Prof Exp:* Lectr elec eng, Coimbatore Inst Technol, 65-66; asst, Univ SC, 68-71; instr, Univ Lowell, 71-72; asst prof elec eng, WVa Univ, 72-75, assoc prof, 75-79; PROF ELEC ENG, UNIV WASH, 79- *Concurrent Pos:* Consult, SC Elec & Gas Co, 69-70; fel, Univ SC, 71; consult, Union Carbide Corp, 77-78. *Mem:* Inst Elec & Electronics Engrs; Am Soc Eng Educ; Sigma Xi; Nat Soc Prof Engrs. *Res:* Six-phase power transmission; mine power system safety; reliability, availability and optimum maintainability; energy conservation; digital and analog simulation of energy systems; electrical power distribution. *Mailing Add:* Dept of Elec Eng Univ Wash Seattle WA 98195

VENKATACHALAM, TARACAD KRISHNAN, b Cochin, India, Apr 28, 37. ORGANIC CHEMISTRY. *Educ:* Univ Bombay, BSc, 58, MSc, 62; Univ Louisville, PhD(chem), 65. *Prof Exp:* Res chemist, 65-69, SR RES CHEMIST, E I DU PONT DE NEMOURS & CO, INC, 69- *Mem:* Am Chem Soc; Indian Chem Soc; Royal Inst Chem. *Res:* Polymer technology; natural and synthetic resins; rubber chemistry; textile fibers; tire cord adhesion and processing; ropes and cables. *Mailing Add:* Indust Prod Res TRL Chestnut Run Wilmington DE 19898

VENKATARAGHAVAN, R, b Madras, India, June 29, 39. ANALYTICAL CHEMISTRY. *Educ:* Univ Madras, BSc, 58, MSc, 60; Indian Inst Sci, Bangalore, PhD(chem), 63. *Prof Exp:* Fel spectros, Nat Res Coun Can, 63-65; NIH res assoc mass spectros, Purdue Univ, Lafayette, 65-69; sr res assoc chem, Cornell Univ, 69-77; mem staff, Res Data Processing, Lederle Labs, Am Cyanamid Co, 77-80. *Concurrent Pos:* Consult, US Army Labs. *Mem:* AAAS; Am Chem Soc; Am Soc Mass Spectros. *Res:* Spectrochemistry; reaction kinetics; structural effects on infrared and ultraviolet spectra; instrumental effects on spectra; computer aided analytical techniques; structure-activity studies; artificial intelligence techniques. *Mailing Add:* Am Cyanamid Co Res Data Processing Lederle Labs Pearl River NY 10965

VENKATARAMIAH, AMARANENI, b Atmakur, India, Aug 16, 28; m 49; c 5. COMPARATIVE PHYSIOLOGY, MARINE ZOOLOGY. *Educ:* Andhra Univ, India, BSc, 55; Sri Venkateswara Univ, India, MSc, 57, PhD(exp ecol), 65. *Prof Exp:* Asst prof zool, Andhra Loyola Col, India, 57-61; asst prof, Sri Venkateswara Univ, India, 65-66; PHYSIOLOGIST & HEAD SECT PHYSIOL, GULF COAST RES LAB, 69- *Concurrent Pos:* Prin investr salinity problems coastal water fauna, Environ Br, US Army Corps, Washington, DC, 70-; prin investr toxicity & impingement-entertainment studies, Ocean Thermal Energy Conversion Plant, Dept Energy, Argonne, Ill. *Mem:* AAAS; Am Fisheries Soc; Am Soc Zoologists; World Mariculture Soc. *Res:* Osmoregulatory, metabolic and nutritional problems of commercial shrimps and prawns in relation to salinity, temperature and dissolved oxygen parameters; oceans; solar energy; heat exchangers; working fluid; biocides; toxicity to marine life. *Mailing Add:* Gulf Coast Res Lab PO Drawer AG Ocean Springs MS 39564

VENKATESAN, DORASWAMY, b Coimbatore, India. SPACE PHYSICS, ASTROPHYSICS. *Educ:* Loyola Col, Madras, India, BSc, 43; Benares Hindu Univ, MSc, 45; Gujarat Univ, India, PhD(cosmic rays), 55. *Prof Exp:* Lectr physics, K P Col, Allahabad, India, 47-48; lectr, Durbar Col, Rewa, 49; sr res asst cosmic rays, Phys Res Lab, Ahmedabad, 49-56; fel, Inst Electron Physics, Royal Inst Technol, Stockholm, 56-57; fel, Nat Res Coun Can, 57-60; res assoc space physics & astrophysics, Univ Iowa, 60-63, asst prof physics, 63-65, consult, High Altitude Balloon Prog, 65; assoc prof physics, Univ Alta, 65-66; assoc prof, 66-69, PROF PHYSICS, UNIV CALGARY, 69- *Mem:* Am Geophys Union; Can Asn Physicists; Can Astron Soc; fel Brit Inst Physics. *Res:* Solar terrestrial relations; astrophysics involving studies of cosmic rays, radiation belts, ionospheric absorption, auroral x-rays, geomagnetism, solar activity, cosmic x-ray sources and interplanetary medium. *Mailing Add:* Dept Physics Univ Calgary Calgary AB T2N 1N4 Can

VENKATESAN, THIRUMALAI, b Madras, India, June 19, 49; m 77. PHYSICS. *Educ:* Indian Inst Technol, Kharagpur, BS, 69, Kanpur, MS, 71; City Univ New York, PhD(physics), 77. *Prof Exp:* Mem tech staff, Optical Commun Res, 77-79, MEM STAFF, RADIATION PHYSICS RES, BELL LABS, 79- *Mem:* Sigma Xi; Am Inst Physics. *Res:* Ion solid interaction, ion beam lithography, germanium selenide resists, metal-insulatory transition; optical properties of semiconductors; optical nonlinear devices; optical communication systems and associated solid state and device physics; laser-solid interaction. *Mailing Add:* 1E 335 Bell Labs Murray Hill NJ 07974

VENKATU, DOULATABAD A, b Bangalore, India, July 31, 36; m 67; c 2. METALLURGY, CERAMICS. *Educ:* Univ Mysore, BSc, 55; Indian Inst Sci, Bangalore, Dipl, 58; Univ Notre Dame, MS, 61, PhD(metall eng & mat sci), 65. *Prof Exp:* Sr res asst metall, Indian Inst Sci, Bangalore, 58-59; res asst metall eng, Univ Notre Dame, 59-64; asst prof, Clemson Univ, 64-67; res assoc, Rensselaer Polytech Inst, 67-68; asst prof, Clemson Univ, 68-69; sr mat scientist, Owens-Ill Inc, 69-73; SR ENG SPECIALIST, GOODYEAR AEROSPACE CORP, 73- *Mem:* Am Soc Metals; Am Inst Mining, Metall & Petrol Engrs; Am Ceramic Soc. *Res:* Fatigue of metals; fracture mechanics; light metals technology; powder metallurgy; high temperature and technical ceramics. *Mailing Add:* 1278 Goldfinch Trail Stow OH 44224

VENKAYYA, VIPPERLA, b Raghudevapuram, Andhra, India, May 16, 31; m 65; c 1. STRUCTURAL ENGINEERING. *Educ:* Andhra Univ, BSc, 52; Indian Inst Technol, BTech, 56; Univ Mo, MS, 59; Univ Ill, Urbana, PhD(struct eng), 62. *Prof Exp:* Asst engr, Damodar Valley Corp, India, 56-57; bridge engr, State Hwy Dept, Pa, 58-59; asst prof struct eng, State Univ NY Buffalo, 62-67; AEROSPACE ENGR, FLIGHT DYNAMICS LAB, WRIGHT-PATTERSON AFB, 67- *Concurrent Pos:* Assoc ed, AIAA J, 78-; adj prof, Air Force Inst Technol, 78- *Mem:* Am Soc Civil Engrs; Am Inst Aeronaut & Astronaut. *Res:* Response of discrete and continuous elastic systems to static and dynamic disturbances, particularly civil and aeronautical structures; stability of elastic systems. *Mailing Add:* 5464 Honeyleaf Way Dayton OH 45424

VENKETESWARAN, S, b Alleppey, Kerala, India, July 21, 31. CELL BIOLOGY, BOTANY. *Educ:* Univ Madras, BSc, 50; Univ Bombay, MSc, 53; Univ Pittsburgh, PhD(bot), 61. *Prof Exp:* Demonstr biol, Jai Hind Col, Univ Bombay, 52-57; ed asst, Coun Sci & Indust Res, Govt India, 57-58; teaching fel & asst, Univ Pittsburgh, 59-61, res assoc, 61-62, instr biol, 62-63, NASA res assoc, 63-65; asst prof, 65-68, ASSOC PROF BIOL, UNIV HOUSTON, 68- *Concurrent Pos:* Am Cancer Soc instnl grant, Univ Pittsburgh, 65; consult & NASA res grant, Lunar Sample Receiving Lab, 66-75; vis scientist, Argonne Nat Lab, 67; NSF travel award, India, 80. *Mem:* AAAS; Bot Soc Am; Soc Develop Biol; Tissue Cult Asn; Am Soc Cell Biol. *Res:* Plant morphogenesis using tissue culture techniques; wood biomass as energy sources; forestry. *Mailing Add:* Dept Biol Univ Houston Houston TX 77004

VENNART, GEORGE PIERCY, b Boston, Mass, Apr 1, 26; m 51; c 3. PATHOLOGY. *Educ:* Wesleyan Univ, AB, 48; Univ Rochester, MD, 53. *Prof Exp:* Asst biol, Wesleyan Univ, 47-48; inetern intern & resident path, NC Mem Hosp, 53-56; asst prof, Col Physicians & Surgeons, Columbia Univ, 56-60; assoc prof path, Univ NC, 60-65; PROF PATH & CHMN DIV CLIN PATH, MED COL VA, 65-, CHMN DEPT PATH, 78- *Concurrent Pos:* Instr, Univ NC, 54-56; asst attend pathologist, Preby Hosp, New York, 56-60. *Res:* Experimental liver disease; platelet agglutination; pulmonary morphology and physiology. *Mailing Add:* Dept Clin Path Box 817 Med Col of Va Sta Richmond VA 23298

VENNES, JACK A, b Wheeler, Wis, June 12, 23. GASTROENTEROLOGY, INTERNAL MEDICINE. *Educ:* Univ Minn, BS, 47, MD, 51. *Prof Exp:* Intern med, Hennepin County Med Ctr, Minneapolis, 51-52; residency, Vet Admin Hosp, Minneapolis, 52-55; pvt pract, St Louis Park Med Ctr, Minneapolis, 57-63; staff physician gastroenterol, 64-67, asst chief med, 67-71, STAFF PHYSICIAN GASTROENTEROL, VET ADMIN HOSP, MINNEAPOLIS, 71- *Concurrent Pos:* Instr med, Univ Minn, 55-57, from asst prof to assoc prof, 65-76, prof med, 76- *Mem:* Am Gastroenterol Asn; Am Soc Gastrointestinal Endoscopy; Am Asn Study Liver Dis; Am Soc Clin Invest; Am Fedn Clin Res. *Res:* Development and applications of fiberoptic endoscopy to improved diagnosis in upper gastrointestinal tract, pancreas and biliary tree; treatment of gastrointestinal hemorrhage; non-surgical endoscopic removal of common duct gallstones; improved teaching methods of fiberoptic endoscopy. *Mailing Add:* Minneapolis Vet Admin Hosp 54th St & 48th Ave South Minneapolis MN 55417

VENNES, JOHN WESLEY, b Grenora, NDak, Aug 28, 24; m 48; c 3. BACTERIOLOGY. *Educ:* Univ NDak, BS, 51, MS, 52; Univ Mich, PhD(bact), 57. *Prof Exp:* Instr bact, Univ NDak, 52-54; asst, Univ Mich, 54-56; from instr to assoc prof, 56-66, actg dean, sch med, 73-75, assoc dean acad affairs, 73-77, PROF BACT, UNIV NDAK, 66-, CHMN, DEPT MICROBIOL, 81- *Mem:* Am Soc Microbiol. *Res:* Bacterial physiology and industrial microbiology. *Mailing Add:* Dept of Microbiol Univ of NDak Grand Forks ND 58201

VENNOS, MARY SUSANNAH, b Oct 14, 31; Can citizen; m 58; c 4. CHEMISTRY. *Educ:* Univ London, BSc, 53; Univ NB, Fredericton, PhD(chem), 56. *Prof Exp:* Instr chem, Univ NB, 56-59; from asst prof to assoc prof, Russell Sage Col, 59-70; assoc prof, 70-80, PROF CHEM, ESSEX COMMUNITY COL, BALTIMORE COUNTY, MD, 80- *Mem:* Am Chem Soc. *Res:* Analytical instrumentation; polarography and chemical kinetics. *Mailing Add:* One Milldale Ct Phoenix MD 21131

VENT, ROBERT JOSEPH, b Ford City, Pa, Feb 13, 40. UNDERWATER ACOUSTICS. *Educ:* San Diego State Univ, BS, 61, MS, 69. *Prof Exp:* Physicist underwater acoust, Navy Electronics Lab, 61-68; supv physicist, Naval Undersea Ctr, 68-77, RES PHYSICIST, ACOUST, NAVAL OCEAN SYSTS CTR, 77- *Mem:* Acoust Soc Am. *Res:* Underwater acoustics, especially attenuation, surface, bottom and volume scattering; applied ocean sciences. *Mailing Add:* Naval Ocean Systs Ctr Code 6352 San Diego CA 92132

VENTER, J CRAIG, b Salt Lake City, Utah, Oct 14, 46; m 81. PROTEIN CHEMISTRY, HYBRIDOMA TECHNOLOGY. *Educ:* Univ Calif, San Diego, BA, 72, PhD(physiol & pharmacol), 75. *Prof Exp:* Res assoc cardiovasc pharmacol, Univ Calif, San Diego, 75-76; asst prof pharmacol, 76-81, ASSOC PROF BIOCHEM, STATE UNIV NY, BUFFALO, 82- *Concurrent Pos:* Mem, Basic Sci Coun, Am Heart Asn. *Mem:* Am Soc Pharmacol & Exp Therapeut; AAAS. *Res:* Purification and molecular characterization of B-adrenergic and muscarinic acetylcholine receptors; production of monoclonal antibodies to each receptor. *Mailing Add:* Dept Biochem State Univ NY 102 Cary Hall Buffalo NY 14214

VENTRES, CHARLES SAMUEL, b Tucson, Ariz, Oct 21, 42. AERONAUTICAL ENGINEERING. *Educ:* Univ Ariz, BSME, 64; Princeton Univ, MA, 67, PhD(eng), 70. *Prof Exp:* Res assoc aeronaut eng, Princeton Univ, 69-70, mem res staff, 70-74; SR CONSULT, BOLT, BERANEK & NEWMAN, INC, 74- *Mem:* Am Inst Aeronaut & Astronaut; Acoust Soc Am. *Res:* Structural dynamics; aeroelasticity; acoustics; physical acoustics; aerodynamics. *Mailing Add:* Bolt Beranek & Newman Inc 50 Moulton St Cambridge MA 02138

VENTRICE, CARL ALFRED, b York, Pa, Aug 7, 30; m 60; c 3. PLASMA PHYSICS, NUCLEAR PHYSICS. *Educ:* Pa State Univ, BS, 56, MS, 58, PhD(physics), 62. *Prof Exp:* Sr analyst, Anal Serv Inc, 63-64; assoc prof physics, Tenn Technol Univ, 64-66; assoc prof elec eng, Auburn Univ, 66-68; PROF ELEC ENG, TENN TECHNOL UNIV, 68- *Mem:* AAAS; Inst Elec & Electronics Engrs; Am Phys Soc. *Res:* Interaction of electromagnetic waves in plasmas; plasma stability; lasers. *Mailing Add:* Dept Elec Eng Tenn Technol Univ Cookeville TN 38501

VENTRICE, MARIE BUSCK, b Allentown, Pa, Oct 17, 40; m 60; c 3. THERMAL & FLUID SCIENCES. *Educ:* Tenn Technol Univ, BSES, 66, PhD(mech eng), 74; Auburn Univ, MS, 68. *Prof Exp:* Instr eng sci, 69-70, asst prof, 74-79, ASSOC PROF MECH ENG, TENN TECHNOL UNIV, 79- *Mem:* Am Soc Mech Engrs; Am Soc Eng Educ; Nat Soc Professional Engrs; Sigma Xi; Am Inst Aeronaut & Astronaut. *Res:* Experimental studies of liquid propellant rocket combustion instabilities using an analog technique. *Mailing Add:* Dept of Mech Eng Tenn Technol Univ Cookeville TN 38501

VENTRIGLIA, ANTHONY E, b New York, NY, June 20, 22; m 53; c 2. ALGEBRA, APPLIED MATHEMATICS. *Educ:* Columbia Univ, AB, 42; Brown Univ, ScM, 43. *Prof Exp:* Instr math, Rutgers Univ, 47; from instr to asst prof, 47-61, ASSOC PROF MATH, MANHATTAN COL, 61- *Concurrent Pos:* Social Sci Res Fel, Stanford Univ, 57, instr, Hunter Col, 61-63; adj asst prof, City Col New York; NSF fel, Inst Math Teachers, Univ Wyo, 59. *Mem:* AAAS; Am Math Soc; Math Asn Am; Am Acad Polit & Soc Sci; Am Asn Univ Prof. *Res:* Linear algebra and analysis. *Mailing Add:* 1 Georgia Ave Bronxville NY 10708

VENTURA, JOAQUIN CALVO, b Cadiz, Spain, Mar 22, 29; Can citizen; m 61; c 2. PATHOLOGY. *Educ:* Univ Seville, MD, 52; Univ Montreal, PhD, 58; FRCP(C), 61. *Prof Exp:* SR LECTR PATH, UNIV MONTREAL, 58-; MEM STAFF, SANTA CABRINI HOSP, 71- *Concurrent Pos:* Chief serv & dir res, St Joseph of Rosemont Hosp, Montreal, 62-69; consult pathologist, Louis H LaFontaine Hosp, Montreal, 69- & Maisonneuve Rosemont Hosp, Montreal, 70-; assoc dir labs, Santa Cabrini Hosp, 69-70. *Mem:* Can Asn Path; NY Acad Sci; Can Med Asn. *Res:* Chronic bronchitis, role of sensitization; pathogenesis of bronchiectasis; effects of pollution on chronic experimental bronchitis. *Mailing Add:* Santa Cabrini Hosp 5655 St Zotique E Montreal PQ H1T 1P7 Can

VENTURA, SHARON MARIE, b Providence, RI, May 6, 44. BIOLOGY, ENDOCRINOLOGY. *Educ:* RI Col, AB, 72; Pa State Univ, MS, 74, PhD(biol), 78. *Prof Exp:* FEL ENDOCRINOL, MILTON S HERSHEY MED CTR, 79- *Mem:* AAAS. *Res:* Steroid hormone; receptor interactions and molecular events associated with hormonal control of gene expression. *Mailing Add:* 414 W Chocolate Ave Hershey PA 17033

VENTURA, WILLIAM PAUL, b Braddock, Pa, Dec 1, 42; m 69; c 1. PHARMACOLOGY. *Educ:* Duquesne Univ, BS, 64, MS, 66; New York Med Col, PhD(pharmacol), 69, Pace Univ, MBA, 80. *Prof Exp:* Res assoc endocrinol, Duquesne Univ, 66; from instr to asst prof pharmacol, New York Med Col, 69-74; assoc prof, 74-81, PROF PHARMACOL & SCI COORDR, GRAD SCH NURSING, PACE UNIV, 81- *Concurrent Pos:* Lalor Found grant, 70; NSF equip grant, 80. *Mem:* Am Physiol Soc; NY Acad Sci; Int Fertil Asn; Am Chem Soc; Am Col Clin Pharm. *Res:* Reproductive pharmacology, male and female reproductive studies. *Mailing Add:* 368 Elm Rd Briarcliff Manor NY 10510

VENUTI, WILLIAM J(OSEPH), b Philadelphia, Pa, Aug 16, 24; m 49; c 6. CIVIL ENGINEERING. *Educ:* Univ Pa, AB, 47; Univ Colo, BS, 50, MS, 55; Stanford Univ, PhD(civil eng), 63. *Prof Exp:* Civil engr, US Bur Reclamation, Colo & Mont, 49-52; instr civil eng, Univ Colo, 52-55; assoc prof, 55-63, PROF CIVIL ENG, SAN JOSE STATE UNIV, 63- *Concurrent Pos:* Sr design engr, Food Mach & Chem Corp, 56-; assoc, Boeing Airplane Co, 59; prof struct eng, SEATO Grad Sch Eng, Bangkok, Thailand, 64-66; vis prof, Stanford Univ, 70-71, 78- & Univ Dundee, 72; NSF int travel grant, India, 72. *Mem:* Fel Am Soc Civil Engrs; Am Soc Eng Educ; fel Concrete Inst; Am Rwy Eng Soc. *Res:* Lightweight prestressed concrete; framed structures; effects of impact loads on structures; fatigue of concrete; structural dynamics; blast loading and effects; prestressed concrete connectors; concrete railroad ties. *Mailing Add:* 16091 Greenwood Rd Monte Sereno CA 95030

VENUTO, PAUL B, b Flushing, NY, Feb 8, 33; m 58; c 3. PETROLEUM PROCESSING, PRODUCTION TECHNOLOGY. *Educ:* Univ Pa, AB, 54, PhD(org chem), 62. *Prof Exp:* Res & develop chemist, Columbian Carbon Co, 57-59; sr res chemist, Mobil Oil Corp, 62-66, group leader heterogeneous catalysis, 66-67, group leader appl res & develop div, 67-69, res assoc, Paulsboro Res Lab, 69-75, mgr anal & spec technol, Cent Res Lab, 75-77, MGR, HEAVY OILS & ENERGY MINERALS, FIELD RES LAB, MOBIL RES & DEVELOP CORP, 77- *Honors & Awards:* Ipatieff Award, Am Chem Soc, 71; Philadelphia Catalysis Club Award, 75. *Mem:* Am Chem Soc; Am Inst Chem Eng; Soc Petrol Engrs. *Res:* Organic heterogeneous catalysis; zeolite technology; process scoping and economics; catalysis in petroleum refining; uranium in-situ leaching; heavy oil and tar sands thermal recovery; petroleum production technology. *Mailing Add:* Mobil Res & Develop Corp Field Res Lab PO Box 900 Dallas TX 75221

VENZKE, WALTER GEORGE, b White Lake, SDak, June 18, 12; m 39; c 1. VETERINARY ANATOMY. *Educ:* Iowa State Col, DVM, 35, PhD(vet anat), 42; Univ Wis, MS, 37. *Prof Exp:* Asst genetics, Univ Wis, 35-37; instr vet anat, Iowa State Col, 37-41, asst prof, 41-42, vet physiol, 42; instr zool, 46, asst prof vet prev med, 46-48, assoc prof vet med, 48-53, PROF VET ANAT & HEAD DEPT, OHIO STATE UNIV, 54-, ASST DEAN & SECY, COL VET MED, 60- *Mem:* Am Vet Med Asn; Am Asn Anat; Conf Res Workers Animal Dis. *Res:* Endocrinology of the thymus and pineal gland. *Mailing Add:* 2535 Andover Rd Columbus OH 43221

VEOMETT, GEORGE ECTOR, b Rochester, NY, Aug 27, 44; m 70; c 4. CELL BIOLOGY. *Educ:* Univ Rochester, AB, 66; Univ Colo, PhD, 72. *Prof Exp:* Res assoc virol, Univ Colo, Boulder, 72-74, res assoc cell biol, 74-76; asst prof, 77-81, ASSOC PROF CELL BIOL, UNIV NEBR, 81- *Concurrent Pos:* Prin investr, Am Cancer Soc & NIH grants, 77- *Mem:* AAAS; Am Soc Cell Biol. *Res:* Control of cellular production of interferon and cellular responses to interferon; involvement of nuclear-cytoplasmic interactions in interferon system and cellular phenotype; mechanisms of cellular senescence. *Mailing Add:* 1031 N 78 Lincoln NE 68505

VERA, HARRIETTE DRYDEN, b Washington, Pa, Feb 22, 09. MEDICAL MICROBIOLOGY. *Educ:* Mt Holyoke Col, AB, 30; Yale Univ, PhD(bact), 38; Am Bd Microbiol, dipl. *Prof Exp:* Asst zool, Mt Holyoke Col, 30-31; teacher high sch, Conn, 31-37; from instr to asst prof physiol & hyg, Goucher Col, 38-43; res bacteriologist, Baltimore Biol Lab, 43-60; dir qual control lab prod, Becton, Dickinson & Co, 60-62, dir qual control, B-D Labs, Inc, 62-75; CONSULT, 75- *Concurrent Pos:* Vis lectr, Goucher Col, 46-51; consult, Becton, Dickinson & Co, 52-60 & US Dept Army, 56- *Honors & Awards:* Barnett L Cohen Award, Am Soc Microbiol, 63. *Mem:* Fel AAAS; fel Am Acad Microbiol; fel Am Pub Health Asn; Am Soc Microbiol; NY Acad Sci. *Res:* Bacterial morphology and physiology, especially nutrition. *Mailing Add:* Apt 414 204 E Joppa Rd Baltimore MD 21204

VERBANAC, FRANK, b Yugoslavia, Jan 12, 20; nat US; m 45; c 2. ORGANIC CHEMISTRY. *Educ:* Wayne State Univ, BS, 41; Univ Ill, PhD(chem), 49. *Prof Exp:* Chemist, Gelatin Prod Corp, 42-46 & Merck & Co, Inc, 49-57; sr res chemist, 57-60, group leader, 60-70, SR SCIENTIST, A E STALEY MFG CO, 70- *Mem:* AAAS; Am Chem Soc. *Res:* N-arylpyrazolines; antibiotics; natural products; carbohydrates; polymers; proteins. *Mailing Add:* 12 Dakota Dr Decatur IL 62526

VERBEEK, EARL RAYMOND, b Philadelphia, Pa, Mar 4, 48; m 69. STRUCTURAL GEOLOGY, MINERALOGY. *Educ:* Pa State Univ, BS, 69, PhD(struct geol), 75. *Prof Exp:* GEOLOGIST, STRUCT GEOL, US GEOL SURV, 74- *Mem:* Geol Asn Can. *Res:* Minor structures of deformed rocks; mechanics of folding, origin of joints in relation to consolidation history of rocks; luminescence spectroscopy of minerals. *Mailing Add:* US Geol Surv MS 913 Fed Ctr Denver CO 80225

VERBER, CARL MICHAEL, b New York, NY, May 20, 35; m 57; c 2. OPTICAL PHYSICS. *Educ:* Yale Univ, BS, 55; Univ Rochester, MA, 58; Univ Colo, PhD(physics), 61. *Prof Exp:* SR PHYSICIST, COLUMBUS LAB, BATTELLE MEM INST, 61- *Mem:* AAAS; Optical Soc Am; Soc Photo-Optical Instrumentation Engrs; Inst Elec & Electronics Engrs. *Res:* Interaction of intense light with solids; optical properties of solids; integrated optics; optical data processing. *Mailing Add:* Dept of Physics Battelle Mem Inst 505 King Ave Columbus OH 43201

VERBER, JAMES LEONARD, b De Pere, Wis, Sept 2, 25; m 60; c 5. PHYSICAL OCEANOGRAPHY. *Educ:* Univ Wis, BS, 49, MS, 50. *Prof Exp:* Instr climat, Ohio State Univ, 50-53; chief hydrographer, Ohio State Div Shore Erosion, 53-60; chief oceanographer, Fed Water Pollution Control Admin, US Dept Interior, 60-67; chief oceanographer, Northeast Marine Health Sci Lab, 67-68, CHIEF, NORTHEAST TECH SERVS UNIT, FOOD & DRUG ADMIN, USPHS, 68- *Mem:* Am Geophys Union; Am Soc Limnol & Oceanog; Marine Technol Soc; Nat Shellfisheries Asn; Int Soc Theoret & Appl Limnol. *Res:* Physical geography; climatology; physical limnology. *Mailing Add:* Northeast Tech Serv Bldg S-26 Food & Drug Admin USPHS Davisville RI 02854

VERBINSKI, VICTOR V, b Shickshinny, Pa, May 7, 22; m 58; c 5. NUCLEAR PHYSICS. *Educ:* Mass Inst Technol, SB, 48; Univ Pa, PhD(physics), 57. *Prof Exp:* Physicist, Gen Elec Co, 57-59, Oak Ridge Nat Lab, 59-67 & Gulf Gen Atomic, 67-74; mem staff, IRT Corp, 74-75; MEM STAFF, SCI APPLN, INC, 75- *Mem:* Am Phys Soc; Am Nuclear Soc. *Res:* Low energy nuclear physics; neutron spectroscopy; nuclear structure physics; photonuclear reactions and fission studies. *Mailing Add:* Sci Appln Inc 4030 Sorrento Valley Blvd San Diego CA 92037

VERBISCAR, ANTHONY JAMES, b Chicago, Ill, Mar 22, 29; m 59; c 3. ORGANIC CHEMISTRY. *Educ:* DePaul Univ, BS, 51; Univ Notre Dame, PhD(org chem), 55. *Prof Exp:* Res chemist, Hercules Powder Co, 54 & Argonne Cancer Res Hosp, Ill, 56-57; vpres res, Regis Chem Co, 57-63; fel, Univ Calif, Los Angeles, 64; PRES, ANVER BIOSCI DESIGN, 64- *Mem:* Am Chem Soc; Am Inst Chemists; Sigma Xi; AAAS; Plant Growth Regulator Soc Am. *Res:* Organic synthesis; medicinal chemistry; drug latentiation, reference standards, biosynthesis in microbial systems; natural products; biogenic amines indole chemistry; metabolism of foreign compounds; plant materials, jojoba, guayule and red aquill; radioactive techniques. *Mailing Add:* Anver Biosci Design Inc 160 E Montecito Ave Sierra Madre CA 91024

VERBIT, LAWRENCE, b Philadelphia, Pa, Dec 14, 35; c 2. ORGANIC CHEMISTRY. *Educ:* Col William & Mary, BS, 59; Bryn Mawr Col, MA, 61, PhD(org chem), 63. *Prof Exp:* USPHS res fel, Univ Calif, Berkeley, 63-64; asst prof org chem, 64-68, assoc prof, 68-76, PROF ORG CHEM, STATE UNIV NY BINGHAMTON, 77- *Concurrent Pos:* NIH grant, 66-72. *Mem:* AAAS; Am Chem Soc; Royal Soc Chem. *Res:* Asymmetric synthetic reactions; determination of molecular geometry by means of optical rotatory dispersion and circular dichroism; synthesis and properties of liquid crystals; science communication to public. *Mailing Add:* Dept of Chem State Univ of NY Binghamton NY 13901

VERBRUGGE, CALVIN JAMES, b Sioux Falls, SDak, July 26, 37; m 61; c 2. POLYMER CHEMISTRY. *Educ:* Calvin Col, BA, 59; Purdue Univ, PhD(org chem), 63. *Prof Exp:* sr res chemist, 63-80, RES ASSOC, S C JOHNSON & SON, INC, 80- *Mem:* Sigma Xi; Am Chem Soc. *Res:* Polymer Emulsion and solution polymerization and coatings therefrom. *Mailing Add:* Polymer Res Dept 1525 Howe St S C Johnson & Son Inc Racine WI 53403

VERBRUGGE, FRANK, b Chandler, Minn, Dec 22, 13; m 40; c 4. ACADEMIC ADMINISTRATION. *Educ:* Calvin Col, BA, 34; Univ Mo, MA, 40, PhD(physics), 42. *Prof Exp:* Instr physics, Univ Mo, 40-41; prof, Northeast Mo State Teachers Col, 41-43; from asst prof to prof, Carleton Col, 43-56; staff mem radiation lab, Mass Inst Technol, 44-46; assoc prof physics, 56-59, actg dean, 66-68, PROF PHYSICS, UNIV MINN, MINNEAPOLIS, 59-, ASSOC DEAN, INST TECHNOL, 59-, DIR, UNIV COMPUTER SERV, 68- *Concurrent Pos:* Consult, Ford Found Sci & Eng, Latin Am, 63-68. *Mem:* AAAS; Am Phys Soc; Am Asn Physics Teachers. *Res:* Absorption spectroscopy; enzyme and vitamin inactivation. *Mailing Add:* 1787 Shryer Ave W St Paul MN 55113

VERBY, JOHN E, b St Paul, Minn, May 24, 23; m 46; c 4. FAMILY MEDICINE, COMMUNITY HEALTH. *Educ:* Carleton Col, BA, 44; Univ Minn, MB, BS, MD, 47. *Prof Exp:* Physician, pvt family pract, Minn, 49-68; PROF FAMILY PRACT & COMMUNITY HEALTH, MED SCH, UNIV MINN, MINNEAPOLIS, 69- *Concurrent Pos:* Sci assoc, Mayo Clin, Rochester, Minn, 67-68. *Mem:* Int Soc Gen Med; Am Asn Family Pract; AMA. *Res:* Thyroid disease. *Mailing Add:* Dept of Family Pract & Community Health Mayo Med Sch Rochester MN 55901

VERCELLOTTI, JOHN R, b Joliet, Ill, May 2, 33; m; c 1. ORGANIC CHEMISTRY, BIOCHEMISTRY. *Educ:* St Bonaventure Univ, BA, 55; Marquette Univ, MS, 60; Ohio State Univ, PhD(chem), 63. *Prof Exp:* Asst chem, Marquette Univ, 58-60; fel Ohio State Univ, 60-63, lectr & vis res assoc, 63-64; asst prof, Marquette Univ, 64-67; asst prof, Univ Tenn, Knoxville, 67-70; assoc prof, Va Polytech Inst & State Univ, 70-74, prof biochem & Nutrit, 74-80. *Concurrent Pos:* Res chemist, Freeman Chem Corp, Wis, 59; consult, US Vet Hosp, Wood, Wis, 65-67 & Oak Ridge Nat Lab, 67-71; vis scientist, Ronzoni Inst, Milan Italy, 77-78. *Mem:* Am Chem Soc; The Chem Soc; Am Soc Biol Chem. *Res:* Biosynthesis and reactivity of glycoproteins and mucopolysaccharides; bacterial and fungal carbohydrate metabolism. *Mailing Add:* 215 E 4th Ave Covington LA 70433

VERCH, RICHARD LEE, b Wakefield, Mich, Feb 15, 37; m 66; c 1. AQUATIC BIOLOGY. *Educ:* Northland Col, BS, 62; Northern Mich Univ, MA, 66; Univ NDak, DA(biol), 71. *Prof Exp:* Asst prof biol, Bay de Noc Col, 66-69; asst prof, 71-75, ASSOC PROF BIOL & CHMN DIV NATURAL SCI, NORTHLAND COL, 75- *Mem:* Am Inst Biol Scientists; Nat Asn Biol Teachers; Nat Asn Sci Teachers. *Res:* Biology teaching, self study units. *Mailing Add:* Dept of Biol Northland Col Ashland WI 54806

VERDERBER, JOSEPH ANTHONY, b Cleveland, Ohio, Nov 30, 38; m 60; c 3. MECHANICAL ENGINEERING. *Educ:* Mass Inst Technol, BME & MME, 61. *Prof Exp:* Res assoc, Addressograph-Multigraph Corp, Ohio, 61-64, res supvr, 64-66, mgr res, 66-70; mgr eng, Varityper Div, 70-72, prod mgr, 72-77, dir advan develop, Multigraphics Div, 77-80, vpres advan bus develop, 80-81, vpres & gen mgr, Am ECRM, 81, PRES, AM VARITYPER, AM CORP, 82- *Concurrent Pos:* Lectr mech eng, Fenn Col, 62-67. *Mem:* Am Soc Mech Engrs. *Res:* Research and development in imaging systems, particularly electrostatic and lithographic systems; business equipment and electromechanical research; electrostatics and reprographic systems; phototypesetting systems. *Mailing Add:* 1800 W Central Rd Mt Prospect IL 60056

VERDERBER, NADINE LUCILLE, b St Louis, Mo, Jan 28, 40. MATHEMATICS EDUCATION. *Educ:* Wash Univ, AB, 62; Univ Mo, MA, 65; Ohio State Univ, PhD(math educ), 74. *Prof Exp:* Teaching asst math, Univ Mo, 63-64; instr, 65-74, asst prof, 74-80, ASSOC PROF MATH, SOUTHERN ILL UNIV, EDWARDSVILLE, 80- *Concurrent Pos:* Teaching asst, Ohio State Univ, 71-72. *Mem:* Nat Coun Teachers Math; Am Asn Univ Prof; Math Asn Am. *Res:* Mathematics education; readability of mathematics texts. *Mailing Add:* Dept of Math Statist & Comput Sci Southern Ill Univ Edwardsville IL 62026

VERDEYEN, JOSEPH T, b Terre Haute, Ind, Aug 15, 32; m 54; c 4. ELECTRICAL ENGINEERING, PLASMA PHYSICS. *Educ:* Rose Polytech Inst, BS, 54; Rutgers Univ, MS, 58; Univ Ill, Urbana, PhD(elec eng), 62. *Prof Exp:* Mem tech staff, Bell Tel Labs, 54-55 & 57; asst instr elec eng, Rutgers Univ, 57-58; from instr to assoc prof, 62-69, PROF ELEC & NUCLEAR ENG, UNIV ILL, URBANA, 69-, DIR, GASEOUS ELECTRONIC LAB, 72- *Concurrent Pos:* Mem tech staff, Stavid Eng, 57-58; mem awards comt, Nat Electronics Conf, 65; consult, Corps Engrs, 70-, Zenith Radio Corp, Chicago, 71-79, Gen Elec Lamp Div, 76- & Lucitron Inc, 79-81. *Mem:* Am Phys Soc; Inst Elec & Electronics Engrs. *Res:* Studies of laser discharges and plasmas used for semiconductor processing. *Mailing Add:* Dept of Elec Eng 607 E Healey Champaign IL 61820

VERDI, JAMES L, b New Haven, Conn, Aug 11, 41; m 63; c 2. PHYSIOLOGY. *Educ:* SConn State Col, BS, 63; Univ Nev, Reno, MS, 65, PhD(biochem & physiol), 71. *Prof Exp:* Instr physiol, New Haven Col, 65-66; assoc prof biochem, Univ Nev, Reno, 66-68; CLIN LAB DIR, VET ADMIN MED CTR, NV, 68-; ASSOC PROF, MED SCH, UNIV NEV, 78- *Concurrent Pos:* Consult, State Lab Syst, Nev, 78. *Mem:* Am Asn Clin Chem; Am Chem Soc; AAAS. *Res:* Immunocompetence in aging; nutrition in aging. *Mailing Add:* 39 E Quail St Sparks NV 89431

VERDIER, PETER HOWARD, b Pasadena, Calif, Feb 16, 31; m 53; c 1. PHYSICAL CHEMISTRY. *Educ:* Calif Inst Technol, BS, 52; Harvard Univ, PhD(phys chem), 57. *Prof Exp:* Res assoc chem, Mass Inst Technol, 57-58; res fel, Harvard Univ, 58-59; res chemist, Union Carbide Res Inst, 59-64, staff consult, 64-65; chemist, 65-70, chief molecular characterization sect, Polymers Div, 70-75, CHEMIST, NAT BUR STAND, 75- *Mem:* Am Phys Soc. *Res:* Chemical physics, especially molecular structure and dynamics; polymer solution properties; polymer chain dynamics; polymer molecular weight determination. *Mailing Add:* Nat Bur Stand Washington DC 20234

VERDINA, JOSEPH, b Palermo, Italy, Dec 7, 21; US citizen; m 60; c 2. MATHEMATICS. *Educ:* Univ Palermo, PhD(math), 49. *Prof Exp:* Prof physics, Harbor Col, Calif, 58-59; PROF MATH, CALIF STATE UNIV, LONG BEACH, 59- *Mem:* Math Asn Am; Ital Math Union. *Res:* Geometrical transformations; computer simulation. *Mailing Add:* Dept of Math Calif State Univ Long Beach CA 90804

VERDON, JOSEPH MICHAEL, b New York, NY, July 4, 41; m 63; c 3. FLUID MECHANICS, DYNAMICAL SYSTEMS. *Educ:* Webb Inst Naval Archit, BS, 63; Univ Notre Dame, MS, 65, PhD(eng sci), 67. *Prof Exp:* Res engr, United Aircraft Res Labs, 67-68; asst prof mech eng, Univ Conn, 68-72; sr res engr, 72-81, PRIN SCIENTIST, UNITED TECHNOL RES CTR, 81- *Concurrent Pos:* Consult, Pratt & Whitney Aircraft, 70-71. *Mem:* Am Soc Mech Engrs; Soc Indust & Appl Math; Am Inst Aeronaut & Astronaut; Sigma Xi; Am Acad Mech. *Res:* Unsteady aerodynamics, viscous flow, random vibrations; applied mathematics. *Mailing Add:* United Technol Res Ctr Silver Lane East Hartford CT 06108

VERDUIN, JACOB, b Orange City, Iowa, Nov 19, 13; m 42; c 5. PLANT PHYSIOLOGY. *Educ:* Iowa State Col, BS, 39, MS, 41, PhD(plant physiol), 47. *Prof Exp:* Instr bot, Iowa State Col, 41-42, instr plant physiol, 45-46; assoc prof bot & head dept, Univ SDak, 46-48; assoc prof hydrobiol, Franz Theodore Inst Hydrobiol, 48-55; prof biol & dept chmn, Bowling Green State Univ, 55-64; PROF BOT, SOUTHERN ILL UNIV, CARBONDALE, 64- *Concurrent Pos:* Consult, Commonwealth Edison, Chicago, 73- & Nat Environ Res Ctr, Environ Protection Agency, Nev, 75- *Mem:* AAAS; Ecol Soc Am; Am Soc Limnol & Oceanog; Am Fisheries Soc; Am Inst Biol Scientists. *Res:* Photosynthesis under natural conditions; respiration; diffusion problems; aquatic ecology. *Mailing Add:* Dept Bot Southern Ill Univ Carbondale IL 62901

VEREEN, LARRY EDWIN, b Loris, SC, Mar 24, 40. MICROBIOLOGY. *Educ:* Clemson Univ, BS, 63, MS, 64; Colo State Univ, PhD(microbiol), 68. *Prof Exp:* Asst prof food sci & biochem, Clemson Univ, 68-70; ASSOC PROF BIOL, LANDER COL, 70- *Mem:* Am Soc Microbiol. *Res:* Behavior of Clostridium perfringens in vacuum-sealed foods. *Mailing Add:* Dept of Biol Lander Col Greenwood SC 29646

VERELL, RUTH ANN, b New York, NY, Mar 8, 35; m 66; c 2. ORGANIC CHEMISTRY. *Educ:* Allegheny Col, BS, 57; Univ Ill, MS, 58; Columbia Univ, PhD(chem), 62. *Prof Exp:* Res chemist, Nat Bur Standards, 62-64; prof asst, 64-65, asst prog dir, Instrnl Sci Equip Prog, 65-68, assoc prog dir, Col Sci Improv Progs, 68-69 & 71-73, proj mgr exp projs & develop progs, NSF, 73-76, prof assoc, Energy Res & Develop Admin, 76-77; MEM PROF STAFF, US DEPT OF ENERGY, 77- *Mem:* AAAS; Am Chem Soc; Sigma Xi. *Res:* Cyclopropenones; alkaline conversions of labeled sugars. *Mailing Add:* 6215 Thornwood Dr Alexandria VA 22310

VERESS, SANDOR A, b Jaszkiser, Hungary, Mar 13, 27; US citizen; m 51; c 2. PHOTOGRAMMETRY, GEODESY. *Educ:* Univ Forestry & Timber Indust, Hungary, BS, 51; Hungarian Tech Univ, Sopron, MS, 56; Laval Univ, DSc(photogram), 68. *Prof Exp:* From instr to asst prof geod & photogram, Univ Forestry & Timber Indust, Hungary, 51-56; asst prof, Univ BC, 56-59; photogrammetrist, Ohio State Hwy Dept, 60-62; asst prof surv & mapping, Purdue Univ, 62-65; PROF CIVIL ENG, UNIV WASH, 65- *Concurrent Pos:* Consult to several pvt & fed photogram orgns, 61- *Mem:* Am Soc Civil Engrs; Am Cong Surv & Mapping; Am Soc Photogram. *Res:* Determination of structural deformations by photogrammetry; biomedical and x-ray photogrammetry. *Mailing Add:* Dept Civil Eng Univ Wash Seattle WA 98195

VERGANO, PETER JOSEPH, b New York, NY, Oct 30, 42; m 65; c 2. MATERIAL SCIENCE. *Educ:* Rutgers Univ, BS & BA, 65; Mass Inst Technol, DSc(mat sci), 69. *Prof Exp:* Sr scientist, Owens-Ill, Inc, 69-72, chief, Glass Sci Sect, 72-73, chief, Glass Technol Sect, 73-80; WITH BURCKWAY GLASS CO, INC, 80- *Mem:* Am Ceramic Soc; Soc Glass Technol. *Res:* Glass properties, composition, preparation; laser glasses. *Mailing Add:* Burckway Glass Co Inc McCullaugh Ave Burckway PA 15824

VERGARA, WILLIAM CHARLES, b Far Rockaway, NY, July 6, 23; m 46. ELECTRONIC ENGINEERING. *Educ:* Rensselaer Polytech Inst, BEE, 45. *Prof Exp:* Engr, Cardwell Mfg Corp, 46-48; proj engr, Commun Div, 48-53, prin engr, 53-58, dir advan res, 58-72, DIR PHYS ELECTRONICS, COMMUN DIV, BENDIX CORP, BALTIMORE, 72- *Concurrent Pos:* Mem, Gov Sci Adv Bd, State of Md, 66- *Mem:* Inst Elec & Electronics Engrs; Nat Asn Sci Writers. *Res:* Physics of thin films; microelectronics; radiowave propagation; radio receiver design. *Mailing Add:* 910 Dunellen Dr Towson MD 21204

VERGHESE, KURUVILLA, b Kottayam, India, June 29, 36; m 64; c 2. NUCLEAR ENGINEERING. *Educ:* Univ Kerala, BSc, 58; Univ Iowa, MS, 60, PhD(nuclear eng), 63. *Prof Exp:* From asst prof to assoc prof, 63-76, PROF NUCLEAR ENG, NC STATE UNIV, 76- *Concurrent Pos:* Consult, various industrial corps; grad adminr, NC State Univ, 76- *Mem:* Am Nuclear Soc. *Res:* Nuclear radiation effects in materials; reactor physics problems; radiation applications. *Mailing Add:* 2112 Burlington Eng Labs NC State Univ Raleigh NC 27607

VERGHESE, MARGRITH WEHRLI, b Davos, Switz, May 12, 39; m 64; c 3. GENETICS, IMMUNOGENETICS. *Educ:* Iowa State Univ, BS, 61, PhD(poultry breeding), 64. *Prof Exp:* Res asst poultry breeding, Iowa State Univ, 62-64; res assoc quant genetics, NC State Univ, 65-68; researcher biostatist, Univ NC, Chapel Hill, 68-69; RES ASSOC, DUKE UNIV, 75- *Honors & Awards:* Nat Res Serv Award, NIH, 75. *Mem:* AAAS; Am Asn Immunologists. *Res:* Quantitative genetics; selection theory for quantitative traits; interaction between artificial and natural selection in genetic populations; simulation of genetic populations; effects of murine anti-H-Z sera and human anti-DrW sera on the human mixed lymphocyte culture reaction; Con-A induced suppression in human cellular immune function. *Mailing Add:* 1228 Kingston Ridge Dr Cary NC 27511

VERGONA, KATHLEEN ANNE DOBROSIELSKI, b Pittsburgh, Pa, Dec 6, 48; m 73; c 1. CELLULAR AGING, PRIMARY LIVER CULTURE. *Educ:* Univ Pittsburgh, BS, 70, PhD(cell biol), 76. *Prof Exp:* Fel res assoc, Cancer Res Unit, Allegheny Gen Hosp, 76; fel, 77-79, RES ASST PROF, SCH MED, UNIV PITTSBURGH, 79-, ASST PROF HISTOL, SCH DENT MED, 76- *Mem:* Am Soc Cell Biol; Tissue Culture Asn; Sigma Xi; Am Asn Dent Res. *Res:* Hormonal regulation of hepatic microsomal glucose-6-phosphatase, in vivo and in primary cell cultures. *Mailing Add:* 627 Salk Hall Sch Med Univ Pittsburgh Pittsburgh PA 15261

VERHALEN, LAVAL MATHIAS, b Knox City, Tex, May 8, 41; m 64; c 2. PLANT BREEDING, PLANT GENETICS. *Educ:* Tex Tech Col, BS, 63; Okla State Univ, PhD(plant breeding, genetics), 68. *Prof Exp:* From instr to assoc prof agron, 67-77, PROF AGRON, OKLA STATE UNIV, 77- *Concurrent Pos:* Chmn, 26th Cotton Improv Conf, 73-74. *Mem:* Sigma Xi; Am Soc Agron; Crop Sci Soc Am. *Res:* Cotton breeding; genetics, particularly population genetics; variety testing; cultural practices. *Mailing Add:* Dept of Agron Okla State Univ Stillwater OK 74078

VERHANOVITZ, RICHARD FRANK, b Walsenburg, Colo, Sept 20, 44; m 67; c 2. THEORETICAL NUCLEAR PHYSICS, SYSTEMS ENGINEERING. *Educ:* Wilkes Col, BS, 66; Lehigh Univ, MS, 69, PhD(physics), 74. *Prof Exp:* Mathematician, Defense Intel Agency, Dept Defense, 66; engr, Univac, Sperry-Rand Corp, 66-67; SR PROGRAMMER, SPACE DIV, GEN ELEC CO, 75-, MGR SYSTS ENG, 80- *Mem:* Am Phys Soc; AAAS; NY Acad Sci; Opers Res Soc. *Res:* Low energy nuclear physics; two and three body interactions; charge symmetry and nuclear coulomb interactions; computer simulation and numerical analysis. *Mailing Add:* Valley Forge Space Ctr Gen Elec Box 8048 Philadelphia PA 19101

VERHEY, ROGER FRANK, b Grand Rapids, Mich, Sept 12, 38; m 60; c 4. MATHEMATICS. *Educ:* Calvin Col, AB, 60; Univ Mich, MA, 61, PhD(math), 66. *Prof Exp:* Lectr, 65-66, from asst prof to assoc prof, 66-72, chmn dept math & statist, 71-77, PROF MATH, UNIV MICH-DEARBORN, 72- *Concurrent Pos:* Fulbright lectr, Univ Ceylon, 69-70. *Mem:* Am Math Soc; Math Asn Am. *Res:* Immersions of the circle into the plane; extension of immersions to the disk from the point of view of the geometry of the image curve. *Mailing Add:* Dept of Math Univ of Mich Dearborn MI 48128

VERHEYDEN, JULIEN P H, b Brussels, Belg, May 22, 33; m 59; c 2. ORGANIC CHEMISTRY, MOLECULAR BIOLOGY. *Educ:* Free Univ Brussels, Lic en sci, 55, PhD(chem), 58. *Prof Exp:* Res assoc, Free Univ Brussels, 58-59; res assoc, Inst Sci Res Indust & Agr, Brussels, Belg, 60-61; fel, 61-63, res chemist, 63-72, head bio-org dept, Syntex Inst Molecular Biol, 70-77, head dept, Syntex Inst Org Chem, 77-81, HEAD DEPT CHEM, SYNTEX INST BIO-ORG CHEM, 81- *Mem:* Am Chem Soc; Chem Soc Belg; Royal Soc Chem. *Res:* Carbohydrates; nucleosides; nucleotides; genetic engineering. *Mailing Add:* Syntex Inst of Bio-Org Chem 3401 Hillview Ave Palo Alto CA 94304

VERHOEK, FRANK HENRY, b Grand Rapids, Mich, Feb 12, 09; m 40; c 3. PHYSICAL CHEMISTRY, CHEMICAL KINETICS. *Educ:* Harvard Univ, SB, 29; Univ Wis, MS, 30, PhD(phys chem), 33; Oxford Univ, DPhil(phys chem), 35. *Prof Exp:* Asst chem, Univ Wis, 29-33; Rhodes scholar, Copenhagen Univ, 35-36; from instr to assoc prof chem, 36-53, supvr res found, 42-65, vchmn dept chem, 60-64 & 66-68, PROF CHEM, OHIO STATE UNIV, 53- *Concurrent Pos:* Res chemist, Gen Elec Co, 38; res assoc, Stanford Univ, 40; consult, Liberty Mirror Div, Libby-Owens-Ford Glass Co, 43-52; prin chemist, Argonne Nat Lab, 47; sr chemist, Olin Mathieson Chem Corp, 55; consult, US Naval Weapons Ctr, 57-62; vis prof, Univ Fla, 58-59; lectr chem bond approach proj, NSF, 59-68; Rhodes scholar, 33-35. *Mem:* Am Chem Soc. *Res:* Solution kinetics; gas kinetics; complex ion equilibria; strength of acids in nonaqueous solvents; solubility of electrolytes in nonaqueous solvents; hydrocarbon oxidation; oxidation of boron alkanes. *Mailing Add:* Dept of Chem Ohio State Univ 140 W 18th Ave Columbus OH 43210

VERHOEK, SUSAN ELIZABETH, b Columbus, Ohio; m. BOTANY, BIOSYSTEMATICS. *Educ:* Ohio Wesleyan Univ, BA, 64; Ind Univ, MA, 66; Cornell Univ, PhD(bot), 75. *Prof Exp:* Herbarium supvr, Mo Bot Garden, 66-70; ASST PROF BIOL, LEBANON VALLEY COL, 74- *Mem:* Am Soc Plant Taxon; Bot Soc Am; Int Asn Plant Taxon; Soc Econ Bot. *Res:* Biosystematics, economic botany, floristics, hybridization and pollination of tribe Polianthеae (Agavaceae). *Mailing Add:* Dept Biol Lebanon Valley Col Annville PA 17003

VERHOEVEN, JOHN DANIEL, b Monroe, Mich, Aug 26, 34; m 62; c 5. METALLURGY. *Educ:* Univ Mich, BS, 57, MS, 59, PhD(metall eng), 63. *Prof Exp:* From asst prof to assoc prof, 63-69, PROF METALL, IOWA STATE UNIV, 69- *Mem:* Am Soc Metals; Am Inst Mining, Metall & Petrol Engrs; Metals Soc; Am Asn Crystal Growth. *Res:* Solidification in metals and metal alloys; physical metallurgy; superconducting alloys. *Mailing Add:* 104 Metall Bldg Iowa State Univ Ames IA 50011

VERHOOGEN, JOHN, b Brussels, Belg, Feb 1, 12; nat US; wid; c 4. GEOPHYSICS. *Educ:* Free Univ Brussels, MinEng, 33; Univ Liege, GeolEng, 34; Stanford Univ, PhD(volcanol), 36. *Prof Exp:* Asst geol, Free Univ Brussels, 36-39; Nat Sci Res Found fel, Belg, 39-40; chief prospecting serv, Kilo-Moto Gold Mines, Congo, 40-43; engr, Belg Congo Govt, 43-46; from assoc prof to prof geol, 47-77, EMER PROF GEOL, UNIV CALIF BERKELEY, 77- *Concurrent Pos:* Guggenheim fel, 53-54, 61. *Honors & Awards:* Day Medal, Geol Soc Am, 58; Day Prize, Nat Acad Sci, 78. *Mem:* Nat Acad Sci; fel Geol Soc Am; fel Am Acad Arts & Sci; fel Am Geophys Union. *Res:* Paleomagnetism; thermodynamics of geologic phenomena; volcanology. *Mailing Add:* Dept Geol & Geophys Univ Calif Berkeley CA 94720

VERINK, ELLIS D(ANIEL), JR, b Peking, China, Feb 9, 20; US citizen; m 42; c 2. METALLURGICAL ENGINEERING. *Educ:* Purdue Univ, BS, 41; Ohio State Univ, MS, 63, PhD(metall eng), 65. *Prof Exp:* Engr, Aluminum Co Am, 46-48, mgr chem sect, Develop Div, 48-59, mgr chem & petrol indust sales, 59-62; assoc prof metall, 65-68, asst chmn dept metall & mat eng, 70-73, PROF METALL, UNIV FLA, 68-, CHMN MAT SCI & ENG DEPT, 73- *Concurrent Pos:* Consult, Aluminum Asn, 67-; pres, Mat Consult, Inc. *Mem:* Am Inst Mining, Metall & Petrol Engrs; fel Am Soc Metals; Am Welding Soc; Nat Asn Corrosion Engrs; Nat Soc Prof Engrs. *Res:* Corrosion; materials selection; metal forming. *Mailing Add:* Dept of Mat Sci & Eng Univ of Fla Gainesville FL 32611

VERITY, MAURICE ANTHONY, b Bradford, Eng, Apr 21, 31; c 3. PATHOLOGY, NEUROPATHOLOGY. *Educ:* Univ London, MB, BS, 56. *Prof Exp:* Intern surg, Paddington Gen Hosp, London, Eng & Portsmouth Group Hosps, 56; intern med, Royal Hosp, Wolverhampton, 57; clin pathologist, United Bristol Hosps, 58-59; vis asst prof pharmacol, 59-60, assoc resident path, Sch Med, 60-61, assoc prof, 68-74, PROF PATH, SCH MED, UNIV CALIF, LOS ANGELES, 74-, MEM, BRAIN RES INST, 67- *Concurrent Pos:* NIH travel award, Int Neuropath-Neurol Cong, Europe, 65 & 70; NIH fel biochem, Med Sch, Bristol Univ, 68-69; Milheim Found grant, Sch Med, Univ Calif, Los Angeles, 70-71, USPHS grant, 71-74. *Mem:* AAAS; Am Soc Exp Path; Am Asn Pathologists & Bacteriologists; for mem Royal Soc Med; Brit Biochem Soc. *Res:* Biochemical and histochemical studies of subcellular organelle function in pathologic states, including mercury intoxication, partial hepatectomy; investigations of neurogenic control of vascular smooth muscle; thyroid hormone modulation of brain development. *Mailing Add:* Dept of Path Univ of Calif Med Ctr Los Angeles CA 90024

VERKADE, JOHN GEORGE, b Chicago, Ill, Jan 15, 35; div; c 3. BIOINORGANIC CHEMISTRY, ORGANOMETALLIC CHEMISTRY. *Educ:* Univ Ill, BS, 56, PhD(inorg chem), 60; Harvard Univ, AM, 57. *Prof Exp:* From instr to assoc prof, 60-70, PROF INORG CHEM, IOWA STATE UNIV, 70- *Concurrent Pos:* Grants, NSF, 61-, Petrol Res Found, 63-66 & NIH, 72-78; Sloan fel, 66-68. *Mem:* Am Chem Soc. *Res:* Spectroscopic studies of coordination compounds containing phosphorus ligands; catalytic studies of transition metal compounds hypervalent non metallic compounds; stereospecific reactions of phosphorus compounds. *Mailing Add:* Dept of Chem Iowa State Univ Ames IA 50010

VERKHOVSKY, BORIS SAMUEL, systems analysis, computer science, see previous edition

VERLANGIERI, ANTHONY JOSEPH, b Newark, NJ, Aug 2, 45; m 67; c 3. BIOCHEMISTRY, TOXICOLOGY. *Educ:* Rutgers Univ, BS, 68; Pa State Univ, PhD(biochem), 73. *Prof Exp:* Asst biochem, Pa State Univ, 68-72; ASST PROF TOXICOL, COOK COL, RUTGERS UNIV, 72- *Concurrent Pos:* Consult toxicologist, Nutrit Int, Inc, 74- *Mem:* Am Col Vet Toxicol; Am Chem Soc. *Res:* Effects of sulfating agents on atherogenesis and the influence of lead intoxication on the central nervous system, behavior and learning; sulfated glycosaminoglycans, analytical methods, role in atherogenesis; endothelial cell culture model systems. *Mailing Add:* Dept of Animal Sci Cook Col Rutgers Univ New Brunswick NJ 08903

VERLEUR, HANS WILLEM, b Hillegom, Holland, July 1, 32; US citizen; m 56; c 4. PHYSICS, MATERIAL SCIENCE. *Educ:* Cooper Union, BS, 63; NY Univ, MS, 64, PhD(physics), 66. *Prof Exp:* SUPVR DISPLAY DEVELOP GROUP, BELL LABS, 60- *Res:* Optoelectronic device research. *Mailing Add:* Bell Labs 2525 N 12th St Reading PA 19604

VERLEY, FRANK A, b Kingston, Jamaica, Dec 18, 33; m 67. GENETICS. *Educ:* Univ Conn, BS, 59; Univ Ill, Urbana, MS, 60, PhD(genetics), 64. *Prof Exp:* Resident res assoc radiation genetics, Argonne Nat Lab, 64-67; from asst prof biol genetics to assoc prof biol genetics, 67-74, PROF BIOL GENETICS, NORTHERN MICH UNIV, 74- *Mem:* Genetics Soc Am; Am Inst Biol Sci; Am Genetics Asn; Biomet Soc Am. *Res:* Genetic effects of a recessive sex-linked lethal gene on prenatal development in mice, copper metabolism in the mottled mice and biosynthesis of metallothionein in mice. *Mailing Add:* 33 West Sci Bldg Dept of Biol Northern Mich Univ Marquette MI 49855

VERMA, DEEPAK KUMAR, b India. METALS PROCESSING, FRACTURE MECHANICS. *Educ:* Bihar Inst Technol, India, BS, 67; Univ Mass, MSME, 70; Ga Inst Technol, PhD(mech eng), 79. *Prof Exp:* Trainee engr, Hindustan Motors Ltd, India, 67-68; res fel mech eng, Univ Mass, 68-71; tech asst, Tata Steel Ltd, India, 71-73; tech exec, Texmaco Ltd, India, 73-74; teaching fel mat eng, Ga Inst Technol, 74-78; res develop engr, Southwire Corp, Ga, 78-80; STAFF ENGR, IBM CORP, 80- *Mem:* Am Soc Mech Engrs; Am Soc Metals; Soc Mfg Engrs; Nat Soc Prof Engrs. *Res:* Processing of metals with emphasis on structure-property relationships, fracture behavior, machining, metal forming, casting, heat treatment, surface finishing, welding and brazing. *Mailing Add:* Dept 573/004-1 IBM Corp Rochester MN 55901

VERMA, DEVI C, b Barsalu-Haryana, India, Apr 30, 46. AGRICULTURAL BIOCHEMISTRY. *Educ:* Punjab Agr Univ, BS, 68; Univ Calif, Davis, MS, 70; State Univ NY Buffalo, PhD(plant biochem), 75. *Prof Exp:* Fel plant tissue cult, W Alton Jones Cell Sci Ctr, 75-78; SR RES FEL, INST PAPER CHEM, 78- *Mem:* Am Soc Plant Physiologists; Int Asn Plant Tissue Cult. *Res:* Biochemistry of cellular differentiation; cell wall formation and development in plant tissue cultures; gymnosperm tissue culture; propagation of forest tree species by tissue culture. *Mailing Add:* Inst of Paper Chem PO Box 1039 Appleton WI 54911

VERMA, GHASI RAM, b Sigari, India, Aug 1, 29; m 54; c 3. APPLIED MATHEMATICS. *Educ:* Birla Eng Col, India, BA, 50; Benaras Hindu Univ, MA, 54; Univ Rajasthan, India, PhD(math), 57. *Prof Exp:* Tutor math, Birla Eng Col, India, 54-57, lectr, 57-58; fel, Courant Inst Math Sci, NY Univ, 58-59; asst prof, Fordham Univ, 59-61; reader, Birla Inst Technol & Sci, India, 61-64; assoc prof, 64-80, PROF MATH, UNIV RI, 80- *Concurrent Pos:* Sr sci res fel, Coun Sci & Indust Res, New Delhi, India, 55-57. *Mem:* Am Math Soc; Math Asn Am; Soc Indust & Appl Math. *Res:* Elasticity; fluid mechanics. *Mailing Add:* Dept of Math Univ of RI Kingston RI 02881

VERMA, PRAMODE KUMAR, b Barauli, India, Sept 1, 41; Can citizen; m 66; c 1. ELECTRICAL ENGINEERING, COMMUNICATION ENGINEERING. *Educ:* Patna Univ, BSc hons, 59; Indian Inst Sci, BEng, 62; Sir George Williams Univ, DEng(elec eng), 70. *Prof Exp:* Sr res asst elec commun eng, Indian Inst Sci, 62-64; asst div engr commun, Indian Posts & Tel, 64-67; asst prof elec eng & comput sci, Sir George Williams Univ, 71; supv engr comput commun, Bell Can, 72-78; mem tech staff comput commun,

Bell Labs, 78-80; DIST MGR, AM TEL & TEL, 80- *Concurrent Pos:* Lectr, Univ Ottawa, 75-78. *Mem:* Sr mem Inst Elec & Electronics Engrs; Commun Soc. *Res:* Computer networks; communication networks. *Mailing Add:* Am Tel & Tel Rm 5322 B1 295 N Maple Ave Basking Ridge NJ 07920

VERMA, RAM D, b May 31, 29; Can citizen; m 62; c 2. SPECTROSCOPY. *Educ:* Univ Agra, BSc, 52, MSc, 54, PhD(physics), 58. *Prof Exp:* Lectr physics, DAV Col, Aligarh, 54-55; res asst, Aligarh Muslim Univ, India, 55-57, sr res fel, 57-58; res assoc, Univ Chicago, 58-61; fel Nat Res Coun Can, 61-63; from asst prof to assoc prof, 63-71, PROF PHYSICS, UNIV NB, 71- *Concurrent Pos:* Can deleg, Int Conf Spectros, 67; vis prof, Univ Calif, Santa Barbara, Univ Stockholm & Bhabha Atomic Res Ctr, Bombay, India. *Mem:* Am Phys Soc; Can Asn Physicists. *Res:* Molecular structure and spectra of stable and free radicals; investigation covering region from near infrared to far ultraviolet. *Mailing Add:* Dept of Physics Univ of NB Fredericton NB E3B 5A3 Can

VERMA, SADANAND, b Muzaffarpur, India, Jan 24, 30. ALGEBRA, TOPOLOGY. *Educ:* Patna Univ, BSc, 50; Univ Bihar, MSc, 52; Wayne State Univ, MS & PhD(math), 58. *Prof Exp:* Hon lectr math, L S Col, Univ Bihar, 52-53, lectr univ, 53-55 & 58-60; asst prof, Univ Windsor, 60-65; assoc prof, Western Mich Univ, 65-67; PROF MATH, UNIV NEV, LAS VEGAS, 67-, CHMN DEPT, 68- *Mem:* Math Asn Am; Can Math Cong; Asn Comput Mach. *Res:* Algebraic topology; homotopy theory; elementary number theory; magnetohydrodynamics; general topology; elementary ordinary differential equations. *Mailing Add:* Dept of Math Univ of Nev Las Vegas NM 89154

VERMA, SURENDRA KUMAR, b India, Jan 1, 43; m 75. CHEMICAL ENGINEERING. *Educ:* Agra Univ, India, BSc, 61; Indian Inst Technol, Kharagpur, BTech, 65; Univ Louisville, MS, 70, PhD(chem eng), 74. *Prof Exp:* Mech engr, Shriram Fertilizers & Chem, India, 65-68; res assoc mech eng, Univ Louisville, 70; res assoc, Universal Restoration, Washington, DC, 73-74; SR RES ENGR TECH CTR, UNION CARBIDE CORP, 74- *Mem:* Am Inst Chem Engrs; Sigma Xi. *Res:* New separation techniques development for energy conservation and process improvement. *Mailing Add:* 5315 Pamela Circle West Gate Charleston WV 25312

VERME, LOUIS JOSEPH, b New York, NY, Jan 24, 24; m 57; c 2. WILDLIFE BIOLOGY, ECOLOGY. *Educ:* Mich State Univ, BS, 50, MS, 53. *Prof Exp:* Fishery aide, US Fish & Wildlife Serv, 51; game biologist, 53-65, GAME RES BIOLOGIST, MICH DEPT NATURAL RESOURCES, 65- *Mem:* Wildlife Soc; Am Soc Mammal. *Res:* Relation of nutrition to reproduction, growth and physiology of deer; habitat quality and management; environmental resistances. *Mailing Add:* Cusino Wildlife Res Sta Shingleton MI 49884

VERMEERSCH, JOYCE ANN, nutrition, community health, see previous edition

VERMEIJ, GEERAT JACOBUS, b Sappemeer, Neth, Sept 28, 46; m 72; c 1. EVOLUTIONARY BIOLOGY, BIOGEOGRAPHY. *Educ:* Princeton Univ, AB, 68; Yale Univ, MPhil, 70, PhD(biol), 71. *Prof Exp:* From instr to asst prof 71-74, assoc prof, 74-80, PROF ZOOL, UNIV MD, COLLEGE PARK, 80- *Concurrent Pos:* J S Guggenheim Mem fel, 75. *Mem:* Soc Study Evolution; Ecol Soc Am; Soc Am Naturalists; Paleont Soc; Neth Malacol Soc. *Res:* Comparative ecology and history of shallow-water benthic marine communities; adaptive morphology, especially molluscs and decapods; temporal patterns of adaptation. *Mailing Add:* Dept of Zool Univ of Md College Park MD 20742

VERMEULEN, CARL WILLIAM, b Chicago, Ill, July 23, 39; div; c 2. MICROBIOLOGY, BIOCHEMISTRY. *Educ:* Hope Col, AB, 61; Univ Ill, Urbana, MS, 63, PhD(microbiol), 66. *Prof Exp:* Asst prof microbiol & biochem, 66-71, ASSOC PROF MICROBIOL & BIOCHEM, COL WILLIAM & MARY, 71- *Concurrent Pos:* Desert soils mapping. *Mem:* Fel Am Inst Chemists; Royal Soc Chem London. *Res:* Microbial genetics; biochemical contributions to soil genesis. *Mailing Add:* Dept Biol Col William & Mary Williamsburg VA 23185

VERMEULEN, THEODORE (COLE), b Los Angeles, Calif, May 7, 16; m 39; c 2. CHEMICAL ENGINEERING, CATALYSIS WATER TECHNOLOGY. *Educ:* Calif Inst Technol, BS, 36, MS, 37; Univ Calif, Los Angeles, PhD(chem), 42. *Prof Exp:* Jr chem engr, Union Oil Co, 37-39; asst chem, Univ Calif, Los Angeles, 39-41; chem engr, Shell Develop Co, 41-47; assoc prof chem eng, 47-51, chmn div, 52-53, Miller res prof, 59-60, PROF CHEM ENG, UNIV CALIF, BERKELEY, 51-, DIR WATER TECHNOL CTR, 80- *Concurrent Pos:* Consult, Lawrence Berkeley Lab, 47-, Savannah River Lab, E I du Pont de Nemours & Co, 61-67, US Borax Res Corp, 63-67, Upjohn Co, 67-71, Teknekron, Inc, 71-76 & Exxon Res & Eng, 80-; Fulbright prof, Univ Liege & Ghent, 53; vis prof, French Petrol Inst, 54, Nat Univ Mex, 67 & South China Inst Technol, 81; consult & dir, Memorex Corp, 63-81; Guggenheim fel, Cambridge Univ, 64; res assoc, Scripps Inst Oceanog, 70-71. *Honors & Awards:* W H Walker Award, Am Inst Chem Engrs, 71. *Mem:* Am Nuclear Soc; fel Am Inst Chem Engrs; Am Chem Soc; Am Inst Aeronaut & Astronaut; Am Water Works Asn. *Res:* Water purification and recovery; magnetochemistry and coal liquefication; multicomponent thermodynamics and diffusion; homogeneous and heterogeneous catalysis; chemical kinetics and reactor design; liquid extraction; agitation and fluidization; ion exchange; adsorption; interfacial phenomena; atmospheric modeling. *Mailing Add:* Dept of Chem Eng Univ of Calif Berkeley CA 94720

VERMILLION, ROBERT EVERETT, b Kingsport, Tenn, Aug 17, 37; m 63; c 2. PHYSICS. *Educ:* King Col, AB, 59; Vanderbilt Univ, MS, 61, PhD(physics), 65. *Prof Exp:* Asst prof physics, 65-70, assoc prof, 70-77, PROF PHYSICS, UNIV NC, CHARLOTTE, 77- *Mem:* Am Phys Soc; Am Asn Physics Teachers. *Res:* Electric shock-tube production of plasmas; techniques and apparatus for teaching undergraduate physics; experimental plasma physics. *Mailing Add:* Dept of Physics Univ of NC at Charlotte Sta Charlotte NC 28223

VERMILYEA, BARRY LYNN, b Dayton, Ohio, Dec 17, 41; m 65; c 2. FOOD SCIENCE, MICROBIOLOGY. *Educ:* Univ Wyo, BS, 64; Iowa State Univ, MS, 67, PhD(food sci), 69. *Prof Exp:* Sr scientist food sci, Gen Mills Inc, 69-70; develop mgr food sci, Cargill Inc, 70-71; TECH MGR FOOD SCI, INT MULTIFOODS INC, 71- 71- *Mem:* Inst Food Technol. *Res:* New foods products, processes and packaging concepts for retail, industrial and institutional areas. *Mailing Add:* Int Multifoods Inc 9449 Sci Ctr Dr New Hope MN 55428

VERMILYEA, D(AVID) A(UGUSTUS), b Troy, NY, Oct 11, 23; m 50; c 3. METALLURGY. *Educ:* Rensselaer Polytech Inst, PhD(metall), 53. *Prof Exp:* Instr, Rensselaer Polytech Inst, 48-51; chemist, 51-58, mgr, Chem Metall Sect, Res Lab, 58-59, metallurgist, Phys Chem Lab, Gen Elec Co, 59-74; energy analyst, Energy Sci & Eng Sector, 74-78, CONSULT, RES & DEVELOP STRATEGIC ANAL, GEN ELEC RES & DEVELOP CTR, 78- *Honors & Awards:* Whitney Award, Nat Asn Corrosion Engrs, 75; Acheson Award. *Mem:* Am Chem Soc; Electrochem Soc. *Res:* Oxidation of metals; crystal growth; electrochemistry; corrosion. *Mailing Add:* 2505 Whamer Lane Schenectady NY 12309

VERMUND, HALVOR, b Norway, Aug 8, 16; nat US; m 43; c 2. RADIOLOGY. *Educ:* Univ Oslo, MD, 43; Univ Minn, PhD(radiol), 51. *Prof Exp:* Fel, Halden Munic & Vestfold County Hosps, Norway, 44-48; Picker Found fel radiol, Univ Minn, 51-53, res assoc radiol, 53, from asst prof to assoc prof, 54-57; prof radiol & dir radiation ther, Univ Wis-Madison Hosps, 57-68; PROF RADIOL & DIR RADIOTHER RES & DEVELOP, UNIV CALIF, IRVINE, 68- *Concurrent Pos:* Mem radiation study sect, NIH, 65-69; mem comt diag & ther of cancer, Am Cancer Soc; mem staff, Norweg Radiumhosp, Oslo, Norway, 78- *Mem:* Fel Am Col Radiol; Soc Exp Biol & Med; Am Radium Soc; Radiol Soc NAm; Am Roentgen Ray Soc. *Res:* Radiation therapy; medical radiology; radioactive isotopes. *Mailing Add:* 19151 Sierra Maria Irvine CA 92715

VERNA, JOHN E, b Everett, Mass, Oct 8, 29; m 54; c 4. BIOLOGY. *Educ:* Northeastern Univ, BS, 52; Univ RI, MS, 54; Brown Univ, PhD(biol), 57. *Prof Exp:* From instr to asst prof microbiol, Med Sch, Univ Minn, 57-65; head, Cell Biol & Viral Oncol Br, Melpar, Inc, Va, 65-70; vpres biosci & bio prod div, 70-74, VPRES & GEN MGR, BIOSCI DIV, MELOY LABS, INC, 74- *Mem:* Am Soc Microbiol; NY Acad Sci. *Res:* Virology, bacteriology, immunology and cancer biology. *Mailing Add:* Meloy Labs Inc 6715 Electronic Dr Springfield VA 22151

VERNADAKIS, ANTONIA (MRS H L OCKERMAN), b Canea, Crete, Greece, May 11, 30; m 61. DEVELOPMENTAL NEUROBIOLOGY. *Educ:* Univ Utah, BA, 55, MS, 57, PhD(anat, pharmacol), 61. *Prof Exp:* Res assoc & res instr anat & pharmacol, Univ Utah Col Med, 61-64; interdisciplinary training prog fel pharmacol, Univ Calif Sch Med, San Francisco Med Ctr, 64-65; asst res physiologist, Univ Calif, Berkeley, 65-67; asst prof, 67-70, assoc prof, 70-78, PROF PSYCHIAT & PHARMACOL, UNIV COLO SCH MED, 78- *Concurrent Pos:* Res scientist develop award, NIMH, 69-79. *Mem:* Am Soc Pharmacol & Exp Therapeut; Am Physiol Soc; Am Neurochem Soc; Int Soc Neurochem; Int Soc Psychoneuroendocrinology. *Res:* Regulatory mechanisms in brain maturation; drugs and hormones; neurotransmission maturation; neural cell growth and differentiation using neural cell culture. *Mailing Add:* Univ of Colo Sch of Med 4200 E Ninth Ave Denver CO 80220

VERNAZZA, JORGE ENRIQUE, b Buenos Aires, Arg, Jan 16, 43; US citizen; m 73; c 2. SOLAR PHYSICS, PLASMA PHYSICS. *Educ:* Univ Buenos Aires, Licenciate, 67; Harvard Univ, PhD(astron), 72. *Prof Exp:* Res fel astron, Harvard Univ, 72-74, res assoc, 74-80; MEM STAFF, LAWRENCE LIVERMORE NAT LAB, 80- *Mem:* Am Astron Soc. *Res:* Solar physics; radiative transfers, data processing and plasma physics. *Mailing Add:* Lawrence Livermore Nat Lab L-481 PO Box 5508 Livermore CA 94550

VERNBERG, FRANK JOHN, b Fenton, Mich, Nov 6, 25; m 45; c 3. MARINE BIOLOGY, PHYSIOLOGICAL ECOLOGY. *Educ:* DePauw Univ, AB, 49, MA, 50; Purdue Univ, PhD(zool), 51. *Prof Exp:* From instr to prof zool, Duke Univ, 51-69, asst dir res, 58-63, asst dir marine lab, 63-69; BARUCH PROF MARINE BIOL & DIR BELLE W BARUCH COASTAL RES INST, UNIV SC, 69- *Concurrent Pos:* Guggenheim fel, 57-58; Fulbright-Hayes res award, Brazil, 65; lectr, Univs Kiel & Sao Paulo; mem comt manned orbital res lab, Am Inst Biol Sci, 66-; dir int biol prog-prog exp anal, Biogeog of the Sea, Nat Acad Sci, 67-69; consult, Environ Protection Agency, 74- *Honors & Awards:* Russell Award, 77. *Mem:* AAAS; Estuarine Res Fedn (pres, 75-77); Am Soc Zoologists (pres, 82); Ecol Soc Am. *Res:* Physiological ecology of marine animals; distribution of decapod crustacea; tissue metabolism; mechanisms of temperature acclimation; physiological diversity of latitudinally separated populations. *Mailing Add:* Belle W Baruch Inst Univ of SC Columbia SC 29208

VERNEKAR, ANANDU DEVARAO, b Hosali, India, July 5, 32; m 59; c 3. METEOROLOGY. *Educ:* Univ Poona, BSc, 55, BSc, 56, MSc, 59; Univ Mich, MS, 63, PhD(meteorol), 66. *Prof Exp:* Sci asst meteorol, Upper Air Sect, India Meteorol Dept, 56-61; res scientist, Travelers Res Ctr, Inc, 67-69; asst prof, 69-73, assoc prof, 73-78, PROF METEOROL, UNIV MD, COLLEGE PARK, 78- *Mem:* AAAS; Am Geophys Union; Am Meteorol Soc. *Res:* Dynamical meteorology; general circulation; theory of climate and statistical meteorology. *Mailing Add:* Dept Meteorol Univ Md College Park MD 20742

VERNER, JAMES HAMILTON, b Hitchin, Eng, Feb 22, 40; Can citizen; m 64; c 3. MATHEMATICS. *Educ:* Queen's Univ, Ont, BSc, 62, MSc, 65; Univ Edinburgh, PhD(comput sci), 69. *Prof Exp:* Lectr math, Royal Mil Col Can, 63-64; External Aids Off teaching adv, Umuahia, Eastern Nigeria, 64-66; res assoc, 69-72, asst prof, 72-77, ASSOC PROF MATH, QUEENS UNIV, ONT, 77- *Concurrent Pos:* Hon lectr math, Univ of Auckland, NZ, 75-76. *Mem:* Soc Indust & Appl Math. *Res:* Numerical analysis, especially numerical solution of initial value problems for ordinary differential equations. *Mailing Add:* Dept Math & Statist Queen's Univ Kingston ON K7M 2M8 Can

VERNER, JARED, b Baltimore, Md, Aug 16, 34; m 58; c 3. ANIMAL ECOLOGY. *Educ:* Wash State Univ, BS, 57; La State Univ, MS, 59; Univ Wash, PhD(zool), 63. *Prof Exp:* Res assoc zool, Univ Calif, Berkeley, 63-65; from asst prof to prof biol, Cent Wash State Col, 65-73; PROF BIOL, ILL STATE UNIV, 73-, ADJ PROF ECOL, 77- *Concurrent Pos:* NSF fel, 63-65, res grant, 66-71. *Mem:* Am Ornith Union; Cooper Ornith Soc; Wilson Ornith Soc; Soc Study Evolution; Ecol Soc Am. *Res:* Evolution and natural selection; avian social organization and communication systems; avian population ecology. *Mailing Add:* Dept of Biol Ill State Univ Normal IL 61761

VERNICK, SANFORD H, pathobiology, see previous edition

VERNIER, ROBERT L, b El Paso, Tex, July 29, 24; m 45; c 4. PEDIATRICS. *Educ:* Univ Dayton, BS, 48; Univ Cincinnati, MD, 52. *Prof Exp:* Clin fel pediat, Univ Ark, 52-54; clin fel pediat, Univ Minn, 54-55, USPHS res fel, 55-57, Am Heart Asn res fel, 57-59; asst prof pediat & Am Heart Asn estab investr, Med Sch, Univ Minn, 59-65; prof, Sch Med, Univ Calif, Los Angeles, 65-68; PROF PEDIAT, MAYO MED SCH, UNIV MINN, 68- *Mem:* AAAS; Am Soc Clin Invest; Am Soc Exp Path; Soc Pediat Res; affil Royal Soc Med. *Res:* Clinical pediatrics; renal disease in childhood; electron microscopy in the kidney. *Mailing Add:* Dept Pediat Mayo Med Sch Univ Minn Box 491 Minneapolis MN 55455

VERNIER, VERNON GEORGE, b Norwalk, Conn, Nov 14, 24; m 55; c 4. PHARMACOLOGY. *Educ:* Univ Ill, BS, 47, MD, 49. *Prof Exp:* Intern, Res & Educ Hosp, Univ Ill, 49-50, res assoc pharmacol, Med Col, 50-51, instr, 51-52; res assoc, Sharpe & Dohme, Inc, 52-54; res assoc physiol, Merck Inst Therapeut Res, 56-63; mgr pharmacol sect, Stine Lab, 63-74, DIR PHARMACOL, E I DU PONT DE NEMOURS & CO, INC, 74- *Concurrent Pos:* Lectr, Sch Med, Temple Univ, 56-66, vis prof, 66- *Mem:* AAAS; Am Soc Pharmacol & Exp Therapeut; Am Col Neuropsychopharmacol; NY Acad Sci. *Res:* Neuropsychopharmacology; psychopharmacology; toxicology. *Mailing Add:* E I du Pont de Nemours & Co Stine Lab PO Box 30 Newark DE 19711

VERNIKOS, JOAN, b Alexandria, Egypt, May 9, 34; m 78; c 2. ENDOCRINE PHARMACOLOGY, STRESS AND COPING. *Educ:* Univ Alexandria, BPharm, 55; Univ London, PhD(pharmacol), 60. *Prof Exp:* Muelhaupt scholar, Ohio State Univ, 60-61, asst prof pharmacol, Col Med, 61-64; res assoc, 64-66, chief human studies br, 72-76, actg dep dir, life sci, 76, actg asst div chief, Biomed Res Div, 81-82, RES SCIENTIST, AMES RES CTR, NASA, 66- *Concurrent Pos:* Assoc ed, Pharmcol Reviews, 77-81; hon clin prof pharmacol, Sch Med, Wright State Univ, Ohio, 75-81. *Honors & Awards:* NASA Medal for Except Sci Achievement, 73. *Mem:* Endocrine Soc; Soc Exp Biol & Med; Am Physiol Soc; Am Soc Pharmacol & Exp Therapeut; Int Brain Res Orgn. *Res:* Stress and the environmental, behavioral and physiological factors that affect the stress response including weightlessness and inactivity; mechanisms regulating pituitary-adrenal function, fluids, electrolytes drug/stress and pain stress interactions. *Mailing Add:* Ames Res Ctr Biomed Res Div NASA Moffett Field CA 94035

VERNON, CARL WAYNE, b Alamosa, Colo, Oct 29, 39; m 58; c 2. ELEMENTARY PARTICLE PHYSICS, PROTEIN CRYSTALLOGRAPHY. *Educ:* Univ Wash, BPhys, 61; Princeton Univ, PhD(physics), 66. *Prof Exp:* Univ Wash, BPhys, 61; asst prof, 66-74, assoc prof, 74-80, PROF PHYSICS, UNIV CALIF, SAN DIEGO, 80- *Res:* Cosmic ray and deep inelastic scattering muons; electron-positron colliding beam physics; x-ray detectors for crystallography. *Mailing Add:* Dept of Physics Univ Calif San Diego La Jolla CA 92093

VERNON, EUGENE HAWORTH, b Mesilla Park, NMex, June 27, 01; m 41; c 4. ANIMAL BREEDING. *Educ:* Iowa State Col, BS, 23, MS, 48, PhD(animal breeding), 50. *Prof Exp:* Animal husbandman & supt-in-chg, Iberia Livestock Exp Farm, USDA, 50-58, animal husbandman, Animal Husb Res Div, 58-65; animal sci adv, NC State AID Mission to Peru, 65-68; dir Guyana Prog, 68-70, EMER PROF ANIMAL SCI, SCH AGR, TUCKEGEE INST, 70- *Mem:* Fel AAAS; Am Genetic Asn. *Res:* Effects of inbreeding on sex ratios and on mortality in swine; crossbreeding of beef cattle. *Mailing Add:* 811 N Maple St Tuskegee AL 36083

VERNON, FRANK LEE, JR, b Dallas, Tex, Sept 16, 27; m 50; c 3. LOW TEMPERATURE PHYSICS, QUANTUM PHYSICS. *Educ:* Southern Methodist Univ, BS, 49; Univ Calif, Berkeley, MS, 52; Calif Inst Technol, PhD(elec eng, physics), 59. *Prof Exp:* Asst recorder geophys prospecting, Tex Co, 49-50; head, Sect Microwave Physics, Hughes Aircraft Co, 51-61; SR STAFF SCIENTIST LOW TEMPERATURE & QUANTUM PHYSICS, AEROSPACE CORP, 61- *Concurrent Pos:* Res fel physics, Calif Inst Technol, 59-60. *Mem:* Am Phys Soc; Inst Elec & Electronics Engrs; Sigma Xi; AAAS. *Res:* Experimental and theoretical investigations in the fields of low temperature, microwave and quantum physics including superconductors, lasers and the interaction of electron tunneling mechanisms with high frequency radiation. *Mailing Add:* 1560 Knollwood Terr Pasadena CA 91103

VERNON, GREGORY ALLEN, b Akron, Ohio, July 27, 47. PHYSICAL CHEMISTRY. *Educ:* Pa State Univ, BS, 69; Univ Ill, MS, 71, PhD(chem), 75. *Prof Exp:* Res anal chemist, Atomic Int Div, Rockwell Int, 75-80; RES CHEMIST, CHINA LAKE NAVAL WEAPONS CTR, 80- *Mem:* Am Chem Soc. *Res:* Detonation physics; thermal hazards; decomposition kinetics. *Mailing Add:* 2006 Mitscher Ridgecrest CA 93555

VERNON, JACK ALLEN, b Kingsport, Tenn, Apr 6, 22; m 45; c 2. PSYCHOPHYSIOLOGY. *Educ:* Univ Va, BA, 48, MA, 50, PhD, 52. *Prof Exp:* From instr psychol to prof psychol, Princeton Univ, 52-66; dir audition lab, 66-76, PROF OTOLARYNGOL, MED SCH, UNIV ORE, 66- *Concurrent Pos:* Consult, Nat Acad Sci, 59- *Mem:* AAAS; Am Acad Otocaryngol; Asn Res Otolaryngol (pres, 77). *Res:* Sensory processes, especially audition and tinnitus. *Mailing Add:* Kresge Hearing Res Lab 3181 SW Sam Jackson Park Rd Portland OR 97201

VERNON, JOHN ASHBRIDGE, b Camden, NJ, Jan 19, 40; m 62; c 3. ORGANIC CHEMISTRY. *Educ:* Rutgers Univ, BS, 61; Univ Md, PhD(org chem), 65. *Prof Exp:* Asst chem, Univ Md, 61-63, Gillette Harris res fel org chem, 63-64; res chemist, E I du Pont de Nemours & Co, Inc, 65-70; plant mgr, Pioneer Labs, Chesebrough-Ponds, Inc, 71-73; mgr labs, Vick Mfg Div, 73-77, QUAL ASSURANCE MGR, VICKS HEALTH CARE DIV, RICHARDSON-VICKS, INC, 77- *Mem:* Am Chem Soc. *Res:* Reactions of organic compounds over alumina; synthesis and reaction of azides; heterocyclic compounds; synthesis of liquid crystals. *Mailing Add:* Box V Hatboro PA 19040

VERNON, LEO PRESTON, b Roosevelt, Utah, Oct 10, 25; m 46; c 5. BIOCHEMISTRY. *Educ:* Brigham Young Univ, BA, 48; Iowa State Col, PhD, 51. *Prof Exp:* Fel, Enzyme Inst, Univ Wis, 51-52; res assoc, Washington Univ, 52-54; assoc prof chem, Brigham Young Univ, 54-61; dir, C F Kettering Res Lab, Kettering Found, Ohio, 61-70; dir res, Brigham Young Univ, 70-74, asst acad vpres res, 74-81; VPRES, BILLINGS ENERGY CORP, 81- *Concurrent Pos:* Researcher, Nobel Inst, Stockholm, Sweden, 60-61. *Mem:* Am Soc Biol Chem; Am Soc Plant Physiol. *Res:* Photosynthesis; cytochrome chemistry; respiratory enzymes. *Mailing Add:* Billings Energy Corp 186000 E 37th Terrace S Independence MO 64057

VERNON, LONNIE WILLIAM, b Dallas, Tex, Mar 16, 22; m 49; c 3. PHYSICAL CHEMISTRY, FUEL SCIENCE. *Educ:* Rice Univ, BA, 48, MA, 50, PhD(chem), 52. *Prof Exp:* SR RES ASSOC, EXXON RES & ENG CO, 52- *Mem:* Am Chem Soc. *Res:* Coal conversion processes; surface chemistry; catalysis. *Mailing Add:* 5017 Ashwood Dr Baytown TX 77521

VERNON, MINA LEE, b Winters, Tex, Apr 12, 27. ANATOMY. *Educ:* Tex State Col Women, BS, 49; Univ Okla, MS, 55, PhD(anat), 58. *Prof Exp:* Jr clerk, Dallas Chem Warfare Procurement Div, Eighth Serv Command, US Dept Army, 44-45; chief technician, Tissue Lab, Univ Hosp, Baylor Univ, 49-54, vis teaching fel, Col Dent, 53-54; asst, Univ Okla, 54-56; USPHS fel, Nat Cancer Inst, 56-58; chief electron micros lab, Hazelton Labs, Inc, 58-68; HEAD ELECTRON MICROS LAB, MICROBIOL ASSOCS, INC, BETHESDA, MD, 68-, PROJ DIR, 68- *Mem:* Am Soc Microbiol; Am Asn Cancer Res; AAAS; Electron Micros Soc Am; NY Acad Sci. *Res:* Histology; cytology; electron microscopy; ultrastructural studies related to viral-chemical oncology and slow latent virus diseases. *Mailing Add:* Grosvenor Park 11-Apt 827 10500 Rockville Pike Rockville MD 20852

VERNON, RALPH JACKSON, b Greenville, SC, Apr 6, 20; m 47; c 3. OCCUPATIONAL HEALTH, SAFETY ENGINEERING. *Educ:* Clemson Univ, BS, 50; Tex A&M Univ, MEd, 51; Univ Iowa, PhD(prev med, environ hyg), 68. *Prof Exp:* Instr safety, Tex A&M Univ, 51-53; safety engr, Liberty Mutual Ins Co, 53-60, loss prev mgr, 60-66; prof eng technol & indust eng, 68-77, PROF INDUST ENG, TEX A&M UNIV, 77-, HEAD INDUST HYG & SAFETY ENG DIV, 68- *Concurrent Pos:* Vpres, Hill, Stocker, Vernon & Assocs, 70-; mem, Bd Cert Safety Prof. *Mem:* Human Factors Soc; Am Inst Indust Engrs; Am Indust Hyg Asn; Am Conf Govt Indust Hyg; Am Pub Health Asn. *Res:* Occupational diseases; accident causation; noise; biodynamics and resulting effects on performance decrement. *Mailing Add:* Dept of Indust Eng Tex A&M Univ College Station TX 77840

VERNON, ROBERT CAREY, b Wilmington, Ohio, Feb 7, 23; m 49; c 2. SOLID STATE PHYSICS. *Educ:* Bates Col, BS, 47; Wesleyan Univ, MA, 49; Pa State Univ, PhD(physics), 52. *Prof Exp:* Asst physics, Pa State Univ, 49-52; instr, Williams Col, 52-54, lectr, 54-55, asst prof, 55-58; asst prof, Clarkson Col Technol, 58-60, assoc prof, 60-61; chmn dept physics, 61-72, PROF PHYSICS, SIMMONS COL, 61- *Mem:* Am Phys Soc; Am Asn Physics Teachers; Geol Soc Am. *Res:* Imperfections in nearly perfect crystals; optical properties of semiconductors. *Mailing Add:* Dept of Physics Simmons Col Boston MA 02115

VERNON, RONALD J, b Chicago, Ill, June 3, 36; m 71. ELECTRICAL ENGINEERING. *Educ:* Northwestern Univ, BS, 59, MS, 61, PhD(elec eng), 65. *Prof Exp:* From asst prof to assoc prof, 65-77, PROF ELEC ENG, UNIV WIS-MADISON, 77- *Concurrent Pos:* NSF res grants, 66 & 68. *Mem:* Inst Elec & Electronics Engrs. *Res:* Electromagnetic field theory; microwave engineering; microwave interaction with solids; semiconductor physics. *Mailing Add:* Dept of Elec Eng Univ of Wis Madison WI 53706

VERNON, RUSSEL, b Chicago, Ill, May 5, 30; m 52; c 4. PLASMA PHYSICS, NUCLEAR ENGINEERING. *Educ:* Univ Chicago, PhB, 48, MS, 51; Univ Calif, Los Angeles, PhD(plasma physics), 60. *Prof Exp:* From physicist to sr tech specialist, Atomics Int Div, NAm Aviation, Inc, 54-67; mem tech staff, Bellcomm, Inc, 67-68, supvr flight exp, 68-72; MEM TECH STAFF SERV ECON DEPT, BELL LABS, 72- *Concurrent Pos:* Guest scientist, Swiss Fed Inst Reactor Res, 62-63. *Mem:* Am Phys Soc. *Res:* Applied mathematics; space applications; plasma physics; software systems; applied statistics. *Mailing Add:* Serv Econ Dept Bell Tel Labs Murray Hill NJ 07974

VERNON, WILLIAM W, b Concord, NH, Nov 1, 25; m 51; c 1. GEOLOGY, ARCHAEOLOGY. *Educ:* Univ NH, BA, 52; Lehigh Univ, MS, 55, PhD, 64. *Prof Exp:* Civil engr, Dept Pub Rds & Hwys, NH, 52-53; geologist, US Geol Surv, 56-57; from asst prof to assoc prof geol, 57-71, chmn dept, 65-74, PROF GEOL, DICKINSON COL, 71- *Mem:* AAAS; Sigma Xi; Nat Asn Geol Teachers; Archaeol Inst Am; Geol Soc Am. *Res:* Mineralogy, petrology and structure of igneous and metamorphic rocks in south-central New Hampshire; archaeological investigations of Early Man in New York State. *Mailing Add:* Dept Geol Dickinson Col Carlisle PA 17013

VERONIS, GEORGE, b New Brunswick, NJ, June 3, 26; m 63; c 2. OCEANOGRAPHY. *Educ:* Lafayette Col, AB, 50; Brown Univ, PhD(appl math), 54. *Hon Degrees:* MA, Yale Univ, 66. *Prof Exp:* Staff meteorologist, Inst Advan Study, 53-56; staff mathematician, Woods Hole Oceanog Inst, 56-63; assoc prof oceanog, Mass Inst Technol, 61-63, res oceanogr, 64-66;

PROF GEOPHYS & APPL SCI, YALE UNIV, 66- *Concurrent Pos:* Guggenheim fel, Stockholm, Sweden, 60-61 & 66-67; sr queen's fel, Australia, 81; ed, J Marine Res, 73- *Mem:* AAAS; fel Am Geophys Union; Am Acad Arts & Sci; Norwegian Acad Arts & Letters. *Res:* Ocean circulations; rotating and stratified fluids. *Mailing Add:* Dept of Geol & Geophys Yale Univ New Haven CT 06520

VEROSUB, KENNETH LEE, b New York, NY, July 10, 44; m 67; c 1. GEOPHYSICS. *Educ:* Univ Mich, BA, 66; Stanford Univ, MS, 71, PhD(physics), 73. *Prof Exp:* Asst prof geophysics, Amherst Col, 72-75; asst prof, 75-80, ASSOC PROF GEOPHYSICS, UNIV CALIF, DAVIS, 80- *Mem:* Am Geophys Union; Geol Soc Am. *Res:* Paleomagnetism of sediments; history of the earth's magnetic field; quaternary seismicity of California and Alaska; physical precursors of earthquakes; geothermal resources in California. *Mailing Add:* Dept of Geol Univ of Calif Davis CA 95616

VERPOORTE, JACOB A, b Utrecht, Neth, Oct 17, 36; m 61; c 2. BIOPHYSICAL CHEMISTRY. *Educ:* Univ Utrecht, MSc, 60; Univ Pretoria, PhD(biochem), 64. *Prof Exp:* Fel phys protein chem, Univ Alta, 64-65 & Harvard Univ, 65-67; asst prof, 67-72, ASSOC PROF PHYS PROTEIN CHEM, DALHOUSIE UNIV, 72- *Concurrent Pos:* Muscular Dystrophy Asn Can fel, 64-66. *Res:* Isolation and characterization of biologically active proteins; physico-chemical studies, including studies on the structure of proteins. *Mailing Add:* Dept Biochem Dalhousie Univ Halifax NS B3H 4H7 Can

VERRALL, RONALD ERNEST, b Ottawa, Ont, Feb 26, 37; m 61; c 2. PHYSICAL CHEMISTRY. *Educ:* Univ Ottawa, Ont, BSc, 62, PhD(phys chem), 66. *Prof Exp:* Nat Res Coun Can-NATO fel, Mellon Inst, Carnegie-Mellon Univ, 66-68, vis fel, 68; from asst prof to assoc prof, 68-77, PROF CHEM, UNIV SASK, 77- *Mem:* Sigma Xi; AAAS. *Res:* Thermodynamic studies of electrolyte and non-electrolyte solutions; fluorescence studies of protein dynamics; ultrasonic studies of liquid phase, particularly microemulsions; effect of high intensity ultrasound on biological systems. *Mailing Add:* Dept Chem Univ Sask Saskatoon SK S7N 0W0 Can

VERRILLO, RONALD THOMAS, b Hartford, Conn, July 31, 27; m 50; c 3. PSYCHOPHYSICS, NEUROSCIENCES. *Educ:* Syracuse Univ, BA, 52; Univ Rochester, PhD(psychol), 58. *Prof Exp:* Asst prof spec educ, 57-62, res assoc, Bioacoust Lab, 59-63, res fel, Lab Sensory Commun, 63-67, assoc prof sensory commun, 67-74, PROF SENSORY SCI, SYRACUSE UNIV, 74- *Concurrent Pos:* NATO sr fel, Oxford Univ, 70-71. *Honors & Awards:* Res Award, Am Personnel & Guid Asn, 62. *Mem:* Acoust Soc Am; AAAS; Psychonomic Soc; Int Asn Study Pain; Soc Neurosci. *Res:* Cutaneous sensitivity; effects of the physical parameters of vibratory stimuli on threshold and suprathreshold responses in humans; sensory characteristics of pain. *Mailing Add:* Inst for Sensory Res Syracuse Univ Merrill Lane Syracuse NY 13210

VERSCHINGEL, ROGER H C, b Jan 19, 28; Can citizen; m 59. CHEMICAL INSTRUMENTATION. *Educ:* Sir George Williams Univ, BSc, 49; McGill Univ, PhD(chem), 55. *Prof Exp:* Lectr chem, Sir George Williams Univ, 54-56, from asst prof to assoc prof, 56-67, PROF CHEM, CONCORDIA UNIV, 67-, CHMN DEPT, 68-, DEAN, SIR GEORGE WILLIAMS FAC SCI, 73- *Mem:* Am Chem Soc; Chem Inst Can. *Res:* Chemical spectroscopy. *Mailing Add:* Sir George Williams Fac Sci 1455 de Maisonneuve Blvd W Montreal PQ H3G 1M8 Can

VERSCHOOR, J(ACK) D(AHLSTROM), b Grand Rapids, Mich, Nov 11, 23; m 47; c 3. HEAT TRANSFER, BUILDING CONSTRUCTION TECHNOLOGY. *Educ:* Univ Mich, BS, 45; Calif Inst Technol, MS, 47. *Prof Exp:* Physicist heat transfer, Johns-Manville Res Ctr, 47-59, proj mgr, Johns-Manville Corp, 59-69, mgr corp planning, 69-72, mgr venture anal & develop, 72-75, RES ASSOC TESTING & CONTRACTS, JOHNS-MANVILLE RES & DEVELOP CTR, 75- *Concurrent Pos:* Teaching fel, Calif Inst Technol, 45-47; instr, Rutgers Univ, 47-58; adv comt mem, US Dept Energy, 79-81. *Mem:* Am Soc Heating Refrig & Airconditioning Engrs; Am Soc Testing & Mat; Sigma Xi. *Res:* Energy construction for industrial and building applications; air leakage; moisture and sound control in building construction; physics of heat transfer in thermal insulations; development of heat transfer test apparatus. *Mailing Add:* 6050 W Mansfield Ave #6 Denver CO 80235

VERSCHUREN, JACOBUS PETRUS, b Delft, Neth, Apr 13, 30; nat Can; m 54; c 2. ENGINEERING, HYDROLOGY. *Educ:* Delft Univ Technol, CE, 52; Univ Alta, MSc, 60; Colo State Univ, PhD, 68. *Prof Exp:* Asst civil eng, Lehigh Univ, 52-53; engr, Howard Needles Tammen & Bergendoff, NY, 53; soil mech, Soil Mech Labs, Delft Univ Technol, 53-54; resident bridge engr, Prov Dept of Hwy, Man, 54-55; lectr, 55-57, from asst prof to assoc prof, 57-70, PROF CIVIL ENG, UNIV ALTA, 70- *Concurrent Pos:* Dir, T Blench & Assocs, Ltd, 59-; spec consult, Northwest Hydraul Consult, Ltd. *Mem:* Am Soc Civil Engrs; Am Geophys Union. *Res:* Engineering and environmental aspects of hydrology. *Mailing Add:* Dept of Civil Eng Univ of Alta Edmonton AB T6G 2E1 Can

VERSCHUUR, GERRIT L, b Capetown, SAfrica, June 6, 37; m 66; c 1. ASTRONOMY. *Educ:* Rhodes Univ, SAfrica, BSc, 57, MSc, 60; Univ Manchester, PhD(radio astron), 65. *Prof Exp:* Jr lectr physics, Rhodes Univ, SAfrica, 60; lectr, Univ Manchester, 64-67; res assoc, Nat Radio Astron Observ, 67-69, asst scientist, 69-72, assoc scientist, 72-73; prof astrogeophys & dir, Fiske Planetarium, Univ Colo, Boulder, 73-80. *Mem:* Am Astron Soc; Int Planetarium Soc; AAAS. *Res:* Interstellar neutral hydrogen studies; interstellar magnetic field measurements. *Mailing Add:* 1111 Maxwell Ave Boulder CO 80302

VERSEPUT, HERMAN WARD, b Grand Rapids, Mich, Sept 25, 21; m 51. PAPER TECHNOLOGY. *Educ:* Yale Univ, BE, 42; Lawrence Univ, MS, 48, PhD(pulp & paper technol), 51. *Prof Exp:* Res chemist, Robert Gair Co, Inc, 51-56, chief appl res sect, Gair Paper Prod Group, Continental Can Co, Inc, 56-61; dir res & develop, Folding Carton Div, Riegel Paper Corp, 61-66; sr develop engr, Beloit Corp, 67-71; RES MGR PAPERBOARD, BOXBOARD RES & DEVELOP ASN, 71- *Mem:* Tech Asn Pulp & Paper Indust; Am Chem Soc. *Res:* Product and process development in the manufacture of packaging materials from recycled fibers. *Mailing Add:* Boxboard Res & Develop Asn 350 S Burdick Mall Kalamazoo MI 49007

VERSES, CHRIST JAMES, b Stamford, Conn, Apr 12, 39; m 66; c 1. PHYSIOLOGY, MOLECULAR BIOLOGY. *Educ:* Valparaiso Univ, BS, 61; Univ Conn, PhD(bact), 67. *Prof Exp:* Fel microbiol, Univ Colo Med Ctr, 66-68; asst prof biol, Moorhead State Col, 68-69; res microbiologist, Pollution Control Industs Inc, 69-72; dir pub health lab, Water & Sewage Anal, State of Conn, 72-73; asst prof, 73-75, dir honors prog, 78-81, ASSOC PROF BIOL, SACRED HEART UNIV, 75-, DIR ALLIED HEALTH SCI, 81- *Concurrent Pos:* Owner anal lab; Lilly vis fac fel, Yale Univ. *Mem:* Fel Am Inst Chemists; Am Asn Univ Prof; Am Soc Microbiologists; Am Inst Biol Sci. *Res:* Pollution survey of municipal harbor systems; mechanism of attachment of phage to a host cell; biochemical reactions; viral genetics; new sterilization device and indicators; heart metabolism; microbiology. *Mailing Add:* 295 Fairview Ave Fairfield CT 06430

VERSIC, RONALD JAMES, b Dayton, Ohio, Oct 19, 42; m 66; c 2. PRODUCT DEVELOPMENT. *Educ:* Univ Dayton, BS, 64; Johns Hopkins Univ, MA, 68; Ohio State Univ, PhD(mat eng), 69. *Prof Exp:* Sr scientist, Standard Register Co, 71-76; dir res & develop, Monarch Marking Systs, Subsidiary of Pitney Bowes, 76-79; EXEC VPRES, RONALD T DODGE CO, 79- *Mem:* Sigma Xi; AAAS; Am Chem Soc; Am Asn Physics Teachers; Soc Photographic Scientists & Engrs. *Res:* Engineering management related to commercial product development in the chemical and paper converting areas. *Mailing Add:* Ronald T Dodge Co PO Box 77 Dayton OH 45409

VER SNYDER, FRANCIS L(OUIS), b Utica, NY, May 27, 25; m 48; c 3. PHYSICAL METALLURGY, METALLURGICAL ENGINEERING. *Educ:* Univ Notre Dame, BS, 50. *Prof Exp:* Tech engr, Thomson Lab, Gen Elec Co, 50-54, supvr, Small Aircraft Engine Dept, 54-55, res assoc, Metall & Ceramics Res Dept, 55-57, specialist, 57-58, metall engr, 58-61; asst dir, Advan Mat Res & Develop Lab, Pratt & Whitney Aircraft Div, 61-64, assoc dir, 64-70, mgr, Mat Eng & Res Lab, 70-77, MGR MAT TECHNOL DIV, RES CTR, UNITED TECHNOLOGIES CORP, 77- *Honors & Awards:* Howe Medal, Am Soc Metals, 54; Arch T Colwell Merit Award, Soc Automotive Engrs, 71; Joseph L Dickson Prize, Carnegie-Mellon Univ, 72. *Mem:* Nat Acad Eng; AAAS; Am Vacuum Soc; fel Am Soc Metals; Am Inst Mining, Metall & Petrol Engrs. *Res:* Phase identification; precipitation processes in alloys; theory of alloying; high temperature creep and fracture; solidification; high temperature alloy and materials development. *Mailing Add:* United Technologies Corp 400 Main St East Hartford CT 06108

VERSTEEGH, LARRY ROBERT, b Minneapolis, Minn, Feb 13, 49; m 70; c 2. DRUG REGULATORY AFFAIRS. *Educ:* Cent Col, Iowa, BA, 71; Iowa State Univ, PhD(biochem), 75. *Prof Exp:* Staff scientist, Procter & Gamble Co, 75-79; ASSOC DIR DRUG REGULATORY AFFAIRS, MEAD JOHNSON PHARMACEUT CO, SUBSIDIARY BRISTOL-MYERS CO, 79- *Concurrent Pos:* Lectr biol sci, Univ Cincinnati, 76-77. *Mem:* AAAS; Am Chem Soc; Regulatory Affairs Profs Soc; Fedn Am Scientists. *Res:* Drug regulatory affairs: central nervous system and cardiovascular drugs; preclinical and clinical pharmacology; toxicology. *Mailing Add:* 2040 Polaris Ave Evansville IN 47715

VER STRATE, GARY WILLIAM, b Metuchen, NJ, Jan 29, 40; m 61; c 2. POLYMER CHEMISTRY, POLYMER PHYSICS. *Educ:* Hope Col, BS, 63; Univ Del, PhD(chem), 67. *Prof Exp:* Sr res chemist, 66-75, RES ASSOC, EXXON CHEM CO, LINDEN, 75- *Mem:* Am Phys Soc. *Res:* Crystallinity; rheological properties; characterization by physical methods; light scattering; kinetics and molecular weight distribution; branching; cationic polymerization; chemical modification of polymers; polymer networks; liquid rubbers. *Mailing Add:* 25 Balmoral Ave Matawan NJ 07747

VERTER, HERBERT SIGMUND, b New York, NY, Jan 30, 36; m 60, 81; c 1. ORGANIC CHEMISTRY. *Educ:* City Col New York, BS, 56; Harvard Univ, MA, 57, PhD(chem), 60. *Prof Exp:* NATO fel, Imp Col, Univ London, 60-61; asst prof chem, Cent Mich Univ, 61-66; assoc prof, Inter-Am Univ, PR, 66-67, dean acad affairs, 73, prof chem, 67-77, chmn dept, 66-72 & 74-77; admin dir, Dept Chem, Brandeis Univ, 77-79; CHMN, SCI DEPT, WOODMERE ACAD, 79- *Mem:* Am Chem Soc; Sigma Xi. *Res:* Chemistry of natural products; organic synthesis; mechanism; carbon oxides. *Mailing Add:* 336 Woodmere Blvd Woodmere NY 11598

VERTES, VICTOR, b Cleveland, Ohio, Sept 10, 27. INTERNAL MEDICINE. *Educ:* Western Reserve Univ, BS, 49, MD, 53; Am Bd Internal Med, dipl, 62. *Prof Exp:* Intern med, Univ Hosps, Cleveland, 53-54; resident, Mt Sinai Hosp, Cleveland, 54-56; fel metab & endocrinol, New York Hosp-Cornell Med Ctr, 56-57; demonstr & instr med, 58-62 & 64, from asst clin prof to assoc clin prof, 64-72, PROF MED, SCH MED, CASE WESTERN RESERVE UNIV, 72-, DIR DEPT MED, MT SINAI MED CTR, 64- *Concurrent Pos:* Assoc vis physician, Mt Sinai Hosp, 58-64, dir metab & endocrine lab, 59-65, proj dir chronic dialysis ctr, 65-68; investr, USPHS, 65-; mem, Coun Hemoglobin-Blood Pressure Res. *Mem:* Fel Am Col Physicians; Am Soc Nephrology; fel Am Col Angiology; dipl mem Pan-Am Med Asn; Europ Dialysis & Transplant Asn. *Res:* Treatment and mechanisms of uremia; role of the kidney in hypertension. *Mailing Add:* 1800 E 105th St Cleveland OH 44106

VERTREES, ROBERT LAYMAN, b Louisville, Ky, Nov 1, 39; m 66; c 3. FOREST SCIENCES, RESOURCE MANAGEMENT. *Educ:* Purdue Univ, BS, 61; Mich State Univ, MS, 67, PhD(resource develop), 74. *Prof Exp:* Instr resource econ, Dept Agr & Food Econ, Univ Mass, 69-72; asst prof, Dept Econ, SDak State Univ, 73-76; ASST PROF RESOURCE DEVELOP, OHIO STATE UNIV, 76- *Mem:* Am Agr Econ Asn; Soil Conserv Soc Am.

Res: Economic and land-use impacts of alternative water and land resource projects; formulation and implementation of public water and land resource projects, policies and programs. *Mailing Add:* Sch of Natural Resources Ohio State Univ Columbus OH 43210

VERVILLE, GEORGE JULIUS, b Chippewa Falls, Wis, May 4, 21; m 43; c 3. GEOLOGY. *Educ:* Univ Wis, PhB, 47, MS, 49, PhD, 51. *Prof Exp:* Paleontologist, Stanolind Oil & Gas Co, Okla, 51-59; sr paleontologist, Pan Am Petrol Corp, 59-65, res group supvr, 65-69, res sect mgr, 69-76, CONSULT PALEONTOLOGIST, AMOCO PROD CO, 76- *Mem:* Am Asn Petrol Geologists; Paleont Soc. *Res:* Fusulinid research; stratigraphy. *Mailing Add:* Amoco Prod Co Amoco Bldg Denver CO 80202

VERVOORT, GERARDUS, b Utrecht, Neth, July 17, 33; Can citizen; m 64; c 2. MATHEMATICS EDUCATION, COMMUNICATIONS SCIENCE. *Educ:* Loras Col, BA, 60; Univ Iowa, MSc, 64, PhD(math), 70. *Prof Exp:* Teacher elem sch, Neth, 53-55 & Indian Sch, Ont, Can, 55-58; itinerant teacher, Dept Northern Affairs, NW Territories, 59-60; teacher sec sch, Dept Indian Affairs, Alta, 60-62; PROF MATH & EDUC, LAKEHEAD UNIV, 70- *Concurrent Pos:* IBM Corp grant, Lakehead Univ, 71-72; consult, Ont Educ Commun Authority, 74-75; dept commun res contract, 74-75 & 75-76. *Mem:* Math Asn Am; Can Asn Prof Educ. *Res:* instructor effectiveness in the teaching of university and college level mathematics courses; satellite communication for delivery of higher education in remote areas. *Mailing Add:* Dept of Math Sci Lakehead Univ Thunder Bay ON P7B 5E1 Can

VERWEY, WILLARD FOSTER, medical microbiology, deceased

VERWOERDT, ADRIAN, b Voorburg, Neth, July 5, 27; US citizen; m 65; c 2. PSYCHIATRY, PSYCHOANALYSIS. *Educ:* Univ Amsterdam, MD, 52; Am Bd Psychiat & Neurol, dipl, 62. *Prof Exp:* Intern, Touro Infirmary, New Orleans, 53-54; resident, 54-55 & 58-60, chief resident, 59-60, from instr to assoc prof, 60-71, dir gero-psychiat training, 66-80, PROF PSYCHIAT, MED CTR, DUKE UNIV, 71-; DIR RESIDENCY TRAINING PSYCHIAT, JOHN UMSTEAD HOSP, BUTNER, 68- *Concurrent Pos:* Consult, Vet Admin Regional Off, Winston-Salem, 61-63, Serv to Aging, NC Dept Pub Welfare, 66-68, Dorothea Dix Hosp, Raleigh, 69-72 & Cherry Hosp, Goldsboro, 72-74; fel psychiat res, Duke Univ Med Ctr, 60-62, NIMH career teacher training award, 64-66; mem, NC Multiversity Comt, 68-; dir residency training psychiat, John Umstead Hosp Hosp, Butner, 68-80, dir, Gero-Psychiat Inst, 80-; corresp ed, J Geriat Psychiat, 70-; instr psychoanal, Duke-Univ NC Psychoanal Inst, 72. *Mem:* Fel Am Psychiat Asn; Geront Soc; Am Psychoanal Asn; Am Geriat Soc; dipl Pan-Am Med Asn. *Res:* Physical illness and depressive symptomatology; psychological reactions in fatal illness; depression in the aged; sexual behavior in senescence; training in geriatric psychiatry; psychiatric education. *Mailing Add:* Dept Psychiat Duke Univ Med Ctr Durham NC 27710

VESELL, ELLIOT S, b New York, NY, Dec 24, 33. PHARMACOGENETICS, MOLECULAR PHARMACOLOGY. *Educ:* Harvard Univ, MD, 59. *Prof Exp:* Intern pediat, Mass Gen Hosp, 59-60; res assoc human genet & asst physician, Rockefeller Inst, 60-62; asst resident med, Peter Bent Brigham Hosp, 62-63; clin assoc, Nat Inst Arthritis & Metab Dis, 63-65, head sect pharmacogenet, Lab Chem Pharmacol, Nat Heart Inst, 65-69; EVAN PUGH PROF PHARMACOL, GENETICS & MED & CHMN DEPT PHARMACOL, COL MED, HERSHEY MED CTR, PA STATE UNIV, 69-, ASST DEAN GRAD STUDIES, 74- *Concurrent Pos:* Clin asst prof, Sch Med, Georgetown Univ, 65-; vis prof, Med Col Ala, 66-67; physician, Johns Hopkins Hosp, 66-70; William N Creasy vis prof clin pharmacol, Sch Med, George Washington Univ, 75, Sch Med, Univ Conn, 79; Pfizer lectr clin pharmacol, Univ Iowa, Med Col Pa, 76, Univ Conn, 77, Med Col Wis, 78, Georgetown Univ, 79, State Univ NY, Buffalo, 81. *Honors & Awards:* Samuel James Meltzer Award, 67; Am Soc Pharmacol & Exp Therapeut Award, 71; Julius W Sturmer Mem lectr. *Mem:* Harvey Soc; Soc Human Genetics; Soc Exp Biol & Med; Am Soc Clin Invest; Am Fedn Clin Res. *Res:* Multiple molecular forms of enzymes; effect of heredity and environmental factors on disposition of drugs; biochemical pharmacology. *Mailing Add:* Hershey Med Ctr Pa State Univ Col Med Hershey PA 17033

VESELY, JOHN ANTHONY, b Prague, Czech, Apr 26, 25; Can citizen; m 59; c 2. ANIMAL BREEDING, GENETICS. *Educ:* Univ BC, BSA, 55, MSA, 57; NC State Univ, PhD(breeding, genetics), 70. *Prof Exp:* Res officer sheep breeding, Res Br, 57-66, RES SCIENTIST SHEEP & DAIRY CATTLE BREEDING, RES BR, CAN DEPT AGR, 69- *Mem:* Am Soc Animal Sci. *Res:* Improvement of livestock production through breeding; population genetics; evolution; statistics. *Mailing Add:* Res Sta Can Dept of Agr Lethbridge AB T1J 4B1 Can

VESIC, A(LEKSANDAR) S, b Resan, Yugoslavia, Aug 8, 24; nat US; m 46. SOIL MECHANICS, STRUCTURAL ANALYSIS. *Educ:* Univ Belgrade, BS, 50, CE, 52, DSc, 56. *Hon Degrees:* DSc, Univ Ghent, Belgium, 81. *Prof Exp:* Technician, Bur Reclamation, Yugoslavia, 42-44; instr, Univ Belgrade, 49-52, lectr, 53-56; struct engr, Large Dam Drina I & Yugoslavian Army, 52-53; res engr, Nat Geotech Inst, Belg, 56-58; from asst prof to assoc prof civil eng, Ga Inst Technol, 58-64; prof, 64-71, dir grad studies, 66-69, chmn dept civil eng, 68-74, JONES PROF CIVIL ENG, DUKE UNIV, 71-, DEAN, SCH ENG, 74- *Concurrent Pos:* Consult, Nat Inst Testing Mat, Yugoslavia, 53-56; chmn comt theory of pavement design & mem, Hwy Res Bd, Nat Acad Sci-Nat Res Coun, 65-70; vis lectr, Europe, 66, 69, 72, 74 & 81, SAm, 67, 77 & 78, Asia, 69, 70 & 78, Mex, 69, 71 & 76, Can, 71 & 80; gen reporter, Third Pan-Am Conf Soil Mech & Found Eng, Caracas, 67 & Fifth Pan-Am Conf Soil Mech Found Eng, Buenos Aires, 75; mem adv panel pavements, Nat Coop Hwy Res Prog, Nat Acad Sci, 67-; consult, Off Chief Engrs, US Army, 68-; fel, Churchill Col, Univ Cambridge, 71-72. *Honors & Awards:* Nat Comt Univs Prize, 49; Nat Acad Sci Hwy Res Bd Award, 69; Thomas Middlebrooks Award, Am Soc Civil Engrs, 74; Transp Res Award, Am Soc Testing & Mat, 81. *Mem:* Fel Am Soc Civil Engrs; Int Soc Soil Mech & Found Engrs; Int Soc Rock Mech. *Res:* Soil mechanics and foundations; bearing capacity and penetration resistance of soils; behavior of piles and pile groups; soil-structure interaction; cratering by explosives. *Mailing Add:* Sch of Eng Duke Univ Durham NC 27706

VESLEY, DONALD, b Astoria, NY, Nov 7, 32; m 62; c 1. ENVIRONMENTAL HEALTH. *Educ:* Cornell Univ, BS, 55; Univ Minn, MS, 58, PhD(environ health), 68. *Prof Exp:* From instr to assoc prof, 60-78, PROF PUB HEALTH, UNIV MINN, MINNEAPOLIS, 78-, DIR ENVIRON HEALTH & SAFETY, 80- *Mem:* Am Soc Microbiol; Am Pub Health Asn. *Res:* Environmental microbiology. *Mailing Add:* Univ Minn Sch Pub Health 1158 Mayo Minneapolis MN 55455

VESSEL, EUGENE DAVID, b Mt Olive, Ill, Dec 1, 27; m 46; c 2. ORGANIC POLYMER CHEMISTRY. *Educ:* Univ Ill, BS, 57; Univ Iowa, MS, 59, PhD(org chem), 60. *Prof Exp:* Res chemist, Chevron Res Corp, Standard Oil Calif, 60-61; sr res chemist, United Tech Ctr, United Aircraft Corp, 61-67; RES SPECIALIST NONMETALLIC MAT, COM AIRPLANE GROUP, BOEING CO, 67- *Mem:* Am Chem Soc. *Res:* Adhesives; elastomers; plastics; composite materials; materials research; fire research and technology. *Mailing Add:* Boeing Co PO Box 3707 7755 E Marginal Way Seattle WA 98124

VESSEL, MATTHEW F, b Chisholm, Minn, Apr 21, 12; m 38; c 2. SCIENCE EDUCATION, BOTANY. *Educ:* St Cloud Teachers Col, BE, 36; Cornell Univ, PhD(sci educ limnol & bot), 40. *Prof Exp:* Teacher high sch, Minn, 36-38; head, Dept Sci Educ, 59-78, assoc dean, Sch Sci, 69-78. prof, 40-43 & 46-78, EMER PROF BIOL & SCI EDUC, SAN JOSE STATE UNIV, 78- *Concurrent Pos:* Field biologist, State Conserv Dept, Minn, 37; consult, San Mateo Schs, 46-49 & Palo Alto Schs, 58-59; dean sch sci, Calif State Univ, San Jose, 66-67, actg dean, 67-69; vis prof, Saipan & Palau, 80-81. *Mem:* AAAS; Am Nature Study Soc; Nat Asn Res Sci Teaching; Nat Sci Teachers Asn. *Mailing Add:* Sch of Sci S-127 San Jose State Univ San Jose CA 95192

VESSELINOVITCH, STAN DUSHAN, b Zagreb, Yugoslavia, Feb 20, 22; Can citizen; m 47; c 3. PHYSIOLOGY, ONCOLOGY. *Educ:* Univ Belgrade, DVM, 49; Univ Toronto, MVSc, 57, DVSc, 58. *Prof Exp:* Lectr physiol, Univ Belgrade, 49-51; res assoc oncol, Univ Toronto, 52-53, asst prof, 54-58; res assoc, Michael Reese Hosp, Chicago, Ill, 59-61, asst dir oncol, 62-64; assoc prof, Chicago Med Sch, 64-69; assoc prof radiol, 69-72, PROF RADIOL & PATH, FRANKLIN MCLEAN MEM RES INST, UNIV CHICAGO, 72-, DIR, SECT RADIATION BIOL & EXP ONCOL, 80- *Concurrent Pos:* Res assoc fel, Nat Cancer Inst Can, 55-57, prin investr res grant, 57-58; co-investr res grant, Nat Cancer Inst, 59-64, prin investr, 64-69, res contracts, 69- *Mem:* AAAS; Am Vet Med Asn; Am Asn Cancer Res; NY Acad Sci. *Res:* Animal physiology; environmental carcinogenesis; factors and mechanisms modifying carcinogenesis. *Mailing Add:* Dept of Radiol Univ of Chicago Chicago IL 60637

VESSEY, ADELE RUTH, b South Charleston, WVa, 47. IMMUNOLOGY, VIROLOGY. *Educ:* Ohio Univ, BS, 69, MS, 72; Case Western Reserve Univ, PhD(microbiol), 76. *Prof Exp:* Fel immunol, Cleveland Clin Found, 76-80. *Mem:* Am Soc Microbiol; Int Asn Comp Res Leukemia & Related Dis. *Res:* Interaction of leukemia viruses with the immunological system; autoaggressive and immunosuppressive properties of lymphomas. *Mailing Add:* PO Box 23572 Rochester NY 14692

VESSEY, STEPHEN H, b Stamford, Conn, Mar 7, 39; m 62. ANIMAL BEHAVIOR, ECOLOGY. *Educ:* Swarthmore Col, BA, 61; Pa State Univ, MS, 63, PhD(zool), 65. *Prof Exp:* Biologist, NIH, 65-69; from asst prof to assoc prof, 69-80, PROF BIOL SCI, BOWLING GREEN STATE UNIV, 80- *Mem:* Am Soc Primatologists; Animal Behav Soc; Am Soc Mammal; AAAS; Int Primatol Soc. *Res:* Social behavior and population dynamics; field studies of non-human primates and small mammals. *Mailing Add:* Dept of Biol Bowling Green State Univ Bowling Green OH 43403

VESSEY, THEODORE ALAN, b St Paul, Minn, June 16, 38; m 65; c 1. MATHEMATICAL ANALYSIS. *Educ:* Univ Minn, BA, 60, PhD(math), 66. *Prof Exp:* Assoc res engr, Honeywell, Inc, 62-63; asst prof math, Univ Wis-Milwaukee, 66-70; asst prof, 70-72, ASSOC PROF MATH, ST OLAF COL, 72- *Mem:* Am Math Soc; Math Asn Am. *Res:* Cluster set theory in determination of boundary behavior of complex functions. *Mailing Add:* Dept of Math St Olaf Col Northfield MN 55057

VESSOT, ROBERT F C, b Montreal, Que, Apr 16, 30; m; c 3. PHYSICS. *Educ:* McGill Univ, BA, 51, MSc, 54, PhD(physics), 57. *Prof Exp:* Mem, Div Sponsored Res Staff, Mass Inst Technol, 56-60; mgr maser res & develop, Varian Assocs, 60-67 & Hewlett-Packard Co, 67-69; physicist, 69-72, MEM STAFF, SMITHSONIAN ASTROPHYS OBSERV, CAMBRIDGE, 72- *Mem:* Am Phys Soc. *Res:* Physical electronics; noise in electron beams; atomic beams; atomic resonance physics; atomic hydrogen maser frequency standard. *Mailing Add:* 334 Ocean Ave Marblehead MA 01945

VEST, CHARLES MARSTILLER, b Morgantown, WVa, Sept 9, 41; m 63; c 2. MECHANICAL ENGINEERING, OPTICS. *Educ:* Univ WVa, BSME, 63; Univ Mich, MSE, 64, PhD(mech eng), 67. *Prof Exp:* From asst prof to assoc prof, 67-72, PROF MECH ENG, UNIV MICH, ANN ARBOR, 77- *Concurrent Pos:* Vis assoc prof aero & elec eng, Stanford Univ, 74-75. *Mem:* Soc Mech Engrs; Optical Soc Am. *Res:* Heat transfer and fluid mechanics; hydrodynamic stability; optical holography and coherent optical measurement techniques. *Mailing Add:* 910 Kuebler Dr Ann Arbor MI 48103

VEST, FLOYD RUSSELL, b Orland, Calif, Feb 12, 34; m 55; c 2. MATHEMATICS EDUCATION. *Educ:* ECent State Col, BSEd, 56; Univ Okla, MA, 59; NTex State Univ, EdD(math), 68. *Prof Exp:* Instr math, ETex State Univ, 59-61; asst prof, 61-74, ASSOC PROF MATH, N TEX STATE UNIV, 74- *Mem:* Math Asn Am. *Res:* Learning theory; curriculum. *Mailing Add:* Dept of Math NTex State Univ Denton TX 76203

VEST, HYRUM GRANT, JR, b Salt Lake City, Utah, Sept 23, 35; m 58; c 5. PLANT PATHOLOGY, PLANT GENETICS. *Educ:* Utah State Univ, BS, 60, MS, 65; Univ Minn, PhD(plant path), 67. *Prof Exp:* Res plant pathologist crops res div, Agr Res Serv, USDA, Md, 67-70; assoc prof hort, Mich State Univ, 70-76; PROF HORT & HEAD DEPT, OKLA STATE UNIV, 76- *Mem:* Am Soc Hort Sci; Am Soc Agron. *Res:* Genetics of nodulation and nitrogen fixation in soybean; breeding and genetics of onions, lettuce and asparagus. *Mailing Add:* Dept of Hort Okla State Univ Stillwater OK 74074

VEST, ROBERT W(ILSON), b Lawrenceburg, Ind, Oct 17, 30; m 52; c 3. PHYSICAL CHEMISTRY, MATERIALS ENGINEERING. *Educ:* Purdue Univ, BS, 52; Iowa State Univ, PhD, 57. *Prof Exp:* Chemist, Nat Lead Co Ohio, 52-53; asst, Ames Lab & Inst Atomic Res, Iowa State Univ, 53-57; res chemist, Monsanto Chem Co, 57-61; sr scientist, Systs Res Labs, Inc, 61-66; PROF ENG, PURDUE UNIV, LAFAYETTE, 66- *Concurrent Pos:* Consult, CTS Microelectronics, Inc, 66 & Gen Motors Corp, 72- *Mem:* Am Soc Metals; Am Ceramic Soc; Nat Inst Ceramic Engrs; Int Soc Hybrid Microelectronics. *Res:* Electrical properties of metal oxides; electroceramics; transport properties on non-metallic materials; hybrid microelectronics. *Mailing Add:* Potter Eng Ctr Purdue Univ Lafayette IN 47907

VESTAL, BEDFORD MATHER, b Gainesville, Tex, Mar 8, 43; m 65; c 2. ANIMAL BEHAVIOR, BEHAVIORAL ECOLOGY. *Educ:* Austin Col, BA, 65; Mich State Univ, MS, 67, PhD(zool), 70. *Prof Exp:* Instr biol, Univ Mo-St Louis, 69-70, asst prof, 70-73; asst prof, 73-80, ASSOC PROF ZOOL, UNIV OKLA, 80- *Concurrent Pos:* Res assoc, Mich State Univ, 70-71; res cur, Oklahoma City Zoo, 73-76. *Mem:* AAAS; Soc Study Evolution; Animal Behav Soc; Ecol Soc Am; Am Soc Mammal. *Res:* Comparative social behavior of mammals; behavioral ecology and behavior development of rodents. *Mailing Add:* Sutton Hall Dept Zool Univ Okla Norman OK 73019

VESTAL, CHARLES RUSSELL, b Moran, Kans, Feb 21, 40; m 62; c 2. CHEMICAL ENGINEERING. *Educ:* Colo Sch Mines, BS, 62, MS, 69, PhD(chem eng), 73. *Prof Exp:* Process design engr, Continental Oil Co, 62-63; assoc engr, 65-69, engr, 69-72, advan engr, 72-74, res engr chem eng, 74-77, adv res engr, 77-80, RES ENGR, DENVER RES CTR, MARATHON OIL CO, 80- *Concurrent Pos:* Adj assoc prof, Colo Sch Mines, 75-; lectr, Univ Colo, Boulder, 75- *Mem:* Am Inst Chem Engrs; Soc Petrol Engrs. *Res:* Numerical analysis and computer simulation of petroleum reservoir engineering and chemical engineering design problems. *Mailing Add:* Denver Res Ctr 7400 S Broadway Littleton CO 80121

VESTAL, CLAUDE KENDRICK, b High Point, NC, Mar 11, 16; m 46. METEOROLOGY, CLIMATOLOGY. *Educ:* Guilford Col, AB, 46. *Prof Exp:* Observer, Weather Bur, NC, 37-39, observer & forecaster, DC, 39-42, proj head climat, NY, 42-43, sect head, DC, 43-50; foreign serv staff officer, Dept State, Monrovia, Liberia, 50-52; sect head, Weather Bur, DC, 52-56, regional climatologist, Tex, 57-71; CONSULT, 71- *Res:* Application of modern statistical methods to climatological data analysis, for design purposes and evaluation of operational risks. *Mailing Add:* 1720 Gun Wood Pl Crofton MD 21114

VESTAL, J ROBIE, b Orlando, Fla, Oct 16, 42; m 67. MICROBIOLOGY. *Educ:* Hanover Col, BA, 64; Miami Univ, MS, 66; NC State Univ, PhD(microbiol), 69. *Prof Exp:* Fed Water Pollution Control Admin res assoc microbiol, Syracuse Univ, 69-71; asst prof, 71-77, ASSOC PROF BIOL SCI, UNIV CINCINNATI, 77- *Concurrent Pos:* Vis prof, Fla State Univ, 80-81. *Mem:* Sigma Xi; Arctic Inst NAm; Am Soc Microbiol; AAAS. *Res:* Functional microbial ecology of aquatic, marine and terrestrial habitats; microbial metabolism; effects of pollutants on microbial habitats. *Mailing Add:* Dept of Biol Sci Univ of Cincinnati Cincinnati OH 45221

VESTER, JOHN WILLIAM, b Cincinnati, Ohio, June 5, 24. BIOCHEMISTRY, INTERNAL MEDICINE. *Educ:* Univ Cincinnati, MD, 47. *Prof Exp:* Porter fel res med, Hosp Univ Pa, 54-56; from asst prof to assoc prof biochem & nutrit, Grad Sch Pub Health, Univ Pittsburgh, 56-61, from asst prof to assoc prof med, Sch Med, 56-67, asst prof biochem, 61-67; assoc prof biochem, 67-74, assoc prof med, 67-71, PROF MED, COL MED, UNIV CINCINNATI, 71-, PROF BIOCHEM, 74-; DIR RES, GOOD SAMARITAN HOSP, 67- *Concurrent Pos:* Asst ward chief, Hosp Univ Pa, 54-56; chief sect isotopes & metab, Vet Admin Hosp, Pittsburgh, Pa, 61-67 & assoc chief of staff, 62-67. *Mem:* Endocrine Soc; Am Fedn Clin Res; Am Diabetes Asn; fel Am Col Physicians; fel Am Col Cardiol. *Res:* Diabetes and mechanism of insulin actions; alcoholism; obesity; muscle diseases. *Mailing Add:* Dept of Med Res Good Samaritan Hosp Cincinnati OH 45220

VESTLING, CARL SWENSSON, b Northfield, Minn, May 6, 13; m 38; c 3. BIOCHEMISTRY. *Educ:* Carleton Col, BA, 34; Johns Hopkins Univ, PhD(biochem), 38. *Prof Exp:* From instr to prof chem, Univ Ill, Urbana, 38-63; prof biochem, Univ Iowa, 63-81, head dept, 63-76; VIS PROF BIOCHEM, UNIV ARIZ, 82- *Concurrent Pos:* Guggenheim fel, Nobel Inst, Sweden, 54. *Mem:* AAAS; Am Chem Soc; Am Soc Biol Chemists; Soc Exp Biol & Med; Brit Biochem Soc. *Res:* Isolation, structure, mechanism, lactate and malate dehydrogenases and certain other liver and hepatoma enzymes. *Mailing Add:* 7981 N Sendero Uno Tucson AZ 85704

VESTLING, MARTHA MEREDITH, b Urbana, Ill, Sept 4, 41. ORGANIC CHEMISTRY. *Educ:* Oberlin Col, AB, 62; Northwestern Univ, Evanston, PhD(chem), 67. *Prof Exp:* Fel, Univ Fla, 67-68; res assoc, Vanderbilt Univ, 68-69; asst prof chem, 70-75, ASSOC PROF CHEM, STATE UNIV NY COL BROCKPORT, 75- *Mem:* Am Chem Soc; AAAS; Am Soc Mass Spectrometry. *Res:* Organosulfur and organonitrogen chemistry; reaction mechanisms; mass spectrometry; chromatography. *Mailing Add:* Dept of Chem State Univ of NY Col Brockport NY 14420

VETELINO, JOHN FRANK, b Westerly, RI, Oct 17, 42; m 67; c 2. ELECTRICAL ENGINEERING, PHYSICS. *Educ:* Univ RI, BS, 64, MS, 66, PhD(elec eng), 69. *Prof Exp:* Prof, 69-78, assoc prof, 78-79, PROF ELEC ENG, UNIV MAINE, ORONO, 79- *Concurrent Pos:* Consult, Navy Underwater Systs Ctr, Allied Chem Corp. *Mem:* Am Phys Soc; Acoust Soc Am; sr mem Inst Elec & Electronics Engrs. *Res:* Microwave acoustics; surface acoustic waves; solid state phenomena; lattice dynamics and related thermodynamic optical and electronic properties of solids; phase transitions and impurity studies; electromagnetic and acoustic wave propagation; switched capacitor filters; sonar signal processing. *Mailing Add:* Dept of Elec Eng Univ of Maine Orono ME 04473

VETHAMANY, VICTOR GLADSTONE, b Servaikaramadam, India, Feb 7, 35; Can citizen; m 62; c 1. BIOLOGY, ANATOMY. *Educ:* Univ Madras, BA, 54, MA, 57; Univ Toronto, PhD(zool), 65. *Prof Exp:* Asst lectr biol, Univ Madras, 57-59; high sch teacher, Ethiopia, 60-61; demonstr zool, Univ Toronto, 61-64; res assoc path, Isaac Albert Res Inst, Kingsbrook Med Ctr, 65-67; asst prof, 67-73, ASSOC PROF ANAT, MED SCH, DALHOUSIE UNIV, 73- *Concurrent Pos:* Fel, Isaac Albert Res Inst, Kingsbrook Med Ctr, NY, 65-67; Med Res Coun vis scientist, Inst Cellular Path, Paris, 73-74. *Mem:* AAAS; Am Asn Anat; Can Asn Anat; NY Acad Sci; Can Soc Cell Biol. *Res:* Ultrastructure and histochemistry of blood cells and blood forming organs; ultrastructural studies on Niemann-Pick disease; comparative ultrastructural studies of blood in vertebrates and invertebrates; chemotaxis and cell injury. *Mailing Add:* Dept of Anat Dalhousie Univ Med Sch Halifax NS B3H 4H7 Can

VETTE, JAMES IRA, b Evanston, Ill, Mar 4, 27; m 51; c 4. PHYSICS. *Educ:* Rice Univ, BS, 52; Calif Inst Technol, PhD(physics), 58. *Prof Exp:* Jr geophysicist, Humble Oil Co, 52; asst physics, Calif Inst Technol, 52-54; staff scientist, Sci Res Lab, Convair Div, Gen Dynamics Corp, 58-62, sr staff scientist, Sci Res Lab, Astronaut Div, 62; mgr nuclear physics, Vela Satellite Prog, Aerospace Corp, 62-63, staff scientist, Space Physics Lab, 63-67; DIR, NAT SPACE SCI DATA CTR, NASA GODDARD SPACE FLIGHT CTR, 67- *Mem:* AAAS; Am Phys Soc; Am Geophys Union; Inst Elec & Electronics Engrs. *Res:* Synchrotron; meson physics; high altitude radiation with balloons; solar physics; high energy physics; cosmic rays; magnetospheric physics; satellite measurements; space physics. *Mailing Add:* Nat Space Sci Data Ctr Code 601 NASA Goddard Space Flight Ctr Greenbelt MD 20771

VETTER, ARTHUR FREDERICK, b De Witt, Iowa, July 26, 18; m 41; c 4. CHEMICAL & NUCLEAR ENGINEERING. *Educ:* Coe Col, BA, 39; NC State Col, MS, 56. *Prof Exp:* Meteorologist, US Air Force, 47-54, res adminr, 56-57, asst prof physics & nuclear eng, Air Force Inst Technol, 57-61, mem staff, Hq, US Air Force, 61-62; ASSOC PROF CHEM ENG, UNIV IOWA, 62- *Concurrent Pos:* With dept nuclear eng, Univ Ill, Urbana, 69-71. *Mem:* Am Inst Chem Engrs; Am Nuclear Soc; Fine Particle Soc. *Res:* Radiation protection; particle morphology. *Mailing Add:* Dept of Chem Eng Univ of Iowa Iowa City IA 52240

VETTER, JAMES LOUIS, b St Louis, Mo, Jan 26, 33; m 54; c 2. FOOD TECHNOLOGY. *Educ:* Washington Univ, AB, 54; Univ Ill, MS, 55, PhD(food technol), 58. *Prof Exp:* Food technologist, Monsanto Chem Co, 58-63; mgr res & develop labs, Keebler Co, Ill, 63-67, dir res & develop, 67-72; corp dir res & develop, Confectionery, Nut & Snack Prod Lab, Planters/Curtiss Div, Standard Brands, Inc, 72-74, vpres & tech dir res & develop lab, 74-75; vpres food sci & technol, Triticale Industs, Inc, Amarillo, Tex, 75-77; dir res, 77-80, VPRES TECH, AM INST BAKING, 81- *Mem:* Am Asn Cereal Chem; Inst Food Technologists. *Res:* Basic, nutrition and applied research on cereal grains and their utilization in processed, grain-based foods. *Mailing Add:* Am Inst of Baking 1213 Bakers Way Manhattan KS 66502

VETTER, RICHARD C, b Homer, Mich, Apr 17, 23; m 51; c 3. OCEANOGRAPHY. *Educ:* Albion Col, BA, 49; Univ Calif, San Diego, MS, 51. *Prof Exp:* Instr col math, Far East Exten Div, Univ Calif, 51; oceanogr, Off Naval Res, 51-57; exec secy comt oceanog, 57-70, EXEC SECY OCEAN SCI BD, NAT ACAD SCI, 70- *Concurrent Pos:* Consult develop oceanog, State Univs, Fla, 64 & Univ Va, 67. *Mem:* AAAS; Marine Technol Soc (vpres, 64-67); Am Geophys Union; Am Soc Limnol & Oceanog. *Res:* Characteristics of surface ocean waves, particularly the two-dimensional ocean wave spectra. *Mailing Add:* Nat Acad Sci Ocean Sci Bd 2101 Constitution Ave NW Washington DC 20418

VETTER, RICHARD J, b Castlewood, SDak, July 17, 43; m 65; c 3. HEALTH PHYSICS, RADIOBIOLOGY. *Educ:* SDak State Univ, BS, 66, MS, 68; Purdue Univ, PhD(bionucleonics), 70. *Prof Exp:* Asst prof biol, Point Park Col, Pittsburgh, 69-70; asst prof bionucleonics, 70-75, assoc prof, 75-80, PROF BIONUCLEONICS, PURDUE UNIV, 80- *Concurrent Pos:* Asst radiol control officer, Purdue Univ, 70- *Mem:* AAAS; Health Physics Soc; Int Radiation Protection Asn; Int Microwave Power Inst. *Res:* Biological effects of ionizing and nonionizing radiation including radioecology; applications of microwaves, especially as a modality in treatment of cancer. *Mailing Add:* Dept of Bionucleonics Purdue Univ West Lafayette IN 47907

VETTER, RICHARD L, b Henry Co, Ill, Dec 28, 30; m 50; c 2. ANIMAL SCIENCE, ENVIRONMENTAL SCIENCES. *Educ:* Univ Ill, BS, 53, MS, 57; Univ Wis, PhD(nutrit, biochem), 60. *Prof Exp:* Asst, Univ Ill, 55-57; asst biochem, Univ Wis, 57-60, fel, 60-61; res nutritionist, Hess & Clark Co Div, Richardson-Merrill, Inc, 61-62; from asst prof to prof animal sci, Iowa State Univ, 72-78; DIR RES, A O SMITH HARVESTORE PROD, INC, 78- *Concurrent Pos:* Researcher, Inst Animal Physiol, Cambridge, Eng, 68-69. *Mem:* Am Soc Animal Sci; Am Soc Dairy Sci; Am Inst Nutrit; Fedn Am Soc Exp Biol. *Res:* Nutrition and metabolic disorders; animal production; chemistry, nutrition and utilization of plant and animal wastes; bioenergy production and nutrient conservation. *Mailing Add:* A O Smith Harvestore Prod Inc 550 W Algonquin Rd Arlington Heights IL 60005

VETTER, WILLIAM J, b Grenfell, Sask. ELECTRICAL ENGINEERING. *Educ:* Univ Toronto, BASc, 59; Univ Waterloo, MASc, 61, PhD(elec eng), 65. *Prof Exp:* Lectr elec eng, Univ Waterloo, 61-65, from asst prof to assoc prof, 65-71; prof, 71-77, PROF ENG & APPL SCI, MEM UNIV NFLD, 77- *Mem:* Inst Elec & Electronics Engrs. *Res:* Theoretical and practical aspects of dynamical systems, particularly modeling, analysis, control and simulation; instrumentation and computer control of industrial systems and processes. *Mailing Add:* Fac of Eng Mem Univ of Nfld St John's NF A1C 5S7 Can

VETTERLING, JOHN MARTIN, b Fitzsimons, Colo, July 21, 34; m 57; c 3. PROTOZOOLOGY, PARASITOLOGY. *Educ:* Colo State Univ, BS, 56, MS, 62; Univ Ill, PhD(vet med sci), 65. *Prof Exp:* Sr res parasitologist, Beltsville Parasitol Lab, Sci & Educ Admin-Agr Res, 65-76, asstt area dir, Sci

& Educ Admin-Agr Res, 76-81, DIR, ROCKY MOUNTAIN AREA, AGR RES SERV, USDA, FT COLLINS, 81- *Mem:* Am Soc Parasitol; World Asn Advan Vet Parasitol. *Res:* Biology and taxonomy of coccidia; cytology, cytochemistry and electron microscopy of intestinal protozoan parasites. *Mailing Add:* Area Dir Off PO Box E Ft Collins CO 80522

VETTERLING, WILLIAM THOMAS, b Greenfield, Mass, July 16, 48. SOLID STATE PHYSICS. *Educ:* Amherst Col, BA, 70; Harvard Univ, MA, 71, PhD(physics), 76. *Prof Exp:* asst prof, 76-80, ASSOC PROF PHYSICS, HARVARD UNIV, 80- *Mem:* Am Phys Soc. *Res:* Mössbauer effect, solid state physics, synchrotron radiation. *Mailing Add:* Lyman Lab Harvard Univ Cambridge MA 02138

VEUM, TRYGVE LAURITZ, b Virogua, Wis, Mar 16, 40; m 67; c 2. ANIMAL NUTRITION, VETERINARY PHYSIOLOGY. *Educ:* Univ Wis, BS, 62; Cornell Univ, MS, 65, PhD(animal nutrit, vet physiol & path), 68. *Prof Exp:* Asst prof, 67-74, assoc prof, 74-80, PROF ANIMAL NUTRIT, UNIV MO-COLUMBIA, 80- *Mem:* Am Soc Animal Sci. *Res:* Swine nutrition. *Mailing Add:* Animal Sci Res Ctr Univ of Mo-Columbia Columbia MO 65201

VEVERKA, JOSEPH F, b Pelrimov, Czech, June 8, 41; Can citizen; m 69; c 1. PLANETARY SCIENCE, ASTRONOMY. *Educ:* Queen's Univ, Kingston, Ont, BSc, 64, MSc, 65; Harvard Univ, MA, PhD(astron), 70. *Prof Exp:* Res assoc, 70-72, sr res assoc space sci, 72-74, asst prof, 74-77, ASSOC PROF ASTRON, CORNELL UNIV, 77- *Mem:* Am Astron Soc; Am Geophys Union; Meteoritical Soc; Royal Astron Soc Can. *Res:* Spacecraft investigation of planetary and satellite surfaces; evolution of planets and satellites. *Mailing Add:* Lab for Planetary Studies Cornell Univ Ithaca NY 14853

VEZINA, CLAUDE, b Oka, Que, Feb 19, 26; m 52; c 3. MICROBIOLOGY. *Educ:* Univ Montreal, BA, 46, BSA, 50, MSc, 52; Univ Wis, PhD(bact), 56. *Prof Exp:* Prof bact & biochem, Oka Agr Inst, Univ Montreal, 50-60; head gen microbiol, Res Labs, Ayerst, McKenna & Harrison, Ltd, 60-64, assoc dir res-microbiol, 64-80, DIR MICROBIOL, AYERST LABS, AM HOME PRODS CORP, 80- *Concurrent Pos:* Nat Res Coun Can res assoc, 57; asst prof, Fac Med, Univ Montreal. *Mem:* Am Soc Microbiol; Mycol Soc Am; Soc Indust Microbiol; Am Chem Soc; Soc Gen Microbiol. *Res:* Microbial genetics and physiology; transformation of steroids; antibiotics; heterokaryosis in fungi; recombination in streptomyces and nocardia; nocardiophages; antitumor agents. *Mailing Add:* Dept Microbiol Ayerst Labs Am Home Prod Corp Box 6115 Montreal PQ H3C 3S1 Can

VEZIROGLU, T NEJAT, b Istanbul, Turkey, Jan 24, 24; m 61; c 2. HEAT TRANSFER, NUCLEAR ENGINEERING. *Educ:* Univ London, BSc, 46, PhD(heat transfer), 51, Imp Col, dipl, 47. *Prof Exp:* Sci adv, Off Soil Prod, Ankara, Turkey, 53-55, assoc dir steel silos, 55-57; eng consult, 57-59; tech dir, M K Veziroglu Construct Co Ltd, Istanbul, 59-62; assoc prof mech eng, 62-66, chmn dept, 71-75, assoc dean res, 75-79, PROF MECH ENG, UNIV MIAMI, 66-, DIR, CLEAN ENERGY RES INST, 74- *Concurrent Pos:* Ed, Int J Hydrogen Energy. *Mem:* AAAS; fel Am Soc Mech Engrs; Am Inst Aeronaut & Astronaut; fel Brit Inst Mech Engrs; Int Asn Hydrogen Energy (pres). *Res:* Thermal conductance of metal surfaces in contact; two-phase flow instabilities; solar and hydrogen energy. *Mailing Add:* 800 Paradiso Ave Coral Gables FL 33146

VEZZETTI, DAVID JOSEPH, statistical mechanics, see previous edition

VEZZOLI, GARY CHRISTOPHER, solid state physics, chemical physics, see previous edition

VIA, FRANCIS ANTHONY, b Frostburg, Md; m 70. CHEMISTRY. *Educ:* WVa Univ, BS, 65; Ohio State Univ, MS, 67, PhD(phys org chem), 70. *Prof Exp:* Teaching asst chem, Ohio State Univ, 65-66, res fel phys org chem, 66-70; from res chemist to sr res chemist, 70-75, MGR INORG CHEM, STAUFFER CHEM CO, 75- *Mem:* Am Chem Soc. *Res:* Synthetic methods and structure-reactivity relationships in organophosphorus chemistry; organic and inorganic photochemistry applied to initiation of polymerization; Zeigler-Natta catalysis. *Mailing Add:* Eastern Res Ctr Stauffer Chem Co Dobbs Ferry NY 10522

VIA, GIORGIO G, b Rome, Italy, Dec 6, 28; US citizen; m 55; c 3. PHYSICS. *Educ:* Univ Pisa, PhD(physics), 57. *Prof Exp:* Assoc physicist res lab, Switz, 58-60, staff physicist fed systs div, NY, 60-61, 63, adv physicist, 64, adv physicist space systs ctr advan progs, 64-68, sr physicist, 68-70, SR PHYSICIST, FED SYST DIV, MANASSAS, IBM CORP, 70- *Res:* Applied research in solid state, semiconductors and magnetics; electron diffraction studies; electronoptics devices and advanced storage techniques; very large scale integration devices technology and fabrication; integrated circuits evaluation and testing; high resolution photolitographic systems; scanning electron microscopy of very large scale integration for process development. *Mailing Add:* 5954 Woodacre Ct McLean VA 22101

VIA, WILLIAM FREDRICK, JR, b Ironton, Ohio, Dec 27, 20; m 47; c 2. PEDODONTICS. *Educ:* Ohio State Univ, DDS, 45; Univ Mich, MS, 53. *Prof Exp:* Instr oper dent, Col Dent, Ohio State Univ, 48-51; instr, Col Dent, Univ Calif, 51-52; mem staff, Henry Ford Hosp, Detroit, Mich, 53-68; chmn dept oral radiol, Sch Dent Med, Univ Conn, 68-69; prof oral diag & chmn dept, Sch Dent, Univ NC, Chapel Hill, 69-80; RETIRED. *Mem:* AAAS; fel Am Col Dentists; fel Am Acad Dent Radiol; Am Acad Pedodontics; Int Asn Dent Res. *Res:* Prenatal, neonatal and post-natal influences upon dental enamel development; healing of dental pulp following bacterial, chemical or mechanical trauma; oral roentgenographic technique. *Mailing Add:* Box 2006 Chapel Hill NC 27514

VIAL, JAMES LESLIE, b Taft, Calif, Dec 19, 24. VETEBRATE BIOLOGY, POPULATION ECOLOGY. *Educ:* Calif State Univ, Long Beach, BA, 52, MA, 54; Univ Southern Calif, PhD, 65. *Prof Exp:* From instr to assoc prof biol, Los Angeles Valley Col, 55-61; vis prof zool, Univ Costa Rica, 61-62, Ford Found Prof ecol, 62-64; asst prof biol, Western Mich Univ, 64-66; from assoc prof to prof, Univ Mo-Kansas City, 66-75, asst dean res & dir res admin, 67-68; PROF BIOL & CHMN FAC NATURAL SCI, UNIV TULSA, 75- *Concurrent Pos:* Assoc dir, Orgn Trop Studies, Inst Trop Ecol, Costa Rica, 63, dir, 64; herpet ed, Am Soc Ichthyologists & Herpetologists, 72- *Mem:* AAAS; Ecol Soc Am; Am Soc Mammal; Soc Study Amphibians & Reptiles; Asn Trop Biol. *Res:* Vertebrate ecology and population dynamics, especially amphibians and reptiles. *Mailing Add:* Fac of Natural Sci Univ of Tulsa Tulsa OK 74104

VIAL, LESTER JOSEPH, JR, b New Orleans, La, Mar 19, 44; m 71. MEDICINE, PATHOLOGY. *Educ:* La State Univ, New Orleans, BS, 66; Med Sch, La State Univ, MD, 70; Am Bd Path, dipl, 74. *Prof Exp:* Intern path, Charity Hosp, New Orleans, 70-71, resident, 71-74; instr, 74-75, ASST PROF PATH, MED SCH, LA STATE UNIV, 75- *Concurrent Pos:* Vis staff, Charity Hosp, New Orleans, 74- *Mem:* AOA; Am Soc Clin Path; Am Soc Cytol. *Mailing Add:* Dept of Path Sch Med La State Univ 1542 Tulane Ave New Orleans LA 70112

VIAL, THEODORE MERRIAM, b Ware, Iowa, Feb 27, 21; m 49; c 5. RUBBER CHEMISTRY. *Educ:* Univ Md, BS, 42; Univ Ill, PhD(chem), 49. *Prof Exp:* Res chemist, Chas Pfizer & Co, 48-50; res chemist, 50-51, tech rep, 51-58, tech mgr rubber chem dept, 58-60, com develop mgr, 60-63, sales develop mgr, 63-66, GROUP LEADER, CHEM RES DIV, AM CYANAMID CO, 66- *Mem:* AAAS; Am Chem Soc; Com Develop Asn. *Res:* Rubber and elastomer compounding; theory and application of vulcanization and protective agents; polyacrylate and other specialty elastomers. *Mailing Add:* Am Cyanamid Co Chem Res Div Bound Brook NJ 08805

VIALE, RICHARD O, b Eureka, Calif, June 9, 40; m 62; c 2. BIOCHEMISTRY, BIOPHYSICS. *Educ:* Chico State Col, AB, 62; Univ Calif, Davis, PhD(biophys), 55. *Prof Exp:* NIH fel, Sch Med, Univ Pa, 66-67; assoc, 67-71, ASST PROF BIOCHEM, SCH MED, UNIV PA, 71- *Mem:* AAAS. *Res:* Applied mathematics in biochemistry; methods of education in biochemistry and medicine; application of computers to biochemistry. *Mailing Add:* 4618 Larchwood Ave Philadelphia PA 19143

VIAMONTE, MANUEL, JR, radiology, see previous edition

VIAN, RICHARD W, geology, see previous edition

VIANNA, NICHOLAS JOSEPH, b New York, NY, Dec 20, 41; m 67; c 2. EPIDEMIOLOGY. *Educ:* St Peter's Col, BS, 63; Cornell Univ Med Col, 67; Albany Med Col, MSPH, 71. *Prof Exp:* Intern & resident med, Montefiore Hosp & Med Ctr, New York, 68-70; clin instr, Albany Med Col, 70-71; fel infectious dis, NJ Col Med & Sloan Kettering Mem Inst, 71-72; DIR BUR OCCUP HEALTH & CHRONIC DIS RES, NY STATE DEPT HEALTH, ALBANY, 72-; ASST PROF, DEPT MED & PREV MED, ALBANY MED COL, 72- *Concurrent Pos:* Asst to the dir, Bur Epidemiol & Cancer, NY State Health Dept, Albany, 69-71; officer epidemiol, Ctr Dis Control, Atlanta, 69-71; consult, Kettering Inst Cancer Res, NY, 72-73 & Cancer Epidemiol Sect, WHO, Geneva, Switz, 72-73; travel fel, WHO, Oxford Univ, 72; dir, Coeymans Med Clin, Albany, NY, 72-; consult infectious dis, Ellis Hosp, Schenectady, NY, 73- *Res:* Epidemiology of lymphoreticular malignancies with major emphasis on etiology. *Mailing Add:* NY State Dept Health Tower Bldg Empire State Plaza Albany NY 12237

VIAVANT, WILLIAM JOSEPH, b San Antonio, Tex, Jan 2, 22; m 50; div. COMPUTER SCIENCE. *Educ:* Univ Tex, BS, 44, PhD(physics), 54. *Prof Exp:* Res physicist, Univ Tex, 51-55; res scientist, Shell Develop Co, 55-57; dir sci comput, Univ Okla, 57-62; NSF sr fel, Cambridge & Regnecentralen, Denmark, 62-63; PROF COMPUT SCI, UNIV UTAH, 64- *Concurrent Pos:* Consult, Owens-Ill Co, 64-71, Gen Elec Co, 66, Univ Jundi Shapur, Ahwaz, Iran, 74-75 & IBM Corp, Nairobi, Kenya, 79; Iran minister of higher educ, 74-75. *Mem:* Asn Comput Mach; Sigma Xi. *Res:* Computer organization and programming; simulation; person-to-machine communication; academic programs in computer science; small computer systems. *Mailing Add:* Dept Comput Sci Univ Utah Salt Lake City UT 84112

VICE, JOHN LEONARD, b Evergreen Park, Ill, Jan 12, 42; m 63. MICROBIOLOGY, BIOCHEMISTRY. *Educ:* Loyola Univ Chicago, BS, 63; Univ Ill, Chicago, MS, 65, PhD(microbiol), 69. *Prof Exp:* Res microbiologist, Nat Cancer Inst, 65-66; dir clin microbiol, Alexian Bros Med Ctr, Ill, 67-68; dir clin microbiol, Med Ctr, Loyola Univ, Chicago, 68-77; SECT HEAD, CLIN MICROBIOL, CITY OF HOPE, NAT MED CTR, DUARTE, CA, 77- *Concurrent Pos:* Consult, Community Gen Hosp, Sterling, Ill, 72- *Mem:* Am Soc Microbiol. *Res:* Immunogenetics of rabbit immunoglobulins; rabbit lymphocyte antigens; immunochemical characterization of gram negative nonfermentative bacteria. *Mailing Add:* City of Hope 1500 E Duarte Rd Duarte CA 91010

VICEPS-MADORE, DACE I, b Esslingen, Ger, Feb 22, 47; US citizen; m 75. CELL BIOLOGY. *Educ:* Univ Rochester, AB, 69; Temple Univ, MA, 71, PhD(biol), 74. *Prof Exp:* Res investr cell biol, Wistar, Inst, 73-75; fel cell biol, Inst Cancer Res, 75-77; fel pharmacol, Yale Univ, 77-80; MEM FAC, DEPT BIOCHEM, UNIV VT, 80- *Mem:* AAAS; Asn Women Sci; Tissue Cult Asn; Sigma Xi. *Res:* The regulation of enzyme activity in eukaryotic cells. *Mailing Add:* Dept Biochem Univ Vt Burlington VT 05401

VICHER, EDWARD ERNEST, b Chicago, Ill, Nov 12, 14; m 50; c 2. BACTERIOLOGY. *Educ:* Univ Ill, BS, 35, MS, 37, PhD(bact), 42. *Prof Exp:* Asst bact, Col Pharm, 35-39, from instr to assoc prof, Col Med, 39-69, prof, 69-78, EMER PROF BACT, COL MED, UNIV ILL, 78-, ASSOC DEPT HEAD MICROBIOL, 76- *Concurrent Pos:* Pharmacist, Ill, 35-; consult res

& educ hosps, 46-; consult, US Vet Admin Hosps, Hines & Chicago, 46-56; consult, Toni Co, 52-72. *Mem:* Am Soc Microbiol; Med Mycol Soc of the Americas. *Res:* Medical microbiology; clinical diagnostic bacteriology; mycology and parasitology; hospital asepsis and disinfection; metabolism of the dermatophytes; cariogenic streptococci. *Mailing Add:* Dept of Microbiol Univ of Ill Col Med Chicago IL 60612

VICHICH, THOMAS E, b Calumet, Mich, Oct 5, 17; m 45; c 2. MATHEMATICS. *Educ:* Mich Col Mining & Technol, BS, 39; Univ Mich, MS, 52. *Prof Exp:* From instr to assoc prof, 41-61, PROF MATH, MICH TECHNOL UNIV, 61- *Res:* Differential and integral calculus; differential equations. *Mailing Add:* Dept of Math Mich Technol Univ Houghton MI 49931

VICK, ALPHONSO ROSCOE, b Wilson Co, NC, Mar 12, 20; m 49; c 2. BOTANY, ZOOLOGY. *Educ:* J C Smith Univ, AB, 42; NC Col Durham, MS, 47; Univ Mich, AM, 56; Syracuse Univ, PhD(bot), 61. *Prof Exp:* Prof biol, Bennett Col, 61-62; prof, Winston-Salem State Col, 62-67, chmn sci dept, 63-67; PROF BIOL, NC A&T STATE UNIV, 67- *Mem:* AAAS; Nat Inst Sci; Inst Biol Sci Med; Sigma Xi. *Res:* A comparison of the accumulation rates of radioactive phosphorus in certain vital organs of fish; radioactive phosphorus is fed the specimens over a given period followed by dissecting out the organs and exposing them to a radioactive detecting machine to ascertain the concentration of the isotope in the respective organs. *Mailing Add:* 1601 S Benbow Rd Greensboro NC 27406

VICK, CHARLES BOOKER, b Seaboard, NC, Sept 15, 32; m 63; c 2. FOREST PRODUCTS. *Educ:* Duke Univ, AB, 54, MF, 58. *Prof Exp:* Forest prod technologist, 58-60, wood scientist, 60-74, PRIN WOOD SCIENTIST, FORESTRY SCI LAB, SOUTHEASTERN FOREST EXP STA, 74- *Honors & Awards:* Cert appreciation, USDA, 73, Cert Merit, 75. *Mem:* Am Soc Testing & Mat; Forest Prod Res Soc; Adhesion Soc. *Res:* Housing research, especially development and application of structural adhesives for more efficient structural design of light-frame constructions. *Mailing Add:* Forestry Sci Lab Carlton St Athens GA 30602

VICK, GEORGE R, b New Waverly, Tex, Dec 18, 20; m 43; c 2. ALGEBRA, GEOMETRY. *Educ:* Sam Houston State Teachers Col, BA, 41, MA, 42; Univ Tex, PhD(math), 64. *Prof Exp:* Teacher high sch, Tex, 41-42; from asst prof to assoc prof math, 46-51, assoc prof, 55-56, actg dir dept, 56-64, dir dept, 64-67, PROF MATH, SAM HOUSTON STATE UNIV, 64- *Mem:* Math Asn Am; Nat Coun Teachers Math. *Res:* Foundations of geometry; mathematical pedagogy at all levels, especially training and re-training teachers. *Mailing Add:* Div Math & Info Sci Sam Houston State Univ Huntsville TX 77340

VICK, GERALD KIETH, b Dixon, Ill, Mar 6, 30; m 50; c 3. ORGANIC CHEMISTRY. *Educ:* Univ Ill, BS, 52; Univ Rochester, PhD(org chem), 56. *Prof Exp:* Res chemist, Esso Res & Eng Co, 55-58, proj leader engine oils, 58-62, sect head motor fuels & lubricants, 62-65, sr staff adv petrol fuels & lubricants, 65-67, dir lubricants & specialties lab, 67-75, sr planning adv, Corp Planning Dept, Exxon Corp, 75-76, SR STAFF ADV, SYNTHETIC FUELS RES, EXXON RES & ENG CO, 76- *Mem:* AAAS; Am Chem Soc; Soc Automotive Eng. *Res:* Liquid fuels and lubricants. *Mailing Add:* Exxon Res & Eng Co PO Box 101 Florham NJ 07932

VICK, JAMES WHITFIELD, b Hope, Ark, Mar 8, 42; m 64; c 2. MATHEMATICS. *Educ:* La State Univ, Baton Rouge, BS, 64; Univ Va, MA, 66, PhD(math), 68. *Prof Exp:* Instr math, Princeton Univ, 68-70; asst prof, 70-73, ASSOC PROF MATH, UNIV TEX, AUSTIN, 73-, ASST DEAN, COL NATURAL SCI, 80- *Mem:* Math Asn Am; Am Math Soc. *Res:* Algebraic and differential topology, K-theory and transformation groups. *Mailing Add:* Dept of Math Univ of Tex Austin TX 78712

VICK, ROBERT LORE, b Courtland, Miss, Sept 1, 29; m 53; c 1. PHARMACOLOGY, PHYSIOLOGY. *Educ:* Univ Miss, BS, 52, MS, 54; Univ Cincinnati, PhD(pharmacol), 57. *Prof Exp:* Actg asst prof pharm, Southwestern Okla State Col, 53; instr, Univ Miss, 53-54; res assoc pharmacol, Univ Cincinnati, 57-58; instr physiol, State Univ NY Upstate Med Ctr, 58-61; from asst prof to assoc prof, 61-72, PROF PHYSIOL, BAYLOR COL MED, 72- *Concurrent Pos:* USPHS career develop award, 66-71. *Mem:* AAAS; Am Physiol Soc; Int Soc Heart Res; Am Soc Pharmacol & Exp Therapeut; Soc Exp Biol & Med. *Res:* Heart and circulation; ion movements; electrophysiology; autonomic nervous system. *Mailing Add:* Dept of Physiol Baylor Col of Med Houston TX 77030

VICKERS, DAVID HYLE, b Sturgis, Miss, Jan 14, 40; m 70; c 2. ENTOMOLOGY, BIOCHEMISTRY. *Educ:* Miss State Univ, BS, 61, MS, 64; La State Univ, PhD(entom), 69. *Prof Exp:* Instr entom, Southeastern La Col, 64-66; asst prof physiol, Fla Technol Univ, 69-72, actg chmn dept, 74-75, chmn, 75-81, ASSOC PROF PHYSIOL, UNIV CENT FLA, 72- *Mem:* AAAS; Am Inst Biol Sci; Entom Soc Am. *Res:* Pollution of natural waters by solid wastes; insect lipids; metabolism of pesticides by insects, particularly chemosterilants; nitrogen metabolism in insects. *Mailing Add:* Dept Biol Sci Univ Cent Fla Orlando FL 32816

VICKERS, FLORENCE FOSTER, b Philadelphia, Pa, Mar 3, 47; m 76. PHARMACOLOGY. *Educ:* Pa State Univ, BS, 69; Hahnemann Med Col, PhD(cardiovasc physiol & pharmacol), 81. *Prof Exp:* Res biologist, Merk Sharp & Dohme Res Labs, 69-74, med writer, 74-78; INSTR, HAHNEMANN MED COL, 79-80. *Mem:* AAAS. *Res:* Cardiovascular physiology and pharmacology; renin-angiotension system; anti hypertensive drugs; beta adrenoceptor antagonists; catecholamines. *Mailing Add:* Box 243 Bedminster PA 18944

VICKERS, FRANK DOW, b Sebastian, Fla, Aug 25, 36; m 60; c 1. COMPUTER SCIENCE. *Educ:* Univ Fla, BS, 58, MS, 59, PhD(elec eng), 64. *Prof Exp:* Assoc prof indust & systs eng, 64-71, ASSOC PROF COMPUT & INFO SCI, UNIV FLA, 71- *Mem:* Inst Elec & Electronics Engrs; Asn Comput Mach. *Res:* Softwave systems design, particularly multiprogramming, time sharing and high level language interpreters; computer aided instruction and training; computer science education. *Mailing Add:* Dept of Comput & Info Sci Univ Fla Weil 512 Gainesville FL 32611

VICKERS, J(OHN) M(ICHAEL) F(RANK), b Dar-es-Salaam, Brit EAfrica, May 2, 23; m 46; c 2. ELECTRICAL ENGINEERING. *Educ:* Univ Birmingham, BSc, 48; Univ Toronto, MASc, 51, PhD, 54. *Prof Exp:* Demonstr, instr & lectr mech eng, Univ Toronto, 48-55; assoc prof, Univ Nebr, 55-61; res specialist, Calif Inst Technol, 61-66, mem tech staff, 66-77, proj engr, Nimbus E & F Microwave Spectrometers & Apollo Gamma Ray Spectrometer, 69-75, task mgr, Nimbus G & Seasat 1 Scanning Multi-Channel Microwave Radiometers, 75-77, task mgr, Shuttle Imaging Radar-A, 77, dep mgt, Radar Sci & Eng Sect, Telecommun Sci & Eng Div, 77-80. *Concurrent Pos:* Engr, Serv Div, A V Roe, Can, 50; consult, Majestic Elec Co, Can, 52-54; engr, McGregor, Anderson & Beynon, 55. *Mem:* Assoc fel Am Inst Aeronaut & Astronaut. *Res:* Radar engineering; microwave radiometry. *Mailing Add:* 5047 Fallhaven Lane La Canada CA 91011

VICKERS, JAMES HUDSON, b Columbus, Ohio, Apr 21, 30; m 64; c 1. VETERINARY MEDICINE, PATHOLOGY. *Educ:* Ohio State Univ, BSc, 52, DVM, 58; Univ Conn, MS, 66; Am Col Vet Pathologists, dipl, 75. *Prof Exp:* Vet, Columbus Zoo, Ohio, 58-60 & Lab Animal Colony, Lederle Labs, Am Cyanamid Co, NY, 60-64, pathologist, 64-66, head dept vet path, 66-68, head dept exp path, 68-70; vpres & dir res, Primelabs, Inc, 70-73; DIR PATH & PRIMATOL BR, BUR BIOL, FOOD & DRUG ADMIN, 73- *Concurrent Pos:* Lectureship, State Univ NY Downstate Med Sch; Food & Drug Admin rep, Interagency Primate Steering Comt, 74-, proj officer, Primate Breeding Colony contracts. *Mem:* Am Vet Med Asn; Am Asn Zool Vets; Am Col Vet Pathologists; Soc Toxicol; Int Acad Pathol. *Res:* Diseases and pathology of primates, laboratory animals and exotic zoological species; testing and quality control of vaccines, especially polio vaccine, toxicological testing and pathology of pharmaceuticals. *Mailing Add:* 2324 Oak Dr Ijamsville MD 21754

VICKERS, PAUL T(HOMAS), b Anderson, Ind, Sept 27, 23; m 48; c 7. MECHANICAL ENGINEERING. *Educ:* Gen Motors Inst, BSME, 48. *Prof Exp:* Student engr, D,elco Remy Div, 41-43, jr engr, Res Lab, 48-51, res engr, 51-54, sr res engr, 54-56, supv heat transfer, 56-71, asst head emissions res dept, 71-73, asst head engine res dept, 73-79, HEAD FLUID DYNAMICS DEPT, RES LAB, GEN MOTORS CORP, 79- *Mem:* Soc Automotive Engrs; fel Am Soc Mech Engrs; Sigma Xi; Combustion Inst. *Res:* Vehicular powerplant research; emission reduction and fuel economy improvement; vehicle aerodynamics; fluid motions in engines. *Mailing Add:* Fluid Dynamics Dept Gen Motors Res Labs 12 Mile & Mound Rd Warren MI 48090

VICKERS, ROGER SPENCER, b Hitchin, Eng, Nov 13, 37; m 67; c 3. REMOTE SENSING, MEASUREMENT TECHNOLOGY. *Educ:* Univ Southampton, BSc, 59, PhD(physics), 63. *Prof Exp:* Res physicist, IIT Res Inst, 63-66 & Stanford Univ, 66-68; res assoc remote sensing, Colo State Univ, 68-69; vpres, Environ Res Assocs, 69-70; assoc prof remote sensing, Colo State Univ, 70-73; SR PHYSICIST, SRI INT, 73- *Concurrent Pos:* Consult, commercial & industrial, 71-81, NSF, 74-79. *Honors & Awards:* IR-100 Award, 76. *Mem:* Soc Explor Geophysicists. *Res:* Remote sensing techniques; infrared absorption and Raman spectroscopy; high resolution radars; subsurface profiling; radar sounding of ice; development of electromagnetic geophysical techniques; airborne ground-penetrating radar. *Mailing Add:* SRI Int Menlo Park CA 94025

VICKERS, STANLEY, b Blackpool, Eng, Sept 27, 39. DRUG METABOLISM. *Educ:* Univ London, BSc, 62; State Univ NY Buffalo, PhD(biochem pharm), 67. *Prof Exp:* Fel, Univ Kans, 66-69; res fel, 69-80, SR RES FEL DRUG METAB, MERCK INST THERAPEUT RES, 80- *Mem:* Am Soc Pharmacol & Exp Therapeut; Am Chem Soc; AAAS; Royal Soc Chem; NY Acad Sci. *Res:* Detoxification mechanisms and metabolic transformations which control the fate of foreign compounds. *Mailing Add:* Merck Inst for Therapeut Res West Point PA 19486

VICKERS, THOMAS J, b Miami, Fla, Mar 29, 39; m 63; c 4. ANALYTICAL CHEMISTRY. *Educ:* Spring Hill Col, BS, 61; Univ Fla, PhD(chem), 64. *Prof Exp:* From asst prof to assoc prof, 66-76, PROF ANAL CHEM, FLA STATE UNIV, 76- *Mem:* Am Chem Soc; Soc Appl Spectros. *Res:* Spectroscopic methods of trace element analysis, atomic emission, absorption and fluorescence flame spectrometry; new excitation sources for emission spectroscopy; non-flame atomization techniques. *Mailing Add:* Dept of Chem Fla State Univ Tallahassee FL 32306

VICKERS, WILLIAM W, b San Francisco, Calif, June 21, 23; m 54; c 3. ATMOSPHERIC PHYSICS. *Educ:* Univ Calif, BA, 54, MA, 56; McGill Univ, PhD(hydrol, meteorol), 65. *Prof Exp:* Res assoc, Inst Polar Studies, Ohio State Univ, 57-61; head geophys res group, Tech Opers, Inc, 61-66; SR SCI EXEC, EG&G, INC & ENVIRON SENSOR SYSTS DIV, MITRE CORP, BEDFORD, 66- *Concurrent Pos:* Mitre Corp grant, 69-70. *Mem:* Am Geophys Union; Am Meteorol Soc; NY Acad Sci; Cosmos Club. *Res:* Weather modification; atmospheric pollution transport; atmospheric refraction; cloud physics; electronic warfare. *Mailing Add:* Indian Hill Prides Crossing MA 01965

VICKERS, ZATA MARIE, b Salem, Ore, Oct 13, 50. FOOD SCIENCE. *Educ:* Ore State Univ, BS, 72; Cornell Univ, PhD(food sci), 75. *Prof Exp:* Asst prof, 75-80, ASSOC PROF FOOD SCI, UNIV MINN, ST PAUL, 80- *Mem:* Inst Food Technol. *Res:* Relationships between the physical, acoustical and sensory properties of foods. *Mailing Add:* Dept of Food Sci & Nutrit Univ Minn St Paul MN 55101

VICKERY, LARRY EDWARD, b Atlanta, Ga, Nov 26, 45; c 2. ENZYMOLOGY, STEROID CHEMISTRTY. *Educ:* Univ Calif, Santa Barbara, BA, 67, PhD(biol), 71. *Prof Exp:* Res assoc biochem, Western Regional Res Lab, USDA, 71; res assoc biophys chem, Lawrence Berkeley Lab, 72; fel, Univ Calif, Berkeley, 73-74, res assoc biophys chem, Dept Chem, 75-76; ASST PROF BIOPHYS, DEPT PHYSIOL, UNIV CALIF, IRVINE, 77- *Concurrent Pos:* Res assoc, Nat Res Coun, Nat Acad Sci, Nat Acad Engr, 71; fel, Nat Inst Gen Med Sci, USPHS, 73-74. *Mem:* Biophys Soc; AAAS. *Res:* Investigations on the molecular mechanisms and regulation of steroid hormone biosynthesis; characterization of enzymes and reaction mechanisms involved; development of inhibitors of steroid synthesis. *Mailing Add:* Dept Physiol & Biophys Univ of Calif Irvine CA 92717

VICKERY, ROBERT KINGSTON, JR, b Saratoga, Calif, Sept 18, 22; m 51; c 2. PLANT EVOLUTION. *Educ:* Stanford Univ, AB, 44, AM, 48, PhD(biol, bot), 52. *Prof Exp:* Instr bot, Pomona Col, 50-51; from instr to assoc prof biol, 52-64, head dept genetics & cytol, 62-65, PROF BIOL, UNIV UTAH, 64- *Concurrent Pos:* Researcher, Carnegie Inst Wash, 48-52; res fel, Calif Inst Technol, 55; vis assoc prof, Harvard Univ, 63; mem gen biol & genetics fel panel, NIH, 65-69, 7th, 12th & 13th Int Bot Cong & 10th-13th Int Gen Cong; assoc ed, Evolution, Soc Study Evolution, 68-72; mem, Int Orgn Plant Biosysts Coun, 75-81. *Mem:* AAAS; Soc Study Evolution (vpres, 77-78); Am Soc Nat; Ecol Soc Am; Genetics Soc Am. *Res:* Cytogenetics, ecologic, numerical and classical taxonomic, and biochemical approaches to problems of the evolutionary mechanisms and patterns of the genus Mimulus, particularly sections Simiolus and Erythranthe. *Mailing Add:* Dept of Biol Univ of Utah Salt Lake City UT 84112

VICKERY, VERNON RANDOLPH, taxonomy, entomology, see previous edition

VICKREY, HERTA MILLER, b San Gregorio, Calif; div; c 4. IMMUNOLOGY, MEDICAL MICROBIOLOGY. *Educ:* Jan Jose State Col, BA, 57; Univ Calif, Berkeley, MA, 63, PhD(bact & immunol), 70. *Prof Exp:* Microbiologist, Viral & Rickettsial Dis Lab, Calif State Dept Pub Health, 57-60, 61-62; res bacteriologist, Univ Calif, Berkeley, 63-64; asst prof immunol, virol & microbiol, Univ Victoria, BC, 70-72; RES ASSOC CANCER IMMUNOL, DEPT RES & EDUC, WAYNE COUNTY GEN HOSP, 72- *Concurrent Pos:* Bacteriologist, Children's Hosp Med Ctr Northern Calif, Oakland, 58-70; res grants, Univ Victoria, BC, 70-72; med staff res & educ grants, 73-81. *Mem:* Am Soc Microbiol; Clin Ligand Assay Soc; Am Soc Clin Path. *Res:* Cellular immunological resistance: tuberculosis and oncogenesis; cell culture assays to autoallergies, oncogenesis and hypersensitivities; tissue culture studies: lymphatic leukemia immunotherapy; growth and metabolic responses of liver cells (canine, rabbit, murine-diabetic versus normal) to hormones, drugs, lectins, medium additives; hybridoma immunological technology. *Mailing Add:* Dept Res & Educ PO Box 549 Wayne County Gen Hosp Wayne MI 48184

VICKROY, DAVID GILL, b San Antonio, Tex, July 5, 41; m 64; c 2. ANALYTICAL CHEMISTRY. *Educ:* Vanderbilt Univ, BA, 63; Rice Univ, MA, 66; Univ Tenn, PhD(inorg chem), 69. *Prof Exp:* Res chemist, 69-72, sr res chemist, 72-75, res assoc anal chem, 75-76, GROUP LEADER, CELANESE FIBERS C0, 76- *Mem:* Sigma Xi; Am Chem Soc; NY Acad Sci. *Res:* Analytical characterization of complex mixtures such as tobacco smoke and environmental samples; development of synthetic alternatives to natural products. *Mailing Add:* Celanese Fibers Co PO Box 32414 Charlotte NC 28232

VICKROY, VIRGIL VESTER, JR, b San Antonio, Tex, Aug 8, 31; m 55; c 2. POLYMER CHEMISTRY, PHYSICAL CHEMISTRY. *Educ:* Auburn Univ, BS, 52; Univ Akron, MS, 62, PhD(polymer sci), 65. *Prof Exp:* Jr chemist, B F Goodrich Co, 55-61; res chemist, Harrison-Morton Labs, Ohio, 61-63; res chemist, Univ Akron, 63-65; sr res chemist, Monsanto Co, 65-73, lab mgr, 73-74; prin chemist, Dart Industs, 74-75; RES CHEMIST, ALLIED CORP, 75- *Mem:* Am Chem Soc; Soc Rheol; NAm Thermal Anal Soc; Soc Plastics Engrs. *Res:* Effect of thermal and thermo-oxidative history on morphological, mechanical and molecular properties of polyolefins; physical chemistry of Ziegler and Phillips catalyst systems. *Mailing Add:* PO Box 53006 Baton Rouge LA 70805

VICTERY, WINONA WHITWELL, b Abilene, Tex, Apr 15, 41; m 63. RENAL PHYSIOLOGY, METAL TOXICOLOGY. *Educ:* Rice Univ, BA, 63; Univ Wis-Madison, MS, 67; Univ Mich, Ann Arbor, PhD(physiol), 78. *Prof Exp:* Res biologist nuclear med, Univ Calif, Los Angeles, 67-74; scholar physiol, Univ Mich, 78-81; SCHOLAR PHARM, NAT INST ENVIRON HEALTH SCI, 81- *Mem:* Am Physiol Soc; Sigma Xi. *Res:* Physiological relationships between essential and toxic trace metals; mechanisms of renal handling of lead and zinc using clearance, stop-flow and membrane vesicle techniques. *Mailing Add:* Nat Inst Environ Health Sci PO Box 12233 Research Triangle Park NC 27709

VICTOR, ANDREW C, b New York, NY, Nov 4, 34; m 55; c 3. ENGINEERING PHYSICS. *Educ:* Swarthmore Col, BA, 56; Univ Md, MS, 61. *Prof Exp:* Physicist, Nat Bur Stand, 56-62; head, Standards Lab, US Naval Ord Test Sta, 62-64, physicist systs anal & rocket plume technol, 64-68, head, Anal Br, 68-73, head Propulsion Anal Br, 73-76, head appl propulsion res, 76-79, coordr independent explor develop, 79-80, proj mgr explosives advan develop, 80-81, HEAD THERMAL/STRUCTURES BR, US NAVAL WEAPONS CTR, 81- *Concurrent Pos:* Chmn plume technology subcomt, JANNAF, 78- *Mem:* Assoc fel Am Inst Aeronaut & Astronaut; Sigma Xi. *Res:* Missile propulsion analysis; rocket exhaust plume; ramjet engine cost analysis; weapon energy utilization. *Mailing Add:* 712 N Peg St Ridgecrest CA 93555

VICTOR, JOE MAYER, b Houston, Tex, Sept 20, 39; m 81; c 4. ELECTRICAL ENGINEERING. *Educ:* Univ Tex, Austin, BS, 62, MS, 64, PhD, 67. *Prof Exp:* Teaching asst elec eng, Univ Tex, Austin, 61-66; sr res engr, Southwest Res Inst, 66-75; ENG MGR, PETROLITE INSTRUMENTS, 75- *Mem:* Nat Soc Corrosion Engrs; Inst Elec & Electronics Engrs. *Res:* Corrosion instrumentation. *Mailing Add:* Petrolite Instruments PO Box 2546 Houston TX 77001

VICTOR, LEONARD BAKER, b Schenectady, NY, Aug 3, 34; m 66; c 2. CLINICAL PATHOLOGY, LEGAL MEDICINE. *Educ:* NY Univ, AB, 53; Univ Brussels, MD, 60; Royal Col Trop Med, TMD, 60. *Prof Exp:* Intern & resident path, Strong Hosp, Univ Rochester, 61-65, sr instr, Univ, 65-67; assoc prof path & lab med, Meharry Med Col, 68-72, assoc prof path, Grad Sch & dir Meharry Multiphasic Lab, 68-72; prof path, Univ Tenn, Memphis & dir clin labs, City of Memphis Hosps, 72-78; prof & chmn, Dept Path, Sch Med, Marshall Univ, 78-80. *Concurrent Pos:* Dep med examr, Monroe County, NY, 65-67; consult, State Hosp, Rochester, NY, 65-67; assoc prof biomed eng, Sch Eng, Vanderbilt Univ, 69-72; chmn, Comt Health Fitness Sci, Nashville, 70-71; chmn, Nat Adv Task Force for Regional Med Prog Eval of Automated Multiphasic Health Testing, 72; med dir & dir, Mid-South Comprehensive Home Health Serv Agency, 73-77; mem bd dirs, Mid-South Regional Blood Ctr, 73-77. *Mem:* Fel Col Am Path; fel Am Soc Clin Path; fel Soc Advan Med Systs; fel Royal Soc Health; AMA. *Res:* Administrative and legal medicine and pathology including curriculum development and interdisciplinary functions; lab medicine and prospective medicine, including automation, computerization and management techniques. *Mailing Add:* 405 11th Ave W Huntington WV 25701

VICTOREEN, JOHN AUSTIN, b Johnstown, Pa, July 4, 02; m 28, 71; c 2. APPLIED PHYSICS, INSTRUMENTATION. *Hon Degrees:* LLD, John Carroll Univ, 49. *Prof Exp:* Vpres, eng, radio mfg, Victoreen Radio Co, 20-29; pres, chmn bd, radiation instruments, Victoreen Instrument Co, 25-50; OWNER, DIR, HEARING PROSTHETICS, VICTOREEN LAB, 50- *Mem:* Acoust Soc Am. *Res:* Radiation instrumentation; acoustical prosthetics. *Mailing Add:* Victoreen Lab 350 N Maitland Ave Maitland FL 32751

VICTORIA, EDWARD JESS, JR, b San Diego, Calif, Sept 11, 41. BIOCHEMISTRY, CELL BIOLOGY. *Educ:* Univ Calif, Los Angeles, AB, 63, MA, 65, PhD(molecular & cell biol), 68. *Prof Exp:* Asst res biologist, Univ Calif, Los Angeles, 68-69; fel, Univ Utrecht, 70-71; spec res fel, Lab Biochem, NIH, 71-73; ASST RES BIOCHEMIST, DEPT OF PATH, UNIV CALIF, SAN DIEGO, 73- *Concurrent Pos:* Res fel, Am Cancer Soc, Biochemisch Laboratorium, Utrecht, The Netherlands, 70-71; USPHS, NIH fel, 71-73; prin investr, NIH res grant, 78- *Mem:* Am Chem Soc; Am Soc Cell Biol; AAAS. *Res:* Membrane biochemistry. *Mailing Add:* Dept of Path T-003 Univ Calif San Diego La Jolla CA 92093

VICTORICA, BENJAMIN (EDUARDO), b Mendoza, Arg, June 9, 36; m 63; c 3. PEDIATRICS. *Educ:* Nat Univ Cuyo, MD, 62; Educ Coun For Med Grad, cert, 63; Am Bd Pediat, dipl, 68, cert pediat cardiol, 71. *Prof Exp:* Intern, MedSch, Nat Univ Cuyo, 63-63 & St Benedict's Hosp, Ogden, Utah, 63-64; from resident pediat to chief resident, 64-66, instr & spec trainee pediat cardiol, 67-70, asst prof, 70-74, assoc prof, 74-79, PROF PEDIAT CARDIOL, COL MED, UNIV FLA, 80- *Mem:* Fel Am Acad Pediat; Am Col Cardiol. *Res:* Pediatric cardiology. *Mailing Add:* Dept Pediat Univ Fla Col Med Gainesville FL 32601

VICTORIUS, CLAUS, b Hamburg, Ger, Aug 24, 23; nat US; m 52; c 2. ORGANIC COATINGS. *Educ:* Guilford Col, BS, 43; Univ NC, MA, 46. *Prof Exp:* RES ASSOC, EXP STA, E I DU PONT DE NEMOURS & CO, INC, WILMINGTON, DEL, 46- *Mem:* Am Chem Soc. *Res:* Organic coatings; automotive finishes; high solids, powder and water-based coatings. *Mailing Add:* 21 Paxon Hollow Rd Media PA 19063

VIDA, JULIUS, b Losonc, Czech, May 30, 28; US citizen; c 3. MEDICINAL CHEMISTRY. *Educ:* Pazmany Peter Univ, Budapest, Dipl, 50; Carnegie Inst Technol, MS, 59, PhD(org chem), 60; Columbia Univ, MBA, 81. *Prof Exp:* Chemist, EGYT Co, (Wander Co), Hungary, 50-56 & Merck & Co, Inc, NJ, 57-58; res fel, Harvard Univ, 61-62; chemist, Worcester Found Exp Biol, Mass, 62-67; group leader, T Clark Lab, Kendall Co, Lexington, Mass, 67-72, sect head, 72-75; asst dir res planning & licensing, Bristol Lab, 75-76; dir chem, 76-79, DIR CHEM RES, DEVELOP & LICENSING, BRISTOL-MYERS CO, INT DIV, 80- *Concurrent Pos:* Adj prof med chem, Grad Sch Pharmaceut Sci, Northeastern Univ, 73-75; lectr ophthal, Columbia Univ, 77- *Mem:* Sigma Xi; Am Chem Soc; AAAS; NY Acad Sci. *Res:* Drugs acting on the central nervous systems; heterocyclic compounds; antibiotics; anticonvulsants; anabolic agents; antiosteoporotics. *Mailing Add:* Bristol-Myers Co Int Div 345 Park Ave New York NY 10022

VIDAL, JACQUES J, b Liege, Belg, Apr 18, 30; div; c 2. COMPUTER SCIENCE, NEUROSCIENCES. *Educ:* Univ Liege, MS, 54; Saclay Nuclear Res Ctr, France, nuclear engr, 58; Univ Paris, PhD(elec eng), 61. *Prof Exp:* Lectr, Univ Liege, 56-63; from asst prof to assoc prof eng, 63-70, PROF ENG, UNIV CALIF, LOS ANGELES, 70- *Concurrent Pos:* Orgn Econ Coop & Develop & NATO res fels, 62-63; consult comput educ, USAID mission to Tunisia, 70-; mem, Brain Res Inst; Res fel, Inst Nat Statistque des Estudes Econ, France, 78-81. *Mem:* Inst Elec & Electronics Engrs; Soc Neurosci; Asn Comput Mach; NY Acad Sci. *Res:* Neuroscience; computer brain and medicine research; biocybernetics; system identification. *Mailing Add:* Dept of Comput Sci BH 3531 Univ of Calif Los Angeles CA 90024

VIDALE, RICHARD F(RANCIS), b Rochester, NY, Apr 22, 36; m 65; c 1. SYSTEMS ENGINEERING. *Educ:* Univ Rochester, BS, 58; Univ Wis, PhD(mech), 64. *Prof Exp:* From asst prof to assoc prof, 64-70, PROF SYSTS ENG & CHMN DEPT, BOSTON UNIV, 70- *Concurrent Pos:* Consult, Space & Info Systs Div, Raytheon Co, Mass, 66- *Mem:* Inst Elec & Electronics Engrs; Am Soc Eng Educ. *Res:* Control system theory and design; systems engineering methodology. *Mailing Add:* Dept of Systs Eng Col of Eng Boston Univ Boston MA 02215

VIDALE, ROSEMARY J, b New Haven, Conn, Mar 27, 31; m 51; c 3. GEOCHEMISTRY, MINERALOGY-PETROLOGY. *Educ:* Oberlin Col, BA, 52; Univ Mich, MS, 54; Yale Univ, PhD(geol), 68. *Prof Exp:* From asst prof to assoc prof geol, State Univ NY Binghamton, 68-75; res fel, Carnegie Inst, Washington, DC, 74-75; staff mem, 75-77, assoc group leader nuclear chem, 78-80, ASSOC GROUP LEADER ISOTOPE GEOCHEM, LOS ALAMOS NAT LAB, 80- *Mem:* Fel AAAS; Geochem Soc; fel Am Mineral Soc; Sigma Xi; fel Geol Soc Am. *Res:* Experimental element transport and retention; geothermal systems. *Mailing Add:* CNC-11 MS-514 Los Alamos Nat Lab Los Alamos NM 87545

VIDAURRETA, LUIS E, b Havana, Cuba, Dec 15, 20; US citizen; m 43; c 2. ANALYTICAL CHEMISTRY. *Educ:* Univ Havana, PhD(chem), 43. *Prof Exp:* Prof anal chem, Univ Havana, 43-65; ASSOC PROF CHEM, LA STATE UNIV, BATON ROUGE, 66- *Mem:* Am Chem Soc. *Res:* Instrumental analysis; gas chromatography; sugar and sugar by-products analysis. *Mailing Add:* Dept of Chem 211 Choppin Hall La State Univ Baton Rouge LA 70803

VIDAURRI, FERNANDO C, JR, b Laredo, Tex, Feb 23, 39; m 67; c 2. CHEMICAL ENGINEERING. *Educ:* Tex Tech Univ, BSChE, 62, MSChE, 65, PhD, 68. *Prof Exp:* Develop engr, Phillips Petrol Co, 62-63; teaching asst, Tex Tech Univ, 64-68; sr develop engr, Phillips Petrol Co, Okla, 68-78, tech mgr, Petrochem Plant, 78-81, OPERS MGR, PETROCHEM PLANT, PHILLIPS CHEM CO, TEX, 81- *Mem:* Am Inst Chem Engrs. *Res:* Process development; kinetics; heat transfer; high temperature polymers; experimental and theoretical thermodynamics; acid gas treating; economic evaluation; mixing and reactor design. *Mailing Add:* Phillips Chem Co PO Box 968 Phillips TX 79071

VIDAVER, ANNE MARIE KOPECKY, b Vienna, Austria, Mar 29, 38; US citizen; m 62; c 2. BACTERIOLOGY. *Educ:* Russell Sage Col, BA, 60; Ind Univ, Bloomington, MA, 62, PhD(bact), 65. *Prof Exp:* Instr bact, 65-66, res assoc plant path, 66-72, asst prof, 72-74, assoc prof plant path, 74-79, PROF, UNIV NEBR-LINCOLN, 79- *Mem:* Am Soc Microbiol; Am Phytopath Soc (secy, 80-83); AAAS. *Res:* Phytopathogenic bacteria; bacteriophages; bacteriocins. *Mailing Add:* Dept of Plant Path Univ of Nebr Lincoln NE 68503

VIDAVER, GEORGE ALEXANDER, b Detroit, Mich, Apr 17, 30; m 62; c 2. BIOCHEMISTRY. *Educ:* Univ Chicago, BA, 51, PhD(biochem), 55. *Prof Exp:* Res assoc biochem, Univ Chicago, 55-56, Inst Enzyme Res, Univ Wis, 56-57, Med Sch, Northwestern Univ, 57-58 & Ind Univ, 58-65; assoc prof, 66-73, PROF CHEM, UNIV NEBR, LINCOLN, 73- *Concurrent Pos:* Nat Found Infantile Paralysis fel, 56-57; NSF fel, 59-60, res grant, 68-70; USPHS fel, 61-62, res grants, 66- *Mem:* AAAS; Am Chem Soc; Am Soc Biol Chem; Fedn Am Socs Exp Biol. *Res:* Active transport of amino acids; membrane structure. *Mailing Add:* Dept of Chem Univ of Nebr Lincoln NE 68588

VIDAVER, WILLIAM ELLIOTT, b San Francisco, Calif, Feb 2, 21; m 51; c 3. PLANT PHYSIOLOGY. *Educ:* San Francisco State Col, AB, 58; Stanford Univ, PhD(biol), 64. *Prof Exp:* Fel plant biol, Carnegie Inst Dept Plant Biol, 63-65; assoc prof biol, 65-69, PROF BIOL, SIMON FRASER UNIV, 69- *Concurrent Pos:* Nat Res Coun Can operating grants, 65- *Mem:* AAAS; Am Soc Plant Physiol; Can Soc Plant Physiol. *Res:* Algal physiology; mechanisms of photosynthesis; mechanisms of phytochrome action; germination and dormancy. *Mailing Add:* Dept of Biol Sci Simon Fraser Univ Burnaby BC V5A 1S6 Can

VIDEON, FRED F(RANCIS), b Hayden, Colo, Oct 4, 34; m 57; c 3. CIVIL ENGINEERING. *Educ:* Colo State Univ, BS, 58, MCE, 60; Univ Ill, PhD(civil eng), 65. *Prof Exp:* From asst prof to assoc prof, 65-75, PROF CIVIL ENG & ENG MECH, MONT STATE UNIV, 75- *Honors & Awards:* Western Elec Award, Am Soc Eng Educ. *Mem:* Am Soc Civil Engrs; Am Soc Eng Educ; Nat Soc Prof Engrs. *Res:* Feasibility of using nuclear explosives for peaceful purposes; brittle fracture of mild steel; state of stress in solids containing cracks; structural mechanics and design; structural design and loading; plate girder behavior; post tensioned concrete systems; design of bridges-steel, concrete and segmental. *Mailing Add:* Dept of Civil Eng & Eng Mech Mont State Univ Bozeman MT 59717

VIDMAR, PAUL JOSEPH, b Vallejo, Calif, May 22, 44. UNDERWATER ACOUSTICS. *Educ:* Univ Notre Dame, BS, 66; Univ Calif, San Diego, MS, 72, PhD(physics), 75. *Prof Exp:* Res assoc physics, Fusion Res Ctr, 75-78, RES ASSOC, APPL RES LAB, UNIV TEX, AUSTIN, 78- *Mem:* Acoust Soc Am; Am Phys Soc. *Res:* Theoretical studies of long-range propagation and bottom interaction in underwater acoustics. *Mailing Add:* 10118 Aspen Austin TX 78758

VIDOLI, VIVIAN ANN, b Bridgeport, Conn, Nov 2, 41. PHYSIOLOGY, NEUROPHYSIOLOGY. *Educ:* Southern Conn State Col, BS, 63; Ariz State Univ, MS, 66, PhD(zool & physiol), 69. *Prof Exp:* Asst prof, 70-73, assoc prof, 73-78, PROF BIOL, CALIF STATE UNIV, FRESNO, 73-, ASST DIR, DIV HEALTH PROFESSIONS, 78-, DEAN, DIV GRAD STUDIES & RES, 80- *Concurrent Pos:* Consult, Area Health Educ Consortium, San Joaquin Valley, Calif, 74- *Mem:* Am Physiol Soc; AAAS; Sigma Xi. *Res:* Anatomical and physiological correlates of sensory mechanisms. *Mailing Add:* Dept of Biol Calif State Univ Shaw & Cedar Ave Fresno CA 93710

VIDONE, ROMEO ALBERT, b Greenwich, Conn, July 1, 30; m 55; c 3. PATHOLOGY. *Educ:* Davis & Elkins Col, BS, 52; Yale Univ, MD, 57. *Prof Exp:* From instr to assoc prof, 59-68, ASSOC CLIN PROF PATH, YALE UNIV, 68-; CHMN DEPT PATH, HOSP ST RAPHAEL, 77- *Concurrent Pos:* Asst clin prof, Health Ctr, Univ Conn, 72-; pvt pract; dir lab, Charlotte Hungerford Hosp, 68-77. *Mem:* Am Soc Clin Path; Col Am Path; AMA; Int Acad Path; Am Cancer Soc. *Res:* Cardiopulmonary physiology and pathology; cancer, clinicopathologic correlation with emphasis on mucin production by tumors. *Mailing Add:* Dept of Path 1450 Chapel St New Haven CT 06511

VIDOSIC, J(OSEPH) P(AUL), b Lovran, Austria, June 10, 09; US citizen; m 35; c 2. ENGINEERING DESIGN. *Educ:* Stevens Inst Technol, ME, 32, MS, 34; Purdue Univ, PhD(mech), 51. *Prof Exp:* Instr elec, Stevens Inst Technol, 32-34; res engr, Keuffel & Esser Co, 35-36; plant engr, Whitlock Cordage Co, 36-37; from instr to assoc prof theoret mech, Ga Inst Technol, 38-49; instr mech eng, Purdue Univ, 49-51; prof, Ga Inst Technol, 51-59, regents' prof, 60-68; dean admin, 68-73, EMER DEAN, MID GA COL, 73-; EMER REGENTS' PROF, GA INST TECHNOL, 73- *Concurrent Pos:* Vis prof, Univ Baghdad, 64-65 & Tuskegee Inst Technol, 67-68. *Honors & Awards:* Am Defense Medal, 45; Recognition Award, Am Soc Mech Engrs, 70. *Mem:* Fel Am Soc Mech Engrs; Am Soc Eng Educ; Soc Exp Stress Anal. *Res:* Stress analysis; lubrication; bearings; vibration; photoelasticity; plastics; design; mechanics; mechanisms; materials science. *Mailing Add:* RD 3 Berry Knoll Cooperstown NY 13326

VIDRINE, MALCOLM FRANCIS, b Eunice, La, June 23, 49; m 70; c 1. ARTHROPOD-VECTORS, AQUATIC MOLLUSKS. *Educ:* La State Univ, BS, 70, MS, 74; Univ Southwestern La, PhD(biol), 80. *Prof Exp:* Biologist, Gulf S Res Inst, 73-76; instr zool & physiol, Univ Southwestern La, 77-80; ASST DIR, JEFFERSON DAVIS PARISH MOSQUITO ABATEMENT DIST, 80- *Concurrent Pos:* Jessup fel, Acad Nat Sci Philadelphia, 78. *Mem:* Sigma Xi; Am Malacol Union; Am Mosquito Control Asn. *Res:* Aquatic ecology; invertebrates in aquatic ecosystems; parasitology; evolution and systematics of fresh-water mollusks and their parasites; evolution and systematics of unionidlid water-mites of the world. *Mailing Add:* Rte 2 Box 732-A Jennings LA 70546

VIDT, EDWARD JAMES, b Pittsburgh, Pa, June 16, 27; m 53; c 2. COAL CONVERSION, COST ENGINEERING. *Educ:* Carnegie Inst Technol, BSc, 48. *Prof Exp:* Sr develop engr chem eng, Air Reduction Co, 59-60; process proj engr, Chem Plants Div, Blaw-Knox Co, 60-65, asst mgr synthetic fuels, 65-72; sr res scientist, 72-74, fel engr, 74-78, ADV ENGR CHEM ENG, RES & DEVELOP CTR, WESTINGHOUSE ELEC CORP, 78- *Concurrent Pos:* Mem, Ad Hoc Comt Data Coal Conversion, Nat Bur Standards, 72-74; mem, Tech Adv Comt, US Off Coal Res, 74-75. *Mem:* Am Inst Chem Engrs; Am Asn Cost Engrs; Am Gas Asn. *Res:* Coal conversion to synthetic fuels for clean, efficient production of heat and power. *Mailing Add:* Res & Develop Ctr Westinghouse Elec Corp Pittsburgh PA 15235

VIDULICH, GEORGE A, b New York, NY, Nov 20, 31. PHYSICAL CHEMISTRY. *Educ:* Univ Conn, BA, 59; Brown Univ, PhD(phys chem), 64. *Prof Exp:* NIH fel phys chem, Max Planck Inst Phys Chem, Ger, 63-64; fel chem, Mellon Inst, 65-66; asst prof chem, 66-73, ASSOC PROF CHEM, HOLY CROSS COL, 73- *Concurrent Pos:* Holy Cross Col fac. *Mem:* AAAS; Am Phys Soc; Biophys Soc; Am Chem Soc. *Res:* Properties and structures of aqueous and electrolyte solutions; precipitation chemistry. *Mailing Add:* Dept of Chem Holy Cross Col Worcester MA 01610

VIDYASAGAR, MATHUKUMALLI, b Guntur, Andhra Pradesh, India, Sept 29, 47. ELECTRICAL ENGINEERING, APPLIED MATHEMATICS. *Educ:* Univ Wis-Madison, BS, 65, MS, 67, PhD(elec eng), 69. *Prof Exp:* Asst prof elec eng, Marquette Univ, 69-70; asst prof & Nat Res Coun Can grants, 70-73, assoc prof, 73-77, PROF ELEC ENG, CONCORDIA UNIV, 77- *Concurrent Pos:* Consult, Alcan Smelters & Chem, Ltd, 75-78; mem grant selection comt for elec engrs, Natural Sci & Eng Res Coun, 78- *Honors & Awards:* Prix George Montefiore, Asn Elec Engrs Belg, 76. *Mem:* Inst Elec & Electronics Engrs; Soc Indust & Appl Math. *Res:* Control and system theory; large-scale systems. *Mailing Add:* Dept of Elec Eng 1455 Blvd de Maisonneuve W Montreal PQ H3G 1M8 Can

VIEBROCK, FREDERICK WILLIAM, b Staten Island, NY, Nov 23, 35; m 56; c 2. BIOCHEMISTRY. *Educ:* Wagner Col, BS, 57; Polytech Inst Brooklyn, MS, 68; Va Polytech Inst & State Univ, PhD(biochem), 74. *Prof Exp:* Res scientist enzymol, Wallerstein Lab, Div Travenol Lab, 58-69; SR SCIENTIST BIOCHEM, JOHNSON & JOHNSON RES CTR, 72- *Mem:* AAAS; Am Chem Soc; Sigma Xi. *Res:* Purification and kinetic analysis of enzymes of the purine metabolic pathways, wound healing, eczematous skin diseases, local anesthetic. *Mailing Add:* 1779 W Circle Rd Martinsville NJ 08836

VIECHNICKI, DENNIS J, b Passaic, NJ, Dec 25, 40; m 65; c 4. CERAMICS, MATERIAL SCIENCE. *Educ:* Rutgers Univ, BS, 62; Pa State Univ, PhD(ceramics), 66. *Prof Exp:* Sr scientist, Westinghouse Res & Develop Labs, 66; GROUP LEADER CERAMICS, US ARMY MAT & MECH RES LAB, 68- *Concurrent Pos:* Nat Sci Res Ctr-NSF France-US exchange of scientists grant, Lab Appl Solid State Chem, Metall Chem Res Ctr, Vitry-sur-Seine, France, 72-73. *Mem:* Am Ceramic Soc. *Res:* Reactions in oxides above 1000 C; eutectoid decomposition; high temperature growth using heat exchanger method of sapphire, spinel, Nd:YAG and eutectics; ceramic-metal seals; radome materials; high energy laser/ceramic interactions. *Mailing Add:* 5 Poplar Rd Wellesley MA 02181

VIEHLAND, LARRY ALAN, b St Louis, Mo, Apr 30, 47; m 69; c 2. CHEMICAL PHYSICS. *Educ:* Mass Inst Technol, BS, 69; Univ Wis-Madison, PhD(chem), 73. *Prof Exp:* Res assoc chem, Brown Univ, 73-76, asst prof (res) chem, 76-77; asst prof, 77-79, ASSOC PROF CHEM, PARKS COL, 79- *Mem:* Sigma Xi. *Res:* Theoretical chemistry and atomic physics, specifically kinetic theory and nonequilibrium statistical mechanics as a tool for understanding intermolecular potentials and other microscopic properties. *Mailing Add:* Dept of Chem Parks Col St Louis Univ Cahokia IL 62206

VIEIRA, DAVID JOHN, b Oakland, Calif, May 5, 50; m 72; c 2. NUCLEAR CHEMISTRY. *Educ:* Ore State Univ, BS, 72; Univ Calif, Berkeley, PhD(nuclear chem), 78. *Prof Exp:* Res & teaching asst nuclear chem, Univ Calif, Berkeley & Lawrence Berkeley Lab, 72-78; res fel nuclear chem, 78-79, STAFF SCIENTIST NUCLEAR CHEM, LOS ALAMOS NAT LAB, 79- *Mem:* Am Chem Soc; Am Phys Soc. *Res:* Nuclear mass measurements; pion-nucleus reactions; decay and reaction studies of light nuclei far from B-stability. *Mailing Add:* CNC-11/LAMPF MS 824 Los Alamos Nat Lab Los Alamos NM 87545

VIEIRA, ERNEST CHARLES, physical chemistry, see previous edition

VIELE, GEORGE WASHINGTON, b Wausau, Wis; m 58; c 2. GEOLOGY, TECTONICS. *Educ:* Yale Univ, BS, 51; Univ Utah, PhD(geol), 60. *Prof Exp:* Geologist, US Geol Surv, 51-56 & Standard Oil Co Calif, 57-59; from asst prof to assoc prof geol, 59-72, PROF GEOL, UNIV MO-COLUMBIA, 72-, CHMN DEPT, 74- *Mem:* Geol Soc Am; Am Asn Petrol Geol; Am Geophys Union. *Res:* Structural geology; regional tectonics; Northern Rocky and Ouachita Mountains. *Mailing Add:* Dept of Geol Univ of Mo Columbia MO 65201

VIER, DWAYNE TROWBRIDGE, b Washington, DC, Sept 17, 14; m 51; c 2. THERMODYNAMICS & MATERIAL PROPERTIES. *Educ:* Univ NH, BS, 37, MS, 39; Columbia Univ, PhD(phys chem), 43. *Prof Exp:* Asst, Univ NH, 37-39, asst Columbia Univ, 39-40, asst chem, 40-42, res chemist, S A M Labs, 43-45; assoc scientist, Manhattan Dist, 45-46, group leader, Los Alamos Sci Lab, 46-70, STAFF MEM, LOS ALAMOS NAT LAB, UNIV CALIF, 70- *Mem:* Am Chem Soc; AAAS. *Res:* Fields in physical chemistry; inorganic chemistry of rare radioactive elements; high temperature chemistry; equation of state. *Mailing Add:* 764 43rd St Los Alamos NM 87544

VIERCK, CHARLES JOHN, JR, b Columbus, Ohio, July 6, 36; m 60; c 2. NEUROSCIENCE, SOMATOSENSATION. *Educ:* Univ Fla, BS, 59, MS, 61, PhD(psychol), 63. *Prof Exp:* Fel neurosci, Inst Neurol Sci, Univ Pa, 63-65; asst prof, 65-71, assoc prof, 71-76, PROF NEUROSCI, COL MED, UNIV FLA, 76-; ADJ RES PROF PHYSIOL, SCH MED, UNIV NC, 75- *Concurrent Pos:* Nat Inst Neurol Dis & Stroke res grant, 67-, mem neurol B study sect, 72-76; assoc ed, J Neurosci, 80-83; mem, Animal Resources Rev Comt, 81-85. *Mem:* Am Psychol Asn; Psychonomic Soc; Soc Neurosci; Int Neuropsychol Soc; Int Asn Study Pain. *Res:* Central nervous system mechanisms relating to somesthetic discrimination; discrimination and perception of pain; recovery of function after nervous system damage. *Mailing Add:* Dept of Neurosci Ctr Neurobiol Sci Univ of Fla Col of Med Gainesville FL 32610

VIERCK, ROBERT K, b Avoca, Iowa, Jan 5, 08; m 33; c 3. ENGINEERING MECHANICS. *Educ:* Univ Iowa, BS, 32, MS, 33. *Prof Exp:* Engr, State of Iowa, 33-34; jr engr, US Bur Reclamation, 34-36; instr eng, Univ Ill, 36-39; from asst engr to assoc engr, Fed Power Comn, 39-43; from asst prof to prof eng mech, 43-73, actg head dept, 65-67, EMER PROF ENG MECH, PA STATE UNIV, 73- *Concurrent Pos:* Consult, Boeing Co, Wash, 54 & N Am Aviation, Inc, Calif, 55. *Mem:* Am Soc Eng Educ; Am Acad Mech. *Res:* Mechanical vibrations; mechanical properties of materials. *Mailing Add:* 299 Nimitz Ave State College PA 16801

VIERECK, LESLIE A, b New Bedford, Mass, Feb 20, 30; m 55; c 3. PLANT ECOLOGY, PLANT TAXONOMY. *Educ:* Dartmouth Col, BA, 51; Univ Colo, MA, 57, PhD(plant ecol), 62. *Prof Exp:* Asst bot, McGill Subarctic Res Sta, 54-55; asst, Herbarium, Univ Colo, 55-57, actg cur, 56-57, res assoc ecol, Inst Arctic & Alpine Res, 55-59; res assoc ecol, Univ Alaska, 59-60, asst prof bot, 60-61; res biologist, Alaska Dept Fish & Game, 61-63; PRIN PLANT ECOLOGIST, INST NORTHERN FORESTRY, 63- *Concurrent Pos:* Affil prof div life sci, Univ Alaska, 75- *Mem:* Fel AAAS; fel Arctic Inst NAm; Ecol Soc Am; Am Bryol & Lichenological Soc. *Res:* Plant ecology and plant taxonomy of arctic, subarctic and alpine regions. *Mailing Add:* 308 Tanana Dr Inst Northern Forestry Fairbanks AK 99701

VIERNSTEIN, LAWRENCE J, b New York, NY, Feb 20, 19; m 69; c 2. BIOMEDICAL ENGINEERING. *Educ:* Okla State Univ, BS, 50, MS, 51; Johns Hopkins Univ, PhD, 70. *Prof Exp:* Mem assoc staff, Appl Physics Lab, Johns Hopkins Univ, 52-57, sr physicsist, 57-59, mem prof staff, Dept Physiol, 61-66, mem prof staff, Wilmer Inst, 66-76, MEM PROF STAFF, NEUROSURG, JOHNS HOPKINS UNIV, 76- & APPL PHYSICS LAB, 59- *Res:* Theoretical biology and biomedical engineering; neurophysiology; artificial intelligence in medicine. *Mailing Add:* Johns Hopkins Univ Appl Physics Lab Johns Hopkins Rd Laurel MD 20810

VIERS, JIMMY WAYNE, b Grundy, Va, Feb 26, 43; m 65; c 2. PHYSICAL CHEMISTRY. *Educ:* Berea Col, AB, 65; Wake Forest Univ, MA, 67; Stanford Univ, PhD(chem), 71. *Prof Exp:* ASST PROF CHEM, VA POLYTECH INST & STATE UNIV, 71- *Mem:* Am Chem Soc. *Res:* Quantum chemistry, electron-atom scattering. *Mailing Add:* Dept Chem Va Polytech Inst & State Univ Blacksburg VA 24061

VIERTL, JOHN RUEDIGER MADER, b New York, NY, Sept 25, 41; m 69; c 2. SOLID STATE PHYSICS, ELECTRICAL ENGINEERING. *Educ:* Fordham Univ, BS, 63; Rutgers Univ, MS, 65; Cornell Univ, PhD(appl physics), 73. *Prof Exp:* Res training prog physics & geophys fission tracks & semiconductors, 67-69, RES PHYSICIST ULTRASONIC PHENOMENA & LASER INTERACTIONS, GEN ELEC TURBINE TECHNOL LAB, 73- *Mem:* Fel Am Phys Soc; Soc Photo-Optical Instrumentation Engrs; Am Soc Nondestructive Testing. *Res:* Optical properties of thin films; point defects in solids; ultrasonic imaging, scattering theory, phenomena, ultrasonic non destructive testing; laser target interactions; ultrasonic transducer design. *Mailing Add:* Gen Elec Turbine Technol Lab Schenectady NY 12345

VIESSMAN, WARREN, JR, b Baltimore, Md, Nov 9, 30; m 53; c 6. HYDROLOGY, WATER RESOURCES. *Educ:* Johns Hopkins Univ, BE, 52, MSE, 58, DEng(water resources), 61. *Prof Exp:* Proj engr, Johns Hopkins Univ, 56-61; from asst prof to assoc prof civil eng, Univ NMex, 61-66; prof civil eng & dir water resources ctr, Univ Maine, 66-68; prof civil eng & dir water resources res inst, Univ Nebr, Lincoln, 68-75; SR SPECIALIST ENG & PUB WORKS, CONG RES SERV, LIBR OF CONG, 75- *Mem:* Am Soc Civil Engrs; Am Water Works Asn; Am Geophys Union. *Res:* Water resources systems and policy. *Mailing Add:* Libr of Cong ENRD Cong Res Serv Washington DC 20540

VIEST, IVAN M, b Czech, Oct 10, 22; nat US; m 53. STRUCTURAL ENGINEERING, ENGINEERING PROMOTION. *Educ:* Slovak Tech Univ, Czech, CE, 46; Ga Inst Technol, MS, 48; Univ Ill, PhD(eng), 51. *Prof Exp:* Asst, Univ Ill, 48-51, from res assoc to res assoc prof, 51-57; bridge res eng, Am Asn State Hwy Off Rd Test, Nat Acad Sci, 57-61; struct engr, 61-67, sr struct consult, 67-70, ASST MGR SALES ENG, BETHLEHEM STEEL CORP, 70- *Concurrent Pos:* Consult, Nelson Student Welding, Ohio, 54-61; mem, Transp Res Bd, Nat Acad Sci-Nat Res Coun. *Honors & Awards:* Wason Medal, Am Concrete Inst, 55; Res Prize, Am Soc Civil Engrs, 58. *Mem:* Nat Acad Eng; hon mem Am Soc Civil Engrs (vpres, 74-75); fel Am Concrete Inst; Int Asn Bridge & Struct Engrs; Soc Automotive Engrs. *Res:* Steel structures; composite construction; reinforced concrete. *Mailing Add:* Sales Eng Div Bethlehem Steel Corp Bethlehem PA 18016

VIETH, JOACHIM, b Hamburg, Ger, Oct 26, 25; m 53; c 2. PLANT MORPHOLOGY. *Educ:* Univ Saarbruecken, Lic natural sci, 53, Dr rer nat, 57; Univ Dijon, DSc(bot), 65. *Prof Exp:* Asst bot, Univ Saarbrücken, 53-57; res fel, Nat Ctr Sci Res, Univ Dijon, 57-65; vis prof, 66-67, assoc prof, 67-77, PROF BOT, UNIV MONTREAL, 77- *Mem:* Bot Soc France; Can Bot Asn. *Res:* Anatomy of flowers and inflorescences, both normal and anomalous; relationship between vegetative and inflorescential regions, between normal and anomalous forms experimentally induced; plant propagation by tissue culture. *Mailing Add:* Inst of Bot 4101 Sherbrooke Est Montreal PQ H1X 2B2 Can

VIETH, WOLF R(ANDOLPH), b St Louis, Mo, May 5, 34; m 57; c 4. CHEMICAL ENGINEERING. *Educ:* Mass Inst Technol, SB, 56, ScD(chem eng), 61; Ohio State Univ, MSc, 58. *Prof Exp:* Res engr, NAm Aviation, Inc, 56-57; Ford fel eng, 61-62; dir practice sch sta, Mass Inst Technol Sta-Am Cyanamid Co, NJ, 62-64; from asst prof to assoc prof chem eng, Mass Inst Technol, 62-68, overall dir sch chem eng practice, 65-68; chmn chem & biochem engr dept, 68-78, PROF CHEM & BIOCHEM ENG, RUTGERS UNIV, NEW BRUNSWICK, 68- *Concurrent Pos:* Consult, Am Cyanamid Co, 63, Ashland Oil Co, 63-, Carter's Ink, 64- & US Army Natick Labs, 65- *Mem:* Am Chem Soc; Am Inst Chem Engrs. *Mailing Add:* Dept of Chem & Biochem Eng Rutgers Univ New Brunswick NJ 08903

VIETMEYER, NOEL DUNCAN, b Wellington, NZ, Nov 9, 40; m 65; c 2. ECONOMIC BIOLOGY, SCIENCE WRITING. *Educ:* Univ Otago, NZ, BSc, 63; Univ Calif, Berkeley, PhD, 67. *Prof Exp:* Lectr org chem, Univ Calif, Berkeley, 67-68; NIH fel, Stanford Univ, 68-69, fel, 68-70; PROF ASSOC, NAT ACAD SCI, 70- *Res:* Organic chemistry; introduction of technology into developing countries; development of neglected plants and animals with promising economic potential. *Mailing Add:* Nat Acad of Sci 2101 Constitution Ave Washington DC 20418

VIETOR, DONALD MELVIN, b Urbana, Ill, Sept 29, 45; m 71; c 2. CROP PHYSIOLOGY. *Educ:* Univ Minn, BS, 67, MS, 69; Cornell Univ, PhD(crop sci), 75. *Prof Exp:* Biol sci asst soil sci, US Army Cold Regions Res & Engr Lab, 69-71; asst prof agron, Univ Mass, 74-76; ASST PROF AGRON, DEPT SOIL & CROP SCI, TEX A&M UNIV, 76- *Mem:* Am Soc Agron; Crop Sci Soc Am. *Res:* Genotypic, environmental, ontogenetic, and management effects on photosynthate distribution in crop plants; photosynthate distribution to the roots and rhizosphere of grasses. *Mailing Add:* Dept of Soil & Crop Sci Tex A&M Univ College Station TX 77843

VIETS, FRANK GARFIELD, JR, b Stanberry, Mo, Apr 3, 16; m 38; c 3. SOIL SCIENCE. *Educ:* Colo Agr & Mech Col, BS, 37; Univ Calif, MS, 39, PhD(plant physiol), 42. *Prof Exp:* Agent div cereal crops, USDA, Calif, 37-39; asst div plant nutrit, Univ Calif, 39-42; supv chemist, Cutter Labs, Calif, 42-44; assoc agr chemist, Exp Sta, SDak State Col, 44-45; agronomist div soil mgt & irrig, USDA, 45-49, soil scientist, Agr Res Serv, 49-53, soil & water conserv res div, 53-74; CONSULT AGR, 80- *Concurrent Pos:* Vis prof, Univ Ill, 59 & Iowa State Univ, 64, Col State Univ, 74 & Univ Saskatchewan, 75; ed in chief, Soil Sci Soc Am, 63-65; agr consult, 74- *Honors & Awards:* Superior Serv Award, USDA, 55, Distinguished Serv Award, 72. *Mem:* Fel AAAS; fel Soil Sci Soc Am (vpres, 66, pres, 67); fel Am Soc Agron; Int Soc Soil Sci. *Res:* Mineral nutrition of plants; zinc deficiency in soils and plants; water pollution by animal wastes, fertilizers and agriculture; soil fertility and productivity; tropical soils. *Mailing Add:* 102 Yale Way Ft Collins CO 80525

VIETS, HERMANN, b Quedlinburg, Ger, Jan 28, 43; US citizen; m 68; c 4. AEROSPACE ENGINEERING, MECHANICAL ENGINEERING. *Educ:* Polytech Inst Brooklyn, BS, 65, MS, 66, PhD(astronaut), 70. *Prof Exp:* Res asst fluid mech res, Polytech Inst Brooklyn, 68-69; group leader, Aerospace Res Labs, US Air Force, 70-75; assoc prof mech eng, Wright State Univ, 76-80, prof, 80-81; PROF MECH ENG & ASSOC DEAN, WVA UNIV, 81- *Concurrent Pos:* NATO res grant, 69-70; fel, von Karman Inst, Brussels, Belg, 69-70; US Air Force Off Aerospace res grant, 77-; consult, US Air Force Aero Propulsion Lab, 76-; chmn bd, Precision Stampings Inc, Beaumont, Calif, 78- *Mem:* Assoc fel Am Inst Aeronaut & Astronaut; Am Helicopter Soc. *Res:* Positive aspects of time dependent flows; fluidically and mechanically generated unsteadiness; advanced ramjet combustors; vortex dynamics; jets and wakes; computational methods; nozzles, diffusers and thrust augmentors. *Mailing Add:* Col Eng WVa Univ Morgantown WV 26506

VIETTE, MICHAEL ANTHONY, b Pittsburg, Kans, Mar 27, 41; m 63; c 1. PHYSICS. *Educ:* Kans State Col Pittsburg, BA, 64, MS, 66; Univ Mo-Rolla, PhD(physics), 72. *Prof Exp:* Res asst cloud physics, Grad Ctr Cloud Physics Res, Univ Mo-Rolla, 66-70; asst prof, 71-80, ASSOC PROF PHYSICS, UNIV MAINE, ORONO, 80- *Concurrent Pos:* NSF res grant, 72- *Mem:* Am Phys Soc; Am Geophys Union; Am Meteorol Soc. *Res:* Condensation and growth of micron sized water droplets. *Mailing Add:* Bennett Hall Univ of Maine Orono ME 04473

VIETTI, TERESA JANE, b Ft Worth, Tex, Nov 5, 27. PEDIATRICS, HEMATOLOGY. *Educ:* Rice Inst, AB, 49; Baylor Univ, MD, 53; Am Bd Pediat, dipl, 59; Bd Pediat Hematol & Oncol, dipl, 74. *Prof Exp:* Instr pediat, Wayne State Univ, 58 & Southwestern Med Sch, Univ Tex, 58-60; vis pediatrician, Hacettepe Children's Hosp, Ankara, Turkey, 60-61; from asst prof to assoc prof pediat, 61-72, PROF PEDIAT, SCH MED, WASHINGTON UNIV, 72-, PROF PEDIAT IN RADIOL, 80- *Concurrent Pos:* Dir hemat labs, attend pediatrician & consult, Tex Children's Hosp, Dallas, 58-60; attend pediatrician & consult, Parkland Mem Hosp, 58-60; Am Cancer Soc fel, 58-59; USPHS trainee, 59-60, grant, 61-; vchmn, Southwest Oncol Group, 61-; asst pediatrician, St Louis Children's Hosp, 61-65, assoc pediatrician, 65-, dir div hemat & oncol, 70-; from asst pediatrician to assoc pediatrician, Barnes & Allied Hosps, 61-65; consult, St Louis County Hosp; assoc in pediat, Mo Crippled Children's Serv; mem, Cancer Clin Invest Rev Comt, 74-78; pediat consult high risk maternity & child care prog, Mo Div Health, 75; chmn Pediat Oncol Group, 81-84. *Mem:* Am Acad Pediat; Am Hemat Soc; Int Soc Hemat; Am Asn Cancer Res; Am Pediat Soc. *Res:* Oncology; cancer chemotherapy. *Mailing Add:* Dept of Pediat PO Box 14871 St Louis MO 63178

VIG, BALDEV K, b India, Oct 1, 35; m; c 2. CYTOGENETICS. *Educ:* Khalsa Col, India, BSAgr, 57; Panjab Univ, India, MS, 61; Ohio State Univ, PhD(genetics), 67. *Prof Exp:* Demonstr agr, Khalsa Col, India, 58-61; assoc prof bot, Rajasthan Col Agr, India, 61-64; res cytogeneticist, Dept Pediat, Children's Hosp, Ohio State Univ, 67-68, res award, 68; asst prof biol, 68-72, res adv grants, 69-79, assoc prof biol, 72-78, PROF GENETICS, UNIV NEV, RENO, 78- *Concurrent Pos:* Consult, Western Environ Res Ctr, Environ Protection Agency; res grant, Environ Protection Agency; prof human & med genetics, Nev Ment Health Inst, 76-81; Humboldt fel & Jones fel. *Mem:* Am Genetics Asn; Genetic Soc Am; Genetics Soc Can; Environ Mutagen Soc. *Res:* Mode and mechanisms of somatic crossingover in Glycine max; chromosome structure and rejoining in human leukocytes in vitro; action of antileukemic drugs on chromosomes; sequence of centromere separation. *Mailing Add:* Dept Biol Genetics Lab Univ Nev Reno NV 89507

VIG, PETER SIEGFRIED, b Vienna, Austria, June 4, 36; Brit citizen; m 70; c 2. ORTHODONTICS, CRANIOFACIAL BIOLOGY. *Educ:* Univ Sydney, BDS, 58; Univ London, PhD(physiol), 68. *Prof Exp:* Sr lectr orthod, Univ London, 67-74, reader, 74-76; assoc prof, 76-80, PROF ORTHOD, UNIV NC, CHAPEL HILL, 80- *Concurrent Pos:* Mem staff, Regional Dent Res Ctr, NC, 76-; investr, NIH grants. *Mem:* Brit Soc Study Orthod; Europ Orthod Soc; Int Asn Dent Res; Am Dent Asn. *Res:* Growth and development and physiologic adaptation to variations in oro-facial complex. *Mailing Add:* Dept of Orthod Univ of NC Sch of Dent Chapel Hill NC 27514

VIGDOR, STEVEN ELLIOT, b New York, NY, July 23, 47; m 70; c 2. EXPERIMENTAL NUCLEAR PHYSICS. *Educ:* City Col NY, BS, 67; Univ Wis-Madison, MS, 69, PhD(physics), 73. *Prof Exp:* Res assoc, Dept Physics, Univ Wis, 73-74; fel appointee, Argonne Nat Lat, 74-76, res assoc, 76; asst prof, 76-79, ASSOC PROF PHYSICS, INDIANA UNIV, 79- *Mem:* Am Phys Soc. *Res:* Nuclear structure and nuclear reactions at intermediate energies; interplay of microscopic and macroscopic aspects of heavy-ion-induced reactions; polarization measurements in nuclear structure studies and tests of fundamental symmetry principles. *Mailing Add:* Dept Physics Ind Univ Bloomington IN 47405

VIGEE, GERALD S, b Crowley, La, Mar 4, 31; m; c 3. PHYSICAL INORGANIC CHEMISTRY. *Educ:* US Mil Acad, BS, 54, La State Univ, Baton Rouge, BS, 60, PhD(chem), 68. *Prof Exp:* Prof engr, NASA, Ala, 60-61; propulsion design engr, Chrysler Corp, 61-64; asst prof chem, Univ Miss, 68-69; ASSOC PROF CHEM, UNIV ALA, BIRMINGHAM, 69- *Res:* Synthesis of coordination complexes, investigation of the magneto chemistry and spectroscopic energy levels of these complexes. *Mailing Add:* Dept of Chem Univ of Ala Birmingham AL 35294

VIGFUSSON, NORMAN V, b Ashern, Man, July 1, 30; m 54; c 5. GENETICS, MEDICAL GENETICS. *Educ:* Univ Man, BSA, 51; Univ Alta, PhD(fungal genetics), 69. *Prof Exp:* Asst prof genetics, 69-72, assoc prof, 72-76, PROF BIOL, EASTERN WASH UNIV, 76- *Concurrent Pos:* Genetic consult, Sacred Heart Med Ctr, Spokane, Wash, 75- *Mem:* Genetics Soc Am; AAAS. *Res:* Sexuality in Neorospora crassa with respect to stages and control of the sexual cycle and attempts to arrive at elucidation of incompatibility control mechanism; human cytogenetics. *Mailing Add:* Dept of Biol Eastern Wash Univ Cheney WA 99004

VIGGERS, ROBERT F, b Tacoma, Wash, Jan 18, 23; m 45; c 3. MECHANICAL ENGINEERING. *Educ:* Univ Wash, BS, 44; Ore State Col, MS, 50. *Prof Exp:* Instr eng, Univ Wash, 46-47 & Ore State Col, 47-49; from instr to prof, 49-70, PROF MECH ENG, SEATTLE UNIV, 70-, CHMN DEPT, 78- *Concurrent Pos:* NSF fac fel, 60-61; head hydraul sect, Reconstructive Cardiovasc Res Lab, Providence Hosp, 61- *Res:* Automatic control; stability problems; cardiovascular hydraulics; machine design. *Mailing Add:* Dept Mech Eng Seattle Univ Seattle WA 98122

VIGIL, EUGENE LEON, b Chicago, Ill, Mar 14, 41; m 63; c 3. CELL BIOLOGY. *Educ:* Loyola Univ Chicago, BS, 63; Univ Iowa, MS, 65, PhD(bot), 67. *Prof Exp:* NIH fel, Univ Wis-Madison, 67-69; trainee cell biol, Univ Chicago, 69-71; asst prof cell biol, Marquette Univ, 71-79; plant cell biologist, Univ Md, 79-82; VIS SCIENTIST, BELTSVILLE AGR RES CTR, USDA, 82- *Concurrent Pos:* Distinguished vis scientist, Dept Physiol & Biophys, Colo State Univ, 74-75. *Mem:* NY Acad Sci; Am Soc Cell Biol; Am Soc Plant Physiol; Histochem Soc. *Res:* Structure and function of animal and plant microbodies; effects of plant growth regulatiors on barley aleurone cells; biogenesis and turnover of microbodies in cotyledons of fatty seeds during germination; cytochemical localization of photosynthetic reactions in chloroplasts; membrane changes in response to chill injury of embryonic organs in seeds. *Mailing Add:* B-00 6 BARC-W Seed Res Lab Rm 103 Beltsville MD 20705

VIGIL, JOHN CARLOS, b Espanola, NMex, Mar 28, 39; m 58; c 4. NUCLEAR ENGINEERING. *Educ:* NMex Inst Mining & Technol, BS, 61; Univ NMex, MS, 63, PhD(nuclear eng), 66. *Prof Exp:* staff mem reactor physics, 63-77, group leader, thermal reactor safety group, asst div leader, energy div, 80-81, ASST TO ASSOC DIR, ENERGY PROG, LOS ALAMOS NAT LAB, 81- *Mem:* Am Nuclear Soc; NY Acad Sci; Sigma Xi. *Res:* Reactor safety, physics, codes and computations; energy technology. *Mailing Add:* PO Box 1663 MS-178 Los Alamos Nat Lab Los Alamos NM 87545

VIGLIERCHIO, DAVID RICHARD, b Madera, Calif, Nov 25, 25; m 67; c 1. NEMATOLOGY. *Educ:* Calif Inst Technol, BS, 50, PhD(bio-org chem), 55. *Prof Exp:* Jr res nematologist, 55-57, asst res nematologist, 57-63, assoc nematologist, 63-69, NEMATOLOGIST, UNIV CALIF, DAVIS, 69-, CHMN NEMATOL, 78- *Concurrent Pos:* Fulbright fel, 64-65, 76-77; J S Guggenheim fel, 65; partic, US Antarctic Prog, 69-70; Nat Acad Sci exchange USSR, 70-71. *Mem:* Am Chem Soc; Soc Nematol; Soc Europ Nematol. *Res:* Chemistry and physiology of plant parasitic and free-living nematodes; host-parasite relationships; physiological methods of nematode control. *Mailing Add:* Dept of Nematol Univ of Calif Davis CA 95616

VIGLIONE, SAM S, b Erie, Pa, July 12, 29; m 57; c 4. ELECTRICAL ENGINEERING. *Educ:* Carnegie Inst Technol, BS, 54; Univ Southern Calif, MS, 56. *Prof Exp:* Electronic engr, Hughes Aircraft Co, 54-58; sr design engr, Astronaut Div, Convair Corp, 58-59; sr res scientist, Aeronutronic Div, Ford Motor Co, 59-61; mgr, Pattern Recognition Systs Dept, McDonnell Douglas Corp, Huntington Beach, 61-76, dir, Res & Develop Directorate, 76-78; SR DIR, S S VIGLIONE & ASSOCS, 78-; DIR, VOICE ENG INTERSTATE ELECTRONICS CORP, 78- *Mem:* sr mem Inst Elec & Electronics Engrs. *Res:* Mathematical procedures for the simulation of pattern recognition systems; pattern recognition systems for classification of photographic and physiologic data; investigation of biological neural networks and their electronic replication; development of speech recognition systems. *Mailing Add:* 551 E Peralta Hills Dr Anaheim CA 92807

VIGNALE, MICHAEL JOSEPH, organic chemistry, see previous edition

VIGNOS, JAMES HENRY, b Cleveland, Ohio, July 27, 33; m 62; c 2. PHYSICS. *Educ:* Case Inst, BS, 55; Yale Univ, MS, 57, PhD(physics), 62. *Prof Exp:* Vis res scientist, Low Temperature Inst, Bavarian Acad Sci, Germany, 62-64; resident res assoc, Chem Div, Argonne Nat Lab, 64-66; asst prof physics, Dartmouth Col, 66-72; SR RES SCIENTIST, RES CTR, FOXBORO CO, 72- *Concurrent Pos:* Fulbright res scholar, 62-63; von Humboldt fel, 63-64. *Mem:* AAAS; Am Asn Physics Teachers; Am Phys Soc. *Res:* Low temperature physics; liquid and solid helium; superconductivity; ultrasonics. *Mailing Add:* Res Ctr Foxboro Co Foxboro MA 02035

VIGNOS, PAUL JOSEPH, JR, b Canton, Ohio, Nov 10, 19; m 46; c 3. MYOLOGY, RHEUMATOLOGY. *Educ:* Univ Notre Dame, BS, 41; Western Reserve Univ, MD, 44. *Prof Exp:* From intern to resident, Univ Hosps, Cleveland, 44-46; resident, Presby Hosp, New York, 48-49; Am Cancer Soc fel, Univ Hosps, Cleveland, 49-50; Rees fel med, Sch Med, 50-51, USPHS fel pharmacol, 51-52, from instr to asst prof, 52-66, assoc prof, 66-81, PROF MED, SCH MED, CASE WESTERN RESERVE UNIV, 81- *Res:* Bioclinical effect of myopathic disease of the locomotor system on skeletal muscle and ambulation; biochemistry of normal and diseased muscle; metabolic effects of corticosteroid on skeletal muscle. *Mailing Add:* Dept of Med Case Western Reserve Univ Cleveland OH 44106

VIGO, TYRONE LAWRENCE, b New Orleans, La, Feb 1, 39; m 63; c 2. POLYMER CHEMISTRY, TEXTILE CHEMISTRY. *Educ:* Loyola Univ, La, BS, 60; Tulane Univ La, MS, 63, PhD(org chem), 69. *Prof Exp:* Res chemist, 63-66, proj leader textile & polymer chem, Southern Regional Res Ctr, Agr Res Serv, USDA, 68-76, DIR & RES LEADER, TEXTILES & CLOTHING LAB, AGR RES SERV, USDA, 76- *Concurrent Pos:* vis prof chem dept, Tulane Univ, La, 70-75. *Mem:* NY Acad Sci; Fiber Soc; Am Chem Soc; Am Asn Textile Chemists & Colorists. *Res:* Chemical modification of polymers and textiles by application of new synthetic techniques; synthetic organic chemistry; polymer chemistry and physics of textiles and polymers; industrial microbiology of polymeric materials. *Mailing Add:* Textiles & Clothing Lab 1303 W Cumberland Ave Knoxville TN 37916

VIGRASS, LAURENCE WILLIAM, b Melfort, Sask, May 9, 29; m 54; c 3. GEOLOGY, ENGINEERING. *Educ:* Univ Sask, BE, 51, MSc, 52; Stanford Univ, PhD(geol), 61. *Prof Exp:* Geologist, Calif Stand Co, 52-55; res geologist, Imp Oil Ltd, 58-65; consult geologist, Western Resources Consult Ltd, 65-68; assoc prof geol, Univ Sask, Regina, 68-73, actg chmn dept, 72-73, PROF GEOL, UNIV REGINA, 73-, DIR ENERGY RES, 76- *Mem:* Geol Asn Can; Can Inst Mining & Metall; Am Asn Petrol Geol; Can Soc Petrol Geologists; Solar Energy Soc Can. *Res:* Sedimentary geology; occurence of petroleum and natural gas; geothermal energy in sedimentary basins; water movement and occurrence in the subsurface. *Mailing Add:* Dept Geol Sci Univ Regina Regina SK S4S 0A2 Can

VIJAY, INDER KRISHAN, b Lahore, India, Dec 25, 40. BIOCHEMISTRY, FOOD SCIENCE. *Educ:* Panjab Univ, BS, 61; Univ Sask, MS, 66; Univ Calif, Davis, PhD(biochem), 71. *Prof Exp:* Prod supvr food prod, Nestle Int, 61-63; fel biochem, Sch Med, Univ Mich, 71-72; NIH trainee & fel, Sch Med, Univ Calif, Davis, 72-75; asst prof, 75-80, ASSOC PROF DAIRY SCI, UNIV MD, 80- *Concurrent Pos:* Multiple grants, 75-; NIH res career develop award, 78-83. *Mem:* AAAS; Am Dairy Sci Asn; Inst Food Technologists; Sigma Xi. *Res:* Biochemistry of glycoproteins; enzyme activities in sterilized milk. *Mailing Add:* Dept of Dairy Sci Univ of Md College Park MD 20742

VIJAYAN, SIVARAMAN, b Thuckalay, Madras, June 14, 45. CHEMICAL ENGINEERING, SURFACE SCIENCE. *Educ:* Madras Univ, BSc, 64; Indian Inst Technol, Madras, B Tech, 67, M Tech, 69; Univ NB, MSc, 71; Swiss Fed Inst Technol, Lausanne, DSc(chem eng), 74. *Prof Exp:* First res asst

& lectr, Swiss Fed Inst Technol, Lausanne, 72-76; ASST PROF CHEM ENG, MCMASTER UNIV, 78- *Concurrent Pos:* Fel McMaster Univ, 76-77; adj asst eng, Univ Fla, 77-78; grant, Schweizerischer Nat Fonds zur forderung der Wissenschaftlichen Forschung, 73-76; consult, Biazzi, SA, Vevey, Switz, 75-76; ed, J Chem Eng 73-76. *Mem:* Can Soc Chem Eng; Can Asn Physicists; Am Inst Chem Eng; Brit Inst Chem Eng; Indian Inst Chem Eng. *Res:* Interfacial phenomena in chemical engineering transport processes; stability of macroemulsions; surface chemistry; surfactants microstructure; dispersion phase separation. *Mailing Add:* Dept Chem Eng McMaster Univ Hamilton ON L8S 4K1 Can

VIJAYAN, VIJAYA KUMARI, b Trivandrum, India, Feb 25, 42; m 66; c 2. HUMAN ANATOMY, NEUROANATOMY. *Educ:* Univ Kerala, MBBS, 65; Univ Calif, Davis, PhD(anat), 72. *Prof Exp:* Tutor human anat, Med Col, Trivandrum, India, 65-68; ASST PROF HUMAN ANAT, MED SCH, UNIV CALIF, DAVIS, 73- *Res:* Biochemistry and ultrastructure of developing and aging nervous system; neuroglial reaction to injury; neurotransmitters. *Mailing Add:* Dept of Human Anat Univ of Calif Sch of Med Davis CA 95616

VIJAYENDRAN, BHEEMA R, b Bangalore, India, 1941; m 70. PHYSICAL CHEMISTRY. *Educ:* Univ Madras, BTech, 63, MTech, 65; Univ Southern Calif, PhD(chem), 69. *Prof Exp:* Lectr, Cent Leather Res Inst, India, 65-66; indust fel surface chem, R J Reynolds Indust, NC, 69-70; mgr res, Copier Prod Div, Pitney Bowes, Inc, 74-75, chemist, 70-77; res assoc, Celanese Res Co, 76-78, PROJ MGR SURFACE & COLLOID CHEM, CELANESE POLYMER SPECIALTY CO, 78- *Concurrent Pos:* Teaching asst, Univ Southern Calif, 66-68; adj fac, Ind Univ, 81- *Mem:* Am Chem Soc; Soc Petrol Engrs. *Res:* Physical chemistry of surfaces; colloidal systems; emulsions; biopolymers and synthetic polymers; interfacial phenomena and their application in graphic arts such as printing, photography, xero-graphy and other reprographic techniques. *Mailing Add:* Celanese Polymer Specialty Co PO Box 99038 Jeffersontown KY 40299

VIKIS, ANDREAS CHARALAMBOUS, b Moni, Cyprus, July 8, 42; Can citizen; m 71; c 2. PHYSICAL CHEMISTRY. *Educ:* Col Emporia, BSc, 64; Kans State Univ, PhD(phys chem), 69. *Prof Exp:* Fel, Univ Toronto, 69-70, lectr & res assoc, 70-74, asst prof & res assoc, 74-75; asst res officer chem, Nat Res Coun Can, 75-79; ASSOC RES OFFICER, ATOMIC ENERGY CAN LTD, WHITESHELL NUCLEAR RES ESTAB, 79- *Mem:* Inter-Am Photochem Soc; Am Chem Soc; Can Inst Chem. *Res:* Energy transfer processes and chemical reactivity of electronically excited atoms and molecules; photochemistry; isotope enrichment; reactions, monitoring and abatement of gas-phase radionuclides. *Mailing Add:* Res Chem Br Atomic Energy Can Ltd Whiteshell Nuclear Res Estab Pinawa MB R0E 1L0 Can

VIKRAM, CHANDRA SHEKHAR, b Payagpur, India, Oct 31, 50; m 75; c 2. OPTICS. *Educ:* Indian Inst Technol, Delhi, MTech, 70, PhD(physics), 73. *Prof Exp:* Sr res fel holography, Indian Inst Technol, Delhi, 70-75, sci pool officer, 75-77; RES ASSOC HOLOGRAPHY, PA STATE UNIV, UNIVERSITY PARK, 77- *Mem:* Optical Soc Am. *Res:* Holography; speckle metrology; particle analysis. *Mailing Add:* Mat Res Lab Pa State Univ University Park PA 16802

VIKSNE, ANDY, b Jan 27, 34. GEOPHYSICS. *Educ:* Harvard Univ, AB, 56; Univ Utah, MS, 58. *Prof Exp:* Geophysicist, Texaco, Inc, 59-65 & Environ Res Corp, Systs Sci Corp, 65-66; scientist, Raytheon Co, Va, 67-68; geophysicist, US Bur Mines, 68-72; HEAD, GEOPHYS SECT, US BUR RECLAMATION, 72- *Mem:* Soc Explor Geophys; Europ Asn Explor Geophysicists. *Res:* Application of geophysical exploration methods in solving geotechnical engineering problems; in situ determination of elastic moduli for earth dams and foundation sites. *Mailing Add:* 7719 S Eaton Way Littleton CO 80123

VILA, SAMUEL CAMPDERROS, b Rubi, Spain, May 7, 30. ASTROPHYSICS. *Educ:* Univ Barcelona, Lic physics, 52; Univ Rochester, PhD(astron), 65. *Prof Exp:* Res assoc astron, Ind Univ, 65-67 & Inst Space Studies, NASA, NY, 67-69; asst prof, 69-74, ASSOC PROF ASTRON, UNIV PA, 74- *Mem:* Am Astron Soc; Int Astron Union. *Res:* Stellar evolution. *Mailing Add:* Dept of Astron Univ of Pa Philadelphia PA 19104

VILCEK, JAN TOMAS, b Bratislava, Czech, June 17, 33; m 62. MICROBIOLOGY, VIROLOGY. *Educ:* Univ Bratislava, MD, 57; Czech Acad Sci, CSc(virol), 62. *Prof Exp:* Res assoc virol, Inst Virol Czech Acad Sci, Bratislava, 57-59, head lab, 62-64; from asst prof to assoc prof microbiol, 65-72, PROF MICROBIOL, SCH MED, NY UNIV, 72- *Concurrent Pos:* Am Cancer Soc grant, 65-66; USPHS grant, 65-82, career develop award, 68-73 & contract, 70-81; Irwin Strasburger Mem Med Found grant, 69-73; ed, Arch Virol 72-74, ed in chief, 75- *Mem:* AAAS; Am Asn Immunol; Am Soc Microbiol; Brit Soc Gen Microbiol. *Res:* Virus interference; interferon; antiviral substances. *Mailing Add:* Dept of Microbiol NY Univ Sch of Med 550 First Ave New York NY 10016

VILCHES, OSCAR EDGARDO, b Mercedes, Arg, Feb 20, 36. PHYSICS. *Educ:* Nat Univ Cuyo, lic physics, 59, Dr en Fisica, 66. *Prof Exp:* Investr physics, Cent Atomico Bariloche, Arg, 60-64; res asst, Univ Ill, Urbana, 64-65, res assoc, 65-67; res assoc, Univ Calif, San Diego, 67-68; asst prof, 68-73, assoc prof, 73-80, PROF PHYSICS, UNIV WASH, 80- *Concurrent Pos:* NSF res grant, 70- *Mem:* Am Phys Soc. *Res:* Properties of liquid and solid helium and helium films; experimental physical adsorption. *Mailing Add:* Dept of Physics Univ of Wash Seattle WA 98195

VILCINS, GUNARS, b Riga, Latvia, May 8, 30; m 61; c 2. ANALYTICAL CHEMISTRY, SPECTROSCOPY. *Educ:* Univ Richmond, BS, 54, MS, 62. *Prof Exp:* Assoc chemist, 57-63, res chemist, 63-77, SR SCIENTIST, PHILIP MORRIS, INC, 77- *Mem:* Am Chem Soc; Soc Appl Spectros; Coblentz Soc. *Res:* Infrared and Raman spectroscopy; cigarette smoke; tobacco; low temperature studies; microanalysis; tunable diode laser spectroscopy; air quality analysis. *Mailing Add:* 2504 Haviland Dr Richmond VA 23229

VILENKIN, ALEXANDER, theoretical physics, see previous edition

VILKER, VINCENT LEE, b Beaver Dam, Wis, Jan 17, 43; m 81. PHYSICAL CHEMISTRY, BIOCHEMISTRY. *Educ:* Univ Wis, Madison, BS, 67; Mass Inst Technol, PhD(chem eng), 76. *Prof Exp:* Res engr, Exxon Res & Eng, 67-70; asst prof, 75-81, ASSOC PROF CHEM ENG, UNIV CALIF, LOS ANGELES, 81- *Concurrent Pos:* Prin investr, Nat Ctr Intermedia Transp Res, Univ Calif, Los Angeles, 80- *Mem:* AAAS; Am Chem Soc; Am Inst Chem Engrs. *Res:* Physical chemistry of solutions of biological macromolecules; membrane transport phenomena; separation processes; movement and fate of toxic materials (viruses, volatile organics) in soils; interfacial transport phenomena. *Mailing Add:* 5531 Boelter Hall Univ Calif Los Angeles CA 90024

VILKITIS, JAMES RICHARD, b Rush, Pa, Oct 31. RESOURCE PLANNING & MANAGEMENT, TERRESTRIAL ECOLOGY. *Educ:* Mich State Univ, BS, 65; Univ Idaho, MS, 68; Univ Mass, PhD(wildlife biol), 70. *Prof Exp:* Res asst, Water Resource Res Ctr, 68-70; leader spec big game wildlife, Dept Inland Fisheries & Game, 70-71; prin ecologist, Carlozzi, Sinton & Vilkitis Inc, 71-79; OWNER & MGR, TLC LEATHER, 76-; ENVIRON SPECIALIST, CALIF POLYTECH STATE UNIV, 80- *Concurrent Pos:* Biostatistician, Regional Plannning & Design Assocs, 69-71; lectr, Univ Mass, 71-79; res assoc ecol, Inst for Man & Environ, 73-74; asst prof biol sci, Mount Holyoke Col, 79-80. *Mem:* Wildlife Soc; Am Forestry Asn; Asn Environ Prof. *Res:* Developing new assessment techniques for managing terrestrial and aquatic ecosystems; waste water and riparian systems; waste water management; coastal resource management. *Mailing Add:* NRM Dept FOB-26N Calif Polytech State Univ San Luis Obispo CA 93407

VILKS, GUSTAVS, b Riga, Latvia, May 7, 29; Can citizen; m 55; c 2. MICROPALEONTOLOGY. *Educ:* McMaster Univ, BSc, 61; Dalhousie Univ, MSc, 66, PhD, 73. *Prof Exp:* MICROPALEONTOLOGIST, BEDFORD INST OCEANOG, 62- *Mem:* AAAS; Geol Asn Can. *Res:* Ecology and paleoecology of Recent Foraminifera in the Canadian Arctic and Gulf of St Lawrence; ecology of planktonic Foraminifera in the North Atlantic; glacial limits off eastern Canada; sedimentary processes on Labrador shelf and Abyssal Plains. *Mailing Add:* Atlantic Geosci Ctr Bedford Inst Oceanog Dartmouth NS B2Y 4A2 Can

VILLA, FRANCESCO, high energy physics, see previous edition

VILLA, JUAN FRANCISCO, b Matanzas, Cuba, Sept 23, 41; US citizen; m 67; c 4. INORGANIC CHEMISTRY. *Educ:* Univ Miami, BS, 65, MS, 67, PhD(inorg chem), 69. *Prof Exp:* Teaching asst chem, Univ Miami, 65-69; res assoc inorg chem, Univ NC, Chapel Hill, 69-71; from asst prof to assoc prof, 71-78, actg dean natural & social sci, 80-81, PROF CHEM, LEHMAN COL, 78- *Concurrent Pos:* George N Shuster fel, Lehman Col, 71-72 & 74-77; Petrol Res Fund fel, 71-73; Fulbright-Hays sr lectr, Colombia, SAm, 76; adj prof, Sarah Lawrence Col, 77 & 78. *Mem:* AAAS; Am Chem Soc; The Chem Soc; Sigma Xi; NY Acad Sci; Am Inst Chemists. *Res:* Study of transition metal coordination compounds of biological importance including synthesis, electron paramagnetic resonance spectroscopy, magnetic susceptibility measurements, electronic and infrared spectra; ligand field and molecular orbital calculations. *Mailing Add:* 14 Clark Dr Spring Valley NY 10977

VILLA, VICENTE DOMINGO, b Laredo, Tex, Dec 1, 40; m 62; c 2. MICROBIAL PHYSIOLOGY. *Educ:* Univ Tex, Austin, BA, 64; Rice Univ, PhD(microbiol), 70. *Prof Exp:* Fel molecular biol, Molecular Biol Lab, Univ Wis, 69-71; res assoc, Rosenstiel Res Ctr, Brandeis Univ, 71-72; asst prof, 72-75, ASSOC PROF BIOL, N MEX STATE UNIV, 76- *Concurrent Pos:* NIH fel, 70-71; ad hoc consult, Minority Biomed Support Prog, NIH, 72-75, mem gen res support prog adv comt, Div Res Resources, 76-80; panelist, NSF Rev Panel-Res Initiation & Support Prog, 76. *Mem:* Am Soc Microbiol. *Res:* Regulation of fermentative and oxidative metabolism in fungi and its relation to the morphogenesis of the organism. *Mailing Add:* Dept of Biol NMex State Univ Las Cruces NM 88003

VILLABLANCA, JAIME ROLANDO, b Chillan, Chile, Feb 28, 29; m 55; c 5. NEUROPHYSIOLOGY, EXPERIMENTAL NEUROLOGY. *Educ:* Univ Chile, Bachelor, 46, Lic Med, 53, Dr(med), 54; Univ Calif, Los Angeles, cert neurophysiol, 68. *Prof Exp:* From instr to prof pathophysiol, Sch Med, Univ Chile, 54-71; assoc res anat & psychiat, 71-72, PROF PSYCHIAT, UNIV CALIF, LOS ANGELES, 72-, PROF ANAT, 77- *Concurrent Pos:* Rockefeller Found fel physiol, Johns Hopkins Univ, 59-61; fel, Neurol Unit, Harvard Med Sch, 61; US Air Force Off Sci res grant, 62-65; NIH int res fel anat, Univ Calif, Los Angeles, 66-68; Found Fund Res in Psychiat grant, 69-72; Nat Inst Child Health & Human Develop prog proj grant, 71-84; mem, Mental Retardation Res Ctr, Univ Calif, Los Angeles; sci adv coun, Inst Inst Res & Advice on Mental Deficiency, Madrid, Spain. *Mem:* NY Acad Sci; Am Physiol Soc; Soc Neurosci; Sigma Xi; Int Brain Res Orgn. *Res:* Neurophysiology of sleep-wakefulness; neurological, behavioral and electrophysiological effects of lesions upon the mature and upon the developing brain; physiology and pathophysiology of the basal ganglia; recovery of function and anatomical reorganization following lesions of the mature and the developing brain; physiology and pathophysiology of the basal ganglia; role of the basal ganglia on the effects of opiates. *Mailing Add:* Dept of Psychiat Univ of Calif Los Angeles CA 90024

VILLACORTE, GUILLERMO VILAR, b Rizal, Philippines, Dec 25, 33; m 61; c 2. ALLERGY, IMMUNOLOGY. *Educ:* Univ St Tomas, Manila, AA, 62, MD, 67; Am Bd Allergy & Immunol, dipl, 74, recert, 80. *Prof Exp:* Asst prof pediat, Sch Med, Creighton Univ, 69-79; MEM STAFF, ALLERGY-IMMUNOL SERV, WILFORD HALL MED CTR, LACKLAND AFB, TEX, 79- *Concurrent Pos:* Fels pediat allergy & immunol, Med Ctr, Univ Cincinnati, 65-69. *Mem:* Fel Am Acad Allergy; Am Thoracic Soc; Am Fedn Clin Res; Asn Military Allergists. *Res:* Etiopathogenesis of allergic and immunodeficiency diseases. *Mailing Add:* 8306 Brixton San Antonio TX 78250

VILLAFRANCA, JOSEPH JOHN, b Silver Creek, NY, Mar 23, 44; m 67; c 2. BIOCHEMISTRY, BIO-ORGANIC CHEMISTRY. *Educ:* State Univ NY Col Fredonia, BS, 65; Purdue Univ, Lafayette, PhD(biochem), 69. *Prof Exp:* USPHS fel, Inst Cancer Res, 69-71; asst prof, 71-76, assoc prof, 76-81, PROF CHEM, PA STATE UNIV, UNIVERSITY PARK, 81- *Concurrent Pos:* Res Corp grant, Pa State Univ, 72-73, NSF grant, 72- & USPHS grant, 74-77, 76-79, 78-81, 79-82, 81-84 & 80-85; estab investr, Am Heart Asn, 78-83. *Mem:* Am Chem Soc; Biophys Soc; Am Soc Biol Chemists. *Res:* Mechanism of enzyme action studied by magnetic resonance techniques; biophysics. *Mailing Add:* Dept of Chem 152 Davey Lab Pa State Univ University Park PA 16802

VILLA-KOMAROFF, LYDIA, b Las Vegas, NMex, Aug 7, 47; m 70. MOLECULAR BIOLOGY, DEVELOPMENTAL BIOLOGY. *Educ:* Goucher Col, AB, 70; Mass Inst Technol, PhD(cell biol), 75. *Prof Exp:* Res fel biol, Harvard Univ, 75-78; asst prof, 78-81, ASSOC PROF MICROBIOL, MED SCH, UNIV MASS, 82- *Concurrent Pos:* Vis fel, Cold Spring Harbor Lab, 76-77; fel, Helen Hay Whitney Found, 75-78. *Mem:* Am Soc Microbiol; Am Soc Cell Biol; AAAS; Fedn Am Sci; Sigma Xi. *Res:* Structure of DNA encoding brain-specific peptides; structure of DNA encoding developmentally regulated genes. *Mailing Add:* Dept of Microbiol 55 Lake Ave N Worcester MA 01605

VILLANI, FRANK JOHN, b Brooklyn, NY, May 9, 21; m 51; c 4. MEDICINAL CHEMISTRY. *Educ:* Brooklyn Col, BA, 41; Fordham Univ, MS, 43, PhD(chem), 46. *Prof Exp:* Org chemist, 46-64, FEL MED CHEM, SCHERING CORP, BLOOMFIELD, 64- *Mem:* AAAS; Am Chem Soc; Am Inst Chem; NY Acad Sci; Int Soc Hetero Chemists. *Res:* Aldehyde condensations; synthetic medicinals; heterocyclic chemistry. *Mailing Add:* 55 McKinley Ave West Caldwell NJ 07006

VILLANUEVA, JOSE, b Santiago de Cuba, Cuba, Mar 31, 37; US citizen; m 61; c 2. ENGINEERING MECHANICS. *Educ:* Ga Inst Technol, BS, 59, MS, 61, PhD(eng mech), 65. *Prof Exp:* Prof docent mech eng, Univ Oriente, Cuba, 61; asst prof eng mech, Ga Inst Technol, 61-68; assoc prof mech eng, 68-77, actg chmn dept, 71-77, PROF MECH ENG, FLA ATLANTIC UNIV, 77- *Concurrent Pos:* Eng consult, Am Art Metals, Ga, 61 & Lockheed-Ga Co, 66- *Honors & Awards:* Ralph R Teetor Award, Soc Automotive Engrs, 67. *Mem:* Am Soc Mech Engrs. *Res:* Continuum mechanics; dynamics and vibrations; sloshing of liquids and design of mechanical models to describe the phenomena. *Mailing Add:* Dept of Mech Eng Fla Atlantic Univ Boca Raton FL 33431

VILLAR, JAMES WALTER, b New York, NY, July 25, 30; m 58; c 3. METALLURGY, GEOLOGY. *Educ:* Mich State Univ, BS, 52, MS, 56, PhD(geol), 64. *Prof Exp:* Geologist, 56-58 & 60-63, sr metallurgist, 63-64, asst chief metallurgist, 64-65, asst mgr res & develop, 65-68, mgr res & develop, 68-78, gen mgr res & develop, 78-79, gen mgr res & eng, 79-81, VPRES RES & ENG, CLEVELAND-CLIFFS IRON CO, 81- *Mem:* Fel Geol Soc Am; Am Inst Mining, Metall & Petrol Engrs. *Res:* Development of beneficiation methods for low grade iron deposits, especially fine grained hematites. *Mailing Add:* Cleveland-Cliffs Iron Co 1460 Union Commerce Bldg Cleveland OH 44115

VILLARD, OSWALD G(ARRISON), JR, b Dobbs Ferry, NY, Sept 17, 16; m 42; c 3. ELECTRONICS, DEFENSE RESEARCH. *Educ:* Yale Univ, AB, 38; Stanford Univ, EE, 43, PhD(radio eng), 49. *Prof Exp:* Actg instr elec eng, Stanford Univ, 41-42; spec res assoc, Radio Res Lab, Harvard Univ, 42-43, mem sr staff, 43-46; actg asst prof elec eng, 46-50, from asst prof to assoc prof, 50-55, dir, Radiosci Lab, 60-73, dir ionospheric dynamics lab, 70-72, PROF ELEC ENG, STANFORD UNIV, 55-, SR SCI ADV, STANFORD RES INST, 72- *Concurrent Pos:* Mem, Air Force Studies Bd, Nat Res Coun, 62-; mem geophys panel, US Air Force Sci Adv Bd, 66-75; mem, Naval Res Adv Comt, 69-75, chmn, 72-75. *Honors & Awards:* Morris Liebmann Mem Award, Inst Elec & Electronics Engrs, 57. *Mem:* Nat Acad Sci; Nat Acad Eng; fel AAAS; fel Inst Elec & Electronics Engrs; Am Geophys Union. *Res:* Ionospheric radio propagation; upper atmosphere research; radar techniques; defense electronic systems. *Mailing Add:* 2887 Woodside Rd Woodside CA 94062

VILLAREJO, MERNA, b New York, NY, June 19, 39; m 59; c 2. BIOCHEMISTRY. *Educ:* Univ Chicago, BS, 59, PhD(biochem), 63. *Prof Exp:* Res assoc & asst prof biochem, Univ Chicago, 63-68; res assoc biol chem, Sch Med, Univ Calif, Los Angeles, 68-75; ASST PROF BIOCHEM, UNIV CALIF, DAVIS, 75- *Concurrent Pos:* USPHS fel, Univ Chicago, 63-65. *Res:* Membrane protein structure and function; isolation and characterization of the lactose permease protein; regulation of Ecoli membrane protein composition by local anesthetics. *Mailing Add:* Dept of Biochem & Biophys Univ of Calif Davis CA 95616

VILLAREJOS, VICTOR MOISES, b La Paz, Bolivia, Sept 4, 18; US citizen; m 41; c 4. EPIDEMIOLOGY, TROPICAL MEDICINE. *Educ:* Univ Heidelberg, MD, 41; Tulane Univ, MPH & TM, 59, DrPH, 61. *Prof Exp:* Chief serv med, Miraflores Gen Hosp, La Paz, 45-58; from assoc prof to prof trop med, Med Sch, Univ La Paz, 47-58; assoc prof trop med, Sch Med, 61-66, chief epidemiol sect, La State Univ Int Ctr Med Res & Training, San Jose, Costa Rica, 62-66, prog coordr, 66-69, PROF TROP MED, SCH MED, LA STATE UNIV, NEW ORLEANS, 66-, DIR, LA STATE UNIV-INT CTR MED RES & TRAINING, SAN JOSE, COSTA RICA, 69- *Concurrent Pos:* Alexander von Humboldt fel, Ger, 41-42; Pan Am Health Orgn fel, 58-59; USPHS & Armed Forces Epidemiol Bd res grants. *Mem:* Am Soc Trop Med & Hyg; Am Soc Parasitol; Am Pub Health Asn. *Res:* Epidemiology of diseases prevalent in tropical areas; pathogenesis of E histolytica; diarrheal diseases; infectious hepatitis. *Mailing Add:* Dept Trop Med Sch Med La State Univ New Orleans LA 70112

VILLAR-PALASI, CARLOS, b Spain, Mar 3, 28; m 57; c 4. PHARMACOLOGY, BIOCHEMISTRY. *Educ:* Univ Valencia, MS, 51; Univ Madrid, PhD(biochem), 55; Univ Barcelona, MPharm, 62. *Prof Exp:* Res assoc biochem, Univ Madrid, 60-63; res assoc, Univ Minn, Minneapolis, 64-65, asst prof, 65-69; assoc prof pharmacol, 69-72, PROF PHARMACOL, UNIV VA, 72- *Concurrent Pos:* Span Res Coun fel, Univ Hamburg, 53-54; NIH fel, Western Reserve Univ, 57-60; NIH grant, Univ Va, 70- *Honors & Awards:* AAAS Res Award, 60; Span Soc Biochem Res Award, 72. *Mem:* AAAS; NY Acad Sci; Am Soc Biol Chemists; Span Soc Biochem; Am Soc Pharmacol & Exp Therapeut. *Res:* Glycogen metabolism and the mechanism of action of cyclic adenosine monophosphate; mechanisms of control, metabolic and hormonal; effects of insulin, epinephrine and glucagon on glycogen metabolism as well as the mechanisms by which epinephrine exerts its effect on muscle contraction. *Mailing Add:* Dept of Pharmacol Univ of Va Charlottesville VA 22903

VILLARREAL, JESSE JAMES, b San Antonio, Tex, Oct 22, 13; m 35; c 2. SPEECH PATHOLOGY. *Educ:* Univ Tex, BA, 35, MA, 37; Northwestern Univ, PhD(speech path, audiol), 47. *Prof Exp:* Dir, Speech & Hearing Clin, Univ Tex, Austin, 39-62, prof, 52-65, chmn, Dept Speech, 62-68, prof speech commun & educ, 65-80. *Mem:* Fel Am Speech & Hearing Asn; Speech Commun Asn. *Res:* English as a second language. *Mailing Add:* 5104 Crestway Austin TX 78731

VILLARREAL, LUIS PEREZ, b Los Angeles, Calif, July 6, 49; m 82. MOLECULAR VIROLOGY. *Educ:* Los Angeles State Univ, BS, 71; Univ Calif, San Diego, PhD(biol), 76. *Prof Exp:* Fel molecular biol, Biochem Dept, Stanford Univ, 76-78; ASST PROF MICROBIOL & VIROL, UNIV COLO HEALTH SCI CTR, 78- *Concurrent Pos:* Res fel, Jane Coffin Childs Mem Res Fund, 76. *Mem:* Am Soc Microbiol. *Res:* Control of gene expression in animal viruses. *Mailing Add:* Dept Microbiol & Immunol B175 Univ Colo Health Sci Ctr Denver CO 80262

VILLARROEL, FERNANDO, b Valparaiso, Chile, Aug 18, 35; US citizen; m 59; c 1. BIOMEDICAL ENGINEERING, CHEMICAL ENGINEERING. *Educ:* Mil Politech Acad, Chile, BS, 60; Univ Md, College Park, MS, 67, PhD(chem eng), 70. *Prof Exp:* Assoc engr, Nat Instrument Lab, 62-66; proj leader, Biomed Eng Group, Harry Diamond Labs, 67-72; prog coordr, Artificial Kidney-Chronic Uremia Prog, Nat Inst Arthritis, Metab & Digestive Dis, 73-80; DIR, DIV GASTROENTEROL-UROL & GEN USE DEVICES, BUR MED DEVICES, US FOOD & DRUG ADMIN, 80- *Mem:* Am Soc Artificial Internal Organs; Am Inst Chem Engrs. *Res:* Artificial internal organs. *Mailing Add:* Bur Med Devices 8757 Georgia Ave (HFK420) Silver Spring MD 20910

VILLARS, FELIX MARC HERMANN, b Biel, Switz, Jan 6, 21; nat US; m 49; c 4. THEORETICAL PHYSICS. *Educ:* Swiss Fed Inst Technol, Dipl, 45, DSc, 46. *Prof Exp:* Res asst physics, Swiss Fed Inst Technol, 46-49; vis mem, Inst Adv Study, 49-50; res assoc 50-52, from asst prof to assoc prof, 52-60, PROF PHYSICS, MASS INST TECHNOL, 60- *Concurrent Pos:* Consult, Lincoln Lab, 54-64, 68-70; Guggenheim fel, 56-57; lectr physics, Harvard Med Sch, 74- *Mem:* Am Phys Soc; Am Acad Arts & Sci. *Res:* Nuclear physics, mainly nuclear models and reactions; quantum field theory; physics of upper atmosphere; turbulence; plasma probes; biophysics. *Mailing Add:* Dept of Physics Rm 6-311 Mass Inst of Technol Cambridge MA 02139

VILLEE, CLAUDE ALVIN, JR, b Lancaster, Pa, Feb 9, 17; m 52; c 4. BIOCHEMISTRY. *Educ:* Franklin & Marshall Col, BS, 37; Univ Calif, PhD(physiol genetics), 41. *Hon Degrees:* AM, Harvard Univ, 57. *Prof Exp:* Res assoc zool, Univ Calif, 41-42; from instr to asst prof, Univ NC, 42-45; from instr to assoc prof biol chem, 46-63, PROF BIOL CHEM, HARVARD UNIV, 63-, ANDELOT PROF, 64-, TUTOR PRECLIN SCI, MED SCH, 47- *Concurrent Pos:* Asst prof, Armstrong Col, 41-42; tech aide, Come Growth, Nat Res Coun, 46; Lalor fel, Marine Biol Lab, Woods Hole, 47 & 48; Guggenheim fel, Denmark, 49-50; res assoc, Boston Lying-in-Hosp, 50-; consult, Mass Gen Hosp, 50- & NSF, 59-; consult, NIH, 58-, mem nat adv child health & human develop coun, 63-65; dir lab reproductive biol, Boston Hosp Women, 66-; mem sci adv comt, Ore Regional Primate Ctr, 70-; distinguished vis prof, Univ Belgrade & Mahidol Univ, Bangkok, 74; consult, March Dimes Found, 78- *Honors & Awards:* Ciba Award, Endocrine Soc, 56; Rubin Award, Am Soc Study Sterility, 57. *Mem:* Hon mem Soc Gynec Invest; hon fel Am Col Obstet & Gynec; hon fel Am Gynec Soc; Am Soc Biol Chemists; Genetic Soc Am. *Res:* Nucleic acid chemistry and metabolism; carbohydrate metabolism; effects of hormones on intermediary metabolism; function of the placenta; biochemical genetics; metabolism of fetal tissues. *Mailing Add:* Dept of Biol Chem Harvard Med Sch Boston MA 02115

VILLEE, DOROTHY, b Charleston, SC, Nov 25, 27; m 52; c 4. ENDOCRINOLOGY, BIOCHEMISTRY. *Educ:* Barnard Col, Columbia Univ, BA, 50; Harvard Med Sch, MD, 55. *Prof Exp:* Instr pediat, 56-60, res fel biochem, 60-61, assoc pediat, 62-74, ASST PROF PEDIAT, HARVARD MED SCH, 74- *Concurrent Pos:* Fel, Mass Gen Hosp, 57-59, USPHS res grant, 64- *Mem:* Endocrine Soc; Am Med Women's Asn. *Res:* Growth and differentiation of normal and abnormal endocrine tissue and in the factors controlling growth and differentiation. *Mailing Add:* Dept of Pediat 25 Shattuck St Boston MA 02115

VILLEGAS, CESAREO, b Montevideo, Uruguay, April 5, 21; Can citizen; m 50; c 4. MATHEMATICAL STATISTICS. *Educ:* Univ de La Repub, Uruguay, Ing Ind, 53. *Prof Exp:* Prof math, Univ de La Repub, Uruguay, 58-68; vis assoc prof, Univ Rochester, 68-70; assoc prof, 70-79, PROF STATIST, SIMON FRASER UNIV, 79- *Mem:* Int Statist Inst; Inst Math Statist; Can Statist Soc. *Res:* Developing a new approach to statistics called logical bayesian inference, and its applications, especially to linear functional models. *Mailing Add:* Dept Math Simon Fraser Univ Burnaby BC V5A 1S6 Can

VILLELLA, JOHN BAPTIST, b Walston, Pa, Mar 31, 15; m 59. ZOOLOGY. *Educ:* Gettysburg Col, AB, 42; Univ Mich, MS, 49, PhD(zool), 54. *Prof Exp:* Jr chemist, USDA, 46-47; asst radiation biol, AEC, 53-55; AEC res assoc parasitol, Univ Mich, 55-57, res assoc, Phoenix Mem Lab, 57-61; mem fac med zool, Sch Trop Med, Univ PR & PR Nuclear Ctr, 61-66; prof biol, Savannah State Col, 66-71; PROF BIOL, INTER-AM UNIV PR, 71- *Mem:* Am Soc Parasitol; Am Micros Soc; Am Inst Biol Sci; AAAS. *Res:* Host-parasite relationships. *Mailing Add:* Dept of Biol Inter-Am Univ of PR San German PR 00753

VILLEMEZ, CLARENCE LOUIS, JR, b Port Arthur, Tex, Sept 6, 38; m 64; c 4. BIOCHEMISTRY. *Educ:* Harvard Univ, AB, 58; Purdue Univ, MS, 61, PhD(biochem), 63. *Prof Exp:* Fel biochem, Purdue Univ, 63-65; asst res biochemist, Univ Calif, Berkeley, 65-66; res assoc biochem, Univ Colo, 66-67; from asst prof to assoc prof, Ohio Univ, 67-72; assoc prof, 72-74, PROF BIOCHEM, UNIV WYO, 74- *Concurrent Pos:* Vis prof microbiol, Univ Tex Health Sci Ctr, Dallas, 79-80. *Mem:* Am Soc Cell Biol; AAAS; Am Soc Biol Chemists; Am Soc Plant Physiologists; NY Acad Sci. *Res:* Polysaccharide biosynthesis; cell wall formation; protein glycosylation; hybridomas; specific cytotoxic reagents. *Mailing Add:* Div Biochem Univ Wyo Laramie WY 82071

VILLEMURE, M PAUL JAMES, b Newberry, Mich, Nov 28, 28. MATHEMATICS. *Educ:* Siena Heights Col, BS, 50; Univ Notre Dame, PhD(math), 58. *Prof Exp:* Teacher high sch, 58-59; instr math & sci, Col San Antonio, 51-54; from instr math to asst prof math, 59-69, PROF MATH, BARRY COL, 69- *Mem:* Math Asn Am. *Mailing Add:* Dept of Math Barry Col Miami FL 33161

VILLENEUVE, A(LFRED) T(HOMAS), b Syracuse, NY, Mar 14, 30; m 56; c 5. ELECTRICAL ENGINEERING. *Educ:* Manhattan Col, BEE, 52; Syracuse Univ, MEE, 55, PhD(elec eng), 59. *Prof Exp:* Res assoc elec eng, Syracuse Univ, 52-56, instr, 56-59, asst prof, 59; mem tech staff, 59-60, staff engr, 60-63, sr staff engr, 63-72, SR SCIENTIST, HUGHES AIRCRAFT CO, 72- *Concurrent Pos:* Lectr, Univ Southern Calif, 59, Loyola Univ, Calif, 62 & Univ Calif, Los Angeles, 69; mem comn B, Int Union Radio Sci. *Mem:* Inst Elec & Electronics Engrs; Sigma Xi. *Res:* Ultra-high-frequency antennas; microwave filters; large aperture antennas; electromagnetic fields in anisotropic media; advanced antenna techniques; satellite antennas; space communications. *Mailing Add:* 8123 Kenyon Ave Los Angeles CA 90045

VILLENEUVE, ANDRE, b Chicoutimi, Que, Sept 17, 32; m 58; c 1. NEUROPSYCHOPHARMACOLOGY. *Educ:* Laval Univ, BA, 52, MD, 58; McGill Univ, MSc, 58; FRCPS(C); FRCPsychiat. *Prof Exp:* Residency psychiat, Cent Islip State Hosp & NY Sch Psychiat, 61-64; researcher phsyciat, Fac Grad Studies, McGill Univ, Montreal & clin fel, Royal Victoria Hosp, 64-66, researcher psychopharmacol, Hosp St Anne & Fac Med, Paris, 66-67; lectr, 68-70, assoc prof, 70-76, PROF, DEPT PSYCHIAT, LAVAL UNIV, QUE, 76- *Concurrent Pos:* Res psychiatrist neuropsychopharmacol, Univ Ctr Hosp Robert Giffard, Beauport, Que, 67-, chief, 67-74 & 79-; dir res, Dept Psychiat, Hosp De L'Enfant-Jesus, Que, 73-; pres, Examining Bd, French Sect, Psychiat Specialty, Royal Col Physicians & Surgeons, Can, 78-; chief, Neuropsychopharmacol Sect, Clinique Roy-Rousseau, Beauport, Que, 82- *Mem:* Fel Am Psychiat Asn; fel Am Col Physicians; fel Col Int Neuro-Psychopharmacol. *Res:* Methodology; clinical trials; pharmacokinetics; drug interactions; extraphyramidal system (side effects, tradive dyskinesia, endorphins, estrogens); neuropsychoendocrinology. *Mailing Add:* Neuropsychopharmacol Univ Ctr Hosp Robert Giffard 2601 De La Canadiere Beauport PQ G1J 2G3 Can

VILLET, RUXTON HERRER, b June 26, 33; Brit citizen; m 60; c 2. BIOCHEMISTRY, BIOCHEMICAL ENGINEERING. *Educ:* Univ Cape Town, BSc, 53; Princeton Univ, MS, 59; Univ Oxford, DPhil(biochem), 68. *Prof Exp:* Chem engr petrol, Mobil Oil Refinery, SAfrica, 53-57; chem engr res, Shell Develop Co, Calif, 59-60; assoc prof chem eng, Univ Witwatersrand, 61-65; maitre de rech assoc biochem, Ctr Nat Rech Sci/Inst Nat de la Sante et de la Rech Medicale, France, 73-75; reader, biochem eng, Massey Univ, NZ, 76-78; SR BIOENGR & SCIENTIST, SOLAR ENERGY, SOLAR ENERGY RES INST, 78- *Concurrent Pos:* Res fel, Calif Inst Technol, 68-70 & Max-Planck Inst, WGer, 71-73. *Mem:* Am Soc Microbiol; Am Inst Chem Engrs; Brit Biophys Soc. *Res:* Biochemical, genetic and chemical engineering research directed toward developing biotechnological processes for the conversion of biomass to fuels and chemicals. *Mailing Add:* Solar Energy Res Inst 1536 Cole Blvd Golden CO 80401

VILMS, JAAK, b Viljandi, Estonia, Jan 30, 37; US citizen; m 62; c 2. MATHEMATICS. *Educ:* Dickinson Col, AB, 59; Columbia Univ, MS, 61, PhD(math), 67. *Prof Exp:* Instr math, Purdue Univ, 65-67, asst prof, 67-71; ASSOC PROF MATH, COLO STATE UNIV, 71- *Mem:* Am Math Soc; Math Asn Am. *Res:* Differential geometry. *Mailing Add:* Dept of Math Colo State Univ Ft Collins CO 80523

VILTER, RICHARD WILLIAM, b Cincinnati, Ohio, Mar 21, 11; m 35; c 1. MEDICINE. *Educ:* Harvard Univ, BA, 33, MD, 37; Am Bd Internal Med, dipl; Am Bd Nutrit, dipl. *Prof Exp:* Intern, Cincinnati Gen Hosp, Ohio, 37-38, sr asst resident, 40-41, chief resident, Med Serv, 41-42; from asst prof to assoc prof med, Col Med, Univ Cincinnati, 42-56, asst to dean, Col Med, 43-45, asst dean, 45-52, asst dir dept, 52-56, dir, Lab Hemat & Nutrit, 45-56, Taylor prof med & dir, Dept Internal Med, 56-78. *Concurrent Pos:* Fel nutrit, Hillman Hosp, Ala, 39-40; attend physician, Cincinnati Gen Hosp, 45-; Musser lectr, Sch Med, Tulane Univ, 65; chmn hemat study sect, NIH, 65-69. *Honors & Awards:* Goldberger Award, AMA, 60, Tehan Award, 78. *Mem:* Am Soc Clin Invest; Am Clin & Climat Asn (vpres, 64-65); Asn Am Physicians; fel Am Col Physicians (secy-gen, 74-77, pres-elect, 78-79, pres, 79-80); Am Soc Hemat. *Res:* Hematology; nutrition; refractory and aplastic anemias; megaloblastic anemias; nutritional anemias. *Mailing Add:* 6067 Col of Med Bldg 231 Bethesda Ave Cincinnati OH 45267

VIMMERSTEDT, JOHN P, b Jamestown, NY, June 5, 31; m 53; c 4. SOIL SCIENCE, FORESTRY. *Educ:* State Univ NY Col Forestry, Syracuse, BS, 53; Yale Univ, MS, 58, DF, 65. *Prof Exp:* Res forester, Southeastern Forest Exp Sta, 55-58; asst prof forest soils, 63-68, ASSOC PROF FOREST SOILS, OHIO AGR RES & DEVELOP CTR, 68- *Mem:* Soil Sci Soc Am; Soc Am Foresters; AAAS; Sigma Xi. *Res:* Cation exchange properties of plant roots; mineral nutrition of trees; reclamation of spoil banks from coal mining; ecological impacts of forest recreation; soil fauna; use of legumes for nitrogen enrichment of forest planting sites. *Mailing Add:* Dept of Forestry Ohio Agr Res & Develop Ctr Wooster OH 44691

VINAL, RICHARD S, b Worcester, Mass, May 5, 38; m 61; c 2. INORGANIC CHEMISTRY. *Educ:* Bates Col, BS, 60; Cornell Univ, PhD(inorg chem), 65. *Prof Exp:* Sr res chemist, 65-71, RES ASSOC, EASTMAN KODAK CO, 71- *Mem:* Am Chem Soc; Soc Photog Scientists & Engrs. *Res:* Transition metal; coordination chemistry; structural studies; photographic science; redox reactions; non-silver photographic systems development. *Mailing Add:* 350 Mt Airy Dr Rochester NY 14617

VINATIERI, JAMES EDWARD, b Yankton, SDak, June 27, 47; m 69; c 2. INTERACTIVE COMPUTER GRAPHICS. *Educ:* Univ SDak, BA, 69; Univ Nebr, PhD(chem), 74. *Prof Exp:* Sr res chemist, 73-81, SYST SPECIALIST, PHILLIPS PETROLEUM CO, 82- *Mem:* Am Chem Soc. *Res:* Chemical and physical properties of surfactant systems for enhanced oil recovery, especially phase behavior and interfacial phenomena. *Mailing Add:* Phillips Petroleum Co 308 TRW Bldg Bartlesville OK 74002

VINCE, ROBERT, b Auburn, NY, Nov 20, 40; m 61; c 2. MEDICINAL CHEMISTRY. *Educ:* Univ Buffalo, BS, 62; State Univ NY Buffalo, PhD(med chem), 66. *Prof Exp:* Asst prof med chem, Col Pharm, Univ Miss, 66-67; from asst prof to assoc prof, 67-73, PROF MED CHEM, COL PHARM, UNIV MINN, 76- *Concurrent Pos:* Vis scientist, Roche Inst Molecular Biol, 74-75; Nat Cancer Inst res career develop award, 72-76. *Honors & Awards:* Lunsford Richardson Grad Res Award, Richarson-Merrell Inc, 66. *Mem:* Am Chem Soc; Am Pharmaceut Asn; Am Soc Biol Chemists; Am Asn Cancer Res. *Res:* Design and synthesis of inhibitors of protein biosynthesis; nucleoside analogs as cancer chemotherapy agents. *Mailing Add:* Col of Pharm Univ of Minn Minneapolis MN 55455

VINCENT, CHARLES L, oceanography, environmental sciences, see previous edition

VINCENT, DAYTON GEORGE, b Hornell, NY, Apr 23, 36; m 59, 75; c 4. METEOROLOGY. *Educ:* Univ Rochester, AB, 58; St Louis Univ, dipl meteorol, 59; Univ Okla, MS, 64; Mass Inst Technol, PhD(meteorol), 70. *Prof Exp:* Weather officer meteorol, Air Weather Serv, US Air Force, 59-62; res asst, Univ Okla Res Inst, 64; res meteorologist, Naval Weapons Lab, Dahlgren, Va, 64-65; res assoc, Mass Inst Technol, 69-70; asst prof atmospheric sci, 70-74, ASSOC PROF ATMOSPHERIC SCI, DEPT GEOSCI, PURDUE UNIV, WEST LAFAYETTE, 74- *Concurrent Pos:* Mem Trop Meteorol Group to study scale interactions, 73-; Int travel grant, Am Meteorol Soc, 74. *Mem:* Am Meteorol Soc; Sigma Xi; Royal Meterol Soc. *Res:* Impact of connection on large-scale circulations in the tropics and mid-latitudes. *Mailing Add:* Dept of Geosci Purdue Univ West Lafayette IN 47907

VINCENT, DIETRICH H(ERMANN), b Leszno, Poland, May 11, 25; m 54; c 2. PHYSICS, NUCLEAR ENGINEERING. *Educ:* Univ Göttingen, dipl phys, 50, Dr rer nat, 56. *Prof Exp:* Sci asst physics, Isotope Lab, Max Planck Inst Med Res, 51-58; resident res assoc, Argonne Nat Lab, 58-60; assoc prof nuclear eng, 60-64, PROF NUCLEAR ENG, UNIV MICH, ANN ARBOR, 64- *Mem:* AAAS; Am Phys Soc; Am Nuclear Soc; Am Soc Metals. *Res:* Radiation effects in solids; Mössbauer spectroscopy; ion implantation; hydrogen in metals. *Mailing Add:* 4795 Bridgeway Ann Arbor MI 48103

VINCENT, DONALD LESLIE, b St John, NB, CAn, July 23, 21; m 49; c 3. ORGANIC CHEMISTRY. *Educ:* Acadia Univ, BSc, 42; McGill Univ, PhD(chem), 53. *Prof Exp:* Instr chem, Acadia Univ, 46-49; asst res officer, Nat Res Coun Can, 53-60; org group leader res lab, Coal Tar Prod Div Dom Tar & Chem Co, Ltd, 60-63; group leader organic chem, 63-79, SR RES SCIENTIST, DOMTAR RES CTR, 79- *Mem:* Chem Inst Can. *Res:* Wood chemistry; lignin; carbohydrates; pulp and paper; natural products; organic synthesis. *Mailing Add:* 153 Douglas Shand Ave Pointe Claire PQ H9R 2E2 Can

VINCENT, GEORGE PAUL, b Cleveland, Ohio, Oct 20, 01; m 68; c 1. CHEMISTRY. *Educ:* Hiram Col, AB, 23; Cornell Univ, MS, 24, PhD(phys chem), 27. *Prof Exp:* Asst chem, Cornell Univ, 23-25; res chemist, Eastman Kodak Co, 27-30; res chemist, Olin Mathieson Chem Corp, NY, 30-33, mgr res lab, 33-34, asst to res dir, 35-38, mgr sales develop, 49-52, mgr sales, Hydrocarbon Div, 52-53, govt serv, 53-67; CONSULT, 67- *Concurrent Pos:* Fed Govt liaison in food additive fields. *Mem:* Am Chem Soc; Am Inst Chem Eng. *Res:* Electrochemistry; sodium chlorite manufacturing methods and uses; inorganic chemistry in alkali-chlorine industry. *Mailing Add:* Chemists Club 52 E 41st St New York NY 10017

VINCENT, GERALD GLENN, b Winnipeg, Man, Apr 13, 34; m 56; c 4. RESEARCH ADMINISTRATION, POLYMER CHEMISTRY. *Educ:* Univ Man, BS, 58, MS, 60, PhD(phys chem), 63. *Prof Exp:* Res chemist adhesion, Dow Chem Co, 63-65, proj mgr adhesives, 65-67; sect leader resins, DeSoto Inc, Des Plaines, 67-69, tech mgr aerospace, 69-72, mgr resin res, 72-73; asst dir res, 73-74, DIR RES, CENT RES, CROWN ZELLERBACH, 74- *Mem:* Am Chem Soc; Sigma Xi; Tech Asn Pulp & Paper Indust; Indust Res Inst. *Res:* Adhesion chemistry. *Mailing Add:* Cent Res Crown Zellerbach Camas WA 98607

VINCENT, HAROLD ARTHUR, b Lake City, Iowa, Jan 19, 30; m 57; c 2. ANALYTICAL CHEMISTRY. *Educ:* Univ Iowa, BS, 53; Univ Nev, MS, 60; Univ Ariz, PhD(chem), 64. *Prof Exp:* Chemist, Mining Anal Lab, Univ Nev, Reno, 56-68; chief chemist, 68-77, dir, Geol Labs, 77-81, MGR GEOL RES, ANACONDA CO, TUCSON, 81- *Mem:* AAAS; Am Chem Soc; Soc Appl Spectros. *Res:* Electroanalytical chemistry; fast neurtron activation analysis; flame emission and absorption spectroscopy; x-ray emission spectroscopy; thermal methods of analysis. *Mailing Add:* Anaconda Co Box 27007 Tucson AZ 85726

VINCENT, JAMES SIDNEY, b Redlands, Calif, Sept 19, 35; m 69; c 1. PHYSICAL CHEMISTRY. *Educ:* Univ Redlands, BS, 57; Harvard Univ, PhD(chem), 63. *Prof Exp:* Fel, Harvard Univ, 63-64 & Calif Inst Technol, 64-65; asst prof chem, Univ Calif, Davis, 65-71; ASSOC PROF CHEM, UNIV MD, BALTIMORE COUNTY, 71- *Mem:* Am Phys Soc. *Res:* Electron paramagnetic resonance of triplet state molecules. *Mailing Add:* Dept of Chem Univ of Md Baltimore County Baltimore MD 21228

VINCENT, JERRY WILLIAM, b Chicago, Ill, June 24, 35; m 59; c 3. PALEONTOLOGY, PALEOECOLOGY. *Educ:* Univ Maine, Orono, BA, 58; Tex A&M Univ, MEd, 66, PhD(geol), 71. *Prof Exp:* Teacher geol & biol, N Yarmouth Acad, 58-61; teacher high sch, Maine, 61-67; assoc prof, 69-80, PROF GEOL, STEPHEN F AUSTIN STATE UNIV, 80- *Mem:* Soc Econ Paleont & Mineral; Nat Asn Geol Teachers. *Res:* Paleoecology of carbonate rocks, numerical taxonomy of various fossil taxa; biostratigraphy of lower Cretaceous rocks of Texas; invertebrate paleontology; earth science education in elementary and secondary schools. *Mailing Add:* Dept of Geol Stephen F Austin State Univ Nacogdoches TX 75962

VINCENT, LEONARD STUART, b Cleveland, Ohio, July 27, 47. ARANEOLOGY. *Educ:* Calif State Univ, Northridge, BA, 70; Univ Calif, Davis, MS, 72; Univ Calif, Berkeley, PhD(entomol), 80. *Prof Exp:* Lectr biol & arachnol, Univ Calif, Berkeley, 80-81; ASST PROF BIOL, GA SOUTHERN COL, 81- *Mem:* Sigma Xi; Am Arachnol Soc; Brit Arachnol Soc; Entomol Soc Am. *Res:* Ecology and natural history of spiders. *Mailing Add:* Dept Biol Ga Southern Col Statesboro GA 30460

VINCENT, LLOYD DREXELL, b DeQuincy, La, Jan 7, 24; m 51; c 2. NUCLEAR PHYSICS. *Educ:* Univ Tex, BS, 52, MA, 53, PhD(physics), 60. *Prof Exp:* From asst prof to assoc prof, Univ Southwestern La, 53-58; instr, Tex A&M, 55-56; res scientist, Tex Nuclear Corp, 59-60, prof & dir physics dept, Sam Houston State Col, 60-65, asst to pres, 65-67; PRES, ANGELO STATE UNIV, 67- *Concurrent Pos:* Bd dir, Asn Tex Col & Univ, 81-; dir, WTex Utilities Co, 78-; bd dir, WTex Rehab Ctr, 77- *Mem:* Am Phys Soc; Am Asn Physics Teachers; Am Asn State Col & Univ; Sigma Xi. *Mailing Add:* President's Off Angelo State Univ San Angelo TX 76909

VINCENT, MONROE MORTIMER, b Cleveland, Ohio, July 28, 12; m 41; c 1. CELL BIOLOGY, IMMUNOBIOLOGY. *Educ:* Case Western Reserve Univ, BA, 34. *Prof Exp:* Res asst parasitol, Univ Chicago, 36-41; vpres, North-Strong Corp, 48-50; vpres, Microbiol Assocs, 51-74; CONSULT, 74-; SR RES ASSOC, DEPT PEDIAT, SCH MED, UNIFORMED SERV UNIV OF THE HEALTH SCI, BETHESDA, MD, 78- *Concurrent Pos:* Assoc ed, In Vitro, 70-79; mem bd dir, Am Found Biol Res, 74-; exec ed, Tissue Cult manual, 74-79; exec ed, Index Tissue Culture, 80- *Mem:* Tissue Culture Asn; Soc Cryobiology (treas, 73-74); Am Soc Cell Biol; Am Soc Trop Med. *Res:* Cell tissue and organ culture, virology, cell-mediated immunity, cryobiology. *Mailing Add:* 3905 Jones Bridge Rd Chevy Chase MD 20815

VINCENT, MURIEL C, b Spokane, Wash, Sept 8, 22. PHARMACY, PHARMACEUTICAL CHEMISTRY. *Educ:* Ore State Col, BS, 44; Univ Wash, MS, 51, PhD, 55. *Prof Exp:* Instr pharm, Univ Wash, 53-54 & Ore State Col, 54-56; from asst prof to assoc prof, 56-58, chmn dept, 58-74, PROF PHARM PRACT, COL PHARM, N DAK STATE UNIV, 58-, ASST DEAN, COL PHARM, 65-, PROF PHARMACEUT, 77- *Concurrent Pos:* Consult, Vet Admin Hosp, 60-74. *Mem:* AAAS; Am Chem Soc; Am Pharmaceut Asn; NY Acad Sci. *Res:* Application of ion exchange resins and chromatography to the analysis of pharmaceutical products; drug absorption. *Mailing Add:* NDak State Univ Col of Pharm Fargo ND 58105

VINCENT, PHILLIP G, b East Machias, Maine, July 18, 41. BIOCHEMISTRY, MICROBIOLOGY. *Educ:* Univ Md, BS, 64, PhD(fungus physiol), 67. *Prof Exp:* Res asst bot, Univ Md, 64, res fel fungus physiol & biochem, 65-67; res phytopathologist, 67-68, res microbiologist, Field Crops & Animal Prod Res Br, Mkt Qual Res Div, 68-78, RES PLANT PHYSIOLOGIST, AGR ENVIRON INST, USDA, 78- *Mem:* AAAS; Am Soc Microbiol; Am Phytopath Soc; Scand Soc Plant Physiol. *Res:* Fungus physiology and biochemistry; mechanism of action of toxicants; phytopathology; plant physiology; biochemical characteristics and mechanisms of quality deterioration of meat; narcotics. *Mailing Add:* Agr Environ Res Inst USDA Agr Res Ctr Beltsville MD 20705

VINCENT, THOMAS LANGE, b Portland, Ore, Sept 16, 35; m; c 2. AEROSPACE ENGINEERING. *Educ:* Ore State Univ, BS, 58, MS, 60; Univ Ariz, PhD(aerospace eng), 63. *Prof Exp:* Res engr, Boeing Airplane Co, Wash, 59-60; from asst prof to assoc prof aerospace & mech eng, 63-68, PROF AEROSPACE & MECH ENG, UNIV ARIZ, 68- *Concurrent Pos:* Guest prof, Tech Univ Munich, 67; NSF sci fac fel, Univ Calif, Berkeley, 69-70; guest lectr, Inst Mech & Appl Mach, Univ Genoa, 70; recipient, US-Australia Coop Sci Prog Award, NSF, 76-77. *Res:* Applications of optimal control theory to problems in aerospace engineering and biological sciences. *Mailing Add:* Dept of Aerospace & Mech Eng Univ of Ariz Tucson AZ 85721

VINCENT, WALTER SAMPSON, JR, b Veneta, Ore, Aug 6, 21; m 42; c 3. ZOOLOGY. *Educ:* Ore State Col, BS, 46, MS, 48; Univ Pa, PhD(zool), 52. *Prof Exp:* Asst zool, Ore State Col, 46; asst instr, Univ Pa, 48; res assoc genetics, Iowa State Col, 51-52; from instr to asst prof anat, Col Med, State Univ NY Upstate Med Ctr, 52-61; assoc prof, Sch Med, Univ Pittsburgh, 61-69; vis prof, Dept Biol, Brooklyn Col, 69-70; prof biol sci & chmn dept, 71-76, PROF CELL & MOLECULAR BIOL, SCH LIFE & HEALTH SCI, UNIV DEL, 76- *Concurrent Pos:* USPHS sr res fel, 59-61, career develop award, 61-63; Lalor fel, Marine Biol Lab, Woods Hole, 55, trustee, 66-, mem exec comt, 71-, mem corp; res prof, Univ Edinburgh, 64, Sci Res Coun sr vis res fel, 67; mem exec comt, Marine Biol Lab, 71-75. *Mem:* AAAS; Am Soc Cell Biol; Genetics Soc Am; Soc Gen Physiol; Int Inst Embryol. *Res:* Chemistry and function of oocytes; biosynthesis of ribosomes; evolution of ribosomal genes. *Mailing Add:* Sch of Life & Health Sci Univ of Del Newark DE 19711

VINCENTI, WALTER G(UIDO), b Baltimore, Md, Apr 20, 17; m 47; c 2. AERONAUTICAL ENGINEERING, HISTORY OF TECHNOLOGY. *Educ:* Stanford Univ, AB, 38. *Prof Exp:* Aeronaut res scientist, Ames Aeronaut Lab, Nat Adv Comt Aeronaut, Calif, 40-57; PROF AERONAUT ENG, STANFORD UNIV, 57- *Concurrent Pos:* Lectr, Stanford Univ, 46-47, 52-54; Rockefeller Pub Serv Award, Univ Cambridge, 55-56; Guggenheim fel, 63; co-ed, Ann Rev Fluid Mech, 70-77. *Mem:* Fel Am Inst Aeronaut & Astronaut; Am Phys Soc; Soc Hist Technol; corresp mem Int Acad Astronaut; Hist Sci Soc. *Res:* High temperature gas dynamics. *Mailing Add:* Dept of Aeronaut & Astronaut Stanford Univ Stanford CA 94305

VINCENZ, STANISLAW ALEKSANDER, b Oskrzesince, Poland, Feb 4, 15; m 49; c 5. GEOPHYSICS. *Educ:* Univ London, ARCS & BSc, 37, DIC, 39, PhD(geophys), 52. *Prof Exp:* Demonstr geophys, Imp Col, London, 48-49, asst lectr, 49-51, res asst, 51-53; geophysicist & head geophys div, Jamaica Indust Develop, Corp, Jamaica, Wis, 53-61; assoc prof geophys & geophys eng, 61-67, PROF GEOPHYS, ST LOUIS UNIV, 67- *Concurrent Pos:* NSF prin investr grants, St Louis Univ, 62-67, 67-68, 69-70, 71-73 & 74-79 & US Geol Surv, 73-76. *Mem:* AAAS; Soc Explor Geophys; Am Geophys Union; fel Royal Astron Soc; Europ Asn Explor Geophys. *Res:* Exploration geophysics; rock magnetism and paleomagnetism; geomagnetism. *Mailing Add:* Dept Earth & Atmospheric Sci St Louis Univ PO Box 8099 Laclede Sta St Louis MO 63156

VINCENZI, FRANK FOSTER, b Seattle, Wash, Mar 14, 38; m 60; c 3. PHARMACOLOGY. *Educ:* Univ Wash, BS, 60, MS, 62, PhD(pharmacol), 65. *Prof Exp:* NSF fel, Berne, 65-67; asst prof, 67-72, ASSOC PROF PHARMACOL, SCHS MED & PHARM, UNIV WASH, 72- *Mem:* AAAS; NY Acad Sci; Am Soc Pharmacol & Exp Therapeut; Biophys Soc; Cardiac Muscle Soc. *Res:* Autonomic transmitters; mechanisms of cardioactive drugs; membrane transport; red blood cell physiology and pathology. *Mailing Add:* Dept of Pharmacol Univ of Wash Seattle WA 98195

VINCETT, PAUL STAMFORD, b Southend, Eng, Jan 23, 44; m 65; c 3. THIN FILM PHYSICS. *Educ:* Univ Cambridge, BA, 65, PhD(physics), 68. *Prof Exp:* Fel physics, Simon Fraser Univ, 68-70; scientist, Corp Lab, ICI Ltd, Runcorn, Eng, 70-74; scientist physics, 74-80, MGR THIN FILM SCI & MEMORY, XEROX RES CTR CAN, 80- *Concurrent Pos:* Tutor, Open Univ, NW Region, Manchester, Eng, 71-74. *Mem:* Can Asn Physicists; Nat Micrographics Asn. *Res:* Solid state and chemical physics, particularly thin film physics and conduction processes in insulating solids and liquids; novel electrophotographic processes; high density information recording; business development of new technologies. *Mailing Add:* Xerox Res Ctr of Can 2480 Dunwin Dr Mississauga ON L5L 1J9 Can

VINCIGUERRA, MICHAEL JOSEPH, b New York, NY, Mar 19, 45; m 70; c 1. PHYSICAL CHEMISTRY. *Educ:* Iona Col, BS, 66; Adelphi Univ, MS, 69, PhD(phys chem), 71. *Prof Exp:* From asst prof to assoc prof, 70-78, PROF CHEM, STATE UNIV NY AGR & TECH COL FARMINGDALE, 78-, CHMN, DIV ARTS & SCI, 76- *Concurrent Pos:* Res asst, Adelphi Univ, 71-72; adj asst prof, St John's Univ, NY, 72; res consult, Unichem Res Assoc, 75- *Mem:* Am Chem Soc; NY Acad Sci. *Res:* Physical properties of bio-polymers; light scattering by biological gels; nuclear magnetic relaxation of polymer solutions. *Mailing Add:* Div of Arts & Sci State Univ of NY Agr & Tech Col Farmingdale NY 11735

VINCOW, GERSHON, b New York, NY, Feb 27, 35; m 64; c 2. PHYSICAL CHEMISTRY. *Educ:* Columbia Univ, AB, 56, MA, 57, PhD(chem), 59. *Prof Exp:* Fel, Hebrew Univ, Israel, 60; NSF fel, Calif Inst Technol, 60-61; from asst prof to prof chem, Univ Wash, 61-71; chmn, Dept Chem, 71-77, vpres res & grad affairs, 77-78, actg dean, 79-80, DEAN, COL ARTS & SCI, SYRACUSE UNIV, 80- *Concurrent Pos:* Sloan Found res fel, 64-67; NSF fel, Harvard Univ, 70-71. *Mem:* Am Chem Soc; Am Phys Soc; AAAS. *Res:* Electron paramagnetic resonance spectroscopy. *Mailing Add:* 300 Hall Lang Syracuse Univ Syracuse NY 13210

VIND, HAROLD PENNINGTON, environmental chemistry, deceased

VINE, ALLYN COLLINS, b Garrettsville, Ohio, June 1, 14; m 40; c 3. OCEANOGRAPHY GEOPHYSICS. *Educ:* Hiram Col, BA, 36; Lehigh Univ, MS, 38. *Hon Degrees:* PhD, Lehigh Univ, 73. *Prof Exp:* Physicist, 40-50, physical oceanographer, 50-63, sr scientist, 63-79, EMER SR SCIENTIST, WOODS HOLE OCEANOG INST, 79- *Concurrent Pos:* Oceanographer, US Navy Bur Ships, 46-49. *Honors & Awards:* Compass Award, Marine Technol Soc, 68; David Stone Award, New Eng Aquarium, 77. *Mem:* Acoust Soc Am; Am Geophys Soc; Marine Technol Soc; AAAS. *Res:* Underwater acoustics; design of deep submersibles and research ships; improved measurement techniques for the floor of the ocean; the ocean as a stabilizing influence in world affairs. *Mailing Add:* Woods Hole Oceanog Inst Woods Hole MA 02543

VINEGAR, RALPH, b New York, NY, June 28, 24; m 48; c 2. PHARMACOLOGY. *Educ:* NY Univ, BA, 49, MS, 50; Cornell Univ, PhD(biol growth, pharm), 57. *Prof Exp:* Head dept cytol, Wallace Labs, Inc, 57-65; SR PHARMACOLOGIST, WELLCOME RES LABS, 65- *Res:* Chemical and phsyical effects on malignant, hematological and reticuloendothelial cells; development of edema and inflammation; mechanism of action of anti-inflammatory and analgesic drugs. *Mailing Add:* 5537 Thayer Dr Raleigh NC 27612

VINES, DARRELL LEE, b Crane, Tex. ELECTRICAL ENGINEERING. *Educ:* McMurry Col, BA, 59; Tex Tech Univ, BS, 59, MS, 60; Tex A&M Univ, PhD(elec eng), 67. *Prof Exp:* Engr, Tex Instruments, 60-62; instr elec eng, Tex Tech Univ, 62-63 & Tex A&M Univ, 63-66; assoc prof, 66-76, PROF ELEC ENG & COMPUT SCI, TEX TECH UNIV, 76- *Mem:* Inst Elec & Electronics Engrs (treas, 69, secy, 70, vpres, 71); Soc Petrol Engrs; Am Soc Eng Educ. *Res:* Computer applications and logic circuit design. *Mailing Add:* Dept of Elec Eng Tex Tech Univ Lubbock TX 79409

VINES, HERBERT MAX, b Ala, Feb 4, 18; m 42; c 2. PLANT PHYSIOLOGY. *Educ:* Ala Polytech Inst, BS, 40; Univ Calif, MS, 49; Univ Calif, Los Angeles, PhD, 59. *Prof Exp:* Specialist postharvest physiol, Univ Calif, 49-53; tech rep nutrit, Shell Chem Co, 53-56; technician plant biochem, Univ Calif, 57-59, fel, 59-60; assoc biochemist, Citrus Exp Sta, Univ Fla, 61-67; PROF PLANT PHYSIOL, UNIV GA, 67- *Mem:* Am Soc Hort Sci; Am Soc Plant Physiol. *Res:* Post-harvest physiology; plant metabolism, especially metabolic blocks in electron transport system. *Mailing Add:* Dept of Hort Plant Sci Bldg Univ of Ga Athens GA 30601

VINEYARD, BILLY DALE, b Clarkton, Mo, Sept 7, 31; m 56; c 1. ORGANIC CHEMISTRY. *Educ:* Southeast Mo State Col, BS, 53; Univ Mo, PhD(org chem), 59. *Prof Exp:* Res chemist, Celanese Corp, 59-60; sr res chemist, Org Div, 60-64, res specialist, 64-68, sci fel, 68-76, SR FEL, MONSANTO CO, 76- *Mem:* Am Chem Soc. *Res:* Catalytic homogeneous asymmetric hydrogenation; food, fine and feed chemicals. *Mailing Add:* Monsanto Co 800 N Lindbergh Blvd St Louis MO 63166

VINEYARD, GEORGE HOAGLAND, b St Joseph, Mo, Apr 28, 20; m 45; c 2. PHYSICS. *Educ:* Mass Inst Technol, BS, 41, PhD(physics), 43. *Hon Degrees:* ScD, Long Island Univ. *Prof Exp:* Mem staff, Radiation Lab, Mass Inst Technol, 42-45; from asst prof to prof physics, Univ Mo, 46-54; from physicist to sr physicist, 54-61, chmn dept physics, 61-66, assoc dir, 66-67, dep dir, 67-72, DIR, BROOKHAVEN NAT LAB, 73- *Concurrent Pos:* Mem solid state sci comt, Nat Res Coun, 65; mem, Advan Res Proj Agency, Mat Res Coun, 67-; mem math & phys sci adv comt, NSF, 68-71. *Mem:* Fel Am Acad Arts & Sci; Sigma Xi; fel Am Phys Soc; fel AAAS. *Res:* Phase transitions; magnetron, klystrons and other microwave devices; theory of x-ray and neutron scattering; structure of liquids; radiation effect; solid state physics. *Mailing Add:* Brookhaven Nat Lab Upton NY 11973

VINGIELLO, FRANK ANTHONY, b New York, NY, Aug 20, 21; m 42; c 3. CHEMISTRY. *Educ:* Polytech Inst Brooklyn, BS, 42; Duke Univ, PhD(org chem), 47. *Prof Exp:* Lab instr org chem, Polytech Inst Brooklyn, 43-44; lab instr, Duke Univ, 44-47; instr, Univ Pittsburgh, 47; res assoc, Northwestern Univ, 47-48; from asst prof chem to assoc prof chem, Va Polytech Inst & State Univ, 48-57, prof org chem, 57-68; PROF ORG CHEM, NORTHEAST LA UNIV, 68- *Concurrent Pos:* Chemist, WVa Ord Works, 42-43; consult chem indust. *Honors & Awards:* J Shelton Horsley Award, Va Acad Sci, 66. *Mem:* Am Chem Soc; NY Acad Sci. *Res:* Organic synthesis in steroids and aromatic molecules; mechanisms of organic reactions; cyclization of o-benzylphenones; synthesis of aromatic hydrocarbons, research in air pollution. *Mailing Add:* Dept of Chem Northeast La Univ Monroe LA 71209

VINH, NGUYEN XUAN, b Yenbay, Viet Nam, Jan 3, 30; m 55; c 4. ANALYSIS & FUNCTIONAL ANALYSIS. *Educ:* Air Inst, France, BS, 53; Univ Marseille, MS, 54; Univ Colo, MS, 63, PhD(aerospace), 65; Univ Paris, DSc(math), 72. *Prof Exp:* Asst prof aerospace eng, Univ Colo, 65-68; assoc prof, 68-72, PROF AEROSPACE ENG, UNIV MICH, ANN ARBOR, 72- *Concurrent Pos:* vis lectr, Univ Calif, Berkeley, 67; vis prof ecol nat statist & admin econ, France, 74; assoc ed, Acta Astronautica, 79-; chair prof, Nat Tsing Hua Univ, Taiwan, 82. *Mem:* Math Asn Am. *Res:* Ordinary differential equations; astrodynamics and optimization of space flight trajectories; theory of non linear oscillations. *Mailing Add:* Dept of Aerospace Eng Univ of Mich Ann Arbor MI 48109

VINICK, FREDRIC JAMES, b Amsterdam, NY, June 18, 47; m 70; c 3. SYNTHETIC ORGANIC CHEMISTRY. *Educ:* Williams Col, BA, 69; Yale Univ, PhD(chem), 73. *Prof Exp:* NIH res fel, Columbia Univ, 73-75; sr scientist org chem, Pharmaceut Div, Ciba-Geigy Corp, 75-78; RES SCIENTIST ORG CHEM, CENT RES, PFIZER, INC, 78- *Mem:* Am Chem Soc. *Res:* Synthesis of biologically and/or medicinally important compounds; development of new synthetic methods. *Mailing Add:* 16 Trumbull Rd Waterford CT 06385

VINING, LEO CHARLES, b Whangarei, NZ, Mar 28, 25; m 53; c 4. BIO-ORGANIC CHEMISTRY, MICROBIOLOGY. *Educ:* Univ NZ, BSc, 48, MSc, 49; Cambridge Univ, PhD, 51. *Prof Exp:* Scholar, Univ Kiel, Ger, 51-53; fel, Rutgers Univ, 53-54, instr, Inst Microbiol, 54-55; asst res off, Prairie Regional Lab, Nat Res Coun Can, 55-58, assoc res off, 58-62, sr res off, Atlantic Regional Lab, 62-69, prin res off, 69-71; PROF BIOL, DALHOUSIE UNIV, 71- *Concurrent Pos:* vis scientist, Mass Inst Technol, 77-78. *Honors & Awards:* Harrison Prize, Royal Soc Can, 72; Can Soc Microbiologists Award, 76; Merck, Sharpe & Dohme lectr, 65. *Mem:* Fel Royal Soc Chem; fel Can Inst Chem; Can Soc Microbiol; Am Soc Microbiol; fel Royal Soc Can. *Res:* Chemistry of antibiotics; fungal metabolites; biosynthesis of natural products; control of secondary metabolism. *Mailing Add:* Dept of Biol Dalhousie Univ Halifax NS B3H 3J5 Can

VINJE, MARY M, b Madison, Wis, Sept 8, 13; m 38. BIOLOGY. *Educ:* Univ Wis, PhD(bot), 38. *Prof Exp:* Asst bot, Univ Wis, 35-38; teacher high schs, 45-48; from asst prof to assoc prof biol, 48-58, prof, 58-77, head dept, 74-77, EMER PROF BIOL, ST AMBROSE COL, 77- *Concurrent Pos:* NSF vis scientist, Iowa High Schs, 60-66. *Mem:* AAAS; Nat Asn Biol Teachers; Nat Sci Teachers Asn; Bot Soc Am; Sigma Xi. *Res:* Aerobiology, particularly the investigation of microbiota in atmosphere; isolation of a fungus from an ozone meter; origin of blue rain. *Mailing Add:* 786 Carlita Circle Rohnert Park CA 94928

VINOCUR, MYRON, b Detroit, Mich, Feb 27, 31; m 58; c 2. MEDICINE, PATHOLOGY. *Educ:* Univ Mich, AB, 53, MD, 56; Am Bd Toxicol, dipl. *Prof Exp:* Intern, Harper Hosp, 56-57; resident path, Wayne State Univ, 57-61; pathologist, Lederle Labs, Am Cyanamid Co, 63-66, head dept path, 66-68; head exp path, Geigy Pharmaceut, 68-72; DIR CLIN PATH & TOXICOL EVAL & ASSOC DIR CLIN RES, BOEHRINGER INGELHEIM LTD, RIDGEFIELD, CONN, 72- *Mem:* Soc Toxicol; Am Soc Clin Path; Int Acad Path; Col Am Toxicologists. *Res:* Anatomical, clinical and experimental pathology; evaluation of drug induced morphological findings; development, preparation and monitoring clinical trials for new drug development, preclinical animal toxicology and pathology studies; toxicology. *Mailing Add:* Box 253 Ridgefield CT 06877

VINOGRADE, BERNARD, b Chicago, Ill, May 7, 15; m 42; c 4. MATHEMATICS. *Educ:* City Col, BS, 37; Univ Mich, MA, 40, PhD(math), 42. *Prof Exp:* Instr math, Univ Wis, 42-44 & Tulane Univ, 44-45; staff mem, Radiation Lab, Mass Inst Technol, 45; from asst prof to assoc prof math, Iowa State Univ, 45-55, prof, 55-80, chmn dept, 61-64, actg head, 60; RETIRED. *Concurrent Pos:* Opers analyst, Standby Unit, US Air Force, 50-; vis prof, San Diego State Col, 59-60 & City Col New York, 64-65. *Mem:* Am Math Soc; Math Asn Am. *Res:* Abstract and linear algebra; field theory; forest resouce management. *Mailing Add:* Dept Math Iowa State Univ Ames IA 50010

VINOGRADOFF, ANNA PATRICIA, b Essex, Eng. PHARMACEUTICAL CHEMISTRY. *Educ:* Univ Calif, Los Angeles, BSc, 76, PhD(chem), 81. *Prof Exp:* Teaching asst org chem, Univ Calif, Los Angeles, 76-77, res assoc, 78-80; SR RES CHEMIST, DOW CHEM USA, 80- *Mem:* Am Chem Soc. *Res:* Organic synthesis with emphasis on molecules of biological interest and natural products. *Mailing Add:* 1135D Kenwal Rd Concord CA 94521

VINOGRADOV, SERGE, b Beirut, Lebanon, Aug 27, 33; US citizen; m; c 2. BIOCHEMISTRY. *Educ:* Am Univ Beirut, BA, 52, MA, 54; Ill Inst Technol, PhD(phys chem), 59. *Prof Exp:* Fel, Univ Alta, 59-62; res assoc, Yale Univ, 62-66; asst prof biochem, 66-68, assoc prof, 68-71, PROF BIOCHEM & ADJ ASSOC PROF BIOL, WAYNE STATE UNIV, 71- *Mem:* Am Soc Biol Chem; The Chem Soc; Am Chem Soc; Biophys Soc. *Mailing Add:* Dept of Biochem Wayne State Univ Sch of Med Detroit MI 48202

VINOKUR, MARCEL, b Moravska-Ostrava, Czech, Feb 16, 29; US citizen; m 54; c 1. FLUID MECHANICS, NUMERICAL ANALYSIS. *Educ:* Cornell Univ, BEngPhys, 51; Princeton Univ, PhD(aeronaut eng), 57. *Prof Exp:* Assoc res scientist, Lockheed Palo Alto Res Lab, 55-59, res scientist, Lockheed Missiles & Space Co, Calif, 59-61, staff scientist, 61-71; lectr mech, 65-75, RES ASSOC MECH ENG, UNIV SANTA CLARA, 75- *Mem:* Am Inst Aeronaut & Astronaut. *Res:* Inviscid flow; radiation gas dynamics; non-equilibrium flow; numerical methods. *Mailing Add:* 919 Channing Ave Palo Alto CA 94301

VINORES, STANLEY ANTHONY, b Pottsville, Pa, July 7, 50; m 78; c 2. ONCOLOGY, DEVELOPMENTAL NEUROBIOLOGY. *Educ:* Pa State Univ, BS, 72; Univ Tex, PhD(zool), 76. *Prof Exp:* Teaching asst biol & zool, Univ Tex, 72-74, trainee carcinogenesis & genetics, 74-76; fel, Ohio State Univ, 77-78; staff fel, NIH, n78-81; RES ASSOC, INST CANCER RES, 81- *Res:* Role of nerve growth factor on neural oncology and neural differentiation; carcinogen-protein interactions. *Mailing Add:* Inst Cancer Res 7701 Burholme Ave Philadelphia PA 19111

VINSON, DAVID BERWICK, b Houston, Tex, Oct 7, 17; m 40; c 1. PSYCHOPHYSIOLOGY. *Educ:* Univ Calif, Los Angeles, BA, 41; Univ London, PhD, 52. *Prof Exp:* Asst psychol, Baylor Col Med, 48-50, asst prof, 52-54; res psychologist, Inst Psychiat, Univ London, 50-52; CONSULT LIFE SCI, 54-; DIR, TEX ACAD ADVAN LIFE SCI, 60-; PRES, ASSESSMENT SYSTS INC, 67-; PRES MICROSET, INC, 78- *Concurrent Pos:* Res psychologist, Med Br, Univ Tex, 48-50; clin psychologist, Vet Admin Regional Off, 48-50; consult, Neurosurg Unit, Netherne Hosp, London, Eng, 50-52. *Mem:* Aerospace Med Asn; Am Inst Aeronaut & Astronaut; Am Psychol Asn; Inst Elec & Electronics Engrs; Soc Biol Psychiat. *Res:* Man-machine systems; neuropsychology. *Mailing Add:* 1107 Fannin Bank Bldg Houston TX 77030

VINSON, JAMES S, b Chambersburg, Pa, May 17, 41; m 67. PHYSICS. *Educ:* Gettysburg Col, BA, 63; Univ Va, MS, 65, PhD(physics), 67. *Prof Exp:* Res asst low temperature physics, Univ Va, 64-67; asst prof physics, MacMurray Col, 69-71; assoc prof, Univ NC, Asheville, 71-75, prof physics, 75-78, chmn dept, 71-78, dir comput ctr, 74-78; DEAN COL ARTS & SCI, UNIV HARTFORD, 78- *Mem:* AAAS; Am Phys Soc; Am Asn Physics Teachers; Nat Sci Teachers Asn; World Future Soc. *Res:* Low temperature physics; scintillations in liquid helium; quantum mechanics; computer based instructions; future studies. *Mailing Add:* Col Arts & Sci Univ Hartford West Hartford CT 06117

VINSON, JOE ALLEN, b Ft Smith, Ark, Nov 16, 41; m 66; c 1. ANALYTICAL CHEMISTRY. *Educ:* Univ Calif, Berkeley, BS, 63; Iowa State Univ, MS, 66, PhD(org & anal chem), 67. *Prof Exp:* Res asst, Anal Chem Sect, Ames Lab, AEC, 66-67; asst prof chem, Shippensburg State Col, 67-68 & Washington & Jefferson Col, 68-72; mem staff, J T Baker Chem Co, 72, prod develop chemist, 72-74; ASSOC PROF CHEM, UNIV SCRANTON, 74- *Concurrent Pos:* Res Corp Cottrell grant, 69-70; Law Enforcement Assistance Admin grant, 71-72; NSF Instruct Sci Equip grant, 75-77. *Mem:* Am Chem Soc; NY Acad Sci. *Res:* Use of dipolar aprotic solvents in organic and anlytical chemistry; clinical, drug and pollution analysis; thin layer chromatography; analysis of marijuana in biological fluids. *Mailing Add:* Dept of Chem Univ of Scranton Scranton PA 18072

VINSON, JOHN WILLIAM, rickettsial diseases, venereal diseases, see previous edition

VINSON, LEONARD J, b New York, NY, May 29, 15; m 42; c 5. BIOCHEMISTRY. *Educ:* Brooklyn Col, AB, 36; Fordham Univ, MS, 37, PhD(biochem), 43. *Prof Exp:* Nutrit Found fel, Fordham Univ, 44; supvr biochem res, Armour Res Found, 45-49; sect cheif biochem, Lever Bros Co, 49-65, res mgr, Biol Dept, 65-74, dir biomed affairs, 74-80; RES CONSULT & PRES, VINTOX ASSOC, INC, 80- *Concurrent Pos:* Lectr, NY Univ Med Ctr, 56- *Mem:* AAAS; Soc Toxicol; Am Chem Soc; Sigma Xi; Soc Invest Dermat. *Res:* Medical, regulatory and clinical developments dealing with human and environmental health and safety. *Mailing Add:* 179 Rodney St Glen Rock NJ 07452

VINSON, PAULA COSPER, b Birmingham, Ala, Mar 4, 47. MEDICAL GENETICS. *Educ:* Birmingham-Southern Col, BS, 69; Univ Ala, Birmingham, MS, 72, PhD(physiol biophys), 74. *Prof Exp:* Fel med genetics, 74-75, res assoc, 75-76, instr physiol & med genetics, 76-78, ASST PROF PHYSIOL & MED GENETICS, UNIV ALA, BIRMINGHAM, 78- *Mem:* Am Soc Human Genetics; Tissue Cult Asn; Sigma Xi. *Res:* Human cytogenetics; drug effects on human chromosomes; prenatal cytogenetic studies. *Mailing Add:* Lab of Med Genetics Univ Sta Birmingham AL 35294

VINSON, RICHARD G, b Prattville, Ala, Nov 18, 31; m 55; c 2. MATHEMATICS. *Educ:* Huntingdon Col, BA, 54; Fla State Univ, MA, 56; Univ Ala, PhD(math), 62. *Prof Exp:* Instr math, Fla State Univ, 55-56, Univ Tenn, 56-58 & Univ Ala, 58-61; prof, Huntingdon Col, 61-69; PROF MATH, UNIV SOUTH ALA, 69- *Concurrent Pos:* Instr state-wide educ TV network, 63-67; dir NSF two-yr col prog. *Mem:* AAAS; Am Math Soc; Math Asn Am. *Res:* Non-Euclidean geometry. *Mailing Add:* Dept of Math Univ South Ala Mobile AL 36688

VINSON, S BRADLEIGH, b Mansfield, Ohio, Apr 8, 38; m 60; c 2. BIOLOGY, CHEMICAL BIOLOGY OF HYMENOPTERA. *Educ:* Ohio State Univ, BS, 61; Miss State Univ, MS, 63, PhD(entom), 65. *Prof Exp:* Res asst entom, Miss State Univ, 64-65, asst prof, 65-69; assoc prof, 69-75, PROF ENTOM, TEX A&M UNIV, 75- *Honors & Awards:* Outstanding Res Award, Am Registry Prof Entomologists, 79. *Mem:* AAAS; Entom Soc Am; Am Inst Biol Sci; Am Soc Zool; Am Chem Soc. *Res:* Vertebrate insecticide resistance; mechanisms of arthropod resistance; insect physiology; parasite-host and predator-host relationships; biology of social insects. *Mailing Add:* Dept of Entom Tex A&M Univ College Station TX 77843

VINSON, WILLIAM ELLIS, b Greensboro, NC, Apr 4, 43; m 63; c 2. POPULATION GENETICS, DAIRY SCIENCE. *Educ:* NC State Univ, BS, 65, MS, 68; Iowa State Univ, PhD(pop genetics), 71. *Prof Exp:* asst prof dairy cattle genetics, 71-80, ASSOC PROF DAIRY SCI, VA POLYTECH INST & STATE UNIV, 71- *Mem:* Am Dairy Sci Asn; Am Genetic Asn; Am Soc Animal Sci; Biomet Soc; Sigma Xi. *Res:* Direct and correlated responses to selection; pedigree evaluation of genetic merit; inheritance of discontinuous characters; genetic evaluations from field data; computer simulation of genetic populations. *Mailing Add:* Dept of Dairy Sci Va Polytech Inst & State Univ Blacksburg VA 24061

VINSONHALER, CHARLES I, b Winfield, Kans, Mar 29, 42. MATHEMATICS. *Educ:* Calif Inst Technol, BS, 64; Univ Wash, PhD(math), 68. *Prof Exp:* Asst prof, 68-76, ASSOC PROF MATH, UNIV CONN, 76- *Mem:* Am Math Soc. *Res:* Ring theory and Abelian groups. *Mailing Add:* Dept of Math Univ of Conn Storrs CT 06268

VINT, LARRY FRANCIS, b Davenport, Iowa, May 12, 41; m 64; c 3. ANIMAL BREEDING, POULTRY BREEDING. *Educ:* Iowa State Univ, BS, 63, MS, 69, PhD(animal breeding), 71. *Prof Exp:* Data processing mgr biomet, Pilch-De Kalb, De Kalb AgRes, 71-72, dir res poultry breeding, 72-73, res investr corp develop, De Kalb AgRes, 73-74; geneticist animal breeding, USDA, 74; ASST DIR RES POULTRY BREEDING, DE KALB AGRES, 74- *Mem:* Am Soc Animal Sci; Poultry Sci Asn; Coun Agr Sci & Technol; AAAS. *Res:* Genetic improvement in poultry populations. *Mailing Add:* De Kalb AgRes Inc Sycamore Rd De Kalb IL 60115

VINTI, JOHN PASCAL, b Newport, RI, Jan 16, 07. CELESTIAL MECHANICS. *Educ:* Mass Inst Technol, SB, 27, ScD(physics), 32. *Prof Exp:* Harrison res fel physics, Univ Pa, 32-34; res asst, Mass Inst Technol, 34-35; instr, Brown Univ, 36-37; asst prof, The Citadel, 37-38; instr, Worcester Polytech Inst, 39-41; physicist ballistic res labs, Aberdeen Proving Ground, 41-57 & Nat Bur Standards, 57-65; prof appl math, NC State Univ, 66; consult, Exp Astron Lab, 67-70, vis assoc prof aeronaut & astronaut, Inst, 69-70, LECTR AERONAUT & ASTRONAUT, MASS INST TECHNOL, 71-, CONSULT, MEASUREMENT SYSTS LAB, 70- *Concurrent Pos:* Lectr, Univ Del, 48-49 & 54-55 & Univ Md, 50-52; consult, Army Chem Ctr, 52; prof lectr, Georgetown Univ, 63-64; adj prof, Cath Univ Am, 65-66; mem, Comn Celestial Mech, Int Astron Union. *Honors & Awards:* Cert Award, Nat Bur Standards, 61. *Mem:* Fel AAAS; fel Am Phys Soc; assoc fel Am Inst Aeronaut & Astronaut; Am Astron Soc; Am Geophys Union. *Res:* Possible effects of variation of the gravitational constant, both in dynamical astronomy and in cosmology. *Mailing Add:* Measurement Systs Lab Rm W91-202 Mass Inst Technol Cambridge MA 02139

VINYARD, GARY LEE, b Harrisburg, Ill, Mar 13, 49; m. AQUATIC ECOLOGY, BEHAVIORAL ECOLOGY. *Educ:* Univ Kans, BA, 71, PhD(biol), 77. *Prof Exp:* Vis asst prof, Sch Biol Sci, Okla State Univ, 76-77; asst prof, Dept Zool, Univ Mont, 77-78; ASST PROF, DEPT BIOL, UNIV NEV, 78- *Mem:* Am Soc Limnol & Oceanog; AAAS; Ecol Soc Am; Sigma Xi. *Res:* Predatory interactions of aquatic organisms, both fish and invertebrates; behavioral ecology of aquatic organisms. *Mailing Add:* Dept of Biol Univ of Nev Reno NV 89507

VINYARD, WILLIAM CORWIN, b McArthur, Calif, Apr 30, 22; m 60. BOTANY. *Educ:* Chico State Col, BA, 42; Mich State Univ, MS, 51, PhD(bot), 58. *Prof Exp:* Instr bot, Univ Okla, 53-54; instr, Mich State Univ, 55-56; instr, Univ Mont, 56-57; asst prof, Univ Kans, 57-58; from asst prof to assoc prof, 58-72, PROF BOT, HUMBOLDT STATE UNIV, 72- *Concurrent Pos:* Algological consult, Calif State Dept Water Resources, 62-64 & Klamath Basin Study, US Dept Interior, 67-68 & Nat Park Serv, 71-72. Phycol Soc Am; Int Asn Plant Taxon; Int Phycol Soc. *Res:* Taxonomy and ecology of freshwater algae; synopsis of the desmids of North America; algae of western North America; relation of algae to water pollution; algal food of herbivorous fishes; eipzoic algae. *Mailing Add:* Dept of Biol Humboldt State Univ Arcata CA 95521

VIOLA, ALFRED, b Vienna, Austria, July 8, 28; nat US; m 63. ORGANIC CHEMISTRY. *Educ:* Johns Hopkins Univ, BA, 49, MA, 50; Univ Md, PhD(chem), 55. *Prof Exp:* Asst instr chem, Johns Hopkins Univ, 49-50; asst, Univ Md, 50-54; res assoc, Boston Univ, 55-57; from asst prof to assoc prof chem, 57-68, PROF CHEM, NORTHEASTERN UNIV, 68- *Mem:* Am Chem Soc; Sigma Xi. *Res:* Preparation and properties of unsaturated organic compounds; thermal rearrangements; stereochemistry; pericyclic reactions of acetylenes. *Mailing Add:* Dept of Chem 360 Huntington Ave Boston MA 02115

VIOLA, JOHN THOMAS, b Haverhill, Mass, Mar 6, 38; m 60; c 2. PHYSICAL CHEMISTRY. *Educ:* Univ NH, BS, 60; Pa State Univ, MS, 61; Mass Inst Technol, PhD(chem), 67. *Prof Exp:* US Air Force, 61-81, nuclear effects res officer thermodyn, Air Force Weapons Lab, Albuquerque, NMex, 61-64, lab proj officer, 67-71; instr & asst prof chem, US Air Force Acad, 71-74, assoc prof & dir advan courses chem, 74-75, prog mgr chem, Directorate Chem Sci, Air Force Off Sci Res, 75-78, dir bus mgt, E-4 Prog Off, 78-80, prog dir, Joint Surveillance Systs, 80-81. *Mem:* Sigma Xi. *Res:* Identification, selection and management of research in chemical dynamics, chemical kinetics and atomic and molecular phenomena. *Mailing Add:* Electronic Systs Div Joint Surveillence Systs Prog Off Statist Control Unit Hanscom AFB MA 01731

VIOLA, VICTOR E, JR, b Abilene, Kans, Apr 8, 35; m 62; c 3. NUCLEAR CHEMISTRY. *Educ:* Univ Kans, AB, 57; Univ Calif, Berkeley, PhD(nuclear chem), 61. *Prof Exp:* Instr & res fel nuclear chem, Univ Calif, Berkeley, 61-62; NSF fel, Europ Orgn Nuclear Res, 63, Ford fel, 64; res assoc chem, Argonne Nat Lab, 64-66; from asst prof to assoc prof chem, Univ Md, College Park, 66-74, prof, 74-80; PROF CHEM, IND UNIV, 80- *Concurrent Pos:* Consult, Argonne Nat Lab, 66-73; vis prof, Univ Calif, Berkeley, 73-74; Guggenheim fel, 80-81. *Mem:* AAAS; AAUP; Am Chem Soc; Am Phys Soc; Sigma Xi. *Res:* Reaction mechanism studies in heavy ion collisions; synthesis of the elements in nature; nuclear fission at moderate excitation energies; systematics of heavy element lifetimes and energetics. *Mailing Add:* Dept of Chem Indiana Univ Bloomington IN 47405

VIOLANTE, MICHAEL ROBERT, b Buffalo, NY, Mar 6, 44; m 77. COLLOID CHEMISTRY, PHYSICAL CHEMISTRY. *Educ:* State Univ NY Buffalo, BA, 66; Fla State Univ, PhD(inorg chem), 70. *Prof Exp:* res scientist pulp & paper, Res & Develop Div, Union-Camp Corp, 70-74; ASST PROF RADIOL, SCH MED & DENT, UNIV ROCHESTER, 74- *Mem:* Am Chem Soc; NY Acad Sci; AAAS; Asn Univ Radiologists; Sigma Xi. *Res:* Development and formulation of particulate drug delivery system; water insoluble drugs can be administered intravenously for selective accumulation in the liver, specifically in kupffer cells; membrane transport phenomena; colloid and solution chemistry. *Mailing Add:* Dept of Radiol PO Box 648 Rochester NY 14642

VIOLET, CHARLES EARL, b Des Moines, Iowa, May 1, 24; m 51; c 5. PHYSICS. *Educ:* Univ Chicago, BS, 48; Univ Calif, AB, 49, PhD(physics), 53. *Prof Exp:* Physicist, 50-57, test group dir, Oper Plumbbob, 57-58, dep test mgr, Oper Hardtack, 58-59, test div leader, 59-61, PHYSICIST, LAWRENCE LIVERMORE LAB, UNIV CALIF, 61- *Mem:* Fel Am Phys Soc. *Res:* Mössbauer resonance spectroscopy; dilute alloy magnetism; nuclear moments; laser plasma interactions. *Mailing Add:* Lawrence Livermore Lab Univ of Calif Box 808 Livermore CA 94550

VIOLETT, THEODORE DEAN, b Great Bend, Kans, Apr, 27, 32; m 53; c 3. PHYSICS. *Educ:* Univ Mo, BS, 53, MA, 54; Univ Colo, PhD(physics), 59. *Prof Exp:* PROF PHYSICS, WESTERN STATE COL COLO, 59- *Mem:* Am Phys Soc; Am Asn Physics Teachers. *Res:* Vacuum ultraviolet radiation and solar spectroscopy. *Mailing Add:* Dept of Physics Western State Col Gunnison CO 81230

VIOLETTE, JOSEPH LAWRENCE NORMAN, b Winslow, Maine, Aug 24, 32; m 57; c 7. ELECTRICAL ENGINEERING. *Educ:* Rensselaer Polytech Inst, BEE, 56; NC State Univ, PhD(elec eng), 71; Auburn Univ, Montgomery, MBA, 72. *Prof Exp:* US Air Force, 56-77, from instr to asst prof elec eng, US Air Force Acad, 62-67, proj mgr tactical air commun systs, Electronic Systs Div, L G Hanscom Field, Mass, 69-71, proj mgr, Advan Res Projs Agency, Washington, DC, 72-73; C3I proj engr, Washington Off, TRW, 77-79; PRIN ENGR, DON WHITE CONSULTS, EMC ENG, 80- *Mem:* Inst Elec & Electronics Engrs. *Res:* Integral equation solution for nonplanar obstacles in coaxial waveguides obtained from dyadic Green's function formulation of boundary value problem; computer solution of singular integral equations so derived. *Mailing Add:* 6927 Tyndale St McLean VA 22101

VIRARAGHAVAN, THIRUVENKATACHARI, b Madras, India, July 15, 34; m 67; c 2. WATER TREATMENT, WASTEWATER TREATMENT. *Educ:* Univ Madras, India, BE, 55; Univ Ottawa, PhD(civil eng), 75. *Prof Exp:* Jr public health engr, Dept Public Health Eng & Municipal Works, Govt Madras, India, 55-61, asst public health engr, 61-65; asst adv public health eng, Ministry Health, Govt India, New Delhi, 65-70; res asst fluid mech, Dept Civil Eng, Univ Ottawa, 70-75; SR ENVIRON ENGR, ADI LIMITED CONSULT ENGRS, NB, CAN, 75- *Concurrent Pos:* Hon res assoc, Univ NB, 78- *Mem:* Fel Inst Engrs; Am Soc Civil Engrs; Can Soc Civil Eng; Am Water Works Asn; Water Pollution Fedn. *Res:* On-site wastewater treatment and disposal; biological treatment of wastewaters, especially anaerobic treatment of wastewaters. *Mailing Add:* ADI Limited PO Box 44 Fredericton NB E3B 4Y2 Can

VIRGILI, LUCIANO, b Carassai, Italy, Mar 15, 48; m 72; c 1. THERMAL ANALYSIS, MICROSCOPY. *Educ:* Univ Firenze, Italy, Dr, 75. *Prof Exp:* SR RES CHEMIST, E R SQUIBB & SONS, INC, 78- *Mem:* Am Chem Soc; NAm Thermal Anal Soc. *Res:* Methods development in pharmaceuticals and related raw materials; problem solving; non routine complaint analysis; materials characterization and properties particle analysis. *Mailing Add:* E R Squibb & Sons Inc PO Box 191 New Brunswick NJ 08903

VIRGO, BRUCE BARTON, b Vancouver, BC, Mar 18, 43; Can citizen; m 69; c 2. TOXICOLOGY, DRUG & STEROID METABOLISM. *Educ:* Univ BC, BSc, 65, MSc, 70, PhD(pharmacol, toxicol), 74. *Prof Exp:* Res biologist econ ornith, Can Wildlife Serv, Govt Can, 65-66, contractee ecol, 67-68; Nat Res Coun fel toxicol, McGill Univ, 74-75; Nat Res Coun fel pharmacol, Univ Montreal, 75; asst prof, 75-81, ASSOC PROF PHYSIOL, UNIV WINDSOR, 81- *Concurrent Pos:* Consult, Govt New Brunswick, 80. *Mem:* Soc Toxicol Can; Pharmacol Soc Can. *Res:* Pharmacology of the hepatic drug and steroid metabolizing enzymes; physiology, pharmacology and toxicology of reproduction processes at all organizational levels; toxicology of environmental chemicals with emphasis on the effects of chronic, low-dose exposure. *Mailing Add:* Dept of Biol Univ of Windsor Windsor ON N9B 3P4 Can

VIRKAR, RAGHUNATH ATMARAM, b Vir, Maharashtra, India, Dec 12, 30; m 53; c 1. PHYSIOLOGY, INVERTEBRATE ZOOLOGY. *Educ:* Univ Bombay, BS, 50, MS, 52; Univ Minn, PhD(zool), 64. *Prof Exp:* Demonstr zool, Wilson Col, Bombay, 52-53; lectr, Vithalbhai Patel Col, 53-61; instr, Univ Minn, 64; asst res biologist, Univ Calif, Irvine, 65-66 & Univ Calif, Riverside, 66; asst prof biol, Wis State Univ-Superior, 66-68; assoc prof, Newark State Col, 68-73, PROF BIOL, KEAN COL NJ, 73-, CHMN DEPT BIOL SCI, 77- *Mem:* AAAS; Am Soc Zool; Am Inst Biol Sci; Sigma Xi. *Res:* Nutritional role of dissolved organic matter in invertebrates; role of free amino acids in osmoregulation. *Mailing Add:* Dept of Biol Kean Col of NJ Union NJ 07083

VIRKKI, NIILO, b Vuoksela, Finland, May 7, 24; m 49; c 2. INSECT CYTOGENETICS. *Educ:* Univ Helsinki, Lic phil, 51, PhD(genetics), 52. *Prof Exp:* Inspector pest animals, Vet Sect, Health Bd, Helsinki, Finland, 49-53; lab keeper, Univ Helsinki, 53-61, asst prof genetics, 55-61; from asst cytogeneticist to assoc cytogeneticist, 61-64, CYTOGENETICIST, AGR EXP STA, UNIV PR, 64- *Concurrent Pos:* Fel fores insect lab, Can Dept Agr, Ont, 55-56; NSF grants, 65-68, Fundacao Amparo de Pesquisa de Sao Paulo grant, 80; vis prof, Univ Estadual Paulista, Brazil, 81. *Res:* Problems concerning evolution of karyotypes in the beetle sub-family Alticimae, especially formation of giant asynaptic sex chromosomes and their mode of orientation and segregation in meiosis; beetle cytogenetics. *Mailing Add:* Crop Protection Dept Agr Exp Sta Rio Piedras PR 00927

VIRNIG, MICHAEL JOSEPH, b Rochester, Minn, Mar 31, 46; m 68; c 3. ORGANIC CHEMISTRY. *Educ:* St Mary's Col, BA, 68; Iowa State Univ, PhD(org chem), 75. *Prof Exp:* Sr res chemist, 75-80, GROUP LEADER, HENKEL CORP, 80- *Mem:* Am Chem Soc; Am Inst Mining Engrs. *Res:* Solvent extraction, process development organic synthesis, natural products. *Mailing Add:* 1365 73rd Ave NE Minneapolis MN 55432

VIRNSTEIN, ROBERT W, b Washington, DC, Mar 19, 43; m 69. MARINE ECOLOGY. *Educ:* Johns Hopkins Univ, BA, 66; Univ SFla, MA, 72; Col William & Mary, PhD(marine sci), 76. *Prof Exp:* Marine scientist, Va Inst Marine Sci, 75-76; fel, Harbor Br Inst, 76-77, ASST RES SCIENTIST, HARBOR BR FOUND, 77- *Mem:* Ecol Soc Am; Int Asn Meiobenthologists; Southeastern Estuarine Res Soc. *Res:* Estuarine benthic ecology; trophic relationships; experimental field ecology; role of predation; benthic invertebrate taxonomy; seagrass growth rates; seagrass communities. *Mailing Add:* Harbor Br Found RR 1 Box 196 Ft Pierce FL 33450

VISCELLI, THOMAS ALFONSE, biochemistry, see previous edition

VISCOMI, B(RUNO) VINCENT, b Philadelphia, Pa, Sept 21, 33; m 58; c 3. MECHANICAL ENGINEERING. *Educ:* Drexel Inst, BS, 56; Lehigh Univ, MS, 57; Univ Colo, PhD(civil eng), 69. *Prof Exp:* Engr, Westinghouse Elec Co, 57; res engr, Philadelphia Elec Co, 58-62, nuclear engr, 62-64; from asst prof to assoc prof eng, 64-75, PROF ENG, LAFAYETTE COL, 75-, HEAD DEPT CIVIL ENG, 72- *Concurrent Pos:* Roy T & Laura Jones fac lectureship, Lafayette Col, 69; NSF fel, Nat Ctr Resource Recovery, 74; consult, Resource Recovery Serv, Woodbridge, NJ & Naval Sea Systs Command, Washington, DC, 81. *Mem:* Am Soc Eng Educ; NY Acad Sci; Am Soc Civil Engrs; Sigma Xi; Am Soc Testing & Mat. *Res:* Dynamic response of elastic mechanisms; structural dynamics. *Mailing Add:* Dept of Civil Eng Lafayette Col Easton PA 18042

VISCONTI, JAMES ANDREW, b St Louis, Mo, Apr 13, 39; m 63; c 2. PHARMACY. *Educ:* St Louis Col Pharm, BS, 61, MS, 63; Univ Miss, PhD(pharm), 69. *Prof Exp:* Resident, John Cochran Vet Admin Hosp, St Louis, Mo, 63, staff pharmacist, 64-66; res pharmacist, Vet Admin Hosp, Long Beach, Calif, 63-64; asst prof pharm, 68-72, ASSOC PROF PHARM, COL PHARM, OHIO STATE UNIV, 72-, DIR DRUG INFO CTR, UNIV HOSPS, 68- *Concurrent Pos:* Lehn & Fink Pharm gold medal award, 61-62; Robert Lincoln McNeil citation fel award, 66-67. *Mem:* Am Soc Hosp Pharmacists; Am Pharmaceut Asn; assoc mem AMA; Drug Info Asn. *Res:* Epidemiology and econmics of adverse drug reactions; pharmacology of drug-drug drug-laboratory tests and drug-food interactions; computerized drug information services; health and disease economics. *Mailing Add:* Drug Info Ctr Ohio State Univ Hosp Dept Pharm 410 W Tenth Ave Columbus OH 43210

VISEK, WILLARD JAMES, b Sargent, Nebr, Sept 19, 22; m 49; c 3. NUTRITION, TOXICOLOGY. *Educ:* Univ Nebr, BSc, 47; Cornell Univ, MSc, 49, PhD(nutrit), 51; Univ Chicago, MD, 57. *Hon Degrees:* DSc, Univ Nebr, 80. *Prof Exp:* Asst animal husb, Cornell Univ, 48-51; AEC fel, Univ-Atomic Energy Agr Res Prog, Tenn, 51-52, res assoc, 52-53; res asst pharmacol, Univ Chicago, 53-57, from asst prof to assoc prof, 57-64; prof nutrit & comp metab, Cornell Univ, 64-75; PROF CLIN SCI, SCH BASIC MED SCI & FOOD SCI, UNIV ILL, URBANA-CHAMPAIGN, 75-, PROF SCH CLIN MED, 78- *Concurrent Pos:* Intern univ hosp & clins, Univ Chicago, 57-59; mem teratol subcomt, Comn Drug Safety, 63 & subcomt animal nutrit, Nat Res Coun-Nat Acad Sci, 65-72, adv coun, Inst Lab Animal Resources, 66-69, subcomt animal care facilities surv, 68-70; consult sect health related facilities, USPHS, 67; assoc ed, Nutrit Rev, 68-71; George Henry Durgin lectr, Bridgewater State Col, 70; Nat Cancer Inst-USPHS spec fel, Mass Inst Technol, 70-71; res fel, Mass Gen Hosp, 70-71; grad fac rep nutrit, Cornell Univ, 74-; mem adv comt, Diet, Nutrit & Cancer Prog, Nat Cancer Inst, 76-; mem inst rev bd, Univ Ill, 76-; mem exec comt, Sch Basic Med Sci & Clin Med, Univ Ill, Urbana-Champaign; consult & mem dean's comt, Danville Vet Admin Hosp, 77-; mem study sect nutrit, NIH, 80- *Mem:* AAAS; Am Soc Pharmacol & Exp Therapeut; Soc Exp Biol & Med; Am Soc Animal Sci; Am Soc Clin Nutrit. *Res:* Effects of ammonia on energy metabolism, area cycle activity and nucleic acid synthesis; interactions of amino acids; enzyme immunity; influence of diet on cancer incidence and toxicity of environmental pollutants. *Mailing Add:* 190 Med Sci Bldg Univ Ill 506 S Mathews Urbana IL 61801

VISELTEAR, ARTHUR JACK, b New York, NY, Mar 19, 38; m 66; c 2. HISTORY OF MEDICINE, PUBLIC HEALTH. *Educ:* Tulane Univ, BA, 59; Univ Calif, Los Angeles, MPH, 63, PhD(hist), 65. *Prof Exp:* Lectr pub health, Univ Calif, Los Angeles, 65-69; from asst prof to assoc prof pub health, 69-79, res assoc hist of sci & med, 74-79, ASSOC PROF HIST MED & PUB HEALTH, SCH MED, YALE UNIV, 79- *Concurrent Pos:* Robert Wood Johnson Health Policy fel, Inst Med, Nat Acad Sci, 74-75. *Mem:* AAAS; Am Asn Hist Med; Am Pub Health Asn. *Res:* History and health policy; social medicine; health services research. *Mailing Add:* Sect Hist Med Yale Univ Sch of Med New Haven CT 06510

VISHER, FRANK N, b Twin Falls, Idaho, Mar 10, 23; m 48; c 4. HYDROLOGY, GEOLOGY. *Educ:* Tex Tech Col, BS, 46 & 47. *Prof Exp:* Apprentice engr, Tex Hwy Dept, 47-48; geologist, 48-56, engr, 56-66, hydrologist, Fla, 66-67, res hydrologist, 67-80, CONSULT HYDROLOGIST, US GEOL SURV, 80- *Mem:* Geol Soc Am. *Res:* Hydrologic studies, especially the principals of occurrence of ground water, water budget studies, fresh-salt water interrelationships, geochemistry of water and relation of geomorphology to ground water; environmental studies. *Mailing Add:* 3351 Vivian St C 1 Wheat Ridge CO 80033

VISHER, GLENN S, b May 20, 30; US citizen; m 53; c 3. GEOLOGY. *Educ:* Univ Cincinnati, BS, 52; Northwestern Univ, MS, 56, PhD(geol), 60. *Prof Exp:* Explorationist, Shell Oil Co, 58-60; res geologist, Sinclair Res, Inc, 60-66; adj asst prof, Univ Tulsa, 64-68, assoc prof geol, 66-71, prof, 71-80; PRES, GEOL SERV & VENTURES INC, 80-; PRES, BNJ OIL PROPERTIES INC, 81- *Concurrent Pos:* Lectr training courses, Domestic & Int Petrol Co Personnel. *Mem:* Am Asn Petrol Geol; fel Geol Soc Am; Soc Econ Paleont & Mineral; Int Asn Sedimentol; fel AAAS. *Res:* Stratigraphic models; depostional processes; physical characteristics of sandstone units; texture of sandstones; petrology of shales and sandstones. *Mailing Add:* Geol Serv & Ventures Inc 2920 E 73rd St Tulsa OK 74136

VISHNIAC, HELEN SIMPSON, b New Haven, Conn, Dec 22, 23; m 51; c 3. MICROBIAL ECOLOGY, MYCOLOGY. *Educ:* Univ Mich, BA, 45; Radcliffe Col, MA, 47; Columbia Univ, PhD(bot), 50. *Prof Exp:* Tutor biol, Queens Col, NY, 48-51, instr, 51-52; lectr microbiol, Sch Med, Yale Univ, 53-61; res assoc biol, Univ Rochester, 74-77; mem staff, 77-80, ASST PROF MICROBIOL, DEPT CELL, MOLECULAR & DEVELOP BIOL, OKLA STATE UNIV, 80- *Concurrent Pos:* Lectr, Nazareth Col Rochester, 75-76; fel, Am Asn Univ Women, 75-76. *Mem:* AAAS; Mycol Soc Am; Soc Gen Microbiol; Am Soc Microbiol. *Res:* Antarctic yeasts, aquatic fungi. *Mailing Add:* Dept of Cell Molecular Univ of Rochester Stillwater OK 14627

VISHNUBHOTLA, SARMA RAGHUNADHA, b Masuli Patam, India, July 7, 46; m 74. COMPUTER SCIENCE. *Educ:* Madras Inst Technol, India, DMIT, 68; Wash Univ, MS, 72, DSc(comput sci), 73. *Prof Exp:* Asst prof, 73-78, ASSOC PROF COMPUT SCI, CENT MICH UNIV, 78- *Mem:* Asn Comput Mach; Inst Elec & Electronics Engrs. *Res:* Computer science education; fault diagnosis in computer hardware and software systems; data structures and data bases. *Mailing Add:* Dept of Comput Sci Cent Mich Univ Mt Pleasant MI 48858

VISICH, MARIAN, JR, b Brooklyn, NY, Jan 8, 30; m 59. AEROSPACE ENGINEERING. *Educ:* Polytech Inst Brooklyn, BAeE, 51, MAeE, 53, PhD, 56. *Prof Exp:* From asst to res assoc aeronaut eng, Polytech Inst Brooklyn, 51-56, from res asst prof to prof, 56-77; ASSOC DEAN, COL ENG & APPL SCI, STATE UNIV NY, STONY BROOK, 77- *Concurrent Pos:* Consult, Curtiss-Wright Corp, 55, Gen Elec Corp, 56, Gen Appl Sci Lab, 56-68, Advan Technol Labs, 69-75 & US Army Res Labs, 69-75. *Mem:* AAAS; Am Inst Aeronaut & Astronaut; Am Soc Eng Educ. *Res:* Physics of fluids; high-speed aerodynamics; aircraft and missile propulsion. *Mailing Add:* Col of Eng & Appl Sci State Univ of NY Stony Brook NY 11794

VISKANTA, RAYMOND, b Lithuania, July 16, 31; US citizen; m 56; c 3. HEAT TRANSFER. *Educ:* Univ Ill, BS, 55; Purdue Univ, MS, 56, PhD(heat transfer), 60. *Prof Exp:* Asst mech engr heat transfer, Argonne Nat Lab, 56-58, assoc mech engr, 60-62; assoc prof, 62-66, PROF MECH ENG, PURDUE UNIV, 66- *Concurrent Pos:* Vis prof mech eng, Univ Calif, Berkeley, 68-69; consult to various pvt & govt orgn, 72-; Alexander von Humbolt Found award, 76-78; guest prof mech eng, Tech Univ Munich, 76-77. *Honors & Awards:* US Sr Scientist Award, Alexander von Humbolt Found, 75; Heat Transfer Mem Award, Am Soc Mech Engrs, 76; Thermophysics Award, Am Inst Aeronaut & Astronaut, 79. *Mem:* Fel Am Soc Mech Engrs; Am Inst Aeronaut & Astronaut. *Res:* Radiation transfer in gases and solids; applied thermodynamics; heat transfer in combustion systems; solar energy utilization; thermal energy storage. *Mailing Add:* Sch of Mech Eng Purdue Univ West Lafayette IN 47907

VISNER, SIDNEY, b New York, NY, Dec 10, 17; m 45; c 2. PHYSICS. *Educ:* City Col New York, BS, 37, MS, 38; Univ Tenn, PhD(physics), 51. *Prof Exp:* Lab asst physics, Columbia Univ, 41-43, res scientist & sect leader, S A M Labs, 43-45; sr res physicist & dept head, Gaseous Diffusion Plant, Carbide & Carbon Chems Corp, 45-50, head physicist, 50-55; mgr physics dept, Nuclear Div, 55-69, DIR PHYSICS & COMPUT ANAL, NUCLEAR POWER DEPT, COMBUSTION ENG, INC, 69- *Mem:* AAAS; Am Phys Soc; fel Am Nuclear Soc. *Res:* Hydrodynamic studies in isotope separation by gaseous diffusion; transport properties of gases at low pressures; neutron reactor physics and analysis; experimental physics; nuclear reactor development. *Mailing Add:* Nuclear Power Dept Combustion Eng Inc Windsor CT 06095

VISOTSKY, HAROLD M, b Chicago, Ill, May 25, 24; m 56; c 2. MEDICINE, PSYCHIATRY. *Educ:* Univ Ill, BS, 48, MD, 51. *Prof Exp:* Coordr psychiat residency training, Med Sch, Univ Ill, Chicago, from asst prof to assoc prof psychiat, 59-69; PROF PSYCHIAT & CHMN DEPT, MED SCH, NORTHWESTERN UNIV, 69-, DIR INST PSYCHIAT, UNIV & MEM HOSP, 75- *Concurrent Pos:* Nat Found Infantile Paralysis res fel, 55-56; chief of serv, Chicago State Psychiat Hosp, 57-59; dir ment health sect, City Bd Health, Chicago, 59-62; dir, Ill Dept Ment Health, 62-69; chmn task force, Joint Comn Ment Health of Children, 66-68; mem adv comt, Secy Dept Health, Educ & Welfare, 66-67; mem eval ment health prog, First Mission to USSR, 67; mem task force, President's Comn Ment Health; dir, Ctr Ment Health & Psychiat Serv, Am Hosp Asn, 79-; chmn, Int Comn Abuse Psychiat & Psychiatrists, Am Psychiat Asn, 80- *Honors & Awards:* Edward A Strecker Award, Inst of Pa Hosp, 69; Bowis Award, Am Col Psychiat, 81. *Mem:* Am Psychosom Soc; AMA; Am Psychiat Asn (vpres, 73-74); NY Acad Sci; Am Orthopsychiat Asn (pres, 76-77). *Res:* Social and milieu psychiatry; effects of hallucinogenic drugs in understanding mental illness; stress: coping and adaptation. *Mailing Add:* Dept of Psychiat Northwestern Univ Med Sch Chicago IL 60611

VISSCHER, MAURICE B, b Holland, Mich, Aug 25, 01; m 25; c 4. PHYSIOLOGY. *Educ:* Hope Col, BS, 22; Univ Minn, MS, 24, PhD(physiol), 25, MD, 31. *Prof Exp:* From fel to asst prof, Univ Minn, 22-25; prof physiol & head dept, Col Med, Univ Tenn, 27-29; prof physiol & pharmacol, Univ Southern Calif, 29-31; prof physiol, Col Med, Univ Ill, 31-36; prof & head dept, 36-60, distinguished serv prof, 60-68, regents prof, 68-71, EMER REGENTS PROF PHYSIOL, UNIV MINN, MINNEAPOLIS, 71- *Concurrent Pos:* Mem subcomt clin invest, Div Med Sci & Comt on UNESCO, Nat Res Coun; secy coun, Int Union Physiol Sci, 53-60; sci co-dir, Italian Med Nutrit Mission, UNRRA & Unitarian Serv Comt, chmn Austrian med teaching. *Honors & Awards:* Res Achievement Award, Am Heart Asn, 62; Distinguished Serv Physiol, Am Physiol Soc, 75. *Mem:* Nat Acad Sci; AAAS; Nat Soc Med Res (pres, 65-76); Am Physiol Soc (secy, 46-48, pres, 48-49); Soc Exp Biol & Med (pres, 67-69). *Res:* Circulation; respiration; physiology of secretion and absorption; cardiovascular physiology; biological transport of materials; ionic factors in cardiac function. *Mailing Add:* Dept Physiol Univ Minn Minneapolis MN 55455

VISSCHER, PIETER BERNARD, b Minneapolis, Minn, Dec 11, 45; m 72; c 2. NON-EQUILIBRIUM STATISTICAL MECHANICS. *Educ:* Harvard Univ, BA, 67; Univ Calif, Berkeley, MA, 68, PhD(solid state physics), 71. *Prof Exp:* Res assoc, Univ Ill, Urbana, 71-73; res physicist, Univ Calif, San Diego, 73-75; asst prof physics, Univ Ore, 75-78; asst prof, 78-80, ASSOC PROF PHYSICS, UNIV ALA, 80- *Mem:* Am Phys Soc; Am Asn Univ Professors. *Res:* Solids (election correlations in graphite and magnetic materials, galvanomagnetic properties of metals); surfaces (reaction rate theory); liquids (developing a discrete formulation of hydrodynamics). *Mailing Add:* Dept Physics & Astron Univ Ala University AL 35486

VISSCHER, SARALEE NEUMANN, b Lewistown, Mont, Jan 9, 29; m 69; c 4. ENTOMOLOGY. *Educ:* Univ Mont, BA, 49; Mont State Univ, MS, 58, PhD(entom), 63. *Prof Exp:* Asst prof entom, Mont State Univ, 62-65; NIH res fel insect develop, Univ Va, 65-66; assoc prof, 67-71, PROF ENTOM, MONT STATE UNIV, 72- *Concurrent Pos:* Co-investr, NIH res grant, 65-69; US-Japan grant, 77-79; AID grant, 79-80; Rockefeller grant, 80-81; Dow Chem grant, 80-81; NSF grant, 80-82. *Mem:* Fel AAAS; Entom Soc Am; Am Soc Zoologists; Soc Develop Biol; Sigma Xi. *Res:* Maternal and neuroendocrine regulation of embryonic morphogenesis and physiology, especially diapause of insects; role of plant growth hormones in regulation of insect growth and reproduction; host plant effects on grasshopper population dynamics. *Mailing Add:* Dept of Biol Mont State Univ Bozeman MT 59715

VISSCHER, WILLIAM M, b Memphis, Tenn, May 16, 28; m 51; c 4. THEORETICAL PHYSICS. *Educ:* Univ Minn, BA, 49; Cornell Univ, PhD(theoret physics), 53. *Prof Exp:* Res assoc physics, Univ Md, 53-56; STAFF MEM THEORET PHYSICS, LOS ALAMOS SCI LAB, 56- *Concurrent Pos:* Vis prof, Univ Wash, 67. *Mem:* Fel Am Phys Soc. *Res:* Meson theory; theory of nuclear structure and spectra; lattice dynamics and Mössbauer effect; particle accelerator physics; solid state physics; statistical mechanics; random packing; transport processes; scattering theory. *Mailing Add:* Theoret Div Los Alamos Sci Lab Los Alamos NM 87545

VISSER, CORNELIS, b Rotterdam, Neth; US citizen. ENGINEERING MECHANICS, CIVIL ENGINEERING. *Educ:* Tech Col, Rotterdam, dipl civil eng, 48; Ohio State Univ, MS, 63, PhD(eng mech), 66. *Prof Exp:* Engr civil eng, J P Van Eesteren, Rotterdam, 50-53; engr, T O Lazarides Lount & Partners, Toronto, 53-58; chief struct engr, Barrett Assoc Engrs, Columbus, 58-64; instr mech, Ohio State Univ, 64-66; sr engr mech, 66-70, mgr anal mech, 70-74, MGR, DEPT MECH, RES & DEVELOP CTR, WESTINGHOUSE ELEC CORP, 74- *Mem:* Am Soc Mech Engrs. *Res:* Structural analysis; numerical analysis; finite element method as applied to structural mechanics. *Mailing Add:* Res & Develop Ctr Beulah Rd Pittsburgh PA 15235

VISSER, DONALD WILLIS, b Holland, Mich, June 8, 15; m 44; c 1. BIOCHEMISTRY. *Educ:* Hope Col, AB, 37; Syracuse Univ, MS, 39; Univ Colo, PhD(biochem), 47. *Prof Exp:* Mem staff chem res, Agfa Ansco, NY, 39-40 & Dow Chem Co, Mich, 40-42; from instr to assoc prof, 47-56, prof, 56-80, EMER PROF BIOCHEM, SCH MED, UNIV SOUTHERN CALIF, 80- *Mem:* AAAS; Am Soc Biol Chemists; Soc Exp Biol & Med; Am Chem Soc. *Res:* Synthesis and biological properties of nucleoside analogs; transport of purines, pyrimidines and nucleosides in bacteria and animal cells. *Mailing Add:* Dept of Biochem Univ of Southern Calif Sch Med Los Angeles CA 90033

VISTE, ARLEN E, b Austin, Minn, Aug 13, 36; m 59; c 3. INORGANIC CHEMISTRY. *Educ:* St Olaf Col, BA, 58; Univ Chicago, PhD(inorg chem), 62. *Prof Exp:* Asst prof chem, St Olaf Col, 62-63; NSF fel, Columbia Univ, 63-64; assoc prof, 64-72, PROF CHEM, AUGUSTANA COL, SDAK, 72- *Concurrent Pos:* Partic fac res participation prog, Argonne Nat Lab, Ill, 70-71. *Mem:* Am Chem Soc; Royal Soc Chem. *Res:* Reaction mechanisms; spectroscopy. *Mailing Add:* 1500 W 30th St Sioux Falls SD 57105

VISVANATHAN, T R, b India, June 4, 22; US citizen. EARTH SCIENCE, STATISTICS. *Educ:* Univ Madras, BS, 41; Fla State Univ, MS, 67; Univ SC, PhD(geol), 73. *Prof Exp:* Asst meteorol, India Meteorol Serv, 43-65; instr geog, Benedict Col, 67-70; asst prof geol & geog, 71-78, ASSOC PROF GEOL & GEOG, UNIV SC, UNION, 78- *Mem:* Am Geophys Union. *Res:* Seismology; earthquake prediction; meteorology; prediction of atmospheric phenomena; solar terrestrial relationship planetary influences on terrestrial phenomena. *Mailing Add:* Dept of Geol & Geog Univ of SC Union SC 29379

VISWANATHA, THAMMAIAH, b Channapatna, India, Sept 22, 26. BIOCHEMISTRY. *Educ:* Univ Mysore, PhD, 55. *Prof Exp:* Rask-Orsted fel, Carlsberg Lab, Denmark, 56-57; res assoc, Univ Minn, 57-58; vis scientist, Nat Inst Arthritis & Metab Dis, 58-62 & Inst Molecular Biol & Dept Chem, Univ Ore, 62-64; PROF CHEM, UNIV WATERLOO, 64- *Res:* Enzymes; proteins; nucleic acids. *Mailing Add:* Dept of Chem Univ of Waterloo Waterloo ON N2L 3J5 Can

VISWANATHAN, C T, b Madras, India; US citizen. BIOPHARMACEUTICS, PHARMACOKINETICS. *Educ:* Presidency Col, BSc, 62, MSc, 64; Marquette Univ, MS, 72; Univ Wis-Madison, MS 74, PhD(pharmacokinetics), 77. *Prof Exp:* Res assoc, Sch Pharm, Univ Ga, 77-78 & Univ Wash, 78-79; REVIEWING SCIENTIST, DIV BIOPHARMACEUT, FOOD & DRUG ADMIN, 79- *Res:* Drug absorption, distribution, metabolism and elimination in humans; phenobarbital; valproic acid; drug interactions; protein binding. *Mailing Add:* 12805 Twinbrook Rockville MD 20851

VISWANATHAN, CHAND R, b Madras, India, Oct 23, 29. SOLID STATE PHYSICS, ELECTRONICS. *Educ:* Univ Madras, BSc, 48, MA, 49; Univ Calif, Los Angeles, MS, 59, PhD(solid state physics), 64. *Prof Exp:* Engr, Res Dept, All India Radio, 49-57; asst prof eng, 62-68, assoc prof eng & appl sci, 68-74, asst dean, Sch Eng & Appl Sci, 74-77, PROF ENG & APPL SCI, UNIV CALIF, LOS ANGELES, 74-, CHMN, ELEC ENG DEPT, 79- *Mem:* Fel Inst Elec & Electronics Engrs; Am Phys Soc. *Res:* Solid state electronics; magnetic properties of materials; electron energy levels in solids; electron emission from solids; semiconductor device physics; integrated electronics; manual override switch. *Mailing Add:* Dept Elec Eng Univ of Calif 7731 Boelter Hall Los Angeles CA 90024

VISWANATHAN, KADAYAM SANKARAN, b Madras, India, Apr 25, 37; m 67. PHYSICS, FIELD THEORY. *Educ:* Univ Madras, BSc, 57; Univ Calif, Riverside, MA, 64, PhD(physics), 65. *Prof Exp:* Res officer crystallog, Atomic Energy Estab, India, 57-60; asst prof, 65-70, assoc prof, 70-81, PROF THEORET PHYSICS, SIMON FRASER UNIV, 81- *Mem:* Am Phys Soc; Can Asn Physicists. *Res:* Gauge and super guage theories of fundamental interactions and rigorous statistical mechanics. *Mailing Add:* Dept Physics Simon Fraser Univ Burnaby BC V5A 1S6 Can

VISWANATHAN, R, b Tenkasi, India, Dec 17, 38; US citizen; m 65; c 2. LOW TEMPERATURE PHYSICS. *Educ:* Univ Madras, India, MA, 60, MSc, 60; Indian Inst Sci, PhD(physics), 64. *Prof Exp:* Res assoc, Univ Ill, 65-66; res physicist, Battelle Mem Inst, 66-67; res assoc, Univ Cincinnati, 67-69; asst scientist, Univ Calif, San Diego, 69-74; assoc scientist, Brookhaven Nat Lab, 74-78; SR STAFF, HUGHES AIRCRAFT CO, 78- *Concurrent Pos:* Vis scientist, Inst Solid State Physics, Ger, 73; prin investr, Hughes Aircraft Co, 78-79. *Mem:* Am Phys Soc; Am Inst Mining & Metal Engrs; Am Vacuum Soc; AAAS. *Res:* Low temperature calorimetry; radiation damage in superconductors and devices; physical property measurements; author or coauthor of over 50 puplications in international journals. *Mailing Add:* 30711 Casilina Dr Rancho Palos Verdes CA 90274

VITAGLIANO, VINCENT J, b New York, NY, Oct 29, 27; m 51; c 9. COMPUTER AIDED DESIGN, INTERACTIVE COMPUTER GRAPHICS. *Educ:* Manhattan Col, BCE, 49; Va Polytech Inst, MS, 51; NY Univ, EngScD, 60. *Prof Exp:* Instr appl mech, Va Polytech Inst, 49-50; struct designer, Praeger-Maguire, Consult Engrs, 50-52 & M W Kellogg Co, Pullman, Inc, NY, 52-54; from instr to assoc prof civil eng, Manhattan Col, 54-63; UNIV CONSULT, IBM CORP, 63- *Concurrent Pos:* Consult, 55-; Smith-Mundt vis lectr, AlHikma Univ Baghdad, 61-62. *Mem:* Am Soc Civil Engrs. *Res:* Structural engineering; electronic computers. *Mailing Add:* Saldi Lane Valhalla NY 10595

VITALE, JOSEPH JOHN, b Boston, Mass, Dec 14, 24; m 49; c 1. NUTRITION, BIOCHEMISTRY. *Educ:* Northeastern Univ, BS, 47; NY Univ, MS, 49; Harvard Univ, DSc(nutrit biochem), 51; Antioquia Univ, Colombia, MD, 66. *Prof Exp:* Res assoc nutrit, Sch Pub Health, Harvard Univ, 51-54, assoc, 54-55, asst prof, 55-66; prof food, nutrit & med, Univ Wis, 66-67; dir nutrit progs, Sch Med, Tufts Univ, 67-72; PROF PATH & COMMUNITY MED, SCH MED, BOSTON UNIV, 72- *Concurrent Pos:*

Res assoc path, Sch Med, Boston Univ, 52-66; spec consult, Interdept Comt Nutrit for Nat Defense, 59-; Claude Bernard prof, Med Sch, Univ Montreal, 60; vis prof, Univ del Valle, Colombia, 60-62. *Mem:* Am Inst Nutrit; Am Soc Clin Nutrit; Brit Nutrit Soc. *Res:* Atherosclerosis, gastrointestinal metabolism, nutritional anemias and public health. *Mailing Add:* 73 Bartlett Somerville MA 02155

VITALE, RICHARD ALBERT, b New Haven, Conn, Sept 7, 44. MATHEMATICS, STATISTICS. *Educ:* Harvard Univ, AB, 66; Brown Univ, PhD(appl math), 70. *Prof Exp:* Asst prof appl math, Brown Univ, 70-76; asst scientist, Math Res Ctr, Madison, 76-77; ASSOC PROF MATH, CLAREMONT GRAD SCH, 77- *Mem:* Sigma Xi; Am Math Soc; Bernoulli Soc Math Statist & Probability; Soc Indust & Appl Math; Inst Math Statist. *Res:* Geometric probability. *Mailing Add:* Dept of Math Claremont Grad Sch Claremont CA 91711

VITALIANO, CHARLES JOSEPH, b New York, NY, Apr 2, 10; m 40; c 2. GEOLOGY. *Educ:* City Col New York, BS, 36; Columbia Univ, AM, 38, PhD(mineral), 44. *Prof Exp:* Asst mineral, Columbia Univ, 37-39, lab instr gems & precious stones, Exten, 39-40; instr ceramic petrog, Rutgers Univ, 40-42; from asst geologist to assoc geologist, US Geol Surv, 42-46; assoc prof, 47-57, PROF GEOL, IND UNIV, BLOOMINGTON, 57- *Concurrent Pos:* Geologist, US Geol Surv, 46-59; Fulbright scholar, NZ Geol Surv, 54-55; NSF grant, 57-60 & 62-67; mem consortium crystalline basement rocks cent US, 80-82. *Mem:* Fel Mineral Soc Am; Soc Econ Geologists; fel Geol Soc Am; Geochem Soc. *Res:* Geology and ore deposits of the Paradise Peak Quadrangle, Nevada; igneous and metamorphic petrography of western Nevada, southern New Zealand and southwest Montana; volcanic rocks of western United States; archaeological geology of Mediterranean regions. *Mailing Add:* Dept of Geol Ind Univ Bloomington IN 47401

VITALIANO, DOROTHY BRAUNECK, b New York, NY, Feb 10, 16; m 40; c 2. GEOLOGY. *Educ:* Barnard Col, AB, 36; Columbia Univ, AM, 38, MPhil, 73. *Prof Exp:* Teaching asst geol, Barnard Col, 36-39; field asst, 42-43, GEOLOGIST, US GEOL SURV, 53- *Concurrent Pos:* Mem-at-large, Sect Comt E Geol & Geog, AAAS, 78-82; Sigma Xi lectr, 81-83. *Mem:* Fel Geol Soc Am; Geosci Info Soc; AAAS. *Res:* Bronze Age eruption of Santorini volcano; scientific basis of Atlantis; geomythology; technical translation; tephrochronology. *Mailing Add:* Geol Bldg Rm 227 1005 E Tenth St Bloomington IN 47401

VITCHA, JAMES F, b Cleveland, Ohio, Mar 5, 10; m 36; c 1. ORGANIC CHEMISTRY. *Educ:* Ohio Wesleyan Univ, BA, 32; Univ Ill, MS, 33. *Prof Exp:* Res chemist, Solvay Process Corp, NY, 33-43; chief chemist, Ohio Chem & Mfg Co, 43-50 & Puritan Compressed Gas Corp, Mo, 50-55; sect head, Cent Res Labs, Airco Inc, 55-65, mgr chem prod develop, Ohio Med Prod Div, 65-75, consult, Ohio Med Prod Div, 75-81. *Mem:* Am Chem Soc. *Res:* Research in anesthetics and anesthetic gases; medical equipment; clinical evaluation of new anesthetics; drug regulatory affairs. *Mailing Add:* 223 SE 45th St Cape Coral FL 33904

VITELLO, PETER ALFONSO JAMES, b Glendale, Calif, Sept 15, 50; m 76. THEORETICAL ASTROPHYSICS. *Educ:* Univ Southern Calif, BS, 72; Cornell Univ, PhD(theoret phys), 77. *Prof Exp:* Fel theoret astrophys, Ctr Astrophys, Harvard Col Observ, 77-80; MEM STAFF, SCI APPLICATIONS, INC, 80- *Mem:* Sigma Xi; Am Astron Soc. *Res:* Theoretical studies of radiation-driven stellar winds in binary x-ray source systems, and of accretion onto black holes. *Mailing Add:* Ctr for Astrophys PO Box 1303 McLean VA 22102

VITERBI, ANDREW J, b Bergamo, Italy, Mar 9, 35; US citizen; m 58; c 3. COMMUNICATIONS. *Educ:* Mass Inst Technol, BS & MS, 57; Univ Southern Calif, PhD(elec eng), 62. *Prof Exp:* Res engr, Commun Res Sect, Jet Propulsion Lab, Calif Inst Technol, 57-62, res group supvr, 62-63; from asst prof to prof eng, Univ Calif, Los Angeles, 63-73; EXEC VPRES, LINKABIT CORP, 73- *Concurrent Pos:* Consult, var indust orgns & govt labs, 63-; mem bd dirs, Linkabit Corp, Calif, 68-; res grants, Air Force Off Sci Res, NASA & Army Electronics Command, 64-73 & Army Res Off, 71- *Honors & Awards:* Inst Elec & Electronics Engrs Award, 62, Ann Award, 68; Columbus Int Commun Award, Ital Nat Res Coun, 75. *Mem:* Nat Acad Eng; fel Inst Elec & Electronics Engrs. *Res:* Communication and information theory; coding; detection; modulation; signal processing. *Mailing Add:* Linkabit Corp 10453 Roselle St San Diego CA 92121

VITKOVITS, JOHN A(NDREW), b Cleveland, Ohio, Apr 7, 21; m 48; c 2. MECHANICAL ENGINEERING. *Educ:* Southern Methodist Univ, BS, 48. *Prof Exp:* Proj engr, Lubrizol Corp, Ohio, 48-49; mech engr, 49-55, asst sect mgr, 55-56, mgr, Standardized Tests Sect, 56-59, dir, Dept Engines, Fuels & Lubricants Eval, 59-72, VPRES, DIV ENGINES, FUELS & LUBRICANTS EVAL, SOUTHWEST RES INST, 72- *Concurrent Pos:* Mem diesel rating panel & comt automatic transmission fluids, Coord Res Coun, Inc, 56-; mem automatic transmission fluid panel, Gen Motors Corp. *Mem:* Soc Automotive Engrs; Am Soc Testing & Mat; Am Soc Lubrication Engrs; Sci Res Soc Am. *Res:* Research and automotive engines; torque converters; high speed and high torque hypoid gear lubricant evaluation; copper-lead, tin overlay and babbitt bearing endurance testing; design of engine research labs. *Mailing Add:* Southwest Res Inst 6220 Culebra Rd San Antonio TX 78284

VITOLS, VISVALDIS ALBERTS, b Riga, Latvia, Aug 24, 36; US citizen; m 63; c 2. ELECTRICAL ENGINEERING, INFORMATION SCIENCE. *Educ:* Iowa State Univ, BS, 58, MS, 59, PhD(elec eng), 62. *Prof Exp:* Asst prof elec eng, Iowa State Univ, 62-63; group scientist, NAm Aviation, Inc, 63-65; mem tech staff comput technol, IBM Corp, 65-68; mgr pattern recognition, Rockwell Int, 68-75; MGR, INFO SCI, 75- *Concurrent Pos:* Consult, Nat Acad Sci, 69-72. *Mem:* Inst Elec & Electronics Engrs; Sigma Xi; Int Asn Identification. *Res:* Pattern recognition and signal processing techniques utilizing general and special purpose digital processors; processor architectures for information classification and retrieval systems; machine recognition of unconstrained speech and image processing; imaged based scene and target recognition. *Mailing Add:* 864 Woodland Ave Orange CA 92669

VITOSH, MAURICE LEE, b Odell, Nebr, Jan 16, 39; m 63; c 1. AGRONOMY, SOIL SCIENCE. *Educ:* Univ Nebr, BS, 62, MS, 64; NC State Univ, PhD(soils), 68. *Prof Exp:* Agronomist, NC Dept Agr, 65-68; EXTEN SPECIALIST SOIL FERTILITY PROF CROP & SOIL SCI, MICH STATE UNIV, 68- *Mem:* Am Soc Agron; Soil Sci Soc Am; Potato Asn Am. *Res:* Soil fertility with potato, corn, soybeans and field beans. *Mailing Add:* Dept Crop & Soil Sci Mich State Univ East Lansing MI 48824

VITOUSEK, MARTIN J, b Honolulu, Hawaii, July 30, 24; m 65; c 4. GEOPHYSICS. *Educ:* Stanford Univ, BS, 49, PhD(math), 54. *Prof Exp:* Radar lab worker, Pearl Harbor, 43-46; asst prof math, Univ Hawaii, 53-55; sr engr, Scripps Inst, Calif, 56-59; from assoc geophysicist to geophysicist, 61-74, SPECIALIST OCEANOG INSTRUMENT, HAWAII INST GEOPHYS, UNIV HAWAII AT MANOA, 74- *Mem:* Marine Technol Soc; Solar Energy Soc. *Res:* Applied mathematics; solid earth geophysics and oceanography; long period ocean waves, instrumentation and analysis. *Mailing Add:* Hawaii Inst of Geophys Univ of Hawaii at Manoa Honolulu HI 96822

VITOUSEK, PETER MORRISON, b Honolulu, Hawaii, Jan 24, 49. ECOLOGY. *Educ:* Amherst Col, BA, 71; Dartmouth Col, PhD(biol sci), 75. *Prof Exp:* Asst prof biol, Ind Univ, Bloomington, 75-79; ASSOC PROF BOT, UNIV NC, CHAPEL HILL, 80- *Mem:* Ecol Soc Am; AAAS; Soil Sci Soc Am. *Res:* Regulation of nutrient cycling in terrestrial ecosystems; land-water interactions. *Mailing Add:* Dept Bot Univ NC Chapel Hill NC 27514

VITOVEC, FRANZ H, b Vienna, Austria, June 7, 21; nat Can; m; c 2. PHYSICAL METALLURGY. *Educ:* Vienna Tech Univ, dipl, 46, Dr tech sci, 47. *Prof Exp:* Docent, Vienna Tech Univ, 51; from asst prof to assoc prof mech & mat, Univ Minn, 52-58; from assoc prof to prof metall eng, Univ, Wis, 58-65; chmn dept mineral eng, 71-80, PROF METALL ENG, UNIV ALTA, 65- *Mem:* Am Soc Metals; fel Am Soc Testing & Mat. *Res:* Relationship between the mechanical behavior of metals and alloys, their microstructure, and the environment. *Mailing Add:* Dept Mech Eng Univ of Alta Edmonton AB T6G 2G8 Can

VITT, DALE HADLEY, b Washington, Mo, Feb 9, 44; c 2. BOTANY, BRYOLOGY. *Educ:* Southeast Mo State Col, BS, 67; Univ Mich, Ann Arbor, MS, 68, PhD(bot), 70. *Prof Exp:* From asst prof to assoc prof, 70-79, PROF BOT, UNIV ALTA, 80- *Mem:* Int Asn Plant Taxon; Am Bryol & Lichenological Soc; Can Bot Soc; Danish Bryol Soc; British Bryol Soc. *Res:* Taxonomic, phylogenetic and ecological studies of bryophytes; monographic treatment of arctic, antarctic and temperate mosses; ecological analyses and productivity of bryophytes in arctic and alpine tundras and in boreal peatlands. *Mailing Add:* Dept of Bot Univ of Alta Edmonton AB T6G 2E1 Can

VITT, LAURIE JOSEPH, b Bremerton, Wash, Aug 20, 45. ECOLOGY, HERPETOLOGY. *Educ:* Western Wash State Col, BA, 67, MS, 71; Ariz State Univ, PhD(zool), 76. *Prof Exp:* Res fel ecol, Academia Brasileira de Ciencas, Brazil, 77-78; scholar ecol, Mus Zool, Univ Mich, 78-79; res assoc fel, Mus Natural Hist, 79-81, RES ASSOC, UNIV GA, 81- *Concurrent Pos:* Res ecologist, Ariz State Univ grant, 73-75; res assoc, Ariz State Univ, 75-76; consult, Desert Plan Off, Bur Land Mgt, 78 & Athene Wildlife Found, 79; adj asst prof, Savannah River Ecol Lab & Univ Ga, 81- *Mem:* Am Soc Ichthyol & Herpet; Soc Study Evolution; Herpet League; Soc Study Amphib & Reptiles; Ecol Soc Am. *Res:* Community structure, competition, predation, reproductive effort, parental investment, demographies, life histories and reproduction of vertebrates, tail autotomy of lizards, resource partitioning of invertebrates, particularly scorpions. *Mailing Add:* Savannah River Ecol Lab Drawer E Aiken SC 29801

VITTI, TRIESTE GUIDO, b Detroit, Mich, May 22, 25; m 53; c 4. BIOPHARMACEUTICS, PHARMACOKINETICS. *Educ:* Univ Detroit, BS, 49, MS, 51; Wayne State Univ, PhD(biochem), 61. *Prof Exp:* Lectr pharmacol, Fac Med, Univ Man, 64-67; chief bioavailability, Upjohn Co, Mich, 67-71; dir clin res, Bur Drugs, Food & Drug Admin, 71-72; PROF BIOPHARMACEUT, FAC PHARM, UNIV MAN, 72- *Concurrent Pos:* USPHS fel, Univ Man, 64-67; consult, Biodecision Labs, Pittsburgh, Pa, 72-76; mem permanent adv expert comt bioavailability, Health & Welfare, Health Progs Bd, Can, 74-; mem bd, Alcohol & Drug Educ Serv, Manitoba, 78-; mem adv res comt, Col Family Physicians, Family Med Ctr, Winnipeg, 78-80. *Mem:* Am Chem Soc; Pharmacol Soc Can; Can Pharmaceut Asn. *Res:* Biochemical pharmacology. *Mailing Add:* Fac of Pharm Univ of Man Winnipeg MB R3T 2N2 Can

VITTITOE, CHARLES NORMAN, b Louisville, Ky, Oct 3, 34; m 58; c 2. ELECTRODYNAMICS. *Educ:* Univ Ky, BS, 56; Univ Wis, MS, 58; Univ Ky, PhD(physics), 63. *Prof Exp:* Instr physics, Univ Ky, 59-60, from res asst to res assoc, 62-63; asst prof, Univ Ohio, 63-66, univ res comt, grant, 66; staff mem, Radiation Phenomena Div, 66-70, STAFF MEM, THEORET DIV, SANDIA LABS, 70- *Mem:* Am Phys Soc. *Res:* Pion-nucleon interactions; reconstruction and identification of bubble chamber tracks; elementary particle physics; nuclear weapon effects; electrodynamics; optical transport theory; central receiver solar energy collection; geological probing by electrical methods. *Mailing Add:* Sandia Labs Sandia Base Br Box 5800 Albuquerque NM 87185

VITTORIA, CARMINE, b Avella, Italy, May 15, 41; US citizen; m 67; c 3. MAGNETISM. *Educ:* Toledo Univ, BS, 62; Yale Univ, MS, 67, PhD(physics), 70. *Prof Exp:* Elec engr bionics, Naval Ord Lab, 62-63; teacher elec eng, Toledo Univ, 63-64; PHYSICIST, NAVAL RES LAB, 70- *Concurrent Pos:* Naval Res Coun adv, Naval Res Lab, 74, res award, 76; mem tech prog comt, Nat Magnetism Conf, 78; consult, Navy Electronic Syst Agencies. *Honors & Awards:* Outstanding Achievement Award, Naval Res Lab, 72 & 74. *Mem:* Am Phys Soc; Inst Elec & Electronics Engrs; Sigma Xi. *Res:* Electromagnetic wave propagation in magnetic materials. *Mailing Add:* Naval Res Lab Code 6453 V Washington DC 20375

VITTUM, MORRILL THAYER, b Haverhill, Mass, May 4, 19; m 41; c 3. HORTICULTURE, AGRONOMY. *Educ:* Univ Mass, BS, 39; Univ Conn, MS, 41; Purdue Univ, PhD(soil sci), 44. *Prof Exp:* Asst agron, Univ Conn, 39-41; asst agron, Purdue Univ, 41-42, tech asst soils, 42-45; from asst prof to assoc prof, 46-59, PROF VEG CROPS, NY STATE AGR EXP STA, CORNELL UNIV, 59-, HEAD DEPT, 60-69 & 71- *Concurrent Pos:* Actg asst olericulturist, Univ Calif, Davis, 56-57; vis prof hort, Ore State Univ, 64; proj leader, Univ Philippines-Cornell Grad Educ Prog, Col Agr, Univ Philippines, 69-71; actg horticulturist, Coop State Res Serv, USDA, 73-74 & 80-81. *Mem:* Am Soc Agron; Soil Sci Soc Am; fel Am Soc Hort Sci; Int Soc Hort Sci; Int Soc Soil Sci. *Res:* Effects of fertilizers, irrigation, rotation and cultural practices on the yield and quality of processing vegetables; evapotranspiration and soil-plant-water relationships. *Mailing Add:* NY State Agr Exp Sta Cornell Univ Geneva NY 14456

VITULLO, VICTOR PATRICK, b Chicago, Ill, Oct 18, 39; m 62; c 1. ORGANIC CHEMISTRY. *Educ:* Loyola Univ, Chicago, BS, 61; Ill Inst Technol, PhD(chem), 65. *Prof Exp:* NSF fel, Mass Inst Technol, 65-66; res chemist, E I du Pont de Nemours & Co, Inc, 66-68; instr, Univ Kans, 68-69; asst prof, 69-74, ASSOC PROF CHEM, UNIV MD, BALTIMORE COUNTY, 69- *Mem:* AAAS; Am Chem Soc. *Res:* Physical organic chemistry; organic reaction mechanisms; acid-base catalysis; transition state structure; isotope effects. *Mailing Add:* Dept of Chem Univ of Md Baltimore County Baltimore MD 21228

VIVIAN, J(OHNSON) EDWARD, b Montreal, Que, July 6, 13; nat US; m 40; c 3. CHEMICAL ENGINEERING. *Educ:* McGill Univ, BEng, 36; Mass Inst Technol, SM, 39, ScD(chem eng), 45. *Prof Exp:* Asst, Can Pulp & Paper Asn, Que, 34-36; asst chem eng, 37-38, asst dir, Bangor Pract Sch, 38-41, from asst prof to assoc prof chem eng, 42-56, dir, Buffalo Pract Sch, 41-43, adminr, Metall Proj, 44-45, res group leader, 45-46, dir, Sch Chem Eng Pract, 46-57, dir, Eng Pract, Sch, Oak Ridge, 48-57, dir, Atomic Energy Comn Proj Separation, 54, prof chem eng, 56-80, EMER PROF CHEM ENG, MASS INST TECHNOL, 80-, SR LECTR, 80- *Concurrent Pos:* Vis prof, Birla Inst Technol & Sci, Pilani, India, 72- *Honors & Awards:* Award, Am Inst Chem Engrs, 48. *Mem:* AAAS; Am Soc Eng Educ; Am Chem Soc; Tech Asn Pulp & Paper Indust; Am Inst Chem Engrs. *Res:* Unit operations; mass transfer; chemical engineering design. *Mailing Add:* Dept of Chem Eng Rm 66-350 Mass Inst of Technol Cambridge MA 02139

VIVIAN, VIRGINIA M, b Barneveld, Wis, July 1, 23. NUTRITION. *Educ:* Univ Wis, BS, 45; Columbia Univ, MS, 47; Univ Wis, PhD(home econ, biochem), 59. *Prof Exp:* Instr foods, nutrit & dietetics, Sch Nursing, Presby Hosp, 48-49; instr foods, nutrit & dietetics, Sch Nursing, Univ Mich, 49-51, asst dir dietary dept, Univ Hosp, 51-55; from asst prof to assoc prof, 59-68, prof home econ, Ohio State Univ & Ohio Agr Res & Develop Ctr, 68-77, chairperson dept human nutrit & food mgt, 77-82, CAROL S KENNEDY DISTINGUISHED PROF NUTRIT, OHIO STATE UNIV, 82- *Mem:* AAAS; Am Home Econ Asn; Am Dietetic Asn; Am Inst Nutrit; NY Acad Sci. *Res:* Amino acid-lipid metabolism with humans, preschool dietary adequacy and nutrition status studies; exercise, diet and metabolism. *Mailing Add:* 1787 Neil Ave Ohio State Univ Columbus OH 43210

VIVILECCHIA, RICHARD, analytical chemistry, see previous edition

VIVONA, STEFANO, b St Louis, Mo, Mar 25, 19; m 50; c 5. PREVENTIVE MEDICINE, PUBLIC HEALTH. *Educ:* St Louis Univ, MD, 43; Harvard Univ, MPH, 52. *Prof Exp:* Chief prev med, 5th Army Corps, US Army, Ger, 52-54, chief prev med, 7th Army, 54-55, actg chief biostatist, Walter Reed Army Inst Res, DC, 55-58, chief prev med res Br, Med Res & Develop Command, 58-60, chief prev med, 8th Army, Korea, 60-61, dir div commun dis & immunol, 62-64, chief med res team, Vietnam, 64-65, dir med component, SEATO, Thailand, 65-67, dir div prev med, Walter Reed Army Inst Res, 67-69; res adminr, 69-70, vpres res grant awards, 70-74, VPRES RES, RES DEPT, AM CANCER SOC, INC, 74- *Concurrent Pos:* Fel biologics res, Walter Reed Army Inst Res, 61-62. *Mem:* AMA; Am Pub Health Asn; Am Asn Cancer Res; Am Col Prev Med. *Res:* Infectious diseases; epidemiologic aspects of biostatistics; cancer. *Mailing Add:* Res Dept Am Cancer Soc Inc 777 Third Ave New York NY 10017

VIZARD, DOUGLAS LINCOLN, b Worcester, Mass, Sept 13, 44; m 62, 77; c 3. BIOPHYSICS, MOLECULAR BIOLOGY. *Educ:* Worcester Polytech Inst, BS, 66; Pa State Univ, MS, 69, PhD(biophys), 71. *Prof Exp:* NIH fel biophys, 71-73, Robert A Welch Found fel, 73-74, fel biochem, 75, NIH fel biophys, 75-76, ASST PHYSICIST, DEPT PHYSICS, M D ANDERSON HOSP & TUMOR INST, 76-; ASST PROF BIOPHYSICS, GRAD SCH BIOMED SCI, UNIV TEX HOUSTON, 76- *Mem:* Biophys Soc; Sigma Xi. *Res:* Organization of viral DNA and RNA genomes; organization of eucaryotic chromatin and DNA sequences; high resolution thermal denaturation. *Mailing Add:* Dept of Physics M D Anderson Hosp & Tumor Inst Houston TX 77030

VIZY, KALMAN NICHOLAS, b Györ, Hungary, July 7, 40; US citizen; m 68; c 2. APPLIED PHYSICS. *Educ:* Cleveland State Univ, BES, 63, BS, 64; John Carroll Univ, MS, 67. *Prof Exp:* Dept head sci, Byzantine Educ Ctr, 64-67; SR RES PHYSICIST, RES LABS, EASTMAN KODAK CO, 67- *Concurrent Pos:* Adj lectr modern physics, Rochester Inst Technol, 67- *Honors & Awards:* Autometric Award, Am Soc Photogram & Am Soc Mech Engrs, 75. *Mem:* Am Soc Mech Engrs; Am Asn Physics Teachers; Am Asn Physicists Med; Am Phys Soc; Soc Photog Scientists & Engrs. *Res:* Research and development on the application of photography for reconnaissance, micrographics, and medical applications; systems designer and analyst. *Mailing Add:* Eastman Kodak Res Labs 199 Lake Ave Rochester NY 14650

VLACH, JIRI, b Praha, Czech, Oct 5, 22; m 49; c 1. ELECTRICAL ENGINEERING. *Educ:* Prague Tech Univ, Dipl Eng, 47, PhD(elec eng), 57. *Prof Exp:* Mem res staff, Res Inst Radiocommun, Czech, 48-67; vis prof elec eng, Univ Ill, 67-69; PROF ELEC ENG, UNIV WATERLOO, 69- *Mem:* fel Inst Elec & Electronics Engrs. *Res:* Network theory; computer aided design. *Mailing Add:* Dept of Elec Eng Univ of Waterloo Waterloo ON N2L 3G1 Can

VLACHOPOULOS, JOHN A(POSTOLOS), b Volos, Greece, Aug 11, 42. CHEMICAL ENGINEERING. *Educ:* Athens Tech Univ, Dipl eng, 65; Washington Univ, St Louis, MS, 68, DSc, 69. *Prof Exp:* Asst prof, 68-74, assoc prof, 74-79, PROF CHEM ENG, MCMASTER UNIV, 82- *Concurrent Pos:* Sabbatical, Univ Stuttgart Ger, 75 & Ecole Des Mines, Paris, France, 81-82. *Mem:* Am Inst Chem Engrs; Soc Plastics Engrs; Soc Rheol; Chem Inst Can; Can Soc Chem Eng. *Res:* Fluid mechanics; polymer processing and polymer rheology; extrudate swell and melt fracture; finite difference and finite element methods for numerical simultions; polymer extrusion; calendering. *Mailing Add:* Dept of Chem Eng McMaster Univ Hamilton ON L8S 4L8 Can

VLADUTIU, ADRIAN O, b Bucharest, Romania, Aug 5, 40; US citizen; m 71; c 2. CLINICAL PATHOLOGY, IMMUNOPATHOLOGY. *Educ:* Spiru Haret, Romania, BS, 56; Bucharest Univ, MD, 62; Jassy Univ, PhD(physiopath), 68. *Prof Exp:* Asst prof physiopath, Sch Med, Univ Bucharest, 68-71; res asst prof microbiol, 69-71, clin assoc prof path, 77-81, RES ASSOC PROF MED, SCH MED, STATE UNIV NY, BUFFALO, 79-, PROF PATH, 81-, MEM, E WITEBSKY CTR IMMUNOL, 81-, PROF MICROBIOL, 82- *Concurrent Pos:* Intern, G Marinesco Hosp, Bucharest, 62-65, Millard Fillmore Hosp, Buffalo, 71-72; Nat Res Award, Ministry Educ, Romania, 65; resident, State Univ NY, Buffalo, E J Meyer & Buffalo Gen Hosp, 72-74; dir, Immunopath Lab, Buffalo Gen Hosp, 74-, assoc pathologist, 79-, dir, Chem Lab, 81-82, pathologist, 82-; consult, path, Niagara Falls Mem Hosp, 76- *Mem:* Am Asn Immunologists; Am Asn Pathologists; Soc Exp Biol & Med; Am Fedn Clin Res; NY Acad Sci. *Res:* Autoimmunity in animals and man; diagnosis, pathogenesis and particularly its genetic control; laboratory medicine particularly isoenzymes, immune complexes, receptor assays and differential diagnosis of pleural effusions. *Mailing Add:* 80 Oakview Dr Amherst NY 14221

VLADUTIU, GEORGIRENE DIETRICH, b Bremerton, Wash, Dec 21, 44; m 71; c 2. MICROBIOLOGY. *Educ:* Syracuse Univ, BS, 66; State Univ NY, Buffalo, MA, 70, PhD(microbiol), 73. *Prof Exp:* Res instr, 76-77, res asst prof, 77-81, RES ASSOC PROF PEDIAT, CHILDREN'S HOSP, BUFFALO, 81- *Concurrent Pos:* Prin investr, NSF, 77-79, NIH, 79-85 & Cystic Fibrosis Found, 81-82. *Mem:* Am Soc Biol Chemists; Am Soc Human Genetics; Soc Pediat Res; Asn Women Sci. *Res:* Transport of lysosomal enzymes in fibroblasts via specific glycosylated recognition markers; hereditary lysosomal storage diseases such as I-cell disease (mucolipidosis II) in which lysosomal enzymes are abnormally glycosylated and excreted; neonatal screening tests for inborn errors of metabolism such as familial hypercholesterolemia and cystic fibrosis. *Mailing Add:* Children's Hosp 219 Bryant St Buffalo NY 14222

VLAHAKIS, GEORGE, b New York, NY, Oct 12, 23; m 49; c 2. GENETICS. *Educ:* Johns Hopkins Univ, AB, 51; Univ Tex, MA, 53. *Prof Exp:* Biologist, NIH, 52-53; chemist, US Testing Co, 54-55; BIOLOGIST, NAT CANCER INST, 55- *Mem:* AAAS; Am Genetic Asn; Am Inst Biol Sci. *Res:* Role of genes and their relationship to non-genetic factors in the development of tumors in mice. *Mailing Add:* 1720 Evelyn Dr Rockville MD 20852

VLAHCEVIC, ZDRAVKO RENO, b Yugoslavia, June 30, 31; US citizen; m 61; c 2. GASTROENTEROLOGY. *Educ:* Univ Zagreb, MD, 67. *Prof Exp:* Instr med, Sch Med, Tufts Univ, 62-64; jr instr, Western Reserve Univ, 65-66; from asst prof to assoc prof, 66-74, PROF MED, MED COL VA, 74-, CHMN, DIV GASTROENTEROL, 79- *Concurrent Pos:* Mem staff, Vet Admin Hosp, Richmond, Va; chief, Gastroenterol Sect, Vet Admin Med Ctr, 66- *Mem:* AAAS; AMA; Am Fedn Clin Res; Am Asn Study Liver Dis; Am Gastroenterol Asn. *Res:* Cholesterol bile acid metabolism and lipoprotein metabolism in man; bile acid biosynthesis pathways. *Mailing Add:* Dept of Gastroenterol Vet Admin Med Ctr Richmond VA 23249

VLAOVIC, MILAN STEPHEN, b Novi Sad, Yugoslavia, Feb 1, 36; m 69; c 2. VETERINARY PATHOLOGY. *Educ:* Univ Belgrade, DVM, 61; Univ Sask, MSc, 70; Univ Mo-Columbia, PhD(vet med), 74. *Prof Exp:* Gen practr, WGer, 65-67; tech officer, Can Dept Agr, 67-68; res asst vet microbiol, Univ Sask, 68-70; res asst, Wash State Univ, 70-71; res assoc, Univ Mo, 71-74; vet pathologist, Frederick Cancer Res Ctr, 74-78; PATHOLOGIST, EASTMAN KODAK CO, 78- *Mem:* Am Vet Med Asn; Am Asn Lab Animal Sci; Soc Pharmacol & Environ Pathologists; Tissue Cult Asn. *Res:* Immunopathology. *Mailing Add:* 7 Bremen Circle Penfield NY 14526

VLASES, GEORGE CHARPENTIER, b New York, NY, Oct 22, 36; m 58; c 3. PLASMA PHYSICS. *Educ:* Johns Hopkins Univ, BES, 58; Calif Inst Technol, MS, 59, PhD(aeronaut), 63. *Prof Exp:* Res fel aeronaut, Calif Inst Technol, 63; from asst prof to assoc prof aerospace eng sci, Univ Colo, Boulder, 63-69; res assoc prof, 69-73, PROF NUCLEAR ENG, AEROSPACE RES LAB, UNIV WASH, 73- *Concurrent Pos:* Consult, Aerospace Corp, Calif, 63 & Math Sci Northwest, Inc. *Mem:* Am Phys Soc. *Mailing Add:* Aerospace Res Lab FL-10 Univ of Wash Seattle WA 98195

VLATTAS, ISIDOROS, b Chios, Greece, Apr 28, 35; US citizen; m 67; c 3. ORGANIC CHEMISTRY. *Educ:* Nat Univ Athens, BS, 59; Univ BC, MsD, 63, PhD(chem), 66. *Prof Exp:* Fel, Harvard Univ, 67-68, res chemist; 68-80, SR STAFF SCIENTIST ORG CHEM, CIBA-GEIGY CORP, 80- *Mem:* Am Chem Soc. *Res:* Natural products; medicinal organic chemistry research. *Mailing Add:* 131 Butler Pkwy Summit NJ 07901

VLCEK, DONALD HENRY, b Holyrood, Kans, Nov 17, 18; m 44; c 4. ELECTRONICS, RESEARCH ADMINISTRATION. *Educ:* US Mil Acad, BA, 43; Stanford Univ, ME, 49. *Prof Exp:* Chief electronic requirements br, HQ, Air Defense Command, US Air Force, 49-51, electronics staff officer to Asst Secy Defense for Res & Develop, 52-54, semi-atomic ground environ proj officer, Air Defense Systs Proj Off, Hq, Air Res & Develop Command, 55-56, chief track test div, Missile Develop Ctr, 56-61, test instrumentation develop div, Hq, Air Force Systs Command, 61-64, dir plans & requirements, Hq, Nat Range Div, 64-67, dir eng, Hq, Ground Electronics Eng Installation

Agency, 67-69, Comdr, Ballistic Missile Early Warning Site, Eng, 69-72; COORDR, CANCER RES CTR, MED SCH, OHIO STATE UNIV, 72-, COORDR & BUS MGR, COMP CANCER CTR, 72- *Mem:* Inst Elec & Electronics Engrs. *Res:* Captive testing and the influence of the rate of change of acceleration upon the behavior of components and systems. *Mailing Add:* 2588 Edgevale Upper Arlington Columbus OH 43221

VLIEKS, ARNOLD EVALD, experimental nuclear physics, astrophysics, see previous edition

VLIET, DANIEL H(ENDRICKS), b New Orleans, La, May 30, 21; m 43; c 3. ELECTRICAL ENGINEERING. *Educ:* Tulane Univ, BSEE, 49; Univ Mich, MSEE, 52; Univ Wis, PhD, 65. *Prof Exp:* Assoc prof, 58-65, PROF ELEC ENG, TULANE UNIV LA, 65- *Mem:* Am Soc Eng Educ; Inst Elec & Electronics Engrs. *Res:* Power system analysis; electrical machinery; automation and control. *Mailing Add:* Dept of Elec Eng Tulane Univ New Orleans LA 70118

VLIET, GARY CLARK, b Bassano, Alta, June 3, 33; US citizen; m 62; c 3. HEAT TRANSFER, SOLAR ENERGY. *Educ:* Univ Alta, BSc, 55; Stanford Univ, MS, 57, PhD(mech eng), 62. *Prof Exp:* Res scientist, Lockheed Missiles & Space Co, 61-71; assoc prof, 71-79, PROF MECH ENG, UNIV TEX, AUSTIN, 79- *Honors & Awards:* Best Paper Award, Am Soc Mech Engrs, 70. *Mem:* Assoc mem Am Soc Mech Engrs; Int Solar Energy Soc. *Res:* Thermal energy systems; solar energy; energy conversion. *Mailing Add:* Dept of Mech Eng Univ of Tex Austin TX 78712

VLITOS, AUGUST JOHN, b Vandergrift, Pa, Mar 30, 23; m 48; c 3. PLANT PHYSIOLOGY. *Educ:* Okla Agr & Mech Col, BS, 48; Iowa State Col, MS, 50; Columbia Univ, PhD(plant physiol, biochem), 53. *Prof Exp:* Asst plant path, Okla Agr & Mech Col, 41-42 & 46-48; asst plant path, Iowa State Col, 49-50; asst plant pathologist, Boyce Thompson Inst Plant Res, 50-51, sr fel plant physiol, 51-59; dir res, Caroni, Ltd & St Madeleine Sugar Co, Ltd, Trinidad, 59-67; CHIEF EXEC, GROUP RES & DEVELOP, PHILIP LYLE MEM RES LAB, TATE & LYLE, LTD, 67- *Concurrent Pos:* Plant physiologist, Carbide & Carbon Chem Co, 51-59; vis prof, Univ Reading, 72- *Mem:* AAAS; Am Phytopath Soc; fel Inst Biol UK. *Res:* Plant growth regulators; biochemistry; chemistry of sugar refining; bioanalysis; chemurgy. *Mailing Add:* Philip Lyle Mem Res Lab Tate & Lyle Ltd Univ Reading Reading RG6 2BX England United Kingdom

VOBACH, ARNOLD R, b Chicago, Ill, Nov 20, 32; m 57; c 2. MATHEMATICS. *Educ:* Harvard Univ, AB, 54, SB, 56; Ill Inst Technol, MS, 59; La State Univ, PhD(math), 63. *Prof Exp:* Instr math, Univ Ga, 62-63, asst prof, 63-68; ASSOC PROF MATH, UNIV HOUSTON, 68- *Mem:* Am Math Soc; Math Asn Am. *Res:* Topology. *Mailing Add:* Dept of Math Univ of Houston Cullen Blvd Houston TX 77004

VOBECKY, JOSEF, b Brno, Czech, Sept 29, 23; m 55; c 3. EPIDEMIOLOGY. *Educ:* Masaryk Univ, Brno, MD, 50; Postgrad Med Sch, Prague, DPH, 56, dipl epidemiol, 60; CSPQ, 74. *Prof Exp:* Epidemiologist, Czech Pub Health Serv, Prague, 50-55, head dept epidemiol, Brno, 56-62; dir dept epidemiol, Inst Epidemiol & Microbiol, Prague, 63-68; asst prof epidemiol, 69-70, assoc prof, 71-78, PROF EPIDEMIOL, MED FAC, UNIV SHERBROOKE, 78-, CHMN DEPT COMMUNITY HEALTH SCI, 78- *Concurrent Pos:* Vis prof, Fac Med, Charles Univ, Prague, 60-62; consult field proj, WHO, Mongolia, 63-65, Iraq, 66, lectr, 66-69; sr lectr, Postgrad Med Sch, Prague, 66-69. *Mem:* Int Epidemiol Asn; Am Col Prev Med; AAAS; Am Pub Health Asn; NY Acad Sci. *Res:* Epidemiology of nutrition; epidemiological surveillance; chronic disease epidemiology; environmental factors; cancer epidemiology. *Mailing Add:* Dept Community Health Sci Fac Med Univ Sherbrooke Sherbrooke PQ J1H 5N4 Can

VOCCI, FRANK JOSEPH, b Baltimore, Md, Aug 13, 24. BIOCHEMISTRY. *Educ:* Loyola Col, Md, BS, 49. *Prof Exp:* Group leader & gen chemist, Aerosol Br, 49-61, chief, Basic Toxicol Br, Toxicol Div, Edgewood Arsenal, 61-76, chief, Whole Animal Toxicol Br, Toxicol Div, 76-80, CONSULT, BUR FOODS, FOOD & DRUG ADMIN, 80- *Mem:* AAAS; Sigma Xi; Am Chem Soc; Am Indust Hyg Asn. *Mailing Add:* Bur Foods Food & Drug Admin Washington DC 20204

VOCKE, MERLYN C, b Milwaukee, Wis, Nov 17, 33; m 61; c 3. ELECTRICAL ENGINEERING. *Educ:* Valparaiso Univ, BS, 55; Univ Notre Dame, MS, 57; Univ Iowa, PhD, 71. *Prof Exp:* From instr to assoc prof, 55-76, PROF ELEC ENG, VALPARAISO UNIV, 76- *Concurrent Pos:* Consult, Naval Weapons Support Ctr. *Mem:* Inst Elec & Electronics Engrs; Am Soc Eng Educ. *Res:* Computer-aided circuit analysis; digital and analog system design. *Mailing Add:* Dept of Elec Eng Valparaiso Univ Valparaiso IN 46383

VODKIN, LILA OTT, b Laurens, SC, Dec 21, 50; m 76. PLANT MOLECULAR BIOLOGY. *Educ:* Univ SC, BS, 73, MS, 75; NC State Univ, PhD, 78. *Prof Exp:* RES GENETICIST, USDA, 78- *Mem:* Genetics Soc Am. *Res:* Gene expression in soybeans. *Mailing Add:* Seed Res Lab BARC West Beltsville MD 20705

VODKIN, MICHAEL HAROLD, b Boston, Mass, Dec 4, 42; m 75. GENETICS. *Educ:* Boston Col, BS, 64, MS, 66; Univ Ariz, PhD(genetics), 71. *Prof Exp:* Fel genetics, Cornell Univ, 71-73; asst prof biol, Univ SC, 73-79; staff fel, NIH, 79-81; MEM STAFF, MED RES INST INFECTIOUS DIS, US ARMY, 81- *Mem:* Sigma Xi; Genetics Soc Am; Am Soc Microbiol. *Res:* Genetics and biochemistry of bacillus anthracis. *Mailing Add:* Div Path USAMRIID Ft Detrick Frederick MD 21701

VOEDISCH, ROBERT W, b Ft Eustis, Va, Nov 5, 24; m 53; c 3. ORGANIC CHEMISTRY. *Educ:* Beloit Col, BS, 48. *Prof Exp:* Res & develop chemist, 50-55, group leader, 55-56, chief chemist, 56-60, tech dir, 60-67, VPRES RES & DEVELOP, LAWTER CHEM, INC, CHICAGO, 67- *Mem:* AAAS; Am Chem Soc; Fedn Socs Paint Technol; Soc Appl Spectros; Am Asn Textile Chem & Colorists. *Res:* Luminescent compounds; ink vehicles; synthetic resins; alkyds, phenolics, maleics, ketone and polyamide resins. *Mailing Add:* 9400 Normandy Ave Morton Grove IL 60053

VOEKS, JOHN FORREST, b Seattle, Wash, Aug 16, 22; m. PHYSICAL CHEMISTRY. *Educ:* Univ Wash, PhD(chem), 51. *Prof Exp:* ASSOC SCIENTIST, DOW CHEM CO, 51- *Res:* Physical chemistry of polymers. *Mailing Add:* Res Dept Dow Chem Co Walnut Creek CA 94598

VOELCKER, HERBERT B(ERNHARD), b Tonawanda, NY, Jan 7, 30; m 54; c 2. COMPUTER & SYSTEMS ENGINEERING. *Educ:* Mass Inst Technol, BS, 51, MS, 54; Imp Col, Univ London, PhD(elec eng), 61. *Prof Exp:* Lectr elec eng, Imp Col, Univ London, 60-61; from asst prof to assoc prof, 61-71, PROF ELEC ENG, UNIV ROCHESTER, 71-, DIR, PROD AUTOMATION PROJ, 72- *Concurrent Pos:* Consult, US Army Signal Corps, 58-60; consult indust, 58-; NATO fel, 67-68. *Honors & Awards:* Inst Elec & Electronics Engrs Award, 67. *Mem:* Fel Inst Elec & Electronics Engrs; Asn Comput Mach; Numerical Control Soc; Am Soc Mech Engrs; Soc Mfg Engrs. *Res:* Automation engineering for design and production in the mechanical goods industries. *Mailing Add:* Prod Automation Proj Univ of Rochester Rochester NY 14627

VOELKER, ALAN MORRIS, b Eau Claire, Wis, Aug 12, 38; m 60; c 2. SCIENCE EDUCATION. *Educ:* Wis State Univ-River Falls, BS, 59; Syracuse Univ, MS, 63; Univ Wis-Madison, PhD(sci educ), 67. *Prof Exp:* Teacher chem, physics, gen sci & math & chmn dept, High Schs, Wis, 59-64; asst prof sci educ, Ohio State Univ, 67-69; asst prof sci educ, Univ Wis-Madison & prin investr cognitive learning, Res & Develop Ctr, 69-73; ASSOC PROF & PROF SCI EDUC, COL EDUC, NORTHERN ILL UNIV, 73- *Concurrent Pos:* Mem adv bd sci educ sect, Educ Resources Info Ctr, Info Anal Ctr Sci, Math & Environ Educ, 72-76. *Mem:* Fel AAAS; Nat Sci Teachers Asn; Nat Asn Res Sci Teaching; Am Educ Res Asn. *Res:* Science concept learning; science teacher education; attitudes toward science; scientific literacy. *Mailing Add:* Gabel Hall Northern Ill Univ De Kalb IL 60115

VOELKER, C(LARENCE) E(LMER), b Two Rivers, Wis, July 6, 23; m 47; c 3. CHEMICAL ENGINEERING. *Educ:* Univ Wis, BS, 49, MS, 50. *Prof Exp:* Process control engr, Food Mach & Chem Corp, 50-52; process engr, 52-56, group leader, Process Eng Dept, 56-57, proj leader polychems, Res Dept, 57-59, from res engr to sr res engr, Process Fundamentals Res Lab, 59-64, sr process engr, Comput Res Lab, 64-65, sr process engr, Process Eng Dept, 65-68, tech expert, 68-70, SR PROCESS SPECIALIST, PROCESS ENG DEPT, DOW CHEM CO, 70- *Mem:* AAAS; Am Chem Soc; Sigma Xi; Am Inst Chem Engrs. *Res:* Heat transfer; fluid dynamics; mathematics; crystallization. *Mailing Add:* Process Eng Dept Dow Chem Co Midland MI 48640

VOELKER, RICHARD WILLIAM, b Stanton, Nebr, July 16, 36; m 61; c 4. VETERINARY PATHOLOGY. *Educ:* Kans State Univ, BS & DVM, 59; Purdue Univ, MS, 64, PhD(vet path), 69; Am Col Vet Pathologists, cert, 70. *Prof Exp:* Vet food inspector, US Army Vet Corps, 59-61; med lab officer, US Armed Forces, Europe, 61-64; instr vet path, Purdue Univ, West Lafayette, 64-68; staff pathologist, Hazleton Labs, 68-71; sect head toxicol, William S Merrell Co, 71-73; DIR PATH, HAZLETON LABS AM, 73- *Concurrent Pos:* Adj asst prof path, Med Sch, Univ Cincinnati, 71-73. *Mem:* Am Vet Med Asn; Int Acad Path; Am Col Vet Pathologists; Soc Pharmacol & Environ Pathologists; Indust Vet Asn. *Res:* Toxocologic pathology in the investigation and description of various tissue responses caused by a wide variety of chemical and pharmaceutical compounds; tumor induction in laboratory animals by a wide variety of environmental chemicals given by various routes of administration. *Mailing Add:* Hazleton Labs Am 9200 Leesburg Turnpike Vienna VA 22180

VOELKER, ROBERT ALLEN, b Palmer, Kans, Jan 24, 43; m 65. GENETICS. *Educ:* Concordia Teachers Col, Nebr, BSEd, 65; Univ Nebr, Lincoln, MS, 67; Univ Tex, Austin, PhD(zool), 70. *Prof Exp:* Asst, Univ Nebr, Lincoln, 67; NSF fel, Univ Ore, 70-71; res assoc genetics, NC State Univ, 71-73; sr staff fel, Lab Environ Mutagenesis, 76-80, RES GENETICIST LAB GENETICS, NAT INST ENVIRON HEALTH SCI, 80- *Concurrent Pos:* Vis asst prof, Dept Genetics, NC State Univ, Raleigh, 73-76. *Mem:* Genetics Soc Am; Soc Study Evolution; Sigma Xi. *Res:* Drosophila population genetics; drosophila salivary gland chromosome cytogenetics; meiotic drive in drosophila; genetic control of the structure and function of RNA ploymerase II in Drosophila. *Mailing Add:* Lab Genetics Nat Inst of Environ Health Sci Research Triangle Park NC 27709

VOELZ, FREDERICK, b Wheaton, Ill, May 22, 27; m 50; c 2. ENVIRONMENTAL ENGINEERING. *Educ:* Ill Inst Technol, BS, 51, MS, 53, PhD(physics, math), 55. *Prof Exp:* Asst, Ill Inst Technol, 51-55; proj chemist, Sinclair Res, Inc, 55-62, sr res physicist, 62-69, sr proj engr spec projs, 69-78, RES ASSOC NEW TECHNOL APPL, ATLANTIC RICHFIELD CO, 78- *Mem:* Soc Automotive Eng; Air Pollution Control Asn. *Res:* Raman and infrared spectroscopy; molecular structure; automotive exhaust emissions instrumentation and testing; ambient air and environmental technology. *Mailing Add:* Harvey Tech Ctr Atlantic Richfield Co Harvey IL 60426

VOELZ, GEORGE LEO, b Wittenberg, Wis, Oct 13, 26; m 50; c 4. OCCUPATIONAL MEDICINE. *Educ:* Univ Wis, BS, 48, MD, 50. *Prof Exp:* AEC fel indust med, 51-52; indust physician, Los Alamos Sci Lab, Univ Calif, 52-57; chief med br, Idaho Opers Off, AEC, 57-63, asst dir, Health Serv Lab, 63-67, dir, 67-70; HEALTH DIV LEADER, LOS ALAMOS SCI LAB, 70- *Concurrent Pos:* Mem, Nat Coun Radiation Protection & Measurements, 75-; ed adv, Occup Health & Safety J. *Mem:* Indust Med Asn; Am Acad Occup Med; Am Col Prev Med; Am Indust Hyg Asn; Health Physics Soc. *Res:* Occupational health problems, especially in the atomic energy industries; radiological health problems; radiobiological research and radiation dosimetry. *Mailing Add:* Health Div Los Alamos Sci Lab PO Box 1663 Los Alamos NM 87545

VOELZ, HERBERT GUSTAV HERMANN, b Kartzig, Ger, Sept 15, 20; US citizen; m 49. MICROBIOLOGY. *Educ:* Univ Greifswald, dipl biol, 56, Dr rer nat(microbiol), 59. *Prof Exp:* Sci asst, Inst Microbiol, Univ Greifswald, 56-59; sci assoc, Inst Hyg & Bact, Wernigerode, Ger, 59-60; fel microbiol, Sch Med, Univ Ind, 60-62, asst prof, 62-64; from asst prof to assoc prof, 64-72, PROF MICROBIOL, SCH MED, WVA UNIV, 72- *Concurrent Pos:* USPHS res grant, 63-72. *Mem:* Am Soc Microbiol; fel Am Acad Microbiol. *Res:* Plasma membrane-associated phospholipases in cancer biology. *Mailing Add:* Dept Microbiol WVa Univ Sch Med Morgantown WV 26505

VOET, DONALD HERMAN, b Amsterdam, Neth, Nov 29, 38; US citizen; m 65; c 2. CRYSTALLOGRAPHY, BIOCHEMISTRY. *Educ:* Calif Inst Technol, BS, 60; Harvard Univ, PhD(chem), 67. *Prof Exp:* Res assoc biol, Mass Inst Technol, 66-69; asst prof, 69-74, ASSOC PROF CHEM, UNIV PA, 74-, ASSOC CHMN DEPT, 77- *Mem:* Am Chem Soc; Am Crystallog Asn. *Res:* X-ray structural determination of molecules of biological interest such as proteins, nucleic acid model compounds, coenzymes and drugs. *Mailing Add:* Dept of Chem Univ of Pa Philadelphia PA 19004

VOET, JUDITH GREENWALD, b New York, NY, Mar 10, 41; m 65; c 2. BIOCHEMISTRY. *Educ:* Antioch Col, BS, 63; Brandeis Univ, PhD(biochem), 69. *Prof Exp:* Res assoc, Haverford Col, 72-74 & Inst for Cancer Res, 75; vis scientist, Univ Oxford, 76; lectr chem, Univ Pa, 76-77; vis asst prof, Univ Del, 77-78; ASST PROF BIOCHEM, SWARTHMORE COL, 78- *Concurrent Pos:* NIH fel, 70-72. *Mem:* Am Chem Soc. *Res:* Mechanisms of enzyme action; chemical modification of enzymes. *Mailing Add:* Dept of Chem Swarthmore Col Swarthmore PA 19081

VOGAN, ERIC LLOYD, b London, Ont, Sept 3, 24; m 51; c 3. PHYSICS. *Educ:* Univ Western Ont, BSc, 46, MSc, 47; McGill Univ, PhD(physics), 52. *Prof Exp:* Sci officer, Defense Res Telecommun Estab, Can, 52-57; Can liaison officer, Lincoln Lab, Mass Inst Technol & Air Force Cambridge Res Ctr, 57-60; sci officer, Defense Res Telecommun Estab, Can, 60-64; assoc prof physics, 64-70, PROF PHYSICS, UNIV WESTERN ONT, 70- *Mem:* Am Asn Physics Teachers; Am Geophys Union; Can Asn Physicists. *Res:* Aeronomy; physics of the upper atmosphere. *Mailing Add:* Dept of Physics Univ of Western Ont London ON N6A 5B8 Can

VOGE, MARIETTA, b Yugoslavia, July 7, 19; nat US; m 42; c 1. PARASITOLOGY. *Educ:* Univ Calif, AB, 44, MA, 46, PhD(zool), 50. *Prof Exp:* From asst to assoc zool, Univ Calif, 44-51; assoc med microbiol, 52-54, from instr to assoc prof, 54-68, PROF MED MICROBIOL, SCH MED, UNIV CALIF, LOS ANGELES, 68- *Mem:* Am Soc Parasitol; Brit Soc Parasitol; Am Soc Trop Med & Hyg; Brazilian Soc Trop Med. *Res:* Helminthology, particularly cestodes; systematics; distribution; ecology; development in vitro; anatomy of digestive tract of mammals. *Mailing Add:* Univ Calif Sch Med Los Angeles CA 90024

VOGEL, ALFRED MORRIS, b New York, NY, Mar 11, 15; m 40; c 2. CHEMISTRY, INSTRUMENTATION. *Educ:* City Col New York, BS, 34; NY Univ, MS, 48, PhD(chem), 50. *Prof Exp:* Jr chemist, US Dept Navy, 36-41; chemist, New York City Bd Transp, 41-47; asst, NY Univ, 47-49; instr, Sch Indust Technol, 49-51; from asst prof chem to prof chem, Adelphi Univ, 50-67, chmn dept, 53-67; PROF CHEM, C W POST COL, LONG ISLAND UNIV, 67-, CHMN DEPT, 74- *Mem:* Am Chem Soc. *Res:* Analytical and chemical instrumentation; methods of assay of pharmaceutical products; coordination compounds. *Mailing Add:* 77 Cedar Rd Malverne NY 11565

VOGEL, F(ERDINAND), L(INCOLN), b Philadelphia, Pa, Nov 30, 22; m 46; c 3. ELECTRONIC MATERIALS. *Educ:* Univ Pa, BS, 48, MS, 39, PhD(metall), 52. *Prof Exp:* Instr metall, Univ Pa, 50-52; mem tech staff, Bell Tel Labs, Inc, 52-59; group leader & sr engr, Semiconductor & Mat Div, Radio Corp Am, 59-60, mgr, 60-63; dir semiconductor res, Sprague Elec Co, Mass, 63-68; vis prof metall & mat sci, Univ Pa, 68-69; head surface & mat sci group, Corp Res Labs, Esso Res & Eng Co, 69-73; RES PROF ELEC ENG & SCI, UNIV PA, 73- *Concurrent Pos:* Mem, Franklin Inst; ed, Synthetic Metals. *Mem:* Am Phys Soc; Am Inst Mining, Metall & Petrol Engrs; Am Inst Elec & Electronic Engrs. *Res:* Deformation of metals; composite materials; electronic properties of materials; high electrical conductivity in graphite intercalation compounds. *Mailing Add:* Moore Sch D2 Univ Pa Philadelphia PA 19104

VOGEL, FRANCIS STEPHEN, b Middletown, Del, Sept 29, 19; m 49; c 5. PATHOLOGY. *Educ:* Villanova Col, AB, 41; Western Reserve Univ, MD, 44; Am Bd Path, dipl, 51. *Prof Exp:* From asst prof to assoc prof path, Med Col, Cornell Univ, 50-61, asst prof path in surg, 50-61; PROF PATH, MED CTR, DUKE UNIV, 61- *Concurrent Pos:* Consult, Vet Admin Hosp, New York. *Mem:* Am Soc Exp Path; Am Asn Pathologists & Bacteriologists. *Res:* Neuropathology; metabolic function of mitochondrial nucleic acids. *Mailing Add:* Dept of Path Duke Univ Med Ctr Durham NC 27710

VOGEL, GEORGE, b Prague, Czech, May 28, 24; nat US; m 50; c 2. ORGANIC CHEMISTRY. *Educ:* Prague Inst Technol, DSc(chem), 50. *Prof Exp:* Lectr chem, Univ Col, Ethiopia, 51-54; res chemist, Monsanto Chem, Ltd, Eng, 54-55; res fel, Ohio State Univ, 55-56; from asst prof to assoc prof, 56-69, PROF CHEM, BOSTON COL, 69- *Mem:* Am Chem Soc. *Res:* Heterocyclic chemistry; steric effects in conjugated systems. *Mailing Add:* Dept of Chem Boston Col Chestnut Hill MA 02167

VOGEL, GERALD LEE, b Janesville, Wis, Feb 6, 43. ANALYTICAL CHEMISTRY. *Educ:* Univ Wis-Madison, BS, 65; Georgetown Univ, MS, 70, PhD(chem), 73. *Prof Exp:* Supvr, Washington Ref Lab, 71-73, Pharmacopathics Res Lab, 73-74; PROJ LEADER, AM DENT ASN HEALTH FOUND, 74- *Mem:* Int Asn Dent Res. *Res:* Dissolution and preparation of biological calcium phosphates as it relates to dental caries. *Mailing Add:* Dept Res Unit Nat Bur Standards Washington DC 20234

VOGEL, GLENN CHARLES, b Columbia, Pa, Mar 7, 43; m 69. INORGANIC CHEMISTRY. *Educ:* Pa State Univ, University Park, BS, 65; Univ Ill, Urbana, MS, 67, PhD(inorg chem), 70. *Prof Exp:* Asst prof, 70-74, assoc prof, 74-82, PROF CHEM, ITHACA COL, 82- *Concurrent Pos:* Grants, Am Chem Soc-Petrol Res Fund, 73, NATO, 79 & Res Corp, 80. *Mem:* Sigma Xi; Am Chem Soc. *Res:* Complex formation of metalloporphyrins; transition metal complexes of oxocarbon ligands; ternary copper catechol complexes. *Mailing Add:* Dept of Chem Ithaca Col Ithaca NY 14850

VOGEL, HENRY, b New York, NY, Sept 2, 16; m 47; c 1. MICROBIOLOGY, SEROLOGY. *Educ:* La State Univ, BS, 40; NY Univ, MS, 49, PhD(biol), 56. *Prof Exp:* Bacteriologist, Jewish Mem Hosp, New York, 45-49; sr bacteriologist, Willard Parker Hosp, New York, 49-52; sr bacteriologist, Bur Labs, New York City Dept Health, 52-66, sr res scientist, 66-79. *Mem:* NY Acad Sci; Brit Soc Appl Bact; Brit Soc Gen Microbiol; Sigma Xi. *Res:* Enteric microbiology; metabolism of cold-blooded acid fast organisms; metabolism of Leptospira; serologic studies of genetic relationships and diagnosis. *Mailing Add:* 2601 Henry Hudson Pkwy New York NY 10463

VOGEL, HENRY ELLIOTT, b Greenville, SC, Sept 16, 25; m 53; c 4. SOLID STATE PHYSICS. *Educ:* Furman Univ, BS, 48; Univ NC, MS, 50, PhD(physics), 62. *Prof Exp:* From instr to assoc prof, 50-65, head dept physics, 67-71, PROF PHYSICS, CLEMSON UNIV, 65-, DEAN, COL SCI, 71- *Mem:* Am Phys Soc; Am Asn Physics Teachers. *Res:* Superconductivity; thin vacuum-deposited films; tunneling between films. *Mailing Add:* Kinard Lab Physics Rm 119 Clemson Univ Clemson SC 29631

VOGEL, HERBERT D(AVIS), b Chelsea, Mich, Aug 26, 00; m 25; c 2. CIVIL ENGINEERING. *Educ:* US Mil Acad, BS, 24; Univ Mich, CE, 33; Univ Calif, MS, 28; Tech Hochsch, Berlin, DIng, 29. *Prof Exp:* Founder & dir US Waterways Exp Sta, Corps Engrs, US Army, 30-34 & Schofield Barracks, Hawaii, 35-38, instr, Eng Sch, Ft Belvoir, Va, 38-40, instr, US Eng Dist, Pittsburgh, 40-43, dep, Australia, 44, chief staff intermediate sect, New Guinea, 44, base comdr, PI, 45, dist engr, Buffalo Dist, NY, 45-49, engr maintenance & Lt Gov, Panama Canal, 49-52, southwest div engr, Dallas, 52-54; chmn bd, Tenn Valley Authority, 54-62; engr adv, Int Bank Reconstruct & Develop, 63-67; CONSULT ENGR RESOURCE DEVELOP, 67- *Concurrent Pos:* Chmn, Ark, White, Red River Comn, 52-54; mem, Miss River Comn, 52-54; mem, Permanent Int Asn Navig Cong & nat comt & int comn, 56-64, hon mem int comn, 67-; mem, Int Comn Large Dams; mem eng comt visitors, Vanderbilt Univ, 75-80. *Mem:* Nat Acad Eng; hon mem Am Soc Civil Engrs; hon mem Soc Am Mil Engrs; Nat Soc Prof Engrs; fel Am Inst Consult Engrs. *Res:* Experimental hydraulics; structures; resource development; flood control engineering; rivers and harbor development. *Mailing Add:* 3033 Cleveland Ave NW Washington DC 20008

VOGEL, HOWARD H, JR, b New York, NY, Nov 30, 14; m 40; c 4. ZOOLOGY. *Educ:* Bowdoin Col, AB, 36; Harvard Univ, MA, 37, PhD(biol), 40. *Prof Exp:* From asst prof to assoc prof, Wabash Col, 41-48, actg head dept, 46; chmn col biol sci, Univ Chicago, 48-50; assoc biol & group leader neutron radiobiol, Argonne Nat Lab, 50-67; PROF RADIOL, PHYSIOL & BIOPHYS & HEAD RADIATION BIOL, DEPT RADIATION ONCOL, CTR HEALTH SCI, UNIV TENN, MEMPHIS, 67-, PROF RADIATION ONCOL, 73- *Concurrent Pos:* Ornithologist, Bowdoin-MacMillan Arctic Exped, 34; assoc, Roscoe B Jackson Mem Lab. *Mem:* AAAS; Am Soc Zool; assoc Am Ornith Union; assoc Arctic Int NAm; Transplantation Soc. *Res:* History of arctic aviation; social behavior of birds and mammals; skin transplantation; radiobiology; biological effects of neutrons; radiation carcinogenesis. *Mailing Add:* Dept of Radiation Oncol Univ of Tenn Ctr for Health Sci Memphis TN 38163

VOGEL, JAMES ALAN, b Snohomish, Wash, Dec 22, 35; m 59; c 3. EXERCISE PHYSIOLOGY, ENVIRONMENTAL MEDICINE. *Educ:* Wash State Univ, BS, 57; Rutgers Univ, PhD(physiol), 61. *Prof Exp:* Res physiologist, US Army Med Res & Nutrit Lab, Fitzsimons Gen Hosp, 61-67, RES PHYSIOLOGIST, US ARMY RES INST ENVIRON MED, 67-, DIR DEPT PHYSIOL, 73- *Honors & Awards:* Civilian Outstanding Performance Award, US Dept Army, 65. *Mem:* Am Physiol Soc; Am Col Sports Med. *Res:* Cardiac output physiology; exercise and physical fitness training; cardiopulmonary physiology of high altitude. *Mailing Add:* US Army Res Inst of Environ Med Natick MA 01760

VOGEL, JAMES JOHN, b Longmont, Colo, June 16, 35; m 60; c 2. BIOCHEMISTRY, NUTRITION. *Educ:* William Jewell Col, AB, 57; Univ Wis, MS, 59, PhD(biochem), 61. *Prof Exp:* Res fel dent biochem, Forsyth Dent Ctr, Harvard Univ, 61-63; res assoc biochem, Med Sch, Univ Minn, 63-67; asst mem, 67-71, ASSOC PROF, UNIV TEX DENT SCI INST, HOUSTON, 71- *Mem:* Int Asn Dent Res; Am Chem Soc. *Res:* Dietary factors involved in dental caries; nutritional and metabolic aspects of magnesium, phosphorus and fluorine with respect to skeletal tissues; microbiologic calcification; phospholipid-protein interactions in calcification. *Mailing Add:* Univ of Tex Dent Sci Inst PO Box 20068 Houston TX 77025

VOGEL, MARTIN, b Los Angeles, Calif, Mar 7, 35; m 63; c 2. ORGANIC CHEMISTRY, POLYMER CHEMISTRY. *Educ:* Calif Inst Technol, BS, 55, PhD(org chem), 61. *Prof Exp:* Asst prof org chem, Rutgers Univ, 60-65; SR RES CHEMIST, ROHM AND HAAS CO, 65- *Honors & Awards:* Otto Haas Award, 80. *Mem:* Am Chem Soc. *Res:* Organic coatings. *Mailing Add:* 550 Pine Tree Rd Jenkintown PA 19046

VOGEL, NORMAN WILLIAM, b Brooklyn, NY, May 17, 17; m 47; c 4. ZOOLOGY. *Educ:* Univ Mich, AB, 40, MS, 43; Univ Ind, PhD(zool), 56. *Prof Exp:* Asst zool, Univ Mich, 42-43; asst physiol, Vanderbilt Univ, 43-44; Lawrason Brown res fel, Saranac Lab, NY, 48-49; instr biol, Champlain Col, 49-52; asst zool, Univ Ind, 52-55; from asst prof biol to assoc prof biol, 56-66, PROF BIOL, WASHINGTON & JEFFERSON COL, 66- *Concurrent Pos:* USPHS res grant, Nat Cancer Inst, 58-59; Fulbright-Hays lectr physiol, Fac

Med, Univ Nangrahar, Afghanistan, 68-69. *Mem:* AAAS; Am Inst Biol Sci. *Res:* Role of the pituitary gland in chick growth and development, prior to hatching by accomplishing hypophysectomy through ablation of the free-head region of the early embryo. *Mailing Add:* Dept of Biol Washington & Jefferson Col Washington PA 15301

VOGEL, PAUL WILLIAM, b Swayzee, Ind, Oct 5, 19; m 48; c 2. ORGANIC CHEMISTRY. *Educ:* DePauw Univ, AB, 41; Ind Univ, PhD(org chem), 46. *Prof Exp:* Asst, Ind Univ, 41-44; res chemist, Lubrizol Corp, 45-46, res supvr, 47-50, tech asst to dir res & develop, 50-53, supvr org & anal res, 53-59, dir testing, 59-62, dir chem res, 62-78; RETIRED. *Mem:* AAAS; Am Chem Soc. *Res:* Synthetic organic chemistry; pyroxonium and pyrylium salts; organic phosphorous compounds; lubricant additives. *Mailing Add:* 1839 Caronia Dr Cleveland OH 44124

VOGEL, PETER, b Prague, Czech, Aug 12, 37. NUCLEAR PHYSICS. *Educ:* Czech Inst Technol, Prague, EngrTechPhysics, 60; Acad Sci USSR, CandSci(physics), 66. *Prof Exp:* Res fel, Joint Inst Nuclear Res, Dubna, USSR, 62-66, Nuclear Res Inst, Rez, Czech, 66-68 & Niels Bohr Inst, Copenhagen, Denmark, 68-69; res assoc, Nordic Inst Theoret Atomic Physics, Univ Bergen, 69-70; sr res fel physics, 70-75, res assoc, 75-81, SR RES ASSOC PHYSICS, CALIF INST TECHNOL, 81- *Mem:* Am Phys Soc. *Res:* Nuclear structure theory; vibrations, rotations and deformations of nuclei; intermediate energy physics, mesonic atoms, neutrions. *Mailing Add:* Phys 34 Norman Bridge Lab Physics Calif Inst of Technol Pasadena CA 91125

VOGEL, PHILIP CHRISTIAN, b Fargo, NDak, Nov 28, 41; m 66. PHYSICAL ORGANIC CHEMISTRY. *Educ:* Lawrence Univ, AB & BS, 63; Ind Univ, PhD(chem), 67. *Prof Exp:* From res assoc to sr res assoc chem, Yeshiva Univ, 67-70; asst prof chem, Col Pharmaceut Sci, Columbia Univ, 70-73; guest scientist, Max Planck Inst Chem, 73-75; res staff scientist, BASF Wyandotte Corp, 75-76, deleg Dyestuff Div, BASF Ag, 76-78, MGR TECH DEVELOP, COLORS & AUXILIARIES DIV, WYANDOTTE CORP, 78- *Mem:* Am Chem Soc. *Res:* Theory of isotope effects in organic reaction mechanisms; theory of structure of aqueous solutions. *Mailing Add:* BASF Wyandotte Corp Riverside Ave Rensselaer NY 12144

VOGEL, RALPH A, b Brooklyn, NY, June 13, 23; m 52; c 3. MICROBIOLOGY. *Educ:* Wagner Col, BS, 46; Univ Buffalo, MS, 49; Duke Univ, PhD(microbiol), 52. *Prof Exp:* Instr bact, Sch Med, Duke Univ, 52-53; from instr to asst prof, 54-76, ADJ ASSOC PROF MICROBIOL, SCH MED, EMORY 76-; MICROBIOLOGIST, VET ADMIN HOSP, 54- *Concurrent Pos:* Fel, Yale Univ, 52; instr, Ga State Col, 53- *Mem:* Fel Am Acad Microbiol; Am Soc Microbiol; Sigma Xi; NY Acad Med. *Res:* Immunology of the mycosis; pathogenesis of bacterial and mycotic diseases. *Mailing Add:* Dept of Microbiol Emory Univ Sch of Med Atlanta GA 30322

VOGEL, RICHARD CLARK, b Ames, Iowa, Jan 28, 18; m 44; c 3. PHYSICAL CHEMISTRY. *Educ:* Iowa State Univ, BS, 39; Pa State Univ, MS, 41; Harvard Univ, AM, 43, PhD(chem), 46. *Prof Exp:* Asst prof chem, Ill Inst Technol, 46-49; sr chemist, Argonne Nat Lab, 49-54, assoc dir, Chem Eng Div, 54-63, div dir, 63-73; MEM STAFF, ELEC POWER RES INST, EXXON NUCLEAR CO, INC, 73- *Mem:* Am Chem Soc; fel Am Nuclear Soc; fel Am Inst Chem Engrs. *Res:* Physical inorganic chemistry; fluorine chemistry; pyrochemical processes; separations processes; chemical problems in nuclear reactor safety. *Mailing Add:* 3412 Hillview Ave PO Box 10412 Elec Power Res Inst Palo Alto CA 94303

VOGEL, RICHARD E, b Chicago, Ill, July 7, 30; m 53; c 2. COMPUTER SCIENCE. *Educ:* Colo State Univ, BS, 53; Univ NMex, MS, 60. *Prof Exp:* Staff scientist, Los Alamos Sci Lab, 57-59; consult statist & comput, Corp Econ & Indust Res, 59-60; dir comput facil, Kaman Nuclear Div, Kaman Aircraft Corp, 60-69; PRES, DATA MGT ASSOCS INC, 69- *Concurrent Pos:* Lectr, Univ Colo, 61-; adj prof, Colo Col, 65- *Mem:* Am Meteorol Soc. *Res:* Statistics; meteorology; mathematics. *Mailing Add:* 2509 Andromeda Dr Colorado Springs CO 80906

VOGEL, STEVEN, b Beacon, NY, Apr 7, 40; m 63 & 74; c 1. ZOOLOGY, PHYSIOLOGY. *Educ:* Tufts Univ, BS, 61; Harvard Univ, AM, 63, PhD(biol), 66. *Prof Exp:* From asst prof to assoc prof, 66-79, PROF ZOOL, DUKE UNIV, 79- *Concurrent Pos:* Vis fac, Marine Biol Lab, 72 & Univ Wash Marine Lab, 79 & 81; jr fel, Harvard Univ, 64-66. *Res:* Fluid flow through and around organisms; induced flow and ventilatory processes in sponges, leaves, burrows and mounds; convective cooling. *Mailing Add:* Dept of Zool Duke Univ Durham NC 27706

VOGEL, THOMAS A, b Janesville, Wis, July 5, 37; m 60; c 3. GEOLOGY. *Educ:* Univ Wis, BS, 59, MS, 61, PhD(geol), 63. *Prof Exp:* Asst prof geol, Rutgers Univ, New Brunswick, 63-68; assoc prof, 68-74, PROF GEOL, MICH STATE UNIV, 74- *Concurrent Pos:* Vis prof, Univ SC, 74-75; vis scientist, Lawrence Livermore Nat Labs, 81-82. *Mem:* Geol Soc Am; Am Geophys Union. *Res:* Evolution of high-level silicic magma chambers; origin of batholiths; igneous rocks of Northwest Africa; coexisting mafic and silicic melts. *Mailing Add:* Dept Geol Mich State Univ East Lansing MI 48824

VOGEL, VERONICA LEE, b New York, NY, Mar 9, 43; m 69. TOXICOLOGY, ANALYTICAL CHEMISTRY. *Educ:* Univ Mich, BS, 64; NY Univ, MS, 67, PhD(phys chem), 72. *Prof Exp:* Res fel chem, NSF, Feltman Res Lab, 72-74; asst prof chem, County Col Morris, 74-75; lectr chem, Rutgers Univ, 75-79; anal chemist, Forensic Toxicol Lab, State NJ Med Examr's Off, 79-81; LAB MGR, SPEC CHEM & TOXICOL LAB, METROP PATH CLIN LABS, TETERBORO, NJ, 81- *Concurrent Pos:* Consult, Energetics Mat Lab, 74-81. *Mem:* Am Chem Soc. *Res:* Theoretical quantum chemistry, approximate molecular orbital calculations; drug analysis. *Mailing Add:* 16 Ridgewood Pkwy E Denville NJ 07834

VOGEL, WILLIS GENE, b Seward, Nebr, Nov 27, 30; m 54; c 4. SURFACE MINE REVEGETATION, RANGE SCIENCE. *Educ:* Univ Nebr, BS, 52; Mont State Col, MS, 61. *Prof Exp:* Range conservationist, Soil Conserv Serv, USDA, Idaho, 59-60, range conservationist, Forest Serv, Mo, 60-63, RANGE SCIENTIST, FOREST SERV, NORTHEASTERN FOREST EXP STA, USDA, 63- *Mem:* Soc Range Mgt; Sigma Xi. *Res:* Revegetation of coal strip mine spoils. *Mailing Add:* Northeastern Forest Exp Sta USDA Rt 2 Berea KY 40403

VOGEL, WOLFGANG HELLMUT, b Dresden, Ger, Aug 4, 30; m 61; c 1. BIOCHEMISTRY, PHARMACOLOGY. *Educ:* Dresden Tech Univ, BS, 49; Stuttgart Tech Univ, MS, 56, PhD(chem), 58. *Prof Exp:* Fel med, State Univ NY Upstate Med Ctr, 58-59; chemist, Farbwerke Hoechst, Ger, 59-61; res assoc biochem pharmacol, Col Med, Univ Ill, 61-63, instr, 63-64; vis scientist, NIH, 64-65; asst prof pharmacol, Col Med, Univ Ill, 65-67; assoc prof pharmacol, Jefferson Med Col, 67-74, prof, 74-80, prof psychiat & human behav, 76-80. *Concurrent Pos:* Med res assoc, L B Mendel Res Lab, Elgin State Hosp, 65-67. *Res:* Biochemistry of mental disorders; biochemical pharmacology; drug-enzyme-interactions; development of drug assays; neurochemical correlates of behavior. *Mailing Add:* 14 Darien Dr Cherry Hill NJ 08003

VOGELBERGER, PETER JOHN, JR, b Youngstown, Ohio, Apr 14, 32; m 54; c 4. NUCLEAR ENGINEERING. *Educ:* US Naval Acad, BS, 54. *Prof Exp:* Assoc nuclear engr, Argonne Nat Lab, 63-65; mgr tech liaison, Isotopes, Inc, 65-67, vpres & gen mgr, Energy Systs Div, Teledyne Isotopes, Inc, 68-76, PRES, TELEDYNE ENERGY SYSTS, TIMONIUM, 76- *Concurrent Pos:* Mem, Md Adv Comn Atomic Energy, 68-78. *Res:* Design, development and production of nuclear and fossil-fuel thermoelectric power systems for space and terrestrial use; electrochemical gas generators and fuel cell; radioactive waste volume reduction and solidification systems. *Mailing Add:* Teledyne Energy Systs 110 W Timonium Rd Timonium MD 21093

VOGELFANGER, ELLIOT AARON, b New York, NY, Apr 5, 37; m 58; c 2. POLYMER SCIENCE, ORGANIC CHEMISTRY. *Educ:* Columbia Univ, BA, 58; Univ Calif, Los Angeles, PhD(phys org chem), 63. *Prof Exp:* Res chemist, Esso Res & Eng Co, 63-66; group leader polymer sci, Celanese Corp, 66-74; MGR RES & DEVELOP, SOLTEX POLYMER CORP, 74- *Concurrent Pos:* Lectr, Hunter Col, 65-71. *Mem:* Am Chem Soc; Soc Plastics Engrs; Am Soc Testing & Mat. *Res:* Polymer rheology; high temperature polymers; physical organic chemistry; polyolefins research, application, development, and catalysis. *Mailing Add:* 27 Hibury Dr Houston TX 77024

VOGELHUT, PAUL OTTO, b Vienna, Austria, Dec 2, 35; m 60; c 3. BIOPHYSICS. *Educ:* Univ Calif, Berkeley, AB, 57, PhD(biophys), 62. *Prof Exp:* Asst prof bioelectronics, Univ Calif, Berkeley, 62-70; sr res physicist, 70-80, PRIN RES SCIENTIST, AMES CO, DIV MILES LABS INC, 80- *Concurrent Pos:* Consult, Electro-Neutronics, 65-68; Ames Co div, Miles Labs Inc, 69-70. *Mem:* AAAS. *Res:* Analysis of constituents of body fluids for clinical diagnosis by automated techniques. *Mailing Add:* Ames Co Div Miles Labs Inc 1127 Myrtle St Elkhart IN 46514

VOGELI, BRUCE R, b Alliance, Ohio, Nov 25, 29; m 56; c 2. MATHEMATICS. *Educ:* Mt Union Col, BS, 51; Kent State Univ, MA, 57; Univ Mich, PhD(math educ), 60. *Prof Exp:* Assoc prof math, Bowling Green State Univ, 59-65; prof math, Teachers Col, 65-76, CLIFFORD BREWSTER UPTON PROF, COLUMBIA UNIV, 76- *Concurrent Pos:* Vis prof, Lenin Inst, Moscow, USSR, 64 & Kurukshetra Univ, India, 65; consult, Ministry Educ, Chile, 66-67 & Silver Burdett Co, 60-; NSF fel; sr Fulbright lectr. *Honors & Awards:* Harold Benjamin Prize. *Mem:* Math Asn Am; Nat Coun Teachers Math. *Res:* Mathematics education; international mathematical activities. *Mailing Add:* Dept of Math Teachers Col Columbia Univ New York NY 10027

VOGELMAN, JOSEPH H(ERBERT), b New York, NY, Aug 18, 20; m 46; c 3. ELECTRONICS, BIOMEDICAL ENGINEERING. *Educ:* City Col New York, BS, 40; Polytech Inst Brooklyn, MEE, 48, DEE, 57. *Prof Exp:* Res analyst, Signal Corps Radar Lab, US Dept Army, 42, proj engr, 42-43, proj engr, Signal Corps Eng Labs, 43-44; chief test equip sect, Watson Labs, US Air Force, 44-47, chief develop br, 47-51; chief scientist gen eng, Rome Air Develop Ctr, NY, 51-52, chief electronic warfare lab, 52-55, dir commun & electronics, 55-59; vpres res & develop, Capehart Corp, 59-64; dir electronics, Chromalloy Am Corp, 64-67, gen mgr, Pocket Fone Div, 65-67, vpres, 67-73; vpres & dir, Cro-Med Bionics Corp, 68-73; vchmn bd & sr vpres, Laser Link Corp, 71-73; PRES, VOGELMAN DEVELOPMENT CO, 73-; CHIEF SCIENTIST, ORENTREICH FOUND ADVAN SCI, 73- *Concurrent Pos:* Mem, Army-Navy Radio Frequency Cable Coord Comt, 44-48; mem test equip comt, Res & Develop Bd, 48-52, chmn waveguide comt, 48-52; chmn commun tech adv comt, Air Res & Develop Command, 58-59, award, 58, consult, 59-; consult, Dept of Defense, 59-67; vpres, ACR Electronics Corp, 66-68; dir & consult, Orentreich Found Advan Sci, 63-73. *Mem:* Fel AAAS; fel Inst Elec & Electronics Engrs; Sigma Xi. *Res:* Radio frequency instrumentation; microwave theory and techniques; bio-medical instrumentation; communications; computers for medicine; biochemistry; radio immune assays; chromatography. *Mailing Add:* 48 Green Dr Roslyn NY 11576

VOGELMANN, HUBERT WALTER, b Buffalo, NY, Nov 13, 28; m 51; c 2. BOTANY. *Educ:* Heidelberg Col, BS, 51; Univ Mich, MA, 52, PhD(bot), 55. *Prof Exp:* Asst prof taxon bot, 59-62, assoc prof, 62-70, PROF BOT, UNIV VT, 70- *Mem:* Ecol Soc Am. *Res:* Ecology of mountain forests; natural areas protection. *Mailing Add:* Dept of Bot Univ of Vt Burlington VT 05401

VOGELSONG, DONALD CLAIR, physical chemistry, polymer chemistry, see previous edition

VOGH, BETTY POHL, b Georgetown, Ohio, Apr 19, 27; m 47; c 4. PHARMACOLOGY, PHYSIOLOGY. *Educ:* Tex Woman's Univ, BA, 46; Univ Fla, PhD(physiol), 64. *Prof Exp:* Res assoc physiol, 65-66, res assoc pharmacol, 66-67, asst prof, 68-74, ASSOC PROF PHARMACOL, COL MED, UNIV FLA, 74- *Res:* Physiology and pharmacology of body fluids; regulation of cerebrospinal fluid. *Mailing Add:* Dept of Pharmacol Univ of Fla Col of Med Gainesville FL 32610

VOGL, OTTO, b Traiskirchen, Austria, Nov 6, 27; nat US; m 55; c 2. POLYMER CHEMISTRY. *Educ:* Univ Vienna, PhD, 50. *Prof Exp:* Instr chem, Univ Vienna, 48-53; res assoc, Univ Mich, 53-55 & Princeton Univ, 55-56; chemist, E I du Pont de Nemours & Co, Del, 56-70; PROF POLYMER SCI ENG, UNIV MASS, AMHERST, 70- *Concurrent Pos:* Vis prof, Kyoto Univ, Osaka Univ, 68 & 80, Royal Inst Technol, Stockholm, 71, Univ Freiburg, 73, Univ Strasburg, 76 & Univ Berlin, 77; comt mem macromol chem, Nat Res Coun-Nat Acad Sci, 75-78, chmn, 78-80. *Mem:* AAAS; Am Chem Soc (treas div polymer chem, 69-72, secy gen macromolecule secretariat, 76); Austrian Chem Soc; Japanese Soc Polymer Sci. *Res:* Ionic and stereoselective polymerization; polyaldehydes; ring opening polymerization; regular copolyamides; reactions on polymers; functional polymers; biologically and ultraviolet active polymers; head to head polymers. *Mailing Add:* Dept of Polymer Sci & Eng Univ of Mass Amherst MA 01002

VOGL, RICHARD J, b Milwaukee, Wis, Jan 19, 32; m 61; c 3. BOTANY, ECOLOGY. *Educ:* Marquette Univ, BS, 53, MS, 55; Univ Wis, PhD(ecol), 61. *Prof Exp:* Instr bot, Marquette Univ, 55-56; res asst, Univ Wis, 58-61; PROF BOT, CALIF STATE UNIV, LOS ANGELES, 61- *Concurrent Pos:* Ed, Ecol Soc Am, 72-75. *Mem:* Ecol Soc Am; Wildlife Soc. *Res:* Plant and fire ecology. *Mailing Add:* Dept of Biol Calif State Univ Los Angeles CA 90032

VOGL, THOMAS PAUL, b Vienna, Austria, July 10, 29; nat US; c 3. BIOMEDICAL SCIENCE, SCIENCE POLICY & ADMINISTRATION. *Educ:* Columbia Univ, BA, 52; Univ Pittsburgh, MS, 57; Carnegie-Mellon Univ, PhD(syst sci), 69. *Prof Exp:* Sr res physicist, Res Lab, Westinghouse Elec Corp, 52-60; head infrared sect, Res Labs, Hughes Aircraft Co, 60-61; mgr optical physics, Res Labs, Westinghouse Elec Corp, 61-69, mgr optics, 69-74; prin staff officer, Assembly Life Sci, Nat Acad Sci, 74-77; exec secy, Nat Comn Digestive Dis, 77-79, NUTRIT COORDR COMT, OFF DIR, NAT INST ARTHRITIS, METAB & DIGESTIVE DIS, NIH, 79- *Concurrent Pos:* Lectr, Univ Calif, Los Angeles, 59-74; mem comt photother in newborn & subcomt bioeng aspects, Div Med, Nat Acad Sci-Nat Res Coun & chmn; adj prof radiation biophysics, Dept Radiol & Pediat, Col Physicians & Surgeons, Columbia Univ, 73-79, mem, Bioeng Inst, 75-79. *Mem:* Optical Soc Am; Environ Mutagen Soc; Am Soc Photobiol. *Res:* Optical imaging and illuminating systems; non-linear optimization; clinical applications of light; phototherapy of hyperbilirubinemia; photobiology. *Mailing Add:* 4857 Battery Lane Bethesda MD 20814

VOGT, ALBERT R, b St Louis, Mo, Apr 6, 38; c 2. PLANT PHYSIOLOGY. *Educ:* Univ Mo, BS, 61, MS, 62, PhD(forestry), 66. *Prof Exp:* Instr forestry, Univ Mo, 65-66; from asst prof tree physiol to assoc prof, 66-76, from actg assoc chmn to assoc chmn, Div Forestry, 69-75, actg chmn, 75-76, PROF TREE PHYSIOL, OHIO AGR RES & DEVELOP CTR, OHIO STATE UNIV, 76-, CHMN, DIV FORESTRY, 76- *Mem:* Am Soc Plant Physiol; Soc Am Foresters. *Res:* Physiology of tree growth and development; bud dormancy in oak; flowering of trees. *Mailing Add:* Dept of Forestry Ohio Agr R&D Ctr Ohio State Univ Wooster OH 44691

VOGT, CLIFFORD MARSHALL, organic chemistry, polymer chemistry, see previous edition

VOGT, DALE WILLIAM, animal breeding, animal genetics, see previous edition

VOGT, EDWARD G(EORGE), b Detroit, Mich, Mar 2, 19; m 41; c 3. CHEMICAL ENGINEERING. *Educ:* Tri-State Col, BS, 38; Univ Mich, MS, 41, PhD(chem eng), 46. *Prof Exp:* Control chemist, Cent Sugar Co, Ind, 39; jr chem engr, Universal Oil Prod Co, Ill, 41-43; asst, Dept Eng Res, Univ Mich, 43-46, res assoc, 46; asst prof chem eng, State Col Wash, 46-50; res engr, M W Kellogg Co, 50-54; res assoc, Universal-Cyclops Steel Corp, 54-59; opers analyst, Opers Eval Group, Off Chief Naval Opers, Washington, DC, 59-71; OPERS ANALYST, KETRON, INC, 71- *Mem:* Am Chem Soc; Opers Res Soc Am. *Res:* Friction in the flow of suspensions of granular solids in gases; liquid-liquid extraction of lube oils; vacuum melting of metals; operations research. *Mailing Add:* 4804 Randolph Dr Annandale VA 22003

VOGT, ERICH W, b Steinbach, Can, Nov 12, 29; m 52; c 5. NUCLEAR PHYSICS, THEORETICAL PHYSICS. *Educ:* Univ Man, BSc, 51, MSc, 52; Princeton Univ, PhD(physics), 55. *Prof Exp:* Nat Res Coun Can fel, Univ Birmingham, 55-56; from asst res officer to sr res officer, Atomic Energy Can Ltd, 56-65; PROF PHYSICS, UNIV BC, 65- *Concurrent Pos:* Vis assoc prof, Univ Rochester, 58-59; Nat Res Coun Can sr travelling fel, Oxford Univ, 71-72; vpres fac & student affairs, Univ BC, 75-81; chmn, Sci Coun BC, 78-80; dir, Triumf Proj, 81- *Honors & Awards:* Centennial Medal Can, 67. *Mem:* Fel Am Phys Soc; fel Royal Soc Can; Can Asn Physicists (pres, 70-71). *Res:* Theory of nuclear reactions, nuclear structure and intermediate energy physics. *Mailing Add:* Dept of Physics Univ of BC Vancouver BC V6T 1W5 Can

VOGT, FRANK CONRAD, pediatrics, deceased

VOGT, HERWART CURT, b Elizabeth, NJ, Sept 14, 29; m 58; c 2. POLYMER CHEMISTRY. *Educ:* Northwestern Univ, 52; Univ Del, MS, 54, PhD(chem), 57; Wayne State Univ, MS, 77. *Prof Exp:* Res chemist, Hercules Inc, 57-59; sr res chemist, 59-66, res assoc, 67-73, supvr, 73-77, corp toxicologist 77-79, MGR ADMIN, BASF WYANDOTTE CORP, 79- *Concurrent Pos:* Vis lectr, Oakland Univ, 66-69 & Wayne State Univ, 69-71; exchange chemist, BASF-AG, WGer, 71-73; adj prof, Upsala Col, 81- *Mem:* Am Chem Soc; AAAS; Sigma Xi. *Res:* Organic phosphorus compounds pertaining to polymers; novel halogen containing unsaturated polyesters; isocyanate and urethane chemistry; chlorine containing elastomers; research and development in noncellular urethane plastics. *Mailing Add:* Administration 100 Cherry Hill Rd Parsippany NJ 07054

VOGT, KRISTIINA ANN, b Turku, Finland, Mar 3, 49; US citizen; m 73. MICROBIAL ECOLOGY. *Educ:* Univ Tex, El Paso, BS, 71; NMex State Univ, MS, 74, PhD(biol), 75. *Prof Exp:* res assoc ecosyst, 76-80, RES ASST PROF, COL FOREST RESOURCES, UNIV WASH, 80- *Mem:* Soc Indust Microbiol; AAAS; Sigma Xi. *Res:* Physiology; decomposition and nutrient cycling; mycorrhizae and below ground root dynamics. *Mailing Add:* Col Forest Resources Univ Wash Seattle WA 98195

VOGT, LESTER HERBERT, JR, b New York, NY, Nov 9, 31. INORGANIC CHEMISTRY. *Educ:* Hofstra Univ, BA, 55; Rensselaer Polytech Inst, MS, 61, PhD(chem), 64. *Prof Exp:* Chemist, US testing Co, 55-56; res chemist, Gen Elec Res Lab, 56-62 & Res & Develop Ctr, 65-70, supvr, Advan Process Lab, Chem Prod Sect, 70-73, MGR PHOSPHORS & CHEMS ENG, QUARTZ & CHEM PROD DEPT, GEN ELEC CO, NY, 73- *Concurrent Pos:* NIH spec fel, Univ Calif, Berkeley, 64-65. *Res:* Silicones; organic semiconductors; coordination compounds; x-ray crystallography; synthetic oxygen-carrying chelates; organic and inorganic phosphors. *Mailing Add:* Quartz & Chem Prod Dept Gen Elec Co 1099 Ivanhoe Rd Cleveland OH 44110

VOGT, MOLLY THOMAS, b Lyndhurst, Eng, Apr 15, 39; div; c 2. BIOCHEMISTRY. *Educ:* Bristol Univ, BSc, 60; Univ Pittsburgh, PhD(biochem), 67. *Prof Exp:* Jr res officer, Toxicol Unit, Med Res Coun, Eng, 60-62; res asst biochem path, Sch Med, 62-63, from asst prof biochem to assoc prof, 70-78, chmn div health related prof interdisciplinary progs, 72-74, PROF BIOCHEM, SCH HEALTH RELATED PROF, UNIV PITTSBURGH, 78-, ASSOC DEAN, 77- *Concurrent Pos:* NIH fel biochem, Sch Med, Univ Pittsburgh, 67-70, Health Res Serv Found grant, 70-71; Am Coun Educ Admin intern, 74-75. *Mem:* AAAS; Am Inst Biol Scientists; Sigma Xi. *Res:* Cell metabolism in health and disease; phagocytic process; mitochondrial metabolism; biochemical effects of typical air pollutants. *Mailing Add:* Sch Health Related Professions Univ of Pittsburgh Pittsburgh PA 15261

VOGT, PETER KLAUS, b Braunau, Ger, Mar 10, 32; US citizen. BIOLOGY, VIROLOGY. *Educ:* Univ Tübingen, PhD, 59. *Prof Exp:* From asst prof to assoc prof path, Sch Med, Univ Colo, 62-67; from assoc prof to prof microbiol, Sch Med, Univ Wash, 67-71; Hastings prof, 71-77, HASTINGS DISTINGUISHED PROF MICROBIOL, SCH MED, UNIV SOUTHERN CALIF, 78-, CHMN DEPT, 80- *Concurrent Pos:* Damon Runyon cancer fel, Virus Lab, Univ Calif, Berkeley, 59-62; res grants, USPHS, 62- & Am Cancer Soc, 63-68; mem virol study sect, NIH, 67-71; mem cell biol & virol adv comt, Am Cancer Soc, 72-76. *Honors & Awards:* Vogeler Prize, Max-Planck-Soc, 76. *Mem:* Nat Acad Sci; NY Acad Sci; Am Soc Microbiol; AAAS; Genetics Soc Am. *Res:* Mechanism of neoplastic cellular transformation induced by viruses. *Mailing Add:* Dept of Microbiol Univ of Southern Calif Sch Med Los Angeles CA 90033

VOGT, PETER RICHARD, b Hamburg, Ger, June 8, 39; US citizen; m 67; c 1. MARINE GEOPHYSICS. *Educ:* Calif Inst Technol, BS, 61; Univ Wis, MA, 65, PhD(oceanog), 68. *Prof Exp:* Geophysicist, US Naval Oceanog Off, 67-75, GEOPHYSICIST, US NAVAL RES LAB, 76-77 & 78- *Concurrent Pos:* Mem staff, Univ Oslo, Norway, 77-78. *Honors & Awards:* Henry A Kaminski Award, Sci Res Soc Am. *Mem:* Am Geophys Union; fel Geol Soc Am. *Res:* Geophysical research on the constitution and history of the crust beneath the sea, especially the analysis of marine magnetic field, gravity, altimetric, and topographic anomalies and mantle hot spot phenomena as related to ocean floor (plate) movement, crustal composition and continental drift. *Mailing Add:* Code 8106 US Naval Res Lab Washington DC 20375

VOGT, ROCHUS E, b Neckarelz, Ger, Dec 21, 29; m 58; c 2. PHYSICS. *Educ:* Univ Chicago, SM, 57, PhD(physics), 61. *Prof Exp:* Res assoc cosmic rays, Univ Chicago, 61-62; from asst prof physics to assoc prof, 62-70, chmn fac, 75-77, chief scientist, Jet Propulsion Lab, 77-78, PROF PHYSICS, CALIF INST TECHNOL, 70-, CHMN DIV PHYSICS, MATH & ASTRON, 78- *Concurrent Pos:* Actg dir, Owens Valley Radio Observ, Calif, 80-81. *Mem:* Fel Am Phys Soc; Am Asn Physics Teachers; AAAS. *Res:* Cosmic rays; astrophysics. *Mailing Add:* Physics 103-33 Calif Inst of Technol Pasadena CA 91125

VOGT, STEVEN SCOTT, b Rock Island, Ill, Dec 20, 49. ASTRONOMY. *Educ:* Univ Calif, Berkeley, AB(physics) &AB(astron), 72; Univ Tex, MA, 75, PhD(astron), 78. *Prof Exp:* Res asst astron, Univ Tex, 72-78; ASST PROF & ASST ASTRONR, LICK OBSERV, UNIV CALIF, SANTA CRUZ, 78- *Mem:* Am Astron Soc; Optical Soc Am; Soc Photo-Optical Instrument Engrs. *Res:* Astronomical instrumentation; solid state imaging detectors, stellar spectroscopy. *Mailing Add:* Lick Observ Univ of Calif Santa Cruz CA 95064

VOGT, THOMAS CLARENCE, JR, b San Antonio, Tex, Sept 21, 32; m 63; c 6. PHYSICAL CHEMISTRY. *Educ:* St Mary's Univ, BS, 54, PhD(phys chem), 61. *Prof Exp:* Res chemist, Mobil Oil Corp, 57; asst, Univ Notre Dame, 57-58, fel diffusion kinetics, Radiation Proj, 58-61; assoc chemist, 61-80, RES ASSOC, FIELD RES LAB, MOBIL RES & DEVELOP CORP, 80- *Mem:* Sigma Xi; Am Chem Soc; Soc Petrol Eng. *Res:* diffusion and recombination of free radicals in liquid systems; effects of high pressure on reaction rates; chemical stimulation of petroleum production wells; in-situ uranium leaching; hydraulic fracturing of subsurface formations; economics of well treatments; in situ coal gasification. *Mailing Add:* Mobil Res & Develop Corp PO Box 900 Dallas TX 75221

VOGT, WILLIAM G(EORGE), b McKeesport, Pa, June 1, 31; m 64; c 2. ELECTRICAL ENGINEERING. *Educ:* Univ Pittsburgh, BS, 53, MS, 57, PhD(elec eng), 62. *Prof Exp:* Res engr, Eng Res Div, Univ Pittsburgh, 53-60; engr, Adv Systs & Eng Div, Westinghouse Elec Corp, 61; assoc prof elec eng, 62-68, PROF ELEC ENG, UNIV PITTSBURGH, 68- *Concurrent Pos:* NASA res assoc, Univ Pittsburgh, 63-64; consult, Astrionics Labs, Marshall Space Flight Ctr, NASA, Ala, 64-67, Fecker Systs Div, Owens-Ill, Pa, 68-74, Contraves-Goerz, 78- & TASC, 78-; NSF fel, 61-62 & NSF sci fac fel, 75-76. *Mem:* Inst Elec & Electronics Engrs; Am Soc Mech Engrs; Instrument Soc Am; Sigma Xi. *Res:* Control and optimization theory; societal systems; electric power systems; microcomputer systems; modeling and simulation. *Mailing Add:* Dept of Elec Eng 348 BEH Univ of Pittsburgh Pittsburgh PA 15261

VOHR, JOHN H, b Laconia, NH, Nov 27, 34; m 56; c 4. MECHANICAL ENGINEERING. *Educ:* Harvard Univ, AB, 56; Columbia Univ, MS, 58, PhD(mech eng), 64. *Prof Exp:* Res engr, Mech Tech Inc, NY, 62-68, supvr anal mech, 68-69; from asst prof to assoc prof mech eng, Rensselaer Polytech Inst, 69-73, chmn mech eng curric, 70-73; SR ENGR, GEN ELEC CO, 73- *Concurrent Pos:* Consult, Gen Elec Co, 69- *Honors & Awards:* Best Paper of Year Award, Lubrication Div, Am Soc Mech Engrs, 67. *Mem:* Am Soc Mech Engrs; Am Soc Lubrication Engrs. *Res:* Analytical studies of hydrodynamic and hydrostatic bearings; heat transfer analysis and two-phase flow studies; experimental studies of flow stability phenomena. *Mailing Add:* 1400 Dean St Schenectady NY 12309

VOHRA, PRAN NATH, b Gwaliar, India, June 11, 19. NUTRITION, BIOCHEMISTRY. *Educ:* Univ Panjab, India, MSc, 42; Wash State Univ, MS, 54; Univ Calif, Davis, PhD(nutrit), 59. *Prof Exp:* Res asst chem, Sci & Indust Res Orgn, India, 42-49; int trainee fermentations, Joseph E Seagram & Sons, Ky, 49-50; specialist nutrit, Dept Poultry Husb, Univ Calif, Davis, 58-59; asst, BO&C Mills, Eng, 59-60; specialist poultry, US AID India, 61-62; asst res nutritionist, Dept Poultry Husb, 62-70, assoc prof avian sci, 70-74, PROF AVIAN SCI, UNIV CALIF, DAVIS, 74- *Honors & Awards:* Award, Am Feed Mfrs Asn. *Mem:* Poultry Sci Asn; Am Inst Nutrit; Brit Biochem Soc; Brit Nutrit Soc. *Res:* Trace elements in nutrition; improvement of nutrition in developing countries; comparative nutrition of avian species; nutrition evaluation of cereals and legumes. *Mailing Add:* Dept Avian Sci Univ Calif Davis CA 95616

VOHS, PAUL ANTHONY, JR, b Kansas City, Kans, Jan 19, 31; m 53; c 5. ZOOLOGY. *Educ:* Kans State Univ, BS, 55; Univ Southern Ill, MA, 58; Iowa State Univ, PhD, 64. *Prof Exp:* Proj leader, Coop Proj, Ill Dept Conserv, Ill Natural Hist Surv & Southern Ill Univ, 55-58; res assoc, Coop Wildlife Res Proj, Univ Southern Ill, 59-61; res asst, Coop Wildlife Res Unit, Iowa State Univ, 61-62, instr zool & entom, 63-64, asst prof zool, 64-68, assoc prof wildlife biol, 68; assoc prof wildlife ecol, Ore State Univ, 68-73, prof & exten wildlife specialist, Coop Exten Serv & Dept Fisheries & Wildlife, 73-74; prof wildlife & fisheries sci & head dept, SDak State Univ, Brookings, 74-76; leader, Okla Coop, Wildlife Res Unit, Okla State Univ, Fish & Wildlife Serv, Stillwater, 76-80; SUPVR, COOPR WILDLIFE RES UNITS, US DEPT INTERIOR-FISH & WILDLIFE SERV, WASHINGTON, DC, 80- *Mem:* AAAS; Wilson Ornith Soc; Wildlife Soc; Am Soc Mammal; Ecol Soc Am. *Res:* Vertebrate ecology; response of birds and mammals to manipulations of habitat; serology; genetics, biology and ecology of wild ungulates. *Mailing Add:* Off Coopr Res Units US Dept Interior Fish & Wildlife Serv Washington DC 20240

VOICHICK, MICHAEL, b Yonkers, NY, May 28, 34; m 60; c 3. MATHEMATICS. *Educ:* Oberlin Col, BA, 57; Brown Univ, PhD(math), 62. *Prof Exp:* Res instr math, Dartmouth Col, 62-64; from asst prof to assoc prof, 64-73, PROF MATH, UNIV WIS-MADISON, 73- *Mem:* Am Math Soc; Math Asn Am. *Res:* Function theory. *Mailing Add:* Dept of Math Univ of Wis Madison WI 58706

VOIGE, WILLIAM HUNTLEY, b Pittsburgh, Pa, Sept 15, 47. BIOCHEMISTRY. *Educ:* Mich State Univ, BS, 69; Case Western Reserve Univ, PhD(biochem), 75. *Prof Exp:* Instr chem, St Olaf Col, 74-75; ASST PROF CHEM, JAMES MADISON UNIV, 75- *Mem:* Am Chem Soc; AAAS. *Res:* Computer-aided instruction in biochemistry; peptidases. *Mailing Add:* Dept Chem James Madison Univ Harrisonburg VA 22807

VOIGHT, BARRY, b Yonkers, NY, Dec 17, 37; m 59; c 2. GEOLOGY. *Educ:* Univ Notre Dame, BS, 59 & 60, MS, 61; Columbia Univ, PhD(struct geol), 65. *Prof Exp:* Asst prof eng geol, 64-70, assoc prof, 70-78, PROF GEOL, PA STATE UNIV, 78- *Concurrent Pos:* vis prof, Delft Technol Inst, 72, Univ Toronto, 73 & Univ Calif, Santa Barbara, 81. *Mem:* Am Soc Civil Eng; Asn Eng Geol; Geol Soc Am; Int Soc Rock Mech; Am Acad Mech. *Res:* Stress measurements; residual stresses in rocks; fault mechanics; engineering geology; rock mechanics; mechanics of landslides; geology of Iceland; geology of Yellowstone Park area. *Mailing Add:* Dept Geosci Pa State Univ University Park PA 16802

VOIGT, CHARLES FREDERICK, b Woodside, NY, Dec 17, 42; m 62; c 3. ORGANIC CHEMISTRY. *Educ:* Univ SFla, Tampa, BA, 65; Duke Univ, PhD(org chem), 70. *Prof Exp:* Assoc indexer org chem, 70-71, sr assoc ed macromolecular chem, 71-73, sr ed appl chem, 73-79, ASST MGR CHEM TECHNOL, CHEM ABSTR SERV, OHIO STATE UNIV, 79- *Mem:* Am Chem Soc. *Res:* Heterocyclic chemistry; polymers; applied chemistry. *Mailing Add:* Chem Abstr Serv Dept 60 Ohio State Univ PO Box 3012 Columbus OH 43210

VOIGT, EVA-MARIA, b Dortmund, WGer, Feb 2, 28; Can citizen. PHYSICAL CHEMISTRY, MOLECULAR PHYSICS. *Educ:* McMaster Univ, BSc, 53, MSc, 54; Univ BC, PhD(phys chem), 63. *Prof Exp:* Head res sect, Aylmer Foods, Inc, 55-56; lectr chem, Mt Allison Univ, 56-57; fel phys chem, Univ Calif, Berkeley, 63-65; asst prof, 66-69, assoc prof, 69-79, PROF CHEM, SIMON FRASER UNIV, 79- *Mem:* AAAS; Am Chem Soc; Am Phys Soc; Chem Inst Can; Can Inst Phys. *Res:* Molecular spectroscopy; charge-transfer interactions; energy transfer. *Mailing Add:* Dept Chem Simon Fraser Univ Burnaby BC U5A 1S6 Can

VOIGT, GARTH KENNETH, b Merrill, Wis, Jan 17, 23; m 46; c 3. SOILS, PLANT NUTRITION. *Educ:* Univ Wis, BS, 48, MS, 49, PhD(soils), 51. *Prof Exp:* From instr to asst prof soils, Univ Wis, 51-55; from asst prof to prof, 55-67, actg dean, Sch Forestry, 70-71 & 75-76, dir admis, 70-75, dir grad studies, Dept Forestry, 71-75, MARGARET K MUSSER PROF FOREST SOILS, YALE UNIV, 67- *Concurrent Pos:* Collabr, Lake States Forest Exp Sta, US Forest Serv, 54-60. *Mem:* Am Soc Plant Physiol; Soil Sci Soc Am; Am Soc Agron. *Res:* Relationships between soil and the growth of plants. *Mailing Add:* Yale Univ Sch Forestry New Haven CT 06511

VOIGT, GERD-HANNES, b Germany; m 75. MAGNETO-HYDRODYNAMICS, SPACE PHYSICS. *Educ:* Brunswick Tech Univ, Dipl, 70, PhD(physics), 75. *Prof Exp:* Scientific asst teach & res, Tech Univ Brunsick, 70-75, Univ Darmstadt, 75-80; ASST RES SCIENTIST, RICE UNIV, 80- *Concurrent Pos:* Mem magnetospheric working group, Int Asn Geomagnetism & Aeronomy, 78- *Mem:* Am Geophys Union; Ger Geophys Soc. *Res:* Theory of planetary magnetospheres; development of computer codes for earth's magnetosphere; development of numerical methods for solving non linear equations in magneto-hydrodynamics; space plasma physics. *Mailing Add:* Space Phys & Astron Rice Univ Houston TX 77251

VOIGT, JOHN WILBUR, b Sullivan, Ind, July 6, 20; m 43; c 2. PLANT ECOLOGY. *Educ:* Univ Nebr, PhD, 50. *Prof Exp:* From asst prof to assoc prof, 50-60, dean gen studies div, 62-75, PROF BOT, SOUTHERN ILL UNIV, CARBONDALE, 60-, ASSOC DEAN COL SCI, 80- *Mem:* Soc Range Mgt; Sigma Xi. *Res:* Geography of southern Illinois vascular plants; vegetation of southern Illinois; prairie and pasture research. *Mailing Add:* Rte 4 Carbondale IL 62901

VOIGT, PAUL WARREN, b Ann Arbor, Mich, Mar 20, 40; m 63; c 3. PLANT BREEDING. *Educ:* Iowa State Univ, BS, 62; Univ Wis, MS, 64, PhD(agron), 67. *Prof Exp:* Res geneticist, Southern Great Plains Field Sta, 67-74, res geneticist, 74-80, SUPVR RES GENETICIST & RES LEADER, GRASSLAND, SOIL & WATER RES LAB, SCI & EDUC AGR RES SERV, USDA, 80- *Concurrent Pos:* Assoc ed, Crop Sci, 80-82. *Mem:* Am Soc Agron; Crop Sci Soc Am; Soc Range Mgt; AAAS; Am Forest & Grassland Coun. *Res:* Forage grass breeding and genetics. *Mailing Add:* Grassland Soil & Water Res Lab PO Box 748 Temple TX 76503

VOIGT, ROBERT GARY, b Olney, Ill, Dec 21, 39; m 62; c 1. NUMERICAL ANALYSIS. *Educ:* Wabash Col, BA, 61; Purdue Univ, West Lafayette, MS, 63; Univ Md, College Park, PhD(math), 69. *Prof Exp:* Res assoc, Comput Sci Dept, Univ Md, 69-70, vis asst prof, 70-71; mathematician, Naval Ship Res & Develop Ctr, Washington, DC, 71-73; ASST DIR, INST COMPUT APPLNS IN SCI & ENG, 73- *Mem:* Soc Indust & Appl Math; Asn Comput Mach; Am Math Soc; AAAS; Inst Elec & Electronic Engrs. *Res:* Numerical analysis for parallel and vector computers and the application of micro processors to scientific computing. *Mailing Add:* ICASE MS-132 C NASA-Langley Res Ctr Hampton VA 23665

VOIGT, ROBERT LEE, b Hebron, Nebr, Nov 23, 24; m 51; c 4. PLANT BREEDING. *Educ:* Univ Nebr, BS, 49, MS, 55; Iowa State Univ, PhD(crop breeding), 59. *Prof Exp:* Instr soybeans, Iowa State Univ, 55-59; from asst prof & asst plant breeder to assoc prof & assoc plant breeder, 59-69, PROF PLANT SCI & PLANT BREEDER, AGR EXP STA, UNIV ARIZ, 69- *Concurrent Pos:* Ed, Sorghum Newsletter, Sorghum Improvement Conf NAm, 72- *Mem:* Am Soc Agron; Crop Sci Soc Am; Nat Asn Cols & Teachers Agr; Coun Agr Sci & Technol. *Res:* Crop breeding; forage and grain sorghum; soybeans. *Mailing Add:* Dept of Plant Sci Univ of Ariz Tucson AZ 85721

VOIGT, WALTER, b Havana, Cuba, Feb 26, 38; US citizen; m 61; c 3. BIOCHEMISTRY, ENDOCRINOLOGY. *Educ:* Univ Villanueva, Cuba, MS, 60; Univ Miami, PhD(biochem), 68. *Prof Exp:* Res assoc skin biochem, 69-70, asst prof dermat, 70-74, ASSOC PROF PATHOL & ONCOL, SCH MED, UNIV MIAMI, 74- *Concurrent Pos:* Fel bile acid metab, Sch Med, Univ Miami, 68-69, Am Cancer Soc grant, 70-71, Nat Cancer Inst grant, 72-75. *Mem:* AAAS; Brit Biochem Soc; Am Chem Soc; Endocrine Soc; Am Fedn Clin Res. *Res:* Mechanism of androgen action and prostatic neoplasia; enzymes of bile acids and steroid metabolism; biochemistry of the skin; membrane electron transport; cancer. *Mailing Add:* Dept of Pathol Univ of Miami Sch of Med Miami FL 33152

VOISARD, WALTER BRYAN, b Dayton, Ohio, Dec 14, 25; m 46; c 4. MECHANICAL ENGINEERING. *Educ:* Univ Cincinnati, BSME, 50. *Prof Exp:* Proj engr, Haines Designed Prod Co, 50-53, proj engr & chief eng, McCauley Industrial Corp, 53-60, CHIEF ENGR, MCCAULEY ASSESSORY DIV, CESSNA AIRCRAFT CO, 60- *Concurrent Pos:* Consult, 68- *Mem:* Soc Automotive Engrs; Am Inst Aeronaut & Astronaut; Soc Air Safety Invest. *Res:* Developmental activity associated with aircraft propellers, propeller deicing, governors and synchrophasers and aircraft wheels and brakes. *Mailing Add:* 1072 Grange Hall Rd Dayton OH 45340

VOITLE, ROBERT ALLEN, b Parkersburg, WVa, May 12, 38; m 75; c 4. POULTRY PHYSIOLOGY. *Educ:* Univ WVa, BS, 62, MS, 64; Univ Tenn, PhD(physiol), 69. *Prof Exp:* From asst prof physiol to assoc prof, Univ Fla & from asst poultry physiologist to assoc poultry physiologist, 69-79; prof physiol & head, Dept Poultry Indust, Calif Polytech State Univ, 79-81; DEAN, SCH AGR, FORESTRY & BIOL SCI, AUBURN UNIV, 81- *Mem:* Poultry Sci Asn. *Res:* Environmental and reproductive physiology with special emphasis on the effect of nutrition and photoperiod; breeding and genetics, especially radiation effects. *Mailing Add:* Sch Agr Forestry & Biol Sci Auburn Univ Auburn AL 36849

VOJNOVICH, THEODORE, b Weirton, WVa, Oct 7, 32; m 58; c 2. CERAMIC ENGINEERING. *Educ:* Iowa State Univ, BS, 59, MS, 61, PhD(ceramic eng), 67. *Prof Exp:* Mgt trainee, Weirton Steel Co Div, Nat Steel Corp, 59-60; planning engr, Western Elec Co, 61-64; SR ENGR, RES LABS, WESTINGHOUSE ELEC CO, 67- *Mem:* Am Ceramic Soc; Nat Inst

Ceramic Engrs; Am Soc Metals. *Res:* Electronic and magnetic properties of materials; high temperature properties of oxides and alloys; materials processing including sintering, chemical vapor deposition and sputtering. *Mailing Add:* 3318 Hermar Dr Murrysville PA 15668

VOKES, EMILY HOSKINS, b Monroe, La, May 21, 30; m 59. INVERTEBRATE PALEONTOLOGY, MALACOLOGY. *Educ:* Tulane Univ, La, BS, 60, MS, 62, PhD(paleont), 67. *Prof Exp:* Cur paleont, Dept Geol, 57-74, assoc prof, 73-81, PROF GEOL, TULANE UNIV, 81-, CHMN DEPT, 74- *Concurrent Pos:* Lectr geog, Tulane Univ, 69-, assoc ed, Tulane Studies Geol & Paleont, 70-; vis prof, Univ Rio Grande do Sul, Brazil, 71- *Mem:* Am Malacol Union; Paleont Soc; Malacol Soc London; Paleont Res Inst. *Res:* Systematic paleontology and zoology of Cenozoic Gastropoda, including both fossil and recent members. *Mailing Add:* Dept Geol Tulane Univ New Orleans LA 70118

VOKES, HAROLD ERNEST, b Windsor, Ont, June 27, 08; nat US; m 32 & 59; c 4. STRATIGRAPHY, INVERTEBRATE PALEONTOLOGY. *Educ:* Occidental Col, BA, 31; Univ Calif, PhD(paleont), 35. *Prof Exp:* Hon fel paleont, Yale Univ, 35-36; asst geologist, State Geol Surv, Ill, 37; from asst cur to assoc cur invert paleont, Am Mus Natural Hist, 37-43, actg chmn dept invert, 43; geologist, US Geol Surv, 43-45; from assoc prof to prof geol, Johns Hopkins Univ, 45-56; prof, 56-72, chmn dept, 57-67 & 70-71, W R Irby prof, 72-77, EMER PROF GEOL, TULANE UNIV, 77- *Concurrent Pos:* Guggenheim fel, Am Univ Beirut, 40; geologist, US Geol Surv, PI, 52-53; vis prof, Univ Rio Grande do Sul, Brazil, 71; mem, Int Comn Zool Nomenclature; trustee, Paleont Res Inst, 72- *Mem:* Fel Geol Soc Am (vpres, 52); Am Asn Petrol Geologists; Paleont Soc (secy, 40-49, pres, 51); Am Malacological Union. *Res:* Cretaceous and Tertiary stratigraphy and molluscan paleontology; fossil and recent pelecypoda. *Mailing Add:* Dept of Geol Tulane Univ New Orleans LA 70118

VOLANTE, RALPH PAUL, b Nelson, Pa, Aug 10, 49; m 75. ORGANIC CHEMISTRY. *Educ:* Pa State Univ, BS, 71; Harvard Univ, MA, 73, PhD(org chem), 76. *Prof Exp:* Fel org chem, Cornell Univ, 76-77; SR RES CHEMIST ORG CHEM, MERCK & CO, 77- *Mem:* Am Chem Soc. *Res:* Synthetic organic chemistry, reaction processes and mechanisms; new synthetic methods. *Mailing Add:* 22 Hawthorne Lane East Windsor NJ 08520

VOLAVKA, JAN, b Prague, Czech, Dec 29, 34; m 64. PSYCHIATRY, ELECTROPHYSIOLOGY. *Educ:* Charles Univ, Prague, BA & MD, 59; Czech Acad Sci, PhD(med sci), 65. *Prof Exp:* Intern internal med, Psychiat Hosp, Horni Berkovice, Czech, 59-60, resident psychiat, 60-63; resident psychiatrist, Psychiat Res Inst, Prague, 63-66; electroencephalographer, London Hosp, Eng, 66-67; resident psychiatrist, Psychiat Res Inst, Prague, 67-68; fel neurophysiol, Max Planck Inst Psychiat, 68-69; asst prof, New York Med Col, 69-73, assoc prof psychiat, 73-76; PROF PSYCHIAT, INST PSYCHIAT, UNIV MO, 76- *Concurrent Pos:* Prin investr, Nat Inst Drug Abuse grant, 73-76. *Mem:* Soc Biol Psychiat; Am Electroencephalog Soc. *Res:* Psychopharmacology; EEG; drug addiction; experimental design; statistics. *Mailing Add:* Inst Psychiat Univ Mo 5400 Arsenal St St Louis MO 63139

VOLBORTH, ALEXIS, b Viipuri, Finland, July 11, 24; nat US; m 47; c 7. GEOCHEMISTRY, ANALYTICAL CHEMISTRY. *Educ:* Univ Helsinki, PhC, 50, PhLic & PhD(geol, mineral), 54. *Prof Exp:* Res asst, Geol Surv, Finland, 50, field asst, 52; asst, Inst Technol, Finland, 50-51; field geologist, Finnish Mineral Co, 53; sr asst geol, Univ Helsinki, 53-54; traveling res fel, Outokumpu Found, 54-55 & Calif Inst Technol, 55-56; from asst mineralogist to mineralogist, Nev Mining Anal Lab, Univ Nev, Reno, 56-68, res assoc & consult, Desert Res Inst, 61-62, assoc prof, Univ, 63, prof, 64-68, mem radioactivity safety bd, 64-66; Killam vis prof geol, Dalhousie Univ, 68-71, Killam res prof, 71-72; vis prof, Lunar Sci Inst, Univ Houston, 72-73; vis res chemist, Univ Calif, Irvine, 73-75; prof geol & chem, NDak State Univ, 75-78; prof geol & scientist, Nuclear Radiation Ctr, Wash State Univ, 78-79; PROF GEOCHEM & CHEM, MONT TECH, BUTTE, MONT, 79- *Concurrent Pos:* Australian Acad Sci sr fel, 65; J S Guggenheim Mem Found fel, 65-66; adj prof geol, Mackay Sch Mines, Univ Nev, Reno, 69-73; prin investr, Stoichiometry Study of Lunar Rocks, NASA, 72-73; Consult, US AEC, 61-63, NASA, 65-73, Anaconda Co, 68 & Johns Manville Corp, Chevron, 80- *Honors & Awards:* White Cross, Finnish Chem Soc, 55. *Mem:* Fel Mineral Soc Am; fel Am Inst Chemists; Am Chem Soc; Am Nuclear Soc; Soc Econ Geologists. *Res:* Geochemistry and analytical chemistry of complex systems, mainly nondestructive instrumental neutron activation and x-ray, fluorescence analysis of major and trace elements; oxygen stoichiometry in rocks, minerals, chemicals and industrial products; mineralogy of and deficiency of oxygen in lunar rocks and fines; nondestructive analysis of coal and lignite. *Mailing Add:* Dept Chem & Geochem Montana Tech Butte MT 59701

VOLBRECHT, STANLEY GORDON, b Lodi, Calif, Sept 12, 23; m 45; c 4. MINING GEOLOGY. *Educ:* Col of the Pac, BA, 53; Stanford Univ, MS, 62. *Prof Exp:* Explor geologist, Am Copper Co, 54-55; instr geol, Stockton Col, 56-61; from asst prof to assoc prof, 61-70, PROF GEOL, UNIV OF THE PAC, 70-, CHMN DEPT GEOL & GEOG, 66- *Mem:* Nat Asn Geol Teachers; Geol Soc Am. *Res:* Economics. *Mailing Add:* Dept of Geol & Geog Univ of the Pac Stockton CA 95204

VOLCANI, BENJAMIN ELAZARI, b Ben-Shemen, Israel, Jan 4, 15; m 48; c 1. MICROBIOLOGY, BIOCHEMISTRY. *Educ:* Hebrew Univ, MSc, 36, PhD, 41. *Prof Exp:* Vis scientist microbiol, Inst Tech, Delft Univ, 37-38 & chem, State Univ Utrecht, 38-39; mem staff, Sieff Res Inst, Weizmann Inst, 39-58; PROF MICROBIOL, SCRIPPS INST OCEANOG, UNIV CALIF, 59- *Concurrent Pos:* Res fel, Univ Calif, Berkeley, 45-46, res assoc biochem, 56-59; res fel microbiol, Hopkins Marine Sta, Stanford Univ, 46-47 & Calif Inst Technol, 47; res fel biochem, Univ Wis, 48; res assoc, Pasteur Inst, Paris, 51; vis prof, Univ Col, Welsh Nat Sch Med, Cardiff, Wales, UK, 73-74. *Mem:* Am Soc Cell Biol; Am Soc Microbiol; Soc Gen Microbiol; Brit Biochem Soc; AAAS. *Res:* Microbial metabolism and ecology; antimetabolites; bacterial pigments; halophilic microorganisms; biochemistry and ultra-fine structure of the diatoms; siliceous organisms and dinoflagellates; silicon metabolism; mineralization in biological systems; role of silicon in life processes and pathogenicity. *Mailing Add:* Scripps Inst of Oceanog Univ of Calif La Jolla CA 92093

VOLCHOK, HERBERT LEE, geochemistry, see previous edition

VOLCKMANN, RICHARD PETER, geology, see previous edition

VOLD, BARBARA SCHNEIDER, b Oakland, Calif, Jan 3, 42. BIOCHEMISTRY, MICROBIOLOGY. *Educ:* Univ Calif, Berkeley, BA, 63; Univ Ill, MS, 64, PhD(cell biol), 67. *Prof Exp:* NIH fel biol, Mass Inst Technol, 67-69; assoc microbiol, Scripps Clin & Res Found, 69-76; MEM STAFF BIOMED RES DEPT, SRI INT, 77- *Concurrent Pos:* Nat Inst Gen Med Sci career develop award, 71-76; consult, Physiol Chem Study Sect, NIH, 73-77. *Mem:* Am Soc Microbiol; Am Soc Biol Chem. *Res:* Structure and function of transfer ribonucleic acids; changes in nucleic acids during development; antibodies to modified nucleosides. *Mailing Add:* Biomed Res Dept 333 Ravenswood Ave Menlo Park CA 94025

VOLD, CARL LEROY, b McVille, NDak, Dec 9, 32; m 61; c 2. SOLID STATE PHYSICS, METALLURGY. *Educ:* Concordia Col, Moorhead, Minn, BA, 54; Iowa State Univ, MS, 59. *Prof Exp:* Jr scientist, Ames Lab, Iowa State Univ, 54-56; RES PHYSICIST, US NAVAL RES LAB, 59- *Mem:* Am Soc Metals; Am Crystallog Asn; Sigma Xi. *Res:* Application of x-ray diffraction techniques to the study of defects in metals; energetics of solid-liquid and solid-solid interfaces in pure metals; crystalline anisotrophy; dislocation energetics. *Mailing Add:* Code 6320 Mat Sci & Technol Div Naval Res Lab Washington DC 20375

VOLD, MARJORIE JEAN, b Ottawa, Ont, Oct 25, 13; US citizen; wid; c 3. COLLOID CHEMISTRY. *Educ:* Univ Calif, BS, 34, PhD(chem), 36. *Prof Exp:* Jr res assoc chem, Stanford Univ, 37-41; res assoc & lectr, 41-58, adj prof, 58-73, EMER PROF CHEM, UNIV SOUTHERN CALIF, 73- *Concurrent Pos:* Res chemist, Union Oil Co Calif, 42-46; Guggenheim Mem fel, State Univ Utrecht, 53-54. *Honors & Awards:* Garvan Medal, Am Chem Soc, 67. *Mem:* Am Chem Soc; Royal Soc Chem; Int Asn Colloid-Interface Scientists; AAAS. *Res:* Association colloids; mesomorphic phases; gels and other colloidal solids; stability of emulsions, foams, films and suspensions; adsorption; rheology; computer simulation of colloidal processes. *Mailing Add:* 17465 Plaza Animado 144 San Diego CA 92128

VOLD, REGITZE ROSENØRN, b Copenhagen, Denmark, July 2, 37; US citizen; m 72. NUCLEAR MAGNETIC RESONANCE, PHYSICAL CHEMISTRY. *Educ:* Tech Univ Denmark, MS, 60, Lic Techn(org chem), 62. *Prof Exp:* Lectr org chem, Tech Univ Denmark, 62; fel chem, Univ NMex, 62-64; staff fel magnetic resonance, NIH, 65-71; RES ASSOC MAGNETIC RESONANCE, UNIV CALIF, SAN DIEGO, 71- *Concurrent Pos:* Fel, NIH, 68-69; guest worker, Nat Bur Standards, 69-71; lectr chem, Univ Calif, San Diego, 72-74; mem bd trustees, Exp Nuclear Magnetic Resonance Conf, 74-78 & 81-84, treas, 75-78, chairwoman, 83; assoc ed, J Am Chem Soc, 77-79. *Mem:* Am Chem Soc; AAAS. *Res:* Nuclear magnetic resonance as used in study of molecular dynamics and liquid structure by means of relaxation in complex spin systems. *Mailing Add:* 14092 Rue Saw Remo Del Mar CA 92014

VOLD, ROBERT DONALD, colloid chemistry, deceased

VOLD, ROBERT LAWRENCE, b Los Angeles, Calif, Sept 20, 42; m 71. CHEMICAL PHYSICS. *Educ:* Univ Calif, Berkeley, BS, 63; Univ Ill, Urbana, MS, 65, PhD(chem), 66. *Prof Exp:* From asst prof to assoc prof, 68-80, PROF CHEM, UNIV CALIF, SAN DIEGO, 80- *Concurrent Pos:* A P Sloan fel, 72-74. *Mem:* Am Inst Physics; Am Chem Soc. *Res:* Nuclear magnetic resonance; relaxation mechanisms; theory and applications of pulsed nuclear magnetic resonance techniques. *Mailing Add:* 14092 Rue San Remo Del Mar CA 92093

VOLDENG, ALBERT NELSON, b Wellington, Kans, Nov 25, 38; m 61; c 2. MEDICINAL CHEMISTRY. *Educ:* Univ Kans, BS, 60, PhD(med chem), 64. *Prof Exp:* Asst prof pharmaceut chem, 64-68, assoc prof med chem, 68-73, chmn dept, 73-77, PROF MED CHEM, COL PHARM, UNIV ARK FOR MED SCI, 73- *Mem:* Am Chem Soc; Am Acad Clin Toxicol; Am Acad Pharm Sci; Am Asn Cols Pharm. *Mailing Add:* Col of Pharm Univ Ark Little Rock AR 72201

VOLENEC, FRANK JERRY, virology, biochemistry, see previous edition

VOLESKY, BOHUMIL, b Prague, Czech, Oct 29, 39; m 67. BIOCHEMICAL ENGINEERING, WATER POLLUTION CONTROL. *Educ:* Prague Tech Univ, MESc, 62; Univ Western Ont, PhD(biochem eng), 71. *Prof Exp:* Proj engr, Cent Res Inst Food Indust, 63-66; res assoc food eng, Prague Tech Univ, 66-67; res asst biochem eng, Univ Western Ont, 67-70, teaching & res fel, Fanshawe Col Arts & Technol, 70-72, lectr, 72-73; ASSOC PROF BIOCHEM ENG, MCGILL UNIV, 73- *Concurrent Pos:* Consult, M M Dillon Consults & Planners, Ont, 71-72, L G L Consult, Que, 73-78 & Can Federal Govt, 80-; vis prof chem eng, Univ PR, Mayaquez, 81- *Mem:* Am Chem Soc; Chem Inst Can; Can Soc Chem Engrs; Eng Inst Can. *Res:* Biotechnology fermentation process engineering and optimization; enzyme applications; biochemical production of combustible gases and industrial solvents; biosorbent recovery of nuclear fuel and metallic elements; single cell protein production; industrial water and air pollution control; environmental studies. *Mailing Add:* Dept of Chem Eng McGill Univ 3480 Univ St Montreal PQ H3A 2A7 Can

VOLGENAU, LEWIS, b Buffalo, NY, Nov 30, 40; m 69; c 2. PAPER CHEMISTRY. *Educ:* Syracuse Univ, BE, 61; Inst Paper Chem, MS, 65, PhD(paper chem), 69. *Prof Exp:* Engr res & develop, Riegel Paper, 61-63; engr pulp & paper, Champion Int, 69-72; MGR RES & DEVELOP, BETZ LABS, INC, 72- *Mem:* Tech Asn Pulp & Paper Indust. *Res:* Corrosion, scale and foam control in aqueous systems; development of biocides and specialty chemical formulations. *Mailing Add:* PO Box 4300 The Woodlands TX 77380

VOLICER, LADISLAV, b Prague, Czech, May 21, 35; m 72; c 1. PHARMACOLOGY, CARDIOVASCULAR DISEASES. *Educ:* Charles Univ, Prague, MD, 59; Czech Acad Sci, PhD(pharmacol), 64. *Prof Exp:* Resident med, Hosp Jindr Hradec, 59-61; instr pharmacol, Sch Pediat, Charles Univ, Prague, 61-65; vis assoc, Nat Heart Inst, Md, 65-66; res assoc & lectr, Inst Pharmacol, Czech Acad Sci, 66-68; res asst prof, Sch Med, Univ Munich, 68-69; from asst prof to assoc prof, 69-77, PROF PHARMACOL, SCH MED & GRAD SCH, BOSTON UNIV, 77-, ASST PROF MED, 75-; CLIN PHARMACOLOGIST, GERIAT RES EDUC CLIN CTR, VET ADMIN HOSP, BEDFORD, 80- *Concurrent Pos:* Asst vis physician, Boston City Hosp, 75- *Mem:* Soc Neurosci; Am Soc Pharmacol & Exp Therapeut; Res Soc Alcoholism. *Res:* Pharmacology of hypertension; pharmacology of alcoholism and aging. *Mailing Add:* Dept Pharmacol Boston Univ Boston MA 02118

VOLIN, RAYMOND BRADFORD, b Kalispell, Mont, May 22, 43; m 64. PLANT PATHOLOGY, PLANT BREEDING. *Educ:* Mont State Univ, BS, 66, MS, 68, PhD(plant path), 71. *Prof Exp:* Trainee agron, Mont State Univ, 66-68, res asst plant path, 68-71; asst prof, 71-77, ASSOC PROF PLANT PATH, AGR RES & EDUC CTR, UNIV FLA, 77- *Mem:* Am Soc Hort Sci; Am Phytopath Soc; Am Soc Crop Sci. *Res:* Genetic improvement of field and vegetable crops; physiological relationship and genetic interaction between plant hosts and plant disease organisms. *Mailing Add:* Dept Plant Path Univ Fla 18905 SW 380 St Homestead FL 33031

VOLK, BOB GARTH, b Auburn, Ala, July 13, 43; m 66; c 4. SOIL CHEMISTRY. *Educ:* Ohio State Univ, BA, 65, MS, 67; Mich State Univ, PhD(soil chem), 70. *Prof Exp:* Asst prof soil chem & asst soil chemist, 70-73, ASSOC PROF SOIL SCI, UNIV FLA & ASSOC SOIL CHEMIST, AGR RES & EDUC CTR, BELLE GLADE, 73- *Mem:* Am Soc Agron. *Res:* Organic soil chemistry; metal-organic interactions; subsidence; acid precipetation. *Mailing Add:* Dept Soil Sci 2169 McCarty Hall Univ of Fla Gainesville FL 32611

VOLK, MURRAY EDWARD, b Cleveland, Ohio, Aug 23, 22; m 49; c 3. ORGANIC CHEMISTRY, RADIOCHEMISTRY. *Educ:* Oberlin Col, BA, 43; Univ Chicago, MS, 48; Temple Univ, PhD(chem), 53. *Prof Exp:* Assoc chemist, Nuclear Instrument & Chem Corp, 53-55; pres, Volk Radiochem Co, 55-65; mkt mgr res prod, Miles Labs, 66-69; PRES, ISOLAB INC, 69- *Mem:* AAAS; Am Chem Soc; Am Asn Clin Chem; Soc Nuclear Med. *Res:* Application of isotopes to biological and chemical research; preparation of radioactive pharmaceuticals; liquid chromatography applied to clinical diagnostic problems. *Mailing Add:* Isolab Inc Drawer 4350 Akron OH 44321

VOLK, RICHARD JAMES, b Tela, Honduras, Nov 5, 28; m 51; c 3. PLANT NUTRITION. *Educ:* Purdue Univ, BS, 50, MS, 51; NC State Univ, PhD(soil chem), 54. *Prof Exp:* Res specialist, Crops Div, Biol Warfare Labs, Ft Detrick, Md, 54-56; from asst prof to assoc prof, 56-66, PROF SOIL SCI, NC STATE UNIV, 66- *Concurrent Pos:* Grants, NSF, 62-64 & 78-80, Am Potash Inst, 63-66 & res contract, USDA, 65-68. *Honors & Awards:* Co-recipient Campbell Award, Am Inst Biol Sci, 65. *Mem:* Am Soc Plant Physiol; Soil Sci Soc Am; Crop Sci Soc Am; Am Soc Agron. *Res:* Application of mass spectrometry and stable isotopes to plant nutrition and biochemistry; absorption and metabolism of ammonium and nitrate nitrogen by plants; regulatory role of mineral nutrition in photosynthesis and respiration. *Mailing Add:* Dept Soil Sci NC State Univ Raleigh NC 27650

VOLK, THOMAS LEWIS, b Dayton, Ohio, Nov 4, 33; m 61; c 4. HUMAN PATHOLOGY, ENDOCRINOLOGY. *Educ:* Univ Dayton, BS, 55; Marquette Univ, MD, 59. *Prof Exp:* Instr path, Ohio State Univ, 65-66; asst prof, Univ Kans, 66-67; asst prof path, Univ Calif, Davis, 68-72; DIR LABS, KAWEAH DELTA DIST HOSP, 72- *Concurrent Pos:* NIH path training grant, 63-65; Am Cancer Soc adv clin fel, 65-66; consult, Vet Admin Hosp, Kansas City, Mo, 67-68 & Sacramento County Hosp, Calif, 68-72. *Mem:* AMA; Int Acad Path; Am Asn Path & Bact. *Res:* Ultrastructural-functional relationships of steroidogenesis in the adrenal cortex and placenta, ovary and testis; ultrastructural changes in the adrenal cortex and placenta, produced by drugs inhibiting steroidogenesis. *Mailing Add:* Kaweah Delta Dist Hosp 400 W Mineral King Visalia CA 93277

VOLK, VERIL VAN, b Montgomery, Ala, Nov 18, 38. SOIL CHEMISTRY. *Educ:* Ohio State Univ, BS, 60, MS, 61; Univ Wis, PhD(soils), 66. *Prof Exp:* Proj assoc soils, Univ Wis, 66; asst prof, 66-74, assoc prof, 74-80, PROF SOILS, ORE STATE UNIV, 80- *Mem:* Am Soc Agron; Weed Sci Soc Am. *Res:* Ion exchange and soil acidity interactions; waste utilization on soils. *Mailing Add:* Dept of Soil Sci Ore State Univ Corvallis OR 97330

VOLK, WESLEY AARON, b Mankato, Minn, Nov 23, 24; m 45; c 2. MICROBIOLOGY. *Educ:* Univ Wash, BS & BS(food technol), 48, MS, 49, PhD, 51. *Prof Exp:* From asst prof to assoc prof, 51-64, PROF MICROBIOL, SCH MED, UNIV VA, 64- *Concurrent Pos:* NIH spec fel, 62-63; spec fel, Max Planck Inst Immunobiol, 69-70. *Mem:* Am Soc Microbiol; Am Soc Biol Chemists. *Res:* Carbohydrate metabolism; structure and function of endotoxins; monoclonal antibodies; virus neutralization. *Mailing Add:* Dept of Microbiol Univ of Va Sch of Med Charlottesville VA 22908

VOLKAN, VAMIK, b Nicosia, Cyprus, Dec 13, 32; US citizen; m; c 4. PSYCHIATRY, PSYCHOANALYSIS. *Educ:* Univ Ankara, MD, 56; Wash Psychoanal Inst, grad, 71; bd cert psychoanal, 73. *Prof Exp:* Staff physician, NC State Hosp, 61-63; from instr to assoc prof, 63-72, PROF PSYCHIAT, SCH MED, UNIV VA, 72-, DIR BLUE RIDGE HOSP DIV, 78- *Concurrent Pos:* Clin instr, Sch Med, Univ NC, 61-63. *Mem:* Am Psychoanal Asn; fel Am Psychiat Asn; Int Psychoanal Asn; Int Soc Polit Psychol. *Res:* Psychotherapy of schizophrenia; pathological grief reactions; psycho-history; psycho-politics. *Mailing Add:* Blue Ridge Hosp Div Univ of Va Charlottesville VA 22901

VOLKER, EUGENE JENO, b Sopron, Hungary, May 13, 42; US citizen. ORGANIC CHEMISTRY. *Educ:* Univ Md, BS, 64; Mass Inst Technol, MS, 67; Univ Del, PhD(chem), 70. *Prof Exp:* Asst prof, 69-75, assoc prof, 75-79, PROF CHEM, SHEPHERD COL, WVA, 79- *Mem:* Am Chem Soc. *Res:* Chemical education. *Mailing Add:* Dept of Chem Shepherd Col Shepherdstown WV 25443

VOLKER, JOSEPH FRANCIS, b Elizabeth, NJ, Mar 9, 13; m 37; c 3. BIOCHEMISTRY, DENTISTRY. *Educ:* Ind Univ, DDS, 36; Univ Rochester, AB, 38, MS, 39, PhD(biochem), 41; FRCS, 61; FRCS(I), 73. *Hon Degrees:* DSc, Univ Med Sci, Bangkok, 67, Ind Univ, 70, Univ Ala, 70, Col Med & Dent NJ, 73, Georgetown Univ, 78, Fairleigh Dickinson Univ, 78; Dr Odontol, Univ Lund, 68; Dr, Louis Pasteur Univ, 72, DS, Univ Rochester, 75. *Prof Exp:* Dent res, Mountainside Hosp, NJ, 36-37; asst prof dent, Sch Med & Dent, Univ Rochester, 41-42; prof clin dent, Sch Dent, Tufts Col, 42-47, dean, 47-49; dean, Sch Dent, Univ Ala, Birmingham, 48-62, dir res & grad study, 55-65, vpres health affairs, 62-66, vpres, Birmingham Affairs & dir med ctr, 66-68, exec vpres univ, 68-69, pres univ, 69-76; CHANCELLOR, UNIV ALA SYST, 76- *Concurrent Pos:* Mem, Unitarian Med Teaching Mission, Czech, 46, Ger, 48; specialist, US Dept State, Thailand, 51-; dir, Ariz Med Sch Study, 60-61; mem, Inst Med, Nat Acad Sci, 71; mem bd regents, Nat Libr Med, 73-77; hon prof, Fed Univ Rio de Janeiro, 77. *Honors & Awards:* Mem, Order of White Lion, Czech, 46; Comdr, Order of Crown, Thailand, 59; Comdr, Order of the Falcon, Repub Iceland, 69. *Mem:* AAAS; Soc Exp Biol & Med; Int Asn Dent Res; Sigma Xi; hon mem Stomatol Soc Czech. *Res:* Dental caries; mineral metabolism; oral physiology of carbohydrates. *Mailing Add:* Univ Ala Syst PO Box BT University AL 35486

VOLKERT, WYNN ARTHUR, b St Louis, Mo, Apr 6, 41; m 67; c 3. RADIOCHEMISTRY, RADIOBIOLOGY. *Educ:* St Louis Univ, BS, 63; Univ Mo-Columbia, PhD(chem), 68. *Prof Exp:* NASA fel, 67-69, asst prof, 69-72, ASSOC PROF RADIOL SCI & BIOCHEM, UNIV MO-COLUMBIA, 72- *Concurrent Pos:* NSF grant, Univ Mo-Columbia, 73-; consult, Vet Admin Hosp, Columbia, 73- *Mem:* Radiation Res Soc; Biophys Soc; Soc Exp Biol & Med; Am Asn Physicists in Med; Soc Nuclear Med. *Res:* Photochemistry of tryptophan; chemistry of Tc-99m macrocyclic-nitrogen compounds. *Mailing Add:* Dept of Radiol Univ of Mo Med Ctr Columbia MO 65201

VOLKIN, ELLIOT, b Mt Pleasant, Pa, Apr 23, 19; m 47; c 2. BIOCHEMISTRY. *Educ:* Pa State Col, BS, 42; Duke Univ, MA, 45, PhD(biochem), 47. *Prof Exp:* Res assoc biochem, Duke Univ, 47-48; sci dir biochem, 48-65, SR RES SCIENTIST, OAK RIDGE NAT LAB, 65- *Concurrent Pos:* Prof, Univ Tenn, 77- *Mem:* Fel AAAS; Am Chem Soc; Am Soc Biol Chem; Am Soc Microbiol; Am Soc Cell Biol. *Res:* Biochemical and biophysical studies of nucleic acids and nucleoproteins. *Mailing Add:* Biol Div Oak Ridge Nat Lab Oak Ridge TN 37830

VOLKMAN, ALVIN, b Brooklyn, NY, June 10, 26; m 47; c 5. PATHOLOGY, IMMUNOLOGY. *Educ:* Union Col, BS, 47; Univ Buffalo, MD, 51; Oxford Univ, DPhil, 63. *Prof Exp:* Asst prof path, Columbia Univ, 60-66; from asst mem to assoc mem, Trudeau Inst, 66-77; assoc chmn dept, 77-80, PROF PATH, SCH MED, EAST CAROLINA UNIV, 77- *Concurrent Pos:* Arthritis & Rheumatism Found fel, 52-54; researcher to sr researcher path, Peter Bent Brigham Hosp; Am Cancer Soc scholar, 61-62; adj assoc prof path, Sch Med, NY Univ, 69-; chmn IMS study sect, NIH, 75- *Mem:* Am Asn Immunol; AAAS; Am Soc Hemat; Am Thoracic Soc; NY Acad Sci. *Res:* Experimental pathology related to the origin and production of white blood cells and their roles in inflammation and immunological processes. *Mailing Add:* Dept of Path East Carolina Univ Sch of Med Greenville NC 27834

VOLKMANN, KEITH ROBERT, b Milwaukee, Wis, May 30, 42; m 65; c 1. MICROBIOLOGY. *Educ:* Univ Rochester, BA, 65, PhD(microbiol), 73; Ga Sch Dent, DMD, 76. *Prof Exp:* Res asst virol, Med Ctr, Univ Rochester, 68-73; ASST PROF ORAL BIOL, MED COL, GA SCH DENT, 76- *Mem:* Int Asn Dent Res. *Res:* Penetration of oral antigens into oral mucosa and connective tissue; effect of endotoxins on the human periodontium. *Mailing Add:* Dept of Oral Biol/Microbiol 1120 15th St Augusta GA 30901

VOLKMANN, ROBERT ALFRED, b Pittsburgh, Pa, Aug 21, 45; m 79; c 1. ORGANIC CHEMISTRY. *Educ:* Lafayette Col, AB, 67; Univ Pittsburgh, PhD(org chem), 72. *Prof Exp:* Res assoc, Stanford Univ, 72-74; RES SCIENTIST ORG CHEM, PFIZER INC, 74- *Concurrent Pos:* Instr, Conn Col, 76- *Mem:* Am Chem Soc. *Res:* Development of novel methodology for the design and or synthesis of biologically active molecules. *Mailing Add:* Pfizer Inc Cent Res Groton CT 06340

VOLKOFF, GEORGE MICHAEL, b Moscow, Russia, Feb 23, 14; Can Citizen; m 40; c 3. THEORETICAL PHYSICS. *Educ:* Univ BC, BA, 34, MA, 36; Univ Calif, PhD(theoret physics), 40. *Hon Degrees:* DSc, Univ BC, 45. *Prof Exp:* Asst prof physics, Univ BC, 40-43; assoc res physicist, Montreal Lab, Nat Res Coun, Can, 43-45, res physicist & head theoret physics br, Atomic Energy Proj, Que & Ont, 45-46; head, Dept Physics, Univ BC, 61-72, prof, 46-79, dean, 72-79, EMER DEAN UNIV BC, 79- *Concurrent Pos:* Ed, Can J Physics, 50-56; mem, Nat Res Coun Can, 69-75. *Honors & Awards:* Mem, Order of the Brit Empire, 46. *Mem:* Fel AAAS; fel Am Phys Soc; Am Asn Physics Teachers; fel Royal Soc Can; Can Asn Physicists (vpres, 61-62, pres, 62-63). *Res:* Theoretical nuclear physics; neutron diffusion; nuclear magnetic and quadrupole resonance. *Mailing Add:* 1776 Western Parkway Vancouver BC V6T 1V3 Can

VOLKOV, ANATOLE BORIS, b San Francisco, Calif, Oct 29, 24; m 50; c 2. NUCLEAR PHYSICS. *Educ:* Univ NC, BS, 48; Univ Wis, MS, 50, PhD(physics), 53. *Prof Exp:* Longwood fel, Univ Del, 53-55; asst prof physics, Univ Miami, 58-59; sr lectr, Israel Inst Technol, 59-62; res intermediate scientist, Weizmann Inst, 62-63; Ford Found fel, Niels Bohr Inst, Copenhagen, Denmark, 63-64; from asst prof to assoc prof, 64-68, PROF PHYSICS, McMASTER UNIV, 68- *Mem:* Fel Am Phys Soc; Can Asn Physicists. *Res:* Theoretical physics, especially low energy nuclear physics and nuclear deformations. *Mailing Add:* Dept Physics McMaster Univ Hamilton ON L8S 4K1 Can

VOLKSEN, WILLI, b Gitter, Ger, Mar 9, 50; m 72; c 1. POLYMER CHEMISTRY, MATERIALS SCIENCE. *Educ:* NMex Inst Mining & Technol, BS, 72; Univ Lowell, PhD(polymer chem), 75. *Prof Exp:* Fel polymer chem, Calif Inst Technol, 75-76; sr scientist, Jet Propulsion Lab, 76-77; MEM RES STAFF POLYMER CHEM, IBM CORP, 77- *Mem:* Am Chem Soc. *Res:* Synthesis of new and novel polymeric materials including polyelectrolytes and polymers of high temperature stability. *Mailing Add:* IBM Corp Res Div 5600 Cottle Rd San Jose CA 95193

VOLL, MARY JANE, b Baltimore, Md, June 29, 33. BACTERIAL GENETICS. *Educ:* Loyola Col, BA, 55; Johns Hopkins Univ, MSc, 61; Univ Pa, PhD(microbiol), 64. *Prof Exp:* Staff fel microbiol, NIH, 64-66, USPHS fel, 66-67, microbiologist, 67-69; res assoc biol, Johns Hopkins Univ, 69-71; asst prof microbiol, 71-76, ASSOC PROF MICROBIOL, UNIV MD, COLLEGE PARK, 76- *Mem:* Am Soc Microbiol. *Res:* Homospecific and heterospecific gene transfer in enteric bacteria; environmental mutagenesis; extrachromosomal elements in vibrio species. *Mailing Add:* Dept of Microbiol Univ of Md College Park MD 20742

VOLLAND, LEONARD ALLAN, b Cleveland, Ohio, Apr 26, 37; m 63; c 2. PLANT ECOLOGY. *Educ:* Univ Idaho, BS, 59; Ore State Univ, MS, 63; Colo State Univ, PhD(quant ecol), 74. *Prof Exp:* Forester natural resources, 59-66, plant ecologist, 66-73, QUANT ECOLOGIST, US FOREST SERV, 73- *Mem:* Soc Am Foresters; Soc Range Mgt. *Res:* Plant community ecology and its application to natural resource management. *Mailing Add:* US Forest Serv PO Box 3623 Portland OR 97208

VOLLE, ROBERT LEON, b Houston, Pa, June 2, 30; m 52; c 5. PHARMACOLOGY. *Educ:* WVa Wesleyan Col, BS, 53; Univ Kans, PhD(pharmacol), 59. *Prof Exp:* From instr to assoc prof pharmacol, Sch Med, Univ Pa, 60-65; prof, Sch Med, Tulane Univ, 65-68; PROF PHARMACOL, SCH MED, UNIV CONN, 68- *Concurrent Pos:* Marsh fel pharmacol, Sch Med, Univ Pa, 59-60, Pa Plan scholar, 60-63; USPHS career develop award, 63-65. *Mem:* Fel AAAS; Am Soc Pharmacol & Exp Therapeut; Soc Neurosci. *Res:* Neuropharmacology. *Mailing Add:* Dept of Pharmacol Univ of Conn Sch of Med Farmington CT 06032

VOLLENWEIDER, RICHARD A, b Zurich, Switz, June 27, 22; m 65. LIMNOLOGY. *Educ:* Univ Zurich, dipl biol, 46, PhD(biol), 51. *Prof Exp:* Teacher undergrad schs, Lucern, Switz, 49-54; fel limnol, Ital Hydrobiol Inst, Palanza, Italy, 54-55 & Swiss Swed Res Coun, Uppsala, 55-56; field expert limnol & fisheries, UNESCO Dept Agr, Egypt, 57-59; res assoc limnol, Ital Hydrobiol Inst, Pallanza, 59-66; consult water pollution, Orgn Econ Coop Develop, Paris, France, 66-68; chief limnologist & head fisheries res bd, 68-70, chief, Lakes Res Div, 70-73, SR SCIENTIST, CAN CENTRE INLAND WATERS, 73- *Concurrent Pos:* Res asst Mc Master Univ, Hamilton, Ont, 78:; consult, Pan Am Health Orgn, Venezuela, 77-80 & Argentina, 80- *Honors & Awards:* Int Award, Premio Cervia/Ambiente, 78. *Mem:* Int Asn Ecol; Int Asn Theoret & Appl Limnol; Int Asn Great Lakes Res. *Res:* Inland water research; biological communities; water chemistry and physics; eutrophication; water pollution. *Mailing Add:* Can Ctr Inland Waters Box 5050 Burlington ON L7R 4A6 Can

VOLLMAR, ARNULF R, b Pluderhausen, Ger, Apr 15, 28. ORGANIC CHEMISTRY. *Educ:* Univ Heidelberg, dipl chem, 55, PhD(org chem), 57. *Prof Exp:* Res assoc, Univ Heidelberg, 57-58; fel, Univ Calif, Los Angeles, 58-60; res chemist, Chevron Res Corp, Calif, 60-64; assoc prof, 65-74, PROF CHEM, CALIF STATE POLYTECH UNIV, POMONA, 74- *Concurrent Pos:* NSF res grant, 69. *Mem:* Am Chem Soc. *Res:* Chemistry of tetrazole ethers and isocyanide. *Mailing Add:* Dept of Chem Calif State Polytech Univ Pomona CA 91768

VOLLMER, ERWIN PAUL, b New York, NY, Jan 16, 06; m 34; c 2. PHYSIOLOGY. *Educ:* Dartmouth Col, AB, 29; NY Univ, MS, 39, PhD(physiol), 41. *Prof Exp:* Bacteriologist, Calco Chem Co Div, Am Cyanamid Co, 37; asst instr biol, NY Univ, 41-42; tutor, Brooklyn Col, 42-43; physiologist, US Naval Med Inst, 47-56; chief endocrinol, Cancer Chemother Nat Serv Ctr, 56-66; chief endocrine eval br, Gen Labs & Clins & exec secy breast cancer task force, Nat Cancer Inst, Bethesda, 66-74; RETIRED. *Mem:* AAAS; Endocrine Soc; NY Acad Sci. *Res:* Physiology of resistance to infection; endocrine factors in hemopoiesis; endocrine etiology and chemotherapy in cancer. *Mailing Add:* 7202 44th St Chevy Chase MD 20815

VOLLMER, JAMES, b Philadelphia, Pa, Apr 19, 24; m 46; c 3. PHYSICS. *Educ:* Union Col, BS, 45; Temple Univ, MA, 51, PhD(physics), 56; Harvard Univ, advan mgt prog, 71. *Prof Exp:* Instr physics, Temple Univ, 46-51; res engr, Indust Div, Honeywell Inc, 51-59; engr appl res, Radio Corp Am, 59, group leader appl plasma physics, 59-63, mgr appl physics, 63-66, mgr appl res, 66-68, dir, Advan Technol Labs, 68-72, gen mgr, Palm Beach Div, 72-74, div vpres & gen mgr, 74-75, div vpres & gen mgr, Govt Commun Systs Div, 75-76, div vpres & gen mgr, Govt Systs Div, 76-79, GROUP VPRES, RCA CORP, 79- *Concurrent Pos:* Lectr, Temple Univ, 57-59; adj prof, Drexel Inst Technol, 64-66; chmn session on low noise technol, Int Conf Commun, 66. *Mem:* Fel AAAS; fel Inst Elec & Electronics Engrs; Am Phys Soc. *Res:* Infrared properties of materials; plasma physics; quantum electronics; microsonics; lasers; photosensors; radiometry. *Mailing Add:* Govt Systs Div Bldg 108-110 RCA Corp Moorestown NJ 08057

VOLLMER, REGIS ROBERT, b Wilkinsburg, Pa, Aug 20, 46; m 67; c 2. CARDIOVASCULAR PHARMACOLOGY, ANTIHYPERTENSIVE DRUGS. *Educ:* St Vincent Col, Latrobe, Pa, BA, 68; Univ Houston, PhD(pharmacol), 75. *Prof Exp:* Res scientist, Squibb Inst Med Res, 75-77; ASST PROF PHARMACOL, SCH PHARM, UNIV PITTSBURGH, 77- *Concurrent Pos:* Prin investr, NIH grant, 81-; mem, Am Heart Asn. *Mem:* Am Soc Pharmacol & Exp Therapeut; AAAS. *Res:* Cardiovascular pharmacology with specific focus upon the role of dietary sodium and its influence on the sympathetic nervous system control of cardiovascular function relating to hypertensive disease. *Mailing Add:* Dept Pharmacol & Toxicol Sch Pharm Univ Pittsburgh Pittsburgh PA 15261

VOLLUM, HOWARD, b 1913; US citizen; m. ENGINEERING. *Educ:* Univ Portland, BA, 36. *Prof Exp:* Mem staff, Murdock Radio & Appliance Co, 36-41; FOUNDER, CHMN & CHIEF EXEC OFFICER, TEKTRONIX, INC, 46- *Concurrent Pos:* Dir, Pac Power & Light Co. *Mem:* Nat Acad Eng. *Mailing Add:* Tektronix Inc PO Box 500 Beaverton OR 97077

VOLMAN, DAVID H, b Los Angeles, Calif, July 10, 16; m 44; c 3. PHYSICAL CHEMISTRY. *Educ:* Univ Calif, Los Angeles, AB, 37, AM, 38; Stanford Univ, PhD(chem), 40. *Prof Exp:* Asst chem, Univ Calif, Los Angeles, 37-38, res chemist, Nat Defense Res Comt Proj, 41-42; asst chem, Stanford Univ, 38-39; instr chem & jr chemist, Exp Sta, Univ Calif, 40-41; res chemist, Off Sci Res & Develop, Northwestern Univ, 41-45 & Univ Ill, 45-46; from asst prof & asst chemist to assoc prof & assoc chemist, Exp Sta, 46-56, chmn dept, 74-80, PROF CHEM, UNIV CALIF, DAVIS, 56- *Concurrent Pos:* Guggenheim fel, Harvard Univ, 49-50. *Mem:* Am Chem Soc; Int-Am Photochem Soc. *Res:* Photochemistry; kinetics; chemistry of the atmosphere. *Mailing Add:* Dept of Chem Univ of Calif Davis CA 95616

VOLOSHIN, ARKADY S, b Kishinev, USSR, Aug 7, 46. ENGINEERING MECHANICS. *Educ:* Leningrad Polytech Inst, USSR, dipl, 69; Tel-Aviv Univ, Israel, PhD(mech), 78. *Prof Exp:* Sr res officer non destructive testing res, Inst Non-Destructive Testing, 69-70; asst exp stress anal, Tel-Aviv Univ, 73-78, fel biomech, 78-79; ASST PROF EXP STRESS ANAL & BIOMECH, IOWA STATE UNIV, 79- *Mem:* Soc Exp Stress Anal. *Res:* Biomechanics of gait and impulse wave propagation through human locomotor system; photoelasticity through digital image analysis--application to fracture mechanics; interaction of stress waves and defects in solids; composite materials. *Mailing Add:* 203 Lab Mech Dept Eng Sci & Mech Iowa State Univ Ames IA 50011

VOLPE, ANGELO ANTHONY, b New York, NY, Nov 8, 38; m 65. ORGANIC CHEMISTRY, POLYMER CHEMISTRY. *Educ:* Brooklyn Col, BS, 59; Univ Md, MS, 62, PhD(org chem), 66. *Hon Degrees:* ME, Stevens Inst Technol, 75. *Prof Exp:* Res chemist, US Naval Ord Lab, 61-66; from asst prof to prof chem, Stevens Inst Technol, 66-77, actg head dept chem & chem eng, 74-75; chmn dept, 77-80, PROF CHEM, EAST CAROLINA UNIV, 77-, DEAN, COL ARTS & SCI, 80- *Mem:* Am Chem Soc; Sigma Xi. *Res:* Correlation of polymer properties to molecular structure; synthesis and mechanisms of formation and degradation of thermally stable polymers; monomer synthesis; synthesis and study of biopolymers; educational administration. *Mailing Add:* Col Arts & Sci East Carolina Univ Greenville NC 27834

VOLPE, ERMINIO PETER, b New York, NY, Apr 7, 27; m 55; c 3. ZOOLOGY. *Educ:* City Col New York, BS, 48; Columbia Univ, MA, 49, PhD(zool), 52. *Prof Exp:* Asst zool, Columbia Univ, 48-51; instr biol, City Col New York, 51-52; from asst prof to assoc prof zool, Newcomb Col, Tulane Univ, 52-60, chmn dept, Col, 54-64, chmn dept, Univ, 64-66, assoc dean, Grad Sch, 67-69, prof, 60-81, chmn dept, 69-81; PROF BASIC MED SCI, SCH MED, MERCER UNIV, 81- *Concurrent Pos:* Mem steering comt, Biol Sci Curric Study, 66-69; consult comn undergrad educ biol sci, NSF, 67-70; US Nat comnr, UNESCO, 68-72; mem exam comt, Col Entrance Exam Bd, Princeton Univ, 69-; chmn advan placement test biol, Educ Testing Serv, 75-81; ed, Am Zoologist, Am Soc Zoologists, 76-81. *Mem:* Fel AAAS; Genetics Soc Am; Soc Study Evolution; Am Soc Zoologists (pres, 81); Soc Syst Zool. *Res:* Embryology, genetics and evolution of amphibians; transplantation immunity and tolerance in anurans. *Mailing Add:* Sch Med Mercer Univ Macon GA 31207

VOLPE, GERALD T, b New York, NY, Feb 15, 35; m 57; c 2. ELECTRICAL ENGINEERING. *Educ:* City Col New York, BEE, 57, MEE, 61; NY Univ, EngScD, 64. *Prof Exp:* Jr engr, Bendix Res Labs, Mich, 57-59; design engr, Loral Electronics Div, Loral Corp, NY, 59-61; instr elec eng, NY Univ, 61-64; sr eng, CBS Labs, Columbia Broadcasting Syst, 64-66, Marchand Electronic Labs, 66-67 & Perkin-Elmer Corp, Conn, 67-68; ASSOC PROF ELEC ENG, COOPER UNION, 68- *Concurrent Pos:* Consult, Perkin-Elmer Corp, 69-78 & Gen Instrument Corp, NY, 73-77. *Mem:* Inst Elec & Electronics Engrs; Optical Soc Am. *Res:* Feedback controls; communication theory; electro-optics and acoustics; circuit theory. *Mailing Add:* 352 E 39th New York NY 10028

VOLPE, P(ETER) J, JR, b New York, NY, Mar 13, 34; m 57; c 4. CHEMICAL ENGINEERING, ECONOMICS. *Educ:* Rice Inst, BA, 56, BS, 57. *Prof Exp:* Jr prod engr, 57-58, from jr engr to engr, 58-60, from res engr to sr res engr, 60-65, group leader chem eng econ & design, 65-66, sect head process develop, 66-71, mgr chem eng, 71-74, tech mgr, 74-76, opers mgr, Bishop Tex Plant, 76-80, mgr facil & admin, Tech Ctr, 80-81, DIR FAC, TECH CTR, CORPUS CHRISTI PLANT, CELANESE CHEM CO, 81- *Mem:* Am Inst Chem Engrs. *Res:* Laboratory and pilot plant process development for bulk organic chemicals, especially nylon salt; economics and process design for new bulk organic chemical products and processes. *Mailing Add:* Celanese Chem Co Box 9077 Corpus Christi TX 78403

VOLPE, ROBERT, b Toronto, Ont, Mar 6, 26; m 49; c 5. ENDOCRINOLOGY. *Educ:* Univ Toronto, MD, 50; FRCP(C), 56. *Prof Exp:* Dept Vet Affairs med res fel, Clin Invest Unit, Sunnybrook Hosp, Toronto, 52-53; Med Res Coun Can fel, Toronto Gen Hosp, 55-57; sr res fel endocrinol, Fac Med, Univ Toronto, 57-65; from clin teacher to assoc prof, 65-71, PROF MED, FAC MED, UNIV TORONTO, 71-; DIR ENDOCRINE RES LAB, WELLESLEY HOSP, 67- *Concurrent Pos:* Physician-in-chief, Dept Med, Wellesley Hosp, Toronto, 74-; gov, Am Col Physicians, 80- *Mem:* Fel Am Col Physicians; Am Thyroid Asn (pres, 80-81); Am Fedn Clin Res; Endocrine Soc; Can Soc Endocrinol & Metab (pres, 72). *Res:* Immune mechanisms in thyroid diseases. *Mailing Add:* 3 Daleberry Pl Don Mills ON M3B 2A5 Can

VOLPERT, EUGENE M, b Koenigsberg, Ger, Feb 15, 25; US citizen. BIOCHEMISTRY, ENDOCRINOLOGY. *Educ:* NY Univ, BA, 45; Univ Wis, MS, 47; Univ Paris, PhD(biochem), 59. *Prof Exp:* Res assoc biochem, Col Physicians & Surgeons, Columbia Univ, 59-65; biochemist, Endocrine Serv, Montefiore Hosp, Bronx, 65-67; assoc scientist, Med Found Buffalo, 67-75; BIOLOGIST, NUCLEAR MED, VET ADMIN HOSP, BROOKLYN, 75-; CLIN ASST PROF RADIOL, DOWNSTATE MED CTR, STATE UNIV NY, 80- *Mem:* Am Chem Soc; Am Thyroid Asn; Endocrine Soc. *Res:* Biochemistry and binding of thyroid hormones; relation of thyroid with pituitary gland and catecholamines; thyroid gland mechanisms. *Mailing Add:* Nuclear Med Vet Admin Hosp Brooklyn NY 11209

VOLPITTO, PERRY PAUL, b Italy, July 9, 05; nat US; m 37; c 3. ANESTHESIOLOGY. *Educ:* Washington & Jefferson Col, BS, 28; Western Reserve Univ, MD, 33; Am Bd Anesthesiol, dipl. *Prof Exp:* From assoc prof to prof anesthesiol, 37-73, chmn dept, 38-72, EMER PROF ANESTHESIOL, MED COL GA, 73- *Concurrent Pos:* Area consult, US Vet Admin, 48-68; consult, US Army Hosp, Ft Gordon, 50-74. *Honors & Awards:* Hardeman Award, 66 & Distinguished Serv Award, 75, Med Asn Ga; Distinguished Serv Award, Am Soc Anesthesiol, 74. *Mem:* Am Soc Anesthesiol (pres, 65); AMA. *Res:* Treatment of barbiturate poisoning; amnesia in labor; treatment of apnea of the newborn; intra-arterial blood pressure in children and during anesthesia; use of stellate ganglion block in cerebral vascular accidents; intravenous barbiturates and muscle relaxants for endotracheal intubation; electronarcosis utilizing a combination of alternating and direct currents. *Mailing Add:* Dept of Anesthesiol Med Col of Ga Augusta GA 30902

VOLPP, GERT PAUL JUSTUS, b Loerrach, Ger, July 30, 30; nat US; m 62; c 4. AGRICULTURAL CHEMISTRY. *Educ:* Univ Basel, PhD(chem), 58. *Prof Exp:* Res fel org chem, Harvard Univ, 58-63; interdisciplinary scientist, 63-65, mgr explor org res, 65-72, mgr prod res, 72-73, tech dir alkali chem, 73-75, asst venture mgr, pyrethroids, 75-76, asst dir res, 76-77, acquisition mgr, 77-79, DIR COMMERCIAL DEVELOP, FMC CORP, 80- *Mem:* Am Chem Soc; Ger Chem Soc; NY Acad Sci. *Res:* Synthetic organic chemistry; intermediates for dyestuffs; additives for plastics; antioxidants; detergent chemistry; agricultural chemistry; manufacturing technology for soda ash, caustic, chlorine, glycerine, allyl alcohol, barium and strontium chemicals; commercial development of pesticides. *Mailing Add:* Chem Res & Develop Ctr FMC Corp PO Box 8 Princeton NJ 08540

VOLTZ, STERLING ERNEST, b Philadelphia, Pa, Apr 17, 21; m 43; c 2. PHYSICAL CHEMISTRY, RESEARCH ADMINISTRATION. *Educ:* Temple Univ, AB, 43, MA, 47, PhD(phys chem), 52. *Prof Exp:* Lab asst, Temple Univ, 46-47; res fel, Univ Pa, 47-48; instr, Temple Univ, 48-51; res chemist, Houdry Process Corp, 51-58; group leader, Sun Oil Co, 58-60; supv chemist, Missile & Space Div, Gen Elec Co, 60-62, consult liaison scientist, 62-68; res assoc, 68-80, ADMIN COORDR, MOBIL RES & DEVELOP CORP, PAULSBORO, NJ, 80- *Mem:* AAAS; Am Chem Soc; Catalysis Soc. *Res:* Catalysis; surface and solid state chemistry; chemical kinetics; electrochemistry; fuel cells; petroleum and petrochemical processes; synthetic fuels; automotive emission control systems; program management; research administration and planning; research contracts. *Mailing Add:* 6 E Glen Circle Media PA 19063

VOLWILER, WADE, b Grand Forks, NDak, Sept 16, 17; m 43; c 3. MEDICINE. *Educ:* Oberlin Col, AB, 39; Harvard Med Sch, MD, 43; Am Bd Internal Med, dipl, 50, recert, 77; Am Bd Gastroenterol, dipl, 54. *Prof Exp:* From intern to resident med, Mass Gen Hosp, Boston, 43-45, asst, 45-48; asst, Harvard Med Sch, 46-48; head, div gastroenterol, 50-81, from instr to assoc prof, 49-59, PROF MED, SCH MED, UNIV WASH, 59- . *Concurrent Pos:* Teaching fel med, Harvard Med Sch, 45-46; res fel gastroenterol, Mass Gen Hosp, Boston, 45-48; Am Gastroenterol Asn res fel, 47; Nat Res Coun fel, 48-49; Markle scholar, 50-55; res assoc, Mayo Found, Univ Minn, 48-49; attend physician, King County Hosp Syst, Seattle, 50- & Vet Admin Hosp, 51-; consult, USPHS Hosp, 55- & Univ Wash Hosp, 60-; mem subspecialty bd gastroenterol, Am Bd Internal Med, 70-76. *Honors & Awards:* Friedenwald Medal, Am Gastroeuterological Asn, 81. *Mem:* Am Soc Clin Invest; Am Gastroenterol Asn (secy, 59-62, pres, 67); Asn Am Physicians; Am Asn Study Liver Dis (pres, 56). *Res:* Liver diseases; gastroenterology; plasma proteins. *Mailing Add:* Dept of Med Univ of Wash Sch of Med Seattle WA 98195

VOLZ, FREDERIC ERNST, b Singen, Ger, Oct 29, 22; m 57; c 3. ATMOSPHERIC PHYSICS. *Educ:* Univ Frankfurt, dipl, 50, PhD(meteorol), 54. *Prof Exp:* Res asst, Lichtklimat Observ Arosa, 50-52; res asst meteorol, Univ Mainz, 52-57; res fel atmospheric physics, Harvard Univ, 57-61 & Astron Inst, Univ Tübingen, 62-67; RES PHYSICIST, AIR FORCE GEOPHYSICS LAB, 67- *Mem:* Am Meteorol Soc; Am Geophys Union; Optical Soc Am; Ger Meteorol Soc. *Res:* Atmospheric optics, optical constants of aerosol, twilight, stratospheric aerosol. *Mailing Add:* Air Force Geophysics Lab Bedford MA 01731

VOLZ, JOHN EDWARD, b Baltimore, Md, March 23, 40; m 61; c 4. ADIPOSE TISSUE, CANCER. *Educ:* Towson State Univ, BS, 69; Univ Md, PhD(anat), 75. *Prof Exp:* ASSOC PROF GROSS ANAT, DENT SCH, TEMPLE UNIV, 73- *Res:* Dipose tissue, especially the effects of diet and exercise on the growth and development of fat stores in rats and mice. *Mailing Add:* Dept Anat Sci Sch Dent Temple Univ 3223 N Broad St Philadelphia PA 19140

VOLZ, MICHAEL GEORGE, b Long Beach, Calif, Nov 30, 45; m 68; c 2. SANITARY MICROBIOLOGY, SOIL BIOCHEMISTRY. *Educ:* Univ Calif, Berkeley, BS, 67, PhD(soil sci, plant physiol), 72. *Prof Exp:* Asst res biochemist, Univ Calif, Berkeley, 72-74, res biochemist, 74-75; asst plant physiologist, Conn Agr Exp Sta, 75-77; ASSOC SANIT MICROBIOLOGIST, SANIT & RADIATION LAB, CALIF STATE DEPT HEALTH, 77- *Mem:* Am Soc Agron; Soil Sci Soc Am; Crop Sci Soc Am; AAAS; Am Chem Soc. *Res:* Assessing the significance of mans waste disposal techinques on the sanitary quality of drinking water supplies and marine shellfish aquaculture. *Mailing Add:* Sanit & Radiation Lab State CA Dept Health Serv 2151 Berkeley Way Berkeley CA 94704

VOLZ, PAUL ALBERT, b Ann Arbor, Mich, Mar 26, 36. MYCOLOGY, BOTANY. *Educ:* Heidelberg Col, BA, 58; Mich State Univ, MS, 62, PhD(mycol), 66. *Prof Exp:* Instr bot, Univ Wis-Milwaukee, 62-63; USPHS res grant, Med Ctr, Ind Univ, 67-68; assoc prof bot & mycol, Purdue Univ, 68-69; asst prof & mycologist, 69-72, assoc prof, 72-80, PROF BOT & MYCOL, EASTERN MICH UNIV, 80- *Concurrent Pos:* Sr res assoc, Nat Res Coun, 71-73; res contractor, NASA Manned Spacecraft Ctr, 71-74; vis prof mycol, Nat Taiwan Univ, 74-75, Wayne State Univ, 80-81. *Mem:* AAAS; Am Inst Biol Sci; Electron Micros Soc Am; Am Fern Soc; Asn Trop Biol. *Res:* Fern anatomy; marine and soil fungi of the Bahamas and The Republic of China; keratinophilic fungi; drug sensitivity and nutritional requirements of fungi; effects of space flight parameters on select fungal species; fungal cytogenetics and morphology. *Mailing Add:* Dept of Biol Eastern Mich Univ Ypsilanti MI 48197

VOLZ, RICHARD A, b Woodstock, Ill, July 10, 37; m 61; c 2. ROBOTICS, REAL TIME COMPUTING. *Educ:* Northwestern Univ, BS, 60, MS, 61, PhD(elec eng), 64. *Prof Exp:* Assoc prof, 64-77, assoc chmn elec & comput eng dept, 78-79, assoc dir comput ctr, 79-82, PROF ELEC & COMPUT ENG, UNIV MICH, ANN ARBOR, 77-, DIR ROBOTICS LAB, 81- *Concurrent Pos:* NSF grants, 65-68 & 70-72; mem prog comt, Nat Electronics Conf, 68. *Mem:* Inst Elec & Electronics Engrs; Asn Comput Mach; Soc Mfg Engrs; Int Inst Robotics. *Res:* Automatic control theory; computational methods of optimal control, particularly the use of hybrid systems for such work; discrete control systems. *Mailing Add:* Dept of Elec & Comput Eng Univ of Mich Ann Arbor MI 48109

VOLZ, WILLIAM BECKHAM, b Chickasha, Okla, July 9, 42; m 66; c 2. ELECTROOPTICS. *Educ:* Okla State Univ, BS, 63, PhD(chem), 70. *Prof Exp:* Assoc scientist, 70-76, SR SCIENTIST MAT SCI, TEX DIV, VARO, INC, 76- *Mem:* Am Chem Soc. *Res:* Thermal imaging based on the quantum counter principle; photocathode sensitivity at 1.06 microns; laser damage; applications of low-light level image intensifiers in medicine, science and military technology. *Mailing Add:* Varo Inc Tex Div 2201 Walnut PO Box 828 Garland TX 75040

VOLZ, WILLIAM K(URT), b Mannheim, Ger, Feb 28, 19; nat US; m 42; c 4. CHEMICAL ENGINEERING. *Educ:* Columbia Univ, BSc, 41. *Prof Exp:* Mem eng staff, Monsanto Co, 41-48, proj engr, 48-55, sect mgr eng, 55-60, asst dir, 60-62, eng dir, Spain, 64-65, mgr int eng, 65-77, mgr eng, 77-79; asst prof chem eng, 79-81, CONSULT & AFFIL PROF, WASHINGTON UNIV, ST LOUIS, 81- *Mem:* Nat Soc Prof Engrs; Instrument Soc Am; Sigma Xi; Am Inst Chem Engrs. *Res:* Management; design and construction of new chemical plant facilities. *Mailing Add:* Wash Univ 46 Morwood Lane St Louis MO 63141

VOMACHKA, ARCHIE JOEL, b Duluth, Minn, Sept 28, 46; m 73. REPRODUCTIVE BIOLOGY, ENDOCRINOLOGY. *Educ:* Univ Minn, Duluth, BA, 68; Mich State Univ, PhD(zool), 76. *Prof Exp:* Fel reprod physiol, Univ Kans Med Ctr, 76-79; lectr exp vert biol, Princeton Univ, 79-81; ASST PROF HUMAN PHYSIOL, MARQUETTE UNIV, 81- *Concurrent Pos:* Res assoc, Princeton Univ, 79-81. *Mem:* Animal Behav Soc; AAAS; Sigma Xi. *Res:* Neural and hormonal regulation of sexual behavior in rodents, including the sexual differentiation of behavior and endocrine physiology in hamsters. *Mailing Add:* Dept Biol Marquette Univ Milwaukee WI 53233

VOMHOF, DANIEL WILLIAM, b Grant, Nebr, Apr 19, 38; m 60, 78; c 3. FORENSIC SCIENCE, CHEMISTRY. *Educ:* Augsburg Col, BA, 62; Univ Ariz, MS, 66, PhD(plant physiol), 67; Am Inst Chemists, cert, 69. *Prof Exp:* Chemist, Ariz Agr Exp Sta, Univ Ariz, 63-67; res chemist, Corn Refiners Asn, 67-69; dir, Region IX Lab, US Bur Customs, Ill, 69-72, forensic scientist, Region VII, 72-74, dir, Lab Div, US Customs Serv, Region IX, Chicago, 74; PRES, EXPERT WITNESS SERV, 74- *Concurrent Pos:* Res assoc, Nat Bur Stand, 67-69. *Mem:* AAAS; Am Chem Soc; fel Am Inst Chemists; Sigma Xi; Am Soc Testing & Mat. *Res:* Accident dynamics; document identification; biomechanics; analytical chemistry; driver behavior. *Mailing Add:* Expert Witness Serv 8381 University Ave La Mesa CA 92041

VOMOCIL, JAMES ARTHUR, b Jacumba, Calif, Sept 12, 26; m 46; c 3. SOIL SCIENCE, AGRONOMY. *Educ:* Univ Ariz, BS, 50; Mich State Univ, MS, 52; Rutgers Univ, PhD, 55. *Prof Exp:* Asst soil sci, Mich State Univ, 50-52, instr, 52; asst, Rutgers Univ, 52-55; instr soil physics, Univ Calif, Davis, 55, from asst prof to assoc prof & assoc exp sta, 55-67; EXTEN SOILS SPECIALIST & PROF SOILS, ORE STATE UNIV, 67- *Mem:* Am Soc Agron; Soil Sci Soc Am; Int Soc Soil Sci. *Res:* Soil physical condition and plant growth; soil strength and deformation. *Mailing Add:* Dept of Soils Ore State Univ Corvallis OR 97331

VON, ISAIAH, b Philadelphia, Pa, Dec 28, 18; m 45; c 3. INDUSTRIAL ORGANIC CHEMISTRY. *Educ:* Univ Buffalo, BA, 40; Univ Pa, MS, 41, PhD(org chem), 43. *Prof Exp:* Res assoc, Nat Defense Res Comt Proj, Univ Pa, 43-45, mem comt on med res proj, 45-46; res chemist, Am Cyanamid Co, 46-53, develop chemist, 53-54, group leader, 54-56, sect chief chemist, 56-64, dep chief chemist, 65-81; CONSULT, 81- *Mem:* Am Chem Soc; Am Asn Textile Chemists & Colorists. *Res:* Dyestuffs; pigments; organic intermediates. *Mailing Add:* Apt 16E 1050 George St New Brunswick NJ 08901

VONA, JOSEPH ALBERT, b Brooklyn, NY, Aug 15, 20; m 46; c 2. ORGANIC CHEMISTRY. *Educ:* Brooklyn Col, BA, 41, MA, 44; Polytech Inst Brooklyn, PhD, 54. *Prof Exp:* Head lab sect plastics res, Barrett Chem Co, 45-46; res & develop chemist, Nat Lead Co, 46-50; asst to tech dir, Baker Castor Oil Co, 50-55; mgr, Tech Serv Lab, 55-69, DIR MTD LAB, CELANESE CHEM CO, 69- *Mem:* Am Chem Soc; Com Develop Asn; Chem Indust Asn; Asn Res Dirs; NY Acad Sci. *Res:* Research and development in radiation technology; new types of coatings; emulsion solution and bulk polymerization of monomers; new compounds which can produce durable coatings. *Mailing Add:* Celanese Chem Co Box 1000 Summit NJ 07901

VON ALMEN, WILLIAM FREDERICK I, b Olney, Ill, May 6, 28; m 50; c 4. PALYNOLOGY, GEOLOGY. *Educ:* Southern Ill Univ, Carbondale, BA, 57; Univ Mo-Columbia, MA, 59; Mich State Univ, PhD(geol), 70. *Prof Exp:* Geologist, Pure Oil Co, 59-60; geologist, Stand Oil Co Tex, 60-64, geologist-palynologist, 66-68, palynologist, Chevron Oil Field Res Co, 68-69, from lead palynologist to div paleontologist, 69-71, SR PALEONTOLOGIST, CHEVRON USA, INC, 71- *Mem:* Am Asn Stratig Palynol. *Res:* Palynology of Devonian-Mississippian Boundary; Mesozoic palynostratigraphy. *Mailing Add:* Chevron USA Inc 1111 Tulane Ave New Orleans LA 70112

VON AMSBERG, HANS J, b Hamburg, WGer, June 5, 35; m 62; c 2. HERBICIDES. *Educ:* Univ Toronto, BSA, 60, MSA, 62; Ore State Univ, PhD(farm crops), 65. *Prof Exp:* Lectr weed control, Ont Agr Col, 60-62; res asst crop physics, Ore State Univ, 62-64; develop supvr, Agr Div, Monsanto Co, 64-66; develop coordr, Dept Chem, 66-70, mgr field res, Dept Agr Chem, 70-75, mgr res & develop, Div Agr Chem, 76-80, DIR RES & DEVELOP, AGR CHEM GROUP, BASF WYANDOTTE CORP, 80- *Mem:* Weed Sci Soc Am; Plant Growth Regulator Soc. *Mailing Add:* BASF Wyandotte Corp 100 Cherry Hill Rd Parsippany NJ 07054

VON ARX, EUGENE F(RANCIS), b Pittsburgh, Pa, Mar 29, 21; m 45; c 2. SYSTEMS & ELECTRICAL ENGINEERING. *Educ:* Pa State Univ, BSEE, 44. *Prof Exp:* Test engr, Hamilton Standard Propellers Div, United Aircraft Corp, 44-45; asst prof eng res, Pa State Univ, 45-48; sr engr, Sperry Gyroscope Co, 49-52, eng sect head, 52-56, eng dept head, 56-59, eng mgr, 59-60, asst chief engr, Air Armament Div, 60-63, chief engr, Inertial Div, 63-65, mgr aircraft inertial navig systs, 65-67, chief engr digital systs, Sperry Gyroscope Div, 67-69, dir eng, 69-71, mgr ocean/mil systs, Sperry Systs Mgt Div, 71-75, vpres, Anti-Submarine Warfare & Navig & Guid Progs, Sperry Gyroscope Div, 75-78, DIR DEVELOP PLANNING, SPERRY DIV, SPERRY RAND CORP, 78- *Concurrent Pos:* Eastern regional vpres, Inst Navig, 73. *Mem:* Inst Elec & Electronics Engrs; Am Defense Preparedness Asn; Nat Security Indust Asn. *Res:* Servomechanisms. *Mailing Add:* Sperry Div Sperry Rand Corp Great Neck NY 11020

VON AULOCK, WILHELM HEINRICH, b Pirna, Ger, Jan 24, 15; US citizen; m 56; c 4. ELECTRICAL & SYSTEMS ENGINEERING. *Educ:* Tech Univ, Berlin, Dipl Eng, 37; Stuttgart Tech Univ, DEng, 53. *Prof Exp:* Div head engr, Torpedoversuchsanstalt Eckernfoerde, Ger, 42-45; physicist, Bur Ships, Navy Dept, Washington, DC, 47-53; mem tech staff, 54-62, dept head nuclear effects, 62-71, dir tech support, Am Bell Int, 77-79, dept head installation studies, 71-79, DEPT HEAD DEVELOP, PLANNING & ANALYSIS, BELL LABS, 79- *Concurrent Pos:* Instr, Postgrad Sch, Univ Md, 51-52. *Mem:* fel Inst Elec & Electronics Engrs. *Res:* Guided acoustic torpedoes; electromagnetic fields in sea water; microwave ferrite materials and devices; phased arrays for radar applications; systems engineering for communication facilities. *Mailing Add:* PO Box 84 Fairview Dr Bedminster NJ 07921

VON BACHO, PAUL STEPHAN, JR, b Rochester, NY, Dec 28, 37; m 60; c 2. PHOTOGRAPHIC CHEMISTRY. *Educ:* Univ Rochester, BS, 65, MS, 71, PhD(mat sci), 76. *Prof Exp:* Res chemist, 65-74, sr res chemist color photog, 74-77, sr anal chemist, Ind Labs, 77-79, SECT SUPVR, IND LABS, EASTMAN KODAK CO RES LABS, 79- *Mem:* Am Chem Soc; Soc Photog Scientists & Engrs. *Res:* Use of analytical, radiotracer and instrumental techniques to study color photographic films and process solutions; management of analytical, chemical and photographic quality control laboratories. *Mailing Add:* 31 Jamestown Terrace Rochester NY 14615

VON BAEYER, HANS CHRISTIAN, b Berlin, Ger, Apr 6, 38; Can citizen; c 2. THEORETICAL PHYSICS. *Educ:* Columbia Univ, AB, 58; Univ Miami, MSc, 61; Vanderbilt Univ, PhD(physics), 64. *Prof Exp:* Res assoc physics, McGill Univ, 64-65, asst prof, 65-68; from asst prof to assoc prof, 68-75, chmn dept, 72-78, PROF PHYSICS, COL WILLIAM & MARY, 75-; DIR, VA ASSOC RES CAMPUS, 79- *Concurrent Pos:* Vis prof, Tri-Univ Meson Facil & Simon Fraser Univ, 78-79. *Mem:* Fel Am Phys Soc; Fedn Am Sci; Am Asn Univ Prof. *Res:* Theory of elementary particles; public understanding of science. *Mailing Add:* Dept of Physics Col of William & Mary Williamsburg VA 23185

VON BARGEN, KENNETH LOUIS, b Alliance, Nebr, Apr 6, 31; div; c 3. AGRICULTURAL & SYSTEMS ENGINEERING. *Educ:* Univ Nebr, Lincoln, BS, 52, MS, 62; Purdue Univ, Lafayette, PhD(agr eng), 70. *Prof Exp:* Design engr, Lockwood Grader Corp, Nebr, 55-56; from instr to asst prof agr eng, 56-69, assoc prof systs eng, 69-77, PROF AGR SYSTS ENG, UNIV NEBR, LINCOLN, 77- *Concurrent Pos:* mem, Nebr Bd Tractor Testing Engrs, 76-80, chmn, 81-; mem bd dirs, Am Forge & Grasslands Coun, 77-80. *Mem:* Sigma Xi; Am Soc Agr Engrs; Am Forage & Grassland Coun. *Res:* Forage and residue harvesting and handling systems and systems engineering of agricultural production systems emphasizing weather and crop response; man-machine performance; energy and optimum tractor-machine sizing. *Mailing Add:* Dept of Agr Eng Univ of Nebr Lincoln NE 68583

VON BECKH, HARALD JOHANNES, b Vienna, Austria, Nov 17, 17; nat US; m 49; c 6. AEROSPACE MEDICINE. *Educ:* Univ Vienna, MD, 40; Nat Bd Cert, Buenos Aires, Arg, cert specialist aviation med, 56. *Prof Exp:* Staff mem & lectr aviation med, Aeromed Acad, Berlin, Ger, 41-43; prof, Nat Inst Aviation Med, Buenos Aires, 47-56; mem sci staff, Aeromed Res Lab, Holloman AFB, NMex, 57-64, chief scientist, 64-70; DIR MED RES, CREW SYSTS DEPT, NAVAL AIR DEVELOP CTR, 70- *Concurrent Pos:* Mem comt bioastronaut, Armed Forces-Nat Res Coun, 58-61; mem bioastronaut comt, Int Astronaut Fedn, 61-; hon mem, Ctr Astronaut Studies Portugal, 61- *Honors & Awards:* Melbourne W Boynton Award, Am Astronaut Soc, 72; Arnold D Tuttle Award, Aerospace Med Asn, 72; Claude Bernard Medal, Fr Asn Astronaut Res, 72; Hermann Oberth Honor Ring, 75; Hubertus Strughold Award, Aerospace Med Asn, 76; Jeffries Med Res Award, Am Inst Aeronaut & Astronaut, 77. *Mem:* Assoc fel Am Inst Aeronaut & Astronaut; fel Aerospace Med Asn; hon mem Hermann Oberth Soc; hon mem Span Soc Aerospace Med. *Res:* Neurophysiology, hemodynamics and deconditioning effect of weightlessness; effects of accelerations on humans and test animals; protective devices against accelerations of space and atmospheric flight. *Mailing Add:* PO Box 1220 Warminster PA 18974

VON BERG, ROBERT L(EE), b Wheeling, WVa, June 14, 18; m 47; c 4. CHEMICAL ENGINEERING. *Educ:* Univ WVa, BSChE, 40, MS, 41; Mass Inst Technol, ScD(chem eng), 44. *Prof Exp:* Instr chem eng, Univ WVa, 39-40; indust engr, E I du Pont de Nemours & Co, Del, 44-46; from asst prof to assoc prof, 46-58, PROF CHEM ENG, CORNELL UNIV, 58- *Concurrent Pos:* Consult, Atomic Energy Comn, 50 & Dow Chem Co, Mich, 53-54; NATO res fel, Delft Univ Technol, 60-61. *Mem:* Am Chem Soc; Am Inst Chem Engrs. *Res:* Chemical processes; liquid-liquid extraction; reaction kinetics and reactor design; nuclear processing; radiation chemistry. *Mailing Add:* Dept of Chem Eng Cornell Univ Ithaca NY 14853

VON BODUNGEN, GEORGE ANTHONY, b New Orleans, La, Oct 12, 40; m 69; c 3. PHYSICAL CHEMISTRY. *Educ:* Loyola Univ, New Orleans, 62; Tulane Univ La, PhD(phys chem), 66. *Prof Exp:* sr res chemist, 66-80, PROCESS DEVELOP GROUP LEADER, COPOLYMER RUBBER & CHEM CORP, 80- *Mem:* Soc Plastics Engrs. *Res:* Synthesis and rheology of impact resistant plastics and thermo plastic elastomers; computer simulations and mathematical models of process and products; applied mathematics; development and scale-up of emulsion products and processes. *Mailing Add:* 3836 Partridge Lane Baton Rouge LA 70809

VON BORSTEL, ROBERT CARSTEN, b Kent, Ore, Jan 24, 25; m 48. GENETICS. *Educ:* Ore State Col, BA, 47, MS, 49; Univ Pa, PhD(zool), 53. *Prof Exp:* Fel, Carnegie Inst, NY, 52-53; biologist, Oak Ridge Nat Lab, 53-71; PROF GENETICS & CHMN DEPT, UNIV ALTA, 71- *Concurrent Pos:* NSF fel, Univ Pavia, 59-60. *Mem:* Genetics Soc Am; Am Soc Naturalists; Genetic Soc Can; Int Asn Environ Mutagen Socs (secy, 73-); Am Environ Mutagen Soc. *Res:* Dominant lethality and cell-killing by radiation; microorganism genetics; spontaneous mutation rates; mutator genes in yeast. *Mailing Add:* 12312 Grandview Dr Edmonton AB T6H 4K4 Can

VON BUN, FRIEDRICH OTTO, b Vienna, Austria, June 22, 25; US citizen; m 52; c 2. PHYSICS, MATHEMATICS. *Educ:* Vienna Tech Univ, MS, 52; Graz Tech Univ, PhD(physics, math), 56. *Prof Exp:* Physicist, US Army Signal Corps, 53-57, chief molecular beam sect, Atomic Resonance Br, 57-59, sr scientist & dir frequency control div, 59-60; consult, Tracking & Data Systs Directorate, 60-61, head plans off, 61-63, chief systs anal off, 63-65, chief mission anal off, 65-67, chief mission & trajectory anal div, 67-71, chief trajectory anal & geodyn div, Mission & Data Opers Directorate, 71-72, CHIEF, GEODYN PROG DIV, GODDARD SPACE FLIGHT CTR, NASA, 72-, ASST DIR APPLN SCI, APPLN DIRECTORATE, 74- *Concurrent Pos:* Mem panel tracking & data anal, Nat Acad Sci, 63-65; spec adv, Range Tech Adv Group, 66-; mem, Steering Comt, Working Group 1, COSPAR, 72-; chmn, Working Group Earth & Ocean Dynamics, Int Astronaut Fedn, 75 & Working Group Global Data Collection, 76. *Mem:* Assoc fel Am Inst Aeronaut & Astronaut; Am Geophys Union; Int Astronaut Fedn. *Res:* Space systems analysis; navigation; geodynamics; ocean dynamics; gravity and magnetic field studies; active and passive microwave observations of the Earth's surface from space; application of space science and technology toward solutions of practical problems. *Mailing Add:* Appln Directorate NASA Code 900 Greenbelt MD 20771

VONDELL, RICHARD M, b Amherst, Mass, Apr 6, 30; m 59; c 4. FOOD SCIENCE. *Educ:* Univ Mass, BS, 52, PhD(food sci), 63; Univ NH, MS, 56. *Prof Exp:* Res assoc animal nutrit, Univ NH, 56-57; asst instr food sci, Univ Mass, 59-62; food technologist, 63-65, dir pilot plant opers, 65-75, DIR CEREAL PROD RES, KELLOGG CO, 75- *Mem:* Inst Food Technologists. *Res:* Cereal technology; vapor-phase destruction of microorganisms. *Mailing Add:* Kellogg Co Battle Creek MI 49016

VONDERHAAR, BARBARA KAY, b Des Moines, Iowa, July 4, 43; m 74; c 2. ENDOCRINOLOGY. *Educ:* Clarke Col, BA, 65; Univ Wis-Madison, PhD(oncol), 70. *Prof Exp:* Fel, McArdle Lab Cancer Res, 70-71; staff fel, Nat Inst Arthritis, Metabol & Digestive Dis, 71-73, sr staff fel, 73-76; cancer expert, 76-80, SR RES CHEMIST, LAB PATHOPHYSICS, NAT CANCER INST, 80- *Mem:* AAAS; Endocrine Soc; Am Soc Cell Biol; Am Soc Biol Chemists; Int Asn Breast Cancer Res. *Res:* Multiple hormone interactions in mammary gland development and milk protein production; the effects of neonatal hormone treatment on development of mammary glands and tumor formation; thyroid hormone and prolactin interactions in breast development. *Mailing Add:* NIH Bldg 10 Rm 5B56 Bethesda MD 20205

VONDER HAAR, RAYMOND A, b St Louis, Mo, Nov 18, 46; m 68; c 2. BIOCHEMISTRY, CELL BIOLOGY. *Educ:* Univ Mo-Columbia, AB, 68; Purdue Univ, PhD(molecular biol), 73. *Prof Exp:* Fel virol & cell biol, Univ Utah, 74-78; ASST PROF MED BIOCHEM, TEX A&M UNIV, 78- *Res:* Frameshift suppression in mammalian cells; mutagenesis in mammalian cells and animal viruses. *Mailing Add:* Dept of Med Biochem Col of Med Tex A&M Univ College Station TX 77843

VONDER HAAR, THOMAS HENRY, b Quincy, Ill, Dec 28, 42; m 80; c 3. METEOROLOGY, SPACE SCIENCE. *Educ:* St Louis Univ, BS, 63; Univ Wis-Madison, MS, 64, PhD(meteorol), 68. *Prof Exp:* Assoc scientist meteorology, Space Sci & Eng Ctr, Univ Wis, 68-70; assoc prof, 70-77, PROF ATMOSPHERIC SCI, COLO STATE UNIV, 77-, HEAD DEPT, 74-, DIR, COOP INST RES, 80- *Concurrent Pos:* Consult, US Army, McDonnell-Douglas Corp, Ball Bros & Res Corp, 69-, NASA; mem int radiation comn, Int Union Geod & Geophys, 75; mem climate res comt, Nat Acad Sci. *Honors & Awards:* Second Half Century Award, Am Meteorol Soc, 81. *Mem:* Am Meteorol Soc. *Res:* Application of measurements from meteorological satellites to problems of atmospheric and environmental science; radiation measurement; air pollution; weather forecasting. *Mailing Add:* Dept of Atmospheric Sci Colo State Univ Ft Collins CO 80523

VON DOHLEN, WERNER CLAUS, b Langen, Ger, Nov 7, 24; nat US; m 47; c 3. SURFACE CHEMISTRY. *Educ:* Rutgers Univ, BSc, 50; Brown Univ, PhD(phys chem), 54. *Prof Exp:* Res chemist, 54-64, PROJ SCIENTIST, UNION CARBIDE CORP, 64- *Concurrent Pos:* Instr, WVa State Col, 59-61, asst prof, 61-62. *Mem:* Am Chem Soc; Am Vacuum Soc. *Res:* Surface science, electron spectroscopy; x-ray crystallography of organic compounds; heterogeneous and homogeneous catalysis; olefin polymerization; kinetics and mechanism of polymerization; polymer morphology and physical properties; structure of catalysts; electron microscopy. *Mailing Add:* Charleston Tech Ctr Res & Develop Union Carbide Corp PO Box 8361 South Charleston WV 25303

VONDRA, CARL FRANK, b Seward, Nebr, June 3, 34; m 55; c 4. GEOLOGY. *Educ:* Univ Nebr, BS, 56, MS, 58, PhD(geol), 63. *Prof Exp:* Develop geologist, Calif Co, 61-62; geologist, Pan Am Petrol Corp, 62-63; from asst prof to assoc prof, 63-71, PROF GEOL, IOWA STATE UNIV, 71- *Mem:* Geol Soc Am; Am Asn Petrol Geol; Paleont Soc; Soc Vert Paleont; Soc Econ Paleont & Mineral. *Res:* Stratigraphy of the Eocene deposits of the Big Horn Basin, Wyoming; stratigraphy of the upper Eocene and Oligocene deposits of Egypt; stratigraphy of the Siwalik deposits in northern India; stratigraphy and sedimentation of the Plio-Pleistocene deposits in the East Rudolf Basin, Kenya. *Mailing Add:* Dept of Earth Sci Iowa State Univ Ames IA 50010

VONDRAK, EDWARD ANDREW, b Chicago, Ill, Nov 12, 38; m 61; c 3. PHYSICS. *Educ:* Knox Col, AB, 60; Vanderbilt Univ, MA, 63, PhD(physics), 65. *Prof Exp:* Teaching fel physics, Vanderbilt Univ, 61-64; from asst prof to assoc prof, 67-72, PROF PHYSICS, IND CENT UNIV, 72- *Mem:* Am Asn Physics Teachers; Math Asn Am. *Mailing Add:* Dept of Math & Physics Ind Cent Univ 1400 E Hanna Ave Indianapolis IN 46227

VON DREELE, ROBERT BRUCE, b Minneapolis, Minn, Dec 10, 43; m 78. SOLID STATE CHEMISTRY, CRYSTALLOGRAPHY. *Educ:* Cornell Univ, BS, 66, PhD(chem), 71. *Prof Exp:* Asst prof, 71-75, assoc prof, 75-81, PROF CHEM, ARIZ STATE UNIV, 81- *Concurrent Pos:* NSF fel dept inorg chem, Oxford Univ, 72-73. *Mem:* Am Chem Soc; Am Crystallog Asn. *Res:* X-ray crystal structure analysis; solid state chemistry of metal oxides; neutron scattering. *Mailing Add:* Dept of Chem Ariz State Univ Tempe AZ 85281

VONEIDA, THEODORE J, b Auburn, NY, Aug 26, 30; m 56; c 3. NEUROBIOLOGY. *Educ:* Ithaca Col, BS, 53; Cornell Univ, MEd, 54, PhD(zool), 60. *Prof Exp:* Res assoc neuroanat, Walter Reed Army Inst Res, 54-56; asst comp neurol, Cornell Univ, 56-59; from assoc prof to prof, Sch Med, Case Western Reserve Univ, 62-76, adj prof anat & biol, 76-78; MEM FAC DEPT ANAT, COL MED, NORTHEASTERN OHIO UNIV, 78-, CHMN DEPT, 80- *Concurrent Pos:* USPHS res fel neurobiol, Calif Inst Technol, 60-62. *Mem:* AAAS; Am Asn Anatomists. *Res:* Utilization of neuroanatomical and behavioral techniques to investigate the central nervous system. *Mailing Add:* Dept of Anat Col of Med Rootstown OH 44272

VON ESCHEN, GARVIN L(EONARD), b Morristown, Minn, July 22, 13; m 38; c 3. AERONAUTICAL ENGINEERING. *Educ:* Univ Minn, BAeroE, 36, MS, 39. *Prof Exp:* Instr, Univ Minn, 36-40, instr aeronaut eng, 40-42, from asst prof to assoc prof, 42-46, consult & proj supvr, Res Found, 46-76, prof & chmn dept, 46-80, EMER PROF AERONAUT & ASTRONAUT ENG, OHIO STATE UNIV, 80- *Concurrent Pos:* Consult, Minneapolis-Honeywell Regulator Corp, 44-46 & Denison Res Found, 57-60. *Mem:* Am Inst Aeronaut & Astronaut; Am Phys Soc; Am Soc Eng Educ. *Res:* Compressible flow; experimental aerodynamics. *Mailing Add:* Dept of Aeronaut & Astronaut Eng Ohio State Univ Columbus OH 43210

VON ESSEN, CARL FRANCOIS, b Tokyo, Japan, May 17, 26; nat US; m 79; c 3. RADIOTHERAPY. *Educ:* Stanford Univ, AB, 48, MD, 52; Am Bd Radiol, dipl, 58. *Prof Exp:* Res fel cancer, Stanford Univ, 57-59; from instr to assoc prof radiol, Yale Univ, 59-69; prof radiol & oncol & dir radiation ther, Univ Calif, San Diego, 69-77; res prof radiol, Univ NMex, 77-78; LEADER, PION THER PROJ, SWISS INST NUCLEAR RES, 78- *Concurrent Pos:* Vis prof, Christian Med Col, Vellore, India, 65-66; mem rev comt, Radiation Study Sect, NIH, 67-69 & Cancer Res Ctr, 70-74; mem staff, Ludwig Inst Cancer Res, 75-76. *Honors & Awards:* Swiss Cancer Prize, 81. *Mem:* Am Soc Ther Radiologists; Radiation Res Soc. *Res:* Biological effects of radiation; clinical and experimental time-dose relationships; pi-meson radiation therapy. *Mailing Add:* Schweizerisches Inst für Nuklearforschung 5234 Villigen Switzerland

VON EULER, LEO HANS, b Stockholm, Sweden, Jan 31, 31; US citizen; m 55; c 2. PATHOLOGY. *Educ:* Williams Col, BA, 52; Yale Univ, MD, 59. *Prof Exp:* Trainee path, Sch Med, Yale Univ, 59-61, trainee pharmacol, 61-63; fel hematol, Dept Clin Path, NIH, 65-66; scientist, Sect Nutrit Biochem, Nat Inst Arthritis & Metab Dis, 66-67, prog adminr path res training progs, 67-72, spec asst to dir, 72-74, DEP DIR, NAT INST GEN MED SCI, 74-, ACTG DIR, PHYSIOL & BIOMED ENG PROG, 78- *Mem:* Am Asn Path. *Res:* Purine and pyrimidine metabolism; orotic acid induced fatty liver in the rat; biochemical and histological changes. *Mailing Add:* Westwood Bldg Rm 926 Nat Inst Gen Med Sci Bethesda MD 20205

VON FISCHER, WILLIAM, b St Paul, Minn, Mar 3, 10; m 37; c 3. CHEMISTRY. *Educ:* Univ Minn, BChem, 32, MS, 33, PhD(anal & phys chem), 37. *Prof Exp:* Asst, Inst Technol, Univ Minn, 33-37; from instr to prof chem, Case Inst Technol, 37-56, asst head dept chem & chem eng, 48, head, 48-56; coordr res & develop, Glidden Co, 56-58, vpres res, 58-60; consult, 60-63; vpres, Day-Glo Color Corp, Ohio, 63-71; res adminr, Inst Environ Studies, Univ Ill, Urbana, 71-74; CONSULTANT, 74- *Mem:* AAAS; Am Chem Soc; Am Inst Chem Eng; Fedn Socs Paint Technol. *Res:* Analytical methods; organic protective coatings; co-precipitation and aging; use of radioactive indicators; preparation of organic indicators; synthetic rubber; environmental studies. *Mailing Add:* 7975 S A1A Hwy Melbourne Beach FL 32951

VON FRANKENBERG, CARL ALEXANDER, b Gera, Germany, Nov 22, 32; US citizen; m 57; c 2. PHYSICAL CHEMISTRY, CHEMISTRY. *Educ:* Swarthmore Col, BA, 56; Univ Pa, PhD(chem), 61. *Prof Exp:* Asst prof, 61-69, ASSOC PROF CHEM, UNIV DEL, 69- *Concurrent Pos:* NSF fel, Cornell Univ, 61. *Mem:* Am Chem Soc. *Res:* Polymer statistics. *Mailing Add:* 409 Apple Rd Newark DE 19711

VON GIERKE, HENNING EDGAR, b Karlsruhe, Ger, May 22, 17; m 50; c 2. BIOACOUSTICS, BIOMECHANICS. *Educ:* Karlsruhe Tech, Dipl Ing, 43, DrEng, 44. *Prof Exp:* Asst acoust, Inst Theoret Elec Eng & commun techniques, Karlsruhe Tech, 44-47, lectr, 46; consult, 47-54, chief bioacoust br, 54-63, DIR BIODYNAMICS & BIONICS DIV, AEROSPACE MED RES LABS, WRIGHT-PATTERSON AFB, 63-; ASSOC PROF, OHIO STATE UNIV, 63- *Concurrent Pos:* Mem comt hearing & bioacoust, Armed Forces Nat Res Coun, 53-, mem bioastronaut comt, 59-61; mem adv comt flight med & biol, NASA, 60-61; mem, White House Ad Hoc Panel Jet Aircraft Noise, 66; clin prof, Wright State Univ, 80- *Honors & Awards:* Distinguished Civilian Serv Award, Dept Defense, 63; Eric LiljenKrantz Award, Aerospace Med Asn, 66 & Arnold D Tuttle Award, 74; Silver Medal, Acoust Soc Am, 81. *Mem:* Nat Acad Eng; fel Aerospace Med Asn (vpres, 66-67); hon fel Inst Environ Sci; cor mem Int Acad Astronaut; fel Acoust Soc Am (pres, 78). *Res:* Physical, physiological and psychological acoustics; biodynamics; effects of noise, vibration and impact on man; communication biophysics; bionics; bioengineering. *Mailing Add:* 1325 Meadow Lane Yellow Springs OH 45387

VON GOELER, EBERHARD, b Berlin, Ger, Feb 22, 30; m 60; c 3. HIGH ENERGY PHYSICS. *Educ:* Univ Ill, MS, 55, PhD(physics), 61. *Prof Exp:* Res assoc physics, Univ Ill, 60-61; res scientist, Deutsches Elektronen Synchrotron, Hamburg, Ger, 61-63; from asst prof to assoc prof, 63-73, PROF PHYSICS, NORTHEASTERN UNIV, 73- *Concurrent Pos:* Vis prof, Univ Hamburg, 67-68; vis scientist, Nat Accelerator Lab, Ill, 71-72 & Stanford Linear Accelerator, Calif, 78-79. *Mem:* Am Phys Soc. *Res:* Surface physics; tests of quantum electrodynamics; photoproduction of vector mesons, antibaryons; meson spectroscopy; high mass bosons; colliding electron beam experiments; counter techniques in high energy physics. *Mailing Add:* Dept of Physics Northeastern Univ Boston MA 02115

VON GONTEN, (WILLIAM) DOUGLAS, b Rockdale, Tex, Feb 15, 34; m 59; c 2. PETROLEUM ENGINEERING. *Educ:* Tex A&M Univ, BS(geol) & BS(petrol eng), 57, MS, 65, PhD(petrol eng), 66. *Prof Exp:* Petrol engr, Mobil Oil Corp, 57-58, 60-62; res engr, 66-67, from asst prof to assoc prof petrol eng, 67-76, PROF PETROL ENG, TEX ENG EXP STA, TEX A&M UNIV, 76-, HEAD DEPT, 76- *Mem:* Soc Petrol Engrs; Am Asn Petrol Geol; Soc Prof Well Log Analysts; Am Soc Eng Educ. *Res:* Subsurface formation evaluation; reservoir engineering. *Mailing Add:* Dept of Petrol Eng Tex A&M Univ College Station TX 77843

VON GRAEVENITZ, ALEXANDER W C, b Leipzig, Ger, Nov 8, 32; US citizen; m 60; c 3. MEDICAL MICROBIOLOGY. *Educ:* Univ Tübingen, BS, 51; Univ Bonn, MD, 56; Am Bd Med Microbiol, dipl, 73. *Prof Exp:* Res fel pharmacol, Univ Bonn, 56; Fulbright travel grant, 57; res fel microbiol, Univ Mainz, 58-60 & Yale Univ, 61-63; asst prof microbiol & lab med, 63-69, assoc prof, 69-73, PROF LAB MED, YALE UNIV, 73-; DIR CLIN MICROBIOL LABS, YALE-NEW HAVEN HOSP, 63- *Concurrent Pos:* Mem standards & exam comt, Am Bd Med Microbiol, 73- *Mem:* Am Acad Microbiol; Am Soc Microbiol; Ger Soc Hyg & Microbiol; Asn Clin Sci. *Res:* Pathogenicity and diagnosis of gram-negative rods. *Mailing Add:* 789 Howard Ave New Haven CT 06504

VON GUTFELD, ROBERT J, b Berlin, Ger, Mar 5, 34; US citizen; m 77; c 1. SOLID STATE PHYSICS. *Educ:* Queens Col, BS, 54; Columbia Univ, MA, 57; NY Univ, PhD(physics), 65. *Prof Exp:* Substitute instr physics, Queens Col, 54-55; engr, Sperry Gyroscope Co, 57-60; RES STAFF MEM, T J WATSON RES CTR, IBM CORP, 60- *Mem:* Fel Am Phys Soc; Am Soc Nondestructive Testing. *Res:* Thermal transport in solids using heat pulse techniques; amorphous semiconductor and dye laser research and applications to optical memories; transverse thermoelectric effects in metallic thin films; laser thermoelastic waves; laser enhanced plating and etching. *Mailing Add:* T J Watson Res Ctr IBM Corp Yorktown Heights NY 10598

VON HAGEN, D STANLEY, b Nashville, Tenn, Dec 21, 37; m 59; c 2. PHARMACOLOGY. *Educ:* Carson-Newman Col, BS, 59; Vanderbilt Univ, PhD(pharmacol), 65. *Prof Exp:* Res assoc pharmacol, Vanderbilt Univ, 65-66, instr, 66; instr, 67-69, ASST PROF PHARMACOL, NJ MED SCH, COL MED & DENT, NJ, 69- *Mem:* AAAS; NY Acad Sci. *Res:* Smooth muscle physiology and pharmacology; physiological role of calcium ion in smooth muscle function. *Mailing Add:* Dept of Pharmacol New Jersey Med Sch Newark NJ 07103

VON HERZEN, RICHARD P, b Los Angeles, Calif, May 21, 30; m 58; c 2. MARINE GEOPHYSICS. *Educ:* Calif Inst Technol, BS, 52; Harvard Univ, AM, 56; Univ Calif, PhD(oceanog), 60. *Prof Exp:* Lab asst oceanog, Scripps Inst Oceanog, 52-53, geophysicist, 58-60, asst res geophysicist, 60-64; dep dir off oceanog, UNESCO, 64-66; assoc scientist, 66-73, SR SCIENTIST, WOODS HOLE OCEANOG INST, 73- *Concurrent Pos:* Assoc ed J Geophys Res, Am Geophys Union, 69-71; vis res geophysicist & lectr, Scripps Inst Oceanog, 74-75. *Mem:* Am Geophys Union. *Res:* Structure and dynamics of the earth beneath the ocean floor especially as evidenced from geothermal studies. *Mailing Add:* Woods Hole Oceanog Inst Woods Hole MA 02543

VON HIPPEL, FRANK, b Cambridge, Mass, Dec 26, 37; div. THEORETICAL PHYSICS. *Educ:* Mass Inst Technol, SB, 59; Oxford Univ, DPhil(physics), 62. *Prof Exp:* Res assoc physics, Univ Chicago, 62-64; res assoc, Cornell Univ, 64-66; asst prof, Stanford Univ, 66-70; mem staff theory group, High Energy Physics Div, Argonne Nat Lab, 70-73; resident fel, Nat Acad Sci, 73-74; res scientist, 74-78, SR RES PHYSICIST, CTR ENVIRON STUDIES, PRINCETON UNIV, 78- *Concurrent Pos:* Sloan Found fel, 67-70; consult nuclear energy policy, Off Technol Assessment, Gen Acct Off, House Interior Comt, US Congress, Nuclear Regulatory Comn, Dept Energy, 75. *Honors & Awards:* Am Phys Soc Award, 77. *Mem:* Am Phys Soc; AAAS; Fedn Am Scientists. *Res:* Nuclear energy policy; energy general policy; nuclear arms control and disarmament. *Mailing Add:* Ctr Environ Studies Princeton Univ Eng Quadrangle Princeton NJ 08540

VON HIPPEL, PETER HANS, b Göttingen, Ger, Mar 13, 31; nat US; m 54; c 3. BIOPHYSICAL CHEMISTRY, MOLECULAR BIOLOGY. *Educ:* Mass Inst Technol, BS, 52, MS, 53, PhD(biophys), 55. *Prof Exp:* Asst phys biochem, Mass Inst Technol, 53, NIH fel, 55-56; phys biochemist, US Naval Med Res Inst, Md, 56-59; asst prof biophys, Dartmouth Med Sch, 59-61, assoc prof biochem, 61-67; res assoc, 67-69, PROF CHEM, UNIV ORE, 67-, DIR INST MOLECULAR BIOL, 69- *Concurrent Pos:* Sr fel, USPHS, 59-67, mem study sect biophys & biophys chem, 63-67; chmn, Gordon Res Conf Physics & Phys Chem of Biopolymers, 68; corp vis comn, Dept Biol, Mass Inst Technol, 73-77; Guggenheim found fel, 73-74; mem bd sci counr, Nat Inst Arthritis, Metab & Digestive Dis, NIH, 74-78. *Mem:* AAAS; Biophys Soc (pres, 73-74); Am Soc Biol Chem; Am Chem Soc; Soc Gen Physiol. *Res:* Physical biochemistry of macromolecules; structure, function and interactions of proteins and nucleic acids; molecular aspects of control of genetic expression. *Mailing Add:* Inst of Molecular Biol Univ of Ore Eugene OR 97403

VON HOERNER, SEBASTIAN, b Goerlitz, Ger, Apr 15, 19; m 42; c 3. ASTRONOMY, ENGINEERING. *Educ:* Univ Göettingen, Ger, Diplom, 49, PhD(physics), 51. *Prof Exp:* Scientist astrophys, Max Planck Inst Physics, Göettingen, 49-57; Fulbright fel, Mt Wilson & Palomar Observ, Pasadena, Calif, 55-56; scientist, Astron Rechen-Inst, Heidelberg, Ger, 57-62; SCIENTIST ASTROPHYS & ENG, NAT RADIO ASTRON OBSERV, GREEN BANK, 62- *Concurrent Pos:* Vis prof, Univ Switz, 62, Univ Calif, Los Angeles, 69, Nat Univ, Mexico City, 71, Max Planck Inst Radioastron, Bonn, 72 & 75, Cornell Univ, Ithaca, NY, 74 & Univ Okla, Norman, 77. *Mem:* Deut Astron Gesellschaft; Max-Planck-Gesellschaft; Ver Deut Wiss; Int Astron Union. *Res:* Astrophysics, star formation, stellar dynamics; radio astronomy, cosmology; antenna design, structural optimization; life in space; interstellar communication. *Mailing Add:* Nat Radio Astron Observ Green Bank WV 24944

VON HUENE, ROLAND, b Los Angeles, Calif, Jan 30, 29; m 53; c 3. GEOLOGY. *Educ:* Univ Calif, Los Angeles, AB, 53, PhD, 60. *Prof Exp:* Gen geologist, US Naval Ord Test Sta, 53-67; GEOPHYSICIST, US GEOL SURV, 67- *Concurrent Pos:* Asst, Univ Calif, Los Angeles, 55-57; Fulbright grant, Innsbruck, 57-58; mem comt Alaska earthquake, Nat Acad Sci; Pac site panel, Joint Ocean Insts for Deep Earth Sampling; dep chief off marine geol, US Geol Surv, 73-75; panel mem active margin & site surv, Int Prog Ocean Drilling, 74-; mem nat comt, US Geodynamics Comt, 75- *Mem:* AAAS; Am Geophys Union; Sigma Xi; Geol Soc Am; Ger Geol Asn. *Res:* Marine gravity; magnetics; seismic profiling; tectonics; structural geology; gravimetry. *Mailing Add:* US Geol Surv 345 Middlefield Rd Menlo Park CA 94025

VON HUNGEN, KERN, b Modesto, Calif, May 2, 40; m 67; c 2. NEUROCHEMISTRY, PSYCHOPHARMACOLOGY. *Educ:* Reed Col, BA, 62; Ind Univ, PhD(biol chem), 68. *Prof Exp:* Fel neurobiochem, Chem Biodynamics Lab, Univ Calif, Berkeley, 68-70; fel neurobiochem, Dept Biol Chem, Univ Calif, Los Angeles, 70-71; res chemist, Neurochem Lab, 76-79, CHIEF, BRAIN BIOCHEM LAB, VET ADMIN MED CTR, SEPULVEDA, CALIF, 79- *Concurrent Pos:* Asst res biochemist, Dept Biol Chem, Univ Calif, Los Angeles, 71- *Mem:* Am Soc Neurochem. *Res:* Functional neurochemistry: regulatory mechanisms involving brain membranes, proteins, neurotransmitters and cyclic nucleotides and the effects of alcohol and age on these systems; biochemical aspects of behavior. *Mailing Add:* Brain Biochem Lab 151-B2 Vet Admin Med Ctr Sepulveda CA 91343

VON KESZYCKI, CARL HEINRICH, b Utrecht, Holland, Sept 4, 22; US citizen; m 56. PHYSICS. *Educ:* Univ Munich, BS, 52, PhD(physics), 59. *Prof Exp:* Res engr, Lockheed-Calif Co, 60-63, scientist, Lockheed-Ga Co, 63-64, dir res, 64-67, sr res & develop engr, 67-70; pres, Sylesia Corp, 70-72; sr fel, Mellon Inst Sci, 72-74; dir phys sci technol, Essex Int, Inc, 72-74; DIR SPEC PROJS, GRUMMAN AEROSPACE CORP, 74- *Mem:* Am Phys Soc; Am Inst Aeronaut & Astronaut. *Res:* Nuclear physics; aeronautical engineering; controlled thermonuclear fusion. *Mailing Add:* 121 Santa Barbara Dr Plainview NY 11803

VON KORFF, RICHARD WALTER, b Davenport, Iowa, Jan 6, 16; m 43; c 3. BIOCHEMISTRY, ENZYMOLOGY. *Educ:* Univ Minn, BA, 47, PhD(physiol chem), 51; Am Bd Clin Chem, dipl, 74. *Prof Exp:* Anal chemist, Testing & Res Lab, Deere & Co, Ill, 37-41; asst & sr sci aide, Anal & Phys Chem Div, Northern Regional Res Lab, USDA, 41-43, jr chemist, Agr Residues Div, 43-45; asst prof pediat & physiol chem, Univ Minn, 55-66; dir biochem res, Friends of Psychiat Res, Spring Grove State Hosp, Baltimore, 66-68; dir biochem res, Md Psychiat Res Ctr, 68-77; RES PROF BIOCHEM, MICH MOLECULAR INST, MIDLAND, MICH, 77- *Concurrent Pos:* Fel, Inst Enzyme Res, Univ Wis, 51-52; Whitney Found fel biochem, Dept Pediat, Heart Hosp, Univ Minn, 52-53, Am Heart Asn fel, 53-55, USPHS sr res fel biochem, 60-66; chmn subcomt enzymes, Comt Biol Chem, Nat Acad Sci-Nat Res Coun, 61-67 & 69-76, adj prof, Dept Med Chem, Sch Pharm, 71-73; adj assoc prof, Dept Macromolecular Sci, Case-Western Univ, 79-; adj prof, Dept Biochem, Dent Sch, Univ Md, 75-77; Adj prof dept chem, Cent Mich Univ, 80- *Mem:* Am Soc Biol Chemists; Am Chem Soc; Nat Acad Clin Biochem; Int Soc Neurochem; Am Soc Neurochem. *Res:* Monomaine oxidase, reaction mechanism, nature of action of reversible inhibitors; enzymic control mechanisms; monoamine oxidase. *Mailing Add:* Mich Molecular Inst 1910 W St Andrews Rd Midland MI 48640

VON LEDEN, HANS VICTOR, b Ger, Nov 20, 18; nat US; m 48; c 2. LARYNGOLOGY. *Educ:* Loyola Univ, Ill, MD, 42; Am Bd Otolaryngol, dipl, 45. *Prof Exp:* Intern, Mercy Hosp-Loyola Univ Clins, 41-42; resident, Presby Hosp, Chicago, 42-43; fel otolaryngol & plastic surg, Mayo Found, Univ Minn, 43-45, first asst, Mayo Clin, 45; clin assoc otolaryngol, Stritch Sch Med, Loyola Univ, Ill, 47-51; from asst prof to assoc prof, Med Sch, Northwestern Univ, 52-61; assoc prof surg, Sch Med, Univ Calif, Los Angeles, 61-66; PROF BIO-COMMUN, UNIV SOUTHERN CALIF, 66- *Concurrent Pos:* Consult, US Navy, 47-; assoc prof, Cook County Grad Sch Med, 49-58; med dir, William & Harriet Gould Found, 55-59; pres, Inst Laryngol & Voice Dis, 59-65, med dir, 65-; vis prof, US & 25 for countries. *Honors & Awards:* Bucranio, Univ Padua, 58; Gold Medal, Ital Res Cross, 59; Hektoen Medal, AMA, 60; Sci Awards, Am Speech & Hearing Asn, 60, 62 & 65; Casselberry Award, Am Laryngol Asn, 62; Manuel Garcia Prize, Int Asn Logoped & Phoniatrics, 68; Gutzmann Medaille, Deut Ges Otolaryngol. *Mem:* Fel AAAS; fel Am Acad Otolaryngol; fel Am Col Surgeons; fel Int Col Surgeons (pres, 72); fel Am Speech & Hearing Asn. *Res:* Voice and speech; laryngology. *Mailing Add:* Inst Laryngol & Voice Dis 10921 Wilshire Blvd Los Angeles CA 90024

VON LICHTENBERG, FRANZ, b Miskolc, Hungary, Nov 29, 19; nat US; m 49; c 6. PATHOLOGY. *Educ:* Nat Univ Mex, MD, 45; Am Bd Path, dipl, 51. *Hon Degrees:* Dr, Nat Univ Nicaragua, 59; MA, Harvard Univ, 68. *Prof Exp:* Pathologist, Hosp Exp Nutrit, Mex, 47; prof path, Nat Univ Mex, 48-52; from asst prof to assoc prof, Univ PR, 53-58; instr, 58-59, assoc, 59-62, from asst prof to assoc prof, 62-74, PROF PATH, HARVARD MED SCH, 74- *Concurrent Pos:* Fel, Mex Dept Health, 46; Kellogg Found, Am Col Physicians & Latin Am fels, 50-51; pathologist, Clin Hosp, Bahia, Brazil, 51-52, Gen Hosp, Mex, 52-53 & San Juan City Hosp, PR, 53-58; assoc pathologist, Peter Bent Brigham Hosp, 58-62, sr assoc, 62-68, pathologist, 68-; assoc mem comn parasitol, Armed Forces Epidemiol Bd, 59, mem, 64-71; consult, Div Parasitic Dis, WHO, 65; mem study sect trop med & parasitol, NIH, 68-73; mem parasitic dis panel, USJapan Coop Med Sci Prof, 71-74, chmn, 74-78; mem steering comn Schistosomiasis, WHO-TDR, 77-; James W McLaughlin vis prof, Univ Tex Med Br, 80. *Mem:* Am Soc Trop Med & Hyg (vpres, 76); Am Asn Path & Bact; Fedn Am Socs Exp Biol. *Res:* Tropical and parasitic diseases; schistosomiasis; filariasis; liver pathology; immunopathology. *Mailing Add:* Peter Bent Brigham Hosp 721 Huntington Ave Boston MA 02115

VON MALTZAHN, KRAFT EBERHARD, b Rostock, Ger, Dec 17, 25; Can citizen; m 49; c 3. BOTANY. *Educ:* Yale Univ, MS, 50, PhD(bot), 54. *Prof Exp:* From asst prof to assoc prof, 54-62, PROF BIOL, DALHOUSIE UNIV, 62-, GEORGE S CAMPBELL PROF & HEAD DEPT, 63- *Mem:* Can Bot Asn; Can Soc Plant Physiol. *Res:* Plant morphogenesis. *Mailing Add:* 15 Wenlock Grove Halifax NS B3P 1P5 Can

VON MEERWALL, ERNST DIETER, b Vienna, Austria, Dec 29, 40. PHYSICS. *Educ:* Northern Ill Univ, BS, 63, MS, 65; Northwestern Univ, Evanston, PhD(physics), 69. *Prof Exp:* Res assoc, Dept Metall & Mat Res Lab, Univ Ill, Urbana, 69-71; asst prof, 71-74, assoc prof, 74-80, PROF PHYSICS, UNIV AKRON, 80- *Mem:* Am Phys Soc; Sigma Xi. *Res:* Solid state experiment; nuclear magnetic resonance, Mössbauer effect and magnetic susceptibility; alloys; nuclear quadrupole effect; polymers; numerical methods. *Mailing Add:* Dept of Physics Univ of Akron Akron OH 44325

VON MOLNAR, STEPHAN, b Leipzig, Ger, June 26, 35; US citizen; m 56; c 2. SOLID STATE PHYSICS. *Educ:* Trinity Col (Conn), BS, 57; Univ Maine, MS, 59; Univ Calif, Riverside, PhD(physics), 65. *Prof Exp:* Mem res staff physics, Polychem Div, Exp Sta, E I du Pont de Nemours & Co, 59-60; MEM RES STAFF PHYSICS, THOMAS J WATSON RES CTR, IBM CORP, 65-, MGR COOP PHENOMENA GROUP, 69- *Concurrent Pos:* Sr res fel, Imp Col, Univ London, 73-74. *Mem:* Am Phys Soc. *Res:* Paramagnetic and ferromagnetic resonance; transport properties of magnetic semiconductors; tunneling spectroscopy of superconductors and semiconductors; low temperature specific heat. *Mailing Add:* Thomas J Watson Res Ctr IBM Corp PO Box 218 Yorktown Heights NY 10598

VONNEGUT, BERNARD, b Indianapolis, Ind, Aug 29, 14; wid; c 5. PHYSICAL CHEMISTRY. *Educ:* Mass Inst Technol, BS, 36, PhD(phys chem), 39. *Prof Exp:* Res assoc, Preston Labs, Pa, 39-40 & Hartford Empire Co, Conn, 40-41; chem eng, Mass Inst Technol, 41-42, meteorol, 42-45; res labs, Gen Elec Co, 45-52; mem staff, Arthur D Little Inc, 52-67; PROF ATMOSPHERIC SCI, STATE UNIV NY ALBANY, 67-, SR RES SCIENTIST ATMOSPHERIC SCI RES CTR, 67- *Mem:* AAAS; Am Meteorol Soc; Am Geophys Union; Meteorol Soc Japan; Royal Meteorol Soc. *Res:* Nucleation phenomena; cloud seeding; surface chemistry; aerosols; atmospheric electricity. *Mailing Add:* Dept of Atmospheric Sci State Univ of NY Albany NY 12222

VON NEIDA, ALLYN ROBERT, b West Reading, Pa, May 7, 32; m 55; c 3. METALLURGY, MATERIALS SCIENCE. *Educ:* Lehigh Univ, BS(elec eng) & BS(metall eng), 55; Yale Univ, PhD(metall), 60. *Prof Exp:* Res metallurgist, Olin Mathieson Chem Corp, 55-57; res asst metall, Yale Univ, 60-61; MEM TECH STAFF, BELL TEL LABS, MURRAY HILL, 61- *Res:* Magnetics; crystal growth. *Mailing Add:* 133 Ashland Rd Summit NJ 07901

VON NOORDEN, GUNTER KONSTANTIN, b Frankfurt, Ger, Mar 19, 28; US citizen; m; c 1. OPHTHALMOLOGY. *Educ:* Univ Frankfurt, MD, 54; State Univ Iowa, MS, 60. *Prof Exp:* Rotating intern, St Vincent Infirmary, Little Rock, Ark, 54-56; fel ophthal, Cleveland Clin, 56-57; resident, Med Ctr, State Univ Iowa, 57-60, asst prof, Sch Med, 61-63; from assoc prof to prof, Johns Hopkins Univ, 63-72; PROF OPHTHAL, BAYLOR COL MED, 72- *Concurrent Pos:* Nat Inst Neurol Dis & Blindness spec trainee, Univ Tübingen, 60-61; Nat Inst Neurol Dis & Blindness spec fel, Univ Iowa, 61-62; mem, Armed Forces Nat Res Coun Vision, 64-68; Int Strabismological Asn Bielschowsky lectr, 70; adj prof neurol sci, Sch Biol Sci, Univ Tex, 72-; pres, Am Orthoptic Coun, 73-74. *Honors & Awards:* Hectoen Gold Medal, AMA, 60; Honor Award, Am Acad Ophthal & Otolaryngol, 70. *Mem:* Am Ophthal Soc; fel Am Acad Ophthal & Otolaryngol; Asn Res Strabismus (secy, 72-73); Int Strabismological Asn (secy-treas, 68-74); Pan Am Ophthal Asn. *Res:* Investigation of clinical and laboratory aspects of neuromuscular anomalies of the eyes, especially amblyopia; improvement of our knowledge of strabismus and the basic morphological and neurophysiological aspects of different forms of amblyopia. *Mailing Add:* Tex Children's Hosp 6621 Fannin Houston TX 77025

VON OHAIN, HANS JOACHIM, b Dessau, Ger, Dec 14, 11; US citizen; m 49; c 4. GAS TURBINE TECHNOLOGY. *Educ:* Univ Goettingen, PhD(physics), 35. *Prof Exp:* Chief scientist, Aero Space Res Lab, US Air Force, 63-75, Propulsion Lab, Wright-Patterson AFB, 75-79; SR RES ENGR, RES INST, UNIV DAYTON, 80- *Concurrent Pos:* Consult aero propulsion, 80-; adj prof, Univ Fla. *Honors & Awards:* Goddard Award, Am Inst Aeronaut & Astronaut, 66. *Mem:* Nat Acad Eng; fel Am Inst Aeronaut & Astronaut. *Res:* Advanced ejector application to aircraft; advanced methods for particle separation in multicomponent flows. *Mailing Add:* 5598 Folkestone Dr Dayton OH 45459

VON OSTWALDEN, PETER WEBER, b Reichenberg, Czech, June 1, 23; m 46; c 1. ORGANIC CHEMISTRY. *Educ:* Univ Graz, Doctorandum, 50; Columbia Univ, MA, 54, PhD(pyridine chem), 58. *Prof Exp:* Process develop chemist, Merck & Co, Inc, Cherokee Plant, Pa, 57-63; from asst prof to assoc prof, 63-77, PROF CHEM, YOUNGSTOWN STATE UNIV, 77- *Concurrent Pos:* Vis assoc, Calif Inst Technol, 70-71; vis fel, Princeton Univ, 79-80. *Mem:* Am Chem Soc; Sigma Xi. *Res:* Pyridine and steroid chemistry; heterocyclic nitrogen oxides; chemistry of heterocyclic compounds; spectroscopy; organic applications. *Mailing Add:* Dept of Chem Youngstown State Univ Youngstown OH 44555

VON REIS, SIRI, b Detroit, Mich, Feb 10, 31; m 63, 75; c 7. BOTANICAL TAXONOMY, ETHNOBOTANY. *Educ:* Univ Mich, AB, 53; Radcliffe Col, MA, 57, PhD(biol), 61. *Prof Exp:* HON CUR ETHNOBOT, NY BOT GARDEN & ASSOC ETHNOPHARMACOL, BOT MUS HARVARD UNIV, 74- *Concurrent Pos:* Nat Inst Ment Health res grants, Bot Mus, Harvard Univ, 64-66; Nat Libr Med Grant, 69; trustee, Radcliffe Col, 70-76; Rockefeller Found grant, NY Bot Garden, 75- *Mem:* AAAS; Am Anthrop Asn; Am Inst Biol Sci; Am Soc Pharmacog; Int Asn Plant Taxon. *Res:* Higher plants which are used by primitive societies for curing, magic or eating and which contain biodynamic agents potentially useful in modern medicine and nutrition. *Mailing Add:* 1107 Fifth Ave New York NY 10028

VON RIESEN, DANIEL DEAN, b Beatrice, Nebr, Nov 20, 43; m 68. ORGANIC CHEMISTRY. *Educ:* Hastings Col, BA, 65; Univ Nebr, PhD(chem), 71. *Prof Exp:* Instr chem, Hastings Col, 70-71; asst prof, Hamilton Col, 71-72; ASST PROF CHEM, ROGER WILLIAMS COL, 72- *Mem:* Am Chem Soc. *Res:* Cycloaddition reactions of heterocumulenes; chemical education. *Mailing Add:* Dept of Chem Roger Williams Col Bristol RI 02809

VON RIESEN, VICTOR LYLE, b Marysville, Kans, Jan 21, 23; m 45; c 2. MEDICAL MICROBIOLOGY. *Educ:* Univ Kans, BA, 48, MA, 50, PhD, 55. *Prof Exp:* Asst instr bact, Univ Kans, 48-49, instr, 49-55, instr med microbiol, Sch Med, 55-56, asst prof, 56-59; from asst prof to assoc prof, 59-69, PROF MED MICROBIOL, UNIV NEBR MED CTR, OMAHA, 69- *Mem:* Am Soc Microbiol; Soc Appl Bact. *Res:* Medical bacteriology; microbial physiology. *Mailing Add:* Dept of Med Microbiol Univ of Nebr Med Ctr Omaha NE 68105

VON ROHR, BEATRICE LOUISE, b St Louis, Mo, Apr 7, 25; m 47. APPLIED MATHEMATICS. *Educ:* Wash Univ, AB, 46; Gonzaga Univ, MS, 64. *Prof Exp:* Asst math, Wash Univ, 46-47, instr, 47-51, res mathematician, Barnes Hosp Div, 51-52, asst math, univ, 52-59; chmn dept math high sch, Mo, 59-60; prof, Hannibal-La Grange Col-St Louis, 61-62; assoc prof, Shelton Col, 67-68; prof, Hannibal-La Grange Campus, 68-69, head dept, St Louis Campus, 69-71, PROF MATH, MO BAPTIST COL, ST LOUIS CAMPUS, 69- *Concurrent Pos:* Vpres, Electrovision Co, 68-; math consult parochial schs, E US, 71- & Electrovision Co, 74-; judge high sch St Louis Post-Dispatch Sci Fair, 71-; lectr high schs, Mo, 72. *Mem:* Math Asn Am; Soc Indust & Appl Math. *Res:* Research for advanced calculus and algebra texts. *Mailing Add:* 1119 Sanford St Louis MO 63139

VON ROHR, OSCAR E, JR, b St Louis, Mo, June 30, 17; m 47. ELECTRICAL ENGINEERING. *Educ:* Wash Univ, BSEE, MSEE, 56; Trinity Col, PhD(physics), 58. *Prof Exp:* Field engr, Brookley Field, 42-46; elec engr, White Rodgers Co, 53-54; teaching asst elec eng, Sever Inst, Wash Univ, 54-56, instr, 56-58; pres consult, Electrovision Co, 58-62; chief elec engr, City St Louis, 58-61; elec engr, Falstaff Brewing Co, 61; res engr, McDonnell Aircraft Co, 61-62; prof elec eng & head dept, Gonzaga Univ, 62-66; prof sci & math & head dept, Shelton Col, 66-67; PRES CONSULT, ELECTROVISION CO, 67- *Concurrent Pos:* Independent expert witness, consult & lectr, 58- *Mem:* Inst Elec & Electronics Engrs. *Res:* Microwaves; antennas; semicircular ridges in rectangular waveguides; relativity; science and the Bible; smoking. *Mailing Add:* 1119 Sanford St Louis MO 63139

VON ROOS, OLDWIG, b Koblenz, Ger, Jan 23, 25; m 53; c 4. THEORETICAL PHYSICS. *Educ:* Univ Marburg, BS, 50, MS, 54, PhD(physics), 56. *Prof Exp:* Staff scientist, Jet Propulsion Lab, 57-61, group supvr physics, 61-65; sr staff scientist, Astrophys Res Co, Calif, 65-72; MEM TECH STAFF, JET PROPULSION LAB, 72- *Concurrent Pos:* Vis prof, Univ Southern Calif, 63-65. *Mem:* AAAS; fel Am Phys Soc. *Res:* Atomic physics; quantum plasma theory; electromagnetic theory; semiconductor device theory. *Mailing Add:* Jet Propulsion Lab 4800 Oak Grove Dr Pasadena CA 91109

VON ROSENBERG, DALE URSINI, chemical & petroleum engineering, see previous edition

VON ROSENBERG, H(ERMANN) E(UGENE), b Austin, Tex, Mar 6, 26; m 57. CHEMICAL ENGINEERING. *Educ:* Univ Tex, BS, 49, MS, 51; Univ Del, PhD(chem eng), 55. *Prof Exp:* Res chem engr, 54-60, sr res chem engr, 60-65, res specialist, 65-72, res assoc, 72-77, HEAD M&C, EXXON RES & ENG CO, 77- *Mem:* Am Chem Soc; Am Inst Chem Engrs. *Res:* Chemical reactor dynamics applied chiefly to the petroleum refining processes; feed, catalyst and process studies in fluid catalytic cracking; coal utilization and gasification. *Mailing Add:* 105 Crow Rd Baytown TX 77520

VON ROSENBERG, JOSEPH LESLIE, JR, b Lockhart, Tex, Aug 22, 32; m 58; c 3. ORGANIC CHEMISTRY. *Educ:* Univ Tex, Austin, BA, 54, PhD(chem), 63. *Prof Exp:* Res chemist, Ethyl Corp, 57-58; res chemist, Celanese Chem Co, 62-64; Robert A Welch fel, Univ Tex, Austin, 64-65; asst prof, 65-69, assoc prof, 69-80, PROF CHEM, CLEMSON UNIV, 80- *Mem:* Am Chem Soc; The Chem Soc. *Res:* Physical organic and organometallic chemistry. *Mailing Add:* Dept of Chem Clemson Univ Clemson SC 29631

VON ROSENVINGE, TYCHO TOR, b Beverly, Mass, Apr 18, 42; m 66; c 3. SPACE PHYSICS. *Educ:* Amherst Col, AB, 63; Univ Minn, PhD(physics), 70. *Prof Exp:* Nat Acad Sci fel, 69-71, ASTROPHYSICIST, HIGH ENERGY ASTROPHYS DIV, GODDARD SPACE FLIGHT CTR, NASA, 71-, PROJ SCIENTIST, INT SUN-EARTH EXPLORER-3, 72- *Mem:* Am Phys Soc. *Res:* Charge composition of solar energetic particles; charge composition, origin and propagation of galactic cosmic rays. *Mailing Add:* Code 661 NASA Goddard Space Flight Ctr Greenbelt MD 20771

VON RUDLOFF, ERNST MAX, organic chemistry, see previous edition

VON RÜMKER, ROSMARIE, b Halberstadt, Ger, July 30, 26; nat US. PESTICIDE EFFICACY. *Educ:* Univ Bonn, Dipl & DAgr(plant path, entom, agr econ), 50. *Prof Exp:* Farm adminr seed breeding, Ger, 50-51; agr res biologist, Farbenfabriken Bayer, Ag, 51-54; dir res, Chemagro Corp, NY, 54-58, vpres res & develop, Kansas City, Mo, 59-71; MANAGING PARTNER, RVR CONSULTS, 71- *Concurrent Pos:* Mem state & nat sci & environ adv comt, Sci Adv Bd, US Environ Protection Agency & Nat Acad Sci. *Mem:* Entom Soc Am; Am Chem Soc; Am Soc Agr Eng; Weed Sci Soc Am; Plant Growth Regulator Soc Am. *Res:* Crop protection; benefits, costs and environmental effects of pesticides; pest management problems and opportunities; pesticide research and development; economics and marketing of pesticides, forecasting. *Mailing Add:* PO Box 553 Shawnee Mission KS 66201

VON SCHONFELDT, HILMAR ARMIN, b Delitzsch, Ger, May 3, 37. PETROLEUM ENGINEERING, ROCK MECHANICS. *Educ:* Clausthal Tech Univ, Dipl Ing, 64; Univ Minn, Minneapolis, PhD(mineral resources), 70. *Prof Exp:* Res engr, Shell Develop Co, 66 & Continental Oil Co, 67; asst prof petrol eng, Univ Tex, Austin, 69-77; MGR MINING RES, OCCIDENTAL RES CORP, 77- *Mem:* Soc Petrol Engrs. *Res:* In situ stress measurement; hydraulic fracturing; drilling; underground caverns; solution mining. *Mailing Add:* Occidental Res Corp C/O Island Cork Coal Lexington KY 40503

VON SCHRILTZ, DON MORRIS, chemistry, see previous edition

VON STRYK, FREDERICK GEORGE, b Pollenhof, Estonia, Sept 6, 12; Can citizen; m 44; c 1. ORGANIC CHEMISTRY. *Educ:* Tartu State Univ, Chem, 34; Univ Leipzig, dipl chem, 38, Dr rer nat(chem), 40. *Prof Exp:* Res asst org chem, Univ Leipzig, 40-41; res chemist, Badische Soda & Anilin Fabrik, Ger, 41-48, Tex Co, Que, 48-51 & Dominion Rubber Co, Ont, 51-65; res scientist, Can Dept Agr, 65-77; RETIRED. *Concurrent Pos:* Consult. *Mem:* Chem Inst Can. *Res:* Plant protection by chemicals, such as insecticides, fungicides and herbicides; translocation of these chemicals in plants and changes in their structure due to plant metabolism. *Mailing Add:* Apartado Postal 228 Palma de Mallorca Spain

VON TERSCH, LAWRENCE W, b Waverly, Iowa, Mar 17, 23; m 48. ELECTRICAL ENGINEERING. *Educ:* Iowa State Univ, BS, 43, MS, 48, PhD(elec eng), 53. *Prof Exp:* From asst prof to prof elec eng, Iowa State Univ, 46-56; chmn dept elec eng, 58-65, assoc dean eng, 65-67, actg dean, 67-68, PROF ELEC ENG & DIR COMPUT LAB, MICH STATE UNIV, 56-, DEAN COL ENG, 68- *Mem:* Inst Elec & Electronics Engrs. *Res:* Computer applications. *Mailing Add:* Col of Eng Mich State Univ East Lansing MI 48824

VON TURKOVICH, BRANIMIR F(RANCIS), b Zagreb, Croatia, Dec 3, 24; US citizen; m 51; c 5. MATERIALS SCIENCE, MECHANICAL ENGINEERING. *Educ:* Univ Naples, BSc, 47; Univ Madrid, MSc & DNav Eng, 51; Univ Ill, Urbana, PhD(mech eng, physics), 62. *Prof Exp:* Naval architect, Forgas & Font SA, Madrid, 50-51; sr res engr, Kearney & Trecker

Corp, Wis, 52-57; lectr mech eng, Univ Ill, Urbana, 57-62, assoc prof mech eng & physics, 62-69, prof mech & indust eng, 69-70; PROF MECH ENG & CHMN DEPT, UNIV VT, 70- *Concurrent Pos:* Lectr, Marquette Univ, 55-57; vis prof, Torino Polytech, Italy, 67-68; consult, Vermont Am Corp, Louisville, Ky, 71-; NATO sr prof, Italy, 76. *Honors & Awards:* Res Medal, Soc Mfg Engrs, 76. *Mem:* Fel Am Soc Mech Engrs; Am Phys Soc; Int Inst Prod Res; Soc Mfg Engrs; Sigma Xi. *Res:* Mechanical and physical metallurgy; production engineering; theoretical and applied mechanics; metal cutting and forming. *Mailing Add:* 201 Votey Bldg Univ of Vt Burlington VT 05405

VON VOIGTLANDER, PHILIP FRIEDRICH, b Jackson, Mich, Feb 3, 46; m 68; c 3. NEUROPHARMACOLOGY. *Educ:* Mich State Univ, BS, 68, DVM, 69, MS, 71, PhD(pharmacol), 72. *Prof Exp:* NIH trainee cent nerv syst pharmacol, Mich State Univ, 69-72; res scientist, 72-80, SR RES SCIENTIST, CENT NERV SYST PHARMACOL, UPJOHN CO, 80- *Mem:* AAAS; Soc Neurosci; Am Soc Pharmacol & Exp Therapeut. *Res:* Development of animal models of psychiatric and neurological diseases for the purpose of studying the mechanisms of action of centrally acting drugs and identification of new therapeutic agents. *Mailing Add:* Upjohn Co Kalamazoo MI 49001

VON WICKLEN, FREDERICK CHARLES, b Mt Vernon, Ohio, Sept 3, 00; m 41; c 1. CHEMISTRY. *Educ:* Univ Louisville, BS, 22, MS, 23; Columbia Univ, MA, 31, PhD(phys chem), 34. *Prof Exp:* Res chemist, Acme White Lead Co, Mich, 23-25; asst chief chemist, Graham-Paige Motors, 25-29; res chemist, Titanium Pigment Co, NY, 34-36; asst, Columbia Univ, 36-37; prof chem, Col Ozarks, 37-39; res chemist, Takamine Lab, NJ, 39-40; prof chem, York Col, 41-46; assoc prof, Univ Omaha, 46-48; prof, Lambuth Col, 49-52; assoc prof, Westminster Col (Mo), 52-53; prof, Panhandle Agr & Mech Col, 54-61; prof, 61-70, EMER PROF CHEM, SOUTHWESTERN STATE COL, 70- *Concurrent Pos:* Instr, Univ Nebr, 44-46. *Mem:* AAAS; fel Am Inst Chem; Am Chem Soc. *Res:* Chemistry of colloidal solutions of chromic chloride; preparation and testing of starch-splitting enzymes

VON WINBUSH, SAMUEL, b Henderson, NC, Aug 2, 32; m 62; c 1. INORGANIC CHEMISTRY, PHYSICAL CHEMISTRY. *Educ:* Tenn State Univ, AB, 53; Iowa State Univ, MS, 56; Univ Kans, PhD(inorg chem), 60. *Prof Exp:* Asst prof chem & chmn dept, Tenn State Univ, 60-62; prof, NC A&T State Univ, 62-65; prof, Fisk Univ, 65-71; prof, 71-80, DISTINGUISHED PROF CHEM, STATE UNIV NY COL OLD WESTBURY, 80- *Concurrent Pos:* Consult metals & ceramics div, Oak Ridge Nat Lab, 66-; vis prof, Wesleyan Univ, 69-70; consult, State Univ NY Col Old Westbury, 70-71. *Mem:* AAAS; Am Chem Soc. *Res:* Coordination chemistry; ligand field and charge transfer spectra; inorganic polymers; unfamiliar oxidation states of metals in molten salts and other nonaqueous solvents. *Mailing Add:* Dept of Chem State Univ NY Old Westbury NY 11568

VON WINKLE, WILLIAM A, b Bridgeport, Conn, Nov 29, 28; m 40; c 8. HYDRODYNAMICS, UNDERWATER ACOUSTICS. *Educ:* Yale Univ, BSEE, 50-52, MSEE, 52; Univ Calif, Berkeley, PhD(eng sci), 61. *Prof Exp:* Asst, Yale Univ, 50-52; electronic engr, US Navy Underwater Sound Lab, 52-61, electronic engr, mgr & dir, Bur Ships Trident Lab, Bermuda, 61-63, head signal processing br, 63-66, assoc tech dir res, 66-70, ASSOC TECH DIR TECHNOL, NAVAL UNDERWATER SYSTS CTR, 70- *Concurrent Pos:* Instr, YMCA Jr Col, 51-52 & Mitchell Jr Col, 54-57; vis lectr, Univ Conn, 54-81; assoc ed, Acoust Signal Processing, Acoust Soc Am, 69-81; adj asst prof, Rensselaer Polytech Inst, 55-65; instr, Univ Md, 62; US Nat Rep to Sci Comn of Nat Rep, NATO, Saclant Res Ctr, 71- *Mem:* Inst Elec & Electronics Engrs; fel Acoust Soc Am; Sigma Xi. *Res:* Acoustics, sonar systems, target characteristics, transducer array design, fire control, submarine weaponry, hydrodynamics, optical signal processing, transient detection and classification, adaptive filtering techniques and holography; boundary layer hydrodynamics with application to naval warfare problems. *Mailing Add:* 324 Great Neck Rd Waterford CT 06385

VON ZELLEN, BRUCE WALFRED, b Ann Arbor, Mich, Feb 14, 22; m 49; c 1. PARASITOLOGY, PROTOZOOLOGY. *Educ:* Northern Mich Col, AB, 47; Univ Mich, MS, 49; Duke Univ, PhD(zool), 59. *Prof Exp:* Lab asst physiol & zool, Univ Mich, 49-50; assoc prof biol sci, Ky Wesleyan Col, 50-57; instr zool, Duke Univ, 57-59; ASSOC PROF BIOL SCI, NORTHERN ILL UNIV, 59- *Concurrent Pos:* Consult, panels on equip grants, NSF, Washington, DC & Chicago. *Mem:* AAAS; Am Soc Trop Med & Hyg; Soc Protozool; Am Soc Parasitol. *Res:* Parasitic protozoa; life history of coccidiosis; blood parasite infection; cell culture. *Mailing Add:* Dept of Biol Sci Northern Ill Univ De Kalb IL 60115

VON ZWECK, ORTWIN HARTMUT, physical oceanography, see previous edition

VOOGT, JAMES LEONARD, b Grand Rapids, Mich, Feb 8, 44; m 66; c 2. PHYSIOLOGY, NEUROENDOCRINOLOGY. *Educ:* Mich Technol Univ, BS, 66; Mich State Univ, MS, 68, PhD(physiol), 70. *Prof Exp:* NIH fel, Med Ctr, Univ Calif, San Francisco, 70-71; asst prof physiol, Univ Louisville, 71-77, NIH res grant, 72-81; ASSOC PROF PHYSIOL, UNIV KANS, 77- *Mem:* Am Physiol Soc; Int Soc Neuroendocrinol; Endocrine Soc; Soc Study Reproduction; Soc Neurosci. *Res:* Control of anterior pituitary function by hypothalamus; feedback systems; hormone analysis; reproduction control. *Mailing Add:* Dept of Physiol Univ of Kans Kansas City KS 66103

VOOK, FREDERICK LUDWIG, b Milwaukee, Wis, Jan 17, 31; m 58; c 2. PHYSICS. *Educ:* Univ Chicago, BA, 51, BS, 52; Univ Ill, MS, 54, PhD(physics), 58. *Prof Exp:* Mem staff, 58-62, div supvr, 62-71, dept mgr, 71-78, DIR, SANDIA LABS, 78- *Mem:* Fel Am Phys Soc. *Res:* Defects in solids, primarily semiconductors; defects investigated by means of radiation damage at low temperatures; infrared absorption; ion implantation in semiconductors; ion backscattering and channeling studies of solids

VOOK, RICHARD WERNER, b Milwaukee, Wis, Aug 2, 29; m 57; c 4. SOLID STATE PHYSICS. *Educ:* Carleton Col, BA, 51; Univ Ill, MS, 52, PhD(physics), 57. *Prof Exp:* Mem res staff, Res Ctr, Int Bus Mach Corp, NY, 57-61; res labs, Franklin Inst, Pa, 61-65; assoc prof metall, 65-70, PROF MAT SCI, SYRACUSE UNIV, 70-, DIR ELECTRON MICROS LAB, 68- *Concurrent Pos:* Consult, Amperex Corp, 72, Carrier Corp, 72-73, Revere Copper & Brass, 77, Inficon Leyboldt-Heraeus, 81; prin investr, Atomic Energy Comn, 66-72, NSF, 66-76, Electron Resources Develop Agency, 77 & Off Naval Res, 79-82; res contract, Westinghouse, 77-79. *Mem:* Am Phys Soc; Am Vacuum Soc; Electron Micros Soc Am; Metal Soc of the Am Inst Metal Engrs; Am Soc Testing Mat. *Res:* Electron microscopy and diffraction; x-ray diffraction; thin films; epitaxial growth; surface physics; imperfections in solids; electrical contact phenomena. *Mailing Add:* Dept of Chem Eng & Mat Sci Syracuse Univ 409 Link Hall Syracuse NY 13210

VOORHEES, BURTON HAMILTON, b Tucson, Ariz, Dec 3, 42. BIOMATHEMATICS. *Educ:* Univ Calif, Berkeley, AB, 64; Univ Ariz, MS, 66; Univ Tex, Austin, PhD(physics), 71. *Prof Exp:* Asst prof math & physics, Pars Col, Iran, 71-73; RES ASSOC MATH, UNIV ALTA, 73- *Res:* Stochastic geometry; quantization of gravitation; black hole physics; mathematical models of evolutive processes; general systems theory. *Mailing Add:* Dept of Math Univ of Alta Edmonton AB T5H 0Z8 Can

VOORHEES, HOWARD R(OBERT), b Eatontown, NJ, Feb 13, 21; m 46; c 3. CHEMICAL ENGINEERING, MATERIALS SCIENCE. *Educ:* Rutgers Univ, BS, 42; Mass Inst Technol, MS, 47; Univ Mich, PhD(chem & metall eng), 56. *Prof Exp:* Asst prof chem eng, Univ Toledo, 48-50; instr chem & metall eng, Univ Mich, 50-55, assoc res engr, 55-63; TECH DIR, MAT TECHNOL CORP, 64- *Honors & Awards:* Award of Merit, Am Soc Testing & Mat, 78. *Mem:* Am Soc Mech Engrs; Am Soc Testing & Mat; Am Soc Metals. *Res:* Creep-rupture of alloys under variable and complex stresses. *Mailing Add:* 2646 Park Ridge Dr Ann Arbor MI 48103

VOORHEES, JOHN E, b Lima, Ohio, Aug 20, 29; m 53; c 2. MECHANICAL & ELECTRICAL ENGINEERING. *Educ:* Univ Toledo, BSME, 51; Ohio State Univ, MSME, 52. *Prof Exp:* Prin mech engr, Battelle Mem Inst, 52-58, asst chief mech res, 58-60, group dir mech dynamics, 60-66, chief mech dynamics, 66-70; mgr res & develop, Minster Mach Co, 70-77; MGR RES, HOBART CORP, 77- *Mem:* Am Soc Mech Engrs. *Res:* Vibrations analysis; design of balancing equip; control system and machine design; development of high speed mechanisms and heavy machines; dynamic analysis of heavy machinery; design of machine foundations and mounts. *Mailing Add:* 1429 Fox Dale Pl Sidney OH 45365

VOORHEES, JOHN JAMES, b Cleveland, Ohio, Dec 5, 38; m 61; c 4. DERMATOLOGY, MEDICAL RESEARCH. *Educ:* Bowling Green State Univ, BS, 60; Univ Mich, Ann Arbor, MD, 63. *Prof Exp:* Intern internal med, 63-64, trainee clin internal med, 66, NIH trainee biochem, 67-68, trainee clin dermat, 67-69, Carl Herzog scholar biochem, 68-70, from instr to assoc prof dermat, 69-74, PROF DERMAT, MED SCH, UNIV MICH, ANN ARBOR, 74-, CHMN DEPT, 75-, CHIEF DERMAT SERV, UNIV HOSP, 75- *Concurrent Pos:* Consult dermat, Dept Med, Wayne County Gen Hosp, 69- & Vet Admin Hosp, Ann Arbor, 71-; assoc ed, J Cutaneous Path, 72-; mem med & sci adv bd, Nat Psoriasis Found, 71-; mem revision panel, 1980 Ed, US Pharmacopeia, 75-80. *Honors & Awards:* Taub Int Mem Award Psoriasis Res, 73; Henry Russell Award Distinguished Res, Univ Mich, 73; Outstanding Serv Award, Nat Psoriasis Found, 73. *Mem:* Am Soc Clin Invest; Am Soc Pharmacol & Exp Therapeut; Am Soc Exp Path; Am Soc Cell Biol; Soc Exp Biol & Med. *Res:* Role of cyclic nucleotides, glucocorticoids, the arachidonate, HETE, thromboxane, prostaglandin cascade and immunology in the molecular pathophysiology and pharmacology of skin diseases with inflammation, induced proliferation and reduced differentiation. *Mailing Add:* Dept of Dermat Med Sch Univ of Mich Ann Arbor MI 48109

VOORHEES, KENT JAY, b Provo, Utah, Sept 7, 43; m 66; c 2. PHYSICAL ORGANIC CHEMISTRY, ANALYTICAL CHEMISTRY. *Educ:* Utah State Univ, BS, 65, MS, 68, PhD(org chem), 70. *Prof Exp:* Res fel phys chem, Mich State Univ, 70-71; instr org chem, Univ Utah, 71-73, asst res prof anal polymer chem, 73-76, assoc res prof, 76-80; MEM FAC, DEPT CHEM, COLO SCH MINES, 80- *Mem:* Am Chem Soc. *Res:* Formulation of complex structures and/or degradation mechanisms by the application of gas chromatography and mass spectrometry in the analysis of thermal decomposition products of oil shale, petroleum and man made polymers. *Mailing Add:* Dept Chem Colo Sch Mines Golden CO 80401

VOORHEES, LARRY DONALD, b Benson, Minn, Dec 23, 46; m 70; c 1. ZOOLOGY, ECOLOGY. *Educ:* Univ Minn, Morris, BS, 70; NDak State Univ, MS, 72, PhD(zool), 76. *Prof Exp:* Instr zool, NDak State Univ, 74-75, res assoc ecol, 75-76; RES ASSOC ECOL, OAK RIDGE LAB-UNION CARBIDE, 76- *Concurrent Pos:* Comt mem, Roadside Maint Transp Res Bd, Nat Res Coun, 78-, Task Force, Wildlife & Fisheries Issues, 81. *Mem:* Wildlife Soc; Am Soc Mammal; Sigma Xi. *Res:* Applied problems in terrestrial community ecology; management of habitat for wildlife, techniques of population estimation and applications of statistics. *Mailing Add:* Environ Sci Div Oak Ridge Nat Lab Oak Ridge TN 37830

VOORHESS, MARY LOUISE, b Livingston Manor, NY, June 2, 26. PEDIATRICS, ENDOCRINOLOGY. *Educ:* Univ Tex, BA, 52; Baylor Univ, MD, 56. *Prof Exp:* From intern to resident pediat, Albany Med Ctr, New York, 56-59; from asst prof to prof pediat, State Univ NY Upstate Med Ctr, 61-76; PROF PEDIAT, STATE UNIV NY BUFFALO, 76- *Concurrent Pos:* Res fel pediat endocrinol & genetics, State Univ NY Upstate Med Ctr, 59-61; Nat Cancer Inst res grant, 62-69, career develop award, 61-71; consult pediat, Roswell Park Mem Inst, Buffalo, 78-; mem, Nat Adv Environ Health Sci Coun, 80- *Mem:* Endocrine Soc; Am Fedn Clin Res; Am Acad Pediat; Lawson Wilkins Pediat Endocrine Soc; Am Pediat Soc. *Res:* Pediatric endocrinology; catecholamine metabolism in children; biochemistry in tumors of neural crest origin. *Mailing Add:* Children's Hosp 219 Bryant St Buffalo NY 14222

VOORHIES, ALEXIS, JR, b New Iberia, La, Sept 8, 99; m 24; c 3. CHEMICAL ENGINEERING, CATALYSIS. *Educ:* St Charles Col, La, AB, 17; La State Univ, BS, 22; Loyola Univ, La, MS, 26. *Hon Degrees:* DSc, Loyola Univ, La, 64. *Prof Exp:* Prof chem, physics & math, Northwestern State Col, La, 22-24 & Loyola Univ, La, 24-30; from chem engr to assoc dir, Baton Rouge Refinery, Esso Res Labs, Humble Oil & Refining Co, 30-47, dir, Esso Res Labs, 47-64; VIS PROF CHEM ENG, LA STATE UNIV, BATON ROUGE, 64- *Concurrent Pos:* Consult, Esso Res & Eng Co, 64- *Honors & Awards:* E V Murphree Award Indust & Eng Chem, Am Chem Soc, 77. *Mem:* Am Chem Soc; Am Inst Chem Engrs; Soc Chem Industs. *Res:* Catalysis in petroleum refining; catalytic reforming; hydrocracking; hydroisomerization. *Mailing Add:* Div of Eng Res La State Univ Baton Rouge LA 70803

VOORHIES, JOHN DAVIDSON, b Hartford, Conn, Nov 26, 33; m 59. SURFACE CHEMISTRY. *Educ:* Princeton Univ, AB, 55, MA, 57, PhD(chem), 58. *Prof Exp:* Res chemist, 58-62, sr res chemist, 62-64, group leader, 64-71, SR RES SCIENTIST, AM CYANAMID CO, 71-, SPECIALIST SAFETY & ENVIRON CONTROL, 78- *Concurrent Pos:* Vis scholar, Dept Chem Eng, Stanford Univ, 70-71. *Mem:* AAAS; Am Chem Soc; Electrochem Soc. *Res:* Electrochemistry; electrochemical power sources; electrochemistry of organic compounds; electroanalytical techniques; chronopotentiometry; polarography; coulometry; interfacial chemistry; heterogeneous catalysis; hydrotreating catalysts. *Mailing Add:* 14 Harrison Ave New Canaan CT 06840

VOORHIES, MICHAEL REGINALD, b Orchard, Nebr, June 17, 41; m 68; c 2. VERTEBRATE PALEONTOLOGY. *Educ:* Univ Nebr, BS, 62; Univ Wyo, PhD(geol), 66. *Prof Exp:* From asst prof to assoc prof geol, Univ Ga, 66-75; assoc cur, 75-80, CUR FOSSIL VERT, UNIV NEBR STATE MUS, 80-; PROF GEOL, UNIV NEBR, 77- *Mem:* Paleont Soc; Soc Vert Paleont; Soc Study Evolution; Soc Syst Zool. *Res:* Taphonomy and population dynamics of Cenozoic mammals; community evolution; neogene stratigraphy of the Great Plains. *Mailing Add:* State Mus Morrill Hall Univ of Nebr Lincoln NE 68508

VOORHOEVE, RUDOLF JOHANNES HERMAN, b Sentang, Sumatra, Indonesia, Oct 4, 38; m 62, 68, 75; c 5. SURFACE CHEMISTRY, PHYSICAL INORGANIC CHEMISTRY. *Educ:* Delft Univ Technol, Ing, 61, Dr(organosilicon & catalytic chem), 64. *Prof Exp:* Instr organosilicon & catalysis chem, Delft Univ Technol, 61-64; res chemist, Nat Defense Res Orgn, 64-66; res chemist, Koninklyke/Shell Lab, Amsterdam, 66-68; mem tech staff, Bell Labs, 68-80; WITH CELANESE RES CO, 80- *Mem:* Am Chem Soc; Am Phys Soc. *Res:* Organosilicon chemistry, especially direct synthesis of organohalosilanes; heterogeneous catalysis, studies by gas-solid kinetics, mechanistic studies; gas-solid reactions for chemical vapors deposition, molecular beams. *Mailing Add:* Celanese Res Co 86 Morris Ave Summit NJ 07901

VOORS, ANTONIE WOUTER, b Opperdoes, Neth, Dec 11, 24; m 56; c 2. EPIDEMIOLOGY. *Educ:* State Univ Utrecht, MD, 51; Univ Amsterdam, cert trop med & hyg, 53; Univ NC, MPH, 56, DrPH, 65. *Prof Exp:* Resident med, Deaconess Hosp, Hilversum, Neth, 51-53; govt physician, Govt Neth, New Guinea, 53-55, chief, Div Health Educ, 56-59, sr govt physician, 60-63; fel epidemiol, Sch Pub Health, Univ NC, Chapel Hill, 63-65; sr resident epidemiol, NY State Dept Health, 65-66; from instr to assoc prof, Sch Pub Health, Univ NC, Chapel Hill, 66-73; assoc prof, 73-79, PROF PREV MED, SCH MED, LA STATEUNIV, NEW ORLEANS, 79- *Concurrent Pos:* Fel coun epidemiol, Am Heart Asn. *Mem:* Am Heart Asn; Am Pub Health Asn; Soc Epidemiol Res; Soc Environ Geochem & Health; NY Acad Sci. *Res:* Determinants of diseases using mathematical models; cardiovascular disease epidemiology. *Mailing Add:* Dept Prev Med La State Univ Sch Med New Orleans LA 70112

VOOS, JANE RHEIN, b Neuremberg, Ger, Oct 2, 27; m 50; c 3. MICROBIOLOGY. *Educ:* Hunter Col, BA, 52; Columbia Univ, PhD(biol sci), 68. *Prof Exp:* Res bacteriologist, Bellevue Hosp, New York, 53-54; instr biol, Stern Col Women, 56-58; from asst prof to assoc prof biol sci, William Patterson Col, NJ, 68-75, asst to dean, 71-72, prof, 75-80, chmn dept, 72-80. *Mem:* AAAS; Bot Soc Am; Mycol Soc Am. *Res:* Electron microscopy of spores and modern pollens. *Mailing Add:* 28 Wenonak Ave Rockaway NJ 07866

VOOTS, RICHARD JOSEPH, b Quincy, Ill, Feb 18, 21; m 45; c 3. ACOUSTICS. *Educ:* NY Univ, BS, 44; Univ Iowa, PhD, 55. *Prof Exp:* Engr, Boeing Aircraft Co, Kans, 46; instr, Burrton High Sch, 47; instr, Benton High Sch, 47-48; physics lab, Univ Wichita, 48; audio technician, Bennett Music House, 49-51; asst psychol, 51-52, res assoc speech path & audiol, 51-61, RES ASST PROF SPEECH PATH, AUDIOL & MUSIC, COL MED, UNIV IOWA, 61-, ASST PROF OTOLARYNGOL & MAXILLOFACIAL SURG, 77- RES ASSOC OTOLARYNGOL, UNIV HOSPS, 55- *Mem:* AAAS; Acoust Soc Am; Am Auditory Soc. *Res:* Otological and musical acoustics; auditory stimulus-response relationship, particularly the frequency-pitch dimension; automated apparatus for sensitivity threshold and differential pitch threshold audiometry; physical acoustics of musical instruments. *Mailing Add:* Dept of Otolaryngol Univ of Iowa Iowa City IA 52242

VOPAT, WILLIAM A, b New York, NY, Mar 8, 10; m 35; c 2. MECHANICAL ENGINEERING. *Educ:* Cooper Union, BS, 31; Univ Mich, MSE, 37. *Hon Degrees:* ME, Cooper Union, 39. *Prof Exp:* Asst sales refrig engr, Lynbrook, NY, 31-32; from instr to prof, 32-76, head dept mech eng, 48-69, dean sch eng & sci, 69-76, EMER PROF MECH ENG & EMER DEAN SCH ENERGY & SCI, 76- *Concurrent Pos:* Consult ed, McGraw-Hill Pub Co, Inc, 38-45; asst engr, Kennedy Van Saun Mfg Co, 42; consult, NY Civil Serv Comn. *Mem:* Am Soc Mech Engrs; Am Soc Eng Educ. *Res:* Applied energy conversion; steam and gas turbines; power station engineering and economy. *Mailing Add:* 150 Park Blvd Malverne NY 11565

VOPICKA, ELLEN VANDERSEE, developmental biology, microbiology, see previous edition

VORBECK, MARIE L, b Rochester, NY, June 24, 33. BIOCHEMISTRY, MICROBIOLOGY. *Educ:* Cornell Univ, BS, 55, PhD(bact biochem), 62; Pa State Univ, MS, 58. *Prof Exp:* Fel biochem, Sch Med & Dent, Univ Rochester, 62-64; asst prof microbiol, Med Sch, Temple Univ, 64-66; asst prof biochem, Jefferson Med Col, 67-68; assoc prof, 68-74, PROF PATH & BIOCHEM, SCH MED, UNIV MO-COLUMBIA, 74- *Mem:* Am Chem Soc; Am Soc Microbiol; NY Acad Sci. *Res:* Structure, function biosynthesis of membrane lipids; role of lipids in membrane processes; role of membrane and organelles in the biology of aging. *Mailing Add:* Dept of Path Univ of Mo Columbia MO 65212

VORCHHEIMER, NORMAN, b Thungen, Ger, Sept 10, 35; US citizen; m 67; c 3. POLYMER CHEMISTRY. *Educ:* Brooklyn Col, BS, 57; Polytech Inst Brooklyn, PhD(org chem), 62. *Prof Exp:* Res chemist textile fibers, E I du Pont de Nemours & Co, 62-67; sr res chemist polymer synthesis, Betz Labs Inc, 67-70; exec vpres, Shasta Fund Inc, 70-71; sr res chemist, 71-73, group leader, 73-77, supvr polymer synthesis, 77-80, SECT HEAD SYNTHESIS/POLYMER APPLN, BETZ LABS INC, TREVOSE, 80- *Mem:* Am Chem Soc; Royal Soc Chem. *Res:* Water-soluble polymers. *Mailing Add:* PO Box 403 Buckingham PA 18912

VORE, MARY EDITH, b Guatemala City, Guatemala, June 27, 47; US citizen. TOXICOLOGY, PHARMACOLOGY. *Educ:* Asbury Col, BA, 68; Vanderbilt Univ, PhD(pharmacol), 72. *Prof Exp:* Fel, Dept Biochem & Drug Metab, Hoffmann-LaRoche Inc, 72-74; asst prof toxicol, Dept Pharmacol, Univ Calif Med Ctr, San Francisco, 74-78; asst prof, 78-81, ASSOC PROF PHARMACOL, COL MED, UNIV KY, 81- *Mem:* Am Soc Pharmacol & Exp Therapeut; Soc Toxicol. *Res:* The biochemical properties of liver and lung microsomal mixed-function oxidases and their role in the metabolism of drugs and xenobiotics to toxic reactive intermediates; hepatic drug elimination in pregnancy. *Mailing Add:* Dept of Pharmacol Univ of Ky Lexington KY 40536

VOREADES, DEMETRIOS, b Athens, Greece, Dec 8, 42; m 76; c 1. APPLIED PHYSICS, ELECTRON MICROSCOPY. *Educ:* Univ Athens, dipl physics, 66; Univ Chicago, MS, 70, PhD(physics), 75. *Prof Exp:* Res asst physics, Univ Athens, 67-68; teaching asst, Univ Chicago, 68-70, res asst, Enrico Fermi Inst, 70-75; res fel biol, Calif Inst Technol, 75-77; syst mgr cytol, Obstet & Gynec Lying-In Hosp, Chicago, 77-78; assoc biophysicist biol, Brookhaven Nat Lab, 78-80; SR ENGR, BURROUGHS CORP, 80- *Mem:* Am Phys Soc; Electron Micros Soc Am; Inst Elec & Electronics Engrs. *Res:* Scanning transmission electron microscopy as analytical tool in biology, physics and materials science. *Mailing Add:* Burroughs Corp MS 701 16701 W Bernardo Dr San Diego CA 92127

VORHAUS, JAMES LOUIS, b St Louis, Mo, Aug 2, 50; m 75; c 1. SOLID STATE PHYSICS. *Educ:* Lehigh Univ, BS, 72; Univ Ill, Champaign-Urbana, MS, 74, PhD(physics), 76. *Prof Exp:* Res asst low temp physics, Dept of Physics, Univ Ill, Champaign-Urbana, 72-76; SR SCIENTIST DEVICE PHYSICS, RES DIV, RAYTHEON CO, 76- *Mem:* Am Phys Soc. *Res:* Design, fabrication and evaluation of galium arsenide monolithic microwave integrated circuits. *Mailing Add:* Raytheon Co Res Div 28 Seyon St Waltham MA 02154

VORHEES, CHARLES V, b Columbus, Ohio, Oct 9, 48; m 69; c 2. PSYCHOTERATOLOGY. *Educ:* Univ Cincinnati, BA, 71; Vanderbilt Univ, MA, 73, PhD(psychopharmacol), 77. *Prof Exp:* Fel res scholar psychoteratology, 76-78, asst prof, 78-82, DIR, PSYCHOTERATOLOGY LAB, CHILDRENS HOSP RES FOUND, INST DEVELOP RES, CINCINNATI, 80-, ASSOC PROF, DEPT PEDIAT, 82- *Concurrent Pos:* Asst prof, Social Sci Prog, Evening Col, Univ Cincinnati, 77- *Mem:* Behav Teratology Soc; Teratology Soc; Int Soc Develop Psychobiol; AAAS; Neurobehav Toxicol Soc. *Res:* Behavioral birth defects; psychoactive drugs and food additives as possible causes of mental retardation or other learning or emotional problems caused by early (usually prenatal) exposure to their agents; developmental psychopharmacology. *Mailing Add:* Inst Develop Res Childrens Hosp Res Found Cincinnati OH 45229

VORHERR, HELMUTH WILHELM, b Alzey, WGer, Feb 6, 28; m 55; c 2. OBSTETRICS & GYNECOLOGY, PHARMACOLOGY. *Educ:* Univ Mainz, MD, 55, specialist obstet & gynec, 62. *Prof Exp:* Mem staff obstet & gynec, Univ Frankfurt, 62-65; res pharmacologist, Cedars-Sinai Med Ctr, Los Angeles, Calif, 65-68; assoc prof, 68-71, PROF OBSTET, GYNEC & PHARMACOL, SCH MED, UNIV NMEX, 71- *Concurrent Pos:* Damon Runyon Mem Fund res fel, Cedars-Sinai Med Ctr & Univ Calif, Los Angeles, 65-66, NIH spec fel, 66-67; asst prof, Sch Med, Univ Calif, Los Angeles, 66-68. *Mem:* Am Fedn Clin Res; Am Soc Pharmacol & Exp Therapeut; Soc Gynec Invest. *Res:* Effects of sex steroid hormones on reproductive tissues; factors influecing embryonic/fetal growth; lactation; pathobiology of breast cancer. *Mailing Add:* Dept of Obstet & Gynec Univ of NMex Albuquerque NM 87131

VORIS, HAROLD CORNELIUS, b Pleasant, Ind, Apr 18, 02; m 31; c 4. NEUROSURGERY. *Educ:* Hanover Col, AB, 23; Univ Chicago, PhD, 29, Rush Med Sch, MD, 30; Univ Minn, MS, 34. *Hon Degrees:* DSc, Hanover Col, 45. *Prof Exp:* Instr biol & physics, Morris Harvey Col, 23-24; instr anat, Univ Chicago, 26-27; fel neurosurg, Mayo Clin, Minn, 31-34; assoc clin prof, Stritch Sch Med, Loyola Univ Chicago, 34-35, clin prof neurol surg, 36-64; prof neurol surg, 64-75, EMER PROF NEUROL SURG, UNIV ILL COL MED, 75-; EMER PROF, RUSH MED SCH, 71- *Concurrent Pos:* Mem staff, Mercy Hosp & Med Ctr, 34-75; consult, Hines Vet Admin Hosp, 55-; consult, Presby-St Lukes Med Ctr, 70-75; pvt pract. *Mem:* Am Asn Neurol Surg; fel Am Asn Surg of Trauma; AMA; fel Am Col Surg; fel Int Col Surg. *Res:* Neuroanatomy. *Mailing Add:* 1550 Lake Shore Drive Chicago IL 60610

VORIS, HAROLD K, b Chicago, Ill, Oct 5, 40. HERPETOLOGY. *Educ:* Hanover Col, BA, 62; Univ Chicago, PhD(biol), 69. *Prof Exp:* Instr biol, Yale Univ, 67-69; asst prof, Dickinson Col, 69-73; ASST CUR, FIELD MUS NATURAL HIST, 73- *Mem:* Am Soc Ichthyol & Herpet; Soc Syst Zool; Ecol Soc Am; Soc Study Evolution. *Res:* Evolution and systematics; ecology; sea snake ecology and systematics; rain forest ecosystems; numerical taxonomy. *Mailing Add:* Div of Reptiles Field Mus of Natural Hist Chicago IL 60605

VORRES, KARL S, b Chicago, Ill, Mar 14, 27; m 52; c 4. PHYSICAL CHEMISTRY. *Educ:* Mich State Univ, BS, 52, MS, 53; Univ Iowa, PhD(phys chem), 58. *Prof Exp:* Org chemist, Isotopes Specialties Co, 55-56; instr phys chem, Univ Iowa, 58-60; asst prof phys & inorg chem, Univ Miami, 60-62; asst prof inorg chem, Purdue Univ, 62-65; chief chem sect, Res Ctr, Babcock & Wilcox Co, 65-69, mgr chem & combustion sect, 69-75; ASSOC DIR PLANNING & DEVELOP, INST GAS TECHNOL, 75- *Concurrent Pos:* Consult, Inst Gas Technol, 59-61 & Babcock & Wilcox Co, 64-65. *Mem:* Am Chem Soc (chmn, Fuel Chem Div, 81); Am Soc Mech Engrs. *Res:* Physical chemistry of solid state; metal oxidation; phase studies; radiochemistry; supervision of research; air pollution; coal gasification; combustion. *Mailing Add:* Inst Gas Technol 3424 S State St Chicago IL 60616

VORST, JAMES J, b Cloverdale, Ohio, Mar 20, 42; m 66; c 3. AGRONOMY, CROP ECOLOGY. *Educ:* Ohio State Univ, BS, 64, MS, 66; Univ Nebr, PhD(agron), 69. *Prof Exp:* Teaching asst agron, Ohio State Univ, 64-66; instr, Univ Nebr, 66-69; MEM FAC, DEPT AGRON, PURDUE UNIV, LAFAYETTE, 69- *Mem:* Am Soc Agron; Crop Sci Soc Am. *Res:* Crop production and physiology; cassava production; teaching methods in agronomy. *Mailing Add:* Dept Agron Purdue Univ West Lafayette IN 47906

VORTMAN, L(UKE) J(EROME), b Springfield, Ill, Apr 18, 20; m 46. PHYSICS, ENGINEERING. *Educ:* Univ Ill, BS, 47, MS, 49. *Prof Exp:* MEM TECH STAFF, SANDIA LABS, 49- *Concurrent Pos:* Mem adv comt civil defense, Nat Acad Sci, 61-73, chmn, Protective Struct Subcomt, 65-66 Blast & Thermal Effects Subcomt, 66-70, mem, NAS Supersonic Transport, Phys Effects Subcomt, 66-71; consult, Boeing Co, 64. *Mem:* AAAS; Am Nuclear Soc. *Res:* Effects of nuclear and chemical explosions in air and underground; peaceful uses of nuclear explosives; protective construction. *Mailing Add:* Div 1111 Sandia Labs PO Box 5800 Albuquerque NM 87115

VOS, KENNETH DEAN, b Oskaloosa, Iowa, Nov 13, 35; m 60; c 2. PHYSICAL CHEMISTRY. *Educ:* Cent Col, Iowa, BA, 57; Mich State Univ, PhD(phys chem), 63. *Prof Exp:* Res asst chem, Los Alamos Sci Lab, 60; staff assoc, John Jay Hopkins Lab, Gen Atomic Div, Gen Dynamics Corp, Calif, 63-68; sr res chemist, 68-72, supvr pressurized prod res sect, 72-76, prod safety dir, 76-78, PHYS SCI MGR & PROD SAFETY DIR, S C JOHNSON & SON, INC, 78- *Mem:* AAAS; Am Chem Soc; Am Phys Soc; 76-; NY Acad Sci. *Res:* Physical chemistry, electron paramagnetic presonance of metalamines and free radicals; semiconductor and high polymer chemistry biomedical research; fine particle and aerosol research; toxicology; product safety. *Mailing Add:* Prod Safety Dept S C Johnson & Son Inc Racine WI 53403

VOSBURG, DAVID LEE, b Enid, Okla, Dec 24, 30; m 60; c 2. STRATIGRAPHY. *Educ:* Phillips Univ, BS, 52; Univ Okla, MS, 54, PhD(geol), 63. *Prof Exp:* From instr to asst prof geol, Univ RI, 60-65; asst prof & chmn dept, Phillips Univ, 65-66; asst prof, 66-67, ASSOC PROF GEOL, ARK STATE UNIV, 67- *Mem:* Am Asn Petrol Geol. *Res:* Occurrence and distribution of subsurface evaporites within shelf sediments related to the Permian Basin, especially economic potential and stratigraphic relations. *Mailing Add:* Dept of Geol Ark State Univ State University AR 72467

VOSBURGH, KIRBY GANNETT, b Pasadena, Calif, May 27, 44; m 67; c 2. APPLIED PHYSICS, EXPERIMENTAL PHYSICS. *Educ:* Cornell Univ, BS, 65, MS, 67; Rutgers Univ, PhD(physics), 71. *Prof Exp:* Res asst applied physics, Cornell Univ, 65-67; mem tech staff accelerator physics, Princeton-Penn Accelerator, Princeton Univ, 67-68; res fel physics, Rutgers Univ, 68-71; mem tech staff & asst to dir particle physics, Princeton Particle Accelerator, Princeton Univ, 71-72; physicist, 72-77, mgr signal electronic systs, Corp Res & Develop, 77-79, mgr electronic mat, 79-80, MGR SILICON PROCESSING, GEN ELEC CO, 80- *Mem:* Am Phys Soc; Inst Elec & Electronics Engrs. *Res:* Solid state electronics; very-large-scale integration devices; silicon process technology; electronic materials; photovoltaics; power generation and transmission; electronic systems, devices and peripherals computer memory systems; medical x-ray imaging; radiation therapy; electron optics. *Mailing Add:* Corp Res & Develop Gen Elec Co PO Box 43 Schenectady NY 12301

VOSBURGH, WILLIAM GEORGE, b Flint, Mich, May 30, 25; m 46; c 6. ORGANIC CHEMISTRY. *Educ:* Mich State Col, BS, 49, MS, 50; Univ Del, PhD, 56. *Prof Exp:* Chemist, 50-51, res chemist, 51-75, SR RES CHEMIST, TEXTILE FIBERS DEPT, E I DU PONT DE NEMOURS & CO, INC, 75- *Mem:* Am Chem Soc; Sigma Xi. *Res:* Organic synthesis; vinyl and condensation polymers; flame proofing; spunbonded nonwoven fabrics; latex development. *Mailing Add:* Textile Fibers Dept E I du Pont de Nemours & Co Inc Wilmington DE 19899

VOSE, GEORGE PARLIN, b Machias, Maine, May 3, 22. FISH & WILDLIFE SCIENCES, NUTRITION. *Educ:* Pa State Univ, BA, 52; Southern Methodist Univ, MS, 56. *Prof Exp:* Res assoc, 52-53, from asst prof to assoc prof human nutrit, 54-65, prof radiographic res, Tex Woman's Univ, 65-77; SR RES ASSOC, CHIHUAHUAN DESERT RES INST, 78- *Mem:* Am Nuclear Soc; Sigma Xi. *Res:* Human ecology and nutrition; bone metabolism; aerial radiotelemetry. *Mailing Add:* Chihuahuan Desert Res Inst Box 1334 Alpine TX 79830

VOSE, JOHN RANDAL, b Cheshire, Eng, June 21, 41; m 67; c 3. BIOTECHNOLOGY. *Educ:* Univ Wales, BSc, 64; Univ Alta, PhD(plant PhD(plant biochem), 68. *Prof Exp:* Nat Res Coun fel biochem, Univ Liverpool, 68-69; fel bot, Univ BC, 69-70; res mgr plant enzymes, Reckitt & Colman Ltd Can, 70-72; assoc res chemist, R T French Co, 72-74, mgr biochem res, 73-74; assoc res officer, Prairie Regional Lab, 75-77, sr res officer, 78-79, sr proj mgr, 79-81, GEN MGR, NAT RES COUN CAN, OTTAWA, 82- *Res:* Starch chemistry and biotechnology; process development. *Mailing Add:* Nat Res Coun Can Montreal Rd Ottawa ON K1J 7B6 Can

VOSHALL, ROY EDWARD, b Beacon, NY, May 29, 33; m 56; c 2. ELECTRICAL ENGINEERING. *Educ:* Carnegie Inst Technol, BS, 56, MS, 57, PhD, 61. *Prof Exp:* From instr to asst prof elec eng, Carnegie Inst Technol, 57-63, lectr, 63-69; sr res scientist, 63-76, FEL ENGR, RES LABS, WESTINGHOUSE ELEC CORP, 76- *Mem:* Inst Elec & Electronics Engrs; Am Phys Soc. *Res:* Electrical gaseous discharges; plasma physics; magnetohydrodynamics; vacuum arcs; vacuum breakdown. *Mailing Add:* Westinghouse Res & Develop Ctr Beulah Rd Pittsburgh PA 15235

VOSKO, SEYMOUR H, b Montreal, Que, Sept 9, 29; m 55; c 2. THEORETICAL PHYSICS. *Educ:* McGill Univ, BEng Phys, 51, MSc, 52; Carnegie Inst Technol, PhD(theoret physics), 57. *Prof Exp:* Instr physics, Carnegie Inst Technol, 56-58, vis asst prof, 58-60; from asst prof to assoc prof, McMaster Univ, 60-64; fel scientist, Westinghouse Res Labs, Pa, 64-70; PROF PHYSICS, UNIV TORONTO, 70- *Mem:* Am Phys Soc; Can Asn Physicists. *Res:* Theoretical solid state physics; applications of many-body perturbation theory; nuclear magnetic resonance in metals and alloys; electron-phonon interaction; phonons in metals; magnetism in metals. *Mailing Add:* Dept of Physics Univ of Toronto Toronto ON M5S 1A7 Can

VOSS, CHARLES HENRY, JR, b Kiangyen, China, Sept 28, 26; US citizen; m 54; c 2. ELECTRICAL ENGINEERING, BIOENGINEERING. *Educ:* La State Univ, BS, 49, MS, 56; NC State Univ, PhD(elec eng), 63. *Prof Exp:* Engr, WJBO-WBRL-FM, 51-53; div transmission engr, Southern Bell Tel Co, 53-54; instr elec eng, La State Univ, 54-56 & NC State Univ, 58-61; assoc prof, 62-67, PROF ELEC ENG, LA STATE UNIV, BATON ROUGE, 67- *Concurrent Pos:* Res Coun fac fel, 65; Delta Regional Primate Ctr consult, 66-70. *Mem:* Inst Elec & Electronics Engrs; Am Asn Advan Med Instrumentation. *Res:* Design of electronic circuits. *Mailing Add:* Dept of Elec Eng La State Univ Baton Rouge LA 70803

VOSS, EDWARD GROESBECK, b Delaware, Ohio, Feb 22, 29. TAXONOMIC BOTANY. *Educ:* Denison Univ, BA, 50; Univ Mich, MA, 51, PhD(bot), 54. *Prof Exp:* Asst syst bot, Biol Sta, 49, bot, univ, 50-51, biol sta, 51-53, res assoc, bot gardens, 54, res asst, Metab Res Lab, Univ Hosp, 54-56, res assoc herbarium, 56-61, from asst prof to assoc prof bot, 60-69, PROF BOT, UNIV MICH, ANN ARBOR, 69- CUR VASCULAR PLANTS, HERBARIUM, 61- *Concurrent Pos:* Secy gen comt on bot nomenclature, 69-, secy ed comt, Int Code of Bot Nomenclature, 69-81, chmn ed comt, 81-; vice rapporteur, Bur of Nomenclature, Int Bot Congresses, 69 & 75, rapporteur, 81. *Mem:* Am Soc Plant Taxon; Soc Syst Zool; Lepidop Soc; Int Asn Plant Taxon; Soc Bibliog Natural Hist. *Res:* Floristics; vascular flora and vegetational history of Great Lakes region; history of biology; nomenclature; Lepidoptera of Michigan; natural areas in Michigan. *Mailing Add:* Herbarium North Univ Bldg Univ of Mich Ann Arbor MI 48109

VOSS, EDWARD WILLIAM, JR, b Chicago, Ill, Dec 2, 33; m 58; c 2. IMMUNOCHEMISTRY, MICROBIOLOGY. *Educ:* Cornell Col, AB, 55; Univ Ind, Indianapolis, MS, 64, PhD(immunol), 66. *Prof Exp:* USPHS fel, Sch Med, Wash Univ, 66-67; from asst prof to assoc prof immunochem, 67-74, PROF MICROBIOL, UNIV ILL, URBANA, 74- *Concurrent Pos:* Fac fel sci, NSF, 75. *Mem:* AAAS; Am Asn Immunol; Sigma Xi; Reticuloendothelial Soc; Fedn Am Scientists; Am Soc Biol Chemists. *Res:* Structure and biosynthesis of immunoglobins; lymphocyte receptors and autoimmune diseases. *Mailing Add:* Dept of Microbiol Univ of Ill 131 Burrill Hall Urbana IL 61801

VOSS, GILBERT LINCOLN, b Hypoluxo, Fla, Feb 12, 18; m 52; c 2. BIOLOGICAL OCEANOGRAPHY, SYSTEMATIC ZOOLOGY. *Educ:* Univ Miami, BS, 51, MS, 52; George Washington Univ, PhD(biol), 55. *Prof Exp:* Asst marine biol, 51-55, from res instr to res assoc prof, 58-61, chmn div biol, 61-73, PROF MARINE SCI, UNIV MIAMI, 61- *Mem:* AAAS; Soc Syst Zool; Am Soc Limnol & Oceanog; Am Soc Zool. *Res:* Biological oceanography; marine ecology; systematics of marine invertebrates, especially biology, systematics and Cephalopod fisheries; deepsea biology. *Mailing Add:* Dept of Biol & Living Resources Univ of Miami Coral Gables FL 33124

VOSS, HENRY DAVID, b Evergreen Park, Ill, Jan 5, 50; m 73; c 4. ATMOSPHERIC PHYSICS, SPACE SCIENCES. *Educ:* Ill Inst Technol, BS, 72; Univ Ill, Urbana-Champaign, MS, 74, PhD(elec eng), 77. *Prof Exp:* res assoc, Aeronomy Lab, Univ Ill, 77-79; RES SCIENTIST, LOCKHEED PALO ALTO RES LAB, 79- *Concurrent Pos:* Consult prof elec, Urbana, 76-78. *Mem:* Am Geophys Union; Inst Elec & Electronics Engrs. *Res:* Upper atmosphere and ionosphere investigations; plasma physics; energetic particles in the magnetosphere and their global precipitation patterns on the atmosphere; rocket-borne instrumentation development; thermal physics; satellite instrumentation development. *Mailing Add:* Lockheed Palo Alto Res Lab 3251 52-12 B255 3251 Hanover St Palo Alto CA 94304

VOSS, JAMES LEO, b Grand Junction, Colo, Apr 7, 34; m 54; c 3. ANIMAL PHYSIOLOGY. *Educ:* Colo State Univ, BS, 56, DVM, 58, MS, 65. *Prof Exp:* From instr to assoc prof med & surg, 58-71, PROF CLIN SCI, COLO STATE UNIV, 72-, HEAD DEPT, 75- *Mem:* Am Vet Med Asn; Soc Study Reproduction; Am Soc Animal Sci; Am Asn Equine Practioners; Am Asn Vet Clinicians. *Res:* Equine reproduction; sexual behavior; artificial insemination; spermatogenesis; female reproductive cycle; ova transfer; pregnancy maintenance and control of ovulation. *Mailing Add:* Dept Clin Sci Colo State Univ Ft Collins CO 80523

VOSS, KENNETH EDWIN, b Hastings, Nebr, Nov 12, 46; m 79. COLLOID SCIENCE. *Educ:* Univ Nebr-Lincoln, BSci, 69; Kans Univ, PhD(inorg chem), 75. *Prof Exp:* Fel res staff, Iowa State Univ, 74-76; res chemist, 76-79, sr res chemist, 79-81, GROUP LEADER, MINERAL & CHEM DIV, ENGELHARD CORP, 81- *Mem:* Am Chem Soc; Am Ceramic Soc. *Res:* Inorganic compounds, particularly industrial minerals and chemicals; characterization of physical, chemical, and colloidal properties and their applications as sorbents, catalysts and pigments in ceramics. *Mailing Add:* 500 Auten Rd 3B Somerville NJ 08876

VOSS, PAUL JOSEPH, b Chicago, Ill, March 10, 43; m 62; c 2. OPERATIONS RESEARCH. *Educ:* Syracuse Univ, BS, 69; Johns Hopkins Univ, MS, 72. *Prof Exp:* Assoc physicist, 69-75, SR PHYSICIST, APPL PHYSICS LAB, JOHNS HOPKINS UNIV, 75- *Res:* Analysis and simulation of missile and radar processing systems. *Mailing Add:* Appl Physics Lab Johns Hopkins Univ Johns Hopkins Rd Laurel MD 20707

VOSS, REGIS D, b Cedar Rapids, Iowa, Jan 4, 31; m 56; c 3. SOIL FERTILITY. *Educ:* Iowa State Univ, BS, 52, MS, 60, PhD(soil fertil), 62. *Prof Exp:* Res asst soil fertil, Iowa State Univ, 57-62; agriculturist, Test Demonstration Br, Tenn Valley Auth, 62-64; from asst prof to assoc prof, 64-69, PROF AGRON, IOWA STATE UNIV, 69- *Concurrent Pos:* Vis prof, Univ Ill, 70-71; consult, Int Maize & Wheat Improvement Ctr, Arg, 71-; bd dir, Am Soc Agron, 77-78. *Mem:* AAAS; Am Soc Agron; Soil Sci Soc Am. *Res:* Effect of uncontrolled factors on the response of field crops to applied fertilizers by using biological statistical methods. *Mailing Add:* Dept of Agron Iowa State Univ Ames IA 50011

VOSS, RICHARD FREDERICK, b St Paul, Minn, Aug 27, 48. NOISE, JOSEPHSON JUNCTIONS. *Educ:* Mass Inst Technol, BS, 70; Univ Calif, Berkeley, PhD(physics), 75. *Prof Exp:* RES STAFF MEM, THOMAS J WATSON RES LAB, IBM, 75- *Mem:* Am Phys Soc. *Res:* Thermal and quantum mechanical limitations to physical devices, particularly Josephson Junctions; intermediate frequency noise and connection with music; computer generation and display of fractal objects. *Mailing Add:* Thomas J Watson Res Lab IBM Corp PO Box 218 Yorktown Heights NY 10598

VOSSEN, JOHN LOUIS, b Philadelphia, Pa, Apr 4, 37; m 63; c 1. PHYSICS. *Educ:* St Joseph's Col, Pa, 58. *Prof Exp:* Engr, RCA Semiconductor & Mat Div, 58-62, group leader thin-film physics, RCA Advan Commun Lab, 62-65, mem tech staff, Process Res Lab, David Sarnoff Res Ctr, 65-78, MGR THIN FILM TECHNOL, RCA LABS, 78- *Honors & Awards:* Achievement Awards, RCA Labs, 68, 69 & 71. *Mem:* Am Vacuum Soc (pres, 80); Am Phys Soc; Electrochem Soc; Inst Elec & Electronic Engrs; Am Inst Physics. *Res:* Study of the methods by which the properties of thin films may be controlled or etched; principally, sputtering, ion plating, plasma anodization, evaporation, plasma deposition and etching; thin film technology. *Mailing Add:* Thin Film Technol David Sarnoff Res Ctr RCA Labs Princeton NJ 08540

VOSTAL, JAROSLAV JOSEPH, b Prague, Czech, Mar 17, 27; m 52; c 4. PHARMACOLOGY, TOXICOLOGY. *Educ:* Charles Univ, Prague, MD, 51; Czech Acad Sci, PhD(med sci), 61. *Prof Exp:* Physician, Regional Inst Nat Health, Jihlava, Czech, 51-55; vis scientist, Nat Inst Pub Health, Stockholm, Sweden, 67-68; assoc prof pharmacol & toxicol, Sch Med, Univ Rochester, 68-77, assoc prof prev med & commun health, 69-77; HEAD BIOMED SCI DEPT, GMC RES LABS, 77- *Concurrent Pos:* Mem, Permanent Comn & Int Asn Occup Health, 66-, mem, Int Subcomt Toxicol Metals, 69-; chmn, Panel Fluorides, Nat Acad Sci-Nat Res Coun, 70-71, mem, Comt Biol Effects Atmospheric Pollutants, 70- *Mem:* AAAS; Am Soc Pharmacol & Exp Therapeut; Fedn Am Soc Exp Biol; Soc Toxicol. *Res:* Pharmacology of organomercurial compounds; toxicology of heavy metals and inorganic poisons, inter-species differences in pharmacokinetics and biotransformation of toxic substances. *Mailing Add:* Biomed Sci Dept GMC Res Labs Warren MI 48090

VOSTI, DONALD CURTIS, b Modesto, Calif, Aug 26, 27; m 51; c 6. ORGANIC CHEMISTRY, FOOD TECHNOLOGY. *Educ:* Univ Calif, BS, 47, PhD, 52. *Prof Exp:* Chemist, E & J Gallo Winery, Calif, 47-52; sr chemist, 52-61, supvr, Container Specif Group, Western Area Lab, 61-62, supvr, Eval & Inspection Group, 62-64, supvr, Packaging Technol Group, 64-66, mgr, Customer Rels Sect, 66-69, proj mgr, Prod Technol Sect, 69-72, assoc dir, Gen Technol Sect, 72-73, proj mgr plastic hot fill foods, 73-76, PROJ MGR PLASTIC TECHNOL, AM CAN CO, 76- *Mem:* Inst Food Technologists. *Res:* Commercialization of new rigid containers developed for foods, non-foods and beverages; container utilization technology involving food processing, microbiological spoilage of food, container corrosion and related problems; container materials and manufacturing process improvments; development of plastic container for hot filled foods. *Mailing Add:* 433 N Northwest Hwy Barrington IL 60010

VOTAW, CHARLES ISAC, b Farris, Okla, Jan 3, 33; m 56; c 2. MATHEMATICS. *Educ:* Okla State Univ, BS, 57; NTex State Univ, MS, 67; Univ Kans, PhD(math), 71. *Prof Exp:* Staff mem, Sandia Corp, 57-60; mkt engr, Raytheon Co, 60-62; prod engr, Tex Instruments, 62-65; prod & test engr, Hunt Electronics, 65-66; ASST PROF MATH, FT HAYS KANS STATE COL, 71- *Mem:* Math Asn Am; Soc Indust & Appl Math; AAAS; Am Math Soc. *Res:* Topology; applied mathematics. *Mailing Add:* Dept Math Ft Hays State Univ 600 Park St Hays KS 67601

VOTAW, CHARLES LESLEY, neuroanatomy, see previous edition

VOTAW, MARTIN JAMES, b St Louis, Mo, Oct 2, 25; m 48; c 6. ELECTRICAL ENGINEERING, COMMUNICATIONS. *Educ:* Univ Va, BEE, 47. *Prof Exp:* Engr wave propagation res br, US Naval Res Lab, 47-55, head satellite transmitter group, Proj Vanguard, 55-58, head satellite tech br, 58-63; dir space segment, Implementation Div, Commun Satellite Corp, 66-71, asst vpres, 71-75, vpres Intelsat Mgt Div, 75-76; vpres tech opers, 77-79, DIR TECH & OPERS, SATELLITE BUS SYSTS, 80- *Mem:* Inst Elec & Electronics Engrs; Am Inst Aeronaut & Astronaut. *Res:* Wave propagation; satellite scientific systems; satellite communications. *Mailing Add:* 7005 Duncraig Ct McLean VA 22101

VOTAW, ROBERT BARNETT, b Cincinnati, Ohio, Oct 19, 39; m 65; c 2. BIOSTRATIGRAPHY, PALEOECOLOGY. *Educ:* Ind Univ, BS, 62, MA, 64; Ohio State Univ, PhD(geol), 71. *Prof Exp:* Geologist, Standard Oil Co, Calif, 64-68; asst prof, 71-77, dept chmn, 73-76, asst dean facs, 76-77, ASSOC PROF GEOL, IND UNIV NORTHWEST, 77- *Mem:* Geol Soc Am; Paleontol Soc. *Res:* Conodont biostratigraphy of the Ordovician rocks of the North American midcontinent; paleoecology of the middle and upper Ordovician rocks of the North American midcontinent. *Mailing Add:* Dept Geosci Ind Univ Northwest 3400 Broadway Gary IN 46408

VOTAW, ROBERT GRIMM, b St Louis, Mo, Sept 13, 38; m 61; c 3. BIOCHEMISTRY, MEDICAL EDUCATION. *Educ:* Wesleyan Univ, BA, 60; Case Western Reserve Univ, PhD(microbiol), 66. *Prof Exp:* Instr microbiol, Sch Med, Case Western Reserve Univ, 66-67; instr biochem, 67-70, asst prof, 70-77, assoc dean med educ, 74-77, ASST PROF RES HEALTH EDUC & DIR COMPUT BASED EDUC, SCH MED, UNIV CONN, 77- *Mem:* AAAS; Am Soc Microbiol; Am Chem Soc; Am Asn Med Cols. *Res:* Medical education; computer based education; use of simulation of teaching and assessing complex behavior, clinical problem solving. *Mailing Add:* Dept of Res in Health Educ Univ of Conn Health Ctr Farmington CT 06032

VOTER, ROGER CONANT, b Boston, Mass, July 10, 22; m 45; c 5. CHEMISTRY. *Educ:* Wesleyan Univ, AB, 44; Iowa State Col, PhD(chem), 51. *Prof Exp:* Polymer res staff, 51-64, MEM PATENTS & CONTRACTS STAFF, E I DU PONT DE NEMOURS & CO, INC, 64- *Res:* Organic analytical reagents; instrumental analysis; physical measurements of polymers; polymer product development; patents; licensing and contracts. *Mailing Add:* RD 2 Box 57A Chadds Ford PA 19317

VOTH, DAVID RICHARD, b St Cloud, Minn, July 11, 41; m 69; c 2. PARASITOLOGY, INVERTEBRATE ZOOLOGY. *Educ:* Univ NDak, BS, 63, MS, 65; Ore State Univ, PhD(zool), 71. *Prof Exp:* Asst prof biol, Haile Selassie I Univ, 66-68; instr zool, Ore State Univ, 69-71; assoc prof, 71-75, PROF BIOL, METROP STATE COL, 75- *Mem:* Nat Asn Biol Teachers; Nat Educ Asn. *Res:* Helminth taxonomy, ecology and natural history. *Mailing Add:* Dept of Biol Box 53 1006 11th St Denver CO 80204

VOTH, HAROLD MOSER, b Newton, Kans, Dec 29, 22; m 46; c 3. PSYCHIATRY. *Educ:* Washburn Univ, BS, 43; Univ Kans, MD, 47; Menninger Sch Psychiat, psychiatrist, 52; Topeka Inst Psychoanal, psychoanalyst, 62. *Prof Exp:* Asst sect chief, Vet Admin Hosp, Topeka, Kans, 52-53, asst chief acute intensive treatment sect, 53-54, chief women's neuropsychiat serv, 54-57; STAFF PSYCHIATRIST, MENNINGER FOUND, 57-; CHIEF OF STAFF, VET ADMIN HOSP, TOPEKA, 80- *Concurrent Pos:* Mem fac, Menninger Sch Psychiat, 55-; NIMH res grant, Menninger Found, 63-72; examr, Am Bd Psychiat & Neurol, 70-71; consult, Walter Reed Army Med Ctr, 72-; assoc chief psychiat for educ, Vet Admin Hosp, Topeka, Kans, 75- *Honors & Awards:* William Porter Award, Am Asn Mil Surgeons, 79. *Mem:* Fel AAAS; fel Am Psychiat Asn; Am Psychoanal Asn; Am Col Psychoanal; AMA. *Res:* Personality organization; psychotherapy; the study of autokinesis as a research and clinical instrument. *Mailing Add:* Chief Staff Vet Admin Hosp Topeka KS 66622

VOTH, RICHARD DAVID, soil science, agronomy, see previous edition

VOTTA, FERDINAND, JR, b Providence, RI, June 8, 16; m 47; c 2. CHEMICAL ENGINEERING. *Educ:* Univ RI, BS, 39, MS, 41; Yale Univ, DEng, 58. *Prof Exp:* Develop engr, Allied Chem & Dye Corp, 41-43; res engr, Manhattan Proj, Columbia, 44-46; from instr to assoc prof, 46-74, PROF CHEM ENG, UNIV RI, 74- *Mem:* Am Inst Chem Engrs. *Res:* Thermodynamics; heat and mass transfer. *Mailing Add:* Dept of Chem Eng Univ of RI Kingston RI 02881

VOUGHT, ELDON JON, b Chicago, Ill, May 21, 35; m 59; c 4. TOPOLOGY. *Educ:* Manchester Col, AB, 57; Univ Mich, Ann Arbor, MA, 58; Univ Calif, Riverside, PhD(math), 67. *Prof Exp:* Instr math, Pomona Col, 60-61; assoc prof math, Calif State Polytech Univ, Pomona, 61-70; PROF MATH, CALIF STATE UNIV, CHICO, 70- *Concurrent Pos:* NSF res fel, 71-73; vis prof math, Ariz State Univ, 75-76; mathematician, Lockheed Aircraft Co, 77, 78, 79, 80 & 81. *Mem:* Am Math Soc; Math Asn Am. *Res:* The study of the invariance of various topological properties of compact, connected metric spaces under certain types of continuous functions, for example, local homeomorphisms and confluent functions. *Mailing Add:* Dept of Math Calif State Univ Chico CA 95926

VOUGHT, ROBERT HOWARD, b Ridgway, Pa, Jan 30, 20; m 49; c 3. PHYSICS. *Educ:* Allegheny Col, BA, 41; Univ Pa, PhD(physics), 46. *Prof Exp:* Res physicist, Univ Pa, 42-46, instr phsyics, 44-46; res assoc, Gen Elec Co, 46-48; asst prof, Union Univ, NY, 48-53, assoc prof, 53-56; SOLID STATE PHYSICIST, GEN ELEC CO, 56- *Concurrent Pos:* Exchange prof, St Andrews Univ, 53-54. *Mem:* Am Phys Soc; Am Asn Physics Teachers; AAAS; Am Nuclear Soc. *Res:* Semiconductors; mass spectrometry; surface physics; corrosion; energy conversion materials and devices; optoelectron devices; reactor technology; radiation damage. *Mailing Add:* 1465 Myron St Schenectady NY 12309

VOULGAROPOULOS, EMMANUEL, b Lowell, Mass, Apr 16, 31; m 59; c 2. PUBLIC HEALTH. *Educ:* Tufts Col, BSc, 52; Cath Univ Louvain, MD, 57; Johns Hopkins Univ, MPH, 62. *Prof Exp:* Med dir, Med Int Corp, Cambodia, 58-60, exec field dir for Asia, Cent Am & Africa, 60-61; dep, Health Serv Develop Proj, Vietnam AID, Saigon, 62-64, chief pub health div, 64-65; assoc prof pub health, 65-68, head, Int Health Prog, 65-70, head, Int Health-Pop & Family Planning Studies Prog, 70-71, assoc dean, 74-79, PROF PUB HEALTH, SCH PUB HEALTH, UNIV HAWAII, MANOA, 68- *Concurrent Pos:* Consult, AID, 62, US Civil Admin Ryuku Islands, 65-67, US Trust Territory Pac Islands, 65-71, Govt of Guam & Govt of Am Samoa, 65-71; consult, Peace Corps, 66-69, SPac Comn, Noumea New Caledonia, 67 & USPHS Global Community, Arlington, Va, 69; vis prof pub health & adv, Udayana Community Health Prog, Udayana State Univ, 71-72; vis prof pub health & adv to fac pub health, Univ Indonesia, 72-73; consult, Ministry Health, Govt Indonesia, 71-72, Ministry Educ & Culture, 71-73 & Ministry Social Welfare, 73; consult, Int Asn Schs Social Work, NY, 73; dir, Lampang

Health Develop Proj, Thailand, 75-79; vis prof pub health & adv, Univ Indonesia, 79-81; adv, Pop & World Bank, USAID, Indonesia, 77-81. *Res:* Health and medical education systems; health delivery systems; international health. *Mailing Add:* Univ Hawaii Manoa 1960 E-W Rd Honolulu HI 96822

VOURNAKIS, JOHN NICHOLAS, b Cambridge, Ohio, Dec 1, 39; m 61; c 1. BIOPHYSICS, MOLECULAR BIOLOGY. *Educ:* Albion Col, BA, 61; Cornell Univ, PhD(chem), 68. *Prof Exp:* Nat Acad Sci exchange fel, Inst Org Chem & Biochem, Prague, Czech, fall 68; NIH fel biol, Mass Inst Technol, 69-71, res assoc, 71-72; res assoc, Harvard Univ, 72-73; ASSOC PROF BIOL, SYRACUSE UNIV, 73- *Concurrent Pos:* Vis assoc prof, Amherst Col, 70-71; NIH res grant gen med, 75. *Mem:* Biophys Soc; Soc Develop Biol. *Res:* Secondary and tertiary structure of eukaryotic mRNA; structure of mapping techniques using enzymes as probes; secondary structure of rRNA. *Mailing Add:* Dept of Biol Res Labs Syracuse Univ 130 College Place Syracuse NY 13210

VOUROS, PAUL, b Thessaloniki, Greece, Apr 1, 38; US citizen; m 65; c 2. ANALYTICAL CHEMISTRY, ORGANIC CHEMISTRY. *Educ:* Wesleyan Univ, BA, 61; Mass Inst Technol, PhD(chem), 65. *Prof Exp:* Staff scientist, Tech Opers, Inc, 66-67, proj mgr, 67-68; asst prof chem, Inst Lipid Res, Col Med, Baylor Univ, 68-74; ASSOC PROF, DEPT CHEM, NORTHEASTERN UNIV, 74- *Mem:* Am Chem Soc; Sigma Xi; Am Soc Mass Spectrometry. *Res:* Organic mass spectrometry; mass spectrometry of biological compounds; gas chromatography-mass spectrometry; photographic ion detection; applications of chromatography and mass spectrometry to forensic problems; high performance liquid chromatography-mass spectrometry. *Mailing Add:* Dept Chem Northeastern Univ Boston MA 02115

VOURVOPOULOS, GEORGE, b June 11, 36; US citizen; m 63; c 3. NUCLEAR PHYSICS. *Educ:* Nat Univ Athens, BS, 58; Fla State Univ, MS, 65, PhD(physics), 67. *Prof Exp:* From assoc prof to prof physics, Fla A&M Univ, 67-76, chmn dept, 74-76; MEM STAFF, TANDEM ACCELERATOR LAB, GREEK ATOMIC ENERGY COMN, 76- *Concurrent Pos:* Res fel, Israel Inst Technol, 69-70; Res Corp grant, Fla A&M Univ, 71-76, NSF grant, 72-74. *Mem:* Am Phys Soc. *Res:* Nuclear reactions; nuclear spectroscopy. *Mailing Add:* Tandem Accelerator Lab Agia Paraskevi Athens Greece

VOUTSAS, ALEXANDER MATTHEW, b New York, NY, Mar 26, 23; m 57; c 2. AERODYNAMICS, THERMODYNAMICS. *Educ:* Rensselaer Polytech Inst, BAeE, 44; US Navy Reserve Northwestern Univ, MS, 45; Harvard Grad Bus Sch, AMP, 69. *Prof Exp:* Aerodynamicist transonic windtunnel, Ames Labs, Nat Aeronaut & Space Admin, 45-56, XP-92, F102 delta wing, Gen Dynamics-Convair, San Diego, Calif, 47-48; proj aerodynamicist hermes intercontinental missile, Gen Elec Co, Schenectady, NY, 48-51; aerodynamicist rigel missile pre polaris, Gruman Corp, Bethpage, NY, 51-52; proj design engr terrapin iono rocket, Republic Aviation Corp, Hicksville, NY, 52-56; res & develop mgr atlas-titan intercontinental ballistic missile instrument ground system, Am Bosch Arma Corp, Garden City, NY, 56-61; mgr mkt commun aerospace syst, Int Tel & Tel Corp, NY, 62-67; PRES ADV AEROSPACE, HELLENIC AEROSPACE INDUST, LTD, 68- *Concurrent Pos:* Guest comt mem, US Naval Bur Ordnance Comt Aerobalastics, 49-; lectr, Am Mgr Asn New York, 68-; mkt consult, ITT Fed Elec Corp New York, 68-72; indust consult & pres adv, Motor Oil Hellas Ltd, New York & Greece, 69-73; aerospace & indust tech consult, A Voutsas Assoc, 73-80; dir, Am Acad Greece Bd Dir, 76-78. *Mem:* Am Inst Aeronaut & Astronaut; Assoc fel Inst Aerospace Sci; sr mem Am Astronaut Soc; Nat Space Inst. *Res:* Ultrasonic c-scan theory and equipment for diagnosis of materials fatigue and cancer growths and its cure; vibrating string accelerometer gravimeter theory and equipment; author or coauthor of over 200 publications. *Mailing Add:* Kalliga 21 Athens Greece

VO-VAN, TRUONG, b Saigon, Viet-Nam, Dec 3, 48; m 71; c 2. THIN FILMS PHYSICS. *Educ:* Polytech Col Montreal, BScA, 70; Univ Moncton, MSc, 72; Univ Toronto, PhD(physics), 76. *Prof Exp:* ASSOC PROF PHYSICS, UNIV MONCTON, 76- *Concurrent Pos:* Nat Res Coun Can grant, 76-, Regional Develop Prog grant, 76- & Coun Res, Univ Moncton, 76- *Mem:* Optical Soc Am; Can Asn Physicists; Asn Can-Fr pour L'Advan Sci. *Res:* Experimental solid state physics; specialization in thin films; optical properties of solids, spectroscopy and optics. *Mailing Add:* Dept of Physics & Math Univ of Moncton Moncton NB E1A 3E9 Can

VOXMAN, WILLIAM L, b Iowa City, Iowa, Feb 1, 39; m 63; c 2. TOPOLOGY. *Educ:* Univ Iowa, BA, 60, MS, 63, PhD(math), 68. *Prof Exp:* Latin Am teaching fel & prof math, Univ Chile, 68-69; prof, Concepcion Univ, 69; Fulbright travel grant & prof, State Tech Univ, Chile, 69-70; asst prof, 70-72, assoc prof, 72-76, PROF MATH, UNIV IDAHO, 76- *Concurrent Pos:* Latin Am teaching fel & prof math, Nat Polytech Sch, Quito, Ecuador, 74-76. *Mem:* Am Math Soc; Sigma Xi. *Res:* General topology, especially upper semicontinuous decompositions of topological spaces. *Mailing Add:* 1118 King Rd Moscow ID 83843

VOYVODIC, LOUIS, b Yugoslavia, Oct 22, 21; US citizen; m 51; c 5. HIGH ENERGY PHYSICS. *Educ:* McGill Univ, BSc, 43, PhD(physics), 48. *Prof Exp:* Physicist cosmic rays, Nat Res Coun Can, 48-56; tech proj dir radiation physics, Isotope Prod Ltd Can, 56-58; physicist, Armour Res Found, Ill Inst Technol, 58-60; physicist, Argonne Nat Lab, 62-72; PHYSICIST, FERMI NAT ACCELERATOR LAB, 72- *Mem:* Am Inst Physics; Am Phys Soc; Fedn Am Scientists. *Res:* Interactions of elementary particles at high energies, particularly as studied by optical track chamber techniques, and development of improved detection techniques. *Mailing Add:* Fermi Nat Accelerator Lab PO Box 500 Batavia IL 60510

VOZOFF, KEEVA, b Minneapolis, Minn, Jan 26, 28; m 57; c 4. EXPLORATION GEOPHYSICS, ENGINEERING GEOPHYSICS. *Educ:* Univ Minn, BPhys, 49; Pa State Univ, MSc, 51; Mass Inst Technol, PhD(geophys), 56. *Prof Exp:* Geophysicist, Nucom-McPhar Geophys, Ltd, 55-58; assoc prof geophys, Univ Alta, 58-64; vpres, Geosci Inc, Mass, 64-69; consult, 69-72; PROF GEOPHYS, MACQUARIE UNIV, AUSTRALIA, 72-, DIR, CTR GEOPHYS EXPLOR RES, 81- *Concurrent Pos:* Mem earth sci ad hoc comt on Soviet-Australian coop, 74-75; Hearst vis prof, Univ Calif, Berkeley, 78-80; pres, Australian Soc Explor Geophysicists, 76-77. *Mem:* Australian Soc Explor Geophys; Am Geophys Union; Europ Asn Explor Geophys; Petrol Explor Soc Australia; Soc Explor Geophys. *Res:* Electrical and electromagnetic methods of determining earth structure; natural electromagnetic fields. *Mailing Add:* Sch of Earth Sci Macquarie Univ Sydney 2113 Australia

VRANA, NORMAN M, b Hudson Heights, NJ, Feb 16, 20; m 42; c 4. ELECTRICAL ENGINEERING. *Educ:* NY Univ, BEE, 47; Cornell Univ, MEE, 51. *Prof Exp:* Sr engr, ADT Co, NY, 40-49; assoc prof elec eng, Cornell Univ, 49-57; sr res engr, Autonetics Co, Calif, 57-58; assoc prof elec eng, Cornell Univ, 58-65; res & develop engr, Hewlett Packard Co, Colo, 65-66; assoc prof, 66-75, PROF ELEC ENG, CORNELL UNIV, 75- *Concurrent Pos:* Commun engr & seminar consult, NY Tel Co, 62-65; consult, Frankford Arsenal, Pa, 68-71 & Ballistics Res Lab, Md, 70- *Mem:* Inst Elec & Electronics Engrs. *Res:* Hybrid computer simulation and computation; communication and instrumentation; electronic design and development; computer and digital systems. *Mailing Add:* Dept of Elec Eng Cornell Univ Ithaca NY 14853

VRANIC, MLADEN, b Zagreb, Yugoslavia, Apr 3, 30; Can citizen; m 57; c 1. PHYSIOLOGY, ENDOCRINOLOGY. *Educ:* Univ Zagreb, MD, 55, DSc(physiol), 62. *Prof Exp:* Fel, Fac Med, Univ Toronto, 63-65, from asst prof to assoc prof, 65-72, PROF PHYSIOL, FAC MED, UNIV TORONTO, 72-, ASSOC PROF MED, 77- *Concurrent Pos:* Mem, Inst Biomed Electronics, Univ Toronto, 71-, Inst Med Sci, 73- & dir, C H Best Found; guest prof, Univ Geneva, 76-77. *Mem:* Endocrine Soc; Can Diabetes Asn; Am Diabetes Asn; Can Physiol Soc; Am Physiol Soc. *Res:* Metabolic roles and interactions of insulin, glucagon, epinephrine, growth hormone, glucocorticoids and glucocorticoid hormones in health and disease-diabetes and obesity; origin, structure and secretion of nonpancreatic glucagon; endocrine responses and effects during exercise; tracer methodology. *Mailing Add:* Dept Physiol Med Sci Bldg Univ Toronto Fac Med Toronto ON M5S 1A8 Can

VRATNY, FREDERICK, b Detroit, Mich, Mar 23, 31; c 2. PHYSICAL CHEMISTRY, ANALYTICAL CHEMISTRY. *Educ:* Univ Mich, BS, 53; Ind Univ, PhD(chem), 57. *Prof Exp:* Asst chem, Ind Univ, 53-56; instr, Purdue Univ, 56-60; MEM STAFF, BELL LABS, INC, 60- *Mem:* Am Phys Soc; Electrochem Soc; Am Vacuum Soc; Am Soc Testing & Mat; NY Acad Sci. *Res:* Solid state reactions; Raman and infrared spectra of solids and adsorbates; thin film; plasma; dielectrics; active thin film devices; electrochemical processes. *Mailing Add:* Bell Labs Murray Hill NJ 07971

VRATSANOS, SPYROS M, b Athens, Greece, Apr 10, 20; US citizen; m 58; c 2. BIOCHEMISTRY, ORGANIC CHEMISTRY. *Educ:* Univ Athens, dipl chem, 50; Adelphi Univ, MS, 56; Fordham Univ, PhD(enzymol, org chem), 61. *Prof Exp:* Asst prof biochem, Adelphi Univ, 61-63; res assoc, 63-65, ASST PROF MICROBIOL, COL PHYSICIANS & SURGEONS, COLUMBIA UNIV, 65- *Mem:* Am Chem Soc; Neuberg Socl Harvey Soc. *Res:* Organophosphorous compounds; origin of life on the earth; proteins; active sites of enzymes; conversion of light energy to chemical signals; chemistry of vision; immunochemistry. *Mailing Add:* 11 Chadwick Rd Syosset NY 11791

VRBA, FREDERICK JOHN, b Cedar Rapids, Iowa, May 25, 49; m 71. ASTRONOMY. *Educ:* Univ Iowa, BA, 71; Univ Ariz, PhD(astron), 76. *Prof Exp:* STAFF ASTRONR, FLAGSTAFF STA, NAVAL OBSERV, 76- *Mem:* Sigma Xi; Am Astron Soc. *Res:* Infrared and polarimetric observations of young stars, dark nebulae, and the general interstellar medium; electronic camera photometry and polarimetry; trigonometric parallaxes of nearby stars. *Mailing Add:* Naval Observ Flagstaff Sta Box 1149 Flagstaff AZ 86001

VRBA, RUDOLF, b Topolcany, Czech, Sept 11, 24; m; c 2. NEUROCHEMISTRY, IMMUNOCHEMISTRY. *Educ:* Prague Tech Univ, IngChem, 49, DrTechnSc, 51; Czech Acad Sci, CSc(chem), 56. *Prof Exp:* Staff mem, Penicillin Factory, Czech, 52-53; mem sci staff, Inst Indust Hyg & Occup Dis, Ministry Health, Czech, 53-58; staff mem, Vet Res Inst, Ministry Agr, Israel, 58-60; mem sci staff, Neuropsychiat Res Unit, Brit Med Res Coun, 60-67; ASSOC PROF PHARMACOL, FAC MED, UNIV BC, 67- *Concurrent Pos:* Rockefeller grant, Neuropsychiat Res Unit, Brit Med Res Coun, 60-62; assoc, Med Res Coun Can, 68-75; vis lectr pharmacol, Harvard Med Sch, 73-75. *Mem:* Brit Biochem Soc; Int Neurochem Soc; Can Biochem Soc. *Res:* Physiological chemistry; biochemical aspects of cancer, diabetes and immunology; neurochemistry. *Mailing Add:* Dept of Pharmacol Univ of BC Fac of Med Vancouver BC V6T 1W5 Can

VREBALOVICH, THOMAS, b Los Angeles, Calif, July 10, 26; m 51; c 2. SPACE PHYSICS, FLUID MECHANICS. *Educ:* Calif Inst Technol, BS, 48, MS, 49, PhD(aeronaut eng), 54. *Prof Exp:* From res scientist to sr res scientist, Jet Propulsion Lab, Calif Inst Technol, 52-61, res specialist, 61-62, Ranger proj scientist, 63-65, group supvr photosci, 65-66, Surveyor assoc proj scientist, 65-67, div rep space sci, 66-67, Voyager landed capsule syst scientist, 67-68, on leave, 68-70, Sci Recommendation Chief, Mariner Mars 1971 proj, 70-73, mission sci coordr, Mariner Jupiter Saturn Proj, 73-74, mgr res, 74-75; mem coun sci & technol affairs, Am Embassy, New Delhi, India, 75-80, MEM COUN SCI & TECHNOL AFFAIR, AM EMBASSY, CAIRO, EGYPT, 80- *Concurrent Pos:* Instr, Univ Southern Calif, 56 & Univ Calif, Los Angeles, 57; consult, Flow Corp, 66-; vis prof aeronaut, Indian Inst Technol, Kanpur, 68-70; mem bd gov, Photog Art & Sci Found, 72-; mem bd dir, US Educ Found in India, 75. *Honors & Awards:* Fairbanks Mem Award, Soc

Photog Instrumentation Engrs, 66; NASA Group Achievement Award for Mariner Mars 71 proj. *Mem:* Am Inst Aeronaut & Astronaut; Sigma Xi; Am Phys Soc; Explorers Club. *Res:* Supersonic aerodynamics; space photography and science. *Mailing Add:* Am Embassy Cairo Box 20 FPO New York NY 09527

VREDEVELD, NICHOLAS GENE, b Hudsonville, Mich, May 5, 29; m 53; c 2. PLANT PATHOLOGY, MICROBIOLOGY. *Educ:* Calvin Col, AB, 51; Mich State Univ, MS, 55, PhD(plant path), 65. *Prof Exp:* Biochemist, St Lawrence Hosp, Lansing, Mich, 62-64; asst prof, 64-67, ASSOC PROF BIOL, UNIV TENN, CHATTANOOGA, 67- *Mem:* Am Phytopath Soc. *Res:* Fungicides and fungus physiology, environmental effect on plant disease distribution; effect of microbiol toxins on plants, whole and in tissue culture. *Mailing Add:* Dept Biol Univ Tenn Chattanooga TN 37401

VREDEVOE, DONNA LOU, b Ann Arbor, Mich, Jan 11, 38; c 1. IMMUNOLOGY, MICROBIOLOGY. *Educ:* Univ Calif, Los Angeles, BA, 59, PhD(microbiol), 63. *Prof Exp:* Instr bact, 63, asst res immunologist, 64-67, asst prof nursing res, 67-70, assoc prof, 70-76, consult lab nuclear med & radiation biol, 67-80, assoc dean, sch nursing, 76-78, PROF NURSING RES, UNIV CALIF, LOS ANGELES, 76-, DIR SPACE PLANNING, CANCER CTR, 74- *Concurrent Pos:* USPHS fel microbiol, Stanford Univ, 63-64; res grants, Calif Inst Cancer Res, Univ Calif, Cancer Res Coord Comt, Am Cancer Soc, Calif Div & Nat Am Cancer Soc, US Dept Energy & USPHS. *Mem:* Am Asn Immunol; Am Soc Microbiol; Am Asn Cancer Res. *Res:* Serotyping for human kidney transplantation; delayed hypersensitivity; immunosuppression; immunotherapy; tumor immunology; mouse lymphoma; effects of metallic ions on the immune response; carcinogenesis. *Mailing Add:* Sch of Nursing Univ of Calif Ctr Health Sci Los Angeles CA 90024

VREDEVOE, LAWRENCE A, b Ann Arbor, Mich, Aug 2, 40; m 66; c 2. ANESTHESIOLOGY. *Educ:* Univ Calif, Los Angeles, BA, 62, MA, 64, PhD(physics), 66; Univ Calif, San Francisco, MD, 75. *Prof Exp:* Mem tech staff theoret physics, Sci Ctr, NAm Rockwell Corp, Calif, 66-70; assoc prof physics, Ind Univ Bloomington, 70-72; mem staff med training, Sch Med, Univ Calif, San Francisco, 72-75, surg resident, 75-77, head & neck surg resident, 77-78, anesthesiol resident, 78-80, ASST PROF ANESTHESIOL, CTR HEALTH SCI, UNIV CALIF, LOS ANGELES, 80- *Mem:* AMA; Am Soc Anesthesiologists; Am Phys Soc. *Mailing Add:* 428 21st St Santa Monica CA 90402

VREELAND, JOHN ALLEN, b Orlando, Fla, Jan 6, 25; m 52; c 2. PHYSICS. *Educ:* Presby Col, BS, 49; Univ Wis, MA, 51, PhD(physics), 56. *Prof Exp:* Asst physicist, Univ Wis, 50-55; fel scientist, Atomic Power Div, Westinghouse Elec Corp, 55-60; sr nuclear specialist, Rocketdyne Div, NAm Aviation, 60-62; mgr nuclear anal dept, nuclear rocket opers, Aerojet-Gen Corp, 62-69; PROF NUCLEAR ENG, SCH ENG, CALIF STATE UNIV, SACRAMENTO, 69- *Concurrent Pos:* Lectr, Univ Calif, 60-; consult, Univ Fla, 62; mem Atomic Indust Forum. *Mem:* Am Physics Soc; Am Nuclear Soc; Am Inst Aeronaut & Astronaut. *Res:* Reactor physics; nuclear structure; analysis and detection of nuclear transport phenomena; systems analysis related to nuclear power plant design. *Mailing Add:* Sch of Eng Calif State Univ Sacramento CA 95819

VREELAND, THAD, JR, b Portland, Ore, Oct 20, 24; m 48; c 3. MATERIALS SCIENCE. *Educ:* Calif Inst Technol, BS, 49, MS, 50, PhD(mech eng), 52. *Prof Exp:* Res fel mech eng, 52-54, from asst prof to assoc prof, 54-63, assoc prof mat sci, 63-67, PROF MAT SCI, CALIF INST TECHNOL, 68- *Res:* Plastic deformation of crystals; dislocation dynamics. *Mailing Add:* W M Keck Lab of Eng Mat 1201 E California St Pasadena CA 91125

VREMAN, HENDRIK JAN, b Soest, Netherlands, Jan 22, 39; US citizen; m 64; c 2. BIOLOGICAL CHEMISTRY. *Educ:* Univ NC, Chapel Hill, BA, 68; Univ Wis-Madison, PhD(bot), 73. *Prof Exp:* Lab asst dairy chem & bact, United Gooi Dairies, Hilversum, Netherlands, 56-57; anal chemist vet med, Lab Medical Vet Medicine, Univ Utrecht, 57-60; anal chemist pub health, Pharmaceut & Toxicol Lab, Nat Inst Pub Health, Utrecht, Netherlands, 60-62; res technician biochem, E R Johnson Found, Univ Pa, 62-64; res technician physiol & pharmacol, Duke Univ, 64-68; res asst bot, Inst Plant Develop, Univ Wis-Madison, 68-73; Nat Res Coun res assoc, Western Regional Res Ctr, Agr Res Serv, USDA, Calif, 73-75; res assoc med, Stanford Univ Serv, Vet Admin Hosp, 75-80, LAB DIR, GEN CLIN RES CTR, SCH MED, STANFORD UNIV, 80- *Mem:* AAAS; Am Soc Plant Physiologists; Am Chem Soc. *Res:* Role of cytokinins in plant growth and development; isolation, separation, identification of naturally occurring cytokinins; plant cell and tissue cultures; acetate metabolism in humans with chronic renal failure; zinc nutrition; atherosclerosis; carbohydrate metabolism; diabetes mellitus in human subjects. *Mailing Add:* Gen Clin Res Ctr Stanford Univ Med Ctr Stanford CA 94305

VRENTAS, JAMES SPIRO, b Danville, Ill, Apr 14, 36; m 75; c 1. CHEMICAL ENGINEERING. *Educ:* Univ Ill, BS, 58; Univ Del, MChE, 61, PhD(chem eng), 63. *Prof Exp:* Res engr, Dow Chem Co Mich, 63-72; from asst prof to assoc prof, 72-76, prof, 76-80, PROF CHEM ENG, PA STATE UNIV, 80- *Honors & Awards:* William H Walker Award, Am Inst Chem Engrs, 81. *Mem:* Am Inst Chem Engrs; Am Chem Soc. *Res:* Transport phenomena; fluid mechanics; diffusion; applied mathematics; polymer science. *Mailing Add:* 119 Fenske Lab Pa State Univ University Park PA 16802

VRIELAND, GAIL EDWIN, b Grand Rapids, Mich, Jan 4, 38; m 63; c 3. INDUSTRIAL CHEMISTRY. *Educ:* Calvin Col, AB, 59; Northwestern Univ, PhD(chem), 63. *Prof Exp:* Res specialist, 63-80, RES ASSOC CHEM, CENT RES LAB, DOW CHEM CO, 80- *Mem:* Am Chem Soc. *Res:* Heterogeneous catalysis and high temperature vapor phase reaction including oxidations and hydrocyanation. *Mailing Add:* Cent Res Labs Dow Chem Co Midland MD 48640

VRIENS, GERARD N(ICHOLS), b New York, NY, July 4, 24; m 47; c 2. CHEMICAL ENGINEERING. *Educ:* Purdue Univ, BSChE, 44, PhD(chem eng), 49. *Prof Exp:* Sr chemist, Process Develop Dept, 49-58, chief chemist, Rubber Chem Dept, 58-65, group leader dyes res & develop, 65-69, mgr process develop, agr div, 69-79, PRIN ENGR, AGR RES DIV, AM CYANAMID CO, 79- *Mem:* Am Chem Soc; Am Inst Chem Engrs. *Res:* Chemical kinetics; thermodynamics. *Mailing Add:* 114 Branch Rd Bridgewater NJ 08807

VRIESEN, CALVIN W, b Elkhart Lake, Wis, Aug 31, 16; m 41; c 2. ORGANIC POLYMER CHEMISTRY, ORGANIC CHEMISTRY. *Educ:* Univ Minn, BS, 39, MS, 47; Purdue Univ, PhD(org chem), 52. *Prof Exp:* Assoc prof chem, Ill Col, 47-49; res chemist, Chattanooga Nylon Plant, E I du Pont de Nemours & Co, 52-56, Chambers Works, 56-58; res chemist, 58-62, staff chemist, 62-68, sr scientist, 68-74, GROUP SUPVR, THIOKOL CORP, ELKTON, MD, 74- *Honors & Awards:* Aerospace Scientist of Year Award, Am Inst Aeronaut & Astronaut, 67. *Mem:* Am Chem Soc. *Res:* Condensation, cationic, anionic polymerization; synthesis of new binders, oxidizers, coolants for solid rocket propellants. *Mailing Add:* 12 Mitchell Circle Newark DE 19713

VRIJENHOEK, ROBERT CHARLES, b Rotterdam, Netherlands, Mar 13, 46; US citizen; m 68; c 2. EVOLUTIONARY BIOLOGY. *Educ:* Univ Mass, BA, 68; Univ Conn, PhD(zool), 72. *Prof Exp:* Asst prof biol, Southern Methodist Univ, 72-74; asst prof, 74-78, ASSOC PROF ZOOL, RUTGERS UNIV, NEW BRUNSWICK, 78- *Concurrent Pos:* NSF grants, 74, 76, 77 & 79; mem, Pop Biol & Physiol Ecol Panel, NSF, 78-81; mem, Conf Biol Diversity, US Dept State, 81. *Mem:* Soc Study Evolution; Am Soc Ichthyol & Herpetol; Genetics Soc Am; Am Genetic Asn; Am Soc Naturalists. *Res:* Population genetic studies of evolutionary relationships and genetic variation in fishes, snails and parasitic helminths; the effects of various sexual and asexual mating systems on the genetic structure and evolutionary potential of populations. *Mailing Add:* Dept of Zool Rutgers Univ Busch Campus New Brunswick NJ 08903

VROMAN, HUGH EGMONT, b Detroit, Mich, Apr 18, 28; m 59. BIOCHEMISTRY. *Educ:* Univ Md, BS, 50, PhD(zool), 62. *Prof Exp:* Biologist, Nat Heart Inst, 57-58, biochemist, 58-61; res biologist, Insect Physiol Lab, Agr Res Serv, USDA, 61-66; biochemist, Dept Dermat, Sch Med, Univ Miami, 66-69; chmn dept biol, Claflin Col, 71-73, prof biol, 69-76; asst prof, 76-81, ASSOC PROF BIOL, CLEVELAND STATE COMMUNITY COL, 81- *Mem:* AAAS; Entom Soc Am; Am Soc Zool; Brit Biochem Soc; Am Inst Biol Sci. *Res:* Cholesterol metabolism; lipid biosynthesis by insects; insect hormones; sterol metabolism by insects; lipid biosynthesis and metabolism in skin. *Mailing Add:* Dept Math & Sci Cleveland State Community Col Cleveland TN 37311

VROMAN, LEO, b Gouda, Holland, Apr 10, 15; nat; m 47; c 2. PHYSIOLOGY, BIOPHYSICS. *Educ:* Jakarta Med Col, Indonesia, Drs, 41; Univ Utrecht, PhD(animal physiol), 58. *Prof Exp:* Asst zool, anat & physiol, Jakarta Med Col, 41; res assoc, St Peter's Gen Hosp, New Brunswick, NJ, 46-55; asst, Mt Sinai Hosp, New York, 56-58; sr physiologist, Stress-Tension Proj, Dept Animal Behav, Am Mus Natural Hist, 58-61; biochemist, 61-78, RES CAREER SCIENTIST, VET ADMIN HOSP, BROOKLYN, 78-; ASSOC PROF BIOPHYS DEPT, STATE UNIV NY, DOWNSTATE MED CTR, 77- *Mem:* Fel NY Acad Sci. *Res:* Behavior of blood at interfaces; biomaterials. *Mailing Add:* 2365 E 13th St Brooklyn NY 11229

VROMEN, BENJAMIN H, b Leeuwarden, Netherlands, June 6, 21; US citizen; m 53; c 2. PHYSICAL CHEMISTRY. *Educ:* Hebrew Univ, MS, 46, PhD(phys chem), 51. *Prof Exp:* Mem staff, Weizman Inst, 49-54; dir lab, Kadimah Chem Co, Israel, 54-58; group leader res & develop, Graver Water Conditioning Co, 58-60; mem tech staff, Bell Tel Labs, NJ, 61-68; ADV CHEMIST, GEN BUS GROUP, IBM CORP, 68- *Concurrent Pos:* Vis lectr, Polytech Inst Brooklyn, 67-68. *Mem:* Electrochem Soc; Am Vacuum Soc; Royal Netherlands Chem Soc. *Res:* Properties of sputtered and evaporated films; anodic reactions; separation processes; diffusion; thin film dielectrics. *Mailing Add:* IBM Corp Dept 424 Bldg 330-89F Route 52 Hopewell Junction NY 12533

VROOM, ALAN HEARD, b Montreal, Que, Can, Oct 5, 20; m 43; c 2. INSTRUMENTATION, MATERIALS SCIENCE. *Educ:* McGill Univ, BSc, 42, PhD(phys chem), 45. *Prof Exp:* Nat Res Coun Can, 44-46; asst dir res pulp & paper, Fraser Co, Ltd, 46-49; Hibbert Mem fel & hon lectr, McGill Univ, 50; res fel bark chem, Pulp & Paper Res Inst Can, 50-51; asst chief appl chem sect, Weyerhaeuser Timber Co, 51-52, chief appl physics sect, 52-54, chief appl chem sect, 54; asst dir res, Consol Paper Corp, Ltd, 55-56, dir res, 56-67, dir res & develop Consol-Bathurst Ltd, 67-71; spec consult, Nat Res Coun Can, 71-73; PRES, SULPHUR INNOVATIONS, LTD, 73- *Concurrent Pos:* Consult, Pulp & Paper Res Inst, Can, 51-54. *Mem:* Am Concrete Inst; fel Chem Inst Can; Can Soc Chem Eng. *Res:* Bark chemistry; pulp and paper; wood and fiber technology; sulfur utilization; development of new sulfur-based construction materials, primarily sulfur concrete. *Mailing Add:* 3015 58th Ave SE Calgary AB T2C 0B4 Can

VROOM, DAVID ARCHIE, b Vancouver, BC, Sept 12, 41; m 69; c 1. POLYMER ENGINEERING, RADIATION TECHNOLOGY. *Educ:* Univ BC, BSc, 63, PhD(phys chem), 67. *Prof Exp:* Nat Res Coun Can overseas fel, 67-68; staff chemist, Atomic Physics Br, Gulf Radiation Technol Div, Gulf Energy & Environ Systs, 68-73; prin scientist, IRT Corp, 73-77, mgr atomic physics dept, 77-81; TECH DIR CORP RES & DEVELOP PROCESS ENG, RAYCHEM CORP, 81- *Mem:* Am Phys Soc; Radiation Res Soc; Am Chem Soc. *Res:* Photoionization and photoelectron spectroscopy; electron impact studies of excitation; dissociation and ionization; low energy ion neutral reactions and pulse radiolysis studies. *Mailing Add:* 300 Constitution Dr Raychem Corp Menlo Park CA 94025

VROOM, KENNETH EDWIN, b Montreal, Can, May 28, 27. MATHEMATICS. *Educ:* McGill Univ, BSc, 48. *Prof Exp:* Supvr statist, Bell Tel Co Can, 48-53; supvr statist methods, 53-60, chmn tech serv dept, 60-69, dir sci & bus serv, 71-76, secy, 67-80, dir, Info Serv Div, 69-80, VPRES ADMIN, PULP & PAPER RES INST CAN, 77- *Res:* Statistical and mathematical analysis; operations and pulping research; applications of computers to research; information science; research administration. *Mailing Add:* Pulp & Paper Res Inst Can 570 St John's Blvd Pointe Claire PQ H9R 3S9 Can

VUCHIC, VUKAN R, b Belgrade, Yugoslavia, Jan 14, 35; US citizen; m 60; c 4. TRANSPORTATION ENGINEERING. *Educ:* Univ Belgrade, dipl transp eng, 60; Univ Calif, Berkeley, MEng, 65, PhD(civil eng, transp), 66; Univ Pa, MA, 71. *Prof Exp:* Planning engr, Hamburger Hochbahn AG, Ger, 60-61; asst & prin engr, Wilbur Smith & Assocs, Conn, 61-63; asst prof civil eng-transp, 67-70, assoc prof transp eng, 70-75, PROF TRANSP ENG, DEPT CIVIL & MECH ENG DEPT, UNIV PA, 75- *Concurrent Pos:* Mem, Transp Res Bd, Nat Acad Sci-Nat Res Coun; consult, Urban Mass Transp Admin, US Dept Transp & Off Technol Assessment, US Cong, 75- *Mem:* Opers Res Soc Am; Am Soc Civil Engrs; assoc mem Inst Traffic Engrs; assoc mem Int Union Pub Transp; Asn Transp & Commun Eng & Technol Yugoslavia. *Res:* Transportation policy, analysis and economics; public transportation systems; city planning and urban development; urban transportation planning, design and operations; traffic engineering. *Mailing Add:* 113 Towne Bldg D3 Univ of Pa Philadelphia PA 19174

VUCICH, M(ICHAEL) G(EORGE), b Bower Hill, Pa, Oct 30, 26; m 57; c 4. ELECTROCHEMISTRY, LUBRICATION. *Educ:* US Merchant Marine Acad, BS, 48; Carnegie Inst Technol, BS, 52. *Prof Exp:* From chem engr to res chem engr, Weirton Steel Co Div, 52-58, res engr, 58-59, sr res engr, 59-73, res assoc, 73-74, SUPVR CORROSION & LUBRICATION RES, RES & DEVELOP DEPT, NAT STEEL CORP, 74- *Mem:* Electrochem Soc; Nat Asn Corrosion Engrs. *Res:* Electrodeposition; surface chemistry and corrosion; lubrication; cold reduction. *Mailing Add:* Res & Develop Dept Nat Steel Corp Weirton WV 26062

VUCKOVIC, VLADETA, b Aleksinac, Yugoslavia, Mar 30, 23; m 54; c 1. MATHEMATICS. *Educ:* Univ Belgrade, MS, 49; PhD(math), Serbian Acad Sci, 53. *Prof Exp:* Instr math, Univ Belgrade, 49-52; sci collabr, Math Inst, Serbian Acad Sci, 52-54; prof math, Teacher Inst, Zrenjanin, Yugoslavia, 54-60; from asst prof to assoc prof, Univ Belgrade, 60-63; asst prof, 63-66, ASSOC PROF MATH, UNIV NOTRE DAME, 66- *Mem:* Math Asn Am; Asn Symbolic Logic. *Res:* Foundations of mathematics; mathematical analysis; summability of divergent series and integrals; theory of recursive functions. *Mailing Add:* Dept of Math Univ of Notre Dame Notre Dame IN 46556

VUILLEMIN, JOSEPH J, b Waco, Tex, July 22, 34; m 57; c 3. PHYSICS. *Educ:* Univ Tex, BS, 56; Baylor Univ, MS, 57; Univ Chicago, PhD(physics), 65. *Prof Exp:* NSF fel, Cambridge Univ, 65-66; asst prof, 66-70, assoc prof, 70-81, PROF PHYSICS, UNIV ARIZ, 81- *Concurrent Pos:* Sci res coun fel, Univ Bristol, 74-75. *Mem:* Am Phys Soc. *Res:* Electronic structure of metals and low temperature physics. *Mailing Add:* Dept Physics Univ Ariz Tucson AZ 85721

VUILLEMIN, VINCENT, high energy physics, see previous edition

VUILLEUMIER, FRANCOIS, b Berne, Switz, Nov 26, 38; m 64, 72; c 2. POPULATION BIOLOGY, BIOGEOGRAPHY. *Educ:* Univ Geneva, Lic nat sci, 61; Harvard Univ, PhD(biol), 67. *Prof Exp:* From instr to asst prof biol, Univ Mass, Boston, 66-71; prof zool & dir inst animal ecol, Univ Lausanne, 71-72; res fel marine biol, Biol Sta Roscoff, France, 72-73; vis prof, Lab Ecol, Ecole Normale Superieure, Univ Paris, 73-74; from assoc cur to CUR ORNITHOL, AM MUS NATURAL HIST, 74- *Concurrent Pos:* Am Mus Natural Hist Chapman fel, 67-68; vis prof, Univ or the Andes, Merida, Venezuela, 81. *Mem:* AAAS; Am Ornith Union; Soc Study Evolution; Soc Syst Zool; Am Soc Naturalists. *Res:* Avian migration; avian speciation in South American Andes; biogeography; patterns of species diversity in continental habitats; ecological genetics of marine molluscs; community ecology; evolution ornithology. *Mailing Add:* Am Mus Natural Hist Central Park W at 79th St New York NY 10024

VUKASOVICH, MARK SAMUEL, b Detroit, Mich, Dec 6, 27; m 54; c 5. CORROSION INHIBITION, LUBRICATION. *Educ:* Wayne State Univ, BS, 51, MS, 53. *Prof Exp:* res scientist friction/wear high temperature mat, Chrysler Corp, 53-61; head fiber optics, pigments & electron mat, Ceramics Dept, Horizons Res Inc, 61-64; res mgr microencapsulated pigments & fluorescent pigments, Sherwin Williams Co, 64-67; dir res & develop, Prof Dent Mat & Prod, Kerr Mfg Co, 67-69; SUPVR CHEM RES, LUBRICATION & CORROSION INHIBITION, CLIMAX MOLYBDENUM CO, 70- *Mem:* Nat Asn Corrosion Engrs; Am Soc Testing & Mat; Am Soc Lubrication Engrs; Am Chem Soc; Fedn Soc Coating Technol. *Res:* Corrosion inhibition; lubrication; pigment synthesis; fiber reinforced composities; fiber optics; microencapsulated products; electronic materials. *Mailing Add:* 1457 Woodland Dr Ann Arbor MI 48103

VUKCEVICH, MILAN RADOJE, b Belgrade, Yugoslavia, Mar 11, 37; US citizen; m 78; c 2. LATTICE DYNAMICS, PHYSICS. *Educ:* Belgrade Inst Technol, Dipl Ing, 63; Mass Inst Technol, MSc, 65, DSc(metall), 67. *Prof Exp:* Asst prof mat sci, Case Western Reserve Univ, 67-73; res scientist physics, Gen Elec Co, 67-80; GEN MGR & RES DIR, EDWARD ARTON JR CERAMIC FOUND, 80- *Concurrent Pos:* Consult, Chase Brass & Copper Co, Cleveland, 67-71. *Res:* Physics of incandescent light sources; optics; theory and uses of ultrasound. *Mailing Add:* Edward Arton Jr Ceramic Found 1445 Summit St PO Box 8309 Columbus OH 43201

VUKOV, RASTKO, b Belgrade, Yugoslavia, June 23, 42; Can citizen; m 66; c 2. ORGANIC & POLYMER CHEMISTRY. *Educ:* Univ Belgrade, BSc, 65; Univ Alta, PhD(chem), 72. *Prof Exp:* Res scientist, Raylo Chem Ltd, 72-76, proj mgr, 76-78, dir indust res, 78-80, mgr contract res, 80-82; SCI ADV, POLYSAR LTD, CAN, 82- *Mem:* Can Inst Chem; Am Chem Soc. *Res:* Investigation of the micro-structure of polymers; studies of polymer reactions; synthesis of novel monomers, antioxidants and cross-linking agents, preparation and characterization of specialty polymers; development of structure-properties correlations for polymers. *Mailing Add:* Polysar Ltd S Vidal St Sarnia ON N7I 1M2 Can

VUKOVICH, FRED MATTHEW, b Chicago, Ill, July 13, 39; m 66; c 3. DYNAMIC METEOROLOGY, PHYSICAL OCEANOGRAPHY. *Educ:* Parks Col Aeronaut Technol, St Louis, BS, 60; St Louis Univ, MS, 63, PhD(meteorol), 66. *Prof Exp:* Res meteorologist, Meteorol Res Inc, 63-64; res meteorologist, 66-68, supvr, 68-71, sr scientist, 71-74, mgr, Geosci Dept, 74-81, MGR OFF GEOSCI, RES TRIANGLE INST, 81- *Concurrent Pos:* Assoc prof, Duke Univ, 67-77. *Mem:* Am Meteorol Soc. *Res:* Dynamic meteorology of urban atmosphere; physical oceanographic studies on continental shelf, Gulf Stream, and Gulf of Mexico; dynamics of synoptic-scale pollution; satellite oceanography; atmospheric gravity waves and synoptic scale energetics. *Mailing Add:* Res Triangle Inst PO Box 12194 Research Triangle Park NC 27709

VUKOVICH, ROBERT ANTHONY, b Hoboken, NJ, Aug 6, 43; m 65; c 3. CLINICAL PHARMACOLOGY, CLINICAL RESEARCH. *Educ:* Allegheny Col, BS, 65; Jefferson Med Col, PhD(pharm), 69. *Prof Exp:* Clin res scientist clin pharmacol, Warner-Lambert Res Inst, 69-70; assoc dir med res, USV Labs, 70-71; dir clin pharmacol, The Sqiubb Inst Med Res, 72-79; DIR CLIN RES, DIV DEVELOP THERAPEUT, RES & DEVELOP DIV, REVLON HEALTH CARE GROUP, 79- *Concurrent Pos:* Co-ed, Clin Res Practices, Marcel Dekker, 81- *Mem:* Am Soc Clin Pharmacol & Therapeut; Am Soc Pharmacol & Exp Therapeut; NY Acad Sci; fel Am Col Clin Pharmacol; AMA. *Res:* Clinical pharmacology; clinical research; new drug development; cardiovascular hypersensitivity; inflammatory, infectious diseases. *Mailing Add:* 33 Ridge Rd Colts Neck NJ 07722

VULLIET, WILLIAM GEORGE, b Pueblo, Colo, July 11, 28; m 51; c 2. ATOMIC PHYSICS, MOLECULAR PHYSICS. *Educ:* San Diego State Col, BS, 49; Univ Iowa, MA, 54. *Prof Exp:* Engr, Collins Radio Co, 53-54; res engr, Gen Dynamics/Convair, 54-59; sr sci adv, IRT Corp, 59-77; SCI STAFF, MISSION RES CORP, 77- *Concurrent Pos:* Consult, Los Alamos Sci Lab, 73- *Res:* Equation of state and radiative opacities; radiative transfer under non-local thermodynamic equilibrium; nuclear weapons effects; pollutant formation kinetics during combustion. *Mailing Add:* Mission Res Corp PO Box 1209 La Jolla CA 92137

VULLO, WILLIAM JOSEPH, b Buffalo, NY, June 14, 33; m 59; c 2. ORGANIC CHEMISTRY. *Educ:* Univ Buffalo, BA, 55; Northwestern Univ, PhD(org chem), 59. *Prof Exp:* Instr gen chem, Northwestern Univ, 59; sr chemist, Hooker Chem Corp, 59-69; mgr textile res, Mohasco Industs, 69-79; MEM STAFF, ENVIRON PROTECTION OPER, GEN ELEC CO, 80- *Mem:* Am Chem Soc; Am Asn Textile Chem & Colorists. *Res:* Organometallic chemistry; organic reaction mechanisms; metal conversion coatings and treatments; cellulose reactive chemicals; organic phosphorus and fluorine chemistry; fire retardants; textile chemicals and finishes. *Mailing Add:* Environ Protection Oper Gen Elec Co 1 River Rd Schenectady NY 12345

VYAS, BRIJESH, b Jodhpur, India, Feb 7, 48. MATERIALS SCIENCE. *Educ:* Indian Inst Technol, BTech, 71; State Univ NY, Stony Brook, PhD(mat sci), 75. *Prof Exp:* ASSOC METALLURGIST MAT SCI, BROOKHAVEN NAT LAB, 75- *Mem:* Nat Asn Corrosion Engrs; Metall Soc; Am Soc Metals; Am Inst Mining, Metall & Petrol Engrs; Electrochem Soc. *Res:* Electrochemistry, corrosion, stress corrosion cracking and erosion of metallic materials; batteries. *Mailing Add:* Bell Labs 600 Mountain Ave Murray Hill NJ 07974

VYAS, GIRISH NARMADASHANKAR, b Aglod, India, June 11, 33; m 62; c 2. IMMUNOLOGY, GENETICS. *Educ:* Univ Bombay, BSc, 54, MSc, 57, PhD(microbiol), 64. *Prof Exp:* Asst res officer, Blood Group Ref Ctr, Indian Coun Med Res, Bombay, 57-64; officer-in-chg, Bombay Munic Blood Ctr, King Edward Mem Hosp, India, 64-65; lectr immunol, 67-69, asst prof path, 69-73, assoc prof, 73-77, PROF LAB MED & DIR BLOOD BANK, SCH MED, UNIV CALIF, SAN FRANCISCO, 77- *Concurrent Pos:* Jr res fel hemat, J J Hosp, Bombay, India, 56-57; fel genetics, Western Reserve Univ, 65-67. *Mem:* AAAS; Am Asn Immunol. *Res:* Microbiology; blood group serology; immunogenetics; blood banking; viral hepatitis; transfusion and circulatory physiology; genetics of gamma globulin and its structure. *Mailing Add:* Univ of Calif Med Ctr San Francisco CA 94143

VYAS, RAVINDRA KANTILAL, b Ahmedabad City, India, Oct 31, 35; m 67. STRUCTURAL ENGINEERING, APPLIED MECHANICS. *Educ:* Univ Bombay, BEng, 56; Stanford Univ, MS, 61, PhD(civil eng), 66. *Prof Exp:* Sub engr, Bombay Munic Corp, India, 57-60; Nat Acad Sci res assoc struct mech, NASA Ames Res Ctr, 66-68; asst prof, 68-72, ASSOC PROF CIVIL ENG, UNIV UTAH, 72- *Concurrent Pos:* NSF grant, 70-73. *Res:* Theory of shells; problems of plane elasticity in multiply-connected domains; non-linear structural analysis; thermally induced stresses in shells; membrane studies in scalloped shells. *Mailing Add:* Dept of Civil Eng Univ of Utah Salt Lake City UT 84112

VYBORNY, CARL JOSEPH, b Oak Park, Ill, Nov 23, 50; m 75; c 1. RADIOLOGY, MEDICAL PHYSICS. *Educ:* Univ Ill, Chicago, BS, 72, Urbana, MS, 73; Univ Chicago, PhD(radiol), 76, MD, 80. *Prof Exp:* Res assoc radiol physics, 78-80, RESIDENT PHYSICIAN RADIOL, UNIV CHICAGO, 80- *Honors & Awards:* Eastman Kodak Sci Award, 76; Itek Award, 79. *Mem:* Am Asn Phys Med; Radiol Soc NAm; Am Col Radiol. *Res:* Applications of x-ray fluorescence to radiographic imaging research; chest radiography. *Mailing Add:* Dept of Radiol Box 429 Univ of Chicago Chicago IL 60637

VYE, MALCOLM VINCENT, b Gary, Ind, Feb 17, 36; m 60; c 1. HEMATOLOGY, PATHOLOGY. *Educ:* Marquette Univ, MD, 61. *Prof Exp:* Asst instr, 62-64, from instr to asst prof path, Univ Ill Col Med, 64-66 & 68-71; ASST PROF PATH, MED SCH, NORTHWESTERN UNIV, EVANSTON, 71-; ASSOC PATHOLOGIST, EVANSTON HOSP, 71- *Concurrent Pos:* Mem staff, Armed Forces Inst Path. *Mem:* AAAS; Am Soc Clin Path; Am Asn Path & Bact; Col Am Pathologists. *Res:* Cell differentiation embryonic muscle; ultrastructure of glycogen; hematology laboratory methodology. *Mailing Add:* Dept Path Northwestern Univ Evanston IL 60201

VYGANTAS, AUSTE MARIJA, biochemistry, organic chemistry, see previous edition

W

WAACK, RICHARD, b Syracuse, NY, May 18, 31; m 60. PHYSICAL CHEMISTRY, POLYMER CHEMISTRY. *Educ:* State Univ NY, BS, 53, MS, 54, PhD, 58. *Prof Exp:* Tech serv rep, Dow Chem Co, Mich, 54-56; chemist, Solvay Process Div, Allied Chem Co, NY, 58-59; res chemist, Eastern Res Lab, Dow Chem Co, Mich, 59-60, res chemist, Phys Res Lab, 67-69; MGR DEVELOP LAB, POLAROID CORP, WALTHAM, MD 69- *Mem:* Am Chem Soc; Soc Photog Sci & Eng. *Res:* Polymer synthesis; spectroscopy; ionic polymerization mechanisms; photographic science; silver halide emulsion technology; colloidal processes; water soluble polymers; diffusion processes. *Mailing Add:* 19 Morrill Dr Wayland MA 01778

WAAG, CHARLES JOSEPH, b Oct 25, 31; US citizen; m 56; c 1. GEOLOGY. *Educ:* Univ Pittsburgh, BS, 56, MS, 58; Univ Ariz, PhD(geol), 68. *Prof Exp:* Sr geologist, Orinoco Mining Co, US Steel Corp, 58-63; sr geologist, Va Div Mineral Resources, 63-64; asst & lectr, Univ Ariz, 64-68; asst prof, 68-71, ASSOC PROF GEOL, GA STATE UNIV, 71- *Concurrent Pos:* Consult hydrogeol, 69- *Mem:* Geol Soc Am. *Res:* Glaciers as models in structural geology; gravity tectonics attendant to mantled gneiss domes in the Basin and Range Province. *Mailing Add:* Dept of Geol Ga State Univ Atlanta GA 30303

WAAG, ROBERT CHARLES, b Upper Darby, Pa, Oct 8, 38; m 61; c 2. ELECTRICAL ENGINEERING, ACOUSTICS. *Educ:* Cornell Univ, BEE, 61, MS, 63, PhD(commun), 65. *Prof Exp:* Mem tech staff, Sandia Sci Labs, 65-66; proj officer commun, Rome Air Develop Ctr, US Air Force, 66-69; ASSOC PROF ELEC ENG & RADIOL, UNIV ROCHESTER, 69- *Concurrent Pos:* NSF grant, 75-; Career Develop Award, NIH, 76- *Mem:* Inst Elec & Electronics Engrs; Acoust Soc Am; Am Inst Ultrasound Med. *Res:* Apply principles of physics and signal processing along with computer-based technology to improve imaging in diagnostic ultrasound and to characterize materials from measurements of ultrasonic scattering. *Mailing Add:* Dept of Elec Eng Univ of Rochester Rochester NY 14627

WAAGE, EDWARD VERN, physical chemistry, see previous edition

WAAGE, JONATHAN KING, b Pueblo, Colo, July 27, 44; m 67. BEHAVIORAL ECOLOGY, EVOLUTIONARY BIOLOGY. *Educ:* Princeton Univ, AB, 66; Univ Mich, PhD(zool), 71. *Prof Exp:* Instr, 72-73, asst prof, 73-79, ASSOC PROF BIOL, BROWN UNIV, 79- *Mem:* Am Soc Naturalists; Soc Study Evolution; Animal Behav Soc; Ecol Soc Am; Societas Internationalis Odonatologics. *Res:* Evolutionary and ecological determinants of reproductive behavior in odonates and other insects; manipultive and comparative field studies of sexual selection, including sperm competition and mating systems. *Mailing Add:* Box G Div Biol & Med Brown Univ Providence RI 02912

WAAGE, KARL MENSCH, b Philadelphia, Pa, Dec 17, 15; m 42; c 2. GEOLOGY. *Educ:* Princeton Univ, AB, 39, MA, 42, PhD(geol), 46. *Prof Exp:* From instr to assoc prof, 46-67, chmn dept geol-geophys, 73-76, dir, Peabody Mus, 79-82, PROF GEOL, YALE UNIV, 67-, CUR INVERT PALEONT, PEABODY MUS, 46- *Concurrent Pos:* Geologist, US Geol Surv, Washington, DC, 42-59. *Mem:* Fel Geol Soc Am; Paleont Soc; AAAS. *Res:* Field exploration for non-metalliferous deposits; stratigraphic geology and paleontology of cretaceous of western interior. *Mailing Add:* Peabody Mus Yale Univ New Haven CT 06520

WAALAND, JOSEPH ROBERT, b San Mateo, Calif, Feb 22, 43; m 69. ALGOLOGY, CYTOLOGY. *Educ:* Univ Calif, Berkeley, BA, 66, PhD(bot), 69. *Prof Exp:* Asst prof bot, Univ Wash, 69-75, assoc prof, 75-80; MEM STAFF, DIV MARINE LAND MGT, WASH DEPT NATURAL RESOURCES, 80- *Mem:* Bot Soc Am; Phycol Soc Am; Int Phycol Soc; Marine Biol Asn UK. *Res:* Development, cytology and ecology of algae; aquaculture of marine algae. *Mailing Add:* Div Marine Land Mgt Wash Dept Natural Resources Olympia WA 98504

WAALKES, T PHILLIP, b Belmond, Iowa, Oct 30, 19; m 45; c 6. PUBLIC HEALTH. *Educ:* Hope Col, AB, 41; Ohio State Univ, PhD(org chem), 45; George Washington Univ, MD, 51. *Prof Exp:* Asst chem, Ohio State Univ, 41-43, res assoc, Res Found, 44, Am Petrol Inst res assoc, Univ, 45, instr chem, 46-47; intern, USPHS Hosp, 51-52, res med, 52-55, Nat Heart Inst, 55-58, asst chief in chg clin activ, Cancer Chemother Nat Serv Ctr, 58-63, assoc dir, Nat Cancer Inst, 63-68, sr investr, 68-75; PROF ONCOL, MED SCH, JOHNS HOPKINS UNIV, 75- *Mem:* Am Asn Cancer Res; Am Soc Clin Oncol; AAAS. *Res:* Organic fluorine compounds; biochemistry; amino acids; fluorinated derivatives of propane and propylene; addition of fluorine to double bonds; cancer chemotherapy; biological markers. *Mailing Add:* 4244 Norbeck Rd Rockville MD 20853

WABECK, CHARLES J, b Montague, Mass, July 16, 38; m 64; c 2. FOOD SCIENCE. *Educ:* Univ Mass, BS, 62; Univ NH, MS, 64; Purdue Univ, PhD(food sci), 66. *Prof Exp:* Res assoc poultry & frozen foods, Armour & Co, 66-69; dir res frozen foods, Ocoma Foods Co, Nebr, 69; asst prof poultry prod, 69-76, ASSOC PROF POULTRY SCI, UNIV MD, COLLEGE PARK, 76- *Mem:* Inst Food Technologists; Poultry Sci Asn. *Res:* Research and development; quality control; frozen foods; poultry and meat products. *Mailing Add:* Dept of Poultry Sci Univ of Md College Park MD 20740

WABER, JAMES THOMAS, b Chicago, Ill, Apr 8, 20; m 51; c 3. ATOMIC PHYSICS, SOLID STATE PHYSICS. *Educ:* Ill Inst Technol, BS, 41, MS, 43, PhD(metall), 46. *Prof Exp:* Res assoc, Ill Inst Technol, 46, asst prof chem, 46-47; assoc metallurgist, Los Alamos Sci Lab, 47-49, staff mem, 49-66; PROF MAT SCI, NORTHWESTERN UNIV, EVANSTON, 67- *Concurrent Pos:* NSF sr fel, Univ Birmingham, 60-61; chmn comt alloy phases, past chmn nuclear metall comt & mem exec comt, Inst Metals Div, NY; partic, Robert A Welch Found Conf on Chem Res XIII Mendeleef Centennial-The Transuranium Elements; Alexander von Humboldt Found sr scientist award, Bonn, Ger. *Honors & Awards:* Turner Prize, Electrochem Soc, 47; Whitney Prize, Nat Asn Corrosion Eng, 63. *Mem:* Am Soc Metals; Electrochem Soc; Am Inst Mining, Metall & Petrol Engrs; Nat Asn Corrosion Engrs; fel Am Phys Soc. *Res:* Corrosion and oxidation of metals; relativistic self-consistent field Dirac-Slater and Hartree-Fock calculations for atoms and ions; energy band calculations; chemistry and physics of superheavy elements; positron annhilation in metals. *Mailing Add:* Dept of Mat Sci & Eng Northwestern Univ Evanston IL 60201

WACASEY, JERVIS WINN, b Clarksville, Tex, Nov 1, 29; m 56; c 2. BIOLOGICAL OCEANOGRAPHY. *Educ:* Tex Technol Col, BS, 54, MS, 55; Mich State Univ, PhD(zool), 61. *Prof Exp:* Instr biol, Eastern Ill Univ, 61-64; NIH fel, Inst Marine Sci, Univ Miami, 64-66; RES SCIENTIST II BIOL OCEANOG, ARCTIC BIOL STA, DEPT FISHERIES & OCEANS CAN, 67- *Mem:* Am Soc Limnol & Oceanog; Soc Syst Zool. *Res:* Ecology of benthic invertebrates in the arctic marine ecosystem. *Mailing Add:* Dept Fisheries & Oceans Arctic Biol Sta 555 St Pierre Blvd Ste-Anne-de-Bellevue PQ H9X 3R4 Can

WACHHOLZ, BRUCE WILLIAM, b Chicago, Ill, Aug 16, 36; m 63; c 1. RADIATION BIOLOGY. *Educ:* Valparaiso Univ, BA, 58; Univ Rochester, MS, 59, PhD(radiation biol), 67. *Prof Exp:* Sr res scientist, Pac Northwest Labs, Battelle Mem Inst, 66-71; RADIATION BIOLOGIST, OFF HEALTH & ENVIRON, ENERGY RES & DEVELOP ADMIN, 71- *Mem:* AAAS; Am Phys Soc; Radiation Res Soc; NY Acad Sci; Geront Soc. *Res:* Pathological, physiological and endocrinological effects of radiation; metabolism and toxicity of radionuclides; gerontology. *Mailing Add:* Off Health & Environ Energy Res & Develop Admin Washington DC 20545

WACHMAN, HAROLD YEHUDA, b Tel Aviv, Israel, Dec 2, 27; nat US; m 54; c 1. SURFACE PHYSICS. *Educ:* City Col New York, BS, 49; Univ Mo, MA, 52, PhD(phys chem), 57. *Prof Exp:* Specialist chem physics, Aerosci Lab, Gen Elec Co, 57-63; vis prof, 63-64, assoc prof, 64-69, PROF AERONAUT & ASTRONAUT, MASS INST TECHNOL, 69- *Concurrent Pos:* Consult, Space Sci Lab, Gen Elec Co; vis sr res fel, Jesus Col, Oxford Univ, 72-73. *Res:* Rarefied gas phenomena; adsorption; high temperature chemical equilibrium studies; gas surface interactions; nucleation phenomena. *Mailing Add:* Dept of Aeronaut & Astronaut Mass Inst of Technol Cambridge MA 02139

WACHMAN, MURRAY, b Tel Aviv, Israel, Feb 1, 31; US citizen; m 58; c 3. MATHEMATICS. *Educ:* Brooklyn Col, BA, 53; NY Univ, MS, 56, PhD(math), 61. *Prof Exp:* Math analyst, Repub Aviation Corp, 57-59; appl mathematician, Gen Elec Co, 59-63, consult mathematician, 63-65, group leader appl math, 65-67; assoc prof, 67-73, PROF MATH, UNIV CONN, 73- *Concurrent Pos:* Consult, Missile & Space Div, Gen Elec Co, 67-69. *Mem:* Soc Indust & Appl Math; Am Math Soc. *Res:* Representation of functions; Boltzmann equation; elliptic partial differential equation; two point boundary value problem; biological and economic models. *Mailing Add:* Dept Math Univ Conn Storrs CT 06268

WACHOWSKI, HILLARD M(ARION), b Chicago, Ill, Dec 10, 26. ELECTRODYNAMICS, APPLIED MATHEMATICS. *Educ:* Northwestern Univ, BS, 48, MS, 50, PhD(elec eng), 52. *Prof Exp:* Asst prof elec eng, Northwestern Univ, 52-53; elec engr, Armour Res Found, Ill Inst Technol, 53-54; sr engr, Raytheon Mfg Co, 54-56; mem tech staff, Ramo-Wooldridge Corp, 56-59; eng consult, Kearfott Div, Gen Precision, Inc, 59-61; mem res staff, Sperry Rand Res Ctr, 61-62; staff engr, 62-80, ENG SPECIALIST, AEROSPACE CORP, 80- *Concurrent Pos:* Exchange scientist, Warsaw, Poland, Nat Acad Sci, 74-75. *Res:* Microwaves; electromagnetic theory; wave propagation; antennas; radar systems; inverse scattering. *Mailing Add:* 605 Toledo St Los Angeles CA 90042

WACHS, GERALD N, b Chicago, Ill, Nov 5, 37; m 62; c 4. DERMATOLOGY. *Educ:* Univ Ill, BS, 58, MD, 62; Am Bd Dermat, dipl, 68. *Prof Exp:* Intern med, Michael Reese Hosp, Ill, 62-63; resident dermat, Univ Calif, 63-65, chief resident, 65-66; mem dept clin invest, 66-67, asst med dir, 67-69, assoc med dir, 69-74, dir new prod planning, 74-78, SR ASSOC MED DIR, SCHERING-PLOUGH CORP, KENILWORTH, NJ, 78- *Concurrent Pos:* Clin asst dermatologist, St Vincent's Hosp, NY, 67-; attend staff dermatologist, Mary Manning Walsh Home, New York, 71-81; attend staff, St Barnabas Med Ctr, Livingston, NJ. *Mem:* Fel Am Col Physicians; fel Am Acad Dermat; fel Am Col Allergists; Int Soc Trop Dermat; Am Acad Allergy. *Res:* Clinical investigation of drugs in dermatology, allergy and ophthamology; development of new concepts in approaching the therapy of difficult clinical diseases in dermatology, allergy and ophthamology. *Mailing Add:* 459 Long Hill Dr Short Hills NJ 07078

WACHSBERGER, PHYLLIS RACHELLE, b New York, NY; m 67; c 1. MOLECULAR BIOLOGY. *Educ:* City Univ New York, BS, 64; Med Col Pa, PhD(physiol & biophys), 71. *Prof Exp:* Res instr muscle biophys, Dept Physiol & Biophys, Med Col Pa, 70-71; RES ASSOC MUSCLE BIOPHYS, DEPT ANAT, UNIV PA, 73- *Concurrent Pos:* NIH fel, Dept Anat, Univ Pa, 71-73; asst prof physiol & biophys, Hahnemann Med Col & Hosp, Philadelphia, 77-81. *Mem:* Biophys Soc; AAAS; Am Inst Biol Sci; Sigma Xi. *Res:* Studies of the self assembly of synthetic vertebrate smooth muscle myosin filaments; comparative studies of molecular substructure of myosin filaments from various muscle types; immunochemical studies of the Myosin Crossbridge; identification of monsclonal antibodies raised to myosin and other myofibrillar proteins. *Mailing Add:* 433 School Lane Strafford Wayne PA 19087

WACHSMAN, JOSEPH T, b New York, NY, July 25, 27; m 60; c 1. MICROBIOLOGY, BIOCHEMISTRY. *Educ:* NY Univ, AB, 48; Univ Calif, PhD(microbiol), 55. *Prof Exp:* USPHS fel, Brussels, Belg, 55-57; asst prof, 57-63, ASSOC PROF MICROBIOL, UNIV ILL, URBANA-CHAMPAIGN, 63- *Concurrent Pos:* USPHS res career develop award, 62- *Mem:* Am Soc Microbiol. *Res:* Biochemistry and molecular biology of mammalian cells; unique properties of malignant cells-emphasis on the plasminogen activator associated with transformed cells-nucleic acid synthesis and repair. *Mailing Add:* Dept of Microbiol Univ of Ill Urbana IL 61801

WACHTEL, ALLEN W, b New York, NY, Aug 13, 25; m 46, 61; c 2. CELL BIOLOGY, CYTOLOGY. *Educ:* Columbia Univ, BS, 53, MA, 54, PhD(zool), 62. *Prof Exp:* Res asst cell biol, Cell Res Lab, Mt Sinai Hosp, New York, 56-63; from asst prof to assoc prof zool, 63-72, PROF BIOL, UNIV CONN, 72- *Mem:* Am Soc Cell Biol; Electron Micros Soc Am; Histochem Soc. *Res:* Histochemistry; cytology of electric organs; receptor structure. *Mailing Add:* Dept of Biol Sci Univ of Conn U-131 Storrs CT 06268

WACHTEL, ANSELM, solid state chemistry, see previous edition

WACHTEL, HOWARD, b New York, NY, July 5, 39; m 67; c 1. BIOMEDICAL ENGINEERING, PHYSIOLOGY. *Educ:* Cooper Union, BSEE, 60; Drexel Inst Technol, MS, 61; NY Univ, PhD(physiol), 67. *Prof Exp:* Res asst biomed eng, NY Univ, 61-67; NSF grant, 68-70, asst prof biomed eng, 68-71, asst prof physiol, 68-78, ASSOC PROF BIOMED ENG, DUKE UNIV, 71-, ASSOC PROF PHYSIOL, 78- *Concurrent Pos:* NIH grant, Duke Univ, 69- & NIMH grant, 71- *Mem:* Am Physiol Soc; Soc Gen Physiol; Biomed Eng Soc. *Res:* Neurophysiology; neuronal basis of behavior; neuronal interactions; slow wave generation in neurons; prolonged synaptic events; organization of neural nets; microwave effects on neurons. *Mailing Add:* Div of Physiol Duke Univ Med Ctr Durham NC 27706

WACHTEL, STEPHEN SHOEL, b Philadelphia, Pa, June 17, 37; m 62; c 2. IMMUNOGENETICS, TRANSPLANTATION IMMUNOBIOLOGY. *Educ:* Kenyon Col, Ohio, AB, 59; Univ Pa, PhD(biol), 71. *Prof Exp:* Fel immunol, 72-73, res assoc, 73-75, assoc, 75-78, ASSOC MEM, MEM SLOAN-KETTERING CANCER CTR, 78-; ASSOC PROF IMMUNOL, MED COL, CORNELL UNIV, 77- *Concurrent Pos:* NIH res career develop award, 76-; prin investr, NIH res grant, 74- & 76-; co-investr, Pop Coun grant, 77-78; co-chmn, Develop Genetics Training Comt, Mem Sloan-Kettering Cancer Ctr, 77- *Mem:* Int Transplantation Soc; Am Asn Immunologists. *Res:* H-Y antigen and differentiation of the vertebrate gonad; immunogenetics of tissue transplantation; immunological tolerance; serological analysis of epidermal cell antigens. *Mailing Add:* Mem Sloan-Kettering Cancer Ctr New York NY 10021

WACHTELL, GEORGE PETER, b New York, NY, Mar 18, 23; div; c 2. PHYSICS. *Educ:* Princeton Univ, PhD(physics), 51. *Prof Exp:* Mem staff, Radiation Lab, Mass Inst Technol, 43-45; asst, Princeton Univ, 45-51; PRIN SCIENTIST, ENERGY ENG LAB, FRANKLIN RES CTR, PHILADELPHIA, 51- *Res:* Optics; supersonics; heat transfer; fluid dynamics. *Mailing Add:* Energy Eng Lab Franklin Res Ctr Philadelphia PA 19103

WACHTELL, RICHARD L(LOYD), b New York, NY, Feb 18, 20; m 41; c 1. ENGINEERING. *Educ:* Columbia Univ, BS, 41. *Prof Exp:* Asst metallurgist, Repub Aviation Corp, NY, 42-46; metall engr, Tech Serv Sect, Res Lab, Air Reduction Co, 46-48; supvr metallog lab, Am Electro-Metals Corp, 48-49, proj engr, 49-51, asst tech dir, 51-52; chief metallurgist, 52-54, tech dir, 54-60, vpres & gen mgr, Chromalloy Div, 60-63, vpres, 63-68, pres, 63-76, pres, Turbine Support Div, 66-76, pres res & tech div & mem bd dirs, 68-71, exec vpres technol, 71-76, div pres, Chromalloy Res & Tech Div, 76-77, chmn, Chromalloy Metal Tectonics, 77-80, CHMN BD, CHROMALLOY AM CORP, 80- *Mem:* Am Soc Metals; Am Ord Asn; Am Inst Mining, Metall & Petrol Engrs; Am Iron & Steel Inst. *Res:* High temperature metallurgy, especially refractory metals and super-alloys and their protection from oxidation damage; coatings by diffusion; metallurgy techniques; intermetallic systems for high temperature service. *Mailing Add:* Chromalloy Am Corp Tuxedo Park NY 10987

WACHTER, RALPH FRANKLIN, b Frederick, Md, Mar 6, 18; m 47; c 3. BIOCHEMISTRY, VIROLOGY. *Educ:* Univ Notre Dame, BS, 39; Catholic Univ, MS, 41; Purdue Univ, PhD(biochem), 50. *Prof Exp:* City chemist, Frederick, Md, 41-43; biochemist, US Army Biol Labs, 50-72; RES CHEMIST, RICKETTSIOL DIV, US ARMY MED RES INST INFECTIOUS DIS, 72- *Mem:* Sigma Xi; Am Soc Microbiol. *Res:* Biochemical aspects of virology; virus stabilization and inactivation; biochemical and biological characterization of rickettsiae; rickettsial vaccines. *Mailing Add:* Aerobiol Div US Army Med Res Inst Infect Dis Frederick MD 21701

WACHTL, CARL, b Vienna, Austria, Oct 3, 06; nat US. ORGANIC CHEMISTRY. *Educ:* Univ Tex, BS, 48; Northwestern Univ, PhD(biochem), 53. *Prof Exp:* Res assoc, Lithographic Tech Found, 48-49; biochemist, Kresge Eye Inst, 53-60; head phys & inorg chem ed, Chem Abstr Serv, Ohio, 60-71; vis scholar chem, Technol Inst, Northwestern Univ, Evanston, 71-73; RETIRED. *Concurrent Pos:* Asst prof, Wayne State Univ. *Mem:* Fel AAAS; Am Chem Soc; Asn Res Vision & Ophthal. *Res:* Synthesis of inhibitors of dental caries; permeability of teeth; lens metabolism; culture of the lens of the eye in natural and synthetic media; radiation cataract; amino acid and protein metabolism of ocular lens. *Mailing Add:* PO Box 1549 Evanston IL 60204

WACHTMAN, JOHN BRYAN, JR, b Conway, SC, Feb 6, 28; m 55. SOLID STATE SCIENCE. *Educ:* Carnegie Inst Technol, BS, 48, MS, 49; Univ Md, PhD(physics), 61. *Prof Exp:* Physicist, 51-62, chief phys properties sect, 62-68, chief inorg mat div, 68-78, DIR CTR MAT SCI, NAT BUR STANDARDS, 78- *Concurrent Pos:* Ed, Ceramics & Glass, 68- & Sci & Technol, 68-; trustee, Edward Orton, Jr Ceramic Found, 70-; mem ceramic eng adv bd, Univ Ill Urbana, 73-76, Alfred Univ, 74-, Pa State Univ, 76-, Northwestern Univ, 77- & Mass Inst Technol, 78-; prog mgr mat, Off Technol Assessment, US Congress, 74-75; mem adv coun ceramics, Univ NY Alfred, 74-; mem mat dept adv comt, State Univ NY, Stonybrook, 79; lectr, Johns Hopkins Univ, 81- *Honors & Awards:* Gold Medal, Dept of Commerce, 71; Sosman Mem Lectr Award, Am Ceramic Soc, 74; Hobart Krauer Award, 78; Stratton Award, 75; Orton Mem Lectr, 81; Dorn Mem Lectr, 81. *Mem:* Nat Acad Eng; Am Ceramic Soc (pres, 78-79); Am Soc Testing & Mat; Nat Inst Ceramic Eng; Fedn Mat Socs (secy/treas, 73, pres-elect, 74, pres, 75). *Res:* Mechanical properties and effective utilization of inorganic materials. *Mailing Add:* Nat Bur of Standards Washington DC 20234

WACK, PAUL EDWARD, b Council Bluffs, Iowa, Apr 28, 19; m 52; c 4. NUCLEAR PHYSICS. *Educ:* Creighton Univ, AB, 41; Univ Notre Dame, MS, 42, PhD(physics), 47. *Prof Exp:* Asst physics, Univ Notre Dame, 41-43, instr, 43-46; res assoc, Off Naval Res, 46-47; dir dept physics, Creighton Univ, 47-49; from asst prof to assoc prof physics, 49-68, head dept, 66-73, PROF PHYSICS, UNIV PORTLAND, 68- *Concurrent Pos:* Res assoc, Off Rubber Reserve, 43-45; res assoc, Gen Tire Co, 45-46. *Mem:* Am Phys Soc; Am Asn Physics Teachers. *Res:* Electron optics; stress relaxation, low temperature behavior, equation of state and electrical conductivity of natural and synthetic rubbers; nuclear spectroscopy. *Mailing Add:* Dept of Physics Univ of Portland Portland OR 97203

WACKER, GEORGE ADOLF, b New York, NY, Aug 18, 39; m 63; c 2. METALLURGY, CORROSION. *Educ:* Polytech Inst, Brooklyn, BSMetE, 62, MSMetE, 64. *Prof Exp:* Foundry metallurgist, Naval Appl Sci Lab, 62, phys metallurgist, 63-65 & Marine Eng Lab, 65-67; metallurgist, 68-71, head metal physics br, 71-77, head, high temperature alloys br, 77-78, HEAD, METALS DIV, NAVAL SHIP RES & DEVELOP CTR, 79- *Mem:* Am Soc Metals; Am Soc Testing & Mat; Nat Asn Corrosion Engrs; Sigma Xi. *Res:* Effects of the marine environment on metals and alloys; physical metallurgy of engineering materials used in saline environments; effects of elevated temperature corrosive environments on engineering materials. *Mailing Add:* Naval Ship Res & Develop Ctr Code 281 Annapolis MD 21402

WACKER, WALDON BURDETTE, b Garrison, NDak, Aug 13, 23; m 55; c 4. IMMUNOLOGY, MICROBIOLOGY. *Educ:* Washington Univ, AB, 49; Univ Mich, MS, 51; Ohio State Univ, PhD(bact), 57. *Prof Exp:* Res assoc virol, Ohio State Univ, 58-59; from asst prof to assoc prof microbiol, 59-80, PROF OPHTHAL RES, UNIV LOUISVILLE, 80- *Concurrent Pos:* NIH career develop award, Univ Louisville, 62-69, NIH res grant, 62- *Mem:* Asn Res Vision & Ophthal; Sigma Xi. *Res:* Autoimmune disease; immunopathology; uveitis. *Mailing Add:* Eye Res Inst Dept Ophthal Univ of Louisville Sch of Med Louisville KY 40202

WACKER, WARREN ERNEST CLYDE, b Brooklyn, NY, Feb 29, 24; m 48; c 2. MEDICINE, BIOCHEMISTRY. *Educ:* George Washington Univ, MD, 51; Harvard Univ, MS, 68. *Prof Exp:* Intern, George Washington Univ Hosp, 51-52, resident, 52-53; resident, Peter Bent Brigham Hosp, 53-55; res fel biophys, Harvard Med Sch & Peter Bent Brigham Hosp, 55-57; from instr to assoc prof med, Harvard Med Sch, 57-71; PROF HYG, HARVARD UNIV, 71- *Concurrent Pos:* Nat Found Infantile Paralysis fel, 55-57; investr, Howard Hughes Med Inst, 57-68. *Mem:* Am Soc Biol Chemists; Am Soc Clin Invest; Biochem Soc; Am Chem Soc; Am Col Physicians. *Res:* Biochemistry of metals; studies of metalloenzymes; use of enzymatic methods in diagnoses; analytical chemistry of metals in biological material. *Mailing Add:* Harvard Univ Health Serv 75 Mount Auburn St Cambridge MA 02138

WACKER, WILLIAM DENNIS, b St Louis, Mo, Dec 5, 41; m 73; c 2. STATISTICS. *Educ:* Wash Univ, BS, 64, MS, 67, DSc(probability), 71. *Prof Exp:* ASSOC PROF MATH, PARKS COL, ST LOUIS UNIV, 68- *Mem:* Sigma Xi; Inst Mgt Sci; Opers Res Soc Am. *Res:* Application of optimization theory and statistics to real world problems. *Mailing Add:* Dept of Math Parks Col of St Louis Univ Cahokia IL 62206

WACKERLE, JERRY DONALD, b Edna, Kans, May 21, 30; m 49; c 4. PHYSICS, MATHEMATICS. *Educ:* Univ Kans, BS, 51, MS, 54, PhD(physics), 56. *Prof Exp:* Staff mem, 56-64, ASST GROUP LEADER, UNIV CALIF, LOS ALAMOS SCI LAB, 64- *Concurrent Pos:* Adj prof physics, Univ NMex, 58-68. *Mem:* Am Phys Soc; AAAS. *Res:* Shock wave physics and equation of state; initiation and detonation of chemical explosives. *Mailing Add:* Group WX-7 Mail Stop 950 Los Alamos Sci Lab Los Alamos NM 87545

WACKERNAGEL, HANS BEAT, b Basel, Switz, Aug 31, 31; US citizen; m 74; c 4. ASTRODYNAMICS, DATA PROCESSING. *Educ:* Univ Basel, PhD(astron), 58. *Prof Exp:* Observer, Observ Neuchatel, 53-54; res asst, Observ Basel, 55-58; astronr, Proj Spacetrack, Air Force Cambridge Res Labs, Mass, 58-59, 496L Syst Proj Off, 60-61, First Aerospace Control Squadron, Ent AFB, Colo, 61-62, Ninth Aerospace Defense Div, 62-68 & Fourteenth

Aerospace Force, 68-73, comput specialist, Hq NAm Air Defense, 73-75, opers res analyst, Second Commun Squadron, Buckley Air Nat Guard Base, 75, mathematician, 75-79, PHYSICIST, HQ N AM AIR DEFENSE, PETERSON AFB, COLO, 79- *Concurrent Pos:* Lectr, Univ Colo, Colorado Springs Ctr, 64-70. *Mem:* Am Astron Soc; fel Brit Interplanetary Soc; Swiss Astron Soc. *Res:* Design and evaluation of advanced space defense systems; applied celestial mechanics. *Mailing Add:* 2939 Country Club Dr Colorado Springs CO 80909

WACKMAN, PETER HUSTING, b Cleveland, Ohio, June 16, 28; m 51; c 3. THEORETICAL PHYSICS. *Educ:* Univ Wis, BS, 51, MS, 53; Univ Pittsburgh, PhD(physics), 60. *Prof Exp:* Sr scientist, Bettis Atomic Power Lab, Westinghouse Elec Corp, 53-60; staff scientist, A-C Spark Plug Div, Gen Motors Corp, 60-61; ASSOC PROF MECH ENG, MARQUETTE UNIV, 61- *Concurrent Pos:* Mem staff, McGraw Edison Power Syst, 69- *Mem:* Am Phys Soc; Am Nuclear Soc. *Res:* Nuclear structure; low energy nuclear physics; nuclear reactor physics; inertial guidance systems; radiation effects; materials science. *Mailing Add:* Dept of Mech Eng Marquette Univ Milwaukee WI 53233

WADA, GEORGE, b Lomita, Calif, Oct 18, 27; m 58; c 2. ELECTRICAL ENGINEERING. *Educ:* Calif Inst Technol, BS, 54; Stanford Univ, MS, 55, PhD(elec eng), 58. *Prof Exp:* Res assoc elec eng, Stanford Univ, 55-58; mem tech staff, Devices Dept, Watkins-Johnson Co, 58-80; STAFF SCIENTIST, HUGHES AIRCRAFT CORP, 80- *Mem:* Inst Elec & Electronics Engrs. *Res:* Microwave electron tubes and devices. *Mailing Add:* Hughes Aircraft Corp 3100 Lomita Blvd Torrance CA 90501

WADA, JAMES YASUO, b Lomita, Calif, May 15, 34; m 57; c 4. LASERS, PLASMA PHYSICS. *Educ:* Univ Calif, Los Angeles, BS, 56; Univ Southern Calif, MS, 58, PhD(elec eng), 63. *Prof Exp:* Sect head, Elec-Gasdyn Lasers, Hughes Res Labs, Malibu, 56-74, SR SCIENTIST & DEPT MGR, HUGHES SPACE-COMMUN GROUP, LOS ANGELES, 74- *Concurrent Pos:* Lectr, Univ Southern Calif, 64, asst prof, 64-66. *Mem:* Inst Elec & Electronics Engrs. *Res:* High power lasers and optics; physical optics; microwave tubes; electromagnetic theory; space communications. *Mailing Add:* Hughes Space-Comm GP Box 92919 Bldg 366 MS 720 Los Angeles CA 90009

WADA, JUHN A, b Tokyo, Japan, Mar 28, 24; nat Can; m 56. MEDICINE. *Educ:* Hokkaido Imp Univ, Japan, MD, 45, DMedSci, 51; FRCPS(C), 72. *Prof Exp:* Asst prof neurol & psychiat, dir labs exp neurol & brain surgeon-in-chief, Univ Hosps, Hokkaido Imp Univ, Japan, 52-57; res assoc neurol, 57-59, asst prof neurol res & psychiat & chief labs EEG & neurophysiol, 60-63, assoc prof med neurol & dir EEG labs, 63-70, PROF NEUROL SCI, UNIV BC & DIR NEUROL & EEG DEPT, HEALTH SCI CTR HOSP, 70- *Concurrent Pos:* Fel, Univ Minn, 54-55 & Montreal Neurol Inst, McGill Univ, 55-56; Can Med Res Coun assoc, 66; attend neurologist & assoc dir EEG dept, Vancouver Gen Hosp. *Mem:* Am Electroencephalog Soc; Am Epilepsy Soc; fel Am Acad Neurol; Can Neurol Soc; Can Soc Electroencephalog. *Res:* Neurological mechanism of human behavior; epilepsy; electrical activity of brain; cerebral speech function. *Mailing Add:* Health Sci Ctr Hosp Univ BC Vancouver BC V6T 1W5 Can

WADA, WALTER W, b Loomis, Calif, Feb 26, 19; m 46; c 4. PHYSICS. *Educ:* Univ Utah, BA, 43; Univ Mich, MA, 46, PhD, 51. *Prof Exp:* Physicist nucleonics div, US Naval Res Lab, 51-66; PROF PHYSICS, OHIO STATE UNIV, 66- *Concurrent Pos:* Lectr, Univ Md, 51-62; vis prof, Northwestern Univ, 62-64. *Mem:* Am Phys Soc. *Res:* Quantum theory of fields and applications in electrodynamics; theoretical high energy physics. *Mailing Add:* Dept of Physics Ohio State Univ Columbus OH 43210

WADDELL, CHARLES NOEL, b Omaha, Nebr, Nov 11, 22; m 45; c 6. PHYSICS. *Educ:* Univ Calif, BA, 50, PhD(physics), 58. *Prof Exp:* Assoc physics, Univ Calif, 50-52, physicist, Radiation Lab, 52-58; asst prof, 58-65, ASSOC PROF PHYSICS, UNIV SOUTHERN CALIF, 65- *Mem:* Am Phys Soc. *Res:* Nuclear reaction mechanisms; semiconductor physics, ion implantation and optical properties. *Mailing Add:* Dept of Physics University Park Los Angeles CA 90007

WADDELL, HENRY THOMAS, b Wilson, Ark, Apr 19, 18; m 45; c 2. BOTANY. *Educ:* Peabody Col, BS, 49, MA, 51; Univ Fla, PhD(plant path), 59. *Prof Exp:* Asst prof biol, Martin Br, Univ Tenn, 49-56; assoc prof, Peabody Col, 59-63; PROF BIOL, LAMAR UNIV, 63- *Mem:* AAAS; Am Phytopath Soc; Mycol Soc Am. *Res:* Plant Pathology; mycology. *Mailing Add:* Dept of Biol Lamar Univ Beaumont TX 77710

WADDELL, ROBERT CLINTON, b Mattoon, Ill, Aug 15, 21; m 60; c 3. PHYSICS. *Educ:* Eastern Ill Univ, BS, 47; Univ Ill, MS, 48; Iowa State Univ, PhD(physics), 55. *Prof Exp:* From instr to assoc prof, 48-60, PROF PHYSICS, EASTERN ILL UNIV, 60- *Concurrent Pos:* Res asst, Iowa State Univ, 53-55. *Mem:* Am Asn Physics Teachers; Am Phys Soc; Sigma Xi. *Res:* Physics education. *Mailing Add:* Dept of Physics Eastern Ill Univ Charleston IL 61920

WADDELL, THOMAS GROTH, b Madison, Wis, July 29, 44; m 67. BIO-ORGANIC CHEMISTRY. *Educ:* Univ Wis-Madison, BS, 66; Univ Calif, Los Angeles, PhD(org chem), 69. *Prof Exp:* Scholar org chem, Univ Calif, Los Angeles, 69; NIH res fel, Univ Calif, Berkeley, 70-71; from asst prof to assoc prof, 71-81, PROF CHEM, UNIV TENN, CHATTANOOGA, 81- *Concurrent Pos:* Vis prof, Univ Denver, 80. *Mem:* Am Chem Soc; AAAS. *Res:* Chemical plant taxonomy; chemical constituents of medicinal plants; synthesis of naturally occurring drugs. *Mailing Add:* Dept Chem Univ Tenn Chattanooga TN 37401

WADDELL, WALTER HARVEY, b Chicago, Ill, Sept 26, 47. PHOTOCHEMISTRY. *Educ:* Univ Ill, Chicago, BS, 69; Univ Houston, PhD(chem), 73. *Prof Exp:* Res assoc chem, Columbia Univ, 73-75; asst prof, 75-79, ASSOC PROF CHEM, CARNEGIE-MELLON UNIV, 79- *Concurrent Pos:* NIH res fel, Nat Eye Inst, 75. *Mem:* Am Chem Soc; Inter-Am Photochem Soc; Am Soc Photobiol. *Res:* Spectroscopic and photochemical investigations of linear polyenes related to vitamin A; photo-polymerization reactions of synthetic polymers based on arylazide initiators; chemistry of the hydroxy and superoxide radicals. *Mailing Add:* Dept of Chem Carnegie-Mellon Univ Pittsburgh PA 15213

WADDELL, WILLIAM JOSEPH, b Commerce, Ga, Mar 16, 29; m 74; c 4. PHARMACOLOGY. *Educ:* Univ NC, AB, 51, MD, 55. *Prof Exp:* From asst prof to assoc prof pharmacol, Univ NC, Chapel Hill, 58-71, assoc prof oral biol, 67-69, prof oral biol & assoc dir dent res ctr, 69-72, assoc div dir, Ctr Res Pharmacol & Toxicol, 66-67; prof pharmacol, Univ Ky, 72-77; PROF PHARMACOL & TOXICOL & CHMN DEPT, UNIV LOUISVILLE, 77- *Concurrent Pos:* USPHS res fel, Univ NC, Chapel Hill, 55-58; NIH spec fel, Royal Vet Col, Sweden, 65-66. *Mem:* Teratology Soc; Int Soc Quantum Biol; Am Soc Pharmacol & Exp Therapeut; Soc Exp Biol & Med; Am Physiol Soc. *Res:* Intracellular pH; teratogenic agents. *Mailing Add:* Dept of Pharmacol & Toxicol Univ of Louisville Louisville KY 40232

WADDELL, WILLIAM RHOADS, b Ft Smith, Ark, Oct 12, 18; m 44; c 4. SURGERY. *Educ:* Univ Ariz, BS, 40; Harvard Univ, MD, 43; Am Bd Surg, dipl, 54; Am Bd Thoracic Surg, dipl, 55. *Prof Exp:* From instr to asst clin prof surg, Harvard Med Sch, 52-61; chmn dept, 61-72, PROF SURG, MED CTR, UNIV COLO, DENVER, 61- *Concurrent Pos:* USPHS res grant, 64-72; asst, Mass Gen Hosp, 52-54, asst surgeon, 55-58, assoc vis surgeon, 58-61; mem courtesy staff, Faulkner Hosp, 53-54, assoc staff, Surg Serv, 55-61; consult, Mass Eye & Ear Infirmary, 56-61 & Vet Admin Hosp, Grand Junction & Denver, Colo, 61-; mem active staff, Denver Gen Hosp, 61-72; consult, Mercy Hosp, 68- & Gen Rose Mem Hosp, 70-; Glover H Copher vis lectr, Sch Med, Washington Univ, 72. *Mem:* AAAS; Am Asn Thoracic Surg; Am Thoracic Soc; fel Am Col Surgeons; Am Surg Asn. *Res:* Surgical physiology; physiological and clinical research on lipid metabolism, gastric physiology, transplantation and clinical surgery; cancer research surgery; enzyme inhibition synthesis. *Mailing Add:* 5745 E Sixth Ave Denver CO 80220

WADDEN, RICHARD ALBERT, b Sioux City, Iowa. ENVIRONMENTAL HEALTH, ENVIRONMENTAL ENGINEERING. *Educ:* Iowa State Univ, BS, 59; NC State Univ, MS, 62; Northwestern Univ, PhD(chem, environ eng), 72, Am Acad Environ Engrs, dipl. *Prof Exp:* Develop engr, Linde Co, Tonawanda, NY, 59-60; engr, Humble Oil & Refining Co, Houston, 62-65; instr chem & mech eng, Pahlavi Univ, Iran, 65-67; tech adv, Ill Pollution Control Bd, Chicago, 71-72; asst dir, Environ Health Resource Ctr, 72-74, asst prof, 72-75, assoc prof, 75-79, PROF ENVIRON HEALTH SCI, SCH PUB HEALTH, UNIV ILL, 79- *Concurrent Pos:* Adv, Northeastern Ill Planning Comn, 73-; lectr, Nat Safety Coun, 74- & Nat Inst Safety & Health, 74-76; mem task force hazardous mat in environ, Am Pub Health Asn, 75-77; vis scientist, Japanese Nat Inst Environ Studies, 78-79. *Mem:* Am Inst Chem Engrs; Am Chem Soc; Air Pollution Control Asn. *Res:* Characterization and modeling of air pollution in inside and outside environments; fine particle modeling and measurements; ozone episode detection; methodologies for predicting pollution source impacts on human health; evaluation of the environmental impact of industrial chemical processes. *Mailing Add:* Univ Ill Sch of Pub Health Box 6998 Chicago IL 60680

WADDILL, VAN HULEN, b Brady, Tex, Aug 24, 47; m 69. ENTOMOLOGY. *Educ:* Tex A&M Univ, BS, 70, MS, 71; Clemson Univ, PhD(entom), 74. *Prof Exp:* Asst prof, 75-80, ASSOC PROF ENTOM, AGR RES & EDUC CTR, INST FOOD & AGR SCI, UNIV FLA, 80- *Mem:* Sigma Xi; Entom Soc Am; Int Orgn Biol Control. *Res:* Management of insect pests of vegetables. *Mailing Add:* Univ Fla Agr Res & Educ Ctr 18905 SW 280th St Homestead FL 33030

WADDINGTON, CECIL JACOB, b Cambridge, Eng, July 6, 29; m 56. PHYSICS, ASTROPHYSICS. *Educ:* Bristol Univ, BSc, 52, PhD(physics), 55. *Prof Exp:* Royal Soc McKinnon res studentship physics, Bristol Univ, 56-59, lectr, 59-62; assoc prof, 62-68, PROF, SCH PHYSICS & ASTRON, UNIV MINN, MINNEAPOLIS, 68- *Concurrent Pos:* Res assoc & lectr, Univ Minn, 57-58; Nat Acad Sci sr fel, Goddard Space Flight Ctr, Md, 61; sr vis fel, Imp Col, Univ London, 72-73; mem, Cosmic Ray Comn, Int Union Pure & Appl Physics, 72-78. *Mem:* AAAS; fel Am Phys Soc; Am Geophys Union; Am Astron Soc. *Res:* Nature and properties of the primary cosmic radiation, particularly electronic and nuclear emulsion detectors, charge and mass composition. *Mailing Add:* Sch of Physics & Astron Univ of Minn Minneapolis MN 55455

WADDINGTON, DAVID, b Colorado Springs, Colo, June 20, 24; m 49; c 2. ELECTRICAL ENGINEERING, MATHEMATICS. *Educ:* Univ Colo, BS, 45, MS, 48. *Prof Exp:* Engr optical interferometry, Nat Adv Comt Aeronaut, Langley Field, Va, 48-49; elec design explosives, Stearns Roger Mfg Co, Colo, 49; eng monitoring br chief, Off Area Eng Coordr, White Sands Proving Ground, 49-56, chief eng, Frequency Coord Div, 56-58; engr & unit head electromagnetic compatibility, 58-59, design specialist & unit head missile syst design anal, 59-63, staff design specialist electromagnetic pulse studies, 63-66, staff engr space generation elec power, Res Div, 67-72, prog mgr, Space Power Labs, 72-76, ENGR, MARTIN MARIETTA CORP, 76- *Mem:* Am Inst Aeronaut & Astronaut. *Res:* Techniques of conversion of solar chemical and thermal energy to electrical power; techniques of electromagnetic compatibility, wind tunnel optical measurements and high energy electrical discharge. *Mailing Add:* 1809 E Tufts Ave Denver CO 80236

WADDINGTON, DONALD VAN PELT, b Norristown, Pa, Dec 31, 31; m 55; c 6. SOIL FERTILITY, PLANT SCIENCE. *Educ:* Pa State Univ, BS, 53; Rutgers Univ, MS, 60; Univ Mass, PhD(agron), 64. *Prof Exp:* Asst chemist, Eastern States Farmer's Exchange, Inc, 56-57; instr agron, Univ Mass, 60-65; asst prof soil technol, 65-68, assoc prof soil sci, 68-75, PROF SOIL SCI, PA STATE UNIV, UNIVERSITY PARK, 75- *Mem:* Am Soc Agron; Soil Sci Soc Am; Int Soil Sci Soc; Soil Conserv Soc; Int Turfgrass Soc. *Res:* Soil physical properties, especially soil modification for turfgrass; turfgrass nutrition; controlled-release fertilizers. *Mailing Add:* RD 1 Box 231 Boalsburg PA 16827

WADDINGTON, JOHN, b Manchester, Eng, Mar 15, 38; Can citizen; m 66; c 1. WEEDS, FORAGE CROPS. *Educ:* Univ Leeds, Eng, BSc, 60; Univ Man, MSc, 62, PhD(agron), 68. *Prof Exp:* RES SCIENTIST FORAGE CROPS, RES BR, AGR CAN, 68- *Mem:* Agr Inst Can; Weed Sci Soc Am; Am Soc Agr; Crop Sci Soc Am. *Res:* Forage crops management, particularly weed control, weed competition and effects of weather on yield and quality of hay and seed. *Mailing Add:* Agr Can Res Sta PO Box 1240 Melfort SK S0E 1A0 Can

WADDLE, BRADFORD AVON, b Tex, Jan 26, 20; m 45. AGRONOMY, PLANT BREEDING. *Educ:* Agr & Mech Col, Tex, BS, 42, MS, 50; Purdue Univ, PhD(plant breeding), 54. *Prof Exp:* Instr, Hunt County Voc Schs, Tex, 46-47; jr agronomist, Greenville Cotton Sta, USDA, 48; instr cotton breeding, Agr Exp Sta, Univ Tex, 50; asst agron, Agr Exp Sta, 51-56, assoc, 56-59, PROF AGRON & ALTHEIMER CHAIR COTTON RES, UNIV ARK, FAYETTEVILLE, 59- *Mem:* Am Soc Agron; Am Genetic Asn. *Res:* Cotton breeding and genetics, especially breeding for resistance to disease and insects. *Mailing Add:* Dept of Agron Univ of Ark Fayetteville AR 72701

WADE, ADELBERT ELTON, b Hilliard, Fla, Apr 29, 26; m 50; c 2. PHARMACOLOGY, BIOCHEMISTRY. *Educ:* Univ Fla, BS, 54, MS, 56, PhD(pharmacol), 59. *Prof Exp:* Asst chemother, Univ Fla, 54-56, asst biochem, 56-57, asst chemother, 57-59; from asst prof to assoc prof, 59-67, PROF PHARMACOL, UNIV GA, 67-, HEAD DEPT, 68- *Mem:* Am Asn Cols Pharm; Soc Exp Biol & Med; Am Soc Pharmacol & Exp Therapeut; Int Soc Biochem Pharmacol; Sigma Xi. *Res:* Influence of diet and drugs on mixed-function oxidases; effects of diet on drug and carcinogen metabolism. *Mailing Add:* Dept of Pharmacol Univ of Ga Sch of Pharm Athens GA 30602

WADE, CAMPBELL MARION, b Elizabethtown, Ky, Nov 25, 30; m 56, 78; c 4. ASTRONOMY. *Educ:* Harvard Univ, AB, 54, AM, 55, PhD(astron), 57. *Prof Exp:* Res officer, Div Radiophysics, Commonwealth Sci & Indust Res Orgn, Australia, 57-59; res assoc, 60-66, SCIENTIST, NAT RADIO ASTRON OBSERV, 66- *Concurrent Pos:* Adv ed, Soviet Astron, Am Inst Physics, 69- *Mem:* Am Astron Soc; Int Astron Union. *Res:* Galactic and extragalactic radio astronomy. *Mailing Add:* 635 Newberry Rd NW Socorro NM 87801

WADE, CHARLES GARY, b Spring City, Pa, Dec 8, 38; m 64; c 2. ORGANIC & INORGANIC CHEMISTRY. *Educ:* Ursinus Col, BS, 60; Univ Del, MS, 68. *Prof Exp:* Chemist, Abex Corp, 66-68; sr chemist, 68-74, res chemist, 74-76, SUPVR, ATLAS POWDER CO, 76- *Honors & Awards:* IR 100 Award, Ind Res Mag, 77. *Mem:* Am Chem Soc. *Res:* Water based explosives based on emulsion technology. *Mailing Add:* Atlas Powder Co PO Box 271 Tamaqua PA 18252

WADE, CHARLES GORDON, b Griggsville, Ill, Apr 5, 37; m 64. PHYSICAL CHEMISTRY. *Educ:* Southern Ill Univ, BA, 60; Mass Inst Technol, PhD(phys chem), 65. *Prof Exp:* Res assoc chem, Enrico Fermi Inst Nuclear Studies, Univ Chicago, 65-67; asst prof chem, Univ Tex, Austin, 67-73, assoc prof, 73-80; APPLN SCIENTIST, IBM INSTRUMENTS, INC, 80- *Mem:* Am Phys Soc; Am Chem Soc; Sigma Xi; AAAS. *Res:* Nuclear magnetic resonance relaxation; electron spin resonance of photo-excited triplet states; computer controlled instrumentation; properties of liquid crystals; fluorescence of carcinogens; chemical carcinogenesis; structure and diffusion in membrane systems; spectroscopic studies of biological systems. *Mailing Add:* IBM Instruments Inc 40 W Brokaw Rd San Jose CA 95110

WADE, CLARENCE W R, b Laurinburg, NC, Mar 31, 27; m 55; c 1. ORGANIC CHEMISTRY. *Educ:* J C Smith Univ, BS, 48; Tuskegee Inst, MS, 50; Georgetown Univ, PhD(org chem), 65. *Prof Exp:* From instr to asst prof chem, St Augustine's Col, 50-57; from chemist to res chemist, Nat Bur Stand, 57-66; res chemist, US Army Med & Biomech Lab, Walter Reed Army Med Ctr, 66-68, chief, Synthesis Br, 68-70, chief mat & applns div, 70-72, chief, Mat & Applns Div, 72-76, SR RES CHEMIST, US ARMY MED & BIOMECH RES & DEVELOP LAB, FT DETRICK, MD, 76-, PROJ AREA MGR CHEM SYSTS, 80- *Concurrent Pos:* Consult, Nat Heart Inst, 68-70; adj prof chem, Univ DC, 75-; prof orthop res, Howard Univ, 77-79. *Mem:* AAAS; Am Chem Soc; NY Acad Sci; Asn Off Anal Chemists. *Res:* Development of inert or degradable implant materials, tissue and bone adhesives, sutures, tendons, vascular tubes, wound and burn dressings, bone repair polymers; mechanisms of implant degradation. *Mailing Add:* US Army Med & Bioeng Res & Develop Lab Ft Detrick Frederick MD 21701

WADE, DALE A, b Buffalo, SDak, May 23, 28; m 53; c 5. WILDLIFE MANAGEMENT. *Educ:* SDak State Univ, BS, 69, PhD(animal sci), 72. *Prof Exp:* Mem staff mammal control, US Fish & Wildlife Serv, 62-65; wildlife specialist, Colo State Univ, 72-74; wildlife specialist, Univ Calif, Davis, 74-78; WILDLIFE SPECIALIST, TEX A&M UNIV, SAN ANGELO, 78- *Concurrent Pos:* Consult, US Environ Protection Agency, 70-75; mem, Eisenhower Consortium, 73-74. *Mem:* Sigma Xi; AAAS; Am Inst Biol Sci; Soc Range Mgt; Wildlife Soc. *Res:* Evaluation of biological, economic conflicts and possible solutions in human, wildlife and agricultural relationships. *Mailing Add:* 3330 Bonargrove Lane San Angelo TX 76901

WADE, DAVID ROBERT, b London, Eng, May 25, 39; m 62; c 3. BIOCHEMISTRY. *Educ:* Univ Cambridge, BA & MA, 63, PhD(biochem), 67. *Prof Exp:* Res assoc physiol, Col Med, Pa State Univ, 67-69; Bank Am Giannini fel biochem, Sch Med, Univ Calif, Davis, 69-71; USPHS grant metab regulation & asst prof physiol, Col Med, Pa State Univ, 71-74; assoc prof physiol, Sch Med, Southern Ill Univ, 74-80. *Res:* Regulation of melanin synthesis. *Mailing Add:* 3006 Kent Dr Carbondale IL 62901

WADE, EARL KENNETH, b Toledo, Iowa, July 13, 14; m 47; c 3. PLANT PATHOLOGY. *Educ:* Univ Wis, BS, 38, MS, 50. *Prof Exp:* Instr high sch, Wis, 38-42; asst potato cert serv, 46-50, prof plant path, 69-79, EXTEN PLANT PATHOLOGIST, UNIV WIS-MADISON, 50-, EMER PROF PLANT PATH, 79- *Mem:* Am Phytopath Soc; Am Potato Asn. *Res:* Vegetable and fruit diseases. *Mailing Add:* Dept of Plant Path Univ of Wis Madison WI 53706

WADE, GLEN, b Ogden, Utah, Mar 19, 21; m 45; c 4. ELECTRICAL ENGINEERING. *Educ:* Univ Utah, BS, 48, MS, 49; Stanford Univ, PhD, 54. *Prof Exp:* Electronic scientist, US Naval Res Labs, Washington, DC, 49-50; res assoc, Microwave Lab, Gen Elec Co, 55; mem sr staff, Electronics Labs, Stanford Univ, 55-60 assoc prof elec eng, 58-60; asst gen mgr, Res Div, Raytheon Co, Mass, 60-63; dir sch elec eng & J Preston Levis prof eng, Cornell Univ, 63-66; PROF ELEC ENG, UNIV CALIF, SANTA BARBARA, 66- *Concurrent Pos:* Consult, Gen Elec Co, 55-58, Diamond Ord Fuze Labs, 57-60, Zenith Radio Corp, 57-60, 63- & EG&G, Inc, 66-; ed, Trans on Electron Devices, Inst Elec & Electronics Engrs, 61-71 & J Quantum Electronics, 65-67; series ed, Harcourt, Brace & World, Inc, 64-; consult mem adv group electron devices, Comt of Dept Defense, 66-; Japan Soc Promotion of Sci vis prof award, Univ Tokyo, 71; Fulbright-Hays fel, Spain, 72-73; ed, Proc of Inst Elec & Electronics Engrs, 77-80; Taiwanese Nat Sci Coun spec chair award, Nat Taiwan Univ, 80-81. *Honors & Awards:* Nat Electronics Conf Annual Award, 59; Distinguished Teaching Award, Univ Calif Santa Barbara Acad Senate, 77. *Mem:* Am Phys Soc; Inst Elec & Electronics Engrs. *Res:* Physical and quantum electronics; ultrasonics; optical systems. *Mailing Add:* Dept Elec Eng Univ Calif Santa Barbara CA 93106

WADE, JAMES JOSEPH, b St Paul, Minn, Jan 7, 46; m 70; c 3. MEDICINAL CHEMISTRY. *Educ:* Col St Thomas, BA, 68; Univ Minn, PhD(org chem), 72. *Prof Exp:* NIH fel org chem, Univ Rochester, 72-73; sr med chemist, 73-76, RES SPECIALIST, RIKER LABS, 3M CO, 76- *Mem:* Am Chem Soc. *Res:* Design and synthesis of organic compounds for possible medicinal use, particularly in the antiallergy and antithrombotic areas. *Mailing Add:* Riker Labs 3M Co 3M Ctr Bldg 270-2S St Paul MN 55144

WADE, LEROY GROVER, JR, b Jacksonville, Fla, Oct 8, 47; m 74; c 2. ORGANIC SYNTHETIC METHODS, CHEMICAL EDUCATION. *Educ:* Rice Univ, BA, 69; Harvard Univ, AM, 70, PhD(chem), 74. *Prof Exp:* Asst prof, 74-80, ASSOC PROF CHEM, COLO STATE UNIV, 80- *Mem:* Am Chem Soc; AAAS; Sigma Xi. *Res:* Organic chemistry; organic synthesis. *Mailing Add:* Chem Dept Colo State Univ Fort Collins CO 80523

WADE, LESTER ARTHUR, b Lansing, Mich, April 9, 43; m 73; c 1. BLOOD-BRAIN BARRIER. *Educ:* Mich State Univ, BS, 65, MS, 67; Univ Kans, PhD(physiol), 71. *Prof Exp:* Res fel neurosci, Albert Einstein Col Med, 71-74, assoc, 74-75; ASST PROF PHYSIOL, SCH MED, TULANE UNIV, 75- *Concurrent Pos:* Prin investr, NIH, 78-81; mem, Stroke Coun, Am Hear. *Mem:* Soc Neurosci; AAAS. *Res:* Amino acid transport systems; cerebral capillary endothelial transport; cerebral capillary permeability. *Mailing Add:* Physiol Dept Sch Med Tulane Univ 1430 Tulane Ave New Orleans LA 70112

WADE, LUTHER IRWIN, b Dallas, Tex, Nov 27, 16; m 36; c 6. MATHEMATICS. *Educ:* Duke Univ, AB, 38, PhD(math), 41. *Prof Exp:* Instr math, Johns Hopkins Univ, 41-42; Nat Res Coun fel, Inst Advan Study, 42-43; from instr to asst prof, Duke Univ, 43-48; prof & head dept, 48-80, EMER PROF MATH, LA STATE UNIV, BATON ROUGE, 80- *Mem:* Am Math Soc; Math Asn Am. *Res:* Number theory of polynomials in finite fields; abstract algebra. *Mailing Add:* Dept of Math La State Univ Baton Rouge LA 70803

WADE, MICHAEL GEORGE, b Watford, Eng, Nov 5, 41; c 1. PHYSICAL EDUCATION, HUMAN FACTORS ENGINEERING. *Educ:* Loughborough Col, DLC, 63; Univ Ill, MS, 68, PhD(phys educ, human factors), 70. *Prof Exp:* Lectr phys educ, Univ Guelph, Can, 65-66; asst, Inst Child Behav & Develop, Univ Ill, 66-70, asst prof leisure studies & spec educ, 70-75, assoc prof, 75-81; PROF PHYS EDUC, SOUTHERN ILL UNIV, 81- *Mem:* NAm Soc Psychol Sport & Phys Activ; Am Asn Mental Deficiency. *Res:* Motor behavior of special populations; mental retardation; play behavior of children; biorhythms. *Mailing Add:* Dept Phys Educ Southern Ill Univ Carbondale IL 62901

WADE, MICHAEL JAMES, b Salt Lake City, UT, May 18, 42; m 71. TOXICOLOGY, NUTRITIONAL TOXICOLOGY. *Educ:* Univ Utah, BS, 64, MS, 67; Wash Univ, PhD(molecular biol), 71. *Prof Exp:* Res assoc biophysics, Max-Planck Inst Med Res, Heidelberg, Ger, 72-73, chem, Boston Univ, 73-75; fel toxicol, Univ Calif, San Francisco, 75-76; staff scientist, Life Sci Res Off, Fedn Am Soc Exp Biol, 76-78; REV SCIENTIST TOXICOL, US FOOD & DRUG ADMIN, 78- *Mem:* Am Col Toxicol; Soc Toxicol & Environ Chem; Am Chem Soc. *Mailing Add:* Div Toxicol Bur Foods Food & Drug Admin 200 C St SW Washington DC 20204

WADE, MICHAEL JOHN, b Evanston, Ill, Oct 21, 49; m 72. POPULATION BIOLOGY, POPULATION GENETICS. *Educ:* Boston Col, BA, 71; Univ Chicago, PhD(theoret biol), 75. *Prof Exp:* Asst prof, 75-82, ASSOC PROF BIOL, UNIV CHICAGO, 82- *Concurrent Pos:* Res career develop award, NIH, 81-86. *Mem:* Soc Am Naturalists; Soc Study Evolution. *Res:* Role of population structure in evolution; evolution of social behaviors. *Mailing Add:* Dept Biol Univ Chicago Chicago IL 60637

WADE, NEIL H(OWARD), civil engineering, soil mechanics, see previous edition

WADE, PETER ALLEN, b Taunton, Mass, Nov 12, 46; m 67. ORGANIC CHEMISTRY. *Educ:* Lowell Technol Inst, BS, 68; Purdue Univ, PhD(org chem), 73. *Prof Exp:* Fel org chem, Univ Groningen, Neth, 73-74; IBM fel, Harvard Univ, 74-76; ASST PROF CHEM, DREXEL UNIV, 76- *Mem:* Am Chem Soc; Nat Math Asn. *Res:* New synthetic methods; cycloaddition reactions; reactive intermediates. *Mailing Add:* Dept of Chem Drexel Univ Philadelphia PA 19104

WADE, PETER CAWTHORN, b Washington, DC, Feb 15, 44; m 66; c 1. MEDICINAL CHEMISTRY, ORGANIC CHEMISTRY. *Educ:* Middlebury Col, AB, 66; Univ Wash, PhD(org chem), 71. *Prof Exp:* res scientist, Squibb Inst Med Res, 71-80; RES ASSOC, DIAMOND SHAMROCK CORP, 80- *Mem:* Am Chem Soc. *Res:* Anxiolytic, antidepressive, neuroleptic and anti-inflammatory, anti-hypertensive and anthelmintic agents; heterocyclic chemistry. *Mailing Add:* PO Box 348 Diamond Shamrock Corp Painesville OH 44077

WADE, RICHARD ARCHER, b Fitchburg, Mass, Aug 16, 30; m 70; c 2. BIOLOGICAL OCEANOGRAPHY. *Educ:* Univ Miami, BS, 56, MS, 62, PhD(biol oceanog), 68. *Prof Exp:* Marine scientist, Ayerst Labs, Div Am Home Prod Corp, 66-68; head dept ecol & pollution, Va Inst Marine Sci, 68-69; chief lab, Environ Protection Agency, Fed Water Qual Admin, 68-69 & 70-71; exec secy, Sport Fishing Inst, 71-72; exec dir, Am Fisheries Soc, 72-75; MARINE ECOLOGIST, US FISH & WILDLIFE SERV, 75- *Concurrent Pos:* Consult, NIH Pesticide Proj, Univ Miami, 66-68; mem, Water Qual Mgt Comt, US Govt Interagency Group, 68-69; mem res subcomt, Fed Comt Pest Control, 68; clin res assoc, Med Univ SC, 70-71; mem, Subcomt Marine Water Qual Criteria, Nat Acad Sci, 71; treas, Sport Fishing Res Found, 71-72. *Mem:* Am Fisheries Soc; Am Soc Ichthyol & Herpet; Gulf & Caribbean Fisheries Inst; Marine Technol Soc. *Res:* Coastal ecosystems of the United States, including dredge disposal, offshore oil and gas development, development of deepwater ports, power plant construction and operation; marine and estuarine water quality problems. *Mailing Add:* 1011 South St Key West FL 33040

WADE, ROBERT CHARLES, b Lakewood, Ohio, May 18, 20; m 44; c 8. INORGANIC CHEMISTRY. *Educ:* Oberlin Col, AB, 42. *Prof Exp:* Res chemist, E I du Pont de Nemours & Co, 42-44 & 46-49; res chemist & group leader, Nat Distillers Prod Corp, 49-53; asst dir res, Metal Hydrides, Inc, 53-59, mgr tech mkt, 59-67, mgr explor develop, 67-68; mgr explor res, 68-74, SR SCIENTIST, VENTRON CORP, 68- *Mem:* Am Chem Soc; Am Inst Chemists; Catalysis Soc; Tech Asn Pulp & Paper Indust. *Res:* Inorganic and organic investigations on sodium metal; reduction of metal chlorides; metal-hydrogen systems; sodium and alumino hydrides; borohydride chemistry; organometallic chemistry; pulp and pulp bleaching; catalysts. *Mailing Add:* 61 S Village Green Ipswich MA 01938

WADE, ROBERT HAROLD, b Opportunity, Wash, Sept 16, 20; m 44; c 2. ORGANIC CHEMISTRY, POLYMER CHEMISTRY. *Educ:* Univ Wash, BS, 46, PhD(chem), 51. *Prof Exp:* Res chemist, M W Kellog Co Div, Pullman, Inc, 51-57; org chemist & proj leader, Stanford Res Inst, 57-63; SR RES SCIENTIST, US NAVAL UNDERSEA CTR, 63- *Res:* Synthesis of polynuclear aromatic compounds; high temperature metal-chelate polymers; physical and chemical fate of fluoride in plants; synthesis and properties of water soluble and friction reducing polymers; marine natural products. *Mailing Add:* 7810 Golfcrest Dr San Diego CA 92119

WADE, ROBERT SIMSON, b Gorrie, Ont, Aug 20, 20; m 43; c 3. CHEMISTRY, RESEARCH ADMINISTRATION. *Educ:* Univ Western Ont, BA, 42, MA, 43. *Prof Exp:* Res chemist, Imp Oil, Ltd, 43-47; chief chemist, Imp Tobacco Co Can, Ltd, 47-53, mgr lab, 53-57, mgr res develop & tech serv, 57-69, mgr res & develop, 69-76, mgr res & lab serv, 76-80, PRESIDENTIAL SCI ADV, IMP TOBACCO LTD, 80- *Mem:* Chem Inst Can; Can Res Mgt Asn; Am Chem Soc. *Res:* Growing, processing and manufacturing of tobacco and tobacco products; development of processes and products; technology of tobacco and tobacco smoke. *Mailing Add:* Res & Develop Dept Imp Tobacco Ltd 3810 St-Antoine Montreal PR H4C 2B5 Can

WADE, THOMAS LEONARD, JR, b Ridgeway, Va, Apr 21, 05; m 31; c 4. MATHEMATICS. *Educ:* Univ Va, BS, 29, MS, 30, PhD(math), 33. *Prof Exp:* Asst instr math, Univ Va, 29-34; prof, Mercer Univ, 34-39; asst prof, Univ Ala, 39-43; prof, 43-75, head dept, 43-64, EMER PROF MATH, FLA STATE UNIV, 75- *Mem:* Am Math Soc; Math Asn Am. *Res:* Algebraic invariants; tensor algebra. *Mailing Add:* 1003 Washington St Tallahassee FL 32303

WADE, WILLIAM H, b San Antonio, Tex, Nov 3, 30; wid. PHYSICAL CHEMISTRY, PETROLEUM ENGINEERING. *Educ:* St Mary's Univ, Tex, BS, 51; Univ Tex, PhD(chem), 55. *Prof Exp:* Res scientist, Univ Calif, Berkeley, 55-58; res scientist, 58-61, from asst prof to assoc prof, 61-72, chmn dept, 74-80, PROF CHEM, UNIV TEX, AUSTIN, 72- *Honors & Awards:* L'Ordre des Palmes Academiques, 80. *Mem:* Am Chem Soc; Soc Petrol Engrs. *Res:* Surface chemistry; emulsions; surfactants for enhanced oil recovery. *Mailing Add:* Dept Chem Univ Tex Austin TX 78712

WADE, WILLIAM HOWARD, b Stoughton, Wis, Apr 18, 23; m 43; c 1. ENTOMOLOGY. *Educ:* Univ Calif, BS, 50, PhD(entom), 56. *Prof Exp:* Res asst, Univ Calif, 50-53; mgr tech serv & prod promotion, Agr Chem Div, 53-72, mgr develop, 72-75, MGR TECH SERV, AGR CHEM GROUP, FMC CORP, 75- *Mem:* Entom Soc Am; Sigma Xi. *Res:* Insect biology; field evaluation of pesticides. *Mailing Add:* 214 W Andrews Fresno CA 93705

WADE, WILLIAM RAYMOND, II, b Los Angeles, Calif, Oct 28, 43; m 65; c 2. MATHEMATICS. *Educ:* Univ Calif, Riverside, BA, 65, MA, 66, PhD(math), 68. *Prof Exp:* From asst prof to assoc prof, 68-78, PROF MATH, UNIV TENN, KNOXVILLE, 78- *Concurrent Pos:* Consult, Oak Ridge Nat Lab, 69-76; vis assoc prof math, Univ Southern Calif, 77; Fulbright prof math, Moscow State Univ, 77-78. *Mem:* Am Math Soc; Math Asn Am. *Res:* Fourier analysis on groups; Haar and Walsh series; sets of uniqueness; harmonic analysis of p-series fields; transform theory. *Mailing Add:* Dept of Math Univ of Tenn Knoxville TN 37916

WADELIN, COE WILLIAM, b Dover, Ohio, Aug 18, 27; m 50; c 1. ANALYTICAL CHEMISTRY. *Educ:* Mt Union Col, BS, 50; Purdue Univ, MS, 51, PhD, 53. *Prof Exp:* Res chemist, 53-65, sect head anal chem, 65-75, sect head spectros, 75-77, MGR RES ANAL SERV, RES DIV, GOODYEAR TIRE & RUBBER CO, AKRON, OHIO, 77- *Concurrent Pos:* Fel, Ctr Advan Eng Study, Mass Inst Technol, 68-69. *Mem:* Am Chem Soc. *Res:* Analysis of polymers and organic chemicals; absorption spectroscopy. *Mailing Add:* 3117 Orchard Rd Cuyahoga Falls OH 44224

WADELL, LYLE H, b Elsie, Mich, Mar 7, 34; m 57; c 4. ANIMAL BREEDING, DATA PROCESSING MANAGEMENT. *Educ:* Mich State Univ, BS, 55, MS, 57; Iowa State Univ, PhD(animal breeding, statist, genetics), 59. *Prof Exp:* Res assoc animal breeding res, 59-60, res animal geneticist, 60-61, admin supvr comput ctr mgt, 61-66, DIR COMPUT CTR MGT, CORNELL UNIV, 66- *Mem:* Am Dairy Sci Asn. *Res:* Computing center management; data processing techniques; statistics. *Mailing Add:* B-24 Morrison Hall Cornell Univ Ithaca NY 14850

WADEY, WALTER GEOFFREY, b Whangarei, NZ, Sept 9, 18; nat US; m 45; c 3. PHYSICS. *Educ:* Univ Mich, BSc, 41, MA, 42, PhD(physics), 47. *Prof Exp:* Res assoc, Radio Res Lab, Harvard Univ, 43-45; instr physics, Yale Univ, 47-50, asst prof, 50-56; prof, Southern Ill Univ, 56-57; mgr sci prog, Remington Rand Univac Div, Sperry Rand Corp, 57-58, tech coordr, 59; physicist, Hughes Aircraft Co, 59-60; mgr advan electromech develop dept, Univac Div, Sperry Rand Corp, 60-62; chief scientist, Bowles Eng Corp, 62-63 & Wash Tech Assocs, 63-64; SR SCIENTIST, OPERS RES, INC, SILVER SPRING, MD, 64- *Mem:* AAAS; Am Phys Soc; Asn Comput Mach; Opers Res Soc Am; Marine Technol Soc. *Res:* Experimental nuclear physics; nuclear spectroscopy; linear electron accelerators; electronics; computer programming and arithmetics; fluid mechanics; electromechanical design; fluid-amplifier technology; operations research; systems analysis; anti-submarine warfare; information systems. *Mailing Add:* 7505 Holiday Terrace Bethesda MD 20817

WADKE, DEODATT ANANT, b July 7, 38; US citizen; m 67; c 1. PHYSICAL PHARMACY. *Educ:* Banaras Hindu Univ, BPharm, 61; Ohio State Univ, MS, 63; State Univ NY Buffalo, PhD(pharmaceut), 67. *Prof Exp:* Res assoc formulations, Merck Sharpe & Dohme Res Labs, 66-69; res investr pharmaceut res & develop, 69-71, sr res investr, 72-73, head, preformulation studies sect, 73-76, head, solid formulation develop sect, 76-79, ASST DIR PHARM RES & DEVELOP, SQUIBB INST MED RES, 79- *Mem:* Am Pharmaceut Asn; Acad Pharmaceut Sci. *Res:* Thermodynamics of dissolution, solubilization and absorption; dissolution of polyphase systems; drug stability; pharmacokinetics. *Mailing Add:* Squibb Inst for Med Res New Brunswick NJ 08903

WADKINS, CHARLES L, b Joplin, Mo, May 8, 29; m 52; c 2. BIOCHEMISTRY. *Educ:* Univ Kans, AB, 51, PhD(biochem), 56. *Prof Exp:* Instr biochem, Univ Kans, 55-56; from instr to assoc prof, Sch Med, Johns Hopkins Univ, 57-66; chmn dept, 66-80, PROF BIOCHEM, MED CTR, UNIV ARK, LITTLE ROCK, 66- *Concurrent Pos:* Fel biochem, Sch Med, Johns Hopkins Univ, 56-57; USPHS sr res fel, 59-64; mem adv panel, NSF; planning officer, Nat Inst Aging, NIH, 80-82. *Mem:* Am Chem Soc; Am Soc Biol Chemists; Brit Biochem Soc. *Res:* Biological oxidation reactions; oxidative phosphorylation; mechanism and control of biological calcification reactions. *Mailing Add:* Dept of Biochem Univ of Ark Med Ctr Little Rock AR 72205

WADLEIGH, CECIL HERBERT, b Gilbertville, Mass, Oct 1, 07; m 30; c 4. PLANT PHYSIOLOGY. *Educ:* Mass Col, BS, 30; Ohio State Univ, MS, 32; Rutgers Univ, PhD(plant physiol), 35. *Prof Exp:* Asst, Rutgers Univ, 33-36; asst prof agron, Univ Ark, 36-41; sr chemist, Regional Salinity Lab, Bur Plant Indust, USDA, 41-42 & Bur Plant Indust, Soils & Agr Eng, 42-48, prin plant physiologist, 48-51, head physiologist in chg div sugar plant invests, 51-54, head sect soils & plant relationships, Soil & Water Conserv Res Br, 54-55, dir, Soil & Water Conserv Res Div, 55-74; RETIRED. *Mem:* Nat Acad Sci; Soil Conserv Soc Am; Am Soc Agron; Soil Sci Soc Am; Am Soc Sugar Beet Technol. *Res:* Mineral nutrition of plants; carbohydrate and nitrogen metabolism of plants; salt tolerance of plants; soil moisture stress. *Mailing Add:* 5621 Whitfield Chapel Rd Lanham MD 20801

WADLEIGH, KENNETH R(OBERT), b Passaic, NJ, March 27, 21; m 48; c 2. MECHANICAL ENGINEERING. *Educ:* Mass Inst Technol, SM & SB, 43, ScD, 53. *Hon Degrees:* MA, Univ Cambridge, Eng, 54. *Prof Exp:* From instr to assoc prof, 46-61, dean student affairs, 61-69, PROF MECH ENG, MASS INST TECHNOL, 61-, V PRES, 69-, DEAN GRAD SCH, 75- *Concurrent Pos:* Lectr, Univ Cambridge, Eng, 53-54. *Honors & Awards:* Goodwin Medal, 52; Bronze Beaver Award, Mass Inst Technol, 69. *Res:* Applied thermodynamics; fluid mechanics; two-phase flows. *Mailing Add:* Rm 3-136 Mass Inst of Technol 77 Massachusetts Ave Cambridge MA 02139

WADLEY, GERALD WELDON, biological oceanography, limnology, see previous edition

WADLEY, MARGIL WARREN, b Cisco, Tex, Dec 4, 31; m 66; c 1. INORGANIC CHEMISTRY. *Educ:* Bethany Nazarene Col, BS, 53; Okla State Univ, MS, 60; Purdue Univ, PhD(inorg chem), 63. *Prof Exp:* Sr chemist, Autonetics Div, NAm Aviation, Inc, 63-64 & Korad Dept, Union Carbide Corp, 64-65; sr res engr, Autonetics Div, NAm Aviation, Inc, 65 & 66-69 & Space Systems Div, Rockwell Int, Inc, 65-66; environ scientist, 69-71, prin chemist, 71-75, supv chemist, Southern Calif Air Pollution Control Dis, 75-77; PRIN CHEMIST, SOUTH COAST AIR QUAL MGT DIST, 77- . *Concurrent Pos:* Mem bd, Henry George Sch Soc Sci, Los Angeles. *Mem:* Am Chem Soc; Sigma Xi. *Res:* Electrochemistry of nonaqueous solvent systems; improved materials for medical and semiconductor applications; political economics; size and mass distribution of airborne particulate matter and associated visibility relationships. *Mailing Add:* 520 E Riverdale Ave Orange CA 92665

WADLINGER, ROBERT LOUIS PETER, b Philadelphia, Pa, Mar 20, 32; m 55; c 3. CHEMISTRY. *Educ:* LaSalle Col, AB, 53; Cath Univ, PhD(photochem kinetics, phys chem), 61. *Prof Exp:* Res asst, Benjamin Franklin Inst Labs, Pa, 53-55; sr res chemist, Mobil Oil Co, Inc, Labs, NJ, 60-62; assoc prof chem, State Univ NY Col Oneonta, 62-65; assoc prof chem, Niagara Univ, 65-76; sales rep, Equitable Life Assurance Soc, USA, 76-77; sr scientist, SCA Serv, Inc, Model City, NY, 77-78; with Recra Res, Inc, Tonawanda, NY, 78-79; assoc prof chem, Elmira Col, Elmira, NY, 80-81;

ASST PROF CHEM, PA STATE UNIV, MIDDDLETOWN, PA, 81- *Concurrent Pos:* Assoc prof chem, Daemen Col, Amherst, NY, 80; consult environ chem, Hooker Chem Corp, Grand Island, NY, 80. *Mem:* Am Chem Soc. *Res:* Zeolite syntheses. *Mailing Add:* Capitol Campus Pa State Univ Middletown PA 17057

WADMAN, W HUGH, b Marlborough, Eng, Sept 18, 26; m 52; c 2. CHEMISTRY, BIOCHEMISTRY. *Educ:* Bristol Univ, BSc, 47, PhD, 51. *Prof Exp:* Res assoc plant biochem, Univ Calif, 51-53; group leader cellulose chem, Rayonier Inc, Wash, 53-55; PROF ORG CHEM, UNIV OF THE PAC, 55- *Mem:* Am Chem Soc. *Res:* Carbohydrate chemistry and chromatographic techniques; origin of life; primitive biochemical systems. *Mailing Add:* Dept of Chem Univ of the Pac Stockton CA 95204

WADSWORTH, DALLAS FREMONT, b Arcadia, Okla, Mar 2, 22; m; c 1. PLANT PATHOLOGY. *Educ:* Okla State Univ, BS, 48, MS, 49; Univ Calif, PhD(plant path), 66. *Prof Exp:* From asst prof to assoc prof, 71-74, PROF BOT & PLANT PATH, OKLA STATE UNIV, 74- *Mem:* Am Phytopath Soc. *Res:* Diseases of peanuts; plant virology. *Mailing Add:* Dept of Plant Path Okla State Univ Stillwater OK 74074

WADSWORTH, DONALD VAN ZELM, b Mamaroneck, NY, July 14, 31. GEOPHYSICS, TELECOMMUNICATIONS. *Educ:* Williams Col, Mass, BA, 53; Mass Inst Technol, PhD(geophys), 58. *Prof Exp:* Dept head, Bell Labs, 58-75; pres, Wadsworth Eng, 75-78; SR SCIENTIST, HUGHES AIRCRAFT CO, 78- *Concurrent Pos:* Consult, Comt Undersea Warfare, Nat Acad Sci, 66-71. *Mem:* Sr mem Inst Elec & Electronics Eng; Am Inst Aeronaut & Astronaut. *Res:* Telecommunications; celestial mechanics. *Mailing Add:* Hughes Res Lab 3011 Malibu Canyon Rd Malibu CA 90265

WADSWORTH, FRANK H, b Chicago, Ill, Nov 26, 15; m 41; c 2. FORESTRY. *Educ:* Univ Mich, BSF & MF, 37, PhD(forestry), 50. *Prof Exp:* STAFF MEM, INST TROP FORESTRY, US FOREST SERV, 42- *Concurrent Pos:* Consult 18 trop countries, 49-80. *Honors & Awards:* Fernow Award, Am Forestry Asn, 73. *Mem:* Soc Am Foresters. *Res:* Multiple forest land use and management, silviculture, growth and yield of naturally regenerated forests and timber plantations in the humid tropics. *Mailing Add:* Sacarello 1016 Urbanizacion San Martin Rio Piedras PR 00924

WADSWORTH, HARRISON M(ORTON), b Duluth, Minn, Aug 20, 24; m 50; c 2. INDUSTRIAL ENGINEERING, STATISTICS. *Educ:* Ga Inst Technol, BIndEng, 50, MS, 55; Case Western Reserve Univ, PhD(statist), 60. *Prof Exp:* Indust engr, Steel Heddle Mfg Co, SC, 52-54; qual control engr, Nat Carbon Co, 54-56; asst prof mech eng, Mich State Univ, 56-57; instr & res assoc statist, Case Western Reserve Univ, 57-60; assoc prof, 60-64, PROF INDUST ENG, GA INST TECHNOL, 64- *Concurrent Pos:* Consult statist, Lockheed-Ga Co, 66-; Orgn Econ Coop & Develop consult, Mid East Tech Univ, Ankara, 67-68; NSF grant, exp design course for eng profs, Univ Wis, 66; ed, J Quality Technol, 79-82. *Honors & Awards:* Brumbaugh Award, Am Soc Qual Control, 71. *Mem:* Fel Am Soc Qual Control; sr mem Am Inst Indust Eng; Am Statist Asn; Sigma Xi; Am Soc Eng Educ. *Res:* Economics of statistical sampling plans; design of experiments; documentation and information retrieval; systems engineering. *Mailing Add:* Sch of Indust & Systs Eng Ga Inst of Technol Atlanta GA 30332

WADSWORTH, JAMES ROGER, b Rochester, NY, Aug 22, 20; m 51; c 4. ANIMAL SCIENCES. *Educ:* Univ Pa, VMD, 44; Univ Ill, MS, 50. *Prof Exp:* Instr surg, Univ Pa, 45-46; vet anat, Univ Ill, 47-50; ANIMAL PATHOLOGIST, UNIV VT, 51- *Concurrent Pos:* Exten vet exten serv, US Dept Agr. *Mem:* Vet Med Asn; Asn Zoo Vets; Am Asn Exten Veterinarians; Sigma Xi. *Res:* Comparative veterinary oncology including neoplastic diseases of wild mammals, reptiles and birds. *Mailing Add:* 21 S Summit St Essex Junction VT 05452

WADSWORTH, JEFFREY, b Hamburg, WGer, May 12, 50; UK citizen; m 76; c 1. METALLURGY. *Educ:* Sheffield Univ, Eng, BMetall, 72, PhD(metall), 75. *Prof Exp:* Fel metall, Stanford Univ, 76-78, res assoc, 78-81; RES SCIENTIST METALL, LOCKHEED PALO ALTO RES LAB, 81- *Concurrent Pos:* Ed, Sheffield Univ Metall Soc J, 74; lectr, Dept Mat Sci, Stanford Univ, 81, consult asst prof, 81-82. *Mem:* Am Inst Mining, Metall & Petrol Engrs; Am Soc Metals; Sigma Xi. *Res:* Metallurgical research into the ambient and high-temperature mechanical properties of metals and alloys with an emphasis on materials of significant technological importance. *Mailing Add:* Lockheed Palo Alto Res Lab 3251 Hanover St B204 0/52-31 Palo Alto CA 94304

WADSWORTH, MILTON E(LLIOT), b Salt Lake City, Utah, Feb 9, 22; m 43; c 6. METALLURGY. *Educ:* Univ Utah, BS, 48, PhD(metall), 51. *Prof Exp:* From instr to assoc prof, 48-66, head dept, 58-66 & 74-76, PROF METALL ENG, UNIV UTAH, 66-, ASSOC DEAN, COL MINES & MINERAL INDUSTS, 76- *Mem:* Am Soc Metals; Am Inst Mining, Metall & Petrol Engrs; Am Soc Eng Educ; Can Metals Soc. *Res:* Surface reactions involved in metallurgical processes, flotation, leaching, oxidation, reduction and corrosion. *Mailing Add:* Dept of Metall & Metall Eng Univ of Utah 412 WBB Salt Lake City UT 84112

WADSWORTH, WILLIAM BINGHAM, b Cortland, NY, Dec 4, 34; m 62; c 2. PETROLOGY, MINERALOGY. *Educ:* Brown Univ, AB, 57; Northwestern Univ, MS, 62, PhD(igneous petrol), 66. *Prof Exp:* Asst prof geol, Univ SDak, 63-66; from asst prof to assoc prof, Idaho State Univ, 66-72; assoc prof, 72-80, PROF GEOL, WHITTIER COL, 80-, CHMN DEPT, 73- *Concurrent Pos:* NSF sci fac fel, Pomona Col, 71-72. *Mem:* Int Asn Math Geol; Geol Soc Am; Soc Econ Paleont & Mineral; Am Geophys Union; Mineral Soc Am. *Res:* Quantitative petrography and geochemistry of igneous rocks; petrology of granitic plutons, especially copper-bearing porphyries; structural petrology and fabric analysis; statistical design in geology. *Mailing Add:* Dept Geol Sci Whittier Col Whittier CA 90608

WADSWORTH, WILLIAM STEELE, JR, b Hartford, Conn, May 6, 27; m 56; c 4. ORGANIC CHEMISTRY. *Educ:* Trinity Col, Conn, BS, 50, MS, 52; Pa State Univ, PhD(chem), 56. *Prof Exp:* Res chemist, Rohm & Haas Co, 56-63; assoc prof, 63-68, PROF CHEM, S DAK STATE UNIV, 68- *Mem:* Am Chem Soc. *Res:* New reactions and mechanisms in organic chemistry; heterocyclic and organophosphorus chemistry. *Mailing Add:* Dept Chem SDak State Univ Brookings SD 57007

WADT, WILLARD ROGERS, b Bayonne, NJ, Jan 6, 49. THEORETICAL CHEMISTRY. *Educ:* Williams Col, BA, 70; Calif Inst Technol, PhD(chem), 75. *Prof Exp:* Sr res chemist, Mound Lab, Monsanto Res Corp, 74-76; mem staff, 76-81, DEP GROUP LEADER & PROJ MGR, LOS ALAMOS NAT LAB, 81- *Mem:* Am Chem Soc; AAAS. *Res:* Ab initio electronic structure theory of molecules; electronic transition lasers; molecular photochemistry; mesic molecules; atmospheric chemistry. *Mailing Add:* Theoret Div Mail Stop 531 Los Alamos Nat Lab Los Alamos NM 87545

WAECH, THEODORE G, physical chemistry, see previous edition

WAEHNER, KENNETH ARTHUR, b Milwaukee, Wis, Apr 12, 26; m 52; c 3. ANALYTICAL CHEMISTRY. *Educ:* Marquette Univ, BS, 52; Univ Wis-Madison, MS, 53. *Prof Exp:* Lab supvr anal chem, Fansteel Metall Corp, Ill, 53-66; MGR SPECTROG LAB, XEROX CORP, 66- *Mem:* Soc Appl Spectros. *Res:* Inorganic analyses; application of emission spectrography and classical chemical analyses to the characterization of semiconductors and refractory metals. *Mailing Add:* Chem Analyses Labs Xerox Corp Webster NY 14580

WAELSCH, SALOME GLUECKSOHN, b Ger, Oct 6, 07; nat US; m 43; c 2. GENETICS, DEVELOPMENTAL BIOLOGY. *Educ:* Univ Freiburg, PhD(zool), 32. *Prof Exp:* Res assoc & lectr zool, Columbia Univ, 36-55; assoc prof anat, 55-58, chmn dept, 63-76, PROF GENETICS, ALBERT EINSTEIN COL MED, 58- *Mem:* Nat Acad Sci; Am Asn Anatomists; Genetics Soc Am; Soc Develop Biol; Am Soc Zoologists. *Res:* Developmental and mammalian genetics; role and control of genes in differentiation. *Mailing Add:* Dept of Genetics Albert Einstein Col of Med Bronx NY 10461

WAESCHE, R(ICHARD) H(ENLEY) WOODWARD, b Baltimore, Md, Dec 20, 30; m 57; c 2. AEROSPACE SCIENCE. *Educ:* Williams Col, BA, 52; Princeton Univ, MA, 62, PhD(aerospace & mech sci), 65. *Prof Exp:* Intermediate scientist, Redstone Arsenal Res Div, Rohm and Haas Co, Ala, 54-59, scientist, 64-66; asst in res aerospace sci, Princeton Univ, 61-64, res aide, 64; sr res engr, Propulsion Applications, United Technol Res Ctr, 66-81; PRIN SCIENTIST ADVAN PROJ, ATLANTIC RES CORP, 81- *Concurrent Pos:* Consult, Goodyear Aircraft Corp, 59 & Princeton Univ, 64-65; assoc ed, J Spacecraft & Rockets, Am Inst Aeronaut & Astronaut, 75-80, ed-in-chief, 80- *Mem:* Am Phys Soc; Am Inst Aeronaut & Astronaut; Combustion Inst. *Res:* Combustion related to chemical propulsion, rockets, ramjets ducted rockets; management of propulsion-related programs; optical spectroscopy; ablation heat transfer; fuel-spray atomization and combustion in a ramjet environment. *Mailing Add:* Atlantic Res Corp 7511 Wellington Rd Gainesville VA 22065

WAFF, HARVE S, geophysics, see previous edition

WAFFLE, ELIZABETH LENORA, b Marion, Iowa, Feb 14, 38. PARASITOLOGY, INVERTEBRATE ZOOLOGY. *Educ:* Cornell Col, BA, 60; Univ Iowa, MS, 63; Iowa State Univ, PhD(parasitol), 67. *Prof Exp:* Assoc prof biol, Armstrong State Col, 66-67; asst prof, Iowa Wesleyan Col, 67-68; asst prof, 68-77, ASSOC PROF BIOL, EASTERN MICH UNIV, 77- *Concurrent Pos:* Consult, Parasitol Prog, Ann Arbor Biol Ctr, 70- *Mem:* Am Soc Parasitol; Am Mosquito Control Asn; Wildlife Dis Asn. *Res:* Dog heartworm and other parasites of dogs; parasites of fish; mosquitoes feeding habits in relation to disease transmission; marine biology. *Mailing Add:* Dept of Biol Eastern Mich Univ Ypsilanti MI 48197

WAGENAAR, EMILE B, b Poerwokerto, Indonesia, Apr 7, 23; Can citizen; m 54; c 3. CELL BIOLOGY, GENETICS. *Educ:* St Agr Univ, Wageningen, Ir, 54; Univ Alta, PhD(genetics), 58. *Prof Exp:* Nat Res Coun Can res fel, 58-60; res scientist, Genetics & Plant Breeding Res Inst, Can Dept Agr, 60-65; res zoologist, Univ Calif, Berkeley, 65-67; assoc prof, 67-69, PROF BIOL, UNIV LETHBRIDGE, 69- *Concurrent Pos:* Vis assoc & sessional lectr, Ottawa, Ont, 64-65. *Mem:* Genetics Soc Am; Genetics Soc Can. *Res:* Cytogenetics and evolution of species in Triticum and Hordeum; chemistry, ultrastructure and behavior of chromosomes in nucleus and during cell division. *Mailing Add:* Dept of Biol Sci Univ of Lethbridge Lethbridge AB T1K 3M4 Can

WAGENAAR, RAPHAEL OMER, b Spokane, Wash, Jan 9, 16; m 51; c 2. DAIRY BACTERIOLOGY. *Educ:* Wash State Univ, BS, 42, MS, 47; Univ Minn, PhD(dairy bact), 51. *Prof Exp:* Asst dairy bact, Univ Minn, 49-51; res assoc, Food Res Inst, Univ Chicago, 51-56; sect leader microbiol, Food Develop Dept, 56-62, RES ASSOC MICROBIOL, FOOD DEVELOP ACTIV, TECHNICAL CTR, GEN MILLS, INC, 62- *Mem:* Am Soc Microbiol; Am Dairy Sci Asn; Inst Food Technologists. *Res:* Bacterial food poisoning; lactic acid bacteria; effect of irradiation on bacterial spores and toxins; psychrophilic bacteria causing food spoilage. *Mailing Add:* Tech Ctr Gen Mills Inc 9000 Plymouth Ave N Minneapolis MN 55427

WAGENBACH, GARY EDWARD, b Barron, Wis, Mar 24, 40; m 60; c 3. PARASITOLOGY, ZOOLOGY. *Educ:* Univ Wis-River Falls, BS, 62; Univ Wis-Madison, MS, 64, PhD(zool), 68. *Prof Exp:* NIH proj assoc, Univ Wis-Madison, 68-69; asst prof, 69-74, ASSOC PROF BIOL, CARLETON COL, 74- *Concurrent Pos:* Vis prof, Stanford Univ, 80. *Mem:* AAAS; Am Soc Parasitol; Sigma Xi. *Res:* Biology of parasites, especially digenetic trematodes. *Mailing Add:* Dept Biol Carleton Col Northfield MN 55057

WAGENET, ROBERT JEFFREY, b Pittsburg, Calif, Aug 10, 50. SOIL PHYSICS, SOIL CHEMISTRY. *Educ:* Univ Calif, Davis, BS, 71, PhD(soil sci), 75; Univ Okla, MS, 72. *Prof Exp:* Staff res assoc, Univ Calif, Davis, 73-74, water scientist, 74-75; asst prof, 76-79, ASSOC PROF SOIL SCI, UTAH STATE UNIV, 79- *Mem:* Am Soc Agron; Am Geophys Union; Sigma Xi; Soil Sci Soc Am; Int Soil Sci Soc. *Res:* Simulation modeling of soil water and solutes; description of transient nitrogen fluxes under field conditions; utilization and improvement of salt-affected soils and saline waters. *Mailing Add:* Dept Soil Sci & Biometeorol Utah State Univ Logan UT 84322

WAGENKNECHT, BURDETTE LEWIS, b Cotter, Iowa, Sept 9, 25; m 51; c 4. BOTANY. *Educ:* Univ Iowa, BA, 48, MS, 54; Univ Kans, PhD(bot), 58. *Prof Exp:* Instr biol & phys sci, Franklin Col, 54-55; asst bot, Univ Kans, 57-58; hort taxonomist, Arnold Arboretum, 58-61; from asst prof to assoc prof biol, Norwich Univ, 61-68; PROF BIOL & HEAD DEPT, WILLIAM JEWELL COL, 68- *Mem:* AAAS; Am Inst Biol Sci. *Res:* Floristics of Washington County, Iowa; Heterotheca; taxonomy of cultivated wood plants; registration of cultivars in the genus Buxus. *Mailing Add:* Dept of Biol William Jewell Col Liberty MO 64068

WAGENKNECHT, JOHN HENRY, b Washington, Iowa, Jan 30, 39; m 60; c 3. ORGANIC CHEMISTRY, ELECTROCHEMISTRY. *Educ:* Monmouth Col, AB, 60; Univ Iowa, PhD(chem), 64. *Prof Exp:* Sr res chemist, 64-70, res specialist, 70-74, SCI FEL, MONSANTO CO, 74- *Mem:* Electrochem Soc; Int Soc Electrochem; Am Chem Soc. *Res:* Synthesis of organic chemicals by electrochemistry; electroanalytical chemistry; electrical discharge chemistry; scale-up of electro-organic processes. *Mailing Add:* Monsanto Co 800 N Lindbergh Blvd St Louis MO 63167

WAGGENER, ROBERT GLENN, b Benton, Ky, June 12, 32; m 59; c 2. MEDICAL PHYSICS, BIOPHYSICS. *Educ:* Univ Tex, Austin, BA, 54, MA, 63; Univ Tex M D Anderson Hosp & Tumor Inst Houston, PhD(biophys), 67; Am Bd Radiol, cert, 72. *Prof Exp:* Res asst physics, Nuclear Physics Lab, Balcones Res Ctr, Univ Tex, Austin, 60-61; pres, Nucleonics Res & Develop Corp, Tex, 61-63; radiol health specialist, Tex State Health Dept, 63-64; Nat Cancer Inst fel physics, Univ Tex M D Anderson Hosp & Tumor Inst Houston, 67-68; asst prof, 68-72, ASSOC PROF RADIOL, UNIV TEX MED SCH SAN ANTONIO, 72-, ASSOC PROF DIAG & ROENTGENOL, 77- *Concurrent Pos:* Consult, Brooke Army Med Ctr, Ft Sam Houston, Tex, 71- *Mem:* Am Asn Physicists in Med; Biophys Soc; Am Col Radiol; Soc Nuclear Med; Radiol Soc NAm. *Res:* Measurement of x-ray spectra; calculation of information content in diagnostic x-rays; dosimetry and measurement of ionizing radiation; computerized tomography. *Mailing Add:* Dept of Radiol Univ of Tex Med Sch San Antonio TX 78284

WAGGENER, RONALD E, b Green River, Wyo, Oct 6, 26; m 48; c 4. RADIOLOGY. *Educ:* Univ Nebr, BS, 49, MS, 53, MD, 54, PhD, 57; Am Bd Radiol, dipl, 59. *Prof Exp:* ASSOC PROF RADIOL, UNIV NEBR MED CTR, OMAHA, 58- *Concurrent Pos:* Radiotherapist, Methodist Hosp, 59- *Mem:* Am Asn Cancer Res; Radiol Soc NAm; Royal Soc Med; Brit Inst Radiol; fel Am Col Radiol. *Res:* Biological effects of radiation stressing the hematological effects of ionizing rays. *Mailing Add:* Nebr Methodist Hosp 8303 Dodge St Omaha NE 68114

WAGGENER, THOMAS RUNYAN, b Indianapolis, Ind, July 20, 38; m 64; c 2. FOREST ECONOMICS, POLICY ANALYSIS. *Educ:* Purdue Univ, BSF, 62; Univ Wash, MF, 63, MA, 65, PhD(forest econ), 66. *Prof Exp:* Asst prof, 67-71, chmn mgt & soc sci div, 72-75, assoc prof, 71-78, PROF FOREST ECON, COL FOREST RESOURCES, UNIV WASH, 78-, ASSOC DEAN INSTR, 78- *Concurrent Pos:* Assoc coordr course in trop forestry, Orgn Trop Studies, Inc, Costa Rica & Honduras, 68 & 71; economist & analyst, Pub Land Law Rev Comn, DC, 68-69. *Mem:* Am Econ Asn; Soc Am Foresters. *Res:* Natural resources economics and analysis of economic impact of resource management policies; regional economic analysis; industrial organization and market structure; forest policy. *Mailing Add:* Col Forest Resources AR-10 Univ of Wash Seattle WA 98195

WAGGENER, WILLIAM COLE, b Princeton, Ky, Feb 5, 17; m 51; c 2. PHYSICAL CHEMISTRY. *Educ:* Centre Col, Ky, AB, 39; Univ Buffalo, PhD(inorg chem), 49. *Prof Exp:* Asst chem, Univ Buffalo, 39-41; supvr, Ammonia Oxidation Plant, Lake Ont Ord Works, 41-42; chemist, Res Lab, Nat Carbon Co, 43-45; MEM STAFF, OAK RIDGE NAT LAB, 49- *Mem:* AAAS; Am Chem Soc; Sigma Xi. *Res:* Chemistry of thorium; inorganic complexes; coordination properties of thiocyanates; solution spectrophotometry over wide ranges of temperature and pressure; near infrared spectroscopy of pure substances in condensed states; liquid effluents from light water-cooled nuclear reactors; heterogeneous calatysis. *Mailing Add:* 524 Avon Circle Knoxville TN 37919

WAGGLE, DOYLE H, b Osborne, Kans, Aug 11, 39; m 60; c 2. CEREAL CHEMISTRY. *Educ:* Ft Hays Kans State Col, BS, 61; Kans State Univ, MS, 63, PhD(milling indust), 66. *Prof Exp:* Res asst feed technol, Kans State Univ, 65-66, res assoc, 66-67; process res chemist, 67-68, mgr process res, 68-72, DIR RES & DEVELOP, VENTURE MGT, RALSTON PURINA CO, 72-, DIV VPRES, 78- *Mem:* Am Asn Cereal Chemists; Inst Food Technologists; Am Chem Soc. *Res:* Chemistry of processes related to foods and feeds. *Mailing Add:* Ralston Purina Co 835 S Eighth St St Louis MO 63188

WAGGONER, ALAN STUART, b Los Angeles, Calif, Jan 8, 42; m 65. BIOPHYSICAL CHEMISTRY. *Educ:* Univ Colo, BA, 65; Univ Ore, PhD(chem), 69. *Prof Exp:* NIH fel, Yale Univ, 69-71; asst prof, 71-77, ASSOC PROF CHEM, AMHERST COL, 77- *Res:* Spectroscopic studies of biological membranes. *Mailing Add:* Dept of Chem Amherst Col Amherst MA 01002

WAGGONER, JACK HOLMES, JR, b Pittsburgh, Pa, Sept 4, 27; m 61. THEORETICAL PHYSICS. *Educ:* Ohio State Univ, BS, 49, PhD(physics), 57. *Prof Exp:* Asst photochem, Res Found, Ohio State Univ, 49-53, res assoc, 58-59, proj assoc supvr, 59, proj supvr, 59, asst physics, Ohio State Univ, 53-55, instr, 57-58, asst prof, 58-59; asst prof, Univ Calif, Riverside, 59-61; asst prof, 61-65, ASSOC PROF PHYSICS, HARVEY MUDD COL, 65- *Concurrent Pos:* Vis assoc, Calif Inst Technol, 67-68. *Mem:* AAAS; Am Phys Soc; Am Inst Physics; Am Asn Physics Teachers. *Res:* Methods of theoretical physics; theory of molecular spectroscopy. *Mailing Add:* Dept of Physics Harvey Mudd Col Claremont CA 91711

WAGGONER, JAMES ARTHUR, b West Lafayette, Ind, Dec 31, 31; m 53; c 4. NUCLEAR PHYSICS. *Educ:* Univ Ill, BS, 53; Cornell Univ, PhD(exp physics), 60. *Prof Exp:* Physicist, Lawrence Radiation Lab, Univ Calif, 60-70, Physics Int Co, Calif, 71 & Maxwell Labs, 71; PHYSICIST, SCHLUMBERGER WELL SERVS, 71- *Concurrent Pos:* Consult, NASA. *Mem:* Am Phys Soc. *Res:* Lunar and planetary surface composition analysis using neutron inelastic scattering; Van Allen zone charged particles; geophysical instrumentation. *Mailing Add:* Schlumberger Well Servs PO Box 2175 Houston TX 77001

WAGGONER, JAMES NORMAN, b Elgin, Ill, Nov 10, 25; m; c 2. AEROSPACE MEDICINE. *Educ:* Ind Univ, BS, 46, MD, 49; Am Bd Prev Med, dipl & cert aviation med, 57. *Prof Exp:* Flight surgeon, United Air Lines, Inc, 52-59; CORP DIR MED SAFETY & LIFE SCI, GARRETT CORP, 59- *Concurrent Pos:* Adj prof, Univ Southern Calif, 58-; Aerospace Med Asn fel, 60; Indust Med Asn fel, 64; sr med consult, Western US, Air France, 72- *Honors & Awards:* Spec Aerospace Med Honor Citation, AMA, 62; Louis H Bauer Founders Award, Eaton Lab-Norwich Pharmacal Co, 68. *Mem:* Aerospace Med Asn (pres, 67-68); Airline Med Dir Asn (pres, 63-64); Am Col Prev Med; Am Inst Aeronaut & Astronaut; Int Acad Aviation & Space Med. *Res:* Effects of microbiological contamination of closed ecological systems; aeroembolism; combined stressors of spaceflight on human and subhuman subjects; effects of trace contaminants on humans and animals. *Mailing Add:* Garrett Corp 9851 Sepulveda Blvd Los Angeles CA 90009

WAGGONER, MARGARET ANN, nuclear physics, history of science, see previous edition

WAGGONER, PAUL EDWARD, b Appanoose Co, Iowa, Mar 29, 23; m 45; c 2. CLIMATOLOGY. *Educ:* Univ Chicago, SB, 46; Iowa State Col, MS, 49, PhD, 51. *Prof Exp:* From asst to assoc plant pathologist, 51-56, chief dept soils & climat, 56-69, vdir, 69-71, DIR, CONN AGR EXP STA, 72- *Concurrent Pos:* Guggenheim fel, 63; lectr, Yale Univ, 62- *Honors & Awards:* Am Meteorol Soc Award, 67. *Mem:* Nat Acad Sci; fel Am Phytopath Soc; Am Meteorol Soc; Ecol Soc Am; Am Soc Plant Physiologists. *Res:* Agriculture; plant pathology; effect of environment on plants, especially plant diseases. *Mailing Add:* Conn Agr Exp Sta PO Box 1106 New Haven CT 06504

WAGGONER, PHILLIP RAY, b Parkersburg, WVa, Apr 4, 43; m 67; c 2. DEVELOPMENTAL BIOLOGY. *Educ:* WVa Univ, BS, 65, MS, 68, PhD(genetics & develop biol), 72. *Prof Exp:* Instr biol, Fairmont State Col, 68 & WVa Univ, 68-69; ASST PROF ANAT, WAYNE STATE UNIV, 72- *Mem:* Am Asn Anat; AAAS; Sigma Xi. *Res:* Development of the vertebrate eye. *Mailing Add:* Dept of Anat Sch of Med Wayne State Univ Detroit MI 48202

WAGGONER, RAYMOND C, b Louisville, Ky, Feb 13, 30; m 54; c 3. CHEMICAL ENGINEERING. *Educ:* Univ Louisville, BChE, 52; Tex A&M Univ, MEng, 61, PhD(chem eng), 64. *Prof Exp:* Prod control engr & sr prod control engr, Dow Chem Co, 56-61; res asst chem engr, Tex A&M Univ, 61-64; sr engr, Humble Oil & Refining Co, 64-65; assoc prof, 65-79, PROF CHEM ENG, UNIV MO-ROLLA, 79- *Concurrent Pos:* Res engr, Savannah River Lab, E I du Pont de Nemours & Co Inc, 81-82. *Mem:* Am Inst Chem Engrs; Am Chem Soc; Am Soc Eng Educ; Instrument Soc Am. *Res:* Development and confirmation of calculational procedures for stagewise separation processes, including distillation and extraction; process dynamics and control. *Mailing Add:* Dept of Chem Eng Univ of Mo Rolla MO 65401

WAGGONER, RAYMOND WALTER, b Carson City, Mich, Aug 2, 01; m 30; c 2. PSYCHIATRY, NEUROLOGY. *Educ:* Univ Mich, MD, 24; Univ Pa, ScD, 30. *Prof Exp:* Intern, Harper Hosp, Detroit, 24-25; resident, Philadelphia Orthop Hosp & Infirmary Nerv Dis, 25-26; lab intern, Pa Hosp, Philadelphia, 26; from asst prof to assoc prof neurol, Med Sch, 29-36, from asst neurologist to neurologist, Univ Hosp, 29-36, chmn dept psychiat, Med Sch, 37-71, prof psychiat & dir neuropsychiat inst, 37-70, EMER PROF PSYCHIAT & EMER DIR NEUROPSYCHIAT INST, MED SCH, UNIV MICH, ANN ARBOR, 70- *Concurrent Pos:* Consult, spec comt rights ment ill, Am Bar Found, 59-66, indust personnel security, Dept Defense, 48-60, Surgeon-Gen, US Army, Selective Serv Syst, Peace Corps, Vet Admin & Social Security Admin, 43-50; mem med adv bd, Social Security Admin, 65-; adv comt, Nat Paraplegic Found; mem test comt psychiat, Nat Bd Med Examr, 65-70; mem, Res Socs Coun, 70-73; vpres bd trustees, Mich Inst Pastoral Care; consult & bd mem, Reproductive Biol Res Found, 70-; consult, Mich State Dept Ment Health, 74-; distinguished vis prof psychiat, Univ Louisville, 74- *Honors & Awards:* E B Bowis Award, Am Col Psychiat, 68. *Mem:* Fel AAAS; Am Acad Psychoanal; fel Am Col Psychiat (vpres, 64-65, pres elect, 65-66, pres, 66-67); Am Geriat Soc; fel Am Psychiat Asn (vpres, 60-61, pres, 69-70). *Res:* Personality studies in chorea; the convulsive state; myopathies; psychotherapy. *Mailing Add:* 3333 Geddes Rd Ann Arbor MI 48105

WAGGONER, TERRY BILL, b Stillwater, Okla, Oct 25, 34; m 66; c 1. ORGANIC CHEMISTRY, BIOCHEMISTRY. *Educ:* Okla State Univ, BS, 57, MS, 59; Mich State Univ, PhD(chem), 64. *Prof Exp:* Instr chem, Okla State Univ, 59-60; sr res chemist, M & T Chem, Inc, 63-66; res chemist, 66-69, mgr biochem res, Chemagro Div, Mobay Chem Corp, 69-78; vpres, Anal Develop Corp, 79-81; MGR REGIST, RHONE-POULENC INC, 81- *Mem:*

Am Chem Soc; Am Inst Chemists. *Res:* Pesticide residues in plants, animals, water, soil; analytical residue methods; metabolism of pesticides in plant and animal systems; chemistry of environmental pollutants; radioactive tracer methods. *Mailing Add:* Rhone-Poulenc Inc PO Box 125 Black Horse Lane Monmouth Junction NJ 08852

WAGGONER, WILBUR J, b Sutherland, Iowa, May 28, 24; m 46; c 3. MATHEMATICS. *Educ:* Buena Vista Col, BA, 47; Drake Univ, MSE, 50; Univ Wyo, EdD, 56. *Prof Exp:* Prin, coach & teacher high sch, 47-51; supt twp sch, 51-55; asst, Univ Wyo, 55-56; from asst prof to assoc prof, 56-62, actg dean, Sch Grad Studies, 73-75, PROF MATH, CENT MICH UNIV, 62- *Mem:* Am Statist Asn; Nat Coun Teachers Math. *Res:* Statistics. *Mailing Add:* Dept of Math Cent Mich Univ Mt Pleasant MI 48858

WAGGONER, WILLIAM CHARLES, b Alma, Mich, Jan 18, 36; m 80; c 8. PHYSIOLOGY, TOXICOLOGY. *Educ:* Hope Col, AB, 58; Mich State Univ, MS, 61, PhD(physiol), 63. *Prof Exp:* Teaching fel physiol & pharmacol, Med Sch, Mich State Univ, 60-63; res physiologist, Colgate-Palmolive Res Ctr, 63-64, res projs coordr oral health, 64-66; asst dir med res, Unimed, Inc, 66-70; assoc dir med serv & govt affairs, Wallace Pharmaceut, NJ, 70-74; mgr med & regulatory affairs, 74-80, DIR GOVT AFFAIRS, BABY PROD CO, JOHNSON & JOHNSON, 80- *Concurrent Pos:* Consult fac mem, Inst Clin Toxicol, 74- *Mem:* Am Physiol Soc; fel Am Acad Clin Toxicol; Soc Toxicol. *Res:* Clinical toxicology and pharmacology. *Mailing Add:* 5 Banner Ct East Brunswick NJ 07060

WAGGONER, WILLIAM HORACE, b Ravenna, Ohio, June 8, 24; m 46; c 1. INORGANIC CHEMISTRY. *Educ:* Hiram Col, AB, 49; Western Reserve Univ, MS, 51, PhD(chem), 53. *Prof Exp:* Asst chem, Hiram Col, 48-49; asst prof, 52-59, ASSOC PROF INORG CHEM, UNIV GA, 59- *Mem:* Am Chem Soc. *Res:* Solubilities in non-aqueous systems; history of chemistry; spectral properties of inorganic materials. *Mailing Add:* Dept of Chem Univ of Ga Athens GA 30602

WAGH, PREMANAND VINAYAK, b Sadashivgad, India, July 9, 34; US citizen; c 3. BIOCHEMISTRY. *Educ:* Univ Bombay, BSc Hons, 54, MSc, 56; Southern Ill Univ, Carbondale, MS, 62; Univ Minn, Minneapolis, PhD(animal sci, biochem), 65. *Prof Exp:* Res assoc biochem, Univ Ill Med Ctr, 65; res assoc, State Univ NY Buffalo, 65-68, instr, 68-69; res biochemist, Vet Admin Hosp, 69-73, chief connective tissue res, 75-77; asst prof biochem, Med Ctr, Univ Ark, Little Rock, 69-76; RES ASSOC PROF, DIV CELL & MOLECULAR BIOL, DEPT BIOL SCI, STATE UNIV NY AMHERST, 79- *Mem:* Soc Complex Carbohydrates; Am Soc Biol Chemists. *Res:* Cardiovascular glycoproteins in Atherosclerosis; structure and function of connective tissue glycoproteins; glycosidases. *Mailing Add:* Div Cell & Molecular Biol State Univ of NY Amherst NY 14260

WAGLE, GILMOUR LAWRENCE, b Staten Island, NY, Nov 17, 22; m 49; c 3. PHARMACOLOGY. *Educ:* Wagner Col, BS, 50; Rutgers Univ, MS, 56; Princeton Univ, MA, 59, PhD(biol), 60. *Prof Exp:* Pharmacologist, Res Dept, Ciba Pharmaceut Prod, Inc, NJ, 48-61; sr pharmacologist, Chas Pfizer & Co, 61-64; asst to dir res admin, Toxicol Res Sect, 64-72, asst dir, Med Controls Br, Off Govt Controls, 72-77, dir, Sci Compliance Qual Assurance Dept, 77-79, res toxicologist, Environ Serv Div, 80, MGR MED REGULATORY SURVEILLANCE, MED RES DIV, LEDERLE LABS, AM CYANAMID CO, 81- *Mem:* Soc Toxicol; Fedn Am Scientists. *Res:* Cardiovascular, renal and central nervous system pharmacology; government regulatory affairs; toxicology. *Mailing Add:* Am Cyanamid Co Lederle Labs Pearl River NY 10965

WAGLE, ROBERT FAY, b Jamestown, NDak, Sept 3, 16. FORESTRY, BOTANY. *Educ:* Univ Minn, BS, 40; Univ Wash, MF, 55; Univ Calif, PhD(bot), 58. *Prof Exp:* Asst forestry, Univ Wash, 47-48; logging engr, Shasta Plywood Co, Calif, 48-49; sr lab asst, Univ Calif, 49-54; asst, Calif Forest & Range Exp Sta, US Forest Serv, 54-57; assoc prof watershed mgt, 57-69, PROF WATERSHED MGT & WATERSHED SPECIALIST, UNIV ARIZ, 69- *Concurrent Pos:* Consult fire & silvicult, Univ Nev, 64, wood technol, Tucson Power, Indust Res Inst, World Bank, forest res, Yeman, Arabia, pulp wood availability, SW Wilburt Assoc, fire & forest regeneration. *Mem:* Fel AAAS; Soc Am Foresters; Ecol Soc Am. *Res:* Silvics, genetics, ecology and silviculture; plant variation and its relationship to environment; nutrient and water relationships of wildland plants; effects of fire on plants and their environments; growth and variation in containerized pine seedling; effect of nutrients and mycorrhizae on containerized pine seedling growth, and root/shoot ratios and field survival; tree species for ornamentals and Christmas trees in the southwest. *Mailing Add:* Sch of Renewable Natural Resources Univ of Ariz Col of Agr Tucson AZ 85721

WAGLE, SHREEPAD R, b Bombay, India, Jan 1, 31; nat US; m 62; c 3. PHARMACOLOGY. *Educ:* Univ Bombay, BS, 52, MS, 55; Univ Ill, PhD(biochem, nutrit), 59. *Prof Exp:* Res chemist, Haffkine Inst, India, 52-55; asst, Univ Ill, 55-59; res chemist, Sigma Lab, India, 60; from res assoc to asst prof, 60-65, assoc prof, 65-68, dir grad progs, 68-80 PROF PHARMACOL, SCH MED, IND UNIV, INDIANAPOLIS, 68- *Mem:* Am Cancer Soc; Am Inst Nutrit; Soc Exp Biol & Med; Am Diabetes Asn; Am Soc Pharmacol & Exp Therapeut. *Res:* Cofactors in protein and RNA biosynthesis; role of hormones and nutritional factors in protein synthesis and cancer cells; protein kinases; lipases and cyclic adenosine monophosphates; metabolism of isolated liver parenchymal and sinusoidal cells. *Mailing Add:* 350 Med Sci Bldg Ind Univ Sch Med Indianapolis IN 46202

WAGLEY, PHILIP FRANKLIN, b Mineral Wells, Tex, Feb 5, 17; m 53. MEDICINE. *Educ:* Southern Methodist Univ, BS, 38; Johns Hopkins Univ, MD, 43; Am Bd Internal Med, dipl. *Prof Exp:* Instr med, 45-47 & 49-64, asst prof, 64-74, ASSOC PROF MED, JOHNS HOPKINS UNIV, 74- *Concurrent Pos:* Am Col Physicians res fel, Harvard Med Sch, 47-48; Nat Res Coun fel med sci, Mass Inst Technol, 48-49. *Mem:* Am Clin & Climat Asn; fel Am Col Physicians; Am Thoracic Soc; Am Soc Hemat. *Res:* Chest disease. *Mailing Add:* 9 E Chase St Baltimore MD 21212

WAGMAN, GERALD HOWARD, b Newark, NJ, Mar 4, 26; m 48; c 2. MICROBIAL BIOCHEMISTRY. *Educ:* Lehigh Univ, BS, 46; Va Polytech Inst, MS, 47. *Prof Exp:* Tech asst antibiotics, Squibb Inst Med Res, 47-49, electronics, 49-54, microbial biochemist, 54-57; from assoc biochemist to sr biochemist, 57-69, sect leader, 69-70, mgr antibiotics dept, 70-74, assoc dir microbiol sci/antibiotics, 74-77, assoc dir, Microbiol Sci/Screening Lab, 77-78, DIR, MIROBIOL STRAIN LAB, SCHERING CORP, 79- *Mem:* AAAS; Am Chem Soc; Am Soc Microbiol; fel Am Inst Chemists; Sigma Xi. *Res:* Antibiotics, especially isolation, identification and evaluation; strain development; fermentation biosynthesis and development; isolation and identification of natural products. *Mailing Add:* Antibiotics Res Schering Corp 2000 Galloping Hill Rd Kenilworth NJ 07033

WAGMAN, NICHOLAS EMORY, astronomy, deceased

WAGNER, ALAN R, b Columbus, Ohio, Aug 20, 23; m 52; c 3. PATHOLOGY. *Educ:* Ohio State Univ, DVM, 46, MSc, 52. *Prof Exp:* Sr veterinarian, UNRRA, 46-47; field veterinarian, USDA, 47; veterinarian, Columbus Health Dept, 47-48; pathologist, Path Serv Labs, Ohio State Dept Agr, 48-56 & Lederle Labs Div, Am Cyanamid Co, 56-58; dir vet med res, Warren-Teed Pharmaceut Inc, 58-69; pres, Arlington Res Labs, Inc, 69-72; dir res & develop, Pet Chem, Inc, 75-78; ASST DIR & PATHOLOGIST, LAB ANIMAL CTR, OHIO STATE UNIV, 72-75, 78- *Mem:* Am Vet Med Asn; Am Asn Lab Animal Sci; NY Acad Sci; Soc Toxicol. *Res:* Pathology in fields of human and animal investigations and clinical as well as histopathological and bacteriological determination; new pharmaceutical and biological products. *Mailing Add:* Lab Animal Ctr Ohio State Univ 5769 Godown Rd Columbus OH 43220

WAGNER, ALBERT FORDYCE, b Rochester, NY, Feb 3, 45; m 69; c 1. CHEMICAL PHYSICS. *Educ:* Boston Col, BS, 66; Calif Inst Technol, PhD(chem), 72. *Prof Exp:* Presidential intern, 72-74, asst chemist, 74-77, CHEMIST, CHEM DIV, ARGONNE NAT LAB, 77- *Mem:* Am Inst Physics. *Res:* Theory and modeling of chemical reactions, ion-pair plasmas, and sputtering phenomena. *Mailing Add:* Chem Div Argonne Nat Lab Argonne IL 60439

WAGNER, ALFRED, b Brooklyn, NY, Apr 9, 50; m 72; c 2. MATERIALS SCIENCE, PHYSICS. *Educ:* Cooper Union, BChE, 71; Cornell Univ, MS, 74, PhD(mat sci), 78. *Prof Exp:* MEM TECH STAFF MAT SCI, BELL LABS, 78- *Mem:* Am Physics Soc; Am Vacuum Soc. *Res:* Ion lithography; field ion microscopy; radiation effects; ion sources. *Mailing Add:* Rm 1E 344 600 Mountain Ave Murray Hill NJ 07974

WAGNER, ANDREW JAMES, b Greenwich, Conn, Apr 12, 34; m 69. METEOROLOGY, CLIMATOLOGY. *Educ:* Wesleyan Univ, BA, 56; Mass Inst Technol, MS, 58. *Prof Exp:* Res meteorologist, Extended Forecast Div, Weather Bur, 65-69, res meteorologist forecasting & interpretation, 69-72, meteorologist long range prediction group, 72-78, METEOROLOGIST CLIMATE ANAL CTR, NAT WEATHER SERV, NAT OCEANIC & ATMOSPHERIC ADMIN, DEPT COM, 78- *Mem:* Am Meteorol Soc; Royal Meteorol Soc; Am Geophys Union; Am Sci Affil. *Res:* Understanding and predicting statistical relationships of monthly and seasonal weather patterns over the northern hemisphere; authored articles in professional journals describing results of these studies. *Mailing Add:* Rm 604 World Weather Bldg Climate Anal Ctr W351 Washington DC 20233

WAGNER, ARTHUR FRANKLIN, b Jersey City, NJ, Oct 25, 22; m 45; c 3. ORGANIC CHEMISTRY. *Educ:* Princeton Univ, AB, 48, MA, 49, PhD(org chem), 51. *Prof Exp:* Sr chemist, 51-61, res assoc org chem, 61-65, SR RES FEL ORG CHEM, MERCK SHARP & DOHME RES LABS, 65- *Mem:* Am Chem Soc; AAAS. *Res:* Synthetic organic chemistry in natural products, isolation, structure determination and synthesis of vitamins and cofactors; synthesis of benzimidazoles; synthesis of peptides, biopolymers and immobilized biopolymers; B-lactam antibiotic synthesis. *Mailing Add:* Synthetic Chem Res Merck Sharp & Dohme Res Labs Rahway NJ 07065

WAGNER, AUBREY JOSEPH, b Hillsboro, Wis, Jan 12, 12; m 33; c 4. ENERGY APPLICATIONS. *Educ:* Univ Wis, BS, 33. *Hon Degrees:* LLD, Newberry Col, 66. *Prof Exp:* Eng aide to chief navig br, Tenn Valley Authority, 34-50, asst gen mgr, 50-54, gen mgr, 54-61, mem bd dir, 61-62, chmn, 62-78; MEM BD, ROY F WESTON, INC, 80- *Concurrent Pos:* Comt mem, Pres Water Resources Pol Comm, 50, Appalachian Regional Comm, 63-65, Pres Coun Recreation & Nat Beauty, 63-65, Pres Coun Cost Reduction Govt, 68-69, Gov Sci Advv Comm, 69-70, Adv Comm 1972 UN Conf, Human Environ, 71-72, AEC Sr Utility Steering Comt, 71-72; vchmn, Breeder Reactor Corp, 72-78 & US Nat Comt of World Energy Conf, 76-78, mem, 78-; vchmn elect, Power Res Inst, 77-78; consult, Tenn Valley Authority, 78- *Honors & Awards:* Walter H Zinn Award, Am Nuclear Soc, 78. *Mem:* Nat Acad Eng; Explorers Club. *Res:* Multiple purpose development and use; role of energy; nuclear energy. *Mailing Add:* 201 Whittington Dr Knoxville TN 37923

WAGNER, BERNARD MEYER, b Philadelphia, Pa, Jan 17, 28; m 51; c 2. PATHOLOGY. *Educ:* Hahnemann Med Col, MD. *Prof Exp:* Dir exp path labs, Hahnemann Med Col, 54-55; asst prof path, Med Sch & Grad Sch Med, Univ Pa, 56-58; assoc prof path & Robert L King chair cardiovasc res, Sch Med, Univ Wash, 58-60; prof path & chmn dept, New York Med Col, 60-67, clin prof, 67-68; CLIN PROF PATH, COLUMBIA UNIV, 68-; DIR LABS, BEEKMAN DOWNTOWN HOSP, NEW YORK, 71-; DIR LABS, OVERLOOK HOSP, SUMMIT, 76- *Concurrent Pos:* Dazian Found Med Res fel, Hahnemann Med Col, 53, Am Heart Asn Southeast Pa fels, 54-55; asst vis chief serv, Philadelphia Gen Hosp, 54-58; pathologist & dir path, Children's Hosp, Philadelphia, 55-58; lectr, Philadelphia Col Pharm, 56-58; attend pathologist, Vet Admin Hosp, 58-; Burroughs Wellcome Fund travel grant & spec investr, Hosp for Sick Children, London, Eng, 59; vpres, Warner Lambert Res Inst, 67-; dir labs, Francis Delafield Hosp, 68-71; ed-in-chief, Human Path, 73-; assoc ed, Conn Tissue Res, 74- & J Environ Path & Toxicol, 76- *Mem:* Am Soc Exp Path; Soc Pediat Res; Fedn Am Soc Exp Biol; Am Asn Path & Bact; Am Rheumatism Asn. *Res:* Diseases of connective tissue; rheumatic heart disease. *Mailing Add:* Overlook Hosp Summit NJ 07901

WAGNER, C(HRISTIAN) N(IKOLAUS) J(OHANN), b Saarbruecken-Dudweiler, Ger, Mar 6, 27; US citizen; m 52; c 3. PHYSICAL METALLURGY, MATERIALS SCIENCE. *Educ:* Univ Saarland, Lic es sc, 51, Dipl Ing, 54, Dr rer nat, 57. *Prof Exp:* Asst x-ray metall, Inst Metall Res, Univ Saarland, 53-55, 57-58, res asst phys metall, 59; from asst prof to assoc prof eng & appl sci, Yale Univ, 59-70; chmn, Mat Dept, 74-79, PROF ENG & APPL SCI, UNIV CALIF, LOS ANGELES, 70- *Concurrent Pos:* Vis prof, Univ Saarbrucken, 79-80. *Mem:* Am Soc Metals; Am Phys Soc; Am Crystallog Asn; Am Inst Mining, Metall & Petrol Engrs; Ger Phys Soc. *Res:* Diffraction studies including x-rays, neutrons, electrons of amorphous materials and liquids, plastic deformation and transformation in alloys, thin films, and biomaterials. *Mailing Add:* Mat Dept 6531-Boelter Hall Univ of Calif Los Angeles CA 90024

WAGNER, CARL GEORGE, b Newark, NJ, Sept 26, 43; m 69. MATHEMATICS. *Educ:* Princeton Univ, AB, 65; Duke Univ, PhD(math), 69. *Prof Exp:* Asst prof, 69-76, ASSOC PROF MATH, UNIV TENN, KNOXVILLE, 76- *Mem:* Am Math Soc. *Res:* Function theory in fields with non-archimedean absolute value; combinatorics; arithmetic functions. *Mailing Add:* Dept of Math Univ of Tenn Knoxville TN 37916

WAGNER, CHARLES EUGENE, b Memphis, Tenn, June 21, 23; m 49; c 3. MORPHOLOGY. *Educ:* Princeton Univ, AB, 47; Ind Univ, PhD(zool), 54. *Prof Exp:* Asst zool, Ind Univ, 48-50; from instr to assoc prof, 52-71, from asst dean to assoc dean, 61-74, PROF ANAT, SCH MED, UNIV LOUISVILLE, 71- *Res:* Experimental morphology; regeneration; movements at synovial joints. *Mailing Add:* Dept of Anat Univ of Louisville Sch of Med Louisville KY 40292

WAGNER, CHARLES KENYON, b Cleveland, Ohio, Mar 11, 43; m 66; c 2. ECOLOGY, BIOLOGY. *Educ:* Emory Univ, BA, 65; Univ Ga, MS, 68, PhD(zool), 73. *Prof Exp:* Lectr zool, Univ Ga, 70-72; asst prof biol, Southwestern at Memphis, 72-77; asst prof, 77-81, ASSOC PROF BIOL, CLEMSON UNIV, 81- *Concurrent Pos:* Consult, Community Develop Task Force, 75-77. *Honors & Awards:* Am Soc Mammalogists Award, 72. *Mem:* Ecol Soc Am; Am Soc Mammalogists; Am Inst Biol Sci; Sigma Xi. *Res:* Bioenergetics of terrestrial populations; microecosystem investigation of population growth. *Mailing Add:* Biol Prog Clemson Univ Clemson SC 29631

WAGNER, CHARLES ROE, b Olivet, SDak, Dec 3, 25; m 50; c 2. ORGANIC CHEMISTRY. *Educ:* SDak Sch Mines & Technol, BSc, 50; Mich State Col, PhD, 55. *Prof Exp:* Res chemist, 55-62, res supvr, Specialty Chem Div, 62-69, mgr process res, 69-71, dir develop, 71-74, DIR, BUFFALO RES LABS, SPECIALTY CHEM DIV, ALLIED CHEM CORP, 74- *Mem:* Am Chem Soc. *Res:* Organic isocyanates; organic acids. *Mailing Add:* Allied Chem Co Buffalo Res Labs 20 Peabody St Buffalo NY 14210

WAGNER, CONRAD, b Brooklyn, NY, Nov 1, 29; m 53; c 2. BIOCHEMISTRY, NUTRITION. *Educ:* City Col New York, BA, 51; Univ Mich, MS, 52, PhD(biochem), 56. *Prof Exp:* USPHS fel biochem, NIH, 59-61; from asst prof to assoc prof biochem, 61-75, PROF BIOCHEM, SCH MED, VANDERBILT UNIV, 75- *Concurrent Pos:* Res biochemist, Vet Admin Hosp, 61-68, chief biochem res, 68-, assoc chief of staff res, 74- *Mem:* Am Soc Biol Chemists; Am Inst Nutrit. *Res:* Gluconeogenesis from lipid in Tetrahymena pyriformis; regulation of tryptophan-niacin relation in animals and microorganisms; sulfonium compounds and one carbon metabolism in bacteria; role and function of natural folate coenzymes; characterization of folate binding proteins; cellular transport of folate and other cofactors; nutritional biochemistry. *Mailing Add:* Dept Biochem Vanderbilt Univ Nashville TN 37232

WAGNER, DANIEL HOBSON, b Jersey Shore, Pa, Aug 24, 25; m 49; c 4. MATHEMATICS. *Educ:* Haverford Col, BS, 47; Brown Univ, PhD(math), 51. *Prof Exp:* Mem sci staff, Opers Eval Group, Mass Inst Technol, 51-56; supvr math anal, Burroughs Corp, 56-58; partner, Kettelle & Wagner, 58-63; PRES, DANIEL H WAGNER ASSOCS, 63- *Concurrent Pos:* Chmn electronics reliability task group, Off Asst Secy Defense Res & Eng, 56; lectr, Swarthmore Col, 58 & Univ Pa, 58 & 61-62; comt appl math training, Nat Acad Sci- Nat Res Coun, 77-78. *Mem:* Am Math Soc; Opers Res Soc Am; Soc Indust & Appl Math; Math Asn Am; Inst Mgt Sci. *Res:* Operations research; constrained optimization; measurable set-valued functions. *Mailing Add:* Station Square One Paoli PA 19301

WAGNER, DAVID DARLEY, b Ft Riley, Kans, Sept 27, 44; m 71; c 2. INTESTINAL ECOLOGY, INTESTINE FUNCTION. *Educ:* Univ Md, BSc, 72, MSc, 74, PhD(nutrit), 77. *Prof Exp:* Res assoc microbiol, Dept Food Sci, NC State Univ, 77; reviewing staff scientist metab drugs, Div Drugs Avian Species, 77-79, biores monitoring prog mgr, toxicol, Off Sci Eval, 79-80, CHIEF, DIV VET RES, ANIMAL NUTRIT RES BR, BUR VET MED, FOOD & DRUG ADMIN, 80- *Mem:* Sigma Xi; Am Soc Animal Sci; Poultry Sci Asn. *Res:* Effects of diet composition on intestine microecology; intestine digestive and absorptive function; intestine mucosal integrity and diet plus drug interactions. *Mailing Add:* Bur Vet Med Med Food & Drug Admin Bldg 328-A Agr Res Ctr Beltsville MD 20705

WAGNER, DAVID KENDALL, b Berkeley, Calif, Aug 7, 45; m 67. EXPERIMENTAL SOLID STATE PHYSICS. *Educ:* Pomona Col, BA, 67; Cornell Univ, PhD(physics), 72. *Prof Exp:* res assoc physics, 72-78, SR RES ASSOC, SCH ELEC ENG, CORNELL UNIV, 78- *Mem:* Am Phys Soc. *Res:* Investigation of electronic scattering mechanisms in metals. *Mailing Add:* Sch Elec Eng Cornell Univ Ithaca NY 14853

WAGNER, DAVID LOREN, b Erie, Pa, Nov 19, 42; m 64; c 1. LOW TEMPERATURE PHYSICS, SOLID STATE PHYSICS. *Educ:* Case Western Reserve Univ, BS, 64, MS, 66, PhD(physics), 70. *Prof Exp:* From asst prof to assoc prof, 70-75, chmn dept, 72-81, PROF PHYSICS, EDINBORO STATE COL, 75- *Concurrent Pos:* NSF acad year exten grant, 71-73, student sci training grant, 75, teacher grant, 78. *Mem:* Am Asn Physics Teachers; AAAS. *Res:* Fermi surface of metals and semi-metals. *Mailing Add:* Dept Chem & Physics Edinboro State Col Edinboro PA 16444

WAGNER, EDWARD D, b Eureka, SDak, June 28, 19; m 42; c 3. PARASITOLOGY. *Educ:* Walla Walla Col, BA, 42; Wash State Univ, MS, 45; Univ Southern Calif, PhD, 53. *Prof Exp:* Instr biol, Atlantic Union Col, 45-47 & Andrews Univ, 47-49; assoc, Univ Southern Calif, 50-52; head dept parasitol, Sch Trop & Prev Med, 50-59, instr microbiol, Sch Med, 53-56, from asst prof to assoc prof, 56-68, PROF MICROBIOL, SCH MED, LOMA LINDA UNIV, 68- *Mem:* Am Soc Trop Med & Hyg; Am Soc Parasitol; Am Micros Soc; Royal Soc Trop Med & Hyg; Japanese Soc Parasitol. *Res:* Schistosomiasis; parasite therapy; helminths. *Mailing Add:* Dept of Microbiol Loma Linda Univ Sch of Med Loma Linda CA 92350

WAGNER, EDWARD KNAPP, b Akron, Ohio, May 4, 40; m 61; c 2. ANIMAL VIROLOGY, BIOCHEMISTRY. *Educ:* Univ Calif, Berkeley, BA, 62; Mass Inst Technol, PhD(biochem), 67. *Prof Exp:* Helen Hay Whitney Found fel, Univ Chicago, 67-70; asst prof, 70-75, assoc prof, 75-80, PROF VIROL, UNIV CALIF, IRVINE, 80- *Concurrent Pos:* Nat Cancer Inst res grant, 70- *Mem:* AAAS; Am Soc Microbiol; Tissue Cult Asn; Am Soc Biol Chemists; Am Soc Cell Biol. *Res:* Control of gene action in animal virus infection; mechanism of viral carcinogenesis; control of information transfer between nucleus and cytoplasm in eucaryotic cells. *Mailing Add:* Dept of Molecular Biol & Biochem Univ of Calif Irvine CA 92664

WAGNER, ERIC G, b Ossining, NY, Oct 1, 31; m 60; c 3. MATHEMATICS. *Educ:* Harvard Univ, BA, 53; Columbia Univ, MA, 59, PhD(math), 63. *Prof Exp:* Tech engr, IBM Corp, 53-54, assoc engr switching theory, 56-58, RES STAFF MEM, T J WATSON RES CTR, IBM CORP, 58- *Concurrent Pos:* Lectr, NY Univ, 64-65, adj asst prof, 65-66; sr vis res fel, Queen Mary Col, Univ London, 73-74. *Mem:* Am Math Soc; Asn Comput Mach; Asn Symbolic Logic; NY Acad Sci; Europ Asn Theoret Comput Sci. *Res:* Computability theory and category theory with emphasis on their relationship to computer science; theory of programming languages and logical design. *Mailing Add:* IBM Watson Res Ctr PO Box 218 Yorktown Heights NY 10598

WAGNER, ERWIN F, b Wolfsberg, Austria, Nov 25, 50; Austria & US citizen. DEVELOPMENTAL BIOLOGY. *Educ:* Univ Graf, Austria, Dipl Ing, 75; Univ Innsbruck, Austria, DR, 78. *Prof Exp:* Max-Planck-fel genetics, Max-Planck-Inst Molecular Genetics, Berlin, 76-78; res assoc biochem, Inst Biochem, Innsbruck, Austria, 78-79; Max-Kade-fel & vis scientist, 79-81, RES ASSOC, INST CANCER RES, 81- *Concurrent Pos:* Lectr, Univ Innsbruck, Austria, 82- *Res:* Regulation of gene expression during development; use of micro manipulation on mouse embryos with totipotent teratocarcinoma cells and direct injection of cloned genes into mouse eggs. *Mailing Add:* Inst Cancer Res Fox Chase Cancer Ctr 7701 Burholme Ave Philadelphia PA 19111

WAGNER, EUGENE ROSS, b Monroe, Wis, Nov 21, 37; m 58; c 2. MEDICINAL CHEMISTRY. *Educ:* Univ Wis, BS, 59, PhD(org chem), 64. *Prof Exp:* Chemist, Spec Assignment Prog, Dow Chem Co, 63-64, Dow Human Res & Develop Labs, Pitman-Moore Div, 64-67, sr res chemist, 67-72, res specialist, Chem Biol Res, 72-75, sr res specialist, Midland, Mich, 75-78, sr res specialist, pharmaceut chem, 78-80; SR RES SPECIALIST, MERRELL DOW, 81- *Mem:* Am Chem Soc. *Res:* Organic synthesis of biologically active compounds; synthesis of hypocholesteremic agents, antidiabetics and radiolabeled compounds. *Mailing Add:* Merrell Dow PO Box 68511 Indianapolis IN 46268

WAGNER, EUGENE STEPHEN, b Gary, Ind, Mar 30, 34; m 62; c 3. BIOLOGICAL CHEMISTRY, PHYSICAL CHEMISTRY. *Educ:* Ind Univ, BS, 59; Purdue Univ, PhD(chem), 64. *Prof Exp:* Instr chem, Purdue Univ, 62-64; sr phys chemist, Eli Lily & Co, Ind, 64-71; asst prof, 71-75, ASSOC PROF CHEM, BALL STATE UNIV & MUNCIE CTR MED EDUC, 75- *Mem:* Am Chem Soc. *Res:* Chemical kinetics; reaction mechanisms; mechanism of penicillin hypersensitivity. *Mailing Add:* Dept of Chem Ball State Univ Muncie IN 47306

WAGNER, FLORENCE SIGNAIGO, b Birmingham, Mich; m 48; c 2. BOTANY. *Educ:* Univ Mich, Ann Arbor, AB, 41, MA, 43; Univ Calif, Berkeley, PhD(bot), 52. *Prof Exp:* Res asst soc sci, Off Coordr Inter-Am Affairs, 43-45 & Off Strategic Serv, 45; from res asst to res assoc bot, 61-73, sr res assoc bot, 73-76, assoc res scientist, 76-80, PROF BIOL SCI, UNIV MICH, ANN ARBOR, 80- *Concurrent Pos:* Lectr, Univ Ctr Adult Educ, Ann Arbor, 71- *Mem:* Am Fern Soc; Brit Pteridological Soc; Bot Soc Am; Am Soc Plant Taxonomists. *Res:* Analysis of chromosomal behavior in ferns and fern hybrids and comparative studies of their morphology. *Mailing Add:* Dept of Bot Univ of Mich Ann Arbor MI 48109

WAGNER, FRANK A, JR, b New Haven, Conn, Apr 19, 32; m 61; c 4. ORGANIC CHEMISTRY. *Educ:* Yale Univ, BS, 58; Rutgers Univ, New Brunswick, PhD(org chem), 68. *Prof Exp:* Chemist, 58-65, res chemist, 65-68, sr res chemist, 68-77, GROUP LEADER, AM CYANAMID CO, 77- *Mem:* Am Chem Soc; AAAS. *Res:* Preparation of compounds as agricultural pesticides; design of procedures for large-scale syntheses. *Mailing Add:* Am Cyanamid Co PO Box 400 Princeton NJ 08540

WAGNER, FRANK S, JR, b Temple, Tex, Aug 26, 25; m 53; c 5. ORGANIC CHEMISTRY. *Educ:* Southwest Tex State Col, BA & MA, 47. *Prof Exp:* Assoc prof chem, Schreiner Inst, Tex, 48-50; analyst, Celanese Corp, 50-52, group leader, 52-53, librn, 53-65, HEAD INFO CTR, TECH CTR, CELANESE CHEM CO, 65- *Mem:* AAAS; Am Chem Soc; Spec Libr Asn; Egypt Explor Soc. *Res:* Application of machine methods to critical literature reviews and commerical intelligence activities; writing of encyclopedic reviews. *Mailing Add:* Celanese Chem Co PO Box 9077 Corpus Christi TX 78408

WAGNER, FREDERIC HAMILTON, b Corpus Christi, Tex, Sept 26, 26; m 49; c 2. BIOLOGY. *Educ:* Southern Methodist Univ, BS, 49; Univ Wis, MS, 53, PhD(wildlife mgt, zool), 61. *Prof Exp:* Refuge asst, US Fish & Wildlife Serv, 45; asst zool & bot, Southern Methodist Univ, 46-49; asst wildlife mgt,

Univ Wis, 49-51; res fel, Wildlife Mgt Inst, 51; res biologist, Wis Conserv Dept, 52-58; asst prof wildlife resources, Utah State Univ, 58-59; res biologist, Wis Conserv Dept, 59-61; assoc prof, 61-66, assoc dean, Col Natural Resources, 70-77, PROF WILDLIFE RESOURCES, UTAH STATE UNIV, 66-, ASSOC DEAN, COL NATURAL RESOURCES, 77- *Concurrent Pos:* Dir Desert Biome, US-Int Biol Prog & mem US Exec Comt, Int Biol Prog, 71-74; mem comt predator control, President's Coun Environ Qual, 71. *Honors & Awards:* Award, Wildlife Soc, 68. *Mem:* Ecol Soc Am; Am Soc Mammal; Wildlife Soc; Am Inst Biol Sci; Cooper Ornith Soc. *Res:* Vertebrate population ecology, especially population dynamics, limiting factors and homeostatic mechanisms; wildlife management; conservation of natural resources; systems ecology. *Mailing Add:* Col of Natural Resources Utah State Univ Logan UT 84321

WAGNER, FREDERICK WILLIAM, b Erie, Pa, Feb 4, 40; m 65. BIOCHEMISTRY. *Educ:* Southwest Tex State Col, BSc, 62; Tex A&M Univ, PhD(biochem), 66. *Prof Exp:* US Air Force res assoc, Brooks AFB, 66-67; res fel biochem & biophys, Tex A&M Univ, 67-68; asst prof biochem & nutrit, 68-73, assoc prof, 73-80, PROF, DEPT AGR BIOCHEM, UNIV NEBR-LINCOLN, 80- *Concurrent Pos:* Vis prof, Biophys Res Lab, Med Sch, Harvard Univ, Boston, 81-82. *Res:* Structure and function of proteins with special emphasis on proteolytic enzymes. *Mailing Add:* Lab Agr Biochem Univ of Nebr Lincoln NE 68583

WAGNER, GEORGE HOYT, b Mulberry, Ark, Dec 28, 14; m 39; c 3. GEOLOGY. *Educ:* Univ Ark, BS, 37, MS, 74; Univ Iowa, MS, 39, PhD(phys chem), 41. *Prof Exp:* Chemist, Univ Ark, 35-37; asst chem, Univ Iowa, 37-41; res chemist, Linde Div, Union Carbide Corp, 41-47, head div phys chem, 47-51, asst to supt, 51-53, res supvr, 53-55, mgr res, 55-59, dir, 59-64, mgr develop, 64-65, dir res, mining & metals div, 65-66, vpres, 66-70, ferroalloy div, 70-71; CONSULT RES & DEVELOP, 71- *Concurrent Pos:* Adj prof, Univ Ark, 74- *Honors & Awards:* Schoellkopf Medal, Am Chem Soc, 60. *Mem:* Am Chem Soc; Geol Soc Am; AAAS. *Res:* Synthetic lubricants; corrosion inhibition; organometallics; geochemistry and economic geology. *Mailing Add:* Box 144 Fayetteville AR 72702

WAGNER, GEORGE JOSEPH, b Buffalo, NY, Sept 15, 43; m 70; c 3. PLANT PHYSIOLOGY, ENVIRONMENTAL SCIENCES, GENERAL. *Educ:* State Univ NY Buffalo, BA, 70, MA, 71, PhD(biol), 74. *Prof Exp:* res assoc, 74-77, asst scientist, 77-79, ASSOC SCIENTIST PLANT BIOCHEM, BROOKHAVEN NAT LAB, 79- *Mem:* Am Soc Plant Physiologists; AAAS; Phytochem Soc NAm; Soc Environ Geochem & Health. *Res:* Study of the physiology and biochemistry of the mature plant cell vacuole, the mechanisms of solute accumulation and the fate of heavy metals in plants. *Mailing Add:* Biol Div Brookhaven Nat Lab Upton NY 11973

WAGNER, GEORGE RICHARD, b Chicago, Ill, Nov 12, 33; m 54; c 3. SOLID STATE PHYSICS. *Educ:* Univ Ill, Urbana, BS, 60; Carnegie-Mellon Univ, MS, 62, PhD(physics), 65. *Prof Exp:* Sr engr, 65-73, FEL SCIENTIST PHYSICS, RES & DEVELOP CTR, WESTINGHOUSE ELEC CORP, 73- *Mem:* Am Phys Soc. *Res:* Alternating current losses, stability and properties which characterize superconducting wires for use in magnets and machines. *Mailing Add:* Res & Develop Ctr Westinghouse Elec Corp Pittsburgh PA 15235

WAGNER, GERALD GALE, b Plainview, Tex, June 3, 41; m 62; c 2. IMMUNOLOGY. *Educ:* Tex Tech Col, BS, 63; Univ Kans, MA, 65, PhD, 68. *Prof Exp:* Microbiologist, Immunol Div, Plum Island Animal Dis Lab, 68-71, microbiologist, Coop Res Div, EAfrican Vet Res Orgn, USDA, 71-77; ASSOC PROF VET MICROBIOL & PARASITOL, TEX A&M UNIV, 77- *Concurrent Pos:* Nat Acad Sci-Agr Res Serv res fel, Plum Island Animal Dis Lab, 68-70. *Mem:* Fedn Am Soc Exp Biol; Am Soc Microbiol; Am Asn Immunol; Am Soc Parasitol. *Res:* Pathogenesis of bacterial and protozoal infections in domestic animals; cellular effector mechanisms of immunity. *Mailing Add:* Dept of Vet Microbiol & Parasitol Tex A&M Univ College Station TX 77843

WAGNER, GERALD ROY, b Evansville, Ind, Feb 14, 28; m 50; c 2. ORGANIC CHEMISTRY, GEOLOGY. *Educ:* Mt Union Col, BS, 50; Univ Ark, MS, 52. *Prof Exp:* Res chemist, Com Solvents Corp, NY, 52-53, Olin Mathieson Chem Corp, 53-55 & Nat Aniline Div, Allied Chem Corp, 55-61; res chemist, 61-66, asst prof, 66, head dept, 66-72, PROF CHEM, ERIE COMMUNITY COL, 66- *Mem:* Am Chem Soc; Nat Asn Geol Teachers; Am Inst Chemists. *Res:* Geological education; chemical education. *Mailing Add:* Dept of Chem Erie Community Col Buffalo NY 14221

WAGNER, HANS, b July 19, 32; US citizen. ORGANIC CHEMISTRY. *Educ:* Univ Iowa, BS, 55; Pa State Univ, PhD(chem), 59. *Prof Exp:* Sr res investr, 59-70, GROUP LEADER CHEM, G D SEARLE & CO, 70- *Mem:* Am Chem Soc. *Res:* Dipolar cycloadditions; mesoionic compounds; heterocyclic azido compounds. *Mailing Add:* Chem Res G D Searle & Co Box 5110 Chicago IL 60680

WAGNER, HARRY HENRY, b San Diego, Calif, Jan 10, 33; m 56; c 3. FISH BIOLOGY, ECOLOGY. *Educ:* Humboldt State Col, BS, 55; Ore State Univ, MS, 59, PhD(fisheries), 70. *Prof Exp:* Fishery res biologist & physiol ecologist, 59-68, fishery res coordr, 69-73, res supvr, 73-78, ASST CHIEF FISHERIES DIV, ORE DEPT FISH & WILDLIFE, 79- *Concurrent Pos:* Courtesy assoc prof, Ore State Univ, 59- *Mem:* Am Fisheries Soc; Am Inst Fishery Res Biol. *Res:* Parr-smolt transformation of anadromous salmonids. *Mailing Add:* Ore Dept Fish & Wildlife 506 SW Mill St PO Box 3503 Portland OR 97208

WAGNER, HARRY MAHLON, b Iola, Kans, June 1, 24; m 44; c 5. MATHEMATICS. *Educ:* Naval Postgrad Sch, BS, 54; Kans State Teachers Col, MS, 64; Univ Ark, EdD(higher educ), 69. *Prof Exp:* Instr math, John Brown Univ, 64-67; res grad asst psychol, Univ Ark, 67-69; asst prof, 69-72, ASSOC PROF MATH, CAMERON UNIV, 72- *Mem:* Math Asn Am. *Mailing Add:* Dept of Math Cameron Univ Lawton OK 73505

WAGNER, HARVEY ARTHUR, b Ann Arbor, Mich, Jan 2, 05; m 29. ENGINEERING. *Educ:* Univ Mich, BS, 27; Lawrence Inst Technol, DEng, 69. *Prof Exp:* Mem staff, Procter & Gamble Co, 27-28; mem staff, Detroit Edison Co, 28-69, exec vpres, 69-70; CONSULT ENGR, 70-; VPRES & DIR, OVERSEAS ADV ASSOCS, INC, 74- *Concurrent Pos:* Trustee, Nat Sanit Found, 65- *Honors & Awards:* Cert Pub Serv, Fed Power Comn, 64; Sesquicentennial Award as Outstanding Exec & Nuclear Power Consult, Univ Mich, 67. *Mem:* Nat Acad Eng; fel Am Soc Mech Engrs; fel Am Nuclear Soc. *Mailing Add:* Overseas Adv Assocs Inc 1300 Washington Blvd Detroit MI 48226

WAGNER, HENRY GEORGE, b Washington, DC, Sept 13, 17; m 45; c 3. NEUROSCIENCES, AEROSPACE MEDICINE. *Educ:* George Washington Univ, AB, 39, MD, 42; Univ Pa, cert ophthal, 49. *Prof Exp:* Intern, Naval Hosp, Brooklyn, NY, 42-43, med officer, Naval Med Sch, Md, 43, flight surgeon, Sch Aviation Med, Naval Air Sta, Fla, 43-44, flight surgeon, Naval Air Base, Guam, 44-45, flight surgeon, Naval Air Sta, Tex, 45-46, asst supt aeromed equip lab, Naval Air Exp Sta, Pa, 46-48, med res investr, Naval Med Res Inst, Md, 51-54, sr med officer, USS Valley Forge, 54-56, head physiol div, Naval Med Res Inst, 56-60, cmndg officer, 60-61, exec officer, 61-64, actg dir physiol sci dept, 61-64, dir aerospace crew equip lab, Naval Air Eng Ctr, Pa, 64-66; dir intramural res, 66-74, CHIEF SECT NEUROANAL INTERACTIONS, LAB NEUROPHYSIOL, NAT INST NEUROL, COMMUNICATIVE DIS & STROKE, 74- *Concurrent Pos:* Fel biophys, Johns Hopkins Univ, 49-51, hon prof, 58-64; mem comt vision, hearing & bioacoust, Nat Acad Sci-Nat Res Coun; vis prof ophthal, Duke Univ, 76- *Mem:* AAAS; Am Physiol Soc; Soc Neurosci; Am Col Prev Med; AMA. *Res:* Neuroscience of the visual system; ophthalmology. *Mailing Add:* Nat Inst of Neurol Commun Dis & Stroke Bethesda MD 20205

WAGNER, HENRY N, JR, b Baltimore, Md, May 12, 27; m 51; c 4. INTERNAL MEDICINE, NUCLEAR MEDICINE. *Educ:* Johns Hopkins Univ, AB, 48, MD, 52. *Hon Degrees:* LLD, Washington Col. *Prof Exp:* From asst prof med & radiol, Sch Med to assoc prof med, radiol & radiol sci, 59-67, assoc prof med, 67-68, PROF RADIOL SCI & RADIOL, SCH MED & SCH HYG & PUB HEALTH, JOHNS HOPKINS UNIV, 67-, PROF MED, 68-, DIR, DIV NUCLEAR MED, 65-, DIR, DIV RADIATION HEALTH SCI, 77- *Honors & Awards:* George Hevesy Medal, 76. *Mem:* Am Fedn Clin Res; Asn Am Physicians; Am Soc Clin Invest; Soc Nuclear Med (past pres); World Fedn Nuclear Med & Biol (past pres). *Mailing Add:* Div of Radiation Health Sci Sch of Hyg & Pub Health Baltimore MD 21205

WAGNER, HERMAN BLOCK, physical chemistry, see previous edition

WAGNER, HERMAN LEON, b New York, NY, Mar 21, 21; wid; c 1. POLYMER CHEMISTRY. *Educ:* City Col, New York, BS, 42; Polytech Inst Brooklyn, MS, 46; Cornell Univ, PhD(chem), 50. *Concurrent Pos:* Chemist, SAM Labs, Manhattan Proj, Columbia Univ, 42-46; res assoc, Cornell Univ, 50-51; phys chemist, E I du Pont de Nemours & Co, 51-55, M W Kellog Co, 55-57 & Celanese Corp Am, 57-68; RES CHEMIST, NAT BUR STANDARDS, 68- *Mem:* Am Chem Soc. *Res:* Physical chemistry of high polymers; dilute solution properties; characterization of high polymers; thermal analysis; composites; melt rheology; fibers; gel permeation chromatography; correlation of molecular structure with physical properties; low shear viscosity of ultra high molecular weight polyethylene solutions. *Mailing Add:* Nat Bur of Standards Washington DC 20234

WAGNER, J(AMES) F(RANCIS), b Waterbury, Conn, Oct 12, 22; m 49; c 7. MECHANICAL ENGINEERING. *Educ:* Rensselaer Polytech Inst, BME, 42; Northwestern Technol Inst, MS, 49. *Prof Exp:* From res engr to sr res engr, 46-69, sect supvr, 69-70, res assoc, 70-78, SR RES ASSOC, GULF RES & DEVELOP CO, 78- *Mem:* Soc Automotive Engrs. *Res:* Exhaust emissions and related fuel and lubricant behavior in current and possible future automotive powerplants. *Mailing Add:* Gulf Res & Develop Co PO Drawer 2038 Pittsburgh PA 15230

WAGNER, JAMES BRUCE, JR, b Hampton, Va, July 28, 27; m 51; c 3. MATERIALS SCIENCE. *Educ:* Univ Va, BS, 50, PhD(chem), 55. *Prof Exp:* Fel metall, Mass Inst Technol, 54-56; asst prof, Pa State Univ, 56-58 & Yale Univ, 58-62; assoc prof, 62-65, prof mat sci, Northwestern Univ, 65-77, dir, Mat Res Ctr, 72-76; PROF, CTR SOLID STATE SCI, ARIZ STATE UNIV, 77-, DIR, 80- *Concurrent Pos:* Ford Found resident engr pract, Semiconductor Prod Div, Motorola, Inc, Ariz, 68-69. *Mem:* Am Phys Soc; Am Inst Mining, Metall & Petrol Eng; Electrochem Soc (vpres, 80-83). *Res:* Oxidation of metals; thermodynamics and transport properties of compound semiconductors; solid electrolytes. *Mailing Add:* Ctr Solid State Sci Ariz State Univ Tempe AZ 85281

WAGNER, JEAMES ARTHUR, b New Praque, Minn, Sept 5, 44; m 79; c 1. ENVIRONMENTAL PHYSIOLOGY, CARDIORESPIRATORY PHYSIOLOGY. *Educ:* St Johns Univ, BSc, 66; Univ SDak, MA, 67; Univ Western Ont, 70. *Prof Exp:* Asst prof physiol, Ind Univ, Bloomington, 69-71; res asst, 71-80, RES ASSOC PHYSIOL, UNIV CALIF, SANTA BARBARA, 80- *Concurrent Pos:* Prog chmn, Int Symposium, Univ Calif, Santa Barbara, 77; lectr, Westmont Col, 77, Univ Calif, Santa Barbara, 71-; prin investr, NIH, 79- *Mem:* AAAS; Am Col Sports Med; Am Physiol Soc; Fedn Am Scientists; NY Acad Sci. *Res:* Environmental and cardiorespiratory physiology, specifically physiological response differences to environmental stressors that are related to age and gender; physiological responses to heat, cold, altitude, air pollution and exercise stressors. *Mailing Add:* Inst Environ Stress Univ Calif Santa Barbara CA 93106

WAGNER, JOHN ALEXANDER, b Kansas City, Mo, Feb 9, 35; m 63; c 2. ENTOMOLOGY. *Educ:* Northwestern Univ, BS, 57, MS, 59, PhD(biol), 62. *Prof Exp:* mem fac, 62-80, PROF BIOL & SCI, KENDALL COL, 80- *Concurrent Pos:* Collabr & consult, Encycl Britannica Films, 62-75; res assoc, Dept Biol Sci, Northwestern Univ, 63-78; mem, Environ Studies Group, Alfred Benesch & Co, Consult Engrs, 74-78; res assoc, Dept of Zool, Div

Insects, Field Mus Natural Hist. *Mem:* Am Inst Biol Sci; Soc Syst Zool; Coleopterists Soc; Nature Conservancy; AAAS. *Res:* Coleoptera, family Pselaphidae, especially nearctic and neotropics. *Mailing Add:* Dept of Biol Kendall Col Evanston IL 60201

WAGNER, JOHN EDWARD, b Springfield, Mo, Oct 11, 27; m 50; c 2. CIVIL ENGINEERING, EARTH SCIENCES. *Educ:* US Mil Acad, BS, 50; Univ Ill, MS, 59, PhD(civil eng), 61; George Washington Univ, MBA, 80. *Prof Exp:* Instr, US Army Eng Sch, Ft Belvoir, Va, 52-53, asst proj engr, Eng Dist, Little Rock, Ark, 53-54, co comdr & staff engr, VII Corps, Europe, 55-58, res engr soil mech, Waterways Exp Sta, Miss, 60-63, staff engr adv, Army Repub Vietnam, 63, dep dir, Nuclear Cratering Group, Lawrence Radiation Labs, Calif, 64-65, chief engr br, Test Command, Defense Atomic Support Agency, NMex, 65-67, comdr & dir, Cold Regions Res & Eng Lab, NH, 67-70, staff engr, First Field Force, Vietnam, 70-71, comdr & dir, Engr Topographic Labs, Ft Belvoir, Va, 71-54, dep dir res, Off Dept Chief Staff, Res Develop & Acquisitions, 74-77, asst for conserv, Off Secy Defense, 77-79, dep dir eng, NAtlantic Div, Corps Engrs, 79-80; EXEC SECY, UN NAT COMT ROCK MECH & TUNNELING TECHNOL, NAT ACAD SCI, WASHINGTON, DC, 81- *Mem:* Sigma Xi; fel Am Soc Civil Engrs; Nat Soc Prof Engrs; Soc Mil Engrs; Am Soc Photogrammetry. *Res:* Soil mechanics especially arching of soils and slope stability; all areas of Army funded research; cold regions research and topographic sciences. *Mailing Add:* 26 S Park Dr Arlington VA 22204

WAGNER, JOHN GARNET, b Weston, Ont, Mar 28, 21; m 46. PHARMACEUTICAL CHEMISTRY, ORGANIC CHEMISTRY. *Educ:* Univ Toronto, PhmB, 47; Univ Sask, BSP, 48, BA, 49; Ohio State Univ, PhD(pharmaceut chem), 52. *Prof Exp:* Instr pharmaceut chem, Ohio State Univ, 51-52, asst prof, 52-53; res scientist, Upjohn Co, Mich, 53-56, sect head, 56-63, sr res scientist, 63-68; asst dir res & develop, Pharm Serv, Univ Hosp, 68-72, PROF PHARM, COL PHARM, UNIV MICH, ANN ARBOR, 68-, MEM STAFF, UPJOHN CTR CLIN PHARMACOL, 73- *Honors & Awards:* Ebert Prize, Am Pharmaceut Asn, 61; Høst-Madsen Medal, Int Pharmaceut Fedn, 72; Propter Merita Medal, Czech Med Soc, 74. *Mem:* AAAS; Am Pharmaceut Asn; Am Fedn Clin Res; Am Soc Clin Pharmacol & Therapeut; Am Soc Pharmacol & Exp Therapeut. *Res:* Pharmacokinetics and biopharmaceutics; absorption, metabolism and excretion of drugs in man. *Mailing Add:* Upjohn Ctr for Clin Pharmacol Univ of Mich Ann Arbor MI 48109

WAGNER, JOHN GEORGE, b Bowmansville, NY, July 9, 42; m 67; c 3. EXPERIMENTAL MECHANICS, TECHNICAL MANAGEMENT. *Educ:* State Univ NY Buffalo, BS, 67; Univ Calif, Berkeley, MS, 65; Brown Univ, PhD(solid mech), 69. *Prof Exp:* Asst prof mech eng, Univ Pittsburgh, 69-75; res engr optical recording, 76-80, PROG LEADER POWDER TECHNOL, PHILIPS LAB, NAM PHILIPS CORP, 80- *Concurrent Pos:* Consult, various law firms, 72-75; prin investr conveyor belt transport anal, US Bur Mines, 75; vis engr, Res Lab, US Steel, 75; vis scientist, Natuurkundig Lab, Neth, 80-81. *Mem:* Am Soc Mech Engrs; Am Soc Metals; Am Powder Metall Inst; Sigma Xi; Soc Exp Stress Anal. *Res:* Theoretical and experimental mechanics of flow and deformation of solid and powdered materials with particular emphasis on constitutive and void behavior. *Mailing Add:* 345 Scarborough Rd Briarcliff Manor NY 10510

WAGNER, JOSEPH EDWARD, b Dubuque, Iowa, July 29, 38; m 59; c 4. LABORATORY ANIMAL SCIENCE, PATHOLOGY OF RESEARCH ANIMALS. *Educ:* Iowa State Univ, DVM, 63; Tulane Univ, MPH, 64; Univ Ill, Urbana, PhD, 67. *Prof Exp:* PROF VET MED, COL VET MED, UNIV MO-COLUMBIA, 69- *Concurrent Pos:* Mem, Animal Resources Adv Comt, Div Res Resources, NIH, 80- *Mem:* Am Vet Med Asn; Am Asn Lab Animal Sci; Am Col Lab Animal Med; Am Soc Lab Animal Practitioners; NY Acad Sci. *Res:* Pathogenesis and etiology of naturally occurring diseases of animals used in human health related research. *Mailing Add:* Col Vet Med Univ Mo Columbia MO 65211

WAGNER, KENNETH A, b Union City, Ind, Nov 30, 19; m 45. BOTANY. *Educ:* DePauw Univ, AB, 41, AM, 46; Univ Mich, PhD, 51. *Prof Exp:* Instr, Univ Tenn, 47-49; asst prof, Fla State Univ, 49-54; prof & head dept biol, Norfolk Div, Col William & Mary, 54-59; botanist & sci coordr, Powell Lab Div, Carolina Biol Supply Co, 59-66; prof biol, NC Wesleyan Col, 66-69; PROF BIOL, FERRIS STATE COL, 69- *Concurrent Pos:* Consult, Army Air Force Trop Test Detachment, Panama, 44; partic, Fla State Archaeol Exped, Cuba, 53; mem, Nat Wildlife Fedn. *Mem:* Nat Asn Biol Teachers; Am Inst Biol Sci. *Res:* North American liverworts; cypress; east coast salt marshes; desert ecology. *Mailing Add:* Dept Biol Ferris State Col Big Rapids MI 49307

WAGNER, KIT KERN, b Chickasha, Okla, Nov 13, 47; m 70. DYNAMIC METEOROLOGY, AIR POLLUTION METEOROLOGY. *Educ:* Univ Okla, BS, 70, MS, 71, PhD(meteorol), 75. *Prof Exp:* Res asst meteorol, Univ Okla Res Inst, 70-75; meteorologist, Nat Severe Storm Lab, Nat Oceanic & Atmospheric Admin, 75; asst prof meteorol, Univ Calif, Davis, 75-80; AIR POLLUTION RES SPECIALIST, CALIF AIR RESOURCES BD, 81- *Mem:* Am Meteorol Soc. *Res:* Mesoscale dynamic meteorology and air pollution modeling. *Mailing Add:* Calif Air Resources Bd PO Box 2815 Sacramento CA 95812

WAGNER, LAWRENCE CARL, b Campbellsport, Wis, Dec 28, 46. HIGH TEMPERATURE CHEMISTRY. *Educ:* Marquette Univ, BS, 68; Purdue Univ, PhD(chem), 74. *Prof Exp:* appointee chem div, Argonne Nat Lab, 74-76; mem tech staff, 76-79, MGR, DEVICE ANAL LAB, TEXAS INSTRUMENTS, 79- *Mem:* Am Chem Soc; Am Soc Mass Spectrometry; Sigma Xi. *Res:* High temperature mass spectrometry; photoelectron spectrometry; diffusion controlled processes; scanning electron microscopy; semiconductor failure analysis. *Mailing Add:* MS 074 PO Box 225012 Dallas TX 75265

WAGNER, MARTIN GERALD, b New York, NY, Mar 19, 42; m 65; c 3. CHEMICAL ENGINEERING, RHEOLOGY. *Educ:* Cooper Union, BChE, 62; Northwestern Univ, Evanston, MS, 64, PhD(chem eng), 67. *Prof Exp:* RES ASSOC, RES & DEVELOP LAB, POLYMER PROD DEPT, E I DU PONT DE NEMOURS & CO, INC, 66- *Mem:* AAAS; Am Inst Chem Engrs; Soc Rheol; Am Chem Soc. *Res:* Polymer processing; polymerization technology. *Mailing Add:* Elastomer Chem Dept Exp Sta Wilmington DE 19898

WAGNER, MARTIN JAMES, b Independence, Kans, Oct 4, 31; m 53; c 3. BIOCHEMISTRY, SCIENCE EDUCATION. *Educ:* Kans State Col Pittsburg, BS, 54; Ind Univ, PhD(biochem), 58. *Prof Exp:* Asst chem, Ind Univ, 54-58; from asst prof to assoc prof, 58-63, PROF BIOCHEM, BAYLOR COL DENT, 63-, CHMN DEPT, 58- *Mem:* Am Chem Soc; Int Asn Dent Res; Sigma Xi; Am Asn Dent Schs; Nutrit Today Soc. *Res:* Intermediary metabolism of inorganic fluoride ion; trace element nutrition; toxicology of trace elements; microcomputer applications in education. *Mailing Add:* Dept of Biochem Baylor Col of Dent Dallas TX 75226

WAGNER, MELVIN PETER, b Nebr, Nov 16, 26; m 53; c 5. ORGANIC CHEMISTRY, POLYMER CHEMISTRY. *Educ:* Creighton Univ, BS, 49, MS, 52; Univ Akron, PhD(polymer chem), 60. *Prof Exp:* Res chemist, 52-60, sr res chemist, 60-64, supvr rubber chem res, 64-78, RES SCIENTIST, BARBERTON LAB, CHEM DIV, PPG INDUSTS, 78- *Mem:* Am Chem Soc. *Res:* High polymers; rubber reinforcement; vulcanization. *Mailing Add:* PPG Industs PO Box 31 Barberton OH 44203

WAGNER, MORRIS, b Chicago, Ill, Aug 6, 17; m 47; c 4. BACTERIOLOGY, IMMUNOLOGY. *Educ:* Cornell Univ, BS, 41; Univ Notre Dame, MS, 46; Purdue Univ, PhD, 66. *Prof Exp:* Asst, 41-43, bacteriologist, Lobund Labs, 43-46, from instr to assoc prof, Univ, 46-69, PROF MICROBIOL & ASST CHMN DEPT, UNIV NOTRE DAME, 69-, RES SCIENTIST, LOBUND LAB, 41-; ADJ PROF MICROBIOL, SCH MED, IND UNIV, 79- *Concurrent Pos:* NSF sci fac fel, 63; mem, Subcomt Stand Gnotobiotics, Nat Acad Sci. *Mem:* Am Soc Microbiol; Asn Gnotobiotics; Am Soc Dent Children; Am Asn Lab Animal Sci. *Res:* Gnotobiotics; experimental dental caries; defined intestinal flora. *Mailing Add:* Dept of Microbiol Univ of Notre Dame Notre Dame IN 46556

WAGNER, NEAL RICHARD, b Topeka, Kans, May 4, 40; m 71. TOPOLOGY. *Educ:* Univ Kans, AB, 62; Univ Ill, Urbana-Champaign, AM, 64, PhD(math), 70. *Prof Exp:* Asst prof math, Univ Tex, El Paso, 69-76, assoc prof, 76-79; CONSULT MODERN CRYPTOGRAPHY, 81- *Concurrent Pos:* Vis assoc prof comput sci, Univ Houston, Tex, 79-81 & Drexel Univ, Philadelphia, 81- *Mem:* Am Math Soc; Math Asn Am. *Res:* Computer sciences in general; software systems; theory; real-time simulation of NASA space shuttle. *Mailing Add:* Math Sci Dept Drexel Univ Philadelphia PA 19104

WAGNER, NORMAN KEITH, b Longview, Wash, Oct 3, 32; m 54; c 2. MICROMETEOROLOGY. *Educ:* Univ Wash, BS, 54, MS, 56; Univ Hawaii, PhD(meteorol), 66. *Prof Exp:* Instr meteorol, Univ Tex, 56-57 & 58-63, res meteorologist, 57-58; asst prof meteorol, Univ Hawaii, 65, asst researcher, 65-66; asst prof, 66-70, dir, Atmospheric Sci Group, 72-76, ASSOC PROF METEOROL, UNIV TEX, AUSTIN, 70- *Mem:* Am Meteorol Soc. *Res:* Meteorological instrumentation; micrometeorology; atmospheric boundary layer. *Mailing Add:* Atmospheric Sci Group Univ of Tex Austin TX 78712

WAGNER, PATRICIA ANTHONY, b Kirksville, Mo, Nov 26, 37; m 59; c 2. NUTRITIONAL SCIENCES. *Educ:* Northeast Mo State Teachers Col, BS, 59; Univ Wis-Madison, MS, 73, PhD(nutrit sci, biochem), 75. *Prof Exp:* Teacher home econ, Mo Pub Sch Syst, 59-69; res asst & NIH trainee nutrit sci, Univ Wis-Madison, 69-75; asst prof, 75-80, ASSOC PROF HUMAN NUTRIT, UNIV FLA, 80- *Concurrent Pos:* Prin investr, NIH-Nat Inst Aging res grant, 77-80; co-prin investr, USDA-Sci & Educ Admin grant, 78-81; prin investr, Area Agency Aging, Older Am Nutrit Proj, 81. *Mem:* Sigma Xi. *Res:* Human nutrition; trace element requirements and metabolism; community nutritional assessment; nutrition and aging. *Mailing Add:* 1510 NW 35th Terrace Gainesville FL 32605

WAGNER, PAUL, b Troy, NY, Dec 27, 23; m 62; c 2. PHYSICAL CHEMISTRY. *Educ:* State Univ NY, AB, 47, AM, 48; Univ Rochester, PhD(phys chem), 52. *Prof Exp:* Asst, Cornell Univ, 48 & Univ Rochester, 49-50; res scientist, Lewis Flight Propulsion Lab, Nat Adv Comt Aeronaut, 52-56; MEM STAFF, LOS ALAMOS NAT LAB, UNIV CALIF, 56- *Concurrent Pos:* Mem bd govrs & secy, Int Thermal Expansion comt, Int Thermal Conductivity Conf. *Mem:* Am Soc Metals; Am Soc Testing & Mat; Sigma Xi. *Res:* All aspects of materials research and development for high temperature reactor application, including advanced high temperature nuclear fuels, chemical reactions and kinetics relating to underground coal gasification, environmental aspects of coal and oil shale extraction and utilization; water pollution assessment and control. *Mailing Add:* Los Alamos Nat Lab MS-734 Univ Calif Los Alamos NM 87545

WAGNER, PETER EWING, b Ann Arbor, Mich, July 4, 29; m 51; c 2. PHYSICS, ENVIRONMENTAL ENGINEERING. *Educ:* Univ Calif, AB, 50, PhD(physics), 56. *Prof Exp:* Asst, Univ Calif, 50-56; physicist, Westinghouse Res Labs, 56-59; from assoc prof to prof elec eng, Johns Hopkins Univ, 59-73; prof & dir, Ctr Environ & Estuarine Studies, Univ Md, 73-80; PROF PHYSICS, UNIV ALA, 80- *Concurrent Pos:* Consult, Radiation Lab & Carlyle Barton Lab, Johns Hopkins Univ, 59-65, Westinghouse Elec Corp, 59-66, Am Cyanamid Co, 64-70 & US Army, 69-; Guggenheim fel, 66-67; physicist, Appl Physics Lab, Johns Hopkins Univ, 71; spec proj engr, State of Md, 71-72; exec secy, Md Power Plant Siting Adv Comt, 72- *Mem:* AAAS; Am Phys Soc. *Res:* Solid state physics; paramagnetic resonance; microwave acoustics; static electrification; environmental measurements. *Mailing Add:* Univ Ala Box 1247 West Sta Huntsville AL 35807

WAGNER, PETER J, b Chicago, Ill, Dec 25, 38; m 63; c 6. PHYSICAL ORGANIC CHEMISTRY, PHOTOCHEMISTRY. *Educ:* Loyola Univ, Ill, BS, 60; Columbia Univ, MA, 61, PhD(chem), 63. *Prof Exp:* Res assoc chem, Columbia Univ, 63-64; NSF fel, Calif Inst Technol, 64-65; from asst prof to assoc prof, 65-70, PROF CHEM, MICH STATE UNIV, 70- *Concurrent Pos:* Sloan fel, 68-70; NSF sr fel, Univ Calif, Los Angeles, 71-72; consult, Hercules, Inc, 73-77; assoc ed, J Am Chem Soc, 75- *Mem:* Sigma Xi; Am Chem Soc. *Res:* Mechanisms of free radical and photochemical reactions; electronic energy transfer; spectroscopy of excited states. *Mailing Add:* Dept of Chem Col of Natural Sci Mich State Univ East Lansing MI 48823

WAGNER, RAYMOND LEE, b Kansas City, Mo, Aug 21, 46; m 69; c 1. THEORETICAL ASTROPHYSICS, ASTRONOMY. *Educ:* Rice Univ, BA, 68; Univ Tex, Austin, PhD(astron), 72. *Prof Exp:* Asst prof astron, Univ Wash, 72-74, res assoc, 73-74; asst prof astron & physics, La State Univ, Baton Rouge, 74-80; WITH FORD AEROSPACE, 80- *Concurrent Pos:* NSF res grant, 75- *Mem:* Am Astron Soc; AAAS; Sigma Xi; Am Asn Univ Prof. *Res:* Stellar structure and evolution; stellar stability; nucleosynthesis; peculiar stars. *Mailing Add:* 2610 Black Diamond Trail Colorado Springs CO 80918

WAGNER, RICHARD CARL, b Orange, NJ, Sept 25, 41. MATHEMATICS. *Educ:* Rutgers Univ, AB, 63; Univ Chicago, MS, 64, PhD(math), 68. *Prof Exp:* From asst prof to assoc prof, 68-79, PROF MATH, FAIRLEIGH DICKINSON UNIV, 79- *Mem:* Asn Comput Mach; Am Math Soc; Math Asn Am; London Math Soc. *Res:* Quadratic forms; algebraic k-theory. *Mailing Add:* Dept of Math Fairleigh Dickinson Univ Madison NJ 07940

WAGNER, RICHARD JOHN, b Barnesville, Minn, Jan 13, 36; m 58; c 2. SOLID STATE PHYSICS. *Educ:* St John's Univ, Minn, BS, 58; Univ Calif, Los Angeles, MS, 60, PhD(physics), 66. *Prof Exp:* Mem tech staff eng, 58-68, staff physicist, 68-69, sr tech staff asst physics, 69-71, sr staff physicist, 71-75, sr scientist, 75-78, dept mgr, Receiver Dept, 78-80, ASST LAB MGR, MICROWAVE SYSTS LAB, HUGHES AIRCRAFT CO, 80- *Concurrent Pos:* Teaching asst, Univ Calif, Los Angeles, 61-63, res asst, 63-66, asst res physicist, 66-67. *Mem:* Am Phys Soc. *Res:* Solid state physics, particularly as applicable to solid state microwave devices. *Mailing Add:* Radar Microwave Lab Hughes Aircraft Co Culver City CA 90230

WAGNER, RICHARD JOHN, b New Ulm, Minn, Dec 3, 32; m 53; c 4. MATHEMATICAL PHYSICS. *Educ:* Univ Minn, BA, 53, MS, 55; Rice Univ, PhD(physics), 58. *Prof Exp:* Mem tech staff theoret physics, Ramo-Wooldridge Corp, 58-59 & TRW Space Tech Labs, 59-61, sect head quantum theory, 62-65, sect head, TRW Systs, 65-66, SECT HEAD WAVE PROPAGATION, TRW SYSTS, 66- *Concurrent Pos:* Cedric K Ferguson Medal, Am Inst Mining, Metall & Petrol Engrs, 58. *Mem:* Am Phys Soc. *Res:* Scattering theory; missile and space vehicle re-entry physics; radio propagation; electromagnetic diffraction theory; radar concealment; underwater acoustics; statistical scattering theory; remote sensing; laser propagation. *Mailing Add:* Res Group Bldg R1-1196 TRW Systs One Space Park Redondo Beach CA 90278

WAGNER, RICHARD LLOYD, b Manitowoc, Wis, May 30, 34; m 56; c 5. POLYMER CHEMISTRY, PHOTOCHEMISTRY. *Educ:* Univ Wis-Madison, BS, 60. *Prof Exp:* Chemist, Hercules Res Ctr, 60-65, res chemist & proj leader mat sci & appl res, 66-71, sr venture analyst, New Enterprise Dept, 71-73, supvr mkt serv, 73-75, mgr eng & develop, Graphic Systs Div, Org Dept, 75-78, MGR, DEVELOP DEPT, HERCULES INC, 78- *Mem:* Am Chem Soc. *Res:* Applications research and product development work related to uses of company products in graphic arts areas and other commercially important areas; product and market development with photochemical systems in graphic arts uses; chemical and equipment systems for graphic arts products involving photopolymers. *Mailing Add:* 2319 Wynnwood Rd Wilmington DE 19810

WAGNER, RICHARD LORRAINE, JR, b Oklahoma City, Okla, July 7, 36; m 58; c 3. PHYSICS, MATHEMATICS. *Educ:* Williams Col, BA, 58; Univ Utah, PhD(physics), 63. *Prof Exp:* Student teacher & res asst physics, Univ Utah, 58-63; physics & defense res, Lawrence Livermore Lab, 63-75, assoc dir, 76-81; ASST SECY DEFENSE, ATOMIC ENERGY, DEPT DEFENSE, 81- *Concurrent Pos:* Mem, Advan Res Projs Agency-Defense Nuclear Agency Long Range Res & Develop Panel, 73-74, Joint Strategic Target Planning Staff Sci Adv Group, Joint Chiefs of Staff, Offutt AFB, Nebr, 73-79, US Army Sci Adv Panel, 76-78 & Defense Sci Bd, Off Under Secy Defense, 79- *Mem:* Am Phys Soc. *Res:* Cosmic rays; high energy physics; nuclear explosive design; weapons effects; antiballistic missile system studies. *Mailing Add:* Asst Secy Defense The Pentagon Rm 3E 1074 Washington DC 20301

WAGNER, RICHARD S(IEGFRIED), b Wels, Austria, July 3, 25; m 57; c 4. MATERIALS SCIENCE. *Educ:* Vienna Tech Univ, MS, 51; Harvard Univ, MS, 57, PhD(appl physics), 59. *Prof Exp:* MEM TECH STAFF MAT SCI, BELL TEL LABS, 59-, DEPT HEAD, 70- *Honors & Awards:* C Mathewson Gold Medal, Am Inst Mining, Metall & Petrol Engrs, 66. *Mem:* AAAS; Am Inst Mining, Metall & Petrol Engrs; Am Phys Soc. *Res:* Physical metallurgy; solidification; crystal growth; defects in solids; vapor phase reactions; semiconductor device and magnetic bubble device technology development. *Mailing Add:* Bell Tel Labs Rm 2D-344 Murray Hill NJ 07974

WAGNER, ROBERT ALAN, b Philadelphia, Pa, Mar 25, 41; m 68. COMPUTER SCIENCE. *Educ:* Mass Inst Technol, BS, 62; Carnegie-Mellon Univ, PhD(comput sci), 69. *Prof Exp:* Programmer, Rand Corp, 62-65; asst prof comput sci, Cornell Univ, 68-71; assoc prof systs & info sci, Vanderbilt Univ, 71-78; assoc prof comput sci, Duke Univ, 78-80; MEM STAFF, DEPT PATH, SCH MED, UNIV NC, CHAPEL HILL, 80- *Mem:* Soc Indust & Appl Math; Asn Comput Mach. *Res:* Algorithms, especially techniques for constructing optimal algorithms; application of dynamic programming to computer-suggested problems; programming languages; operating systems. *Mailing Add:* Dept Path Sch Med Univ NC Chapel Hill NC 27514

WAGNER, ROBERT E(ARL), b Baltimore, Md, July 30, 20; m 49; c 3. CHEMICAL ENGINEERING. *Educ:* Drexel Inst, BS, 46; Princeton Univ, MS, 48, PhD(chem eng), 55. *Prof Exp:* Lab asst chem, E I du Pont de Nemours & Co, 39-41 & Lever Bros Co, 41-42; thermodynamist, Glenn L Martin Co, 46; from asst prof to assoc prof, 49-62, PROF CHEM ENG, WORCESTER POLYTECH INST, 62- *Concurrent Pos:* Consult, New Eng Gas & Elec Asn. *Mem:* Am Chem Soc; Am Inst Chem Engrs. *Res:* Distillation; vapor liquid equilibria. *Mailing Add:* Dept of Chem Eng Worcester Polytech Inst Worcester MA 01609

WAGNER, ROBERT EDWIN, b Akron, Ohio, May 5, 20; m 52; c 2. ORGANIC CHEMISTRY. *Educ:* Mass Inst Technol, SB, 42; Princeton Univ, MA, 49, PhD(chem), 51. *Prof Exp:* Jr technologist, Shell Oil Co, 43-47; res chemist, 53-60, TECH SERV SUPVR, EXP STA LAB, E I DU PONT DE NEMOURS & CO, INC, 60- *Concurrent Pos:* Mem, Nat Defense Res Comt, 42. *Res:* Cellulose and polymer chemistry. *Mailing Add:* Burnt Mill Rd Chadds Fonds PA 19317

WAGNER, ROBERT G, b Kansas City, Mo, Apr 2, 34; m 57; c 3. SOLID STATE PHYSICS, DIGITAL IMAGE ANALYSIS. *Educ:* Grinnell Col, AB, 56; Univ Mo, MS, 60, PhD(physics), 66. *Prof Exp:* Res engr, NAm Aviation, Inc, 56-58; res asst solid state physics, 60-66, from res scientist to assoc scientist, 66-71, sr group engr electronics, 71-76, sr tech specialist, 76-81, PRIN TECH SPECIALIST, MCDONNELL DOUGLAS CORP, 81- *Concurrent Pos:* Asst prof, Univ Mo-St Louis, 71- *Mem:* AAAS; Inst Elec & Electronics Engrs; Am Phys Soc; Sigma Xi. *Res:* Thins films; device physics. *Mailing Add:* McDonnell Douglas Corp PO Box 516 St Louis MO 63166

WAGNER, ROBERT H, b Peru, Ind, Aug 11, 21; m 45; c 6. BIOCHEMISTRY. *Educ:* DePauw Univ, AB, 43; Univ Cincinnati, PhD(biochem), 50. *Prof Exp:* Asst, DePauw Univ, 43-44; asst, Res Found, Children's Hosp, 46-50; res assoc path & instr biochem, 53-56, asst prof path & biochem, 57-61, assoc prof, 61-67, PROF PATH, SCH MED, UNIV NC, CHAPEL HILL, 67-, PROF BIOCHEM, 72- *Concurrent Pos:* USPHS sr fel, 59-63, res career develop fel, Univ NC, Chapel Hill, 64-69. *Honors & Awards:* Muray Thelin Hemophilia Award; Int Prize French Asn Hemophilia. *Mem:* AAAS; Am Chem Soc; Soc Exp Biol & Med; Am Inst Chemists; Am Soc Exp Path. *Res:* Plasma proteins; enzymes; blood clotting; antihemophilic factors. *Mailing Add:* Dept Path Univ NC Sch Med Chapel Hill NC 27514

WAGNER, ROBERT MARVIN, physical organic chemistry, see previous edition

WAGNER, ROBERT PHILIP, b New York, NY, May 11, 18; m 47; c 3. GENETICS. *Educ:* City Col New York, BS, 40; Univ Tex, PhD(genetics), 43. *Prof Exp:* Instr zool, Univ Tex, 43-44; res biologist, Nat Cotton Coun, Dallas, 44-45; from asst prof to assoc prof, 45-56, prof, 56-77, EMER PROF ZOOL, UNIV TEX, AUSTIN, 77- *Concurrent Pos:* Nat Res Coun fel, Calif Inst Technol, 46; Guggenheim fel, 57; mem genetics panel, NSF, 61-64 & prog projs comt, 64-68 & Genetics Training Grant Comt, Nat Inst Gen Med Sci, 70-73; consult, Los Alamos Nat Lab, 78- *Mem:* AAAS; Soc Study Evolution; Genetics Soc Am (secy, 65-66, vpres, 70, pres, 71); Am Soc Naturalists; Am Soc Biol Chemists. *Res:* Physiological and biochemical aspects of Neurospora; genetics and biochemistry of mitochondria; mammalian cell genetics. *Mailing Add:* 313 Los Arboles Dr Santa Fe NM 87501

WAGNER, ROBERT RODERICK, b New York, NY, Jan 5, 23. VIROLOGY, MICROBIOLOGY. *Educ:* Yale Univ, MD, 46. *Prof Exp:* Intern med, New Haven Hosp, 46-47, asst resident, 49-50; instr med, Yale Univ, 51-53, asst prof, 53-55; from asst prof to prof microbiol, Johns Hopkins Univ, 56-67, from asst dean to assoc dean med fac, 57-63; PROF MICROBIOL & CHMN DEPT, UNIV VA, 67- *Concurrent Pos:* USPHS fel, Nat Inst Med Res, London, 50-51; vis fel, All Souls Col, Oxford Univ, 67; vis scientist, Dept Path, Oxford Univ, 67; ed-in-chief, J Virol, 66-; consult, NIH, NSF & Am Cancer Soc; Josiah Macy Jr Found Fac Scholar, Oxford Univ, 75-76. *Mem:* Am Soc Microbiol; Am Soc Clin Invest; Asn Am Med Cols; Asn Am Physicians; Am Soc Biol Chemists. *Res:* Biochemistry of viruses. *Mailing Add:* Dept of Microbiol Univ of Va Charlottesville VA 22901

WAGNER, ROBERT THOMAS, b Winona, Minn, July 15, 23; m; c 3. NUCLEAR PHYSICS. *Educ:* US Mil Acad, BS, 46; Univ Va, PhD(nuclear physics), 55. *Prof Exp:* Staff mem, Los Alamos Sci Lab, 55-64; prof physics, St Mary's Col, Minn, 64-66; chief tech develop div, Nike-X Syst Off, US Army, 66-67; prof & head physics dept, Northern Mich Univ, 67-75; dean fac, Sch Sci & Math, Univ Southern Colo, 75-78; ACAD DEAN, NMEX MILITARY INST, 78- *Mem:* AAAS; Am Phys Soc; Sigma Xi. *Res:* Ferroelectric ceramics; particle accelerators; fission physics; nuclear decay schemes; neutron and x-ray transport and diffusion; theoretical mechanics; scintillation radiation detectors. *Mailing Add:* NMex Military Inst Roswell NM 88201

WAGNER, ROBERT WANNER, b Nesquehoning, Pa, May 5, 13; m 42; c 3. MATHEMATICS. *Educ:* Ohio Univ, AB, 34; Univ Mich, AM, 35, PhD(math), 37. *Prof Exp:* Instr math, Univ Wis, 37-39; from instr to assoc prof, Oberlin Col, 39-50; assoc dean, Col Arts & Sci, 61-70, actg dir, Off Instnl Studies, 70-72, PROF MATH, UNIV MASS, AMHERST, 50- *Mem:* Am Math Soc; Math Asn Am. *Res:* Differential equations; function theory of linear algebras. *Mailing Add:* Dept of Math & Statist Univ of Mass Amherst MA 01002

WAGNER, ROGER CURTIS, b Aitkin, Minn, May 4, 43; m 68; c 1. CELL BIOLOGY. *Educ:* Hamline Univ, BS, 65; Ohio Univ, MS, 67; Univ Minn, Minneapolis, PhD(cell biol), 71. *Prof Exp:* Teaching asst zool, anat & hist, Ohio Univ, 65-67; teaching asst biol & physiol, Univ Minn, Minneapolis, 67-68, res asst electrophysiol, St Paul, fel cell biol, Med Sch, Yale Univ, 71-74; asst prof biol sci, 74-77, ASSOC PROF LIFE & HEALTH SCI, UNIV DEL, 77- *Concurrent Pos:* Nat Heart Lung & Blood Inst, 76-84. *Honors & Awards:* Res Career Develop Award. *Mem:* AAAS; Am Soc Cell Biol; Biophys Soc;

Am Inst Biol Sci. *Res:* Mechanism and function of macropinocytosis and micropinocytosis in mammalian cells; biomembranes; cell and molecular biology; histology. *Mailing Add:* Sch Life & Health Sci Univ Del Newark DE 19711

WAGNER, ROMEO BARRICK, b Hopewell, Va, Dec 14, 17; m 48; c 1. ORGANIC CHEMISTRY. *Educ:* Gettysburg Col, AB, 38; Pa State Univ, MS, 40, PhD(chem), 41. *Prof Exp:* Asst chem, Pa State Univ, 41-42, instr, 42-45, asst prof, 45-51; res chemist, Res Ctr, Hercules, Inc, 51-56, res supvr, 56-59, mgr, Naval Stores Res Div, 60-61, tech asst to dir res, 61-64, tech asst to dir, Res Ctr, 64-79; RETIRED. *Res:* Synthetic organic chemistry; steroids; penicillin; insecticides; cellulose; resin acids; terpenes; phenols. *Mailing Add:* 400 Snuff Mill Rd Wilmington DE 19807

WAGNER, ROSS IRVING, b Los Angeles, Calif, Apr 8, 25; m 49; c 3. SYNTHETIC INORGANIC & ORGANOMETALLIC CHEMISTRY. *Educ:* Univ Calif, Los Angeles, BS, 47; Univ Southern Calif, MS, 50, PhD(chem), 53. *Prof Exp:* Asst chem, Univ Southern Calif, 49-53; sr res chemist, Am Potash & Chem Corp, 53-63; MEM TECH STAFF, ROCKETDYNE DIV, ROCKWELL INT, 63- *Mem:* Am Chem Soc. *Res:* Chemistry of boron and phosphorus sulfur and fluorine. *Mailing Add:* Rocketdyne Div Rockwell Int D/522-6633 Canoga Ave Canoga Park CA 91304

WAGNER, RUSSEL OLSON, b Racine, Wis, Feb 18, 18; m 40; c 2. ECOLOGY, BOTANY. *Educ:* Univ Wis, BS, 40, MS, 47, PhD(bot), 60. *Prof Exp:* Teacher high schs, Wis, 40-42; instr biol, 47-53, asst prof biol sci, 53-57, assoc prof, 57-60, head dept life sci, 63-68, PROF BIOL SCI, UNIV WIS-PLATTEVILLE, 60- *Concurrent Pos:* Dir Wis univ biol sessions, Pigeon Lake Field Sta, 70-73. *Mem:* Ecol Soc Am; Entom Soc Am. *Res:* Influence of reproduction on distribution pattersn of prairie plants; ecology of a mound building ant found in prairie remnants, Formica cinerea. *Mailing Add:* Dept of Biol Sci Univ of Wis Platteville WI 53818

WAGNER, THOMAS CHARLES GORDON, b Pittsburgh, Pa, Jan 9, 16; m 42; c 3. ELECTRICAL ENGINEERING. *Educ:* Harvard Univ, SB, 37; Univ Md, MA, 40, PhD(math), 43. *Prof Exp:* With W Jett Lauck, DC, 37-38; asst mathematician, Univ Md, College Park, 38-40, instr, 40-45, prof elec eng, 46-80; PRES, TCG INC, 80- *Concurrent Pos:* Consult, Wash Inst Technol, Md, 40-46, Minneapolis-Honeywell Regulator Co, 47-59, Litton Industs, Inc, 59-62, Keltec Industs, Inc, 62-67 & Aero Geo Astro Div, Aiken Industs, Inc, 67- *Mem:* Inst Elec & Electronics Engrs. *Res:* Circuit analysis; timing devices; topology of networks. *Mailing Add:* TCG Inc 201 W Montgomery Ave Rockville MD 20850

WAGNER, THOMAS EDWARDS, b Cleveland, Ohio, Nov 29, 42; m 66; c 1. BIOCHEMISTRY, ENDOCRINOLOGY. *Educ:* Princeton Univ, BS, 64; Northwestern Univ, PhD(biochem), 66. *Prof Exp:* Asst prof chem, Wellesley Col, 66-68; asst prof biochem, Med Col, Cornell Univ, 68-70; asst prof chem, 70-77, PROF CHEM, OHIO UNIV, 77- *Concurrent Pos:* Petrol Res Fund grant, 67-70; assoc endocrinol, Sloan-Kettering Inst Cancer Res, 68-70. *Mem:* Am Chem Soc. *Res:* Study of weak interactions due to hydrophobic groups and their role in enzyme and hormone mechanism. *Mailing Add:* Dept of Chem Ohio Univ Athens OH 45701

WAGNER, TIMOTHY KNIGHT, b Pearl River, NY, July 5, 39; m 65; c 3. SOLID STATE PHYSICS. *Educ:* Univ Rochester, BS, 61; Univ Md, PhD(physics), 68. *Prof Exp:* Assoc solid state physic, Ames Lab, AEC, Iowa, 67-68, asst physicist, 68-70; from instr to asst prof, Iowa State Univ, 68-70; assoc prof, 70-74, chmn dept, 74-79, PROF PHYSICS, EAST STROUDSBURG STATE COL, 74- *Mem:* Sigma Xi; Am Phys Soc; Am Asn Physics Teachers. *Res:* Fermi surface measurements using radio-frequency size effect; ferromagnetic resonance in rare earth metals. *Mailing Add:* Dept of Physics East Stroudsburg State Col East Stroudsburg PA 18301

WAGNER, VAUGHN EDWIN, b Sharon, Pa, Sept 5, 42; m 68; c 1. ENVIRONMENTAL HEALTH, MEDICAL ENTOMOLOGY. *Educ:* Grove City Col, BS, 64; Pa State Univ, MS, 67; Mich State Univ, PhD(med entom), 75. *Prof Exp:* Sanitarian, Allegheny Co Health Dept, Pa, 64-65; res assoc, USDA, 67-68; med entomologist, Dutchess Co Health Dept, NY, 68-71; res assoc environ health, Mich State Univ, 74-75; asst prof environ health, York Col, City Univ New York, 75-76; exec dir, Saginaw-Bay Mosquito Control Comn, 77-80; WITH WAGNER & ASSOCS, 80- *Mem:* Sigma Xi; AAAS; Entom Soc Am; Am Mosquito Control Asn. *Res:* Epidemiology of arthropod-borne diseases; ecology and population dynamics of invertebrate disease vectors. *Mailing Add:* Wagner & Assocs 185 W Washington West Chicago IL 60185

WAGNER, WARREN HERBERT, JR, b Washington, DC, Aug 29, 20; m 48; c 2. BOTANY. *Educ:* Univ Pa, AB, 42; Univ Calif, PhD, 50. *Prof Exp:* Res fel, Harvard Univ, 50-51; from instr to assoc prof, 51-61, dir bot gardens, 66-71, chmn dept, 75-78, PROF BOT & NATURAL RESOURCES, UNIV MICH, ANN ARBOR, 61-, CUR HERBARIUM, 62- *Concurrent Pos:* Mem, Ad Hoc Comt Plant Taxon, Nat Acad Sci, 56-57, Plant Sci Planning Comt, 64-65, dep for bot, Subcomt Syst Biogeog, US Nat Comt, Int Biol Prog, 65-68; trustee, Cranbrook Inst Sci, 63-78; mem, Fairchild Trop Garden Res Comt, 66-69; mem, Smithsonian Inst Coun, 67-72 & Panel Syst Biol, NSF; consult mem, Int Union Conserv Nature & Natural Resources, 72-; hon mem, Smithsonian Coun, Curado Asn ad hon Herbario Nacional de Costa Rica. *Mem:* Fel AAAS (secy, 63-67, vpres bot sci sect, 68); Soc Study Evolution (vpres, 66, pres, 72); Am Soc Plant Taxon (pres, 66); Am Fern Soc (secy, 51-53, cur, 57-, pres, 70-71); Bot Soc Am (vpres, 72, pres, 77). *Res:* Morphology, life cycles, evolution and systematics of vascular plants, especially pteridophytes; science education; biology of higher plants, especially ferns. *Mailing Add:* Dept Bot Univ Mich Ann Arbor MI 48109

WAGNER, WILLIAM CHARLES, b Elma, NY, Nov 12, 32; m 54; c 4. ENDOCRINOLOGY. *Educ:* Cornell Univ, DVM, 56, PhD(physiol), 68. *Prof Exp:* Res vet, Col Vet Med, Cornell Univ, 57-65, fel physiol, Dept Animal Sci, 65-68; from asst prof to assoc prof physiol, Col Vet Med Iowa State Univ, 68-77; PROF & HEAD, DEPT VET BIOSCI, UNIV ILL COL VET MED, 77- *Concurrent Pos:* Vis prof, Inst Physiol, Tech Univ Munich, WGer, 73-74; consult, Res Adv Bd, Morris Animal Found, 78-81; Alexander von Humboldt Found sr US scientist award, 73. *Mem:* Am Col Theriopenology (pres, 77-78); Am Physiol Soc; Am Vet Med Asn; Am Soc Animal Sci; Soc Study Reproduction. *Res:* Physiology of parturition and the postpartem female, especially in regard to ruminants; mechanism of stress-induced infertility and role of the adrenal. *Mailing Add:* Dept Vet Biosci Col Vet Med Univ Ill 2001 S Lincoln Urbana IL 61801

WAGNER, WILLIAM EDWARD, JR, b New York, NY, June 17, 25; m 63; c 2. CLINICAL PHARMACOLOGY. *Educ:* Princeton Univ, BA, 45; Columbia Univ, MD, 50; Am Bd Family Pract, dipl, 70. *Prof Exp:* Instr clin med, Med Sch, NY Univ, 60-77; SR FEL CLIN PHARMACOL, PHARMACEUT DIV, CIBA-GEIGY CORP, 51-; INSTR CLIN MED, MED SCH, COLUMBIA UNIV COL PHYSICIANS & SURGEONS, 77- *Mem:* AMA; Am Soc Clin Pharmacol & Therapeut; fel Am Acad Family Pract. *Res:* Drug metabolism; pharmacokinetics; biopharmaceuticals. *Mailing Add:* 3301 Valley Rd Millington NJ 07946

WAGNER, WILLIAM FREDERICK, b Canton, Mo, Sept 13, 16; m. CHEMISTRY. *Educ:* Culver-Stockton Col, AB, 38; Univ Chicago, SM, 40; Univ Ill, PhD(anal chem), 47. *Prof Exp:* Asst chemist, State Geol Surv, Ill, 40-45; asst chem, Univ Ill, 45-47; asst prof, Hanover Col, 47-49; from instr to assoc prof, 49-58, chmn dept, 65-68, PROF CHEM, UNIV KY, 58-, CHMN DEPT, 76- *Mem:* AAAS; Am Chem Soc. *Res:* X-ray applied to chemical analysis; solvent extraction of metal chelates; thermal methods of analysis. *Mailing Add:* Dept of Chem Univ of Ky Lexington KY 40506

WAGNER, WILLIAM GERARD, b St Cloud, Minn, Aug 22, 36; m 68; c 4. THEORETICAL PHYSICS, QUANTUM ELECTRONICS. *Educ:* Calif Inst Technol, BS, 58, PhD(physics), 62. *Prof Exp:* Mem tech staff, Res Labs, Hughes Aircraft Co, 62-65, sr staff physicist, 65-70; assoc prof, 66-69, PROF PHYSICS & ELEC ENG, UNIV SOUTHERN CALIF, 69- *Concurrent Pos:* Consult, Rand Corp, 60-65; Tolman res fel theoret physics, Calif Inst Technol, 62-65; asst prof, Univ Calif, Irvine, 65-66; consult, Janus Mgt Corp, 70-71 & Croesus Capital Corp, 71-74; dean, Div Natural Sci & Math, Col Letters, Arts & Sci, Univ Southern Calif, 73-, spec asst, Acad Record Serv, 75-81. *Mem:* Am Phys Soc; Financial Mgt Asn. *Res:* Investment analysis; computer applications. *Mailing Add:* Div Natural Sci & Math LAS Univ Southern Calif Los Angeles CA 90007

WAGNER, WILLIAM JOHN, b Gary, Ind, Mar 29, 38; m 62; c 5. ASTROPHYSICS. *Educ:* John Carroll Univ, BS, 60, MS, 62; Univ Colo, PhD(astro-geophys), 69. *Prof Exp:* Sr physicist, Rocketdyne Div, NAm Aviation, Inc, 62-64, sci eng fel, 64-69; astrophysicist & Big Dome facil sect chief, Sacramento Peak Observ, Air Force Geophys Lab, 69-76; coronagraph-polarimeter exp scientist, 76-81, STAFF SCIENTIST, HIGH ALTITUDE OBSERV, NAT CTR ATMOSPHERIC RES, 81- *Concurrent Pos:* mem sub comn solar physics, Comt on Space Res, 81- *Mem:* Fel AAAS; Int Astron Union; Am Astron Soc; Am Phys Soc; Am Geophys Union. *Res:* Observational research concerning solar physics, solar activity, the corona and solar wind; solar-terrestrial physics; spectroscopy. *Mailing Add:* High Altitude Observ PO Box 3000 Boulder CO 80307

WAGNER, WILLIAM S, b Cincinnati, Ohio, Apr 8, 36; m 65. ELECTRICAL ENGINEERING. *Educ:* Univ Ky, BS, 59; Case Western Reserve Univ, MS, 61; Univ Cincinnati, PhD, 67. *Prof Exp:* Instr, 61-67, ASST PROF ELEC ENG, UNIV CINCINNATI, 67- *Concurrent Pos:* Ford Found yr in residency prog grant, 68-69. *Res:* Nonlinear system analysis; network synthesis; electronics; control systems. *Mailing Add:* Univ Cincinnati Cincinnati OH 45221

WAGNER, WILLIAM SHERWOOD, b Mora, Minn, Sept 21, 28; m 62. ORGANIC CHEMISTRY. *Educ:* Univ Minn, BChem, 49; Univ Mo, PhD(org chem), 52. *Prof Exp:* Sr res chemist, Chemstrand Corp, Ala, 52-59; mgr org res paper prod, Fiber Prod Res Ctr, Inc, 59-62, asst dir paper prod, 62-63; res assoc, Celanese Res Co, 63-65, head spinning res sect, 65-70; group mgr, 70-71, mgr res & labs, 71-72, dir develop, 72-81, DIR FIBER TECHNOL, HOECHST RIBERS INDUST, 81- *Mem:* Am Chem Soc; Am Inst Chemists. *Res:* Synthetic fibers; polymers; organic synthesis. *Mailing Add:* 696 Perrin Dr Spartanburg SC 29302

WAGNER, WILTZ WALKER, JR, b New Orleans, La, July 7, 39; m 67; c 1. PULMONARY PHYSIOLOGY. *Educ:* Colo State Univ, PhD(physiol), 74. *Prof Exp:* Res fel physiol, 60-67, res assoc, 67-74, instr, 74-80, ASST PROF MED, UNIV COLO MED CTR, DENVER, 80- *Concurrent Pos:* Site vis, NIH, 74; consult, Med Sch, Univ Calif, Los Angeles, 74 & Univ Calif, La Jolla, 75, Med Sch, Univ Calif, San Francisco, 70 & 79, Harvard Med Sch, Boston, 79. *Mem:* Fel Royal Micros Soc; Sigma Xi; Am Physiol Soc; Microcirc Soc; Am Heart Asn. *Res:* Pulmonary microcirculation using methods for direct visualization of capillary perfusion in vivo; capillary control mechanisms and functional implications in health and disease; collateral ventilation and relation to ventilation-perfusion balance; athletic amenorrhea. *Mailing Add:* CVP Lab Univ Colo Med Ctr Denver CO 80262

WAGONER, DALE E, b Niagara Falls, NY, Oct 12, 36; m 65, 74; c 3. GENETICS, BIOLOGY. *Educ:* Ind Univ, AB(music) & AB(zool), 59, MA, 64, PhD(genetics), 65. *Prof Exp:* Res asst Drosophila genetics, H J Muller Lab, Ind Univ, 60; Res geneticist, Metab & Radiation Res Lab, USDA, 64-75; PROF BIOL, MAHARISHI INT UNIV, 75- *Concurrent Pos:* From asst prof to assoc prof entom, Grad Fac, NDak State Univ, 68-75. *Mem:* Sigma Xi; Genetics Soc Am; Geront Soc Am; Am Genetic Asn. *Res:* Basic formal genetics of house flies; karyotype-linkage group relationship; insect control by the use of genetic mechanisms, such as chromosomal translocation, meiotic drive, hybrid sterility, cytoplasmic incompatability, compound chromosomes and conditional lethal mutations; aging and oxygen consumption research in practitioners of the transcendental meditation and TM Sidhis Program. *Mailing Add:* Dept of Biol Maharishi Int Univ Fairfield IA 52556

WAGONER, DAVID EUGENE, b Clarinda, Iowa, July 8, 49; m 82. EXPERIMENTAL HIGH ENERGY PHYSICS. *Educ:* Iowa State Univ, BS, 71; Cornell Univ, MS, 78, PhD(exp physics), 81. *Prof Exp:* Teaching asst, Dept Physics, Cornell Univ, 75-76, res asst, Lab Nuclear Studies, 76-81; RES ASSOC, DEPT PHYSICS, FERMI NAT ACCELERATOR LAB, 81- *Mem:* Am Phys Soc; AAAS. *Res:* Experimental high energy physics research on strong, weak, and electromagnetic elementary particle interactions; production and decay of resonant and non-resonant high mass states; Monte Carlo computer simulations. *Mailing Add:* Dept Physics Fermi Nat Accelerator Lab MS122 PO Box 500 Batavia IL 60510

WAGONER, GLEN, b Terreton, Idaho, July 28, 27; m 52; c 1. PHYSICS. *Educ:* Idaho State Col, BS, 49; Univ Chicago, MS, 52; Univ Calif, PhD(physics), 57. *Prof Exp:* PHYSICIST, RES LABS, UNION CARBIDE CORP, 57- *Concurrent Pos:* Prof lectr, Case Inst Technol, 59-61. *Mem:* Am Phys Soc. *Res:* Solid state physics; magnetic resonance; electronics; electric arcs. *Mailing Add:* Parma Tech Ctr Union Carbide Corp PO Box 6116 Cleveland OH 44101

WAGONER, ROBERT H, II, b Columbus, Ohio, Jan 8, 52. MECHANICAL METALLURGY, FORMABILITY MECHANICS. *Educ:* Ohio State Univ, BS, 74, MS, 75, PhD(metall eng), 76. *Prof Exp:* Res scientist, 77-80, STAFF RES SCIENTIST, PHYSICS DEPT, GEN MOTORS RES LABS, 80- *Concurrent Pos:* NSF fel, Univ Oxford, 76-77. *Honors & Awards:* Rossiter W Raymond Mem Award & Robert Lansing Hardy Gold Medal, Am Inst Mining, Metall & Petrol Engrs, 81. *Mem:* Am Inst Mining, Metall & Petrol Engrs. *Res:* Metal elasticity and plasticity; sheet metal forming; deformation testing, dislocation modelling; mechanical equation of state studies. *Mailing Add:* Physics Dept Gen Motors Res Labs Warren MI 48090

WAGONER, ROBERT VERNON, JR, b Teaneck, NJ, Aug 6, 38; m 63; c 2. THEORETICAL ASTROPHYSICS & GRAVITATION. *Educ:* Cornell Univ, BME, 61; Stanford Univ, MS, 62, PhD(physics), 65. *Prof Exp:* Res fel physics, Calif Inst Technol, 65-68; from asst prof to assoc prof astron, Cornell Univ, 68-73; assoc prof, 73-77, PROF PHYSICS, STANFORD UNIV, 77- *Concurrent Pos:* Sloan res fel, 69-71; Guggenheim fel, 79; George Ellery Hale distinguished vis prof, Univ Chicago, 78; mem comt space astron & astrophys; prin investr, Nat Sci Found & NASA. *Mem:* Fel Am Phys Soc; Int Astron Union; Am Astron Soc; Sigma Xi. *Res:* Relativistic astrophysics; cosmology; gravitation theory; nucleosynthesis. *Mailing Add:* Dept of Physics Stanford Univ Stanford CA 94305

WAGONER, RONALD LEWIS, b Fairfield, Calif, Aug 4, 42; m 60; c 2. MATHEMATICS. *Educ:* Fresno State Col, BA, 65, MA, 66; Univ Ore, PhD(math), 69. *Prof Exp:* Asst prof, 69-74, assoc prof, 74-77, PROF MATH, CALIF STATE UNIV, FRESNO, 77- *Concurrent Pos:* Math specialist, Fresno City Unified Sch Dist, 70-71. *Res:* Ring theory: associative rings with identity. *Mailing Add:* 5794 E Nees Clovis CA 93612

WAGREICH, PHILIP DONALD, b New York, NY, July 25, 41; m 62; c 3. PURE MATHEMATICS. *Educ:* Brandeis Univ, BA, 62; Columbia Univ, PhD(math), 66. *Prof Exp:* Lectr math, Brandeis Univ, 66-68; asst prof, Univ Pa, 68-74; assoc prof, 74-80, PROF, UNIV ILL, CHICAGO CIRCLE, 80- *Concurrent Pos:* Off Naval Res fel, 68-69; mem, Inst Advan Study, 68-70; NSF res grants, 74- *Mem:* Am Math Soc. *Res:* Algebraic geometry; topology; transformation groups. *Mailing Add:* Dept of Math Box 4348 Univ of Ill at Chicago Circle Chicago IL 60680

WAGSTAFF, DAVID JESSE, b Lehi, Utah, Feb 22, 35; m 63; c 3. TOXICOLOGY. *Educ:* Utah State Univ, BS, 59, PhD(toxicol), 70; Cornell Univ, DVM, 62. *Prof Exp:* Vet epidemiologist, USPHS, 62-64; vet meat inspector, USDA, 64-65; vet epidemiologist, USPHS, 65-66; asst prof toxicol, Univ Mo-Columbia, 69-73; toxicologist, 73-77, EPIDEMIOLOGIST, FOOD & DRUG ADMIN, 77- *Concurrent Pos:* NIH fel toxicol, Utah State Univ, 66-69; mem, Am Bd Vet Toxicol. *Mem:* Soc Toxicol; Am Col Vet Toxicol; Am Vet Med Asn. *Res:* Induction of liver microsomal enzymes; drug toxicity; environmental contaminants; toxicants in natural foods; interaction of toxicology with other fields; toxicant interactions; poisonous plants; food safety epidemiology. *Mailing Add:* 200 C St SW Washington DC 20705

WAGSTAFF, SAMUEL STANDFIELD, JR, b New Bedford, Mass, Feb 21, 45. COMPUTATIONAL NUMBER THEORY. *Educ:* Mass Inst Technol, BS, 66; Cornell Univ, PhD(math), 70. *Prof Exp:* Instr math, Univ Rochester, 70-71; vis mem, Inst Advan Study, 71-72; vis lectr, Univ Ill, 72-75, asst prof math, 75-81; ASSOC PROF STATIST & COMPUT SCI, UNIV GA, 81- *Mem:* Am Math Soc; Math Asn Am; Soc Actuaries. *Res:* Factoring; primality testing; diophantine equations; computational complexity. *Mailing Add:* Dept Statist & Comput Sci Univ Ga Athens GA 30602

WAH, THEIN, b Rangoon, Burma, Apr 11, 19; nat US; m 52; c 3. MECHANICS, STRUCTURAL ENGINEERING. *Educ:* Univ Rangoon, BS, 41; Univ Utah, MS, 48; Harvard Univ, MS, 49; Univ Ill, PhD(eng), 53. *Prof Exp:* Asst engr, Burma Rwy, 41-47; bridge designer, State Div, Hwys, Ill, 52-53; asst prof civil eng & mech, Lehigh Univ, 53-54 & Univ Conn, 54-57; sr res engr, Southwest Res Inst, Tex, 57-61, staff scientist, 62-71; PROF CIVIL & MECH ENG, TEX A&I UNIV, 71- *Concurrent Pos:* Vis prof, Indian Inst Technol, Kharagpur, 61-62. *Mem:* AAAS; Am Soc Mech Engrs; Am Soc Eng Educ; Sigma Xi. *Res:* Elasticity; plasticity; vibrations; creep; thermoelasticity. *Mailing Add:* Dept of Civil & Mech Eng Tex A&I Univ Kingsville TX 78363

WAHAB, JAMES HATTON, b Bridgeton, NC, Aug 29, 20; m 47; c 2. MATHEMATICS. *Educ:* Col William & Mary, BS, 40; Univ NC, AM, 50, PhD(math), 51. *Prof Exp:* Instr math & eng, Norfolk Div, Col William & Mary, 40-42 & 46-47, asst prof, 47-48; instr math, Univ NC, 50-51; from asst prof to assoc prof, Ga Inst Technol, 51-58; prof, La State Univ, 58-61, chmn dept, 60-61; prof, NC State Col, 61-63; prof & chmn dept, Univ NC, Charlotte, 63-68, actg acad dean, 64-68; head dept, 68-73, dir undergrad studies math, 77-80, PROF MATH, UNIV SC, 68- *Mem:* Am Math Soc; Math Asn Am. *Res:* Irreducibility of legendre polynomials; algebra; statistics; numerical analysis. *Mailing Add:* Dept of Math Univ of SC Columbia SC 29208

WAHBA, ALBERT J, b Alexandria, Egypt, Feb 27, 28; US citizen; m 65; c 3. BIOCHEMISTRY. *Educ:* Univ Calif, Berkeley, AB, 51; Univ Tex, MA, 54; Tufts Univ, PhD(biochem & pharamacol), 61. *Prof Exp:* Instr, Dept Biochem, Sch Med, NY Univ, 63, asst prof, 63-65, assoc prof, 66-69; prof & dir biochem, Lab Molecular Biol, Can, 70-77; PROF & CHMN, DEPT BIOCHEM, UNIV MISS MED CTR, 77- *Concurrent Pos:* Jane Coffin Childs Fund med res fel, Dept Biochem, Sch Med, NY Univ, 62; vis scientist, Salk Inst Biol Studies, 66; Med Res Coun Assoc, Can, 70-77. *Mem:* Am Soc Biol Chemists; AAAS; Sigma Xi; Am Chem Soc; Am Soc Microbiol. *Res:* Nucleic acids and protein synthesis; molecular mechanisms and regulation during early embryonic development; transcriptional and translated control of gene expression during development of brine shrimp Artemia embryos; author or coauthor of over 70 publications. *Mailing Add:* Dept Biochem Med Ctr Univ Miss 2500 North State St Jackson MS 39216

WAHBA, GRACE, b Washington, DC. MATHEMATICAL STATISTICS. *Educ:* Cornell Univ, BA, 56; Univ Md, College Park, MA, 62; Stanford Univ, PhD(math statist), 66. *Prof Exp:* Res mathematician, Opers Res, Inc, 57-61; systs analyst, Int Bus Mach Corp, 61-66; res assoc math statist, Stanford Univ, 66-67; from asst prof to assoc prof, 67-74, PROF STATIST, UNIV WIS-MADISON, 75- *Concurrent Pos:* Assoc ed, Annals Statist, 74-80; mem int ed bd, Communications in Statist, 71-; fel St Cross Col; sr vis fel, Oxford Univ, 74-75; Lady Davis fel, tech, 80; mem, Coun Soc Indust & Appl Math, 80-82, Coun Inst Math Statist, 78-80, adv panel, math sci, Nat Sci Found, 80-82, Peer Review Panel, 81. *Mem:* Inst Math Statist; Am Statist Asn; Am Math Soc; Soc Indust & Appl Math. *Res:* Estimation of functions of one or several variables, given discrete, noisy data both direct and indirect and on the determination of good or optival experimental designs connected with indirect sensing experiments; approximation theory. *Mailing Add:* Dept of Statist Univ of Wis Madison WI 53705

WAHL, A(RTHUR) J, b Saxman, Kans, Feb 5, 20; m 50; c 2. ELECTRICAL ENGINEERING. *Educ:* Univ Kans, BS, 42; Princeton Univ, PhD(elec eng), 50. *Prof Exp:* Mem tech staff, 53-56, SUPVR SEMICONDUCTOR DEVICE DEVELOP, BELL TEL LABS, 56- *Mem:* Inst Elec & Electronics Engrs. *Res:* Semiconductor device development. *Mailing Add:* Div 21 Bell Tel Labs 2525 N 11th St Reading PA 19604

WAHL, ARTHUR CHARLES, b Des Moines, Iowa, Sept 8, 17; m 43; c 1. INORGANIC & NUCLEAR CHEMISTRY. *Educ:* Iowa State Univ, BS, 39; Univ Calif, PhD(chem), 42. *Prof Exp:* Res assoc, Manhattan Proj, Univ Calif, 42-43, group leader, Los Alamos Sci Lab, 43-46; assoc prof chem, 46-53, FARR PROF RADIOCHEM, WASHINGTON UNIV, 53- *Concurrent Pos:* Consult, Los Alamos Sci Lab, 50-; NSF fel, 67. *Honors & Awards:* Am Chem Soc Award, 66; Humboldt Award, 77. *Mem:* Am Chem Soc. *Res:* Nuclear-charge distribution in fission; rapid electron-transfer reactions. *Mailing Add:* Dept of Chem Washington Univ St Louis MO 63130

WAHL, EBERHARD WILHELM, b Berlin, Ger, May 24, 14; US citizen; m 46; c 2. METEOROLOGY, SPACE SCIENCES. *Educ:* Univ Berlin, PhD(astron), 37. *Prof Exp:* Asst prof meteorol, Meteorol Inst, Univ Berlin, 37-45; scientist, N W Ger Weather Serv, 46-49; proj scientist, Geophys Res Directorate, US Air Force, 49-58, astronr, Proj Spacetrack, 58-61, tech dir, 61-63; chmn dept, 70-73, PROF METEOROL, UNIV WIS-MADISON, 63- *Concurrent Pos:* Fel astron, Observ, Univ Berlin, 37-41; vis prof, Univ Wis, 62-63; trustee, Univ Corp Atmospheric Res, Boulder, Colo, 75- *Mem:* Fel AAAS; Am Meteorol Soc; Am Geophys Union; Ger Meteorol Soc. *Res:* Meteorology of large scale circulation; dynamic climatology; satellite meteorology. *Mailing Add:* Dept of Meteorol Univ of Wis Madison WI 53706

WAHL, FLOYD MICHAEL, b Hebron, Ind, July 7, 31; m 53; c 4. MINERALOGY. *Educ:* DePauw Univ, AB, 53; Univ Ill, MA, 57, PhD(mineral & geochem), 58. *Prof Exp:* Instr geol, Univ Ill, Urbana, 58-59, res asst prof, 59-60, from asst prof to assoc prof, 60-69; prof & chmn dept, 69-73, dir div phys sci & math, 71-73, ASSOC DEAN, GRAD SCH & ASSOC DIR RES, UNIV FLA, 73-, PROF GEOL, 80- *Mem:* Fel Geol Soc Am; Mineral Soc Am; Geochem Soc; Clay Minerals Soc; Am Inst Prof Geologists. *Res:* Clay mineralogy and sedimentary geochemistry; development of mineral resources; chemical alteration and those factors that lead to and control element concentration; phase changes in minerals at elevated temperatures. *Mailing Add:* 237 Grinter Hall Univ of Fla Gainesville FL 32611

WAHL, GEOFFREY MYLES, molecular biology, see previous edition

WAHL, GEORGE HENRY, JR, b New York, NY, Sept 17, 36; m 58; c 3. STRUCTURAL CHEMISTRY. *Educ:* Fordham Univ, BS, 58; NY Univ, MS, 61, PhD(org chem), 63. *Prof Exp:* Res chemist, Pittsburgh Plate Glass Chem Co, Ohio, 58-59; NIH res fel org chem, Cornell Univ, 63-64; from asst prof to assoc prof, 64-75, PROF ORG CHEM, NC STATE UNIV, 75- *Concurrent Pos:* Guest prof, Swiss Fed Inst, Zurich, 73-74; consult, Environ Protection Agency, 78- *Honors & Awards:* Sigma Xi Res Award, 74. *Mem:* Am Chem Soc; Royal Soc Chem. *Res:* Organic stereochemistry; nuclear magnetic resonance spectroscopy; mass spectrometry; synthesis of unusual structures for physical investigation; synthesis and structure of adamantane and biphenyl derivatives. *Mailing Add:* Dept of Chem NC State Univ Raleigh NC 27650

WAHL, JOHN SCHEMPP, b Tungjen, China, Aug 8, 20; US citizen; m 43; c 3. NUCLEAR PHYSICS. *Educ:* Iowa State Teachers Col, BA, 41; Univ Iowa, MS, 44, PhD(physics), 52. *Prof Exp:* Asst, Sylvania Elec Prod Co, Pa, 41; res assoc, Physics Eng, Develop Proj, Iowa, 44-45; instr physics, Univ Iowa, 47-48; mem res staff, Los Alamos Sci Lab, Univ Calif, 49-54; MEM RES STAFF, SCHLUMBERGER-DOLL RES CTR, 54- *Mem:* Am Phys Soc; AAAS. *Res:* Nuclear physics; neutron and gamma ray interactions in extended media. *Mailing Add:* Schlumberger-Doll Res Ctr Box 307 Ridgefield CT 06877

WAHL, JONATHAN MICHAEL, b Washington, DC, Jan 29, 45; m 70. MATHEMATICS. *Educ:* Yale Univ, BS & MA, 65; Harvard Univ, PhD(math), 71. *Prof Exp:* Instr math, Univ Calif, Berkeley, 70-72; vis, Inst Advan Study, Princeton Univ, 72-73, 79; from asst prof to assoc prof, 73-81, PROF MATH, UNIV NC, CHAPEL HILL, 81- *Concurrent Pos:* NSF res grant, 71- *Mem:* Am Math Soc. *Res:* Singularities; deformation theory; algebraic geometry. *Mailing Add:* Dept of Math Univ of NC Chapel Hill NC 27514

WAHL, PATRICIA WALKER, b La Grande, Ore, Dec 6, 38; m 63; c 1. BIOSTATISTICS. *Educ:* San Jose State Col, BA, 60; Univ Wash, PhD(biostatist), 71. *Prof Exp:* Res analyst comput programming, Lockheed Missiles, Lockheed Aircraft Corp, 60-62; systs analyst, Control Data Corp, 63-64; head programmer, 64-66, instr biostatist, 71-73, asst prof, 74-76, ASSOC PROF BIOSTATIST, UNIV WASH, 77- *Mem:* Am Statist Asn; Biomet Soc. *Res:* Use of regression analysis and other multivariate statistical techniques for exploratory data analysis; effect on classification by discriminant analysis when model assumptions fail. *Mailing Add:* 700 SE Shoreland Dr Bellevue WA 98004

WAHL, SHARON KNUDSON, b Mt Vernon, Wash, Mar 16, 45; m 71; c 2. IMMUNOLOGY. *Educ:* Pac Lutheran Univ, BS, 67; Univ Wash, PhD(biol struct), 71. *Prof Exp:* Fel path, Sch Med, Univ Wash, 71-72; fel cellular immunol, 72-74, staff fel humoral immunity, 74-75, sr staff fel humoral immunity, 75-76, RES MICROBIOLOGIST, NAT INST DENT RES, 76- *Mem:* Am Asn Immunol; Sigma Xi; Reticuloendothelial Soc. *Res:* Mechanisms of activation and characterization of T and B lymphocyte participation in cellular immune reactions and effect of immunosuppressive agents on these responses; influence of immune system on connective tissue metabolism. *Mailing Add:* Nat Inst Dent Res Bldg 30 Rm 332 9000 Rockville Pike Bethesda MD 20014

WAHL, WERNER HENRY, b Buffalo, NY, Oct 1, 30; m 51; c 2. NUCLEAR CHEMISTRY, RADIOCHEMISTRY. *Educ:* Univ Buffalo, BA, 54; Purdue Univ, MS, 56, PhD(phys inorg chem), 57. *Prof Exp:* Chem operator, Pathfinder Chem Corp, 49; asst, Linde Co Div, Union Carbide Co, 51-53; asst, Durez Plastics, Inc, 53; asst chem, Purdue Univ, 54-57; res chemist, Union Carbide Nuclear Corp, 57-61, group leader, 61-65, asst mgr res, 65-66, dir radiopharmaceut, Neisler Labs, Inc, Union Carbide Corp, NY, 66-69; dir opers, Mallinckrodt/Nuclear, Mo, 69-70; vpres & gen mgr, Amersham-Searle Corp, Ill, 70, exec vpres, 71, pres, 71-75; vpres new bus develop, Searle Diag, Inc, 75-78; PRES, NUCLEAR DIAGNOSTICS, INC, 78- *Concurrent Pos:* Asst chem, Univ Buffalo, 53. *Mem:* Fel AAAS; Am Chem Soc; Am Asn Physicists Med; Clin Radio Assay Soc; fel Am Inst Chem. *Mailing Add:* Nuclear Diagnostics Inc 575 Robbins Dr Troy MI 48084

WAHLBECK, PHILLIP GLENN, b Kankakee, Ill, Mar 29, 33; m 56; c 3. HIGH TEMPERATURE CHEMISTRY, SURFACE CHEMISTRY. *Educ:* Univ Ill, BS, 54, PhD(chem), 58. *Prof Exp:* Asst chem, Univ Ill, 54-58; res assoc, Univ Kans, 58-60; from instr to assoc prof, 60-72, chmn dept, 72-78, PROF CHEM, WICHITA STATE UNIV, 72- *Concurrent Pos:* Vis prof, Tech Univ Norway, 70 & 78. *Mem:* Am Sci Affil; AAAS; Am Chem Soc. *Res:* Molecular beams; thermodynamics at high temperatures; transition metal hydrides, oxides, selenides and tellurides; vapor pressure measurements; effusion of gases; gas-surface interactions adsorption phenomena; mean residence times; surface diffusion; spatial distributions of restituted molecules. *Mailing Add:* Dept of Chem Wichita State Univ Wichita KS 67208

WAHLERT, JOHN HOWARD, b New York, NY, May 12, 43; m 69; c 3. VERTEBRATE PALEONTOLOGY. *Educ:* Amherst Col, BA, 65; Harvard Univ, MA, 66, PhD(geol), 72. *Prof Exp:* Curatorial asst vert paleont, 72-77, ASSOC, DEPT VERT PALEONT, AM MUS NATURAL HIST, 76- *Concurrent Pos:* Vis asst prof biol, Franklin & Marshall Col, 77-78, cur mammal, North Mus, 78-81; asst prof biol, Millersville State Col, 80-81; asst prof biol, Baruch Col, 81- *Mem:* Soc Vert Paleont; Am Soc Mammal. *Res:* Cenozoic rodents and their anatomy, taxonomy and phylogeny. *Mailing Add:* Dept Vert Paleont Am Mus Natural Hist New York NY 10024

WAHLGREN, MORRIS A, b Wildrose, NDak, May 31, 29; m 55; c 3. ENVIRONMENTAL CHEMISTRY. *Educ:* Jamestown Col, BS, 51; Univ Mich, PhD(chem), 61. *Prof Exp:* Radiochemist, Atomic Energy Div, Phillips Petrol Co, Idaho, 53-56; asst chemist, Chem Div, 61-66, assoc chemist, 66-72, chemist, Radiol & Environ Res Div, 72-80, CHEMIST, CHEM ENG DIV, ARGONNE NAT LAB, 80- *Mem:* AAAS; Am Chem Soc; fel Am Inst Chemists; Int Soc Limnol. *Res:* Nuclear and analytical chemistry; radiochemical separations; chemical limnology; behavior of artificial radionuclides in the Great Lakes. *Mailing Add:* Argonnne Nat Lab D205 L190 9700 S Cass Ave Argonne IL 60439

WAHLIG, CHARLES F, physics, deceased

WAHLIG, MICHAEL ALEXANDER, b New York, NY, Oct 21, 34; m 56; c 4. ENERGY CONVERSION. *Educ:* Manhattan Col, BS, 55; Mass Inst Technol, PhD(physics), 62. *Prof Exp:* Res assoc physics, Mass Inst Technol, 62-66; res staff physics, 66-72, MEM RES STAFF SOLAR ENERGY, ENERGY & ENVIRON DIV, LAWRENCE BERKELEY LAB, UNIV CALIF, BERKELEY, 72- *Mem:* Am Phys Soc; Int Solar Energy Soc; AAAS. *Res:* Research, development and analysis of the availability, conversion, and use of solar energy for providing heating, cooling and electric power. *Mailing Add:* Lawrence Berkeley Lab Univ of Calif Berkeley CA 94720

WAHLS, HARVEY E(DWARD), b Evanston, Ill, Aug 8, 31; m 60; c 2. CIVIL ENGINEERING, SOIL MECHANICS. *Educ:* Northwestern Univ, BS, 54, MS, 55, PhD(civil eng), 61. *Prof Exp:* From instr to asst prof civil eng, Worcester Polytech Inst, 55-60; from asst prof to assoc prof, 60-69, PROF CIVIL ENG, NC STATE UNIV, 69- *Concurrent Pos:* Instr, Northwestern Univ, 57-59; mem, Hwy Res Bd, Nat Acad Sci-Nat Res Coun, 64- *Mem:* Am Soc Civil Engrs; Am Soc Testing & Mat; Am Soc Eng Educ; Int Soc Soil Mech & Found Engrs. *Res:* Consolidation theory for cohesive soils; settlement analysis; compaction process and the behavior of compacted soils; soil dynamics. *Mailing Add:* Dept of Civil Eng NC State Univ Raleigh NC 27650

WAHLSTROM, LAWRENCE F, b Aurora, Wis, Feb 4, 15; m 38; c 2. MATHEMATICS. *Educ:* Lawrence Col, BA, 36; Univ Wis, MA, 37, PhD(math educ), 50. *Prof Exp:* Pub sch teacher, Ill, 37-41, chmn dept math, jr high sch, 41-45; chmn dept, Elgin Acad, 45-47; asst, Univ Wis, 47-48; PROF MATH & CHMN DEPT, UNIV WIS-EAU CLAIRE, 48- *Concurrent Pos:* NSF fac sci grant, 57-58. *Mem:* Math Asn Am. *Res:* Geometry. *Mailing Add:* Dept of Math Univ of Wis Eau Claire WI 54701

WAHLSTROM, RICHARD CARL, b Craig, Nebr, Feb 13, 23; m 47; c 3. ANIMAL SCIENCE. *Educ:* Univ Nebr, BS, 48; Univ Ill, MS, 50, PhD(animal nutrit), 52. *Prof Exp:* Asst animal husb, Univ Ill, 48-51; res assoc nutrit, Merck Inst Therapeut Res, 51-52; assoc prof animal husb, 52-59, head dept, 60-67, PROF ANIMAL HUSB, SDAK STATE UNIV, 59- *Concurrent Pos:* Vis prof, Univ Nottingham & Nat Inst Res, Dairying, Eng, 74-75. *Mem:* Am Soc Animal Sci; Am Inst Nutrit. *Res:* Swine nutrition; antibiotics; selenium poisoning; protein levels and amino acid requirements; high protein cereals; mineral nutrition; by-product feeds. *Mailing Add:* Dept of Animal Sci SDak State Univ Brookings SD 57007

WAHNSIEDLER, WALTER EDWARD, b Ind, Jan 23, 47; m 69; c 1. CHEMICAL PHYSICS. *Educ:* Purdue Univ, BS, 67, PhD(chem physics), 75. *Prof Exp:* Vis scholar mat sci, Northwestern Univ, 74; SR SCIENTIST PHYS CHEM, ALUMINUM CO AM, 75- *Mem:* Am Chem Soc. *Res:* Theoretical solid state studies; numerical modelling of chemical processes; properties of oxides; aluminum smelting; environmental impact of industry. *Mailing Add:* 16 Oakwood Terr Oakmont PA 15139

WAHR, JOHN CANNON, b Ann Arbor, Mich, Apr 2, 26; m 49; c 2. PHYSICS. *Educ:* Univ Mich, BSE, 48, MS, 49, PhD(physics), 53. *Prof Exp:* Asst, Univ Mich, 48-49; physicist, Cent Res, Dow Chem Co, 53-80. *Mem:* AAAS; Am Phys Soc; Optical Soc Am. *Res:* Quantum electronics; holography; atomic and molecular physics; surface physics. *Mailing Add:* 705 Crescent Dr Midland MI 48640

WAHRHAFTIG, AUSTIN LEVY, b Sacramento, Calif, May 5, 17; m 57. MASS SPECTROMETRY. *Educ:* Univ Calif, AB, 38; Calif Inst Technol, PhD(phys chem), 41. *Prof Exp:* Fel, Calif Inst Technol, 41-45; res chemist, Dr W E Williams, 45-46; univ fel, Ohio State Univ, 46-47; from asst prof to assoc prof chem, 47-59, PROF CHEM, UNIV UTAH, 59- *Concurrent Pos:* Vis prof, Latrobe Univ, Australia, 72 & 80. *Mem:* AAAS; Am Chem Soc; Am Phys Soc; Am Soc Mass Spectrometry. *Res:* Molecular spectra; mass spectrometry; kinetics of gas-phase ion reactions; dense (supercritical) gas chromatography. *Mailing Add:* Dept Chem Univ Utah Salt Lake City UT 84112

WAHRHAFTIG, CLYDE (ADOLPH), b Fresno, Calif, Dec 1, 19. GEOLOGY. *Educ:* Calif Inst Technol, BS, 41; Harvard Univ, MA, 47, PhD, 53. *Prof Exp:* Jr geologist, US Geol Surv, 41 & 42-43, asst geologist, 43-45; assoc prof, 60-67, PROF GEOL, UNIV CALIF, BERKELEY, 67-; GEOLOGIST, US GEOL SURV, 45- *Concurrent Pos:* Am Geol Inst vis geoscientist, 69; mem comt geol sci, Nat Acad Sci, 70-72; consult, Conserv Found, 71-72. *Honors & Awards:* Kirk Bryan Award, Geol Soc Am, 67. *Mem:* AAAS; fel Geol Soc Am; Am Geophys Union. *Res:* Geomorphology; igneous petrology; stratigraphy and sedimentation; geology applied to land use; geology of California and Alaska. *Mailing Add:* Dept of Geol & Geophys Univ of Calif Berkeley CA 94720

WAI, CHIEN MOO, b China, Aug 8, 37; m 65; c 2. NUCLEAR CHEMISTRY, GEOCHEMISTRY. *Educ:* Nat Taiwan Univ, BS, 60; Univ Calif, Irvine, PhD(chem), 67. *Prof Exp:* Fel, Univ Calif, Los Angeles, 66-69; from asst prof to assoc prof chem & geol, 69-78, PROF CHEM, UNIV IDAHO, 78- *Concurrent Pos:* Vis assoc prof, Inst Geophys & Planetary Physics, Univ Calif, Los Angeles, 75-76. *Mem:* AAAS; Am Chem Soc; Geochem Soc. *Res:* Chemical effects of nuclear transformation; origin of meteorites; heavy metal pollution. *Mailing Add:* Dept Chem Univ Idaho Moscow ID 83843

WAIBEL, PAUL EDWARD, b Hawthorne, NJ, June 22, 27; m 71; c 3. POULTRY NUTRITION. *Educ:* Rutgers Univ, BS, 48; Univ Wis, MS, 51, PhD(poultry nutrit, biochem), 53. *Prof Exp:* Teaching asst poultry husb, Univ Wis, 49-53; res assoc poultry nutrit, Cornell Univ, 53-54; res assoc, 54-55, from asst prof to assoc prof, 55-64, PROF POULTRY NUTRIT, UNIV MINN, ST PAUL, 64- *Honors & Awards:* Nat Turkey Fedn Res Award; Am Feed Manufacturers Poultry Nutrit Res Award. *Mem:* AAAS; Am Inst Nutrit; Am Chem Soc; Poultry Sci Asn; NY Acad Sci. *Res:* Nutrition of turkeys. *Mailing Add:* Dept of Animal Sci Univ Minn 1404 Gortner Ave St Paul MN 55108

WAIBLER, PAUL JOHN, b Odebolt, Iowa, Mar 18, 13; m 49; c 2. MECHANICAL ENGINEERING. *Educ:* Kans State Univ, BS, 43; Yale Univ, ME 44; Univ Ill, PhD, 58. *Prof Exp:* Instr mech eng, Yale Univ, 44-49; asst prof, Univ Utah, 49-51; res assoc, Univ Ill, 53-54; assoc prof, 54-59, PROF MECH ENG, UNIV WASH, 59- *Mem:* Am Soc Mech Engrs. *Res:* Thermodynamics and heat transfer. *Mailing Add:* Dept of Mech Eng Univ of Wash FU-10 Seattle WA 98195

WAID, MARGARET COWSAR, b Baton Rouge, La, Feb 21, 41; m 63; c 2. APPLIED MATHEMATICS. *Educ:* La State Univ, Baton Rouge, BS, 61, MS, 63; Tex Tech Univ, PhD(math), 71. *Prof Exp:* Teacher pub schs, La, 65-67; instr math, Tex Tech Univ, 67-71; asst prof math, DC Teachers Col, 71-72; assoc prof math, Univ Del, 72-81; SR DEVELOP ENGR, ENG INTERPRETATION, SCHLUMBERGER WELL SERV, 81- *Concurrent Pos:* Vis assoc prof math, Univ Tex, 79-80. *Mem:* Am Math Soc; Soc Indust & Appl Math; Asn Women in Math; Sigma Xi. *Res:* Partial differential equations, including applications to fluid flow through porous media analysis; applications to well log analysis, especially pressure measurements and production logging. *Mailing Add:* Schlumberger Well Serv PO Box 2175 Houston TX 77001

WAID, REX A(DNEY), b Dardanelle, Ark, Jan 14, 33; m 59; c 3. ELECTRICAL ENGINEERING. *Educ:* William Jewell Col, BA, 54; Univ Mo-Columbia, BS, 58, MS, 59; Univ Wis-Madison, PhD(elec eng), 68. *Prof Exp:* From instr to asst prof elec eng, Univ Mo-Columbia, 59-63; asst prof, Univ Wis-Madison, 65-66; asst prof, 66-76, PROF ELEC ENG, UNIV MO-COLUMBIA, 76- *Concurrent Pos:* Consult, Univ Mo Network Analyzer, 62-63. *Mem:* Inst Elec & Electronics Engrs; Am Soc Eng Educ; Simulation Coun. *Res:* Pattern recognition; data acquisition and processing; computer design and development. *Mailing Add:* Dept of Elec Eng Univ of Mo Columbia MO 65201

WAID, TED HENRY, b Warsaw, Poland, Mar 28, 25; Can citizen; m 58; c 2. CHEMICAL ENGINEERING, ORGANIC CHEMISTRY. *Educ:* Univ Caen, BSc, 50, BEng, 51; McGill Univ, PhD(org chem), 57. *Prof Exp:* Chemist, Sherwin-Williams Co, Can, 52-53; sr res chemist, Monsanto Can Ltd, 57-60, res group leader surface finishes, 60-64, develop specialist, 64-65; PRES, CHEMOR INC, 65- *Concurrent Pos:* Mem Can Govt Specifications Bd, 63- *Mem:* Am Chem Soc; Sigma Xi. *Res:* Syntheses of nitrogen containing steroids, chloromethylated aromatic hydrocarbons, aromatic polyamides and sulphur containing heterocyclic compounds; chemical coatings and adhesives; polymer chemistry. *Mailing Add:* 10520 Bois de Boulogne Montreal PQ H4N 1K7 Can

WAIDE, JACK BOID, b El Paso, Tex, Aug 29, 47; m 67; c 2. ECOLOGY. *Educ:* Univ Tex, Austin, BA, 70; Univ Ga, PhD(ecol), 79. *Prof Exp:* Asst biol & zool, Univ Tex, Austin, 68-70; res asst ecol, Univ Ga, 73-76; asst prof zool, Clemson Univ, 76-80; MEM STAFF, ENVIRON SCI DIV, OAK RIDGE NAT LAB, 80- *Mem:* Ecol Soc Am; AAAS; Am Inst Biol Sci; Asn Southeastern Biologists; Sigma Xi. *Res:* Ecosystem theory; systems ecology; bioecochemistry of terrestrial and fresh water ecosystems; ecosystems and their response to perturbation; soil biota and substrate quality as regulators of terrestrial decomposition processes; systems and decomposition processes; forest defoliation. *Mailing Add:* Environ Sci Div Oak Ridge Nat Lab Oak Ridge TN 37830

WAIDELICH, D(ONALD) L(ONG), b Allentown, Pa, May 3, 15; m 39; c 1. ELECTRICAL ENGINEERING. *Educ:* Lehigh Univ, BS, 36, MS, 38; Iowa State Univ, PhD(elec eng), 46. *Prof Exp:* Asst, Lehigh Univ, 36-38; from instr to assoc prof, 38-47, chmn dept, 60-61, assoc dir eng exp sta, 54-58, PROF ELEC ENG, UNIV MO-COLUMBIA, 47- *Concurrent Pos:* Elec engr, US Naval Ord Lab, 44-45; Fulbright grant & vis prof, Univ Cairo, 51-52; Fulbright res grant, Univ Australia, 61-62; vis prof, Univ New South Wales, 61-62; consult, US Navy Electronics Lab, 49-52, UNESCO, Egypt, 52, Argonne Nat Lab, 53-56, 65-72, Bendix Aviation Corp, 57, Int Tel & Tel Co Labs, 58-59, Midwest Res Inst, 60-61, Goddard Space Flight Ctr, NASA, 62-67, US Naval Underwater Systs Ctr, 71 & Hughes Aircraft Co, 72-82. *Mem:* Am Soc Eng Educ; Nat Soc Prof Engrs; fel Inst Elec & Electronics Engrs; Am Soc Nondestructive Testing; Am Soc Testing & Mat. *Res:* Electromagnetic fields; nondestructive testing. *Mailing Add:* Dept of Elec Eng Univ of Mo Columbia MO 65211

WAIFE, SHOLOM OMI, b New York, NY, Feb 20, 19; m 42; c 2. INTERNAL MEDICINE, MEDICAL EDUCATION. *Educ:* Johns Hopkins Univ, AB, 40; NY Univ, MD, 43; Am Bd Internal Med, dipl, 51. *Prof Exp:* Res assoc med, Sch Med, Yale Univ, 45; resen resident physician, Long Island Col Hosp, 45-46; asst med, Med Sch, Johns Hopkins Univ, 46-48; instr, Sch Med, Univ Pa, 48-52; assoc, 52-60, asst prof, 60-68, ASSOC PROF MED, SCH MED, IND UNIV, INDIANAPOLIS, 68-; DIR MED SERV DIV, RES LAB, ELI LILLY & CO, 64- *Concurrent Pos:* Ed-in-chief, Am J Clin Nutrit, 52-62; head med educ dept, Eli Lilly & Co, 52-64; co-ed, Perspectives Biol & Med, 58-64. *Mem:* Am Diabetes Asn; Am Med Writers' Asn; fel Am Col Physicians; Am Fedn Clin Res. *Res:* Metabolism; diabetes; obesity; vitamins. *Mailing Add:* Lilly Res Labs 307 E McCarty St Indianapolis IN 46225

WAILES, JOHN LEONARD, b Loveland, Colo, Oct 9, 23; m 47; c 3. PHARMACY. *Educ:* Univ Colo, BS, 47, MS, 50, PhD(pharm), 54. *Prof Exp:* Chemist, US Food & Drug Admin, 47-48; pharmacist, Park-Hill Drug Co, Colo, 48-50; instr pharm, Univ Colo, 50-54; from asst prof to assoc prof, 43-61, PROF PHARM, UNIV MONT, 61- *Concurrent Pos:* USPHS grant, 59; with Merck Sharp & Dohme Div, Merck & Co, Colo, 51-54. *Mem:* Am Pharmaceut Asn; Asn Cols Pharm. *Res:* Respiration of mold and yeast in the presence and absence of inhibitors and antagonists using the Warburg apparatus; preservation of pharmaceutical products; synergism and antagonism of various preservatives and their possible inactivation; complexing of macromolecules. *Mailing Add:* Dept of Pharm Univ of Mont Missoula MT 59812

WAINBERG, MARK ARNOLD, b Montreal, Que, Apr 21, 45; m 69; c 2. CANCER. *Educ:* McGill Univ, BSc, 66; Columbia Univ, PhD(microbiol), 72. *Prof Exp:* Lectr immunol, Hebrew Univ-Hadassah Med Sch, 72-74; STAFF INVESTR TUMOR IMMUNOL, LADY DAVIS INST MED RES, JEWISH GEN HOSP, MONTREAL, 74- *Concurrent Pos:* Europ Molecular Biol Orgn res fel, 72-74; Que Med Res Coun res scholar, 75-; Nat Cancer Inst Can res grant, 75-; researcher, Dept Microbiol & Immunol, Univ Montreal, 75- *Mem:* Am Soc Microbiol; Sigma Xi; Can Soc Immunol; NY Acad Sci; Can Oncol Soc. *Res:* Cellular and humoral anti-tumor immunity of chickens bearing tumors induced by Rous sarcoma virus; development of monoclonal anti-viral antibodies; viral gene expression at different stages of tumor growth. *Mailing Add:* Lady Davis Inst for Med Res 3755 Cote Ste Catherine Rd Montreal PQ H3T 1E2 Can

WAINE, MARTIN, b Berlin, Ger, Apr 8, 33; US citizen; m 63; c 2. PHYSICS. *Educ:* Columbia Univ, BS, 58; Yale Univ, MS, 59, PhD(physics), 65. *Prof Exp:* Asst prof physics, Mt Holyoke Col, 64-70; prin engr, MRC Corp, Md, 71-72; chief engr, Diamondex Enterprises Inc, 72-74; vpres mfg, Evershield Prod Inc, 74-75; prin engr, MRC Corp, 75-80. *Mem:* Am Phys Soc. *Res:* Dynamic nuclear orientation; nuclear magnetic resonance; instrumentation and control theory. *Mailing Add:* 29 Coventry Lane Riverside CT 06878

WAINER, ARTHUR, b Cincinnati, Ohio, Jan 28, 38; m 57; c 3. BIOCHEMISTRY. *Educ:* Univ Miami, BS, 57; Univ Fla, PhD(biochem), 61. *Prof Exp:* Instr biochem, Univ Fla, 61-62; from instr to assoc prof, Bowman Gray Sch Med, 62-70; PROF CHEM, EDINBORO STATE COL, 70-, CHMN DEPT, 80- *Mem:* AAAS; Am Chem Soc; Am Soc Biol Chemists; Am Asn Clin Chemists. *Res:* Sulfur amino acid metabolism, ion exchange column chromatography. *Mailing Add:* Dept of Chem Edinboro State Col Edinboro PA 16412

WAINER, IRVING WILLIAM, b Detroit, Mich, March 27, 44. STEREOCHEMICAL SEPARATIONS, PHARMACOKINETICS. *Educ:* Wayne State Univ, BS, 65; Cornell Univ, PhD(chem), 70. *Prof Exp:* Fel, Inst Molecular Biol, Univ Ore, 70-72; res assoc, Dept Pharmacol, Thomas Jefferson Univ, 72-78; RES CHEMIST ORG CHEM, DIV DRUG CHEM, FOOD & DRUG ADMIN, 78- *Concurrent Pos:* Harry chair prof, Hartwick Col, 81. *Mem:* Am Chem Soc; AAAS; Asn Off Anal Chemists. *Res:* Separation of steroisomers; development of assays for isomeric purity of drug substances; application of these assays to the study of the pharmacokinetics of drug substance in humans. *Mailing Add:* Food & Drug Admin HFD-420 200 C St Southwest Washington DC 20204

WAINERDI, RICHARD E(LLIOTT), b New York, NY, Nov 27, 31; m 56; c 2. NUCLEAR ACTIVATION ANALYSIS. *Educ:* Univ Okla, BS, 52; Pa State Univ, MS, 55, PhD, 58. *Prof Exp:* Jr exploitation engr, Shell Oil Co, 52; asst petrol eng, Pa State Univ, 53-55; coordr nuclear activities, Dresser Industs, Inc, 56-57; assoc prof petrol & nuclear eng, Tex A&M Univ, 57-61, supvr training reactor facil & radiol safety off, 57-58, head nuclear sci ctr, Eng Exp Sta, 57-59, head activation anal res lab, 58-77, asst to dean eng, 59-62, prof chem eng, 61-77, assoc dean eng, 62-72, vpres acad affairs, 72-77; SR VPRES & DIR OF SPEC PROJ, 3D/INT, INC, 77- *Mem:* Am Nuclear Soc; Nat Soc Prof Engrs. *Res:* Activation analysis and isotope utilization. *Mailing Add:* 1635 Warwickshire Dr Houston TX 77077

WAINFAN, ELSIE, b New York, NY, Aug 2, 26; m 47; c 2. BIOCHEMISTRY. *Educ:* City Col New York, BS, 47; Univ Southern Calif, PhD(biochem), 54. *Prof Exp:* Res technician, NY Psychiat Inst, 47-49; USPHS fel, Med Sch, Univ Ore, 55-56; res assoc biochem, Cornell Univ, 56-59; res assoc, Col Physicians & Surgeons, Columbia Univ, 59-67; asst prof, Univ Southern Calif, 67-68; assoc investr, 68-80, INVESTR, NY BLOOD CTR, 80- *Concurrent Pos:* Assoc scientist, Sloan-Kettering Inst Cancer Res, 77- *Mem:* Am Chem Soc; Am Soc Biol Chemists; Am Soc Microbiologists; Am Asn Cancer Res. *Res:* Carcinogenesis, nucleic acids, enzymes; metabolic inhibitors. *Mailing Add:* New York Blood Ctr New York NY 10021

WAINIO, WALTER W, b Astoria, Ore, Sept 8, 14; m 49; c 1. ENZYMOLOGY, BIOCHEMISTRY. *Educ:* Univ Mass, BS, 36; Pa State Univ, MS, 40; Cornell Univ, PhD(physiol), 43. *Prof Exp:* Asst animal nutrit, Pa State Univ, 36-38, instr, 38-41; asst prof physiol, Med Col, Cornell Univ, 41-43; asst prof, Col Dent, NY Univ, 43-48; assoc res specialist, 48-50, assoc prof biochem, 50-59, chmn dept physiol & biochem, 60-63 & 66-67, chmn dept biochem, 67-72 & 75-78, PROF BIOCHEM, RUTGERS UNIV, 59- *Concurrent Pos:* Mem, Marine Biol Labs, Woods Hole. *Mem:* AAAS; Am Soc Biol Chemists; fel NY Acad Sci; Brit Biochem Soc. *Res:* Cytochromes. *Mailing Add:* Nelson Biol Labs Box 1059 Rutgers Univ Dept of Biochem Piscataway NJ 08854

WAINWRIGHT, LILLIAN K (SCHNEIDER), b Brooklyn, NY, June 30, 23; m 52; c 2. GENETICS. *Educ:* Brooklyn Col, BA, 43; Columbia Univ, MA, 51, PhD(zool), 56. *Prof Exp:* Res asst zool, Columbia Univ, 43-52; from asst prof to assoc prof biol, 57-70, PROF BIOL, MT ST VINCENT UNIV, 70-, CHMN DEPT, 79- *Mem:* Genetics Soc Am; Can Soc Cell Biol; Sigma Xi; Can Fedn Biol Soc. *Res:* Organ cultures as models of tissues in vivo. *Mailing Add:* Dept Biol Mt St Vincent Univ Halifax NS B3M 2J6 Can

WAINWRIGHT, RAY M, b Deep River, Iowa, July 24, 13; m 52; c 3. ELECTRICAL ENGINEERING. *Educ:* Mont State Univ, BSEE, 36; Univ Ill, MSEE, 49. *Prof Exp:* Asst elec engr, Mont Power Co, 36-38; elec engr, Mont-Dakota Utilities Co, 38-42, res engr, 45-46; res engr, US Signal Corps, 42-45; from asst prof to assoc prof elec eng, Univ Ill, 46-56; dir eng, Good-All Elec Mfg Co, 56-61; mgr res, Capacitor Div, TRW, Inc, 61-63; prof elec eng, Colo State Univ, 63-66; prof elec eng & coordr continuing educ, Univ Denver, 66-74; STAFF ENGR, STEARNS-ROGER INC, 74- *Mem:* Nat Asn Corrosion Engrs; sr mem Inst Elec & Electronics Engrs. *Res:* Cathodic protection; reliability engineering; engineering economy. *Mailing Add:* 3715 S Niagara Way Denver CO 80237

WAINWRIGHT, RICHARD ADOLPH, b Creston, Iowa, Apr 15, 31; m 76; c 7. ELECTRONIC ENGINEERING. *Educ:* Capitol Inst Technol, BSET, 54. *Hon Degrees:* SciD, Capitol Inst Technol, 76. *Prof Exp:* Consult eng res, Rixon Electronics, 58-60; res engr, Telona Eng Co, 60-62; pres & eng dir, I-TEL, Inc, 62-71; sr partner, 71-73, OWNER, CHMN BD & CONSULT ENG RES, CIRQTEL INC, 73- *Concurrent Pos:* Lectr math & eng, Emerson Inst, 53-54; sr lectr, Capitol Inst Technol, 53-56; asst dept head antennas,

Page Commun Eng, 56-58; mem bd trustees, Capitol Inst Technol, 68-, vchmn, 75, chmn, 76-80. *Mem:* Inst Elec & Electronics Engrs; Numerical Control Soc; Am Photo-optical Soc; AAAS; NY Acad Sci. *Res:* Electric wave filters; antennas; network synthesis and analysis. *Mailing Add:* CIRQTEL Inc 10504 Wheatley St Kensington MD 20795

WAINWRIGHT, STANLEY D, b Hull, Eng, Apr 15, 27; Can citizen; m 52; c 2. NEUROCHEMISTRY, BIOLOGICAL CLOCKS. *Educ:* Cambridge Univ, BA, 47; Univ London, PhD(biochem), 50. *Prof Exp:* Brit Med Res Coun exchange scholar biochem, Physiol Microbiol Serv, Pasteur Inst, Paris, 50-51; res assoc microbial genetics, Columbia Univ, 51-52; Nat Res Coun Can & Atomic Energy Can, Ltd fel, Biol Div, Atomic Energy Can, Ltd, 52-55; res assoc microbial physiol, Yale, 55-56; res asst prof & Med Res Coun assoc biochem, 56-58, res assoc prof & Med Res Coun assoc, 58-64, PROF BIOCHEM, DALHOUSIE UNIV, 65- *Concurrent Pos:* Career investr, Med Res Coun, 65- *Mem:* AAAS; Genetics Soc Am; Am Soc Cell Biologists; Can Biochem Soc; Can Soc Cell Biol (pres, 75-76). *Res:* Biochemical neuroendocrinology of the developing chick pineal gland. *Mailing Add:* Dept Biochem Fac Med Dalhousie Univ Halifax NS B3H 3J5 Can

WAINWRIGHT, STEPHEN ANDREW, b Indianapolis, Ind, Oct 9, 31; m 56; c 4. INVERTEBRATE ZOOLOGY. *Educ:* Duke Univ, BS, 53; Univ Cambridge, BA, 58, MA, 63; Univ Calif, Berkeley, PhD(zool), 62. *Prof Exp:* NSF fel med physics, Karolinska Inst, Sweden, 62-63; NSF fel biol, Woods Hole Oceanog Inst, 63-64; assoc prof zool, 64-76, PROF ZOOL, DUKE UNIV, 76- *Mem:* Soc Exp Biol & Med; Am Soc Enol; Marine Biol Asn UK. *Res:* Functional morphology of supportive systems of animals and plants from the macromolecular through the organism levels of organization. *Mailing Add:* Dept of Zool Duke Univ Durham NC 27706

WAINWRIGHT, THOMAS EVERETT, b Seattle, Wash, Sept 22, 27; m 59; c 5. PHYSICS. *Educ:* Mont State Col, BS, 50; Univ Notre Dame, PhD(physics), 54. *Prof Exp:* Instr physics, Univ Notre Dame, 53-54; STAFF PHYSICIST, LAWRENCE LIVERMORE LAB, UNIV CALIF, 54- *Honors & Awards:* Lawrence Award, US AEC, 73. *Mem:* Fel Am Phys Soc; Am Geophys Union. *Res:* Statistical mechanics; applied physics. *Mailing Add:* 955 S L St Livermore CA 94550

WAINWRIGHT, WILLIAM LLOYD, b Fostoria, Ohio; m 51; c 4. ENGINEERING. *Educ:* Purdue Univ, West Lafayette, BS, 51, MS, 54; Univ Mich, Ann Arbor, PhD(eng mech), 58. *Prof Exp:* Assoc prof mech, US Naval Postgrad Sch, 58-61; res asst, Univ Calif, Berkeley, 61-63, asst prof, 63-64; ASSOC PROF MECH, UNIV COLO, BOULDER, 64- *Mem:* AAAS; Soc Eng Sci. *Res:* Continuum mechanics. *Mailing Add:* 4305 Chippewa Dr Boulder CO 80303

WAISMAN, JERRY, b Borger, Tex, Sept 14, 34; m 58; c 3. PATHOLOGY. *Educ:* Univ Tex, BA, 56, MD, 60. *Prof Exp:* Pathologist & chief lab div path, US Air Force Hosp, Sheppard AFB, Tex, 62-64; fel path, Univ Utah, 64-65, instr path, 65-68; from asst prof to assoc prof, Univ Calif, Los Angeles, 68-76, prof path, 76-81; DIR LAB, UNIV HOSP, NEW YORK UNIV MED CTR, 81- *Concurrent Pos:* Attend physician, Ft Douglas Vet Admin Hosp, Salt Lake City, 67, part-time sr physician, 67-68; consult, Sepulveda Vet Admin Hosp, 76- *Mem:* Int Acad Path; Am Asn Path; Electron Micros Soc Am. *Res:* Ultrastructure of benign and malignant neoplasms. *Mailing Add:* Dept of Path NY Univ Sch Med 550 First Ave New York NY 10016

WAISMAN, JOSEPH L, b Racine, Wis, Mar 10, 19; m 40; c 1. METALLURGICAL ENGINEERING, MATERIALS SCIENCE. *Educ:* Univ Ill, MetE, 40; Univ Calif, Los Angeles, PhD(eng), 69. *Prof Exp:* Asst chief metallurgist, Douglas Aircraft Co, Calif, 45-57; western mgr, Tatnall Measuring Systs Div, Budd Co, 57-59; chief metallurgist, Douglas Aircraft Co, Calif, 59-60, chief mat res & prod methods, 60-62, asst chief engr, missiles & space systs, 62-64, asst dir res & develop, 64-66, dir, 66-67, dir res & develop, McDonnell Douglas Astronaut Co, Huntington Beach, 67-68, dir res & develop, 68-73, dir advan prod applns, 73-80, dir cryogenic insulation prog, 80-81, DIR ENERGY PROG, MCDONNELL DOUGLAS ASTRONAUT CO WEST, 81- *Concurrent Pos:* Consult, Metals Adv Bd, NSF, 63-66. *Mem:* Fel Am Soc Metals; assoc fel Am Inst Aeronaut & Astronaut; Soc Exp Stress Anal; Am Inst Mining, Metall & Petrol Engrs; Am Soc Testing & Mat. *Res:* Fatigue of metals; stress corrosion cracking; residual stresses. *Mailing Add:* 25 Redwood Tree Lane Irvine CA 92715

WAISS, ANTHONY C, JR, b China, Sept 30, 36; US citizen; m 58; c 3. ORGANIC CHEMISTRY, NATURAL PRODUCTS. *Educ:* Univ Calif, Berkeley, BS, 58; Univ Calif, Los Angeles, PhD(chem), 62. *Prof Exp:* Res fel chem, Harvard Univ, 62-63; RES LEADER, WESTERN REGION RES CTR, AGR RES SERV, USDA, 63- *Mem:* Am Chem Soc; Royal Soc Chem; Phytochem Soc NAm; Entom Soc Am. *Res:* Isolation and structural determination of biologically active compounds; chemical basis of host plant resistance to insects and diseases; crop protection. *Mailing Add:* Western Region Res Ctr USDA Albany CA 94710

WAIT, DAVID FRANCIS, b Sidney, Nebr, Sept 28, 33; m 56; c 4. METROLOGY. *Educ:* Colo State Univ, BS, 55, MS, 57; Univ Mich, PhD(physics), 63. *Prof Exp:* Instr & res asst physics, Univ Mich, 62-63; sr scientist, Laser Systs Ctr, Lear Siegler, Inc, 63; PHYSICIST, NAT BUR STAND, 63- *Mem:* Sigma Xi; Inst Elec & Electronics Engrs; Microwave Theory & Tech Soc. *Res:* Noise in communications; radiometers; microwave cryogenic noise standards. *Mailing Add:* 325 Broadway Boulder CO 80302

WAIT, JAMES RICHARD, b Ottawa, Can; US citizen. GEOENVIRONMENTAL SCIENCE. *Educ:* Univ Toronto, BASc, 48, MASc, 49, PhD(elec eng), 51. *Prof Exp:* Consult appl physics, US Dept Com, Boulder, Co, 65-80; PROF ELEC ENG, UNIV ARIZ, 80- *Concurrent Pos:* Mem nat comt, Int Union Radio Sci, 58-61 & 65-68, secy, US Nat Comt, 75-78; adj prof elec eng, Univ Colo, Boulder, 61-, fel, Coop Inst Res Environ Sci, 68- *Honors & Awards:* Gold Medal, US Dept Commerce, 58; Flemming Award, US Chamber Commerce, 64; Harry Diamond Award, Inst Elec & Electronics Eng, 64; NOAA Res & Achievement Award, Nat Oceanic & Atmospheric Admin, 73; Van der Pol Gold Medal, Int Union Radio Sci, 77. *Mem:* Nat Acad Eng; fel Inst Elec Engrs; Am Geophys Union; fel Inst Elec & Electronics Eng; Int Union Radio Sci. *Res:* Applications of electromagnetic theory to problems in geophysics and telecommunications. *Mailing Add:* Dept Elec Eng Bldg 20 Univ Ariz Tucson AZ 95721

WAIT, JOHN V, b Chicago, Ill, Oct 1, 32; m 61; c 2. ELECTRICAL ENGINEERING. *Educ:* Univ Iowa, BSEE, 55; Univ NMex, MSEE, 59; Univ Ariz, PhD, 63. *Prof Exp:* Res engr, RCA Labs, 55; instr, Univ NMex, 57-59; res engr & instr, Univ Ariz, 59-63; asst prof, Univ Calif, Santa Barbara, 63-64; assoc prof grad eng educ syst, Univ Fla, 64-66; assoc prof, 66-71, PROF ELEC ENG, UNIV ARIZ, 71- *Res:* Electronics; computers; signal processing. *Mailing Add:* Dept of Elec Eng Univ of Ariz Tucson AZ 85721

WAIT, SAMUEL CHARLES, JR, b Albany, NY, Jan 26, 32; m 57; c 2. PHYSICAL CHEMISTRY. *Educ:* Rensselaer Polytech Inst, BS, 53, MS, 55, PhD(chem), 56. *Prof Exp:* Fulbright fel, Univ Col, London, 56-57, asst lectr chem, 57-58; res fel, Univ Minn, 58-59; asst prof, Carnegie Inst Technol, 59-60; chemist, Nat Bur Stand, 60-61; from asst prof to assoc prof chem, 61-71, asst dean sch sci, 72-74, actg dean, 78-79, PROF CHEM, RENSSELAER POLYTECH INST, 71-, ASSOC DEAN SCI, 74- *Concurrent Pos:* Mem adv coun sci & math, Schenectady County Community Col, 75-83, chmn adv coun, 76-78; mem, Schenectady County Fire Adv Bd, 76-81, vchmn, 78; mem bd fire comnrs, Niskayuna Dist Two, 78-83. *Mem:* Am Chem Soc; Optical Soc Am; Coblentz Soc. *Res:* High resolution ultraviolet, infrared and Raman spectroscopy; asymmetric rotor theory and calculation; quantum biology; molecular orbital theory; vibrational and fine structural analyses; theoretical methods; simple and polyatomic systems. *Mailing Add:* Sch Sci Rensselaer Polytech Inst Troy NY 12181

WAITE, ALBERT B, b Holbrook, Ariz, Mar 4, 36; m 60; c 4. REPRODUCTIVE PHYSIOLOGY, GENETICS. *Educ:* Utah State Univ, BS, 61, MS, 62; Univ Mo, PhD(reprod physiol), 66. *Prof Exp:* Instr reprod physiol, Univ Mo, 66-67; asst prof animal husb, 67-71, assoc prof agr, 71-74, PROF AGR, CENT MO STATE UNIV, 74- *Mem:* Am Fertil Soc; Brit Soc Study Fertil. *Res:* Estrus synchronization in sheep and swine; embryonic mortality in domestic animals. *Mailing Add:* Dept of Agr Cent Mo State Univ Warrensburg MO 64093

WAITE, DANIEL ELMER, b Grand Rapids, Mich, Feb 19, 26; m 48; c 4. ORAL SURGERY, MAXILLOFACIAL SURGERY. *Educ:* Univ Iowa, DDS, 53, MS, 55; Am Bd Oral Surg, dipl, 59. *Prof Exp:* Resident oral surg, Univ Hosp, Univ Iowa, 53-55, from instr to prof & head dept, Col Dent, 55-59, assoc prof, Hosp Dent Dept, Univ Hosps, 57-63; asst prof dent, Mayo Grad Sch Med, 63-68, PROF ORAL SURG, CHMN DIV & HEAD HOSP DENT, SCH DENT, UNIV MINN, MINNEAPOLIS, 68- *Concurrent Pos:* Mem staff, Proj Hope, Peru, Ceylon & Haiti; trustee, Park Col, Mo. *Mem:* Am Soc Oral Surg; Am Dent Asn; Am Col Dent; Int Asn Dent Res. *Mailing Add:* Div of Oral & Maxillofacial Surg Univ of Minn Sch of Dent Minneapolis MN 55455

WAITE, JOHN HENRY, b St Cloud, Minn, Aug 6, 33; m 42; c 5. SURGERY. *Educ:* State Univ NY Buffalo, MD, 47; Ohio State Univ, MMSc, 53. *Prof Exp:* Instr surg, Ohio State Univ, 50-53; investr, NIH, 54-57; clin instr surg, Univ Wash, 59-61; clin asst prof, Tulane Univ, 61-64, clin assoc prof, 64-67; assoc prof, 67-72, PROF SURG, LA STATE UNIV, BATON ROUGE, 73- *Mem:* Am Col Surg. *Res:* Clinical cancer therapy. *Mailing Add:* Earl K Long Mem Hosp 5825 Airline Hwy Baton Rouge LA 70805

WAITE, LEONARD CHARLES, b Reynoldsville, Pa, Sept 10, 41; m 60; c 3. PHARMACOLOGY. *Educ:* Alderson-Braddus Col, BS, 65; WVa Univ, MS, 67; Univ Mo-Columbia, PhD(pharmacol), 69. *Prof Exp:* Asst prof, 70-74, ASSOC PROF PHARMACOL, SCH MED, UNIV LOUISVILLE, 74- *Mem:* Endocrine Soc; Am Soc Pharmacol & Exp Therapeut. *Res:* Endocrinology; physiology; calcium metabolism. *Mailing Add:* Dept Pharmacol Univ Louisville Sch Med Louisville KY 40208

WAITE, MARILYNN RANSOM FAIRFAX, b Mt Vernon, NY, May 1, 42. VIROLOGY. *Educ:* Bryn Mawr Col, BA, 63; Dartmouth Col, PhD(molecular biol), 71. *Prof Exp:* Instr microbiol, Dartmouth Med Sch, 73; ASST PROF MICROBIOL, UNIV TEX, AUSTIN, 73- *Concurrent Pos:* Anna Fuller Fund fel, Med Sch, Dartmouth Col, 71-73; NIH fel, 73. *Mem:* AAAS; Am Soc Microbiol. *Res:* Replication of RNA tumor viruses and Sindbis virus; interaction of viral proteins with membranes of infected cells. *Mailing Add:* Dept of Microbiol Univ of Tex Austin TX 78712

WAITE, MOSELEY, b Durham, NC, Oct 22, 36; m 59; c 3. BIOCHEMISTRY, ORGANIC CHEMISTRY. *Educ:* Rollins Col, BS, 58; Duke Univ, PhD(biochem), 63. *Prof Exp:* Asst prof, 67-71, assoc prof, 71-76, PROF BIOCHEM, BOWMAN GRAY SCH MED, 76-, CHMN, 78- *Concurrent Pos:* Am Cancer Soc fel biochem, Duke Univ, 62-65; Am Heart Asn advan fel, Univ Utrecht, 65-67; grants, Am Heart Asn, 66-69, USPHS, 67-81 & NC Heart Asn, 70-73; USPHS res career develop award, 73-78 & Environ Protection Agency, 80-82. *Mem:* AAAS; Am Chem Soc; Am Soc Biol Chemists. *Res:* Phospholipid and fatty acid metabolism; enzyme purification and characterization; relation of metabolism of lipids to certain morphological changes, especially mitochondrion; prostaglandin synthesis. *Mailing Add:* Dept Biochem Bowman Gray Sch Med Winston-Salem NC 27103

WAITE, PAUL J, b New Salem, Ill, June 21, 18; m 43; c 2. CLIMATOLOGY. *Educ:* Western State Univ, BEd, 40; Univ Mich, MS, 66. *Prof Exp:* Meteorologist, US Air Force, 42-46; meteorologist & climatologist, Nat Weather Bur, 48-74; dep mgr Lacie Proj, Environ Data Serv, 74-76; CLIMATOLOGIST, IOWA DEPT AGR, 76- *Concurrent Pos:* Teacher & coach, Ill schs, 38-39 & 40-42; coach & instr, Ill High Schs, 46-48; adj prof geol & geog, Drake Univ, 70-75 & 77- *Mem:* Am Asn State Climatologists (secy, 76-77; pres, 77-78); Am Meteorol Soc; AAAS; Nat Weather Asn. *Res:* Iowa storm climatology; agricultural climatology; climatology for decision making and descriptive climatology. *Mailing Add:* 6657 NW Timberline Dr Des Moines IA 50313

WAITE, WILLIAM MCCASTLINE, b New York, NY, Jan 14, 39; m 60; c 1. COMPUTER SCIENCE, ELECTRICAL ENGINEERING. *Educ:* Oberlin Col, AB, 60; Columbia Univ, MS, 62, PhD(elec eng), 65. *Prof Exp:* Res asst, Electronics Res Labs, Columbia Univ, 62-65; NSF fel, 65-66; from asst prof to assoc prof, 66-75, PROF ELEC ENG, UNIV COLO, BOULDER, 75- *Concurrent Pos:* Vis lectr, Dept Info Sci, Monash Univ, Australia, 70-71; temp res assoc, Culham Lab, UK Atomic Energy Auth, Eng, 71; newslett ed, Spec Interest Group on Operating Systs, Asn Comput Mach, 72-; mem staff, Inst fu6r Informatik, Univ Karlsruhe, Ger, 80. *Mem:* Asn Comput Mach; Brit Comput Soc. *Res:* Programming languages and software system design. *Mailing Add:* Dept Elec Eng Univ Colo Boulder CO 80309p

WAITER, SERGE-ALBERT, b Paris, France, Feb 8, 30; US citizen; m 53; c 1. MATHEMATICS, GAS DYNAMICS. *Educ:* Univs Lille & Paris, Lic es Sci, 51; Univ Paris, Dr es Sci, Univ Paris, 54. *Prof Exp:* Res engr, Off Aeronaut & Astronaut Res, France, 49-51; flight test engr, Fouga Aircraft, 51-53; mgr prototype dept, Sud Aviation, 53-59; res scientist plasma physics, Eng Ctr, Univ Southern Calif, 59-62; PRIN SR SCIENTIST, SPACE DIV, NORTH AM ROCKWELL CORP, 62- *Mem:* Assoc fel Am Inst Aeronaut & Astronaut; Sigma Xi; Soc Civil Engrs France. *Res:* Fluid dynamics; plasma physics; space sciences. *Mailing Add:* Space Div Rockwell Int Downey CA 90241

WAITES, ROBERT ELLSWORTH, b Middletown, Ohio, Apr 28, 16; m 45; c 2. ENTOMOLOGY. *Educ:* Otterbein Col, BS, 41; Ohio State Univ, MS, 46, PhD(entom), 49. *Prof Exp:* Asst entomologist, 51-68, ASSOC ENTOMOLOGIST, AGR EXP STA, UNIV FLA, 68-, ASSOC PROF ENTOM, 74- *Mem:* Am Registry Prof Entomologists; Coleopterists Soc; Sigma Xi; Entom Soc Am. *Res:* Chemical control of insects on vegetable crops; systematics and biology of the Coccinellidae; insects on peanuts and field corn. *Mailing Add:* Dept Entom Univ Fla Gainesville FL 32611

WAITHE, WILLIAM IRWIN, b New York, NY, May 3, 37; c 4. CELL PHYSIOLOGY, NUCLEAR PROTEINS. *Educ:* St Francis Col, BS, 58; NY Univ, MS, 63, PhD(cell biol), 69. *Prof Exp:* Res asst med genetics, Sch Med, NY Univ, 58-66; res assoc immunol & cell biol, Mt Sinai Sch Med, City Univ NY, 66-68, instr genetics, 68-71; asst prof, 71-77, ASSOC PROF IMMUNOL & CELL BIOL, FAC MED, UNIV LAVAL, 77- *Concurrent Pos:* Scholar, Med Res Coun Can, 71-76. *Mem:* Can Biochem Soc; Can Soc Cell Biol. *Res:* Regulation of growth by nuclear and cytoplasmic proteins; biochemical mechanisms controlling lymphocyte activation in vitro; the role of serum factors in controlling the in vitro immune response. *Mailing Add:* Hotel Dieu de Quebec 11 Cote du Palais Quebec PQ G1R 2J6 Can

WAITKINS, GEORGE RAYMOND, b Glasgow, Scotland, Feb 28, 11; nat US; m 37; c 2. PHYSICAL CHEMISTRY. *Educ:* Syracuse Univ, 33, MS, 34, PhD(chem), 38. *Prof Exp:* Res engr, Battelle Mem Inst, 38-43; chemist, Mutual Chem Co Am, 43; chem supvr, Can Copper Refiners, Ltd, Que, 44-45; res chemist, Calco Div, Am Cyanamid Co, 45-52; asst mgr res dept, Am Zinc Lead & Smelting Co, 52-62; phys chemist, Mattin Labs, Mearl Corp, Ossining, 62-76; RETIRED. *Mem:* Am Chem Soc; Am Inst Chemists; AAAS. *Res:* Inorganic, organic and nacreous pigments; crystal growth. *Mailing Add:* 1 Hughes St Croton-on-Hudson NY 10520

WAITS, BERT KERR, b New Orleans, La, Dec 21, 40; m 63; c 2. MATHEMATICS. *Educ:* Ohio State Univ, BSc, 62, MSc, 64, PhD(math educ), 69. *Prof Exp:* Asst to chmn dept math, 65-69, asst prof math, 69-75, ASSOC PROF MATH, OHIO STATE UNIV, 75- *Mem:* Math Asn Am; Nat Coun Teachers Math. *Res:* Mathematics education; individualized instruction at the college level; calculator based instruction; audiovisual pedagogical experimentation. *Mailing Add:* Dept of Math Ohio State Univ Columbus OH 43210

WAITZ, JAY ALLAN, b Elizabeth, NJ, Nov 26, 35; m 60; c 2. CHEMOTHERAPY. *Educ:* Univ Idaho, BS, 57, MS, 59; Univ Ill, PhD(parasitol), 62. *Prof Exp:* Assoc res parasitologist, Parke, Davis & Co, 62-65, res parasitologist, 65-66; sr microbiologist, 66-68, sect head, 69-70, mgr chemother dept, 70-73, assoc dir microbiol, 73-77, dir antibiotic res, 77-81, VPRES MICROBIOL RES, SCHERING CORP, 81- *Mem:* Am Soc Parasitol; Am Micros Soc; Am Soc Microbiol; Am Soc Trop Med & Hyg; Soc Protozool. *Res:* Chemotherapy of parasitic, bacterial and fungal diseases; parasite physiology and histochemistry. *Mailing Add:* Dept Microbiol Schering Corp Bloomfield NJ 07003

WAITZMAN, MORTON BENJAMIN, b Chicago, Ill, Nov 8, 23; m 49; c 3. PHYSIOLOGY, BIOCHEMISTRY. *Educ:* Univ Miami, BS, 48; Univ Ill, MS, 50, PhD(physiol), 53. *Prof Exp:* Res asst physiol, Univ Ill, 51-54; res assoc, Dept Pharmacol & Lab Res Ophthal, Sch Med, Western Reserve Univ, 54-56, instr, 56-59, asst prof ophthalmic res & pharmacol & dir lab res ophthal, 59-62; assoc prof, 62-68, inst, 78-79, ASST PROF CARDIAC SURG, UNIV CALIF, SAN FRANCISCO, 79- *Mem:* AAAS; Asn Res Vision & Ophthal; Am Asn Univ Prof; Am Physiol Soc; NY Acad Sci. *Res:* Ophthalmic research; metabolic and hormonal aspects of aqueous humor and cerebrospinal fluid production; glaucoma; metabolic aspects of diabetes mellitus; neuro-chemistry; autonomic nature of ocular extracts. *Mailing Add:* Lab for Ophthalmic Res Emory Univ Sch of Med Atlanta GA 30322

WAIWOOD, KENNETH GEORGE, b St Boniface, Man, Feb 12, 47; m 72. FISHERIES SCIENCE, AQUATIC TOXICOLOGY. *Educ:* Sir George Williams Univ, BSc, 68; Queen's Univ, MSc, 72; Univ Guelph, PhD(zool), 77. *Prof Exp:* RES SCIENTIST MARINE FISH BIOL, DEPT FISHERIES & OCEANS, 77- *Mem:* Can Soc Zoologists. *Res:* Eco-physiology of marine fishes in support of fisheries management; bioenergetics; physiology of reproduction, feeding and growth. *Mailing Add:* Fisheries & Oceans Res Br Marine Fish Div Biol Sta St Andrews NB E0G 2X0 Can

WAJDA, EDWARD STANLEY, b Schenectady, NY, Oct 31, 24; m 50; c 2. PHYSICS. *Educ:* Union Col, NY, BS, 45; Cornell Univ, MS, 48; Rensselaer Polytech Inst, PhD(physics), 53. *Prof Exp:* Instr physics, Amherst Col, 46-47; Col, instr, Union Col, NY, 48-49, asst prof, 53-55; SR PHYSICIST, IBM CORP, 55- *Mem:* Inst Elec & Electronics Engrs. *Res:* Solid state physics; semiconductors. *Mailing Add:* 39 Spy Hill Poughkeepsie NY 12603

WAJDA, ISABEL, b Cracow, Poland, Apr 3, 13; US citizen; m 34. PHARMACOLOGY, NEUROCHEMISTRY. *Educ:* Jagiellonian Univ, BSc, 36; Univ Birmingham, PhD(pharmacol), 51. *Prof Exp:* Res pharmacologist, Oxford Univ, 43-46; res pharmacologist, Med Sch, Univ Birmingham, 46-51; head dept pharmacol, Med Sch, Univ Mendoza, Arg, 53-55; instr, New York Med Col, Flower & Fifth Ave Hosps, 55, asst prof, 56-59; sr res scientist, NY State Psychiat Inst, 59-66, assoc res scientist, 66-68; ASSOC RES SCIENTIST, NY STATE CTR NEUROCHEM & DRUG ADDICTION, 68- *Concurrent Pos:* Assoc prof pharmacol & chmn dept, Sch Dent, Fairleigh Dickinson Univ, 68-74. *Mem:* Am Soc Pharmacol & Exp Therapeut; Am Soc Neurochem; Brit Pharmacol Soc; Int Soc Neurochem. *Res:* Biological standardization; biochemistry and pharmacology of the central nervous system related to neurochemical transmission; enzyme metabolism in experimental autoimmune diseases; metabolism of neurotransmitters in drug addiction; dopamine and opiate receptor binding and effects of psychotropic drugs. *Mailing Add:* NY State Ctr Neurochem Ward's Island NY 10035

WAKADE, ARUN RAMCHANDRA, b Wai, India, Dec 3, 40. PHARMACOLOGY. *Educ:* Univ Bombay, BS, 61; State Univ NY Downstate Med Ctr, MS, 64, PhD(pharmacol), 67. *Prof Exp:* Govt India sr sci fel pharmacol, Med Col, Univ Baroda, 68-70; from instr to assoc prof pharmacol, 70-77, PROF PHARMACOL, STATE UNIV NY DOWNSTATE MED CTR, 77- *Mem:* Am Soc Pharmacol & Exp Therapeut; Indian Asn; Physiol & Pharmacol. *Res:* Adrenergic mechanism in peripheral autonomic nervous system. *Mailing Add:* Dept of Pharmacol State Univ of NY Downstate Med Ctr Brooklyn NY 11203

WAKE, DAVID BURTON, b Webster, SDak, June 8, 36; m 62; c 1. EVOLUTIONARY BIOLOGY. *Educ:* Pac Lutheran Univ, BA, 58; Univ Southern Calif, MSc, 60, PhD(biol), 64. *Prof Exp:* Asst biol, Univ Southern Calif, 58-59, head lab assoc, 62-63, instr, 63-64; instr anat & biol, Univ Chicago, 64-66, asst prof, 66-69; assoc prof zool, 69-73, assoc cur, Mus Vert Zool, 69-71, PROF ZOOL, UNIV CALIF, BERKELEY, 73-, DIR, MUS VERT ZOOL, 71-, CUR HERPET, 73- *Concurrent Pos:* Fel, John Simon Guggenheim Mem Found, 81-82. *Honors & Awards:* Quantrell Award, Univ Chicago, 67. *Mem:* AAAS; Am Soc Ichthyologists & Herpetologists; Soc Syst Zool; Am Soc Zoologists; Soc Study Evolution (pres-elect, 82). *Res:* Functional and evolutionary morphology of lower vertebrates; evolution, systematics and zoogeography of modern Amphibia, with emphasis on salamanders; evolutionary theory. *Mailing Add:* Mus of Vert Zool Univ of Calif Berkeley CA 94720

WAKE, MARVALEE H, b Orange, Calif, July 31, 39; m 62; c 1. VERTEBRATE BIOLOGY. *Educ:* Univ Southern Calif, BA, 61, MS, 64, PhD(biol), 68. *Prof Exp:* Teaching asst biol, Univ Ill, Chicago, 64-66, instr, 66-68, asst prof, 68-69; lectr, 69-73, asst prof, 73-76, assoc prof, 76-80, PROF BIOL, UNIV CALIF, BERKELEY, 80- *Concurrent Pos:* Prin investr, NSF, 77-; vis prof, Univ Bremen, 82. *Mem:* AAAS; Am Inst Biol Sci; Am Soc Ichthyologists & Herpetologists; Soc Study Evolution; Soc Study Amphibians & Reptiles. *Res:* Evolution of vertebrates; morphology; reproductive biology. *Mailing Add:* Dept Zool 4079 LSB Univ Calif Berkeley CA 94720

WAKEFIELD, ERNEST HENRY, b Vermilion, Ohio, Feb 11, 15; m 39; c 2. ELECTRICAL ENGINEERING. *Educ:* Univ Mich, BS, 38, MS, 39, PhD, 52. *Prof Exp:* Instr elec eng, Univ Tenn, 39-41; assoc physicist, Mass Inst Technol, 42; assoc physicist, Manhattan Proj, Chicago, 43-46; pres, RCL, Inc, 46-62 & RCL Calif, Inc, 59-62; PRES, LINEAR ALPHA, INC, 62-; CHMN, THIRD WORLD ENERGY INST INT, 78-; CHMN, INT INST MGT & APPROPRIATE TECHNOL FOR EMERGING NATIONS, 81- *Concurrent Pos:* Hon prof, Cent Univ Ecuador, 58; dir, Atomic Indust Forum, 60-62; pres, Evanston Bd Educ, 66-67. *Honors & Awards:* Presidential Citation, 46. *Res:* Data processing systems; electronic controls; technology for third world; electric vehicle design. *Mailing Add:* 630 Dartmouth St Evanston IL 60201

WAKEFIELD, KENNETH EARL, b Pipestone, Minn, June 14, 19; m 43; c 2. ENGINEERING, PLASMA PHYSICS. *Educ:* St Mary's Col, Minn, BS, 42; Purdue Univ, BS, 47. *Prof Exp:* Engr, Gen Eng & Develop Lab, Gen Elec Co, NY, 47-58; assoc div head & eng mgr major device fabrication, 58-80, HEAD, ADVAN PROJ DESIGN & ANAL DIV, PLASMA PHYSICS LAB, PRINCETON UNIV, 80- *Res:* Large volume, high magnetic fields, especially pertaining to fusion research; design, development and fabrication of fusion research devices and reactors. *Mailing Add:* Plasma Physics Lab PO Box 451 Princeton NJ 08544

WAKEFIELD, LUCILLE MARION, b Dayville, Conn, June 13, 25. NUTRITION. *Educ:* Univ Conn, BS, 49, MS, 56; Ohio State Univ, PhD(nutrit), 65. *Prof Exp:* Intern dietetics, Mt Auburn Hosp, 49-50; therapeut dietitian, New Brit Gen Hosp, 50-52, admin dietitian, 52-53; dir dietetics, Auburn Mem Hosp, 53-57; asst prof food & nutrit, Univ Vt, 57-65, head dept nutrit & inst mgt, 62-65; prof foods & nutrit & head dept, Kans State Univ, 65-75; prof food & nutrit & head dept, Fla State Univ, 75-79; CHMN, DEPT FOOD & NUTRIT, UNIV NC, GREENSBORO, 79- *Mem:* AAAS; fel Am Inst Chemists; Am Dietetic Asn; Am Pub Health Asn; Am Inst Nutrit. *Res:* Nutritional, sociological, psychological aspects of humans and their body composition as it relates to population groups and nutritional status; clinical nutrition and community health problems; nutrition in aging; food patterning. *Mailing Add:* Dept of Foods & Nutrit Univ NC Greensboro NC 27411

WAKEFIELD, ROBERT CHESTER, b Providence, RI, Sept 14, 25; m 49; c 3. AGRONOMY. *Educ:* Univ RI, BS, 50; Rutgers Univ, MS, 51, PhD, 54. *Prof Exp:* Res assoc farm crops, Rutgers Univ, 51-54; from asst prof to assoc prof agron, 54-65, chmn dept, 61-70, PROF AGRON, UNIV RI, 65- *Res:* Crop ecology; landscape ecology. *Mailing Add:* Dept of Plant & Soil Sci Univ of RI Kingston RI 02881

WAKEFIELD, SHIRLEY LORRAINE, b Milwaukee, Wis, Nov 20, 34; m 57; c 2. SOLID STATE CHEMISTRY. *Educ:* Univ Wis-Madison, BS, 57; Univ Cincinnati, PhD(phys chem), 69; Xavier Univ, MBA, 76. *Prof Exp:* Chemist, Forest Prod Lab, US Forest Serv, 57-58; lab technician, Pulmonary Dis Res Lab, Vet Admin Hosp, 59-62; staff engr, Avco Electronics, 69-73; spec progs mgr, Measurements & Sensors Develop, 73-75, mgr composites, Mat & Processes Technol Progs, 75-81, MGR SURVIVABILITY & EXHAUST SYST MAT, ADVAN ENG & TECHNOL PROG DEPT, AIRCRAFT ENGINE GROUP, GEN ELEC CO, 81- *Mem:* Am Chem Soc; Am Phys Soc; Am Soc Nondestructive Testing; Soc Advan Mat & Process Eng. *Res:* Infrared detectors; nuclear quadrupole resonance spectroscopy; pulmonary disease; gas chromatography; high energy x-ray, Raman spectroscopy; ceramics; high temperature alloy development; countermeasure materials. *Mailing Add:* Gen Elec Aircraft Engine Group MD H-6 175 & Bypass 50 Cincinnati OH 45215

WAKEHAM, HELMUT, b Hamburg, Ger, Apr 15, 16; US citizen; m 39; c 3. PHYSICAL CHEMISTRY. *Educ:* Univ Nebr, BA, 36, MA, 37; Univ Calif, PhD(phys chem), 39. *Prof Exp:* Asst chem, Univ Nebr, 36-37; asst, Univ Calif, 37-39; res chemist, Stand Oil Co, Calif, 39-41; res chemist, Southern Regional Res Lab, USDA, 41-47; from res assoc to proj head & dir res, Chem Physics Sect, Textile Res Inst, NJ, 49-56; dir, Ahmedabad Textile Industs Res Asn, India, 56-58; staff asst to vpres & chief opers & subsidiaries, Res Ctr, Philip Morris, Inc, 58-60, dir, Res Ctr, 60-66, vpres res & develop, 61-82; RETIRED. *Concurrent Pos:* Mem, Tobacco Working Group, 68-; mem, Nat Cancer Plan, 71; mem bd dir, Indust Res Inst, Inc, 71-72. *Mem:* Fel AAAS; Am Chem Soc; Fiber Soc; Soc Rheol; fel Am Inst Chemists. *Res:* Agricultural and food chemistry; technical management. *Mailing Add:* 8905 Norwick Rd Richmond VA 23229

WAKELAND, WILLIAM RICHARD, b Mound City, Ill, Nov 14, 21; m 45; c 4. ELECTRICAL ENGINEERING, CONTROL SYSTEMS. *Educ:* US Naval Acad, BS, 43; US Naval Postgrad Sch, BS, 50, MS, 51; Univ Houston, PhD(elec eng), 68. *Prof Exp:* Dir astronaut directorate, Naval Missile Ctr, Point Mugu, Calif, 61-62; mgr Gemini-agena develop, Manned Spacecraft Ctr, NASA, Houston, 62-64; dir aeronaut elec dept, Naval Air Develop Ctr, Pa, 64-65; instr, Univ Houston, 65-68; asst prof, 68-77, ASSOC PROF ENG SCI, TRINITY UNIV, TEX, 77-; PROF & HEAD, ELEC SURG DEPT, LAMAR UNIV, 78- *Mem:* Inst Elec & Electronics Engrs; Nat Soc Prof Engrs; Am Soc Eng Educ. *Res:* Control system design; optimal design; weighting factor for quadratic performance index. *Mailing Add:* Box 10029 Lamar Univ Beaumont TX 77710

WAKELEY, JAMES STUART, b Raleigh, NC, July 8, 50; m 73. WILDLIFE ECOLOGY. *Educ:* Univ Calif, Santa Barbara, BA, 71; Univ Maine, MS, 73; Utah State Univ, PhD(wildlife ecol), 76. *Prof Exp:* ASST PROF WILDLIFE ECOL, SCH FOREST RESOURCES, PA STATE UNIV, 76- *Mem:* Wildlife Soc; Am Ornithologists' Union; Ecol Soc Am; Raptor Res Found. *Res:* Ecology and management of game and nongame birds; applied population biology. *Mailing Add:* 205 Forest Resources Lab Pa State Univ University Park PA 16802

WAKELEY, JAY TOWNSEND, b Honesdale, Pa, July 19, 19; m 41; c 2. OPERATIONS RESEARCH, APPLIED STATISTICS. *Educ:* Iowa State Univ, BS, 41; NC State Univ, MS, 46, PhD(exp statist), 50. *Prof Exp:* Asst statistician, NC State Univ, 46-48, asst prof statist, 48-51; oper analyst, A F Spec Weapons Ctr, 51-54; mathematician, Rand Corp, 54-63; mgr opers anal, NAm Aviation, Inc, 63-66; dir new progs, Gen Res Corp, 66-69; dir opers res & econ div, 69-71, dir ctr health studies, 71-78, SR SCIENTIST, RES TRIANGLE INST, 78- *Concurrent Pos:* Adj prof, NC State Univ, 70-, consult, Ctr Alcohol Studies, 74- *Mem:* AAAS; Opers Res Soc Am; Am Pub Health Asn. *Res:* Operations research and statistics as applied to health services delivery and health systems research. *Mailing Add:* Res Triangle Inst Research Triangle Park NC 27709

WAKELIN, DAVID HERBERT, b Southampton, Eng, Dec 8, 40; m 66; c 2. METALLURGICAL ENGINEERING. *Educ:* Univ London, BSc, 62, ARSM, 62, PhD(eng metall) & DIC, 66. *Prof Exp:* Res engr, Graham Res Lab, 66-68, sr res engr, 68-70, res assoc metall, 70-74, develop engr ironmaking, 74-79, SUPERVR IRONMAKING ENG, GRAHAM RES LAB, JONES & LAUGHLIN STEEL CORP, 79- *Mem:* Am Inst Mining, Metall & Petrol Engrs; Iron & Steel Soc; Am Soc for Metals. *Res:* Primary steelmaking processes and energy requirements. *Mailing Add:* Graham Res Lab 900 Agnew Rd Pittsburgh PA 15227

WAKELIN, JAMES HENRY, JR, b Holyoke, Mass, May 6, 11; m 38, 74; c 3. PHYSICS. *Educ:* Dartmouth Col, AB, 32; Cambridge Univ, BA, 34, MA, 39; Yale Univ, PhD(physics), 40. *Prof Exp:* Sr physicist, B F Goodrich Co, Ohio, 39-43; dir res, Eng Res Assocs, Inc, DC & Minn, 46-48; assoc dir res, Textile Res Inst, NJ, 48-51, dir res, 51-54; founding dir & vpres, Chesapeake Instrument Corp, Md, 54-59; asst secy res & develop, Dept Navy, 59-64; chmn adv bd, Teledyne Ryan Aeronaut, Calif, 64-68, mem adv bd, 68-71; asst secy sci & technol, Dept Com, 71-72; pres, Res Anal Corp, McLean, Va, 72-75, chmn bd dirs, 65-71. *Concurrent Pos:* Independent consult, 54-59; dir, Nassau Fund, Princeton, NJ, 55-59; pres, Sci Eng Inst, Waltham, Mass, 64-67; consult, United Aircraft Corp, Conn, 67-69; dir, Greyrad Corp, NJ, 67-69, Oceans Gen, Inc, Fla, 68-71, Aqua Int, Calif, 69-70 & Wellington & Assoc Mutual Funds, Del, 70-71; spec asst to Gov Del for Marine & Coastal Affairs, 70-71; head US deleg, Intergovt Conf Oceanog, Copenhagen, 60 & Intergovt Oceanog Comn, UNESCO, Paris, 61; chmn, Interagency Comt Oceanog, 60-64; mem, Naval Res Adv Comt, Dept Navy, 64-71; chmn bd, Oceanic Found, Honolulu, Hawaii, 66-71; mem corp, Woods Hole Oceanog Inst, 66-71; chmn, President's Task Force Oceanog, 69 & Com Tech Adv Bd, 71-72; mem, Fed Coun Sci & Technol, Off of the President, 71-72; chmn, Interagency Comt Atmospheric Sci, 71-72 & Comt Govt Patent Policy, 71-72; mem, Comt Res Appl to Nat Needs, 71-72; mem bd trustees, Comt Res & Explor, Nat Geog Soc, 63-; overseers' vis comt, Dept Astron, Harvard Univ, 64-69 & 70-75; chmn bd overseers, Thayer Sch Eng, Dartmouth Col, 67-70; mem bd adv to President, Naval War Col, 70-74; mem vis comt, Dept Ocean Eng, Mass Inst Technol, 71-75; pres, Grad Sch Asn & mem, Alumni Bd, Yale Univ, 71-, chmn comt phys sci, Univ Coun, 73-78. *Honors & Awards:* Distinguished Pub Serv Awards, Dept Navy, 61 & 64; Rear Admiral William S Parsons Award, Navy League of US, 65. *Mem:* Hon mem Nat Security Indust Asn; hon mem Marine Technol Soc (pres, 66-68); Am Phys Soc. *Res:* Magnetization near boundaries; x-ray diffraction of natural rubber and synthetic polymers; mathematical computing devices; physics of textile fibers; oceanography. *Mailing Add:* 1809 45th St NW Washington DC 20007

WAKELYN, PHILLIP JEFFREY, b Akron, Ohio, Apr 29, 40. TEXTILE CHEMISTRY. *Educ:* Emory Univ, BS, 63; Ga Inst Technol, MS, 68; Univ Leeds, PhD(textile chem), 71. *Prof Exp:* Res chemist, Fibers Div, Dow Chem Co, 63-66 & Dow-Badische Co, 66-67; res assoc textile chem, Textile Res Ctr, Tex Tech Univ, 71-73, head chem res, 73; MGR ENVIRON/SAFETY TECHNOL, NAT COTTON COUN, 73- *Concurrent Pos:* Lectr textile chem, Tex Tech Univ, 72-73, adj prof chem eng, 74- *Mem:* Am Chem Soc; Sigma Xi; sr mem Am Asn Textile Chemists & Colorists; NY Acad Sci; assoc Brit Textile Inst. *Res:* Physical and chemical properties of textile fibers; additives to fibers; antistats; lubricants; fire retardants; chemistry of wool and cotton; environmental, health and safety problems; cotton dust and occupational diseases. *Mailing Add:* Nat Cotton Coun Box 12285 Memphis TN 38112

WAKEMAN, CHARLES B, b New Haven, Conn, Aug 4, 27; m 48; c 3. ELECTRONICS. *Educ:* Yale Univ, BE, 50, ME, 52, PhD(elec eng), 55. *Prof Exp:* Res engr, Magnetics Inc, 55-57, dir res & develop, 57-61, vpres res & develop, 61-62; dir electronics res, Corning Glass Works, 62-66, dir phys res, 66-72, dir corp develop, 72-74, dir res & develop Europe, 74-78, dir tech & admin serv, 78-80; VPRES RES & DEVELOP, SIECOR CORP, 80- *Mem:* AAAS; Inst Elec & Electronics Engrs. *Res:* Magnetic domain effects in highly rectangular hysteresis loop magnetic materials of interest in magnetic switching, memory and similar devices. *Mailing Add:* SIECOR Corp Box 489 Hickory NC 28601

WAKEMAN, DONALD LEE, b Lebanon, Mo, Nov 17, 29; m 50; c 3. ANIMAL HUSBANDRY. *Educ:* Okla State Univ, BSA, 51; Univ Fla, MSA, 55. *Prof Exp:* Instr animal sci, Univ Tenn, 51; instr, 55-57, asst prof, Univ & asst animal husbandman, Agr Exp Sta, 57-67, assoc prof, Univ, 67-75, PROF ANIMAL SCI, UNIV FLA, 75-, ASSOC ANIMAL HUSBANDMAN, AGR EXP STA, 67- *Mem:* Am Soc Animal Sci. *Res:* Animal production and nutrition; beef cattle production. *Mailing Add:* Dept of Animal Sci Univ of Fla Gainesville FL 32601

WAKEMAN, JOHN MARSHALL, b Victoria, Australia, June 12, 37; m 70; c 2. FISH & WILDLIFE SCIENCES. *Educ:* Southern Ill Univ, BS, 73; Univ Ala, MS, 75; Univ Tex, Austin, PhD(zool), 78. *Prof Exp:* Res scientist, Maricult Ctr, Univ Tex, 78-79; ASST PROF ANIMAL PHYSIOL, LA TECH UNIV, 79- *Concurrent Pos:* Res scientist, Marine Consortium, La Tech Univ, 80, Marine Sci Inst, Univ Tex, Austin, 81. *Mem:* Sigma Xi; Am Fisheries Soc; Gulf Estuarine Res Soc. *Res:* Swimming energetics and physiological responses of fishes with respect to salinity variations and to environmental pollutants; spawning and culture of marine fishes; closed-system aquaculture and mericulture. *Mailing Add:* Dept Zool La Tech Univ Ruston LA 71272

WAKIL, SALIH J, b Kerballa, Iraq; nat US; m 52; c 4. BIOCHEMISTRY. *Educ:* Am Univ Beirut, BSc, 48; Univ Wash, PhD(biochem), 52. *Prof Exp:* Res assoc, Inst Enzyme Res, Univ Wis, 52-56, asst prof, Univ, 56-59; from asst prof to prof biochem, Sch Med, Duke Univ, 59-71; PROF BIOCHEM & CHMN DEPT, BAYLOR COL MED, 71- *Concurrent Pos:* Vis prof, Pasteur Inst Paris, 68-69; John Simon Guggenheim fel, 68-69; ad hoc mem physiol study sect, NIH, 71; mem metab biol panel, NSF, 71-74. *Honors & Awards:* Am Chem Soc Award, 67. *Mem:* Am Chem Soc; Am Soc Biol Chemists; Sigma Xi; Am Soc Neurochem; Am Soc Microbiol. *Res:* Genetic and metabolic control of fatty acid metabolism. *Mailing Add:* Dept Biochem Baylor Col Med Houston TX 77025

WAKIM, KHALIL GEORGES, b Sidon, Lebanon, July 17, 07; nat US; m 36. INTERNAL MEDICINE. *Educ:* Am Univ Beirut, BA, 29, MD, 33; Univ Minn, PhD(physiol), 41. *Prof Exp:* Instr physiol, Am Univ Beirut, 33-38; actg prof, Col Med, Univ Iowa, 40; from assoc prof to prof, Sch Med, Ind Univ, 41-46; prof, 46-71, EMER PROF PHYSIOL, MAYO GRAD SCH MED, UNIV MINN, 71-, EMER CONSULT, MAYO CLIN & MAYO FOUND, ROCHESTER, MINN, 71-; PROF CLIN PHYSIOL, SCH MED, IND UNIV, INDIANAPOLIS, 71-; COORDR MED EDUC, TERRE HAUTE MED EDUC FOUND, 71- *Concurrent Pos:* Consult, Mayo Clin, 46-71; consult, Off Surgeon Gen, US Army. *Honors & Awards:* First Order Merit, Repub Syria, 50; Highest Order Merit, Repub Lebanon, 50, Knight, Order of the Cedar, Lebanon, 67. *Mem:* AAAS; Am Physiol Soc; Soc Exp Biol & Med; Am Soc Trop Med & Hyg; Am Soc Pharmacol & Exp Therapeut. *Res:* Liver and gastrointestinal tract; heart and circulation; effects of physical agents; kidney; neurophysiology; muscle physiology. *Mailing Add:* Terre Haute Med Educ Found 2153 Ohio Blvd Terre Haute IN 47803

WAKSBERG, ARMAND L, b Paris, France, Oct 11, 34; Can citizen; m 60; c 1. MATHEMATICS, PHYSICS. *Educ:* McGill Univ, BS, 56, MS, 60. *Prof Exp:* Scientist, Canadair, Ltd, 56-58 & Can Aviation Electronics, 60-63; sr mem sci staff, 63-77, SR SCIENTIST RES DEPT, RCA LTD, 77- *Mem:* Inst Elec & Electronics Engrs. *Res:* Lasers, including sidelight spectroscopy, laser noise and phase locking phenomena; laser communications and propagation; laser systems. *Mailing Add:* MPB Technol PO Box 160 Ste-Anne-de-Bellevue PQ H9X 3L5 Can

WAKSBERG, JOSEPH, b Kielce, Poland, Sept 20, 15; US citizen; m 41; c 2. APPLIED STATISTICS. *Educ:* City Col New York, BS, 36. *Prof Exp:* Jr mathematician, US Navy Dept, 37-38; asst proj dir math, US Works Proj Admin, 38-40; asst proj dir, US Bur Census, 40-59, asst chief construction statist div, 59-63, chief statist methods div, 63-71, assoc dir statist, Bur, 72-73; VPRES, WESTAT INC, 73- *Concurrent Pos:* Instr statist, USDA Grad Sch, 63-73; consult, CBS News, 66- *Honors & Awards:* Gold Medal for Distinguished Contrib, US Dept Com, 68. *Mem:* Fel Am Statist Asn; Inst Math Statist; Pop Asn Am; Int Asn Surv Statist. *Res:* Sample design for surveys; research in survey methodology, especially sampling and response errors. *Mailing Add:* 6302 Tone Dr Bethesda MD 20817

WAKSMAN, BYRON HALSTEAD, b New York, NY, Sept 15, 19; m 44; c 2. IMMUNOLOGY. *Educ:* Swarthmore Col, BA, 40; Univ Pa, MD, 43. *Prof Exp:* Intern, Michael Reese Hosp, Ill, 44; res assoc neuropath, Harvard Med Sch, 49-52, assoc bact & immunol, 52-57, asst prof, 57-63; prof microbiol, 63-74, PROF PATH, YALE UNIV, 74- *Concurrent Pos:* Fel, Mayo Clin, 46-48; NIH fel, Columbia Univ, 48-49; res fel neuropath, Mass Gen Hosp, 49-52; assoc bacteriologist, Mass Gen Hosp, 52-63; consult assoc bacteriologist, Mass Eye & Ear Infirmary, 57-63; mem microbiol fels panel, NIH, 61-64, mem study sect B on allergy & Immunol, 65-69; mem res rev panel, Nat Multiple Sclerosis Soc, 61-66; mem expert adv panel immunol, WHO, 63-68; chmn dept microbiol, Yale Univ, 64-70 & 72-74. *Mem:* Fel AAAS; Am Asn Immunol (secy-treas, 61-64, pres, 70-71); Am Soc Microbiol; Soc Exp Biol & Med; Am Rheumatism Asn. *Res:* Role of thymus and lymphocytes in immune responses; immunologic tolerance; delayed hypertensitivity; mechanism of action of suppressor T-cells and lymphokines; immunologic and pathologic character of experimental autoallergic diseases. *Mailing Add:* Dept of Path Yale Univ New Haven CT 06510

WALASZEK, EDWARD JOSEPH, b Chicago, Ill, July 4, 27:; m 55; c 2. PHARMACOLOGY. *Educ:* Univ Ill, BSc, 49; Univ Chicago, PhD(pharmacol), 53. *Prof Exp:* Asst prof neurophysiol & biochem, Univ Ill, 55-56; asst prof, 57-59, assoc prof, 59-62, PROF PHARMACOL, UNIV KANS MED CTR, KANSAS CITY, 62-, CHMN DEPT, 64- *Concurrent Pos:* Res fel, Univ Edinburgh, 53-55; USPHS spec res fel, 56-61, res career develop award, 61-63, res career award, 63-64; mem health study sect med chem, NIH, 62-66, mem res career award study sect, Nat Inst Gen Med Sci, 66-70; mem adv coun, Int Union Pharmacol, 72-76; mem, Health Study Sect Pharmacol-Toxicol, 74-78; mem comt teaching of sci, Int Coun Sci Unions. *Honors & Awards:* Bela Issekutz medal, Hungarian Acad Sci. *Mem:* AAAS; Am Chem Soc; Soc Neurosci; Am Soc Pharmacol & Exp Therapeut; fel Am Soc Clin Pharmacol & Therapeut. *Res:* Pharmacologically active pôlypeptides; neurohumoral substances; naturally-occurring biogenic amines; pharmacology and physiology of the central nervous system. *Mailing Add:* Dept of Pharmacol Univ of Kans Med Ctr Kansas City KS 66103

WALAWENDER, MICHAEL JOHN, b Auburn, NY, Dec 16, 39; m 67. PETROLOGY, GEOLOGY. *Educ:* Syracuse Univ, BS, 65; SDak Sch Mines & Technol, MS, 67; Pa State Univ, University Park, PhD(petrol), 72. *Prof Exp:* Res asst mineral, SDak Sch Mines & Technol, 65-67; asst petrol, Pa State Univ, University Park, 67-72; asst prof geol, 72-77, ASSOC PROF GEOL, SAN DIEGO STATE UNIV, 77- *Mem:* Geol Soc Am. *Res:* Igenous and metamorphic petrology; mineralogy; planetology. *Mailing Add:* Dept of Geol San Diego State Univ San Diego CA 92182

WALBA, DAVID MARK, b Oakland, Calif, June 29, 49. ORGANIC CHEMISTRY. *Educ:* Univ Calif, Berkeley, BS, 71; Calif Inst Technol, PhD(chem), 75. *Prof Exp:* Fel, Univ Calif, Los Angeles, 75-77; ASST PROF CHEM, UNIV COLO, BOULDER, 77- *Mem:* Am Chem Soc. *Res:* Total synthesis of natural products; host-guest chemistry. *Mailing Add:* Dept of Chem Univ of Colo Boulder CO 80309

WALBA, HAROLD, b Chelsea, Mass, Mar 10, 21; m 46; c 2. ORGANIC CHEMISTRY. *Educ:* Univ Mass, BS, 46; Univ Calif, PhD(chem), 49. *Prof Exp:* From instr to assoc prof, 49-58, chmn dept, 61-64, PROF CHEM, SAN DIEGO STATE UNIV, 58- *Mem:* AAAS; Am Chem Soc; The Chem Soc. *Res:* Substituent effects and their transmission in organic molecules; tautomerism; acid-base strengths. *Mailing Add:* Dept of Chem San Diego State Univ San Diego CA 92182

WALBERG, CLIFFORD BENNETT, b Watkins, Minn, Feb 24, 15; m 46; c 4. CLINICAL CHEMISTRY. *Educ:* Univ Sask, BS, 39; Univ Southern Calif, AB, 43, MS, 45, PhD(biochem), 57. *Prof Exp:* Asst prof path, 69-76, CLIN CHEMIST, TOXICOL LAB, LOS ANGELES COUNTY-UNIV SOUTHERN CALIF MED CTR, 57-, ASSOC PROF PATH, SCH MED, UNIV SOUTHERN CALIF, 76- *Mem:* Am Asn Clin Chem. *Res:* Clinical biochemistry; toxicology. *Mailing Add:* Toxicol Lab Med Ctr Univ Southern Calif 1200 N State St Box 780 Los Angeles CA 90033

WALBORG, EARL FREDRICK, JR, b Chicago, Ill, Nov 13, 35; m 58; c 3. BIOCHEMISTRY. *Educ:* Austin Col, BA, 58; Baylor Univ, PhD(biochem), 62. *Prof Exp:* Asst biochemist & asst prof biochem, 65-70, assoc prof biochem, 70-73, assoc biochemist & chief sect protein structure, 70-77, prof biochem, M D Anderson Hosp & Tumor Inst, Houston, 73-77, PROF BIOCHEM, UNIV TEX SYST CANCER CTR, SCI PARK-RES DIV, SMITHVILLE, 77-; MEM GRAD FAC, UNIV TEX GRAD SCH BIOMED SCI, HOUSTON, 70- *Concurrent Pos:* USPHS res fel physiol chem, Univ Lund, 62-65; Eleanor Roosevelt Int Cancer fel biochem, Neth Cancer Inst, Amsterdam, 74. *Mem:* AAAS; Am Chem Soc; fel Am Inst Chem; Am Asn Cancer Res; Am Soc Biol Chem. *Res:* Chemistry of the cell-surface, glyoproteins, hepatocarcinogenesis. *Mailing Add:* Sci Park Res Div Univ Tex Syst Cancer Ctr PO Box 389 Smithville TX 78957

WALBORN, NOLAN REVERE, b Bloomsburg, Pa, Sept 30, 44; m 75; c 1. ASTRONOMY. *Educ:* Gettysburg Col, BA, 66; Univ Chicago, PhD(astron, astrophys), 70. *Prof Exp:* Fel, Yerkes Observ, Univ Chicago, 71 & David Dunlap Observ, Univ Toronto, 71-73; staaff astronr, Cerro Tololo Inter-Am Observ, 73-81; NAT RES COUN SR RES ASSOC, GODDARD SPACE FLIGHT CTR, NASA, 81- *Mem:* Am Astron Soc; Can Astron Soc; Int Astron Union. *Res:* Stellar spectroscopy; spectral classification; early-type stars; galactic structure; interstellar lines; Magellanic clouds. *Mailing Add:* Lab Astron & Solar Physics Code 683 Goddard Space Flight Ctr Greenbelt MD 20771

WALBORSKY, HARRY M, b Lodz, Poland, Dec 25, 23; nat US; m 53; c 4. ORGANIC CHEMISTRY. *Educ:* City Col New York, BS, 45; Ohio State Univ, PhD(chem), 49. *Prof Exp:* Res assoc, Calif Inst Technol, 48; res assoc, Atomic Energy Proj, Univ Calif, Los Angeles, 49-50; from asst prof to assoc prof chem, 50-59, PROF CHEM, FLA STATE UNIV, 59- *Concurrent Pos:* USPHS fel, Basel, Switz, 52-53. *Mem:* Am Chem Soc; Royal Soc Chem. *Res:* Small ring compounds; organometallics; asymmetric synthesis; electrolytic and dissolving metal reductions; synthetic methods. *Mailing Add:* Dept Chem Fla State Univ Tallahassee FL 32306

WALBOT, VIRGINIA ELIZABETH, US citizen. DEVELOPMENTAL BIOCHEMISTRY. *Educ:* Stanford Univ, AB, 67; Yale Univ, MPhil, 69, PhD(biol), 72. *Prof Exp:* NIH fel, Univ Ga, 72-75; asst prof biol, Washington Univ, 75-80; ASSOC PROF BIOL SCI, STANFORD UNIV, 80- *Mem:* AAAS; Bot Soc Am; Soc Develop Biol; Am Soc Plant Physiol; Am Soc Cell Biol. *Res:* Plant biochemistry and development; cell biology; botany. *Mailing Add:* Dept Biol Sci Stanford Univ Stanford CA 94305

WALBRICK, JOHNNY MAC, b Wichita Falls, Tex, Sept 14, 41; m 64; c 2. INDUSTRIAL ORGANIC CHEMISTRY. *Educ:* Midwestern Univ, BS, 63; Univ Fla, PhD(chem), 67. *Prof Exp:* NSF fel, Univ Fla, 67-68; res chemist, Res Labs, 70-74, mgr res, 73-77, DIR RES, MERICHEM CO, 77- *Mem:* Am Chem Soc; Royal Soc Chem; Indust Res Inst; Am Mgt Asn. *Res:* Mechanism of electroorganic reaction processes; new industrial processes for organic chemicals. *Mailing Add:* Merichem Co Res Ctr 1503 Cent Houston TX 77012

WALBURG, CHARLES HERMAN, b Mankato, Minn, June 9, 26; m 49; c 2. FISH BIOLOGY. *Educ:* Univ Minn, BS, 49. *Prof Exp:* Fishery res biologist, Atlanta Coast Shad & Blue Crab Prog, Biol Lab, US Bur Com Fisheries, NC, 50-61, fishery res biologist, NCent Reservoir Invests, US Bur Sport Fisheries & Wildlife, 62-75, chief n cent, 75-78, CHIEF E CENT, RESERVOIR INVESTS, US FISH & WILDLIFE SERV, 78- *Mem:* Am Fisheries Soc; fel Am Inst Fishery Res Biologists; Sigma Xi. *Res:* Population dynamics; estuarine and freshwater ecology; biology of reservoirs; effect of reservoir operation on tailwater ecology; effect of industrial development on aquatic biota; author of forty journal publications. *Mailing Add:* E Cent Reservoir Invests Fed Bldg Bowling Green KY 42101

WALBURG, HARRY E, JR, b Newark, NJ, Feb 6, 32; m 54; c 4. VETERINARY MEDICINE. *Educ:* Dartmouth Col, AB, 53; Va Polytech Inst, MS, 58; Univ Ga, DVM, 58; Univ Ill, PhD(radiobiol), 61. *Prof Exp:* Biologist, 61-73, DIR COMP ANIMAL RES LAB, OAK RIDGE NAT LAB, 73- *Honors & Awards:* Animal Care Panel Res Award, 65. *Mem:* Radiation Res Soc; Geront Soc; Am Asn Cancer Res; Am Vet Med Asn. *Res:* Radiation carcinogenesis and radiation induced life-shortening and aging. *Mailing Add:* Prog Ecol Univ Tenn Knoxville TN 27916

WALCH, HENRY ANDREW, JR, b Minneapolis, Minn, June 3, 22; m 53; c 2. MYCOLOGY. *Educ:* Univ Calif, Los Angeles, BA, 50, PhD(microbiol), 54. *Prof Exp:* Mycol technician, Univ Calif, Los Angeles, 50-54, res asst, 54-55; from instr to assoc prof microbiol, 55-64, chmn dept, 60-64 & 72-75, PROF MICROBIOL, SAN DIEGO STATE UNIV, 64- *Concurrent Pos:* Res grants, San Diego Imp Counties Tuberc & Respiratory Health Asn, 57-72 & Respiratory Dis Asn Calif, 72-73; consult & lectr, Sharp Mem Hosp, San Diego, 58- & US Naval Hosp, 64-; consult, Palomar Mem Hosp, Escondido, Calif; NIH spec fel, Mycol Unit, Commun Dis Ctr, Atlanta, Ga. *Mem:* Am Soc Microbiol; Mycol Soc Am; Am Inst Biol Sci; AAAS. *Res:* Human and animal pathogenic fungi, particularly virulence factors, immunology and ecology. *Mailing Add:* Dept of Microbiol San Diego State Univ San Diego CA 92182

WALCHER, DWAIN N, b Ill, Apr 7, 15; m 39; c 2. PEDIATRICS, HUMAN DEVELOPMENT. *Educ:* Univ Chicago, BS, 38, MD, 40. *Prof Exp:* Instr pediat, Sch Med, Yale Univ, 43-46; asst prof, Med Ctr, Ind Univ, 47-52, assoc prof, 52-62, prof, 62-63; prog dir growth & develop, Nat Inst Child Health & Human Develop, 63-66, assoc dir prog planning & eval, 66-69; PROF HUMAN DEVELOP & DIR INST STUDY HUMAN DEVELOP, PA STATE UNIV, 69- *Mem:* Soc Pediat Res; Am Acad Pediat; Infectious Dis Soc Am; Int Orgn Study Human Develop (exec secy-treas). *Res:* Infectious diseases in children. *Mailing Add:* Col of Human Develop Pa State Univ University Park PA 16802

WALCHLI, HAROLD E(DWARD), b Warren, Pa, Nov 13, 22; m 45; c 2. ENGINEERING, PHYSICS. *Educ:* Pa State Univ, BS, 44; Univ Tenn, MS, 54. *Prof Exp:* Field engr, Bell Tel Co, Pa, 41; instr preradar, Pa State Univ, 42-43, staff asst elec eng, 43, asst instr physics, 43-44; asst engr, Tenn Eastman Corp, 44-47; engr, Carbide & Carbon Chem Co, 47-55; asst to tech dir, 56-57, mgr eng serv, Atomic Power Dept, 57-58, asst proj mgr, Yankee Atomic Plant Proj, 58-60, fuel serv supvr, 60-64, fuel serv mgr, Nuclear Fuel Div, 64-71, mgr & adv engr, pressurized water reactor systs, Nuclear Servs Dept, Nuclear Energy Systs, 71-77, mgr strategic progs, Nuclear Serv Div, 77-80, FACIL & FINANCIAL PLANNING, FEL ENGR DATA & COMMUN SERV, WESTINGHOUSE ELEC CORP, PITTSBURGH, 80-; PRES, HAL-COM ASSOCS, 80- *Concurrent Pos:* Chmn, Adv Comt Radioactive Mat, Hazardous Substances Transp Bd, Commonwealth Pa, 72-77. *Mem:* Am Soc Mech Engrs; Inst Elec & Electronics Engrs; Inst Nuclear Mat Mgt. *Res:* Nuclear magnetic resonance spectroscopy; electronic circuit design; radioactive materials transport; nuclear materials management; engineering management; computerized data communications; atomic plant design and construction; atomic fuel cycle services. *Mailing Add:* 1329 Foxboro Dr Monroeville PA 15146

WALCOTT, BENJAMIN, b Boston, Mass, May 31, 41; m 72. COMPARATIVE PHYSIOLOGY. *Educ:* Harvard Univ, BA, 63; Univ Ore, PhD(biol), 68. *Prof Exp:* USPHS physiol trainee, Univ Ore, 64-67, instr biol, 67-68; vis res fel biol, Res Sch Biol Sci, Australian Nat Univ, 69-71, fel biol, 71-72; asst prof, 72-79, ASSOC PROF ANAT, HEALTH SCI CTR, STATE UNIV NY STONY BROOK, 79- *Mem:* Am Soc Cell Biol; foreign mem Brit Soc Exp Biol; Soc Gen Physiol; Biophys Soc; Soc Neurosci. *Res:* Structure and physiology of sensory systems and the control of muscle activity; correlation between molecular structure and mechanical responses of muscles from different vertebrates and invertebrates. *Mailing Add:* Dept Anat Sci Sch Med Health Sci Ctr State Univ NY Stony Brook NY 11794

WALCOTT, CHARLES, b Boston, Mass, July 19, 34; m 76; c 2. BEHAVIORAL PHYSIOLOGY. *Educ:* Harvard Univ, AB, 56; Cornell Univ, PhD, 59. *Prof Exp:* Asst, Cornell Univ, 56-58; res fel biol, Harvard Univ, 59-60, asst prof appl biol, Div Eng & Appl Physics, 60-65; asst prof biol, Tufts Univ, 65-67; assoc prof biol, 67-74, actg dir, Ctr Curriculum Develop, 67-71, chmn dept cellular & comp biol, 71-76, PROF BIOL, STATE UNIV NY STONY BROOK, 74-; PROF BIOL & EXEC DIR, LAB ORNITHOL, CORNELL UNIV, 81- *Concurrent Pos:* Dir, Natural Sci TV Proj, 59-60; dir elem sci study, Educ Develop Ctr, Inc, 65-67; dir, Content Res 3-2-1 Contact, Children's Television Workshop, 78-80. *Mem:* AAAS; Am Soc Zoologists; Animal Behav Soc. *Res:* Neurophysiology; animal behavior and orientation. *Mailing Add:* Lab Ornithol Cornell Univ 159 Sapsucker Woods Rd Ithaca NY 14850

WALCZAK, HUBERT R, b South Saint Paul, Minn, Jan 21, 34; m 61; c 3. MATHEMATICS. *Educ:* Col St Thomas, BA, 55; Univ Minn, PhD(math), 63. *Prof Exp:* Asst prof, 63-72, assoc prof, 72-77, PROF MATH, COL ST THOMAS, 77- *Mem:* Math Asn Am. *Res:* Analysis and quasiconformal mappings. *Mailing Add:* Dept of Math Col of St Thomas St Paul MN 55105

WALD, FRANCINE JOY, b Brooklyn, NY, Jan 13, 38; m 64; c 2. SOLID STATE PHYSICS, SCIENCE EDUCATION. *Educ:* City Col New York, BEE, 60; Polytech Inst Brooklyn, MS, 62, PhD(chem physics), 69. *Prof Exp:* Engr solid state physics, Remington Rand Univac Div, 60; instr physics, Polytech Inst Brooklyn, 62-64, adj res assoc, 69-70; sci consult physics & biol, 72-75, SCI INSTR, FRIENDS SEM, 75-, CHAIRPERSON DEPT SCI, 76- *Concurrent Pos:* Lectr phys sci, New York Community Col, 69 & 70. *Mem:* Am Phys Soc; Sigma Xi; Am Asn Physics Teachers; Nat Sci Teachers Asn. *Res:* Investigating how children of various ages respond to science, particularly physics, how they assimilate the concepts and language encountered. *Mailing Add:* 520 La Guardia Pl New York NY 10012

WALD, FRITZ VEIT, b Dieringhausen, WGer, Apr 28, 33; m 59; c 3. SOLID STATE CHEMISTRY, MATERIALS SCIENCE. *Educ:* Sch Tech Chem, Cologne, Ger, BS, 55. *Prof Exp:* Tech chemist, Ed Doerrenberg Soehne, Steelworks Ruenderoth, WGer, 55-57; res asst metall & solid state chem, Philips Cent Lab Aachen, 57-61; res metallurgist, Frigistors Ltd Que, Can, 61-63; sr scientist, Tyco Labs Inc, 63-69, head, Mat Sci Dept, Corp Technol Ctr, 69-75, assoc tech dir, 75-80, DIR RES, MOBIL TYCO SOLAR ENERGY CORP, 80- *Concurrent Pos:* Mem bd dirs, Radiation Monitoring Devices Inc, 76- *Honors & Awards:* Indust Res Award, 70. *Mem:* AAAS; Metall Soc; Am Inst Mining, Metall & Petrol Engrs; Int Microstruct Anal Soc; Am Chem Soc. *Res:* Solid state chemistry; electronic materials; photovoltaic solar energy conversion; crystal growth. *Mailing Add:* Mobil Tyco Solar Energy Corp 516 Hickory Dr Waltham MA 02154

WALD, MILTON M, b San Francisco, Calif, Oct 29, 25; m 56; c 2. CHEMISTRY. *Educ:* Univ Calif, Los Angeles, BS, 49; Univ Southern Calif, PhD(chem), 54. *Prof Exp:* Res assoc, Brookhaven Nat Lab, 54-56; CHEMIST, SHELL DEVELOP CO, 56- *Mem:* Am Chem Soc. *Res:* Organic and catalytic chemistry; petroleum chemistry. *Mailing Add:* Shell Develop Co PO Box 1380 Houston TX 77001

WALD, NIEL, b New York, NY, Oct 1, 25; m 53; c 2. PUBLIC HEALTH, RADIATION MEDICINE. *Educ:* Columbia Univ, AB, 45; NY Univ, MD, 48. *Prof Exp:* Intern & resident med affiliated hosps, NY Univ, 48-49, 50-52; sr hematologist & head radioisotope lab, Atomic Bomb Casualty Comn, Japan, 54-57; head biologist, Health Physics Div, Oak Ridge Nat Lab, 57-58; assoc res prof, 58-60, assoc prof, 60-62, chmn dept occup health, 75-76, chmn dept indust environ health sci, 76-77, PROF RADIATION HEALTH, GRAD SCH PUB HEALTH, UNIV PITTSBURGH, 62-, CHMN DEPT, 69-76 & 77-, PROF RADIOL, SCH MED, 65- *Concurrent Pos:* Fel immunohemat, NY Univ affiliated hosps, 49-50; asst prof med, Sch Med, Univ Pittsburgh, 58-65; mem Pa Governor's Adv Comt Atomic Energy Develop & Radiation Control, 66-, chmn, 74-76; consult, Div Oper Safety, US AEC, 68-75, Div Compliance, 69-75, US Navy Submarine & Radiation Med Div, 73-, US Energy Res & Develop Admin, 75-77, US Nuclear Regulatory Comn, 75- & Dept of Energy, 78-80; mem, Nat Coun Radiation Protection, 70- *Mem:* Health Physics Soc (pres, 73-74); Radiation Res Soc; Environ Mutagen Soc; Soc Human Genetics; AMA. *Res:* Diagnosis and treatment of radiation injury; health physics; cytogenetics; automatic biomedical image processing. *Mailing Add:* Grad Sch of Pub Health Univ of Pittsburgh Pittsburgh PA 15261

WALD, ROBERT MANUEL, b New York, NY, June 29, 47. THEORETICAL PHYSICS. *Educ:* Columbia Univ, AB, 68; Princeton Univ, PhD(physics), 72. *Prof Exp:* Res assoc physics, Univ Md, 72-74; res assoc, 74-76, asst prof, 76-80, ASSOC PROF PHYSICS, UNIV CHICAGO, 80- *Mem:* Am Phys Soc. *Res:* General relativity and gravitation; black holes; quantum field theory in curved spacetime. *Mailing Add:* Enrico Fermi Inst Univ of Chicago Chicago IL 60637

WALD, SAMUEL STANLEY, b New York, NY, Feb 5, 06; m 32; c 2. ROENTGENOLOGY. *Educ:* NY Univ, DDS, 28. *Prof Exp:* CLIN PROF RADIOL, DIAG & ORAL CANCER, COL DENT, NY UNIV, 28-, ASSOC PROF ROENTGENOL, 54-, CLIN PROF RADIOL, SCH MED & POSTGRAD MED SCH, 30- *Concurrent Pos:* Head dept roentgenol & diag, Guggenheim Dent Clin & Sch Dent Hyg, 30-42; consult, Dent Clins, Community Serv Soc, NY, 30-; spec lectr, US Naval Hosp, St Albans, 48- & Vet Admin, Brooklyn, 51-; chmn adv comt radiol, State Dept Health, NY & mem, Mayor's Adv Comt Radiation & Dent, New Yor, 56-; vis prof, NJ Col Med & Dent, 58-; consult radiol, diag & oral med, Mem Hosp Cancer & Allied Dis, New York. *Mem:* Fel Royal Soc Health; Sci Res Soc Am; Am Dent Asn; Asn Mil Surg US; fel Am Col Dent. *Res:* Radiology and diagnosis; oral surgery and oral cancer; dental medicine. *Mailing Add:* 420 E 72nd St New York NY 10021

WALDBAUER, EUGENE CHARLES, b Philadelphia, Pa, July 4, 26; m 56; c 5. NATURAL HISTORY. *Educ:* East Stroudesburg State Col, BS, 52; Pa State Univ, MS, 56; Cornell Univ, PhD(wildlife biol, natural hist & parasitol), 66. *Prof Exp:* From asst prof to assoc prof, 56-69, PROF BIOL, STATE UNIV NY COL CORTLAND, 69- *Mem:* Wilderness Soc. Sigma Xi. *Res:* Flora of Cortland County, New York; pollen analysis of central New York bogs; ferns and lycopodiums of central New York. *Mailing Add:* Dept of Biol State Univ NY Col Cortland NY 13045

WALDBAUER, GILBERT PETER, b Bridgeport, Conn, Apr 18, 28; m 55; c 2. ENTOMOLOGY. *Educ:* Univ Mass, BS, 53; Univ Ill, MS, 56, PhD, 60. *Prof Exp:* Asst, 53-58, from instr to assoc prof, 58-71, PROF ENTOM, UNIV ILL, URBANA, 71- *Mem:* AAAS; Entom Soc Am; Ecol Soc Am. *Res:* Ecology, behavior and physiology of insects; mimicry. *Mailing Add:* Dept of Entom Univ of Ill Urbana IL 61803

WALDBILLIG, RONALD CHARLES, b Iron Mountain, Mich, Mar 17, 43; m 61; c 2. MEMBRANE BIOPHYSICS, ELECTRO-OPTICAL DIELECTRICS. *Educ:* Northern Mich Univ, BS, 67; Univ Rochester, PhD(neurobiol), 73. *Prof Exp:* Res fel, Anat Dept, Duke Univ, 74-76; ASST PROF BIOPHYSICS, PHYSIOL DEPT, MED BR, UNIV TEX, 76- *Mem:* Biophys Soc; AAAS. *Res:* Molecular and physical aspects of membrane function and structure; electrical and optical analysis of the insulating characteristics of single lipid bilayer membranes. *Mailing Add:* Physiol & Biophysics Dept Med Br Univ Tex Galveston TX 77550

WALDE, RALPH ELDON, b Perham, Minn, Mar 8, 43; div; c 2. MATHEMATICS. *Educ:* Univ Minn, Minneapolis, BA, 64; Univ Calif, Berkeley, PhD(math), 67. *Prof Exp:* Asst prof math, Univ Minn, Minneapolis, 67-72; ASST PROF MATH, TRINITY COL, CONN, 72- *Res:* Lie algebras; non-associative algebras. *Mailing Add:* Dept of Math Trinity Col Hartford CT 06106

WALDEN, C(ECIL) CRAIG, b Guernsey, Sask, Apr 19, 21; m 41; c 4. POLLUTION CONTROL, MICROBIOLOGY. *Educ:* Univ Sask, BA, 40, MA, 41; Univ Minn, PhD(agr biochem), 54. *Prof Exp:* Chemist & supvr munitions, Defence Industs, Ltd, 41-44; chemist in charge cereal chem, Quaker Oats Co Can, Ltd, 44-50; assoc res chemist, BC Res Coun, 50-51; asst prof cereal chem, Univ Sask, 51-54; res chemist, 54-61, head div appl biol, 61-70, ASSOC DIR, BC RES, 70- *Concurrent Pos:* Hon prof chem eng, Univ BC. *Mem:* Fed Asns Can Environ; Can Pulp & Paper Asn. *Res:* Water quality and effluent treatment; mineral microbiology; marine biology. *Mailing Add:* 4008 Quensel Vancouver BC V6L 2X2 Can

WALDEN, CLYDE HARRISON, b Kansas City, Mo, Dec 19, 21; m 46; c 3. SCIENCE ADMINISTRATION. *Educ:* William Jewell Col, BA, 42; Univ Colo, MS, 46, PhD(phys chem), 49. *Prof Exp:* Mgr uranium accountability, Mallinckrodt Chem Co, 48-51; sr scientist sec recovery oil, Phillips Petrol Co, 51; mgr qual control, Nat Lead Co, Ohio, 51-57; dir qual control, Gen Tire & Rubber Co, 57-64; DIR PROCESS TECHNOL, KAISER ALUMINUM & CHEM CORP, 64- *Mem:* Am Chem Soc; fel Am Soc Qual Control. *Res:* Administration of technical and engineering functions; heats of chemical reactions. *Mailing Add:* 50 Bellevue Ave Piedmont CA 94611

WALDEN, DAVID BURTON, b New Haven, Conn, Mar 29, 32; m; c 2. PLANT GENETICS, CYTOGENETICS. *Educ:* Wesleyan Univ, BA, 54; Cornell Univ, MSc, 58, PhD(genetics), 59. *Prof Exp:* Fel bot, Ind Univ, 59-61; from asst prof to assoc prof, 61-71, actg chmn dept, 71-73, PROF PLANT SCI, UNIV WESTERN ONT, 71- *Concurrent Pos:* Vis prof, Dept Genetics, Univ Birmingham, 73-74 & 81 & Dept Genetics & Develop & Dept Agron, Univ Ill, 74; pres, Biol Coun Can, 74-75; assoc ed, Can J Genetics & Cytol, 78- *Mem:* AAAS; Crop Sci Soc Am; Genetics Soc Am; Genetics Soc Can (pres, 81-82); Am Inst Biol Sci. *Res:* Pollen biology; corn genetics; plant and human cytogenetics; somatic cell genetics; heat shock and stress proteins. *Mailing Add:* Dept of Plant Sci Univ of Western Ont London ON N6A 5B8 Can

WALDEN, GEORGE ELLIS, physical chemistry, analytical chemistry, see previous edition

WALDEN, JACK M, b Sheridan, Wyo, July 1, 22; m 46; c 5. ELECTRICAL ENGINEERING, COMPUTER SCIENCE. *Educ:* SDak Sch Mines & Technol, BS, 44; Okla State Univ, MS, 62, PhD(eng), 65. *Prof Exp:* Chief engr, Midnight Sun Broadcasting, Alaska, 48-53; vpres & tech dir, Northern TV, Inc, 53-60; from instr to assoc prof elec eng, Okla State Univ, 60-69; eng group leader, Calculator Prod Div, Hewlett-Packard Co, 69-78; SECT TECH DIR, FISCAL INFO COLO, INC, 78- *Mem:* Sr mem Inst Elec & Electronics Engrs; Asn Comput Mach. *Res:* Computer logic design; computer programming of operating systems and compilers; engineering applications of computers; computer-aided instruction. *Mailing Add:* Fiscal Info Inc 1529 W Eisenhower Blvd Suite 3 Loveland CO 80537

WALDEN, ROBERT HENRY, b New York, NY, May 24, 39; m 63; c 2. SEMICONDUCTORS, LARGE SCALE INTEGRATED CIRCUITS. *Educ:* NY Univ, BES, 62, MEE, 63, PhD(eng sci), 66. *Prof Exp:* Mem tech staff, Bell Tel Labs Inc, 66-78; sr proj engr, 78-80, sect head, 80-81, MGR TECH DEPT, HUGHES AIRCRAFT CO, 81- *Mem:* Inst Elec & Electronics Engrs. *Res:* Semi-custom digital large-scale integration, switched capacitor. *Mailing Add:* Hughes Aircraft Co 8433 Fallbrook Ave Canoga Park CA 91304

WALDEN, WILLIAM EARL, computer sciences, mathematics, see previous edition

WALDERN, DONALD E, b Lacombe, Alta, June 8, 28; m 53; c 4. ANIMAL NUTRITION, BIOCHEMISTRY. *Educ:* Univ BC, BSA, 51, MSA, 54; Wash State Univ, PhD(nutrit, biochem), 62. *Prof Exp:* Res scientist, Exp Sta, Can Dept Agr, 53-57 & 61-62; assoc prof dairy nutrit, Wash State Univ, 62-67; res scientist, 67-73, dir, Res Sta, 73-78, prog specialist, 78-80, DIR, LACOMBE RES STA, WEST REGION RES BR, AGR CAN, 80- *Concurrent Pos:* Coordr, agr res progs, WCan. *Mem:* Am Dairy Sci Asn; Am Soc Animal Sci; Agr Inst Can; Can Soc Animal Sci. *Res:* Nutritive value of forages and cereal grains for dairy and beef cattle; complete feeds for dairy cows and early weaned calves; relationship of blood biochemical parameters to performance factors in dairy and beef cows; nutritional management systems for beef cows grazing grassland and forested rangeland. *Mailing Add:* Agr Can Res Br Lacombe Res Sta Box 1420 Lacombe AB T0C 1S0 Can

WALDHALM, DONALD GEORGE, b Enderlin, NDak, Jan 6, 24; m 45; c 4. VETERINARY MICROBIOLOGY. *Educ:* Univ Minn, BA, 48, MS, 50; Univ Ill, PhD, 53. *Prof Exp:* Res scientist microbiol, Res Labs, Swift & Co, Ill, 53-54; med bacteriologist, Rocky Mountain Lab, USPHS, Mont, 54-56; asst prof biol, Carroll Col, Mont, 56-60; asst prof bact, 60-66, ASSOC VET MICROBIOLOGIST, UNIV IDAHO, 66-, ASSOC RES PROF VET SCI, 68- *Mem:* Am Soc Microbiologists. *Res:* Microbial physiology; pathogenic microorganisms; abortion diseases in livestock; diseases of neonatal calves and lambs. *Mailing Add:* Univ of Idaho Exp Sta Rte 8 Caldwell ID 83605

WALDHAUSEN, JOHN ANTON, b New York, NY, May 22, 29; m 57; c 3. SURGERY. *Educ:* Col Great Falls, BS, 50; St Louis Univ, MD, 54. *Prof Exp:* Intern, Johns Hopkins Hosp, Baltimore, 54-55, resident, 56-57; surgeon, Nat Heart Inst, Md, 57-59: resident, Hosp, Univ Pa, 59-60; resident, Med Ctr, Ind Univ, Indianapolis, 60-62, instr surg, Sch Med, 62-63, asst prof, 63-66; assoc prof, Sch Med, Univ Pa, 66-70; interim provost & dean, Col Med, 72-73, PROF SURG & CHMN DEPT, HERSHEY MED CTR, PA STATE UNIV, 70- *Concurrent Pos:* Surg fel, Johns Hopkins Hosp, Baltimore, Md, 55-56; NIH career develop award, Sch Med, Ind Univ, Indianapolis, 63-66; assoc surgeon, Children's Hosp, Philadelphia, 66-70 & Hosp Univ Pa, 66-70; mem surg study sect B, NIH, 74-78. *Mem:* Soc Univ Surg; Am Col Cardiol (secy, 81-); Am Surg Asn; Am Asn Thoracic Surg; Am Col Surg. *Res:* Effects of operative repair of congenital heart defects on pulmonary circulation; newer methods in repair of congenital heart defects; effects of cardiac surgery on ventricular function. *Mailing Add:* Milton S Hershey Med Ctr Pa State Univ Hershey PA 17033

WALDICHUK, MICHAEL, b Mitkau, Roumania, Oct 23, 23; nat Can; m 55; c 3. OCEANOGRAPHY. *Educ:* Univ BC, BA, 48, MA, 50; Univ Wash, PhD, 55. *Prof Exp:* Assoc scientist, Pac Biol Sta, Fisheries Res Bd Can, Nanaimo, BC, 54-58, sr scientist, 58-63, prin scientist, 63-66, oceanogr-in-chg, 66-69; oceanog consult & secy, Can Comt Oceanog, Ottawa, 69-70; prog head, 70-77, SR SCIENTIST, WEST VAN LAB, FISHERIES & OCEANS, CAN, 77- *Concurrent Pos:* Mem, Intergovt Maritime Consult, Orgn-Food & Agr Orgn-UNESCO-World Meteorol Orgn-Int Atomic Energy Agency-UN Joint Group Experts Sci Aspects of Marine Pollution, 69-77, chmn, 70-73; partic coastal wastes mgt study session, Nat Acad Sci, Wyo, 69, workshop on marine environ qual, 71; mem panel marine aquatic life & wildlife, Comt Water Qual Criteria, Nat Acad Sci, Washington, DC, 71-73. *Mem:* AAAS; Can Meteorol & Oceanog Soc; Am Geophys Union; Am Soc Limnol & Oceanog; fel Chem Inst Can. *Res:* Chemical and physical oceanography; industrial wastes and marine pollution. *Mailing Add:* Fisheries & Marine Serv Pac Environ Inst 4160 Marine Dr Vancouver BC V7V 1N6 Can

WALDINGER, HERMANN V, b Vienna, Austria, June 17, 23; US citizen; m 48; c 2. MATHEMATICS. *Educ:* Pomona Col, BA, 43; Brown Univ, MS, 44; Columbia Univ, PhD(math), 51. *Prof Exp:* Res engr, Repub Aviation Corp, 45-46; appl mathematician, M W Kellogg Co, 46-53; sr mathematician, Nuclear Develop Corp Am, 53-59; sr scientist, Repub Aviation Corp, 59-61; ASSOC PROF MATH, POLYTECH INST NEW YORK, 61- *Mem:* AAAS; Am Math Soc; Math Asn Am. *Res:* Group theory. *Mailing Add:* Dept of Math Polytech Inst of New York Brooklyn NY 11201

WALDINGER, RICHARD J, b Brooklyn, NY, Mar 1, 44. COMPUTER SCIENCE. *Educ:* Columbia Univ, AB, 64; Carnegie-Mellon Univ, PhD(comput sci), 69. *Prof Exp:* Res mathematician, 69-76, sr comput scientist, 76-81, STAFF SCIENTIST, ARTIFICIAL INTEL CTR, SRI INT, 81- *Concurrent Pos:* Vis instr, Stanford Univ, 73, vis scholar, 79- *Res:* Artificial intelligence; automatic program synthesis and verification; mechanical theorem proving; robotics. *Mailing Add:* Artificial Intel Ctr SRI Int Menlo Park CA 94025

WALDMAN, ALAN A, cell biology, hematology, see previous edition

WALDMAN, BERNARD, b New York, NY, Oct 12, 13; m 42, 64; c 4. NUCLEAR PHYSICS. *Educ:* NY Univ, AB, 34, PhD(physics), 39. *Prof Exp:* Asst physics, NY Univ, 35-38; res assoc, Univ Notre Dame, 38-40, instr, 40-42, asst prof, 42-43; staff mem & group leader, Los Alamos Sci Lab, 43-45; assoc prof physics, 45-51, assoc dean, Col Sci, 64-67, PROF PHYSICS, UNIV NOTRE DAME, 51-, DEAN, COL SCI, 79-; PROF, MICH STATE UNIV, 79- *Concurrent Pos:* Mem staff, Midwestern Univs Res Asn, 58-59, vpres, 59-60, 65-, lab dir, 60-65; mem physics adv panel, NSF, 65-68, chmn, 68; trustee, Univs Res Asn, Inc, 65-71; assoc dir, Nat Superconducting Cyclotron Lab, 79- *Mem:* Fel Am Phys Soc; Am Asn Physics Teachers. *Res:* Medium energy electrons and x-rays; electrostatic and high energy accelerators. *Mailing Add:* Col of Sci Univ of Notre Dame Notre Dame IN 46556

WALDMAN, GEORGE D(EWEY), b Hartford, Conn, Aug 5, 32. AERONAUTICAL ENGINEERING. *Educ:* Trinity Col, BS, 54; Brown Univ, MS, 57, PhD(appl math), 59. *Prof Exp:* Staff scientist, Res & Adv Develop Div, 59-65, SR STAFF SCIENTIST, SYSTS DIV, AVCO CORP, 65- *Mem:* Am Inst Aeronaut & Astronaut. *Res:* Theory of flows at high speeds; pressure and heat transfer distributions over reentering vehicles; aerodynamic stability and control; multiphase flows and pollution. *Mailing Add:* Avco Systs Div 201 Lowell St Wilmington MA 01887

WALDMAN, JOSEPH, b Philadelphia, Pa, May 12, 06; m; c 3. OPHTHALMOLOGY. *Educ:* Jefferson Med Col, MD, 30; Am Bd Ophthal, dipl, 35. *Prof Exp:* Prof, 30-80, EMER PROF OPHTHAL, JEFFERSON MED COL, 30- *Mem:* AMA. *Mailing Add:* Dept of Ophthal Jefferson Med Col Philadelphia PA 19107

WALDMAN, L(OUIS) A(BRAHAM), b Toledo, Ohio, Oct 13, 29; m 61; c 2. NUCLEAR REACTOR TECHNOLOGY. *Educ:* Univ Toledo, BS, 51; Carnegie Inst Technol, MS, 56; Univ Pittsburgh, PhD(chem eng), 64. *Prof Exp:* Student-employee, Oak Ridge Sch Reactor Tech, Oak Ridge Nat Lab, Union Carbide & Carbon Chem Corp, 51-52; FEL ENGR, BETTIS ATOMIC POWER LAB, WESTINGHOUSE ELEC CORP, 52- *Concurrent Pos:* Lectr, Carnegie Inst Technol, 65-66. *Mem:* Am Inst Chem Engrs; Am Nuclear Soc. *Res:* Heat and mass transfer; corrosion; erosion; fretting wear; release, transport and deposition of fission products from nuclear fuels; investigation of materials for nuclear reactors. *Mailing Add:* 6550 Lilac St Pittsburgh PA 15217

WALDMAN, ROBERT H, b Dallas, Tex, Dec 21, 38; m 63; c 3. IMMUNOLOGY. *Educ:* Rice Inst, BA, 59; Wash Univ, MD, 63. *Prof Exp:* Intern, Johns Hopkins Hosp, 64, resident, 65; clin assoc, Nat Inst Allergy & Infectious Dis, 65-67; prof & actg chmn dept med, Col Med, Univ Fla, 67-76; PROF & CHMN DEPT MED, SCH MED, WVA UNIV, 76- *Concurrent Pos:* Consult, cholera, WHO, 69, vis scientist, Int Res & Training Ctr Immunol, 69-70; mem cholera adv comt, NIH. *Honors & Awards:* Alexandre Besredka Prize, Ger Immunol Soc, 77. *Mem:* Am Soc Clin Invest; Am Fedn Clin Res; Am Asn Immunol; Am Soc Microbiol; fel Am Col Physicians. *Res:* Immunology of viral respiratory infections; study of the secretory immunologic system; immunization by application of antigen to mucous surfaces; host defense mechanisms resident on mucosal surfaces. *Mailing Add:* Dept of Med WVa Univ Med Ctr Morgantown WV 26506

WALDMANN, THOMAS A, b New York, NY, Sept 21, 30; m 58; c 3. MEDICINE, IMMUNOLOGY. *Educ:* Univ Chicago, AB, 51; Harvard Univ, MD, 55. *Prof Exp:* Intern, Mass Gen Hosp, 55-56; clin assoc, 56-58, sr investr, Metab Br, 59-65, HEAD IMMUNOPHYSIOL SECT, NAT CANCER INST, 65-, CHIEF METAB BR, 71- *Concurrent Pos:* Am Heart Asn fel, Nat Cancer Inst, 58-59; mem, Nat Cancer Plan Comt, 72; consult, Fed Trade Comn & WHO; assoc ed, J Immunol. *Honors & Awards:* Michael Heidelberger lectr, Columbia Univ; Irvin Strasberger lectr, Cornell Univ; Lucy Klein Mem lectr, Northwestern Univ; Merril lectr, Thomas Jefferson Univ; Phillips McMaster Mem lectr, Rockefeller Univ; Bela Schick Award, Am Col Allergists; Henry M Stratton Medal, Am Soc Hematol; Larry S Bernton Award, Allergy Soc; Kroc Honor Award, Am Asn Physicians; G Burroughs Mider Award, NIH. *Mem:* Am Asn Immunologists; Am Fedn Clin Res; Am Soc Clin Invest; Asn Am Physicians; Am Physiol Soc. *Res:* Factors controlling the human immune responses; discovery of the diseases intestinal lymphangiectasia, allergic enteropathy and familial hypercatabolic hypoproteinemia; new mechanisms of human disease including abnormalities of suppressor and helper T cells in the pathogenesis of primary immune deficiency disease, immunodeficiency associated with cancer and autoimmune disease. *Mailing Add:* Metab Br Nat Cancer Inst Bethesda MD 20014

WALDNER, MICHAEL, b St Louis, Mo, Mar 21, 24; m 55; c 5. ENGINEERING PHYSICS. *Educ:* Wash Univ, St Louis, BS, 44; Cornell Univ, MS, 48, PhD(eng physics), 54. *Prof Exp:* Test engr, McQuay Norris Co, Mo, 44-45; res engr, Northrop Aircraft Corp, Calif, 48-50; physicist, Gen Elec Co, NY, 53-59 & Hughes Aircraft Co, Calif, 59-61; mem tech staff, NAm Aviation Sci Ctr, 61-68; sr staff physicist, 68-80, SR SCIENTIST, HUGHES RES LABS, 80- *Mem:* Inst Elec & Electronics Engrs. *Res:* Semiconductor devices and surfaces; optical properties of semiconductors; thin film insulators; acousto-electric devices; semiconductor integrated circuits. *Mailing Add:* Hughes Res Labs 3011 Malibu Canyon Rd Malibu CA 90265

WALDO, GEORGE VAN PELT, JR, b Montgomery, Ala, July 20, 40; m 66. ENGINEERING PHYSICS. *Educ:* Johns Hopkins Univ, AB, 61; Univ Md, PhD(physics), 72. *Prof Exp:* PHYSICIST, DAVID TAYLOR NAVAL SHIP RES & DEVELOP CTR, MD, 62- *Concurrent Pos:* Prin investr, David Taylor Naval Ship Res & Develop Ctr, 70- *Res:* Statistical mechanics of phase transitions; cavitation induced by shock waves; interaction of shock waves with structures; monte-carlo simulation of ship vulnerability; perturbation theory of phase transitions; underwater explosions. *Mailing Add:* David Taylor Naval Ship Res Develop Ctr Code 1750-2 Bethesda MD 20084

WALDO, WILLIS HENRY, b Detroit, Mich, Sept 27, 20; m 49; c 5. INORGANIC CHEMISTRY. *Educ:* Washington & Jefferson Col, BS, 42; Univ Md, MS, 50. *Prof Exp:* Chemist, E I du Pont de Nemours & Co, 42-45; chemist, Socony Vacuum Oil Co, 45-46; asst chem, Univ Md, 46-49; tech ed, Monsanto Chem Co, 49-60, admin mgr agr div, Monsanto Co, 60-77, ed, Monsanto Tech Rev, 56-77; opers mgr, Indust Res Inst, Res Corp, St Louis, 77-80. *Concurrent Pos:* Mem, Nat Acad Sci-Nat Res Coun Comt on Mod Methods Handling Chem Info, 62-66; lectr, Southern Ill Univ, Edwardsville, 72-74. *Mem:* Soc Tech Commun; Am Chem Soc; Sigma Xi; Am Soc Info Sci. *Res:* Chromium complexes; sulfur; machine documentation. *Mailing Add:* 15 Balmagoun Lane St Louis MO 63122

WALDON, EDGAR F, audiology, deceased

WALDREN, CHARLES ALLEN, b Syracuse, Kans, June 2, 34; m 61; c 3. BIOPHYSICS. *Educ:* Univ Colo, Boulder, BA, 59; Univ Colo Med Ctr, Denver, MS, 65, PhD(biophys), 72. *Prof Exp:* Chemist, 60-61, fel, 61-65, res tech III, 65-67, instr, 67-75, ASST PROF BIOPHYS & GENETICS, UNIV

COLO MED CTR, 75-; SR FEL, ELEANOR ROOSEVELT INST CANCER RES, 74-; ASSOC PROF, DEPT RADIOL, UNIV COLO HEALTH SCI CTR, 80- *Concurrent Pos:* Vis scientist & fel, Dept Zool, Div Cell Biol, Univ Cambridge, 72-73, 75-76 & 81. *Mem:* Sigma Xi; Am Soc Cell Biol; Human Genetics Soc; Radiation Res Soc; Tissue Culture Asn. *Res:* Genetic-biochemical analysis of mutagenesis and genome repair mechanisms in somatic mammalian cells. *Mailing Add:* Eleanor Roosevelt Inst Cancer Res Box B129 4200 E Ninth Ave Denver CO 80262

WALDREN, RICHARD PAUL, agronomy, see previous edition

WALDREP, ALFRED CARSON, JR, b Orange, Tex, Apr 17, 23; m; c 4. ORAL SURGERY, DENTISTRY. *Educ:* Loyola Univ, La, DDS, 46; Baylor Univ, BS, 59, MS, 61; Am Bd Oral Surg, dipl, 63. *Prof Exp:* Oral surgeon, Valley Forge Gen Hosp, Valley Forge Pa Hq, US Army, San Antonio, Tex, 46-54, dent surgeon, Task Force 7, Cent Pac, 54-55, chief hosp surg dent, US Army Hosp, Ft Polk, La, 55-58, resident oral surg, Hosp, Baylor Univ, 58-59, resident, Brooks Army Med Ctr, 59-61, consult, US Army Med Area, Stuttgart, Ger, 61-64, chief host dent, US Army Hosp, Ft Polk, La, 64-68; asst dean extramural affairs, Col Dent Med, 76-77, PROF ORAL SURG, MED UNIV SC, 68-, ASST DEAN CURRIC & EXTRAMURAL AFFAIRS, COL DENT MED, 77- *Concurrent Pos:* Fel, Hosp, Baylor Univ, 58-59 & Brooks Army Med Ctr, 59-61; consult, Vet Admin Hosp, Charleston, SC, 68-, US Navy Hosp, 69- & SC Dept Corrections, 69-; coordr dent activ, SC Area Health Educ Ctr, 72. *Mem:* Am Dent Asn; Am Soc Oral Surg; assoc Brit Asn Oral Surg. *Res:* Dental education; precautions for patients on drug therapy; oral surgery for patients on anticoagulant therapy. *Mailing Add:* Dept of Oral Surg Med Univ of SC Charleston SC 29401

WALDREP, THOMAS WILLIAM, b Madison, Fla, Feb 14, 34; m 55; c 2. PLANT PHYSIOLOGY. *Educ:* Univ Fla, BSA, 61; Univ Ky, MSA, 63; NC State Univ, PhD(crop sci), 67. *Prof Exp:* Instr crop sci, NC State Univ, 66-67, asst prof, 67-69; RES SCIENTIST, LILLY RES LABS, ELI LILLY & CO, 69- *Mem:* Weed Sci Soc Am. *Res:* Basic and applied research in plant physiology; growth regulators and herbicides; herbicide research. *Mailing Add:* 1501 Chapman Dr Greenfield IN 46140

WALDRON, ACIE CHANDLER, b Malad, Idaho, Feb 4, 30; m 57; c 5. AGRONOMY, ENTOMOLOGY. *Educ:* Brigham Young Univ, BSc, 57; Ohio State Univ, MSc, 59, PhD(agron), 61. *Prof Exp:* Res asst agron, Agr Exp Sta, Ohio State Univ, 57-61; develop chemist, Agr Div, Am Cyanamid Co, NJ, 61-66; exten specialist pesticide chem & state coordr agr chem, Ohio Coop Exten Serv, 66-77, COORDR, N CENT REGION PESTICIDE IMPACT ASSESSMENT PROG, OHIO AGR RES & DEVELOP CTR, OHIO STATE UNIV, 77- *Concurrent Pos:* State IR-4 rep, Ohio State Univ & Ohio Agr Res & Develop Ctr, 73-; pesticide appln educ training coordr, Ohio Coop Exten Serv, 75-77. *Mem:* Am Chem Soc; Am Soc Agron; Coun Agr Sci & Technol; Soil Sci Soc Am; AAAS. *Res:* Pesticide residue chemistry; pesticide residues in plant and animal crops, in soil and water; pesticide safety; administration of regional research for pesticide impact assessment; chemistry of organic nitrogen and phosphorous in soil organic matter. *Mailing Add:* Pesticide Impact Assessment Prog Ohio State Univ 1735 Neil Ave Columbus OH 43210

WALDRON, CHARLES A, b Minneapolis, Minn, July 16, 22; m 43; c 2. ORAL PATHOLOGY. *Educ:* Univ Minn, DDS, 45, MSD, 51; Am Bd Oral Path, dipl, 52. *Prof Exp:* From asst prof to prof path, Sch Dent Wash Univ, 50-57; PROF PATH, SCH DENT, EMORY UNIV, 57- *Concurrent Pos:* Consult, Vet Admin Hosp, Ga, 57 & Dent Intern Prog, Ft Benning, 59; mem med bd dirs, Am Bd Oral Path, 59-70; sci adv bd consult, Armed Forces Inst Path, 70-75. *Mem:* Am Dent Asn; fel Am Col Dent; Am Acad Oral Path (pres, 59, ed, 70-76). *Res:* Oral tumors; diagnostic oral pathology. *Mailing Add:* Sch of Dent Emory Univ Atlanta GA 30322

WALDRON, HAROLD FRANCIS, b Manchester, Ohio, Sept 24, 29; m 49; c 1. APPLIED CHEMISTRY. *Educ:* Capital Univ, BS, 52; Purdue Univ, West Lafayette, MS, 54. *Prof Exp:* Chemist, Uranium Div, Mallinckrodt Chem Works, 54-62, supvr anal methods develop, 62-66, supvr anal res, Opers Div, 66-67, res group leader, Indust Chem Div, 67-69, res mgr chem group, 69-73, res & develop mgr, 73-75, res assoc, Food Prod Div, 75-78, SCIENTIST, MALLINCKRODT, INC, 78- *Mem:* Am Chem Soc. *Res:* Chemical analytical methods, especially the use of vacuum techniques and application of complex ion formation; design and application of electronic instrumentation; general inorganic and uranium chemistry; process research and development. *Mailing Add:* 6 Garden Lane Kirkwood MO 63122

WALDRON, HOWARD HAMILTON, b Nampa, Idaho, Nov 6, 17; m 43; c 3. GEOLOGY. *Educ:* Univ Wash, BS, 40. *Prof Exp:* Photogrammetrist, US Hydrographic Off, Washington, DC, 42-46; geologist, US Geol Surv, 46-73; STAFF CONSULT GEOL, SHANNON & WILSON, INC, 73- *Concurrent Pos:* Tech adv, Geol Surv Indonesia, 60-62, Costa Rica, 64 & Colo Eng Coun, 65-73; eng geol consult & adv, AEC, 67-72 & Vet Admin, 71-73; mem, Earthquake Eng Res Inst. *Mem:* Fel AAAS; Am Geophys Union; Asn Eng Geol; fel Geol Soc Am; Am Soc Civil Eng. *Res:* Engineering geology; areal and glacial geology of Pacific Northwest; urban and environmental geology; geologic and earthquake hazards evaluations. *Mailing Add:* 1105 N 38th St Seattle WA 98103

WALDRON, INGRID LORE, b Nyack, NY, Dec 8, 39. PSYCHOSOMATIC MEDICINE. *Educ:* Radcliffe Col, AB, 61; Univ Calif, Berkeley, PhD(biol), 67. *Prof Exp:* NSF fel, Univ Cambridge, 67-68; ASSOC PROF BIOL, UNIV PA, 68- *Concurrent Pos:* NIH grant, Univ Pa, 69-72; social security grant, Univ Pa, 79-80. *Res:* Human biology; sex differences; social and psychological origins of disease. *Mailing Add:* Dept of Biol Univ of Pa Philadelphia PA 19104

WALDRON, KENNETH JOHN, b Sydney, Australia, Feb 11, 43; m 68; c 2. MECHANICAL ENGINEERING. *Educ:* Univ Sydney, BE, 64, MEngSci, 65; Stanford Univ, PhD(mech eng), 69. *Prof Exp:* Res asst mech eng, Stanford Univ, 65-68, actg asst prof, 68-69; lectr, Univ New SWales, 69-73, sr lectr, 73-74; assoc prof, Univ Houston, 74-80; MEM FAC, DEPT MECH ENG, OHIO STATE UNIV, 80- *Honors & Awards:* Ralph R Teetor Award, Soc Automotive Engrs, 77. *Mem:* Am Soc Mech Engrs; Soc Automotive Engrs; Sigma Xi; US Coun Theory Mach & Mechanisms (treas, 76-78). *Res:* Mechanism kinematics; manipulator design and control; design of active solar collectors. *Mailing Add:* Dept of Mech Eng Ohio State Univ Columbus OH 43210

WALDROP, ANN LYNEVE, b Winters, Tex, Oct 9, 39; m 64. CRYSTALLOGRAPHY. *Educ:* McMurry Col, BA, 61; Vanderbilt Univ, MA, 65; Mass Inst Technol, PhD(crystallog), 70. *Prof Exp:* Teacher high sch, Mass, 64-65; ASST PROF CHEM, SIENA COL, NY, 70- *Mem:* Am Crystallog Asn; Am Chem Soc. *Res:* Determination of crystal and molecular structure by x-ray crystallography; relationship between structure and properties; polymorphism. *Mailing Add:* Dept of Chem Siena Col Londonville NY 12211

WALDROP, FRANCIS N, b Asheville, NC, Oct 5, 26; m 50; c 2. MEDICINE. *Educ:* Univ Minn, AB, 46; George Washington Univ, MD, 50. *Prof Exp:* Intern med, Univ Hosp, George Washington Univ, 50-51; resident psychiat, US Dept Health, Educ & Welfare, 51-54, med officer, 54-59, assoc dir res, 59-65, dir prof training psychiat, 63-71, dir, Clin & Behav Studies Res Ctr, St Elizabeth's Hosp, 65-79, dep adminr, Alcohol, Drug Abuse & Ment Health Admin, 75-79; RETIRED. *Concurrent Pos:* Clin asst prof, George Washington Univ, 62-65, clin assoc prof, 65-; spec asst res & training, Nat Inst Ment Health, 66-68, dep dir, Nat Ctr Ment Health Serv, Training & Res, 68-71, from assoc dir to dir, Div Manpower & Training Progs, 71-75. *Honors & Awards:* Vestermark award, Am Psychiat Asn, 80. *Mem:* AAAS; AMA; fel Am Psychiat Asn. *Res:* Clinical psychiatry; psychopharmacology; drug dependence; basic biological sciences in relation to psychiatric disorders. *Mailing Add:* 1775 Elton Rd Silver Spring MD 20903

WALDROP, MORGAN A, b Ft Worth, Tex, Jan 8, 37. SOLID STATE PHYSICS, ATOMIC PHYSICS. *Educ:* Rice Inst, BA, 59, MA, 62, PhD(physics), 64. *Prof Exp:* SR RES PHYSICIST, PHILLIPS PETROL CO, 63- *Mem:* Am Phys Soc. *Res:* Nuclear magnetic and electron paramagnetic resonance in solids; atomic aspects of heterogeneous catalysis. *Mailing Add:* 1330 Melmart Bartlesville OK 74003

WALDROUP, PARK WILLIAM, b Maryville, Tenn, Oct 17, 37; m 61; c 3. NUTRITION, BIOCHEMISTRY. *Educ:* Univ Tenn, Knoxville, BS, 59; Univ Fla, MS, 62, PhD(nutrit, biochem), 65. *Prof Exp:* Res assoc poultry nutrit, Univ Fla, 64-65, asst prof, 65-66; from asst prof to assoc prof, 66-75, PROF POULTRY NUTRIT, UNIV ARK, FAYETTEVILLE, 75- *Honors & Awards:* Nat Broiler Coun Award, 80. *Mem:* Poultry Sci Asn; Am Inst Nutrit; Animal Nutrit Res Coun. *Res:* Studies concerned with nutrient requirements of poultry in terms of nutrient balance and interrelationships of nutrients; effects of processing on nutritive value of feeds. *Mailing Add:* Dept of Animal Sci Univ of Ark Fayetteville AR 72701

WALDSTEIN, SHELDON SAUL, b Chicago, Ill, June 23, 24; m 52; c 3. INTERNAL MEDICINE, ENDOCRINOLOGY & METABOLISM. *Educ:* Northwestern Univ, BS, 46, MD, 47, MS, 51; Am Bd Internal Med, dipl. *Prof Exp:* Intern & resident internal med, Cook County Hosp, 47-51; from clin asst to assoc prof, 51-66, PROF INTERNAL MED, MED SCH, NORTHWESTERN UNIV, CHICAGO, 66- *Concurrent Pos:* Res assoc, Hektoen Inst & assoc attend physician, Cook County Hosp, 54-57, attend physician, 57-, chief, Northwestern Med Div, 59-62, exec dir dept med, 62-64, chmn dept med, 64-69; exec dir, NSuburban Asn Health Resources, Northbrook, 69-; exec dir, Cook County Grad Sch Med, 77- *Mem:* AAAS; Endocrine Soc; AMA; Am Col Physicians; Am Fedn Clin Res. *Res:* Endocrinology. *Mailing Add:* Northwestern Univ 222 E Superior St Chicago IL 60611

WALECKA, JERROLD ALBERTS, b Highland Park, Ill, Aug 30, 30; m 53; c 2. ORGANIC CHEMISTRY. *Educ:* Lawrence Col, BS, 51, MS, 53, PhD(pulp & paper), 56. *Prof Exp:* Asst tech dir, WVa Pulp & Paper Co, 55-59; res chemist, Mead Corp, 59-63, assoc res dir new prod develop, 63-70; gen mgr res & develop, Forest Prod Group, Continental Can Co, 70-77; MGR BROWNBOARD RES & DEVELOP, WEYERHAEUSER CO, 77- *Mem:* Tech Asn Pulp & Paper Indust. *Res:* Pulp and paper industry; new products; cellulose and plastic chemistry; photochemistry; reproduction processes; graphic arts; information handling; electronic data processing; packaging. *Mailing Add:* Weyerhaeuser Co Tacoma WA 98477

WALECKA, JOHN DIRK, b Milwaukee, Wis, Mar 11, 32; m 54; c 3. THEORETICAL PHYSICS. *Educ:* Harvard Col, BA, 54; Mass Inst Technol, PhD(physics), 58. *Prof Exp:* NSF fel, Europ Orgn Nuclear Res, Switz, 58-59; NSF fel, Stanford, 59-60, from asst prof to assoc prof physics, 60-66, assoc dean humanities & sci, 70-72, chmn acad senate, 73-74, chmn, Dept Physics, 77-82, PROF PHYSICS, STANFORD UNIV, 66- *Concurrent Pos:* A P Sloan Found fel, 62-66; mem sci prog adv comts, Bates Linac, Mass Inst Technol, 71-76, Nevis Cyclotron, Columbia Univ, 71-76, & Los Alamos Meson Physics Facil, 74-76; mem ad hoc panel on future nuclear sci, Nat Res Coun-Nat Acad Sci, 75-77; mem Nuclear Sci Adv Comt, 77; mem vis comt, Lab Nuclear Sci, Nat Inst Technol, 80- *Mem:* Fel Am Phys Soc. *Res:* Nuclear structure; high energy physics. *Mailing Add:* Dept of Physics Stanford Univ Stanford CA 94305

WALES, CHARLES E, b Chicago, Ill, Dec 20, 28; m 53; c 3. EDUCATIONAL ENGINEERING. *Educ:* Wayne State Univ, BS, 53; Univ Mich, MS, 54; Purdue Univ, PhD, 65. *Prof Exp:* From instr to assoc prof chem eng, Wayne State Univ, 54-65; asst prof, Purdue Univ, 65-67; assoc prof eng, Wright State Univ, 67-69; dir freshman eng, 69-81, PROF ENG, WVA

UNIV, 72-, DIR, CTR GUIDED DESIGN, 81- *Concurrent Pos:* Am Oil fel, 64. *Honors & Awards:* George Westinghouse Teaching Award, Am Soc Eng Educ, 71. *Mem:* Int Cong Individualized Instruction; Am Soc Eng Educ. *Res:* Engineering education; programmed learning; guided and educational systems design. *Mailing Add:* WVa Univ Eng Sci Bldg Morgantown WV 26506

WALES, DAVID BERTRAM, b Vancouver, BC, July 31, 39; m 61; c 2. COMBINATORICS, FINITE MATHEMATICS. *Educ:* Univ BC, BSc, 61, MA, 62; Harvard Univ, PhD(math), 67. *Prof Exp:* Bateman res fel, 67-68, from asst prof to assoc prof, 68-77, assoc dean, 76-80, PROF MATH, CALIF INST TECHNOL, 77-, DEAN STUDENTS, 80- *Mem:* Am Math Soc. *Res:* Representation theory of finite groups. *Mailing Add:* Dept of Math Calif Inst of Technol Pasadena CA 91109

WALES, WALTER D, b Oneonta, NY, Aug 2, 33; m 55; c 2. PHYSICS. *Educ:* Carleton Col, BA, 54; Calif Inst Technol, MS, 55, PhD(physics), 60. *Prof Exp:* From instr to assoc prof, 59-72, PROF PHYSICS, UNIV PA, 72-, CHMN DEPT, 73- *Concurrent Pos:* Assoc dir, Princeton Pa Accelerator, 68-71; physicist, AEC, 72-73. *Mem:* Am Phys Soc. *Res:* Particle physics. *Mailing Add:* Dept of Physics Univ of Pa Philadelphia PA 19174

WALFORD, LIONEL ALBERT, fish biology, deceased

WALFORD, LIONEL K, b Cardiff, UK, May 19, 39; m 63. SOLID STATE PHYSICS. *Educ:* Univ Wales, BSc, 60; Univ Cambridge, PhD(physics), 63. *Prof Exp:* Chmn dept physics, 75-77, PROF PHYSICS, SOUTHERN ILL UNIV, EDWARDSVILLE, 63- *Concurrent Pos:* Consult res div, McDonnell Co, Mo, 64-71. *Mem:* Am Crystallog Asn; fel Brit Inst Physics. *Res:* X-ray crystallography; defects in semiconductors; structure of intermetallic compounds; charge transfer in alloys; amorphous phases; general properties of material. *Mailing Add:* Dept of Physics Southern Ill Univ Sch Sci & Tech Edwardsville IL 62026

WALFORD, ROY LEE, JR, b San Diego, Calif, June 29, 24; m 50; c 3. PATHOLOGY. *Educ:* Univ Chicago, BS, 46, MD, 48. *Prof Exp:* Intern, Gorgas Hosp, CZ, 50-51; resident path, Vet Admin Hosp, Los Angeles, 51-52; chief lab, Chanute AFB Hosp, Ill, 52-54; from asst prof to prof path, 54-70, PROF PATH & HEMATOPATH, SCH MED, UNIV CALIF, LOS ANGELES, 70- *Concurrent Pos:* Attend physician, Brentwood Vet Admin Hosp, 55-56; consult, Los Angeles Harbor Gen Hosp, 59- *Mem:* Am Soc Exp Path; Am Asn Path & Bact. *Res:* Hematologic pathology; immunology of the white blood cell; structure, metabolism and diseases of elastic tissue; homograft immunity; gerontology. *Mailing Add:* Dept of Path Univ of Calif Sch of Med Los Angeles CA 90024

WALGENBACH, DAVID D, b Marshall, Minn, Sept 4, 37; m 61; c 4. ENTOMOLOGY, AGRONOMY. *Educ:* Iowa State Univ, BS, 59; Univ Wis-Madison, MS, 62, PhD(entom), 65. *Prof Exp:* Asst prof biol, Stout State Univ, 64-65; field tech specialist entom, Chevron Chem Co, 65-66, crop specialist, Agr Chem Res, 66-67, sr res specialist, 67-73; MEM FAC, DEPT OF ENTOM & ZOOL, S DAK STATE UNIV, 73- *Mem:* AAAS; Entom Soc Am; Am Soc Agron. *Res:* Foreward agricultural chemical research; plant physiology. *Mailing Add:* Dept of Entom & Zool SDak State Univ Brookings SD 57006

WALI, KAMESHWAR C, b Bijapur, India, Oct 15, 27; m 52; c 3. THEORETICAL PHYSICS. *Educ:* Univ Bombay, BSc, 48; Benares Hindu Univ, MSc, 52, MA, 54; Univ Wis, PhD(theoret physics), 59. *Prof Exp:* Res asocxthassoc theoret physics, Univ Wis, 59-60 & Johns Hopkins Univ, 60-62; from asst physicist to sr physicist, Argonne Nat Lab, 62-69; PROF PHYSICS, SYRACUSE UNIV, 69- *Concurrent Pos:* Co-ed, Int Conf Weak Interactions, Argonne Nat Lab, 65; vis mem, Inst Advan Sci Study, Bures-sur-Yvette, France, 71-72 & 75-76; co-ed, Int Symp Nucleon-Nucleon Annihilations, Syracuse, 75; vis scientist, Int Inst Theoret Physics, Trieste, Italy, 67. *Mem:* Am Phys Soc; Sigma Xi. *Res:* Elementary particles; high energy physics; higher symmetries; dispersion theory. *Mailing Add:* Dept Physics Syracuse Univ Syracuse NY 13210

WALI, MOHAN KISHEN, b Srinagar, India, Mar 1, 37; m 60; c 2. PLANT ECOLOGY, ENVIRONMENTAL BIOLOGY. *Educ:* Univ Jammu & Kashmir, India, BSc, 57; Allahabad Univ, MSc, 60; Univ BC, PhD(plant ecol), 69. *Prof Exp:* Demonstr bot, S P Col, Srinagar, India, 61-63, lectr, 63-65; teaching asst biol, Univ BC, 66-67, teaching asst plant ecol, 68-69; asst prof, 69-73, assoc prof, 73-79, PROF BIOL, UNIV NDAK, 79-, SPEC ASST UNIV PRES, 77- *Concurrent Pos:* Res asst, Nat Res Coun Can, 67-69; dir, Proj Reclamation, 75-; sr ed, Reclamation Rev, 76-81, chief ed, Reclamation & Revegetation res, 82- *Honors & Awards:* Sigma Xi Award, Univ NDak, 75; B C Gamble Award, 77. *Mem:* Ecol Soc Am; Can Bot Asn; Am Inst Biol Sci; Brit Ecol Soc; Int Asn Ecol. *Res:* Environmental ecology; influence of water, nutrients, temperature and light on plant populations and communities; nutrient cycling; ecosystem model building; soil-plant relationship; pollution; phytosociology; systems approach to the reclamation of strip mined areas. *Mailing Add:* Dept of Biol Univ of NDak Grand Forks ND 58201

WALIA, AMRIK SINGH, b Punjab, India, Aug 6, 47; m 74; c 2. IMMUNOLOGY, CHEMISTRY. *Educ:* Punjab Univ, BS, 65; Meerut Univ, MS, 68; Loyola Univ, PhD(chem), 75. *Prof Exp:* Lectr chem, GMN Col, Ambala India, 68-70; instr, Loyola Univ, 74-75; tumor immunologist, Dept Surg, 75-77, ASST RES PROF, DEPT SURG, SCH MED, UNIV ALA, 80- *Concurrent Pos:* Fel, Univ Ala Cancer Ctr, 77-78; NIH fel, Nat Cancer Inst, 78-80. *Honors & Awards:* ICRETT Award, Int Union Against Cancer, 78. *Mem:* AAAS; Am Chem Soc; Sigma Xi; Am Asn Immunologists. *Res:* Immune response to polyoma induced tumors, IgG, IgM, and C3 receptors for T cells; biological and biochemical characterization of C3 receptors. *Mailing Add:* 740 LHR Univ of Ala Birmingham AL 35294

WALIA, JASJIT SINGH, b Lahore, India, Mar 19, 34; m 66; c 2. ORGANIC CHEMISTRY. *Educ:* Univ Punjab, India, BS(hons), 55, MS(hons), 56; Univ Southern Calif, PhD(org chem), 60. *Prof Exp:* Res assoc org chem, Univ Southern Calif, 60; res assoc, Mass Inst Technol, 60-61; lectr, Benaras Hindu Univ, 62-66; assoc prof, 66-73, PROF CHEM, LOYOLA UNIV, LA, 73- *Mem:* Am Chem Soc; Royal Soc Chem; Int Soc Heterocyclic Chem. *Res:* New reactions of organic nitrogen compounds; new synthetic reactions; heterocumulene intermediates; carbanion chemistry; electronic interaction through N H...N bond; cyanide ion-catalyzed reactions; enamino carbonyl compounds; mechanism of reactions; new compounds of potential therapeutic and/or other commercial importance. *Mailing Add:* Dept of Chem Loyola Univ New Orleans LA 70118

WALING, J(OSEPH) L(EE), b Brook, Ind, Mar 17, 16; m 42; c 4. STRUCTURAL ENGINEERING. *Educ:* Purdue Univ, BS, 38, MSE, 40; Univ Ill, PhD, 52. *Prof Exp:* Asst appl mech, Purdue Univ, 38-40, instr, 40-41; naval architect, Norfolk Navy Yard, 41-45; from asst prof to assoc prof eng mech, 45-54, prof eng sci, 54-55, asst dean grad sch, 60-63, PROF STRUCT ENG, PURDUE UNIV, 55-, ASSOC DEAN GRAD SCH, 63-, DIR DIV SPONSORED PROGS, 66- *Concurrent Pos:* Mem Nat Coun Univ Res Adminr. *Mem:* AAAS; Am Soc Civil Engrs; Am Soc Eng Educ; Am Concrete Inst; Int Asn Shell Struct. *Res:* Photoelasticity; structural mechanics; reinforced concrete; shell structures. *Mailing Add:* 3731 Capilano Dr West Lafayette IN 47906

WALKE, RAYMOND HENRY, biogeochemistry, environmental engineering, see previous edition

WALKENSTEIN, SIDNEY S, b Philadelphia, Pa, Dec 21, 20; m 46; c 1. DRUG METABOLISM. *Educ:* Temple Univ, BS, 42, AM, 50, PhD(biochem), 53. *Prof Exp:* Biochemist, Mold Metab, Pitman-Dunn Labs, 52-53; chief radiochemist drug metab, Wyeth Inst Med Res, 53-58; pharmaceut specialist, Union of Burma Appl Res Inst, 58-60; sr res scientist, Wyeth Labs, Inc, 60-62, mgr radiochem sect, 62-67; ASSOC DIR BIOL RES, SMITH KLINE & FRENCH LABS, 67- *Concurrent Pos:* Consult, Burma pharmaceut indust, 58-60. *Mem:* Am Soc Pharmacol & Exp Therapeut; Am Pharmaceut Asn; Int Soc Biochem Pharmacol; NY Acad Sci. *Res:* Metabolism of aldehydes and fatty acids; effects of toxins on yeast respiration; pantothenate-deficient yeast metabolism; utilization of hydrocarbons by molds; biotransformation and physiological disposition of isotopically-labeled drugs; medicinal plants; mechanism of drug action; trace drug analysis; pharmacokinetics; biopharmaceutics. *Mailing Add:* Smith Kline & French Labs Philadelphia PA 19101

WALKER, ALAN, b Bridlington, Eng, Apr 30, 37; m 62. INORGANIC CHEMISTRY. *Educ:* Univ Nottingham, BSc, 59, PhD(inorg chem), 62. *Prof Exp:* Dept Indust & Sci Res res fel inorg chem, Univ Nottingham, 62-63; resident res assoc fel chem, Argonne Nat Lab, 63-65; ASSOC PROF CHEM & ASSOC DEAN, UNIV TORONTO, 65- *Concurrent Pos:* Nat Res Coun Can res grant, 65- *Mem:* Fel Royal Soc Chem. *Res:* Nonaqueous solvent chemistry, particularly of nitrates; inorganic spectroscopy; reactions of coordinated ligands to platinum group metals. *Mailing Add:* Dept of Chem Univ of Toronto Toronto ON M5S 2R8 Can

WALKER, ALAN KENT, b Albert Lea, Minn, Jan 23, 50; m 73; c 2. AGRONOMY. *Educ:* Univ Minn, BS, 72; Univ Md, MS, 74; Iowa State Univ, PhD(plant breeding), 77. *Prof Exp:* Res asst soybean breeding, Univ Md, 72-74; res assoc, Iowa State Univ, 75-77; ASST PROF SOYBEAN BREEDING, OHIO AGR RES & DEVELOP CTR, 77- *Mem:* Am Soc Agron; Crop Soc Agron. *Res:* Breeding for Phytophthora stem and root rot resistance and tolerance in soybeans; development of superior cultivars of soybeans. *Mailing Add:* Dept of Agron Ohio Agr Res & Develop Ctr Wooster OH 44691

WALKER, ALMA TOEVS, b Charlson, NDak, Aug 6, 11; m 41. BOTANY. *Educ:* Iowa State Col, BS, 40, PhD, 52; Tex State Col Women, MA, 43. *Prof Exp:* Asst prof home econ, Col Idaho, 40-42; anal chemist, Armour & Co, Inc, Tex, 44; asst prof home econ, Utah, 45-46; asst, Ohio State Univ, 46-48; microbiologist, Tuberc Res Lab, Vet Admin Hosp, Atlanta, Ga, 57-58; assoc investr zool, Univ Ga, 59-62, res physiologist, 62-77; RETIRED. *Concurrent Pos:* Grants in aid, Am Acad Arts & Sci, 62 & Sigma Xi, 65. *Mem:* AAAS; Sigma Xi. *Res:* Fungus physiology; catalase of mycobacteria; lipid deposition in migratory birds; lichens; medicinal plants; conservation and environmental concerns. *Mailing Add:* Rte 2 Box 153 Lexington GA 30648

WALKER, ARTHUR BERTRAM CUTHBERT, JR, b Cleveland, Ohio, Aug 24, 36; m 59; c 1. SPACE PHYSICS, ASTRONOMY. *Educ:* Case Inst Technol, BS, 57; Univ Ill, Urbana, MS, 58, PhD(physics), 62. *Prof Exp:* Mem tech staff, Space Physics Lab, Aerospace Corp, 65-68, staff scientist, 68-70, sr staff scientist, 70-72, dir, Space Astron Proj, 72-73, ASSOC PROF APPL PHYSICS, STANFORD UNIV, 74-, ASSOC DEAN GRAD STUDIES, 75- *Concurrent Pos:* Mem exec comt, Inst Plasma Res, Stanford Univ, 75-, chmn, Astron Course Prog, 76- *Mem:* Sigma Xi; Am Phys Soc; Am Geophys Union; Am Astron Soc; Int Astron Union. *Res:* Solar physics; solar coronal structure; solar x-rays; solar abundances; high energy astrophysics; stellar x-ray sources; interstellar medium; physics of the upper atmosphere. *Mailing Add:* Dept of Appl Physics Stanford Univ Stanford CA 94305

WALKER, ARTHUR EARL, b Winnipeg, Man, Mar 12, 07; nat US. MEDICINE. *Educ:* Univ Alta, BA, 26, MD, 30. *Hon Degrees:* LLD, Univ Alta, 52. *Prof Exp:* Intern, Toronto Western Hosp, 30-31; Smith fel, Univ Chicago, 31, res neurol & neurosurg, 31-34, instr neurol, 37-38, from instr to assoc prof neurol surg, 38-45, prof & chief div, 46-47; instr neurosurg, Univ Iowa, 34; Rockefeller fel, Yale Univ, Univ Amsterdam & Brussels, 35-37; prof neurol surg, 47-72, EMER PROF NEUROL SURG, JOHNS HOPKINS UNIV, 72- *Concurrent Pos:* Vis prof, Sch Med, Univ NMex, 71- *Mem:* Soc Neurol Surg (pres, 66); Am Asn Neurol Surg (pres, 69); Am Electroencephalog Soc (pres, 54); Am Neurol Asn (pres, 65-); fel Am Col

Surg. *Res:* Neurophysiological basis of epilepsy; anatomy and physiology of thalamus; experimental physiology of cerebral cortex; cerebello-cerebral relationships; visual mechanisms; neurosurgical therapy of pain; physiology of cerebral injuries; cerebral death; intracranial pressure; epidemiology of brain tumors; history of neurosurgery. *Mailing Add:* 2211 Lomas Blvd NE Albuquerque NM 87131

WALKER, AUGUSTUS CHAPMAN, b Brooklyn, NY, Oct 2, 23; m 47; c 4. RESEARCH ADMINISTRATION, ACADEMIC ADMINISTRATION. *Educ:* Harvard Univ, BS, 48. *Prof Exp:* Asst biochemist, Thanhauser Lab, New Eng Med Ctr, 48-51; res chemist high polymers, Cryovac Div, W R Grace Co, 52-57; res assoc, Plastics Lab, Mass Inst Technol, 57-58; lectr, Lowell Technol Inst, 57-59, asst prof chem, 58-59; consult, group leader, sect chief & asst to gen mgr, Res & Adv Develop Div, Avco Corp, 59-65; dir res, Polymer Corp, Pa, 65-70; dir res, Resin Products Div, PPG Indust, Inc, 70-73; PRES, EFFECTIVE RES, PITTSBURGH, 73-; consult & actg dir, Off Post-Col Prof Educ, Carnegie Inst Technol, 75-80, SR LECTR ENG MGT, CARNEGIE-MELLON UNIV, 74- *Honors & Awards:* Award, Am Inst Chem Engrs, 63. *Mem:* Am Chem Soc; Soc Plastic Engrs; Am Soc Eng Educ. *Res:* Methods of managing technical activities. *Mailing Add:* Effective Res 141 Westland Dr Pittsburgh PA 15217

WALKER, BENNIE FRANK, b Mt Pleasant, Tex, Sept 19, 37. PHYSICAL CHEMISTRY. *Educ:* Sam Houston State Col, BS, 59, MA, 62; Univ Tex, Austin, PhD(phys chem), 70. *Prof Exp:* Instr chem, Sam Houston State Col, 59-62; asst prof, 68-72, assoc prof, 72-79, PROF CHEM, STEPHEN F AUSTIN STATE UNIV, 79- *Mem:* Am Chem Soc. *Res:* Kinetics; hydrogen bonding; applications of computers in chemistry. *Mailing Add:* Dept of Chem Stephen F Austin State Univ Nacogdoches TX 75962

WALKER, BOYD WALLACE, b Manhattan, Kans, May 26, 17; m 43; c 4. ICHTHYOLOGY. *Educ:* Univ Mich, AB, 40, MS, 42; Univ Calif, Los Angeles, PhD, 49. *Prof Exp:* From asst prof to assoc prof, 48-60, PROF ZOOL, UNIV CALIF, LOS ANGELES, 60- *Mem:* AAAS; Am Soc Ichthyologists & Herpetologists; Soc Study Evolution; Am Fisheries Soc; Soc Syst Zool. *Res:* Systematics, zoogeography, ecology and behavior of fishes, especially the fauna of eastern tropical Pacific. *Mailing Add:* Dept of Biol 2203 Life Sci Bldg Univ of Calif Los Angeles CA 90024

WALKER, BRIAN LAWRENCE, b Liverpool, Eng, Jan 4, 37; m 64; c 3. BIOCHEMISTRY, NUTRITION. *Educ:* Univ Ill, PhD(food sci), 62. *Prof Exp:* Lab asst chem, Albright & Wilson, Mfg Chemists, 54-57; res assoc lipid chem, Univ Ill, 62-64; from asst prof to assoc prof nutrit, 64-75, PROF NUTRIT, UNIV GUELPH, 75- *Concurrent Pos:* Grants, Nat Res Coun Can, 65- & Med Res Coun Can, 66-68. *Honors & Awards:* Borden Award, 75. *Mem:* Fel Royal Soc Chem UK; Am Inst Nutrit; Am Oil Chem Soc; Can Soc Nutrit Sci; Nutrit Today Soc. *Res:* Lipid chemistry and biochemistry; essential fatty acids; lipids and cell membranes; perinatal nutrition and development; nutrition-genetic interactions. *Mailing Add:* Dept of Nutrit Univ of Guelph Guelph ON N1G 2W1 Can

WALKER, BRUCE EDWARD, b Montreal, Que, June 17, 26; m 48; c 4. ANATOMY. *Educ:* McGill Univ BSc, 47, MSc, 52, PhD(genetics), 54; Univ Tex, MD, 66. *Prof Exp:* Lectr anat, McGill Univ, 54-57; from asst prof to assoc prof, Univ Tex Med Bd, Galveston, 57-67; prof anat & chmn dept, 67-75; PROF ANAT, MICH STATE UNIV, 75- *Mem:* Am Asn Anat; Teratology Soc. *Res:* Experimental teratology; carcinogenesis; cell differentiation. *Mailing Add:* Dept Anat Mich State Univ East Lansing MI 48823

WALKER, CAROL L, b Martinez, Calif, Aug 19, 35; m 62; c 4. MATHEMATICS. *Educ:* Univ Colo, BME, 57; NMex State Univ, MS, 61, PhD(math), 63. *Prof Exp:* Mem math, Inst Advan Study, 63-64; from asst prof to assoc prof, 64-72, PROF MATH, N MEX STATE UNIV, 72- *Concurrent Pos:* NSF fel, 63-64, NSF grants, 64-72. *Mem:* Am Math Soc. *Res:* Algebra, primarily Abelian group theory and homological algebra. *Mailing Add:* Dept of Math NMex State Univ Las Cruces NM 88003

WALKER, CEDRIC FRANK, b Stanford Univ, BS, 72, MS, 72; Duke Univ, PhD(biomed eng, 78. NEUROPROSTHESES, MICROPROCESSORS. *Prof Exp:* Res assoc, Div Neurosurg, Duke Med Ctr, 77; asst prof, 77-82, ASSOC PROF BIOMED ENG, TULANE UNIV, 82- *Concurrent Pos:* Adj prof, Dept Orthop Surg & Dept Psychiat & Neurol, Tulane Univ, 78-; prin investr, NSF, 78-80 & Nat Inst Neurol & Comn Disordeers & Stroke, NIH, 82- *Mem:* Am Bd Clin Eng; Inst Elec & Electronics Engrs; Biomed Eng Soc. *Res:* Neuroprosthetic devices, particularly for cerebellar stimulation; bioeffects of low frequency electromagnetic fields. *Mailing Add:* Dept Biomed Eng Tulane Univ New Orleans LA 70118

WALKER, CHARLES A, b Foreman, Ark, Dec 14, 35; m 57; c 3. NEUROPHARMACOLOGY. *Educ:* Ark Agr, Mech & Normal Col, BS, 57; Wash State Univ, MS, 59; Loyola Univ, PhD(pharmacol), 69. *Prof Exp:* Res asst, Wash State Univ, 57-59; asst prof biol, Ft Valley State Col, 59-63; asst prof physiol, Tuskegee Inst, 63-65, assoc prof pharmacol, 68-71, prof vet pharmacol & chmn dept pharmacol, 71-74; PROF PHARM & DEAN SCH PHARM, FLA A&M UNIV, 74- *Mem:* AAAS; Am Asn Clin Chem; NY Acad Sci; Am Soc Pharmacol & Exp Therapeut; Int Soc Chronobiol. *Res:* Circadian rhythms of biogenic amines in the central nervous system. *Mailing Add:* 3113 Shamrock S Tallahassee FL 32308

WALKER, CHARLES A(LLEN), b Wise Co, Tex, June 18, 14; m 42; c 3. CHEMICAL ENGINEERING. *Educ:* Univ Tex, BSChE, 38, MSChE, 40; Yale Univ, DEng, 48. *Prof Exp:* Asst prof chem, Tex Col Arts & Indust, 40-41 & Univ Ark, 41-42; from instr to assoc prof, 42-56, master, Berkeley Col, 59-69, dept chmn, 74-76, PROF CHEM ENG, YALE UNIV, 56-, DEPT CHMN, 81- *Concurrent Pos:* Mem adv bd, Petrol Res Fund, 70-72, chmn, 72-81. *Mem:* AAAS; Am Chem Soc; Sigma Xi; Am Soc Eng Educ; Am Inst Chem Engrs. *Res:* Water quality control; technology and the social sciences; role of the social sciences in energy policy; nuclear waste management. *Mailing Add:* 300 Mason Lab Yale Univ New Haven CT 06520

WALKER, CHARLES CAREY, organic polymer chemistry, see previous edition

WALKER, CHARLES EDWARD, JR, b Kosciusko, Miss, June 16, 39; m 67; c 1. PHYSICS. *Educ:* Univ Calif, Berkeley, BA, 61; Univ Ill, Urbana, MS, 63; Univ Wyo, PhD(physics), 68. *Prof Exp:* Asst prof physics, Univ Wyo, 68; asst prof, 68-75, ASSOC PROF PHYSICS, UNIV WIS-RIVER FALLS, 75- *Mem:* Am Phys Soc. *Res:* Non-mesic decay of heavy hypernuclei. *Mailing Add:* Dept of Physics Univ of Wis River Falls WI 54022

WALKER, CHARLES EUGENE, cereal chemistry, see previous edition

WALKER, CHARLES R, b Chicago, Ill, Dec 18, 28; m 50; c 4. BIOCHEMISTRY, FISH BIOLOGY. *Educ:* Southern Ill Univ, BA, 51, MA, 52. *Prof Exp:* Biochemist & fishery biologist, Mo Conserv Comn, 52-61; biochemist, Fish Control Lab, US Fish & Wildlife Serv, 61-67, chief br pest control res, Div Fishery Res, 67-72, chief off environ assistance, 72-75, sr environ scientist, 75-81; CONSULT ENVIRON CONTAMINANTS & TOXICOL, 81- *Concurrent Pos:* Consult fishery biol, hazardous mat, pesticides & pond cult, 54-82; lectr, Viterbo Col, 64-65; instr, USDA Grad Sch, 69-; mem adj fac environ systs mgt, Am Univ, 75- *Mem:* Am Chem Soc; Am Fisheries Soc; Weed Sci Soc Am; Am Soc Testing & Mat; Am Soc Limnol & Oceanog. *Res:* Fishery research; aquatic ecology, fish-pesticide relationships; pollution biology; pond culture; aquatic herbicides; toxicity; efficacy residues of drugs and pest control agents for fisheries; analytical chemistry; limnology; soil science; environment impact statements control; environmental impact assessments; biological testing methods and hazard assessment of toxic substances; monitoring environmental contaminants. *Mailing Add:* 4613 Dixie Hill Rd Fairfax VA 22030

WALKER, CHARLES ROBERT, developmental biology, see previous edition

WALKER, CHARLES THOMAS, b Chicago, Ill, Sept 5, 32; m 73; c 3. SOLID STATE PHYSICS. *Educ:* Univ Louisville, AB, 56, MS, 58; Brown Univ, PhD(physics), 61. *Prof Exp:* Res asst physics, Brown Univ, 58-60; res assoc, Cornell Univ, 61-63; asst prof, Northwestern Univ, Evanston, 63-67, assoc prof, 67-71; PROF PHYSICS, ARIZ STATE UNIV, 71-, CHMN DEPT, 81- *Concurrent Pos:* Guggenheim fel, Oxford Univ, 67-68; vis prof, Munich Tech Univ, 71; consult, Motorola, Inc, 74-; vis prof, Univ Sao Paulo, 76 & Univ Regensburg, 77; dir, Ctr Solid State Sci, Ariz State Univ, 76-78; Alexander von Humboldt fel, Max-Planck Inst, Stuttgart, 78-79. *Mem:* AAAS; fel Am Phys Soc; Am Asn Physics Teachers. *Res:* Light scattering; lattice dynamics and impurity studies in solids; magnetism. *Mailing Add:* Dept of Physics Ariz State Univ Tempe AZ 85287

WALKER, CHARLES WAYNE, b Oberlin, Ohio, Mar 27, 47; m 69. DEVELOPMENTAL BIOLOGY. *Educ:* Miami Univ, BA, 69; Cornell Univ, MS, 73, PhD(invertebrate zool), 76. *Prof Exp:* Lectr embryol, Cornell Univ, 75-76; asst prof, 76-80, ASSOC PROF EMBRYOL OF INVERTEBRATES, UNIV NH, 80- *Concurrent Pos:* Hubbard Fund grant, 78-80, NSF grant, 80-81, NATO grant, 80-81. *Mem:* Am Soc Zoologists; Sigma Xi; Soc Develop Biol; Int Soc Invertebrate Reproduction. *Res:* Physiological and ultrastructural aspects of cellular interaction during spermatogenesis and regeneration; comparative aspects of invertebrate development. *Mailing Add:* Dept Zool Univ NH Durham NH 03824

WALKER, CHRISTOPHER BLAND, b Lakeland, Fla, July 25, 25; m 61; c 3. PHYSICS. *Educ:* Davidson Col, BS, 48; Mass Inst Technol, PhD(physics), 51. *Prof Exp:* Fulbright scholar, France, 51-52; instr physics, Mass Inst Technol, 52-53; from asst prof to assoc prof, Inst Metals, Chicago, 53-63; RES PHYSICIST, ARMY MAT & MECH RES CTR, 63- *Concurrent Pos:* Guggenheim fel, 63-64. *Mem:* Am Phys Soc; Am Crystallog Asn; Fr Soc Mineral & Crystallog. *Res:* X-ray diffraction; imperfections in crystals; thermal vibrations; neutron inelastic scattering. *Mailing Add:* Army Mat & Mech Res Ctr Watertown MA 02172

WALKER, DAN B, b Connersville, Ind, Apr 18, 45. PLANT ANATOMY. *Educ:* Ind Univ, Bloomington, AB, 68; Univ Calif, Berkeley, PhD(bot), 74. *Prof Exp:* Lectr bot, Univ Calif, Berkeley, 73-74; asst prof bot, Univ Ga, 74-78; ASST PROF BIOL, UNIV CALIF, LOS ANGELES, 78- *Mem:* Sigma Xi; AAAS; Bot Soc Am; Am Soc Plant Physiologists; Soc Develop Biol. *Res:* Investigations of structure-function and developmental problems at the cellular level in higher plants, especially on the mechanisms of intercellular transport and communication in plants. *Mailing Add:* Dept Biol Univ Calif Los Angeles CA 90024

WALKER, DANIEL ALVIN, b Cleveland, Ohio, Dec 18, 40; m 70; c 3. SEISMOLOGY. *Educ:* John Carroll Univ, BS, 63; Univ Hawaii, MS, 65, PhD(geophys), 71. *Prof Exp:* Res asst seismol, 63-68, jr seismologist, 69-71, asst geophysicist, 72-76, ASSOC GEOPHYSICIST, HAWAII INST GEOPHYSICS, UNIV HAWAII, 76- *Mem:* Seismol Soc Am; Am Geophys Union; AAAS. *Mailing Add:* Hawaii Inst Geophys Univ of Hawaii Honolulu HI 96822

WALKER, DAVID, b Troy, New York, NY, Aug 9, 46. PETROLOGY. *Educ:* Oberlin Col, AB, 68; Harvard Univ, AM, 70, PhD(geol), 72. *Prof Exp:* Lectr geol, 73-74, res fel geophysics, 72-77, SR RES ASSOC, HARVARD UNIV, 78- *Honors & Awards:* F W Clarke Medal, Geochem Soc, 75. *Mem:* Geol Soc Am; Am Geophys Union; Geochem Soc; Mineral Soc Am; AAAS. *Res:* General geology with specialty in petrology, particularly experimental petrology studies of lunar basaltic samples. *Mailing Add:* Hoffman Lab Harvard Univ 20 Oxford St Cambridge MA 02138

WALKER, DAVID CROSBY, b York, Eng, June 16, 34; m 78; c 3. PHYSICAL CHEMISTRY. *Educ:* Univ St Andrews, BSc, 55, Hons, 56; Univ Leeds, PhD(chem), 59. *Hon Degrees:* DSc, Univ St Andrews, 74. *Prof Exp:* Fel chem, Nat Res Coun Can, 59-61; res lectr, Univ Leeds, 61-64; asst prof,

64-67, assoc prof, 67-75, PROF CHEM, UNIV BC, 75- *Mem:* Fel Chem Inst Can; fel Royal Soc Chem; Am Chem Soc; Am Inst Physics; Radiation Res Soc. *Res:* Radiation chemistry of water and organic liquids; muonium chemistry; solvated electron studies in polar liquids; orgins of optical activity in nature. *Mailing Add:* Dept of Chem Univ of BC Vancouver BC V6T 1Y6 Can

WALKER, DAVID KENNETH, b Youngstown, Ohio, Apr 4, 43; m 67. PHYSICS. *Educ:* Pa State Univ, University Park, BS, 65; WVa Univ, MS, 68, PhD(physics), 71. *Prof Exp:* Instr physics, WVa Univ, 69-71; asst prof, 71-75, ASSOC PROF PHYSICS, WAYNESBURG COL, 75- *Mem:* Electrostatics Soc Am; Am Phys Soc; Am Asn Physics Teachers. *Res:* Electrophysics, electrostatics; atmospheric electric field; operation of motors from atmospheric field; electrets; electromechanical devices; windmills. *Mailing Add:* Dept of Chem & Physics Waynesburg Col Waynesburg PA 15370

WALKER, DAVID NORTON, b Yuba City, Calif, Aug 17, 43; m 68; c 2. PLASMA PHYSICS, SPACE SCIENCE. *Educ:* Univ Md, BS, 65; Univ NH, MA, 72, PhD(physics), 75. *Prof Exp:* Engr, McDonnell-Douglas Corp, 66-67; assoc engr, Elec Assoc Inc, 68-70; instr physics, Univ NH, 70-75; analyst, Anal Servs Inc, 75-77; PHYSICIST, NAVAL RES LAB, 77- *Mem:* Am Phys Soc; Am Geophys Union; Am Acad Sci. *Res:* Plasma physics as related to magnetospheric research. *Mailing Add:* Naval Res Lab Washington DC 20375

WALKER, DAVID RUDGER, b Ames, Iowa, Sept 15, 29; m 48; c 10. POMOLOGY. *Educ:* Utah State Univ, BS, 51, MS, 52; Cornell Univ, PhD, 55. *Prof Exp:* From asst prof to assoc prof hort, NC State Col, 55-60; assoc prof, 60-65, PROF PLANT SCI, UTAH STATE UNIV, 65- *Honors & Awards:* Shepard Award, Am Pomol Soc; Stark Award, Am Soc Hort Sci. *Mem:* Fel Am Soc Hort Sci; Am Pomol Soc; AAAS. *Res:* Plant hardiness; mineral nutrition; growth substances. *Mailing Add:* Dept of Plant Sci Utah State Univ Logan UT 84321

WALKER, DAVID TUTHERLY, b Huntington, WVa, July 10, 22; m 57; c 1. MATHEMATICS. *Educ:* Wofford Col, BS, 49; Univ Ga, MS, 51, PhD, 55. *Prof Exp:* Asst math, Univ Ga, 51-53; instr, Univ SC, 53-54; asst, Univ Ga, 54-55; from asst prof to assoc prof, 55-67, PROF MATH, MEMPHIS STATE UNIV, 67- *Mem:* Sigma Xi. *Res:* Mathematical analysis; modern algebra; theory of numbers; geometry. *Mailing Add:* Dept Math Memphis State Univ Memphis TN 38111

WALKER, DAVID WHITMAN, entomology, see previous edition

WALKER, DENNIS KENDON, b Sacramento, Calif, Aug 1, 38; m 60; c 4. BOTANY. *Educ:* Humboldt State Col, BA, 60; Univ Calif, Davis, MS, 64, PhD(bot), 66. *Prof Exp:* Asst prof, 65-70, assoc prof, 70-76, PROF BOT, HUMBOLDT STATE UNIV, 76- *Mem:* Electron Micros Soc Am. *Res:* Plant morphology; developmental plant anatomy and plant ultrastructure, specifically the ultrastructure of differentiating elements of vascular tissues. *Mailing Add:* Dept of Biol Humboldt State Univ Arcata CA 95521

WALKER, DON WESLEY, b Ft Worth, Tex, July 30, 42; m 64; c 2. NEUROSCIENCE, NEUROPHARMACOLOGY. *Educ:* Univ Tex, Arlington, BA, 64; Tex Christian Univ, MA & PhD(psychol), 68. *Prof Exp:* Asst prof, 70-75, assoc prof, 75-80, PROF NEUROSCI & PSYCHOL, UNIV FLA, 80-; RES INVESTR, VET ADMIN HOSP, GAINESVILLE, 70- *Concurrent Pos:* Nat Inst Ment Health training grant, Col Med, Univ Fla, 68-70, NIH res grant neurosci, 72-; Vet Admin res fund grant, Vet Admin Hosp, Gainesville, 70- *Mem:* AAAS; Soc Neurosci; Am Psychol Asn. *Res:* Neurobiology of drug dependence; chronic effects of ethanol on the brain; neural mechanisms of feeding behavior and weight regulation. *Mailing Add:* Dept of Neurosci Univ of Fla Col of Med Gainesville FL 32601

WALKER, DONALD EVERETT, b Green Bay, Wis, Nov 22, 28; m 48; c 3. COMPUTER SCIENCE, LINGUISTICS. *Educ:* Univ Chicago, PhD(psychol), 55. *Prof Exp:* Asst prof psychol, Rice Univ, 53-61; head lang & text processing, The MITRE Corp, 61-71; PROJ LEADER LANGUAGE UNDERSTANDING, SRI INT, 71- *Concurrent Pos:* Vis asst prof, Univ Chicago, 55; res psychologist, Vet Admin Hosp, Houston, 57-61; NIMH res grant & clin asst prof, Col Med, Baylor Univ, 59-60; vis scholar & guest, Res Lab Electronics, Mass Inst Technol, 61-67; secy & mem bd dirs, Am Fedn Info Processing Socs, 67-72 & 79-; coun mem, gen chmn, trustee & secy-treas, Int Joint Conf Artificial Intel, 69-; panel comt mem & chmn, Nat Acad Sci, 70-72 & 74-81; consult, Off Sci Info Serv, Nat Sci Found, 71-72; comt vchmn & chmn, Int Fedn Doc, 73- *Mem:* Asn Comput Mach; Asn Comput Ling (pres & vpres, 67-68, secy-treas, 77-); Am Soc Info Sci; Ling Soc Am; Asn Artificial Intel (secy-treas, 79-). *Res:* Computational linguistics; natural language understanding; artificial intelligence; information science; organization and use of information. *Mailing Add:* 855 Chimalus Dr Palo Alto CA 94306

WALKER, DONALD F, b Brush, Colo, July 16, 23; m 44; c 1. VETERINARY MEDICINE. *Educ:* Colo State Univ, DVM, 44. *Prof Exp:* Pvt pract, Grassland Hosp, 45-58; assoc prof, 58-66, PROF LARGE ANIMAL SURG & MED, AUBURN UNIV, 66-, DEPT HEAD, 78- *Mem:* Am Col Theriogenology. *Res:* Urogenital surgery; ultrasonic therapy. *Mailing Add:* Dept of Large Animal Surg & Med Auburn Univ Auburn AL 36830

WALKER, DONALD GREGORY, anatomy, deceased

WALKER, DONALD I, b Lombard, Ill, Jan 13, 22; m 44; c 3. ANALYTICAL CHEMISTRY, CHEMICAL MICROSCOPY. *Educ:* Univ Ill, BS, 48; Univ Colo, PhD(chem), 56. *Prof Exp:* Asst chem, Univ Colo, 48-50, asst instr, 53-56; res chemist, Los Alamos Sci Lab, Univ Calif, 50-53; dep dir health & safety div, Idaho Opers Off, AEC, 56-57, dir licensee compliance div, 57-60, dir region VIII, Div Compliance, 60-62, dir region IV, 62-70, dir, Health Serv Lab, Idaho Opers Off, Energy Res & Develop Admin, 70-76; EXEC DIR, ASSOC WESTERN UNIVS, INC, 76- *Concurrent Pos:* Consult, Rocky Flats Div, Dow Chem Co, 54. *Mem:* AAAS; Am Chem Soc; Health Physics Soc; Am Inst Chemists. *Res:* Administration of environmental monitoring, radiation dosimetry, ecology. *Mailing Add:* Suite 200 142 E 200 South Salt Lake City UT 84111

WALKER, DUARD LEE, b Bishop, Calif, June 2, 21; m 45; c 4. VIROLOGY, MICROBIOLOGY. *Educ:* Univ Calif, Berkeley, AB, 43, MA, 47; Univ Calif, San Francisco, MD, 45; Am Bd Med Microbiol, dipl. *Prof Exp:* Asst resident physician internal med, Stanford Univ Serv, San Francisco Hosp, 50-52; assoc prof, 52-59, chmn dept, 70-76, PROF MED MICROBIOL, MED SCH, UNIV WIS-MADISON, 59-, CHMN DEPT, 81- *Concurrent Pos:* Nat Res Coun fel, Rockefeller Inst, New York, 47-49; USPHS fel, George Williams Hooper Found, Univ Calif, San Francisco, 49-50, res assoc, 50-51; consult, Naval Med Res Unit 4, Great Lakes, Ill, 58-74; mem microbiol training comt, Nat Inst Gen Med Sci, 66-70; mem, Nat Adv Allergy & Infectious Dis Coun, 70-74, study group on papovaviridae, Int Comt Taxon Viruses, 76-, adv comt blood prog res, Am Red Cross, 78-79 & bd sci adv, Delta Regional Primate Ctr, Tulane Univ, 80-83. *Mem:* Am Asn Immunol; Am Soc Microbiol; fel Am Acad Microbiol; Reticuloendothelial Soc; Soc Exp Biol & Med. *Res:* Persistent and chronic viral infections; host response to viral infection. *Mailing Add:* Dept of Med Microbiol Univ of Wis Med Sch Madison WI 53706

WALKER, EDWARD BELL MAR, b Ogden, Utah, Mar 19, 52; m 75; c 2. PHOTOCHEMISTRY, PHOTOBIOLOGY. *Educ:* Weber State Col, BA, 76; Tex Tech Univ, PhD(chem), 80. *Prof Exp:* Grad student chem, Tex Tech Univ, 76-80; scholar biochem pharm, Stanford Univ Med Ctr, 80-81; ASST PROF BIOCHEM, WEBER STATE COL, 81- *Mem:* Am Soc Photobiol; Am Chem Soc; Am Soc Plant Physiologists; Sigma Xi. *Res:* Photochemistry and photobiology, particularly the mechanisms of photoreception in both plants and animals. *Mailing Add:* Dept Chem Weber State Col Ogden UT 84408

WALKER, EDWARD JOHN, b Detroit, Mich, Apr 16, 27; m 60; c 1. SOLID STATE PHYSICS. *Educ:* Univ Mich, BSE, 49; Yale Univ, PhD(physics), 60. *Prof Exp:* Asst electronics, Tube Lab, Nat Bur Stand, 49-53; PHYSICIST, RES CTR, IBM CORP, 60- *Res:* Semiconductor physics. *Mailing Add:* Spring Valley Rd Ossining NY 10562

WALKER, EDWARD ROBERT, b Winnipeg, Man, July 29, 22; m 54; c 3. METEOROLOGY. *Educ:* Univ Manitoba, BSc, 43; Univ Toronto, MA, 49; McGill Univ, PhD(meteorol), 61. *Prof Exp:* Meteorologist, Meteorol Serv Can, 43-59; res asst meteorol, McGill Univ, 59-60; res micrometeorologist, Defence Res Bd, Can, 61-67; RES ARCTIC METEOROLOGIST, CAN DEPT ENVIRON, 67- *Mem:* Am Meteorol Soc; Royal Astron Soc Can; fel Royal Meteorol Soc. *Res:* Arctic meteorology; oceanography. *Mailing Add:* 3350 Woodburn Ave Victoria BC V8P 5C1 Can

WALKER, ELBERT ABNER, b Huntsville, Tex, Mar 11, 30; m 51; c 3. MATHEMATICS. *Educ:* Sam Houston State Col, BA, 50, MA, 52; Univ Kans, PhD(math), 55. *Prof Exp:* High sch teacher, Tex, 50-52; mathematician, US Dept Defense, Washington, DC, 55-56; asst prof math, Univ Kans, 56-57; from asst prof to assoc prof, 57-63, PROF MATH, NMEX STATE UNIV, 63- *Mem:* Am Math Soc; Math Asn Am; Am Statist Asn. *Res:* Abelian group theory; category theory; ring theory; statistics. *Mailing Add:* Dept of Math Sci NMex State Univ Las Cruces NM 88003

WALKER, ELIZABETH REED, b Rochester, Pa, July 2, 41; m 67; c 1. HUMAN ANATOMY. *Educ:* Mich State Univ, BA, 63; WVa Univ, MS, 71, PhD(human anat), 75. *Prof Exp:* Res asst microbiol, Rockefeller Univ, 64-66; technologist electron micros, 67-71, lectr human anat, 74-75, INSTR HUMAN ANAT, W VA UNIV, 75- *Res:* Investigation of rheumatology by transmission and scanning electron microscopy, particularly pathogenesis of rheumatoid arthritis and other connective tissue diseases, and pulmonary research, with emphasis on macrophage uptake of respirable mineral particulates. *Mailing Add:* Dept of Anat WVa Univ Sch of Med Morgantown WV 26506

WALKER, ERIC A(RTHUR), b Long Eaton, Eng, Apr 29, 10; nat US; m 37; c 2. ELECTRICAL ENGINEERING. *Educ:* Harvard Univ, BS, 32, SM, 33, ScD(elec eng), 35. *Hon Degrees:* LLD, Temple Univ & Lehigh Univ, 57, Hofstra Col, Lafayette Col & Univ Pa, 60, Univ RI, 62; LHD, Elizabethtown Col, 58; LittD, Jefferson Med Col, 60; DL, St Vincent Col, 68; ScD, Wayne State Univ, 65, Thiel Col, 66, Univ Notre Dame, 68, Univ Pittsburgh, 70 & Univ Bridgeport, 72. *Prof Exp:* Instr elec eng & math, Tufts Col, 34-38, asst prof math, 38-39, chmn dept elec eng, 39-40; assoc prof elec eng & head dept, Univ Conn, 40-42; assoc dir, underwater sound lab, Harvard Univ, 42-45; prof elec eng & head dept, 45-51, dir, Ord Res Lab, 45-52, dean col eng & archit, 51-56, vpres, 56, pres, 56-70, EMER PRES, PA STATE UNIV, 70-; V PRES, ALUMINUM CO AM, 70- *Concurrent Pos:* Mem & former chmn, Comt Undersea Warfare, Nat Res Coun; chmn comt eng, NSF, 51-53, mem, Nat Sci Bd; exec secy, Res & Develop Bd, US Dept Defense, 50-51; mem sci adv panel, US Dept Army, 56-58; chmn res adv comt, US Dept Navy, 71-; vchmn, President's Comt Scientists & Engrs, 56-58; gen chmn, President's Conf Technol & Distribution Res for Benefit of Small Bus, 57; mem exec comt, Am Asn Land Grant Cols & State Univs; bd vis, US Naval Acad, 58-60; trustee, Inst Defense Anal, 58-; dir, Aluminum Co Am, 71-75. *Honors & Awards:* Presidential Cert Merit, 48; Distinguished Civilian Serv Award, US Dept Navy, 58; Bliss Award, Am Soc Mil Engrs, 59; Horatio Alger Award; Lamme Award, Am Soc Eng Educ. *Mem:* Nat Acad Eng (pres, 66-70); fel Am Phys Soc; fel Acoust Soc Am; Am Soc Eng Educ (vpres, 52-54, pres, 60-61); fel Inst Elec & Electronics Engrs. *Res:* Acoustic properties of liquids; high voltage insulation; electrostatics precipitation. *Mailing Add:* Pa State Univ 222-A Hammond Bldg University Park PA 16802

WALKER, EUGENE HOFFMAN, b New York, NY, Mar 28, 15; m 47; c 3. ECONOMIC GEOLOGY. *Educ:* Harvard Univ, BA, 37, MA, 42, PhD(geol), 47. *Prof Exp:* Geologist, Shell Oil Co, Tex, 37-39; geologist, Patino Mines, Bolivia, 42-45; instr geol, Univ Mich, 45-49; geologist, US Geol Surv, 49-80. *Mem:* Geol Soc Am. *Res:* Ground water geology and hydrology; geomorphology; glacial geology. *Mailing Add:* 14 Chestnut St Concord MA 01742

WALKER, FRANCIS EDWIN, b Morris, Ill, Nov 29, 31; m 51; c 3. AGRICULTURAL ECONOMICS. *Educ:* Univ Ill, BS, 54, MS, 58, PhD(agr econ), 60. *Prof Exp:* Asst prof agr econ, Purdue Univ, 60-61; from asst prof to assoc prof, 61-68, PROF AGR ECON, OHIO STATE UNIV, 68- *Mem:* Am Statist Asn; Am Agr Econ Asn. *Res:* International trade policy; interregional competition. *Mailing Add:* Dept of Agr Econ Ohio State Univ 2120 Fyffe Rd Columbus OH 43210

WALKER, FRANCIS H, b San Francisco, Calif, Jan 15, 36; m 66; c 2. ORGANIC CHEMISTRY. *Educ:* Stanford Univ, BS, 58, MS, 60. *Prof Exp:* Chemist, 60-76, SR RES CHEMIST, STAUFFER CHEM CO, 76- *Res:* Organic synthesis of agricultural chemicals. *Mailing Add:* Stauffer Chem Co 1200 S 47th St Richmond CA 94804

WALKER, GENE B(ERT), b Gladewater, Tex, Feb 24, 32; m 56; c 4. ELECTRICAL ENGINEERING. *Educ:* Univ Tex, BS, 59, MS, 62, PhD(elec eng), 64. *Prof Exp:* Res engr, Elec Eng Res Lab, Univ Tex, 59-64; sr res engr, Southwest Res Inst, 64-67; from asst prof to assoc prof, 67-77, PROF ELEC ENG, UNIV OKLA, 77- *Concurrent Pos:* Consult, Nat Severe Storms Lab, Nat Oceanic & Atmospheric Admin, 69-78. *Mem:* Inst Elec & Electronics Engrs; Sigma Xi. *Res:* Radios wave propagation; radio direction finding; radar sounding of troposphere; acoustic sounding of the troposphere. *Mailing Add:* 2408 Cypress Ave Norman OK 73069

WALKER, GEORGE EDWARD, b Chillicothe, Ohio, Nov 5, 40; m 64; c 3. THEORETICAL NUCLEAR PHYSICS. *Educ:* Wesleyan Univ, BA, 62; Case Western Reserve Univ, MS, 64, PhD(physics), 66. *Prof Exp:* Res assoc physics, Los Alamos Sci Lab, 66-68; res assoc, Stanford Univ, 68-70; asst prof, 70-73, assoc prof, 73-76, PROF PHYSICS, IND UNIV, BLOOMINGTON, 76- *Concurrent Pos:* Vis staff mem, Los Alamos Sci Lab, 68- *Mem:* fel Am Phys Soc; Am Asn Physics Teachers. *Res:* Nuclear theory; electron scattering; meson-nucleus interactions; nucleon-nucleus interactions; heavy ion scattering. *Mailing Add:* Dept of Physics Ind Univ Bloomington IN 47401

WALKER, GEORGE ROBERT, b New York, NY, Jan 13, 26; m 51; c 3. TITANIUM DIOXIDE PIGMENTS, FINE PARTICLE TECHNOLOGY. *Educ:* Rensselaer Polytech Inst, RCHE, 49. *Prof Exp:* Develop engr, Nat Lead Co, 49-61; mgr develop, Pigments Div, The Glidden Co, 61-64, tech dir, 64-68; DIR RES & DEVELOP, GLIDDEN PIGMENTS, SCM CORP, 68- *Mem:* Int Fine Particle Res Inst (vpres, 81-); Indust Res Inst. *Res:* Titanium, cadium and silicon chemistry related to the production of pigmentary materials from these elements. *Mailing Add:* 11 Sunset Dr Severna Park MD 21146

WALKER, GLENN KENNETH, b South Weymouth, Mass, May 15, 48. CELL BIOLOGY, PROTOZOOLOGY. *Educ:* Univ Mass, Amherst, BS, 70; Northern Ariz Univ, MS, 72; Univ Md, College Park, PhD(cell biol), 75. *Prof Exp:* Teaching asst biol, Northern Ariz Univ, 70-72; teaching asst zool, cell biol & protozool, Univ Md, College Park, 72-75; NIH res fel, Cell Chem Lab, Univ Mich, Ann Arbor, 75-76; asst prof, 76-80, ASSOC PROF BIOL, EASTERN MICH UNIV, 80- *Concurrent Pos:* Adj prof, Med Sch, Univ Mich, 82- *Mem:* Am Micros Soc; Sigma Xi. *Res:* Examination of the molecular mechanisms associated with pathologies which may represent abnormalities in skeletal muscle differentiation; ultrastructural and cytochemical examination of protozoan encystment and differentiation. *Mailing Add:* Dept Biol Eastern Mich Univ Ypsilanti MI 48197

WALKER, GORDON ARTHUR HUNTER, b Kinghorn, Scotland, Jan 30, 36; m 62; c 2. ASTROPHYSICS. *Educ:* Univ Edinburgh, BSc, 58; Univ Cambridge, PhD(astrophys), 62. *Prof Exp:* Nat Res Coun fel astrophys, Dept Mines & Technol Surv, Dom Astrophys Observ, 62-63, res scientist II, 63-69; assoc prof, 69-74, dir inst astron & space sci, 72-78, PROF, UNIV BC, 74- *Mem:* Can Astron Soc; fel Royal Soc Can; Am Astron Soc. *Res:* Interstellar materials, particularly interstellar dust; early type stars, their distance, luminosity and rotational velocities; telescope auxilliary instrumentation; low light level multichannel detection systems. *Mailing Add:* Dept of Geophysics & Astron Univ of BC Vancouver BC V6T 1W5 Can

WALKER, GRAYSON HOWARD, b North Wilkesboro, NC, Dec 9, 38; m 71. STATISTICAL MECHANICS, CHEMICAL PHYSICS. *Educ:* Univ NC, BS, 61; Univ Ill, MS, 62; Ga Inst Technol, PhD(physics), 69. *Prof Exp:* From instr to prof physics, Clark Col, 67-77; prof, 77-81, UNIV CHATTANOOGA FOUND PROF PHYSICS & DIR ENVIRON STUDIES PROG, UNIV TENN, CHATTANOOGA, 81- *Mem:* Am Phys Soc; Am Meteorol Soc; Am Asn Physics Teachers. *Res:* Applications of the methods of statistical physics to problems in chemical physics, atomospheric research, planetary atmospheres; nonlinear systems. *Mailing Add:* Dept Physics & Astron Univ Tenn Chattanooga TN 37402

WALKER, GUSTAV ADOLPHUS, b Locust Grove, Ga, Dec 5, 44; m 70; c 2. BIOCHEMISTRY, MICROBIOLOGY. *Educ:* Clark Col, BS, 67; Purdue Univ, PhD(biochem), 74. *Prof Exp:* NIH fel, 74-76 & Med Sch, St Louis Univ, 76-77; RES SCIENTIST, UPJOHN CO, 77- *Mem:* Am Chem Soc; Am Soc Microbiologists; AAAS. *Res:* Protein chemistry; assay design and development of pharmaceutical products, including liquid chromatography, electrophoresis, and spectrophotometric techniques. *Mailing Add:* Upjohn Co 7171 S Portage Rd Kalamazoo MI 49001

WALKER, HARRELL LYNN, b Minden, La, May 14, 45; m 75; c 2. PLANT PATHOLOGY, BIOLOGICAL CONTROL. *Educ:* La Tech Univ, BS, 66; Univ Ky, MS, 69, PhD(plant path), 70. *Prof Exp:* Plant pathologist, Plant Indust Div, Ala Dept Agr, 74-75, asst dir, 75-76; RES PLANT PATHOLOGIST, SOUTHERN WEED SCI LAB, SCI & EDUC ADMIN-USDA, 76- *Mem:* Am Phytopath Soc; Weed Sci Soc Am; Sigma Xi. *Res:* Biological control of weeds. *Mailing Add:* Southern Weed Sci Lab PO Box 225 Stoneville MS 38776

WALKER, HOMER FRANKLIN, b Beaumont, Tex, Sept 7, 43; m 70. MATHEMATICS. *Educ:* Rice Univ, BA, 66; NY Univ, MS, 68, PhD(math), 70. *Prof Exp:* From asst prof to assoc prof math, Tex Tech Univ, 70-74; vis assoc prof, Univ Denver, 73-74; vis assoc prof, 74-75, assoc prof, 75-80, PROF MATH, UNIV HOUSTON, 80- *Concurrent Pos:* Vis assoc prof comput sci, Cornell Univ, 78; vis prof math, Univ NMex, 81-82. *Mem:* Soc Indust & Appl Math; Am Math Soc; Math Asn. *Res:* Partial differential equations; scattering theory; statistical pattern recognition; numerical analysis. *Mailing Add:* Dept Math Univ Houston Houston TX 77004

WALKER, HOMER WAYNE, b Saxonburg, Pa, May 22, 25; m 63; c 1. FOOD MICROBIOLOGY. *Educ:* Pa State Univ, BS, 51; Univ Wis, MS, 53, PhD(bact), 55. *Prof Exp:* Asst bact, Univ Wis, 51-55; from asst prof to assoc prof, 55-66, PROF FOOD TECHNOL, IOWA STATE UNIV, 66- *Mem:* Am Soc Microbiol; Inst Food Technologists; AAAS; Int Asn Milk, Food & Environ Sanit; Brit Soc Appl Bact. *Res:* Resistance of bacterial spores to heat and chemicals; bacterial toxins; antibiotics in foods and use as preservatives; microbiology of processed poultry and meats; sanitary bacteriology of food and water; mycotoxins. *Mailing Add:* Dept of Food Technol Iowa State Univ Ames IA 50011

WALKER, HOWARD DAVID, b New York, NY, May 7, 25; m 47; c 3. BIOCHEMISTRY. *Educ:* NY Univ, BA, 47, MS, 48; Univ Calif, Los Angeles, PhD(biochem), 55. *Prof Exp:* USPHS fel biochem, Am Meat Inst Found, Chicago, 55-56; instr, Northwestern Univ, 56-57; from asst prof to assoc prof chem, 57-68, PROF CHEM, CALIF POLYTECH STATE UNIV, SAN LUIS OBISPO, 68- *Concurrent Pos:* Group leader, Vet Admin Hosp, Downey, Ill, 56-57. *Mem:* Am Chem Soc. *Res:* Chemistry of pesticides and foods. *Mailing Add:* Dept of Chem Calif Polytech State Univ San Luis Obispo CA 93407

WALKER, HOWARD GEORGE, JR, b Oak Park, Ill, Aug 1, 21; m 48; c 4. AGRICULTURAL CHEMISTRY. *Educ:* Duke Univ, BS, 43, PhD(chem), 47. *Prof Exp:* Res assoc, Univ Ill, 46-47 & Univ Calif, Los Angeles, 47-48; CHEMIST, AGR RES SERV, WESTERN REGION, USDA, 48- *Mem:* Am Chem Soc; Am Soc Animal Sci. *Res:* Sugar beet, synthetic organic, physical and cereal chemistry, ruminant feeding. *Mailing Add:* Western Regional Res Ctr Agr Res Serv USDA Berkeley CA 94710

WALKER, HUGH S(ANDERS), b Mooringsport, La, July 31, 35; m 58; c 4. MECHANICAL ENGINEERING, APPLIED MECHANICS. *Educ:* La State Univ, BS, 57, MS, 60; Kans State Univ, PhD(mech eng), 65. *Prof Exp:* Instr eng mech, La State Univ, 57-60; res asst, 60-64, from instr to assoc prof, 64-76, PROF MECH ENG, KANS STATE UNIV, 76-, ASSOC DIR INST COMPUT RES IN ENG, 69- *Concurrent Pos:* NSF res grant, 66-67. *Mem:* Am Soc Mech Engrs; Am Inst Aeronaut & Astronaut; Soc Exp Stress Anal; Am Soc Eng Educ. *Res:* Analytical and experimental investigations in stress analysis, vibrations and acoustics; numerical analysis and computer techniques. *Mailing Add:* Dept of Mech Eng Kans State Univ Manhattan KS 66506

WALKER, IAN GARDNER, b Saskatoon, Sask, Apr 20, 28; m 52, 80; c 4. BIOCHEMISTRY, CELL BIOLOGY. *Educ:* Univ Sask, BA, 48; Univ Toronto, MA, 51, PhD(biochem), 54. *Prof Exp:* Defense sci serv officer, Defence Res Med Labs, Toronto, 54-60, spec lectr, Fac Pharm, Univ Toronto, 54-62; from asst prof to assoc prof, 66-74, PROF BIOCHEM, CANCER RES LAB & DEPT BIOCHEM, UNIV WESTERN ONT, 74- *Concurrent Pos:* Nat Cancer Inst Can fel, Ont Cancer Inst, 60-62; Eleanor Roosevelt Int Cancer fel, 68-69. *Mem:* Am Asn Cancer Res; Can Biochem Soc; Can Soc Cell Biol. *Res:* Biochemistry of nucleic acids, cell division, anticancer agents; biochemistry and toxicology of omega-fluorinated compounds; repair synthesis of DNA; toxicity of oxygen at high pressures; biochemistry of uremia. *Mailing Add:* Dept of Biochem Univ of Western Ont London ON N6A 5C1 Can

WALKER, IAN MUNRO, b Toronto, Ont, Aug 18, 40; US citizen; m 66. INORGANIC CHEMISTRY. *Educ:* Bowdoin Col, BA, 62; Brown Univ, PhD(chem), 67. *Prof Exp:* NIH fel chem, Univ Ill, Urbana, 67-68; asst prof, 68-73, ASSOC PROF CHEM, YORK UNIV, 73- *Mem:* Am Chem Soc. *Res:* Structure of ion-aggregates in solution; low symmetry fields in transition-metal complexes. *Mailing Add:* Dept of Chem York Univ Downsview ON L7G 3A7 Can

WALKER, J CALVIN, b Mooresville, NC, Jan 16, 35; m 58; c 3. NUCLEAR PHYSICS, SOLID STATE PHYSICS. *Educ:* Harvard Univ, AB, 56; Princeton Univ, PhD(physics), 61. *Prof Exp:* Instr physics, Princeton Univ, 61-62; fel, Atomic Energy Res Estab, Harwell, Eng, 62-63; from asst prof to assoc prof, 63-70, PROF PHYSICS, JOHNS HOPKINS UNIV, 70- *Concurrent Pos:* Alfred P Sloan Found fel, 66-68. *Mem:* Fel Am Phys Soc. *Res:* Atomic beam studies of radioactive nuclei; solid state and nuclear studies using gamma resonance techniques. *Mailing Add:* Dept of Physics Johns Hopkins Univ Baltimore MD 21218

WALKER, JACK, b Derbyshire, Eng, June 30, 29; Can citizen. PHYSICAL CHEMISTRY, CHEMICAL ENGINEERING. *Educ:* Univ Birmingham, BSc, 50, PhD(chem eng), 56. *Prof Exp:* Lectr chem eng, Univ Toronto, 54-55; chemist, Husky Oil & Ref Ltd, Can, 55-57; from chemist to sr res chemist, 57-70, res adv lube process, 70-74, mgr lube process, 74-75, mgr process res, Imp Oil Enterprises Ltd, 75-77; dir, Lubricants & Specialties Res Lab, Prod Res Div, Exxon Res & Eng Co, 77-80; mgr technol div, Logistics Dept, 80-81, ASST MGR, RES DEPT, IMP OIL LTD, 81- *Mem:* Fel Chem Inst Can; assoc Royal Inst Chemists; Can Soc Chem Eng. *Res:* Petroleum processing technology; lubricating oil processing. *Mailing Add:* Imp Oil Ltd PO Box 3022 Linden ON N7T 7M1 Can

WALKER, JAMES BENJAMIN, b Dallas, Tex, May 15, 22; m 56; c 3. BIOCHEMISTRY. *Educ:* Rice Inst, BS, 43; Univ Tex, MA, 49, PhD(biochem), 52. *Prof Exp:* Res scientist, Biochem Inst, Univ Tex, 52-55; Nat Cancer Inst fel biochem, Univ Wis, 55-56; from asst prof to assoc prof, Baylor Col Med, 56-64; PROF BIOCHEM, RICE UNIV, 64- *Concurrent Pos:* USPHS sr res fel, 57-64. *Mem:* Am Soc Biol Chemists; Am Chem Soc; Am Soc Microbiol. *Res:* Enzymes involved in biosynthesis of creatine and certain antibiotics especially gentamicin, spectinomycin and streptomycin and their regulation; physiological effects of introduction of synthetic phosphagens into brain, heart, muscle and tumor cells; feedback repression during embryonic development. *Mailing Add:* Dept of Biochem Rice Univ Houston TX 77001

WALKER, JAMES CALLAN GRAY, b Johannesburg, SAfrica, Jan 31, 39; m 59; c 2. ATMOSPHERIC CHEMISTRY & EVOLUTION. *Educ:* Yale Univ, BS, 60; Columbia Univ, PhD(geophys), 64. *Prof Exp:* Res assoc aeronomy, Inst Space Studies, New York, 64-65; res fel, Queen's Univ, Belfast, 65-66; res assoc, Goddard Space Flight Ctr, NASA, 66-67; asst prof geol, Yale Univ, 67-70, assoc prof geophys, 70-74; sr res assoc, Nat Astron & Ionosphere Ctr, 74-80; PROF ATMOSPHERIC SCI & ASSOC DIR, SPACE PHYSICS RES LAB, UNIV MICH, 80- *Concurrent Pos:* Adj asst prof, NY Univ, 64-65; mem comt solar terrestrial res, Geophys Res Bd, Nat Acad Sci, 71-76 & comt on planetary & lunar exploration, Space Sci Bd, 77-78; assoc ed, J Geophys Res, 74-76; mem Int Comn Planetary Atmospheres & Evolution, 78-; mem, Comt Planetary Biol & Chem Evolution, Space Sci Bd, 79-; mem, Atmospheric Sci Adv Comt, NSF, 80-; mem Planetary Atmospheres Mgt Oper Working Group, NASA, 81- *Mem:* AAAS; Am Geophys Union; Sigma Xi; Am Asn Univ Professors; Fedn Am Scientists. *Res:* Aeronomy; atmospheric physics; ionospheric physics; evolution of the atmosphere. *Mailing Add:* Space Physics Res Lab Univ Mich Ann Arbor MI 48109

WALKER, JAMES DON, chemical engineering, see previous edition

WALKER, JAMES ELLIOT CABOT, b Bryn Mawr, Pa, Sept 28, 26:; m 65; c 1. INTERNAL MEDICINE. *Educ:* Williams Col, BA, 49; Univ Pa, MD, 53; Harvard Univ, MS, 66. *Prof Exp:* Intern, Univ Wis Hosp, 53-54; resident med, Univ Mich Hosp, 54-55; res fel, Harvard Med Sch, 57-60; sr resident, Peter Bent Brigham Hosp, 59-60, asst to assoc dir ambulatory serv, 60-65; prof med & soc, 65-67, prof clin med & health care & chmn dept, 67-71, PROF MED & CHMN DEPT COMMUNITY MED & HEALTH CARE, SCH MED, UNIV CONN, 71- *Concurrent Pos:* Mass Heart Asn fel, 58-59; Commonwealth Fund traveling fel, 65-66; from instr to lectr, Harvard Med Sch, 60-66; dir div med care res, Dept Med, Peter Bent Brigham Hosp, 63-66; consult, Univ Wis Hosp & Univ NB Hosp, 65; chief med serv, Univ Conn Health Ctr, McCook Div & actg chief med serv, Vet Admin Hosps, Newington, Univ Conn, 69-71; pres, Can Am Health Coun, 79-; dir, Ctr Int Community Health Studies, 81- *Mem:* AAAS; Asn Am Med Cols; fel Am Col Physicians; Am Fedn Clin Res; AMA. *Res:* Pulmonary physiology; airway temperatures; delivery of health care services; responsibilities of medical education and the university to medical care and society. *Mailing Add:* Univ of Conn Sch of Med Farmington CT 06032

WALKER, JAMES FREDERICK, b Riverton, Ala, July 30, 04; m 27; c 1. PHYSIOLOGY, HISTOLOGY. *Educ:* Univ Miss, AB, 27, MS, 31; Univ Iowa, PhD(zool), 35. *Prof Exp:* Instr sci, Miss Southern Col, 26-30, actg head dept, 29-30, assoc prof, 30-31; asst zool, Univ Iowa, 31-32; assoc prof sci, Miss Southern Col, 32-33 & 35-41; instr naval aviation ground sch, Boston Univ, 41-43; instr naval preflight sch, Univ Iowa, 43-44; from assoc prof to prof anat, Univ Calif-Calif Col Med, 44-45; prof biol, 45-72, head div biol sci, 46-57, chmn dept biol, 57-68, assoc dean arts & sci, 68-70, distinguished univ prof biol, 72-80, EMER PROF BIOL, UNIV SOUTHERN MISS, 80- *Concurrent Pos:* Researcher zool, Univ Calif, Los Angeles, 62-63. *Mem:* Fel AAAS; assoc Am Physiol Soc; Sigma Xi. *Res:* Experimental histology; marine biology; histology and cytology of invertebrates; physiology of vertebrates and invertebrates; histology and histochemistry of the commercial shrimp integument and the phenomena of black spotting in shrimp integument; transverse fission of two types in hydra; correlation of excess ive bud formation and excessive tentacles in individual hydra. *Mailing Add:* Dept of Biol Univ of Southern Miss Box 8145 Hattiesburg MS 39401

WALKER, JAMES FREDERICK, JR, b Minneapolis, Minn, July 22, 37; m 59; c 3. NUCLEAR THEORY, INTERMEDIATE ENERGY REACTIONS. *Educ:* Univ Minn, BPhys, 59, MS, 61, PhD(physics), 64. *Prof Exp:* Asst res scientist, NY Univ, 64-66; mem res staff, Mass Inst Technol, 66-68; asst prof, 68-74, ASSOC PROF PHYSICS, UNIV MASS, AMHERST, 74- *Mem:* Am Phys Soc. *Res:* Pion interactions with nuclei; nuclear reaction theories. *Mailing Add:* Dept of Physics & Astron Univ of Mass Amherst MA 01003

WALKER, JAMES HARRIS, b Washington, DC, Oct 13, 44; m 69; c 2. SPECTRORADIOMETRY, RADIOMETRIC PHYSICS. *Educ:* Univ Md, BS, 70. *Prof Exp:* Physics technician optical pyrometry, 65-69, PHYSICIST RADIOMETRY, NAT BUR STANDARDS, 70- *Mem:* Optical Soc Am. *Mailing Add:* Nat Bur of Standards Bldg 221 Rm A223 Washington DC 20234

WALKER, JAMES JOSEPH, b Philadelphia, Pa, Dec 29, 33; m 57; c 3. THEORETICAL PHYSICS. *Educ:* Univ NMex, BS, 59; Univ SC, PhD(physics), 65. *Prof Exp:* Gen mgr, EG&G, Inc, NMex, 65-75; GROUP LEADER NEUTRON PHYSICS, LOS ALAMOS SCI LAB, J-16, 75- *Mem:* Sigma Xi. *Res:* Integral equations; holography; nuclear physics. *Mailing Add:* 1300 Camino Amparo NW Albuquerque NM 87101

WALKER, JAMES KING, b Greenock, Scotland, Oct 9, 35; m 60; c 2. PARTICLE PHYSICS. *Educ:* Glasgow Univ, BSc, 57, PhD(physics), 60. *Prof Exp:* Res scientist, Ecole Normale Superieure, Paris, 60-62; res assoc physics, Harvard Univ, 62-64, from asst prof to assoc prof, 64-69; SCIENTIST, NAT ACCELERATOR LAB, 69- *Concurrent Pos:* Consult, Pilot Chem Co, 67-69. *Res:* Electromagnetic and weak properties and structure of elementary particles; elementary particle physics. *Mailing Add:* Physics Dept Nat Accelerator Lab PO Box 500 Batavia IL 60510

WALKER, JAMES LESTER, agronomy, soil science, see previous edition

WALKER, JAMES MARTIN, b Jonesboro, La, Oct 21, 38; m 61; c 2. HERPETOLOGY. *Educ:* La Polytech Inst, BS, 60, MS, 61; Univ Colo, PhD(zool), 66. *Prof Exp:* Assoc prof, 65-76, PROF ZOOL, UNIV ARK, FAYETTEVILLE, 76- *Mem:* Am Soc Ichthyologists & Herpetologists; Herpetologists League. *Res:* Reptiles and amphibians of North America, with special interest in the ecology and systematics of lizards of the genus Cnemidophorus of the family Teiidae. *Mailing Add:* Dept of Zool Univ of Ark Fayetteville AR 72701

WALKER, JAMES RICHARD, b Boise, Idaho, Feb 26, 33; m 61; c 3. PHYSIOLOGY. *Educ:* Ariz State Univ, BS, 56; Univ Miss, PhD(physiol), 65. *Prof Exp:* Instr, 65-66, ASST PROF PHYSIOL, UNIV TEX MED BR, GALVESTON, 66-, ASST DIR INTEGRATED FUNCTIONAL LAB, 74- *Concurrent Pos:* Mem staff, Commun Sci Lab, Univ Fla, 72-73. *Mem:* Acoust Soc Am; Am Inst Physics. *Res:* Auditory neurophysiology, biological control systems. *Mailing Add:* Dept of Physiol Univ of Tex Med Br Galveston TX 77550

WALKER, JAMES ROY, b Chestnut, La, Nov 8, 37; m 59; c 2. MICROBIOLOGY. *Educ:* Northwestern State Col, La, BS, 60; Univ Tex, PhD(microbiol), 63. *Prof Exp:* Nat Cancer Inst fel biochem sci, Princeton Univ, 65-67; asst prof microbiol, 67-71, assoc prof, 71-78, PROF MICROBIOL, UNIV TEX, AUSTIN, 78-, CHMN DEPT, 81- *Concurrent Pos:* Res assoc dept chem, Harvard Univ, 72-73. *Mem:* Genetics Soc Am; Am Soc Microbiol. *Res:* Microbial genetics; regulation of cell division. *Mailing Add:* Dept of Microbiol Univ of Tex Austin TX 78712

WALKER, JAMES WILLARD, b Taylor, Tex, Mar 23, 43; m 73. EVOLUTIONARY BIOLOGY. *Educ:* Univ Tex, Austin, BA, 64; Harvard Univ, PhD(biol), 70. *Prof Exp:* Asst prof, 69-75, ASSOC PROF BOT, UNIV MASS, AMHERST, 75- *Honors & Awards:* George R Cooley Award, Am Soc Plant Taxon, 72. *Mem:* AAAS; Bot Soc Am; Am Soc Plant Taxon; Am Inst Biol Sci; Linnean Soc London. *Res:* Angiosperm systematics; morphology, phylogeny and evolution of primitive angiosperms; pollen morphology of ranalean dicots. *Mailing Add:* Dept of Bot Univ of Mass Amherst MA 01003

WALKER, JAMES WILSON, b NC, July 17, 22; m 45; c 2. MATHEMATICAL STATISTICS. *Educ:* Univ NC, PhD(math statist), 57. *Prof Exp:* Intel specialist, US Dept Air Force, 50-55; asst statist, Univ NC, 55-56; from asst prof to assoc prof math, 56-64, res assoc eng exp sta, 58-65, PROF MATH, GA INST TECHNOL, 64- *Concurrent Pos:* Consult, WVa Pulp & Paper Co, 66-68 & Union Camp, Inc, 74-75. *Mem:* Am Statist Asn; Math Asn Am. *Res:* Statistical inference from grouped data; optimal grouping of statistical data; inefficiency of certain estimates based on grouped data. *Mailing Add:* Dept Math Ga Inst Technol Atlanta GA 30332

WALKER, JEAN TWEEDY, b Dublin, Ireland, Mar 3, 44; m 72. MICROBIAL GENETICS, ELECTRON MICROSCOPY. *Educ:* Trinity Col, Ireland, BA, 65; Univ Reading, Eng, PhD(microbiol), 71. *Prof Exp:* Res demonstr, Univ Reading, 65-67; from asst prof to assoc prof, Trinity Col, 67-72; asst res scientist, 72-75, ASSOC RES SCIENTIST, UNIV IOWA, 75- *Mem:* Soc Gen Microbiol; Am Soc Microbiol; Royal Microscopical Soc; Genetics Soc of Am. *Res:* Bacterial and phage genetics and molecular biology; morphogenesis of phage; plasmids. *Mailing Add:* Dept of Microbiol Univ of Iowa Iowa City IA 52242

WALKER, JEARL DALTON, b Pensacola, Fla, Jan 20, 45; div; c 3. OPTICS. *Educ:* Mass Inst Technol, BS, 67; Univ Md, PhD(physics), 73. *Prof Exp:* Asst prof, 73-77, assoc prof, 77-81, PROF PHYSICS, CLEVELAND STATE UNIV, 81- *Concurrent Pos:* Assoc ed, Am J Physics, 77-80; mem staff, Sci Am, 77- *Honors & Awards:* Glover Award, Dickinson Col, 81. *Mem:* Am Asn Physics Teachers. *Res:* Scattering of light from particles. *Mailing Add:* Dept of Physics Cleveland State Univ Cleveland OH 44115

WALKER, JERRY, b Michigantown, Ind, Mar 6, 37; m 57; c 2. VETERINARY MEDICINE, MICROBIOLOGY. *Educ:* Mich State Univ, BS, 59, DVM, 61; Univ Mich, MS, 65. *Prof Exp:* Vet practitioner, Bardens Small Animal Hosp, 61-62; vet process develop div, Ft Detrick, 62-63, prin investr, 65-68, chief dept vet med, 9th Med Lab, Vietnam, 68-69, asst chief virol div, US Army Med Res Inst Infectious Dis, 69-70, chief dept rickettsial dis, US Army Med Res Univ, Inst Med Res, Kuala Lumpur, Malaysia, 70-72, chief div aerobiol, US Army Med Res Inst Infectious Dis, Vet Corps, US Army, 72-76; BIOL SAFETY OFFICER, PLUM ISLAND ANIMAL DIS CTR, 76- *Honors & Awards:* Outstanding Res Award, Sci Res Soc Am, 66. *Mem:* Infectious Dis Soc Am; Am Vet Med Asn; Am Soc Microbiol; Am Acad Microbiol. *Res:* Pathogenesis and therapy of infectious diseases, both bacterial and viral; biological safety. *Mailing Add:* Plum Island Animal Dis Ctr Greenport NY 11944

WALKER, JERRY ARNOLD, b Olney, Ill, Mar 4, 48. SYNTHETIC ORGANIC CHEMISTRY. *Educ:* Univ Ill, BS, 69; Mass Inst Technol, PhD(org chem), 73. *Prof Exp:* Fel org chem, Univ Calif, Los Angeles, 73-74 & Calif Inst Technol, 74-75; RES CHEMIST, UPJOHN CO, 75- *Mem:* Am Chem Soc; Royal Soc Chem. *Res:* Research and development of methods for the synthesis of biologically active compounds. *Mailing Add:* Upjohn Co Portage Rd Kalamazoo MI 49001

WALKER, JERRY TYLER, b Cincinnati, Ohio, Sept 7, 30; m 53; c 2. PLANT PATHOLOGY. *Educ:* Univ Miami, Ohio, BA, 52; Ohio State Univ, MSc, 57, PhD, 60. *Prof Exp:* Asst, Ohio State Univ, 55-59, asst agr exp sta, 59-61; plant pathologist, Brooklyn Bot Garden, 61-69; assoc prof, 69-80, PROF PLANT PATH & HEAD DEPT, AGR EXP STA, GA STA, UNIV GA, 80- *Concurrent Pos:* NSF grant, 63-66; actg chmn res, Kitchawan Lab, NY, 67-69. *Mem:* Am Phytopath Soc; Soc Nematol. *Res:* Phytonematology, including control; diseases of ornamentals; fungicides; air pollution effects on plants. *Mailing Add:* Dept of Plant Path Agr Exp Sta Univ Ga Ga Sta Experiment GA 30212

WALKER, JIMMY NEWTON, b Eldorado, Okla, Mar 6, 24; m 49; c 2. CHEMICAL ENGINEERING, CHEMISTRY. *Educ:* Okla State Univ, BS, 49; Univ Chicago, MBA, 63. *Prof Exp:* Engr, US Gypsum Co, 49-50; prod foreman paint plant, Tex, 50-51; res chemist, 57-58, sect mgr joint compounds, 58-61, div mgr, Formulated Prod, 61-63 & Fiber & Formulated Prod, 63-66, dir res & develop, 66-72, VPRES RES & DEVELOP, US GYPSUM CO, LIBERTYVILLE, 72- *Concurrent Pos:* Indust Res Inst seminar comt, 69- *Mem:* Am Chem Soc; Indust Res Inst. *Res:* Development of flat latex paints; dissociation of gypsum; industrial resin tooling products; advanced joint compounds and systems; research and project evaluation. *Mailing Add:* US Gypsum Co 700 N Hwy 45 Libertyville IL 60048

WALKER, JOAN MARION, b New Plymouth, NZ, May 21, 37; NZ & Can citizen. MORPHOMETRIC ARTICULATIONS. *Educ:* Univ Man, BPT, 71, MA, 73; McMaster Univ, PhD(med sci), 77. *Prof Exp:* Lectr phys ther, Univ Toronto, 63-66, Univ Witwatersrand, 66-69, Univ Man, 70-71; lectr anat, McMaster Univ, 73-76; asst prof, 78-81, ASSOC PROF GROWTH & DEVELOP ARTHROLOGY, DEPT PHYS THER, UNIV SOUTHERN CALIF, 81- *Mem:* Am Phys Ther Asn; Can Physiol Ther Asn; Can Asn Phys Arthropology; AAAS. *Res:* Realtionships between growth of the human fetal and infant hip joint and congenital hip disease; aging mechanisms in synovial joints including range of motion studies. *Mailing Add:* Dept Phys Ther Univ Southern Calif 12933 Erickson Ave Downey CA 90242

WALKER, JOANNE GILLESPIE, physiology, see previous edition

WALKER, JOE AARON, b San Augustine, Tex, Sept 21, 21; m 46; c 3. MEDICINE, ANESTHESIOLOGY. *Educ:* Stephen F Austin State Col, BS, 43; Univ Tex, MD, 46. *Prof Exp:* From instr to assoc prof, 59-72, PROF ANESTHESIOL, UNIV TEX MED BR, GALVESTON, 72- *Mem:* Am Soc Anesthesiol. *Res:* Cardiovascular effects of anesthetic drugs and methods of treating different types of peripheral myoneural blocks. *Mailing Add:* Dept of Anesthesiol Univ of Tex Med Br Galveston TX 77550

WALKER, JOE M, b Baxter Springs, Kans, Mar 8, 30; m 53; c 2. ANALYTICAL CHEMISTRY. *Educ:* Kans State Col Pittsburg, BS, 51, MS, 53; Kans State Univ, PhD(chem), 58. *Prof Exp:* Instr sci, Kans State Col Pittsburg, 50-53; asst prof chem, Univ Ottawa, 54-56; from asst prof to assoc prof, 57-61, PROF CHEM, PITTSBURG STATE UNIV, 61- *Mem:* Am Chem Soc. *Res:* Instrumental methods; high frequency methods in analytical chemistry; trace carbon analysis; gas chromatography; analytical chemistry of boron. *Mailing Add:* Dept of Chem Pittsburg State Univ Pittsburg KS 66762

WALKER, JOHN A, mechanical engineering, see previous edition

WALKER, JOHN J, b Alma, Nebr, July 4, 35; m 60. ORGANIC CHEMISTRY. *Educ:* Univ Nebr, Lincoln, BS, 58; Atlanta Univ, MS, 68; Ga Inst Technol, PhD(org chem), 73. *Prof Exp:* Instr, Ga Inst Technol, 70-73; tech dir, Dettelbach Chem Corp, 73-81; DIR RES & DEVELOP, I SCHNEID, 81- *Concurrent Pos:* Adj prof, DeKalb Community Col, 73- *Mem:* Am Chem Soc; fel Am Inst Chemists; AAAS. *Res:* Synthesis of physiologically active barbiturates. *Mailing Add:* 2952 Greenrock Trail Doraville GA 30340

WALKER, JOHN LAWRENCE, JR, b Whitewater, Wis, Dec 12, 31; m 56; c 2. PHYSIOLOGY. *Educ:* Univ Wis, BS, 56; Duke Univ, MA, 58; Univ Minn, Minneapolis, PhD(physiol), 63. *Prof Exp:* Instr physiol, Univ Minn, Minneapolis, 62-64, asst prof, 64-65; asst prof, 66-71, assoc prof, 75-76, PROF PHYSIOL, UNIV UTAH, 76- *Concurrent Pos:* USPHS fel, 64-66, res grant, 66. *Res:* Mechanism of movement of ions and molecules through membranes, especially permeation of ions and electrical properties of membranes; ion selective microelectrodes. *Mailing Add:* Dept of Physiol Univ of Utah Salt Lake City UT 84112

WALKER, JOHN MARTIN, b Norfolk, Va, July 6, 35; m 55; c 2. WATER POLLUTION, SOIL SCIENCE. *Educ:* Rutgers Univ, BS, 57, MS, 59, PhD(agron), 61. *Prof Exp:* Asst soil fertility and plant nutrit, Purdue Univ, 57-60; NATO fel soil chem, Rothamsted Exp Sta, Eng, 61-62; res soil scientist soils lab plant indust sta, Soil & Water Conserv Res Div, Agr Res Serv, USDA, 63-72, soil scientist biol waste mgt lab, 72-74, actg chief, 75; regional sci adv wastewater, sludge & soil, Off Res & Develop, 75-77, PHYS SCIENTIST, OFF WATER PROGS OPERS, US ENVIRON PROTECTION AGENCY, 77- *Concurrent Pos:* Adj prof dept crop & soil sci, Mich State Univ, 75-77. *Mem:* Fel AAAS; Am Soc Agron; Soil Sci Soc Am; Int Soc Soil Sci; Water Pollution Control Fedn. *Res:* Utilization of sewage sludge and wastewater treatment and use on land; soil temperature effects on movement and uptake of water and ions; plant response to controlled environments. *Mailing Add:* Off of Water Progs Opers WH-547 Washington DC 20460

WALKER, JOHN NEAL, b Erie, Pa, Feb 19, 30; m 54; c 2. AGRICULTURAL & ENVIRONMENTAL ENGINEERING. *Educ:* Pa State Univ, BS, 51, MS, 58; Purdue Univ, PhD(agr eng), 61. *Prof Exp:* Exten agr engr, Pa State Univ, 54-58; asst agr eng, Purdue Univ, 58-60; from asst prof to assoc prof, 60-66, dept chmn agr eng, 74-81, PROF AGR ENG, UNIV KY, 66-, ACTG DIR, INST MINING & MINERALS RES, 81- *Concurrent Pos:* Vis scientist, Nat Inst Agr Eng, England, 70. *Mem:* Fel Am Soc Agr Eng; Am Soc Eng Educ. *Res:* Environmental and structural problems associated with plant and animal structures, especially greenhouse problems. *Mailing Add:* Agr Eng Bldg Univ of Ky Lexington KY 40506

WALKER, JOHN ROBERT, b Newbern, Tenn, Nov 27, 31; m 55; c 1. ENTOMOLOGY, RESEARCH ADMINISTRATION. *Educ:* La State Univ, BS, 55, MS, 59; Iowa State Univ, PhD(entom), 62. *Prof Exp:* Asst prof, 62-65, asst to vpres res, 66-68, asst to vpres instr & res, 66-80, ASSOC PROF ENTOM, LA STATE UNIV, BATON ROUGE, 65-, ASST VPRES ACAD AFFAIRS, UNIV SYST, 80- *Mem:* AAAS; Entom Soc Am; Nat Conf Advan Res; Nat Coun Univ Res Adminr; Sigma Xi. *Res:* Effects of ionizing radiations on reproductive system of insects. *Mailing Add:* Off of VPres Acad Affairs La State Univ Syst Baton Rouge LA 70893

WALKER, JOHN SCOTT, b Washington, DC, May 25, 44; m 70. FLUID MECHANICS, NUCLEAR ENGINEERING. *Educ:* Webb Inst Naval Archit, BS, 66; Cornell Univ, PhD(fluid mech), 70. *Prof Exp:* Res assoc, Cornell Univ, 70-71; from asst prof to assoc prof, 71-78, assoc dean, Col Eng, 80-81, PROF, DEPT THEORET & APPL MECH, UNIV ILL, 78- *Concurrent Pos:* NSF grants, 73-74, 75-78, 76-77 & 79-81; consult, Oak Ridge Nat Lab, 78-80 & IBM Res Lab & Westinghouse Res & Develop Ctr, 81- *Mem:* Am Acad Mech; Am Soc Mech Engrs; Am Nuclear Soc; Am Soc Eng Educ; Sigma Xi. *Res:* Liquid-metal magnetohydrodynamic flows with strong magnetic fields; flows in fusion reactor cooling blankets; rotating flows; waterhammer waves; ferrohydrodynamic flows. *Mailing Add:* Dept Theoret & Appl Mech 216 Talbot Lab 104 S Wright St Urbana IL 61801

WALKER, JOSEPH, b Rockford, Ill, Dec 28, 22; m 44; c 4. ANALYTICAL CHEMISTRY, ORGANIC CHEMISTRY. *Educ:* Beloit Col, BS, 43; Univ Wis, MS, 48, PhD(chem), 50. *Prof Exp:* Sr res chemist res ctr, Pure Oil Co, Ill, 50-51, proj technologist, 51-56, sect supvr phys chem, 56-58, dir anal res & serv div, 58-64, res coordr, 64-65, dir res, 65-66, assoc dir res, 66-78, VPRES CHEM RES DEPT, UNION OIL CO CALIF, BREA, 78- *Mem:* Am Chem Soc. *Res:* Petroleum technology; analysis of petroleum products; petrochemicals research; fuels development; petroleum research administration. *Mailing Add:* 3010 Anacapa Place Fullerton CA 92635

WALKER, KEITH GERALD, b Carthage, Mo, Aug 22, 41; m 63; c 2. ATOMIC PHYSICS, MOLECULAR PHYSICS. *Educ:* Bethany Nazarene Col, BS, 63; Ohio State Univ, MS, 66; Univ Okla, PhD(physics), 71. *Prof Exp:* Technician, State of Ohio, summer 64; instr physics, 65-67, from asst prof to assoc prof, 67-72, PROF PHYSICS, BETHANY NAZARENE COL, 72- *Mem:* Am Asn Physics Teachers; Optical Soc Am. *Res:* Electron-atom impact and resulting cross-sections. *Mailing Add:* Dept of Physics Bethany Nazarene Col Box 339 Bethany OK 73008

WALKER, KELSEY, JR, b Columbus, Tex, Nov 16, 25; m 45; c 5. THEORETICAL GAS DYNAMICS, APPLIED MATHEMATICS. *Educ:* Rensselaer Polytech Inst, BAE, 50; Mass Inst Technol, SM, 52. *Prof Exp:* Res scientist, Douglas Aircraft Co, 52-54; sr scientist, Lockheed Missile Systs Div, 54-55 & Aeronutronic Systs, Inc, 56-57; sect head syst anal, Space Tech Labs, 57-61; dept mgr systs eng, Aerospace Corp, 61-66; mgr sr staff, Los Angeles Opers, 66-72, asst prog mgr site defense, Ballistic Missile Defense Bus Area, 72-75, asst mgr adv defense systs, 75, PROG MGR, BALLISTIC MISSILE DEFENSE BUS AREA, TRW SYSTS, REDONDO BEACH, 75- *Mem:* Am Inst Aeronaut & Astronaut; Sigma Xi. *Res:* Transonic gas dynamics; supersonic wing body interference; hypersonic gas dynamics; reentry body ablation theory; flight mechanics of reentry vehicles and ballistic missiles; systems analysis and design of ballistic missiles and space craft. *Mailing Add:* TRW Systs One Space Park Mail Sta R2/1062 Redondo Beach CA 90278

WALKER, KENNETH MERRIAM, b Blaine, Ore, Mar 30, 21; m 41; c 4. BIOLOGY. *Educ:* Ore State Col, BS, 42, MS, 49, PhD(zool), 55. *Prof Exp:* From instr to asst prof biol, Univ Puget Sound, 51-57; from asst prof to assoc prof, 57-69, PROF BIOL, WESTERN ORE STATE COL, 69- *Mem:* Am Soc Mammalogists. *Res:* Vertebrate taxonomy and ecology. *Mailing Add:* Dept of Biol Western Ore State Col Monmouth OR 97361

WALKER, KENNETH RUSSELL, b Spartanburg, SC, June 21, 37; div; c 3. STRATIGRAPHY, PALEOECOLOGY. *Educ:* Univ NC, Chapel Hill, BS, 59, MS, 64; Yale Univ, MPh, 67, PhD(paleoecol), 69. *Prof Exp:* Asst prof geol, 68-72, assoc prof, 72-75, PROF GEOL, UNIV TENN, KNOXVILLE, 75-, HEAD DEPT, 77- *Mem:* Paleont Soc; Am Asn Petrol Geol; Soc Econ Paleont & Mineral; Geol Soc Am. *Res:* Ancient marine organic communities; lower paleozoic paleoenvironments; trophic relationships in organic communities; Cambro-Ordovician problems; Holocene and ancient carbonate environments; invertebrate paleontology; carbonate geochemistry. *Mailing Add:* Dept of Geol Sci Univ of Tenn Knoxville TN 37916

WALKER, LAURENCE COLTON, b Washington, DC, Sept 8, 24; m 48; c 4. SILVICULTURE, SOILS. *Educ:* Pa State Univ, BS, 48; Yale Univ, MF, 49; State Univ NY, PhD(silvicult, soils), 53. *Prof Exp:* Forester, US Forest Serv, 58-51; asst, State Univ NY Col Forestry, Syracuse, 51-53; res forester, US Forest Serv, 53-54; prof silvicult res, Univ Ga, 54-63; prof forestry & dean sch, 63-76, HUNT PROF FORESTRY, STEPHEN F AUSTIN STATE UNIV, 76- *Concurrent Pos:* Consult, Nat Plant Food Inst, forest industry, educational insts. *Mem:* Fel AAAS; fel Soc Am Foresters; Am Sci Affil. *Res:* Silvicides for hardwood control; soil-water relationships in forests; forest fertilization; natural resource policy; technology transfer; transferring technical information for ready use by professional foresters and layman. *Mailing Add:* Sch of Forestry Stephen F Austin State Univ Nacogdoches TX 75962

WALKER, LEON BRYAN, JR, b Gulfport, Miss, June 9, 25; m 47; c 1. ANATOMY. *Educ:* Univ Houston, BS, 50, MS, 52; Duke Univ, PhD(anat), 55. *Prof Exp:* Asst biol, Univ Houston, 50-52; asst anat, Duke Univ, 53-55; instr, Sch Med, Temple Univ, 55-59; from asst prof to assoc prof, 59-71, PROF ANAT, SCH MED, TULANE UNIV, 71- *Mem:* Am Asn Anatomists. *Res:* Muscle innervation; morphology of neuromuscular spindles; stress-strain studies in tendon. *Mailing Add:* Dept of Anat Tulane Univ New Orleans LA 70118

WALKER, LEROY HAROLD, b Union, Utah, Sept 24, 33; m 63; c 3. MATHEMATICS, COMPUTER SCIENCE. *Educ:* Univ Utah, BS, 55; Mass Inst Technol, SM, 57, EE, 58; Univ Calif, Los Angeles, PhD(math), 68. *Prof Exp:* Res assoc opers res ctr, Mass Inst Technol, 58-60; asst prof math, Brigham Young Univ, 68-73; sr programmer & analyst, Univ Utah, 73-81; SYST ANALYST, INTERMOUNTAIN CONSUMER POWER ASN, 81- *Concurrent Pos:* Fac res fel, Brigham Young Univ, 69-70. *Mem:* Inst Math Statist; Math Asn Am; Am Math Soc; Asn Comput Mach. *Res:* Stopping rules for stochastic processes. *Mailing Add:* Intermountain Consumer Power Asn 8722 S 300 W Sandy UT 84070

WALKER, M LUCIUS, JR, b Washington, DC, Dec 16, 36; m 60; c 2. MECHANICAL ENGINEERING. *Educ:* Howard Univ, BSME, 57; Carnegie Inst Technol, MSME, 58, PhD(mech eng), 66. *Prof Exp:* Teaching asst, Carnegie Inst Technol, 57-58; instr eng, Howard Univ, 58-59 & Carnegie Inst Technol, 61-63; from asst prof to assoc prof eng, 63-68, asst dean, 65-66, actg head dept, 66-67, head, 67-68, assoc dean, Sch Eng, 73-74, actg dean, 77-78, PROF MECH ENG, HOWARD UNIV, 70-, DEAN, SCH ENG, 78- *Concurrent Pos:* Vis sr staff mem, Int Res & Technol Corp, Washington, DC, 69-70; Ford teaching fel, Carnegie Inst Technol; mem eng manpower comn, Accrediting Bd Eng & Technol & Biotechnol Resources Rev Comt, Nat Inst Health, 72-; mem bd trustees, Carnegie-Mellon Univ. *Mem:* Sigma Xi; NY Acad Sci; Am Soc Mech Engrs; Am Soc Eng Educ. *Res:* New transportation systems planning and economics; cardiovascular mechanics. *Mailing Add:* Sch of Eng Howard Univ Washington DC 20059

WALKER, MARSHALL JOHN, b Bath, NY, Jan 23, 12; m 37; c 2. OPTICS. *Educ:* Cornell Univ, BChem, 33, AM, 36; Pa State Univ, PhD(physics), 50. *Prof Exp:* Asst physicist photo prods dept, E I du Pont de Nemours & Co, 36-39, asst chemist, 39-42; assoc physicst, Nat Bur Standards, 42-44; assoc physicist, Allegany Ballistics Lab, 44-45; asst, Pa State Univ, 46-49; from asst prof to assoc prof physics, 49-63, prof, 63-77, EMER PROF PHYSICS, UNIV CONN, 77- *Mem:* Am Phys Soc; Optical Soc Am; Am Asn Physics Teachers. *Res:* Philosophy of science. *Mailing Add:* Star Route Chaplin CT 06235

WALKER, MATTHEW, surgery, see previous edition

WALKER, MERLE F, b Pasadena, Calif, Mar 3, 26; m 59; c 1. ASTRONOMY. *Educ:* Univ Calif, AB, 49, PhD(astron), 52. *Prof Exp:* Asst astron, Univ Calif, 49-52, jr res astronr, 55-56; Carnegie fel, Mt Wilson & Palomar Observ, 52-54; res assoc, Yerkes Observ, Univ Chicago, 54-55; instr, Warner & Swasey Observ, Case Inst Technol, 56-57; from asst astronr to assoc astronr, 57-71, PROF ASTRON & ASTRONOMER, LICK OBSERV, UNIV CALIF, SANTA CRUZ, 71- *Concurrent Pos:* Sr resident astronr, Cerro Tololo Interam Observ, 68-69. *Mem:* Int Astron Union; Am Astron Soc. *Res:* Photoelectric photometry of short period variable stars; photoelectric magnitudes and colors of stars; stellar spectra and radial velocities; electronic image intensification; astronomical seeing and observatory sites. *Mailing Add:* Lick Observ Univ of Calif Santa Cruz CA 95060

WALKER, MICHAEL BARRY, b Regina, Sask. PHYSICS. *Educ:* McGill Univ, BEng, 61; Oxford Univ, PhD, 65. *Prof Exp:* Fel, 66-68, assoc prof, 68-77, PROF PHYSICS, UNIV TORONTO, 77- *Honors & Awards:* Herzberg Medal, 77. *Mem:* Can Asn Physicists. *Res:* Theoretical solid state physics. *Mailing Add:* Dept Physics Univ Toronto Toronto ON M5S 1A7 Can

WALKER, MICHAEL DIRCK, b New York, NY, Jan 24, 31; m 53; c 3. NEUROSURGERY. *Educ:* Yale Univ, BA, 56; Boston Univ, MD, 60. *Prof Exp:* Intern surg, Mass Mem Hosps, 60-61; resident neurosurg, Boston City Hosp & Lahey Clin, 61-65; sr investr pharmacol, Nat Cancer Inst, 65-67; chief sect neurosurg, Baltimore Cancer Res Ctr, 67-80, chief ctr, 71-80; DIR STROKE & TRAUMA PROG, NAT INST NEUROL & COMMUN DISORDERS & STROKE, NIH, 80- *Concurrent Pos:* Chmn, Brain Tumor Study Group, 67; assoc dir, Div Cancer Treatment, Nat Cancer Inst, 73-; assoc prof neurosurg, Sch Med, Univ Md, 73-; asst prof neurol surg, Sch Med, Johns Hopkins Univ, 74- *Mem:* Am Asn Cancer Res; Am Acad Neruol; Am Soc Clin Oncol; Cong Neurol Surg; NY Acad Sci. *Res:* Neurological surgery; analysis and treatment of human brain tumors with cytotoxic agents able to penetrate the blood-brain barrier. *Mailing Add:* Fed Bldg Rm 8A08 7550 Wis Ave Bethesda MD 20205

WALKER, MICHAEL SIDNEY, b Hull, Eng, Sept 13, 40; m 66; c 2. PHOTOPHYSICS. *Educ:* Univ Sheffield, BS, 62, PhD(chem), 65. *Prof Exp:* AEC fel dept chem, Univ Minn, Minneapolis, 65-67; scientist res labs, 67-71, MGR LABS, XEROX CORP, 71- *Res:* Photophysics of organic molecules including semiconductors and photoconductors; materials characterization. *Mailing Add:* 256 Council Rock Ave Rochester NY 14610

WALKER, MICHAEL STEPHEN, b Detroit, Mich, Dec 16, 39; m 70; c 2. ENGINEERING PHYSICS, EXPERIMENTAL SOLID STATE PHYSICS. *Educ:* Mass Inst Technol, BS, 61; Carnegie Inst Technol, MS, 64; Carnegie Mellon Univ, PhD(physics), 71. *Prof Exp:* Sr engr, Westinghouse Elec Corp, 61-75; MGR MAT & DEVICE DEVELOP, INTERMAGNETICS GEN CORP, 76- *Mem:* Am Phys Soc; Inst Elec & Electronics Engrs; Sigma Xi. *Res:* Research and development on superconducting materials and devices, including the development of niobium-tin multifilament conductors and superconducting magnets for machinery, energy storage and for plasma confinement for fusion devices. *Mailing Add:* Intermagnetics Gen Corp PO Box 566 Guilderland NY 12084

WALKER, NATHANIEL, b Cincinnati, Ohio, Apr 9, 09; m 34; c 2. FOREST MANAGEMENT, FOREST ECONOMICS. *Educ:* Colo Col, BS, 33; Pa State Univ, MS, 55; NC State Univ, PhD, 70. *Prof Exp:* Dist forest ranger, US Forest Serv, 33-44; asst exten forester, Exten Serv, 44-47, from assoc prof to prof forestry, 47-74, EMER PROF FORESTRY, OKLA STATE UNIV, 74- *Mem:* Fel Soc Am Foresters. *Res:* Frequency analyses and measurements; development and yield of cottonwood and red cedar; stand structures and valuation in several species of forest trees; forest soil-site evaluations. *Mailing Add:* 1906 W Admiral Stillwater OK 74074

WALKER, NEIL ALLAN, b Flint, Mich, May 4, 24; m 53; c 2. ACAROLOGY. *Educ:* Southern Methodist Univ, BS, 47; Univ Mich, MA, 48; Univ Calif, Berkeley, PhD(entom), 64. *Prof Exp:* Fisheries res technician inst fisheries res, Mich Dept Conserv, 49-50; from asst prof to assoc prof zool, 58-67, chmn dept biol sci & agr, 70-73, prof biol, 67-80, PROF BIOL EXTENDED MED LEARE, FT HAYS STATE UNIV, 80- *Concurrent Pos:* Consult, Dept Sci & Indust Res, NZ, 65 & 72. *Mem:* Entom Soc Am; Acarol Soc Am. *Res:* Taxonomy; biogeography; ecology of ptyctimous Oribatei; biology of Opiliones. *Mailing Add:* Dept of Biol Sci Ft Hays State Univ Hays KS 67601

WALKER, PETER ROY, b Batley, Eng, Nov 24, 45; m 81; c 1. BIOCHEMISTRY, MOLECULAR BIOLOGY. *Educ:* Univ Sheffield, BSc Hons, 64, PhD(biochem), 70. *Prof Exp:* Damon Runyon Mem Fund fel oncol, McArdle Lab, Univ Wis, 70-73; hon lectr biochem, Univ Sheffield, 73-75; RES OFFICER BIOL, NAT RES COUN, 75- *Concurrent Pos:* Med Res Coun grant, Brit Empire Cancer Campaign grant & Wellcome Found grant, Univ Sheffield, 73-75. *Res:* Factors involved in the regulation of cell proliferation in vivo with particular reference to the changes in gene expression during prereplicative development. *Mailing Add:* Animal & Cell Physiol Group Bldg M54 Montreal Rd Ottawa ON K1A 0R6 Can

WALKER, PHILIP CALEB, b Pittsburgh, Pa, Nov 26, 11; m 40; c 4. BIOLOGY, PALYNOLOGY. *Educ:* Univ Pittsburgh, BS, 34, PhD, 58. *Prof Exp:* Asst bot & biol, Univ Pittsburgh, 34-40; park naturalist, Bur Parks, Pittsburgh, Pa, 40-43; asst prof biol, WVa Inst Technol, 46-51; PROF BIOL, STATE UNIV NY COL PLATTSBURGH, 51- *Concurrent Pos:* Instr bot, Geneva Col, 37-38; panelist instrnl sci equip prog, NSF. *Mem:* AAAS. *Res:* Forest ecology and sequence; palynology and forest sequence studies in pleistocene and post-Wisconsin glacial bogs in New York, Pennsylvania and New Jersey; forest sequence of Hartstown bog area in Pennsylvania; palynology of Adirondack bogs and anemophilous and zoophilous pollen transport in the atmosphere. *Mailing Add:* Dept of Biol State Univ of NY Col Plattsburgh NY 12901

WALKER, PHILIP L(EROY), JR, b Baltimore, Md, Jan 10, 24; m 49; c 3. MATERIALS SCIENCE. *Educ:* Johns Hopkins Univ, BS, 47, MS, 48; Pa State Univ, PhD(fuel technol), 52. *Prof Exp:* Control chemist, Lever Bros Co, 48-49; from asst prof to assoc prof, 52-55, head dept fuel technol, 54-59, chmn div mineral technol, 59-65, head dept mat sci, 67-78, prof fuel technol, 55-74, EVAN PUGH PROF MAT SCI, PA STATE UNIV, UNIVERSITY PARK, 74- *Concurrent Pos:* Chmn, Am Carbon Comt, 62-70; ed, Chem Physics of Carbon, 62-81; assoc ed, Carbon, 64-81. *Honors & Awards:* Henry H Storch Award, Am Chem Soc, 69; George Skakel Mem Award, 71. *Mem:* Am Chem Soc; Am Phys Soc; Am Ceramic Soc; Am Carbon Soc. *Res:* Catalysis; adsorption; kinetics; crystal growth; solid state chemistry; heterogeneous reactions; pollution control; carbon and coal science. *Mailing Add:* Dept of Mat Sci & Eng Pa State Univ University Park PA 16802

WALKER, RAYMOND JOHN, b Los Angeles, Calif, Oct 26, 42. SPACE PHYSICS. *Educ:* San Diego State Univ, BA, 64; Univ Calif, Los Angeles, MS, 69, PhD(planetary & space physics), 73. *Prof Exp:* Res assoc physics, Univ Minn, Minneapolis, 73-77; asst res geophysics, 77-80, ASSOC RES GEOPHYSICS, UNIV CALIF, LOS ANGELES, 80- *Mem:* Am Geophys Union; AAAS. *Res:* Magnetospheric physics; the magnetospheres of the earth and Jupiter; the dynamics of charged particles in the magnetosphere; numerical studies of magnetospheric convection; quantitative modeling of magnetospheric magnetic fields; organization and analysis of multi-parameter satellite data sets. *Mailing Add:* Inst of Geophysics Univ of Calif Los Angeles CA 90024

WALKER, RICHARD ALDEN, b Chicago, Ill, Jan 15, 21; m 54; c 4. UNDERWATER ACOUSTICS, OCEAN ENGINEERING. *Educ:* Iowa State Col, PhD(physics), 52. *Prof Exp:* Res assoc, Iowa State Col, 50-52; MEM TECH STAFF, BELL TEL LABS, INC, 52- *Mem:* AAAS. *Res:* Underwater acoustics; seismology; communications engineering; ultrasonics; re-entry physics. *Mailing Add:* Bell Tel Labs Whippany NJ 07981

WALKER, RICHARD BATTSON, b Tennessee, Ill, Oct 24, 16; m 40; c 3. BOTANY. *Educ:* Univ Ill, BS, 38; Univ Calif, PhD(bot), 48. *Prof Exp:* From instr to assoc prof, 48-60, chmn dept, 62-71, dir biol educ, 75-82, PROF BOT, UNIV WASH, 60- *Mem:* Fel AAAS; Ecol Soc Am; Bot Soc Am; Am Soc Plant Physiologists. *Res:* Mineral nutrition and water relations of conifers; comparative calcium-magnesium nutrition; iron nutrition. *Mailing Add:* Dept of Bot Univ of Wash Seattle WA 98195

WALKER, RICHARD DAVID, b Washington, DC, Feb 19, 31; m 53; c 3. CIVIL ENGINEERING. *Educ:* Univ Md, BS, 53; Purdue Univ, MSCE, 55, PhD(civil eng), 61. *Prof Exp:* Asst civil eng, Purdue Univ, 53-55; from instr to assoc prof, 57-68, actg head dept, 69-70, PROF CIVIL ENG, VA POLYTECH INST & STATE UNIV, 68-, HEAD DEPT, 70- *Concurrent Pos:* Mem comt A2-E1 & A2-H03 & chmn comt A3-E5, Transp Res Bd, Nat Acad Sci-Nat Res Coun, 70-76. *Mem:* Am Soc Civil Engrs; Am Soc Eng Educ; Am Soc Testing & Mat. *Res:* Highway materials; durability of concrete; design of flexible pavements; lime-stabilization; identification of aggregates causing poor concrete performance when frozen. *Mailing Add:* Dept of Civil Eng Va Polytech Inst & State Univ Blacksburg VA 24061

WALKER, RICHARD E, b Cincinnati, Ohio, Dec 24, 23; m 46; c 2. CHEMICAL ENGINEERING, RHEOLOGY. *Educ:* Purdue Univ, BS, 45; Bucknell Univ, MS, 48; Iowa State Col, PhD(chem eng), 52. *Prof Exp:* Res chem engr, Stand Register Co, 46-47; from asst to instr, Bucknell Univ, 47-48; res assoc, Iowa Eng Exp Sta, 48-52; res engr, Jersey Prod Res Co, Stand Oil Co NJ, 52-63; PROF CHEM ENG, LAMAR UNIV, 63- *Mem:* Am Inst Chem Engrs; Am Inst Mining, Metall & Petrol Engrs; Soc Rheol. *Res:* Means of drilling for and producing oil; rheology of elastic and non-elastic liquids; non-Newtonian flow applications. *Mailing Add:* Dept of Chem Eng PO Box 10053 Beaumont TX 77704

WALKER, RICHARD FRANCIS, b South Amboy, NJ, Dec 14, 39. GERONTOLOGY, REPRODUCTIVE ENDOCRINOLOGY. *Educ:* Rutgers Univ, BS, 61, PhD(endocrinol), 72; NMex State Univ, MS, 68. *Prof Exp:* Asst prof biol, Clemson Univ, 72-76; trainee gerontol, Duke Univ, 77-78; fel neuroendocrinol, Univ Calif, Berkeley, 78-80; ASST PROF ANAT, MED CTR, UNIV KY, 80- *Mem:* Endocrine Soc; Am Asn Anatomists; Gerontol Soc; Int Soc Develop Neurosci. *Res:* Role of hypothalamic monoamines, specifically in suprachismatic nucleus, on aging in the female reproductive system. *Mailing Add:* Dept Anat Med Ctr Univ Ky Lexington KY 40536

WALKER, RICHARD V, b Pueblo, Colo, Mar 8, 18; m 45; c 3. MEDICAL BACTERIOLOGY, IMMUNOLOGY. *Educ:* Univ Calif, Berkeley, BS, 49, MPH, 52, PhD(bact), 60. *Prof Exp:* Assoc & instr, Pub Health Lab, Sch Pub Health, Univ Calif, Berkeley, 49-57; from grad res immunologist to asst res immunologist, George Williams Hooper Found, Med Ctr, Univ Calif, San Francisco, 57-65; asst res immunologist, Nat Ctr Primate Biol, Univ Calif, Davis, 65-67; ASSOC PROF ZOOL, OHIO UNIV, 67- *Mem:* Am Soc Microbiol. *Res:* Bacterial toxins; immunochemistry; fluorescent antibody; Salmonella-Shigella diagnosis. *Mailing Add:* Dept of Zool & Microbiol Ohio Univ Athens OH 45701

WALKER, ROBERT BRIDGES, b Houston, Tex, Sept 24, 46; m 71. THEORETICAL CHEMISTRY, CHEMICAL PHYSICS. *Educ:* La State Univ, New Orleans, BS, 68; Univ Tex, Austin, PhD(chem), 73. *Prof Exp:* Res assoc, James Franck Inst, Univ Chicago, 73-76; appointee, 76-77, STAFF MEM, LOS ALAMOS NAT LAB, 77- *Mem:* AAAS; Am Phys Soc. *Res:* Quantum reactive scattering of light atom-diatom systems; quantum and classical description of infrared multiple photon excitation dynamics of polyatomic molecules. *Mailing Add:* Group T-12 MS531 Los Alamos Nat Lab Los Alamos NM 87545

WALKER, ROBERT D(IXON), JR, b Atlanta, Ga, Mar 6, 12; m 35; c 3. CHEMICAL ENGINEERING. *Educ:* Ga Inst Technol, BS, 35; Univ Fla, MS, 51. *Prof Exp:* Res chemist, Eastman Kodak Co, NY, 35-44; PROF CHEM ENG, UNIV FLA, 44- *Mem:* Am Chem Soc; Electrochem Soc; Soc Petrol Engrs; Am Inst Chem Engrs. *Res:* Adsorption fractionation; electrochemistry and thermodynamics of fused salt systems; transport phenomena; electrochemical engineering; solubility and diffusion in biological systems; fuel cells; thermal batteries; enhanced oil recovery. *Mailing Add:* Dept of Chem Eng Univ of Fla Gainesville FL 32611

WALKER, ROBERT HUGH, b O'Donnell, Tex, Sept 8, 35; m 55; c 4. PHYSICS. *Educ:* Tex Christian Univ, BS, 57, MS, 59; Mass Inst Technol, PhD(physics), 62. *Prof Exp:* Asst prof physics, 64-67, assoc dean col arts & sci, 73-74, ASSOC PROF PHYSICS, UNIV HOUSTON, 67-, DEAN COL NATURAL SCI & MATH, 74- *Concurrent Pos:* Lectr, Baylor Col Med, 66-; consult, Int Inst Educ, 67-69. *Mem:* Am Phys Soc; Am Asn Physics Teachers. *Res:* Theoretical physics; solid state physics; atomic physics. *Mailing Add:* Col of Natural Sci & Math Univ of Houston Houston TX 77004

WALKER, ROBERT LEE, b St Louis, Mo, June 29, 19; m 46. PHYSICS. *Educ:* Univ Chicago, BS, 41; Cornell Univ, PhD(exp physics), 48. *Prof Exp:* Asst metall lab, Univ Chicago, 42-43; scientist, Los Alamos Sci Lab, 43-46; res assoc, Cornell Univ, 48-49; from asst prof to assoc prof, 49-59, PROF PHYSICS, CALIF INST TECHNOL, 59- *Mem:* Am Phys Soc. *Res:* Photoproduction experiments and analyses; interaction of gamma rays with matter; high energy physics. *Mailing Add:* Lauritsen Lab 356-48 Calif Inst of Technol Pasadena CA 91109

WALKER, ROBERT MOWBRAY, b Philadelphia, Pa, Feb 6, 29; m 51; c 2. SPACE PHYSICS. *Educ:* Union Univ, NY, BS, 50; Yale Univ, MS, 51, PhD(physics), 54. *Hon Degrees:* DSc, Union Univ, NY, 67; Dr, Univ Clermont-Ferrond, 75. *Prof Exp:* Res assoc, Gen Elec Co, 54-66; dir lab space physics, 66-75, McDONNELL PROF PHYSICS, WASH UNIV, 66-, DIR, McDONNELL CTR SPACE SCI, 75- *Concurrent Pos:* NSF sr fel, 62; vis prof, Univ Paris, 62-63; adj prof, Rensselaer Polytech Inst, 65-66; mem, Lunar Sample Anal Planning Team, 68-70; mem, Lunar Sample Rev Bd, 70-72; vis prof, Calif Inst Technol, 72; mem bd dirs, Vols Tech Assistance; mem bd dirs, Univs Space Res Asn, 69-71; mem, Lunar Sci Inst Adv Comt, 72-, mem bd sci & technol for int develop, Nat Acad Sci, 74-77, mem comt lunar & planetary explor, 77-; vis phys res lab, Ahmedabad, India & Inst Astron, Paris, 81. *Honors & Awards:* Am Nuclear Soc Award, 64; Yale Eng Asn Award, 66; NASA Medal Except Sci Achievement, 70; E O Lawrence Award, AEC, 71. *Mem:* Nat Acad Sci; fel Am Phys Soc; fel Meteoritical Soc; fel Am Geophys Union; Am Astron Soc. *Res:* Radiation effects in solids; development of dielectric nuclear track detectors and their application to nuclear science; geochronology; space science; cosmic rays; meteorites; astrophysics; planetary surfaces; archeometry; laboratory studies of interplanetary dust. *Mailing Add:* Dept of Physics Wash Univ St Louis MO 63130

WALKER, ROBERT PAUL, b Washington, DC, Mar 15, 43; m 65; c 2. MATHEMATICS. *Educ:* Univ Md, BS, 65; Mass Inst Technol, PhD(math), 68. *Prof Exp:* Asst prof math, Univ NC, Chapel Hill, 68-73; prof & chmn dept, Talladega Col, 73-76; assoc prof & dir, Bowie State Col, 76-79; MEM RES STAFF, SYST PLANNING CORP, 79- *Mem:* Am Math Soc; Math Asn Am; Nat Asn Mathematicians. *Res:* Algebraic topology; mathematics education; operations research; strategic systems analysis. *Mailing Add:* Syst Planning Corp 1500 Wilson Blvd Rosslyn VA 22209

WALKER, ROBERT W, b Arlington, Mass, Mar 15, 33; m 59; c 1. MICROBIOLOGY. *Educ:* Univ Mass, BS, 55, MS, 59; Mich State Univ, PhD(microbiol), 63. *Prof Exp:* Hatch fel, 63-64; instr, 64-65, asst prof, 65-74, ASSOC PROF ENVIRON SCI, UNIV MASS, AMHERST, 74- *Res:* environmental microbiology. *Mailing Add:* Dept of Environ Sci Marshall Hall Univ of Mass Amherst MA 01003

WALKER, ROBERT WINN, b Montgomery, Ala, Jan 5, 25; m 49; c 3. PHYSICAL CHEMISTRY. *Educ:* Auburn Univ, BS, 48; Mass Inst Technol, PhD(phys chem), 52. *Prof Exp:* Res chemist, Redstone Labs, 52-53, group leader propellant res, 53-59, sect head phys & polymer chem, 59-65, lab head ion exchange appln res div, 65-73, mgr ion exchange res dept, 73-76, PROJ LEADER FLUID PROCESS CHEM RES, ROHM AND HAAS CO, 76- *Mem:* Am Chem Soc. *Res:* Molecular structure; chemical thermodynamics; rocket propulsion; ion exchange resins; adsorbents; flocculants. *Mailing Add:* 6008 Cannon Hill Rd Ft Washington PA 19034

WALKER, ROGER GEOFFREY, b London, Eng, Mar 26, 39; m 65; c 2. SEDIMENTOLOGY. *Educ:* Oxford Univ, BA, 61, DPhil(geol), 64. *Prof Exp:* NATO fel geol, Johns Hopkins Univ, 64-66; from asst prof to assoc prof, 66-73, PROF GEOL, McMASTER UNIV, 73- *Honors & Awards:* Past Pres' Medal, Geol Asn Can, 75. *Mem:* Geol Soc Am; Soc Econ Paleont & Mineral; Int Asn Sedimentol; Am Asn Petrol Geologists; Geol Asn Can. *Res:* Sedimentary facies analysis; sedimentology of turbidites; quantitative basin analysis; sedimentology of Western Canadian Cretaceous clastic wedge; sedimentology of Archaean greenstone belts. *Mailing Add:* Dept of Geol McMaster Univ Hamilton ON L8S 4L8 Can

WALKER, ROLAND, b Stellenbosch, SAfrica, Feb 8, 07; US citizen; wid; c 2. FISH PATHOLOGY. *Educ:* Oberlin Col, AB, 28, AM, 29; Yale Univ, PhD(zool), 34. *Prof Exp:* Asst biol, Yale Univ, 29-31; instr physiol, Oberlin Col, 31-32; instr biol, 34-42, from asst prof to assoc prof, 42-54, prof, 54-72, EMER PROF BIOL, RENSSELAER POLYTECH INST, 72- *Mem:* AAAS; Am Soc Zool; Wildlife Dis Asn. *Res:* Neurology of fish and crustacea; fish parasitology; ultrastructure of fish blood and tumor cells with virus. *Mailing Add:* Dept of Biol Rensselaer Polytech Inst Troy NY 12181

WALKER, RONALD ELLIOT, b Avon, SDak, Mar 14, 29; m 53; c 2. PHYSICS, PHYSICAL CHEMISTRY. *Educ:* SDak Sch Mines & Technol, BS, 50; Univ Md, MS, 55, PhD(physics), 58. *Prof Exp:* Assoc physicist, 51-55, sr physicist, Johns Hopkins Univ, 55-60, prin staff physicist, Appl Physics Lab, 60-79; SR SCIENTIST, SCI APPLN, INC, 79- *Concurrent Pos:* Instr eve col, Johns Hopkins Univ, 66-78. *Mem:* Am Phys Soc. *Res:* Atomic and molecular physics; laser and optical physics; bioengineering. *Mailing Add:* 4980 E Calle Guebabl Tucson AZ 85718

WALKER, RUDGER HARPER, soil science, deceased

WALKER, RUSSELL GLENN, b Cincinnati, Ohio, May 3, 31; US citizen; m 53; c 2. ASTRONOMY, INFRARED PHYSICS. *Educ:* Ohio State Univ, BSc, 53, MSc, 54; Harvard Univ, PhD(astron), 67. *Prof Exp:* Staff scientist Fourier spectros, Block Assocs, 60-61; physicist infrared physics, Air Force Cambridge Res Labs, 61-66, chief, Infrared Physics Br, 67-75; astronr, Int Sci Sta, Jungfraujoch, Switz, 66-67; staff scientist astrophys, Ames Res Ctr, NASA, 75-81; ASSOC SCIENTIST, JAMIESON SCI & ENG, INC, 81- *Concurrent Pos:* Consult, Smithsonian Astrophys Observ, 65-66 & TOM subgroup, Dir of Defense Res & Eng Reentry Progs, 68-69; mem, Infrared Panel Astron Study Group, Nat Acad Sci, 71-72; mem, Space Sci Bd Infrared & Submillimeter Astron, 74-75. *Honors & Awards:* Sci Achievement Award, US Air Force, 70. *Mem:* Am Astron Soc; fel Optical Soc Am. *Res:* Infrared astronomy; cryogenically cooled telescopes and instruments for space research; infrared sky surveys, atmospheric infrared phenomena. *Mailing Add:* 3680 Park Blvd #6B Palo Alto CA 94306

WALKER, RUSSELL WAGNER, b Fredericktown, Ohio, Nov 14, 24; m 46; c 3. ORGANIC CHEMISTRY, PHYSICAL CHEMISTRY. *Educ:* Ohio Wesleyan Univ, BS, 47; Ohio State Univ, PhD(org chem), 52. *Prof Exp:* Res assoc, Am Petrol Inst, 48-52; res chemist, Sinclair Res, Inc, 53-57, group leader, 57-60, div dir, 60-66, res dir, Sinclair Petrochem, Inc, 66-67, tech mgr, Sinclair Res, Inc, 67-68, vpres & dir assoc opers, Sinclair Petrochem, 68-69, mgr res & develop, Sinclair-Koppers Co, 69-74; DIR RES & DEVELOP, ARCO POLYMERS INC, 74- *Mem:* AAAS; Am Chem Soc; Indust Res Inst. *Res:* Relation of hydrocarbon structure to combustion characteristics; biodegradation and environmental pollution. *Mailing Add:* 28 Forestview Rd Wallingford PA 19086

WALKER, RUTH ANGELINA, b New York, NY, July 11, 20. ORGANIC CHEMISTRY. *Educ:* Vassar Col, BA, 42; Yale Univ, PhD(org chem), 45. *Prof Exp:* Asst chem, Chas Pfizer & Co, NY, 45; asst chemist, Col Med, NY Univ, 45-50; sr res chemist, Celanese Corp Am, 50-56; sr res chemist, Johnson & Johnson, 57; instr chem, Hunter Col, Bronx, 57-60, asst prof, Hunter Col, Bronx, 61-68, assoc prof, Lehman Col, 69-71, dir, Health Prof Inst, 77-78, PROF CHEM, LEHMAN COL, CITY UNIV NEW YORK, 71-, ASSOC DEAN HEALTH PROFESSION, 79- *Concurrent Pos:* Sigma Delta Epsilon grant-in-aid metal complexes hydroxyanthraquinones, Hunter Col, 63, Sigma Xi grant-in-aid res, 65, George N Shuster fel grant, 65, City Univ New York res grant, 65; chmn, Lehman Col Comt Curric, 68-77. *Honors & Awards:* Award, Am Asn Textile Chem & Colorists, 60. *Mem:* Sigma Xi; Am Chem Soc; fel NY Acad Sci; fel Am Inst Chem; Sci Res Soc Am. *Res:* Synthesis of medicinal products; dyestuff synthesis; organometallic complexes of 1,4-dihydroxynathraquinones; methods of teaching; development of interdisciplinary programs to teach the team delivery of health care. *Mailing Add:* Lehman Col City Univ New York Bedford Park Blvd W Bronx NY 10468

WALKER, SHEPPARD MATTHEW, b Perkinston, Miss, Feb 2, 09; m 32; c 1. PHYSIOLOGY, BIOPHYSICS. *Educ:* Western Ky Univ, BS, 32, AM, 33; La State Univ, PhD(physiol), 41. *Prof Exp:* Instr biol, Perkinston Jr Col, 33-38; asst prof sci, Delta State Teachers Col, Miss, 41-42; from instr to asst prof physiol, Sch Med, Wash Univ, 42-49; assoc prof, 49-62, prof, 62-74, EMER PROF PHYSIOL, SCH MED, UNIV LOUISVILLE, 74- *Concurrent Pos:* Mem, Spec Rev Muscle Contraction, 60 & 67; actg chmn dept physiol & biophys, Sch Med, Univ Louisville, 65-67. *Mem:* Soc Exp Biol & Med; Am Physiol Soc; Biophys Soc. *Res:* Muscle structure and function; development of fine structures in muscle fibers; neurophysiology. *Mailing Add:* Health Sci Ctr Dept Physiol Sch Med Univ Louisville Louisville KY 40201

WALKER, STROTHER HOLLAND, b Denver, Colo, Jan 19, 14; m 40; c 3. MATHEMATICS, STATISTICS. *Educ:* Harvard Col, SB, 34; Georgetown Univ, MA, 62; Johns Hopkins Univ, PhD(biostatist), 65. *Prof Exp:* Res group chmn, Opers Res Off, Johns Hopkins Univ, 54-61, res group chmn, Res Anal Corp, 61-66; div head biostatist, 66-74, PROF BIOMET & CHMN DEPT, UNIV COLO MED CTR, DENVER, 74- *Concurrent Pos:* NIH spec fel biostatist sch hyg & pub health, Johns Hopkins Univ, 62-65. *Mem:* Am Math Soc; Math Asn Am; Am Statist Asn; Opers Res Soc Am. *Res:* Development of mathematical and statistical models of biomedical processes and of methods of estimating risk in cardiovascular disease. *Mailing Add:* Dept Biomet Univ Colo Med Ctr 4200 E Ninth Ave Denver CO 80262

WALKER, TERRY M, b Chicago, Ill, Dec 15, 38; m 60; c 2. COMPUTER SCIENCE. *Educ:* Fla State Univ, BS, 61; Univ Ala, PhD(statist), 66. *Prof Exp:* Asst prof comput sci & economet, Ga State Col, 65-67; assoc prof comput sci, Univ Houston, 67-72; PROF COMPUT SCI & HEAD DEPT, UNIV SOUTHWESTERN LA, 72- *Concurrent Pos:* Lectr & Ford Found consult, Atlanta, 66-67. *Mem:* Asn Comput Mach. *Res:* Simulation of industrial processes; computer programming languages. *Mailing Add:* 618 Brentwood Blvd Lafayette LA 70503

WALKER, THEODORE ROSCOE, b Madison, Wis, Feb 8, 21; m 49; c 4. GEOLOGY. *Educ:* Univ Wis, PhB, 47, PhD, 52. *Prof Exp:* Asst geologist, State Geol Surv, Ill, 52-53; from asst prof to assoc prof geol, 53-65, fac res lectr, 72-73, chmn dept geol sci, 72-75, PROF GEOL, UNIV COLO, BOULDER, 65- *Concurrent Pos:* NSF sr fel, 62-63, grants, 65-; Am Asn Petrol Geol distinguished lectr, 65. *Mem:* AAAS; Geol Soc Am; Soc Econ Paleont & Mineral; Am Asn Petrol Geologists. *Res:* Sedimentation; sedimentary petrology. *Mailing Add:* Dept of Geol Sci Univ of Colo Boulder CO 80309

WALKER, THOMAS CARL, b Teaneck, NJ, Aug 13, 44; m 70; c 1. BIOMATERIALS, INSTRUMENTATION. *Educ:* Fairleigh Dickinson Univ, BS, 70; Univ Va, MS, 72, PhD(mat sci), 75. *Prof Exp:* Res technician seismol, Lamont-Doherty Geol Observ, Columbia Univ, 66-70; res assoc physics, Univ Va, 75-76; res assoc, Dept Physiol, 76-77, fel, Dept Med, 77-78, INSTR, DEPT PHYSIOL, MED COL, VA COMMMONWEALTH UNIV, 78- *Mem:* Am Asn Physics Teachers. *Res:* Improvements of the ultra sensitive magnetic susceptometer; using this susceptometer to conduct measurements on heme proteins; electrophysiological studies of ion transport across epithelial cell membranes. *Mailing Add:* 1205 Bridle Lane Richmond VA 23229

WALKER, THOMAS EUGENE, b Glendale, Calif, Feb 1, 48; m 73. BIOCHEMISTRY. *Educ:* Westmar Col, BA, 69; Univ Iowa, PhD(biochem), 74. *Prof Exp:* Res assoc, Mich State Univ, 74-75; fel, 75-77, STAFF MEM, LOS ALAMOS NAT LAB, 77- *Mem:* Am Chem Soc. *Res:* The synthesis by chemical and biosynthetic techniques and nuclear magnetic resonance and mass spectral analysis of carbon 13, nitrogen 15, oxygen 17 and oxygen 18 enriched compounds of biological interest. *Mailing Add:* Los Alamos Nat Lab CNC-4 MS-C346 Los Alamos NM 87544

WALKER, THOMAS JEFFERSON, b Dyer Co, Tenn, July 24, 31; m 59; c 2. ENTOMOLOGY. *Educ:* Univ Tenn, BA, 53; Ohio State Univ, MSc, 54, PhD(entom), 57. *Prof Exp:* From asst prof to assoc prof biol sci & entom, 57-68, PROF BIOL SCI & ENTOM, UNIV FLA, 68- *Concurrent Pos:* Res assoc dept tropic res, NY Zool Soc, 66; res assoc, Fla State Collection Arthropods, 63-; ed, Fla Entomologist, 64-66. *Mem:* Fel AAAS; Entom Soc Am; Soc Study Evolution; Soc Syst Zool. *Res:* Acoustical behavior of insects; systematics, behavior, ecology and evolution of Gryllidae and Tettigoniidae. *Mailing Add:* Dept of Entom & Nematol Univ of Fla Gainesville FL 32611

WALKER, WALDO SYLVESTER, b Fayette, Iowa, June 12, 31; m 52; c 2. BOTANY. *Educ:* Upper Iowa Univ, BS, 53; Univ Iowa, MS, 57, PhD(bot), 59. *Prof Exp:* From asst prof to assoc prof biol, 58-68, assoc dean, 63-65, dean admin, 69-73, dean col, 73-80, PROF BIOL, GRINNEL COL, 68, EXEC VPRES, 80- *Res:* Ultrastructure of plants; experimental morphology; plant physiology. *Mailing Add:* Off of the Dean Grinnell Col Grinnell IA 50112

WALKER, WALTER W(YRICK), b Winslow, Ariz, Jan 14, 24; m 52. PHYSICAL METALLURGY, PHYSICAL CHEMISTRY. *Educ:* Univ Ariz, BSc, 50, MSc, 62, PhD(metall), 68. *Prof Exp:* Asst metallurgist, Buick Motor Div, Gen Motors Corp, 50-51; res engr, Oak Ridge Nat Lab, 51-52; tech supvr metall, Livermore Res Lab, AEC, 52-53; sr metallurgist, Tucson Div, Hughes Aircraft Co, 53-56, tech supvr metall engr, 56-59; lectr metall, Univ Ariz, 59-62; group leader metall eng, Tucson Div, Hughes Aircraft Co, 62-63, group head mat eng, 63-66; assoc prof metall eng, Univ Ariz, 67-73; sr process engr, Tucson Div, 73-78, STAFF ENGR, TUCSON ENG LABS, HUGHES AIRCRAFT, 78- *Concurrent Pos:* Assoc instr, Pima Community Col, 74- *Mem:* AAAS; fel Am Inst Chemists; Nat Asn Corrosion Engrs; Am Soc Metals; Am Inst Mining, Metall & Petrol Engrs. *Res:* Nucleation and solidification of metals; crystal growth phenomena; thermodynamics and kinetics of condensed systems; metallurgy of meteorites; plasticity of ionic crystals; surface chemistry and physics of solid interfaces; novel optical materials. *Mailing Add:* 729 N Richey Blvd Tucson AZ 85716

WALKER, WARREN ELLIOTT, b New York, NY, Apr 7, 42; m 70; c 2. OPERATIONS RESEARCH, PUBLIC POLICY ANALYSIS. *Educ:* Cornell Univ, BA, 63, MS, 64, PhD(opers res), 68. *Prof Exp:* Pres, Compuvisor, Inc, 68-70; sr opers res analyst & proj dir, NY City-Rand Inst, Rand Corp, 70-75; asst vpres, Chem Bank, 75-76; dep dir, Urban Acad, 76-77; SR POLICY ANALYST, RAND CORP, 77- *Concurrent Pos:* Consult, US Environ Protection Agency Off Solid Waste Mgt Progs, 68-72; adj prof opers res, Columbia Univ, 71-77; ed, Pub Sect Applns Dept, Mgt Sci. pres, Urbatronics, Inc, 75- *Honors & Awards:* Lanchester Prize, Opers Res Soc Am, 74; NATO Systs Sci Prize, 76. *Mem:* Inst Mgt Sci; Opers Res Soc Am. *Res:* Applying quantitative methods to the analysis of problems in governmental management and operations; water management, fire department deployment, the criminal justice system and military manpower. *Mailing Add:* The Rand Corp 1700 Main St Santa Monica CA 90406

WALKER, WARREN FRANKLIN, JR, b Malden, Mass, Sept 27, 18; m 44; c 4. ZOOLOGY. *Educ:* Harvard Univ, SB, 41, PhD(zool), 46. *Prof Exp:* Instr anat sch med, Boston Univ, 45-47; instr zool, 47-48, from asst prof to assoc prof, 49-57, actg provost, 74-75, chmn dept biol, 67-74, PROF BIOL, OBERLIN COL, 57- *Mem:* AAAS; Am Asn Anat; Am Soc Zool; Soc Syst Zool; Am Soc Ichthyol & Herpet. *Res:* Herpetology of South America; vertebrate anatomy and evolution; myology; vertebrate locomotion. *Mailing Add:* Dept of Biol Oberlin Col Oberlin OH 44074

WALKER, WELLINGTON EPLER, b Owenton, Ky, July 20, 31; m 64; c 2. INDUSTRIAL CHEMISTRY, ORGANIC CHEMISTRY. *Educ:* Univ Ky, BS, 53; Marshall Univ, MS, 58. *Prof Exp:* Chemist, 53-65, PROF SCIENTIST, TECH CTR, UNION CARBIDE CORP, 65- *Res:* Homogeneous catalysis via organometallic complexes of transition metals, especially group VIII complexes. *Mailing Add:* Tuppers Creek 8361 South Charleston WV 25303

WALKER, WILBUR GORDON, b Lena, La, Sept 18, 26; m 47; c 4. INTERNAL MEDICINE. *Educ:* Tulane Univ, MD, 51. *Prof Exp:* Intern med, Osler Med Serv, Johns Hopkins Hosp, 51-52; resident, Tulane Serv, Charity Hosp, La, 52-53; asst resident, Osler Med Serv, Hosp, 53-54, Am Heart Asn fel, 54-56, resident physician, 56-57, from asst prof to assoc prof, Univ, 58-68, PROF MED, SCH MED, JOHNS HOPKINS UNIV, 68-, PHYSICIAN, JOHNS HOPKINS HOSP, 57-, DIR CLIN RES CTR, 60-, DIR RENAL DIV, 58- *Concurrent Pos:* Estab investr, Am Heart Asn, 57-60; consult, Vet Admin Hosp, Loch Raven; dir renal div, Johns Hopkins & Good Samaritan Hosps; physician-in-chg, Dept Res Med, Good Samaritan Hosp; mem urol & renal dis training grant comt, Nat Inst Arthritis, Metab & Digestive Dis, 68-72; mem gen clin res ctrs comt, Div Res Resources, NIH, 72-76, chmn, 75-76; mem, Kidney Comn of Md, 72-79, 81-, chmn, 75-78. *Mem:* Am Physiol Soc; Am Soc Nephrology; Am Soc Clin Invest; Am Fedn Clin Res. *Res:* Renal function and renal diseases; electrolyte metabolism; renal ion exchange mechanisms; metabolic investigations in renal disease; energy metabolism and protein synthesis in isolated glomeruli; capillary and glomerular permeability to protein; renin-angiotensin-aldosterone physiology; factors influencing biological calcification. *Mailing Add:* Johns Hopkins Hosp Baltimore MD 21205

WALKER, WILLIAM CHARLES, b Santa Barbara, Calif, Aug 22, 28; m 51; c 3. SOLID STATE PHYSICS. *Educ:* Univ Calif, AB, 50; Univ Southern Calif, MS, 53, PhD(physics), 55. *Prof Exp:* Asst physics, Univ Southern Calif, 50-52, res assoc, 52-55; instr, 55-57, from asst prof to assoc prof, 57-68, chmn dept, 72-75, PROF PHYSICS, UNIV CALIF, SANTA BARBARA, 68- *Concurrent Pos:* Consult, Servomechanisms, Inc, 59-60; Nat Acad Sci-NASA fel, Goddard Space Flight Ctr, 63-64; consult, Sloan Technol, 68-74. *Mem:* AAAS; Am Phys Soc; Optical Soc Am. *Res:* Solid state and ultraviolet spectroscopy; optical properties of solids. *Mailing Add:* Dept of Physics Univ of Calif Santa Barbara CA 93106

WALKER, WILLIAM COMSTOCK, b Milwaukee, Wis, July 6, 21; m 45; c 2. PAPER CHEMISTRY, PHYSICAL CHEMISTRY. *Educ:* Lehigh Univ, BS, 43, MS, 44, PhD(phys chem), 46. *Prof Exp:* Inst res fel, Lehigh Univ, 46-47; dir, Nat Printing Ink Res Inst, 47-55, res asst prof chem, 53-55; res dir, 55-65, TECH ASST TO CORP VPRES RES, WESTVACO CORP, NEW YORK, NY, 64- *Concurrent Pos:* Instr, Muhlenberg Col, 46-47. *Mem:* Am Chem Soc; Tech Asn Graphic Arts; Tech Asn Pulp & Paper Indust; Can Pulp & Paper Asn. *Res:* Printability of paper; novel crop systems; paper production technology; printing inks; adsorption of gases on solids; removal of sulfur oxides from flue gases. *Mailing Add:* Westvaco Corp Westvaco Bldg 229 Park Ave New York NY 10171

WALKER, WILLIAM DELANY, b Dallas, Tex, Nov 23, 23; m 46, 75; c 3. PARTICLE PHYSICS. *Educ:* Rice Inst, BA, 44; Cornell Univ, PhD(cosmic ray physics), 49. *Prof Exp:* Physicist, US Naval Res Lab, 44-45; asst prof physics, Rice Inst, 49-51; lectr, Univ Calif, 51-52; asst prof, Univ Rochester, 52-54; asst prof, Univ Wis, Madison, 54-57, from assoc prof to prof, 57-67, Max Mason prof, 67-71, chmn dept, 64-66; chmn dept, 75-81, PROF PHYSICS, DUKE UNIV, 71- *Concurrent Pos:* Mem physics panel, NSF, 64-67; mem high energy surv comt, Nat Acad Sci, 64-65; chmn, Argonne User's Group, 64-66; mem user's exec comt, Fermilab, 72-75; chmn, Fermilab User's Exec Comt, 73-74; mem bd dir, Oak Ridge Assoc Univ, 80- *Mem:* Fel Am Phys Soc. *Res:* Strong interaction physics; technology of bubble chambers. *Mailing Add:* Dept of Physics Duke Univ Durham NC 27706

WALKER, WILLIAM F(RED), b Sherman, Tex, Dec 1, 37; m 60; c 2. MECHANICAL ENGINEERING, BIOMEDICAL ENGINEERING. *Educ:* Univ Tex, BS, 60, MS, 61; Okla State Univ, PhD(mech eng), 66. *Prof Exp:* Aerodyn engr, Ling-Temco-Vought, Inc, 61-62; from asst prof to assoc prof, 65-75, PROF AEROSPACE ENG, RICE UNIV, 75-, CHMN, DEPT MECH ENG & MAT SCI, 76- *Mem:* Am Inst Aeronaut & Astronaut; Am Soc Mech Engrs; Am Soc Artificial Internal Organs. *Res:* Compressible turbulent boundary layers; separated and reattached jet flows; transpiration and ablation cooling. *Mailing Add:* Dept of Mech Eng Rice Univ Houston TX 77001

WALKER, WILLIAM HAMILTON, b Brookline, Mass, Dec 28, 34; m 62; c 2. CIVIL ENGINEERING, STRUCTURAL DYNAMICS. *Educ:* Univ Mass, BS, 56; Univ Ill, Urbana, MS, 58, PhD(civil eng), 63. *Prof Exp:* Res asst civil eng, 56-61, from instr to asst prof, 61-68, asst head dept, 73-76, ASSOC PROF CIVIL ENG, UNIV ILL, URBANA, 68- *Concurrent Pos:* Mem comt bridge dynamics, Transp Res Bd, Nat Acad Sci, 65- *Mem:* Am Soc Civil Engrs; Am Soc Eng Educ; Seismol Soc Am. *Res:* Structural mechanics with emphasis on dynamics; dynamic response of bridges by means of field tests and computer analysis; earthquake engineering. *Mailing Add:* Dept Civil Eng Univ Ill 208 N Romine Urbana IL 61801

WALKER, WILLIAM M, b Savannah, Tenn, Sept 17, 28; m 51; c 4. SOIL FERTILITY, BIOMETRICS. *Educ:* Florence State Col, BS, 50; Univ Tenn, MS, 57; Iowa State Univ, PhD(soil fertil), 61. *Prof Exp:* Res assoc agron, Iowa State Univ, 57-61; asst agronomist, Univ Tenn, 61-66; from asst prof to assoc prof, 66-75, PROF BIOMET, UNIV ILL, URBANA, 75- *Mem:* Am Soc Agron; Coun Soil Testing & Plant Anal. *Res:* Application of biomathematics to soil-plant relationships. *Mailing Add:* Dept of Agron 501C Turner Hall Univ of Ill Urbana IL 61801

WALKER, WILLIAM R, b Lincoln, Nebr, June 8, 25; m 49; c 3. CIVIL ENGINEERING, LAW. *Educ:* Univ Nebr, Lincoln, BSCE, 49, JD, 52; Univ NC, Chapel Hill, MSSE, 64. *Prof Exp:* DIR WATER RESOURCES RES CTR, VA POLYTECH INST & STATE UNIV, 65- *Concurrent Pos:* Vis scholar, Bd Rivers & Harbors, Corps Engrs, 70-71; mem exec bd, Univ Coun on Water Resources. *Mem:* AAAS; Am Soc Civil Engrs; Am Soc Eng Educ; Water Pollution Control Fedn; Am Water Works Asn. *Res:* Legal and institutional arrangements for water resources. *Mailing Add:* Water Resources Res Ctr Va Polytech Inst & State Univ Blacksburg VA 24060

WALKER, WILLIAM STANLEY, b Glendale, Calif, Apr 21, 40; m 64; c 2. IMMUNOLOGY, MICROBIOLOGY. *Educ:* Univ Southern Calif, AB, 63, PhD(microbiol), 68. *Prof Exp:* Lectr bact, Univ Southern Calif, 64-65; sci officer first class, Dept Immunohaemat, Acad Hosp, State Univ Leiden, 71; asst mem labs virol & immunol, 72-74, ASSOC MEM DIV IMMUNOL, ST JUDE CHILDREN'S RES HOSP, 75- *Concurrent Pos:* Fel immunol, Pub Health Res Inst City New York, Inc, 68-71. *Mem:* Reticuloendothelial Soc; Am Asn Immunologists. *Res:* Polymorphonuclear leukocyte chemotaxis; immunobiology of macrophages. *Mailing Add:* St Jude Children's Res Hosp 332 N Lauderdale Memphis TN 38101

WALKER, WILLIAM WALDRUM, b Alexander City, Ala, Jan 16, 33; m 58; c 3. PHYSICS. *Educ:* Auburn Univ, BS, 55; Univ Va, MA, 57, PhD(physics), 59. *Prof Exp:* Asst prof physics, Col William & Mary, 59-60; physicist, Signal Res & Develop Lab, US Army, NJ, 60; from asst prof to assoc prof physics, 61-71, PROF PHYSICS, UNIV ALA, 71- *Mem:* Am Phys Soc; Am Asn Physics Teachers. *Res:* Positron life-times; low energy nuclear physics. *Mailing Add:* Dept of Physics Univ of Ala University AL 35486

WALKER-NASIR, EVELYNE, b Geneva, Switz, Mar 16, 36; m 74; c 1. CARBOHYDRATE CHEMISTRY. *Educ:* Col Geneva, Switz, BA, 55; Univ Geneva, BSc, 57, Fed Dipl, 61, PhD & Pharm D, 66. *Prof Exp:* Asst pharmacist, Switz, 58-59; pharmacist, Switz, 61-62; res asst carbohydrate chem, Lab Carbohydrate Res, Mass Gen Hosp, Boston, 62-64; chemist pharmaceut & med chem, Labs, Vifor SA, Switz, 66-67, head sci dept, 67-70; res fel biol chem, Harvard Med Sch, 71-73; res fel biochem, 71-73, ASST BIOCHEM, MASS GEN HOSP, BOSTON, 73-; ASSOC BIOL CHEM, HARVARD MED SCH, 73- *Mem:* Soc Complex Carbohydrates. *Res:* Chemistry of carbohydrates with biological interest; study of mammalian cell surface-glycoproteins; synthesis of muramic acid derivatives, of glycopeptides and of oligosaccharide-lipid derivatives; structure of glycosaminoglycuronans. *Mailing Add:* Lab for Carbohydrate Res Mass Gen Hosp Boston MA 02114

WALKIEWICZ, THOMAS ADAM, b Erie, Pa, Dec 25, 39; m 62; c 3. NUCLEAR PHYSICS, SOLID STATE PHYSICS. *Educ:* Xavier Univ, Ohio, BS, 62; Pa State Univ, PhD(physics), 69. *Prof Exp:* Asst prof physics, East Stroudsburg State Col, 69; physicist, Picatinny Arsenal, NJ, 69-70; ASSOC PROF PHYSICS, EDINBORO STATE COL, 70- *Concurrent Pos:* AEC collab researcher, Oak Ridge Nat Lab, 71-77, consult, 75-76. *Mem:* Am Phys Soc; Am Asn Physics Teachers. *Res:* Experimental low-energy nuclear physics, especially gamma ray spectroscopy; neutron and charged particle reactions; experimental solid state physics, especially electrooptical and radiation effects in amorphous semiconductors. *Mailing Add:* Dept of Physics Edinboro State Col Edinboro PA 16444

WALKINGTON, DAVID L, b Waukegan, Ill, July 20, 30; m 55; c 1. BOTANY. *Educ:* Ariz State Univ, BA, 57, MS, 59; Claremont Grad Sch, PhD(bot), 65. *Prof Exp:* Instr bot, Ariz State Univ, 59-60; res assoc, 60-63, lectr, 62-63, from asst prof to assoc prof biol, 63-72, actg assoc dean sch math, sci & eng, 73-74, actg dean, 74-75 & 77-78, assoc dean, 75-77, actg assoc vpres, 78-80, PROF BIOL, CALIF STATE UNIV, FULLERTON, 72-, ASSOC VPRES, 80- *Concurrent Pos:* NSF res grant, 65-66; pres bd trustees, Mus Asn NOrange County, 75- *Mem:* Nat Asn Biol Teachers; Cactus & Succulent Soc Am; Am Inst Biol Sci. *Res:* Morphology and chemistry of pollen; chemotaxonomy of cacti; naturally occurring antibiotics in plants especially bryophytes and cacti. *Mailing Add:* Off of Continuing Educ Eng Calif State Univ Fullerton CA 92634

WALKINSHAW, CHARLES HOWARD, JR, b Blairsville, Pa, Nov 14, 35; m 57; c 3. PHYTOPATHOLOGY. *Educ:* Univ Fla, BSA, 57; Univ Wis, PhD(plant path), 60. *Prof Exp:* Asst plant path, Univ Wis, 57-60, proj assoc, 60-61, trainee biochem & path sch med, 61-63; plant pathologist, Southern Forest Exp Sta, US Forest Serv, Miss, 63-65; asst prof microbiol sch med, Univ Miss, 65-68; plant pathologist med support br, NASA-Manned Spacecraft Ctr, 68-73; PRIN PLANT PATHOLOGIST, SOUTHERN FOREST EXP STA, US FOREST SERV, 73- *Mem:* AAAS; Am Phytopath Soc; Am Soc Cell Biol; Sigma Xi. *Res:* Plant diseases; plant tissue culture; fungus diseases of pines; biochemistry of plant diseases. *Mailing Add:* Forestry Sci Lab Box 2008 GMF Gulfport MS 39503

WALKLING, ROBERT ADOLPH, b Philadelphia, Pa, Sept 11, 31; m 59; c 2. ACOUSTICS. *Educ:* Swarthmore Col, BA, 53; Harvard Univ, SM, 54, PhD(acoustics), 62. *Prof Exp:* Res fel appl physics, Harvard Univ, 62-63; asst prof physics, Bowdoin Col, 63-69; ASSOC PROF PHYSICS, UNIV SOUTHERN MAINE, 69- *Mem:* AAAS; Acoust Soc Am; Audio Eng Soc; Am Sci Affiliation; Am Asn Physics Teachers. *Res:* Electroacoustics; noise and vibration; architectural and musical acoustics. *Mailing Add:* Dept of Earth Sci Physics & Eng Univ of Southern Maine Portland ME 04103

WALKLING, WALTER DOUGLAS, b Baltimore, Md, Feb 27, 39; m 61; c 2. PHARMACY. *Educ:* Univ Md, BS, 61, MS, 63, PhD(pharm), 66. *Prof Exp:* Pharmacist, Yager Drug Co, 64-66; Nat Inst Gen Med Sci fel, Swiss Fed Inst Technol, 66-67; sr pharmaceut chemist, Eli Lilly & Co, 67-70; sr scientist, 70-72, group leader, 72-76, SECT HEAD, PHARM RES DEPT, MCNEIL PHARMACEUT, 76- *Mem:* Fel Acad Pharmaceut Sci; Am Pharmaceut Asn; Am Chem Soc. *Res:* Design and evaluation of pharmaceutical dosage forms. *Mailing Add:* Chem & Pharm Develop Dept McNeil Pharmaceut Spring House PA 19477

WALKOWIAK, EDMUND FRANCIS, b Webster, Mass, June 12, 35; m 60; c 2. PHYSIOLOGY. *Educ:* Boston Univ, AB, 58; Univ Conn, PhD(zool), 67. *Prof Exp:* Instr biol, Salem State Col, 59-62; from asst prof to assoc prof, Augusta Col, 66-69; assoc prof, 70-74, PROF PHYSIOL, NEW ENG COL OPTOM, 74-, DIR, INSTNL AFFAIRS, 74- *Concurrent Pos:* Mem biol curric comt, Univ Syst Ga, 69. *Mem:* Am Inst Biol Sci; Am Soc Mammal. *Res:* Application of serological and electrophoretic techniques to the study of tear films. *Mailing Add:* Dept of Physiol New Eng Col of Optom Boston MA 02115

WALL, CHARLES EPHRAIM, b Chandler, Okla, Jan 21, 14; m 35; c 5. CHEMISTRY. *Educ:* Okla State Univ, BS, 35, MS, 58, EdD, 67. *Prof Exp:* Instr pub schs, Okla, 35-39; mgr, Wall & Sons' Farms, 39-56; instr pub schs, Okla, 56-60; NSF traveling sci teacher, Okla State Univ, 60-61, teaching asst chem, 61-63, instr, 64-66; assoc prof, Langston Univ, 66-68, prof phys sci, 68-78; RETIRED. *Mem:* Am Chem Soc; Am Asn Physics Teachers; Nat Sci Teachers Asn. *Res:* Course content and method of presentation for students in beginning chemistry and physics. *Mailing Add:* RR 1 Box 318 Perkins OK 74059

WALL, CONRAD, III, b Boston, Mass, June 13, 39; m 61; c 2. BIOENGINEERING. *Educ:* Tulane Univ, BS, 62, MS, 68; Carnegie-Mellon Univ, PhD(bioeng), 75. *Prof Exp:* Proj officer elec eng, US Army AV Labs, 63-65; mem tech staff appl physics, Boeing Co, 65-70; NIH res assoc sensory physiol, Dept Otolaryngol, Med Sch, 75-77, SCI DIR, HUMAN VESTIBULAR LAB, UNIV PITTSBURGH, 76- *Mem:* Soc Neurosci; Inst Elec & Electronics Engrs; Barany Soc; Sigma Xi. *Res:* Information processing in the vestibular and visual systems; digital signal processing of clinical and experimental sensory systems data. *Mailing Add:* Eye & Ear Hosp of Pittsburgh 230 Lothrop St Pittsburgh PA 15213

WALL, DONALD DINES, b Kansas City, Mo, Aug 13, 21; m 43; c 3. COMPUTER SCIENCES. *Educ:* Univ Calif, PhD(math), 49. *Prof Exp:* Instr, Santa Barbara Col, 49-51; appl sci rep, IBM Corp, 51-74, mkt analyst, 74-81; pres, Datamaps Consult Co, 81- *Mem:* Math Asn Am. *Res:* Number theory; computing machines. *Mailing Add:* 260 Burdett Rd Atlanta GA 30327

WALL, EDWARD THOMAS, b Brooklyn, NY, May 16, 20; m 47; c 4. ELECTRICAL ENGINEERING, CONTROL SYSTEMS. *Educ:* Purdue Univ, West Lafayette, BS, 47; Lehigh Univ, MS, 49; Univ Denver, PhD(elec eng), 67. *Prof Exp:* Instr elec eng, Univ Maine, 49; engr, Pac Gas & Elec Co, 49-51; asst prof elec eng, Calif State Polytech Col, 51-54; anal engr, Gen Elec Co, 54-57; staff engr, Martin-Marietta Corp, 57-64; res elec engr, US Bur Reclamation, 64-66; assoc prof, 66-73, PROF ELEC ENG, UNIV COLO, DENVER, 66- *Concurrent Pos:* NSF grants, Univ Colo, Denver, 68-71. *Mem:* AAAS; Inst Elec & Electronics Engrs. *Res:* Stability theory design of digital control systems using application to aerospace microprocessors; nonlinear control systems; microwave retorting of oil shale and fossil fuels; power system stability. *Mailing Add:* Dept of Elec Eng Univ of Colo Denver CO 80202

WALL, FRANCIS JOSEPH, b Moss Point, Miss, Mar 22, 27; m 50; c 3. BIOSTATISTICS, APPLIED STATISTICS. *Educ:* Sul Ross State Col, BS, 47; Univ Colo, MS, 56; Univ Minn, PhD, 61. *Prof Exp:* Sr statistician, Dow Chem Co, 52-57; statistician, Remington Rand Univac Div, Sperry Rand Corp, 57-61; sr res mathematician, Dikewood Corp, 61-69; biostatistician, Lovelace Found Med Educ & Res, 69-71; CONSULT BIOSTATIST & STATIST ANAL, 72- *Concurrent Pos:* Consult, Shell Oil Co, Colo, 56; vis lectr, Univ NMex, 67, adj asst prof sch med, 70-74, clin assoc, 68-69. *Mem:* Biomet Soc; Am Statist Asn; Sigma Xi. *Res:* Application of statistical methods to biomedical research; design and analysis of clinical trials; applications of statistical methods especially experimental design to the pharmaceutical, chemical and electronic industries. *Mailing Add:* 290 Alamosa Rd NW Albuquerque NM 87107

WALL, FREDERICK THEODORE, b Chisholm, Minn, Dec 14, 12; m 40; c 2. PHYSICAL CHEMISTRY. *Educ:* Univ Minn, BCh, 33, PhD(chem), 37. *Prof Exp:* Instr chem, Univ Ill, Urbana, 37-39, assoc, 39-41, from asst prof to assoc prof, 41-46, prof, 46-64, dean grad col, 55-63; prof chem & chmn dept, Univ Calif, Santa Barbara, 64-66, vchancellor res, 65-66; vchancellor grad studies & res & prof chem, Univ Calif, San Diego, 66-69; exec dir, Am Chem Soc, 69-72; prof chem, Rice Univ, 72-78; prof chem, San Diego State Univ, 79-82. *Honors & Awards:* Award, Am Chem Soc, 45. *Mem:* Nat Acad Sci; AAAS; Am Acad Arts & Sci; Am Chem Soc (ed, J Phys Chem, 65-69); Am Phys Soc. *Res:* Physical chemistry of macromolecular configurations; theory of reaction rates. *Mailing Add:* Dept of Chem San Diego State Univ San Diego CA 92182

WALL, GREGORY JOHN, b Toronto, Ont, Aug 16, 44; m 68; c 3. SOIL SCIENCE. *Educ:* Univ Guelph, BSA, 67, MSc, 69; Ohio State Univ, PhD(soil sci), 73. *Prof Exp:* Res officer soil sci, Agr Can, 67-70; teaching asst agron, Ohio State Univ, 70-71, res assoc soil mineral, 71-73; SOIL SCIENTIST, AGR CAN, 73- *Mem:* Can Soc Soil Sci; Am Soc Agron; Int Asn Great Lakes Res; Int Soc Soil Sci; Soil Conserv Soc Am. *Res:* Sources and magnitude of water pollution by sediment in agricultural regions; mineralogy and exchange properties of fluvial sediments; variability of soil physical and engineering properties in the mineralogy of soils; interpretation of soil survey data. *Mailing Add:* Dept Land Resource Sci Agr Can Univ Guelph Guelph ON N1G 2W1 Can

WALL, JAMES ROBERT, b Lenoir, NC, Dec 7, 29; m 57; c 1. PLANT GENETICS. *Educ:* Va Polytech Inst, BS, 51; Cornell Univ, PhD, 55. *Prof Exp:* Geneticist, USDA, 56-62; asst prof biol, La State Univ, New Orleans, 62-66; from asst prof to assoc prof, Tex Tech Univ, 66-69; assoc prof, 68-74, PROF BIOL, GEORGE MASON UNIV, 74- *Mem:* Bot Soc Am; Genetics Soc Am; Soc Study Evolution; Sigma Xi. *Res:* Interspecific hybridization in Cucurbita and mechanisms of speciation in Phaseolus; experimental evolution. *Mailing Add:* Dept of Biol George Mason Univ Fairfax VA 22030

WALL, JOHN HALLETT, b St Stephen, NB, Aug 10, 24; m 61; c 1. MICROPALEONTOLOGY. *Educ:* Univ NB, BSc, 45; Univ Alta, MSc, 51; Univ Mo, PhD(geol), 58. *Prof Exp:* Asst geologist, NB Dept Mines, 43; asst geologist, Geol Surv Can, 44; jr geologist, Imp Oil Ltd, 45-46, subsurface geologist & micropaleontologist, 47-51; subsurface geologist, J C Sproule & Assocs, Explor Consults, 52; micropaleontologist, Calif Standard Co, 53; res officer, Res Coun Alta, 57-74; RES SCIENTIST, GEOL SURV CAN, 74- *Concurrent Pos:* Lectr geol, Univ Alta, 60-72. *Mem:* fel Geol Soc Am; Soc Econ Paleont & Mineral; Paleont Soc; fel Geol Asn Can. *Res:* Mesozoic microfossils of western and arctic Canada. *Mailing Add:* 3303 33rd St NW Geol Surv Can Calgary AB T2L 2A7 Can

WALL, JOHN K(LIEWER), engineering management, see previous edition

WALL, JOSEPH S, b Madison, Wis, Nov 17, 42. BIOPHYSICS. *Educ:* Univ Wis-Madison, BS, 64; Univ Chicago, PhD(biophys), 71. *Prof Exp:* Fel biophys, Univ Chicago, 71-73; assoc biophysicist, 73-78, BIOPHYSICIST DEPT BIOL, BROOKHAVEN NAT LAB, 78- *Res:* Development and biological application of the high resolution scanning transmission electron microscope. *Mailing Add:* Dept Biol Brookhaven Nat Lab Upton NY 11973

WALL, JOSEPH SENNEN, b Chicago, Ill, June 2, 23; m 50; c 3. BIOCHEMISTRY, PROTEIN CHEMISTRY. *Educ:* Univ Chicago, BS, 46, MS, 49; Univ Wis, PhD(biochem), 52. *Prof Exp:* Instr chem, Lincoln Col, 47-49; asst biochem, Univ Wis, 50-52; instr pharmacol sch med, NY Univ, 52-56; head chem reactions & structure invests, 56-72, RES LEADER CEREAL PROTEINS RES UNIT, CEREAL SCI & FOODS LAB, NORTHERN REGIONAL RES CTR, USDA, PEORIA, ILL, 72- *Mem:* AAAS; Am Chem Soc; Am Soc Biol Chemists; Am Asn Cereal Chemists; Inst Food Technologists. *Res:* Mechanism of nitrogen fixation by bacteria; isolation of natural products; hormonal regulation of carbohydrate metabolism in mammals; protein chemistry; cereal chemistry; nutrition; enzymology. *Mailing Add:* Northern Regional Res Ctr USDA Peoria IL 61604

WALL, LEONARD WONG, b Tallulah, La, Nov 7, 41; m 68; c 3. PHYSICS. *Educ:* La Tech Univ, BS, 63; Iowa State Univ, PhD(physics), 69. *Prof Exp:* Vis asst prof, Univ Kans, 68-69; PROF PHYSICS, CALIF POLYTECH STATE UNIV, 69- *Mem:* Am Phys Soc; Am Asn Physics Teachers; AAAS; Sigma Xi. *Res:* Physics of energy; energy usage in buildings; passive solar. *Mailing Add:* Dept of Physics Calif Polytech State Univ San Luis Obispo CA 93407

WALL, MALCOLM JEFFERSON, JR, b Meridian, Miss, Jan 25, 41; m 65; c 2. PHYSIOLOGY. *Educ:* Lamar Univ, BS, 63; Univ Tex Med Br, Galveston, PhD(physiol), 70; NTex State Univ, MA, 67. *Prof Exp:* Asst biol, NTex State Univ, 63-66; from instr to asst prof physiol & med, Med Col Wis, 70-74; res assoc physiol & biophys, 74-76, surg internship, 76-77, RESIDENT PHYSICIAN, DIV ORTHOPED SURG, UNIV TEX MED BR, GALVESTON, 74- *Concurrent Pos:* USPHS grant, Med Col Wis, 72-74; lectr, Univ Wis-Milwaukee, 72. *Mem:* AAAS; Am Inst Biol Sci; Biophys Soc; Assoc Am Physiol Soc. *Res:* Intestinal transport mechanisms for electrolytes, orgainc solutes and water. *Mailing Add:* Dept of Physiol & Biophys Univ of Tex Med Br Galveston TX 77550

WALL, MONROE ELIOT, b Newark, NJ, July 25, 16; m 41; c 2. BIOCHEMISTRY. *Educ:* Rutgers Univ, BS, 36, MS, 38, PhD(biochem), 39. *Prof Exp:* Chemist, NJ Exp Sta, 39-40; res chemist, Wallerstein Labs, 40; res assoc, Barrett Co, 41; from asst chemist to supvr plant steroid units eastern regional res lab, Bur Agr & Indust Chem, USDA, 41-53, supvr eastern utilization res br, Agr Res Serv, 53-60; head natural prod lab, 60-66, dir chem & life sci lab, 66-71, VPRES PHYS & LIFE SCI DIV, RES TRIANGLE INST, 71- *Concurrent Pos:* Adj prof, NC State Univ, 62- & Univ NC, Chapel Hill, 66-; NSF vis scientist, Am Col Pharmacists, 64-; consult, NIH, 62- *Honors & Awards:* Merck, Sharp & Dohme Res Achievement Award Natural Prod, Am Pharmaceut Asn, 70. *Mem:* AAAS; Am Chem Soc; fel Acad Pharmaceut Sci; NY Acad Sci; Soc Econ Bot (pres, 75). *Res:* Plant chemistry; steroids; cancer chemotherapy; drug metabolism; chemistry and metabolism of cannabinoids. *Mailing Add:* Life Sci Div Res Triangle Inst PO Box 12194 Res Triangle Park NC 27709

WALL, NATHAN SANDERS, nuclear physics, deceased

WALL, ROBERT ECKI, b Aurora, Ill, Aug 1, 35; m 63; c 3. GEOPHYSICS. *Educ:* Carleton Col, AB, 57; Columbia Univ, PhD(geophys), 65. *Prof Exp:* Res assoc marine geophys, Lamont Geol Observ, Columbia Univ, 65-66; sci officer marine geol & geophys, Off Naval Res, 66-70; prog dir submarine geol & geophys, 70-75, head oceanog sect, 75-81, HEAD OCEAN SCI RES SECT, NSF, 81- *Mem:* AAAS; Am Geophys Union; Geol Soc Am; Soc Explor Geophys. *Res:* Marine geophysics; geological oceanography. *Mailing Add:* Ocean Sci Res Sect 1800 G St NW Washington DC 20550

WALL, ROBERT GENE, b Mo, Nov 17, 37; m 64; c 3. ORGANIC CHEMISTRY. *Educ:* Ore State Univ, BS, 61, MS, 63; Univ Wis-Madison, PhD(org chem), 66. *Prof Exp:* NIH fel, Univ Mich, Ann Arbor, 66-67; res chemist, 67-72, sr res chemist, 72-81, SR RES ASSOC CHEMIST, CHEVRON RES CO, RICHMOND, CALIF, 81- *Mem:* AAAS; Am Chem Soc; Soc Petrol Engrs. *Res:* Physical organic chemistry; catalysis and surfactants. *Mailing Add:* 2826 Wright Ave Pinole CA 94564

WALL, ROBERT LEROY, b Doylestown, Pa, July 7, 21; m 52; c 4. MEDICINE. *Educ:* Oberlin Col, AB, 43; Temple Univ, MD, 46; Am Bd Internal Med, dipl, 55. *Prof Exp:* Intern, Bryn Mawr Hosp, 46-47, resident clin path, 47-48; mem staff med res, Univ Hosp, 50-52, asst prof med & dir lymphoma clin, Col Med, 52-57, assoc prof med, 57-65, asst dean res & secy col med, 71-73, PROF MED, COL MED, OHIO STATE UNIV, 65- *Concurrent Pos:* Consult, Dayton Vet Hosp, 54-; mem plasma proteins comt, Nat Res Coun, 63-71. *Mem:* AAAS; Am Soc Hemat; AMA; Am Asn Cancer Res; Am Fedn Clin Res. *Res:* Blood preservation; plasma protein fractionation; qualitative changes in globulins of diseased plasma. *Mailing Add:* Univ Hosp Rm N1016 410 Tenth Ave Columbus OH 43210

WALL, RONALD EUGENE, b Dryden, Ont, Feb 19, 36; m 57; c 3. PLANT PATHOLOGY. *Educ:* Ont Agr Col, BSA, 58; Univ Wis, PhD(plant path), 62. *Prof Exp:* Plant pathologist, Can Dept Agr, 62-66; plant pathologist, 66-73, RES SCIENTIST, DEPT ENVIRON, CAN DEPT FORESTRY, 73- *Mem:* Am Phytopath Soc; Can Phytopath Soc. *Res:* Decays of maturing plants; trunk rots of forest trees; diseases of conifer seedlings. *Mailing Add:* Dept of Fisheries & the Environ Maritimes Forest Res Ctr Fredericton NB E3B 5P7 Can

WALL, THOMAS RANDOLPH, b Lakeland, Fla, Mar 23, 43. MOLECULAR BIOLOGY, IMMUNOLOGY. *Educ:* Univ SFla, AB, 65; Ind Univ, PhD(microbiol), 70. *Prof Exp:* Res assoc cell & molecular biol, Columbia Univ, 70-72; asst prof, 72-78, assoc prof, 78-79, PROF MICROBIOL & IMMUNOL, SCH MED, UNIV CALIF, LOS ANGELES, 79- *Concurrent Pos:* Damon Runyon Mem Fund Cancer Res fel, Columbia Univ, 70-72; assoc mem, Molecular Biol Inst, Univ Calif, Los Angeles, 72- *Mem:* Am Soc Microbiol. *Res:* Organization, expression and regulation of viral and cellular genes in eukaryotic cells; molecular analysis of the nature and expression of immunoglobulin genes; developmental aspects of the immune response. *Mailing Add:* Dept Microbiol & Immunol Univ Calif Sch Med Los Angeles CA 90024

WALL, WILLIAM JAMES, b Northampton, Mass, June 25, 21; m 46; c 1. ENTOMOLOGY. *Educ:* Univ Mass, BS, 42, MS, 49; Univ Calif, PhD(entom), 52. *Prof Exp:* Instr biol, Univ Mass, 46-49; asst, Univ Calif, 49-52; instr biol, State Univ NY Albany, 52-54, asst prof, 54-56; PROF BIOL, BRIDGEWATER STATE COL, 56- *Concurrent Pos:* NIH-USPHS-Nat Commun Dis Ctr res grant, Cape Cod, Mass, 67-70; entomologist, Cape Cod Mosquito Control Proj, 58-; mem sci adv panel, Volta River Basin Area, WAfrica, WHO, 74-79. *Mem:* AAAS; Entom Soc Am; Am Mosquito Control Asn; Am Asn Univ Professors; Sigma Xi. *Res:* Biology, life history, control and taxonomy of Thysanura, Tabanidae, Ceratopogonidae and Culicidae. *Mailing Add:* Dept Biol Bridgewater State Col Bridgewater MA 02324

WALLACE, AARON, b New York, NY, June 2, 23; m 56; c 1. HEALTH SYSTEMS, PHYSICS. *Educ:* City Col New York, BEE, 49; NY Univ, MS, 65. *Prof Exp:* Inspector, NY Ord Dist, US Army, 42-43 & Signal Corps Inspection, 43-46; engr-aide, Watson Labs, US Air Force, 46-47; sr engr, Mat Lab, US Navy, 47-51; sr scientist, W L Maxson Corp, 51-54; res assoc physics, NY Univ, 54-55; sr scientist, W L Maxson Corp, 55-60 & Kollsman Instrument Corp, 60-70; MEM RES STAFF, RIVERSIDE RES INST, 77-; CONSULT, WALLACE TECH ASSOCS, 71- *Concurrent Pos:* Prin investr res contracts, US Air Force, 58-60 & 62-63 & 62-63, US Army, 59-60 & NASA, 64-65; pvt lectr amateur bionics, 67-68; staff engr, Perkin-Elmer Corp, 75-76. *Mem:* Inst Elec & Electronics Engrs; Am Phys Soc; Am Inst Aeronaut & Astronaut; NY Acad Sci. *Res:* Navigation and radar systems; electrooptical and laser systems; cybernetic and bionic systems; scientific and alternative healing systems. *Mailing Add:* 440 West End Ave 10B New York NY 10024

WALLACE, ALEXANDER CAMERON, b St Thomas, Ont, Aug 27, 21; m 48; c 4. MEDICINE, PATHOLOGY. *Educ:* Univ Western Ont, BA, 47, MD, 48; FRCP(C), 72. *Prof Exp:* Clin intern, Victoria Hosp, London, Ont, 48-49; intern path, New Haven Hosp, 49-51; resident, 51-52; lectr med res, Univ Western Ont, 52-53, asst prof, 53-55; assoc prof path, Univ Man, 55-61; dir cancer res lab, 61-65, head dept path, 65-74, PROF PATH, FAC MED, UNIV WESTERN ONT, 65- *Concurrent Pos:* Markle Found scholar, 52-57; pathologist, Winnipeg Munic Hosp, 55-61; mem res adv comt, Nat Cancer Inst Can, 60-68, dir, 69-80; consult, Westminster Hosp, London, 63-78; pathologist, Univ Hosp, London, 72- *Mem:* Fel Am Col Physicians; Am Asn Cancer Res; Can Asn Path; Int Acad Path. *Res:* Cancer research; biology of neoplasia; metastases; renal pathology; immunopathology. *Mailing Add:* Dept Path Univ Western Ont Fac Med London ON N6A 5B8 Can

WALLACE, ALFRED THOMAS, b Cranford, NJ, Nov 26, 35; m 58; c 3. ENVIRONMENTAL ENGINEERING. *Educ:* Rutgers Univ, BS, 59, Univ Wis, MS, 60, PhD(sanit eng), 65. *Prof Exp:* Asst engr, Triangle Conduit & Cable Co, 57-58 & Am Oil Co, 60-62; instr sanit eng, Univ Wis, 62-65; asst prof environ eng, Clemson Univ, 65-67; assoc prof, 67-72, PROF CIVIL ENG, UNIV IDAHO, 72- *Concurrent Pos:* Lectr, Calumet Ctr, Purdue Univ, 60-62. *Mem:* Am Water Works Asn; Water Pollution Control Fedn; Am Soc Civil Engrs. *Res:* Unit operations of environmental engineering; industrial wastes; ground water pollution. *Mailing Add:* Dept of Civil Eng Univ of Idaho Moscow ID 83843

WALLACE, ALTON SMITH, b New Bern, NC, Jan 3, 44; m 69; c 2. OPERATIONS RESEARCH. *Educ:* NC A&T State Univ, BS, 66; Pa State Univ, MS, 68; Univ Md, PhD(math), 74. *Prof Exp:* Eng officer, US Army Corps Engrs, 68-70; sr scientist, BDM Corp, Va, 73-75; ASSOC DIR, SYST PLANNING CORP, VA, 75- *Res:* Development of military weapons systems and surveilance systems; test and evaluation of systems; survivability assesments; weapons effectiveness. *Mailing Add:* 4105 Blacksnake Dr Hillcrest Heights MD 20748

WALLACE, ANDREW GROVER, b Columbus, Ohio, Mar 22, 35; m 57; c 3. INTERNAL MEDICINE, CARDIOVASCULAR PHYSIOLOGY. *Educ:* Duke Univ, BS, 58, MD, 59. *Prof Exp:* Intern med, Med Ctr, Duke Univ, 59-60, asst resident, 60-61; investr cardiovasc physiol, Nat Heart Inst, 61-63; chief resident med, 63-64, assoc, 64-65, from asst prof to assoc prof, 65-70, dir cardiac intensive care unit, 65-70, PROF MED, ASST PROF PHYSIOL, ASST DIR GRAD MED EDUC & CHIEF CARDIOL DIV, MED CTR, DUKE UNIV, 70-, ASSOC VPRES & CHIEF EXEC OFFICER, MED CTR, 81- *Concurrent Pos:* Fel cardiol, Duke Univ, 61; Markle scholar acad med, 65-70; USPHS career develop award, 65-70. *Mem:* Am Fedn Clin Res; Am Heart Asn. *Res:* Cardiology; electrocardiology; electrophysiology of the heart. *Mailing Add:* 3413 Rugby Rd Durham NC 27707

WALLACE, ANDREW HUGH, b Glasgow, Scotland, June 14, 26. MATHEMATICS. *Educ:* Univ Edinburgh, MA, 46; St Andrews Univ, PhD(math), 49. *Prof Exp:* Asst lectr math, Univ Col, Dundee, 46-49, lectr, 49-50; Commonwealth Fund fel, Univ Chicago, 50-52; lectr, Univ Col, Dundee, 52-53; from lectr math to sr lectr, Univ Col, NStaffordshire, 53-57; asst prof, Univ Toronto, 57-59; asst prof, Ind Univ, 59-61, prof, 61-64; grant in aid, Inst Adv Study, 64-65; PROF MATH, UNIV PA, 65- *Concurrent Pos:* Vis prof & assoc dir, Univ Pa Group, Pahlavi Univ, Iran, 71-72. *Mem:* Am Math Soc; Can Math Cong; London Math Soc. *Res:* Algebra; algebraic geometry and topology. *Mailing Add:* Dept of Math Univ of Pa Philadelphia PA 19104

WALLACE, ARTHUR, b Bear River, Utah, Jan 4, 19; m 43; c 4. PLANT NUTRITION, PLANT PHYSIOLOGY. *Educ:* Utah State Univ, BS, 43; Rutgers Univ, PhD, 49. *Prof Exp:* Chief div environ biol, 66-72, asst chief div environ biol, 72-79, PROF PLANT NUTRIT, UNIV CALIF, LOS ANGELES, 49- *Mem:* Am Soc Plant Physiol; Am Chem Soc; Am Soc Hort Sci; fel Am Soc Agron. *Res:* Inorganic plant nutrition and related physiology; major cations, nitrogen and micronutrient elements including their supply to plants by synthetic chelating agents; comparative mineral nutrition of plants; ecophysiology; trace element toxicity. *Mailing Add:* Lab Biomed & Environ Sci Univ of Calif Los Angeles CA 90024

WALLACE, BRUCE, b McKean, Pa, May 18, 20; m 45. GENETICS. *Educ:* Columbia Univ, AB, 41, PhD(genetics), 49. *Prof Exp:* Res assoc dept genetics, Carnegie Inst, 47-49; res assoc, LI Biol Asn, 49-58; assoc prof genetics, Cornell Univ, 58-61, prof genetics, 61-81; PROF BIOL, VA POLYTECH INST & STATE UNIV, 81- *Mem:* Soc Study Evolution (pres, 74); Genetics Soc Am (secy, 68-70, pres, 74); Am Acad Arts & Sci; Am Soc Naturalists (secy, 56-58, pres, 70); AAAS. *Res:* Population dynamics and speciation of Drosophila. *Mailing Add:* Dept Biol Va Polytech Inst & State Univ Blacksburg VA 24061

WALLACE, C(HARLES) E(DWARD), b Portland, Ore, Apr 19, 29; m 65; c 2. ENGINEERING MECHANICS, PHYSICS. *Educ:* Lewis & Clark Col, BS, 51; Ore State Univ, MS, 54; Stanford Univ, PhD(eng mech), 59. *Prof Exp:* Engr, Douglas Aircraft Co, 53-55; asst prof eng sci, 58-59, from assoc prof to prof & chmn dept, 59-67, prof eng mech & mat & chmn dept, 67-74, prof & chmn aerospace eng & eng sci, 74-82, PROF MECH & AEROSPACE, ARIZ STATE UNIV, 82- *Concurrent Pos:* Consult, Gen Elec Co, 59 & NAm Aviation, Inc, 60-; Nat Res Coun sr resident res associateship, NASA-Langley Res Ctr, 68-69. *Mem:* Am Inst Aeronaut & Astronaut; Acoust Soc Am; Am Soc Eng Educ; Am Acad Mech. *Res:* Plasticity of anisotropic materials; thermoelasticity of plates; vibration of aircraft structure; acoustic fatigue and damping; community noise control; radiation resistance. *Mailing Add:* Col Eng & Appl Sci Ariz State Univ Tempe AZ 85291

WALLACE, CARL J, b Lane's Prairie, Mo, Feb 11, 38; m 61; c 2. CHEMICAL ENGINEERING. *Educ:* Mo Sch Mines, BS, 61, MS, 62, PhD(chem eng), 66. *Prof Exp:* Teaching asst chem, Sch Mines, Univ Mo-Rolla, 61-62, 63-64 & 65-66; from asst prof to assoc prof chem eng, SDak Sch Mines & Technol, 66-75; GROUP LEADER, JET PROPULSION LAB, CALIF INST TECHNOL, 75- *Concurrent Pos:* Lectr, NSF Summer Inst, 67; NSF res initiation grant, 69-70. *Mem:* Am Inst Chem Engrs; Am Chem Soc; Am Soc Eng Educ; AAAS; Sigma Xi. *Res:* Biochemical engineering; chemical processing by ultraviolet and ultrasonic energy; bioconversion; energy recovery from wastes; environmental engineering. *Mailing Add:* Jet Propulsion Lab Calif Inst Technol 4800 Oak Grove Dr Pasadena CA 91103

WALLACE, CHESTER ALAN, b Rockville Centre, NY, Oct 1, 42; m 68; c 2. STRATIGRAPHY, SEDIMENTARY PETROLOGY. *Educ:* Antioch Col, BA, 65; Univ Calif, Santa Barbara, PhD(geol), 72. *Prof Exp:* Asst prof geol, Ga Southwestern Col, 69-74; GEOLOGIST, US GEOL SURV, 74- *Mem:* Geol Soc Am; Soc Econ Paleontologists & Mineralogists. *Res:* Stratigraphy, sedimentology, paleocurrent analysis, and diagenesis of clastic sedimentary rocks; tectonic history and sedimentary basin analysis of Precambrian sedimentary rocks in the western United States. *Mailing Add:* US Geol Surv Cent Environ Geol Box 25046 Denver CO 80225

WALLACE, CRAIG KESTING, b Woodbury, NJ, Dec 4, 28; m 60; c 2. MEDICINE. *Educ:* Princeton Univ, AB, 50; NY Med Col, MD, 55. *Prof Exp:* Instr med, Jefferson Med Col Hosp, 60-64; from asst prof to assoc prof, Sch Med & Sch Hyg & Pub Health, Johns Hopkins Univ, 64-72, assoc dir, Ctr Med Res & Training, 67-72; cmndg officer, US Naval Med Res Unit, Ethiopia, 72-76, prog mgr infectious dis, Naval Med Res & Develop Command, 76-78, chief internal med, Camp Pendleton, 78-80, DIR CLIN SERV, NAVAL REGIONAL MED CTR, JACKSONVILLE, FLA, 80- *Concurrent Pos:* Clin investr, US Naval Med Res Unit, Taiwan, 60-63; adv & consult, WHO, 62-; consult, Magee Mem Hosp, Philadelphia, Pa, 63-64; resident coordr & head med prog, Ctr Med Res & Training, Calcutta, India, 64-66; asst physician, Johns Hopkins Hosp, 66-69, physician, 69-72; physician & consult, Vet Admin Hosp, Perry Point, Md, 67-72; mem bact & mycol study sect, NIH, 68-72, chmn, 71-72; physician, Good Samaritan Hosp, Baltimore, Md, 69-72. *Mem:* AAAS; fel Am Col Physicians; Infectious Dis Soc Am; Am Soc Microbiol; Am Soc Trop Med & Hyg. *Res:* Pathophysiology and treatment of infectious diseases, especially in the areas of tropical enteric infections; physician training and research in international medicine. *Mailing Add:* Naval Regional Med Ctr Jacksonville FL 32214

WALLACE, DAVID H, b Cambridge, Mass, May 15, 37; m 63. LARGE SCALE CULTURE OF MICROORGANISMS. *Educ:* Harvard Univ, AB, 58; Mass Inst Technol, SM, 63, ScD(food sci & eng), 66. *Prof Exp:* Dep dir, New Eng Enzyme Ctr, Tufts Univ, 66-80; MICROBIOLOGIST, NEW ENGLAND BIOLABS, 80- *Res:* Carry out large scale culture of microorganisms, optimize growth conditions and improve methods for large scale purification. *Mailing Add:* 61 Donazette St Wellesley MA 02181

WALLACE, DAVID LEE, b Homestead, Pa, Dec 24, 28; m 55; c 3. STATISTICS. *Educ:* Carnegie Inst Technol, BS, 48, MS, 49; Princeton Univ, PhD(math), 53. *Prof Exp:* Moore instr math, Mass Inst Technol, 53-54; from asst prof to assoc prof statist, 54-67, PROF STATIST, UNIV CHICAGO, 67- *Concurrent Pos:* Fel, Ctr Advan Study in Behav Sci, 60-61; mem comput & biomath sci study sect, NIH, 70-74. *Mem:* Fel Am Statist Asn; Inst Math Statist; Biometric Soc; Asn Comput Mach; fel Royal Statist Soc. *Res:* Theoretical statistics; computer methods. *Mailing Add:* Dept Statist Univ Chicago Chicago IL 60637

WALLACE, DONALD HOWARD, b Driggs, Idaho, June 27, 26; m 49; c 5. PLANT GENETICS. *Educ:* Utah State Agr Col, BS, 53; Cornell Univ, PhD(plant breeding), 58. *Prof Exp:* Asst plant breeding, 53-55 & 57, actg asst prof plant breeding & veg crops, 55-57, from asst prof to assoc prof, 58-71, PROF PLANT BREEDING & VEG CROPS, CORNELL UNIV, 71- *Concurrent Pos:* Vis prof, Mich State Univ, 78-79. *Honors & Awards:* Campbell Award, 70; Asgrow Award, 81. *Mem:* Am Soc Hort Sci; Crop Sci Soc Am; Am Soc Plant Physiol. *Res:* Development of hybrid and improved varieties of vegetables; physiological genetics of crop plants. *Mailing Add:* Dept of Plant Breeding Cornell Univ Ithaca NY 14850

WALLACE, DONALD MACPHERSON, JR, b Montclair, NJ, June 24, 34; m 60; c 2. MECHANICAL ENGINEERING. *Educ:* Univ Vt, BSME, 60; Univ Ill, Urbana, MS, 62; Columbia Univ, EngScD(mech eng), 68. *Prof Exp:* Instr mech eng, Univ Ill, 60-62; ASSOC PROF, NORWICH UNIV, 62- *Concurrent Pos:* Engr, Allis-Chalmers Corp, 73-74. *Mem:* Am Soc Mech Engrs; Am Soc Eng Educ. *Res:* Kinematics of spatial mechanisms. *Mailing Add:* RD 1 Box 156 Terrace Rd Northfield VT 05663

WALLACE, DOUGLAS CECIL, b Cumberland, Md, Nov 6, 46. MITOCHONDRIAL GENETICS. *Educ:* Cornell Univ, BS, 68; Yale Univ, MPh, 72, PhD(somatic cell genetics), 75. *Prof Exp:* Res microbiologist, USPHS Northwestern Water Hyg Lab, Gig Harbor, Wash, 68-70; NIH fel, Sch Med, Yale Univ, 75-76; ASST PROF, SCH MED, STANFORD UNIV, 76- *Mem:* Sigma Xi; Am Soc Microbiol; AAAS. *Res:* Study of the genetics, biogenesis and phylogenetic relationships of mammalian mitochondria using the techniques of somatic cell genetics and molecular biology. *Mailing Add:* Dept Genetics Stanford Univ Sch Med Stanford CA 94305

WALLACE, EDITH WINCHELL, b Jersey City, NJ, Oct 3, 35; m; c 3. HYDROBIOLOGY. *Educ:* Montclair State Col, BA, 56, MA, 61; Rutgers Univ, PhD(zool), 69. *Prof Exp:* Instr biol, Westwood Bd Educ, NJ, 56-61; instr sci, Englewood Hosp Sch Nursing, 65-68; ASSOC PROF BIOL, WILLIAM PATERSON COL, NJ, 68- *Mem:* AAAS; NY Acad Sci; Soc Study Reproduction. *Res:* Morphological, histological, transmission electron microscope andphysiologicaal investigations in selenium and zinc deficient rodents of the roles of these trace elements in spermatogenesis. *Mailing Add:* Dept Biol William Paterson Col 300 Pompton Rd Wayne NJ 07470

WALLACE, EDWIN GARFIELD, b Akron, Ohio, Jan 27, 17; m 44; c 6. ORGANIC CHEMISTRY. *Educ:* Univ Miami, Ohio, AB, 38; Ohio State Univ, PhD(chem), 42. *Prof Exp:* Res chemist, Eastman Kodak Co, NY, 42-47; res chemist, US Naval Ord Test Sta, Calif, 47-48; res chemist & group leader, Shell Chem Corp, 48-54; from asst to vpres res to mgr chem res, 54-65, lab dir, 65-67, SR RES ASSOC, WESTERN RES CTR, STAUFFER CHEM CO, 67- *Mem:* Am Chem Soc. *Res:* Agricultural chemicals; industrial organic chemicals and products; polymers; fluorine chemicals. *Mailing Add:* 133 Sleepy Hollow Lane Orinda CA 94563

WALLACE, FELIX A(NTHONY), b Pittsburgh, Pa, May 10, 11; m 44. CIVIL ENGINEERING. *Educ:* Polytech Inst Brooklyn, BCE, 39, MCE, 42; Carnegie Inst Technol, PhD(civil eng), 52. *Prof Exp:* From rodman to asst engr, Brooklyn Manhattan Transit Syst, 29-42; mem staff eng design & drafting, Pittsburgh & Lake Erie RR, 45-46; instr civil eng, Carnegie Inst Technol, 46-47, asst struct & surv, 51-52; prof eng & head dept eng struct & mech, Col of Pac, 47-51 & 52-58; asst to dean eng, 58-59, asst dean, 59-63, prof civil eng, 58-74, head dept, 59-74, assoc dean sch eng & sci, 68-74, res coordr, 70-74, EMER PROF CIVIL ENG, COOPER UNION, 74- *Concurrent Pos:* Vis lectr, Carnegie Inst Technol, 57; dir, NSF grant; consult, 50-57 & 74- *Mem:* Fel Am Soc Civil Engrs; Am Soc Eng Educ; Sigma Xi. *Res:* Structures and mechanics; concrete industry; engineering and engineering education. *Mailing Add:* 223 B Columbia Ave Whiting NJ 08759

WALLACE, FRANKLIN GERHARD, b Deer River, Minn, Apr 3, 09; m 35, 75; c 4. PARASITOLOGY. *Educ:* Carleton Col, BA, 28; Univ Minn, MA, 30, PhD(zool), 33. *Prof Exp:* Asst prof biol, Lingnam Univ, 33-37; from instr to assoc prof zool, 37-63, prof zool, 63-77, EMER PROF ZOOL, UNIV MINN, MINNEAPOLIS, 77- *Concurrent Pos:* Consult, Vet Admin Hosp, 46-73; mem trop med & parasitol study asst, NIH, 70-74; consult, Brazil, 77, 79 & 81. *Mem:* Am Micros Soc (vpres, 66); Am Soc Parasitol (vpres, 74); Am Soc Trop Med & Hyg; Soc Protozool (pres, 77). *Res:* Trypanosomatid flagellates and parasites of insects. *Mailing Add:* 2603 Cohansey St St Paul MN 55113

WALLACE, FREDERIC ANDREW, b Boston, Mass, Apr 28, 33; m 54; c 2. PHYSICAL CHEMISTRY, ANALYTICAL CHEMISTRY. *Educ:* Harvard Univ, AB, 58; Calif Inst Technol, MS, 60; Tufts Univ, PhD(chem), 67. *Prof Exp:* GROUP LEADER PHYS & ANAL CHEM RES, CENT ANAL LAB, RES DIV, POLAROID CORP, 67- *Concurrent Pos:* Chemist, Monsanto Chem Co, 70-74. *Mem:* Am Chem Soc. *Res:* Investigations of structure and bonding of organo-silver complexes and salts; measurement of stability constants, and solubility products of same; chemical analysis and method development for photographic chemicals. *Mailing Add:* Polaroid Corp 750 Main St 3-D Cambridge MA 02139

WALLACE, GARY DEAN, b Pasadena, Calif, Jan 4, 46; m 77; c 2. PLANT SYSTEMATICS, PLANT ANATOMY. *Educ:* Calif State Univ, BA, 67, MA, 72; Claremont Grad Sch, PhD(bot), 75. *Prof Exp:* Biologist, Los Angeles Count Aboretum, 75-81; ASSOC CURATOR & BOTANIST, NATURAL HIST MUS, LOS ANGELES, 82- *Concurrent Pos:* Exten Instr, Univ Calif, Los Angeles, 76- *Mem:* Am Soc Plant Taxonomists; Int Asn Plant Taxonomy; Bot Soc Am; AAAS; Asn Trop Biol. *Res:* Taxonomy of the monotropoidese (ericpase); checklist of the flora of the offshore islands of Southern California; ecological word anatomy of arctostaphylos (ericpase). *Mailing Add:* Bot Sect Nat Hist Mus 900 Exposition Blvd Los Angeles CA 90007

WALLACE, GARY OREN, b Stewart Co, Tenn, Apr 2, 40; m 62; c 2. ECOLOGY. *Educ:* Austin Peay State Univ, BS, 62; Univ Tenn, MS, 64, PhD(zool), 70. *Prof Exp:* Teacher biol, Maryville Col, 64-65; ASST PROF BIOL, MILLIGAN COL, 67-68 & 71- *Concurrent Pos:* Ed, The Migrant, 71-81. *Mem:* Wilson Ornith Soc; Nat Audubon Soc; Sigma Xi. *Res:* Abundance and distribution of certain bird populations. *Mailing Add:* Rte 7 Sunrise Dr Elizabethtown TN 37643

WALLACE, GEORGE JOHN, b Waterbury, Vt, Dec 9, 06; m 34; c 2. ORNITHOLOGY. *Educ:* Univ Mich, AB, 32, MA, 33, PhD(zool), 36. *Hon Degrees:* ScD, Cent Mich Univ, 70. *Prof Exp:* Biologist, Vt Fish & Game Serv, 36-37; dir, Pleasant Valley Sanctuary, Mass, 37-42; game ecologist game div, Mich Dept Conserv, 42; instr zool, 42-45, from asst prof to assoc prof, 45-54, prof, 54-72, EMER PROF ZOOL, MICH STATE UNIV, 72- *Concurrent Pos:* Consult AEC, Argonne Nat Lab, 74-75. *Mem:* Wilson Ornith Soc; Cooper Ornith Soc; Nat Audubon Soc; Am Ornith Union; Nat Wildlife Fedn. *Res:* Predatory birds; effects of insecticides on birds; neotropical thrushes; conservation of natural resources; books and encyclopedia articles on birds. *Mailing Add:* Route 1 Box 1638 Grayling MI 49738

WALLACE, GERALD WAYNE, b Sault Ste Marie, Mich, July 20, 33; m 54; c 3. ANALYTICAL CHEMISTRY, PHYSICAL CHEMISTRY. *Educ:* Univ Mich, BS, 55; Purdue Univ, MS, 57, PhD(anal chem), 59. *Prof Exp:* Sr chemist, Esso Res & Eng Co, 59-60; sr anal chemist, 60-65, res scientist, 65-67, head anal develop phys, 67-71, dir, Phys Chem Res Div, 71-79, dir pharmaceut res, 79-80, DIR ANAL DEVELOP, ELI LILLY & CO, 80- *Mem:* Am Chem Soc; AAAS. *Res:* Spectroscopy; fluorescence; photochemistry. *Mailing Add:* Lilly Res Lab 307 E McCarty St Indianapolis IN 46285

WALLACE, GORDON DEAN, b Los Angeles, Calif, Dec 17, 27; m 52; c 2. EPIDEMIOLOGY. *Educ:* Colo State Univ, BS, 52, DVM, 54; Univ Calif, MPH, 62. *Prof Exp:* Epidemiologist, Commun Dis Ctr, USPHS, 54-61, med researcher, 61-79, ASST SCI DIR, NAT INST ALLERGY & INFECTIOUS DIS, 79- *Mem:* AAAS; Am Soc Trop Med & Hyg. *Res:* Epidemiology of infectious diseases, including eosinophilic meningitis, influenza and toxoplasmosis. *Mailing Add:* Bldg 5 Rm 135 Nat Inst Health Bethesda MD 20205

WALLACE, GORDON THOMAS, b Chicago, Ill, Sept 22, 42; m 69; c 1. CHEMICAL OCEANOGRAPHY, ATMOSPHERIC CHEMISTRY. *Educ:* Antioch Col, BS, 65; Univ RI, PhD(oceanog), 76. *Prof Exp:* Anal chemist, Geigy Chem Corp, 62-63; chemist, Naval Res Lab, 63-69; res asst, Univ RI, 72-76; res assoc, 75-76, ASST PROF, SKIDAWAY INST OCEANOG, 76- *Concurrent Pos:* Consult, Amos T Shaler Inc, 73-74, Knoll Atomic Power Labs; adj asst prof, Ga Inst Technol, 78- *Mem:* Am Soc Limnol & Oceanog; AAAS; Am Geophys Union. *Res:* Biogeochemistry of metals in the marine environment; trace metal-organic interactions; chemical fractionation at the sea-air interface; chemical composition of marine aerosols. *Mailing Add:* Skidaway Inst of Oceanog PO Box 13687 Savannah GA 31406

WALLACE, GRAHAM FRANKLIN, b Santa Rosa, Calif, Mar 27, 35; m 59; c 2. COMPUTER SCIENCE. *Educ:* Pomona Col, BA, 57; Univ Calif, Berkeley, MA, 60. *Prof Exp:* Mathematician, Math Sci Dept, 60-64, res mathematician, 64-66, asst mgr admin, 66-70, sr systs programmer, Info Sci Lab, 70-74, SR RES ENGR, SYSTS TECH LAB, STANFORD RES INST, 74- *Concurrent Pos:* Chmn seventh symposium gaming & chmn steering comt, Nat Gaming Coun, 68; vchmn tech prog eight int conf, Inst Elec & Electronics Engrs Comput Soc, 74. *Mem:* AAAS; Sigma Xi. *Res:* Theory and application of simulation in the study of systems; design, analysis and evaluation of computer-based information systems. *Mailing Add:* 1331 Hillview Dr Menlo Park CA 94025

WALLACE, HAROLD DEAN, b Walnut, Ill, June 8, 22; m 45; c 4. ANIMAL NUTRITION. *Educ:* Univ Ill, BS, 45, MS, 47; Cornell Univ, PhD(animal nutrit), 50. *Prof Exp:* From asst prof to assoc prof, 50-61, PROF ANIMAL NUTRIT, UNIV FLA, 61-, CHMN ANIMAL SCI, 76- *Honors & Awards:* Am Feed Mfrs Award, 62. *Mem:* AAAS; Am Soc Animal Sci; Am Dairy Sci Asn; Am Inst Nutrit. *Res:* Swine nutrition; vitamins; antibiotics; amino acids; carcass quality. *Mailing Add:* Dept Animal Sci Univ Fla Gainesville FL 32611

WALLACE, HELEN M, b Hoosick Falls, NY, Feb 18, 13. PUBLIC HEALTH. *Educ:* Wellesley Col, AB, 33; Columbia Univ, MD, 37; Harvard Univ, MPH, 43. *Prof Exp:* With New York Dept Health, 43-55; prof prev med, New York Med Col, 55-56; prof maternal & child health, Univ Minn, 56-59; chief child health studies, US Children's Bur, 59-62; prof maternal, child & family health, Sch Pub Health, Univ Calif, Berkeley, 62-80; DISTINGUISHED LECTR & PROF, GRAD SCH PUB HEALTH, SAN DIEGO STATE UNIV, 80- *Concurrent Pos:* WHO traveling fel, 57; consult, WHO, Uganda, 61, Philippines, 66, India, 68 & 69, Turkey, 69, Geneva, 70 & 74 & Iran, 72; Ford Found consult, Sch Pub Health, Univ Antioquaia, Colombia, 71; consult, Health Bur, Panama Canal Co, 72, India, Thailand, Burma & Ceylon, 75; dir Uganda Prog, Univ Calif, India, 81 & Thailand, 81. *Mem:* Asn Teachers Maternal & Child Health (pres); Am Pub Health Asn. *Res:* Maternal and child health. *Mailing Add:* San Diego State Univ Grad Sch Pub Health San Diego CA 92182

WALLACE, HERBERT WILLIAM, b Brooklyn, NY, Dec 11, 30; m 54; c 3. BIOCHEMISTRY, SURGERY. *Educ:* Harvard Univ, AB, 52; Tufts Univ, MD, 56, MS, 60; Wharton Sch Univ Pa, MBA, 81. *Prof Exp:* Asst attend surgeon, Elmhurst Gen Hosp Div, Mt Sinai Hosp, 65-66; assoc, 66-70, from asst prof to assoc prof surg & assoc prof physiol, Sch Med, 70-79, assoc prof bioeng, Col Eng & Appl Sci, 74-76, PROF SURG & PHYSIOL, SCH MED & PROF BIOENG, COL ENG & APPL SCI, UNIV PA, 76-; RES ASSOC, DIV CARDIOL, PHILADELPHIA GEN assoc 71- *Concurrent Pos:* Res fel, Nat Heart Inst, 58-59; teaching fel surg, Sch Med, Univ Pittsburgh, 61-62; Am Thoracic Soc fel, 62-65; John Polachek Found Med Res fel, Div Cardio-Thoracic Surg, Mt Sinai Hosp, New York, 65-66; asst surgeon, Grad Hosp, Univ Pa, 66-74, assoc surg, 74-, assoc dir, Gen Clin Res Ctr, 67-70, actg dir, 70-73. *Mem:* AAAS; Asn Acad Surg; Am Chem Soc; Am Col Surg; Am Fedn Clin Res. *Res:* Biochemistry and physiology of extracorporeal circulation and respiration; lung metabolism; hemoglobin; artificial red cell; cardiac metabolism; cancer immunology; management and marketing of medical services. *Mailing Add:* Dept Surg Univ Pa Grad Hosp Philadelphia PA 19146

WALLACE, JACK E, b Harrisburg, Ill, Jan 5, 34; m 55; c 2. ANALYTICAL BIOCHEMISTRY. *Educ:* Univ Southern Ill, BA, 55, MA, 57; Purdue Univ, PhD(biochem), 62. *Prof Exp:* Instr chem, Univ Southern Ill, 55-57; instr biochem, Purdue Univ, 59-61; chemist anal lab, State Chemist's Lab, Ind, 57-59; chief forensic toxicol br, US Air Force Sch Aerospace Med, 61-72; assoc prof, 72-79, PROF PATH, UNIV TEX HEALTH SCI CTR, SAN ANTONIO, 79- *Concurrent Pos:* Consult, Army Med Lab, Ft Sam Houston, Tex, Audie Murphy Vet Admin Hosp, San Antonio, Tex, Wilford Hall US Air Force Med Ctr, Lackland AFB, Tex, Southwest Bioclin Lab, San Antonio, Tex & Harris Med Labs, Ft Worth, Tex. *Mem:* Sr mem Am Chem Soc; fel Am Inst Chem; fel Am Acad Forensic Sci; Am Acad Clin Toxicol; Am Asn Clin Chemists. *Res:* Forensic toxicology; enzymology; drug metabolism; drug analysis in biological specimens; pharmacology; clinical chemistry; biochemical pathology. *Mailing Add:* Dept of Path Univ of Tex Health Sci Ctr San Antonio TX 78284

WALLACE, JAMES, b New Brunswick, NJ, Oct 6, 32; m 58; c 5. OPTICS, FLUID MECHANICS. *Educ:* US Merchant Marine Acad, BS, 54; Univ Notre Dame, MS, 59; Brown Univ, PhD(fluid mech), 63. *Prof Exp:* Res engr, Bendix Corp, 58-59; prin res scientist optics, Fluid Mech, Avco Everett Res Lab & Avco Systs Div, 63-73; PRES, FAR FIELD, INC, 73- *Mem:* Optical Soc Am; Inst Elec & Electronics Engrs. *Res:* Theoretical optics; lasers; fluid mechanics. *Mailing Add:* 6 Thoreau Way Sudbury MA 01776

WALLACE, JAMES BRUCE, b Williamsburg Co, SC, Mar 2, 39; m 62; c 1. ENTOMOLOGY, HYDROBIOLOGY. *Educ:* Clemson Univ, BS, 61; Va Polytech Inst, MS, 63, PhD(entom), 67. *Prof Exp:* Res asst entom, Va Polytech Inst, 61-66; asst prof, 67-71, assoc prof, 71-77, PROF ENTOM, UNIV GA, 77-, MEM STAFF, INST ECOL, 69- *Concurrent Pos:* Environ Protection Agency res grant, Univ Ga, 68-72; NSF res grant, 74-81; vis scientist, Univ Lund, Sweden, 80. *Mem:* AAAS; Royal Entom Soc London; Am Entom Soc; Entom Soc Am; NAm Benthol Soc. *Res:* Immature insects; aquatic entomology; taxonomy and biology; ecology and biology of filter feeding insects. *Mailing Add:* Dept of Entom Univ of Ga Athens GA 30602

WALLACE, JAMES ROBERT, b Magnolia, Ark, Nov 9, 38; m 63; c 3. HYDROLOGY, FLUID MECHANICS. *Educ:* Ga Inst Technol, BCivE, 61, MS, 63; Mass Inst Technol, ScD, 66. *Prof Exp:* Res asst civil eng, Mass Inst Technol, 62-66; asst prof, 66-69, ASSOC PROF CIVIL ENG, GA INST TECHNOL, 69- *Mem:* Am Geophys Union; Am Soc Civil Engrs. *Res:* Flow of fluids in open channels; design and operation of water resource systems; computer simulation of hydrologic processes. *Mailing Add:* 2680 Peppermint Dr Tucker GA 30084

WALLACE, JAMES WILLIAM, JR, b Cincinnati, Ohio, July 31, 40; m 62; c 2. PLANT BIOCHEMISTRY, PLANT PHYSIOLOGY. *Educ:* Miami Univ, BS, 62, MS, 64; Univ Tex, Austin, PhD(plant biochem), 67. *Prof Exp:* Technician, Kimberly-Clarke Corp, 62; asst prof, 67-72, assoc prof, 72-77, PROF BIOL, WESTERN CAROLINA UNIV, 78- *Concurrent Pos:* Sr res fel, NZ Nat Res Adv Coun, 76-77. *Mem:* Am Chem Soc; Bot Soc Am; Phytochem Soc NAm. *Res:* Flavanoids, biosynthesis and physiology. *Mailing Add:* Dept of Biol Western Carolina Univ Cullowhee NC 28723

WALLACE, JOAN M, b Rochester, NY, Mar 7, 28. PLANT BIOCHEMISTRY, TOXICOLOGY. *Educ:* Cornell Univ, BS, 51; Rutgers Univ, MS, 54, PhD(plant physiol), 57. *Prof Exp:* Res fel biol, Calif Inst Technol, 58-63; RES CHEMIST, WESTERN REGIONAL RES LAB, USDA, 63- *Mem:* AAAS; Am Inst Biol Sci; Sigma Xi. *Res:* Toxicology of natural plant constituents; effects of fumigants on food composition. *Mailing Add:* Western Regional Res Lab 800 Buchanan St Berkeley CA 94710

WALLACE, JOHN F(RANCIS), b Boston, Mass, Oct 26, 19; m 43; c 3. METALLURGY, FOUNDRY TECHNOLOGY. *Educ:* Mass Inst Technol, BS, 41, MS, 53. *Prof Exp:* Asst metallurgist, Watertown Arsenal, Mass, 41-42, metallurgist, 46-47, sr metallurgist, 47-52, prin metallurgist, 52-54; from assoc prof to prof, 54-80, REP STEEL PROF METALL, CASE WESTERN RESERVE UNIV, 80-, CHMN DEPT METALL & MAT SCI, 74- *Concurrent Pos:* Consult, 55; Hoyt Mem lectr, Am Foundrymen's Soc, 75. *Honors & Awards:* Pangborn Gold Medal, Foundrymen's Soc, 62; Award of Merit, Steel Founders' Soc Am, 67; Nyselius Award, Am Die Casting Inst, 67; Gold Medal, Gray & Ductile Iron Founders' Soc, 70; Howard Taylor Award, Am Foundry Men's Soc, 81. *Mem:* Foundrymen's Soc; Am Soc Metals; Am Inst Mining, Metall & Petrol Engrs; Soc Die Casting Engrs; Sigma Xi. *Res:* Cast metals; control of casting processes, including solidification behavior, gating, rising, mold selection and behavior; die casting; heat treatment of metals; welding; metal forming and mechanical behavior of metals. *Mailing Add:* Dept Metall & Mat Sci Case Western Reserve Univ Cleveland OH 44106

WALLACE, JOHN HOWARD, b Cincinnati, Ohio, Mar 8, 25; m 45, 79; c 2. MICROBIOLOGY, IMMUNOLOGY. *Educ:* Howard Univ, BS, 47; Ohio State Univ, MS, 49, PhD(bact), 53. *Prof Exp:* Asst virol, Children's Hosp Res Found, Cincinnati, 47 & 49-51; asst bact, Ohio State Univ, 51-53, asst instr, 53; asst bacteriologist, Leonard Wood Mem Lab & res assoc bact & immunol, Harvard Univ Med Sch, 55-59; from asst prof to prof microbiol, Meharry Med Col, 59-66; from assoc prof to prof, Sch Med, Tulane Univ, 66-70; prof, Ohio State Univ, 70-72; PROF MICROBIOL & IMMUNOL & CHMN DEPT MICROBIOL, SCH MED, UNIV LOUISVILLE, 72- *Concurrent Pos:* USPHS fel, Ohio State Univ, 54-55; USPHS sr res fel, 59-61; NIH career res develop award, 61-66; mem bd sci counrs, Nat Inst Allergy & Infectious Dis, 72-75, chmn, 75-76; prof microbiol & immunol & chmn dept & assoc dean for acad affairs, Sch Med, Morehouse Col, 79-80; mem cancer res manpower rev comn, Nat Cancer Inst, 77-81; mem microbiol & infectious dis adv comn, Nat Inst Allergy & Infectious Dis, 82- *Mem:* Am Asn Immunol; Transplantation Soc; fel Am Acad Microbiol; Am Asn Cancer Res; Soc Exp Biol & Med. *Res:* Virus modified erythrocytes; in vitro cultivation of murine leprosy bacilli; tissue culture in agar systems; delayed hypersensitivity; immunology of leprosy; tissue transplantation; tumor immunology; effects of tobacco smoke on immune responses; regulation of the immune response. *Mailing Add:* Sch of Med Univ Louisville Health Sci Ctr Louisville KY 40292

WALLACE, JOHN LONGSTREET, b Philadelphia, Pa, Dec 14, 45; m 64; c 2. EXPERIMENTAL SOLID STATE PHYSICS. *Educ:* Temple Univ, AB, 64; Calif Inst Technol, MS, 66, PhD(physics), 71. *Prof Exp:* RES SCIENTIST, AIL, DIV CUTLER HAMMER INC, 71- *Res:* The development of gallium arsenide microwave semiconductor devices. *Mailing Add:* 43 Reynolds St Huntington Station NY 11746

WALLACE, JOHN M, JR, b Cincinnati, Ohio, Dec 29, 24; m 66. ELECTRICAL ENGINEERING. *Educ:* Rensselaer Polytech Inst, BEE, 51; Ga Inst Technol, MS, 55. *Prof Exp:* From instr to asst prof, 52-65, assoc prof, 65-80, PROF ELEC ENG, GA INST TECHNOL, 80- *Mem:* Am Soc Eng Educ; Am Asn Univ Prof. *Res:* Engineering education; instrumentation; digital hardware. *Mailing Add:* Sch of Elec Eng Ga Inst of Technol Atlanta GA 30332

WALLACE, JOHN MICHAEL, b Flushing, NY, Oct 28, 40; c 2. METEOROLOGY. *Educ:* Webb Inst Naval Archit, BS, 62; Mass Inst Technol, PhD(meteorol), 66. *Prof Exp:* From asst prof to assoc prof, 66-77, PROF ATMOSPHERIC SCI, UNIV WASH, 77- *Concurrent Pos:* Adj assoc prof environ studies, Univ Wash, 73- *Honors & Awards:* Macelwane Award, Am Geophys Union, 72. *Mem:* Am Meteorol Soc; Am Geophys Union; Meteorol Soc Japan. *Res:* General circulation; tropical meteorology. *Mailing Add:* Dept of Atmospheric Sci Univ of Wash Seattle WA 98115

WALLACE, JON MARQUES, b Pensacola, Fla, Dec 21, 43; m 70; c 2. PHYSICS. *Educ:* Univ Calif, Berkeley, AB, 66; Harvard Univ, PhD(physics), 71. *Prof Exp:* Fel physics, Univ Md, 71-73; STAFF MEM, LOS ALAMOS NAT LAB, 73- *Mem:* Am Phys Soc. *Res:* Nuclear scattering theory; transport theory; hydrodynamics; inertial confinement fusion; cosmic ray theory. *Mailing Add:* Los Alamos Nat Lab MS 531 PO Box 1663 Los Alamos NM 87545

WALLACE, JOSEPH E(UGENE), b Scranton, Pa, Mar 16, 26. PHYSICS, ELECTRICAL ENGINEERING. *Educ:* Univ Scranton, BS, 50; Fordham Univ, MS, 51; Syracuse Univ, MS, 68. *Prof Exp:* Design engr, 51-55, assoc engr, 55-56, staff engr, 56-58, adv engr, 58-62, SR ENGR, IBM CORP, 62- *Res:* Computer input-output equipment, particularly magnetic devices. *Mailing Add:* 1200 Queen's Rd Charlotte NC 28207

WALLACE, KYLE DAVID, b Nancy, Ky, Apr 3, 43; m 64; c 2. MATHEMATICS. *Educ:* Eastern Ky State Col, BS, 63; Vanderbilt Univ, MS, 65, PhD(math), 70. *Prof Exp:* Instr math, Easten Ky Univ, 65-67; asst prof, 70-75, assoc prof, 75-80, PROF MATH, WESTERN KY UNIV, 80- *Mem:* Am Math Soc; Math Asn Am. *Res:* Infinite Abelian groups; structure and classification of groups. *Mailing Add:* Dept of Math Western Ky Univ Bowling Green KY 42101

WALLACE, LARRY J, b South Lyon, Mich, Sept 17, 37; m 58; c 3. ORTHOPEDIC SURGERY. *Educ:* Mich State Univ, BS, 60, DVM, 62, MS, 64; Am Col Vet Surgeons, dipl. *Prof Exp:* Asst instr surg & med, Mich State Univ, 62-63; asst prof exp path, Lab Animal Med, Univ Fla, 63-66; asst prof surg, Kans State Univ, 66-69, assoc prof, 69-72; assoc prof, 72-74, PROF ORTHOP SURG, UNIV MINN, 74- *Concurrent Pos:* Dir surg residencies, Col Vet Med, Univ Minn, 72-, head, Div Small Animal Surg, 73-78; consult vet, Cardiac Pacemakers, Inc, St Paul, 78-; lectr orthop sur, Ohio State Univ, 82. *Mem:* Am Vet Med Asn; Am Animal Hosp Asn; Vet Orthop Soc; Sigma Xi. *Res:* Joint transplantation; bone grafting; bone healing; methods for the fixation of fractures; arthritis; reconstructive surgery; joint prostheses; growth deformities of bone; hip dysplasia; bone banking; bone infections; experimental surgery. *Mailing Add:* 233 17th Ave New Brighton MN 55112

WALLACE, MICHAEL DWIGHT, b Columbia, SC, Feb 15, 47; m 68; c 2. PROCESS CONTROL ENGINEERING, CHEMICAL ENGINEERING. *Educ:* Ga Inst Technol, BChE, 68; Univ Fla, ME, 69; Ohio State Univ, MBA, 82. *Prof Exp:* Asst chem eng, Univ Fla, 68-69; develop engr, Celanese Plastics Co, 70-73; process control engr, Brunswick Pulp & Paper Co, 73-76, group leader, 76-78, mgr, 78; mgr systs-process eng, 78-81, MGR OPERS TECHNOL, MEAD CENT RES, 81- *Mem:* Tech Asn Pulp & Paper Indust; Am Mgt Asn. *Res:* Process development and control. *Mailing Add:* Mead World Hq Ct House Plaza Northeast Chillicothe OH 45601

WALLACE, PAUL FRANCIS, b Tyrone, Pa, June 11, 27; m 52; c 3. SURFACE CHEMISTRY. *Educ:* Pa State Univ, BS, 50, MS, 52. *Prof Exp:* Res asst ceramics, Pa State Univ, 50-52; res engr, Res Labs, Carborundum Co, 52-54; res engr, Alloy Tech Div, 54-70, sr scientist, 70-80, staff scientist, 80-81, TECH SPECIALIST, PROCESS CHEM & PHYSICS DIV, ALCOA RES LABS, ALUMINUM CO AM, 81- *Mem:* Sigma Xi; Am Chem Soc. *Res:* Surface chemistry of aluminum and aluminum alloys as related to fabricating processes and end uses of fabricated products. *Mailing Add:* 200 McLaughlin Dr New Kensington PA 15068

WALLACE, PAUL WILLIAM, b Cork, Ireland, Dec 27, 36; m 64; c 4. MECHANICAL ENGINEERING, MANUFACTURING ENGINEERING. *Educ:* Col Technol, Dublin, BS, 58; Univ Salford, MS, 62; Univ Bristol, PhD(mech eng), 65. *Prof Exp:* Engr, Unidare Ltd, Dublin, 58-60; res asst, Univ Salford, 60-62; res engr, Univ Bristol, 62-65; res metallurgist, IIT Res Inst, Chicago, 65-68; mgr, Mat Develop, 68-69, mgr, Irish Lab, 70-76, DIR RES & DEVELOP, SPS TECHNOL, 76- *Mem:* Inst Mech Engrs, London. *Res:* Mechanics; metallurgy; machine tools; metal working; automatic control; adhesive and mechanical fastening. *Mailing Add:* SPS Technol Jenkintown PA 19046

WALLACE, PHILIP RUSSELL, b Toronto, Ont, Apr 19, 15; m 40; c 3. THEORETICAL PHYSICS. *Educ:* Univ Toronto, BA, 37, MA, 38, PhD, 40. *Prof Exp:* Instr math, Univ Cincinnati, 40-42; instr, Mass Inst Technol, 42; assoc res physicist, Atomic Energy Div, Nat Res Coun, 43-46; from assoc prof to prof appl math, 46-63, dir inst theoret physics, 66-70, PROF PHYSICS, RUTHERFORD PHYSICS BLDG, MCGILL UNIV, 63- *Concurrent Pos:* Mem comn higher educ, Super Coun Educ, Que, 70-73; mem grant selection comt physics, Nat Res Coun Can, 71-74; ed, Can J Physics, 73- *Mem:* Am Phys Soc; Am Asn Physics Teachers; Can Asn Physicists; Europ Phys Soc; fel Royal Soc Can. *Res:* Theoretical and solid state physics; physics of semiconductors and semimetals in intense magnetic fields. *Mailing Add:* Dept of Physics Rutherford Physics Bldg McGill Univ Montreal PQ H3A 2T8 Can

WALLACE, RICHARD KENT, b Washington, DC, Jan 29, 54; m 76; c 1. NUCLEAR ASTROPHYSICS, RADIATION HYDRODYNAMICS. *Educ:* La State Univ, Baton Rouge, BS, 75; Univ Calif, Santa Cruz, MS, 77, PhD(astrophysics), 81. *Prof Exp:* MEM STAFF, LOS ALAMOS NAT LAB, 81- *Mem:* Am Astron Soc. *Res:* Basic thermonuclear burn physics; laser fusion target physics; applications to astrophyscics includes nucleosynthesis and nuclear sources for novae, supernovae and x- and gamma-ray bursts. *Mailing Add:* X-2 MS B-220 Los Alamos Nat Lab Los Alamos NM 87545

WALLACE, RICHARD MAITHA, b Ellwood City, Pa, Sept 29, 21; m 42; c 5. PHYSICAL CHEMISTRY. *Educ:* Bethany Col, WVa, BS, 43; Univ Kans, PhD(chem), 53. *Prof Exp:* Chemist, Hercules Powder Co, 43-45; instr chem, ETenn State Col, 48-50; chemist, 52-62, RES ASSOC, SAVANNAH RIVER LAB, E I DU PONT DE NEMOURS & CO, INC, 62- *Mem:* Am Chem Soc. *Res:* Membrane equilibrium; ruthenium chemistry; nuclear waste disposal; actinide chemistry; uranium geochemistry. *Mailing Add:* Savannah River Lab E I du Pont de Nemours & Co Aiken SC 29801

WALLACE, ROBERT ALLAN, b Chicago, Ill, Aug 23, 30. BIOCHEMISTRY, ORGANIC CHEMISTRY. *Educ:* Northern Ill Univ, BS, 53; Univ Bonn, MS, 57, PhD(org chem), 59. *Prof Exp:* Fel, Calif Inst Technol, 60-62; assoc prof biochem, 62-71, PROF BIOCHEM, HUMBOLDT STATE UNIV, 71- *Mem:* AAAS; Am Chem Soc; Soc Ger Chem; Ger Soc Nature Study. *Res:* Enzyme and pteridine chemistry. *Mailing Add:* Dept of Chem Humboldt State Univ Arcata CA 95521

WALLACE, ROBERT B, b Stoneham, Mass, Jan 16, 37. PSYCHOBIOLOGY, NEUROANATOMY. *Educ:* Boston Univ, AB, 60, AM, 61, PhD(psychol), 66. *Prof Exp:* Instr psychol, 66-67, lectr, 67-68; asst prof, 68-72, ASSOC PROF PSYCHOL, UNIV HARTFORD, 72- *Concurrent Pos:* Res assoc, Mass Inst Technol, 66-68 & Inst Living, 71-; vis assoc prof, Univ Conn Health Ctr, 74-77, res assoc, 78. *Mem:* AAAS; Am Asn Anat; Soc Neurosci; Psychonomic Soc; NY Acad Sci. *Res:* Relation of central nervous system structure to behavior; plasticity of mammalian nervous system; postnatal neurogenesis; neuraltransplantation. *Mailing Add:* Dept of Psychol Univ of Hartford 200 Bloomfield Ave West Hartford CT 06117

WALLACE, ROBERT BRUCE, thoracic surgery, cardiovascular surgery, see previous edition

WALLACE, ROBERT BRUCE, b Vancouver, BC, Jan 28, 50; m 71; c 2. RECOMBINANT DNA. *Educ:* Simon Fraser Univ, BSc, 72; McMaster Univ, PhD(biochem),75. *Prof Exp:* Res asst biol & chem, Simon Fraser Univ, 70; student biochem, McMaster Univ, 71-75, fel, 75; fel biol, Calif Inst Technol, 75-77 & 77-78; ASSOC RES SCIENTIST, DEPT MOLECULAR GENETICS, CITY OF HOPE RES INST, 78- *Concurrent Pos:* Prin investr, NIH, 79- *Mem:* AAAS. *Res:* Molecular basis of human genetic disease; genes of the murine major histocompatibility complex and other multigene families; gene evolution; application of synthetic DNA. *Mailing Add:* Dept Molecular Genetics City of Hope Res Inst Duarte CA 91010

WALLACE, ROBERT EARL, b New York, NY, July 16, 16; m 45; c 1. GEOLOGY. *Educ:* Northwestern Univ, BS, 38; Calif Inst Technol, MS, 40, PhD(struct geol, vert paleont), 46. *Prof Exp:* Geologist, 42-70, chief southwestern br, 60-65, chief, Nat Ctr Earthquake Res, 72-73, regional geologist, 70-73, CHIEF SCIENTIST, OFF EARTHQUAKE STUDIES, US GEOL SURV, 73- *Concurrent Pos:* From asst prof to assoc prof, Wash State Univ, 46-51; vis lectr, Stanford Univ, 60; mem comt seismol, Nat Acad Sci-Nat Res Coun; chmn, US/USSR Environ Agreement, US Working Group Earthquake Prediction; mem eng criteria rev bd, San Francisco Bay Conserv & Develop Comn, 78-, chmn, 81- *Mem:* Fel Geol Soc Am; Soc Econ Geol; Seismol Soc Am; Earthquake Eng Res Inst. *Res:* Active faults; tectonics; earthquakes; engineering geology and environment; mineral deposits. *Mailing Add:* US Geol Surv Menlo Park CA 94025

WALLACE, ROBERT HENRY, b Cleveland, Ohio. MEDICAL PHYSICS. *Educ:* Transylvania Col, BA, 64; Purdue Univ, West Lafayette, MS, 68, PhD(bionucleonics), 70. *Prof Exp:* Assoc radiol health physicist, Ky State Dept Health, 65-66; ASST PROF RADIOL, ALBANY MED COL, 70-,

RADIATION PHYSICIST, ALBANY MED CTR HOSP, 70- *Mem:* Am Asn Physicists in Med; Health Physics Soc. *Res:* Radiation dosimetry and protection; nuclear medicine instrumentation. *Mailing Add:* 186 Second Ave N Troy NY 12180

WALLACE, ROBERT WILLIAM, b Central Falls, RI, Jan 1, 43; m 65; c 2. SCIENCE EDUCATION, ENVIRONMENTAL CHEMISTRY. *Educ:* Providence Col, BS, 64; Niagara Univ, MS, 66; Boston Univ, PhD(chem), 73. *Prof Exp:* ASST PROF CHEM, BENTLEY COL, 72- *Mem:* Am Chem Soc; AAAS. *Res:* Air and water quality as well as the quality of consumer products, including chemical composition versus the list of ingredients. *Mailing Add:* 19 Coolidge Ave Westford MA 01886

WALLACE, ROBIN A, b Chicago, Ill, Nov 11, 33; m 55; c 2. REPRODUCTIVE BIOLOGY. *Educ:* Columbia Univ, BA, 55, PhD(zool), 61. *Prof Exp:* Res assoc, Sloan-Kettering Inst, NY, 57; consult, Oak Ridge Nat Lab, 60-61, USPHS fel, 61-63, staff mem biol div, 63-81; MEM STAFF ANAT DEPT, COL MED, UNIV FLA, GAINESVILLE, 81- *Concurrent Pos:* Vis investr, Nat Res Coun Can, 63-64; mem, Marine Biol Lab Corp; dir reprod biol prog, Marine Biol Lab, Woods Hole, 74 & 75; co-ed, Develop Biol, 72-74; mem develop biol panel, NSF, 75-76. *Mem:* AAAS; Am Soc Cell Biol; Soc Develop Biol; Fedn Am Sci; Soc Gen Physiol. *Res:* Comparative biochemical studies on yolk proteins and the mechanisms of oocyte growth. *Mailing Add:* Dept Anat Col Med Univ Fla Gainsville FL 32610

WALLACE, RONALD GARY, b Cadiz, Ohio, July 6, 38; m 65; c 1. GEOMORPHOLOGY. *Educ:* Kent State Univ, BS, 61; Ohio State Univ, MS, 64, PhD(geol), 67. *Prof Exp:* Petroleum geologist, Standard Oil Co, Tex, 67-69; asst prof geol, Ohio State Univ, 69-70; ASST PROF GEOL, EASTERN ILL UNIV, 70- *Mem:* Geol Soc Am. *Res:* Alpine mass movement; strip mine erosion. *Mailing Add:* Dept of Geog & Geol Eastern Ill Univ Charleston IL 61920

WALLACE, RONALD RICHARD, fresh water ecology, see previous edition

WALLACE, SIDNEY, b Philadelphia, Pa, Feb 26, 29; m; c 3. RADIOLOGY. *Educ:* Temple Univ, BA, 49, MD, 54; Am Bd Radiol, dipl, 62. *Prof Exp:* Intern, Philadelphia Gen Hosp, 54-55; resident radiol, Hosp, Jefferson Med Col, 59-62, from instr to asst prof, Col, 62-66; assoc prof, 66-69, prof, 69-80, ASHBEL SMITH PROF RADIOL, UNIV TEX M D ANDERSON HOSP & TUMOR INST HOUSTON, 80- *Concurrent Pos:* Fel radiol, Univ Lund, 63-64. *Mem:* AMA; Am Col Radiol; Int Soc Lymphology. *Res:* Lymphangiography and angiography. *Mailing Add:* M D Anderson Hosp & Tumor Inst 6723 Bertner Ave Houston TX 77025

WALLACE, STEPHEN JOSEPH, b Youngstown, Ohio, May 10, 39; m 61; c 2. THEORETICAL NUCLEAR PHYSICS. *Educ:* Case Inst Technol, BS, 61; Univ Wash, MS, 69, PhD(physics), 71. *Prof Exp:* Res engr, Boeing Co, 61-68; res asst physics, Univ Wash, 68-71; res assoc, Univ Fla, 71-72 & Harvard Univ, 72-74; from asst prof to assoc prof, 74-82, PROF PHYSICS, UNIV MD, COLLEGE PARK, 82- *Mem:* Am Phys Soc. *Res:* Intermediate to high energy nuclear multiple scattering theory; Eikonal expansion methods. *Mailing Add:* Dept Physics & Astron Univ Md College Park MD 20742

WALLACE, STEWART RAYNOR, b Freeport, NY, Mar 31, 19; m 46; c 2. GEOLOGY. *Educ:* Dartmouth Col, BA, 41; Univ Mich, MS, 48, PhD(geol), 53. *Prof Exp:* Geologist, US Geol Surv, 48-55; resident geologist, Climax Molybdenum Co, 55-58, chief geologist, 58-64, chief geol & explor, 64-69; pres & dir explor, Mine Finders, Inc, 70-75; CONSULT, 76- *Honors & Awards:* D C Jackling Award, Am Inst Mining, Metal & Petrol Engrs, 74. *Mem:* Geol Soc Am; Geochem Soc; Am Inst Mining, Metall & Petrol Engrs; Soc Econ Geol; Asn Explor Geochemists. *Res:* Genesis of metallic ore deposits; igneous and metamorphic structure and petrology related to ore deposits. *Mailing Add:* 8700 W 14th Ave Lakewood CO 80215

WALLACE, SUSAN SCHOLES, b Brooklyn, NY, Jan 10, 38; m 60; c 3. MOLECULAR BIOLOGY, BIOPHYSICS. *Educ:* Marymount Col, NY, BS, 59; Univ Calif, Berkeley, MS, 61; Cornell Univ, PhD(biophys), 65. *Prof Exp:* USPHS fel, Columbia Univ, 65-67; instr biol sci, Lehman Col, 67-68, asst prof, 69-73, assoc prof, 73-76; assoc prof, 76-79, PROF MICROBIOL, NY MED COL, 79- *Concurrent Pos:* City Univ New York res grant, Lehman Col, 68-76, NIH res grant, 72-; vis prof, Albert Einstein Col Med, 74-75; scholar, Am Cancer Soc, 74-75; mem, NIH Radiation Study Sect, 77-81. *Mem:* AAAS; Biophys Soc; Radiation Res Soc; Am Soc Microbiologists; Am Soc Biol Chemists. *Res:* Radiation repair processes in bacteria and bacteriophages; in vivo and in vitro enzymatic repair of ionizing radiation damage. *Mailing Add:* Dept Microbiol NY Med Col Valhalla NY 10595

WALLACE, TERRY CHARLES, b Phoenix, Ariz, May 18, 33; m 55; c 5. MATERIALS CHEMISTRY, CHEMICAL TECHNOLOGY. *Educ:* Ariz State Univ, BS, 55; Iowa State Univ, PhD(phys chem), 58. *Prof Exp:* Mem staff, 58-70, alt group leader, 70-79, GROUP LEADER, LOS ALAMOS NAT LAB, UNIV CALIF, 79- *Concurrent Pos:* Chief tech projs br, Environ Test Div, Dugway Proving Ground. *Mem:* AAAS; Am Chem Soc. *Res:* Structural properties and mass transport of materials at high temperature; materials synthesis; materials characterrization; high temperature thermodynamics; chemical vapor deposition; modeling of high temperature chemical processes. *Mailing Add:* Los Alamos Nat Labs CMB-3/MS-348 PO Box 1663 Los Alamos NM 87544

WALLACE, THOMAS PATRICK, b Washington, DC, Apr 11, 35; m 59; c 3. PHYSICAL CHEMISTRY, POLYMER SCIENCE. *Educ:* State Univ NY Col Potsdam, BS, 58; Syracuse Univ, MS, 61; St Lawrence Univ, MS, 64; Clarkson Col Technol, PhD(phys chem), 68. *Prof Exp:* Asst prof chem, State Univ NY Col Potsdam, 61-67; from asst prof to prof chem, Rochester Inst Technol, 68-78, head, Dept Chem, 70-72, assoc dean, Col Sci, 72-73, dean, Col Sci, 73-78; PROF CHEM SCI & DEAN, SCH SCI & HEALTH PROF, OLD DOMINION UNIV, NORFOLK, VA, 78- *Mem:* AAAS; Am Chem Soc; NY Acad Sci; Sigma Xi. *Res:* Light scattering; polymer latex systems and characterization; size distribution analysis; statistical thermodynamics of dilute polymer solutions. *Mailing Add:* Sch Sci & Health Prof Old Dominion Univ Norfolk VA 23508

WALLACE, TRACY I, b Irvine, Ky, Nov 20, 24; m 51; c 3. INTERNAL MEDICINE. *Educ:* Univ Ky, BS, 46; Univ Cincinnati, MD, 49. *Prof Exp:* Staff physician, Vet Admin Hosp, McKinney, Tex, 55-57, asst chief med serv, 57-59, CHIEF MED SERV, TEMPLE VET ADMIN HOSP, 61- *Mem:* AMA. *Res:* Adrenal function in patients with pulmonary emphysema and other hypoxic states. *Mailing Add:* 3609 Deer Tr Temple TX 76501

WALLACE, VICTOR LEW, b Brooklyn, NY, Mar 20, 33; m 62; c 2. COMPUTER SCIENCE. *Educ:* Polytech Inst Brooklyn, BS, 55; Univ Mich, PhD(elec eng), 69. *Prof Exp:* Mem tech staff syst eng, Bell Tel Labs, 55-56; mathematician-programmer, IBM Corp, 56-57; instr elec eng, Univ Mich, 57-62; assoc res scientist, 62-69; assoc prof comput sci, Univ NC, 69-76; PROF & CHMN COMPUT SCI, UNIV KANS, 76- *Concurrent Pos:* Vis scientist, Imp Col, Univ London, 70. *Mem:* Asn Comput Mach; Inst Elec & Electronics Engrs; Inst Mgt Sci; Am Asn Univ Profs. *Res:* Computer system modeling; operating system theory; computer graphics software; man-machine interface in computer-aided design. *Mailing Add:* Dept of Comput Sci Strong Hall Univ of Kans Lawrence KS 66044

WALLACE, VOLNEY, b Idaho Falls, Idaho, Oct 9, 25; m 44; c 5. AGRICULTURAL CHEMISTRY. *Educ:* Univ Idaho, BS, 46; Purdue Univ, MS, 49, PhD(agr chem), 53. *Prof Exp:* Asst agr chem, Purdue Univ, 47-53; res assoc, Wash State Univ, 53-55; asst prof biochem, SDak State Col, 55-61; RES CHEMIST, DUGWAY PROVING GROUND, 61- *Concurrent Pos:* Vpres, Terracopia. *Mem:* Am Chem Soc. *Res:* Geo-agricultural and analytical chemistry; environmental energy and gardening. *Mailing Add:* Box 1 West Terra Dugway UT 84022

WALLACE, WILLIAM, b Manchester, Eng, Oct 15, 40; m 64; c 3. MATERIALS ENGINEERING, METALLURGY. *Educ:* Manchester Univ, BSc, 63; Victoria Univ Manchester, PhD(metall), 66. *Prof Exp:* Lectr, John Dalton Col Technol, 66-67; asst res officer, 67-70, assoc res officer, 70-76, head, Mat Sect, 76-81, HEAD, STRUCT & MAT LAB, NAT AERONAUT ESTAB CAN, NAT RES COUN CAN, 81- *Concurrent Pos:* Hon adj prof, Dept Mech & Aeronaut Eng, Carleton Univ, Ottawa. *Mem:* Inst Metals; Inst Metallurgists; Am Soc Metals. *Res:* Metal processing; powder metallurgy; isothermal and superplastic forging; mechanical behavior, creep, fatigue, and fracture. *Mailing Add:* Struct & Mat Lab Montreal Rd Ottawa ON K1A 0R6 Can

WALLACE, WILLIAM DONALD, b Detroit, Mich, Sept 19, 33. SOLID STATE PHYSICS. *Educ:* Eastern Mich Univ, BA, 55; Univ Md, College Park, MS, 60; Wayne State Univ, PhD(physics), 66. *Prof Exp:* Asst prof physics, Eastern Mich Univ, 59-62; res asst, Cornell Univ, 67-70; asst prof, 70-74, ASSOC PROF PHYSICS, OAKLAND UNIV, 74- *Concurrent Pos:* Leverhulme vis fel, Univ Essex, 66-67. *Mem:* AAAS; Am Phys Soc; Am Asn Physics Teachers. *Res:* Ultrasonic properties and magnetic properties of solids; metals and low temperature physics. *Mailing Add:* Dept of Physics Oakland Univ Rochester MI 48063

WALLACE, WILLIAM EDWARD, b Fayette, Miss, Mar 11, 17; m 47; c 3. SOLID STATE CHEMISTRY. *Educ:* Miss Col, BA, 36; Univ Pittsburgh, PhD(chem), 41. *Prof Exp:* Asst, Univ Pittsburgh, 36-40; Carnegie Found fel, 40-42, sr res fel, 42-44; res assoc, Ohio State Univ, 44-45; from asst res prof to assoc res prof chem, 45-53, chmn dept, 63-77, PROF CHEM, UNIV PITTSBURGH, 53-, DISTINGUISHED SERV PROF, 77- *Mem:* AAAS; Am Chem Soc. *Res:* Magnetic behavior and hydrogen absorption of intermetallic compounds containing lanthanides; photoelectrolysis of water and solar energy utilization; heterogeneous catalysis and surface science. *Mailing Add:* Dept of Chem Univ of Pittsburgh Pittsburgh PA 15213

WALLACE, WILLIAM EDWARD, JR, b Charleston, WVa, Sept 25, 42; m 70; c 1. CHEMICAL PHYSICS, BIOPHYSICS. *Educ:* WVa Univ, BS, 63, MS, 67, PhD(physics), 69. *Prof Exp:* Nat Res Coun-US Bur Mines res assoc, Morgantown Energy Res Ctr, US Bur Mines, 70-71, res physicist, 71-74, SUPVRY RES PHYSICIST, MORGANTOWN ENERGY RES CTR, US ENERGY RES & DEVELOP ADMIN, 74- *Res:* Chemical and surface physics studies of solids removal from coal derived liquids; biophysics studies of pulmonary surfactant interactions with solids. *Mailing Add:* Morgantown Energy Res Ctr US Energy Res & Develop Admin Morgantown WV 26505

WALLACE, WILLIAM ELDRED, b Wichita, Kans, Feb 8, 17; m 41; c 3. CHEMISTRY. *Educ:* Univ Wichita, BS, 50; Univ Ill, MS, 42, PhD(org chem), 44. *Prof Exp:* Res chemist, Chem Div, GAF Corp, 44-78; mem staff, BASF Wyandotte, 78-80; RETIRED. *Mem:* Am Chem Soc; Am Asn Textile Chemists & Colorists. *Res:* Grignard reaction; Friedel-Crafts reaction; synthetic organic chemicals; azoic dyes; synthetic dyestuffs. *Mailing Add:* RD 1 Box 190A Rensselaer NY 12144

WALLACE, WILLIAM J, b Knoxville, Tenn, July 27, 35; m 58; c 2. INORGANIC CHEMISTRY. *Educ:* Carson-Newman Col, BS, 56; Purdue Univ, PhD(inorg chem), 61. *Prof Exp:* Asst prof inorg chem, Univ Miss, 60-63; from asst prof to assoc prof inorg & phys chem, 63-72, actg chmn dep, 68-69, coordr, Sci Div, 72-76, PROF INORG & PHYS CHEM, MUSKINGUM COL, 72- *Concurrent Pos:* Res grants, Res Corp, 61-63; res grants, Am Acad Arts & Sci, 62-63; dir, NSF Res Partic High Sch Teachers, 66, 67 & 68; res fel with P S Braterman, Univ Glasgow, 70-71; fac fel & res grants, Lewis Res Ctr, NASA, 78-80. *Mem:* AAAS; Am Chem Soc. *Res:* Study of systems using polyether solvents with inorganic compounds, especially solubility, reaction and spectral phenomena; iron carbonyl reactions with Lewis bases; electrocatalysis of chronium; reduction in flow cell. *Mailing Add:* Dept Chem Muskingum Col New Concord OH 43762

WALLACE, WILLIAM JAMES LORD, b Salisbury, NC, Jan 13, 08; m 29; c 1. PHYSICAL CHEMISTRY. *Educ:* Univ Pittsburgh, BS, 27; Columbia Univ, AM, 31; Cornell Univ, PhD(phys chem), 37; Livingstone Col, LLD, 59; Concord Col, LHD, 70; Alderson Broaddus Col, DSc, 71. *Prof Exp:* Instr chem, Livingston Col, 27-32; instr, Lincoln Univ, Mo, 32-33; instr, 33-34, from asst prof to assoc prof, 34-43, prof, 43-75, actg admin asst to pres, 44-45, admin asst, 45-50, actg pres, 52-53, pres, 53-73, EMER PRES, WVA STATE COL, 73- *Honors & Awards:* Outstanding Civilian Serv Medal, Dept Army, 72; Annual Award, Educ Comn States, 75. *Mem:* Am Chem Soc. *Res:* Freezing points of aqueous solutions of alpha amino acids; teaching problems in general chemistry. *Mailing Add:* WVa State Col PO Box 416 Institute WV 25112

WALLACE-HAAGENS, MARY JEAN, endocrinology, reproductive physiology, see previous edition

WALLACH, DONALD P, b New York, NY, Sept 16, 27; m 51. BIOCHEMISTRY, PHARMACOLOGY. *Educ:* Mich State Univ, BS, 47, MS, 48; Univ Wis, PhD(pharmacol), 53. *Prof Exp:* RES ASSOC PHARMACOL, UPJOHN CO, 56- *Concurrent Pos:* Fel pharmacol, Alumni Res Found, Univ Wis, 53-54; USPHS fel enzyme chem, Univ Kans Med Ctr, Kansas City, 54-56. *Mem:* Am Soc Pharmacol & Exp Therapeut; Am Soc Biol Chem. *Res:* Applications of enzymology to problems in pharmacology. *Mailing Add:* Upjohn Co Dept of Exp Biol 301 Henrietta St Kalamazoo MI 49001

WALLACH, EDWARD E, b Brooklyn, NY, Oct 8, 33; m 56; c 2. OBSTETRICS & GYNECOLOGY. *Educ:* Swarthmore Col, BA, 54; Cornell Univ, MD, 58. *Prof Exp:* Intern internal med, Cornell Med Div, Bellevue Hosp, New York, 58-59; resident obstet & gynec, Kings County Hosp, 59-63; assoc, 65-66, from asst prof to assoc prof, 66-71, PROF OBSTET & GYNEC, SCH MED, UNIV PA, 71-; DIR OBSTET & GYNEC, PA HOSP, 71- *Concurrent Pos:* Res fel reprod physiol, Worcester Found Exp Biol, 61-62; Josiah Macy, Jr Found fel, 65-; Lalor Found awards, 67-69. *Mem:* Am Col Obstetricians & Gynecologists; Soc Gynec Invest; Am Fertil Soc; Soc Study Reprod; Endocrine Soc. *Res:* Reproductive biology; ovarian physiology; gynecologic endocrinology; infertility; family planning. *Mailing Add:* Dept of Obstet & Gynec Pa Hosp Philadelphia PA 19107

WALLACH, JACQUES BURTON, b New York, NY, Jan 25, 26; m 53; c 3. MEDICINE, PATHOLOGY. *Educ:* Long Island Col Med, MD, 47; Am Bd Path, dipl, 55. *Prof Exp:* From instr to asst prof, 54-59, VIS ASST PROF PATH, ALBERT EINSTEIN COL MED, 59-; CLIN PROF PATH, STATE UNIV NY DOWNSTATE MED CTR, BROOKLYN, 79- *Concurrent Pos:* Resident fel & asst pathologist, Queens Gen Hosp Ctr, New York, 48-55; asst vis pathologist, Bronx Munic Hosp Ctr, 54-59; consult, NY Zool Park, 54-; vis asst prof, Rutgers Med Sch, Col Med & Dent NJ, 69-72, vis assoc prof, 72- *Mem:* Fel Am Soc Clin Path; fel Col Am Path; fel Am Col Physicians; NY Acad Sci. *Res:* Rheumatic heart disease; clinical pathology; comparative pathology; histochemistry; cardiology; cancer; computers in interpretative medical laboratory reporting. *Mailing Add:* 18 Dartmouth Rd Cranford NJ 07016

WALLACH, MARSHALL BEN, b Buffalo, NY, June 15, 42; m 63; c 3. NEUROPHARMACOLOGY. *Educ:* Columbia Univ, BS, 62; Univ Minn, PhD(pharmacol), 67. *Prof Exp:* Assoc res scientist neuropharmacol, Dept Psychiat, Med Ctr, NY Univ, 68-70, res scientist, 70-71, instr, 71-72; staff researcher II, 73-76, sr staff researcher, 76-79, PRIN SCIENTIST, SYNTEX RES, 79- *Concurrent Pos:* Consult, New York City Rand Inst, 71-72. *Mem:* AAAS; Am Soc Exp Pharmacol & Therapeut; Western Pharmacology Soc. *Res:* Models of psychiatric and neurological diseases; electrophysiology of sleep; neurohumoral mechanisms; anorexigens; antidepressants; neuroleptics; analgesics; antiparkinsonian agents; anticonvulsants; antitussives and psychotomimetic agents. *Mailing Add:* Dept Exp Pharmacol Syntex Res 3401 Hillview Ave Palo Alto CA 94304

WALLACH, STANLEY, b Brooklyn, NY, Dec 10, 28; m 54, 73; c 3. MEDICINE. *Educ:* Cornell Univ, AB, 48; Columbia Univ, MA, 49; State Univ NY Downstate Med Ctr, MD, 53. *Prof Exp:* Intern med, Univ Med Serv, Kings County Hosp, Brooklyn, 53-54; resident, Col Med, Univ Utah, 54-56; clin & res fel, Mass Gen Hosp, 56-57; from instr to prof, State Univ NY Downstate Med Ctr, 57-73, prog dir, USPHS Clin Res Ctr, 66-73; PROF MED & ASST CHMN DEPT, ALBANY MED COL, 73-; CHIEF MED, VET ADMIN MED CTR, 73- *Concurrent Pos:* Vis physician, Kings County Hosp, Brooklyn, 57-73; career scientist, Health Res Coun City of New York, 61-71; consult, St Johns Episcopal Hosp, Brooklyn, 65-73; attend physician, State Univ Hosp, Brooklyn, 66-73; consult & lectr, US Naval Hosp, St Albans, NY, 66-73; attend, physician, Albany Med Ctr, 73-; res collabr, Med Dept, Brookhaven Nat Lab, 69- *Honors & Awards:* Hektoen Silver Award, AMA, 59. *Mem:* Endocrine Soc; Am Soc Clin Invest; Am Fedn Clin Res; Harvey Soc; fel Am Col Physicians. *Res:* Endocrine and metabolic diseases; radioisotopes; calcium, magnesium and mineral metabolism; metabolic bone disease. *Mailing Add:* Vet Admin Med Ctr Albany NY 12208

WALLACH, SYLVAN, b San Antonio, Tex, Jan 9, 14; m 38; c 5. MATHEMATICS. *Educ:* Rutgers Univ, BS, 34; Johns Hopkins Univ, PhD(math), 48. *Prof Exp:* Chemist Mass & Waldstein Co, NJ, 36-38; patent examr, US Patent Off, Washington, DC, 38-42; indust analyst, War Prod Bd, 42-45; instr math, Johns Hopkins Univ, 48-49; sr scientist atomic power div, Westinghouse Elec Corp, 49-52; sr scientist, Walter Kidde Nuclear Labs, Inc, 52-57; asst proj mgr, Gibbs & Cox, Inc, 57-61; chmn dept math, 62-72, PROF MATH, C W POST COL, LI UNIV, 62- *Mem:* AAAS; Am Math Soc; Math Asn Am. *Mailing Add:* 101 Central Park W 12A New York NY 10023

WALLACK, PAUL MARK, b Girard, Kans, Aug 3, 27; m 50, 80; c 6. INDUSTRIAL ENGINEERING. *Educ:* Univ Tulsa, BS, 50; Okla State Univ, MS, 56, PhD(indust eng), 67. *Prof Exp:* Div engr, Pure Oil Co, 50-55; supvr, Sandia Labs, 56-59; asst prof, Ariz State Univ, 59-62; assoc prof, Kans State Univ, 62-64; supvr, Space Div, Rockwell Corp, 64-67; staff specialist, Autonetics Div, 67-69, mgr prod eng, 69-74, mgr indust eng, Admiral Div, 74-75, staff specialist, Strategic Systs Div, 76-78, MGR, AUTONETICS STRATEGIC SYSTS DIV, ROCKWELL INT, 78- *Concurrent Pos:* Dir, Traveling Sci Inst, Ariz Acad Sci, 60-62; consult, Sandia Corp, 63; lectr, Calif State Univ, Fullerton, 72-74 & 79-80. *Mem:* Am Inst Indust Engrs; Am Soc Qual Control. *Res:* Production design economics and forecasting; sources and statistics associated with inspector error; organization behavior and the management process. *Mailing Add:* 2306 Arbutus St Newport Beach CA 92660

WALLANDER, JEROME F, b Cato, Wis, Aug 29, 39; m 65; c 3. FOOD SCIENCE, BIOCHEMISTRY. *Educ:* Univ Wis, BS, 62, MS, 65, PhD(food sci), 68. *Prof Exp:* Sr scientist, Mead Johnson Nutritionals, 67-71, ASSOC DIR FOOD PROD DEVELOP, MEAD JOHNSON & CO, 71- *Mem:* Sigma Xi; Am Dairy Sci Asn; Inst Food Technol. *Res:* Milk lipase and milk protein studies. *Mailing Add:* Food Prod Develop Mead Johnson & Co Evansville IN 47721

WALLBANK, ALFRED MILLS, b Farmington, Mich, May 13, 25; m 49; c 3. VIROLOGY. *Educ:* Mich State Univ, BS, 48, MS, 53, PhD, 57. *Prof Exp:* Bacteriologist, Barry Labs, Inc, Mich, 48-50; bacteriologist, Blood Sterilization Proj, Henry Ford Hosp, Detroit, 50-52; asst microbiol & pub health, Mich State Univ, 53-56; res assoc & microbiologist, Dept Surg, Duke Univ, 56-59; res asst prof microbiol & virologist, Sch Vet Med, Univ Pa, 59-66; head dept virol, Va Inst Sci Res, 66-67; ASSOC PROF MICROBIOL, MED COL, UNIV MAN, 67- *Mem:* Am Soc Microbiol; Am Asn Cancer Res; Can Col Microbiologists; Tissue Cult Asn; Am Acad Microbiol. *Res:* Virucides, disinfectants and biohazards. *Mailing Add:* Dept of Med Microbiol Univ of Man Med Col Winnipeg MB R3E 0W3 Can

WALLBRUNN, HENRY MAURICE, b Chicago, Ill, Apr 30, 18; m 53; c 4. ZOOLOGY. *Educ:* Univ Chicago, BS, 40, PhD, 51. *Prof Exp:* Instr zool, Univ Chicago, 50; asst prof biol, 51-62, ASSOC PROF ZOOL, UNIV FLA, 63- *Concurrent Pos:* Fel statist & zool, Univ Chicago, 53-54. *Mem:* Genetics Soc Am; Soc Study Evolution. *Res:* Genetics; genetics and evolution of orchids. *Mailing Add:* Dept of Zool Univ of Fla Gainesville FL 32611

WALLCAVE, LAWRENCE, b Schenectady, NY, Apr 21, 26; m 65. BIOCHEMISTRY. *Educ:* Univ Calif, Berkeley, BS, 48; Calif Inst Technol, PhD, 53. *Prof Exp:* Assoc prof biochem, Eppley Inst Med Ctr, Univ Nebr, Omaha, 68-74, res prof, 74-81; CONSULT, CALSEC CONSULTS, INC, BERKELEY, CALIF, 81- *Res:* Chemical carcinogenesis; analytical biochemistry. *Mailing Add:* 6578 Birch Dr Santa Rosa CA 95404

WALLEIGH, ROBERT S(HULER), b Washington, DC, Mar 31, 15; m 38; c 2. ELECTRICAL ENGINEERING. *Educ:* George Washington Univ, BS, 36. *Prof Exp:* Test engr, Gen Elec Co, 36-37; lighting & power apparatus specialist, Gen Elec Supply Corp, DC, 37-38; rating exam, US Civil Serv Comn, 38-39, secy, Bd US Civil Serv Exam, US Pub Rd Admin, 39-43; elec engr, Lab, Nat Bur Standards, 43, phys sci adminr, 43-53; phys sci adminr, Diamond Ord Fuze Labs, Ord Corps, US Dept Army, 53-55; assoc dir admin, 55-74, actg dep dir, 75-78, SR ADV INT AFFAIRS, NAT BUR STANDARDS, 78- *Concurrent Pos:* Consult, Inst Elec & Electronics Engrs, 79- *Honors & Awards:* Gold Medal, Dept Com, 67. *Mem:* AAAS; Inst Elec & Electronics Engrs. *Res:* Radio; illumination engineering; electric apparatus and machinery; electronics management. *Mailing Add:* 5701 Springfield Dr Bethesda MD 20816

WALLEN, CLARENCE JOSEPH, b Phoenix, Ariz, Oct 17, 16. MATHEMATICS. *Educ:* St Louis Univ, BA, 45, MS, 46, PhD(math), 56; Alma Col, STL, 52. *Prof Exp:* Instr math, 46-48 & 56-57, from asst prof to assoc prof, 57-70, chmn dept, 70-73, PROF MATH, LOYOLA MARYMOUNT UNIV, LOS ANGELES, 70-, MEM BD TRUSTEES, 67- *Mem:* AAAS; Am Math Soc; Math Asn Am. *Res:* Limit theory in mathematics. *Mailing Add:* Dept of Math Loyola Marymount Univ 7101 W 80th Los Angeles CA 90045

WALLEN, CYNTHIA ANNE, b Asheville, NC, June 27, 52. CELL KINETICS, RADIOBIOLOGY. *Educ:* Univ NC, BA, 74; Univ Rochester, MS, 78, PhD(biophysics), 80. *Prof Exp:* Fel, 80-81, RES ASSOC, UNIV UTAH, 81- *Mem:* Radiation Res Soc; Sigma Xi. *Res:* Development of proliferating and quiescent subpopulations in tumors, and the control of these populations and their interactions with various anti-tumor therapies such as radiation, heat and drugs. *Mailing Add:* Dept Radiol Univ Utah Salt Lake City UT 84132

WALLEN, DONALD GEORGE, b Ont, Can, July 6, 33; m 65; c 2. ECOLOGY, CELL PHYSIOLOGY. *Educ:* Dalhousie Univ, BS, 61, MEd, 62; Simon Fraser Univ, MS, 67, PhD(algal physiol & ecol), 70. *Prof Exp:* asst prof, 70-75, ASSOC PROF BIOL, UNIV WINDSOR, 75- *Mem:* Am Soc Limnol & Oceanog; Phycol Soc Am; Can Soc Plant Physiol; Int Asn Theoret Appl Limnol. *Res:* Interrelationship between light quality, intensity and temperature on growth, photosynthesis and metabolism of algae; toxic substances, polychlorinated biphenyl and actachlorostyrene in lakes Erie and St Clair; heterotrophic utiization of amino acids by algae. *Mailing Add:* Dept of Biol Univ of Windsor Windsor ON N9B 3P4 Can

WALLEN, IRVIN EUGENE, oceanography, see previous edition

WALLEN, LOWELL LAWRENCE, b Rockford, Ill, May 22, 21; m 49; c 2. BIO-ORGANIC CHEMISTRY. *Educ:* Wheaton Col, Ill, BS, 44; Univ Ark, MS, 48; Iowa State Col, PhD, 54. *Prof Exp:* Asst chemist, Goodyear Tire & Rubber Co, Ohio, 44-46; asst, Univ Ark, 46-48; asst, Iowa State Col, 51-54; BIOCHEMIST, NORTHERN REGIONAL RES CTR, USDA, 54- *Mem:* Am Chem Soc; Coblentz Soc; Am Oil Chem Soc. *Res:* Chemistry of fermentation products; microbiological type reactions; oxidation; reduction; fermentations; chemical structure elucidation; bio-organic chemistry; infrared spectroscopy; fatty acid chemistry; mycotoxin chemistry. *Mailing Add:* 2929 N Gale Ave Peoria IL 61604

WALLEN, STANLEY EUGENE, b Lincoln, Nebr, Jan 31, 48; m 70; c 2. DAIRY SCIENCE, FOOD SAFETY. *Educ:* Univ Nebr, BS, 69; Iowa State Univ, PhD(food technol statist), 76. *Prof Exp:* Vet food inspector, US Army, 69-72; grad res & teaching asst, Dept Food Technol, Iowa State Univ, 72-76; food technologist, Res & Develop Command, US Army, 76-77; EXTEN FOOD SCIENTIST, DEPT FOOD SCI TECHNOL, UNIV NEBR, LINCOLN, 77- *Mem:* Inst Food Technologists; Int Asn Milk, Food & Environ Sanitarians; Am Dairy Sci Asn. *Res:* Milk quality: factors affecting iodine concentration, beta-carotene concentration, somatic cell count, bacteria count and flavor of milk; mastitis control in dairy cattle. *Mailing Add:* Dept Food Sci & Technol 134 Filley Hall Univ Nebr Lincoln NE 68583

WALLEN, VICTOR REID, plant pathology, see previous edition

WALLENBERGER, FREDERICK THEODORE, b St Peter, Austria, Aug 28, 30; nat US. ORGANIC POLYMER CHEMISTRY. *Educ:* Fordham Univ, MS, 56, PhD(chem), 58. *Prof Exp:* Instr chem, Fordham Univ, 57-58; res fel, Harvard Univ, 58-59; res chemist pioneerins res div, 59-63, res supvr, Carothers Res Lab, Nylon Tech Div, 63-69, res supvr, Textile Res Lab, 68-72, prod develop supvr, Cristina Lab, res supvr, Textile Res Lab, 72-78, RES ASSOC, TEXTILE FIBERS DEPT, E I DU PONT DE NEMOURS & CO, INC, 78- *Concurrent Pos:* Gen chmn 5th mid Atlantic regional meeting, Am Chem Soc, 70, chmn 1st conf chem & environ, 70; lectr, Fiber Soc, 80-81. *Honors & Awards:* Gordon Conf lectr, 64 & 75. *Mem:* AAAS; Am Chem Soc; NY Acad Sci; Am Asn Textile Chemists & Colorists. *Res:* Organic polymer synthesis; new carpet fibers; textile technology; kinetics; ozonization; high performance fibers; foam and pneumacel technology. *Mailing Add:* Textile Fibers Dept E I du Pont de Nemours & Co Inc Wilmington DE 19898

WALLENFELDT, EVERT, b Stanton, Iowa, June 26, 04; m 28; c 2. FOOD SCIENCE. *Educ:* Iowa State Col, BS, 26; Cornell Univ, MS, 29. *Prof Exp:* Instr high sch, Wis, 26-28; dairy fieldman, Borden Farm Prod Co, Ill, 29-31, supvr spec prod & tech probs, 31-34; supvr, Borden-Wieland Co, 34-37; res bacteriologist, Borden Co, 37-38; prof dairy indust, 38-70, EMER PROF FOOD SCI, UNIV WIS-MADISON, 70- *Mem:* AAAS; Am Dairy Sci Asn; Nat Environ Health Asn; Int Asn Milk, Food & Environ Sanitarians. *Res:* Market milk; butter manufacturing; concentrated milks and related products. *Mailing Add:* Dept of Food Sci Univ of Wis Madison WI 53706

WALLENFELS, MIKLOS, b Budapest, Hungary, July 14, 34; US citizen; m 57; c 2. MECHANICAL ENGINEERING. *Educ:* Budapest Tech Univ, BS, 56; Univ Buffalo, MS, 62. *Prof Exp:* Engr, 59-62, res engr, 62-69, SR ENGR, YERKES RES & DEVELOP, E I DU PONT DE NEMOURS & CO, INC, 69- *Mem:* Soc Plastics Engrs. *Res:* Process development for manufacturing and coating thermoplastic films. *Mailing Add:* Yerkes Plant Sta B Buffalo NY 14207

WALLENIUS, ROGER WYNN, b Baltimore, Md, Oct 21, 41; m 68; c 2. ANIMAL NUTRITION. *Educ:* Pa State Univ, BS, 63; Ohio State Univ, MS, 65, PhD(animal nutrit), 69. *Prof Exp:* asst prof animal sci, Wash State Univ, 70-80. *Mem:* Am Dairy Sci Asn; Am Soc Animal Sci. *Res:* Ruminant nutrition; nutritional aspects of maximizing production in dairy cattle. *Mailing Add:* 13817 Thomas Ave S Burnsville MN 55337

WALLENMEYER, WILLIAM ANTON, b Evansville, Ind, Feb 3, 26; m 52; c 4. HIGH ENERGY PHYSICS. *Educ:* Purdue Univ, BS, 50, MS, 54, PhD(physics), 57. *Prof Exp:* Asst physics, Purdue Univ, 50-54 & 56; jr res assoc high energy particle interactions, Brookhaven Nat Lab, 54-55; asst prof physics, Wabash Col, 55-56; physicist, Midwestern Univs Res Asn, Wis, 56-60, div dir particle accelerators, 60-62; physicist res div, US AEC, 62-66, asst dir high energy physics, 66-75, asst dir, 75-77, DIR HIGH ENERGY PHYSICS, DIV PHYS RES, US ENERGY RES & DEVELOP ADMIN, 77- *Mem:* AAAS; fel Am Phys Soc. *Res:* elementary particle physics; accelerator physics. *Mailing Add:* Div Phys Res Energy Res & Develop Admin Washington DC 20545

WALLENTINE, MAX V, b Paris, Idaho, Apr 19, 31; m 53; c 8. ANIMAL SCIENCE. *Educ:* Utah State Univ, BS, 55; Cornell Univ, MS, 56, PhD(animal sci & physiol), 60. *Prof Exp:* Asst animal sci, Cornell Univ, 55-56 & 58-60, res assoc meat sci, 60-61; asst prof meat & animal sci, Purdue Univ, 61-62, dir agr, 68-82, asst dean, Col Biol & Agr, 71-82, PROF MEAT & ANIMAL SCI, BRIGHAM YOUNG UNIV, 71-, DIR FARMS, 82- *Mem:* Am Soc Animal Sci; Am Meat Sci Asn. *Res:* Ultrasonic evaluation of live meat animals; carcass effects from stilbestrol and pelleted roughages; early breeding of ewe lambs; effects of nutritional level. *Mailing Add:* 301 Widstoe Bldg Brigham Young Univ Provo UT 84602

WALLER, COY WEBSTER, b Dover, NC, Feb 25, 14; m; c 4. PHARMACEUTICAL CHEMISTRY. *Educ:* Univ NC, BS, 37; Univ Buffalo, MS, 39; Univ Minn, PhD(pharmaceut chem), 42. *Prof Exp:* Instr pharm, State Col Wash, 42-44; dir org chem, Lederle Labs, Am Cyanamid Co, 44-57; dir chem res, Mead Johnson & Co, 57-61; vpres res, Res Ctr, 61-68; assoc dir, Res Inst Pharmaceut Sci, 68-69, PROF PHARM, UNIV MISS, 68-, DIR, RES INST PHARMACEUT SCI, 69- *Mem:* Am Chem Soc; Am Pharmaceut Asn; Royal Soc Chem. *Res:* Structural determination of natural organic compounds. *Mailing Add:* Res Inst of Pharmaceut Sci Univ of Miss Sch of Pharm University MS 38677

WALLER, DAVID PERCIVAL, b Buffalo, NY, Jan 18, 43; m 78; c 1. ORGANIC CHEMISTRY, PHOTOGRAPHIC CHEMISTRY. *Educ:* Tex Christian Univ, BS, 64; Northeastern Univ, MS, 75. *Prof Exp:* Res asst chem, Res Found, Tex Christian Univ, 64-65; from asst scientist to assoc scientist chem, 65-74, scientist, 74-80, SR SCIENTIST CHEM, POLAROID CORP, 80- *Mem:* Am Chem Soc; Royal Soc Chem. *Res:* Organic synthesis; novel photographic systems; dye chemistry. *Mailing Add:* Polaroid Corp 730 Main St Cambridge MA 02139

WALLER, DONALD MACGREGOR, b Northampton, Mass, Oct 15, 51. PLANT ECOLOGY, POPULATION BIOLOGY. *Educ:* Amherst Col, AB, 73; Princeton Univ, PhD(biol), 78. *Prof Exp:* Asst instr biol, Princeton Univ, 74-75; ASST PROF BOT, UNIV WIS-MADISON, 78- *Concurrent Pos:* Res fel bot, Gray Herbarium, Harvard Univ, 77-78. *Mem:* AAAS; Bot Soc Am; Soc Study Evolution; Sigma Xi. *Res:* Ecology; competitive and reproductive strategies of plants; evolution; adaptive significance of various breeding systems of plants. *Mailing Add:* Dept of Bot Birge Hall 430 Lincoln Dr Madison WI 53706

WALLER, ERNEST FREDERICK, b Stewartsville, Mo, Aug 17, 08; m 33; c 2. VETERINARY PATHOLOGY. *Educ:* Iowa State Col, DVM, 31, MS, 38. *Prof Exp:* Diagnostician, Dept Vet Med, Univ Minn, 31-34; asst prof vet path, Iowa State Col, 34-40, jr vet in-chg Bangs Dis Lab, Bur Animal Indust, USDA, 35-40; asst prof poultry husb, Univ NH & poultry pathologist, Exp Sta, 40-45; prof animal path, Univ Vt, 45-50; prof animal & poultry indust & head dept, Univ Del, 50-59; dir extramural res animal husb, Sterling-Winthrop Res Inst, NY, 60-68; tech dir, Sterwin Labs Inc, 68-70; DIR, GA POULTRY LAB 6, 70- *Mem:* Am Vet Med Asn; Poultry Sci Asn; Am Asn Avian Path; Indust Vet Asn. *Res:* Virology of poultry diseases; veterinary pharmacology. *Mailing Add:* Ga Poultry Lab 6 Coastal Exp Sta Tifton GA 31794

WALLER, FRANCIS JOSEPH, b Rome, NY, Mar 12, 43; m 69. ORGANIC CHEMISTRY, ORGANOMETALLIC CHEMISTRY. *Educ:* Niagara Univ, BS, 65; Univ Vt, PhD(org chem), 70. *Prof Exp:* Res investr low temperature kinetics, St Louis Univ, 70-71; vis asst prof org chem, St Lawrence Univ, 71-72; asst prof, Simmons Col, 72-74; res chemist, Polymer Prod Dept & Petrochem Dept, 74-79, STAFF SCIENTIST, CENT RES & DEVELOP DEPT, E I DU PONT DE NEMOURS & CO INC, 79- *Mem:* AAAS; Am Chem Soc; NY Acad Sci. *Res:* Homogeneous catalysis; process development. *Mailing Add:* Cent Res & Develop Dept E I du Pont de Nemours & Co Inc Wilmington DE 19898

WALLER, GEORGE ROZIER, JR, b Clinton, NC, July 14, 27; m 47; c 3. BIOCHEMISTRY. *Educ:* NC State Univ, BS, 50; Univ Del, MS, 52; Okla State Univ, PhD(biochem), 61. *Prof Exp:* Instr agr & biol chem, Univ Del, 50-53; res chemist, Imp Paper & Color Div, Hercules Powder Co, NY, 53-56; from asst prof to assoc prof, 56-67, asst dir, Agr Exp Sta, 69-76, PROF BIOCHEM, OKLA STATE UNIV, 67- *Concurrent Pos:* NIH fel, Nobel Med Inst & Karolinska Inst, Sweden, 63-64; Seydell-Woolley lectr, Ga Inst Technol, 68; mem, Okla Environ Qual Task Force & Gov Task Force on Recommending Sci Policy Struct for State of Okla, 70; pres, Midcontinent Environ Ctr Asn, 69-75; sabbatical leave, Swed Food Inst, Univ Zurich & Univ London; ed, Mass Spectrometry Rev, 81-; head, USA team for USA & Taiwan sem, NSF, 82; mgr nat meeting, Phytochem Soc NAm & Am Soc Pharmacog, 78. *Mem:* AAAS; Am Soc Biol Chemists; Am Soc Mass Spectrometry; Am Chem Soc; Phytochem Soc NAm (pres, 78-79). *Res:* Plant biochemistry, autotoxicity and allelopathy in plants; Maillard reaction products; biochemical applications of mass spectrometry; alkaloid metabolism; author of numerous publications. *Mailing Add:* Dept of Biochem Okla State Univ Stillwater OK 74074

WALLER, GORDON DAVID, b Gale, Wis, July 19, 35; m 59; c 2. APICULTURE. *Educ:* Wis State Univ-River Falls, BS, 59; Utah State Univ, MS, 67, PhD(entom, statist), 73. *Prof Exp:* Sci teacher, Pub Schs, Wis, 62-64; RES ENTOMOLOGIST, BEE RES LAB, AGR RES SERV, USDA, 67-; ASST PROF ENTOM, UNIV ARIZ, 69- *Mem:* Bee Res Asn; Entom Soc Am; Int Comn Bee Bot; Int Union Study Social Insects. *Res:* Applied pollination ecology with special emphasis on honey bee responses to olfactory and gustatory stimuli and the evaluation of foraging behavior of honey bees subjected to different management practices. *Mailing Add:* Univ Ariz 238 Bentley Ave Tucson AZ 85716

WALLER, HARDRESS JOCELYN, b San Diego, Calif, Aug 27, 28; m 53; c 3. NEUROSCIENCE. *Educ:* San Diego State Col, AB, 50; Univ Wash, PhD(physiol), 57. *Prof Exp:* From instr to assoc prof physiol, Albert Einstein Col Med, Yeshiva Univ, 58-73; ASSOC PROF NEUROSCI, MED COL OHIO, 73- *Mem:* Soc Neurosci; AAAS; Am Physiol Soc. *Res:* Electrical activity of central nervous system. *Mailing Add:* Dept of Neurosci CS 10008 Med Col Ohio Toledo OH 43699

WALLER, JAMES R, b Eureka, Mont, Dec 8, 31; m 55; c 8. MICROBIOLOGY, BIOCHEMISTRY. *Educ:* St John's Univ, Minn, BA, 57; Univ Minn, MS, 60, PhD(microbiol), 64. *Prof Exp:* Res assoc microbial physiol, Univ Cincinnati, 63-66; asst prof, 66-70, ASSOC PROF MICROBIOL, UNIV NDAK, 70- *Mem:* Am Soc Microbiol; Sigma Xi. *Res:* Physiology and mechanisms of vitamin transport in microorganisms and tissue cultures; water quality of impounded waters used for recreation; clinical microbiology. *Mailing Add:* Dept of Microbiol Univ of NDak Grand Forks ND 58201

WALLER, JOHN WAYNE, b Johnson City, Tenn, Dec 15, 37. ELECTRICAL ENGINEERING, ELECTRONICS. *Educ:* Univ Tenn, PhD(eng sci). *Prof Exp:* Asst prof, 64-80, ASSOC PROF ELEC ENG, UNIV TENN, KNOXVILLE, 80- *Mem:* Inst Elec & Electronics Engrs; Am Soc Eng Educ. *Res:* Electronic solid state circuits. *Mailing Add:* Dept of Elec Eng Ferris Hall 203 Univ of Tenn Knoxville TN 37916

WALLER, JULIAN ARNOLD, b New York, NY, Apr 17, 32; m 56; c 2. MEDICINE, PUBLIC HEALTH. *Educ:* Columbia Univ, AB, 53; Boston Univ, MD, 57; Harvard Univ, MPH, 60; Am Bd Prev Med, dipl, 65. *Prof Exp:* Intern, Mary Fletcher Hosp, Burlington, Vt, 57-58; resident, Contra Costa Health Dept, Calif, 58-59; regional consult chronic dis & voc rehab, USPHS, 60-62; resident, Calif Dept Pub Health, 62, coordr accident prev, 62-63, med officer occup health, 64-66, med officer chronic dis, 66-67, chief emergency health serv, 68; prof community med, 68-72, prof & chmn, Dept Epidemiol & Environ Med, 72-79, PROF MED, UNIV VT, 79- *Concurrent Pos:*

Consult, US Dept Transp, 67-80, Vt State Health Dept, 68-79 & Vt Dept Ment Health, 70-78; mem safety & occup health study sect, Dept Health, Educ & Welfare, 68-71; mem, Nat Hwy Safety Adv Comt, 69-72; adv, WHO, 78- *Honors & Awards:* Metrop Life Award of Merit Accident Res, 72. *Mem:* AAAS; fel Am Pub Health Asn; Am Asn Automotive Med (pres elect, pres, 73); Int Asn Accident & Traffic Med; fel Am Col Epidemiol. *Res:* Epidemiology and control of highway and non-highway injury; emergency health services; epidemiology and control of problem drinking; program evaluation. *Mailing Add:* Dept Med Given Bldg Univ Vt Burlington VT 05405

WALLER, MARION VAN NOSTRAND, b Flushing, NY, Jan 6, 19; m 64; c 2. SEROLOGY, IMMUNOLOGY. *Educ:* Hunter Col, BA, 40; Med Col Va, MS, 53, PhD(immunol), 59. *Prof Exp:* Dir blood grouping res lab, 52-61, dir blood bank, 57-61, from asst prof to assoc prof med, 61-73, PROF MED, MED COL VA, 73-, DIR SEROL STUDIES, CONNECTIVE TISSUE DIV, 61- *Concurrent Pos:* Arthritis & Rheumatism Asn fel, Lister Inst Prev Med, London, 61-62; dir serol studies for child develop study, Connective Tissue Div, Med Col, Va, 57-66, asst prof clin path, 60-61. *Mem:* Am Rheumatism Asn; Int Soc Hemat; Am Soc Hemat. *Res:* Antiglobulin antibodies in human sera; humoral antibodies in patients with renal transplants, influence of infection on antiglobulin antibodies, serum agglutinators. *Mailing Add:* Dept of Med Med Col of Va Richmond VA 23298

WALLER, RAY ALBERT, b Grenola, Kans, Mar 4, 37; m 60; c 2. MATHEMATICAL STATISTICS. *Educ:* Southwestern Col, BA, 59; Kans State Univ, MS, 63; Johns Hopkins Univ, PhD(math statist), 67. *Prof Exp:* Instr math, St John's Sch, PR, 60-61; asst prof math, Towson State Col, 66-67; from asst prof to assoc prof statist, Kans State Univ, 67-74; STAFF MEM, LOS ALAMOS NAT LAB, 74-, DEP DIV LEADER, 80- *Concurrent Pos:* Consult, White Sands Missile Range, 68-72. *Mem:* Am Statist Asn. *Res:* Bayesian inference and reliability estimation. *Mailing Add:* MS 606 Los Alamos Nat Lab Los Alamos NM 87545

WALLER, RICHARD CONRAD, b Victory, Wis, Sept 24, 15; m 48; c 5. CHEMICAL ENGINEERING, PHYSICAL CHEMISTRY. *Educ:* Wash State Univ, BS, 38; Iowa State Univ, PhD(phys chem), 42. *Prof Exp:* Res chemist, E I du Pont de Nemours & Co, Inc, 42-48; res scientist fibers, Goodyear Tire & Rubber Co, 48-53, sect head polymer, 53-58, mgr, 58-65, dir res & develop polymer, 65-76, vpres res, 76-80; CONSULT, 80- *Mem:* Am Chem Soc; Fiber Soc. *Res:* Polymer; fiber. *Mailing Add:* 123 Leland St SE Port Charlotte FL 33952

WALLER, ROGER MILTON, b Taylor, Wis, Dec 30, 26; m 55; c 3. GROUNDWATER GEOLOGY. *Educ:* Univ Wis, BS, 50; Univ Ariz, MS, 69. *Prof Exp:* Jr computer seismic explor, Nat Geophys Co, 50-51; groundwater geologist, 51-55, admin hydrologist, Alaska Dist, 56-63, res hydrologist, Alaska Earthquake Effects, 64-65, hydrologist, NY, 66-68, Wis, 68-71, assoc dist chief, Ohio Dist, 72-73, HYDROLOGIST, US GEOL SURV, NY, 73- *Concurrent Pos:* Hydrol panel mem, Nat Acad Sci Comt Alaska Earthquake, 64-74. *Mem:* Geol Soc Am; Am Geophys Union. *Res:* Groundwater resources of glacial deposits. *Mailing Add:* US Geol Surv PO Box 1350 Albany NY 12201

WALLER, STEVEN SCOBEE, b Indianapolis, Ind, Aug 29, 47; m 70; c 2. RANGE SCIENCE, PLANT ECOLOGY. *Educ:* Purdue Univ, BSc, 70; Tex A&M Univ, PhD(range sci), 75. *Prof Exp:* Res asst, Tex A&M Univ, 71-73, teaching asst, 73-74, res fel, 74-75; asst prof, SDak State Univ, 75-77, asst to dir resident instr & asst prof, 77-78; ASSOC PROF RANGE SCI, UNIV NEBR, 78- *Mem:* Soc Range Mgt; Sigma Xi. *Res:* Development of successful range improvement practices within the field of range science. *Mailing Add:* Keim Hall 347 E Campus Lincoln NE 68583

WALLER, THOMAS RICHARD, b Chicago, Ill, July 18, 37; m 59; c 2. MALACOLOGY, EVOLUTION. *Educ:* Univ Wis, BS, 59, MS, 61; Columbia Univ, PhD(geol), 66. *Prof Exp:* assoc cur, 66-74, CUR TERTIARY MOLLUSCA, SMITHSONIAN INST, 74- *Mem:* AAAS; Paleont Soc; Soc Syst Zool. *Res:* Cenozoic and living mollusca; evolution; zoogeography; bivalve morphology and development; upper Cenozoic biostratigraphy of eastern North America and Caribbean. *Mailing Add:* Dept of Paleobiol Smithsonian Inst Washington DC 20560

WALLER, WILLIAM T, b Girard, Kans, Apr 29, 41; m 61; c 2. AQUATIC BIOLOGY, LIMNOLOGY. *Educ:* Kans State Col, BS, 65, MS, 67; Va Polytech Inst & State Univ, PhD(biol), 71. *Prof Exp:* Res asst, Kans State Col, 65-67, Univ Kans, 68, Va Polytech Inst & State Univ, 68-71 & Region VII, Environ Protection Agency, 72; assoc res scientist environ med, Med Ctr, NY Univ, 72-75; ASSOC PROF, GRAD SCH ENVIRON SCI, UNIV TEX, DALLAS, 75- *Mem:* Am Fisheries Soc. *Res:* Organismic, population and community structure and function as it relates to acute and chronic stresses. *Mailing Add:* Grad Sch of Environ Sci Univ of Tex at Dallas PO Box 688 Richardson TX 75080

WALLERSTEIN, DAVID VANDERMERE, b New York, NY, Nov 19, 37; m 72; c 1. APPLIED MECHANICS, SYSTEMS ANALYSIS. *Educ:* Mich Technol Univ, BS, 60, MS, 61, PhD(eng mech), 69. *Prof Exp:* Design specialist, Lockheed Calif Co, 69-71; asst prof res, Va Polytech Inst, 71-72; sr opers res specialist, Lockheed Calif Co, 72-81; SR STAFF ENGR, MACNEAL-SCHWENDLER CORP, 82- *Concurrent Pos:* Adj assoc prof aerospace eng, Univ Southern Calif, 82- *Mem:* Am Inst Mining, Metall & Petrol Engrs. *Res:* Structuring of engineering systems into mathematical models; development of solutions that yield optimal values of system measures of desirability; finite element analysis. *Mailing Add:* 667 W California Blvd Pasadena CA 91105

WALLERSTEIN, EDWARD PERRY, b New York, NY, May 23, 28; m 51; c 3. OPTICAL SYSTEM DESIGN. *Prof Exp:* Engr, Perkin-Elmer Corp, 51-55; res asst, Phys Res Labs, Boston Univ, 55-58; engr, Itek Corp, 58-60; founder & exec, Diffraction Limited, Inc, 60-69; mgr systs group, Valpey Corp, 70-74; ENGR-GROUP LEADER, LAWRENCE LIVERMORE NAT LAB, 74- *Concurrent Pos:* Consult design optical systs, 55- *Honors & Awards:* IR 100 Award, Indust Res & Develop, 79. *Mem:* Optical Soc Am; Soc Photo-Optical Instrumentation Engrs. *Res:* Design and manufacture of advanced high precision optical systems for reconnaisance, astronomy and laser fusion; large operture frequency conversion with nonlinear materials. *Mailing Add:* 1742 Beachwood Way Pleasanton CA 94566

WALLERSTEIN, GEORGE, b New York, NY, Jan 13, 30. ASTRONOMY. *Educ:* Brown Univ, AB, 51; Calif Inst Technol, PhD, 58. *Prof Exp:* From instr to assoc prof astron, Univ Calif, Berkeley, 58-64; PROF ASTRON, UNIV WASH, 65- *Concurrent Pos:* Bd trustees, Brown Univ, 75-80. *Mem:* Am Astron Soc; Royal Astron Soc; Arctic Inst NAm; Astron Soc Pac; AAAS. *Res:* Spectra of variable stars; abundances of the elements in stellar atmospheres; interstellar absorption lines. *Mailing Add:* Dept of Astron Univ of Wash Seattle WA 98195

WALLERSTEIN, ROBERT SOLOMON, b Berlin, Ger, Jan 28, 21; US citizen; m 47; c 3. PSYCHIATRY, PSYCHOANALYSIS. *Educ:* Columbia Univ, BA, 41, MD, 44. *Prof Exp:* Intern med, Mt Sinai Hosp, New York, 44-45, asst resident, 45-46, resident, 48, resident psychiat, 49; resident, Vet Admin Hosp, Topeka, Kans, 49-51, chief psychosom sect, 51-53; assoc dir dept res, Menninger Found, Kans, 54-65, dir dept, 65-66; clin prof psychiat, Sch Med & Langley-Porter Neuropsychiat Inst, 67-75, PROF PSYCHIAT & CHMN DEPT, SCH MED & DIR, LANGLEY PORTER INST, UNIV CALIF, SAN FRANCISCO, 75- *Concurrent Pos:* Lectr psychiat, Menninger Sch Psychiat, Kans, 51-66; lectr, Topeka Inst Psychoanal, 59-66, training & supv analyst, 65-66; fel, Ctr Advan Studies Behav Sci, Stanford, Calif, 64-65 & 81-82; training & supv analyst, San Francisco Psychoanal Inst, 66-; mem res sci career develop comn, NIMH, 66-70, chmn, 68-70; vis prof psychiat, Sch Med, La State Univ & New Orleans Psychoanal Inst, 72-73 & Sch Med, Pahlavi Univ, Iran, 77; chief, Dept Psychiat, Mt Zion Hosp, San Francisco, 66-78. *Honors & Awards:* Heinz Hartmann Award, New York Psychoanal Inst, 68. *Mem:* Am Psychoanal Asn (pres, 71-72); Int Psychoanal Asn (vpres, 77-); fel Am Psychiat Asn; fel Am Col Physicians; fel Am Orthopsychiat Asn. *Res:* Psychotherapy research, especially the processes and outcomes of psychoanalytic therapy; supervision processes; alcoholism; psychosomatic medicine. *Mailing Add:* Langley-Porter Inst 401 Parnassus San Francisco CA 94143

WALLES, WILHELM EGBERT, b Enschede, Neth, May 25, 25; nat US; m 51; c 5. ORGANIC CHEMISTRY, POLYMER CHEMISTRY. *Educ:* Univ Amsterdam, MSc, 48, PhD(org chem, physics), 51, DSc, 53. *Prof Exp:* Asst indust res, Univ Amsterdam, 49-51; Nat Res Coun Can fel, 51-53; dir res, N V Neth Refining Co, 53-55; assoc scientist, 55-67, ASSOC RES SCIENTIST PLASTICS, CENT RES LAB, DOW CHEM CO, 67- *Honors & Awards:* IR 100 Award, 74. *Mem:* Am Chem Soc. *Res:* Synthesis and physical properties of high polymers; surface reactions of polymers; polymolecular complexes; magneto-organic chemistry; aerosol physics; surface chemistry of plastic films, fibers and articles. *Mailing Add:* Cent Res Lab 1702 Bldg Dow Chem Co Midland MI 48640

WALLEY, WILLIS WAYNE, b Brooklyn, Miss, July 26, 34; m 66. ZOOLOGY, ECOLOGY. *Educ:* Southern Miss Univ, BS, 56; Miss State Univ, MS, 61, PhD(zool)j 65. *Prof Exp:* Pub sch teacher, Miss, 56-61; asst prof biol, Southeastern La Col, 64-68; PROF BIOL & CHMN DEPT & CHMN DIV III, BELHAVEN COL, 68- *Mem:* AAAS; Am Inst Biol Sci; Nat Audubon Soc; Sigma Xi. *Res:* Absorption, metabolism and excretion of chlorinated hydrocarbons in birds; in vitro metabolism of dichloro-diphenyl-trichloro-ethane by various tissues of the common grackle; biogeochemical cycling of boron; site fertility and primary production in hydrosoils. *Mailing Add:* Dept of Biol Belhaven Col Jackson MS 39202

WALLICK, EARL TAYLOR, b Monticello, Ark, Jan 11, 38; m 62; c 2. BIOLOGICAL CHEMISTRY. *Educ:* Miss State Univ, BS, 60, MS, 62; Rice Univ, PhD(org chem), 66. *Prof Exp:* Res chemist, Dacron Res Lab, E I du Pont de Nemours & Co, Inc, 66-67; assoc prof chem, King Col, 67-71; trainee myocardial biol, Baylor Col Med, 71-73, instr cell biophys, 73-76, asst prof, 76-77; asst prof, 77-78, ASSOC PROF PHARMACOL & CELL BIOPHYSICS, COL MED, UNIV CINCINNATI, 78- *Concurrent Pos:* Mem pharmacol study sect, NIH. *Mem:* Am Chem Soc; Am Soc Pharmacol & Exp Therapeut. *Res:* Isotope effects; cardiac glycosides, adenosine triphosphatase. *Mailing Add:* Dept Pharmacol & Cell Biophysics Col Med Univ Cincinnati 231 Bethesda Ave Cincinnati OH 45267

WALLICK, EDWARD ISRAEL, geochemistry, hydrogeology, see previous edition

WALLICK, GEORGE CASTOR, b Grand Rapids, Mich, July 2, 23; m 45; c 2. PHYSICS. *Educ:* Univ Mich, BS, 43, MS, 46, PhD(physics), 52. *Prof Exp:* Radio engr radar res & develop, US Naval Res Lab, 44-45; sr res technologist appl math, 51-59, RES ASSOC, FIELD RES LAB, MOBIL RES & DEVELOP CORP, DALLAS, 59- *Mem:* Am Phys Soc; Am Asn Physics Teachers. *Res:* Petroleum production; flow of fluids through porous media; non-Newtonian flow; heat transfer; numerical analysis; computer programming and utilization; geophysics; underground coal gasification. *Mailing Add:* 518 Towne Pl Duncanville TX 75116

WALLIN, JACK ROBB, b Omaha, Nebr, Nov 21, 15; m; c 2. PLANT PATHOLOGY. *Educ:* Iowa State Col, BS, 39, PhD(plant path), 44. *Prof Exp:* Asst bot, Univ Mo, 39-41 & N Iowa Agr Exp Asn, 41-44; collabr, E May Seed Co, 44-45; res asst prof, Iowa State Col, 45-47; plant pathologist, Agr Res Serv, USDA, 47-58, sr plant pathologist, Iowa State Univ, 59-75; PROF PLANT PATH, UNIV MO-COLUMBIA, 75-; RES PLANT

PATHOLOGIST, USDA, 80- *Concurrent Pos:* Mem working group, Comn Instruments & Methods Observation, World Meteorol Orgn; mem aerobiol comt, Nat Acad Sci, 76- *Honors & Awards:* William F Peterson Award, Int Soc Biometeorol, 67. *Mem:* Am Phytopath Soc; Am Meteorol Soc; Int Soc Biometoerol. *Res:* Investigating the cause of epidemics of corn diseases and experimental forecasts of these diseases especially Csperzillus fluous and genetic resistance to the fungus and levels of aflatoxin; epidemiology; disease forecasting; aerobiology; corn diseases. *Mailing Add:* Dept of Plant Path Univ Mo 312 Curtis Hall Columbia MO 65201

WALLIN, JOHN DAVID, b Pasadena, Calif, June 30, 37; m 59; c 2. NEPHROLOGY, RENAL PHYSIOLOGY. *Educ:* Stanford Univ, BS, 58; Sch Med, Yale Univ, MD, 62. *Prof Exp:* Intern & resident med, Naval Regional Med Ctr, PR, 62-66, chief med, 66-70; res fel nephrol, Southwest Med Sch, Univ Tex, 70-72; dir clin invest, Naval Regional Med Ctr, Calif, 72-78; CHIEF NEPHROL & PROF INTERNAL MED, SCH MED, TULANE UNIV, 78- *Concurrent Pos:* Instr internal med, Univ Puerto Rico, 67-70; chief nephrol, Vet Admin Hosp, New Orleans, 78-81. *Mem:* fel Am Col Physicians; Am Soc Nephrol; Am Fedn Clin Res; Int Soc Nephrol. *Res:* Examination of homeostasis of water metabolism with specific reference to control of vasopresion release from hypophysis and its end organ effects in renal tubule. *Mailing Add:* 1430 Tulane Ave New Orleans LA 70112

WALLIN, RICHARD FRANKLIN, b Chicago, Ill, Jan 31, 39; m 61; c 2. TOXICOLOGY, LABORATORY ANIMAL MEDICINE. *Educ:* Univ Ill, BS, 61, DVM, 63, MS, 64, PhD(vet med sci), 66. *Prof Exp:* Physiologist, McDonnell Aircraft Corp, 66-67; sr res pharmacologist, Baxter Labs, Inc, Morton Grove, 67-70, dir res admin, 70-72, actg dir pharm & microbiol res, 72-73, assoc dir pharmacol res, 73-77; sci dir, 77-78, vpres & sci dir, 78-81, PRES, NORTH AM SCI ASSOCS, INC, 81- *Concurrent Pos:* NIH fel, 63-66; adj assoc prof, Med Col Ohio; lectr, Ctr Prof Advan, East Brunswick, NJ. *Mem:* Am Vet Med Asn; Am Soc Vet Physiol & Pharmacol; Am Asn Lab Animal Sci; Am Soc Pharmacol & Exp Therapeut; Soc Biomat. *Res:* Anesthesiology; biomaterials; medical devices; biocompatibility of materials; inhalation anesthetics. *Mailing Add:* 29969 St Andrews Dr Perrysburg OH 43551

WALLING, CHEVES, b Evanston, Ill, Feb 28, 16; m 40; c 5. PHYSICAL ORGANIC CHEMISTRY. *Educ:* Harvard Univ, BA, 37; Univ Chicago, PhD(org chem), 39. *Prof Exp:* Res chemist, Jackson Lab, E I du Pont de Nemours & Co, 39-42 & Gen Labs, US Rubber Co, 43-49; res assoc, Lever Bros Co, 49-52; prof chem, Columbia Univ, 52-70, chmn dept, 63-66; DISTINGUISHED PROF, UNIV UTAH, 70- *Concurrent Pos:* Tech aide, Comt Med Res, Off Sci Res & Develop, 45-46; chmn div chem & chem technol, Nat Res Coun, 72-; ed, J Am Chem Soc, 75- *Honors & Awards:* James Flack Norris Award, Am Chem Soc, 70. *Mem:* Nat Acad Sci; Am Acad Arts & Sci; AAAS; Am Chem Soc. *Res:* Organic reaction mechanisms; free radical reactions; polymerization; peroxides and autoxidation. *Mailing Add:* Dept of Chem Univ of Utah Salt Lake City UT 84112

WALLING, DERALD DEE, b Granger, Iowa, Feb 14, 37; m 58; c 3. MATHEMATICS. *Educ:* Iowa State Univ, BS, 58, MS, 61, PhD(math), 63. *Prof Exp:* Mathematician, Ames Lab, US AEC, 62-63; asst prof math, Univ Ariz, 63-66; ASSOC PROF MATH, TEX TECH UNIV, 66- *Mem:* Am Math Soc. *Res:* Numerical analysis; least squares; statistics; probability. *Mailing Add:* Dept of Math Tex Tech Univ Lubbock TX 79409

WALLINGFORD, ERROL E(LWOOD), b Ottawa, Ont, Jan 25, 28; m 54; c 3. COMMUNICATIONS. *Educ:* Carleton Col, BSc, 53; Univ Ottawa, MSc, 61. *Prof Exp:* Inspector, Dept Nat Defense Inspection Servs, 52-57; lectr physics, Waterloo Col, 57-58; from lectr to asst prof, 61-68, ASSOC PROF ELEC ENG, ROYAL MIL COL CAN, 68- *Concurrent Pos:* Defence Res Bd Can grants, 65- *Mem:* Inst Elec & Electronics Engrs. *Res:* Primary source redundancy identification; removal and replacement using secondary source data to maintain a block code structure; method applicable to both first and second order redundancies. *Mailing Add:* Dept of Elec Eng Royal Mil Col Kingston ON K7L 2W3 Can

WALLINGFORD, JOHN STUART, b El Paso, Tex, Apr 13, 35; m 70; c 2. PHYSICS. *Educ:* Univ Minn, Minneapolis, BPhys, 61; Fla State Univ, MS, 66, PhD(physics), 67. *Prof Exp:* Instr physics, Fullerton Jr Col, 61-62 & Cerritos Col, 62-63; asst, Fla State Univ, 63-66; from asst prof to assoc prof, Fla A&M Univ, 66-69; vis assoc prof, Temple Univ, 69-70; assoc prof, 70-75, PROF PHYSICS, PEMBROKE STATE UNIV, 75- *Mem:* Am Asn Physics Teachers; Am Inst Physics. *Res:* Consequences of general relativity theory; making science interesting and accessible to all; hydrolysis of organic wastes; computer assisted tomography (reconstruction techniques); linear programming (simplex algorithm Kachiyan's algorithm); personal (micro-) computer programming and interfacing. *Mailing Add:* Dept of Physical Sci Pembroke State Univ Pembroke NC 28372

WALLIS, ANTHONY, computer science, mathematics, see previous edition

WALLIS, CLIFFORD MERRILL, b Waitsfield, Vt, Mar 7, 04; m 28; c 2. ELECTRONICS, RADIO ENGINEERING. *Educ:* Univ Vt, BS, 26; Mass Inst Technol, MS, 28; Harvard Univ, ScD(eng), 41. *Prof Exp:* Mem staff eng training course, Gen Elec Co, Mass, 26-28; from instr to prof elec eng, 28-70, chmn dept, 47-68, EMER PROF ELEC ENG, UNIV MO-COLUMBIA, 70- *Concurrent Pos:* Res assoc, Underwater Sound Lab, Harvard Univ, 44-45; Fulbright lectr, Ankara, 60-61, award, Taiwan, 67-68; dir prof develop, US Navy Underwater Systs Ctr, Conn, 70-72. *Honors & Awards:* Distinguished Serv in Eng, Col of Eng & Eng Found, Univ Mo, 73. *Mem:* Am Soc Eng Educ; fel Inst Elec & Electronics Engrs. *Res:* Rectifier analysis; half wave gas rectifier circuits; single phase full wave rectifier circuits; current division in tetrode and pentode power tubes; low frequency constant time delay lines; solid state theory of semiconductors. *Mailing Add:* Moretown VT 05660

WALLIS, DONALD DOUGLAS JAMES H, b Brandon, Man, Apr 20, 43. IONOSPHERIC PHYSICS. *Educ:* Univ Alta, Calgary, BSc, 65; Univ Calgary, MSc, 68; Univ Alaska, PhD(geophys), 74. *Prof Exp:* Fel geophys, Univ Alta, 73-75; res assoc geophys, Univ Calgary, 75-76; res assoc, 76-81, RES OFFICER SPACE PHYS, NAT RES COUN CAN, 81- *Mem:* Can Asn Physicists; Am Geophys Union. *Res:* Auroral spectroscopy; ionospheric winds and currents; atmospheric changes; magnetospheric physics. *Mailing Add:* Herzberg Inst Astrophys Nat Res Coun Can Ottawa ON K1A 0R6 Can

WALLIS, GRAHAM B, b Rugby, Eng, Apr 1, 36; m 59; c 4. ENGINEERING. *Educ:* Cambridge Univ, BA, 57, MA, 61, PhD(eng), 61; Mass Inst Technol, SM, 59. *Prof Exp:* Res fel, UK Atomic Energy Authority, 59-62; from asst prof to assoc prof, 62-72, PROF ENG, DARTMOUTH COL, 72- *Concurrent Pos:* Sr vis res fel, Heriot-Watt Univ, 64; vis reader, Univ Warwick, 70-71. *Mem:* Am Soc Mech Engrs. *Res:* Two-phase and multicomponent flow; heat and mass transfer; boiling and condensation. *Mailing Add:* Dept of Eng Sci Dartmouth Col Hanover NH 03755

WALLIS, ORTHELLO LANGWORTHY, ecology, natural science, see previous edition

WALLIS, PETER MALCOLM, b London, Eng, May 9, 52; Can citizen; m 76; c 2. ORGANIC GEOCHEMISTRY. *Educ:* Univ Toronto, BSc, 74; Univ Waterloo, MSc, 75, PhD(biol), 78. *Prof Exp:* Fel, 78-79, res assoc, 79-80, PROF ASSOC, KANANASKIS CTR, UNIV CALGARY, 80- *Mem:* NAm Benthological Soc; Soc Int Limnol; Freshwater Biol Asn. *Res:* Microbiology; organic and inorganic chemistry of groundwater and streams; isotope geochemistry; chemical evolution of groundwater. *Mailing Add:* Kananaskis Ctr Environ Res Seebe AB T0L 1X0

WALLIS, RICHARD FISHER, b Washington, DC, May 14, 24; m 55. SOLID STATE PHYSICS. *Educ:* George Washington Univ, BS, 45, MS, 48; Cath Univ, PhD(chem), 52. *Prof Exp:* Fel, Inst Fluid Dynamics, Univ Md, 51-53; chemist, Appl Physics Lab, Johns Hopkins Univ, 53-56; physicist, US Naval Res Lab, 56-58, from actg head to head semiconductors br, 58-66; prof physics, Univ Calif, Irvine, 66-67; head semiconductors br, US Naval Res Lab, 67-69; PROF PHYSICS, UNIV CALIF, IRVINE, 69-, CHMN DEPT, 72- *Concurrent Pos:* Consult, Res Labs, Gen Motors Corp, 58- *Mem:* Fel Am Phys Soc. *Res:* Quantum and statistical mechanics. *Mailing Add:* Dept of Physics Univ of Calif Irvine CA 92650

WALLIS, ROBERT CHARLES, b West Burlington, Iowa, Oct 30, 21; m 53; c 2. MEDICAL ENTOMOLOGY, PARASITOLOGY. *Educ:* Ohio Univ, BS, 48, MS, 50; Johns Hopkins Univ, DSc, 53. *Prof Exp:* Asst zool, Ohio Univ, 48-49, asst parasitol, Sch Hyg & Pub Health, Johns Hopkins Univ, 50-52; from asst prof to prof entom, Agr Exp Sta, Univ Conn, 53-63; assoc prof, 63-79, PROF EPIDEMIOL, SCH MED, YALE UNIV, 79-, CHIEF SECT MED ENTOM, 63- *Concurrent Pos:* Consult, US Army, 62-72. *Mem:* Am Soc Trop Med & Hyg; Am Soc Parasitol; Entom Soc Am; Am Mosquito Control Asn. *Res:* Epidemiology and natural history of eastern encephalitis; ecology and physiology of arthropod vectors of disease; mosquito biology and control. *Mailing Add:* Dept of Epidemiol & Pub Health Yale Univ Sch of Med New Haven CT 06520

WALLIS, ROBERT L, b Sheridan, Wyo, Sept 22, 34; m 60; c 2. PHYSICS. *Educ:* Univ Colo, BA, 56, MA, 58, PhD(physics), 62. *Prof Exp:* From asst prof to assoc prof, 62-75, PROF PHYSICS, BALDWIN-WALLACE COL, 75-, CHMN DEPT, 70- *Mem:* AAAS; Am Phys Soc; Am Asn Physics Teachers. *Res:* Educational techniques. *Mailing Add:* Dept Physics Baldwin-Wallace Col Berea OH 44017

WALLIS, THOMAS GARY, b Paducah, Ky. ORGANIC CHEMISTRY, PHOTOGRAPHIC SCIENCE. *Educ:* Murray State Univ, BA, 70; Duke Univ, PhD(org chem), 74. *Prof Exp:* Assoc chemist, Ohio State Univ, 74-76; RES CHEMIST, EASTMAN KODAK CO, 76- *Mem:* Am Chem Soc. *Res:* Synthesis of photographically active compounds; image structure improvement in color films. *Mailing Add:* Eastman Kodak Co Res Lab Rochester NY 14650

WALLMAN, JOSHUA, b New York, NY, July 4, 43. NEUROBIOLOGY. *Educ:* Harvard Univ, AB, 65; Tufts Univ, PhD(biol), 72. *Prof Exp:* Fel neurophysiol, Inst Animal Behav, Rutgers Univ, 72-74; asst prof, 74-79, ASSOC PROF BIOL, CITY COL NEW YORK, 80- *Concurrent Pos:* Nat Inst Neurol Dis & Stroke, NIH fel, 72-73; res grants, Nat Eye Inst, NIH, 78-81 & 81-86. *Mem:* Asn Res Vision Opthal; Soc Neurosci; Sigma Xi; Animal Behav Soc. *Res:* Neurophysiology of the accessory optic system; physiological and behavioral studies of the development of the oculomotor and visual systems in birds; studies on experimentally-induced myopia. *Mailing Add:* Dept Biol City Col New York New York NY 10031

WALLMARK, J(OHN) TORKEL, b Stockholm, Sweden, June 4, 19; nat US; m 49; c 2. ELECTRONICS. *Educ:* Royal Inst Technol, Sweden, Civilingenjor, 44, Techn lic, 47, Techn dr, 53. *Prof Exp:* Asst electronics, Royal Inst Technol, Sweden, 44; engr, A B Standard Radio Mfg Co, Stockholm, 44-45; asst electronics, Royal Inst Technol, Sweden, 45-47; trainee, RCA Labs, 47-48; asst electronics, Royal Inst Technol, 49-53; res engr, RCA Labs, 53-68; PROF ELECTRONICS, CHALMERS UNIV TECHNOL, SWEDEN, 68- *Concurrent Pos:* Secy, State Tech Res Coun, Stockholm, 50-51; res engr, Elektrovarme Inst, Sweden, 52-53; consult, Royal Swedish Air Force, 52-53; prof, Chalmers Univ Technol, 64-66. *Honors & Awards:* L J Wallmark Award, Royal Acad Sci Sweden, 54; David Sarnoff Team Achievement Award, 64. *Mem:* Am Phys Soc; fel Inst Elec & Electronics Engrs; Royal Swedish Acad Eng Sci; Royal Swedish Acad Sci & Humanities; fel AAAS. *Res:* Integrated circuits; solid state devices. *Mailing Add:* Chalmers Univ of Technol Gothenburg Sweden 40220

WALLMO, OLOF CHARLES, b CarsonCity, Iowa, July 1, 19; m 45; c 3. VERTEBRATE ECOLOGY. *Educ:* Utah State Agr Col, BS, 47; Univ Wis, MS, 49; Agr & Mech Col, Tex, PhD(wildlife mgt), 57. *Prof Exp:* Res biologist, US Fish & Wildlife Serv, 47; biologist, Ariz Game & Fish Dept, 48-51 & Tex Game & Fish Comn, 53-54; from asst prof to assoc prof wildlife mgt, Agr & Mech Col Tex, 55-62; res biologist, Ariz Game & Fish Dept, 62-64; RES WILDLIFE BIOLOGIST, ROCKY MOUNTAIN FOREST & RANGE EXP STA, US FOREST SERV, 64- *Concurrent Pos:* Fac affil, Grad Sch, Colo State Univ. *Mem:* AAAS; Wildlife Soc; Sigma Xi. *Res:* Wildlife habitat management research. *Mailing Add:* 1220 S Tracy Bozeman MT 59715

WALLNER, EDWARD PETER, b Louisville, Ky, Jan 11, 27; m 49; c 3. SYSTEMS ANALYSIS, ELECTRICAL ENGINEERING. *Educ:* Univ Louisville, BEE, 47; Rensselaer Polytech Inst, MEE, 50. *Prof Exp:* Proj engr, Sperry Gyroscope Co, 50-55; sr mem guid & control, Airborne Syst Div, RCA Corp, 55-58, leader, 58-62, sr eng scientist, Aerospace Syst Div, 63-74; PRIN SYSTS ENGR, ADVAN ANAL, OPTICAL SYSTS DIV, ITEK CORP, 74- *Honors & Awards:* Samuel M Burka Award, Inst Navig, 61-62. *Mem:* Sigma Xi; Optical Soc Am. *Res:* Analysis and design of electro-optical and adaptive optics systems. *Mailing Add:* Optical Systs Div ITEK Corp 10 Maguire Rd Lexington MA 02173

WALLNER, STEPHEN JOHN, b Sioux Falls, SDak, Mar 22, 45; m 69; c 2. PLANT PHYSIOLOGY. *Educ:* SDak State Univ, BS, 67, MS, 69; Iowa State Univ, PhD(plant physiol), 73. *Prof Exp:* Plant physiologist, US Army Natick Labs, 73-75; asst prof hort physiol, Pa State Univ, University Park, 75-80; ASSOC PROF PLANT PHYSIOL, COLO STATE UNIV, 80- *Mem:* Am Soc Plant Physiologists; Am Inst Biol Sci; Sigma Xi; AAAS; Int Asn Plant Tissue Cult. *Res:* Postharvest physiology, especially involving cell wall changes during fruit ripening. *Mailing Add:* Hort Dept Colo State Univ Ft Collins CO 80523

WALLNER, WILLIAM E, b Greenfield, Mass, Nov 25, 36; m 64; c 2. ENTOMOLOGY, PLANT PATHOLOGY. *Educ:* Univ Conn, BS, 59; Cornell Univ, PhD, 65. *Prof Exp:* Res asst entom, Cornell Univ, 59-65; exten entomologist, Mich State Univ, 65-76, assoc prof entom, 69-74, prof, 74-76; RES PROJ LEADER, FOREST INSECT & DIS LAB, US FOREST SERV, 76- *Mem:* Entom Soc Am; Soc Am Foresters; Sigma Xi. *Res:* Biology and control of forest ornamental and plantation insects with emphasis on population suppression and pest management of insects for forest-recreational areas; gypsy moth. *Mailing Add:* Forest Insect & Dis Lab US Forest Serv Hamden CT 06514

WALLRAFF, EVELYN BARTELS, b Chicago, Ill, Oct 21, 20. MICROBIOLOGY, IMMUNOLOGY. *Educ:* Rosary Col, BS, 40; Univ Chicago, MS, 42; Univ Ariz, PhD(virol, immunol), 61. *Prof Exp:* Res technician bact & immunol, Univ Chicago & Zoller Dent Clin, 41-43; from instr to asst prof bact, Univ Ariz, 43-47, res assoc med res, Univ Ariz & Southwestern Clin & Res Inst, 47-51; res microbiologist, Vet Admin Hosp, 61-71; RES ASSOC MICROBIOL & MED TECHNOL, UNIV ARIZ, 70-; PROF MICROBIOL & LIFE SCI, PIMA COL, 72- *Concurrent Pos:* Consult, Vet Admin Hosp, Tucson, 71- *Mem:* AAAS; Am Soc Microbiol; Am Asn Immunol; Reticuloendothelial Soc; Am Thoracic Soc. *Res:* Coccidioidinn hypersensitivity used for study of mechanisms of delayed hypersensitivity in man; cellular and transplantation immunology; anti-macrophage serum. *Mailing Add:* 2708 E Mabel Tucson AZ 85716

WALLS, HUGH A(LAN), b Wellsboro, Pa, Feb 14, 34; m 71; c 3. CHEMICAL ENGINEERING, MECHANICAL ENGINEERING. *Educ:* Univ Okla, BS, 57, MChE, 58, PhD(chem eng), 63. *Prof Exp:* Res asst chem & metall eng, Res Inst, Univ Okla, 58-62, proj dir inst & asst prof metall eng, 62-63; res engr, Bur Eng Res, 63-65, asst prof, 64-68, assoc prof, 68-80, PROF MECH ENG, UNIV TEX, AUSTIN, 68-, ASSOC DIR, 77- *Concurrent Pos:* NSF res initiation grant, 65-67. *Mem:* AAAS; Am Soc Mech Engrs; NY Acad Sci; Am Inst Chemists; Am Chem Soc. *Res:* Liquid structure and transport phenomena, fluid mechanics; heat transfer, materials science; thermodynamics; engineering design; numerical methods. *Mailing Add:* Off Anal & Planning Univ Tex Austin TX 78712

WALLS, KENNETH W, b Ft Lauderdale, Fla, Dec 4, 28; m 56. IMMUNOLOGY, PARASITOLOGY. *Educ:* Ind Univ, AB, 49 & 50; Univ Mich, MS, 52, PhD(bact), 55. *Prof Exp:* Lab chief parasitol & mycol serol, 55-59, lab chief toxoplasmosis, 59-66, CHIEF PARASITOL SEROL UNIT, CTR DIS CONTROL, 66- *Mem:* AAAS; Am Soc Trop Med & Hyg. *Res:* Immunology, serology and epidemiology of parasitic diseases with special emphasis on toxoplasmosis and related diseases. *Mailing Add:* Parasitol Sect Ctr Dis Control 1600 Clifton Rd Atlanta GA 30333

WALLS, NANCY WILLIAMS, b Johnstown, Pa, Sept 19, 30; div. BACTERIOLOGY. *Educ:* Univ Mich, BS, 52, MS, 53, PhD(bact), 59. *Prof Exp:* Instr bact, Emory Univ, 58-59; asst res biologist, 59-61, res asst prof, 62-67, sr res biologist, 67-69, actg dir sch biol, 69-70, ASSOC PROF BIOL, GA INST TECHNOL, 69- *Mem:* AAAS; Am Soc Microbiol; Radiation Res Soc; Am Inst Biol Sci; NY Acad Sci. *Res:* Physiology of Clostridium botulinum; marine microbial ecology; anaerobic bacterial spores; mechanisms of bacterial toxin formation. *Mailing Add:* Sch of Biol Ga Inst of Technol Atlanta GA 30332

WALLS, ROBERT CLARENCE, b Batesville, Ark, Mar 9, 34; m 66; c 3. BIOMETRICS & BIOSTATISTICS, STATISTICS. *Educ:* Harding Col, BS, 59; Univ Ark, MS, 61; Okla State Univ, PhD(statist), 67. *Prof Exp:* Mathematician, Res & Technol Dept, Texaco Inc, 61-64; asst prof biomet, 67-72, assoc prof, 72-77, PROF & HEAD BIOMET, SCH MED SCI, UNIV ARK, LITTLE ROCK, 77- *Mem:* Am Statist Asn; Math Asn Am; Biomet Soc. *Res:* Nonparametric statistics; graphical methods in statistics; mathematical models in biology and medicine. *Mailing Add:* Div of Biomet Univ of Ark Med Ctr Little Rock AR 72201

WALMSLEY, FRANK, b New Bedford, Mass, June 26, 35; m 59; c 2. INORGANIC CHEMISTRY. *Educ:* Univ NH, BS, 57; Univ NC, Chapel Hill, PhD(chem), 62. *Prof Exp:* From asst prof to assoc prof, 62-75, PROF CHEM, UNIV TOLEDO, 75- *Concurrent Pos:* Vis prof, Mich State Univ, 79-80. *Mem:* Am Chem Soc; Royal Soc Chem; Am Sci Affil; Sigma Xi. *Res:* Spectral and magnetic properties of coordination compounds; heteropolyions. *Mailing Add:* Dept of Chem Univ of Toledo Toledo OH 43606

WALMSLEY, JUDITH ABRAMS, b Oak Park, Ill, Feb 6, 36. INORGANIC CHEMISTRY. *Educ:* Fla State Univ, BA, 58; Univ NC, Chapel Hill, PhD(chem), 62. *Prof Exp:* Res scientist chem, Owens-Ill, Inc. 63-66; vis res assoc, 73-75, SR RES ASSOC CHEM, UNIV TOLEDO, 74-, ASST PROF CHEM, 81- *Mem:* Am Chem Soc; AAAS; Sigma Xi. *Res:* Chemistry of metal complexes of biological significance; transition metal complexes of organophosphorus ligands; self-association of hydrogen-bonding molecules in nonpolar solvents; solute-solvent interactions. *Mailing Add:* Dept of Chem Univ of Toledo Toledo OH 43606

WALMSLEY, PETER N(EWTON), b Oldham, Eng, Mar 11, 36; m 56; c 3. CHEMICAL ENGINEERING. *Educ:* Univ Manchester, BScTech, 57, PhD(chem eng), 60. *Prof Exp:* Engr, Sabine River Works, 60-63, engr, Plastics Dept, Exp Sta, 63-67, sr res engr, 67-70, res supvr, 70-74, sr res supvr, 74-75, prin consult, Corp Plans Dept, 75-79, MGR ACQUISTIONS & CORP STUDIES, CORP PLANS DEPT, E I DU PONT DE NEMOURS & CO, INC, 79- *Mem:* Brit Inst Chem Engrs. *Mailing Add:* E I du Pont de Nemours & Co Inc Wilmington DE 19898

WALNE, PATRICIA LEE, b Newark, NJ, Nov 27, 32. BOTANY. *Educ:* Hanover Col, BS, 54; Ind Univ, MS, 59; Univ Tex, PhD(phycol, cell biol), 65. *Prof Exp:* Res fel, Cell Res Inst, Univ Tex, 65-66; from asst prof to assoc prof, 66-73, PROF BOT, UNIV TENN, KNOXVILLE, 73- *Concurrent Pos:* Ed, Phycol Soc Am Newslett, 66-69; consult, Biol Div, Oak Ridge Nat Lab, 66-74; Fulbright-Hays res scholar, Denmark, Coun Int Exchange; Am Asn Univ Women sr fel, 74-75; vis res prof, Univ Copenhagen, 76, 77, 82 & Nencki Inst Exp Biol, Warsaw, 81. *Honors & Awards:* Darbaker Prize, Bot Soc Am, 78. *Mem:* Am Soc Cell Biol; Soc Evolutionary Protistology; Phycol Soc Am (secy, 69-72, vpres, 73, pres, 74); Am Soc Plant Physiologists; Int Phycol Soc. *Res:* Cell biology, experimental phycology and cytology; ultrastructure and development of algae; photoreceptors and sensory transduction in algal flagellates; correlation of structure and function; systematic and evolutionary biology. *Mailing Add:* Dept of Bot Univ of Tenn Knoxville TN 37996

WALNUT, THOMAS HENRY, JR, b Philadelphia, Pa, May 22, 24; m 70; c 2. QUANTUM CHEMISTRY. *Educ:* Harvard Univ, AB, 47; Brown Univ, PhD(chem), 51. *Prof Exp:* Instr, Inst Study Metals, Univ Chicago, 50-52; from asst prof to assoc prof, 52-63, PROF CHEM, SYRACUSE UNIV, 63- *Mem:* Am Chem Soc; Am Phys Soc. *Res:* Magnetic susceptibility of molecules; quantum chemistry; development of shapes in biological systems. *Mailing Add:* Dept of Chem Syracuse Univ Syracuse NY 13210

WALPER, JACK LOUIS, b Excel, Alta, Nov 29, 16; nat US; m 43. GEOLOGY. *Educ:* Univ Okla, BS, 47, MS, 49; Univ Tex, PhD(geol), 58. *Prof Exp:* Asst geol, Univ Okla, 47-48; asst prof, Univ Tulsa, 48-54; instr, Univ Tex, 55-58; assoc prof, Univ Tulsa, 58-63; PROF GEOL, TEX CHRISTIAN UNIV, 63- *Concurrent Pos:* Consult & mem bd dirs, Tex Archit Aggregate Co & Empresa Centro Americana, 74- *Mem:* Am Geophys Union; Asn Eng Geologists; Am Asn Petrol Geologists; Geol Soc Am; Nat Asn Geol Teachers. *Res:* Field exploration; tectonics, especially Central American tectonics. *Mailing Add:* Dept of Geol Tex Christian Univ Ft Worth TX 76129

WALPERT, GEORGE W, b Monett, Mo, Dec 10, 24; m 48; c 6. CHEMICAL ENGINEERING. *Educ:* Mo Sch Mines, BS, 47; Univ Colo, MS, 51, PhD(chem eng), 54. *Prof Exp:* Chem engr, Koppers Co, Inc, 47-50; sr engr, Monsanto Chem Co, 53-57; group leader atomic fuel recovery, Phillips Petrol Co, 57-58; dir res, Wigton Develop Lab, 58-59; mgr process develop, Kordite Co Div, Nat Distillers & Chem Corp, 59-62, USI Film Prod Div, 62-63 & Kordite Co Div, Socony Mobil Oil Co, Inc, 63-64; mgr mat eng, 64-68, MGR OPERS REV STAFF, XEROX CORP, ROCHESTER, 68- *Mem:* Am Chem Soc; Soc Plastics Engrs. *Res:* Process and materials development in fields of coal byproducts, plastics and intermediates, pure metals, packaging materials and consumables for office machinery. *Mailing Add:* 99 Wheelock Rd Penfield NY 14526

WALPOLE, RONALD EDGAR, b Wiarton, Ont, June 19, 31; m 64; c 1. MATHEMATICS, STATISTICS. *Educ:* McMaster Univ, BA, 54, MSc, 55; Va Polytech Inst, PhD, 58. *Prof Exp:* From asst prof to assoc prof, 57-61, PROF MATH & STATIST, ROANOKE COL, 61- *Concurrent Pos:* Consult, White Sands Missile Range, 50-63. *Mem:* Inst Math Statist; Am Statist Asn; Biomet Soc. *Res:* Statistical design of experiments. *Mailing Add:* Dept of Math & Statist Roanoke Col Salem VA 24153

WALRADT, JOHN PIERCE, b Caldwell, Idaho, Feb 12, 42; m 64; c 4. FOOD SCIENCE, ANALYTICAL CHEMISTRY. *Educ:* Univ Idaho, BS, 65; Ore State Univ, MS, 67, PhD(food sci), 69. *Prof Exp:* Sr chemist, 69-71, proj leader, 71-73, group leader, 73-76, SR GROUP LEADER, INT FLAVORS & FRAGRANCES, INC, 76- *Mem:* Am Chem Soc; Inst Food Technologists. *Res:* Flavor chemistry, gas chromatography, natural component identification and associated analytical techniques. *Mailing Add:* Int Flavors & Fragrances Inc 1515 Hwy 36 Union Beach NJ 07735

WALSBERG, GLENN ERIC, b Long Beach, Calif, June 25, 49; m 74. PHYSIOLOGICAL ECOLOGY, ORNITHOLOGY. *Educ:* Calif State Univ, BS, 71; Univ Calif, Los Angeles, PhD(biol), 75. *Prof Exp:* NIH fel, Wash State Univ, 76-78; ASST PROF ZOOL, ARIZ STATE UNIV, 78- *Mem:* Am Ornithologists' Union; Ecol Soc Am; Cooper Ornith Soc; Am Soc Zoologists; Sci Res Soc NAm. *Res:* Avian ecological energetics; physiological ecology of desert birds. *Mailing Add:* Dept of Zool Ariz State Univ Tempe AZ 85281

WALSER, ARMIN, b Walzenhausen, Switz, Apr 6, 37; m 57; c 3. MEDICINAL CHEMISTRY. *Educ:* Swiss Fed Inst Technol, Dipl Ing Chem, 60, PhD(org chem), 63. *Prof Exp:* Fel org chem, Stanford Univ, 63-64; sr chemist, Nutley, NJ, 64-66, Basel, Switz, 66-69 & Nutley, NJ, 69-72, res fel med chem, 72-74, group chief med chem, 74-79, SR RES FEL, HOFFMANN-LA ROCHE, INC, 79- *Mem:* Am Chem Soc. *Res:* Synthesis of new compounds of potential pharmaceutical interest, in particular compounds acting on central nervous system. *Mailing Add:* Hoffmann-La Roche Inc Nutley NJ 07110

WALSER, MACKENZIE, b New York, NY, Sept 19, 24; m 65; c 4. MEDICINE. *Educ:* Yale Univ, BA, 44; Columbia Univ, MD, 48; Am Bd Internal Med, dipl, 56. *Prof Exp:* Intern med, Mass Gen Hosp, 48-49, asst resident, 49-50; from instr to asst prof, Univ Tex Southwestern Med Sch, Dallas, 50-52; investr, Nat Heart Inst, 54-57; from asst prof to assoc prof med & pharmacol, 57-70, PROF MED & PHARMACOL, SCH MED, JOHNS HOPKINS UNIV, 70- *Concurrent Pos:* Resident, City-County Hosp, Dallas, Tex, 50-52; physician, Johns Hopkins Hosp, 60- *Mem:* Am Physiol Soc; Am Soc Clin Invest; Am Soc Pharmacol & Exp Therapeut; Am Inst Nutrit; Asn Am Physicians. *Res:* Medical, Physiological, and pharmacological aspects of electrolyte, amino acid, metabolism and renal function. *Mailing Add:* Dept Pharmacol Sch Med Johns Hopkins Univ Baltimore MD 21205

WALSER, RONALD HERMAN, b Juarez, Mex, Jan 24, 44; m 67; c 5. HORTICULTURE, PLANT PHYSIOLOGY. *Educ:* Brigham Young Univ, BS, 68; Utah State Univ, PhD(crop physiol), 75. *Prof Exp:* Mgr res & develop, Hyponex Co, 75-76; asst prof, Univ Ky, 76-78; ASST PROF HORT, TEX TECH UNIV, 78- *Mem:* Am Soc Hort Sci. *Res:* Environmental physiology of fruits and vegetables. *Mailing Add:* Dept of Plant & Soil Sci Tex Tech Univ Lubbock TX 79409

WALSH, ALEXANDER HAMILTON, b Montclair, NJ, June 2, 31; m 57; c 2. VETERINARY PATHOLOGY. *Educ:* Cornell Univ, DVM, 57; Univ Wis-Madison, PhD(path), 74. *Prof Exp:* Veterinarian, Del-Tor Clin, Lexington, Ky, 57-59, Animal Rescue League of Boston, 59-61 & Green Mountain Animal Hosp, South Burlington, Vt, 61-69; res asst path, Univ Wis-Madison, 69-72; pathologist, Pfizer, Inc, 72-79, dir, Path Bioassay Systs Corp, Woburn, Mass, 79-81; MGR PATH, ETHICON, INC, SOMERVILLE, NJ, 81- *Concurrent Pos:* Lectr fish path, NY State Vet Col, 72-; consult pathobiol, Univ Conn, 73-75; discussant, Charles Louis Davis Found Advan Vet Path, 73-, mem directorate, 75-; adj prof animal path, Univ RI, 76; vpres, Environ Path Lab, Inc, 76- *Mem:* Am Col Vet Path; AAAS; Wildlife Dis Asn; Soc Toxicol; AAAS. *Res:* Evaluation of the toxic and carcinogenic potential of environmental chemicals on laboratory animals, particularly neurocarcinogens and the carcinogenic potential of that group of compounds upon fish. *Mailing Add:* Ethicon Res Found Somerville NJ 08876

WALSH, BERTRAM (JOHN), b Lansing, Mich, May 7, 38; m 60. MATHEMATICAL ANALYSIS. *Educ:* Univ Mich, PhD(math), 63. *Prof Exp:* Lectr math, Univ Mich, 63; from asst prof to assoc prof, Univ Calif, Los Angeles, 63-70; assoc prof, 70-71, PROF MATH, RUTGERS UNIV, NEW BRUNSWICK, 71- *Concurrent Pos:* Vis asst prof, Univ Wash, 66-67. *Mem:* Am Math Soc. *Res:* Functional analysis, locally convex spaces, linear transformations and spectral theory; measure theory; potential theory. *Mailing Add:* Dept of Math Rutgers Univ New Brunswick NJ 08903

WALSH, CHRISTOPHER THOMAS, b Boston, Mass, Feb 16, 44; m 66. BIOCHEMISTRY. *Educ:* Harvard Univ, BA, 65; Rockefeller Univ, PhD(life sci), 70. *Prof Exp:* Helen Hay Whitney Found fel, Brandeis Univ, 70-72; ASST PROF CHEM & BIOL, MASS INST TECHNOL, 72- *Res:* Enzymatic reaction mechanisms, phosphoryl and pyrophosphoryl transfers; flavin-dependent enzymes; membrane biochemistry and mechanism of active transport. *Mailing Add:* Dept of Chem Rm 18-288 Mass Inst of Technol Cambridge MA 02139

WALSH, DAVID ALLAN, b Schenectady, NY, Aug 3, 45; m 67; c 2. ORGANIC CHEMISTRY, MEDICINAL CHEMISTRY. *Educ:* Clarkson Col Tech, NY, BS, 67; Univ NH, MS, 70, PhD(org chem), 73. *Prof Exp:* Sr res chemist, 74-79, GROUP MGR, A H ROBINS CO INC, 79- *Concurrent Pos:* NIH fel, Dept Med Chem, Sch Pharm, Univ Kans, 73-74. *Mem:* Am Chem Soc. *Res:* Synthesis of new nonsteroidal anti-inflammatory agents; synthesis of various nitrogen-containing heterocydes including piperidines, pyrrolidines, isoquinolines, and quinolines. *Mailing Add:* A H Robins Co Inc Box 26609 Richmond VA 23261

WALSH, DAVID ERVIN, b DeGraff, Minn, Aug 7, 39; m 63; c 2. CEREAL CHEMISTRY, BIOCHEMISTRY. *Educ:* St Cloud State Col, BS, 61; NDak State Univ, MS, 63, PhD(cereal chem), 69. *Prof Exp:* Proj leader cereal prod, Squibb Beech-Nut Corp, 63-65; instr cereal chem, NDak State Univ, 65-69, assoc prof cereal chem & technol, 69-77; STAFF MEM, GEN NUTRIT CORP, 77- *Mem:* Am Asn Cereal Chemists; Inst Food Technologists. *Res:* Macaroni products; industrial engineering; computer applications to food processes; protein compositional studies of wheat. *Mailing Add:* Gen Nutrit Corp Box 349 Fargo ND 58102

WALSH, DON, b Berkeley, Calif, Nov 2, 31; m 62; c 2. PHYSICAL OCEANOGRAPHY, OCEAN ENGINEERING. *Educ:* US Naval Acad, BS, 54; Tex A&M Univ, MS, 67, PhD(oceanog), 68; San Diego State Col, MA, 68. *Prof Exp:* Officer-in-chg bathyscaphe Trieste, Navy Electronics Lab, US Navy, San Diego, Calif, 58-62, prin investr remote sensor oceanog proj, Tex A&M Univ, 65-68, sci liaison officer ocean eng, Submarine Develop Group One, San Diego, 69-70, spec asst to Asst Secy Navy Res & Develop, Navy Dept, Washington, DC, 70-73, dep dir, Navy Labs, Hq Naval Mat Command, 74-75; PROF OCEAN ENG & DIR INST MARINE & COASTAL STUDIES, UNIV SOUTHERN CALIF, 75- *Concurrent Pos:* Partic, Deep Freeze, Antarctic, 71; fel, Woodrow Wilson Int Ctr Scholars, Smithsonian Inst, 72-74; mem US adv comt, Eng Comt Ocean Resources, Nat Acad Eng, 72-; dir, US Naval Inst, 74-75; ed, Marine Technol Soc J, 75-80; chmn comt aquacult, Nat Res Coun, 76-78; pres & mem bd dirs, Int Maritime, Inc, 76-; mem, State Dept Law of Sea Adv Group, 79-, Nat Adv Comt Oceans & Atmosphere, 79-; mem comt maritime indust opportunities & requirements for develop ocean resources, Nat Res Coun, Nat Acad Sci, 78-80. *Mem:* AAAS; Am Geophys Union; fel Marine Technol Soc (vpres, 75-79); Soc Naval Architects & Marine Engrs; fel Explorers Club. *Res:* Application of deep submersibles to ocean sciences; deep ocean engineering research and development; application of remote sensors to oceanography; ocean resource planning and policy; author of numerous publications. *Mailing Add:* Inst for Marine & Coastal Studies Univ Southern Calif Los Angeles CA 90007

WALSH, EDWARD JOHN, b Brooklyn, NY, Aug 29, 42; m 64; c 2. INORGANIC CHEMISTRY, POLYMER CHEMISTRY. *Educ:* Franklin & Marshall Col, BA, 64; Middlebury Col, MS, 66; Pa State Univ, University Park, PhD(inorg chem), 70. *Prof Exp:* ASST PROF CHEM, PA STATE UNIV, SHENANGO VALLEY CAMPUS, 70- *Mem:* Am Chem Soc; The Chem Soc. *Res:* Phosphazene derivatives; germazanes; trace elements in water aseneazenes. *Mailing Add:* 735 Robertson Rd Hermitage PA 16146

WALSH, EDWARD JOSEPH, b Woonsocket, RI, June 13, 41. ELECTRICAL ENGINEERING. *Educ:* Northeastern Univ, BS, 63, PhD(elec eng), 67. *Prof Exp:* Instr elec eng, Northeastern Univ, 66-67; aerospace technologist, Electronics Res Ctr, 67-70, AEROSPACE TECHNOLOGIST, WALLOPS FLIGHT CTR, NASA, 70- *Mem:* Am Geophys Union; Inst Elec & Electronics Engrs. *Res:* Electromagnetic theory; radio wave propagation and scattering; radio oceanography; radar altimetry. *Mailing Add:* DAS NASA/Wallops Flight Ctr Wallops Island VA 23337

WALSH, EDWARD JOSEPH, JR, b Philadelphia, Pa, Aug 2, 35; m 59; c 2. ORGANIC CHEMISTRY. *Educ:* State Univ NY Albany, BS, 60; Univ NH, PhD(chem), 64. *Prof Exp:* Teaching asst, State Univ NY Albany, 60-61; asst prof, 64-86, assoc prof, 68-70, PROF CHEM & DEPT CHMN, ALLEGHENY COL, 70- *Concurrent Pos:* NSF sci fac grant, Mass Inst Technol, 69-70. *Mem:* Am Chem Soc. *Res:* Free radical reactions involving the acyl radical; free radical reactions of certain organotin hydrides. *Mailing Add:* Dept of Chem Allegheny Col Meadville PA 16335

WALSH, EDWARD KYRAN, b Philadelphia, Pa, Feb 19, 31; m 52; c 6. ENGINEERING SCIENCE, APPLIED MECHANICS. *Educ:* Union Col, BME, 63; Brown Univ, PhD(appl math), 67. *Prof Exp:* Engr, Mech Technol Inc, 62-63; res fel, Mellon Inst Sci, 66-68; asst prof civil eng, Carnegie-Mellon Univ, 67-70; assoc prof, 70-74, PROF ENG SCI, UNIV FLA, 74- *Concurrent Pos:* Consult, Gen Eng & Consult Lab, Gen Elec Co, 64-65, Sandia Labs, Albuquerque, 69- *Mem:* Soc Natural Philos. *Res:* Continuum mechanics; dynamic material response; wave propagation; bioengineering. *Mailing Add:* Dept of Eng Sci Univ of Fla Gainesville FL 32611

WALSH, EDWARD L(ENORD), aeronautical engineering, theoretical mechanics, see previous edition

WALSH, EDWARD NELSON, b Chicago, Ill, Nov 22, 25; m 50; c 2. ORGANIC CHEMISTRY. *Educ:* Ill Inst Technol, BS, 48, PhD, 65; DePaul Univ, MS, 52. *Prof Exp:* Chemist, Swift & Co, Ill, 48-51 & Victor Chem Works, 51-59; supvr org res, 59-63, mgr chem res, 63-65, mgr chem prod develop sect, Dobbs Ferry, 65-69, sr sect mgr org res, 69-75, MGR CHEM DEPT, STAUFFER CHEM CO, DOBBS FERRY, 75- *Mem:* AAAS; Am Chem Soc. *Res:* Organophosphorus compounds; agricultural chemicals; solvents; surfactants; flame retardants; synthetic lubricants; pharmaceutical intermediates; organometallics; photochemistry; catalysts; inorganic phosphorus compounds. *Mailing Add:* 33 Concord Dr New City NY 10956

WALSH, GARY LYNN, b Fremont, Nebr, June 30, 40; m 64. AIR POLLUTION, ENVIRONMENTAL SCIENCES. *Educ:* Midland Lutheran Col, BS, 62; Univ Nebr, MS, 65; Univ SDak, PhD(zool), 69. *Prof Exp:* Asst prof zool, Ind Univ Northwest, 69-70; air pollution control chief, Michigan City, Ind, 70-72; admin asst to air pollution control officer, 72-74, supvr, Air Pollution Control Sect, 74-79, ASST CHIEF, DIV ENVIRON HEALTH, LINCOLN LANCASTER COUNTY HEALTH DEPT, 79- *Mem:* Air Pollution Control Asn. *Res:* Role of vitamin B12, biotin and thiamine on seasonal fluctuations of euglenophyte populations; taxonomy of Antarctic freshwater and soil amoeba. *Mailing Add:* Div Environ Health Lincoln-Lancaster Co Health Dept Lincoln NE 68502

WALSH, GERALD MICHAEL, b Portland, Ore, Sept, 1, 44; m 70; c 2. PHARMACOLOGY. *Educ:* Univ Santa Clara, BS, 66; Ore State Univ, PhD(pharmacol), 71. *Prof Exp:* Res asst pharmacol, Ore State Univ, 67-69; asst prof, Univ Ga, 70-74; asst prof res med, Sch Med, Univ Okla, 74-80; GROUP LEADER, DEPT PHARMACOL, G D SEARLE & CO, 80- *Concurrent Pos:* NSF instnl res grant, Univ Ga, 72-73. *Res:* Cardiovascular pharmacology and toxicology; hypertension. *Mailing Add:* G D Searle & Co Box 5110 Chicago IL 60680

WALSH, GERALD PETER, experimental medicine, microbiology, see previous edition

WALSH, JAMES ALOYSIUS, b Brooklyn, NY, Dec 15, 33; m 60. PHYSICAL ORGANIC CHEMISTRY. *Educ:* Fordham Univ, BS, 55; Purdue Univ, MS, 58, PhD(org chem), 63. *Prof Exp:* Instr chem, Purdue Univ, 60-63; from asst prof to assoc prof, 63-73, chmn dept, 77-81, PROF CHEM, JOHN CARROLL UNIV, 73- *Concurrent Pos:* Res assoc, Univ Calif, Santa Cruz, 73. *Mem:* Am Chem Soc; Sigma Xi. *Res:* Chemistry of organo-sulfur compounds, especially sulfoxides and derivatives of sulfurtrioxide; phthalocyanines. *Mailing Add:* Dept of Chem John Carroll Univ Cleveland OH 44118

WALSH, JAMES PAUL, b Fall River, Mass, Apr 3, 17; m 42; c 3. ENGINEERING. *Educ:* Stevens Inst Technol, ME, 38; Univ Md, MS, 50. *Hon Degrees:* EngD, Stevens Inst Technol, 58. *Prof Exp:* Sect head, US Naval Res Lab, 42-55, dep dir proj Vanguard, 55-59; dir dept, C-E-I-R, Inc, 60-63; pres & chmn bd, Matrix Corp, 63-69; supt ocean technol, Naval Res Lab, Washington, DC, 69-78; CONSULT OCEAN ENG, SHOCK & VIBRATION, DYNAMICS, 78- *Concurrent Pos:* Consult, US Naval Res Lab. *Res:* Shock vibration; dynamics of structures; instrumentation; space research and operations; systems analysis; computer sciences; ocean technology; ocean operations. *Mailing Add:* Box 946 Sherwood Forest MD 21405

WALSH, JOHN EDMOND, b New York, NY, Aug 20, 39; m 66; c 3. PLASMA PHYSICS. *Educ:* NS Tech Col, BSc, 62; Columbia Univ, MSc, 65, DSc, 68. *Prof Exp:* Res engr, US Army Signal Res & Develop Lab, Ft Monmouth, 62-65; asst prof, 68-74, assoc prof, 74-790, PROF PHYSICS, DARTMOUTH COL, 79- *Mem:* Am Phys Soc; Sigma Xi. *Res:* Diffusion of turbulent plasmas; electron scattering in turbulent plasmas; nonlinear interactions in plasmas; millimeter and submillimeter radiation sources. *Mailing Add:* Dept of Physics Dartmouth Col Hanover NH 03755

WALSH, JOHN JOSEPH, b Cambridge, Mass, Sept 11, 42; m 69. ECOLOGY, OCEANOGRAPHY. *Educ:* Harvard Univ, AB, 64; Univ Miami, MS, 68, PHD(marine sci), 69. *Prof Exp:* Fel, Univ Wash, 69-70, res asst prof oceanog, 70-75; HEAD DIV OCEANOG SCI, BROOKHAVEN NAT LAB, 75- *Honors & Awards:* Gold Medal Sci, Univ de Liege, 80. *Mem:* AAAS; Am Soc Limnol & Oceanog. *Res:* Shelf ecosystems; systems analysis; statistics; phytoplankton ecology; mathematical models; theoretical ecology. *Mailing Add:* Div of Oceanog Sci Bldg 318 Upton NY 11973

WALSH, JOHN JOSEPH, b New York, NY, July 31, 24; wid; c 3. CARDIOLOGY. *Educ:* Long Island Col Med, MD, 48; Am Bd Internal Med, dipl, 58. *Prof Exp:* Intern USPHS Hosp, NY, 48-49, resident med, Seattle, Wash, 51-54, asst chief med, New Orleans, La, 54-56, dep chief, 56; from instr med to asst prof clin med, 57-60, dean sch med & coordr health serv, 68-69, PROF MED, SCH MED, TULANE UNIV, 60-, VPRES HEALTH AFFAIRS, 69-, CHANCELLOR MED CTR, 72- *Concurrent Pos:* Fel cardiol, Sch Med, Tulane Univ, 57-58, instr, 55-; vis physician, Charity Hosp, 55-; chief res activities, USPHS, 58-64, chief med, 63-64, med officer in charge, 64-66, dir div direct health serv, 66-68. *Mem:* Am Thoracic Soc; AMA; fel Am Col Cardiol; fel Am Col Physicians; fel Am Col Chest Physicians. *Res:* Cardiopulmonary diseases. *Mailing Add:* Tulane Univ Med Ctr 1430 Tulane Ave New Orleans LA 70112

WALSH, JOHN LAWRENCE, b San Francisco, Calif, Apr 5, 28. SOLID STATE PHYSICS. *Educ:* Univ Calif, BS, 50, MA, 52, PhD(physics), 65. *Prof Exp:* Physicist, Los Alamos Sci Lab, 52 & US Naval Electronics Lab, 53; mem tech staff, Hughes Aircraft Co, 56-60, mem tech staff, Res Labs, 60-62; mem tech staff, Sci & Tech Div, Inst Defense Anal, 62-70; PHYSICIST, NAVAL RES LAB, 70- *Concurrent Pos:* Lectr, Univ Southern Calif, 61-62. *Mem:* Am Phys Soc; Sigma Xi; Optical Soc Am; Inst Elec & Electronics Engrs. *Res:* Solid state and gaseous laser physics; solid state physics research, using nuclear magnetic resonance as an experimental tool. *Mailing Add:* Naval Res Lab Code 4109 Washington DC 20375

WALSH, JOHN M, b Wichita Falls, Tex, Nov 6, 23; m 52; c 3. PHYSICS, CONTINUUM DYNAMICS. *Educ:* Univ Tex, BS, 47, PhD(physics), 50. *Prof Exp:* Staff mem, Los Alamos Sci Lab, 50-60; staff mem, Gen Atomic Div, Gen Dynamics Corp, 60-67; mgr continuum mech div, Systs Sci & Software, 67-74; MEM STAFF, LOS ALAMOS SPACE LAB, 74- *Mem:* Am Phys Soc. *Res:* Shock hydrodynamics; shock wave physics; properties of materials at extreme pressures; experimental, theoretical and numerical work in these areas and supervision of groups so involved; fluid dynamics. *Mailing Add:* Los Alamos Sci Lab Los Alamos NM 87544

WALSH, JOHN PAUL, b Rochester, NY, Dec 29, 42; c 2. ORGANIC CHEMISTRY. *Educ:* Purdue Univ, Lafayette, BS, 64; Univ Wis-Madison, MS, 66; Univ Tex, Austin, PhD(org chem), 70. *Prof Exp:* Sr res chemist, Org Res Dept, Pennwalt Corp, Pa, 69-74; res chemist, Para-Chem Inc, 74-76; SR APPL CHEMIST, CELANESE CHEM CO, INC, 76- *Mem:* Am Chem Soc. *Res:* Organic synthesis; organosulfur, nitrogen and phosphorus; alkyds; polyesters; urea-formaldehyde resins. *Mailing Add:* Celanese Chem Co Inc 86 Morris Ave Summit NJ 07901

WALSH, JOHN RICHARD, b San Francisco, Calif, Aug 22, 20; m 44; c 5. INTERNAL MEDICINE. *Educ:* Creighton Univ, BS, 43, MD, 45, MSc, 51; Am Bd Internal Med, dipl, 53. *Prof Exp:* Actg asst med, Sch Med, Creighton Univ, 51-52, asst, 52-53, from instr to assoc prof, 53-57, prof & dir dept, 57-60; PROF MED, MED SCH, UNIV ORE, 60- *Concurrent Pos:* Ward physician, Vet Admin Hosp, Omaha, Nebr, 51-52, asst chief med serv, 52-53, actg chief, 53-54, chief, 54-56, chief, Portland, Ore, 60-, actg chief radioisotope serv, 62-70; assoc, Col Med, Univ Nebr, 53-55, asst prof, 55-56. *Mem:* Am Soc Hemat; Am Fedn Clin Res; fel Am Col Physicians; Int Soc Hemat. *Res:* Hematology. *Mailing Add:* Health Sci Ctr Sch of Med Univ of Ore Portland OR 97201

WALSH, JOHN THOMAS, b Lincoln, RI, Dec 23, 27; m 52; c 3. ANALYTICAL CHEMISTRY. *Educ:* Providence Col, BS, 50; Univ RI, MS, 52, PhD(chem), 65. *Prof Exp:* Res chemist, Rumford Chem Works, RI, 52-54; RES CHEMIST, US ARMY NATICK LABS, 54- *Mem:* Am Chem Soc; Am Soc Testing & Mat. *Res:* Analytical instrumentation research in the areas of gas chromatography and mass spectrometry; applications have been the composition study of natural products such as foods and biologicals; investigation of toxic pollutants in air, water and solid wastes by analytical methods of gas and liquid chromatography and mass spectrometry; fourier transform infrared spectroscopy as an area of analytical instrumentation research; bacterial degradation products of military materials such as foods, clothing and munitions. *Mailing Add:* 15 Ridgeland Dr Cumberland RI 02864

WALSH, JOSEPH BROUGHTON, b Utica, NY, Sept 5, 30; m 62; c 1. GEOLOGY, GEOPHYSICS. *Educ:* Mass Inst Technol, SB, 52, SM, 54, ME, 56, ScD(mech eng), 58. *Prof Exp:* Engr, Foster Miller Assocs, Inc, 57-59, A-b DeLaval Ljungstrom Angturbin, 59-60 & Woods Hole Oceanog Inst, 60-63; part-time vis prof, 63-64; res assoc geol & geophys, 63-72, SR RES SCIENTIST, DEPT EARTH & PLANETARY SCI, MASS INST TECHNOL, 72- *Res:* Theoretical analysis of various properties of rock, especially strength, elastic moduli and seismic attenuation, and analysis of how these properties should affect behavior in situ. *Mailing Add:* Rm 54-720 Mass Inst Technol 77 Massachusetts Ave Cambridge MA 02139

WALSH, KENNETH ALBERT, b Yankton, SDak, May 23, 22; m 44; c 5. CHEMICAL METALLURGY, CERAMICS. *Educ:* Yankton Col, BA, 42; Iowa State Univ, PhD(chem), 50. *Prof Exp:* Asst prof chem, Iowa State Univ, 50-51; mem staff, Los Alamos Sci Lab, 51-57; supvr inorg chem res, Int Minerals & Chem Corp, 57-60; ASSOC DIR CORP TECHNOL, BRUSH WELLMAN INC, ELMORE, 60- *Mem:* AAAS; Am Chem Soc; Am Soc Metals; Am Ceramic Soc. *Res:* Beryllium metal extraction; role of trace elements in properties of beryllium; beryllium chemicals, ecology, and electronic materials. *Mailing Add:* 2624 Fangboner Rd Fremont OH 43420

WALSH, KENNETH ANDREW, b Hemmingford, Que, Aug 7, 31; m 53; c 3. BIOCHEMISTRY. *Educ:* McGill Univ, BSc, 51; Purdue Univ, MS, 53; Univ Toronto, PhD, 59. *Prof Exp:* Jr res officer, Nat Res Coun Can, 53-55; res instr, 59-62, asst prof, 62-65, assoc prof biochem, 65-68, PROF BIOCHEM, UNIV WASH, 68- *Mem:* Am Soc Biol Chemists. *Res:* Structure and function of proteins; mechanisms of zymogen activation and protease action; amino acid sequence and protein conformation; molecular evolution; biochemistry of fertilization. *Mailing Add:* Dept of Biochem Univ of Wash Seattle WA 98195

WALSH, LEO MARCELLUS, b Moorland, Iowa, Jan 16, 31; m 58. SOIL FERTILITY, SOIL SCIENCE. *Educ:* Iowa State Univ, BS, 52; Univ Wis, MS, 57, PhD(soils), 59. *Prof Exp:* Asst prof & exten specialist, 59-64, assoc prof, 64-68, chmn, 72-79, PROF SOILS, UNIV WIS-MADISON, 68-, DEAN, COL AGR & LIFE SCI, 79- *Mem:* Soil Sci Soc Am (pres, 79); fel AAAS; Fel Am Soc Agron; Soil Conserv Soc Am. *Res:* Use of nitrogen and sulfur fertilizers; use of zinc, manganese and other micronutrients; soil fertility, especially for corn and other cash crops; disposal of wastes on agricultural land; soil conservation. *Mailing Add:* Univ Wis 1450 Linden Dr Madison WI 53706

WALSH, LINDA JANE, b London, Eng, June 18, 50; Can & Brit citizen. IMMUNOLOGY. *Educ:* Univ Toronto, BSc, 72, MSc, 75; Queens Univ, Kingston, PhD(genetics), 80. *Prof Exp:* Fel, Hosp Sick Children, Toronto, 79-81; RES SCIENTIST, MT SINAI HOSP, 81- *Concurrent Pos:* Lectr, Univ Toronto, 80-81. *Res:* Identification of disease resceptibility genes; isolating the etiological agent in non-A and non-B hepatitis. *Mailing Add:* Res Dept Rm 138D Mt Sinai Hosp 600 University Ave Toronto ON M5G 1X5 Can

WALSH, MICHAEL ANTHONY, b Burlington, Iowa, Mar 7, 41; m 63, 76; c 3. BOTANY, PLANT ANATOMY. *Educ:* Western Ill Univ, BSEd, 64; Univ Mo, MA, 67; Univ Wis, PhD(bot), 72. *Prof Exp:* Instr bot, Wis State Univ, 67-68; asst prof, Univ Pittsburgh, 72-76; ASST PROF BIOL & BOT, UTAH STATE UNIV, 76- *Mem:* Bot Soc Am; Am Inst Biol Sci; AAAS. *Res:* Light and electron microscope study of phloem structure and development in monocotyledons and parasitic angiosperms. *Mailing Add:* Dept of Biol UMC 45 Utah State Univ Logan UT 84322

WALSH, PATRICK NOEL, b New York, NY, Dec 7, 30; m 62; c 5. HIGH TEMPERATURE CHEMISTRY. *Educ:* Fordham Univ, BS, 51, MS, 52, PhD(chem), 56. *Prof Exp:* Res assoc high temperature chem, Ohio State Univ, 56-60; mem staff, Union Carbide Res Inst, NY, 60-66 & Space Sci & Eng Lab, 66-68, res assoc, Linde Div, 68-81, CONSULT, ENG PROD DIV, UNION CARBIDE CORP, 82- *Mem:* Am Soc Metals; Electrochem Soc; Am Chem Soc. *Res:* Thermodynamics and kinetics of high temperature chemical processes. *Mailing Add:* Union Carbide Corp 1500 Polco St Indianapolis IN 46224

WALSH, PETER, b New York, NY, Aug 21, 29; m 52; c 4. PHYSICS. *Educ:* Fordham Univ, BS, 51; NY Univ, MS, 53, PhD(physics), 60. *Prof Exp:* Sr scientist, Westinghouse Lamp Div, NY, 51-61; instr physics & math, Eve Sch, Wagner Col, 57-63; supvr physics res, Am Stand Res Lab, NJ, 61-63; PROF PHYSICS, FAIRLEIGH DICKINSON UNIV, 63- *Concurrent Pos:* Dir, NSF Undergrad Partic Prog, Fairleigh Dickinson Univ, 63-; consult, S-F-D Labs, 63-66, Am Standard, 63, Belock Instr, 63-64, Nuclear Res Assocs, 64-65, Thiokol Chem, 64, US Army Res Off, 64-71, 77, 80, Curtiss Wright Corp, 65, Singer Corp, 68, Picatinny Arsenal, 70-74, Corning Glass, 71, Columbus Labs, Battelle Mem Inst, 74-75, Duro Test Corp, 76-, Xerox Corp, 79-, Mass Inst Technol, 80 & Polaroid, 81; vis res scientist, Mass Inst Technol, 77; vis prof, Univ Sheffield, 78 & 79. *Mem:* AAAS; Am Phys Soc; Optical Soc Am. *Res:* Amorphous semiconductors; lasers; quantum physics; optics; plasmas. *Mailing Add:* Dept of Physics Fairleigh Dickinson Univ Teaneck NJ 07666

WALSH, PETER NEWTON, b Chicago, Ill, Apr 16, 35; m 58; c 3. HEMATOLOGY. *Educ:* Amherst Col, BA, 57; Washington Univ, MD, 61; Oxford Univ, DPhil(med), 72; Am Bd Internal Med, dipl, 68. *Prof Exp:* Intern internal med, Barnes Hosp, St Louis, 61-62, resident, 62-63; fel hemat, Sch Med, Washington Univ, 63-69; res fel blood coagulation, Oxford Haemophilia Ctr, Churchill Hosp, 69-72; asst prof, 72-74, ASSOC PROF INTERNAL MED, HEALTH SCI CTR, TEMPLE UNIV, 75- *Concurrent Pos:* Sr resident, Palo Alto Stanford Hosp, 64-65; chief resident, Sch Med, Washington Univ, 65-66; asst physician, Barnes Hosp, 65-66; med liaison officer, Nat Heart Inst, 66-69; NIH res fel, 69-72; hon sr registr med, United Oxford Hosps, 69-72; assoc ed, Thrombosis et Diathesis Haemorrhagica, 76-; mem Exec Comt Coun Thrombosis, Am Heart Asn. *Honors & Awards:* First Int Prize, Viviana Luckhaus Found, Arg, 72; Res Career Develop Award, Nat Heart & Lung Inst, 72; Jane Nugent Cochems Prize, Univ Colo Sch Med, 74. *Mem:* Int Soc Thrombosis & Haemostasis; Am Physiol Soc; Soc Exp Med &

Biol; Am Soc Clin Invest. *Res:* Role of blood platelets in blood coagulation, hemostasis and thrombosis; coagulation factor purification; mechanisms of binding of coagulation factors to platelets; role of platelet coagulant activities in thrombosis. *Mailing Add:* Spec Ctr Thrombosis Res Temple Univ Health Sci Ctr Philadelphia PA 19140

WALSH, PHILIP REGIS, b Pittsburgh, Pa, July 9, 44; m 71; c 3. CLINICAL CHEMISTRY, BIOCHEMISTRY. *Educ:* Gannon Col, Pa, BA, 66; Univ Pittsburgh, PhD(biochem), 71. *Prof Exp:* Fel clin chem, Dept Lab Med, Univ Wash, 71-73; chief chemist, 73-75, head, Dept Chem, 75-79, MGR, DEPT CHEM, LAB PROCEDURES EAST INC, 79- *Concurrent Pos:* NIH fel, 71-73; vis asst prof biochem, Hahnemann Med Col & Hosp, Philadelphia, 77-80, assoc prof, 80- *Mem:* Am Asn Clin Chem; Am Soc Clin Pathologists; Clin Liband Assay Soc. *Res:* Development of analytical methods for the clinical chemistry laboratory. *Mailing Add:* Lab Procedures East Inc 1075 First Ave King of Prussia PA 19406

WALSH, RAYMOND ANTHONY, chemistry, see previous edition

WALSH, RAYMOND ROBERT, b Denver, Colo, Apr 9, 25; m 52; c 6. PHYSIOLOGY. *Educ:* Cornell Univ, AB, 50, PhD(zool), 53. *Prof Exp:* Assoc res physiologist, Brookhaven Nat Lab, 53-55; from instr to assoc prof physiol, Sch Med, Univ Colo, Denver, 55-71; prof, Sch Dent, Southern Ill Univ, 71-72; PROF BIOL & CHMN DEPT, ST LOUIS UNIV, 72- *Mem:* Am Physiol Soc; Am Soc Zoologists; Soc Exp Biol & Med. *Res:* Neurobiology; comparative physiology. *Mailing Add:* Dept of Biol St Louis Univ St Louis MO 63103

WALSH, ROBERT JEROME, b Chicago, Ill, Jan 12, 29. SEMICONDUCTOR MATERIALS, CHEMO-MECHANICAL POLISHING. *Educ:* Univ Wis, BS, 50. *Prof Exp:* Res engr, 51-55, sr res engr, 55-58, res group leader, 58-62, sr res group leader, 62-70, fel, 70-81, SR FEL, MONSANTO CO, 81- *Mem:* Am Inst Chem Engrs; Electrochem Soc; AAAS. *Res:* Semiconductor materials technology including growth of single crystals, epitaxial deposition, damage free polished surfaces and ultracleaning of surfaces. *Mailing Add:* 356 Sudbury Lane Ballwin MO 63011

WALSH, ROBERT MICHAEL, b Wilmington, Del, Jan 28, 38; m 61; c 4. PHYSICAL CHEMISTRY. *Educ:* Univ Del, BS, 60; Univ Calif, Berkeley, PhD(chem), 65. *Prof Exp:* Res chemist, 65-72, sr res chemist, 72-80, RES SCIENTIST, HERCULES INC, 80- *Mem:* Soc Photog Scientists & Engrs; Am Chem Soc. *Res:* Photoprocesses in materials; photographic systems. *Mailing Add:* 1800 Mt Salem Lane Wilmington DE 19806

WALSH, ROBERT R(EDDINGTON), b Wilmington, Del, Nov 4, 27. ELECTRICAL ENGINEERING, PHYSICS. *Educ:* St Mary's Col, Md, AB, 53. *Prof Exp:* Engr, E I du Pont de Nemours & Co, 54-59, res engr, 59-60; asst to dir appl physics, All Am Eng Co, 60-61, dir mkt & prod develop, Div, 61-63, dir res, 63-66; exec vpres & gen mgr, Technidyne, Inc, 67-71; pub rels asst, 71-72; electronics consult, Advan Technol Prod, Inc, Newark, 73-76; tech planning staff mem, 76-79, ASST VPRES TECH PLANNING, WILMINGTON TRUST CO, 80- *Concurrent Pos:* Chief engr, Reynolds Broadcasting Co, 57-60; teacher, Adult Prog, Wilmington Pub Schs, 56-60; 56-60. *Mem:* Inst Elec & Electronics Engrs; AAAS. *Res:* Circuit logic; systems; automata; memory and computing circuits; design of cybernetic systems; instruments for medical applications and devices and systems for instrumentation, control and automation of industrial processes; engineering applications of lasers; data and communication networks; energy management. *Mailing Add:* 1301 N Harrison St Wilmington DE 19806

WALSH, SCOTT WESLEY, b Wauwatosa, Wis, July 23, 47; m 81. PERINATAL PHYSIOLOGY, REPRODUCTIVE ENDOCRINOLOGY. *Educ:* Univ Wis-Milwaukee, BS, 70; Univ Wis-Madison, MS, 72, PhD(endocrinol, reproductive physiol), 75. *Prof Exp:* asst prof physiol, Sch Med Univ NDak, 75-76; asst scientist perinatal physiol, Ore Regional Primate Res Ctr, 76-80; asst prof dept physiol, Health Sci Ctr, Sch Med, Univ Ore, 78-80; ASST PROF DEPT PHYSIOL, MICH STATE UNIV, 80- *Mem:* Soc Study Reproduction; Sigma Xi; Endocrine Soc; Am Physiol Soc; Soc Gynec Invest. *Mailing Add:* Dept Physiol Giltner Hall Mich State Univ East Lansing MI 78824

WALSH, STEPHEN G, b Brooklyn, NY, Apr 23, 47. BIOCHEMISTRY. *Educ:* Cath Univ Am, BA, 69; State Univ NY Buffalo, MA, 80, PhD(biochem), 81. *Prof Exp:* Teacher sci & math, St Thomas Community Sch, 69-73; teacher chem, La Salle Acad, 73-77; ASST PROF CHEM, COL MT ST VINCENT, 81- *Mem:* AAAS; Am Chem Soc; Sigma Xi. *Res:* Protein chemistry and immunochemistry of venom allergens investigated by biochemical and immunochemical methods. *Mailing Add:* Chem Dept Manhattan Col Bronx NY 10471

WALSH, THOMAS DAVID, b Chicago, Ill, Oct 30, 36; m 58; c 2. CHEMISTRY. *Educ:* Univ Notre Dame, AB, 58; Univ Calif, PhD(chem), 62. *Prof Exp:* Asst prof chem, Univ Ga, 62-67; vis asst prof, Ohio State Univ, 67-68; assoc prof, Univ SDak, 68-70; asst prof, 70-72, ASSOC PROF CHEM, UNIV NC, CHARLOTTE, 72- *Concurrent Pos:* Danforth Found assoc, 64-; res assoc, Univ NC, Chapel Hill, 69-70. *Mem:* Am Chem Soc. *Res:* Organic reaction mechanisms; stereochemistry; organometallic chemistry; photochemistry; electrochemistry. *Mailing Add:* Dept of Chem Univ of NC Charlotte NC 28223

WALSH, WALTER MICHAEL, JR, b Los Angeles, Calif, July 28, 31; m 56; c 2. SOLID STATE PHYSICS. *Educ:* Harvard Univ, AB, 54, AM, 55, PhD(physics), 58. *Prof Exp:* Res fel solid state physics, Harvard Univ, 58-59; mem tech staff, Bell Labs, 59-67 & 77, dept head, 67-77, head, Solid State & Physics Metals Res Dept, 67-77. *Mem:* Fel Am Phys Soc. *Res:* Experimental physics of solids using microwave resonance techniques; effects of pressure and temperature on solids; resonance and wave propagation phenomena in metals and organic conductors. *Mailing Add:* Bell Labs Murray Hill NJ 07974

WALSH, WILLIAM J, b Saginaw, Mich, Oct 2, 36; m 62; c 5. CHEMICAL & NUCLEAR ENGINEERING. *Educ:* Notre Dame Univ, BS, 58; Univ Mich, MS, 60, MS, 61; Iowa State Univ, PhD(chem eng), 64. *Prof Exp:* Res asst, Univ Mich Res Inst, 58-61; res asst, Inst Atomic Res, Ames, Iowa, 61-64; assoc engr, Argonne Nat Lab, 64-77; MEM STAFF, DIAMOND SHAMROCK CORP, 77- *Mem:* Am Inst Chem Engrs. *Res:* High temperature battery development; nuclear fuels reprocessing; liquid metal distillation, nuclear criticality; radiotracer experiments; mass transfer; heat transfer; high vacuum experiments; fast breeder reactor design and economics. *Mailing Add:* Diamond Shamrock Corp 1100 Superior Ave Cleveland OH 44114

WALSH, WILLIAM K, b Columbus, Ohio, Sept 29, 32. TEXTILE CHEMISTRY, CHEMICAL ENGINEERING. *Educ:* Univ SC, BS, 54; NC State Univ, PhD(chem eng), 67. *Prof Exp:* Engr, Celanese Corp Am, SC, 59-60; res asst, 60-67, asst prof, 67-72, assoc prof, 72-77, prof textile chem, 77-80, asst dean res, Sch Textiles, 80-81, ASSOC DEAN, RES & GRAD EDUC, SCH TEXTILES, NC STATE UNIV, 81- *Mem:* AAAS; Am Chem Soc; Am Asn Textile Chemists & Colorists; Fiber Soc. *Res:* Applications of ionizing radiation to textile chemistry; radiation graft copolymerization, cross-linking, mechanical properties of textiles; physical and surface chemistry of polymers. *Mailing Add:* Sch Textiles NC State Univ Raleigh NC 27650

WALSKE, (MAX) CARL, b Seattle, Wash, June 2, 22; m 46; c 3. PHYSICS. *Educ:* Univ Wash, BS, 44; Cornell Univ, PhD(physics), 51. *Prof Exp:* Mem staff, Los Alamos Sci Lab, 51-55, asst leader theoret div, 55-56; dep res dir, Atomics Int Div, NAm Aviation, Inc, 56-59; mem US deleg, Conf Suspension Nuclear Tests, Geneva, Switz, 59-61; sci rep, AEC, London, Eng, 61-62; theoret physicist, Rand Corp, 62-63; sci attache, US Missions to NATO & Orgn Econ Coop & Develop, Paris, France, 63-65; staff mem, Los Alamos Sci Lab, 65-66; asst to secy defense & chmn mil liaison comt, US Dept Defense, 66-73; PRES, ATOMIC INDUST FORUM, INC, 73- *Concurrent Pos:* Consult, Los Alamos Sci Lab, 56-59 & 62-63. *Mem:* Am Phys Soc; Am Nuclear Soc; fel Explorers Club. *Res:* Nuclear and reactor physics. *Mailing Add:* 10125 Bevern Lane Potomac MD 20854

WALSTAD, JOHN DANIEL, b Minneapolis, Minn, Aug 22, 44; m 66; c 2. FOREST PROTECTION. *Educ:* Col William & Mary, BS, 66; Duke Univ, MF, 68; Cornell Univ, PhD(entom), 71. *Prof Exp:* Forest scientist, Weyerhaeuser Co, 71-76, admin asst res, 76-77, res mgr forestry, 77-80; ASSOC PROF FOREST VEGETATION MGT, ORE STATE UNIV, 80- *Mem:* Soc Am Foresters; Weed Sci Soc Am; Entom Soc Am; AAAS. *Res:* Forest vegetation management. *Mailing Add:* Forest Sci Dept Sch Forestry Ore State Univ Corvallis OR 97331

WALSTEDT, RUSSELL E, b Minneapolis, Minn, June 12, 36; m 64; c 2. SOLID STATE PHYSICS. *Educ:* Mass Inst Technol, BS, 58; Univ Calif, Berkeley, PhD(physics), 62. *Prof Exp:* NSF fel, Clarendon Lab, Eng, 61-62; asst res physicist, Univ Calif, Berkeley, 62-65; MEM TECH STAFF SOLID STATE MAGNETISM, BELL LABS, 65- *Mem:* Am Phys Soc. *Res:* Nuclear magnetic resonance and its application to the study of magnetism and atomic motion in the solid state; computer modeling of amorphous magnetic systems. *Mailing Add:* Room 1d362 Box 261 Bell Labs Murray Hill NJ 07974

WALSTON, CLAUDE ELLSWORTH, electrical engineering, see previous edition

WALSTON, DALE EDOUARD, b Woodsboro, Tex, Dec 1, 30. MATHEMATICS. *Educ:* Tex A&M Univ, BA, 52; Univ Tex, MA, 59, PhD(math), 61. *Prof Exp:* Asst prof, 61-72, ASSOC PROF MATH, UNIV TEX, AUSTIN, 72- *Concurrent Pos:* Consult, Manned Space Ctr, NASA, 66. *Mem:* Am Math Soc; Math Asn Am. *Res:* Numerical solution of differential equations. *Mailing Add:* Dept of Math Univ of Tex Austin TX 78712

WALSTON, WILLIAM H(OWARD), JR, b Salisbury, Md, Apr 13, 37; m 62; c 2. MECHANICAL ENGINEERING. *Educ:* Univ Del, BME, 59, MME, 61, PhD(appl sci), 64. *Prof Exp:* Asst prof, 65-67, ASSOC PROF MECH ENG, UNIV MD, COLLEGE PARK, 67- *Mem:* Am Soc Mech Engrs. *Res:* Signal propagation; shock and vibrations analysis; applied mathematics; design; automotive drag reduction, acoustics, noise control. *Mailing Add:* Dept of Mech Eng Univ of Md College Park MD 20742

WALSTROM, ROBERT JOHN, b Omaha, Nebr, Apr 24, 22; m 44; c 2. ENTOMOLOGY. *Educ:* Univ Nebr, BS, 47, MS, 49; Iowa State Univ, PhD, 55. *Prof Exp:* State entomologist, State Dept Agr & Inspection, Nebr, 48-50; exten entomologist, Iowa State Univ, 50-55; PROF ENTOM, SDAK STATE UNIV, 55- *Mem:* AAAS; Entom Soc Am. *Res:* Control of beneficial and injurious legume insects; apiculture. *Mailing Add:* 1409 First St Brookings SD 57006

WALT, ALEXANDER JEFFREY, b Cape Town, SAfrica, June 13, 23; US citizen; c 3. SURGERY. *Educ:* Univ Cape Town, MB & ChB, 48; FRCS(C), 55; Univ Minn, MS, 56; FRCS, 56; Am Bd Surg, dipl, 62. *Prof Exp:* Lectr path, Univ Cape Town, 49-50; registr surg, St Martin's Hosp, Bath, Eng, 56-57; asst surgeon, Groote Schuur Hosp, Cape Town, 57-61; asst chief surg, Vet Admin Hosp, Allen Park, Mich, 61-62; from asst prof to assoc prof, 61-66, from asst dean to assoc dean med, 64-70, PROF SURG & CHMN DEPT, SCH MED, WAYNE STATE UNIV, 66- *Concurrent Pos:* Consult div physician manpower & clin cancer training comt, NIH, 72-73. *Mem:* Am Surg Asn; Int Soc Surg; Soc Surg Alimentary Tract; Am Asn Surg of Trauma. *Res:* Studies of the effects and clinical management of severe trauma of the liver and stomach of humans. *Mailing Add:* Dept of Surg Wayne State Univ Sch of Med Detroit MI 48201

WALT, MARTIN, b West Plains, Mo, June 1, 26; m 50; c 4. SPACE PLASMA PHYSICS, GEOPHYSICS. *Educ:* Calif Inst Technol, BS, 50; Univ Wis, MS, 51, PhD(physics), 53. *Prof Exp:* Mem staff, Los Alamos Sci Lab, 53-56; mem sci staff, 56-65, mgr physics, 65-71, DIR PHYS SCI, LOCKHEED MISSILES & SPACE CO, 71- *Mem:* Am Phys Soc; Am Geophys Union; Am Inst Aeronaut & Astronaut. *Res:* Experiments and theory of interaction of fast neutrons with nuclei; space research, including measurements and theory on geomagnetically trapped radiation belts, aurora and cosmic rays; diffusion of ions and electrons in plasmas; cosmic rays. *Mailing Add:* 12650 Viscaino Ct Los Altos Hills CA 94022

WALTCHER, AZELLE BROWN, b New York, NY, Mar 27, 25; m 55; c 2. MATHEMATICS. *Educ:* Columbia Univ, BA, 45, MA, 46; NY Univ, PhD(math, educ), 54. *Prof Exp:* Asst math, Barnard Col, Columbia Univ, 45-46; instr, Hollins Col, 46-48; teacher, Calhoun Sch, NY, 48-52; from instr to assoc prof, Univ, 52-72, teaching fel, New Col, 61-72, PROF MATH, HOFSTRA UNIV, 72- *Concurrent Pos:* Mem fac, Sarah Laurence Col, 53-55. *Mem:* Am Math Soc; Math Asn Am. *Res:* Logic and foundations of mathematics; number theory; group theory. *Mailing Add:* Dept of Math Hofstra Univ Hempstead NY 11550

WALTCHER, IRVING, b Newport, RI, Mar 6, 17. POLYMER CHEMISTRY. *Educ:* Univ RI, BS, 38; Duke Univ, MA, 40; Ohio State Univ, PhD(org chem), 47. *Prof Exp:* Chemist, War Ord Dept, Ala, 41-42; res chemist, B F Goodrich Co, Ohio, 42-44; asst org chem, Res Found, Ohio State Univ, 44-47; res assoc chem, Polytech Inst Brooklyn, 47-48; assoc prof, State Univ NY Col Forestry, Syracuse, 48-55; asst prof, 55-58, ASSOC PROF CHEM, CITY COL NEW YORK, 58, DEP CHMN DEPT, 74- *Mem:* Am Chem Soc. *Res:* Selective hydrogenation of acetylenes; preparation and characterization of graft copolymers. *Mailing Add:* Dept of Chem City Col of New York New York NY 10031

WALTER, CARLTON H(ARRY), b Willard, Ohio, July 22, 24; m 48; c 2. ELECTRICAL ENGINEERING, PHYSICS. *Educ:* Ohio State Univ, BEE, 48, MS, 51, PhD(elec eng), 57. *Prof Exp:* Res assoc, 48-54, from instr to assoc prof, 54-65, asst supvr lab, 54-57, assoc supvr, 57-69, PROF ELEC ENG, ELECTRO SCI LAB, OHIO STATE UNIV, 65-, TECH AREA DIR ANTENNAS, 69- *Concurrent Pos:* Mem bd dirs, Ladar Systs, Inc, 64-71. *Mem:* Fel Inst Elec & Electronics Engrs. *Res:* Microwave, traveling wave, Luneberg lens and electrically small antennas. *Mailing Add:* Electro Sci Lab Ohio State Univ Columbus OH 43210

WALTER, CHARLES FRANK, b Sarasota, Fla, June 19, 36. BIOCHEMISTRY, TECHNICAL AND PATENT LAW. *Educ:* Ga Inst Technol, BS, 57; Fla State Univ, MS, 59, PhD(chem), 62; Univ Houston, JD, 79. *Prof Exp:* NIH fel, Med Sch, Univ Calif, San Francisco, 62-64; from asst prof to assoc prof biochem, Med Sch, Univ Tenn, Memphis, 64-70; assoc prof biomath & biochem, M D Anderson Hosp & Tumor Inst, Univ Tex, Houston, 70-74; prof chem eng, Univ Houston, 74-77; PATENT & TRADEMARK ATTY, 79- *Concurrent Pos:* NIH career develop award, Med Sch, Univ Tenn, Memphis, 65-70. *Mem:* Biophys Soc; Am Soc Eng Educ; Soc Math Biol; Am Soc Biol; Chem Fed Soc Exp Biol. *Res:* Solar energy conversion; biological control; enzyme mechanisms and kinetics; biochemical engineering; photoproduction of hydrogen coenzyme conformation; real-time computer applications; legal problems and other issues related to technology. *Mailing Add:* 9131 Timberside Houston TX 77025

WALTER, CHARLES ROBERT, JR, b Charlottesville, Va, Oct 31, 22; m 50; c 3. ORGANIC CHEMISTRY. *Educ:* Univ Va, BA, 43, PhD(chem), 49. *Prof Exp:* Res asst chem, Univ Ill, 49-50; asst prof, Univ NC, 50-52; sr res chemist, Nitrogen Div, Allied Chem Corp, 52-58, supvry res chemist, 58-60, mgr res, 60-66; PROF CHEM & CHMN DEPT, GEORGE MASON UNIV, 66- *Mem:* Am Chem Soc. *Res:* Synthetic organic chemistry; Diels-Alder reaction of quinoneimides; industrial process development; organic nitrogen chemicals; vapor phase catalysis; chlorination of olefins. *Mailing Add:* 6120 Sherborn Lane Springfield VA 22152

WALTER, CHARLTON M, b Altoona, Pa, July 1, 23; m 47; c 2. INFORMATION SCIENCE. *Educ:* Columbia Univ, BA, 49; Harvard Univ, MA, 51. *Prof Exp:* Mathematician, Commun Lab, Air Force Cambridge Res Ctr, 51-54, chief simulation & eval br, Comput & Math Sci Lab, 54-63, chief dynamic processes br, Data Sci Lab, 63-70, chief multisensor processing br, data sci lab, Air Force Cambridge Res Labs, 70-73, chief anal & simulation br, Comput Ctr, 73-76; SR SYSTS ANAL, DIR RES SERVS, AIR FORCE GEOPHYS LAB, 76- *Mem:* AAAS; Inst Elec & Electronics Engrs; Soc Gen Syst Res. *Res:* Development of interactive, computer-based, display-oriented signal processing systems, with applications to environmental sensor data collection; statistical data reduction; dynamic modelling; simulation and systems evaluation. *Mailing Add:* Air Force Geophys Lab Hanscom Air Force Base Bedford MA 01731

WALTER, EDWARD JOSEPH, b St Louis, Mo, Dec 6, 14; m 39; c 8. GEOPHYSICS. *Educ:* St Louis Univ, BS, 37, MS, 40, PhD(geophys), 44. *Prof Exp:* Seismic computer, Root Petrol Co, Ark, 37; asst seismologist, Shell Oil Co, 38, seismologist, 45-46; assoc prof math & asst dir seismol observ, 46-50, dir dept, 57-59, dir seismol observ, 62, PROF MATH, JOHN CARROLL UNIV, 50- *Mem:* AAAS; Seismol Soc Am; Soc Explor Geophys; Am Geophys Union; Geol Soc Am. *Res:* Seismology; local earthquakes; crustal structure; wave motion; attenuation coefficients; volcanology; engineering seismology; environmental acoustics and vibration. *Mailing Add:* Seismol Observ John Carroll Univ Cleveland OH 44118

WALTER, EUGENE LEROY, JR, b St Thomas, VI, Aug 14, 22; m 64; c 4. MEDICAL MICROBIOLOGY, VIROLOGY. *Educ:* Univ Calif, Los Angeles, BA, 47; Univ Southern Calif, MS, 58; Univ Wis, PhD(med microbiol), 64. *Prof Exp:* Eng asst, Los Angeles Bur Standard, 47-51; microbiologist, Epidemic Dis Control Unit, Pearl Harbor, 51-56; med microbiologist med res units, Berkeley, Calif, Great Lakes, Ill, Cairo, Egypt, Washington, DC, 56-69; HEALTH SCI ADMINR, NIH, 71- *Concurrent Pos:* Instr bact, US Navy Hosp Corps Sch, 53-54. *Mem:* AAAS; Am Soc Microbiol. *Res:* Bacteriophage; papilloma virus; infectious hepatitis diagnosed by fluorescent antibody; latent herpes simplex virus; leptospirosis; environmental engineering; health science administration. *Mailing Add:* NIH Bethesda MD 20014

WALTER, EVERETT L, b Rensselaer, Ind, July 1, 29; m 51; c 4. MATHEMATICS. *Educ:* Ariz State Univ, BS, 51; NMex State Univ, MS, 57, PhD(math), 61. *Prof Exp:* Dir comput, Army Field Forces, Ft Bliss, Tex, 54-56; instr math, NMex State Univ, 56-60; res mathematician, White Sands Missile Range, 61-62; assoc prof, 62-68, PROF MATH, NORTHERN ARIZ UNIV, 68- *Mem:* Math Asn Am; Am Math Soc. *Res:* Functional analysis, particularly in the study of generalized conjugate spaces. *Mailing Add:* Dept of Math Northern Ariz Univ Flagstaff AZ 86001

WALTER, GERALD JOSEPH, organic chemistry, see previous edition

WALTER, HARRY, b Vienna, Austria, May 15, 30; m 56; c 3. BIOCHEMISTRY, CELL BIOLOGY. *Educ:* City Col New York, BS, 51; Ind Univ, MS, 53, PhD(biochem), 55. *Prof Exp:* Teaching asst chem, Ind Univ, 51-52, res asst biochem, 52-55, res assoc, 55-57; prin scientist, Vet Admin Hosp, Brooklyn, NY, 57-62; RES CHEMIST, LAB CHEM BIOL, VET ADMIN MED CTR, LONG BEACH, CALIF, 62-, RES CAREER SCIENTIST, 78- *Concurrent Pos:* Asst clin prof, Dept Biol Chem, Sch Med, Univ Calif, Los Angeles, 62-75; clin prof, Dept Physiol, Col Med, Univ Calif, Irvine, 75-79, prof in residence, Dept Physiol & Biophys, 79- *Mem:* Am Soc Biol Chemists; Am Soc Cell Biol; Biophys Soc; Swed Biochem Soc. *Res:* Characterization of membrane surface properties by cell partitioning in two-polymer aqueous phase systems. *Mailing Add:* Lab of Chem Biol Vet Admin Med Ctr Long Beach CA 90822

WALTER, HARTMUT, b Stettin, Ger, July 13, 40; m 69. BIOGEOGRAPHY, ORNITHOLOGY. *Educ:* Univ Bonn, Dr rer nat(bird ecol), 67. *Prof Exp:* Harkness fel geog, Univ Calif, Berkeley, 67-68 & Univ Chicago, 68; assoc regional expert ecol & conserv for Africa, UNESCO Field Sci Off, Nairobi, Kenya, 70-72; actg asst prof, 72-73, asst prof, 73-74, assoc prof biogeog, 74-80, PROF GEOG, UNIV CALIF, LOS ANGELES, 80- *Honors & Awards:* Hoerlein Prize, Ger Biol Asn, 60. *Mem:* AAAS; Ecol Soc Am; Asn Am Geogr; Int Asn Ecol; Brit Ecol Soc. *Res:* Mediterranean and tropical ecosystem dynamics; evolutionary ecology; raptor ecology; wildlife in urban and other man-modified environments. *Mailing Add:* Dept Geog Univ Calif Los Angeles CA 90024

WALTER, HENRY ALEXANDER, b Muehlhausen, Ger, Jan 8, 12; nat US; m 39; c 4. ORGANIC CHEMISTRY. *Educ:* Univ Heidelberg, dipl, 39. *Prof Exp:* Res chemist, Plaskon Co, 39-42; asst prof chem, Univ Mo, 42-44; res specialist, Monsanto Chem Co, 44-62; sr scientist, Plastic Coating Corp, Scott Paper Co, 62-71, consult, Scott Graphics, Inc, 71-76; CONSULT CHEMIST, CATAUMET, MASS, 76- *Concurrent Pos:* Assoc mem, Woodshole Oceanog Inst. *Mem:* AAAS; Am Chem Soc. *Res:* Polymer chemistry; technical information services; patent liaison. *Mailing Add:* PO Box 86 Cataumet MA 02534

WALTER, HENRY CLEMENT, b Boston, Mass, Sept 12, 19; m 54; c 6. ORGANIC CHEMISTRY. *Educ:* Mass Inst Technol, SB, 41, PhD(org chem), 46. *Prof Exp:* Asst, Mass Inst Technol, 42-43 & 44-45; RES CHEMIST, EXP STA, E I DU PONT DE NEMOURS & CO, INC, 46- *Mem:* Am Chem Soc. *Res:* Elastomers; adhesives. *Mailing Add:* 310 Hampton Rd Sharpley Wilmington DE 19803

WALTER, JOHN F(ITCH), nuclear engineering, see previous edition

WALTER, JOHN FITLER, b Philadelphia, Pa, Mar 19, 43; m 68; c 3. APPLIED PHYSICS, ELECTRO-OPTICS. *Educ:* Drexel Univ, BSEE, 66, MS, 68, PhD(physics), 70. *Prof Exp:* PHYSICIST, APPL PHYSICS LAB, JOHNS HOPKINS UNIV, 70- *Res:* Electro-optics applications to missle navigation and control; laser physics with applications to missle guidance. *Mailing Add:* Appl Physics Lab Johns Hopkins Rd Laurel MD 20707

WALTER, JOHN HARRIS, b Los Angeles, Calif, Dec 14, 27; m 55; c 3. ALGEBRA. *Educ:* Calif Inst Technol, BS, 51; Univ Mich, MS, 53, PhD, 54. *Prof Exp:* From instr to asst prof math, Univ Wash, 54-61; assoc prof, 61-66, PROF MATH, UNIV ILL, URBANA, 66- *Concurrent Pos:* NSF fel, 57-58; vis asst prof, Univ Chicago, 60-61, vis assoc prof, 65-66; res assoc, Harvard Univ, 67-68 & Cambridge Univ, 72-73. *Mem:* Am Math Soc. *Res:* Finite groups; classical groups; representation theory. *Mailing Add:* Dept of Math Univ of Ill Urbana IL 61801

WALTER, JOSEPH DAVID, b Merchantville, NJ, July 6, 39; m 62; c 3. ENGINEERING MECHANICS, MECHANICAL ENGINEERING. *Educ:* Va Polytech Inst, BS, 62, MS, 64, PhD(eng mech), 66. *Prof Exp:* Asst, Va Polytech Inst, 65-66; res physicist, Cent Res Labs, 66-69, mgr physics & math res, 69-74, ASST DIR, CENT RES LABS, FIRESTONE TIRE & RUBBER CO, 74- *Concurrent Pos:* Adj prof, Dept Mech Eng, Univ Akron, 75- *Mem:* Am Chem Soc; Fiber Soc; Am Soc Mech Engrs; Soc Exp Stress Anal; Am Inst Aeronaut & Astronaut. *Res:* Composite materials; anisotropic viscoelasticity and elasticity; stress analysis; tire mechanics. *Mailing Add:* 343 Barnstable Rd Akron OH 44313

WALTER, JOSEPH L, b Braddock, Pa, Jan 23, 30. INORGANIC CHEMISTRY. *Educ:* Duquesne Univ, BS, 51; Univ Pittsburgh, PhD(chem), 55. *Prof Exp:* ASSOC PROF INORG CHEM, UNIV NOTRE DAME, 60- *Concurrent Pos:* NIH fels, 62-70; AEC fel, 63-67. *Mem:* Am Chem Soc; Soc Appl Spectros; Am Asn Med Col. *Res:* Normal coordinate analysis of inorganic coordination compounds using the Urey-Bradley Force Field calculations and the thermodynamic studies of metal chelate formation. *Mailing Add:* Dept of Chem Univ of Notre Dame Notre Dame IN 46556

WALTER, LOUIS S, b New York, NY, Aug 11, 33; m 57; c 2. GEOCHEMISTRY. *Educ:* City Col New York, BS, 54; Univ Tenn, MS, 55; Pa State Univ, PhD(geochem), 60. *Prof Exp:* Res fel geochem, Pa State Univ, 60-62; res assoc, Nat Acad Sci, 62-63; geochemist, 63-73, asst div chief, Earth Sci Div, 73-74, CHIEF EARTH SURV APPLN DIV, GODDARD SPACE FLIGHT CTR, NASA, 74- *Mem:* Am Geophys Union; Geochem Soc; Mineral Soc Am; Meteoritical Soc. *Res:* Experimental petrology and mineralogy; crystal chemistry; phase equilibria; petrography; electron microprobe analyses; planetology; theoretical petrology; application of remote sensing to agriculture, geology; use of geophysical measurements from space for tectonic studies and oil and mineral exploration. *Mailing Add:* Goddard Space Flight Ctr NASA Code 920 Greenbelt MD 20771

WALTER, PAUL HERMANN LAWRENCE, b Jersey City, NJ, Sept 22, 34; m 56; c 2. INORGANIC CHEMISTRY. *Educ:* Mass Inst Technol, SB, 56; Univ Kans, PhD(inorg chem), 60. *Prof Exp:* Res chemist, Cent Res Dept, E I du Pont de Nemours & Co, 60-66, col rels rep, Employee Rels Dept, 66-67; asst prof, 67-70, assoc prof, 70-78, PROF CHEM, SKIDMORE COL, 78-CHMN DEPT, 75- *Concurrent Pos:* Guest, Univ Stuttgart, 64-65. *Mem:* AAAS; Am Chem Soc; Am Meteorol Soc; fel Am Inst Chemists. *Res:* Solid state inorganic chemistry; chemical education; rhenium chemistry; inorganic analytical chemistry; environmental chemistry. *Mailing Add:* Dept of Chem Skidmore Col Saratoga Springs NY 12866

WALTER, REGINALD HENRY, b St John's, Antigua, Feb 13, 33; m 65. FOOD CHEMISTRY. *Educ:* Tuskegee Inst, BS, 60, MS, 63; Univ Mass, PhD(food sci), 67. *Prof Exp:* Asst food technologist, Univ PR, 67-68; sr chemist, Int Flavors & Fragrances, Inc, 68-71; asst prof, 71-77, ASSOC PROF FOOD SCI, CORNELL UNIV, 77- *Mem:* Am Chem Soc. *Res:* Food waste; carbohydrate polymers. *Mailing Add:* Food Res Lab Cornell Univ Geneva NY 14456

WALTER, RICHARD D, b Alameda, Calif, Aug 16, 21; m 47. MEDICINE. *Educ:* St Louis Univ, MD, 46; Am Bd Psychiat & Neurol, cert psychiat, 55, cert neurol, 60. *Prof Exp:* From instr to assoc prof, 55-70, PROF NEUROL & CHMN DEPT, MED CTR, UNIV CALIF, LOS ANGELES, 70- *Concurrent Pos:* Res fel psychiat, Langley Porter Clin, Univ Calif, Los Angeles, 53-55; dir, Reed Neurol Res Ctr. *Mem:* Am Acad Neurol; fel Am EEG Soc; Am Psychiat Asn; Am Neural Asn. *Res:* Clinical neurophysiology and electroencephalography as it relates to the convulsive disorders. *Mailing Add:* Neuropsychiat Inst Univ of Calif Med Ctr Los Angeles CA 90024

WALTER, RICHARD L, b Chicago, Ill, Nov 1, 33; m 58; c 3. NUCLEAR PHYSICS. *Educ:* St Procopius Col, BS, 55; Univ Notre Dame - PhD(physics), 60. *Prof Exp:* Res assoc nuclear physics, Univ Wis, 59-61, instr physics, 61-62; from asst prof to assoc prof, 62-74, PROF PHYSICS, DUKE UNIV, 74- *Concurrent Pos:* Vis prof, Max Planck Inst Nuclear Physics, Heidelberg, Ger, 70-71; Fulbright res fel, 70-71; vis scientist, Los Alamos Sci Lab, 75. *Mem:* Am Phys Soc; Sigma Xi. *Res:* Neutron physics; polarization of nucleons produced in reactions; scattering of polarized nucleons; low energy accelerator physics; studies involving trace metals in the environment. *Mailing Add:* Dept of Physics Duke Univ Durham NC 27706

WALTER, RICHARD WEBB, JR, b West Chester, Pa, Oct 5, 44; m 67; c 2. MICROBIAL BIOCHEMISTRY, FERMENTATION. *Educ:* Pa State Univ, BS, 66; Mich State Univ, PhD(biochem), 72. *Prof Exp:* Fel biochem, Univ Colo Med Ctr, Denver, 72-74; sr res biochemist, 74-80, PROJ LEADER, DOW CHEM CO, 80- *Mem:* Am Soc Microbiol; Am Chem Soc; AAAS. *Res:* Biochemical transformation and synthesis of sterospecific molecules that are of interest to both the chemical and pharmaceutical industries and are difficult to synthesize by normal chemical means; fermentation process design and optimization. *Mailing Add:* 1701 Bldg Dow Chem Co Midland MI 48640

WALTER, ROBERT IRVING, b Johnstown, Pa, Mar 12, 20. PHYSICAL ORGANIC CHEMISTRY. *Educ:* Swarthmore Col, AB, 41; Johns Hopkins Univ, MA, 42; Univ Chicago, PhD(chem), 49. *Prof Exp:* Asst, Swarthmore Col, 40-41 & Johns Hopkins Univ, 41-42; res chemist, Wyeth, Inc, 42-44; instr chem, Univ Colo, 49-51; from res asst prof to res assoc prof, Rutgers Univ, 51-53; instr chem, Univ Conn, 53-55; assoc physicist, Brookhaven Nat Lab, 55-56; from asst prof to prof chem, Haverford Col, 56-68; PROF CHEM, UNIV ILL, CHICAGO CIRCLE, 68- *Concurrent Pos:* NSF fac fel, 60-61; mem, Adv Coun Col Chem, 66-70, sr staff assoc, 67; vis prof, Stanford Univ, 67; acad guest, Inst Phys Chem, Univ Zurich, 75-76. *Mem:* AAAS; Am Chem Soc. *Res:* Equilibria in porphyrin systems; preparation and properties of stable organic free radicals. *Mailing Add:* Dept of Chem Univ of Ill Box 4348 Chicago IL 60680

WALTER, RODERICH, b Darmstadt, Ger, July 16, 37; m 74; c 2. CHEMISTRY, PHYSIOLOGY. *Educ:* Univ Giessen, Vordiplom, 61; Univ Cincinnati, PhD(chem, physiol), 64. *Prof Exp:* Res assoc biochem, Med Col, Cornell Univ, 64-65; res assoc physiol, Mt Sinai Hosp, 65-66; from assoc prof to prof physiol & biophys, Mt Sinai Sch Med, 66-74, co-dir dept, Grad Sch, 66-74; PROF PHYSIOL & HEAD DEPT, UNIV ILL MED CTR, 74- *Mem:* AAAS; Am Chem Soc; Soc Exp Biol & Med; Biophys Soc; Soc Appl Spectros. *Res:* Membrane and transport phenomena; mechanism of hormone action; peptide and orgainc synthesis; sequence and conformational analysis of peptides and proteins; endocrinol. *Mailing Add:* Dept of Physiol PO Box 6998 Chicago IL 60612

WALTER, THOMAS JAMES, b Dodgeville, Wis, Aug 20, 39; m 65; c 3. ORGANIC CHEMISTRY. *Educ:* Univ Wis-Madison, BS, 61; Cornell Univ, MST, 69; Univ Ga, PhD(chem), 73. *Prof Exp:* Pub sch teacher, Wis, 65-68; res chemist, 73-78, sr res chemist, 78-80, SUPVR, ETHYL CORP, 80- *Mem:* Am Chem Soc. *Res:* Paracyclophanes, synthesis of heterocycles; synthesis of drugs and drug intermediates (chemical intermediates, transition metal catalysis). *Mailing Add:* Ethyl Corp Res & Develop Lab PO Box 341 Baton Rouge LA 70821

WALTER, TREVOR JOHN, b West Bromwich, Eng, June 9, 44; US citizen. BIOCHEMISTRY. *Educ:* Univ Hull, Eng, BS, 65; Univ Manchester, Eng, PhD(biochem), 68. *Prof Exp:* Res assoc biochem, Dept Bot, Univ Md, 68-69 & Dept Biochem, Univ Fla, 69-70; chemist, A Guinness Son & Co Ltd, 70-74 & Dept Biochem, Univ Fla, 74-76; res assoc, Dept Biochem, Univ Minn, 76-79; GROUP LEADER FOOD BIOCHEM, RES & DEVELOP, KRAFT INC, 79- *Res:* Food chemistry. *Mailing Add:* Res & Develop Kraft Inc 801 Waukegan Rd Glenview IL 60025

WALTER, WILBERT GEORGE, b Lingle, Wyo, Nov 16, 33; m 55; c 2. PHARMACOGNOSY, MEDICINAL CHEMISTRY. *Educ:* Univ Colo, BA, 55, BS & MS, 58; Univ Conn, PhD(pharmaceut chem), 62. *Prof Exp:* Asst, Univ Colo, 55-58; asst, Univ Conn, 58-61, spec res technologist, 60; res assoc pharmacog & asst prof pharmaceut chem, Sch Pharm, Univ Tenn, 61-63; assoc prof, Sch Pharm, Univ Miss, 63-68; chmn dept, 68-77, PROF PHARMACOG & BIOL, COL PHARM, MED UNIV SC, 68-, CHMN FINAL AID DEPT, 77- *Mem:* Am Pharmaceut Asn; Am Soc Pharmacog; Am Chem Soc; Soc Econ Bot. *Res:* Organic medicinal chemistry; natural product chemistry. *Mailing Add:* Dept of Biol Med Univ of SC Charleston SC 29401

WALTER, WILLIAM ARNOLD, JR, b Pittsburgh, Pa, May 17, 22; m 46; c 2. EPIDEMIOLOGY. *Educ:* Ind Univ, AB, 43, MD, 45; Johns Hopkins Univ, MPH, 51. *Prof Exp:* Med officer, Ky State Bd Health, Louisville, 48-50; dir, Venereal Dis Control Div, Fla State Bd Health, Jacksonville, 51-53, assoc dir, Bur Prev Dis, 53-55; epidemiologist, Epidemiol Sect, Nat Cancer Inst, 55-57; med officer in-chg, Houston Pulmonary Cytol Proj, Univ Tex M D Anderson Hosp & Tumor Inst, 57-59; med officer in-chg uterine cancer cytol proj, Women's Med Col Pa, 59-60; res grants adminr, Grants & Training, 60-66, chief, Spec Prog Br, Extramural Activ, 66-77, dep dir, Div Cancer Res Resource & Centers, 77-80, ACTG DIR & DEP DIR, DIV EXTRAMURAL ACTIV, NAT CANCER INST, NIH, 80- *Mem:* Am Pub Health Asn; AMA. *Res:* Chronic disease epidemiology with special interest in geographic pathology of leukemia. *Mailing Add:* Nat Cancer Inst NIH Div Cancer Res Resources & Centers Bethesda MD 20014

WALTER, WILLIAM GOFF, b Lake Placid, NY, Nov 1, 14; m 41; c 4. MICROBIOLOGY. *Educ:* Cornell Univ, BS, 38, MS, 41; Mich State Univ, PhD, 52; Am Bd Med Microbiol, dipl. *Prof Exp:* Spec investr, NY Exp Sta, Geneva, 40-41, asst, 41-42; from asst prof to assoc prof, 42-61, head dept microbiol, 68-77, PROF MICROBIOL, MONT STATE UNIV, 51-, ACTG V PRES, ACAD AFFAIRS, 77- *Honors & Awards:* Walter S Mangold Award, Nat Environ Health Asn, 72. *Mem:* Am Soc Microbiol; fel Am Pub Health Asn; fel Am Acad Microbiol; Nat Environ Health Asn (pres, Nat Asn Sanitarians, 62); Am Acad Environ Engrs. *Res:* Environmental and public health; surface contamination. *Mailing Add:* Dept of Microbiol Mont State Univ Bozeman MT 59715

WALTER, WILLIAM MOOD, JR, b Sumter, SC, Nov 20, 36; m 59; c 1. FOOD SCIENCE. *Educ:* The Citadel, BS, 58; Univ Ga, PhD(org chem), 63. *Prof Exp:* Res asst, Univ Ga, 60-63; asst prof, 65-70, assoc prof, 70-77 PROF FOOD SCI, NC STATE UNIV, 77- RES CHEMIST, AGR RES SERV, USDA, 65- *Mem:* Am Chem Soc; Inst Food Technologists. *Res:* Effect of processing and storage on organic constituents of food; emphasis on quality and nutritional value of processed foods. *Mailing Add:* Dept of Food Sci NC State Univ Raleigh NC 27650

WALTER, WILLIAM TRUMP, b Jamaica, NY, Dec 28, 31; m 60; c 4. ELECTROPHYSICS. *Educ:* Middlebury Col, AB, 53; Mass Inst Technol, PhD(physics), 62. *Prof Exp:* Res asst, Res Lab Electronics, Mass Inst Technol, 59-62; sr scientist, TRG, Inc, 62-67; res scientist, 67-79, RES ASSOC PROF, POLYTECH INST NEW YORK, 79- *Concurrent Pos:* Guest, Res Lab Electronics, Mass Inst Technol, 62-63; pres, Laser Consults, Inc, 68- *Mem:* Am Phys Soc; Optical Soc Am; NY Acad Sci; Soc Photo-Optical Instrumentation Engrs; Am Asn Physics Teachers. *Res:* Wave-matter interactions; metal vapor lasers; laser research development and applications; microwaves; gas discharges; atomic physics; resonance phenomena in dilute gases, including optical pumping, orientation and nuclear magnetic resonance; optical and radiofrequency spectroscopy. *Mailing Add:* Dept of Elec Eng & Microwave Res Inst Polytech Inst of New York Rte 110 Farmingdale NY 11735

WALTERS, CARL JOHN, b Albuquerque, NMex, Sept 14, 44. SYSTEMS ECOLOGY. *Educ:* Humboldt State Col, BS, 65; Colo State Univ, MS, 67, PhD(fisheries), 69. *Prof Exp:* Res asst fisheries biol, Colo Coop Wildlife Unit, Colo State Univ, 66-67, NSF fel, 67-69, consult, 68-70; ASSOC PROF ZOOL & ANIMAL RESOURCE ECOL, UNIV BC, 69- *Concurrent Pos:* Can Dept Environ & Natural Resources consult, 71-; res scholar, Int Inst Appl Systs Anal, Austria, 74-75. *Res:* Dynamics of ecological communities; application of mathematical models and computer simulation techniques to problems in resource ecology. *Mailing Add:* Inst of Animal Resource Ecol Univ of BC Hut B8 Vancouver BC V6T 1W5 Can

WALTERS, CHARLES PHILIP, b Kansas City, Mo, May 1, 15; m 36; c 3. ASTROGEOLOGY. *Educ:* Kans State Univ, BS, 36, MS, 38; Cornell Univ, PhD, 57. *Prof Exp:* Asst geologist, Continental Oil Co, 44-48; from asst prof to assoc prof, 45-72, PROF GEOL, KANS STATE UNIV, 72- *Concurrent Pos:* Ford Found fac fel, 51-52; mem comt exam natural sci test & geol subj matter test, Educ Testing Serv, 62-70. *Mem:* AAAS; Am Asn Petrol Geologists; Am Quaternary Asn; Meteoritical Soc. *Res:* Structural and tectonic geology; geophysics; planetology; environmental geology; deterioration of Kansas salt beds; tektites from cryptovolcanic eruptions; paleoclimatology; climate change. *Mailing Add:* Dept of Geol Kans State Univ Manhattan KS 66506

WALTERS, CHARLES SEBASTIAN, b Detroit, Mich, Aug 18, 13; m 39; c 2. FORESTRY. *Educ:* Purdue Univ, BS, 38; Yale Univ, DFor, 57. *Prof Exp:* Asst, Tenn Valley Authority, 40 & Univ Ill, 40-41; proj forester, Timber Prod War Proj, Ill, 41-45; asst chief wood technol & utilization in forestry, Univ Ill, Urbana, 45-47, from asst prof to assoc prof, 47-57, prof, 57-79; CONSULT, 79- *Concurrent Pos:* Consult, Indonesia, 71; adv, Nat Bur Standards, 71-78; mem standing comt hardboard, US Bur Standards, 74-78. *Honors & Awards:* Wood Salute, Wood & Wood Prod, 70. *Mem:* AAAS; Sigma Xi; Forest Prod Res Soc; Soc Wood Sci & Technol; Am Soc Testing & Mat. *Res:* Technology of wood and its use; wood preservation. *Mailing Add:* Dept Forestry 109 Mumford Hall Univ Ill Urbana IL 61801

WALTERS, CRAIG THOMPSON, b Columbus, Ohio, July 23, 40; m 62; c 1. PLASMA PHYSICS, LASERS. *Educ:* Ohio State Univ, BS & MS, 63, PhD(physics), 71. *Prof Exp:* From res physicist to sr physicist, 63-71, assoc fel plasma physics, 71-73, sr researcher laser effects, 73-75, ASSOC SECT MGR LASER EFFECTS & ELECTROMAGNETICS, BATTELLE COLUMBUS LABS, BATTELLE MEM INST, 75- *Concurrent Pos:* Mem adv panel laser-supported absorption waves, Defense Advan Proj Agency, 74. *Honors & Awards:* NASA Tech Brief Award, 69; Distinguished Inventor Awards, Battelle Mem Inst, 73 & 74. *Mem:* Am Phys Soc; AAAS; Am Inst Aeronaut & Astronaut. *Res:* Generation, propagation and material interaction of intense energy beams consisting of electromagnetic radiation or fundamental particles; study of plasma produced in laser beam interaction with condensed matter. *Mailing Add:* Battelle Columbus Labs 505 King Ave Columbus OH 43201

WALTERS, CURLA SYBIL, b Jamaica, June 3, 29. IMMUNOLOGY, MICROBIOLOGY. *Educ:* Andrews Univ, BA, 61; Howard Univ, MSc, 64; Georgetown Univ, PhD(microbiol & immunol), 69. *Prof Exp:* From instr to asst prof immunol, Med Ctr, Univ Colo, Denver, 71-74; assoc prof dept med, Med Ctr, Howard Univ, 74-77; MEM STAFF, DEPT OF MED, HOWARD UNIV HOSP, 77- *Concurrent Pos:* Am Asn Univ Women fel, Karolinska Inst, Sweden, 69-70; NIH training grant, Med Ctr, Univ Colo, 71. *Mem:* AAAS; Am Asn Immunol. *Res:* Basic and tumor immunology. *Mailing Add:* Dept of Med 2041 Georgia Ave Washington DC 20060

WALTERS, DANIEL ALFRED, communication engineering, electrical engineering, deceased

WALTERS, DAVID ROYAL, cell biology, developmental biology, see previous edition

WALTERS, DOUGLAS BRUCE, b Brooklyn, NY, Apr 6, 42; div; c 1. CHEMICAL HEALTH & SAFETY, ANALYTICAL CHEMISTRY. *Educ:* Long Island Univ, BS, 63, MS, 65; Univ Ga, PhD(chem), 71. *Prof Exp:* Res chemist, Farbewerke Hoechst A G, Frankfurt, Ger, 65 & Southeast Water Lab, Environ Protection Agency, Ga, 69-71; res chemist, Russell Res Lab, USDA, 71-77; tech progs mgr chem, NIH/HEW, 77-80, PROG LEADER/ CHEM HEALTH & SAFETY, NAT TOXICOL PROG, NAT INST ENVIRON HEALTH SCI, NIH/NAT HEALTH SERV, 80- *Mem:* Am Chem Soc; Am Indust Hyg Asn. *Res:* Organophosphorus chemistry; nuclear magnetic resonance; inorganic chemistry; chelation; food and flavor chemistry; development of analytical methods; pollution chemistry; phase diagrams; tobacco chemistry; separation techniques; safety and health; chemistry aspects of in vitro and in vivo bioassay techniques; safe handling chemistry carcinogens; wasted disposal of hazardous chemicals; industrial hygiene. *Mailing Add:* Nat Inst Environ Health Sci PO Box 12233 Research Triangle Park NC 30604

WALTERS, EDWARD ALBERT, b Whitefish, Mont, Jan 2, 40; m 64; c 3. ENVIRONMENTAL CHEMISTRY. *Educ:* Pac Lutheran Univ, BS, 62; Univ Minn, Minneapolis, PhD(org chem), 66. *Prof Exp:* Res assoc chem, Cornell Univ, 66-68; from asst prof to assoc prof, 68-74, PROF CHEM, UNIV N MEX, 74- *Concurrent Pos:* Res Corp grant, Univ NMex, 69-70, NSF grant, 69-72. *Mem:* AAAS; Am Chem Soc. *Res:* Fast proton transfer reactions in solution; kinetic isotope effects; potential energy surfaces for reactive collisions; photoionization mass spectrometry of cluster molecules. *Mailing Add:* Dept Chem Univ NMex Albuquerque NM 87131

WALTERS, FRED HENRY, b Owen Sound, Ont, Aug 8, 47. ANALYTICAL CHEMISTRY. *Educ:* Univ Waterloo, BSc, 71; Univ Mass, PhD(chem), 75. *Prof Exp:* Res asst, Toronto Gen Hosp, Kitchener Waterloo Hosp & Ashland Oil Can, 66-71; teaching asst chem, Univ Mass, 71-75; res assoc chem, Univ Windsor, 75-76; asst prof, Quinnipiac Col, Hamden, Conn, 76-79; MEM STAFF, UNIV SOUTHWESTERN LA, 79- *Mem:* Am Chem Soc; Sigma Xi. *Res:* Electrochemical synthesis of inorganic compounds; high pressure liquid chromatography; organometallic chemistry; metals in biological systems. *Mailing Add:* Dept Chem Univ Southwestern La Lafayette LA 70504

WALTERS, GEOFFREY KING, b Baton Rouge, La, Aug 23, 31; m 54; c 3. ATOMIC PHYSICS. *Educ:* Rice Univ, BA, 53, PhD(physics), 56. *Prof Exp:* NSF fel, Duke, 56-57; br mgr & physicist, Tex Instruments, Inc, 57-62, corp res assoc, 62-63; prof physics, 63-64, actg dean sci & eng, 68-69 & 72-73, chmn dept physics, 73-77, PROF PHYSICS & SPACE SCI, RICE UNIV, 64-, DEAN NAT SCI, 80- *Concurrent Pos:* Actg chief fire technol div, Nat Bur Standards, 71-72; Guggenheim Found fel, Stanford Univ, 77-78. *Mem:* Fel AAAS; fel Am Phys Soc; Am Geophys Union. *Res:* Magnetic resonance; low temperature, solid state, atomic collisions and reactions, surface physics; optical pumping and dynamic nuclear orientation; solar-terrestrial relationships; radio-astronomy. *Mailing Add:* Dept of Physics Rice Univ Houston TX 77001

WALTERS, HELEN VANDERVORT, b Williamsport, Pa, June 25, 23; m 46; c 2. CHEMISTRY. *Educ:* Pa State Univ, BS, 44. *Prof Exp:* Lab technician silicone chem, 44-47, lab technician chem durability, 59-62, sr technician, 63-71, chemist, 70-73, SR CHEMIST, SURFACE ANAL, CORNING GLASS WORKS, 74- *Mem:* Am Ceramic Soc; Am Soc Testing & Mat. *Res:* Mechanism of interactions between materials (glass, ceramics, metals, minerals and glasses) and chemical environments. *Mailing Add:* Corning Glass Works Sullivan Park Corning NY 14830

WALTERS, HUBERT JACK, b Spring, Tex, Nov 2, 15; m 47; c 3. PLANT PATHOLOGY. *Educ:* NMex Col, BS, 41; Univ Ill, MS, 48; Univ Nebr, PhD(plant path), 51. *Prof Exp:* Asst prof plant path & asst plant pathologist, Univ Wyo, 50-54; from asst prof plant path & asst plant pathologist to assoc prof plant path & assoc plant pathologist, 54-62, PROF PLANT PATH & PLANT PATHOLOGIST, UNIV ARK, FAYETTEVILLE, 62- *Mem:* Am Phytopath Soc. *Res:* Virus diseases; beetle transmission of plant viruses; diseases of soybeans. *Mailing Add:* Dept of Plant Path Univ of Ark Fayetteville AR 72701

WALTERS, JACK HENRY, b Toronto, Ont, Apr 2, 25; m 49; c 3. OBSTETRICS, GYNECOLOGY. *Educ:* Univ Western Ont, BA, 46, MD, 51; FRCPS(C), 57; FRCOG, 67. *Prof Exp:* Chief dept obstet & gynec & dir cytol, St Joseph's Hosp, London, Ont, 58-73; prof obstet & gynec, Univ Western Ont, 66-73; prof obstet & gynec & chmn dept, Med Col Ohio, 73-78; PROF & CHMN, DEPT OBSTET & GYNEC, UNIV OTTAWA, 78- *Concurrent Pos:* Can Cancer Soc McEachern traveling fel, 56-57; chief obstet & gynec, Ottawa Gen Hosp, 78- *Mem:* Can Med Asn; Soc Obstet & Gynaec Can; Am Soc Cytol; fel Am Col Obstet & Gynec. *Res:* Gynecological, particularly hormonal cytology; screening programs; perinatal mortality, particularly statistical research in computer programs; manpower studies; obstetrics-gynecology health care; delivery systems. *Mailing Add:* Dept Obstet & Gynec Ottawa Gen Hosp 501 Symth Rd Ottawa ON K1H 8L6 Can

WALTERS, JAMES CARTER, b Zeeland, Mich, June 27, 48; m 71; c 2. GEOLOGY. *Educ:* Grand Valley State Col, Mich, BA, 70; Rutgers Univ, MPhil, 74, PhD(geol), 75. *Prof Exp:* ASST PROF GEOL, UNIV NORTHERN IOWA, 75- *Concurrent Pos:* Res assoc, Ctr Northern Studies, 75- *Mem:* Geol Soc Am; Am Quaternary Asn; Nat Asn Geol Teachers. *Res:* Glacial and periglacial geomorphology; Quaternary geology. *Mailing Add:* Dept of Earth Sci Univ of Northern Iowa Cedar Falls IA 50614

WALTERS, JAMES LEE, cytogenetics, deceased

WALTERS, JAMES VERNON, b Dublin, Ga, May 13, 33; m 55; c 2. CIVIL ENGINEERING, SANITARY ENGINEERING. *Educ:* Ga Inst Technol, BCE, 55, MS, 58; Univ Fla, PhD(sanit eng), 63. *Prof Exp:* Res asst, State Hwy Dept Ga, 55-56; jr asst & asst sanit engr, Atlanta Regional Off, USPHS, 56-59; from asst prof to assoc prof civil eng, 59-70, PROF CIVIL ENG, UNIV ALA, TUSCALOOSA, 70- *Concurrent Pos:* Ford Found eng resident, Southern Kraft Div, Int Paper Co, 66-67. *Mem:* Am Chem Soc; Am Soc Civil Engrs; Am Water Works Asn; Tech Asn Pulp & Paper Indust; Water Pollution Control Asn. *Res:* Water supply and sewerage; water, sewage and industrial waste treatment; hydrology; sanitary nematology. *Mailing Add:* PO Box AB University AL 35486

WALTERS, JOHN LINTON, b Washington, DC, Mar 8, 24; m 48; c 5. ELECTRICAL ENGINEERING. *Educ:* US Naval Acad, BS, 44; Harvard Univ, MS, 49; Johns Hopkins Univ, DrEng(elec eng), 59. *Prof Exp:* Res asst, Los Alamos Sci Lab, 49-51, staff mem, 51-52; res staff asst, Radiation Lab, Johns Hopkins Univ, 52-57, res assoc, 57-59; assoc elec engr, Brookhaven Nat Lab, 59-62; res scientist, Carlyle Barton Lab, Johns Hopkins Univ, 62-70; supvry electronic engr, Radar Div, Naval Res Lab, Washington, DC, 70-78; sci adv, Staff Comdr Sixth Fleet, Italy, 78-80; ENGR SPEC SERV, GEN DYNAMICS CORP, 80- *Concurrent Pos:* Teacher, Exten Div, Univ Calif, Los Angeles, 52; lectr, Johns Hopkins Univ, 64-65, instr, 68. *Mem:* Inst Elec & Electronics Engrs. *Res:* Particle accelerators; electrical breakdown of gases; microwave structures; radar. *Mailing Add:* Gen Dynamics Corp Pierre Laclede Ctr St Louis MO 63105

WALTERS, JOHN PHILIP, b Elgin, Ill, July 4, 38; m 61; c 2. ANALYTICAL CHEMISTRY, SPECTROSCOPY. *Educ:* Purdue Univ, BS, 60; Univ Ill, Urbana, PhD(chem), 64. *Prof Exp:* Res assoc spectros, Univ Ill, Urbana, 64-65; asst prof, 65-72, PROF ANAL CHEM, UNIV WIS-MADISON, 72- *Honors & Awards:* Am Chem Soc Award Chem Instrumentation; Meggers Award; Lester W Strock Award. *Mem:* Soc Appl Spectros; Am Soc Testing & Mat; Am Chem Soc; fel AAAS; Optical Soc Am. *Res:* Time-resolved emission spectroscopy; mechanisms of spectroscopic discharges; spectrochemical methods and instrumentation. *Mailing Add:* Dept of Chem Univ of Wis Madison WI 53706

WALTERS, JOHN PHILIP, b Manhattan, Kans, Sept 26, 41; m 63; c 4. PHYSICAL CHEMISTRY. *Educ:* Kans State Univ, BS, 63; Iowa State Univ, PhD(phys chem), 68. *Prof Exp:* Sr res chemist, Phillips Petrol Co, Okla, 68-70; res chemist, Phillips Fiber Corp, Greenville, SC, 70-76; RES CHEMIST, PHILLIPS PETROL CO, 76- *Mem:* AAAS; Am Chem Soc; Am Phys Soc. *Res:* Polymer physics. *Mailing Add:* 4809 SE Barlow Dr Bartlesville OK 74003

WALTERS, LEE RUDYARD, b New York, NY, Jan 20, 28; m 50; c 2. ORGANIC CHEMISTRY. *Educ:* Bucknell Univ, BS, 54; Univ Kans, PhD(chem), 58. *Prof Exp:* Asst org chem, Univ Kans, 55-58; res chemist, Atlas Powder Co, Del, 58-59; ASST PROF CHEM, LAFAYETTE COL, 59- *Mem:* Am Chem Soc. *Res:* Nitrogen heterocyclic and organometallic compounds; chemistry of natural products. *Mailing Add:* Dept of Chem Lafayette Col Easton PA 18042

WALTERS, LEON C, b Butte, Mont, Jan 6, 40; m 61; c 3. MATERIALS SCIENCE, METALLURGICAL ENGINEERING. *Educ:* Purdue Univ, BA, 61, MS, 63, PhD(mat sci, metall eng), 66. *Prof Exp:* Staff mem, Sandia Labs, 66-69; assoc metall eng, 69-73, mgr reactor & mfg mat support sect & metall engr, Fuels & Mat Dept, 73-78, ASSOC DIR, FUELS & MAT DEPT, EBR-II PROJ, ARGONNE NAT LAB, IDAHO, 78- *Concurrent Pos:* Prin investr for Argonne Nat Lab, Nat Cladding/Duct Mat Develop Prog, 78- *Mem:* Am Inst Mining, Metall & Petrol Engrs; Am Soc Metals; Am Nuclear Soc. *Res:* Formation and diffusion of point defects in compounds; effects of irradiation on the mechanical properties of metals. *Mailing Add:* EBR-II Proj Argonne Nat Lab Idaho Falls ID 83401

WALTERS, LESTER JAMES, JR, b Tulsa, Okla, June 3, 40; m 67. GEOCHEMISTRY. *Educ:* Univ Tulsa, BS, 62; Mass Inst Technol, PhD(geochem), 67. *Prof Exp:* Res scientist, Marathon Oil Co, 67-69; tech assistance expert, Int Atomic Energy Agency, 69; from asst prof to prof geol, Bowling Green State Univ, 70-81; PRIN RES SCIENTIST, ARCO OIL & GAS CO, 81- *Mem:* Am Chem Soc; Am Asn Petrol Geologists; Geochem Soc; Soc Explor Paleontologists & Mineralogists. *Res:* Geochemical cycle of iodine, bromine, and chlorine in sediments; neutron activation analysis; stable isotope geochemistry; heavy metal pollution in Lake Erie; exploration geochemistry. *Mailing Add:* 2804 Glencliff Dr Plano TX 75075

WALTERS, LOWELL EUGENE, b Freedom, Okla, Jan 13, 19; m 42; c 2. ANIMAL SCIENCE. *Educ:* Okla State Univ, BS, 40; Univ Mass, MS, 42; Okla State Univ, PhD(animal nutrit), 53. *Prof Exp:* Instr animal husb, La State Univ, 42-44; asst prof, Univ Mass, 44-46; from asst prof to assoc prof, 46-57, PROF ANIMAL HUSB, OKLA STATE UNIV, 58- *Mem:* Am Meat Sci Asn. *Res:* Meats; beef quality; carcass composition of beef, pork and lamb; potassium 40 techniques in live animal and carcass evaluation; growth and performance in slaughter livestock; systems analysis methods as applied to efficient beef production. *Mailing Add:* Meat Sci Lab Okla State Univ Stillwater OK 74074

WALTERS, MARTA SHERMAN, b Los Angeles, Calif, Aug 11, 14; m 41. CYTOGENETICS. *Educ:* Univ Calif, Berkeley, BA, 35, MS, 37, PhD(genetics), 44. *Prof Exp:* Biologist, Radiation Lab, Univ Calif, 47; cytol asst, Div Genetics, Univ Calif, Berkeley, 48, Guggenheim fel & univ res fel, 49-50; RES ASSOC BIOL SCI, UNIV CALIF, SANTA BARBARA, 49-; RES ASSOC, SANTA BARBARA BOT GARDEN, 49- *Concurrent Pos:* USPHS res career develop award, 63-69. *Mem:* Am Soc Cell Biol; Bot Soc Am; Soc Study Evolution; Genetics Soc Am. *Res:* Chromosome cytology. *Mailing Add:* Santa Barbara Bot Garden 1212 Mission Canyon Rd Santa Barbara CA 93105

WALTERS, MARTHA I, b Logan, Ohio, Oct 21, 25. CLINICAL CHEMISTRY. *Educ:* Ohio State Univ, BSc, 47, MSc, 59, PhD(clin path), 70. *Prof Exp:* Supvr biochem labs, Ohio State Univ Hosp, 49-59, instr clin path, Univ, 55-59; sr res asst, Bellevue Med Ctr, NY Univ, 59-62; dir biochem, St Francis Hosp, Bronx, NY, 63-67 & Ohio Valley Hosp, Steubenville, 71-73; supvr endocrinol & toxicol, Consol Biomed Labs, 73-80; DIR THERAPEUT DRUG MONITORING, OHIO STATE UNIV HOSP, 80- *Mem:* Am Chem Soc; Am Asn Clin Chemists; Sigma Xi. *Res:* Relationship between metabolism and function in erythrocytes and leukocytes. *Mailing Add:* 952 Chelsea Ave Columbus OH 43209

WALTERS, RANDALL KEITH, b Cheyenne, Wyo, Aug 15, 43; m 63; c 2. MATHEMATICS, STATISTICS. *Educ:* Univ Wyo, BS, 65; Univ Tex, El Paso, MS, 69; NMex State Univ, PhD(math), 75. *Prof Exp:* Res mathematician, White Sands Missle Range, 65-70; math economist, El Paso Natural Gas Co, 75-77; INSTR MATH, COL REDWOODS, 77- *Mem:* Am Statist Asn; Am Math Soc; Math Asn Am. *Res:* Torsion-free abelian groups, non commutative ring theory and homological algebra; non-parametric time series analysis. *Mailing Add:* 1631 C St Eureka CA 95501

WALTERS, RICHARD FRANCIS, b Teleajen, Romania, Aug 30, 30; US citizen; m 52; c 2. INFORMATION SCIENCE, MEDICAL EDUCATION. *Educ:* Williams Col, BA, 52, Univ Wyo, MA, 53; Univ Bordeaux, dipl natural sci, 55; Stanford Univ, PhD(geol), 57. *Prof Exp:* Res geologist, Humble Oil & Ref Co, 56-67; asst prof, 67-73, assoc prof community health, 73-78, PROF COMMUNITY HEALTH, SCH MED, UNIV CALIF, DAVIS, 78- & PROF ELEC & COMPUT ENG, 80- *Mem:* AAAS; Biomed Eng Soc; Asn Comput Mach; Inst Elec & Electronics Engrs. *Res:* Interactive information systems; machine-independent implementation of high-level languages; computerized problem-oriented medical record systems. *Mailing Add:* Univ of Calif Sch of Med Davis CA 95616

WALTERS, ROLAND DICK, b Portland, Ore, Jan 30, 20; m 45; c 3. ORTHODONTICS. *Educ:* Walla Walla Col, BA, 47; Ore State, MS, 49; Loma Linda Univ, DDS, 57, MS, 67. *Prof Exp:* Instr biol, Walla Walla Col, 47-49; asst prof biol, 49-53, instr oral med, 65-67, asst prof anat, 68-69, PROF ORTHOD & CHMN DEPT, SCH DENT, LOMA LINDA UNIV, 69- *Concurrent Pos:* Ed, SDA Dentist, 63; mem, Bd Trustees, Loma Linda Univ, 63-65; vchmn, Bd Dir, Kern Acad, 64; chmn, Tri-County Dent Soc, 71-73; consult, Jerry L Pettis Mem Vet Hosp, 78- *Mem:* Found Orthod Res; Am Dent Asn; Sigma Xi. *Res:* Facial changes and bone growth; transplantation of human teeth; retraction of the maxillae using orthopedic force; mandibular dental arch; surgical orthodontic expansion. *Mailing Add:* Orthod Dept Sch Dent Loma Linda Univ Loma Linda CA 92350

WALTERS, RONALD ARLEN, b Greeley, Colo, Apr 25, 40; m 69; c 2. BIOCHEMISTRY, RADIOBIOLOGY. *Educ:* Colo State Univ, BS, 62, MS, 64, PhD(radiation biol), 67. *Prof Exp:* Engr radiation biol, Gen Elec Co, 62-63; STAFF MEM BIOCHEM, LOS ALAMOS SCI LAB, UNIV CALIF, 67-, DEP GROUP LEADER, 81- *Mem:* AAAS; Am Chem Soc; Am Soc Biol Chemists; Radiation Res Soc; Am Soc Cell Biol. *Res:* Cellular biology; gene structure and function; trace metal metabolism; radiation biology. *Mailing Add:* 545 Totavi Los Alamos NM 87544

WALTERS, THOMAS RICHARD, b Milwaukee, Wis, May 9, 29. PEDIATRICS, HEMATOLOGY. *Educ:* Marquette Univ, MD, 54. *Prof Exp:* Instr pediat, Stanford Univ, 61-62; asst prof, Univ Kans Med Ctr, Kansas City, 62-67; assoc prof, Univ Tenn, Memphis, 67-71; assoc prof, 71-76, PROF PEDIAT & DIR DIV HEMAT-ONCOL, NJ MED SCH, 76- *Concurrent Pos:* Assoc mem hemat, St Jude Children's Res Hosp, Memphis, 67-71. *Mem:* Am Soc Hemat; Am Acad Pediat; Am Asn Cancer Res. *Res:* Multi-disciplinary chemotherapy programs; clinical nematology-oncology. *Mailing Add:* Dept of Pediat NJ Med Sch Newark NJ 07103

WALTERS, VIRGINIA F, b New York, NY, May 26, 25; m 45; c 2. PHYSICS. *Educ:* Smith Col, AB, 47; Western Reserve Univ, MA, 58, PhD(physics), 65. *Prof Exp:* Physicist, DeMornay Budd, Inc, 47-49; res asst microwave components, Radiation Lab, Columbia Univ, 49-50; lectr elem physics, Adelphi Col, 50-51; physicist, Servo Corp Am, 51; asst physics, Western Reserve Univ, 54-65, fel, 65-66; asst prof, Cleveland State Univ, 66-67; res physicist, Carnegie-Mellon Univ, 67-68; asst prof phys sci, Point Park Col, 68-69; teacher physics & math, Western Reserve Acad, 69-74; lectr physics, Cleveland State Univ, 75-80. *Concurrent Pos:* Vis asst prof, Dept Physics, Cleveland State Univ, 77- *Mem:* Am Phys Soc; Am Asn Physics Teachers. *Res:* Positron annihilation; nuclear instrumentation. *Mailing Add:* PO Box 155 Ellicottville NY 14731

WALTERS, WILLIAM BEN, b Highland, Kans, Apr 26, 38; m 62; c 2. NUCLEAR CHEMISTRY, PHYSICAL CHEMISTRY. *Educ:* Kans State Univ, BS, 60; Univ Ill, PhD(chem), 64. *Prof Exp:* Res assoc chem, Mass Inst Technol, 64-65, asst prof, 65-70; assoc prof, 70-77, PROF CHEM, UNIV MD, COLLEGE PARK, 77- *Concurrent Pos:* Vis prof physics, Katolieke Univ Leuven, Belg, 78. *Mem:* Am Chem Soc; Am Phys Soc. *Res:* Radioactive decay; nuclear spectroscopy; new isotopes and isomers; nuclear reactions; positron annihilation; nuclear structure; neutron-capture gamma-ray spectroscopy. *Mailing Add:* Dept of Chem Univ of Md College Park MD 20742

WALTERS, WILLIAM LE ROY, b Racine, Wis, Mar 30, 32; m 55; c 4. PHYSICS. *Educ:* Univ Wis, BS, 54, MS, 58, PhD(physics), 61. *Prof Exp:* From asst prof to prof physics, 61-68, assoc dean sci, Col Lett & Sci, 65-68, exec asst chancellor, 68-70, actg dean col appl sci & eng, 70, VCHANCELLOR, UNIV WIS-MILWAUKEE, 71- *Concurrent Pos:* Exec comt coun for acad affairs, Nat Asn State Univs & Land-grant col, 76-79, chmn Coun, 78. *Mem:* AAAS; Am Asn Physics Teachers; Am Phys Soc; Am Vacuum Soc. *Res:* Vacuum and surface physics; science communications. *Mailing Add:* Univ Wis Milwaukee WI 53201

WALTHER, ADRIAAN, b The Hague, Holland, Apr 22, 34; m 60; c 2. OPTICS. *Educ:* Delft Univ Technol, PhD(physics), 59. *Prof Exp:* Mem res staff, Diffraction Ltd Inc, 60-72; PROF ENG & SCI, WORCESTER POLYTECH INST, 72- *Concurrent Pos:* Am Optical vis prof, Worcester Polytech Inst, 68-69. *Mem:* Optical Soc Am; Neth Phys Soc. *Res:* Geometrical and physical optics. *Mailing Add:* 20 Whittier Dr Acton MA 01720

WALTHER, ALINA, b Rosenthal, USSR, Aug 15, 23; Can citizen. PLANT PHYSIOLOGY, PLANT ECOLOGY. *Educ:* Sir George Williams Univ, BCom, 53, BSc, 61; McGill Univ, MSc, 63; Univ Toronto, PhD(plant physiol), 68. *Prof Exp:* Spec lectr, 67-68, asst prof, 68-72, ASSOC PROF BIOL, UNIV REGINA, 72- *Mem:* AAAS; Phytochem Soc NAm; Am Soc Plant Physiologists; Can Soc Plant Physiologists; Ecol Soc Am. *Res:* Plant senescence, especially metabolic changes in developing and senescing sunflower cotyledons and leaves; seed production and germination in native prairie plants (opuntia polyacantha and glycyrrhiza lepiolola); betalaines in emergent cactus seedlings. *Mailing Add:* Dept of Biol Univ of Regina Regina SK S4S 0A2 Can

WALTHER, CARL H(UGO), b Baltimore, Md, June 4, 11; m 36. ENGINEERING MECHANICS, CIVIL ENGINEERING. *Educ:* Johns Hopkins Univ, BE, 31, MCE, 33; Univ Md, PhD(eng mech), 67. *Prof Exp:* From instr to prof civil eng, 39-62, asst dean eng, 45-51 & 57-62, prof eng & appl sci, 62-76, asst vpres acad affairs, 66-76, EMER PROF ENG & APPL SCI, GEORGE WASHINGTON UNIV, 76- *Concurrent Pos:* Struct consult, Res & Develop Br, Off Qm Gen, 44-45; tech adv, Int Training Admin, 45; chmn subcomt struct mech, Nat Res Coun Comt on Qm Res & Develop, 46-50; expert mem, Nat Inventors' Coun, Dept Com, 50-62. *Mem:* Am Soc Civil Engrs; Am Soc Eng Educ. *Res:* Impact behavior of materials and dynamic response of structures; photoelasticity and experimental stress analysis. *Mailing Add:* 1337-27th St NW Washington DC 20007

WALTHER, FRANK H, b Williamsport, Pa, Aug 4, 30; m 54; c 3. MINERALOGY. *Educ:* Franklin & Marshall Col, BSc, 52. *Prof Exp:* Mgr mineral res, 56-72, mgr res, 72-78, DIR RES, HARBISON-WALKER REFRACTORIES, 78- *Mem:* Fel Am Ceramic Soc. *Res:* Mineralogical aspects of refractory technology. *Mailing Add:* Harbison-Walker Refractories Garber Res Ctr West Mifflin PA 15122

WALTHER, FRITZ R, b Chemnitz, Ger, Sept 8, 21. ANIMAL BEHAVIOR. *Educ:* Univ Frankfurt, BS, 44, MS, 56, PhD(zool), 63. *Prof Exp:* Teacher, Fed Ministry Educ, Ger, 51-59; sci dir res & admin, Opel Zoo, 63-63; res scientist, Zurich Zool, Switz, 64 & Serengeti Nat Park, Tanzania, 65-67; assoc prof zool, Univ Mo-Columbia, 67-70; PROF WILDLIFE, TEX A&M UNIV, 70- *Concurrent Pos:* Grants, Ger Res Soc, 63, Gertrud Ruegg Found, 64 & 67, Fritz Thyssen Found, 65-67 & 74-75, Res Coun Univ Mo, 69-70, Smithsonian Foreign Currency, 70-72 & Caesar Kleberg Found, 74-75, 78. *Mem:* Am Soc Mammalogists; Ger Soc Mammalogists; Animal Behav Soc. *Res:* Ethology of game animals, especially horned ungulates. *Mailing Add:* Dept of Wildlife & Fisheries Sci Tex A&M Univ College Station TX 77843

WALTHER, JAMES EUGENE, b Spokane, Wash, May 16, 32; m 54; c 2. CHEMICAL ENGINEERING. *Educ:* Univ Wash, BS, 54; Univ Ill, Urbana, MS, 56, PhD(chem eng), 57. *Prof Exp:* Res engr, Stand Oil Co Calif, 57-62; res engr, 62-70, SR RES ENGR, CROWN ZELLERBACH CORP, CAMAS, 70- *Mem:* Am Inst Chem Engrs; Am Chem Soc. *Res:* Air pollution control from pulp and paper industry; instrumentation development for air pollution control. *Mailing Add:* 700 Umatilla Way Vancouver WA 98661

WALTKING, ARTHUR ERNEST, b New York, NY, Nov 7, 37; m 61; c 2. ANALYTICAL CHEMISTRY, FOOD CHEMISTRY. *Educ:* Lehigh Univ, BA, 59. *Prof Exp:* Asst chemist, 59-64, chemist, 64-66, group leader anal res, 66-67, sect head anal serv, 67-72, mgr anal serv, 72-79, ASSOC RES

SCIENTIST, BEST FOODS DIV, CPC INT INC, 79- *Concurrent Pos:* Assoc referee oxidized oils, Asn Off Anal Chemists, 71-; rep, Am Oil Chemists Soc, Joint Am Oil Chemists Soc-Asn Off Anal Chemists-Am Asn Cereal Chemists Comt Mycotoxins, 75-; US rep, comn oils, fats & derivatives, Int Union Pure & Appl Chem, 80- *Honors & Awards:* Golden Peanut Award, Nat Peanut Coun, 71. *Mem:* Am Oil Chemists Soc; Am Chem Soc; Asn Off Anal Chemists; Soc Rheol; NAm Thermal Anal Soc. *Res:* The development of analytical methodology for analysis of food products for mycotoxins, flavor volatiles, texture, rheological properties, essential fatty acids and polymers derived from oxidation of heat abuse of vegetable oils. *Mailing Add:* Best Foods Res Ctr 1120 Commerce Ave Box 1534 Union NJ 07083

WALTMAN, PAUL E, b St Louis, Mo, Oct 17, 31; m 53; c 3. MATHEMATICAL ANALYSIS, BIOMATHEMATICS. *Educ:* St Louis Univ, BS, 52; Baylor Univ, MA, 54; Univ Mo, MA, 60, PhD(math), 62. *Prof Exp:* Staff mem, Lincoln Lab, Mass Inst Technol, 57-58, Mitre Corp, 62-63 & Sandia Corp, 63-65; from asst prof to assoc prof, 65-68, PROF MATH, UNIV IOWA, 68- *Mem:* AAAS; Soc Indust & Appl Math. *Res:* Ordinary differential equations; mathematical models in biological science. *Mailing Add:* Dept of Math Univ of Iowa Iowa City IA 52240

WALTMANN, WILLIAM LEE, b Cedar Falls, Iowa, July 5, 34; m 58; c 3. MATHEMATICS. *Educ:* Wartburg Col, BA, 56; Iowa State Univ, MS, 58, PhD(math), 64. *Prof Exp:* Instr math, Wartburg Col, 58-61 & Iowa State Univ, 63-64; assoc prof, 64-72, PROF MATH, WARTBURG COL, 72-, CHMN DEPT, 71- *Mem:* Am Math Soc; Math Asn Am; Soc Indust & Appl Math. *Res:* Inversion of matrices; non-associative rings; tridiagonalization of matrices. *Mailing Add:* Dept of Math Wartburg Col Waverly IA 50677

WALTNER, ARTHUR, b Moundridge, Kans, Nov 28, 14; m 41; c 2. NUCLEAR PHYSICS. *Educ:* Bethel Col, Kans, AB, 38; Kans State Col, MS, 43; Univ NC, PhD, 49. *Prof Exp:* High sch teacher, 38-41; instr elec theory, Naval Training Sch, Ky State Teachers Col, Morehead, 42-43; lectr physics, Univ NC, 43-46, instr, 46-48; from asst prof to assoc prof, 48-56, PROF PHYSICS, NC STATE UNIV, 56- *Concurrent Pos:* Exchange physicist, A B Atomenergie, Stockholm, Sweden, 52-53. *Mem:* AAAS; fel Am Phys Soc. *Res:* Nuclear instrumentation; nuclear reactions due to heavy ions; x-ray production cross sections. *Mailing Add:* Dept of Physics NC State Univ Raleigh NC 27607

WALTON, ALAN, b Durham, Eng, May 29, 32; m 56; c 3. CHEMICAL OCEANOGRAPHY, GEOCHEMISTRY. *Educ:* Univ Durham, BSc, 53, PhD(chem), 56; Glasgow Univ, DSc, 71. *Prof Exp:* Res scientist nuclear chem, Isotopes Inc, NJ, 59-65; lectr, Glasgow Univ, 65-67, sr lectr, 67-70; head chem oceanog div, Atlantic Oceanog Lab, Bedford Inst Oceanog, 70-78; DIR INT MARINE POLICY, DEPT FISHERIES & OCEANS, 78- *Mem:* Fel Royal Inst Chem; Am Geophys Union; Geochem Soc. *Res:* Air-sea exchange; isotope applications in marine environment; carbon 14 dating; marine and atmospheric pollution. *Mailing Add:* 14 Kimdale Nepean Ottawa ON K2G 0W9 Can

WALTON, ALAN GEORGE, b Birmingham, Eng, Apr 3, 36; m 77; c 4. BIOPHYSICAL CHEMISTRY. *Educ:* Univ Nottingham, BSc, 57, PhD(chem), 60, DSc(biophys chem), 73. *Prof Exp:* Res assoc chem, Ind Univ, 60-62; from asst prof to assoc prof macromolecular sci, Case Western Reserve Univ, 62-71, prof, 71-81; PRES, UNIV GENETICS CO, 81- *Concurrent Pos:* Vis lectr, Harvard Med Sch, 71; mem, Pres Task Force Sci & Technol Policy, 75-76. *Mem:* NY Acad Sci; Am Chem Soc; Biophys Soc. *Res:* Conformation and structure of synthetic biopolymers and fibrous proteins; molecular hematology; cell adhesion; genetic engineering; cartilage research; drug release. *Mailing Add:* 537 Newtown Ave PO Box 6080 Univ Genetics Co Norwalk CT 44106

WALTON, BARBARA ANN, b Baltimore, Md, Mar 30, 40; m 70. VERTEBRATE EMBRYOLOGY, HISTOLOGY. *Educ:* Ind Univ Pa, BSEd, 62; Univ Okla, MNatSci, 66, PhD(zool), 70. *Prof Exp:* Teacher, Franklin Twp Sch Dist, Pa, 62-63 & Bethel Park Jr High Sch, 63-65; ASST PROF BIOL, UNIV TENN, CHATTANOOGA, 70- *Mem:* Am Inst Biol Sci; Am Soc Zoologists. *Res:* Development of the chicken embryo following x-irradiation and application of other teratogens; histology and histochemistry of embryonic development. *Mailing Add:* Dept of Biol Univ of Tenn Chattanooga TN 37401

WALTON, BRYCE CALVIN, b Lead, SDak, June 5, 23; m 46; c 4. PARASITOLOGY. *Educ:* Univ Southern Calif, MS, 50; Univ Md, PhD(zool, parasitol), 56. *Prof Exp:* US Army, 50-, res parasitologist, Walter Reed Army Inst Res, 52-56, chief dept med zool, 406th Med Gen Lab, 56-59, parasitologist, Third Army Med Lab, 59-62, chief parasitic dis sect, Middle Am Res Unit, 62-65, cmndg officer, Med Res Unit, Panama, CZ, 65-69 & US Army Res & Develop Group Far East, 69-72, cmndg officer, Army Med Res Unit-Panama, 72-76; regional adv parasitic dis, Pan Am Health Orgn-WHO, 76-80; Am Soc Trop Med & Hyg; fel Royal Soc Trop Med & Hyg; Am Micros Soc. *Res:* American trypanosomiasis and leishmaniasis; toxoplasmosis; immuno-diagnosis of parasitic disease; systematics. *Mailing Add:* 312 Baltimore St Gettysburg PA 17325

WALTON, CHARLES ANTHONY, b Auburn, Ala, Apr 3, 26; m 46; c 2. PHARMACY, PHARMACOLOGY. *Educ:* Auburn Univ, BS, 49; Purdue Univ, MS, 50, PhD, 56. *Prof Exp:* Instr, Ala Polytech Inst, 49; from asst prof to prof mat med, Col Pharm, Univ Ky, 50-72, head dept, 56-66, dir drug info ctr, 66-72, prof oral biol, Col Dent, 72-73; PROF & ASSOC DEAN, COL PHARM, UNIV TEX AUSTIN, 73- *Concurrent Pos:* Fulbright prof, Univ Cairo, 64-65; prof pharmacol, Univ Tex Health Sci Ctr, San Antonio, 73- *Mem:* Am Soc Hosp Pharmacists; fel Am Col Clin Pharmacol; Am Coun Pharmaceut Educ. *Res:* Clinical pharmacy and drug information services. *Mailing Add:* Clin Pharm Progs Univ Tex San Antonio TX 40506

WALTON, CHARLES MICHAEL, b Hickory, NC, June 28, 41; m 63; c 4. TRANSPORTATION ENGINEERING, POLICY PLANNING. *Educ:* Va Mil Inst, BS, 63; NC State Univ, MCE, 69, PhD(civil eng), 71. *Prof Exp:* Asst civil eng, NC State Univ, 67-71; asst prof, 71-76, ASSOC PROF CIVIL ENG, UNIV TEX, AUSTIN, 76- *Concurrent Pos:* Consult, Res Triangle Inst, NC, 70, Off Econ Opportunity, 70-71 & Radian Corp, Tex, 71-; mem & prog chmn, Transp Res Bd, Nat Acad Sci-Nat Res Coun; mem, Governor's Interagency Transp Coun, Tex, 72-; transp consult, Parsons, BrinckerHoff, Quade, Douglas, Inc, NY, 73-; mem exec comn, Urban Transp Div, Am Soc Civil Engrs, 81-; consult, Asn Am Railroads, Washington, DC, 81-; assoc dir, Ctr Transp Res, Univ Tex, Austin, 80- *Mem:* Am Soc Civil Engrs; Inst Transp Engrs; Soc Am Mil Engrs; Opers Res Soc Am. *Res:* Transportation and land use planning; airport access and capacity; rural development; traffic safety; public transportation; supertanker terminal planning; application of light rail transit; truck use of highways; human service transportation planning and management; truck size and weight issues. *Mailing Add:* ECJ Hall Suite Univ of Tex Austin TX 78712

WALTON, CHARLES WILLIAM, b Carlinville, Ill, Apr 3, 08; m 33; c 3. CHEMISTRY. *Educ:* Univ Ill, BS, 30; Univ Mich, MS, 31, PhD(chem), 33. *Hon Degrees:* DSc, Blackburn Col, 65. *Prof Exp:* Lectr & lab asst, Univ Mich, 30-31; res chemist, Goodyear Tire & Rubber Co, 33-39, supvr phys chem, 40-41, mgr & tech coordr, Synthetic Rubber Div, 41-44, mgr, Chem Prod Develop Div, 44-46; asst to exec vpres, 47, mgr, New Prod Div, 48-51, gen mgr, Adhesives & Coatings Div, 52-59, div vpres & gen mgr, Adhesives, Coatings & Sealers Div, 59-61, vpres res, 61-62, vpres res & develop, 62-69, consult, 69-73, DIR, MINN MINING & MFG CO, 73- *Concurrent Pos:* Trustee, Blackburn Col, 67-74. *Mem:* Am Chem Soc; Soc Chem Indust; Commercial Develop Asn. *Res:* Synthetic rubber; high polymers; surface chemistry and solids. *Mailing Add:* PO Box 136 Sugarloaf Shores FL 33044

WALTON, DANIEL C, b Philadelphia, Pa, May 16, 34; m 60; c 2. PLANT BIOCHEMISTRY, PLANT PHYSIOLOGY. *Educ:* Univ Del, BS, 55; State Univ NY Col Forestry, Syracuse Univ, PhD(plant physiol), 62. *Prof Exp:* Chem engr, E I du Pont de Nemours & Co, 55-58; fel, Univ Tex, 62-63; from asst prof to assoc prof, 63-74, PROF BIOCHEM, STATE UNIV NY COL FORESTRY, SYRACUSE UNIV, 74- *Concurrent Pos:* Vis mem, Dept Bot, Univ Col Wales, 71-72 & 78-79. *Mem:* AAAS; Am Chem Soc; Plant Growth Regulator Soc; Am Soc Plant Physiologists. *Res:* Seed germination; plant growth regulation. *Mailing Add:* Dept of Biol Col Environ Sci Forestry Syracuse NY 13210

WALTON, DEREK, b Sao Paulo, Brazil, Mar 1, 31; nat US; m 54; c 4. PHYSICS, GEOPHYSICS. *Educ:* Univ Toronto, MSc, 54; Harvard Univ, PhD(appl physics), 58. *Prof Exp:* Asst res engr, Univ Calif, 57-58; sr physicist, Convair Div, Gen Dynamics Corp, 58-60; res assoc eng physics, Cornell Univ, 60-62; physicist, Oak Ridge Nat Lab, 62-68; assoc prof, 68-74, PROF PHYSICS, McMASTER UNIV, 74- *Mem:* Am Phys Soc. *Res:* Solidification, nucleation and growth; phonon-defect interactions; thermal conductivity; spin-phonon interactions; phase transformations; amorphous materials; archaeomagnetism; physics in archaeology; rock magnetism. *Mailing Add:* Dept of Physics McMaster Univ Hamilton ON L8S 4M1 Can

WALTON, EDWARD, b Mt Carmel, Pa, May 11, 21; m 46; c 2. ORGANIC CHEMISTRY. *Educ:* Univ Md, BS, 42, PhD(org chem), 48. *Prof Exp:* Res chemist, Off Emergency Mgt & Comt Med Res Contract, Univ Md, 43-46; RES CHEMIST, MERCK SHARPE & DOHME RES LABS, 47- *Concurrent Pos:* Vis scientist, Univ Basel, 59-60; mem subcomt carbohydrates & related compounds, Nat Res Coun, 69- *Mem:* AAAS; Am Chem Soc. *Res:* Synthetic antimalarials; vitamins; antibiotics; peptides; nucleosides; carbohydrates. *Mailing Add:* Merck Sharp & Dohme Res Labs 126 E Lincoln Ave Rahway NJ 07065

WALTON, GEORGE, b Edmunton, Eng, Aug 14, 14; nat US; m 49; c 1. PHYSICAL CHEMISTRY, FORENSIC SCIENCE. *Educ:* San Diego State Col, AB, 36; Columbia Univ, MA, 39, PhD(phys chem), 41. *Prof Exp:* Asst, Columbia Univ, 40-41; asst prof chem, Col Pharm, Univ Cincinnati, 41-44, assoc prof, 46-47; consult chemist, 47-50; sr res chemist, Drackett Co, 50-52, tech adminr, 52-57, sr scientist, 57-62; geochem prospecting, 62-66; asst dir, Southwestern NMex Media Ctr, Western NMex Univ, 66-68, asst prof phys sci, 68-74, assoc prof, 75-80. *Res:* X-ray crystallography applied to chemical problems; paper chromatography of metal ions; silver in ores by atomic absorption spectroscopy. *Mailing Add:* 1312 S Silver Ave Deming NM 88030

WALTON, GERALD STEVEN, b Kansas City, Kans, July 23, 35; m 56; c 5. PLANT PATHOLOGY. *Educ:* Wabash Col, AB, 57; Rutgers Univ, PhD(plant path), 61. *Prof Exp:* From asst plant pathologist to assoc plant pathologist, 61-77, PLANT PATHOLOGIST, CONN AGR EXP STA, 77- *Mem:* Am Phytopath Soc. *Res:* Nature of resistance to plant diseases, methods of disease control and determination of causal factor of a disease when unknown. *Mailing Add:* Dept of Plant Path Conn Agr Exp Sta PO Box 1106 New Haven CT 06504

WALTON, HAROLD FREDERIC, b Tregony, Eng, Aug 25, 12; nat US; m 38; c 3. ANALYTICAL CHEMISTRY. *Educ:* Oxford Univ, BA, 34, PhD(chem), 37. *Prof Exp:* Procter vis fel, Princeton Univ, 37-38; res chemist, Permutit Co, 38-40; from instr to asst prof chem, Northwestern Univ, 40-46; from asst prof to assoc prof, 47-56, chmn dept, 62-66, PROF CHEM, UNIV COLO, BOULDER, 56- *Concurrent Pos:* Vis Fulbright-Hays lectr, Trujillo, 66-67 & 70 & Lima, 66-67; vis prof, Pedag Inst, Caracas, Venezuela, 72. *Mem:* AAAS; Am Chem Soc; Royal Soc Chem; corresp mem Chem Soc Peru. *Res:* Ion exchange; chromatography. *Mailing Add:* Dept of Chem Univ of Colo Boulder CO 80309

WALTON, HAROLD V(INCENT), b Christiana, Pa, June 17, 21; m 46; c 3. AGRICULTURAL ENGINEERING. *Educ:* Pa State Univ, BS, 42, MS, 50; Purdue Univ, PhD, 61. *Prof Exp:* Engr, Gen Elec Co, 43-45; prof agr eng, Pa State Univ, 47-62; prof, Univ Mo-Columbia, 62-76, chmn dept, 62-69, prof

& chief party, India Contract, 69-71; PROF AGR ENG & HEAD DEPT, PA STATE UNIV, UNIVERSITY PARK, 76- *Mem:* Inst Food Technologists; Am Soc Eng Educ; fel Am Soc Agr Engrs. *Res:* Physical properties of poultry egg and meat products. *Mailing Add:* Dept of Agr Eng Pa State Univ University Park PA 16802

WALTON, HARRIETT J, b Claxton, Ga, Sept 19, 33; m 58; c 4. MATHEMATICS. *Educ:* Clark Col, AB, 52; Howard Univ, MS, 54; Syracuse Univ, MA, 57; Ga State Univ, PhD(math educ), 79. *Prof Exp:* Instr math, Hampton Inst, 54-55, asst prof, 57-58; PROF MATH, MOREHOUSE COL, 58- *Concurrent Pos:* Proj dir, Atlanta Univ, 70-73 & Atlanta Univ Ctr, Inc, 81-82. *Mem:* Math Asn Am; Nat Asn Math (secy/treas, 80-). *Res:* Remediation in mathematics at the college level. *Mailing Add:* Morehouse Col Atlanta GA 30318

WALTON, HENRY MILLER, b Frankfurt am Main, Ger, May 7, 12; nat US; m 50; c 2. ORGANIC CHEMISTRY. *Educ:* Univ Frankfurt, PhD(philos), 34; Univ Chicago, PhD(org chem), 38. *Prof Exp:* Res chemist, Continental Carbon Co, NY, 39; Chas Pfizer & Co fel, Columbia Univ, 40-42; sr res chemist, Warner Inst Therapeut Res, 43-47; group leader fundamental res lab, Nat Dairy Res Labs, Inc, 47-57; sr res chemist, A E Staley Mfg Co, 57-61, res assoc, 61-69, patent chemist, 69-72; patent consult, 72-74; prof philos, Richland Community Col, 74-75; RETIRED. *Mem:* Am Chem Soc; Am Philos Asn; Philos Sci Asn. *Res:* Vitamins A and E; unsaturated aliphatics; condensation polymers; free radical polymerization reactions; starches; sugars; enzymes; immobilized enzymes; philosophy of science. *Mailing Add:* 115 S Stevens Ave Decatur IL 62522

WALTON, JOHN JOSEPH, b Sterling, Ill, Aug 25, 34; m 59; c 2. ATMOSPHERIC PHYSICS. *Educ:* Northwestern Univ, BS, 56; Univ Kans, PhD(physics), 61. *Prof Exp:* Physicist, Lawrence Radiation Lab, 61-72, PHYSICIST, LAWRENCE LIVERMORE LAB, 72- *Concurrent Pos:* Lectr appl sci, Univ Calif, 67-71. *Res:* Regional and global atmospheric modeling with emphasis on transport processes. *Mailing Add:* Atmosperhic & Geophys Sci Div Lawrence Livermore Lab L-142 Livermore CA 94550

WALTON, KENNETH NELSON, b Winnipeg, Man, May 1, 35; US citizen; m; c 4. MEDICINE. *Educ:* Univ Man, MD, 59; Am Bd Urol, dipl, 68. *Prof Exp:* Intern, Winnipeg Gen Hosp, 59-60, resident surg & path, 60-61; jr asst resident urol, Johns Hopkins Hosp, 61-62, res fel, 62-63, sr asst resident, 63-64, co-head resident, 64-65; from instr to asst prof urol, Dept Surg, Med Ctr, Univ Ky, 65-69, chmn div urol, 68-69; chmn, Dept Urol, 69-80, LOUIS MCDONALD ORR PROF SURG, SCH MED, EMORY UNIV, 69- *Concurrent Pos:* Am Cancer Soc res fel, 63-64. *Mem:* Am Col Surgeons; AMA; Am Soc Nephrology; Am Urol Asn; Pan-Am Med Asn. *Res:* Kidney transplants; factors influencing renal oxygen consumption; effect of hypothermia and the inhibition of the tubular transport of sodium; difference in carbohydrate metabolism between prostatic cancers which are endocrine sensitive and those which are not. *Mailing Add:* Emory Univ Sch of Med Atlanta GA 30322

WALTON, PETER DAWSON, b Leeds, Eng, Oct 18, 24; Can citizen; m 49; c 4. PLANT BREEDING. *Educ:* Univ Durham, BSc, 49, MSc, 53; Univ Lancaster, PhD(pop genetics), 61. *Prof Exp:* Plant breeder, Res Div, Ministry of Agr, Sudan, 50-55; sr plant breeder, Empire Cotton Growing Corp, 55-63; lectr agr & bot, Ahmadu Bello Univ, Nigeria, 63-67; assoc prof plant sci, Univ Sask, 67-69; chmn dept, 75-80, PROF PLANT SCI, UNIV ALTA, 69- *Mem:* Brit Inst Biol; Am Soc Agron; Genetics Soc Can; Am Forage & Grassland Coun. *Res:* Forage crop breeding with special reference to the study of genotype by environment interaction. *Mailing Add:* Dept Plant Sci Univ Alta Edmonton AB T6H 2B3 Can

WALTON, PHILIP WILSON, medical physics, see previous edition

WALTON, RAY DANIEL, JR, b Ogden, Utah, Jan 26, 21; m 44; c 6. CHEMICAL & NUCLEAR ENGINEERING, OPERATIONS RESEARCH. *Educ:* Ore State Univ, BS, 43, MS, 48. *Prof Exp:* Chem engr, Hanford Labs, Gen Elec Co, 47-56; chem engr, Idaho Opers Off, US Atomic Energy Comn, 56-60, tech analyst, Div Oper Anal & Forecasting, 60-64; chem engr, Int Atomic Energy Agency, 64-66; chief eng br, Div Oper Anal & Forecasting, US Atomic Energy Comn, 66-70, mat & process control engr, Div Waste & Scrap Mgt, 70-71, chem engr, Develop Br, Div Waste Mgt & Transp, 71-74; proj engr, US Energy Res & Develop Admin, 74-77; actg chief technol br, Div Waste Prod, 77-78, eng prog mgr, Technol Div, Off Waste Oper(s) & Technol, 79-81, ENG PROG MGR, OFF DEFENSE WASTE & BYPRODUCTS, US DEPT ENERGY, 81- *Concurrent Pos:* Leader, Int Atomic Energy Agency nuclear power mission, Turkey. *Mem:* Am Sci Affiliation; Am Inst Chem Engrs. *Res:* Technical and economic aspects of the nuclear fuel cycle, irradiated reactor fuel processing and disposal of radioactive waste; initiation, funding, direction and evaluation of nuclear waste management research and development projects. *Mailing Add:* 19205 Germantown Rd Germantown MD 20767

WALTON, ROBERT BRUCE, b Jersey City, NJ, Nov 30, 15; m 39; c 4. MICROBIOLOGY. *Educ:* Rutgers Univ, BSc, 48, PhD(microbiol), 53. *Prof Exp:* From asst res microbiologist to assoc res microbiologist, Merck Sharp & Dohme Res Labs, 40-53, sr res microbiologist, 53-78, res fel, 78-81; RETIRED. *Mem:* AAAS; Am Soc Microbiol; Am Chem Soc; Soc Indust Microbiol. *Res:* Antibiotics; vaccines; immunology; microbial nutrition and physiology; fermentations; actinophage. *Mailing Add:* 798 Central Ave Rahway NJ 07065

WALTON, ROBERT EUGENE, b Shattuck, Okla, Jan 15, 31; m 59. ANIMAL BREEDING, ANIMAL GENETICS. *Educ:* Okla State Univ, BS, 52, MS, 56; Iowa State Univ, PhD, 61. *Prof Exp:* Farm mgr, Westhide Farms, Eng, 53-54; asst prof dairy sci, Univ Ky, 58-62; geneticist, 68, PRES & CHIEF EXEC OFFICER, AM BREEDERS SERV, 68- *Concurrent Pos:* Mem prog mgt develop, Harvard Univ, 70. *Mem:* Am Soc Animal Sci; Am Dairy Sci Asn; Biomet Soc; Nat Asn Animal Breeders (pres, 72-74). *Res:* Application of genetical and statistical tools to problems of animal breeding and improvement; estimation of parameters of domestic large animal populations; genetic evaluation of dairy sires. *Mailing Add:* 4066 Vinburn Rd De Forest WI 53532

WALTON, RODDY BURKE, b Goldthwaite, Tex, Dec 9, 31; m 61; c 1. NUCLEAR PHYSICS. *Educ:* Tex A&M Col, BS, 52; Univ Wis, MS, 54, PhD(nuclear physics), 57. *Prof Exp:* Nuclear res officer, Air Force Weapons Lab, 57-59; staff physicist, Gen Atomic Div, Gen Dynamics Corp, 59-67; STAFF MEM, LOS ALAMOS SCI LAB, 67- *Mem:* Am Phys Soc; Inst Nuclear Mat Mgt; fel Am Nuclear Soc. *Res:* Neutron physics; photonuclear research; positron production with an electron linear accelerator; delayed gamma rays and delayed neutrons from fission; non-destructive assay applications. *Mailing Add:* A-1 Los Alamos Sci Lab Los Alamos NM 87545

WALTON, THEODORE ROSS, b Takoma Park, Md, Feb 26, 31; m 56; c 4. ORGANIC CHEMISTRY. *Educ:* Univ Md, BS, 55; Ohio State Univ, PhD(org chem), 60. *Prof Exp:* Proj dir chem, Atlantic Res Corp, 60-63; res chemist, Author W Sloan Found Va, 63-64; RES CHEMIST, US NAVAL RES LAB, WASHINGTON, DC, 64- *Mem:* Am Chem Soc. *Res:* Organic and polymer synthesis and chemistry; thermally stable organic polymers; electrical conducting organic polymers; rocket motor case thermal insulation and material compatibility; fire retardant coating systems; water based paints; adhesive bonding. *Mailing Add:* US Naval Res Lab 4555 Overlook Ave SW Washington DC 20375

WALTON, THOMAS PEYTON, III, b Archer, Fla, Dec 7, 22; m 64; c 3. SURGERY. *Educ:* Tulane Univ, MD, 50; Am Bd Surg, dipl, 64. *Prof Exp:* Intern, Charity Hosp La, New Orleans, 50-51; physician for Seminole Indian Nation, Fla, 51-52; resident surg, Baptist Hosp, Nashville, Tenn, 52-55; chief resident, Nashville Gen Hosp, 55-56; pvt pract surg, Tampa, Fla, 57-67; asst prof, La State Univ Med Ctr New Orleans, 68-69; vchief surg, Vet Admin Hosp, Big Spring, Tex, 69-70; clin dir & chief surg, Lafayette Charity Hosp, 70-77; assoc prof, 77-80, PROF SURG, LA STATE UNIV, 80- *Concurrent Pos:* VChief surg, Tampa Gen Hosp, Fla, 61-62; chief of staff, Clara Frye Hosp, Tampa, 62-63; asst prof surg, Med Sch, Univ New Orleans, 70-73; guest examr, Am Bd Surg, 71. *Mem:* Fel Am Col Surgeons. *Res:* Emergency treatment of upper gastrointestinal bleeding by comparison of vagotomy and drainage with vagotomy and resection. *Mailing Add:* La State Univ Sch of Med 1542 Tulane Ave New Orleans LA 70112

WALTON, VINCENT MICHAEL, b Spokane, Wash, Oct 23, 49. SPACECRAFT & POINTING PAYLOAD, ALTITUDE CONTROL. *Educ:* Univ Wash, BS, 73, MS, 75. *Prof Exp:* Mem tech staff, Boeing Aerospace Co, 73-75; mem tech staff, 75-80, MEM STAFF, TRW SYSTS GROUP, 80- *Mem:* Am Inst Aeronaut & Astronaut; Inst Elec & Electronics Engrs. *Res:* Systems engineering; design, analysis and simulation of automatic control sytems for spacecraft; orbitor gimballed payloads; gimbulled optical pointer trackers; laser hot antoalignment. *Mailing Add:* 2116 Bataan Rd B Redondo Beach CA 90278

WALTON, WARREN LEWIS, b La, Dec 13, 14; m 43; c 3. ORGANIC CHEMISTRY. *Educ:* Millsaps Col, BS, 35; La State Univ, MS, 37; Univ Ill, PhD, 41. *Prof Exp:* Br chemist, The Coca-Cola Co, 37-38; res & develop chemist, Hercules Co, 41-46; res & develop chemist silicone synthesis, Gen Elec Co, NY, 46-50, head anal unit, Insulating Mat Dept, 50-69, instrumental anal chemist, 50-71; SELF-EMPLOYED, 71- *Concurrent Pos:* Consult, Schenectady Chem Inc, 78-79. *Mem:* Am Chem Soc. *Res:* Infrared spectroscopy; microscopy, gas and gelpermeation chromatography, nuclear magnetic resonance spectroscopy. *Mailing Add:* 3017 Sunset Lane Schenectady NY 12303

WALTON, WAYNE J A, JR, b Chariton, Iowa, Apr 6, 41; m 70; c 2. LUNAR GEOLOGY. *Educ:* Drury Col, AB, 64; Univ Ariz, MS, 66; Ohio State Univ, Columbus, PhD(mineral), 72. *Prof Exp:* Teaching asst geol, Univ Ariz, 64-66; teaching assoc mineral, Ohio State Univ, 69-71; instr geol, Capital Univ, 71-72, asst prof, 72-74; instr, Univ Houston, 76-79; ASST PROF GEOL, MIDWESTERN STATE UNIV, 79- *Concurrent Pos:* Geologist, US Geol Surv, Ariz, 64, Am Metal Climax, 65; photo chemist, Kitt Peak Nat Observ, 64-65; res assoc, Univ Ariz, 65; res chemist, Minn Mining & Mfg Co, 66-69; vis instr geol Ohio State Univ, 72; sr res analysis, Northrop Serv, Inc, 74-78. *Mem:* Meteoritical Soc; Can Mineral Soc; Mineral Soc Gt Brit. *Res:* High temperature ceramic bodies. *Mailing Add:* Dept Geol & Geophysics Midwestern State Univ Wichita Falls TX 76308

WALTON, WILLIAM RALPH, b Ft Worth, Tex, Apr 11, 23; m 49; c 2. GEOLOGICAL OCEANOGRAPHY. *Educ:* Amherst Col, BA, 49; Univ Calif, MS, 52, PhD(oceanog), 54. *Prof Exp:* Paleoecologist, Gulf Res & Develop Co, 53-57; paleoecologist & sedimentologist, Pan Am Petrol Corp, 57-60, div consult geologist, 60-63, geol & geochem res dir, Amoco Prod Co, Okla, 63-73, chief geologist, 73-75, chief geologist, Amoco Int Oil Co, Ill, 75-81explor mgr, 77-81, . *Concurrent Pos:* Mem bd dirs, Gulf Univs Res Consortium, 67-; mem Pres oil spill panel & coord subcomt, Nat Petrol Coun Comt Environ Conserv, 69-; mem vis comt, Univ Okla, 69-72 & Brown Univ, 74; mem steering comt, Hillcrest Hosp Assoc, 67-73; distinguished lectr, Am Asn Petrol Geologists, 72-73; mem offshore explor & prod task group, Nat Petrol Coun Comt Ocean Petrol Resources, 74. *Honors & Awards:* Pres Award, Am Asn Petrol Geol, 57. *Mem:* Soc Econ Paleontologists & Mineralogists; Geol Soc Am; Paleont Soc; Sigma Xi; Am Asn Petrol Geologists. *Res:* Biostratigraphy of gulf coast tertiary; paleoecology, marine geology and sedimentology. *Mailing Add:* 2815 Main St Barnstable MA 02630

WALTRUP, PAUL JOHN, b Baltimore, Md, June 12, 45. ENGINEERING, MATERIALS SCIENCE. *Educ:* Univ Md, BS, 67, MS, 68; Va Polytech Inst, PhD(aeronaut eng), 71. *Prof Exp:* Fel, 71-72, sr staff engr, 72-74, SUPVR, APPL PHYSICS LAB, JOHNS HOPKINS UNIV, 74- *Concurrent Pos:*

Consult, McGraw Hill Info Systs, 77-; instr, Univ Md, 78- *Mem:* Assoc fel Am Inst Aeronaut & Astronaut; Combustion Inst. *Res:* Ramjet-Scramjet propulsion. *Mailing Add:* Appl Physics Lab Johns Hopkins Rd Laurel MD 20810

WALTZ, ARTHUR G, b Irwin, Pa, Feb 14, 32; m. NEUROLOGY, CARDIOVASCULAR DISEASES. *Educ:* Univ Mich, BS, 52, MD, 55; Am Bd Psychiat & Neurol, dipl neurol, 62. *Prof Exp:* Rotating intern, Hosp Univ Pa, 55-56; asst resident neurol, Neurol Unit, Boston City Hosp, Mass, 56-57, sr resident, 57-58; res assoc, Sch Med, Wayne State Univ, 58-59, instr, 59; from instr to assoc prof, Mayo Grad Sch Med, Univ Minn, 62-71; prof neurol, Med Sch, Univ Minn, Minneapolis, 71-74; chmn, Dept Neurol, Pac Med Ctr, 75-81; CLIN PROF NEUROL, UNIV CALIF, 81- *Concurrent Pos:* Teaching fel neurol, Harvard Med Sch, 56-58; asst to staff neurol, Mayo Clin, 61, consult, 62-71; adj prof neurol, Univ of the Pac, 75-80; fel stroke coun, Am Heart Asn. *Mem:* Fel Am Acad Neurol; Am Neurol Asn; Asn Res Nerv & Ment Dis. *Res:* Cerebral circulation, including blood flow, microcirculation and fluid balance, in normal and ischemic brain. *Mailing Add:* 4141 Geary Blvd #415 PO Box 7999 San Francisco CA 94118

WALTZ, MAYNARD CARLETON, b Damariscotta, Maine, Aug 19, 16; m 41; c 2. SEMICONDUCTORS. *Educ:* Colby Col, BA, 38; Wesleyan Univ, MA, 40. *Prof Exp:* Mem staff, Radiation Lab, Mass Inst Technol, 42-45; mem tech staff, NJ, 45-55, supvr, Pa, 55-69, DEPT HEAD, BELL TEL LABS, INC, NJ, 69- *Mem:* Inst Elec & Electronics Eng. *Res:* Measurement of log decrement of crystal quartz; measurement and measuring techniques for microwave noise; noise theory of reflex klystrons; varistors and transistors; integrated circuits; reliability of solid-state devices; technical relations information; solar heating. *Mailing Add:* Bell Tel Labs Mountain Ave Murray Hill NJ 07974

WALTZ, WILLIAM LEE, b Berkeley, Calif, June 3, 40; m 63; c 2. PHOTOCHEMISTRY, RADIATION CHEMISTRY. *Educ:* Miami Univ, BS, 62; Northwestern Univ, PhD(phys inorg chem), 67. *Prof Exp:* Res assoc chem, Univ Southern Calif, 66-68; sr chemist, Cent Res Lab, 3M Co, Minn, 68-69; asst prof, 69-73, assoc prof, 73-80, PROF CHEM, UNIV SASK, 80- *Concurrent Pos:* Vis assoc prof chem, Ohio State Univ, 77-78; guest scientist, Hahn-Meitner Inst Nuclear Res, West Berlin, Ger, 78. *Mem:* Sigma Xi; Am Chem Soc; The Chem Soc; Can Inst Chem. *Res:* Inorganic materials. *Mailing Add:* Dept of Chem & Chem Eng Univ of Sask Saskatoon SK S7N 0W0 Can

WALUM, HERBERT, b Bremerton, Wash, Aug 14, 36; m 59; c 2. MATHEMATICS. *Educ:* Reed Col, BA, 58; Univ Colo, PhD(math), 62. *Prof Exp:* Asst prof math, Harvey Mudd Col, 62-64; asst prof, 64-71, ASSOC PROF MATH, OHIO STATE UNIV, 71- *Mem:* Am Math Soc; Math Asn Am. *Res:* Number theory. *Mailing Add:* Dept of Math Ohio State Univ Columbus OH 43210

WALVEKAR, ARUN GOVIND, b Belgaum, India, May 7, 42. APPLIED MATHEMATICS, OPERATIONS RESEARCH. *Educ:* Univ Bombay, BE, 63 & 64; Ill Inst Technol, MS, 66, PhD(opers res), 67. *Prof Exp:* Instr math, Northeastern Ill State Col, 67-68; asst prof indust eng, 68-71, ASSOC PROF INDUST ENG & STATIST, TEX TECH UNIV, 71- *Mem:* Opers Res Soc Am; Am Inst Indust Engrs. *Res:* Multistage decision processes; calculus of variations; complex variables. *Mailing Add:* Dept of Indust Eng Tex Tech Univ Lubbock TX 79409

WALWICK, EARLE RICHARD, b San Diego, Calif, Oct 9, 29; m 51; c 2. CLINICAL CHEMISTRY. *Educ:* Univ Calif, Berkeley, AB, 52, PhD(biochem), 58. *Prof Exp:* Biochemist, US Naval Sch Aviation Med, Fla, 52-53; aviation physiologist, Naval Air Sta, 53-55; biochemist, Naval Hosp, Oakland, Calif, 57-58, biochemist, Naval Radiol Defense Lab, San Francisco, 58-61; supvr res, Aeronutronic Div, Philco-Ford Corp, 61-71; mem staff, US Govt, 71-72; clin chemist & hosp-pathologist, Cent Lab of Orange County, Inc, 74-77; CHIEF CLIN CHEMIST, JERRY L PETTIS MEM VET HOSP, 77- *Concurrent Pos:* NIH fel path, Univ Calif, Irvine, 72-74. *Mem:* Am Asn Clin Chem. *Mailing Add:* 1317 Olive Ave Redlands CA 92373

WALZ, ALVIN EUGENE, b Hot Springs, SDak, Jan 12, 19. PHYSICAL CHEMISTRY, ANALYTICAL CHEMISTRY. *Educ:* Northern State Teachers Col, BS, 43; Univ Iowa, MS, 45, PhD(phys chem), 50. *Prof Exp:* Teacher, High Sch, Iowa, 43-48; from asst prof to prof chem, Mankato State Col, 50-63; PROF CHEM, CALIF LUTHERAN COL, 63-, CHMN DEPT, 66- *Mem:* AAAS; Am Chem Soc. *Res:* Reaction rates; electron affinity; methyl stibine. *Mailing Add:* 119 Sirius Circle Thousand Oaks CA 91360

WALZ, ARTHUR JOSEPH, b Calif, June 28, 18; m 43; c 5. ECONOMIC ENTOMOLOGY. *Educ:* Univ Calif, BS, 42, MS, 48. *Prof Exp:* Asst entomologist, Br Exp Sta, Univ Idaho, 48-56; mem staff, Asgrow Seed Co, 56-67; EXTEN PROF & EXTEN POTATO SPECIALIST, PARMA RES & EXTEN CTR, UNIV IDAHO, 67- *Mem:* Entom Soc Am; Potato Asn Am. *Res:* Insects affecting onions and potatoes. *Mailing Add:* Res & Exten Ctr Univ of Idaho Parma ID 83660

WALZ, DANIEL ALBERT, b Rochester, NY, July 30, 44; m 66; c 3. PHYSIOLOGY, BIOCHEMISTRY. *Educ:* St John Fisher Col, BS, 66; Wayne State Univ, PhD(physiol), 73. *Prof Exp:* Instr, 73-74, asst prof, 74-79, ASSOC PROF PHYSIOL, WAYNE STATE UNIV, 79- *Mem:* Am Chem Soc; Int Soc Thrombosis & Harmostasis; Am Heart Asn; AAAS. *Res:* Properties of macromolecules; protein structure; coagulation biochemistry. *Mailing Add:* Sch of Med 540 E Canfield Detroit MI 48201

WALZ, DONALD THOMAS, b Newark, NJ, Oct 25, 24; m 59; c 3. PHARMACOLOGY. *Educ:* Upsala Col, BS, 50; Rutgers Univ, MS, 51; Georgetown Univ, PhD(pharmacol), 59. *Prof Exp:* Jr pharmacologist, Hoffmann-La Roche, Inc, 51-55; sr investr pharmacol, 60-68, from asst dir to assoc dir pharmacol, 68-77, ASSOC DIR RES, SMITH, KLINE & FRENCH LABS, 77- *Concurrent Pos:* Nat Inst Neurol Dis & Blindness fel, Sch Med, Georgetown Univ, 59-60. *Mem:* AAAS; Am Diabetes Asn; Am Soc Pharmacol & Exp Therapeut; Acad Pharmaceut Sci; Fedn Am Socs Exp Biol. *Res:* Biochemical neuropharmacology metabolism; carbohydrate metabolism; cardiovascular-autonomic pharmacology. *Mailing Add:* Smith Kline & French Labs 1500 Spring Garden St Philadelphia PA 19101

WALZ, FREDERICK GEORGE, b Brooklyn, NY, May 11, 40; m 62; c 7. BIOCHEMISTRY. *Educ:* Manhattan Col, BS, 62; State Univ NY Downstate Med Ctr, PhD(biochem), 66. *Prof Exp:* NIH res fel biochem, Cornell Univ, 66-68; asst prof, State Univ NY Albany, 68-75; asst prof chem, 75-77, ASSOC PROF CHEM, KENT STATE UNIV, 77-; RES ASSOC PROF MOLECULAR PATH, COL MED, NORTHEAST OHIO UNIVS, 77- *Concurrent Pos:* NSF res grant, State Univ NY Albany, 69-75 & Kent State Univ, 76-80. *Mem:* Am Soc Biochem; Am Chem Soc; Biophys Soc. *Res:* Liver endoplasmic reticulum proteins, cytochrome P-450, albumin secretion; ribonuclease mechanisms and substrate recognition. *Mailing Add:* Dept of Chem Kent State Univ Kent OH 44242

WAMBACH, ROBERT F, b Detroit, Mich, Sept 29, 30; m 52; c 3. FOREST ECONOMICS, RESOURCE ADMINISTRATION. *Educ:* Univ Mont, BSF, 57; Univ Mich, MF, 59, PhD(forest econ), 67. *Prof Exp:* Forester, Forest Inventory, Intermountain Forest Exp Sta, US Forest Serv, 57-58, res forester silvicult northern conifers, Lake State Forest Exp Sta, 59-62, res proj leader plantation mgt, 62-64, res proj leader silvicult northern conifers, NCent Forest Exp Sta, 64-67; assoc prof forest econ, Univ Mont, 67-71, prof forestry, 71-76, dean, Forestry Sch & dir, Forest & Conserv Exp Sta, 72-76; DIR, MONT DEPT FISH & GAME, 77- *Mem:* AAAS; Soc Am Foresters; Am Econ Asn. *Res:* Growth and yield studies in northern conifers; silviculture of northern conifers; economic aspects of forest management, especially forest plantation management; development of methodology for decision-making in forestry. *Mailing Add:* 1804 Virginia Dale Ave Helena MT 59601

WAMBOLD, JAMES CHARLES, b Emmaus, Pa, Nov 24, 32; m 60; c 4. MECHANICAL ENGINEERING, ENGINEERING MECHANICS. *Educ:* Pa State Univ, BS, 59; Carnegie Inst Technol, MS, 60; Univ NMex, PhD(mech eng), 67. *Prof Exp:* Staff mem, Sandia Corp, 58-62; instr mech eng, Univ NMex, 62-67; asst prof, 67-77, assoc prof, 77-81, PROF MECH ENG, PA STATE UNIV, 81- *Concurrent Pos:* Aircraft mech consult to indust & lawyers. *Mem:* Am Soc Mech Engrs; Am Soc Eng Educ; Analog/Hybrid Comput Educ Soc; Am Soc Testing & Mat. *Res:* Random signal processing; roughness effects on vehicle performances; application of solid mechanics to engineering design; modeling of physical systems for computer solution and control system design. *Mailing Add:* Rm 301 Dept Mech Eng Pa State Univ University Park PA 16802

WAMPLER, DALE LEE, b Boones Mill, Va, June 25, 36; m 62; c 2. STRUCTURAL CHEMISTRY, INORGANIC CHEMISTRY. *Educ:* Bridgewater Col, BA, 57; Univ Wis, PhD(chem), 62. *Prof Exp:* From instr to assoc prof, 61-69, chmn dept, 65-68, PROF CHEM, JUNIATA COL, 69- *Concurrent Pos:* Sr vis fel, Univ Cambridge, 69-70. *Mem:* Am Chem Soc; Am Crystallog Asn. *Res:* Thermodynamics and kinetics of adsorption of hydrocarbon gases on Devonion shales; single crystal x-ray diffraction techniques. *Mailing Add:* Dept of Chem Juniata Col Huntingdon PA 16653

WAMPLER, E JOSEPH, b Taiku, China, Jan 27, 33; US citizen; m 56; c 3. ASTRONOMY. *Educ:* Univ Va, BA, 58; Univ Chicago, MS, 59, PhD(astron), 62. *Prof Exp:* Res asst astron, Univ Chicago, 62-63; fel in residence, Miller Inst Basic Res in Sci, 63-65, actg asst astronomer, Observ, 65-66, asst astronomer, 66-70, assoc astronomer, 70-73, ASTRONOMER, LICK OBSERV, UNIV CALIF, 73- *Concurrent Pos:* Dir, Anglo-Australian Observ, 74-76. *Mem:* Am Astron Soc; Int Astron Union. *Res:* Quasi stellar sources; extra-galactic astronomy; instrumentation. *Mailing Add:* Lick Observ Univ of Calif Santa Cruz CA 95064

WAMPLER, FRED BENNY, b Kingsport, Tenn, Apr 2, 43; m 63; c 3. PHYSICAL CHEMISTRY, PHOTOCHEMISTRY. *Educ:* Univ Tenn, Knoxville, BS, 65; Univ Mo-Columbia, PhD(phys chem), 70. *Prof Exp:* Fel phys chem, Ohio State Univ, 70-72; sr scientist, Allison Div, Gen Motors Corp, 72-74; staff mem, 74-79, asst group leader, 79-81, DEP GROUP LEADER, LOS ALAMOS NAT LAB, 81- *Mem:* Am Chem Soc; Inter-Am Photochem Soc. *Res:* Kinetics; application of lasers to chemical problems; energy transfer; laser spectroscopy; atmospheric chemistry; optical instrumentation. *Mailing Add:* 479 Pruitt Ave Los Alamos NM 87544

WAMPLER, JESSE MARION, b Harrisonburg, Va, Oct 31, 36; m 62; c 2. NUCLEAR GEOCHEMISTRY, GEOCHRONOLOGY. *Educ:* Bridgewater Col, BA, 57; Columbia Univ, PhD(geochem), 63. *Prof Exp:* Res asst geochem, Lamont Geol Observ, NY, 60-63; res assoc, Brookhaven Nat Lab, 63-65; asst prof, 65-69, ASSOC PROF GEOPHYS SCI, GA INST TECHNOL, 69- *Mem:* Geochem Soc; Am Geophys Union; Sigma Xi; Nat Asn Geol Teachers. *Res:* Nuclear geochemistry; geochemistry of argon and potassium; potassium-argon geochronology; lead isotope geochemistry. *Mailing Add:* Sch of Geophys Sci Ga Inst of Technol Atlanta GA 30332

WAMPLER, JOE FORREST, b Chanute, Kans, Dec 13, 26; m 49; c 2. MATHEMATICS. *Educ:* Univ Kans, AB, 50, MA, 52; Univ Nebr, PhD, 67. *Prof Exp:* Head dept math & physics, York Col, 51-53, head dept math & registr, 53-54; assoc prof, 54-66, chmn div natural sci, 71-76, PROF MATH, NEBR WESLEYAN UNIV, 66-, HEAD DEPT, 54- *Concurrent Pos:* Woods Found grant, 60-61; NSF coop teacher develop grant, 66. *Mem:* Math Asn Am. *Res:* Liouville's methods; use of various measures of aptitude to predict achievement in college mathematics. *Mailing Add:* Dept of Math Nebr Wesleyan Univ Lincoln NE 68504

WAMPLER, STANLEY NORMAN, b Irwin, Pa, Dec 9, 31. VETERINARY MEDICINE, RADIOBIOLOGY. *Educ:* Pa State Univ, BS, 53; Univ Pa, VMD, 56; Univ Rochester, MS, 61. *Prof Exp:* Vet, US Army, 56-60, radiobiologist, Walter Reed Inst Res, 61-65; res sr vet, Pesticide Res Lab,

USPHS, 65-67; asst prof lab animal med, Sch Vet Med, Univ Pa, 67-76. *Concurrent Pos:* Lectr, Col Med, Univ Miami, 65-67; from asst prof to assoc prof, Hahnemann Med Col, 67-76; asst prof, Sch Med, Temple Univ & Med Col Pa, 67-76; dir lab animal med, Fed Med Resources, 67-76. *Mem:* Sigma Xi. *Res:* Veterinary laboratory animal medicine. *Mailing Add:* PO Box 876 Jensen Beach FL 33457

WAMSER, CARL CHRISTIAN, b New York, NY, Aug 10, 44; c 2. ORGANIC CHEMISTRY, PHOTOCHEMISTRY. *Educ:* Brown Univ, ScB, 66; Calif Inst Technol, PhD(chem), 69. *Prof Exp:* US Air Force Off Sci Res-Nat Res Coun fel, Harvard Univ, 69-70; from asst prof to assoc prof chem, 70-77, PROF CHEM, CALIF STATE UNIV, FULLERTON, 77- *Concurrent Pos:* Vis assoc prof, Univ Southern Calif, 75-76; vis prof, Univ Hawaii, 80. *Mem:* Am Chem Soc. *Mailing Add:* Dept of Chem Calif State Univ Fullerton CA 92634

WAMSER, CHRISTIAN ALBERT, b Long Island City, NY, July 15, 13; m 40; c 2. INORGANIC CHEMISTRY. *Educ:* Cooper Union, BS, 34. *Prof Exp:* Anal chemist, J F Jelenko & Co, Inc, NY, 34-41; supvr anal group, Gen Chem Div, Allied Chem Corp, 41-48; res chemist, Vitro Corp Am, NJ, 53-62; res chemist, Gen Chem Div, 62-65, res scientist, 65-69, res scientist, Syracuse Tech Ctr, 69-74, RES ASSOC, INDUST CHEM DIV, SYRACUSE TECH CTR, ALLIED CHEM CORP, NY, 74- *Mem:* Am Chem Soc. *Res:* Industrial inorganic chemistry, uranium, fluorine, chromium and aluminum compounds. *Mailing Add:* 207 Rebhahn Dr Camillus NY 13031

WAMSLEY, ROBERT ALAN, b Cameron, Mo, Aug 8, 27; m 54; c 2. PAPER CHEMISTRY. *Educ:* Cent Mo State Col, BS, 51. *Prof Exp:* Res chemist, Crossett Co, Ark, 55-61; res assoc, Int Paper, 61-65; mgr tech serv paper, Celanese Coatings Co, 65-73, PROD MGR RESINS, STEINHALL DIV, CELANESE CORP, 73-, CHEMIST, 77- *Mem:* Tech Asn Pulp & Paper Indust. *Res:* Pulp and paper; paper coatings; adhesives; electrophotographic coating; colloid chemistry. *Mailing Add:* Celanese Polymer Spec Sta E PO Box 8248 Louisville KY 40208

WAMSLEY, W(ELCOME) W(ILLARD), b Leavenworth, Wash, July 18, 25; m 47; c 3. CHEMICAL ENGINEERING. *Educ:* Univ Wash, BS, 49, PhD(chem eng), 53. *Prof Exp:* Instr, Univ Wash, 51-53; chem engr, 53-60, tech supvr, 60-61, sr tech supvr, 61-64, spec asst, 64-65, supt process control, 65-75, ASST PLANT MGR, E I DU PONT DE NEMOURS & CO, INC, 75- *Mem:* Am Chem Soc; assoc Am Inst Chem Engrs. *Res:* Heat transfer; gas-solid fluidization; coating and drying of photographic emulsions. *Mailing Add:* RD 1 Box 408A Ulster PA 18850

WAN, ABRAHAM TAI-HSIN, b Tsingtao, China, Oct 14, 28; US citizen; m 59; c 2. CLINICAL CHEMISTRY, ENDOCRINOLOGY. *Educ:* Nat Taiwan Univ, BS, 55; Univ Minn, Minneapolis, MS, 60; Univ Nebr, Omaha, PhD(med biochem), 64. *Prof Exp:* Biochemist, Dept Pub Health, Sask, Can, 63-64 & Sunland Hosp, Orlando, 64-67; assoc dir clin chem, Clin Lab, Dept Path, Norfolk Gen Hosp, 67-74; asst prof, Eastern Va Med Sch, 74; DEP DIR DEPT BIOCHEM, ALFRED HOSP, 74- *Concurrent Pos:* NIH grant, Sunland Hosp, Orlando, Fla, 64-67 & Norfolk Gen Hosp, 72-74; adj prof, Old Dom Univ, 69-74. *Mem:* Am Chem Soc; Am Asn Clin Chemists; Am Soc Clin Pathologists; Australia Asn Clin Biochemists; NY Acad Sci. *Mailing Add:* Dept Biochem Alfred Hosp Prahran Victoria Australia 3181

WAN, CHUNG-NAN, b Taipei, Taiwan, Dec 12, 48; m 74; c 1. ORGANIC CHEMISTRY, NUCLEAR MEDICINE. *Educ:* Fu-Jen Univ, Taiwan, BS, 70; Rutgers Univ, MS, 74, PhD(chem), 77. *Prof Exp:* Chemist, Cooper Lab, Inc, 77-79; CHEMIST ORG CHEM, BERLEX LAB, INC, 79- *Concurrent Pos:* Res assoc, Brookhaven Nat Labs, Assoc Univ, Inc, 76-77. *Mem:* Am Chem Soc. *Res:* Medicinal chemistry. *Mailing Add:* Berlex Lab Inc 110 E Hanover Ave Cedar Knolls NJ 07927

WAN, FREDERIC YUI-MING, b Shanghai, China, Jan 7, 36; US citizen; m 60. APPLIED MATHEMATICS, SOLID MECHANICS. *Educ:* Mass Inst Technol, SB, 59, SM, 63, PhD(math), 65. *Prof Exp:* Staff mem struct mech, Lincoln Lab, Mass Inst Technol, 59-62, staff assoc, 62-65, from instr to assoc prof appl math, 65-74; PROF MATH & DIR INST APPL MATH & STATIST, UNIV BC, 74- *Concurrent Pos:* Sloan Found fel, 73; mem comt appl math, Can Math Soc, 75-77; Univ BC Killam sr fel, 79. *Mem:* Am Soc Mech Eng; Soc Indust & Appl Math; Can Math Soc; Can Appl Math Soc. *Res:* Classical elasticity; shell theory; random vibrations; stochastic ordinary and partial differential equations; natural resource economics; bio-mathematics. *Mailing Add:* Dept of Math Univ of BC Vancouver BC V6T 1W5 Can

WAN, JEFFREY KWOK-SING, b Hong Kong, June 4, 34; m 62; c 2. PHYSICAL CHEMISTRY. *Educ:* McGill Univ, BSc, 58; Univ Alta, PhD(phys chem), 62. *Prof Exp:* Fel, Univ Alta, 62-63; asst res chemist, Univ Calif, 63-65; Nat Res Coun Can fel chem, 65-66; from asst prof to assoc prof, 66-74, PROF CHEM, QUEEN'S UNIV, 74- *Concurrent Pos:* Hon prof, Univ Lanzhou, China, 81- *Mem:* Chem Inst Can. *Res:* Photochemistry and electron paramagnetic resonance spectroscopy. *Mailing Add:* Dept of Chem Queen's Univ Kingston ON K7L 3N6 Can

WAN, PETER J, b Shantong, China, Jan 1, 29, 43; US citizen; m 70; c 2. PROCESS DEVELOPMENT, METHODS DEVELOPMENT. *Educ:* Cheng-Kung Univ, China, BSE, 65; Ill Inst Technol, MS, 70; Tex A&M Univ, PhD(phys chem), 73. *Prof Exp:* Fel, Chem Dept, Tex A&M Univ, 74-75, proj leader & asst res chemist, Res & Develop Ctr Food Protein, 75-79; sr res chemist, Best Foods, CPC Int, 79-80; RES ASSOC, ANDERSON CLAYTON FOODS, 80- *Mem:* Inst Food Technologists; Am Oil Chemists Soc; Am Chem Soc. *Res:* Improve and assure the equality of product; improve process efficiency; develop new methods and new processes. *Mailing Add:* Anderson Clayton Foods 3333 N Cent Expressway Richardson TX 75080

WAN, PETER JANSSEN, b Wei-Hai-Wey, Shantung, China, Jan 29, 43; US citizen; m 70; c 2. PHYSICAL CHEMISTRY, CHEMICAL ENGINEERING. *Educ:* Cheng-Kung Univ, Taiwan, BSE, 65; Ill Inst Technol, MS, 70; Tex A&M Univ, PhD(chem), 73. *Prof Exp:* NSF fel biophys chem, Tex A&M Univ, 74-75, asst res chemist basic & appl res foods & food ingredients, Food Protein Res & Development Ctr, 75-79; SR MAT SCIENTIST ANAL RES MAT SCI, BEST FOODS/CPC INT, NJ, 79- *Concurrent Pos:* Asst res chemist, USDA grants, 76-79 & Cotton Inc grants, 75-79. *Mem:* Inst Food Technologists; Am Oil Chemists Soc; Am Asn Cereal Chemists. *Res:* Physical chemistry of macromolecules; rheological properties of materials; analytical methods of natural products; chemical kinetics and thermodynamics of interacting systems; process and product development of oilseed proteins. *Mailing Add:* Best Foods PO Box 1534 1120 Commerce Union NJ 07083

WAN, SUK HAN, b Malaysia. PHARMACODYNAMICS, CLINICAL PHARMACOLOGY. *Educ:* Univ Singapore, BPharm(Hons), 65; Univ Calif, San Francisco, PhD(pharm chem), 71. *Prof Exp:* Res assoc pharmacokinetics, Univ Kans Med Ctr, Kansas City, 71-74; ASST PROF PHARM, UNIV SOUTHERN CALIF, 74- *Mem:* Am Pharmaceut Asn; Acad Pharmaceut Sci. *Res:* The distribution, metabolism, excretion and absorption of drugs in man and animals, and factors affecting the above processes. *Mailing Add:* Sch of Pharm Univ Southern Calif 1985 Zonal Ave Los Angeles CA 90033

WAN, YIEH-HEI, b China, Feb 17, 47; m 75. TOPOLOGY. *Educ:* Nat Taiwan Univ, BS, 68; Univ Calif, Berkeley, PhD(math), 73. *Prof Exp:* Asst prof, 73-74, GEORGE WILLIAM HILL INSTR MATH, STATE UNIV NY BUFFALO, 74- *Res:* Application of global analysis to the study of general competitive equilibrium theory in mathematical economics; bifurcation theory for dynamical systems. *Mailing Add:* Dept Math 106 Diefendorf Hall State Univ NY Amherst NY 14214

WAN, YIEH-PING, organic chemistry, biochemistry, see previous edition

WANAT, STANLEY FRANK, b Nanticoke, Pa, Dec 31, 39; m 64; c 2. ORGANIC CHEMISTRY. *Educ:* Rutgers Univ, AB, 63; Seton Hall Univ, MS, 69, PhD(org chem), 71. *Prof Exp:* Develop chemist agr chem, Shell Chem Co, 64-65; instr chem & math, Union County Col Syst, NJ, 65-67; process develop chemist agr chem, Ciba-Geigy Corp, 67-70; asst, Seton Hall Univ, 70-71; instr org chem, Upsala Col, 71-73; GROUP LEADER GRAPHIC ARTS CHEM, TECH INFO SYSTS DIV, AM HOECHST CORP, 73- *Concurrent Pos:* Teacher chem, Union County Schs, 71-73. *Mem:* Am Chem Soc. *Res:* Development of photosensitive lithographic products, printing plates, color proofing systems and chemicals; study of surface chemistry of substrates suitable for coating lithographic materials; coating technology. *Mailing Add:* 3 Frances Lane Scotch Plains NJ 07076

WAND, RONALD HERBERT, b Gloucester, NSW, Australia, July 20, 37; m 72; c 3. IONOSPHERIC PHYSICS. *Educ:* Univ Sydney, BSc, 58, PhD(physics), 65. *Prof Exp:* Res assoc ionospheric physics, Cornell Univ, 65-69; sr res fel, Univ Sydney, 70-71; staff scientist radiophysics, Lincoln Lab, Mass Inst Technol, 72-80; WITH HAYSTACK OBSERV, 80- *Concurrent Pos:* Mem Comn III, Int Union Radio Sci. *Mem:* Am Geophys Union. *Res:* Ionospheric research using incoherent scatter radars and radar propagation studies. *Mailing Add:* NE Radio Observ Corp Haystack Observ Westford MA 01886

WANDER, JOSEPH DAY, b Columbus, Ohio, July 20, 41; m 67. ORGANIC CHEMISTRY. *Educ:* Case Inst Technol, BS, 63; Ohio State Univ, PhD(chem), 70. *Prof Exp:* Res fel chem, Tulane Univ, 70-71, La State Univ, Baton Rouge, 71-72 & Ohio State Univ, 72-74; dir Charles B Stout neurosci lab, Univ Tenn Ctr Health Sci, Memphis, 74-77; ASST PROF CHEM, UNIV GA, 78- *Mem:* Am Chem Soc. *Res:* Applications of analytical spectroscopic methods to problems of molecular structure and stereochemistry; thiosugars. *Mailing Add:* Dept of Chem Univ of Ga Athens GA 30602

WANDERER, PETER JOHN, JR, b Monroe, La, Aug 5, 43; m 72; c 3. HIGH ENERGY PHYSICS. *Educ:* Univ Notre Dame, BS, 65; Yale Univ, PhD(physics), 70. *Prof Exp:* Res assoc high energy physics, Lab Nuclear Studies, Cornell Univ, 70-73 & Univ Wis-Madison, 73-75; assoc scientist, 75-78, SCIENTIST HIGH ENERGY PHYSICS, BROOKHAVEN NAT LAB, 78- *Mem:* Am Phys Soc. *Res:* Experimental research in neutrino-nucleon interactions; construction of high field superconducting magnets for Isabelle accelerator. *Mailing Add:* Bldg 902B Brookhaven Nat Lab Upton NY 11973

WANDMACHER, CORNELIUS, b Brooklyn, NY, Sept 1, 11; m 36; c 3. CIVIL ENGINEERING. *Educ:* Polytech Inst Brooklyn, BCE, 33, MCE, 35. *Hon Degrees:* DEng, Polytech Inst Brooklyn, 69 & Rose-Hulman Inst, 75. *Prof Exp:* Civil engr, Plant Eng Dept, WVa Pulp & Paper Co, NY, 36-37; from instr to assoc prof civil eng, Polytech Inst Brooklyn, 37-51, dir eve session & asst to pres, 43-51; William Thomas prof & head dept, 51-58, from assoc dean to dean, Col Eng, 57-74, prof civil eng, 58-81, EMER DEAN, UNIV CINCINNATI, 81- *Concurrent Pos:* Designer & detailer, Off Struct Engr, NY Cent RR, 39; eng examr, Munic Civil Serv Comn, New York, 39-51; struct designer, Phelps Dodge Corp, 40; mem, Bd Regist Prof Engrs, Ohio, 62-72. *Mem:* Hon mem Am Soc Civil Engrs; hon mem Am Soc Eng Educ; Nat Soc Prof Engrs; Am Nat Metric Coun (dir, 76-82). *Res:* Professional engineering education. *Mailing Add:* Col of Eng Univ of Cincinnati Cincinnati OH 45221

WANDS, RALPH CLINTON, b Norwich, NY, May 12, 19; m 42; c 3. TOXICOLOGY, INDUSTRIAL HYGIENE. *Educ:* Kent State Univ, BS, 41; Univ Minn, MS, 48; Am Bd Indust Hyg, dipl. *Prof Exp:* Chemist, Firestone Tire & Rubber Co, 41-42, develop engr, 42-43; res chemist, Minn Mining & Mfg Co, 51-61, res chemist, Indust Hyg & Toxicol, 61-64; prof assoc, Nat Acad Sci, 64-66, dir, Adv Ctr Toxicol, 66-77; dir cosmetic ingredient rev, Cosmetic Toiletry & Fragrance Asn, 77-79; head, Off Info, Chem Indust Inst Toxicol, 79-80; GROUP LEADER HAZARDOUS SUBSTANCES EVAL,

THE MITRE CORP, 80- *Honors & Awards:* Herbert E Stokinger Award. *Mem:* AAAS; Am Chem Soc; Am Indust Hyg Asn; Soc Toxicol; Am Conf Govt Indust Hygienists. *Res:* Toxicology data evaluation and risk assessment for occupational and public environments and development of acceptable exposure limits; chemistry. *Mailing Add:* The Mitre Corp 1820 Dolley Madison Blvd McLean VA 22102

WANE, MALCOLM T(RAFFORD), b Pittston, Pa, Jan 2, 21; m 46; c 1. MINING ENGINEERING. *Educ:* Lehigh Univ, BS, 50, Columbia Univ, MS, 54. *Prof Exp:* Res technician & mineral engr, US Steel Corp, 50-53; assoc, 53-59, from asst prof to assoc prof, 59-69, PROF MINING, COLUMBIA UNIV, 69- *Concurrent Pos:* NSF fac fel, Royal Sch Mines, 65-66; consult biologist, New York City Transit Authority & New York City Bd Water Resource Develop. *Mem:* Am Inst Mining, Metall & Petrol Engrs. *Res:* Rock mechanics; failure of brittle solids; earth vibration and blasting problems. *Mailing Add:* Henry Krumb Sch of Mines Columbia Univ New York NY 10027

WANER, JOSEPH LLOYD, microbiology, see previous edition

WANG, ALBERT SHO-DWO, b Chifoo, China, July 13, 37; m 67; c 2. APPLIED MECHANICS, COMPOSITE MATERIALS. *Educ:* Univ Taiwan, BS, 59; Univ Nev, MS, 63; Univ Del, PhD(aerospace eng), 67. *Prof Exp:* Fel, Univ Del, 67; from asst prof to assoc prof, 67-77, PROF APPL MECH, DREXEL UNIV, 77- *Concurrent Pos:* Consult, Lockheed Corp, Lawrence Livermore Lab & Gen Motors Corp. *Res:* Stress analysis of composite materials, including failure, fracture, fatigue and reliability. *Mailing Add:* Dept Mech & Eng Drexel Univ Philadelphia PA 19104

WANG, AN, b Shanghai, China, Feb 7, 20; US citizen; m; c 3. PHYSICS, ENGINEERING. *Educ:* Chiao-Tung Univ, BS, 40; Harvard Univ, MSc, 46, PhD(appl physics, eng), 48. *Hon Degrees:* DSc, Lowell Technol Inst, 71 & Southeastern Mass Univ, 81; Dr Commercial Sci, Suffolk Univ, 80. *Prof Exp:* Teacher, Chiao-Tung Univ, 40-41; engr, Cent Radio Works, China, 41-45; res fel, Harvard Univ, 48-51; owner, Wang Labs, 51-55, PRES, WANG LABS, INC, 55- *Mem:* Fel Inst Elec & Electronics Engrs; fel Am Acad Arts & Sci. *Res:* Original development of basic components and systems of digital computing machines. *Mailing Add:* Wang Labs Inc One Industrial Ave Lowell MA 01851

WANG, AN-CHUAN, b Tsing Tao City, China, Dec 28, 36; m 65; c 2. IMMUNOGENETICS. *Educ:* Nat Taiwan Univ, BS, 59; Univ Tex, PhD(genetics), 66. *Prof Exp:* Sec teacher, Taiwan, 61; res assoc genetics, Univ Tex, 66-67; asst prof genetics, Med Ctr, Univ Calif, San Francisco, 70-72, assoc prof microbiol & assoc researcher med, 72-75; assoc prof immunol, 75-76, PROF IMMUNOL, MED UNIV SC, 76- *Concurrent Pos:* Fel, Med Ctr, Univ Calif, San Francisco, 67-70; USPHS & NSF res grants, 70-; USPHS career development award, 74; Am Cancer Soc fac res award, 74-79; adv ed, Immunochem, 78- *Mem:* AAAS; Am Soc Human Genetics; Genetics Soc Am; Am Asn Immunol. *Res:* Biochemical and genetical analyses of human plasma proteins, with special emphasis on immunoglobulins; immunology. *Mailing Add:* Dept of Basic & Clin Med Univ of SC Charleston SC 29401

WANG, AUGUSTINE WEISHENG, b China, Jan 5, 37; US citizen; m 63; c 3. MICROBIOLOGY. *Educ:* Nat Taiwan Univ, BS, 60; Ore State Univ, MS, 65; Syracuse Univ, PhD(microbiol), 69. *Prof Exp:* NIH fel, Case Western Reserv Univ, 69-70; asst prof microbiol, 70-73, ASSOC PROF MICROBIOL, MISS STATE UNIV, 73- *Mem:* Am Soc Microbiol. *Res:* Physiology of blue-green algae and other autotrophs. *Mailing Add:* Dept of Biol Sci Miss State Univ State College MS 39762

WANG, BIN CHING, b Taipei, Taiwan, July 11, 41; m 65; c 2. PHYSIOLOGY, BIOLOGY. *Educ:* Nat Taiwan Normal Univ, BEd, 63; Northwestern State Univ La, MS, 71; Univ Kans, PhD(physiol), 75. *Prof Exp:* Health educator, Nat Tuberc Asn, Taiwan, 63-66; res asst, Vet Gen Hosp, Taiwan, 66-70; res physiologist, St Luke's Hosp, 75-78; asst prof physiol, Univ Tenn Med Ctr, 79-81; SR SCIENTIST, ST LUKE'S HOSP, 81- *Concurrent Pos:* Adj instr physiol, Univ Kans Med Ctr, 75, adj asst prof, 78. *Mem:* AAAS; assoc mem Am Physiol Soc. *Res:* Cardiovascular physiology, especially control of blood pressure. *Mailing Add:* Div Exp Med St Luke's Hosp 44th & Wornall Rd Kansas City MO 64111

WANG, C(HIAO) J(EN), b China, Mar 24, 18; nat US; m 45; c 1. AERONAUTICS, MECHANICAL ENGINEERING. *Educ:* Chiao Tung Univ, China, BS, 42; Mass Inst Technol, MSME, 46; Johns Hopkins Univ, PhD, 53. *Prof Exp:* Instr, Johns Hopkins Univ, 49-53; res & eng specialist, NAm Aviation, Inc, 53-56; assoc mgr aerophys dept & mgr propulsion systs dept, Space Technol Labs, Inc, 56-60; head propulsion dept & dir advan studies, Aerospace Corp, 60-65; dep dir combined arms res off, Booz-Allen Appl Res, Inc, Kans, 65-66; DIR OFF ADVAN ENG, ADVAN RES PROJS AGENCY, US DEPT DEFENSE, DC, 66- *Res:* Aeronautical and space science and technology; systems analysis; operations research. *Mailing Add:* 1300 Army-Navy Dr Arlington VA 22202

WANG, CARL C T, b Hankow, China, Dec 2, 35; m 63; c 3. ELECTRICAL ENGINEERING. *Educ:* Univ Ill, BS, 58, MS, 59, PhD(elec eng), 64. *Prof Exp:* Res asst plasma physics, Univ Ill, 60, res asst microwave, 60-64; mem res staff electron-optics, T J Watson Res Ctr, Int Bus Mach Corp, 64-67; res assoc biomed eng & elec engr, Columbia Univ, 67-69; sr engr, Micro-Bit Corp, 69-75; vpres eng, Berkeley Bio-Eng, Inc, 75-79; vpres eng, Cooper Med Device Corp, 79-81; PRES, MED INSTRUMENT DEVELOP LABS INC, 81- *Concurrent Pos:* Tech consult, NIMH, 68-75. *Mem:* Inst Elec & Electronics Engrs; Asn Advan Med Instrumentation; Sigma Xi. *Res:* Maser; ultra-microwave; electromagnetohydrodynamics; electron-optics; display systems; man-machine systems; physical electronics; physiological system simulation; bio-medical instrumentation. *Mailing Add:* Med Instrument Develop Labs 2999 Teagarden St San Leandro CA 94577

WANG, CHANG-YI, b Kweichow, China, Aug 26, 39; US citizen; m 66; c 3. APPLIED MATHEMATICS. *Educ:* Nat Taiwan Univ, BS, 60; Mass Inst Technol, MS, 63, PhD, 66. *Prof Exp:* Fel appl math, Calif Inst Technol, 66-67, assoc appl math, Jet ProPropulsion Lab, 67-68; asst prof math, Univ Calif, Los Angeles, 68-69; asst prof, 69-70, assoc prof, 70-80, PROF MATH, MICH STATE UNIV, 80- *Concurrent Pos:* Vis prof, Nat Taiwan Univ, 71-72. *Mem:* Soc Indust & Appl Math. *Res:* Fluid mechanics. *Mailing Add:* Dept of Math Mich State Univ East Lansing MI 48824

WANG, CHAO-CHENG, b Rep. of China, July 20, 38; m 63; c 2. CONTINUUM MECHANICS. *Educ:* Nat Taiwan Univ, BS, 59; Johns Hopkins Univ, PhD(mech), 65. *Prof Exp:* Res asst math, Chinese Acad Sci, 60-61; instr mech, Johns Hopkins Univ, 63-64, lectr & fel, 65-66, from asst prof to assoc prof, 66-68; PROF MECH, RICE UNIV, 68-, NOAH HARDING PROF MATH SCI, 79- *Concurrent Pos:* NSF res grant, 66-81. *Mem:* Am Acad Mech; Soc Natural Philos. *Mailing Add:* 11007 Albury Houston TX 77096

WANG, CHARLES C(HEN-DING), b Hankow, China, Sept 4, 33; m 61; c 3. ELECTRICAL ENGINEERING, PHYSICS. *Educ:* Taiwan Col Eng, BS, Brown Univ, MS, 58; Stanford Univ, PhD, 60. *Prof Exp:* Asst prof elec eng, Univ Wash, 60-63; res specialist, Philco Res Lab, 63-65; prin res scientist assoc, 66-68, staff scientist, 68-77, PRIN RES SCIENTIST, FORD SCI LAB, 77- *Mem:* Fel Am Phys Soc; Inst Elec & Electronics Engrs. *Res:* Nonlinear optics, quantum electronics; laser spectroscopy; atomic and molecular physics; detection of oxygen hydrogen in the atmosphere. *Mailing Add:* Ford Sci Lab PO Box 2053 Dearborn MI 48121

WANG, CHARLES T P, b Shantung, China, May 6, 30; US citizen; m 60; c 2. PHYSICS. *Educ:* Taiwan Norm Univ, BS, 55; Southern Ill Univ, Carbondale, MS, 59; Wash Univ, PhD(physics), 66. *Prof Exp:* Lectr physics, Southern Ill Univ, Edwardsville, 59-62; from asst prof to assoc prof, Parks Col, St Louis Univ, 65-67; PROF PHYSICS, STATE UNIV NY COL ONEONTA, 67- *Concurrent Pos:* NSF res participation fel, La State Univ, Baton Rouge, 69 & 71. *Mem:* Am Asn Physics Teachers; Sigma Xi; Am Phys Soc. *Res:* Strong dynamical correlations in nuclear matter. *Mailing Add:* Dept of Physics State Univ of NY Col Oneonta NY 13820

WANG, CHEN-SHOW, b Taiwan; US citizen; c 3. SOLID STATE PHYSICS, QUANTUM ELECTRONICS. *Educ:* Nat Taiwan Univ, BS, 59; Univ Iowa, MS, 64; Univ Calif, San Diego, PhD(physics), 68. *Prof Exp:* Fel physics, Univ Calif, San Diego, 68-69; res fel, Harvard Univ, 69-72; asst prof physics, Bartol Res Found, Univ Del, 72-78, assoc prof, 78-79; MGR RES & DEVELOP, GEN OPTRONICS CORP, 79- *Mem:* Am Phys Soc; Sigma Xi. *Res:* Solid state physics and quantum electronics, in particular surface physics, lattice dynamics, nonlinear optics laser light scattering, solid state lasers, gas lasers and semiconductor lasers. *Mailing Add:* Gen Optronics Corp 3005 Hadley Rd South Plainfield NJ 07080

WANG, CHIA PING, b Philippines; US citizen. NUCLEAR RADIATION PHYSICS, THERMAL PHYSICS. *Educ:* Univ London, BSc, 50; Univ Malaya, MSc, 51; Univs Malaya & Cambridge, PhD(physics), 53. *Hon Degrees:* DSc, Univ Singapore, 72. *Prof Exp:* Asst lectr, Univ Malaya, 51-53; assoc prof physics, Nankai Univ, 54-56, head electron physics & electronics div, 55-58, prof, 56-58; head electrophysics div, Lanchow Proj, 58; sr lectr, prof & actg head, Depts Physics & Math, Hong Kong Univ & Chinese Univ Hong Kong, 58-63; res assoc, Lab Nuclear Studies, Cornell Univ, 63-64; assoc prof space sci & physics, Cath Univ, 64-66; assoc prof physics, Case Inst Technol & Case Western Reserve Univ, 66-70; vis scientist & vis prof, Univs Cambridge & Louvain, US Naval Res Lab, Univ Md & Mass Inst Technol, 70-75; RES PHYSICIST, US ARMY NATICK RES & DEVELOP LABS, 75- *Mem:* Am Phys Soc; Inst Physics, London; AAAS; Sigma Xi; NY Acad Sci. *Res:* Nuclear, ratiation physics; cosmic rays; neutrinos;space atmospheric science; dosimetry; quantum mechanics; quantum electrodynamics; nucleon sub-structure; particle production; nucleon cascades; Hartree-Fock methods; atomic and molecular stopping power; thermodynamics heat transfer; microbiology kill; electronics; computer science. *Mailing Add:* Res & Develop Labs USA Army Natick MA 01760

WANG, CHIA-LIN JEFFREY, b China, June 24, 49; m 73. CHEMISTRY. *Educ:* Nat Taiwan Univ, BS, 71; Univ Pittsburgh, PhD(chem), 77. *Prof Exp:* Res assoc, Dept Chem, Univ Pittsburgh, 77, Harvard Univ, 78-79; RES CHEMIST, CENT RES & DEVELOP DEPT, E I DU PONT NEMOURS & CO, INC, 79- *Mem:* Am Chem Soc. *Res:* Synthesis of medicinally interesting compounds. *Mailing Add:* Cent Res & Develop Dept Exp Sta E I du Pont de Nemours & Co Inc 328-306 Wilmington DE 19898

WANG, CHIEN YI, b Fengshan, Taiwan, Nov 22, 42; US citizen; c 2. POSTHARVEST PHYSIOLOGY, HORTICULTURE. *Educ:* Nat Taiwan Univ, BS, 64; Ore State Univ, PhD(hort), 69. *Prof Exp:* Res assoc fruits, Ore State Univ, 69-76; RES HORTICULTURIST, USDA, 76- *Mem:* Am Soc Hort Sci. *Res:* Postharvest physiology of horticultural crops; basic and applied problems concerning physiological and pathological deterioration and quality maintenance of fruits, vegetables and flowers after harvest. *Mailing Add:* Bldg 002 Agr Res Ctr-West Beltsville MD 20705

WANG, CHIH CHUN, b Peking, China, Oct 9, 32; m 59; c 3. MATERIALS SCIENCE, PHYSICAL CHEMISTRY. *Educ:* Nat Taiwan Univ, BSc, 55; Kans State Univ, MSc, 59; Colo State Univ, PhD(phys chem), 62. *Prof Exp:* Res assoc, High Temp Phys Chem Res Lab, Univ Kans, 62-63; mem tech staff solid state mat res, 63-73, FEL TECH STAFF, RCA LABS, DAVID SARNOFF RES CTR, RCA CORP, PRINCETON, 73- *Mem:* Am Chem Soc; Electrochem Soc; Am Phys Soc. *Res:* Electronic materials; thin films; crystal growth; chemical vapor deposition; high pressure and high temperautre chemistry; thermodynamics; x-ray crystallography; vidicon materials and devices; tribology. *Mailing Add:* 41 Maple Stream Rd Hightstown NJ 08520

WANG, CHIH HSING, b Shanghai, China, Sept 20, 17; nat US; m 58; c 1. RADIOCHEMISTRY. *Educ:* Shantung Univ, China, BS, 37; Ore State Univ, MS, 47, PhD(chem), 50. *Prof Exp:* From asst prof to assoc prof, 51-58, PROF CHEM, ORE STATE UNIV, 58-, DIR RADIATION CTR, 62-, DIR INST NUCLEAR SCI & ENG, 64-, HEAD DEPT NUCLEAR ENG, 74- *Concurrent Pos:* Consult, NSF, 65-69; chmn, Ore Nuclear & Thermal Energy Coun, 72-73. *Mem:* Fel AAAS; Am Chem Soc; Am Soc Biol Chem; Am Soc Plant Physiol; Am Nuclear Soc. *Res:* Nuclear education; radiotracer methodology. *Mailing Add:* Radiation Ctr Ore State Univ Corvallis OR 97331

WANG, CHIH-CHUNG, b Wusih, China, Mar 8, 22; US citizen; m 53; c 2. METALLURGY. *Educ:* Tang Shan Eng Col, BS, 45; Ill Inst Technol, MS, 50; Mass Inst Technol, DSc, 53. *Prof Exp:* Sr engr, Sylvania Elec Prod, Inc, 53-55; dir, Mat & Metall Dept, Clevite Transistor Prod, Inc, 55-63; staff scientist, Ledgemont Lab, Kennecott Copper Corp, 63-78, mgr metal prod, Lexington Develop Ctr, 78-80; CHIEF METALLURGIST, DURACELL INT, 81- *Mem:* Am Inst Mining, Metall & Petrol Engrs; Am Soc Metals; Electrochem Soc. *Res:* Solidification of metals; crystal growing; materials research; extractive metallurgy; electroplating. *Mailing Add:* 9 Gould Rd Lexington MA 02173

WANG, CHI-HUA, b Peking, China, Apr 18, 23; m 49; c 1. ORGANIC CHEMISTRY. *Educ:* St John's Univ, China, BS, 45; Cath Univ, China, MS, 47; St Louis Univ, PhD(org chem), 51. *Prof Exp:* Fel, Brandeis Univ, 51-53, from instr to assoc prof chem, 53-62; sr chemist, Arthur D Little, Inc, 62-64; assoc prof chem, Wellesley Col, 64-68; assoc prof, 68-70, PROF CHEM, UNIV MASS, HARBOR CAMPUS, 70- *Mem:* Am Chem Soc; Sigma Xi. *Res:* Chemistry of free radicals in solution; mechanism of organic reactions. *Mailing Add:* Dept of Chem Univ of Mass Boston MA 02125

WANG, CHIN HSIEN, b Taiwan, Sept 4, 39; US citizen; m 63; c 4. CHEMISTRY. *Educ:* Nat Taiwan Univ, BS, 61; Utah State Univ, MS, 64; Mass Inst Technol, PhD(phys chem), 67. *Prof Exp:* Mem tech staff, Bell Tel Labs, 67-69; from asst prof to assoc prof phys chem, 69-76, PROF CHEM, UNIV UTAH, 76- *Concurrent Pos:* Petrol Res Fund grant, 70-78; Res Corp grant, 72-73; Alfred P Sloan Found fel, 73; Off Naval Res grants, 74-78 & 78-82; NSF grants, 77-79 & 79-82; adj prof mat sci, Univ Utah, 81- *Honors & Awards:* David P Gardner Award, 81. *Mem:* Am Phys Soc; Am Chem Soc. *Res:* Light scattering and Raman spectroscopy; polymer physics; statistical mechanics; using laser light scattering as an experimental technique to a investigate; relaxation and orientation behavior of polymer chairs in solution and in bulk; studies of the glass transition phenomena in supercooled liquids and solids using light scattering and non-equilibrium statistical mechanics are also in progress. *Mailing Add:* Dept of Chem Univ of Utah Salt Lake City UT 84112

WANG, CHING CHUNG, b Peking, China, Feb 10, 36; m 63; c 2. BIOCHEMISTRY, PARASITOLOGY. *Educ:* Nat Taiwan Univ, BS, 58; Univ Calif, Berkeley, PhD(biochem), 66. *Prof Exp:* Fel biochem, Col Physicians & Surgeons, Columbia Univ, 66-67; res assoc, Princeton Univ, 67-69; sr res biochemist, Merck Inst Therapeut Res, 69-72, res fel, 72-75, sr res fel, 75-78, sr investr, 78-81; PROF CHEM & PHARMACEUT CHEM, DEPT PHARMACEUT CHEM, SCH PHARM, UNIV CALIF, SAN FRANCISCO, 81- *Res:* Enzymes and active transport in microorganisms; biochemistry and development of protozoan parasites; invertebrate neurobiology. *Mailing Add:* 22 Miraloma Dr San Francisco CA 94127

WANG, CHING-PING SHIH, b Shanghai, China, Feb 16, 47; m 71. THEORETICAL SOLID STATE PHYSICS. *Educ:* Tung-Hai Univ, Taiwan, BS, 69; La State Univ, Baton Rouge, MS, 71, PhD(physics), 74. *Prof Exp:* Res assoc physics, Dept Physics & Astron, La State Univ, Baton Rouge, 74-76; res assoc physics, Dept Physics & Astron, Northwestern Univ, Evanston, 76-79; ASST PROF, DEPT PHYSICS & ASTRON, UNIV MD, 79- *Concurrent Pos:* Off Naval Res contract, 79-81, Naval Res Lab contract, 81-82. *Mem:* Am Phys Soc. *Res:* Self-consistent band structure and other properties of ferromagnetic metals, of magnetic metal surfaces, of surface with adsorbed atoms and of semiconductors. *Mailing Add:* Dept Physics & Astron Univ Md College Park MD 20742

WANG, CHI-SUN, b Shanghai, China, Oct 8, 42; m 73; c 1. BIOCHEMISTRY. *Educ:* Nat Taiwan Univ, BS, 66; Univ Okla, PhD(biochem), 71. *Prof Exp:* Staff scientist, 74-75, ASST MEM MEMBRANE BIOCHEM, OKLA MED RES FOUND, 75- *Honors & Awards:* Eason Award, 77; Merrick Award, 81. *Res:* Lipoprotein lipase; bile salt-activated lipase; tissue lipases. *Mailing Add:* 825 NE 13th St Oklahoma City OK 73104

WANG, CHIU-CHEN, b Canton, China, Nov 5, 22; US citizen; m 55; c 1. RADIOTHERAPY. *Educ:* Nat Kwei-Yang Med Col, China, MD, 48; Am Bd Radiol, dipl, 53. *Prof Exp:* Rotation intern, Canton Hosp, China, 47-48, asst resident med, 48-49; intern, Univ Hosp, Syracuse, NY, 49-50; asst resident radiol, Mass Gen Hosp, Boston, 50-51, resident, 52, clin fel, 53-56; asst radiol, 58-60, instr, 60-61, clin assoc, 62-67, asst clin prof, 68-69, asst prof, 69-70, from asst prof to assoc prof radiation ther, 70-75, PROF RADIATION THER, HARVARD MED SCH, 75-; RADIATION THERAPIST & HEAD CLIN SERV, MASS GEN HOSP, 73- *Concurrent Pos:* Damon Runyon res grant, Donner Lab, Univ Calif, Berkeley, 61-62; consult radiologist, Lawrence Berkeley Lab, Univ Calif, Berkeley, 62-65 & Mass Eye & Ear Infirmary, Waltham Hosp, Emerson Hosp & Malden Hosp, Mass, 62-; mem comt disaster planning, Mass Gen Hosp, 62; guest examr, Am Bd Radiol, 66. *Mem:* Fel Am Col Radiol; Am Radium Soc; Radiol Soc NAm; Am Soc Therapeut Radiol. *Res:* Clinical radiation oncology; radiobiology. *Mailing Add:* Dept of Radiation Med Mass Gen Hosp Boston MA 02114

WANG, CHIU-SEN, b Taichung, Formosa, Dec 3, 37; m 67; c 3. CHEMICAL ENGINEERING, ENVIRONMENTAL HEALTH ENGINEERING. *Educ:* Taiwan Univ, BS, 60; Kans State Univ, MS, 63; Calif Inst Technol, PhD(chem eng), 66. *Prof Exp:* Res fel chem eng, Calif Inst Technol, 66-68; asst prof environ med, Med Ctr, NY Univ, 68-69; assoc prof chem eng, 69-74, PROF CHEM ENG, SYRACUSE UNIV, 74- *Concurrent Pos:* Assoc res scientist, Med Ctr, NY Univ, 66; vis prof, Kyoto Univ, Japan, 78. *Mem:* Soc Powder Technol Japan; Air Pollution Control Asn; Am Inst Chem Engrs; Am Indust Hyg Asn; Am Asn Aerosol Res. *Res:* Systems optimization; aerosol physics and physiology; gas-particle separations. *Mailing Add:* Dept of Chem Eng Syracuse Univ Syracuse NY 13210

WANG, CHI-WU, b Tientsin, China, May 4, 13; nat US; m 56; c 3. FOREST GENETICS. *Educ:* Nat Tsing-Hua Univ, China, BS, 33; Yale Univ, MS, 47; Harvard Univ, PhD(biol), 53. *Prof Exp:* Res asst, Fan Mem Inst Biol, China, 33-43; assoc prof, Nat Kwangsi Univ, 43-46; res assoc, Harvard Forest, Harvard Univ, 53-54; from asst prof to assoc prof forestry, Univ Fla, 54-60; PROF FOREST GENETICS, UNIV IDAHO, 60- *Concurrent Pos:* Res assoc, Sch Forestry, Univ Minn, 58-59. *Mem:* AAAS; Ecol Soc Am; Soc Am Foresters; Soc Study Evolution; Am Genetic Asn. *Res:* Forest genetics and tree improvement; silvics; ecology; silviculture. *Mailing Add:* Univ of Idaho Col of Forestry Moscow ID 83843

WANG, CHU PING, b China, Mar 25, 31; m 61; c 3. COMPUTER SYSTEMS, INFORMATION SCIENCE. *Educ:* Taiwan Univ, BSc, 54; Univ Toronto, MASc, 56; Stanford Univ, PhD(microwave electronics), 61. *Prof Exp:* Asst prof elec eng, San Jose State Col, 60-61; res staff mem, Thomas J Watson Res Ctr, IBM Corp, 61-67; vis assoc prof, Wash Univ, 67-68; res staff mem, San Jose Res Lab, 68-76, RES STAFF MEM, THOMAS J WATSON RES CTR, IBM CORP, 76- *Mem:* Inst Elec & Electronics Engrs. *Res:* Information system design and evaluation methodology; computer performance evaluation; data base organization. *Mailing Add:* Thomas J Watson Res Ctr IBM Corp Yorktown Heights NY 10598

WANG, CHUN-JUAN KAO, b Mukden, China, Jan 10, 28; m 55; c 3. MYCOLOGY. *Educ:* Nat Taiwan Univ, BS, 50; Vassar Col, MS, 52; Univ Iowa, PhD(mycol), 55. *Prof Exp:* Asst, Univ Iowa, 52-55; res assoc, Clin Labs, Jewish Hosp, Cincinnati, Ohio, 55-58; from asst prof to assoc prof, 59-72, PROF FOREST BOT & PATH, NY STATE COL ENVIRON SCI & FORESTRY, SYRACUSE UNIV, 72- *Concurrent Pos:* Instr, Sch Med, Univ Cincinnati, 57-58. *Mem:* Mycol Soc Am; Brit Mycol Soc. *Res:* Medical mycology; soil fungi; pulp and paper fungi; imperfect fungi. *Mailing Add:* Dept of Forest Bot & Path NY State Col Envrn Sci & Forest Syracuse NY 13210

WANG, DANIEL I-CHYAU, b Nanking, China, Mar 12, 36; US citizen; m 66; c 1. CHEMICAL & BIOCHEMICAL ENGINEERING. *Educ:* Mass Inst Technol, BS, 59, SM, 61; Univ Pa, PhD(chem eng), 63. *Prof Exp:* Process engr, US Army Biol Labs, 63-65; asst prof, 65-76, PROF BIOCHEM, MASS INST TECHNOL, 76- *Concurrent Pos:* Consult, Environ Protection Agency. *Honors & Awards:* Food, Pharmaceut & Bioeng Award, Am Inst Chem Engrs. *Mem:* Am Chem Soc; Am Inst Chem Engrs; Inst Food Technol; Am Soc Microbiol. *Res:* Kinetics of biological systems; mass transfer in fermentation process; membrane processes; microbial sterilization; hydrocarbon fermentation; fermentation recovery. *Mailing Add:* Dept of Nutrit & Food Sci Mass Inst of Technol Cambridge MA 02139

WANG, DONG-PING, physical oceanography, see previous edition

WANG, DUEN-PAO, b Amoy, China, Oct 9, 33; m 65. ENGINEERING SCIENCE, HYDRODYNAMICS. *Educ:* Nat Taiwan Univ, BS, 56; Va Polytech Inst, MS, 58; Calif Inst Technol, PhD(eng sci), 62. *Prof Exp:* Res fel eng sci, Calif Inst Technol, 62-65, sr res fel, 65-66; vis mem, Courant Inst Math Sci, NY Univ, 66-67; assoc prof aerospace & atmospheric sci, Cath Univ Am, 67-72; CONSULT, 72- *Res:* Unsteady cavity flows; high-speed hydrofoils; water entry problems. *Mailing Add:* 2525 N Tenth St No 324 Arlington VA 22201

WANG, EDWARD YEONG, b Nantung, China, July 30, 33; m 60; c 3. SOLID STATE ELECTRONICS. *Educ:* Morningside Col, BS, 54; Purdue Univ, MS, 59; Tufts Univ, PhD(physics), 66. *Prof Exp:* Jr physicist, Nat Semiconductor Co, Ill, 54-56; assoc staff mem, Res Div, Raytheon Co, Mass, 59-61; sr res Electronics Corp Am, 61-63 & Gen Motors Res Lab, Mich, 66-70; assoc prof elec eng, Wayne State Univ, 70-77, prof elec & comput eng, 77-79; PROF ELEC & COMPUT ENG, ARIZ STATE UNIV, TEMPE, 79- *Mem:* Am Phys Soc. *Res:* Electrical and optical properties of solids; optoelectronics. *Mailing Add:* Elec & Comput Eng Ariz State Univ Tempe AZ 85281

WANG, FRANCIS WEI-YU, b Peikang, Taiwan, July 21, 36; US citizen; m 66; c 3. POLYMER SCIENCE. *Educ:* Calif Inst Technol, BS, 61, MS, 62; Univ Calif, San Diego, PhD(chem), 71. *Prof Exp:* Chemist, Pac Soap Co, 62-66; USPHS fel, 71-72; RES CHEMIST, POLYMERS DIV, NAT BUR STANDARDS, 72- *Mem:* Am Chem Soc; Am Phys Soc. *Res:* Thermodynamic and frictional properties of polymer solutions; photophysical processes in polymer molecules; ultracentrifugal analysis of macromolecules; diffusion in polymers. *Mailing Add:* Rm A313 Bldg 224 Polymers Div Nat Bur Standards Washington DC 20234

WANG, FRANK FENG HUI, b Hopeh, China, Mar 21, 24; nat US; m 58; c 3. MARINE GEOLOGY. *Educ:* Nat Southwestern Assoc Univ, China, BS, 45; Univ Wash, PhD(geol), 55. *Prof Exp:* Asst geol, Nat Southwestern Assoc Univ, China, 45-46; instr, Nat Peking Univ, 46-48; asst, Univ Wash, 50-54; sedimentalogist-stratigrapher, Western Gulf Oil Co, 54-57; res geologist, Gulf Res & Develop Co, 57-63; marine geologist, Int Minerals & Chem Corp, 64-67; MARINE GEOLOGIST, US GEOL SURV, 67- *Concurrent Pos:* Spec consult, Chinese Petrol Corp, 58; vis scholar, Northwestern Univ, 64; tech adv, UN, 67-, spec adv & sr marine geologist, UN Develop Prog on Regional Offshore Prospecting in E Asia, 72-74, prin marine geologist, 74-; vchmn marine geol panel, US-Japan Coop Prog Natural Resources, 70- *Mem:* Am Asn Petrol Geol; Am Geophys Union; Marine Technol Soc. *Res:* Marine mineral resources; ocean mining; sea-floor geological mapping; regional marine geology of eastern Asia. *Mailing Add:* US Geol Surv Off Marine Geol 345 Middlefield Rd Menlo Park CA 94025

WANG, FRANKLIN FU-YEN, b China, Sept 19, 28; nat US; m 56; c 2. MATERIALS SCIENCE. *Educ:* Pomona Col, BA, 51; Univ Toledo, MS, 53; Univ Ill, PhD(ceramics), 56. *Prof Exp:* Asst dir res, Glascote Prod, Inc, 56-58; res scientist, A O Smith Corp, 58-61; res staff mem, Sperry Rand Res Ctr, 61-66; assoc prof mat sci, 66-72, chmn dept, 72-74, PROF MAT SCI, STATE UNIV NY STONY BROOK, 72- *Mem:* Am Phys Soc; fel Am Ceramic Soc; Am Chem Soc; Am Soc Metals; Inst Elec & Electronics Engrs. *Res:* Magnetic materials; transport properties; dielectric materials; physical ceramics; glass systems; high temperature materials; engineering education; semiconductor processing; crystal growth. *Mailing Add:* Dept of Mat Sci & Eng State Univ of NY Stony Brook NY 11790

WANG, FREDERICK E, b She-Tou, Formosa, Aug 1, 32; US citizen; m 61; c 2. CHEMISTRY, PHYSICS. *Educ:* Memphis State Univ, BS, 56; Univ Ill, MS, 57; Syracuse Univ, PhD(phys chem), 60. *Prof Exp:* Fel, Harvard Univ, 60-61; res assoc metal alloys, Syracuse Univ, 61-63; chemist, US Naval Surface Weapons Ctr, 63-80; PRES, INNOVATIVE TECHNOL INT, INC, 80- *Concurrent Pos:* Fulbright exchange lectr, 67-68. *Mem:* Am Phys Soc; Am Crystallog Asn; AAAS. *Res:* Metal and alloy physicsl order-disorder phenomena; superconductivity. *Mailing Add:* Innovative Technol Int Inc 10747-3 Tucker St Beltsville MD 20705

WANG, GUANG TSAN, b Taiwan, China, Mar 6, 35; US citizen; m 62; c 2. VETERINARY MEDICINE, PARASITOLOGY. *Educ:* Nat Taiwan Univ, DVM, 58; Univ Ill, Urbana, MS, 64, PhD(vet med sci), 68. *Prof Exp:* Vet, Taiwan Serum Vaccine Labs, 60-62; res asst parasitol, Univ Ill, 62-68; res vet, 68-74, group leader parasitol discovery, 74-77, prog mgr, Agr Div, 77-81, DIR, ANIMAL INDUST RES & DEVELOP, AMERICAS/FAR EAST, AGR RES DIV, AM CYANAMID CO, PRINCETON, 81- *Mem:* Am Soc Parasitol; Am Vet Med Asn. *Res:* Toxicity and efficacy of anthelmintics, anticoccidials and antibiotics in domestic animals; industrial parasitic chemotherapy; research administration. *Mailing Add:* 41 Slayback Dr Princeton Junction NJ 08550

WANG, GWO-CHING, b Hu-Pei Prov, China, Oct 10, 46. SURFACE PHYSICS. *Educ:* Cheng Kung Univ, Taiwan, BS, 68; Northern Ill Univ, MS, 73; Univ Wis-Madison, PhD(mat sci), 78. *Prof Exp:* Teaching asst, Fu-Jen Univ, Taiwan, 68-69, Univ Wyo, 69-71; res asst, Northern Ill Univ, 71-73, Univ Wis-Madison, 73-78; physicist, Nat Bur Standards, 78-80; PHYSICIST, SOLID STATE PHYS DIV, OAK RIDGE NAT LAB, 80- *Mem:* Sigma Xi. *Res:* Geometric properties of surfaces; chemisorption and phase transitions using low energy electron diffraction and spin polarized low energy electron diffraction. *Mailing Add:* Solid State Physics Div Oak Ridge Nat Lab PO Box X Oak Ridge TN 37832

WANG, H E FRANK, b China, Oct 23, 29; US citizen; m 55; c 2. FLUID PHYSICS, SYSTEMS ENGINEERING. *Educ:* Nat Taiwan Univ, BS, 52; Bucknell Univ, MS, 54; Brown Univ, PhD(gas dynamics), 59. *Prof Exp:* Res engr gas dynamics, Boeing Co, 58-60; mem tech staff & prog mgr aerophys & systs eng, 60-77, dir, 76-81, PRIN DIR, SPACE TEST PROGS, AEROSPACE CORP, 81- *Mem:* Assoc fel Am Inst Aeronaut & Astronaut. *Mailing Add:* 27241 Sunnyridge Rd Rolling Hills CA 90274

WANG, HAO, b Tsinan, China, May 20, 21; m 48, 77; c 3. MATHEMATICS. *Educ:* Nat Southwestern Assoc Univ, China, BS, 43; Tsing Hua Univ, MA, 45; Harvard Univ, PhD, 48; Oxford Univ, MA, 56. *Prof Exp:* Soc Fels fel, Harvard Univ, 48-51, asst prof philos, 51-56; reader philos of math, Oxford Univ, 56-61; Gordon McKay prof math logic & appl math, Harvard Univ, 61-67; PROF MATH, ROCKEFELLER UNIV, 67- *Concurrent Pos:* Res engr, Burroughs Corp, 53-54; fel, Rockefeller Found, 54-55; John Locke lectr philos, Oxford Univ, 55; mem tech staff, Bell Tel Labs, 59-60; res scientist, IBM Res Ctr, 73-74; vis, Inst Advan Study, Princeton, 75-76. *Mem:* Asn Symbolic Logic; fel Am Acad Arts & Sci; foreign fel Brit Acad. *Res:* Mathematical logic; epistemology; philosophy of mathematics; general philosophy; contemporary China; author or coauthor of over 100 articles and three books. *Mailing Add:* Rockefeller Univ New York NY 10021

WANG, HERBERT FAN, b Shanghai, China, Sept 14, 46; US citizen; m 68; c 3. GEOPHYSICS. *Educ:* Univ Wis-Madison, BA, 66; Harvard Univ, AM, 68; Mass Inst Technol, PhD(geophys), 71. *Prof Exp:* Res assoc geophys, Mass Inst Technol, 71-72; asst prof, 72-77, ASSOC PROF GEOPHYS, UNIV WIS-MADISON, 77- *Concurrent Pos:* Geoscientist, Dept Energy, 80-81. *Mem:* Am Geophys Union. *Res:* Elasticity of minerals and rocks; rock mechanics applied to earthquake mechanism; groundwater modeling. *Mailing Add:* Dept Geol & Geophys Univ Wis 1215 W Dayton St Madison WI 53706

WANG, HOWARD HAO, b Shanghai, China, Jan 24, 42; m 63; c 2. NEUROSCIENCES, BIOCHEMICAL PHARMACOLOGY. *Educ:* Calif Inst Technol, BS, 63; Univ Calif, Los Angeles, PhD(neurophysiol), 68. *Prof Exp:* USPHS fel, Univ Calif, Berkeley, 68-69; resident scientist, Neurosci Res Prog, Mass Inst Technol, 69-70; asst prof, 70-77, ASSOC PROF BIOL, STEVENSON COL, UNIV CALIF, SANTA CRUZ, 77-, FEL, 70- *Mem:* AAAS; Am Asn Anat; Biophys Soc; Soc Neurosci. *Res:* Mechanism of local anesthetic action and drug-membrane interaction; effect of environmental chemicals on membrane structure and function; molecular and cellular mechanisms of brain function. *Mailing Add:* Div of Natural Sci Univ of Calif Santa Cruz CA 95064

WANG, HSIANG, b China, Jan 20, 36; m 64; c 2. FLUID MECHANICS. *Educ:* Taiwan Univ, BS, 58; Univ Mass, MS, 63; Univ Iowa, PhD(fluid mech), 65. *Prof Exp:* Res asst fluid mech, Iowa Inst Hydraul Res, 62-63, res assoc, 63-65; res engr ocean, US Naval Civil Eng Lab, 65-67; mem tech staff, Nat Eng Sci Div, Fluor Corp Int, 67, mem sr staff, 67-69; sr engr, Tatra-Technol Inc, 69-70; assoc prof civil eng, Univ Del, 70-75, prof, 75-81, actg chmn, 78-79; VPRES, COASTAL & OTTSHIRE ENG & RES, INC, 77-; CHMN & PROF COASTAL & OCEAN ENG, UNIV FLA, 81- *Concurrent Pos:* Vis prof, Tech Univ Braunschweig. *Mem:* Am Soc Civil Engrs. Fluid mechanics and ocean engineering; submarine wake study; offshore structure and offshore oil exploration; coastal and estuarine research. *Mailing Add:* Dept Coastal & Ocean Eng Univ Fla Gainsville FL 32611

WANG, HSIEN-YIEN, physical chemistry, radiation chemistry, see previous edition

WANG, HSIN-PANG, b Nanking, China, Apr 11, 46; US citizen; m 73. COMPUTER AIDED ENGINEERING, COMPUTATIONAL MECHANICS. *Educ:* Cheng-Kung Univ, BS, 69; Univ Fla, MS, 72; Univ RI, PhD(mech eng), 76. *Prof Exp:* Res asst, Univ RI, 73-76; MECH ENGR, GEN ELEC RES & DEVELOP CTR, 76- *Mem:* Am Soc Mech Engrs; Am Physical Soc. *Res:* Computer simulation of manufacturing processes, fluid flow and heat transfer by using the finite element method. *Mailing Add:* Gen Elec Res & Develop Ctr PO Box 43 Schenectady NY 12301

WANG, HSUEH-HWA, b Peiping, China, July 10, 23; US citizen; m 48; c 3. PHARMACOLOGY, PHYSIOLOGY. *Educ:* Nat Cent Univ, Nanking, China, MB, 46. *Prof Exp:* assoc prof, 70-80, PROF PHARMACOL, COL PHYSICIANS & SURGEONS, COLUMBIA UNIV, 80- *Concurrent Pos:* NY Heart fel, 53-54. *Mem:* AAAS; Am Physiol Soc; Am Soc Pharmacol & Exp Therapeut. *Res:* Coronary circulation; effects of endogenous mediators (prostaglandins, antidiuretic hormone, angiotensen) on peripheral circulation and blood pressure control. *Mailing Add:* Col of Physicians & Surgeons Columbia Univ Dept of Pharmacol New York NY 10032

WANG, HWA LIH, b Chekiang, China, Nov 29, 21; m 49; c 2. BIOCHEMISTRY. *Educ:* Nat Cent Univ, China, BS, 45; Univ Wis, MS, 50, PhD(biochem), 52. *Prof Exp:* Asst biochem, Med Sch, Nat Cent Univ, China, 45; res assoc, Med Sch, Marquette Univ, 53-55, Med Sch, Univ Wis, 56-61 & Wash Univ, 61-62; RES CHEMIST, NORTHERN REGIONAL LAB, AGR RES SERV, USDA, 63- *Mem:* Am Inst Nutrit; Am Chem Soc; Inst Food Technologists. *Res:* Biochemistry and physiology of molds used in soybean and cereal food fermentation; nutritional value of fermented food products. *Mailing Add:* Fermentation Lab USDA Northern Regional Res Lab Peoria IL 61604

WANG, I-TUNG, atmospheric physics, nuclear physics, see previous edition

WANG, JAMES C, b China, Nov 18, 36; m 61; c 2. BIOCHEMISTRY, MOLECULAR BIOLOGY. *Educ:* Nat Taiwan Univ, BS, 59; Univ SDak, MA, 61; Univ Mo, PhD(chem), 64. *Prof Exp:* Res fel chem, Calif Inst Technol, 64-66; from asst prof to prof chem, Univ Calif, Berkeley, 66-77; PROF BIOCHEM & MOLECULAR BIOL, HARVARD UNIV, 77- *Concurrent Pos:* Mem biophys & biochem study sect, NIH, 72-76; mem adv comt physiol, cellular & molecular biol, NSF, 80- *Mem:* Am Soc Biol Chem; Biophys Soc. *Res:* Structures and functions of DNAs. *Mailing Add:* Dept Biochem & Molecular Biol Harvard Univ Cambridge MA 02138

WANG, JAMES TING-SHUN, b Nanking, China, Feb 8, 31; US citizen; m 63; c 1. ENGINEERING MECHANICS. *Educ:* Nat Taiwan Univ, BS, 54; Univ Kans, MS, 58; Purdue Univ, PhD(civil eng), 61. *Prof Exp:* Instr eng mech, Univ Kans, 56-58; from asst prof to assoc prof, 61-69, PROF ENG MECH, GA INST TECHNOL, 69- *Concurrent Pos:* Spec lectr, George Washington Univ, 63; consult, Lockheed-Ga Co, 65-66, aircraft develop engr specialist, 66-67. *Mem:* Am Soc Civil Engrs; Am Soc Eng Educ; Soc Rheology. *Res:* Structural mechanics; plate and sheil theory. *Mailing Add:* Sch of Eng Mech Ga Inst of Technol Atlanta GA 30332

WANG, JAW-KAI, b Nanking, China, Mar 4, 32; m 57; c 3. AGRICULTURAL ENGINEERING. *Educ:* Nat Taiwan Univ, BSAE, 53; Mich State Univ, MSAE, 56, PhD, 58. *Prof Exp:* Lectr farm mach, Prov Taoyaun Agr Inst, 54-55; asst farm processing, Mich State Univ, 55-58; from asst prof to assoc prof agr eng, 59-68, chmn dept, 64-75, PROF AGR ENG, UNIV HAWAII, 68- *Concurrent Pos:* Consult, US Army, Okinawa, 65, Taiwan Sugar Co, 66, Int Rice Res Inst, 71, Pac Concrete & Rock Co, 73, USAID, 73, The World Bank, 81 & 82, Am Bankers Asn Int, 81 & Univ Tankship, Del, 80 & 81; sr fel, Food Inst, East-West Ctr, 73-74; co dir, Int Sci & Educ Coun, 79; vis assoc dir, Int Prog & Studies Off, Nat Asn State Univ & land-grant col, 79; vis prof, Univ Calif, Davis, 80. *Mem:* Nat Soc Prof Engrs; Am Soc Agr Engrs; Chinese Soc Agr Engrs; World Mariculture Soc; Sigma Xi. *Res:* Irrigated rice production system design; aquacultural engineering, especially fresh water prawn and oyster; agricultural production systems design and analysis. *Mailing Add:* Dept of Agr Eng Univ of Hawaii 3050 Maile Way Honolulu HI 96822

WANG, JEN YU, b Foochow, China, Mar 3, 15; c 1. METEOROLOGY. *Educ:* Fukien Christian Univ, China, BS, 38; Univ Chicago, cert, 54; Univ Wis, MS, 55, PhD(meteorol), 58. *Prof Exp:* Instr math & physics, Cols, China & Hong Kong, 38-42; prin meteorologist, Weather Bur, China, 42-47; assoc prof physics, Fukien Christian Univ, 47-50; asst meteorol, Weather Forecasting Res Ctr, Univ Chicago, 53-54; asst, Univ Wis, 54-57, res assoc, 57-60, asst prof, 60-64; assoc prof, 64-68, PROF METEOROL & DIR ENVIRON SCI INST, SAN JOSE STATE UNIV, 68- *Concurrent Pos:* Fel, United Bd Higher Educ in Asia, US, 50-54; consult, 10th Weather Squadron, US Air Force, China, 45, US Weather Bur, Washington, DC, 58, AEC Proj, 65 & Stanford Res Inst, 66-67; pres, Milieu Info Serv, 71-, Blackwell Land Mgt Co, 74- & Sierra-Misco, Inc, 81- *Mem:* Am Meteorol Soc; Am Soc Agron; Int Soc Biometeorol; fel Am Geog Soc. *Res:* New techniques in the investigation of environmental relationships between animals and plants; agricultural meteorology; ecology; phenology; phytoclimatology; environmental assessment studies. *Mailing Add:* San Jose State Univ Dept of Meteorol San Jose CA 95192

WANG, JERRY HSUEH-CHING, b Nanking, China, Mar 12, 37; m 62; c 2. BIOCHEMISTRY. *Educ:* Nat Taiwan Univ, BSc, 58; Iowa State Univ, PhD(biochem), 65. *Prof Exp:* From asst prof to assoc prof, 66-78, PROF BIOCHEM, FAC MED, UNIV MAN, 78- *Concurrent Pos:* Nat Res Coun Can fel biochem, 65-66; Med Res Coun scholar, 66- *Mem:* Can Biochem Soc; Am Soc Biol Chemists. *Res:* Quaternary structure and regulatory property of enzymes. *Mailing Add:* Dept of Biochem Univ of Man Fac of Med Winnipeg MB R3T 2N2 Can

WANG, JI CHING, b Kobe, Japan, Nov 29, 38; m 70; c 1. ENGINEERING SCIENCE. *Educ:* Osaka Inst Technol, BS, 61; Univ Calif, Berkeley, MS, 65, PhD(mech eng), 69. *Prof Exp:* Design engr, Shinippon Koki, Japan, 61-62; res asst mech eng, Univ Calif, Berkeley, 64-65 & Naval Biol Lab, Oakland, 65-66; res engr, Kaiser Eng, 66-67; from asst prof to assoc prof, 69-82, PROF MECH ENG, SAN JOSE STATE UNIV, 82- *Concurrent Pos:* NSF grants, 70-71; consult, Ames Res Ctr, NASA, 70-71 & 74-82. *Mem:* Inst Elec & Electronics Engrs; Am Soc Mech Engrs. *Res:* System control engineering. *Mailing Add:* Dept of Mech Eng San Jose State Univ San Jose CA 95192

WANG, JIA-CHAO, b China, Mar 17, 39; m 66; c 2. SOLID STATE PHYSICS, THEORETICAL PHYSICS. *Educ:* Tunghai Univ, BS, 62; Nat Chiao Tung Univ, Taiwan, MS, 65; Univ NC, PhD(physics), 73. *Prof Exp:* Res assoc, Dept Physics & Astron, Univ NC, 73-75 & Wright-Patterson Air Force Base, 75-77; STAFF MEM, SOLID STATE DIV, OAK RIDGE NAT LAB, 77- *Concurrent Pos:* Res assoc, Nat Res Coun, 75-77. *Mem:* Am Phys Soc; Electrochem Soc; Sigma Xi; Sci Res Soc. *Res:* Solid electrolytes or superionic conductors; laser annealing of ion-implanted semiconductors; electronic density of states of disordered systems. *Mailing Add:* Solid State Div Oak Ridge Nat Lab Oak Ridge TN 37830

WANG, JIN TSAI, b Inchon, Korea, Apr 7, 31; US citizen; m 58; c 2. INORGANIC CHEMISTRY, ANALYTICAL CHEMISTRY. *Educ:* Ore State Univ, BS, 57; Carnegie Inst Technol, PhD(chem), 68. *Prof Exp:* Instr, Pa State Univ, 68; asst prof, 68-77, ASSOC PROF CHEM, DUQUESNE UNIV, 77- *Res:* Infrared and polarographic studies of metal complexes. *Mailing Add:* Dept of Chem Duquesne Univ Pittsburgh PA 15219

WANG, JIN-LIANG, b Chu-Nan, Taiwan, Aug 18, 37; US citizen; div; c 2. POLYMER CHEMISTRY. *Educ:* Taipei Inst Technol, dipl, 58; Kent State Univ, MS, 66; Univ Akron, PhD(polymer chem), 71. *Prof Exp:* Sr chem engr, Hua Min Paper Mill, Taiwan, 60-61; res chem engr, Taiwan Prov Tobacco & Wine Monopoly Bur, 61-63; SR RES CHEMIST, RES DIV, GOODYEAR TIRE & RUBBER CO, 66- *Mem:* Am Chem Soc; Sigma Xi. *Res:* Polymer synthesis, characterization and applications; polymerization mechanism and kinetics. *Mailing Add:* Res Div Goodyear Tire & Rubber 142 Goodyear Blvd Akron OH 44316

WANG, JOHN LING-FAI, b Amoy, China, Sept 21, 42; US citizen; m 70. PHYSICAL CHEMISTRY, CHEMICAL METALLURGY. *Educ:* Hope Col, BA, 65; Univ Calif, Berkeley, PhD(chem), 69. *Prof Exp:* Fel ceramics, Lawrence Radiation Lab, 69-70; fel high temperature chem, Rice Univ, 70-74; STAFF SCIENTIST HIGH FIELD SUPERCONDUCTOR MAT, LAWRENCE BERKELEY LAB, 74- *Mem:* Am Chem Soc; Am Phys Soc; Am Soc Metals; Am Powder Metall Inst; Sigma Xi. *Res:* High field superconducting materials and powder metallurgy; application of fundamental principles of materials science and high temperature chemistry to the design of new materials required in advanced technologies. *Mailing Add:* Lawrence Berkeley Lab Bldg 62 Berkeley CA 94720

WANG, JUI HSIN, b Peking, China, Mar 16, 21; nat US; m 49; c 2. BIOCHEMISTRY. *Educ:* Nat Southwest Assoc Univ, China, BSc, 45; Wash Univ, PhD(chem), 49. *Hon Degrees:* MA, Yale Univ, 60. *Prof Exp:* Fel radiochem, Wash Univ, 49-51; res fel chem, Yale Univ, 51-52, res asst, 52-53, from instr to prof, 53-62, Eugene Higgins Prof, 62-72; EINSTEIN PROF, UNIV NY BUFFALO, 72- *Concurrent Pos:* Guggenheim fel, Cambridge Univ, 60-61; mem biophys & biochem study sect, NIH, 65-69; Kennedy lectr, Wash Univ, 72; distinguished vis prof, Miss State Univ, 80. *Mem:* AAAS; Am Chem Soc; Am Soc Biol Chemists; Am Acad Arts & Sci; Am Soc Photobiol. *Res:* Diffusion in liquids; hemoglobin; mechanisms of enzyme action, particularly those related to oxidative phosphorylation, photosynthesis and ion-transport through biological membranes; electrochemistry. *Mailing Add:* Bioenergetics Lab State Univ NY Buffalo NY 14214

WANG, JU-KWEI, b Peiping, China, Feb 15, 34. MATHEMATICS. *Educ:* Nat Taiwan Univ, BS, 55; Stanford Univ, PhD(math), 60. *Prof Exp:* Assoc researcher math, Acad Sinica, 60-62; vis assoc prof, Univ Calif, Berkeley, 62-63; vis lectr, Yale Univ, 63-65; from assoc prof to prof, Nat Taiwan Univ, 65-68; assoc prof, 68-70, PROF MATH, UNIV MASS, AMHERST, 70- *Mem:* Am Math Soc. *Res:* Functional analysis, including harmonic analysis; Banach algebras and function algebras. *Mailing Add:* Dept of Math & Statist Univ of Mass Amherst MA 01003

WANG, KANG-LUNG, b Taiwan, China, July 3, 41; m 68. ELECTRICAL ENGINEERING, SEMICONDUCTOR PHYSICS & DEVICES. *Educ:* Cheng Kung Univ, Taiwan, BS, 64; Mass Inst Technol, MS, 66, PhD(elec eng), 70. *Prof Exp:* Res assoc, Div Sponsored Res, Mass Inst Technol, 70-71, asst prof elec eng, 71-72; scientist, Res & Develop Ctr, Gen Elec Co, 72-79, physicist, 78-80; ASSOC PROF, ENG DEPT, UNIV CALIF, LOS ANGELES, 79- *Concurrent Pos:* Adj prof, Physics Dept, State Univ NY Albany; consult, Xero Corp, El Segundo, Calif, 79-, Rockwell Int, Thousand Oaks, Calif. *Mem:* Sr mem Inst Elec & Electronics Engrs; Am Phys Soc; Am Vacuum Soc; Inst Elec Engrs Repub China. *Res:* Studies of semiconductor surface and heterojunction interface phonemena; physics and modeling of small geometry devices; semiconductor defect study and characterization using transient charge spectroscopy and electron spectroscopies. *Mailing Add:* 7731 Boelter Hall Elec Eng Dept Univ Calif Los Angeles CA 90024

WANG, KE-CHIN, b Chekiang, China, Dec 8, 30; US citizen; m 55; c 2. HIGH TEMPERATURE CHEMISTRY, CERAMICS. *Educ:* Univ Wis-Madison, BA, 58, MS, 60; Ill Inst Technol, PhD(chem), 66. *Prof Exp:* Res assoc high temperature chem, Okla State Univ, 67-69 & Ill Inst Technol, 69-70; dir res, Ceramtec Industs, Inc, 70-71, vpres, 71-72; RES MGR INDUST CERAMICS, HARBISON-WALKER REFRACTORIES CO, DIV DRESSER INDUSTS, INC, 73- *Mem:* Am Chem Soc; Am Ceramic Soc. *Res:* Advanced ceramic materials and forming processes. *Mailing Add:* Garber Res Ctr Harbison-Walker Refractories Co Pittsburgh PA 15227

WANG, KEN HSI, b Shanghai, China, July 4, 34; m 62; c 3. NUCLEAR PHYSICS. *Educ:* Int Christian Univ, Tokyo, BA, 58; Yale Univ, PhD(physics), 63. *Prof Exp:* Res fel physics, Harvard Univ, 63-66; asst prof, 66-69, ASSOC PROF PHYSICS, BAYLOR UNIV, 69- *Concurrent Pos:* Assoc res scientist, Tex A&M Univ, 80-81. *Mem:* Am Phys Soc; Am Asn Physics Teachers. *Res:* Nuclear reaction and scattering. *Mailing Add:* Dept of Physics Baylor Univ Waco TX 76798

WANG, KIA K, b Soochow, China, Oct 10, 24; nat US; m 43; c 3. GEOLOGY, STRATIGRAPHY. *Educ:* Nat Southwestern Assoc Univ, China, BS, 43; La State Univ, MS, 47, PhD, 51. *Prof Exp:* Geologist, Calif Oil Co, La, 46; res geologist, State Geol Surv, La, 47-50; asst prof, 50-70, ASSOC PROF GEOL, BROOKLYN COL, 70- *Concurrent Pos:* Asst, La State Univ, 46-50. *Mem:* Geol Soc Am; Soc Econ Paleontologists & Mineralogists; Am Asn Petrol Geologists. *Res:* Petroleum geology; micropaleontology. *Mailing Add:* Dept of Geol Brooklyn Col Brooklyn NY 11210

WANG, KUNG-PING, b China, Mar 11, 19; nat US; m; c 1. MINING ENGINEERING, METALLURGICAL ENGINEERING. *Educ:* Yenching Univ, China, BS, 40; Mo Sch Mines, BS, 42; Columbia Univ, MS, 43, PhD(mining), 46. *Hon Degrees:* Prof Mining Engr, Mo Sch Mines, 61. *Prof Exp:* Jr engr, Wah Chong Corp, 42 & Hudson Coal Co, 43-44; surveyor, NJ Zinc Co, 44-45; engr, Warren Pipe & Foundry Corp, 46; chief engr & asst gen mgr, Ping-Hsing Coal Co, 46-48; prof, Peiyang Univ, 48; chief specialist int activities, US Bur Mines, 60-69, supvry phys scientist nonmetallic minerals, 70-75, supvry phys scientist asia minerals, 75-80; PRES, K P WANG ASSOCS, 80- *Concurrent Pos:* Part-time asst to sci adv, Dept Interior, 64-67; adj assoc prof, Krumb Sch Mines, Columbia Univ, 67-70; consult to UN, 69-71. *Mem:* Am Inst Mining, Metall & Petrol Engrs. *Res:* Mineral economics; international natural resources, particularly in developing countries. *Mailing Add:* 1402 Longhill Dr Potomac MD 20854

WANG, KUO KING, b Wutsin, China, Oct 8, 23; c 3. ENGINEERING. *Educ:* Nat Cent Univ, Nanking, BS, 47; Univ Wis-Madison, MS, 62, PhD(mech eng), 68. *Prof Exp:* Engr, Taiwan Shipbuilding Corp, 47-57; mgr eng, Ingalls-Taiwan Shipbuilding Corp, 57-60; supvr shipbuilding, United Tanker Corp, 60-61; proj engr, Walker Mfg Co, 62-66; asst prof mech eng, Univ Wis-Madison, 68-70; assoc prof, 70-77, PROF MECH ENG, CORNELL UNIV, 77- *Honors & Awards:* Blackall Award, Am Soc Mech Engrs, 68; Adams Mem Award, Am Welding Soc, 76. *Mem:* Am Soc Mech Engrs; fel Am Welding Soc; Soc Mfg Engrs. *Res:* Materials processing; numerical control; computer-aided manufacturing systems; engineering. *Mailing Add:* Sch of Mech Eng Cornell Univ Ithaca NY 14853

WANG, LAWRENCE CHIA-HUANG, b Wusih, China, Apr 5, 40; m 66. PHYSIOLOGY, ZOOLOGY. *Educ:* Taiwan Norm Univ, BSc, 63; Rice Univ, MA, 67; Cornell Univ, PhD(physiol), 70. *Prof Exp:* Vis asst prof biol, Univ Ore, 69-70; asst prof zool, 70-74, assoc prof, 74-80, PROF ZOOL, UNIV ALTA, 80- *Concurrent Pos:* operating grant, Nat Res Coun Can, 71- & Nat Defence Res Bd Can, 73-76. *Mem:* AAAS; Can Soc Zool; Can Physiol Soc; Soc Cryobiol; Am Soc Zoologists. *Res:* Physiology of temperature regulation; hypothermia and hibernation in mammals. *Mailing Add:* Dept Zool Univ Alta Edmonton AB T6G 2E9 Can

WANG, LEON RU-LIANG, b Canton, China, June 15, 32; US citizen; m 61; c 3. STRUCTURAL ENGINEERING. *Educ:* Cheng Kung Univ, Taiwan, BS, 57; Univ Ill, MS, 61; Mass Inst Technol, ScD(struct), 65. *Prof Exp:* Res asst struct eng, Mass Inst Technol, 61-65, res engr, 65; asst prof struct, Rensselaer Polytech Inst, 65-69, assoc prof, 69-80; PROF CIVIL ENG, UNIV OKLA, 80- *Concurrent Pos:* Tech consult, Watervliet Arsenal, 66- & Nat Sci Coun, Taiwan, 75-; lectr, Am Inst Steel Construct, 69 & 71; NSF vis scientist, Cheng Kung Univ, Taiwan, 72-73; tech rev, NSF, 76-; vis scholar, Public Works Res Inst, Japan, 81. *Mem:* AAAS; Am Concrete Inst; Am Soc Civil Engrs; Am Soc Eng Educ; Chinese Inst Eng. *Res:* Structural mechanics; dynamics; stability; buckling; computer applications; model analysis; plate and shell theories; steel and reinforced concrete construction; earthquake engineering. *Mailing Add:* Sch Civil Eng & Environ Sci Univ Oklahoma Norman OK 93019

WANG, LI CHUAN, b Kaiyuan, China; US citizen; m; c 2. BIOCHEMISTRY, SOIL FERTILITY. *Educ:* Nat Cent Univ, Nanking, China, BS, 45; Univ Wis-Madison, PhD, 52, MS, 58. *Prof Exp:* Teaching asst, Nat Cent Univ, Nanking, 45-48; fel biochem, Univ Wis-Madison, 58-60; res chemist, Monsanto Chem Co, 60-62; assoc prof chem, Univ Alaska, 62-63; PRIN CHEMIST, NORTHERN REGIONAL RES LAB, USDA, 63- *Mem:* Am Chem Soc; Am Soc Plant Physiologists; Inst Food Technologists. *Res:* Soybean proteins, their utilization, flavor and functionalities. *Mailing Add:* 7013 N Teton Dr Peoria IL 61614

WANG, LIN-SHU, b Shanghai, China, Feb 14, 38; m 65; c 2. ENGINEERING. *Educ:* Univ Calif, Berkeley, PhD(eng), 66. *Prof Exp:* From asst prof to assoc prof eng, 65-76, ASSOC PROF MECH ENG, STATE UNIV NY STONY BROOK, 77- *Concurrent Pos:* Vis mem, Ctr Earth & Planetary Physics, Harvard Univ, 72. *Mem:* AAAS. *Res:* Radiative heat transfer. *Mailing Add:* Dept of Mech Eng State Univ of NY Stony Brook NY 11794

WANG, MAW SHIU, b Chang Hwa, Formosa, Nov 1, 25; m 51; c 3. AGRONOMY, SPECTROCHEMISTRY. *Educ:* Prov Agr Col, Formosa, BS, 51; Okla State Univ, MS, 56; Univ Ill, PhD, 59. *Prof Exp:* Jr engr, Chem Lab, Pingtong Sugar Exp Sta, Formosa, 51-54; asst soil chem, Univ Ill, Urbana, 55-59, res assoc, 59-61; sr res chemist, Cent Res Dept, 61-68, res specialist, 68-77, FEL, MONSANTO CO, 78- *Concurrent Pos:* Adj prof, St Louis Univ, 70- *Honors & Awards:* Megger's Award, Soc Appl Spectros, 73. *Mem:* Am Soc Testing & Mat; Soc Appl Spectros. *Res:* Emission spectroscopy; spectrochemical analysis of major and minor elements in agricultural material; traces in semiconductors and related materials; surface analysis, cleaning, and packaging of semiconductors. *Mailing Add:* Monsanto Co 800 N Lindbergh St Louis MO 63166

WANG, NAI-SAN, b Changhua, Taiwan, Jan 20, 36; Can citizen; m 63; c 4. PATHOLOGY. *Educ:* Nat Taiwan Univ, MD, 60; McGill Univ, MS, 69, PhD(path), 71. *Prof Exp:* Teaching & res fel, 67-71, asst prof, 71-74, ASSOC PROF PATH, McGILL UNIV, 74- *Concurrent Pos:* Consult, Mesothelum Ref Panel Can, Tumor Ref Ctr, 74-81. *Mem:* Am Asn Pathologists; Am Thoracic Soc; Can Thoracic Soc; Int Asn Pathologists. *Res:* Ultrastructural studies of the lung and pleura in normal and diseased conditions. *Mailing Add:* Dept Path McGill Univ 3775 University Ave Montreal PQ H3A 2B4 Can

WANG, NANCY YANG, b Peiping, China, Jan 20, 26; m 49; c 1. ORGANIC CHEMISTRY. *Educ:* Cath Univ, Peiping, BS, 45; St Louis Univ, MS, 51; Boston Univ, PhD(org chem), 65. *Prof Exp:* Fel biol, Mass Inst Technol, 64-65, fel nutrit, 65-66, res assoc chem, 66-68; res assoc, Retina Found, Boston Univ, 68-71; res assoc, 71-73, lectr, 73-75, RES ASSOC CHEM, UNIV MASS, BOSTON, 75- *Mem:* Sigma Xi. *Res:* Biochemistry and organic reaction mechanisms. *Mailing Add:* Dept of Chem Univ of Mass Boston MA 02125

WANG, P(AUL) K(ENG) C(HIEH), b Nanking, China, July 23, 34. ELECTRICAL ENGINEERING. *Educ:* Calif Inst Technol, BS, 55, MS, 56; Univ Calif, Berkeley, PhD(elec eng), 60. *Prof Exp:* Mem res staff, Res Lab, Int Bus Mach Corp, 59-64; asst prof elec eng, Univ Southern Calif, 64-67; assoc prof eng, 67-73, PROF ENG & APPL SCI, UNIV CALIF, LOS ANGELES, 73- *Concurrent Pos:* Vis mem res staff, Dept Physique du Plasma et Fusion Controlee, Centre d'Etudes Nucleaires, France, 74-75; consult, Jet Propulsion Lab, Calif Inst Technol, 81- *Mem:* Inst Elec & Electronics Engrs; Soc Indust & Appl Math; Am Phys Soc; Am Math Soc. *Res:* Automatic control system theory; plasma physics; distributed system. *Mailing Add:* Dept Syst Sci Univ Calif Los Angeles CA 90024

WANG, PAUL KUO UN, b Fukien, China, Oct 5, 38; m 64; c 2. NETWORK TOPOLOGY, COMPUTER AIDED DESIGN. *Educ:* Taipei Inst Technol, Taiwan, BS, 58; Lehigh Univ, MS, 62; Univ Cincinnati, PhD(elec eng), 67. *Prof Exp:* From instr to asst prof, Univ Cincinnati, 62-74, dir grad studies, 75-77, assoc prof elec eng, 74-81; SR PRIN DESIGN AUTOMATION ENGR, HONEYWELL INC, 81- *Concurrent Pos:* Vis prof, Taipei Inst Technol, 77-78; fac res fel, IBM Corp, 69. *Mem:* Inst Elec & Electronics Engrs; Am Soc Eng Educ; Tensor Soc Gt Britain. *Res:* Application of Kron's method of tearing to power systems and electronic circuits, and applications to modern topology to network theory; computer-aided network design; large scale networks. *Mailing Add:* Solid State Electronics Div Honeywell Inc 12001 State Hwy 55 Plymouth MN 55441

WANG, PETER CHENG-CHAO, b Shantung, China, Jan 11, 37; US citizen; m 60; c 2. STATISTICS. *Educ:* Pac Lutheran Univ, BA, 60; Wayne State Univ, MA, 62, PhD(math), 66. *Prof Exp:* Instr math, Wayne State Univ, 64-66; asst prof statist, Mich State Univ, 66-67; from asst prof to assoc prof, Univ Iowa, 67-70; ASSOC PROF STATIST, NAVAL POSTGRAD SCH, 70- *Concurrent Pos:* Vis assoc prof statist, Stanford Univ, 69-70; consult, B D M Serv Co, Tex, 71- *Mem:* Am Math Soc; Inst Math Statist; London Math Soc. *Res:* Stochastic models; combinatorics; forecast models for military systems; sound propagation models. *Mailing Add:* Code 53 Naval Postgrad Sch Monterey CA 93940

WANG, PING CHUN, b Kiangsu, China, Mar 10, 20; US citizen; m 55; c 2. ENGINEERING. *Educ:* Nat Cent Univ China, BS, 43; Univ Ill, MS, 48, PhD(eng), 51. *Prof Exp:* Engr, China Bridge Co, 43-47; struct designer, Ammann & Whitney Consult Engrs, 51-52; struct supvr, Seelye, Stevenson, Value & Knecht Consult Engrs, 52-60; assoc prof eng, Stevens Inst Technol, 60-63; PROF CIVIL ENG, POLYTECH INST NEW YORK, 63- *Concurrent Pos:* Dir & vpres, Omnidata Serv Inc, 71-72. *Mem:* Fel Am Soc Civil Engrs; Am Concrete Inst; Am Soc Eng Educ. *Res:* Discrete systems approach in structural mechanics. *Mailing Add:* Dept Civil Eng 333 Jay St Brooklyn NY 11201

WANG, RICHARD I H, b Shanghai, China, Oct 12, 24; US citizen; m 58; c 2. PHARMACOLOGY, INTERNAL MEDICINE. *Educ:* St John's Univ, BS, 45; Utah State Univ, MS, 49; Univ Ill, PhD(pharmacol), 52; Northwestern Univ, MD, 55. *Prof Exp:* Intern, Presby Hosp, Chicago, Ill, 55-56; resident, Indianapolis Gen Hosp, Ind, 56-58; prin scientist, Roswell Park Mem Inst, 61-63; assoc prof pharmacol & med, 63-70, PROF CLIN PHARMACOL, MED COL WIS, 70-, ASSOC PROF MED, 77-; CHIEF DRUG TREATMENT CTR, WOOD VET'S ADMIN CTR, 77- *Concurrent Pos:* Chief clin pharmacol serv, Wood Vet Admin Hosp, 63-, dir drug abuse treatment & rehab prog, 71-; consult physician, Milwaukee County Gen Hosp, 64-; attend physician, Milwaukee County Ment Health Ctr, 65- *Mem:* Am Soc Pharmacol & Exp Therapeut; Fedn Am Socs Exp Biol; Radiation Res Soc; Am Soc Clin Pharmacol & Therapeut. *Res:* Clinical pharmacology; radiation biology. *Mailing Add:* Wood Vet Admin Ctr 5000 W Nat Ave Milwaukee WI 53193

WANG, RICHARD J, b Chungking, China, Oct 23, 41; US citizen; m 66; c 3. CELL BIOLOGY, GENETICS. *Educ:* Harvard Univ, BA, 64; Univ Colo, PhD(biophys), 68. *Prof Exp:* Fel cell biol, NY Univ, 68-70; res assoc biol, Mass Inst Technol, 70-71; asst prof, 71-76, ASSOC PROF BIOL, UNIV MO, COLUMBIA, 76- *Concurrent Pos:* NIH res career develop award, 72-77; biochem consult, Cancer Res Ctr, Columbia, Mo, 73-; res investr, Dalton Res Ctr, Univ Mo, Columbia, 74- *Mem:* Am Soc Cell Biol; Tissue Cult Asn; AAAS. *Res:* Biochemical genetics of human and mammalian cells in culture; effect of near-ultraviolet and visible light on human cells. *Mailing Add:* Dalton Res Ctr Univ of Mo Columbia MO 65211

WANG, RICHARD JINCHI, b Tainan, Formosa, Apr 24, 32; m 63; c 1. ELECTRICAL ENGINEERING. *Educ:* Purdue Univ, BS, 55; Kans State Univ, MS, 58; Univ Kans, PhD(elec eng), 65. *Prof Exp:* Res engr, Indust Condenser Corp, Ill, 55-56; asst prof elec eng, Univ Bridgeport, 60-64; sr res engr, Amoco Prod Co, 65-69, staff res engr, 69-80; PRES, PAC HOUSE, INC, 80- *Concurrent Pos:* Adj assoc prof, Univ Tulsa, 71- *Mem:* Inst Elec & Electronics Engrs; Soc Explor Geophys; NY Acad Sci. *Res:* Research and development in signal processing of seismic data. *Mailing Add:* Pac House Inc PO Box 1261 Tulsa OK 74101

WANG, ROBERT T, b Chung King, China, Aug 3, 41; US citizen; m 68; c 2. INORGANIC CHEMISTRY, PHYSICAL CHEMISTRY. *Educ:* Taiwan Cheng Kung Univ, BS, 62; Johns Hopkins Univ, PhD(chem), 68. *Prof Exp:* Fel inorg chem, Iowa State Univ, 68-70; asst prof, 70-76, ASSOC PROF CHEM, SALEM STATE COL, 76- *Concurrent Pos:* Consult, US Summit Corp, New York, NY, 72- *Mem:* Am Chem Soc. *Res:* The studies of kinetics and mechanisms of inorganic transition metal complexes reactions; synthesis of bioinorganic compounds. *Mailing Add:* Dept of Chem Salem State Col Salem MA 01970

WANG, RU-TSANG, b Changhua, China, Sept 13, 28; US citizen; m 55; c 2. PHYSICS OF LIGHT SCATTERING, MICROWAVE ELECTRONICS. *Educ:* Nat Taiwan Univ, BSc, 50; Rensselaer Polytech Inst, PhD(physics), 68. *Prof Exp:* Res asst physics, Rensselaer Polytech Inst, 68-70; res assoc, Dudley Observ, 70-76; res assoc physics, Space Astron Lab, State Univ NY Albany, 77-81; ASSOC RES SCIENTIST, SPACE ASTRON LAB, UNIV FLA, GAINESVILLE, 81- *Mem:* Sigma Xi; Optical Soc Am. *Res:* Scattering of light and other electromagnetic radiations; associated mivrowave techniques. *Mailing Add:* 1810 NW 6th St Univ Fla Gainesville FL 32601

WANG, SAN-PIN, b Taiwan, Nov 7, 20; m 46; c 5. MEDICAL MICROBIOLOGY. *Educ:* Keio Univ, Japan, MD, 44; Univ Mich, MPH, 52. *Hon Degrees:* Dr Med Sci, Keio Univ, Japan, 59. *Prof Exp:* Asst bact, Sch Med, Keio Univ, Japan, 44-46; chief dept bact, Taiwan Prov Hyg Lab, 46-51; chief dept virol, Taiwan Serum Vaccine Lab, 52-58; med officer virus immunol, US Naval Med Res Unit, 58-64; vis assoc prof prev med, Sch Med, 64-66, assoc prof, 66-70, PROF PATHOBIOL, SCH PUB HEALTH & COMMUNITY MED, UNIV WASH, 70- *Res:* Biological products, rabies and smallpox vaccines; research on tropical diseases, rabies, influenza, encephalitis and trachoma. *Mailing Add:* Dept of Pathobiol SC-38 Univ of Wash Seattle WA 98195

WANG, SHAO-FU, b Dairen, China, Aug 26, 22; m 44; c 3. THEORETICAL PHYSICS, CONDENSED MATTER PHYSICS. *Educ:* Nagoya Univ, PhD(physics), 64. *Prof Exp:* Lectr physics, Ching Kung Univ, Taiwan, 48-52, assoc prof, 52-56; from assoc prof to prof, Tunghai Univ, Taiwan, 56-65; assoc prof, 65-68, PROF PHYSICS, UNIV WATERLOO, 68- *Concurrent Pos:* Res assoc, Univ Ill, 61-63, vis assoc prof, 67. *Mem:* Am Phys Soc; Can Asn Physicists. *Res:* Theoretical study of electronic processes in condensed matter. *Mailing Add:* Dept Physics Univ Waterloo Waterloo ON N2L 3G1 Can

WANG, SHIEN TSUN, b Changsha, China, Aug 24, 38; m 69; c 2. STRUCTURAL ENGINEERING, ENGINEERING MECHANICS. *Educ:* Nat Taiwan Univ, BS, 60; Mich State Univ, MS, 64; Cornell Univ, PhD(struct eng), 69. *Prof Exp:* Civil eng, Nat Taiwan Univ, 61-62 & Mich State Univ, 62-64; struct engr, Cornell Univ, 64-68, res assoc & instr, 68-69; asst prof, 69-75, ASSOC PROF CIVIL ENG, UNIV KY, 75- *Concurrent Pos:* Fac res & teaching fels, Univ Ky, 70-72; NSF fel, Syracuse Univ, 71; various consulting work. *Mem:* Am Soc Civil Engrs; Structural Stability Res Coun; Am Soc Eng Educ. *Res:* Structural stability and dynamics; thin-walled structures; computerized structural analysis and design; experimental stress analysis; numerical methods; nonlinear structural analysis; finite element methods; metal structures. *Mailing Add:* Dept of Civil Eng Univ of Ky Lexington KY 40506

WANG, SHIH YI, b Peiping, China, June 15, 23; nat US; m 47; c 2. ORGANIC CHEMISTRY. *Educ:* Nat Peking Univ, China, BS, 44; Univ Wash, PhD(org chem), 52. *Prof Exp:* Fel org chem, Boston Univ, 52-54; res fel, Harvard Univ, 54-55; res assoc, Sch Med, Tufts Univ, 55-56, asst prof physiol, 56-61; from asst prof to assoc prof biochem, 61-66, PROF BIOCHEM, JOHNS HOPKINS UNIV, 66- *Concurrent Pos:* Dir div radiation chem, Johns Hopkins Univ, 76-78, actg head prog environ chem, Dept Environ Health Sci, 77- *Mem:* AAAS; Am Chem Soc; Royal Soc Chem. *Res:* Photochemistry of nucleic acids and related compounds; chemistry of heterocyclic nitrogen containing compounds; synthesis and structure of natural products; polynuclear aromatic compounds. *Mailing Add:* Sch Hyg & Pub Health Johns Hopkins Univ 3100 Wyman Park Dr Bldg 6 Baltimore MD 21211

WANG, SHIH-CHI, b Taiwan, June 12, 46; m 73; c 1. WOOD SCIENCE, WOOD TECHNOLOGY. *Educ:* Chung-Hsing Univ, BSF, 68; Univ Fla, MSF, 72; Mich State Univ, PhD(bot plant path & forestry), 77. *Prof Exp:* Asst wood sci, Univ Fla, 71-72, bot, Mich State Univ, 73-77; fel, 78-79, ASST RES SCIENTIST FORESTRY, UNIV FLA, 79- *Mem:* Forest Prod Res Soc; Soc Econ Bot. *Res:* Utilization of plant biomass for energy and chemicals; tree extractives and their biological significance; wood deterioration and forest products protection. *Mailing Add:* 5929 NW 32nd St Gainesville FL 32606

WANG, SHIOW YING, b Tainan, Taiwan, Sept 21, 40; US citizen; m 68; c 2. PLANT PHYSIOLOGY, HORTICULTURE. *Educ:* Nat Taiwan Univ, BS, 64; Univ Calif, Davis, MS, 66; Ore State Univ, PhD(plant physiol), 69. *Prof Exp:* Res assoc fruits, Ore State Univ, 69-72; PLANT PHYSIOLOGIST, USDA, 77- *Mem:* Am Soc Plant Physiologists. *Res:* Postharvest physiology and biochemistry of fruits, vegetables and flowers; ethylene and other plant hormones in growth, development, maturation, senescence and aging of plants; respiratory metabolism in plants. *Mailing Add:* Bldg 002 USDA Agr Res Ctr-West Beltsville MD 20705

WANG, SHOU-LING, b Shanghai, China, Oct 17, 24; nat US; div; c 3. STRUCTURAL MECHANICS. *Educ:* St John's Univ, China, BS, 46; Yale Univ, ME, 48; Univ Ill, PhD(theoret & appl mech), 52. *Prof Exp:* Designer, D B Steinman, 52-55; asst prof civil eng, Clarkson Tech Inst, 55-57; assoc prof, Univ Mo, 57-60; vis assoc prof eng mech, NC State Univ, 60-67; struct engr, 67-78, SUPVRY STRUCT ENGR, DAVID TAYLOR NAVAL SHIP RES & DEVELOP CTR, 78- *Concurrent Pos:* Lectr weapon effects and ship protection, Mass Inst Technol, 76- *Mem:* Am Soc Civil Engrs; Am Acad Mech. *Res:* Structural dynamics; weapon effects; protective design. *Mailing Add:* 9132 Kirkdale Rd Bethesda MD 20817

WANG, SHU LUNG, b Szechwan, China, May 2, 25; m 47; c 2. COMPUTER APPLICATIONS. *Educ:* Wash Univ, St Louis, BS, 49, MS, 50, DSc(chem eng), 53. *Prof Exp:* From asst prof to assoc prof chem eng, Kans State Univ, 52-57; sect head eng systs develop & dir comput lab, Linde Div, 57-66, mgr, Niagara Frontier Regional Comput Ctr, 66-69, MGR COMPUT APPLNS, SCI, UNION CARBIDE CORP, 69- *Mem:* Am Inst Chem Eng; Am Chem Soc; Am Soc Eng Educ; Asn Comput Mach. *Res:* Information system development and data processing management; process control systems engineering; adsorption and cryogenic gas separation processes; vapor-liquid equilibrium data. *Mailing Add:* Tarrytown Tech Ctr Union Carbide Corp Tarrytown NY 10591

WANG, SHU-YI, b Chungking, China, Sept 21, 36; m 66; c 2. MECHANICAL ENGINEERING, AEROSPACE SCIENCES. *Educ:* Cheng Kung Univ, Taiwan, BSc, 59; Univ Rochester, MSc, 65, PhD(mech & aerospace sci), 68. *Prof Exp:* Design engr, Yue Loong Motor Co Ltd, 60-61; asst mech, Cheng Kung Univ, 61-63; asst fluid mech, Univ Rochester, 63-64, asst aerospace sci, 64-67; asst prof, 67-72, assoc prof, 72-81, PROF ENG, UNIV MISS, 81- *Concurrent Pos:* Res assoc, Stanford Univ, 68; vis scientist, Johnson Space Ctr, NASA, 73-74 & Aero Propulsion Lab, US Air Force, 75; gen chmn & organizer, 3rd Int Conf on Finite Elements in Water Resources, Univ Miss, 80. *Honors & Awards:* Ralph R Teetor Award, Soc Automotive Engrs, 75. *Mem:* Assoc fel Am Inst Aeronaut & Astronaut; Am Soc Civil Engrs; Am Soc Eng Educ; Am Soc Mech Engrs; Soc Natural Philos. *Res:* Fluid mechanics including hypersonic flow theory, boundary layer theory, hydrodynamic stability, magnetohydrodynamics, plasma physics and physics of fluids; computer simulation of fluid flows. *Mailing Add:* Sch of Eng Univ of Miss University MS 38677

WANG, SHYH, b China, June 15, 25. ELECTRONICS, PHYSICS. *Educ:* Chiao Tung Univ, BS, 45; Harvard Univ, MA, 49, PhD(appl physics), 51. *Prof Exp:* Res fel appl physics, Harvard Univ, 51-53; eng specialist, Semiconductor Div, Sylvania Elec Prod Co, 53-58; assoc prof elec eng, 58-64, PROF ELEC ENG & COMPUT SCI, UNIV CALIF, BERKELEY, 64- *Mem:* Am Phys Soc; fel Inst Elec & Electronics Engrs; Optical Soc Am. *Res:* Solid state physics and quantum electronics; semiconducting devices and materials; magnetic properties of solids at microwave frequencies. *Mailing Add:* Dept of Elec Eng & Comput Sci Univ of Calif Berkeley CA 94720

WANG, SOO RAY, b Tainan, Taiwan, Aug 2, 40; m 69; c 3. ALLERGY, IMMUNOLOGY. *Educ:* Kaohsiung Med Col, Taiwan, MD, 67; Univ Ill Med Ctr, PhD(immunol), 73. *Prof Exp:* Intern, Shadyside Hosp, Pittsburgh, 68-69; jr residency, Hahnemann Med Col Hosp, Philadelphia, 73-74; residency, Atlantic City Hosp, NJ, 74-75; clin fel, Hosp Univ Pa, 75-77, res fel, 77-78; DIR DIV ALLERGY & IMMUNOL, DEPT INTERNAL MED, CHANG GUNG MEM HOSP, TAIWAN, 78-; PROF MED & MICROBIOL, KAOHSIUNG MED COL, TAIWAN, 80- *Mem:* Sigma Xi; Am Acad Allergy; Am Acad Allergist. *Res:* Histamine and corticosteroid suppression on human lymphocyte proliferation; slow-reacting substance of anaphylaxis in asthmatics. *Mailing Add:* Chang Gung Mem Hosp Taipei Taiwan

WANG, SU-SUN, biochemistry, see previous edition

WANG, TAITZER, b Taiwan, Feb 2, 39; m 68; c 1. BIOCHEMISTRY. *Educ:* Nat Univ Taiwan, BS, 61; Rice Univ, PhD(org chem), 67. *Prof Exp:* Res asst prof cell biophysics, Baylor Col Med, 75-77; ASST PROF PHARMACOL & CELL BIOPHYSICS, COL MED, UNIV CINCINNATI, 77- *Concurrent Pos:* Nat Inst Arthritis & Metab Dis res fel org chem, Fla State Univ, 67-69; US Dept Defense res fel inorg chem, Univ Ky, 69-71; Welch fel biochem, Baylor Col Med, 71-73; Welch fel, Rice Univ, 73-74; NIH spec res fel cell biophys, Baylor Col Med, 74-75. *Mem:* Am Chem Soc; AAAS; NY Acad Sci. *Res:* Enzyme kinetics and synthetic chemistry; cell biophysics. *Mailing Add:* Dept of Pharmacol & Cell Biophys Univ of Cincinnati Col of Med Cincinnati OH 45267

WANG, THEODORE JOSEPH, b Chicago, Ill, Dec 8, 06; m 36; c 2. PHYSICS. *Educ:* Univ Ill, BS, 32, PhD(physics), 39. *Prof Exp:* Asst physics, Univ Ill, 35-39; physicist, Oakes Prod Corp, Ill, 39-40; fel, Univ Minn, 41; from instr to asst prof elec eng, Ohio State Univ, 42-48; physicist, Nat Bur Standards, 48-49; biophysicist, Nat Cancer Inst, 49-50; physicist, George Washington Univ, 50-52; asst prof physics, Univ Mass, 52-55; prof & head dept, SDak Sch Mines & Technol, 55-56; prof, Howard Univ, 56-59; analyst, Opers Res Off, Res Anal Corp, 59-62; prin scientist, Booz, Allen Appl Res, 62-66; DIR, INST CREATIVE STUDIES, 67- *Concurrent Pos:* Consult physicist, 50-52; analyst, Opers Res Off, Johns Hopkins Univ, 57; analyst, Res Anal Corp, 57-58; prof, Howard Univ, 60-64, lectr, 64- *Res:* Radiation physics. *Mailing Add:* Inst Creative Studies 4700 Essex Ave Chevy Chase MD 20015

WANG, THOMAS NIE-CHIN, b Shanghai, China, Feb 17, 38; m 67; c 2. ELECTRICAL ENGINEERING, APPLIED MATHEMATICS. *Educ:* Cheng Kung Univ, Taiwan, BSEE, 60; Univ NMex, MSEE, 64; Stanford Univ, PhD(elec eng), 70. *Prof Exp:* RES ENGR, RADIO PHYSICS LAB, STANFORD RES INST, 67- *Concurrent Pos:* Vis prof, Cheng Kung Univ, Taiwan, 71-72; mem US nat comt, Comn 6, Int Union Radio Sci, Washington, DC, 72. *Mem:* Inst Elec & Electronics Engrs; Int Union Radio Sci. *Res:* Radiation and waves in scattering and diffraction of electromagnetic waves; propagation in magnetosphere and ionosphere. *Mailing Add:* 1294 Bedford Ct Sunnyvale CA 94086

WANG, TING-I, b Chekiang, China, Jan 11, 44; m 71; c 1. APPLIED PHYSICS, ATMOSPHERIC REMOTE SENSING. *Educ:* Nat Taiwan Univ, BA, 66; Dartmouth Col, MA, 70, PhD(radiophys), 73. *Prof Exp:* Vis fel & res assoc optical remote sensing, Coop Inst Res Environ Sci, Univ Colo, 73-75; PHYSICIST OPTICAL REMOTE SENSING, WAVE PROPAGATION LAB, NAT OCEANIC & ATMOSPHERIC ADMIN, 75- *Mem:* Fel Optical Soc Am; Am Inst Physics; Am Geophys Union; Sigma Xi. *Res:* The use of optical effects to develop novel techniques of remote sensors to probe the atmosphere, including turbulence, wind and precipitation. *Mailing Add:* Optical Propagation R45-1 Nat Oceanic & Atmospheric Admin Boulder CO 80303

WANG, TSUEY TANG, b Tainan, Taiwan, Nov 12, 32; US citizen; m 65; c 3. MECHANICS. *Educ:* Cheng Kung Univ, Taiwan, BSc, 55; Brown Univ, MSc, 61, PhD(appl mech), 65. *Prof Exp:* Res group leader appl mech, Polytech Inst Brooklyn, 65-66, asst prof, 66-67; MEM TECH STAFF, BELL TEL LABS, 67- *Mem:* Am Phys Soc; Soc Rheol; Am Acad Mech; NY Acad Sci. *Res:* Mechanical behavior of polymers and polymer composites; structures and properties; piezoelectricity in polymers. *Mailing Add:* Bell Tel Labs 600 Mountain Ave Murray Hill NJ 07974

WANG, TUNG YUE, b Peking, China, Oct 27, 21; US citizen; m 48. BIOCHEMISTRY. *Educ:* Nat CheKiang Univ, BSc, 42; Univ Mo, MA, 49, PhD(biochem), 51. *Prof Exp:* Res fel, Jewish Hosp, St Louis, 51-53; res assoc, Washington Univ, St Louis, 53-57, asst prof, 57-59, assoc prof, 59-63; PROF, DEPT BIOL SCI, STATE UNIV NY, BUFFALO, 63- *Mem:* Am Soc Biol Chemists; Am Soc Cell Biol; Am Chem Soc; AAAS. *Res:* Mechanism of androgen action. *Mailing Add:* Dept Biol Sci State Univ NY Buffalo Amherst NY 14260

WANG, VICTOR KAI-KUO, b Quei-Chow, China, Mar 18, 44; m 69; c 2. PHYSICAL CHEMISTRY, INDUSTRIAL CHEMISTRY. *Educ:* Chung Yuan Col Sci & Eng, Taiwan, BS, 65; State Univ NY Binghamton, MS, 68; Univ Minn, PhD(phys chem), 73. *Prof Exp:* Res asst phys chem, State Univ NY Binghamton, 66-68; teaching assoc, Univ Minn, 68-73; res chemist, 73-80, SR RES CHEMIST, E I DU PONT DE NEMOURS & CO, INC, 81- *Mem:* Am Chem Soc. *Res:* Process research, kinetics and catalysis. *Mailing Add:* Photo Prod Dept E I du Pont de Nemours & Co Inc Cheese-Quake Rd Parlin NJ 08859

WANG, VIRGINIA LI, b Canton, China, Apr 2, 33; US citizen; c 3. PUBLIC HEALTH. *Educ:* NY Univ, MA, 56; Univ NC, MPH, 65, PhD, 68. *Prof Exp:* Res dietitian, Montefiore Hosp, 56; instr nutrit, Univ NC, 62-64; health educ specialist, Univ Md, 68-74; assoc prof, 74-82, PROF PUB HEALTH EDUC, JOHNS HOPKINS UNIV, 82- *Concurrent Pos:* Temp consult, Pan Am Health Orgn, 74; consult, WHO, UN, 74, 76 & 82, Nat Cancer Inst, NIH, Dept Health, Educ & Welfare, 74-77. *Mem:* Am Dietetic Asn; Am Pub Health Asn; Soc Pub Health Educ. *Res:* Evaluation of nutrition and health education programs in developed and developing societies; health care delivery and health education in the Peoples Republic of China; planning, development and evaluation of continuing education for the health professions; smoking cessation research; rural development. *Mailing Add:* Sch Hyg & Pub Health Johns Hopkins Univ Baltimore MD 21205

WANG, WAYNE LUNG, b I-Lan City, Taiwan, Jan 24, 44; US citizen; m 67; c 2. NUCLEAR PHYSICS, NUCLEAR ENGINEERING. *Educ:* Taipei Inst Technol, Taiwan, dipl mech eng, 64; Mass Inst Technol, PhD(nuclear eng), 71. *Prof Exp:* Fel physics, Carnegie-Mellon Univ, 71-73; res physicist nuclear physics, Lawrence Berkeley Lab, 73-75; asst engr nuclear eng, 75-78, NUCLEAR ENGR, ARGONNE NAT LAB, 78- *Mem:* Am Nuclear Soc; Am Phys Soc; Sigma Xi. *Res:* Nuclear structure and reactions, photonuclear reactions; nuclear reactor safety studies; nuclear fuel pin performance analysis, transient behavior and failure modeling. *Mailing Add:* 814 Albany Lane Darien IL 60559

WANG, WEI-YEH, b Sian, China, Oct 10, 44; m 69; c 2. BIOCHEMICAL GENETICS, PLANT PHYSIOLOGY. *Educ:* Nat Taiwan Univ, BS, 66; Univ Mo, Columbia, PhD(genetics), 72. *Prof Exp:* Fel genetics, Duke Univ, 72-75; asst prof, 75-80, ASSOC PROF BOT, UNIV IOWA, 80- *Concurrent Pos:* Vis prof, Carlsberg Lab, Copenhagen, 80-81. *Mem:* Genetics Soc Am; Am Soc Cell Biol; Am Soc Plant Physiologists; Sigma Xi. *Res:* Genetic regulation of chlorophyll and heme biosynthesis. *Mailing Add:* Dept of Bot Univ of Iowa Iowa City IA 52242

WANG, WUN-CHENG, b Taichung, China, Mar 10, 36; m 62; c 3. AQUATIC TOXICOLOGY. *Educ:* Nat Taiwan Univ, BS, 58, MS, 61; Univ Wis-Madison, PhD(water chem), 68. *Prof Exp:* Asst prof scientist, 67-70, assoc prof scientist, 70-80, PROF SCIENTIST, WATER QUAL SECT, ILL STATE WATER SURV, 81- *Mem:* Int Asn Water Pollution Res; Am Soc Testing & Mat; Am Fisheries Soc. *Res:* Water qualtiy; eutrophication; algal growth; suspended solid, natural particulate matter. *Mailing Add:* Ill State Water Surv PO Box 717 Peoria IL 61601

WANG, YANG, b Tangshan, China, May 12, 23; US citizen; m 66; c 4. CARDIOLOGY. *Educ:* Nat Med Col Shanghai, MB; Harvard Univ, MD, 52; Am Bd Internal Med, dipl, Am Bd Cardiovasc Dis, dipl. *Prof Exp:* Intern & resident med, Mass Gen Hosp, 52-54 & 56-57; from instr to assoc prof, 59-64,

PROF MED, MED SCH, UNIV MINN, MINNEAPOLIS, 74-, DIR CARDIAC CATHETERIZATION LABS & DIR CARDIAC CLINS, UNIV HOSPS, 60- *Concurrent Pos:* P D White fel cardiol, Mass Gen Hosp, Boston, 57-58; fel physiol, Mayo Grad Sch Med, Univ Minn, 58-59; consult, Vet Admin Hosp, Minneapolis, 67; fel coun clin cardiol & circulation, Am Heart Asn; attend physician, Univ Minn Hosps, Minneapolis, 59-, dir, Cardiac Clin, 80- *Mem:* Fel AAAS; Am Fedn Clin Res; fel Am Col Physicians; Soc Exp Biol & Med; Asn Univ Cardiol. *Res:* Cardiovascular and exercise physiology; cardiac catheterization in humans. *Mailing Add:* Dept of Med Univ of Minn Hosps Minneapolis MN 55455

WANG, YA-YEN LEE, b Peking, China, Mar 1, 30; US citizen; m 56; c 3. MATHEMATICS, COMPUTER SCIENCE. *Educ:* Villa Maria Col, BS, 56; Univ Fla, MS, 58; Univ Idaho, PhD(math), 65. *Prof Exp:* Instr math, 60-62, asst prof, 65-72, acting dir comput ctr, 67, ASSOC PROF MATH, UNIV IDAHO, 72- *Mem:* Am Math Soc; Math Asn Am; Asn Comput Mach; Sigma Xi; Am Asn Univ Prof. *Res:* Differential geometry and equations; calculus of variations; numerical analysis; computer languages. *Mailing Add:* Dept of Math Univ of Idaho Moscow ID 83843

WANG, YEN, b Dairen, China, Oct 21, 28; m 62. RADIOLOGY, NUCLEAR MEDICINE. *Educ:* Nat Taiwan Univ, MD, 53; Univ Pa, DSc(med), 62. *Prof Exp:* Asst prof, 63-65, assoc prof, 65-75, CLIN PROF RADIOL, UNIV PITTSBURGH, 75-; DIR RADIOL, HOMESTEAD HOSP, 66-; DIR NUCLEAR MED, MAGEE-WOMENS HOSP, PITTSBURGH, 67- *Concurrent Pos:* Res fel, Picker Found Acad Sci, 61-63; vis scientist, Protein Found, 62-64; ed, Critical Rev Clin Radiol & Nuclear Med. *Mem:* AMA; Soc Nuclear Med; Am Roentgen Ray Soc; Am Physiol Soc; Am Radium Soc; Radiol Soc NAm. *Res:* Physiology; protein chemistry. *Mailing Add:* South Hill Health Syst Homestead PA 15120

WANG, YEU-MING ALEXANDER, b Chungking, China, May 2, 42; m 73. BIOCHEMISTRY, HEMATOLOGY. *Educ:* Taiwan Chung-Hsing Univ, BS, 65; Vanderbilt Univ, PhD(biochem), 71. *Prof Exp:* Res asst biochem, Med Sch, Vanderbilt Univ, 66-71, res assoc, 71-73, instr pediat & hemat, 73; ASST PROF PEDIAT & ASST BIOCHEMIST, M D ANDERSON HOSP & TUMOR INST, UNIV TEX SYST CANCER CTR, 73- *Mem:* Am Assoc Cancer Res; AAAS. *Res:* Biochemistry of erythrocytes metabolism and function; biochemistry and pharmacology of cancer drugs. *Mailing Add:* M D Anderson Hosp & Tumor Inst 6723 Bertner Ave Houston TX 77030

WANG, YU, b Shee-ann, China, May 5, 43; Can & Chinese citizen. CRYSTALLOGRAPHY, INORGANIC CHEMISTRY. *Educ:* Nat Taiwan Univ, BSc, 66; Univ Ill, MSc, 70, PhD(chem), 73. *Prof Exp:* Fel, Dept Chem, State Univ NY, Buffalo, 73-74; fel, Nat Res Coun, 74-75, res assoc crystallog & chem, Chem Div, 75-79; PROF, DEPT CHEM, NAT TAIWAN UNIV, 79- *Mem:* Am Crystallog Asn. *Res:* Structural crystallographic work on metal, organometallic and organic compounds; bonding density studies of transition metal complexes; computerized data bank. *Mailing Add:* Dept Chem Nat Taiwan Univ Taipei 107 Taiwan

WANG, YUAN REAU, computer science, electrical engineering, see previous edition

WANG, YUNG-LI, b Canton, China, Jan 8, 37; m 63; c 1. SOLID STATE PHYSICS. *Educ:* Nat Taiwan Univ, BS, 59; Nat Tsing Hua Univ, Taiwan, MS, 61; Univ Pa, PhD(physics), 66. *Prof Exp:* Res assoc physics, Univ Pa, 66-67 & Univ Pittsburgh, 67-68; asst prof, 68-72, assoc prof, 72-77, PROF PHYSICS, FLA STATE UNIV, 77- *Mem:* Am Phys Soc. *Res:* Many body theory of spin systems, magnetic phase transitions; crystal-field effects and impurities in magnetic systems. *Mailing Add:* Dept of Physics Fla State Univ Tallahassee FL 32306

WANGAARD, FREDERICK FIELD, b Minneapolis, Minn, Jan 3, 11; m 36; c 3. FOREST PRODUCTS. *Educ:* Univ Minn, BS, 33; State Univ NY, MS, 35, PhD(wood technol), 39. *Hon Degrees:* MA, Yale Univ, 52. *Prof Exp:* Instr forestry, Univ Wash, 36-39, asst prof wood technol, 39-42; technologist, Forest Prod Lab, US Forest Serv, 42-45; from asst prof to prof forest prod, Yale Univ, 45-67; head dept forest & wood sci, Colo State Univ, 68-76; CONSULT, 76- *Concurrent Pos:* Adv, Food & Agr Orgn, Philippines, 57; Fulbright res scholar, Norway, 58. *Mem:* Forest Prod Res Soc (pres, 75); Soc Am Foresters; Soc Wood Sci & Technol (pres, 64); Int Acad Wood Sci. *Res:* Thermal conductivity of wood; properties of wood in relation to growth; properties of tropical woods; plywood and laminated wood; technology of wood fibers; wood structure and properties. *Mailing Add:* 1609 Hillside Dr Ft Collins CO 80524

WANGBERG, JAMES KEITH, b Oakland, Calif, Sept 6, 46. ENTOMOLOGY. *Educ:* Humboldt State Col, Calif, BA, 69; Calif State Univ, Humboldt, MA, 73; Univ Idaho, PhD(entom), 76. *Prof Exp:* Vis instr, 75-76, asst prof, 76-81, ASSOC PROF ENTOM, TEX TECH UNIV, 81- *Concurrent Pos:* Co-prin investr, Smithsonian Inst res grant, 78- *Mem:* AAAS; Entom Soc Am; Soc Range Mgt. *Res:* Rangeland entomology with emphasis on insects affecting native shrubs; gall insect biology. *Mailing Add:* Dept of Entom Tex Tech Univ Lubbock TX 79409

WANGEMANN, ROBERT THEODORE, b Rhinelander, Wis, Apr 27, 33; m 54; c 2. BIOPHYSICS. *Educ:* Univ Wis-Madison, BS, 55; Univ Rochester, MS, 64; Med Col Va, PhD(biophys), 74. *Prof Exp:* Pharmacist, Northgate Drugs & Southside Drugs, 55-57; med supply officer, 57-62, health physicist, 64-67, instr nuclear sci, 67-70, chief, Laser-Microwave Div, 73-77, dir radiation & environ sci, 77-78, consult, Off Surgeon Gen, 78-81, COMDR, ENVIRON HYG AGENCY, US ARMY, 81- *Concurrent Pos:* Mem C95 comt, Am Nat Standards Inst, 73- *Mem:* AAAS; Bioelectromagnetics Soc; Health Physics Soc; Am Conf Govt Indust Hygienists; Am Asn Physicists in Med. *Res:* Biological effects of electromagnetic radiation; interactions of microwave and radio frequency energy at the biomolecular level and the photochemical aspects of vision and optical radiation effects. *Mailing Add:* Environ Hyg Agency US Army Aberdeen Proving Ground MD 21010

WANGENSTEEN, OVE DOUGLAS, b St Paul, Minn, Mar 15, 42; m 65; c 2. RESPIRATORY PHYSIOLOGY, MICROVASCULAR EXCHANGE. *Educ:* Univ Minn, Minneapolis, BS, 64, PhD(physiol), 68. *Prof Exp:* Res assoc physiol, Sch Med & Dent, State Univ NY, Buffalo, 68-70; asst prof, 70-76, ASSOC PROF PHYSIOL, MED SCH, UNIV MINN, MINNEAPOLIS, 76- *Mem:* Am Physiol Soc. *Res:* Respiratory and cardiovascular physiology; transcapillary exchange; lung fluid balance. *Mailing Add:* Dept Physiol 6-255 Millard Hall Univ Minn 435 Delaware St SE Minneapolis MN 55455

WANGENSTEEN, OWEN H(ARDING), surgery, deceased

WANGENSTEEN, STEPHEN LIGHTNER, b Minneapolis, Minn, Aug 30, 33; m 56; c 4. SURGERY. *Educ:* Univ Minn, BA, 54, BS, 55; Harvard Univ, MD, 58. *Prof Exp:* Instr surg, Columbia-Presby Med Ctr, 64-65; from asst prof to prof surg, Univ Va, 67-76; PROF & HEAD DEPT SURG, UNIV ARIZ, 76- *Concurrent Pos:* Vascular fel, Columbia-Presby Med Ctr, 58-59, USPHS fel, 60-63. *Mem:* Asn Acad Surg (vpres, 67-68); Soc Univ Surg; Am Surg Asn. *Res:* Gastrointestinal pathophysiology; circulatory shock; vascular surgery. *Mailing Add:* Dept of Surg Univ of Ariz Health Sci Ctr Tucson AZ 85724

WANGERSKY, PETER JOHN, b Woonsocket, RI, Aug 26, 27; m 59. OCEANOGRAPHY. *Educ:* Brown Univ, ScB, 49; Yale Univ, PhD(zool), 58. *Prof Exp:* Marine chem technician, Scripps Inst, Univ Calif, 49-50; chemist, Chem Corps, US Dept Army, 50-51; chem oceanogr, US Fish & Wildlife Serv, 51-54; res asst prof marine sci, Marine Lab, Univ Miami, 58-61; res assoc, Bingham Oceanog Lab, Yale Univ, 61-65; assoc prof chem, 65-68, chmn dept oceanog, 77-80, PROF OCEANOG, DALHOUSIE UNIV, 68- *Concurrent Pos:* Guggenheim fel, John Simon Guggenheim Found, 71-72; ed in chief, Marine Chem, 74- *Mem:* AAAS; Am Soc Limnog & Oceanog; Am Chem Soc; Ecol Soc Am; Am Mat Soc. *Res:* Mechanisms of marine sedimentation; chemical oceanography; organic metabolites in sea water; population dynamics. *Mailing Add:* Dept of Oceanog Dalhousie Univ Halifax NS B3H 4J1 Can

WANG-IVERSON, PATSY, b Shanghai, China, Jan 6, 47; m 76; c 1. CELL BIOLOGY, LIPID BIOCHEMISTRY. *Educ:* Mt Holyoke Col, BA, 68; Bowman Gray Sch Med, 70, PhD(biochem), 75. *Prof Exp:* Res asst enzyme, Burroughs Wellcome & Co, 70-71; fel bact & immunol, Sch Med, Univ NC, 75-77, fel cellular physiol & immunol, Rockefeller Univ, 77-79; ASST PROF BIOCHEM, MT SINAI SCH MED, 79- *Concurrent Pos:* Mem, Coun Arteriosclerosis. *Mem:* Sigma Xi; NY Acad Sci. *Res:* Human monocyte; macrophage function, specifically its contribution to lipoprotein metabolism. *Mailing Add:* Mt Sinai Sch Med Annenberg 24-50 1 Gustave Levy Pl New York NY 10029

WANGLER, THOMAS P, b Bay City, Mich, Aug 2, 37. PHYSICS. *Educ:* Mich State Univ, BS, 58; Univ Wis, PhD(physics), 64. *Prof Exp:* Res assoc physics, Univ Wis, 64-65 & Brookhaven Nat Lab, 65-66; asst physicist, Argonne Nat Lab, 66-80; MEM STAFF, LOS ALAMOS NAT LAB, 80- *Mem:* Am Phys Soc. *Res:* Experimental high energy physics; cosmic rays; environmental science; nuclear physics. *Mailing Add:* Los Alamos Nat Lab AT-1 MS-817 PO Box 1663 Los Alamos NM 87545

WANGSNESS, PAUL JEROME, b Madison, Wis, Mar 27, 44; m 67; c 2. ANIMAL NUTRITION. *Educ:* Univ Wis-Madison, BS, 66; Iowa State Univ, PhD(nutrit & physiol), 71. *Prof Exp:* NDEA fel nutrit, Iowa State Univ, 66-69, NSF fel, 69-71; asst prof, 72-75, assoc prof, 75-81, PROF NUTRIT & HEAD, DEPT DAIRY & ANIMAL SCI, PA STATE UNIV, 81- *Mem:* Am Dairy Sci Asn; Am Soc Animal Sci; Am Inst Nutrit. *Res:* Regulatory mechanisms involved in the control of food intake and the regulation of energy balance in lean and obese animals. *Mailing Add:* 303 Animal Indust Bldg Pa State Univ University Park PA 16802

WANGSNESS, ROALD KLINKENBERG, b Sleepy Eye, Minn, July 24, 22; m 44; c 2. PHYSICS. *Educ:* Univ Minn, BA, 44; Stanford Univ, PhD(physics), 50. *Prof Exp:* Asst physics, Univ Minn, 42-44; jr scientist, Los Alamos Sci Lab, 44-45; asst physics, Univ Minn, 45-46; asst physics, Stanford Univ, 46-48; asst prof, Univ Md, 50-51, prof, 53-59; PROF PHYSICS, UNIV ARIZ, 59- *Concurrent Pos:* Physicist, Naval Ord Lab, Md, 51-59. *Mem:* Fel AAAS; fel Am Phys Soc; Sigma Xi; Am Asn Physics Teachers. *Res:* Nuclear induction; nuclear moments; ferrimagnetic resonance; anti-ferromagnetism; atomic spectra. *Mailing Add:* Dept of Physics Univ of Ariz Tucson AZ 85721

WANI, JAGANNATH K, b Maharashtra, India, Sept 10, 34; m 59; c 3. STATISTICS. *Educ:* Univ Poona, BSc, 58, Hons, 59, MSc, 60; McGill Univ, PhD(math statist), 67. *Prof Exp:* Lectr math, Col Agr, Dhulia, India, 60-61; res asst statist, Gokhale Inst Econ, Poona, India, 61-62; res asst math statist, McGill Univ, 62-65; asst prof math, Univ Lethbridge, 65-66; from asst prof to assoc prof, St Mary's Univ, NS, 66-69; ASSOC PROF STATIST, UNIV CALGARY, 69- *Concurrent Pos:* Nat Res Coun Can fel, St Mary's Univ & Univ Calgary, 67-72; Can Math Cong fel, McGill Univ, Queen's Univ & Univ Alta, 69-71. *Mem:* Inst Math Statist; Am Statist Asn; Statist Soc Can. *Res:* Distribution theory and statistical inference. *Mailing Add:* Dept Statist Univ Calgary Calgary AB T2N 1N4 Can

WANIEK, RALPH WALTER, b Milan, Italy, June 1, 25; nat US; m 53; c 1. PHYSICS. *Educ:* Univ Vienna, PhD(physics), 50. *Prof Exp:* Res assoc nuclear physics, Inst Radium Res, Univ Vienna, 48-50; asst prof physics & math, Newton Col, 50-56; sr physicist, Cambridge Electron Accelerator, Harvard Univ & Mass Inst Technol, 50-58; dir res, Plasmadyne Corp, 58-60; PRES & DIR RES, ADVAN KINETICS, INC, 60- *Concurrent Pos:* Res fel, Synchrocyclotron Lab, Harvard Univ, 50-55; consult, Transistor Prod, Inc, 52-55 & Allied Res Assocs, 56-57; lectr, Boston Col, 56-58 & Exten, Univ Calif, Los Angeles, 59-67. *Mem:* Am Phys Soc; Am Inst Aeronaut & Astronaut; Inst Elec & Electronics Eng. *Res:* Plasma, laser, space and nuclear physics; solid state; production of very intense magnetic fields; problems of space propulsion. *Mailing Add:* Advan Kinetics Inc 1231 Victoria St Costa Mesa CA 92627

WANIELISTA, MARTIN PAUL, b Taylor, Pa, Dec 7, 41; m 66; c 1. ENVIRONMENTAL ENGINEERING, WATER RESOURCES. *Educ:* Univ Detroit, BS, 64; Manhattan Col, MS, 65; Cornell Univ, PhD(environ eng), 71. *Prof Exp:* From asst prof to assoc prof, 70-76, PROF ENG & GORDON J BARNETT PROF ENVIRON SYSTS & MGT, FLA TECHNOL UNIV, 76-, ACTG CHMN DEPT CIVIL & ENVIRON ENG, 78- *Concurrent Pos:* Dir, Environ Systs Eng Inst, 71-74; NSF grant, 72-73; pres, STE Inc, 73- *Mem:* Am Soc Civil Engrs; Am Soc Eng Educ; Asn Environ Eng Prof; Am Water Works Asn; Am Water Resources Asn. *Res:* Optimization models for water and solid waste systems; lake restoration; mathematical models of surface water systems; atmospheric pollution measurements and control methods. *Mailing Add:* Col Eng Box 25000 Orlando FL 32816

WANKAT, PHILLIP CHARLES, b Oak Park, Ill, July 11, 44; m 80. SEPARATIONS. *Educ:* Purdue Univ, West Lafayette, BS, 66; Princeton Univ, PhD(chem eng), 70. *Prof Exp:* Assoc prof, 74-78, PROF CHEM ENG, PURDUE UNIV, WEST LAFAYETTE, 78- *Concurrent Pos:* NSF eng grants, 72- *Mem:* Am Inst Chem Engrs; Am Chem Soc; Am Soc Eng Educ. *Res:* Separation techniques; cascade theory; parametric pumping and cycling zone adsorption; chromatography; biochemical separations; high gradient magnetic separations. *Mailing Add:* Sch of Chem Eng Purdue Univ West Lafayette IN 47907

WANKE, SIEGHARD ERNST, b Herrenstein, Ger, July 31, 42; Can citizen; m 69. CHEMICAL ENGINEERING. *Educ:* Univ Alta, BSc, 64, MSc, 66; Univ Calif, Davis, PhD(chem eng), 69. *Prof Exp:* Engr, Chemcell Ltd, Alta, 65-66; res engr, Celanese Res Co, 69-70; asst prof, 70-77, ASSOC PROF CHEM ENG, UNIV ALTA, 78- *Mem:* Chem Inst Can; Can Soc Chem Eng. *Res:* Heterogeneous catalysis; supported metal catalysts; chemical kinetics; modeling of reaction networks. *Mailing Add:* Dept of Chem Eng Univ of Alberta Edmonton AB T6G 2E1 Can

WANLESS, HAROLD ROGERS, b Champaign, Ill, Feb 14, 42; m 65; c 3. SEDIMENTOLOGY, MARINE GEOLOGY. *Educ:* Princeton Univ, AB, 64; Univ Miami, MS, 68; Johns Hopkins Univ, PhD(geol), 73. *Prof Exp:* Res scientist, 71-73, res asst prof, 73-75, asst prof, 75-81, ASSOC PROF MARINE GEOL, SCH MARINE & ATMOSPHERIC SCI, UNIV MIAMI, 81- *Mem:* Soc Econ Paleontologists & Mineralogists. *Res:* Environments and processes of modern coastal and shelf sediments; petrology and paleoenvironmental reconstruction of ancient sedimentary rocks; fine-grained sediment dynamics; biotic influences on sediments; economic and environmental application. *Mailing Add:* Rosenstiel Sch of Marine & Atmos Sci Univ of Miami Miami FL 33149

WANN, DONALD FREDERICK, b St Louis, Mo, Mar 28, 32; m 53; c 1. ELECTRICAL ENGINEERING. *Educ:* Yale Univ, BE, 53; Washington Univ, MS, 57, DSc(elec eng), 61. *Prof Exp:* Control engr, Glenn L Martin Aircraft Co, 53-54; from asst prof to assoc prof, 61-69, assoc chmn dept, 65-70, PROF ELEC ENG, WASHINGTON UNIV, 69- *Mem:* Inst Elec & Electronics Engrs; Asn Comput Mach; Am Soc Eng Educ. *Res:* Design of special purpose digital computers for analysis of biological images; development of digital design automation aids. *Mailing Add:* Dept of Elec Eng Washington Univ St Louis MO 63130

WANN, ELBERT VAN, b Grange, Ark, Dec 29, 30; m 50; c 1. GENETICS, PLANT BREEDING. *Educ:* Univ Ark, BS, 59, MS, 60; Purdue Univ, PhD(genetics), 62. *Prof Exp:* Res assoc veg crops, Univ Ill, 62-63; GENETICIST, USDA, 63-, LAB DIR, 72- *Honors & Awards:* Asgrow Award, Am Soc Hort Sci, 72. *Mem:* Am Soc Hort Sci; Am Soc Agron; Crop Sci Soc Am. *Res:* Genetics and breeding of sweet corn and tomatoes, as related to disease and insect resistance and the improvement of consumer quality. *Mailing Add:* US Veg Lab 2875 Savannah Hwy Charleston SC 29407

WANNAMAKER, LEWIS WILLIAM, b Matthews, SC, May 19, 23; m 48; c 4. PEDIATRICS, MICROBIOLOGY. *Educ:* Duke Univ, MD, 46. *Prof Exp:* Pediat intern & resident, Duke Univ & Willard Parker Hosps, 46-48; res asst prev med, Western Reserve Univ, 48-50, res assoc, 50-52; from instr to assoc prof pediat, 52-58, PROF PEDIAT, MED SCH, UNIV MINN, MINNEAPOLIS, 58-, PROF MICROBIOL, 65-; CAREER INVESTR, AM HEART ASN, 58- *Concurrent Pos:* Mem, Streptococcal Dis Lab, Wyo, 48-50, asst dir, 50-52; vis investr, Rockefeller Inst, 55-57; guest investr, Cent Pub Health Lab & Nat Inst Med Res, Eng, 66-67 & Hyg Inst, Univ Kölm, 73-74; mem streptococcal & staphylococcal comn, Armed Forces Epidemiol Bd & dir, 67-72. *Mem:* Am Soc Clin Invest; Am Soc Microbiol; Soc Pediat Res; Am Asn Immunol; Am Fedn Clin Res. *Res:* Streptococcal and other infectious diseases; rheumatic fever; nephritis; biology of streptococci and staphylococci; bacterial nucleases and other extracellular enzymes. *Mailing Add:* Dept of Pediat Box 296 Univ of Minn Med Sch Minneapolis MN 55455

WANNEMACHER, ROBERT, JR, b Hackensack, NJ, Jan 12, 29; m 71. BIOCHEMISTRY, NUTRITION. *Educ:* Wagner Col, BS, 50; Rutgers Univ, MS, 51, PhD(biochem, nutrit), 60. *Prof Exp:* From res asst to res assoc nutrit & biochem, Bur Biol Res, Rutgers Univ, 51-60, from asst res prof to assoc res prof, 60-69; SR BIOCHEMIST, PHYS SCI DIV, US ARMY MED RES INST INFECTIOUS DIS, 69- *Mem:* AAAS; Am Inst Nutrit; Am Chem Soc; Biophys Soc; Soc Exp Biol & Med; Am Soc Biol Chem. *Res:* Protein and RNA metabolism; infectious diseases; regulatory mechanisms; endocrinology, cancer and radiation. *Mailing Add:* US Army Med Res Inst for Infectious Dis Ft Detrick Frederick MD 21701

WANNIER, GREGORY HUGH, b Basel, Switz, Dec 30, 11; nat US; m 39; c 2. THEORETICAL PHYSICS. *Educ:* Univ Basel, PhD(math physics), 35. *Prof Exp:* Asst, Univ Geneva, 35-36; Swiss-Am exchange fel, Princeton Univ, 36-37; instr, Univ Pittsburgh, 37-38; lectr, Bristol Univ, 38-39; instr, Univ Tex, 39-41; lectr physics, Univ Iowa, 41-46; res assoc, Theoret Physics Lab, Socony-Vacuum Oil Co, 46-49; mem tech staff, Bell Labs, 49-60; prof physics, 61-77, EMER PROF PHYSICS, UNIV ORE, 77- *Concurrent Pos:* Prof, Univ Geneva, 55-56. *Mem:* Fel Am Phys Soc; Swiss Phys Soc. *Res:* Theoretical molecular and crystal structure; magnetism; statistical mechanics; gas discharges; electron and solid state physics. *Mailing Add:* Dept of Physics Univ of Ore Eugene OR 97403

WANNIER, PETER GREGORY, b Iowa City, Iowa, Sept 14, 46; m 78. RADIO ASTRONOMY. *Educ:* Stanford Univ, BS, 68; Princeton Univ, PhD(astron), 75. *Prof Exp:* Tech consult radio astron, Bell Tel Labs, 74-75; asst prof astron & elec eng, Univ Mass, 75-76; asst prof, 76-78, PROF RADIO ASTRON, CALIF INST TECHNOL, 78- *Concurrent Pos:* Mem comn J, Int Union Radio Sci, 77-78. *Mem:* Am Astron Soc; Int Astron Union. *Res:* Millimeter-wave and centimeter-wave studies of the interstellar medium, especially of dense clouds, with special interest in nuclear processing of material in the galaxy. *Mailing Add:* Dept of Astron Code 102-24 Calif Inst of Technol Pasadena CA 91125

WANTLAND, EVELYN KENDRICK, b Suffolk, Va, June 22, 17; m 39, 64; c 1. MATHEMATICS. *Educ:* Univ Ill, BA, 48, MA, 49, PhD(math), 58. *Prof Exp:* Asst, Univ Ill, 48-49; prof math, Ferrum Jr Col, 49-51; asst prof, Ill Wesleyan Univ, 51-57; asst prof, Kans State Univ, 57-62; assoc prof, Univ Miss, 62-64; prof math & head dept, Ill Wesleyan Univ, 64-76; RETIRED. *Mem:* Am Math Soc; Math Asn Am. *Res:* Complex variables. *Mailing Add:* 110 E Beecher St Bloomington IL 61701

WAPLES, DOUGLAS WENDLE, b Oklahoma City, Okla, July 29, 45; m 68. ORGANIC GEOCHEMISTRY. *Educ:* DePauw Univ, AB, 67; Stanford Univ, PhD(org chem), 71. *Prof Exp:* Alexander von Humboldt fel, Geochem Inst, Univ Göttingen, 71-72; org geochemist, Empresa Nacional del Petroleo, Chile, 72-73; res chemist, Chevron Oil Field Res Co, Standard Oil Calif, 73-76; ASST PROF GEOCHEM, COLO SCH MINES, 76- *Concurrent Pos:* Fulbright travel grant, 72; Latin Am teaching fel & prof chem, Cath Univ Valparaiso, Chile, 72-73. *Res:* Application of chemical methods to petroleum exploration; development of theoretical models for the process of petroleum formation. *Mailing Add:* 7204 W 26th Ave Lakewood CO 80215

WAPPNER, REBECCA SUE, b Mansfield, Ohio, Feb 25, 44. PEDIATRICS, BIOCHEMICAL GENETICS. *Educ:* Ohio Univ, BS, 66; Ohio State Univ, MD, 70; Am Bd Pediat, dipl, 75. *Prof Exp:* Intern pediat, Children's Hosp, Columbus, Ohio, 70-71, resident, 71-72, asst chief resident, 72-73; fel pediat metab & genetics, 73-75, asst prof, 75-77, ASSOC PROF PEDIAT, SCH MED, IND UNIV, INDIANAPOLIS, 77- *Mem:* Am Acad Pediat; Sigma Xi; Am Soc Human Genetics; Am Med Women's Asn. *Res:* Inborn errors of metabolism; lysosomal storage disorders. *Mailing Add:* Dept Pediat Riley A-36 Ind Univ Sch Med Indianapolis IN 46223

WARAVDEKAR, VAMAN SHIVRAM, b Varavda, India, May 11, 14; nat US; m 60; c 2. BIOCHEMISTRY. *Educ:* Univ Bombay, MSc, 40, PhD(chem), 42. *Prof Exp:* Res assoc, V J Tech Inst, India, 42-45; res officer carcinogenesis, Tata Mem Hosp, Bombay, 45-48; prin investr, Georgetown Univ, 50-52; vis scientist, Nat Cancer Inst, 52-57; prof biochem, All-India Inst Med Sci, 57-58; chief biochem br, Armed Forces Inst Path, 58-65; dir cancer chemother dept, Microbial Assocs, Inc, DC, 65-72; res chemist, Off of Assoc Dir Drug Res & Develop, Div Cancer Treatment, 72-73, RES PLANNING OFFICER, NAT CANCER INST, 73- *Concurrent Pos:* Res fel chemother of cancer, Nat Cancer Inst, 48-50; lectr grad sch, Georgetown Univ, 50-55. *Mem:* AAAS; Soc Exp Biol & Med; Am Soc Pharmacol & Exp Therapeut; Am Chem Soc; Am Asn Cancer Res. *Res:* Cellular chemistry; metabolism; enzymology; fatty acid oxidation; protein synthesis; chemotherapy; cancer research. *Mailing Add:* Res Planning Off Nat Cancer Inst Bethesda MD 20014

WARBURTON, DAVID LEWIS, b Hackensack, NJ, Aug 10, 47; m 75. GEOCHEMISTRY. *Educ:* Univ Calif, San Diego, BA, 69; Univ Chicago, PhD(geochem), 78. *Prof Exp:* ASST PROF GEOL, FLA ATLANTIC UNIV, 75- *Mem:* Am Geophys Union; AAAS; Mineral Soc Am; Sigma Xi; Sci Res Soc. *Res:* Synthetic samples of olivine prepared for examination by Mossbauer technique to determine iron ion distribution at the two nonequivalent distorted octahedral sites. *Mailing Add:* Dept of Geol Fla Atlantic Univ Boca Raton FL 33431

WARBURTON, DOROTHY, b Toronto, Ont, Jan 12, 36; m 57; c 4. HUMAN GENETICS. *Educ:* McGill Univ, BSc, 57, PhD(genetics), 61. *Prof Exp:* From res asst to res assoc human genetics, Montreal Children's Hosp & McGill Univ, 58-63; res assoc obstet & gynec, Col Physicians & Surgeons, Columbia Univ, 64-67; dir genetics serv, St Luke's Hosp Ctr, 67-68; instr obstet & gynec, 68-69, assoc human genetics & develop, 69-71, asst prof human genetics & develop, 71-75, asst prof pediat, 74-75, ASSOC PROF CLIN PEDIAT, COL PHYSICIANS & SURGEONS, COLUMBIA UNIV, 75-; DIR GENETICS DIAG LAB, PRESBY HOSP, 69- *Mem:* Am Soc Human Genetics. *Res:* Cytogenetics; congenital malformations; genetics of obstetrical variables; dermatoglyphics. *Mailing Add:* Col of Physicians & Surgeons Columbia Univ New York NY 10032

WARBURTON, ERNEST KEELING, b Worcester, Mass, Apr 26, 28; m 47; c 3. NUCLEAR PHYSICS. *Educ:* Miami Univ, BA, 49; Mass Inst Technol, SB, 51; Univ Pittsburgh, PhD(physics), 57. *Prof Exp:* From instr to asst prof physics, Princeton Univ, 58-61; assoc physicist, 61-63, physicist, 63-68, SR PHYSICIST, BROOKHAVEN NAT LAB, 68- *Concurrent Pos:* NSF fel, Oxford Univ, 63-64 & 68-69; consult, Lawrence Livermore Nat Lab; assoc ed, Phys Rev Letters, 82- *Mem:* Fel Am Phys Soc. *Res:* Experimental and theoretical investigations of nuclear structure primarily using a tandem Van de Grooff accelerator. *Mailing Add:* 12 Harbor Hills Dr Port Jefferson NY 11777

WARD, ALFORD L, b Rockville, Md, Aug 14, 19. PHYSICS. *Educ:* Univ Md, BS, 49, PhD, 54. *Prof Exp:* PHYSICIST, HARRY DIAMOND LABS, US ARMY ELECTRONICS RES & DEVELOP COMMAND, ADELPHI, 54- *Mem:* Fel AAAS; fel Am Phys Soc. *Res:* Gaseous electronics; semiconductors. *Mailing Add:* 3804 Underwood St Chevy Chase MD 20815

WARD, ANTHONY THOMAS, b London, Eng, Mar 9, 41; m 66; c 2. PHYSICAL CHEMISTRY. *Educ:* Univ London, BSc, 62; Rensselaer Polytech Inst, MS, 64, PhD(phys chem), 66. *Prof Exp:* MEM TECH STAFF, XEROX CORP, 66- *Mem:* Electrochem Soc; Am Phys Soc. *Mailing Add:* Joseph C Wilson Ctr for Technol W-114 Xerox Corp Webster NY 14580

WARD, ARTHUR ALLEN, JR, b Manipay, Ceylon, Feb 4, 16; US citizen; m 41. NEUROSURGERY. *Educ:* Yale Univ, BA, 38, MD, 42. *Prof Exp:* Demonstr path, McGill Univ, 43, demonstr neruol & neruosurg, 44-45; asst physiol, Yale Univ, 45; asst, Ill Neuropsychiat Inst, 46; instr neurosurg, Univ Louisville, 46-48; from asst prof to prof surg, 48-65, chmn dept, 65-81, PROF NEUROSURG, MED SCH, UNIV WASH, 65- *Concurrent Pos:* Fel, McGill Univ, 43. *Honors & Awards:* Lennox Award, 76. *Mem:* Soc Neurol Surgery (pres, 74); Am Acad Neurol Surgery (pres, 77-78); Am Epilepsy Soc (vpres, 49, pres, 72); Am Physiol Soc; Am EEG Soc (pres, 59-60). *Res:* Epilepsy; function of animal and human cerebral cortex; reticular formation of the midbrain. *Mailing Add:* Dept of Neurosurg Univ of Wash Med Sch Seattle WA 98195

WARD, BENNIE FRANKLIN LEON, b Millen, Ga, Oct 19, 48. THEORETICAL HIGH ENERGY PHYSICS, MICROELECTRONIC DEVICE PHYSICS. *Educ:* Mass Inst Technol, BS(physics) & BS(math), 70; Princeton Univ, MA, 71, PhD(physics), 73. *Prof Exp:* Instr physics, Princeton Univ, 73; res assoc physics, Stanford Linear Accelerator Ctr, Stanford Univ, 73-75; asst prof physics, Purdue Univ, West Lafayette, 75-78; staff engr, Intel Corp, 78-79; res specialist, 80-82, STAFF ENGR, LOCKHEED MISSILES & SPACE CO, 82- *Concurrent Pos:* Vis scientist, Stanford Linear Accelerator Ctr, 78-, res assoc, 78. *Mem:* Am Phys Soc; Inst Elec & Electronics Engrs; NY Acad Sci. *Res:* Continued development of the theory of previously introduced sources in the renormalization group equations; the applications of a previously introduced Lorentz invariant formulation of strong coupling theory. *Mailing Add:* Lockheed Missiles & Space Co Stanford Univ PO Box 4349 Stanford CA 94305

WARD, CALVIN HERBERT, b Strawberry, Ark, Mar 1, 33; m 54; c 3. PLANT PATHOLOGY, PHYSIOLOGY. *Educ:* NMex State Univ, BS, 55; Cornell Univ, MS, 58, PhD(plant path), 60; Univ Tex, MPH, 78. *Prof Exp:* Res biologist, US Air Force Sch Aerospace Med, 60-63, plant physiologist, 63-65; assoc prof biol, 66-70, PROF BIOL & ENVIRON SCI & CHMN DEPT ENVIRON SCI & ENG, RICE UNIV, 70-, CO-DIR, NAT CTR GROUNDWATER RES, 79- *Concurrent Pos:* Grants, NASA, 63-66 & 70-, Environ Protection Agency, 66- & US Dept Air Force, 68-70; mem environ biol adv panel, Am Inst Biol Sci, 66-71, chmn, 69-71, mem comt space shuttle impact eval, 74-; mem bd dirs, Southwest Ctr Urban Res, 69-, chmn, 77-78; mem life sci comt, NASA, 71-78; vis prof, Univ Tex Sch Pub Health Houston, 73-74, adj prof environ health, 74-; ed-in-chief, Environ Toxicol & Chem, 81- *Mem:* AAAS; Am Phytopath Soc; Soc Nematol; Soc Indust Microbiol; Phycol Soc Am. *Res:* Algal and plant physiology; bioregeneration; environmental microbiology; ground water contamination and pollution control. *Mailing Add:* Depts of Biol & Environ Sci & Eng Rice Univ Houston TX 77001

WARD, CALVIN LUCIAN, b Yancey, Tex, Jan 30, 28; m 66; c 2. GENETICS. *Educ:* Univ Tex, BA, 47, MA, 49, PhD(zool), 51. *Prof Exp:* AEC fel, Oak Ridge Nat Lab, 51-52; from instr to assoc prof zool, 52-78, PROF ZOOL, DUKE UNIV, 78- *Mem:* Genetics Soc Am; Soc Study Evolution. *Res:* Cytology and genetics of Drosophila; speciation; radiation genetics. *Mailing Add:* Dept of Zool Duke Univ Durham NC 27706

WARD, CHARLES ALBERT, b Bailey, Tex, May 28, 39; m 59. MECHANICAL ENGINEERING, BIOMEDICAL ENGINEERING. *Educ:* Univ Tex, Arlington, BSc, 62; Northwestern Univ, PhD(mech eng), 67. *Prof Exp:* From asst prof to assoc prof, 67-77, PROF MECH ENG, UNIV TORONTO, 77- *Concurrent Pos:* Res assoc, Res Inst, Hosp Sick Children, 72- *Res:* Phase changes, transport phenomena, energy conversion, fuel cells, biomedical engineering, biocompatibility of synthetic materials. *Mailing Add:* Dept of Mech Eng Univ of Toronto Toronto ON M5S 1A4 Can

WARD, CHARLES BRADLEY, JR, b Pittsburgh, Pa, Apr 1, 20; m 49; c 2. INDUSTRIAL MICROBIOLOGY. *Educ:* Univ Southern Calif, BS, 49; Okla State Univ, MS, 50; Iowa State Univ, PhD(food technol), 56. *Prof Exp:* Bacteriologist, Arden Farms Co, Calif, 56-59, Dugway Proving Ground, Chem Corps, US Dept Army, 59-61 & Truesdail Labs, Calif, 61-64; BIOL CHEMIST, ARROWHEAD PURITAS WATERS, 65- *Mem:* Am Chem Soc; Am Soc Microbiol. *Res:* Water, dairy and general industrial bacteriology. *Mailing Add:* 4929 Lauderdale Ave La Crescenta CA 91214

WARD, CHARLES EUGENE WILLOUGHBY, b Madison, Wis, Sept 8, 38; m 61; c 2. COMPUTER SOFTWARE DESIGN. *Educ:* Northwestern Univ, BS, 61; Mass Inst Technol, PhD(physics), 67. *Prof Exp:* Res assoc, Lab Nuclear Sci, Mass Inst Technol, 67-68; appointee, Argonne Nat Lab, 68-70, asst physicist, High Energy Physics Div, 70-73, physicist, 74-79; MEM TECH STAFF, BELL LABS, 79- *Mem:* Inst Elec & Electronics Engrs-Comput Soc; Sigma Xi. *Res:* Design of computer software systems for switching systems and other telecommunications applications. *Mailing Add:* Dept 55446 Bell Labs Warrenville & Naperville Rd Naperville IL 60566

WARD, CHARLES RICHARD, b Tahoka, Tex, Mar 25, 40; m 61; c 2. ENTOMOLOGY. *Educ:* Tex Tech Col, BS, 62, MS, 64; Cornell Univ, PhD(med entom), 68. *Prof Exp:* From asst prof to assoc prof entom, Tex Tech Univ, 72-76; assoc prof, Tex Agr Exp Sta, 76; entom specialist, Consortium for Int Develop, Bolivia, 76-78; res assoc, 78-80, ASSOC PROF ENTOM, NMEX STATE UNIV, 78-, PEST MGT SPECIALIST, 80- *Concurrent Pos:* Consult, Consortium for Int Crop Protection, Indonesia, 81. *Mem:* AAAS; Entom Soc Am. *Res:* Pest management research and extension; biology and control of rangeland pests and ecology of desert and grasslands insects; biological control; insect resistance to pesticides. *Mailing Add:* Southeastern Br Exp Sta NMex State Univ Rte 1 Box 1231 Las Cruces NM 88003

WARD, CHARLOTTE REED, b Lexington, Ky, Feb 19, 29; m 51; c 4. PHYSICAL CHEMISTRY. *Educ:* Univ Ky, BS, 49; Purdue Univ, MS, 51, PhD(phys chem), 56. *Prof Exp:* Instr gen sci, Ala Educ TV, 58-60, 61-62 & 63-72, from instr to asst prof physics, Univ, 61-75, ASSOC PROF PHYSICS, AUBURN UNIV, 75- *Concurrent Pos:* Abstractor, Che Abstr, 58- *Mem:* Am Asn Physics Teachers; Sigma Xi. *Res:* Molecular spectroscopy; development of physical science courses. *Mailing Add:* 134 Norwood Ave Auburn AL 36830

WARD, COLEMAN YOUNGER, b Millican, Tex, Sept 20, 28; m 47; c 3. AGRONOMY, PHYSIOLOGY. *Educ:* Tex Tech Univ, BS, 50, MS, 54; Va Polytech Inst & State Univ, PhD(agron), 62. *Prof Exp:* Instr agricult, Eastern NMex Univ, 50-51; soil scientist, Soil Conserv Serv, USDA, 51-52; instr agron, Tex Tech Univ, 52-54; asst agronomist, Univ Fla, 54-55 & Va Agr Exp Sta, 55-61; from assoc prof to prof crop sci, Miss State Univ, 61-74; prof agron & chmn dept, Univ Fla, 74-80. *Honors & Awards:* Merit Award, Am Forage & Grassland Coun, 70. *Mem:* Fel Am Soc Agron; Sigma Xi; Crop Sci Soc Am. *Res:* Physiology and ecology of turfgrasses and forage crops. *Mailing Add:* 3809 Heritage Pl Opelika AL 36801

WARD, CURTIS HOWARD, b Round Bottom, Ohio, June 21, 27; m 51; c 4. PHYSICAL CHEMISTRY. *Educ:* Ind State Teachers Col, BS, 47; Univ Ky, MS, 50; Purdue Univ, PhD(phys chem), 54. *Prof Exp:* Res chemist, Linde Co Div, Union Carbide Corp, 53-57; assoc prof chem, Auburn Univ, 57-60; sr staff scientist, Avco Corp, 60-61; assoc prof, 61-65, PROF CHEM, AUBURN UNIV, 65- *Mem:* Am Chem Soc. *Res:* Thermodynamics; molecular spectroscopy; organometallic chemistry. *Mailing Add:* Dept of Chem Auburn Univ Auburn AL 36830

WARD, DANIEL BERTRAM, b Crawfordsville, Ind, Mar 20, 28; m 56; c 4. PLANT TAXONOMY. *Educ:* Wabash Col, AB, 50; Cornell Univ, MS, 53, PhD(plant taxon), 59. *Prof Exp:* From asst prof to assoc prof, 58-75, PROF BOT, UNIV FLA, 75- *Mem:* Int Asn Plant Taxon; Am Soc Plant Taxonomists. *Res:* Vascular flora of Florida; methods of population analysis; preservation of endangered species. *Mailing Add:* Dept Bot Univ Fla Gainesville FL 32611

WARD, DARRELL N, b Logan, Utah, Jan 22, 24; m 46; c 7. BIOCHEMISTRY. *Educ:* Utah State Univ, BS, 49; Stanford Univ, MS, 51; PhD(biochem), 53. *Prof Exp:* Res assoc & instr biochem, Med Col, Cornell Univ, 52-55; from asst biochemist to assoc biochemist, 55-61, PROF BIOCHEM, HEAD DEPT & BIOCHEMIST, UNIV TEX M D ANDERSON HOSP & TUMOR INST, HOUSTON, 61-; from chmn to pres grad fac, 78-80, MEM GRAD FAC, GRAD SCH BIOMED SCI, UNIV TEX, HOUSTON, 61- *Concurrent Pos:* Asst prof, Univ Tex Dent Br, Houston, 56-60; from asst clin prof to assoc clin prof, Baylor Col Med, 56-62; mem reproductive biol study sect, NIH, 67-71, consult, Ctr Pop Res. 69-71; chmn, Biochem Endocrinol Study, NIH, 79-81. *Honors & Awards:* Ayerst Award, Endocrine Soc, 78. *Mem:* AAAS; Am Chem Soc; Am Asn Cancer Res; Am Soc Biol Chem; Endocrine Soc. *Res:* Protein purification; protein and peptide hormones; gonzdotropins amino acid sequence; functional group substitution and effects of biological activity; biochemistry of glycoprotein hormones. *Mailing Add:* Dept Biochem Univ Tex M D Anderson Hosp & Tumor Inst Houston TX 77030

WARD, DAVID, b Wakefield, Eng, Aug 5, 40; Can citizen. EXPERIMENTAL NUCLEAR PHYSICS. *Educ:* Univ Birmingham, BSc, 61; Univ Manchester, PhD(nuclear physics), 65. *Prof Exp:* Fel nuclear physics, Univ Manchester, 65-66 & Univ Calif, Berkeley, 66-68; PHYSICIST, CHALK RIVER NUCLEAR LABS, ATOMIC ENERGY CAN, 68- *Concurrent Pos:* Vis scientist nuclear physics, Univ Calif, Berkeley, 74-75; vis fel nuclear physics, Australian Nat Univ, 81-82. *Mem:* Am Phys Soc. *Res:* Reactions and coulomb excitation with heavy ions; lifetimes and magnetic moments of short-lived nuclear states; atomic phenomena in nuclear physics; stopping powers for heavy ions. *Mailing Add:* Nuclear Physics Br Chalk River Nuclear Labs Chalk River ON K0J 1J0 Can

WARD, DAVID ALOYSIUS, b Joliet, Ill, Nov 13, 30; m 53; c 9. MECHANICAL & NUCLEAR ENGINEERING. *Educ:* Univ Ill, BSME, 53. *Prof Exp:* Res engr, Savannah River Lab, 53-65, engr, Savannah River Plant, 65-67, sr supvr, 67-69, area supvr, 69-72, chief tech supvr, 72-75, supt, Reactor Technol Dept, 75-78, supt, Reactor & Reactor Mat Technol Dept, 78-80, RES MGR NUCLEAR ENG, SAVANNAH RIVER PLANT, E I DU PONT DE NEMOURS & CO, INC, 80- *Concurrent Pos:* Mem adv comt reactor safeguards, US Nuclear Regulatory Comn. *Mem:* Am Nuclear Soc. *Res:* Nuclear reactor heat transfer; hydraulics; safety analysis; engineering management. *Mailing Add:* E I du Pont de Nemours & Co Inc Savannah River Plant Aiken SC 29801

WARD, DAVID CHRISTIAN, b Sackville, NB, May 22, 41; m 62; c 1. VIROLOGY, BIOCHEMISTRY. *Educ:* Mem Univ Nfld, BSc, 61; Univ BC, MSc, 63; Rockefeller Univ, PhD(biochem), 69. *Prof Exp:* ASST PROF MOLECULAR BIOPHYS & BIOCHEM, SCH MED, YALE UNIV, 71- *Concurrent Pos:* Leukemia Soc Am fel, Imp Cancer Res Fund, Eng, 69-71. *Mem:* AAAS. *Res:* Replication and genetic analysis of animal viruses; mammalian genetics, fractionation and properties of metaphase chromosomes; conformational properties of nucleic acid polymerases. *Mailing Add:* Dept of Molecular Biophys Yale Univ Sch of Med New Haven CT 06510

WARD, EDMUND WILLIAM BESWICK, b Stockport, Eng, May 30, 30; m 53; c 3. MICROBIOLOGY, PLANT PATHOLOGY. *Educ:* Univ Wales, BSc, 52; Univ Alta, MSc, 54, PhD, 58. *Prof Exp:* Res officer, Alta, 57-61, head lab, 61-73, PLANT PATHOLOGIST, LONDON RES INST, PLANT PATH LAB, CAN DEPT AGR, 73- *Mem:* Bot Soc Am; Am Phytopath Soc; Can Soc Phytopath. *Res:* Physiology of fungi; diseases resistance in plants. *Mailing Add:* London Res Inst Can Dept Agr Univ West Ont London ON N6A 5B7 Can

WARD, EDWARD HILSON, b Milton, Fla, Sept 15, 30; m 54; c 2. INORGANIC CHEMISTRY, ANALYTICAL CHEMISTRY. *Educ:* Troy State Col, BS, 58; Univ Miss, PhD(chem), 63. *Prof Exp:* Fel chem, Fla State Univ, 63-65; assoc prof, 65-68, PROF CHEM, TROY STATE UNIV, 68-, CHMN DEPT PHYS SCI, 70- *Mem:* Am Chem Soc. *Res:* Inorganic complexes; non-aqueous solvent systems; co-precipitation. *Mailing Add:* Dept of Phys Sci Troy State Univ Troy AL 36082

WARD, FRANCES ELLEN, b Freedom, Maine, Mar 21, 39. IMMUNOGENETICS. *Educ:* Clark Univ, AB, 61; Brown Univ, PhD(biol), 65. *Prof Exp:* Instr, 67-69, asst prof, 69-73, assoc prof immunol, 73-79, PROF IMMUNOL, DUKE UNIV MED CTR, 79- *Concurrent Pos:* NIH fel statist, Iowa State Univ, 66-67; dir, Transplant Lab, Durham Vet Admin Hosp, 69-79; assoc scientist, The Wistar Inst, 80-81. *Mem:* Genetics Soc Am; AAAS; Transplantation Soc; Am Asn Clin Histocompatibility Testing; Am Asn Immunologists. *Res:* Genetics of the major human histocompatibility complex; immunogenicity of gene products of the major histocompatibility complex as measured by organ and tissue rejection. *Mailing Add:* Div Immunol Duke Univ Med Ctr Box 3010 Durham NC 27710

WARD, FRANK KERNAN, b Brockton, Mass, Jan 19, 31; m 56; c 3. ORGANIC CHEMISTRY, POLYMER CHEMISTRY. *Educ:* Boston Col, BS, 54; Mass Inst Technol, PhD(org chem), 58. *Prof Exp:* Res asst chem, Mass Inst Technol, 54-57; res chemist, Celanese Corp, 57-59; scientist, Avco Corp, 59-60, sr scientist, 60-61; sr chemist, 61-64, res chemist, 64-67, group leader, 67-71, environ technologist, 71-78, COORDR, TEXACO INC, BEACON, 78- *Mem:* Sigma Xi; Am Chem Soc. *Res:* Synthetic polymer chemistry; organometallics; environmental affairs; fuel and lubricant additives; petrochemicals. *Mailing Add:* Deerwood Dr RD-3 Hopewell Junction NY 12533

WARD, FRASER PRESCOTT, b Lancaster, Pa, Aug 22, 40; m 63; c 3. ECOLOGY, VETERINARY MEDICINE. *Educ:* Univ Pa, VMD, 65; Johns Hopkins Univ, PhD(pathobiol), 79. *Prof Exp:* Vet practr, Tredyffrin Vet Hosp, Paoli, Pa, 65-66; Captain, Vet Corps, 66-69, chief, Ecol Br, 69-81, chief, Toxicol Br, 81-82, CHIEF SCIENTIST, RES DIV, US ARMY CHEM SYSTS LAB, ABERDEEN PROVING GROUND, MD, 82- *Concurrent Pos:* Mem path comt, Raptor Res Found, 70-; comnr, Md Chesapeake Bay & Coastal Zone Adv Bd, 73-; proj sci coordr, US/USSR Agreement on Coop Environ Protection, 73- *Mem:* Raptor Res Found; Wildlife Soc; Wildlife Dis Asn. *Res:* Global population dynamics of peregrine falcons; diseases of birds of prey; ecology of turtles; toxicology with emphasis on pesticides; assessment of environmental impacts; endangered species. *Mailing Add:* Chief Ecol Br Chem Systs Lab Aberdeen Proving Ground MD 21010

WARD, FREDERICK EDMUND, US citizen. MEDICINAL CHEMISTRY. *Educ:* Goshen Col, BA, 71; Univ Notre Dame, PhD(org chem), 74. *Prof Exp:* Asst res chemist, 70-71, res chemist, 74-77, SR RES CHEMIST, MILES LABS, INC, 77- *Mem:* Am Chem Soc. *Res:* Antifungal agents; anti-inflammatory agents. *Mailing Add:* Miles Labs Inc 1127 Myrtle St Elkhart IN 46514

WARD, FREDERICK ROGER, b Cleveland, Miss, Oct 30, 40; m 64; c 2. MATHEMATICS. *Educ:* Col William & Mary, BS, 62; Univ Colo, MS, 65; Va Polytech Inst & State Univ, PhD(math), 69. *Prof Exp:* Instr math, Va Polytech Inst & State Univ, 65-69; asst prof, 69-72, ASSOC PROF MATH, BOISE STATE UNIV, 72- *Mailing Add:* Dept of Math Boise State Univ Boise ID 83725

WARD, FREDRICK JAMES, b Alert Bay, BC, Jan 22, 28; m 56; c 3. LIMNOLOGY, FISH BIOLOGY. *Educ:* Univ BC, BA, 52, MA, 57; Cornell Univ, PhD(conserv), 62. *Prof Exp:* Biologist, Int Pac Salmon Fisheries Comn, 52-57, proj supvr, 57-64; from asst prof to assoc prof, 64-73, PROF LIMNOL & INVERT ZOOL, UNIV MAN, 73- *Mem:* Am Fisheries Soc; Am Soc Limnol & Oceanog; Can Soc Wildlife & Fishery Biol; Int Asn Theoret & Appl Limnol. *Res:* Limnology, particularly secondary production; dynamics of Pacific salmon populations. *Mailing Add:* Dept of Zool Univ of Man Winnipeg MB R3T 2N2 Can

WARD, GEORGE A, b Chicago, Ill, Feb 17, 36; m 57; c 4. ANALYTICAL CHEMISTRY. *Educ:* Univ Ill, BS, 57; Northwestern Univ, PhD(anal chem), 61. *Prof Exp:* Sr res chemist, 60-75, mgr, Anal Div, 75-78, dir, Anal & Tech Servs, 78-80, DIR, CHEM LAB, RES CTR, HERCULES, INC, 80- *Mem:* Am Chem Soc. *Res:* Electrochemistry; nuclear magnetic resonance; organic analysis. *Mailing Add:* Hercules Res Ctr Wilmington DE 19899

WARD, GEORGE HENRY, b Withrow, Wash, Nov 28, 16; m 46; c 2. SYSTEMATIC BOTANY. *Educ:* State Col Wash, BS, 40, MS, 48; Stanford Univ, PhD(biol), 52. *Prof Exp:* Teacher, Wash High Sch, 40-42; asst bot & taxon, State Col Wash, 42 & 46-48; asst bot & biol, Stanford Univ, 48-52, instr biol, 52-54, curatorial asst, Dudley Herbarium, 49; from asst prof to assoc prof, 54-66, PROF BIOL, KNOX COL, ILL, 66- *Mem:* AAAS. *Res:* Cyto-taxonomy of Artemisia; arctic flora; stripmine spoilbank ecology. *Mailing Add:* Dept of Biol Knox Col Galesburg IL 61401

WARD, GEORGE MERRILL, b New Haven, Vt, June 4, 19; m 48; c 3. DAIRYING, NUTRITION. *Educ:* Univ Vt, BS, 41; Rutgers Univ, MS, 47; Mich State Univ, PhD(dairy nutrit), 51. *Prof Exp:* Asst, Rutgers Univ, 46; asst, Mich State Univ, 48-50, asst prof dairy, 50-55; assoc prof dairy sci, 55-66, PROF DAIRY SCI, KANS STATE UNIV, 66- *Mem:* Am Dairy Sci Asn. *Res:* Dairy cattle nutrition; roughage evaluation; mineral nutrition. *Mailing Add:* Dept of Animal Sci & Indust Kans State Univ Manhattan KS 66506

WARD, GERALD MADISON, b Thorndike, Maine, Nov 2, 21; m 48; c 2. ANIMAL SCIENCE. *Educ:* Univ Maine, BS, 47; Univ Wis, MS, 48; Wash State Univ, PhD(animal sci), 51. *Prof Exp:* Asst prof dairy sci, Univ Maine, 48-49; exten specialist, Kans State Univ, 51-52 & Wash State Univ, 52-53; from asst prof to assoc prof, Colo State Univ, 53-60; scientist, Los Alamos Sci Lab, Univ Calif, 60-61; PROF ANIMAL SCI, COLO STATE UNIV, 61- *Concurrent Pos:* Head animal prod & health sect, Joint Div Food & Agr Orgn-Int Atomic Energy Agency, UN, Vienna, Austria, 68-70. *Mem:* AAAS; Am Dairy Sci Asn; Am Inst Nutrit; Am Soc Animal Sci. *Res:* Applications of radioisotope technique to animal nutrition; environmental problems of animal agriculture; nutrition of ruminant animals; systems analysis of livestock production. *Mailing Add:* Dept of Animal Sci Colo State Univ Ft Collins CO 80523

WARD, GERALD T(EMPLETON), b Harrow, Eng, Apr 15, 26; Can citizen; m 63; c 3. RENEWABLE ENERGY RESOURCES, ENERGY IN AGRICULTURE. *Educ:* Glasgow Univ, BSc, 46; Univ Durham, PhD(agr eng), 52. *Prof Exp:* Sci officer animal physiol, Rowett Res Inst, Agr Res Coun, Aberdeen, Scotland, 51-52; proj engr, Colonial Develop Corp, Tawau, Brit NBorneo, 52-53; lectr physics, Univ Malaya, 53-55 & eng, 55-57, sr lectr, 58-60; dir res, Brace Res Inst & prof eng, McGill Univ, 60-71; head dept, 71-77, PROF AGR ENG, LINCOLN COL, UNIV CANTERBURY & DIR NZ AGR ENG INST, 71- *Concurrent Pos:* Vis prof, Univ Calif, Berkeley, 57-58; Carnegie Corp & Asia Found grants, 58; consult, UN Food & Agr Orgn, 58-60; mem adv comt, Univ West Indies, 63-68; mem water control bd, soil conserv bd & smoke control bd, Govt Barbados, WI, 63-68; rep for Malaya, Nat Inst Agr Eng, England, 50; vis prof, Univ SPac, WSamoa, 78; vis fel, Int Inst Appl Syst Anal, Laxenburg, Austria, 80-81. *Honors & Awards:* Clayton Prize, Brit Inst Mech Eng, 57. *Mem:* Am Soc Mech Engrs; Am Soc Agr Engrs; Am Soc Heat, Refrig & Air-Conditioning Engrs; Solar Energy Soc (vpres); fel Brit Inst Mech Eng. *Res:* Rural development, especially arid areas; desalination; solar energy utilization; irrigation; drainage; design of water pumps; vapor compressors; airscrew windmills; environmental control; drying; processing rural products. *Mailing Add:* Dept of Agr Eng Lincoln Col PO Box 102 Canterbury New Zealand

WARD, GERTRUDE LUCKHARDT, b Mt Vernon, NY, May 27, 23. ENTOMOLOGY. *Educ:* Mt Holyoke Col, AB, 44; Univ Mich, MS, 48; Purdue Univ, PhD(entom), 70. *Prof Exp:* Teaching asst zool, Iowa State Univ, 44-46; reporter-ed, Palladium-Item, Ind, 46-47; teaching asst zool, Univ Mich, 48-49; instr biol, 49-61, lectr, 61-67, from asst prof to assoc prof, 67-75, PROF BIOL, EARLHAM COL, 75-, ASST DIR MUS, 52- *Mem:* Am Micros Soc; Entom Soc Am. *Res:* Wasp-spider relationships; Chalybion zimmermanni; parasitism of the bagworm; bat populations in Indiana. *Mailing Add:* Dept of Biol Earlham Col Richmond IN 47374

WARD, GRAY (GOVINDA), b Des Moines, Iowa, Dec 24, 34; div; c 2. ATMOSPHERIC PHYSICS. *Educ:* Univ Va, BEE, 56; Univ Calif, Los Angeles, MS, 58; Univ Colo, Boulder, MA, 62; Univ Md, College Park, PhD(physics), 70. *Prof Exp:* Mem tech staff, Hughes Aircraft Co, Calif, 56-58; physicist, Nat Bur Stand, Colo, 58-62; asst prof physics, Univ Redlands, 62-64, chmn dept, 63-64; asst prog dir, Off Int Sci Activ, NSF, Washington, DC, 64-65, consult, 65-66; asst prof, Univ Fla, 70-75, assoc prof physics & elec eng, 75-78; ASSOC DIR, KRIPALU INST, 78- *Concurrent Pos:* Consult, Off Int Sci Activ, NSF, 63-64. *Mem:* Am Phys Soc; Inst Elec & Electronics Engrs. *Res:* Microwave and plasma physics; scientific applications of laser scattering; remote measurements of atmospheric properties; psychophysical stress; science education. *Mailing Add:* Kripalu Inst PO Box 120 Summit Station PA 17979

WARD, HAROLD NATHANIEL, b Evanston, Ill, Apr 29, 36; m 59; c 3. MATHEMATICS. *Educ:* Swarthmore Col, BA, 58; Harvard Univ, MA, 59, PhD(math), 62. *Prof Exp:* From instr to asst prof math, Brown Univ, 62-67; asst prof, 67-69, ASSOC PROF MATH, UNIV VA, 69- *Mem:* Am Math Soc; Math Asn Am; Soc Indust Appl Math. *Res:* Finite groups; representations of groups; coding theory. *Mailing Add:* Dept Math Astro Bldg Univ of Va Charlottesville VA 22903

WARD, HAROLD RICHARD, b Lancaster, NY, July 31, 31; m 60; c 3. ELECTRICAL ENGINEERING. *Educ:* Clarkson Col Technol, BEE, 53; Univ Southern Calif, MSEE, 57. *Prof Exp:* Engr electronics, Hughes Aircraft Co, 53-54 & 56-57; res engr radar, Sylvania Elec Prod, 57-64; CONSULT SCIENTIST RADAR, RAYTHEON CO, 64- *Mem:* Am Inst Elec & Electronics Engrs. *Res:* Radar system design. *Mailing Add:* 23 Hilltop Dr Bedford MA 01730

WARD, HAROLD ROY, b Mt Vernon, Ill, Nov 3, 35. ENVIRONMENTAL CHEMISTRY. *Educ:* Southern Ill Univ, AB, 57; Mass Inst Technol, PhD(org chem), 61; Harvard Univ, JD, 75. *Prof Exp:* NSF fel, 61-62; NATO fel, 62-63; from asst prof to assoc prof, 63-71, assoc dean, 76-80, PROF CHEM, BROWN UNIV, 71-, DIR, CTR ENVIRON STUDIES, 76- *Concurrent Pos:* Spec fel, Environ Protection Agency, 72-75. *Mem:* Am Chem Soc. *Res:* Public interest chemistry; environmental law. *Mailing Add:* Dept of Chem Brown Univ Providence RI 02912

WARD, HELEN LAVINA, parasitology, deceased

WARD, HERBERT BAILEY, b Texarkana, Tex. ALGAL PHYSIOLOGY, PLANT PHYSIOLOGY. *Educ:* NTex State Univ, BS, 65, MS, 66; Univ Tex, Austin, PhD(bot), 71. *Prof Exp:* Asst biol, NTex State Univ, 63-66; instr, Univ Tex, Arlington, 66-67; res scientist II bot, Lab Algal Physiol, Univ Tex, Austin, 68-71; asst prof, 71-75, ASSOC PROF BIOL, UNIV MISS, 75- *Mem:* Sigma Xi; Phycol Soc Am; Am Soc Plant Physiologists. *Res:* General physiology of microalgae; photosynthesis, nutrition, metabolism and physiological ecology of aquatic algae and plants; microbiology. *Mailing Add:* Dept Biol Univ Miss University MS 38677

WARD, HOWARD LEON, b New York, NY, 46; m 76; c 2. PERIODONTOLOGY, PREVENTIVE DENTISTRY. *Educ:* NY Univ, BA, 46, DDS, 49, MA, 69; Am Bd Periodont & Am Bd Oral Med, dipl. *Prof Exp:* Prof periodont & chmn dept, 71-72, PROF PREV DENT & CHMN DEPT, NY UNIV, 72-, HEAD DIV HEALTH MGT SERV ORAL DIAG, RADIOL, 77-, ASST DEAN CLIN AFFAIRS, COL DENT, 78- *Concurrent*

Pos: Pvt pract periodont, 49-; consult, Nassau Co Med Ctr, 70 & NY State Educ Dept; mem, Northeast Regional Bd Dent Examrs, 76-; attend, Dept Surg, NY Univ Med Ctr, 77. *Honors & Awards:* Hirschfeld Award; S C Miller Award. *Mem:* Am Acad Periodont; fel Am Acad Oral Med; Res Soc Am; Am Asn Dent Examrs; fel Am Pub Health Asn. *Res:* Clinical research. *Mailing Add:* 150 Central Park S New York NY 10019

WARD, INGEBORG L, b Rötha, Ger, Aug 14, 40; US citizen; m 63; c 2. PHYSIOLOGICAL PSYCHOLOGY. *Educ:* Westhampton Col, BS, 60; Tulane Univ, MS, 65, PhD(psychol), 67. *Prof Exp:* ASSOC PROF PSYCHOL, VILLANOVA UNIV, 66- *Concurrent Pos:* NSF res grant, 68-69; Nat Inst Child Health & Human Develop res grant, 70-80; mem ment health small grant comt, NIMH, res career develop award, 75-80; mem, Bio-Psychol Study Sect, NIH, 78-82; consult ed, J Comp & Physiol Psychol. *Mem:* Fel Am Psychol Asn; Soc Study Reproduction; AAAS. *Res:* Hormonal and environmental determinants of reproductive behavior, neural and pharmacological bases of sexual behavior. *Mailing Add:* Dept of Psychol Villanova Univ Villanova PA 19085

WARD, IRL EUGENE, organic chemistry, physical chemistry, see previous edition

WARD, JACK A, b Lebanon, Ore, Sept 2, 35. ZOOLOGY, ANIMAL BEHAVIOR. *Educ:* Willamette Univ, BS, 57; Univ Wash, MS, 60; Univ Ill, Urbana, PhD(animal behav), 65. *Prof Exp:* Instr zool, Olympic Col, 60-62; from asst prof to assoc prof animal behav, 65-75, PROF ETHOLOGY, ILL STATE UNIV, 75- *Concurrent Pos:* Res grants, Ill State Univ, Ill Acad Sci, NIH & NSF, 65- *Mem:* Am Soc Zoologists; Animal Behav Soc; Am Soc Ichthyologists & Herpetologists; Am Inst Biol Sci. *Res:* Behavior of fish; development and regulation of behavior in cichlid fish. *Mailing Add:* Dept of Biol Sci Ill State Univ Normal IL 61761

WARD, JAMES ANDREW, b Pittsburgh, Pa, May 11, 38; m 66; c 5. PHYSICAL CHEMISTRY. *Educ:* St Vincent Col, BS, 60; Univ Notre Dame, PhD(phys chem), 64. *Prof Exp:* Res scientist radiation chem, Babcock & Wilcox Co, 64-65; RES SCIENTIST RADIATION CHEM, UNION CARBIDE CORP, 65- *Mem:* Am Chem Soc; Sigma Xi. *Res:* Radiation chemistry; effects of radiation on polymers in solution, polymer degradation and stabilization; radiation polymerization, hydrogels. *Mailing Add:* Union Carbide Corp PO Box 324 Tuxedo NY 10987

WARD, JAMES AUDLEY, b Timmonsville, SC, May 19, 10; m 35; c 3. MATHEMATICS, COMPUTER SCIENCE. *Educ:* Davidson Col, BA, 31; La State Univ, MS, 34; Univ Wis, PhD(math), 39. *Prof Exp:* Asst prof math, Davidson Col, 37-38 & Tenn Polytech Inst, 39-40; prof, Delta State Col, 40-42; from assoc prof to prof, Univ Ga, 46-49; prof, Univ Ky, 49-55; mathematician, US Air Force Missile Develop Ctr, 55-57, chief digital comput br, 57-59; spec asst to vpres, Univac Div, Sperry Rand Corp, 59-62; staff specialist electronic comput, Off Dir Defense Res & Eng, Dept of Defense, 62-69; staff asst comput progs, Naval Sea Systs Command, 69-76; RETIRED. *Concurrent Pos:* Consult, Proj Scamp, Univ Calif, Los Angeles, 52 & Tube Turns, Ky, 53-55; consult, Appl Physics Lab, 76-78. *Mem:* Math Asn Am; Am Math Soc; Soc Indust & Appl Math; Asn Comput Mach; sr mem Inst Elec & Electronics Eng. *Res:* Digital computers; research in hardware and software; mathematical research in linear algebra and in numerical analysis. *Mailing Add:* 5106 Marlyn Dr Washington DC 20016

WARD, JAMES B, b Clio, Ky, May 5, 31; m 65. POULTRY NUTRITION, BIOCHEMISTRY. *Educ:* Berea Col, BS, 57; Univ Ky, MS, 58; Mich State Univ, PhD(poultry nutrit), 62. *Prof Exp:* Proj leader, Exten Poultry, Univ Tenn, 62-66; assoc prof, NC State Univ, 66-70; dir nutrit, Nash Johnson & Sons, 70-72; PROF POULTRY, NC STATE UNIV, 72- *Concurrent Pos:* Consult nutritionist, All-In-One Feeds, 59-62 & Armour Foods, 74-; mem, Coun Agr Sci & Technol. *Mem:* Poultry Sci Asn; AAAS; World Poultry Sci Asn. *Mailing Add:* Dept of Poultry Sci NC State Univ Box 5307 Raleigh NC 27607

WARD, JAMES EDWARD, III, b Greenville, SC, Sept 20, 39; m 62; c 3. MATHEMATICS. *Educ:* Vanderbilt Univ, BA, 61; Univ Va, MA, 64, PhD(math), 68. *Prof Exp:* Asst to pres, George Peabody Col, 61-62; teaching asst math, Univ Va, 62-64, jr instr, 66-68, asst prof, 68-73, dir sr ctr, 71-76, assoc prof, 73-79, chmn dept, 78-80, PROF MATH, BOWDOIN COL, 73-79. *Mem:* Am Math Soc; Math Asn Am. *Res:* Jordan algebras of characteristic two; structure of two-groups. *Mailing Add:* Dept of Math Bowdoin Col Brunswick ME 04011

WARD, JAMES VERNON, b Minneapolis, Minn, Mar 27, 40; m 63. STREAM ECOLOGY, LIMNOLOGY. *Educ:* Univ Minn, Minneapolis, BS, 63; Univ Denver, MS, 67; Univ Colo, PhD(limnol), 73. *Prof Exp:* ASSOC PROF STREAM ECOL, DEPT ZOOL & ENTOM, COLO STATE UNIV, 73- *Mem:* Am Soc Limnol & Oceanog; Soc Int Limnol, Ecol Soc Am; Entom Soc Am; NAm Benthological Soc. *Res:* Stream ecology and limnology, especially aquatic macroinvertebrates and factors influencing their distribution and community structure; effects of reservoirs on river systems. *Mailing Add:* Dept Zool & Entom Colo State Univ Ft Collins CO 80523

WARD, JERROLD MICHAEL, b New York, NY, Oct 29, 42; m 71. VETERINARY PATHOLOGY. *Educ:* Cornell Univ, DVM, 66; Univ Calif, Davis, PhD(comp path), 70. *Prof Exp:* Res pathologist, Univ Calif, Davis, 66-68; vet pathologist, Environ Protection Agency, 70-72; vet pathologist, 72-78, chief, tumor pathol, Nat Toxicol Prog, 79-81, ACTG CHIEF, TUMOR PATHOL BR, CARCINOGENESIS TESTING PROG, NAT CANCER INST, 78- *Mem:* Am Vet Med Asn; Int Acad Pathol. *Res:* Pathology; cancer research; hematopoietic pathology; rodent pathology. *Mailing Add:* 10513 Wayridge Dr Gaithersburg MD 20879

WARD, JOHN C(LAYTON), b Ft Worth, Tex, July 23, 34; m 57; c 2. SANITARY ENGINEERING. *Educ:* Univ Okla, BS, 57, ME, 58, PhD(eng sci), 61; Environ Eng Intersoc Bd, dipl. *Prof Exp:* Health physicist, Univ Okla, 59-60; asst prof civil eng, Univ Ark, 61-65; assoc prof, 65-71, PROF CIVIL ENG, COLO STATE UNIV, 71- *Mem:* Am Chem Soc; Am Soc Civil Engrs; Water Pollution Control Fedn; Am Water Works Asn; Am Asn Prof Sanit Engrs. *Res:* Water quality hydrology; experimental nucleonics; thermal pollution; water pollution from cattle feedlots; water pollution potential of oil shale development; evaporation of wastewater; trickling filter cooling towers; pure oxygen aeration. *Mailing Add:* Dept of Civil Eng Eng Res Ctr Colo State Univ Ft Collins CO 80523

WARD, JOHN E(RWIN), b Toledo, Ohio, Jan 4, 20; m 49; c 4. ELECTRICAL ENGINEERING. *Educ:* Mass Inst Technol, BS, 43, MS, 47. *Prof Exp:* Mem res staff, Radiation Lab, 43-45, res asst control systs, 45-47, proj engr, 47-55, exec officer, 55-59, asst dir, 59-66, dep dir, Electron Systs Lab, 66-74, RES STAFF MEM, MASS INST TECHNOL, 66-, LECTR, ELEC ENG INST, 64- *Concurrent Pos:* Pres, Am Automatic Control Coun, 63-65; mem comt comput-aided design tech, Am Ord Asn-Dept Defense, 66-78; mem subcomt automation, Nat Acad Sci-Off Emergency Planning, 66-68. *Mem:* AAAS; fel Inst Elec & Electronics Engrs. *Res:* Control engineering; airborne radar and gunlaying systems; servomechanisms; cable television system design; digital instrumentation; analog-to-digital convertors; numerical machine-tool control; computer-aided design; computer-controlled displays; man-machine communication. *Mailing Add:* Rm 35-402 Mass Inst of Technol Cambridge MA 02139

WARD, JOHN EDWARD, b Chicago, Ill, Feb 7, 23; m 46; c 6. ORGANIC CHEMISTRY. *Educ:* Wabash Col, AB, 44; Lawrence Col, MS, 48, PhD, 51. *Prof Exp:* Res chemist, P H Glatfelter Co, Pa, 50-51, from chief chemist paper chem lab to tech mgr foreign dept, Nopco Chem Co, NJ, 51-59, MANAGING DIR, DIAMOND SHAMROCK CHIMIE, SA, 59- *Mem:* Am Chem Soc; Tech Asn Pulp & Paper Indust. *Res:* Pulp and paper technology, especially the production of pigment coated papers; market research, product development and international marketing of industrial chemical specialties, especially for the particular requirements of various European markets. *Mailing Add:* 24 Route de la Veveyse CH-1700 Fribourg Switzerland

WARD, JOHN EVERETT, JR, b Mocksville, NC, Feb 23, 41; m 64; c 2. MYCOLOGY, ECOLOGY. *Educ:* High Point Col, BS, 63; Wake Forest Univ, MA, 65; Univ SC, PhD(biol), 70. *Prof Exp:* Asst prof biol, Gaston Col, NC, 65-67; asst prof, 70-74, assoc prof, 74-81, PROF BIOL, HIGH POINT COL, 81- *Mem:* Mycol Soc Am. *Res:* Taxonomy and ecology of mushrooms; ecology of soil fungi. *Mailing Add:* Dept of Biol High Point Col High Point NC 27262

WARD, JOHN F, b Blyth, Northumberland, Eng, Aug 26, 35; m 75; c 2. RADIATION CHEMISTRY, RADIATION BIOCHEMISTRY. *Educ:* Durham Univ, BSc, 56, PhD(radiation chem), 60. *Prof Exp:* Demonstr chem, Kings Col, Durham Univ, 60-62; asst res biophysicist, Lab Nuclear Med & Radiation Biol, Univ Calif, Los Angeles, 62-69; assoc res chemist, 69-79, assoc prof path, Sch Med, 74-78, PROF RADIOL, SCH MED, UNIV CALIF, SAN DIEGO, 78-, CHIEF RADIOBIOL, 80- *Concurrent Pos:* Mem radiation study sect, NIH, 74-78; counr chem, Radiation Res Soc, 78-81; assoc ed, Radiation Res, 81- *Mem:* The Chem Soc; Biophys Soc; Radiation Res Soc; Asn Radiation Res. *Res:* Studies of radiation chemical destruction of biologically significant molecules; molecular mechanisms of cell killing; measurement of repair of DNA damage in mammalian cells. *Mailing Add:* Dept of Radiol Univ Calif M027 La Jolla CA 92093

WARD, JOHN FRANK, b London, Eng, May 14, 34; m 60; c 2. PHYSICS. *Educ:* Oxford Univ, BA, 57, MA & DPhil(physics), 61. *Prof Exp:* From lectr to asst prof physics, Univ Mich, 61-64; Assoc Elec Industs res fel, Oxford Univ & lectr, Wadham Col, Univ Oxford, 64-67; assoc prof, 67-74, PROF PHYSICS, UNIV MICH, ANN ARBOR, 74- *Concurrent Pos:* Consult, Lear-Siegler Laser Systs Ctr, 62-64, Royal Radar Estab, 66, Photon Sources, 67- & KMS Fusion Inc, 81- *Mem:* Am Phys Soc. *Res:* Nonlinear optics; lasers. *Mailing Add:* Dept of Physics Univ of Mich Ann Arbor MI 48109

WARD, JOHN HENRY, b Springfield, Mass, Oct 10, 50; m. ATMOSPHERIC SCIENCE. *Educ:* Worcester Polytech Inst, BS, 73; Purdue Univ, MS, 75, PhD(atmospheric sci), 78. *Prof Exp:* Asst atmospheric sci, Purdue Univ, 73-78; FEL NUMERICAL WEATHER PREDICTION, NAT WEATHER SERV, 78- *Mem:* Am Meteorol Soc; AAAS. *Res:* Numerical weather prediction, particularly diagnostic analyses of data assimilation systems. *Mailing Add:* Nat Meteorol Ctr W32 WWB Rm 204 Washington DC 20233

WARD, JOHN K, b Litchfield, Nebr, July 1, 27; m 53; c 3. ANIMAL NUTRITION. *Educ:* McPherson Col, BS, 50; Kans State Univ, BS, 54, PhD, 61. *Prof Exp:* Asst animal husb, Okla State Univ, 54-56; asst prof agr, McPherson Col, 56-66; assoc prof, 67-74, PROF ANIMAL SCI, UNIV NEBR-LINCOLN, 74- *Res:* Beef cattle management. *Mailing Add:* Dept of Animal Sci Baker 235 Univ of Nebr Lincoln NE 68508

WARD, JOHN ROBERT, b Boston, Mass, Jan 10, 29; m 55; c 2. ELECTRICAL ENGINEERING. *Educ:* Univ Sydney, BSc, 49, BE, 52, PhD(aeronaut eng), 58. *Prof Exp:* Aerodynamicist, Vickers-Armstrongs, Ltd, Eng, 51-52; lectr, Univ Sydney, 57; asst prof elec eng, Brown Univ, 58-62; assoc prof, 62-68, PROF ELEC ENG, NAVAL POSTGRAD SCH, 68- *Mem:* Inst Elec & Electronics Engrs; Am Soc Eng Educ. *Res:* Educational technology, programmed instruction; systems dynamics, circuits and control. *Mailing Add:* Dept of Elec Eng Naval Postgrad Sch Monterey CA 93940

WARD, JOHN ROBERT, b Salt Lake City, Utah, Nov 23, 23; m 48; c 4. MEDICINE. *Educ:* Univ Utah, BS, 44, MD, 46; Univ Calif, Berkeley, MPH, 67. *Prof Exp:* Resident internal med, Salt Lake County Gen Hosp, 49-51; from instr to assoc prof med, 57-70, chmn dept prev med, 66-70, PROF MED & CHIEF RHEUMATOLOGY DIV, COL MED, UNIV UTAH, 70- *Concurrent Pos:* Res fel physiol, Col Med, Univ Utah, 48-49; res fel med, Salt Lake County Gen Hosp, 53-54; fel med & rheumatic dis, Mass Gen Hosp & res fel rheumatic dis, Harvard Med Sch, 55-57; consult, Vet Admin Hosp, 57-; sr investr, Arthritis & Rheumatism Found, 59; mem arthritis training grants comt, Nat Inst Arthritis & Metab Dis. *Mem:* AAAS; AMA; Am Rheumatism Asn; Am Col Physicians; NY Acad Sci. *Res:* Biology of mycoplasmatales; experimental arthritis; immunology; epidemiology. *Mailing Add:* Rheumatology Div Univ of Utah Med Ctr Salt Lake City UT 84112

WARD, JOHN WESLEY, b Martin, Tenn, Apr 8, 25; m 47; c 4. PHARMACOLOGY. *Educ:* George Washington Univ, BS & MS, 55; Georgetown Univ, PhD(pharmacol), 59. *Prof Exp:* Res assoc pharmacol, Hazleton Labs, Inc, 50-56, head dept pharmacol, 56-58, chief dept pharmacol & biochem, 58, res appln specialist, 59; prin pharmacologist, 59-60, dir pharmacol, 60-71, dir pharmacol develop, 71-72, dir toxicol, 73-77, dir good lab practs, 77-78, dir biol res, 78-80, dir res, 80-81, VPRES RES, A H ROBINS CO, 82- *Concurrent Pos:* Lectr, Med Col Va, 60-65. *Mem:* AAAS; Am Chem Soc; Soc Toxicol; NY Acad Sci; Am Soc Pharmacol & Exp Therapeut. *Res:* Structure-activity relationships; general pharmacodynamics; autonomics; toxicology. *Mailing Add:* A H Robins Co 1407 Cummings Dr PO Box 26609 Richmond VA 23261

WARD, JOHN WILLIAM, b Moline, Ill, Oct 16, 29; m 52, c 4. HIGH TEMPERATURE CHEMISTRY. *Educ:* Augustana Col, Ill, BA, 52; Wash Univ, MA, 55; Univ NMex, PhD(phys chem), 66. *Prof Exp:* STAFF MEM, LOS ALAMOS NAT LAB, 56- *Concurrent Pos:* Consult, US Army Nuclear Defense Lab, Edgewood Arsenal, 66-; sr fel, Alexander von Humboldt Found, Inst Transuranium Elements, Ger, 72-73. *Mem:* Am Chem Soc; Am Vacuum Soc; fel Am Inst Chem. *Res:* Vapor pressure theory; Monte Carlo computer simulation of experiment; electrochemistry; gas-surface reactions. *Mailing Add:* Group CMB-5 MS 730 Los Alamos Nat Lab Los Alamos NM 87545

WARD, JOHN WILLIAM, b Wigan, Eng, Aug 4, 37; m 69; c 4. PHYSICAL CHEMISTRY. *Educ:* Univ Manchester, BSc, 59, MSc, 60; Cambridge Univ, PhD(phys chem), 62. *Prof Exp:* Res coun Alta fel, 62-63; res scientist, 63-66, sr res scientist, 66-70, res assoc, 70-77, sr res assoc, 77-79, STAFF CONSULT, UNION OIL CO CALIF, 79- *Mem:* Am Chem Soc; Catalysis Soc; Royal Soc Chem; assoc Royal Inst Chem. *Res:* Application of spectroscopic techniques to the study of surface chemistry and catalysis; heterogeneous catalysis; hydrocarbon conversions; petroleum processing, especially hydrotreating, hydrocracking and reforming petrochemical processing; molecular sieves. *Mailing Add:* Union Oil Co Calif Res Dept PO Box 76 Brea CA 92621

WARD, JOHN WILLIAM, b Rochester, NY, Aug 28, 30; m 50; c 8. OPTICS. *Prof Exp:* Sr prod designer, 74, res physicist, 74-81, SR RES PHYSICIST, EASTMAN KODAK CO, 82- *Mem:* Optical Soc Am. *Res:* Development of optical systems to be used for future products or as research tools. *Mailing Add:* Res Labs Eastman Kodak Co Rochester NY 14650

WARD, JONATHAN BISHOP, JR, b Tacoma, Wash, Oct 13, 43; m 69; c 2. GENETICS, TOXICOLOGY. *Educ:* Whitman Col, AB, 65; Univ Idaho, MS, 68; Cornell Univ, PhD(microbiol), 72. *Prof Exp:* Fel somatic cell genetics, Mass Gen Hosp, 72-74; sr res assoc human genetics, 74-78, ASST PROF GENETIC TOXICOL, UNIV TEX MED BR, 78- *Mem:* Am Soc Cell Biol; Sigma Xi; Environ Mutagen Soc. *Res:* Mutagenicity of environmental chemicals in cultured mammalian cells; membrane function in cystic fibrosis fibroblasts; human population monitoring for genetic damage from environmental agents. *Mailing Add:* Div Environ Toxicol Univ Tex Med Br Galveston TX 77550

WARD, JOSEPH RICHARD, b Salt Lake City, Utah, Dec 7, 42. CHEMISTRY. *Educ:* Univ Del, BS, 64; State Univ NY Stony Brook, PhD(chem), 69. *Prof Exp:* RES CHEMIST, US ARMY BALLISTIC RES LABS, ABERDEEN PROVING GROUND, 71- *Mem:* Am Chem Soc. *Res:* Erosion of gun barrels, combustion of solid propellants; effect of propellant combustion in the near-wake of supersonic projectiles. *Mailing Add:* Ballistic Res Labs Aberdeen Proving Ground MD 21005

WARD, KEITH BOLEN, JR, b Paducah, Tex, Feb 20, 43. BIOPHYSICS. *Educ:* Tex A&M Univ, BS, 65; Johns Hopkins Univ, PhD(biophys), 74. *Prof Exp:* Res assoc physics, Appl Res Lab, Gen Dynamics Corp, 65-66; Nat Res Coun res assoc, Lab Struct Matter, Naval Res Lab, 74-76; asst prof, 76-81, ASSOC PROF CHEM, UNIV WIS-PARKSIDE, 82- *Mem:* AAAS; Am Crystallog Asn. *Res:* Study of the relationship between the structure and function of proteins by using x-ray diffraction analysis; oxygen transport pigments; phospholipases; bioluminescent. *Mailing Add:* Sci Div Wood Rd Kenosha WI 53141

WARD, KYLE, JR, b Beaumont, Tex, Sept 2, 02; m 29. CELLULOSE CHEMISTRY, PULP & PAPER TECHNOLOGY. *Educ:* Univ Tex, BA & BS, 23; George Washington Univ, MS, 26; Univ Berlin, PhD(chem), 32. *Hon Degrees:* MS, Lawrence Univ, 68. *Prof Exp:* Instr, Univ Tex, 23-24; jr chemist, Bur Chem & Soils, USDA, 24-28, collabr, 36-38, sr chemist, Southern Regional Res Lab, Bur Agr & Chem Eng, 38-41, prin chemist, Bur Agr & Indust Chem, 41-51; res chemist, Hercules Powder Co, 28-36; res assoc, 51-59, leader cellulose group, 59-66, chmn dept chem, 59-68, leader carbohydrate group & chmn sect org chem, 66-68, EMER PROF, INST PAPER CHEM, 68- *Concurrent Pos:* Res chemist, Chem Found, 36-38; True Mem lectr, 63; consult, Joint Chiefs of Staff, 45 & Am Can Co, 73-75; mem Am-Egyptian chem workshop, 77. *Honors & Awards:* Citation, VI Int Symp Carbohydrate Chem, 72; Anselme Payen Award, 77. *Mem:* AAAS; Am Chem Soc; Fiber Soc; fel Tech Asn Pulp & Paper Indust. *Res:* Cellulose and derivatives; terpenes and related fields; chlorination and oxidation; cotton fiber properties; textiles; high polymers. *Mailing Add:* 1821 S Carpenter St Appleton WI 54911

WARD, LAIRD GORDON LINDSAY, b Wellington, NZ, Dec 6, 31; US citizen. INORGANIC CHEMISTRY. *Educ:* Univ NZ, BSc, 56, MSc, 57; Univ Pa, PhD(inorg chem), 61. *Prof Exp:* Res chemist, Fabrics & Finishes Dept, E I du Pont de Nemours & Co, 61-63; res fel, Mellon Inst Sci, 63-64; res chemist, Int Nickel Co, Inc, NY, 64-71; res assoc chem, Univ Ga, 72; sr chemist, Colonial Metals, Inc, 72-74; RES ASSOC & MEM CHEM FAC, CEND, UNIV DEL, 75-; GROUP LEADER RES & DEVELOP, JOHNSON MATTHEY INC, 75- *Mem:* Am Chem Soc; Royal Soc Chem; fel Am Inst Chemists. *Res:* Hydrometallurgical and pyrometallurgical processes related to refining and recovery of platinum group metals; kinetics of release of carbon-14 and tritium labeled molecules from biosorbable polymers; synthesis of inorganic complexes, especially platinum group metals; organometallic chemistry with group five elements; inorganic pigment applications of non-stoichiometric transition metal oxides. *Mailing Add:* Johnson Matthey Inc Malvern PA 19355

WARD, LAWRENCE MCCUE, b Canton, Ohio, Dec 11, 44; c 2. PSYCHOPHYSICS, VISION. *Educ:* Harvard Univ, AB, 66; Duke Univ, PhD(exp psychol), 71. *Prof Exp:* Asst prof psychol, Rutgers Univ, 70-73; vis asst prof, 73-74, asst prof, 74-77, ASSOC PROF PSYCHOL, UNIV BC, 77- *Concurrent Pos:* Consult, Dept Hwys, State NJ, 72; assoc, Acoust Eng, Vancouver, BC, 75-; res fel, Harvard Univ, 78-79. *Mem:* AAAS; Am Psychol Asn; Psychonomic Soc; Soc Math Psychol; Can Psychol Asn. *Res:* Psychophysical scaling; information processing models of psychophysical judgment; sequential dependencies and context effects in psychophysical judgement; decision theory; environment perception/cognition; attention and feature processing in auditory and visual pattern recognition; visual illusions. *Mailing Add:* Dept of Psychol Univ of BC Vancouver BC V6T 1W5 Can

WARD, LAWRENCE W(ATERMAN), b Flushing, NY, Feb 21, 26; m 55; c 3. APPLIED & FLUID MECHANICS. *Educ:* Univ Mich, BS, 48; Stevens Inst Technol, MS, 51, DSc(appl mech), 62. *Prof Exp:* Technician, Gibbs & Cox, Inc, NY, 48-50, res engr, 51-55; res engr, Stevens Inst Technol, 55-58; PROF ENG, WEBB INST NAVAL ARCHIT, 58- *Concurrent Pos:* NSF sci fac fel, 65-66. *Mem:* Soc Naval Architects & Marine Engrs; Am Soc Naval Engrs; Am Soc Eng Educ; Ger Ship Bldg Soc. *Res:* Ship wave pattern and spectra; experimental determination of wave resistance from wave pattern; ship anti-rolling tanks; ship maneuvering; hull impact. *Mailing Add:* Dept of Eng Webb Inst of Naval Archit Glen Cove NY 11542

WARD, LEWIS EDES, JR, b Arlington, Mass, July 20, 25; m 49; c 3. MATHEMATICS. *Educ:* Univ Calif, AB, 49; Tulane Univ, MS, 51, PhD(math), 53. *Prof Exp:* Instr math, Univ Nev, 53-54; asst prof, Univ Utah, 54-56; mathematician, US Naval Ord Test Sta, Univ Calif, 56-59; assoc prof, 59-65, PROF MATH, UNIV ORE, 65- *Mem:* Am Math Soc; Math Asn Am. *Res:* Topology, especially ordered spaces and fixed point theory. *Mailing Add:* Dept of Math Univ of Ore Eugene OR 97403

WARD, LOUIS EMMERSON, b Mt Vernon, Ill, Jan 19, 18; m 42; c 4. MEDICINE. *Educ:* Univ Ill, AB, 39; Harvard Univ, MD, 43; Univ Minn, MS, 49. *Prof Exp:* From instr med to prof clin med, Mayo Grad Sch Med, Univ Minn, 51-73, PROF MED, MAYO MED SCH, 73-; chmn bd gov, 64-75, CONSULT SECT MED, MAYO CLIN, 50- *Mem:* Inst of Med of Nat Acad Sci; Am Rheumatism Asn (past pres); AMA; Nat Soc Clin Rheumatol. *Res:* Rheumatic diseases. *Mailing Add:* 200 First St SW Rochester MN 55901

WARD, MAX, b Mt Zion, WVa, May 14, 14; m; c 2. BOTANY, MORPHOLOGY. *Educ:* Glenville State Col, AB, 40; Harvard Univ, MA, 47, PhD(bot), 50. *Prof Exp:* Teacher, pub schs, Calhoun County, WVa, 34-35 & 36-38, high sch, 40-43 & 45-46; prof bot & chmn div sci & math, Glenville State Col, 48-69; vis prof biol, Univ Akron, 69-70; vis prof bot, Ohio Univ, 70-71; MGR STUDENT-ORIENTED PROG, DIV SCI PERSONNEL IMPROV, NSF, 71- *Concurrent Pos:* NSF res grant, Harvard Univ, 58-60. *Mem:* AAAS; Bot Soc Am; Am Bryol & Lichenological Soc; Int Soc Plant Morphol. *Res:* Morphogenesis and developmental morphology in the ferns and mosses. *Mailing Add:* 5432 Connecticut Ave NW Washington DC 20015

WARD, OSCAR GARDIEN, b Denver, Colo, Feb 16, 32; m 55; c 2. GENETICS. *Educ:* Univ Ariz, BS, 58, MS, 60; Purdue Univ, PhD(genetics), 66. *Prof Exp:* Instr biol, Purdue Univ, 60-64; asst prof, 66-74, lectr, 74-77, ASSOC PROF, BIOL SCI, UNIV ARIZ, 77- *Concurrent Pos:* Fogarty sr int fel, Mexico, 80. *Mem:* AAAS; Genetics Soc Am; Am Soc Human Genetics; Am Soc Mammalogists; Am Genetic Asn. *Res:* plant and animal cytogenetics with emphasis on mammalian systems including man; chromosome identification by banding patterns with application to karyotype evolution; role of chromosomes during development; human cytogenetics. *Mailing Add:* Dept of Ecol & Evolutionary Biol Univ of Ariz Tucson AZ 85721

WARD, PAUL H, b Lawrence, Ind, Apr 24, 28; m 52; c 2. OTOLARYNGOLOGY. *Educ:* Anderson Col, AB, 53; Johns Hopkins Univ, MD, 57; Am Bd Otolaryngol, dipl, 62. *Prof Exp:* Intern, Henry Ford Hosp, Detroit, 57-58; resident otolaryngol, Univ Chicago, 58-61, NIH spec res fel, 61-62, asst prof, 62-64; assoc prof surg & chief div otolaryngol, Sch Med, Vanderbilt Univ, 64-68; PROF SURG & CHIEF HEAD & NECK SURG, CTR HEALTH SCI, UNIV CALIF, LOS ANGELES, 68- *Concurrent Pos:* USPHS res grant, 63-69; Deafness Res Found res grant, 65-67; NIH res grant, 66-70; attend otolaryngologist, Nashville Metrop Gen Hosp, Tenn, 64-68; consult, Thayer Vet Admin Hosp, 64-68 & Surgeon Gen of US Navy, 74-; mem bd dirs, Bill Wilkerson Hearing & Speech Ctr, 64-68. *Mem:* AAAS; Am Otol Soc; Am Acad Ophthal & Otolaryngol; Am Laryngol Soc; Am Laryngol, Rhinol & Otol Soc. *Res:* Cochlear, vestibular and laryngeal physiology; temporal bone pathology; velopharyngeal corrective techniques; laryngeal and palatal reconstruction. *Mailing Add:* Dept Surg Sch Med Univ Calif Los Angeles CA 90024

WARD, PAUL J, b Blairstown, Mo, Oct 30, 21; m 44; c 3. DAIRY BACTERIOLOGY. *Educ:* Univ Mo, BS, 46, MS, 47. *Prof Exp:* Res technician cheese, Kraft Foods Res Lab, 48-53, group leader, 53-59; mgr dairy prod res, Res & Develop Div, Nat Dairy Prod Corp, 59-69; prod mgr natural cheese cutting & contract suppliers, 69-71, nat prod mgr contract suppliers, 71-74, nat prod mgr cream cheese & frozen foods, Kraftco Corp, 74-76, NAT PROD MGR FOOD SERV, KRAFT INC, 76- *Mem:* Am Dairy Sci Asn; Inst Food Technol. *Res:* Dairy manufacturing; cheese and all other dairy products. *Mailing Add:* Kraftco Corp 500 Peshtigo Ct Chicago IL 60690

WARD, PETER A, b Winsted, Conn, Nov 1, 34. PATHOLOGY, IMMUNOLOGY. *Educ:* Univ Mich, BS, 58, MD, 60. *Prof Exp:* Intern med, Third Div, Bellevue Hosp, New York, 60-61; resident path, Hosp, Univ Mich, Ann Arbor, 61-63; res fel immunopath, Div Exp Path, Scripps Clin & Res Found, La Jolla, Calif, 63-65; chief immunobiol, Armed Forces Inst Path, Washington, DC, 65-70; prof path, Sch Med, Univ Conn, 71-80, chmn dept, 73-80; PROF & CHMN DEPT PATH, MED SCH, UNIV MICH, 80- *Mem:* Am Asn Path; Am Asn Immunologists; Am Soc Clin Invest. *Res:* Immunopathology; inflammation; biological role of complement; antibody formation. *Mailing Add:* Dept Path Box 045 Univ Mich Med Sch 1355 E Catherine St Ann Arbor MI 48109

WARD, PETER LANGDON, b Washington, DC, Aug 10, 43; m 65, 78; c 4. SEISMOLOGY, VOLCANOLOGY. *Educ:* Dartmouth Col, BA, 65; Columbia Univ, MA, 67, PhD(geophys), 70. *Prof Exp:* Asst seismol, Columbia Univ, 65-70, res scientist, 70-71; geophysicist, 71-75, chief br seismol, 75, chief br earthquake mech & prediction, 75-77, coordr earthquake prediction prog, 77-78, GEOPHYSICIST SEISMOL, US GEOL SURV, 78- *Concurrent Pos:* Mem adv panel magma energy res, Sandia Labs, 74-; mem, Earth Dynamics Adv Subcomt, NASA, 76-77; mem geophys prediction panel, Nat Acad Sci, 77-78. *Mem:* Int Asn Volcanol & Chem of Earth's Interiors; AAAS; Am Geophys Union; Seismol Soc Am; Geol Soc Am. *Res:* Analysis of earthquakes related to volcanoes, geothermal areas and tectonic features; earthquake seismology; earthquakes and ground deformation near volcanoes; geothermal exploration with seismic techniques; seismic instrumentation; computer techniques; earthquake prediction and hazard reduction. *Mailing Add:* US Geol Surv NCER 345 Middlefield Rd Menlo Park CA 94025

WARD, RAYMOND LELAND, b San Pedro, Calif, Feb 12, 32; m 58; c 4. PHYSICAL CHEMISTRY. *Educ:* Univ Calif, BSc, 53; Washington Univ, St Louis, PhD(chem), 56. *Prof Exp:* Chemist, Lawrence Radiation Lab, Univ Calif, 56-64; NSF sr fel, Harvard Univ, 64-65; CHEMIST, LAWRENCE LIVERMORE NAT LAB, UNIV CALIF, 65- *Mem:* Am Chem Soc. *Res:* Magnetic resonance studies of molecular interactions. *Mailing Add:* Dept Chem Lawrence Livermore Nat Lab Univ Calif Livermore CA 94550

WARD, RICHARD BERNARD, b Felixstowe, Eng, Jan 3, 32; m 63; c 2. ORGANIC CHEMISTRY. *Educ:* Univ Birmingham, BSc, 53, PhD, 56. *Prof Exp:* Atomic Energy Auth fel, Univ Birmingham, Eng, 56-58; Corn Indust Res Found fel, Ohio State Univ, 58-59; res org chemist, 59-65, res supvr, 65-68, prod supvr, 68-70, sr res chemist, 70-75, RES ASSOC & TECH CONSULT, E I DU PONT DE NEMOURS & CO, INC, 75- *Mem:* Am Chem Soc; Royal Soc Chem. *Res:* Permeation through polymers; fluorine; dye manufacture; fluorocarbons; environmental and toxicological consulting. *Mailing Add:* E I Du Pont de Nemours & Co Inc Petrochemicals Dept N9510 Wilmington DE 19898

WARD, RICHARD FLOYD, b New York, NY, July 5, 27; m 49; c 3. GEOLOGY. *Educ:* Bradley Univ, BS, 50; NY Univ, MS, 56; Bryn Mawr Col, PhD, 58. *Prof Exp:* Geologist, Del State Geol Surv, 54-58; ASSOC PROF GEOL, WAYNE STATE UNIV, 59- *Mem:* Geol Soc Am; Geochem Soc. *Res:* Metamorphic and igneous petrology; evolution of crystalline terrains. *Mailing Add:* Dept of Geol Wayne State Univ Detroit MI 48202

WARD, RICHARD JOHN, b Seattle, Wash, Aug 7, 25; m 50; c 3. ANESTHESIOLOGY. *Educ:* Gonzaga Univ, BSc, 46; St Louis Univ, MD, 49; Seattle Univ, MEd, 72; Am Bd Anesthesiol, dipl. *Prof Exp:* Chief anesthesiol serv, Air Force Hosp, Weisbaden, Ger, 54-57; asst chief anesthesiol, Lackland AFB, 57-60, chief, 60-61; chief anesthesiol, Ballard Gen Hosp, 62-63; from instr to assoc prof anesthesiol, 63-72, PROF ANESTHESIOL, SCH MED, UNIV WASH, 72-, CHIEF STAFF, UNIV HOSP, 77- *Concurrent Pos:* NIH res fel, 64-65; consult, Surgeon Gen, US Air Force in Europe, 54-57; chief surg res lab, Lackland AFB, 58-61; admin officer, Sch Med, Univ Wash, 66; consult, Madigan Gen Hosp, 72- *Mem:* AAAS; Am Soc Anesthesiol; AMA; Asn Mil Surg US; fel Am Col Anesthesiol. *Res:* Pharmacology and physiology of anesthetized man. *Mailing Add:* Dept of Anesthesiol Univ of Wash Sch of Med Seattle WA 98195

WARD, RICHARD LEO, b Bozeman, Mont, Nov 16, 42; m 66; c 2. VIROLOGY. *Educ:* Mont State Univ, BS, 65; Univ Calif, PhD(biochem), 69. *Prof Exp:* Fel molecular biol, Max Planck Inst Biochem, 69-70; fel animal virol, Roche Inst Molecular Biol, 70-72; asst res virologist, Sch Med, Univ Calif, Los Angeles, 72-74; mem tech staff, Sandia Labs, Albuquerque, 74-80; chief viral disease, Health & Environ Res Lab, US Environ Protection Agency, Cincinnati, 81-81; ASSOC MEM, CHRIST HOSP INST MED RES, CINCINNATI, 81- *Mem:* Am Soc Microbiol; AAAS. *Res:* Enteric viral diseases; environmental virology; herpes viruses; chemical carcinogenesis; radiation biology. *Mailing Add:* 2282 Spinningwheel Lane Cincinnati OH 45244

WARD, RICHARD S, b Beirut, Lebanon, Oct 9, 20; m 60; c 3. PSYCHIATRY, PEDIATRICS. *Educ:* Amherst Col, BA, 42; Columbia Univ, MD, 45, cert, 57. *Prof Exp:* Clin dir, Child Guid Inst, Jewish Bd Guardians, NY, 56-61; assoc prof, 60-63, PROF PSYCHIAT, SCH MED, EMORY UNIV, 63-, ASSOC PROF PEDIAT, 76- *Concurrent Pos:* Rockefeller fel child psychiat, Babies Hosp, Columbia Univ, 48-50. *Mem:* Am Psychoanal Asn; Am Psychiat Asn; fel Am Orthopsychiat Asn; Am Acad Child Psychiat. *Res:* Child development; psychoanalysis. *Mailing Add:* Emory Univ Sch of Med Atlanta GA 30307

WARD, RICHARD THEODORE, b Avoca, Nebr, Sept 10, 25; m 53; c 2. PLANT ECOLOGY. *Educ:* Univ Nebr, BSc, 48; Univ Minn, MSc, 51; Univ Wis, PhD, 54. *Prof Exp:* Asst plant ecol, Univ Wis, 53-54; from instr to asst prof biol, Beloit Col, 54-57; from asst prof to prof bot & plant path, 57-75, chmn dept, 66-75, PROF PLANT ECOL, COLO STATE UNIV, 75- *Concurrent Pos:* Mem, Mined Land Reclam Bd, Colo & Gov's Sci & Technol Adv Coun. *Mem:* Ecol Soc Am; Sigma Xi. *Res:* Alpine vegetation; ecologic race differentiation; ecological races and (for) mined land reclamation; ecology of the American beech. *Mailing Add:* Dept of Bot & Plant Path Colo State Univ Ft Collins CO 80521

WARD, ROBERT C, b Mt Clemens, Mich, Mar 9, 32; c 4. OSTEOPATHY, BIOMECHANICS. *Educ:* Kansas City Col Osteop Med, DO, 57. *Prof Exp:* Intern, Mt Clemens Gen Hosp, 57-58, staff mem family med, 58-71; preceptor, Col Osteop Med & asst prof family med, 70-71, prof family med & chmn dept, 72-74, prof med educ res & develop, 74-71, PROF BIOMECHANICS, MICH STATE UNIV, 81-; STAFF MEM, LANSING GEN HOSP, 72- *Concurrent Pos:* Off Med Educ fel, Mich State Univ, 72-73. *Mem:* Am Osteop Asn; Am Asn Study Headache; Am Acad Osteop. *Res:* Family medicine curriculum design; osteopathic therapeutics; community based medical education; stress management education. *Mailing Add:* Off Med Educ Res & Develop Mich State Univ East Lansing MI 48823

WARD, ROBERT CARL, b Swansea, Wales, July 4, 44; US citizen; m 66. ENVIRONMENTAL ENGINEERING, AGRICULTURAL ENGINEERING. *Educ:* Miss State Univ, BS, 66; NC State Univ, MS, 68, PhD(agr eng), 70. *Prof Exp:* Asst prof agr eng, 70-75, assoc prof, 75-80, PROF AGR & CHEM ENG, COLO STATE UNIV, 80- *Concurrent Pos:* Guest researcher, Water Qual Inst, Denmark, 76; systs engr, US Environ Protection Agency, 77. *Honors & Awards:* Durrell Award, Colo State Univ, 74; Gunlogson Award, Am Soc Agr Engrs, 76. *Mem:* Nat Water Well Asn; Water Pollution Control Fedn; Am Soc Agr Engrs; Am Water Resources Asn; Am Geophys Union. *Res:* Water quality management; design of water quality monitoring systems; on-site home sewage disposal; data use for regulatory water quality management. *Mailing Add:* Dept Agr & Chem Eng Colo State Univ Ft Collins CO 80523

WARD, ROBERT CLEVELAND, b Sparta, Tenn, Dec 7, 44; m 65; c 2. NUMERICAL ANALYSIS. *Educ:* Tenn Technol Univ, BS, 66; Col William & Mary, MS, 69; Univ Va, PhD(appl math), 74. *Prof Exp:* Mathematician, Langley Res Ctr, Nasa, 66-74; res staff mem math, 74-77, HEAD MATH RES SECT, COMPUT SCI DIV, NUCLEAR DIV, UNION CARBIDE CORP, 77- *Mem:* Sigma Xi; AAAS; Soc Indust & Appl Math; Asn Comput Mach. *Res:* Developing, analyzing and improving numerical techniques in the areas of numerical linear algebra and computational statistics. *Mailing Add:* Nuclear Div Union Carbide Corp Bldg 9704-1 PO Box Y Oak Ridge TN 37830

WARD, ROBERT T, b Jersey City, NJ, Feb 7, 20; m 60. ZOOLOGY, CYTOLOGY. *Educ:* NJ State Teachers Col, AB, 42; Columbia Univ, MA, 52, PhD(zool), 60. *Prof Exp:* Res assoc zool, Columbia Univ, 52-57; ASST PROF ANAT, STATE UNIV NY DOWNSTATE MED CTR, 60- *Concurrent Pos:* NSF res grant, 62-66. *Mem:* AAAS; Electron Micros Soc Am; Am Soc Cell Biol; Am Asn Anat. *Res:* Electron microscopy; histochemistry. *Mailing Add:* Dept of Anat State Univ NY Downstate Med Ctr Brooklyn NY 11203

WARD, RONALD ANTHONY, b New York, NY, Jan 25, 29; m 50; c 2. MEDICAL ENTOMOLOGY. *Educ:* Cornell Univ, BSc, 50; Univ Chicago, PhD(zool), 55; Univ London, MSc, 67. *Prof Exp:* Instr biol, Gonzaga Univ, 55-58; MED ENTOMOLOGIST, WALTER REED ARMY INST RES, 58- *Concurrent Pos:* US Secy of Army fel, London Sch Hyg & Trop Med, 66-67; res assoc, Smithsonian Inst, Washington, DC, 77-; ed, Mosquito News, 81- *Mem:* Coun Biol Ed; Am Soc Trop Med & Hyg; Am Mosquito Control Asn; Royal Soc Trop Med & Hyg; Entom Soc Am. *Res:* Genetic and ecologic factors affecting susceptibility and resistance of arthropods to infectious agents; host adaptation of malaria parasites; mosquito biosystematics; mosquito control. *Mailing Add:* Dept Entom Walter Reed Army Inst Res Washington DC 20012

WARD, RONALD WAYNE, b Johnson City, Tenn, Dec 17, 43; m 66. AGRICULTURAL ECONOMICS, ECONOMETRICS. *Educ:* Univ Tenn, BS, 65; Iowa State Univ, MS, 67, PhD(econ & statist), 70. *Prof Exp:* Res asst agr econ, Univ Tenn, summer 65; res asst, Iowa State Univ, 65-69; coop agent, USDA, 69-70; assoc prof, 70-80, PROF ECON, DEPT FOOD & RESOURCE ECON, UNIV FLA, 80- *Concurrent Pos:* Res economist, Fla Dept Citrus, 70-; USDA mkt struct res grant, Univ Fla, 71-72. *Mem:* Am Econ Asn; Am Agr Econ Asn. *Res:* Price analysis; marketing; advertising; market structures. *Mailing Add:* 1099 McCarty Hall Univ of Fla Gainesville FL 32611

WARD, RONALD WAYNE, b Burbank, Calif, Sept 20, 44; m 76; c 1. APPLIED SEISMOLOGY, EARTHQUAKE SEISMOLOGY. *Educ:* Mass Inst Technol, BS, 66, PhD(geophysics), 71. *Prof Exp:* Res scientist, Tex Instruments, Inc, 65; res geophysicist, Ray Geophys, Inc, Houston, Tex, 66, Geosci, Inc, 67 & Lincoln Lab, 68; sr res scientist geophysics, Amoco Prod Co, Tulsa, Okla, 71-74; ASSOC PROF GEOPHYSICS, UNIV TEX DALLAS, 74-, DIR, CTR LITHOSPHERIC STUDIES, 81- *Concurrent Pos:* Chmn, Tech Adv Comt Seismic Methods, Dept Energy, 77-; adv, External Proposal Rev Panel, US Geol Survey, 78-79, co-covener, Workshop Seismic Model for the Geysers-Clear Lake Geothermal Region, Pajaro Dunes, Calif, 79; distinguished lectr, Phillips Petrol Seminars, 80. *Mem:* Am Geophys Union; Soc Explor Geophysicists; Seismol Soc Am; European Asn Explor Geophysicists; AAAS. *Res:* Three-dimensional and long-range seismic reflection/refracion surveys of the earth's crust; development of new signal processing techniques; seismic modeling techniques, and seismic inversion techniques; seismic studies of geothermal areas, especially the attenuation of seismic waves; seismic velocity studies in partially melted rock. *Mailing Add:* PO Box 688 MS FA3 1 Richardson TX 75080

WARD, ROSCOE FREDRICK, b Boise, Idaho, Dec 5, 30; m 63; c 2. CIVIL ENGINEERING. *Educ:* Col of Idaho, BA, 53; Ore State Col, BS, 59; Wash State Univ, MS, 61; Washington Univ, DSc(environ & sanit eng), 64; Environ Engrs Intersoc, dipl, 69. *Prof Exp:* Design engr, Standard Oil Co Calif, 59-60; asst prof civil eng, Univ Mo-Columbia, 63-65 & Robert Col, Istanbul, 65-67; assoc prof, Asian Inst Technol, 67-68; assoc prof civil eng & asst dean sch eng, Univ Mass, Amherst, 68-75; br chief, Fuels From Biomass Systs Br, Dept Energy, 75-80. *Concurrent Pos:* Prof, Istanbul Tech Univ, 66-67; consult, Democ, 66-67; prog mgr undergrad instrnl progs & res appl to nat needs, NSF, 72-73; prof civil eng, Bogazici Univ, Istanbul, 74-75. *Mem:* Am Acad Environ Eng; Am Soc Civil Engrs; Water Pollution Control Fedn. *Res:* Water supply, wastewater treatment, solid waste disposal and clean energy production from biomass. *Mailing Add:* 93 Deerfield Lane N Pleasantville NY 10570

WARD, SAMUEL, b Los Angeles, Calif, Sept 29, 44; m 66; c 2. BIOCHEMISTRY. *Educ:* Princeton Univ, AB, 65; Calif Inst Technol, PhD(biochem), 71. *Prof Exp:* Tutor biochem sci, Harvard Col, 73-74; asst prof biol chem, Harvard Med Sch, 72-77; MEM STAFF, DEPT EMBRYOL, CARNEGIE INST WASHINGTON, 77-; ASSOC PROF BIOL, JOHNS HOPKINS UNIV, 77- *Concurrent Pos:* NSF fel, Med Res Coun Lab Molecular Biol, Cambridge, Eng, 70-71, NIH spec fel, 71-72. *Mem:* Am Soc Genetics; AAAS; Am Soc Cell Biol; Am Soc Develop Biol. *Res:* Genetic control of cell structure and morphology; nematode sperm development. *Mailing Add:* Carnegie Inst Washington 115 W University Pkwy Baltimore MD 21210

WARD, SAMUEL ABNER, b Binghamton, NY, Apr 27, 23; m 46; c 2. ELECTRONIC PHYSICS. *Educ:* Cornell Univ, BEE, 44, MEE, 46, PhD(electronics, physics), 53. *Prof Exp:* Elec radio engr, US Naval Res Lab, 44-45; asst physics, Cornell Univ, 46-50; res engr, Electron Tubes, Nat Union Radio Corp, 50-51, A B Du Mont Labs, Inc, 51-52 & Electron Tubes & Devices, RCA Labs, Inc, 52-56; physicist, Gen Elec Co, 56-57; chief physicist, Machlett Labs, Inc, 57-61; sr eng physicist, Perkin-Elmer Corp, 61-64; sr scientist, CBS Labs, Stamford, Conn, 64-75; sr engr, Machlett Labs, Div Raytheon, 75-78; sr physicist, Coulter Systs Corp, Bedford, 78-80; PRIN SCIENTIST, RES DIV, RAYTHEON CO, 80- *Mem:* Am Phys Soc; Inst Elec & Electronics Engrs; Sigma Xi. *Res:* Solid state physics; physical electronics; electron devices; sputtering of insulating films; photoelectric emission from semiconductors and metals; photoeffects in solids; ion implantation doping of semiconductors; electron and ion optics. *Mailing Add:* Res Div Raytheon Co 28 Seyon St Waltham MA 02154

WARD, STANLEY HARRY, b Vancouver, BC, Jan 16, 23; m 43; c 1. GEOPHYSICS. *Educ:* Univ Toronto, BASc, 49, MA, 50, PhD(geophys), 52. *Prof Exp:* Geophysicist, Int Nickel Co Can, Ltd, 49; chief geophysicist & managing dir, McPhar Geophys, Ltd, 49-53, exec vpres, 53-54; chief geophysicist & managing dir, Nucom Ltd, 54-58; consult geophysicist, Univ Toronto, 58-59; assoc prof mineral explor, Univ Calif, Berkeley, 59-64, prof geophys eng, 64-70; PROF GEOL SCI & CHMN DEPT GEOL & GEOPHYS, UNIV UTAH, 70- *Mem:* Soc Explor Geophys; Am Geophys Union; Am Inst Mining, Metall & Petrol Engrs; Inst Elec & Electronics Engrs; Can Inst Mining & Metall. *Res:* Variation magnetic and electric fields; rock physics; mineral exploration. *Mailing Add:* Dept of Geol Sci Univ of Utah Salt Lake City UT 84112

WARD, THOMAS EDMUND, b Los Angeles, Calif, Nov 10, 44; m 78; c 1. NUCLEAR CHEMISTRY, NUCLEAR PHYSICS. *Educ:* Northeastern State Col, BSEd, 65; Univ Ark, Fayetteville, MS, 69, PhD(nuclear chem), 71. *Prof Exp:* Res assoc nuclear chem, Brookhaven Nat Lab, 70-72; STAFF CHEMIST, DEPT PHYSICS, IND UNIV, BLOOMINGTON, 72- *Concurrent Pos:* Vis assoc chemist, Brookhaven Nat Lab, 72-75; vis fac mem, Dept Chem, Ind Univ, 81- *Mem:* Am Chem Soc; Am Phys Soc; NY Acad Sci. *Res:* Nuclear spectroscopy and radioactive decay; intermediate energy nuclear reactions; pion production; cosmic rays; environmental nuclear chemistry. *Mailing Add:* Dept of Physics Ind Univ Bloomington IN 47401

WARD, THOMAS J(ULIAN), b Amsterdam, NY, Aug 14, 30. CHEMICAL ENGINEERING, PROCESS CONTROL. *Educ:* Clarkson Col Technol, BChE, 52; Univ Tex, MS, 56; Rensselaer Polytech Inst, PhD(chem eng), 59. *Prof Exp:* Asst to Dr E J Weiss, Austin, Tex, 53-56; mem staff, Rensselaer Polytech Inst, 56-59; asst prof, 59-61, assoc prof, 61-82, PROF CHEM ENG, CLARKSON COL TECHNOL, 61- *Mem:* Am Inst Chem Engrs; Am Nuclear Soc; sr mem Instrument Soc Am. *Res:* Process control; optimization; design; ceramic materials; nuclear engineering. *Mailing Add:* Box 178 Colton NY 13625

WARD, TRUMAN L, b Ft Worth, Tex, Oct 21, 25; m 45; c 3. PHYSICS, PHYSICAL CHEMISTRY. *Educ:* Tulane Univ, BS, 48. *Prof Exp:* Assoc physicist, 48-63, RES PHYSICIST, SOUTHERN REGIONAL LAB, AGR RES SERV, USDA, 63- *Honors & Awards:* Awards, Sustained Outstanding Performance, Agr Res Serv, 61, Cert Merit & Dept Agr Superior Serv, 74, Fed Sci Distinguished Serv Award, 78. *Mem:* Am Chem Soc; Sigma Xi; fel Am Inst Chem; Am Asn Textile Chem & Colorists. *Res:* Physical properties of vegetable fats and oils; reaction mechanisms and kinetics; synthesis and reactions of thiorane and epoxy compounds; development of new instrumental procedures; glassification of cellulose; low temperature plasmas; polymers; ion exchanges. *Mailing Add:* Southern Regional Ctr USDA PO Box 19687 New Orleans LA 70179

WARD, WALLACE DIXON, b Pierre, SDak, June 30, 24; m 49; c 4. PSYCHOACOUSTICS. *Educ:* SDak Sch Mines & Technol, BS, 44; Harvard Univ, PhD(exp psychol), 53. *Hon Degrees:* ScD, SDak Sch Mines & Technol, 71. *Prof Exp:* Asst scientist, Rosemount Res Ctr, Univ Minn, 49; asst, Harvard Univ, 49-53; res engr, Baldwin Piano Co, 53-54; res scientist, Cent Inst Deaf, 54-57; res assoc subcomt noise, Comt Conserv Hearing, Am Acad Ophthal & Otolaryngol, 57-62; PROF OTOLARYNGOL & COMMUN DIS, 62- & ENVIRON HEALTH, UNIV MINN, MINNEAPOLIS, 72- *Concurrent Pos:* Fels, Acoust Soc Am, 61 & Am Speech & Hearing Asn, 66; chmn exec coun, Comt Hearing, Bioacoust & Biomech, Nat Acad Sci-Nat Res Coun, 71-73; consult, Off Noise Abatement & Control, Environ Protection Agency, 72-73, Air Transport Asn Am, 73- & Edgewood Arsenal, US Army. *Mem:* Am Otol Soc; Psychonomic Soc; Int Soc Audiol (vpres, 76-78, pres, 78-80); Am Audiol Soc (vpres, 73-75, pres, 76-77); Int Comt Biol Effects Noise (co-chmn, 73-78). *Res:* Auditory fatigue and noise-induced hearing loss; musical perception; musical psychoacoustics. *Mailing Add:* Hearing Res Lab 2630 Univ Ave SE Minneapolis MN 55414

WARD, WALTER FREDERICK, b Darlington, Wis, June 23, 40; m 59; c 3. PHYSIOLOGY, ENDOCRINOLOGY. *Educ:* Univ Wis-Platteville, BSc, 64; Marquette Univ, PhD(physiol), 70. *Prof Exp:* Asst prof physiol, Col Med, Pa State Univ, 73-78; asst prof, 78-80, ASSOC PROF PHYSIOL, HEALTH SCI CTR, UNIV TEX, SAN ANTONIO, 80- *Concurrent Pos:* USPHS fel, Brown Univ, 71-73. *Mem:* AAAS; Am Physiol Soc. *Res:* Regulation of protein metabolism; mechanisms of hormone action. *Mailing Add:* Dept of Physiol Univ of Tex Health Sci Ctr San Antonio TX 78284

WARD, WILLIAM CRUSE, b Waco, Tex, Apr 26, 33; m 57; c 3. SEDIMENTARY PETROLOGY. *Educ:* Univ Tex, Austin, BS, 55, MA, 57; Rice Univ, PhD(geol), 70. *Prof Exp:* Geologist, Humble Oil & Refining Co, 57-66; asst prof, 70-73, assoc prof, 73-78, PROF GEOL, UNIV NEW ORLEANS, 78- *Mem:* Soc Econ Paleontologists & Mineralogists; Am Asn Petrol Geologists. *Res:* Petrology and diagenesis of Quaternary limestones of eastern Yucatan; sandstone petrology and diagenesis. *Mailing Add:* Dept of Earth Sci Univ of New Orleans New Orleans LA 70122

WARD, WILLIAM FRANCIS, b Erie, Pa, June 19, 28. PARASITOLOGY. *Educ:* Gannon Col, BS, 50; Univ Notre Dame, MS, 55. *Prof Exp:* Instr biol, Col St Mary, Utah, 55-57; asst prof, 57-66, from actg chmn dept to chmn dept, 64-72, chmn div natural sci & math, 76-79, ASSOC PROF BIOL, ROSEMONT COL, 66- *Mem:* Am Soc Microbiol; Sigma Xi; AAAS; Am Soc Parasitol; Am Inst Biol Sci. *Res:* Interrelationships between intestinal parasites and the bacterial flora. *Mailing Add:* Dept of Biol Rosemont Col Rosemont PA 19010

WARD, WILLIAM J, III, b Paterson, NJ, Oct 4, 39; m 62; c 2. CHEMICAL ENGINEERING. *Educ:* Pa State Univ, BS, 61; Univ Ill, MS, 63, PhD(chem eng), 65. *Prof Exp:* RES ENGR, GEN ELEC CO, 65- *Mem:* AAAS; Am Inst Chem Engrs. *Res:* Research and development of membrane separation processes; catalysis. *Mailing Add:* Gen Elec Corp Res & Develop Ctr Box 8 Schenectady NY 12301

WARDE, CARDINAL, b Barbados, July 14, 45. SOLID STATE PHYSICS, OPTICAL ENGINEERING. *Educ:* Stevens Inst Technol, BSc, 69; Yale Univ, MPhil, 71, PhD(physics), 74. *Prof Exp:* Asst prof, 74-79, ASSOC PROF ELEC ENG, MASS INST TECHNOL, 79- *Concurrent Pos:* Vinton Hayes fel, Mass Inst Technol, 75-76; prin investr, NSF grants, 76- & Air Force Off Sci Res grant, 77-; consult, Lincoln Lab, Mass Inst Technol, 77-, Rome Air Develop Ctr, 81- & Hamamatsu TV Co, Japan, 80-; State Univ NY res grant, 80-81. *Mem:* Optical Soc Am; Inst Elec & Electronics Engrs; Soc Photo-Optical Instrumentation Engrs. *Res:* Optical signal processing and storage devices; adaptive optical systems; optical properties of electron-beam-addressed materials. *Mailing Add:* Rm 13-3134 Mass Inst of Technol Cambridge MA 02139

WARDE, CHARLES JOSEPH, b Castlebar, Ireland, July 3, 40; US citizen; m 69; c 3. ELECTROCHEMISTRY. *Educ:* Univ Col, Dublin, BSc, 63, PhD(electrochem), 69. *Prof Exp:* Engr, Res Labs, Westinghouse Elec Corp, 68-69, sr engr, 69-76; mgr load-leveling batteries, 76-78, dir battery res & develop, 78-80, VPRES RES & DEVELOP, ENERGY DEVELOP ASSOCS, MICH, 80- *Mem:* Electrochem Soc; Am Chem Soc. *Res:* Zinc-chlorine batteries; fuel cells, metal-air batteries, hydrogen generation, electro-analysis, corrosion and energy storage. *Mailing Add:* 7290 Glengrove Birmingham MI 48010

WARDELL, JOE RUSSELL, JR, b Omaha, Nebr, Nov 11, 29; m 52; c 3. PHARMACOLOGY, PHYSIOLOGY. *Educ:* Creighton Univ, BS, 51; Univ Nebr, MSc, 59, PhD(pharmacol, physiol), 62. *Prof Exp:* Sr pharmacologist, 62-65, group leader pharmacol, 64-68, asst dir pharmacol, 68-71, assoc dir pharmacol & mission dir cardiopulmonary res area, 71-75, assoc dir biol res & mission dir cardiovasc res area, 75-78, sci dir new prod eval, Res & Mission dir cardiovasc res area, 78-81, DIR NEW COMPOUND EVAL, SMITH KLINE & FRENCH LABS, 81- *Mem:* AAAS; Am Chem Soc; NY Acad Sci; Am Soc Pharmacol & Exp Therapeut; Am Acad Allergy. *Res:* Cardiovascular and respiratory pharmacology; immunopharmacology; autonomic pharmacology; regulation of biosynthesis and secretion of respiratory mucus. *Mailing Add:* Res & Develop Div PO Box 7929 Smith Kline & French Labs Philadelphia PA 19101

WARDELL, WILLIAM MICHAEL, b Christchurch, NZ, Nov 15, 38; m 65; c 2. CLINICAL PHARMACOLOGY. *Educ:* Oxford Univ, BA, 61, DPhil(pharmacol), 64, BM & BCh, 67, DM, 73. *Prof Exp:* Intern med, Radcliffe Infirmary, Oxford, 67; intern med & surg, Dunedin Hosp, Univ Otago, NZ, 68; med res officer clin pharmacol & toxicol, NZ Med Res Coun, 69; lectr clin pharmacol, Med Sch, Univ Otago, NZ, 70; instr clin pharmacol, 71-73, asst prof, 73-76, ASSOC PROF PHARMACOL, TOXICOL & MED, MED CTR, UNIV ROCHESTER, 76- *Concurrent Pos:* Hon clin asst, Otago Hosp Bd, Dunedin, NZ, 69-70. *Mem:* Am Soc Pharmacol & Exp Therapeut; Am Soc Clin Pharmacol & Therapeut; Am Col Clin Pharmacol; Australasian Soc Clin & Exp Pharmacol. *Res:* Design, methodology and analysis of drug studies in man; analgesic and hypnotic drugs in man; regulation and drug development; adverse drug reactions. *Mailing Add:* Dept of Pharmacol & Toxicol Univ of Rochester Med Ctr Rochester NY 14642

WARDEN, HERBERT EDGAR, b Cleveland, Ohio, Aug 30, 20; m 58; c 4. SURGERY, THORACIC SURGERY. *Educ:* Washington & Jefferson Col, BS, 42; Univ Chicago, MD, 46; Am Bd Surg, dipl, 58; Bd Thoracic Surg, dipl, 63. *Prof Exp:* Intern, Clin, Univ Chicago, 46-47; asst resident surg, Hosps, Univ Minn, 51-56, res asst, 53-55, res asst physiol, 55-56, clin instr surg, 55-57, chief resident, 56-57, instr surg, 57-60; assoc prof, 60-62, PROF SURG, MED CTR, W VA UNIV, 62- *Concurrent Pos:* Coordr, USPHS Cardiovasc Surg Training Prog, Univ Minn, 56-60; consult, Anoka State Hosp, Minn, 58-59. *Honors & Awards:* Cert of Merit, AMA, 55 & 58, Hektoen Gold Medal, 57; Lasker Award, Am Pub Health Asn, 55; Citation of Merit, Am Col Surgeons, 57. *Mem:* Soc Univ Surgeons; Am Asn Thoracic Surgeons; Am Surg Asn; Soc Thoracic Surgeons; fel Am Col Surgeons. *Res:* Cardiovascular surgery and physiology. *Mailing Add:* Dept of Surg WVa Univ Med Ctr Morgantown WV 26506

WARDEN, JOSEPH TALLMAN, b Huntington, WVa, Aug 7, 46. BIOPHYSICAL CHEMISTRY. *Educ:* Furman Univ, BS, 68; Univ Minn, PhD(phys chem), 72. *Prof Exp:* Vis scientist biophys, State Univ Leiden, 72-73; chemist, Univ Calif, Berkeley, 73-75; asst prof, 75-80, ASSOC PROF CHEM, RENSSELAER POLYTECH INST, 80- *Concurrent Pos:* Vis prof, Univ Col, London, 81. *Mem:* AAAS; Am Chem Soc; Am Soc Photobiol; Biophys Soc. *Res:* Electron spin resonance investigations of electron transfer components and mechanisms in photosynthesis and mitochondrial respiration; structure and function of heme proteins; photochemistry; solid state chemistry. *Mailing Add:* Dept of Chem Rensselaer Polytech Inst Troy NY 12181

WARDEN, WILLIAM KENT, poultry nutrition, see previous edition

WARDER, DAVID LEE, b Akron, Ohio, June 17, 40; m 63; c 2. CIVIL ENGINEERING. *Educ:* Univ Akron, BSCE, 63; Mich State Univ, MS, 65, PhD(civil eng), 69. *Prof Exp:* Assoc prof civil eng, Tri-State Col, 69-76; SOILS ENGR, ATEC ASSOCS, INC, 76- *Mem:* Am Soc Civil Engrs. *Res:* Use of artificially frozen soil for temporary support; structure-foundation interaction. *Mailing Add:* 11344 Fieldstone Ct Carmel IN 46032

WARDER, RICHARD C, JR, b Nitro, WVa, Sept 30, 36; m 64; c 2. ASTRONAUTICAL SCIENCES, MECHANICAL ENGINEERING. *Educ:* SDak Sch Mines & Technol, BS, 58; Northwestern Univ, MS, 59, PhD(mech eng, astronaut sci), 63. *Prof Exp:* Asst prof mech eng & astronaut sci, Northwestern Univ, 63-65; mgr energy processes res, Space Sci Labs, Litton Industs, Inc, Calif, 65-68; assoc prof, 68-72, PROF MECH & AEROSPACE ENG, UNIV MO-COLUMBIA, 72- *Concurrent Pos:* Prof staff mem, Nat Sci Found, 74-76. *Mem:* AAAS; Am Soc Eng Educ; Am Phys Soc; Am Inst Aeronaut & Astronaut; Am Soc Mech Engrs. *Res:* Gas dynamics; plasma physics. *Mailing Add:* Dept of Mech & Aerospace Eng Univ of Mo Columbia MO 65211

WARDESKA, JEFFREY GWYNN, b Irondale, Ohio, June 13, 41; m 65; c 2. INORGANIC CHEMISTRY. *Educ:* Mt Union Col, BSc, 63; Ohio Univ, PhD(inorg chem), 67. *Prof Exp:* Asst prof, 67-73, ASSOC PROF CHEM, E TENN STATE UNIV, 73- *Mem:* Am Chem Soc. *Res:* Coordination chemistry; reactions of coordination compounds of transition metals; thiocyanate complexes; aminoalcohol complexes. *Mailing Add:* Dept of Chem E Tenn State Univ Johnson City TN 37601

WARDI, AHMAD HASSAN, biochemistry, analytical chemistry, deceased

WARDLAW, JANET MELVILLE, b Toronto, Ont, June 20, 24. NUTRITION, HOME ECONOMICS. *Educ:* Univ Toronto, BA, 46; Univ Tenn, MS, 50; Pa State Univ, PhD(nutrit), 63. *Prof Exp:* Dietition, Can Red Cross Soc, Toronto, 47-49; nutritionist, Mich Dept Health, 50-53 & Toronto Dept Pub Health, 53-56; asst prof nutrit, Fac Household Sci, Univ Toronto, 56-60 & 63-64, assoc prof, Fac Food Sci, 64-66; assoc dean-dean designate, 67-68, PROF NUTRIT, COL FAMILY & CONSUMER STUDIES, UNIV GUELPH, 66-, DEAN, 69- *Honors & Awards:* Stuart's Branded Foods Ltd Award, Can Dietetic Asn, 71. *Mem:* AAAS; Am Dietetic Asn; Nutrit Soc Can; Can Dietetic Asn (treas, 65-67). *Res:* Sodium regulation during pregnancy; body composition and feeding frequency; community nutrition. *Mailing Add:* Col Family & Consumer Studies Univ Guelph Guelph ON N1G 2W1 Can

WARDLAW, NORMAN CLAUDE, b Trinidad, Brit WI, Nov 22, 35. GEOLOGY. *Educ:* Univ Manchester, BSc, 57; Univ Glasgow, PhD(geol), 60. *Prof Exp:* Spec lectr sedimentation, Univ Sask, 60-62, from asst prof to assoc prof geol, 62-72; assoc prof, 72-74, PROF GEOL, UNIV CALGARY, 74- *Honors & Awards:* Link award, Can Petrol Geologists. *Mem:* Soc Econ Paleontologists & Mineralogists; Geol Soc Am; Am Asn Petrol Geologists. *Res:* Petrophysics of oil and gas reservoirs and petroleum recovery; petrology and geochemistry of evaporites. *Mailing Add:* Dept of Geol Univ of Calgary Calgary AB T2N 1N4 Can

WARDLAW, WILLIAM PATTERSON, b Los Angeles, Calif, Mar 3, 36; m 63; c 1. MATHEMATICS. *Educ:* Rice Inst, BA, 58; Univ Calif, Los Angeles, MA, 64, PhD(math), 66. *Prof Exp:* Asst prof, Univ Ga, 66-72; ASST PROF MATH, US NAVAL ACAD, 72- *Mem:* Am Math Soc; Math Asn Am. *Res:* Lie algebras and Chevalley groups; universal algebra. *Mailing Add:* Dept of Math US Naval Acad Annapolis MD 21402

WARDLE, JOHN FRANCIS CARLETON, b Hemel Hempstead, Eng, May 8, 45; m 71. RADIO ASTRONOMY. *Educ:* Univ Cambridge, BA, 66; Univ Manchester, MSc, 68, PhD(radio astron), 69. *Prof Exp:* Res asst radio astron, Nat Radio Astron Observ, 69-71; from instr to asst prof astrophys, 71-78, ASSOC PROF ASTROPHYS, BRANDEIS UNIV, 78- *Mem:* Am Astron Soc; Royal Astron Soc. *Res:* Extragalactic radio astronomy; cosmology. *Mailing Add:* Dept of Physics Brandeis Univ Waltham MA 02154

WARDNER, CARL ARTHUR, b Fisher, Minn, July 13, 04; m 30; c 2. ORGANIC CHEMISTRY. *Educ:* Univ NDak, BS, 27, MS, 29; Univ Pittsburgh, PhD, 32. *Prof Exp:* Res chemist, Daugherty Ref Co, Pa, 31-35 & Flaat Co, NDak, 35-57; from asst prof to prof chem, 58-71, EMER PROF CHEM, UNIV N DAK, 71- *Concurrent Pos:* Dir, Sci Inst, Univ NDak, 67-71, res assoc limnol, 71-75. *Mem:* Am Chem Soc; Nat Sci Teachers Asn. *Res:* Fixation of plant nutrients in alkaline soils; humic acids; soil and precipitation nutrients and their limnological significance; science education. *Mailing Add:* 3720 Cherry St N-56 Grand Forks ND 58201

WARDOWSKI, WILFRED FRANCIS, II, b Pontiac, Mich, May 23, 37; m 74; c 1. HORTICULTURE. *Educ:* Mich State Univ, BS, 59, MS, 61, PhD(pomol), 66. *Prof Exp:* Foreman fruit prod, Blossom Orchard, Leslie, Mich, 61-63; midwest rep tech exten agr chem, Agr Div, Upjohn Co, 66-69; assoc prof, 69-80, PROF EXTEN SERV, CITRUS HARVESTING & HANDLING, AGR RES & EDUC CTR, UNIV FLA, 80- *Concurrent Pos:* Consult, UN Food & Agr Orgn develop prog, Bhutan, 80. *Mem:* Am Soc Hort Sci. *Res:* Nutrition and histology of apples; agricultural chemicals research and development; harvesting and handling of fresh market citrus. *Mailing Add:* Agr Res & Educ Ctr 700 Exp Sta Rd Lake Alfred FL 33850

WARE, ALAN ALFRED, b Portsmouth, Eng, Dec 4, 24; US citizen; m 52; c 4. PLASMA PHYSICS. *Educ:* Imp Col, Univ London, BSc & ARCS, 44, PhD(physics) & DIC, 47. *Prof Exp:* Res asst plasma physics, Imp Col, Univ London, 47-51; sect leader, Res Lab, Assoc Elec Industs, UK, 51-63; consult, Gen Atomic, San Diego, 60-61; group leader plasma physics, Culham Lab, UK Atomic Energy Authority, 63-65; asst mgr res oper plasma physics, Aerojet Gen Corp, 65-69; RES SCIENTIST PLASMA PHYSICS, UNIV TEX, AUSTIN, 69- *Concurrent Pos:* Consult, Los Alamos Sci Lab, 71- *Mem:* Am Phys Soc. *Res:* Theory of Tokamak plasmas in research aimed at controlled nuclear fusion power. *Mailing Add:* Fusion Res Ctr Univ of Tex Austin TX 78712

WARE, ARNOLD GRASSEL, b Butler, Ill, June 1, 15; m 41; c 3. BIOCHEMISTRY. *Educ:* Carthage Col, BA, 37; Univ Colo, MS, 39, PhD(biochem), 42. *Prof Exp:* Asst biochem, Sch Med, Univ Colo, 38-42; res assoc, Col Med, Wayne State Univ, 46-49; from asst prof to assoc prof biochem, 49-56, PROF PATH, SCH MED, UNIV SOUTHERN CALIF, 56-; PRES, BIOCON LABS. *Concurrent Pos:* Head clin biochemist, Los Angeles County-Univ Southern Calif Med Ctr, 49-72. *Mem:* AAAS; Am Soc Biol Chemists; Am Chem Soc; Am Asn Clin Chemists. *Res:* Blood coagulation; clinical chemistry. *Mailing Add:* 4044 Park Vista Pasadena CA 91107

WARE, CAROLYN BOGARDUS, b Baltimore, Md, Oct 15, 30; div; c 1. NEUROANATOMY, PHYSIOLOGICAL PSYCHOLOGY. *Educ:* Western Reserve Univ, BA, 52; Columbia Univ, cert phys ther, 53; Univ Buffalo, MEd, 63; Duke Univ, PhD(psychol), 71. *Prof Exp:* Instr phys ther, Univ NC, 63-66; instr anat, State Univ NY Downstate Med Ctr, 70-75, asst prof & asst dean, Sch Health Related Professions, State Univ NY, Buffalo, 75-78; ASST VPRES FOR ACAD AFFAIRS, STATE UNIV NY, BINGHAMTON, 78- *Mem:* Soc Neurosci; Am Asn Univ Professors; Sigma Xi. *Res:* Comparative neuroanatomy, visual system and cerebellum; central nervous system and behavior, especially visual discrimination. *Mailing Add:* Asst VPres for Acad Affairs State Univ of NY Binghamton NY 13901

WARE, CHARLES HARVEY, JR, b New York, NY, July 8, 27; m 52; c 2. CHEMICAL ENGINEERING. *Educ:* Princeton Univ, BSE, 49; Univ Pa, MS, 57, PhD(chem eng), 59. *Prof Exp:* Chem engr, Texaco Res Ctr, 59-60, sr chem engr, 60-61, group leader exp lube process res, 61-65, sr res chem engr, 65-70, group leader process anal, 70-74; CONSULT, COMMERCIALIZATION INSIGHTS, 74- *Concurrent Pos:* Adj assoc prof, Columbia Univ, 68-69; adj prof, Manhattan Col, 78-80. *Mem:* Fel Am Inst Chem Engrs; Am Chem Soc; Am Statist Asn. *Res:* Chemical reaction engineering; research methodology; mathematical modelling; design methods; petroleum processing. *Mailing Add:* Commercialization Insights 13902 N Dale Mabry Hwy Tampa FL 33618

WARE, CHESTER DAWSON, b Grundy Center, Iowa, Feb 26, 20; m 45; c 2. MECHANICAL ENGINEERING, HEAT TRANSFER. *Educ:* Iowa State Univ, BScME, 47. *Prof Exp:* Engr, Procter & Gamble Co, Ohio, 47-52; develop engr, Trane Co, 52-54, sr develop engr, 54-63, chief develop engr, 63-65, chief engr heat transfer prod, Develop Eng Sect, 65-68, mgr & chief engr, 68-78, eng mgr & sr staff engr, heat transfer prods, CACD Develop Eng, 78-79, ENGR MGR & SR STAFF ENGR HEAT TRANSFER TECHNOL ADVAN DEVELOP ENGR, TRANE CO, 79- *Mem:* Am Soc Heating, Refrig & Air-Conditioning Engrs. *Res:* Heat transfer and fluid flow; air handling; refrigeration machinery; development and design of heat exchangers for heating, air conditioning, refrigeration and cryogenic equipment. *Mailing Add:* Advan Develop Eng Heat Transfer Technol Trane Co La Crosse WI 54601

WARE, DONNA MARIE EGGERS, b Springfield, Mo, Oct 1, 42; m 68. PLANT TAXONOMY. *Educ:* Southwest Mo State Col, BA, 64; Vanderbilt Univ, PhD(biol), 69. *Prof Exp:* HERBARIUM CUR VASCULAR PLANTS, COL WILLIAM & MARY, 69- *Concurrent Pos:* NSF grant-in-aid, Highlands Biol Sta, NC, 70. *Mem:* Am Soc Plant Taxon. *Res:* Floristics; revisional and biosystematic taxonomy. *Mailing Add:* Herbarium Dept Biol Col William & Mary Williamsburg VA 23185

WARE, DOUGLAS ROBERT, b Huntington, Ind, Nov 10, 47; m 71. ANIMAL NUTRITION. *Educ:* Purdue Univ, BS, 70; Iowa State Univ, MS, 75, PhD(animal nutrit), 76. *Prof Exp:* PROD DEVELOP MGR, DOW CHEM CO, 76- *Mem:* Am Soc Animal Sci; AAAS. *Res:* Protein and energy requirements of high producing animals; interaction of growth stimulant effects with plane of nutrition. *Mailing Add:* 3104 Noeske St Midland MI 46750

WARE, FREDERICK, b Omaha, Nebr, June 16, 28; m 50, 78; c 5. PHYSIOLOGY, INTERNAL MEDICINE. *Educ:* Univ Nebr, BS, 49, MS, 53, PhD & MD, 56. *Prof Exp:* Instr physiol, 53-56, instr internal med, 55-56, asst prof physiol & pharmacol, 60-62, assoc prof physiol & asst prof internal med, 62-70, PROF PHYSIOL, BIOPHYS & INTERNAL MED, COL MED, UNIV NEBR, OMAHA, 70- *Mem:* Am Physiol Soc; Am Soc Nephrology; Int Soc Nephrology; Am Col Physicians; Am Soc Artificial Internal Organs. *Res:* Membrane electrophysiology of skeletal muscle and heart; principles of electrocardiography; biophysics of renal function. *Mailing Add:* Dept of Physiol-Biophys Univ of Nebr Col of Med Omaha NE 68105

WARE, GEORGE HENRY, b Avery, Okla, Apr 27, 24; m 55; c 4. PLANT ECOLOGY. *Educ:* Univ Okla, BS, 45, MS, 48; Univ Wis, PhD(bot), 55. *Prof Exp:* From asst prof to prof bot, Northwestern State Univ, 48-68; ECOLOGIST & DENDROLOGIST, MORTON ARBORETUM, 68-, RES GROUP ADMINR, 76- *Mem:* AAAS; Ecol Soc Am; Int Soc Arboriculture; Am Inst Biol Sci. *Res:* Vegetation of the Southeastern United States; ecology of swamp and floodplain forests; ecology of urban trees. *Mailing Add:* Morton Arboretum Lisle IL 60532

WARE, GEORGE WHITAKER, JR, b Pine Bluff, Ark, Aug 27, 27; m 52; c 3. ENTOMOLOGY. *Educ:* Univ Ark, BS, 51, MS, 52; Kans State Univ, PhD(entom), 56. *Prof Exp:* Assoc prof entom, Ohio State Univ, 56-66; PROF ENTOM & HEAD DEPT, UNIV ARIZ, 67- *Concurrent Pos:* Consult, Environ Protection Agency, Washington & Coun Grad Schs US, 74-, Dames & Moore, Phoenix, 75-, USAID, Univ Calif, Berkeley, 78- & Nat Agr Chem Asn, 80- *Mem:* Entom Soc Am; Am Chem Soc; Soc Toxicol. *Res:* Insect toxicology; pesticide chemistry, metabolism and residues. *Mailing Add:* Dept Entom Univ Ariz Tucson AZ 85721

WARE, GLENN OREN, b Athens, Ga, Dec 8, 41; m 67; c 2. APPLIED STATISTICS, OPERATIONS RESEARCH. *Educ:* Univ Ga, BSF, 63, PhD(forest biomet), 68; Yale Univ, MF, 64. *Prof Exp:* Res forester, Hudson Pulp & Paper Corp, 64-65; asst prof statist, 66-74, ASSOC PROF FORESTRY, UNIV GA, 77-, STA STATISTICIAN, EXP STA, 74- *Mem:* Soc Am Foresters. *Res:* Application of mathematical and statistical techniques in the physical and biological sciences. *Mailing Add:* Marshall Hill Rd Athens GA 30603

WARE, JAMES GARETH, b Baltimore, Md, Aug 19, 29; m 55; c 1. MATHEMATICS. *Educ:* Duke Univ, BS, 50; George Peabody Col, MA, 51, PhD(math), 62. *Prof Exp:* Teacher, McCallie Sch, Tenn, 52-54 & 59-60, dept chmn, 60-65; assoc prof, 67-73, PROF MATH, UNIV TENN, CHATTANOOGA, 73-, CHMN DEPT, 68- *Mem:* Nat Coun Teachers Math; Am Asn Univ Profs; Math Asn Am. *Res:* Mathematics education; geometry. *Mailing Add:* Dept of Math Univ of Tenn Chattanooga TN 37402

WARE, JAMES H, b Detroit, Mich, Oct 27, 41; m 72; c 1. MATHEMATICAL STATISTICS. *Educ:* Yale Univ, BA, 63; Stanford Univ, MA, 65, PhD(statist), 69. *Prof Exp:* Instr statist, Calif State Col, Hayward, 69-70; math statistician, NIH, 71-80; MEM FAC, DEPT BIOSTATIST, HARVARD SCH PUBLIC HEALTH, 80- *Concurrent Pos:* Assoc ed, J Am Statist Asn, 73-75; adj prof statist, George Washington Univ, 75- *Mem:* Am Statist Asn; Biomet Soc. *Res:* Interest in the areas of nonparametric methods and sequential analysis; survival data analysis and methods for data analysis in clinical trials of chronic disease. *Mailing Add:* Dept Biostatist Harvard Sch Public Health Boston MA 02115

WARE, KENNETH DALE, b Webster Springs, WVa, Aug 30, 35; m 57; c 2. FOREST BIOMETRICS, SURVEY SAMPLING. *Educ:* WVa Univ, BS, 56; Yale Univ, MS, 57, PhD(biomet), 60. *Prof Exp:* Res forester, Northeastern Forest Exp Sta, US Forest Serv, 58-61; asst prof forestry, Iowa State Univ, 61-64, assoc prof, 65-68, prof, 69-71; CHIEF MENSURATIONIST, SOUTHEASTERN FOREST EXP STA, US FOREST SERV, 71- *Concurrent Pos:* Vis scientist, Nat Sci Found & Soc Am Forests; adj prof, Sch Forest Resources, Univ Ga, 71- *Mem:* Soc Am Forests; Biomet Soc; Am Statist Asn. *Mailing Add:* Forest Sci Lab Carlton St Athens CA 30602

WARE, LAWRENCE L, JR, b Montgomery, WVa, Sept 12, 20; m 46; c 3. MEDICAL MICROBIOLOGY. *Educ:* Roosevelt Univ, BS, 50. *Prof Exp:* Res asst bact, Univ Chicago, 46-49; bacteriologist, Med Bact Div, US Army Chem Corp, Ft Detrick, Md, 51-53, Process Res Div, 53-57, bio-eng br, Pilot Plant, 59; lab dir, Div Indian Health, USPHS, Ariz, 59-63, area lab dir, 63-65; microbiologist & sci info specialist, 65-72, CHIEF, SCI & TECH INFO DIV, US ARMY MED RES & DEVELOP COMMAND, 72- *Concurrent Pos:* Ed, newsletter, Nat Registry Microbiol, 65- *Mem:* Am Soc Microbiol; NY Acad Sci; Asn Mil Surg US; Soc Indust Microbiol; Am Soc Info Sci. *Res:* Medical microbiology and immunology; microbial fermentations; medical information and documentation storage and retrieval. *Mailing Add:* 9224 Kristin Lane Fairfax VA 22032

WARE, ROGER PERRY, b San Francisco, Calif, Apr 2, 42; m 65; c 2. ALGEBRA. *Educ:* Univ Calif, Berkeley, AB, 65; Univ Calif, Santa Barbara, MA, 68, PhD(math), 70. *Prof Exp:* Asst prof math, Northwestern Univ, Evanston, 70-72 & Univ Kans, Lawrence, 72-74; assoc prof, 74-80, PROF MATH, PA STATE UNIV, 80- *Concurrent Pos:* NSF grants, 71-72, 73, 74 & 76-82; vis prof math, Univ Calif, Berkely, 80-81. *Mem:* Am Math Soc; Math Asn Am. *Res:* Quadratic forms; field theory. *Mailing Add:* Dept Math Pa State Univ University Park PA 16802

WARE, STEWART ALEXANDER, b Stringer, Miss, Aug 20, 42; m 68. PLANT ECOLOGY. *Educ:* Millsaps Col, BA, 64; Vanderbilt Univ, PhD(biol), 68. *Prof Exp:* Asst prof, 67-72, chmn dept, 76-82, ASSOC PROF BIOL, COL WILLIAM & MARY, 72- *Concurrent Pos:* Ed, Jeffersonia, Va Bot Newsletter, 69-74 & Va J Sci, 79- *Mem:* Ecol Soc Am; Torrey Bot Club. *Res:* Vegetation of the southeastern United States; Quercus systematics and ecology; physiological ecology of rock outcrop plants; ecology and distribution of Talinum. *Mailing Add:* Dept of Biol Col of William & Mary Williamsburg VA 23185

WARE, W(ILLIS) H(OWARD), b Atlantic City, NJ, Aug 31, 20; m 43; c 3. COMPUTER SCIENCE, ELECTRONIC ENGINEERING. *Educ:* Univ Pa, BS, 41; Mass Inst Technol, SM, 42; Princeton Univ, PhD(elec eng), 51. *Prof Exp:* Res engr, Hazeltine Electronics Corp, 42-46 & Inst Advan Study, 46-51; head comput sci dept, 51-71, dep vpres, 71-73, CORP RES STAFF, RAND CORP, 73- *Concurrent Pos:* Mem & vchmn, Privacy Protection Study Comn, 75-77. *Mem:* AAAS; Asn Comput Mach; fel Inst Elec & Electronics Engrs. *Res:* Electronic digital computers; applications of computers to military and civil information processing problems; computer system research; societal impact of information technology. *Mailing Add:* 1115 Georgina Ave Santa Monica CA 90402

WARE, WALTER ELISHA, b Jacksonville, Fla, June 1, 33; m 55; c 3. PHYSICS. *Educ:* US Naval Acad, BS, 55; Univ Colo, PhD(physics), 62. *Prof Exp:* From instr to assoc prof physics, US Air Force Acad, 62-65, tenure assoc prof, 65-66; res scientist, Nuclear Technol Lab, Kaman Sci Corp, 66-80; DIV MGR, MISSION RES CORP, 80- *Concurrent Pos:* Proj consult, Kaman Nuclear, 62-66. *Mem:* Am Asn Physics Teachers; Inst Elec & Electronics Engrs. *Res:* Nuclear structure theory; effects of nuclear weapons; electromagnetic theory; quantum theory. *Mailing Add:* Mission Res Corp 3720 Sinton Rd Colorado Springs CO 80907

WARE, WILLIAM ROMAINE, b Portland, Ore, June 13, 31; m 54. PHYSICAL CHEMISTRY. *Educ:* Reed Col, BA, 53; Univ Rochester, PhD, 58. *Prof Exp:* Res chemist, Parma Res Ctr, Union Carbide Corp, 57-60; res assoc chem, Univ Minn, Minneapolis, 61; from asst prof to assoc prof, San Diego State Col, 62-66; from assoc prof to prof, Univ Minn, Minneapolis, 67-71; PROF CHEM, UNIV WESTERN ONT, 71- *Mem:* Am Chem Soc; Am Phys Soc; fel Chem Inst Can. *Res:* Molecular photochemistry and photophysics. *Mailing Add:* 14 Metamora Cerscent London ON N6G 1R3 Can

WAREHAM, ELLSWORTH EDWIN, b Avinger, Tex, Oct 3, 14; m 50; c 5. THORACIC SURGERY. *Educ:* Col Med Evangelists, MD, 42; Am Bd Surg, dipl, 54; Bd Thoracic Surg, dipl, 55. *Hon Degrees:* LLD, Andrews Univ, 72. *Prof Exp:* From asst prof to assoc prof, 58-64, PROF SURG, SCH MED, LOMA LINDA UNIV, 64- *Mem:* Am Asn Thoracic Surgeons; Am Col Surgeons; Am Col Cardiol; Soc Thoracic Surg; AMA. *Res:* Cardiovascular surgery; open heart surgery; use of heart-lung machine. *Mailing Add:* Dept of Surg Loma Linda Univ Sch of Med Loma Linda CA 92354

WAREN, ALLAN D(AVID), b Toronto, Ont, Nov 23, 35; m 62; c 4. OPERATIONS RESEARCH, COMPUTER SCIENCE. *Educ:* Univ Toronto, BASc, 60; Case Inst Technol, MS, 62, PhD(eng), 64. *Prof Exp:* Electronics engr, Electronic Res Div, Clevite Corp, 63-64, sr electronics engr, 64-66, staff engr, 66; from asst prof to assoc prof elec eng, Cleveland State Univ, 66-69; founder & pres, Com-Share Ltd, 69-71; chmn dept, 71-76, PROF COMPUT & INFO SCI, CLEVELAND STATE UNIV, 71- *Concurrent Pos:* Consult, Cleveland Court Mgt Proj, Environ Econ, Gould & Cleveland legal firms; consult, Gould Inc Ocean Systs Div, 77-, Cleveland Pub Utilities, 80, Sci Systs Inc, 80-, Gould Elastomer Prods Div, 79-80 & The World Bank 79; res grants, NSF, 75-78, Off Naval Res, 73-, NASA, 80- & Environ Protection Res Inst, 81- *Mem:* Asn Comput Mach; Inst Elec & Electronics Engrs; Math Programming Soc. *Res:* Computer-aided design of engineering systems; optimization methods and mathematical programming. *Mailing Add:* Dept of Comput & Info Sci Cleveland State Univ Cleveland OH 44115

WARF, JAMES CURREN, b Nashville, Tenn, Sept 1, 17; m 65; c 3. INORGANIC CHEMISTRY. *Educ:* Univ Tulsa, BS, 39; Iowa State Univ, PhD(inorg chem), 46. *Prof Exp:* Jr chemist, Phillips Petrol Co, Okla, 40-41; instr chem, Univ Tulsa, 41-42; group leader, Manhattan Proj, Iowa State Univ, 42-47; Guggenheim fel, Univ Berne, 47-48; from asst prof to assoc prof, 48-70, PROF CHEM, UNIV SOUTHERN CALIF, 70- *Concurrent Pos:* Vis prof, Univ Indonesia, 57-59, Airlangga Univ, Indonesia, 62-64, Tech Univ Vienna, 69-70 & Nat Univ Malaysia, Kuala Lumpur, 74-75; consult, Jet Propulsion Lab, Calif Inst Technol, Hasanuddin Univ & Andalas Univ, Indonesia, 78-79, Nat Univ Malaysia, Sabah, 82- *Mem:* Am Chem Soc; Fedn Am Sci. *Res:* Hydrides of heavy metals; chemistry in liquid ammonia; chemistry of europium and ytterbium. *Mailing Add:* Dept of Chem Univ of Southern Calif Los Angeles CA 90007

WARFEL, DAVID ROSS, b Pana, Ill, Sept 25, 42; m 65; c 1. ORGANIC CHEMISTRY, POLYMER CHEMISTRY. *Educ:* Carthage Col, BA, 64; Univ Tenn, Knoxville, PhD(chem), 70; Univ Pittsburgh, MBA, 76. *Prof Exp:* Scientist polymer chem, Koppers Co, Inc, Monroeville, 69-74; sr scientist polymer chem, Arco/Polymers, Inc, Monroeville, 74, SR RES SCIENTIST POLYMER CHEM, ARCO CHEM CO, 74- *Mem:* Am Chem Soc. *Res:* Influence of catalysis on the reactivity of organometallic compounds. *Mailing Add:* 463 Spruce Dr Exton PA 19341

WARFEL, JOHN HIATT, b Marion, Ind, Mar 3, 16; m 42; c 3. ANATOMY. *Educ:* Capital Univ, BSc, 38; Ohio State Univ, MSc, 41; Western Reserve Univ, PhD, 48. *Prof Exp:* Asst, Western Reserve Univ, 46-48; instr, 49-54, assoc, 54-56, asst prof, 56-70, ASSOC PROF ANAT, SCH MED, STATE UNIV NY BUFFALO, 70- *Mem:* Am Asn Anatomists. *Res:* Gross anatomy. *Mailing Add:* 153 Walton Dr Buffalo NY 14226

WARFIELD, ALBERT HARRY, organic chemistry, see previous edition

WARFIELD, CAROL LARSON, b Oldham, SDak, June 6, 41; m 62; c 3. TEXTILE CHEMISTRY. *Educ:* SDak State Univ, BS, 62; Univ Ill, Urbana, MS, 67, PhD(family econ), 77. *Prof Exp:* Teacher home econ, Bridgewater Pub Sch, SDak, 63, Rock Island Pub Sch, Ill, 63-65; instr textiles, Univ Ill, Urbana, 69-77; ASST PROF TEXTILE SCI, AUBURN UNIV, 77- *Mem:* Sigma Xi; Am Asn Textile Chemists & Colorists; Am Soc Testing & Mat; Am Home Econ Asn; Asn Col Professors Textiles & Clothing. *Res:* Consumer attitudes relating to textiles and textile regulation; end-use performance characteristics of textiles and the effect of maintenance on these characteristics; economic aspects of regulation, selection, use and care. *Mailing Add:* Dept Consumer Affairs Auburn Univ Auburn AL 36830

WARFIELD, GEORGE, b Piombino, Italy, Apr 21, 19; nat US; m 45; c 3. SOLID STATE ELECTRONICS, PHOTO VOLTAICS. *Educ:* Franklin & Marshall Col, BS, 40; Cornell Univ, PhD(physics), 49. *Prof Exp:* From asst prof to prof elec eng, Princeton Univ, 49-74; prof elec eng & exec dir, Inst Energy Conversion, Univ Del, 74-78; assoc dir technol dissemination, Solar Energy Res Inst, 78-80; CONSULT PHOTOVOLTAICS, 80- *Mem:* Am Phys Soc; Inst Elec & Electronics Engrs; Int Solar Energy Soc. *Res:* Photovoltaic cells; solid state device physics; insulator electronics; behavior of electrons in insulators. *Mailing Add:* Box 264 Hallock Rd 2 Vergennes VT 05491

WARFIELD, J(OHN) N(ELSON), b Sullivan, Mo, Nov 21, 25; m 48; c 3. SYSTEMS ENGINEERING, APPLIED MATHEMATICS. *Educ:* Univ Mo, AB & BSEE, 48, MSEE, 49; Purdue Univ, PhD, 52. *Prof Exp:* Instr elec eng, Univ Mo, 48; from instr to assoc prof, Pa State Univ, 49-55; from asst prof to assoc prof, Univ Ill, 55-57; assoc prof, Purdue Univ, 57-58; from assoc prof to prof, Univ Kans, 58-66; sr adv, Battelle Mem Inst, 66-74; chmn, Dept Elec Eng, 75-78, HARRY DOUGLAS FORSYTH PROF, UNIV VA, 75-, DIR, CTR INTERACTIVE MGT, 81- *Concurrent Pos:* Consult, Ramo-Wooldridge Corp, 56-57, Sylvania Data Systs, 59-60 & Wilcox Elec Co, 62-66, IBM Corp, 79- , NSF, 79-; adj prof, Ohio State Univ, 66-71. *Honors & Awards:* Western Elec Fund Award, 66; Outstanding Contrib Award, Inst Elec & Electronics Engrs, 77. *Mem:* AAAS; Am Soc Eng Educ; fel Inst Elec & Electronics Engrs; World Future Soc; Soc Gen Systs Res (pres, 80-). *Res:* Interdisciplinary research methodology & modeling; science education; systems planning; environmental education; bureaucracy. *Mailing Add:* Dept of Elec Eng Univ of Va Charlottesville VA 22901

WARFIELD, PETER FOSTER, b Rye, NY, Aug 4, 18; m 42; c 3. ORGANIC CHEMISTRY. *Educ:* Hamilton Col, BS, 40; Univ Ill, MS, 41, PhD(org chem), 44. *Prof Exp:* Asst chem, Univ Ill, 42-44; res chemist, Bakelite Corp, NJ, 44-45; from res chemist to sr res chemist, Ansco Div, Gen Aniline & Film Corp, 45-49, develop specialist, 49-52; chemist, 52-60, tech serv rep, 60-63, res chemist, 63-68, sr res chemist, 69-78, RES ASSOC, PHOTO PRODS DEPT, E I DU PONT DE NEMOURS & CO, INC, 78- *Mem:* Am Chem Soc; Soc Photog Sci & Eng. *Res:* Hindered Grignard reactions; aliphatic polyamines; phenolic resins; synthetic peptides; restrainers for photographic gelatin; photographic emulsions; cyanine dyes; color photography; color formers; color processing; photopolymer printing plates. *Mailing Add:* Photo Prods Dept EI du Pont de Nemours & Co Inc Parlin NJ 08859

WARFIELD, ROBERT BRECKINRIDGE, JR, b Lexington, Ky, Aug 20, 40; m 64; c 3. ALGEBRA. *Educ:* Haverford Col, BA, 62; Harvard Univ, PhD(math), 67. *Prof Exp:* Fel, NMex State Univ, 67-68; from asst prof to assoc prof, 68-74, PROF MATH, UNIV WASH, 74- *Concurrent Pos:* NSF res grant, Univ Wash, 69-; consult, Proj Seed, Seattle Pub Schs, 71. *Mem:* Math Asn Am; Am Math Soc. *Res:* Commutative and noncommutative rings; module theory; infinite Abelian groups; nilpotent and solvable groups. *Mailing Add:* Dept of Math Univ of Wash Seattle WA 98195

WARFIELD, ROBERT WELMORE, b Asbury Park, NJ, Oct 11, 26; m 55; c 2. POLYMER CHEMISTRY. *Educ:* Univ Va, BS, 50. *Prof Exp:* Chemist, US Bur Mines, Md, 50-55; chemist, 55-64, SR SCIENTIST, NAVAL SURFACE WEAPONS CTR, WHITE OAK, 64- *Honors & Awards:* Meritorious Serv Award, US Dept Interior, 54; Honor Citation, Secy Interior, 55; Meritorious Civilian Serv Award, Naval Ord Lab, 61. *Mem:* Am Chem Soc. *Res:* Patentee in field; chemistry and physics of the solid state of polymers; compressibility and electrical properties of polymers; transitions of polymers; polymerization kinetics. *Mailing Add:* 22712 Ward Ave Hereford Hills Germantown MD 20874

WARFIELD, VIRGINIA MCSHANE, b Charlottesville, Va, Sept 30, 42; m 64; c 3. MATHEMATICAL ANALYSIS. *Educ:* Bryn Mawr Col, AB, 63; Brown Univ, MA, 65, PhD(math), 71. *Prof Exp:* Seattle dir math, Spec Elem Educ Disadvantaged Proj, 70-73; LECTR MATH, UNIV WASH, 73- *Mem:* Sigma Xi. *Res:* Stochastic integrals and stochastic control theory. *Mailing Add:* Dept Math Univ Wash Seattle WA 98195

WARGA, JACK, b Warsaw, Poland, Dec 5, 22; nat US; m 49; c 2. MATHEMATICS. *Educ:* NY Univ, PhD(math), 50. *Prof Exp:* Assoc mathematician, Reeves Instrument Corp, 51-52; prin engr, Repub Aviation Corp, 52-53; sr mathematician & head math dept, Electrodata Div, Burroughs Corp, 54-56; fel, Weizmann Inst Sci, Israel, 56-57; sr staff mathematician & mgr math dept, Res & Adv Develop Div, Avco Corp, 57-66; PROF MATH, NORTHEASTERN UNIV, 66- *Concurrent Pos:* Ed, J Control, Soc Indust & Appl Math. *Mem:* AAAS; Am Math Soc; Soc Indust & Appl Math. *Res:* Mathematical control theory; nonsmooth analysis. *Mailing Add:* Dept of Math Northeastern Univ Boston MA 02115

WARGEL, ROBERT JOSEPH, b Evansville, Ind, Dec 24, 40; m 70. BIOCHEMISTRY, FOOD SCIENCE & TECHNOLOGY. *Educ:* Univ Evansville, BA, 66; Northwestern Univ, PhD(chem), 70. *Prof Exp:* Chemist, City of Evansville, Ind, 64-66 & Mead Johnson & Co, 66; group leader, 70-80, SR GROUP LEADER, KRAFT INC, 80- *Mem:* Am Chem Soc; Am Soc Microbiol; Am Dairy Sci Asn; Inst Food Technologists. *Res:* Enzyme use in dairy products; biochemistry of cheese; metabolism of dairy culture; new dairy product development and implementation; technical management; research administration. *Mailing Add:* Kraft Inc 801 Waukegan Rd Glenview IL 60025

WARING, DEREK MORRIS HOLT, b Northern Ireland, June 16, 25; nat US; m 50; c 2. ORGANIC CHEMISTRY. *Educ:* Queen's Univ, Belfast, BSCh, 46, MSc, 47, PhD(chem), 49. *Prof Exp:* Res chemist, Albright & Wilson, Eng, 50-52; from res chemist to res assoc, 52-67, SR SUPVR RES & DEVELOP, E I DU PONT DE NEMOURS & CO, INC, 67- *Res:* Stereochemistry; polynuclear aromatic hydrocarbons; polymer intermediates and chemistry. *Mailing Add:* Plastics Dept Chestnut Run Lab EI du Pont de Nemours & Co Inc Wilmington DE 19898

WARING, GEORGE HOUSTOUN, b Denver, Colo, July 15, 39; m 62; c 3. ANIMAL BEHAVIOR, VERTEBRATE ZOOLOGY. *Educ:* Colo State Univ, BS, 62, PhD(zool), 66; Univ Colo, MA, 64. *Prof Exp:* Asst prof, 66-72, ASSOC PROF ANIMAL BEHAV, SOUTHERN ILL UNIV, CARBONDALE, 72- *Concurrent Pos:* Guest prof, Univ Munich, 72-73; res prog dir, US Marine Mammal Comn, 74-75. *Mem:* AAAS; Animal Behav Soc; Am Soc Mammal; Ecol Soc Am; Am Ornith Union. *Res:* Communicative behaviors of vertebrates; development of intraspecies and interspecies relationships of horses; social behaviors; vertebrate natural history; wildlife ecology; applied ethology. *Mailing Add:* Dept of Zool Southern Ill Univ Carbondale IL 62901

WARING, GEORGE O, III, b Buffalo, NY, Feb 21, 41; m 65; c 3. OPHTHALMOLOGY. *Educ:* Wheaton Col, BS, 63; Baylor Med Col, MD, 67; Am Bd Ophthal, dipl, 78. *Prof Exp:* Sr asst surgeon, USPHS Indian Hosp, Winnebago, NB, 68-70; resident, Wills Eye Hosp, Philadelphia, Pa, 70-73, Heed fel, 73-74; asst prof ophthal, Univ Calif, Davis, 74-79; ASSOC PROF OPHTHAL, EMORY UNIV, 79- *Concurrent Pos:* Attend physician ophthal, Ship of Hope, Natal, Brazil, 72; consult, Vet Admin Hosp, Martinez, Calif, 74-79 & Travis AFB, Fairfield, Calif, 74-78; surg dir, Sacramento Valley Eye Bank, 75-79; res consult, Calif Comn Peace Officer Standards & Training, Sacramento, 76-78; chmn, Corneal & External Dis Sect, Found SSysts Postgrad Educ in Ophthal, 76- *Honors & Awards:* Physician's Recognition Award, AMA, 76. *Mem:* Am Acad Ophthal; Am Soc Contemporary Ophthal; Asn Res Vision & Ophthal; AMA. *Res:* Clinico-pathologic correlations in corneal diseases; corneal basement membrane; corneal lipid metabolism. *Mailing Add:* Dept of Ophthal Emory Univ Med Sch Atlanta GA 30322

WARING, RICHARD C, b Excelsior Springs, Mo, Mar 25, 36; m 62; c 3. PHYSICS. *Educ:* William Jewell Col, BA, 58; Univ Ark, MS, 61. *Prof Exp:* From instr to asst prof, 60-72, ASSOC PROF PHYSICS, UNIV MO-KANSAS CITY, 72- *Concurrent Pos:* AEC grants, 63 & 66; NSF grant, 67; Off Water Resources Res grant, 72. *Mem:* Sigma Xi. *Res:* Infrared reflectance spectroscopy. *Mailing Add:* Dept of Physics Univ of Mo Kansas City MO 64110

WARING, RICHARD H, b Chicago, Ill, May 17, 35; m 57; c 2. PLANT ECOLOGY. *Educ:* Univ Minn, St Paul, BS, 57, MS, 59; Univ Calif, Berkeley, PhD(bot), 63. *Prof Exp:* Asst prof, 63-72, PROF FOREST ECOL, ORE STATE UNIV, 76- *Concurrent Pos:* Dep dir, Coniferous Forest Biome, 73- *Mem:* AAAS; Ecol Soc Am. *Res:* Ecosystem analysis of watersheds; environmental classification; physiological ecology; plant-water relationships. *Mailing Add:* Forest Res Lab Ore State Univ Corvallis OR 97330

WARING, ROBERT KERR, JR, b Palmerton, Pa, Aug 18, 28; m 54; c 4. PIGMENT OPTICS, COLOR IMAGING. *Educ:* Va Mil Inst, BS, 50; Yale Univ, PhD, 55. *Prof Exp:* RES PHYSICIST, E I DU PONT DE NEMOURS & CO, INC, 55- *Mem:* Am Phys Soc. *Res:* Measurement and interpretation of the optical properties of colored pigments; general color imaging; measurement and interpretation of the magnetic properties of assemblies of single domain ferromagnetic particles. *Mailing Add:* Cent Res & Develop Dept EI du Pont de Nemours & Co Inc Wilmington DE 19898

WARING, WILLIAM WINBURN, b Savannah, Ga, July 20, 23; m 52; c 5. PEDIATRICS. *Educ:* Harvard Univ, MD, 47. *Prof Exp:* Intern pediat, Children's Hosp, Boston, Mass, 47-48; intern, Johns Hopkins Hosp, Md, 48-49, asst res, 49-50, chief res outpatient dept, 50-51, chief res, Hosp, 51-52; from instr to assoc prof, 57-65, PROF PEDIAT, SCH MED, TULANE UNIV, 65-, LECTR PHYSIOL, 66- *Concurrent Pos:* Pulmonary dis adv comt, Nat Heart & Lung Inst, 71-73; vchmn gen med & sci adv coun, Cystic Fibrosis Found, 72-73. *Mem:* Am Pediat Soc; Am Acad Pediat; Am Col Chest Physicians; Am Thoracic Soc (vpres, 72-73). *Res:* Respiratory disease and physiology in infants and children; cystic fibrosis. *Mailing Add:* Dept of Pediat Tulane Univ Sch of Med New Orleans LA 70112

WARING, WORDEN, b Washington, DC, Jan 8, 15; m 49; c 1. BIOMEDICAL ENGINEERING. *Educ:* Cornell Univ, BChem, 36; Mass Inst Technol, PhD(phys chem), 40. *Prof Exp:* Instr chem, Tulane Univ, 40-42, asst prof, 42-43; engr, Shell Develop Co, 43-53; engr opers res group, Arthur D Little, Inc, 53-54; chemist, Semiconductor Div, Raytheon Mfg Co, 54-58; head chem sect, Fairchild Semiconductor Corp, 58-64; prin investr human systs design ctr, Rancho Los Amigos Hosp, Downey, Calif, 64-69; assoc prof biomed eng, 69-72, PROF BIOMED ENG, SCHS MED & ENG, UNIV CALIF, DAVIS, 72- *Mem:* AAAS; Biomed Eng Soc; Am Chem Soc; Electrochem Soc; Inst Elec & Electronics Engrs. *Res:* Thermodynamics; phase rule; industrial operations research; surface chemistry; diffusion; electrochemistry; biomedical engineering. *Mailing Add:* 3 Patwin Rd Davis CA 95616

WARINNER, DOUGLAS KEITH, b Little Falls, Minn, Jan 20, 40; m 67; c 2. NUCLEAR ENGINEERING. *Educ:* Univ Calif, Davis, BS, 65, MS, 68; Purdue Univ, PhD(mech eng), 73. *Prof Exp:* Teaching asst fluid mech & aerodyne rocket propulsion, Univ Calif, Davis, 65-67; mech engr aerodynamics, Naval Weapons Ctr, 67-68; teaching asst heat transfer & measurements, Purdue Univ, 69-71; asst prof thermosci, Fla Atlantic Univ, 71-75; MECH ENGR THERMOHYDRAULICS, ARGONNE NAT LAB, 75- *Concurrent Pos:* Instr, Ill Inst Technol, 77-; mem safety comn, US Dept Energy, 78-80. *Mem:* AAAS; Sigma Xi; Am Soc Mech Engrs; Am Soc Eng Educ. *Res:* Analytical study of the in-care behavior and atmospheric consequences of a nuclear research reactor meltdown or loss of coolant accident: prediction of the in core thermohydraulics (natural circulation and natural conversion) and the atmospheric dispersion and decay of nuclid. *Mailing Add:* CEN/207 RERTR Argonne Nat Lab Argonne IL 60439

WARITZ, RICHARD STEFEN, b Portland, Ore, Apr 1, 29; m 50; c 4. TOXICOLOGY. *Educ:* Reed Col, BA, 51; Stanford Univ, PhD(chem), 57; Am Bd Toxicol, dipl, 80. *Prof Exp:* Actg instr gen chem & biochem, Wash State Univ, 54-55; sr res chemist, E I du Pont de Nemours & Co, Inc, 56-62, sr res scientist, 62-64, sect chief inhalation toxicol, 64-70, res mgr, Biosci Group, 70-75; sr toxicologist, 75-77, MGR TOXICOL, HERCULES INC, 78- *Mem:* AAAS; Am Chem Soc; Am Indust Hyg Asn; Int Union Toxicol Soc; Soc Toxicol (treas, 81-83). *Res:* Pulmonary toxicology and pharmacology; biochemical measures of chemical exposure; organometallic biochemistry; mechanisms of toxic actions of chemicals. *Mailing Add:* 2613 Turnstone Dr Brookmeade 2 Wilmington DE 19808

WARK, DAVID QUENTIN, b Spokane, Wash, Mar 25, 18. METEOROLOGY, ASTROPHYSICS. *Educ:* Univ Calif, AB, 41, PhD(astron), 59. *Prof Exp:* Aviation forecaster, US Weather Bur, 46-58, res meteorologist, 58-65, SR RES SCIENTIST, OFF OF RES NAT ENVIRON SATELLITE SERV, NAT OCEANIC & ATMOSPHERIC ADMIN, 65- *Honors & Awards:* Gold Medal, Dept Com, 69; NASA Medal for Exceptional Sci Achievement, 69; Second Half Century Award, Am Meteorol Soc, 70; Lloyd V Berkner Space Utilization Award, Am Astronaut Soc, 70; Robert M Losey Award, Am Inst Aeronaut & Astronaut, 72. *Mem:* Am Meteorol Soc; Am Astron Soc; Am Inst Aeronaut & Astronaut; Am Geophys Union; Optical Soc Am. *Res:* Satellite meteorology; radiative transfer; physical meteorology; planetary meteorology; spectroscopy; airglow. *Mailing Add:* 53 FB 4 Rm 0125 Nat Oceanic & Atmospheric Admin Washington DC 20233

WARK, KENNETH, JR, b Indianapolis, Ind, Jan 2, 27; m 55; c 3. THERMODYNAMICS. *Educ:* Purdue Univ, BS, 50, PhD(mech eng), 55; Univ Ill, MS, 51. *Prof Exp:* Res engr, Atlantic Refining Co, Tex, 51-53; ASSOC PROF MECH ENG, PURDUE UNIV, WEST LAFAYETTE, 55- *Concurrent Pos:* Consult, US Steel Corp, 57-58 & Rovac Corp, 76-78; NSF sci fac fel, Stanford Univ, 62-63. *Mem:* Am Chem Soc; Am Soc Eng Educ; Combustion Inst. *Res:* Air pollution control; alternative and innovative energy conversion systems. *Mailing Add:* Dept of Mech Eng Purdue Univ West Lafayette IN 47907

WARKANY, JOSEF, b Vienna, Austria, Mar 25, 02; US citizen; m 37; c 2. PEDIATRICS. *Educ:* Univ Vienna, MD, 26. *Hon Degrees:* DSc, Thomas Jefferson Med Col, 74; DSc, Univ Ill, 75. *Prof Exp:* Intern, Univ Pediat Clin, Vienna, 26-27; asst, Fed Inst Mothers & Children, 27-31; from asst prof to prof, 32-72, EMER PROF RES PEDIAT, UNIV CINCINNATI, 72-; DIR MENT RETARDATION RES, INST DEVELOP RES, CHILDREN'S HOSP RES FOUND, 66- *Concurrent Pos:* Scholar, Children's Hosp Res Found, 31-34, asst attend pediatrician, 34-35, attend pediatrician & fel, 35-; prog consult, Nat Inst Child Health & Human Develop. *Honors & Awards:* Howland Award, Am Pediat Soc, 70; Child Health Award, Charles H Hood Found, 72. *Mem:* Am Pediat Soc; Soc Pediat Res; hon mem Harvey Soc; cor mem Fr Soc Pediat; hon mem Europ Teratology Soc. *Res:* Nutritional deficiencies; congenital malformations in children; experimental teratology; mental retardation; experimental oncology. *Mailing Add:* Children's Hosp Res Found Elland Ave Cincinnati OH 45229

WARKENTIN, BENNO PETER, b Man, Can, June 21, 29; m 56; c 3. ENVIRONMENTAL MANAGEMENT. *Educ:* Univ BC, BSA, 51; Wash State Univ, MS, 53; Cornell Univ, PhD(soils), 56. *Prof Exp:* Nat Res Coun Can Overseas fel, Oxford Univ, 56-57; asst prof agr physics, 57-62, assoc prof soil sci, 62-70, dir environ studies, 72-75, MacDonald Col, McGil Univ, 70-78; PROF & HEAD DEPT SOIL SCI, ORE STATE UNIV, CORVALLIS, 78- *Mem:* Am Soc Agron; Can Soc Soil Sci (pres, 65-66); Int Soc Soil Sci. *Res:* Physical and chemical properties of clay minerals; physical properties of soils; water in clay soils; solid waste disposal. *Mailing Add:* Dept Soil Sci Ore State Univ Corvallis OR 97331

WARKENTIN, JOHN, b Grunthal, Man, Aug 18, 31; m 57; c 3. ORGANIC CHEMISTRY. *Educ:* Univ Man, BS, 54, MS, 55; Iowa State Univ, PhD(chem), 59. *Prof Exp:* Fel chem, Calif Inst Technol, 59 & Harvard Univ, 59-60; from asst prof to assoc prof, 60-71, PROF CHEM, McMASTER UNIV, 71- *Concurrent Pos:* Assoc ed, Can J Chem, 76-81. *Mem:* Am Chem Soc; Chem Inst Can. *Res:* Synthetic and mechanistic investigations in organic chemistry. *Mailing Add:* Dept Chem McMaster Univ Hamilton ON L8S 4M1 Can

WARLICK, CHARLES HENRY, b Hickory, NC, May 08, 30; m 58; c 1. MATHEMATICS, COMPUTER SCIENCE. *Educ:* Duke Univ, BS, 52; Univ Md, MA, 55; Univ Cincinnati, PhD(math), 64. *Prof Exp:* Mathematician, US Dept Army, 52-53; programmer, Int Bus Mach Corp, 54; appl mathematician, Gen Elec Co, 55-57, supvr appl math, 57-62, supvr appl math & comput softwar develop, 63-65; lectr comput sci & dir, Comput Ctr, Univ Tex, Austin, 65-80. *Concurrent Pos:* Vpres, VIM Users Orgn Control Data Corp 6000 Series Comput, 68-70, pres, 70-71. *Mem:* Asn Comput Mach. *Res:* Numerical solution of partial differential equations; fundamental solutions of finite difference equations; computer executive operating systems; algorithmic languages. *Mailing Add:* 4509 Edgemont Dr Austin TX 78731

WARMACK, ROBERT JOSEPH, molecular physics, see previous edition

WARMAN, JAMES CLARK, b Morgantown, WVa, May 27, 27; m 53; c 3. HYDROGEOLOGY. *Educ:* WVa Univ, BA, 50, MS, 52. *Prof Exp:* Geologist, US Geol Surv, 52-65; ASSOC PROF CIVIL ENG, AUBURN UNIV, 70-, DIR WATER RESOURCES RES INST, 65- *Concurrent Pos:* Grants, Auburn Univ, Water Resources Planning, US Water Resources Coun, 68-, Econ of Pollution Abatement, US Dept Interior, 71-73 & Res Mgt, 72-74; mem work group hydrol maps, US Nat Comt for Int Hydrol Decade, 70-73; consult, Study of Nat Water Res Probs & Priorities, Univs Coun Water Resources for US Dept Interior, 71-72 & Harmon Eng, 75-; chmn tech div & vpres, Nat Water Well Asn, 71-72. *Honors & Awards:* Ross L Oliver Award, Nat Water Well Asn, 74. *Mem:* Fel Am Water Resources Asn (pres, 76); Am Geophys Union; fel Geol Soc Am. *Res:* Occurrence and availability of ground water; water resources planning; research management; waste heat storage by injection into a confined aquifer. *Mailing Add:* Water Resources Res Inst Auburn Univ Auburn AL 36830

WARMAN, PHILIP ROBERT, b Jersey City, NJ, Aug 10, 46; Can citizen; m 70; c 1. SOIL BIOCHEMISTRY, SOIL-PLANT RELATIONSHIPS. *Educ:* Rutgers Univ, BSc, 68; Univ Guelph, MSc, 72, PhD(soil biochem), 77. *Prof Exp:* Lectr, Univ Guelph, 76-77; lectr, Macdonald Col, McGill Univ, 77-78, from auxiliary prof to asst prof, 78-81; ASST PROF SOIL SCI, NS AGR COL, 81- *Concurrent Pos:* Auxiliary prof & res dir, McGill Univ, 81- *Mem:* Am Soc Agron; Soil Sci Soc Am; Int Soil Sci Soc; Agr Inst Can; Can Soil Sci Soc. *Res:* Effects of organic amendments on soil chemistry, soil fertility, crop nutrition and crop production; effects of pesticides and heavy metals on soils and crops. *Mailing Add:* NS Agr Col PO Box 550 Truro NS B2N 5E3 Can

WARMBRODT, ROBERT DALE, b Boonville, Mo, Aug 30, 47. PLANT ANATOMY, PHLOEM TRANSPORT. *Educ:* Univ Mo, Columbia, AB, 70; Univ Wis-Madison, MS, 73, PhD(bot & hort), 78. *Prof Exp:* Res assoc, Dept Bot, Univ Wis-Madison, 78-79; ASST PROF PLANT ANAT & BOT, OHIO STATE UNIV, 80- *Concurrent Pos:* Alexander von Humboldt fel, Dept Forest Bot, Univ Gottingen, 79-80; prin investr grant, Develop Biol Prog, NSF, 81-84, co-prin investr, Multi-use Equip Prog, 81. *Mem:* AAAS; Bot Soc Am; Am Inst Biol Sci; Am Fern Soc. *Mailing Add:* Dept Bot Ohio State Univ 1735 Neil Ave Columbus OH 43210

WARME, JOHN EDWARD, b Los Angeles, Calif, Jan 16, 37; div; c 2. PALEOECOLOGY. *Educ:* Augustana Col, Ill, BA, 59; Univ Calif, Los Angeles, PhD(geol), 66. *Prof Exp:* Fulbright scholar, Scotland, 66-67; W Maurice Ewing prof oceanog, Rice Univ, 67-79; PROF GEOL, COLO SCH MINES, 79- *Mem:* Fel AAAS; Am Asn Petrol Geol; Int Asn Sedimentologists; Palaeont Asn; fel Geol Soc Am. *Res:* Depositional systems; submarine bio-erosion by invertebrates; burrowing marine invertebrates and trace fossils; population and paleopopulation dynamics; shelled invertebrate community identification and analysis; modern and fossil reef ecology; molluscan ecology; lagoonal and deep marine ecology and sedimentation. *Mailing Add:* Dept of Geol Colo Sch Mines Golden CO 80401

WARME, PAUL KENNETH, b Westbrook, Minn, Jan 23, 42; m 62; c 1. BIOCHEMISTRY. *Educ:* Univ Minn, Minneapolis, BCh, 64; Univ Ill, Urbana, PhD(biochem), 69. *Prof Exp:* Fel protein chem, Cornell Univ, 69-72; asst prof biochem, Pa State Univ, University Park, 72-79; PRES, INTERACTIVE MICROWARE, INC, 79- *Concurrent Pos:* NIH fel, Cornell Univ, 69-71. *Mem:* Am Soc Biol Chemists; Inst Elec & Electronics Engrs; Asn Comput Mach. *Res:* Heme proteins and peptides; conformational energy calculations on proteins; computer applications in biochemistry; chemical synthesis of biologically active polypeptides; structure-function relationships of proteins; micro-computer software and hardware for laboratory use. *Mailing Add:* 135 N Gill St Interactive Microware Inc State College PA 16801

WARMKE, HARRY EARL, b Twin Falls, Idaho, Aug 29, 07; m 33, 46; c 3. PLANT CYTOLOGY, PLANT GENETICS. *Educ:* Stanford Univ, AB, 31, PhD(plant cytogenetics), 35. *Prof Exp:* Prof & head dept biol, Seton Hall Col, 35-38; asst genetics, Carnegie Inst, 38-40, cytologist, 41-45; head dept cytogenetics, Inst Trop Agr, Univ PR, 45-47; plant breeder, Fed Exp Sta, USDA, 47-53, officer chg, 53-63, plant geneticist, 64-77; prof, 64-77, EMER PROF AGRON, UNIV FLA, 77- *Mem:* Am Soc NAm; Am Genetic Asn. *Res:* Experimental polyploidy; cytogenetics of sex determination; tropical agriculture; mechanism of cytoplasmic male sterility in plants; electron microscopy of plant viruses and viral inclusions. *Mailing Add:* 1711 SW 43rd Ave Gainesville FL 32608

WARNE, RONSON JOSEPH, b East Orange, NJ, June 14, 32; m 50. MATHEMATICS. *Educ:* Columbia Univ, AB, 53; NY Univ, MS, 55; Univ Tenn, PhD(math), 59. *Prof Exp:* Asst & instr math, Univ Tenn, 55-59; asst prof, La State Univ, 59-63; assoc prof, Va Polytech Inst, 63-64; prof, WVa Univ, 64-69; PROF MATH, UNIV ALA, BIRMINGHAM, 69- *Res:* Algebraic theory of semigroups. *Mailing Add:* Dept of Math Univ of Ala Birmingham AL 35294

WARNE, THOMAS MARTIN, b Chicago, Ill, Sept 27, 39; m 61; c 3. ORGANIC CHEMISTRY, PETROLEUM CHEMISTRY. *Educ:* Yale Univ, BA, 61; Univ Ill, MS, 63; Northwestern Univ, PhD(org chem), 70. *Prof Exp:* Asst prof org chem, Alliance Col, 63-66; res chemist, 70-80, SR RES CHEMIST, AMOCO OIL CO, DIV STANDARDS OIL CO IND, 80- *Mem:* Am Soc Lubrication Engrs; Am Chem Soc; Am Soc Testing & Mat. *Res:* Development of industrial lubricants, particularly hydraulic oils and additives; development of products based upon waxes and petrolatums; product toxicity. *Mailing Add:* 1219 N Main Wheaton IL 60187

WARNECKE, MELVIN OSCAR, b Delphos, Ohio, July 26, 39; m 62; c 3. FOOD SCIENCE. *Educ:* Ohio State Univ, BS, 61, MS, 62; Univ Ga, PhD(food sci), 68; Northwestern Univ, MBA, 74. *Prof Exp:* Res & develop coordr, Food Div, US Army Natick Labs, Mass, 63-64; scientist, Food Res Div, Armour & Co, Ill, 67-69; group leader, Moffett Tech Ctr, CPC Int, Inc, 69-70, sect leader, 70-74; dir res & develop, 74-77, TECH DIR, E J BRACH & SONS, 77- *Mem:* AAAS; Inst Food Technologists; Sigma Xi; Am Asn Candy Technol. *Res:* Research and development in the food science field; fresh and processed meats; carbohydrates in confection, snacks, baking and canning. *Mailing Add:* E J Brach & Sons Box 802 Chicago IL 60690

WARNER, ALDEN HOWARD, b Central Falls, RI, July 2, 37; m 60; c 4. DEVELOPMENTAL BIOLOGY. *Educ:* Univ Maine, BA, 59; Univ Southern Ill, MA, 61, PhD(physiol), 64. *Prof Exp:* USPHS fel biol & biochem, Biol Div, Oak Ridge Nat Lab, 64-65; from asst prof to assoc prof, 65-72, PROF BIOL, UNIV WINDSOR, 72-, HEAD DEPT, 79- *Concurrent Pos:* Consult, Biol Div, Oak Ridge Nat Lab, 74-75. *Mem:* AAAS; Am Soc Biol Chemists; Soc Develop Biol; Can Soc Cell Biol. *Res:* Nucleic acid and nucleotide metabolism in relation to control of protein synthesis during embryonic development; proteases and their control in development and the onset of muscular dystrophy. *Mailing Add:* Dept Biol Univ Windsor Windsor ON N9B 3P4 Can

WARNER, ALEXANDER CARL, b Mentor, Ohio, Aug 25, 40; m 60; c 3. PHYSIOLOGY, ECOLOGY. *Educ:* Cent Mo State Col, BS, 61, MA, 64; Kent State Univ, PhD(biol), 70. *Prof Exp:* Teacher pub sch, Mo, 61-63; asst prof biol, Col Sch of the Ozarks, 64-66; instr, Kent State Univ, 69-70; asst prof physiol, Southern Ill Univ, Carbondale, 70-74; asst prof zool, Howard Univ, 75-80. *Mem:* AAAS; Am Soc Zoologists. *Res:* Hormonal control of calcium shifts in arthropods. *Mailing Add:* 5057 1st St NW Washington DC 20011

WARNER, ANN MARIE, clinical chemistry, see previous edition

WARNER, BERT JOSEPH, b Ardmore, Okla, June 15, 25; m 52; c 2. CHEMICAL ENGINEERING. *Educ:* Rice Univ, BS, 49. *Prof Exp:* Chem engr, Colombian Petrol Co, 50-53, petrol eng lab mgr, 53-55; res technologist, 55-58, sr res technologist, 58-64, eng assoc, 64-77, MGR RECOVERY PROCESSES, FIELD RES LAB, MOBIL OIL CORP, 78- *Mem:* Soc Petrol Engrs. *Res:* Hydrocarbon phase behavior, processing and production. *Mailing Add:* Field Res Lab Mobil Oil Corp PO Box 900 Dallas TX 75221

WARNER, CAROL MILLER, b New York, NY, Sept 26, 46; m 66; c 2. BIOCHEMISTRY, IMMUNOBIOLOGY. *Educ:* Queens Col, NY, BA, 66; Univ Calif, Los Angeles, PhD(biochem), 70. *Prof Exp:* Fel, Yale Univ, 70-71; asst prof, 71-76, assoc prof, 76-80, PROF BIOCHEM, IOWA STATE UNIV, 80- *Mem:* Soc Develop Biol; Fedn Am Scientists; Sigma Xi; Am Soc Biol Chemists; Am Asn Immunologists. *Res:* Preimplantation mouse embryo development; immune response of allophenic mice. *Mailing Add:* Dept of Biochem Iowa State Univ Ames IA 50011

WARNER, CECIL F(RANCIS), b Parker, Ind, June 13, 15; m 39; c 2. MECHANICAL ENGINEERING. *Educ:* Purdue Univ, BS, 39, PhD(heat transfer), 45; Lehigh Univ, MS, 41. *Prof Exp:* Instr mech eng, Lehigh Univ, 40-42; from instr to assoc prof, 42-55, PROF MECH ENG, PURDUE UNIV, WEST LAFAYETTE, 55- *Concurrent Pos:* Staff mem, Aerojet Gen Corp. *Mem:* Am Soc Mech Engrs; Air Pollution Control Asn. *Res:* Problems in air pollution; heat transfer; jet and rocket propulsion; heat transfer characteristics of liquid film cooling. *Mailing Add:* Dept of Mech Eng Purdue Univ West Lafayette IN 47907

WARNER, CHARLES D, b Mt Hope, WVa, Mar 25, 45; m 66; c 1. ORGANIC CHEMISTRY. *Educ:* Univ Mo-Columbia, BS, 67, PhD(org chem), 71. *Prof Exp:* Asst prof chem, Mo Valley Col, 71-74; asst prof, 74-79, ASSOC PROF CHEM, HASTINGS COL, 79-, HEAD DEPT, 78- *Mem:* Am Chem Soc. *Res:* Synthetic organometallic chemistry. *Mailing Add:* Dept Chem Hastings Col Hastings NE 68901

WARNER, CHARLES ROBERT, b Aug 24, 31; Can citizen. MATHEMATICS. *Educ:* Univ Toronto, BA, 55; Rochester Univ, MS, 57, PhD(math), 62. *Prof Exp:* Instr math, Univ Conn, 58-59; asst prof, Mich State Univ, 62-64; asst prof, 64-69, ASSOC PROF MATH, UNIV MD, COLLEGE PARK, 69- *Concurrent Pos:* Vis assoc prof, Univ Calif, Irvine, 70-71, vis prof, Mittag-Leffler Inst, Djursholm, Sweden, 77, Univ Paris, Orsay, 77-78 & Univ Lausanne, Switz, 78. *Mem:* Am Math Soc; Math Asn Am. *Res:* Banach algebras and harmonic analysis. *Mailing Add:* Dept of Math Univ of Md College Park MD 20742

WARNER, CHARLES Y, b Pocatello, Idaho, Sept 4, 34. MECHANICAL ENGINEERING. *Educ:* Brigham Young Univ, BES, 57, MS, 63; Univ Mich, PhD(mech eng), 66. *Prof Exp:* Design engr, Hewlett-Packard, Calif, 57; test prog engr, Nat Reactor Test Sta, Gen Elec Co, Idaho, 58; from instr to assoc prof, 61-77, PROF MECH ENG, BRIGHAM YOUNG UNIV, 77- *Concurrent Pos:* Consult, Eimco Corp, Utah & Rich's Soft Cushion Bumper Co, 67- *Mem:* Am Soc Mech Engrs; Am Soc Eng Educ. *Res:* Automotive safety; heat transfer; engineering design. *Mailing Add:* Dept of Mech Eng Brigham Young Univ Provo UT 84602

WARNER, DANIEL DOUGLAS, b Mobile, Ala, Sept 1, 42; m 68; c 2. NUMERICAL ANALYSIS. *Educ:* Ariz State Univ, BS, 65, MA, 66; Univ Calif, San Diego, PhD(math), 74. *Prof Exp:* Programmer, Process Comput Sect, Gen Elec Co, 63-65; comput analyst, Airesearch Corp, 66; mem tech staff, Bell Tel Labs, 74-80; ASSOC PROF MATH, CLEMSON UNIV, 80- *Mem:* Am Math Soc; Soc Indust & Appl Math; Asn Comput Mach. *Res:* Theory of Hermite interpolation with rational functions; numerical solution of stiff systems of ordinary differential equations. *Mailing Add:* Clemson Univ Clemson SC 29631

WARNER, DAVID CHARLES, b Granite City, Ill, Apr 27, 42; m 64. MATHEMATICAL PHYSICS, PLASMA PHYSICS. *Educ:* Univ Mo-Columbia, BS, 65, MS, 67, PhD(physics), 70. *Prof Exp:* Asst prof physics, Lincoln Univ, 70-78; ASST PROF PHYSICS, COLUMBIA COL, MO, 78- *Mem:* Am Asn Physics Teachers; Am Phys Soc. *Res:* Quantum kinetic equations of plasma physics; density matrix formalism applied to damping of plasma waves. *Mailing Add:* Dept of Sci & Math Columbia Col Columbia MO 65216

WARNER, DON LEE, b Norfolk, Nebr, Jan 4, 34; m 57; c 2. HYDROGEOLOGY, GEOLOGICAL ENGINEERING. *Educ:* Colo Sch Mines, Geol Engr, 56, MSc, 61; Univ Calif, Berkeley, PhD(eng sci), 64. *Prof Exp:* Res geologist, R A Taft Sanit Eng Ctr, Ohio, 64-69; assoc prof, 69-72, prof geol eng, 72-81, DEAN SCH MINES & METALL, UNIV MO, ROLLA, 81- *Concurrent Pos:* Consult; ed, Ground Water, 80-; ed, Ground Water Monitoring Review, 80- *Mem:* Am Inst Mining, Metall & Petrol Eng; Geol Soc Am; Am Asn Petrol Geol; Asn Prof Geol Scientists; Nat Water Well Asn. *Res:* Mineral exploration and exploitation, areal geology; stratigraphic geology and geophysics; geohydrology; water pollution control; engineering geology. *Mailing Add:* 103 Mining Bldg Univ of Mo Rolla MO 65401

WARNER, DONALD R, b Winston, Mo, July 6, 18; m 60; c 3. ANIMAL HUSBANDRY, ANIMAL NUTRITION. *Educ:* Univ Mo, BS, 42, MS, 49, PhD(animal nutrit & ed), 60. *Prof Exp:* Mem staff, Mo Agr Exten Serv, 45-47; instr animal husb, Univ Mo, 47-49 & Univ Nebr, 49-56; assoc prof animal sci, 60-78, PROF ANIMAL SCI, IOWA STATE UNIV, 78- *Concurrent Pos:* Livestock judging team coach, Iowa State Univ. *Mem:* Am Soc Animal Sci. *Res:* Swine feeding investigations; antibiotics; protein supplements for pigs on pasture and in dry lot; methods of feeding and effects on carcass value; bloat studies of sheep; breeding, feeding and management of sheep. *Mailing Add:* Dept of Animal Sci 119 Kildee Hall Iowa State Univ Ames IA 50011

WARNER, DONALD THEODORE, b Holland, Mich, Apr 7, 18; m 45; c 2. BIOCHEMISTRY. *Educ:* Hope Col, AB, 39; Univ Ill, PhD(biochem), 43. *Prof Exp:* Res chemist, Gen Mills, Inc, 43-52; res chemist, Upjohn Co, 52-82; RETIRED. *Mem:* Am Chem Soc. *Res:* Amino acids; isolation and synthesis; amino acid diets; isolation and properties of threonine; organic synthesis, 1, 4 addition reactions; polysaccharides; peptide synthesis; protein conformation studies; antiasthmatic drugs. *Mailing Add:* Res Dept Upjohn Co Kalamazoo MI 49006

WARNER, DWAIN WILLARD, b Cottonwood Co, Minn, Sept 1, 17; m 40, 66; c 5. ZOOLOGY. *Educ:* Carleton Col, BA, 39; Cornell Univ, PhD(ornith), 47. *Prof Exp:* Lab asst bot, Carleton Col, 38-39; asst zoologist, Cornell Univ, 41, asst, 42-43 & 46, instr 46-47; from asst prof to assoc prof, 47-67, PROF ZOOL, UNIV MINN, MINNEAPOLIS, 67-, CUR BIRDS, BELL MUS NATURAL HIST, 47- *Mem:* Assoc Am Ornith Union; Cooper Ornith Soc; Wilson Ornith Soc; AAAS. *Res:* Birds of Mexico and New Caledonia; zoogeography; biology and ecology of avifauna. *Mailing Add:* Bell Mus Natural Hist Univ of Minn Minneapolis MN 55455

WARNER, ELDON DEZELLE, b Whitewater, Wis, Oct 5, 11; m; c 3. ENDOCRINOLOGY. *Educ:* Wis State Teachers Col, BEd, 32; Univ Wis, PhM, 38, PhD(zool), 41. *Prof Exp:* Asst prof sci, Adams State Teachers Col, 41-43; from instr to assoc prof, 46-58, chmn dept, 56-58, 59-61 & 66-69, prof zool, 58-78, EMER PROF ZOOL, UNIV WIS, MILWAUKEE, 78- *Concurrent Pos:* NSF fel, 58-59. *Mem:* AAAS; Am Soc Zool. *Res:* Lower vertebrate endocrinology. *Mailing Add:* Dept of Zool Univ of Wis Milwaukee WI 53201

WARNER, EMORY DEAN, b North English, Iowa, July 5, 05; m 30; c 3. PATHOLOGY. *Educ:* Univ Iowa, BS, 27, MD, 29; Am Bd Path, dipl. *Prof Exp:* Asst resident path, Univ Rochester, 29-30; asst, Col Med, Univ Iowa, 30-31, from instr to prof, 31-70, head dept, 45-70; prof path, Col Med, Univ Ariz, 70-76; EMER PROF PATH, UNIV IOWA, 73- *Concurrent Pos:* Pathologist, Mercy Hosp, 30-33; asst hosp pathologist, Univ Hosps, Iowa, 33-45, pathologist, 45-70. *Honors & Awards:* Gold Headed Cane Award, Am Asn Pathologists, 80. *Mem:* AAAS; Am Soc Clin Pathologists; Am Soc Exp Pathologists (pres, 57-58); Soc Exp Biol & Med; Am Asn Pathologists & Bacteriologists. *Res:* Physiology of blood clotting; hemorrhagic diseases; role of the liver in prothrombin production; methods for measuring prothrombin; vitamin K prothrombin; transfusion nephritis; pathophysiology of hypercoagualability and thrombosis. *Mailing Add:* 1402 E Court St Iowa City IA 52240

WARNER, FRANCIS JAMES, b Chicago, Ill, Oct 3, 97. ANATOMY. *Educ:* Loyola Univ Chicago, MD, 19; Univ Iowa, BA, 22; Univ Mich, MA, 25; Am Bd Path, dipl, 52. *Prof Exp:* Instr neurol, Univ Mich, 32-33; instr med sci, Univ Md, 38-39; mem res staff neuroanat, Med Sch, Univ Calif, 42-44; mem res staff neuropath & neuroanat, Med Sch, Columbia Univ, 44-45; lectr neuroanat, Univ Utah, 46-49; guest investr, Sch Med, Yale Univ, 49-50; fel neurol, Henry Ford Hosp, Detroit, Mich, 51-52; guest investr, Cornell Univ, 53-55 & Univ Col, Univ London, 56-57; instr clin neurol, 57-75, ASST PROF NEUROL, SCH MED, TEMPLE UNIV, 75- *Mem:* Am Psychiat Asn; Am Micros Soc; Am Soc Ichthyologists & Herpetologists; Am Soc Zoologists; Am Asn Anatomists. *Res:* Comparative neuroembryology; neuropathology of the malformation in the human brain in adult and fetal material; teratological brain malformations in the human form. *Mailing Add:* PO Box 523 Philadelphia PA 19105

WARNER, FRANK WILSON, III, b Pittsfield, Mass, Mar 2, 38; m 58; c 2. DIFFERENTIAL GEOMETRY, RIEMANNIAN GEOMETRY. *Educ:* Pa State Univ, BS, 59; Mass Inst Technol, PhD(math), 63. *Prof Exp:* Instr math, Mass Inst Technol, 63-64; actg asst prof math, Univ Calif, Berkeley, 64-65, asst prof, 65-68; assoc prof, 68-73, PROF MATH, UNIV PA, 73- *Mem:* Am Math Soc; Math Asn Am; AAAS; Sigma Xi. *Res:* Applications of partial differential equations to differential geometry. *Mailing Add:* Dept of Math E1 Univ of Pa Philadelphia PA 19104

WARNER, FREDERIC COOPER, b Whitesboro, NY, Jan 28, 15; m 40; c 2. GEOMETRY. *Educ:* Col Wooster, BA, 37; Univ Buffalo, MA, 50, PhD, 53. *Prof Exp:* Teacher high schs, NY, 37-46; instr math, Univ Buffalo, 46-53; from asst prof to assoc prof math, St Lawrence Univ, 53-60, prof, 60-80. *Mem:* Am Math Soc; Sigma Xi; Math Asn Am. *Res:* Operations research. *Mailing Add:* 10 Jay St Canton NY 12207

WARNER, GEORGE S, b Montgomery, Ala, June 18, 20; m 46; c 3. MICROBIOLOGY, IMMUNOLOGY. *Educ:* Miss State Univ, BS, 42; Univ Md, MS, 46, PhD(microbiol), 51. *Prof Exp:* Res microbiologist, 50-53, dir biol qual control lab, 53-76, DIR QUAL ASSURANCE, CONTROL LAB, HYNSON, WESTCOTT & DUNNING, INC, 76- *Honors & Awards:* Unit Award for Superior Serv, USDA. *Mem:* Am Soc Microbiol; US Animal Health Asn; Am Asn Lab Animal Sci. *Res:* Antiseptics; sterility; microbic and biologic test of pharmaceuticals; serologic studies on Neisseria, Brucella, Trichinella and animal diseases. *Mailing Add:* Hynson Westcott & Dunning Inc BQC Lab Charles & Chase Sts Baltimore MD 21201

WARNER, H JACK, US citizen. FOOD TECHNOLOGY. *Educ:* Ohio State Univ, BS, 65. *Prof Exp:* Qual control mgr, Chung King Corp, 65-67; food inspector, US Army, 67-69; food technologist develop, 69-72, dir tech serv, Spec Foods Div, 72-78, asst gen mgr, 79-80, GEN MGR, BEATRICE FOODS CO, 81- *Mem:* Inst Food Technol; Am Asn Cereal Chemists. *Res:* Spray dehydration of foods. *Mailing Add:* Beatrice Foods Co 525 Cross St Beloit WI 53511

WARNER, HARLOW LESTER, b Greenport, NY, Aug 26, 42; m 63; c 3. PLANT PHYSIOLOGY, PLANT BREEDING. *Educ:* Cornell Univ, BS, 64; Univ Idaho, MS, 66; Purdue Univ, PhD(plant physiol), 70. *Prof Exp:* SR SCIENTIST PLANT PHYSIOL, ROHM & HAAS CO, 69- *Mem:* Am Soc Hort Sci; Am Soc Plant Physiologists. *Res:* Agricultural chemicals, specifically plant growth regulators and herbicides; plant growth regulators for developing hybrid seeds. *Mailing Add:* Rohm & Haas Co Res Labs Spring House PA 19477

WARNER, HAROLD, b Philadelphia, Pa, June 6, 17; m 43; c 2. BIOMEDICAL ENGINEERING, ELECTRONICS SCIENCE. *Prof Exp:* Chief engr, Microwave Div, Frankford Arsenal, 48-56, Teledynamics, Inc, 56-58; consult engr, Missile & Space Div, Gen Elec Co, 58-65; CLIN ASST PROF PSYCHIAT, RES PROF BIOMED ENG & CHIEF, BIOMED ENG LAB, EMORY UNIV, 65- *Mem:* Sigma Xi; Alliance Eng Med & Biol; Neurosci Soc; Asn Advan Med Instrumentation. *Res:* Application of electronics, physics and mechanics to the fields of reproductive biology, the neurosciences and psychology. *Mailing Add:* Yerkes Regional Primate Res Ctr Emory Univ Atlanta GA 30322

WARNER, HOMER R, b Salt Lake City, Utah, Apr 18, 22; m 46; c 6. PHYSIOLOGY, BIOENGINEERING. *Educ:* Univ Utah, BA, 46, MD, 49; Univ Minn, PhD(physiol), 53. *Hon Degrees:* DSc, Brigham Young Univ, 71. *Prof Exp:* Intern, Parkland Hosp, Dallas, 49-50; resident med, Univ Minn Hosp, 50-51; fels, Mayo Clin, 51-52 & Univ Minn, 52-53; instr med, 53-54, asst res prof physiol, 57-64, PROF BIOPHYS & BIOENG & CHMN DEPT MED BIOPHYS & COMPUT, UNIV UTAH, 64-, RES PROF SURG, 66- *Concurrent Pos:* Dir, Cardiovasc Lab, Latter-Day Saints Hosp, 54-; estab investr, Am Heart Asn, 59-64; mem adv comt comput res, NIH, 61-63, chmn comput res study sect, 63-66; Nat Heart Inst res career award, 62-; ed, Comput & Biomed Res, 66-; vis prof, Univ Hawaii, 68 & Univ Southern Calif, 72; mem, President's Adv Comt Redeploying Scientists & Engrs into Health Ctrs, 71. *Mem:* Am Physiol Soc. *Res:* Control of cardiovascular system; application of computers to medicine. *Mailing Add:* Dept of Med Biophys & Comput Univ of Utah Salt Lake City UT 84112

WARNER, HUBER RICHARD, b Glendale, Ohio, May 16, 36; m 61; c 2. BIOCHEMISTRY. *Educ:* Ohio Wesleyan Univ, BA, 58; Mass Inst Technol, BS, 58; Univ Mich, PhD(biochem), 62. *Prof Exp:* NSF fel biochem, Mass Inst Technol, 62-64; from asst prof to assoc prof, 64-72, PROF BIOCHEM, UNIV MINN, ST PAUL, 72- *Concurrent Pos:* vis prof, Univ Calif, Berkeley, 79. *Mem:* Am Soc Biol Chem; Am Soc Microbiol. *Res:* Biochemistry of bacteriophage infection and replication; DNA repair. *Mailing Add:* Dept of Biochem Univ of Minn St Paul MN 55108

WARNER, JAMES HOWARD, b Angola, Ind, Dec 24, 38. BOTANY, PLANT ECOLOGY. *Educ:* Manchester Col, BS, 61; Univ Wis, Madison, MS, 63; Univ Utah, PhD(biol), 71. *Prof Exp:* Teaching asst bot, Univ Wis, Madison, 61-63; ASSOC PROF BIOL, UNIV WIS, LA CROSSE, 63- *Mem:* AAAS; Am Inst Biol Sci; Ecol Soc Am; Sigma Xi. *Res:* Development of indices of site quality in forest management and plant association. *Mailing Add:* Dept of Biol Univ of Wis La Crosse WI 54601

WARNER, JEFFREY, b Queens, NY, May 19, 39. PLANETARY SCIENCES. *Educ:* City Col New York, BS, 60; Harvard Univ, AM, 62, PhD(geol), 67. *Prof Exp:* Instr geol, Univ Alaska, 64-65; asst prof, Franklin & Marshall Col, 67-68; geologist, Lunar Receiving Lab, Manned Spacecraft Ctr, 68-74, chief geochem, 74-78, PLANETARY GEOLOGIST, JOHNSON SPACE CTR, NASA, 78- *Mem:* Linnean Soc; AAAS; Mineral Soc Am; Am Geophys Union. *Res:* Geology of Maine; metamorphism of calcsilicate rocks, lunar geology; petrology of lunar igneous and metamorphic rocks; petrogenesis of impact produced rocks; planetary tectonics; Mars geology; Venus lithosphere and geology. *Mailing Add:* Code TN-7 Johnson Space Ctr Houston TX 77058

WARNER, JOHN CHRISTIAN, b Goshen, Ind, May 28, 97; m 25; c 2. CHEMISTRY. *Educ:* Univ Ind, AB, 19, MA, 20, PhD(chem), 23. *Hon Degrees:* Fourteen from US cols & univs. *Prof Exp:* Res chemist, Barrett Co, Pa, 18 & Cosdon Co, Okla, 20-21; instr chem, Univ Ind, 19 & 21-24; res chemist, Wayne Chem Co, 25-26; from instr to asst prof chem, 26-33, assoc prof theoret chem, 33-36 & metall, 36-38, prof chem & head dept, 38-49, dean grad studies, 45-50, from vpres to pres, 49-65, EMER PRES, CARNEGIE INST TECHNOL, 65- *Concurrent Pos:* Res assoc, Manhattan Proj, 43-45; consult, Found & Indust Trustee, Carnegie Inst, Carnegie-Mellon Univ; mem gen adv comt, AEC, 52-64; consult, Scaife Family Charities, 65-79; chmn, Educ Projs, Inc, 66-76. *Honors & Awards:* Pittsburgh Award, Am Chem Soc, 45; Gold Medal, Am Inst Chem, 53. *Mem:* Nat Acad Sci; AAAS; Am Chem Soc (pres, 56); Electrochem Soc (pres, 52-53); Am Soc Eng Educ. *Res:* Kinetics of reactions in solutions, salt and medium effects, electrostatic contribution to activation energies; thermodynamic properties of solutions; acid-base properties of mixed solvents; thermodynamics, rates and mechanism of corrosion reactions; educational and research administration; scientific and technological education. *Mailing Add:* 4742 Center Ave Apt 301 Pittsburgh PA 15213

WARNER, JOHN NORTHRUP, b Los Angeles, Calif, May 19, 19; m 42; c 3. PLANT BREEDING, AGRONOMY. *Educ:* Univ Hawaii, BS, 41; Univ Minn, PhD(plant genetics), 50. *Prof Exp:* Asst, Univ Minn, 48-50; asst agronomist, Exp Sta, Hawaiian Sugar Planters' Asn, 41-46, from asst geneticist to prin geneticist & head dept genetics & path, 46-66; consult agronomist, 66-68, VPRES & DIR AGR SERV, HAWAIIAN AGRONOMICS, 68- *Mem:* Sigma Xi; AAAS; Am Soc Agron. *Res:* Sugarcane breeding; field experiment design; pathology; tropical agriculture and agribusiness management. *Mailing Add:* Hawaiian Agronomics 745 Fort St Suite 1826 Honolulu HI 96813

WARNER, JOHN SCOTT, b Woodstown, NJ, Oct 25, 28; m 61; c 4. CHROMATOGRAPHIC METHODS, ENVIRONMENTAL ANALYSIS. *Educ:* Rensselaer Polytech Inst, BS, 49; Cornell Univ, PhD(org chem), 52. *Prof Exp:* Anal chemist, Socony Vacuum Oil Co, 49; asst, Cornell Univ, 49-52; prin chemist, 52-57, proj leader, 57-62, sr res chemist, 62-81, RES LEADER, ORG CHEM DIV, COLUMBUS LABS, BATTELLE MEM INST, 62- *Mem:* AAAS; Am Chem Soc. *Res:* Development of methods for determining organic compounds in water, sludge and solid wastes; application of gas and liquid chromatography; determination of petroleum components and pesticides in environemntal samples. *Mailing Add:* Battelle Columbus Labs 505 King Ave Columbus OH 43201

WARNER, JOHN WARD, b Dubuque, Iowa, Oct 17, 44; m 66; c 2. ASTRONOMY, PROGRAM MANAGEMENT. *Educ:* Kalamazoo Col, BA, 66; Ohio State Univ, PhD(astron), 72. *Prof Exp:* Res fel terrestrial magnetism, Carnegie Inst Washington, 72-74; asst prof astron, Sch Physics & Astron, Univ Minn, Minneapolis, 74-78; asst proj scientist, Space Telescope, Marshall Space Flight Ctr, Ala, 78-80, MGR, GAMMA RAY OBSERV, NASA HQ, WASHINGTON, DC, 80-82. *Mem:* Am Astron Soc; Int Astron Union. *Res:* Infrared and optical studies of gas and dust and its relation to star formation and death, including planetary nebulae, galactic H II regions and galactic nuclei. *Mailing Add:* NASA Code TA-01 Marshall Space Flight Ctr AL 55455

WARNER, JOHN WARD, JR, b Davenport, Iowa, Feb 4, 18; m 42; c 5. MATHEMATICS. *Educ:* Taylor Univ, AB, 40; Univ Iowa, MS, 58; Ohio State Univ, PhD(math ed), 64. *Prof Exp:* Assoc athletics dir, Asbury Col, 40-41; teacher math & coach high sch, Tenn, 41-42; from instr to asst prof, Dubuque Univ, 42-45, bus mgr, 45-47; bus mgr, Taylor Univ, 47-48; bus mgr, Dubuque Univ, 48-53; pvt bus, Davenport, Iowa, 53-56; asst math, Univ Iowa, 56-58; from instr to assoc prof, 58-68, PROF MATH, COL WOOSTER, 68- *Concurrent Pos:* Consult, Ohio Coun Teachers Math, 62-65; Nat Defense Educ Act, Ohio, 62-67. *Mem:* Math Asn Am. *Mailing Add:* Dept of Math Col of Wooster Wooster OH 44691

WARNER, JONATHAN ROBERT, b New York, NY, Feb 19, 37; m 58; c 2. MOLECULAR BIOLOGY, CELL BIOLOGY. *Educ:* Yale Univ, BS, 58; Mass Inst Technol, PhD(biophys), 63. *Prof Exp:* Res assoc biophys, Mass Inst Technol, 63-64; res assoc biochem, 64-65, from asst prof to assoc prof, 65-74, PROF BIOCHEM & CELL BIOL, ALBERT EINSTEIN COL MED, 74-, DIR SUE GOLDING GRAD SCH, 72- *Concurrent Pos:* NSF fel, 64-65; career scientist, Health Res Coun, City New York, 65-72; Guggenheim fel, 71-72; Am Cancer Soc fac res award, 72-77; mem sci adv bd, Damon Runyon-Walter Winchell Cancer Fund, 73-77; mem molecular cytol study sect, NIH, 75-77. *Mem:* Am Soc Biol Chemists; Am Soc Cell Biol; Am Soc Microbiol. *Res:* synthesis and assembly of ribosomes and its regulation in yeast and mammalian cells; ribosomal protein genes; nuclear-cytoplasmic interactions. *Mailing Add:* Dept Biochem Albert Einstein Col Med Bronx NY 10461

WARNER, JUDITH SAUVE, ecology, see previous edition

WARNER, KENDALL, b Westfield, Mass, Oct 2, 27; m 70; c 1. FISHERIES. *Educ:* Univ Maine, BS, 50; Cornell Univ, MS, 52. *Prof Exp:* Fishery aide, US Fish & Wildlife Serv, 50; asst fishery biol, Cornell Univ, 51-52; regional fishery biologist, 52-68, CHIEF RES BIOLOGIST, FISHERY DIV, MAINE DEPT INLAND FISHERIES & WILDLIFE, 68- *Mem:* Am Fisheries Soc; fel Am Inst Fishery Res Biologists. *Res:* Fresh water fisheries; landlocked salmon; brook trout. *Mailing Add:* 34 Idaho Ave Bangor ME 04401

WARNER, LAURANCE BLISS, b Brooklyn, NY, Dec 29, 31; m 52; c 3. NUCLEAR PHYSICS. *Educ:* Rensselaer Polytech Inst, BS, 53; Johns Hopkins Univ, MS, 58; Fla State Univ, PhD(physics), 62. *Prof Exp:* US Navy, 53-, instr physics & electronics, US Naval Acad, 56-58, terrier battery officer, USS Long Beach CGN-9, 62-64, exec officer, USS Benjamin Stoddert DDG-22, 64-66, physicist, Lawrence Radiation Lab, 66-69, weapons officer, USS Galveston CLG-3, 69-70, mem staff, Chief Naval Opers, Washington, DC, 70-77; MEM STAFF, LOS ALAMOS SCI LAB, 77- *Concurrent Pos:* Instr physics, Fed City Col, Washington, DC, 71- *Mem:* Am Phys Soc. *Res:* Nuclear decay and reaction spectroscopy; deformed nuclei; fast electronics instrumentation; computer applications; neutron transport; radiative transfer; missile systems analysis. *Mailing Add:* 465 Camino Cereza Los Alamos NM 87544

WARNER, LAWRENCE ALLEN, b Monroe, Ohio, Apr 20, 14; m 42; c 2. GEOLOGY. *Educ:* Univ Miami, Ohio, AB, 37; Johns Hopkins Univ, PhD(geol), 42. *Prof Exp:* Geologist, US Antarctic Exped, Marie Byrd Land, 39-41 & Alaskan Br, US Geol Surv, 42-46; from asst prof to prof, Univ Colo, Boulder, 46-82; RETIRED. *Concurrent Pos:* Geologist, US Geol Surv, 46-52; res consult, Univ Boston, 52-54; consult, Denver Water Bd, 55- *Honors & Awards:* Congressional Medal for Sci & Explor. *Mem:* AAAS; Geol Soc Am; Am Geophys Union; Asn Eng Geol; Mineral Soc Am. *Res:* Antarctic and Alaskan geology; structure and tectonics of eastern Rocky Mountains; environmental and engineering geology. *Mailing Add:* Dept of Geol Sci Univ of Colo Boulder CO 80309

WARNER, LOUISE, b Dixon, Ill, Aug 14, 16. ANATOMY. *Educ:* Univ Chicago, SB, 38, PhD(anat), 49. *Prof Exp:* Asst prev med, Col Med, Univ Tenn, 41-42; asst anat, Univ Chicago, 42-45, asst, Metall Lab, 45-46, asst anat, 46-48; physiologist, Naval Med Res Inst, Nat Naval Med Ctr, 48-53; ASST PROF ANAT, SCH MED, GEORGETOWN UNIV, 53- *Mem:* Am Asn Anatomists; Microcirc Soc. *Res:* Living capillaries; electron microscopy; cinephotomicrography; electronic image processing; television applied to medical research. *Mailing Add:* 4644 Reservoir Rd NW Washington DC 20007

WARNER, MARK CLAYSON, b Nephi, Utah, Aug 30, 39; m 62; c 6. AQUATIC BIOLOGY. *Educ:* Utah State Univ, BS, 66, MS, 69; Okla State Univ, PhD(zool), 72. *Prof Exp:* Aquatic biologist, Tenn Valley Authority, 70-74; aquatic biologist, Med Bioeng Res & Develop Lab, Environ Protection Res Div, US Army, Ft Detrick, 74-80; AQUATIC BIOLOGIST, SPORT FISH DIV, ALASKA FISH & GAME 80- *Mem:* Am Fisheries Soc; Wildlife Dis Asn; Am Soc Testing & Mat. *Res:* Aquatic bioassy toxicity studies; review and evaluate research proposals in areas of aquatic biology. *Mailing Add:* Sport Fish Dept Alaska Fish & Game Juneau AK 99801

WARNER, MARLENE RYAN, b Philadelphia, Pa, Apr 30, 38; m 69; c 2. ENDOCRINOLOGY. *Educ:* Univ Calif, Berkeley, AB, 61, MA, 66; Univ Calif, Davis, PhD(anat), 72. *Prof Exp:* Res asst anat, Univ Calif, Davis, 68-69; res assoc cell biol, 72-75, instr cell biol, 75-77, ASST PROF OBSTET & GYNEC & CELL BIOL, BAYLOR COL MED, 77- *Mem:* Am Asn Cancer Res; Tissue Cult Asn; Endocrine Soc; Soc Study Reproduction; Am Soc Zoologists. *Res:* Tumor biology; reproductive physiology; differentiation; tumor-endocrinology. *Mailing Add:* Dept Obstet & Gynec Baylor Col Med Houston TX 77030

WARNER, MONT MARCELLUS, b Fillmore, Utah, Oct 9, 19; m 47. GEOLOGY. *Educ:* Brigham Youn Univ, AB, 47, MA, 49; Univ Iowa, PhD(geol), 63. *Prof Exp:* Geologist, Shell Oil Co, 49-55; consult petrol geol, La & Utah, 55-59; instr geol, Brigham Young Univ, 59-61; asst prof, Ariz State Univ, 63-67, res grant, 64-66; chmn dept ecol, 67-70, PROF GEOL, BOISE STATE COL, 67- *Concurrent Pos:* Idaho state rep in geothermal matters, 70-72; res & legis work in geothermal resources, 70-72; mem exec comt & comt info educ, Geothermal Resources Coun, 70-72. *Mem:* Am Asn Petrol Geologists; Nat Asn Geol Teachers; Ecol Soc Am; Nat Inst Prof Geol. *Res:* Sedimentation; structural and petroleum geology. *Mailing Add:* Boise State Univ Boise ID 83725

WARNER, NANCY ELIZABETH, b Dixon, Ill, July 8, 23. PATHOLOGY. *Educ:* Univ Chicago, SB, 44, MD, 49; Am Bd Path, dipl, 54. *Prof Exp:* From intern to asst resident path, Univ Chicago Clins, 49-50; resident, Cedars of Lebanon Hosp, Los Angeles, Calif, 53-54, asst pathologist, 54-58; from asst prof to assoc prof path, Univ Chicago, 58-65, dir lab surg path, Univ Clins, 59-65; assoc clin prof path, Univ Southern Calif, 65-66; assoc prof, Sch Med, Univ Wash, 66-67; assoc prof, 67-69, PROF PATH, UNIV SOUTHERN CALIF, 69-, CHMN DEPT, 72-, ASSOC DEAN ACAD AFFAIRS, 77- *Concurrent Pos:* Assoc dir labs, Cedars-Sinai Med Ctr, Los Angeles, 65-66; chief pathologist, Women's Hosp, Los Angeles County-Univ Southern Calif Med Ctr, 68-72, dir labs & path, 72- *Mem:* Fel Col Am Pathologists; Endocrine Soc; Am Asn Anatomists; Microcirc Soc; fel Am Soc Clin Pathologists. *Res:* Pathology of endocrine glands; comparative pathology of tumors of the gonads; microcirculation in experimental mammary tumors; effect of toxins on the microcirculation. *Mailing Add:* Dept Path Univ Southern Calif Los Angeles CA 90033

WARNER, PAUL LONGSTREET, JR, b New York, NY, June 20, 40; c 2. MEDICINAL CHEMISTRY. *Educ:* Ursinus Col, BS, 62; Pa State Univ, MS, 64; State Univ NY Buffalo, PhD(med chem), 69. *Prof Exp:* dir patents & prod liaison, 68-77, DIR CHEM RES, WESTWOOD PHARMACEUT INC, 77- *Mem:* Am Pharmaceut Asn; AAAS; Am Chem Soc; NY Acad Sci. *Res:* Antimicrobial agents; sunscreen agents; design and synthesis of antipsoriatics; antimetabolites; design and synthesis of anti-inflammatory agents. *Mailing Add:* 5200 Band St Clarence NY 14031

WARNER, PETER, b Winnipeg, Man, Apr 22, 20; m 52; c 6. MICROBIOLOGY. *Educ:* Univ London, MB & BS, 44, MD, 48, PhD(path), 51. *Prof Exp:* Asst pathologist, Bland-Sutton Inst Path, Middlesex Hosp, London, Eng, 43-44 & 46-52; pathologist, Winnipeg Gen Hosp, 53-54; assoc prof path, Fac Med, Univ Man, 54-55; head med res div, Inst Med Sci, Australia, 55-58; assoc prof med bact, Fac Med, Univ Man, 58-74; ASST REGIONAL DIR, MAN MED SERVS BR, HEALTH & WELFARE CAN, 74- *Concurrent Pos:* Brit Empire Cancer Campaign traveling scholar, Walter Reed Army Med Ctr, DC, 48-49; asst dep minister health, Man Govt, 67-71; chmn, Man Clean Environ Comn, 71-72; consult, Man Inst Tech; ed, Man Med Rev. *Mem:* Fel, Am Acad Microbiol; fel Am Soc Clin Path; Can Soc Microbiol; Can Asn Path; Path Soc Gt Brit & Ireland. *Res:* Medical microbiology; experimental pathology; health administration. *Mailing Add:* 3202-55 Nassau Winnipeg MB R3L 2G8 Can

WARNER, PHILIP MARK, b New York, NY, Nov 5, 46. ORGANIC CHEMISTRY. *Educ:* Columbia Univ, BA, 66; Univ Calif, Los Angeles, PhD(chem), 70. *Prof Exp:* NSF fel, Yale Univ, 70-71; from instr to asst prof, 71-77, ASSOC PROF ORG CHEM, IOWA STATE UNIV, 77- *Mem:* Am Chem Soc; Royal Soc Chem. *Res:* Strained ring compounds; carbonium ions; synthesis. *Mailing Add:* Dept of Chem Iowa State Univ Ames IA 50011

WARNER, R(ICHARD) E(LMORE), b Canton, Ohio, May 7, 21; m 43. CHEMICAL ENGINEERING. *Educ:* Miami Univ, AB, 42; Ohio State Univ, MSc, 48, PhD(chem eng), 51. *Prof Exp:* Asst chem eng, Ohio State Univ, 47-49, res assoc, Res Found, 50-51; res chem engr, Olin Mathieson Chem Corp, 51-53, sr chem engr, 53-56, process develop sect chief, 56-58, tech rep, 58-59, asst to vpres & tech dir energy div, 59-61; consult, 65-66; PROF MECH ENG, UNIV IDAHO, 66- *Concurrent Pos:* Vpres, Techno Fund Inc, 61-65; dir, Wallace Expanding Mach, Inc, Ind, 62-70; assoc dir eng, Exp Sta, Univ Idaho, 66-74. *Mem:* Nat Soc Prof Engrs; Int Solar Energy Soc. *Res:* Corrosion; phosphate fertilizer chemistry; organic and inorganic process development; market development; process economics; production engineering; solar energy utilization. *Mailing Add:* 605 Ridge Rd Moscow ID 83843

WARNER, RAY ALLEN, b Davis, Calif, May 5, 38; m 65. EXPERIMENTAL NUCLEAR PHYSICS. *Educ:* Univ Calif, Berkeley, BS, 61; Univ Calif, Davis, PhD(physics), 69. *Prof Exp:* Res assoc, 69-71, asst prof chem & physics, Cyclotron Lab, Mich State Univ, 72-77; SR RES SCIENTIST ANAL & NUCLEAR RES, BATTELLE MEM INST, PAC NORTHWEST DIV, 77- *Mem:* Am Phys Soc; AAAS. *Res:* Experiments in collective and intrinsic nuclear structure, parity mixing, beta strength functions, fission yields and properties of delayed neutron emitters; instrumentation for radio-analytical and laser-analytical chemistry. *Mailing Add:* Pac Northwest Div Battelle Mem Inst PO Box 999 Richland WA 99352

WARNER, RAYMOND M, JR, b Barberton, Ohio, Mar 21, 22; m 48; c 3. PHYSICS. *Educ:* Carnegie Inst Technol, BS, 47; Case Univ, MS, 50, PhD(physics), 52. *Prof Exp:* Lab asst, Pittsburgh Plate Glass Co, Ohio, 41 & 42; lab instr physics, Carnegie Inst Technol, 43; jr physicist, Res Lab, Corning Glass Works, NY, 47-48; instr physics, Case Univ, 51-52; mem tech staff semiconductor device develop, Bell Tel Labs, Inc, NJ, 52-59; chief engr diode develop, Semiconductor Prod Div, Motorola, Inc, Ariz, 59-61, mgr mat res, 61-63, dir eng, 63-65; mgr metal-oxide-semiconductor devices prog, Semiconductor Components Div, Tex Instruments Inc, 65-67; dir res, Semiconductor Div, Int Tel & Telegraph Corp, Fla, 67-69; dir technol, Semiconductor Dept, Union Carbide Corp, Calif, 69-70; prof elec eng & chmn microelectronics comt, Univ Minn, Minneapolis, 70-80. *Mem:* AAAS; Am Phys Soc; fel Inst Elec & Electronics Engrs. *Res:* Semiconductor device physics and engineering; solid-state electronics. *Mailing Add:* Dept of Elec Eng Univ of Minn Minneapolis MN 55455

WARNER, RICHARD DUDLEY, b Pittsfield, Mass, Aug 3, 44; m 74; c 1. GEOLOGY. *Educ:* Mass Inst Technol, SB, 66; Stanford Univ, PhD(geol), 71. *Prof Exp:* Res assoc geol, Univ Md, 73-74; RES ASSOC GEOL, UNIV NMEX, 74- *Concurrent Pos:* Resident res assoc, Goddard Space Flight Ctr, NASA, 71-73. *Mem:* Mineral Soc Am. *Res:* Petrology of lunar samples; petrology of terrestrial mafic and ultramafic rocks; experimental petrology. *Mailing Add:* Dept Geol Univ NMex Albuquerque NM 87131

WARNER, RICHARD G, b Washington, DC, Nov 1, 22; m 49; c 4. ANIMAL NUTRITION. *Educ:* Ohio State Univ, BSc, 47, MS, 48; Cornell Univ, PhD(animal nutrit), 51. *Prof Exp:* PROF ANIMAL NUTRIT, CORNELL UNIV, 51- *Concurrent Pos:* Consult dairy nutrit, Empresa Brasileira Pesquisa Agropecuaria, Brazil. *Mem:* Am Soc Animal Sci; Am Dairy Sci Asn; Am Inst Nutrit. *Res:* Calf and ruminant nutrition; laboratory animal nutrition; food intake physiology. *Mailing Add:* Dept Animal Sci Cornell Univ Ithaca NY 14853

WARNER, ROBERT, b Buffalo, NY, Feb 16, 12; m 39; c 2. PEDIATRICS. *Educ:* Harvard Univ, AB, 35; Univ Chicago, MD, 39; Am Bd Pediat, dipl, 49. *Prof Exp:* Intern, Buffalo Gen Hosp, 39-40; spec intern pediat, Buffalo Children's Hosp, 40-41, res, 46-47; asst, Cincinnati Children's Hosp & Res Found, 47-48; pvt pract, 48-55; ASSOC PROF PEDIAT, SCH MED, STATE UNIV NY BUFFALO, 56-; CLIN ASSOC PROF REHAB MED, 76-; MED DIR CHILDREN'S REHAB CTR, BUFFALO CHILDREN'S HOSP, 56- *Concurrent Pos:* Vis teacher, Buffalo Gen Hosp; attend, Buffalo Children's Hosp; ed, Acta Geneticae Medecae et Genellologiae. *Mem:* Am Soc Human Genetics; fel Am Pub Health Asn; fel Am Acad Pediat; fel Am Acad Cerebral Palsy; Am Acad Neurol. *Res:* Etiologics and relationships for prevention and prognostication of congenital anomalies and mental retardation, especially Down's Syndrome; endocrinology; human genetics; rehabilitation of children with neuromuscular disease cerebral palsy; juvenile amputee; reading and learning problems; treatment of phenylketonuria. *Mailing Add:* 936 Delaware Ave Buffalo NY 14209

WARNER, ROBERT COLLETT, b Denver, Colo, Aug 31, 13; m 36, 69; c 3. BIOCHEMISTRY. *Educ:* Calif Inst Technol, BS, 35; NY Univ, MS, 37, PhD(biochem), 41. *Prof Exp:* Chemist protein chem, Eastern Regional Lab, USDA, Philadelphia, 41-46; from asst prof to prof biochem, Sch Med, NY Univ, 46-69; chmn dept, 69-77, PROF MOLECULAR BIOL & BIOCHEM, UNIV CALIF, IRVINE, 69- *Concurrent Pos:* Mem panel plasma, Nat Res Coun, 52-57; Guggenheim Mem Found fel, Carlsberg Lab, Copenhagen, Denmark, 58; mem study sect biophys & biophys chem, NIH, 60-64; chmn study sect biochem, 72-74; assoc ed, J Biol Chem, 68-72. *Mem:* Am Soc Biol Chemists; Biophys Soc; Am Chem Soc. *Res:* Physical biochemistry of nucleic acids and proteins; mechanism of genetic recombination in small DNA containing bacteriophages; properties of circular DNA; bacterial plasmids. *Mailing Add:* Dept Molecular Biol & Biochem Univ of Calif Irvine CA 92717

WARNER, ROBERT EDSON, b Pomeroy, Ohio, Apr 11, 31; c 4. PHYSICS. *Educ:* Antioch Col, BS, 54; Univ Rochester, PhD(physics), 59. *Prof Exp:* From instr to asst prof physics, Univ Rochester, 59-61; asst prof, Antioch Col, 61-63; from asst prof to assoc prof, Univ Man, 63-65; assoc prof, 65-72, PROF PHYSICS, OBERLIN COL, 72- *Concurrent Pos:* NSF sci fac fel, Oxford Univ, 71-72. *Mem:* Am Phys Soc. *Res:* Nuclear scattering and reactions; nucleon-nucleon scattering; final-state interactions; angular correlations. *Mailing Add:* Dept of Physics Oberlin Col Oberlin OH 44074

WARNER, ROBERT LEWIS, b Redwood Falls, Minn, June 16, 37; m 64; c 2. AGRONOMY, PLANT PHYSIOLOGY. *Educ:* Univ Minn, BS, 62, MS, 64; Univ Ill, PhD(plant physiol & agron), 68. *Prof Exp:* Res asst agron, Univ Minn, 62-64 & Univ Ill, 64-68; asst prof, 68-74, assoc prof, 74-80, PROF AGRON, WASH STATE UNIV, 80- *Mem:* Am Soc Agron; Am Soc Plant Physiol. *Res:* Factors involved in cold resistance of alfalfa; inheritance and physiological studies of nitrate reductase. *Mailing Add:* Dept of Agron & Soils Wash State Univ Pullman WA 99163

WARNER, ROBERT RONALD, b Long Beach, Calif, Oct 28, 46. MARINE ECOLOGY. *Educ:* Univ Calif, Berkeley, AB, 68, Univ Calif, San Diego, PhD(marine ecol), 73. *Prof Exp:* Fel biol, Smithsonian Trop Res Inst, 73-75; ASST PROF BIOL, UNIV CALIF, SANTA BARBARA, 75- *Mem:* Soc Study Evolution; Ecol Soc Am; Am Soc Naturalists; Animal Behav Soc; Am Soc Ichthyologists & Herpetologists. *Res:* Reproductive strategies of marine organisms. *Mailing Add:* Dept of Biol Sci Univ of Calif Santa Barbara CA 93106

WARNER, SETH L, b Muskegon, Mich, July 11, 27; m 62; c 3. ALGEBRA. *Educ:* Yale Univ, BS, 50; Harvard Univ, MA, 51, PhD(math), 55. *Prof Exp:* From res instr to assoc prof, 55-65, PROF MATH, DUKE UNIV, 65- *Concurrent Pos:* NSF fel, Inst Advan Study, 59-60; vis res prof, Reed Col, 70-71. *Mem:* Am Math Soc; Math Asn Am. *Res:* Topological algebra; abstract analysis. *Mailing Add:* Dept of Math Duke Univ Durham NC 27706

WARNER, THEODORE BAKER, b Chicago, Ill, Mar 6, 31; m 55, 80; c 3. PHYSICAL CHEMISTRY, CHEMICAL OCEANOGRAPHY. *Educ:* Williams Col, BA, 52; Univ Ind, Bloomington, PhD(phys chem), 63. *Prof Exp:* Lectr chem, Univ Ind, 62; Nat Acad Sci resident res assoc, 63-64, res chemist, Electrochem Br, 64-67 & Chem Oceanog Br, 67-69, HEAD ELECTROCHEM SECT, ENVIRON CHEM BR, NAVAL RES LAB, 69- *Mem:* AAAS; Am Chem Soc; Am Geophys Union; Am Soc Limnol & Oceanog. *Res:* Aerosol chemistry; electroanalytical chemistry; computer-controlled analyses; geochemistry of fluorine; in situ chemical sensors; specific ion electrodes; mechanisms and kinetics of electrode processes; adsorption; catalysis; fused salts. *Mailing Add:* Code 4334 Environ Chem Br Naval Res Lab Washington DC 20375

WARNER, THOMAS CLARK, JR, b Waterbury, Conn, Nov 20, 19; m 42; c 2. MECHANICAL ENGINEERING, ELECTRICAL ENGINEERING. *Educ:* Yale Univ, BE, 42; Mass Inst Technol, MS, 47. *Prof Exp:* Res & develop officer, US Air Force, Wright Patterson AFB, Ohio, 42-45 & Hq, Washington, DC, 47-52; chief develop engr, MB Electronics Div, Textron Inc, 52-62; chmn dept math, 62-64 & dept mech eng, 62-65, dean, Sch Eng, 65-77, PROF MECH ENG, UNIV NEW HAVEN, 65- *Concurrent Pos:* Consult, MB Electronics Div, Textron Inc, 62- *Mem:* Am Soc Mech Engrs; Am Soc Eng Educ; Inst Environ Sci; Nat Soc Prof Engrs; Am Inst Aeronaut & Astronaut. *Res:* Vibration analysis and instrumentation; electro-mechanical design. *Mailing Add:* Dept of Mech Eng Univ of New Haven West Haven CT 06516

WARNER, THOMAS GARRIE, b El Paso, Tex, July 7, 48. BIOCHEMISTRY. *Educ:* Univ Tex, El Paso, BS, 70; Univ Calif, San Diego, PhD(chem), 75. *Prof Exp:* Res chemist, Scripps Inst Oceanog, 75-77; US Dept Pub Health fel, Neurosci Dept, Univ Calif, 77-78; asst res neuroscientist, 78-79, ASST PROF IN RESIDENCE, DEPT NEUROSCI, UNIV CALIF, 79- *Mem:* Am Chem Soc; Am Oil Chemists Soc; AAAS. *Res:* Human biochemical genetics; lysosomal storage diseases; complex carbohydrates structure and function analysis and relation to disease states; chemical anthesis of lipids and phospholipids; hydrophobic enzymes. *Mailing Add:* Dept Neurosci M-008 Univ Calif San Diego La Jolla CA 92093

WARNER, VICTOR DUANE, b Coulee Dam, Wash, Sept 9, 43; m 68. MEDICINAL CHEMISTRY. *Educ:* Univ Wash, BS, 66; Univ Kans, PhD(med chem), 70. *Prof Exp:* Asst prof med chem, Col Pharm & Allied Health Sci, Northern Univ, 70-74, assoc prof, 74-80, prof, 80-81, actg chmn, Dept Med Chem & Pharmacol, 75-76, chmn, 76-79, actg dean, Col Pharm & Allied Heatlh, 77-78, actg assoc univ provost, 78-79, assoc provost, 79-81; PROF MED CHEM & DEAN, COL PHARM, UNIV PR, 81- *Mem:* Am Chem Soc; Am Pharmaceut Asn. *Res:* Antibacterial agents for inhibition of dental plaque. *Mailing Add:* Col Pharm Univ PR GPO Box 5067 San Juan PR 00936

WARNER, WALTER CHARLES, b Barberton, Ohio, June 2, 20; m 47; c 2. POLYMER CHEMISTRY. *Educ:* Oberlin Col, AB, 41; Case Western Reserve Univ, MS, 43, PhD(org chem), 50. *Prof Exp:* Chem engr, Firestone Tire & Rubber Co, 43-47; sr res chemist, 49-55, group leader anal & testing, 55-62, sect head, Tech Serv, 62-71, sect head, Phys Testing Res & Serv, 71-77, res ctr adminr, 78-80, HEAD, INFO CTR, GEN TIRE & RUBBER CO, 80- *Mem:* Am Chem Soc; Soc Rheology; Am Soc Testing & Mat; Spec Libraries Asn; Am Soc Info Sci. *Mailing Add:* Gen Tire & Rubber Co Akron OH 44329

WARNER, WILLIAM HAMER, b Pittsburgh, Pa, Oct 6, 29; m 57; c 1. APPLIED MATHEMATICS. *Educ:* Carnegie Inst Technol, BS, 50, MS, 51, PhD(math), 53. *Prof Exp:* Asst math, Carnegie Inst Technol, 50-53; res assoc appl math, Brown Univ, 53-55; from asst prof to assoc prof mech, 55-68, PROF AEROSPACE ENG & MECH, UNIV MINN, MINNEAPOLIS, 68- *Mem:* Soc Indust & Appl Math; Am Math Soc; Math Asn Am; Soc Natural Philos. *Res:* Continuum mechanics; dynamic stability; energy methods; nonlinear systems; optimization of structures. *Mailing Add:* Dept Aerospace Eng & Mech Univ of Minn Minneapolis MN 55455

WARNER, WILLIS L, b Endicott, NY, Jan 28, 30. MEDICINE. *Educ:* Syracuse Univ, BA, 50; State Univ NY, MD, 60. *Prof Exp:* Res investr biochem, US Naval Radiol Defense Lab, 52-55; intern, San Francisco Hosp, 60-61; resident obstet, St Mary's Hosp, San Francisco, 61-63; assoc clin res, Baxter Labs, Ill, 63-68, assoc dir clin res, 68-71; dir clin res-biol, Hoechst Pharmaceut, Inc, 71-75; dir clin res, 75-76, dir med opers, Cutter Labs, Inc, 77-79; DIR & PRES, CONSULTS FOR HEALTH CARE, 79- *Concurrent Pos:* Ed, Plasma Forum, 79- *Mem:* Am Soc Pharmacol Therapeut; Am Soc Hemat; World Fed Hemophilia. *Mailing Add:* 39 Bret Harte Rd San Rafael CA 94901

WARNES, DENNIS DANIEL, b Stephen, Minn, June 14, 33; m 56; c 3. AGRONOMY, WEED SCIENCE. *Educ:* NDak State Univ, BSc, 55; Univ Minn, St Paul, MSc, 60; Univ Nebr-Lincoln, PhD(plant breeding), 69. *Prof Exp:* Technician agron, NDak State Univ, 51-55; teaching asst agron, Univ Minn, Minneapolis, 57-60; instr agron & outstate testing, Univ Nebr-Lincoln, 60-66, supvr, Mead Field Lab, 66-69; AGRONOMIST, W CENT EXP STA, UNIV MINN, MINNEAPOLIS, 69- *Mem:* Am Soc Agron; Weed Sci Soc Am. *Res:* Variety testing, weed control, row spacing, plant population, disease and insect control in corn, soybeans, field beans, sunflowers, small grains and forage crops; principles of weed control with specific weeds. *Mailing Add:* W Cent Exp Sta Morris MN 56267

WARNES, RICHARD HARRY, b Chicago, Ill, Apr 23, 33; m 55; c 2. PHYSICS, OPTICS. *Educ:* DePauw Univ, BA, 55; Stanford Univ, MS, 57. *Prof Exp:* STAFF MEM PHYSICS, LOS ALAMOS NAT LAB, 57- *Mem:* Am Phys Soc. *Res:* Shock wave phenomena; dynamic equation of state; constitutive relations; mechanics. *Mailing Add:* Group M-4 MS-940 Los Alamos Nat Lab Los Alamos NM 87545

WARNHOFF, EDGAR WILLIAM, b Knoxville, Tenn, May 5, 29; m 56; c 3. ORGANIC CHEMISTRY. *Educ:* Wash Univ, St Louis, AB, 49; Univ Wis, PhD(chem), 53. *Prof Exp:* Nat Res Coun fel, Birkbeck Col, Eng, 53-54; asst scientist, Nat Heart Inst, 54-57; NSF fel, Fac Pharm, Univ Paris, 57-58; res assoc chem, Mass Inst Technol, 58-59; asst prof, Univ Southern Calif, 59-62; from asst prof to assoc prof, 62-66, PROF CHEM, UNIV WESTERN ONT, 66- *Concurrent Pos:* Mem ed adv bd, J Org Chem, 70-74 & Can J Chem, 75-77; ed, Can J Chem, 82- *Honors & Awards:* Merck, Sharp & Dohme Lect Award, Chem Inst Can, 69. *Mem:* Chem Inst Can; Am Chem Soc; Royal Soc Chem. *Res:* Organic nitrogen chemistry; mechanisms of organic reactions, especially alpha-substituted carbonyl compounds. *Mailing Add:* Dept of Chem Univ of Western Ont London ON N6A 5B7 Can

WARNICK, ALVIN CROPPER, b Hinckley, Utah, Nov 15, 20; m 47; c 3. PHYSIOLOGY. *Educ:* Utah State Agr Col, BS, 42; Univ Wis, MS, 47, PhD(physiol of reprod), 50. *Prof Exp:* Asst animal husb & genetics, Univ Wis, 46-50; asst prof, Ore State Col, 50-53; from asst physiologist to assoc physiologist, 53-62, PHYSIOLOGIST, UNIV FLA, 62- *Mem:* Am Soc Animal Sci; Am Soc Study Reproduction; Genetic Asn. *Res:* Physiology of reproduction; effect of nutrition on fertility. *Mailing Add:* Dept of Animal Sci Univ of Fla Gainesville FL 32611

WARNICK, EDWARD GEORGE, b Chicago, Ill, Nov 1, 05; m 30. RADIOLOGY. *Educ:* Loyola Univ, Ill, MD, 37; Am Bd Radiol, dipl, 42. *Prof Exp:* Intern, St Agnes Hosp, Fond du Lac, Wis, 36-37; asst phys med, Sch Med, Loyola Univ, Ill, 37-43, from asst clin prof to assoc clin prof, Stritch Sch Med, 46-57, roentgenologist, Univ Hosp, 48-50; ASSOC PROF RADIOL, MED SCH, NORTHWESTERN UNIV, CHICAGO, 57-; CHIEF DIAG RADIOL, VET ADMIN RES HOSP, 57- *Concurrent Pos:* Assoc, Cook County Hosp, 37-40, fel, 40-43; consult, Induction Ctr, US Army & US Air Force, 43, 46-53; roentgenologist, Cook County Hosp, 46-53; chief dept radiol, West Side Vet Admin Hosp, 53-57. *Mem:* Radiol Soc NAm; Soc Nuclear Med; AMA; fel Am Col Radiol. *Res:* Clinical diagnostic radiology. *Mailing Add:* 5316 Wellington Ave Chicago IL 60641

WARNICK, JORDAN EDWARD, b Boston, Mass, Mar 21, 42; m 70; c 1. NEUROPHARMACOLOGY. *Educ:* Mass Col Pharm, BS, 63; Purdue Univ, Lafayette, PhD(pharmacol), 68. *Prof Exp:* USPHS trainee pharmacol, Sch Med, State Univ NY Buffalo, 68-70 & spec awardee, 70-71, asst prof biochem pharmacol, Sch Pharm, 71-74; asst prof, 74-80, ASSOC PROF PHARMACOL & EXP THERAPEUT, SCH MED, UNIV MD, BALTIMORE CITY, 80- *Mem:* AAAS; NY Acad Sci; Am Soc Pharmacol & Exp Therapeut; Soc Neurosci. *Res:* Physiology and pharmacology of muscular dystrophy and allied neuromuscular disorders; trophic influence of nerve on muscle; degeneration and regeneration in the peripheral and central nervous systems; pharmacology of neurotoxins; effects of drugs on nicotinic recptor-channel complex. *Mailing Add:* Dept Pharmacol & Exp Therapeut Univ of Md Sch of Med Baltimore MD 21201

WARNICK, ROBERT ELDREDGE, b Pleasant Grove, Utah, July 10, 29; m 53; c 6. NUTRITION. *Educ:* Brigham Young Univ, BS, 55; Utah State Univ, MS, 63, PhD(poultry nutrit), 70. *Prof Exp:* Agr inspector, Utah State Dept Agr, 58-59; lab technician chem anal, 59-60, res asst poultry res, 60-76, RES ASST PROF TURKEY RES, UTAH STATE UNIV, 76- *Mem:* Poultry Sci. *Res:* Nutrition and management of growing turkeys. *Mailing Add:* Snow Field Sta Utah State Univ Ephraim UT 84627

WARNKE, DETLEF ANDREAS, b Berlin, Ger, Jan 29, 28; m 64; c 2. EARTH SCIENCES. *Educ:* Freiburg Univ, dipl, 53; Univ Southern Calif, PhD(geol), 65. *Prof Exp:* Res asst geol, Aachen Tech Univ, 55-56; jr exploitation engr, Shell Oil Co, 57-58; res asst oceanog, Alan Hancock Found, 59-61; from res assoc to asst prof oceanog & geol, Fla State Univ, 65-71; asst prof, 71-73, actg chmn dept, 73-74, assoc prof, 73-77, prof earth sci, 77-80, PROF GEOL SCI, CALIF STATE UNIV, HAYWARD, 80- *Concurrent Pos:* Exchange prof, Free Univ Berlin, 80-81. *Mem:* Am Geophys Union; Soc Econ Paleont & Mineral; Am Soc Limnol & Oceanog; Geol Soc Am; Ger Geol Asn. *Res:* Marine geology; geomorphology; beach erosion; geochemistry. *Mailing Add:* Dept of Geol Sci Calif State Univ Hayward CA 94542

WARNOCK, JOHN EDWARD, b Freeport, Ill, Aug 20, 32; m 55; c 2. ZOOLOGY. *Educ:* Univ Ill, BS, 54; Univ Wis, MS, 58, PhD(zool), 63. *Prof Exp:* Field asst wildlife res, Ill Natural Hist Surv, 54 & Southern Ill Univ & Ill Natural Hist Surv, 54-55; res assoc, Ill Natural Hist Surv & Univ Ill, 62-64; from asst prof to assoc prof, 64-72, PROF BIOL SCI, WESTERN ILL UNIV, 72-, DIR, INST ENVIRON MGT, 79- *Mem:* AAAS; Am Soc Mammal; Animal Behav Soc; Ecol Soc Am; Wildlife Soc. *Res:* Mammalogy; animal behavior; vertebrate ecology; ornithology; ecology of small mammal populations, especially the relationships of behavior, physiological condition, density and physical factors of the environment; biology and management of small game animals. *Mailing Add:* Dept of Biol Sci Western Ill Univ Macomb IL 61455

WARNOCK, LAKEN GUINN, b Newton Falls, Ohio, Apr 19, 28; m 53; c 2. BIOCHEMISTRY. *Educ:* Milligan Col, BS, 57; Vanderbilt Univ, PhD(biochem), 62. *Prof Exp:* Instr biochem, Okla State Univ, 62-64; ASST PROF BIOCHEM, VANDERBILT UNIV, 64-; BIOCHEMIST, VET ADMIN HOSP, 64- *Concurrent Pos:* Consult, Interdept Comt Nutrit, Nat Defense Nutrit Surv, Lebanon, 61. *Mem:* Am Inst Nutrit. *Res:* Carbohydrate metabolism in vitamin deficiencies; vitamin nutriture in hemodialysis. *Mailing Add:* Res Lab Vet Admin Hosp Nashville TN 37203

WARNOCK, MARTHA L, b Detroit, Mich, July 19, 34; m 59; c 2. PATHOLOGY. *Educ:* Oberlin Col, AB, 56; Harvard Univ, MD, 60. *Prof Exp:* From instr to prof path, Univ Chicago, 65-78; PROF PATH, UNIV CALIF, SAN FRANCISCO, 78- *Mem:* AAAS; Am Thoracic Soc; Int Acad Path. *Mailing Add:* HSW595 Univ of Calif San Francisco CA 94143

WARNOCK, ROBERT G, b Salt Lake City, Utah, Mar 28, 25; m 48; c 3. PARASITOLOGY. *Educ:* Univ Utah, BS, 49, MS, 51, PhD(parasitol), 62. *Prof Exp:* Instr biol, Univ Utah, 62-63; from asst prof to assoc prof, 63-71, PROF BIOL, WESTMINSTER COL, UTAH, 71- *Mem:* Am Soc Parasitol. *Mailing Add:* Dept of Biol Westminster Col Salt Lake City UT 84105

WARNOCK, ROBERT LEE, b Portland, Ore, Feb 20, 30; m 59; c 2. THEORETICAL HIGH ENERGY PHYSICS. *Educ:* Reed Col, BA, 52; Harvard Univ, AM, 55, PhD(physics), 59. *Prof Exp:* Res assoc, Boston Univ, 59-60 & Univ Wash, Seattle, 60-62; from asst prof to assoc prof, 62-69, PROF THEORET PHYSICS, ILL INST TECHNOL, 69- *Concurrent Pos:* Asst physicist, Argonne Nat Lab, 64-67, assoc physicist, 67-71; vis scientist, Int Ctr Theoret Physics, Italy, 67; vis prof, Imperial Col, Univ London & Univ Bonn, 72; sci assoc, Inst Theoret Phys, Univ Groningen, 76; participating guest, Lawrence Berkeley Lab, 78- *Mem:* Am Phys Soc; Soc Indust & Appl Math. *Res:* Theory of elementary particles; dynamics and symmetries of strong interactions; construction of the S matrix; nonlinear analysis in mathematical physics. *Mailing Add:* Bldg 50A Rm 3115 Lawrence Berkeley Lab Berkeley CA 94720

WARPEHOSKI, MARTHA ANNA, b Wausau, Wis, Feb 22, 49; div. ORGANIC CHEMISTRY, POLYMER SCIENCE. *Educ:* Mass Inst Technol, SB, 71, PhD(org chem), 77; Johns Hopkins Univ, MA, 75. *Prof Exp:* Res assoc biomat, Dept Mech Eng, Mass Inst Technol, 77-79; SCIENTIST, UPJOHN CO, 81- *Mem:* Am Chem Soc; Sigma Xi. *Res:* Biological responses to polymeric materials; properties and modifications of biopolymers; oxidation of organic molecules; chemiluminescence of organic molecules; organic synthesis; medicinal chemistry. *Mailing Add:* Rte 2 Box 27 Hatley WI 54440

WARR, WILLIAM BRUCE, b Providence, RI, June 24, 33; m 59; c 2. NEUROANATOMY. *Educ:* Brown Univ, BA, 57, MA, 58, PhD(physiol psychol), 63. *Prof Exp:* NIH fel neurophysiol & neuroanat, Eaton-Peabody Lab Auditory Physiol, Mass Eye & Ear Infirmary, 63-64, res assoc neurophysiol & neuroanat, 64-67; assoc prof anat, Sch Med, Boston Univ, 67-78; RES ASSOC & DIR, NEUROANAT LAB, BOYS TOWN INST COMMUN DISORDERS CHILDREN, 78-; PROF HUMAN COMMUN, SCH MED, CREIGHTON UNIV, 78- *Concurrent Pos:* Asst, Harvard Med Sch, 67. *Mem:* AAAS; Am Asn Anatomists. *Res:* Neuroanatomy of the auditory system. *Mailing Add:* Boys Town Inst 555 N 30th St Omaha NE 68131

WARREN, BRUCE ALBERT, b Sydney, Australia, Nov 2, 34; m 64; c 2. PATHOLOGY. *Educ:* Univ Sydney, BSc, 57, MB, BS, 59; Oxford Univ, PhD(path), 64, MA, 67; FRCPath Australia, 72; MRCPath, UK, 73. *Prof Exp:* Brit Commonwealth scholar, Sir William Dunn Sch Path, Oxford Univ, 62-64; res fel, Div Oncol, Inst Med Res, Chicago Med Sch, 64-65; lectr cardiovasc res, Nuffield Dept Surg, Oxford Univ, 66-68, tutor path, Oxford Med Sch, 67-68; vis asst prof anat, 68, asst prof path, 68-69, assoc prof, 69-74, PROF PATH, UNIV WESTERN ONT, 74- *Concurrent Pos:* Consult, Westminster Hosp, London, Ont, 68-77; consult, Univ Hosp, London, Ont, 72-; dir cytopath serv, Univ Hosp, 76-; assoc ed, Biosci Commun & Companion Life Sci. *Mem:* AAAS; Can Asn Pathologists; Microcirc Soc; fel Royal Micros Soc; fel Royal Soc Med. *Res:* Thrombosis and athero-embolism; platelet aggregation; fibrinolysis; function of endothelium; microvasculature of tumors; transplantation and growth of tumors; tumor emboli in bloodstream. *Mailing Add:* Dept of Path Univ of Western Ont London ON N6L 3K7 Can

WARREN, BRUCE ALFRED, b Waltham, Mass, May 14, 37. PHYSICAL OCEANOGRAPHY. *Educ:* Amherst Col, BA, 58; Mass Inst Technol, PhD(phys oceanog), 62. *Prof Exp:* Res asst phys oceanog, 62-63, from asst scientist to assoc scientist, 63-78, SR SCIENTIST, WOODS HOLE OCEANOG INST, 78- *Concurrent Pos:* co-ed, J Phys Oceanog, 80- *Mem:* Am Geophys Union. *Res:* Dynamics of ocean currents; water-mass structures; general ocean circulation. *Mailing Add:* Dept of Phys Oceanog Woods Hole Oceanog Inst Woods Hole MA 02543

WARREN, CHARLES EDWARD, b Portland, Ore, Oct 26, 26; m 48; c 3. ECOLOGY, FISH BIOLOGY. *Educ:* Ore State Col, BS, 49, MS, 51; Univ Calif, PhD(zool), 61. *Prof Exp:* Asst prof, 53-59, assoc prof, 59-65, PROF FISHERIES, ORE STATE UNIV, 65-; GEN COORDR BIOL, DEPT FISHERIES & WILDLIFE, OAK CREEK LAB, 57- *Concurrent Pos:* Actg head, Dept Fisheries & Wildlife, Ore State Univ, 70-74. *Mem:* Sigma Xi. *Res:* Water pollution biology; autecology; population ecology; community ecology; theoretical ecology; resource management; philosophy of science. *Mailing Add:* Dept of Fisheries & Wildlife 104 Nash Hall Ore State Univ Corvallis OR 97331

WARREN, CHARLES O, JR, mycology, plant physiology, see previous edition

WARREN, CHARLES PRESTON, b Chicago, Ill, Apr 7, 21; m 45; c 2. BIOLOGICAL ANTHROPOLOGY. *Educ:* Northwestern Univ, BS, 47; Ind Univ, MA, 50; Univ Chicago, MA, 61. *Prof Exp:* Phys anthropologist, Am Graves Regist Serv Group, US Dept Army, Philippines & Japan, 51-55; from instr to asst prof, 57-76, ASSOC PROF ANTHROP, UNIV ILL, CHICAGO CIRCLE, 76-; RES ASSOC, PHILIPPINE STUDIES PROG, UNIV CHICAGO, 56- *Concurrent Pos:* Prin investr, Fulbright res award, Philippines, 50-51; co-investr, USPHS grant, Cook County Hosp & Chicago Undergrad Div, Univ Ill, 58-60; prin investr, NSF sci fac fel, Univ Chicago, 63-64; phys anthropologist, US Army Cent Identification Lab, Sattahip, Thailand, 73-75; consult phys & forensic anthrop, Sheriff of Cook County, Off Med Examiner & US Army Mem Affairs Agency, Washington, DC. *Honors & Awards:* Meritorious Civilian Serv Award, Dept Army, US Army Cent Identification Lab, Thailand, 75. *Mem:* Am Anthrop Asn; Am Asn Phys Anthrop; Am Ethnol Soc; fel Soc Appl Anthrop. *Res:* Philippine and Southeast Asian ethnography; forensic anthropology; identification of human remains; cognitive learning in non-western societies, Afro and Latin American urban studies. *Mailing Add:* Dept of Anthrop Box 4348 Univ of Ill at Chicago Circle Chicago IL 60680

WARREN, CHARLES REYNOLDS, b Kyoto, Japan, Sept 24, 13; US citizen; m 45. PLEISTOCENE GEOLOGY. *Educ:* Yale Univ, BS, 35, PhD(geol), 39. *Prof Exp:* Jr geologist, Socony-Vacuum Oil Co, Venezuela, 39-40; jr geologist, US Geol Surv, Calif & Ore, 40-41, asst geologist, NY, 46; instr geol, Yale Univ, 46-47; asst prof, Washington & Lee Univ, 47-52; geologist, US Geol Surv, 52-80; CONSULT. *Mem:* Fel AAAS; fel Geol Soc Am. *Res:* Geomorphology; glacial geology. *Mailing Add:* 3606 Whitehaven Pkwy NW Washington DC 20007

WARREN, CHRISTOPHER DAVID, b Luton, Eng, Apr 24, 38; m 66; c 2. CARBOHYDRATE CHEMISTRY. *Educ:* Univ Sheffield, BS, 60, PhD(carbohydrate chem), 63; Royal Inst Chem, ARIC, 64. *Prof Exp:* Mem sci staff lipid & carbohydrate chem, Med Res Coun, Nat Inst Med Res, London, 63-69; res fel biol chem, 69-70, assoc, 70-73, PRIN ASSOC BIOL CHEM, HARVARD MED SCH, 73-; ASST BIOCHEMIST, MASS GEN HOSP, 72- *Concurrent Pos:* Res fel biochem, Mass Gen Hosp, 69-72. *Mem:* Fel Royal Soc Chem; Asn Biol Chemists; AAAS; Soc Complex Carbohydrates; Am Chem Soc. *Res:* Synthesis of glycosyl phosphates, polyisoprenyl phosphates and glycosyl polyprenyl phosphate and pyrophosphate diesters, and the investigation of the role of these compounds in the biosynthesis of glycoproteins. *Mailing Add:* Lab for Carbohydrate Res Harvard Med Sch-Mass Gen Hosp Boston MA 02114

WARREN, CLAUDE EARL, b Columbus, Ohio, Jan 11, 14; m 39; c 2. ELECTRICAL ENGINEERING. *Educ:* Ohio State Univ, BEE, 38; Mass Inst Technol, MS, 40. *Prof Exp:* Meter tester, Ohio Power Co, 38; asst, Mass Inst Technol, 38-40; engr cent sta, Westinghouse Elec Corp, Pa, 40-45; from asst prof to assoc prof, 45-54, supvr res found, 46, PROF ELEC ENG, OHIO STATE UNIV, 54- *Mem:* Sr mem Inst Elec & Electronics Engrs. *Res:* Analog computers; circuit theory. *Mailing Add:* Dept of Elec Eng Ohio State Univ Columbus OH 43210

WARREN, CRAIG BISHOP, b Philadelphia, Pa, Oct 21, 39; m 64; c 2. PHYSICAL ORGANIC CHEMISTRY. *Educ:* Franklin & Marshall Col, AB, 61; Villanova Univ, BS, 63; Cornell Univ, PhD(org chem), 70. *Prof Exp:* Fel prebiol evolution, Corp Res Dept, Monsanto Co, 68-69, sr res chemist, 69-73, res specialist, 73-75; group leader,75-77, sr group leader, 77-80, DIR, INT FLAVORS & FRANGRANCES RES & DEVELOP, 80- *Mem:* Am Chem Soc; Sigma Xi; Soc Cosmetic Chem; Am Soc Testing & Mat. *Res:* Structure-activity relationships of fragrance molecules; reaction of molecules with oxygen; quantitative sensory evaluation of flavors and fragrances. *Mailing Add:* Int Flavors & Fragrances 1515 Hwy 36 Union Beach NJ 07735

WARREN, DAVID HENRY, b Ithaca, NY, June 9, 30; m 62; c 4. GEOPHYSICS, SEISMOLOGY. *Educ:* Rensselaer Polytech Inst, BS, 51; Columbia Univ, AM, 56. *Prof Exp:* Res asst marine geophys, Lamont Geol Observ, Columbia Univ, 51-53; geophysicist, Stand Oil Soc Calif, 53-61 & Alpine Geophys Assocs, Inc, 61-62; GEOPHYSICIST, US GEOL SURV, 63- *Mem:* Am Geophys Union; Soc Explor Geophys; Seismol Soc Am. *Res:* Explosion seismology studies of the earth's crust and upper mantle; seismic data processing and display techniques; geologic interpretation of geophysical data. *Mailing Add:* US Geol Surv 345 Middlefield Rd Menlo Park CA 94025

WARREN, DON CAMERON, b Saratoga, Ind, July 16, 90; m 10; c 1. GENETICS. *Educ:* Univ Ind, AB, 14, AM, 17; Columbia Univ, PhD(genetics), 23. *Hon Degrees:* Hon Dr, Univ Ind, 72. *Prof Exp:* Sci asst, Carnegie Inst, 14-15; field agent entom, Exp Sta, Ala Polytech Inst, 17-19; asst state entomologist, State Bd Entom, Ga, 19-21; from asst prof to prof poultry genetics, Kans State Col, 23-48; nat coord poultry breeding, USDA, 48-56; geneticist, 56-68, EMER GENETICIST, KIMBER FARMS, INC, CALIF, 68- *Concurrent Pos:* Consult, US Dept of State, India, 55. *Honors & Awards:* Award, Poultry Sci Asn, 33; Borden Award, 40; Superior Serv Award, USDA, 54; Poultry Hist Soc Hall of Fame, 71; Distinguished Serv Award, Kans State Univ, 72. *Mem:* Fel AAAS; Am Soc Nat; fel Poultry Sci Asn; Am Genetic Asn. *Res:* Genetics of Drosophila and fowl; physiology of reproduction in the fowl. *Mailing Add:* 4446 Grover Dr Fremont CA 94536

WARREN, DONALD, b Carbondale, Pa, Nov 30, 24; m 46; c 3. METALLURGY. *Educ:* Univ Ky, BS, 48; Lehigh Univ, MS, 49, PhD(metall eng), 52. *Prof Exp:* Res engr, 51-56, res proj engr, 56-60, res assoc, Eng Mat Lab, 60-67, SR CONSULT, ENG TEST CTR, E I DU PONT DE NEMOURS & CO, INC, 74- *Mem:* Am Soc Metals. *Res:* Constitution and corrosion of stainless steels. *Mailing Add:* E I Du Pont de Nemours & Co Inc Eng Test Ctr Wilmington DE 19898

WARREN, DONALD W, b Brooklyn, NY, Mar 22, 35; m 56; c 2. DENTISTRY. *Educ:* Univ NC, BS, 56, DDS, 59; Univ Pa, MS, 61, PhD(physiol), 63. *Prof Exp:* From asst prof to assoc prof dent, 63-69, prof oral biol, 69-70, PROF DENT ECOL & CHMN DEPT, SCH DENT & PROF, DEPT SURG, SCH MED, UNIV NC, CHAPEL HILL, 70-, DIR, ORAL FACIAL & COMMUNICATIVE DISORDERS PROG, 63-, KENAN PROF, 80- *Concurrent Pos:* Asst secy gen, Int Cong Cleft Palate, 66-69; consult, Joint Comt Dent & Speech Path-Audiol, Am Dent Asn & Am Speech & Hearing Asn, 67-71; pres, Am Cleft Palate Educ Found, 76-77. *Mem:* Am Dent Asn; Int Asn Dent Res; fel Am Speech & Hearing Asn; Am Cleft Palate Asn (vpres, 67-68, pres, 81-82). *Res:* Physiology of speech; effects of oral-facial disorders on the speech process; effects of breathing on facial morphology. *Mailing Add:* Dept of Dent Ecol Univ of NC Sch of Dent Chapel Hill NC 27514

WARREN, DOUGLAS ROBSON, b Fenelon Falls, Ont, July 16, 16; m 42; c 1. OCCUPATIONAL MEDICINE, ENVIRONMENTAL MEDICINE. *Educ:* Univ Toronto, MD, 41, dipl pub health, 47; Can Bd Occup Med, cert, 81. *Prof Exp:* Indust physician & consult, Can, 47-67; DIR & PARTNER, INDUST MED CONSULT, LTD, 67- *Concurrent Pos:* Assoc prof indust health, Sch Hyg, Univ Toronto, 67-75, spec lectr, Fac Med, 68-71 & 82-, mem staff hearing conserv course, Div Exten, 69-; mem assoc comt sci criteria for environ qual, Nat Res Coun Can, 71-78; Can med dir, Occidental Life Calif, 71-81; chmn, Continued Educ Can Coun Occup Med, 75-; mem, Environ Qual Comt, Metrop Toronto Bd Trade, 75- *Res:* Industrial medicine, related occupational and environmental subjects; hearing conservation and noise control; administration studies related to sickness absence control; metals in the environment and health factors. *Mailing Add:* PO Box 670 Fenelon Falls ON K0M 1N0 Can

WARREN, DWIGHT WILLIAM, III, b Los Angeles, Calif, Dec 21, 42; m 65; c 1. ENDOCRINOLOGY, REPRODUCTION. *Educ:* Univ Calif, AB, 64; Univ Southern Calif, PhD(physiol), 72. *Prof Exp:* Instr, 72-75, asst prof, 75-78, ASSOC PROF PHYSIOL & BIOPHYSICS, UNIV SOUTHERN CALIF, 78- *Concurrent Pos:* Consult, Amvac Chem Corp, 79-81; Nat Res Serv sr fel, NIH, 80-81. *Mem:* Endocrine Soc; Soc for Study Reprod; Am Soc Andrology; AAAS; NY Acad Sci. *Res:* Development of the fetal testis and regulation of androgen production by this organ by both internal and external modulators. *Mailing Add:* Dept Physiol & Biophysics Sch Med Univ Southern Calif 2025 Zonal Ave Los Angeles CA 90033

WARREN, FRANCIS A(LBERT), b Ashfield, Mass, May 16, 17; m 55. CHEMICAL ENGINEERING. *Educ:* Mass State Col, BS, 39; Va Polytech Inst, BS, 44; Ohio State Univ, MS, 49. *Prof Exp:* Lab supvr, Ciba Co, Inc, NY, 40-42; physicist, Hercules Powder Co, 42-45; res engr chem dept, Battelle Mem Inst, 45-49; supvry chem engr & head internal ballistics br, US Naval Ord Test Sta, Calif, 49-54; propellant technologist, Southwest Res Inst, 54-57, mgr spec projs sect, Dept Chem & Chem Eng, 57-58 & propellants sect, 58-60; sr tech specialist, Eng Dept, Rocketdyne Div, NAm Rockwell Corp, 60-80. *Mem:* AAAS; Am Inst Aeronaut & Astronaut; Sigma Xi; Am Chem Soc; Am Ord Asn. *Res:* Solid propellants; internal ballistics of solid-fuel rockets; gas generators. *Mailing Add:* 2133 Lake James Waco TX 76710

WARREN, FRANCIS SHIRLEY, b Winnipeg, Man, Oct 26, 20; m 43; c 6. AGRONOMY. *Educ:* Ont Agr Col, BSA, 46; Univ Minn, MSc, 48, PhD(plant genetics & path), 49. *Prof Exp:* Asst corn breeding, Univ Minn, 47-49; res officer, Exp Farm Can Dept Agr, Ont, 49-53, head forage & cereal sect, NS, 53-66, RES SCIENTIST, FORAGE CROPS SECT, CENT EXP FARM, CAN DEPT AGR, 66- *Mem:* Can Soc Agron; Agr Inst Can. *Res:* Cereal and forage crop production. *Mailing Add:* 45 Rockfield Crest Ottawa ON K2E 5L6 Can

WARREN, GEORGE FREDERICK, b Ithaca, NY, Sept 23, 13; m 44; c 3. WEED SCIENCE. *Educ:* Cornell Univ, BS, 35, PhD(veg crops), 45. *Prof Exp:* Dist county agr agent, Maine, 35-38; asst nutrit veg crops, Cornell Univ, 38-42; asst prof hort, Univ Wis, 45-48; assoc prof hort, Purdue Univ, 49-55, prof, 55-79; CONSULT AGR, 79- *Concurrent Pos:* Exec comt mem, Coun Agr Sci & Technol, 75-76, pres, 77-78. *Honors & Awards:* Campbell Award, Am Inst Biol Sci, 66. *Mem:* Fel AAAS; fel Weed Sci Soc Am (pres, 64-66); fel Am Soc Hort Sci; Weed Sci Soc Am. *Res:* Basis of selective action of herbicides; fate of herbicides in soil; control of weeds in horticultural crops. *Mailing Add:* 1130 Cherry Lane West Lafayette IN 47906

WARREN, GEORGE HARRY, b Morrisville, Pa, Sept 7, 16; m 46; c 1. MICROBIOLOGY, CHEMOTHERAPY. *Educ:* Temple Univ, BA, 39, MA, 40; Princeton Univ, PhD(microbiol), 44. *Prof Exp:* Lab instr microbiol, Princeton Univ, 41-42; instr bact-immunol, Jefferson Med Col, 44-46; head dept antibiotics-bact, Wyeth Inst Med Res, 47-59, dir dept microbiol, 60-79, DIR CLIN MICROBIOL, WYETH LABS, 81-; PROF MICROBIOL, JEFFERSON MED COL, THOMAS JEFFERSON UNIV, 66- *Mem:* Am Soc Microbiol; Soc Exp Biol & Med; Am Asn Cancer Res; fel Royal Soc Trop Med & Hyg; fel NY Acad Sci. *Res:* Antimicrobial agents and chemotherapy; tumor research; enzymes; mucopolysaccharides; immunostimulatory agents; host response mechanisms. *Mailing Add:* Wyeth Labs Box 8299 Philadelphia PA 19101

WARREN, GUYLYN REA, b Butte, Mont, Aug 16, 41. MOLECULAR BIOLOGY, SYNTHETIC INORGANIC CHEMISTRY. *Educ:* Mont State Col, BS, 63; Mont State Univ, PhD(genetics), 67. *Prof Exp:* NIH fel radiation repair, Palo Alto Med Res Found, Stanford Univ, 68-70, res assoc, 70-72; res assoc vet res, 73-74, asst prof, 74-76, adj asst prof, 76-80, ADJ ASSOC PROF CHEM, MONT STATE UNIV, 80- *Concurrent Pos:* Prin investr, USDA, 74-76 & 79-81, Mont Air Pollution Study, 78-80, Smelter Environ Res Assoc, 76-77, Proctor & Gamble, 79-81 & NIH Cancer Inst, 80-82; sci consult, Dept Energy, 77-78. *Mem:* Environ Mutagen Soc; AAAS; Am Soc Microbiol. *Mailing Add:* Chem Dept Johnson Hall Mont State Univ Bozeman MT 59717

WARREN, HALLECK BURKETT, JR, b St Louis, Mo, Sept 3, 22; m 51; c 2. BACTERIOLOGY. *Educ:* Univ St Louis, BS, 43; Univ Ill, MS, 49, PhD(bact), 51. *Prof Exp:* Asst dairy bact, Univ Ill, 49-50; res microbiologist, Res Div, Abbott Labs, 51-57; head bact, Res Labs, Pet Inc, 57-68, mgr food sci & eng, 68-70; mgr food sci, Fairmont Foods Co, 70-72; mgr food sci, 72-77, dir food sci & qual assurance, 77-78, V PRES & DIR TECH SERV, INTERSTATE BRANDS CORP, 78- *Mem:* Am Asn Cereal Chem; Am Soc Microbiol. *Res:* Microbial physiology of flavor components; bacteriology of foods and dairy products; antibiotic action, production and assay; food preservation. *Mailing Add:* Interstate Brands Corp PO Box 1627 Kansas City MO 64141

WARREN, HAROLD HUBBARD, b Derry, NH, July 5, 22. ORGANIC CHEMISTRY. *Educ:* Univ NH, BS, 44, MS, 47; Princeton Univ, MA, 49, PhD(chem), 50. *Prof Exp:* From instr to prof chem, 50-72, HALFORD R CLARK PROF NATURAL SCI, WILLIAMS COL, 72- *Mem:* AAAS; Sigma Xi; Am Chem Soc. *Res:* Determination of structure of natural products and synthesis and evaluation of structural variants. *Mailing Add:* Thompson Chem Lab Williams Col Williamstown MA 01267

WARREN, HARRY VERNEY, b Anacortes, Wash, Aug 27, 04; m 34. GEOLOGY, MINERALOGY. *Educ:* Univ BC, BA, 26, MASc, 27; Oxford Univ, BSc, 28, DPhil, 29. *Hon Degrees:* DSc, Univ Waterloo, 75, Univ BC, 78; FRCGP, Gt Brit, 73. *Prof Exp:* Commonwealth Fund fel, Calif Inst Technol, 29-32; from lectr to prof, 32-71, PROF MINERAL & PETROL, UNIV BC, 71-; GEOCHEM ADV, PLACER DEVELOP LTD, VANCOUVER, 71- *Concurrent Pos:* Exec mem, BC & Yukon Chamber Mines, 39-, from vpres to pres, 39-54; exec mem, UN Asn Can, 48-, pres, 55-58. *Honors & Awards:* Order of Can, CM, 71, OC, 72. *Mem:* Fel Geol Soc Am; Am Inst Mining, Metall & Petrol Eng; fel Royal Soc Can; fel Geol Asn Can; Can Inst Mining & Metall. *Res:* Lead and zinc deposits in southwestern Europe; precious and base metal relationships in western and North America; rarer metals; precious and base metal deposits of British Columbia; trace elements in relation to mineral exploration and epidemiology; relationship existing between geology and health. *Mailing Add:* Dept of Geol Univ of BC Vancouver BC V6T 1W5 Can

WARREN, HERBERT DALE, b Houston, Tex, Apr 8, 32; div; c 1. ANALYTICAL CHEMISTRY, INORGANIC CHEMISTRY. *Educ:* Rice Univ, BA, 54; Univ Idaho, MS, 59; Ore State Univ, PhD(anal chem), 66. *Prof Exp:* Tech grad chem, Hanford Atomic Prod Oper, Gen Elec Co, Wash, 56-58, chemist II, 58, tech librn, 59; tech asst chem, Los Alamos Sci Lab, 61; res asst, Union Oil Res Ctr, Calif, 62; from instr to asst prof, 63-74, ASSOC PROF CHEM, WESTERN MICH UNIV, 74- *Mem:* Am Chem Soc; Hist Sci Soc. *Res:* Organic reagents for spectrophotometric analysis; equilibrium constants of coordination compounds; extraction chromatography of inorganic systems; history of chemistry. *Mailing Add:* Dept of Chem Western Mich Univ Kalamazoo MI 49008

WARREN, HERBERT G(USTAVUS), b Epps, La, June 4, 30; m 56; c 2. PETROLEUM ENGINEERING. *Educ:* La Polytech Inst, BS, 54, MS, 62; Miss State Univ, PhD(eng), 65. *Prof Exp:* Petrol engr, Union Prod Co, United Gas Corp, 54-61; instr petrol eng, La Polytech Inst, 61-62; from instr to asst prof, Miss State Univ, 62-65; from asst prof to assoc prof, Mont Col Mineral Sci & Technol, 65-70, res assoc, 70-71, educ consult, 72-76; vpres, Billings Bus Col, 72-76; assoc prof petrol eng, Miss State Univ, 76-80; WITH AMOCO CHEM CORP, 80- *Mem:* Soc Petrol Engrs; Am Soc Eng Educ; Nat Soc Prof Engrs. *Res:* Production of methane gas from household garbage under anaerobic conditions; chemically combining water with gasoline in a microemulsion to reduce pollution in internal combustion engines. *Mailing Add:* Amoco Chem Corp 200 E Randolph Chicago IL 60601

WARREN, HERMAN LECIL, b Tyler, Tex, Nov 13, 32; m 63; c 3. PLANT PATHOLOGY. *Educ:* Prairie View Agr & Mech Col, BS, 53; Mich State Univ, MS, 62; Univ Minn, St Paul, PhD(plant path), 69. *Prof Exp:* Res scientist plant path, Olin Mathieson Chem Corp, 62-67; PLANT PATHOLOGIST, AGR RES SERV, USDA, 69- *Concurrent Pos:* Asst prof, Purdue Univ, Lafayette, 71-77, assoc prof, 77- *Mem:* Am Phytopath Soc; Mycol Soc Am. *Res:* Relationship of soilborne diseases to stalk rot of corn; survival mechanism of soilborne pathogens; effects of light and temperature on spore germination, growth and production of fungi; physiology of host parasites. *Mailing Add:* Dept of Bot & Plant Path Purdue Univ West Lafayette IN 47907

WARREN, HOLLAND DOUGLAS, b Wilkes Co, NC, July 31, 32; m 55; c 3. PHYSICS. *Educ:* Wake Forest Col, BS, 59; Univ Va, MS, 61, PhD(nuclear physics), 63. *Prof Exp:* Develop physicist, Celanese Corp Am, 63-64; sr physicist, 64-70, RES SPECIALIST, BABCOCK & WILCOX CORP, 70- *Mem:* Am Phys Soc; Am Nuclear Soc. *Res:* Neutron spectroscopy; nuclear physics; nuclear instrumentation; neutron radiography; reactor instrumentation. *Mailing Add:* Lynchburg Res Ctr Babcock & Wilcox Corp Lynchburg VA 24505

WARREN, J(OSEPH) E(MMET), b Chicago, Ill, Aug 19, 26; wid; c 5. PETROLEUM ENGINEERING. *Educ:* Univ Pittsburgh, BS, 51; Univ Pa, MS, 54, PhD(petrol eng), 60. *Prof Exp:* Res engr, Stanolind Oil & Gas Co, 51-52; res assoc petrol eng, Pa State Univ, 55-56; sect head reservoir eng appln, Gulf Res & Develop Co, 56-63; gen supt reservoirs, Kuwait Oil Co, 63-66; div dir prod, Gulf Res & Develop Co, Pa, 66-67, dept dir explor & prod, 67-70; vpres opers, Santa Fe Int Corp, 70-76; PLANNING ADV, GULF OIL CORP, 76- *Mem:* Soc Indust & Appl Math; Asn Comput Mach; Soc Petrol Engrs; Inst Mgt Sci; Brit Inst Petrol. *Res:* Energy management; economics; production systems; computer applications; optimization methods; transportation. *Mailing Add:* Gulf Oil Corp 107 Nantucket Dr Pittsburgh PA 15238

WARREN, JAMES C, b Oklahoma City, Okla, May 13, 30; m 51; c 4. ENDOCRINOLOGY, BIOCHEMISTRY. *Educ:* Univ Wichita, AB, 50; Univ Kans, MD, 54; Univ Nebr, PhD(biochem), 61. *Prof Exp:* Fel, Nat Inst Child Health & Human Develop, 59-61; from asst prof to prof obstet & gynec, Univ Kans, 61-70, from instr to assoc prof biochem, 61-70; PROF BIOL CHEM, PROF OBSTET & GYNEC & HEAD DEPT, SCH MED, WASHINGTON UNIV, 70- *Concurrent Pos:* Markle scholar med sci, 61. *Res:* Biosynthesis; metabolism and mechanism of action of free and conjugated steroids; kinetics of steroid interconverting enzymes; biochemistry of menstruation. *Mailing Add:* Dept of Obstet & Gynec Washington Univ Sch of Med St Louis MO 63103

WARREN, JAMES DONALD, b Ludlow, Mass, June 10, 48; m 74. MEDICINAL CHEMISTRY, SYNTHETIC ORGANIC CHEMISTRY. *Educ:* Western New Eng Col, BS, 70; Brown Univ, PhD(chem), 74. *Prof Exp:* Nat Cancer Inst fel, Temple Univ, 73-74; SR RES CHEMIST, LEDERLE LABS, AM CYANAMID CO, 74- *Mem:* Am Chem Soc. *Res:* Organic synthesis and evaluation of antitumor drug candidates. *Mailing Add:* CPRD-697 Am Cyanamid Co Rte 46 Clifton NJ 07015

WARREN, JAMES VAUGHN, b Columbus, Ohio, July 1, 15; m 54. INTERNAL MEDICINE. *Educ:* Ohio State Univ, BA, 35; Harvard Med Sch, MD, 39; Am Bd Internal Med, dipl. *Hon Degrees:* DSc, Emory Univ, 74. *Prof Exp:* Med house officer, Peter Bent Brigham Hosp, Mass, 39-41, asst resident med, 41-42; instr internal med, Sch Med, Emory Univ, 42-46; asst prof med, Sch Med, Yale Univ, 46-47; from assoc prof to prof physiol med, Sch Med, Emory Univ, 47-52; prof med, Sch Med, Duke Univ, 52-58; prof internal med & chmn dept, Univ Tex Med Br, 58-61; chmn dept, 61-79, PROF MED, COL MED, OHIO STATE UNIV, 61- *Mem:* Nat Inst Med; Am Soc Clin Invest; Am Physiol Soc; Am Heart Asn; master Am Col Physicians. *Res:* Cardiovascular diseases. *Mailing Add:* Dept of Med Ohio State Univ Col of Med Columbus OH 43210

WARREN, JAMES WALTER, JR, b Lincolnton, NC, Aug 17, 44; m 64; c 2. PHARMACEUTICS, INDUSTRIAL PHARMACEUTICAL TECHNOLOGY. *Educ:* Univ SC, BS, 67; Butler Univ, MS, 73; Univ Ga, PhD(pharmaceut), 76. *Prof Exp:* Pharm supvr, Greenville Gen Hosp, SC, 67-69; pharm chemist, Eli Lilly & Co, Indianapolis, 69-73; instr, Univ Ga, 73-76; asst prof, 76-81, ASSOC PROF PHARM, MED UNIV SC, 81- *Concurrent Pos:* SC Appropriation Gen Med Res grant, 78-79. *Mem:* Am Pharmaceut Asn; Acad Pharmaceut Sci; Sigma Xi. *Res:* Pharmaceut dosage form design and formulation; dissolution of drugs from solid dosage forms; drug product stability; biopharmaceutics and pharmacokinetics. *Mailing Add:* Med Univ of SC Col of Pharm Charleston SC 29403

WARREN, JOEL, b New York, NY, 1914; m 42; c 2. CANCER RESEARCH. *Educ:* Yale Univ, AB, 36; Columbia Univ, AM, 38, PhD(bact), 40. *Prof Exp:* Res assoc pediat, Childrens' Hosp, Cincinnati, Ohio, 29-42; chief virus res sect, US Army Med Sch, DC, 46-51, dept bact, 51-54; sci attache for Scandinavia, US Dept State, Sweden, 54-56; virologist, Div Biol Stand, NIH, 56-58; dir biol res, Chas Pfizer & Co, 58-68; dir, Life Sci Ctr, Nova Univ, 68-80; DIR, GOODWIN INST CANCER, 67- *Concurrent Pos:* Nat Res Coun fel, 42-43; vis prof, Ohio State Univ, 49-50 & Univ Md, 51-58; vis res fel, Univ Uppsala, 51; mem microbiol study sect, Grant-in-Aid Div, NIH, 53-55. *Mem:* Soc Exp Biol & Med; Am Asn Immunol; Am Acad Microbiol; Am Asn Cancer Res. *Res:* Viruses and viral diseases; biophysical methodology; toxoplasmosis; instrumentation; immunology of viral infections; cancer chemotherapy and immunology. *Mailing Add:* Life Sci Ctr Nova Univ Ft Lauderdale FL 33314

WARREN, JOHN BERNARD, b London, Eng, Nov 4, 14; Can citizen; m 51; c 4. PHYSICS. *Educ:* Univ London, BSc, 34, Imp Col, dipl & PhD(physics), 36. *Prof Exp:* Jr sci officer, Dept Sci & Indust Res, UK, 37-39; lectr appl physics, Southampton Univ, 39; sr sci officer, Telecommun Res Estab, 40-45; sr sci officer, UK Atomic Energy Proj, 45-46; lectr physics, Glasgow Univ, 46-47; PROF PHYSICS, UNIV BC, 47- *Concurrent Pos:* Res fel, Australian Nat Univ, 55-56; res fel, Rutherford Lab, Abingdon, Eng, 65-66; dir, TRIUMF Proj, Univ BC, 68-71; vis, Europ Orgn Nuclear Res, 72-73. *Mem:* Am Phys Soc; Can Asn Physicists; fel Royal Soc Can; Brit Inst Physics. *Res:* Nuclear physics. *Mailing Add:* Dept of Physics Univ of BC Vancouver BC V6T 1W5 Can

WARREN, JOHN LUCIUS, b Chicago, Ill, Dec 17, 32; m 58; c 2. ACCELERATOR PHYSICS. *Educ:* Univ Chicago, BA, 53; Univ Md, PhD(physics), 59. *Prof Exp:* Asst prof physics, De Pauw Univ, 59-61; mem staff, 61-73, asst to assoc dir res, 73-75, asst div leader, Ctr Div, 75-77, STAFF MEM, LOS ALAMOS NAT LAB, UNIV CALIF, 77- *Mem:* Am Phys Soc. *Res:* Lattice dynamics using inelastic neutron scattering; group theory applied to lattice dynamics. *Mailing Add:* MS H808 Los Alamos Nat Lab Univ Ga Los Alamos NM 87544

WARREN, JOHN RUSH, b Columbus, Ohio, July 20, 19. BOTANY. *Educ:* Marietta Col, AB, 41; Ohio State Univ, MS, 49, PhD, 50. *Prof Exp:* Asst plant pathologist, Agr Exp Sta, Ohio State Univ, 42-46; asst prof, Duke Univ, 46-52; plant pathologist, Standard Fruit & Steamship Co, Honduras, 52-55, dir trop res, 55-59, dir statist qual control, La, 59-60; assoc prof biol sci & chmn dept, Tenn Technol Univ, 60-61; dean grad sch, 64-72, PROF BIOL SCI, MARSHALL UNIV, 64- *Concurrent Pos:* Consult, Atomic Energy Comn, 66; Fulbright lectr & consult, Nat Univ Honduras, 68-69 & Univ Guayaquil, Ecuador, 80. *Mem:* Sigma Xi; NY Acad Sci; fel Explorers Club. *Res:* Microbiology; ecology; tropical agriculture. *Mailing Add:* Dept of Biol Sci Marshall Univ Huntington WV 25701

WARREN, JOHN STANLEY, b Ithaca, NY, Dec 19, 37; div; c 1. GEOLOGY. *Educ:* Cornell Univ, BA, 60; Stanford Univ, PhD(geol), 67. *Prof Exp:* Asst prof geol, Univ Cincinnati, 65-72; assoc prof geol, Thomas Jefferson Col, Grand Valley State Col, 72-79; vis fac, Evergreen State Col, 79-80; MEM FAC, MARLBORO COL, 80- *Mem:* Paleont Soc; Sigma Xi; AAAS. *Res:* Invertebrate paleontology; micropaleontology; palynology. *Mailing Add:* Marlboro Col Marlboro VT 05344

WARREN, KENNETH S, b New York, NY, June 11, 29; m 59; c 2. TROPICAL MEDICINE. *Educ:* Harvard Univ, AB, 51, MD, 55; Univ London, dipl, 59. *Prof Exp:* Intern med, Boston City Hosp, Mass, 55-56; mem staff med res, Lab Parasitic Dis, NIH, 56-63; from asst prof to assoc prof prev med, Sch Med, Case Western Res Univ, 63-70, from asst prof to assoc prof med, 63-75, adj prof lib sci, 72-75, assoc prof geog med, 70-76, dir div geog med, 73-76, prof med & prof lib sci, 75-77; DIR HEALTH SCI, ROCKEFELLER FOUND, NY, 76- *Concurrent Pos:* NIH res career develop award, 66-71. *Honors & Awards:* Bailey K Ashford Award, 74; Squibb Award, 75. *Mem:* Inst of Med of Nat Acad Sci; Am Soc Trop Med & Hyg; Am Asn Immunologists; Infectious Dis Soc Am; Asn Am Physicians. *Res:* Schistosomiasis; pathophysiology; immunology; control. *Mailing Add:* Rockefeller Found 1133 Ave of the Americas New York NY 10036

WARREN, LEONARD, b Toronto, Can, Sept 23, 24; US citizen; m 47; c 3. BIOCHEMISTRY. *Educ:* Univ Toronto, BA, 47, MD, 51; Mass Inst Technol, PhD(biochem), 57. *Prof Exp:* Vis scientist biochem, NIH, 57-63; PROF, DEPT ANAT, UNIV PA, 63- *Concurrent Pos:* Vis scientist, Pasteur Inst, Paris, France, 63-64 & Imperial Cancer Res Fund, Eng, 70-71; inst prof, Wistar Inst, Philadelphia, Pa, 75-; prof, Am Cancer Soc, 80- *Mem:* Am Soc Biol Chem; Soc Gen Physiologists. *Res:* Glycoproteins of membrane, in normal and pathological cells (malignancy, metabolic and other diseases); changes in the structure of the carbohydrate groups of glycoproteins with changing conditions. *Mailing Add:* Wistar Inst 36th & Spruce St Philadelphia PA 19104

WARREN, LIONEL GUSTAVE, b New York, NY, May 5, 26; m 52; c 3. PARASITOLOGY, MOLECULAR BIOLOGY. *Educ:* Syracuse Univ, AB, 48, MA, 53; Johns Hopkins Univ, ScD(parasitol), 57. *Prof Exp:* Res assoc biol, Rice Univ, 57-60; vis Int Atomic Energy Agency prof parasitol, Sci Res Inst, Caracas, Venezuela, 60-63; assoc prof med parasitol, 63-79, assoc prof trop med, 77-79, PROF MED PARASITOL & TROP MED, LA STATE UNIV MED CTR, NEW ORLEANS, 79- *Concurrent Pos:* USPHS grant, 64-70; scientist, Charity Hosp La, New Orleans, 67-; coordr grad studies, Dept Trop Med, La State Univ Med Ctr, 80-; Pfizer Latin Am grant, 81-82. *Mem:* Am Soc Parasitologists; Am Soc Trop Med & Hyg; Am Soc Cell Biol. *Res:* Carbohydrate and oxidative metabolism of endoparasitic animals; immunology of endoparasites; biochemistry of endemic amoebae and related organisms. *Mailing Add:* Dept of Trop Med La State Univ Med Ctr New Orleans LA 70112

WARREN, LLOYD OLIVER, b Fayetteville, Ark, Dec 27, 15; m 42; c 3. ENTOMOLOGY. *Educ:* Univ Ark, BS, 47, MS, 48; Kans State Col, PhD, 54. *Prof Exp:* Instr & jr entomologist, Univ Ark, 47-51; instr entom, Kans State Univ, 53-54; from asst prof & asst entomologist to prof entom & entomologist, 54-73, DIR, ARK AGR EXP STA, UNIV ARK, FAYETTEVILLE, 73- *Mem:* Entom Soc Am. *Res:* Forest insects; apiculture. *Mailing Add:* Dept of Entom Univ of Ark Fayetteville AR 72701

WARREN, MCWILSON, b Wayne Co, NC, Aug 29, 29; m 75; c 1. MALARIOLOGY, TROPICAL MEDICINE. *Educ:* Univ NC, BA, 51, MSPH, 52; Rice Univ, PhD(parasitol), 57. *Prof Exp:* Asst prof prev med & pub health, Sch Med, Univ Okla, 57-59, assoc prof & vchmn dept, 59-61; scientist, Lab Parasite Chemother, NIH, USPHS, 61-69, scientist, Far East Res Proj, Kuala Lumpur, Malaysia, 61-64, officer-in-chg, 63-64, officer-in-chg, Sect Cytol, Chamblee, Ga, 64-65, head sect chemother, Nat Inst Allergy & Infectious Dis, 66-69, parasitologist, Cent Am Malaria Res Sta, Ctr Dis Control, 69-74, scientist dir, Ctr Dis Control, 72-79, parasitologist, Vector Biol & Control Div, 74-79, dir, Cent Am Res Sta, El Salvador, 79-81, DIR, WHO SECRETARIAT FOR MALARIA TRAINING & APPL RES, BUR TROP DIS, KUALA LUMPUR, MALAYSIA, 82- *Concurrent Pos:* China Med Bd fel trop med, Cent Am, 57; consult various orgns, 66-; res assoc, Sch Trop Med & Hyg, Univ London, 67-68; adj prof, Sch Med, Tulane Univ, 78- *Mem:* Am Soc Trop Med & Hyg; Am Soc Parasitol; Soc Protozool; Royal Soc Trop Med & Hyg; Am Mosquito Control Asn. *Res:* Ecology and immunity of the primate malarias; parasite physiology; pathophysiology of infectious disease agents; global and institutional epidemiology and human ecology; field studies on sero-epidemiology of malaria; genetics of malaria vectors; field problems in chemotherapy of malaria; biology of malaria parasites. *Mailing Add:* Parasitic Dis Div Ctr Dis Control Atlanta GA 30333

WARREN, MASHURI LAIRD, b Findlay, Ohio, Jan 12, 42; div; c 2. ENVIRONMENTAL PHYSICS, PLASMA PHYSICS. *Educ:* Ohio Wesleyan Univ, BA, 61; Univ Calif, Berkely, MA, 63, PhD(plasma physics), 68. *Prof Exp:* Asst prof physics, Calif State Univ, Hayward, 68-74; lectr, San Francisco State Univ, 76-78; science writing, 74-78; STAFF SCIENTIST, SOLAR ENERGY GROUP, LAWRENCE BERKELEY LAB, 78- *Mem:* Am Phys Soc; Int Solar Energy Soc. *Res:* Solar energy physics of environmental problems; atomic collisions of fusion; transport problems in plasma physics. *Mailing Add:* Solar Energy Group-90-2021 Lawrence Berkeley Lab Berkeley CA 94720

WARREN, MITCHUM ELLISON, JR, b Paris, Tenn, Nov 10 34; m 61; c 2. ORGANIC CHEMISTRY. *Educ:* Vanderbilt Univ, BA, 56, PhD(org chem), 63. *Prof Exp:* NIH fel, 63-66; asst prof chem, George Peabody Col, 66-71, assoc prof, 71-79; CONSULT, WARREN ENTERPRISES, 79- *Mem:* AAAS; Am Chem Soc. *Res:* Stereochemistry; optically active compounds; alkaloids. *Mailing Add:* Warren Enterprises 2500 Belmont Blvd Nashville TN 37212

WARREN, PAUL HORTON, b Bay Shore, NY, July 19, 43. PLANETOLOGY, ASTROGEOLOGY. *Educ:* State Univ NY Oswego, BS, 75; Univ Calif, Los Angeles, PhD(geochem), 79. *Prof Exp:* Fel, Inst Geophysics & Planetary Physics, Univ Calif, Los Angeles, 79; FEL, INST METEORITICS, UNIV NMEX, 79- *Mem:* Meteorit Soc; Mineral Soc Am; Planetary Soc; Sigma Xi. *Res:* Early igneous differentiation of the moon: pristine, endogenous, unadulteraterated, nonmare rock samples and analyzation to learn about the formation of the moon's crust. *Mailing Add:* Inst Meteoritics Univ NMex Albuquerque NM 87131

WARREN, PETER, b New York, NY, Sept 30, 38; m 70. MATHEMATICS, BIOMATHEMATICS. *Educ:* Univ Calif, Berkeley, BA, 60; Univ Wis-Madison, MA, 65, PhD(math), 70. *Prof Exp:* Mem tech staff, IBM Nordic Labs, 61-63; invited fel theory of traffic control, Thomas J Watson Res Labs, 64; lectr math, Med Sch, Univ Wis-Madison, 65-66; asst prof, 70-74, ASSOC PROF MATH, UNIV DENVER, 74- *Concurrent Pos:* Statist consult, 73- *Mem:* Am Math Soc; Math Asn Am. *Res:* Probability theory; epidemiology; probability theory in Banach spaces. *Mailing Add:* Dept of Math Univ of Denver Denver CO 80210

WARREN, RICHARD HAWKS, b Binghamton, NY, Feb 16, 34; m 61; c 2. MATHEMATICS. *Educ:* US Naval Acad, BS, 56; Univ Mich, Ann Arbor, MS, 64; Univ Colo, Boulder, PhD(math), 71. *Prof Exp:* Maintenance officer, US Air Force, 56-62, from instr to assoc prof math, US Air Force Acad, 64-69, dep dir, Appl Math Res Lab, Aerospace Res Lab, 72-75, res mathematician, Aerospace Med Res Lab, Wright-Patterson AFB, 76-77, chief, Appl Math Group, Air Force Flight Dynamics Lab, 75-76; assoc prof math, Univ Nebr, Omaha, 77-80; SR SYSTS ANAL, GEN ELEC CO, 80- *Mem:* Math Asn Am; Am Math Soc. *Res:* General topology; proximity spaces; fuzzy topological spaces; uniformities; applied mathematics. *Mailing Add:* Gen Elec Co PO Box 8048 Philadelphia PA 19101

WARREN, RICHARD JOSEPH, b Lowell, Mass, Dec 25, 31; m 58; c 4. ANALYTICAL CHEMISTRY. *Educ:* Merrimack Col, BS, 53; Univ Pa, MS, 58. *Prof Exp:* Anal chemist, 56-61, sr anal chemist, 61-73, sr investr, 73-80, ASST DIR, SMITH KLINE & FRENCH LABS, 80- *Mem:* Am Chem Soc; Soc Appl Spectros. *Res:* Infrared, ultra violet and nuclear magnetic resonance spectroscopy; mass spectroscopy; x-ray diffraction. *Mailing Add:* Anal Chem 1500 Spring Garden St Philadelphia PA 19101

WARREN, RICHARD JOSEPH, b Oklahoma City, Okla, June 30, 33; m 69; c 1. HUMAN GENETICS, CYTOGENETICS. *Educ:* Okla City Univ, AB, 58; St Louis Univ, PhD(microbiol), 67. *Prof Exp:* NIH fel, Harvard Med Sch-Mass Gen Hosp, 67; NIH fel, Wash Univ, 67-69, asst prof pediat & med, Med Sch, 67-70; asst prof pediat, Univ Miami, 70-74; PRES & DIR BIOCHEM TESTING LABS, GENETICS ASSOCS, 74- *Concurrent Pos:* dir, Palm Beach Genetics Clin, 73-76; chmn ad hoc comt, NIH Contract-Cytogenetics Registries, 73-81; genetics consult, Bur Health & Rehab, State of Fla, 74-81. *Mem:* Am Soc Human Genetics; AAAS; Mammalian Cell Genetics Soc; Am Tissue Cult Asn; Am Soc Cell Biol. *Res:* Human cytogenetics; molecular biology; cellular regulation. *Mailing Add:* Genetics Assocs 7821 Coral Way Miami FL 33155

WARREN, RICHARD SCOTT, b Malden, Mass, Oct 21, 42; m 67. PLANT PHYSIOLOGY. *Educ:* Defiance Col, BA, 65; Univ NH, MS, 68, PhD(plant sci), 70. *Prof Exp:* Sigma Xi grant-in-aid res, 70-71, ASST PROF BOT, CONN COL, 70- *Mem:* AAAS; Bot Soc Am; Am Inst Biol Sci. *Res:* Physiological ecology of Halophytes; physiology of disease resistance. *Mailing Add:* Conn Col 360 Mahegan Ave New London CT 06320

WARREN, ROBERT HOLMES, b Austin, Tex, Feb 20, 41; div. CELL BIOLOGY. *Educ:* Rice Univ, BA, 62, MA, 63; Harvard Univ, PhD(cell biol), 69. *Prof Exp:* NIH fels, Cambridge Univ, 69-70 & Univ Tex, Austin, 70-71; asst prof biol struct, 71-75, ASSOC PROF ANAT, MED SCH, UNIV MIAMI, 75- *Mem:* Am Soc Cell Biol; Soc Develop Biol. *Res:* Ultrastructural and biochemical basis of cell motility. *Mailing Add:* 33 SW 18th Terr Miami FL 33129

WARREN, S REID, JR, b Philadelphia, Pa, Jan 31, 08; m 30; c 2. ELECTRICAL ENGINEERING, RADIOLOGIC PHYSICS. *Educ:* Univ Pa, BS, 28, MS, 29, ScD(elec eng), 37; Am Bd Radiol, dipl, 47. *Prof Exp:* From instr to prof elec eng, 33-76, asst vpres eng, 54-73, EMER PROF ELEC ENG & RADIOL, UNIV PA, 76-, PROF RADIOLOGIC PHYSICS, SCH MED, 58- *Concurrent Pos:* Consult radiol physicist, Vet Admin, Pub Health Serv, Hosps, 36-70. *Mem:* Assoc fel Am Col Radiol; fel Inst Elec & Electronics Engrs; fel AAAS; Soc Hist Technol. *Res:* Electric circuits and fields; radiologic physics. *Mailing Add:* 45 Server Lane Springfield PA 19064

WARREN, SHIELDS, pathology, deceased

WARREN, WALTER R(AYMOND), JR, b New York, NY, Nov 25, 29; m 54; c 10. AERONAUTICAL ENGINEERING. *Educ:* NY Univ, BSE, 50; Princeton Univ, MSE, 52, PhD(aeronaut eng), 57. *Prof Exp:* Asst aeronaut eng, Princeton Univ, 50-55; assoc res scientist, Missiles & Space Div, Lockheed Aircraft Corp, 55-56; mgr aeromech & mat lab, Missile & Space Div, Gen Elec Co, Pa, 56-68; dir aerophysics, Aerospace Corp, Los Angeles, 68-81; PRES, PACIFIC APPLIED RES, LOS ANGELES, 81- *Concurrent Pos:* Lectr, Univ Pa, 62-68; mem sci adv bd comt, US Air Force, 69-75; mem fluid mech subcomt, NASA, 70; assoc ed, Am Inst Aeronaut & Astronaut J, 72-74. *Mem:* fel Am Inst Aeronaut & Astronaut. *Res:* High energy lasers; fluid dynamics; plasma dynamics; atmospheric entry; shock tube/tunnel and plasma jet development and application; lasers. *Mailing Add:* 6 Crestwind Dr Rancho Palos Verdes CA 90274

WARREN, WILLIAM A, b Findlay, Ohio, Mar 29, 36; m 59; c 3. BIOCHEMISTRY. *Educ:* Amherst Col, AB, 58; Western Reserve Univ, MD, 62; Univ Mass, PhD, 68. *Prof Exp:* Staff assoc biochem, Nat Inst Arthritis & Metab Dis, Md, 66-68; assoc res physician, Mary Imogene Bassett Hosp, Cooperstown, NY, 68-77; MEM STAFF, DIV LABS & RES, NY STATE DEPT HEALTH, 77- *Concurrent Pos:* USPHS fel biochem, Dartmouth Med Sch, 64-65; fel, Amherst Col, 65-66. *Mem:* Am Chem Soc; Am Asn Clin Chemists; Am Soc Biol Chemists. *Res:* Protein structure and function; chemistry of pyridine nucleotides and glyoxylate; mast cell tumor biochemistry. *Mailing Add:* 12 Paxwood Rd Delmar NY 12054

WARREN, WILLIAM ERNEST, b Rochester, NY, Aug 11, 30; m 55; c 2. APPLIED MATHEMATICS. *Educ:* Univ Rochester, BS, 56, MS, 59; Cornell Univ, PhD(eng mech), 62. *Prof Exp:* From instr to asst prof mech & mat, Cornell Univ, 57-62; STAFF MEM, SOLID DYNAMICS RES DEPT, SANDIA LAB, 62- *Concurrent Pos:* Mem, NMex House Rep, 71-; chmn, Legis Sch Study Comt, 75-76. *Honors & Awards:* Public Serv Award, Am Soc Mech Engrs, 76. *Mem:* Am Inst Aeronaut & Astronaut; Am Math Soc; Am Soc Mech Engrs; Soc Indust & Appl Math. *Res:* Plane elastic systems; thermal stress concentrations; electric field effects on solid dielectrics, particularly dielectric breakdown; wave propagation; solid-fluid interacting systems. *Mailing Add:* 7712 La Condesa N E Albuquerque NM 87110

WARREN, WILLIAM MICHAEL, b Bancroft, Mich, July 5, 17; m 45; c 5. ANIMAL HUSBANDRY, ANIMAL BREEDING. *Educ:* Mich State Col, BS, 40; Agr & Mech Col Tex, MS, 48; Univ Mo, PhD(animal breeding), 52. *Prof Exp:* From instr to assoc prof animal husb, Tex A&M Univ, 41-55; assoc prof animal husb & assoc animal breeder, 55-57, prof & head dept, 57-80, EMER PROF ANIMAL SCI, AUBURN UNIV, 57- *Mem:* Am Soc Animal Sci. *Res:* Improvement of livestock through selection and breeding. *Mailing Add:* Dept of Animal-Dairy Sci Auburn Univ Auburn AL 36830

WARREN, WILLIAM WILLARD, JR, b Seattle, Wash, Nov 7, 38; m 65; c 2. NUCLEAR MAGNETIC RESONANCE. *Educ:* Stanford Univ, BS, 60; Wash Univ, PhD(physics), 65. *Prof Exp:* Asst res physicist, Univ Calif, Los Angeles, 65-68; MEM TECH STAFF, BELL LABS, INC, 68- *Honors & Awards:* US Sr Scientist Award, Alexander von Humboldt Found, 74. *Mem:* AAAS; Am Phys Soc. *Res:* Application of nuclear magnetic resonance to the study of electronic structure and atomic dynamics of liquids and solids, especially metals and semiconductors; metal-nonmetal transitions in liquids; electronic transport properties of liquids. *Mailing Add:* Bell Labs Inc Dept 11525 Murray Hill NJ 07974

WARRICK, ARTHUR W, b Kellerton, Iowa, Dec 4, 40; m 62; c 2. SOIL PHYSICS, MATHEMATICS. *Educ:* Iowa State Univ, BS, 62, MS, 64, PhD(soil physics), 67. *Prof Exp:* Res assoc soil physics, Iowa State Univ, 66-67; asst prof, 67-71, assoc prof, 71-81, PROF SOIL PHYSICS, UNIV ARIZ, 81-, RES SCIENTIST, AGR EXP STA, 71- *Mem:* Soil Sci Soc Am; Am Soc Agron; Am Geophys Union. *Res:* Drainage; soil water flow; porous media flow; potential theory. *Mailing Add:* Dept of Soils Water & Eng Univ of Ariz Tucson AZ 85721

WARRICK, EARL LEATHEN, b Butler, Pa, Sept 23, 11; m 40; c 2. PHYSICAL CHEMISTRY. *Educ:* Carnegie Inst Technol, BS, 33, MS, 34, DSc(phys chem), 43. *Prof Exp:* Asst, Mellon Inst Sci, 35-37, fel organosilicon chem, 37-46, sr fel, 46-56; asst dir res, Dow Corning Corp, 57-59, mgr hyper-pure silicon div, 59-62, gen mgr electronic prod div, 62-68, mgr new proj bus, 68-72, sr mgt consult, 72-76; RETIRED. *Concurrent Pos:* Lectr, Univ Pittsburgh, 47-48; interim dean sci & eng technol, Saginaw Valley State Col, 79-80. *Honors & Awards:* Charles Goodyear Medal & Award, 76. *Mem:* Am Chem Soc. *Res:* Glass composition; chemical kinetics; gas phase; organosilicon and radiation chemistry; physical chemistry of polymers. *Mailing Add:* 508 Crescent Dr Midland MI 48640

WARRICK, PERCY, JR, b South Bend, Ind, Aug 6, 35; m 61; c 2. PHYSICAL ORGANIC CHEMISTRY. *Educ:* Wabash Col, 57; Univ Rochester, PhD(org chem), 61. *Prof Exp:* Fel phys org chem, Univ Minn, 60-62; res assoc, Mass Inst Technol, 62-63; from asst prof to assoc prof, 63-77, PROF CHEM, WESTMINSTER COL, PA, 77- *Concurrent Pos:* Fel, Univ Utah, 70-71; vis prof, Univ Kent, Canterbury, Eng, 78-79. *Mem:* Am Chem Soc; Royal Soc Chem. *Res:* Mechanisms of reactions between metals and solutions; general-acid catalysis; solvent isotope effects in organic reactions; relaxation kinetics; acid-base reactions in mixed solvents. *Mailing Add:* Dept of Chem Westminster Col New Wilmington PA 16142

WARRINGTON, PATRICK DOUGLAS, b Winnipeg, Man, Mar 21, 42; m 65; c 2. AQUATIC PLANTS DISTRIBUTION & ECOLOGY. *Educ:* Univ BC, BSc, 64, PhD(bot), 70. *Prof Exp:* Consult bot, 72-73; res officer aerial satellite photog, 73-75, BIOLOGIST, BC GOVT, 75- *Mem:* Can Bot Asn; Asn Prof Biologists BC; Int Asn Aquatic Vascular Plant Biologists. *Res:* All aspects of the biology of aquatic plants. *Mailing Add:* Aquatic Studies Br Parliament Bldg Victoria BC V8L 3S1 Can

WARRINGTON, TERRELL L, b Baltimore, Md, June 5, 40; m 64. PHYSICAL CHEMISTRY, BIOCHEMISTRY. *Educ:* Yale Univ, BA, 61; Purdue Univ, PhD(phys chem), 66. *Prof Exp:* ASST PROF CHEM, MICH TECHNOL UNIV, 67- *Mem:* Am Chem Soc. *Res:* Physical chemistry of biological macromolecules concentrating mainly on conformational studies. *Mailing Add:* Dept of Chem Mich Technol Univ Houghton MI 49931

WARSCHAUER, DOUGLAS MARVIN, physics, energy conversion, see previous edition

WARSH, CATHERINE EVELYN, b San Diego, Calif, Apr 19, 43; m 70. OCEANOGRAPHY. *Educ:* Old Dominion Col, BA, 65; Fla State Univ, MS, 71. *Prof Exp:* Teacher math, Kempsville Jr High Sch, Virginia Beach, Va, 65-66; researcher marine biol, Duke Univ, NC, 66-67; teacher marine biol & math, First Colonial High Sch, Virginia Beach, 67-68; researcher limnol, Fla State Univ, Tallahassee, 71-72, res programmer biol oceanog, 72, environ specialist pollution & limnol, Dept Pollution Control, 73; admin oceanogr, Nat Oceanic & Atmospheric Admin-Nat Marine Fisheries Serv, 74-75, RES OCEANOGR, DEPT COMMERCE, NAT OCEANIC & ATMOSPHERIC ADMIN-NAT OCEAN SURV, WASHINGTON, DC, 75- *Concurrent Pos:* Teacher math & phys sci, Griffin Middle Sch, Tallahassee, Fla, 71; phys oceanogr researcher, Dept Commerce, Nat Oceanic & Atmospheric Admin-Nat Marine Fisheries Serv, Washington, DC, 74; task team oil spill trajectory models, Environ Res Labs-Nat Oceanic & Atmospheric Admin, Boulder, Colo, 75- *Res:* Study of surface circulation, near-shore dynamics over the continental shelf in the middle Atlantic bight; study of circulation, water properties and transport in Gulf of California; pollution monitoring water chemistry and physics for the northeast monitoring program. *Mailing Add:* Nat Oceanic & Atmospheric Admin C2X7 6001 Executive Blvd Rockville MD 20852

WARSH, KENNETH LEE, b Chicago, Ill, Oct 17, 36; m 70. COMPUTER SCIENCE. *Educ:* Univ Notre Dame, BS, 58, MS, 60; Fla State Univ, PhD(physics), 62; Univ Md, JD, 82. *Prof Exp:* Physicist, Lockheed-Ga Co, 63-64; asst prof physics, Jacksonville Univ, 64-66; asst prof oceanog, Fla State Univ, 66-73; sr staff physicist, Appl Physics Lab, Johns Hopkins Univ, 73-78; systs analyst, Mantech Int Corp, 78-81; SYSTS ANALYST, OAO CORP, 81- *Concurrent Pos:* Lectr, Morehouse Col, 63-64. *Mem:* Am Meteorol Soc; Am Asn Physics Teachers. *Res:* Marine meteorology; environmental management. *Mailing Add:* OAO Corp Greenbelt MD 20810

WARSHAUER, STEVEN MICHAEL, b New York, NY, May 20, 45. STRATIGRAPHY, PALEOECOLOGY. *Educ:* Queens Col, NY, BA, 67; Univ Cincinnati, MS, 69, PhD(geol), 73. *Prof Exp:* Asst prof geol, WVa Univ, 72-77, assoc prof, 77-81; EXPLOR GEOLOGIST, TENNECO OIL, 81- *Concurrent Pos:* Consult, WVa Geol Econ Surv, Champlin Petrol, Dept Energy & Amoco Oil. *Mem:* Int Paleont Union; Am Asn Petrol Geologists; Paleont Soc; Soc Econ Paleontologists & Mineralogists; Sigma Xi. *Res:* Lower Paleozoic Ostracoda; carbonate depositional models; multivariate statistical methods in paleoecology and stratigraphy. *Mailing Add:* Frontier Projs Tenneco Oil PO Box 2511 Houston TX 77001

WARSHAW, CHARLOTTE MARSH, b Newark, NJ, Feb 5, 20; m 48. GEOCHEMISTRY, MINERALOGY. *Educ:* Smith Col, AB, 41; Bryn Mawr Col, MA, 42; Pa State Univ, PhD(geochem), 57. *Prof Exp:* Chemist, Geophys Lab, Carnegie Inst Wash, 42-46; ed asst, Off Sci Res & Develop, 46; geologist & chemist, US Geol Surv, 46-53; mineralogist, Gulf Res & Develop Co, 53-57; asst, Pa State Univ, 51-53; res assoc, 57-60; sr scientist, Tem-Pres Res, Inc, Pa, 60-61; consult geochemist, 61-71; GEOLOGIST, US GEOL SURV, 71- *Mem:* Mineral Soc Am. *Res:* Clay mineralogy; mineral synthesis; phase equilibria in silicate systems; mineralogy of volcanic rocks. *Mailing Add:* US Geol Surv 12201 Sunrise Valley Reston VA 22090

WARSHAW, ISRAEL, b Brooklyn, NY, Nov 30, 25; m 48. MATERIALS SCIENCE. *Educ:* Alfred Univ, BA, 51; Pa State Univ, MS, 53, PhD, 61. *Prof Exp:* Sci aide & chem lab asst, Water Resources Br, US Geol Surv, 42-43, chem lab asst, Geochem & Petrol Br, 46-51, chemist, 51-53; asst geochem, Pa State Univ, 51-53 & 57-58; group leader, Glass Res Labs, Pittsburgh Plate Glass Co, 53-57; assoc res dir, Tem-Pres Res, Inc, Pa, 59-60; assoc prog dir, NSF, 60-63, dir eng mat prog, 63-71, actg dir, Eng Div, 71-74, dep dir, 72-76; PHYS SCI ADMINR, DEPT ENERGY, 77- *Concurrent Pos:* Lectr, Univ Pittsburgh, 56-57. *Res:* Phase equilibrium studies of silicate, aluminate and oxide systems at high temperatures and pressures; synthesis of refractory compounds, particularly those of the rare earths; silicate glasses; materials research. *Mailing Add:* 3703 Stewart Dr Chevy Chase MD 20815

WARSHAW, STANLEY I(RVING), b Boston, Mass, Nov 5, 31; m 55; c 2. PRODUCT ENGINEERING, MATERIAL SCIENCE. *Educ:* Ga Inst Technol, BCerE, 57; Mass Inst Technol, ScD(ceramics), 61. *Prof Exp:* Res asst, Ga Inst Technol, 56-57 & Mass Inst Technol, 57-61; sr res scientist, Raytheon Mfg Co, 61-64; res supvr, Ceramics & Metall Sect, Am Standard Inc, 64-68, mgr ceramic technol, Res & Develop Ctr, 68-69, mgr mat & chem dept, 69-72, gen mgr, Prod Develop & Eng Lab, 72-75; DIR, CTR FOR CONSUMER PROD TECHNOL, NAT BUR STANDARDS, 75- *Honors & Awards:* Sigma Xi. *Mem:* Am Ceramic Soc; Am Soc Testing & Mat; Metall Soc. *Res:* Product performance and safety analysis and test method design. *Mailing Add:* Nat Bur of Standards Bldg 225 Rm B154 Washington DC 20234

WARSHAW, STEPHEN I, b New York, NY, Mar 26, 39; m 64; c 2. PHYSICS, COMPUTER SCIENCE. *Educ:* Polytech Inst Brooklyn, BSc, 60; Johns Hopkins Univ, PhD(physics), 66. *Prof Exp:* Teaching asst physics, Polytech Inst Brooklyn, 56-60; res asst, Johns Hopkins Univ, 60-66; res assoc, Univ Ill, Urbana-Champaign, 66-68; SR PHYSICIST, LAWRENCE LIVERMORE NAT LAB, UNIV CALIF, 68- *Mem:* Am Phys Soc; Sigma Xi. *Res:* Experimental low energy nuclear physics; computer modeling of hydrodynamic phenomena; theoretical atmospheric acoustics; geometrical algorithms for digital computers; interpolation methods; ionospheric radio progagation theory. *Mailing Add:* Lawrence Livermore Nat Lab L-71 Univ of Calif PO Box 808 Livermore CA 94550

WARSHAWSKY, HERSHEY, b Montreal, Que, Feb 6, 38; m 60; c 3. HISTOLOGY. *Educ:* Sir George Williams Univ, BSc, 59; McGill Univ, MSc, 61, PhD(anat), 66. *Prof Exp:* Lectr anat, McGill Univ, 63-66; res fel orthop res, Harvard Univ, 66-67; from asst prof to assoc prof, 67-77, PROF ANAT, MCGILL UNIV, 77- *Concurrent Pos:* Vis prof, Univ Sao Paulo. *Mem:* Am Asn Anat; Can Asn Anat. *Res:* Use of the enamel organ in the rat incisor as a model system for structural and radioautographic studies of secretory processes, cell renewal and mineralization. *Mailing Add:* Dept Anat McGill Univ 3640 University St Montreal PQ H3A 2B2 Can

WARSHAWSKY, JAY, b Chicago, Ill, Mar 27, 27; m 54; c 3. ELECTRICAL ENGINEERING. *Educ:* Ill Inst Technol, BS, 48; Purdue Univ, MS, 50; Northwestern Univ, PhD(elec eng, biomed eng), 63. *Prof Exp:* Dir servomech sect, Cook Res Labs, 51-56; tech dir mech res div, Am Mach & Foundry Co & Gen Am Transp Corp, 56-65; dir res & develop dept, 65-77, V PRES RES & DEVELOP FULLER CO, GATX CORP, 77- *Concurrent Pos:* Lectr, Grad Sch, Ill Inst Technol, 54, lectr, Med Sch, 63, res asst, 63. *Mem:* AAAS; Inst Elec & Electronics Engrs; Air Pollution Control Asn; Water Pollution Control Fedn; Instrument Soc Am. *Res:* Automatic control systems; analog and digital computers; electronic instrumentation; accommodation in the human eye; automatic focusing devices; physiological optics. *Mailing Add:* 2616 Gordon St Allentown PA 18104

WARSHAY, MARVIN, b Tel Aviv, Israel, Jan 12, 34; US citizen; m 62; c 3. ELECTROCHEMICAL SYSTEMS, ENERGY TECHNOLOGY. *Educ:* Rensselaer Polytech Inst, BChE, 55; Ill Inst Technol, MS, 57, PhD(chem eng), 60. *Prof Exp:* Res engr, Esso Res & Eng Co, 60-62; res engr, Lewis Res Ctr, NASA, 62-78, MGR FUEL CELL PROJ, NASA/DEPT ENERGY, 78- *Concurrent Pos:* Lectr, Cleveland State Univ, 67-, adj prof chem eng, 74- *Mem:* Am Chem Soc; Am Inst Chem Engrs; Electrochem Soc. *Res:* Drop motion; chemical reactions in nozzles; chemical reactions and colloidal phenomena in oil additive formation and in muffler corrosion; shock tubes; high temperature chemical kinetics of gases; electrochemical systems; batteries; fuel cells. *Mailing Add:* Lewis Res Ctr NASA MS 49-5 21000 Brookpark Rd Cleveland OH 44135

WARSHEL, ARIEH, b Sde-Nahom, Israel, Nov 20, 40; m 66; c 2. CHEMICAL PHYSICS, MOLECULAR BIOLOGY. *Educ:* Israel Inst Technol, BSc, 66; Wiezmann Inst Sci, MSc, 67, PhD(chem), 69. *Prof Exp:* Res assoc chem, Harvard Univ, 70-72; res assoc, Wiezmann Inst, 72-73, sr scientist, 73-74; vis scientist, Med Res Coun Lab Molecular Biol, Cambridge, Eng, 74-76; ASST PROF CHEM, UNIV SOUTHERN CALIF, 76- *Res:* Theoretical study of the early steps of the visual process; resonance Raman of large molecules; simulation of protein folding; simulation of enzymatic reactions. *Mailing Add:* Dept of Chem Univ of Southern Calif Los Angeles CA 90007

WARSHOWSKY, BENJAMIN, b New York, NY, Jan 21, 19; m 57; c 3. ANALYTICAL CHEMISTRY. *Educ:* City Col New York, BS, 40; Univ Minn, MS, 42, PhD(biochem), 45. *Prof Exp:* Anal res chemist, Publicker Industs, Inc, Pa, 45-46; chief anal chem sect, Biol Labs, US Army Chem Corps, Ft Detrick, 47-54, prog coord officer, 54-56, decontamination br, 56-57, spec asst to dir med res, 57-60, chief phys detection br, 60-64, chief rapid warning officer, 64-72, chief biol defense br, Edgewood Arsenal, 72-75; PROF, FREDERICK COMMUNITY COL, FREDERICK, MD, 73- *Mem:* Am Chem Soc; Sci Res Soc Am. *Res:* Microbiological detection techniques; instrument development; administration of chemical and biological research; administration of research and development program on rapid detection of microbiological aerosols. *Mailing Add:* 315 W College Terr Frederick MD 21701

WARSI, NAZIR AHMED, b Sheopur, Uttar Pradesh, India, June 30, 39; m 66. MATHEMATICAL PHYSICS. *Educ:* St Andrew's Col, Gorakhpur, India, BSc, 57; Gorakhpur Univ, MSc, 59, PhD(shock wave), 61. *Prof Exp:* Asst prof math, Gorakhpur Univ, India, 59-63; assoc prof physics & math, Savannah State Col, 63-64; prof physics & math, 64-66, PROF MATH, ATLANTA UNIV, 66-, ACTG CHMN DEPT, 70- *Mem:* Am Math Soc; Tensor Soc. *Res:* Shock waves in ideal and magneto-gas-dynamic flows; nonlinear functional analysis; optimization. *Mailing Add:* Dept of Math Atlanta Univ Atlanta GA 30314

WARSI, ZAHIR U A, b Uttar Pradesh, India, July 7, 36; m 58; c 5. APPLIED MATHEMATICS, AERONAUTICS. *Educ:* Univ Lucknow, BSc, 54, MSc, 56, PhD(math), 65. *Prof Exp:* Scientist, Cent Bldg Res Inst, Roorkee, India, 62-67; fel aerodyn, 67-70, asst prof, 70-73, assoc prof, 73-80, PROF AEROSPACE ENG, MISS STATE UNIV, 80- *Honors & Awards:* Am Soc Eng Educ Res Award, 75. *Mem:* Sigma Xi. *Res:* Numerical fluid dynamics; solutions of compressible and turbulent incompressible flow equations in general coordinates. *Mailing Add:* Dept Aerospace Eng Miss State Univ Mississippi State MS 39762

WARSON, SAMUEL R, b St John, NB, Oct 1, 09; US citizen; c 2. PSYCHIATRY. *Educ:* McGill Univ, BA, 30, MD, 34. *Prof Exp:* Instr psychiat, Yale Univ, 37-39; assoc, Univ Louisville, 39-40; asst prof, Wash Univ, 40-50; prof, Ind Univ, 50-54; PROF PSYCHIAT, UNIV FLA, 67- *Res:* Psychiatric theory and practice. *Mailing Add:* 495 Golden Gate Point 4E Sarasota FL 33577

WARTELL, ROGER MARTIN, b New York, NY, Feb 24, 45; m 68; c 2. BIOPHYSICS. *Educ:* Stevens Inst Technol, BSc, 66; Univ Rochester, PhD(physics), 71. *Prof Exp:* NIH fel & res assoc biochem, Univ Wis-Madison, 71-73; asst prof, 74-77, ASSOC PROF PHYSICS/BIOL, SCH PHYSICS, GA INST TECHNOL, 78- *Concurrent Pos:* NIH career develop award, 79-84. *Mem:* Biophys Soc; AAAS; Am Phys Soc. *Res:* Conformational properties of DNA gene regulatory sites; influence of cooperative interactions along DNA on genetic processes; Raman spectroscopy. *Mailing Add:* Sch Physics Ga Inst Technol Atlanta GA 30332

WARTEN, RALPH MARTIN, b Bielefeld, Ger, Jan 6, 26; US citizen; m 50. MATHEMATICS. *Educ:* Brooklyn Col, BS, 57; Purdue Univ, MS, 59, PhD(math), 61. *Prof Exp:* Staff mathematician, IBM Corp, NY, 61-65, adv mathematician, 65-66, staff mem sci ctr, Calif, 66-68; assoc prof, 68-73, PROF MATH, CALIF POLYTECH STATE UNIV, SAN LUIS OBISPO, 73- *Mem:* AAAS; Am Math Soc; Math Asn Am; NY Acad Sci. *Res:* Ordinary differential equations and numerical analysis. *Mailing Add:* Dept of Math Calif Polytech State Univ San Luis Obispo CA 93407

WARTER, JANET KIRCHNER, b Greensburg, Pa, July 27, 33; m 62. PALYNOLOGY, SCIENCE EDUCATION. *Educ:* Pa State Univ, BS, 55, MEd, 60; La State Univ, PhD(bot), 65. *Prof Exp:* Lectr bot, Calif State Col, Fullerton, 65-66; LECTR GEOL, CALIF STATE UNIV, LONG BEACH, 66-68, & 70- *Concurrent Pos:* Res assoc, Los Angeles County Mus Natural Hist. *Mem:* Am Asn Stratig Palynologists. *Res:* Tertiary palynology; Pleistocene seeds and pollen; archeological macro-plant analysis. *Mailing Add:* 17841 Still Harbor Lane Huntington Beach CA 92647

WARTER, STUART L, b New York, NY, Apr 9, 34; m 62. ORNITHOLOGY, VERTEBRATE PALEONTOLOGY. *Educ:* Univ Miami, Fla, BS, 56, MS, 58; La State Univ, PhD(zool), 65. *Prof Exp:* Instr zool, La State Univ, 64-65; from asst prof to assoc prof, 65-75, PROF BIOL, CALIF STATE UNIV, LONG BEACH, 75- *Concurrent Pos:* Res assoc vert paleont, Los Angeles County Mus Natural Hist, 66- *Mem:* Am Ornith Union; Cooper Ornith Soc; Wilson Ornith Soc; Soc Vert Paleont. *Res:* Avian paleontology, morphology and systematics; osteology and relationships of suboscine passerine birds. *Mailing Add:* Dept of Biol 1250 Bellflower Blvd Long Beach CA 90840

WARTERS, MARY, b Rome, Ga, Oct 18, 02. GENETICS. *Educ:* Shorter Col, AB, 23; Ohio State Univ, MA, 25; Univ Tex, PhD(cytogenetics), 43. *Prof Exp:* Asst zool, Ohio State Univ, 23-25; instr biol, Winthrop Col, 25-27; from instr to prof, 27-71, head dept, 47-69, EMER PROF ZOOL, CENTENARY COL, 71- *Concurrent Pos:* Vis scientist, Jackson Mem Lab, 51; res partic biol div, Oak Ridge Nat Lab, 59-61. *Mem:* Fel AAAS. *Res:* Bryozoa; cytogenetics of Drosophila; chromosomal aberrations in wild populations of Drosophila; x-autosomal translocations. *Mailing Add:* 3568 Greenway Place Shreveport LA 71105

WARTERS, RAYMOND LEON, b Atlanta, Ga, Nov 22, 45; m 78. MOLECULAR BIOLOGY, RADIATION BIOLOGY. *Educ:* Emory Univ, BA, 67; Fla State Univ, MS, 72, PhD(molecular biol), 76. *Prof Exp:* Nat Cancer Inst fel, 76-78, RES ASST PROF RADIATION BIOL, UNIV UTAH, 78- *Mem:* Sigma Xi; Radiation Res Soc; Am Soc Cell Biol. *Res:* Effect of enviromental agents, including radiations and chemicals, on molecular and cellular biology and biochemistry, especially with respect to the eukaryotic genetic apparatus. *Mailing Add:* Dept of Radiol Univ of Utah Col of Med Salt Lake City UT 84112

WARTERS, WILLIAM DENNIS, b Des Moines, Iowa, Mar 22, 28; m 52; c 2. MICROWAVE ELECTRONICS. *Educ:* Harvard Univ, AB, 49; Calif Inst Technol, MS, 50, PhD(physics), 53. *Prof Exp:* Asst, Calif Inst Technol, 50-52; mem tech staff guided wave res, 53-61, head repeater res dept, 61-67, dir transmission systs res ctr, 67-69, exec dir tech, Staff Employment, Educ & Salary Admin Div, 69-70, dir, Millimeter Wave Syst Lab, 70-76, dir, Toll Transmission Lab, 76-80, DIR, SATELLITE TRANSMISSION LAB, BELL TEL LABS, INC, 80- *Mem:* Am Phys Soc; fel Inst Elec & Electronics Engrs; Am Inst Aeronaut & Astronaut. *Res:* Multi-mode wave guides; millimeter waves; microwaves; transmission systems; communications satellites. *Mailing Add:* 514 Sunnyside Rd Lincroft NJ 07738

WARTHEN, JOHN DAVID, JR, b Baltimore, Md, Mar 8, 39; m 69. NATURAL PRODUCT CHEMISTRY. *Educ:* Univ Md, BS, 60, PhD(pharmaceut chem), 66. *Prof Exp:* RES CHEMIST, SCI & EDUC ADMIN-AGR RES, USDA, 65- *Mem:* Am Chem Soc. *Res:* Isolation and synthesis of biologically active natural products; insect attractants, antifeedants, repellants and insecticides. *Mailing Add:* USDA South Lab 306 BARC East Rm 316 Beltsville MD 20705

WARTIK, THOMAS, b Cincinnati, Ohio, Oct 1, 21; m 52; c 2. INORGANIC CHEMISTRY. *Educ:* Univ Cincinnati, AB, 43; Univ Chicago, PhD(chem), 49. *Prof Exp:* From asst prof to prof chem & head dept, 50-71, DEAN COL SCI, PA STATE UNIV, 71- *Concurrent Pos:* Vis scientist radiation lab, Univ Calif, 57, 59, 61; mem, Fulbright selection comt chem, Nat Acad Sci-Nat Res Coun, 66-72, chmn, 70-72; mem adv bd, Am Chem Soc-Petrol Res Fund, 68-71; consult, Radiation Lab, Callery Chem Co, Koppers Co, Inc & NY Bd Regents, 73-74. *Mem:* AAAS; Am Chem Soc. *Res:* Chemistry of boron and aluminum compounds; light metal hydrides; organometallic chemistry. *Mailing Add:* 211 Whitmore Lab Pa State Univ University Park PA 16802

WARTMAN, WILLIAM BECHMANN, b Philadelphia, Pa, June 26, 07; m 40; c 2. PATHOLOGY. *Educ:* Univ Pa, BS, 29, MD, 32; Am Bd Path, 41. *Prof Exp:* Intern, Lankenau Hosp, Philadelphia, Pa, 33-35; demonstr path, Case Western Reserve Univ, 35-37, from instr to asst prof, 37-46; Morrison prof, Northwestern Univ, Chicago, 46-69; prof path, Univ Va, 69-77; RETIRED. *Concurrent Pos:* Pathologist in chg, Univ Hosps, Case Western Reserve Univ, 29-46, Hanna res fel, 38-39; dir labs, Passavant Mem Hosp & Wesley Mem Hosp, 46-; secy-treas, Am Bd Path, 51-55, pres, 59-60; consult, Sci Adv Bd, Armed Forces Inst Path; mem comt path, Nat Res Coun; mem spec adv group, Vet Admin, chmn, 65-66. *Mem:* Am Soc Exp Pathologists (pres, 58); Am Asn Pathologists & Bacteriologists (pres, 64-65); Am Asn Cancer Res; Am Asn Hist Med; Int Soc Geog Path. *Res:* Chemotropism of leukocytes; venous blood pressure; occlusion of coronary artery; myocardial infarction, history of tumors; filariasis; carcinogenesis. *Mailing Add:* Williston Court West Leigh Charlottesville VA 22901

WARTZOK, DOUGLAS, b Lansing, Mich, May 10, 42; m 66. PHYSIOLOGICAL ECOLOGY. *Educ:* Andrews Univ, BA, 63; Univ Ill, MS, 65; Johns Hopkins Univ, PhD(biophysics), 71. *Prof Exp:* Fel, 71-72, asst prof, 72-78, ASSOC PROF ECOL & BEHAV, JOHNS HOPKINS UNIV, 78- *Res:* Physiological ecology and behavior of captive and wild marine mammals, in particular, visual discrimination, spectral sensitivity and vocalization of captive seals; hauling-out behavior, population age structure, remote sensing and distribution of walrus, radio tagging of large whales. *Mailing Add:* Dept Pathobiol Johns Hopkins Univ 615 N Wolfe St Baltimore MD 21205

WARWICK, EVERETT JAMES, b Aledo, Ill, May 2, 17; m 42; c 3. ANIMAL SCIENCE. *Educ:* Univ Ill, BS, 39; Univ Wis, MS, 42, PhD(genetics, animal husb), 43. *Prof Exp:* Teacher high sch, Ill, 39-40; asst genetics & physiol, Univ Wis, 40-42; from instr to assoc prof animal husb, Wash State Univ, 43-47; agent, USDA, 47-50, geneticist, 50-55, head cattle res sect, Agr Res Serv, 55-57, chief beef cattle res br, Animal Husb Res Div, 57-68, asst dir div, 68-72, mem nat prog staff, Sci & Educ Admin-Agr Res, 72-80; VIS PROF ANIMAL HUSBANDRY, GADJAH MADA UNIV, YOGYAKARTA, INDONESIA, 80- *Concurrent Pos:* Asst prof, Purdue Univ, 47-50; prof, Univ Tenn, 50-55; livestock adv, Ministry Agr & Natural Resources, Tehran, Iran, 73-75. *Mem:* AAAS; Am Soc Animal Sci. *Res:* Endocrinology of reproduction in animals; nutrition and genetics of farm animals; breeding systems. *Mailing Add:* c/o Rockefeller Found 1133 Ave Americas New York NY 10036

WARWICK, JAMES WALTER, b Toledo, Ohio, May 22, 24; m 47, 66; c 6. RADIO ASTRONOMY. *Educ:* Harvard Univ, AB, 47, AM, 48, PhD(astron), 51. *Prof Exp:* Asst prof astron, Wellesley Col, 50-52; mem res staff, Sacramento Peak Observ, 52-55; mem sr sci staff, High Altitude Observ, 55-61, PROF ASTRO-GEOPHYS, UNIV COLO, BOULDER, 61- *Concurrent Pos:* Prin investr, Voyager Missions Planetary Radio Astron Exp, NASA, 73-82. *Mem:* Am Astron Soc; AAAS; Am Geophys Union. *Res:* Theoretical astrophysics; stellar and planetary magnetism; solar physics; solar-terrestrial physics. *Mailing Add:* Dept of Astro-Geophys Univ of Colo Boulder CO 80309

WARWICK, SUZANNE IRENE, b Winnipeg Beach, Man, Dec 10, 52. PLANT TAXONOMY. *Educ:* Univ Man, BSc, 74; Univ Cambridge, Eng, PhD(bot), 77. *Prof Exp:* RES SCIENTIST, BIOSYSTS RES INST, AGR CAN, 77- *Mem:* Can Bot Asn; Am Inst Biol Sci; Am Soc Plant Taxonomists. *Res:* Weed genecology; weed taxonomy. *Mailing Add:* Biosyst Res Inst Agr Can Wm Saunders Bldg CEF Ottawa ON K1A 0C6 Can

WARWICK, WARREN J, b Racine, Wis, Jan 27, 28; m 52; c 2. PEDIATRICS. *Educ:* St Olaf Col, BA, 50; Univ Minn, MD, 54. *Prof Exp:* Med fel pediat, 55-57, med fel specialist, 59-60, from instr to assoc prof, 60-78, PROF PEDIAT, UNIV MINN, MINNEAPOLIS, 78- *Concurrent Pos:* Alpha Omega Phi fel cardiovasc res, 55-57; Am Heart Asn res fel, 59-60; USPHS res career develop award, 61-66; mem ctr prog comt, Nat Cystic Fibrosis Res Found, 64-66, chmn med care comt, 66-71, coop study comt, 71-72; mem exec bd, Sci-Med Comt, Int Cystic Fibrosis (Mucoviscidosis) Asn, 70; mem, Nat Data Registry Comt, Cystic Fibrosis Found, 72- *Res:* Pulmonary diseases; experimental pathology; immunology; cystic fibrosis. *Mailing Add:* Dept of Pediat Box 184 Univ of Minn Minneapolis MN 55455

WARZEL, L(AWRENCE) A(LFRED), b Ft Scott, Kans, Sept 26, 25; m 50; c 3. CHEMICAL ENGINEERING. *Educ:* Univ Tulsa, BS, 47; Univ Mich, MS, 52, PhD(chem eng), 55. *Prof Exp:* Res proj engr, Ethyl Corp, 47-51; res assoc, Eng Res Inst, Univ Mich, 53-55; theoret develop engr, NY, 55-60, sect mgr, 60-65, tech rep proj develop, Int Dept, 65-68, sr proj mgr, NJ, 68-76, SR PROJ MGR, PHILLIPS PETROL CO, OKLA, 76- *Mem:* AAAS; Am Chem Soc; Am Inst Chem Engrs. *Res:* Mass transfer; separations; systems engineering; phase equilibria; thermodynamics; mathematical analysis of engineering data and scale-up problems; international projects development. *Mailing Add:* Phillips Petrol Co Pawhusha Rd Bartlesville OK 74004

WASACZ, JOHN PETER, b Brooklyn, NY, Sept 11, 44; m 70; c 3. ORGANIC CHEMISTRY. *Educ:* St John's Univ, NY, BS, 65; Univ Pa, PhD(org chem), 69. *Prof Exp:* Asst prof, 69-74, ASSOC PROF CHEM, MANHATTAN COL, 74- *Concurrent Pos:* Asst mgr NY sect, Am Chem Soc, 73-77, mgr, 77- NSF fac fel, Columbia Univ, 75-77; vis scholar, NY Univ, 80. *Mem:* Am Chem Soc; AAAS; Sigma Xi; Coblentz Soc. *Res:* Organic synthesis; photochemistry of heterocyclic molecules; synthesis of natural products. *Mailing Add:* Dept of Chem Manhattan Col Bronx NY 10471

WASAN, DARSH T, b Sarai Salah Hazara, India, July 15, 38; m 66; c 2. CHEMICAL ENGINEERING. *Educ:* Univ Ill, Urbana, BSChE, 60; Univ Calif, Berkeley, PhD(chem eng), 64. *Prof Exp:* From asst prof to assoc prof, 64-70, PROF CHEM ENG, ILL INST TECHNOL, 70-, CHMN DEPT, 71- *Concurrent Pos:* Consult, Inst Gas Technol, 65-, res inst, Ill Inst Technol, 66-, Chicago Bridge & Iron Co, 67-71, Ill Environ Protection Agency, 71-, Continental Can Co, 72-, Exxon Res & Eng Co, 77- & Stauffer Chem Co, 80- *Honors & Awards:* Western Elec Fund Award, Am Soc Eng Educ, 72. *Mem:* AAAS; Am Inst Chem Engrs; Am Chem Soc; Am Soc Eng Educ; Am Inst Physics. *Res:* Mass transfer; interfacial phenomena; particle science and technology; enhanced oil recovery; synthetic fuels; interfacial rkeology. *Mailing Add:* Dept of Chem Eng Ill Inst of Technol Chicago IL 60616

WASAN, MADANLAL T, b Saraisaleh, WPakistan, July 13, 30; m 60; c 4. STATISTICS. *Educ:* Univ Bombay, BA, 52, MA, 54; Univ Ill, PhD(statist), 60. *Prof Exp:* From asst prof to assoc prof, 59-68, PROF MATH, QUEEN'S UNIV, ONT, 68- *Concurrent Pos:* Vis assoc prof, Stanford Univ, 65 & Univ Bombay, 65-66; statist consult, Du Pont of Can, 62-65. *Mem:* Inst Math Statist. *Res:* Sequential estimation; stochastic approximation; stochastic processes and applied probability. *Mailing Add:* Dept of Math Queen's Univ Kingston ON K7L 3N6 Can

WASBAUER, MARIUS SHERIDAN, b Rockford, Ill, Sept 29, 28; m 69; c 3. INSECT TAXONOMY. *Educ:* Univ Calif, Berkeley, BS, 50, PhD(entom), 61. *Prof Exp:* SYST ENTOMOLOGIST, CALIF DEPT FOOD & AGR, 59- *Concurrent Pos:* Collabr, Animal & Plant Health Inspection Serv, USDA, 59-; res assoc, Univ Calif, Berkeley, 73-, mem, Robert Gordon Sproul Assocs, 77-; fel, Calif Acad Sci, 76- *Mem:* Sigma Xi; Int Orgn Biosystematists. *Res:* Biosystematics of New World Pompilidae and of North American Tiphiidae; larval systematics and biology of North American Tephritidae. *Mailing Add:* Lab Serv Entom Calif Dept Food & Agr 1220 N St Sacramento CA 95814

WASCOM, EARL RAY, b Corbin, La, Nov 26, 30; m 51; c 2. ECOLOGY. *Educ:* Southeastern La State Col, BS, 56; La Polytech Inst, MS, 62; La State Univ, PhD(bot), 67. *Prof Exp:* From instr to assoc prof, 58-68, head dept, 68-76, PROF BIOL SCI, SOUTHEASTERN LA UNIV, 69- *Mem:* Am Inst Biol Sci; Ecol Soc Am; Am Soc Plant Taxon; Bot Soc Am. *Res:* Taxonomy of angiosperms; plant ecology. *Mailing Add:* Dept of Biol Sci Southeastern La Univ Hammond LA 70402

WASE, ARTHUR WILLIAM, b Jersey City, NJ, Nov 15, 19; m 40; c 2. BIOCHEMISTRY. *Educ:* Columbia Col, AB, 47; Rutgers Univ, PhD, 51. *Prof Exp:* From instr to assoc prof, 51-68, PROF BIOCHEM, HAHNEMANN MED COL, 68-; SR RES FEL BIOCHEM ENDOCRINOL, MERCK INST THERAPEUT RES, 75- *Concurrent Pos:* Fulbright prof, Univ Brussels & Inst Jules Bordet, Belgium, 56-57; consult, Colgate Biol Res Labs, 58- & pub sect, Radio Corp Am; res fel biochem endocrinol, Merck Inst Therapeut Res, 63-75, head dept health physics, 76- *Mem:* Am Cancer Soc; Am Heart Asn Coun Thrombosis. *Res:* Radiobiochemistry as applied to cancer research and neuropsychopharmacology; bone metabolism; biochemistry and endocrinology of atherosclerosis. *Mailing Add:* 213 Valentine St Highland Park NJ 08904

WASER, PETER MERRITT, b Pasadena, Calif, Dec 12, 45. BEHAVIORAL ECOLOGY. *Educ:* Stanford Univ, BS, 68; Rockefeller Univ, PhD(biol), 74. *Prof Exp:* NIH fel, Rockefeller Univ, 74-75; asst prof, 75-80, ASSOC PROF BIOL, PURDUE UNIV, 80- *Concurrent Pos:* Grants, EAfrican Wildlife Soc, 74-75, Am Philos Soc, 76-77, NIMH, 77-78, NSF, 78- & NIH, 80-82. *Mem:* Animal Behav Soc; Int Primate Soc; Ecol Soc Am; AAAS; Am Soc Mammalogist. *Res:* Adaptive aspects of animal social behavior; animal communication; territoriality and resource use. *Mailing Add:* Dept Biol Sci Purdue Univ West Lafayette IN 47907

WASFI, SADIQ HASSAN, b Basrah, Iraq, July 1, 37; m 68; c 2. INORGANIC CHEMISTRY. *Educ:* Univ Baghdad, BS, 61; Georgetown Univ, MS, 66, PhD(inorg chem), 71. *Prof Exp:* From lectr to asst prof chem, Col Sci, Basrah Univ, Iraq, 71-75; res assoc chem, Univ Hawaii, Manoa, 75-76; res assoc, Georgetown Univ, 76-78; assoc prof, Montgomery Col, Md, 78-80; ASSOC PROF CHEM, DEL STATE COL, 80- *Mem:* Am Chem Soc; Iraqi Chem Soc; Sigma Xi. *Res:* Transition metal complexes of organic thiols and disulfides; organic derivatives of heteropoly tungstates and molybdates; heteropoly tungstate and molybdate anions containing several transition metal ions. *Mailing Add:* Dept Chem Del State Col Dover DE 19901

WASHA, GEORGE WILLIAM, b Milwaukee, Wis, May 6, 09; m 34; c 3. MECHANICS. *Educ:* Univ Wis, BS, 30, MS, 32, PhD(mech), 38. *Prof Exp:* Instr, 30-40, chmn dept, 53-75, PROF MECH, UNIV WIS-MADISON, 40- *Honors & Awards:* Wason Medal, Am Concrete Inst, 41 & 76. *Mem:* Nat Acad Sci; Am Soc Test & Mat; fel Am Concrete Inst. *Res:* Durability, permeability and plastic flow of concrete; light weight agregates and concrete; vibrated concrete; masonry cements; properties of ferrous metals; concrete block. *Mailing Add:* 1114 Shorewood Blvd Madison WI 53705

WASHAM, CLINTON JAY, b Pryor, Okla, June 23, 41; m 69; c 3. MICROBIOLOGY. *Educ:* Okla State Univ, BS & MS, 63; Ore State Univ, PhD(microbiol), 68. *Prof Exp:* Res asst microbiol, Ore State Univ, 63-67, instr, 67-68; vis lectr food technol, Iowa State Univ, 68-70; assoc prof biol, Southwestern Union Col, 70-73; vpres, Tolibia Cheese, Inc, Wis, 73-75; asst prof dairy sci, Univ Ga, 75-78; vpres, Miss Valley Milk Producers Asn, Iowa, 78-81; RES DIR, MALLINCKRODT, INC, ST LOUIS, MO, 81- *Concurrent Pos:* Res & develop consult, Tolibia Cheese, Inc, 75-; qual assurance consult, McKee Baking Co, Tenn. *Mem:* Am Soc Microbiol; Int Asn Milk, Food & Environ Sanitarians; Sigma Xi; Am Dairy Sci Asn; AAAS. *Res:* Dairy starter cultures; blue cheese; culture media; bacterial metabolism; electron microscopy of dairy products; flavor and aroma compounds in dairy products; artificial cheese; factors affecting cheese ripening. *Mailing Add:* Systs Lab Mallinckrodt Inc St Louis MO 63134

WASHBURN, ALBERT LINCOLN, b New York, NY, June 15, 11; m 35; c 3. GEOMORPHOLOGY, QUATERNARY GEOLOGY. *Educ:* Dartmouth Col, AB, 35; Yale Univ, PhD(geol), 42. *Prof Exp:* Mem, Nat Geog Soc exped, Mt McKinley, 36; asst geologist, Boyd E Greenland exped, 37; geol invests, Can Arctic, 38-41, 49 & 81; exec dir, Arctic Inst NAm, 45-51; dir snow, ice & permafrost res estab, Corps Engrs, US Army, 52-53; prof northern geol, Dartmouth Col, 54-60; prof geol, Yale Univ, 60-66; prof, 66-76, EMER PROF GEOL, UNIV WASH, 76- *Concurrent Pos:* Consult, Res & Develop Bd, US Dept Defense, 46-53 & Corps Engrs, US Army, 54-60; hon lectr, McGill Univ, 48-50; mem, US Nat Comt, Int Geophys Year, 53-59, Panel Glaciol, Nat Acad Sci, 59-65 & 67-71; chmn bd, Polar Res, 78-81; mem geol expeds, Greenland, 54-58, 60 & 64; dir, Quaternary Res Ctr, Univ Wash, 67-75; vpres, Int Quaternary Union, 73- *Honors & Awards:* Kirk Bryan Award, Geol Soc Am, 71; Medaile Andre H Dumont, Geol Soc Belg, 73. *Mem:* Fel Am Geog Soc; hon mem Int Glaciol Soc; fel Geol Soc Am; Am Geophys Union; hon mem Arctic Inst NAm. *Res:* Periglacial studies. *Mailing Add:* Quaternary Res Ctr Univ of Wash Seattle WA 98195

WASHBURN, HAROLD W(ILLIAMS), b Jacksonville, Ore, June 23, 02; m 56; c 2. PHYSICS, ELECTRICAL ENGINEERING. *Educ:* Univ Calif, BS, 24, PhD(elec eng), 32; Mass Inst Technol, MS, 27. *Prof Exp:* From instr to asst prof elec eng, Univ Calif, 28-31; instr, Mass Inst Technol, 32-33; chief physicist in charge res lab, Western Geophys Co, Calif, 33-37; vpres in charge res, Consol Electrodyne Corp, 37-60; from chief exp space sci to staff scientist, Jet Propulsion Lab, Calif Inst Technol, 60-65; prof, 65-76, EMER PROF ELEC ENG, CALIF STATE UNIV, LONG BEACH, 77- *Concurrent Pos:* Consult, Jet Propulsion Lab, Calif Inst Technol. *Honors & Awards:* Beckman Award, Am Chem Soc, 56. *Mem:* AAAS; Am Soc Testing & Mat; Am Geophys Union. *Res:* Mass spectroscopy; lunar atmosphere and surface characteristics; electric circuits. *Mailing Add:* 102 Rivo Alto Canal Long Beach CA 90803

WASHBURN, JACK, b Mt Vernon, NY, Apr 30, 21; m 47; c 3. PHYSICAL METALLURGY. *Educ:* Univ Calif, BS, 49, MS, 50, PhD, 54. *Prof Exp:* Res engr, Inst Eng Res, 49-52, from instr to assoc prof metall, 52-61, chmn dept, 67-70, PROF MAT SCI & ENG, UNIV CALIF, BERKELEY, 61- *Concurrent Pos:* Sr fel, Univ Cambridge, 59-60; res prof, Miller Inst Basic Res Sci, 61-62; sr fel, Univ Paris, 65. *Honors & Awards:* Mathewson Gold Medal, Am Inst Mining, Metall & Petrol Engrs, 56. *Mem:* Am Soc Metals; Am Inst Mining, Metall & Petrol Engrs. *Res:* Relation between properties and structure of solid materials, particularly the characterization and effects of crystal imperfections. *Mailing Add:* Dept of Mat Sci & Eng Univ of Calif Berkeley CA 94720

WASHBURN, KENNETH W, b Martinsville, Va, June 21, 37; m 59; c 2. POULTRY GENETICS. *Educ:* Va Polytech Inst, BS, 59, MS, 62; Univ Mass, PhD(poultry), 65. *Prof Exp:* Res asst poultry genetics, Va Polytech Inst, 60-62; instr, Univ Mass, 62-65; assoc prof, 65-75, PROF POULTRY GENETICS, UNIV GA, 75- *Honors & Awards:* Poultry Sci Jr Res Award, Poultry Sci Asn, 75. *Mem:* Poultry Sci Asn. *Res:* Genetic-nutrition interrelationships; compensatory growth; feed efficiency; egg shell strength; egg cholesterol; hemoglobins. *Mailing Add:* Dept Poultry L P Bldg Univ of Ga Athens GA 30602

WASHBURN, LEE CROSS, b Paducah, Ky, Jan 10, 47; m 69; c 3. ORGANIC CHEMISTRY, NUCLEAR MEDICINE. *Educ:* Murray State Univ, BA, 68; Vanderbilt Univ, PhD(org chem), 72. *Prof Exp:* Assoc scientist, 72-77, SCIENTIST RADIOPHARMACEUT DEVELOP, MED & HEALTH SCI DIV, OAK RIDGE ASSOC UNIVS, 77- *Mem:* Soc Nuclear Med. *Res:* Synthesis and testing of short-lived radiopharmaceutical tumor-scanning and organ-imaging agents; chelation therapy. *Mailing Add:* Oak Ridge Assoc Univs PO Box 117 Oak Ridge TN 37830

WASHBURN, RICHARD HANCORNE, b Cadillac, Mich, Mar 25, 19; m 42; c 4. ECONOMIC ENTOMOLOGY. *Educ:* Mich State Univ, BS, 41; Cornell Univ, PhD, 48. *Prof Exp:* Asst entom, Cornell Univ, 45-48; asst prof, Univ Ga, 48-49; entomologist hq, US Army Engrs, Alaska, 49; res entomologist, 50-52, exten entomologist, 52-56, assoc prof entom, 59-78, SR ENTOMOLOGIST, USDA AGR EXP STA, UNIV ALASKA, 58-, ADJ PROF ENTOM, 78- *Concurrent Pos:* Res entomologist, NC Region Sci & Educ Admin-Agr Res, USDA, 68- *Mem:* AAAS; Entom Soc Am; Am Hort Soc; Int Plant Propagators Soc. *Res:* Insect toxicology, ecology and physiology. *Mailing Add:* PO Box 823 Palmer AK 99645

WASHBURN, ROBERT HENRY, b Lincoln, Nebr, Nov 27, 36; m 66. STRATIGRAPHY, STRUCTURAL GEOLOGY. *Educ:* Univ Nebr, BS, 59, MS, 61; Columbia Univ, PhD(geol), 66. *Prof Exp:* Instr geol, Brooklyn Col, 64-66; from asst prof to assoc prof, 66-77, PROF GEOL, JUNIATA COL, 77- *Mem:* AAAS; Geol Soc Am; Am Asn Petrol Geologists; Soc Econ Paleont & Mineral. *Res:* Paleozoic stratigraphy; structural geology of central Nevada and Pennsylvania. *Mailing Add:* Dept of Geol Juniata Col Huntingdon PA 16652

WASHBURN, ROBERT LATHAM, b Malone, NY, June 22, 21; m 74; c 4. MECHANICAL ENGINEERING, POLYMER ENGINEERING. *Educ:* Clarkson Col Technol, BE, 47; Mass Inst Technol, MS, 48. *Prof Exp:* Chief engr design develop, Sklenar Furnace & Mfg Co, 46-47; mgr eng tech sect, 48-53, asst supt, 53-55, supt, 55-58, sr supvr res & develop, 58-68, sr supvr res plastics prod div, 68-72, supt res lab, 68-72, polymer prod div, 72-78, sr supvr admin & eng res, 78-80, SR TECH SUPVR TECH SERV & MKT DEVELOP, ETHYLENE COPOLYMER DIV, E I DU PONT DE NEMOURS & CO, INC, 80- *Mem:* Sigma Xi; Am Soc Mech Engrs; Tech Asn Pulp & Paper Indust. *Res:* Concept development, resultant program derivation, and subsequent engineering new polymer systems encompassing process, product and equipment; synthesis, rheology, morphology and conformational alterations such as orientation. *Mailing Add:* 3250 Landsdowne Dr Cardiff Wilmington DE 19898

WASHBURN, WILLIAM H, b Milwaukee, Wis, Oct 14, 20; m 42; c 3. ANALYTICAL CHEMISTRY. *Educ:* Univ Wis, BA, 41. *Prof Exp:* CHEMIST, ABBOTT LABS, 46- *Mem:* Soc Appl Spectros; Am Chem Soc; Coblentz Soc; Sigma Xi. *Res:* Infrared spectroscopy, materials purity and chemical structure analysis. *Mailing Add:* 120 Hawthorne Ct Lake Bluff IL 60044

WASHBURNE, STEPHEN SHEPARD, b Hartford, Conn, Sept 6, 42; m 70. ORGANIC CHEMISTRY. *Educ:* Trinity Col, Conn, BS, 63; Mass Inst Technol, PhD(org chem), 67. *Prof Exp:* Asst prof, 67-73, asst chmn dept, 74-78, ASSOC PROF CHEM, TEMPLE UNIV, 73- *Concurrent Pos:* NSF fel, 64-66; NIH fel, 67; chief consult, Petrarch Systs, Inc, 70-; Fulbright sr lectr, Portugal, 80. *Mem:* Am Chem Soc. *Res:* Organosilicon chemistry; cancer chemotherapy; organometallic chemistry of the elements of group IV. *Mailing Add:* Dept of Chem Temple Univ Philadelphia PA 19122

WASCHCECK, PAUL HOWARD, b Oklahoma City, Aug 12, 40; m 60; c 2. INDUSTRIAL ORGANIC CHEMISTRY. *Educ:* Univ Okla, BS, 62, PhD(org chem), 67. *Prof Exp:* Chemist, 66-70, GROUP LEADER, EXPLOR SECT, PETROCHEM DIV, CONTINENTAL OIL CO, 66- *Mem:* Am Chem Soc. *Res:* Organic synthesis in petrochemical field; sesquiterpenoids found in octocorallia; industrial organic chemistry as applied to process and product research and development. *Mailing Add:* Petrochem Div Drawer 1267 Ponca City OK 74601

WASHINGTON, ARTHUR CLOVER, b Tallulah, La, Aug, 19, 39; m 62; c 3. DEVELOPMENTAL BIOLOGY. *Educ:* Tex Col Tyler, BS, 61; Tuskegee Inst, Ala, MS, 63; Ill Inst Technol, PhD(biol), 71. *Prof Exp:* Res scientist plant path, Wash State Univ, 63-64; instr biol, Talladega Col, 65-67; assoc prof, Amundsen-Mayfair Col, 67-72; assoc prof, Langston Univ, Okla, 72-74; PROF BIOCHEM, PRAIRIE VIEW A&M UNIV, 74- *Concurrent Pos:* Res scientist, Pfizer Chem Co, Conn, 66; univ admin trainee, Univ Wis-Extension, Madison, 73; prin investr, NSF res initiation award, 73-74, USDA Tri-Co Nutrit, Prairrie View, 74-79, Robert A Welch Found award, 76-, NIH awards, 76-; sci develop consult, Paul Quinn Col, Tex, 76- *Mem:* Nat Inst Sci; Am Soc Microbiologists; AAAS; Sigma Xi. *Res:* Mechanisms which seem to regulate morphogenesis in the cellular slime mold, Dictyostelium discoideum; DNA, RNA folic acid and mitochondrial enzyme metabolism. *Mailing Add:* 10303 Green Creek Houston TX 77070

WASHINGTON, DONALD R(EED), engineering, see previous edition

WASHINGTON, ELMER L, b Houston, Tex, Oct 18, 35; m 60; c 2. PHYSICAL CHEMISTRY. *Educ:* Tex Southern Univ, BS, 57, MS, 58; Ill Inst Technol, PhD(thermodyn), 66. *Prof Exp:* Asst proj engr, Pratt & Whitney Aircraft Div, United Aircraft Corp, Conn, 65-67, res assoc advan mat res & develop lab, 67-69; asst prof phys sci, 69-72, dean natural sci & math, 72-74, assoc prof, 72-77, PROF CHEM & V PRES RES & DEVELOP, CHICAGO STATE UNIV, 77-, DEAN COL ARTS & SCI, 74- *Mem:* Electrochem Soc; Am Chem Soc. *Res:* Thermodynamics of non-electrolytes; electrochemistry as related to fuel cell technology. *Mailing Add:* Col of Arts & Sci Chicago State Univ Chicago IL 60628

WASHINGTON, JAMES M(ACKNIGHT), b Hackensack, NJ, Dec 1, 38; m 56; c 4. CHEMICAL ENGINEERING. *Educ:* Clemson Univ, BS, 61; Va Polytech Inst, MS, 64, PhD, 69. *Prof Exp:* Asst prof chem eng, Univ NB, 65-66; res engr, E I du Pont de Nemours & Co, 66-68; sr scientist, Allied Chem Corp, 68-72; res engr, 72-80, ASSOC SR ENGR, PHILIP MORRIS RES CTR, 80- *Mem:* Am Inst Chem Engrs. *Res:* Chemical reactor engineering, particularly non-ideal mixing of fluids. *Mailing Add:* Philip Morris Res Ctr Richmond VA 23261

WASHINGTON, JOHN A, II, b Istanbul, Turkey, May 29, 36; US citizen; m 59; c 3. CLINICAL MICROBIOLOGY, CLINICAL PATHOLOGY. *Educ:* Univ Va, BA, 57; Johns Hopkins Univ, MD, 61. *Prof Exp:* From intern to asst resident surg, Med Ctr, Duke Univ, 61-63; Nat Cancer Inst fel, 63-65; resident clin path, Clin Ctr, NIH, 65-67; assoc consult, 67-68, assoc prof microbiol & lab med, 72-76, CONSULT MICROBIOL, MAYO CLIN, 68-, HEAD SECT CLIN MICROBIOL, 71-, PROF MICROBIOL & LAB MED, MAYO MED SCH, 76- *Concurrent Pos:* Asst prof microbiol, Mayo Grad Sch Med, 70-72; ed, J Clin Microbiol, 74-75; ed, Antimicrobiol Agents & Chemother, 81- *Mem:* Fel Am Soc Clin Path; Am Soc Microbiol; fel Am Col Physicians; fel Am Acad Microbiol; fel Infectious Dis Soc Am. *Res:* Antimicrobial agents; antimicrobial susceptibility tests; methodology in clinical bacteriology. *Mailing Add:* Sect of Clin Microbiol 200 SW First St Rochester MN 55901

WASHINGTON, WARREN MORTON, b Portland, Ore, Aug 28, 36. METEOROLOGY. *Educ:* Ore State Univ, BS, 58, MS, 60; Pa State Univ, PhD(meteorol), 64. *Prof Exp:* Res asst meteorol, Pa State Univ, 61-63; SCIENTIST, NAT CTR ATMOSPHERIC RES, 63- *Concurrent Pos:* Adj prof metoerol & oceanog, Univ Mich, 69-71; mem var panels, Nat Acad Sci & NSF, 69-; mem, Gov Sci Adv Comt, State Colo, 75-78; Presidential appointment, Nat Adv Comt, Oceans & Atmosphere, 78- *Mem:* AAAS; Am Meteorol Soc. *Res:* Numerical modeling of the atmosphere. *Mailing Add:* Nat Ctr for Atmospheric Res PO Box 3000 Boulder CO 80307

WASHINGTON, WILLIE JAMES, b Madison, Fla, Dec 26, 42; m 70. PLANT GENETICS, CYTOGENETICS. *Educ:* Fla A&M Univ, BS, 64; Univ Ariz, MS, 66; Univ Mo-Columbia, PhD(plant genetics, cytogenetics), 70. *Prof Exp:* Asst prof biol, Tougaloo Col, 70-71 & Cent State Univ, Ohio, 71-72; D F Jones fel agron, NDak State Univ, 72-73; asst prof, 73-77, ASSOC PROF BIOL, CENT STATE UNIV, OHIO, 77- *Concurrent Pos:* Prin investr, Mutagenic/Teratological Potential Lab Solvents, Minority Biomed Support Prog, NIH, 80-83 & Careers in Natural Resources for Urban Minorities, Forest Serv, US Dept Agr, 81-83. *Mem:* Orgn Black Scientists; Nat Inst Sci; Cent Asn Adv for Health Prof; AAAS. *Res:* Genetics and cytogenetics of higher plants and animals; application of genetical and cytogentical analysis to the improvement of economic crops; mammalian tissue culture and immunological assays; environmental mutagenesis. *Mailing Add:* Dept of Biol Cent State Univ Wilberforce OH 45384

WASHINO, ROBERT K, b Sacramento, Calif, Mar 14, 32; m 56; c 3. ENTOMOLOGY, PUBLIC HEALTH. *Educ:* Univ Calif, Berkeley, BS, 54; Univ Calif, Davis, MS, 56, PhD(entom), 67. *Prof Exp:* Assoc-sr specialist, Calif State Dept Pub Health, 59-65; asst specialist, 65-67, assoc prof, 67-81, PROF ENTOM, UNIV CALIF, DAVIS, 81-, LECTR & ASST ENTOMOLOGIST, 67- *Concurrent Pos:* NIH grant, 71-73. *Mem:* Entom Soc Am; Am Soc Trop Med & Hyg; Am Mosquito Control Asn (vpres). *Res:* Studies regarding the various aspects of insect biology which affect their role as vectors of human and animal pathogens; sociological as well as entomological studies of mosquito pest problems. *Mailing Add:* Dept of Entom Univ of Calif Davis CA 95616

WASHKO, FLOYD VICTOR, b New Brunswick, NJ, Oct 17, 22; m 47; c 2. VETERINARY PATHOLOGY. *Educ:* Mich State Univ, DVM, 44; Purdue Univ, MS, 48, PhD, 50. *Prof Exp:* Vet pract, NJ, 44-45; assoc prof vet sci, Purdue Univ, 46-53; mem staff, Plum Island Animal Dis Lab, USDA, 53-54; VET PATHOLOGIST, MERCK, SHARP & DOHME RES LABS, 54-, SR INVESTR, 74- *Mem:* Am Vet Med Asn; NY Acad Sci; Am Asn Avian Pathologists; Am Asn Vet Lab Diagnosticians; US Animal Health Asn. *Res:* Brucellosis of swine and cattle; virus diseases of the bovine; veterinary therapeutics. *Mailing Add:* Merck Sharp & Dohme Res Labs Rahway NJ 07065

WASHKO, PHILIP WAYNE, nutritional biochemistry, toxicology, see previous edition

WASHKO, WALTER WILLIAM, b New Brunswick, NJ, July 29, 20; m 55; c 4. AGRONOMY. *Educ:* Rutgers Univ, BS, 41, MS, 47, Univ Wis, PhD(agron, bot), 58. *Prof Exp:* Agronomist, Tex Res Found, 47-53 & Eastern States Farmers Exchange, 53-64; EXT AGRONOMIST & PROF AGRON, UNIV CONN, 64- *Mem:* Am Soc Agron; Am Inst Biol Sci. *Res:* Crop production. *Mailing Add:* Dept of Plant Sci Univ of Conn Storrs CT 06268

WASIELEWSKI, MICHAEL ROMAN, b Chicago, Ill, June 7, 49; m 75; c 1. PHOTOSYNTHESIS. *Educ:* Univ Chicago, BS, 71, MS, 72, PhD(chem), 75. *Prof Exp:* Fel chem, Columbia Univ, 74-75; res assoc, 75-76, asst chemist, 76-81, CHEMIST, ARGONNE NAT LAB, 81- *Mem:* Am Chem Soc; Biophys Soc; Am Soc Photobiol. *Res:* Mechanism of the primary events of photosynthesis; light induced electron transfer reactions; biomimetic modelling of natural biophysical chemistry. *Mailing Add:* Chem Div Argonne Nat lab Argonne IL 60439

WASIELEWSKI, PAUL FRANCIS, b Bay Shore, NY, Oct 21, 41; m 67; c 3. TRANSPORTATION SCIENCE, PHYSICS. *Educ:* Georgetown Univ, BS, 63; Yale Univ, MS, 65, PhD(physics), 69. *Prof Exp:* SCIENTIST, DEPT TRANSP & TRAFFIC SCI, GEN MOTORS RES LAB, 69- *Mem:* Opers Res Soc Am; Am Phys Soc. *Res:* Transportation and traffic science; affect of traffic conditions on fuel consumption; mathematical models of traffic; traffic accident research. *Mailing Add:* 25474 Wareham Dr Huntington Woods MI 48070

WASILEWSKI, ROMAN J(ERZY), b Warsaw, Poland, Oct 6, 19; m 48; c 3. MATERIALS SCIENCE. *Educ:* Cambridge Univ, BA, 48; Columbia Univ, PhD(phys metall), 53. *Prof Exp:* Res metallurgist, Murex, Ltd, Eng, 48-50, sr res metallurgist, 53; chief metallurgist, Edibrac, Ltd, 54; lectr phys metall, Univ Liverpool, 55-56; res supvr, E I du Pont de Nemours & Co, Inc, Del, 56-62, res assoc, 62-67; sr tech adv, Battelle Mem Inst, Ohio, 67-71; HEAD MAT RES LAB SECT, NAT SCI FOUND, 71- *Mem:* Sigma Xi; Am Soc Metals; Am Inst Mining, Metall & Petrol Engrs; Brit Metals Soc; fel Brit Inst Metallurgists. *Res:* Refractory metals and compounds; intermetallic compounds; martensitic transformations and shape memory phenomena; elastic-plastic deformation. *Mailing Add:* Mat Res Lab Sect Nat Sci Found Washington DC 20550

WASILIK, JOHN H(UBER), b Franklin, NC, Feb 9, 25; m 51; c 6. SOLID STATE PHYSICS, MICROWAVE ENGINEERING. *Educ:* Manhattan Col, BS, 47; Cath Univ Am, PhD(physics), 57. *Prof Exp:* Physicist, Nat Bur Standards, 50-67; PHYSICIST, HARRY DIAMOND LABS, 67- *Mem:* Am Phys Soc; Inst Elec & Electronics Engrs. *Res:* Elastic and dielectric properties, their pressure and temperature dependence; associated loss mechanisms; excitons; microwave acoustics; lattice attenuation; theory and experiment; piezoelectricity; electrostriction; bulk and surface wave microwave acoustic delay lines. *Mailing Add:* Harry Diamond Labs 2800 Powder Mill Rd Adelphia MD 20783

WASLEY, RICHARD J(UNIOR), b Oakland, Calif, June 24, 31; m 60; c 3. MECHANICAL & CIVIL ENGINEERING. *Educ:* Univ Calif, Berkeley, BS, 54; Stanford Univ, MS, 58, PhD(civil eng), 60. *Prof Exp:* Sanit engr, Bur Sanit Eng, Calif Dept Pub Health, 55-56; civil engr, Alameda County Surveyor Off, 57; ENGR, LAWRENCE LIVERMORE LAB, UNIV CALIF, 60- *Honors & Awards:* Alfred Noble Prize, 62. *Mem:* Am Soc Civil Engrs; Nat Soc Prof Engrs; Am Soc Mech Engrs. *Res:* Dynamic mechanical properties of materials; elastic and viscoelastic waves; fluid mechanics; shock wave phenomena. *Mailing Add:* 4290 Colgate Way Livermore CA 94550

WASLIEN, CAROL IRENE, b Mayville, NDak, Sept 24, 40; m 70. NUTRITION EDUCATION, NUTRITION ASSESSMENT. *Educ:* Univ Calif, Santa Barbara, BA, 61; Cornell Univ, MS, 63; Univ Calif, Berkeley, PhD(nutrit), 68. *Prof Exp:* NIH res training fel, Vanderbilt Univ, Naval Med Res Unit-3, Egypt, 68-69; res assoc nutrit, Vanderbilt Univ, 69-72; assoc prof & head dept nutrit & foods, Auburn Univ, 72-77; chief nutrit planning proj, USAID, 77-79; exec dir, League Int Food Educ, 79-81; PROF & HEAD HOME ECON, NUTRIT DEPT, HUNTER COL, CITY UNIV NEW YORK, 81- *Concurrent Pos:* Res consult biochem dept, Vanderbilt Univ, 72- *Mem:* Am Asn Cereal Chemists; Am Inst Nutrit; Am Dietetic Asn; Inst Food Tech. *Res:* Human requirements for protein, vitamins and trace minerals; use of micro-organisms as food sources for man; assessment of nutritional status in health and disease; nutrition program evaluation. *Mailing Add:* Home Econ Nutrit Dept Hunter Col City Univ New York New York NY 10021

WASON, SATISH KUMAR, b Lyallpur, India, Feb 24, 40; m 70; c 3. PHYSICAL INORGANIC CHEMISTRY. *Educ:* Univ Delhi, BSc, 59, MSc, 61; Cornell Univ, PhD(phys chem), 65. *Prof Exp:* Scientist, Coun Sci & Indust Res, New Delhi, India, 65-66; res assoc phys chem, Boston Univ, 66-67; res chemist, E I du Pont de Nemours & Co, Inc, Del, 67-69; res scientist, 69-73, sect leader, 73-79, SECT MGR, COM DEVELOP, J M HUBER CORP, 80- *Mem:* Am Chem Soc; Soc Cosmetic Chemists; Sigma Xi; Soc Plastic Indust; Soc Plastic Engrs. *Res:* High temperature thermodynamic and spectroscopic studies; photochemistry and mercury photosensitized reactions; chemistry of synthetic silicas and silicates; surface chemistry, structure and applications of fine-particle synthetic silicas and silicates in paper, rubber, paints, plastics, dentrifices, cosmetics, pharmaceutical and specialty industries. *Mailing Add:* J M Huber Corp PO Box 310 Havre De Grace MD 21078

WASOW, WOLFGANG RICHARD, b Vevey, Switz, July 25, 09; nat US; m 39, 59; c 3. MATHEMATICS. *Educ:* NY Univ, PhD(math), 42. *Prof Exp:* Instr math, Goddard Col, 39-40, Conn Col for Women, 41-42 & NY Univ, 42-46; asst prof, Swarthmore Col, 46-49; mathematician numerical anal res, Univ Calif, Los Angeles, 49-55; math res ctr, US Dept Army, Wis, 56-57; prof, 57-80, EMER PROF MATH, UNIV WIS-MADISON, 80- *Concurrent Pos:* Fulbright fel, Rome, Italy, 54-55 & Haifa, Israel, 62. *Mem:* Am Math Soc; Math Asn Am; Soc Indust & Appl Math. *Res:* Asymptotic theory and numerical solution of differential equations. *Mailing Add:* Dept of Math Univ of Wis Madison WI 53706

WASS, MARVIN LEROY, b Worthington, Minn, Apr 24, 22; m; c 3. ZOOLOGY, BOTANY. *Educ:* Winona State Col, BS, 49; Fla State Univ, MS, 53; Univ Fla, PhD, 59. *Prof Exp:* Cur, Pinellas County Marine Mus, St Petersburg, Fla, 53-55; asst prof biol, Western Carolina Col, 59-60; assoc marine scientist, 60-71, SR MARINE SCIENTIST & HEAD DEPT, VA INST MARINE SCI, 72- *Concurrent Pos:* Assoc prof, Sch Marine Sci, Col William & Mary, 60-; partic, US Prog Biol, Int Indian Ocean Exped, 64. *Mem:* Am Soc Limnol & Oceanog. *Res:* Marine ecology; marine invertebrates; biogeography; wetlands; ornithology. *Mailing Add:* Va Inst of Marine Sci Gloucester Point VA 23062

WASS, WALLACE M, b Lake Park, Iowa, Nov 19, 29; m 53; c 4. VETERINARY MEDICINE, VETERINARY SURGERY. *Educ:* Univ Minn, BS, 51, DVM, 53, PhD(vet med), 61. *Hon Degrees:* Vet Med, Nat Univ Colombia, 63. *Prof Exp:* From instr to asst prof vet med, Univ Minn, 58-63; res assoc lab animal med, Brookhaven Nat Lab, 63-64; PROF VET CLIN SCI & HEAD DEPT, IOWA STATE UNIV, 64- *Mem:* Am Vet Med Asn. *Res:* Large animal medicine and surgery; metabolic diseases of domestic animals; bovine porphyria. *Mailing Add:* Dept of Vet Clin Sci Iowa State Univ Ames IA 50010

WASSARMAN, PAUL MICHAEL, b Milford, Mass, Mar 26, 40; c 4. DEVELOPMENTAL BIOLOGY, DEVELOPMENTAL BIOCHEMISTRY. *Educ:* Univ Mass, BS, 61, MS, 64; Brandeis Univ, PhD(biochem), 68. *Prof Exp:* Helen Hay Whitney Found fel, Molecular Res Ctr Lab, Eng, 67-69; asst prof, Dept Biol Sci, Purdue Univ, 69-72; lectr & special res fel, Harvard Med Sch & Rockefelller Found, 72-73, asst prof, 73-76, ASSOC PROF, DEPT BIOL CHEM, HARVARD MED SCH, 76- *Concurrent Pos:* Mem, Exec Comt, Prog Cell & Develop Biol, Harvard Med Sch, 75-, Molecular Cytol Study Sect, NIH, 78-82, Bd Tutors biochem sci, 75- *Mem:* Am Soc Biol Chem; Am Soc Cell Biol; Soc Develop Biol; AAAS.

Res: Gene expression during early mammalian development; sperm-egg interaction during mammalian fertilization; structure and replication of eukaryotic chromosomes. *Mailing Add:* Dept Biol Chem Bldg C2-467 Harvard Med Sch Boston MA 02115

WASSER, CLINTON HOWARD, b Phoenix, Ariz, Nov 11, 15; m 39; c 3. RANGE ECOLOGY. *Educ:* Univ Ariz, BS, 37; Univ Nebr, MS, 47; Colo State Univ, MF, 48. *Prof Exp:* Res asst southwestern forest & range exp sta, US Forest Serv, 37-38; instr range sci & asst range mgt, Colo State Univ, 38-43, from asst prof to assoc prof, 43-52, prof, 52-80. *Concurrent Pos:* Asst range conservationist, Colo State Univ, 43-47, actg head dept range mgt, 47-50, head, 50-57, chief range conservationist & chief forestry and range mgt sect, Agr Exp Sta, 47-52, dean col forestry & natural resources, 52-69, pres, Res Found, 57-59; collabr, State Prod & Mkt Admin, Colo, 43-44 & Rocky Mt Forest & Range Exp Sta, US Forest Serv, 54-60; consult, Bowes & Hart, Inc, 47; admin tech rep, McIntire Stennis Coop State Forestry Prog, 63-69. *Honors & Awards:* Accievement Serv Award, Soc Range Mgt, 69. *Mem:* Soc Am Foresters; Soc Range Mgt (pres-elect, 64, pres, 65); AAAS; Ecol Soc Am. *Res:* Range management, ecology and seeding; alpine plant ecology. *Mailing Add:* 1400 S Shields Ft Collins CO 80521

WASSER, RICHARD BARKMAN, b Oshkosh, Wis, Sept 26, 36; m 68; c 2. PAPER CHEMISTRY, PHYSICAL CHEMISTRY. *Educ:* Univ Wis, BS, 59; Inst Paper Chem, MS, 61, PhD(paper chem), 64. *Prof Exp:* From res chemist to sr res chemist, 64-73, proj leader paper chem, 73-78, mgr paper chem res & develop, 78-80, PRIN RES SCIENTIST, AM CYANAMID CO, 80- *Mem:* Tech Asn Pulp & Paper Indust; Am Chem Soc. *Res:* Physical chemistry of paper and its modification with chemical additives. *Mailing Add:* Stamford Res Labs 1937 W Main St Stamford CT 06904

WASSERBURG, GERALD JOSEPH, b New Brunswick, NJ, Mar 25, 27; m 51; c 2. GEOLOGY, GEOPHYSICS. *Educ:* Univ Chicago, BSc, 51, MS, 52, PhD(geol), 54. *Prof Exp:* from asst prof to assoc prof, 55-62, PROF GEOL & GEOPHYS, CALIF INST TECHNOL, 62- *Concurrent Pos:* Vis prof, Univ Kiel, 60, Harvard Univ, 62, Univ Berne, 66 & Swiss Fed Inst Technol, 67; Vinton Hayes sr fel, Harvard, 80; Smithsonian Regents' fel, 82. *Honors & Awards:* Arthur L Day Medal, Geol Soc Am, 70; Except Sci Achievement Award, NASA 70 & Distinguished Pub Serv Medal, 72 & 78; J F Kemp Medal, Columbia Univ, 73; Leonard Medal, Meteoritical Soc, 75; V M Goldschmidt Medal, Geochem Soc, 78; Jaeger-Hales lectr, Australian Nat Univ, 80; Harold Jeffreys lectr, Royal Astron Soc, 81; Arthur L Day Prize and lectr, Nat Acad Sci, 81. *Mem:* Nat Acad Sci; fel Am Geophys Union; Geol Soc Am; fel Am Acad Arts & Sci. *Res:* Application of methods of chemical physics to geologic problems; measurement of absolute geologic time, solar system and planetary time scales; nucleosynthesis and variations in isotopic abundances due to long and short lived natural radioactivities and cosmic ray interactions in nature. *Mailing Add:* Arms Lab Calif Inst of Technol Pasadena CA 91125

WASSERMAN, AARON E, b Philadelphia, Pa, Dec, 28, 21; m 44; c 2. FOOD CHEMISTRY. *Educ:* Philadelphia Col Pharm, BSc, 42, ScD(bact), 48; Mass Inst Technol, MSc, 47. *Prof Exp:* Instr bact, Pa State Col Optom, 47; res assoc, Sharp & Dohme, Inc, 48-54; head, Meat Composition & Qual Invest, Meat Lab, 63-77, CHEMIST & BIOCHEMIST, EASTERN REGIONAL RES CTR, USDA, 54-, CHIEF, MEAT LAB, 77- *Mem:* Am Meat Sci Asn; Am Chem Soc; Inst Food Technol. *Res:* Flavor chemistry; organoleptic and sensory evaluation of food products; isolation and identification techniques; food processing; meat technology; bacterial physiology and metabolism; food safety. *Mailing Add:* 600 E Mermaid Lane Philadelphia PA 19118

WASSERMAN, AARON OSIAS, b New York, NY, Oct 15, 27; m 69; c 1. VERTEBRATE ZOOLOGY. *Educ:* City Col New York, BS, 51; Univ Tex, PhD(zool), 56. *Prof Exp:* From asst prof to assoc prof, 63-74, PROF BIOL, CITY COL NEW YORK, 74- *Mem:* Soc Study Evolution; Am Soc Ichthyol & Herpet; Am Soc Zool; Sigma Xi. *Res:* Speciation problems in anuran amphibians; cytogenetics of anurans. *Mailing Add:* Dept Biol City Col Convent Ave & 138th St New York NY 10031

WASSERMAN, AARON REUBEN, b Philadelphia, Pa, Apr 14, 32; m 63; c 2. BIOCHEMISTRY. *Educ:* Univ Pa, AB, 53; Univ Wis, MS, 57, PhD(biochem), 60. *Prof Exp:* Asst Univ Wis, 57-59; fel plant biochem, Johnson Found Med Physics, Univ Pa, 60-61, res assoc, Dept Chem, 61-62; fel, Enzyme Inst, Univ Wis-Madison & Dept Molecular Biol, Vanderbilt Univ, 63-65; asst prof, 65-72, ASSOC PROF BIOCHEM, McGILL UNIV, 72- *Mem:* Can Biochem Soc. *Res:* Biomembranes; membrane proteins; cytochromes; bioenergetics; photosynthesis. *Mailing Add:* 500 Pine W Montreal PQ H2W 1S6 Can

WASSERMAN, ALBERT J, b Richmond, Va, Jan 25, 28; m 48; c 3. CLINICAL PHARMACOLOGY, INTERNAL MEDICINE. *Educ:* Univ Va, BA, 47; Med Col Va, MD, 51. *Prof Exp:* Instr, 56-57, assoc, 57-60, from asst prof to assoc prof, 60-67, asst dean curric, 78-80, PROF MED, MED COL VA, 67-, ASSOC DEAN CURRIC, 80- *Mem:* Am Col Physicians; Am Col Chest Physicians; Am Soc Clin Pharmacol & Therapeut; Am Fedn Clin Res. *Res:* Cardiovascular pharmacology; human pharmacology and drug trials. *Mailing Add:* Med Col of Va Richmond VA 23298

WASSERMAN, ALLEN LOWELL, b New York, NY, Dec 7, 34; m 58; c 2. SOLID STATE PHYSICS. *Educ:* Carnegie Inst Technol, BS, 56; Iowa State Univ, PhD(physics), 63. *Prof Exp:* Res assoc, Princeton Univ, 63-65; asst prof, 65-71, ASSOC PROF PHYSICS, ORE STATE UNIV, 71- *Concurrent Pos:* Consult, Lawrence Radiation Lab, 65- *Mem:* Am Phys Soc. *Res:* Optical properties of solids; electron gas models of solid behavior. *Mailing Add:* Dept of Physics Ore State Univ Corvallis OR 97331

WASSERMAN, ARTHUR GABRIEL, b Bayonne, NJ, Nov 10, 38; m 64, 74; c 2. MATHEMATICS. *Educ:* Mass Inst Technol, BS, 60; Brandeis Univ, PhD(math), 65. *Prof Exp:* Pierce instr math, Harvard Univ, 65-68; asst prof, 68-70, assoc prof, 70-80, PROF MATH, UNIV MICH, ANN ARBOR, 80- *Concurrent Pos:* Mem, Inst Advan Study, Princeton Univ, 71-72; vis prof, Unicamp, Campinas, Brazil, 80 & Univ Oporto, Portugal, 81. *Mem:* Am Math Soc. *Res:* Topology; transformation groups; applied mathematics. *Mailing Add:* Dept Math 3009 Angell Hall Univ of Mich Ann Arbor MI 48109

WASSERMAN, DAVID, b New York, NY, Apr 6, 17; m 46; c 2. POLYMER CHEMISTRY. *Educ:* Brooklyn Col, AB, 37; Columbia Univ, PhD(org chem), 43. *Prof Exp:* Irvington Varnish & Insulator Co fel chem, Columbia Univ, 43-46; sr chemist, Irvinton Varnish & Insulator Div, Minn Mining & Mfg Co, 46-58, res assoc, Merck, Sharp & Dohme Res Div, 58-64; sr res scientist, 64-68, PROJ LEADER ETHICON, INC, 68- *Honors & Awards:* P B Hoffman Award for Res, Johnson & Johnson, Inc, 74. *Mem:* AAAS; NY Acad Sci; Am Chem Soc. *Res:* Synthetic polymers; organic synthesis; natural products; pharmaceutical chemistry; developed new synthetic absorbable suture. *Mailing Add:* Polymer Dept Ethicon Inc Div of Johnson & Johnson Inc Somerville NJ 08876

WASSERMAN, EDEL, b New York, NY, July 29, 32; m 55; c 2. THEORETICAL CHEMISTRY, ORGANIC CHEMISTRY. *Educ:* Cornell Univ, BA, 53; Harvard Univ, AM, 54, PhD(chem), 59. *Prof Exp:* Mem tech staff, Bell Tel Labs, Inc, 57-76; prof chem, Rutgers Univ, 67-76; dir, Chem Res Ctr, Allied Chem, 76-78, dir, Corp Res Ctr, 78-80; MEM RES STAFF, E I DU PONT DE NEMOURS & CO, INC, 80- *Concurrent Pos:* Vis prof, Cornell Univ, 62-63; adv ed, Chem Phys Letters, 68-79, J Am Chem Soc, 71-76 & Chem Rev, 82-; regent's lectr, Univ Calif, Irvine, 73. *Mem:* Am Chem Soc; Am Phys Soc. *Res:* Complex organic systems; inorganic chemistry. *Mailing Add:* 1904 Academy Place Wilmington DE 19806

WASSERMAN, EDWARD, b New York, NY, Jan 13, 21. PEDIATRICS. *Educ:* Johns Hopkins Univ, BA, 41; NY Med Col, MD, 46. *Prof Exp:* From clin asst to instr, 51-54, asst, 54-55, clin assoc, 55-56, from asst prof to assoc prof, 56-64, PROF PEDIAT, NEW YORK MED COL, FLOWER & FIFTH AVE HOSPS, 64-, CHMN DEPT, 66- *Concurrent Pos:* Mem pediat adv comt, Dept Health, New York, 64- *Mem:* Fel Am Fedn Clin Res; Am Acad Pediat. *Res:* Renal diseases. *Mailing Add:* Dept of Pediat New York Med Col New York NY 10029

WASSERMAN, HARRY H, b Boston, Mass, Dec 1, 20; m 47; c 3. ORGANIC CHEMISTRY. *Educ:* Mass Inst Technol, BS, 41; Harvard Univ, MS, 42, PhD(org chem), 49. *Prof Exp:* Res asst, Off Sci Res & Develop, 45; from instr to assoc prof, 48-62, chmn dept, 62-65, PROF CHEM, YALE UNIV, 62- *Concurrent Pos:* Guggenheim fel, 59-60; Am ed, Tetrahedron & Tetrahedron Letters, 60- ; mem study sect med chem, NIH, 62-66; postdoctoral rev panel, NSF, 63-65. *Mem:* Am Acad Arts & Sci; Am Chem Soc. *Res:* Natural products; reactions of organic systems with oxygen; cyclopropanones. *Mailing Add:* Sterling Chem Lab Yale Univ New Haven CT 06520

WASSERMAN, JACK F, b Dayton, Ohio, July 29, 41; m 75; c 3. BIOMECHANICS, BIOACOUSTICS. *Educ:* Purdue Univ, BS, 64; Univ Cincinnati, MS, 71, PhD(mech eng & biomed optics), 75. *Prof Exp:* Design engr, Gen Elec Co, 65-71; assoc dir, Stroke Res Lab, Univ Cincinnati, 75-79; ASSOC PROF BIOMECH SIGNAL PROCESSING, DEPT ENG SCI & MECH, UNIV TENN, 79- *Concurrent Pos:* Adj assoc prof, Mech Eng Dept, Univ Cincinnati, 75-79; consult, Surg Appliances, Inc, 78-81, Patricia Neal Rehab Ctr, 80-81; prin investr, IBM, 82- *Mem:* Am Soc Mech Eng; Orthop Res Soc; Am Soc Biomech. *Mailing Add:* Dept Eng Sci & Mech 317 Perkins Hall Univ Tenn Knoxville TN 37996

WASSERMAN, KARLMAN, b Brooklyn, NY, Mar 12, 27; m 53; c 4. PHYSIOLOGY, MEDICINE. *Educ:* Upsala Col, BA, 48; Tulane Univ, PhD(physiol), 51, MD, 58. *Prof Exp:* Intern, Johns Hopkins Univ, 58-59; sr res fel med, Univ Calif, San Francisco, 59-61; asst prof med, Stanford Univ, 61-67, dir respiratory function lab & chest clin, 61-67; assoc prof, 67-72, PROF MED, MED SCH, UNIV CALIF, LOS ANGELES, 72-; CHIEF DIV RESPIRATORY DIS, LOS ANGELES HARBOR GEN HOSP, TORRANCE, 67- *Mem:* Am Physiol Soc; Am Fedn Clin Res. *Res:* Respiratory, circulatory and renal physiology; respiratory disease. *Mailing Add:* Div Resp Physiol & Med Harbor Gen Hosp 1000 W Carson St Torrance CA 90509

WASSERMAN, LAWRENCE HARVEY, b Bronx, NY, Oct 19, 45; m 70; c 3. PLANETARY ASTRONOMY. *Educ:* Rensselaer Polytech Inst, BS, 67; Cornell Univ, MS, 71, PhD(astron), 73. *Prof Exp:* Res assoc astron, Lab Planetary Studies, Cornell Univ, 73-74; fel, 74-77, ASTRONOMER, LOWELL OBSERV, 77- *Mem:* Am Astron Soc; Sigma Xi. *Res:* Studies of planets, satellites and asteroids by occultation techniques; astronomical image processing; photographic astrometry. *Mailing Add:* Lowell Observ PO Box 1269 Flagstaff AZ 86002

WASSERMAN, LOUIS ROBERT, b New York, NY, July 11, 10; m 39, 57. MEDICINE. *Educ:* Harvard Univ, AB, 31; Rush Med Col, MD, 35; Am Bd Internal Med, dipl, 46. *Prof Exp:* Intern, Michael Reese Hosp, 35-37; res fel, Mt Sinai Hosp, 37-39, clin asst, 40-42, adj physician physiol hemat, 47-50, assoc physician, 50-54, hematologist & dir dept hemat, 54-72; prof med, 66-72, chmn, Dept Clin Sci, 68-72, distinguished serv prof, 72-79, Albert A & Vera G List prof, 77-79, EMER PROF MED & ALBERT A & VERA G LIST PROF, MT SINAI SCH MED, 79. *Concurrent Pos:* Res fel, Donner Lab Med Physics, Univ Calif, 46-49, consult, Radiation Lab, 48-51; asst clin prof, Col Physicians & Surgeons, Columbia Univ, 51-60, assoc prof, 60-66; res collabr, Brookhaven Nat Lab, 60-72; chmn polycythemia vera study group, Nat Cancer Inst, 67-, mem nat cancer planning comt, 72-73, mem cancer control comt, 72-73; diag rev adv group, 72-75, mem cancer treatment adv comt, 72-74 & chmn, 74-76; mem blood & hemopoietic syst res eval comt, Vet Admin, 69-72. *Mem:* Fel Am Col Physicians; Int Soc Hemat (vpres, 70-74); Am Soc Hemat (vpres, 67-68, pres, 68-69); Asn Am Physicians; Am Asn Cancer Res. *Res:* Diseases of the blood. *Mailing Add:* Mt Sinai Sch of Med 19 E 98th St Apt 5-B New York NY 10029

WASSERMAN, MARTIN ALLAN, b Newark, NJ, Nov 20, 41; m 66; c 2. PHARMACOLOGY, PHYSIOLOGY. *Educ:* Rutgers Univ, BS, 63; Univ Tex Med Br Galveston, MA, 71, PhD(pharmacol), 72. *Prof Exp:* Pharmacist, Shor's Med Serv Ctr, 63-68; res assoc pharmacol, Upjohn Co, 72-81; instr, Kalamazoo Valley Community Col, 78-81; ASSOC DIR PHARMACOL, SMITH KLINE & FRENCH LAB, 81- *Concurrent Pos:* Res asst, Univ Tex Med Br, 68-70, McLaughlin fel, 70-72; mem, Am Heart Asn. *Honors & Awards:* Mead-Johnson Excellence in Res Award, 72; Sigma Xi Award, 73. *Mem:* Am Soc Pharmacol & Exp Therapeut; Am Thoracic Soc. *Res:* Prostaglandins and pulmonary function and disease; pharmacology of asthma; leukotriene biology; calcium channel blockers. *Mailing Add:* Dept of Hypersensitivity Dis Res Upjohn Co Kalamazoo MI 49001

WASSERMAN, MARTIN S, b New York, NY, Jan 19, 38; m 63, 76; c 2. CHILD PSYCHIATRY. *Educ:* Columbia Col, AB, 59; State Univ NY Downstate Med Ctr, MD, 63. *Prof Exp:* Intern med, Albany Med Ctr, Union Univ, 64; resident psychiat, Kings County Gen Hosp, 64-67; instr, State Univ NY Downstate Med Ctr, 66-68; fel child psychiat, Univ Mich-Childrens Psychiat Hosp, 69-70; asst prof & assoc dir grad educ, Med Sch, 70-75, ASSOC CLIN PROF PSYCHIAT, UNIV SOUTHERN CALIF, 75- *Concurrent Pos:* Asst adj prof soc sci, Long Island Univ, 66-69; staff psychiatrist, Cath Charities, New York, 66-69; consult, Oper Headstart, Off Econ Opportunity, San Diego, Calif, 67-69, Ctr Forensic Psychiat, Mich, 69-70 & Bur Prisons, USPHS, 69-70; dir & fac mem, Los Angeles Psychoanal Soc & Inst, 76-78, secy, 77-78; psychiat consult, MGM, Columbia & 20th Century Fox Film Studios, 77-81. *Mem:* Fel Am Psychiat Asn; Am Col Psychiat; assoc Am Psychoanal Asn; Am Acad Child Psychiat. *Res:* College health; psychiatric education; socio-cultural factors in human development; film as developmental organizer. *Mailing Add:* Westwood Ctr 1100 Glenden Ave Los Angeles CA 90024

WASSERMAN, MARVIN, b New York, NY, Feb 2, 29; m 64; c 2. EVOLUTIONARY BIOLOGY. *Educ:* Cornell Univ, BS, 50; Univ Tex, MA, 52, PhD(biol), 54. *Prof Exp:* Res assoc biol, Univ Tex, 56-60; sr lectr zool, Univ Melbourne, 60-62; from asst prof to assoc prof, 62-67, PROF BIOL, QUEENS COL, NY, 67- *Mem:* Am Genetic Asn; Genetics Soc Am; Am Soc Nat; Soc Study Evolution; Soc Syst Zool. *Res:* Evolution and genetics of Drosophila; chromosomal polymorphism. *Mailing Add:* Dept of Biol Queen's Col Flushing NY 11367

WASSERMAN, MELVIN L, chemical engineering, see previous edition

WASSERMAN, MOE STANLEY, b Hampton, Va, May 31, 27; m 52; c 3. PHYSICAL CHEMISTRY. *Educ:* Univ Va, BS, 46, MS, 47; Univ Mich, PhD(phys chem), 55. *Prof Exp:* Develop engr, Gen Elec Co, 47-49; adv res engr, Sylvania Elec Prod, Inc, 55-61; sect head chem electronics, 61-64, group head advan mat & devices, 64-76, MGR ADVAN MAT & DEVICES, GTE LABS, INC, 76- *Mem:* Electrochem Soc; Inst Elec & Electronics Engrs; Am Vacuum Soc; Am Inst Chemists; AAAS. *Res:* Electron diffraction and microscopy; photoconductivity; electroluminescence; information display; semiconductor and dielectric materials and devices; preparation and electronic properties of thin-film materials. *Mailing Add:* 3 Fawn Rd Sherborn MA 01770

WASSERMAN, ROBERT H, b Chicago, Ill, Jan 3, 23; m 48; c 1. APPLIED MATHEMATICS. *Educ:* Univ Chicago, BS, 43; Univ Mich, MS, 46, PhD(math), 57. *Prof Exp:* Aeronaut res scientist, Nat Adv Comt Aeronaut, 43-57; from asst prof to assoc prof, 57-70, PROF MATH, MICH STATE UNIV, 70- *Mem:* Am Math Soc; Math Asn Am. *Res:* Fluid mechanics. *Mailing Add:* Dept of Math Mich State Univ East Lansing MI 48824

WASSERMAN, ROBERT HAROLD, b Schenectady, NY, Feb 11, 26; m 50; c 3. PHYSIOLOGY, BIOCHEMISTRY. *Educ:* Cornell Univ, BS, 49, PhD(nutrit), 53; Mich State Univ, MS, 51. *Prof Exp:* Asst bact, Mich State Univ, 49-50; asst animal nutrit, Cornell Univ, 51-53; res assoc biochem, Univ Tenn-AEC agr res prog, 53-55; sr scientist, Oak Ridge Inst Nuclear Studies, 55-57; assoc prof, 57-63, PROF PHYSIOL, NY STATE VET COL, CORNELL UNIV, 63-, ACTG CHMN DEPT, 74- *Concurrent Pos:* Consult, Oak Ridge Inst Nuclear Studies, 57-59; chmn, Conf Calcium & Strontium Transport, 62; Guggenheim fel, 64 & 72; vis fel, Inst Biol Chem, Denmark, 64-65; Orgn Econ Coop & Develop-NSF fel, 65; mem gen med B study sect, NIH, 68-71; mem organizing comt, Conf Calcium Transfer Mechanisms, 70, chmn, Conf Calcium-Binding Proteins, 77, mem adv comt, 83; mem, Nutrit Educ Comt, Nat Nutrit Consortium, 77- *Honors & Awards:* Mead-Johnson Award Nutrit, Am Inst Nutrit, 69. *Mem:* Nat Acad Sci; Soc Exp Biol & Med; Am Physiol Soc; Biophys Soc; AAAS. *Res:* Ion transport; mineral metabolism; vitamin D action; intestinal absorption. *Mailing Add:* Dept of Phys Biol Cornell Univ Ithaca NY 14850

WASSERMAN, STANLEY, b Louisville, Ky, Aug 29, 51; m 74; c 1. APPLIED STATISTICS, STATISTICAL METHODOLOGY. *Educ:* Univ Pa, BS & MA, 73; Harvard Univ, AM, 74, PhD(statists), 77. *Prof Exp:* Instr psychol, Harvard Univ, 76; vis instr urban & pub affairs, Carnegie-Mellon Univ, 76-77; ASST PROF STATIST, UNIV MINN, 77- *Concurrent Pos:* Res assoc social sci, Columbia Univ, 78; fel, Social Sci Res Coun, 78-79; co prin investr grants, NSF, 79, prin investr, 80-81; assoc ed, Sociol Methodology, 80-82; assoc mem, Dept Sociol, Univ Minn, 81- *Mem:* Am Sociol Asn; Am Statist Asn; Inst Math Statist; Royal Statist Soc; Sigma Xi. *Res:* Categorical data analysis; mathematical sociology; applied stochastic processes. *Mailing Add:* Dept Appl Statists Univ Minn 1994 Buford Ave St Paul MN 55108

WASSERMAN, WILLIAM JACK, b New York, NY, Apr 27, 25; m 59; c 2. ORGANIC POLYMER CHEMISTRY. *Educ:* Univ Calif, Los Angeles, BS, 47; Univ Southern Calif, MS, 50; Univ Wash, PhD(org chem), 54. *Prof Exp:* Asst prof chem, Humboldt State Col, 54-57; sr res chemist, Martin-Marietta Corp, Wash, 57-62 & Truesdail Labs, Los Angeles, Calif, 62-63; asst prof chem, San Jose State Col, 63-67; INSTR CHEM, SEATTLE CENT COMMUNITY COL, 67- *Concurrent Pos:* Dir, NSF Inst Polymer Chem for Col Teachers, San Jose State Col, 67; mem writing team, Am Chem Soc Chemtec Proj, 70-72. 70-72. *Mem:* Am Chem Soc. *Res:* Synthesis and evaluation of condensation polymers; emphasis on epoxies, polyesters, polyamides, polyurethanes; cross-linking agent synthesis and evaluation; aldol condensations with unsaturated ketones; furanoid ring-opening reactions. *Mailing Add:* Div of Sci & Math Seattle Cent Community Col Seattle WA 98122

WASSERMAN, WILLIAM JOHN, b Toronto, Ont, Feb 27, 47. CELL BIOLOGY, DEVELOPMENTAL BIOLOGY. *Educ:* Univ Toronto, BSc, 69, MSc, 72, PhD(biol), 76. *Prof Exp:* Fel, Purdue Univ, 76-80; ASST PROF BIOL, UNIV ROCHESTER, 80- *Concurrent Pos:* Prin investr, Univ Rochester, 81- *Mem:* AAAS; Am Soc Cell Biologists. *Res:* Determining the molecular mechanisms involved in controlling meiosis and mitosis, in oocytes and embryos. *Mailing Add:* Dept Biol Univ Rochester River Campus Rochester NY 14627

WASSERMANN, FELIX EMIL, b Bamberg, Ger, Aug 7, 24; US citizen; m 53; c 3. VIROLOGY, EPIDEMIOLOGY. *Educ:* Univ Wis, BS, 49, MS, 50; NY Univ, PhD(microbiol), 57. *Prof Exp:* Res assoc microbiol, Univ Chicago, 58; asst virol, Pub Health Res Inst City New York, Inc, 58-60, from asst to assoc epidemiol, 60-65; from asst prof to assoc prof, 65-77, actg chmn dept, 70-76, PROF VIROL, NY MED COL, 77- *Mem:* Am Soc Microbiol. *Res:* Virus-host cell interaction; viral genetics; epidemiology; biomedical ethics. *Mailing Add:* Dept of Microbiol NY Med Col Valhalla NY 10595

WASSERSUG, RICHARD JOEL, b Boston, Mass, Apr 13, 46. EVOLUTIONARY BIOLOGY. *Educ:* Tufts Univ, BS, 67; Univ Chicago, PhD(evolutionary biol), 73. *Prof Exp:* Asst prof syst & ecol & asst cur, Mus Natural Hist, Univ Kans, 73-74; asst prof anat & comt evolutionary biol, Univ Chicago, 74-81; ASSOC PROF ANAT, DALHOUSIE UNIV, 81- *Mem:* Soc Study Evolution; Am Soc Ichthyologists & Herpetologists; AAAS; Ecol Soc Am; Am Soc Zoologists. *Res:* Feeding adaptations of anuran larvae, or tadpoles, and of fish; studies on the evolution of complex life cycles and on the evolution of diversity. *Mailing Add:* Dept Anat Sir Charles Tupper Bldg Dalhousie Univ Halifax NS B3H 4H7 Can

WASSHAUSEN, DIETER CARL, b Jena, Ger, Apr 15, 38; US citizen; m 61; c 2. SYSTEMATIC BOTANY. *Educ:* George Washington Univ, BS, 63, MS, 66, PhD(bot), 72. *Prof Exp:* From asst cur to assoc cur dept bot, 69-76, CUR & CHMN DEPT BOT, MUS NATURAL HIST, SMITHSONIAN INST, 76- *Mem:* Int Asn Plant Taxon. *Res:* Taxonomy of Acanthaceae and flowering plants of Am Asn Plant Taxon; the New World tropics. *Mailing Add:* Dept of Bot Mus of Natural Hist Smithsonian Inst Washington DC 20560

WASSMUNDT, FREDERICK WILLIAM, b Oak Park, Ill, Aug 6, 32; div; c 1. ORGANIC CHEMISTRY. *Educ:* DePauw Univ, BA, 53; Univ Ill, PhD(chem), 56. *Prof Exp:* Instr chem, Univ Calif, 56-58; from instr to asst prof, 58-69, ASSOC PROF CHEM, UNIV CONN, 69- *Concurrent Pos:* Sabbatical leave, Univ Heidelberg, 66-67; invited lectr, Chemische Gesellschaft zu Heidelberg, 74. *Mem:* NY Acad Sci; Am Chem Soc; Royal Soc Chem. *Res:* Exploratory synthesis; reactions of organic nitrogen compounds; diazonium salts; bridged bicyclic compounds. *Mailing Add:* Dept of Chem Univ of Conn Storrs CT 06268

WASSOM, CLYDE E, b Osceola, Iowa, Feb, 6, 24; m 45; c 3. AGRONOMY. *Educ:* Iowa State Col, BS, 49, MS, 51, PhD(crop breeding), 53. *Prof Exp:* Technician agron, Iowa State Col, 47-51, res assoc, 51-54; asst prof, 54-62, assoc prof, 62-76, PROF KANS STATE UNIV, 76- *Concurrent Pos:* Temp staff mem, Int Ctr Improv Corn & Wheat, Mexico City, 67. *Mem:* Am Soc Agron. *Res:* Forage breeding; research and breeding for improvement of red clover and other legumes; corn breeding and genetics research. *Mailing Add:* Dept Agron Throckmorton Hall Kans State Univ Manhattan KS 66506

WASSON, JAMES A(LLEN), b Tyrone, Pa, July 5, 26; div; c 2. PETROLEUM ENGINEERING. *Educ:* Pa State Univ, BS, 51 & 52, MS, 57. *Prof Exp:* Jr petrol engr, Humble Oil & Refining Co, 56-58; asst prof petrol eng, La Polytech Inst, 58-60; asst prof, 60-69, assoc prof, 69-80, PROF PETROL ENG, COL MINERAL & ENERGY RESOURCES, WEST VA UNIV, 80-, CHMN DEPT, 77- *Concurrent Pos:* Staff res adv, US Dept Energy, WVa, 60- *Mem:* Am Inst Mining, Metall & Petrol Engrs; Am Meteorol Soc; Petrol Soc; Can Inst Mines; Am Soc Eng Educ. *Res:* Petroleum reservoir engineering; secondary recovery of oil; natural gas engineering. *Mailing Add:* Col Mineral & Energy Resources WVa Univ Morgantown WV 26506

WASSON, JOHN R, b St Louis, Mo, Aug 22, 41; m 63; c 2. PHYSICAL CHEMISTRY, INORGANIC CHEMISTRY. *Educ:* Univ Mo-Columbia, BS, 63, MA, 66; Ill Inst Technol, PhD(phys chem), 70. *Prof Exp:* Instr chem, Southern State Col, 65-66; asst prof chem, Univ Ky, 69-75; vis sr scientist, Univ NC, Chapel Hill, 75-78; dir, Chem Div, res dept, Lithium Corp Am, 78-81; PRES, KINGS MOUNTAIN SPECIALTIES, INC, 81- *Mem:* Am Chem Soc; Royal Soc Chem; Am Asn Textile Chemists & Colorists; Electrochem Soc. *Res:* Electron spin resonance; semi-empirical molecular orbital theory; change-transfer complexation; transition metal complexes; higher oxidation states of silver; polymers; electrolytes; lithium chemistry. *Mailing Add:* 3101 Gardner Park Dr Gastonia NC 28052

WASSON, JOHN TAYLOR, b Springtown, Ark, July 4, 34; m 60; c 2. COSMOCHEMISTRY, PLANETOLOGY. *Educ:* Univ Ark, BS, 55; Mass Inst Technol, PhD(nuclear chem), 58. *Prof Exp:* NSF fel tech physics lab, Munich Technol Univ, 58-59; res chemist geophys res directorate, Air Force Cambridge Res Labs, 59-63; NIH spec fel phys inst, Univ Berne, 63-64; from asst prof to assoc prof, 64-72, PROF, UNIV CALIF, LOS ANGELES, 72- *Concurrent Pos:* Guggenheim fel, Max Planck Inst Chem, 70-71. *Mem:* AAAS; Am Phys Soc; Am Geophys Union; Geochem Soc; Meteoritical Soc (pres, 79-80). *Res:* Compostition and origin of the meteorites; formation of lunar rocks and surface materials; geochemistry; solar nebula formation and evolution. *Mailing Add:* Inst Geophys & Univ of Calif Los Angeles CA 90024

WASSON, L(OERWOOD) C(HARLES), b Denning, Ark, Feb 27, 09; m 36; c 1. CORROSION SCIENCE, BIO-MEDICAL. *Educ:* Univ Ark, BSEE, 33. *Prof Exp:* Shop foreman, Hydraul Lab, Tenn Valley Authority, 35-36; develop engr, Milwaukee Gas Specialty Co, 36-42, prod engr, 42-46, res engr, 46-48; asst chief engr, Durant Mfg Co, 48-49; elec res engr, A O Smith Corp, 49-52, dir, Electrochem Lab, 52-60, mat engr, 60-65, res scientist, 65-74; PRES, L C WASSON CO, 74- *Mem:* Nat Asn Corrosion Engrs; Inst Elec & Electronics Engrs. *Res:* Cathodic protection theory and application; corrosion mechanisms and corrosion prevention techniques; electrochemistry of corrosion. *Mailing Add:* 8322 Avon Ct Wauwatosa WI 53213

WASSON, OREN A, b Wooster, Ohio, Mar 27, 35; m 59; c 2. NUCLEAR PHYSICS. *Educ:* Col Wooster, BA, 57; Yale Univ, MS, 59, PhD(physics), 64. *Prof Exp:* Res staff physicist, Yale Univ, 63-65; from res assoc physics to physicist, Brookhaven Nat Lab, 65-73; PHYSICIST, NAT BUR STAND, 73- *Concurrent Pos:* Vis mem, Oak Ridge Nat Lab, 71-72; tech expert, Int Atomic Energy Agency, Greece, 75. *Mem:* AAAS; Am Phys Soc; Sigma Xi. *Res:* Experimental nuclear physics; neutron and photon reaction mechanisms; heavy ion studies; computer programming; neutron cross sections and dosimetry. *Mailing Add:* Nat Bur Stand Washington DC 20234

WASSON, RICHARD LEE, b Farmington, Ill, May 19, 32; m 55; c 2. ORGANIC CHEMISTRY. *Educ:* Univ Ill, BS, 53; Mass Inst Technol, PhD, 56. *Prof Exp:* Asst org chem, Mass Inst Technol, 53-56; sr res chemist, 56-63, res specialist, 63-66, res group leader, 66-71, mgr flavor-fragrance res, 71-76, mgr commercial develop, 76-77, mgr new prod/process res, 77-78, mgr technol planning, 78-80, DIR TECHNOL SUPPORT, MONSANTO CO, 80- *Mem:* Am Chem Soc: Inst Food Technol; Am Inst Chem; NY Acad Sci. *Res:* Preparation and rearrangements of epoxides; halogenation and carboxylation of aromatic compounds; aromatic nitro compounds; basic condensations; organophosphate compounds; isolation and identification of natural products; food chemistry; organic analysis; environmental hazard assessment. *Mailing Add:* Monsanto Co 800 N Lindbergh St Louis MO 63166

WASSON, ROBERT GORDON, b Great Falls, Mont, Sept 22, 98; m 26; c 2. ETHNOMYCOLOGY. *Educ:* Columbia Univ, BLitt, 20. *Hon Degrees:* DSc, Univ Bridgeport, 74. *Prof Exp:* HON RES FEL ETHNOMYCOL, BOT MUS, HARVARD UNIV, 57- *Concurrent Pos:* Corresp, Nat Mus Natural Hist, Paris & hon researcher, NY Bot Garden, 57- *Honors & Awards:* Sarah Gildersleeve Fife Mem Award, NY Bot Garden, 58. *Mem:* Sigma Xi. *Res:* Every aspect of ethnomycology. *Mailing Add:* 42 Long Ridge Rd Danbury CT 06810

WASSON, W(ALTER) DANA, b NB, Can, Apr 2, 34; m 59. COMPUTER SCIENCE, ELECTRICAL ENGINEERING. *Educ:* Univ NB, BSc, 56; Mass Inst Technol, SM, 58; Univ Waterloo, PhD, 72. *Prof Exp:* From asst prof to assoc prof, 58-70, head comput sci dept, 69-74, PROF ELEC ENG, UNIV NB, FREDERICTON, 70-, DIR COMPUT CTR, 64-, DIR SCH COMPUT SCI, 74- *Mem:* Inst Elec & Electronics Engrs; Eng Inst Can; Asn Comput Mach; Can Info Processing Soc; Pattern Recognition Soc. *Res:* Computer hardware and software; pattern recognition and active circuit analysis. *Mailing Add:* Sch of Comput Sci PO Box 4400 Fredericton NB E3B 5A3 Can

WASTI, KHIZAR, b Jan 27, 48; m 76; c 1. TOXICOLOGY. *Educ:* Univ Punjab, Pakistan, BSc, 66; Univ Peshawar, MSc, 69; Marshall Univ, MS, 72; Univ Pa, PHD(chem), 76. *Prof Exp:* Sr lectr chem, Edwardes Col, Pakistan, 69-71; teaching asst, Marshall Univ, 71-72; teaching fel, Univ Pa, 73-75; res chemist, McNeil Labs, Fort Washington, Pa, 74, Campbell Soup Co, Camden, NJ, 74-75; proj mgr & sr info analyst, Toxicol Dept, Res Labs, Franklin Inst, 75-78; TOXICOLOGIST, VA STATE DEPT HEALTH, RICHMOND, 78- *Mem:* Am Col Toxicol; Am Chem Soc; Fel Am Inst Chemists; Royal Soc Chem; AAAS. *Mailing Add:* Bur Toxic Substances Info Va State Dept Health 109 Governor St Richmond VA 23219

WASYLISHEN, RODERICK ERNEST, b Elk Point, Alta, July 6, 44; m 68. CHEMISTRY. *Educ:* Univ Waterloo, BSc, 68; Univ Manitoba, MSc, 70, PhD(phys chem), 72. *Prof Exp:* Res fel, Nat Inst Health, Bethesda, Md, 72-74; asst prof, Univ Winnipeg, 74-79; assoc prof chem, Univ Winnipeg, 79-82; ASSOC PROF CHEM, DALHOUSIE UNIV, 82- *Mem:* Chem Inst Can; Am Chem Soc; Sigma Xi; Royal Soc Chem; Int Soc Magnetic Resonance. *Res:* Applications of nuclear magnetic resonance spectroscopy; molecular motion in liquids and orientationally disordered solids. *Mailing Add:* Dept Chem Univ Winnipeg Winnipeg MB R3B 2E9 Can

WASYLKIWSKYJ, WASYL, b Kowel, Ukraine, Feb 12, 35; US citizen; m 60; c 2. ELECTROMAGNETICS. *Educ:* City Col New York, BEE, 57; Polytech Inst Brooklyn, MS, 65, PhD(elec eng), 68. *Prof Exp:* Microwave component design engr, Missiltron Inc, NY, 59-60; Consult & Designers, NY, 60-62; sr tech specialist, ITT Defense Commun Div, Int Tel & Tel Corp, NJ, 62-69; MEM TECH STAFF, INST DEFENSE ANAL, 69- *Concurrent Pos:* Consult, ITT Fed Labs, NJ, 63-65; prof lectr, George Washington Univ, 70-; mem comns B & C, Int Union Radio Sci. *Honors & Awards:* Spec Commendation Award, Inst Elec & Electronics Engrs Antennas & Propagation Soc, 72. *Mem:* Inst Elec & Electronics Engrs. *Res:* Electromagnetic radiation and diffraction, guided wave and cavity theory; antenna theory, particularly antenna arrays; microwave technology, particularly parametric and solid state microwave devices. *Mailing Add:* Inst for Defense Anal 400 Army Navy Dr Arlington VA 22202

WASYLYK, JOHN STANLEY, b Passaic, NJ, Feb 15, 42; m 69; c 2. GLASS TECHNOLOGY, CERAMIC SCIENCE. *Educ:* Rutgers Univ, BS, BA, 64, PhD(ceramics sci), 70. *Prof Exp:* Pres & tech dir, Glass Container Indust Res Corp, 69-76; TECH DIR, AM GLASS RES INC, 76- *Mem:* Am Ceramic Soc; Am Soc Testing & Mat; Soc Glass Technol; Microbeam Anal Soc; Nat Inst Ceramic Engrs. *Res:* Glass technology; heat transfer during forming and relation to workability; glass microanalysis; lubricating coatings on glass surfaces; glass strength; glass fracture analysis. *Mailing Add:* Am Glass Res Inc PO Box 149 Butler PA 16001

WAT, BO YING, b Honolulu, Hawaii, Feb 15, 25; m 48; c 4. MEDICINE. *Educ:* Col Med Evangelists, MD, 49; Am Bd Path, dipl. *Prof Exp:* From asst to assoc prof, 58-62, PROF PATH, SCH MED, LOMA LINDA UNIV, 62- *Mem:* Am Soc Clin Pathologists; AMA. *Mailing Add:* Dept of Path Loma Linda Univ Sch of Med Loma Linda CA 92354

WAT, EDWARD KOON WAH, b Honolulu, Hawaii, Aug 27, 40; m 69; c 3. ORGANIC CHEMISTRY. *Educ:* Univ Hawaii, BA, 62; Stanford Univ, PhD(chem), 66. *Prof Exp:* NIH fel chem, Harvard Univ, 65-66; res chemist, Cent Res Dept, 66-77, RES CHEMIST, BIOCHEM DEPT, EXP STA, E I DU PONT DE NEMOURS & CO, INC, 77- *Mem:* Am Chem Soc. *Res:* Synthetic organic chemistry and process development for agricultural and pharmaceutical applications. *Mailing Add:* Biochem Dept E335 E I du Pont de Nemours & Co Inc Wilmington DE 19898

WATABE, NORIMITSU, b Kure City, Japan, Nov 29, 22; m 52; c 2. ELECTRON MICROSCOPY. *Educ:* Tohoku Univ, Japan, MS, 48, DSc(biocrystallog), 60. *Prof Exp:* Res investr biocrystallog pearl cult, Fuji Pearl Res Lab, Japan, 48-52; asst fac fisheries, Mie Prefectural Univ, Japan, 52-55, lectr, 55-59, consult, Fisheries Exp Sta, 53-59; res assoc calcification electron micros, Duke Univ, 57-70; assoc prof, 70-72, NAT INST DENT RES & NSF GRANTS, ELECTRON MICROS CTR, 71-, PROF BIOL & MARINE SCI, UNIV SC, 72-, DIR ELECTRON MICROS CTR, 70- *Concurrent Pos:* Asst, Tohoku Univ, Japan, 48-49; consult, Ford Found Off Latin Am & Caribbean, 68 & SC State Develop Bd, 75-; Russel res award, Univ SC, 80. *Mem:* AAAS; Electron Micros Soc Am; Am Soc Zool; Royal Micros Soc. *Res:* Microanatomy; ultrastructural and physiological aspects of mechanism of calcification in invertebrates, algae and fish. *Mailing Add:* 3510 Greenway Dr Columbia SC 29206

WATADA, ALLEY E, b Platteville, Colo, July 20, 30; m 56; c 2. HORTICULTURE, PLANT PHYSIOLOGY. *Educ:* Colo State Univ, BS, 52, MS, 53; Univ Calif, Davis, PhD(plant physiol), 65. *Prof Exp:* Lab technician, Univ Calif, Davis, 56-65; from asst prof to assoc prof hort, WVa Univ, 65-71; invests leader, 71-72, proj leader, 72-81, res food technologist, 71-81, CHIEF HORT CROPS QUAL LAB, HORT SCI INST, AGR RES SERV, USDA, 81- *Mem:* Am Soc Hort Sci; Am Soc Plant Physiol; Inst Food Technol; Am Inst Biol Sci. *Res:* Postharvest physiology of fruits and vegetables; evaluation of chemical composition and physical and sensory measurement of fruits and vegetables for developing nondestructive method of measuring quality and maturity. *Mailing Add:* ARMI Bldg 002 Rm 113 Sci & Educ Admin-Agr Res USDA Beltsville MD 20705

WATANABE, AKIRA, b Vancouver, BC, Sept 17, 35; m 57; c 5. COMMUNICATIONS SCIENCE. *Educ:* McMaster Univ, BSc, 57; Univ Toronto, MA, 62, PhD(molecular physics), 64. *Prof Exp:* Sci off, 57-69, RES SCIENTIST, DEPT COMMUN, DEFENCE RES TELECOMMUN ESTAB, 69- *Concurrent Pos:* Sci counr, Can Embassy, Tokyo, 76-79. *Mem:* Can Asn Physicists; Optical Soc Am. *Res:* Optical communications, thin-film waveguides and spectroscopy; laser physics. *Mailing Add:* 13 Lismer Circle Kanata ON K2K 1A1 Can

WATANABE, DANIEL SEISHI, b Honolulu, Hawaii, Oct 30, 40; m 66. COMPUTER SCIENCE. *Educ:* Harvard Univ, AB, 62, AM, 67, PhD(appl math), 70. *Prof Exp:* Mathematician, Baird-Atomic, Inc, 63-64; asst prof, 70-76, ASSOC PROF COMPUT SCI, UNIV ILL, URBANA, 76- *Concurrent Pos:* Vis scholar, Tokyo Univ, 79. *Mem:* Soc Indust & Appl Math. *Res:* Numerical software; simulation of semiconductor devices. *Mailing Add:* Dept of Comput Sci Univ of Ill Urbana IL 61801

WATANABE, HOWARD T, b Bear River, Utah, May 18, 20. NUCLEAR ENGINEERING, MECHANICAL ENGINEERING. *Educ:* Univ Utah, BS, 43. *Prof Exp:* Proj engr, Phillips Petrol Co, Idaho, 52-57, supvr hot cells, 57-58; supvr in-reactor eng, Aerojet Gen Corp, Calif, 58-63, supvr test planning, Nuclear Engine for Rocket Vehicle Applns, 63-69, supvr opers planning, Idaho Nuclear Corp, Idaho, 69-71, supvr opers planning, Aerojet Nuclear Corp, 71-72; prin engr, Nuclear Energy Bus Group, 72-80, PROG MGR, NUCLEAR ENERGY BUS OPER, GEN ELEC CO, SAN JOSE, CALIF, 80- *Mem:* Am Nuclear Soc. *Res:* Formulate test specifications for ground testing of NERVA nuclear rocket; design, fabrication, inpile testing and evaluation of nuclear fuel elements for small electrical power plant application; post irradiation examination of irradiated materials for radiation effects. *Mailing Add:* Gen Elec Co 175 Curtner Ave M/C 682 San Jose CA 95125

WATANABE, ITARU S, b Sapporo, Japan, June 20, 33; US citizen; m 59; c 3. NEUROPATHOLOGY. *Educ:* Keio Univ Sch Med, MD, 58, DMSc, 63. *Prof Exp:* Fel, Sch Med, Ind Univ, 64-69, asst prof, 69-72; assoc prof, Sch Med, Univ Kans, 72-77; UNIT DIR, PATH, VET ADMIN MED CTR, 72-; PROF PATH, SCH MED, UNIV KANS, 77- *Mem:* Am Asn Neuropathologists; Soc Neurosci; Int Congress Neuropath; Am Asn Pathologists; AMA. *Res:* Neuropathologic studies of various brain disorders, particularly their ultrastructural aspects. *Mailing Add:* Vets Admin Med Ctr 4801 Linwood Blvd Kansas City MO 64128

WATANABE, KYOICHI A, b Amagasaki, Japan, Feb 28, 35; m 62; c 6. ORGANIC CHEMISTRY, BIOCHEMISTRY. *Educ:* Hokkaido Univ, BA, 58, MA, 60, PhD(chem), 63. *Prof Exp:* Lectr chem, Sophia Univ, Japan, 63; res assoc, Sloan-Kettering Inst, 63-66; res fel, Univ Alta, 66-68; from asst to assoc mem, 68-80, MEM CHEM, SLOAN-KETTERING INST, 80-, PROF, SLOAN-KETTERING DIV, GRAD SCH MED SCI, CORNELL UNIV, 81- *Concurrent Pos:* Assoc prof, Sloan-Kettering Div, Grad Sch Med Sci, Cornell Univ, 72-80. *Mem:* Pharm Soc Japan; Am Chem Soc; Am Asn Cancer Res; Int Asn Heterocyclic Chem. *Res:* Structure, syntheses, reactions and stereochemistry of nitrogen heterocyclics, carbohydrates, nucleosides and antibiotics of potential biological activities; medicinal chemistry; antitumor and antiviral compounds. *Mailing Add:* Walker Lab Sloan-Kettering Inst 145 Boston Post Rd Rye NY 10580

WATANABE, MAMORU, b Vancouver, BC, Mar 15, 33. MEDICINE, BIOCHEMISTRY. *Educ:* McGill Univ, BSc, 55, MD, CM, 57, PhD, 63; FRCPS(C), 63. *Prof Exp:* Assoc molecular biol, Albert Einstein Col Med, 65-66, asst prof, 66-67; from assoc prof med & biochem to prof med, Univ Alta, 67-73; head div med, 74-76, assoc dean educ, 76-80, assoc dean res, 80-81, PROF MED, UNIV CALGARY, 73-, ACTG DEAN, 81- *Concurrent Pos:* Ayerst fel, Endocrine Soc, 63-64; res fel, Am Col Physicians, 64-67; dir dept med, Foothills Hosp, Calgary, Alta. *Mem:* Am Soc Microbiol; Can Med Asn. *Res:* Secretion rate of aldosterone in normal and abnormal pregnancy; replication of RNA bacteriophages; transport of steroids across cell membranes, using Pseudomonas testosteroni as a model system. *Mailing Add:* Dept of Med Univ of Calgary Calgary AB T2N 1N4 Can

WATANABE, MICHAEL SATOSI, b Tokyo, Japan, May 26, 10; m 37; c 1. THEORETICAL PHYSICS, INFORMATION SCIENCE. *Educ:* Univ Tokyo, BS, 33, DSc, 40; Univ Paris, DSc, 35. *Prof Exp:* Mem res staff, Inst Physics, Univ Leipzig, 37-39; assoc prof, Eng Sch, Univ Tokyo, 42-45; adv, Far East Command, Allied Powers, 46-47; prof physics & chmn physics dept, St Paul's Univ, 49-50; assoc prof, Wayne Univ, 50-52; prof, US Naval Postgrad Sch, 52-56; sr physicist, Res Ctr, Int Bus Mach Corp, NY, 56-64; prof eng & philos, Yale Univ, 64-66; prof, 66-76, EMER PROF PHYSICS & INFO SCI, UNIV HAWAII, 76- *Concurrent Pos:* Vis prof, Yale Univ, 59-60; adj prof, Columbia Univ, 60-61, univ panel mem, 65- *Mem:* Fel Am Phys Soc; fel Inst Elec & Electronics Engrs; Int Acad Philos Sci (vpres); Int Soc Study Time (pres, 69-73). *Res:* Quantum theory; statistical mechanics; information theory; philosophy of science; pattern recognition. *Mailing Add:* 242 Kaalawi Pl Honolulu HI 96816

WATANABE, PHILIP GLEN, b Inglewood, Calif, Mar 23, 47. TOXICOLOGY, PHARMACOLOGY. *Educ:* Univ Calif, BS, 69; Utah State Univ, PhD(toxicol), 74; Am Bd Toxicol, dipl, 80. *Prof Exp:* ASSOC SCIENTIST, TOXICOL LAB, HEALTH & ENVIRON RES, DOW CHEM CO, 74- *Concurrent Pos:* Vis lectr, Sch Pub Health, Univ Mich, 68-79; toxicol comt, Nat Acad Sci-Nat Res Coun, 78-82. *Honors & Awards:* F R Blood Award, Soc Toxicol, 78. *Mem:* Soc Toxicol; Int Soc Biochem Pharmacol; AAAS; Sigma Xi. *Res:* Molecular toxicology; interaction of chemicals with intracellular macromolecules to facilitate the assessment of hazards of chemical exposure. *Mailing Add:* Toxicol Bldg 1803 Midland MI 48640

WATANABE, RONALD S, BIOCHEMISTRY. *Educ:* Wash State Univ, BS, 47, Ms, 49; Univ Okla, PhD(chem), 62. *Prof Exp:* Assoc prof, 62-70, PROF CHEM, CALIF STATE UNIV, SAN JOSE, 70- *Mem:* AAAS; Am Chem Soc. *Res:* Enzymes. *Mailing Add:* Dept Chem Calif State Univ San Jose CA 95192

WATANABE, TOMIYA, b Koriyama, Japan, Aug 3, 27; m 59; c 2. AERONOMY, PLASMA PHYSICS. *Educ:* Tohoku Univ, Japan, BSc, 53, PhD(geophys), 61. *Prof Exp:* Res asst physics, Univ Md, 60-61; lectr, 61-63, from asst prof to assoc prof, 63-72, PROF GEOPHYS, UNIV BC, 72- *Concurrent Pos:* Mem, working group of magnetospheric field variations, comt IV, Int Asn Geomag & Aeronomy, 67-; vis assoc res physicist, Space Sci Lab, Univ Calif, Berkeley, 69; sr res fel, Nat Res Coun Can, 69-70, mem assoc comt space physics, 78-82. *Mem:* Am Geophys Union; Soc Terrestrial Magnetism & Elec Japan; Am Phys Soc; Can Asn Physicists. *Res:* Geomagnetism; generation and propagation of hydromagnetic waves in the terrestrial magnetosphere; electrostatic waves in the ionosphere. *Mailing Add:* Dept of Geophys & Astron Univ of BC Vancouver BC V6T 1N5 Can

WATANAKUNAKORN, CHATRCHAI, internal medicine, infectious diseases, see previous edition

WATENPAUGH, KEITH DONALD, b Amarillo, Tex, Sept 3, 39; m 63; c 3. PHYSICAL CHEMISTRY, BIOCHEMISTRY. *Educ:* Univ Idaho, BS, 62; Mont State Univ, PhD(chem), 67. *Prof Exp:* Sr fel, 66-69, res assoc, 69-72, asst prof, 72-78, ASSOC PROF BIOCHEM & MOLECULAR STRUCT, UNIV WASH, 78- *Mem:* Am Chem Soc; Am Crystallog Asn; AAAS. *Res:* Structure and mechanisms of electron transport proteins, protein-substrate interactions, and various metalloproteins; computer modelling of molecular structure and interactions. *Mailing Add:* Dept Biol Struct Univ Wash Seattle WA 98195

WATERBURY, GLENN RAYMOND, b Canon City, Colo, Oct 28, 20; m 53; c 2. ANALYTICAL CHEMISTRY. *Educ:* Colo Agr & Mech Col, BS, 44; Iowa State Col, PhD(phys chem), 52. *Prof Exp:* Mem staff anal chem, 46-48, 52-72, GROUP LEADER, LOS ALAMOS NAT LAB, 72- *Mem:* Am Chem Soc; fel Am Inst Chemists. *Res:* Special methods of analysis. *Mailing Add:* 1503 41st St Los Alamos NM 87544

WATERBURY, LOWELL DAVID, b Lansing, Mich, Jan 8, 42. PHARMACOLOGY. *Educ:* Univ Mich, BS, 64; Univ Vt, PhD(pharmacol), 68. *Prof Exp:* Technician, Univ Mich, 62-64, asst lab instr bot, 62; from instr to asst prof biochem, Inst Lipid Res, Col Med, Baylor Univ, 67-69; asst prof pharmacol, Bowman Gray Sch Med, Wake Forest Univ, 69-74; staff researcher, 74-80, SR STAFF RESEARCHER, DEPT EXP PHARMACOL, SYNTEX RES, 80- *Mem:* AAAS; Am Soc Pharmacol & Exp Therapeut; Am Chem Soc; Am Fedn Clin Res; Asn Res Vision & Ophthal. *Res:* Biochemical pharmacology; ocular pharmacology; drugs affecting diabetic retinopathy, cataracts, and ocular inflammation; drugs affecting gastric mucus production and plasma renin activity; determination of mechanism of action of newly synthesized therapeutic agents. *Mailing Add:* Dept Exp Pharmacol Syntex Res 3401 Hillview Ave Palo Alto CA 95014

WATERHOUSE, HOWARD N, b Bethel, Maine, Apr 19, 32. ANIMAL NUTRITION. *Educ:* Univ Maine, BS, 54; Univ Ill, Urbana, MS, 58, PhD(animal sci), 60. *Prof Exp:* Group leader animal nutrit, Gen Mills, Inc, 60-62, proj leader, 62-67; mgr poultry nutrit res & tech serv, Allied Mills Inc, 67-70; dir nutrit & res, Robin Hood Multifoods Ltd, Can, 70-74; sr poultry scientist, Cent Soya, Inc, Decatur, Ind, 74-78; DIR NUTRIT, BELL GRAIN & MILLING, 78- *Mem:* Poultry Sci Asn. *Res:* Amino acid studies with chicks; dog and cat management and nutrition; applied animal husbandry; poultry nutrition; sales and dealer training; egg quality studies. *Mailing Add:* 2837 Sandberg St Riverside CA 92506

WATERHOUSE, JOHN P, b Kent, Eng, Dec 4, 20; m 44; c 3. PATHOLOGY, HISTOLOGY. *Educ:* Univ London, MB, BS, 51, BDS, 56, MD, 63. *Prof Exp:* From jr lectr to sr lectr dent path, London Hosp Med Col, Univ London, 56-66, univ reader oral path, 66-67; actg head dept histol, Col Dent, 68-69, PROF ORAL PATH & HEAD DEPT, COL DENT, UNIV ILL MED CTR, 67-, PROF PATH, COL MED, 68- *Honors & Awards:* Robert Caldwell mem lectr, Univ Glasgow, Scotland, 76. *Mem:* Am Acad Oral Pathologists; Brit Soc Periodont (hon ed, 64, hon secy, 66); Int Asn Dent Res (asst secy-treas, 73-). *Res:* Electron microscopy; cytochemistry; lysosomes; stereology; normal and damaged oral mucosa. *Mailing Add:* Dept of Oral Path Univ of Ill at the Med Ctr Chicago IL 60612

WATERHOUSE, JOSEPH STALLARD, b Toronto, Ont, Apr 28, 29; m 54; c 3. HUMAN ANATOMY, HUMAN PHYSIOLOGY. *Educ:* Univ Guelph, BSc, 54; Wash State Univ, MSc, 57, PhD(entom), 62. *Prof Exp:* Aide entom & zool, Wash State Univ, 54-60; asst prof biol, State Univ NY Col Arts & Sci Plattsburgh, 60-64; Ford of Can res fel zool, Carleton Univ, 64-65; assoc prof biol, 65-72, chmn dept biol sci, 74-75, PROF BIOL, STATE UNIV NY COL PLATTSBURGH, 72- *Mem:* AAAS; Am Inst Biol Sci; Entom Soc Am; Entom Soc Can. *Res:* Biology of the garden symphylan, Scutigerella immaculata; ecology and taxonomy of the carabidae (ground beetles) in upper New York state; incidence of hypertension in upper New York State; entomology. *Mailing Add:* Dept of Biol Sci State Univ of NY Col Plattsburgh NY 12901

WATERHOUSE, KEITH R, b Derby, Eng, May 10, 29; US citizen; m 55; c 5. UROLOGY, SURGERY. *Educ:* Cambridge Univ, BA, 50, MA, 57; Oxford Univ, MB & BChir, 53. *Prof Exp:* Instr urol, Kings County Hosp Ctr, 59-61; from asst prof to assoc prof, 61-65, PROF UROL SURG, STATE UNIV NY DOWNSTATE MED CTR, 65- *Concurrent Pos:* Consult, Vet Admin Hosp, Brooklyn, NY, St Mary's Hosp, Passaic, NJ & Paterson Gen Hosp, 65-, Samaritan Hosp, Brooklyn, NY, 66- & St Charles Hosp, Port Jefferson, St Francis Hosp, Poughkeepsie, Arden Hill Hosp, Goshen & Brookhaven Mem Hosp, Patchogue, 67- *Mem:* Am Urol Asn; Am Col Surgeons; Am Acad Pediat; Am Fertil Soc; Int Soc Urol. *Res:* Investigation, diagnosis and treatment of congenital anomalies of the urinary tract in children and the subsequent treatment of these patients when they develop chronic renal failure. *Mailing Add:* Dept of Urol State Univ NY Downstate Med Ctr Brooklyn NY 11203

WATERHOUSE, RICHARD (VALENTINE), b Eng, Feb 28, 24; nat US; m 51; c 4. PHYSICS. *Educ:* Oxford Univ, MA, 49; Cath Univ, PhD, 59. *Prof Exp:* Res physicist, Royal Navy Torpedo Exp Estab, Scotland, 44-46, Paint Res Asn, London, 46-49 & Nat Bur Stand, 51-59; PROF PHYSICS, AM UNIV, 61- *Concurrent Pos:* Vis prof, Univ Calif, Berkeley, 69-70 & Univ Delft, Neth, 75-76; consult, US Navy. *Mem:* Fel Acoust Soc Am. *Res:* Waves and vibrations; theoretical physics; acoustics. *Mailing Add:* Dept of Physics Am Univ Washington DC 20016

WATERHOUSE, WILLIAM CHARLES, b Galveston, Tex, Dec 31, 41; m 80. MATHEMATICS. *Educ:* Harvard Univ, AB, 63, AM, 64, PhD(math), 68. *Prof Exp:* Res assoc math, Off Naval Res & Cornell Univ, 68-69; asst prof, Cornell Univ, 69-75; assoc prof, 75-80, PROF MATH, PA STATE UNIV, UNIVERSITY PARK, 80- *Mem:* Am Math Soc; Math Asn Am. *Res:* Algebraic number theory; algebraic geomtry, especially group schemes; history of mathematics. *Mailing Add:* Dept of Math Pa State Univ University Park PA 16802

WATERLAND, LARRY R, b St Louis, Mo, Aug 11, 48; m 70; c 2. ENVIRONMENTAL SCIENCES. *Educ:* Calif Inst Technol, BS, 70; Stanford Univ, MS, 72, PhD(chem eng), 75. *Prof Exp:* Staff engr, 75-78, sect leader, 78-79, PROJ MGR, ACUREX CORP, 79- *Mem:* Am Inst Chem Engrs; Air Pollution Control Asn; Combustion Inst. *Res:* Technologies for the control of combustion source air pollutant emissions, with emphasis on the formation and control of the oxides of nitrogen and potential organic and inorganic hazardous air pollutants. *Mailing Add:* 485 Clyde Ave Mountain View CA 94042

WATERMAN, ALAN T(OWER), JR, b Northampton, Mass, July 8, 18; m 46; c 4. ELECTRICAL ENGINEERING. *Educ:* Princeton Univ, BA, 39; Calif Inst Technol, BS, 40; Harvard Univ, MA, 49, PhD(eng sci, appl physics), 52. *Prof Exp:* Meteorologist, Am Airlines, 40-41; instr, Univ Minn, 41-42; res assoc, Calif Inst Technol, 42-45; res scientist, Columbia Univ, 45; chief meteorologist, Univ Tex, 45-46; asst, Harvard Univ, 46-52; res assoc, 52-57, assoc prof, 58-65, PROF ELEC ENG, STANFORD UNIV, 65- *Concurrent Pos:* Consult, Weapons Systs Eval Group, US Dept Defense, 56-61, Nat Security Agency, 58-68, Stanford Res Inst, 58-, Inst Sci & Technol, Univ Mich, 58-61, Missile Systs Div, Lockheed Aircraft Corp, 58-59, Sylvania Elec Prods Co, Inc, 58-59 & Norair Res Coun, 63-68; chmn comn II, Int Sci Radio Union, 61-64; secy, US Nat Comt, 64-67, vchmn, 67-69, chmn, 69-72. *Mem:* Am Meteorol Soc; fel Inst Elec & Electronics Engrs. *Res:* Radio wave and optical propagation; physics of the atmosphere. *Mailing Add:* Radio Sci Lab Stanford Univ Stanford CA 94305

WATERMAN, DANIEL, b New York, NY, Oct 24, 27; m 60; c 3. MATHEMATICS. *Educ:* Brooklyn Col, BA, 47; Johns Hopkins Univ, MA, 48; Univ Chicago, PhD, 54. *Prof Exp:* Res assoc, Cowles Comn Res in Econ, 51-52; Fulbright fel, Univ Vienna, 52-53; from instr to asst prof math, Purdue Univ, 53-59; asst prof, Univ Wis-Milwaukee, 59-61; prof, Wayne State Univ, 61-69; PROF MATH, SYRACUSE UNIV, 69- *Mem:* Am Math Soc; Math Asn Am. *Res:* Fourier analysis; real variables; functional analysis; orthogonal series. *Mailing Add:* Dept of Math Syracuse Univ Syracuse NY 13210

WATERMAN, FRANK MELVIN, b Delhi, NY, Nov 3, 38; m 61; c 4. MEDICAL PHYSICS. *Educ:* Hartwick Col, BA, 60; Clarkson Technol Col, MS, 69, PhD(physics), 73. *Prof Exp:* Res assoc nuclear physics, Kent State Univ, 72-75; RES ASSOC & ASST PROF, MED PHYSICS, DEPT RADIOL, UNIV CHICAGO, 75- *Mem:* Am Phys Soc; Am Asn Physicists Med. *Res:* Applications of neutron physics to biology and medicine; neutron dosimetry; nuclear instrumentation. *Mailing Add:* Dept of Radiol Univ of Chicago Chicago IL 60637

WATERMAN, MICHAEL ROBERTS, b Tacoma, Wash, Nov 23, 39; m 66; c 2. MOLECULAR BIOLOGY, PROTEIN CHEMISTRY. *Educ:* Willamette Univ, BA, 61; Univ Ore, PhD(biochem), 69. *Prof Exp:* Fel biochem, Johnson Res Found, Sch Med, Univ Pa, 68-70; asst prof, 70-75, ASSOC PROF BIOCHEM, HEALTH SCI CTR, UNIV TEX, 75- *Mem:* Am Chem Soc; Am Soc Biol Chem; Am Soc Hemat. *Res:* Synthesis of cytochrome P-450; regulation of steroidogenesis in the adrenal cortex; hemoglobin structure and function relationship. *Mailing Add:* Dept of Biochem Univ Tex Health Sci Ctr Dallas TX 75235

WATERMAN, MICHAEL S, b Coquille, Ore, June 28, 42; m 62; c 1. MATHEMATICS, STATISTICS. *Educ:* Ore State Univ, BS, 64, MS, 66; Mich State Univ, MA, 68, PhD(probability, statist), 69. *Prof Exp:* Teaching asst math, Ore State Univ, 64-66; from asst prof to assoc prof, Idaho State Univ, 69-75, NSF res grant, 71-73; STAFF MEM, LOS ALAMOS SCI LAB, 75- *Concurrent Pos:* Vis prof, Univ Hawaii, 79-80 & Med Sch, Univ Calif, San Francisco, 82. *Mem:* Am Statist Asn; AAAS; Math Asn Am; Inst Math Statist. *Res:* Ergodic theory; probabilistic and computational number theory; mathematical biology; combinations and finite mathematics. *Mailing Add:* Statics Group Los Alamos Sci Lab Los Alamos NM 87545

WATERMAN, TALBOT HOWE, b East Orange, NJ, July 3, 14. COMPARATIVE PHYSIOLOGY. *Educ:* Harvard Univ, AB, 36, MA, 38, PhD(zool), 43; Yale Univ, MA Privatim, 58. *Prof Exp:* Jr fel, Harvard Univ Soc of Fels, 38-40, res assoc, Psychoacoustic Lab, Off Sci Res & Develop, Harvard Univ, 41-43; staff mem, Radiation Lab, Mass Inst Technol, 43-45; sci consult, Off Sci Res & Develop, Off Field Serv, US Navy Dept & US Army Air Force, 45; secy comt res, Sigma Xi, 46; instr biol, 46-47, from asst prof to prof zool, 47-58, PROF ZOOL, YALE UNIV, 58- *Concurrent Pos:* Exec fel, Trumbull Col, 46-56; instr invert zool, Marine Biol Lab, Woods Hole, 47-52, mem corp, 48-; secy corp, Bermuda Biol Sta, 51-61, trustee, 62-75 & 76-80; mem Am Inst Biol Sci Adv Comt Hydrobiol, Off Naval Res, 59-65; Guggenheim fel, 62-63; Sigma Xi nat lectr, 64-65; vis prof, Sch Med, Keio Univ, Japan, 68; assoc ed, J Exp Zool, 71-75; vis prof, Japan Soc Promotion Sci, 74; vis lectr & investr, Woods Hole Oceanog Inst, 76-; vis prof, Sophia Univ, Japan, 77-78 & 80. *Mem:* AAAS; Soc Gen Physiol; Marine Biol Asn UK; Am Physiol Soc; Am Soc Zool. *Res:* Visual physiology and spatial orientation; deepsea plankton and vertical migrations; compound eye fine structure and information processing; photoreceptor membrane turnover in compound eyes; polarized light behavior in the sea. *Mailing Add:* Dept of Biol 610 Kline Biol Tower Yale Univ New Haven CT 06520

WATERMEIER, LELAND A, b Carlinville, Ill, Dec 27, 27; m 50; c 4. PHYSICAL CHEMISTRY, PHYSICS. *Educ:* Blackburn Col, BA, 50; Univ Del, MS, 55; Univ London, DIC, 65. *Prof Exp:* Res chemist, 51-56, supvry aero-fuels res chemist, 56-60, supvry res chemist, 60-66, asst to tech dir weapons technol, 66-68, chief interior ballistics lab, 68-77, chief, Propulsion Div, 77-80, CHIEF INTERIOR BALLISTICS, US ARMY BALLISTICS RES LABS, 80- *Concurrent Pos:* Army mem tech steering comt, Propulsion Comt, 76- Propulsion Group, 62-67. *Mem:* Combustion Inst; Am Defense Preparedness Asn. *Res:* Stable and unstable combustion mechanisms in solid and liquid propellants; weapons technology, including large and small caliber weapons; complete interior ballistics and propulsion cycle of all caliber of weapons. *Mailing Add:* Interior Ballistics US Army Ballistics Res Lab Aberdeen Proving Ground MD 21005

WATERS, AARON CLEMENT, b Waterville, Wash, May 6, 05; m 40; c 2. GEOLOGY. *Educ:* Univ Wash, Seattle, BSc, 26, MSc, 27; Yale Univ, PhD(geol), 30. *Prof Exp:* Instr geol, Yale Univ, 28-30; from asst prof to prof, Stanford Univ, 30-38; prof, Johns Hopkins Univ, 38-63 & Univ Calif, Santa Barbara, 63-67; prof, 67-72, EMER PROF GEOL, UNIV CALIF, SANTA CRUZ, 72-; STAFF GEOLOGIST, EARTH & SPACE SCI DIV, LOS ALAMOS NAT LAB, 80- *Concurrent Pos:* Geologist, US Geol Surv, 30, 42-45 & 52-78; Guggenheim fel, 37-38; bicentennial lectr, Columbia Univ, 54; S F Emmons lectr, 58; NSF sr fel, 60; Condon lectr, 66; vis prof, Ore State Univ, 74 & Univ Tex, El Paso, 73, 78 & 79; distinguished vis prof, Calif State Univ, Los Angeles, 78. *Mem:* Nat Acad Sci; Geol Soc Am; Am Acad Arts & Sci. *Res:* Petrology; field geology; geology of the United States Pacific Northwest. *Mailing Add:* Mail Stop 570 Los Alamos Nat Lab Los Alamos NM 87544

WATERS, DEAN ALLISON, b Jersey City, NJ, May 2, 36; c 3. ENGINEERING, MATERIALS SCIENCE. *Educ:* Yale Univ, BE, 57, BS, 58; NC State Univ, MS, 60. *Prof Exp:* Dept head, 67-75, prog mgr, 75-77, DEP DIV DIR, NUCLEAR DIV, UNION CARBIDE CORP, 77- *Honors & Awards:* E O Lawrence Award, Dept of Energy, 78. *Mem:* Nat Soc Prof Engrs. *Res:* Materials, applied mechanics, stress analysis, vibration, machine dynamics, and systems engineering. *Mailing Add:* Nuclear Div Union Carbide Corp PO Box P Oak Ridge TN 37830

WATERS, DONALD HILTON, b Palm Beach, Fla, Dec 31, 43; m 67; c 2. NEUROPHARMACOLOGY. *Educ:* Philadelphia Col Pharm & Sci, BS, 67; Cornell Univ, PhD(pharmacol), 73. *Prof Exp:* Instr pharmacol, Mt Sinai Sch Med, 72-73, assoc, 73-74; ASST PROF BIOCHEM PHARMACOL, STATE UNIV NY BUFFALO, 74- *Mem:* AAAS; NY Acad Sci. *Res:* Drug abuse; physical dependence; barbiturates; ethanol dependence; neuromuscular pharmacology. *Mailing Add:* Dept of Biochem Pharmacol State Univ of NY Sch of Pharm Buffalo NY 14260

WATERS, IRVING WADE, b Baldwyn, Miss, June 19, 31; m 54; c 2. PHARMACOLOGY. *Educ:* Delta State Col, BS, 58; Auburn Univ, MS, 60; Univ Fla, PhD(pharmacol), 63. *Prof Exp:* From asst prof to assoc prof, 66-74, PROF PHARMACOL, UNIV MISS, 74- *Mem:* Am Soc Pharmacol & Exp Therapeut. *Res:* Drug metabolism; toxicology. *Mailing Add:* Dept Pharmacol Univ Miss Sch Pharm University MS 38677

WATERS, JAMES AUGUSTUS, b Postville, Iowa, June 23, 31; m 57; c 4. ORGANIC CHEMISTRY. *Educ:* Univ Iowa, BS, 53, PhD(pharmaceut chem), 59; Purdue Univ, MS, 57. *Prof Exp:* Res assoc org chem, Univ Mich, 59-60; RES CHEMIST, NAT INST ARTHRITIS, METAB & DIGESTIVE DIS, 60- *Mem:* Am Chem Soc. *Res:* Structure elucidation of natural products; steroid biosynthesis; medicinal chemistry; photochemistry; electrolytic oxidations; synthesis of nucleosides and polynucleotides as anti-tumor and interferon-inducing agents. *Mailing Add:* Lab of Chem Metab & Digestive Dis Bethesda MD 20014

WATERS, JAMES FREDERICK, b Oak Park, Ill, Mar 17, 38; m 65. VERTEBRATE ANATOMY. *Educ:* Stanford Univ, BA, 59; Univ Wash, PhD(zool), 69. *Prof Exp:* From asst prof to assoc prof, 66-75, PROF ZOOL, HUMBOLDT STATE UNIV, 75- *Mem:* Am Soc Ichthyologists & Herpetologists; Soc Study Evolution; Soc Vert Paleont; Am Soc Zoologists. *Res:* Functional locomotor anatomy of lizards and snakes. *Mailing Add:* Dept of Biol Humboldt State Univ Arcata CA 95221

WATERS, JOHN ALBERT, b Norwich, Eng, Nov 7, 35; c 4. PHYSICAL ORGANIC CHEMISTRY, CATALYSIS. *Educ:* Univ London, BS, 57; Leicester Univ, PhD(org chem), 60. *Prof Exp:* Sr res chemist, Monsanto, 63-75; res specialist, 75-78, RES ASSOC CHEM, MERICHEM CO, 78- *Mem:* Am Chem Soc; fel Am Inst Chemists; Catalyst Soc. *Res:* Organometallics; organic reactions. *Mailing Add:* Merichem Res Ctr 1503 Central Ave Houston TX 77012

WATERS, JOSEPH HEMENWAY, b Brockton, Mass, Dec 23, 30. VERTEBRATE ZOOLOGY. *Educ:* Univ Mich, BS, 54, MS, 55; Univ Conn, PhD(zool), 60. *Prof Exp:* Instr biol, Mass State Col Bridgewater, 59-61, Duke Univ, 62-63, Univ RI, 63-64 & Roanoke Col, 64-65; instr, 65-81, ASST PROF BIOL, VILLANOVA UNIV, 81- *Mem:* Fel AAAS; Am Soc Mammal; Am Soc Ichthyologists & Herpetologists; Sigma Xi. *Res:* Ecology and systematics of vertebrates in eastern North America. *Mailing Add:* Dept of Biol Villanova Univ Villanova PA 19085

WATERS, KENNETH LEE, b Monroe, Va, Jan 24, 14; m 39. PHARMACY, MEDICINAL CHEMISTRY. *Educ:* Lynchburg Col, AB, 35; Univ Ga, MS, 37; Univ Md, PhD(pharmaceut chem), 45. *Prof Exp:* Instr chem, Transylvania Col, 36-37 & Univ Ga, 37-39; from jr chemist to asst chemist, US Food & Drug Admin, Md, 39-43; fel, Mellon Inst, 43-47; tech dir, Zemmer Co, 47-48; dean, 48-77, EMER DEAN SCH PHARM, UNIV GA, 77- *Concurrent Pos:* Lectr, Sch Pharm, Univ Pittsburgh, 45-47. *Mem:* AAAS; Am Chem Soc; Am Pharmaceut Asn. *Res:* Drug standardization; preparation of alpha-akloximino acids and their derivatives. *Mailing Add:* Sch of Pharm Univ of Ga Athens GA 30606

WATERS, LARRY CHARLES, b Glenville, Ga, July 1, 39; m 60; c 1. BIOCHEMISTRY. *Educ:* Valdosta State Col, BS, 61; Univ Ga, MS, 64, PhD(biochem), 65. *Prof Exp:* Am Cancer Soc fel biochem res, 65-67, STAFF BIOCHEMIST, BIOL DIV, OAK RIDGE NAT LAB, 67- *Concurrent Pos:* Lectr, Univ Tenn, Knoxville. *Mem:* Am Soc Biol Chemists. *Res:* Chemistry and biochemistry of nucleic acids; molecular mechanisms of mutagenesis including metabolic activation of mutagens and repair of DNA; viral carcinogenesis. *Mailing Add:* Biol Div Oak Ridge Nat Lab PO Box Y Oak Ridge TN 37830

WATERS, MELVIN EUGENE, b Screven Co, Ga, Apr 7, 28; m 53; c 2. FOOD SCIENCE. *Educ:* Univ Ga, BS, 57, MS, 67. *Prof Exp:* Food technologist, SeaPak Corp, Ga, 57-59; res food technologist, Bur Com Fisheries, US Dept Interior, 59-70; RES FOOD TECHNOLOGIST, US DEPT COM, NAT MARINE FISHERIES SERV, NAT OCEANIC & ATMOSPHERIC ADMIN, 70- *Honors & Awards:* Spec Serv Award, US Dept Com, 71; Serv to Indust Award, Am Shrimp Canners Asn, 70; Spec Act Award, US Dept Interior, 69. *Mem:* Inst Food Technologists; Atlantic Fisheries Technol Conf; Tropical & Subtropical Fisheries Technol Conf. *Res:* Fishery research; chemistry, microbiological and process technology; product quality improvements and storage stability; processing systems; consumer acceptance of new products. *Mailing Add:* US Dept Com NOAA PO Box 12607 Charleston SC 29412

WATERS, MICHAEL DEE, b Charlotte, NC, Apr 17, 42; m 64; c 2. GENETIC TOXICOLOGY, BIOCHEMISTRY. *Educ:* Davidson Col, BS, 64; Univ NC, Chapel Hill, PhD(biochem), 69. *Prof Exp:* Lab chief biochem, Biophys Lab, Edgewood Arsenal, Md, 69-71; unit chief cellular physiol, Cellular Biol Sect, 71-72, sect chief cellular physiol, Pathobiol Res Br, 72-75, chief cellular biochem sect, Biomed Res Br, 75-76, chief, Biochem Br, 76-79, coordr genetic toxicol prog, 78-79, DIR, GENETIC TOXICOL DIV, ENVIRON RES CTR, ENVIRON PROTECTION AGENCY, 79- *Concurrent Pos:* Clin instr, George Washington Univ, 71-72; adj prof, Univ NC, Chapel Hill, 80-83. *Honors & Awards:* Bronze Medal, Environ Protection Agency, 80. *Mem:* NY Acad Sci; Am Chem Soc; Tissue Cult Asn; Sigma Xi; Environ Mutagen Soc. *Res:* Microbial, mammalian cell, organ culture and whole animal systems for studies of genetic, biochemical and physiological effects of environmental pollutants. *Mailing Add:* Genetic Toxicol Div Environ Protection Agency Research Triangle Park NC 27711

WATERS, NORMAN DALE, b Twin Falls, Idaho, May 1, 22; m 54; c 2. ENTOMOLOGY. *Educ:* Univ Calif, Berkeley, BS, 49, PhD, 55. *Prof Exp:* Mem staff for parasite introd, India, Pakistan, Nepal & Afghanistan, USDA, 49-51; entomologist, Cashewnut Improv Comn, India, 52-53; pest control supvr citrus, Limonera Co, Calif, 55-57; ENTOMOLOGIST, EXP STA, UNIV IDAHO, 57-, ASSOC RES PROF ENTOM, 70- *Mem:* Entom Soc Am; Int Orgn Biol Control. *Res:* Biological control; legume forage insects; pollinating insects. *Mailing Add:* Exp Sta Univ of Idaho Parma ID 83660

WATERS, ROLLAND MAYDEN, b Tucson, Ariz, Apr 7, 26; m 59; c 3. ORGANIC CHEMISTRY. *Educ:* Univ Ark, BS, 48; Yale Univ, PhD(org chem), 54. *Prof Exp:* Sr res chemist gen org chem, Dow Chem Co, 53-63; RES CHEMIST PHEROMONES, USDA, 63- *Concurrent Pos:* Lectr chem, Univ Md-Univ Col, 72- *Mem:* Am Chem Soc; AAAS. *Res:* Isolation, structure elucidation, and synthesis of chemicals affecting the behavior of insects; the goal is alternative methods of controlling insects to reduce our use of pesticides. *Mailing Add:* Rm 305 Bldg 306 BARC-E USDA Beltsville MD 20705

WATERS, THOMAS FRANK, b Hastings, Mich, May 17, 26; m 53; c 3. AQUATIC ECOLOGY, FISHERIES. *Educ:* Mich State Univ, BS, 52, MS, 53, PhD(fishery biol), 56. *Prof Exp:* Supvr, Pigeon River Trout Res Sta, Mich Dept Conserv, 56-57; from asst prof to assoc prof, 58-68, PROF FISHERY BIOL, UNIV MINN, ST PAUL, 68- *Mem:* Am Fisheries Soc; Ecol Soc Am; Am Inst Fishery Res Biol; NAm Benthological Soc (pres, 75). *Res:* Limnology; ecology of aquatic invertebrates and stream fish populations. *Mailing Add:* Dept Entom Fisheries & Wildlife Univ Minn St Paul MN 55108

WATERS, WILLIAM E, b Springfield, Mass, July 2, 22; m 43, 76; c 4. FOREST ENTOMOLOGY. *Educ:* State Univ NY Col Forestry, Syracuse, BS, 48; Duke Univ, MF, 49; Yale Univ, PhD, 58. *Prof Exp:* Entomologist, Bur Entom & Plant Quarantine, USDA, 49-53, entomologist, Forest Serv, 53-59, chief div forest insect res, 59-63, div forest insect & dis res, 63-65, asst dir insects & dis, 65-66, chief forest insect & dis lab & prin ecologist, Northeastern Forest Exp Sta, Conn, 66-68, chief forest insect res, Div Forest Insect & Dis Res, 68-73, chief scientist, Pac Southwest Forest & Range Exp Sta, 73-75; dean, Col Natural Resources, 75-77, PROF FORESTRY & ENTOM, UNIV CALIF, BERKELEY, 77- *Concurrent Pos:* Instr, Quinnipiac Col, 61-64; lectr, Yale Univ, 64-68; mem pop dynamics working party & chmn impact of destructive agents proj group, Int Union Forest Res Orgn; chmn working party on forest insects & dis, Food & Agr Orgn-NAm Forestry Comn; assoc dir, Calif Agr Res Sta, Univ Calif, Berkeley, 75-77; mem fed comn wood protection, Nat Acad Sci-Nat Res Coun. *Mem:* Entom Soc Am; Soc Am Foresters; Sigma Xi. *Res:* Forest insect ecology; population dynamics; biometrics; insect genetics and behavior; forest pest management. *Mailing Add:* Col of Natural Resources Univ of Calif Berkeley CA 94720

WATERS, WILLIAM EDWARD, b Lexington, Ky, July 16, 23; m 47; c 3. PHYSICS. *Educ:* Univ Ky, BS, 47, MS, 49; Univ Md, PhD(physics), 57. *Prof Exp:* Electronics scientist, Diamond Ord Fuse Labs, Washington, DC, 48-56, res supvr microwave tubes, 56-60; sr engr, Microwave Electronics Corp, 60-65, sr engr, Varian Assocs, 65-66; dir res & develop, Phys Electronics Labs, 66-67; prin engr, Ford-Aerospace Corp, Eng Serv Div, Palo Alto, 67-80. *Concurrent Pos:* Secy Army study & res fel, Stanford Univ, 58-59. *Res:* Microwave electron tubes, particularly oscillators; electron optics, including electron guns, beams and focusing systems; low noise microwave solid-state amplifiers and solid-state oscillators; satellite communications receiving and transmitting equipment. *Mailing Add:* 825 La Crosse St Sunnyvale CA 94087

WATERS, WILLIAM F, b Dayton, Ohio, Apr 25, 43. PSYCHOLOGY, PSYCHOPHYSIOLOGY. *Educ:* Tulane Univ, AB, 64; Case Western Reserve Univ, MS, 66, PhD(psychol), 69, Am Bd Prof Psychol, dipl, 73. *Prof Exp:* Assoc prof med psychol, Dept Phychiat, Univ Mo-Columbia, 68-79, assoc prof psychol, Dept Psychol, 78-79; PROF & DIR CLINC TRAINING, DEPT PSYCHOL, LA STATE UNIV, 79- *Concurrent Pos:* Dir psychol serv, Mid-Mo Mental Health Ctr, 68-74. *Mem:* Am Psychol Asn; Soc Psychophysiol Res. *Res:* Psychophysiology of selective attention, emotion, habituation. *Mailing Add:* Dept Psychol Audubon Hall La State Univ Baton Rouge LA 70803

WATERS, WILLIAM LINCOLN, b Columbus, Ohio, Nov 7, 38; div; c 2. ORGANIC CHEMISTRY, ORGANOMETALLIC CHEMISTRY. *Educ:* Kenyon Col, BA, 61; Univ Hawaii, PhD(org chem), 66. *Prof Exp:* Instr & res fel chem, Univ Calif, Irvine, 66-68; from asst prof to assoc prof chem, Univ Mont, 68-78; appln specialist, 78-80, NUCLEAR MAGNETIC RESONANCE PROD MGR, VARIAN INSTRUMENT DIV, 80- *Concurrent Pos:* NSF grant, 70-72. *Res:* Organic mechanisms; nuclear magnetic resonance; electrophilic additions to olefins; organomercurials; stereochemistry; ozone reactions. *Mailing Add:* Varian Instrument Div 611 Hansen Way Palo Alto CA 94303

WATERS, WILLIE ESTEL, b Smith Town, Ky, Sept 19, 31; m 52; c 3. HORTICULTURE. *Educ:* Univ Ky, BS, 54, MS, 58; Univ Fla, PhD(veg crops), 60. *Prof Exp:* Asst county agr agent, Ky, 54; asst soils, Univ Ky, 56-58; asst veg crops, 58-60, from asst ornamental horticulturist to assoc ornamental horticulturist, 60-68, horticulturist & head Agr Res Ctr, Apopka, Fla, 68-70, HORTICULTURIST & DIR AGR RES & EDUC CTR, UNIV FLA, 70- *Mem:* Am Soc Hort Sci. *Res:* Soil and plant nutrition; weed control and physiology of ornamental crops. *Mailing Add:* Agr Res & Educ Ctr Univ Fla Bradenton FL 33508

WATERSON, JOHN R, b Decatur, Ill, May 11, 44; m; c 4. HUMAN GENETICS, PEDIATRICS. *Educ:* Univ Mich, BS, 66, MD, 75; Yale Univ, PhD(biophysics), 71. *Prof Exp:* Instr, 79, ASST PROF PEDIAT, UNIV MICH, 80- *Mem:* Am Soc Human Genetics; Am Acad Pediat. *Res:* Human gene structure and chromosomal organization. *Mailing Add:* 4997 Starak Ann Arbor MI 48105

WATERWORTH, HOWARD E, b Randolph, Wis, Sept 3, 36; m 66; c 3. PLANT VIROLOGY. *Educ:* Univ Wis, BS, 58, PhD(plant path), 62. *Prof Exp:* RES PLANT PATHOLOGIST, SCI & EDUC ADMIN-AGR RES, USDA, 64-, CHIEF, GERMPLASM RESOURCES LAB, RES CTR, BELTSVILLE, 80- *Mem:* Am Inst Biol Sci; Brit Asn Appl Biol; Am Phytopath Soc; Indian Phytopath Soc. *Res:* Testing of new apple, pear, and woody ornamentals for the presence of viruses; basic research on these viruses, including purification, study of chemical and physical properties, preparation of antisera, identification of new viruses and screening for resistance to them. *Mailing Add:* Plant Introd Sta US Dept of Agr Glenn Dale MD 20769

WATKINS, ALLEN HARRISON, b Charlottesville, Va, Apr 25, 38; m 62; c 2. TECHNICAL MANAGEMENT. *Educ:* Va Polytech Inst, BS, 61. *Prof Exp:* Prog mgt space syst, Manned Spacecraft Ctr, NASA, 62-70, prog mgt earth resources, 70-73; DIR, EARTH RESOURCES OBSERV SYST DATA CTR, DEPT INTERIOR, 73- *Mem:* Am Soc Photogram; Am Inst Aeronaut & Astronaut. *Mailing Add:* Dept of Interior Sioux Falls SD 57198

WATKINS, CHARLES B, b Petersburg, Va, Nov 20, 42; m 64; c 2. HEAT TRANSFER, FLUID MECHANICS. *Educ:* Howard Univ, BSME, 64; Univ NMex, MS, 66, PhD(mech eng), 70. *Prof Exp:* Staff mem, Sandia Labs, 64-71; from asst prof to assoc prof, 73-79, PROF MECH ENG, HOWARD UNIV, 79-, CHMN DEPT, 73- *Concurrent Pos:* Mem, Eng Chem & Energetics Adv Panel, NSF, 75-78; mem, Selection Panel Nat Res Coun Post Doctoral Fel Prog, 80; consult, US Army, US Navy & Sandia Labs, 67- *Honors & Awards:* Ralph R Teetor Award, Soc Automotive Engrs, 80. *Mem:* Am Soc Mech Engrs; Am Inst Aeronaut & Astronaut; Soc Automotive Engrs; Nat Soc Prof Engrs; Sigma Xi. *Res:* Heat transfer; fluid mechanics; gas bearing dynamics; mechanical design; truck wheels; product liability; author or coauthor of 25 publications. *Mailing Add:* Dept Mech Eng Howard Univ Washington DC 20059

WATKINS, CHARLES H(ENRY), b Henshaw, Ky, Mar 21, 13; m 40; c 4. CHEMICAL ENGINEERING. *Educ:* Univ Louisville, BS, 35, MS, 36; Purdue Univ, PhD(chem eng), 39. *Prof Exp:* Res engr, Standard Oil Develop Co, NJ, 39-46; div coordr, Universal Oil Prod Co, 46-60, div coordr, Eng Res & Develop, 60-77; RETIRED. *Concurrent Pos:* Consult eng res & develop, Universal Oil Prod Process Div, 77- *Mem:* Am Chem Soc; Am Inst Chem Engrs. *Res:* Olefin production; aromatics; polymerization of hydrocarbons; alkyllation of isoparaffines with ethylene, propylene and butenes; hydrogenation; inorganic reactions in organic solvents; hydrofining; hydrocracking. *Mailing Add:* 8033 SW 103 Lane Ocala FL 32670

WATKINS, CHARLES LEE, b Fairfield, Ala, Oct 27, 42; m. CHEMISTRY. *Educ:* Univ Ala, Tuscaloosa, BS, 64; Univ Fla, MS, 66, PhD(chem), 68. *Prof Exp:* Lab asst gen chem, Univ Ala, Tuscaloosa, 63-64; res assoc, Univ NC, Chapel Hill, 69-70; asst prof, 70-74, ASSOC PROF CHEM, UNIV ALA, BIRMINGHAM, 74- *Mem:* Am Chem Soc. *Mailing Add:* Dept of Chem Univ of Ala Birmingham AL 35294

WATKINS, DARRELL DWIGHT, JR, b Woodbine, Iowa, Mar 7, 43; m 64; c 2. ORGANOMETALLIC CHEMISTRY. *Educ:* Univ Nebr, Omaha, BA, 68; Univ Nebr, Lincoln, PhD(chem), 73. *Prof Exp:* Asst instr chem, Univ Nebr, Omaha, 68-70; res assoc, Ohio State Univ, 73-76; SR RES CHEMIST, MONSANTO CO, 76- *Mem:* Am Chem Soc. *Res:* Synthesis of new and novel organometallic compounds and the use of those compounds in homogeneous catalysis. *Mailing Add:* Q4B Monsanto 800 N Lindbergh Blvd St Louis MO 63166

WATKINS, DAVID HYDER, b Denver, Colo, Nov 26, 17; m 41; c 2. THORACIC SURGERY. *Educ:* Univ Colo, AB, 37, MD, 40; Univ Minn, MS, 47, PhD(surg), 49; Am Bd Surg, dipl; Am Bd Thoracic Surg, dipl. *Prof Exp:* Asst surgeon, Mayo Clin, 44-49; instr surg, Ohio State Univ, 49-51; from assoc prof to prof, Sch Med, Univ Colo, 51-67; CLIN PROF SURG, COL MED, UNIV IOWA, 67-; DIR SURG, IOWA METHODIST HOSP-BROADLAWNS HOSP, DES MOINES, 68- *Concurrent Pos:* Attend thoracic surgeon, Colo Gen Hosp, 51-67; chief surg serv, Denver Gen Hosp, 52-67; consult, Fitzsimons Army Hosp, Denver & Vet Admin Ctr, Des Moines. *Mem:* Am Asn Thoracic Surgery; fel AMA; fel Am Heart Asn; fel Am Col Surgeons; fel Am Col Chest Physicians. *Res:* Surgery of thorax, great vessels, heart and esophagus; assisted circulation; shock and hemorrhage; experimental surgery. *Mailing Add:* 6039 N Waterbury Rd Des Moines IA 50312

WATKINS, DEAN ALLEN, b Omaha, Nebr, Oct 23, 22; m 44; c 3. ELECTRICAL ENGINEERING. *Educ:* Iowa State Col, BS, 44; Calif Inst Technol, MS, 47; Stanford Univ, PhD(elec eng), 51. *Prof Exp:* Engr, Collins Radio Co, Iowa, 47-48; staff mem, Los Alamos Sci Lab, 48-49; head microwave tube sect, Res & Develop Labs, Hughes Aircraft Co, 51-53; from assoc prof to prof elec eng, Stanford Univ, 53-64, dir electron devices lab, 55-64; pres, 57-67, CHMN BD & CHIEF EXEC OFFICER, WATKINS-JOHNSON CO, 67- *Concurrent Pos:* Lectr, Stanford Univ, 64-69. *Mem:* Nat Acad Eng; Am Phys Soc; fel Inst Elec & Electronics Engrs. *Res:* Microwave devices and systems. *Mailing Add:* Watkins-Johnson Co 3333 Hillview Ave Palo Alto CA 94304

WATKINS, DON WAYNE, b Louisville, Ky, June 9, 40; m 66; c 3. PHYSIOLOGY. *Educ:* Univ Louisville, BChE, 63; Univ Wis-Madison, PhD(physiol), 68. *Prof Exp:* Lectr physiol, Med Sch, Makerere Univ, Uganda, 68-70; asst prof, 70-75, ASSOC PROF PHYSIOL, MED SCH, GEORGE WASHINGTON UNIV, 75- *Mem:* Am Physiol Soc. *Res:* Membrane transport, physiology, epithelia; kidney salt and water; frog skin; trace element and mineral metabolism. *Mailing Add:* Dept of Physiol George Washington Univ Med Sch Washington DC 20037

WATKINS, DUDLEY T, b Youngstown, Ohio, May 2, 38; m 60; c 3. ANATOMY. *Educ:* Oberlin Col, AB, 60; Western Reserve Univ, MD, 66, PhD(anat), 67. *Prof Exp:* Fel anat, 66-67, asst prof, 67-72, assoc prof, 72-80, PROF ANAT, HEALTH CTR, UNIV CONN, 80- *Mem:* AAAS; Am Diabetes Asn; Am Asn Anatomists. *Res:* Mechanism of action of alloxan in the production of diabetes; mechanism of insulin secretion. *Mailing Add:* Dept Anat Univ Conn Health Ctr Farmington CT 06032

WATKINS, ELTON, JR, b Portland, Ore, Aug 16, 21. SURGERY, CANCER. *Educ:* Reed Col, BA, 41; Univ Ore, MD, 44. *Prof Exp:* Asst path, Med Sch, Univ Ore, 41-43, biochem, 43-44, resident thoracic surg, Hosps & Clins, 45-48, instr physiol, Med Sch, 49-50; Ore Heart Asn res fel, Children's Hosp Med Ctr, Boston, Mass, 51-53; from instr to asst prof surg, Harvard Med Sch, 54-57; sr surgeon, div res, 64-67, SR SURGEON & DIR SIAS

SURG LAB, LAHEY CLIN FOUND, 57-, CHMN DIV RES, 64- *Concurrent Pos:* Surgeon, Children's Hosp Med Ctr, Boston, Mass, 56-57; asst surgeon, Peter Bent Brigham Hosp, Boston, Mass, 57; consult, Blood Preservation Lab, US Naval Hosp, Boston, 56-; USPHS grant organ transplantation, Sias Surg Lab, Lahey Clin Found, 59-65, USPHS grant cancer immunother, 72-; lectr, Royal Col Surgeons Eng, 63. *Mem:* AAAS; Am Asn Cancer Res; Transplantation Soc; Am Fedn Clin Res; Int Soc Surgeons. *Res:* Cardiovascular physiology and surgery; pancreatic transplantation; regional cancer chemotherapy; experimental manipulation of host immune response to cancer. *Mailing Add:* Sias Res Lab Lahey Clin Found 605 Commonwealth Ave Boston MA 02215

WATKINS, GEORGE DANIELS, b Evanston, Ill, Apr 28, 24; m 49; c 3. PHYSICS. *Educ:* Randolph-Macon Col, BS, 43; Harvard Univ, AM, 47, PhD(physics), 52. *Hon Degrees:* DSc, Randolph-Macon Col, 76- *Prof Exp:* Physicist, Res & Develop Ctr, Gen Elec Co, 52-75; SHERMAN FAIRCHILD PROF PHYSICS, LEHIGH UNIV, 75- *Concurrent Pos:* Adj prof, Rensselaer Polytech Inst, 62-65; NSF fel, Oxford Univ, 66-67; adj prof, State Univ NY Albany, 70-71. *Honors & Awards:* Oliver E Buckley Prize Solid State Physics, 78. *Mem:* Fel Am Phys Soc; fel AAAS. *Res:* Nuclear and electron spin resonance studies; information theory; solid state physics; radiation effects and point defects in solids. *Mailing Add:* Dept of Physics Lehigh Univ Bethlehem PA 18015

WATKINS, IVAN WARREN, b Minneapolis, Kans, Jan 14, 34; m 55; c 4. PHYSICS. *Educ:* Univ Kans, BS, 55, MS, 57; Tex A&M Univ, PhD, 68. *Prof Exp:* Instr physics, Ft Hays Kans State Col, 58-62; from asst prof to prof physics, 63-74, PROF GEOG & EARTH SCI, ST CLOUD STATE COL, 74- *Mem:* Am Asn Physics Teachers. *Res:* Theoretical molecular spectroscopy; student attitudes about sciences and how the attitudes correlate with success in science courses. *Mailing Add:* St Cloud State Col St Cloud MN 56301

WATKINS, JACKIE LLOYD, b Melvin, Tex, Jan 16, 32; m 55; c 4. GEOLOGY. *Educ:* Southern Methodist Univ, BS, 52, MS, 54; Univ Mich, PhD(geol), 58. *Prof Exp:* Assoc prof, 58-72, PROF GEOL, MIDWEST UNIV, 72-, CHMN DEPT, 77- *Concurrent Pos:* Chmn bd, Watkins Mineral Corp. *Mem:* AAAS; Paleont Soc; Soc Econ Paleont & Mineral; Geol Soc Am; Nat Asn Geol Teachers. *Res:* Invertebrate paleontology; tetracorals and tabulate corals. *Mailing Add:* Dept of Geol Sci Midwestern Univ Wichita Falls TX 76308

WATKINS, JOEL SMITH, JR, b Poteau, Okla, May 27, 32; m 56; c 2. GEOPHYSICS, SEISMOLOGY. *Educ:* Univ NC, AB, 53; Univ Tex, PhD(geol), 61. *Prof Exp:* Geophysicist, Regional Geophys Br, US Geol Surv, 61-64, Astrogeol Br, 64-66; res assoc geophys, Mass Inst Technol, 66-67; from assoc prof to prof, Univ NC, Chapel Hill, 67-73; prof geophys, Univ Tex Marine Sci Inst, 73-77; sr res assoc, Gulf Res & Develop Co, Houston, 77-79, mgr, Geol Interpreters Dept, Gulf Sci & Tech Co, Pittsburgh, 79-81, MGR GEOL, CENT EXP GROUP INT, GULF OIL E&P CO, HOUSTON, 81- *Concurrent Pos:* Co-investr, Apollo Active Seismic Exp, 65-72, Apollo Lunar Seismic Profiling Exp, 71-73; mem adv comt, Int Phase Ocean Drilling, 74-; co-chief, Deep Sea Drilling Proj, 79. *Honors & Awards:* Spec Commendation, Geol Soc Am, 73. *Mem:* Am Geophys Union; Soc Explor Geophysicists; Geol Soc Am. *Res:* Marine geophysics; explosion seismology. *Mailing Add:* Gulf Res & Develop Co PO Box 36506 Houston TX 77036

WATKINS, JULIAN F, II, b Marvell, Ark, Mar 18, 36; m 54; c 2. ENTOMOLOGY. *Educ:* Univ Ark, BSA, 56; Kans State Univ, MS, 62, PhD(entom), 64. *Prof Exp:* Asst county agent, Ark Agr Exten Serv, 56-60; asst prof, 64-68, assoc prof, 68-79, actg chmn, 79-81, PROF BIOL, BAYLOR UNIV, 79-, VCHMN, 81- *Mem:* Entom Soc Am. *Res:* Taxonomy and behavior of army ants. *Mailing Add:* Dept of Biol Baylor Univ Waco TX 76798

WATKINS, KAY ORVILLE, b Nunn, Colo, Apr 28, 32; m 61; c 3. INORGANIC CHEMISTRY, PHYSICAL CHEMISTRY. *Educ:* Adams State Col, BA, 55; Vanderbilt Univ, PhD(inorg chem), 61. *Prof Exp:* From asst prof to assoc prof, 61-70, PROF CHEM, ADAMS STATE COL, 70-, CHMN, DIV SCI & MATH, 77- *Concurrent Pos:* NSF acad year exten grant, 63-65 & res grant, 65-68; NSF high sch lectr, 66-67; vis scientist, Brookhaven Nat Lab, 68-69 & Argonne Nat Lab, 73; NSF fac develop fel, 78; vis prof, Univ Utah, 81. *Mem:* Am Chem Soc. *Res:* Equilibria and kinetic studies of inorganic systems in solution. *Mailing Add:* Dept Chem Adams State Col Alamosa CO 81101

WATKINS, KENNETH WALTER, b Philadelphia, Pa, Apr 22, 39; m 62. PHYSICAL CHEMISTRY. *Educ:* Kans State Univ, BS, 61, PhD(chem), 65. *Prof Exp:* Fel chem, Univ Wash, 65-66; ASST PROF CHEM, COLO STATE UNIV, 66- *Mem:* Am Chem Soc; AAAS. *Res:* Chemical kinetics; chemical education. *Mailing Add:* Dept of Chem Colo State Univ Ft Collins CO 80523

WATKINS, LINDA ROTHBLUM, b Norfolk, Va, June 29, 54; m 76. NEUROANATOMY, NEUROPHYSIOLOGY. *Educ:* Va Polytech Inst & State Univ, BS, 76; Med Col Va, PhD(physiol), 80. *Prof Exp:* LECTR NEUROSCI, DEPT PHYSIOL, MED COL VA, 81- *Concurrent Pos:* Fel, Dept Physiol, Med Col Va, 81- *Mem:* Int Asn Study Pain. *Res:* Behavioral, neuroanatomical and neuropharmacological investigations of endogennous opiate and non-opiate pain inhibitory systems which are activated by brain stimulation, morphine or environmental stimuli. *Mailing Add:* Dept Physiol Med Col Va Box 551 Richmond VA 23298

WATKINS, MARK E, b New York, NY, Apr 13, 37; m 61; c 3. MATHEMATICS. *Educ:* Amherst Col, AB, 59; Yale Univ, MA, 61, PhD(math), 64. *Prof Exp:* Instr math, Univ NC, Chapel Hill, 63-64; asst prof, 64-68, assoc prof, 68-76, PROF MATH, SYRACUSE UNIV, 76- *Concurrent Pos:* Vis assoc prof, Univ Waterloo, 67-68 & 80; vis prof, Vienna Tech Univ, 73-74; Ger Acad exchange serv grant, West Berlin, 80. *Mem:* Am Math Soc. *Res:* Problems related to vertex-connectivity in graphs; imbedding of graphs; automorphism groups of graphs and systems. *Mailing Add:* Dept of Math Syracuse Univ Syracuse NY 13210

WATKINS, MARY LOUISE, biochemical pharmacology, see previous edition

WATKINS, MAURICE, b East Chicago, Ind, Aug 8, 46; m 76. METALLURGICAL ENGINEERING. *Educ:* Ill Inst Technol, BS, 68, PhD(metall eng), 73. *Prof Exp:* Engr eng mat, Res & Develop Labs, Continental Can Co, 68-69; sr res engr, 73-80, GROUP LEADER, MAT RES, EXXON PROD RES CO, 80- *Concurrent Pos:* Vis lectr, Black Exec Exchange Prog, Urban League, 76-; indust adv & prog coordr for Jets Club, Houston Independent Sch Dist, 78-; Exxon rep, Nat Asn Corrosion Engrs & Am Petrol Inst. *Mem:* Am Soc Metals; Nat Asn Corrosion Engrs; Am Petrol Inst. *Res:* Welding, corrosion, stress corrosion cracking, hydrogen embrittlement and fatigue of materials used in the manufacture of equipment for oil and gas exploration and production. *Mailing Add:* 5623 Bent Bough Houston TX 77088

WATKINS, NANCY CHAPMAN, b Bowling Green, Ky, Mar 19, 39; m 62; c 1. PHYSICS, POLYMER SCIENCE. *Educ:* Univ Ky, BS, 61; Rensselaer Polytech Inst, PhD(chem eng), 67. *Prof Exp:* sr res scientist fiber struct, Am Enka Corp, 67-80; STAFF ENGR, IBM CORP, 80- *Mem:* Am Chem Soc. *Res:* Thermal analysis, scanning electron microscopy, x-ray diffraction and computer applications to fiber structural studies; cross-linking technique applied to thermal studies. *Mailing Add:* One Warwick Lane Frankfort KY 40601

WATKINS, PAUL DONALD, b Carterville, Ill, Oct 25, 40. MICROBIOLOGY, BIOCHEMISTRY. *Educ:* Southern Ill Univ, Carbondale, BA, 63, PhD(microbiol), 70. *Prof Exp:* Sr microbiologist, Schering Corp, 69-72; SR MICROBIOLOGIST, HOFFMANN-LA ROCHE INC, 72- *Mem:* AAAS; Am Soc Microbiol; Genetics Soc Am; Am Genetic Asn. *Res:* Antibiotics; genetics; regulatory mechanisms. *Mailing Add:* PO Box 56 Verona NJ 07044

WATKINS, ROBERT ARNOLD, b Boston, Mass, Aug 3, 26; m 48; c 2. ELECTROOPTICS, MILITARY SYSTEMS. *Educ:* Brown Univ, ScB, 47; Ohio State Univ, MS, 48, PhD(physics), 53. *Prof Exp:* Instr physics, Univ WVa, 48-49; engr, Zenith Radio Corp, 52-54; sr engr, 54-57, sect mgr, 57-60, dept mgr, 60-63, prin engr, 63-80, DEPT MGR, RAYTHEON CO, GOLETA, 80- *Mem:* Inst Elec & Electronics Engrs; Optical Soc Am. *Res:* Optical systems design with associated electronic and mechanical configurations; laser effects on materials; combined radio frequency and optical systems; digital based radio frequency systems. *Mailing Add:* 4575 Camino Molinero Santa Barbara CA 93110

WATKINS, SALLIE ANN, b Jacksonville, Fla, June 27, 22. PHYSICS. *Educ:* Notre Dame Col, Ohio, BS, 45; Catholic Univ, MS, 54, PhD(physics), 58. *Prof Exp:* Instr chem & physics, Notre Dame Acad, Ohio, 45-49, Elyria Dist Cath High Sch, Ohio, 49-50; instr physics, Notre Dame Col, Ohio, 50-53, prof, 57-66; teaching asst, Catholic Univ, 55-56; PROF PHYSICS, UNIV SOUTHERN COLO, 66- *Concurrent Pos:* NSF res grant biophys, 60-63; Oak Ridge Asn Univs res partic fel, Savannah River Lab, 66-68. *Mem:* Am Phys Soc; Am Asn Physics Teachers. *Res:* Nuclear reactor physics; ultrasonics and biophysics. *Mailing Add:* Dept of Physics Univ of Southern Colo Pueblo CO 81001

WATKINS, SPENCER HUNT, b Mayfield, Ky, Sept 15, 24; m 46; c 3. ORGANIC CHEMISTRY. *Educ:* Univ Ill, BS, 47; Univ Wis, PhD(chem), 50. *Prof Exp:* Res chemist, 50-55, res supvr, 55-57, tech rep, 57-60, asst sales mgr, 60-63, mgr tech serv, 63-65, mgr mkt develop, 65-74, dir develop, pine & paper chem dept, 74-78, DIR TECHNOL, HERCULES, INC, 78- *Mem:* Am Chem Soc; Tech Asn Pulp & Paper Indust; Com Develop Asn; Am Asn Textile Chem & Colorists. *Res:* Paper chemicals, rosin chemistry; urea-formaldehyde resins. *Mailing Add:* Organics Dept Hercules Inc 910 Market St Wilmington DE 19899

WATKINS, STANLEY READ, b University Park, NMex, June 22, 29; m 52; c 2. ANALYTICAL CHEMISTRY, ENVIRONMENTAL CHEMISTRY. *Educ:* NMex State Univ, BS, 51; Univ Colo, PhD(anal chem), 58. *Prof Exp:* Chemist, E I du Pont de Nemours & Co, 51-54; PROF CHEM, COE COL, 58- *Mem:* Am Chem Soc. *Res:* Metal binding properties of human blood proteins, nuclear magnetic resonance studies of metal complexes, analysis of trace metals in biological systems. *Mailing Add:* Dept of Chem Coe Col Cedar Rapids IA 52402

WATKINS, STEVEN F, b Amarillo, Tex, May 14, 40; m 66; c 2. STRUCTURAL CHEMISTRY, CRYSTALLOGRAPHY. *Educ:* Pomona Col, BA, 62; Univ Wis, PhD(phys chem), 67. *Prof Exp:* Res fel, Bristol Univ, 67-68; asst prof, 68-73, ASSOC PROF CHEM, LA STATE UNIV, BATON ROUGE, 73- *Mem:* AAAS; Am Chem Soc; Am Crystallog Asn; Royal Soc Chem. *Res:* Molecular structure of organometallic, inorganic and organic biological molecules in the solid state by means of x-ray and neutron crystallography. *Mailing Add:* Dept of Chem La State Univ Baton Rouge LA 70803

WATKINS, TERRY ANDERSON, b Brady, Tex, June 29, 38. STATISTICS. *Educ:* WTex State Univ, BS, 61; Ill Inst Technol, MS, 64; Tex Tech Univ, PhD(math statist), 72. *Prof Exp:* Instr math, WTex State Univ, 64-65, asst prof, Angelo State Univ, 66-68, 71-72; instr, Tex Tech Univ, 70-71, asst prof, 72-77; ASSOC PROF MATH STATIST, UNIV NEW ORLEANS, 77- *Mem:* Am Statist Asn. *Res:* Estimation; jackknifing procedures. *Mailing Add:* Dept of Math Univ of New Orleans New Orleans LA 70122

WATKINS, WILLIAM, b Los Angeles, Calif, July 7, 42. MATHEMATICS, STATISTICS. *Educ:* Univ Calif, Santa Barbara, BA, 64, MA, 68, PhD(math), 69. *Prof Exp:* Assoc prof, 69-77, PROF MATH, CALIF STATE UNIV, NORTHRIDGE, 77- *Mem:* Am Math Soc; Math Asn Am. *Res:* Linear and multilinear algebra. *Mailing Add:* Dept of Math Calif State Univ Northridge CA 91324

WATLING, HAROLD, b Hayle, Eng, July 22, 17; nat US; m 41; c 2. ZOOLOGY. *Educ:* Univ Idaho, BS, 41, MS, 44; Ore State Univ, PhD, 62. *Prof Exp:* Instr army specialized training prog, Univ Idaho, 44; from instr to assoc prof comp anat, histol & embryol, 45-65, PROF ZOOL, MONT STATE UNIV, 65- *Res:* Vertebrate anatomy and embryology. *Mailing Add:* Dept of Biol Mont State Univ Bozeman MT 59717

WATLINGTON, CHARLES OSCAR, b Midlothian, Va, Apr 9, 32; m 55; c 2. MEDICINE, PHYSIOLOGY. *Educ:* Va Polytech Inst, BS, 54; Med Col Va, Va Commonwealth Univ, MD, 58, PhD(physiol), 68. *Prof Exp:* Intern med, Univ Calif, San Francisco, 58-59, asst resident, 60-62; from instr to asst prof, 62-69, assoc prof, 69-76, PROF MED, MED COL VA, VA COMMONWEALTH UNIV, 76- *Concurrent Pos:* Fel endocrinol, Univ Calif, San Francisco. *Mem:* Am Physiol Soc; Am Fedn Clin Res; Endocrine Soc; Am Diabetes Asn; Am Soc Nephrology. *Res:* Regulation of ion transport; sodium and calcium homeostasis; cellular mechanism of action of hormones. *Mailing Add:* Endocrine Div Dept of Med Med Col of Va Health Sci Div Richmond VA 23219

WATNE, ALVIN LLOYD, b Shabbona, Ill, Jan 13, 27; m 66; c 4. SURGERY. *Educ:* Univ Ill, BS, 50, MD, 52, MS, 56. *Prof Exp:* Intern, Indianapolis Gen Hosp, Ind, 52-53; res asst surg, Univ Ill, 53-54; resident, Res & Educ Hosp, Univ Ill, 54-58; assoc cancer res surgeon, Roswell Park Mem Inst, 58-59, assoc chief cancer res surgeon, 59-62; assoc prof, 62-67, PROF SURG, W VA UNIV, 67-, CANCER COORDR, 62-, CHMN SURG, 74- *Mem:* Am Asn Cancer Res; Am Col Surgeons; Soc Univ Surgeons; NY Acad Sci. *Res:* Cancer metastases, including dissemination of tumor cells via the blood and lymph and their lodgement and growth; etiology and prevention of polyposis and coli and colon cancer. *Mailing Add:* Dept of Surg WVa Univ Med Ctr Morgantown WV 26506

WATNICK, ARTHUR SAUL, b Brooklyn, NY, Feb 4, 30; m 57; c 2. ENDOCRINOLOGY. *Educ:* Brooklyn Col, BS, 53, MA, 56; NY Univ, PhD(physiol), 63. *Prof Exp:* Biochemist, Sloan-Kettering Inst, 53-54, Beth-El Hosp, Brooklyn, NY, 54-56; from asst chemist to assoc chemist, 56-62, from scientist to sr scientist, 62-70, ASSOC DIR, BIOL RES, SCHERING CORP, 70-, MGR DEPT PHYSIOL, 77-, ASSOC DIR, DEPT ALLERGY & INFLAMMATION, 81- *Concurrent Pos:* Lectr endocrinol, Fairleigh Dickenson Univ, 66- & Rutgers Univ, 71- *Mem:* AAAS; Soc Exp Biol & Med; Am Chem Soc; Endocrine Soc; NY Acad Sci; Reticuloendothelial Soc. *Res:* Reproductive physiology; immunology. *Mailing Add:* 27 Harding Dr South Orange NJ 07079

WATRACH, ADOLF MICHAEL, b Poland, Jan 7, 18; nat US; m 55. VETERINARY PATHOLOGY. *Educ:* Royal (Dick) Vet Col, Scotland, MRCVS, 48; Glasgow Univ, PhD(path), 58. *Prof Exp:* Asst vet path, Vet Sch, Glasgow Univ, 49-51; from instr to assoc prof, 51-62, PROF VET PATH, COL VET MED, UNIV ILL, URBANA, 62- *Mem:* AAAS; Electron Micros Soc Am; Am Col Vet Path; Vet Med Asn; Int Acad Path. *Res:* Ultrastructural pathology; virus-cell relationship; viral oncogenesis; mammary tumor biology; cell pathobiology. *Mailing Add:* Col Vet Med Univ Ill Urbana IL 61801

WATREL, WARREN GEORGE, b Brooklyn, NY, Jan 5, 35; m 60; c 3. MICROBIOLOGY, BIOCHEMISTRY. *Educ:* Syracuse Univ, BS, 57, MS, 58. *Prof Exp:* Asst to dir of NSF, Syracuse Univ, 57, instr, 57-58; pharmaceut sales & mkt staff, Lederle Labs, Am Cyanamid Co, 60-62; biochem specialist, M&T Chem, Am Can Co, 62-64; sales mgr, Pharmacia Fine Chem, Inc, 64-65, dir mkt & gen mgr, 65-72; vpres, Vineland, Vista Labs, Inc, Ideal & Nickolson Inst, Damon Corp, 72-74; vpres, Pharmachem Corp, 74-75; exec vpres, Newton Industs Inc, 76-79; VPRES, SECAL INC & SELOMAS INC, 79- *Concurrent Pos:* Am Cyanamid Co study grants, 57-58. *Honors & Awards:* Mkt Award, Am Chem Soc. *Mem:* AAAS; Am Chem Soc; Am Mkt Asn; Am Soc Microbiol; NY Acad Sci. *Res:* Application research and development of products biologically active for use in commercial products; research and development of products to be used in gel filtration chromatography; development, manufacture and sale of veterinarian, pharmacy, human, industrial chemicals and medical electronic instruments. *Mailing Add:* 506 Collins Ave Hasbrouck Heights NJ 07604

WATROUS, JAMES JOSEPH, b Cleveland, Ohio, July 20, 42; m 70; c 2. PHYSIOLOGY. *Educ:* Univ Dayton, BSEd, 65, MS, 69; Georgetown Univ, PhD(biol), 72. *Prof Exp:* Teacher sec sch, Ohio, 64-67; teaching asst biol, Univ Dayton, 67-69 & Georgetown Univ, 69-72; asst prof, 72-80, ASSOC PROF BIOL, ST JOSEPH'S UNIV, 80-, CHMN DEPT, 77- *Mem:* Am Phys Soc; NY Acad Sci; AAAS; Sigma Xi; Am Soc Zoologists. *Res:* Transport of materials across biological membranes; nerve muscle physiology. *Mailing Add:* Dept of Biol St Joseph's Univ 54th & City Ave Philadelphia PA 19131

WATSCHKE, THOMAS LEE, b Charles City, Iowa, Apr 12, 44; m 65. AGRONOMY, HORTICULTURE. *Educ:* Iowa State Univ, BS, 67; Va Polytech Inst & State Univ, MS, 69, PhD(agron), 71. *Prof Exp:* assoc prof agron, 70-80, PROF TURFGRASS SCI, PA STATE UNIV, UNIVERSITY PARK, 80- *Mem:* Am Soc Agron; Crop Sci Soc Am. *Res:* Turfgrass physiology, weed control and growth regulation. *Mailing Add:* Dept of Agron 16 Tyson Bldg Pa State Univ University Park PA 16802

WATSON, ALAN KEMBALL, b Vernon, BC, Sept 1, 48; m 71; c 3. WEED SCIENCE, ECOLOGY. *Educ:* Univ BC, BSc, 70, MSc, 72; Univ Sask, PhD(weed sci), 75. *Prof Exp:* asst prof, 75-80, ASSOC PROF AGRON, MACDONALD CAMPUS, MCGILL UNIV, 80- *Mem:* Weed Sci Soc Am; Soc Nematologists; Agr Inst Can; Can Phytopath Soc. *Res:* Biology and control of weeds with emphasis on biological control utilizing plant pathogens and insects. *Mailing Add:* Dept of Plant Sci McGill Univ 21111 Lakeshore Rd Ste-Anne-de-Bellevue PQ H9X 1C0 Can

WATSON, ANDREW JOHN, b Mich, Aug 1, 21; m 50, 68. WEED SCIENCE. *Educ:* Mich State Univ, PhD(soil sci), 49. AGRONOMIST, DOW CHEM CO, 49- *Mem:* Weed Sci Soc Am. *Res:* Herbicide development. *Mailing Add:* Legal Dept Dow Chem Co Washington St Bldg Midland MI 48640

WATSON, ANDREW SAMUEL, b Highland Park, Mich, May 2, 20; m 67; c 2. PSYCHIATRY. *Educ:* Univ Mich, BS, 42; Temple Univ, MD, 50, MS, 51. *Prof Exp:* From instr to asst prof psychiat, Med Sch, Univ Pa, 45-59, assoc prof, Law Sch, 55-59; from asst prof psychiat & asst prof law to assoc prof psychiat & assoc prof law, 59-66, PROF PSYCHIAT, MED SCH, UNIV MICH, ANN ARBOR, & PROF LAW, LAW SCH, 66- *Concurrent Pos:* Lectr social work, Sch Social Work, Bryn Mawr Col, 55-59; psychiat consult, Mich Dept Corrections, 59-; comnr, Mich Law Enforcement Criminal Justice Comn, 68-72; mem, Adv Comt Divorce, Nat Conf Comnr Uniform State Laws, 69-70; mem, Surgeon's Gen Sci Adv Comn TV & Social Behav, 69-72. *Honors & Awards:* Issac Ray Award, Am Psychiat Asn, 78. *Mem:* Group Advan Psychiat. *Res:* Family treatment; professionalizing process of lawyers; applications of psychiatric concepts to law. *Mailing Add:* CPH Univ Hosp Ann Arbor MI 48104

WATSON, ANNETTA PAULE, b Pleasure Ridge Park, Ky, May 2, 48; m 75. TERRESTRIAL ECOLOGY, ENTOMOLOGY. *Educ:* Purdue Univ, West Lafayette, BS, 70; Univ Ky, PhD(entom), 76. *Prof Exp:* Consult res, Oak Ridge Nat Lab, Union Carbide Corp, 75-76; vis scientist, Div Entom, Commonwealth Sci & Indust Res Orgn, Australia, 76; guest scientist, 77, RES ASSOC, OAK RIDGE NAT LAB, UNION CARBIDE CORP, 77- *Mem:* Ecol Soc Am; Entom Soc Am; AAAS; Sigma Xi. *Res:* Assessment of energy technologies on human systems, human ecology, insect ecology and entomology; litter decomposition; analysis of occupational and public health and safety as a function of energy; industry development. *Mailing Add:* Health & Safety Res Div Bldg 7509 PO Box X Oak Ridge TN 37830

WATSON, BARRY, b Middlesbrough, Eng, Dec 2, 40. BIOPHYSICAL CHEMISTRY. *Educ:* Univ Bradford, BSc, 65, PhD(phys chem), 68. *Prof Exp:* Scientist, Unilever Res Ltd, 66-68; Off Saline Water fel, Mellon Inst Sci, 69-72; RES CHEMIST, OWENS-ILL INC, 72- *Mem:* Royal Soc Chem; Am Chem Soc. *Res:* Thermodynamics of aqueous solutions; electrochemistry; biomedical research. *Mailing Add:* Owens-Ill Inc Tech Ctr 1700 N Westwood Ave Toledo OH 43607

WATSON, CECIL JAMES, b Minneapolis, Minn, May 31, 01; m 25. MEDICINE. *Educ:* Univ Minn, BS, 23, MB, 24, MS, 25, MD, 26, PhD(path), 28; Am Bd Internal Med, dipl, 37. *Hon Degrees:* MD, Univ Mainz, 63 & Univ Munich, 72. *Prof Exp:* Instr path, Univ Minn, 26-28; instr path & internal med, Northwest Clin, Minot, NDak, 28-30; res chemist, Univ Munich, 30-32, Nat Res Coun fel, 31-32; fel med & resident physician, Minneapolis Gen Hosp & Univ Minn Hosp, 32-33; from instr to prof med, 33-61, dir div internal med, 36-40, chmn dept med, 43-66, dir, Unit for Teaching & Res Internal Med, Northwest Hosp, 66-72, DISTINGUISHED SERV PROF MED, UNIV MINN, MINNEAPOLIS, 61-, REGENTS PROF, 68- *Concurrent Pos:* Pathologist, Minneapolis Gen Hosp, 26-28; vis prof & assoc dir health div, Metall Labs, Univ Chicago, 43-46; mem, Life Ins Med Res Coun, 46-49; dir comn liver dis, Armed Forces Epidemiol Bd, 48-54; mem coun, Nat Inst Arthritis & Metab Dis, 51-54; scholar in residence, Fogarty Int Ctr, NIH, 72; hon prof, Lima & Chile; mem comt med & surg, Nat Res Coun; adv comt metab, Surgeon Gen, US Dept Army; mem, Am Bd Internal Med, 44-49. *Honors & Awards:* Wilson Medal, Am Clin & Climat Asn, 47; Phillips Medal, Am Col Physicians, 57; Modern Med Award, 59; Order of Merit, Chile, 60; Kober Medal, Asn Am Physicians, 72. *Mem:* Nat Acad Sci; Am Soc Clin Invest (pres, 46); hon fel Royal Col Physicians & Surgeons Can; Asn Am Physicians (pres, 60-61); master Am Col Physicians. *Res:* Liver and biliary tract disease; jaundice and anemia; urobilin and porphyrin metabolism. *Mailing Add:* Abbott-Northwestern Hosp 800 E 28th St Minneapolis MN 55407

WATSON, CHARLES S, b Chicago, Ill, Aug 16, 32; c 4. PSYCHOACOUSTICS. *Educ:* Ind Univ, AB, 58, PhD(psychol), 63. *Prof Exp:* Teaching assoc psychol, Ind Univ, 59-61; asst prof, Univ Tex, 62-65; from assoc prof to prof, Wash Univ, 67-76; sr res assoc, Cent Inst for Deaf, St Louis, 66-76; DIR RES, BOYS TOWN INST COMMUN DISORDERS IN CHILDREN, 76-; PROF HUMAN COMMUN, MED SCH, CREIGHTON UNIV, 76- *Concurrent Pos:* Ed assoc, Perception & Psychophysics, 68-73; mem, Comt Hearing & Bioacoust, Nat Res Coun-Nat Acad Sci, 70-, chmn, 81-83; assoc ed, J Acoust Soc Am, 73-78; mem, NSF Rev Panel Sensory Physiol & Perception, 78- *Mem:* Fel Acoust Soc Am; fel Am Psychol Asn; AAAS; Sigma Xi; Asn Res Otolaryngol. *Res:* Hearing and deafness; perception of complex sounds; psychophysical methods; learning, memory and selective attention in auditory perception. *Mailing Add:* Boys Town Inst 555 N 30th St Omaha NE 68131

WATSON, CLARENCE ELLIS, JR, b Stillwater, Okla, Apr 13, 51; m 72; c 1. PLANT BREEDING, EXPERIMENTAL STATISTICS. *Educ:* NMex State Univ, BS, 72, MS, 74; Ore State Univ, PhD(crop sci), 76. *Prof Exp:* Res asst, NMex State Univ, 73-74; res asst, Ore State Univ, 74-76; asst prof, 76-81, ASSOC PROF AGRON, MISS STATE UNIV, 81- *Mem:* Am Soc Agron; Crop Sci Soc Am. *Res:* Forage grass breeding; genetics; management with particular emphasis on host-plant resistance. *Mailing Add:* Agron Dept PO Box 5248 Mississippi State MS 39762

WATSON, CLAYTON WILBUR, b Neosho, Mo, Feb 24, 33; m 55; c 3. NUCLEAR ENGINEERING. *Educ:* Wash Univ, BS, 54; Iowa State Univ, MS, 55, PhD(nuclear eng), 60. *Prof Exp:* Engr, Westinghouse Atomic Power, 55-57; res assoc, Rocketdyne, 60-62; asst prof nuclear eng, Univ Fla, 62-63; MEM STAFF, LOS ALAMOS SCI LAB, UNIV CALIF, 63- *Mem:* Am Nuclear Soc. *Res:* Monte Carlo analysis; nuclear reactor physics and applications; radiation environmental analysis; nuclear applications in space; advanced space systems; nuclear weapons; advanced-technology assessment; systems analysis and evaluation; technology development planning. *Mailing Add:* Los Alamos Sci Lab Box 1663 MS 632 Los Alamos NM 87545

WATSON, CLIFFORD ANDREW, b Barr, Mont, Sept 5, 29; m 54; c 2. CEREAL CHEMISTRY. *Educ:* Mont State Univ, BS, 56; Kans State Univ, MS, 58, PhD(cereal chem), 64. *Prof Exp:* From instr to assoc prof cereal chem, Mont State Univ, 56-67; res chemist field crops & animal prod res br, Md, 67-68, invests leader mkt qual res div, Kans, 68-72, actg dir, & location leader & res leader, US Graing Mktg Res Ctr, Manhattan, Kans, 72-74, RES CHEMIST, SCI & EDUC ADMIN-AGR RES, USDA, N DAK, 74-, ADJ PROF CEREAL CHEM, N DAK STATE UNIV, 77- *Mem:* Sigma Xi. *Res:* Agricultural biochemistry; biochemistry of wheat and barley. *Mailing Add:* Dept of Cereal Chem NDak State Univ Fargo ND 58102

WATSON, DAVID GOULDING, b Toronto, Ont, May 7, 29; nat US; m 61; c 5. PEDIATRICS. *Educ:* Univ Toronto, MD, 52. *Prof Exp:* From asst prof to assoc prof, 59-75, PROF PEDIAT, MED CTR, UNIV MISS, 75- *Concurrent Pos:* NIH spec fel, Univ Fla, 72-73. *Mem:* Am Acad Pediat; Am Col Cardiol; Royal Col Physicians Can. *Res:* Pediatric cardiology. *Mailing Add:* Dept of Pediat Univ of Miss Med Ctr Jackson MS 39216

WATSON, DAVID LIVINGSTON, b Burlington, Ont, Oct 22, 26; US citizen; m 51; c 3. ENTOMOLOGY. *Educ:* Univ Guelph, BSA, 51; Cornell Univ, PhD(entom), 56. *Prof Exp:* Res specialist, Chevron Chem Co, 55-59, coordr indust res, 59-61, res supvr, 61-66; assoc dir indust res, 66-70, DIR PROD DEVELOP DIV, VELSICOL CHEM CORP, CHICAGO, 70- *Mem:* AAAS; Entom Soc Am; Am Phytopath Soc; Weed Sci Soc Am. *Res:* Genetic relationship of phosphate resistance in mites; development of crop protection chemicals in agriculture and related fields. *Mailing Add:* Velsicol Chem Corp 341 E Ohio Chicago IL 60611

WATSON, DENNIS RONALD, b Overton, Tex, Dec 7, 41; m 70; c 1. CHEMISTRY. *Educ:* Howard Payne Col, BA, 64; Univ Colo, Boulder, MS, 67, PhD(chem), 70. *Prof Exp:* Asst prof, 70-75, assoc prof, 75-81, PROF CHEM, LA COL, 81-, CHMN DEPT, 70- *Res:* Air and water pollution topics that can be performed by senior level students dealing with local problems and conditions. *Mailing Add:* Dept of Chem La Col Pineville LA 71360

WATSON, DENNIS WALLACE, b Morpeth, Ont, Apr 29, 14; nat US; m 41; c 2. MICROBIOLOGY. *Educ:* Univ Toronto, BSA, 34; Dalhousie Univ, MSc, 37; Univ Wis, PhD(bact), 41. *Hon Degrees:* DSc, Univ Wis-Madison, 81. *Prof Exp:* Asst, Biol Bd Can, NS, 35-37, sci asst, 37-38; asst bact, Univ Wis, 38-41, Alumni Res Found fel, 41-42, res assoc, 42; vis investr, Rockefeller Inst, 42; vis investr, Connaught Labs, Toronto, 42-44; asst prof bact, Univ Wis, 46-49; from assoc prof to prof bact, 49-64, Regents prof, 80, PROF MICROBIOL & HEAD DEPT, MED SCH, UNIV MINN, MINNEAPOLIS, 64- *Concurrent Pos:* Med consult, Fed Security Agency, Washington, DC, 44; assoc mem comn immunization, Armed Forces Epidemiol Bd, 46-59; vis prof, Med Sch, Univ Wash, 50; mem allergy & immunol study sect, NIH, 54-58, mem bd sci counr, Div Biol Standards, 57-59, mem allergy & immunol training grant comt, Nat Inst Allergy & Infectious Dis, 58-60 & 64-66, chmn, 66, mem nat adv coun, 67-71; USPHS spec res fel, WGer, 60-61; mem ad hoc comt med microbiol, Div Med Sci, Nat Acad Sci; vis investr, Osaka Univ, Japan, 71; vis instr, WHO Immunol Course, High Inst Public Health, Alexandria, Egypt, 81. *Mem:* AAAS; Am Chem Soc; Am Soc Microbiol (vpres, 67-68, pres, 68-69); Soc Exp Biol & Med (pres, 75-76); Infectious Dis Soc Am. *Res:* Host-parasite relationships; chemistry and immunology of microbial toxins; pathogenesis of group A streptococci; mechanisms of nonspecific resistance to infection. *Mailing Add:* Med Sch Dept of Microbiol Univ of Minn Box 196 Mayo Minneapolis MN 55455

WATSON, DONALD GORDON, b Moscow, Idaho, Mar 12, 21; m 50; c 3. AQUATIC ECOLOGY. *Educ:* Univ Wash, BS, 48. *Prof Exp:* Biologist, Wash State Dept Game, 49 & Gen Elec Co, 49-65; STAFF SCIENTIST, PAC NORTHWEST LAB, BATTELLE MEM INST, 65- *Mem:* Am Fisheries Soc; Am Inst Fishery Res Biol. *Res:* Effects of ionizing radiation on aquatic organisms; mineral cycling in aquatic systems; effects of thermal power stations on aquatic organisms; ecological effects of radioactive waste management; environmental effects of electrical power production. *Mailing Add:* Battelle Mem Inst Pac Northwest Lab PO Box 999 Richland WA 99352

WATSON, DONALD PICKETT, b Port Credit, Ont, May 20, 12; nat US; m 55. HORTICULTURE. *Educ:* Univ Toronto, BSA, 34; Univ London, MSc, 37; Cornell Univ, PhD(plant anat), 48. *Prof Exp:* Instr hort, State Univ NY Agr Inst, Long Island, 37-42; from asst prof to prof hort & head ornamental hort, Mich State Univ, 48-63; prof hort, 63-75, head dept, 63-66, urban horticulturist, 66-75, EMER PROF HORT, UNIV HAWAII, 75- *Mem:* Am Hort Soc. *Res:* Plant science and anatomy; horticultural television and therapy. *Mailing Add:* 5443 Drover Dr San Diego CA 92115

WATSON, DUANE CRAIG, b Enid, Okla, Dec 8, 30; m 51; c 3. ANALYTICAL CHEMISTRY. *Educ:* Eastern NMex Univ, BA, 51, BS, 56, MS, 57. *Prof Exp:* Res chemist, El Paso Natural Gas Prod, Tex, 57-63; prof res chemist, Philip Morris, Inc, 63-74, SR SCIENTIST, PHILIP MORRIS, USA, 74- *Concurrent Pos:* Lectr, Univ Tex, El Paso, 61-63. *Res:* Smoke chemistry; trace analyses; pollution; process instrumentation; gas chromatography. *Mailing Add:* Philip Morris USA Box 26583 Richmond VA 23261

WATSON, EARL EUGENE, b Sterling, Ill, July 27, 39; m 78; c 5. ACOUSTICS. *Educ:* Fla State Univ, BS, 62, MS, 63; Pa State Univ, PhD(eng acoust), 71. *Prof Exp:* Res engr, Piezeo-Technol, 62; instr eng sci, Fla State Univ, 63-67; res asst, Pa State Univ, 71-74, asst prof acoust, 74-75; mgr acoust, Wolverine Div, UOP Inc, 75-78; PROG MGR, WYLE LAB, 78- *Concurrent Pos:* Res engr, Recon, Inc, 63-65. *Mem:* Audio Eng Soc Inc. *Res:* Acoust holography; noise control. *Mailing Add:* Wyle Lab 128 Maryland El Segundo CA 90245

WATSON, EDNA SUE, b Batesville, Miss, July 8, 45; m 65; c 3. IMMUNOLOGY. *Educ:* Univ Miss, BA, 67, MS, 70, PhD(biol), 75. *Prof Exp:* RES ASSOC, RES INST PHARMACEUT SCI, SCH PHARM, UNIV MISS, 74- *Mem:* AAAS; Can Soc Immunol; Brit Soc Immunol. *Res:* Poison ivy dermatitis, desensitization and immunoprophylaxis; cellular immunology, manipulation of the immune response by cyclic nucleotides. *Mailing Add:* Rte 2 Oxford MS 38655

WATSON, ERNEST L(LOYD), b Saskatoon, Sask, Apr 3, 17; m 41; c 2. AGRICULTURAL ENGINEERING. *Educ:* Univ BC, BASc, 40; Univ Calif, MSc, 55. *Prof Exp:* Plant supvr, Can Industs, Ltd, 40-46; engr, Pac Coop Union, 46-52; PROF AGR ENG, UNIV BC, 52- *Mem:* Am Soc Agr Engrs; Inst Food Technol; Can Soc Agr Engrs; Agr Inst Can. *Res:* Application of engineering to food and agricultural products processing. *Mailing Add:* Univ of BC Bio Res Eng 4959 College Highroad Vancouver BC V6T 1W5 Can

WATSON, FLETCHER GUARD, b Baltimore, Md, Apr 27, 12; m 35; c 4. SCIENCE EDUCATION. *Educ:* Pomona Col, AB, 33; Harvard Univ, MA, 35, PhD(astron), 38. *Prof Exp:* Instr & asst astron, Harvard Univ, 33-38, exec secy & res assoc, 38-41; instr, Radcliffe Col, 41; tech aide, Nat Defense Res Corp Radiation Lab, Mass Inst Technol, 42-43; from asst prof to assoc prof sci educ, 46-57, prof educ, 57-66, Henry Lee Shattuck prof, 66-78, EMER PROF EDUC, HARVARD UNIV, 78- *Concurrent Pos:* Ford Found fel, Europe, 64-65; co-dir, Harvard Proj Physics, 64-; prof educ, NY Univ, 78-81. *Honors & Awards:* Distinguished Serv Citation, Nat Sci Teachers Asn, 72. *Mem:* AAAS; Nat Sci Teachers Asn; Am Asn Physics Teachers; Nat Asn Res Sci Teaching; Asn Educ Teachers in Sci (pres, 63-64). *Res:* Development and evaluation of new high school physics course; studies of development of science teachers and influence of various teacher-types on pupils. *Mailing Add:* 24 Hastings Rd Belmont MA 02178

WATSON, FRANK YANDLE, b Charlotte, NC, May 18, 25; m 49; c 4. PATHOLOGY. *Educ:* Univ Md, MD, 49; Am Bd Path, dipl, 58. *Prof Exp:* Res physician path, Charlotte Mem Hosp, NC, 52-56; from instr to asst prof path, Col Med, State Univ NY Downstate Med Ctr, 56-61; assoc pathologist, 61-72, DIR LABS, MOUNTAINSIDE HOSP, NJ, 72-; CLIN ASST PROF PATH, COL MED, STATE UNIV NY DOWNSTATE MED CTR, 61- *Concurrent Pos:* Surg pathologist, Inst Path, Kings County Med Ctr, NY, 56-61. *Mem:* Fel Col Am Pathologists; fel Am Soc Clin Pathologists; AMA; Asn Am Med Col. *Res:* General and surgical pathology. *Mailing Add:* Mountainside Hosp Bay & Highland Ave Montclair NJ 07042

WATSON, GEOFFREY STUART, b Bendigo, Australia, Dec 3, 21; m 53; c 4. MATHEMATICAL STATISTICS. *Educ:* Univ Melbourne, BA, 42; NC State Col, PhD, 52. *Hon Degrees:* DSc, Univ Melbourne, 67. *Prof Exp:* Res officer, Commonwealth Sci & Indust Res Orgn, Australia, 43; tutor math, Trinity Col, Univ Melbourne, 44-47; res officer appl econ, Cambridge Univ, 49-51; sr lectr statist, Univ Melbourne, 51-54; sr fel, Australian Nat Univ, 55-58; res assoc math, Princeton Univ, 58-59; assoc prof, Univ Toronto, 59-62; prof statist & chmn dept, Johns Hopkins Univ, 62-68; on leave to inst genetics, Univ Pavia, 68-69; chmn dept, 70-79, PROF STATIST, PRINCETON UNIV, 70- *Concurrent Pos:* Guggenheim fel, 76-77. *Mem:* Fel AAAS; fel Inst Math Statist; fel Am Statist Asn; fel Royal Statist Soc; fel Int Statist Inst. *Res:* Application of mathematics, especially probability theory, stochastic processes and statistics, to science; statistical methods in geophysics. *Mailing Add:* Dept of Statist Fine Hall Princeton Univ Princeton NJ 08540

WATSON, GEORGE E, III, b New York, NY, Aug 13, 31; m 66; c 2. ZOOLOGY, ORNITHOLOGY. *Educ:* Yale Univ, BA, 53, MS, 61, PhD(biol), 64. *Prof Exp:* From asst cur to cur ornith, 62-67, chmn dept vert zool, 67-72, CUR VERT ZOOL, NAT MUS NATURAL HIST, SMITHSONIAN INST, 72-; ASSOC PATHOBIOL, SCH PUB HEALTH & HYG, JOHNS HOPKINS UNIV, 70- *Concurrent Pos:* Mem, Seabird Comt, 66-, Nomenclature Comt, 78-, Int Ornith Cong & Comt Res & Explor, Nat Geog Soc, 75- *Mem:* Fel AAAS; fel Am Ornith Union (secy, 73-77); Brit Ornith Union; cor mem Ger Ornith Soc. *Res:* Marine ornithology, especially Antarctica; systematics of birds of Palearctic and Oriental realms. *Mailing Add:* Dept of Vert Zool Birds Smithsonian Inst Washington DC 20560

WATSON, HAL, JR, b Jacksonville, Tex, Dec 27, 39; m 63; c 2. ENGINEERING MECHANICS. *Educ:* Columbia Univ, BA, 62; Univ Tex, Austin, MS, 65, PhD(eng mech), 67. *Prof Exp:* Res engr, Eng Mech Res Lab, Univ Tex, Austin, 64-67; from asst prof to assoc prof solid mech, 67-76, ASSOC PROF CIVIL & MECH ENG, INST TECHNOL, SOUTHERN METHODIST UNIV, 77- *Concurrent Pos:* NSF study grant, 68-69; Dept Defense-Off Naval Res consult grant, Dept Statist, Southern Methodist Univ. *Mem:* Am Soc Mech Engrs; Soc Exp Stress Anal; Am Inst Aeronaut & Astronaut; Am Soc Eng Educ. *Res:* Acoustics; wave propagation in solids; dynamic properties of materials in high pressure and high temperature environments. *Mailing Add:* Inst of Technol Southern Methodist Univ Dallas TX 75222

WATSON, HUGH ALEXANDER, b Ottawa, Ont, Oct 8, 26; US citizen; m 58; c 2. PHYSICS. *Educ:* Univ Toronto, BS, 48; McGill Univ, MS, 49; Mass Inst Technol, PhD(physics), 52. *Prof Exp:* Mem staff div indust coop, Mass Inst Technol, 51-52; mem tech staff, 52-81, dept head mask lab & micrographics dept, 73-77, dept head, Integrated Circuit Technol Eval Dept, 77-80, DEPT HEAD, DIGNOSTICS & LITHOGRAPHIC PROCESS DEVELOPMENT DEPT, BELL LABS, 80- *Mem:* Sr mem, Inst Elec & Electronics Engrs. *Res:* Electron lithography and x-ray lithography. *Mailing Add:* Bell Labs Inc Murray Hill NJ 07974

WATSON, J(AMES) KENNETH, b Ada, Okla, Sept 23, 29; m 58; c 3. ELECTRICAL ENGINEERING. *Educ:* Univ Okla, BS, 51; Mass Inst Technol, SM, 55; Rice Univ, PhD, 66. *Prof Exp:* Observer, Seismic Eng Co, 51-52; teaching asst elec eng, Mass Inst Technol, 52-54; electronics engr, Gen Electronic Labs, Inc, 54-56; proj engr, Systron-Donner Co, 56-58; asst prof elec eng & proj engr, OSAGE Comput Lab, Univ Okla, 58-63, consult dept prev med & pub health, Med Ctr, 61-63; chief engr, Rice Comput Proj, Rice Univ, 63-66; assoc prof, 66-81, PROF ELEC ENG, UNIV FLA, 81- *Concurrent Pos:* Vis res physicist, Magnetism & Metall Div, US Naval Ord Lab, Md, 72-73; vis prof elec eng, Calif Inst Technol, 80-81. *Mem:* Sr mem Inst Elec & Electronics Engrs. *Res:* Modeling of magnetic materials for device and circuit applications; thin magnetic films; magnetic bubble devices; digital electronics; power electronics. *Mailing Add:* Dept of Elec Eng Univ of Fla Gainesville FL 32611

WATSON, JACK ELLSWORTH, b Robertsdale, Pa, Apr 17, 38; m 62; c 3. GENETICS, HUMAN GENETICS. *Educ:* Shippensburg State Col, BS, 61; Purdue Univ, MS, 63, PhD(genetics), 67. *Prof Exp:* From asst prof to assoc prof, 65-77, PROF ZOOL & ENTOM, AUBURN UNIV, 77- *Concurrent Pos:* Lectr, St Bernard Col, 70; consult, Pub Sch Sci Prog, Miss. *Mem:* Southern Genetics Group; Genetics Soc Am; Am Genetic Asn; Sigma Xi. *Res:* Structure, function and manipulation of human metaphose chromosomes; effects of heterochromatin on chromosome pairing; genetics and cytogentics of sickle cell families; inheritance of threshold characters in plants and animals. *Mailing Add:* Dept of Zool & Entom Auburn Univ Auburn AL 36830

WATSON, JACK SAMUEL, b Oliver Springs, Tenn, Oct 18, 35; m 60; c 2. CHEMICAL ENGINEERING. *Educ:* Univ Tenn, BS, 58, MS, 62, PhD(chem eng), 67. *Prof Exp:* DEVELOP ENGR, CHEM TECHNOL DIV, OAK RIDGE NAT LAB, 58- *Mem:* Am Inst Chem Engrs. *Res:* Mass transfer; ion exchange; solvent extraction; fluid mechanics; heat transfer. *Mailing Add:* Chem Technol Div Oak Ridge Nat Lab PO Box X Oak Ridge TN 37830

WATSON, JACK THROCK, b Casey, Iowa, May 2, 39; m 66; c 2. ANALYTICAL CHEMISTY. *Educ:* Iowa State Univ, BS, 61; Mass Inst Technol, PhD(anal chem), 65. *Prof Exp:* Res chemist, US Air Force Sch Aerospace Med, 65-68; asst prof, Sch Med, Vanderbilt Univ, 69-72, assoc prof pharmacol, 73-79; PROF BIOCHEM & CHEM, MICH STATE UNIV, 80- *Concurrent Pos:* Fel, Univ Strasbourg, 68-69. *Mem:* Am Soc Mass Spectrometry; Am Chem Soc. *Res:* Gas chromatography in separation and mass spectrometry in elucidation of structure of biologically significant molecules; prostaglandins; biogenic amines; selective detection of drugs with gas chromatography-mass spectrometry computer systems; biochemical applications of gas chromatography. *Mailing Add:* Biochemistry Mich State Univ East Lansing MI 48824

WATSON, JAMES DEWEY, b Chicago, Ill, Apr 6, 28. MOLECULAR BIOLOGY. *Educ:* Univ Chicago, BS, 47; Ind Univ, PhD, 50. *Hon Degrees:* DSc, Univ Chicago, 61, Ind Univ, 63, Long Island Univ, 70, Adelphi Univ, 72, Brandeis Univ, 73, Albert Einstein Col Med, 74, Hofstra Univ, 76 & Harvard Univ, 78; LLD, Univ Notre Dame, 65; Rockefeller Univ, 80. *Prof Exp:* Nat Res Coun fel, Copenhagen Univ, 50-51 & Cambridge Univ, 51-52; Nat Found Infantile Paralysis fel, 52-53; sr res fel biol, Calif Inst Technol, 53-55; from asst prof to assoc prof, 56-61, PROF BIOL, HARVARD UNIV, 61-; DIR, COLD SPRING HARBOR LAB, 68- *Concurrent Pos:* Mem, Nat Cancer Bd, 72-74. *Honors & Awards:* Co-recipient, Nobel Prize in Med, 62; John Collins Warren Prize, Mass Gen Hosp, 59; Eli Lilly Biochem Award, 60; Lasker Prize, Am Pub Health Asn, 60; co-recipient, Res Corp Prize, 62; John J Carty Medal, Nat Acad Sci, 71; Presidential Medal of Freedom, 77. *Mem:* Nat Acad Sci; Am Acad Arts & Sci; Royal Danish Acad; Am Soc Biol Chemists; Am Asn Cancer Res. *Res:* Induction of cancer by viruses. *Mailing Add:* Cold Spring Harbor Lab Cold Spring Harbor NY 11724

WATSON, JAMES E, JR, b Red Springs, NC, Jan 10, 38; m 62. HEALTH PHYSICS, RADIATION PROTECTION. *Educ:* NC State Univ, BS, 60, MS, 62; Univ NC, PhD(environ sci & eng), 70. *Prof Exp:* Nuclear engr, US Army Ballistic Res Labs, 62-67; health physicist, Oak Ridge Nat Lab, 67; br chief health physics, Tenn Valley Authority, 70-74; ASSOC PROF HEALTH PHYSICS, UNIV NC, 75- *Concurrent Pos:* Mem, Task Force Low-Level Radioactive Waste Mgt, US Dept Energy, 80-81; vchmn, NC Radiation Protection Comn, 79- *Mem:* Health Physics Soc; Am Pub Health Asn; Sigma Xi. *Res:* Radiological impact assessments of natural sources of radiation, nuclear power generation and low-level radioactive waste management; environmental radiation surveillance. *Mailing Add:* Dept Environ Sci & Eng Univ NC Chapel Hill NC 27514

WATSON, JAMES FREDERIC, b Port Huron, Mich, Aug 26, 31; m 52; c 3. METALLURGY, CERAMICS. *Educ:* Univ Mich, BS, 53, MS, 56, PhD(metall eng), 58. *Prof Exp:* Metallurgist, Magnesium Div, Dow Chem Co, Mich, 53 & Ballistic Res Lab, Aberdeen Proving Ground, Md, 54-55; staff scientist, Convair-Astronaut Div, Gen Dynamics Corp, 58-62; asst chmn metall, 62-68, mgr mat & processes lab, 68-70, assoc dir res & develop div, 70-71, DEPT MGR MAT SCI, GULF GEN ATOMIC, 71- *Concurrent Pos:* Lectr, Univ Calif, Los Angeles, 59-60, 61-62; mem mat adv bd, comt eval mat, Nat Acad Sci, 60-61. *Mem:* Am Soc Metals; Brit Inst Metals. *Res:* High temperature materials for nuclear reactors; materials and processes for components of steam power plants; properties of materials for missiles and spacecraft at cryogenic temperatures. *Mailing Add:* 4961 Quincy Pacific Beach CA 92109

WATSON, JAMES KEATLEY, b Montreal, Que, Feb 26, 21; c 3. ORGANIC CHEMISTRY, CHEMICAL ENGINEERING. *Educ:* Queen's Univ, Ont, BSc, 50. *Prof Exp:* DIR PLANNING, CIP RES LTD, 50- *Mem:* Can Pulp & Paper Asn; Chem Inst Can; Soc Plastics Engrs. *Res:* Mechanical and chemical wood pulping; papermaking. *Mailing Add:* CIP Res Ltd Hawkesbury ON K6A 2H4 Can

WATSON, JAMES RAY, JR, b Anniston, Ala, Dec 6, 35; m 60; c 3. PLANT TAXONOMY. *Educ:* Auburn Univ, BS, 57, MS, 60; Iowa State Univ, PhD(bot), 63. *Prof Exp:* Res asst agron, Auburn Univ, 58-60; asst prof bot, 63-68, assoc prof bot, 68-78, PROF BIOL SCI, MISS STATE UNIV, 78- *Concurrent Pos:* NSF fel, 64-65. *Mem:* Sigma Xi. *Res:* Woody flora of Mississippi. *Mailing Add:* Dept Biol Sci Miss State Univ PO Drawer GY Mississippi State MS 39762

WATSON, JEFFREY, b Butterknowle, Eng, Oct 4, 40. RESOURCE MANAGEMENT, INFORMATION SCIENCE. *Educ:* Univ Durham, BSc, 62, dipl educ, 63, PhD(zool), 66. *Prof Exp:* Scientist, 66-71, dep ed, Off of the Ed, 71-79, ED-IN-CHIEF, CAN J FISH & AQUATIC SCI, FISHERIES RES BD CAN, 79- *Concurrent Pos:* Consult. *Mem:* Am Fisheries Soc; Am Soc Info Sci; Coun Biol Ed (pres, 81-82). *Mailing Add:* Sci Info & Publ Br Fisheries & Oceans Can Ottawa ON K1A 0C6 Can

WATSON, JERRY M, b Independence, Kans, June 26, 42; m 62. EXPERIMENTAL HIGH ENERGY PHYSICS, ACCELERATOR DEVELOPMENT. *Educ:* Univ Chicago, BS, 64, MS, 65, PhD(physics), 71. *Prof Exp:* Asst physicist, 70-77, PHYSICIST, ARGONNE NAT LAB, 77-, GROUP LEADER, HEAVY ION FUSION & ACCELERATOR DEVELOP, 80- *Mem:* Am Phys Soc; AAAS; Sigma Xi. *Res:* The development of large streamer chambers for high energy physics experiments, including the study of hyperon beta decay and meson spectroscopy; development of heavy ion accelerators for inertial confinement fusion research; development of polarized proton sources and preaccelerators. *Mailing Add:* Accelerator Res Facil Div Argonne Nat Lab Argonne IL 60439

WATSON, JOE MOORE, b Bedford, Ind, Oct 7, 24; m 45; c 4. ENGINEERING. *Educ:* Purdue Univ, BSEE, 49. *Prof Exp:* Asst engr, Va Elec & Power Co, 49-53; engr, Flight Propulsion Div, Ohio, 53-58, mgr automated anal unit, 58-61, COMPUT SYSTS ENGR, RES & DEVELOP CTR, GEN ELEC CO, 61- *Res:* Computational systems engineering. *Mailing Add:* 2101 Rankin Rd Schenectady NY 12309

WATSON, JOHN ALFRED, b Chicago, Ill, May 21, 40; m 60; c 4. BIOCHEMISTRY. *Educ:* Ill Inst Technol, BS, 64; Univ Ill, Chicago, USPHS fel & PhD(biochem), 67. *Prof Exp:* USPHS fel biochem, Brandeis Univ, 67-69; asst prof, 69-76, assoc dean admis med, 73-80, PROF BIOCHEM, UNIV CALIF, SAN FRANCISCO, 76- *Concurrent Pos:* From asst dean, to assoc dean student affairs, 69-73; estab investr, Am Heart Asn, 80- *Mem:* Am Oil Chem Soc; Am Soc Biol Chemists; Sigma Xi; Tissue Cult Asn; Nat Inst Sci. *Res:* Regulation of sterol and non-sterol isopentenoid synthesis in isolated cultured vertebrate and invertebrate cells. *Mailing Add:* Dept Biochem & Biophys Univ Calif San Francisco CA 94143

WATSON, JOHN ERNEST, b Kansas City, Mo, May 31, 25; m 52; c 2. AUDIOLOGY. *Educ:* Univ Denver, BA, 52, MA, 57, PhD(audiol), 60. *Prof Exp:* Fel med audiol, Univ Iowa, 60-64; chief audiol serv, Vet Admin Ctr, San Juan, PR, 64-66; dir audiol sect, Speech & Hearing Ctr, Memphis, Tenn, 66-67; CHIEF AUDIOL SERV, VET ADMIN HOSP, 67- *Mem:* Acoust Soc Am; Am Speech & Hearing Asn; Am Psychol Asn. *Res:* Auditory physiology; clinical testing of pathological conditions of the vestibular and auditory systems. *Mailing Add:* Vet Admin Hosp 3801 Miranda Blvd Palo Alto CA 94304

WATSON, JOHN THOMAS, b Indianapolis, Ind, Jan 9, 40; m 64; c 2. CARDIOVASCULAR PHYSIOLOGY, BIOMEDICAL ENGINEERING. *Educ:* Univ Cincinnati, BSME, 62; Southern Methodist Univ, MSME, 66; Univ Tex Southwestern Med Sch, PhD(physiol), 72. *Prof Exp:* Student engr, Indianapolis Power & Light Co, 57-59; design consult, Nat Cash Register Co, 59-62; systs engr, Ling-Temco Vought, Inc, 62-66; teaching asst physiol, Univ Tex Health Sci Ctr, Dallas, 66-69, adj instr, 69-71, instr thoracic & cardiovasc surg & physiol, 71-74, asst prof surg & physiol, 74-76, asst prof, Grad Sch Biomed Sci, 73-80. *Concurrent Pos:* Chief devices & technol br, Nat Heart, Lung & Blood Inst, 76- *Mem:* Am Heart Asn; Am Soc Artificial Internal Organs; Am Soc Mech Engrs; Am Fedn Clin Res. *Res:* Circulatory assistance, ischemic heart diseases. *Mailing Add:* 103 N Dwight Dallas TX 75211

WATSON, JOSEPH ALEXANDER, b Pittsburgh, Pa, July 23, 26; m 50; c 2. RADIOBIOLOGY, MICROBIOLOGY. *Educ:* Univ Pittsburgh, BS, 50, MS, 52, PhD(microbiol), 62. *Prof Exp:* Res asst radiation health, Univ Pittsburgh, 51-56; res biochemist, Radioisotope Serv, Vet Admin Hosp, Pittsburgh, Pa, 56-57; res assoc radiation health, 57-59, asst prof, 61-67, assoc prof, 67-74, PROF RADIOBIOL, GRAD SCH PUB HEALTH, UNIV PITTSBURGH, 74-, ASSOC PROF RADIOL, SCH MED, 72-, DIR RADIATION HEALTH TRAINING PROG, 68-, DIR MED PHYSICS TRAINING PROG, 74- *Mem:* Radiation Res Soc; Am Soc Microbiol; Am Pub Health Asn. *Res:* Pulmonary clearance of radioactive dusts; radiation effects on the lungs; metabolic control mechanisms in the cell. *Mailing Add:* Dept of Radiation Health Grad Sch of Pub Health 130 De Soto St Pittsburgh PA 15213

WATSON, KENNETH, b Montreal, Que, July 25, 35; m 59; c 2. GEOPHYSICS. *Educ:* Univ Toronto, BA, 57; Calif Inst Technol, MS, 59, PhD(geophys), 64. *Prof Exp:* Geophysicist, 63-76, CHIEF, BR PETROPHYS & REMOTE SENSING, US GEOL SURV, 76-, GEOPHYSICIST, 80- *Concurrent Pos:* Lectr, Northern Ariz Univ, 66-67; prin investr, NASA, 77-81. *Mem:* AAAS; Soc Explor Geophysicists; Am Geophys Union; Sigma Xi. *Res:* Planetary science; behavior of volatiles on the lunar surface; infrared emission and visible light reflection; terrestrial remote sensing investigations; thermal modeling; analysis of satellite thermal infrared data. *Mailing Add:* US Geol Surv MS 964 Denver Fed Ctr PO Box 25046 Denver CO 80225

WATSON, KENNETH DE PENCIER, b Vancouver, BC, July 19, 15; m 41; c 3. GEOLOGY. *Educ:* Univ BC, BASc, 37; Princeton Univ, PhD(geol), 40. *Prof Exp:* Instr econ geol, Princeton Univ, 40-43; assoc mining engr, Dept Mines, BC, 43-46; from assoc prof to prof geol & geog, Univ BC, 46-50; prof geol, Univ Calif, Los Angeles, 50-57; chief geologist, Dome Explor Ltd, Can, 57-58; PROF GEOL, UNIV CALIF, LOS ANGELES, 58- *Concurrent Pos:* Dir, Sigma Mines Ltd, 66- *Mem:* Fel Geol Soc Am; fel Mineral Soc Am; Soc Econ Geol; Geochem Soc; Mineral Asn Can. *Res:* Petrology and mineral deposits. *Mailing Add:* Dept of Earth & Space Sci Univ of Calif Los Angeles CA 90024

WATSON, KENNETH FREDRICK, b Pasco, Wash, Feb 17, 42; m 64; c 2. BIOCHEMISTRY, MOLECULAR VIROLOGY. *Educ:* Northwest Nazarene Col, AB, 64; Ore State Univ, PhD(biochem), 69. *Prof Exp:* Res assoc molecular virol, Inst Cancer Res, Columbia Univ, 69-71, instr, Col Physicians & Surgeons, 71-72; res assoc virol, Robert Koch Inst, 72-73; asst prof, 73-77, ASSOC PROF BIOCHEM, UNIV MONT, 77- *Concurrent Pos:* Fel, Nat Cancer Inst, 69-71; res fel, Int Agency Res Cancer, 72-73; fac res award, Am Cancer Soc, 76-81. *Mem:* Am Soc Microbiol; Sigma Xi. *Res:* Replication of viral nucleic acids; mechanism of RNA tumor virus replication and virus-induced cell transformation; characterization of reverse transcriptase and its use in gene synthesis; role of protein phosphorylation in virus life cycle. *Mailing Add:* Dept of Chem Univ of Mont Missoula MT 59812

WATSON, KENNETH MARSHALL, b Des Moines, Iowa, Sept 7, 21; m 46; c 2. PHYSICS. *Educ:* Iowa State Col, BS, 43; Univ Iowa, PhD(physics), 48. *Hon Degrees:* DSc, Indiana Univ, 76. *Prof Exp:* Lab instr, Iowa State Col, 42-43; radio engr, US Naval Res Lab, Washington, DC, 43-46; instr physics, Univ Iowa, 48 & Princeton Univ, 48; AEC fel, Inst Advan Study & Radiation Lab, Univ Calif, 48-50; asst prof physics, Ind Univ, 51-53; assoc prof, Univ Wis, 53-59; prof physics, Univ Calif, Berkeley, 59-81; PROF OCEANOG, UNIV CALIF, SAN DIEGO, 81-, DIR, MARINE PHYS LAB, SCRIPPS INST OCEANOG, 81- *Concurrent Pos:* Staff mem, Lawrence Berkeley Lab; consult, Phys Dynamics, Inc, SRI Int, La Jolla Inst & Sci Applications, Inc. *Mem:* Am Phys Soc; Am Geophys Union; Nat Acad Sci. *Res:* Scattering theory; statistical mechanics; atomic and plasma physics. *Mailing Add:* Scripps Inst Oceanog Univ Calif Mail Code A-005 La Jolla CA 92093

WATSON, MARSHALL TREDWAY, b Blacksburg, Va, Dec 27; 22; m 52; c 2. PHYSICAL CHEMISTRY, TEXTILE CHEMISTRY. *Educ:* Va Polytech Inst, BS, 43; Princeton Univ, MA, 48, PhD(phys chem), 49. *Prof Exp:* Asst, Princeton Univ, 46-48; from res chemist to sr res chemist, 49-63, res assoc, 63-68, head fibers res div, 68-76, DIR FIBERS RES DIV, TENN EASTMAN CO, 76- *Mem:* Am Chem Soc; Am Asn Textile Technol. *Res:* Mechanism of protein denaturation; mechanical and rheological properites of polymers; processing of polymers into fibers; structure and properties of fibers. *Mailing Add:* Res Labs Tenn Eastman Co Kingsport TN 37662

WATSON, MARTHA F, b Janesville, Wis, Feb 2, 35. MATHEMATICS. *Educ:* Murray State Col, AB, 56; Univ Ky, MA, 58, PhD(math), 62. *Prof Exp:* Assoc prof, 62-74, PROF MATH, WESTERN KY UNIV, 74- *Mem:* Am Math Soc; Math Asn Am. *Res:* Complex analysis. *Mailing Add:* Dept of Math Western Ky Univ Bowling Green KY 42101

WATSON, MAXINE AMANDA, b New Rochelle, NY, May 8, 47. PLANT POPULATION BIOLOGY. *Educ:* Cornell Univ, BS, 68; Yale Univ, MDH, 70, PhD(population biol), 74. *Prof Exp:* Asst prof, Univ Utah, 75-80; ASST PROF POPULATION BIOL, IND UNIV, 80- *Mem:* Soc Study Evolution; Ecol Soc Am; Bot Soc Am; Am Bryological & Lichenological Soc; Aquatic Plant Mgt Soc. *Res:* Regulation of population structure in clonal plants using demographic and physiological approaches; investigation of patterns of resource allocation in plants designed to identify relevant currencies. *Mailing Add:* Dept Biol Ind Univ Bloomington IN 47405

WATSON, MICHAEL DOUGLAS, b St Thomas, Ont, July 27, 36; m 59; c 3. AERONOMY. *Educ:* Univ Western Ont, BSc, 57, MS, 59, PhD(physics), 61. *Prof Exp:* Asst res officer, Herzberg Inst Astrophysics, 61-67, assoc res officer, 67-77, sr res officer, 77-81; DIR ASST, CAN CTR SPACE SCI, NAT RES COUN CAN, 81- *Res:* Shock-tube excitation of powdered solids; plasma jet diagnostics; optical studies of aurora; observational studies of infrasonic waves from meteors. *Mailing Add:* Can Ctr Space Sci Nat Res Coun Ottawa ON K1A 0R6 Can

WATSON, NATHAN DEE, b Westfield, NC, Oct 14, 35; m 57; c 1. HEAT TRANSFER, DYNAMICS. *Educ:* NC State Univ, BS, 62; Polytech Inst, MS, 68; NC State Univ, PhD, 77. *Prof Exp:* SUPVR AEROSPACE ENGR, NASA LANGLEY RES CTR, 62- *Res:* Thermal design and analysis of hypersonic aircraft and spacecraft; development of mathematical analysis techniques to predict the rigid and flexible body responses of large aerospace aircraft. *Mailing Add:* NASA Langley Res Ctr Hampton VA 23665

WATSON, P(ERCY) KEITH, b Staffordshire, Eng, Dec 22, 27; m 53; c 4. ELECTRICAL ENGINEERING, PHYSICS. *Educ:* Univ Birmingham, BSc, 48, PhD(elec eng), 52. *Prof Exp:* Engr, English Elec Co, 53-54; fel, Nat Res Coun Can, 54-56; physicist res lab, Gen Elec Co, 56-62; engr, English Elec Co, 62-63; STAFF MEM, XEROX CORP, 63- *Res:* Dielectrics and electrostatics; electrical conduction and breakdown in liquids, solids and gases; electrophotography; electrical insulation. *Mailing Add:* Xerox Corp 800 Phillips Rd W-114 Webster NY 14580

WATSON, PHILIP DONALD, b Leeds, Eng, Oct 20, 41; m 65; c 2. MAMMALIAN CARDIOVASCULAR PHYSIOLOGY, CAPILLARY PERMEABILITY. *Educ:* Univ Leeds, BSc, 64; Univ Southern Calif, MS, 71, PhD(biomed eng), 75. *Prof Exp:* Res engr, Western Gear Corp, Calif, 66-69; fel physiol, Univ Calif, Davis, 75-77; asst prof, 77-80, ASSOC PROF PHYSIOL, UNIV SC, 80- *Concurrent Pos:* NIH fel, 72-75, 75-77; Pharmacia travel award, Microcirculatory Soc, 81. *Mem:* Microcirculatory Soc; Am Physiol Soc. *Res:* Solute and water movement between blood and tissue. *Mailing Add:* Dept of Physiol Univ SC Columbia SC 29208

WATSON, RALPH A, exploration geology, mineral economics, deceased

WATSON, RAND LEWIS, b Denver, Colo, Aug 29, 40; m 62; c 2. CHEMICAL PHYSICS. *Educ:* Colo Sch Mines, BS, 62; Univ Calif, Berkeley, PhD(nuclear chem), 66. *Prof Exp:* Res assoc, Lawrence Radiation Lab, Univ Calif, 66-67; from asst prof to assoc prof, 69-77, PROF CHEM, TEX A&M UNIV, 77-, ASST DEAN SCI, 80- *Concurrent Pos:* Vis prof, Univ Calif, Berkeley, 78-79. *Mem:* Am Phys Soc; Am Chem Soc. *Res:* Fast electron rearrangement following multiple ionization in heavy-ion-collisions; excited state distributions in fast ions penetrating solids and gases; x-ray spectroscopy of few-electron ions. *Mailing Add:* Col Sci Tex A&M Univ College Station TX 77843

WATSON, RICHARD ELVIS, b Carterville, Ill, Apr 9, 12; m 36; c 2. PHYSICS. *Educ:* Southern Ill Norm Univ, BEd, 32; Univ Ill, AM, 35, PhD(physics), 38. *Prof Exp:* Instr physics, Eastern Ill Teachers Col, 38-39; sci ed, Coop Test Serv, NY, 39-40; asst prof physics, Southern Ill Teachers Col, 40-42; res technologist, Elec Div, Leeds & Northrup Co, 46-58; PROF PHYSICS, SOUTHERN ILL UNIV, CARBONDALE, 58-, CHMN DEPT, 76- *Mem:* Am Phys Teachers; Inst Elec & Electronics Eng. *Res:* Scattering of neutrons by light nuclei; scattering of fast electrons by Coulomb field; electrometer amplifiers and recorders; automatic electrical controllers; economic loading of power systems; modelling human visual response. *Mailing Add:* Dept of Physics Southern Ill Univ Carbondale IL 62901

WATSON, RICHARD LEE, b Philadelphia, Pa, May 3, 43. SEDIMENTOLOGY. *Educ:* Lehigh Univ, AB, 65; Univ Tex, Austin, MA, 68, PhD(geol), 75. *Prof Exp:* Res sci assoc geol, Univ Tex Marine Sci Inst, 72-77; CONSULT, 77- *Res:* Hydrodynamics of sediment transport; longshore transport systems; inlet stability; coastal engineering geology; natural hazards affecting development of the coastal zone. *Mailing Add:* Box 1040 Port Aransas TX 78373

WATSON, RICHARD WHITE, JR, b Indiana, Pa, Apr 13, 33; m 58; c 3. CLINICAL LABORATORY MANAGEMENT. *Educ:* Cornell Univ, BS, 59; Rutgers Univ, MS, 61, PhD(bact), 64. *Prof Exp:* Sr lab technician, Rutgers Univ, 61-62; res microbiologist, Anheuser-Busch, Inc, 64-67 & Esso Res & Eng Co, 67-71; LAB DIR, NAT HEALTH LABS, INC, MOUNTAINSIDE, 71- *Mem:* AAAS; Am Soc Microbiol; Am Chem Soc. *Res:* Analytical biochemistry. *Mailing Add:* 16 Walnut St New Providence NJ 07974

WATSON, RICHARD WILLIAM, b Wheeling, WVa, Aug 15, 27. PHYSICS. *Educ:* Carnegie Inst Technol, BS, 62. *Prof Exp:* Jr res physicist, Explosives Res Group, Carnegie Inst Technol, 54-57, from asst proj supvr to proj supvr, 57-62; res physicist, Explosives Res Ctr, US Bur Mines, 62-70, supvry res physicist & proj coord, 70-71, RES res supvr, Pittsburgh Mining & Safety Res Ctr, 71-77; LECTR, UNIV CALIF, DAVIS, 77- *Mem:* Am Phys Soc; Combustion Inst; Am Soc Test & Mat. *Res:* Explosives physics and chemistry; hazardous materials. *Mailing Add:* Dept of Appl Sci Univ of Calif Davis CA 95616

WATSON, ROBERT BARDEN, b Champaign, Ill, Apr 14, 14; m 41; c 3. PHYSICS, LASERS. *Educ:* Univ Ill, AB, 34; Univ Calif, Los Angeles, MA, 36; Harvard Univ, PhD(physics), 41. *Prof Exp:* Asst physics, Univ Calif, Los Angeles, 35-36; asst, Harvard Univ, 36-37, instr, 37-38, physics & commun eng, 38-40, res assoc physics, 40-41, spec res assoc, Underwater Sound Lab, 41-45; res physicist, Defense Res Lab, Univ Tex, 45-52, mil physics res lab, 52-57, from asst prof to assoc prof physics, Univ Tex, 46-60; chief, Physics, Electronics & Mech Br, Phys & Eng Sci Div, Off Chief Res & Develop, Dept Army, 60-72, chief, Phys & Eng Sci Div, 72-75, staff officer, Directorate Army Res, Off Dept Chief Staff Res, Develop & Acquisition, 75-76; CONSULT, 76- *Mem:* Fel AAAS; fel Acoust Soc Am; Am Asn Physics Teachers; Inst Elec & Electronics Eng; Optical Soc Am. *Res:* Electronic circuits; architectural and musical acoustics; propagation of high frequency electromagnetic radiation; semiconductors; management of broad research programs in physical and engineering sciences. *Mailing Add:* 1176 Wimbledon Dr McLean VA 22101

WATSON, ROBERT DALE, b Elko, Nev, Dec 19, 34; m 59; c 4. ENVIRONMENTAL PHYSICS. *Educ:* Ariz State Univ, BS, 56, MS, 61. *Prof Exp:* Assoc engr, Boeing Airplane Co, Kans, 58-59, res engr, Wash, 61; res asst, Ariz State Univ, 59-61; physicist, Cent Radio Propagation Lab, Nat Bur Stand, Colo, 61-63 & Nat Ctr Atmospheric Res, Colo, 63-67; PHYSICIST, BR EXPLOR RES, US GEOL SURV, 67- *Res:* Remote sensing of environment; electromagnetic wave propagation in gases and solids; scattering properties of polydispersed suspensions of aerosols; optical properties of terrestial surface; luminescence properties of natural materials. *Mailing Add:* 2853 E Pebble Beach Dr Flagstaff AZ 86001

WATSON, ROBERT FLETCHER, b Charlottesville, Va, Jan 24, 10; m 46; c 2. MEDICINE. *Educ:* Univ Va, MD, 34. *Prof Exp:* Intern, House of the Good Samaritan, Boston, Mass, 34; intern, Mass Gen Hosp, 35-36; from asst to instr, Med Col, Cornell Univ, 36-39; from asst mem to assoc mem, Rockefeller Inst, 39-46; assoc prof med, 46-50, from assoc prof to prof clin med, 50-75, EMER PROF CLIN MED, MED COL, CORNELL UNIV, 75-; CONSULT, NY HOSP, 75- *Concurrent Pos:* Asst resident, NY Hosp, 36-38, resident physician, 38, assoc attend physician, 46-50, attend physician & chief-of-serv, Vincent Astor Diag Serv, 50-75; asst resident, Hosp, Rockefeller Inst, 39-41, resident physician, 41-46; clin prof med, Med Col, Cornell Univ, 75-78. *Mem:* AAAS; Am Soc Clin Invest; Harvey Soc; Am Heart Asn; Am Rheumatism Asn. *Res:* Cardiovascular physiology; hemolytic streptococcal infection; rheumatic fever and collagen diseases. *Mailing Add:* 2230 Westover Circle Charlottesville VA 22901

WATSON, ROBERT FRANCIS, b Knoxville, Tenn, Nov 20, 36; m 58; c 3. CHEMISTRY, SCIENCE EDUCATION. *Educ:* Col Wooster, AB, 58; Univ Tenn, Knoxville, PhD(chem), 63. *Prof Exp:* From asst prof to assoc prof chem, Memphis State Univ, 63-68; from asst prog dir to assoc prog dir, Undergrad Educ in Sci, 68-73, prog mgr, Off Exp Proj & Progs, 73-75, prog dir, Undergrad Instrnl Improvement Progs, 75-78, dep dir, 78-81, ACTG DIV DIR, DIV SCI EDUC DEVELOP & RES, NSF, 81- *Concurrent Pos:* Nat Acad Sci res assoc, Naval Stores Lab, USDA, Fla, 67-68; on leave, Off Mgt & Budget, Exec Off Pres, 82-83. *Mem:* Am Chem Soc; AAAS. *Res:* Chemistry of indanes; nonclassical ions; physical properties of sulfoxides; federal programs for support of science education and scientific research; federal science policy, administration and budget analysis; science policy. *Mailing Add:* Div of Sci Educ Develop & Res NSF Washington DC 20550

WATSON, ROBERT JOSEPH, b Detroit, Mich, Apr 5, 31; m 53; c 2. GEOPHYSICS. *Educ:* Wayne State Univ, BS, 52; Pa State Univ, PhD(geophys), 58. *Prof Exp:* Res engr, Boeing Co, 58-59; sr res geophysicist, Field Res Lab, Mobil Oil Corp, Tex, 59-63; asst prof geophys, Pa State Univ, 63-65; sr res geophysicist, Field Res Lab, Mobil Oil Corp, Tex, 65-66, res assoc geophys, 66-68, geophys sect supvr, 68-71, corp chief geophysicist, Mobil Oil Corp, NY, 71-75, mgr Field Res Lab, Mobil Res & Develop Corp, 75-80, GEN MGR EXPLOR, MOBIL EXPLOR & PROD SERV INC, DALLAS, 80- *Mem:* Soc Explor Geophysicists; Europ Asn Explor Geophysicists. *Res:* Geophysical data analysis, especially applications of information theory. *Mailing Add:* Mobil Explor & Prod Serv Inc PO Box 900 Dallas TX 75221

WATSON, ROBERT LEE, b Scribner, Nebr, Dec 17, 31; m 53; c 4. EPIDEMIOLOGY, PUBLIC HEALTH. *Educ:* Iowa State Univ, DVM, 55; Univ Minn, MPH, 63, PhD, 73. *Prof Exp:* Jr asst vet, Ga State Dept Health, USPHS, 55-57, asst vet, Md State Dept Health, 57, vet epidemiologist, 57-60, sr asst vet, Univ Minn, 60-61, vet epidemiologist, Miss State Bd Health, 61-63; trainee epidemiol, Sch Pub Health, Univ Minn, 63-64; instr med, 64-67, asst prof epidemiol, 67-70, asst prof med & prev med, 70-71, assoc prof prev med, 71-78, chief div epidemiol & biostatist, 77, PROF PREV MED, MED CTR, UNIV MISS, 78- *Concurrent Pos:* Trainee epidemiol, Sch Pub Health, Univ Minn, 64-67; co-investr, NIH grants, 66-73, 77-82, contract, 71-76. *Mem:* Soc Epidemiol Res; Asn Teachers Prev Med. *Res:* Health and health care statistics; socio-cultural-economic factors related to blood pressure levels; toxemia of pregnancy. *Mailing Add:* Dept of Prev Med Univ of Miss Med Ctr Jackson MS 39216

WATSON, ROBERT LEE, b Plainview, Ark, Nov 8, 34; m 65; c 3. ENTOMOLOGY. *Educ:* Univ Ark, Fayetteville, BS, 56, MS, 63; Auburn Univ, PhD(entom), 68. *Prof Exp:* Instr zool, Auburn Univ, 66-67; asst prof, 67-71, ASSOC PROF BIOL, UNIV ARK, LITTLE ROCK, 71-, CHMN DEPT, 73- *Mem:* Entom Soc Am; Am Inst Biol Sci. *Res:* Taxonomy and ecology of Tabanidae aquatic ecology. *Mailing Add:* Dept of Biol Univ of Ark Little Rock AR 72204

WATSON, RONALD ROSS, b Tyler, Tex, Dec 9, 42; m 66; c 4. IMMUNOLOGY, NUTRITION. *Educ:* Brigham Young Univ, BS, 66; Mich State Univ, PhD(biochem), 71. *Prof Exp:* Res fel immunol & microbiol, Sch Pub Health, Harvard Univ, 71-73; asst prof microbiol, Med Ctr, Univ Miss, 73-74; asst prof microbiol & immunol, Sch Med, Ind Univ, Indianapolis, 74-78; assoc prof immunol & nutrit, Purdue Univ, West Lafayette, 78-82. *Concurrent Pos:* Collabr & vis scientist, Int Ctr Med Res, Cali, Colombia, 73-80; res adv, NIH Postdoctoral Training Prog Sexually Transmitted Dis, Ind Univ, 74-76; vis prof immunol, Brigham Young Univ, 77 & nutrit, Washington State Univ, 79; vis nutritionist & immunologist, Egyption Nutrit Inst, Cairo, Egypt, 79 & 80. *Mem:* Am Asn Immunologists; Am Soc Microbiol; Am Inst Nutrit; Sigma Xi; AAAS. *Res:* Malnutrition's effects on secretory immunity; effect of malnutrition on immune systems in aged mice and humans synthesis and action of apiose compounds on viruses. *Mailing Add:* Dept of Food & Nutrit Purdue Univ West Lafayette IN 47907

WATSON, SIMEON E(LISHA), JR, electrical engineering, see previous edition

WATSON, STANLEY ARTHUR, b Los Angeles, Calif, Aug 30, 15; m 42; c 4. AGRICULTURAL AND FOOD CHEMISTRY, CROP TECHNOLOGY. *Educ:* Pomona Col, AB, 39; Univ Ill, AM, 42, PhD(agron), 49. *Prof Exp:* Asst bot, Univ Ill, 38-42, agron, 46-48; from jr chemist to asst chemist Northern Regional Res Lab, Bur Agr & Indust Chem, USDA, 42-46; sect leader, Res Dept, CPC Int, Inc, 48-68, asst dir, Explor Res Dept, 68-75, res scientist, Agron & Milling Dept, 75-78; COORDR NORTH-CENT REGIONAL PROJ GRAIN QUAL, OHIO RES & DEVELOP CTR, 78- *Mem:* Am Chem Soc; Am Soc Agron; Am Asn Cereal Chem; Sigma Xi. *Res:* Composition, structure, agronomics and processing of cereal grains; industrial corn wet milled process and products. *Mailing Add:* Ohio Agr Res & Develop Ctr Wooster OH 44691

WATSON, STANLEY W, b Seattle, Wash, Jan 3, 21; m 52. BACTERIOLOGY. *Educ:* Univ Wash, BS, 49, MS, 51; Univ Wis, PhD(bact), 57. *Prof Exp:* Fisheries biologist, US Fish & Wildlife Serv, Wash, 52-54; res assoc, 57-71, SR SCIENTIST, WOODS HOLE OCEANOG INST, 71- *Mem:* Am Soc Microbiol; Brit Soc Gen Microbiol; Am Soc Limnol & Oceanog. *Res:* Marine microbiology; nitrification; marine slime molds; fish diseases; myxobacteria. *Mailing Add:* Woods Hole Oceanog Lab Woods Hole MA 02543

WATSON, THEO FRANKLIN, b Plainview, Ark, July 2, 31; m 60; c 4. ENTOMOLOGY, ECOLOGY. *Educ:* Univ Ark, BS, 53, MS, 58; Univ Calif, Berkeley, PhD(entom), 62. *Prof Exp:* From asst prof to assoc prof entom, Auburn Univ, 62-66; assoc prof, 66-70, PROF & ENTOMOLOGIST, AGR EXP STA, UNIV ARIZ, 70- *Mem:* Entom Soc Am. *Res:* Agricultural entomology and ecology; ecology of cotton insects and the integrated approach to pest control in cotton. *Mailing Add:* Dept Entom Univ Ariz Tucson AZ 85721

WATSON, VANCE H, b Kennett, Mo, Nov 25, 42; m 64; c 2. AGRONOMY. *Educ:* Southeast Mo State Univ, BS, 64; Univ Mo-Columbia, MS, 66; Miss State Univ, PhD(agron), 69. *Prof Exp:* Soil conservationist, Soil Conserv Serv, USDA, 63-64; res asst agron, Univ Mo-Columbia, 64-66; from asst prof to assoc prof, 66-77, PROF AGRON, MISS STATE UNIV, 77- *Mem:* Am Soc Agron; Crop Sci Soc Am; Am Forage & Grassland Coun. *Res:* Forage crop ecology and management. *Mailing Add:* Dept of Agron Miss State Univ Box 5248 Mississippi State MS 39762

WATSON, VELVIN RICHARD, b Streator, Ill, June 2, 32; m 58; c 3. GAS DYNAMICS, NUMERICAL ANALYSIS. *Educ:* Univ Calif, Berkeley, BS, 59, MS, 61; Stanford Univ, PhD(plasma physics), 69. *Prof Exp:* RES SCIENTIST GAS DYNAMICS & NUMCERICAL ANAL, AMES RES CTR, NASA, 61- *Concurrent Pos:* Instr, San Jose State Univ, 74-79. *Mem:* Am Inst Aeronaut & Astronaut; Asn Comput Mach; Inst Elec & Electronics Engrs. *Res:* Improving our understanding of plasma dynamics and gas dynamics by utilizing numerical analysis and computer simulations. *Mailing Add:* Mail Stop 245-3 Ames Res Ctr NASA Moffett Field CA 94035

WATSON, WILLIAM CRAWFORD, b Glasgow, Scotland, Dec 20, 27; m 54; c 4. INTERNAL MEDICINE, GASTROENTEROLOGY. *Educ:* Glasgow Univ, MB, ChB, 50, MD, 60, PhD(med), 64; FRCPS(G), 66. *Prof Exp:* Resident surg, Ballochmyle Hosp, 50-51; resident med, Glasgow Royal Infirmary, 53, sr house officer, 53-54, sr house officer cardiol, 54-55, sr registr med, 55-60, lectr, 61-66; prof, Univ EAfrica, 66-67; consult, Glasgow Royal Infirmary, 67-69; assoc prof, 69-72, PROF MED, UNIV WESTERN ONT, 72-; DIR GASTROENTEROL, VICTORIA HOSP, 69- *Concurrent Pos:* EAfrican Med Res Coun fel, Nairobi, Kenyatta Nat Hosp, 66-67. *Mem:* Brit Soc Gastroenterol; Can Asn Gastroenterol; Can Soc Clin Invest; Am Gastroenterol Asn. *Res:* Biophysical and biochemical aspects of intestinal structure and function. *Mailing Add:* Fac of Med Univ of Western Ont London ON N6A 4G5 Can

WATSON, WILLIAM DOUGLAS, b Memphis, Tenn, Jan 12, 42; m 69. ASTROPHYSICS. *Educ:* Mass Inst Technol, BS, 64, PhD(physics), 68. *Prof Exp:* Res assoc, Mass Inst Technol, 68-70; res assoc, Cornell Univ, 70-72; from asst prof to assoc prof physics & astron, 72-77, PROF PHYSICS & ASTRON, UNIV ILL, URBANA, 77- *Concurrent Pos:* A P Sloan Res fel, 74. *Mem:* Am Astron Soc; Am Phys Soc; Int Astron Union. *Res:* Theoretical astrophysics; theory of the interstellar medium; atomic and molecular processes. *Mailing Add:* Depts Physics & Astron Univ Ill Urbana IL 61801

WATSON, WILLIAM HAROLD, JR, b Tex, Sept 2, 31; m 56; c 2. STRUCTURAL CHEMISTRY, NATURAL PRODUCTS CHEMISTRY. *Educ:* Rice Univ, BA, 53, PhD(chem), 58. *Prof Exp:* From asst prof to assoc prof, 57-64, PROF CHEM, TEX CHRISTIAN UNIV, 64-, DIR FASTBIOS LAB, 72-, CHMN, 81- *Concurrent Pos:* Vis prof, Inst Technol, Monterrey, 75-; guest prof, Univ Bonn & Heidelberg, 79. *Mem:* Am Soc Pharmacog; Am Chem Soc; Am Phys Soc; NAm Phytochem Soc; The Chem Soc. *Res:* Structure of biologically active molecules; phytochemical investigations of Central and South America plants; structure and reactivity of molecule exhibiting deformed pi-election system. *Mailing Add:* 6024 Wonder Dr Ft Worth TX 76133

WATSON, WILLIAM HARRISON, b Anniston, Ala, Dec 25, 27; m 50; c 4. POLYMER CHEMISTRY. *Educ:* Emory Univ, AB, 48, MS, 49, PhD(org chem), 52. *Prof Exp:* Res chemist, Carothers Res Lab, 52-54, res chemist, Dacron Res Lab, NC, 54-61, sr res chemist, 61-65, res supvr, 65-69, supvr technol, 69-71, sr res chemist, 71-75, RES ASSOC, DACRON RES LAB, E I DU PONT DE NEMOURS & CO, INC, 75- *Res:* Preparation and evaluation of linear condensation polymers as textile and industrial fibers involving synthetic work in preparation of monomers; product development in synthetic yarns and staples; new polymer preparations and evaluation. *Mailing Add:* E I du Pont de Nemours & Co Inc PO Box 800 Kinston NC 28501

WATSON, WILLIAM MARTIN, JR, b Annapolis, Md, May 10, 46; m 73; c 2. COATINGS POLYMERS, LASER CHEMISTRY. *Educ:* Ga Inst Technol, BS, 68; Univ Ill, MS, 72, PhD(phys chem), 73. *Prof Exp:* RES CHEMIST, ROHM & HAAS CO, 73- *Mem:* AAAS; Am Chem Soc; Sigma Xi. *Res:* Coatings applications; instrumental analysis; laser chemistry; environmental monitoring. *Mailing Add:* Rohm & Haas Res Labs Springhouse PA 19477

WATSON, WYNNFIELD YOUNG, b Toronto, Ont, Feb 5, 24; m 50; c 3. ENTOMOLOGY, INVERTEBRATE ZOOLOGY. *Educ:* Univ Toronto, BA, 50, PhD(entom), 55. *Prof Exp:* Res officer, Fed Dept Forestry, 50-61; from assoc prof to prof zool, Laurentian Univ, 61-74, chmn dept biol, 67-71, dir grad studies, 69-74; chmn dept biol, 74-80, PROF ZOOL, WILFRID LAURIER UNIV, 80- *Concurrent Pos:* Nat Res Coun Can grants, 65-67. *Mem:* Entom Soc Can; Coleopterists Soc. *Res:* Systematics of Coccinellidae; carabidae of eastern North America. *Mailing Add:* Dept Biol Wilfrid Laurier Univ Waterloo ON N2L 3L5 Can

WATT, DANIEL FRANK, b High River, Alta, Feb 9, 38; m 72. METALLURGY. *Educ:* Univ Alta, BSc, 61; McMaster Univ, PhD(metall), 68. *Prof Exp:* Sr scientist, Dept Mines & Tech Surv, Ont, Can, 61-63; Nat Res Coun fel, Cavendish Lab, Eng, 67-69; asst prof eng mat, Univ Windsor, 69-76; gen mgr, Curtis-Hoover Industs, Houston, 77-78; ASSOC PROF ENG MAT, UNIV WINDSOR, 79- *Concurrent Pos:* Consult, Dominion Foundries & Steel Ltd, Ont, Can, 71. *Res:* Metal fatigue; mechanical metallurgy. *Mailing Add:* Dept of Eng Mat Univ of Windsor Windsor ON N9B 3P4 Can

WATT, DAVID MILNE, JR, b Cincinnati, Ohio, July 7, 42; m 67; c 2. SURFACE CHEMISTRY, CATALYSIS. *Educ:* Princeton Univ, BSE, 64; Univ Calif, Berkeley, PhD(chem eng), 69. *Prof Exp:* Asst prof chem eng, Cornell Univ, 69-71; prod develop chemist, Procter & Gamble Co, Cincinnati, 71-77; PROJ LEADER, CLOROX TECH CTR, 77- *Concurrent Pos:* Petrol Res Fund initiation grant, Cornell Univ, 69-71, NSF starter grant, 70-71. *Mem:* Am Chem Soc. *Res:* Chemical engineering; formulation of household cleaning products. *Mailing Add:* Clorox Tech Ctr PO Box 493 Pleasanton CA 94566

WATT, DEAN DAY, b McCammon, Idaho, Sept 21, 17; m 46; c 5. BIOCHEMISTRY. *Educ:* Univ Idaho, BS, 42; Iowa State Col, PhD(bact physiol), 49. *Prof Exp:* Res chemist, Westvaco Chlorine Prod, Inc, 42-44; instr bact, Iowa State Col, 47-49; asst microbiologist, Agr Exp Sta, Purdue Univ,

49-53; assoc prof biochem, Tulane Univ La, 53-60; assoc prof zool, Ariz State Univ, 60-63; mem staff, Midwest Res Inst, Mo, 63-69; PROF BIOCHEM, SCH MED, CREIGHTON UNIV, 69- *Concurrent Pos:* Sr res biochemist & head dept physiol sci, Southeast La Hosp, Mandeville, La, 53-60. *Mem:* AAAS; Int Soc Toxinology. *Res:* Metabolism of bacteria; pigments of fungi; biochemistry of mental disease; chemistry of animal venoms. *Mailing Add:* Dept of Biochem Creighton Univ Sch of Med Omaha NE 68178

WATT, JAMES PETER, b Truro, NS, Sept 22, 49. GEOLOGY, APPLIED PHYSICS. *Educ:* Dalhousie Univ, BSc, 71, MSc, 72; Harvard Univ, PhD(appl physics), 78. *Prof Exp:* Vis res fel, Coop Inst Res Environ Sci, Univ Colo, 78-79; res fel, Seismol Lab, Calif Inst Technol, 79-81; ASST PROF GEOL, RENSSELAER POLYTECH INST, 81- *Mem:* Am Geophys Union; Can Geophys Union; Soc Explor Geophysicists; AAAS; Sigma Xi. *Res:* Mechanical propeties of rocks and minerals. *Mailing Add:* Dept Geol Rensselaer Polytech Inst Troy NY 12181

WATT, JOSEPH T(EE), JR, b Honolulu, Hawaii, July 16, 33; m 71. ELECTRICAL ENGINEERING. *Educ:* Rice Univ, BA, 54, BS, 55; Univ Tex, MS, 63, PhD(elec eng), 65. *Prof Exp:* Eng trainee, Gen Elec Co, 55-56, engr adv eng prog, 57-59, analyst comput sci & info retrieval, 59-60; res asst elec eng, Univ Tex, 61-65; asst prof, 65-67, ASSOC PROF ELEC ENG, LAMAR UNIV, 67- *Mem:* Inst Elec & Electronics Engrs; Asn Comput Mach. *Res:* Automatic control theory including system identification and adjustment of adaptive systems; digital systems; operations research. *Mailing Add:* Dept of Elec Eng Box 10029 Beaumont TX 77710

WATT, KENNETH EDMUND FERGUSON, b Toronto, Ont, July 13, 29; m 55; c 2. ECOLOGY. *Educ:* Univ Toronto, BA, 51; Univ Chicago, PhD(zool), 54. *Hon Degrees:* LLD, Simon Fraser Univ, 70. *Prof Exp:* Biometrician, Ont Dept Lands & Forests, 54-57; sr biometrician, Statist Res & Serv, Res Br, Can Dept Agr, 57-61; head statist res & serv, Can Dept Forestry, 61-63; assoc prof zool, 63-64, PROF ZOOL, UNIV CALIF, DAVIS, 65- *Concurrent Pos:* Consult, Sci Secretariat, Can Privy Coun, 66; sr fel, East-West Ctr, Honolulu, 75. *Honors & Awards:* Fish Ecol & Mgt Award, Wildlife Soc, 61; Entom Soc Can Gold Medal, 69. *Mem:* Ecol Soc Am; Soc Gen Systs Res; Soc Comput Simulation; Japanese Soc Pop Ecol. *Res:* Theoretical, experimental and field ecology of fish and insects; biomathematics; applied statistics; computer simulation studies for evaluating resource management strategies; epidemiology; regional and global modelling and simulation. *Mailing Add:* Dept Zool Univ Calif Davis CA 95616

WATT, LYNN A(LEXANDER) K(EELING), b Winnipeg, Man, Oct 25, 24; m 48; c 4. ELECTRICAL ENGINEERING. *Educ:* Univ Man, BSc, 47; Univ Chicago, SM, 51; Univ Minn, PhD(elec eng), 59. *Prof Exp:* Lectr physics, Univ Man, 48-49, 51-52; asst res off, Atomic Energy Can, Ltd, 52-55; from asst prof to prof elec eng, Univ Wash, 59-66; prof, 66-72, DEAN GRAD STUDIES, UNIV WATERLOO, 72- *Mem:* Am Phys Soc; Inst Elec & Electronics Engrs. *Res:* Diffusion in III-IV compounds; imperfections in semiconductors; physical properties of semiconductor devices. *Mailing Add:* Grad Studies Off Univ Waterloo Waterloo ON N2L 3G1 Can

WATT, ROBERT DOUGLAS, b Santa Paula, Calif, July 7, 19; m 46; c 2. EXPERIMENTAL HIGH ENERGY PHYSICS, PHYSICS ENGINEERING. *Educ:* Univ Calif, BS, 42. *Prof Exp:* Physicist, Lawrence Radiation Lab, Univ Calif, 46-67; GROUP LEADER, STANFORD LINEAR ACCELERATOR CTR, STANFORD UNIV, 67- *Concurrent Pos:* Consult, Argonne Nat Lab & Lawrence Radiation Lab. *Mem:* AAAS; Am Phys Soc. *Res:* Particle accelerator development and operation; development and use of liquid hydrogen bubble chambers for detection of high energy particles of nuclear physics; research to prove existence of magnetic monopoles. *Mailing Add:* 11117 Palos Verde Dr Cupertino CA 95014

WATT, ROBERT M, b Springfield, Ill, Aug 8, 51; m 78; c 1. IMMUNOCHEMISTRY. *Educ:* Univ Ill, Urbana-Champaign, BS, 73, MS, 76, PhD(microbiol & immunol), 78. *Prof Exp:* Teaching asst immunochem, Univ Ill, Urbana-Champaign, 74-77; NIH fel biochem, Med Ctr, Duke Univ, 78-81; ASST PROF MICROBIOL & IMMUNOL, UPSTATE MED CTR, STATE UNIV NY, 81- *Mem:* Am Chem Soc; NY Acad Sci. *Res:* The structure and organization of apoprotein B of human low density lipoprotein; the role of cell surface immunoglobulions in the activation of B lymphocytes. *Mailing Add:* Dept Microbiol Upstate Med Ctr State Univ NY 766 Irving Ave Syracuse NY 13210

WATT, WARD BELFIELD, b Washington, DC, Oct 21, 40; m 79; c 2. EVOLUTIONARY BIOLOGY. *Educ:* Yale Univ, BA, 62, MS, 64, PhD(biol), 67. *Prof Exp:* Asst prof, 69-75, ASSOC PROF BIOL, STANFORD UNIV, 75- *Concurrent Pos:* Mem bd trustees, Rocky Mountain Biol Lab, 71-75, 77-81, 82-, vpres, 82; mem adv panel syst biol, NSF, 73-75. *Mem:* Am Soc Naturalists; Genetics Soc Am; Soc Study Evolution; AAAS; Arctic Inst NAm. *Res:* Study of adaptive mechanisms and microevolutionary processes in natural insect populations from perspectives of physiology, genetics and ecology. *Mailing Add:* Dept of Biol Sci Stanford Univ Stanford CA 94305

WATT, WILLIAM JOSEPH, b Carbondale, Ill, Dec 15, 25; m 56; c 3. INORGANIC CHEMISTRY. *Educ:* Univ Ill, BS, 49; Cornell Univ, MS, 51, PhD, 56. *Prof Exp:* Asst prof chem, Davidson Col, 51-53; from asst prof to assoc prof, 55-65, from asst dean to assoc dean col, 66-71, PROF CHEM, WASHINGTON & LEE UNIV, 65-, DEAN COL, 71- *Mem:* AAAS; Am Chem Soc; Chem Soc France. *Res:* Magnesium fluoride gels; inorganic polymers; boron compounds; molten salts. *Mailing Add:* Washington & Lee Univ Lexington VA 24450

WATT, WILLIAM RUSSELL, b Camden, NJ, June 28, 20; m 46; c 3. POLYMER CHEMISTRY, COATINGS. *Educ:* Univ Pa, BA, 49; Univ Del, MS, 52, PhD(chem), 55. *Prof Exp:* Instr gen chem, Philadelphia Col Textiles & Sci, 49-51; res chemist, Am Viscose Corp, 54-60; sr res chemist, Avisun Corp, 60-64; sr res assoc polymer chem, 64-74, RES FEL AM CAN CO, 77- *Mem:* Am Chem Soc. *Res:* Photochemistry; organic coatings; ultraviolet curable coatings; cellulose derivatives; stereospecific polymerization; catalysis. *Mailing Add:* Am Can Co Princeton Labs PO Box 50 Princeton NJ 08540

WATT, WILLIAM STEWART, b Perth, Scotland, Feb 25, 37; US citizen; m 62; c 3. PHYSICAL CHEMISTRY, SPECTROSCOPY. *Educ:* Univ St Andrews, Scotland, BSc, 59; Univ Leeds, PhD(phys chem), 62. *Prof Exp:* Cornell Prof Exp: Fel, Cornell Univ, 62-64; res chemist, Cornell Aeronaut Lab, Buffalo, NY, 64-71; head chem laser sect, Naval Res Lab, 71-73, dep head laser physics br, 73-76, head laser physics br, Optical Sci Div, 76-79; gen mgr, Washington Opers, 79-80, VPRES CORP OPERS, W J SCHAFER ASSOCS, 80- *Concurrent Pos:* Assoc ed, Inst Elec & Electronics Engrs J Quantum Electronics, 78-81. *Mem:* Am Phys Soc; Combustion Inst; Sigma Xi; Inst Elec & Electronics Engrs. *Res:* Laser physics and development; laser-induced chemistry; energy transfer and reaction rate measurements; optical diagnostics. *Mailing Add:* W J Schafer Assocs 1901 N Fort Myer Dr Arlington VA 22209

WATTENBERG, ALBERT, b New York, NY, Apr 13, 17; m 43; c 3. PHYSICS. *Educ:* City Col New York, BS, 38; Columbia Univ, MA, 39; Univ Chicago, PhD(physics), 47. *Prof Exp:* Spectroscopist, Schenley Prod, Inc, NY, 39-41; asst, Off Sci Res & Develop, Columbia Univ, 41-42; group leader, Metall Lab, Univ Chicago, 42-46; sr physicist & group leader, Argonne Nat Lab, 47-50; vis asst prof, Univ Ill, 50-51; res physicist, Nuclear Sci Lab & lectr, Mass Inst Technol, 51-58; res prof, 58-66, PROF PHYSICS, UNIV ILL, URBANA, 66- *Concurrent Pos:* Actg dir nuclear physics div, Argonne Nat Lab, 49-50; NSF fel, Univ Rome, 62-63; vis prof, Stanford Univ, 73 & 80-81. *Mem:* Am Phys Soc; Sigma Xi; AAAS. *Res:* Spectroscopy; nuclear chain reactors; photoneutron techniques; photonuclear reactions; elementary particle physics. *Mailing Add:* Dept of Physics Univ of Ill Urbana IL 61803

WATTENBERG, FRANKLIN ARVEY, b New York, NY, May 16, 43; m 64; c 2. MATHEMATICS. *Educ:* Wayne State Univ, BS, 64; Univ Wis-Madison, MS, 65, PhD(math), 68. *Prof Exp:* Benjamin Peirce asst prof math, Harvard Univ, 68-71; from asst prof to assoc prof, 71-79, PROF MATH, UNIV MASS, 79- *Mem:* Am Math Soc. *Res:* Differential topology; nonstandard analysis; algebraic topology; probability. *Mailing Add:* Dept Math Univ Mass Amherst MA 01003

WATTENBERG, LEE WOLFF, b New York, NY, Dec 22, 21; m 45; c 6. PATHOLOGY. *Educ:* City Col New York, BS, 41; Univ Minn, Minneapolis, BM, 49, MD, 50; Am Bd Path, dipl, 56. *Prof Exp:* From instr to assoc prof, 56-66, Hill prof, 59-66, PROF PATH, MED SCH, UNIV MINN, MINNEAPOLIS, 66- *Concurrent Pos:* Lederle med fac award, 57-59. *Mem:* Histochem Soc (vpres, 66); Soc Exp Biol & Med; Am Soc Exp Path; Am Asn Pathologists & Bacteriologists; Am Asn Cancer Res. *Res:* Histochemistry; cancer research; experimental pathology. *Mailing Add:* Dept of Path Univ of Minn Sch of Med Minneapolis MN 55455

WATTERS, CHRISTOPHER DEFFNER, b Ironton, Ohio, Dec 7, 39; m 67. CELL BIOLOGY. *Educ:* Univ Notre Dame, BS, 61; Princeton Univ, MA, 64, PhD(biol), 66. *Prof Exp:* Instr biol, Princeton Univ, 64-66; res assoc cell biol prog, Univ Minn, St Paul, 66-68; from asst prof to assoc prof, 73-78, PROF BIOL, MIDDLEBURY COL, 78-, CHMN DEPT, 75- *Concurrent Pos:* Vis scientist, Physiol Lab, Cambridge Univ, 73-74; vis assoc prof, Dartmouth Col, 75; vis prof, Med Sch, Univ Colo, 80-81. *Mem:* NY Acad Sci; Am Soc Cell Biologists; Am Soc Zool. *Res:* Lactation; structural and functional organization of cell membranes; cellular aspects of development. *Mailing Add:* Dept Biol Middlebury Col Middlebury VT 05753

WATTERS, EDWARD C(HARLES), JR, b Monroe, Mich, Feb 16, 23; m 46; c 3. MATHEMATICS, ELECTRONICS. *Educ:* Univ Notre Dame, BSEE, 43, MS, 46; Univ Md, PhD, 54. *Prof Exp:* Asst prof math, US Naval Acad, 46-55; sr engr, Bendix Aviation Corp, 55-57; fel engr, 57, supv engr, 57-58, adv engr, 58-59 & weapon control dept, 59-61, consult engr, Surface Div, 61-70, CONSULT ENGR, ELECTRONIC SYSTS DIV, WESTINGHOUSE ELEC CORP, BALTIMORE, 70- *Res:* Radar; weapon systems; signal processing. *Mailing Add:* 126 Academy St Annapolis MD 21401

WATTERS, GARY Z, b Gilson, Ill, Oct 11, 35; m 57; c 3. FLUID MECHANICS, HYDRODYNAMICS. *Educ:* Chico State Col, BS, 57; Stanford Univ, MS, 58, PhD(civil eng), 63. *Prof Exp:* From instr to asst prof civil eng, Chico State Col, 58-61; from asst prof to assoc prof civil eng, Utah State Univ, 63-77, prof, 77-80, asst dean, 72-74, assoc dean, 74-76; DEAN ENG, COMPUT SCI & TECHNOL, CALIF STATE UNIV, CHICO, 80- *Concurrent Pos:* Am Soc Eng Educ/Ford Found resident in eng pract, 71. *Mem:* Am Soc Civil Engrs; Am Soc Eng Educ; Nat Soc Prof Engrs. *Res:* Free-surface hydrodynamics; hydraulic transients; finite element methods in fluid mechanics; economic design of irrigation systems. *Mailing Add:* Sch Eng Comput Sci & Technol Calif State Univ Chico CA 95929

WATTERS, GORDON VALENTINE, b Winnipeg, Man, Apr 8, 28; m 57; c 3. NEUROLOGY, PEDIATRICS. *Educ:* Univ Minn, Minneapolis, BA, 51; Univ Man, MD, 57. *Prof Exp:* Asst prof neurol, Winnipeg Children's Hosp, Univ Man, 63-65; asst prof, Children's Med Ctr, Harvard Univ, 65-69; PROF NEUROL & PEDIAT, MONTREAL CHILDREN'S HOSP, McGILL UNIV, 69- *Mem:* Am Acad Neurol; Can Neurol Soc. *Res:* Degenerative disease of nervous system; cerebrospinal fluid dynamics. *Mailing Add:* Montreal Children's Hosp Montreal PQ H3H 1P3 Can

WATTERS, JAMES I, b Broadus, Mont, Apr 4, 08; m 38; c 4. CHEMISTRY. *Educ:* Univ Minn, BS, 31, PhD(anal chem), 43. *Prof Exp:* Instr, Cornell Univ, 41-43; res assoc, Metall Lab, Univ Chicago, 43-44, head anal div, 44-45; from asst prof to assoc prof chem, Univ Ky, 45-48; from assoc prof to prof, 48-78, EMER PROF CHEM, OHIO STATE UNIV, 78- *Mem:* AAAS; Am Chem Soc. *Res:* Equilibria of complex species; mixed ligand complexes; acids and complexes of polyphosphates; theory of electrode reactions; applications of potentiometry; absorption and emission spectroscopy; polarography; theory of titrimetry. *Mailing Add:* Dept Chem Ohio State Univ 140 W 18th Ave Columbus OH 43210

WATTERS, KENNETH LYNN, b Iowa City, Iowa, Jan 21, 39; m 64; c 3. INORGANIC CHEMISTRY, BIOINORGANIC CHEMISTRY. *Educ:* Univ Ill, Urbana, BS, 62; Brown Univ, PhD(chem), 70. *Prof Exp:* Res assoc chem, State Univ NY Buffalo, 69-70; asst prof, 70-76, ASSOC PROF CHEM, UNIV WIS-MILWAUKEE, 76- *Mem:* Am Chem Soc. *Res:* Spectroscopic studies of transition metal complexes and metallo-enzymes; Raman, resonance Raman, and infrared spectroscopies; studies of catalytic properties of transition metal complexes and metal cluster compounds. *Mailing Add:* Dept of Chem Univ of Wis Milwaukee WI 53201

WATTERS, NEIL ARCHIBALD, b Glenbrook, Conn, Sept 14, 21; Can citizen; m 47; c 4. SURGERY. *Educ:* Univ Toronto, MD, 44; FRCPS(C), 52. *Prof Exp:* SURGEON-IN-CHIEF, WELLESLEY HOSP, 63-; PROF SURG, UNIV TORONTO, 69- *Concurrent Pos:* Chmn, Interhosp Comt Gen Surg, Univ Toronto, 70-; mem exec comt, Ont Cancer Treat & Res Found, 72- *Mem:* Fel Am Col Surgeons. *Res:* Clinical research; colon carcinoma; breast carcinoma; pilonidal disease. *Mailing Add:* 172 Rosedale Heights Dr Toronto ON M4T 1C8 Can

WATTERS, ROBERT JAMES, b Glasgow, Scotland, July 22, 46. GEOLOGICAL ENGINEERING, ENGINEERING GEOLOGY. *Educ:* Univ Strathclyde, BS, 69; Univ London, MS, 70, PhD(eng geol), 72. *Prof Exp:* Resident eng geologist, Sir Alexander Gibb & Partners Consult Engrs, London, 72-74; proj geol engr, Dames & Moore Consult Engrs, Los Angeles, 74-77; asst prof, 78-80, ASSOC PROF GEOL ENG, MACKAY SCH MINES, UNIV NEV, 80- *Mem:* Int Soc Rock Mech; Inst Civil Engrs; Brit Geotech Soc; Geol Soc London; Asn Eng Geologists. *Res:* Rock mechanics applied to the design of surface and underground excavations; geotechnical documentation and analyses of soil and rock masses; site investigation techniques; ground improvement and instrumentation. *Mailing Add:* Mackay Sch of Mines Univ of Nev Reno NV 89557

WATTERS, ROBERT LISLE, b Everett, Wash, June 25, 25; m 48; c 2. RADIOCHEMISTRY, HEALTH PHYSICS. *Educ:* Univ Wash, BS, 50, PhD(chem), 63; Harvard Univ, MS, 59; Am Bd Health Physics, dipl, 66; recert, 81. *Prof Exp:* Engr asst, Hanford Atomic Prod Oper, Gen Elec Co, Wash, 50-52, supvr bioassay lab, 52-56, supvr radiation monitoring, 56-58; engr, Boeing Co, 59-60; res specialist radiol hazard eval, Atomic Int Div, NAm Aviation, Inc, Calif, 63-65; assoc prof radiochem, Colo State Univ, 65-72; ENVIRON RADIOACTIVITY SPECIALIST, DIV BIOMED & ENVIRON RES, US DEPT OF ENERGY, 72-, GROUP LEADER LAND & FRESHWATER RES, 73-, PHYS SCIENTIST, 79- *Concurrent Pos:* Lectr, Mobile Radioisotope Lab, Oak Ridge Inst Nuclear Studies, 66- *Mem:* AAAS; Health Physics Soc. *Res:* Translocation of plutonium and americium in the body; environmental behavior of polonium; environmental behavior of octinides. *Mailing Add:* Off of Health & Environ Res US Dept of Energy Washington DC 20545

WATTERSON, ARTHUR C, JR, b Ellwood City, Pa, Apr 19, 38. ORGANIC CHEMISTRY, POLYMER CHEMISTRY. *Educ:* Geneva Col, BS, 60; Brown Univ, PhD(org chem), 65. *Prof Exp:* Res assoc chem, Johns Hopkins Univ, 64-65; PROF CHEM, LOWELL TECHNOL INST, 65- *Mem:* Am Chem Soc; Royal Soc Chem. *Res:* Polymer stereochemistry; nuclear magnetic resonance of macromolecules; synthesis of natural products; decomposition of n-nitroso amides; deamination reactions; nitrogen heterocycles. *Mailing Add:* Dept of Chem Lowell Technol Inst Lowell MA 01854

WATTERSON, JON CRAIG, b Kalamazoo, Mich, Nov 25, 44; m 67; c 2. PLANT PATHOLOGY. *Educ:* Carleton Col, BA, 66; Univ Wis, MS, 71. *Prof Exp:* Res asst veg path, Univ Wis, 66-71, res assoc cranberry path, 71-72; HEAD PATH DEPT, PETOSEED CO INC, 72- *Mem:* Am Phytopath Soc. *Res:* Genetics of disease resistance in vegetable corps; breeding for disease resistance in vegetable crops. *Mailing Add:* Petoseed Res Ctr Petoseed Co Inc Rte 4 Box 1255 Woodland CA 95695

WATTERSON, KENNETH FRANKLIN, b London, Eng, July 16, 29; m 68; c 2. INORGANIC CHEMISTRY. *Educ:* Univ London, BSc, 52, PhD(chem), 59. *Prof Exp:* Lect demonstr chem, Birkbeck Col, Univ London, 52-58, res asst, Imp Col, 58-60; res assoc, Cornell Univ, 60-62; sr res chemist, Pennsalt Chem Corp, 62-66; engr, Homer Res Labs, Bethlehem Steel Corp, 66-77; sr scientist photochem, Azoplate Div, Am Hoechst Corp, 78-80. *Mem:* Am Chem Soc; Am Soc Metals; Soc Appl Spectros; Am Soc Mass Spectrometry. *Res:* Metal-gas reactions; surface analysis; ion microprobe spectrometry; auger spectroscopy; corrosion. *Mailing Add:* RD 1 Box 301A Hellertown PA 18055

WATTERSON, RAY LEIGHTON, b Greene, Iowa, Apr 15, 15; m 41; c 1. EMBRYOLOGY. *Educ:* Coe Col, AB, 36; Univ Rochester, PhD(embryol), 41. *Prof Exp:* Asst embryol, Univ Rochester, 37-40; asst, Johns Hopkins Univ, 40-41; instr comp anat & embryol, Dartmouth Col, 41-42; asst prof zool, Univ Calif, 42-46; from asst prof to assoc prof, Univ Chicago, 46-49; from assoc prof to prof biol, Northwestern Univ, 49-61, chmn admin comt, 56-58, chmn dept biol, 58-61; prof exp embryol, 61-72, PROF GENETICS & DEVELOP & BASIC MED SCI, UNIV ILL, URBANA, 72- *Concurrent Pos:* Actg asst prof, Stanford Univ, 45-46; vis prof, Univ Wash, 54 & Univ Iowa, 68; mem fel panel cell biol, NIH, 61-64; Leslie B Arey lectr, Med Sch, Northwestern Univ, 65; guest lectr, Bermuda Biol Sta, 66; secy subcomt embryol, Int Anat Nomenclature Comt, 71-72. *Mem:* AAAS; Soc Develop Biol; Am Soc Cell Biol; Soc Exp Biol & Med; Am Soc Zoologists. *Res:* Analysis of development of pigment cells in down feathers; neural tube; intraneural vascularity; glycogen body; vertebral column and ribs; hatching muscle; endocrine glands and hormone dependent structures of avian embryos; drug action liver, heart, kidneys and neural tube; myeloschisis; invertebrate embryology. *Mailing Add:* Dept Genetics & Develop Univ Ill Urbana IL 61801

WATTERSTON, KENNETH GORDON, b Rockville Centre, NY, Apr 9, 34; m 61; c 2. FOREST SOILS, ENVIRONMENTAL MANAGEMENT. *Educ:* State Univ NY Col Forestry, Syracuse, BS, 59, MS, 62; Univ Wis, PhD(soils), 66. *Prof Exp:* Res asst forest soils, State Univ NY Col Forestry, Syracuse, 59-61; res asst soils, Univ Wis, 61-65; from asst prof to assoc prof forest soils, 65-75, PROF FOREST SOILS, STEPHEN F AUSTIN STATE UNIV, 75- *Mem:* Soil Sci Soc Am; Ecol Soc Am; Soc Am Foresters. *Res:* Forest soil-site relationships; forest soil classification; soil pollution and reclamation. *Mailing Add:* Sch of Forestry Box 6109 SFA Sta Nacogdoches TX 75962

WATTHEY, JEFFREY WILLIAM HERBERT, b London, Eng, Dec 6, 37; m 61; c 3. ORGANIC CHEMISTRY, MEDICINAL CHEMISTRY. *Educ:* Imp Col, Univ London, BSc, 59; St Catherine's Col, Oxford, DPhil(org chem), 62. *Prof Exp:* Res fel, Dept Chem, Univ Calif, Los Angeles, 62-63; SR STAFF SCIENTIST, PHARMACEUT DIV, CIBA-GEIGY CORP, ARDSLEY, 64- *Mem:* Am Chem Soc. *Res:* Organic synthesis; synthesis of biologically active substances with emphasis on central nervous system and antihypertensive agents. *Mailing Add:* 61 Deepwood Dr Chappaqua NY 10514

WATTON, ARTHUR, b Dudley, Eng, Feb 12, 43. SOLID STATE PHYSICS, NUCLEAR MAGNETIC RESONANCE. *Educ:* Univ London, BSc, 65; McMaster Univ, PhD(physics), 71; Univ Chicago, SM, 75. *Prof Exp:* Fel physics, Univ Waterloo, 71-74; asst prof, 75-81, ASSOC PROF PHYSICS, UNIV VICTORIA, 81- *Concurrent Pos:* Nat Res Coun Can Grant, 75- *Mem:* Can Asn Physicists. *Res:* NMR studies of molecular motions in the solid state; solid-solid phase transitions; low temperature rotational quantum effects of molecules. *Mailing Add:* Dept Physics Univ Victoria Victoria BC V8Y 2L7 Can

WATTS, ALVA BURL, animal nutrition, deceased

WATTS, CHARLES EDWARD, b Mo, Mar 21, 28; m 57; c 2. MATHEMATICS. *Educ:* Drury Col, MusB, 50; Univ Calif, MA, 56, PhD, 57. *Prof Exp:* Instr math, Univ Chicago, 57-69, NSF fel, 60-61; from asst prof to assoc prof, 61-69, chmn dept, 76-78, PROF MATH, UNIV ROCHESTER, 69- *Mem:* Am Math Soc; Math Asn Am. *Res:* Algebraic topology; homological algebra. *Mailing Add:* Dept of Math Univ of Rochester Rochester NY 14627

WATTS, DANIEL JAY, b East Cleveland, Ohio, Oct 19, 43; m 73; c 2. CHEMISTRY, BOTANY. *Educ:* Ohio State Univ, BSc, 65; Ind Univ, Bloomington, AM, 68, PhD(org chem), 69. *Prof Exp:* res investr org chem, E R Squibb & Sons, Inc, 69-77; res assoc org chem, 77-81, SR RES ASSOC ORG CHEM, AM CAN CO, 81- *Mem:* AAAS; Am Chem Soc; Water Pollution Control Fedn. *Res:* Antibiotics; anti-infective agents; organic synthesis; chemotaxonomy; natural products; resource recovery; waste water treatment; oil field chemicals. *Mailing Add:* Am Can Co Princeton Lab PO Box 50 Princeton NJ 08540

WATTS, DANIEL THOMAS, b Wadesboro, NC, July 31, 16; m 63; c 2. PHARMACOLOGY. *Educ:* Elon Col, AB, 37; Duke Univ, PhD(physiol), 42. *Prof Exp:* Asst zool & physiol, Duke Univ, 39-42; physiologist, Naval Air Exp Sta, Pa, 46-47; from asst prof to assoc prof pharmacol, Med Sch, Univ Va, 47-53; prof & head dept, Med Ctr, WVa Univ, 53-66; PROF PHARMACOL & DEAN SCH BASIC SCI, MED COL VA, 66- *Concurrent Pos:* Consult, Walter Reed Army Inst Res, 58-67. *Mem:* Am Soc Pharmacol & Exp Therapeut; Soc Exp Biol & Med; AAAS. *Res:* Central nervous system depressants; cardiovascular drugs; experimental shock; aerospace physiology. *Mailing Add:* Sch of Basic Sci Med Col of Va Va Commonwealth Univ Richmond VA 23298

WATTS, DENNIS RANDOLPH, b Riverside, Calif, Dec 7, 43; div; c 2. PHYSICAL OCEANOGRAPHY. *Educ:* Univ Calif, Riverside, BA, 66; Cornell Univ, PhD(physics), 73. *Prof Exp:* Res assoc phys oceanog, Yale Univ, 72-74; asst prof, 74-80, ASSOC PROF PHYS OCEANOG, SCH OCEANOG, UNIV RI, 80- *Mem:* AAAS; Am Geophys Union; Sigma Xi. *Res:* Descriptive and dynamical study of ocean currents, their fluctuation such as eddies, and other processes controlling the oceanic thermocline. *Mailing Add:* Sch of Oceanog Univ of RI Kingston RI 02881

WATTS, DONALD GEORGE, b Winnipeg, Man, Dec 4, 33; m 58; c 2. APPLIED STATISTICS. *Educ:* Univ BC, BASc, 56, MASc, 58; Univ London, PhD(elec eng), 62. *Prof Exp:* Systs analyst, DeHavilland Aircraft Co, Can, 62-64; vis asst prof math, Univ Wis-Madison, 64-65, assoc prof statist, 65-70; PROF STATIST, QUEEN'S UNIV, ONT, 70- *Honors & Awards:* Heaviside Premium Award, Brit Inst Elec Engrs, 61. *Mem:* Fel Am Statist Asn; Int Statist Inst. *Res:* Time series analysis, control and applications of statistics in many disciplines; teaching methods; nonlinear estimation. *Mailing Add:* Dept of Math & Statist Queen's Univ Kingston ON K7L 3N6 Can

WATTS, EXUM DEVER, b Nashville, Tenn, Mar 19, 26; m 48; c 3. ORGANIC CHEMISTRY. *Educ:* George Peabody Col, BS & MA, 48; Vanderbilt Univ, PhD, 54. *Prof Exp:* Instr chem, Florence State Col, 48-49; asst prof, Harding Col, 52-54; from asst prof to assoc prof, 54-60, PROF CHEM, MID TENN STATE UNIV, 60-, PROF PHYSICS, 77- *Mem:* AAAS; Am Chem Soc; Nat Sci Teachers Asn. *Res:* Organic mercurials; ultraviolet spectra; interpretation of organic spectra. *Mailing Add:* Dept of Chem Mid Tenn State Univ Murfreesboro TN 37130

WATTS, HARRY, physical chemistry, see previous edition

WATTS, JOHN ALBERT, JR, b Brooklyn, NY, Nov 30, 48. CELLULAR PHYSIOLOGY, PHARMACOLOGY. *Educ:* Drew Univ, BA, 71; Univ Md, PhD(zool), 77. *Prof Exp:* Teaching asst marine biol, Drew Univ, 69; teaching asst physiol, Univ Md, 71-77; fel physiol, M S Hershey Med Ctr, 77-79; ASST PROF PHYSIOL, UNIV NC, CHARLOTTE, 79- *Concurrent Pos:* Instr seashore life, Children's Sch Sci, 71. *Mem:* Am Physiol Soc; AAAS; Am Soc

Zoologists. *Res:* Possible roles of calcium and changes in mitochondrial function in the causes of cell death from myocardirl ischemic injury; interaction of dimethylsulfoxide with cholinergil function. *Mailing Add:* Dept Biol Univ NC Charlotte NC 28223

WATTS, JUDITH ELIZABETH CULBRETH, b Greenville, SC, Apr 28, 43; div. SOFTWARE SYSTEMS. *Educ:* Furman Univ, BS, 65; Univ Md, College Park, PhD(inorg chem), 71. *Prof Exp:* Teaching asst chem, Univ Md, College Park, 65-68; instr, Northern Va Community Col, 68-69; from jr instr to instr, Univ Md, College Park, 69-72; clin chemist, Diag Labs, 73-80; ENGR DIGITAL SYSTS, GEN ELEC CO, 80- *Mem:* AAAS; Am Chem Soc; Sigma Xi. *Res:* Computer calculation of group electronegatives; correlation of computed charges to observed physical and chemical properties; development of clinical chemistry assays for drugs; heavy metals. *Mailing Add:* 1854 Briarwood Rd Wilmington DC 28405

WATTS, MALCOLM S M, b New York, NY, Apr 30, 15; m 47; c 4. INTERNAL MEDICINE. *Educ:* Harvard Univ, AB, 37, MD, 41. *Prof Exp:* From asst clin prof to assoc clin prof med, 53-71, coordr cardiovasc bd, 52-56, actg dir cardiovasc res inst, 56-57, asst dean, 56-66, spec asst to chancellor, 63-71, CLIN PROF MED, SCH MED, UNIV CALIF, SAN FRANCISCO, 71-, ASSOC DEAN, 66-, DIR EXTENDED PROGS MED EDUC, 74- *Concurrent Pos:* Ed, Calif Med, 68-73; ed, Western J Med, 74-; proj dir, Calif Area Health Educ Ctr Syst, 79-; vpres, Hospice San Francisco, 79- *Mem:* Nat Inst Med; AAAS; fel Am Col Physicians; Am Soc Internal Med (pres, 65). *Res:* Private practice of internal medicine; examination of the role of the physician in modern society; medical education. *Mailing Add:* San Francisco Sch Med Univ Calif San Francisco CA 94143

WATTS, PLATO HILTON, JR, b Florence, SC, May 30, 41; m 75; c 1. CLINICAL CHEMISTRY, PHYSICAL CHEMISTRY. *Educ:* Furman Univ, BS, 65; Univ Md, PhD(chem), 70. *Prof Exp:* Res assoc & fel biophys, Sch Med, Univ Md, 70-71, asst prof chem, 72; res assoc mat sci, Ctr Mat Res, 71-72; teacher chem, Char-Meck Sch, 72-75; assoc dir clin chem, Diag Labs, 75-80. *Mem:* AAAS; Sigma Xi; Am Chem Soc; Am Asn Clin Chemists. *Res:* Application of analytical and radioimmunologic techniques to problems in clinical chemistry. *Mailing Add:* 109 S Franklin Dr Florence SC 29501

WATTS, RAYMOND FREDERICK, III, b Bay Shore, NY, Sept 8, 48; m 70; c 1. ORGANIC CHEMISTRY. *Educ:* Clarkson Col Technol, BS, 70, MS, 76, PhD(org chem), 77. *Prof Exp:* RES SCIENTIST ORG CHEM, CORP RES, UNIROYAL, INC, 78- *Mem:* Am Chem Soc; Sigma Xi; Int Soc Heterocyclic Chem. *Res:* Synthesis of medicinal agents; synthetic fluids and antioxidants. *Mailing Add:* Palmer Rd Southbury CT 06488

WATTS, RODERICK KENT, solid state physics, deceased

WATTS, TERENCE LESLIE, b Leicester, Eng, May 5, 35; m 62; c 2. PHYSICS. *Educ:* Univ London, BSc, 57; Yale Univ, PhD(physics), 63. *Prof Exp:* Res asst nuclear physics, Yale Univ, 63; res assoc particle physics, Duke Univ, 63-64; mem res staff, Lab Nuclear Sci, Mass Inst Technol, 64-65, asst prof physics, 65-70; ASSOC PROF PHYSICS, RUTGERS UNIV, NEW BRUNSWICK, 70- *Mem:* Am Phys Soc. *Res:* Experimental particle physics; phenomenology; data processing of bubble chamber photographs; interactive use of computers. *Mailing Add:* Dept Physics Rutgers Univ New Brunswick NJ 08903

WATTS, WILLIAM WILBUR, academic administration, institutional research, deceased

WATTSON, ROBERT K(EAN), JR, b Kansas City, Mo, Oct 18, 22; m 43; c 5. MECHANICAL ENGINEERING. *Educ:* Okla Agr & Mech Col, BS, 46; Mass Inst Technol, SM, 48. *Prof Exp:* Under eng aide, US Engrs, Mo, 41-42; instr mech eng, Okla Agr & Mech Col, 46-47; asst aeronaut eng, Mass Inst Technol, 47-48; assoc prof mech eng, NDak Agr Col, 48-53; proj engr res dept, Cessna Aircraft Co, 53-56; assoc prof aeronaut eng, Univ Wichita, 56, chief engr & head eng res dept, 57-60; mgr short take-off & landing aerodyn, Boeing Co, Wichita Div, 60-61, mgr vertical take-off & landing aerodyn, 61-63; chief aerodyn, Lear Jet Industs, Inc, 63-64, chief tech staff, 64, chief res & develop, Aircraft Div, 64-67; design specialist adv design-com, Beech Aircraft Corp, 67-70; assoc chmn dept aeronaut eng, Tri-State Col, 70-78; STAFF TECH SPECIALIST, GATES LEAR-JET CORP, 78- *Mem:* Soc Automotive Engrs; Am Inst Aeronaut & Astronaut; Sigma Xi. *Res:* Vertical/short takeoff and landing aerodynamics; preliminary aerodynamic design. *Mailing Add:* 7300 W 11th St Wichita KS 67213

WATWOOD, VERNON BELL, JR, b Opelika, Ala, Sept 24, 35; m 58; c 3. STRUCTURAL ENGINEERING. *Educ:* Auburn Univ, BCE, 57; Cornell Univ, MS, 61; Univ Wash, PhD(eng), 66. *Prof Exp:* Asst prof civil eng, Miss State Univ, 61-62; engr, Boeing Co, Wash, 62-64; sr res engr, Esso Prod Res Co, Tex, 66-67; eng assoc, Pac Northwest Labs, Battelle Mem Inst, 67-70; lab mgr, Res Labs, Franklin Inst, Pa, 70-73; assoc prof, 73-80, PROF CIVIL ENG & CHMN DEPT, MICH TECHNOL UNIV, 80- *Concurrent Pos:* Lectr, Grad Res Ctr, Wash, 69-70; consult, mining indust, 73- *Mem:* Am Soc Civil Engrs. *Res:* Finite element methods in stress analysis and dynamic response of structures; surface mining machinery. *Mailing Add:* Dept Civil Eng Mich Technol Univ Houghton MI 49931

WATZKE, ROBERT COIT, b Madison, Wis, Dec 19, 22; m 56; c 2. OPHTHALMOLOGY. *Educ:* Univ Wis, BS, 50, MD, 52; Am Bd Ophthal, dipl, 57. *Prof Exp:* Intern, Med Ctr, Ind Univ, 52-53; resident, Univ Wis, 56; res asst ophthal, Harvard Med Sch, 56-57; from asst prof to assoc prof, 66-73, PROF OPHTHAL, COL MED, UNIV IOWA, 73- *Mem:* Fel Am Acad Ophthal. *Res:* Clinical ophthalmology; retinal detachment and the vitreous humor of the eye. *Mailing Add:* Dept of Ophthal Univ of Iowa Col of Med Iowa City IA 52240

WATZMAN, NATHAN, b Powhattan Point, Ohio, Feb 15, 26; m 59; c 3. PSYCHOPHARMACOLOGY, PHYSIOLOGY. *Educ:* Univ Pittsburgh, BS, 47 & 55; MS, 57, PhD(muscular dystrophy), 61. *Hon Degrees:* DSc, 77. *Prof Exp:* Asst prof pharmacol, Sch Pharm, Northeast La State Col, 59-63; res assoc prof, Sch Pharm, Univ Pittsburgh, 63-68; health sci adminr, Div Res Grants, NIH, 68-69, health sci adminr, Bur Health Manpower Educ, 69-74; assoc dir regional progs, Div Assoc Health Professions, Health Resource Admin, 74-78, chief spec progs, 78-81; EXEC SECY, DIV RES GRANTS, NIH, 81- *Mem:* Am Soc Pharmacol & Exp Therapeut; Acad Pharmaceut Sci. *Res:* Drug interaction with stress and other environmental modifications of behavior. *Mailing Add:* NIH 218 Westwood Bldg Bethesda MD 20205

WAUCHOPE, ROBERT DONALD, b Atlanta, Ga, Aug 31, 42; m 78; c 6. AGRICULTURAL CHEMISTRY, ANALYTICAL CHEMISTRY. *Educ:* Univ NC, Chapel Hill, BS, 65; NC State Univ, MS, 68, PhD(phys chem), 70. *Prof Exp:* Agr chemist, Ore State Univ, 70-72; RES CHEMIST, SOUTHERN WEED SCI LAB, SCI & EDUC ADMIN-AGR RES, USDA, 72- *Mem:* Am Chem Soc; Sigma Xi; AAAS. *Res:* Aqueous chemistry and soil behavior of pesticides; pesticide residue analysis; environmental behavior of arsenic. *Mailing Add:* USDA Southern Weed Sci Lab Stoneville MS 38776

WAUD, BARBARA E, b Kitchener, Ont, May 18, 31; US citizen; m 56; c 3. ANESTHESIOLOGY. *Educ:* Univ Western Ont, MD, 56, cert, Am Bd Anesthesiol, 66. *Prof Exp:* Instr anesthesia, Sch Med, Boston Univ, 64-66; instr, Harvard Med Sch, 66-71, asst prof, 71-76; prof anesthesiol, 76-77, PROF PHARMACOL, MED SCH UNIV MASS, 77- *Mem:* Asn Soc Anesthesiologists. *Res:* Mechanism of action and kinetics of drugs acting at the neuromuscular junction. *Mailing Add:* Dept Anesthesiol Med Sch Univ Mass 55 Lake Ave N Worcester MA 01605

WAUD, DOUGLAS RUSSELL, b London, Ont, Oct 21, 32; m 56; c 3. PHARMACOLOGY. *Educ:* Univ Western Ont, MD, 56; Oxford Univ, DPhil(pharmacol), 64. *Prof Exp:* Intern, St Joseph's Hosp, London, Ont, 56-57; instr pharmacol, Harvard Med Sch, 59-60; demonstr, Oxford Univ, 61-63; from assoc to assoc prof, Harvard Med Sch, 63-74; PROF PHARMACOL, MED SCH, UNIV MASS, 74- *Concurrent Pos:* USPHS career develop award, 66- *Mem:* Am Soc Pharmacol & Exp Therapeut; AAAS; Brit Pharmacol Soc; Brit Physiol Soc. *Res:* Mechanisms of drug action at molecular level; autonomic and cardiovascular pharmacology; neuromuscular junction physiology and pharmacology; anesthetic agents; uptake and distribution of drugs. *Mailing Add:* Dept of Pharmacol Univ of Mass Med Sch Worcester MA 01605

WAUER, ROLAND H, b Idaho Falls, Idaho, Mar 22, 34; m 66. ECOLOGY, ORNITHOLOGY. *Educ:* San Jose State Col, BS, 57; Sul Ross State Univ, MS, 71. *Prof Exp:* Park naturalist, Death Valley Nat Monument, Calif, 57-62 & Zion Nat Park, Utah, 62-66; chief naturalist, Big Bend Nat Park, 66-72; regional chief scientist, Off Natural Sci, Southwest Region, Nat Park Serv, 72-76, chief natural resources mgt & sci, 76-78, CHIEF DIV NATURAL RESOURCES, NAT PARK SERV, DEPT INTERIOR, 78- *Mem:* Am Ornith Union; Cooper Ornith Soc; Wilson Ornith Soc. *Mailing Add:* Div of Natural Resources Nat Park Serv Dept of Interior Washington DC 20240

WAUGH, DAVID FLOYD, b Kirkwood, Mo, Jan 6, 15; m 37; c 3. BIOLOGY. *Educ:* Washington Univ, AB, 35, PhD(physiol), 40. *Prof Exp:* Asst zool, Washington Univ, 36-38, instr, 39-41; from asst prof to assoc prof phys biol, 41-54, PROF BIOPHYS, MASS INST TECHNOL, 54- *Concurrent Pos:* Mem comt cardiovasc syst & subcomt thrombosis & hemorrhage, Div Med Sci, Nat Acad Sci-Nat Res Coun; mem biophys & biophys chem study sect, NIH, 58-60, chmn, 60-63. *Honors & Awards:* Borden Award, Am Chem Soc, 62. *Mem:* AAAS; Am Chem Soc; Am Physiol Soc; Am Soc Biol Chem; Biophys Soc; Am Acad Arts & Sci. *Res:* Molecular interactions in the development of fibrin clot structure and the bioconversion of prothrombin into thrombin; human platelet characteristics; processes which lead to thrombus formation on implant surfaces. *Mailing Add:* Dept of Biol 56-335 Mass Inst Technol Cambridge MA 02139

WAUGH, DOUGLAS OLIVER WILLIAM, b Hove, Eng, Mar 21, 18; m 46. MEDICAL EDUCATION, PATHOLOGY. *Educ:* McGill Univ, MD, CM, 42, MSc, 48, PhD(path), 50; Royal Col Physicians & Surgeons Can, cert path, 54; FRCP, 64. *Prof Exp:* Demonstr & asst surg pathologist, Path Inst, McGill Univ, 46-47, assoc prof path, 51-57, Miranda Fraser assoc prof comp path, 57; assoc prof path, Univ & asst pathologist, Hosp, Univ Alta, 50-51; from assoc prof to prof, Queen's Univ, Can, 58-64; prof & head dept, Dalhousie Univ, 64-70; prof path & dean fac med, Queen's Univ, Ont, 70-75; EXEC DIR, ASN CAN MED COLS, 75- *Concurrent Pos:* Asst prov pathologist, Alta, 50-51; mem cancer diag clin, Alta Dept Health, 50-51; mem comt consults, Can Tumor Registry, 55-62; med mem adv comt tumor registry, Nat Cancer Inst, 56-62, dir inst, 65, pres, 74-76; dir labs, Hotel Dieu Hosp, Kingston, 58-64; chmn, Can Cytol Coun, 64-65. *Mem:* Am Soc Exp Pathologists; Am Asn Pathologists & Bacteriologists; Can Asn Pathologists; Int Acad Pathologists. *Res:* Renal diseases; hypertension; lesions of experimental hypersensitivity. *Mailing Add:* Asn of Can Med Cols 151 Slater St Ottawa ON K1P 5H3 Can

WAUGH, JOHN BLAKE-STEELE, b Sydney, Australia, Nov 19, 23; m 54; c 3. ELECTRONICS, PHYSICS, GENERAL. *Educ:* Univ Sydney, BS, 48; Univ NSW, MS, 56. *Prof Exp:* Res officer, Atomic Energy Can, Ltd, 56-60; fel electronics, Australian Nat Univ, 60-63; assoc scientist, Brookhaven Nat Lab, 63-64; sr res assoc, Univ Rochester, 64-69; mgr imaging, Xerox Corp, 69-71; corp staff scientist electronics, Singer Co, Fairfield, 71-79; ASST DIR, AIRCO, MURRAY HILL, NJ, 80- *Mem:* Inst Elec & Electronics Engrs; Brit Inst Physics; Inst Elec Engrs Gt Brit. *Res:* Computers; signal processing; instrumentation. *Mailing Add:* 144 Lookout Rd Mountain Lakes NJ 07046

WAUGH, JOHN DAVID, b Charleston, WVa, Sept 20, 32; m 54; c 3. SOLID MECHANICS. *Educ:* Univ SC, BS, 54; Yale Univ, MS, 62. *Prof Exp:* Stress analyst missiles div, Bendix Corp, 56-58; assoc dean, Col Eng, 68-78, PROF ENG, UNIV SC, 58-, DEAN, COL ENG, 78- *Concurrent Pos:* Bd dirs, Assoc Media-based Continuing Eng Educ, 76- *Mem:* Am Soc Eng Educ; Am Soc Civil Engrs. *Mailing Add:* Univ of SC Col of Eng Columbia SC 29208

WAUGH, JOHN LODOVICK THOMSON, b Avonhead, Scotland, Nov 13, 22; m 49; c 4. PHYSICAL INORGANIC CHEMISTRY. *Educ:* Univ Glasgow, BSc, 43, PhD(inorg chem), 49. *Prof Exp:* Plant supt, Imp Chem Industs, Ltd, 43-46; asst lectr, Univ Glasgow, 46-49; Climax Molybdenum Co res fel, Calif Inst Technol, 49-50, inst res fel, 51-53; asst prof chem, Univ Hawaii, 50-51; res chemist, Pac Coast Borax Co, 53-56; assoc prof chem, 56-72, PROF CHEM, UNIV HAWAII, 72- *Concurrent Pos:* Prog dir, NSF Undergrad Res Partic Prog, 60-63; assoc res officer, Neutron Physics Br, Atomic Energy Can, Ltd, Ont, 62-63. *Mem:* NY Acad Sci; fel The Chem Soc; assoc Royal Inst Chem. *Res:* Isopoly and heteropoly compounds; boron and boron compounds; x-ray crystallography; intermetallic compounds; lattice dynamics. *Mailing Add:* Dept Chem Univ Hawaii Honolulu HI 96822

WAUGH, JOHN STEWART, b Willimantic, Conn, Apr 25, 29; m 54; c 2. PHYSICAL CHEMISTRY. *Educ:* Dartmouth Col, AB, 49; Calif Inst Technol, PhD(chem, physics), 53. *Prof Exp:* From instr to prof, 53-73, A A NOYES PROF CHEM, MASS INST TECHNOL, 73- *Concurrent Pos:* Sloan res fel, 58-62; assoc, Retina Found, 61-70; vis scientist, USSR Acad Sci, Moscow, 62 & 75; Guggenheim fel & res assoc physics, Univ Calif, Berkeley, 63-64; consult, Lawrence Radiation Lab, Univ Calif, 64-75; ed, Advan Magnetic Resonance, 65-; Robert A Welch Found lectr, Univ Tex, 69; mem chem rev panel, Argonne Nat Lab, 70-74, chmn, 73-74; vis prof & Humboldt fel, Max Planck Inst Med Res, 72; Falk-Plaut lectr, Columbia Univ, mem fel adv panel, Alfred P Sloan Found, 77-; mem adv comt, Stanford Magnetic Resonance Lab, 76-, Nat Magnetic Lab, 76-80, Magnetic Resonance Ctr, Univ SC, 78- & Lawrence Berkeley Lab, 80-; Reilly lectr, Univ Notre Dame, 78; Lucy Pickett lectr, Mt Holyoke Col, 78. *Honors & Awards:* Irving Langmuir Award, Am Chem Soc, 76. *Mem:* Nat Acad Sci; fel Am Acad Arts & Sci; Am Phys Soc. *Res:* Magnetic resonance. *Mailing Add:* Dept of Chem Mass Inst of Technol Cambridge MA 02139

WAUGH, WILLIAM HOWARD, b New York, NY, Mar 13, 25; m 52; c 3. PHYSIOLOGY, INTERNAL MEDICINE. *Educ:* Tufts Col, MD, 48. *Prof Exp:* Intern internal med, Long Island Col Hosp, 48-49, asst resident, 50-51; asst resident med, Univ Md Hosp, 51-52; cardiovasc trainee, Med Col Ga, 54-55, asst res prof physiol, 55-60, USPHS sr res fel, 59-60, assoc med, 57-60; from assoc prof to prof med, Col Med, Univ Ky, 60-71, head renal div, 60-68, Ky Heart Asn chair cardiovasc res, 63-71; dir clin sci, 71-76, PROF MED & PHYSIOL, SCH MED, EAST CAROLINA UNIV, 71- *Concurrent Pos:* Estab investr, Ga Heart Asn, Med Col Ga, 58, physician in chg hemodialysis sect, 59-60. *Mem:* Microcirc Soc; Am Soc Nephrology; Am Physiol Soc; Am Heart Asn; fel Am Col Physicians. *Res:* Hemodynamics; circulatory and renal physiology; nephrology. *Mailing Add:* East Carolina Univ Sch Med Greenville NC 27834

WAVE, HERBERT EDWIN, b Portsmouth, NH, Oct 13, 23; m 47; c 1. ENTOMOLOGY, PLANT PATHOLOGY. *Educ:* Univ Maine, BS, 52; Rutgers Univ, MS, 60, PhD(entom), 61. *Prof Exp:* Entomologist, USDA, 52-58; res asst entom, Rutgers Univ, 58-61; entomologist, USDA, 61-62; asst prof entom, Univ Mass, 62-67; ASSOC PROF PLANT & SOIL SCI, UNIV MAINE, 67- *Mem:* Entom Soc Am; Am Soc Hort Sci; Weed Sci Soc Am. *Res:* Biology and ecology of potato infesting species of aphids; extension pest control for tree and small fruits; orchard herbicides and growth regulators. *Mailing Add:* Dept of Plant & Soil Sci Univ of Maine Rangeley Rd Orono ME 04473

WAVRIK, JOHN J, b New York, NY, Mar 17, 41; m 61. GEOMETRY. *Educ:* Johns Hopkins Univ, AB, 61, MA, 64; Stanford Univ, PhD(math), 66. *Prof Exp:* Joseph Fells Ritt instr math, Columbia Univ, 66-69; ASSOC PROF MATH, UNIV CALIF, SAN DIEGO, 69- *Mem:* Am Math Soc. *Res:* Algebraic geometry; complex analytic spaces and deformations of complex structures. *Mailing Add:* Dept of Math Univ of Calif San Diego La Jolla CA 92093

WAWERSIK, WOLFGANG R, b Frankenholz, Ger, Apr 23, 36; US citizen; m 65; c 2. ROCK MECHANICS. *Educ:* Tech Col Aachen, Ger, Dipl-Ing, 61; Univ Minn, MS, 63, PhD(mineral eng & roch mech), 68. *Prof Exp:* Res asst mining mech & rock res, Sch Mining & Metall Eng, Univ Minn, 61-65; res assoc, Dept Earth & Planetary Sci, Mass Inst Technol, 68-69; from asst prof to assoc prof mech eng, Dept Mech & Indust Eng, Univ Utah, 69-74; MEM TECH STAFF ROCK MECH RES & DEVELOP, GEOMECH DIV, SANDIA NAT LABS, 74- *Concurrent Pos:* Consult, Re/Spec Inc, Terra Tek Inc, State Utah Hwy Dept & Agbabian & Assoc, 69-74; from asst prof to assoc prof mining eng, Dept Mining, Metall & Fuels, Univ Utah, 70-76; vis scientist, Fed Inst Geosci & Natural Resources, Hannover, Ger, 80; mem ad hoc panels mining & radioactive waste disposal, US Dept Energy, US Nat Rock Mech Comt, Nat Acad Sci & Off War Info. *Mem:* Am Inst Mining, Metall & Petrol Engrs; Am Geophys Union; Int Soc Rock Mech. *Res:* Experimental rock mechanics. *Mailing Add:* 7512 Pickard Ave NE Albuquerque NM 87110

WAWNER, FRANKLIN EDWARD, JR, b Petersburg, Va, Dec 12, 33; m 53; c 3. MATERIALS SCIENCE. *Educ:* Randolph-Macon Col, BS, 59; Univ Va, MS, 68, PhD(mat sci), 71. *Prof Exp:* Physicist, Army Eng Res & Develop Lab, 59-61; sr physicist, Texaco Exp Inc, 61-66; RES ASSOC PROF COMPOSITE MAT, DEPT MAT SCI, UNIV VA, 71- *Concurrent Pos:* Consult, Avco Spec Mat Div, Avco Corp, 69- *Res:* Composite materials; chemical vapor deposition; characterization of mechanical properties; fracture; structure; microstructure. *Mailing Add:* Dept Mat Sci Thornton Hall Univ Va Charlottesville VA 22901

WAWSZKIEWICZ, EDWARD JOHN, b North Smithfield, RI, Feb 10, 33. MICROBIOLOGY, BIOCHEMISTRY. *Educ:* Harvard Univ, AB, 54; Univ Calif, Berkeley, PhD, 61. *Prof Exp:* Asst microbiol, Hopkins Marine Sta, Stanford Univ, 54-55; res asst microbiol, Univ Calif, Berkeley, 55-61; USPHS fel, Max Planck Inst Cell Chem, Ger, 61-63; resident res assoc, Argonne Nat Lab, 64-66; asst mem, Inst Biomed Res, 66-70; ASSOC PROF MICROBIOL, UNIV ILL MED CTR, 70- *Mem:* AAAS; Am Soc Microbiol; fel Am Inst Chemists; Am Inst Biol Sci; Am Chem Soc. *Res:* Metabolism of thiobacilli; erythritol metabolism by propionibacteria; propionate metabolism; erythromycin biosynthesis; mouse salmonellosis, iron metabolism; pacifarins; enology. *Mailing Add:* Dept of Microbiol Univ Ill Med Ctr PO Box 6998 Chicago IL 60680

WAWZONEK, STANLEY, b Valley Falls, RI, June 23, 14; m 43; c 3. ORGANIC CHEMISTRY. *Educ:* Brown Univ, BS, 35; Univ Minn, PhD(org chem), 39. *Prof Exp:* Chemist, Univ Minn, 39-40; Nat Res Coun fel, Univ Ill, 40-41, instr chem, 41-43; instr, Univ Tenn, 43-44; from asst prof to assoc prof, 44-52, chmn dept, 62-68, PROF CHEM, UNIV IOWA, 52- *Mem:* AAAS; Am Chem Soc; Electrochem Soc. *Res:* Organic polarography and synthesis; medicinal chemistry; organic nitrogen heterocycles; aminimides. *Mailing Add:* Dept of Chem Univ of Iowa Iowa City IA 52240

WAX, HARRY, b Boston, Mass, June 17, 18; m 50; c 2. BIOCHEMISTRY. *Educ:* Univ Calif, Los Angeles, MA, 41; Iowa State Col, PhD(chem), 49. *Prof Exp:* Dir fine chems div, Wm T Thompson Co, 40-44; res chemist, Dr Geo Piness Allergy Group, 49-53; res chemist pharmaceuts, Stuart Co, 53-59, mgr prod develop, 59-69, Stuart Pharmaceut Res Dept, Atlas Chem Indust, 69-74; WITH ARCHON PURE PROD CORP, 74- *Concurrent Pos:* Instr, Univ Calif, Los Angeles, 51-52. *Mem:* AAAS; Am Chem Soc; Am Pharmaceut Asn. *Res:* Enzymatic synthesis of peptide bonds; application of ion exchange resins and filter paper electrophoresis to the separation of allergens; organosynthesis; pharmaceutical manufacturing processes. *Mailing Add:* Archon Inc 345 N Baldwin Park Blvd City of Industry CA 91746

WAX, JOAN, b Detroit, Mich, Sept 14, 21. CLINICAL INVESTIGATION, PHARMACOLOGY. *Educ:* Wayne State Univ, BA, 43; Univ NC, MS, 47. *Prof Exp:* From res asst to asst res pharmacologist to res pharmacologist, Parke, Davis & Co, 47-76, sr scientist & clin pharmacologist, 77-80, CLIN SCIENTIST, WARNER-LAMBERT/PARKE-DAVIS PHARMACEUT RES DIV, 80- *Mem:* AAAS; Am Soc Pharmacol & Exp Therapeut; Am Chem Soc. *Res:* Analgetic and anti-inflammatory agents; narcotic antagonists; drug-induced gastrointestinal ulcerogenesis; clinical investigation regarding drugs in arthritis, dysmenorrhea. *Mailing Add:* PO Box 1047 Ann Arbor MI 48106

WAX, NELSON, b Philadelphia, Pa, Apr 2, 17; m 42; c 3. ELECTRICAL ENGINEERING. *Educ:* Univ Pa, BS, 37, MS, 38; Ohio State Univ, PhD(elec eng), 42. *Prof Exp:* Asst, Ohio State Univ, 38-39, instr elec eng, 42; mem tech staff, Bell Tel Labs, Inc, 42-48; from asst prof to assoc prof, 48-53, PROF ELEC ENG & RES, UNIV ILL, URBANA, 53- *Concurrent Pos:* Guggenheim fel, 54-55; consult, Rand Corp, 58-68; assoc mem, Ctr Adv Study, Univ Ill, 64-65; vis prof, Univ Tex, 65-66; vis scientist, Weirman Inst, 78. *Res:* Microwave electronics; communication theory; non-linear oscillations. *Mailing Add:* Dept Elec Eng Univ Ill Urbana IL 61801

WAX, RICHARD GERALD, b New York, NY, Oct 24, 34; m 64; c 3. MICROBIAL GENETICS. *Educ:* Polytech Inst Brooklyn, BChE, 56; Yale Univ, MS, 61; Pa State Univ, PhD(biophys), 63. *Prof Exp:* Nuclear engr, Combustion Eng Co, 56-57; staff fel, NIH, 64-67; NIH spec fel, Weizmann Inst Sci, 67-69; FEL FERMENTATION RES, MERCK RES LABS, 69- *Mem:* AAAS; Am Soc Microbiol. *Res:* Molecular biology of the bacterial spore; protein synthesis; antibiotic development. *Mailing Add:* 16 Saratoga Dr Colts Neck NJ 07722

WAX, ROBERT LEROY, b Des Moines, Iowa, July 7, 38. SPACE PHYSICS. *Educ:* Calif Inst Technol, BS, 60; Univ Ill, Urbana, MS, 61; Univ Calif, Berkeley, PhD(physics), 65. *Prof Exp:* Mem tech staff, TRW Systs Group, 66-71; physicist, Space Environ Lab, Nat Oceanic & Atmospheric Admin, 71-73; consult physicist, 73-78, SR STAFF SYST ENGR, DEFENSE & SPACE SYSTS GROUP, TRW INC, 78- *Mem:* Am Geophys Union. *Mailing Add:* 201 S Poinsettia Manhattan Beach CA 90266

WAXDAL, MYRON JOHN, b San Francisco, Calif, Dec 8, 37; div; c 2. BIOCHEMISTRY, IMMUNOLOGY. *Educ:* Univ Wash, BS, 60, PhD(biochem), 65. *Prof Exp:* Res assoc, Rockefeller Univ, 65-69, asst prof, 69-72; sr staff fel immunol, 72-74, RES CHEMIST, NAT INST ALLERGY & INFECTIOUS DIS, 74- *Mem:* AAAS; Am Asn Immunologists; Am Asn Biol Chemists; Sigma Xi; NY Acad Sci. *Res:* Structure and function, especially of proteins, cell membranes and organelles; immunology, especially biochemistry of cell activation or stimulation. *Mailing Add:* Lab of Immunol Nat Inst of Allergy & Infect Dis Bethesda MD 20014

WAXLER, GLENN LEE, b Olney, Ill, Feb 24, 25; m 46; c 2. VETERINARY PATHOLOGY. *Educ:* Univ Ill, BS, 51, DVM, 53; Mich State Univ, MS, 59, PhD(vet path), 61. *Prof Exp:* Pvt pract, 53-57; from instr to assoc prof vet path, 57-66, PROF PATH, MICH STATE UNIV, 66- *Mem:* Am Vet Med Asn; Am Col Vet Path; Asn Gnotobiotics; Conf Res Workers Animal Dis; Am Soc Exp Path. *Res:* Germ-free research; Enteric disease of swine; histopathology of diseases of domestic animals. *Mailing Add:* Dept Path Mich State Univ East Lansing MI 48824

WAXMAN, ALAN DAVID, b New York, NY, Mar 9, 38; m 61; c 3. NUCLEAR MEDICINE. *Educ:* Univ Southern Calif, BA, 58, MD, 63. *Prof Exp:* Intern med, Los Angeles County Gen Hosp, 63-64; resident med, Los Angeles Vet Admin Hosp, 64-65; res assoc metab, Metab Serv, Cancer Inst, NIH, 65-67; asst prof, 68-70, ASSOC PROF RADIOL, SCH MED, UNIV SOUTHERN CALIF, 70-; DIR NUCLEAR MED, CEDARS-SINAI MED CTR, 77- *Concurrent Pos:* Staff physician radiol, Los Angeles County-Univ Southern Calif Med Ctr, 78- *Mem:* Soc Nuclear Med; Am Fedn Clin Res; AMA; fel Am Col Physicians; Am Col Nuclear Physicians. *Res:* Applications of nuclear medicine technology in the detection and evaluation of disease processes, primarily in oncology and hepatic disease. *Mailing Add:* Cedars-Sinai Med Ctr 8700 Beverly Blvd Los Angeles CA 90048

WAXMAN, DAVID, b Albany, NY, Feb 7, 18; m 50; c 6. INTERNAL MEDICINE, CARDIOLOGY. *Educ:* Syracuse Univ, BS, 42; Syracuse Col Med, MD, 50. *Prof Exp:* Instr internal med, 61-64, asst prof, 64-69, asst dean, 70-71, assoc dean, 71-72, dean, 72-74, vchancellor students, 74-76, vchancelor, 76-77, dep exec vchancellor, 77, EXEC VCHANCELLOR, MED CTR, UNIV KANS, 77- *Concurrent Pos:* Consult, Vet Admin Hosp, 61- & Muson Army Hosp, 79-; assoc prof internal med, Med Ctr, Univ Kans, 69-77, dir med outpatient serv, 70-74 & prof internal med, 77-; major gen mobilization & augmentee to surgeon gen, US Air Force, 70-78, nat consult educ to surgeon gen, 80- *Mem:* AMA; Am Soc Internal Med; Fel Am Col Physicians. *Res:* Non-invasive methods and techniques for the evaluation and assessment of cardiac disfunction; drug inhibition of fatty acid mobilization and catecholamine-induced metabolic changes in humans. *Mailing Add:* Col Health Sci & Hosp Univ Kans 39th & Rainbow Blvd Kansas City KS 66103

WAXMAN, HERBERT SUMNER, b Boston, Mass, Sept 1, 36; m 60; c 3. MEDICINE, HEMATOLOGY. *Educ:* Mass Inst Technol, BS, 58; Harvard Univ, MD, 62; Am Bd Internal Med, dipl, 69, dipl hemat, 74. *Prof Exp:* From intern to resident med, Mass Gen Hosp, Boston, 62-64; res assoc biochem, Nat Cancer Inst, 64-66; resident, Mass Gen Hosp, Boston, 66-67; from asst prof to prof med, Sch Med, Temple Univ, 68-77, dep chmn dept, 75-77; chmn, Dept Med, Baystate Med Ctr, Springfield, Mass, 77-79; prof med, Tufts Univ, 77-79; CHMN, DEPT MED, ALBERT EINSTEIN MED CTR, 79-; DEP CHMN, DEPT MED, SCH MED, TEMPLE UNIV, 79- *Concurrent Pos:* Mead Johnson scholar, Am Col Physicians, 66-67; NIH trainee hemat, Sch Med, Washington Univ, 67-68; advan clin fel, Am Cancer Soc, 68-71. *Mem:* Am Fedn Clin Res; Am Soc Hemat; fel Am Col Physicians. *Res:* Control of protein synthesis in blood cells; clinical studies in sickle cell and related diseases. *Mailing Add:* Albert Einstein Med Ctr York & Taylor Rds Philadelphia PA 19140

WAXMAN, SIDNEY, b Providence, RI, Nov 13, 23; m 48; c 3. ORNAMENTAL HORTICULTURE. *Educ:* Univ RI, BS, 51; Cornell Univ, MS, 54, PhD(ornamental hort), 57. *Prof Exp:* PROF ORNAMENTAL HORT, UNIV CONN, 57- *Mem:* Am Soc Hort Sci; Int Plant Propagators Soc; Int Asn Plant Tissue Culture. *Res:* Photoperiodism; plant propagation; seed and bud dormancy; selection of dwarf forms of Conifers-their introduction and propagation. *Mailing Add:* Dept of Plant Sci Univ of Conn Storrs CT 06268

WAXMAN, STEPHEN GEORGE, b Newark, NJ, Aug 17, 45; m 68; c 2. NEUROLOGY. *Educ:* Harvard Univ, AB, 67; Albert Einstein Col Med, PhD(med sci), 70, MD, 72. *Prof Exp:* Clin fel neurol, Boston City Hosp, 72-75; from asst prof to assoc prof neurol, Harvard Med Sch, 75-78; asst neurologist, Beth Israel Hosp, Boston, 75-78; PROF NEUROL, STANFORD UNIV MED SCH, 78-; CHIEF NEUROL, VET ADMIN HOSP, PALO ALTO, CALIF, 78-; PROF & VCHMN, DEPT NEUROL, MED SCH, STANFORD UNIV, 81- *Concurrent Pos:* Guest lectr, Upsala Col, 68-70; sci investr, Marine Biol Lab, Woods Hole, 71; NIH fel, Harvard Univ, 72-75; vis res fel biol, Mass Inst Technol, 74-75, vis asst prof, 75-77, vis assoc prof, 77-78; NIH career develop award, 75; assoc ed, J Neurocytol, 77-; mem, Nat Adv Comt, Nat Multiple Sclerosis Soc, 80-, Sci Adv Bd, Paralyzed Vets Am, 80- & Res Group, neuromuscular dis, World Fedn Neurol, 81-; sci counr, Fifth Int Cong Neuromuscular Dis, 81-82. *Honors & Awards:* Trygve Tuve Annual Mem Award, NIH Found Advan Educ in Sci, 74. *Mem:* Am Soc Cell Biol; Int Brain Res Orgn; Am Acad Neurol; Am Neurol Asn. *Res:* Basic and clinical neurosciences; electron microscopy; neurophysiology; biology and pathophysiology of cell membranes; demyelirating diseases; peripteral nerve diseases. *Mailing Add:* Neurol Unit 127 3801 Miranda Ave Vet Admin Hosp Palo Alto CA 94304

WAXWEILER, RICHARD JAMES, b Middletown, Ohio, Jan 23, 47. OCCUPATIONAL EPIDEMIOLOGY, CANCER EPIDEMIOLOGY. *Educ:* Univ Mich, BSE, 69, MSIE, 70; Univ NC, PHD(epidemiol), 78. *Prof Exp:* Res asst, Syst Res Lab, 69-71; teaching fel comput programming, Univ Mich, 71; epidemiologist, Nat Inst Occupational Health, 71-73, asst dir, Div Field Studies, 73-75, chief, Epidemiol Sect, 77-82; EPIDEMIOLOGIST & GUEST SCIENTIST, LOS ALAMOS NAT LAB, 82- *Concurrent Pos:* Adj assoc prof, Med Sch, Univ NMex, 82- *Mem:* Soc Occupational & Environ Health; Int Epidemiologic Asn; Int Occupational Health Comn. *Res:* Occupational and other environmental risk factors for cancer, respiratory diseases, and other chronic diseases. *Mailing Add:* PO Box 722 Los Alamos NM 87544

WAY, E LEONG, b Watsonville, Calif, July 10, 16; m 44; c 2. PHARMACOLOGY, TOXICOLOGY. *Educ:* Univ Calif, BS, 38, MS, 40, PhD(pharmaceut chem), 42. *Prof Exp:* Asst pharmacol, Univ Calif, 42; pharmaceut chemist, Merck & Co, Inc, NJ, 42-43; from instr to asst prof pharmacol, Med Sch, George Washington Univ, 43-48; from asst prof to assoc prof, 49-57, vchmn dept, 57-67, chmn dept, 73-78 PROF PHARMACOL & TOXICOL, MED CTR, UNIV CALIF, SAN FRANCISCO, 57- *Concurrent Pos:* USPHS spec res fel, Univ Bern, 55-56; China Med Bd res fel, Univ Hong Kong, 62-63; consult, Attorney Gen, Calif, 59-60 & Dept Corrections, Calif, 64-70; mem, Comt on Probs Drug Safety, Nat Acad Sci-Nat Res Coun, 65-71 & Comt on Probs Drug Dependence, 68-74; mem comt on abuse of depressant & stimulant drugs, Dept Health, Educ & Welfare, 66-68, mem pharmacol study sect, 66-70, chmn, 68-70, mem comt on narcotic addiction & drug abuse rev, 70-74, chmn, 71-74; mem sci adv comt drugs, Bur Narcotics & Dangerous Drugs, 68-74; mem alcohol & drug dependence serv adv group & merit rev bd, Vet Admin, 71-76; mem controlled substances adv comt, Food & Drug Admin, 74-78; Sullivan-Sterling distinguished vis prof, Morehouse Sch Med, 81-82. *Honors & Awards:* Am Pharmaceut Found Award, 62; Ebert Prize Cert, Am Pharmaceut Asn, 62; Kauffman lectr, Ohio State Univ, 66; Forbes lectr, Va Commonwealth Univ, 78; Cultural Citation & Gold Medal, Ministry Educ, Repub China, 78. *Mem:* Fel AAAS; Am Soc Pharmacol & Exp Therapeut (pres, 76-77); Am Pharmaceut Asn; fel Am Col Neuropsychopharmacol; Fed Am Soc Exp Biol (pres, 77-78). *Res:* Drug metabolism; pharmacology analgetics, and endophins; drug tolerance and physical dependence mechanisms. *Mailing Add:* Dept Pharmacol Univ Calif Med Ctr San Francisco CA 94143

WAY, FREDERICK, III, b Sewickley, Pa, Jan 4, 25; m 48; c 2. COMPUTER SCIENCE. *Educ:* Univ Pittsburgh, BS, 50. *Prof Exp:* Physicist, Babcock & Wilcox Co, 51-54, anal eng, Res Lab, 54-56; assoc prof, 56-70, assoc dir, Comput Ctr, 56-80, PROF COMPUT ENG & SCI, CASE WESTERN RESERVE UNIV, 70-, DIR, JENNINGS COMPUT CTR, 80- *Concurrent Pos:* Consult, Thompson Ramo Wooldridge Co, 59 & Bailey Meter Co, 60- *Mem:* Soc Indust & Appl Math; Asn Comput Mach; Math Asn Am. *Res:* Investigation and implementation of automatic programming methods for digital computers. *Mailing Add:* Dept of Comput & Info Sci Case Western Reserve Univ Cleveland OH 44106

WAY, JAMES LEONG, b Watsonville, Calif, Mar 21, 27; m 47; c 3. PHARMACOLOGY, TOXICOLOGY. *Educ:* Univ Calif, Berkeley, BA, 51; George Washington Univ, PhD(pharmacol), 55. *Prof Exp:* USPHS fel pharmacol, Univ Wis, 55-57; USPHS sr fel, 57-58; from instr to asst prof pharmacol, Univ Wis, 59-62; assoc prof, Med Col Wis, 62-67; PROF PHARMACOL, WASH STATE UNIV, 67- *Concurrent Pos:* USPHS career develop award, 58-62, spec res fel, 73-75; mem fed task group toxicol eval pesticide in mammalian species, Environ Protection Agency, 73-75; mem toxicol study sect, NIH, 74-78, mem toxicol data bank rev comt, 74-82; vis scientist, Div Molecular Pharmacol, Nat Inst Med Res, London, 73-75; mem sci adv bd, Nat Ctr Toxicol Res, 79-82; vis prof, NSF, 81-82. *Mem:* AAAS; Am Chem Soc; Am Soc Pharmacol & Exp Therapeut; Soc Toxicol; NY Acad Sci. *Res:* Cancer; nucleic acid; drug metabolism and anticholinesterase alkylphosphate antagonists; cyanide, nitrite and alkylphosphate poisoning; molecular and marine pharmacology; environmental toxicology. *Mailing Add:* Dept of Pharmacol Wash State Univ Pullman WA 99164

WAY, KATHARINE, b Sewickley, Pa, Feb 20, 03. PHYSICS. *Educ:* Columbia Univ, BS, 32; Univ NC, PhD(physics), 38. *Prof Exp:* Huff res fel, Bryn Mawr Col, 38-39; from instr to asst prof physics, Univ Tenn, 39-42; physicist, US Naval Ord Lab, 42, Manhattan Proj, Oak Ridge Nat Lab, 42-48 & Nat Bur Stand, 49-53; dir nuclear data proj, Nat Res Coun, 53-63 & Oak Ridge Nat Lab, 64-68; ADJ PROF PHYSICS, DUKE UNIV, 68-; ED, ATOMIC DATA & NUCLEAR DATA TABLES, 73- *Concurrent Pos:* Ed, Nuclear Data Tables, 65-73, ed, Atomic Data, 69-73. *Mem:* Fel Am Phys Soc; fel AAAS. *Res:* Nuclear fission; radiation shielding; nuclear constants. *Mailing Add:* Dept of Physics Duke Univ Durham NC 27706

WAY, LAWRENCE WELLESLEY, b St Louis, Mo, Nov 15, 33; m 71; c 2. SURGERY. *Educ:* Cornell Univ, AB, 55; Univ Buffalo, MD, 59. *Prof Exp:* Clin instr, 67-69, from asst prof to assoc prof, 69-75, PROF SURG, SCH MED, UNIV CALIF, SAN FRANCISCO, 75-, VCHMN DEPT, 72-; CHIEF SURG SERV, VET ADMIN HOSP, SAN FRANCISCO, 72- *Concurrent Pos:* Fel gastrointestinal physiol, Univ Calif, San Francisco, 67-68 & Vet Admin Ctr, Univ Calif, Los Angeles, 68-69; dir surg out patient dept, Univ Calif, San Francisco, 69-72. *Mem:* Am Col Surg; Am Gastroenterol Asn; Am Surg Asn; Soc Surg Alimentary Tract; Soc Univ Surgeons. *Res:* Gastrointestinal secretion; bile formation. *Mailing Add:* Surg Serv Vet Admin Med Ctr 4150 Clement St San Francisco CA 94121

WAY, ROGER DARLINGTON, b Port Matilda, Pa, Nov 7, 18; m 53; c 4. POMOLOGY. *Educ:* Pa State Univ, BS, 40, MS, 42; Cornell Univ, PhD(pomol), 53. *Prof Exp:* Res assoc pomol, Exp Sta, State Univ NY Col Agr, 49-50; asst, Cornell Univ, 50-53; from asst prof to assoc prof, 53-70, PROF POMOL, EXP STA, NY STATE COL AGR & LIFE SCI, CORNELL UNIV, 70- *Mem:* Am Soc Hort Sci. *Res:* Cherry varieties; winter hardiness; apple varieties and breeding. *Mailing Add:* NY Agr Exp Sta Geneva NY 14456

WAY, WALTER, b Rochester, NY, June 27, 31; m 55; c 3. ANESTHESIOLOGY, PHARMACOLOGY. *Educ:* Univ Buffalo, BS, 53; State Univ NY, MD, 57; Univ Calif, MS, 62. *Prof Exp:* USPHS trainee pharmacol, 60-61; from instr to asst prof anesthesia, 61-63, from asst prof to assoc prof anesthesia & pharmacol, 63-74, PROF ANESTHESIA & PHARMACOL, MED CTR, UNIV CALIF, SAN FRANCISCO, 74- *Mem:* Am Soc Pharmacol & Exp Therapeut; Asn Univ Anesthetists. *Res:* Narcotic and clinical pharmacology. *Mailing Add:* Dept Anesthesia & Pharmacol Univ Calif Med Ctr San Francisco CA 94143

WAYGOOD, EDWARD BRUCE, b Macclesfield, Eng, Dec 15, 45; Can citizen; m 73; c 2. BIOCHEMISTRY, MICROBIOLOGY. *Educ:* Univ Man, BSc, 68, MSc, 69; Univ Toronto, PhD(med biol), 73. *Prof Exp:* Fel biol, Johns Hopkins Univ, 74-77; ASST PROF BIOCHEM, UNIV SASK, 77- *Concurrent Pos:* Med Res Coun Can grant, 74-76 & 76-78. *Res:* Microbial physiology; microbial transport; metabolic regulation; bacterial sugar-phosphotransference system. *Mailing Add:* Dept of Biochem Univ of Sask Saskatoon SK S7H 0W0 Can

WAYGOOD, ERNEST ROY, b Bramhall, Eng, Oct 26, 18; m 50; c 1. PLANT PHYSIOLOGY, BIOCHEMISTRY. *Educ:* Ont Agr Col, BSc, 41; Univ Toronto, MSc, 47, PhD, 49. *Prof Exp:* Assoc prof plant physiol, McGill Univ, 49-54; prof, 54-79, EMER PROF BOT, UNIV MAN, 79- *Mem:* Can Soc Plant Physiol (pres, 59-60); fel Chem Inst Can; fel Royal Soc Can; Am Soc Plant Physiol; Sigma Xi. *Res:* Enzyme mechanisms in respiration and photosynthesis; physiology of host parasite relationships. *Mailing Add:* 9925 Quarry Rd Chilliwack BC V2P 3M3 Can

WAYLAND, BRADFORD B, b Lakewood, Ohio, Dec 14, 39; m 59; c 1. INORGANIC CHEMISTRY. *Educ:* Western Reserve Univ, AB, 61; Univ Ill, PhD(inorg chem), 64. *Prof Exp:* From asst prof to assoc prof, 64-75, PROF CHEM, UNIV PA, 75- *Mem:* Am Chem Soc; Royal Soc Chem. *Res:* Transition metal ion complexes; molecular complexes; thermodynamics; magnetic resonance; metalloporphyrin species; metal ions in biological systems; surface complexes; metal site catalysis. *Mailing Add:* Dept Chem Univ Pa Philadelphia PA 19104

WAYLAND, J(AMES) HAROLD, b Boise, Idaho, July 2, 09; m 33; c 2. BIOENGINEERING. *Educ:* Univ Idaho, BS, 31; Calif Inst Technol, MS, 35, PhD(physics), 37. *Hon Degrees:* DrSci, Univ Idaho, 77. *Prof Exp:* Asst math, Calif Inst Technol, 31-34; instr, Univ Idaho, 34-35; asst prof physics, Univ Redlands, 38-45; physicist, US Naval Ord Test Sta, Calif, 45-48; from assoc prof to prof appl mech, 49-63, prof, 63-79, EMER PROF ENG SCI, CALIF INST TECHNOL, 79- *Concurrent Pos:* Fel, Calif Inst Technol, 38-41, war res fel, 44-45; contract employee, US Naval Ord Lab, 41-42 & 11th Naval Dist, US Dept Navy, 42-44; Guggenheim fel, Univ Strasbourg, 53-54; mem int comn microcirculation & capillary exchange, Int Union Physiol Sci, 78-; vis prof, Univ Limburg, Holland, 79; Alexander von Humboldt sr scientist award, 82. *Honors & Awards:* Ehrenmitglied Ges, Mikrozircultation, 80; Eugene M Landis Award, Microcirculatory Soc, 81. *Mem:* Soc Rheology; Am Soc Eng Educ; Am Soc Enol; Am Asn Physics Teachers; Am Phys Soc. *Res:* Biological engineering science; hemorheology; biophysics and bioengineering of the peripheral circulation; microcirculation. *Mailing Add:* Div of Eng & Appl Sci Calif Inst of Technol (104-44) Pasadena CA 91125

WAYLAND, JAMES ROBERT, JR, b Plainview, Tex, May 3, 37; m 61; c 2. ASTROPHYSICS, AGRICULTURAL PHYSICS. *Educ:* Univ of the South, BS, 59; Univ Ariz, PhD(physics), 67. *Prof Exp:* Res assoc astrophys, Univ Md, 67-70; asst prof astrophysics & agr physics, Tex A&M Univ, 70-74; MEM TECH STAFF, SANDIA LABS, 74- *Honors & Awards:* IR-100 Award. *Mem:* Am Phys Soc. *Res:* Cosmic ray physics; environmental impact of energy generating systems; health physics; petroleum engineering. *Mailing Add:* Sandia Labs Albuquerque NM 87115

WAYLAND, ROSSER LEE, JR, b Charlottesville, Va, Dec 30, 30; m 53; c 3. TEXTILE CHEMISTRY. *Educ:* Univ Va, BS, 49, MS, 50, PhD(chem), 52. *Prof Exp:* Res chemist, 51-54, group leader, Res Div, 54-60, asst dir res, 60-74, mgr, Chem Prod Dept, 74-78, vpres, 78-79, TECH DIR, CHEM PROD DIV, DAN RIVER, INC, 79- *Honors & Awards:* Olney Medal, Am Asn Textile Chemists & Colorists, 75. *Mem:* Am Asn Textile Chemists & Colorists; Am Chem Soc. *Res:* Organic synthesis; thermosetting textile resins. *Mailing Add:* 319 W Main St Danville VA 24541

WAYLAND, RUSSELL GIBSON, b Treadwell, Alaska, Jan 23, 13; m 43, 65; c 2. MINING GEOLOGY, ENGINEERING. *Educ:* Univ Wash, BS, 34; Univ Minn, MS, 35, PhD(econ geol), 39; Harvard Univ, AM, 37. *Prof Exp:* Geologist & engr, Homestake Mining Co, SDak, 30-39; geologist, US Geol Surv, 39-42; minerals specialist, Army-Navy Munitions Bd, 42-45; mining indust control officer, Off Mil Govt for Ger, 45-48; US chmn combined coal control group, Allied High Comn, Ger, 48-52; staff engr, Off of Dir, 52-58, regional geologist, Conserv Div, Los Angeles, 58-66, asst chief, Conserv Div, DC, 66-67, chief, Conserv Div, Reston, Va, 67-78, res, Off Dir, 78-80, ENERGY MINERALS CONSULTANT, US GEOL SURV, ARLINGTON, VA, 80- *Concurrent Pos:* Res asst, Univ Minn, 34-36, instr, 37-39; geologist & engr, Alaska Juneau Gold Mining Co, 37. *Mem:* Fel Mineral Soc Am; Am Inst Mining, Metall & Petrol Engrs; Geol Soc Am; Soc Econ Geologists; Am Inst Prof Geologists. *Res:* Industrial minerals; coal and petroleum; mine evaluation; mineral land appraisal. *Mailing Add:* 4660 N 35th Arlington VA 22207

WAYMAN, C(LARENCE) MARVIN, b Wheeling, WVa, Aug 12, 30; m 56; c 2. METALLURGY. *Educ:* Purdue Univ, BS, 52, MS, 55; Lehigh Univ, PhD(metall), 57. *Prof Exp:* From asst prof to assoc prof, 57-64, PROF METALL, UNIV ILL, URBANA, 64- *Concurrent Pos:* Guggenheim fel, 69; overseas fel, Churchill Col, Cambridge Univ, 69. *Honors & Awards:* Zay Jeffries Award, Am Soc Metals, 77; Matthewson Gold Medal, Am Inst Mining & Metall Engrs, 78. *Mem:* Fel Am Soc Metals; Am Inst Mining & Metall Engrs; Inst Metallurgists Gt Brit; Japan Inst Metals. *Res:* Solid state phase transformations; growth and properties of thin films; transmission electron microscopy. *Mailing Add:* 115B Metall & Mining Bldg Univ of Ill Urbana IL 61801

WAYMAN, COOPER H, b Trenton, NJ, Jan 29, 27; m 51; c 2. ENVIRONMENTAL MANAGEMENT. *Educ:* Rutgers Univ, BS, 51; Univ Pittsburgh, MS, 54; Mich State Univ, PhD(geochem), 59; Univ Denver, JD, 67. *Prof Exp:* Mining engr, Am Agr Chem Co Div, Continental Oil Co, 51-52; explor geologist, Lone Star Steel Co, 52-53; supv technologist, Appl Res Lab, US Steel Corp, 53-54, 59-60; res chemist, Denver Lab, US Geol Surv, 60-65; from asst prof to assoc prof chem, Colo Sch Mines, 65-71; regional gen counsel, 72-74, DIR OFF ENERGY, ENVIRON PROTECTION AGENCY, 74- *Concurrent Pos:* Consult, US Geol Surv, 65-71 & US Fish & Wildlife Serv, 66-72; atty-at-law, Colo, 69-; mem, US Dept Interior Oil Shale Environ Adv Panel, 74-77; adj prof law, Univ Denver, 81-; asst dir, ecol inst & adj sen lectr, Colo Sch Mines, 78-81, asst dir, Mineral Res Inst, 80-81. *Mem:* AAAS; Am Chem Soc; Am Soc Agron; Water Pollution Control Fedn. *Res:* Waste water chemistry; water pollution research on detergents and pesticides both legal and scientific; production of gases and nutrients in lakes and reservoirs; legal aspects of hazardous waste regulation. *Mailing Add:* Environ Protection Agency 1860 Lincoln St Denver CO 80203

WAYMAN, MICHAEL LASH, b Kingston, Ont, Feb 1, 43; m 65; c 2. METALLURGY. *Educ:* Univ BC, BASc, 64; McMaster Univ, MSc, 66; Cambridge Univ, PhD(metall), 68. *Prof Exp:* Res assoc metall, Univ Toronto, 68-69; from asst prof to assoc prof, 69-77, PROF METALL, UNIV ALTA, 78- *Mem:* Am Soc Metals; Can Inst Mining & Metall. *Res:* Effects of environment on structure and on mechanical properties of metals and alloys. *Mailing Add:* Dept of Mining & Metall Univ of Alberta Edmonton AB T6G 0L5 Can

WAYMAN, MORRIS, b Can, Mar 19, 15; m 37; c 2. ORGANIC CHEMISTRY, BIOCHEMICAL ENGINEERING. *Educ:* Univ Toronto, BA, 36, MA, 37, PhD(chem), 41. *Prof Exp:* Asst chem, Univ Toronto, 36-40; res chemist, Dye & Chem Co, Can, 41-43 & Can Int Paper Co, 43-48; mem staff, Indust Cellulose Res Ltd, 48-52; tech dir, Columbia Cellulose Co, Ltd, 52-59; res dir, Sandwell & Co, Ltd, 59-63; PROF CHEM ENG & APPL CHEM, UNIV TORONTO, 63-, PROF FORESTRY, 73- *Mem:* Fel AAAS; Am Chem Soc; Tech Asn Pulp & Paper Indust; Can Soc Microbiologists. *Res:* Chemistry of wood; lignin; pulp and paper; cellulose to alcohol conversion; microbiology conversion of carbon dioxide to fuels and chemicals; feasibility and economic impact analysis. *Mailing Add:* 17 Noel Ave Toronto ON M4G 1B2 Can

WAYMAN, OLIVER, b Logan, Utah, Jan 8, 16; m 43; c 5. ANIMAL PHYSIOLOGY, ANIMAL NUTRITION. *Educ:* Utah State Agr Col, BS, 47; Cornell Univ, PhD, 51. *Prof Exp:* Asst animal husbandman, 51-52, assoc animal scientist, 52-57, chmn dept animal sci, 54-60, animal scientist, 57-80, EMER ANIMAL SCIENTIST, UNIV HAWAII, 80- *Concurrent Pos:* Res assoc psychoenergetic lab, Univ Mo, 60-61; Rockefeller Found grant, Colombian Land & Cattle Inst, 69; USDA Coop State Res Serv grant, Honolulu, 71-74; Dept Planning & Econ Develop grant, Hawaii, 75-77. *Mem:* Am Soc Animal Sci; Soc Study Reproduction. *Res:* Influence of tropical environment upon growth, development and reproduction of cattle; improvement of feeding value of tropical by-products and forage; use of the whole pineapple plant as ruminant feed. *Mailing Add:* Dept of Animal Sci Univ of Hawaii Honolulu HI 96822

WAYMIRE, JACK CALVIN, b Dayton, Ohio, Jan 10, 41; m 67; c 1. NEUROBIOLOGY, NEUROCHEMISTRY. *Educ:* Earlham Col, BA, 63; Ohio State Univ, PhD(physiol), 69. *Prof Exp:* Res assoc, Med Ctr, Univ Colo, 69-73; asst prof neurochem, Univ Calif, Irvine, 73-78; ASSOC PROF NEUROBIOL, MED SCH, UNIV TEX, HOUSTON, 78- *Concurrent Pos:* Prin investr, Nat Inst Neurol & Commun Disorders & Stroke, 74- & Nat Inst Aging, 76-78. *Mem:* Soc Neurosci; Sigma Xi. *Res:* Cellular basis for regulation of monoamine synthesis, secretion and plasticity; aging of the nervous system. *Mailing Add:* Dept of Neurobiol & Anat Box 20708 Houston TX 77025

WAYMOUTH, CHARITY, b London, Eng, Apr 29, 15. CELL BIOLOGY, BIOCHEMISTRY. *Educ:* Univ London, BSc, 36; Aberdeen Univ, PhD(biochem), 44. *Prof Exp:* Technician, Crumpsall Hosp, Manchester, Eng, 37-39; biochemist, Manchester Gen Hosps, 39-41; mem sci staff & head tissue cult dept, Chester Beatty Res Inst, Royal Cancer Hosp, 47-53; res assoc, 55-57, staff scientist, 57-63, asst dir training, 69-72, sr staff scientist, 63-81, asst dir res, 76-77, assoc dir sci affairs, 77-80, intermim dir, 80-81, EMER STAFF SCIENTIST, JACKSON LAB, 81- *Concurrent Pos:* Beit mem fel, Aberdeen Univ, 44-47, Nat Inst Med Res, London, 45, Carlsberg Biol Found, Copenhagen, 46 & St Thomas' Hosp Med Sch, Eng, 46-47; Am Cancer Soc-Brit Cancer Campaign exchange fel, Jackson Lab, 52-53, res fel, 53-55; hon lectr, Univ Maine, 64-80; ed in chief, In Vitro, Tissue Cult Asn, 68-75; Rose Morgan vis prof, Univ Kans, 71. *Mem:* AAAS; Tissue Cult Asn (pres, 60-62); NY Acad Sci. *Res:* Nucleic acids and growth; synthetic nutrients for cells; carcinogenesis in vitro; cell metabolism and differentiation. *Mailing Add:* Jackson Lab Bar Harbor ME 04609

WAYMOUTH, JOHN FRANCIS, b Ingenio Barahona, Dominican Repub, May 24, 26; m 49; c 4. APPLIED PHYSICS. *Educ:* Univ of the South, BS, 47; Mass Inst Technol, PhD(physics), 50. *Prof Exp:* Lab asst, Univ of the South, 43-44 & 46-47; asst, Mass Inst Technol, 49-50; sr engr, Sylvania Elec Prod, Inc Div, 50-58, sect head, 58-65, mgr physics lab, 65-69, DIR RES SYLVANIA LIGHTING PROD GROUP, GEN TEL & ELECTRONICS CORP, 69- *Concurrent Pos:* Consult, Magnet Lab, Mass Inst Technol, 58-65; mem, US Govt Adv Comt, Tech Electron Prod Radiation Safety Standards Comt, 77-79 & Adv Comt Physics, NSF, 81-83. *Honors & Awards:* W Elenbaas Award, Eindhoven Tech Univ, Dutch Phys Soc & N V Philips Co, 73. *Mem:* Am Phys Soc; Illum Eng Soc. *Res:* Oxide cathodes; electroluminescent phosphors; gaseous electronics. *Mailing Add:* Sylvania Lighting Prod 100 Endicott St Danvers MA 01923

WAYNE, BURTON HOWARD, b Acton, Mass, Nov 18, 24; m 47; c 3. ELECTRICAL ENGINEERING. *Educ:* Mich State Univ, BS, 51, MS, 54, PhD(elec eng), 60. *Prof Exp:* Instr elec eng, Mich State Univ, 55-64; assoc prof, 64-71, PROF ENG ANAL & DESIGN & CHMN DEPT, UNIV NC, CHARLOTTE, 71- *Mem:* Inst Elec & Electronics Engrs; Am Soc Eng Educ; Nat Soc Prof Engrs. *Res:* Circuit theory. *Mailing Add:* Dept of Eng Anal & Design Univ of NC Univ Sta Charlotte NC 28223

WAYNE, GEORGE JEROME, b New York, NY, NY, Sept 13, 14; m 41; c 2. PSYCHIATRY, PSYCHOANALYSIS. *Educ:* Brooklyn Col, BS, 34; Univ Western Ont, MD, 39; Southern Calif Psychoanal Inst, PhD(psychoanal), 77; Am Bd Psychiat & Neurol, dipl, 50. *Prof Exp:* Med dir, Los Angeles Neurol Inst, 45-56; CLIN PROF PSYCHIAT, SCH MED, UNIV CALIF, LOS ANGELES, 53- *Concurrent Pos:* Consult, Vet Admin Hosp, 50; teaching analyst, Inst Psychoanal Med Southern Calif, 53-; med dir, Edgemont Hosp, 56-81; consult, Camarillo & Metrop State Hosp, 57; US Info Agency, 59-; pres, Nat Asn Pvt Psychiat Hosps, 75. *Mem:* Fel Geront Soc; fel Am Psychiat Asn; Am Psychoanal Asn; Aerospace Med Asn; fel Am Col Physicians. *Res:* Psychotherapy and somatic therapies in schizophrenia; psychiatric explorations of aged people; cause and treatment of psychoses; research in teaching methods. *Mailing Add:* 4815 Hollywood Blvd Suite 23 Los Angeles CA 90027

WAYNE, LAWRENCE GERSHON, b Los Angeles, Calif, Mar 11, 26; m 48, 62; c 5. MICROBIOLOGY. *Educ:* Univ Calif, Los Angeles, BS, 49, MA, 50, PhD(microbiol), 52. *Prof Exp:* Chief bact res lab, Vet Admin Hosp, San Fernando Calif, 52-71; CHIEF TUBERC RES LAB, VET ADMIN HOSP, LONG BEACH, 71-; ASSOC CLIN PROF MED MICROBIOL, UNIV CALIF, IRVINE-CALIF COL MED, 70- *Concurrent Pos:* Asst clin prof, Univ Calif, Irvine-Calif Col Med, 52-70; clin instr sch med, Univ Calif, Los Angeles, 58-67, lectr, Sch Pub Health, 68-; mem infectious dis res prog comt, Vet Admin, 61-64, mem pulmonary dis res prog comt, 64; mem lab comt, Vet Admin-Armed Forces Coop Study Chemother Tuberc, 61-66; consult, Calif Dept Pub Health, 63-69; mem mycobacterium taxon subcomt, Int Asn Microbiol Socs, 66-, chmn, 76-; mem adv comt actinomycetes, Bergey's Manual Trust, 67-; mem judicial comn, Int Comt Syst Bact, 73-86, chmn, 78-;

mem bact & mycol study sect, Nat Inst Allergy & Infectious Dis, 71-74. *Mem:* AAAS; fel Am Acad Microbiol; Am Soc Microbiol; Am Thoracic Soc (secy-treas, 72-74). *Res:* Natural history and diagnostic techniques of tuberculosis and fungus diseases; physiology and classification of mycobacteria. *Mailing Add:* VA Hosp Tuberc Res Lab 5901 E Seventh St Long Beach CA 90822

WAYNE, LOWELL GRANT, b Washington, DC, Nov 27, 18; m 42; c 2. AIR POLLUTION, ENVIRONMENTAL HEALTH. *Educ:* Univ Calif, Berkeley, BS, 37; Calif Inst Technol, PhD(inorg chem), 49; Am Bd Indust Hyg, dipl. *Prof Exp:* Fel petrol refining, Mellon Inst, 49-52; sr phys chemist, Stanford Res Inst, 53-54; indust health engr, Univ Calif, Los Angeles, 54-56; res photochemist, Air Pollution Control Dist, Los Angeles, 56-62; res analyst, Allan Hancock Found, Univ Southern Calif, 62-69, res assoc comput sci, 63-65, res biol sci, 65-69, sector head, Air Pollution Control Inst, 65-72, res assoc, Sch Pub Admin, 69-72; VPRES & DIR RES, PAC ENVIRON SERV, INC, 72- *Concurrent Pos:* Prof consult, Comt Motor Vehicles Emissions, Nat Acad Sci-Nat Res Coun, 71- *Mem:* Fel AAAS; fel Am Inst Chemists; Am Chem Soc; Air Pollution Control Asn. *Res:* Kinetics and photochemistry of gas phase reactions, especially chemical reactions in polluted urban atmospheres; oxides of nitrogen; air quality modelling; air quality evaluation; atmospheric chemistry. *Mailing Add:* 3292 Grand View Blvd Los Angeles CA 90066

WAYNE, WILLIAM JOHN, b Cass Co, Mich, Apr 23, 22; m 46; c 3. GEOLOGY. *Educ:* Ind Univ, AB, 43, MA, 50, PhD(geol), 52. *Prof Exp:* Head glacial geologist, State Geol Surv, Ind, 52-68; assoc prof geol, 68-71, PROF GEOL, UNIV NEBR, LINCOLN, 71- *Concurrent Pos:* Vis prof, Univ Wis, 66-67; res, Inst Argentino de Nivologia y Glaciologia, 80; NSF grant, Int Progs, 80. *Mem:* AAAS; Geol Soc Am; Arctic Inst NAm; Ger Quaternary Asn; Am Quaternary Asn. *Res:* Quaternary stratigraphy and paleontology; geomorphology; environmental geology; age and origin of Nebraska sandhills; alpine geomorphology in Nevada and Argentina; geomorphology and Pleistocene stratigraphy in eastern Nebraska. *Mailing Add:* Dept of Geol 433 Morrill Hall Univ of Nebr Lincoln NE 68588

WAYNER, MATTHEW JOHN, b Clifton, NJ, Sept 7, 27. NEUROSCIENCES, PSYCHOPHARMACOLOGY. *Educ:* Dartmouth Col, AB, 49; Tufts Univ, MS, 50; Univ Ill, PhD(psychol), 53. *Prof Exp:* From asst prof to assoc prof, 53-63, PROF PSYCHOL, BRAIN RES LAB, SYRACUSE UNIV, 63- *Concurrent Pos:* Vis prof, Fla State Univ, 63, Kanazawa Univ, Japan, 67, Ariz State Univ, 69 & Latrobe Univ, Australia, 74; ed-in-chief, Physiol & Behav, Pharmacol, Biochem & Behav, Brain Res Bulletin & Neurosci Biobehav Rev. *Mem:* Am Psychol Asn; Am Physiol Soc; Int Brain Res Orgn; Soc Neurosci; Am Col Neuropsychopharmacol. *Res:* Hypothalamic mechanisms and ingestive behavior; neural mechanisms of ingestive behavior and drug action. *Mailing Add:* Brain Res Lab 601 University Ave Syracuse Univ Syracuse NY 13210

WAYNER, PETER C, JR, b Taunton, Mass, Aug 18, 34; m 63; c 3. CHEMICAL ENGINEERING. *Educ:* Rensselaer Polytech Inst, BSChE, 56; Mass Inst Technol, SM, 60; Northwestern Univ, PhD(chem eng), 63. *Prof Exp:* Res engr, United Aircraft Res Labs, Conn, 63-65; from asst prof to assoc prof, 65-75, PROF CHEM ENG, RENSSELAER POLYTECH INST, 75- *Concurrent Pos:* Consult heat transfer & fluid mech. *Mem:* Am Inst Chem Engrs; Am Chem Soc. *Res:* Use of interfacial phenomena to control transport phenomena; heat and mass transfer; fluid mechanics; boiling. *Mailing Add:* Dept of Chem & Environ Eng Rensselaer Polytech Inst Troy NY 12181

WAYNICK, ARTHUR H(ENRY), b Spokane, Wash, Nov 9, 05; m 35; c 3. AERONOMY, ELECTRICAL ENGINEERING. *Educ:* Wayne State Univ, BS, 35, MS, 36; Harvard Univ, ScD(commun eng), 43. *Prof Exp:* Radio engr, Reno Radio Co, Mich, 22-35; instr physics, Wayne State Univ, 35-37; demonstr, Cambridge Univ, 39; asst prof, Wayne State Univ, 39-40; electronic engr, Underwater Sound Lab, Harvard Univ, 40-45, res assoc, 41-43; prof eng res, Col Eng, 45-48, A W Nolle prof aeronomy, 48-58, prof elec eng & head dept, 49-71, dir ionospheric res lab, 50-71, EMER PROF ELEC ENG, COL ENG, PA STATE UNIV, UNIVERSITY PARK, 71-; LIAISON SCIENTIST, OFF NAVAL RES, US DEPT NAVY, LONDON, 72- *Concurrent Pos:* Guggenheim fel, Cambridge Univ, 54-55; prog dir eng sci, NSF, 58-59; mem, US Nat Comt, Tech Panel Ionospheric Physics & Working Group Ionospheric Measurements Technol Panel Rockets & Satellites, Int Geophys Year; treas, hon mem & past chmn, US Nat Comt, Int Union Radio Sci; chmn adv comt radio & adv comt, Boulder Labs, Nat Bur Standards; chmn panel atmospheric sci, NSF; mem sci adv coun, Picatinny Arsenal; mem comt atmospheres of earth and planets, Space Sci Bd; mem NSF adv panel, Spec Comt Int Years of Quiet Sun; mem, Working Group, Ionization Panel, Defense Atomic Support Agency; mem, Arecibo Adv Comt, Air Force Off Sci Res; chmn space data ctr panel, Geophys Res Bd, Nat Acad Sci & reporter, Int Years Quiet Sun comt on ionosphere; hon adv bd, English Educ Elektrichestvo. *Honors & Awards:* Navy Ord Develop Award, 45; Off Sci Res & Develop Award, 45. *Mem:* Nat Acad Eng; fel Inst Elec & Electronics Engrs; fel Am Geophys Union; Am Soc Eng Educ. *Res:* Upper atmosphere research; electronics; instruments; guidance systems; radio wave propagation. *Mailing Add:* 833 Thomas St State College PA 16801

WAYRYNEN, ROBERT ELLIS, b Lake Norden, SDak, Oct 24, 24; m 46; c 2. PHOTOGRAPHIC CHEMISTRY. *Educ:* SDak State Col, BS, 48; Univ Utah, PhD(chem), 53. *Prof Exp:* From chemist to sr chemist, Photo Prod Dept, 52-62, res supvr, 62-65, tech serv group supvr, 65-66, field sales mgr, 66-69, TECH MGR PHOTO PROD DEPT, E I DU PONT DE NEMOURS & CO, INC, 69- *Mem:* Am Chem Soc; Soc Photog Sci & Eng; Soc Photo-Optical. *Res:* Photosynthesis; photography. *Mailing Add:* Photo Prod Dept E I du Pont de Nemours & Co Inc Wilmington DE 19898

WAZIRI, RAFIQ, b Afghanistan, Dec 11, 33; US citizen; m 67; c 3. NEUROBIOLOGY, PSYCHIATRY. *Educ:* Am Univ, Beirut, BS, 56, MD, 60. *Prof Exp:* Res fel neurophysiol, Med Sch, Harvard Univ, 64-66; asst prof psychiat, Col Med, Univ Iowa, 66-68; asst prof physiol & assoc prof psychiat, Col Med, Univ Tenn, 70-72; ASSOC PROF PSYCHIAT, COL MED, UNIV IOWA, 72- *Res:* Neurotransmission in the CNS of aplysia; lithium effects on the nervous system; alcohol effects on neural tissues in culture. *Mailing Add:* Dept of Psychiat Univ of Iowa Col of Med Iowa City IA 52242

WAZZAN, AHMED R(ASSEM), b Lattakia, Syria, Oct 17, 35; US citizen; m 59; c 3. NUCLEAR ENGINEERING, FLUID MECHANICS. *Educ:* Univ Calif, Berkeley, BS, 59, MS, 61, PhD(eng sci), 62. *Prof Exp:* From asst prof to assoc prof eng, 62-74, PROF ENG & APPL SCI, UNIV CALIF, LOS ANGELES, 74-, ASSOC DEAN, SCH ENG, 81- *Concurrent Pos:* Guggenheim fel, Copenhagen, 66; consult, McDonnell Douglas Corp, 62-71, Lawrence Radiation Lab, 65-67, Westinghouse Elec Corp, 74-76, NAm Aviation, 75-78, Honeywell, 76-78 & Rand Corp, 75-; reviewer heat & mass transfer, thermodyn & quantum mech, fluid mech & nuclear eng, Appl Mech Rev, 71-; vis scholar with EDF, Paris & Off of Comnr Atomic Energy, Saclay, France, 73 & 79. *Res:* Modeling of fuel elements for fast breeder reactor; stability and transition of laminar flows; thermodynamics of solids and of dense gases; thermal hydraulics of pressurized water reactors. *Mailing Add:* Sch Eng & Appl Sci Univ Calif Los Angeles CA 90024

WEAD, WILLIAM BADERTSCHER, b Columbus, Ohio, Mar 11, 40; m 62; c 3. CARDIOVASCULAR PHYSIOLOGY. *Educ:* Wabash Col, BA, 62; Ohio State Univ, MS, 67, PhD(physiol), 69. *Prof Exp:* Res & teaching asst physiol, Ohio State Univ, 63-69; asst prof, 69-81, basic sci coordr nursing & allied health, 75-80, ASSOC PROF PHYSIOL, SCH MED, UNIV LOUISVILLE, 81- *Concurrent Pos:* Mem, Am Heart Asn. *Mem:* AAAS; NY Acad Sci. *Res:* Myocardial contractility, stress relaxation. *Mailing Add:* Dept of Physiol & Biophys Univ of Louisville Sch of Med Louisville KY 40292

WEAKLEY, MARTIN LEROY, b Piedmont, WVa, June 5, 25; m 50; c 4. RESEARCH ADMINISTRATION, AGRICULTURAL CHEMISTRY. *Educ:* Antioch Col, BS, 51. *Prof Exp:* Lab asst, Nat Cash Register Co, Ohio, 49-51; chemist, Celanese Corp Am, Tex, 51-54 & John Deere Chem Co, Okla, 54-65; chemist, Res & Develop Dept, Nipak Inc, 65-67, mgr chem appln, 67-78; RETIRED. *Mem:* Am Chem Soc; AAAS. *Res:* Product and process development and use application in agricultural field; fertilizer chemistry; scientific education. *Mailing Add:* Rte 2 Box 145 Pryor OK 74361

WEAKLIEM, HERBERT ALFRED, JR, b Newark, NJ, Mar 24, 26; m 55; c 4. PHYSICAL CHEMISTRY. *Educ:* Rutgers Univ, BSc, 53; Cornell Univ, PhD(phys chem), 58. *Prof Exp:* Assoc chemist, Allied Chem & Dye Corp, 53-54; MEM TECH STAFF, RCA LABS, 58- *Concurrent Pos:* Vis prof physics, Univ Calif, Los Angeles, 72-73. *Mem:* Am Chem Soc; Am Phys Soc; Am Crystallog Asn. *Res:* Structures of solids; solid state and molecular spectroscopy; plasma chemistry. *Mailing Add:* RCA Labs Princeton NJ 08540

WEAKS, THOMAS ELTON, b Cumberland City, Tenn, Sept 12, 34; m 59; c 2. PLANT PHYSIOLOGY. *Educ:* Austin Peay State Univ, BS, 56; George Peabody Col, MA, 60; Univ Tenn, Knoxville, PhD(bot), 71. *Prof Exp:* High sch instr, Fla, 58-65; instr biol, Brevard Jr Col, 66-67; asst prof, 71-77, ASSOC PROF BOT, MARSHALL UNIV, 77- *Concurrent Pos:* Sigma Xi res grant, 74; instnl res grant, Marshall Univ, 75. *Mem:* Am Soc Plant Physiologists; Sigma Xi; Scand Soc Plant Physiologists. *Res:* Inhibitory action of canavanine in higher plants; phytotoxin effects on fungus diseases of legumes. *Mailing Add:* Div of Biol Sci Marshall Univ Huntington WV 25701

WEAR, JAMES OTTO, b Francis, Okla, Oct 25, 37; m 59; c 2. PHYSICAL CHEMISTRY, BIOPHYSICS. *Educ:* Univ Ark, BS, 59, MS, 60, PhD(phys chem), 62. *Prof Exp:* Staff mem, Sandia Corp, 61-65; res chemist, Southern Res Support Ctr, Vet Admin, 65-66, dir opers, 66-68, actg chief, 67-68, CHIEF CENT RES INSTRUMENT PROG, VET ADMIN HOSP, LITTLE ROCK, 66-, DIR ENG TRAINING CTR, 72-; PROF BIOMED INSTRUMENTATION TECHNOL & CHMN DEPT, COL HEALTH RELATED PROF, UNIV ARK, LITTLE ROCK, 72- *Concurrent Pos:* Abstractor, Chem Abstr Servs, 62-65; prof, Philander Smith Col, 66-; asst prof, Grad Inst Technol, Univ Ark, 66-69, asst prof, Med Sch, 68-75, assoc prof, 75-; mem, Vet Admin Comt Res Instrumentation, 67; consult, Ark State Health Planning, 68; mem, Ark Gov Sci & Technol Coun; pres, Ark Sci Assocs, 69-73; chmn, Ark Sci & Technol Coun, 73-75. *Mem:* AAAS; Am Chem Soc; Asn Advan Med Instrumentation; Soc Advan Med Systs; Instrument Soc Am. *Res:* Chemical kinetics; electrochemistry; complex ions; solution chemistry; radiochemistry; electron spin resonance; trace metals in biological systems; science education; research support and management; hospital instrumentation maintenance; health and social planning and program evaluation. *Mailing Add:* Vet Admin Med Ctr NLR Div North Little Rock AR 72114

WEAR, JOHN BREWSTER, JR, urology, deceased

WEAR, ROBERT LEE, b Princeville, Ill, Feb 28, 24; m 46; c 2. ORGANIC POLYMER CHEMISTRY. *Educ:* Univ Ill, BS, 46; Univ Nebr, MS, 48, PhD(chem), 50. *Prof Exp:* Sr res chemist, 49-55, group supvr, 55-61, res specialist, 62-67, SR RES SPECIALIST, MINN MINING & MFG CO, 67- *Mem:* Am Chem Soc. *Res:* Condensation polymers. *Mailing Add:* 93 Kraft Rd West St Paul MN 55118

WEARDEN, STANLEY, b Goliad, Tex, Oct 1, 26; m 51; c 5. STATISTICS. *Educ:* St Louis Univ, BS, 50; Univ Houston, MS, 51; Cornell Univ, PhD, 57. *Prof Exp:* Asst biol, Univ Houston, 50-51, instr, 51-53; asst animal husb, Cornell Univ, 53-57; asst prof math, Kans State Univ, 57-59, from assoc prof to prof statist, 59-66; dir div statist, 66-69, chmn, Dept Statist & Comput Sci, 69-73, PROF STATIST, WVA UNIV, 66-, DEAN, GRAD SCH, 72- *Concurrent Pos:* Hon res fel, Birmingham Univ, 63-64; USPHS spec fel, 63-64. *Mem:* Am Statist Asn; Am Soc Animal Sci; Biomet Soc. *Res:* Statistical methods in study of quantitative inheritance; low temperature biology; statistics in agricultural research and genetics. *Mailing Add:* Off of the Dean Grad Sch WVa Univ Morgantown WV 26506

WEARE, JOHN H, b Boston, Mass, Mar 8, 40; m 63; c 1. CHEMISTRY. *Educ:* Harvey Mudd Col, BS, 62; Johns Hopkins Univ, PhD(chem), 67. *Prof Exp:* NSF grant, Air Force Off Sci Res, 68-69; asst prof, 69-80, ASSOC PROF PHYS CHEM, UNIV CALIF, SAN DIEGO, 80- *Res:* Theoretical chemistry, particularly molecular and atomic structure and interactions and the study of irreversible processes. *Mailing Add:* Dept of Chem Univ of Calif San Diego La Jolla CA 92037

WEARN, RICHARD BENJAMIN, b Newberry, SC, Aug 1, 16; m 40; c 5. ORGANIC CHEMISTRY. *Educ:* Clemson Col, BS, 37; Univ Ill, MS, 39, PhD(org chem), 41. *Prof Exp:* Asst, Nat Starch Prod, Inc, NY, 37-38; asst chem, Univ Ill, 39-40; res chemist, Eastman Kodak Co, NY, 41-42; res chemist, Southern Res Inst, 46-47, head org chem div, 47-48; asst res dir, Res & Develop Dept, Colgate-Palmolive Peet Co, 48-52, assoc dir, Colgate-Palmolive Int, Inc, 52-57, dir res & develop, Household Prod Div, 57-65, dir prod develop, 65-67, tech dir, 67-71, vpres res & develop, 71-77; RETIRED. *Mem:* Am Chem Soc. *Res:* Heterogeneous catalytic reactions; terpene derivatives; diene addition products of diaroyl ethylenes; structure of cannabinol and of cannabidiol; isolation and synthesis of active principle in marihuana; utilization of soaps and synthetic detergents. *Mailing Add:* PO Box 4327 Columbia SC 29240

WEART, HARRY W(ALDRON), b Seneca Falls, NY, July 10, 27; m 53; c 3. PHYSICAL METALLURGY. *Educ:* Rensselaer Polytech Inst, BMetE, 51; Univ Wis, MS, 52, PhD(metall), 57. *Prof Exp:* Instr foundry metall, Univ Wis, 53-56; res engr metal physics, Res Lab, Westinghouse Elec Corp, 56-60; asst prof phys metall, Cornell Univ, 60-64; prof metall eng & chmn dept, 64-69, PROF METALL ENG & CHMN DEPT, UNIV MO-ROLLA, 71- *Concurrent Pos:* Am Coun Educ intern acad admin, Univ Calif, Berkeley, 70-71. *Mem:* AAAS; Am Soc Eng Educ; Am Soc Metals; Am Inst Mining, Metall & Petrol Engrs. *Res:* Phase transformations; diffusion, especially surface diffusion; crystal growth. *Mailing Add:* Dept of Metall & Nuclear Eng Univ of Mo Rolla MO 65401

WEART, RICHARD CLAUDE, b Brandon, Iowa, July 20, 22; m 46; c 3. STRATIGRAPHY, PALEONTOLOGY. *Educ:* Cornell Col, BA, 43; Syracuse Univ, MS, 48; Univ Ill, PhD(geol), 50. *Prof Exp:* Asst prof geo, Tex Tech Col, 50-52; from paleontologist & paleogeologist to asst chief geologist, Latin Am Div, Sun Oil Co, 52-60, head staff geologist, 60-62, mgr geol res, 63-71, mgr geol, 71-75, mgr strategic explor, 75-78; MGR EXPLOR RES & DEVELOP, SUNMARK EXPLOR CO, 78- *Mem:* Am Asn Petrol Geologists. *Res:* Petroleum geology. *Mailing Add:* Sunmark Explor Co PO Box 30 Dallas TX 75221

WEART, SPENCER RICHARD, b Detroit, Mich, Mar 8, 42; m 71; c 2. PHYSICS HISTORY. *Educ:* Cornell Univ, BA, 63; Univ Colo, PhD(physics & astrophys), 68. *Prof Exp:* Teaching & res asst physics, Joint Inst Lab Astrophys, Univ Colo, 63-68; res asst astron, Hawaii Inst Astrophys, Univ Hawaii, 66-67; fel solar physics, Mt Wilson & Palomer Observ, 68-71; res assoc hist, Univ Calif, Berkeley, 71-74; DIR CTR HIST PHYSICS, AM INST PHYSICS, 74- *Concurrent Pos:* Teaching asst, Calif Inst Technol, 69-70; res apprenticeship, Inst Int Studies, 72-73. *Mem:* Am Astron Soc; Hist Sci Soc. *Res:* Solar chromosphere; origins of sunspots; space telescopes; history of nuclear physics, French science, and modern astrophysics and cosmology. *Mailing Add:* Am Inst of Physics 335 E 45th St New York NY 10017

WEART, WENDELL D, b Brandon, Iowa, Sept 24, 32; m 54; c 3. GEOPHYSICS. *Educ:* Cornell Col, BA, 53; Univ Wis, PhD(geophys), 61. *Prof Exp:* Geophysicist, Ballistics Res Lab, 56-59; geophysicist, Sandia Corp, 59-69, supvr underground physics div, 69-75, DEPT MGR, NUCLEAR WASTE SYSTS, SANDIA LABS, 75- *Mem:* AAAS; Am Geophys Union. *Res:* Earth physics relating to underground explosion; nuclear waste disposal in geologic media, particular emphasis on salt. *Mailing Add:* Sandia Labs Waste Mgt Systs Dept 4510 Albuquerque NM 87185

WEARY, MARLYS E, b Chicago, Ill, Mar 13, 39. MICROBIOLOGY, ANATOMY. *Educ:* Valparaiso Univ, BA, 60; Univ Ill, MS, 62; Lake Forest Sch Mgt, MBA, 81. *Prof Exp:* Pharmacologist, 62-66, supvr biol control, Baxter Labs, Inc, 66-81, MGR MICROBIOL TECH SERV, BAXTER TRAVENOL LABS, INC, 81- *Mem:* NY Acad Sci; Pharmaceut Mfrs Asn. *Res:* Amphibian regeneration; anticonvulsant research; biologic control and pyrogen testing. *Mailing Add:* Baxter Travenol Labs Inc 6301 Lincoln Morton Grove IL 60053

WEARY, PEYTON EDWIN, b Evanston, Ill, Jan 10, 30; m 52; c 3. DERMATOLOGY. *Educ:* Univ Va, MD, 55. *Prof Exp:* Intern, Univ Hosps Cleveland, 55-56; from asst resident to resident, 58-61, from instr to assoc prof, 61-70, PROF DERMAT, SCH MED, UNIV VA, 70-, VCHMN DEPT, 75- *Concurrent Pos:* Chmn, Coun Nat Prog Dermat, 72-75. *Mem:* Am Dermat Asn; Am Acad Dermat; Soc Invest Dermat. *Res:* Exploration of the keratinolytic abilities of various dermatophyte fungal organisms and investigation of ecology of certain lipophilic yeast organisms on the skin surface. *Mailing Add:* Dept of Dermat Univ of Va Hosp Charlottesville VA 22901

WEAST, CLAIR ALEXANDER, b Modesto, Calif, Oct 13, 13; m 40; c 2. FOOD CHEMISTRY. *Educ:* Univ Calif, BS, 37, MS, 39, PhD(agr chem), 42. *Prof Exp:* Asst, Univ Calif, 37-42; chemist, USDA, 42-44; chief chemist, Pacific Can Co, 44-46; res dir, Tillie Lewis Foods, Inc, 46-78; RETIRED. *Res:* Food products; chlorophyllase. *Mailing Add:* 16127 S Cottage Ave Manteca CA 95336

WEATHERBEE, CARL, b Michigan City, Ind, Nov 21, 16; m 50; c 5. ORGANIC CHEMISTRY. *Educ:* Hanover Col, AB, 40; Univ Ill, AM, 46; Univ Utah, PhD(chem), 50. *Prof Exp:* Asst chem, Univ Ill, 46; instr, Reed Col, 50; asst prof, Univ Hawaii, 50-51; prof chem & chmn dept, Millikin Univ, 52-82; RETIRED. *Concurrent Pos:* Researcher, Univ Utah, 59-60. *Mem:* AAAS; Am Chem Soc; Am Inst Chemists. *Res:* Mannich bases; nitrogen mustards. *Mailing Add:* 1360 W Macon St Decatur IL 62522

WEATHERBY, GERALD DUNCAN, b Neodesha, Kans, Mar 13, 40; m 68; c 2. BIOCHEMISTRY. *Educ:* Univ Kans, BS, 62 & 63, PhD(biochem), 69. *Prof Exp:* Teacher high sch, Kans, 63-65; asst prof chem, Lake Superior State Col, 69-77, assoc prof, 77-81; chmn dept chem, 81, ASSOC PROF CHEM, OKLA CITY UNIV, 81- *Res:* Mechanism of riboflavin catalyzed carbon-carbon bond oxidations; extrapolation of these model system studies to elucidate mechanisms of flavoenzyme catalysis. *Mailing Add:* Dept of Chem Okla City Univ Oklahoma City OK 73106

WEATHERFORD, THOMAS WALLER, III, b Uriah, Ala, Mar 12, 30; m 57; c 2. PERIODONTOLOGY. *Educ:* Auburn Univ, DVM, 54; Univ Ala, Birmingham, DMD, 61, MSD, 69; Am Bd Periodont dipl, 76. *Prof Exp:* Intern pedodontics, Sch Dent, 61-62, instr dent, 62-69, from asst prof to assoc prof periodont, 69-77, PROF PERIODONT, SCH DENT, UNIV ALA, 77-, DIR POSTDOCTORAL EDUC, 70-, ASST PROF COMP MED, SCH MED, SR SCIENTIST, INST DENT RES, SCH DENT, 77- *Concurrent Pos:* NIH trainee, 61-62; staff dentist, Birmingham Vet Admin Hosp, 62-65, resident periodont, 66-68, res assoc, 68-70; resident periodont, Sch Dent, Univ Ala, 66-68; consult, Dept Animal Serv, Univ Ala, 67-69; investr, Inst Dent Res, 70-; mem, Am Asn Dent Schs; consult, Birmingham Vet Admin Hosp & Tuskegee Vet Admin Hosp. *Mem:* AAAS; Am Dent Asn; Int Asn Dent Res; Am Acad Periodont; Am Asn Lab Animal Sci. *Res:* Animal models in periodontal research; dental plaque control; histochemistry of the periodontium. *Mailing Add:* Univ of Ala Sch of Dent 1919 Seventh Ave S Birmingham AL 35233

WEATHERFORD, W(ILLIAM) D(EWEY), JR, b Orange, Tex, Nov 20, 23; m 45; c 2. CHEMICAL ENGINEERING, COMBUSTION. *Educ:* Univ Tex, BS, 44; Univ Pittsburgh, MS, 49, PhD(chem eng), 54. *Prof Exp:* Tutor chem eng, Univ Tex, 44-45; asst process engr, Neches Butane Prod Co, 45-47; jr fel, Mellon Inst, 47-54, fel, 54-58; sr res engr, 58-60, sect mgr, 60-68, staff engr, 68-71, mgr fuel safety & combustion, 71-80, MGR ENERGY SYSTMS RES DIV, SOUTHWEST RES INST, 80- *Concurrent Pos:* Consult, Appl Physics Lab, Johns Hopkins Univ, 54-56. *Mem:* Combustion Inst; Am Inst Chem Engrs. *Res:* Principles and applications of fluid flammability, combustion and fire safety; fire research; principles and applications of diffusional processes; fire-resistant fuels; thermophysical properties of alkali metals. *Mailing Add:* Southwest Res Inst PO Drawer 28510 San Antonio TX 78284

WEATHERLEY, ALAN HAROLD, b Sydney, Australia, Mar 28, 28. FISH & POLLUTION BIOLOGY. *Educ:* Univ Sydney, BSc, 49; Univ Tasmania, MSc, 59; Univ Glasgow, PhD(zool), 61. *Prof Exp:* Res fel physiol, Univ Sydney, 49-51; res scientist fishery biol, Commonwealth Sci & Indust Res Orgn, 51-57; asst lectr zool, Univ Glasgow, 58-59, acting lectr, 59-60; lectr zool, Australian Nat Univ, 60-62, sr lectr, 62-71, reader, 71-72; prof fisheries biol, Inst Biol & Geol, Univ Tromso, 74-75; PROF ZOOL, LIFE SCI DIV, SCARBOROUGH COL, UNIV TORONTO, 75- *Concurrent Pos:* Vis fel, Leverhulme Trust, 70. *Honors & Awards:* Hilary Jolly Award, Australian Soc Limnol, 74. *Mem:* Can Soc Zool; Am Fisheries Soc; Australian Soc Limnol (pres 65-66); Fel Int Acad Fishery Scientists. *Res:* Studies on freshwater fish in fields of ecology, distribution, taxonomy, physiology, especially thermal tolerance and somatic growth, conservation and heavy metal pollution. *Mailing Add:* Scarborough Col Univ of Toronto Toronto ON M1C 1A4 Can

WEATHERLY, GEORGES LLOYD, OCEANOGRAPHY. *Educ:* Univ Va, BS, 64; Harvard Univ, MA, 66, MEng, 67; Nova Univ, PhD(phys oceanography), 71. *Prof Exp:* Fel, Nova Univ, 71-72; Exchange scientist, Inst Oceanog, USSR Acad Sci, 72-73; asst prof, 73-78, ASSOC PROF OCEANOG, FLA STATE UNIV, 78- *Concurrent Pos:* Prin investr, Off Naval Res, 73, NSF, 75-77; comt appointee, NSF, 79-80, Nat Res Coun, 79-82. *Mem:* Am Geophys Union; AAAS. *Res:* Near bottom currents and deep circulation in the ocean; oceans bottom boundary layer; suspended sediment transport dynamics in the oceans; turbulent processes in the ocean. *Mailing Add:* Dept Oceanog Fla State Univ Tallahassee FL 32306

WEATHERLY, NORMAN F, b Elkton, Ore, June 22, 32; m 52; c 6. MEDICAL PARASITOLOGY. *Educ:* Ore State Univ, BS, 53, MS, 60; Kans State Univ, PhD(parasitol), 62. *Prof Exp:* NIH trainee parasitol, 62-63, from asst prof to assoc prof, 63-72, PROF PARASITOL, SCH PUB HEALTH, UNIV NC, CHAPEL HILL, 72- *Concurrent Pos:* Consult, Nat Inst Gen Med Sci, 76-80. *Mem:* Am Soc Parasitol; Am Soc Trop Med & Hyg; Am Micros Soc. *Res:* General immunobiology of helminth parasites; cell mediated responses of hosts to helminth parasites. *Mailing Add:* Dept of Parasitol Sch of Pub Health Univ of NC Chapel Hill NC 27514

WEATHERLY, THOMAS LEVI, b Greenville, Miss, Jan 14, 24; m 52; c 3. PHYSICS. *Educ:* Ohio State Univ, PhD(physics), 51. *Prof Exp:* Assoc prof, 52-61, PROF PHYSICS, GA INST TECHNOL, 61- *Mem:* Fel Am Phys Soc. *Res:* Microwave and radio-frequency spectroscopy. *Mailing Add:* Sch of Physics Ga Inst of Technol Atlanta GA 30332

WEATHERRED, JACKIE G, b Pampa, Tex, Mar 14, 34; m 60; c 3. PHYSIOLOGY. *Educ:* Univ Tex, DDS, 59, PhD(physiol), 65. *Prof Exp:* Dent consult, Tex Inst Rehab & Res, 60-62; instr physiol & res assoc oral path, Med Col Va, 62-63; from asst prof to assoc prof physiol, Dent Sch, Univ Md, Baltimore, 63-69; PROF & COORDR PHYSIOL, SCH DENT, MED COL GA, 69- *Concurrent Pos:* Mem test construction comt, Coun Nat Bd Dent Examr; basic sci consult, Coun Dent Educ; Am Col Dent fel, 71; mem oral biol & med study sect, NIH, 76-80; chmn coun of fac, Am Asn Dent Sch, 78-79; vpres fac, Am Asn Dent Sch, 79-82. *Mem:* AAAS; Int Asn Dent Res; NY Acad Sci. *Res:* Plasma kinins and oral physiology; circulation in of dental pulp; predisposing factors in experimental carcinoma of the hamster cheek pouch; membrane transport in oral epithelium. *Mailing Add:* Sch of Dent Med Col of Ga Augusta GA 30902

WEATHERS, DWIGHT RONALD, b Milledgeville, Ga, Aug 14, 38; m 75; c 4. ORAL PATHOLOGY. *Educ:* Emory Univ, DDS, 62, MSD, 66. *Prof Exp:* Asst prof, 67-70, assoc prof, 70-79, PROF ORAL PATH, SCH DENT, EMORY UNIV, 79- *Mem:* Am Acad Oral Path; Am Dent Asn. *Res:* Herpes simplex virus; neoplasia of oral cavity. *Mailing Add:* Emory Univ Sch Dent 1462 Clifton Rd NE Atlanta GA 30322

WEATHERS, LEWIS GLEN, b Sunset, Utah, July 5, 25; m 46; c 4. PLANT PATHOLOGY. *Educ:* Utah State Col, BS, 49, MS, 51; Univ Wis, PhD(phytopath), 53. *Prof Exp:* Asst bot, Utah State Univ, 49-51; asst plant path, Univ Wis, 51-53; vchmn dept plant path, 71-73, chmn dept, 73-77,

PROF PLANT PATH & PLANT PATHOLOGIST, UNIV CALIF, RIVERSIDE, 53-, ASSOC DEAN, COL NAT & AGR SCI, 77- *Concurrent Pos:* Guggenheim fel, 61-62; Rockefeller fel, 63; NATO fel, 73. *Mem:* Am Phytopath Soc; Int Orgn Citrus Virol; Sigma Xi. *Res:* Citrus and virus diseases; scion and rootstock uncongenialities in citrus; effect of environmental factors on virus diseases; interactions of unrelated viruses in mixed infections. *Mailing Add:* Dept of Plant Path Univ of Calif Riverside CA 92502

WEATHERS, WESLEY WAYNE, b Homer, Ill, Sept 28, 42. ENVIRONMENTAL PHYSIOLOGY. *Educ:* San Diego State Col, BS, 64; Univ Calif, Los Angeles, MA, 67, PhD(zool), 69. *Prof Exp:* USPHS cardiovasc scholar, Sch Med, Univ Calif, Los Angeles, 69-70; from asst prof to assoc prof physiol, Rutgers Univ, New Brunswick, 70-75; asst prof physiol, 75-76, ASSOC PROF PHYSIOL, UNIV CALIF, DAVIS, 76- *Mem:* Am Physiol Soc; Am Soc Zoologists; Sigma Xi; Cooper Ornith Soc; Am Ornith Union. *Res:* Comparative physiology of temperature regulation and vertebrate ecological energetics. *Mailing Add:* Dept of Avian Sci Univ of Calif Davis CA 95616

WEATHERSBY, AUGUSTUS BURNS, b Pinola, Miss, May 19, 13; m 45; c 2. MEDICAL ENTOMOLOGY, PARASITOLOGY. *Educ:* La State Univ, AB, 38, MS, 40, PhD(entom), 54. *Prof Exp:* Asst dist entomologist, State Dept Agr, La, 40-42; entomologist-parasitologist, Naval Med Res Inst, 47-62; PROF ENTOM, UNIV GA, 62- *Mem:* AAAS; Entom Soc Am; Am Soc Parasitol; Am Soc Trop Med & Hyg; Am Mosquito Control Asn. *Res:* Medical entomology; innate immunity of mosquitoes to malaria; malaria survey, control and parasitology; drug action and immunity in malaria; life cycles of malaria; exoerythrocytic stage tissue culture and time-lapse cinephotomicrography; cryobiology. *Mailing Add:* Dept Entom Univ Ga Athens GA 30601

WEATHERSPOON, CHARLES PHILLIP, b Tucson, Ariz, Dec 1, 42; m 64; c 2. SILVICULTURE, FUELS MANAGEMENT. *Educ:* Univ Ariz, BS, 64; Duke Univ, PhD(plant physiol), 68. *Prof Exp:* Res botanist remote sensing, US Army Eng Topog Labs, 70-73; forester silviculture, Kaibab Nat Forest, 73-76, forester timber inventory, Southwestern Region, 76-78, RES FORESTER FUELS MGT & SILVICULTURE RES, PAC SOUTHWEST FOREST & RANGE EXP STA, US FOREST SERV, 78- *Concurrent Pos:* Consult, Nat Acad Sci, Comt Effects Herbicides, Vietnam, 72-73. *Mem:* Soc Am Foresters; Am Soc Plant Physiol; AAAS. *Res:* Establishment and growth of forest stands in relation to their environment and effects of cultural treatment, especially prescribed fire, on this environment. *Mailing Add:* Pac Southwest Exp Sta 2400 Washington Ave Redding CA 96001

WEAVER, ALBERT BRUCE, b Mont, May 27, 17; m 45; c 3. PHYSICS, ACADEMIC ADMINISTRATION. *Educ:* Univ Mont, AB, 40; Univ Idaho, MS, 41; Univ Chicago, PhD(physics), 52. *Prof Exp:* Physicist, US Naval Ord Lab, 42-45; res assoc physics, Univ Chicago, 52-53 & Univ Wash, 53-54; from asst prof to assoc prof, Univ Colo, 54-58, chmn dept, 56-58; head dept, 58-70, assoc dean, Col Lib Arts, 61-70, provost acad affairs, 70-72, PROF PHYSICS, UNIV ARIZ, 58-, EXEC VPRES, 72- *Mem:* AAAS; fel Am Phys Soc. *Res:* Cosmic rays. *Mailing Add:* Admin 512 Univ of Ariz Tucson AZ 85721

WEAVER, ALFRED CHARLES, b Johnson City, Tenn, July 18, 49. COMPUTER SCIENCE. *Educ:* Univ Tenn, BS, 71; Univ Ill, MS, 73, PhD(comput sci), 76. *Prof Exp:* Vis asst prof, Univ Ill, 76-77; ASST PROF COMPUT SCI, UNIV VA, 77- *Concurrent Pos:* Consult, Gen Elec, Struthers-Dunn, Inc, 72- *Mem:* Asn Comput Mach; Inst Elec & Electron Eng; Sigma Xi. *Res:* Microcomputer technology applied to industrial process control; computer networks. *Mailing Add:* Thornton Hall Univ Va Charlottesville VA 22901

WEAVER, ALLEN DALE, b Galesburg, Ill, Nov 15, 11; m 40; c 2. PHYSICS. *Educ:* Knox Col, BS, 33; Univ Mich, MS, 47; NY Univ, PhD(sci educ), 54. *Prof Exp:* High sch teacher, Ill, 35-37; jr high sch teacher, 37-40; instr physics, phys sci & math, Md State Teachers Col, Salisbury, 47-55; assoc prof phys sci, Northern Ill Univ, 55-60, prof physics, 60-81; RETIRED. *Mem:* Nat Sci Teachers Asn; Am Asn Physics Teachers; Nat Asn Res Sci Teaching. *Res:* Science education. *Mailing Add:* 591 Garden Rd De Kalb IL 60115

WEAVER, ANDREW ALBERT, b Sarasota, Fla, Dec 10, 26; m 51; c 4. ENTOMOLOGY. *Educ:* Col Wooster, BA, 49; Univ Wis, MS, 51, PhD(zool), 55. *Prof Exp:* Asst prof biol, 56-66, PROF BIOL, COL WOOSTER, 66- *Mem:* AAAS; Am Micros Soc; Entom Soc Am; Am Soc Zoologists; Soc Syst Zool. *Res:* Taxonomy of centipedes and copepods. *Mailing Add:* Dept Biol Col Wooster Wooster OH 44691

WEAVER, CHARLES EDWARD, b Lock Haven, Pa, Jan 27, 25; m 46; c 3. GEOCHEMISTRY, SEDIMENTOLOGY. *Educ:* Pa State Univ, BS, 48, MS, 50, PhD(mineral), 52. *Prof Exp:* Res assoc mineral, Pa State Univ, 52; res assoc mineral, Shell Res & Develop Co, 52-55, res scientist, 55-59; res group leader mineral, Continental Oil Co, 59-63; assoc prof, 63-65, dir, Sch Geophys Sci, 70-81, PROF MINERAL, GA INST TECHNOL, 65- *Concurrent Pos:* Sigma Xi res award, 72. *Honors & Awards:* Mineral Soc Am Award, 58. *Mem:* Clay Minerals Soc (vpres, 66, pres, 67); Mineral Soc Am; Geochem Soc; Geol Soc Am; Soc Econ Paleontologists & Mineralogists. *Res:* Clay mineralogy and petrology; geochemistry of sediments; clay-water chemistry; radioactive dating of sediments; geothermometry of shales. *Mailing Add:* Sch of Geophys Sci Ga Inst of Technol Atlanta GA 30332

WEAVER, CHARLES HADLEY, b Tenn, Jan 27, 20; m 44; c 4. ELECTRICAL ENGINEERING. *Educ:* Univ Tenn, BS, 43, MS, 48; Univ Wis, PhD(elec eng), 56. *Prof Exp:* Engr & supvr, Tenn Eastman Corp, 43-46; from instr to prof elec eng, Univ Tenn, 46-59; Westinghouse prof, Auburn Univ, 59-63, head prof, 63-65; dean eng, 65-68, chancellor, 68-71, vpres continuing educ, 71-81, dean, Space Inst, 75-81, PROF ELEC ENG, UNIV TENN, KNOXVILLE, 82- *Concurrent Pos:* Consult, Sverdrup & Parcel, Inc, 53-54 & Oak Ridge Nat Lab, 55-64. *Mem:* Inst Elec & Electronics Engrs; Am Soc Eng Educ. *Mailing Add:* 402 Commun Bldg Univ Tenn Knoxville TN 37916

WEAVER, CHARLES R, b Springfield, Mo, June 9, 23; m 54; c 1. BIOLOGY, CHEMISTRY. *Educ:* Drury Col, BS, 48. *Prof Exp:* Fishery biologist, Bur Com Fisheries, US Fish & Wildlife Serv, 50-66, prog leader, Fisheries-Eng Res Lab, 66-72, chief, Fish Facil Br, Environ & Tech Serv Div, Nat Marine Fisheries Serv, 72-79; CONSULT, 79- *Mem:* Am Fisheries Soc; Inst Fishery Res Biol. *Res:* Performance, behavior and swimming abilities of adult salmonids in relation to fish passage problems at dams on the Columbia and tributary rivers. *Mailing Add:* PO Box 295 Stevenson WA 98648

WEAVER, CONNIE MARIE, b LaGrande, Ore, Oct 29, 50; m 71; c 3. FOOD SCIENCE. *Educ:* Ore State Univ, BS, 72, MS, 74; Fla State Univ, PhD(foods & nutrit), 78. *Prof Exp:* Instr foods & nutrit, Grossmont Col, 74-75; res food chem, Univ RI, 75; teaching & res asst fel, Fla State Univ, 75-78; ASST PROF FOODS & NUTRIT, PURDUE UNIV, 78- *Mem:* Sigma Xi; Inst Food Technol; Am Chem Soc. *Res:* Cereals and legumes; mineral uptake bioavailability and removal by processing. *Mailing Add:* Dept of Foods & Nutrit Purdue Univ West Lafayette IN 47907

WEAVER, DAVID DAWSON, b Twin Falls, Idaho, Feb 12, 39; m 67. MEDICINE, HUMAN GENETICS. *Educ:* Col Idaho, BS, 61; Univ Ore, MS & MD, 66. *Prof Exp:* Intern med, Milwaukee County Gen Hosp, Wis, 66-67; biogeneticist, Arctic Health Res Ctr, 67-70, pediat residency, Med Sch, Univ Ore, 70-72; USPHS fel human genetics, Med Sch, Univ Wash, 72-74; March of Dimes fel, Genetics & Metab Dis, Dept Pediat, Univ Ore Health Sci Ctr, Portland, 74-76; asst prof, 76-81, ASSOC PROF, DEPT MED GENETICS, SCH MED, IND UNIV, 81-, DIR CLIN SERV, 76- *Concurrent Pos:* Lectr genetics & cell biol, Univ Alaska, 68-70. *Mem:* Am Soc Human Genetics; Sigma Xi. *Res:* Dysmorphology; conditions affecting head growth; computerization of syndromes. *Mailing Add:* Dept of Med Genetics Ind Univ Sch of Med Indianapolis IN 46202

WEAVER, DAVID LEO, b Albany, NY, Apr 18, 37; m 66. THEORETICAL PHYSICS. *Educ:* Rensselaer Polytech Inst, BS, 58; Iowa State Univ, PhD(physics), 63. *Prof Exp:* Res assoc physics, Iowa State Univ, 63-64; from asst prof to assoc prof, 64-77, PROF PHYSICS, TUFTS UNIV, 77- *Concurrent Pos:* NATO fel physics, Europ Orgn Nuclear Res, Switz, 65-66; Nat Nuclear Energy Comt fel, Frascati Nat Lab, Italy, 68-69. *Mem:* Am Phys Soc. *Res:* Theoretical elementary particle physics; mathematical physics; molecular biophysics. *Mailing Add:* Dept of Physics Tufts Univ Medford MA 02155

WEAVER, DONALD K(ESSLER), JR, b Great Falls, Mont, July 18, 24; m 48; c 2. ELECTRICAL ENGINEERING. *Educ:* Stanford Univ, BS, 48, MS, 49, EE, 50, PhD(elec eng), 59. *Prof Exp:* Asst, Stanford Univ, 48-50; sr res engr, Stanford Res Inst, 50-56; assoc prof elec eng & dir electronics lab, 56-64, dir eng exp sta, 64-69, PROF ELEC ENG, MONT STATE UNIV, 64- *Mem:* Am Soc Eng Educ; Inst Elec & Electronics Engrs. *Res:* Network theory; communication theory. *Mailing Add:* Dept of Elec Eng Mont State Univ Bozeman MT 59715

WEAVER, EDWIN SNELL, b Hartford, Conn, Jan 30, 33; m 55; c 5. PHYSICAL CHEMISTRY. *Educ:* Yale Univ, BS, 54; Cornell Univ, PhD(chem), 59. *Prof Exp:* Asst chem, Cornell Univ, 55-57; from asst prof to assoc prof, 58-71, chmn dept, 72-78, PROF CHEM, MT HOLYOKE COL, 71- *Concurrent Pos:* NSF sci fac fel & vis prof, Univ Calif, San Diego, 64-65; vis prof, Univ Conn, 71-72; vis fel, Yale Univ, 78-79; NSF Sci Fac fel, 78-79. *Mem:* AAAS; Am Chem Soc. *Res:* Physical chemistry of polymers and proteins; neutron activation analysis. *Mailing Add:* Dept of Chem Mt Holyoke Col South Hadley MA 01075

WEAVER, ELLEN CLEMINSHAW, b Oberlin, Ohio, Feb 18, 25; m 44; c 3. PLANT PHYSIOLOGY. *Educ:* Western Reserve Univ, AB, 45; Stanford Univ, MA, 52; Univ Calif, PhD(genetics), 59. *Prof Exp:* Staff mem, Carnegie Inst Dept Plant Biol, 61-62; res assoc, Biophys Lab, Stanford Univ, 62-67; resident res assoc, Ames Res Ctr, NASA, 67-69; dir off sponsored res, 74-77, assoc prof biol sci, 69-77, interium exec vpres, 78-79, PROF BIOL SCI, SAN JOSE STATE UNIV, 78- *Mem:* AAAS; Am Soc Plant Physiol; Biophys Soc; Asn Women in Sci. *Res:* Mechanisms of photosynthesis, using wild type and mutant strains of algae; light-induced electron transport as monitored by means of electron paramagnetic resonance spectroscopy; evolution of photosynthesis. *Mailing Add:* Dept of Biol Sci San Jose State Univ San Jose CA 95192

WEAVER, ERVIN EUGENE, b Centralia, Wash, Mar 12, 23; m 48; c 3. ENVIRONMENTAL CHEMISTRY. *Educ:* Manchester Col, BA, 45; Univ Ill, MA, 47; Western Reserve Univ, PhD(inorg chem), 51. *Prof Exp:* Asst, Univ Ill, 45-47; asst prof chem, Baldwin-Wallace Col, 47-51; asst prof, Wabash Col, 51-53, assoc prof, 53-61; res scientist, Chem Dept Sci Lab, 61-66, consult, 60-61, res scientist, Vehicle Emissions, Prod Res, 66-72, supvr catalysts develop & testing, Engine & Foundry Div, 72-73, EMISSION PLANNING ASSOC, AUTOMOTIVE EMISSIONS & FUEL ECON OFF, FORD MOTOR CO, 73- *Concurrent Pos:* Consult, Argonne Nat Lab, 56-59. *Mem:* Soc Automotive Engrs; Air Pollution Control Asn; Am Chem Soc; Sigma Xi. *Res:* Hexafluorides of heavy metals; xenon fluorides; nonaqueous solvents; air pollution; catalytic control of automotive emissions. *Mailing Add:* Environ & Safety Eng Staff Ford Motor Co Dearborn MI 48121

WEAVER, GEORGE THOMAS, b Anna, Ill, Mar 11, 39; m 60; c 3. FOREST ECOLOGY, SILVICULTURE. *Educ:* Southern Ill Univ, Carbondale, BA, 60, MSEd, 62; Univ Tenn, Knoxville, PhD(bot), 72. *Prof Exp:* Instr bot, 70-71, asst prof forestry, 71-77, ASSOC PROF FORESTRY, SOUTHERN ILL UNIV, CARBONDALE, 77- *Mem:* Ecol Soc Am; Am Inst Biol Sci. *Res:* Dry matter production and nutrient cycling in forest ecosystems; soil-site relationships of forests. *Mailing Add:* Dept of Forestry Southern Ill Univ Carbondale IL 62901

WEAVER, GERALD MACKNIGHT, plant breeding, cytogenetics, see previous edition

WEAVER, HAROLD FRANCIS, b San Jose, Calif, Sept 25, 17; m 39; c 3. ASTRONOMY. *Educ:* Univ Calif, AB, 40, PhD(astron), 42. *Prof Exp:* Nat Res Coun fel, Yerkes Observ, Chicago & McDonald Observ, 42-43; tech aide, Nat Defense Res Comt, DC, 43-44; physicist, Radiation Lab, 44-45, from asst astronr to assoc astronr, Lick Observ, 45-51, assoc prof, 51-56, dir radio astron lab, 58-72, PROF ASTRON, UNIV CALIF, BERKELEY, 56- *Concurrent Pos:* Mem, US Army Air Force-Nat Geog Soc eclipse exped, Brazil, 47. *Mem:* Int Astron Union; Am Astron Soc. *Res:* Spectroscopy of peculiar stars; star clusters; galactic structure; radio astronomy. *Mailing Add:* Dept of Astron Univ of Calif Berkeley CA 94720

WEAVER, HARRY EDWARD, JR, b Philadelphia, Pa, Feb 1, 23; m 44; c 2. EXPERIMENTAL PHYSICS. *Educ:* Case Inst Technol, BS, 43, MS, 48; Stanford Univ, PhD(physics), 52. *Prof Exp:* Physicist, Manhattan Proj, Tenn, 44-46; instr physics, Case Inst Technol, 46-48; asst, Stanford Univ, 48-52; asst, Physics Inst, Zurich, 52-54; physicist, Varian Assocs, Calif, 54-69; PHYSICIST, HEWLETT-PACKARD CO, 69- *Concurrent Pos:* Vis lectr, Univ Zurich, 59-61. *Mem:* Am Phys Soc; Sigma Xi. *Res:* Nuclear magnetic and electron resonance, especially in solids; cryogenic engineering and application of high field superconductive materials in high field solenoids for high resolution nuclear magnetic resonance; trajectory analysis of ions in electric fields produced by quadrupole structures of finite length and with imperfections as applied to the design of mass spectrometers; x-ray photoelectron spectroscopy; super critical fluid, especially CO2; roman spectroscopy of simple molecules & solvents effects of chromophores. *Mailing Add:* Hewlett-Packard Co 1501 Page Mill Rd Palo Alto CA 94304

WEAVER, HARRY TALMADGE, b Brewton, Ala, Dec 15, 38; m 59; c 3. SOLID STATE PHYSICS. *Educ:* Auburn Univ, BS, 60, MS, 61, PhD(physics), 69. *Prof Exp:* Mem staff eng, Humble Oil & Refining Co, 62-63; MEM STAFF PHYSICS, SANDIA LABS, 68- *Mem:* Am Phys Soc; Inst Elec & Electronics Engrs; AAAS. *Res:* Design and development of radiation tolerent integrated circuits. *Mailing Add:* Sandia Labs Albuquerque NM 87185

WEAVER, HENRY D, JR, b Harrisonburg, Va, May 5, 28; m 52; c 4. PHYSICAL CHEMISTRY. *Educ:* George Washington Univ, BS, 50; Univ Del, MS & PhD(phys chem), 53. *Prof Exp:* Assoc prof chem, Eastern Mennonite Col, 51-57; assoc prof, Goshen Col, 57-71, actg dean, 70-72, prof chem, 71-79, provost, 72-79; DEP DIR EDUC ABROAD, UNIV CALIF, SANTA BARBARA, 79-, ADJ LECTR CHEM, 80- *Concurrent Pos:* Tech adv, Lima, Peru, 64-65; Fulbright lectr, Tribhuvan Univ, Nepal, 69-70. *Mem:* AAAS; Am Chem Soc; Am Sci Affil (pres, 62). *Res:* Heterogenous kinetics; metal; acid systems; kinetics of complex ion formation. *Mailing Add:* 4885 Old Oak Place Santa Barbara CA 93111

WEAVER, JAMES B, JR, b Hartwell, Ga, Jan 28, 26; m 49; c 1. GENETICS, AGRONOMY. *Educ:* Univ Ga, BSA, 50, NC State Univ, MS, 52, PhD(genetics, agron), 55. *Prof Exp:* Asst county agt, Univ Ga, 52-53, asst prof agron, 55-58; dir cotton res, DeKalb Agr Res Inc, 58-63; dir cotton res, Cotton Hybrid Res, Inc, 63-65; supt grounds & agronomist, 65-67, asst prof, 67-72, assoc prof, 72-80, PROF AGRON, UNIV GA, 80- *Mem:* Am Soc Agron; Crop Sci Soc Am; Entom Soc Am. *Res:* Basic research on cotton improvement; utilization of hybrid vigor in cotton; insect resistance. *Mailing Add:* Dept of Agron Univ of Ga Plant Sci Bldg Athens GA 30602

WEAVER, JAMES COWLES, b Faribault, Minn, Sept 8, 40; m 66; c 2. BIOPHYSICS, MEDICAL PHYSICS. *Educ:* Carleton Col, BS, 62; Yale Univ, MS, 63, PhD(physics), 69. *Prof Exp:* Fel physics, Res Lab Electronics, 69-72, res assoc, 72-74, staff physicist, 74-78, LECTR PHYSICS, 74- & RES ASSOC BIOPHYS, DEPT NUTRITION & FOOD SCI, MASS INST TECHNOL, 78- *Concurrent Pos:* Lectr med physics, Harvard-MIT, Div Health Sci & Technol, 78- *Mem:* Am Phys Soc; Am Chem Soc; Am Soc Mass Spectrometry; AAAS; Sigma Xi. *Res:* Biophysics and medical physics. *Mailing Add:* Mass Inst of Technol Cambridge MA 02139

WEAVER, JEREMIAH WILLIAM, b New Orleans, La, Sept 29, 16; m 44; c 4. ORGANIC CHEMISTRY. *Educ:* Loyola Univ, La, BS, 38; Univ Detroit, MS, 40; Tulane Univ La, PhD(chem), 53. *Prof Exp:* Instr chem, Univ Detroit, 40-41; asst analyst, State Health Dept, La, 41-42; chemist, Southern Regional Res Lab, USDA, 45-56; res scientist, Koppers Co, Inc, 56-60; asst mgr, Cent Lab, Cone Mills Corp, NC, 60-61, mgr lab, 61-68; PROF TEXTILES, UNIV DEL, 68- *Mem:* AAAS; Am Chem Soc; Am Asn Textile Chemists & Colorists. *Res:* Cellulose chemistry; textile flammability. *Mailing Add:* Alison Hall Col Human Resources Univ Del Newark DE 19711

WEAVER, JOHN ARTHUR, inorganic chemistry, see previous edition

WEAVER, JOHN HERBERT, b Cincinnati, Ohio, Sept 16, 46. SOLID STATE PHYSICS. *Educ:* Univ Mo, BS, 67, MS, 69; Iowa State Univ, PhD(physics), 73. *Prof Exp:* Fel physics, Mat Res Ctr, Univ Mo-Rolla, 73; res assoc physics, 74-75, asst scientist, 75-77, ASSOC SCIENTIST, SYNCHROTRON RADIATION CTR, PHYS SCI LAB, UNIV WIS, MADISON, 77-, ADJ PROF MATS SCI PROG, 81- *Concurrent Pos:* Assoc, Ames Lab, US Dept Energy, 75- *Mem:* Am Phys Soc; Sigma Xi. *Res:* Optical properties of solids; electronic structure of metals and alloys; hydrogen in metals; photoemission and surface physics. *Mailing Add:* Phys Sci Lab Univ Wis 3725 Schneider Rd Stoughton WI 53589

WEAVER, JOHN MARTIN, b Sallisaw, Okla, Apr 9, 23; m 51, 57; c 2. BIOCHEMISTRY, MICROBIOLOGY. *Educ:* Univ Okla, BS, 48; Univ Tex, PhD(biochem), 55. *Prof Exp:* Sr res chemist, Cent Res Dept, Anheuser-Busch Inc, 55-59; res biochemist, Med Res Labs, Chas Pfizer & Co, 59-62, asst dir res, Paul-Lewis Div, 62-63; sr res assoc biol, 63-66, sect chief biochem & microbiol, 66-75, MGR BIOCHEM & MICROBIOL, LEVER BROS CO, 75- *Mem:* AAAS; Int Asn Dent Res; NY Acad Sci; Am Soc Microbiologists. *Res:* Biodegradation and bioconsequences of detergent constituents; purine biosynthesis; vitamin B-12 fermentation; carboxyanhydrides in peptide bond synthesis; commercial enzyme separation; oral biology. *Mailing Add:* 62 Van Allen Rd Glen Rock NJ 07452

WEAVER, JOHN RICHARD, b Goshen, Ind, Sept 3, 20; m 43; c 7. PHYSICAL CHEMISTRY. *Educ:* Bluffton Col, AB, 42; Univ Mich, MS, 50, PhD, 54. *Prof Exp:* From asst prof to assoc prof, 50-60, PROF PHYSICS & CHEM, BLUFFTON COL, 60-, REGISTRAR, 77- *Concurrent Pos:* Consult, Univ Mich, 56-; vis prof, Univ PR, 63-64. *Mem:* Am Chem Soc. *Res:* Electrode kinetics; streaming mercury electrode; molecular structure; dipole moments. *Mailing Add:* Dept of Chem & Physics Bluffton Col Bluffton OH 45817

WEAVER, JOHN SCOTT, b Rochester, NY, Jan 13, 40; m 61; c 3. GEOPHYSICS. *Educ:* Univ Rochester, BS, 63, MS, 70, PhD(geol), 71. *Prof Exp:* Res asst physics, Univ Rochester, 59-61, instr geol & mineral, 68, asst lectr geol, 68-70; asst prof physics, Queens Col, NY, 71-75, assoc prof, 76-80. *Concurrent Pos:* Guest technician, Brookhaven Nat Lab, 59-61. *Mem:* Am Geophys Union; AAAS. *Res:* Geophysics of the solid earth; theoretical and experimental studies of the equation of state of solids at high pressure. *Mailing Add:* 302 Melbourne Ave Mamaroneck NY 10543

WEAVER, JOHN TREVOR, b Birmingham, Eng, Nov 5, 32; m 60; c 3. GEOPHYSICS. *Educ:* Bristol Univ, BSc, 53; Univ Sask, MSc, 55, PhD(physics), 59. *Prof Exp:* From instr to asst prof math, Univ Sask, 58-61; leader appl math group, Defence Res Estab Pac, BC, 61-66; from asst prof to assoc prof physics, 66-72, PROF PHYSICS, UNIV VICTORIA, 72- *Concurrent Pos:* Lectr math, Univ Victoria, 62-64; Nat Sci Eng Res Coun Can res grants, 66-; travel fel, Univ Cambridge, 72-73; actg chmn physics, Univ Victoria, 78-79; vis fel, Univ Edinburgh, 79-80; chmn physics, Univ Victoria, 80- *Mem:* Am Geophys Union; Can Asn Physicists; Brit Inst Physics; fel Royal Astron Soc; Can Geophys Union. *Res:* Electromagnetic induction in the earth; electromagnetic theory; geomagnetic variations. *Mailing Add:* Dept of Physics Univ Victoria Victoria BC V8W 2Y2 Can

WEAVER, KENNETH NEWCOMER, b Lancaster, Pa, Jan 16, 27; m 50; c 2. GEOLOGY. *Educ:* Franklin & Marshall Col, BS, 50; Johns Hopkins Univ, MA, 52, PhD(geol), 54. *Prof Exp:* Geologist, Medusa Portland Cement Co, 56-61, mgr geol & quarry dept, 61-63; DIR, MD GEOL SURV, 63- *Concurrent Pos:* Governor's rep, Interstate Oil Compact Comn, 64- & Interstate Mining Compact, 74-; mem, Md Mining Coun, 73-, chmn, 77-; mem, Mid-Atlantic Gov Coastal Resources Coun, 74-; mem, Subcomt Mgt Major Underground Projs, US Nat Comt Tunneling Technol, Nat Res Coun, 77-79, Comt Surface Mining & Reclamation, 78-80, Comt Disposal Excess Spoil, 80-81; chmn, Md Land Reclamation Comt, 68-76 & 79-, Topographic Mapping Comn, 76-, mem, Md-Del Joint Boundary Comn, 74-; mem adv bd, Outer Continental Shelf Res, 74-79; mem, Groundwater Interagency Taskforce, Sci & Technol Comts, US House Rep. *Mem:* Fel AAAS; fel Geol Soc Am; Am Inst Mining, Metall & Petrol Eng; Am Inst Prof Geologists; Asn Am State Geol (vpres, 71, pres, 73). *Res:* Geology of industrial minerals; environmental and structural geology; research administration. *Mailing Add:* Md Geol Surv Johns Hopkins Univ Baltimore MD 21218

WEAVER, L(ELLAND) A(USTIN) C(HARLES), b Winnipeg, Man, Sept 29, 37; m 58; c 3. ELECTRICAL ENGINEERING. *Educ:* Univ Toronto, BASc, 60; Univ Ill, MS, 62, PhD(elec eng), 66; Univ Pittsburgh, MBA, 76. *Prof Exp:* Instr elec eng, Univ Ill, 62-66; sr engr, Optical Physics Dept, 66-74, mgr gas laser res, 74-77, prog mgr excimer laser technol, 77-79, ASST TO DIR POWER SYSTS RES & DEVELOP, WESTINGHOUSE RES LABS, 79- *Mem:* Sr mem Inst Elec & Electronics Engrs; Am Phys Soc. *Res:* Gaseous and quantum electronics; gas lasers; research planning; technology assessment. *Mailing Add:* 216 Harwick Dr Pittsburgh PA 15235

WEAVER, LAWRENCE CLAYTON, b Bloomfield, Iowa, Jan 23, 24; m 49; c 4. PHARMACOLOGY. *Educ:* Drake Univ, BS, 49; Univ Utah, PhD(pharmacol), 53. *Prof Exp:* Asst pharmacol, Univ Utah, 49-53; pharmacologist, Res Dept, Pitman-Moore Co, 53-58, dir pharmacol labs, 59-60, assoc dir pharmacol res, 60-61, head biomed res, Pitman-Moore Div, Dow Chem Co, 61-64, asst dir res & develop labs, 64-65, asst to gen mgr, 65-66; PROF PHARMACOL & DEAN COL PHARM, UNIV MINN, MINNEAPOLIS, 66- *Honors & Awards:* Am Pharmaceut Asn Found Res Achievement Award, 63. *Mem:* Am Soc Pharmacol; Soc Exp Biol & Med; Am Pharmaceut Asn; Am Pub Health Asn; Acad Pharmaceut Sci. *Res:* Combinations and assay of anticonvulsant drugs; pharmacology of cardiovascular and central nervous system drugs; social and administrative pharmacy; health care delivery systems. *Mailing Add:* 703 Forest Dale Rd New Brighton MN 55112

WEAVER, LEO JAMES, b Springfield, Mo, Apr 18, 24; m 49. ORGANIC CHEMISTRY. *Educ:* Drury Col, BS, 49; Univ Mich, MS, 50. *Prof Exp:* Res chemist, Org Chems Div, Monsanto Chem Co, 50-54, res chemist, Inorg Chem Div, 54-56, res group leader detergents & surfactants, 56-60, asst dir res, 60-62, dir prod sales, 62-64, dir commercial develop, 64-65, dir res & develop, 65-69, pres, Monsanto Enviro-Chem Systs, Inc, 69-72; EXEC VPRES, CALGON CORP, 72- *Concurrent Pos:* Mem, Indust Res Inst. *Honors & Awards:* Monsanto du Bois Res Award, 54. *Mem:* AAAS; Am Mgt Asn; Am Chem Soc; NY Acad Sci. *Res:* Alkylation reactions of aromatics and olefins; sulfonation and sulfation of organics; detergents and surfactants. *Mailing Add:* Calgon Corp PO Box 1346 Pittsburgh PA 15230

WEAVER, LESLIE O, b St John, NB, Nov 16, 10; nat US; m 39; c 1. PLANT PATHOLOGY. *Educ:* Ont Agr Col, BSA, 34; Cornell Univ, PhD(plant path), 43. *Prof Exp:* Instr bot, Univ Toronto, 34-37; asst, NY Exp Sta, Geneva, 37-43; asst exten plant pathologist, Pa State Col, 43-48; exten plant pathologist, 48-80, EMER PROF, UNIV MD, COLLEGE PARK, 80- *Res:* Diseases of fruit crops; effect of temperature and relative humidity on occurrence of blossom blight of stone fruits. *Mailing Add:* Dept of Plant Path Univ of Md College Park MD 20742

WEAVER, LYNN E(DWARD), b St Louis, Mo, Jan 12, 30; m; c 5. ELECTRICAL ENGINEERING, NUCLEAR ENGINEERING. *Educ:* Univ Mo, BSEE, 51; Southern Methodist Univ, MSEE, 55; Purdue Univ, PhD(elec eng), 58. *Prof Exp:* Develop engr, McDonnell Aircraft Corp, 52-53; aerophys engr, Convair Corp, 53-55; instr elec eng, Purdue Univ, 55-58; assoc prof, Univ Ariz, 58-59, prof nuclear eng & head dept, 59-69; assoc dean, Univ Okla, 69-70; exec asst to pres & dir off environ studies, Argonne Univs Asn, 70-72; DIR, SCH NUCLEAR ENG & HEALTH PHYSICS, GA INST TECHNOL, 72- *Concurrent Pos:* Consult, Argonne Nat Lab, 62-, Lewis Res Lab, NASA, 66- & Jet Propulsion Lab, Calif Inst Technol, 67-; mem, Gov Comt Atomic Energy, Ariz, 62-64 & Ariz Atomic Energy Comn, 64-69; mem adv comt space power & propulsion, NASA, 71-73; exec ed, Ann Nuclear Energy, 78-; chmn coord comt energy, Advan Aircraft Elec Syst, 80-81. *Mem:* Am Soc Eng Educ; fel Am Nuclear Soc; Inst Elec & Electronics Engrs. *Res:* Nuclear reactor dynamics and control. *Mailing Add:* Sch of Nuclear Eng Ga Inst of Technol Atlanta GA 30332

WEAVER, MICHAEL JOHN, b London, Eng, Mar 30, 47. ELECTROCHEMISTRY, ANALYTICAL CHEMISTRY. *Educ:* Univ London, BSc, 68, PhD(chem) & DIC, 72. *Prof Exp:* Res fel chem, Calif Inst Technol, 72-75; asst prof, 75-80, ASSOC PROF CHEM, MICH STATE UNIV, 80- *Mem:* Am Chem Soc. *Res:* Kinetics of electrode processes; structure of electrode-electrolyte interfaces; measurement of rapid electrochemical reaction rates; theories of electron transfer kinetics; chemistry of metal macrocyles. *Mailing Add:* Dept of Chem Mich State Univ East Lansing MI 48824

WEAVER, MILO WESLEY, b Lufkin, Tex, Feb 16, 13; m 34; c 5. MATHEMATICS. *Educ:* Univ Tex, BA, 35, MA, 50, PhD, 56. *Prof Exp:* Pub sch teacher, Tex, 34-45; from instr to assoc prof math, 45-77, EMER ASSOC PROF MATH, UNIV TEX, AUSTIN, 77- *Concurrent Pos:* NSF res fel, 58-59. *Mem:* Am Math Soc; Math Asn Am. *Res:* Theory of semigroups; mappings on a finite set; associative algebras. *Mailing Add:* 3104 White Way Austin TX 78757

WEAVER, MORRIS EUGENE, b Morrison, Okla, June 10, 29; m 50; c 4. ANATOMY, ZOOLOGY. *Educ:* York Col, Nebr, BS, 51; Univ Omaha, BS, 53; Ore State Univ, MA, 56, PhD(zool), 59. *Prof Exp:* From instr to assoc prof, 58-72, PROF ANAT, DENT SCH, UNIV ORE HEALTH SCI CTR, 72- *Concurrent Pos:* Nat Inst Dent Res fel, Inst Animal Physiol, Eng, 66-67; vis reader, Med Sch, Univ Ibadan, 72-73; NATO fel, Med Sch, Bristol, England, 79-80. *Mem:* Am Asn Anatomists; Int Asn Dent Res; Sigma Xi. *Res:* Cell biology and mitosis; dental research using swine as experimental animals; microcirculation and temperature regulation; tooth eruption. *Mailing Add:* Dept of Anat Sch of Dent Univ of Ore Health Sci Ctr Portland OR 97201

WEAVER, NEILL KENDALL, b Tariff, WVa, Oct 3, 19; m 45; c 3. MEDICINE. *Educ:* Oberlin Col, AB, 41; Harvard Med Sch, MD, 44; Am Bd Internal Med, dipl, 52; Am Bd Prev Med, dipl, 59. *Prof Exp:* Intern med, Med Sch, Pittsburgh & Allegheny Gen Hosp, 44-45; resident, Med Col, Univ Ala & Jefferson Hillman Hosp, 47-49; NIH fel, Sch Med, Tulane Univ & Charity Hosp, La, 49-51; instr med, Sch Med, Tulane Univ, 51-56, asst prof clin & prev med & pub health, 56-58, assoc prof clin & occup med, 58-66; asst med dir, Baton Rouge Refinery, Humble Oil & Refining Co, 56-66, asst med dir, Tex, 66-69; assoc med dir, Exxon Co, 69-73; MED DIR, AM PETROL INST, 73- *Concurrent Pos:* Vis physician, Charity Hosp, La, 51-65, sr vis physician, 65-; intern, Esso Standard Oil Co, 51-54, asst med dir, Refinery, 54-56; mem consult staff, Baton Rouge Gen Hosp, 56-66; clin prof med & assoc prof prev med, Sch Med, Tulane Univ, 66- *Mem:* Am Heart Asn; fel Indust Med Asn; fel Am Col Physicians; Am Fedn Clin Res; Am Acad Allergy. *Res:* Internal and occupational medicine. *Mailing Add:* Am Petrol Inst Med & Biol Sci Dept 2101 L St NW Washington DC 20037

WEAVER, NEVIN, b Navasota, Tex, Jan 4, 20; m 62; c 3. INSECT PHYSIOLOGY. *Educ:* Southwestern Univ, AB, 41; Tex A&M Univ, MS, 43, PhD(entom), 53. *Prof Exp:* Asst biol, Southwestern Univ, 38-41; asst, Tex A&M Univ, 41-43; beekeeper, 46-48; asst entom, Tex A&M Univ, 48-51, from instr to assoc prof, 41-65; chmn dept biol, 65-68 & 74-76, chmn campus planning, 69-70, PROF BIOL, UNIV MASS, BOSTON, 65- *Concurrent Pos:* Secy, Am comt, Bee Res Asn, 58; fel biol, Harvard Univ, 59-60. *Mem:* AAAS; Bee Res Asn; Animal Behav Soc. *Res:* Honeybee and stingless bee dimorphism, development, physiology, biochemistry, especially lipids, pheromones and behavior. *Mailing Add:* Dept Biol Univ Mass Boston MA 02125

WEAVER, OLIVER LAURENCE, b Birmingham, Ala, Feb 6, 43; div; c 2. MATHEMATICAL PHYSICS, NUCLEAR PHYSICS. *Educ:* Calif Inst Technol, BS, 65; Duke Univ, PhD(physics), 70. *Prof Exp:* Instr & res assoc, Duke Univ, 69-70; asst prof, 70-77, ASSOC PROF PHYSICS, KANS STATE UNIV, 77- *Mem:* Sigma Xi; Am Phys Soc. *Res:* Applications of group theory in nuclear physics; atomic and nuclear scattering theory; electromagnetic transitions in molecules and solids. *Mailing Add:* Dept of Physics Kans State Univ Manhattan KS 66506

WEAVER, PAUL FRANKLIN, b Allentown, Pa, Feb 11, 26; m 64; c 3. ELECTRICAL ENGINEERING. *Educ:* Cornell Univ, PhD(elec eng), 59. *Prof Exp:* Mem tech staff, Bell Tel Labs, 47-52; asst prof elec eng, Cornell Univ, 59-65; assoc prof, 65-72, PROF ELEC ENG, UNIV HAWAII, 72- *Concurrent Pos:* Staff mem, Space Environ Lab, Nat Oceanic & Atmospheric Admin, Boulder, Colo, 71-72; mem comn III, Int Union Radio Sci; fac fel & consult, GTE Labs, 78- *Mem:* Inst Elec & Electronics Engrs; Am Geophys Union. *Res:* Radio wave propagation; ionospheric physics. *Mailing Add:* Dept of Elec Eng Univ of Hawaii Honolulu HI 96822

WEAVER, QUENTIN CLIFFORD, b Harrisburg, Pa, Mar 22, 23; m 48; c 4. PAPER CHEMISTRY. *Educ:* Gettysburg Col, BA, 47; Pa State Univ, MS, 49. *Prof Exp:* Asst anal & qual org chem, Pa State Col, 47-49; res group leader, 49-53, coordr, Staff Tech Serv, 53-56, prod mgr, 56-57, asst dir res div, 58-72, mgr res & eng serv, 72-80, DIR RES & ENG SERV, SCOTT PAPER CO, 80- *Mem:* Am Chem Soc; Tech Asn Pulp & Paper Indust. *Res:* Colloidal properties of cellulose; high polymers; paper coatings; plasticizers; research management; planning and control systems; high melting hydrocarbons. *Mailing Add:* Scott Paper Co Res & Eng Serv Scott Plaza-3 Philadelphia PA 19113

WEAVER, R(OBERT) E(DGAR) C(OLEMAN), b New Orleans, La, Mar 30, 32; m 65; c 1. CHEMICAL ENGINEERING. *Educ:* Tulane Univ, BS, 53, MS, 55; Princeton Univ, MA, 57, PhD(chem eng), 58. *Prof Exp:* Process design engr, Ethyl Corp, 58-60; from asst prof to assoc prof chem eng, Tulane Univ, 60-66, prof & chmn dept, 66-81; PROF CHEM, METALL & POLYMER ENG & DEAN, COL ENG, UNIV TENN, 81- *Concurrent Pos:* Consult, Ethyl Corp, 60-65, Humble Oil & Refining Co, 65-73 & Dept Nat Resources, State of La, 74- *Mem:* Am Chem Soc; Am Inst Chem Engrs; Soc Petrol Engrs. *Res:* Heterogeneous catalysis; diffusion; automatic control; process dynamics and simulation; biomedical engineering; fluidization; applied econommics; resource management; environmental engineering; coal technology; reservior engineering New Orleans, Louisiana and Knoxville, Tennessee. *Mailing Add:* Dean Col Eng Univ Tenn Knoxville TN 37996

WEAVER, RICHARD WAYNE, b Twin Falls, Idaho, June 25, 44; m 64; c 1. SOIL MICROBIOLOGY. *Educ:* Utah State Univ, BS, 66; Iowa State Univ, PhD(soil microbiol), 70. *Prof Exp:* ASSOC PROF SOIL MICROBIOL, TEX A&M UNIV, 70- *Mem:* Soil Sci Soc Am; Am Soc Agron; Am Soc Microbiol. *Res:* Soil nitrogen; microbial ecology; nitrogen fixation; waste disposal. *Mailing Add:* Dept of Soil & Crop Sci Tex A&M Univ College Station TX 77843

WEAVER, ROBERT F, b Topeka, Kans, July 18, 42; m 65; c 2. BIOCHEMISTRY. *Educ:* Col Wooster, BA, 64; Duke Univ, PhD(biochem), 69. *Prof Exp:* NIH fel, Univ Calif, San Francisco, 69-71; from asst prof to assoc prof, 71-81, PROF BIOCHEM, UNIV KANS, 81- *Concurrent Pos:* Res grants, NIH, 72-75, 75-78 & 78-81 & Am Cancer Soc, 75-77 & 81-82; Am Cancer Soc res scholar, Univ Zurich, Switz, 78-79. *Res:* Structure and function of eucaryotic RNA polymerases; transcription control. *Mailing Add:* Dept of Biochem Univ of Kans Lawrence KS 66044

WEAVER, ROBERT HINCHMAN, b Buckhannon, WVa, Dec 2, 31; m 58; c 1. BIOCHEMISTRY. *Educ:* WVa Wesleyan Col, BS, 53; Univ Md, MS, 55, PhD(biochem), 57. *Prof Exp:* Fel, Enzyme Inst, Univ Wis, 57-61; assoc prof, 61-70, PROF CHEM, UNIV WIS-STEVENS POINT, 70- *Mem:* AAAS; Am Chem Soc. *Res:* Amine and carbohydrate metabolism; enzyme chemistry. *Mailing Add:* Dept of Chem Univ of Wis Stevens Point WI 54481

WEAVER, ROBERT JOHN, b Lincoln, Nebr, Sept 23, 17; m 51; c 2. PLANT PHYSIOLOGY. *Educ:* Univ Nebr, AB, 39, MS, 40; Univ Chicago, PhD(plant physiol), 46. *Prof Exp:* Res assoc bot, Univ Chicago, 46-48; from asst viticulturist to assoc viticulturist, Exp Sta, 48-58, VITICULTURIST, EXP STA, UNIV CALIF, DAVIS, 58-, PROF VITICULTURE, UNIV, 58- *Concurrent Pos:* Fulbright sr res scholar, Superior Col Agr, Greece, 56; vis res worker, Res Inst Grapevine Breeding, Ger, 63; Fulbright sr res scholar, Indian Agr Res Inst, New Delhi, 69; res fel, Enol & Viticult Res Inst, SAfrica, 73; res fel grapes, Foreign Agr Orgn, UN, Cyprus, 79. *Mem:* AAAS; Sm Soc Plant Physiol; Bot Soc Am; Am Soc Enol; Am Soc Hort Sci. *Res:* Plant hormones and regulators; physiology of the grapevine. *Mailing Add:* Dept Viticulture & Enol Univ Calif Davis CA 95616

WEAVER, ROBERT MICHAEL, b Goshen, Ind, June 23, 42. CLAY MINERALOGY, SOIL SCIENCE. *Educ:* Berea Col, BA, 64; Mich State Univ, MS, 66; Univ Wis-Madison, PhD(soil sci), 70. *Prof Exp:* Asst prof soil sci, Cornell Univ, 71-78; MEM STAFF, CLAY DIV, J M HUBER CORP, 78- *Mem:* Soil Sci Soc Am; Clay Minerals Soc. *Res:* Genesis of clay minerals; clay mineralogy of tropical soils. *Mailing Add:* Clay Div J M Huber Corp Huber GA 31040

WEAVER, ROBERT PAUL, b Binghamton, NY, July 19, 52; m 73. ASTROPHYSICS, PHYSICS. *Educ:* Colgate Univ, AB, 74; Univ Colo, MS, 76, PhD(astrophys), 77. *Prof Exp:* Res asst physics, Univ Calif Los Alamos Sci Lab, 75; res asst astrophys, Univ Colo, 75-77; res assoc, Nat Acad Sci- Nat Res Coun, 77-78; STAFF MEM PHYSICS, LOS ALAMOS NAT LAB, 78- *Mem:* Am Astron Soc. *Res:* Transfer of radiation, especially in the x-ray regime; interstellar dynamics. *Mailing Add:* Los Alamos Nat Lab Mail Stop 625 X-7 Los Alamos NM 87545

WEAVER, SYLVIA SHORT, b Concord, Mass, Oct 22, 27; m 53; c 2. MARINE BIOLOGY. *Educ:* Smith Col, BA, 49; NY Univ, MS, 70, PhD(marine biol), 75. *Prof Exp:* Teaching fel invert zool & elem biol, 71-72 & 73-75, RES ASSOC BIOL, NY UNIV, 75-, ADJ ASST PROF, 76-; RES ASSOC, HASKINS LABS, PACE UNIV, 75- *Concurrent Pos:* Adj asst prof invertebrate zool, Pace Univ, 78-79. *Mem:* Am Soc Limnol & Oceanog; Int Oceanog Found; Am Littoral Soc; Sigma Xi. *Res:* Plankton communities in inlets as representative of offshore-estuarine interaction and therefore as monitoring sites for environmental conditions. *Mailing Add:* 50 W 72nd St New York NY 10023

WEAVER, WARREN ELDRED, b Sparrows Point, Md, June 5, 21; m 45; c 4. CHEMISTRY. *Educ:* Univ Md, BS, 42, PhD(pharmaceut chem), 47. *Prof Exp:* Asst pharm, Univ Md, 42, asst antigas prep, Off Sci Res & Develop, 42-44; asst insecticides, 44-45; chemist, US Naval Res Lab, 45-50; assoc prof chem & pharmaceut chem, 50-54, from actg chmn to chmn dept, 50-56, dean, Sch Pharm, 56-81, PROF CHEM & PHARMACEUT CHEM, MED COL VA, 54-, EMER DEAN, SCH PHARM, 81- *Concurrent Pos:* Mem pharm rev comt, NIH, 68-72; mem bd dirs, Am Found Pharm Educ, 69-73; mem, Secretary's Comn to rev Report of President's Task Force on Prescription Drugs, 70; mem, Am Coun Pharmaceut Educ, 74-80. *Mem:* AAAS; Am Chem Soc; Am Pharmaceut Asn; Am Inst Hist Pharm; Am Asn Cols Pharm (vpres, 67-68, pres, 68-69). *Res:* Synthetic peptides; insecticides; correlation of structure with fungicidal activity. *Mailing Add:* Sch of Pharm Med Col of Va Richmond VA 23298

WEAVER, WILLIAM JUDSON, b Twin Falls, Idaho, May 7, 36; m 65; c 2. CRYOBIOLOGY. *Educ:* Col Idaho, BS, 58; Univ Ore, MS, 65, PhD(exp path), 71. *Prof Exp:* RES ASSOC SURG, ORE HEALTH SCI UNIV, 71- *Concurrent Pos:* Sci consult, Res Industs Corp, Utah, 75- *Mem:* AAAS; Soc Cryobiol; NY Acad Sci. *Res:* Chemistry; pharmacology and toxicology of dimethyl sulfoxide. *Mailing Add:* 24 Del Prado Lake Oswego OR 97034

WEAVER, WILLIAM MICHAEL, b Lima, Ohio, Feb 18, 31; m 66. ORGANIC CHEMISTRY. *Educ:* Johns Carroll Univ, BS, 53; Purdue Univ, MS, , 56, PhD, 58. *Prof Exp:* Asst org chem, Purdue Univ, 53-58; from instr to assoc prof, 58-70, PROF ORG CHEM, JOHN CARROLL UNIV, 70- *Mem:* Am Chem Soc. *Res:* Aliphatic nitrocompound; kinetics; reactions in aprotic solvents. *Mailing Add:* Dept of Chem John Carroll Univ Cleveland OH 44118

WEBB, ALAN WENDELL, b Enid, Okla, Sept 20, 39; m 61; c 4. PHYSICAL INORGANIC CHEMISTRY. *Educ:* Brigham Young Univ, BS, 63, PhD(phys chem), 69. *Prof Exp:* RES CHEMIST, US NAVAL RES LAB, 68- *Concurrent Pos:* Nat Acad Sci-Nat Res Coun resident res associateship, 68-70. *Mem:* Am Chem Soc. *Res:* High pressure and high temperature synthesis of inorganic compounds; study of solid ionic conductors; layered-structure transition metal dichalcogenides; high pressure and low temperature study of metals; use of syndrotron radiation for high pressure structural studies. *Mailing Add:* Phase Transformation Sect US Naval Res Lab Washington DC 20375

WEBB, ALBERT DINSMOOR, b Victorville, Calif, Oct 10, 17; m 43; c 2. ENOLOGY. *Educ:* Univ Calif, BS, 39, PhD(chem), 48. *Prof Exp:* From asst prof to assoc prof enol, Col Agr, 48-60, from asst chemist to assoc chemist, Exp Sta, 48-60, PROF ENOL, COL AGR, UNIV CALIF DAVIS, 60-, CHMN DEPT VITICULTURE & ENOL, 73-, CHEMIST, EXP STA, 60- *Concurrent Pos:* Fulbright res scholar, Australia, 58, Alko Res Labs, Helsinki, Finland, 69; NATO scholar, Bordeaux, 62; vis res prof, Univ Stellenbosch, SAfrica, 70. *Mem:* Am Chem Soc; AAAS; Am Soc Enologists (pres, 74-75). *Res:* Identification of aroma and flavor compounds in grapes and wines. *Mailing Add:* Dept of Viticult & Enol Univ of Calif Davis CA 95616

WEBB, ALFREDA JOHNSON, b Mobile, Ala, Feb 21, 23; m 59; c 3. VETERINARY MEDICINE. *Educ:* Tuskegee Inst, BS, 43, DVM, 49; Mich State Univ, MS, 51. *Prof Exp:* From instr to assoc prof anat, Tuskegee Inst, 50-59; PROF BIOL, NC A&T STATE UNIV, 59- *Mem:* Am Asn Vet Anat. *Res:* Histology; cytology; embryology. *Mailing Add:* 137 N Dudley St Greensboro NC 27401

WEBB, ALLEN NYSTROM, b Wichita, Kans, Dec 14, 21; m 43; c 3. PHYSICAL CHEMISTRY. *Educ:* Kans State Univ, BS, 43; Univ Calif, Berkeley, PhD(phys chem), 49. *Prof Exp:* Jr chemist, Boston Consol Gas Co, 43; res chemist, Stand Oil Co, Ind, 44-46; res asst chem, Univ Calif, 46-49; from res chemist to sr res chemist, Texaco Inc, 49-66, res assoc, 66-80; RETIRED. *Concurrent Pos:* Chmn, Gordon Res Conf Catalysis, 70; mem adv bd, Petrol Res Fund, 70-72. *Mem:* Am Chem Soc. *Res:* Catalysis; chemisorption; molecular spectra; fuel cells; exchange reactions; kinetics; hydrodesulfurization. *Mailing Add:* Am Chem Soc 8302 Puerta Vista Austin TX 78759

WEBB, ANDREW CLIVE, b Bishop's Stortford, Eng, Feb 17, 47; m 80; c 1. DEVELOPMENTAL BIOLOGY. *Educ:* Southampton Univ, BSc, 69, PhD(biol), 73. *Prof Exp:* Fel biol, Purdue Univ, West Lafayette, 73-75, asst prof, 75-81, ASSOC PROF BIOL SCI, WELLESLEY COL, 81- *Concurrent Pos:* Prin investr, NIH, 80-82. *Mem:* Brit Soc Develop Biol; AAAS; Sigma Xi. *Res:* ultrastructure and biochemistry of amphibian oogenesis with special reference to the organization and expression of the mitochondrial genome. *Mailing Add:* Dept Biol Sci Wellesley Col Wellesley MA 02181

WEBB, ARTHUR HARPER, b Washington, DC, Dec 28, 15; m 42; c 2. BACTERIOLOGY. *Educ:* Univ Ill, AB, 39, MS, 40, PhD(bact), 44. *Prof Exp:* Asst animal path, Univ Ill, 42-43; from instr to assoc prof bact, Col Med, Howard Univ, 44-60; prof biol, Md State Col, Princess Anne, 60-61; prof biol & chmn, Div Sci, Southern Univ, 61-68; PROF BIOL, UNIV DC, 68- *Concurrent Pos:* Bacteriologist & chief, Pub Health Labs, US Opers Mission, Gondar, Ethiopia, 54-56. *Mem:* AAAS; Am Soc Microbiol. *Res:* Physiology of yeasts; radioactive amino acids; hospital staphylococci; parasitism; medical education in Ethiopia. *Mailing Add:* 1005 Lagrande Rd Silver Spring MD 20903

WEBB, BILL D, b Ralls, Tex, June 13, 28; m 54; c 3. PLANT BIOCHEMISTRY. *Educ:* Tex A&M Univ, BS, 56, MS, 59, PhD(biochem & nutrit), 61. *Prof Exp:* RES CHEMIST, AGR RES SERV, USDA, 61- *Mem:* Am Asn Cereal Chem; Inst Food Technologists. *Res:* Physicochemical properties of the rice grain and their relation to rice milling, cooking, processing and nutritive quality. *Mailing Add:* USDA Regional Rice Qual Lab Rte 7 Box 999 Beaumont TX 77706

WEBB, BURLEIGH C, b Greensboro, NC, Jan 9, 23; m 49; c 3. AGRONOMY, PLANT PHYSIOLOGY. *Educ:* Agr & Tech Col, NC, BS, 43; Univ Ill, MS, 47; Mich State Univ, PhD, 52. *Prof Exp:* Instr agron, Tuskegee Inst, 47-49; asst prof, Ala Agr & Mech Col, 51-52; assoc prof, Tuskegee Inst, 52-59; PROF AGRON, NC A&T STATE UNIV, 59-, DEAN SCH AGR, 63- *Mem:* AAAS; Am Soc Agron. *Res:* Plant physiology and ecology of forage crop plants; role of growth regulators in developmental and growth phenomena in crop plants. *Mailing Add:* 137 N Dudley St NC A&T State Univ Greensboro NC 27401

WEBB, BYRON KENNETH, b Cross Anchor, SC, Feb 2, 34; m 61. AGRICULTURAL ENGINEERING. *Educ:* Clemson Univ, BS, 55, MS, 62; NC State Univ, PhD(agr eng), 66. *Prof Exp:* From asst prof to assoc prof, 55-72, PROF AGR ENG, CLEMSON UNIV, 72-, HEAD DEPT, 77- *Mem:* Am Soc Agr Engrs; Am Soc Eng Educ. *Res:* Fruit and vegetable mechanization. *Mailing Add:* Dept of Agr Eng Clemson Univ Clemson SC 29631

WEBB, CHARLES ALAN, b Charlottesville, Va, July 23, 47; m 74. PHYSICAL CHEMISTRY. *Educ:* Lehigh Univ, BA, 69; Univ Miami, PhD(phys chem), 74. *Prof Exp:* Chemist, Textile Fibers Dept, E I du Pont de Nemours & Co, Inc, Old Hickory, Tenn, 69-70, res chemist, 75-78; MKT REP, PLASTIC PROD & RESINS DEPT, E I DU PONT DE NEMOURS & CO, INC, 78- *Mem:* Am Chem Soc; Electrochem Soc; Int Oceanog Found. *Res:* Electrochemical corrosion of copper in chloride and amino acid solutions; spunbonded nonwoven polymer technology; stabilization, polyethylene and Surlyn product development; polypropylene stabilization. *Mailing Add:* Ethylene Polymers Div E I du Pont de Nemours & Co Inc Chicago IL 60638

WEBB, CYNTHIA ANN GLINERT, b New York, NY, Oct 24, 47; US & Israel citizen; m 70; c 3. DEVELOPMENT BIOLOGY, CELL BIOLOGY. *Educ:* Technion Israel Inst Technol, BSc, 68, MSc, 70; Weizmann Inst Sci, PhD(biochem), 75. *Prof Exp:* Fel, Rockefeller Univ, 75-77; res fel, 77-79, SR SCIENTIST, WEIZMANN INST SCI, 80- *Mem:* Israel Immunol Soc; Am Soc Cell Biol; Int Soc Develop Biol. *Res:* Early embryonic development in mammals; cellular and molecular aspects of differentiation of embryonic cells and teratocarcinomas; immunology of embryonic antigens; glycoproteins on gametes and early mammalian embryos. *Mailing Add:* Dept Hormone Res Weizmann Inst Sci Rehovot 76100 Israel

WEBB, DAVID R, JR, b Taft, Calif, Nov 10, 44; m 66; c 2. IMMUNOLOGY, BIOCHEMISTRY. *Educ:* Calif State Univ, BA, 66, MS, 68; Rutgers Univ, PhD(microbiol), 71. *Prof Exp:* Res immunologist, Univ Calif, San Francisco, 71-73; asst mem, 73-78, ASSOC MEM IMMUNOL, ROCHE INST MOLECULAR BIOL, 78- *Concurrent Pos:* Dernham Jr fel, Am Cancer Soc, 72; adj prof, Grad Dept Biochem, City Univ New York, 76-78 & Dept Zool, Rutgers Univ, 78-; adj assoc prof, Col Physicians & Surgeons, Columbia Univ, 80- *Mem:* Am Asn Immunol; Am Soc Microbiol; Sigma Xi; NY Acad Sci. *Res:* Structure and function of antigen-specific/helper factors; purification and biochemical analysis of immune mediators. *Mailing Add:* Dept of Cell Biol Roche Inst of Molecular Biol Nutley NJ 07110

WEBB, DAVID THOMAS, b Darby, Pa, Aug 2, 45; m 76. PHOTOMORPHOGENESIS, PLANT TISSUE CULTURE. *Educ:* West Chester State Col, BA, 67; Univ Mont, PhD(bot), 78. *Prof Exp:* Asst prof biol, Simmons Col, 78-80; ASST PROF BOT, UNIV PUERTO RICO, 80- *Mem:* Bot Soc Am; Am Asn Plant Physiologists; Int Soc Plant Morphologists; Cycad Soc; Torrey Bot Club. *Res:* Effects of light on cycad root growth and nodulation; cycad-Nostoc cymbiosis in virto; clonal propagation of economically important gymnosperms. *Mailing Add:* Dept Biol Univ Puerto Rico Rio Piedras PR 00931

WEBB, DENIS CONRAD, b Skowheghan, Maine, May 12, 38; m 73. APPLIED PHYSICS, ELECTRICAL ENGINEERING. *Educ:* Univ Mich, BSE, 60, MS, 61; Stanford Univ, PhD(appl physics), 71. *Prof Exp:* From assoc to sr engr electromagnetics, Westinghouse Defense & Space Ctr, 61-66; engr magnetics, Phys Electron Lab, 71-72; supvr electron eng acoust, 72-80, SUPVR ELECTRON ENG, NAVAL RES LAB, 80- *Mem:* Inst Elec & Electronic Engrs. *Res:* Magnetoelastic propagation in highly magnetostrictive materials; excitation and propagation of magnetostatic surface waves; near millimeter wave sources and detectors. *Mailing Add:* Naval Res Lab Code 6853 Washington DC 20375

WEBB, DONALD WAYNE, b Brandon, Man, July 12, 39; m 61; c 2. ENTOMOLOGY. *Educ:* Univ Manitoba, BSc, 61, MSc, 63. *Prof Exp:* Lectr, St Paul's Col, Manitoba, 62-63; asst taxonomist, 66-75, ASSOC TAXONOMIST, ILL NATURAL HIST SURV, 75- *Res:* Aquatic insect ecology and the taxonomy of the mature and immature stages of the Chironomidae; systematics of mecoptera and diptera. *Mailing Add:* Ill Natural Hist Surv 607 E Peabody Champaign IL 61820

WEBB, FRED, JR, b Hinton, WVa, Feb 23, 35; m 56; c 2. GEOLOGY. *Educ:* Duke Univ, AB, 57; Va Polytech Inst, MS, 59, PhD(struct geol), 65. *Prof Exp:* Asst geol, Va Polytech Inst, 59-60, instr, Eng Exp Sta, 61-63, instr, Inst, 63-66, resident dir summer field sta, 65; assoc prof geol, Catawba Col, 66-68; from asst prof to assoc prof.prof, 68-73, PROF GEOL, APPALACHIAN STATE UNIV, 73-, CHMN DEPT, 72- *Concurrent Pos:* Vis prof, Va Polytech Inst & State Univ, 71- *Res:* Stratigraphy and tectonics of southern Appalachians; middle Ordovician turbidites; Ordovician paleotopography; modal fold analysis. *Mailing Add:* Dept Geol Appalachian State Univ Boone NC 28608

WEBB, GEORGE DAYTON, b Oak Park, Ill, June 22, 34; m 57; c 3. NEUROPHYSIOLOGY. *Educ:* Oberlin Col, AB, 56; Yale Univ, MAT, 57; Univ Colo, PhD(physiol), 62. *Prof Exp:* High sch teacher, DC, 57-58; asst prof, 66-69, ASSOC PROF PHYSIOL, UNIV VT, 69- *Concurrent Pos:* Vis fel biochem, Univ Copenhagen, 62-63; vis fel neurol & biochem, Columbia Univ, 63-66. *Mem:* Am Physiol Soc; Am Soc Neurochem; Soc Gen Physiol; NY Acad Sci; Soc Neurosci. *Res:* Molecular physiology of synaptic and conducting membranes, especially cholinergic mechanisms and ion transport; sodium and potassium transport in red blood cells; essential hypertension. *Mailing Add:* Dept of Physiol & Biophys Given Med Bldg Univ of Vt Burlington VT 05405

WEBB, GEORGE N, b Fredericktown, Ohio, Mar 24, 20; m 46; c 2. CLINICAL ENGINEERING, ELECTRICAL SAFETY ENGINEERING. *Educ:* Univ Toledo, BE, 47; NC State Col, MS, 52. *Prof Exp:* Instr elec eng, Univ Toledo, 47-49; instr NC State Col, 49-51, res engr, 51-52; electronics engr, 52-57, asst, 57- 61, instr, 61-64, ASST PROF BIOMED ENG, SCH MED, JOHNS HOPKINS UNIV, 64-, CLIN ENGR, HOSP, 71- *Concurrent Pos:* Secy gen, Int Fedn Med Electronics & Biol Engrs, 67-71, mem conf planning & policies comt, 69-; chmn const comt, Alliance for Engrs in Med & Biol, 69-; mem instrumentation group, Int Soc Comn Heart Dis Resources, 70-; partic, appl physiol & bioeng study sect, NIH, 72-76. *Mem:* AAAS; Inst Elec & Electronics Engrs; Asn Advan Med Instrumentation; Int Fedn Med

Electronics & Biol Engrs; Biomed Eng Soc. *Res:* Instruments for data acquisition; processing and display for intensive care; electro-cardiogram, cardiac pressure, respiratory function; methodology for assuring quality of performance and safe operation of patient related electrical equipment; codes and standards for electrical safety. *Mailing Add:* Dept of Biomed Eng Johns Hopkins Sch of Med Baltimore MD 21205

WEBB, GEORGE RANDOLPH, b Norfolk, Va, Feb 25, 38; m 59; c 4. ENGINEERING SCIENCE, STABILITY. *Educ:* Mass Inst Technol, BS, 59; Va Polytech Inst, PhD(eng mech), 64. *Prof Exp:* From asst prof to assoc prof mech eng, Tulane Univ, 64-73; assoc prof physics, 73-76, PROF PHYSICS, CHRISTOPHER NEWPORT COL, 76- *Concurrent Pos:* NSF vis scientist, Univ Va, 71-72, NSF pub serv resident, Smithfield Times, 77-78. *Mem:* Soc Naval Archit & Marine Eng; Soc Natural Philos; Am Soc Mech Engrs; Am Soc Eng Educ. *Res:* Theories of stability; bifurcation theory and catastrophe theory applications. *Mailing Add:* Christopher Newport Col Newport News VA 23606

WEBB, GLENN FRANCIS, b Cleveland, Ohio, Sept 30, 42; m 73. MATHEMATICAL ANALYSIS. *Educ:* Ga Inst Technol, BS, 65; Emory Univ, MS, 66, PhD(math), 68. *Prof Exp:* From asst prof to assoc prof, 68-79, PROF MATH, VANDERBILT UNIV, 79- *Concurrent Pos:* Vis assoc prof math, Univ Ky, 73; Ital Nat Coun Res fel, Univ Rome, 74; vis prof math, Univ Padova, 80 & Univ Graz, 81. *Mem:* Am Math Soc; Math Asn Am. *Res:* Differential equations and functional analysis. *Mailing Add:* Dept of Math Vanderbilt Univ Nashville TN 37235

WEBB, GLENN R, b Chicago, Ill, May 22, 18; m 53; c 1. MALACOLOGY. *Educ:* Univ Ill, BS, 48, MS, 49; Univ Okla, PhD, 60. *Prof Exp:* Res asst, Univ Ill, 48-49 & Univ Okla, 53-56; instr biol, Henderson State Teachers Col, 56-57; fishery res biologist, US Fish & Wildlife Surv, Ft Worth, Tex, 58-59; instr biol, Coastal Carolina Jr Col, 59-60 & SC, Florence & Conway Branches, 60-62; asst prof, High Point Col, 62-63; PROF BIOL, KUTZTOWN STATE COL, 63- *Mem:* Am Malacol Union. *Res:* Pulmonate land snails life histories with special regard to sexology as a clue to phylogeny; snail autoecology; Polygyridae-Helicoidea; inter-species hybridization. *Mailing Add:* Dept Biol Kutztown State Col Kutztown PA 19530

WEBB, GREGORY WORTHINGTON, b Englewood, NJ, July 29, 26; m 50; c 4. GEOLOGY. *Educ:* Columbia Univ, AB, 48, MA, 50, PhD(stratig), 54. *Prof Exp:* Instr, Rutgers Univ, 51-52; geologist, Standard Oil Co, Calif, 52-56; from instr to asst prof geol, Amherst Col, 56-59; from asst prof to assoc prof, 59-71, PROF GEOL, UNIV MASS, AMHERST, 71- *Concurrent Pos:* Vis lectr, Univ Mass, Amherst, 58-59. *Mem:* Geol Soc Am; Am Asn Petrol Geologists; Am Geophys Union; Soc Econ Paleont & Mineral. *Res:* Strike-slip faults and associated structural and stratigraphic geology; petroleum geology; distribution patterns and petroleum reservoir properties of turbidity current deposits. *Mailing Add:* Dept of Geol & Geog Univ of Mass Amherst MA 01003

WEBB, HAROLD DONIVAN, b Franklin, Ind, Sept 23, 09; m 37; c 4. ELECTRICAL ENGINEERING, APPLIED PHYSICS. *Educ:* Franklin Col, AB, 31; Ind Univ, AM, 32, PhD(physics), 39. *Prof Exp:* Teacher math & sci, Needham Sch, Ind, 34-35; teacher physics & chem, Baylor Sch, Tenn, 35-36; teacher math, chem & physics, Franklin High Sch, Ind, 36-39; prof math & physics, West Liberty Col, WVa, 39-42; elec eng physicist radar, Evans Signal Lab, NJ, 42-47; from asst prof to prof, 47-77, EMER PROF ELEC ENG DEPT, UNIV ILL, 77- *Mem:* Inst Elec & Electronics Engrs; fel AAAS; Am Geophys Soc; Int Union Radio Sci. *Res:* First radar contact with the moon; work in radio direction finding, chiefly with matched channel receivers; used moon reflection data and satellite data to measure and study the electron content of the ionosphere and the moon surface. *Mailing Add:* 812 Delaware Ave Urbana IL 61801

WEBB, HELEN MARGUERITE, b Nova Scotia, July 7, 13; nat US. INVERTEBRATE PHYSIOLOGY. *Educ:* Northwestern Univ, BS, 46, MS, 48, PhD(zool), 50. *Prof Exp:* Asst prof biol, Boston Col, 50-52; asst prof physiol, 52-59, assoc prof biol sci, 59-66, prof, 66-79, EMER PROF BIOL SCI, GOUCHER COL, 79- *Concurrent Pos:* Mem corp, Marine Biol Lab, Woods Hole. *Mem:* Am Soc Zoologists; Soc Gen Physiol; Ecol Soc Am; Int Soc Chronobiol. *Res:* Biological rhythms; crustacean endocrinology. *Mailing Add:* Marine Biol Lab Woods Hole MA 02543

WEBB, JAMES L A, b Webb, Miss, Nov 17, 17; m 46; c 3. ORGANIC CHEMISTRY. *Educ:* Washington & Lee Univ, BS, 39; Johns Hopkins Univ, PhD(org chem), 43. *Prof Exp:* Jr instr chem, Johns Hopkins Univ, 39-43, instr, 43-45; from asst prof to prof, Southwestern at Memphis, 45-59; PROF CHEM, GOUCHER COL, 59-, CHMN DEPT, 65- *Concurrent Pos:* Res chemist, Chapman Chem Co, 51-59. *Mem:* Am Chem Soc. *Res:* Organic heterocyclic compounds; theory and antidotes for heavy metal poisoning; disubstituted pyridines; bipyrryls and pyrrole pigments; asphalt additives. *Mailing Add:* Dept of Chem Goucher Col Baltimore MD 21204

WEBB, JAMES R, b Lafayette, Ind, Sept 18, 45; m 74; c 3. ELECTRICAL ENGINEERING, COMPUTER SCIENCES. *Educ:* Univ Colo, BS, 69. *Prof Exp:* Technician, Colo Inst Inc, 61-69; group leader, ESSA|NOAA, McMurdo Sta, 69-71; electronic engr, Colo Instr Inc, 71-72; pres, Commodore Eng Corp, 72-73; dir engr prod develop, Commodore Bus Mach, 73-74; staff engr new prod, Data Pathing Inc, 74-76; staff engr space telescope, Ball Brothers Res Corp, 76-77; V PRES ENG, DATA RAY CORP, 77- *Mem:* Inst Elec & Electronics Engrs. *Res:* Patents relative to keyboards and calculators. *Mailing Add:* Data Ray Corp 5469 Western Ave Boulder CO 80301

WEBB, JERRY GLEN, b Rosefield, La, Feb 17, 38; m 61; c 3. THEORETICAL PHYSICS. *Educ:* Northeast La State Col, BS, 61; Univ Ark-Fayetteville, MS, 64; Tex A&M Univ, PhD(physics), 69. *Prof Exp:* Instr physics, Cent State Col, Okla, 62-65; assoc prof, 69-75, head, Dept Phys Sci, 78-80, PROF PHYSICS, UNIV ARK, MONTICELLO, 75- *Concurrent Pos:* Res partic, Savannah River Lab, Aiken, SC, 70. *Mem:* Am Asn Physics Teachers. *Res:* Three particle scattering problem. *Mailing Add:* Dept of Physics Univ of Ark Monticello AR 71655

WEBB, JOHN RAYMOND, b Morgantown, WVa, Sept 18, 20. AGRONOMY. *Educ:* WVa Univ, BS, 40, MS, 42; Purdue Univ, PhD(agron), 53. *Prof Exp:* Instr & asst soils, WVa Univ, 41-43; soil surveyor, Soil Conserv Serv, USDA, 46-47; instr & asst soils, WVa Univ, 47-48; asst agron, Purdue Univ, 49-52; asst prof, 52-56, assoc prof soils, Agr Exp Sta, 56-80, PROF AGRON, DEPT AGRON, IOWA STATE UNIV, 80- *Mem:* Am Soc Agron; Soil Sci Soc Am. *Res:* Soil fertility. *Mailing Add:* Dept of Agron Iowa State Univ Ames IA 50010

WEBB, KENNETH EMERSON, JR, b Hamilton, Ohio, Feb 26, 43; m 66; c 2. ANIMAL NUTRITION. *Educ:* Ohio Univ, BS, 65; Univ Ky, MS, 67, PhD(animal sci), 69. *Prof Exp:* Asst prof, 69-76, ASSOC PROF RUMINANT NUTRIT, VA POLYTECH INST & STATE UNIV, 76- *Mem:* Am Soc Animal Sci; Am Inst Nutrit; Animal Nutrit Res Coun; Agr Res Inst. *Res:* Ruminant nutrition, protein, mineral and solid waste utilization by ruminants. *Mailing Add:* 3020 Animal Sci Va Polytech Inst & State Univ Blacksburg VA 24061

WEBB, KENNETH L, b Old Fort, Ohio, July 18, 30; m 73. MARINE BIOLOGY, BIOLOGICAL OCEANOGRAPHY. *Educ:* Antioch Col, BA, 53; Ohio State Univ, MSc, 54, PhD(plant physiol), 59. *Prof Exp:* Res assoc, Marine Inst, Univ Ga, 60-65; assoc marine scientist, Va Inst Marine Sci, 65-79; from asst prof to assoc prof, 65-78, PROF MARINE SCIENCE, COL WILLIAM & MARY, 78-; SR MARINE SCIENTIST, VA INST MAINE SCI, 79- *Concurrent Pos:* Vis assoc prof, Ohio State Univ, 65, Dept Oceanog, Univ Hawaii, 72-73; mem, Adv Comt Ocean Sci, Nat Sci Found, 78-81. *Mem:* AAAS; Am Soc Limnol & Oceanog; Am Soc Zoologists; Estuarine Res Fedn; Phycol Soc Am. *Res:* Intedisciplinary investigations related to energy flow and nutrient cycling in marine environments including estuaries, salt marshes, seagrass systems, and coral reefs; physiology of marine organisms. *Mailing Add:* Col William & Mary Va Inst Marine Sci Gloucester Point VA 23062

WEBB, LELAND FREDERICK, b Hollywood, Calif, July 27, 41; m 63; c 1. MATHEMATICS EDUCATION. *Educ:* Univ Calif, Santa Barbara, BA, 63; Calif State Polytech Univ, San Luis Obispo, MA, 68; Univ Tex, Austin, PhD(math & educ), 71. *Prof Exp:* Lectr math & educ, Calif State Polytech Univ, San Luis Obispo, 67-68; curric writer math, Southwest Educ Develop Lab, 70; teaching asst math, Univ Tex, Austin, 71; res assoc math, Res & Develop Ctr Teacher Educ, Austin, 71; from asst prof to assoc prof math, 71-78, PROF MATH & MATH EDUC, CALIF STATE COL, BAKERSFIELD, 78- *Concurrent Pos:* Consult, Educ Develop Ctr, Newton, Mass, 71-76, Greenfield Sch Dist, Bakersfield, 73- & Maricopa Sch Dist, Calif, 74-75; NSF sec sch math & sci grant, 73-75 & 74-75; sabbatical leave, Agderr Reg Col, Kristiansand, Norway, 80; consult, Bishop Union Elem Sch Dist, 80-; vis lectr, NSP Inst, Tokyo, Japan, 75. *Mem:* Sigma Xi; Nat Coun Teachers Math; Am Educ Res Asn; Sch Sci & Math Asn. *Res:* Learning in science and mathematics education. *Mailing Add:* Dept of Math Calif State Col Bakersfield CA 93309

WEBB, MAURICE BARNETT, b Neenah, Wis, May 14, 26; m 56; c 2. PHYSICS. *Educ:* Univ Wis, BS, 50, MS, 52, PhD, 56. *Prof Exp:* With Proj Lincoln, Mass Inst Technol, 52-53; with res lab, Gen Elec Co, 56-61; assoc prof, 61-65, PROF PHYSICS, UNIV WIS-MADISON, 65- *Mem:* Am Phys Soc. *Res:* Solid state physics; x-ray scattering; surface physics; low energy electron diffraction. *Mailing Add:* Dept of Physics Univ of Wis Madison WI 53706

WEBB, MORGAN CHOFIELD, III, b North Bend, Ore, Mar 4, 20; m 44; c 6. ENTOMOLOGY, ECOLOGY. *Educ:* Park Col, AB, 42; Univ Nebr, PhD(entom), 61. *Prof Exp:* Surv entomologist, Univ Nebr, 59; asst prof biol, Whitworth Col, Wash, 61-65; asst prof, Morningside Col, 65-72, assoc prof biol, 72-80. *Mem:* Wilson Ornith Soc; Cooper Ornith Soc. *Res:* Ecological aspects of bumblebee biology, including the distribution of certain species. *Mailing Add:* 1325 S Newton Sioux City IA 51106

WEBB, NATHANIEL CONANT, JR, b Glen Ridge, NJ, Aug 29, 27; m 56; c 2. PREVENTIVE MEDICINE, MEDICAL STATISTICS. *Educ:* Harvard Univ, AB, 50, MD, 54. *Prof Exp:* Intern & med resident, Colo Gen Hosp, 54-57; instr biophys, Sch Med, Univ Colo, 57-59; from asst prof to assoc prof prev med, NJ Col Med, 59-67; STAFF MEM, HEALTH CARE GROUP, ARTHUR D LITTLE, INC, CAMBRIDGE, 67- *Concurrent Pos:* Baker lectr, Sch Pub Health, Univ Mich, 65. *Res:* Cost and benefit evaluation in public health and health care; medical data processing systems; management systems in tuberculosis, including epidemiologic modeling and data systems. *Mailing Add:* Health Care Group 25 Acorn Park Cambridge MA 02140

WEBB, NEIL BROYLES, b Junta, WVa, May 19, 30; m 53; c 5. BIOCHEMISTRY, MICROBIOLOGY. *Educ:* WVa Univ, BS, 53; Univ Ill, MS, 57; Univ Mo, PhD(food sci), 59. *Prof Exp:* Asst prof food sci, Mich State Univ, 59-62; dir food tech, Eckert Packing Co, Ohio, 62-66; assoc prof food sci, NC State Univ, 66-77; PRES, WEBB FOODLAB, INC, 72- *Mem:* Inst Food Technol; Am Meat Sci Asn; Am Chem Soc. *Res:* Food processing systems; product development; nutritional quality foods. *Mailing Add:* Webb Foodlab Inc 3309 Drake Circle Raleigh NC 27607

WEBB, NORVAL ELLSWORTH, JR, b Indianapolis, Ind, Oct 17, 27; m 50; c 3. PHARMACY, PHARMACEUTICAL CHEMISTRY. *Educ:* Purdue Univ, BS, 50, MS, 52, PhD(pharm), 56. *Prof Exp:* Asst pharm, Purdue Univ, 50-52; from instr to assoc prof, SDak State Col, 52-62; CHEMIST, PHARMACEUT RES & DEVELOP DEPT, MERRELL-DOW PHARMACEUT DIV, DOW CHEM CO, INC, 80- *Mem:* Am Pharmaceut Asn; Acad Pharmaceut Sci. *Res:* Interaction of pharmaceutical dose forms with packaging materials; dose form development. *Mailing Add:* Pharmaceut Res Merrell-Dow Pharmaceut Dow Chem Co 110 E Amity Rd Cincinnati OH 45215

WEBB, PATRICIA ANN, b Cambridge, Eng, Apr 5, 25; US citizen; m 49; c 2. VIROLOGY, PEDIATRICS. *Educ:* Agnes Scott Col, BA, 45; Tulane Univ, MD, 50. *Prof Exp:* Rotating intern, St Joseph's Mercy Hosp, Pontiac, Mich, 50-51; from jr resident to sr resident pediat, Kern Gen Hosp, Bakersfield, Calif, 51-53; mem staff pediat, Well-Baby & Specialty Clins, Dept Maternal & Child Welfare, Washington, DC, 53-54; asst instr exp pediat, Univ Md, 54-55; mem staff, US Army Med Res Unit, Inst Med Res, Kuala Lumpur, Malaysia, 55-61; consult virus & rickettsial dis sect, Nat Inst Allergy & Infectious Dis, 61-62, sr surgeon, Lab Infectious Dis, 62-63, sr surgeon, Mid Am Res Unit, 63-65, med dir, Mid Am Res Unit, 65-75, MED DIR, CTR FOR DIS CONTROL, USPHS, 75-, MED DIR, VECTOR BORNE DIS DIV, 81- *Concurrent Pos:* Pvt pract pediat, Bakersfield, Calif, 54-55; mem organizing comt, Cent Am Cong Microbiol, Panama, 68; virologist, Lassa Fever Res Proj, Kenema, Sierra Leone, 78-79, dir, 79-80. *Mem:* Am Soc Trop Med & Hyg; Soc Microbiol Panama (vpres, 69); Panamanian Asn Microbiol. *Res:* Hemorrhagic fevers; arenaviruses; arboviruses. *Mailing Add:* Vector Borne Dis Div PO Box 2087 Ft Collins CO 80522

WEBB, PAUL, b Hemel Hempstead, Eng, Dec 23, 45; m 70; c 2. BIOMECHANICS, PHYSIOLOGICAL ECOLOGY. *Educ:* Univ Bristol, BSc, 67, PhD(zool), 71. *Prof Exp:* Nat Res Coun fel, Pac Biol Sta, 70-72; from asst prof to assoc prof, 72-80, PROF NATURAL RESOURCES, SCH NATURAL RESOURCES, UNIV MICH, 80- *Concurrent Pos:* NSF grants, 75-83; consult, Calif Inst Tech & Detroit Edison. *Mem:* AAAS; Am Fisheries Soc; Am Soc Zool; Can Soc Zool; Soc Exp Biol. *Res:* Functional morphology, biomechanics and behavior of animals, particularly fish; whole animal bioenergetics and energetic correlates of environmental adaptation, including responses to manmade stress. *Mailing Add:* Sch of Natural Resources 430 E University Ann Arbor MI 48109

WEBB, PETER NOEL, b Wellington, NZ, Dec 14, 36; m 78. GEOLOGY, MICROPALEONTOLOGY. *Educ:* Victoria Univ Wellington, BSc, 59, MSc, 60; State Univ Utrecht, PhD(geol), 66. *Prof Exp:* Micropaleontologist, NZ Geol Surv, 60-73; prof micropaleont & chmn dept, Northern Ill Univ, 73-80; PROF MICROPALEONT & CHEM DEPT, OHIO STATE UNIV, 80- *Concurrent Pos:* Vis micropaleontologist, Hebrew Univ Jerusalem, 67 & Fed Geol Surv, Hanover, Ger, 69; secy, Nat Comt Geol, NZ, 70-73; Late Cenozoic Working Group, Sci Comt Antarctic Res, 72-77, convenor, Ice Shelf Drilling Group, 73-78. *Honors & Awards:* Hamilton Prize, Royal Soc NZ, 60; Cotton Prize, Victoria Univ Wellington, 60. *Mem:* Royal Soc NZ; Soc Econ Paleontologists & Mineralogists; Sigma Xi; Geol Soc New Zealand; Explorers Club. *Res:* Cretaceous, Tertiary and recent Foraminifera from Southern Hemisphere, particularly New Zealand, Antarctica, South America and intervening areas, with special emphasis on biostratigraphy, population compositions and climate relationship. *Mailing Add:* Dept Geol & Minerol Ohio State Univ Columbus OH 43210

WEBB, PHILIP GILBERT, b Norwich, NY, Oct 17, 43; m 68; c 3. INDUSTRIAL ORGANIC CHEMISTRY. *Educ:* Hamilton Col, AB, 65; Univ Rochester, PhD(org chem), 70. *Prof Exp:* Res chemist org pigments, Pigments Div, Am Cyanamid Co, 69-74; plant tech mgr, Chemetron Corp, 74-76, plant mgr, 76-79, TECHNOL SERV MGR PIGMENTS, BASF WYANDOTTE CORP, 79- *Mem:* Am Chem Soc. *Res:* New and improved organic pigments; dispersability and lightfastness of organic compounds in inks, paints and plastics. *Mailing Add:* Pigments Div BASF Wyandotte Corp 491 Columbia Ave Holland MI 49423

WEBB, PHYLLIS MARIE, b Paw Paw, Mich. IMMUNOLOGY. *Educ:* Mich State Univ, BS, 57; Univ Minn, MS, 64, PhD(immunol), 73. *Prof Exp:* Med technologist, Butterworth Hosp, Grand Rapids, Mich, 57-60; res asst immunol, Univ Minn, 60-62; Univ Calif Med Sch, San Francisco vis fac, Univ Airlangga, Indonesia, 64-65; res assoc leucocyte typing, State Univ Leiden, 65-67; asst prof immunol, Univ Notre Dame, 73-82; DIR, CLIN PATH LAB & RES SCIENTIST, TOXICITY RES LABS LTD, MUSKEGON, MICH, 82- *Concurrent Pos:* Vis prof, Dept Allied Health, Univ Wis, 81. *Honors & Awards:* Nat Warner Chilcott Award, Am Soc Med Technol, 60. *Mem:* Am Soc Microbiol; AAAS; Asn Gnotobiotics; Am Soc Clin Pathologists; Am Soc Med Technologists. *Res:* Immunological studies on germfree radiation induced chimeric mice, their mitogen responses and restoration of thymus cell functions; immunological studies on germfree mice fed antigen-free diet; xenogenic transplatnation of bone marrow from donor mice to recipient rats. *Mailing Add:* 565 Lake Forest Lane Muskegon MI 49441

WEBB, R CLINTON, b Evansville, Ind, Dec, 31, 48; m 71; c 2. CARDIOVASCULAR PHYSIOLOGY, HYPERTENSION. *Educ:* Southern Ill Univ, BA, 71, MS, 73; Univ Iowa, PhD(anal), 76. *Prof Exp:* Fel physiol, Univ Mich, 76-78, fel pharmacol, Univ Instelling Antwerpen, 78-79; res scientist, 79-80, ASST PROF PHYSIOL, UNIV MICH, 80- *Honors & Awards:* C & F Demuth Award, Int Soc Hypertension, 82. *Mem:* Am Physiol Soc. *Res:* Physiology of vascular smooth muscle, with particular emphasis placed on: vascular reactivity in hypertension and diabetes, cellular and subcellular mechanisms of contraction and relaxation and adrenesqic neurotransmission in vascular smooth muscle. *Mailing Add:* Dept Physiol Med Sch Univ Mich Ann Arbor MI 48109

WEBB, RALPH L, b Parker, Kans, Feb 22, 34; m 61; c 2. MECHANICAL ENGINEERING, HEAT TRANSFER. *Educ:* Kans State Univ, BS, 57; Rensselaer Polytech Inst, MS, 62; Univ Minn, PhD(mech eng), 69. *Prof Exp:* Instr mech eng, Kans State Univ, 57; exp engr, Knolls Atomic Power Lab, 60-62; mgr heat transfer res dept, The Trane Co, 63-77; assoc prof, 77-80, PROF MECH ENG, PA STATE UNIV, 80- *Concurrent Pos:* Assoc tech ed, J Heat Transfer, 73-76; tech ed, Heat Transfer Eng, 77- & J Heat Recovery Systs, 82- *Mem:* Fel Am Soc Mech Engrs; Am Inst Chem Engrs; Am Soc Heating & Refrig Engrs. *Res:* Applied research on enhanced heat transfer, including convection, two-phase flow, boiling and condensation; design of heat exchangers. *Mailing Add:* Dept of Mech Eng Pa State Univ University Park PA 16801

WEBB, RICHARD C(LARENCE), b Omaha, Nebr, Sept 2, 15; m 41; c 1. ELECTRICAL ENGINEERING. *Educ:* Univ Denver, BS, 37; Purdue Univ, MS, 44, PhD(elec Eng), 51. *Prof Exp:* Traffic trainee, Mountain States Tel & Tel Co, 37-39; instr elec eng, Purdue Univ, 39-45; res engr labs, Radio Corp Am, 45-50 & 52; prof elec eng, Iowa State Univ, 50; prof elec eng, Univ Denver & sect head, Denver Res Inst, 52-56; pres, Colo Res Corp, 56-61; pres & tech dir, Colo Instruments, Inc, 61-73; PRES, WEBB ENG CO, 73-; PRES, DATA RAY CORP, 75- *Mem:* Fel Inst Elec & Electronics Engrs. *Res:* Communication and information theory; electro-mechanical and electrooptical instruments; television; digital data systems. *Mailing Add:* 4906 Club House Ct Boulder CO 80301

WEBB, RICHARD LANSING, b Mountain Lakes, NJ, July 28, 23; m 49; c 3. POLYMER CHEMISTRY. *Educ:* Mass Inst Technol, BS, 48; Columbia Univ, MA, 49. *Prof Exp:* Jr chemist, Cent Labs, Gen Foods Corp, NJ, 48 & 49-50; res chemist, Cent Res Div, 50-60, sr res chemist, 60-69, group leader, Lederle Labs Div, NY, 69-76, SR RES CHEMIST, CHEM RES DIV, AM CYANAMID CO, CT, 76- *Mem:* Am Chem Soc. *Res:* Reactions of acrylonitrile and derivatives; hydrogen cyanide polymerization; x-ray induced addition reactions of olefins including polymerization; synthesis of polymers for biological applications. *Mailing Add:* 5 Stephanie Lane S Darien CT 06820

WEBB, ROBERT BRADLEY, b Guy, Ark, Nov 20, 27; m 50; c 2. MICROBIOLOGY, GENETICS. *Educ:* Harding Col, BS, 47; Univ Okla, MS, 50, PhD(microbiol), 56. *Prof Exp:* Instr biol, Harding Col, 49-50 & Univ Tenn, 50-52; Nat Res Coun fel radiation biol, 56-58, ASSOC SCIENTIST, DIV BIOL & MED RES, ARGONNE NAT LAB, 58- *Concurrent Pos:* Adj assoc prof, Northern Ill Univ. *Mem:* AAAS; Am Soc Photobiol; Biophys Soc; Am Soc Microbiol; Genetics Soc Am. *Res:* Microbial genetics and photobiology; molecular basis of photodynamic inactivation and mutagenesis with acridine dyes; mechanisms of protection against ultraviolet light with acridine dyes; molecular basis of mutagenesis and lethality by near ultraviolet and visible light. *Mailing Add:* Div Biol & Med Res Argonne Nat Lab Argonne IL 60439

WEBB, ROBERT CARROLL, b Petersburg, Va, Mar 6, 47; c 3. HIGH ENERGY PHYSICS. *Educ:* Univ Pa, BA, 68; Princeton Univ, MA, 70, PhD(physics), 72. *Prof Exp:* Adj asst prof high energy physics, Univ Calif, Los Angeles, 72-74; res assoc, Princeton Univ, 75-76, asst prog high energy physics, 76-80; ASSOC PROF PHYSICS, TEX A&M UNIV, 80- *Mem:* Am Phys Soc. *Res:* Experiments to test charge symmetry violation at large momentum transfers and to search for new particle states in proton-antiproton annihilations. *Mailing Add:* Physics Dept Tex A&M Univ College Station TX 08540

WEBB, ROBERT G, b Long Beach, Calif, Feb 18, 27. VERTEBRATE ZOOLOGY. *Educ:* Univ Okla, BS, 50, MS, 52; Univ Kans, PhD(zool), 60. *Prof Exp:* Instr biol, WTex State Univ, 57-58; PROF BIOL, UNIV TEX EL PASO, 62- *Mem:* Am Soc Ichthyol & Herpet; Soc Study Amphibians & Reptiles. *Res:* Systematics, zoogeography and evolution of amphibians and reptiles, especially in the southwestern United States and northern Mexico. *Mailing Add:* Dept of Biol Sci Univ of Tex El Paso TX 79968

WEBB, ROBERT HOWARD, b Burlington, Vt, Oct 17, 34; m 53; c 2. MEDICAL PHYSICS. *Educ:* Harvard Univ, AB, 55; Rutgers Univ, PhD(physics), 59. *Prof Exp:* Res assoc physics, Stanford Univ, 59-63; asst prof, Tufts Univ, 63-69; sr staff scientist, Block Eng Inc, 69-78; ASSOC SCI, EYE RES INST RETINA FOUND, 78- *Mem:* Asn Res Vision & Ophthal; Am Asn Physics Teachers. *Res:* Medical diagnostic instrumentation; optics; chemical and solid state physics; electron and nuclear spin resonance; low temperatures. *Mailing Add:* Eye Res Inst of Retina Found 20 Staniford St Boston MA 02114

WEBB, ROBERT LEE, b Topeka, Kans, Nov 19, 26; m 52; c 2. ORGANIC CHEMISTRY. *Educ:* Washburn Univ, BS, 49. *Prof Exp:* Anal chemist, I H Milling Co, 49-50; res chemist, Org Chem Dept, Glidden Co, 50-56, mgr res lab, 56-59, prod mgr, 59-61, asst tech dir, 61-62, vpres, Terpene Res Inst, 62-64; asst mgr aromatic chem develop, 64-65, supt mfg tech serv terpenes, 65-68, gen mgr terpene & aromatic chem, 68-75, VPRES, UNION CAMP CORP, 75-, GEN MGR, CHEM GROUP, 75- *Mem:* Am Chem Soc. *Res:* Terpene and resin chemistry; synthesis and manufacture of flavor and perfumery chemicals from terpenes; composition and reconstitution of essential oils. *Mailing Add:* 2479 Holly Point Rd E Orange Park FL 32073

WEBB, ROBERT MACHARDY, b Hamilton, Ohio, Dec 2, 15; m 62. PHYSICAL GEOGRAPHY. *Educ:* Memphis State Col, BS, 49; Ohio State Univ, MA, 50; Univ Kans, PhD(geog), 62. *Prof Exp:* Instr geog, Ohio Wesleyan Univ, 52-53; prof geog, Univ Southwestern La, 56-80, coordr, 75-80; RETIRED. *Concurrent Pos:* Consult, Dept Educ, State of La, 67-68. *Mem:* Asn Am Geog; Int Geog Union; Nat Coun Geog Educ. *Res:* Agricultural land use; climatology. *Mailing Add:* Box 40861 Univ of Southwestern La Lafayette LA 70504

WEBB, ROBERT WALLACE, b Los Angeles, Calif, Nov 2, 09; m 33; c 3. GEOLOGY. *Educ:* Univ Calif, Los Angeles, AB, 31; Calif Inst Technol, MS, 32, PhD(geol), 37. *Prof Exp:* Asst geol, Univ Calif, Los Angeles, 32-36, assoc, 36-37, from instr to assoc prof, 37-48, coordr, Army Specialized Training Prog, 43-45 & Vet Affairs, 45-47, univ coordr, 47-52; lectr, Exten Div, 36-75, from assoc prof to prof, 48-75, chmn dept phys sci, 53-58, dir Exp Prog, Instrs for Cols, 60-63, EMER PROF GEOL, UNIV CALIF, SANTA BARBARA, 75- *Concurrent Pos:* Exec secy, Div Geol & Geog, Nat Res Coun, 53; exec dir, Am Geol Inst, Washington, DC, 53. *Honors & Awards:* Neil Miner Award, Nat Asn Geol Teachers, 73, Robert Wallace Webb Award, 73. *Mem:* Fel Geol Soc Am; fel Mineral Soc Am; fel Meteoritical Soc (secy, 37-41); Nat Asn Geol Teachers. *Res:* Petrology; geomorphology; mineralogy; Southern Sierra Nevada of California. *Mailing Add:* Dept of Geol Sci Univ of Calif Santa Barbara CA 93106

WEBB, RODNEY A, b Eng, July 23, 46; Can citizen; m 70. INVERTEBRATE PHYSIOLOGY, NEUROENDOCRINOLOGY. *Educ:* Univ London, BSc, 68; Univ Toronto, PhD(zool), 72. *Prof Exp:* Demonstr zool, Univ Toronto, 68-72; Nat Res Coun Can fel parasitol, Inst Parasitol, MacDonald Col, McGill Univ, 72-74; asst prof zool, Univ NB, 74-75; res assoc zool, 75-77, asst prof, 77-81, ASSOC PROF BIOL, YORK UNIV, 81- *Mem:* Can Soc Zoologists; Am Soc Parasitologists. *Res:* Fine structure, physiology and biochemistry of parasitic helminths; neurobiology and neuroendocrinology of annelids and helminths; endocrine control of spermatogenesis in leeches. *Mailing Add:* Dept Biol York Univ Downsview ON M3J 1P3 Can

WEBB, ROGER P(AUL), b Cedar City, Utah, Dec 28, 36; m 57. ELECTRICAL ENGINEERING. *Educ:* Univ Utah, BSEE, 57; Univ Southern Calif, MSEE, 59; Ga Inst Technol, PhD(elec eng), 64. *Prof Exp:* Engr, Douglas Aircraft Corp, 57-59; proj engr, Sperry Phoenix Co, 59-60; from asst prof to assoc prof, 63-77, ASSOC DIR & GA POWER PROF ELEC ENG, GA INST TECHNOL, 78- *Concurrent Pos:* Consult, Lockheed-Ga Co, 66- *Mem:* Inst Elec & Electronics Engrs. *Res:* Automatic control systems. *Mailing Add:* Dept of Elec Eng Ga Inst of Technol Atlanta GA 30332

WEBB, ROSEANNA AILEEN DARBY, organic chemistry, see previous edition

WEBB, ROY E, b Reading, Pa, Aug 28, 21; m 45; c 3. CHEMICAL ENGINEERING. *Educ:* City Col New York, BChE, 47; Columbia Univ, MS, 48. *Prof Exp:* Chem engr, Nat Aniline Div, Allied Chem Corp, NY, 48-54, sect mgr, 54-58; mgr develop, van Amerigen Haebler Co, 58-60; mgr develop eng, Union Beach Plant, 60-67, dir develop, Corp Res & Develop, 67-72, asst to dir, 72-75, mgr tech info servs & budgetary control, Res & Develop, 75-79, MGR ADMIN SERV, INT FLAVORS & FRAGRANCES INC, 79- *Mem:* Am Inst Chem Engrs. *Res:* Chemical process development, process engineering and chemical engineering research related to organic chemical processing in the production of dyestuffs, detergents, aroma and flavor chemicals. *Mailing Add:* 24 Leland Terr New Shrewsbury NJ 07724

WEBB, RYLAND EDWIN, b Dondi, Angola, Africa, Jan 24, 32; US citizen; m 58; c 3. NUTRITIONAL BIOCHEMISTRY. *Educ:* Univ Ill, BS, 54, PhD(nutrit), 61. *Prof Exp:* Res scientist, Lederle Labs, Am Cyanamid Co, 61-63; from asst prof to assoc prof biochem & nutrit, 63-73, HEAD & PROF HUMAN NUTRIT & FOODS, VA POLYTECH INST & STATE UNIV, 73- *Mem:* Am Inst Nutrit; Am Dietetic Asn. *Res:* Nutrition and toxicant interactions; applied international nutrition programs. *Mailing Add:* Dept Human Nutrit & Foods Va Polytech Inst & State Univ Blacksburg VA 24061

WEBB, SAWNEY DAVID, b Los Angeles, Calif, Oct 31, 36; m 58; c 2. PALEONTOLOGY, ANATOMY. *Educ:* Cornell Univ, BA, 58; Univ Calif, Berkeley, MA, 61, PhD(paleont), 64. *Prof Exp:* Instr paleont, Univ Calif, Berkeley, 63-64; from asst cur & asst prof to assoc cur mus & assoc prof zool, 64-70, CUR FOSSIL VERTEBRATES FLA STATE MUS & PROF GEOL & ZOOL, UNIV FLA, 70- *Concurrent Pos:* NSF grants; Guggenheim fel; assoc ed, Paleobiology, 75-78 & Soc Vert Paleont New Bulletin, 79-82; mem, US Nat Comn Internal Quaternary Asn, 78-82. *Mem:* Soc Vert Paleont (pres, 79-); Soc Study Evolution; Am Soc Mammal; Int Quaternary Asn; Sigma Xi. *Res:* Fossil mammals, evolution, paleoecology and functional morphology. *Mailing Add:* Fla State Museum Univ Fla Gainesville FL 32603

WEBB, STEPHEN RICHARD, b Franklin, Ind, July 3, 38; div; c 3. ENGINEERING STATISTICS. *Educ:* Univ Ill, BS, 59; Univ Chicago, MS, 60, PhD(statist), 62. *Prof Exp:* Specialist statist, Rocketdyne Div, NAm Aviation, Inc, Calif, 62-63, prin scientist, 63-68; br mgr, Math Sci Dept, McDonnell Douglas Astronaut Co, 68-71, chief scientist advan math, Advan Info Systs Subdiv, 72-75; independent consult indust, 75-77; SR SYSTS ANALYST, TELEDYNE BROWN ENG, 77- *Mem:* Am Statist Asn; Inst Math Statist. *Res:* Statistical design of experiments; signal processing. *Mailing Add:* Suite 205 125 Baker Costa Mesa CA 92626

WEBB, SYDNEY JAMES, b London, Eng, July 25, 25; m 48; c 4. BIOPHYSICS, MICROBIOLOGY. *Educ:* Univ London, BSc, 52, MSc, 54, DIC, 55, PhD(biophys), 59, DSc, 68. *Prof Exp:* Asst lectr biol, Univ London, 52-55; res sect leader microbiol, Boots Pure Drug Co, Eng, 55-56; sci officer, Defence Res Bd, Can, 56-60; prof microbiol, Univ Sask, 60-74; PROF PHYSICS & BIOPHYSICS, UNIV S FLA, 74- *Concurrent Pos:* Consult & grantee, Defence Res Bd, Can, 60-; Nat Res Coun Can grantee, 64- *Mem:* Can Soc Cell Biol; Brit Soc Gen Microbiol; Brit Soc Appl Bact; Biophys Soc; Am Soc Photobiol. *Res:* Influence of bound water on structure of macromolecules; effects of nutrition on in-vivo energy states and on the action of microwave radiations. *Mailing Add:* Dept of Physics Univ SFla Tampa FL 33620

WEBB, THEODORE STRATTON, JR, b Oklahoma City, Okla, Mar 4, 30; m 52; c 2. APPLIED PHYSICS, AEROSPACE ENGINEERING. *Educ:* Univ Okla, BS, 51; Calif Inst Technol, PhD(physics), 55. *Prof Exp:* Dir aerospace tech dept, 69-74, vpres res & eng, 74-80, VPRES F-16 PROG, GEN DYNAMICS, 80- *Concurrent Pos:* Adj prof physics, Tex Christian Univ, 55-71. *Mem:* Am Phys Soc; Am Inst Aeronaut & Astronaut; Soc Automotive Engrs; AAAS. *Res:* Management of research and development; aircraft design and development; propulsion systems; nuclear shielding and reactor theory; low energy particle physics. *Mailing Add:* Gen Dynamics PO Box 748 Ft Worth TX 76101

WEBB, THOMAS EVAN, b Edmonton, Alta, Mar 4, 32; m 61; c 2. BIOCHEMISTRY. *Educ:* Univ Alta, BSc, 55, MSc, 57; Univ Toronto, PhD(biochem), 61. *Prof Exp:* Nat Res Coun Can fels, Nat Res Coun, Ont, 61-63 & Univ Wis-Madison, 63-65; asst prof biochem, Med Sch, Univ Man, 65-66; asst prof, Cancer Res Unit, McGill Univ, 66-70, actg dir, 69-70; assoc prof, 70-74, PROF PHYSIOL CHEM, COL MED, OHIO STATE UNIV, 74- *Concurrent Pos:* Prin investr, NIH grants. *Mem:* AAAS; Am Asn Cancer Res; Am Soc Biol Sci; Fedn Am Socs Exp Biol. *Res:* Identification of normal cellular controls and the biochemistry of cancer. *Mailing Add:* Dept of Physiol Chem Ohio State Univ Col of Med Columbus OH 43210

WEBB, THOMAS HOWARD, b Norfolk, Va, July 16, 35; m 57; c 2. ORGANIC CHEMISTRY, LUBRICATION ENGINEERING. *Educ:* Univ Va, BA, 57; Duke Univ, MA, 60, PhD(org chem), 61. *Prof Exp:* Res chemist, Sinclair Res, Inc, 61, proj leader lubricant additives, 63-65, group leader, 65-66, asst sect leader indust oils, 66-69; supvr lubricants, asphalts & waxes, BP Oil Corp, 69-70; sr proj leader indust oils res, 70-72, res assoc lubricants & lubrication, 72-80, RES ASSOC, EXPLOR & PROD, STANDARD OIL CO (OHIO), 81- *Concurrent Pos:* Sr res scientist, Sinclair Oil Corp, 68. *Mem:* AAAS; Am Soc Testing & Mat; Am Soc Lubrication Eng; Am Chem Soc. *Res:* Additives for lubricants; synthesis and structure-property correlations; lubricant formulation and product design. *Mailing Add:* Standard Oil Co 4440 Warrensville Center Rd Cleveland OH 44128

WEBB, THOMPSON, III, b Los Angeles, Calif, Jan 13, 44; m 69; c 2. PALYNOLOGY, CLIMATOLOGY. *Educ:* Swarthmore Col, BA, 66; Univ Wis-Madison, PhD(meteorol), 71. *Prof Exp:* Inst Sci & Technol fel, Univ Mich, Ann Arbor, 70-71, asst res paleocologist, Great Lakes Res Div, 71-72; asst res prof, 72-75, ASSOC PROF GEOL SCI, BROWN UNIV, 75- *Concurrent Pos:* Vis fel, Clare Hall & Bot Sch, Cambridge Univ, England, 77-78; ed, Review Palaeobot & Palynology, 80- *Mem:* AAAS; Am Meteorol Soc; Am Quaternary Asn; Am Asn Stratig Palynologists. *Res:* Use of multivariate statistical techniques for calibrating quaternary pollen data in vegetational and climatic terms; production of paleoclimatic and paleovegetation maps. *Mailing Add:* Dept Geol Sci Box 1846 Brown Univ Providence RI 02912

WEBB, WATT WETMORE, b Kansas City, Mo, Aug 27, 27; m 50; c 3. CONDENSED MATTER PHYSICS. *Educ:* Mass Inst Technol, ScB, 47, ScD(metall), 55. *Prof Exp:* Res engr, Union Carbide Metals Co, 47-52, res scientist, 55-59, coordr fundamental res, 59-60, asst dir res, 61; assoc prof eng, 61-65, PROF APPL & ENG PHYSICS, CORNELL UNIV, 65- *Concurrent Pos:* Consult; mem var adv panels Nat Res Coun, NSF, 58-; John Simon Guggenheim Found fel, 74-75; assoc ed, Phys Rev Letters, 75-; exec comt, Div Biol Physics, Am Phys Soc, 75-78; mem publ comt, Biophys J. *Mem:* Fel Am Phys Soc; AAAS; Biophys Soc; Metall Soc; Inst Elec & Electronics Engrs. *Res:* Critical and collective phenomena; fluctuations; superconductivity; membrane and cellular biophysics; biophysical processes; fluid dynamics; chemical kinetics; phase transformations; crystal defects and composite materials. *Mailing Add:* Sch Appl & Eng Phys Clark Hall Cornell Univ Ithaca NY 14850

WEBB, WATTS RANKIN, b Columbia, Ky, Sept 8, 22; m 44; c 4. SURGERY. *Educ:* Univ Miss, BA, 42; Johns Hopkins Univ, MD, 45; Am Bd Surg, dipl, 52; Am Bd Thoracic Surg, dipl, 53. *Prof Exp:* Chief surgeon, Miss State Sanatorium, 52-63; prof surg & chmn, Div Thoracic & Cardiovasc Surg, Univ Tex Southwest Med Sch Dallas, 64-70; prof surg & chmn dept, State Univ NY Upstate Med Ctr, 70-77; PROF SURG & CHMN DEPT, SCH MED, TULANE UNIV, 77- *Concurrent Pos:* Prof, Sch Med, Univ Miss, 55-63. *Mem:* Fel Am Col Surgeons; Am Asn Thoracic Surgeons; fel Am Col Chest Physicians; Am Col Cardiol; Am Soc Artificial Internal Organs. *Res:* Shock; cardiac-pulmonary transplantation; organ preservation; hypothermia; myocardial physiology. *Mailing Add:* Dept of Surg Tulane Univ Sch Med New Orleans LA 70112

WEBB, WILLIAM ALBERT, b Paterson, NJ, Mar 10, 44; m 66; c 2. MATHEMATICS. *Educ:* Mich State Univ, BS, 65; Pa State Univ, University Park, PhD(math), 68. *Prof Exp:* Res instr math, Pa State Univ, 68-69; asst prof, 69-75, ASSOC PROF MATH, WASH STATE UNIV, 75- *Mem:* Am Math Soc; Math Asn Am. *Res:* Analytic and elementary number theory; number theoretic questions concerning polynomial rings over finite fields. *Mailing Add:* Dept of Math Wash State Univ Pullman WA 99164

WEBB, WILLIAM GATEWOOD, b Charleston, SC, July 17, 25; m 52; c 3. MEDICINAL CHEMISTRY. *Educ:* Univ of South, BS, 50; Univ Rochester, PhD(org chem), 54. *Prof Exp:* Res chemist, Columbia-Southern Chem Corp, WVa, 54-55; res assoc, Res Div, 55-57 & Patent Div, 57-61, patent agent, 61-65, SR PATENT AGENT, STERLING-WINTHROP RES INST, 65- *Mem:* Am Chem Soc. *Res:* Synthetic organic chemistry. *Mailing Add:* Patent Div Sterling-Winthrop Res Inst Rensselaer NY 12144

WEBB, WILLIAM LOGAN, b Chattanooga, Tenn, Feb 13, 30; c 5. PSYCHIATRY. *Educ:* Princeton Univ, AB, 51; Johns Hopkins Univ, MD, 55. *Hon Degrees:* MA, Univ Pa, 71. *Prof Exp:* From instr to asst prof psychiat, Sch Med, Johns Hopkins Univ, 61-64; from asst prof to prof psychiat, Univ Pa, 64-74; PROF PSYCHIAT & CHMN DEPT, UNIV TENN, MEMPHIS, 74- *Mem:* Am Psychiat Asn; AMA; Acad Psychosom Med; Am Pain Soc; Am Psychosom Soc. *Mailing Add:* Memphis Ment Health Inst 865 Poplar Ave Memphis TN 38104

WEBB, WILLIAM PAUL, b Bismarck, NDak, Dec 30, 22; m 47; c 4. ORGANIC CHEMISTRY. *Educ:* Univ Notre Dame, BS, 44 & 47; Univ Minn, PhD(org chem), 51. *Prof Exp:* SR RES ASSOC, CHEVRON RES CO, STANDARDS OIL CO CALIF, SAN FRANCISCO, 51- *Mem:* Am Chem Soc. *Res:* Petrochemicals; patent liaison. *Mailing Add:* 16 Chestnut Ave San Rafael CA 94901

WEBB, WILLIS KEITH, b McCoy, Va, Apr 21, 28; m 50; c 5. REGULATORY VETERINARY MEDICINE. *Educ:* Tex A&M Univ, DVM, 57. *Prof Exp:* Vet livestock inspector, Animal Dis Eradication Div, USDA, 57; vet, US Food & Drug Admin, 57-62; res assoc, Mead Johnson & Co, Ind, 62-70; VET MED OFFICER, USDA, 70- *Res:* Regulatory veterinary medicine; eradication of disease from domestic animals; animal welfare; interstate movement of livestock. *Mailing Add:* Rte 3 Box 136 Christiansburg VA 24073

WEBB, WILLIS LEE, b Nevada, Tex, July 9, 23; m 42; c 1. METEOROLOGY. *Educ:* Southern Methodist Univ, BS, 52; Univ Okla, MS, 70; Colo State Univ, PhD, 72. *Prof Exp:* Meteorol observer, US Weather Bur, 42-43, meteorologist, 46-52, physicist, 52-55; meteorologist & chief scientist, Atmospheric Sci Lab, US Army Electronics Command, 55-80; MEM STAFF, SCHELLENGER RES LAB, UNIV TEX, EL PASO, 80- *Concurrent Pos:* Mem upper atmosphere rocket res comt, Space Sci Bd, Nat Acad Sci, 59-65; chmn meteorol rocket network comt, Inter-Range Instrumentation Group, 60-; consult, Cath Univ, 60-61; adj prof physics, Univ Tex, El Paso, 63-; mem air blast subcomt, Inter-Oceanic Canal Studies Group, 64-74; Army adv, Nat Comt Clear Air Turbulence, 65-66. *Honors & Awards:* Meritorious Civilian Serv Award, US Army, 58, Commendation, 61. *Mem:* Am Meteorol Soc; Am Geophys Union; Am Inst Aeronaut & Astronaut; Am Phys Soc. *Res:* Synoptic exploration of the 25-100 kilometer region with small rocket vehicles to determine the circulation, thermal and composition structure; development of meteorological satellite techniques for mesoscale applications such as severe storm, air pollution, and combat on a global basis. *Mailing Add:* Schellenger Res Lab Univ Tex El Paso TX 79968

WEBBER, CHARLES LEWIS, JR, b Bay Shore, NY, July 26, 47; m 70; c 2. MEDICAL PHYSIOLOGY, RESPIRATORY PHYSIOLOGY. *Educ:* Taylor Univ, AB, 69; Loyola Univ, Chicago, PhD(physiol), 74. *Prof Exp:* Fel physiol, Max Planck Inst Physiol & Clin Res, Bad Nauheim, 73-75; asst prof, 75-81, ASSOC PROF PHYSIOL, LOYOLA UNIV, CHICAGO, 81- *Concurrent Pos:* Sect leader prog proj grant, Nat Heart, Lung & Blood Inst, 75-80. *Mem:* Am Physiol Soc; Soc Neurosci; Sigma Xi. *Res:* Central nervous system regulation of cardiopulmonary mechanisms; structure function correlations in the central nervous system; application of laboratory computer systems to biological problem solving. *Mailing Add:* Dept of Physiol 2160 S First Ave Maywood IL 60153

WEBBER, DONALD SALYER, b Los Angeles, Calif, Jan 15, 17; m 51; c 2. PHYSICS. *Educ:* Univ Calif, Los Angeles, BA, 38, MA, 41, PhD(physics), 54; Calif Inst Technol, MS, 42. *Prof Exp:* Assoc physics, Univ Calif, Los Angeles, 49-54, instr, 54-55; mem tech staff, Ramo-Wooldridge Div, Thompson Ramo Wooldridge, Inc, 55-60, mem sr staff, 60-61, assoc mgr photo equip dept, 61; mgr solar physics prog, Calif Div, Lockheed Aircraft Corp, 61-63, mgr astron sci lab, 64-65; sr staff engr, 65-80, CONSULT PHYSICIST, TRW SYSTS GROUP, 80- *Mem:* Am Phys Soc; Optical Soc Am. *Res:* Infrared spectroscopy of crystals; photo-optical instrumentation; solar physics; remote sensing. *Mailing Add:* 3551 Knobhill Dr Sherman Oaks CA 91423

WEBBER, EDGAR ERNEST, b Worcester, Mass, Sept 11, 32; m 58; c 2. BOTANY. *Educ:* Univ Mass, BS, 55, PhD(bot), 67; Cornell Univ, MS, 61. *Prof Exp:* Instr bot, Wellesley Col, 61-62; asst prof, Pa State Univ, Behrend Campus, 65-67; from asst prof to assoc prof, 67-74, PROF BIOL, KEUKA COL, 74- *Concurrent Pos:* Am Philos Soc grant, 68; teaching/res, Marine Sci Inst, Nahant, Mass, 68-80. *Mem:* Phycol Soc Am; Int Phycol Soc; Brit Phycol Soc. *Res:* Ecology and systematics of benthic salt marsh algae; culture and life history studies; morphology. *Mailing Add:* Dept of Biol Keuka Col Keuka Park NY 14478

WEBBER, GAYLE MILTON, b Sioux City, Iowa, Aug 30, 31; m 60; c 3. ORGANIC CHEMISTRY. *Educ:* Morningside Col, BS, 53; Univ Iowa, MS, 58. *Prof Exp:* Sr res asst, 58-74, RES INVESTR, G D SEARLE & CO, 74- *Mem:* Am Chem Soc. *Res:* Steroids. *Mailing Add:* G D Searle & Co Box 5110 Chicago IL 60680

WEBBER, GEORGE ROGER, b Toronto, Ont, Nov 2, 26; m 54. GEOLOGY. *Educ:* Queen's Univ, Can, BSc, 49; McMaster Univ, MSc, 52; Mass Inst Technol, PhD(geol), 55. *Prof Exp:* Res assoc, 55-59, asst prof, 59-66, ASSOC PROF GEOL, McGILL UNIV, 66- *Mem:* Geol Soc Am; Geochem Soc; Spectros Soc Can; Asn Explor Geochem; Geol Asn Can. *Res:* Geochemistry; x-ray and optical spectrography. *Mailing Add:* Dept of Geol Sci McGill Univ Montreal PQ H3A 2A7 Can

WEBBER, HERBERT H, b Vancouver, BC, Oct 15, 41; m 63. BIOLOGY. *Educ:* Univ BC, BSc, 63, PhD(zool), 66. *Prof Exp:* NATO fel, Can for Study at Hopkins Marine Sta Stanford, 66-68; asst prof biol, Wake Forest Univ, 68-72; asst prof biol, 72-74, ASSOC PROF MARINE RESOURCES, HUXLEY COL ENVIRON STUDIES, WESTERN WASH UNIV, 74- *Mem:* AAAS. *Res:* Invertebrate physiology; reproductive physiology of Gastropoda Mollusca. *Mailing Add:* Huxley Col Environ Studies Western Wash Univ Bellingham WA 98225

WEBBER, JOHN ALAN, b Chicago, Ill, Aug 14, 40. MEDICINAL CHEMISTRY. *Educ:* Univ Colo, BA, 62; Stanford Univ, PhD(org chem), 67. *Prof Exp:* RES SCIENTIST, ELI LILLY & CO, 66- *Mem:* Am Chem Soc; Am Soc Microbiol. *Res:* Structural modification and synthesis of natural products and complex organic molecules; medicinal chemistry of agents with antibiotic activity. *Mailing Add:* Eli Lilly & Co M 705 Indianapolis IN 46285

WEBBER, LARRY STANFORD, b New Orleans, La, Apr 1, 45; m 67; c 2. BIOMETRICS, BIOSTATISTICS. *Educ:* La State Univ, BS, 67; Yale Univ, MPhil, 70, PhD(epidemiol & pub health), 73. *Prof Exp:* Nat Acad Sci statistician, Atomic Bomb Casualty Comn, 72-74; asst prof, 74-79, ASSOC PROF, MED CTR, LA STATE UNIV, 79- *Mem:* Am Statist Asn; Biomet Soc; Am Heart Asn; Am Pub Health Asn. *Res:* Design, implementation and analysis of an ongoing longitudinal research study of cardiovascular risk factor variables in an entire community. *Mailing Add:* Dept Med Specialized Ctr Res La State Univ 1542 Tulane Ave New Orleans LA 70112

WEBBER, MARION GEORGE, b Golden, Colo, Dec 8, 21; m 45; c 9. PHARMACEUTICAL CHEMISTRY. *Educ:* Univ Colo, BS, 47, MS, 48; Univ Fla, PhD(pharm), 51. *Prof Exp:* Instr pharm & pharmaceut chem, Univ Fla, 50-51; asst prof pharmaceut chem, 51-52, assoc prof pharm, 53-72, PROF PHARM, UNIV HOUSTON, 72- *Mem:* Am Col Apothecaries; Am Pharmaceut Asn. *Res:* Tillandsia usneoides; pharmaceutical formulation and stability studies. *Mailing Add:* Univ of Houston Col of Pharm 4800 Calhoun Houston TX 77004

WEBBER, MILO M, b Los Angeles, Calif, Sept 27, 30; m 55; c 2. RADIOLOGY, NUCLEAR MEDICINE. *Educ:* Univ Calif, Los Angeles, BA, 52, MD, 55; Am Bd Radiol, dipl, 61; Am Bd Nuclear Med, dipl, 72. *Prof Exp:* Intern surg serv, 55-56, resident radiol, 56-57 & 59-60, instr, 60-61, lectr, 61-62, from asst prof to assoc prof, 62-74, PROF RADIOL SCI, SCH MED, UNIV CALIF, LOS ANGELES, 74- *Concurrent Pos:* Consult, Queen of Angels Hosp, Los Angeles, 65-77; res radiologist, Lab Nuclear Med & Radiation Biol, Sch Med, Univ Calif, Los Angeles, 65-78. *Mem:* Am Col Radiol; AMA; Soc Nuclear Med; Radiol Soc NAm. *Res:* Development and refinement of organ radioisotope scanning procedures, including development of thrombosis localization techniques; application of telecommunications to the practice of radiology and nuclear medicine. *Mailing Add:* Nuclear Med AR 144B Ctr Health Sci Univ of Calif Los Angeles CA 90024

WEBBER, MUKTA MALA (MAINI), b India, Dec 5, 37; m 63; c 1. ONCOLOGY, CELL BIOLOGY. *Educ:* Agra Univ, BSc, 57, MSc, 59; Queen's Univ, Kingston, Ont, PhD, 63; Univ Toronto, dipl electron micros, 68. *Prof Exp:* Cancer res scientist, Roswell Park Mem Inst, NY State Dept Health, 62-63; lectr histol & embryol, Sch Med, Queen's Univ, Ont, 63-65, res assoc, Dept Urol, Queen's Univ & Kingston Gen Hosp, 65-68; sr instr urol, 71, asst prof, Div Urol, 72-78, asst prof, Dept Biochem, Biophys & Genetics, 77-79, DIR RES, DIV UROL, SCH MED, UNIV COLO HEALTH SCI CTR, DENVER, 71-, MEM GRAD FAC, 77-, ASSOC PROF UROL, 78- *Concurrent Pos:* Res assoc, Inst Arctic & Alpine Res, Univ Colo, Boulder, 69-78; mem, Nat Prostatic Cancer Proj, Nat Organ Site Cancer Progs, Nat Cancer Inst, NIH, 79-; award, Int Cancer Res Technol Transfer Prog, Int Union Against Cancer, 80. *Mem:* Am Soc Cell Biol; Am Asn Cancer Res; Electron Micros Soc Am; NY Acad Sci; Tissue Cult Asn. *Res:* Cell biology, etiology and prevention of human prostatic neoplasia; in vitro cell models for studies on aging, carcinogenesis, cell nutrition, growth, differentiation and toxicity testing; growth regulation; tumor promoters; cell ultrastructure; effects of trace metals, electric fields and microwaves on cells. *Mailing Add:* Div Urol Box C319 Univ Colo Health Sci Center Denver CO 80262

WEBBER, PATRICK JOHN, b Bedfordshire, UK, Feb 24, 38; m 63; c 1. ECOLOGY, BIOLOGY. *Educ:* Univ Reading, BSc, 60; Queen's Univ, Ont, MSc, 63, PhD, 71. *Prof Exp:* Asst prof biol, York Univ, 66-69; from asst prof to assoc prof, 69-78, PROF BIOL, UNIV COLO, BOULDER, 78-, MEM FAC, INST ARCTIC & ALPINE RES, 69-, DIR, 79- *Mem:* AAAS; Ecol Soc Am; Arctic Inst NAm; Can Bot Asn; fel Artic Inst NAm. *Res:* Primary productivity, phenology and phytosociology of arctic and alpine tundras; effects of vehicle damage, oil spills; snowfences and weather modification on tundra ecosystem; gradient analysis of vegetation. *Mailing Add:* Inst of Arctic & Alpine Res Univ of Colo Boulder CO 80309

WEBBER, RICHARD HARRY, b Camillus, NY, Jan 2, 24; m 46; c 7. ANATOMY. *Educ:* St Benedict's Col, BS, 48; Univ Notre Dame, MS, 49; St Louis Univ, PhD(anat), 54. *Prof Exp:* Instr biol, St Benedict's Col, 48; instr, Niagara Univ, 49-51; asst anat, Sch Med, St Louis Univ, 51-54; asst prof, Sch Med, Creighton Univ, 54-59; assoc prof, Sch Med, Temple Univ, 59-61; assoc prof, 61-70, PROF ANAT, SCH MED, STATE UNIV NY BUFFALO, 70- *Concurrent Pos:* Lederle med fac scholar, 56-59; from chmn elect to chmn, Sect Anat Sci, Am Asn Dent Schs, 71-73; mem, Am Benedictine Acad; fel, Human Biol Coun. *Mem:* Am Asn Anatomists; Sigma Xi; Cajal Club. *Res:* Peripheral autonomic nervous system. *Mailing Add:* Dept Anat Sci 319 Farber Hall State Univ of NY Buffalo NY 14214

WEBBER, RICHARD LYLE, b Akron, Ohio, Nov 2, 35; m 56; c 2. PHYSIOLOGICAL OPTICS, DENTISTRY. *Educ:* Albion Col, AB, 58; Univ Mich, Ann Arbor, DDS, 63; Univ Calif, Berkeley, PhD(physiol optics), 71. *Prof Exp:* Intern dent, USPHS Hosp, Seattle, Wash, 63-64, clin investr, Mat & Technol Br, Dent Health Ctr, Div Dent Health, USPHS, 64-68, lectr, Univ Calif, Berkeley, 70-71, staff investr, Diag Systs, Oral Med & Surg Br, 71-75, chief diag methodology sect, 75-77, CHIEF CLIN INVEST BR, NAT INST DENT RES, 75-, CHIEF, DIAG SYST BR, 78- *Mem:* AAAS; Am Acad Dent Radiol; Int Asn Dent Res; Soc Photo-Optical Instrument Eng. *Res:* Image processing and the study of factors influencing diagnostic systems. *Mailing Add:* Clin Invest Br Nat Inst of Dent Res Bethesda MD 20014

WEBBER, STANLEY EUGENE, b Boston, Mass, June 8, 19; c 4. ELECTRICAL ENGINEERING. *Educ:* Mass Inst Technol, BS, 41, MS, 42. *Prof Exp:* Res assoc, Gen Elec Co, 42-57, mgr eng, 57-64; mgr eng, 64-67, mgr linear beam dept, Electron Tube Div, 67-76, vpres, 72-76, PRES, LITTON INDUSTS, INC, 76- *Mem:* Fel Inst Elec & Electronics Engrs. *Res:* Design and manufacture of ultra high frequency vacuum tubes. *Mailing Add:* Litton Electron Tube Div 960 Industrial Ave San Carlos CA 94070

WEBBER, STEPHEN EDWARD, b Springfield, Mo, Sept 19, 40; m 62; c 3. PHYSICAL CHEMISTRY, POLYMER SPECTROSCOPY. *Educ:* Wash Univ, AB, 62; Univ Chicago, PhD(chem), 65. *Prof Exp:* NSF fel, Univ Col, Univ London, 65-66; asst prof, 66-71, ASSOC PROF CHEM, UNIV TEX, AUSTIN, 71- *Mem:* Am Chem Soc; Sigma Xi. *Res:* Molecular excitons; electronic relaxation phenomena; energy transfer in polymers; polymer photochemistry. *Mailing Add:* Dept Chem Univ Tex Austin TX 78712

WEBBER, THOMAS GRAY, b Oct 12, 12; US citizen; m 41; c 2. ORGANIC CHEMISTRY. *Educ:* Brown Univ, ScB, 33; Univ Ill, MS, 34; Harvard Univ, PhD(org chem), 40. *Prof Exp:* Chemist, Am Cyanamid Co, NJ, 35-36 & Nopco Chem Co, 36-37; asst chem, Harvard Univ, 38-40; chemist, Jackson Lab, E I du Pont de Nemours & Co, Inc, Del, 40-41, supvr, Ill, 41-43, chem engr, 42-43, chemist, Wash, 43-45, chief chem engr, Ind, 45, chemist, 45-52, head, Lake Div, Tech Lab, 52-62, color specialist, Plastics Dept, 62-73; CONSULT & ED, 73- *Mem:* Am Chem Soc; Soc Plastics Engrs; Inter-Soc Color Coun. *Res:* Polynuclear hydrocarbons; phthalocyanine pigments; dyes and pigments; plastics colcration; color. *Mailing Add:* 1722 Forest Hill Dr Vienna WV 26105

WEBBER, WILLIAM A, b Nfld, Can, Apr 8, 34; m 58; c 3. HISTOLOGY, PHYSIOLOGY. *Educ:* Univ BC, MD, 58. *Prof Exp:* Intern, Vancouver Gen Hosp, 58-59; fel physiol, Med Col, Cornell Univ, 59-61; from asst prof to assoc prof anat, 61-69, assoc dean med, 71-77, PROF ANAT, UNIV BC, 69-, DEAN MED, 77- *Mem:* Am Asn Anatomists; Can Asn Anatomists. *Res:* Renal physiology; kidney structure. *Mailing Add:* Dept of Anat Univ of BC Vancouver BC V6T 1W5 Can

WEBBER, WILLIAM R, b Bedford, Iowa, June 9, 29; m 61; c 1. PHYSICS, ASTROPHYSICS. *Educ:* Coe Col, BS, 51; Univ Iowa, MS, 54, PhD(physics), 57. *Prof Exp:* Asst prof physics, Univ Md, 58-59; NSF fel, Imp Col, Univ London, 59-61; from asst prof to assoc prof, Univ Minn, Minneapolis, 61-69; PROF PHYSICS & DIR, SPACE SCI CTR, UNIV NH, 69- *Concurrent Pos:* Co-ed, J Geophys Res, Am Geophys Union, 61-; mem Fields & Particles Subcomt, NASA, 63-66; consult, Boeing Aircraft Co & NAm Aviation, Inc, 63-; vis prof, Univ Adelaide, 68-69; vis prof, Danish Space Res Ctr, 71. *Mem:* Am Phys Soc; Am Geophys Union; Am Astron Soc. *Res:* Charge composition and energy spectrum of cosmic rays; motion of charged particles in the earths magnetic field; solar-terrestrial relationships; particle detectors; ray astronomy. *Mailing Add:* Dept Physics Univ NH Durham NH 03824

WEBBINK, RONALD FREDERICK, b Hutchinson, Kans, Sept 21, 45; m 70; c 2. ASTROPHYSICS. *Educ:* Mass Inst Technol, BS, 67; Univ Cambridge, PhD(astron), 75. *Prof Exp:* Res assoc, 75-77, res asst prof, 77-78, ASST PROF ASTRON, UNIV ILL, 78- *Mem:* Am Astron Soc; Royal Astron Soc. *Res:* Structure and evolution of close binary stars; mass and angular momentum loss from stars; stellar interiors; cataclysmic variable stars; globular star clusters. *Mailing Add:* Dept of Astron Univ of Ill Urbana IL 61801

WEBBON, BRUCE WARREN, b Bridgeport, Conn, June 7, 45; div; c 2. BIOENGINEERING, MECHANICAL ENGINEERING. *Educ:* Ga Inst Technol, BSME, 68; Univ Fla, MSME, 69; Univ Mo, PhD(mech eng), 78. *Prof Exp:* Turbine aerodyn engr jet engines, Pratt & Whitney Aircraft Co, 67-68; res asst mech eng, Univ Fla, 68-69; sr thermodyn engr life support syst, LTV Aerospace Corp, 69-72; res assoc mech eng, Univ Mo, 72-75; res scientist life sci, Ames Res Ctr, NASA, 75-81; SR RES ENGR, SRI INT, 81- *Mem:* Am Inst Aeronaut & Astronaut; AAAS. *Res:* Zero gravity fluid mechanics and phase change processes; human thermoregulation. *Mailing Add:* EL 141 SRI Int Menlo Park CA 94025

WEBER, ALBERT VINCENT, b Pittsburgh, Pa, Jan 30, 25; m 48; c 3. BOTANY. *Educ:* Duquesne Univ, BEd, 50, MSc, 52; Univ Minn, PhD(bot), 57. *Prof Exp:* Asst bot, Duquesne Univ, 50-52; asst, Univ Minn, 52-56; from instr to assoc prof, 56-63, co-dir summer session, 69-74, PROF BIOL, UNIV WIS-LA CROSSE, 64-, ASSOC DEAN, COL LETTERS & SCI, 67-, DIR, SCH HEALTH & HUMAN SERV, 74- *Mem:* Sigma Xi; Bot Soc Am. *Res:* Plant anatomy, morphology and morphogenesis. *Mailing Add:* 105 Main Hall Univ Wis La Crosse WI 54601

WEBER, ALFONS, b Dortmund, Ger, Oct 8, 27; nat US; m 55; c 3. PHYSICS. *Educ:* Ill Inst Technol, BS, 51, MS, 53, PhD, 56. *Prof Exp:* Asst physics, Ill Inst Technol, 51-53, instr, 53-56; fel, Nat Res Coun Can, 56-57; from asst prof to assoc prof physics, Fordham Univ, 57-66, chmn dept, 64-69, prof, 66-81; PHYSICIST, NAT BUR STANDARDS, 77- *Mem:* Fel Am Phys Soc; Am Asn Physics Teachers; Optical Soc Am. *Res:* Raman and infrared spectroscopy; molecular mechanics; optics. *Mailing Add:* Molecular Spectroscopy Div 545 Rm B268 Bldg 221 Nat Bur Standards Washington DC 20234

WEBER, ALFRED HERMAN, b Philadelphia, Pa, Jan 15, 06; m 32; c 7. NUCLEAR PHYSICS, SPACE PHYSICS. *Educ:* St Joseph's Col, Pa, AB, 28, MA, 31; Univ Pa, PhD(physics), 36. *Hon Degrees:* DSc, St Joseph's Col, Pa, 68. *Prof Exp:* Instr physics & math, St Joseph's Col, Pa, 28-34, from asst prof to prof physics & head dept, 34-39; from asst prof to prof, 39-74, tech dir, US Army Air Force Radio Sch, 42-43, chmn dept physics, 51-74, EMER PROF PHYSICS & CHMN DEPT, ST LOUIS UNIV, 74- *Concurrent Pos:* Sigma Xi, Res Corp, NSF, Army Res Off, AEC, Am Cancer Soc & Dept Defense grants; consult, Argonne Nat Lab, 47-57, US Army Ballistic Missile Agency, 57-60 & Marshall Space Flight Ctr, NASA, 60-70; vpres, Assoc Midwest Univs, Argonne Nat Lab, 60, pres, 61; prof physics, Univ Ala, 63-67; consult, 74- *Mem:* Fel Am Phys Soc; Am Asn Univ Prof; Am Asn Physics Teachers; Sigma Xi. *Res:* Electron emission and diffraction; properties of thin metallic films; x-ray diffraction; neutron diffraction and scattering; nuclear spectroscopy; plasma and space physics. *Mailing Add:* 1047 Chevy Chase Dr Sarasota FL 33580

WEBER, ALLEN HOWARD, b Lorenzo, Idaho, May 15, 38; m 59; c 3. ATMOSPHERIC DIFFUSION, MICROMETEOROLOGY. *Educ:* Brigham Young Univ, BS, 60; Univ Ariz, MS, 62; Univ Utah, PhD(meteorol), 66. *Prof Exp:* Asst prof meteorol, Univ Okla, 66-68 & meteorol & environ health, 68-69; consult, Nat Severe Storms Lab, 69; from asst prof to assoc prof meteorol, NC State Univ, 69-77; STAFF METEOROLOGIST, SAVANNAH RIVER LAB, 77- *Concurrent Pos:* NSF grant, Univ Okla, 68-69; res meteorologist, Environ Protection Agency, Nat Environ Res Ctr, 70-72; Environ Protection Agency grant, NC State Univ & NC Water Resources Res Inst, 72-77 & turbulence & diffusion res, Savannah River Lab, 77- *Mem:* Am Meteorol Soc. *Res:* Atmospheric turbulence: physical meteorology. *Mailing Add:* Environ Sci Div Savannah River Lab Aiken SC 29808

WEBER, ALLEN THOMAS, b Long Prairie, Minn, Sept 7, 43; m 69; c 2. MICROBIOLOGY. *Educ:* Univ Mich, Ann Arbor, BS, 65; Univ Wis-Madison, MS, 67, PhD(bact), 70. *Prof Exp:* Asst prof, 70-73, ASSOC PROF BIOL, UNIV NEBR AT OMAHA, 73- *Mem:* AAAS; Am Soc Microbiol; Brit Soc Gen Microbiol. *Res:* Morphogenesis and development of microorganisms; cellular slime molds; microbial genetics. *Mailing Add:* Dept of Biol 60th & Dodge St Omaha NE 68182

WEBER, ALVIN FRANCIS, b Hartford, Wis, Mar 13, 18; m 45; c 3. CYTOLOGY. *Educ:* Iowa State Col, DVM, 44; Univ Wis, BA, 46, MS, 48, PhD(vet sci), 49. *Prof Exp:* Instr vet sci, Univ Wis, 44-49; from asst prof to assoc prof, 49-55, head dept, 65-73, PROF VET ANAT, UNIV MINN, ST PAUL, 55- *Concurrent Pos:* USPHS spec fel, Univ Giessen, 59; NIH fel, Univ Bern, 72. *Mem:* Am Asn Anat. *Res:* Bovine uterine histology, histological and cytochemical changes of the adrenal gland and structure of secretory components of the udder; electron microscopic studies of the hematopoietic organs of domestic animals. *Mailing Add:* Dept of Vet Anat Univ of Minn St Paul MN 55101

WEBER, ANNEMARIE, b Rostock, Ger, Sept 11, 23; US citizen. PHYSIOLOGY, BIOCHEMISTRY. *Educ:* Univ Tubingen, MD, 50. *Prof Exp:* Res asst physiol, Univ Tubingen, 50-51; res fel biophys, Univ Col, London & physiol, Univ Md, 51; Rockefeller fel phys chem, Harvard Med Sch, 52; res fel physiol, Univ Tubingen, 53-54; res assoc neurol, Columbia Univ, 54-59; asst mem physiol, Inst Muscle Dis, New York, 59-63, assoc mem, 63-65; prof biochem, St Louis Univ, 65-72; PROF BIOCHEM, UNIV PA, 72- *Mem:* Am Physiol Soc; Soc Gen Physiol; Biophys Soc; Am Soc Biol Chemists. *Res:* Regulation of muscular activity. *Mailing Add:* Dept of Biochem Univ of Pa Philadelphia PA 19104

WEBER, ARTHUR GEORGE, b St Joseph, Mo, Jan 14, 03; m 30; c 4. CHEMISTRY. *Educ:* Univ Kans, BS, 27; Univ Wis, PhD(gen chem), 30. *Prof Exp:* Asst instr chem, Univ Wis, 27-30; res chemist, Ammonia Dept, Exp Sta, E I du Pont de Nemours & Co, Inc, 30-34, proj leader, 34-39, group leader, 39-44, lab dir, 44-50, mgr, Admin & Serv Sect, Polychem Dept, Res Div, 50-56, mgr personnel sect, Personnel & Employee Rels Div, Plastics Dept, 56-68; SPECIALIST COUNSR, TECH SERV DIV, UNIV DEL, 68- *Mem:* Am Chem Soc. *Res:* High pressure synthesis; oxidation and hydrogenation reactions; phosphoric acids; process development. *Mailing Add:* 1514 Brandywine Blvd Wilmington DE 19809

WEBER, BARBARA C, b Prairie du Chien, Wis, Nov 15, 47. ENTOMOLOGY. *Educ:* Viterbo Col, BA, 69; Univ Minn, St Paul, MS, 71; Southern Ill Univ Carbondale, PhD, 82. *Prof Exp:* Conserv forest pest specialist entom, Minn Dept Natural Resources, 73-74; entomologist Dutch elm dis, Minn Dept Agr, 74-75; RES ENTOMOLOGIST, FOREST SERV, USDA, 75- *Mem:* Entom Soc Can; Entom Soc Am; Soc Am Foresters; Am Phytopath Soc; Sigma Xi. *Res:* Insect pests of black walnut; disease transmission by insects; taxonomy of scolytid insects; silvicultural management of black walnut to control insect problems. *Mailing Add:* Forestry Sci Lab Southern Ill Univ Carbondale IL 62901

WEBER, BRUCE HOWARD, b Cleveland, Ohio, June 8, 41. BIOCHEMISTRY, NEUROCHEMISTRY. *Educ:* San Diego State Univ, BS, 63; Univ Calif, San Diego, PhD(chem), 68. *Prof Exp:* Am Cancer Soc fel, Molecular Biol Inst, Univ Calif, Los Angeles, 68-70; asst prof, 70-72, assoc prof, 72-76, PROF CHEM, CALIF STATE UNIV, FULLERTON, 76- *Concurrent Pos:* NIH res fel, 75; res scientist, Div Neurosci, City of Hope Nat Med Ctr, 75-77. *Mem:* AAAS; Am Chem Soc; Brit Soc Hist Sci; Am Soc Biol Chemists; Sigma Xi. *Res:* Structure, function, and evolution of proteins; history of biochemistry. *Mailing Add:* Dept of Chem Calif State Univ Fullerton CA 92634

WEBER, CARL JOSEPH, b Evanston, Ill, Nov 7, 54; m 77. CHEMICAL PROCESSES. *Educ:* Univ Calif, Santa Barbara,BS, 76; Univ Mass, MS, 80, PhD(chem), 81. *Prof Exp:* Develop engr electron mat develop, Thick Film Systs, Subsid Ferro Corp, 76-78; fel inorg & polymer chem, Univ Mass, Amherst, 81-82; RES CHEMIST PROCESS RES, US BORAX RES CORP, DIV US BORAX CHEMICALS CORP, 81- *Mem:* Am Chem Soc; AAAS; Sigma Xi. *Mailing Add:* 3776 Howard Ave Los Alamitos CA 90720

WEBER, CHARLES L, b Dayton, Ohio, Dec 2, 37. COMMUNICATION SYSTEMS, RADAR SYSTEMS. *Educ:* Univ Dayton, BSEE, 58; Univ Southern Calif, MSEE, 60; Univ Calif, Los Angeles, PhD, 64. *Prof Exp:* Mem tech staff, Hughes Aircraft Co, Calif, 58-62; from asst prof to assoc prof, 64-79, PROF ELEC ENG, UNIV SOUTHERN CALIF, 79- *Concurrent Pos:* Consult. *Mem:* Inst Elec & Electronics Engrs. *Mailing Add:* Dept of Elec Eng Univ of Southern Calif Los Angeles CA 90007

WEBER, CHARLES WALTER, b Harold, SDak, Nov 30, 31; m 61; c 2. BIOCHEMISTRY, NUTRITION. *Educ:* Colo State Univ, BS, 56, MS, 58; Univ Ariz, PhD(biochem, nutrit), 66. *Prof Exp:* Res chemist, Univ Colo, 60-63; from asst prof to assoc prof, 66-73, PROF BIOCHEM NUTRIT, UNIV ARIZ, 73- *Mem:* Inst Food Technologists; Poultry Sci Asn; Am Soc Clin Nutrit; NY Acad Sci; Am Inst Nutrit. *Res:* Trace minerals metabolism and toxicity; interaction between trace elements, fiber and trace element requirements of mice; evaluation of desert plants for nutritional quality. *Mailing Add:* Dept Nutrit & Food Sci Rm 309 Agr Sci Bldg Univ Ariz Tucson AZ 85721

WEBER, CHARLES WILLIAM, b Streator, Ill, Dec 28, 22; m 48; c 3. ANALYTICAL CHEMISTRY, ENVIRONMENT MONITORING. *Educ:* Northwestern Univ, BS, 49; Ind Univ, PhD(anal chem), 53. *Prof Exp:* Anal chemist, 53-58, Sect Anal Develop, 58-62, dept head chem anal, Oak Ridge Gaseous Diffusion Plant, 62-77, ENVIRON MEASUREMENTS FOUR-PLANT COORDR, NUCLEAR DIV, UNION CARBIDE CORP, 77- *Mem:* AAAS; Sigma Xi; fel Am Inst Chem; Am Chem Soc. *Res:* Instrument development; gas analysis; automation; laboratory management; process control; personnel development. *Mailing Add:* 1021 W Outer Dr Oak Ridge TN 37830

WEBER, DARLENE MARIE, b Brackenridge, Pa, Nov 17, 39; m 64; c 2. HEALTH SCIENCES. *Educ:* State Univ NY, Cortland, BS, 61; Ind Univ, MS, 63; DHlth & Safety, 64. *Prof Exp:* Instr health & phys educ, State Univ NY, Buffalo, 61-62; teaching assoc health, 62-63, vis lectr, Ind Univ, 63-64; instr health & phys educ, Martinsville, Ind, 64-65; dir pub health educ, Ind

Heart Asn, 65-66; ASST PROF HEALTH, ILL STATE UNIV, 68- *Concurrent Pos:* Lectr, Weight Watchers Int, 70-74; dir grant, Parent Peer Educ Drug Use & Values, 78-79; consult, Sch Syst, 70-79. *Mem:* Am Pub Health Asn; Am Sch Health Asn. *Res:* Weight control through diet modification and behavior modification; drug education; alcohol and drug early intervention through preventative education for parents of young children; health care needs as perceived by consumers. *Mailing Add:* Dept of Health Sci Ill State Univ Normal IL 61761

WEBER, DARRELL J, b Thornton, Idaho, Nov 16, 33; m 62; c 7. BIOCHEMISTRY, PLANT PATHOLOGY. *Educ:* Univ Idaho, BS, 58, MS, 59; Univ Calif, PhD(plant path), 63. *Prof Exp:* Res asst agr chem, Univ Idaho, 57-59; res asst plant path, Univ Calif, 59-63; res assoc biochem, Univ Wis, 63-65, asst prof, 65-69; assoc prof, 69-73, PROF BOT, BRIGHAM YOUNG UNIV, 73- *Concurrent Pos:* Fels, Univ Wis, 63-65; consult, NASA, 66-67; grants, USDA, 66-68, NASA, 67-68, NIH, 68-71 & NSF, 71-78; fel biochem, Mich State Univ, 75-76, NSF, 76-79 & USDA, 80-81. *Honors & Awards:* Maeser Award, 74. *Mem:* AAAS; Am Phytopath Soc; Am Bot Soc; Am Inst Biol Sci; Am Soc Microbiol. *Res:* Phytochemistry; mode of action of fungicides; metabolism of fungal spores; biochemistry of host-parasite complexes; salt tolerance of plants; toxic compounds in plants. *Mailing Add:* Dept of Bot 285 Widtsoe Brigham Young Univ Provo UT 84602

WEBER, DAVID ALEXANDER, b Lockport, NY, Mar 6, 39; m 61; c 2. MEDICAL PHYSICS. *Educ:* St Lawrence Univ, BS, 60; Univ Rochester, PhD(medical physics), 71. *Prof Exp:* Teaching asst physics, Univ Buffalo, 60-61; asst attend physicist, Mem Sloan-Kettering Cancer Ctr, 61-68; AEC grad lab fel radiation biol & biophys, 68-70, asst prof radiol, 70-75, asst prof radiation biol & biophys, 70-80, ASSOC PROF RADIATION BIOL & BIOPHYS, SCH MED & DENT, UNIV ROCHESTER, 80-, ASSOC PROF RADIOL, 75- *Concurrent Pos:* Clin fac, Sch Health Related Prof, Rochester Inst Technol, 76-; vis scientist, Lund Univ Hosp, Sweden, 78-79; Fogarty Sr Int fel, NIH, 78-79. *Mem:* Soc Nuclear Med; Am Asn Physicists in Med; Health Physics Soc; Am Col Nuclear Physicians. *Res:* Radioactive tracers for the study of bone; metabolic radionuclide studies; nuclear medicine imaging systems, instrumentation and computer-assisted imaging. *Mailing Add:* Dept Radiol Univ Rochester Sch Med & Dent Rochester NY 14642

WEBER, DAVID FREDERICK, b North Terre Haute, Ind, Nov 18, 39; m 63; c 1. CYTOGENETICS. *Educ:* Purdue Univ, BS, 61; Ind Univ, MS, 63, PhD(genetics), 67. *Prof Exp:* Asst prof, 67-72, assoc prof, 72-78, PROF GENETICS, ILL STATE UNIV, 78- *Concurrent Pos:* Dept of Energy contract, 70-79. *Mem:* AAAS; Sigma Xi; Genetics Soc Am. *Res:* Analysis of meiosis in monosomics; cytological behavior of univalents; effects of a monosomic chromosome on recombination; study of the frequency and types of spontaneous chromosome abberations arising in monosomics; determination of effects of monosomy on lipid content in Zea mays; screening for ultrastructureal differences in monosomics; determination of free amino acid profiles in monosomics. *Mailing Add:* Dept of Biol Sci Ill State Univ Normal IL 61761

WEBER, DAVID JAMES, b Cincinnati, Ohio, Mar 29, 47; m 80. MICROWAVE ENGINEERING, AMPLIFIER DESIGN. *Educ:* Hiram Col, BA, 69; Univ Minn, MS, 73, PhD(nuclear physics), 76. *Prof Exp:* Res assoc, Cyclotron Facil, Mich State Univ, 76-79; MEM TECH STAFF, ELECTRONICS RES LAB, AEROSPACE CORP, 79- *Res:* Experimental nuclear spectroscopy; gallium arsenide field effect transistor microwave amplifier and fabrication; computer device modeling; measurement of device electrical characteristics. *Mailing Add:* MS M1-110 Aerospace Corp PO Box 92957 Los Angeles CA 90009

WEBER, DEANE FAY, b Aberdeen, SDak, May 17, 25; m 50; c 3. SOIL MICROBIOLOGY. *Educ:* Jamestown Col, BS, 50; Kans State Univ, MS, 52, PhD, 59. *Prof Exp:* Biochemist & bacteriologist, Quain & Ramstad Clin, Bismarck, NDak, 52-55; asst vet bact, pathogenic bact & virol, Kans State Univ, 57-58; soil scientist, Soil & Water Conserv Br, Agr Res Serv, USDA, 58-64 & IRI Res Inst, Campinas, Brazil, 64-66, microbiologist soybean invests, Crops Res Div, 67-72, MICROBIOLOGIST, CELL CULTURE & NITROGEN FIXATION LAB, AGR RES SERV, USDA, 72- *Mem:* Fel AAAS; Soil Sci Soc Am; Am Soc Microbiol; Am Soc Agron. *Res:* Legume microbiology; nitrogen fixation. *Mailing Add:* Cell Cult & Nitrogn Fixation Lab Agr Res Ctr-W USDA Beltsville MD 20705

WEBER, DENNIS JOSEPH, b Kalamazoo, Mich, Mar 30, 34; m 53; c 6. DRUG METABOLISM, PHARMACOKINETICS. *Educ:* Western Mich Univ, BS, 58, MA, 62; Univ Fla, PhD(pharm), 67. *Prof Exp:* Res asst phys & anal chem, Upjohn Co, 58-62; mgr anal chem, Syntex Labs, Calif, 67-70; res scientist phys & anal chem, 70-79, RES SCIENTIST DRUG METAB RES, UPJOHN CO, 79- *Mem:* Am Pharmaceut Asn; Acad Pharmaceut Sci; The Chem Soc; Am Chem Soc. *Res:* Kinetics of hydrolysis of drugs; correlation of spectra and structure of hydrazones; structure and stability constants of metal complexes of thiouracils; partition chromatography of steroids; high pressure liquid chromatography; pharmacokinetics. *Mailing Add:* Upjohn Co Kalamazoo MI 49001

WEBER, EDWARD JOSEPH, b Troy, NY, July 17, 48. AURORAL PHYSICS, SPACE PHYSICS. *Educ:* Union Col, BS, 70; Boston Col, PhD(physics), 75. *Prof Exp:* Res asst physics, Boston Col, 70-74; RES PHYSICIST IONOSPHERIC PHYSICS, AIR FORCE GEOPHYS LAB, US AIR FORCE, 74- *Honors & Awards:* Air Force Sci Achievement Award, US Air Force, 78. *Mem:* Am Geophys Union; Sigma Xi. *Res:* Auroral dynamics; ionospheric structure and dynamics; optical detection of aurora and airglow; magnetospheric dynamics inferred from the aurora. *Mailing Add:* Air Force Geophys Lab Ionospheric Dynamics Br Hanscom AFB MA 01731

WEBER, ERNST, b Vienna, Austria, Sept 6, 01; nat US; m 36; c 2. ELECTRICAL ENGINEERING. *Educ:* Vienna Tech Univ, dipl, 24, DSc(elec mach), 27; Univ Vienna, PhD(physics), 26. *Hon Degrees:* DSc, Pratt Inst, 58, Univ Long Island, 63; DEng, Newark Col, 59, Univ Mich, 64 & Polytech Inst Brooklyn, 69. *Prof Exp:* Res engr, Oesterreichische Siemens-Schuckert-Werke, Austria, 24-29 & Siemens-Schuckert-Werke, Ger, 29-30; vis prof, 30-31, res prof elec eng, 31-41, off investr, Off Sci Res & Develop contract, 42-45, prof elec eng & head dept & dir, Microwave Res Inst, 45-57, pres, Inst, 57-69, EMER PRES, POLYTECH INST BROOKLYN, 69- *Concurrent Pos:* Secy, Polytech Res & Develop Co, Inc, 44-52, pres, 52-60; chmn div eng, Nat Res Coun, 70-74; mem, Comn Sociotech Systs, Nat Res Coun, 74-78, consult, 78- *Mem:* Nat Acad Sci; Nat Acad Eng; AAAS; fel Am Phys Soc; fel Inst Elec & Electronics Engrs (pres, 59 & 63). *Res:* Electromagnetic theory; circuit analysis; conformal mapping; microwave measurements. *Mailing Add:* PO Box 1619 Tryon NC 28782

WEBER, ERWIN WILBUR, b Chicago, Ill, Oct 8, 31. ELECTRICAL ENGINEERING. *Educ:* Ill Inst Technol, BS, 58, MS, 59, PhD(network theory), 64. *Prof Exp:* Res engr, 60-61, from instr to asst prof, 61-70, ASSOC PROF ELEC ENG, ILL INST TECHNOL, 70-, RES ENGR, RES INST, 66- *Concurrent Pos:* Assoc engr, Armour Res Found, 62-63. *Mem:* AAAS; Inst Elec & Electronics Engrs. *Res:* Network theory; electrical network synthesis; computer aided circuit design. *Mailing Add:* Dept of Elec Eng Ill Inst of Technol Chicago IL 60616

WEBER, EVELYN JOYCE, b Tower Hill, Ill, Nov 9, 28. LIPID CHEMISTRY. *Educ:* Univ Ill, BS, 53; Iowa State Univ, PhD(biochem), 61. *Prof Exp:* Asst biochem, Iowa State Univ, 56-61; res assoc, Univ Ill, 61-65; asst prof, 65-72, ASSOC PROF PLANT BIOCHEM, UNIV ILL, URBANA, 72-, RES CHEMIST, USDA, 65- *Mem:* AAAS; Am Chem Soc; fel Am Inst Chem; Am Oil Chem Soc; Am Soc Plant Physiol. *Res:* Identification and characterization of complex lipids; biosynthesis of fatty acids and lipids in corn and other plants; identification and biosynthesis of vitamin E and other natural antioxidants. *Mailing Add:* USDA Agr Res S-320 Turner Hall Univ Ill 1102 S Goodwin St Urbana IL 61801

WEBER, FAUSTIN N, b Toledo, Ohio, Nov 5, 11; m 37; c 4. ORTHODONTICS. *Educ:* Univ Mich, DDS, 34, MS, 36; Am Bd Orthod, dipl. *Prof Exp:* From asst prof to assoc prof, 36-51, chmn dept, 51-78, prof, 78-82, EMER PROF ORTHOD, UNIV TENN CTR HEALTH SCI, MEMPHIS, 81- *Concurrent Pos:* Prof dent hyg, Univ Tenn Ctr Health Sci, Memphis, 72, mem craniofacial anomalies group, Child Develop Ctr; consult, Kennedy Gen Vet Hosp; mem, Am Asn Dent Schs. *Honors & Awards:* Albert H Ketham Award, 80. *Mem:* Am Assoc Orthod; Am Cleft Palate Asn; AAAS; fel Am Col Dent; fel Int Col Dent. *Res:* Child growth and development. *Mailing Add:* Dept Orthod Univ Tenn Ctr Health Sci Memphis TN 38163

WEBER, FLORENCE ROBINSON, b Milwaukee, Wis, Aug 26, 21; m 59. GEOLOGY. *Educ:* Univ Chicago, BS, 43, MS, 48. *Prof Exp:* Lab instr & librn, Univ Chicago, 42-43, librn, 47; subsurface geologist, Shell Oil Co, Tex, 43-47 & State Geol Surv, Mo, 47; geologist, Alaska Br, 49-54, DC, 54-59 & Alaska Br, 54-59, GEOLOGIST-IN-CHARGE, COL OFF, ALASKA BR, US GEOL SURV, 59-; DISTINGUISHED LECTR GEOL, UNIV ALASKA, FAIRBANKS, 59- *Concurrent Pos:* Arctic Inst NAm grant, 56. *Mem:* AAAS; Geol Soc Am; Am Asn Petrol Geol; Arctic Inst NAm. *Res:* Stratigraphy; structure; geomorphology; glaciology; petrology; paleontology; petroleum geology. *Mailing Add:* Alaskan Geol Br US Geol Surv Box 80586 Fairbanks AK 99708

WEBER, FRANK E, b Chicago, Ill, Feb 1, 35; m 57; c 3. FOOD SCIENCE. *Educ:* Ill Inst Technol, BS, 57; Univ Ill, MS, 63, PhD(food sci), 64. *Prof Exp:* Res scientist-leader, Chem Sect, R T French Co, 64-71, mgr prod develop, 71-73, mgr tech res, 73-76, tech dir, 76-80; DIR RES & DEVELOP, RECKITT & COLMAN NORTH AM INC, 80- *Mem:* Am Chem Soc; Inst Food Technologists; Am Asn Cereal Chemists; Sigma Xi. *Res:* Product development; quality control; natural and artificial flavorings; isolation and analysis of flavor substances; food analysis methodology product development; industrial waste treatment. *Mailing Add:* Reckitt & Colman NAm Inc One Mustard St Rochester NY 14609

WEBER, FREDERICK, JR, b Hilgen, Ger, Feb 14, 23; nat US; m 46; c 3. MICROBIOLOGY, PUBLIC HEALTH. *Educ:* Univ RI, BS, 48; Pa State Univ, MS, 50; Mich State Univ, PhD, 56. *Prof Exp:* Instr, Wartburg Col, 50-51 & Wayne State Univ, 51-53; mem res staff, Swift & Co, 56-59; MEM RES STAFF, JOSEPH E SEAGRAM & SONS, INC, 59- *Mem:* Am Soc Microbiol. *Res:* Psychiophiles in dairy products; flavor development by microorganisms in foods; aerobic digestion of wastes; alcoholic fermentations. *Mailing Add:* 9927 Silverwood Lane Louisville KY 40272

WEBER, GEORGE, b Budapest, Hungary, Mar 29, 22; nat US; m 58; c 3. ONCOLOGY, PHARMACOLOGY. *Educ:* Queen's Univ, Ont, BA, 50, MD, 52. *Hon Degrees:* Dr Med & Surg, Univ Chieti, Italy. *Prof Exp:* Nat Cancer Inst Can fel, Univ BC, 52-53; Cancer Res Soc sr fel, Montreal Cancer Inst, 53-58, head dept path chem, 56-59; assoc prof biochem & microbiol, 59-60, assoc prof pharmacol, 60-61, PROF PHARMACOL, SCH MED, IND UNIV, INDIANAPOLIS, 61-, CANCER COORDR BASIC RES, 62-, DIR LAB EXP ONCOL, 74- *Concurrent Pos:* Ed, Adv in Enzyme Regulation, 62-; Oxford Biochem Soc lectr, 69; assoc ed, Cancer Res, 70-; rapporteur, Int Cancer Cong, Tex, 70; mem sci adv comt, Pharmacol B Study Sect, USPHS, 70-74, chmn exp therapeut study sect, Nat Cancer Inst, 76-78; mem, Tiberine Acad, 71-; mem sci adv, Damon Runyon Mem Fund, 71-75; mem adv comt instnl grants, Am Cancer Soc, 72-76; Aaron Brown lectureship, Case Western Reserve Univ, 77; mem, US Nat Organizing Comt & Prog Comt, 13th Int Cancer Cong, 79-82. *Honors & Awards:* Alecce Award, Cancer Res, Rome, Italy, 71; G H A Clowes Award, Am Asn Cancer Res, 82. *Mem:* Am Soc Pharmacol & Exp Therapeut; hon mem, All-Union Biochem Soc, USSR Nat Acad Sci; Am Asn Cancer Res; hon mem Hungarian Cancer Soc; fel Royal Soc Med. *Res:* Oncology; biochemical pharmacology; regulation of enzymes and metabolism; neoplasia; chemotherapy; liver, kidney and colon tumors of different growth rates; hormone action; nutrition. *Mailing Add:* Lab for Exp Oncol Ind Univ Sch of Med Indianapolis IN 46223

WEBER, GEORGE RUSSELL, b Novinger, Mo, Dec 29, 11; m 47; c 2. BACTERIOLOGY. *Educ:* Univ Mo, BS, 35; Iowa State Col, PhD(sanit & food bact), 40. *Prof Exp:* Asst chemist, Exp Sta, Univ Mo, 35-36; instr, Iowa State Col, 40-42; bacteriologist, USPHS, 46, sr asst scientist, 47-49, scientist, 49-53, chief sanitizing agents unit, 51-53; proj leader, US Indust Chem Co, Nat Distillers & Chem Corp, 53-73, sr res microbiologist, Res Div, 73-75, res assoc, 75-76; RETIRED. *Concurrent Pos:* Asst, Iowa State Col, 36-40; lectr, Eve Col, Univ Cincinnati, 69-70. *Mem:* AAAS; Am Soc Microbiol; fel Am Pub Health Asn; NY Acad Sci; fel Royal Soc Health. *Res:* Sanitary and food bacteriology; germicidal efficiency of hypochlorites, chloramines and quaternary ammonium compounds; antibiotics; fermentations; yeast hybridization; ruminant and chinchilla nutrition; biological metal corrosion. *Mailing Add:* 1525 Burney Lane Cincinnati OH 45230

WEBER, GREGORIO, b Buenos Aires, Arg, July 4, 16; m 47; c 3. BIOCHEMISTRY, BIOPHYSICS. *Educ:* Univ Buenos Aires, MD, 43; Cambridge Univ, PhD(biochem), 47. *Prof Exp:* Beit mem fel biochem, Cambridge Univ, 48-52; lectr, Univ Sheffield, 53-60, reader biophys, 60-62; PROF BIOCHEM, UNIV ILL, URBANA, 62- *Honors & Awards:* Rumford Prize, 80. *Mem:* Nat Acad Sci; Am Soc Biol Chem; Am Chem Soc; Am Acad Arts & Sci. *Res:* Physical chemistry of proteins; fluorescence methods; excited states. *Mailing Add:* 397 Roger Adams Lab Dept Biochem Univ Ill Urbana IL 61801

WEBER, HANS JURGEN, b Berlin, Ger, May 3, 39; m 66; c 1. THEORETICAL NUCLEAR PHYSICS. *Educ:* Univ Frankfurt, BS, 60, MS, 61, PhD(theoret physics), 65. *Prof Exp:* Res assoc theoret nuclear physics, Duke Univ, 66-67; asst prof, 68-71, assoc prof, 71-76, PROF THEORET NUCLEAR PHYSICS, UNIV VA, 77- *Concurrent Pos:* Sesquicentennial assoc, Max Planck Inst, Mainz & Univ Frankfurt, 72-73. *Mem:* Am Phys Soc. *Res:* Medium energy physics; photonuclear physics; group theory. *Mailing Add:* Dept of Physics Univ of Va Charlottesville VA 22901

WEBER, HARRY A(NTHONY), b Indianapolis, Ind, July 13, 21; m 49; c 3. INDUSTRIAL MANAGEMENT, ELECTRICAL ENGINEERING. *Educ:* Purdue Univ, BSEE, 42. *Prof Exp:* Dept mgr, Delco-Remy Div, Gen Motors Corp, 43-44; proj engr, US Naval Ord Plant, 46-50; chief, Prog Sect, US Atomic Energy Comn, 50-54, chief, Opers Br, 54, dir, Develop & Prod Div, 54-56, dir, Non-Nuclear Div, 56-57, dir, Plant Opers, 57-60, DIR WEAPONS PROD, US DEPT ENERGY, 60- *Concurrent Pos:* Gen partner, Big Bend Co, Colo. *Mem:* Nat Soc Prof Engrs; Am & Int mem Inst Elec & Electron Engrs. *Res:* Technical administration. *Mailing Add:* 7133 Kiowa Ave NE Albuquerque NM 87110

WEBER, HARRY P(ITT), b Pittsburgh, Pa, June 20, 31; m 52; c 3. ELECTRICAL ENGINEERING, PHYSICS. *Educ:* Univ Pittsburgh, BSEE, 58, MSEE, 61, DSc(elec eng), 64. *Prof Exp:* Res asst, Mellon Inst Indust Res, 56-59; asst prof elec eng, Univ Pittsburgh, 59-64; sr syst analyst, Radio Corp Am Missile Test Proj, Patrick AFB, 64-65; head dept elec eng, 66-71, dean eng & sci, 71-79, DEAN, GRAD SCH, FLA INST TECHNOL, 68-, ASSOC VPRES ACAD AFFAIRS, 80- *Concurrent Pos:* Staff engr, Radio Corp Am Missile Test Proj, Patrick AFB, 65-71. *Mem:* Sigma Xi; Inst Elec & Electronics Engrs. *Res:* Mathematical and experimental analysis of solid state circuit devices; calibration of radio frequency tracking instrumentation using orbital bodies. *Mailing Add:* 310 Greenway Ave Satellite Beach FL 32935

WEBER, HEATHER ROSS, b Passaic, NJ, Mar 7, 43; m 63; c 3. BIOCHEMISTRY. *Educ:* Boston Univ, BA, 65; Univ Southern Calif, PhD(cellular & molecular biol), 74. *Prof Exp:* Res asst hemat, Peter Bent Brigham Hosp, 65-67; res asst biophys, Harvard Med Sch, 67-68; res assoc biochem, 73-74, NIH cancer training grant, 74-76, NIH fel biochem, 76-79, RES SCIENTIST, MED SCH, UNIV SOUTHERN CALIF, 79- *Mem:* AAAS; Am Chem Soc. *Res:* Transcriptional regulation of eucaryotic gene expression; cyclia nucleotide phosphodiesterases and ageing; nucleic acid metabolism of neoplastic cells; effects of 5-bromodeoxyuridine on rat hepatona tissue culture cells. *Mailing Add:* Dept of Molecular Biol University Park Los Angeles CA 90007

WEBER, HELMUT E(RNST), fluid dynamics, thermodynamics, see previous edition

WEBER, J ARTHUR, b Pana, Ill, Jan 19, 21; m 54; c 2. AGRICULTURAL ENGINEERING. *Educ:* Univ Ill, BS, 42, MS, 48. *Prof Exp:* Designer, Int Harvester Co, 42-43; asst, 46-55, from asst prof to assoc prof, 55-64, PROF AGR ENG, UNIV ILL, URBANA, 64- *Mem:* Soc Automotive Engrs; Am Soc Agr Engrs; Am Soc Eng Educ. *Res:* Farm tractor maintenance and performance; hydraulics; soil dynamics; relation of soil properties to design of tillage tools and earthmoving and traction devices. *Mailing Add:* Dept of Agr Eng Univ of Ill Urbana IL 61801

WEBER, JAMES H(AROLD), b Pittsburgh, Pa, Nov 21, 19; m 43; c 3. CHEMICAL ENGINEERING. *Educ:* Univ Pittsburgh, BS, 41, MS, 47, PhD(chem eng), 48. *Prof Exp:* Asst, Univ Pittsburgh, 46-48; from instr to prof chem eng, 48-64, chmn dept, 58-71, REGENTS PROF CHEM ENG, UNIV NEBR, LINCOLN, 64- *Concurrent Pos:* Consult, Phillips Petrol Co, 52-79, Natural Gas Processors Asn, 59 & 64 & C F Braun & Co, 65. *Mem:* Am Chem Soc; Am Inst Chem Engrs; Soc Hist Technol. *Res:* Non-adiabatic absorption of ammonia in a wetted wall tower; applied thermodynamics; distillation; absorption; kinetics. *Mailing Add:* Dept Chem Eng Univ Nebr Lincoln NE 68508

WEBER, JAMES HAROLD, b Madison, Wis, July 21, 36; m 61; c 3. INORGANIC CHEMISTRY. *Educ:* Marquette Univ, BS, 59; Ohio State Univ, PhD(chem), 63. *Prof Exp:* Asst prof, 63-70, assoc prof, 70-77, PROF CHEM, UNIV NH, 77- *Mem:* Am Chem Soc. *Res:* Coordination chemistry; organometallic chemistry; chemistry of natural water. *Mailing Add:* Parsons Hall Univ NH Durham NH 03824

WEBER, JANET CROSBY, b Chicago, Ill, June 1, 23; m 49; c 3. COMPUTER SCIENCE, SOFTWARE SYSTEMS. *Educ:* Iowa State Univ, BS, 45; Univ Ill, Urbana, PhD(chem), 48. *Prof Exp:* Asst prof vet res, Mont State Univ, 48-50; res assoc, 60-63, instr, 63-69, ASST PROF OPHTHAL, MED CTR, IND UNIV, INDIANAPOLIS, 69- *Mem:* Am Chem Soc; Asn Res Vision & Ophthal. *Res:* Computer methods in clinical and research studies; development of computer programs for statistical analysis; microcomputers for research; application of statistics and computers to ophthalmic research. *Mailing Add:* Dept of Ophthal Ind Univ Med Ctr Indianapolis IN 46202

WEBER, JEAN ROBERT, b Thun, Switz, Apr 28, 25; Can citizen; m 54; c 3. GEOPHYSICS. *Educ:* Swiss Fed Inst Technol, Prof Eng, 52; Univ Alta, PhD(physics), 60. *Prof Exp:* Res engr, PTT Res Labs, Berne, Switz, 51-53; lectr, Univ Alta, 57-58; geophysicist-in-chg, Oper Hazen, Int Geophys Year, 58-59; RES SCIENTIST, DOM OBSERV, DEPT ENERGY, MINES & RESOURCES, CAN, 60- *Concurrent Pos:* Mem Arctic Inst NAm Baffin Island Exped, 53 & Univ Toronto, Salmon Glacier Exped, 56; leader, Dom Observ NPole Exped, 67. *Mem:* Am Geophys Union; Soc Explor Geophys; fel Arctic Inst NAm; Glaciol Soc. *Res:* Communications electronics; dosimetry of beta radiation and biological effects on allium cepa roots; regional gravity interpretations; continental margins; upper mantle, Arctic Ocean; application of geophysics to glaciology. *Mailing Add:* Dom Observ 3 Observ Crescent Ottawa ON K1A 0Y3 Can

WEBER, JEROME BERNARD, b Claremont, Minn, Sept 19, 33; m 56; c 4. SOIL CHEMISTRY, WEED SCIENCE. *Educ:* Univ Minn, BS, 57, MS, 59, PhD(soil chem), 63. *Prof Exp:* Assoc prof soil pesticide chem, 62-71, PROF SOIL PESTICIDE CHEM & WEED SCI, NC STATE UNIV, 71- *Concurrent Pos:* NSF lectr, Clemson Univ, 79; consult, WHO, Venezuela, 80. *Honors & Awards:* Sigma Xi Res Award; Res Award, Weed Sci Soc Am. *Mem:* AAAS; Am Soc Agron; Weed Sci Soc Am; Am Chem Soc; Clay Minerals Soc. *Res:* Chemistry of soil, fate and biological availability of applied organic compounds, especially herbicides; effects of pesticides on environmental quality; weed ecology studies; behavior of gases in soil. *Mailing Add:* Dept of Crop Sci Weed Sci Ctr NC State Univ Raleigh NC 27607

WEBER, JOHN DONALD, b Lagon, La, Nov 1, 34; m 62; c 2. PHARMACEUTICAL CHEMISTRY. *Educ:* Xavier Univ La, BS, 57; Univ Notre Dame, MS, 61; Georgetown Univ, PhD(org chem), 72. *Prof Exp:* Instr chem, Southern Univ New Orleans, 62-63; anal chemist, Food & Drug Admin, 63-68, res chem, 68-78; mem staff organic synthesis, USDA, 78-79; RES CHEMIST, FOOD & DRUG ADMIN, 79- *Mem:* Am Chem Soc; Sigma Xi; Asn Off Anal Chemists; NY Acad Sci. *Res:* Pharmaceutical analyses; chromatograph, nuclear magnetic resonance fluorimetric techniques; optical purity of drugs; stereochemistry and chemical kinetics; problems of relationships between stereoisomerism and physiological activity. *Mailing Add:* 7204 Seventh St NW Washington DC 20012

WEBER, JOHN R, b Ft Madison, Iowa, Mar 18, 24; m 48; c 2. PLANT PHYSIOLOGY. *Educ:* Univ Iowa, AB, 48, MS, 49. *Prof Exp:* Prin lab technician, Citrus Exp Sta, Univ Calif, 52-56; plant physiologist, 56-67, mem spec projs egg handling systs, 67-76, INT MGR, CITRUS MACH DIV, FMC CORP, 76- *Res:* Post-harvest physiology of fruits and vegetables. *Mailing Add:* 2102 Oak Crest Dr Riverside CA 92506

WEBER, JOSEPH, b Paterson, NJ, May 17, 19; m 42, 72; c 4. PHYSICS. *Educ:* US Naval Acad, BS, 40; Cath Univ Am, PhD(physics), 51. *Prof Exp:* PROF PHYSICS, UNIV MD, COLLEGE PARK, 48- *Concurrent Pos:* Vis prof, Univ Calif, Irvine; Nat Res Coun & Guggenheim fels, 55-56; fel, Inst Advan Study, 55-56, 62-63 & 69-70 & Lorentz Inst Theoret Physics, State Univ Leiden, 56. *Honors & Awards:* Gravity Res Found First Prize, 59; Sigma Xi Award, 70; Boris Pregel Prize, NY Acad Sci, 73. *Mem:* Fel Am Phys Soc; fel Inst Elec & Electronics Engrs. *Res:* General relativity; microwave spectroscopy; irreversibility; scattering. *Mailing Add:* Dept of Physics & Astron Univ of Md College Park MD 20742

WEBER, JOSEPH, b Budapest, Hungary, Oct 10, 39; Can citizen; m 64, 73; c 2. VIROLOGY. *Educ:* Univ BC, BSc, 64, MSc, 66; McMaster Univ, PhD(virol), 69. *Prof Exp:* Nat Cancer Inst res assoc virol, Ohio State Univ, 69-70; asst prof microbiol, 70-75, assoc prof, 75-80, PROF MICROBIOL, UNIV SHERBROOKE, 80- *Concurrent Pos:* Lectr, Ohio State Univ, 69-70; Med Res Coun Can scholar, 71-76; Nat Cancer Inst Can scholar, 76-80, res assoc, 80- *Mem:* Can Soc Microbiol; Am Soc Microbiol; Can Soc Microbiol. *Res:* Viral oncology; chromatin structure; adenovirus genetics. *Mailing Add:* Dept Microbiol Univ Ctr Hosp Sherbrooke PQ J1H 1R0 Can

WEBER, JOSEPH T, b Brooklyn, NY, Jan 1, 38; m 77; c 1. NEUROANATOMY, NEURODEVELOPMENT. *Educ:* Univ Calif, Berkeley, AB, 73; Univ Wis, PhD(anat), 78. *Prof Exp:* Fel neuroanat, Med Sch, Univ Wis, 78-80; ASST PROF NEUROANAT, MED SCH, TULANE UNIV, 80- *Concurrent Pos:* Ad hoc reviewer, NSF, 81-; prin investr, NIH, 81- *Mem:* Soc Neurosci; Am Asn Anatomists; AAAS; Sigma Xi. *Res:* Anatomical studies of extrageniculate visual pathways; mechanisms involved in the control of head and eye movements; development of visual centers. *Mailing Add:* Tulane Med Sch 1430 Tulane Ave New Orleans LA 70112

WEBER, JULIUS, b Brooklyn, NY, Apr 8, 14; m 47; c 4. CYTOLOGY, PHOTOGRAPHY. *Hon Degrees:* DSc, Jersey City State Col, 74. *Prof Exp:* Asst, Brooklyn Jewish Hosp, New York, 33-35; chief histol technician, Kingston Ave Hosp Infectious Dis, 35-36 & Israel Zion Hosp, Brooklyn, 36-39; head dept med photog, Columbia-Presby Med Ctr, New York, 39-49; HEAD DEPT PHOTOG RES, BETH ISRAEL HOSP, 49- *Concurrent Pos:* Mem training div, Inst Inter-Am Affairs, US Dept State, 46; consult, Western Union Tel Co, 46-48, Chem Corps, US Army, 47-50, Ansco Div, Gen Aniline & Film Corp, 47-48, Nat Film Bd Can, 51, US Naval Hosp, St Albans, NY, 51-52, St Francis Hosp, New York, 59, Perkin-Elmer Corp, 60 & Ehrenreich

Photo-Optical Industs, Inc, 63; lectr, Sch Med, Univ Calif, Los Angeles, 48; guest lectr, Col Physicians & Surgeons, Columbia Univ, 50, Sch Eng, 60; dir med photog, William Douglas McAdams, Inc, 52-59; head dept med photog, Hosp Joint Dis, 53-73; res assoc, Waldemar Med Res Found, 55-; lectr, Grad Sch Pub Admin, NY Univ, 55-57; head dept med photog, Misericordia Hosp, 56-; med photographer, Knickerbocker Hosp, 58-63; assoc, Dept Mineral, Am Mus Natural Hist, 60; ed, Image Dynamics Sci & Med, 69-71; dir, Wildcliff Natural Sci Ctr, 69-74; res assoc, Dept Mineral, Royal Ont Mus, Toronto, 71-; res assoc, Dept Med, Einstein Sch Med, 76- *Mem:* Soc Photog Sci & Eng; assoc Photog Soc Am; fel Biol Photog Asn; fel Royal Micros Soc; fel Royal Photog Soc Gt Brit. *Res:* Photographic instrumentation for endoscopy, micromineralogy; time lapse photomicrography and cinematography; ultraviolet, infrared and interference photomicrography and photomacrography; neurocytology and neuropathology photoimpregnation techniques. *Mailing Add:* 1040 Cove Rd Mamaroneck NY 10543

WEBER, KENNETH C, b Cold Spring, Minn, June 30, 37; m 57; c 4. PULMONARY PHYSIOLOGY. *Educ:* Univ Minn, BSEE, 63, PhD(physiol), 68. *Prof Exp:* USPHS trainee physiol, Univ Minn, 62-68; asst prof, 68-72, assoc prof, 72-76, PROF PHYSIOL, WVA UNIV, 76- *Concurrent Pos:* Chief physiol sect, Appalachian Lab Occup Respiratory Dis, Nat Inst Occup Safety & Health, 68-; chmn, Gordon Res Conf Non-Ventilatory Lung Function, 75; vpres, Am Heart Asn, 81-82. *Mem:* AAAS; Am Physiol Soc; Am Thoracic Soc; Sigma Xi. *Res:* Cardiopulmonary hemodynamics; respiration physiology; non-ventilatory lung function; lung metabolism. *Mailing Add:* Dept Physiol & Biophys WVa Univ Med Ctr Morgantown WV 26506

WEBER, LAVERN J, b Isabel, SDak, June 7, 33; m 59; c 4. PHARMACOLOGY, ACADEMIC ADMINISTRATION. *Educ:* Pac Lutheran Univ, BA, 58; Univ Wash, MS, 62, PhD(pharmacol), 64. *Prof Exp:* From instr to asst prof pharmacol, Sch Med, Univ Wash, 64-69; assoc prof pharmacol & toxicol, 69-75, asst dean, Grad Sch, 74-77, PROF PHARMACOL & TOXICOL, SCH PHARM, ORE STATE UNIV, 75-, DIR, MARINE SCI CTR, 77-, DIR, MARINE & FRESHWATER BIOMED CTR, 78- *Mem:* Am Soc Pharmacol & Exp Therapeut; Soc Toxicol; Soc Exp Biol & Med; Sigma Xi; Am Asn Lab Animal Sci. *Res:* Marine sciences; biochemistry of autonomic nervous system; comparative pharmacology, physiology and toxicology; comparative pharmacology of the autonomic nervous system; liver toxicology; comparative neuromuscular pharmacology. *Mailing Add:* Ore State Univ Marine Sci Ctr Newport OR 97365

WEBER, LEON, b Detroit, Mich, Feb 4, 31; m 52; c 3. SURFACE CHEMISTRY, PHYSICAL CHEMISTRY. *Educ:* Wayne State Univ, BS, 52, MS, 54; Carnegie-Mellon Univ, MS & PhD(phys chem), 67. *Prof Exp:* Chemist, Wayne County Rd, Comn, 51-54; res chemist, Shell Develop Co, 54-56; scientist nuclear chem, Westinghouse Atomic Power Co, 56-57; sr res chemist, Gulf Res & Develop Co, 57-67; SCIENTIST SURFACE CHEM, CHEM DIV, SCM CORP, 67- *Mem:* AAAS; Am Chem Soc; Fedn Socs Paint Technol. *Res:* Colloid and surface chemistry of pigments; gas-solid sorption phenomena; reaction kinetics by thermal analysis. *Mailing Add:* Chem Div SCM Corp 3901 Glidden Rd Baltimore MD 21226

WEBER, LESTER GEORGE, b St Louis, Mo, July 23, 24; m 49; c 5. CHEMICAL ENGINEERING. *Educ:* Purdue Univ, BS, 49; Wash Univ, MS, 54. *Prof Exp:* Analyst, Uranium Div, Mallinckrodt Chem Works, Mo, 49-50, engr pilot plant, 50-51, supvr metal pilot plant, 51-54, asst mgr plant design liaison group, Uranium Div, 54-57, tech supt mfg dept, 57-58, supvr prod tech dept, 58-60, asst mgr, 60-62, asst mgr develop dept, 62-63; res engr, Yerkes Res & Develop Lab, NY, 63-65, res engr, Circleville Res & Develop Lab, Ohio, 65-66, staff engr, 66, res supvr, 66-69, tech supt cellophane, Clinton Film Plant, 69-73, customer serv mgr, Plastic Prod & Resins Dept, Packaging Films Div, BIVAC Meat Packaging Systs, 73-76, STAFF ENGR, POLYMER PROD DEPT, MFG DIV, WASHINGTON WORKS, E I DU PONT DE NEMOURS & CO, INC, 76- *Mem:* Am Inst Chem Engrs; Am Soc Plastics Engrs. *Mailing Add:* 26 North Hills Dr Parkersburg WV 26101

WEBER, LOUIS RUSSELL, b St Joseph, Mo, Oct 15, 01; m 26; c 2. EXPERIMENTAL PHYSICS. *Educ:* Park Col, AB, 25; Univ Mich, AM, 26, PhD(physics), 31. *Prof Exp:* Prof physics & head dept, Friends Univ, 26-38; prof & head dept, 38-65, EMER PROF PHYSICS, COLO STATE UNIV, 65- *Concurrent Pos:* Fulbright lectr physics, Col Sci, Baghdad, Iraq, 52-53, De LaSalle Col, Manila, 65 & Univ of the East, 65-66; adv & prof physics & basic sci, Univ Peshawar, Pakistan, Int Coop Admin, 58-60; consult, Palomar Col, San Marcos, Calif, 68-69; Fulbright vis prof, Univ Antioquia, Colombia, 69-71. *Honors & Awards:* Distinguished Serv Citation, Am Asn Physics Teachers, 65. *Mem:* Am Phys Soc; fel Optical Soc Am; Acoust Soc Am; Am Asn Physics Teachers; Sigma Xi. *Res:* Infrared absorption of water vapor beyond 10 microns; rotational infrared absorption water; piezoelectric-direct study of quartz crystals; spectrographic study of trace metals in plants and soils; atmospheric ozone. *Mailing Add:* PO Box 448 Ft Collins CO 80522

WEBER, MARTIN E, chemical engineering, see previous edition

WEBER, MARVIN JOHN, b Fresno, Calif, Feb 26, 32; m 57; c 2. LASERS, SPECTROSCOPY. *Educ:* Univ Calif, Berkeley, AB, 54, MA, 56, PhD(physics), 59. *Prof Exp:* Asst physics, Univ Calif, 54-59; prin res scientist, Res Div, Raytheon Co, 59-73; GROUP LEADER, LAWRENCE LIVERMORE NAT LAB, 73- *Concurrent Pos:* Vis res assoc, Stanford Univ, 66; consult, Div Mat Res, NSF, 73-76. *Mem:* Fel Am Phys Soc; Optical Soc Am; Am Ceramics Soc. *Res:* Magnetic resonance; optical spectroscopy of solids; luminescence materials; quantum electronics; lasers; solid state physics. *Mailing Add:* Lawrence Livermore Nat Lab Univ of Calif PO Box 808 Livermore CA 94550

WEBER, MICHAEL JOSEPH, b New York, NY, Aug 23, 42; m 67. VIROLOGY, CELL BIOLOGY. *Educ:* Haverford Col, BSc, 63; Univ Calif, San Diego, PhD(biol), 68. *Prof Exp:* Am Cancer Soc Dernham jr fel, Univ Calif, Berkeley, 68-70; asst prof, 70-75, ASSOC PROF MICROBIOL, UNIV ILL, URBANA, 75- *Concurrent Pos:* NIH res career develop award, 75. *Mem:* Am Soc Microbiol; Tissue Cult Asn; Soc Gen Physiologists; Am Soc Biol Chemists. *Res:* Control of growth of animal cells and malignant transformation; tumor virus-induced cell surface changes. *Mailing Add:* Dept Microbiol Univ Ill 407 S Goodwin Urbana IL 61801

WEBER, MORTON M, b New York, NY, May 26, 22; m 55; c 2. MICROBIOLOGY, BIOCHEMISTRY. *Educ:* City Col New York, BS, 49; Johns Hopkins Univ, ScD(microbiol), 53. *Prof Exp:* Instr zool & parasitol, St Francis Col, 49; instr med microbiol, Johns Hopkins Univ, 51-55; instr bact & immunol, Harvard Med Sch, 56-59; from asst prof to assoc prof, 56-63, PROF MICROBIOL, SCH MED, ST LOUIS UNIV, 63-, CHMN DEPT, 64- *Concurrent Pos:* Am Cancer Soc fel, McCollum-Pratt Inst, Johns Hopkins Univ, 53-56; mem microbial chem study sect, NIH, 69-73; vis prof, Oxford Univ, 70-71. *Mem:* Fel AAAS; Am Soc Biol Chemists; Am Soc Microbiol; Am Acad Microbiol; NY Acad Sci. *Res:* Physiology and biochemistry of microorganisms; pathways and mechanisms of electron transport; mode of action of antibiotics and other antimicrobial agents; biochemical regulatory mechanisms. *Mailing Add:* Dept Microbiol Sch Med St Louis Univ St Louis MO 63104

WEBER, NEAL ALBERT, b Towner, NDak, Dec 14, 08; m 40; c 3. ENTOMOLOGY, ECOLOGY. *Educ:* Univ NDak, AB, 30, MS, 32; Harvard Univ, AM, 33, PhD(zool), 35. *Hon Degrees:* ScD, Univ NDak, 58. *Prof Exp:* Assoc prof biol, Univ NDak, 36-43 & anat, Sch Med, 43-47; from assoc prof to prof, 47-74, EMER PROF ZOOL, SWARTHMORE COL, 74- *Concurrent Pos:* Mem expeds, W Indies, 33-36, Trinidad, BWI, 34-36, Orinoco Delta, 35, Brit Guiana, 35-36, Barro Colo Island, CZ & Columbia, 38; Anglo-Egyptian Sudan, Uganda & Kenya, 39; biologist, Am Mus Natural Hist Exped, Cent Africa, 48, Middle East, 50-52, Trop Am, 54- & Europ Mus, 57; consult, Arctic Res Lab, Alaska, 48-50; mem dept zool, Col Arts & Sci Univ Baghdad, Iraq, 50-52; vis prof, Univ Wis, 55-56; mem panel biol & med sci, Comt Polar Res, Nat Acad Sci, 58-60, panel fels, 64-66; mem & US del spec comt Antarctic res, Int Coun Sci Unions, Australia, 59; sci attache, Am Embassy, US Dept State, Buenos Aires, Arg, 60-62; mem, Latin Am Colloquium, Arg, 65 & Brazil, 68; consult, Venezuelan Univs, 72; adj prof biol sci, Fla State Univ, Tallahassee, 74- *Honors & Awards:* John F Lewis Prize, Am Philos Soc, 73. *Mem:* AAAS; fel Entom Soc Am; Ecol Soc Am; Mycol Soc Am; Am Soc Zool. *Res:* Tropical ecology; fungus-growing ants and their fungi; zoogeography. *Mailing Add:* 2606 Mission Rd Tallahassee FL 32304

WEBER, NORMAN, b San Luis Obispo, Calif, Nov 25, 34; m 71; c 6. THERMAL SCIENCES. *Educ:* Calif State Polytech Univ, BS, 57; Univ Southern Calif, MS, 67; Mont State Univ, PhD(mech eng), 71. *Prof Exp:* From res engr to sr res engr heat transfer res, Rocketdyne, Div Rockwell Int, 57-68; res asst, Mont State Univ, 68-71; sr develop engr II nuclear safety prog mgr, Westinghouse Hanford Co, 71-74; supvr thermal & hydraul anal, 74-81, ASST HEAD, NUCLEAR SAFEGUARDS & LICENSING DIV, SARGENT & LUNDY ENGRS, 81- *Mem:* Am Nuclear Soc; Am Soc Mech Engrs; AAAS; NY Acad Sci. *Res:* Natural and forced convection heat transfer. *Mailing Add:* 1041 E Porter Ave Naperville IL 60540

WEBER, PAUL VAN VRANKEN, b Highland Park, Ill, Mar 12, 21; m 48; c 3. PLANT PATHOLOGY. *Educ:* Cornell Univ, BS, 43; Univ Wis, PhD(plant path), 49. *Prof Exp:* Asst plant pathologist, Ohio Agr Exp Sta, 49-52; asst plant pathologist & geneticist, Campbell Soup Co, 52-59; CHIEF, BUR PLANT PATH, STATE DEPT AGR, NJ, 59- *Mem:* Am Phytopath Soc; Am Inst Biol Sci. *Res:* Plant disease and insect surveys; administration. *Mailing Add:* 41 Charles Bossert Dr Bordentown NJ 08505

WEBER, PETER B, b Berlin, Ger, July 31, 34; c 1. BIOCHEMISTRY. *Educ:* Univ Cologne, DNatSc(biol, chem), 61. *Prof Exp:* NIH grants, Univ Ill, Chicago, 64-65; NSF grants, State Univ NY Buffalo, 65-68; asst prof biochem, 68-77, ASSOC PROF BIOCHEM, ALBANY MED COL, 77- *Mem:* Fedn Am Socs Exp Biol; Soc Complex Carbohydrates; Sigma Xi. *Res:* Biochemistry of membrane glycoproteins and bacterial polysaccharides. *Mailing Add:* Dept of Biochem Albany Med Col Albany NY 12208

WEBER, RICHARD GERALD, b Newport News, Va, Dec 20, 39. ENTOMOLOGY. *Educ:* Eastern Mennonite Col, BS(biol) & BA(foreign lang), 69; Univ Del, MS, 71; Kans State Univ, PhD(entom), 75. *Prof Exp:* Instr insect morphol, insect taxonomy, gen entomology, Kans State Univ, 75-77; INSTR INSECT STRUCTURE, INSECT PHOTOGRAPHY, NATURAL HIST INSECTS, DEPT ENTOM & APPL SCI, UNIV DEL, 77- *Mem:* Entom Soc Am. *Res:* insect morphology in relation to behavior; mosquito oviposition behavior; photographic and electronics applications for entomological research. *Mailing Add:* Dept Entom & Appl Ecol Univ Del Newark DE 19711

WEBER, RICHARD RAND, b Columbia, Pa, July 28, 38; m 65; c 3. RADIO ASTRONOMY, INSTRUMENTATION. *Educ:* Franklin & Marshall Col, AB, 60; Univ Md, MS, 68. *Prof Exp:* Teacher physics & math, Wilson High Sch, West Lawn, Pa, 60-61; RES SCIENTIST RADIO ASTRON, GODDARD SPACE FLIGHT CTR, NASA, 64- *Mem:* Am Astron Soc; Am Geophys Union; Int Union Radio Sci. *Res:* Radio experiments on spacecraft; low frequency; studies of galactic, solar, planetary radio emissions; microwave studies of cosmic background radiation. *Mailing Add:* Goddard Space Flight Ctr Code 725 Greenbelt MD 20771

WEBER, ROBERT EMIL, b Oshkosh, Wis, Dec 17, 30; m 53; c 3. POLYMER CHEMISTRY. *Educ:* Wis State Col Oshkosh, BS, 53; Univ Iowa, PhD, 59. *Prof Exp:* Res chemist, Res & Develop Ctr, Wis, 58-66, sr res scientist, 66-68, mgr prod develop lab, Munising Div, Mich, 68-71, group leader, Advan Develop Lab, Res & Eng Ctr, Neenah, 71-75, DIR RES &

DEVELOP, MUNISING PAPER DIV, KIMBERLY-CLARK CORP, 75- *Mem:* Am Chem Soc. *Res:* Physical properties of polymers solutions; physical-chemical properties of fiber-elastomer composites. *Mailing Add:* 1807 N McDonald St Appleton WI 54911

WEBER, ROBERT HARRISON, b Wauseon, Ohio, Feb 8, 19; m 41; c 2. GEOLOGY. *Educ:* Ohio State Univ, BSc, 41; Univ Ariz, PhD(geol), 50. *Prof Exp:* Geologist, Shell Oil Co, 41-42; econ geologist, 50-66, SR GEOLOGIST, NMEX BUR MINES & MINERAL RESOURCES, 66- *Concurrent Pos:* Fac assoc, NMex Inst Mining & Technol, 65- *Mem:* Fel AAAS; fel Geol Soc Am; Soc Econ Geol; Soc Am Archaeol; Am Quaternary Asn. *Res:* Mineral deposits; petrography and petrology of volcanic rocks; Quaternary stratigraphy and geomorphology of the Southwest; meteoritics; early man in the New World. *Mailing Add:* Box 2046 Campus Sta Socorro NM 87801

WEBER, THOMAS ANDREW, b Tiffin, Ohio, June 8, 44; m 68; c 5. THEORETICAL CHEMISTRY. *Educ:* Univ Notre Dame, BS, 66; Johns Hopkins Univ, PhD(chem), 70. *Prof Exp:* MEM TECH STAFF CHEM COMPUT, BELL TEL LABS, INC, 70- *Mem:* AAAS; Am Phys Soc. *Res:* Computer simulation and modeling of chemical systems; quantum chemistry; molecular dynamics; kinetics of air pollution in the troposphere; polymer and photoresist modeling; minicomputer and data acquisition systems in chemistry. *Mailing Add:* Rm 1A364 Bell Labs 600 Mountain Ave Murray Hill NJ 07974

WEBER, THOMAS BYRNES, b Oklahoma City, Okla, Sept 1, 25; m 58; c 4. BIOCHEMISTRY. *Educ:* Okla State Univ, BS, 48; La State Univ, PhD(biochem), 54. *Prof Exp:* Res scientist, Animal Dis Res Ctr, Agr Res Ctr, USDA, 54-57; head biochem dept, US Navy Dent Res Inst, 57-59; head atmospheric & gas anal, US Air Force Sch Aerospace Med, 59-62; head adv res med develop, Beckman Instruments, Inc, 62-67; pres, Biosci Planning Inc, 67-69; pres, Med Patents, Inc, 69-74; pres, Weber Dent Prod, 74-77, PRES, GENERICS INT, 74- *Concurrent Pos:* Life sci consult to indust, 58-62; consult, Life Sci & Instrumentation, US Govt, 63-; mem bd dirs, Metab Dynamic Found, 64- *Mem:* AAAS; Am Chem Soc. *Res:* Life support systems; multiphasic screening methods; biochemical and physiological instrumentation; monitoring in closed ecological systems; body fluid analysis; automation of testing tools; handling of ethical pharmaceuticals; heat transfer; high temperature combustion and incineration. *Mailing Add:* Generics Int 3390 Wellesly Ave San Diego CA 92122

WEBER, THOMAS W(ILLIAM), b Orange, NJ, July 15, 30; m 66; c 2. CHEMICAL ENGINEERING. *Educ:* Cornell Univ, BChE, 53, PhD(chem eng), 63; Newark Col Eng, MS, 58. *Prof Exp:* Instr chem eng, Cornell Univ, 61-62; asst prof, 63-66, ASSOC PROF CHEM ENG, STATE UNIV NY BUFFALO, 66-, ASSOC CHMN, DEPT CHEM ENG, 80- *Concurrent Pos:* Nat Sci Found grant, 66-68. *Honors & Awards:* Prof Achievement Award, Western NY Sect, Am Inst Chem Engrs, 78. *Mem:* Fel Am Inst Chem Engrs; Am Soc Eng Educ. *Res:* Dynamics and control of chemical engineering equipment and processes; gaseous adsorption in granular solids, especially adiabatic and isothermal adsorption in packed beds. *Mailing Add:* Dept of Chem Eng Furnas Hall Amherst NY 14260

WEBER, WALDEMAR CARL, b Chicago, Ill, May 4, 37; m 69. MATHEMATICS. *Educ:* US Naval Acad, BSc, 59; Univ Ill, Urbana, MSc, 64, PhD, 68. *Prof Exp:* Asst prof, 68-72, ASSOC PROF MATH, BOWLING GREEN STATE UNIV, 72-, ASST CHAIR, DEPT MATH & STATIST, 77- *Mem:* Am Math Soc; Math Asn Am. *Res:* Geometry; applied mathematics. *Mailing Add:* Dept Math & Statist Bowling Green State Univ Bowling Green OH 43403

WEBER, WALLACE RUDOLPH, b Murphysboro, Ill, Aug 1, 34; m 60; c 2. SYSTEMATIC BOTANY. *Educ:* Southern Ill Univ, BA, 56, MS, 59; Ohio State Univ, PhD(bot), 68. *Prof Exp:* Instr biol, Otterbein Col, 59-62; teaching assoc bot, Ohio State Univ, 63-67; asst prof, 67-70, assoc prof, 70-79, PROF LIFE SCI, SOUTHWEST MO STATE UNIV, 79- *Mem:* Bot Soc Am; Am Soc Plant Taxon; Int Asn Plant Taxon; Sigma Xi. *Res:* Floristics of Missouri Ozarks; biosystematic studies. *Mailing Add:* Dept of Life Sci Southwest Mo State Univ Springfield MO 65802

WEBER, WALTER J, JR, b Pittsburgh, Pa, June 16, 34; m 55; c 4. WATER RESOURCES ENGINEERING. *Educ:* Brown Univ, ScB, 56; Rutgers Univ, ScM, 59; Harvard Univ, AM, 61, PhD(water resources eng), 62; Am Acad Environ Engrs, dipl, 75. *Prof Exp:* Engr, Caterpillar Tractor Co, 56-57; instr civil eng, Rutgers Univ, 57-60; fel water resources eng, Harvard Univ, 62-63; from asst prof to prof civil & water resources eng, 63-78, DISTINGUISHED PROF CIVIL & WATER RESOURCES ENG, UNIV MICH, ANN ARBOR, 78-, DIR, UNIV PROG WATER RESOURCES, 68- *Concurrent Pos:* Engr, Soil Conserv Serv, 59; vis scholar, Univ Calif, Berkeley & Univ Melbourne, 71. *Honors & Awards:* Award, Am Chem Soc, 63; Award, Am Asn Prof Environ Engrs, 68; John R Rumsey Mem Award, Water Pollution Control Fedn, 75; Rudolph Hering Medal, Am Soc Civil Engrs, 80; Willard F Shephard Award, Mich Water Pollution Control Asn, 80. *Mem:* AAAS; Am Chem Soc; Am Inst Chem Engrs; Am Soc Civil Engrs; Water Pollution Control Fedn. *Res:* Water quality and pollution control; water and wastewater treatment; water resources systems design, modeling and water basin management. *Mailing Add:* 181 Water Resources Eng Bldg 1-A Univ of Mich Ann Arbor MI 48109

WEBER, WENDELL W, b Maplewood, Mo, Sept 2, 25; m 52; c 2. PHARMACOLOGY, PEDIATRICS. *Educ:* Cent Methodist Col, BA, 45; Northwestern Univ, PhD(phys chem), 50; Univ Chicago, MD, 59. *Prof Exp:* Asst prof chem, Univ Tenn, 49-51; opers res analyst, Off of Chief Chem Officer, Dept Army, Washington, DC, 51-55; from resident to chief resident pediat, Univ Calif, San Francisco, 60-62; NIH spec fel human genetics, Univ Col, Univ London, 62-63; from instr to prof pharmacol, Sch Med, NY Univ, 63-74; PROF PHARMACOL, UNIV MICH, ANN ARBOR, 74- *Concurrent Pos:* NIH spec fel biochem, Sch Med, NY Univ, 63-65; Health Res Coun NY career scientist award, 65-70 & 70-; mem pharmacol-toxicol comt, Nat Inst Gen Med Sci, 69-73. *Mem:* Am Chem Soc; Am Soc Pharmacol & Exp Therapeut; Am Soc Human Genetics; NY Acad Sci. *Res:* Physical chemistry; protein-small ion interactions; human genetics; cytogenetics; biochemical genetics and pharmacogenetics; drug metabolism and toxicity. *Mailing Add:* Dept of Pharmacol Univ of Mich Ann Arbor MI 48109

WEBER, WILFRIED T, b Rosenheim, Ger, Feb 10, 36; US citizen; m 60; c 2. PATHOLOGY, IMMUNOLOGY. *Educ:* Cornell Univ, BS, 59, DVM, 61; Univ Pa, PhD(path), 66. *Prof Exp:* From asst prof to assoc prof, 66-75, PROF PATH & HEAD LAB PATH, SCH VET MED, UNIV PA, 75- *Concurrent Pos:* NIH res grants, 67-83. *Honors & Awards:* Lindback Award, 75. *Mem:* AAAS; Am Vet Med Asn; Reticuloendothelial Soc; Am Asn Pathologists. Hematology; immunopathology; cancer research; tissue culture of lymphoid cells and macrophages. *Mailing Add:* Dept of Pathobiol Univ Pa Sch of Vet Med Philadelphia PA 19174

WEBER, WILLES HENRY, b Reno, Nev, Sept 22, 42; m 65. SOLID STATE PHYSICS. *Educ:* Calif Inst Technol, BS, 64; Univ Wis, MS, 65, PhD(physics), 68. *Prof Exp:* Prin res scientist assoc, 68-78, STAFF SCIENTIST, ENG & RES STAFF, FORD MOTOR CO, 78- *Concurrent Pos:* Assoc ed, Optics Letters, Optical Soc Am, 77-80; adj assoc prof physics, Univ Mich, Ann Arbor, 77- *Mem:* Am Phys Soc; fel Optical Soc Am. *Res:* Atomic and molecular physics; semiconductor physics, injection phenomena, instabilities, lasers, luminescence; plasma effects in metals and semiconductors; infrared laser spectroscopy; optical effects at surfaces. *Mailing Add:* Eng & Res Staff Ford Motor Co Dearborn MI 48121

WEBER, WILLIAM ALFRED, b New York, NY, Nov 16, 18; m 40; c 3. BOTANY. *Educ:* Iowa State Col, BS, 40; State Col Wash, MS, 42, PhD(bot), 46. *Prof Exp:* Asst prof, 46-70, PROF NATURAL HIST & CUR HERBARIUM, UNIV COLO, BOULDER, 70- *Concurrent Pos:* Cur, Lichen Herbarium, Am Bryol & Lichenological Soc, 54-70. *Mem:* AAAS; Bot Soc Am; Am Bryol & Lichenol Soc; Am Soc Plant Taxon; Int Asn Plant Taxon. *Res:* Lichen and bryophyte flora of Colorado, Galapagos Islands and Australasia; boreal and arctic elements in the Rocky Mountain flora. *Mailing Add:* Campus Box 218 Univ Colo Mus Boulder CO 80309

WEBER, WILLIAM MARK, b Great Bend, Kans, Nov 24, 41; m 64; c 2. QUATERNARY GEOLOGY. *Educ:* Colo Col, BS, 63; Mont State Univ, MS, 65; Univ Wash, PhD(geol), 71. *Prof Exp:* Lab technician, Lincoln DeVore Testing Lab, 59-63, consult geologist, 65-67; instr geol, Colo Col, 67-68; asst prof, Minot State Col, 70-74; mem staff, Dept Geol, Univ Mont, 74-77; GEOLOGIST, LEWIS & CLARK NAT FOREST, 77-; PRES, WEBER & ASSOC, INC, 77- *Concurrent Pos:* Instr, Univ Colo, Cragmoor Campus, 66-68; co-dir exp col, Minot State Col, 71-72, NSF grant, 71-72. *Mem:* Geol Soc Am; Asn Prof Geol Scientists. *Mailing Add:* Lewis & Clark Nat Forest PO Box 871 Great Falls MT 59403

WEBER, WILLIS W, b Waseca, Minn, Nov 23, 34. CHEMICAL ENGINEERING. *Educ:* Univ Minn, BChE, 57. *Prof Exp:* Develop engr, High Energy Fuels Div, Olin Mathieson Chem Corp, 57-59, group leader, 59-60, develop engr, Chem Div, 60-62; develop engr, Linde Div, 62-65, sr develop engr, 65-68, group leader, 68-69, develop assoc, Mat Systs Div, Tarrytown, 69-77, SR CONSULT, LINDE DIV, UNION CARBIDE CORP, TARRYTOWN, 77- *Mem:* Fel Am Inst Chemists. *Res:* Silicate chemistry; zeolites; clay mineralogy; hypochlorites; alkyl borohydrides; zeolite based catalysts; crystallization; reaction kinetics; phase equilibria. *Mailing Add:* Box 612 South Salem NY 10590

WEBERG, BERTON CHARLES, b St Paul, Minn, Dec 23, 30; m 58; c 4. ORGANIC CHEMISTRY. *Educ:* Hamline Univ, BS, 54; Univ Colo, PhD(org chem), 58. *Prof Exp:* Sr res chemist, Abrasives Lab, Minn Mining & Mfg Co, 58-64; PROF CHEM, MANKATO STATE UNIV, 64- *Mem:* Am Chem Soc. *Res:* Chemistry of hindered ketones and vinyl ethers; polymer chemistry. *Mailing Add:* Dept of Chem Mankato State Univ Mankato MN 56001

WEBERS, GERALD F, b Racine, Wis, Apr 14, 32; m 58; c 2. PALEONTOLOGY. *Educ:* Lawrence Univ, BS, 54; Univ Minn, MS, 61, PhD(geol), 64. *Prof Exp:* Res assoc geol, Univ Minn, 64-66; PROF GEOL, MACALESTER COL, 66- *Mem:* Geol Soc Am; Paleont Soc. *Res:* Evolution, taxonomy and paleoecology of Paleozoic invertebrate fossil faunas, especially trilobites, primitive mollusks and conodonts; antarctic geology. *Mailing Add:* Dept of Geol Macalester Col St Paul MN 55101

WEBERS, VINCENT JOSEPH, b Racine, Wis, Apr 28, 22; m 49; c 6. ORGANIC CHEMISTRY. *Educ:* Univ Wis, BS, 43; Univ Minn, PhD(org chem), 49. *Prof Exp:* Lab asst, Univ Minn, 43-45; chemist, Wyeth Inst Appl Biochem, 46; lab asst, Univ Minn, 47; chemist, Cent Res Dept, 49-53, res chemist, Photo Prod Dept, 53-65, res assoc, 65-66, res assoc, Org Chem Dept, 66-67, res supvr, Photo Prod Dept, 67-73, res assoc, 73-76, RES FEL, PHOTO PROD DEPT, E I DU PONT DE NEMOURS & CO, INC, 76- *Honors & Awards:* V F Payne Award, Am Chem Soc, 65. *Mem:* Am Chem Soc; Sigma Xi; Soc Photog Scientist & Engrs. *Res:* Polymer chemistry; lithography; photochemistry; photopolymerization; sensitometry; photosensitive systems; metal coating and plating. *Mailing Add:* Bldg 352 Du Pont Exp Sta Wilmington DE 19898

WEBERT, HENRY S, b New Orleans, La, Jan 21, 29. BOTANY. *Educ:* Loyola Univ, Ill, BS, 51, MEd, 53; La State Univ, MS, 62, PhD(bot), 65. *Prof Exp:* Teacher high sch, Ill, 54-59; partic biol, NSF Acad Year Inst, Brown Univ, 59-60; res asst bot, La State Univ, 60-64; from asst prof to assoc prof, 64-70, PROF BIOL, NICHOLLS STATE UNIV, 70- *Res:* Plant growth and development. *Mailing Add:* Dept of Biol Sci Nicholls State Univ Thibodaux LA 70301

WEBSTER, BARBARA DONAHUE, b Winthrop, Mass, May 19, 29; m 56; c 1. PLANT MORPHOGENESIS. *Educ:* Univ Mass, BS, 50; Smith Col, MA, 52; Radcliffe Col, PhD, 57. *Prof Exp:* Instr plant sci, Vassar Col, 52-54; instr biol, Tufts Univ, 57-58; instr agron, 58-72, res morphologist & lectr agron & range sci, 72-79, PROF & ASSOC DEAN BIOL SCI, UNIV CALIF, DAVIS, 79- *Concurrent Pos:* Res investr, Brookhaven Nat Lab, 52-53 & 55; NSF fel, Purdue Univ, 58-59 & mgt fel, Univ Calif, Davis, 80; mgt fel, Univ Calif, Davis, 80. *Mem:* Bot Soc Am (pres elect, 82); Am Soc Plant Physiol; Int Soc Plant Morphol. *Res:* Plant growth regulators and abscission; morphology and physiology of plant growth; reproductive biology and pollination mechanisms. *Mailing Add:* Dept Agron & Range Sci Univ Calif Davis CA 95616

WEBSTER, BURNICE HOYLE, b Leeville, Tenn, Mar 3, 10; m 39; c 3. THORACIC DISEASES. *Educ:* Vanderbilt Univ, BA, 36, MD, 40. *Hon Degrees:* DSc, Holy Trinity Col, 71; PhD, Fla Res Inst, 72, Dr Humanities, 80. *Prof Exp:* Prof anat & path, Gupton-Jones Col Mortuary Sci, 36-42; intern & resident, St Thomas Hosp, 40-43; ASSOC INTERNAL MED & CHEST DIS, MED SCH, VANDERBILT UNIV, 43-; PROF MED & MED CONSULT, GUPTON SCH MORTUARY SCI, 44- *Concurrent Pos:* Vis physician, Chest Clin, Vanderbilt Univ, 43-48; consult, Vet Admin, 44-; dir, Nashville Chest Clin, 45-48; pres med staff, Protestant Hosp, 47; pres, Holy Trinity Col, 69-; lectr, St Thomas & Baptist Hosps. *Mem:* AAAS; fel Am Thoracic Soc; fel Am Geriat Soc; Am Soc Trop Med & Hyg; fel AMA. *Res:* Parasitic and fungus disease of the lung; changes in fungi following multiple animal passages; pathogenic mutation; thoracology. *Mailing Add:* 2315 Valley Brook Rd Nashville TN 37215

WEBSTER, CLYDE LEROY, JR, b Colorado Springs, Colo, Nov 15, 44; m 65; c 2. INORGANIC CHEMISTRY, GEOCHEMISTRY. *Educ:* Walla Walla Col, BSc, 68; Colo State Univ, PhD(chem), 72. *Prof Exp:* Consult chem, Accu-Labs Res Inc, 73-74; asst mgr chem, Instrument Anal Div, Com Testing & Eng, 74-75; asst prof chem, Loma Linda Univ, 75-78, assoc chmn dept, 77-80; ASSOC PROF CHEM & CHMN DEPT, WALLA WALLA COL, 80- *Concurrent Pos:* Consult, Geosci Res Inst, 75- *Mem:* Am Chem Soc. *Res:* Ore body genesis and processes of fossilization as related to the great deluge theory. *Mailing Add:* Dept of Chem Walla Walla Col College Place WA 99324

WEBSTER, CURTIS CLEVELAND, b Roxbury, Vt, Sept 22, 22; m 47; c 5. MATHEMATICS, NUCLEAR ENGINEERING. *Educ:* Univ Vt, AB, 47; Mo Sch Mines, MS, 50. *Prof Exp:* Lab asst physics, Case Inst Technol, 47-48; instr, Mo Sch Mines, 48-50; scientist, Oak Ridge Nat Lab, 50-56; sr scientist, Radiation & Nucleonics Lab, Mat Eng Dept, Westinghouse Elec Corp, 56-58, sr scientist, Atomic Power Dept, 58-59, proj engr, Testing Reactor, 59-60, hazards eval engr, 60-62; develop engr, Develop Dept Opers Div, 62-70, COMPUT APPLNS SPECIALIST, MATH DIV, OAK RIDGE NAT LAB, 70- *Mem:* AAAS. *Res:* Neutron radiation effects; reactor fuel element development; reactor power measurement by activation of oxygen in coolant; heat transfer problems in water cooled reactor; safety problems in nuclear reactors; reactor physics; application of computers to science and engineering. *Mailing Add:* 105 Ontario Lane Oak Ridge TN 37830

WEBSTER, D(ONALD) S(TEELE), b Wellsboro, Pa, Nov 27, 17; m 56; c 4. CHEMICAL ENGINEERING. *Educ:* Pa State Univ, BS, 40. *Prof Exp:* Jr engr, Eng Serv Div, E I du Pont de Nemours & Co, 40-42, engr, US Army contract, Metall Lab, Chicago, 42-43, engr, Clinton Lab, Tenn, 43-44, engr, Hanford Eng Works, Wash, 44-45, engr, Eng Serv Div, Titanium Plant, Del, 45-46, engr, Eng Res Lab, Exp Sta, 46-52, res supvr, Savannah River Lab, SC, 54-56, sr res supvr, 56-62, res mgr chem eng, 62-69; assoc dir, 69-76, DEP DIR, CHEM ENG DIV, ARGONNE NAT LAB, 76- *Mem:* Am Inst Chem Engrs; Am Chem Soc; Am Nuclear Soc; AAAS. *Res:* Fluid dynamics; solvent extraction methods; radiochemical processing; fluidized-bed combustion. *Mailing Add:* Chem Eng Div Argonne Nat Lab Argonne IL 60439

WEBSTER, DALE ARROY, b St Clair, Mich, Jan 11, 38; m 59; c 1. BIOCHEMISTRY. *Educ:* Univ Mich, BS, 60; Univ Calif, Berkeley, PhD(biochem), 65. *Prof Exp:* Res fel med, Mass Gen Hosp & Harvard Med Sch, 65-68; from asst prof to assoc prof, 68-78, PROF BIOL, ILL INST TECHNOL, 78- *Mem:* Japanese Soc Plant Physiol; Am Soc Biol Chemists. *Res:* Respiratory cytochromes in microbes. *Mailing Add:* Dept of Biol Ill Inst of Technol Chicago IL 60616

WEBSTER, DAVID DYER, b Grand Rapids, Minn, May 27, 18; m 46; c 2. MEDICINE, NEUROLOGY. *Educ:* Univ Minn, BS, 42, MD, 51; Am Bd Psychiat & Neurol, dipl, 60. *Prof Exp:* PROF NEUROL, MED SCH, UNIV MINN, MINNEAPOLIS, 57- *Concurrent Pos:* Staff neurologist & dir neurophysiol lab, Minneapolis Vet Hosp, 55-, chief neurol serv, 76- *Mem:* AAAS; AMA; Am Acad Neurol. *Res:* Movement disorders; medical electronics. *Mailing Add:* Minneapolis Vet Hosp 54th & 48th St Minneapolis MN 55417

WEBSTER, DAVID HENRY, b Berwick, NS, Oct 29, 34; m 60; c 2. HORTICULTURE. *Educ:* Acadia Univ, BSc, 54, MSc, 55; Univ Calif, Davis, PhD(plant physiol), 65. *Prof Exp:* Mem res staff, NS Res Found, 58-62; RES SCIENTIST, CAN DEPT AGR, 65- *Mem:* Am Soc Hort Sci. *Res:* Fruit tree physiology; nutrition; soil physical properties. *Mailing Add:* Can Dept of Agr Res Sta Kentville NS B4N 2P4 Can

WEBSTER, DENNIS BURTON, b Covington, Va, Dec 14, 42. INDUSTRIAL ENGINEERING. *Educ:* WVa Univ, BSIE, 65, MSIE, 66; Purdue Univ, Lafayette, PhD(indust eng), 69. *Prof Exp:* Field studies analyst, Am Viscose Div, FMC Corp, 64, indust engr, 66; asst prof, 70-75, assoc prof, 75-80, PROF INDUST ENG, AUBURN UNIV, 81- *Concurrent Pos:* Mem, Col Indust Coun Mat Handling Educ. *Mem:* Am Inst Indust Engrs. *Res:* Materials flow models; simulation models and simulation optimization; scheduling and production control. *Mailing Add:* Dept Indust Eng Auburn Univ Auburn AL 36849

WEBSTER, DOUGLAS B, b Fond du Lac, Wis, Jan 14, 34; m 55; c 2. OTORHINOLARYNGOLOGY. *Educ:* Oberlin Col, AB, 56; Cornell Univ, PhD(zool), 60. *Prof Exp:* Fel psychobiol, Calif Inst Technol, 60-62; from asst prof to prof biol, NY Univ, 62-73, actg chmn dept, 67-68; PROF OTORHINOLARYNGOL & ANAT, LA STATE UNIV MED CTR, NEW ORLEANS, 73-, CLIN PROF AUDIOL & SPEECH PATH, SCH ALLIED HEALTH, 74- *Concurrent Pos:* NIH grants, NY Univ, 63-65, NY Univ & La State Univ Med Ctr, 65-75 & La State Univ Med Ctr, 73-74; ed, Am Soc Zoologists Newslett, 69-75. *Mem:* AAAS; Am Asn Anatomists; Soc Neurosci; Soc Study Evolution; Am Soc Zoologists (secy, 69-75). *Res:* Morphology, behavior and physiology of hearing in vertebrates. *Mailing Add:* Dept of Otorhinolaryngol La State Univ Med Ctr New Orleans LA 70119

WEBSTER, DWIGHT ALBERT, b Manchester, Conn, Feb 2, 19; m 41; c 3. BIOLOGY. *Educ:* Cornell Univ, BS, 40, PhD(fishery biol), 43. *Prof Exp:* Asst aquatic biologist, Conn Bd Fisheries & Game, 37-41; instr limnol, 41-45, asst prof limnol & fisheries, 46-49, assoc prof fishery biol, 49-57, head dept, 67-71, PROF NATURAL RESOURCES, CORNELL UNIV, 57- *Concurrent Pos:* Pres, NE Div Am Fisheries Soc, 61 & 69; sci adv comt, Great Lakes Fishery Comn. *Mem:* AAAS; Am Fisheries Soc; Am Soc Limnol & Oceanog. *Res:* Population dynamics of freshwater fish, especially the role of hatchery fish in management; ecology and life history of fishes, especially salmonids in the Finger Lakes and Adirondacks of New York State. *Mailing Add:* Dept of Natural Resources Fernow Hall Cornell Univ Ithaca NY 14850

WEBSTER, EDWARD WILLIAM, b London, Eng, Apr 12, 22; nat US; m 50, 61; c 6. MEDICAL PHYSICS. *Educ:* Univ London, BSc, 43, PhD(elec eng), 46. *Prof Exp:* Res engr, Eng Elec Co, UK, 45-49; guest researcher, Mass Inst Technol, 49-50, radiation physicist, 50-51; lectr elec eng & nuclear energy, Queen Mary Col, Univ London, 52-53; PHYSICIST, MASS GEN HOSP, 53-, PROF RADIOL, HARVARD MED SCH, 75-, PROF RADIOL, HARVARD-MASS INST TECHNOL DIV HEALTH SCI & TECHNOL, 78- *Concurrent Pos:* London County Coun Blair traveling fel, Mass Inst Technol, 49-50; from asst to asst prof, Harvard Med Sch, 53-67, assoc clin prof physics in radiol, 67-69, assoc prof radiol, 69-75; USPHS spec fel, 65-66; lectr med radiation physics, Sch Pub Health, Harvard Univ, 71- Consult, Mass Eye & Ear Infirmary, 57- & Int Atomic Energy Agency, 60-61; mem comt radiol, Nat Acad Sci, 62-68; consult, Children's Hosp Med Ctr, Boston, 62-; mem, Nat Coun Radiation Protection & Measurements, 64-, bd dirs, 81-; consult, WHO, 65 & 67; consult, USPHS, 61-63; chmn physics credentials comt, Am Bd Radiol, 66-76; mem radiol health study sect, Dept Health, Educ & Welfare, 69-72, radiol training grant comt, NIH, 69- & adv comt med uses of isotopes, US Nuclear Regulatory Comn, 71-; mem comt biol effects ionizing radiation, Nat Acad Sci, 77-80 & US Nat Comt, Int Union Pure & Appl Biophys, 71-74; secy-gen, Second Int Conf Med Physics, 69. *Honors & Awards:* Garland lectr, Calif Radiol Soc, 80. *Mem:* Am Asn Physicists in Med (pres, 63-64); RadiolSoc NAm (vpres 77-78); fel Am Col Radiol; Health Physics Soc; Soc Nuclear Med (trustee, 73-77). *Res:* Radiological physics; application of radiation, radioisotopes and electronic methods to medical diagnosis and therapy; radiation protection. *Mailing Add:* Dept of Radiol Mass Gen Hosp Boston MA 02114

WEBSTER, ELEANOR RUDD, b Cleveland, Ohio, Oct 11, 20. ORGANIC CHEMISTRY, HISTORY OF SCIENCE. *Educ:* Wellesley Col, AB, 42; Mt Holyoke Col, MA, 44; Radcliffe Col, MA, 50, PhD(chem), 52. *Prof Exp:* Asst chem, Mt Holyoke Col, 42-44; chemist synthetic org res, Eastman Kodak Co, 44-47; from instr to assoc prof, 52-67, dean of freshmen & sophomores, 56-60, chmn dept chem, 64-67, dir inst chem, 64-72, dir continuing educ, 69-70, PROF CHEM, WELLESLEY COL, 67- *Concurrent Pos:* Fulbright grant, Belg, 51-52; NSF sci fac fel, 60-61. *Mem:* Am Chem Soc; Hist Sci Soc; Brit Soc Hist Sci. *Res:* Physical organic chemistry; dissemination of science, the public's understanding since 1850. *Mailing Add:* Dept of Chem Wellesley Col Boston MA 02181

WEBSTER, EMILIA, b Arad, Romania, Oct, 27, 50; US citizen. OPTICAL COMMUNICATIONS, OPTICS. *Educ:* Univ Calif, Los Angeles, BS, 74, MS, 78, PhD(physics), 80. *Prof Exp:* Teaching assoc physics, Univ Calif, Los Angeles, 74-79; mem tech staff electro-optics, 80-81, MEM TECH STAFF ADVAN SPACE COMMUN, AEROSPACE CORP, 81- *Mem:* Am Phys Soc; Optical Soc Am; Inst Elec & Electronics Engrs; Soc Photo-Optical Instrumentation Engrs; Soc Photog Scientists & Engrs. *Res:* Laser communications; lasers; optics; communications theory. *Mailing Add:* PO Box 25023 Los Angeles CA 90025

WEBSTER, FERRIS, b St Boniface, Man, Aug 7, 34; m 57. PHYSICAL OCEANOGRAPHY. *Educ:* Univ Alta, BSc, 56, MSc, 57; Mass Inst Technol, PhD(geophys), 61. *Prof Exp:* Res asst phys oceanog, Woods Hole Oceanog Inst, 59-62, res assoc, 62-63, asst scientist, 63-65, assoc scientist, 65-70, chmn dept phys oceanog, 71-73, sr scientist, 70-78, assoc dir, 73-78; ASST ADMINR RES & DEVELOP, NAT OCEANIC & ATMOSPHERIC ADMIN, 78- *Concurrent Pos:* Asst prof, Mass Inst Technol, 66-68. *Mem:* AAAS; Am Geophys Union. *Res:* Ocean currents; oceanic variability; oceanographic data processing and time-series analysis. *Mailing Add:* Nat Oceanic & Atmospheric Admin Rockville MD 20852

WEBSTER, GARY DEAN, b Hutchinson, Kans, Feb 15, 34; m 64; c 2. GEOLOGY, PALEONTOLOGY. *Educ:* Univ Okla, BS, 56; Univ Kans, MS, 59; Univ Calif, Los Angeles, PhD(geol), 66. *Prof Exp:* Geologist, Amerada Petrol Corp, 56-57; geologist, Belco Petrol Corp, 60; geologist, Shell Oil Co, 63; lectr phys geol, Calif Lutheran Col, 63-64; mus scientist, Univ Calif, Los Angeles, 64-65; asst prof geol & paleont, San Diego State Col, 65-68; from asst prof to assoc prof, 68-77, PROF GEOL, WASH STATE UNIV, 77-, CHMN DEPT, 80- *Concurrent Pos:* Mem, Am Geol Inst, Int Field Inst, Spain, 71. *Mem:* AAAS; Soc Econ Paleont & Mineral; Paleont Soc; Geol Soc Am; Brit Palaeont Asn. *Res:* Late Paleozoic paleontology and stratigraphy, especially crinoids and conodonts; stratigraphy sedimentation. *Mailing Add:* Dept Geol Wash State Univ Pullman WA 99164

WEBSTER, GEORGE CALVIN, b South Haven, Mich, July 17, 24; m 60; c 2. BIOCHEMISTRY. *Educ:* Western Mich Univ, BS, 48; Univ Minn, MS, 49, PhD(biol), 52. *Prof Exp:* Res fel, Calif Inst Technol, 52-55; from assoc prof to prof biochem, Ohio State Univ, 55-61; vis prof enzyme chem, Univ Wis, 61-65; chief chemist, Aerospace Serv Div, Cape Kennedy, Fla, 65-70; PROF BIOL SCI & HEAD DEPT, FLA INST TECHNOL, 70- *Concurrent Pos:* USPHS spec res fel, 61-63; Am Heart Asn estab investr, 63-65. *Mem:* AAAS; Am Soc Biol Chemists; Sigma Xi; Am Soc Cell Biol; Brit Biochem Soc. *Res:* Molecular biology of aging, nitrogen metabolism and protein synthesis. *Mailing Add:* Dept of Biol Sci Fla Inst of Technol Melbourne FL 32901

WEBSTER, GORDON RITCHIE, b Kindersley, Sask, Jan 7, 22; m 50; c 2. SOIL CHEMISTRY. *Educ:* Univ BC, BSA, 49, MSA, 51; Univ Ore, PhD(soils), 58. *Prof Exp:* Res officer soil sci, Can Dept Agr, 49-60; assoc prof, 60-70, PROF SOIL SCI, UNIV ALTA, 70- *Mem:* Can Soc Soil Sci. *Res:* Reclamation of solonetzic soils; poor alfalfa growth second time in rotation; reclamation of salt spills. *Mailing Add:* Dept of Soil Sci Univ of Alta Edmonton AB T6G 2E3 Can

WEBSTER, GRADY LINDER, b Ada, Okla, Apr 14, 27; m 56; c 1. PLANT TAXONOMY. *Educ:* Univ Tex, BA, 47, MA, 49; Univ Mich, PhD(bot), 54. *Prof Exp:* Lectr trop bot, Harvard Univ, 53, NSF fel biol, 53-55, instr bot, 55-58; asst prof biol sci, Purdue Univ, 58-62, assoc prof biol sci, 62-66; PROF BOT, UNIV CALIF, DAVIS, 66- *Concurrent Pos:* Guggenheim fel bot, State Univ Utrecht, 64-65; prog dir systematic biol, Nat Sci Found, 81-82. *Mem:* Am Soc Plant Taxon; Soc Study Evolution; Bot Soc Am; Asn Trop Biol; Int Asn Plant Taxon. *Res:* Evolution and systematics of vascular plants, especially Euphorbiaceae; vegetational and floristic plant geography; pollination ecology. *Mailing Add:* Dept of Bot Univ of Calif Davis CA 95616

WEBSTER, HAROLD FRANK, b Buffalo, NY, June 25, 19; m 51; c 3. PHYSICS. *Educ:* Univ Buffalo, BA, 41, MA, 44; Cornell Univ, PhD(physics), 53. *Prof Exp:* Mem staff, Radiation Lab, Mass Inst Technol, 43-45; asst, Cornell Univ, 45-51; PHYSICIST, RES LAB, GEN ELEC CO, 51- *Concurrent Pos:* US del gen assembly, Int Sci Radio Union, 60; mem adv comt, Physics Today, 77-80. *Honors & Awards:* Baker Award, Inst Elec & Electronics Eng, 58. *Mem:* Am Phys Soc; Inst Elec & Electronics Eng. *Res:* Thermionic emission from single crystal surfaces; metal surface wetting; electron beam dynamics; cesium plasma; energy conversion; ultraviolet sensors; solid state science; microelectronics. *Mailing Add:* Gen Elec Corp Res & Develop Ctr PO Box 43 Schenectady NY 12301

WEBSTER, HARRIS DUANE, b Lansing, Mich, Jan 14, 20; m 43; c 2. VETERINARY PATHOLOGY. *Educ:* Mich State Col, DVM, 43, MS, 51. *Prof Exp:* Vet, US Regional Poultry Res Lab, East Lansing, 44 & 46-47; gen pract, Mich, 47-48; instr animal path, Mich State Col, 48-52; RES SCIENTIST PATH & TOXICOL, UPJOHN CO, 52- *Mem:* Am Vet Med Asn; Am Col Vet Path; Int Acad Pathologists. *Res:* Toxicologic, experimental pathologic studies and laboratory animal health consultation and service. *Mailing Add:* 715 Jenks Blvd Kalamazoo MI 49007

WEBSTER, HENRY DEFOREST, b New York, NY, Apr 22, 27; m 51; c 5. NEUROLOGY, NEUROPATHOLOGY. *Educ:* Amherst Col, BA, 48; Harvard Med Sch, MD, 52; Am Bd Psychiat & Neurol, dipl & cert neurol, 59. *Prof Exp:* Intern & asst resident med, Harvard Serv, Boston City Hosp, 52-54; asst resident & resident neurol, Mass Gen Hosp, 54-56, res fel neuropath, 56-58; asst instr & assoc neurol, Harvard Med Sch, 58-66, asst prof neuropath, 66; assoc prof neurol, Sch Med, Univ Miami, 66-69, prof, 69; HEAD SECT CELLULAR NEUROPATH & ASSOC CHIEF, LAB NEUROPATH & NEUROANAT SCI, NAT INST NEUROL & COMMUN DISORDERS & STROKE, 69- *Concurrent Pos:* Prin investr, Nat Inst Neurol Dis & Stroke grants, 62-69, partic neuroanat vis scientist prog, 64-65; assoc neurologist & asst neuropathologist, Mass Gen Hosp, 63-66; secy gen, VIII Int Cong Neuropath, 78. *Mem:* Am Asn Neuropath (vpres, 76-77, pres, 78-79); Am Soc Cell Biol; Asn Res Nerv & Ment Dis; Am Acad Neurol; Am Neurol Asn. *Res:* Experimental neuropathology utilizing electron microscopy and immunocytochemistry, especially the formation and breakdown of myelin. *Mailing Add:* Nat Inst Neurol & Commun Disorders & Stroke Bldg 36 Bethesda MD 20014

WEBSTER, ISABELLA MARGARET, b Chicago, Ill, Jan 22, 11. PUBLIC HEALTH. *Educ:* Northwestern Univ, BA, 32; Univ Minn, PhD(org chem), 36; Woman's Med Col Pa, MD, 47; Univ Liverpool, dipl, 65; Univ Hawaii, MPH, 69. *Prof Exp:* Asst chem, Univ Minn, 32-36, instr org chem, 36-37; intern, Mary Immaculate Hosp, NY, 47-48; intern obstet & gynec, Georgetown Univ Hosp, 48; mem med staff, Holy Family Hosp, Mandar, India, 48-54; doctor chg, Archbishop Attipetty Jubilee Mem Hosp, S India, 54-57; chief med servs, Kokofu Leprosarium, Ghana Leprosy Serv, 58-68; consult pub health, Atat Hosp, Ethiopia, Nangina Hosp, Nangina, Kenya, Virika Hosp, Ft Portal, Uganda & Lower Shire Mobile Health Unit, Chiromo, Malawi, 69-71; dist superior, Med Mission Sisters, Ghana, 71-73, mem, Cent Med Mission Sisters, Rome, 73-79; DIOCESAN MED COORDR, DIOCESE KAKAMEGA, KENYA, EAST AFRICA, 81- *Concurrent Pos:* Consult primary health, Med Mission Sisters; chmn health working group, SEDOS, Rome. *Res:* Organic chemistry; bacteriology; obstetrics and gynecology; leprosy. *Mailing Add:* Diocese Kakamega PO Box 712 Kakamega Kenya

WEBSTER, JACKSON DAN, b Tacoma, Wash, Feb 26, 19; m 44; c 3. PARASITOLOGY, ORNITHOLOGY. *Educ:* Whitworth Col, Wash, BSc, 39; Cornell Univ, MSc, 41; Rice Inst, PhD(parasitol), 47. *Prof Exp:* Field researcher ornith, Alaska, 40 & 46; asst prof biol, Jamestown Col, 47-49; assoc prof, 49-53, PROF BIOL, HANOVER COL, 53- *Concurrent Pos:* Field researcher ornith, 72, 75 & 77. *Mem:* Soc Parasitol; assoc Wilson Ornith Soc; assoc Cooper Ornith Soc; Am Ornith Union. *Res:* Septematics, distribution and populations of birds; systematics of tapeworms. *Mailing Add:* Dept of Biol Hanover Col Hanover IN 47243

WEBSTER, JACKSON ROSS, b Brigham City, Utah, May 3, 45; m 68; c 2. STREAM ECOLOGY, SYSTEMS ECOLOGY. *Educ:* Wabash Col, BA, 67; Univ Ga, PhD(ecol, zool), 75. *Prof Exp:* Asst prof, 75-81, ASSOC PROF ZOOL, VA POLYTECH INST & STATE UNIV, 81- *Concurrent Pos:* Vis scientist, Oak Ridge Nat Lab, 81-82. *Mem:* Ecol Soc Am; Am Soc Limnol & Oceanog; NAm Benthological Soc; Int Asn Theoret & Appl Limnol. *Res:* Nutrient and energy dynamics in stream ecosystems; ecosystem modeling. *Mailing Add:* Dept of Biol Va Polytech Inst & State Univ Blacksburg VA 24061

WEBSTER, JAMES ALBERT, b Mineola, NY, June 2, 28; m 51; c 4. ORGANIC CHEMISTRY. *Educ:* Col Wooster, BA, 51; Univ Pittsburgh, MS, 56. *Prof Exp:* Res chemist, Res & Eng Div, Monsanto Chem Co, 56-61, res chemist, Monsanto Res Corp, 61-66, sr res chemist, 66-71, sr group leader, 71-75, SR RES SPECIALIST, MONSANTO RES CORP, 75- *Mem:* Am Chem Soc; AAAS. *Res:* Silicone chemistry; polymer synthesis; fluorine chemistry. *Mailing Add:* 7611 Eagle Creek Dr Dayton OH 45459

WEBSTER, JAMES ALLAN, b Lincoln, Nebr, May 1, 39; m 67; c 2. ENTOMOLOGY. *Educ:* Univ Ky, BS, 61, MS, 64; Kans State Univ, PhD(entom), 68. *Prof Exp:* RES ENTOMOLOGIST, AGR RES SERV, USDA, 68-; ASSOC PROF, DEPT ENTOM, OKLA STATE UNIV, 81- *Concurrent Pos:* Asst prof, Dept Entom, Mich State Univ, 68-74, assoc prof, 74-81. *Mem:* Entom Soc Am; Am Soc Agron. *Res:* Insect resistance in grain and forage crops. *Mailing Add:* Plant Sci Res Facil Agr Res Serv USDA PO Box 1029 Stillwater OK 74076

WEBSTER, JAMES RANDOLPH, JR, b Chicago, Ill, Aug 25, 31; m 54; c 3. PULMONARY PHYSIOLOGY. *Educ:* Northwestern Univ, Chicago, BS, 53, MS & MD, 56. *Prof Exp:* From asst prof to assoc prof, 67-77, PROF MED, MED SCH, NORTHWESTERN UNIV, CHICAGO, 77- *Concurrent Pos:* USPHS fel pulmonary physiol, Med Sch, Northwestern Univ, Chicago, 62-64; assoc dir inhalation ther, Chicago Wesley Mem Hosp, 65-66, dir pulmonary function lab, 66-; chief med, Northwestern Mem Hosp, 72- *Mem:* Am Thoracic Soc; Am Fedn Clin Res; Am Col Physicians. *Res:* Diseases of the chest. *Mailing Add:* Dept of Med Northwestern Univ Med Sch Chicago IL 60611

WEBSTER, JOHN GOODWIN, b Plainfield, NJ, May 27, 32; m 54; c 4. MEDICAL INSTRUMENTATION, ELECTRODES. *Educ:* Cornell Univ, BEE, 53; Univ Rochester, MSEE, 65, PhD(elec eng), 67. *Prof Exp:* Res engr, NAm Aviation, Inc, 54-55; head instrumentation, Boeing Airplane Co, 55-59; head telemetry, Radiation, Inc, 59-61; staff engr, Mitre Corp, 61-62; staff engr, Int Bus Mach Corp, 62-63; res assoc elec eng, Univ Rochester, 67; from asst prof to assoc prof, 67-73, PROF ELEC & ENG, UNIV WIS-MADISON, 73- *Concurrent Pos:* NSF res grant, 68-70; NIH res career develop grant, 71-76; NASA res grant, 72-73; NIH res grant, 76-83; dir, Biomed Eng Ctr, 76-80; assoc ed, Trans Biomed Eng, Inst Elec & Electronics Engrs, 78- *Honors & Awards:* Donald P Eckman Educ Award, Instrument Soc Am, 74. *Mem:* Inst Elec & Electronics Engrs; Instrument Soc Am; Biomed Eng Soc; Asn Advan Med Instrumentation; Am Soc Eng Educ. *Res:* Medical instrumentation; electrodes for monitoring and stimulation; amplifiers; artifacts; interference; ambulatory arrhythmia monitors; electrical impedance plethysmography. *Mailing Add:* Dept Elec & Comput Eng Univ Wis 1415 Johnson Dr Madison WI 53706

WEBSTER, JOHN H, b Belleville, Ont, Dec 17, 28; m 53; c 3. RADIOTHERAPY. *Educ:* Queen's Univ, Ont, MD, 55. *Prof Exp:* Sr cancer res radiologist, Roswell Park Mem Inst, 59-62, assoc cancer res radiologist, 62-63, assoc chief cancer res radiologist, 63-64, chief cancer res radiologist, 64-74; prof therapeut radiol & chmn dept, McGill Univ, 74-80; PROF, DEPT RADIOL, ONCOL CTR, UNIV PITTSBURGH, 80- *Concurrent Pos:* USPHS grants; therapeut radiologist-in-chief, Montreal Gen Hosp, Royal Victoria Hosp, Montreal Children's Hosp & Jewish Gen Hosp, 74-79; sr consult radiotherapist, Montreal Neurol Hosp, 74-79; consult radiotherapist, Presby Univ Hosp & Mazec Womens Hosp, 79- *Mem:* Am Col Radiol; Am Soc Therapeut Radiol; Can Med Asn; Soc Chmn Acad Radiation Oncol Progs; Can Asn Radiologists. *Res:* Experimental radiotherapy and allied fields; oncologically related research; cancer patient care systems. *Mailing Add:* Joint Radiation Oncol Ctr Univ Pittsburgh 230 Lothergs St Pittsburgh PA 15213

WEBSTER, JOHN MALCOLM, b Wakefield, Eng, May 5, 36. BIOLOGY, PARASITOLOGY. *Educ:* Univ London, BSc & ARCS, 58, PhD(zool) & DIC, 62. *Prof Exp:* Sci officer nematol, Rothamsted Exp Sta, Eng, 61-66; sci officer parasitol, Can Dept Agr Res Inst, Belleville, 66-67; assoc prof, 67-71, chmn dept biol sci, 74-76, dean sci, 76-80, PROF BIOL, SIMON FRASER UNIV, 71-, ASSOC VPRES ACADEMIC, 80- *Mem:* Can Soc Zool; Soc Nematol (vpres, 81-); Soc Invert Path; Entom Soc Can; Brit Soc Exp Biol. *Res:* Physiology of host-parasite relationships, especially those of nematode parasites of plants and insects; economic applications of plant nematology and invertebrate pathology; ultrastructure of host response. *Mailing Add:* Dept of Biol Sci Simon Fraser Univ Burnaby Vancouver BC U5A 1S6 Can

WEBSTER, JOHN ROBERT, b Riverdale, Calif, May 5, 16; m 43; c 3. FOOD SCIENCE. *Educ:* Calif State Univ, Fresno, AB, 39. *Prof Exp:* DIR RES & DEVELOP, LINDSAY OLIVE GROWERS, 40- *Mem:* Am Chem Soc; Inst Food Technologists. *Res:* Improving nutrition, improving quality, and decreasing process cost of olives, cherries, pimiento and pickled peppers. *Mailing Add:* 386 Alameda St Lindsay CA 93247

WEBSTER, JOHN THOMAS, b Fond du Lac, Wis, Sept 12, 27; m 55; c 3. STATISTICS. *Educ:* Ripon Col, BA, 51; Purdue Univ, MS, 55; NC State Col, PhD(statist), 60. *Prof Exp:* Statistician, Westinghouse Elec Corp, 55-57; asst prof statist, Bucknell Univ, 60-62; assoc prof, 62-76, PROF STATIST, SOUTHERN METHODIST UNIV, 76- *Mem:* Am Statist Asn; Biomet Soc; Am Soc Qual Control. *Res:* Design and analysis of experiments. *Mailing Add:* Dept of Statist Southern Methodist Univ Dallas TX 75275

WEBSTER, KARL SMITH, b Orleans, Vt, Aug 18, 24; m 53; c 2. MECHANICAL ENGINEERING, ENGINEERING MECHANICS. *Educ:* Univ Vt, BSME, 49; Pa State Univ, MS, 58. *Prof Exp:* Test engr, Gen Elec Co, NY, 49-50, appln eng, Mass, 50-52; chief engr, W J Nolan Co, 52-53; develop engr, Fels Gear Shaper Co, 53-54; res asst mech eng, Pa State Univ, 54, instr, 54-58; asst prof, Univ NH, 58-62, assoc prof mech design technol, Tech Inst, 62-65; Dept Interior consult, River Syst as Reactor Proj, Univ Water Resources, 67-69, asst to vpres acad affairs, Univ, 70-72, assoc prof mech eng, Univ Maine, Orono, 65-77, assoc prof, 77-80, PROF MECH ENG TECHNOL, SCH ENG TECHNOL, COL ENG & SCI, UNIV MAINE, ORONO, 80- *Mem:* Am Soc Eng Educ; Soc Mfg Engrs. *Res:* Internal combustion engine projects; industrial and manufacturing engineering. *Mailing Add:* Rm 218 Boardman Hall Univ of Maine Orono ME 04469

WEBSTER, LARRY DALE, b Westfall, Kans, Feb 8, 39; m 63; c 1. MECHANICS, MATERIALS SCIENCE. *Educ:* Colo Sch Mines, MetE, 61; Cornell Univ, PhD(mat sci), 65. *Prof Exp:* Chmn sci dept, Lamar Community Col, 65-67; res scientist weapons effects, Kaman Sci Corp, 67-73; sr engr reactor technol, Bettis Atomic Power Lab, Pa, 73-77; RES SCIENTIST ACOUST DEVICES, KAMAN SCI CORP, 77- *Res:* Finite element analyses of coupled structural and electromagnetic fields; model development for piezoelectric devices and for magnetically driven flyer plates associated with impact test facilities. *Mailing Add:* Kaman Sci Corp 1500 Garden of the Gods Rd Colorado Springs CO 80907

WEBSTER, LEE ALAN, b Mt Holly, NJ, June 30, 41; m 64; c 2. TRANSPORTATION & TRAFFIC ENGINEERING. *Educ:* Univ Del, BCE, 63; Univ Ill, Urbana, MSc, 65, PhD(traffic eng), 68. *Prof Exp:* Asst prof civil eng, Univ Mass, Amherst, 68-76; transp engr, Curran Assocs, 76-80; MEM FAC, GREENFIELD COMMUNITY COL, 80- *Concurrent Pos:* Mem, Hwy Res Bd, Nat Acad Sci-Nat Res Coun. *Mem:* Am Soc Civil Engrs; Inst Traffic Engrs; Am Soc Eng Educ. *Res:* Transportation and traffic engineering education; transportation planning; computer applications to engineering and education. *Mailing Add:* Greenfield Community Col Greenfield MA 01301

WEBSTER, LESLIE T, JR, b New York, NY, Mar 31, 26; m 55; c 4. PHARMACOLOGY. *Educ:* Amherst Col, BA, 47; Harvard Med Sch, MD, 48; Am Bd Internal Med, dipl, 57. *Prof Exp:* Demonstr med, Sch Med, Case Western Reserve Univ, 55-57, instr, 57-60, from sr instr to asst prof biochem, 58-66, asst prof med, 60-70, from asst prof to assoc prof pharmacol, 66-70; prof pharmacol & chmn dept, Med & Dent Schs, Northwestern Univ, Chicago, 70-76; CHICAGO, J H HORD PROF PHARMACOL & CHMN DEPT, SCH MED, CASE WESTERN RESERVE UNIV, 76- *Concurrent Pos:* Nat Vitamin Found Wilder fel, 56-59; sr investr, USPHS, 59-61, res career develop award, 61-69; mem gastroenterol & nutrit training grants comt, Nat Inst Arthritis & Metab Dis, 65-69; consult, NIH, 71-, WHO, 77 & Rockefeller Found, 78-; Macy fac scholar, 80-81. *Mem:* Am Col Physicians; Am Soc Clin Invest; Am Soc Biol Chemists; Am Soc Pharmacol & Exp Therapeut; Am Soc Trop Med & Hyg. *Res:* Enzymology; pharmacoparasitology; immunopharmacology; clinical pharmacology; drug metabolism. *Mailing Add:* Case Western Reserve Univ 2119 Abington Rd Cleveland OH 44106

WEBSTER, MERRITT SAMUEL, b Cheyney, Pa, June 5, 09; m 36; c 3. MATHEMATICS. *Educ:* Swarthmore Col, AB, 31; Univ Pa, AM, 33, PhD(math), 35. *Prof Exp:* Asst instr math, Univ Pa, 31-33; instr, Univ Nebr, 35-38; from instr to prof, 38-75, EMER PROF MATH, PURDUE UNIV, WEST LAFAYETTE, 75- *Mem:* Am Math Soc; Math Asn Am. *Res:* Orthogonal polynomials; interpolation. *Mailing Add:* 225 Connolly St West Lafayette IN 47906

WEBSTER, ORRIN JOHN, b Arkansas City, Kans, June 26, 13; m 36; c 3. AGRONOMY. *Educ:* Univ Nebr, BSc, 34, MSc, 40; Univ Minn, PhD(plant breeding & genetics), 50. *Prof Exp:* Agronomist, Soil Conserv Serv, USDA, 35-36, Dryland Agr Div, 36-43 & Cereal Corps Res Br, Agr Res Serv, 43-63, dir-coordr major cereal proj, Orgn For African Unity, 63-71, proj leader corn, sorghum & millet res, Fed Exp Sta, PR, 71-74; ADJ PROF AGRON, UNIV ARIZ, 74- *Concurrent Pos:* Adv corn & sorghum breeding, Govt Nigeria, Liberia, Sudan & Africa, 51; secy sorghum res comt, USDA, 53-67; mem comt preserv indigenous strains sorghum, Nat Acad Sci, 61- *Mem:* Am Soc Agron. *Res:* Plant breeding of sorghum; genetics and cytogenetics of sorghum. *Mailing Add:* Dept of Agron Univ of Ariz Tucson AZ 85721

WEBSTER, OWEN WRIGHT, b Devils Lake, NDak, Mar 25, 29; m 53; c 5. ORGANIC CHEMISTRY. *Educ:* Univ NDak, BS, 51; Pa State Univ, PhD(chem), 55. *Prof Exp:* Res chemist, 55-80, RES SUPVR, E I DU PONT DE NEMOURS & CO, INC, 80- *Mem:* Am Chem Soc; Sigma Xi. *Res:* Synthetic organic chemistry; adamantanes; cyanocarbons; hydrogen cyanide; polymers. *Mailing Add:* 2106 Navaro Rd Wilmington DE 19803

WEBSTER, PAUL DANIEL, III, b Mt Airy, NC, Apr 26, 30; m 57; c 2. MEDICINE, GASTROENTEROLOGY. *Educ:* Univ Richmond, BS, 52; Bowman Gray Sch Med, MD, 56. *Prof Exp:* Fel med, Univ Minn, 60-63; fel gastroenterol, Sch Med, Duke Univ, 63-66, asst prof med, Med Ctr, 67-68; assoc prof, 68-71, PROF MED, MED COL GA, 71-, CHMN DEPT, 77- *Concurrent Pos:* USPHS fel, 65-66; chief med serv, Vet Admin Hosp, Augusta, Ga, 73. *Mem:* Am Gastroenterol Asn; Am Physiol Soc; Am Col Gastroenterol; Am Inst Nutrit; Am Soc Clin Invest. *Res:* Hormonal control of pancreatic protein synthesis; pancreatic structure and function; cancer of pancreas. *Mailing Add:* Dept of Med Med Col of Ga Augusta GA 30912

WEBSTER, PORTER GRIGSBY, b Wheatley, Ky, Nov 25, 29; m 61. MATHEMATICS. *Educ:* Georgetown Col, BA, 51; Auburn Univ, MS, 56, PhD(math), 61. *Prof Exp:* PROF MATH, UNIV SOUTHERN MISS, 61- *Mem:* Am Math Soc; Math Asn Am. *Mailing Add:* Southern Sta Box 226 Dept Math Univ of Southern Miss Hattiesburg MS 39401

WEBSTER, ROBERT EDWARD, b New Haven, Conn, May 31, 38; m 60; c 3. MOLECULAR BIOLOGY, MOLECULAR GENETICS. *Educ:* Amherst Col, BA, 59; Duke Univ, PhD(microbiol), 65. *Prof Exp:* NSF fel genetics, Rockefeller Univ, 65-66, from asst prof to assoc prof molecular biol, 66-76, PROF BIOCHEM, MED CTR, DUKE UNIV, 76- *Mem:* AAAS; Am Soc Cell Biol; Am Soc Biol Chemists. *Res:* Protein synthesis; phage genetics and morphogenesis; membrane structure and synthesis; structural elements of mammalian cells. *Mailing Add:* Dept of Biochem Med Ctr Duke Univ Durham NC 27710

WEBSTER, ROBERT G, b Balclutha, NZ, July 5, 32; Australian citizen; m; c 3. VIROLOGY, IMMUNOLOGY. *Educ:* Otago Univ, BS, 55, MS, 57; Australian Nat Univ, PhD(microbiol), 62. *Prof Exp:* Virologist, NZ Dept Agr, 58-59; Fulbright scholar, Dept Epidemiol, Sch Pub Health, Univ Mich, Ann Arbor, 62-63; res fel, Dept of Microbiol, John Curtin Med Sch, Australian Nat Univ, 64-66, fel, 66-67; assoc mem, Lab Immunol, St Jude Children's Res Hosp, 68-69; assoc prof, 68-74, CLIN PROF MICROBIOL, UNIV TENN CTR HEALTH SCI MEMPHIS, 74-; MEM LABS VIROL & IMMUNOL, ST JUDE CHILDREN'S RES HOSP, 69- *Concurrent Pos:* Coordr, US-USSR Joint Comt Health Coop, Ecol of Human Influenza & Animal Influenza Rels to Human Infection, 74- *Mem:* Am Soc Microbiol; Am Asn Immunologists. *Res:* Structure and immunology of influenza viruses. *Mailing Add:* Dept of Microbiol Ctr for Health Sci Univ of Tenn Memphis TN 38163

WEBSTER, ROBERT K, b Solomonville, Ariz, Jan 15, 38; m 59; c 3. PHYTOPATHOLOGY. *Educ:* Utah State Univ, BS, 61; Univ Calif, Davis, PhD(plant path), 66. *Prof Exp:* Res assoc plant path, NC State Univ, 66; from asst prof to assoc prof, 66-75, PROF PLANT PATH, UNIV CALIF, DAVIS, 75- *Mem:* Mycol Soc Am; Am Phytopath Soc; Am Soc Naturalists. *Res:* Genetics of plant pathogenic fungi; field crop diseases. *Mailing Add:* Dept of Plant Path Univ of Calif Davis CA 95616

WEBSTER, STEPHEN RUSSELL, b Centralia, Wash, Oct 27, 42; m 65. FOREST SOILS. *Educ:* Wash State Univ, BS, 65; Ore State Univ, MS, 67; NC State Univ, PhD(soils), 74. *Prof Exp:* RES SCIENTIST, FORESTRY RES CTR, WEYERHAEUSER CO, CENTRALIA, 72-, MGR, 80- *Mem:* Soil Sci Soc Am; Soc Am Foresters. *Res:* Forest fertiliztion, forest tree nutrition and soil survey. *Mailing Add:* Weyerhaeuser Co Forestry Res Ctr Centralia WA 98531

WEBSTER, TERRY R, b Hamilton, Ohio, Feb 10, 38; m 64; c 1. BOTANY, PLANT MORPHOLOGY. *Educ:* Miami Univ, BA, 60; Univ Sask, MA, 62, PhD(bot), 65. *Prof Exp:* Asst prof bot, 65-71, ASSOC PROF BIOL, UNIV CONN, 71- *Mem:* Am Fern Soc (secy, 73-76); 73-78); Soc Am. *Res:* Morphology of the genus Selaginella. *Mailing Add:* Biol Sci Group Univ of Conn Storrs CT 06268

WEBSTER, THOMAS G, b Topeka, Kans, Jan 23, 24; m 48; c 3. PSYCHIATRY, ACADEMIC ADMINISTRATION. *Educ:* Ft Hays Kans State Col, AB, 46; Wayne State Univ, MD, 49. *Prof Exp:* Commonwealth fel col ment health, Mass Inst Technol, 54-56; Nat Inst Ment Health career teacher grant, Harvard Med Sch, 56-58, instr psychiat, 59-63; training specialist, Psychiat Training Br, Nat Inst Ment Health, 63-66, chief, Continuing Educ Br, 66-72; prof psychiat & behav sci & chmn dept, 72-75, prof child develop & health, 75-80, PROF PSYCHIAT & CHILD HEALTH & DEVELOP, GEORGE WASHINGTON UNIV, 75- *Concurrent Pos:* Dir, Presch Retard Children's Prog Greater Boston, 58-62; vis prof phychiat, Harvard Med Sch, 80-82. *Mem:* AAAS; Am Psychiat Asn; Am Col Psychiat; Am Acad Child Psychiat; Group Advan Psychiat. *Res:* Psychiatric education; child development; psychopathology; health policy, international; program evaluation in fields of manpower and training. *Mailing Add:* Dept of Psychiat & Behav Sci George Washington Univ Med Ctr Washington DC 20037

WEBSTER, WILLIAM JOHN, JR, b New York, NY, May 3, 43; m 80; c 1. PLANETARY SCIENCES. *Educ:* Univ Rochester, BS, 65; Case Western Reserve Univ, PhD(astron), 69. *Prof Exp:* Res assoc astron, Nat Radio Astron Observ, Va, 68-70; Nat Acad Sci-Nat Res Coun resident res assoc, Solar Physics Lab, 70-71, staff scientist, Meteorol & Earth Sci Lab, 71-74, STAFF SCIENTIST, GEOPHYS BR, GODDARD SPACE FLIGHT CTR, 74- *Mem:* Am Astron Soc; Am Inst Aeronaut & Astronaut. *Res:* Radio interferometry; gaseous nebulae; radio spectroscopy; continuum mapping of radio sources; microwave observation of earth; precision geodesy by radio interferometry; earthquake prediction; seismology. *Mailing Add:* Geophys Br Code 922 Goddard Space Flight Ctr Greenbelt MD 20771

WEBSTER, WILLIAM MERLE, b Warsaw, NY, June 13, 25; m 47; c 2. PHYSICS. *Educ:* Union Col, NY, BS, 45; Princeton Univ, PhD(elec eng), 54. *Prof Exp:* Res engr, Labs, 46-54, mgr adv develop, RCA Semiconductor & Mat Div, 54-59, dir electronic res lab, RCA Labs, 59-66, staff vpres mat & devices res, 66-68, VPRES LABS, RCA LABS, RCA CORP, 68- *Honors & Awards:* Ed Award, Inst Radio Eng, 53. *Mem:* Nat Acad Eng; fel Inst Elec & Electronics Engrs. *Res:* Solid state and gaseous electronics; electron physics. *Mailing Add:* RCA Labs Princeton NJ 08540

WEBSTER, WILLIAM PHILLIP, b Mt Airy, NC, Apr 26, 30; m 52; c 4. DENTISTRY. *Educ:* Univ NC, Chapel Hill, BS, 56, DDS, 59, MS, 68. *Prof Exp:* Instr prosthodont, 59-61, asst prof periodont & oral path, 61-65, asst prof periodont, oral path & path, 65-67, trainee, 67-68, assoc prof path, 69-71, assoc prof dent ecol, 69-73, PROF PATH & DENT ECOL, SCHS MED & DENT, UNIV NC, CHAPEL HILL, 72-; GHIEF, DIV ORAL MED, HOSP DENT SERV, NC MEM HOSP, 68- *Concurrent Pos:* Res assoc, Sch Med, Univ NC, Chapel Hill, 59-65; mem med adv bd, Nat Hemophilia Found, 62-72; mem med adv comt, Vet Admin Hosp, Fayetteville, NC & sci adv comt, World Fedn Hemophilia. *Honors & Awards:* Achievement Recognition Award, NC Heart Asn, 77. *Mem:* Am Acad Forensic Sci; Am Dent Asn; Am Soc Exp Path; NY Acad Sci; Int Soc Thrombosis & Haemostasis. *Res:* Transplantation; biology; blood coagulation; pathology; oral medicine; oral oncology; hematology. *Mailing Add:* Dept of Dent Ecol Univ of NC Sch of Dent Chapel Hill NC 27514

WECHSLER, MARTIN T, b New York, NY, July 27, 21; m 53; c 3. MATHEMATICS. *Educ:* Queen's Col, NY, BS, 42; Univ Mich, MA, 46, PhD(math), 52. *Prof Exp:* Physicist, Nat Bur Standards, 42-45; instr math, Wayne State Univ, 51-52 & Princeton Univ, 52-53; from instr to asst prof, Wash State Univ, 53-56; from inst to assoc prof, 56-70, chmn dept, 68-75, PROF MATH, WAYNE STATE UNIV, 70-, ASSOC DEAN, COL LIBERAL ARTS, 75- *Mem:* Am Math Soc. *Res:* Topology; groups of homeomorphisms. *Mailing Add:* Off of the Dean Col Liberal Arts Wayne State Univ Detroit MI 48202

WECHSLER, MONROE S(TANLEY), b New York, NY, May 1, 23; m 50; c 3. MATERIALS SCIENCE, SOLID STATE PHYSICS. *Educ:* City Col New York, BS, 44; Columbia Univ, MA, 50, PhD(physics), 53. *Prof Exp:* Elec engr, US Naval Air Magnetics Lab, 47-48; mem sci staff, Columbia Univ, 51-54; physicist, Oak Ridge Nat Lab, 54-69; prof metall, Univ Tenn, 65-69; chmn dept metall, Univ, 70-75, chief metall div, Ames Lab, US Atomic Energy Comn, 70-75, SR METALLURGIST, AMES LAB, US DEPT ENERGY, IOWA STATE UNIV, 70-, PROF, DEPT MAT SCI & ENG, UNIV, 70- *Concurrent Pos:* Ed, Nuclear Eng Mat Handbk, 77- *Mem:* Fel Am Phys Soc; Am Inst Mining, Metall & Petrol Engrs; Am Soc Metals; Am Nuclear Soc; Am Soc Eng Educ. *Res:* Irradiation effects on metals; materials for nuclear reactors; phase transformations; shape-memory alloy heat engines. *Mailing Add:* Ames Lab Iowa State Univ Ames IA 50011

WECHSLER, STEVEN LEWIS, b Bronx, NY, May 30, 48; m 74; c 1. MOLECULAR GENETICS, VIROLOGY. *Educ:* City Col New York, BS, 70; Univ NC, Chapel Hill, PhD(molecular genetics), 75. *Prof Exp:* RES FEL MEASLES VIRUS, DEPT MICROBIOL, HARVARD MED SCH, 75- *Mem:* Am Soc Microbiol. *Res:* Molecular genetics of measles virus and its relationship to persistent infections and chronic diseases such as subacute sclerosing panencephalites and multiple sclerosis. *Mailing Add:* Dept of Microbiol & Harvard Med Sch Cambridge MA 02115

WECHTER, MARGARET ANN, b Chicago, Ill, Sept 30, 35. ANALYTICAL CHEMISTRY, RADIOCHEMISTRY. *Educ:* Mundelein Col, BS, 62; Iowa State Univ, PhD(anal chem), 67. *Prof Exp:* Fel chem, Purdue Univ, 67-68, asst prof chem, Calumet Campus, 69-73; ASSOC PROF CHEM, SOUTHEASTERN MASS UNIV, 73-; mem staff, Ames Lab, Iowa State Univ, 70-80; MEM FAC, DEPT CHEM, SOUTHEASTERN MASS UNIV, 80- *Mem:* Am Chem Soc; Sigma Xi. *Res:* Development, analytical applications and electrochemistry of the tungsten bronze electrodes; activation analysis. *Mailing Add:* Dept of Chem Southeastern Mass Univ North Dartmouth MA 02747

WECHTER, WILLIAM JULIUS, b Louisville, Ky, Feb 13, 32; m 52; c 3. ORGANIC CHEMISTRY. *Educ:* Univ Ill, AB, 53, MS, 54; Univ Calif, Los Angeles, PhD, 57. *Prof Exp:* Asst chem, Univ Ill, 54; asst org chem, Univ Calif, Los Angeles, 55-56; res assoc, Dept Chem, 57-68, res head, 68-79, RES MGR HYPERSENSITIVITY DIS, UPJOHN CO, 79- *Concurrent Pos:* Vis scholar, Depts Chem & Med Microbiol, Stanford Univ, 67-68; vchmn, Gordon Conf Med Chem, 72, chmn, 73; sect ed biol, Annual Reports Med Chem, 72-74; adj prof biochem, Kalamazoo Col, 74-; vis lectr path, Harvard Med Sch, 77-78. *Mem:* AAAS; Am Asn Cancer Res; Am Chem Soc; Transplantation Soc; Am Asn Immunologists. *Res:* Synthesis, mechanisms and isotopic labeling of nucleic acid components; immuno-modulatory and anti-cancer drugs; pharmacological control of cell mediated immunity; gene therapy; transplantation. *Mailing Add:* Hypersensitivity Dis Res Upjohn Co Kalamazoo MI 49001

WECK, FRIEDRICH JOSEF, b Puettlingen, Ger, Nov 10, 18; nat US; m 56; c 2. ORGANIC CHEMISTRY, PHYSICAL CHEMISTRY. *Educ:* Univ Bonn, MS, 50; Univ Saarland, PhD(natural sci), 54. *Prof Exp:* Assistantship, Univ Saarland, 51-52; res assoc, Nat Ctr Sci Res, France, 52-55; head res & develop lab, Saar Water Asn, Ger, 55-57; from group leader new prod & processes sect, to res specialist, Am Potash & Chem Corp, 57-64; dir chem res, Garett Res & Develop Co, 64; PRES, F J WECK CO, 64- *Concurrent Pos:* Consult, Union Saarbruecken, 54-57. *Honors & Awards:* Bronze Medal, Chem Soc France, 57. *Mem:* Am Chem Soc; Ger Chem Soc; fel Am Inst Chem. *Res:* Organic-inorganic synthesis; mono-polymers; photosensitive materials; environmental safety; food and water; liquid and solid ion exchangers; saline mineral chemistry; extraction-crystallization of salts; product and process development and testing; instrumental analyses for industry and government. *Mailing Add:* F J Weck Co 14859 E Clark Ave Industry CA 91745

WECKER, LYNN, b New York, NY, Sept 27, 47. NEUROPHARMACOLOGY, CHOLINERGIC PHARMACOLOGY. *Educ:* State Univ NY, Cortland, BS, 69; Univ Fla, PhD(pharmacol), 72. *Prof Exp:* Lab technologist pharmacol, Col Med, Univ Fla, 69; fel, 73-74, instr, Sch Med, Vanderbilt Univ, 74-75; asst prof, Col Pharm, Northeastern Univ, 75-76; asst prof, Sch Med, Vanderbilt Univ, 76-78; asst prof pharmacol, 78-80, PROF PHARMACOL & PSYCHIAT, SCH MED, LA STATE UNIV, 80- *Concurrent Pos:* Prin investr biomed res support grant, Vanderbilt Univ, 77-78; co-investr, Muscular Dystrophy Asn, 76-77 & 77-78; prin investr, NIMH grant, 79-83, NIH grant, 79-82. *Honors & Awards:* Teacher-scientist Award, Andrew W Mellon Found, 75. *Mem:* NY Acad Sci; AAAS; Soc Neurosci; Am Soc Neurochem Int; Soc Neurochem. *Res:* Cholinergic mechanisms in the central and peripheral nervous systems; relationship between neurotransmitter substrate availability and central cholinergic functions; neurotrophic relationships; acetylcholine analogues. *Mailing Add:* Dept Pharm La State Univ Med Ctr 1901 Perdido St New Orleans LA 70112

WECKER, STANLEY C, b New York, NY, Apr 29, 33; m 64. VERTEBRATE ECOLOGY, APPLIED ECOLOGY. *Educ:* City Col New York, BS, 55; Univ Mich, MS, 57, PhD(zool), 62. *Prof Exp:* Asst prof biol, Hofstra Univ, 62-63; from instr to asst prof, 63-70, assoc prof, 70-82, PROF BIOL, CITY COL NEW YORK, 82-, DIR, ENERGY, ECOL, ENVIRON PROG, 76- *Concurrent Pos:* Res grants, Sigma Xi, 63 & NSF, 64-68; US Dept Health, Educ & Welfare Off Educ grant & staff ecologist, Environ Educ Proj, North Westchester-Putnam Coop Educ Serv, NY, 71-72; spec consult, NY State Educ Dept, 72; mem, Environ Defense Fund, NASA, 75-77. *Honors & Awards:* Award, Am Soc Mammal, 61. *Mem:* Fel AAAS; Am Inst Biol Sci; Ecol Soc Am; Am Soc Mammal; NY Acad Sci. *Res:* Behavioral ecology of deer mice, especially habitat orientation; application of satellite data to coastal zone management. *Mailing Add:* Dept Biol City Col New York New York NY 10031

WECKESSER, LOUIS BENJAMIN, b Baltimore, MD, Feb 22, 28; m 49; c 3. HEAT TRANSFER, MECHANICAL ENGINEERING. *Educ:* Univ MD, BS, 52, MS, 56. *Prof Exp:* SECT SUPVR THERMAL ANAL APPL PHYSICS LAB, JOHNS HOPKINS UNIV, 52- *Mem:* Am Inst Aeronaut & Astronaut. *Res:* Tactical missile thermal design; thermal insulation development; missile radome design and test. *Mailing Add:* Appl Physics Lab Johns Hopkins Rd Laurel MD 20707

WECKLER, GENE PETER, b San Francisco, Calif, July 3, 32; m 56; c 4. ELECTRICAL ENGINEERING. *Educ:* Utah State Univ, BS, 58; San Jose State Col, MS, 64; Stanford Univ, DEng, 68. *Prof Exp:* Jr engr, Convair Astronaut, 58-59; elec engr, Shockley Transistor Corp, 59-62; develop engr, Opto-Electronic Devices, Inc, 62-63; mem tech staff, Fairchild Semiconductor Div, 63-71; DIR ENG, RETICON CORP, 71- *Mem:* Inst Elec & Electronics Engrs. *Res:* Development of silicon p-n junction photodetectors, especially integrated arrays for image sensing; development and application of solid state devices. *Mailing Add:* EG&G-Reticon 345 Potrero Ave Sunnyvale CA 94086

WECKOWICZ, THADDEUS EUGENE, b Iskorst, USSR, Oct 10, 18; Can citizen; m 66. PSYCHIATRY. *Educ:* Univ Edinburgh, MB & ChB, 45; Univ Leeds, DPM, 52; Univ Sask, PhD(psychol), 62. *Prof Exp:* Registr psychiat, Univ Leeds, 53-54, sr registr, Bolton Group Hosps, Eng, 54-55; sr resident, Hosp, Univ Sask, 55-56; res psychiatrist, Weyburn Ment Hosp, Sask, 56-59; res assoc psychiat & sessional lectr psychol, 62, from asst prof to assoc prof, 62-74, PROF PSYCHIAT & PSYCHOL, UNIV ALTA, 74- MEM STAFF, CTR ADVAN STUDY THEORET PSYCHOL, 66- *Concurrent Pos:* Fel, Hosp, Univ Sask, 55-56. *Mem:* Can Psychiat Asn. *Res:* Psychological and biological aspects of schizophrenia; psychotropic drug research, particularly hallucinogenic drugs; psychopharmacology; multivariate study of depression; studies of learned helplessness retardation in depression. *Mailing Add:* Dept of Psychol & Psychiat Univ of Alta Edmonton AB T6G 0B8 Can

WECKSUNG, GEORGE WILLIAM, b Muscatine, Iowa, Oct 31, 31; m 61; c 3. COMPUTER IMAGE PROCESSING, APPLIED MATHEMATICS. *Educ:* Univ Iowa, BA, 58; Calif State Univ, Long Beach, MA, 63. *Prof Exp:* Comput engr inertial navig, Autonetics, 61-64; sci specialist digital signal processing EG&G, Inc, Las Vegas, 64-69; res engr inertial navig, Teledyne Systs Co, 69-70; sci specialist comput image processing EG&G, Inc, Los Alamos, 70-74; STAFF MEM, COMPUT IMAGE PROCESSING, LOS ALAMOS NAT LAB, 74- *Mem:* Soc Photo-optical Instrumentation Engrs. *Res:* Remote sensing; computer image processing; stereo imagery and photogrammetry; digital holography; computed tomography. *Mailing Add:* Los Alamos Nat Lab PO Box 1663 Los Alamos NM 87545

WECKWERTH, VERNON ERVIN, b Herman, Minn, Apr 29, 31; m 55; c 5. BIOSTATISTICS, HOSPITAL ADMINISTRATION. *Educ:* Univ Minn, BS, 54, MS, 56, PhD(biostatist), 63. *Prof Exp:* Teaching asst biostatist, Univ Minn, 54-56, instr, 56-58; head res & statist, Am Hosp Asn, 58-60; from lectr to assoc prof, 60-68, PROF HOSP & HEALTH CARE ADMIN, COORDR CONTINUING HOSP EDUC & PROF FAMILY PRACT, MED SCH, UNIV MINN, MINNEAPOLIS, 68- *Concurrent Pos:* Assoc dir, Hosp Res & Educ Trust, 58-60; mem adv comt to Nat Ctr for Health Servs Res & Develop, 69- *Mem:* Am Statist Asn; Biomet Soc; Am Hosp Asn; Am Pub Health Asn. *Res:* Continuing education of health care workers including professionals; health care delivery systems research; teaching research and statistics in health care. *Mailing Add:* 1260 Mayo Bldg Univ of Minn Minneapolis MN 55455

WEDBERG, HALE LEVERING, b Redlands, Calif, Feb 10, 33; m 59; c 2. PLANT TAXONOMY, EVOLUTION. *Educ:* Calif State Col Los Angeles, BA, 56; Univ Calif, Los Angeles, PhD(plant sci), 62. *Prof Exp:* Instr zool, 59-60, from asst prof to assoc prof bot, 60-67, PROF BOT, SAN DIEGO STATE UNIV, 67- *Mem:* AAAS; Soc Study Evolution. *Res:* Chromosomal variation in natural populations of Clarkia Williamsonii. *Mailing Add:* Dept of Bot San Diego State Univ San Diego CA 92182

WEDBERG, STANLEY EDWARD, b Bridgeport, Conn, Aug 28, 13; m 41; c 2. MICROBIOLOGY. *Educ:* Univ Conn, BS, 37; Yale Univ, PhD(bact), 40. *Prof Exp:* Instr immunol, Sch Med, Yale Univ, 40-41; from instr to assoc prof bact, 41-59, head dept, 55-66, prof, 59-69, fac coordr educ TV, 67-69, prof biol, 68-69, EMER PROF BIOL, UNIV CONN, 69- *Concurrent Pos:* Consult bacteriologist, Windham Community Mem Hosp, Conn, 46-57; biologist, Southwestern Col, Calif, 69-80; lectr, San Diego Paramedic Prog, 79- & San Diego Health Dept. *Mem:* AAAS; Sigma Xi; Am Soc Microbiol; Am Acad Microbiol. *Res:* Microbial thermogenesis; bacterial capsule staining; antihistamines on antibody production of rabbits; germicidal gases. *Mailing Add:* 3361 Ullman St Point Loma San Diego CA 92106

WEDDELL, DAVID S(TOVER), b Philadelphia, Pa, Mar 8, 17; m 43; c 4. CHEMICAL ENGINEERING. *Educ:* Pa State Col, BS, 38; Mass Inst Technol, ScD(chem eng), 41. *Prof Exp:* Chem engr, Ala, 41-44, 45-47, develop dir, Wash, 49-50, develop dept, Mo, 50-52, asst dir, 53-54, European tech rep, 54-60, asst dir develop, Overseas Div, 60-62, dir, 63-64, DIR PROJ EVAL, INT DIV, MONSANTO CO, 65- *Concurrent Pos:* Mem Nat Defense Res Comt, Ohio, 44-45, Mo, 47-48. *Mem:* Am Chem Soc; Am Inst Chem Engrs. *Res:* Turbulent mixing in flames and its reproduction in liquid models; process design; application of phosphate chemicals; commercial chemical development; investment analysis and planning; international operations. *Mailing Add:* Monsanto Co 800 N Lindbergh Blvd St Louis MO 63166

WEDDELL, GEORGE G(RAY), b Baltimore, Md, Jan 30, 23; m 56. CHEMICAL ENGINEERING. *Educ:* Pa State Univ, BS, 44. *Prof Exp:* Asst, SAM Labs, Columbia Univ, 44-45; asst, Carbide & Carbon Chem Co, NY, 45-46, chem engr, Tenn, 46-47; fel, Mellon Inst, 47-52; vpres, Geotic Industs, Inc, 52-53, pres, 54-55; asst mgr, O Hommel Co, 55-56; fel engr, 56-66, supvr, 66-71, MGR, BETTIS ATOMIC POWER LAB, WESTINGHOUSE ELEC CORP, 71- *Mem:* Am Chem Soc; Am Nuclear Soc. *Res:* Utilization of fine particles; manufacture and application of perlite; radioactive waste disposal; thermal and hydraulic nuclear engineering; nuclear fuel cycle. *Mailing Add:* Bettis Atomic Power Lab PO Box 79 West Mifflin PA 15122

WEDDELL, JAMES BLOUNT, b Evanston, Ill, Apr 29, 27. SPACE PHYSICS. *Educ:* Drew Univ, AB, 49; Northwestern Univ, MS, 51, PhD(physics), 53. *Prof Exp:* Asst physics, Northwestern Univ, 49-53; res engr, Westinghouse Elec Corp, 53-57; sr scientist, Martin-Marietta Co, 57-62; supvr, 62-80, MGR, ROCKWELL INT CORP, 80- *Mem:* Am Phys Soc; assoc fel Am Inst Aeronaut & Astronaut; Sigma Xi. *Res:* Space shutle payload of cargo integration; solar physics; magnetosphere; nuclear reactions; radiation shielding; solar-electric propulsion systems. *Mailing Add:* 936 S Peregrine Pl Anaheim CA 92806

WEDDING, BRENT (M), b Walnut, Ill, May 3, 36; m 69; c 2. EXPERIMENTAL PHYSICS. *Educ:* Hamilton Col, AB, 58; Univ Ill, Urbana, MS, 61, PhD(physics), 67. *Prof Exp:* Lectr physics, Southern Ill Univ, Carbondale, 62-63; res supvr, 75-76, SR PHYSICIST, CORNING GLASS WORKS, 67-, DEVELOP ASSOC PHYSICS, 76-, MGR PHYS PROPERTIES RES, 79- *Mem:* Am Phys Soc; Optical Soc Am; Am Ceramic Soc. *Res:* Optical glass development. *Mailing Add:* Tech Staffs Div Corning Glass Works Corning NY 14830

WEDDING, RANDOLPH TOWNSEND, b St Petersburg, Fla, Nov 6, 21; m 43; c 2. BIOCHEMISTRY. *Educ:* Univ Fla, BSA, 43, MS, 47; Cornell Univ, PhD(plant physiol), 50. *Prof Exp:* Tech asst, Agr Exp Sta, Univ Fla, 41-43, 46-47; teaching asst bot, Cornell Univ, 47-49, instr plant physiol, 49-50; jr plant physiologist, 50-52, asst plant physiologist, 52-58, assoc plant physiologist & lectr, 58-61, assoc prof biochem & assoc biochemist, 61-63, chmn dept, 66-75, PROF BIOCHEM & BIOCHEMIST, UNIV CALIF, RIVERSIDE, 63- *Concurrent Pos:* Agr Res Coun fel, Oxford Univ, 59-60, Orgn Econ Coop & Develop sr sci fel, 64; sr sci fel, Natural Environ Res Coun, 71-72. *Mem:* Am Soc Plant Physiol; Am Soc Biol Chem; Brit Soc Exp Biol; Brit Biochem Soc; Scand Soc Plant Physiol. *Res:* Metabolic control; mechanisms of enzyme action and control. *Mailing Add:* Dept Biochem Univ Calif Riverside CA 92521

WEDDLETON, RICHARD FRANCIS, b Boston, Mass, Oct 10, 39; m 62; c 3. POLYMER CHEMISTRY. *Educ:* Mass Inst Technol, BS, 61; Ind Univ, Bloomington, MS, 63, PhD(org chem), 65. *Prof Exp:* Chemist, Mat & Processes Lab, Gen Elec Co, 65-73; mgr insulation eng, Nat Elec Coil Div, McGraw-Edison Co, 73-77; sr engr, 77-80, ASST TO GEN MGR, WESTINGHOUSE ELEC CORP, 80- *Mem:* Am Chem Soc; Inst Elec & Electronics Eng. *Res:* Project management, development and testing of insulation system for use in electrical rotating machinery. *Mailing Add:* Westinghouse Elec Corp G 305 Stgd PO Box 9175 Lester Br Philadelphia PA 19113

WEDEGAERTNER, DONALD K, b Kingsburg, Calif, Sept 9, 36; m 58; c 2. ORGANIC CHEMISTRY. *Educ:* Univ Calif, Berkeley, BS, 58; Univ Ill, Urbana, PhD(org chem), 62. *Prof Exp:* Res asst org chem, Iowa State Univ, 62-63; from asst prof to assoc prof, 63-71, chmn dept chem, 74-80, PROF ORG CHEM, UNIV PAC, 71- *Concurrent Pos:* Res asst org chem, Univ Rochester, 69-70, vis prof, 78-79. *Mem:* Am Chem Soc; Royal Soc Chem. *Res:* Reaction mechanisms; chemistry of allenes. *Mailing Add:* Dept of Chem Univ of the Pac Stockton CA 95211

WEDEKIND, GILBERT LEROY, b Zion, Ill, Feb 28, 33; m 53; c 2. MECHANICAL ENGINEERING. *Educ:* Univ Ill, BS, 59, MS, 61, PhD(mech eng), 65. *Prof Exp:* Res assoc mech eng, Univ Ill, 65-66; from asst prof to assoc prof, 66-77, PROF ENG, OAKLAND UNIV, 77- *Concurrent Pos:* NSF eng res grants, 67-69, 72-74 & 80-82; consult, Propulsion Systs Lab, US Army Tank-Automotive Command, 67-70, Climate Control Opers, Ford Motor Co, 71-73 & Mfg Develop, Gen Motors Tech Ctr, 73- *Mem:* Am Soc Mech Engrs; Am Soc Eng Educ; AAUP; Sigma Xi. *Res:* Thermal modeling of spacecraft; experimental and theoretical study of transient two-phase evaporating and condensing flow phenomena; modeling components; processes and systems which utilize fluid and thermal phenomena for their operation. *Mailing Add:* Dept Eng Oakland Univ Rochester MI 48063

WEDEL, ARNOLD MARION, b Lawrence, Kans, Jan 31, 28; m 54; c 3. MATHEMATICS. *Educ:* Bethel Col, Kans, AB, 47; Univ Kans, MA, 48; Iowa State Col, PhD(math), 51. *Prof Exp:* PROF MATH, BETHEL COL, KANS, 51- *Mem:* Math Asn Am; Am Math Soc. *Res:* Hypergeometric series and volterra transforms. *Mailing Add:* Dept of Math Bethel Col North Newton KS 67117

WEDEL, RICHARD GLENN, electrochemistry, see previous edition

WEDEMEYER, GARY ALVIN, b Fromberg, Mont, Oct 15, 35; m 57; c 2. FISHERIES, BIOCHEMISTRY. *Educ:* Univ Wash, BS, 57, MS, 63, PhD(fisheries), 65. *Prof Exp:* BIOCHEMIST, FISH PHYSIOL, NAT FISHERIES RES CTR, US DEPT INTERIOR, 65- *Concurrent Pos:* Affil prof, Col Fisheries, Univ Wash, 65- *Mem:* Am Inst Fishery Res Biol; Am Fisheries Soc. *Res:* Biochemistry and physiology of fishes; pollution, disease, aquaculture; tolerance of fish and fish populations to environmental stress. *Mailing Add:* Nat Fisheries Res Ctr Dept Interior Bldg 204 Sand Point Naval Air Sta Seattle WA 98115

WEDGWOOD, RALPH JOSIAH PATRICK, b Eng, May 25, 24; nat US; m 43; c 3. PEDIATRICS, RHEUMATOLOGY. *Educ:* Harvard Med Sch, MD, 47; Am Bd Pediat, dipl, 55. *Prof Exp:* Res fel pediat, Harvard Med Sch, 49-51; sr instr pediat & biochem, Western Reserve Univ, 53-57, asst prof pediat & prev med, Sch Med, 57-62; assoc prof, 62-63, chmn dept, 62-72, PROF PEDIAT, SCH MED, UNIV WASH, 63- *Concurrent Pos:* Spec consult & mem gen clin res ctr comt, NIH, 62-66, mem nat adv res resources coun, 66-70; mem sci adv comn, Nat Found, 69-; mem sci adv bd, St Jude's Children's Res Hosp, Memphis, 70-76. *Mem:* Am Asn Immunologists; Am Rheumatism Asn; Heberden Soc; Am Pediat Soc; Infectious Dis Soc Am. *Res:* Immunobiology; natural resistance factors; infectious and rheumatic diseases in children; general pediatrics. *Mailing Add:* Dept of Pediat RD-20 Univ of Wash Sch of Med Seattle WA 98195

WEDIN, WALTER F, b Frederic, Wis, Nov 28, 25; m 55; c 2. AGRONOMY. *Educ:* Univ Wis, BS, 50, MS, 51, PhD(agron, soils), 53. *Prof Exp:* Wis Alumni Res Found assistantship agron, Univ Wis, 50-53, proj assoc hort, 53, asst prof, 53-57; res agronomist, Forage & Range Res Br, Crops Res Div, Agr Res Serv, USDA, Minn, 57-61; assoc prof, 61-64, dir, World Food Inst, 73-77, PROF AGRON, IOWA STATE UNIV, 64- *Concurrent Pos:* Asst prof, Inst Agr, Univ Minn, 59-61; consult, US Agency Int Develop-Iowa State Univ, Uruguay, 64; consult, Coop States Res Serv, USDA, 64, 70, 72 & 74, prin agronomist, 68. *Honors & Awards:* Merit Cert, Am Forage & Grassland Coun, 72. *Mem:* AAAS; fel Am Soc Agron; Crop Sci Soc Am; Am Soc Animal Sci. *Res:* Evaluation of forage crops, especially utilization as pasture, hay or silage; techniques involved in measurement of forage nutritive value; animal intake and digestibility; grassland development, international. *Mailing Add:* Dept of Agron Iowa State Univ Ames IA 50011

WEDLER, FREDERICK CHARLES OLIVER, b Philadelphia, Pa, June 10, 41; m 67; c 2. BIOCHEMISTRY. *Educ:* Univ NC, Chapel Hill, BS, 63; Northwestern Univ, Evanston, PhD(biochem), 68. *Prof Exp:* Molecular Biol Inst fel biochem, Univ Calif, Los Angeles, 68-70; from asst prof to assoc prof chem & biochem, Rensselaer Polytech Inst, 70-78; res chemist, NIH, 77-78; ASSOC PROF BIOCHEM & BIOPHYS, PA STATE UNIV, UNIVERSITY PARK, 79- *Concurrent Pos:* Petrol Res Fund grant, Rensselaer Polytech Inst, 71-, NSF res grant, 72-74, 75-76, 76-78 & 78-81; NASA res grant, 74-79; NIH res grants, 78-79 & 79-82; fac res award, Am Cancer Soc, 80-84. *Mem:* AAAS; Am Chem Soc; Am Soc Biol Chemists. *Res:* Enzymology; kinetics and mechanisms of action of key regulatory enzymes; development of new probe systems for protein structures; thermophilic proteins. *Mailing Add:* Dept of Biochem & Biophys Pa State Univ University Park PA 16802

WEDLICK, HAROLD LEE, b Detroit, Mich, Feb 26, 36; m 59; c 2. HEALTH PHYSICS, ENVIRONMENTAL HEALTH. *Educ:* Wayne State Univ, BS, 61, MS, 63; Am Bd Health Physics, cert, 74. *Prof Exp:* Chemist, City of Detroit Health Dept, Mich, 61-63; res assoc environ health, Univ Mich, 64-66; assoc prof radiol sci, Lowell Technol Inst, 66-75; res assoc, Occupational & Environ Safety Dept, Northwest Labs, Battell Mem Inst, 75-80; OWNER & DIR, WEDLICK'S EDUC DEVELOP SYSTS SAFETY, 80- *Mem:* Health Physics Soc; Conf Radiol Health; Am Nuclear Soc. *Res:* Transfer mechanisms and measurements of radionuclides in the environment. *Mailing Add:* 411 26th Pl Kennewick WA 99336

WEDLOCK, BRUCE D(ANIELS), b Providence, RI, Mar 20, 34; m 58; c 2. ELECTRICAL ENGINEERING, SOLID STATE PHYSICS. *Educ:* Mass Inst Technol, SB & SM, 58, ScD(elec eng), 62. *Prof Exp:* From instr to assoc prof elec eng, Mass Inst Technol, 60-71; staff scientist, Block Eng, Inc, Mass, 71-72; DIR LOWELL INST SCH, 73- *Concurrent Pos:* Ford Found fel, 62-64. *Mem:* Inst Elec & Electronics Engrs; Am Soc Eng Educ. *Res:* Physical electronics of solid state devices; development of two-year technical school curricula in emerging technologies. *Mailing Add:* Mass Inst Technol Rm E19-734 Cambridge MA 02139

WEDMAN, ELWOOD EDWARD, b Harper, Kans, Aug 22, 22; m 46; c 3. VETERINARY MICROBIOLOGY. *Educ:* Kans State Univ, DVM, 46; Univ Minn, MPH, 57, PhD(microbiol), 64. *Prof Exp:* Pvt pract, 45-47, 49-50; vet in charge Mex-US Campaign Eradication Foot & Mouth Dis, Mex, 47-49; vet in charge Wichita Union Stockyards, Animal Dis Eradication Div, Agr Res Serv, USDA, DC, 52-54, staff vet, Lab Serv, 58-61, res assoc, Univ Minn & USDA, 54-58, chief vet diag serv, Animal Dis Labs, USDA, Iowa, 61-64; assoc dir vet med res inst, Col Vet Med, Iowa State Univ, 64-72; DEAN, SCH VET MED, ORE STATE UNIV, 72- *Concurrent Pos:* Consult, USDA, 63-64, 65-66 & 67 & Pan-Am Health Orgn, 65, 67; mem, Nat Conf Vet Lab Diagnosticians. *Honors & Awards:* Cert Merit, USDA, 61, 63 & 66. *Mem:* Am Vet Med Asn; US Animal Health Asn; Am Col Vet Microbiol; Conf Res Workers Animal Dis. *Res:* Microbiology and epidemiology of animal diseases. *Mailing Add:* Sch of Vet Med Ore State Univ Corvallis OR 97331

WEDMID, GEORGE YURI, b Stockach, Ger, Feb 18, 48; US citizen; m 74. BIOLOGICAL CHEMISTRY. *Educ:* Rutgers Univ, BS, 69, PhD(biochem), 75. *Prof Exp:* Res asst lipid chem, Rutgers Univ; res assoc, Hormel Inst, Univ Minn, Austin, 74-81; SECT LEADER, NATURAL PROD RES, FRITZSCHE, DODGE & OLCOTT, 81- *Mem:* Am Oil Chemists Soc; Am Chem Soc. *Res:* Nuclear magnetic resonance and biochemical studies of lipid components in natural and model membranes; isolation and structure-function studies of natural products. *Mailing Add:* Box 511A Jerrys Lane Howell NJ 07731

WEDRAL, ELAINE, b Detroit, Mich, Feb 29, 44. FOOD CHEMISTRY, RESEARCH ADMINISTRATION. *Educ:* Purdue Univ, BS, 66; Cornell Univ, MS, 68; Purdue Univ, PhD(food microbiol), 70. *Prof Exp:* Technologist qual control, Morton House, 64-66; chemist, Campbell Soup Co, 66-70; group leader prod develop, Western Farmers Asn, 70-71; coordr nutrit & prod develop, Libby, McNeill & Libby, 71-73, assoc dir res & develop, 73-76, dir, 76-78, vpres res & develop, 78-81; PRES & DIR, WESTRECO, INC, 81- *Concurrent Pos:* Tech adv, OTA-Senate Select Subcomt on Grade Labeling, 76-77; sci res comt, Am Meat Inst, 76-77 & Am Meat Canners Asn, 77-; tech rep, Grocery Mfg Am, 75-77; nutrit labeling comt, Giant Foods Labeling Comt, 76-77; open date labeling comt, 76-78, Wash Lab Comt, 76-78, sci adv comt, Nat Food Processors Asn, 77-78; sci adv comt, Am Meat Inst, 77-78. *Honors & Awards:* Poultry Egg Nat Bd Res Award, Poultry Sci Asn, 69. *Mem:* Inst Food Technologists; Am Mgt Asn. *Res:* Development of new food products; packaging; new or improved food processing technologies. *Mailing Add:* Westreco Inc Boardman Rd New Milford CT 06776

WEE, ELIZABETH LIU, biophysical chemistry, polymer chemistry, see previous edition

WEE, WILLIAM GO, b Iloilo City, Philippines, Sept 9, 37; m 67; c 1. ELECTRICAL ENGINEERING. *Educ:* Mapua Inst Technol, BSEE, 62; Purdue Univ, Lafayette, MS, 65, PhD(elec eng), 67. *Prof Exp:* Prin res engr, Honeywell Systs & Res Ctr, 67-71; assoc prof, 71-80, PROF ELEC & COMPUT ENG, UNIV CINCINNATI, 80- *Mem:* Inst Elec & Electronics Engrs. *Res:* Theory and application of pattern recognition; adaptive and learning systems; automata theory; picture processing; linguistic approach to picture analysis and related areas in computer science. *Mailing Add:* 5721 Sprucewood Dr Cincinnati OH 45241

WEED, ELAINE GREENING AMES, b Detroit, Mich, Mar 15, 32; m 53; c 3. GEOLOGY. *Educ:* Mt Holyoke Col, BA, 53. *Prof Exp:* GEOLOGIST, US GEOL SURV, 57- *Mem:* Geol Soc Am; Am Asn Petrol Geologists; AAAS. *Res:* Geology and resources of United States Atlantic Margin; subsurface geology of southeastern Massachusetts; impacts of resource development. *Mailing Add:* 7121 Thrasher Rd McLean VA 22101

WEED, GRANT B(ARG), b Salt Lake City, Utah, Aug 19, 35; m 64; c 4. CERAMICS ENGINEERING, METALLURGY. *Educ:* Univ Utah, BS, 61, PhD(ceramic eng), 67. *Prof Exp:* Source engr, Hercules Powder Co, Utah, 60-61; res chemist, Exp Sta, E I du Pont de Nemours & Co, 66-72; res engr, Cent Res Labs, NL Industs, 72-73, supvr mat equip develop, Tech Dept, Magnesium Div, 73-80; WITH MAGNESIUM DIV, AMAX SPECIALITY METALS CORP, 80- *Mem:* Am Ceramic Soc; Nat Inst Ceramic Engrs. *Res:* High temperature ceramics and ceramic-metal composites; refractories for molten salt containment. *Mailing Add:* Magnesium Div Amax Speciality Metals Corp 238 N 2200 West Salt Lake City UT 84116

WEED, HERMAN ROSCOE, b Union City, Pa, Aug 5, 22; m 46; c 3. ELECTRICAL ENGINEERING, BIOMEDICAL ENGINEERING. *Educ:* Pa State Col, BS, 45; Ohio State Univ, MS, 48. *Prof Exp:* Instr elec eng, Pa State Col, 43-46; from instr to assoc prof, 46-59, PROF ELEC ENG, OHIO STATE UNIV, 59-, DIR, BIOMED ENG CTR, 71-, PROF PREVENTIVE MED, 78- *Concurrent Pos:* Mem staff, Westinghouse Elec Corp, 49; mem staff, Res Found, Ohio State Univ, 48-50, mem staff, Exp Sta, 52-53, consult, 51-; mem staff & consult, Robbins & Myers Co, 53-78; US deleg, Am Control Coun, Int Fedn Automatic Control Cong, Russia, 60, London, 66, chmn systs comt, Am Automatic Control Coun; consult, Solid-State Controls, Inc, 61-65 & Am Inst Biol Sci, 77-80; vis prof, Univ Cairo Egypt, Univ Karlsruhe, WGer, 79. *Honors & Awards:* Top Ten Eng Accomplishments in US, Nat Soc Prof Engrs, 70. *Mem:* Inst Elec & Electronics Engrs; Am Soc Eng Educ; Asn Advan Med Instrumentation. *Res:* Automatic control; bioelectrical instrumentation; electronics; systems; non-invasive diagnosis; ultrasound; physiological systems; biomedical-clinical engineering education. *Mailing Add:* Bio-Med Eng Ctr Ohio State Univ 2015 Neil Ave Columbus OH 43210

WEED, HOMER CLYDE, b Sun City, Kans, Mar 30, 20; m 58. PHYSICAL CHEMISTRY. *Educ:* Univ Ariz, BS, 42; Ohio State Univ, MS, 48, PhD(chem), 57. *Prof Exp:* Assoc develop chemist, Tenn Eastman Corp, 42-46; asst chem, Ohio State Univ, 46-47, 48, 49, res found, 47-48, 49, 53-57, metall, 50-53; chemist, Inorg Mat Div, 57-76, CHEMIST EARTH SCI DIV, LAWRENCE LIVERMORE NAT LAB, UNIV CALIF, 76- *Mem:* AAAS; Am Chem Soc; Am Geophys Union. *Res:* High temperature chemistry; electrical properties and high pressure mechanical properties of rock; radionuclide transport in earth materials by water; oxygen-18 diffusion in silicates. *Mailing Add:* Earth Sci Div Box 808 Univ Calif Lawrence Livermore Nat Lab Livermore CA 94550

WEED, JOHN CONANT, b Lake Charles, La, July 7, 12; m 39; c 4. OBSTETRICS & GYNECOLOGY. *Educ:* Tulane Univ, BS, 33, MD, 36, MS, 40; Am Bd Obstet & Gynec, dipl, 46. *Prof Exp:* Instr anat, 39-41, assoc clin prof, 53-60, CLIN PROF OBSTET & GYNEC, SCH MED, TULANE UNIV, 60- *Concurrent Pos:* Mem staff, Ochsner Clin, 45-; chmn dept obstet & gynec, Ochsner Found Hosp, 63-73; bd trustees, Alton Ochsner Med Found. *Mem:* AMA; Am Fertil Soc (pres, 73-74); Am Col Obstet & Gynec; Am Col Surgeons; Sigma Xi. *Res:* Infertility. *Mailing Add:* 1514 Jefferson Hwy New Orleans LA 70121

WEED, LAWRENCE LEONARD, b Troy, NY, Dec 26, 23; m 52; c 5. COMPUTER SCIENCE, MEDICINE. *Educ:* Hamilton Col, BA, 45, Col Physicians & Surgeons, MD, 47. *Prof Exp:* Asst prof med & pharmacol, Sch Med, Yale Univ, 54-56; dir, Med Educ, Eastern Maine Gen Hosp, Bangor, 56-60; asst prof microbiol, Case Western Reserve Univ, 61-64, assoc prof, 64-69; PROF COMMUN MED, COL MED, UNIV VT, 69- *Concurrent Pos:* Prof med & dir, Outpatient Clin, Cleveland Metrop Gen Hosp, 64-69; dir, Promis Lab, 69-81, chief scientist, Promis Info Systs, Inc, 81-82. *Mem:* Am Col Physicians; Am Soc Microbiol. *Res:* Problem oriented medical information system. *Mailing Add:* RFD 1 Box 630 Cambridge VT 05444

WEED, STERLING BARG, b Salt Lake City, Utah, Mar 25, 26; m 49; c 2. SOIL CHEMISTRY. *Educ:* Brigham Young Univ, AB, 51; NC State Col, MS, 53, PhD(soils), 55. *Prof Exp:* Asst prof soils, Cornell Univ, 55-56; from asst prof to assoc prof, 56-70, PROF SOILS, N C STATE UNIV, 70- *Mem:* Soil Sci Soc Am; Clay Minerals Soc; Int Soc Soil Sci; Int Clay Minerals Soc. *Res:* Clay mineralogy; clay-organic interactions. *Mailing Add:* Dept of Soil Sci NC State Univ Raleigh NC 27607

WEEDEN, ROBERT BARTON, b Fall River, Mass, Jan 8, 33; m 59. ZOOLOGY. *Educ:* Univ Mass, BSc, 53; Univ Maine, MSc, 55; Univ BC, PhD(zool), 59. *Prof Exp:* Asst, Univ Maine, 53-55; asst, Univ BC, 55-58; instr zool, Wash State Univ, 58-59; RES BIOLOGIST, ALASKA DEPT FISH & GAME, 59-, PROF WILDLIFE MGT, UNIV ALASKA, 68- *Mem:* Arctic Inst NAm; Cooper Ornith Soc; Wildlife Soc; Am Ornith Union. *Res:* Avian ecology, particularly of Tetraonidae and alpine-arctic environments; resource policy and land use. *Mailing Add:* Box 80425 College AK 99708

WEEDON, ALAN CHARLES, b Oxford, Eng, Mar 29, 51. ORGANIC CHEMISTRY. *Educ:* London Univ, BSc, 73, PhD(chem) & DIC 76; ARCS, 73. *Prof Exp:* Res assoc, 77-80, ASST PROF CHEM, UNIV WESTERN ONT, 80- *Concurrent Pos:* Mem, Photochem Unit, Univ Western Ont, 80-, actg dir, 82. *Mem:* Can Inst Chem; Royal Soc Chem; Am Chem Soc. *Res:* Organic photochemistry and synthetic organic chemistry; applications of photochemistry to organic synthesis; mechanistic photochemistry; light induced-electron transfer. *Mailing Add:* Chem Dept Univ Western Ont London ON N6A 5B7 Can

WEEDON, GENE CLYDE, b Washington, DC, June 11, 36; m 61; c 3. POLYMER CHEMISTRY. *Educ:* Va Polytech Inst & State Univ, BS, 59. *Prof Exp:* Res chemist, Esso Res & Eng Co, 60-66; res chemist, 66-71, RES MGR, FIBERS & PLASTICS CO, ALLIED CORP, 71- *Mem:* Am Chem Soc; Res Soc Am; Soc Plastics Engrs; Sigma Xi. *Res:* Development of modified polymers and processes for applications in films, fibers, and moldings area. *Mailing Add:* Fibers & Plastics Co Tech Ctr PO Box 31 Petersburg VA 23804

WEEGE, RANDALL JAMES, b May 14, 26; US citizen; m 51; c 3. GEOLOGY. *Educ:* Univ Wis-Madison, BS, 51, MS, 55. *Prof Exp:* Geologist, Anaconda Co, 55-56; geologist-engr, Uranium Div, Calumet & Hecla, Inc, 56-60, resident geologist, Calumet Div, 60-61, asst chief geologist, 61-65, dir geol, 65-68; dir geol, 68-74, dir explor, 74, dir mineral develop, Mineral Sci Div, 74-81, DIR MINERAL EXP, UNIVERSAL OIL PROD CO, 82- *Concurrent Pos:* Mineral consult, Parsons-Jurden Corp, 66- *Mem:* Soc Econ Geologists; Am Inst Mining, Metall & Petrol Eng; fel Geol Soc Am; Soc Geol Appl Mineral Deposits. *Res:* Mineral exploration techniques and methods. *Mailing Add:* Universal Oil Prod Inc 40 Universal Oil Prod Plaza Des Plaines IL 60016

WEEKES, TREVOR CECIL, b Dublin, Ireland, May 21, 40; m 64; c 3. ASTROPHYSICS. *Educ:* Nat Univ Dublin, BSc, 62, PhD(physics), 66; Nat Univ Ireland, DSc, 78. *Prof Exp:* Lectr III physics, Univ Col, Dublin, 64-66; fel astrophys, 66-67, resident dir, Mt Hopkins Observ, 69-76, ASTROPHYSICIST, SMITHSONIAN INST, 67- *Concurrent Pos:* Consult, Atomic Energy Res Estab, Harwell, 64-66; vis prof, Dublin Inst Advan Studies, 71 & Univ Ariz, 72 & 74; res assoc, Harvard Col Observ, 67- & Steward Observ, Univ Ariz, 76-; vis prof, Royal Greenwich Observ, 80. *Mem:* AAAS; Am Astron Soc; Royal Astron Soc. *Res:* Gamma ray astronomy; cosmic ray physics; meteor detection; atmospheric Cerenkov and fluorescence radiation; transient astronomy; extragalactic astronomy. *Mailing Add:* Mt Hopkins Observ Box 97 Amado AZ 85640

WEEKMAN, GERALD THOMAS, b Jamestown, NY, Apr 2, 31; m 54; c 2. ENTOMOLOGY. *Educ:* Gustavus Adolphus Col, BS, 53; Iowa State Univ, MS, 56, PhD(entom), 57. *Prof Exp:* From asst to assoc prof entom, Univ Nebr, 57-66; exten assoc prof, 66-71, EXTEN PROF ENTOM, N C STATE UNIV, 71- *Concurrent Pos:* Expert, Opers Div, Off Pesticide Progs, US Environ Protection Agency, 74-75. *Mem:* Entom Soc Am. *Res:* Economic entomology. *Mailing Add:* Entom Ext 2309 Gardner Hall NC State Univ Raleigh NC 27607

WEEKMAN, VERN W(ILLIAM), JR, b Jamestown, NY, June 28, 31; m 55; c 2. CHEMICAL ENGINEERING. *Educ:* Purdue Univ, BS, 53, PhD(chem eng), 63; Univ Mich, MS, 54. *Prof Exp:* Chem engr, Mobil Oil Corp, 54-55, res chem engr, Res Dept, 57-60, fel, 60-63, sr res chem engr, 63-65, eng assoc, 66-67, mgr, Systs Res, 67-76, mgr, Spec Proc, 76-77, mgr, Catalyst Res, 77-79, mgr, Proc Res & Develop, 79-80; PRES, MOBIL TYCO SOLAR ENERGY CORP, 80- *Concurrent Pos:* Ed, Indust & Eng Chem Ann Rev, Am Chem Soc, 71-75. *Mem:* Am Inst Chem Engrs; Am Chem Soc; Sigma Xi. *Res:* Chemical reaction kinetics; diffusion and heat transfer in catalysis; process dynamics and control; solar photovoltaics. *Mailing Add:* Mobil Tyco Solar Energy Corp 16 Hickory Dr Waltham MA 02254

WEEKS, CHARLES MERRITT, b Buffalo, NY, Mar 23, 44. BIOPHYSICS. *Educ:* Cornell Univ, BS, 66; State Univ NY Buffalo, PhD(biophys), 70. *Prof Exp:* ASST RES SCIENTIST, X-RAY CRYSTALLOG, MED FOUND BUFFALO, 70- *Mem:* Am Crystallog Asn. *Res:* Direct methods of phase determination in x-ray crystallography; crystal structures of steroids and related biological materials; protein crystallography. *Mailing Add:* Med Found of Buffalo 73 High St Buffalo NY 14203

WEEKS, CONNIE JEAN, mathematics, see previous edition

WEEKS, DAVID LEE, b Boone, Iowa, June 24, 30; m 57; c 4. EXPERIMENTAL STATISTICS. *Educ:* Okla State Univ, BS, 52, MS, 57, PhD(statist), 59. *Prof Exp:* Asst math, 54-57, from asst to assoc prof statist, 57-66, PROF STATIST, OKLA STATE UNIV, 66- *Concurrent Pos:* Consult, Air Force Armament Lab, 69-73 & 78-81 & Phillips Petrol Co, 61-81; NSF fac fel, Cornell Univ, 67-68; statist consult, RCA, Albuquerque, 73; vis prof NMex State Univ, 76-77. *Mem:* Am Statist Asn; Biomet Soc; Sigma Xi. *Res:* Experimental design; linear models; optimization techniques; design and analysis of experiments. *Mailing Add:* Dept of Statist Okla State Univ Stillwater OK 74074

WEEKS, DONALD PAUL, b Terre Haute, Ind, Feb 15, 41; m 64; c 4. MOLECULAR BIOLOGY, PHYSIOLOGY. *Educ:* Purdue Univ, BSA, 63; Univ Ill, PhD(agron), 67. *Prof Exp:* Res assoc, 67-68, NIH fel, 68-70, res assoc, 70-74, asst mem, 74-78, ASSOC MEM MOLECULAR BIOL, INST CANCER RES, 78- *Mem:* AAAS; Am Soc Plant Physiol; Am Soc Cell Biol. *Res:* Protein synthesis; gene regulation; plant cell transformation. *Mailing Add:* Inst for Cancer Res 7701 Burholme Ave Fox Chase Philadelphia PA 19111

WEEKS, DOROTHY WALCOTT, b Philadelphia, Pa, May 3, 93. PHYSICS. *Educ:* Wellesley Col, BA, 16; Mass Inst Technol, MS, 23, PhD(math), 30; Simmons Col, SM, 25. *Hon Degrees:* DSc, Med Col Pa, 77; Regis, 81. *Prof Exp:* Asst exam, US Patent Off, 17-20; asst physics, Mass Inst Technol, 20-21, res assoc, 21-22, instr, 22-24; employment supvr women, Jordan Marsh Co, Mass, 25-27; instr physics, Wellesley Col, 28-29; prof & head dept, Wilson Col, 30-43, 45-56; physicist, Army Ord Mat Res Off, Watertown Arsenal, 56-62, Army Mat Res Agency, 62-64; spectroscopist, Harvard Col Observ, 64-76. *Concurrent Pos:* Asst, Nat Bur Standards, 20; instr, Buckingham Sch, Cambridge, 23-24; tech aide, Off Sci Res & Develop, 43-46; Guggenheim fel, 49-50; grants, Am Acad Sci, 38, Am Philos Soc, 40, 48 & Res Corp, 53; consult, NSF, 53-56; lectr, Newton Col Sacred Heart, 66-71. *Mem:* Am Phys Soc; Optical Soc Am; Am Asn Physics Teachers. *Res:* Atomic spectroscopy; Lande g values; vacuum ultraviolet; Zeeman patterns of FeI and FeII; coherency matrices; radiological shielding. *Mailing Add:* 28 Dover Rd Wellesley MA 02181

WEEKS, GEORGE ELIOT, b Montgomery, Ala, July 10, 39; m 62; c 2. AEROSPACE ENGINEERING. *Educ:* Univ Ala, BS, 60, MS, 61; Va Polytech Inst, PhD(mech), 66. *Prof Exp:* Stress analyst aircraft, Hayes Int, 61; asst prof aerospace eng, Miss State Univ, 61-63; aerospace technologist, NASA Langley Field, 63-67; asst prof, 67-71, assoc prof, 71-77, PROF AEROSPACE ENG, UNIV ALA, 77- *Concurrent Pos:* Consult, US Army Missile Command, Hayes Int Corp, Remtech, Inc. *Mem:* Am Inst Aeronaut & Astronaut. *Res:* Structural dynamics; stress analysis; numerical mathematics. *Mailing Add:* Univ of Ala PO Box 2908 University AL 35486

WEEKS, GERALD, b Birmingham, Eng, Feb 5, 41. BIOCHEMISTRY. *Educ:* Birmingham Univ, BSc, 62, PhD(biochem), 66. *Prof Exp:* Res assoc biochem, Duke Univ Med Ctr, 66-69; res fel, Leicester Univ, 69-71; asst prof, 71-78, ASSOC PROF MICROBIOL, UNIV BC, 78- *Mem:* Am Soc Microbiol; Can Biochem Soc. *Res:* Molecular basis of cell-cell interaction during the differentiation of the cellular slime mould, Dictyostelium discoideum. *Mailing Add:* Dept of Microbiol Univ of BC Vancouver BC V6T 1W5 Can

WEEKS, GREGORY PAUL, b Seattle, Wash, July 16, 47. TEXTILE CHEMISTRY, INSTRUMENTATION. *Educ:* Univ Wash, BS, 69; Univ Ill, Urbana, PhD(phys chem), 74. *Prof Exp:* Res chemist, E I du Pont de Nemours & Co, Inc, 74-80. *Res:* Development of instrumentation for on-line automated analysis of polymer solutions used in synthetic textile fiber manufacture; synthetic textile technology generally, with emphasis on infrared engineering technology for instrumentation. *Mailing Add:* 16 Lamatan Newark DE 19711

WEEKS, HARMON PATRICK, JR, b Orangeburg, SC, Oct 4, 44; m 65; c 2. WILDLIFE ECOLOGY. *Educ:* Univ Ga, BSF, 67, MS, 69; Purdue Univ, PhD(wildlife ecol), 74. *Prof Exp:* Lectr wildlife ecol, Yale Univ, 73-74; asst prof, 74-79, ASSOC PROF WILDLIFE MGT, PURDUE UNIV, WEST LAFAYETTE, 79- *Mem:* Wildlife Soc; Am Soc Mammalogists; Am Ornithologists Union. *Res:* Effects of silvicultural practices on wildlife populations; adaptations of homeothermic vertebrates to sodium deficiencies; avian breeding biology. *Mailing Add:* Dept Forestry & Nat Resources Purdue Univ West Lafayette IN 47907

WEEKS, JAMES ROBERT, b Des Moines, Iowa, Aug 13, 20; m 43; c 3. PHARMACOLOGY. *Educ:* Univ Nebr, BSc, 41, MS, 46; Univ Mich, PhD(pharmacol), 52. *Prof Exp:* From instr pharm to prof pharmacol, 46-57; RES ASSOC, UPJOHN CO, 57- *Mem:* AAAS; Am Soc Pharmacol & Exp Therapeut; Soc Exp Biol & Med. *Res:* Cardiovascular pharmacology; hypertension; prostaglandins; experimental addiction. *Mailing Add:* Cardiovascular Dis Res Upjohn Co Kalamazoo MI 49001

WEEKS, JOHN DAVID, b Birmingham, Ala, Oct 11, 43. CHEMICAL PHYSICS. *Educ:* Harvard Col, BA, 65; Univ Chicago, PhD(chem physics), 69. *Prof Exp:* Res fel chem, Univ Calif, San Diego, 69-71; res fel physics, Cambridge Univ, 72; MEM TECH STAFF MAT PHYSICS, BELL TEL LABS, 73- *Mem:* Am Phys Soc. *Res:* Statistical physics; theory of crystal growth; diffusion in semiconductors. *Mailing Add:* 1D-148 Bell Labs Murray Hill NJ 07094

WEEKS, JOHN LEONARD, b Bath, Eng, May 10, 26; m 52; c 5. OCCUPATIONAL HEALTH. *Educ:* Univ London, MB, BS, 53, MD, 75; Royal Col Obstet & Gynaec, dipl, 54; Royal Col Physicians & Surgeons, DIH, 57; MFOM (Eng), 78; Can Bd Occup Med, cert, 80. *Prof Exp:* Intern, St Thomas's Hosp, London, Eng, 53-54; sr intern, St Helier Hosp, London, 54-55; indust physician, London Transport Exec, 55-58; med officer, Dept Health, Nfld, 58-60; med officer, Int Nickel Co, 60-62; supt, Health & Safety Br, 62-68, DIR HEALTH & SAFETY DIV, HI DIV, WHITESHELL NUCLEAR RES ESTAB, ATOMIC ENERGY CAN, LTD, 68- *Concurrent Pos:* Hon prof, Univ Man, 66. *Mem:* Can Med Asn. *Res:* Industrial and health toxicology, particularly organic coolants; radiation protection and biology. *Mailing Add:* Whiteshell Nuclear Res Estab Atomic Energy of Can Ltd Pinawa MB R0E 1L0 Can

WEEKS, JOHN R(ANDEL), IV, b Orange, NJ, Oct 30, 27; m 51; c 2. METALLURGY. *Educ:* Colo Sch Mines, EMet, 49; Univ Utah, MS, 50, PhD(metall), 53. *Prof Exp:* Asst metall eng, Univ Utah, 49-52; assoc metallurgist, Brookhaven Nat Lab, 53-59, metallurgist, 59-72; sr metallurgist, US Atomic Energy Comn, 72-74; LEADER, CORROSION SCI GROUP, BROOKHAVEN NAT LAB, 74- *Concurrent Pos:* Adj assoc prof, State Univ NY Stony Brook, 62-63; consult, Aerojet-Gen Corp, 65-71 & US Nuclear Regulatory Comn, 75-; adj prof metall & nuclear eng, Polytech Inst NY, 78- *Mem:* Am Soc Metals; Am Inst Mining, Metall & Petrol Engrs; Am Nuclear Soc; Nat Asn Corrosion Engrs; Electrochem Soc. *Res:* Corrosion in aqueous solutions; liquid metal corrosion; reactor metallurgy; corrosion and stress corrosion cracking of nuclear reactor materials. *Mailing Add:* Brookhaven Nat Lab Upton NY 11973

WEEKS, L(ORAINE) H(UBERT), b Mt Lake Park, Md, Feb 27, 18; m 41; c 2. ELECTRICAL ENGINEERING. *Educ:* Univ Md, BS, 40. *Prof Exp:* Elec engr, Copper Wire Eng Asn, DC & Mo, 40-43; elec engr, Frank Horton & Co, Mo, 46-48; dist design engr, Monongahela Power Co, WVa, 48-50, planning engr, 50-63, mgr planning eng, 63-68; mgr syst transmission planning, 68-69, mgr spec planning studies, 70-73, EXEC DIR, ALLEGHENY POWER SERV CORP, 73- *Mem:* Inst Elec & Electronics Engrs; Nat Soc Prof Engrs. *Res:* Electric utility planning of generation and transmission facilities. *Mailing Add:* Allegheny Power Serv Corp 800 Cabin Hill Dr Greensburg PA 15601

WEEKS, LEO, b Norman Park, Ga, June 18, 25; m 54; c 2. GENETICS. *Educ:* Ga Southern Col, BS, 48; George Peabody Col, MA, 51; Univ Nebr, PhD(zool), 54. *Prof Exp:* Teacher & asst prin pub sch, Ga, 48-50; instr biol, George Peabody Col, 50-51; instr & asst, Univ Nebr, 51-54; asst prof biol, Austin Peay State Col, 54-56; prof & head dept, Berry Col, 56-62; prof biol, Ga Southern Col, 62-67; HEAD DEPT BIOL, HIGH POINT COL, 68- *Mem:* Am Genetic Asn; Am Inst Biol Sci; Sigma Xi. *Res:* Drosophila melanica and other species. *Mailing Add:* Dept of Biol High Point Col High Point NC 27262

WEEKS, LESLIE VERNON, b Lazear, Colo, July 24, 18; m 44; c 3. SOIL SCIENCE. *Educ:* Univ Calif, Berkeley, BS, 52; Univ Calif, Riverside, PhD(soil sci), 66. *Prof Exp:* Sr lab technician, Univ Calif, Riverside, 51-56, prin lab technician, 56-70, staff res assoc soil sci, 70-78, lectr soil sci, 75-78; RETIRED. *Mem:* Am Soc Agron; Soil Sci Soc Am. *Res:* Water movement in liquid and vapor phases due to water potential and thermal gradients in unsaturated soils; use of computers in water movement studies under transient flow conditions. *Mailing Add:* 5496 Jurupa Ave Riverside CA 92504

WEEKS, MAURICE HAROLD, b Germantown, NY, Nov 9, 21; m 48; c 2. TOXICOLOGY. *Educ:* Union Col, BS, 49, MS, 50. *Prof Exp:* Collab path, Forest Prod Lab, US Forest Serv, Wis, 49; chemist, Hanford Works, Gen Elec Co, 50-55; pharmacologist, Directorate Med Res, Army Chem Ctr, 55-66; PHARMACOLOGIST, US ARMY ENVIRON HYG AGENCY, ABERDEEN PROVING GROUNDS, 66- *Mem:* AAAS; Sci Res Soc Am; Am Indust Hyg Asn; Soc Toxicol. *Res:* Animal metabolism studies of administered chemicals; toxicology and hazard evaluation of inhaled aerosols and vapors. *Mailing Add:* 27 Idlewild Bel Air MD 21014

WEEKS, PAUL MARTIN, b Clinton, NC, June 11, 32; m 57; c 6. SURGERY. *Educ:* Duke Univ, AB, 54; Univ NC, MD, 58. *Prof Exp:* From instr to prof surg, Med Ctr, Univ Ky, 64-70; CHIEF DIV PLASTIC SURG, DEPT SURG, SCH MED, WASHINGTON UNIV, 71- *Mem:* Am Col Surgeons; Soc Univ Surgeons; Am Chem Soc; Plastic Surg Res Coun. *Res:* Interrelationships of collagen and mucopolysaccharides in determining tissue compliance; effects of environment in cell synthesis, particularly regarding mucopolysaccharide or collagen synthesis; effects of irradiation on collagen and mucopolysaccharide synthesis. *Mailing Add:* Div of Plastic Surg Washington Univ Sch of Med St Louis MO 63110

WEEKS, RICHARD W(ILLIAM), b Los Angeles, Calif, Mar 21, 22; m 47; c 1. ELECTRICAL ENGINEERING. *Educ:* Calif Inst Technol, BS, 52; Stanford Univ, MS, 58. *Prof Exp:* Assoc engr, Res Lab, Int Bus Mach Corp, 52-55; lectr elec eng, San Jose State Col, 55-56, assoc prof, 58-60; develop engr, Pick Labs, 56-58; asst prof elec eng, Mont State Univ, 60-63; supv bioeng lab, Presby Med Ctr, 63-65; assoc prof elec eng, Nat Resources Res Inst, 65-71, ASSOC PROF ELEC ENG, UNIV WYO, 71- *Concurrent Pos:* Consult various indust concerns. *Mem:* Am Soc Eng Educ; Inst Elec & Electronics Engrs. *Res:* Applications of bioengineering to wildlife management and domestic livestock husbandry; general electronic instrumentation and telemetry. *Mailing Add:* Dept of Elec Eng Box 3295 University Sta Laramie WY 82070

WEEKS, RICHARD WILLIAM, b Borger, Tex, April 12, 42; m 68; c 2. AQUEOUS CORROSION, NUCLEAR FUELS. *Educ:* Swarthmore Col, BS, 64; Calif Inst Technol, MS, 65; Univ Ill, PhD(theoret & appl mech), 68; Univ Chicago, MBA, 82. *Prof Exp:* Asst mech engr, 68-71, group leader fatigue & fracture, 71-73, ASSOC DIV DIR, MAT SCI DIV, ARGONNE NAT LAB, 73- *Concurrent Pos:* Mem, Environ Protection Res Inst, 76-; sr mech engr, Argonne Nat Lab, 79- *Mem:* Sigma Xi. *Res:* Aqueous stress corrosion cracking in light water reactor systems; high temperature mechanical properties including creep-fatigue interactions; computer modelling of nuclear fuel element performance. *Mailing Add:* 342 Fourth St Downers Grove IL 60515

WEEKS, ROBERT A, b Birmingham, Ala, Aug 23, 24; m 48; c 4. SOLID STATE PHYSICS. *Educ:* Birmingham-Southern Col, BS, 48; Univ Tenn, MS, 51; Brown Univ, PhD(physics), 66. *Prof Exp:* Physicist, Solid State Div, Oak Ridge Nat Lab, NASA, 51-68, prin investr lunar mat, 68-74; PRIN INVESTR, REDOX EQUILIBRIA IN OPTICAL WALEGUIDE MAT, VANDERBILT UNIV, 81- *Concurrent Pos:* Distinguished vis prof, Am Univ Cairo, 68, 70-71; res fel, Univ Reading, 71; consult, Dept Phys Sci & Mat Eng, Am Univ Cairo, 71-; assoc ed, J Geophys Res, 68-74; Fulbright short term lectr, 80; prof invite, Ecole Polytechnique Federale de Lausanne, 81; adj prof Geophys, Univ Pa, 77-; consult, Kuwait Inst Sci Res, Technol Develop Coop, 76- & Spectran Corp, 82-; adj prof, Univ Pa, 77- & Vanderbilt Univ, 79- *Mem:* AAAS; Am Phys Soc; Sci Res Soc Am; Am Ceramic Soc. *Res:* Optical and magnetic properties of intrinsic and extrinsic defects of crystalline and glassy solids; effects of photon and particle irradiation upon the properties of diamagnetic non-conducting solids; magnetic properties of extraterrestrial solids; transport in solids. *Mailing Add:* Oak Ridge Mat Lab Box X Oak Ridge TN 37830

WEEKS, ROBERT JOE, b Quapaw, Okla, Feb 19, 29; m 48; c 3. MYCOLOGY, MEDICAL MICROBIOLOGY. *Educ:* Southwest Mo State Col, BS, 61. *Prof Exp:* Mycologist, Kans City Field Sta, Commun Dis Ctr, Bur Labs, USPHS, 62-64, microbiologist, 64-67, chief soil ecol unit, Mycoses Sect, Kansas City Labs, Ecol Invests Prog, Ctr Dis Control, 67-74, microbiologist, microbiol sect, Proficiency Testing Br, 74-79; MICROBIOLOGIST, MYCOTIC DIS DIV, CTR INFECTIOUS DIS, CTR DIS CONTROL, ATLANTA, GA, 79- *Mem:* AAAS; Mycol Soc Am. *Res:* Relationship of the pathogenic fungi to their soil environment. *Mailing Add:* 1799 Killian Hill Rd Lilburn GA 30247

WEEKS, STEPHAN JOHN, b Minneapolis, Minn, Apr 13, 50; m 77; c 1. ANALYTICAL SPECTROMETRY, PETROLEUM CHEMISTRY. *Educ:* St Olaf Col, BA, 72; Univ Fla, PhD(chem), 77. *Prof Exp:* res chemist lasers spectros, 77-79, RES CHEMIST, TRIBOLOGY, NAT BUR STANDARDS, 79- *Concurrent Pos:* Res assoc, Nat Res Coun, 77-79. *Mem:* Am Chem Soc; Soc Appl Spectros; Am Soc Testing & Mat. *Res:* Use of analytical instrumentation for petroleum chemistry; method development; chemiluminescence; trace atomic analysis; computer data correlations; tribology. *Mailing Add:* Nat Bur of Standards Washington DC 20234

WEEKS, THOMAS F, b Wheeling, WVa, Apr 12, 35; m 55; c 2. PLANT PHYSIOLOGY. *Educ:* West Liberty State Col, AB, 63; Purdue Univ, MS, 67, PhD(develop bot), 70. *Prof Exp:* Mem staff sec educ, Ohio County Bd Educ, WVa, 63-64; guest lectr biol, Purdue Univ, 70-71; assoc prof, 71-80, PROF BIOL, UNIV WIS-LA CROSSE, 80- *Mem:* AAAS; Bot Soc Am; Am Soc Plant Physiol. *Res:* Plant growth regulators; control mechanisms in plants. *Mailing Add:* Dept of Biol Univ Wis La Crosse WI 54601

WEEKS, THOMAS JOSEPH, JR, b Tarrytown, NY, Aug 31, 41; m 67; c 2. PHYSICAL INORGANIC CHEMISTRY. *Educ:* Colgate Univ, BA, 63; Univ Colo, PhD(chem), 67. *Prof Exp:* Res chemist, Res & Eng Ctr, Johns-Manville Corp, Manville, NJ, 66-68; sr res chemist, Union Carbide Corp, Tarrytown, NY, 70-72, proj chemist, 72-73, sr staff chemist, 73-75, supvr, 75-78; group leader, 78-80, SECT MGR, ASHLAND CHEM CORP, 80- *Mem:* Am Chem Soc; Catalysis Soc; AAAS. *Res:* Synthesis, testing and manufacturing of heterogeneous catalysts; surface analysis of catalysts and composites; pilot plant start-up and operation. *Mailing Add:* 2655 Camden Rd Columbus OH 43221

WEEKS, WILFORD FRANK, b Champaign, Ill, Jan 8, 29; m 52; c 2. GLACIOLOGY, HYDROLOGY. *Educ:* Univ Ill, BS, 51, MS, 53; Univ Chicago, PhD(geol), 56. *Prof Exp:* Geologist, Mineral Deposits Br, US Geol Surv, 52-55; glaciologist, US Air Force Cambridge Res Ctr, 55-57; asst prof, Wash Univ, 57-62; GLACIOLOGIST, COLD REGIONS Res & ENG LAB, 62- *Concurrent Pos:* Adj assoc prof, Dartmouth Col, 62-72, adj prof, 72-; mem, Polar Res Bd & chmn panel on glaciol, Nat Acad Sci, 71-77; chmn, Div River, Lake & Sea Ice, Int Comn Snow & Ice; Japan soc promotion sci vis prof, Inst Low Temp Sci, Hokkaido Univ, Japan, 73; mem, adv panel, Jet Propulsion Lab; lectr, Advan Study Inst Air, Sea & Ice Interactions, NATO. *Mem:* Nat Acad Eng; fel Arctic Inst NAm; Am Geophys Union; Int Glaciol Soc (vpres, 69-72, pres, 72-75); fel Geol Soc Am. *Res:* Geophysics of sea, lake and river ice. *Mailing Add:* Cold Regions Res & Eng Lab 72 Lyme Rd Hanover NH 03755

WEEKS, WILLIAM THOMAS, b Portchester, NY, Mar 28, 32; m 54; c 3. COMPUTER SCIENCES. *Educ:* Williams Col, BA, 54; Univ Mich, MS, 56, PhD(physics), 60. *Prof Exp:* Assoc physicist, Data Systs Div, 60-61, staff physicist, Systs Develop Div, 61-64, adv physicist, Components Div, 64-68, SR ENGR COMPONENTS DIV, IBM CORP, 68- *Res:* Scientific computation and numerical analysis as applied to design of electronic digital computers. *Mailing Add:* Innsbruck Blvd Hopewell Junction NY 12533

WEEMS, CHARLES WILLIAM, b Greeneville, Tenn, March 1, 41; m 66; c 3. BIOCHEMISTRY, NUTRITION. *Educ:* East Tenn State Univ, BS, 64, MA, 66; WVa Univ, PhD(reproductive endocrinol), 75. *Prof Exp:* Captain chem corps res microbiol, US Army, Fort Detrick, Md, 66-68; instr biol & physiol, Fairmont State Col, WVa, 68-71, asst prof, 71-74, assoc prof, 74-76; assoc prof, 76-79, PROF AGR & ENDOCRINOL, ARIZ STATE UNIV, TEMPE, 79- *Concurrent Pos:* Lectr, Meat Animal Res Ctr, 77, Northwestern Univ Med Sch, 77, Univ Ariz Med Sch, 78, Sch Med, Tulane Univ, 80, Sch Med, La State Univ, 81 & USDA Res Sta, Md, 82; prin investr, UpJohn Co, Inc, 76- *Mem:* NY Acad Sci; Soc Study Reprod; Endocrine Soc; Am Soc Animal Sci; Sigma Xi. *Res:* Uterine and ovarian regulation of corpus luteum; embryo transfer; uterine capacity; survival of embryos; molecular regulation of receptors for hormonal regulationof ovarian steroidogenesis; freezing of embryos. *Mailing Add:* 6708 Sikenwood Lane Tempe AZ 85283

WEEMS, HOWARD VINCENT, JR, b Rome, Ga, Apr 11, 22; m 50; c 5. ENTOMOLOGY. *Educ:* Emory Univ, BA, 46; Univ Fla, MS, 48; Ohio State Univ, PhD(entom), 53. *Prof Exp:* Asst entom, Univ Fla, 46-47; instr biol, Univ Miss, 48-49; res asst, Ohio Biol Surv, Ohio State Univ, 49-53; TAXON ENTOMOLOGIST, DIV PLANT INDUST, FLA DEPT AGR & CONSUMER SERV, 53-; PROF ENTOM, UNIV FLA, 73- *Concurrent Pos:* Cur, Fla State Collection Arthropods, 54-; assoc arthropods, Fla State Mus, 59-; ed, Arthropods of Fla & Neighboring Land Areas, Fla Dept Agr & Consumer Serv, 65-; assoc prof entom, Univ Fla, 66-73. *Mem:* Fel AAAS; Asn Trop Biol; Entom Soc Am; assoc Ecol Soc Am; Soc Syst Zool. *Res:* Taxonomy and ecology of syrphid flies; identifications of Florida arthropods. *Mailing Add:* Fla Dept Agr & Consumer Serv PO Box 1269 Gainesville FL 32602

WEEMS, MALCOLM LEE BRUCE, b Nashville, Kans, Dec 8, 45; m 72; c 1. PHYSICS. *Educ:* Kans State Teachers Col, BSE, 67, MS, 69; Okla State Univ, PhD(physics), 72. *Prof Exp:* Lectr physics, Kans State Teachers Col, 68-69; instr, 72-75, DIR SCI LAB PROG FOR BLIND, EAST CENTRAL STATE UNIV, 74-, ASST PROF PHYSICS, 75-, CHMN, DEPT PHYSICS, 81- *Mem:* Am Inst Physics; Am Asn Physics Teachers. *Res:* Stellar atmospheres; educational innovation. *Mailing Add:* Dept of Phys East Cent State Univ Ada OK 74820

WEERTMAN, JOHANNES, b Fairfield, Ala, May 11, 25; m 50; c 2. PHYSICS. *Educ:* Carnegie Inst Technol, BS, 48, DSc(physics), 51. *Prof Exp:* Fulbright fel, Ecole Normal Superieure, Paris, 51-52; solid state physicist, US Naval Res Lab, 52-58. sci liaison officer, US Off Naval Res US Embassy, Eng Lab, 58-59; from assoc prof to prof, 59-68, WALTER P MURPHY PROF MAT SCI, NORTHWESTERN UNIV, EVANSTON, 68-, PROF GEOPHYS, 63- *Concurrent Pos:* Consult, US Army Cold Regions Res & Eng Lab, 60-75, US Naval Res Lab, 60-67, Bain Lab, US Steel Co, 60-62 & Oak Ridge Nat Lab, 63-68; vis prof, Calif Inst Technol, 64; consult, Los Alamos Sci Lab, 67-; vis prof, Scott Polar Res Inst, Cambridge Univ, 71-72; Guggenheim fel, 71-72. *Honors & Awards:* Horton Award, Sect Hydrol, Am Geophys Union, 62; Mathewson Gold Medal, Am Inst Mining, Metall & Petrol Eng, 77. *Mem:* Nat Acad Eng; AAAS; fel Geol Soc Am; fel Am Phys Soc; fel Am Soc Metals. *Res:* Creep of crystals; dislocation theory; internal friction; theory of glacier movement; metal physics; glaciology; geophysics; fatigue. *Mailing Add:* Dept of Mat Sci Northwestern Univ Evanston IL 60201

WEERTMAN, JULIA RANDALL, b Muskegon, Mich, Feb 10, 26; m 50; c 2. SOLID STATE PHYSICS. *Educ:* Carnegie Inst Technol, BS, 46, MS, 47, DSc(physics), 51. *Prof Exp:* Rotary Int fel, Ecole Normale Superieure, Univ Paris, 51-52; physicist, US Naval Res Lab, 52-58; vis asst prof, 72-73, asst prof, 73-78, ASSOC PROF MAT SCI, NORTHWESTERN UNIV, EVANSTON, 78- *Mem:* Am Phys Soc; Am Inst Phys; Am Soc Metals; Am Inst Mining, Metall & Petrol Eng; Am Crystallographic Asn. *Res:* Dislocation theory; high temperature fatigue; small angle neutron scattering. *Mailing Add:* Dept Mat Sci & Eng Northwestern Univ Evanston IL 60201

WEESE, RICHARD HENRY, b Hyer, WVa, Dec 13, 38; m 68. ORGANIC POLYMER CHEMISTRY. *Educ:* WVa State Col, BS, 64; Bucknell Univ, MS, 67. *Prof Exp:* Scientist chem, 67-74, sr scientist chem, 74-78, RES SECT MGR, RES LABS, ROHM AND HAAS CO, BRISTOL, 78- *Mem:* Soc Plastic Engrs. *Res:* Synthesis and application of organic polymers, including additives or modifiers. *Mailing Add:* RR 1 Glenwood Dr Washington Crossing PA 18977

WEET, JOHN FREEMAN, b Medina, NY, Mar 24, 48; m 72. PHYSIOLOGY, PHARMACOLOGY. *Educ:* St Lawrence Univ, BS, 70; Ohio State Univ, MS, 74, PhD(physiol), 75. *Prof Exp:* Fac assoc physiol, Univ Iowa, 75-76; res investr, 76-81, RES SCIENTIST PHARMACOL, G D SEARLE & CO, 81- *Mem:* Am Heart Asn; AAAS. *Res:* Effects of vasodilators and diuretics on renal function and hemodynamics. *Mailing Add:* Dept of Biol Res Box 5110 Chicago IL 60680

WEETALL, HOWARD H, b Chicago, Ill, Nov 17, 36; m 62; c 2. IMMUNOCHEMISTRY, ENZYMOLOGY. *Educ:* Univ Calif, Los Angeles, BA, 59, MA, 61. *Prof Exp:* Scientist, Jet Propulsion Lab, Calif Inst Technol, 61-65; sr res biologist, Space Gen Corp, 65-66; immunochemist, Bionetics Res Corp, 66-67; res biochemist, 67-71, res assoc, 71-73, sr res assoc biochem, 73-78, MGR BIOMED RES, CORNING GLASS WORKS, 78-, MGR BIOSCI RES, 78- *Mem:* AAAS; Am Chem Soc; Am Soc Microbiol; NY Acad Sci; Am Soc Biol Chemists. *Res:* Immobilized biologically active molecules, including antigens, antibodies and enzymes and the characteristics of such materials. *Mailing Add:* Corning Glass Works Corning NY 14830

WEETE, JOHN DONALD, b Dallas, Tex, June 14, 42. PLANT PHYSIOLOGY, PLANT BIOCHEMISTRY. *Educ:* Stephen F Austin State Univ, BS, 65, MS, 68; Univ Houston, PhD(biol), 70. *Prof Exp:* Fel, Baylor Col Med, 69-70; vis scientist, Lunar Sci Inst, 70-71, staff scientist, 71-72, NASA prin investr lunar sample anal, 72; asst prof, 72-76, ASSOC PROF BOT & MICROBIOL, AUBURN UNIV, 76- *Concurrent Pos:* Spec lectr, La State Univ, New Orleans, 70-71. *Honors & Awards:* Res Award, Am Phytopath Soc, 68. *Mem:* Am Phytopath Soc; Am Soc Plant Physiol; Soc Study Origin of Life; Sigma Xi. *Res:* Fungus physiology and biochemistry; lipid composition and metabolism of fungi and higher plants; organic pollutants of water. *Mailing Add:* Dept of Bot & Microbiol Auburn Univ Auburn AL 30836

WEETMAN, DAVID G, b Poughkeepsie, NY, Feb 20, 38; m 65; c 1. ORGANIC CHEMISTRY. *Educ:* Pa State Univ, BS, 59; Univ Minn, PhD(org chem), 68. *Prof Exp:* RES CHEMIST, TEXACO RES LAB, TEXACO, INC, 68- *Mem:* Am Chem Soc. *Res:* Synthesis and reactions of dihalocyclopropanes derived from 2- and 3- methyl substituted 4-ethoxy-2H-1-benzothiopyrans. *Mailing Add:* 3 Prentiss Dr Box 116 RD 7 Hopewell Junction NY 12533

WEETMAN, GORDON FREDERICK, b York, Eng, Apr 24, 33; Can citizen. FORESTRY. *Educ:* Univ Toronto, BScF, 55; Yale Univ, MS, 58, PhD(forestry), 62. *Prof Exp:* Res forester, Pulp & Paper Res Inst Can, 55-72; prof silvicult, Fac Forestry, Univ NB, Fredencton, 72-78, PROF SILVICULTURE, FAC FORESTRY, UNIV BC, VANCOUVER, 78- *Concurrent Pos:* Ed, Forestry Chronicle, Can Inst Forestry, 67-71. *Mem:* Can Inst Forestry (pres, 73-74). *Res:* Blockage of the nitrogen cycle by raw humus accumulations in boreal forests; nitrogen fertilization; nutrient losses in logging; silviculture. *Mailing Add:* Fac of Forestry Univ of BC Vancouver BC V6T 1W5 Can

WEFEL, JOHN PAUL, b Cleveland, Ohio, Apr 28, 44; m 67; c 2. PHYSICS, ASTROPHYSICS. *Educ:* Valparaiso Univ, BS, 66; Wash Univ, MA, 68, PhD(physics), 71. *Prof Exp:* Nat Acad Sci-Nat Res Coun resident res assoc astrophys, Naval Res Lab, 71-73, res physicist, 73-75; Robert R McCormick fel, Enrico Fermi Inst, Univ Chicago, 75-77, sr res assoc, 77-82; ASST PROF PHYSICS, LA STATE UNIV, 82- *Mem:* AAAS; Am Phys Soc; Sigma Xi. *Res:* Cosmic ray astrophysics; utilized both passive and electronic detectors to measure element and isotopic abundances; studied nuclear fragmentation reactions of importance in cosmic ray propagation calculations; nucleosynthesis studies; instrument development. *Mailing Add:* Dept Physics & Astron Louisiana State Univ Baton Rouge LA 70803

WEFERS, KARL, b Bonn, Ger, Aug 4, 28; m 57; c 2. CRYSTALLOGRAPHY, SURFACE CHEMISTRY. *Educ:* Univ Bonn, Dr rer nat, 58. *Prof Exp:* Group leader crystallog & struct chem, Vereinigte Aluminum Werke, Bonn, Ger, 58-66; sci assoc, Alcoa Res Labs, 67-80, FEL, CORP RES & DEVELOP, ALCOA LABS, ALCOA TECH CTR, 80- *Res:* Physical chemistry and structural chemistry of extractive metallurgy of aluminum; surface chemistry of aluminum. *Mailing Add:* Alcoa Labs Alcoa Tech Ctr Alcoa Center PA 15069

WEG, JOHN GERARD, b New York, NY, Feb 16, 34; m 56; c 6. PULMONARY DISEASES. *Educ:* Col Holy Cross, AB, 55; New York Med Col, MD, 59. *Prof Exp:* Actg chief pulmonary, Wilford Hall, Lackland Air Force Base, US Air Force Hosp, 63-64, chief pulmonary & inhalation therapy sect, 64-66, pulmonary & infectious dis, 66-67; asst prof pulmonary & internal med, Baylor Col Med, 67-71, assoc prof, 71; assoc prof internal med, 71-74, PHYSICIAN IN CHARGE PULMONARY DIV, PULMONARY & INTERNAL MED & PROF INTERNAL MED, MED SCH, UNIV MICH, 74- *Concurrent Pos:* Clin dir pulmonary & internal med, Jefferson Davis Hosp, 67-71; consult, Area Consult Surgeon Gen, Methodist Hosp, Houston, Tex & Med Adv Comt, Assoc Degree Prog Health Sci, South Tex Jr Col, 68-71, Vet Admin Hosp, Ann Arbor, Mich, 72- & Wayne Count Gen Hosp, 73- *Mem:* Am Col Chest Physicians; Int Acad Chest Physicians; Am Thoracic Soc; Am Bd Internal Med. *Res:* Correlation of clinical, physiologic, biochemical-immunologic, and pathologic mechanisms of pulmonary disease; acute respiratory failure; pulmonary emboli; diffuse interstitial disease; sarcoidosis. *Mailing Add:* Pulmonary Box 55 Univ Hosp Box 55 1405 E Ann St Ann Arbor MI 48109

WEG, RUTH BASS, b New York, NY, Oct 12, 20; c 3. GERONTOLOGY. *Educ:* Hunter Col, BA, 40; Univ Southern Calif, MS, 54, PhD(zool), 58. *Prof Exp:* Res assoc, dept biochem, 58-59, biol & physiol, 60-70, biochemist, 62-64, biologist in residence, Air Pollution Control Inst, 66, assoc prof biol, Univ & assoc dir educ & training, 68-74, MEM TEACHING FAC, SUMMER INST STUDY GERONT, ANDRUS GERONT CTR, UNIV SOUTHERN CALIF, 68-, DIR, 69-, ASSOC PROF BIOL & GERONT, 75- *Concurrent Pos:* Consult, Rossmoor-Cortese Inst Study Retirement & Aging, Univ Southern Calif, 67, pre-med adv, Univ, 70-, asst dean student affairs, Leonard Davis Sch Geront, 75- *Mem:* AAAS; Am Inst Biol Sci; Fedn Am Socs Exp Biol; Geront Soc. *Res:* Molecular bases for physiological phenomena; blood groups of mammals; iron metabolism in liver; mechanism of action of air pollutants on cellular activities; sexuality and aging; nutrition and age; health maintenance and age; curriculum development in gerontology; processes of aging on a molecular/organism level. *Mailing Add:* 5410 Vanalden Ave Tarzana CA 91536

WEGE, WILLIAM RICHARD, b Shawano, Wis, Mar 31, 26; m 50; c 3. RADIOLOGY. *Educ:* Marquette Univ, DDS, 52; Univ Ala, MS, 67. *Prof Exp:* Assoc prof radiol, 67-76, PROF ORAL MED & RADIOL, MED COL GA, 76- *Concurrent Pos:* NIH spec fel, Med Col Ga, 67-68; consult, US Army, Ft Jackson, SC, 67- & Vet Admin, 68- *Mem:* Fel Am Acad Dent Radiol (treas, 72); Int Asn Dent Res (pres, 71); fel Am Col Dent. *Res:* Cytogenetics in relation to radiation. *Mailing Add:* Dept of Radiol Med Col of Ga Augusta GA 30902

WEGENER, HORST ALBRECHT RICHARD, b Brooklyn, NY, May 9, 27; m 50; c 4. SOLID STATE SCIENCE. *Educ:* Columbia Univ, BS, 51; Polytech Inst Brooklyn, MS, 55, PhD(inorg chem), 65. *Prof Exp:* Lab asst, Patterson Moos & Co, Inc, 49-50, proj engr, 50-55; scientist, Tung-Sol Elec, Inc, 55-57, supvr res, 57-60, group leader, 60-64; staff mem, Sperry Rand Res Ctr, 64-65, group leader, 65-66, dept head, 66-77; AREA MGR, XEROX CORP, 77- *Mem:* Sr mem Inst Elec & Electronics Eng. *Res:* Imperfections in crystals; x-ray diffraction crystal structure synthesis; properties and structure of semiconductor compounds; semiconductor device theory, design and processing; volatile and non-volatile large scale integrated memory circuit design and fabrication. *Mailing Add:* Apt 19 132 Country Manor Way Webster NY 14580

WEGENER, PETER PAUL, b Berlin, Ger, Aug 29, 17; nat US. FLUID PHYSICS, GAS DYNAMICS. *Educ:* Univ Berlin, Dr rer nat(physics, geophys), 43; Univ Karlsruhe, Dr Ing, 79. *Prof Exp:* Mem & head basic res group supersonic wind tunnels, Ger, 43-45; mem res group hypersonic wind tunnel design & res, US Naval Ord Lab, 46-53; chief gas dynamics res sect, Jet Propulsion Lab, Calif Inst Technol, 53-59; prof appl sci, 60-72, chmn dept, 66-71, HAROLD HODGKINSON PROF ENG & APPL SCI, YALE UNIV, 72- *Concurrent Pos:* Humboldt Award, 79. *Mem:* Fel Am Phys Soc; Sigma Xi; Combustion Inst. *Res:* Gas dynamics; fluid dynamics; chemical physics related to flow problems such as chemical kinetics and condensation. *Mailing Add:* Mason Lab Yale Univ New Haven CT 06520

WEGENER, WARNER SMITH, b Cincinnati, Ohio, June 23, 35; m 58; c 3. MICROBIOLOGY, BIOCHEMISTRY. *Educ:* Univ Cincinnati, BS, 57, PhD(microbiol), 64. *Prof Exp:* Asst mem, Res Labs, Albert Einstein Med Ctr, 64-68; asst prof, 68-72, ASSOC PROF MICROBIOL, SCH MED, IND UNIV, INDIANAPOLIS, 72- *Concurrent Pos:* NIH fel, 65-66. *Mem:* Am Soc Microbiol. *Res:* Intermediary metabolism and cellular regulatory processes; biochemical basis of microbial pathogenicity. *Mailing Add:* Dept of Microbiol Ind Univ Sch of Med Indianapolis IN 46202

WEGGEL, JOHN RICHARD, b Philadelphia, Pa, Nov 29, 41; m 64; c 3. ENGINEERING, HYDRAULICS. *Educ:* Drexel Inst Technol, BS, 64; Univ Ill, MS, 66, PhD(civil eng), 68. *Prof Exp:* Asst prof, Univ Ill, Urbana, 68-71; hydraulic engr, 71-73, spec asst to dir, 73-77, CHIEF EVAL BR, COASTAL ENG RES CTR, US ARMY, 77- *Concurrent Pos:* Mem steering comt, Deep Draft Harbor Study, NAtlantic Div, Corp Engrs, US Army, 72-; mem, PIANC Waves Comn, 73-76; prof lectr, George Washington Univ, 74- *Mem:* Am Soc Civil Engrs; Am Geophys Union. *Res:* Coastal engineering; civil engineering; coastal processes and ocean engineering; development of design criteria for coastal works and littoral processes. *Mailing Add:* Coastal Eng Res Ctr Kingman Bldg Ft Belvoir VA 22060

WEGGEL, ROBERT JOHN, b Cleveland, Ohio, Mar 16, 43. ELECTROMAGNETISM, ENGINEERING PHYSICS. *Educ:* Mass Inst Technol, BS, 64. *Prof Exp:* MEM SPONSORED RES STAFF MAGNET DESIGN, FRANCIS BITTER NAT MAGNET LAB, MASS INST TECHNOL, 61- *Concurrent Pos:* Consult magnet design, var companies & individuals, 66-76. *Mem:* Sigma Xi. *Res:* Designer of world's most intense continuous field electromagnets employing water-cooled solenoids separately or in combination with superconducting coils (hybrid magnets), or long-duration pulse coils precooled with liquid nitrogen. *Mailing Add:* Mass Inst of Technol Rm NW 14-3212 Cambridge MA 02139

WEGMAN, EDWARD JOSEPH, b Terre Haute, Ind, July 4, 43; m 67; c 2. MATHEMATICAL STATISTICS. *Educ:* St Louis Univ, BS, 65; Univ Iowa, MS, 67, PhD(statist), 68. *Prof Exp:* From asst prof to assoc prof statist, Univ NC, 68-78; vis prof math, Manchester Univ, 76-77; DIR STATIST & PROBABILITY PROG, OFF NAVAL RES, 78- *Concurrent Pos:* Res assoc, NSF, 68-72 & Off Naval Res, 72-74; prin investr, Air Force Off Sci Res, 74-78; sr fac fel, NSF, 76-77; consult, Naval Coastal Syst Lab, 72-74, NC State Utilities Comn, 74, Gov James Hunt NC, 75, Am Rose Soc, 75, NC Dept Pub Instr, 76-77 & US Off Mgt & Budget, 80-81. *Mem:* Inst Math Statist; Am Statist Asn; Royal Statist Soc; Inst Elec & Electronics Engrs; Soc Indust Appl Math. *Res:* Statistical inference under order restrictions, time series analysis; probability density estimation. *Mailing Add:* Off of Naval Res Code 436 Arlington VA 22217

WEGMAN, MYRON EZRA, b Brooklyn, NY, July 23, 08; m 36; c 4. PUBLIC HEALTH, PEDIATRICS. *Educ:* City Col New York, BA, 28; Yale Univ, MD, 32; Johns Hopkins Univ, MPH, 38. *Prof Exp:* From asst to instr pediat, Sch Med, Yale Univ, 32-36; pediat consult, State Dept Health, Md, 36-41; asst prof child hyg, Sch Trop Med, Univ PR, 41-42; dir training & res, Dept Health, New York, 42-46, dir, Sch Health Serv, 43-46; prof pediat & head dept, Sch Med, La State Univ, 46-52; dir div educ & training, Pan Am Sanit Bur, WHO, 52-56, secy gen, Pan Am Health Orgn, 57-60; dean, Sch Pub Health, 60-74, prof pub health & prof pediat, 60-78, EMER DEAN, SCH PUB HEALTH, MED SCH, UNIV MICH, ANN ARBOR, 74-, JOHN G SEARLE EMER PROF PUBLIC HEALTH & EMER PROF PEDIAT & COMMUN DIS, 78- *Concurrent Pos:* From intern to resident, New Haven Hosp, Conn, 32-36; lectr, Maternal & Child Health, Johns Hopkins Univ, 39-46; asst prof, Col Physicians & Surgeons, Columbia Univ, 41-44; asst prof, Med Col, Cornell Univ, 42-46; pediatrician-in-chief, Charity Hosp, New Orleans, 46-52, pres, Vis Staff, 50-51; consult, Children's Hosp, Washington, DC, 53-60; spec lectr, Sch Med, George Washington Univ, 54-60; pres, Asn Sch Pub Health, 63-66; WHO vis prof, Univ Malaya, 74; mem, Soc of Scholars, Johns Hopkins Univ, 75; John G Searle prof pub health, Univ Mich, 75-78; chmn comt pediat hosp rates, Nat Res Coun, 75-77; consult & lectr, Univ Mich, Ann Arbor, 78- *Honors & Awards:* Grulee Award, Am Acad Pediat, 58; Townsend Harris Medal, City Col New York, 61; Bronfman Prize, 67; Walter P Reuther Award, United Automobile Workers, 74; Sedgwick Medal, Am Pub Health Asn, 74. *Mem:* Fel AAAS; Am Pub Health Asn (pres, 72); Am Pediat Soc; Soc Exp Biol & Med; fel AMA. *Res:* Infant mortality; prepaid health care; international health organization. *Mailing Add:* Sch of Pub Health Univ of Mich Ann Arbor MI 48109

WEGMANN, THOMAS GEORGE, b Milwaukee, Wis, Sept 29, 41; m 65; c 1. GENETICS, IMMUNOLOGY. *Educ:* Univ Wis, BA, 63, PhD(med genetics), 68. *Prof Exp:* From asst prof to assoc prof biol, Harvard Biol Labs, 69-74; assoc prof, 74-76, PROF IMMUNOL & PRIN INVESTR, MED RES COUN IMMUNOBIOL UNIT, UNIV ALTA, 76- *Res:* Genetics and the immune response; immunological tolerance and developmental analysis of genetically-marked chimeric systems. *Mailing Add:* Med Res Coun Transplantation Unit Univ of Alta Edmonton AB T6G 2H7 Can

WEGNER, GENE H, b Madison, Wis, Aug 30, 30; m 53; c 4. PETROLEUM MICROBIOLOGY, SINGLE CELL PROTEIN. *Educ:* Univ Wis, BS, 53, MS, 57, PhD(bact, biochem), 62. *Prof Exp:* Asst bact, Univ Wis, 55-57; microbiologist, Eli Lilly & Co, 57-59; asst bact, Univ Wis, 59-60, dept fel, 60-61; sr res microbiologist, 62-80, BIOTECHNOL SECT SUPVR, PHILLIPS PETROL CO, 80- *Mem:* Am Soc Microbiol; Am Chem Soc. *Res:* Hydrocarbon microbiology; fatty acid metabolism; microbial lipids; single cell protein; continuous culture; pilot plant development; biopolymers; biotechnology. *Mailing Add:* 94-H Phillips Res Ctr Phillips Petrol Co Bartlesville OK 74003

WEGNER, HARVEY E, b Tacoma, Wash, Aug 12, 25; m 49; c 3. NUCLEAR PHYSICS. *Educ:* Univ Puget Sound, BS, 48; Univ Wash, MS, 51, PhD(physics), 53. *Prof Exp:* Asst physicist, Brookhaven Nat Lab, 53-56; physicist, Los Alamos Sci Lab, 56-62; physicist, 62-66, co-dir, Tandem Van de Graff Facility, 70-75, CONSTRUCTION MGR, TANDEM VAN DE GRAFF FACILITY, BROOKHAVEN NAT LAB, 66-, SR PHYSICIST, 68- *Concurrent Pos:* Consult, Radiation Dynamics, Inc, 63- & Gen Ionex, 74- *Mem:* Fel Am Phys Soc; Am Asn Physics Teachers. *Res:* Accelerator construction; cyclotrons in nuclear physics and machine development; semiconductor detectors; low energy accelerator construction and development; heavy ion reaction and fusion physics. *Mailing Add:* Dept of Phys Brookhaven Nat Lab Upton NY 11973

WEGNER, KARL HEINRICH, b Pierre, SDak, Jan 5, 30; m 57; c 3. MEDICINE, PATHOLOGY. *Educ:* Yale Univ, BA, 52; Harvard Med Sch, MD, 59. *Prof Exp:* prof path & chmn dept, Sch Med, Univ SDak, 68-73, dean sch med & vpres health affairs, Univ, 73-79; PATHOLOGIST & MED DIR, LAB CLIN MED & SIOUX VALLEY HOSP, 62- *Mem:* Col Am Path; Am Soc Clin Path; Int Acad Path. *Mailing Add:* Sunnymede S Minnesota Rd Sioux Falls SD 57101

WEGNER, MARCUS IMMANUEL, b South Haven, Mich, Mar 3, 15; m 41; c 4. BIOCHEMISTRY, NUTRITION. *Educ:* St Norbert Col, BS, 36; Univ Wis, PhD(nutrit biochem), 41. *Prof Exp:* Asst chemist, Exp Sta, Agr & Mech Col, Univ Tex, 41-43; asst nutritionist, Exp Sta, NDak Col, 43-44; res chemist, Mead Johnson & Co, Ind, 44-48; asst res dir, Res Div, Oscar Mayer & Co, 48-51; nutritionist, Pet Milk Co, 51-59, sect leader new prod develop, 59-60, group mgr, 60-61; res dir, Ward Foods, Inc, 61-64; asst res dir, Best Foods Div, Corn Prod Co, 64-71; br chief & diet appraisal, Consumer & Food Economics Div, Agr Res Serv, USDA, 69-71, asst dir, Eastern Regional Res Lab, 71-80; CONSULT FOOD SCI & NUTRIT, 80- *Mem:* Am Asn Cereal Chem; Am Chem Soc; Inst Food Technol. *Res:* Chemistry and nutrition of protein hydrolysates; bakery products; food and diet appraisal; new and wider uses for American farm commodities; meats and dairy products; convenience frozen foods; new product development. *Mailing Add:* 1151 Hagues Mill Rd Ambler PA 19002

WEGNER, PATRICK ANDREW, b South Bend, Ind, Nov 14, 40. ORGANOMETALLIC CHEMISTRY. *Educ:* Northwestern Univ, Evanston, BA, 62; Univ Calif, Riverside, PhD(chem), 66. *Prof Exp:* Res chemist, E I du Pont de Nemours & Co, Inc, 66-68; vis prof chem, Harvey Mudd Col, 68-69; from asst prof to assoc prof, 69-74, PROF CHEM, CALIF STATE UNIV, FULLERTON, 75-, CHMN DEPT, 78- *Concurrent Pos:* Grants, Petrol Res Corp, Calif State Univ, Fullerton, 68-72, 74-78. Res Corp, 70-72, NASA, 72-74; Alexander von Humboldt fel, 77-78. *Mem:* Am Chem Soc. *Res:* Boron hydride chemistry; transition metal organometallic chemistry. *Mailing Add:* Dept of Chem 800 N State College Calif State Univ Fullerton CA 92634

WEGNER, PETER, b Aug 20, 32; US citizen; m 56; c 4. COMPUTER SCIENCE. *Educ:* Univ London, BSC, 53, PhD(comput sci), 68; Pa State Univ, MA, 59. *Prof Exp:* Res assoc, Comput Ctr, Mass Inst Technol, 59-60; asst dir statist lab, Harvard Univ, 60-61; lectr comput sci, London Sch Econ, 61-64; asst prof, Pa State Univ, 64-66; assoc prof, Cornell Univ, 66-69; ASSOC PROF COMPUT SCI, BROWN UNIV, 69- *Concurrent Pos:* Assoc ed, Comput Surveys, 76- *Mem:* Asn Comput Mach; Math Asn Am. *Res:* Programming language theory and implementation; computer science education; semantics of programming languages; theory of computation. *Mailing Add:* Dept of Appl Math Brown Univ Providence RI 02912

WEGNER, ROBERT CARL, b New York, NY, Jan 7, 44; m 69; c 2. GEOPHYSICS, GEOLOGY. *Educ:* Queen's Col, NY, BA, 67; Lehigh Univ, MS, 72; Rice Univ, PhD(geophys), 78. *Prof Exp:* Vis lectr geol, Am Geol Inst, 68; geophys interpreter, Exxon Co USA, 69-70, res specialist, 74-80, SUPVR GEOPHYS, EXXON PROD RES CO, 80- *Concurrent Pos:* Cities Serv fel, 70; adj prof, Rice Univ, 81-82. *Mem:* Am Geophys Union; Soc Explor Geophysicists; Sigma Xi. *Res:* Geophysical research in reflection seismology applied to the exploration of oil and gas reservoirs. *Mailing Add:* Exxon Prod Res Co Box 2189 Houston TX 77001

WEGNER, THOMAS NORMAN, b Cleveland, Ohio, July 8, 32; m 62; c 1. ANIMAL PHYSIOLOGY, BIOCHEMISTRY. *Educ:* Mich State Univ, BS, 54; Colo State Univ, MS, 56; Univ Calif, Davis, PhD(animal physiol), 64. *Prof Exp:* Asst animal pathologist, 64-66, asst prof dairy sci, 67-76, LECTR & RES ASSOC ANIMAL SCI, AGR EXP STA, UNIV ARIZ, 76- *Mem:* Am Dairy Sci Asn. *Res:* Carbohydrate metabolism in ruminant animals; pathogenesis of coccidioidomycosis, biochemistry of the immune responses; physiology of abnormal milk production and heat stress on dairy cows. *Mailing Add:* Dept of Dairy & Food Sci Univ of Ariz Tucson AZ 85721

WEGST, W(ALTER) F(REDERICK), b Philadelphia, Pa, Nov 20, 09; m 33; c 2. CHEMICAL ENGINEERING. *Educ:* Drexel Inst Technol, BS, 31. *Prof Exp:* Chemist, Philadelphia Quartz Co, 31-41; group leader, BASF Wyandotte Corp, 41-54, res supvr, 54-64, res assoc, 64-73; RETIRED. *Mem:* Am Chem Soc. *Res:* Silicate manufacture; formulation of detergents and sanitizing agents; inhibition alkali action on glass by use of berylliate, zincate and organics. *Mailing Add:* 8151 Wood Grosse Ile MI 48138

WEGST, WALTER F, JR, b Philadelphia, Pa, Dec 26, 34; div; c 2. RADIOLOGICAL HEALTH. *Educ:* Univ Mich, BSE, 56, MSE, 57, PhD(environ health), 63; Am Bd Health Phys, Dipl, 66; Bd Cert Safety Prof, Cert. *Prof Exp:* Reactor health physicist, Phoenix Mem Lab, Univ Mich, 57-58, lab health physicist, 58-59, lab supvr, 59-60; inst health physicist, Calif Inst Technol, 63-68, safety mgr, 68-71, mgr security, 71-73, mgr safety, 71-79; DIR RES & OCCUPATIONAL SAFETY, UNIV CALIF, LOS ANGELES, 79- *Concurrent Pos:* Consult, City of Hope Nat Med Ctr, Atomics Int Div Rockwell Int, 74-, Southern Calif Edison, Genetech & Training Resources Div, Nuclear Support Serv. *Mem:* Health Phys Soc; Am Indust Hyg Asn; Sigma Xi; AAAS; Am Health Physics Soc. *Res:* Radiobiological studies on mammalian cells; secondary electron production by charged particle passage through matter; university health physics problems. *Mailing Add:* Univ Calif Dept Community Safety 405 Hilgard Los Angeles CA 90024

WEGSTEIN, JOSEPH HENRY, b Washburn, Ill, Apr 7, 22. COMPUTER SCIENCE, APPLIED MATHEMATICS. *Educ:* Univ Ill, BS, 44, MS, 48. *Prof Exp:* MATHEMATICIAN COMPUT, NAT BUR STANDARDS, 51- *Honors & Awards:* Silver Medal Award, Dept Com, 73. *Res:* Development of automatic fingerprint identification systems; application of pattern recognition; development of computer programming languages. *Mailing Add:* Div 650 Nat Bur Standards Washington DC 20234

WEGWEISER, ARTHUR E, b New York, NY, Feb 20, 34; m 58; c 2. GEOLOGY. *Educ:* Brooklyn Col, BA, 55; Hofstra Univ, MS, 58; Wash Univ, St Louis, PhD(geol), 66. *Prof Exp:* Sci teacher, Island Trees High Sch, 58-61; chmn, Dept Earth Sci, 69-75, PROF GEOL, EDINBORO STATE COL, 65-, DIR MARINE SCI CONSORTIUM, 68- *Concurrent Pos:* Adj lectr, Hofstra Univ, 58-61; fel, Woods Hole Oceanog Inst & Washington Univ, St Louis, Mo. *Mem:* Soc Econ Paleont & Mineral; Sigma Xi; Nat Asn Geol Teachers. *Res:* Micropaleontology-ecology of recent Foraminifera; environments of deposition. *Mailing Add:* Dept of Earth Sci Edinboro State Col Edinboro PA 16444

WEHAUSEN, JOHN VROOMAN, b Duluth, Minn, Sept 23, 13; m 38; c 4. MECHANICS. *Educ:* Univ Mich, BS, 34, MS, 35, PhD(math), 38. *Prof Exp:* Instr math, Brown Univ, 37-38, Columbia Univ, 38-40 & Univ Mo, 40-44; consult opers res group, Off Field Serv, Off Sci Res & Develop, US Dept Navy, 44-46, mathematician, David Taylor Model Basin, 46-49, actg head mech br, Off Naval Res, 49-50; assoc res mathematician, Inst Eng Res, 56-57, res mathematician, Dept Naval Archit, 57-58, assoc prof eng sci, 58-59, PROF ENG SCI, UNIV CALIF, BERKELEY, 59- *Concurrent Pos:* Lectr, Univ Md, 45-50; exec ed, Math Rev, Am Math Soc, 50-56; vis prof, Univ Hamburg, 60-61, Flinders Univ SAustralia, 67, Univ Nantes, 73, Univ Grenoble, 79, Technion, 82, Univ Tel Aviv, 82 & Chalmers Univ, Sweden, 82. *Mem:* Nat Acad Eng; Soc Naval Archit & Marine Eng; Math Asn Am; Am Math Soc. *Res:* Fluid mechanics, especially theory of water waves and hydrodynamics of ships. *Mailing Add:* Dept of Naval Archit Univ of Calif Berkeley CA 94720

WEHE, ROBERT L(OUIS), b Topeka, Kans, Apr 14, 21; m 42; c 5. MECHANICAL ENGINEERING. *Educ:* Univ Kans, BS, 48; Univ Ill, MS, 51. *Prof Exp:* Instr mech eng, Univ Ill, 48-51; asst prof, 51-57, ASSOC PROF MECH ENG, CORNELL UNIV, 57- *Concurrent Pos:* NSF fac fel, Univ Ill, 59-60; proj engr, Corning Glass Works, 57-58, consult, 55-59; consult, Lycoming Div, Avco, Inc, 56. *Mem:* Am Soc Mech Engrs; Am Soc Eng Educ. *Res:* Hydrodynamic lubrication; design of automatic machinery. *Mailing Add:* Dept of Mech Eng Cornell Univ Ithaca NY 14850

WEHINGER, PETER AUGUSTUS, b Goshen, NY, Feb 18, 38; m 67. ASTRONOMY. *Educ:* Union Col, NY, BS, 60; Ind Univ, MA, 62; Case Western Reserve Univ, PhD(astron), 66. *Prof Exp:* Res asst astron, Ind Univ, 60-62; NASA fel, Warner & Swasey Observ, Case Western Reserve Univ, 63-65; from instr to asst prof, Univ Mich, 65-70; assoc prof, Univ Kans, 70-72; vis assoc prof, Tel-Aviv Univ, 72-75; prin res fel, Royal Greenwich Observ, 75-77; vis sr scientist, Max Planck Inst Astron, Heidelberg, 78-80; DISCIPLINE SCIENTIST, INT HALLEY WATCH, NASA, 82- *Concurrent Pos:* NSF res grant, Kitt Peak Nat Observ, 66; sr res assoc, Ohio State Univ, 78-79; vis prof, Physics Dept, Ariz State Univ, 81- & Physics-Astron Dept, Northern Ariz Univ, 81- *Mem:* Am Astron Soc; Royal Astron Soc; Int Astron Union. *Res:* Astronomical instrumentation; stellar spectroscopy; Galilean satellites; cometary spectroscopy; spectroscopy of galaxies and quasars. *Mailing Add:* Dept Physics Ariz State Univ Tempe AZ 85287

WEHLAU, AMELIA W, b Berkeley, Calif, Feb 5, 30; m 50; c 4. ASTRONOMY. *Educ:* Univ Calif, Berkeley, AB, 49, PhD(astron), 53. *Prof Exp:* Lectr, 65-71, asst prof, 71-78, ASSOC PROF ASTRON, UNIV WESTERN ONT, 78- *Concurrent Pos:* Mem, Can Comt, Int Astron Union, 67-70. *Mem:* Am Astron Soc; Royal Astron Soc Can; Can Astron Soc; Int Astron Union. *Res:* Variable stars in globular clusters. *Mailing Add:* Dept Astron Univ Western Ont London ON N6A 3K7 Can

WEHLAU, WILLIAM HENRY, b San Francisco, Calif, Apr 7, 26; m 50; c 4. ASTRONOMY. *Educ:* Univ Calif, AB, 49, PhD(astron), 53. *Prof Exp:* Instr astron, Case Inst Technol, 53-55; assoc prof, 55-65, PROF ASTRON, UNIV WESTERN ONT, 65-, HEAD DEPT, 55- *Mem:* Am Astron Soc; Royal Astron Soc Can; Can Astron Soc. *Res:* Stellar spectroscopy and photometry; astrophysics. *Mailing Add:* Dept of Astron Univ of Western Ont London ON N6A 5B9 Can

WEHLE, LOUIS BRANDEIS, JR, b Washington, DC, Dec 28, 18; m 46; c 4. AERONAUTICAL ENGINEERING. *Educ:* Harvard Univ, BS, 40. *Prof Exp:* Stress analyst, 41-48, head struct methods group, 48-56, head nuclear sect, 56-59, staff engr, 61-72, CHIEF SCIENTIST, GRUMMAN AEROSPACE CORP, BETHPAGE, 72- *Mem:* Am Phys Soc; Am Inst Aeronaut & Astronaut. *Res:* Stress analysis; structural mechanics. *Mailing Add:* Camel Hollow Rd Huntington NY 11743

WEHMAN, ANTHONY THEODORE, b Jamaica, NY, June 6, 42. ORGANIC CHEMISTRY, ORGANOMETALLIC CHEMISTRY. *Educ:* Univ Detroit, BChE, 65; Univ Del, PhD(chem), 69. *Prof Exp:* NIH fel chem, Mass Inst Technol, 69-70; instr, Univ Del, 70-71; asst prof, 71-76, ASSOC PROF CHEM, US COAST GUARD ACAD, 76-, ASST DEAN ACAD, 76- *Concurrent Pos:* Comt mem panel on hazardous mat, Nat Acad Sci, 71-75. *Mem:* Am Chem Soc; The Chem Soc. *Res:* Aromatic metal complexes; organic photochemical reactions; benzyne chemistry. *Mailing Add:* Dept of Phys Sci US Coast Guard Acad New London CT 06320

WEHMAN, HENRY JOSEPH, b Cincinnati, Ohio, Dec 21, 37; div; c 2. COMPARATIVE NEUROLOGY, PSYCHIATRY. *Educ:* Spring Hill Col, BS, 63; Johns Hopkins Univ, PhD(biol), 69; Pa State Univ, MD, 82. *Prof Exp:* Lab scientist electron micros, Rosewood State Hosp, 69-73; asst prof biol,

King's Col, Pa, 73-78. *Concurrent Pos:* Res assoc prof pediat, Sch Med, Univ Md, 70-73; mem bd dirs, Tech Info Proj, Washington, DC, 74-78. *Mem:* AAAS; Am Soc Cell Biol; Soc Neurosci. *Res:* Electron microscopy of the developing nervous system in mammalian fetuses; effects of maternally introduced agents on the development of fetal nerves. *Mailing Add:* Milton S Hershey Med Ctr Pa State Univ Hershey PA 17033

WEHMANN, ALAN AHLERS, b New York, NY, Dec 28, 40; m 68; c 1. PARTICLE PHYSICS. *Educ:* Rensselaer Polytech Inst, BS, 62; Harvard Univ, MA, 63, PhD(physics), 68. *Prof Exp:* Res assoc physics, Univ Rochester, 67-69; PHYSICIST I, MESON LAB SECT, FERMI ACCELERATOR LAB, 69- *Mem:* Am Phys Soc. *Res:* Experimental high energy particle physics. *Mailing Add:* Fermi Nat Accelerator Lab PO Box 500 Batavia IL 60510

WEHNER, ALFRED PETER, b Wiesbaden, Ger, Oct 23, 26; US citizen; m 55; c 4. MEDICINE. *Educ:* Gutenberg Univ, Dr Med Dent, 53. *Prof Exp:* Pvt pract, WGer, 51-53; Dr med dent, Guggenheim Dent Clin, 53-54; Dr med dent, 7100th Hosp, US Air Force, Europe, 54-56; res asst microbiol, Field Res Lab, Mobil Oil Co, Tex, 57-62; sr res scientist biomed res, Biomet Instrument Corp, 62-64; dir & pres, Electro-Aerosol Inst, Inc, 64-67; prof biol & chmn dept sci, Univ Plano, 66-67; res assoc inhalation toxicol, 67-77, mgr, Environ & Indust Toxicol, 78-80, TASK LEADER, INDUST TOXICOL, PAC NORTHWEST LABS, BATTELLE MEM INST, 80- *Concurrent Pos:* Fel clin pedodontia, Guggenheim Dent Clin, 53-54; consult, Vet Admin Hosp, McKinney, Tex, 63-65; US rep, Int Soc Biometeorol, 72- *Mem:* Int Soc Biometeorol; Int Soc Aerosols Med; Am Inst Med Climatol; Sigma Xi. *Res:* Inhalation toxicology; biological effects of electro-aerosols and air ions; bioclimatology. *Mailing Add:* Dept Biol Pac Northwest Labs Battelle Mem Inst Richland WA 99352

WEHNER, DONALD C, b Middletown, NY, Apr 1, 29; m 50; c 3. WATER POLLUTION, ENVIRONMENTAL SCIENCES. *Educ:* Univ Bridgeport, BA, 51. *Prof Exp:* Biologist, Lederle Div, 51-54 & 56-58, res biologist, Indust Chem Div, 58-69, asst to dept head, Water Treating Chem Dept, 69-70. microbiologist-field engr, 70-74, dist sales mgr, 74-75, TECH SPECIALIST, PAPER CHEMS DEPT, AM CYANAMID CO, 75- *Concurrent Pos:* Mem subcomt biol anal of waters for sub-surface injection, Am Petrol Inst, 59-64. *Mem:* Soc Indust Microbiol(treas, 66-68, vpres, 69-70, pres, 71-72); Am Inst Biol Sci; Water Pollution Control Fedn; Tech Asn Pulp & Paper Indust. *Res:* Research and development of industrial algicides, bactericides and fungicides. *Mailing Add:* Am Cyanamid Co PO Box 868 Mobile AL 36601

WEHNER, GOTTFRIED KARL, b Ger, Sept 23, 10; nat US; m 39; c 3. PHYSICS. *Educ:* Inst Technol, Munich, Ger, dipl, 36, DrIng, 39. *Prof Exp:* Physicist, Inst Technol, Munich, 39-45, Wright-Patterson Air Force Base, Ohio, 47-55 & Gen Mills, Inc, 55-63; dir appl sci div, Litton Industs, Inc, 63-68; PROF ELEC ENG, UNIV MINN, MINNEAPOLIS, 68- *Honors & Awards:* Welch Medal, Am Vacuum Soc, 71. *Mem:* Fel Am Phys Soc; fel Inst Elec & Electronics Engrs; hon mem Am Vacuum Soc; Ger Phys Soc; Europ Phys Soc. *Res:* Plasma and surface physics; thin films; vacuum physics; sputtering. *Mailing Add:* Dept Elec Eng Univ Minn Minneapolis MN 55455

WEHNER, J(OHN) FRANCIS, b Wapakoneta, Ohio, June 1, 29; m 56; c 2. CHEMICAL ENGINEERING. *Educ:* Univ Dayton, BChE, 51; Cath Univ, PhD(phys chem), 54. *Prof Exp:* Res asst chem kinetics, Forrestal Res Ctr, Princeton Univ, 54-55; from instr to asst prof chem eng, Cath Univ, 55-59; vis asst prof, Johns Hopkins Univ, 59-63; assoc prof, Univ Notre Dame, 63-66; res engr, Chambers Works, 66-78, CHEMIST, E I DU PONT DE NEMOURS & CO, INC, 78- *Mem:* Am Inst Chem Engrs. *Res:* Molecular physics, flames and detonations; kinetics and reactor design; polymerizations and polymer properties. *Mailing Add:* Exp Sta E I du Pont de Nemours & Co Inc Wilmington DE 19898

WEHNER, PHILIP, b Chicago, Ill, July 21, 17; m 43; c 2. INDUSTRIAL ORGANIC CHEMISTRY. *Educ:* Univ Chicago, PhD(org chem), 43. *Prof Exp:* Res chemist, Gen Aniline & Film Corp, Pa, 43-46; assoc chemist, Argonne Nat Lab, 46-52; chemist, Ciba States Ltd, 52-55; chemist, Toms River-Cincinnati Chem Corp, 55-60, mgr res & develop, 60-64, vpres, 64-68, pres, 68-72; vpres prod & tech develop, 72-78, VPRES TECH AFFAIRS, DYESTUFFS & CHEM DIV, CIBA-GEIGY CORP, 78- *Mem:* Am Chem Soc; Am Asn Textile Chem & Colorists. *Mailing Add:* Dyestuffs & Chem Div Ciba-Geigy Corp Box 11422 Greensboro NC 27409

WEHR, ALLAN GORDON, b Brooklyn, NY, July 31, 31; m 51; c 2. CHEMICAL ENGINEERING, MATERIALS ENGINEERING. *Educ:* Mo Sch Mines, BS, 58; Univ Mo, PhD(metall eng), 62. *Prof Exp:* Res engr, P R Mallory Co, 59-60; assoc prof metall eng, 61-62, prof mat eng & head dept, 62-73, PROF CHEM ENG, MISS STATE UNIV, 73- *Mem:* Am Soc Metals; Am Soc Eng Educ; Am Inst Chem Engrs. *Res:* Fracture; magnetohydrodynamics; mechanical behavior of materials; corrosion; nitrogen oxide generation and control. *Mailing Add:* PO Box AW Mississippi State MS 39762

WEHR, CARL TIMOTHY, b San Francisco, Calif, Feb 15, 43; m 66; c 2. BIOCHEMISTRY, GENETICS. *Educ:* Whitman Col, BA, 65; Ore State Univ, PhD(microbial physiol), 69. *Prof Exp:* Fel microbiol, Dept Bact, Univ Calif, Davis, 69-71; res biologist molecular biol, Virus Lab, Univ Calif, Berkeley, 71-75; dir res chem, Agr Sci Labs, 75-78; sr chemist biochem, 78-80, MGR, HIGH PERFORMANCE LIQUID CHROMATOGRAPHY LAB, VARIAN INSTRUMENTS, 80- *Concurrent Pos:* Jane Coffin Childs Mem Fund Med Res fel, 69-71. *Mem:* AAAS; Am Soc Microbiol; Inst Food Technol. *Res:* Bacterial genetics; development of analytical methods in food agricultural chemistry and biomedical research. *Mailing Add:* Varian Instruments 2700 Mitchell Dr Walnut Creek CA 95498

WEHR, HERBERT MICHAEL, b San Francisco, Calif, Feb 15, 43; m 67; c 1. FOOD SCIENCE, MICROBIOLOGY. *Educ:* Univ Calif, Berkeley, BS, 66; Ore State Univ, MS, 68, PhD(biochem), 72. *Prof Exp:* Supvr microbiol & food chem, 71-73, asst adminr, 73-77, ADMINR, LAB SERV, ORE DEPT AGR, 78- *Concurrent Pos:* Mem, Conf on Interstate Milk Shipments, Nat Lab Comn, 77-; chmn, Ore Comt Synthetic Chem Environ, 77-; chmn, Ore Interagency Pesticides Coun, 79- *Mem:* Inst Food Technologists; Asn Off Anal Chemists; Int Asn Milk, Food & Environ Sanitarians; Am Chem Soc. *Res:* Food microbiology; food biochemistry; methods development in food chemistry and microbiology. *Mailing Add:* Lab Serv Ore Dept of Agr Salem OR 97310

WEHRENBERG, JOHN P, b Springfield, Ill, Aug 10, 27; m 66. MINERALOGY. *Educ:* Univ Mo, BS, 50; Univ Ill, MS, 52, PhD, 56. *Prof Exp:* From asst prof to assoc prof, 55-66, PROF GEOL, UNIV MONT, 66- *Mem:* Mineral Soc Am; Geochem Soc; Am Crystallog Asn. *Res:* Solid state processes in geology; crystallography; infrared spectra of minerals. *Mailing Add:* Dept of Geol Univ of Mont Missoula MT 59801

WEHRENBERG, PAUL JAMES, atomic physics, space physics, see previous edition

WEHRING, BERNARD WILLIAM, b Monroe, Mich, Aug 3, 37; m 59; c 4. NUCLEAR ENGINEERING, NUCLEAR PHYSICS. *Educ:* Univ Mich, BSE(physics) & BSE(math), 59; Univ Ill, MS, 61, PhD(nuclear eng), 66. *Prof Exp:* From asst prof to assoc prof, 66-77, PROF NUCLEAR ENG, UNIV ILL, URBANA, 77-, ASST DEAN ENG, 81- *Concurrent Pos:* Consult, Appl Physics Div, Argonne Nat Lab, 77-79 & Theoretical Div, Los Alamos Sci Lab, 77-79; mem, Cross Sect Eval Working Group, Brookhaven Nat Lab & Am Nuclear Standards Comt. *Mem:* Am Nuclear Soc; Am Soc Eng Educ; Am Phys Soc. *Res:* Fission physics; interaction of radiation with matter; radiation detection. *Mailing Add:* 214 Nuclear Eng Lab Univ Ill 103 S Goodwin Ave Urbana IL 61801

WEHRLE, LOUIS, JR, b Santa Monica, Calif, Apr 2, 35; m 63. FOOD MICROBIOLOGY. *Educ:* Univ Toledo, BS, 57; Ohio State Univ, MS, 67, PhD(microbiol), 69. *Prof Exp:* Asst prof microbiol, Ohio State Univ, 69-72; SR RES SCIENTIST, CENT STATES CAN CORP, MASSILLON, 72- *Mem:* Inst Food Technologists. *Res:* Thermoprocessing of food products. *Mailing Add:* Cent State Can Corp 700 16 St SE Massillon OH 44646

WEHRLE, PAUL F, b Ithaca, NY, Dec 18, 21; m 44; c 4. PEDIATRICS, MICROBIOLOGY. *Educ:* Univ Ariz, BS, 47; Tulane Univ, MD, 47. *Prof Exp:* Clin instr pediat, Univ Ill Col Med, 50-51; res assoc epidemiol & microbiol, Grad Sch Pub Health, Univ Pittsburgh, 51-53; res assoc, Poliomyelitis Lab, Johns Hopkins Univ, 53-55; from asst prof to assoc prof pediat, Col Med, State Univ NY Upstate Med Ctr, 55-61, actg chmn dept microbiol, 59-61; prof, 61-71, HASTINGS PROF PEDIAT, SCH MED, UNIV SOUTHERN CALIF, 71- *Concurrent Pos:* Asst med supt, Chicago Munic Contagious Dis Hosp, Ill, 50-51; head physician contagious dis serv, Los Angeles County-Univ Southern Calif Med Ctr, 61-63, chief physician, Children's Div, 63- *Mem:* Am Acad Pediat; Soc Pediat Res; Am Soc Microbiol; Am Pub Health Asn; Am Asn Immunologists. *Res:* Viral infections in man, especially enteroviruses; antibiotic action; epidemiology of infectious diseases. *Mailing Add:* Los Angeles County-Univ of Southern Calif Med Ctr Los Angeles CA 90033

WEHRLI, PIUS ANTON, b Bazenheid, Switz, July 27, 33; m 62; c 1. CHEMISTRY. *Educ:* Swiss Fed Inst Technol, Dipl Chem Eng, 64, PhD(chem), 67. *Prof Exp:* Sr chemist, 67-69, res fel, 69-70, res group chief, 70-73, res sect chief, 73-78, DIR, KILO LAB & PROCESS RES, CHEM RES DEPT, HOFFMANN-LA ROCHE INC, 78- *Mem:* Am Chem Soc; Swiss Chem Soc; Soc Ger Chem. *Res:* Development in synthetic organic chemistry. *Mailing Add:* Chem Res Dept Kingsland Rd Hoffmann-La Roche Inc Nutley NJ 07110

WEHRLY, THOMAS EDWARD, b Richmond, Ind, Nov 5, 47; m 76. STOCHASTIC MODELLING, DIRECTIONAL DATA ANALYSIS. *Educ:* Univ Mich, BS, 69; Univ Wis-Madison, MA, 70, PhD(statist), 76. *Prof Exp:* ASST PROF STATIST, INST STATIST, TEX A&M UNIV, 76- *Mem:* Am Statist Asn; Biometrics Soc; Inst Math Statist; Royal Statist Soc. *Res:* Stochastic modelling for biological systems and statistical inference for these stochastic models; inference for directional data; estimation theory; nonparametric inference. *Mailing Add:* Inst Statist Tex A&M Univ College Station TX 77843

WEHRMEISTER, HERBERT LOUIS, b Chicago, Ill, Nov 8, 20; m 53; c 3. CHEMISTRY. *Educ:* Ill Inst Technol, BS, 44; Northwestern Univ, MS, 46, PhD(chem), 48. *Prof Exp:* Lab asst, Portland Cement Asn, Ill, 38-40; control chemist, W H Barber Co, 40-44; res chemist, Miner Labs, 44-46; res chemist, Com Solvents Corp, 49-77, RES CHEMIST, IMC CORP, 77- *Mem:* Sigma Xi; Am Chem Soc. *Res:* Organic chemistry; derivatives of sulfenic acids; syntheses in the thiazole series; nitoparaffin and hydroxylamine derivatives; zearalenone and derivatives. *Mailing Add:* Res Dept IMC Corp Terre Haute IN 47808

WEHRY, EARL L, JR, b Reading, Pa, Feb 13, 41. ANALYTICAL CHEMISTRY. *Educ:* Juniata Col, BS, 62; Purdue Univ, PhD(chem), 65. *Prof Exp:* Instr chem, Ind Univ, 65-66, asst prof, 66-70; from asst prof to assoc prof, 70-77, PROF CHEM, UNIV TENN, KNOXVILLE, 77- *Mem:* AAAS; Soc Appl Spectros; Am Chem Soc. *Res:* Fluorescence and phosphorescence; photochemistry. *Mailing Add:* Dept of Chem Univ of Tenn Knoxville TN 37916

WEHUNT, RALPH LEE, b Atlanta, Ga, Dec 2, 22; m 43; c 2. SOIL FERTILITY, PLANT PHYSIOLOGY. *Educ:* Univ Ga, BSA, 46, MSA, 48; Rutgers Univ, New Brunswick, PhD(soil chem), 53. *Prof Exp:* Educ mgr agron, Chilean Nitrate Educ Bur, Inc, 53-55; soils & fertilizer specialist, Agr

Exten Serv, Univ Ga, 55-59; agronomist, Tenn Valley Auth, 59-62, head educ & commun serv, 62-65; chief agronomist, Cities Serv Co, 65-68, mgr personnel develop, CFS Div, 68-71; acct supvr, 71-77, prod group mgr, 77-80, DIR OPER, DOANE AGR SERV, 80- *Concurrent Pos:* Consult with several large corps. *Mem:* Am Soc Agron; Soil Sci Soc Am; Am Soc Training & Develop; Am Mgt Asn. *Res:* Soil chemistry; educational psychology of farmers; market research. *Mailing Add:* 12943 Ambois St Louis MO 63141

WEI, CHIN HSUAN, b Yuanlin, Taiwan, Oct 25, 26; m 54; c 2. X-RAY CRYSTALLOGRAPHY. *Educ:* Cheng Kung Univ, BS, 50; Purdue Univ, MS, 58; Univ Wis, Madison, PhD(phys chem), 62. *Prof Exp:* Asst phys chem, Cheng Kung Univ, 50-55, instr gen chem, 55-56; res assoc struct chem, Univ Wis, Madison, 62-65, sr spectroscopist, 65-66; BIOPHYSICIST, OAK RIDGE NAT LAB, 66- *Concurrent Pos:* Vis prof, Cheng Kung Univ, 70-71. *Mem:* Am Chem Soc; Am Crystallog Asn. *Res:* Structure determination of organometallic complexes and compounds of biological interest; isolation, purification, characterization and crystalliation of proteins. *Mailing Add:* Biol Div Oak Ridge Nat Lab Oak Ridge TN 37830

WEI, CHUNG-CHEN, b Taiwan, Apr 9, 40; m 65; c 1. ORGANIC CHEMISTRY, PHOTOCHEMISTRY. *Educ:* Nat Taiwan Univ, BS, 63; Colo State Univ, PhD(org chem), 69. *Prof Exp:* Fel org chem, Johns Hopkins Univ, 69-71; res assoc bio-org chem, Yale Univ, 71-73; assoc chemist, Midwest Res Inst, 73; SR CHEMIST, HOFFMANN-LA ROCHE INC, 74- *Mem:* Am Chem Soc. *Res:* Synthesis of heterocyclic compounds and natural products; organic photochemistry. *Mailing Add:* Chem Res Dept Hoffmann-La Roche Inc Nutley NJ 07110

WEI, DIANA YUN DEE, b Che-Kiang, China, June 8, 30; m 62; c 1. MATHEMATICS. *Educ:* Taiwan Norm Univ, BS & BEd, 53; Univ Nebr, MS, 60; McGill Univ, PhD(math), 67. *Prof Exp:* Lectr math, Taipei Inst Technol, Taiwan, 53-58; teaching asst, Univ Nebr, 58-60 & Univ Wash, 60-62; lectr, McGill Univ, 62-65; asst prof, Marianopolis Col, 65-68 & Sir George Williams Univ, 68-72; prof, Sch Comn Baldwin-Cartier, 72-75; PROF MATH, NORFOLK STATE UNIV, 75- *Concurrent Pos:* Nat Res Coun Can grant award, 69, 70, 71. *Mem:* Am Math Soc; Can Math Cong. *Res:* Groups, rings and modules; homology; category; linear algebra. *Mailing Add:* Dept Math Norfolk State Univ Norfolk VA 23502

WEI, E T F, b Shanghai, China, Dec 6, 44; m 66; c 2. PHARMACOLOGY, TOXICOLOGY. *Educ:* Univ Calif, Berkeley, AB, 65; Univ Calif, San Francisco, PhD(pharmacol), 69. *Prof Exp:* Nat Inst Arthritis & Metab Dis fel, Stanford Univ, 69-70; from asst prof to assoc prof, 70-80, PROF TOXICOL, SCH PUB HEALTH, UNIV CALIF, BERKELEY, 80- *Concurrent Pos:* Nat Inst Drug Abuse fel, 70-81; Nat Inst Environ Health Sci fel, 74-76; assoc prof toxicol, Dept Pharmacol, Univ Calif, San Francisco, 75-80, prof, 80- *Mem:* AAAS; Soc Toxicol; Am Soc Pharmacol & Exp Therapeut. *Res:* Biological mechanisms of morphine dependence; toxic chemicals and their mechanisms of action. *Mailing Add:* Sch of Pub Health Univ of Calif Berkeley CA 94720

WEI, ENOCH PING, b Shanghai, China, July 19, 42; US citizen; m 69; c 2. CEREBRAL MICROCIRCULATION, PERIPHERAL CIRCULATION. *Educ:* Univ NC, Chapel Hill, BA, 67, PhD(physiol), 72. *Prof Exp:* Fel, 71-73, RES ASSOC MED, MED COL VA, 73-, DIR RES, 81- *Mem:* Am Physiol Soc; Int Soc Cerebral Blood Flow & Metab; Am Fedn Clin Res. *Res:* Local regulatory mechanisms of the cerebral circulation in areas related to high blood pressure, and to percussion-type brain injuries. *Mailing Add:* Dept Med Box 281 Med Col Va Richmond VA 23298

WEI, GUANG-JONG JASON, b Fu-Chou, China, Mar 14, 46; m 71. PHYSICAL BIOCHEMISTRY. *Educ:* Cheng Kung Univ, Taiwan, BS, 68; Univ Ill, Urbana, PhD(phys chem), 74. *Prof Exp:* Res assoc, 74-75, NIH fel phys biochem, Mich State Univ, 75-77; res specialist, 77-80, SCIENTIST, UNIV MINN, ST PAUL, 80- *Mem:* Am Chem Soc. *Res:* Physical chemistry of macromolecules; dynamic light scattering. *Mailing Add:* Dept of Biochem Univ of Minn St Paul MN 55108

WEI, JAMES, b Macau, China, Aug 14, 30; nat US; m 56; c 4. CHEMICAL ENGINEERING. *Educ:* Ga Inst Technol, BChE, 52; Mass Inst Technol, MS, 54, ScD(chem eng), 55. *Prof Exp:* Res assoc, Socony Mobil Oil Co, Inc, 55-65, sr res assoc, Mobil Oil Corp, 65-68, sr scientist, Mobil Res & Develop Corp, 68-69, mgr anal, LRAS Group, Mobil Oil Corp, NY, 69-71; Allan P Colburn prof chem eng, Univ Del, 71-77; WARREN K LEWIS PROF & HEAD DEPT CHEM ENG, MASS INST TECHNOL, 77- *Concurrent Pos:* Consult, Mobil Oil Corp; chmn, catalyst panel, Comt Motor Vehicle Emission, Nat Acad Sci; consult ed, Chem Eng Ser, McGraw-Hill; vis prof, Princeton Univ, 62-63 & Calif Inst Technol, 65; mem, Sci Adv Bd, Environ Protection Agency, 76-79; Fairchild scholar, Calif Inst Technol, 77; chief ed, Adv Chem Eng, 80- *Honors & Awards:* Petrol Chem Award, Am Chem Soc, 66; Prof Progress Award, Am Inst Chem Engrs, 70; William H Walker Award, Am Inst Chem Engrs, 80. *Mem:* Nat Acad Eng; Am Chem Soc; Am Inst Chem Engrs. *Res:* Catalysis and kinetics; chemical reactors; applied mathematics; structure of chemical processing industries. *Mailing Add:* Dept of Chem Eng Mass Inst of Technol Cambridge MA 02139

WEI, L(ING) Y(UN), b Hangyang, China, May 23, 20; Can citizen; m 44; c 4. SOLID STATE PHYSICS, ELECTRICAL ENGINEERING. *Educ:* Northwestern Col Eng, China, BS, 42; Univ Ill, MS, 49, PhD(solid state physics), 58. *Prof Exp:* Engr, Directorate Gen Telecommun, China & Formosa, 42-56; asst prof elec eng, Univ Wash, 58-60; assoc prof, 60-63, PROF ELEC ENG, UNIV WATERLOO, 63- *Mem:* AAAS; Biophys Soc; Inst Elec & Electronics Engrs. *Res:* Semiconductor materials; physics of thin films and physical mechanisms of nerve conduction. *Mailing Add:* 56 High Waterloo ON N2L 3X8 Can

WEI, LEE-JEN, b China, Apr 2, 48; m; c 1. BIOSTATISTICS. *Educ:* Fu Jen Univ, Taiwan, BS, 70; Univ Wis, Madison, PhD(statist), 75. *Prof Exp:* Asst prof statist, Univ SC, 75-79, assoc prof, 79-80; cancer expert, Nat Cancer Inst, 80-81; PROF STATIST, GEORGE WASHINGTON UNIV, 81- *Concurrent Pos:* Comt mem, Nat Res Coun, 82- *Mem:* Am Statist Asn. *Mailing Add:* Dept Statist George Washington Univ Washington DC 20052

WEI, LESTER YEEHOW, b Foochow, China, Sept 4, 44; US citizen; m 72; c 1. ANALYTICAL CHEMISTRY. *Educ:* Cheng Kung Univ, BSE, 67; ETex State Univ, MS, 70, EdD(chem), 74. *Prof Exp:* Res assoc chem, Emory Univ 74-76 & Ill Geol Surv, 76-77; asst chemist, 77-80, ASST PROF SCIENTIST, ILL NATURAL HIST SURV, 80- *Mem:* Am Chem Soc. *Res:* Chemistry and analysis of pesticides; gas chromatography; mass spectroscopy. *Mailing Add:* Ill Natural Hist Surv 607 E Peabody Champaign IL 61820

WEI, LUN-SHIN, b Hou-long, Formosa, Jan 14, 29; m 56; c 4. FOOD SCIENCE. *Educ:* Taiwan Prov Col Agr, BS, 51; Univ Ill, MS, 55, PhD, 58. *Prof Exp:* Asst agron, 55-57, sci analyst, 57-59, res assoc food sci, 59-64, assoc prof, 64-76, PROF FOOD SCI, UNIV ILL, URBANA, 76- *Honors & Awards:* Educ & Res Award, Land of Lincoln Soybean Asn, 73. *Mem:* AAAS; Am Chem Soc; Inst Food Technologists. *Res:* Foods and plant materials analysis; food processing and preservation; product development; food utilization of soybeans. *Mailing Add:* 309 McHenry St Urbana IL 61801

WEI, PAX SAMUEL PIN, b Chungking, China, Nov 11, 38; US citizen; m 64; c 3. PHYSICAL CHEMISTRY. *Educ:* Nat Taiwan Univ, BS, 60; Univ Ill, Urbana, MS, 63; Calif Inst Technol, PhD(chem), 68. *Prof Exp:* Mem tech staff, Bell Tel Labs, NJ, 67-69; res scientist, Boeing Sci Res Labs, 69-71, RES SCIENTIST, BOEING AEROSPACE CO, 72- *Mem:* Am Chem Soc; Am Phys Soc. *Res:* Atomic and molecular spectroscopy; surface science; electron diffraction; laser effects. *Mailing Add:* Boeing Aerospace Co PO Box 3999 Seattle WA 98124

WEI, PETER HSING-LIEN, b Shantung, China, Feb 11, 22; m 48; c 4. MEDICINAL CHEMISTRY. *Educ:* St John's Univ, China, BS, 48; Columbia Univ, MA, 53; Univ Pa, PhD, 69. *Prof Exp:* Res chemist, Norwich Pharmacal Col, 52-60; res chemist, 60-69, sr res chemist, 69-77, GROUP LEADER, WYETH LABS, INC, 77- *Mem:* Am Chem Soc. *Res:* Pharmaceuticals; synthesis of heterocyclic compounds of biological interest. *Mailing Add:* Rm 4079 Med Chem Dept Wyeth Labs Inc Radnor PA 19087

WEI, ROBERT, b Apr 16, 39; US citizen; m 76; c 1. BIOCHEMISTRY, IMMUNOLOGY. *Educ:* George Washington Univ, BA, 69, PhD(biochem), 74; Georgetown Univ, MS, 72. *Prof Exp:* Prin res chemist clin chem, Wash Ref Lab Inc, 74-75; sr res scientist clin chem, Electro-Nucleonics, Inc, 75-76, sr res scientist immunol, 76-78; ASSOC PROF BIOCHEM, CLEVELAND STATE UNIV, 78- *Concurrent Pos:* Mem adj staff, Cleveland Clin Found, 78- *Mem:* Am Asn Clin Chemists; Am Asn Immunol. *Res:* Detection, isolation and purification of endogenous biological components involved in immune response. *Mailing Add:* Dept of Chem 1983 E 24th St Cleveland OH 44115

WEI, ROBERT PEH-YING, b Nanking, China, Sept 16, 31; m 54; c 2. APPLIED MECHANICS, MATERIALS SCIENCE. *Educ:* Princeton Univ, BSE, 53, MSE, 54, PhD(mech eng), 60. *Prof Exp:* Instr mech eng, Princeton Univ, 54-57, res asst aeronaut eng, 58-59; assoc technologist, fracture mech, Appl Res Lab, US Steel Corp, 59-61, technologist, 61-62, sr res engr, 62-64, assoc res consult, 64-66; assoc prof mech, 66-70, PROF MECH, LEHIGH UNIV, 70- *Mem:* Am Soc Testing & Mat. *Res:* Fracture mechanics; mechanics and metallurgical aspects of fatigue crack growth and stress corrosion cracking; experimental stress analysis. *Mailing Add:* Dept of Mech Eng & Mech Lehigh Univ Bethlehem PA 18015

WEI, STEPHEN HON YIN, b Shanghai, China, Sept 17, 37; US citizen; m 63; c 2. PEDODONTICS, HISTOLOGY. *Educ:* Univ Adelaide, BDS, 61, Hons, 62, MDS, 65; Univ Ill, Chicago, MS, 67; Univ Iowa, DDS, 71. *Prof Exp:* Dent surgeon, Royal Adelaide Hosp, Univ Adelaide, 63-64, teaching registr, Queen Elizabeth Hosp, 65; res asst pedodontics, Univ Ill, Chicago, 65-66, instr, 67; from asst prof to assoc prof, 67-74, PROF PEDODONTICS, COL DENT, UNIV IOWA, 74- *Concurrent Pos:* Dentist, Vet Admin Hosp, 69-, consult, 74; consult, Res Comt, Am Acad Pedodont, 71-, ed, 78-; mem res comt, Off Maternal & Child Health, Bur Community Health Serv, HEW. *Mem:* Am Dent Asn; Am Asn Hosp Dent; Int Asn Dent Res; Am Acad Pedodontics; Am Soc Dent for Children. *Res:* Preventive dentistry; remineralization of teeth; systemic and topical fluoride therapy; electron optical studies of dental and other hard tissues; clinical research in pedodontics and dental caries. *Mailing Add:* Rm 203 Col of Dent Univ of Iowa Iowa City IA 52242

WEI, WHUA FU, b Laipor, China, Oct 27, 20; US citizen; m 66; c 3. SOLID STATE PHYSICS. *Educ:* Nat Chekiang Univ, BS, 43; Okla State Univ, MS, 51, PhD(physics), 65. *Prof Exp:* Instr gen physics, Nat Chekiang Univ, 43-49; physicist, Delco Radio Div, Gen Motors Corp, 55-58; res asst semiconductor, Univ Colo, 58-60 & Okla State, 62-64; res physicist, Brown Eng, 65-66; ASSOC PROF PHYSICS, ARK STATE UNIV, 66- *Mem:* Am Physics Soc. *Res:* Magnetic and optical properties of semiconductors. *Mailing Add:* Dept of Math & Physics Ark State Univ State University AR 72467

WEI, WU-SHYONG WILLIAM, b Shin-Chu, Taiwan, June 2, 40; m 71; c 3. STATISTICS, MATHEMATICS. *Educ:* Nat Taiwan Univ, BA, 66; Univ Ore, BA, 69; Univ Wis-Madison, PhD(statist), 74. *Prof Exp:* Asst prof, 74-78, ASSOC PROF STATIST, TEMPLE UNIV, 78-, DIR BUS STATIST, SCH BUS ADMIN, 77- *Mem:* Am Statist Asn; Inst Math Statist. *Res:* Time series analysis, forecasting, statistical modelling and statistical applications in business and economics. *Mailing Add:* Dept Statist N Broad St & Montgomery Ave Philadelphia PA 19122

WEIBEL, ARMELLA, b Ewing, Nebr, Feb 7, 20. MATHEMATICS, SCIENCE EDUCATION. *Educ:* Alverno Col, BSE, 46; Univ Wis, MS, 52. *Prof Exp:* Teacher, St Clara Sch, Ill, 38-48; teacher, Frankenstein High Sch, Mo, 48-50; from instr to asst prof, 52-53, ASSOC PROF MATH, ALVERNO COL, 56- *Concurrent Pos:* Dir, Alverno Ctr, NSF Minn Math & Sci Teaching Proj, 63-70. *Mem:* Nat Coun Teachers Math. *Res:* Math education. *Mailing Add:* 3401 S 39th St Milwaukee WI 53215

WEIBEL, DALE ELDON, b De Witt, Nebr, Dec 14, 20; m 42; c 4. AGRONOMY. *Educ:* Univ Nebr, BSc, 42, MSc, 47; Iowa State Univ, PhD(plant breeding, path), 55. *Prof Exp:* Res agronomist, Div Cereal Crops & Dis, USDA, Kans, 47-53, field crops res br, Tex, 53-58; assoc prof, 58-61, PROF AGRON, OKLA STATE UNIV, 61- *Mem:* Crop Sci Soc Am; Am Soc Agron. *Res:* Sorghum breeding and genetics. *Mailing Add:* Dept of Agron Okla State Univ Stillwater OK 74074

WEIBEL, G(ERHARD) E(MANUEL), solid state electronics, see previous edition

WEIBEL, MICHAEL KENT, biochemistry, enzymology, see previous edition

WEIBELL, FRED JOHN, b Murray, Utah, Oct 18, 27; m 49; c 4. BIOMEDICAL ENGINEERING, COMPUTER SCIENCES. *Educ:* Univ Utah, BS, 53; Univ Calif, Los Angeles, MS, 69, PhD(eng), 77. *Prof Exp:* Staff mem eng, Sandia Corp, 53-57, sect supvr, 57-62; chief biomed eng sect, Vet Admin Western Res Support Ctr, 62-67, asst chief biomed eng & comput sci, Vet Admin Western Res Support Ctr, 67-72, CHIEF, VET ADMIN BIOMED ENG & COMPUT CTR, 72- *Mem:* Biomed Eng Soc (secy-treas, 69-); Instrument Soc Am. *Res:* Electrical safety in the hospital. *Mailing Add:* Biomed Eng & Comput Ctr Vet Admin Med Ctr Sepulveda CA 91343

WEIBLEN, PAUL WILLARD, b Miller, SDak, Feb 15, 27; m 67; c 1. GEOLOGY, PETROLOGY. *Educ:* Wartburg Col, BA, 50; Univ Minn, MA, 52, MS & PhD(geol), 65. *Prof Exp:* Asst prof, 65-71, assoc prof, 71-80, PROF GEOL, UNIV MINN, MINNEAPOLIS, 80- *Mem:* Electron Probe Anal Soc Am; Sigma Xi. *Res:* Petrology, especially the study of gabbroic rocks and associated mineralization; lunar petrology; Precambrian geology; application of electron probe analysis to problems in mineralogy, geochemistry and petrology. *Mailing Add:* Dept of Geol & Geophys Univ of Minn Minneapolis MN 55455

WEIBRECHT, WALTER EUGENE, b New York, NY, June 25, 37. INORGANIC CHEMISTRY. *Educ:* Franklin & Marshall Col, BS, 59; Cornell Univ, PhD(chem), 64. *Prof Exp:* Am Oil fel chem, Harvard Univ, 63-64; asst prof, Mich State Univ, 64-66; asst prof, 66-77, ASSOC PROF CHEM, UNIV MASS, BOSTON, 77- *Mem:* AAAS; Am Chem Soc; The Chem Soc. *Res:* Studies involving borazine as a Lewis acid; B-hydroxyborazines; synthesis; silicon-nitrogen bond cleavage in symmetrically and unsymmetrically alkoxylated silazanes; silicon, germanium and tin transamination equilibria. *Mailing Add:* Dept of Chem Univ of Mass Boston MA 02116

WEIBUST, ROBERT SMITH, b Newport, RI, May 6, 42. GENETICS, ZOOLOGY. *Educ:* Colby Col, AB, 64; Univ Maine, Orono, MS, 66, PhD(zool), 70. *Prof Exp:* Nat Cancer Inst fel, Jackson Lab, 64-65, Nat Inst Gen Med Sci fel, Jackson Lab & Univ Maine, Orono, 68-70, fel, Jackson Lab, 70; asst prof, 70-75, assoc prof, 75-81, PROF BIOL, MOORHEAD STATE UNIV, 81- *Mem:* AAAS; Am Genetic Asn; Sigma Xi; Genetics Soc Am. *Res:* Mammalian genetics. *Mailing Add:* Dept of Biol Moorhead State Univ Moorhead MN 56560

WEICHEL, HUGO, b Selz, Ukraine, July 23, 37; US citizen; m 61; c 2. LASERS. *Educ:* Portland State Univ, BS, 60; US Air Force Inst Technol, MS, 65; Univ Ariz, PhD, 72. *Prof Exp:* US Air Force, 60-, res physicist nuclear rocket propulsion, Edwards Air Force Base, Calif, 61-63, student arc plasmas, Aeronaut Res Lab, Ohio, 64-65, proj officer laser produced plasmas, Air Force Weapons Lab, NMex, 65-69, asst prof physics, US Air Force Inst Technol, 72-78, chief, Flight Eqip Div, 78-80, DIR PROD ASSURANCE, AERONAUT SYST DIV, AIR FORCE SYSTS COMMAND, 80- *Res:* Lasers; optics; solid state; plasmas. *Mailing Add:* Aeronaut Syst Div ENFE Wright-Patterson AFB OH 45433

WEICHENTHAL, BURTON ARTHUR, b Stanton, Nebr, Nov 7, 37; m 60; c 1. ANIMAL NUTRITION. *Educ:* Univ Nebr, BS, 59; SDak State Univ, MS, 62; Colo State Univ, PhD(nutrit), 67. *Prof Exp:* Beef cattle exten specialist, 67-80, ASSOC PROF ANIMAL SCI, UNIV ILL, URBANA, 80- *Mem:* Am Soc Animal Sci. *Res:* Ruminant nutrition and physiology. *Mailing Add:* Dept of Animal Sci Univ of Ill Urbana IL 61801

WEICHERT, DIETER HORST, b Breslau, Ger, May 2, 32; Can citizen; m 62; c 2. SEISMOLOGY. *Educ:* Univ BC, BASc, 61, PhD(geophys), 65; McMaster Univ, MSc, 63. *Prof Exp:* Res asst geophys, Univ BC, 60-61, elec eng, Nat Res Coun Can, 61 & geophys, Univ Toronto, 63; res scientist, Earth Physics Br, Dept Energy, Mines & Resources, 65-78, Pac Geosci Ctr, 78- *Concurrent Pos:* Vis scientist, Geophys Inst, Univ Karlsruhe, 70, UK Atomic Energy Authority, 71, Inst, Frankfurt Univ, 71 & Fed Rep Ger Seismol Ctr, Graefenberg, 76. *Mem:* Seismol Soc Am; Am Geophys Union; Can Geophys Union. *Res:* Geophysics. *Mailing Add:* Pac Geosci Ctr Dept of Energy Mines & Resources Sidney BC V8L 4B2 Can

WEICHLEIN, RUSSELL GEORGE, b Dayton, Ohio, Apr 23, 15; m 48; c 1. MICROBIOLOGY. *Educ:* St Mary's Univ, Tex, BS, 39; Trinity Univ, Tex, MS, 55. *Prof Exp:* Tester, Ref Lab, Tex Co, 47; asst biologist, Found Appl Res, 48-52; assoc res bacteriologist, Sanit Sci Dept, Southwest Res Inst, 53-58, dept chem res, 58-65; from instr to assoc prof, 65-80, EMER ASSOC PROF BIOL SCI, SAN ANTONIO COL, 80- *Res:* Microbial genetics; biology; bacteriology. *Mailing Add:* 306 Waxwood Lane San Antonio TX 78216

WEICHMAN, FRANK LUDWIG, b Liegnitz, Ger, Sept 23, 30; Can citizen; m 58; c 2. EXPERIMENTAL SOLID STATE PHYSICS. *Educ:* Brooklyn Col, BS, 53; Northwestern Univ, PhD(physics), 59. *Prof Exp:* From asst prof to assoc prof, 58-70, PROF PHYSICS, UNIV ALTA, 70- *Concurrent Pos:* Mem fac, Univ Strasbourg, 65-66; vis prof, Technion, Haifa, Israel, 73-74; sr indust fel, Bell Northern Res Ltd, Ottawa, 81-82. *Mem:* Can Asn Physicists; Am Phys Soc. *Res:* Optical and electrical properties of oxide semiconductors with an emphasis on the role of excitons and defect structure on photoconductivity, luminescence and electroluminescence of oxygen; solar energy as applied to photovoltaics and greenhouses. *Mailing Add:* Dept of Phys Univ of Alta Edmonton AB T6G 2E1 Can

WEICHSEL, MORTON E, JR, b Pueblo, Colo, June 17, 33; m 62; c 3. PEDIATRICS, NEUROLOGY. *Educ:* Univ Colo, Boulder, BA, 55; Univ Buffalo, MD, 62; Am Bd Pediat, dipl & cert; Am Bd Psychiat & Neurol, dipl & cert child neurol. *Prof Exp:* Intern pediat, Buffalo Children's Hosp, NY, 63; resident, Med Ctr, Stanford Univ, 63-65, fel pediat neurol, 65-67; fel Med Ctr, Univ Colo, 67-68; clin instr pediat, Med Ctr, Stanford Univ, 68-69, fel develop neurochem, 69-71; asst prof human develop & med, Col Human Med, Mich State Univ, 71-74; assoc prof, 74-80, PROF PEDIAT & NEUROL, HARBOR GEN HOSP & SCH MED, UNIV CALIF, LOS ANGELES, 80- *Mem:* Soc Neurosci; Am Acad Neurol; Soc Pediat Res; Child Neurol Soc; Am Fedn Clin Res. *Res:* Developmental neurochemistry. *Mailing Add:* Harbor Gen Hosp 1000 W Carson St Torrance CA 90509

WEICHSEL, PAUL M, b New York, NY, July 22, 31; m 55; c 3. MATHEMATICS. *Educ:* City Col New York, BS, 53; NY Univ, MS, 54; Calif Inst Technol, PhD(math), 60. *Prof Exp:* From instr to asst prof math, Univ Ill, Urbana, 60-65; NATO fel, Math Inst, Oxford Eng, 61-62; res fel, Inst Advan Studies, Australian Nat Univ, 65-66; from asst prof to assoc prof, 66-75, PROF MATH, UNIV ILL, URBANA, 75- *Concurrent Pos:* Part time consult, Argonne Nat Lab, 63-64; vis prof, Hebrew Univ, Jerusalem, 70-71 & Univ Tel Aviv, Israel, 71-72; math coordr, Nat Coord Ctr Curric Develop, Dept Technol & Soc, Col Eng, State Univ NY Stony Brook, 76-78. *Mem:* Am Math Soc; Math Asn Am. *Res:* Theory of finite groups; algebra; theory of graphs. *Mailing Add:* Dept of Math Univ of Ill Urbana IL 61801

WEICHSELBAUM, THEODORE EDWIN, b Macon, Ga, Mar 22, 08; m 34; c 2. BIOCHEMISTRY. *Educ:* Emory Univ, BS, 30; Univ Edinburgh, PhD(biochem), 35; Am Bd Clin Chem, dipl. *Prof Exp:* Assoc biochemist, Jewish Hosp, St Louis, Mo, 36-40; res dir, A S Aloe Co, 46-47; asst prof exp surg, Sch Med, Wash Univ, 48-53, assoc prof, 53-71; corp sr scientist, 66-80, SR SCIENTIFIC CONSULT, SHERWOOD MED INDUSTS INC, 80- *Concurrent Pos:* Consult, St Luke's & St Louis City Hosps, 50- *Mem:* Am Chem Soc; Am Soc Biol Chemists; Soc Exp Biol & Med. *Res:* Sulfur amino acids; ketone body metabolism; estimation of proteins; instrumentation in flame photometry; electrolyte metabolism; metabolism of fructose in man; metabolism and isolation of adrenocortical steoids. *Mailing Add:* Sherwood Med Industs Inc 5373 Bermuda Rd St Louis MO 63121

WEICK, CHARLES FREDERICK, b Buffalo, NY, Jan 19, 31; m 59; c 2. INORGANIC CHEMISTRY. *Educ:* Mt Union Col, BS, 53; Univ Rochester, PhD, 59. *Prof Exp:* assoc prof, 58-80, PROF CHEM, UNION COL, NY, 80- *Concurrent Pos:* Fel, Univ Kent, Canterbury, Eng, 71-72. *Mem:* Am Chem Soc. *Res:* Coordination chemistry; radiochemistry. *Mailing Add:* Dept of Chem Union Col Schenectady NY 12308

WEICKMANN, HELMUT K, b Munich, Ger, Mar 10, 15; US citizen; m 45; c 4. ATMOSPHERIC PHYSICS, METEOROLOGY. *Educ:* Univ Frankfurt, PhD(geophys), 39. *Hon Degrees:* Dr, Univ Clermont-Ferrand, France, 75. *Prof Exp:* Flight meteorologist, Ger Flight Inst, 39-45; dir high altitude observ, Ger Weather Serv, 45-49; physicist, Atmospheric Physics Br, US Army Electronics Command, 49-61, chief, 61-65; dir atmospheric physics & chem lab, Nat Oceanic & Atmospheric Admin, 65-79; RES ASSOC, COOP INST RES ENVIRON SCI, UNIV BOULDER, 79- *Concurrent Pos:* Co-ed, J Atmospheric Sci. *Honors & Awards:* Tech Achievement Award, Signal Corps, US Army, 61, Cert of Achievement, Electronics Command, 62. *Mem:* Fel Am Meteorol Soc; Am Geophys Union; fel AAAS; hon mem Int Asn Meteorol & Atmospheric Physics; Int Union Geod & Geophys. *Res:* Meteorological research; cloud and weather modification; geophysics. *Mailing Add:* Atmospheric Physics & Chem Lab Nat Oceanic & Atmospheric Admin Boulder CO 80303

WEIDANZ, WILLIAM P, b Jackson Heights, NY, Jan 30, 35; m 60; c 6. IMMUNOLOGY, MEDICAL MICROBIOLOGY. *Educ:* Rutgers Univ, BS, 56; Univ RI, MS, 58; Tulane Univ, PhD(microbiol), 61. *Prof Exp:* NIH fel, 61-64; asst prof immunol & pathogenic bact, La State Univ, 64-66; from asst prof to assoc prof, 66-77, PROF MICROBIOL, HAHNEMANN MED COL, 77- *Concurrent Pos:* NIH res grant, 64-67 & 75-78; fac res coun fel, La State Univ, 65; Eleanor Roosevelt Int Cancer fel, Fibiger-Laboratoriet, Copenhagen, Denmark, 75-76. *Mem:* Am Asn Immunologists; Am Soc Microbiol. *Res:* immunity to malaria. *Mailing Add:* Dept of Microbiol Hahnemann Med Col Philadelphia PA 19102

WEIDEN, MATHIAS HERMAN JOSEPH, b Narrowsburg, NY, Nov 3, 23; m 54; c 4. INSECT TOXICOLOGY. *Educ:* Manhattan Col, BS, 46; Cornell Univ, PhD(entom), 54. *Prof Exp:* Chemist, Lederle Labs, Am Cyanamid Co, 46-47; asst entom, Cornell Univ, 47-48 & 51-52, asst prof insecticide chem, 54-59; entomologist, 59-66, RES SCIENTIST, EXPLOR INSECTICIDE RES, UNION CARBIDE AGR CHEM CO, 66- *Mem:* Entom Soc Am; Am Chem Soc; NY Acad Sci. *Res:* Action of insecticides and detoxication mechanisms in insects; insecticide research and development. *Mailing Add:* Union Carbide Agr Chem Co PO Box 12014 Research Triangle Park NC 27709

WEIDENBAUM, SHERMAN S, b New York, July 8, 25; m 48; c 3. CHEMICAL ENGINEERING. *Educ:* Columbia Univ, BS, 47, MS, 48, PhD(chem eng), 53. *Prof Exp:* Asst chem eng, Columbia Univ, 48-49; sr chem engr, Corning Glass Works, 52-56, sr melting engr, 56-58, res chem engr, 58-66, managing dir UN Proj, Israel Ceramic & Silicate Inst, Haifa, 62-65, proj engr, Corning Glass Works, 65-66, mgr tech serv, Latin Am Area, Corning Glass Int, 66-68; prof phys sci, 68-70, proj mgr & dir, 70-77, PROF PHYS SCI, US COAST GUARD ACAD, 77- *Mem:* Electrochem Soc; Am Soc Qual Control; Am Chem Soc; Am Inst Chem Engrs. *Res:* Solids mixing and processing; paste mixing; pelletizing; applications to glass batch preparation; glass melting; theoretical and practical aspects of solids mixing; industrial statistics; international technical assistance. *Mailing Add:* US Coast Guard Acad New London CT 06320

WEIDENSAUL, T CRAIG, b Reedsville, Pa, Apr 4, 39; m 65; c 2. PLANT PATHOLOGY. *Educ:* Gettysburg Col, BA, 62; Duke Univ, MF, 63; Pa State Univ, PhD(plant path), 69. *Prof Exp:* Plant pathologist, USDA Forest Serv, 63-66; res asst, Pa State Univ, 66-69, fel scholar, 69-70; from asst prof to assoc prof, 70-79, PROF PLANT PATH & FORESTRY, OHIO STATE UNIV, 79- & DIR LAB ENVIRON STUDIES, OHIO AGR RES & DEVELOP CTR, 70- *Concurrent Pos:* Consult forester & plant pathologist. *Mem:* Am Inst Biol Sci; Am Phytopath Soc; Soc Am Foresters; Am Soc Agron. *Res:* Epidemiology of fusarium canker of sugar maple; precipitation quality and effects on terrestrial ecoupterus; effects of gaseous and metallic air pollutants on plants and plant disease. *Mailing Add:* Ohio Agr Res & Develop Ctr Wooster OH 44691

WEIDENSCHILLING, STUART JOHN, b Montclair, NJ, Sept 22, 46; m 73. PLANETARY SCIENCE, ASTRONOMY. *Educ:* Mass Inst Technol, BS, 68, MS, 69, PhD(earth & planetary sci), 76. *Prof Exp:* Fel, Dept Terrestrial Magnetism, Carnegie Inst 76-78; RES SCIENTIST, PLANETARY SCI INST, SCI APPLNS, INC, 78- *Mem:* Am Geophys Union; Am Astron Soc. *Res:* Origin and evolution of the solar system. *Mailing Add:* Planetary Sci Inst 2030 E Speedway Suite 201 Tucson AZ 85719

WEIDHAAS, DONALD E, b Northampton Mass, Feb 12, 28; m 53; c 2. MEDICAL ENTOMOLOGY. *Educ:* Univ Mass, BS, 51; Cornell Univ, NY, PhD(entom), 55. *Prof Exp:* Med entomologist, 56-62, asst chief, 62-67, actg chief, 67, DIR INSECTS AFFECTING MAN & ANIMALS RES LAB, SCI & EDUC ADMIN-AGR RES, USDA, 67- *Mem:* Entom Soc Am; Am Mosquito Control Asn. *Res:* Chemical and alternative methods of control, resistance studies, physiology, toxicology and biology of insects affecting man or of medical importance; integrated control; dynamics and modelling. *Mailing Add:* Sci & Educ Admin-Agr Res USDA Box 14565 Gainesville FL 32604

WEIDHAAS, JOHN AUGUST, JR, b Northampton, Mass, Oct 13, 25; m 48, 75; c 5. ENTOMOLOGY. *Educ:* Univ of Mass, BS, 49, MS, 52, PhD(entom), 59. *Prof Exp:* Instr entom, Univ Mass, 51 & 53-59; from asst prof to assoc prof, Cornell Univ, 59-67; ASSOC PROF ENTOM & EXTEN SPECIALIST, VA POLYTECH INST & STATE UNIV, 67- *Concurrent Pos:* Collabr, Agr Res Serv, USDA; consult, Elm. *Mem:* Entom Soc Am; Entom Soc Can; Int Soc Arboriculture (past pres); hon mem Soc Munic Arborists; Arboricultural Res & Educ Acad (past pres). *Res:* Forest, shade tree, ornamental and beneficial insects; Acarina. *Mailing Add:* Dept of Entom 315 Price Hall Va Polytech Inst & State Univ Blacksburg VA 24061

WEIDIE, ALFRED EDWARD, b New Orleans, La, July 31, 31; m 60; c 3. GEOLOGY. *Educ:* Vanderbilt Univ, BA, 53; La State Univ, MS, 58, PhD(geol), 61. *Prof Exp:* From asst prof to assoc prof, 61-71, chmn dept earth sci, 67-73, PROF GEOL, UNIV NEW ORLEANS, 71- *Res:* Structural geology and physical stratigraphy. *Mailing Add:* Dept of Earth Sci Univ New Orleans New Orleans LA 70148

WEIDIG, CHARLES FERDINAND, b Houston, Tex, Oct 24, 45; m 67; c 2. INORGANIC CHEMISTRY, PETROLEUM CHEMISTRY. *Educ:* Tex Christian Univ, BS, 69, PhD(chem), 74; Sam Houston State Univ, MA, 71. *Prof Exp:* Anal chemist, Indust Labs, Ft Worth, 66-69; assoc biochem, Edsel B Ford Inst Med Res, 74-76; RES CHEMIST, ETHYL CORP, 76- *Mem:* Am Chem Soc; Sigma Xi. *Res:* Rapid reaction kinetics and mechanisms of enzyme-catalyzed reactions; synthesis, kinetics and mechanism of hydrolysis of nitrogen base adducts of substituted boranes; transition metal chemistry; homogeneous and heterogeneous catalysis; lubricant additives; fuel additives; polymer synthesis. *Mailing Add:* Ethyl Corp 1600 W Eight Mile Rd Ferndale MI 48220

WEIDLER, DONALD JOHN, b Fredericksburg, Iowa, Sept 26, 33; m 58; c 2. INTERNAL MEDICINE, CLINICAL PHARMACOLOGY. *Educ:* Wartburg Col, BA, 59; Univ Iowa, MS, 62, MD, 65, PhD(physiol, biophys), 69. *Prof Exp:* Intern internal med, Boston City Hosp, 65-66; instr physiol & biophys, Univ Iowa, 66-69; from asst prof & mem grad fac to assoc prof physiol & biophys, Univ Nebr Med Ctr, 69-72; resident internal med, Sch Med, Univ Mich, 72-74, instr pharmacol, 73-77, asst prof internal med, 74-79; ASSOC PROF & CHIEF DIV CLIN PHARMACOL, SCH MED, UNIV MIAMI, 79- *Concurrent Pos:* NIH fel, Univ Iowa, 66-69. *Mem:* Am Physiol Soc; Am Col Physicians; Am Soc Clin Pharmacol & Therapeut; Am Soc Internal Med; Am Col Clin Pharmacol. *Res:* Clinicial pharmacology; clinical pharmacodynamics; clinical pharmacokinetics. *Mailing Add:* Med Sch Univ Miami Box 015996 Miami FL 33101

WEIDLICH, JOHN EDWARD, JR, b Akron, Ohio, July 31, 19; m 69; c 1. MATHEMATICS. *Educ:* Stanford Univ, BS, 48, MS, 50; Univ Calif, Berkeley, PhD(math), 61. *Prof Exp:* Instr math, Univ Santa Clara, 49-51; from assoc res scientist to res scientist, Lockheed Missile & Space Co, 59-64; from asst prof to assoc prof, 64-70, actg chmn dept, 66-67, res sabbatical, 71-72, PROF MATH, CALIF STATE UNIV, HAYWARD, 70- *Concurrent Pos:* Consult, Lockheed Missile & Space Co, 64-65. *Mem:* Am Math Soc; Math Asn Am; Soc Indust & Appl Math. *Res:* Pure mathematics in analysis, differential equations and asymtotics; mathematical nature of physical phenomena, including work in theoretical orbit mechanics and trajectory studies in the n-body problem. *Mailing Add:* Dept of Math Calif State Univ Hayward CA 94542

WEIDMAN, ROBERT MCMASTER, b Missoula, Mont, Mar 20, 23; m 51; c 4. GEOLOGY. *Educ:* Calif Inst Technol, BS, 44; Univ Ind, MA, 49; Univ Calif, PhD, 59. *Prof Exp:* Geologist, Stand Oil Co, Calif, 44-47 & State Geol Surv, Ind, 48; instr, Fresno State Col, 49-50; from instr to assoc prof, 53-68, PROF GEOL, UNIV MONT, 68- *Mem:* Geol Soc Am; Am Asn Petrol Geologists. *Res:* Structural and petroleum geology. *Mailing Add:* Dept of Geol Univ of Mont Missoula MT 59821

WEIDMAN, ROBERT STUART, b Philadelphia, Pa, Feb 17, 54. BAND THEORY, SURFACE PHYSICS. *Educ:* Univ Del, BS, 76; Univ Ill, PhD(physics), 80. *Prof Exp:* Res assoc, Univ Ill, 80; ASST PROF PHYSICS, MICH TECHNOL UNIV, 80- *Mem:* Am Phys Soc; Sigma Xi. *Res:* Band theory and optical properties of semiconductors and insulators; electronic structure of point defects and impurities; theory of heterogeneous catalysis. *Mailing Add:* Dept Physics Mich Technol Univ Houghton MI 49931

WEIDNER, BRUCE VANSCOYOC, b Pottstown, Pa, Oct 29, 08; m 34; c 2. CHEMISTRY. *Educ:* Pa State Col, BS, 31, MS, 32, PhD(inorg chem), 35. *Prof Exp:* Asst chem, Pa State Col, 32-35, instr arts & sci, Hazleton Undergrad Ctr, 35-37; instr, Univ Alaska, 37-39, asst prof chem, 39-42; asst prof chem, Middlebury Col, 42-46; assoc prof, Utah State Agr Col, 46-47; from assoc prof to prof chem, Miami Univ, 47-79; RETIRED. *Concurrent Pos:* Dir, NSF Summer Sec-Sci Insts Teachers, 60-73. *Mem:* Am Chem Soc; Soc Appl Spectros; AAAS. *Res:* Quantitative and inorganic chemistry. *Mailing Add:* 308 University Ave Oxford OH 45056

WEIDNER, JERRY R, b Bloomington, Ill, July 19, 38; m 62. GEOCHEMISTRY. *Educ:* Miami Univ, BA, 60, MS, 63; Pa State Univ, University Park, PhD(geochem), 68. *Prof Exp:* Res assoc geochem, Stanford Univ, 67-68; asst prof geol, Univ Md, College Park, 70-77, assoc prof, 77-80; MEM FAC, BOWIE STATE COL, 80- *Concurrent Pos:* Nat Res Coun fel NASA Goddard Space FLight Ctr, Md, 68-70. *Mem:* AAAS; Am Geophys Union; Mineral Soc Am; Geochem Soc. *Res:* Experimental petrology. *Mailing Add:* Bowie State Col MacKell Hall Bowie MD 20715

WEIDNER, MICHAEL GEORGE, JR, b Birmingham, Ala, July 18, 22; m 60; c 1. SURGERY. *Educ:* Vanderbilt Univ, BA, 44, MD, 46; Am Bd Surg, dipl, 56. *Prof Exp:* Instr surg, Sch Med, Vanderbilt Univ, 53-57; from sr instr to asst prof, Sch Med, Western Reserve Univ, 57-62; asst dean student affairs, 70-72, assoc prof, 62-68, assoc dean student affairs & proj dir, Area Health Educ Ctr, 72-76, PROF SURG, MED UNIV SC, 68-, ASSOC DEAN, 76-; CHIEF OF STAFF, VET ADMIN HOSP, 76- *Concurrent Pos:* Res fel, Vanderbilt Univ, 54-57; chief surg serv, Vet Admin Hosp, Charleston, SC, 66-72. *Mem:* AAAS; Am Col Surgeons; Soc Univ Surgeons; Soc Exp Biol & Med; NY Acad Sci. *Res:* Hemorrhagic shock; animal and human gastrointestinal physiology, especially ulcer disease. *Mailing Add:* Vet Admin Med Ctr 109 Bee St Charleston SC 29403

WEIDNER, RICHARD TILGHMAN, b Allentown, Pa, Mar 31, 21; m 47; c 3. PHYSICS, MAGNETIC RESONANCE. *Educ:* Muhlenberg Col, B BS, 43; Yale Univ, MS, 43, PhD(physics), 48. *Prof Exp:* Physicist, US Naval Res Lab, 44-46; lab asst & instr physics, Yale Univ, 43-44, asst, 46-47; from instr to assoc prof, 47-63, asst dean col arts & sci, 66-70, assoc dean, Rutgers Col, 70-77 & actg dean, 77-78, PROF PHYSICS, RUTGERS UNIV, NEW BRUNSWICK, 63- *Mem:* Fel Am Phys Soc; Am Asn Physics Teachers; Sigma Xi. *Res:* Electron spin resonance; texts in elementary physics; general physics. *Mailing Add:* Dept Physics Rutgers Univ New Brunswick NJ 08903

WEIDNER, TERRY MOHR, b Allentown, Pa, May 31, 37; m 62; c 3. PLANT PHYSIOLOGY. *Educ:* West Chester State Col, BSEd, 59; Ohio State Univ, MS, 61, PhD(bot), 64. *Prof Exp:* From asst prof to assoc prof, 64-74, PROF BOT, EASTERN ILL UNIV, 74-, CHMN DEPT, 76- *Mem:* Am Inst Biol Sci; Am Soc Plant Physiol. *Res:* Carbohydrate translocation in higher plants; active ion uptake by roots of higher plants; sulfur dioxide effects on mosses. *Mailing Add:* Dept Bot Eastern Ill Univ Charleston IL 61920

WEIDNER, VICTOR RAY, b Clarion, Pa, Jan 4, 32; m 67. OPTICAL PHYSICS. *Educ:* Clarion State Col, BS, 60. *Prof Exp:* PHYSICIST, NAT BUR STANDARDS, 60- *Mem:* Optical Soc Am. *Res:* Infrared spectrophotometry; development of research spectrophotometers and spectrophotometric standards. *Mailing Add:* Nat Bur Standards Washington DC 20234

WEIDNER, WILLIAM JEFFREY, b Michigan City, Ind, Jan 21, 47; m 71. PHYSIOLOGY, EXPERIMENTAL BIOLOGY. *Educ:* Mich State Univ, BA, 68, MS, 71, PhD(physiol), 73. *Prof Exp:* Res assoc physiol, Mich State Univ, 73-74; fel, UniY Calif, San Francisco, 74-75; ASST PROF PHYSIOL, UNIV CALIF, DAVIS, 75- *Mem:* AAAS; Am Physiol Soc; Sigma Xi; Aerospace Med Asn. *Res:* Cardiopulmonary physiology; acceleration biology; history of science. *Mailing Add:* Dept of Animal Physiol Univ of Calif Davis CA 95616

WEIER, RICHARD MATHIAS, b Streator, Ill, July 18, 40; m 69; c 2. ORGANIC CHEMISTRY. *Educ:* Loras Col, BS, 62; Wayne State Univ, PhD(org chem), 67. *Prof Exp:* Res chemist, Ash-Stevens, Inc, Mich, 66-67; res chemist, Res & Develop Div, Kraftco Corp, 68-69; RES SCIENTIST, G D SEARLE & CO, 69- *Mem:* AAAS; Am Chem Soc. *Res:* Synthesis of steroids and natural products; aldosterone blockade; diuretics; anti-hypertensives. *Mailing Add:* Chem Res Dept G D Searle & Co Box 5110 Chicago IL 60680

WEIFFENBACH, CONRAD VENABLE, b Oak Park, Ill, Aug 25, 42. NUCLEAR PHYSICS. *Educ:* Univ Mich, BS, 64, PhD(physics), 70. *Prof Exp:* Res fel, Foster Radiation Lab, McGill Univ, 71-74; vol physics, US Peace Corp, King Mongkut Inst Technol, Bangkok, 76-78; asst prof physics, Kean Col NJ, 78-80; MEM FAC, PHYSICS DEPT, UNIV MAINE, 80- *Res:* Experimental nuclear structure physics. *Mailing Add:* Dept Physics Univ Maine Orono ME 04469

WEIFFENBACH, GEORGE CHARLES, b Newark, NJ, June 20, 21; m 49; c 5. EXPERIMENTAL PHYSICS. *Educ:* Harvard Univ, AB, 49; Cath Univ, PhD(physics), 58. *Prof Exp:* Asst, Cath Univ, 49-51; sr physicist, Appl Physics Lab, Johns Hopkins Univ, 51-69; DIR GEOASTRON PROGS, SMITHSONIAN ASTROPHYS OBSERV, 69- *Mem:* Am Phys Soc; Am Geophys Union. *Res:* Microwave spectroscopy; time and frequency standards; space systems engineering; geodesy; geophysics. *Mailing Add:* 60 Garden St Cambridge MA 02138

WEIGAND, WILLIAM ADAM, b Chicago, Ill, Oct 26, 38. CHEMICAL ENGINEERING. *Educ:* Ill Inst Technol, BS, 62, MS, 63, PhD(chem eng), 68. *Prof Exp:* Engr res, Esso Res Labs, 63-64; asst prof, 67-72, ASSOC PROF CHEM ENG, PURDUE UNIV, 72- *Concurrent Pos:* Prog dir, NSF, 76-77. *Mem:* Am Inst Chem Eng; Am Chem Soc; Sigma Xi. *Res:* Growth kinetics; dynamic modeling; optimal fermentor type and operation; automatic digital control of bioreactors. *Mailing Add:* Sch of Chem Eng Purdue Univ West Lafayette IN 47907

WEIGANG, OSCAR EMIL, JR, physical chemistry, see previous edition

WEIGEL, PAUL HENRY, b New York, NY, Aug 11, 46; m 68; c 1. CELL SURFACE RECEPTORS, GLYCOPROTEINS. *Educ:* Cornell Univ, BA, 68; Johns Hopkins Univ Sch Med, MA, 69, PhD(biochem), 75. *Prof Exp:* Nat Cancer Inst fel, Biol Dept, Johns Hopkins Univ, 75-78; asst prof, 78-82, ASSOC PROF BIOCHEM, UNIV TEX MED BR, GALVESTON, 82- *Mem:* Am Chem Soc; Am Soc Cell Biol; Am Soc Biol Chemists; AAAS; NY Acad Sci. *Res:* Receptor mediated endocytosis; the role of complex carbohydrates in cell motility and growth control; cell surface receptors for extra cellular matrix molecules; cell recognition and responses to external complex carbohydrate molecules. *Mailing Add:* Div Biochem Univ Tex Med Br Galveston TX 77550

WEIGEL, ROBERT DAVID, b Buffalo, NY, Dec 31, 23. VERTEBRATE ZOOLOGY. *Educ:* Univ Buffalo, BA, 49, MA, 55; Univ Fla, PhD(zool), 58. *Prof Exp:* Instr gen biol, Univ Fla, 57; asst prof biol, Howard Col, 58-59; assoc prof, 59-64, PROF BIOL, ILL STATE UNIV, 64- *Mem:* AAAS; Soc Study Evolution; Soc Vert Paleont; Paleont Soc; Am Soc Mammal. *Res:* Avian paleontology; ornithology; osteology. *Mailing Add:* Dept of Biol Ill State Univ Normal IL 61761

WEIGEL, RUSSELL C(ORNELIUS), JR, b Teaneck, NJ, Dec 10, 40. PLANT PHYSIOLOGY. *Educ:* Univ Del, BA, 62; George Washington Univ, BS, 63; Univ Md, College Park, MS, 68, PhD(plant physiol), 70. *Prof Exp:* Agr res investr, E I du Pont de Nemours & Co, Inc, 64-65; teaching asst bot & plant physiol, Univ Md, 65-69; res biologist, 69-80, SR RES BIOLOGIST, BIOCHEM DEPT, PLANT RES LAB, E I DU PONT DE NEMOURS & CO, INC, 80- *Mem:* Am Soc Plant Physiol; Sigma Xi; Am Hort Soc. *Res:* Plant growth regulants; selective herbicides. *Mailing Add:* 808 Princeton Rd Wilmington DE 19807

WEIGENSBERG, BERNARD IRVINE, b Montreal, Que, Feb 6, 26; m 50; c 3. EXPERIMENTAL PATHOLOGY. *Educ:* McGill Univ, BSc, 49, MSc, 51, PhD(biochem), 53. *Prof Exp:* Res asst biochem, 49-54, res assoc path chem, 54-62, asst prof, 62-74, ASSOC PROF EXP PATH, McGILL UNIV, 74- *Concurrent Pos:* Res assoc, Can Heart Found, 58-66; mem coun arteriosclerosis & coun thrombosis, Am Heart Asn. *Mem:* Fel Am Soc Study Arteriosclerosis; Am Soc Exp Path. *Res:* Atherosclerosis from cholesterol and lipoproteins; atherosclerosis from white mural non-occlusive thrombisis; myointimal thickenings from injury; lipid and connective tissue metabolism. *Mailing Add:* Path Inst Rm 205 McGill Univ 3775 University St Montreal PQ H3A 2B4 Can

WEIGER, ROBERT W, b Grantwood, NJ, Nov 23, 27; m 57; c 1. MEDICINE. *Educ:* Northwestern Univ, BS, 51, MD, 55. *Prof Exp:* Intern med, Passavant Mem Hosp, Northwestern Univ, 55-56; clin assoc & resident, Nat Cancer Inst, 56-58, physician div hosps, USPHS, 58-59, resident internal med, USPHS Hosp, Baltimore, Md, 59-62, med scientist, Cancer Chemother Nat Serv Ctr, Nat Cancer Inst, 62, asst dir inst & asst to dir, NIH, 64-65, prog coordr clin pharmacol, Nat Inst Gen Med Sci, 65-76, DIR MED PHARMACOL & TOXICOL PROGS, NIH, 76- *Concurrent Pos:* Staff fel med, Sch Med, Johns Hopkins Univ & Johns Hopkins Hosp, 62; chief officer pesticides, Bur State Serv, 65-66; mem, US-Japanese Comt Health & Nat Acad Sci-Nat Res Coun. *Mem:* AAAS; Am Col Physicians; Am Math Asn; Am Chem Soc; The Chem Soc. *Res:* Research and science administration, particularly in medical research. *Mailing Add:* Off of the Dir Nat Insts of Health Bethesda MD 20014

WEIGHT, FORREST F, b Waynesboro, Pa, Apr 17, 36; m 61; c 3. NEUROSCIENCES, NEUROPHYSIOLOGY. *Educ:* Princeton Univ, AB, 58; Columbia Univ Col Physicians & Surgeons, MD, 62. *Prof Exp:* Resident med, Mary Imogene Bassett Hosp, 63-64; res assoc, NIMH, 64-68; vis scientist, Univ Goteborg, Sweden, 68-69; chief sect synaptic pharmacol, NIMH, 69-78; CHIEF LAB PRECLIN STUDIES, NAT INST ALCOHOL ABUSE & ALCOHOLISM, 78- *Concurrent Pos:* Vis fel, Swedish Med Res Coun, 68-69; secy assembly scientists, NIMH, 77-78; Heritage vis lectr & Int Brain Res Orgn vis lectr. *Mem:* AAAS; Am Physiol Soc; Am Soc Pharmacol & Exp Therapy; Soc Neurosci; Soc Biol Psychiat. *Res:* Cellular mechanisms of communication and information processing in the nervous system; mechanisms of synaptic transmission, mechanisms controlling nerve cell excitability, identification of neurotransmitters and molecular basis of membrane permability changes. *Mailing Add:* Lab of Preclin Studies Nat Inst Alcohol Abuse & Alcoholism Rockville MD 20852

WEIGL, JOHN WOLFGANG, b Vienna, Austria, Aug 1, 26; nat US; m 46; c 3. PHYSICAL CHEMISTRY. *Educ:* Columbia Univ, BS, 46; Univ Calif, PhD(chem), 49. *Prof Exp:* Res chemist, Lawrence Radiation Lab, Univ Calif, 47-49; fel chem, Univ Minn, 50-51; res assoc physics, Ohio State Univ, 51-55, asst prof, 55-57; sr res chemist & res mgr, Ozalid Div, Gen Aniline & Film Corp, NY, 57-62; res mgr, Imaging Mat Area, 62-72, CORPS RES & DEVELOP STAFF, XEROX CORP, 72- *Mem:* Fel AAAS; fel Soc Photog Scientists & Engrs; NY Acad Sci; Am Chem Soc; Am Phys Soc. *Res:* Photochemistry; kinetics; isotopic tracers; organic photoconductors and optical sensitization; electrophotography. *Mailing Add:* 534 Wahlmont Dr Webster NY 14580

WEIGL, PETER DOUGLAS, b New York, NY, Nov 9, 39; m 68. ECOLOGY, ANIMAL BEHAVIOR. *Educ:* Williams Col, AB, 62; Duke Univ, PhD(vert ecol), 69. *Prof Exp:* Asst prof, 68-74, assoc prof, 74-80, PROF BIOL, WAKE FOREST UNIV, 80- *Mem:* AAAS; Am Soc Zoologists; Am Soc Mammal; Ecol Soc Am; Soc Study Evolution. *Res:* Vertebrate zoology; evolution; energetics of behavior, species interactions, functional morphology. *Mailing Add:* Dept of Biol Wake Forest Univ Winston-Salem NC 27109

WEIGLE, JACK LEROY, b Montpelier, Ohio, Sept 5, 25; m 54; c 4. PLANT BREEDING. *Educ:* Purdue Univ, BS, 50, MS, 54; Mich State Univ, PhD, 56. *Prof Exp:* Asst prof hort, Colo State Univ, 56-61; from asst prof to assoc prof, 61-73, PROF HORT, IOWA STATE UNIV, 73- *Mem:* Am Soc Hort Sci; Am Genetic Asn. *Res:* Genetic, cytogenetic and physiological investigations and development of new cultivars of ornamental plants. *Mailing Add:* Dept of Hort Iowa State Univ Ames IA 50011

WEIGLE, ROBERT EDWARD, b Shiloh, Pa, Apr 27, 27; m 49; c 1. APPLIED MECHANICS, APPLIED MATHEMATICS. *Educ:* Rensselaer Polytech Inst, BCE, 51, MS, 57, PhD, 59. *Prof Exp:* Eng consult, 52-54; construct supt, Long Serv Co, Inc, 54-55; assoc res scientist, Dept Mech, Rensselaer Polytech Inst, 55-59; res dir, Res Lab, 59-62, tech dir, Benet Weapons Lab, 62-69, dir lab, Watervliet Arsenal, 69-77, chief scientist, Benet Weapons Lab, 70-77, TECH DIR, ARMAMENT RES & DEVELOP COMMAND, US ARMY, 77- *Concurrent Pos:* Consult high pressure technol comt, Nat Res Coun, 60-61, Army mem gun tube technol comt, Mat Adv Bd, 67-69; mem, Adv Panel Weapons & Mat, NATO, 60-67, consult, Adv Group Aeronaut Res & Develop-Struct & Mat Panel, 71; mem, Dept Defense Forum Phys & Eng Sci; mem, Army Res Coun, 68-70; consult cannon wear & erosion, Mat Adv Bd, 77-78. *Honors & Awards:* Presidential Citation, Secy Army, 65, Civilian Meritorious Serv Award, Dept Army, 65; Cert of Achievement, Asst Secy Army Res & Develop, 69 & 70. *Mem:* Nat Soc Prof Eng; Soc Exp Stress Anal; Am Soc Mech Eng; Am Soc Testing & Mat; Am Acad Mech. *Res:* Fatigue and fracture behavior of high strength alloy steels as applied to high performance, large caliber weapons and related equipment. *Mailing Add:* PO Box 43 US Army Blairstown NJ 07825

WEIGLE, WILLIAM O, b Monaca, Pa, Apr, 28, 27; div; c 2. IMMUNOLOGY, CELL BIOLOGY. *Educ:* Univ Pittsburgh, BS, 50, MS, 51, PhD(bact), 56. *Prof Exp:* Res technician, Dept Path, Sch Med, Univ Pittsburgh, 51-52, res assoc, 55-58, asst res prof, 58-59, asst prof immunochem, 59-61; assoc mem, 61-63, MEM DEPT IMMUNOPATHOL, SCRIPPS CLIN & RES FOUND, 63-, CHMN DEPT, 78- *Concurrent Pos:* USPHS fel, 56-59, sr res fel, 59-61, career res award, 62-; adj prof biol, Univ Calif, San Diego. *Honors & Awards:* Parke-Davis Award, Am Soc Exp Path, 67. *Mem:* Am Soc Microbiol; Am Asn Immunologists; Am Soc Exp Path; Am Acad Allergy; NY Acad Sci. *Res:* Mechanisms involved in immunity and diseases of hypersensitivity; immunochemistry; immunopathology. *Mailing Add:* Dept of Immunopath Scripps Clin & Res Found La Jolla CA 92037

WEIGMAN, BERNARD J, b Baltimore, Md, Nov 18, 32; m 60; c 4. ENGINEERING PHYSICS, COMPUTER SCIENCE. *Educ:* Loyola Col, Md, BS, 54; Univ Notre Dame, PhD(physics), 59. *Prof Exp:* From instr to assoc prof physics, 58-67, chmn dept math, 60-64, chmn dept physics & eng, 64-73, PROF PHYSICS, LOYOLA COL, MD, 67- *Concurrent Pos:* Consult, Martin Co, 59-61 & Westinghouse Corp, 74-, dir, Master Eng Sci Digital Systs. *Mem:* Am Asn Physics Teachers. *Res:* Optical and electrical properties of thin films; behavior of an aerosol system; thermoelectric, photoelectric and field emission of electrons; properties of molecules; small computer systems; real time data collection. *Mailing Add:* Dept of Physics & Eng Loyola Col 4501 N Charles St Baltimore MD 21210

WEIHAUPT, JOHN GEORGE, b La Crosse, Wis, Mar 5, 30; m 61. ASTROGEOLOGY, OCEANOGRAPHY. *Educ:* Univ Wis, BS, 52, MS, 53 & 71, PhD(geomorphol), 73. *Prof Exp:* Teaching asst geol, Univ Wis, 52-53, res asst, 53-54; explor geologist, Anaconda Co, 56-57; seismologist, United Geophys Corp, 57-58; geophysicist, Arctic Inst NAm, 58-63; chmn dept phys & biol sci, US Armed Forces Inst, Dept Defense, 63-73; dean acad affairs, Sch Sci, Ind Univ-Purdue Univ, 73-78, asst dean grad sch, 75-78; ASSOC ACADEMIC VPRES & DEAN GRAD STUDIES & RES, SAN JOSE STATE UNIV, 78- *Concurrent Pos:* Explor geologist, Am Smelting & Ref Co, 53; codiscoverer, USARP Range, Antarctica, 59-60 & Mt Weihaupt named in his honor, 66; lectr, Univ Wis-Madison, 63-73; hon mem, Exped Polaire Francais; mem, Man/Environ Commun Ctr, Community Coun Pub TV & Int Coun Correspondence Educ; sci consult, McGraw-Hill Book Co, 65, geol consult, 68-; sci consult, Holt, Rinehart & Winston, Inc, 65-; ed & consult, John Wiley & Sons, 68. *Mem:* AAAS; Am Geophys Union; fel Geol Soc Am; Asn Am Geog; Int Soc Study Time. *Res:* Antarctic geology and geophysics in regions of Victoria Land and the South Pole in Antarctica; geophysical-biological periodic relationships; marine geology and geophysics; fluvial, glacial and coastal geomorphology; channels and paleoclimate of Mars; meteorite crater and impact phenomena. *Mailing Add:* Grad Off San Jose State Univ San Jose CA 95192

WEIHE, JOSEPH WILLIAM, b Reno, Nev, Sept 23, 21; m 42; c 2. MATHEMATICS. *Educ:* Univ Nev, BS, 46, MS, 48; Univ Calif, PhD(math), 54. *Prof Exp:* Asst math, Univ Nev, 46-47, instr, 47-48; instr, Univ Calif, 48-51, assoc, 51-53; staff mem, Math Res Dept, Sandia Corp, NMex, 54-57, supvr systs anal div, 57-63, mgr math dept, 63-68, mgr systs anal dept, 68-69, MGR ANAL SCI DEPT, SANDIA CORP, CALIF, 69- *Concurrent Pos:* Vis lectr, Univ NMex, 59-60. *Mem:* Am Math Soc; Opers Res Soc; Am Soc Indust & Appl Math; Math Asn Am; Asn Comput Mach. *Res:* Weapons systems analysis; operations research; real variable measure theory and integration; generalized Stieltjes integrals; computer science. *Mailing Add:* 1166 Dunsmuir Pl Livermore CA 94550

WEIHER, JAMES F, b Waverly, Iowa, Mar 30, 33. SURFACE CHEMISTRY, SURFACE PHYSICS. *Educ:* Carleton Col, BA, 55; Iowa State Univ, PhD(phys chem), 61. *Prof Exp:* Res chemist, Study Group Radiochem, Max Planck Inst, Mainz, Germany, 55-57; res asst, Inst Atomic Res, Iowa State Univ, 57-61; fel, 61-62, RES CHEMIST, CENT RES DEPT, E I DU PONT DE NEMOURS & CO, INC, 62- *Mem:* Fel Am Inst Chem; Am Chem Soc; Am Phys Soc. *Res:* Nuclear chemistry and radiochemistry; kinetics; molecular structure; solid state; Mössbauer effect; magnetic susceptibility. *Mailing Add:* 1230 Riverside Dr Wilmington DE 19809

WEIHING, JOHN LAWSON, b Rocky Ford, Colo, Feb 26, 21; m 48; c 4. PLANT PATHOLOGY. *Educ:* Colo Agr & Mech Col, BS, 42; Univ Nebr, MS, 49, PhD(bot), 54. *Prof Exp:* Assoc plant path, 49-50, exten plant pathologist, 50-64, PROF PLANT PATH, AGR EXTEN, UNIV NEBR, LINCOLN, 60-, DIR PANHANDLE STA, 71- *Concurrent Pos:* Mem Univ Nebr group, Agency Inst Develop, 64- *Mem:* Bot Soc Am; Am Phytopath Soc; AAAS; Am Inst Biol Sci. *Res:* Epidemiology of plant diseases. *Mailing Add:* Univ of Nebr Panhandle Sta 4502 Ave I Scottsbluff NE 69361

WEIHING, ROBERT RALPH, b Ft Collins, Colo, Jan 14, 38. BIOCHEMISTRY, CELL BIOLOGY. *Educ:* Rice Univ, BA, 59; Johns Hopkins Univ, PhD(biochem), 65, MD, 67. *Prof Exp:* Staff assoc biochem, NIH, 68-71; staff scientist, 71-77, SR SCIENTIST CELL BIOL, WORCESTER FOUND EXP BIOL, 77- *Concurrent Pos:* Am Cancer Soc res scholar, 77-80. *Mem:* Am Soc Cell Biol; Biophys Soc; Am Soc Biol Chemists. *Res:* Molecular basis of movement in non-muscle cells. *Mailing Add:* Worcester Found for Exp Biol Shrewsbury MA 01545

WEIJER, JAN, b Heerenveen, Neth, Jan 28, 24; m 52. GENETICS. *Educ:* Univ Groningen, BSc, 51, MSc, 52, DSc, 54. *Prof Exp:* Asst genetics, Univ Groningen, 46-52 & exp embryol, 51-52; geneticist, Firestone Bot Res Inst, 52-54, Can, 55-57; prof hort, 57-59, chmn dept genetics, 67-69, PROF GENETICS, UNIV ALTA, 60- *Concurrent Pos:* Lectr, Neth, 59; consult, US AEC, 67; mem coun, Int Orgn Pure & Appl Biophys. *Mem:* AAAS; Radiation Res Soc; Am Genetic Asn; Genetics Soc Am; NY Acad Sci. *Res:* Microbial genetics and cytology, especially fine structure of the gene; biochemical genetics and mutation; biological assessment of radiation damage in humans. *Mailing Add:* Dept of Genetics Biol Sci Bldg Univ of Alta Edmonton AB T6G 2E1 Can

WEIK, MARTIN H, JR, b New York, NY, Oct 5, 22; m 43; c 6. PHYSICS, ELECTRICAL ENGINEERING. *Educ:* City Col New York, BS, 49; Columbia Univ, MS, 51; George Washington Univ, DSc, 79. *Prof Exp:* Asst eng, Columbia Univ, 49-52; designer electronic digital comput, Ballistic Res Labs, Aberdeen Proving Ground, Md, 53-64; chief res & eng systs br & off chief res & develop, US Army Res Off, 64-69, chief data mgt div, 69-73; eng systs analyst, US Mil Commun Electronics Bd, Defense Commun Agency, 73-79; SYSTS ANALYST, DYNAMIC SYSTS, INC, 81- *Concurrent Pos:* Chief US deleg, Int Orgn Standardization Tech Comt 97, subcomt 1 vocabulary, 61-; chmn, Am Nat Standards Inst Tech Comt X3K5 Vocabulary. *Mem:* AAAS; Inst Elec & Electronics Engrs; Asn Advan Med Instrumentation. *Res:* Logical design of electronic digital computers; design and development of technical information systems; information processing and computer language and vocabulary development. *Mailing Add:* 2200 Columbia Pike Arlington VA 22204

WEIKEL, JOHN HENRY, JR, b Palmerton, Pa, June 14, 29. TOXICOLOGY. *Educ:* Trinity Col, Conn, BS, 51; Univ Rochester, PhD(pharmacol), 54. *Prof Exp:* Res assoc, AEC Proj, Univ Rochester, 51-54; pharmacologist, Div Pharmacol, Food & Drug Admin, 54-56; sr pharmacologist, 56-58, group leader, 58-59, sect leader, 59-61, asst dept dir, Res Ctr, 61-62, dir chem pharmacol & safety eval, 62-68, DIR PATH & TOXICOL, MEAD JOHNSON & CO, 68- *Mem:* Am Chem Soc; Soc Exp Biol & Med; Am Soc Pharmacol & Exp Therapeut; Soc Toxicol; NY Acad Sci. *Res:* Inorganic metabolism; drug metabolism; toxicology. *Mailing Add:* Mead Johnson Pharmaceutical Div Evansville IN 47721

WEIKSNORA, PETER JAMES, b New York, NY, Jan 12, 50; m 72; c 1. GENE EXPRESSION, SOMATIC CELL HYBRIDS. *Educ:* Brooklyn Col, BS, 72; Brandeis Univ, PhD(biol), 77. *Prof Exp:* Fel, Albert Einstein Col Med, 77-81; ASST PROF GENETICS, MILWAUKEE DEPT ZOOL, UNIV WIS, 81- *Mem:* Am Soc Cell Biol; Am Soc Microbiol. *Res:* Molecular biology; control of eukaryotic gene expression particularly ribosomal RNA and protein genes; gene control in somatic cell hybrids. *Mailing Add:* Dept Zool Univ Wis 3201 N Maryland Ave Milwaukee WI 53201

WEIL, ANDREW THOMAS, b Philadelphia, Pa, June 8, 42. ETHNOPHARMACOLOGY, MEDICINE. *Educ:* Harvard Col, AB, 64; Harvard Med Sch, MD, 68. *Prof Exp:* RES ASSOC ETHNOPHARMACOL, HARVARD BOT MUS, 71- *Concurrent Pos:* Inst Current World Affairs fel, 71-75; adj prof addiction studies, Health Sci Ctr, Univ Ariz, 78-; pres, Beneficial Plant Res Assocs, 79- *Mem:* Fel Linnean Soc London. *Res:* Ethnopharmacology, especially native uses of psychoactive and medicinal plants; drug abuse; herbal medicine; alternative and holistic medicine; altered states of consciousness; mind body interactions. *Mailing Add:* Bot Mus of Harvard Univ Oxford St Cambridge MA 02138

WEIL, BENJAMIN HENRY, b St Joseph, Mo, July 8, 16; m 44; c 3. CHEMICAL ENGINEERING, COMMUNICATIONS. *Educ:* St Joseph Jr Col, AS, 37; Univ Mo-Columbia, BS, 39; Univ Wis-Madison, MS, 40. *Prof Exp:* Head info sect chem div, Gulf Res & Develop Co, 40-45; res prof mgr tech info div, Ga Tech Eng Exp Sta, 45-50; mgr tech info div, Ethyl Corp Res Lab, 50-57; head tech info sect, 57-72, SR STAFF ADV, EXXON RES & ENG CO, 72- *Concurrent Pos:* Trustee, Eng Index Inc, 64-79, dir, 65-68 & vpres, 66-68; chmn, Eng Found Conf, 75-; US Nat rep abstracting bd int coun sci unions, Nat Acad Sci-Nat Res Coun, 78-; Miles Conrad lectr, Nat Fedn Abstracting & Indexing Serv, 78. *Honors & Awards:* Cert of Merit, Am Chem Soc, 56 & Patterson-Crane Award, 77; Herman Skolnik Award, 81; Miles Conrad lectr award, 78. *Mem:* Am Chem Soc; Nat Fedn Abstracting & Indexing Serv (secy, 68-69 & 72-73, treas, 71-72, pres, 75-76); Am Soc Info Sci. *Res:* Technical writing and editing; micrographics; information retrieval. *Mailing Add:* Exxon Res & Eng Co PO Box 121 Linden NJ 07036

WEIL, CARROL S, b St Joseph, Mo, Dec 16, 17; m 40; c 2. TOXICOLOGY. *Educ:* Univ Mo, BA, 39, MA, 40. *Prof Exp:* Bacteriologist, Anchor Serum Co, Mo, 41-42; unit head, Manhattan Div, Univ Rochester, 43-45; res assoc & toxicologist, Carnegie-Mellon Univ, 42-43, fel, 45-52, chief toxicologist & inst fel, Carnegie-Mellon Inst Res, 52-80; CORP FEL, BUSHY RUN RES CTR, UNION CARBIDE CORP, 80- *Mem:* Am Chem Soc; Am Indust Hyg Asn; Biomet Soc; fel Soc Toxicol (secy, 63-67, pres, 68-69). *Res:* Chemical hygiene and toxicology; biometrics. *Mailing Add:* Bushy Run Res Ctr Rd 4 Mellon Rd Export PA 15632

WEIL, CLIFFORD EDWARD, b East Chicago, Ind, Nov 19, 37; m 60; c 3. REAL ANALYSIS. *Educ:* Wabash Col, BA, 59; Purdue Univ, MS, 61, PhD(math), 63. *Prof Exp:* Instr math, Princeton Univ, 63-64 & Univ Chicago, 64-66; from asst prof to assoc prof, 66-78, PROF MATH, MICH STATE UNIV, 78- *Concurrent Pos:* Vis prof math, Philipps-Univ, W Ger, 73-74. *Mem:* Am Math Soc; Math Asn Am. *Res:* Functions of a real variable. *Mailing Add:* Dept of Math Mich State Univ East Lansing MI 48823

WEIL, EDWARD DAVID, b Philadelphia, Pa, June 13, 28; m 52; c 2. ORGANIC CHEMISTRY. *Educ:* Univ Pa, BS, 50; Univ Ill, MS, 51, PhD(org chem), 53; Pace Univ, MBA, 82. *Prof Exp:* Res & develop chemist, Hooker Electrochem Co, 53-56, supvr agr chem res, Hooker Chem Corp, 56-65; supvr org res, 65-69, sr res assoc, 69-76, SR SCIENTIST, STAUFFER CHEM CO, DOBBS FERRY, 76- *Honors & Awards:* IR-100 Award, Indust Res Inst, 74. *Mem:* Am Chem Soc. *Res:* Vinyl polymers; organic sulfur; chlorine derivatives; pesticides; organic phosphorus; rubber chemicals; flame retardants; textile chemicals; polymer additives; research planning. *Mailing Add:* 6 Amherst Dr Hastings-on-Hudson NY 10706

WEIL, FRANCIS ALPHONSE, b Selestat, France, Nov 5, 38; Can citizen; m 64; c 2. PARTICLE PHYSICS. *Educ:* Univ Strasbourg, BSc, 58; Univ Paris, DiplEng, 61; Dalhousie Univ, MSc, 62, PhD(physics), 68. *Prof Exp:* Teaching asst math, Univ Paris at the Sorbonne, France, 60-61; res asst physics, Saclay Nuclear Res Ctr, France, 66-67; PROF PHYSICS, UNIV MONCTON, 68- *Concurrent Pos:* Fel, Killam Found, 68; Nat Res Coun grant, Univ Moncton, 69-70, Univ Res Coun, 70-72. *Mem:* Can Asn Physicists; Fr-Can Asn Advan Sci; Am Asn Physics Teachers. *Res:* Quantum field theory. *Mailing Add:* Dept of Physics & Math Fac of Sci Univ of Moncton Moncton NB E1A 3E9 Can

WEIL, HERSCHEL, b Rochester, NY, July 26, 21; m 43:; c 2. APPLIED MATHEMATICS, ELECTRICAL ENGINEERING. *Educ:* Univ Rochester, BS, 43; Brown Univ, ScM, 45, PhD(appl math), 48. *Prof Exp:* Optical engr, Bausch & Lomb Optical Co, 43-44; asst appl math, Brown Univ, 46-47, res assoc, 47-48; engr, Gen Elec Co, 48-52; res assoc, 52-53, assoc res engr, 53-55, res engr, 55-60, lectr, 58-60, assoc prof elec eng, 60-67, PROF ELEC ENG, UNIV MICH, ANN ARBOR, 67- *Concurrent Pos:* Vis assoc prof, Univ Paris-Orsay, 64-65; sr fel, Nat Ctr Atmospheric Res, 77-78. *Mem:* Int Union Radio Sci; Inst Elec & Electronics Engrs; Optical Soc Am. *Res:* Electromagnetic theory and applications to engineering and space science. *Mailing Add:* Dept of Elec & Comput Eng Univ of Mich Ann Arbor MI 48104

WEIL, JESSE LEO, b Ann Arbor, Mich, Dec 9, 31; m 60; c 2. NUCLEAR PHYSICS. *Educ:* Calif Inst Technol, BS, 52; Columbia Univ, PhD(physics), 59. *Prof Exp:* Res asst nuclear physics, Columbia Univ, 54-58; res assoc, Rice Univ, 59-60 & 61-63 & Univ Hamburg, 60-61; from asst to assoc prof, 63-73, PROF NUCLEAR PHYSICS, UNIV KY, 73- *Concurrent Pos:* Res assoc, Rutherford High Energy Lab, 71-72. *Mem:* Am Asn Univ Prof; Am Phys Soc. *Res:* Nuclear reactions; scattering of nucleons and nuclei; nuclear energy level studies; radioactivity and fission studies beta decay and nuclear masses; neutron polarization. *Mailing Add:* Dept of Physics Univ of Ky Lexington KY 40506

WEIL, JOHN A, b Hamburg, Ger, Mar 15, 29; nat US; m 47; c 2. CHEMICAL PHYSICS. *Educ:* Univ Chicago, MS, 50, PhD(chem), 55. *Prof Exp:* Res chemist, Inst Study Metals, Univ Chicago, 49-52, Inst Nuclear Studies, 53-54; Corning fel chem, Princeton Univ, 55-56, instr phys chem, 56-59; assoc scientist, Argonne Nat Lab, Ill, 59-71, sr scientist, 71; PROF CHEM & CHEM ENG, UNIV SASK, 71- *Concurrent Pos:* Fulbright scholar physics, Univ Canterbury, NZ, 67; vis prof, Univ Chicago, 80. *Mem:* Fel Chem Inst Can; Am Phys Soc; Brit Int Physics & Phys Soc. *Res:* Paramagnetic resonance; quantum chemistry; electronic structure of inorganic complexes; defect structure of silicates and other solids; organic free radicals. *Mailing Add:* Dept of Chem & Chem Eng Univ of Sask Saskatoon SK S7N 0W0 Can

WEIL, JOHN VICTOR, b Detroit, Mich, May 10, 35; m 64; c 1. INTERNAL MEDICINE. *Educ:* Yale Univ, BS, 57, MD, 61. *Prof Exp:* Intern path, Sch Med, Yale Univ, 61-62, intern med, 62-63, asst resident, 63-64 & 67-68; asst prof, 68-72, ASSOC PROF MED, MED CTR, UNIV COLO, DENVER, 72- *Concurrent Pos:* NIH res fel cardiol, Univ Colo, Denver, 66-67. *Res:* Physiological responses to hypoxia; peripheral circulation, erythropoiesis, ventilation, oxygen transport. *Mailing Add:* 4200 E Ninth Ave Denver CO 80220

WEIL, JON DAVID, b Evansville, Ind, Mar 24, 37; div; c 2. MOLECULAR GENETICS, CLINICAL PSYCHOLOGY. *Educ:* Swarthmore Col, BA, 58; Univ Calif, Davis, PhD(genetics), 63. *Prof Exp:* NSF fel molecular biol, Univ Ore, 63-65; NIH fel, Harvard Univ, 65-67; from asst prof to assoc prof molecular biol, Vanderbilt Univ, 67-77; res geneticist pediat, Univ Calif, San Francisco, 77- *Concurrent Pos:* Lectr, Calif Sch Prof Psychol, 77. *Mem:* Am Soc Human Genetics; AAAS. *Res:* Activities; Developmental consequences of aneuploidy; psychological consequences of genetic diseases. *Mailing Add:* 1608 Belvadere 94702

WEIL, MARVIN LEE, b Gainesville, Fla, Sept 28, 24; m 54; c 3. PEDIATRIC NEUROLOGY, VIROLOGY. *Educ:* Univ Fla, BS, 43; Johns Hopkins Univ, MD, 46; Am Bd Pediat, dipl; Am Bd Psychiat & Neurol, dipl. *Prof Exp:* Intern, Duke Univ Hosp, 46-47; asst resident pediat, 47-48; resident, Children's Hosp, Cincinnati, 50-52, res assoc, Res Found, 52-53; clin asst prof pediat, Sch Med, Univ Miami, 58-65; Nat Inst Neurol Dis & Stroke spec fel, Johns Hopkins Univ & Univ Calif, Los Angeles, 65-68; from asst prof to assoc prof, 68-78, PROF PEDIAT & NEUROL, UNIV CALIF, LOS ANGELES, 78- *Concurrent Pos:* Attend pediatrician, Cincinnati Gen Hosp, 52-53; pvt pract, 53-65; chief div pediat neurol, Harbor Gen Hosp, 68-; sr int fel, Fogarty Int Ctr, Karolinska Inst, NIH, Stockholm, Sweden, 76-77. *Mem:* AAAS; Am Asn Immunologists; fel Am Acad Pediat; Am Acad Neurol; Am Asn Ment Deficiency. *Res:* Growth characteristics, genetics, neurotropic behavior of mammalian viruses; immune responses of central nervous system. *Mailing Add:* Div of Pediat Neurol Harbor-Univ Calif Los Angeles Mes Ctr Torrance CA 90509

WEIL, MAX HARRY, b Baden, Switz, Feb 9, 27; nat US; m 55; c 2. CARDIOVASCULAR DISEASES, BIOMEDICAL ENGINEERING. *Educ:* Univ Mich, AB, 48; State Univ NY Downstate Med Ctr, MD, 52; Univ Minn, PhD(med), 57; Am Bd Internal Med, dipl, 62. *Prof Exp:* Intern internal med, Cincinnati Gen Hosp, Ohio, 52-53; resident, Univ Hosps, Univ Minn, 53-55; asst clin prof, Sch Med, Univ Southern Calif, 57-59, from asst prof to assoc prof, 59-71, dir, Ctr Critically Ill, 68-80, clin prof med, 71-81, clin prof biomed eng, 72-81; DIR, INST CRITICAL CARE MED, LOS ANGELES, 76-, CHMN DEPT MED, UNIV HEALTH SCI, CHICAGO MED SCH, 82-, PROF MED & PHYSIOL, 82- *Concurrent Pos:* Vis prof, Univ Pittsburgh; chief cardiol, City of Hope Med Ctr, Duarte, Calif, 57-59, consult, 59-63; attend physician, Los Angeles County Gen Hosp, 58-, sr attend cardiologist, Children's Div, 68-; consult physician, Cedars-Sinai Med Ctr, 65-; chmn comt emergency med care, Bd Supvrs, County Los Angeles, 68-73; past mem comt shock, Nat Acad Sci-Nat Res Coun; fel coun circulation & coun thrombosis, Am Heart Asn; pres, Int Critical Care Med, Inc, 75- *Mem:* Fel Am Col Cardiol; fel Am Col Physicians; Am Soc Nephrol; Am Soc Pharmacol & Exp Therapeut; Inst Elec & Electronics Engrs. *Res:* Clinical cardiology and cardiorespiratory physiology; critical care medicine; studies on circulatory shock, both experimental and clinical; biomedical instrumentation and automation; applications of computer techniques to bedside medicine. *Mailing Add:* Dept Med Univ Healh Sci Chicago Med Sch 3333 Green Bay Rd North Chicago IL 60064

WEIL, NICHOLAS A, b Budapest, Hungary, Apr 15, 26; nat US; m 70; c 2. MECHANICS. *Educ:* Tech Univ Budapest, BS, 47; Univ Ill, MS, 48, PhD, 52; Univ Santa Clara, MBA, 71. *Prof Exp:* Asst, Univ Ill, 48-52; develop engr, M W Kellogg Co, NY, 52-56, head mech develop div, 56-57, chief develop engr, 57-59; dir mech res, Res Inst, Ill Inst Technol, 59-63; vpres res, Cummins Engine Co, Ind, 63-68; tech adv to chmn, FMC Corp, 68-71, dir planning & ventures, 71-74; DIR CORP TECHNOL, INGERSOLL-RAND CO, 74- *Concurrent Pos:* From adj asst prof to adj assoc prof, NY Univ, 55-59; lectr, Grad Sch Bus, Univ Santa Clara, 71-74. *Mem:* Soc Automotive Eng; Am Soc Mech Eng; Nat Soc Prof Eng; Sigma Xi. *Res:* Internal combustion engines; drive line components; applied mechanics; rheology of materials; fracture dynamics; fluid flow; combustion; stress analysis; heat transfer; process equipment; materials conveying; fuel injection systems; process kinetics. *Mailing Add:* Ingersoll-Rand Co Box 301 Princeton NJ 08540

WEIL, PETER H, thoracic surgery, see previous edition

WEIL, RAOUL BLOCH, b La Paz, Bolivia; US citizen; m 56; c 2. PHYSICS. *Educ:* Univ La Paz, Bachiller, 45; Univ Ill, Urbana, BSEE, 49; Univ Calif, Riverside, MA, 63, PhD(physics), 66. *Prof Exp:* Trainee, Allis Chalmers Mfg Co, 49-51; consult engr, Bolivian Com Corp, 51-53, head tech dept, 53-55; prof elec eng, Univ La Paz, 56-60; res asst cosmic ray physics, Univ Chicago, 60-61; solid state physics, Univ Calif, 61-65; res physicist, Monsanto Co, 65-67, proj leader, 67-69; assoc prof elec eng, Washington Univ, 69-71; ASSOC PROF PHYSICS, ISRAEL INST TECHNOL, 71- *Concurrent Pos:* Res assoc, Cosmic Physics Lab, Chacaltaya, 57-60; vis assoc prof, Univ Ill, Urbana, 77-78; ed-in-chief, Annals Israel Phys Soc, 80- *Mem:* Am Phys Soc; Inst Elec & Electronics Engrs; Israel Laser & Electrooptics Soc (secy, 73-75, pres, 76-); Israel Phys Soc (secy, 76-77). *Res:* Solar cells; optical properties of semiconductors in the infrared; lasers; superionic conductors. *Mailing Add:* Physics Dept Technion Israel Inst Technol Haifa Israel

WEIL, ROLF, b Neunkirchen, Ger, Aug 5, 26; nat US. METALLURGY. *Educ:* Carnegie Inst Technol, BS, 46, MS, 49; Pa State Univ, PhD(metall), 51. *Hon Degrees:* ME, Stevens Inst Technol, 67. *Prof Exp:* Metallurgist, Duquesne Smelting Corp, 46-48; grad asst, Pa State Univ, 49-51; assoc metallurgist, Argonne Nat Lab, 51-54; from asst prof to assoc prof, 56-67, PROF METALL, STEVENS INST TECHNOL, 67- *Mem:* Electrochem Soc; Am Inst Mining, Metall & Petrol Engrs; Am Electroplaters Soc; fel Brit Inst Metal Finishing; Am Soc Testing & Mat. *Res:* Structure and properties of electrodeposited metals; electron microscopy; metal strengthening mechanisms; corrosion. *Mailing Add:* Dept of Mat & Metall Eng Castle Point Sta Hoboken NJ 07030

WEIL, THOMAS ANDRE, b Ft Riley, Kans, June 27, 44; m 70; c 2. INORGANIC CHEMISTRY. *Educ:* State Univ NY Col Oswego, BA, 66; Univ Cincinnati, PhD(chem), 70. *Prof Exp:* Nat Res Coun fel, US Bur Mines, Pa, 70-71; asst prof chem, Trenton State Col, 71-72; NIH fel, Univ Chicago, 72-74; RES SUPVR, AMOCO CHEM CORP, 74- *Concurrent Pos:* NSF exchange fel, US-USSR Sci & Technol, 74. *Mem:* Am Chem Soc. *Res:* Catalysis; heterogeneous and homogeneous catalysis; transition metal complexes; metals in organic synthesis; mechanisms of metal catalyzed reactions; energy related research. *Mailing Add:* Amoco Chem Corp Box 400 Naperville IL 60540

WEIL, THOMAS P, b Mt Vernon, NY, Oct 2, 32; m 65. PUBLIC HEALTH, HOSPITAL ADMINISTRATION. *Educ:* Union Col, NY, AB, 54; Yale Univ, MPH, 58; Univ Mich, PhD(med care orgn), 65. *Prof Exp:* S S Goldwater fel hosp admin, Mt Sinai Hosp, New York, 57-58; assoc consult, John G Steinle & Assocs, Mgt Consults, 58-61; asst prof, Sch Pub Health, Univ Calif, Los Angeles, 62-65; assoc dir & consult, Touro Infirmary, New Orleans, 64-66; prof grad studies health serv mgr & dir, Schs Med, Bus & Pub Admin, Univ Mo-Columbia, 66-71; vpres & prin, E D Rosenfeld Assocs, Inc, New York, 71-75; PRES, BEDFORD HEALTH ASSOCS, INC, 75- *Concurrent Pos:* Consult to numerous hosps, planning agencies & med ctrs; vis prof & W K Kellogg Found grant, Univ New South Wales, 69. *Mem:* Fel Am Pub Health Asn; Am Hosp Asn; Am Col Hosp Adminr; Am Asn Hosp Consult. *Res:* Management, organization and financing of health services, especially hospital and medical care administration. *Mailing Add:* Bedford Health Assocs Inc 223 Katonah Ave Katonah NY 10536

WEIL, WILLIAM B, JR, b Minneapolis, Minn, Dec 3, 24; m 49; c 2. PEDIATRICS. *Educ:* Univ Minn, BA, 45, BS, 46, MB, 47, MD, 48. *Prof Exp:* USPHS & univ res fels, Harvard Univ, 51-52; sr instr pediat, Western Reserve Univ, 53-57, asst prof, 57-63; assoc prof, Col Med, Univ Fla, 63-65, E I Dupont prof for handicapped children, 65-68; chmn dept, 68-79, PROF HUMAN DEVELOP, MICH STATE UNIV, 68- *Mem:* AAAS; Soc Pediat Res (secy-treas, 62-69, pres, 69-70); Am Pediat Soc; Am Acad Pediat; NY Acad Sci. *Res:* Renal disease; diabetes; nutrition. *Mailing Add:* Dept Human Develop Mich State Univ East Lansing MI 48824

WEILER, EDWARD JOHN, b Chicago, Ill, Jan 15, 49. ASTRONOMY. *Educ:* Northwestern Univ, BA, 71, MS, 73, PhD(astron), 76. *Prof Exp:* Res assoc astron, Avionics Lab, Northwestern Univ, 73-74; RES ASSOC, PRINCETON UNIV-NASA GODDARD SPACE FLIGHT CTR, 76- *Mem:* AAAS. *Res:* Chromospheric activity in late-type binary stars and the evolution of galaxies. *Mailing Add:* 3101 Teton Lane Bowie MD 20715

WEILER, ERNEST DIETER, b Neuwied, Ger, June 30, 39; US citizen; m 67. ORGANIC CHEMISTRY. *Educ:* Univ Minn, BChem, 62; Univ Nebr, PhD(org chem), 66; Temple Univ, MBA, 74. *Prof Exp:* Fel, Univ Basel, 66-67; chemist, 67-73, chemist animal health res, 73-74, proj leader animal health res, 74-75, proj leader process res, 75-77, DEPT MGR, PLASTICS INTERMEDIATES, ROHM AND HAAS CO, 77- *Mem:* Am Chem Soc. *Mailing Add:* Rohm and Haas Co Bristol PA 19007

WEILER, IVAN-JEANNE MAYFIELD, immunology, psychobiology, see previous edition

WEILER, JOHN HENRY, JR, b Lincoln, Nebr, July 8, 25; m 58; c 2. PLANT TAXONOMY. *Educ:* Univ Nebr, BSc, 58; Univ Calif, Berkeley, PhD(taxon), 62. *Prof Exp:* PROF PLANT SCI, CALIF STATE UNIV, FRESNO, 62- *Mem:* Am Soc Plant Taxon; Bot Soc Am; Int Asn Plant Taxon. *Res:* Biosystematics; floristics of central California. *Mailing Add:* Dept of Biol Calif State Univ Fresno CA 93710

WEILER, LAWRENCE STANLEY, b Middleton, NS, July 11, 42; m 64; c 3. ORGANIC CHEMISTRY. *Educ:* Univ Toronto, BSc, 64; Harvard Univ, PhD(org chem), 68. *Prof Exp:* asst prof, 68-75, assoc prof, 75-80, PROF CHEM, UNIV BC, 80- *Mem:* Am Chem Soc; Chem Inst Can; Royal Soc Chem; Swiss Chem Soc. *Res:* Synthesis and study of novel organic compounds; synthesis of natural products and organic metals. *Mailing Add:* Dept Chem Univ BC Vancouver BC V6T 1W5 Can

WEILER, MARGARET HORTON, b Sewickley, Pa, Apr 30, 41; m 62; c 2. PHYSICS. *Educ:* Radcliffe Col, AB, 62; Univ Maine, MS, 64; Mass Inst Technol, PhD(physics), 77. *Prof Exp:* Instr physics, Univ Maine, 64-65; comput programmer linguistics, Harvard Computation Ctr, Harvard Univ, 65; res staff mem, Francis Bitter Nat Magnet Lab, 65-74, ASST PROF PHYSICS, MASS INST TECHNOL, 77- *Mem:* AAAS; Am Phys Soc. *Res:* Study of the electronic properties of semiconductors using optical and electron energy loss spectroscopy. *Mailing Add:* Rm 13-2145 Mass Inst Technol Cambridge MA 02139

WEILER, ROLAND R, b Estonia, Feb 23, 36; Can citizen; m 65; c 3. GEOCHEMISTRY. *Educ:* Univ Toronto, BA, 59, MA, 60; Dalhousie Univ, PhD(oceanog), 65. *Prof Exp:* Res scientist, Bedford Inst Oceanog, Can Dept Energy, Mines & Resources, 64-67 & Can Ctr for Inland Waters, 67-80. *Mem:* AAAS; Am Soc Limnol & Oceanog; Int Asn Gt Lakes Res. *Res:* Chemical limnology and geochemistry of sediments. *Mailing Add:* 37 Mercer St Dundas ON L9H 2N8 Can

WEILER, THOMAS JOSEPH, b St Louis, Mo, May 5, 49. ELEMENTARY PARTICLES PHYSICS. *Educ:* Stanford Univ, BS, 71; Univ Wis, PhD(physics), 76. *Prof Exp:* Sr res asst, Univ Liverpool, 76-78; res assoc theoret physics, Northeastern Univ, 78-81; asst res physicist II, Univ Calif, San Diego, 81- *Concurrent Pos:* Vis theoret physics, Ctr Europ Nuclear Res, Rutherford Lab, 77, Aspen Ctr, 80, 81. *Res:* Work towards the description of the ultimate subunits of matter and the forces by which they interact and combine; implications of particle physics for cosmology. *Mailing Add:* Dept of Physics Univ Calif San Diego La Jolla CA 92093

WEILER, WILLIAM ALEXANDER, b Milwaukee, Wis, Nov 8, 41; m 63; c 3. BACTERIOLOGY, MICROBIAL ECOLOGY. *Educ:* Dartmouth Col, AB, 63; Purdue Univ, PhD(microbiol), 69. *Prof Exp:* Instr microbiol, Purdue Univ, 66-69; asst prof, 69-74, assoc prof, 74-80, PROF BOT, EASTERN ILL UNIV, 80- *Mem:* Am Soc Microbiol. *Res:* Herbicide effects on soil microflora; petroleum degradation in soil and water ecosystems. *Mailing Add:* Dept of Bot Eastern Ill Univ Charleston IL 61920

WEILL, CAROL EDWIN, b Brooklyn, NY, Dec 12, 18; m 47; c 2. ORGANIC CHEMISTRY. *Educ:* City Col New York, BS, 39; Columbia Univ, AM, 43, PhD(chem), 44. *Prof Exp:* Res chemist, Div War Res, Columbia Univ, 44-45 & Takamine Lab, 45-47; from instr to assoc prof, 47-60, PROF CHEM, RUTGERS UNIV, NEWARK, 60- *Mem:* Am Chem Soc. *Res:* Enzymes; carbohydrates. *Mailing Add:* Dept of Chem Rutgers Univ Newark NJ 07102

WEILL, DANIEL FRANCIS, b Paris, France, Nov 29, 31; US citizen; m 57; c 3. PETROLOGY, GEOCHEMISTRY. *Educ:* Cornell Univ, AB, 56; Univ Ill, MS, 58; Univ Calif, PhD(geol), 62. *Prof Exp:* Res assoc geochem, Univ Calif, Berkeley, 62-63; asst prof geol, Univ Calif, San Diego, 63-66; assoc prof, 66-70, dir ctr volcanology, 69-70, assoc dean arts & sci, 76-78, PROF GEOL, UNIV ORE, 70- *Concurrent Pos:* Grants, NSF, 65-66, 66-68, & 79, NASA, 68-78, 71-78 & 79-81 & Am Chem Soc, 70-72; Fulbright-Hays sr res fel, UK, 72-73. *Mem:* Mineral Soc Am; Royal Soc Chem. *Res:* Physical chemistry of geological systems; silicate liquid density, viscosity; diffusion; lunar sample analysis; redox equilibria in silicate melts; experimental trace element distribution; thermodynamic properties of mineral and liquid silicate systems. *Mailing Add:* Dept of Geol Univ of Ore Eugene OR 97403

WEILL, GEORGES GUSTAVE, b Strasbourg, France, Apr 9, 26. MATHEMATICAL ANALYSIS, APPLIED MATHEMATICS. *Educ:* Univ Paris, DSc(physics), 55; Univ Calif, Los Angeles, PhD(math), 60. *Prof Exp:* Res scientist, Gen Radio Co, France, 52-56; res fel, Calif Inst Tech, 56-59; res fel math, Harvard Univ, 60-62; lectr & res fel, Yale Univ, 62-64; asst prof, Yeshiva Univ, 64-65; PROF, POLYTECH INST N Y, 66- *Concurrent Pos:* Consult, Electro-Optical Systs, Inc, 59-60 & Raytheon Co, 61-62. *Mem:* Am Math Soc; sr mem Inst Elec & Electronics Eng; Math Soc France. *Res:* Complex analysis; Riemann surfaces; diffraction theory; antennas; theoretical and applied electromagnetics. *Mailing Add:* Dept of Math Polytech Inst of N Y 333 Jay St Brooklyn NY 11201

WEILL, HANS, b Berlin, Ger, Aug 31, 33; US citizen; m; c 3. MEDICINE, PHYSIOLOGY. *Educ:* Tulane Univ, BA, 55, MD, 58; Am Bd Internal Med, dipl & Am Bd Pulmonary Dis, dipl, 65. *Prof Exp:* From instr to assoc prof, 62-71, PROF MED, SCH MED, TULANE UNIV, 71- *Concurrent Pos:* Attending staff, Vet Admin Hosp, New Orleans, 63-; consult, USPHS Hosp, 64-; dir, Specialized Ctr Res & consult to task force environ lung dis, Nat Heart, Lung & Blood Inst, 72-; mem, Pulmonary Dis Adv Comt, Nat Heart Lung & Blood Inst, 81, chmn, 82; mem, Pulmonary Dis Bd, Am Bd Internal Med, 80- *Mem:* Am Thoracic Soc (pres, 76-77); fel Am Col Chest Physicians; fel Am Col Physicians; Am Fedn Clin Res; fel Royal Soc Med. *Res:* Applied pulmonary physiology; occupational respiratory diseases; environmental health sciences. *Mailing Add:* Sch Med Tulane Univ 1700 Perdido St New Orleans LA 70112

WEIMANN, LUDWIK JAN, b Lipnica, Ger, May 24, 41; m 72; c 2. PHOTOCHEMISTRY, POLYMER CHEMISTRY. *Educ:* Univ Poznan, MS, 63, PhD(photochem), 70. *Prof Exp:* Instr photochem & radiochem, Univ Poznan, 63-70; fel theoret chem, Kans Univ, 70-72; fel vision chem, Univ Mo-Kansas City, 72-73, instr phys & gen chem, 73-75, vis asst prof phys chem, 75-76; res & develop dir polymer photochem, K C Coatings Inc, 76-80; WITH JONERGIN INC, 80- *Mem:* Am Chem Soc; Soc Mfg Eng. *Res:* Radical and catonic photopolymerization; application in ink making area; kinetics of photopolymerization and physicochemical properties of ultraviolet-cured films. *Mailing Add:* Jonergin Inc 110 Lake St St Albans VT 05478

WEIMAR, VIRGINIA LEE, b Condon, Ore, Oct 23, 22. PHYSIOLOGY. *Educ:* Ore State Col, MS, 47; Univ Pa, PhD(physiol), 51. *Prof Exp:* Physiologist, US Dept Navy, 51; res assoc biochem, Wills Eye Hosp, Philadelphia, Pa, 52-54; researcher ophthal, Col Physicians & Surgeons, Columbia Univ, 55-58, res assoc, 58-59, asst prof, 59-61; res assoc, 61-63, asst prof, 63-68, ASSOC PROF OPHTHAL, MED SCH, ORE HEALTH SCI UNIV, PORTLAND, 68- *Concurrent Pos:* Nat Cancer Inst fel, Univ Pa, 54-55; NIH travel award; deleg, Int Cong Ophthal, Belg, 58 & Jerusalem Conf Prevention of Blindness, 71. *Mem:* Harvey Soc; Am Physiol Soc; Asn Res Vision & Ophthal; Soc Gen Physiol; Am Soc Cell Biol. *Res:* Biochemistry and physiology of trauma; wound healing; inflammation; corneal wound healing; cellular ultramicrochemistry; biomathematics. *Mailing Add:* Dept Ophthal Ore Health Sci Univ Portland OR 97201

WEIMBERG, RALPH, b San Diego, Calif, Dec 22, 24; m 52; c 2. PHYSIOLOGY, PLANT BACTERIOLOGY. *Educ:* Univ Calif, AB, 49, MA, 51, PhD(bact), 55. *Prof Exp:* Fel, Biol Div, Oak Ridge Nat Labs, 55-56; instr microbiol, Sch Med, Western Reserve Univ, 56-58; biochemist, Northern Utilization Res & Develop Div, 58-65, BIOCHEMIST US SALINITY LAB, AGR RES SERV, US DEPT AGR, 65- *Concurrent Pos:* Vis assoc prof, Univ Calif, Davis, 64; vis res scientist, Bot Dept, Hebrew Univ, Jerusalem, 77 & 81. *Mem:* AAAS; Am Soc Microbiol; Am Soc Plant Physiol; Am Soc Biol Chemists; NY Acad Sci. *Res:* Plant physiology and metabolism; properties and location of enzymes; biochemistry. *Mailing Add:* US Dept Agr US Salinity Lab 4500 Glenwood Dr Riverside CA 92501

WEIMER, DAVID, b Marion, Ind, Oct 13, 19; m 44; c 4. GAS DYNAMICS. *Educ:* Ohio State Univ, BS, 41, MS, 46. *Prof Exp:* Res asst physics, Princeton Univ, 41-45; prof, Am Col SIndia, 46-47; res assoc, Princeton Univ, 47-52; res engr, Armour Res Found, Ill, 52-55 & Am Mach & Foundry Co, 55-56; sr staff scientist physics, Lockheed Corp, Calif, 56-58, 60-64; asst prof, Ohio Northern Univ, 64-68; staff scientist, Martin-Marietta Corp, Colo, 68-69; ASSOC PROF PHYSICS, OHIO NORTHERN UNIV, 69- *Concurrent Pos:* Sr staff engr, Martin-Marietta Corp, Colo, 72-73. *Mem:* Am Phys Soc. *Res:* Gas physics and shock wave phenomena; dissociation and ionization of gas at high temperatures; radiation of excited species in planetary atmospheres. *Mailing Add:* Dept of Physics Ohio Northern Univ Ada OH 45810

WEIMER, F(RANK) CARLIN, b Dayton, Ohio, July 27, 17; m 44; c 3. ELECTRICAL ENGINEERING. *Educ:* Univ Ohio, BS, 38; Ohio State Univ, MSc, 39, PhD(elec eng), 43. *Prof Exp:* Asst, 39-41, from instr to assoc prof, 41-58, PROF ELEC ENG, OHIO STATE UNIV, 58-, V CHMN DEPT, 68- *Concurrent Pos:* Consult, Battelle Mem Inst, 57- *Mem:* AAAS; Am Soc Eng Educ; Nat Soc Prof Engrs; Inst Elec & Electronics Engrs. *Res:* Servomechanisms; magnetic fields in machinery; permeance analysis; automatic control; signal processing. *Mailing Add:* Dept of Elec Eng Ohio State Univ 2015 Neil Ave Columbus OH 43210

WEIMER, HENRY EBEN, b Continental, Ohio, May 13, 14; m 41. IMMUNOCHEMISTRY. *Educ:* Wittenberg Col, AB, 35; Univ Southern Calif, MS, 48, PhD(biochem), 50. *Prof Exp:* Teacher high sch, Ohio, 35-41; res assoc, 50-51, from instr to assoc prof microbiol & immunol, 51-77, prof, 77-80, EMER PROF IMMUNOCHEM, SCH MED, UNIV CALIF, LOS ANGELES, 80- *Mem:* Am Soc Exp Path; Am Asn Immunol. *Res:* Acute phase proteins in inflammatory states; embryonic serum proteins in health and disease; tumor and fetal antigens. *Mailing Add:* Dept of Microbiol & Immunol Sch of Med Univ of Calif Los Angeles CA 90024

WEIMER, JOHN THOMAS, b McKeesport, Pa, Mar 14, 30; m 57; c 3. BIOLOGY, TOXICOLOGY. *Educ:* St Vincent Col, BA, 52. *Prof Exp:* RES BIOLOGIST TOXICOL, CHEM SYSTS LAB, US ARMY, 56- *Mem:* Soc Toxicol; Sigma Xi. *Res:* Inhalation toxicology, pharmacology, aerosol technology. *Mailing Add:* Bldg 3265 Res Div Chem Systs Lab Aberdeen Proving Ground MD 21010

WEIMER, PAUL KESSLER, b Wabash, Ind, Nov 5, 14; m 42; c 3. PHYSICS. *Educ:* Manchester Col, AB, 36; Univ Kans, AM, 38; Ohio State Univ, PhD(physics), 42. *Hon Degrees:* DSc, Manchester Col, 68. *Prof Exp:* Asst, Univ Kans, 36-37; prof physics, Tabor Col, 37-39; asst, Ohio State Univ, 39-42; res engr, RCA Labs, 42-64, fel tech staff, 64-81; CONSULT. *Honors & Awards:* Award, TV Broadcasters Asn, 46; Zworykin Prize, Inst Elec & Electronics Eng, 59, Morris Liebmann Mem Prize, 66. *Mem:* Nat Acad Eng; Am Phys Soc; fel Inst Elec & Electronics Eng. *Res:* Nuclear physics; electron optics; photoconductivity; secondary emission; semiconductor devices; television camera tubes and solid state image sensors. *Mailing Add:* 112 Random Rd Princeton NJ 08540

WEIMER, ROBERT FREDRICK, b Wheeling, WVa, Jan 16, 40. CHEMICAL ENGINEERING. *Educ:* Mass Inst Technol, SB, 61; Univ Calif, Berkeley, PhD(chem eng), 65. *Prof Exp:* Staff engr, Air Prod & Chem Inc, 67-73, process mgr, 73-76, develop mgr, 76-78, dir develop, Corp Res & Develop Dept, 78-81; CHIEF ENGR, INT COAL REFINING CO, 81- *Mem:* AAAS; Am Inst Chem Engrs; Am Chem Soc. *Res:* Energy conversion; fluid flow; heat transfer; cryogenics; thermodynamics; coal liquefaction. *Mailing Add:* Int Coal Refining Co PO Box 2752 Allentown PA 18001

WEIMER, ROBERT J, b Glendo, Wyo, Sept 4, 26; m 48; c 3. GEOLOGY. *Educ:* Univ Wyo, BA, 48, MA, 49; Stanford Univ, PhD, 53. *Prof Exp:* Dist geologist, Union Oil Co Calif, Mont, 53-54; consult res geologist, 54-57; from asst prof to assoc prof, 57-72, head dept, 64-69, PROF GEOL, COLO SCH MINES, 72-, GETTY PROF GEOL ENG, 78- *Concurrent Pos:* Exchange prof, Univ Colo, 60; Fulbright lectr, Univ Adelaide, 67; vis prof, Univ Calgary, 70; mem res assoc comt, Nat Acad Sci, 70-73; mem, Inst Technol, Bandung, Indonesia, 75. *Honors & Awards:* Distinguished Serv Award, Am Asn Petrol Geol, 75. *Mem:* AAAS; Geol Soc Am; Am Asn Petrol Geol; Soc Econ Paleont & Mineral (secy-treas, 66-68, vpres, 71, pres, 72). *Res:* Stratigraphic research in the application of modern sedimentation studies to the geologic record; regional framework of sedimentation in the Cretaceous, Jurassic and Pennsylvanian rock systems; tectonics and sedimentation; geologic history of the Rocky Mountain region. *Mailing Add:* Dept of Geol Colo Sch of Mines Golden CO 80401

WEIN, ROSS WALLACE, b Exeter, Ont, Oct 29, 40; m 67. PLANT ECOLOGY. *Educ:* Univ Guelph, BSA, 65, MSc, 66; Utah State Univ, PhD(ecol), 69. *Prof Exp:* Can Nat Res Coun fel, Univ Alta, 69-71, vis asst prof plant ecol, 71-72; asst prof, 72-74, assoc prof, 74-78, PROF PLANT ECOL, UNIV NB, FREDERICTION, CAN, 78-, DIR, FIRE SCI CTR, 78- *Mem:* Ecol Soc Am; Am Soc Range Mgt; Can Bot Asn. *Res:* Plant production and nutrient cycling following wildfire; plant community dynamics; boreal and arctic ecology. *Mailing Add:* Dept of Biol Univ of N B Fredericton NB E3B 5A3 Can

WEINACHT, RICHARD JAY, b Union City, NJ, Dec 10, 31; m 55; c 6. MATHEMATICS. *Educ:* Univ Notre Dame, BS, 53; Columbia Univ, MS, 55; Univ Md, PhD(math), 62. *Prof Exp:* NSF fel math, Courant Inst Math Sci, NY Univ, 62-63; from asst prof to assoc prof, 63-74, PROF MATH, UNIV DEL, 74- *Concurrent Pos:* Vis assoc prof, Rensselaer Polytech Inst, 69-70; Fulbright fel & vis prof, Darmstadt Tech Univ, 76-77. *Mem:* Am Math Soc; Soc Indust & Appl Math. *Res:* Partial differential equations; singular perturbations. *Mailing Add:* Dept of Math Sci Univ of Del Newark DE 19711

WEINBACH, EUGENE CLAYTON, b Pine Island, NY, Nov 5, 19; m 38; c 2. BIOCHEMISTRY. *Educ:* Univ Md, BS, 42, PhD(org med chem), 47. *Prof Exp:* Res chemist, US Naval Res Lab, Washington, DC, 47; USPHS & Nat Cancer Inst fel, Sch Med, Johns Hopkins Univ, 47-48, instr physiol chem, 48-50; RES CHEMIST, NIH, 50-, HEAD, SECT PHYSIOL & BIOCHEM, LAB PARASITIC DIS, NAT INST ALLERGY & INFECTIOUS DIS, 69- *Concurrent Pos:* Guest worker, Wenner-Gren Inst, Stockholm, Sweden, 60-62. *Mem:* Am Chem Soc; Am Soc Biol Chemists. *Res:* Biochemical mechanisms of drug action; intermediary metabolism of parasites and their hosts; biological oxidations and phosphorylations; biochemistry of mitochondria. *Mailing Add:* Lab Parasitic Dis NIH Bethesda MD 20014

WEINBAUM, CARL MARTIN, b Manchester, Eng, Jan 16, 37; US citizen; m 63; c 4. MATHEMATICS. *Educ:* Queens Col, NY, BS, 58; Harvard Univ, AM, 60; NY Univ, PhD(math), 63. *Prof Exp:* Asst prof math, Univ Calif, Los Angeles, 63-68; assoc prof, Univ Hawaii, 68-70; assoc prof, Hawaii Loa Col, 70-77; fac mem, Woodmere Acad, 77-78; mem tech staff, Newtwork Anal Corp, 78-80. *Mem:* Am Math Soc. *Res:* Infinite groups, particularly word problems and small cancellation and knot groups. *Mailing Add:* 2444 Westlake Ave Oceanside NY 11572

WEINBAUM, GEORGE, b Brooklyn, NY, July 27, 32; m 63; c 4. BIOCHEMISTRY, MICROBIOLOGY. *Educ:* Univ Pa, AB, 53; Pa State Univ, MS, 55, PhD(biochem), 57. *Prof Exp:* Chief biochem labs, Geisinger Med Ctr, 57-61; asst mem, Res Labs, 61-66, assoc mem, 66-71, BIOSCIENTIST, DEPT PULMONARY DIS, ALBERT EINSTEIN MED CTR, 71-; RES ASSOC PROF MICROBIOL, HEALTH SCI CTR, TEMPLE UNIV, 73- *Concurrent Pos:* Fulbright res fel, Tokyo, 59-61; NIH res career develop award, 69. *Mem:* AAAS; Am Soc Biol Chemists; Am Soc Exp Path; Am Soc Microbiol; Am Chem Soc. *Res:* Membrane structure, synthesis and function; role of glycoproteins in organization of cell surface; etiology of emphysema; action of proteinases on cell membranes. *Mailing Add:* Korman Bldg Temple Univ Philadelphia PA 19141

WEINBAUM, SHELDON, b Brooklyn, NY, July 26, 37; m 62; c 1. FLUID PHYSICS, BIOMECHANICS. *Educ:* Rensselaer Polytech Inst, BAE, 59; Harvard Univ, SM, 60, PhD(eng), 63. *Prof Exp:* Mem res staff, Sperry Rand Res Ctr, 63-64; prin scientist, Avco Everett Res Lab, 64; theoret aerodynamicist, Gen Elec Space Sci Lab, 64-67, prin scientist, 67; assoc prof mech eng, 67-72, prof, 72-80, HERBERT G KAYSER CHAIR PROF ENG, CITY COL NEW YORK, 80- *Concurrent Pos:* Consult, Avco Everett Res Lab, 60-61, Wilmer Eye Inst, Sch Med, Johns Hopkins Univ, 67-70, Gen Elec Co, 68-69 & Boeing Sci Res Labs, 68-70; Russell Springer vis prof mech eng, Univ Calif, Berkeley, 79; vis prof mech eng, Mass Inst Technol, 80-81. *Mem:* Am Inst Aeronaut & Astronaut; Am Soc Mech Engrs. *Res:* Fluid mechanics; biofluid mechanics; epithelial membrane transport; hemodynamics; two phase flow; low Reynolds number flow; high speed gas dynamics; interacting boundary layers and wakes; heat transfer. *Mailing Add:* Dept of Mech Eng 140th St & Convent Ave New York NY 10031

WEINBERG, ALFRED FLOYD, b Milwaukee, Wis, Aug 16, 31; m 51; c 4. PHYSICAL METALLURGY. *Educ:* Ill Inst Technol, BS, 52, MS, 53, PhD(metall eng), 60. *Prof Exp:* Metallurgist, Ill Inst Tech Res Inst, 53-54, res metallurgist, 57-59; sr res engr, Solar Div, Int Harvester Co, 59-60; sr staff engr, Gulf Gen Atomic Inc, 60-76; PROF, DEPT METALL, UNIV BC, 76- *Mem:* Am Soc Metals; Am Inst Mining, Metall & Petrol Engrs; Metall Soc; Am Nuclear Soc. *Res:* Advanced reactor concepts with emphasis on high temperature and nuclear materials. *Mailing Add:* Dept of Metall Univ of BC Vancouver BC V6T 1W5 Can

WEINBERG, ALVIN MARTIN, b Chicago, Ill, Apr 20, 15; m 40, 74; c 2. NUCLEAR PHYSICS. *Educ:* Univ Chicago, AB, 35, MS, 36, PhD(physics), 39. *Hon Degrees:* LLD, Univ Chattanooga, 63, Alfred Univ & Denison Col, 67; ScD, Univ of the Pac, 66, Worcester Polytech Inst, 71, Univ Rochester & Butler Univ, 73, Wake Forest Univ, 74 & Univ Louisville, 78; EngD, Stevens Inst Technol, 73. *Prof Exp:* Asst math biophys, Univ Chicago, 39-41, physicist, Metall Lab, 41-45; physicist, Clinton Labs, Tenn, 45-48; dir physics div, Oak Ridge Nat Lab, 48-49, res dir, 49-55, dir, 55-74; dir off energy res & develop, Fed Energy Admin, 74; DIR INST ENERGY ANAL, OAK RIDGE ASSOC UNIVS, 75- *Concurrent Pos:* Mem sci adv bd, US Air Force, 56-59; mem, President's Sci Adv Comt, 60-62; Regents' lectr, Univ Calif, 66 & 78. *Honors & Awards:* Atoms for Peace Award, 60; Lawrence Mem Award, US AEC, 60; Heinrich Hertz Prize, Univ Karlsruhe, 75; Award, NY Acad Sci; Enrico Fermi Award, 80. *Mem:* Nat Acad Sci; Nat Acad Eng; Am Philos Soc; fel Am Nuclear Soc (pres, 59-60); Royal Neth Acad Sci. *Res:* Nuclear energy; mathematical theory of nerve function; science policy; energy analysis. *Mailing Add:* 111 Moylan Lane Oak Ridge TN 37830

WEINBERG, BARBARA LEE HUBERMAN, b New York, NY, Nov 28, 34; m 57; c 3. MOLECULAR BIOLOGY. *Educ:* City Col New York, BS, 55; Yale Univ, MS, 58; Duke Univ, PhD(biochem), 64. *Prof Exp:* Asst prof org chem & microbiol, Marymount Col, 79-80; fel endocrine res, Res Inst Hosp Joint Dis, 80-81; FEL BIOCHEM, NEW YORK MED COL, 81- *Res:* Recombinant plasmids have been constructed to study synthesis and regulation of expression of genes for initiation factor-3 and other synthetases; analysis of molecular mechanisms at level of transcriptional or translational control. *Mailing Add:* 35 Secor Rd Scarsdale NY 10583

WEINBERG, BERND, b Chicago, Ill, Jan 30, 40; m 65. SPEECH PATHOLOGY. *Educ:* State Univ NY, BS, 61; Ind Univ, MA, 63, PhD, 65. *Prof Exp:* Prof otolaryngol, Sch Med & prof speech path, Sch Dent, Ind Univ, 64-66; res fel speech sci, Nat Inst Dent Res, 66-68; dir speech res lab, Med Ctr, Ind Univ, Indianapolis, 68-74; PROF SPEECH PATH & SPEECH SCI, PURDUE UNIV, WEST LAFAYETTE, 74- *Mem:* Acoust Soc Am; Am Speech & Hearing Asn; Am Cleft Palate Asn. *Res:* Speech acoustics; speech physiology. *Mailing Add:* Dept Speech Path & Speech Sci Purdue Univ West Lafayette IN 47906

WEINBERG, DANIEL I, b New York, NY, July 11, 28; m 57; c 3. COMPUTER ENGINEERING, ELECTROMAGNETIC FIELD CONTROL. *Educ:* Clarkson Col Technol, BEE, 48; Duke Univ, MS, 62, PhD(physiol), 69. *Prof Exp:* Engr, Fairchild Engine & Airplane Corp, 48-51; sr engr, Atomic Prod Div, Gen Elec Co, 51-57; assoc, Astra, Inc, Conn & NC, 57-59, mgr med eng, 59-64; staff engr, Adv Systs Develop Div, 64-70, adv systs engr, Data Processing Div, 70-75, adv systs engr, Gen Systs Div, 75-78, adv systs analyst, 78-80, SR ENGR, INTERNAL TELECOMMUN, IBM CORP, 81- *Concurrent Pos:* Consult, 57-64; res assoc, Med Ctr, Duke Univ, 60-64; assoc, Col Physicians & Surgeons, Columbia Univ, 65-79; adv lab safety, Bd Educ, Scarsdale, NY, 81- *Mem:* Inst Elec & Electronics Engrs. *Res:* Application of engineering to solution of biological research and medical problems; computers in medicine and instrumentation; electrical safety in medicine; cardiac electrophysiology; physiological monitoring; instrumentation and measurement; communications systems control; control of nonioninzing electromagnetic fields from industrial facilities; radio communications systems and licensing. *Mailing Add:* 35 Secor Rd Scarsdale NY 10583

WEINBERG, DAVID SAMUEL, b St Louis, Mo, Feb 15, 38; m 61; c 1. ORGANIC CHEMISTRY, ANALYTICAL CHEMISTRY. *Educ:* Univ Ariz, BS, 60, PhD(phys org chem), 65. 64. *Prof Exp:* Res assoc, Stanford Univ, 64-65; res chemist, Phillips Petrol Co, Okla, 65-71; GROUP LEADER, TECH CTR, OWENS-ILL CO, 71- *Mem:* Am Chem Soc. *Res:* Environmental chemistry; materials analysis; molecular spectroscopy; separation technology. *Mailing Add:* 5713 Candlestick Court Toledo OH 43615

WEINBERG, DONALD LEWIS, b New York, NY, Aug 1, 31. INFRARED DETECTORS, LASERS. *Educ:* Harvard Univ, AB, 52, AM, 53, PhD(appl physics), 59. *Prof Exp:* Res physicist, Res & Develop Div, Corning Glass Works, 59-64; res assoc, Lincoln Lab, Mass Inst Technol, 64-67; res physicist, Electronics Res Ctr, Nat Aeronaut & Space Admin, 67-70; mem tech staff, Eng Res Ctr, Western Elec Co, 70-71; RES PHYSICIST, NAVAL RES LAB, 71- *Mem:* Inst Elec & Electronics Engrs. *Res:* Nuclear magnetic resonance in alloys; small angle x-ray scattering; non-linear optics; physical electronics of television pick-up tubes, image intensifiers, silicon charge-coupled devices, and infrared charge-injection devices. *Mailing Add:* Code 6552 Naval Res Lab Washington DC 20375

WEINBERG, ELLIOT CARL, b Chicago, Ill, Aug 17, 32; m 62, 79; c 2. MATHEMATICS. *Educ:* Purdue Univ, BA, 56, MS, 58, PhD(math), 61. *Prof Exp:* From instr to asst prof, 60-66, ASSOC PROF MATH, UNIV ILL, URBANA, 66- *Mem:* Am Math Soc. *Res:* Ordered algebraic structures. *Mailing Add:* Dept of Math Univ of Ill Urbana IL 61801

WEINBERG, ELLIOT HILLEL, b Duluth, Minn, Dec 28, 24; m 47; c 2. SOLID STATE PHYSICS. *Educ:* Univ Mich, BS & MS, 47; Univ Iowa, PhD(physics), 53. *Prof Exp:* Asst, Univ Mich, 42-43, res assoc, 47-48; res physicist, Mass Inst Technol, 48-49; from instr to assoc prof physics, Univ Minn, 49-58; prof & chmn dept, NDak State Univ, 58-62; chief scientist, San Francisco Br, 62-67, dir div phys sci, 67-71, liaison scientist, London, 65-66, DIR RES, OFF NAVAL RES, 71- *Concurrent Pos:* Mem, Col Physics Comn Rev, 62. *Mem:* AAAS; Am Phys Soc; Am Soc Eng Educ; Am Asn Physics Teachers. *Res:* Solid state physics; meteoroology; atmospheric and underwater optics; laser physics and applications. *Mailing Add:* Off of Naval Res Code 401 Arlington VA 22217

WEINBERG, ERICK JAMES, b Ossining, NY, Aug 29, 47; m 72; c 1. QUANTUM FIELD THEORY. *Educ:* Manhattan Col, BS, 68; Harvard Univ, MA, 69, PhD(physics), 73. *Prof Exp:* Mem, Inst Advan Study, 73-75; asst prof, 75-81, ASSOC PROF PHYSICS, COLUMBIA UNIV, 81- *Concurrent Pos:* Alfred P Sloan Found fel, 78-80. *Mem:* Am Phys Soc. *Res:* Theoretical elementary particle physics and quantum field theory, including the study of the very early universe. *Mailing Add:* Physics Dept Columbia Univ New York NY 10027

WEINBERG, EUGENE DAVID, b Chicago, Ill, Mar 4, 22; m 49; c 4. MEDICAL MICROBIOLOGY. *Educ:* Univ Chicago, BS, 42, MS, 48, PhD(microbiol), 50. *Prof Exp:* Asst instr microbiol, Univ Chicago, 47-50; from instr to assoc prof, 50-61, assoc dean res & grad develop, 77-79, PROF MICROBIOL & MED SCI, IND UNIV, BLOOMINGTON, 61- *Mem:* AAAS; Am Soc Microbiol; fel Am Acad Microbiol. *Res:* Roles of trace metals and of metal-binding agents in microbial physiology and in chemotherapy; nutritional immunity; antimicrobial compounds; environmental control of secondary metabolism. *Mailing Add:* Dept Biol Ind Univ Bloomington IN 47401

WEINBERG, FRED, b Poland, Apr 3, 25; nat Can; m 56; c 1. PHYSICS. *Educ:* Univ Toronto, BASc, 47, MA, 48, PhD(metall), 51. *Prof Exp:* Res scientist, Phys Metall Div, Mines Br, Can Dept Energy, Mines & Resources, 51-67, head metal physics sect, 61-67; PROF METALL, UNIV BC, 67- *Concurrent Pos:* Vis prof, Cavendish Lab, Cambridge Univ, 62-63 & Hebrew Univ, Jerusalem, 75-76; head, Dept Metall Eng, Univ BC, 80. *Honors & Awards:* Robert Woolson Hunt Award, Am Inst Mech Engrs, 80; Alcan Award, Can Inst Mining & Metall, 80. *Mem:* Am Inst Mining, Metall & Petrol Eng. *Res:* Metal physics; deformation and solidification of metals. *Mailing Add:* Dept Metall Univ BC Vancouver BC V6T 1W5 Can

WEINBERG, I JACK, b New York, NY, May 25, 35; m 58; c 2. COMPUTER SCIENCE, APPLIED MATHEMATICS. *Educ:* Yeshiva Univ, BA, 56; Mass Inst Technol, SM, 58, PhD(math), 61. *Prof Exp:* Mgr math, Avco Corp, 61-70; assoc prof math, Lowell Technol Inst, 70-73, prof, 73-80; PROF, UNIV LOWELL, 80- *Concurrent Pos:* Instr, Northeastern Grad Sch Arts & Sci, 64-69. *Mem:* Am Math Soc; Soc Indust & Appl Math; Asn Comput Mach; Math Asn Am. *Res:* Numerical analysis; differential equations; theory of elasticity. *Mailing Add:* 84 Rawson Rd Brookline MA 02146

WEINBERG, IRVING, b New York, NY, July 3, 18; m 47; c 1. PHYSICS. *Educ:* Stanford Univ, BS, 50; Univ Colo, MS, 52, PhD, 58. *Prof Exp:* Physicist, Midway Labs, Chicago, 52-53; instr physics, Univ Colo, 54-57; sr physicist, Mobil Oil Co, NJ & Tex, 58-59; sr res physicist, Aeronutronic Div, Ford Motor Co, 59-64; res physicist, Jet Propulsion Lab, 64-67; physicist, Div Res, 67-72, PHYSICIST, MAT PROG, NASA, 72- *Concurrent Pos:* Consult, Magnolia Petrol Co, Tex. *Mem:* Am Phys Soc; Sigma Xi. *Res:* Space physics; radio frequency spectroscopy of the solid state; transport phenomena in solids; energy band theory; interaction of radiation with matter. *Mailing Add:* NASA Lewis Res Ctr MS 302-1 21000 Brookpark Rd Cleveland OH 44135

WEINBERG, JERRY L, b Detroit, Mich, Dec 2, 31; m 61; c 2. ASTROPHYSICS, ATMOSPHERIC PHYSICS. *Educ:* St Lawrence Univ, BS, 58; Univ Colo, PhD(astrophys, atmospheric physics), 63. *Prof Exp:* Res asst astrophys, High Altitude Observ, Boulder, Colo, 59-63; astrophysicist, Haleakala Observ, Univ Hawaii, 63-68; astrophysicist, Dudley Observ, State Univ NY, Albany, 68-73, assoc dir, 70-73, res prof astron, 73-80, dir, Space Astron Lab, 73-80; ADJ PROF ASTRON & DIR, SPACE ASTRON LAB, UNIV FLA, 80- *Concurrent Pos:* Mem organizing comt, Comn 21, Int Astron Union; mem, Int Comt Space Res, Int Coun Sci Unions; mem working group photom, Int Asn Geomag & Aeronomy. *Honors & Awards:* Significant Sci Achievement Medal, NASA, 74. *Mem:* AAAS; Am Astron Soc; Int Astron Union; Am Geophys Union; Astron Soc Pac. *Res:* Space astronomy; instrumentation, interplanetary medium; night sky research; atmospheric optics. *Mailing Add:* Space Astron Lab 1810 NW 6th St Gainesville FL 32601

WEINBERG, LOUIS, b New York, NY, July 15, 19; m 51; c 3. ELECTRICAL ENGINEERING, APPLIED MATHEMATICS. *Educ:* Brooklyn Col, AB, 41; Harvard Univ, MS, 47; Mass Inst Technol, ScD(elec eng), 51. *Prof Exp:* Instr elec eng, Mass Inst Technol, 47-51; res physicist & head commun & networks res sect, Hughes Aircraft Co, 51-61; vpres info processing, Conductron Corp, 61-64; vis prof elec eng, Univ Mich, 64-65; PROF ELEC ENG, CITY COL NEW YORK, 65- *Concurrent Pos:* Lectr, Univ Calif, Los Angeles, 52-54; vis assoc prof, Univ Southern Calif, 55-56; vis prof, Calif Inst Technol, 58-59; vchmn comn VI, Int Union Radio Sci, 60-; NSF grant, City Col New York, 66-68, Res Found grant, 70-72; consult, Gen Elec Co & IBM, T J Watson Res Ctr; vis prof math eng, Univ Tokyo, 79. *Mem:* Fel AAAS; Am Soc Eng Educ; fel Inst Elec & Electronics Engrs. *Res:* Network analysis; synthesis of lumped networks and lumped-distributed networks; graphs and matroids; games, computers, and switching networks; fault detection and test pattern generation. *Mailing Add:* 11 Woodland St Tenafly NJ 07670

WEINBERG, MARC STEVEN, b Boston, Mass, Aug 9, 48; m 71; c 1. MECHANICAL ENGINEERING, AERONAUTICAL ENGINEERING. *Educ:* Mass Inst Technol, BS & MS, 71, ME, 73, PhD(mech eng), 74. *Prof Exp:* Res asst ground transport, Mech Eng Dept, Mass Inst Technol, 71-74; mil officer gas turbine engines, Aeronaut Syst Div, US Air Force, 74-75; STAFF ENGR INERTIAL GUID, CHARLES STARK DRAPER LAB, 75- *Mem:* Am Soc Mech Engrs; Am Inst Navig. *Res:* Inertial navigation gyroscopes and accelerometers, applied control and estimation. *Mailing Add:* 119 Broad Meadow Rd Needham MA 02192

WEINBERG, MYRON SIMON, b New York, NY, July 18, 30; m 54; c 3. TOXICOLOGY, RESEARCH ADMINISTRATION. *Educ:* NY Univ, BA, 50; Fordham Univ, BS, 54; Univ Md, MS, 56, PhD(med chem, pharmacol), 58. *Prof Exp:* Res assoc med, Sinai Hosp, Baltimore, 56-58; chemist, Ortho Res Found, NJ, 58-59; chief chemist, Norwalk Hosp, Conn, 59-65; assoc dir biol opers, Food & Drug Res Labs, NY, 65-67; dir biol sci lab, Foster D Snell, Inc, 67-68, exec vpres, 69-70, pres, 70-73; vpres, Church & Dwight Co, Inc, 73-77; SR VPRES, BOOZ, ALLEN & HAMILTON, INC, 77- *Concurrent Pos:* Prof, Med Sch, Georgetown Univ, lectr, City Col New York & Fairfield Univ. *Mem:* Fel Royal Soc Health; Am Soc Clin Pharmacol & Chemother; Am Chem Soc; AAAS; fel Am Inst Chem. *Res:* Human and animal testing of chemicals; pharmaceuticals; cosmetics; governmental liaison and regulatory advice; research management; regulatory administration and compliance; biology; new uses for chemicals; new business opportunities. *Mailing Add:* Booz Allen & Hamilton Inc 66 Hanover Rd Florham Park NJ 07932

WEINBERG, NORMAN, b New York, NY, Nov 24, 20; m 46; c 2. ELECTRICAL ENGINEERING, UNDERWATER ACOUSTICS. *Educ:* City Col New York, BEE, 43; Univ Rochester, MS, 50; Univ Md, PhD(elec eng), 64. *Prof Exp:* Fel engr, Aerospace Div, Westinghouse Elec Corp, Md, 54-64; assoc prof, 64-74, PROF ELEC ENG, UNIV MIAMI, 74- *Mem:* Acoust Soc Am. *Res:* Signal analysis and processing; network theory; applied mathematics. *Mailing Add:* Dept of Elec Eng Univ of Miami Coral Gables FL 33124

WEINBERG, PHILIP, b New York, NY, Dec 13, 25; m 47; c 3. COMMUNICATIONS, ELECTRICAL ENGINEERING. *Educ:* Univ Denver, BSEE, 50; Stanford Univ, MSEE, 51. *Hon Degrees:* LHD, Bradley Univ, 71. *Prof Exp:* Instr elec eng, Univ NMex, 52; asst prof, Univ Utah, 53-56; prof & head dept, 56-77, DEAN COL COMMUN & FINE ARTS, BRADLEY UNIV, 78- *Concurrent Pos:* Pres, Ill Valley Pub Telecommun Corp, 69-; dir, West Cent Ill Educ Telecommun Corp, 77- *Res:* Urban telecommunications; information utilities. *Mailing Add:* Col Commun & Fine Arts Bradley Univ Peoria IL 61625

WEINBERG, ROBERT A, b Pittsburgh, Pa, Nov 11, 42; m 76; c 2. MOLECULAR BIOLOGY. *Educ:* Mass Inst Technol, BS, 64, PhD(biol), 69. *Prof Exp:* Fel, Weizmann Inst, 69-70 & Salk Inst, 70-72; res assoc, 72-73, asst prof, 73-76, ASSOC PROF BIOL, MASS INST TECHNOL, 76- *Concurrent Pos:* Fel, Helen Hay Whitney Found, 70; res scholar award, Am Cancer Soc, 74; scholar, Rita Allen Found, 76. *Res:* Gene transfer, allowing the detection and isolation of a series of genes from human tumor cells, each of which is capable of inducing the normal cell to undergo conversion to a tumor cell. *Mailing Add:* Mass Inst Technol Ctr Cancer Res E17-517 77 Mass Ave Cambridge MA 02139

WEINBERG, ROGER, b New York, NY, Jan 1, 31. BIOSTATISTICS. *Educ:* Univ Tex, PhD(genetics), 54; Univ Mich, Ann Arbor, PhD(comput sci), 70. *Prof Exp:* USPHS fel microbiol, Calif Inst Technol, 57-58; from instr to asst prof bact, Univ Pittsburgh, 58-65; USPHS spec fel biostatist, Univ Mich, Ann Arbor, 65-68, res assoc logic of comput, 68-70; assoc prof comput sci, Kans State Univ, 70-72; ASSOC PROF BIOMET, MED CTR, LA STATE UNIV, NEW ORLEANS, 72- *Mem:* Biometric Soc; Asn Comput Mach. *Res:* Computer applications to medicine. *Mailing Add:* Dept of Biomet Med Ctr La State Univ New Orleans LA 70112

WEINBERG, SIDNEY B, b Philadelphia, Pa, Sept 13, 23; m 51; c 3. PATHOLOGY. *Educ:* Univ Buffalo, MD, 50; Am Bd Path, dipl, 59. *Prof Exp:* Asst med examr forensic path, New York, 54-59; CHIEF MED EXAMR, SUFFOLK COUNTY, 60-; PROF FORENSIC PATH, STATE UNIV NY STONY BROOK, 70- *Concurrent Pos:* Attend pathologist, Vet Admin Hosp, Brooklyn, 54-55; instr, Col Med & Post-Grad Med Sch, NY Univ, 55-57, asst prof, 57-70; lectr, Columbia Univ, 57-73; res assoc, Med Sch, Cornell Univ, 58-59; consult, Brookhaven Mem & Huntington Hosps, 61-, Southside & Good Samaritan Hosps, 65- & Cent Suffolk Hosp, 66-; dir labs, Brunswick Hosp. *Mem:* AAAS; fel Am Soc Clin Path; AMA; Col Am Path; fel Am Acad Forensic Sci. *Res:* Forensic pathology, especially sudden death and coronary artery disease; automotive trauma; narcotic addiction and industrial poisoning. *Mailing Add:* 34 Winoka Dr Huntington Station NY 11746

WEINBERG, SIDNEY R, b New York, NY, Sept 2, 12; m 38; c 3. UROLOGY. *Educ:* NY Univ, BS, 33, MD, 37. *Hon Degrees:* MD, Univ Madrid, 62. *Prof Exp:* Clin instr urol, Post-Grad Sch, NY Univ, 49-52; from instr to assoc prof, Col Med, State Univ NY Downstate Med Ctr, 54-63, clin prof, 63-74; chief urol serv, Jewish Hosp Brooklyn, 63-74. *Concurrent Pos:* Asst attend urologist, Gouverneur Hosp, 41-50 & Maimonides Hosp, 45-63; attend, Kings County Hosp, 53-74; asst attend, Long Island Col Hosp, 53-60, attend, 60-74; consult, Vet Admin Hosp, 59 & Samaritan & Peninsula Gen Hosps, 62-74. *Mem:* Am Urol Asn; AMA; Am Col Surgeons; fel NY Acad Med; Int Soc Urol. *Res:* Physiology of the ureter; use of the bowel in bladder surgery. *Mailing Add:* Box 6H Sunny Isle Christiansted St Croix VI 00820

WEINBERG, STEVEN, b New York, NY, May 3, 33; m 54; c 1. THEORETICAL PHYSICS. *Educ:* Cornell Univ, AB, 54; Princeton Univ, PhD(physics), 57. *Hon Degrees:* DSc, Knox Col & Univ Chicago, 78, Univ Rochester & Yale Univ, 79, City Univ New York, 80, Clark Univ, 82. *Prof Exp:* Instr physics, Columbia Univ, 57-59; res assoc, Lawrence Radiation Lab, Univ Calif, Berkeley, 59-60, from asst prof to prof physics, 60-69; prof, Mass Inst Technol, 69-73; HIGGINS PROF PHYSICS, HARVARD UNIV, 73-; JOSEY PROF SCI, UNIV TEX, AUSTIN, 82- *Concurrent Pos:* Consult, Inst Defense Anal, 60-73; Sloan Found fel, 61-65; Morris Loeb lectr, Harvard Univ, 66-67; vis prof, Mass Inst Technol, 67-68; consult, US Arms Control & Disarmament Agency, 71-73; counr, Am Phys Soc, 72-75; consult, Stanford Res Inst, 73-; sr scientist, Smithsonian Astrophys Observ, 73-; Richtmeyer lectr, Am Asn Physics Teachers, 74; Scott lectr, Cavendish Lab, Cambridge Univ, 75; Silliman lectr, Yale Univ, 77; Lauritsen lectr, Calif Inst Technol, 79; Shalit lectr, Weizmann Inst, 79; Henry lectr, Princeton Univ, 79; Schild lectr, Univ Tex, 79. *Honors & Awards:* J R Oppenheimer Prize, Univ Miami, 73; Dannie Heineman Prize, 77; Am Inst Physics-US Steel Found Sci Writing Award, 77. 73; Nobel Prize, Physics, 79; Elliot Cresson Medal, Franklin Inst, 79. *Mem:* Nat Acad Sci; Am Acad Arts & Sci; Am Phys Soc; Am Astron Soc; Royal Soc London. *Res:* Elementary particles; field theory; cosmology. *Mailing Add:* Dept of Physics Harvard Univ Cambridge MA 02138

WEINBERG, WILLIAM HENRY, b Columbia, SC, Dec 5, 44. CHEMICAL ENGINEERING, CHEMICAL PHYSICS. *Educ:* Univ SC, BS, 66; Univ Calif, Berkeley, PhD(chem eng), 71. *Prof Exp:* NATO fel phys chem, Cambridge Univ, 71-72; from asst prof to assoc prof chem eng, 72-77, PROF CHEM ENG & CHEM PHYSICS, CALIF INST TECHNOL, 77-; CHEVRON DISTINGUISHED PROF CHEM ENG & CHEM PHYSICS, CALIF INST TECH, 81- *Concurrent Pos:* Prin investr, US-USSR Exchange Prog Chem Catalysis, 74-; vis prof chem, Harvard Univ, 80. *Honors & Awards:* Wayne B Nottingham Prize, Phys Electronics Conf, Am Phys Soc, 72; Alfred P Sloan Found Fel, 76; Camille & Henry Dreyfus Found Teacher-Scholar, 76; A P Colburn Award, Am Inst Chem Engrs, 81. *Mem:* AAAS; Am Chem Soc; Am Inst Chem Engrs; Am Vacuum Soc; Am Phys Soc. *Res:* Physics and chemistry of solids and solid surfaces; gas-surface interactions; chemical adsorption and heterogeneously catalyzed surface reactions. *Mailing Add:* Div Chem & Chem Eng Calif Inst of Technol Pasadena CA 91125

WEINBERGER, CHARLES BRIAN, b Macon, Ga, Jan 31, 41; m 76; c 2. CHEMICAL ENGINEERING. *Educ:* Univ Calif, Berkeley, BS, 63; Univ Mich, Ann Arbor, MSE, 64, PhD(chem eng), 70. *Prof Exp:* Engr, Shell Develop Co, 64-66; res engr, Eng Tech Lab, E I du Pont de Nemours & Co, Inc, 70-72; asst prof, 72-78, actg dept head, 81-82, ASSOC PROF CHEM ENG, DREXEL UNIV, 78- *Mem:* Am Inst Chem Engrs; Soc Rheol; Sigma Xi. *Res:* Extension flow of non-Newtonian fluids; polymer processing; fluid mechanics. *Mailing Add:* Dept of Chem Eng Drexel Univ Philadelphia PA 19104

WEINBERGER, EDWARD BERTRAM, b Pittsburgh, Pa, Mar 21, 21; m 44; c 3. COMPUTER SCIENCE. *Educ:* Mass Inst Technol, BS, 41; Univ Pittsburgh, MS, 47, PhD(math), 50. *Prof Exp:* Phys chemist, Gulf Res & Develop Co, 43-51, mathematician, 51-52, head comput anal sect, 53-62, res assoc, 62-66, sr scientist, 66-71; systs analyst comput ctr, 72-73, SR SYSTS ANALYST, ADMIN SYSTS DEPT, CARNEGIE-MELLON UNIV, 73- *Concurrent Pos:* Lectr, Univ Pittsburgh, 47-73. *Mem:* AAAS; Asn Comput Mach. *Res:* Digital computers; programming languages; numerical analysis; data processing. *Mailing Add:* 6380 Caton St Pittsburgh PA 15217

WEINBERGER, HANS FELIX, b Vienna, Austria, Sept 27, 28; nat US; m 57; c 3. APPLIED MATHEMATICS. *Educ:* Carnegie Inst Technol, BS & MS, 48, ScD, 50. *Prof Exp:* Fel, Inst Fluid Dynamics & Applied Math, Univ Md, 50-51, res assoc, 51-53, from asst res prof to assoc res prof, 53-60; assoc prof, 60-61, head, Sch Math, 67-69, PROF MATH, UNIV MINN, MINNEAPOLIS, 61-, DIR, INST MATH & APPLICATIONS, 81- *Concurrent Pos:* Vis mem, Courant Inst Math Sci, NY Univ, 66-67; vis prof, Univ Ariz, 70-71 & Stanford Univ, 72-73. *Mem:* Am Math Soc; Soc Natural Philos; Soc Indust & Appl Math. *Res:* Approximation of eigenvalues, quadratic functionals and solutions of partial differential equations. *Mailing Add:* Dept of Math Vincent Hall 206 Church St SE Minneapolis MN 55455

WEINBERGER, HAROLD, b New York, NY, Mar 24, 10; m 37; c 4. ORGANIC CHEMISTRY. *Educ:* Polytech Inst Brooklyn, BSc, 31, MS, 33, PhD(org chem), 36. *Prof Exp:* Asst chem, Polytech Inst Brooklyn, 31-35; instr, Long Island Univ, 36-42 & City Col New York, 42-44; proj leader, Gen Chem Co, NY, 44-46; chief chemist, Glyco Prods Inc, 46-48 & Heyden Chem Corp, 48-52; dir res, Fine Organics, Inc, 52-59; assoc prof, 59-62, chmn dept, 60-69, dir career ctr, Col Sci & Eng, 71-73, prof, 62-76, fac leader, Teaneck-Hackensack Campus, 75-76, EMER PROF CHEM, FAIRLEIGH DICKINSON UNIV, 76- *Concurrent Pos:* Asst, Long Island Univ, 31-33; instr, Brooklyn Col, 41-42; consult, 76- *Mem:* Fel AAAS; Am Chem Soc; fel Am Inst Chem; NY Acad Sci. *Res:* Resin chemistry; germicides; fatty acid derivatives. *Mailing Add:* 309 Johnson Ave Teaneck NJ 07660

WEINBERGER, LEON WALTER, b New York, NY, Aug 28, 23; m 50; c 3. SANITARY ENGINEERING. *Educ:* Cooper Union, BCE, 43; Mass Inst Technol, MS, 47, ScD(sanit eng), 49. *Prof Exp:* Eng draftsman, N Am Aviation, Inc, 43; asst, Mass Inst Technol, 47-48, res assoc, 48-49; from asst prof to assoc prof civil & sanit eng, Case Inst Technol, 49-62; chief basic & appl sci br, Div Water Supply & Pollution Control, USPHS, 63-66; asst comnr res & develop, Fed Water Pollution Control Admin, 66-68; vpres environ control mgt, Zurn Industs Inc, 68-70; PRES, LEON W WEINBERGER & ASSOC, LTD & PRES, ENVIRON QUAL SYSTS INC, 71- *Concurrent Pos:* Nat Found Fels Consult engr, 49-62; chmn, Am Sci Team, Am-Ger Coop Exchange Water Pollution; mem exec comt, Package Sewage Treatment Plant Proj, Nat Sanit Found; US rep, Comt Water Pollution, Orgn Econ Coop & Develop; mem expert adv panel environ health; WHO; mem comts water & pollution, Nat Acad Sci; US rep, Int Oceanog comt; mem, Comt Water Resources Res; prof, Nat Grad Univ & univ seminar assoc, Columbia Univ, 68-; mem adv bd, State of Md Dept Natural Resources, 74-77. *Honors & Awards:* Meritorious Serv Award, US Dept Interior, 68. *Mem:* Fel Am Soc Civil Engrs; Water Pollution Control Fedn; Am Water Works Asn; Am Asn Environ Engrs. *Res:* Water supply and treatment; waste water treatment; water pollution control. *Mailing Add:* 1160 Rockville Pike Rockville MD 20852

WEINBERGER, LESTER, organic chemistry, electrophotography, see previous edition

WEINBERGER, MILES, b McKeesport, Pa, June 23, 38; m 64; c 3. MEDICINE, PULMONARY DISEASE. *Educ:* Univ Pittsburgh, MD, 65. *Prof Exp:* assoc prof pediat & pharmacol, 75-80, PROF PEDIAT, UNIV IOWA, 80-, CHMN PEDIAT ALLERGY & PULMONARY DIV & DIR, CYSTIC FIBROSIS CTR, 75- *Mem:* Fel Am Acad Allergy; fel Am Acad Pediat; fel Soc Pediat Res; Am Thoracic Soc. *Res:* Pharmacotherapy of asthma; clinical pharmacology of antiasthmatic drugs; pediatric allergy. *Mailing Add:* Dept of Pediat Univ of Iowa Hosp Iowa City IA 52242

WEINBERGER, MYRON HILMAR, b Cincinnati, Ohio, Sept 21, 37; m 60; c 3. INTERNAL MEDICINE, HYPERTENSION. *Educ:* Ind Univ, AB, 59, MD, 63. *Prof Exp:* Intern internal med, Sch Med, Ind Univ, 63-64, resident, 64-66; res fel endocrinol, Sch Med, Stanford Univ, 66-69; from asst prof to assoc prof, 69-76, PROF MED, SCH MED, IND UNIV, 76- *Concurrent Pos:* Investr, Specialized Ctr Res Hypertension, Ind Univ, 70-75, prin investr-dir, 75-; mem prog comt, Coun High Blood Pressure Res, 78. *Mem:* Am Heart Asn; Am Fedn Clin Res; Endocrine Soc. *Res:* Blood pressure control; salt and water metabolism, hormones; circulation; kidney; adrenal; high blood pressure. *Mailing Add:* Ind Univ Sch of Med 1100 W Michigan St Indianapolis IN 46223

WEINBERGER, NORMAN MALCOLM, b Cleveland, Ohio, Aug 10, 35; m 54; c 7. PSYCHOBIOLOGY, NEUROPHYSIOLOGY. *Educ:* Western Reserve Univ, AB, 57, MS, 59, PhD(psychol), 61. *Prof Exp:* Corresp instr psychol, Univ Calif, Berkeley, 62-64; res physiologist, Univ Calif, Los Angeles, 64; from asst prof to assoc prof, 65-74, chmn, 75-78, PROF PSYCHOBIOL, UNIV CALIF, IRVINE, 74- *Concurrent Pos:* Consult ed, Physiol Psychol; assoc ed, Exp Neurol. *Mem:* AAAS; Soc Neurosci; Int Brain Res Orgn. *Res:* Neurobiological bases of learning and attention; neurobiology of alcoholism. *Mailing Add:* Dept of Psychobiol Univ of Calif Irvine CA 92717

WEINBERGER, PEARL, b Derby, Eng, Apr 20, 26; Can citizen; m 48; c 2. PLANT PHYSIOLOGY, ENVIRONMENTAL BIOLOGY. *Educ:* Univ Manchester, BSc, 48, MSc, 51; Univ Ottawa, PhD(biol), 62. *Prof Exp:* Demonstr bot, Leeds Univ, 48-49; ed asst, Can J Res, 49-50; res officer, Nat Res Coun, Ottawa, 50-52; from lectr to asst prof, 52-67, assoc prof, 67-79, PROF BOT, UNIV OTTAWA, 79- *Mem:* Can Soc Plant Physiol; Can Soc Cell Biol; Can Bot Asn; Am Soc Plant Physiol; Fr-Can Asn Advan Sci. *Res:* Environmental stress physiology (plants), with special reference to xenobiotics and ultrasound. *Mailing Add:* Dept Biol Univ Ottawa Ottawa ON K1N 6N5 Can

WEINBERGER, PETER JAY, b New York, NY, Aug 6, 42. MATHEMATICS, COMPUTER SCIENCE. *Educ:* Swarthmore Col, BA, 64; Univ Calif, Berkeley, PhD(math), 69. *Prof Exp:* Mem tech staff, Bellcomm Inc, 69-70; asst prof math, Univ Mich, Ann Arbor, 70-76; MEM STAFF COMP SCI RES, BELL LABS, 76- *Mem:* Am Math Soc; Asn Comput Mach; Math Asn Am. *Res:* Number theory; computer-assisted typesetting, especially of mathematics; data bases and distributed computing. *Mailing Add:* Bell Labs Murray Hill NJ 07974

WEINBRANDT, RICHARD M, b Lexington, Nebr, July 20, 44; m 67. PETROLEUM ENGINEERING. *Educ:* Univ Calif, Berkeley, BS, 67, MS, 68; Stanford Univ, PhD(petrol eng), 72. *Prof Exp:* Res engr, Chevron Oil Field Res, 68-69 & Union Oil Co, 71-76; mgr eng, Aminoil, 76-81; CONSULT, ENHANCED OIL RECOVERY, 81- *Concurrent Pos:* Teaching asst, Univ Calif, Berkeley, 68 & Stanford Univ, 71; consult, Alcoa, Aminoil, Dow Chem, Gary Energy, PQ Energy Serv Sci Software & Westinghouse. *Mem:* Am Inst Mining, Metall & Petrol Engrs; Soc Petrol Engrs. *Res:* Improved oil recovery methods; reservoir simulation; fluid flow in porous media. *Mailing Add:* Enhanced Oil Recovery 909 Canyon View Dr Laguna Beach CA 92651

WEINDLING, JOACHIM I(GNACE), b Antwerp, Belg, Feb 18, 27; US citizen; m 54; c 3. OPTIMIZATION, ENGINEERING ECONOMY. *Educ:* City Col New York, BME, 48; Columbia Univ, MS, 49, PhD(opers res), 67. *Prof Exp:* Lectr mech eng, City Col New York, 48-51; chief engr, Korfund Dynamics, Inc, 51-59; vpres eng, Vibration Mountings & Controls, Inc, 59-61; assoc prof mech eng, Drexel Inst, 61-67; prof eng, PMC Cols, 67-69; chmn, Dept Opers Res & Syst Anal, 73-74, PROF SYSTS ENG, POLYTECH INST NEW YORK, 69-, DIR OPERS RES PROG, 70- *Concurrent Pos:* Lectr, City Col New York, 51-61; adj assoc prof, NY Univ, 58-61; indust consult, 61- *Mem:* Am Soc Mech Engrs; Opers Res Soc Am; Am Soc Eng Educ; Am Inst Indust Engrs. *Res:* Markov chains; reliability; computer-aided optimum designs; shock and vibration controls; mathematical programming; technology utilization and education in developing countries. *Mailing Add:* 204 Fairfield Dr Wallingford PA 19086

WEINER, CHARLES, b Brooklyn, NY, Aug 11, 31; div; c 1. HISTORY OF PHYSICS, HISTORY OF BIOLOGY. *Educ:* Case Inst Technol, BS, 60, MA, 63, PhD(hist of sci), 65. *Prof Exp:* Dir proj hist of recent physics in US, Am Inst Physics, 64-65, dir, Ctr for Hist of Physics, 65-74, PROF HIST OF SCI & TECHNOL, MASS INST TECHNOL, 74-, DIR, ORAL HIST PROG, 75- *Concurrent Pos:* NSF grants, 65-79 & 81; mem adv comt, Nat Union Catalog of Manuscript Collections, Libr of Cong, 65-71; vis lectr, Polytech Inst Brooklyn, 66; proj dir comt hist of contemp physics, Joint Am Inst Physics-Am Acad Arts & Sci, 66-74; Guggenheim fel, Niels Bohr Inst, Copenhagen, Denmark, 70-71. *Honors & Awards:* Distinguished Serv Citation, Am Asn Physics Teachers, 74. *Mem:* Fel AAAS; Hist Sci Soc; Soc Hist Technol; Am Hist Asn; Orgn Am Historians. *Res:* History of twentieth century science; social impact of science and technology; development of the physical sciences in the United States; history of genetic engineering and of university-industry relations; ethical issues in science and engineering. *Mailing Add:* Prog Sci Technol & Soc Mass Inst Technol E51-206 Cambridge MA 02139

WEINER, DANIEL LEE, b Dayton, Ky, April 13, 50; m 74; c 1. PHARMACOKINETICS, BIOASSAY. *Educ:* Univ Ky, BS, 72, MS, 73, PhD(statist), 76. *Prof Exp:* Biostatistician, Merrell Nat Labs, 76-78, sr biostatistician, 78-82; MGR, BIOSTATIST, MERRELL DOW PHARMACEUT, DIV DOW CHEM CO, 82- *Concurrent Pos:* Adj asst prof, Dept Environ Health, Div Epidemiol & Biostat, Col Med, Univ Cincinnati, 79-81, adj assoc prof, 82- *Mem:* Am Statist Asn; Biomet Soc. *Res:* Bioavailability and pharmacokinetics in relation to biological response; application of statistics to the preclinical evaluation of drugs. *Mailing Add:* Merrell Dow Pharmaceut 2110 E Galbraith Rd Cincinnati OH 45215

WEINER, EUGENE ROBERT, b Pittsburgh, Pa, Sept 16, 28; m 52, 81; c 4. PHYSICAL CHEMISTRY. *Educ:* Ohio Univ, BS, 50; Univ Ill, MS, 57; Johns Hopkins Univ, PhD(chem), 63. *Prof Exp:* Sect chief appl physics sect, Interior Ballistics Lab, Aberdeen Proving Grounds, Md, 50-55; instr, McCoy Col, 62-63; sr scientist, Johnston Labs, Inc, 63-65; asst prof, 65-67, ASSOC PROF CHEM, UNIV DENVER, 67- *Concurrent Pos:* Consult, US Geol Surv, 70- *Mem:* Am Chem Soc; Am Phys Soc. *Res:* Atomic and molecular collisions; radiation chemistry; gas phase ion-molecule reactions, free radical reactions, gas kinetics and energetics; laser Raman spectroscopy; remote sensing of pollutants; solid surface catalysis. *Mailing Add:* Dept Chem Univ Denver Denver CO 80210

WEINER, HENRY, b Cleveland, Ohio, May 18, 37; m 60; c 2. ORGANIC CHEMISTRY, BIOCHEMISTRY. *Educ:* Case Inst Technol, BS, 59; Purdue Univ, PhD(org chem), 63. *Prof Exp:* Res assoc biol, Brookhaven Nat Lab, 63-65; NIH res fel biochem, Karolinska Inst, Sweden, 65-66; from asst prof to assoc prof, 66-76, PROF BIOCHEM & MED CHEM, PURDUE UNIV, LAFAYETTE, 76- *Mem:* Res Soc Alcoholism; Am Soc Biol Chem; Am Chem Soc; Am Asn Univ Prof. *Res:* Enzymology; protein chemistry; neurotransmitter metabolism; effects of ethanol on metabolism; acetaldehyde metabolism. *Mailing Add:* Dept Biochem Purdue Univ West Lafayette IN 47907

WEINER, HERBERT, b Vienna, Austria, Feb 6, 21; nat US; m 53; c 3. PSYCHIATRY, NEUROLOGY. *Educ:* Harvard Univ, AB, 43; Columbia Univ, MD, 46. *Prof Exp:* Exchange fel neurol, 50; USPHS fel psychiat, 52-53; instr psychiat, Sch Med & Dent, Univ Rochester, 53-54; guest lectr, Wash Sch Psychiat, 54-55; from instr to assoc prof, 55-66, PROF PSYCHIAT, ALBERT EINSTEIN COL MED, 66-, PROF NEUROSCI, 74- *Concurrent Pos:* Asst vis psychiatrist & chief adult psychiat in-patient serv, Bronx Munic Hosp Ctr, 55-56, asst vis physician, 56-61, assoc vis psychiatrist, 56-; consult, Home Care Dept, Montefiore Hosp, 55-59; USPHS fel ment health, 56-58 & res career develop award, 62-65; Stern fel, 59-62; mem bd trustees, Scarborough Country Day Sch, 62-; mem ment health study sect, Div Res Grants, NIH, 62-, chmn, 66-67; attend psychiatrist & dir educ prog, Div Psychiat, Montefiore Hosp & Med Ctr, New York, 65-69, chmn dept psychiat, 69-; fel, Ctr Advan Study Behav Sci, Stanford Univ, Guggenheim Mem Found fel & Commonwealth Fund grant-in-aid, 72-73; ed-in-chief, Psychosom Med, 72- *Mem:* AAAS; Am Acad Neurol; Am Psychosom Soc (pres, 71-72); Asn Res Nerv & Dis (pres, 79-80); Psychiat Res Soc; Am Col Psychiat. *Res:* Neurophysiology; psychophysiology. *Mailing Add:* Dept of Psychiat Montefiore Hosp & Med Ctr New York NY 10467

WEINER, HOWARD JACOB, b Chicago, Ill, Aug 26, 37; m 71. PROBABILITY. *Educ:* Ill Inst Technol, BSEE, 58; Univ Chicago, MS, 60; Stanford Univ, PhD(statist), 64. *Prof Exp:* Actg asst prof statist, Univ Calif, Berkeley, 64; asst prof, Stanford Univ, 64-65; from asst prof to assoc prof, 65-72, PROF MATH, UNIV CALIF, DAVIS, 72-, VCHMN DEPT, 77- *Concurrent Pos:* Vis assoc prof statist, Stanford Univ, 76, vis res assoc, 77 & 78. *Mem:* Math Asn Am. *Res:* Age dependent branching processes; sequential random packing. *Mailing Add:* Dept Math Univ Calif Davis CA 95616

WEINER, IRWIN M, b New York, NY, Nov 5, 30; m 61; c 2. PHARMACOLOGY. *Educ:* Syracuse Univ, AB, 52; State Univ NY, MD, 56. *Prof Exp:* Fel pharmacol, Sch Med, Johns Hopkins Univ, 56-58, from instr to asst prof pharmacol & exp therapeut, 58-66; assoc prof, 66-68, PROF PHARMACOL & CHMN DEPT, STATE UNIV NY UPSTATE MED CTR, 68- *Concurrent Pos:* Fel pharmacol & exp therapeut, Sch Med, Johns Hopkins Univ, 58-60; vis prof molecular biol, Albert Einstein Col Med, 64-65; USPHS res career develop award, 64-66; mem study sect pharmacol & exp therapeut, NIH, 65-69; ed, J Pharmacol & Exp Therapeut, 65-72; consult, Sterling Winthrop Res Inst. *Mem:* AAAS; Am Soc Pharmacol & Exp Therapeut; NY Acad Sci. *Res:* Pharmacology of diuretics and uricosuric agents; renal excretion of drugs; intestinal absorption of bile salts; bacterial cell wall biosynthesis. *Mailing Add:* Dept of Pharmacol State Univ of NY Upstate Med Ctr Syracuse NY 13210

WEINER, JACOB, b Brooklyn, NY, Dec 24, 47. PLANT ECOLOGY, BOTANY. *Educ:* Antioch Col, BA, 70; Univ Mich, MS, 74; Univ Ore, PhD(biol), 78. *Prof Exp:* Instr ecol, Eastern Oregon State Col, 77; ASST PROF BIOL, SWARTHMORE COL, 78- *Concurrent Pos:* Trainee syst biol, NIH, 77-78; vis scholar, Harvard Univ, 81; vis scientist, Univ Col North Wales, 81-82. *Mem:* AAAS; Ecol Soc Am; Botanical Soc Am; Sigma Xi. *Res:* Plant population biology. *Mailing Add:* Dept of Biol Swarthmore Col Swarthmore PA 19081

WEINER, JEROME HARRIS, b New York, NY, Apr 5, 23; m 50; c 2. APPLIED MATHEMATICS. *Educ:* Cooper Union, BME, 43; Columbia Univ, AM, 47, PhD(math), 52. *Prof Exp:* Asst tech dir heat & mass flow analyzer lab, Columbia Univ, 51-57, asst prof civil eng & eng mech, 52-56, prof mech eng, 56-68; L HERBERT BALLOU UNIV PROF ENG & PHYSICS, BROWN UNIV, 68- *Mem:* Am Math Soc; Am Phys Soc. *Res:* Thermal stresses; crystal defects. *Mailing Add:* Div of Eng Brown Univ Providence RI 02912

WEINER, JOHN, b Malvern, NY, Apr 14, 43. CHEMICAL PHYSICS. *Educ:* Pa State Univ, BS, 64; Univ Chicago, PhD(chem), 70. *Prof Exp:* Fel & lectr chem, Yale Univ, 70-73; asst prof chem, Dartmouth Col, 73-78; ASSOC PROF CHEM, UNIV MD, 78- *Concurrent Pos:* Vis fel, Univ Paris, 77-78. *Mem:* Am Chem Soc; Am Phys Soc; AAAS. *Res:* Reactive and inelastic collision processes in ion-molecule systems; internal state excitation leading to chemiluminescence phenomena; laser-induced excitation; ionization and reactive collisions in crossed-beam studies. *Mailing Add:* Dept of Chem Univ of Md College Park MD 20742

WEINER, JOSEPH GEORGE, b Los Angeles, Calif, Sept 24, 15; m 38; c 2. CHEMICAL ENGINEERING. *Educ:* Univ Calif, Los Angeles, BA, 36. *Prof Exp:* Chemist, Univ Calif, Los Angeles, 36, Richfield Oil Corp, 37 & US Gypsum Co, 41-43; develop supvr & asst mgr plant tech serv, Filtrol Corp, 43-55; group leader, Aerojet-Gen Corp, 55-56; sr chem engr, Ralph M Parsons Co, 56-62; chem eng specialist & mgr chem processes sect, McDonnell-Douglas Corp, 62-70; SR PROJ MGT, RALPH M PARSONS CO, 70- *Mem:* Am Inst Chem Engrs. *Res:* Design and detailed engineering of petro chemical processing facilities; development of processes and special equipment requirements. *Mailing Add:* 1511 Malcolm Ave Los Angeles CA 90024

WEINER, LAWRENCE MYRON, b Milwaukee, Wis, May 21, 23; m 44; c 2. MICROBIOLOGY, IMMUNOLOGY. *Educ:* Univ Wis, BA, 47, MS, 48, PhD(med microbiol), 51. *Prof Exp:* From instr to assoc prof, 51-65, chmn dept & assoc dean, 70-72, dep dean, 72-79, dean, 79-81, PROF MICROBIOL, SCH MED, WAYNE STATE UNIV, 65- *Concurrent Pos:* Pres, Mich State Bd Examr in Basic Sci, 62-68. *Mem:* Am Soc Microbiol; Soc Exp Biol & Med. *Res:* Immunology of infectious diseases; hypersensitivity to chemical agents; tumor immunology. *Mailing Add:* Off of Dep Dean Wayne State Univ Sch of Med Detroit MI 48201

WEINER, LOUIS I, b Philadelphia, Pa, May 3, 13; m 36; c 1. TEXTILE ENGINEERING. *Educ:* Temple Univ, BS, 36; Lowell Tech Inst, MS, 65. *Prof Exp:* Technologist, Res & Develop Lab, Philadelphia Qm Depot, 43-50, chief, Textile Eng Lab, 50-58; asst chief res, Textile Clothing & Footwear Div, Res & Eng Command, US Dept Army, 58-63, gen phys scientist, 63-67, head fibrous mat res group, Clothing & Org Mat Div, Natick Labs, 67-69, res phys scientist, Clothing & Personal Life Support Equip Lab, 69-72; RETIRED. *Concurrent Pos:* Vis prof, Lowell Technol Inst, 65-72; expert, UN Indust Develop Orgn, 68. *Mem:* Fiber Soc; Sigma Xi. *Res:* Wear resistance; heat transfer; fiber and fabric structure and performance. *Mailing Add:* 36 Morrill St West Newton MA 02165

WEINER, LOUIS MAX, b Chicago, Ill, Nov 11, 26; m 57; c 3. ALGEBRA. *Educ:* Univ Chicago, SB, 47, SM, 48, PhD(math), 51. *Prof Exp:* Asst, Univ Chicago, 48; personnel examr, Chicago Civil Serv Comn, 51-52; asst prof math, DePaul Univ, 52-58; res engr, Mech Res Div, Am Mach & Foundry Co, 58-62, supvr, Anal Sect, Gen Am Res Div, 62-64; assoc prof, 64-68, chmn dept, 68-74, PROF MATH, NORTHEASTERN ILL UNIV, 68- *Concurrent Pos:* Instr, Amundsen Br, Chicago City Jr Col, instr, Oakton Community Col, 77- *Mem:* Am Math Soc; Math Asn Am. *Res:* Algebra; linear algebras; operations research; slide rule type computers. *Mailing Add:* 3144 Greenleaf Wilmette IL 60091

WEINER, MILTON LAWRENCE, b Detroit, Mich, Dec 3, 21; m 50; c 4. POLYMER CHEMISTRY, PLASTICS CHEMISTRY. *Educ:* Wayne State Univ, BS, 47, PhD, 52. *Prof Exp:* Res chemist, Ethyl Corp, 52-56 & Gen Elec Co, 56-59; res chemist, 59-69, RES ASSOC, PLASTICS DIV, TECH CTR, MOBIL CHEM CO, 69- *Res:* Polymers; morphology; rheology. *Mailing Add:* Plastics Div Tech Ctr Mobil Chem Co Macedon NY 14502

WEINER, MURRAY, b New York, NY, Apr 18, 19; m 51; c 1. MEDICINE. *Educ:* City Col New York, BS, 39; NY Univ, MS & MD, 43. *Prof Exp:* From instr to asst prof med, Col Med, NY Univ, 54-72; vpres & dir biol res, Geigy Res Labs, NY, 67-72; vpres res & sci affairs, Merrell-Nat Labs, 72-81; DIR CLIN PHARMACOL, UNIV CINCINNATI, 81- *Concurrent Pos:* Asst vis physician & consult, Bellevue Hosp, NY, 49-72, Univ Hosp, 53-72, Long Island Jewish Hosp, 54-57 & North Shore Hosp, NY, 55-72; assoc vis physician, Willard Parker Hosp, NY, 52-57 & Goldwater Mem Hosp, NY, 56-72; vis staff, Cincinnati Gen Hosp & Christian Holmes Hosp, Ohio, 72-; clin prof med, Univ Cincinnati, 72- *Mem:* Soc Exp Biol & Med; Am Physiol Soc; AMA; Am Heart Asn. *Res:* Clotting mechanism; anticoagulant and anti-inflammatory drugs; drug disposition. *Mailing Add:* 8915 Spooky Ridge Lane Cincinnati OH 45242

WEINER, MYRON, b Baltimore, Md, May 27, 43; m 64; c 2. PHARMACOLOGY. *Educ:* Univ Md, Baltimore City, BS, 66, PhD(pharmacol), 71. *Prof Exp:* Instr pharmacol, Sch Nursing, Univ Md, Baltimore City, 67-68; instr anat & physiol, Sch Nursing, St Agnes Hosp, 68-70; instr, Catonsville Community Col, Md, 70-71; asst prof pharmacol, Sch Pharm, Univ Southern Calif, 71-77; ASSOC PROF PHARMACOL, SCH PHARM, UNIV MD, 77- *Concurrent Pos:* Gen res support grant, Univ Southern Calif, 71-73, Cancer Ctr grant, 74-75; Nat Cancer Inst grant, 73-76. *Mem:* AAAS; NY Acad Sci; Am Col Clin Pharmacol; Am Pharmaceut Asn; Am Asn Cols Pharm. *Res:* Alteration of drug biotransformation caused by cyclic nucleotides; Mechanisms of altered drug metabolism (oxidative and conjugative) caused by cancer, diabetes, and aging. *Mailing Add:* Dept Pharmacol Univ Md Sch Pharm Baltimore MD 21201

WEINER, NORMAN, b Rochester, NY, July 13, 28; m 55; c 5. PHARMACOLOGY. *Educ:* Univ Mich, BS, 49; Harvard Med Sch, MD, 53. *Prof Exp:* Intern, Harvard Med Serv, Boston City Hosp, 53-54, instr pharmacol, Harvard Med Sch, 56-58, assoc, 58-61, asst prof, 61-67; chmn dept, 67-77, PROF PHARMACOL, MED CTR, UNIV COLO, DENVER, 67- *Concurrent Pos:* Dir neuropharmacol lab, Mass Ment Health Ctr, 64-67. *Mem:* AAAS; Am Soc Pharmacol & Exp Therapeut; Am Soc Neurochem; Am Col Neuropsychopharmacol; Asn Med Sch Pharmacologists. *Res:* Metabolism of biologically active amines; regulation of synthesis of neurotransmitters; synthesis, storage and release of tissue amines; effect of drugs on energy metabolism of brain; ionization of drugs, drug distribution and relation to biological activity. *Mailing Add:* Sch Med Univ Colo 4200 E Ninth Ave Denver CO 80262

WEINER, PETER DOUGLAS, b Whitinsville, Mass, Mar 21, 29; m 50; c 4. MECHANICAL ENGINEERING. *Educ:* Tex A&M Univ, BSME, 54, MSME, 61, PhD(eng), 68. *Prof Exp:* Maintenance engr, Magnolia Petrol Co, 54-55; utilization engr, Lone Star Gas Co, 55-56; from instr to prof mech eng, Tex A&M Univ, 56-76; vpres eng res & tech develop, Weatherford-Lamb Inc, 76-78; PROF MECH ENG, TEX A&M UNIV, 78- *Concurrent Pos:* Consult, Rockwell Valves, 56, Humble Oil & Refinery Co, 57-, Gray Tool Co, 66-68, Gen Dynamics Corp, 67-68, Esso Prod Res, 68- & Trans Alaska Pipeline Syst, 69-; mem bd dirs, Global Eng Inc, Petrol Instrumentation Inc & Tubular Make-up Specialist Inc. *Mem:* Am Soc Mech Engrs; Am Soc Eng Educ; Soc Exp Stress Anal; Am Soc Mining, Metall & Petrol Engrs; Nat Soc Prof Engrs. *Res:* Prevention of leakage in tubular connections and other problems related to thick shelled connections, including theoretical and experimental analysis. *Mailing Add:* Drawer GA College Station TX 77841

WEINER, RICHARD, b Brooklyn, NY, Aug 21, 36; m 60; c 2. PHYSIOLOGY. *Educ:* Long Island Univ, BS, 58; NY Univ, PhD(physiol), 65. *Prof Exp:* USPHS fel microcirc, NY Univ Med Ctr, 65, asst res scientist, 66; from instr to asst prof, 66-72, ASSOC PROF PHYSIOL, NEW YORK MED COL, 73- *Mem:* AAAS; Am Physiol Soc; Microcirc Soc. *Res:* Regulation of vascular smooth muscle. *Mailing Add:* Dept of Physiol NY Med Col Basic Sci Bldg Valhalla NY 10595

WEINER, RICHARD IRA, b New York, NY, Nov 6, 40. NEUROENDOCRINOLOGY. *Educ:* Pa State Univ, BS, 63, MS, 65; Univ Calif, San Francisco, PhD(endocrinol), 69. *Prof Exp:* Fel, Brain Res Inst, Univ Calif, Los Angeles, 69-71; asst prof physiol, Univ Tenn Med Units, 71-72; asst prof anat, Sch Med, Univ Southern Calif, 72-74; assoc prof, 74-80, PROF OBSTET & GYNEC & PHYSIOL, SCH MED, UNIV CALIF, SAN FRANCISC0, 80- *Concurrent Pos:* Mem biochem endocrinol study sect, NIH; adv, grad prog endocrinol, Univ Calif, San Francisco. *Mem:* Endocrine Soc; Int Neuroendocrine Soc; Soc Neurosci; Am Physiol Soc. *Res:* Role of brain catecholamines in the neuroendocrine regulation of the secretion of luteinizing hormone and prolactin. *Mailing Add:* Dept of Obstet & Gynec Univ of Calif Sch of Med San Francisco CA 94143

WEINER, ROBERT ALLEN, b New York, NY, Apr 3, 40; m 61; c 2. REACTOR MATERIALS, FUEL PIN MODELLING. *Educ:* Columbia Univ, AB, 61; Harvard Univ, AM, 62, PhD(physics), 67. *Prof Exp:* Asst res physicist, Univ Calif, San Diego, 67-69; asst prof physics, Carnegie-Mellon Univ, 69-75; SR SCIENTIST, ADVAN REACTORS DIV, WESTINGHOUSE ELEC CO, 75- *Mem:* Am Nuclear Soc; AAAS; Am Phys Soc. *Res:* Irradiation damage mechanisms in metals and alloys; fast breeder reactor fuel; cladding model development. *Mailing Add:* Advan Reactors Div Westinghouse Elec Co Madison PA 15663

WEINER, ROBERT SAMUEL, physical chemistry, see previous edition

WEINER, RONALD MARTIN, b Brooklyn, NY, May 7, 42; m 64; c 3. MICROBIOLOGY. *Educ:* Brooklyn Col, BS, 64; LI Univ, MS, 67; Iowa State Univ, PhD(microbiol), 70. *Prof Exp:* Bacteriologist, Greenpoint, Coney Island Hosps, NY, 64-66; teaching asst, Iowa State Univ, 67-68, instr, 69-70; asst prof, 70-75, ASSOC PROF MICROBIOL, UNIV MD, COLLEGE PARK, 76- *Mem:* AAAS; Am Soc Microbiol; Am Inst Biol Sci. *Res:* Morphogenesis of Hyphomicrobium; DNA replication and cell division; microbial ecology. *Mailing Add:* Dept of Microbiol Univ of Md College Park MD 20742

WEINER, STEPHEN DOUGLAS, b Philadelphia, Pa, Jan 1, 41; m 61; c 2. APPLIED PHYSICS. *Educ:* Mass Inst Technol, BS, 61, PhD(physics), 65. *Prof Exp:* Mem staff, 65-73, ASSOC GROUP LEADER, LINCOLN LAB, MASS INST TECHNOL, 73- *Res:* Missile defense research; reentry physics; electromagnetic scattering and propagation; operations research. *Mailing Add:* Lincoln Lab Mass Inst of Technol Lexington MA 02173

WEINER, STEVEN ALLAN, b New York, NY, June 6, 42; m 71; c 1. PHYSICAL ORGANIC CHEMISTRY. *Educ:* Columbia Univ, AB, 63; Iowa State Univ, PhD(org chem), 67. *Prof Exp:* Res assoc, Calif Inst Technol, 67-68; staff scientist, 68-74, proj mgr, Res Staff, 74-77, PRIN STAFF ENGR, FORD MOTOR CO, 77- *Concurrent Pos:* Lectr, Univ Mich-Dearborn, 70-71. *Honors & Awards:* Leibmann Mem Award, Am Chem Soc, 59. *Mem:* Opers Res Soc Am; Am Chem Soc; AAAS; Sigma Xi. *Res:* Photochemistry; free radical kinetics; combustion products and reactions; sodium-sulfur battery; energy storage and conversion; metal casting and heat treating; energy management; process modeling and control; manufacturing process development. *Mailing Add:* Research Staff 24500 Glendale Ave Detroit MI 48239

WEINFELD, HERBERT, b New York, NY, Feb 7, 21; m 46; c 1. BIOCHEMISTRY. *Educ:* City Col New York, BS, 42; Univ Mich, MS, 48, PhD(biochem), 52. *Prof Exp:* Asst biochem, Univ Mich, 47-49, asst, Sloan-Kettering Inst, 53-54; instr, Inst Indust Med, NY Univ-Bellevue Med Ctr, 54-55; assoc cancer res scientist, 55-65, PRIN CANCER RES SCIENTIST, DEPT MED, ROSWELL PARK MEM INST, 65-; res prof & chmn, Dept Biochem, 71-80, EMER PROF, ROSWELL PARK GRAD DIV, STATE UNIV NY BUFFALO, 80- *Concurrent Pos:* Res prof, State Univ NY Buffalo, 72-80, emer prof, 80- *Mem:* AAAS; Am Chem Soc; Am Soc Biol Chemists. *Res:* Metabolism of nucleosides, nucleotides and nucleic acids; cellular agents controlling mitotic events. *Mailing Add:* 51 Brookville Dr 666 Elm St Tonawanda NY 14150

WEINGARTEN, DONALD HENRY, b Boston, Mass, Feb 16, 45; m 71; c 2. THEORETICAL PHYSICS. *Educ:* Columbia Col, AB, 65; Columbia Univ, PhD(physics), 70. *Prof Exp:* Res assoc theoret particle physics, Fermi Nat Accelerator Lab, 69-71; res fel, Niels Bohr Inst, Univ Copenhagen, 71-73; res assoc, Lab Theoret Physics, Univ Paris XI, 73-74; res assoc, Univ Rochester, 74-76; asst prof, 76-80, ASSOC PROF PHYSICS, IND UNIV, BLOOMINGTON, 80- *Res:* Theoretical particle physics; mathematical physics. *Mailing Add:* Dept Physics Ind Univ Bloomington IN 47405

WEINGARTEN, VICTOR I, b New York, NY, Jan 18, 31; m 54; c 2. ENGINEERING MECHANICS, CIVIL ENGINEERING. *Educ:* City Col New York, BME, 52; NY Univ, MSME, 54; Univ Calif, Los Angeles, PhD(eng mech), 64. *Prof Exp:* Stress analyst, Northrop Corp, 56-59; mem tech staff eng mech, TRW Systs, Inc, 59-61; mem tech staff eng mech, Aerospace Corp, 61-64; assoc prof civil eng, 64-71, PROF CIVIL ENG, UNIV SOUTHERN CALIF, 71-, CHMN DEPT, 73- *Concurrent Pos:* Consult, Aerojet-Gen Corp, 64-65, Northrup Norair, 64-71 & Hughes Aircraft Co, 67- *Mem:* Am Soc Mech Engrs; Am Soc Civil Engrs. *Res:* Buckling of nuclear containment vessels; elastic stability and free vibrations of plates and shells; fluid-structure interaction problem; application of visco-elastic finite element techniques to biomechanics problems. *Mailing Add:* Dept of Civil Eng University Park Los Angeles CA 90265

WEINGARTNER, DAVID PETER, b Escanaba, Mich, Mar 13, 39; m 64; c 2. PHYTOPATHOLOGY, PLANT NEMATOLOGY. *Educ:* Univ Mich, BS, 62; Mich State Univ, PhD(plant path), 69. *Prof Exp:* Teacher high sch, Inkster, Mich, 62-64; asst prof & asst plant pathologist, 69-75, ASSOC PROF & ASSOC PLANT PATHOLOGIST, AGR RES CTR, INST FOOD & AGR, UNIV FLA, 75- *Concurrent Pos:* Res award, Fla Fruit & Vegetable Asn, 75. *Mem:* Soc Nematol; Am Phytopath Soc; Potato Asn Am. *Res:* Nematode and disease control in vegetables; nematode population dynamics; epidemiology; disease forecasting; rest management; potato corky ringspot. *Mailing Add:* Agr Res Ctr Univ of Fla Hastings FL 32045

WEINGARTNER, HERBERT, b Karlsruhe, Ger, Apr 4, 35; US citizen; m 67; c 2. PSYCHOBIOLOGY, PSYCHOPHARMACOLOGY. *Educ:* City Univ New York, BS, 56; Johns Hopkins Univ, MA, 62, PhD(exp psychol), 66. *Prof Exp:* Teacher math & sci, Bd Educ, New York City, 56-58; clin psychologist & lectr, Sheppard & Enoch Pratt Hosp, 61-63; from instr to asst prof psychol & assoc dir med psychol, Sch Med, Johns Hopkins Univ, 64-70; from assoc prof to prof psychol, Univ Md, 70-77; res psychologist, 77-78, ACTG CHIEF PSYCHOL, LAB PSYCHOL & PSYCHOTHER, NIMH, 78- *Concurrent Pos:* Vis scientist psychol, NIMH, 74-75 & 76-77; Gilman fel, Johns Hopkins Univ; NIH res fel; mem, Huntington's Comn, 77- *Mem:* Am Psychol Asn; Sigma Xi. *Res:* Biology of learning and memory; cognitive psychology; mood disturbance; state dependent learning. *Mailing Add:* Lab Psychol & Psychother 9000 Rockville Pike Bethesda MD 20014

WEINGOLD, ALLAN BYRNE, b New York, NY, Sept 2, 30; m 52; c 4. OBSTETRICS & GYNECOLOGY. *Educ:* Oberlin Col, BA, 51; New York Med Col, MD, 55; Am Bd Obstet & Gynec, dipl, 64. *Prof Exp:* From asst prof to prof obstet & gynec, New York Med Col, 70-73, asst chmn dept, 71-73; PROF OBSTET & GYNEC & CHMN DEPT, SCH MED, GEORGE WASHINGTON UNIV, 73- *Concurrent Pos:* Am Cancer Soc fel gynec malignancy, 60-61; training dir, USPHS grant, 66-68; chief obstet & gynec, Metrop Hosp, New York, 67-70; consult, NIH Cancer Ctr, Walter Reed Army Med Ctr, Columbia Hosp for Women & Fairfax Hosp; mem sub-spec bd, Maternal Fetal Med, 76- *Mem:* Fel Am Col Obstet & Gynec; Am Gynec Soc; Soc Perinatal Obstetricians; Perinatal Res Soc; fel Am Col Surgeons. *Res:* Studies on monitoring of the fetal environment by endocrine, biochemical and biophysical indices. *Mailing Add:* Dept of Obstet & Gynec George Washington Univ Sch Med Washington DC 20037

WEINHOLD, ALBERT RAYMOND, b Evans, Colo, Feb 14, 31; m 52; c 2. PLANT PATHOLOGY. *Educ:* Colo State Univ, BS, 53, MS, 55; Univ Calif, PhD(plant path), 58. *Prof Exp:* Res asst, Univ Calif, Davis, 55-57, from instr & jr plant pathologist to assoc prof & assoc plant pathologist, 59-72, PROF PLANT PATH & PLANT PATHOLOGIST, EXP STA, UNIV CALIF, BERKELEY, 72-, CHMN DEPT, 76- *Concurrent Pos:* Sr ed, Phytopath, 70-73, ed-in-chief, 73-75. *Mem:* AAAS; Am Phytopath Soc. *Res:* Disease and pathogen physiology; soil-borne pathogens; root diseases; potato diseases. *Mailing Add:* Dept of Plant Path Univ of Calif Berkeley CA 94720

WEINHOLD, PAUL ALLEN, b Evans, Colo, Sept 23, 35; m 56; c 4. BIOCHEMISTRY. *Educ:* Colo State Univ, BS, 57; Univ Wis, PhD(biochem), 61. *Prof Exp:* Asst prof biochem & internal med, Med Sch, Univ Mich, Ann Arbor, 65-72; biochemist, Vet Admin Hosp, 65-77; ASSOC PROF BIOL CHEM, MED SCH, UNIV MICH, ANN ARBOR, 72-; SUPV RES BIOCHEMIST, VET ADMIN HOSP, 77- *Concurrent Pos:* USPHS res fel biochem, Harvard Med Sch, 63-65. *Mem:* AAAS; Am Soc Biol Chemists. *Res:* Biochemistry of development, phospholipid metabolism and control mechanisms in metabolism. *Mailing Add:* Med Res Vet Admin Hosp 2215 Fuller Rd Ann Arbor MI 48105

WEINHOUS, MARTIN S, atomic physics, see previous edition

WEINHOUSE, SIDNEY, b Chicago, Ill, May 21, 09; c 3. BIOCHEMISTRY, CANCER. *Educ:* Univ Chicago, BS, 33, PhD(chem), 36. *Hon Degrees:* DSc, Med Col Pa, 72, Temple Univ, 76; Dr Med & Surg, Univ Chieti, Italy, 79. *Prof Exp:* Coman fel org chem, Univ Chicago, 41-44; head biochem res, Houdry Process Corp, Pa, 44-47; biochem res dir, Res Inst, 47-50, prof chem & biol, chmn div biochem, Inst Cancer Res & head dept metab chem, Lankenau Hosp Res Inst, 50-57, dir Fels Res Inst, 63-74, prof, 57-79, EMER PROF BIOCHEM, SCH MED, TEMPLE UNIV, 80- *Concurrent Pos:* Mem biochem study sect, NIH, 53-58 & nat adv coun, Nat Cancer Inst, Dept Health, Educ & Welfare, 58-62; assoc dir, Fels Res Inst, 61-63; chmn comt biol chem, Div Chem & Chem Technol, Nat Acad Sci-Nat Res Coun, 62-64; co-ed, Advan Cancer Res, 60-, ed, Cancer Res, 69-79; mem sci adv comt, Damon Runyon Mem Fund, 52-60 & Environ Health Sci Adv Comt, 68-72; assoc ed, J Environ Pathol & Toxicol, J Oncofetal Develop. *Honors & Awards:* Philadelphia Sect Award, Am Chem Soc, 66; G H A Clowes Award, Am Asn Cancer Res, 72; Papanicolaou Award, 76; Lucy Wortham James Award, Soc Surg Oncol, 79; Nat Award, Am Cancer Soc. *Mem:* Nat Acad Sci; Am Soc Biol Chemists; Am Asn Cancer Res; Soc Exp Biol & Med; Am Chem Soc. *Res:* Carbohydrate and fatty acid metabolism in normal and neoplastic cells; dietary and hormonal regulation of enzymes of carbohydrate and fatty acid metabolism in liver tumors; effects of hormones on gluconeogenesis; comparative studies on control of respiration and glycolysis in liver and liver tumors. *Mailing Add:* Fels Res Inst Temple Univ Sch of Med Philadelphia PA 19140

WEINIG, SHELDON, b New York, NY, Jan 15, 28; m 74. METALLURGY. *Educ:* NY Univ, BME, 51; Columbia Univ, MS, 53, DEngSc, 55. *Prof Exp:* PRES, MAT RES CORP, 57- *Concurrent Pos:* Mem adv comt, US Dept Com, 76-78; dir, Semiconductor Equip & Mat Inst, 76-; mem adv comt, Polytech Univ NY, 77-; mem, US-Japan Coop Sci Comt. *Mem:* AAAS; Am Soc Metals; Am Inst Mining, Metall & Petrol Engrs; Am Phys Soc. *Res:* Electronic materials. *Mailing Add:* Mat Res Corp Rte 303 Orangeburg NY 10962

WEININGER, STEPHEN JOEL, b New York, NY, Mar 28, 37; m 61; c 3. ORGANIC CHEMISTRY. *Educ:* Brooklyn Col, BA, 57; Univ Pa, PhD(org chem), 64. *Prof Exp:* Sr demonstr phys chem, Univ Durham, 64-65; asst prof, 65-70, assoc prof, 70-77, PROF CHEM, WORCESTER POLYTECH INST, 77- *Concurrent Pos:* Danforth Assoc, 79-85. *Mem:* Am Chem Soc; Am Asn Univ Professors. *Res:* Carbene chemistry; chemistry of hot intermediates; organic synthesis. *Mailing Add:* Dept of Chem Worcester Polytech Inst Worcester MA 01609

WEINKAM, ROBERT JOSEPH, b Cincinnati, Ohio, Dec 27, 42. MEDICINAL CHEMISTRY. *Educ:* Xavier Univ, Ohio, BS, 64; Duquesne Univ, PhD(chem), 68. *Prof Exp:* Fel, Sya Res Inst Calif, 68-69; fel, Sch Med, Univ Calif, San Francisco, 69-70, asst prof, Pharmaceut Chem, 71-80, asst prof neurosurg, 78-80; ASSOC PROF MED CHEM, PURDUE UNIV, WEST LAFAYETTE, 80- *Concurrent Pos:* Res career develop award, NIH, 75-80. *Mem:* Am Chem Soc; Am Soc Mass Spectros; Am Asn Cancer Res. *Res:* Biomedical application of mass spectrometry; chemotherapeutic agents, mechanisms of drug action. *Mailing Add:* Dept of Pharmaceut Chem Univ of Calif San Francisco CA 94122

WEINLAND, BERNARD THEODORE, b Scarsdale, NY, July 2, 22; m 47; c 4. APPLIED STATISTICS. *Educ:* Purdue Univ, BS, 48, MS, 61, PhD(poultry genetics), 66. *Prof Exp:* Poultry plant supt, Ind Farm Bur Coop, 48-49; flock inspector, State Poultry Asn, Ind, 49-51; asst farm supt, Ind Poultry Breeders, Inc, 51-55; farm supt, Regional Poultry Breeding Lab, Agr Res Serv, 55-66, statistician, Biomet Serv, 66-72, REGIONAL CONSULT STATISTICIAN, NORTHEAST REGION, AGR RES SERV, USDA, 72- *Mem:* Poultry Sci Asn; Am Dairy Sci Asn; Am Soc Animal Sci; Biomet Soc. *Res:* Gene frequency stability in a random bred poultry population; genetic correlations between purebred and crossbred progeny of the same sires; statistical problems of animal scientist. *Mailing Add:* Bldg 173 Agr Res Ctr E Beltsville MD 20705

WEINLESS, MICHAEL HOWARD, mathematics, see previous edition

WEINMAN, LESLIE STUART, b Brooklyn, NY, July 4, 45; m 69. MATERIALS SCIENCE. *Educ:* NY Univ, BES, 67; Mass Inst Technol, PhD(mat sci), 71. *Prof Exp:* Res physicist, Naval Res Lab, 71-78; researcher, Honey Corp Res, 78-81; MGR WAFER FABRICATION, OPTIC INFO SYSTS, 81- *Mem:* Am Phys Soc; Am Soc Metals. *Res:* Superconducting resonators and bulk circuits for high frequency communication; critical-current measurements on A15 alloys; pinning in type-II superconductors; author or coauthor of over 30 publications. *Mailing Add:* Optic Info Syts 350 Executive Blvd Elmsford NY 10523

WEINMANN, CLARENCE JACOB, b Oakland, Calif, May 27, 25; m 57; c 2. PARASITOLOGY. *Educ:* Univ Calif, BS, 50, PhD(parasitol), 58. *Prof Exp:* Instr microbiol, Col Med, Univ Fla, 58-60; res fel biol, Rice Univ, 60-62; from asst prof to assoc prof, 62-75, PROF ENTOM & PARASITOL, UNIV CALIF, BERKELEY, 75- *Concurrent Pos:* Fel trop med & parasitol, Univ Cent Am, 59. *Mem:* AAAS; Am Soc Parasitol; Entom Soc Am; Am Soc Trop Med & Hyg; Wildlife Dis Asn. *Res:* Immunity in helminth infections; arthropod-borne helminthiases. *Mailing Add:* Div of Entom & Parasitol Univ of Calif Berkeley CA 94720

WEINREB, EVA LURIE, b New York, NY; m 50. BIOLOGICAL STRUCTURE, CELL BIOLOGY. *Educ:* NY Univ, BA, 48; Univ Wis, MA, 49, PhD(zool), 55. *Prof Exp:* Asst zool, Univ Wis, 49 & 51-55; res assoc path, Sch Med, Marquette Univ, 55-56; dir basic sci, St Mary's Hosp, Sch Nursing, Milwaukee, 56-57; head animal res, Kolmer Res Ctr, 57-58; asst prof biol, Milwaukee-Downer Col, 59-60; fel cell biol & res assoc anat, Med Col, Cornell Univ, 61-63; asst prof biol, Washington Square Col, NY Univ, 63-69; cell biologist & sr res scientist, Biomed Sect, Geometric Data Corp, 71-72; assoc prof, 73-80, PROF BIOL, COMMUNITY COL PHILADELPHIA, 80- *Concurrent Pos:* Consult, Volu-Sol Med Industs, Inc, 72-73. *Mem:* AAAS; Am Asn Anatomists; Am Soc Cell Biol; Am Soc Zool; Am Soc Allied Health Prof. *Res:* Comparative histology; hematology; pathology; electron microscopy; anatomy. *Mailing Add:* Community Col of Philadelphia 1600 Spring Garden St Philadelphia PA 19130

WEINREB, MICHAEL PHILIP, b Lakewood, NJ, Feb 2, 39; m 66; c 2. ATMOSPHERIC PHYSICS. *Educ:* Univ Pa, BA, 60; Brandeis Univ, PhD(physics), 66. *Prof Exp:* Instr physics, Brandeis Univ, 64-65; physicist, Electronics Res Ctr, NASA, Mass, 65-70; PHYSICIST, NAT EARTH SATELLITE SERV, NAT OCEANIC & ATMOSPHERIC ADMIN, 70- *Mem:* Am Meteorol Soc; Optical Soc Am. *Res:* Radiative transfer theory; atomic and molecular physics; remote sensing of atmospheric temperature and constituent profiles. *Mailing Add:* FOB-4 Nat Earth Satellite Serv Nat Oceanic & Atmospheric Admin Suitland MD 20233

WEINREB, SANDER, b New York, NY, Dec 9, 36; m 57; c 2. RADIO ASTRONOMY, MICROWAVE ENGINEERING. *Educ:* Mass Inst Technol, BSEE, 58, PhD(elec eng), 63. *Prof Exp:* Staff mem, Lincoln Lab, Mass Inst Technol, 63-65; scientist electonics, 65-77, assoc head, 77-80, HEAD ELECTRONICS DIV, NAT RADIO ASTRON OBSERV, 80- *Concurrent Pos:* Foreign adv, Neth Found Radio Astron, 72-77; adv, Nat Astron & Ionospheric Observ, 72-78. *Mem:* Sigma Xi; fel Inst Elec & Electronics Engrs. *Res:* Low noise receivers; millimeter wave devices. *Mailing Add:* Nat Radio Astron Observ 2015 Ivy Rd Charlottesville VA 22903

WEINREB, STEVEN MARTIN, b Brooklyn, NY, May 10, 41; m 65; c 2. ORGANIC CHEMISTRY. *Educ:* Cornell Univ, AB, 63; Univ Rochester, PhD(chem), 67. *Prof Exp:* NIH fel, Columbia Univ, 66-67; NIH fel, Mass Inst Technol, 67-68, res assoc, 68-70; from asst prof to assoc prof chem, Fordham Univ, 70-78; assoc prof, 78-80, PROF CHEM, PA STATE UNIV, 80- *Concurrent Pos:* Res fel, Alfred P Sloan Found, 75-79; res career develop award, NIH, 75-80. *Mem:* Am Chem Soc; The Chem Soc. *Res:* Structure determination and synthesis of natural products. *Mailing Add:* Dept of Chem Pa State Univ University Park PA 16802

WEINREICH, DANIEL, b Claremont, France, June 6, 42; US citizen; m 36; c 2. NEUROBIOLOGY. *Educ:* Bethany Col, BS, 64; Univ Utah, PhD(pharmacol), 70. *Prof Exp:* Res asst neuropharmacol, Sandoz Pharmaceut, Inc, 64-65; NSF fel, City of Hope Nat Med Ctr, 70-72, NIMH fel, 73-74; asst prof, 74-77, ASSOC PROF PHARMACOL, SCH MED, UNIV MD, BALTIMORE, 74- *Concurrent Pos:* Extramural reviewer, NSF, 73-, Neurobiol Study Sect, 80-81; NSF res grant, 74-83. *Mem:* Neurosci Soc. *Res:* Identification and regulation of neurotransmitter and neuromodulator substances in single nerve cells; cellular autonomic neuropharmacology. *Mailing Add:* Dept Pharmacol & Exp Therapeut Med Sch Univ Md Baltimore MD 21201

WEINREICH, GABRIEL, b Vilna, Poland, Feb 12, 28; nat US; m 51, 71; c 5. PHYSICS. *Educ:* Columbia Univ, AB, 48, MA, 49, PhD(physics), 54. *Prof Exp:* Asst physics, Columbia Univ, 49-51; mem tech staff, Bell Tel Labs, 53-60; vis assoc prof, 60, assoc prof, 60-64, prof, 64-74, col prof, 74-76, PROF PHYSICS, UNIV MICH, ANN ARBOR, 76- *Mem:* Acoust Soc Am. *Res:* Atomic spectra; solid state theory; electron-phonon interactions; nonlinear optics; thermodynamics; electron-atom scattering; musical acoustics; atomic beam kinetics. *Mailing Add:* Randall Lab Physics Univ Mich Ann Arbor MI 48109

WEINRICH, MARCEL, b Jendiesow, Poland, July 23, 27; nat US; div; c 1. PHYSICS. *Educ:* Bethany Col, WVa, BS, 46; Univ WVa, MS, 48; Columbia Univ, PhD, 57. *Prof Exp:* Instr physics, Univ WVa, 47-49; physicist, Res & Develop Ctr, Gen Elec Co, 57-69; chmn dept, 69-73, PROF PHYSICS, JERSEY CITY STATE COL, 69- *Concurrent Pos:* Coordr gen studies review, Jersey City State Col, co-chmn, Pres Task Force for the 1980's. *Mem:* Fel AAAS; Am Inst Physics; Am Asn Physics Teachers; Nat Sci Teachers Asn; Am Phys Soc. *Res:* Meson and plasma physics; breakdown of parity conservation in meson decays; controlled fusion reactors. *Mailing Add:* Dept Physics Jersey City State Col 2039 Kennedy Blvd Jersey City NJ 07305

WEINRYB, IRA, b New York, NY, Nov 20, 40; m 67; c 2. BIOCHEMISTRY, PHARMACOLOGY. *Educ:* Columbia Univ, BS, 61; Yale Univ, MEng, 62, MS, 65, PhD(molecular biophys), 67. *Prof Exp:* Nat Acad Sci-Nat Res Coun resident res assoc, Lab Phys Biochem, Naval Med Res Inst, Nat Naval Med Ctr, 67-69; from res investr to sr res investr, Dept Biochem Pharmacol, Squibb Inst Med Res, 69-73, head biochem sect, 73-75, res fel, Dept Pharmacol, 75; dir biochem & drug disposition, USV Pharamaceut Corp, 75-81; ASSOC DIV DIR, BIOLOGICAL RES & DEVELOP, REVLON HEALTH CARE GROUP, 75-81. *Concurrent Pos:* Chmn, Biochem Pharmacol Discussion Group. *Mem:* Am Soc Biol Chem; NY Acad Sci; Am Chem Soc. *Res:* Enzyme kinetics and mechanism; spectroscopy of biological molecules; biochemical pharmacology; mechanism of drug action. *Mailing Add:* Revlon Health Care Group Res & Develop 1 Scarsdale Rd Tuckahoe NY 10707

WEINSHANK, DONALD JEROME, b Chicago, Ill, Apr 29, 37; m 59; c 2. NATURAL SCIENCE, COMPUTER LITERACY. *Educ:* Northwestern Univ, BA, 58; Univ Wis-Madison, MS, 61, PhD(biochem), 69. *Prof Exp:* From instr to asst prof nat sci, 67-72, assoc prof, 72-77, prof, 77-81, PROF COMPUT SCI & NAT SCI, UNIV COL, MICH STATE UNIV, 81- *Mem:* AAAS; And Comput Mach; Am Chem Soc. *Res:* Computer assisted instruction; computer literacy; concordances to works of Charles Darwin. *Mailing Add:* Dept of Nat Sci Univ Col Mich State Univ East Lansing MI 48824

WEINSHENKER, NED MARTIN, b Brooklyn, NY, Oct 13, 42; m 66; c 2. ORGANIC CHEMISTRY. *Educ:* Polytech Inst Brooklyn, BSc, 64; Mass Inst Technol, PhD(org chem), 69. *Prof Exp:* NIH fel, Harvard Univ, 68-69; asst prof chem, Univ Md, College Park, 69-70; dir phys sci & prin scientist, Alza Corp, 70-72; VPRES RES, DYNAPOL, 72- *Concurrent Pos:* Lectr, Stanford Univ, 71; guest lectr, Dept Human Biol, Stanford Univ, 79, 81. *Mem:* Am Chem Soc; The Chem Soc; NY Acad Sci. *Res:* Synthetic organic chemistry; new synthetic methods and physiologically active compounds; polymeric reagents and membrane structure; creation of new safe non-toxic food additives; new drug delivery systems. *Mailing Add:* Dynapol 1454 Page Mill Rd Palo Alto CA 94304

WEINSHILBOUM, RICHARD MERLE, b Eldorado, Kans, Mar 31, 40; m 65; c 2. PHARMACOLOGY, INTERNAL MEDICINE. *Educ:* Univ Kans, BA, 62, MD, 67. *Prof Exp:* Intern internal med, Mass Gen Hosp, 67-68, asst resident, 68-69; res assoc pharmacol, Lab Clin Sci, NIMH, 69-71; sr resident internal med, Mass Gen Hosp, 71-72; consult asst prof pharmacol & internal med, 72-75, assoc prof pharmacol, 76-79, assoc prof internal med, 77-79, CHIEF CLIN PHARMACOL UNIT, MAYO CLIN, 74-, PROF PHARMACOL & INTERNAL MED & WILLIAM L MCKNIGHT-3M PROF NEUROSCI, MAYO MED SCH, 79- *Concurrent Pos:* Consult, Mayo Clin, 72-; Pharmaceut Mfg Asn Fedn fac develop award, 73-75; estab investr, Am Heart Asn, 76-81; Burroughs-Wellcome scholar clin pharmacol, 81- *Honors & Awards:* Rawls-Palmer Award, Am Soc Clin Pharmacol Therapeut, 79. *Mem:* Am Soc Pharmacol & Exp Therapeut; Am Soc Clin Pharmacol & Therapeut; Am Fedn Clin Res; Am Soc Neurochem; Soc Neurosci. *Res:* Neurochemistry, biogenic amines; pharmacogenetics; biochemical genetics and clinical pharmacology. *Mailing Add:* Dept Pharmacol 200 First St SW Rochester MN 55901

WEINSIEDER, ALLAN, b Montevideo, Uruguay, Jan 11, 39; US citizen; m 69; c 2. CELL BIOLOGY. *Educ:* Bates Col, BS, 61; Univ Vt, MS, 65, PhD(zool), 73. *Prof Exp:* Asst to dir, Fisheries Res Bd Can Biol Sta, St Andrews, NB, 65-69; Nat Eye Inst fel, Oakland Univ, 72-73; asst prof anat, Sch Med, Wayne State Univ, 73-80; ASST PROF OPHTHAL, UNIV LOUISVILLE, 80- *Mem:* Asn Res Vision & Ophthal; Soc Exp Biol & Med; Am Soc Cell Biol; AAAS. *Res:* Regulation of growth in the vertebrate lens; wound healing. *Mailing Add:* Ky Lions Eye Res Inst Univ Louisville Sch Med Louisville KY 40202

WEINSTEIN, ABBOTT SAMSON, b Troy, NY, Apr 20, 24; m 49. BIOSTATISTICS. *Educ:* Union Col, BA, 45; Cornell Univ, MA, 47. *Prof Exp:* Intern pub admin, NY State Dept Audit & Control, 47-48; jr statistician social res, NY State Dept Social Welfare, 49-51; statistician & sr statistician bus res, NY State Dept Com, 50-57; asst dir statist serv, NY State Dept Ment Hyg, 57-61; dir biomet br, Saint Elizabeth's Hosp, Washington, DC, 61-66; dir statist & clin info systs, NY State Dept Ment Hyg, 66-76; DIR ANAL SERV, NY STATE OFF MENTAL HEALTH, 76- *Concurrent Pos:* Statist consult oncol & cytol, Albany Med Col, 58-61; statist consult, Judicial Conf DC Circuit, 63-64; grant, Nat Inst Ment Health co-prin investr multi-state info syst psychiat patients, Res Found Ment Hyg, Inc, NY, 67-72; mem epidemiol studies rev comt, Nat Inst Ment Health, 71-75. *Honors & Awards:* Superior Serv Award, US Dept Health, Educ & Welfare, 64; Distinguished Serv Award, NY State Dept Ment Hyg, 70. *Mem:* Am Statist Asn; fel Am Pub Health Asn. *Res:* Statistical research in mental health; analysis of systems of service for the mentally disabled; epidemiology of mental disability; data processing administration. *Mailing Add:* 10 Village Dr Delmar NY 12054

WEINSTEIN, ALAN DAVID, b New York, NY, June 17, 43; m 67; c 1. GEOMETRY. *Educ:* Mass Inst Technol, BS, 64; Univ Calif, Berkeley, MA, 66, PhD(math), 67. *Prof Exp:* Vis fel, Inst Advan Sci Studies, France, 67; C L E Moore instr math, Mass Inst Technol, 67-68; NATO fel, Math Inst, Univ Bonn, 68-69; from asst prof to assoc prof, 69-76, PROF MATH, UNIV CALIF, BERKELEY, 76- *Concurrent Pos:* Sloan fel, 71-73; vis prof, Rice Univ, 78-79. *Mem:* Am Math Soc; Math Asn Am. *Res:* Symplectic manifolds; fourier integral operators; Hamiltonian dynamical systems; riemannian geometry. *Mailing Add:* Dept of Math Univ of Calif Berkeley CA 94720

WEINSTEIN, ALAN IRA, b New York, NY, Apr 7, 40; m 66; c 2. METEOROLOGY. *Educ:* City Col New York, BS, 60; Pa State Univ, MS, 63, PhD(meteorol), 68. *Prof Exp:* Res meteorologist, Meteorol Res Inc, 63-66; res asst meteorol, Pa State Univ, 66-68; res scientist, Meteorol Res Inc, Cohu Electronics Inc, 69-71; res physicist, 71-74, br chief stratiform cloud physics, Air Force Geophys Labs, 74-77; DIR RES NAVAL ENVIRON PREDICTION RES FACIL, 77- *Mem:* Am Meteorol Soc; Royal Meteorol Soc; Sigma Xi; AAAS; Nat Weather Asn. *Res:* Manage weather analysis and prediction techniques development of environmental satellite data processing and display methods; techniques to assess effect of atmosphere on Navy systems. *Mailing Add:* Naval Environ Prediction Res Facil Monterey CA 93940

WEINSTEIN, ALEXANDER, b Astrakhan, Russia, Nov 22, 93; nat US; m 17; c 1. GENETICS, HISTORY OF SCIENCE. *Educ:* Columbia Univ, BS, 13, AM, 14, PhD(zool), 17. *Prof Exp:* Asst zool, Columbia Univ, 16-17, Sigma Xi res fel, 21-22, lectr, 28; res asst genetics, Carnegie Inst, 17-19; mem ed staff, Am Men Sci, 20-21; Johnston scholar, Johns Hopkins Univ, 22-23, Nat Res Coun fel, 23-24, assoc zool & hist sci, 30-36; Int Ed Bd fel, Cambridge Univ, 24-25; assoc zool, Univ Ill, 26-27; prof genetics, Univ Minn, 28-29;

researcher, Am Philos Soc grant, Columbia Univ, 37-42; instr physics, City Col New York, 42-49; res fel biol, 51-54, RESEARCHER, COMMONWEALTH FUND GRANT, HARVARD UNIV, 51- *Mem:* AAAS; Am Soc Nat; Am Soc Zool; Genetics Soc Am; Hist Sci Soc. *Res:* Crossing over and multiple-strand theory; radiation genetics; human genetics; heredity and development; comparative genetics of Drosophila; history of biology and physics; ancient and modern science; environmental and genetic factors in the history of science. *Mailing Add:* Biol Labs Harvard Univ Cambridge MA 02138

WEINSTEIN, ALVIN SEYMOUR, b Lynn, Mass, June 12, 28; m 52; c 3. MECHANICAL ENGINEERING. *Educ:* Univ Mich, BS, 51; Carnegie Inst Technol, MS, 53, PhD(mech eng), 55. *Prof Exp:* PROF MECH ENG & PUB POLICY, CARNEGIE MELLON UNIV, 55- *Concurrent Pos:* Res award, Am Soc Test & Mat, 65; partner, Tech Eng Consults, 76- *Honors & Awards:* Melville Medal, Am Soc Mech Engrs, 72; Western Elec Teaching Award, Am Soc Eng Educ, 73. *Mem:* Am Soc Mech Engrs; Am Soc Testing & Mat; Asn Iron & Steel Engrs. *Res:* Materials forming; technical aspects of products liability litigation; methodology for developing product safety standards. *Mailing Add:* Dept of Mech Eng Carnegie Mellon Univ Pittsburgh PA 15213

WEINSTEIN, ARTHUR HOWARD, b Brooklyn, NY, Jan 20, 24; m 46; c 2. ORGANIC POLYMER CHEMISTRY, RUBBER CHEMISTRY. *Educ:* Queens Col, NY, BS, 44; Ohio State Univ, MS, 48, PhD(org chem), 50. *Prof Exp:* Asst path chemist, Bellevue Hosp, New York, 46; anal chemist, Dept of Purchase, New York, 50; SR RES CHEM RESIST, ELASTOMER & CHEM DIV, GOODYEAR TIRE & RUBBER CO, 51- *Mem:* Am Chem Soc. *Res:* Mixed organic acid anhydrides; aminocellulose derivatives; synthesis of aromatic sulfur compounds; polydienes with terminal functionality; polymerization modifiers; castable elastomers; elastomers self-resistant to oxidation or to combustion; specialty rubbers. *Mailing Add:* 2400 Cambridge Dr Hudson OH 44236

WEINSTEIN, BERNARD ALLEN, b Bridgeport, Conn, Nov 15, 46; m 70; c 2. SOLID STATE PHYSICS. *Educ:* Univ Rochester, BS, 68; Brown Univ, PhD(physics), 74. *Prof Exp:* Fel, Max Planck Inst Solid State Res, Stuttgart, 71-73; res assoc solid state mat, Nat Bur Standards, 73-75; asst prof physics, Purdue Univ, West Lafayette, 75-78; RES SCIENTIST, XEROX CORP, 78- *Concurrent Pos:* Alfred P Sloan res fel, 75-77. *Mem:* Am Phys Soc; Fedn Am Scientists. *Res:* Optical properties of solids, with specific work in Raman scattering, visible and infrared spectroscopy and ultra-high pressure research. *Mailing Add:* Xerox Corp WRC-114 800 Phillips Rd Webster NY 14580

WEINSTEIN, BERNARD IRA, biochemistry, see previous edition

WEINSTEIN, BERTHOLD WERNER, b New York, NY, Oct 11, 47. GENERAL PHYSICS, MATHEMATICS. *Educ:* Brigham Young Univ, BS, 71; Univ Ill, Urbana, MS, 73, PhD(physics), 75. *Prof Exp:* RES PHYSICIST LASER FUSION, LAWRENCE LIVERMORE NAT LAB, UNIV CALIF, 74- *Mem:* Am Phys Soc; Am Vacuum Soc. *Res:* Inertial fusion target fabrication and measurement; liquid metal ion beam sources; computer simulation and analysis of high energy physics experiments; electrohydrodynamics, particularly ion spraying; high energy physics. *Mailing Add:* Lawrence Livermore Nat Lab Y Div L-482 PO Box 5508 Livermore CA 94550

WEINSTEIN, BORIS, b New Orleans, La, Mar 31, 30; m 53; c 2. ORGANIC CHEMISTRY, BIO-ORGANIC CHEMISTRY. *Educ:* La State Univ, BS, 51; Purdue Univ, MS, 53; Ohio State Univ, PhD(org chem), 59. *Prof Exp:* Jr chemist, Motor Fuels Lab, La State Univ, 49-51; chemist, United Gas Corp, 51-52; asst, Res Found, Ohio State Univ, 55-56; fel, Univ Calif, 59-60; chemist, Stanford Res Inst, 60-61; lab dir, Stanford Univ, 61-67; assoc prof, 67-74, PROF CHEM, UNIV WASH, 74- *Mem:* AAAS; Am Chem Soc; fel NY Acad Sci; Royal Soc Chem; Am Soc Neurochem. *Res:* Synthesis of biologically active peptides and proteins; phytochemical and phylogenetic relationships; structure and synthesis of natural products; heterocyclic compounds; applications of nuclear magnetic resonance; marine chemistry; neurochemistry. *Mailing Add:* Dept Chem BG-10 Univ Wash Seattle WA 98195

WEINSTEIN, CONSTANCE DE COURCY, b London, Eng, Aug 31, 24; US citizen; m 59; c 3. BIOCHEMISTRY. *Educ:* Univ London, BSc, 48, PhD(biochem), 53. *Prof Exp:* Res biochemist, Hosp Sick Children, London, 53-54; res fel biochem, Jefferson Med Col, Philadelphia, 55-56; sr instr biochem, Med Sch, Western Reserve Univ, Cleveland, 56-61; res scientist cancer, City of Hope, Duarte, Calif, 70-74; health sci adminr, 75-79, HEALTH SCI ADMINR, DIV RES GRANTS, NAT HEART, LUNG & BLOOD INST, NIH, 79- *Mailing Add:* Nat Heart Lung & Blood Inst NIH Westwood Bldg Westbard Ave Bethesda MD 20014

WEINSTEIN, DAVID, b New York, NY, June 24, 28; m 54; c 2. BACTERIOLOGY, CYTOGENETICS. *Educ:* City Col New York, BS, 50; Brooklyn Col, MA, 54; Purdue Univ, PhD(bact), 59. *Prof Exp:* Asst bacteriologist, Queens Gen Hosp, New York, 53-54; bacteriologist, US Army Chem Corps, Ft Detrick, Md, 54-55; asst bact, Purdue Univ, 55-59; res assoc microbiol, Sch Med, Duke Univ, 59-62; res assoc, Merck Res Inst, Pa, 62-63; assoc, Wistar Inst, Philadelphia, 63-68; sr scientist, 68-75, asst res group chief, 75-78, RES GROUP CHIEF, HOFFMANN-LA ROCHE, INC, 78- *Mem:* AAAS; Am Soc Microbiol; Tissue Cult Asn; NY Acad Sci; Sigma Xi. *Res:* Oncogenic virology; clastogenic, mutagenic and carcinogenic chemicals; tissue culture; transformation. *Mailing Add:* 78 Luddington Rd West Orange NJ 07052

WEINSTEIN, DAVID ALAN, b New York City, NY, Mar 26, 51. NUTRIENT CYCLING, COMPUTER MODELING. *Educ:* Darmouth Col, BA, 73; Univ NH, MS, 76; Univ Tenn, PhD(ecol), 82. *Prof Exp:* Grad res fel, Environ Sci Div, Oak Ridge Nat Lab, 77-81; RES ASSOC, ECOSYST RES CTR, ENVIRON PROTECTION AGENCY CTR EXCELLENCE, CORNELL UNIV, 81- *Mem:* Ecol Soc Am; Sigma Xi. *Res:* Mechanisms of response of ecosystems to perturbations through the analysis of nutrient cycling patterns by computer simulation techniques. *Mailing Add:* Ecosyst Res Ctr 141 Biol Sci Bldg Cornell Univ Ithaca NY 14853

WEINSTEIN, HAREL, b Bucarest, Rumania, June 5, 45; m 67; c 1. BIOPHYSICAL CHEMISTRY, QUANTUM CHEMISTRY. *Educ:* Israel Inst Technol, BSc, 66, MSc, 68, DSc(quantum chem), 71. *Prof Exp:* Asst chem, Israel Inst Technol, 66-68, sr res asst, 68-71, lectr, 71-73; res assoc, Johns Hopkins Univ, 73-74; asst prof, 74-76, assoc prof, 76-79, PROF PHARMACOL, MT SINAI SCH MED, 79- *Concurrent Pos:* Consult res assoc biochem, Tel-Aviv Univ, 73-78; vis scientist genetics, Med Ctr, Stanford Univ, 74-75; mem ed & adv bd, Molecular Pharmacol; Irma T Hirschl Trust res career scientist, 78-82; Alcohol, Drug Abuse & Mental Health Admin res grant, 79-83; consult, Merck Sharp & Dohme, 79-81; res scientist develop award, Alcohol, Drug Abuse & Mental Health Admin, 79-83. *Mem:* Royal Soc Chem; Am Soc Pharmacol Exp Therapists; Europ Phys Soc; Am Chem Soc; Int Soc Quantum Biol. *Res:* Development of theoretical methods to study molecular reactivity and interactions between biological molecules; molecular recognition in drug action and energy transfer and storage; receptor theory and molecular mechanisms of neurotransmmission. *Mailing Add:* Dept of Pharmacol Mt Sinai Sch of Med New York NY 10029

WEINSTEIN, HERBERT, b Brooklyn, NY, Mar 10, 33; m 57; c 3. FLUIDIZATION, CHEMICAL REACTOR ENGINEERING. *Educ:* City Col New York, BEChE, 55; Purdue Univ, MSChE, 57; Case Inst Technol, PhD(eng), 63. *Prof Exp:* Staff mem, Los Alamos Sci Lab, 56-68; res engr, Lewis Lab, NASA, 59-63; asst prof chem eng, Ill Inst Technol, 63-66, assoc prof, 66-72, prof, 72-77; PROF CHEM ENG, CITY UNIV NEW YORK, 77- *Concurrent Pos:* Vis res assoc, Michael Reese Hosp & Med Ctr, 65-77; vis prof mech eng, Technion Israel Inst Technol, 72-73, biomed eng, Rush Med Col, 73-76. *Mem:* Am Inst Chem Engrs; Sigma Xi. *Res:* Chemical reactor engineering: fluidization, tracer methods, heat and mass transfer in catalysts; fluid mechanics; biomedical engineering: tracer methods in the circulation and glucose sensors. *Mailing Add:* Dept Chem Eng City Univ New York New York NY 10031

WEINSTEIN, HOWARD, b New York, NY, Nov 9, 27. NEUROCHEMISTRY, CELL PHYSIOLOGY. *Educ:* Cornell Univ, BA, 49; State Univ Iowa, PhD(zool), 56. *Prof Exp:* Instr zool & physiol, Wis State Univ-Stevens Point, 56-57; USPHS fel neuroendocrinol, Case Western Reserve Univ, 58-61; res scientist, City of Hope Med Ctr, Duarte, Calif, 61-74; STAFF SCIENTIST, NAT INST NEUROL DIS & STROKE, 74- *Concurrent Pos:* USPHS grants, 68- *Mem:* Soc Neurosci; Am Soc Neurochem; Int Soc Neurochem; Am Soc Zoologists. *Res:* Membrane transport processes in central nervous system. *Mailing Add:* 14012 Eagle Court Rockville MD 20853

WEINSTEIN, HYMAN GABRIEL, b Worcester, Mass, June 15, 20; m. BIOCHEMISTRY, PHYSIOLOGY. *Educ:* Worcester Polytech Inst, BS, 42; Univ Ill, Urbana, MS, 47; Nat Registry Clin Chem, cert. *Prof Exp:* Res asst, Univ Ill, Urbana, 48-49; res asst, Rheumatic Fever Res Inst, Med Sch, Northwestern Univ, 49-50, res assoc, 50-53; res biochemist, Neurol Res Lab, Vet Admin Hosp, Hines, Ill, 53-54; supvry res biochemist, Vet Admin West Side Hosp, Chicago, 54-64; supvry res biochemist, Geriat Res Lab, 64-65, CHIEF RES-IN-AGING LAB, VET ADMIN HOSP, DOWNEY, ILL, 65-, LECTR, COUN ON ALCOHOLISM, 68- *Concurrent Pos:* Lectr, Northeastern Ill Univ, 75- *Mem:* AAAS; Am Chem Soc; Soc Complex Carbohydrates; NY Acad Sci; Sigma Xi. *Res:* Proteoglycans and related macromolecules in human development, aging and disease; research administration. *Mailing Add:* Res-in-Aging Lab Vet Admin Hosp North Chicago IL 60064

WEINSTEIN, I BERNARD, b Madison, Wis, Sept 9, 30; m 52; c 3. MEDICINE. *Educ:* Univ Wis, BS, 52, MD, 55. *Prof Exp:* Nat Cancer Inst spec res fel bact & immunol, Harvard Med Sch & Mass Inst Technol, 59-61; asst attend physician, 66-78, ATTEND PHYSICIAN, PRESBY HOSP, NEW YORK, 80-; PROF MED & PUB HEALTH & DIR, DIV ENVIRON SCI, COLUMBIA UNIV, 78- *Concurrent Pos:* Career scientist, Health Res Coun, City of New York, 61-72; Europ Molecular Biol Orgn travel fel, 70-71; adv lung cancer segment, Carcinogenesis Prog, Nat Cancer Inst, 71-74; mem interdisciplinary commun prog, Smithsonian Inst, 71-74; mem pharmacol B study sect, NIH, 71-75; vis physician, Francis Delafield Hosp, New York; adv, Roswell Park Mem Inst, Buffalo, NY, Brookhaven Nat Lab, Div Cancer Cause & Prevention, Nat Cancer Inst, Coun on Anal & Projs, Am Cancer Ctr, Int Agency for Res on Cancer, WHO, Lyon, France. *Honors & Awards:* Meltzer Medal, 64. *Mem:* Inst Med-Nat Acad Sci; Am Soc Microbiol; Int Soc Quantum Biol; Am Asn Cancer Res; AAAS. *Res:* Oncology; cellular and molecular aspects of carcinogenesis; environmental carcinogenesis; control of gene expression. *Mailing Add:* Inst Cancer Res Columbia Univ 701 W 168th St New York NY 10032

WEINSTEIN, IRA, b Oak Park, Ill, Jan 30, 28; m 54; c 3. ENDOCRINOLOGY, BIOCHEMICAL PHARMACOLOGY. *Educ:* Roosevelt Univ, BS, 49; Univ Ill, MS, 52; George Washington Univ, PhD(microbiol), 60. *Prof Exp:* From instr to asst prof pharmacol, Vanderbilt Univ, 60-69; assoc prof, Sch Med, Univ Fla, 69-75; assoc prof pharmacol, Sch Med, Univ Mo-Columbia, 75-80, prof, 80-81; PROF, UNIV TENN CTR HEALTH SCI, MEMPHIS, 81- *Concurrent Pos:* Fel pharmacol, Med Sch, Vanderbilt Univ, 60-63; USPHS fels, 60-64; Olson Mem Fund fel, 65-66; vis lectr, Hebrew Univ Israel, 65-66; Am Heart Asn advan res fel, 65-67; fel coun on arteriosclerosis, Am Heart Asn. *Mem:* Sigma Xi; Am Soc Microbiol; Am Soc Pharmacol & Exp Therapeut. *Res:* Bacterial physiology, endocrines and drug effects upon lipid metabolism. *Mailing Add:* Dept of Pharmacol Univ Tenn Ctr Health Sci Memphis TN 38163

WEINSTEIN, IRAM J, b Brooklyn, NY, Oct 17, 36; m 70; c 3. RADAR SYSTEMS ANALYSIS. *Educ:* Rensselaer Polytech Inst, BS, 56; Northeastern Univ, MSEE, 61; Stanford Univ, PhD(elec eng), 67. *Prof Exp:* Sr engr, Raytheon Corp, 56-60; sr res engr, Stanford Res Inst, 60-68, dir syst eval, 68-72, dir, Ctr Anal Public Serv, 72-76; MEM RES STAFF, SYST PLANNING CORP, 78- *Concurrent Pos:* Lectr, Stanford Univ, 67-79. *Mem:* Inst Elec & Electronics Engrs; Operations Res Soc Am. *Res:* Analysis and evaluation of large scale systems to support decision makers to identify appropriate alternatives and to select among them. *Mailing Add:* Syst Planning Corp 1500 Wilson Blvd Arlington VA 22209

WEINSTEIN, IRWIN M, b Denver, Colo, Mar 5, 26; m 51; c 2. HEMATOLOGY, INTERNAL MEDICINE. *Educ:* Univ Colo Med Ctr Denver, MD, 49. *Prof Exp:* Instr med, Univ Chicago, 53-54, asst prof, 54-55; assoc prof, 55-59, assoc clin prof, 59-70, CLIN PROF MED, UNIV CALIF, LOS ANGELES, 70- *Concurrent Pos:* Chief hemat, Vet Admin Ctr, Wadsworth Hq, Los Angeles, 55-59; chief staff, Cedars-Sinai Med Ctr, Los Angeles, 72-75. *Mem:* Inst Med-Nat Acad Sci; Am Soc Hemat; fel Am Col Physicians; Am Fedn Clin Res. *Res:* Mechanisms of anemia; radioactive chromium and iron for studying red cell production and distruction. *Mailing Add:* 8635 W 3rd St Los Angeles CA 90048

WEINSTEIN, JEREMY SAUL, b Brooklyn, NY, Apr 9, 44; m 67; c 3. OPERATIONS RESEARCH, COMPUTER SCIENCE. *Educ:* City Col New York, BE, 66; Purdue Univ, Lafayette, MSIE, 68, PhD(indust eng), 71. *Prof Exp:* Res engr, 70-72, mgr bus planning, Laundry Group, 72-76, mgr prod scheduling & mis, 76-79, MGR INDUST ENG & MIS, MARION DIV, WHIRLPOOL CORP, 79- *Concurrent Pos:* Instr, Benton Harbor Exten, Mich State Univ, 70- *Mem:* Inst Mgt Sci; Inst Indust Engrs. *Res:* Application of operations research and computers to inventory and process control. *Mailing Add:* Whirlpool Corp Marion-Agosta Rd Marion OH 43302

WEINSTEIN, JOHN NEWMAN, biophysics, medicine, see previous edition

WEINSTEIN, LEONARD HARLAN, b Springfield, Mass, Apr 11, 26; m 50; c 2. PLANT PHYSIOLOGY, ENVIRONMENTAL BIOLOGY. *Educ:* Pa State Univ, BS, 49; Univ Mass, MS, 50; Rutgers Univ, PhD(plant physiol), 53. *Prof Exp:* Fel soils, Rutgers Univ, 53-54; from assoc plant physiologist to plant physiologist, 55-63, prog dir plant chem, 63-69, PROG DIR ENVIRON BIOL, BOYCE THOMPSON INST PLANT RES, 69-, MEM BD DIRS, 73-, TRUSTEE, 78- *Mem:* AAAS; Am Soc Plant Physiol; Air Pollution Control Asn; Fedn Am Scientists; Am Inst Biol Sci. *Res:* Air pollution; aromatic metabolism; plant nutrition; plant senescence; environmental biology; effects of atmospheric pollutants on plant growth, development, productivity, and quality. *Mailing Add:* Boyce Thompson Inst Plant Res at Cornell Tower Rd Ithaca NY 14853

WEINSTEIN, LOUIS, b Bridgeport, Conn, Feb 26, 09; m 34. INTERNAL MEDICINE, INFECTIOUS DISEASES. *Educ:* Yale Univ, BS, 28, MS, 30, PhD(bact), 31; Boston Univ, MD, 43; ScD, 73. *Prof Exp:* Instr bact, Med Sch, Yale Univ, 37-39; res assoc immunol, Sch Med, Boston Univ, 39-44, asst med, 43-44, from instr to assoc prof, 44-57; lectr pediat, Med Sch, Tufts Univ, 50-57, prof med, 57-75; chief infectious dis serv, Vet Admin Hosp, West Roxbury, Mass, 75-78; PHYSICIAN, BRIGHAM & WOMEN'S HOSP, BOSTON, 75- *Concurrent Pos:* Asst, Harvard Med Sch, 45-46, instr, 46-49, lectr, 49-75, vis prof med, 75-; chief infectious dis serv, Mass Mem Hosp, 47-57 & New Eng Ctr Hosp & Boston Floating Hosp, 57-75; assoc physician, Med Serv, Mass Gen Hosp, 58-75; assoc physician in chief, New Eng Med Ctr Hosps, 62-71; vis prof med, Harvard Univ, 75- *Honors & Awards:* Finland Award & Bristol Award, Am Soc Infectious Dis. *Mem:* Am Acad Arts & Sci; AAAS; AMA; Am Soc Microbiol; Am Soc Infectious Dis. *Res:* Chemotherapy of infection; host factors in infectious disease. *Mailing Add:* 75 Frances St Boston MA 02115

WEINSTEIN, MARVIN, b Bronx, NY, June 7, 42; m 67; c 1. THEORETICAL HIGH ENERGY PHYSICS. *Educ:* Columbia Univ, BS, 63, MS, 64, PhD(physics), 67. *Prof Exp:* Physics mem, Inst Advan Study, 67-69; vis asst prof physics, Yeshiva Univ, 69-70 & NY Univ, 70-72; sr res assoc physics, Stanford Linear Accelerator Ctr, Stanford Univ, 72-80. *Res:* Current algebra; gauge theories of strong, weak and electromagnetic interactions; non-perturbatic methods in quantum field theory. *Mailing Add:* PO Box 4557 Hauula HI 96717

WEINSTEIN, MARVIN STANLEY, b New York, NY, May 24, 27; m 52; c 2. ACOUSTICS. *Educ:* St Louis Univ, BS, 48; Univ Md, MS, 51, PhD, 56. *Prof Exp:* Asst, Univ Md, 48-49; physicist, US Naval Ord Lab, 49-59; vpres, 59-62, pres, 62-74, CHMN BD, UNDERWATER SYSTS, INC, 75- *Mem:* AAAS; Am Phys Soc; Acoust Soc Am; Inst Elec & Electronics Eng. *Res:* Underwater acoustics; propagation at long and short range in deep and shallow water, noise, sinusoidal and explosive signals; ultrasonics; ultrasonic modeling; electronics. *Mailing Add:* 14305 Northwyn Dr Silver Spring MD 20904

WEINSTEIN, NORMAN J(ACOB), b Rochester, NY, Dec 31, 29; m 57; c 3. POLLUTION CONTROL SYSTEMS. *Educ:* Syracuse Univ, BChE, 51, MChE, 53; Ore State Univ, PhD(chem eng), 56. *Prof Exp:* Chem engr, Esso Res & Eng Co, 56-61, sr engr, 61-66, eng assoc, 66; eng & develop asst dir, Princeton Chem Res Inc, 66-67, eng & develop dir, 67-69; PRES, RECON SYSTS, INC, 69- *Concurrent Pos:* Adj prof, Newark Col Eng, 63-66. *Mem:* Am Chem Soc; Am Inst Chem Engrs; Am Soc Testing & Mat; NY Acad Sci. *Res:* Air and water pollution control; petroleum, petrochemical and metallurgical processes; catalysis; fluidized solids; hydrocarbon and coal gasification; economic evaluation; liquid and solid waste disposal and recycling. *Mailing Add:* 105 Reimer St Somerville NJ 08876

WEINSTEIN, PAUL P, b Brooklyn, NY, Dec 9, 19; m 54; c 2. PARASITOLOGY. *Educ:* Brooklyn Col, AB, 41; Johns Hopkins Univ, ScD(hyg), 49. *Prof Exp:* Jr parasitologist, USPHS, St Bd Health, Fla, 42-44, sr asst sanitarian, Washington, DC, Ga & PR, 44-46, from scientist to scientist dir & chief lab parasitic dis, NIH, 49-68; chmn dept, 69-75, PROF BIOL, UNIV NOTRE DAME, 75- *Concurrent Pos:* Vis scientist, Nat Inst Med Res, Eng, 62-63; mem parasitic dis panel, US-Japan Coop Med Sci Prog, 65-69, chmn, 69-73; mem comt int ctr med res & training, NIH, 70-73; mem adv sci bd, Gorgas Mem Inst Trop Prev Med, 72-; mem nat adv comt, Primate Res Ctr, Univ Calif, Davis, 73-77; mem microbiol & infectious dis adv comt, NIH, 78-81; consult, Walter Reed Army Inst Res, US Army, 77-79. *Honors & Awards:* Ashford Award, Am Soc Trop Med & Hyg, 57; Award of Honor, Brooklyn Col, 58. *Mem:* Fel AAAS; Am Soc Trop Med & Hyg; Am Soc Parasitol (pres, 72); Japanese Soc Parasitol. *Res:* Cultivation and physiology of parasitic helminths; host-parasite relationships. *Mailing Add:* Dept of Biol Univ of Notre Dame Notre Dame IN 46556

WEINSTEIN, RONALD S, b Schenectady, NY, Nov 20, 38; m 64; c 2. EXPERIMENTAL PATHOLOGY, ELECTRON MICROSCOPY. *Educ:* Union Col, NY, BS, 60; Tufts Univ, MD, 65; Am Bd Path, dipl. *Prof Exp:* Res asst electron micros, Mass Gen Hosp, 62-63; instr path, Sch Med, Tufts Univ, 67-69, assoc prof, 72-75; PROF PATH & CHMN DEPT, RUSH MED COL, 75- *Concurrent Pos:* From intern to resident path, Mass Gen Hosp, 65-70, head, Mixter Lab Electron Micros, 66-70; teaching fel, Harvard Med Sch, 65-70; investr toxicol, Aerospace Med Res Lab, Wright-Patterson AFB, 70-72; chmn dept, Rush-Presbyterian-St Lukes Med Ctr. *Mem:* Soc Develop Biol; NY Acad Sci; Am Asn Anatomists; Soc Toxicol; Am Asn Path. *Res:* Development and application of high resolution electron microscopy techniques to the study of biological membrane ultrastructure; comparative and functional studies on normal and neoplastic cell membranes; environmental toxicology. *Mailing Add:* Dept of Path Rush Med Col Chicago IL 60612

WEINSTEIN, SAM, b Omaha, Nebr, May 24, 16; m 46; c 2. ORTHODONTICS. *Educ:* Creighton Univ, DDS, 41; Northwestern Univ, MSD, 48; Am Bd Orthod, dipl. *Prof Exp:* From asst prof to prof orthod, Col Dent, Univ Nebr, 54-71, chmn dept, 63-71; PROF ORTHOD, UNIV CONN, 71- *Concurrent Pos:* Mem dent study sect, NIH, 69-73; consult, Coun Dent Educ, Am Dent Asn, 69-76; examr, Coun on Educ, Can Dent Asn, 74-77. *Mem:* Fel AAAS; Sigma Xi; Int Asn Dent Res; Int Soc Cranio-Facial Biol. *Res:* Theoretical mechanics application to soft tissue forces and tooth movement; cleft palate embryology; growth. *Mailing Add:* Univ of Conn Health Ctr Farmington CT 06032

WEINSTEIN, STANLEY EDWIN, b New York, NY, Apr 26, 42; m 64. MATHEMATICS, COMPUTER SCIENCE. *Educ:* Hunter Col, BA, 62; Mich State Univ, MS, 64, PhD(math), 67. *Prof Exp:* Teaching asst math, Mich State Univ, 62-67; from asst prof to assoc prof math, Univ Utah, 67-75; PROF & CHMN, DEPT MATH & COMPUT SCI, OLD DOMINION UNIV, 75- *Concurrent Pos:* US Air Force Off Sci Res grant, Univ Utah, 72-73; vis assoc prof, Dept Math, Ariz State Univ, 72-73. *Mem:* Soc Indust & Appl Math; Asn Comput Mach; Am Math Soc. *Res:* Approximation theory; numerical analysis; solution of nonlinear equations. *Mailing Add:* Dept of Math & Comput Sci Old Dominion Univ Norfolk VA 23508

WEINSTEIN, STEPHEN HENRY, b Bronx, NY, Apr 14, 37; m 66; c 1. DRUG METABOLISM. *Educ:* Queens Col, NY, BS, 58; Adelphi Col, MS, 61; Adelphi Univ, PhD(biochem), 67. *Prof Exp:* Scientist, Warner-Lambert Res Inst, 67-68; sr biochemist, 68-73, group leader, Endo Labs, Inc, 73-77; sr res biochmist, E I Du Pont de Nemours & Co, Inc, 77-80; SECT HEAD, SQUIBB INST MED RES, 80- *Mem:* AAAS; NY Acad Sci; Am Soc Pharmacol & Exp Therapeut. *Res:* Metabolism and function of phosphatides; mechanisms of membrane transport; pharmacokinetics; drug metabolism; biochemical pharmacology. *Mailing Add:* Squibb Inst Med Res PO Box 4000 Princeton NJ 08540

WEINSTOCK, ALFRED, b Toronto, Ont, May 3, 39; m 65. CELL BIOLOGY, PERIODONTOLOGY. *Educ:* Univ Toronto, DDS, 62; Harvard Univ, cert periodont, 66; McGill Univ, PhD(anat), 69. *Prof Exp:* Res fel dent med, Forsyth Dent Ctr, Boston, 62-63; Nat Res Coun Can res fel periodont, Sch Dent Med, Harvard Univ, 63-66; Nat Res Coun Can res fel anat sci, Sch Med, McGill Univ, 66-67, from lectr to asst prof, 67-70; assoc prof, 70-76, chmn sect periodont, 71-74, CLIN PROF DENT & ANAT, SCH DENT & SCH MED, CTR HEALTH SCI, UNIV CALIF, LOS ANGELES, 77-MEM, DENT RES INST, 73- *Concurrent Pos:* Nat Res Coun Can res scholar, Sch Med, McGill Univ, 67-69, Med Res Coun Can res scholar, 69-70; NIH res grant, Univ Calif, Los Angeles, 71-79; consult, Vet Admin Hosp, Brentwood & Sepulveda, Calif, 72-; mem staff, Univ Calif, Los Angeles Med Ctr Hosp, Cedars-Sinai Med Ctr, 76- *Honors & Awards:* Res Award, Can Dent Asn, 71. *Mem:* AAAS; Am Acad Periodont; Am Asn Anatomists; Am Dent Asn; Sigma Xi. *Res:* Structural and functional aspects of secretory cells involved in the elaboration of collagen, enamel and other glycoproteins, mainly in mineralizing tissues; histology; experimental pathology; periodontal disease. *Mailing Add:* Univ of Calif Sch of Dent Ctr for Health Sci Los Angeles CA 90024

WEINSTOCK, BARNET MORDECAI, b Brooklyn, NY, Oct 10, 40; m 66. MATHEMATICS. *Educ:* Columbia Univ, BA, 62; Mass Inst Technol, PhD(math), 66. *Prof Exp:* From instr to asst prof math, Brown Univ, 66-73; assoc prof math, Univ Ky, 73-77; assoc prof, 77-80, PROF MATH, UNIV NC, CHARLOTTE, 80, CHMN DEPT, 81- *Concurrent Pos:* Acting chmn, Univ SC, Charlotte, 80-81. *Mem:* Am Math Soc; Math Asn Am. *Res:* Functional analysis; several complex variables. *Mailing Add:* Dept of Math Univ of NC Charlotte NC 28223

WEINSTOCK, BERNARD, physical chemistry, deceased

WEINSTOCK, HAROLD, b Philadelphia, Pa, Dec 25, 34; m 61; c 2. SOLID STATE PHYSICS, LOW TEMPERATURE PHYSICS. *Educ:* Temple Univ, BA, 56; Cornell Univ, PhD(helium three), 62. *Prof Exp:* From res asst to res assoc physics, Cornell Univ, 56-62; asst prof, Mich State Univ, 62-65; assoc prof, 65-73, PROF PHYSICS, ILL INST TECHNOL, 73-, DIR, EDUC TECHNOL CTR, 79- *Concurrent Pos:* Vis prof, Cath Univ Louvain, 70 & Cath Univ Nijmegen, 72-73; vis staff mem, Los Alamos Sci Lab, 72-; mem staff, Off Naval Res, 79-82. *Mem:* Am Geophys Union; fel Am Phys Soc; Nat Sci Teachers Asn; Am Asn Physics Teachers. *Res:* Thermal and electrical conductivity and specific heat of solids; radiation damage in solids; superconductivity; computer use in science education. *Mailing Add:* Dept of Physics Ill Inst of Technol Chicago IL 60616

WEINSTOCK, IRWIN MORTON, b New York, NY, July 17, 25; m 56; c 3. BIOCHEMISTRY. *Educ:* Univ Okla, BS, 47; Univ Ill, MS, 48, PhD(chem), 51. *Prof Exp:* Res assoc biochem, Dept Psychiat, Med Col, Cornell Univ, 51-57; res assoc, New York Med Col, 57-59; from asst mem to assoc mem, Inst Muscle Dis, 64-74; dir spec neurol lab, Nassau County Med Ctr, 74-80; MEM STAFF, RES TEST LABS INC, 80- *Concurrent Pos:* Lectr, Hunter Col, 53-54 & Columbia Univ, 68-75; adj assoc prof med, Health Sci Ctr, State Univ NY, Stony Brook, 76. *Mem:* AAAS; Harvey Soc. *Res:* Intermediary metabolism and enzymology of muscle wasting conditions. *Mailing Add:* Res Test Labs Inc 44-07 Little Neck Pkwy Little Neck NY 11363

WEINSTOCK, JEROME, b Brooklyn, NY, Sept 12, 33; m 55; c 3. PLASMA PHYSICS, FLUID MECHANICS. *Educ:* Cooper Union, BChE, 55; Cornell Univ, PhD(phys chem), 59. *Prof Exp:* Sr scientist, Nat Bur Standards, 59-65; SR SCIENTIST, NAT OCEANIC & ATMOSPHERIC ADMIN, 65- *Concurrent Pos:* Nat Res Coun-Nat Acad Sci res fel, 59-62; assoc ed, Physics of Fluids; Emil Schweingerg scholarship. *Mem:* Am Phys Soc; Am Geophys Union. *Res:* Statistical mechanics; turbulence theory; transport theory; fluctuation theory; molecular collision theory; basic research in turbulence theory, atmospheric waves, and plasma physics; statistical physics. *Mailing Add:* Plasma Physics Nat Oceanic & Atmospheric Admin Boulder CO 80302

WEINSTOCK, JOSEPH, b New York, NY, Jan 30, 28; m 52; c 10. MEDICINAL CHEMISTRY, PHARMACOLOGY. *Educ:* Rutgers Univ, BS, 49; Univ Rochester, PhD(chem), 52. *Prof Exp:* Res assoc chem, Northwestern Univ, 52-54, instr, 54-56; sr chemist, 56-62, group leader, 62-67, sr investr, 67-76, ASSOC DIR CHEM, SMITH KLINE & FRENCH LABS, 76- *Mem:* AAAS; Am Chem Soc; NY Acad Sci. *Res:* Medicinal and synthetic organic chemistry; organic reaction mechanisms; pteridines; diuretic, anti-inflammatory, antihypertensive agents; drug metabolism and identification of metabolites; dopamine agonists. *Mailing Add:* Chem F31 Smith Kline & French Labs 1500 Spring Garden St Philadelphia PA 19101

WEINSTOCK, LEONARD M, b Passaic, NJ, Jan 30, 27; m 60; c 2. ORGANIC CHEMISTRY. *Educ:* Rutgers Univ, BS, 50; Ind Univ, PhD(chem), 58. *Prof Exp:* DIR PROCESS RES, MERCK & CO, 78- *Mem:* Am Chem Soc. *Res:* Chemistry of heterocyclic compounds and beta-lactam antibiotics. *Mailing Add:* Knickerbocker Dr Belle Mead NJ 08502

WEINSTOCK, MANUEL, b Philadelphia, Pa, Apr 15, 27; m 54; c 3. MECHANICAL ENGINEERING, AERONAUTICAL ENGINEERING. *Educ:* Drexel Inst, BS, 47; Univ Pa, MS, 50. *Prof Exp:* Struct designer, Widdicombe Eng Co, Pa, 47-50; stress analyst, Piasecki Helicopter Corp, 50-51; aeronaut engr, Naval Air Develop Ctr, 51-54; ord engr, Frankford Arsenal, 54-57, supvry ord engr, 57-58, mech engr, 58-62, supvry mech engr, Mech Eng Propellant Actuated Devices Dept, 62-76, SUPVR IND ENG, US ARMY, 76- *Concurrent Pos:* Mem working group design automation, Interagency Chem Rocket Propulsion Group, 63- *Mem:* Am Soc Mech Engrs; Aerospace Med Asn; Sigma Xi. *Res:* Interior ballistics; digital and analog simulation of the performance of propellant actuated devices and complete systems used for emergency escape from military aircraft. *Mailing Add:* USA Arradcom/Lou-P US Army Dover NJ 07801

WEINSTOCK, MELVYN, b Toronto, Ont, Feb 23, 41. BIOLOGICAL STRUCTURE. *Educ:* Univ Toronto, DDS, 64; Harvard Univ, cert, 69; McGill Univ, PhD(anat), 72, Med Res Coun Can, FRCD(C), 78. *Prof Exp:* Clin fel dent med, Forsyth Dent Ctr, 64-65; res fel ortho & biol, Harvard Univ, 65-69; asst prof anat, 72-78, ASSOC PROF ANAT, MCGILL UNIV, 78-, LECTR ORTHOD, 73-, ASST PROF ORTHOD, 75- *Concurrent Pos:* Nat Res Coun fel, Med Res Coun Can, 65-69, Med Res Coun Can scholar, 73-78; Que Med Res Coun scholar, 78-; affil staff mem, Montreal Gen Hosp, 79- *Mem:* Am Asn Anatomists; Am Soc Cell Biol; Int Asn Dent Res; Am Asn Orthodontists; Can Dent Asn. *Res:* Elaboration of collagen and other matrix components of dentin and bone by odontoblasts and osteoblasts as revealed by electron microscope radioautography and freeze fracture techniques. *Mailing Add:* Dept Anat & Orthodontics Strathcona Anat & Dent Bldg Montreal PQ H3A 2B2 Can

WEINSTOCK, ROBERT, b Philadelphia, Pa, Feb 2, 19; m 50; c 2. MATHEMATICAL PHYSICS. *Educ:* Univ Pa, AB, 40; Stanford Univ, PhD, 43. *Prof Exp:* Instr physics, Stanford Univ, 43-44, math, 46-50, actg asst prof, 50-54; res assoc radar countermeasures, Radio Res Lab, Harvard Univ, 44-45; from asst prof to assoc prof math, Univ Notre Dame, 54-59; vis assoc prof, 59-60, assoc prof, 60-66, PROF PHYSICS, OBERLIN COL, 66- *Concurrent Pos:* NSF fel, Oxford Univ, 65-66. *Mem:* AAAS; Am Phys Soc; Am Asn Physics Teachers. *Res:* Mathematical physics; statistical mechanics; calculus of variations. *Mailing Add:* Dept of Physics Oberlin Col Oberlin OH 44074

WEINSWIG, MELVIN H, b Lynn, Mass, Feb 2, 35; m 60; c 3. PHARMACEUTICAL CHEMISTRY. *Educ:* Mass Col Pharm, BS, 55, MS, 57; Univ Ill, PhD(pharmaceut chem), 61. *Prof Exp:* From asst prof to assoc prof pharmaceut chem, Butler Univ, 61-69; assoc dean, 71-76, PROF PHARM & CHMN EXTEN SERV PHARM, SCH PHARM, UNIV WIS-MADISON, 69- *Concurrent Pos:* Consult, Continuing Co, Educ Health Prof. *Mem:* Am Chem Soc; Am Pharmaceut Asn. *Res:* Novel analytical approach to combination pharmaceutical products; drug abuse education and research. *Mailing Add:* Rm 2308 Pharm Bldg Sch of Pharm Univ of Wis Madison WI 53706

WEINTRAUB, BRUCE DALE, b Buffalo, NY, Sept 19, 40; m 68; c 1. ENDOCRINOLOGY, INTERNAL MEDICINE. *Educ:* Princeton Univ, AB, 62; Harvard Med Sch, MD, 66. *Prof Exp:* Intern med, Peter Bent Brigham Hosp, Boston, Mass, 66-67, resident, 67-68; clin assoc endocrinol, Nat Inst Arthritis & Metab Dis, 68-71; instr med, Harvard Med Sch, 71-72; SR INVESTR ENDOCRINOL, NAT INST ARTHRITIS, METAB & DIGESTIVE DIS, 72- *Concurrent Pos:* Clin & res fel, Nat Inst Arthritis & Metab Dis, 68-71; USPHS res grant & asst med, Mass Gen Hosp, Boston, 71-72. *Mem:* Am Fedn Clin Res; Endocrine Soc. *Res:* Structure and properties of hormones secreted by tumors; applications of affinity chromatography to endocrinology; subunits of glycoprotein hormones. *Mailing Add:* Bldg 10 8N 316 Nat Inst of Arthritis Metab & Digestive Dis Bethesda MD 20014

WEINTRAUB, HERBERT D, b New York, NY, Feb 17, 30; m 63; c 3. ANESTHESIOLOGY, MEDICAL EDUCATION. *Educ:* NY Univ, BA, 50; Oxford Univ, MA, 58, BM, BCh, 59. *Prof Exp:* Intern rotating, Strong Mem Hosp, Univ Rochester, 59-61; resident anesthesiol, Columbia Presby Hosp & Med Ctr, New York, 61-63, NIH res fel, 63-64; asst prof, Med Sch, Univ Pa, 64-69; asst prof, Med Sch, Univ Chicago, 69-71; assoc prof, 71-74, dir med educ, Dept Anesthesia, Med Ctr, 71-78, PROF ANESTHESIOL, GEORGE WASHINGTON UNIV, 74-, ASSOC CHMN, DEPT ANESTHESIA, MED CTR, 79-, DIR OPER RM, 76- *Concurrent Pos:* Mem sr staff, Hosp Univ Pa, 64-69; assoc dir, Dept Anesthesiol, Michael Reese Hosp, Chicago, 69-71. *Mem:* Asn Univ Anesthetists; Am Soc Anesthesiol; Int Anesthesia Res Soc; Soc Neurosurg Anesthetists & Neurol Supportive Care; Soc Cardiovascular Anesthesiologists. *Res:* Anesthesia for cardio-thoracic surgery; educational methods as applied to anesthesiology. *Mailing Add:* Dept of Anesthesiol George Washington Univ Med Ctr Washington DC 20037

WEINTRAUB, HERSCHEL JONATHAN R, b Cincinnati, Ohio, Aug 19, 48; m 81. MOLECULAR GRAPHICS, DRUG DESIGN. *Educ:* Case Inst Technol, BS, 70; Case Western Reserve Univ, MS, 73, PhD(macromolecular sci), 75. *Prof Exp:* Res assoc, Dept Med Chem, Purdue Univ, 75-76, dir comput based educ, Sch Pharm, 76-77, asst prof med chem, 77-82; SR PHYS CHEMIST, LILLY RES LABS, ELI LILLY & CO, 82- *Concurrent Pos:* Nat Library Med fel, Dept Comput Sci, Univ Ill, Urbana, 78; prin investr, NIH grants, dept med chem, Purdue Univ, 79-81, adj prof med chem, 82-; consult, various pharmaceut & chem co, 78- *Mem:* Am Chem Soc; Inst Elec & Electronics Engrs; Biophys Soc; Int Soc Quantum Biol. *Res:* Drug design, with emphasis on solution conformational properties of drugs; modeling drug-receptor interactions; development of drug design software systems. *Mailing Add:* Lilly Res Labs Dept MC525 Eli Lilly & Co Bldg 88/1 307 E McCarty St Indianapolis IN 46285

WEINTRAUB, HOWARD STEVEN, b New York, NY, June 6, 43; m 65; c 2. BIOPHARMACEUTICS. *Educ:* Columbia Univ, BS, 66; State Univ NY Buffalo, PhD(biopharmaceut), 71. *Prof Exp:* Sr scientist phys pharm, Ciba-Geigy Corp, 71-73; group leader phys pharm, 73-75, group leader biopharmaceut, 75-77, sect head drug diposition, 77-80, DIR DRUG METAB, ORTHO PHARMACEUT CORP, 80- *Concurrent Pos:* Adj asst prof biopharmaceut, Col Pharmaceut Sci, Columbia Univ, 74-75. *Mem:* AAAS; NY Acad Sci; Am Pharmaceut Asn; Acad Pharmaceut Sci. *Res:* Metabolism and pharmacodynamics of drug substances in man, with emphasis on the mathematical quantitation of these phenomena. *Mailing Add:* Ortho Pharmaceut Corp Rte 202 Raritan NJ 08869

WEINTRAUB, JOEL D, b New York, NY, May 2, 42; m 68; c 2. ANIMAL BEHAVIOR. *Educ:* City Col New York, BS, 63; Univ Calif, Riverside, PhD(zool), 68. *Prof Exp:* Dir environ studies, 72-75, from asst prof to assoc prof, 68-77, PROF ZOOL, CALIF STATE UNIV, FULLERTON, 77- *Mem:* Am Soc Ichthyol & Herpet; Sigma Xi; Ecol Soc Am. *Res:* Ecology of amphibians and reptiles; homing and orientation of vertebrates; urban ecology. *Mailing Add:* Dept of Biol Sci Calif State Univ Fullerton CA 92634

WEINTRAUB, LEONARD, b New York, NY, Apr 21, 26; m 50; c 2. ORGANIC CHEMISTRY, PHARMACEUTICAL CHEMISTRY. *Educ:* City Col New York, BS, 48; Polytech Inst Brooklyn, MS, 54, PhD(org chem), 68. *Prof Exp:* Org chemist, Francis Delafield Hosp, New York, 50-54; org chemist, 54-62, group leader, 62-68, dept head org chem, 68-69, DIR CHEM RES, BRISTOL MYERS CO, 69- *Mem:* AAAS; Am Chem Soc; Royal Soc Chem; NY Acad Sci; Am Pharmaceut Asn. *Res:* Heterocyclic chemistry; molecular complexes in organic chemistry; salicylate chemistry; synthetic methods; pharmaceutical and cosmetic analysis. *Mailing Add:* Bristol Myers Co 1350 Liberty Ave Hillside NJ 07205

WEINTRAUB, LESTER, b New York, NY, Feb 1, 24; m 50; c 2. ORGANIC POLYMER CHEMISTRY. *Educ:* City Col New York, BS, 46; Fordham Univ, MS, 49; NY Univ, PhD(org chem), 54. *Prof Exp:* Sr chemist, Atomic Energy Comn Proj, Columbia Univ, 53-55, group leader, 55-58; group leader, Adv Res Proj Agency Proj, NY Univ, 58-59; sr chemist, Cent Res Labs, Air Reduction Co, Inc, NJ, 59-71; group leader polymer res, 71-73, TECH MGR RESINS, PANTASOTE CO, INC, 73- *Mem:* Am Chem Soc; Am Inst Chem; Soc Plastics Eng. *Res:* Organic polymer synthesis and structure determination; polyvinyl chloride technology. *Mailing Add:* 8 Tarlton Dr Livingston NJ 07039

WEINTRAUB, LEWIS ROBERT, b New York, NY, Aug 15, 34; m 67; c 2. HEMATOLOGY. *Educ:* Dartmouth Col, AB, 55; Harvard Med Sch, MD, 58. *Prof Exp:* Intern med, Hosp, Univ Pa, 58-59; asst resident res in med, Hosp, Univ Mich, 59-61; fel hemat, Mt Sinai Hosp, New York, 61-62; res hematologist, Walter Reed Army Inst Res, 62-65; from asst prof to assoc prof med, Sch Med, Tufts Univ, 65-72; ASSOC PROF MED, SCH MED, BOSTON UNIV, 72- *Concurrent Pos:* Asst chief hemat, Walter Reed Gen Hosp, 62-65; asst hematologist & asst physician, New Eng Med Ctr Hosps, 65-72; assoc vis physician, Boston Univ Hosp, 72- *Mem:* AAAS; AMA; Am Soc Hemat. *Res:* Clinical hematology and research in field of iron metabolism. *Mailing Add:* 75 E Newton Boston MA 02118

WEINTRAUB, MARVIN, b Radom, Poland, Oct 17, 24; nat Can; m 48; c 4. PLANT VIROLOGY. *Educ:* Univ Toronto, BA, 47, PhD(bot), 50. *Prof Exp:* Demonstr bot, Univ Toronto, 45-50; prin res scientist & head virus chem & physiol sect, Res Br, Can Dept Agr, 50-71, DIR, RES STA, AGR CAN, 71- *Concurrent Pos:* Hon prof, Univ BC, 71- *Mem:* AAAS; Am Phytopath Soc; Can Phytopath Soc; fel NY Acad Sci; Int Soc Plant Morphol. *Res:* Metabolism and cytology of virus-infected plants; fine structure and electron microscopy; virus inhibitors; movement in plants. *Mailing Add:* Res Sta Agr Can 6660 NW Marine Dr Vancouver BC V7W 2S9 Can

WEINTRAUB, PHILIP MARVIN, b Cleveland, Ohio, Feb 22, 39; m 61; c 3. ORGANIC CHEMISTRY. *Educ:* Ohio State Univ, BSc, 60, MSc, 63, PhD(chem), 64. *Prof Exp:* Res chemist, Pioneering Res Lab, Textile Fibers Dept, E I du Pont de Nemours & Co, Inc, 64-66; sr chemist, Hess & Clark, 66-70, SR CHEMIST, MERRELL-DOW PHARMACEUTICALS, 70- *Mem:* Am Chem Soc; NY Acad Sci. *Res:* Steroids; heterocycles; strained ring polycyclic systems; prostaglandins. *Mailing Add:* Org Chem Dept Merrell-Dow Pharmaceuticals 2110 E Galbraith Cincinnati OH 45215

WEINTRAUB, ROBERT LOUIS, b Washington, DC, May 9, 12; m 38; c 3. PLANT & CELL PHYSIOLOGY. *Educ:* George Washington Univ, BS, 31, MA, 33, PhD(plant physiol), 38. *Prof Exp:* Biochemist, Div Radiation & Organisms, Smithsonian Inst, 37-47; supvry plant physiologist, Army Biol Labs, Ft Detrick, 47-59, phys sci adminr, Army Gen Staff, 59-63; prof bot, 63-77, EMER PROF BOT, GEORGE WASHINGTON UNIV, 77- *Concurrent Pos:* Plant physiologist, Smithsonian Radiation Biol Lab, 66-76; lectr bot, NC State Univ, 79- *Mem:* AAAS; Am Chem Soc; Am Inst Biol Sci; Am Soc Plant Physiol; Sigma Xi. *Res:* Effects of radiant energy on plants; plant growth regulators; microbial physiology. *Mailing Add:* 408 Brooks Ave Raleigh NC 27607

WEINTRAUB, SOL, b Luxembourg, July 3, 37; US citizen; m 60; c 3. MATHEMATICS. *Educ:* City Col New York, BS, 58; Temple Univ, MA, 60, PhD(physics), 64. *Prof Exp:* Sr mathematician, Appl Data Res, Inc, 60-65; asst prof, 65-73, assoc prof, 73-82, PROF MATH, QUEENS COL, NY, 82- *Concurrent Pos:* Consult, Appl Data Res, Inc, 65-67. *Mem:* Asn Comput Mach; Am Math Soc. *Res:* Computational mathematics; number theory; statistics. *Mailing Add:* Dept of Math Queens Col Flushing NY 11367

WEINZIMMER, FRED, b New York, NY, May 29, 25; m 47; c 2. NUCLEAR ENGINEERING, MECHANICAL ENGINEERING. *Educ:* Clarkson Col Technol, BME, 50; Polytech Inst Brooklyn, MME, 55. *Prof Exp:* Draftsman diesel design, US Dept Navy, NY, 43; engr, Am Gas & Elec Co, 50-51; asst proj engr, R R Popham, 51-52; engr, Ebasco Serv, Inc, 52-54; systs engr, Bettis Plant, Westinghouse Elec Corp, 54-55, lead systs engr, 55-56; systs tech supvr, Atomic Power Equip Dept, Gen Elec Co, 56-57, lead systs engr, 57-62, specialist, Vallecitos Exp Superheat Reactor Prog & Design, 62-65, prin engr, ECPL proj, 65-66, mgr proj anal, 67, proj mgr, Shoreham Proj, 67-71, proj mgr, Nine Mile Pt Unit 2, 71-74, proj mgr, Nuclear Energy Div, Somerset 1 & 2 Proj, 74-76, proj mgr, BWRSD-High Flow Hydraul Facil, 76-78, proj mgr, NPD-Clinton 1 & 2 Proj, 78-81; DIR, PROJ ENG, GPU NUCLEAR, PARSIPPANY, NJ, 81- *Res:* Major nuclear power plant design, layout and construction for utility application. *Mailing Add:* 28 Puddingstone Dr Boonton NJ 07005

WEINZWEIG, AVRUM ISRAEL, b Toronto, Ont, Apr 22, 26; m 53, 63; c 5. MATHEMATICS. *Educ:* Univ Toronto, BASc, 50; Harvard Univ, AM, 53, PhD(math), 57. *Prof Exp:* Res physicist, Weizmann Inst, 48-49; asst chief geophysicist, Weiss Geophys Corp, 50-52; instr math, Univ Calif, Berkeley, 57-59, actg asst prof, 59-60; asst prof, Northwestern Univ, 60-65; ASSOC PROF MATH, UNIV ILL, CHICAGO CIRCLE, 65- *Concurrent Pos:* Consult, Solomon Schechter Day Schs, Ill. *Mem:* Am Math Soc; Math Asn Am; Math Soc France. *Res:* Algebraic topology, particularly fiber spaces; category theory; learning theory; learning and acquisition of mathematical concepts; mathematics education. *Mailing Add:* Dept of Math Univ of Ill Chicago Circle Box 4348 Chicago IL 60680

WEIPERT, EUGENE ALLEN, b Monroe, Mich, Nov 17, 31; m 60; c 8. INDUSTRIAL ORGANIC CHEMISTRY. *Educ:* Univ Detroit, BS, 52, MS, 54; Iowa State Univ, PhD(org chem), 57. *Prof Exp:* Res supvr, Wyandotte Chem Corp, Mich, 58-72; tech mgr, Southern Sizing Co, 72-82; LAB MGR, MAZER CHEM CO, 82- *Res:* Alkylene oxides, amines; organometallics; organic reaction mechanisms; surfactants. *Mailing Add:* 3938 Porett Dr Mazer Chem Co Gurnee IL 60031

WEIR, ALEXANDER, JR, b Crossett, Ark, Dec 19, 22; m 46; c 3. CHEMICAL ENGINEERING. *Educ:* Univ Ark, BSChE, 43; Polytech Inst Brooklyn, MChE, 46; Univ Mich, PhD, 54. *Prof Exp:* Analyst, W Bauxite Plant, Am Cyanamid & Chem Corp, Ark, 41, chemist, Berger Plant, 42, chem engr, Stanford Res Labs, Am Cyanamid Co, Conn, 43-47; from asst to proj supvr, Aircraft Propulsion Lab, Univ Mich, 48-57, lectr chem & metall eng, 54-56, asst prof, 56-58; from consult to asst mgr, Atlas Prog Off, Space Tech Labs, Ramo-Wooldridge Corp, 56-60; corp sr sci & tech adv res & develop mgt, Northrop Corp, 60-67, dir plans & progs, Corp Labs, 67-70; prin scientist air qual, 70-76, MGR CHEM SYSTS RES & DEVELOP, SOUTHERN CALIF EDISON CO, 76- *Mem:* AAAS; Am Geophys Union; Am Chem Soc; Combustion Inst; Am Inst Chem Engrs. *Res:* Effects of beta radiation on combustion; spectroscopic investigation of flames, temperatures and compositions behind detonation waves; flow through sonic orifices; location of Mach discs in supersonic jets; development of sulfur dioxide and nitrogen oxide removal systems for electric generating stations; fluegas desulferization; coal gasification (cool water project); solar central thermal power (solar one); solar salt ponds. *Mailing Add:* Southern Calif Edison Co PO Box 800 Rosemead CA 91770

WEIR, C EDITH, nutrition, food technology, see previous edition

WEIR, DONALD DOUGLAS, b Sussex, Wis, June 27, 28; m 48; c 3. INTERNAL MEDICINE. *Educ:* Drake Univ, BA, 48; Univ Iowa, MD, 53. *Prof Exp:* Intern med, Philadelphia Gen Hosp, 53-54; from asst resident to resident, Johns Hopkins & Baltimore City Hosps, 54-57; fel, Johns Hopkins Hosp, 57-58; from instr to assoc prof med, Sch Med, Univ NC, Chapel Hill, 58-69; med dir rehab ctr, St Luke's Methodist Hosp, 69-78; clin assoc prof rehab med, Col Med, Univ Iowa, 69-78; MED DIR REGIONAL REHAB CTR, PITT MEM HOSP, 78-; PROF REHAB MED & CHMN DEPT, SCH MED, E CAROLINA UNIV, 78- *Concurrent Pos:* Attend physician, Hosp Univ Iowa, 69-78; consult, Vet Admin Hosp, Iowa City & Iowa Soldiers Home, Marshalltown, Iowa, 69-78. *Mem:* AAAS; Am Rheumatism Asn; AMA. *Res:* Rheumatology; chronic illness and patient care; rehabilitation. *Mailing Add:* Regional Rehab Ctr Pitt Mem Hosp Greenville NC 27834

WEIR, EDWARD EARL, II, b St Petersburg, Fla, Mar 9, 45. ENVIRONMENTAL CHEMISTRY. *Educ:* Ga Inst Technol, BS, 67; Fla State Univ, PhD(biochem), 72. *Prof Exp:* Res assoc biochem, Fla State Univ, 67-72; res assoc oncol, Univ Ala, 72-73, instr biochem, 73-74; res assoc oncol, Johns Hopkins Hosp, 74-77; anal lab mgr & qual asurance coordr, Hittman Assocs, 77-81; ANAL QUAL ASSURANCE COORDR, STANDARD LABS, 82- *Concurrent Pos:* Fels, NIH, 72-74, Am Cancer Soc, 74-76 & USPHS, 76-77. *Res:* Quality assurance coordinator as well as laboratory manager for organic and inorganic analytical laboratories dealing in coal, synthetic fuels, water and other media; computer programs dealing with data reduction,d ata base (particularly quality assurance), cost analysis and purchasing; biochemical ecology and pesticide fate and effects. *Mailing Add:* Rt 5 Box 408 Dade City FL 33525

WEIR, JAMES HENRY, III, b East Orange, NJ, Sept 25, 32; m 58; c 3. MEDICAL RESEARCH. *Educ:* Princeton Univ, AB, 54; Columbia Univ, MD, 58. *Prof Exp:* From med res assoc to dir med serv, 63-75, DIR MED RES, WARNER-LAMBERT CO, 75-, VPRES REGULATORY & MED AFFAIRS, 81. *Concurrent Pos:* Macy teaching fel obstet-gynec, Col Physicians & Surgeons, Columbia Univ, 62-63. *Mem:* Am Fertil Soc; Am Fedn Clin Res; Sigma Xi. *Res:* Clinical investigation of new drugs and instrumentation devices; administration of government regulatory affairs and medical affairs. *Mailing Add:* Warner-Lambert Co 201 Tabor Rd Morris Plains NJ 07950

WEIR, JAMES ROBERT, JR, b Middletown, Ohio, Dec 29, 32; m 52; c 5. METALLURGICAL ENGINEERING. *Educ:* Univ Cincinnati, BS, 55; Univ Tenn, MS, 61. *Prof Exp:* Metallurgist, 55-57, 59-60, group leader metall, 60-66, asst sect chief, 67-70, sect chief, 70-73, DIR, METALS & CERAMICS DIV, OAK RIDGE NAT LAB, 73- *Honors & Awards:* E O Lawrence Award, Atomic Energy Comn, 73. *Mem:* Fel Am Soc Metals; fel AAAS. *Res:* High-temperature properties of metals; fatigue; radiation damage in metals, fuel element design. *Mailing Add:* Metals & Ceramics Div Oak Ridge Nat Lab PO Box X Oak Ridge TN 37830

WEIR, JOHN ARNOLD, b Saskatoon, Sask, Apr 5, 16; nat US; m 46; c 2. GENETICS. *Educ:* Univ Sask, BSA, 37; Iowa State Col, MS, 42, PhD(genetics), 48. *Prof Exp:* Asst animal breeding, Dom Exp Sta, Alta, 37-40; instr, Univ Sask, 42, assoc prof animal husb, 48-50; from asst prof to assoc prof, 50-62, PROF GENETICS, UNIV KANS, 62- *Concurrent Pos:* Consult, Animal Resources Adv Comt, USPHS, 64-67; USPHS spec fel & hon res assoc hist sci, Harvard Univ, 66-67. *Mem:* Genetics Soc Am; Am Genetic Asn. *Res:* Mammalian genetics; sex ratio and behavior of mice; history of genetics; history of aeronautics. *Mailing Add:* Hall Lab of Mammalian Genetics Div of Biol Univ of Kans Lawrence KS 66045

WEIR, ROBERT JAMES, JR, b Washington, DC, Nov 26, 24; m 47; c 3. TOXICOLOGY. *Educ:* Univ Md, College Park, BS, 48, MS, 50, PhD, 55. *Prof Exp:* Asst physiol, Univ Md, 48-51; res assoc toxicol, Hazleton Labs, Va, 51-56, head agr chem dept, 56-58, res applns specialist, 58-62, dir, Hazleton Labs, SA, Lausanne, Switz, 62-65, vpres, Inst Indust & Biol Res, Cologne, Ger, 63-66, vpres, Mkt, Hazleton Labs, Va, 67-69; VPRES, LITTON BIONETICS, INC, 69- *Mem:* AAAS; Am Chem Soc (secy-treas, Agr & Food Div, 67-68); Soc Cosmetic Chemists; Environ Mutagen Soc; Soc Toxicol. *Res:* Toxicology; biochemistry; pharmacology; safety evaluation of drug, cosmetic, food chemical and pesticide development. *Mailing Add:* Litton Bionetics Inc 5516 Nicholson Lane Kensington MD 20795

WEIR, RONALD DOUGLAS, b St John, NB, Jan 10, 41; m 63; c 2. PHYSICAL CHEMISTRY, MATERIALS SCIENCE. *Educ:* Univ NB, BSc, 63; Univ London, DIC & PhD, 66. *Prof Exp:* Nat Res Coun Can fel, 66-68, asst prof chem eng, 68-75, assoc prof, 75-81, PROF CHEM ENG, ROYAL MIL COL CAN, 81- *Concurrent Pos:* Sr vis inorganic chem, Oxford Univ, 78-79. *Mem:* Chem Inst Can; Can Soc Chem Engrs; fel Royal Soc Chem; Am Soc Eng Educ. *Res:* Thermodynamic properties and orientational disorder in crystals; low temperature calorimetry; heats of mixing; dielectrics; equations of state and intermolecular forces. *Mailing Add:* Dept of Chem & Chem Eng Royal Mil Col Can Kingston ON K7L 2W3 Can

WEIR, WILLIAM CARL, b Lakeview, Ore, Aug 24, 19; m 46; c 2. ANIMAL NUTRITION. *Educ:* Ore State Col, BS, 40; Univ Wis, MS, 41, PhD(animal husb, biochem), 48. *Prof Exp:* Asst, Univ Wis, 45-46, instr, 47; assoc prof animal sci, Ore State Col, 48; from asst prof to prof, 48-73, dean students, 58-65, prof nutrit & chmn dept, 73-81, ASSOC PROG DIR, SMALL RUMINANT PROG, UNIV CALIF, DAVIS, 81- *Concurrent Pos:* Fulbright res grant, Univ Western Australia, 65-66; mem comt sheep nutrit, Nat Acad Sci-Nat Res Coun; vis scientist & Univ Calif rep, Univ Chile-Univ Calif Coop Prog, Santiago, Chile, 70-72. *Mem:* Am Soc Animal Sci; Soc Range Mgt; Am Inst Nutrit; Soc Nutrit Educ. *Res:* Sheep nutrition; sheep and goat management. *Mailing Add:* Dept of Nutrit Univ of Calif Davis CA 95616

WEIR, WILLIAM DAVID, b Oakland, Calif, Mar 15, 41; c 2. PHYSICAL CHEMISTRY. *Educ:* Occidental Col, AB, 62; Princeton Univ, AM, 63, PhD(chem), 65. *Prof Exp:* Instr chem, Harvard Univ, 65-68; asst prof, 68-71, ASSOC PROF CHEM, REED COL, 71- *Concurrent Pos:* Consult, indust & govt. *Mem:* Am Chem Soc; Electrochem Soc; Asn Comput Machinery; Inst Elec & Electronics Engrs. *Res:* Chemical kinetics; kinetics and mechanisms of electrochemical reactions and dynamics of membrane function; relaxation methods; instrumentation and computation in chemical research; theoretical protein dynamics; computer graphics and interactive modelling applications in chemistry. *Mailing Add:* Dept of Chem Reed Col Portland OR 97202

WEIR, WILLIAM THOMAS, b Wildwood, NJ, Dec 23, 31; m 54; c 4. SYSTEMS ENGINEERING, OPERATIONS RESEARCH. *Educ:* Drexel Univ, BSEE, 54, MS, 58; Univ Pa, PhD(systms eng, opers res), 72. *Prof Exp:* Component engr elec eng, RCA Corp, 54-56; mgr syst eng, Gen Elec Co, 56-73; PRES & CHMN BD DIRS, EVAL ASSOCS, INC, 73- *Concurrent Pos:* Adj prof physics, Drexel Univ, 58-, adj prof eng mgt, 63-; mem, US Sci Deleg, Peoples Repub China, 79. *Mem:* Sr mem Inst Elec & Electronics Engrs (vpres); Oper Res Soc Am. *Res:* Reliability. *Mailing Add:* Eval Assocs Inc 1 Belmont Ave Bala Cynwyd PA 19004

WEIRES, RICHARD WILLIAM, JR, b Faribault, Minn, Feb 3, 44; m 67; c 2. FRUIT ENTOMOLOGY. *Educ:* Bowling Green State Univ, BA, 66, MA, 68; Univ Minn, PhD(entom), 72. *Prof Exp:* Res fel, Univ Minn, 72-74; res assoc, 74-75, asst prof, 75-81, ASSOC PROF, HUDSON VALLEY LAB, CORNELL UNIV, 81- *Concurrent Pos:* Consult, Fundacion Chile, 79- *Mem:* Sigma Xi; Entom Soc Am; Int Orgn Biol Control. *Res:* Applied insect ecology; practical insect and mite control programs for pome fruit crops. *Mailing Add:* Hudson Valley Lab NY State Agr Exp Sta PO Box 727 Highland NY 12528

WEIRICH, WALTER EDWARD, b Saginaw, Mich, Nov 20, 38; m 60; c 2. VETERINARY SURGERY. *Educ:* Mich State Univ, BS, 61, DVM, 63; Univ Wis, MS, 70, PhD(vet sci, cardiol), 71; Am Col Vet Surgeon, dipl, 78. *Prof Exp:* Officer in chg, Vet Corps, US Army, 63-65; pract vet, Madison Vet Clin, 65-68; NIH fel cardiol, Univ Wis-Madison, 68-71; from asst prof to assoc prof cardiol & surg, 71-75, actg head dept cardiol & surg, 75-76, HEAD DEPT SMALL ANIMAL CLIN, SCH VET MED, PURDUE UNIV, WEST LAFAYETTE, 76-, PROF CARDIOL & SURG, 78- *Concurrent Pos:* Mem cardiol comt, Am Animal Hosp Assoc, 73-; rev, J Am Vet Med Asn. *Mem:* Am Vet Med Asn; Am Acad Vet Cardiol; Am Asn Vet Med Cols. *Res:* Hypothermia for cardiac arrest surgery; myocardial infarctions and vascular surgery in the canine. *Mailing Add:* Dept of Small Animal Clin Sch of Vet Med Purdue Univ West Lafayette IN 47907

WEIRICH, GUNTER FRIEDRICH, b Eisenach, Ger, Feb 17, 34; m 68. INSECT ENDOCRINOLOGY. *Educ:* Univ Munich, PhD(zool), 63. *Prof Exp:* Res assoc endocrinol, Philipps Univ, Marburg, Ger, 64-65; res fel insect physiol, Biol Div, Oak Ridge Nat Lab, 65-66; res assoc endocrinol, Philipps Univ, 66-70; sr scientist biol chem, Zoecon Corp, 70-73; res assoc biol chem, Tex A&M Univ, 73-77; RES ENTOMOLOGIST BIOL CHEM, BELTSVILLE AGR RES CTR-EAST, USDA, 77- *Mem:* AAAS; Ger Soc Biol Chem. *Res:* Transport and metabolism of insect hormones. *Mailing Add:* Insect Physiol Lab Bldg 467 Beltsville Agr Res Ctr-East USDA Beltsville MD 20705

WEIS, DALE STERN, b Cleveland, Ohio, Oct 11, 24; m 70; c 2. MICROBIOLOGY, PROTOZOOLOGY. *Educ:* Western Reserve Univ, BS, 45, MS, 51; Yale Univ, PhD, 55. *Prof Exp:* Instr bact, Albertus Magnus Col, 53-54; res assoc plant physiol, Univ Minn, 55-57; res assoc biochem, Univ Chicago, 57-58; from instr to asst prof biol, Univ Col, 58-64; chmn natural sci 2, Shimer Col, 64-66; from asst prof to assoc prof, 66-77, PROF BIOL, CLEVELAND STATE UNIV, 77- *Concurrent Pos:* Charles F Kettering fel, Univ Minn, 55-57. *Mem:* AAAS; Soc Protozool; Am Soc Microbiol; Am Soc Cell Biol. *Res:* Metabolism of algae; symbiosis; host-symbiote interaction; cell-cell interaction and recognition during infection. *Mailing Add:* Dept of Biol Cleveland State Univ Cleveland OH 44115

WEIS, JERRY SAMUEL, b Salina, Kans, Dec 23, 35; m 61; c 3. BIOLOGY. *Educ:* Kans Wesleyan Univ, AB, 58; Univ Kans, MA, 60, PhD(bot), 64. *Prof Exp:* Asst prof biol, Univ Minn, 64-65; NIH fel biol, Yale Univ, 65-66; asst prof, 66-71, asst dir div biol, 69-73, ASSOC PROF BIOL, KANS STATE UNIV, 72-, ASSOC DIR DIV BIOL, 75- *Mem:* AAAS; Inst Soc Ethics & Life Sci; Am Asn of Higher Educ. *Res:* Bioethics. *Mailing Add:* Div Biol Kans State Univ Manhattan KS 66506

WEIS, JUDITH SHULMAN, b New York, NY, May 29, 41; m 62; c 2. DEVELOPMENTAL BIOLOGY, AQUATIC BIOLOGY. *Educ:* Cornell Univ, BA, 62; NY Univ, MS, 64, PhD(biol), 67. *Prof Exp:* Lectr biol, Hunter Col, 64-67; asst prof, 67-71, assoc prof, 71-76, PROF ZOOL, RUTGERS UNIV, NEWARk, 76- *Concurrent Pos:* Rutgers Res Coun grant, 67-76, NJ sea grant, Nat Oceanic & Atmospheric Admin, 77- *Mem:* Am Soc Zoologists; Am Inst Biol Sci; Soc Develop Biol; Am Fisheries Soc; Asn Women Sci. *Res:* limb regeneration; marine biology; effects of pollutants on aquatic animals; ecology. *Mailing Add:* Dept Zool & Physiol Rutgers Univ Newark NJ 07102

WEIS, LEONARD WALTER, b New York, NY, June 23, 23; m 55; c 2. GEOLOGY. *Educ:* Harvard Univ, SB, 43; Mass Inst Technol, SM, 47; Univ Wis, PhD(geol), 65. *Prof Exp:* Res observer, Blue Hill Meteorol Observ, 43; asst meteorol, Mass Inst Technol, 44-47; instr geol & geog, Univ RI, 47-49; asst prof geol & actg chmn dept, Coe Col, 53-54; asst prof, Lawrence Univ, 55-65; ASST PROF GEOL, UNIV WIS CTR-FOX VALLEY, 65- *Mem:* Am Meteorol Soc; Geol Soc Am; Am Geophys Union; Geochem Soc; NY Acad Sci. *Res:* Igneous and metamorphic petrology; glacial geology, including petrography of sediments; paleoclimatology; meteorological instruments and observations. *Mailing Add:* Dept of Geol Univ Wis Ctr-Fox Valley Menasha WI 54952

WEIS, PAUL LESTER, b Chicago, Ill, June 22, 22; m 45, 69; c 2. GEOLOGY. *Educ:* Univ Wis, BS, 47, PhD(geol), 52. *Prof Exp:* Geologist, US Geol Surv, 50-51; asst prof geol, Univ Va, 51-53; geologist, US Geol Surv, 53-81; RETIRED. *Mem:* Am Inst Prof Geologists; fel Geol Soc Am; Soc Econ Geol. *Res:* Mineral resources; areal geology of northwestern United States; graphite commodity geology; metallic mineral deposits in sedimentary rocks. *Mailing Add:* S 5106 Sunward Dr Spokane WA 99203

WEIS, PEDDRICK, b South Paris, Maine, June 4, 38; m 62; c 2. ANATOMY, EMBRYOLOGY. *Educ:* NY Univ, DDS, 63. *Prof Exp:* NSF res fel, 63-64; instr anat, Col Dent, NY Univ, 64-67; from asst prof to assoc prof, 67-78, PROF ANAT, NJ MED SCH, UNIV MED & DENT NJ, 78- *Mem:* AAAS; Am Asn Anat; Electron Micros Soc Am; Soc Develop Biol. *Res:* Ultrastructural and cytochemical effects of environmental pollutants, especially heavy metals; effects of pollutants on nervous system development and behavior. *Mailing Add:* Dept Anat NJ Med Sch Univ Med & Dent of NJ Newark NJ 07103

WEIS, ROBERT E(DWARD), b Ark, May 11, 18; m 48; c 4. CHEMICAL ENGINEERING. *Educ:* Univ Cincinnati, MS, 41. *Prof Exp:* Asst chem eng, Univ Cincinnati, 40-41; asst chem engr, Phillips Petrol Co, 41-42, assoc chem engr, 42-43, master chem engr, 43-44, sr chem engr, 44-48, pilot plant mgr, 48-51, asst supt, Philtex Exp Sta, 51, supt, 51-53, mgr, Bartlesville Develop Pilot Plant, 53-60, asst to mgr, Process Develop Div, 60-61, systs eng adminr, 61-63, mgr, Process Optimization Br, 63-68; dir, Process Optimization Dept, Appl Automation, Inc, 68-77; res & develop proj coordr, Phillips Petrol Co, Bartlesville, 77-82. *Mem:* AAAS; Am Chem Soc; Am Inst Chem Engrs. *Res:* Process optimization; development and application of digital computer systems with on-line instrumentation and control to test, model, evaluate, and optimize operations and profitability of complex petroleum and chemical processes. *Mailing Add:* Phillips Res Ctr Phillips Petrol Co Bartlesville OK 74004

WEISBACH, JERRY ARNOLD, b New York, NY, Dec 23, 33; m 58; c 3. ORGANIC CHEMISTRY, MEDICINAL CHEMISTRY. *Educ:* Brooklyn Col, BS, 55; Harvard Univ, MA, 56, PhD(chem), 59. *Prof Exp:* Sr med chemist, Smith Kline & French Labs, 60-65, group leader, 65-67, assoc dir chem, 67-71, assoc dir res, US Pharmaceut Prod, 71-75, dep dir res, 75-77, vpres res, 77-79; PRES, PARKE DAVIS PHARMACEUT RES DIV, WARNER LAMBERT CORP, 79-, VPRES, WARNER LAMBERT CORP, 81- *Concurrent Pos:* Sect ed, Ann Reports Med Chem. *Mem:* AAAS; Am Chem Soc; Acad Pharmaceut Sci; NY Acad Sci; Am Soc Microbiol. *Res:* Structure, isolation and synthesis of natural products, particularly antibiotics, alkaloids and lipids; organic biochemistry and synthetic medicinal chemistry. *Mailing Add:* Parke Davis Pharmaceut Res Div Warner Lambert Corp2800 Plymouth Rd Ann Arbor MI 48105

WEISBART, MELVIN, b Toronto, Ont, Dec 28, 38; m 63; c 3. COMPARATIVE ENDOCRINOLOGY, COMPARATIVE PHYSIOLOGY. *Educ:* Univ Toronto, BSc, 61, MA, 63; Univ BC, PhD(physiol), 67. *Prof Exp:* Nat Res Coun Can fel, Fisheries Res Bd Can, 68-69; asst prof biol, Wayne State Univ, 69-76; asst prof, 76-77, ASSOC PROF BIOL, ST FRANCIS XAVIER UNIV, 77- *Concurrent Pos:* Fac res award, Wayne State Univ, 70. *Mem:* AAAS; Am Soc Zoologists; Can Soc Zoologists; Sigma Xi; Am Physiol Soc. *Res:* Fish physiology and endocrinology. *Mailing Add:* Dept Biol Campus Box 136 Antigonish NS B2G 1C0 Can

WEISBECKER, HENRY B, b Kassel, Ger, July 20, 25; US citizen; m 72. ELECTRICAL ENGINEERING. *Educ:* Pratt Inst, BEE, 45; NY Univ, MEE, 48; Munich Tech Univ, Dr Ing(elec eng), 57. *Prof Exp:* Sr engr, A B Dumont Labs, 50-51; sr engr, W L Maxson Corp, 52-54; sr engr, Simmonds Aerocessories, 54-58; dir res elec eng, Manson Labs, Conn, 58-59; dir res elec eng, Loral, Inc, 60; sr prin engr, Litton Industs, 60-66; ASSOC PROF ELEC ENG, NJ INST TECHNOL, 66- *Concurrent Pos:* Independent consult engr. *Mem:* Sr mem Inst Elec & Electronics Engrs. *Res:* Transistors; servos; infrared techniques; communications. *Mailing Add:* 712 Tenth St Union City NJ 07087

WEISBERG, HERBERT, b New York, NY, June 30, 31. MEDICINE. *Educ:* City Col New York, BS, 53; Univ Lausanne, MD, 58. *Prof Exp:* From instr to asst prof med, NY Med Col-Flower & Fifth Ave Hosp, 64-71, assoc prof anat & med, 71-76; PRECEPTOR FAMILY MED, UNIV CALIF, DAVIS, 77- *Concurrent Pos:* USPHS trainee gastroenterol, NY Med Col-Flower & Fifth Ave Hosp, 62-64, USPHS spec fel electron micros, 66-68; vis prof, Sch Med, NY Univ, 71. *Mem:* Am Fedn Clin Res; Am Gastroenterol Asn. *Res:* Intracellular pathway of absorption for nutrients in the intestine, especially vitamin B-12. *Mailing Add:* 510 Cypress St Ft Bragg CA 95437

WEISBERG, HERBERT IRA, b New York, NY, Mar 9, 44. STATISTICS. *Educ:* Columbia Univ, BA, 65; Harvard Univ, MA, 66, PhD(statist), 70. *Prof Exp:* Asst prof statist, NY Univ, 69-72; SR RES ASSOC, HURON INST, 72- *Concurrent Pos:* Vis lectr statist, Univ Kent, 71-72; lectr statist, Boston Univ, 74- *Mem:* Am Statist Asn; Biomet Soc; Am Educ Res Asn. *Res:* Social research methodology; design and analysis of social program evaluations; data analysis; statistical inference; analysis of data on child development, child abuse and education. *Mailing Add:* Huron Inst 119 Mt Auburn St Cambridge MA 02138

WEISBERG, HOWARD LOUIS, b Cleveland, Ohio, Nov 12, 39; m 65; c 2. PHYSICS. *Educ:* Calif Inst Technol, BS, 60; Brandeis Univ, PhD(physics), 65. *Prof Exp:* Physicist, Univ Calif, Berkeley, 65-70, NSF fel, 65-67; asst prof physics, Univ Pa, 70-76; PHYSICIST, BROOKHAVEN NAT LAB, 77- *Mem:* AAAS; Am Phys Soc. *Res:* Experimental elementary particle physics. *Mailing Add:* Accelerator Dept Brookhaven Nat Lab Upton NY 11973

WEISBERG, JOSEPH SIMPSON, b Jersey City, NJ, June 7, 37; m 64; c 2. OCEANOGRAPHY, METEROLOGY. *Educ:* Jersey City State Col, BA, 60; Montclair State Col, MA, 64; Columbia Univ, EdD(earth sci educ), 69. *Prof Exp:* Teacher pub schs, NJ, 60-64; PROF GEOSCI, JERSEY CITY STATE COL, 60-, CHMN DEPT, 73- *Concurrent Pos:* Sci consult, US Off Educ, 68-69; adv, NJ Dept Environ Protection, 75- *Honors & Awards:* Award Merit, US Environ Protection Agency, 78. *Mem:* AAAS; Geol Soc Am; Am Meteorol Soc; Nat Asn Geol Teachers; Nat Sci Teachers Asn. *Res:* Use of visual aids in science teaching; inquiry and learning; environmental aspects of the geosciences; author of various works on oceanography and meteorology. *Mailing Add:* Dept of Geosci Jersey City State Col Jersey City NJ 07305

WEISBERG, ROBERT H, b Brooklyn, NY, May 20, 47. PHYSICAL OCEANOGRAPHY. *Educ:* Cornell Univ, BS, 69; Univ RI, MS, 72, PhD(phys oceanog), 75. *Prof Exp:* Res asst, Grad Sch Oceanog, Univ RI, 69-74, res assoc phys oceanog, 74-76; PROF, DEPT MARINE, EARTH & ATMOSPHERIC SCI, NC STATE UNIV, 76- *Mem:* Am Geophys Union; Am Meteorol Soc. *Res:* Estuarine and equatorial circulation. *Mailing Add:* Dept Marine Earth & Atmospheric Sci NC State Univ PO Box 5923 Raleigh NC 27650

WEISBERG, SANFORD, US citizen. APPLIED STATISTICS. *Educ:* Univ Calif, AB, 69; Harvard Univ, AM, 70, PhD(statist), 73. *Prof Exp:* ASSOC PROF APPL STATIST, UNIV MINN, ST PAUL, 72- *Mem:* Am Statist Asn; Inst Math Statist; Biomet Soc; Royal Statist Soc. *Res:* Data analysis and methods; linear models, categorical models; statistical computing. *Mailing Add:* Dept of Appl Statist Univ of Minn St Paul MN 55108

WEISBERG, STANLEY HERBERT, dermatology, see previous edition

WEISBERG, STEPHEN BARRY, b New York, NY, Apr 19, 54. POPULATION BIOLOGY, ICHTHYOLOGY. *Educ:* Univ Mich, BGS, 74; Univ Del, PhD(biol), 81. *Prof Exp:* Res asst nutrient dynamics, Univ Del, 77-80; instr ecol & wildlife biol, West Chester State Col, 80-81; RES SCIENTIST FISH ECOL, MARTIN MARIETTA ENVIRON CTR, 81- *Mem:* Ecol Soc Am; Am Soc Zoologists; Am Fisheries Soc; Atlantic Estuarine Res Soc; Estuarine Res Fedn. *Res:* Population dynamics and feeding ecology of freshwater and estuarine fish; impacts of fish feeding on population dynamics of prey species. *Mailing Add:* Martin Marietta Environ Ctr 1450 S Rolling Rd Baltimore MD 21227

WEISBERGER, WILLIAM I, b New York, NY, Dec 20, 37; m 61; c 3. THEORETICAL HIGH ENERGY PHYSICS. *Educ:* Amherst Col, BA, 59; Mass Inst Technol, PhD(physics), 64. *Prof Exp:* Res assoc physics, Stanford Linear Accelerator Ctr, 64-66; asst prof, Princeton Univ, 66-70; PROF PHYSICS, STATE UNIV NY STONY BROOK, 70- *Concurrent Pos:* Sloan Found fel, 67-69; vis scientist, Weizmann Inst Sci, 68-69 & 74-75; Guggenheim fel, 74-75; vis prof, Univ Wash, 78-79. *Mem:* Fel Am Phys Soc; AAAS. *Mailing Add:* Inst Theoret Physics State Univ of NY at Stony Brook Stony Brook NY 11794

WEISBLAT, DAVID IRWIN, b Coshocton, Ohio, Aug 11, 16; m 42; c 3. ORGANIC CHEMISTRY. *Educ:* Ohio State Univ, AB, 37, PhD(org chem), 41. *Hon Degrees:* Dr Med, Karolinska Inst, Stockholm, Sweden, 80. *Prof Exp:* Asst org chem, Ohio State Univ, 37-41, res assoc & Hoffmann-La Roche fel, Res Found, 41-43; res chemist, Nutrit Div, 43-45, chem group leader, 45-47, sect leader, Chem Div, 47-50, head chem dept, 50-52, asst dir res, 52-56, dir chem res, 56-62, dir biochem res, 62-68, VPRES PHARMACEUT RES & DEVELOP, UPJOHN CO, 68-, MEM, BD DIRS, 73- *Concurrent Pos:* Investr, Tech Indust Intel Comt, Fed Repub Ger. *Mem:* AAAS; Am Chem Soc. *Res:* Chemistry of simple carbohydrates, heparin, synthetic vitamins and amino acids; steroids and antibiotics; prostaglandin chemistry and clinical application. *Mailing Add:* 11185 Hawthorne Galesburg MI 49053

WEISBORD, NORMAN EDWARD, b Jersey City, NJ, Oct 1, 01; m 39. GEOLOGY, INVERTEBRATE PALEONTOLOGY. *Educ:* Cornell Univ, AB, 23, MS, 26. *Prof Exp:* Paleontologist & geologist, Atlantic Refining Co, 23-32; sr field geologist, Standard Oil Co, Arg, 32-34; sr geologist & asst chief geologist, Standard-Vacuum Oil Co, 34-42; chief geologist, Socony-Vacuum Oil Co, Venezuela, 42-57; res assoc, 57-65, PROF GEOL, FLA STATE UNIV, 65- *Concurrent Pos:* Instr, Cornell Univ, 26; trustee, Paleont Res Inst, 51-63, vpres, 57-59, pres, 59-61; consult, Mobil Oil Corp. *Mem:* Fel AAAS; fel Geol Soc Am; fel Am Geog Soc; fel Sigma Xi; Paleont Res Inst. *Res:* Conchology; invertebrate paleontology; stratigraphy; taxonomy and distribution of the barnacles Cirripedia and corals Scleractinia of Florida; taxonomy and distribution of acrothoracican, rhizocephalan and scalpellid barnacles of Florida and surrounding waters; taxonomy and stratigraphy of Paleocene and Eocene barnacles of Alabama. *Mailing Add:* PO Box 1082 Tallahassee FL 32302

WEISBROD, ALAN RICHARD, vertebrate zoology, evolutionary biology, see previous edition

WEISBRODT, NORMAN WILLIAM, b Cleves, Ohio, June 30, 42; m 65; c 3. PHYSIOLOGY, PHARMACOLOGY. *Educ:* Univ Cincinnati, BS, 65; Univ Mich, Ann Arbor, PhD(pharmacol), 70. *Prof Exp:* USPHS res fel, Univ Iowa, 70-71; from instr to asst prof physiol, 71-75, ASSOC PROF PHYSIOL & PHARMACOL, UNIV TEX MED SCH HOUSTON, 75- *Concurrent Pos:* Fel, Univ Iowa, 70-71; assoc prof, Univ Tex Grad Sch Biomed Sci, 71-; res scientist develop, Nat Inst Drug Abuse, 76-81; assoc ed, Am J Physiol, 77-80. *Mem:* Am Asn Clin Res; Am Physiol Soc; Soc Exp Biol & Med; Am Gastroenterol Asn. *Res:* Smooth muscle physiology and pharmacology; gastrointestinal motility. *Mailing Add:* 12210 Charing Cross Dr Houston TX 77031

WEISBROT, DAVID R, b Brooklyn, NY, Dec 29, 31; m 60; c 2. POPULATION GENETICS. *Educ:* Brooklyn Col, BS, 53, MA, 58; Columbia Univ, PhD(zool), 63. *Prof Exp:* Substitute instr biol, Brooklyn Col, 56-58; res asst genetics, Univ Conn, 58-59 & Long Island Biol Asn, 59-60; instr biol, City Col New York, 60-62; fel genetics, Univ Calif, Berkeley, 63-64; asst prof biol, Tufts Univ, 64-69; assoc prof, State Univ NY Binghamton, 69-72; assoc prof, 72-78, PROF BIOL, WILLIAM PATERSON COL, NJ, 78- *Concurrent Pos:* Adj assoc prof, Columbia Univ, 76- *Mem:* AAAS; Genetics Soc Am; Am Genetic Asn; Am Soc Human Genetics. *Res:* Genotypic interactions among competing strains of Drosophila; relationship of genetic and morphological differences among sibling species. *Mailing Add:* 1103 Sussex Rd Teaneck NJ 07666

WEISBROTH, STEVEN H, b New York, NY, Sept 16, 34; m 58; c 3. LABORATORY ANIMAL MEDICINE, COMPARATIVE PATHOLOGY. *Educ:* Cornell Univ, BS, 58; Wash State Univ, MS, 60, DVM, 64; Am Col Lab Animal Med, dipl. *Prof Exp:* NIH fel lab animal med, NY Univ Med Ctr, 64-66; asst prof path & dir animal facilities, Rockefeller Univ, 66-69; asst prof path & dir, Dept Lab Animal Med, State Univ NY Stony Brook, 69-70, assoc prof path & dir, Div Lab Animal Resources, 70-78; PRES, ANIMAL MED LABS, INC, 70- *Concurrent Pos:* NIH fel lab animal med, Rockefeller Univ, 69-; mem coun, Am Asn Accreditation of Lab Animal Care, 75-79. *Honors & Awards:* Res award, Am Asn Lab Animal Sci, 72. *Mem:* Am Vet Med Asn; Am Asn Lab Animal Sci; Am Soc Exp Path. *Res:* Spontaneous diseases in laboratory animals. *Mailing Add:* Animal Med Labs Inc 1804 Plaza Ave New Hyde Park NY 11040

WEISBURGER, ELIZABETH KREISER, b Greenlane, Pa, Apr 9, 24; m 47; c 3. ONCOLOGY, TOXICOLOGY. *Educ:* Lebanon Valley Col, BS, 44; Univ Cincinnati, PhD(org chem), 47. *Prof Exp:* Res assoc, Univ Cincinnati, 47-49; res fel, 49-51, res org chemist, Biochem Lab, 51-61, carcinogen screening sect, 61-72, chief, Carcinogen Metab & Toxicol Br, 73-78, chief, Lab Carcinogen Metab, 78-81, ASST DIR CHEM CARCINOGEN, DIV CANCER CAUSE & PREVENTION, NAT CANCER INST, 81- *Concurrent Pos:* Asst chief ed, J Nat Cancer Inst, 71- *Honors & Awards:* Hillebrand Prize & Garvan Medal, Am Chem Soc, 81. *Mem:* AAAS; Am Asn Cancer Res; Am Chem Soc; Royal Soc Chem; Soc Toxicol. *Res:* Metabolism of chemical carcinogens, carcinogen testing, chemical carcinogenesis and toxicology. *Mailing Add:* 5309 McKinley St Bethesda MD 20814

WEISBURGER, JOHN HANS, b Stuttgart, Ger, Sept 15, 21; nat US; c 3. BIOCHEMICAL PHARMACOLOGY, ONCOLOGY. *Educ:* Univ Cincinnati, AB, 47, MS, 48, PhD(org chem), 49; Umea Univ, Sweden, MD, 80. *Prof Exp:* Fel, Nat Cancer Inst, 49-50, head phys-org chem unit, Lab Biochem, 50-61, head carcinogen screening sect, 61-72, dir bioassay segment, 71-72; VPRES RES, AM HEALTH FOUND, 72- *Concurrent Pos:* Mem biochem & nutrit rev panel, NIH, 58-59, mem interdept tech panel on carcinogens, 62-71, chmn subcomt, Nat Cancer Progs Strategic Plan, 71-74, chmn carcinogenesis group, Nat Large Bowel Cancer Proj, 72-75; mem expert panel nitrites & nitrosamines, USDA, 73-77; res prof path, New York Med Col, 73- Assoc ed, J Nat Cancer Inst, 60-62; assoc ed, Cancer Res, 69-76, ed, Arch Toxicol, 75- *Honors & Awards:* Nat Defense Serv Medal, USPHS, 64 & Meritorious Serv Medal, 70. *Mem:* Am Asn Cancer Res; Am Soc Biol Chemists; Am Soc Pharmacol & Exp Therapeut; Soc Exp Biol & Med; Soc Toxicol. *Res:* Etiology of cancer, mechanisms of carcinogenesis; bioassay and metabolism of carcinogens and drugs; host factors in cancer induction; nutrition, endocrinology, immunology, cancers of the endocrine, digestive and excretory organs; preventive medicine. *Mailing Add:* Am Health Found Naylor Dana Inst for Dis Prev Valhalla NY 10595

WEISE, CHARLES MARTIN, b Bridgeville, Pa, July 8, 26; m 51; c 5. POPULATION ECOLOGY, ORNITHOLOGY. *Educ:* Ohio Univ, BS, 50; Univ Ill, MS, 51, PhD(zool), 56. *Prof Exp:* Asst prof biol, Fisk Univ, 53-56; from asst prof to assoc prof, 56-66, PROF ZOOL, UNIV WIS-MILWAUKEE, 66-, CHMN DEPT, 78- *Mem:* AAAS; Cooper Ornith Soc; Wilson Ornith Soc; Am Soc Zoologists; Am Ornith Union. *Res:* Annual Physiological and reproductive cycles in birds; field ornithology; animal populations and population ecology. *Mailing Add:* Dept of Zool Univ of Wis-Milwaukee Milwaukee WI 53201

WEISE, JURGEN KARL, b Nov 7, 37; US citizen; m 64; c 3. POLYMER CHEMISTRY, ORGANIC CHEMISTRY. *Educ:* Univ Bonn, BS, 60; Polytech Inst Brooklyn, PhD(polymer chem), 66. *Prof Exp:* Ger Res Asn fel chem, Univ Mainz, 66-67; res chemist, Central Res Dept, E I du Pont de Nemours & Co, 67-71, res chemist, Elastomer Chem Dept, 71-77; MGR RES LAB, BOSTIK TECH CTR, EUROPE, 77- *Mem:* Am Chem Soc. *Res:* Reactions of polymers; polymer structures and their effects on properties; ring-opening polymerization; fluoro-polymers; specialty elastomers; adhesives and sealants development. *Mailing Add:* Bostik Tech Ctr Europe PO Box 528 Taunus Oberursel D637 West Germany

WEISEL, GEORGE FERDINAND, JR, b Missoula, Mont, Mar 21, 15; m 50; c 2. ZOOLOGY. *Educ:* Univ Mont, BS, 41, MA, 42; Univ Calif, Los Angeles, PhD(zool), 49. *Prof Exp:* Asst zool, Univ Mont, 41-42, Univ Mich, 42-43 & Scripps Inst Oceanog, Univ Calif, San Diego, 47-48; from instr to assoc prof comp anat & gen zool, 47-69, PROF COMP ANAT & ICHTHYOL, UNIV MONT, 69- *Mem:* Am Soc Ichthyol & Herpet; Am Soc Zoologists. *Res:* Anatomy, histology, sex organs, life histories, osteology and endocrinology of fish. *Mailing Add:* Dept of Zool Univ of Mont Missoula MT 59812

WEISENBERG, RICHARD CHARLES, b Columbus, Ohio, Apr 2, 41. CELL BIOLOGY. *Educ:* Univ Calif, Santa Barbara, BA, 63; Univ Chicago, PhD(biophys), 68. *Prof Exp:* USDA trainee, Brandeis Univ, 68-70; asst prof, 71-73, ASSOC PROF BIOL, TEMPLE UNIV, 73- *Concurrent Pos:* Investr, Marine Biol Lab, Woods Hole, 71- *Mem:* Am Soc Cell Biol. *Res:* Cell division and motility; biochemistry of microtubules. *Mailing Add:* Dept of Biol Temple Univ Philadelphia PA 19122

WEISENBORN, FRANK L, b Portland, Ore, Feb 26, 25; m 45; c 4. ORGANIC CHEMISTRY. *Educ:* Reed Col, BA, 45; Univ Wash, PhD(chem), 49. *Prof Exp:* AEC fel, Harvard Univ, 49-50, USPHS fel, 50-51; sr res chemist, Riker Labs, Inc, 51-53; res assoc, Univ Calif, Los Angeles, 53; sr res chemist, 53-59, from res assoc to sr res assoc, 59-63, dir org chem, 63-81, DIR SCI INFO, SQUIBB INST MED RES, E R SQUIBB & SONS, INC, 81- *Concurrent Pos:* Chmn, Gordon Res Conf Natural Prod, 75-76. *Mem:* Am Chem Soc; Royal Soc Chem; Swiss Chem Soc. *Res:* Structure and synthesis of antibiotics, steroids and alkaloids; natural and synthetic hypotensive agents; computer assisted molecular modeling. *Mailing Add:* Dept of Org Chem E R Squibb & Sons PO Box 4000 Princeton NJ 08540

WEISER, ALAN, b Houston, Tex, July 16, 55; m 78. NUMERICAL ANALYSIS. *Educ:* Rice Univ, BA, 76; Yale Univ, MS, 77, PhD(comput sci), 81. *Prof Exp:* RES MATHEMATICIAN, EXXON PROD RES CO, 81- *Mem:* Soc Indust & Appl Math; Am Math Soc. *Res:* Theoretical and applied work on adaptive methods for the computer solution of elliptic partial differential equations. *Mailing Add:* 2475 Underwood #377 Houston TX 77030

WEISER, CONRAD JOHN, b Middlebury, Vt, June 20, 35. PLANT STRESS PHYSIOLOGY. *Educ:* NDak State Univ, BS, 57; Ore State Univ, PhD(hort), 60. *Prof Exp:* Asst prof, Hort Dept, Univ Minn, 61-63, assoc prof, 63-66, prof, 66-73; PROF HORT & DEPT HEAD, ORE STATE UNIV, 73- *Honors & Awards:* Alex Laurie Award, Am Soc Hort Sci, 66, J H Gourley Award, 73. *Mem:* Fel Am Soc Hort Sci (vpres, 79-80, pres-elect, 79-80, pres, 80-81); Am Soc Plant Physiol; Soc Cryobiology; Am Asn Adv Sci; Coun Agr Sci Tech. *Res:* Crop stress physiology, plant freezing injury and physiological responses which permit plants to acclimate in response to environmental stimuli. *Mailing Add:* Dept Hort Ore State Univ Corvallis OR 97331

WEISER, DANIEL, b St Louis, Mo, July 10, 33; m 54; c 4. MATHEMATICS. *Educ:* Rice Univ, BA, 54, MA, 56, PhD(math), 58. *Prof Exp:* Asst math, Rice Univ, 57-58; sr res mathematician, Field Res Lab, Mobil Res & Develop Co, 58-77, STATISTICIAN, MOBIL EXPLOR & PROD SERV, INC, 77- *Mem:* Soc Indust & Appl Math. *Res:* Applied mathematics and political science. *Mailing Add:* 3851 Rugged Circle Dallas TX 75224

WEISER, DAVID W, b Omaha, Nebr, Sept 13, 21; m 42; c 3. INORGANIC CHEMISTRY. *Educ:* Drury Col, AB, 42; Univ Chicago, MS, 47, PhD(chem), 56. *Prof Exp:* Asst prof chem, Drake Univ, 50-51; from instr to asst prof natural sci, Univ Chicago, 51-57; dean fac, Shimer Col, 57-63, chmn dept natural sci, 64-67; vis prof chem, Cornell Univ, 67-68; ASSOC PROF CHEM, STATE UNIV NY STONY BROOK, 69-, DIR CTR CURRICULUM DEVELOP, 68- *Concurrent Pos:* Consult & examr, NCent Asn Cols & Univs, 58-; NSF res fel, Yale Univ, 63-64; dir, Ctr Curriculum Develop, State Univ NY Stony Brook, 69-70; instr math, Wyandanch Col, 70-72. *Mem:* Am Chem Soc; Am Educ Res Asn. *Res:* Behavior of the aquocobaltic ion; nature of solutions with ionic solutes; epistemology and history of chemistry; science education. *Mailing Add:* Dept of Chem State Univ of NY Stony Brook NY 11794

WEISER, HERMAN JOSHUA, JR, b Harrisburg, Pa, Dec 9, 24; m 47; c 2. ANALYTICAL CHEMISTRY. *Educ:* Lebanon Valley Col, BS, 47; Univ Cincinnati, MS, 49, PhD(chem), 51. *Prof Exp:* ANAL GROUP LEADER, PROCTER & GAMBLE CO, 51- *Mem:* Am Chem Soc. *Res:* Thermal analysis; gas chromatography of fats, oils and related materials; analysis of detergent raw materials and products. *Mailing Add:* Procter & Gamble Co 6110 Center Hill Ave Cincinnati OH 45224

WEISER, KURT, b Vienna, Austria, Dec 24, 24; US citizen; m 57; c 3. PHYSICS. *Educ:* Harvard Univ, BA, 49; Cornell Univ, PhD(phys chem), 54. *Prof Exp:* Mem tech staff, RCA, 54-58 & T J Watson Ctr, IBM Corp, 58-73; PROF DEPT ELEC ENG & DIR, SOLID STATE INST, TECHNION, 73- *Mem:* Fel Am Phys Soc. *Res:* Solid state physics with emphasis on semiconductors. *Mailing Add:* Solid State Inst Technion Haifa Israel

WEISER, MARY ANN, b Savannah, Ga, Apr 13, 56; m 78. ULTRASONICS, APPLIED MECHANICS. *Educ:* Univ SC, BS, 76; Yale Univ, MS, 77, PhD(appl mech), 81. *Prof Exp:* RES ENGR, EXXON PROD RES CO, 81- *Mem:* Acoust Soc Am; Soc Petrol Engrs; Soc Women Engrs. *Res:* Development and application of techniques and procedures for measuring the chemical and physical properties of colloidal suspensions used in drilling (otherwise referred to as drilling fluids). *Mailing Add:* 2475 Underwood #377 Houston TX 77030

WEISER, PHILIP CRAIG, b Portland, Ore, Oct 26, 41; m 66; c 1. PHYSIOLOGY. *Educ:* Univ Wash, BS, 63; Univ Minn, MS, 67, PhD(physiol), 69. *Prof Exp:* Adj prof biol, Univ Colo, Boulder, 70-76; clin asst prof prev med, Med Ctr, Univ Colo, Denver, 76-80; dir, Dept Physiol, Nat Asthma Ctr, Denver, 77-80; PROG DIR, COMMUNITY FITNESS CTR, INST HEALTH EDUC, WHEAT RIDGE COLO, 80- *Concurrent Pos:* Res physiologist, Physiol Div, Med Res & Nutrit Lab, Fitzsimons Army Med Ctr, Med Serv Corps, US Army, 68-71, chief mil performance br, 71-73; res fel, Cardiovasc Pulmonary Res Lab, Med Ctr, Univ Colo, Denver, 73-75; res fel, Dept Clin Physiol, Nat Asthma Ctr, Denver, 75-76. *Mem:* AAAS; Am Physiol Soc; Am Thoracic Soc; Am Col Sports Med. *Res:* Biological adaptation to stress, particularly the psychophysiological factors limiting physical performance in normoxic and hypoxic environments. *Mailing Add:* Inst Health Educ 8400 W 38th Ave Wheat Ridge CO 80033

WEISER, ROBERT B(RUCE), b Ashley, Ohio, July 19, 27; m 53, 72; c 5. CHEMICAL ENGINEERING, ORGANIC CHEMISTRY. *Educ:* Ohio State Univ, BS & MS, 51, PhD, 54. *Prof Exp:* Res engr, Exp Sta, Polychem Dept, Del, 54-58, RES ENGR, RES & DEVELOP LAB, WASHINGTON WORKS, E I DU PONT DE NEMOURS & CO, INC, 58- *Concurrent Pos:* Lectr, Marietta Col, 61- *Mem:* Am Inst Chem Engrs. *Res:* Reaction kinetics; diffusional operations; fluid mechanics. *Mailing Add:* 1 Fox Hill Dr Parkersburg WV 26101

WEISER, RUSSELL SHIVLEY, b Grimes, Iowa, Sept 28, 06; m 31; c 1. BACTERIOLOGY, IMMUNOLOGY. *Educ:* NDak Col, BS, 30, MS, 31; Univ Wash, PhD(bact), 34. *Prof Exp:* Assoc bact & path, 34-36, from instr to assoc prof & actg exec officer, 36-45, assoc prof microbiol, 45-49, prof, 49-77, EMER PROF IMMUNOL, SCHS MED & DENT, UNIV WASH, 77- *Concurrent Pos:* Mem leprosy res panel, US-Japan Coop Med Sci Prog. *Mem:* Am Asn Immunologists; Reticuloendothelial Soc; Brit Soc Immunol; Transplantation Soc. *Res:* Immunology of syphilis; immunology of cancer; immunologic tissue injury; macrophages; cell-mediated immunity. *Mailing Add:* 5741 60th Ave NE Seattle WA 98105

WEISFEILER, BORIS, b Moscow, USSR, Apr 19, 41; US citizen. ALGEBRAIC GROUPS, LIE ALGEBRAS. *Educ:* Moscow State Univ, AB & MS, 63; Steklow Math Inst, PhD(math), 70. *Prof Exp:* Sr researcher comput, Inst Control Probs, Moscow, 68-74; asst math, Inst Advan Study, Princeton Univ, 75-76; assoc prof, 76-81, PROF MATH, PA STATE UNIV, 81- *Mem:* Am Math Soc. *Res:* Theory of algebraic groups; lie algebras, primarily in positive characteristics. *Mailing Add:* McAllister Bldg University Park PA

WEISGERBER, DAVID WENDELIN, b Delphos, Ohio, May 20, 38; m 65; c 2. INFORMATION SCIENCE. *Educ:* Bowling Green State Univ, BS, 60; Univ Ill, PhD(org chem), 65. *Prof Exp:* Chemist res, E I du Pnt de Nemours & Co, Inc, 64-69; assoc indexer, 69-71, group leader compound name data base, 71-72, sr indexer, 72-73, asst to ed, 73-77, mgr chem substance handling, 77-79, DIR ED OPERS, CHEM ABSTRACTS SERV, 79- *Mem:* Am Chem Soc; NY Acad Sci. *Res:* Synthetic organic chemistry; chemical nomenclature; scientific information storage and retrieval. *Mailing Add:* Chem Abstracts Serv PO Box 3012 Columbus OH 43210

WEISGERBER, GEORGE AUSTIN, b Philadelphia, Pa, Dec 31, 18; m 47; c 2. PETROLEUM CHEMISTRY. *Educ:* Philadelphia Col Pharm, BSc, 40; Univ Del, MSc, 50, PhD(org chem), 51. *Prof Exp:* Res chemist, Johnson & Johnson, NJ, 40-48; from res chemist to sr chemist, Esso Res & Eng Co, 51-60, from res assoc to sr res assoc, 60-74, SR RES ASSOC, EXXON RES & ENG CO, 74- *Mem:* Am Chem Soc; Tech Asn Pulp & Paper Indust; Am Soc Testing & Mat. *Res:* Petroleum product research; additives, burner fuels, industrial and motor lubricants; wax; asphalt. *Mailing Add:* Exxon Res & Eng Co PO Box 51 Linden NJ 07036

WEISGRABER, KARL HEINRICH, b Norwich, Conn, July 13, 41; m 64; c 2. ORGANIC CHEMISTRY, BIOCHEMISTRY. *Educ:* Univ Conn, BA, 64, PhD(org chem), 69. *Prof Exp:* Staff fel, Nat Inst Arthritis & Metab Dis, 69-70 & Nat Res Coun Res Assoc, USDA, Calif, 70-71; prin scientist, Meloy Labs, Va, 71-72; sr staff fel, Nat Heart & Lung Inst, 72-81. *Mem:* Am Chem Soc; The Chem Soc; NY Acad Sci. *Res:* Experimental atherosclerosis; study of serum lipoproteins; mechanism of transport of serum constituents across aortic endothelium. *Mailing Add:* 1018 Rudgear Rd Walnut Creek CA 94596

WEISHAUPT, CLARA GERTRUDE, b Lynchburg, Ohio, July 20, 98. BOTANY. *Educ:* Ohio State Univ, BS, 24, MS, 32, PhD, 35. *Prof Exp:* Asst bot, Ohio State Univ, 32-35; from asst to assoc prof sci, Ala State Teachers Col, 35-46; instr, 46-51, cur herbarium, 49-67, from asst prof to assoc prof, 51-68, EMER ASSOC PROF BOT, OHIO STATE UNIV, 68- *Mem:* Am Soc Plant Taxon; Int Asn Plant Taxon. *Res:* Grasses of Ohio. *Mailing Add:* 328 N Maple Ave Fairborn OH 45324

WEISHEIT, JON CARLETON, b Mt Vernon, Wash, Oct 10, 44; m 65; c 2. ATOMIC PHYSICS, ASTROPHYSICS. *Educ:* Univ Tex, El Paso, BS, 66; Rice Univ, MS, 69, PhD(physics), 70. *Prof Exp:* Res fel astron, Harvard Univ, 70-72, lectr astron, 71-72; physicist, Lawarence Livermore Nat Lab, Univ Calif, 72-79, group leader atomic physics, 78-79; res physicist, plasma physics lab, Princeton Univ, 79-81, lectr astron, 80-81; STAFF SCIENTIST, LAWRENCE LIVERMORE NAT LAB, 81- *Mem:* Am Phys Soc; Am Astron Soc; Int Astron Union. *Res:* Atomic processes in laboratory and cosmic plasmas; physics of the interstellar medium and gaseous nebulae; spectra of galaxies and quasars. *Mailing Add:* Lawrence Livermore Nat Lab PO Box 808 Livermore CA 94550

WEISIGER, JAMES RICHARD, b Oakwood, Ill, Jan 5, 18; m 44; c 2. BIOCHEMISTRY. *Educ:* Univ Ill, AB, 38, MA, 39; Johns Hopkins Univ, PhD(physiol chem), 43. *Prof Exp:* Spec investr, Rockefeller Inst, 45, from asst to assoc, 46-56; prof assoc, Nat Acad Sci-Nat Res Coun, 56-61; sci rep, Richardson-Merrell, Inc, 61-62; METAB PROG DIR, NAT INST ARTHRITIS, METAB & DIGESTIVE DIS, 63-, DIR DIABETES, 80- *Concurrent Pos:* Fel, Harvard Med Sch, 42-45. *Mem:* Am Soc Biol Chemists. *Res:* Organic and biological chemistry of nitrogen compounds; isolation, structure and synthesis of natural products; metabolic regulation; polyamine metabolism; pharmaceuticals; biologicals; cystic fibrosis and genetic metabolic diseases. *Mailing Add:* Extramural Prog Nat Inst of Arthritis Metab & Digestive Dis NIH Westwood Bldg Rm 620 Bethesda MD 20014

WEISLEDER, DAVID, b New York, NY, Sept 30, 39; c 1. ORGANIC CHEMISTRY, NUCLEAR MAGNETIC RESONANCE. *Educ:* City Col New York, BS, 61; Univ Cincinnati, PhD(chem), 66. *Prof Exp:* RES CHEMIST, NORTHERN REGIONAL RES CTR, SCI & EDUC ADMIN-AGR RES, USDA, 66- *Mem:* Am Chem Soc. *Res:* Nuclear magnetic resonance spectroscopy of natural products and their derivatives or analogs. *Mailing Add:* 1815 N University St Peoria IL 61604

WEISLER, LEONARD, b Rochester, NY, Sept 9, 12; m 42; c 4. ORGANIC CHEMISTRY. *Educ:* Univ Rochester, BS, 34, MS, 36, PhD(org chem), 39. *Prof Exp:* Asst, Univ Rochester, 35-38; anal chemist, Distillation Prod, Inc, 42-53; org res & develop chemist, Paper Serv Div, Eastman Kodak Co, 53-78; RETIRED. *Concurrent Pos:* Sr lectr chem, Univ Rochester, 54-; adj prof chem, Monroe Community Col, Rochester, NY, 79- *Mem:* Am Chem Soc. *Res:* Alkylation of nitro compounds; chemistry and biochemistry of vitamin E; synthesis of A; fats, oils and hydrocarbons; metallurgy; photographic chemistry. *Mailing Add:* 6 Eastland Ave Rochester NY 14618

WEISLOW, OWEN STUART, b Cleveland, Ohio, Mar 11, 38. IMMUNOLOGY, MICROBIOLOGY. *Educ:* Delaware Valley Col Sci & Agr, BS, 65; Thomas Jefferson Univ, MS, 68, PhD(microbiol), 70. *Prof Exp:* Fel immunol, Albert Einstein Med Ctr, Philadelphia, 70-71; fel immunol & virol, Thomas Jefferson Univ, 71-73, instr, 73-74; assoc found scientist immunol, Southwest Found Res & Educ, 74-76; scientist III, 76-80, SR SCIENTIST IMMUNOL, FREDERICK CANCER RES CTR, LITTON BIONETICS INC, 80- *Mem:* Am Soc Microbiol; AAAS; Am Asn Immunologists. *Res:* Immunobiology of oncogenic viruses; tumor immunology; regulation of cell proliferation. *Mailing Add:* Litton Bionetics Inc Frederick Cancer Res Ctr Frederick MD 21701

WEISMAN, GARY RAYMOND, b Cincinnati, Ohio, Apr 17, 49; m 71; c 2. ORGANIC CHEMISTRY, PHYSICAL CHEMISTRY. *Educ:* Univ Ky, BS, 71; Univ Wis, PhD(org chem), 76. *Prof Exp:* Res chemist org chem, Univ Calif, Los Angeles, 76-77; ASST PROF ORG CHEM, UNIV NH, 77- *Concurrent Pos:* Prin investr, Petrol Res Found grant, 78-81 & res corp grant, 79- *Mem:* Am Chem Soc; Sigma Xi. *Res:* Organic host guest chemistry; conformational analysis; applications of nuclear magnetic resonance; structure and chemistry of radical ions; organic electrochemistry and electron spin resonance in mechanistic investigations. *Mailing Add:* Dept Chem Univ NH Durham NH 03824

WEISMAN, HAROLD, b Brooklyn, NY, Oct 24, 28; m; c 2. ANESTHESIOLOGY. *Educ:* Univ Calif, Los Angeles, BA, 52, DO, 56, MD, 62. *Prof Exp:* Intern, Pac Hosp, Long Beach, Calif, 56-57; pvt pract gen med, 57-66; resident anesthesia, 66-68, asst prof in residence surg anesthesia, 69-71, ASST PROF ANESTHESIOL, SCH MED, UNIV CALIF, LOS ANGELES, 71- *Concurrent Pos:* Parke-Davis grant, 70; McNeil Labs grant, 71; secy-treas, Community Hosp North Hollywood, Calif, 59-61, from asst chief of staff to chief of staff, 61-63; mem consult staff, Bel Air Mem Hosp, 68, Valley Presby Hosp, Van Nuys, 68-69, Vet Admin Wadsworth Gen Hosp, 71 & Mt Sinai Hosp, Los Angeles, 72-; mem fac, Jules Stein Eye Inst. *Honors & Awards:* Physicians Recognition Award, AMA, 69. *Mem:* AMA; AAAS; Am Soc Anesthesiologists; Int Anesthesia Res Soc; fel Am Col Anesthesiologists. *Res:* Effect of various anesthetic agents on the oculocardiac reflex; effect of general anesthetics on intraocular pressure; retinal artery flow during anesthesia and surgery; determination of damage to retina with Doppler microwave energy output in New Zealand albino rabbits exposed chronically. *Mailing Add:* 4159 Adlon Pl Encino CA 91436

WEISMAN, HARVEY, b Winnipeg, Man, Feb 25, 27; m 57; c 2. HISTOLOGY, NEUROPHARMACOLOGY. *Educ:* Univ Man, BSc, 53, MSc, 55, PhD(histol), 69. *Prof Exp:* Lectr zool, 58-65, asst prof, 65-72, ASSOC PROF PHARMACOL, FAC MED, UNIV MAN, 72-, SPEC LECTR PEDIAT, 71- *Mem:* Can Asn Anatomists. *Res:* Histological, cytological and biochemical reorganization of the central nervous system in mammals as a result of psychopharmacological drugs; histopathology of primary and secondary cardiomyopathics; pathological effects of maternal smoking on fetal growth and health. *Mailing Add:* Dept of Pharmacol & Therapeut Univ of Man Fac of Med Winnipeg MB R3T 2N2 Can

WEISMAN, JOEL, b New York, NY, July 15, 28; m 55. CHEMICAL ENGINEERING, NUCLEAR ENGINEERING. *Educ:* City Col New York, BChE, 48; Columbia Univ, MS, 49; Univ Pittsburgh, PhD, 68. *Prof Exp:* Chem engr, Etched Prod Corp, NY, 50-51; assoc chem engr, Brookhaven Nat Lab, 51-54; from engr to sr engr, Atomic Power Dept, Westinghouse Elec Corp, 54-57, supvry engr, 58-59; sr engr, Nuclear Develop Corp Am, NY, 59-60; fel engr, Atomic Power Dept, Westinghouse Elec Corp, Pa, 60-66, mgr thermal & hydraulic anal, 67-68; from asst prof to assoc prof, 68-72, PROF NUCLEAR ENG, UNIV CINCINNATI, 72- *Mem:* Fel Am Nuclear Soc; Am Inst Chem Engrs. *Res:* Nuclear power reactor technology; experimental heat transfer and fluid flow; design of large scale experiments; system optimization. *Mailing Add:* Dept Chem & Nuclear Eng Univ Cincinnati Cincinnati OH 45221

WEISMAN, ROBERT A, b Kingston, NY, Dec 16, 36; m 63; c 3. BIOCHEMISTRY. *Educ:* Union Univ, NY, BS, 58; Mass Inst Technol, PhD(biochem), 63. *Prof Exp:* Staff fel biochem, Sect Cellular Physiol, Lab Biochem, Nat Heart Inst, 63-66; asst prof biochem, Med Col Pa, 66-68; from asst prof to assoc prof, 68-74, prof biochem, Univ Tex Health Sci Ctr San Antonio, 74-77; PROF BIOCHEM & CHMN DEPT, SCH MED & COL SCI & ENG, WRIGHT STATE UNIV, 77-, DIR, BIOMED SCI PHD PROG, 81- *Mem:* Am Soc Biol Chemists. *Res:* Endocytosis and differentiation mechanisms; biochemistry of protozoa. *Mailing Add:* Dept of Biochem Wright State Univ Sch of Med Dayton OH 45435

WEISMAN, RUSSELL, b Cleveland, Ohio, Jan 20, 22; m 47; c 4. MEDICINE, HEMATOLOGY. *Educ:* Western Reserve Univ, AB, 44, MD, 46. *Prof Exp:* Res fel med, 52-54, instr, 54-55, sr instr clin med & path, 55-57, asst prof, 57-63, assoc prof, 63-80, PROF MED, CASE WESTERN RESERVE UNIV, 80- *Mem:* AAAS; Am Soc Hemat; Am Fedn Clin Res. *Res:* Hemolytic anemia; immunohematology; relation of the spleen and blood destruction. *Mailing Add:* Dept of Med Case Western Reserve Univ Cleveland OH 44106

WEISMANN, THEODORE JAMES, b Pittsburgh, Pa, Apr 21, 30. PHYSICAL CHEMISTRY. *Educ:* Duquesne Univ, BS, 52, MS, 54, PhD(phys chem), 56. *Prof Exp:* RES DIR, GULF RES & DEVELOP CO, 56- *Mem:* Am Chem Soc; Geochem Soc; Am Phys Soc; Am Soc Mass Spectrometry; AAAS. *Res:* Boron chemistry; mass spectrometry; organic and isotopic geochemistry; marine geochemistry; molecular structure of organic radicals; magnetic susceptibilities; geochronometry. *Mailing Add:* 106 Short St Pittsburgh PA 15237

WEISMILLER, RICHARD A, b Elwood, Ind, Feb 23, 42; m 66; c 2. AGRONOMY. *Educ:* Purdue Univ, BS, 64, MS, 66; Mich State Univ, PhD(soil chem, clay mineral), 69. *Prof Exp:* Spec scientist soil stabilization, US Air Force Weapons Lab, 69-73; RES AGRONOMIST, PURDUE UNIV, WEST LAFAYETTE, 73- *Mem:* Am Soc Agron; Soil Sci Soc Am; Clay Minerals Soc; Soil Conserv Soc Am; Sigma Xi. *Res:* Relation of spectral reflectance of soils to their physicochemical properties; application of remote sensing to soils mapping, land use inventories and change detection as related to land use. *Mailing Add:* Lab Applns Remote Sensing Purdue Univ 1220 Potter Dr West Lafayette IN 47906

WEISS, A(DOLPH) KURT, b Graz, Austria, Mar 22, 23; nat US; m 48; c 1. PHYSIOLOGY. *Educ:* Okla Baptist Univ, BS, 48; Univ Tenn, MS, 50; Univ Rochester, PhD(physiol), 53. *Prof Exp:* Asst zool, Univ Tenn, 48-50; from instr to assoc prof physiol, Univ Miami, 53-61; prof biol & head dept, Oklahoma City Univ, 61-64; assoc prof, 64-66, PROF PHYSIOL & BIOPHYS, COL MED, UNIV OKLA, 67- *Concurrent Pos:* Investr, Howard Hughes Med Inst, 55-58; vis prof, Univ of the West Indies, 60; NIH res career develop award, 64-69; pres, Int Found Study Rat Genetics & Rodent Pest Control, 74- *Mem:* Fel AAAS; Am Physiol Soc; Soc Exp Biol & Med; Endocrine Soc; fel Geront Soc (vpres, 70-71). *Res:* Aging; metabolism; hypertension; stress; thyroid function; cold exposure. *Mailing Add:* Health Sci Ctr Univ Okla PO Box 26901 Oklahoma City OK 73190

WEISS, ALVIN H(ARVEY), b Philadelphia, Pa, Apr 28, 28; c 2. CHEMICAL ENGINEERING, PHYSICAL CHEMISTRY. *Educ:* Univ Pa, BS, 49, PhD(phys chem), 65; Newark Col Eng, MS, 55. *Prof Exp:* Chem engr, Fiber Chem Co, 49-51, US Army Chem Ctr, Edgewood Proving Ground, 51-53, Colgate Palmolive Co, 53-55 & Houdry Process Corp, 55-63; res assoc interdisciplinary res, Inst Coop Res, Univ Pa, 63-65, res investr, 65-66; assoc prof, 66-68, PROF CHEM ENG, WORCESTER POLYTECH INST, 68- *Concurrent Pos:* Lectr, Univ Pa, 64-66. *Mem:* AAAS; fel Am Inst Chem Engrs; Am Chem Soc; Catalysis Soc (secy, 68-); Deutsche Gesellschaft fuer Chemisches Apparatewesen. *Res:* Petroleum and petrochemical processing; hydrodealkylation; hydrodechlorination; dehydrogenation; kinetics and mechanisms of complex reactions; catalysis. *Mailing Add:* Dept Chem Eng Worcester Polytech Inst Worcester MA 01609

WEISS, ANDREW W, b Streator, Ill, Mar 13, 30; m 61; c 2. ATOMIC PHYSICS, MOLECULAR PHYSICS. *Educ:* Univ Detroit, BS, 52, MS, 54; Univ Chicago, PhD(atomic physics), 61. *Prof Exp:* PHYSICIST, NAT BUR STANDARDS, 61- *Mem:* AAAS; Am Phys Soc. *Res:* Application of electronic computers to the determination of the electronic structure and properties of atoms and simple molecules. *Mailing Add:* Div 222 07 Nat Bur of Standards Washington DC 20234

WEISS, ARTHUR JACOBS, b Philadelphia, Pa, Apr 11, 25; m 52; c 3. INTERNAL MEDICINE. *Educ:* Pa State Col, BS, 45; Univ Pa, MD, 50. *Prof Exp:* Instr, 57-62, ASST PROF MED, JEFFERSON MED COL, 62- *Concurrent Pos:* Am Heart Asn advan res fel, 57- *Mem:* Am Asn Cancer Res; Am Soc Hemat; Am Soc Pharmacol & Exp Therapeut; Am Col Physicians; Am Soc Clin Oncol. *Res:* Long-term storage of various tissues; hematology; malignant diseases; oncology. *Mailing Add:* 111 S 11th St Suite 6146 Philadelphia PA 19107

WEISS, BENJAMIN, b Newark, NJ, Nov 16, 22; m 47; c 6. BIOCHEMISTRY, ORGANIC CHEMISTRY. *Educ:* Univ Iowa, BS, 44; Univ Ill, PhD(biochem), 49. *Prof Exp:* Asst inorg chem, Univ Ill, 47-49; res biochemist, Harper Hosp, 49-53; res assoc, Columbia Univ, 53-65, asst prof brain metab, Col Physicians & Surgeons & mem staff, NY State Psychiat Inst, 53-76; RES SCIENTIST, INST NEUROCHEM, WARD'S ISLAND, NY, 76- *Mem:* Am Chem Soc; Am Soc Biol Chemists. *Res:* Chemistry and biochemistry of long chain bases; synthesis of long chain base antimetabolites; lipid metabolism; chemical modification of enzymes; isolation of natural products. *Mailing Add:* Inst of Neurochem Ward's Island NY 10035

WEISS, BERNARD, b New York, NY, May 27, 25; m 78; c 2. PSYCHOPHARMACOLOGY, TOXICOLOGY. *Educ:* NY Univ, BA, 49; Univ Rochester, PhD(psychol), 53. *Prof Exp:* Res assoc psychol, Univ Rochester, 53-54; exp & physiol psychologist, Sch Aviation Med, US Air Force, 54-56; instr med, Sch Med, Johns Hopkins Univ, 56-65, from instr to asst prof pharmacol, 59-65; assoc prof radiation biol & biophys & brain res, 65-67, prof radiation biol & biophys, Psychol & Brain Res, Sch Med & Dent, 67-79, PROF TOXICOL & DEP DIR, ENVIRON HEALTH SCI CTR, UNIV ROCHESTER, 79- *Concurrent Pos:* Mem behav pharmacol comt, NIMH, 65-67; mem comt biol effects of atmospheric pollutants, Nat Acad Sci-Nat Res Coun, 71-74; partic, US-USSR Environ Health Exchange Prog, 73-79; mem comt, Toxicol Study Sect, NIH. *Mem:* AAAS; Am Soc Pharmacol & Exp Therapeut; Am Psychol Asn; Behav Pharmacol Soc (pres, 61-64); Soc Toxicol. *Res:* Chemical influences on behavior. *Mailing Add:* Dept of Radiation Biol & Biophys Div Toxicol Univ Rochester Sch of Med & Dent Rochester NY 14642

WEISS, C DENNIS, b Oklahoma City, Okla, July 27, 39; m 62. COMPUTER SCIENCE, ENGINEERING. *Educ:* Stanford Univ, BS, 61; Columbia Univ, MS, 62, PhD(elec eng), 66. *Prof Exp:* Asst prof elec eng, Johns Hopkins Univ, 66-72; MEM TECH STAFF, BELL TEL LABS, INC, 72- *Mem:* Inst Elec & Electronics Engrs. *Res:* Computers; communication systems; software engineering. *Mailing Add:* Bell Tel Labs Inc Rm 1B 402 Holmdel NJ 07733

WEISS, CHARLES, JR, b San Francisco, Calif, Dec 20, 37; m 69. SCIENCE POLICY, BIOPHYSICS. *Educ:* Harvard Univ, AB, 59, PhD(chem physics, biochem), 65. *Prof Exp:* Teaching fel, Harvard Univ, 62-64; NIH fel biophys, Lab Chem Biodyn, Lawrence Radiation Lab, Univ Calif, 67-69; biophysicist, IBM Watson Lab, Columbia Univ, 69-71; SCI & TECHNOL ADV, INT BANK RECONSTRUCT & DEVELOP, 71- *Concurrent Pos:* Mem corp bd, Vols Tech Assistance, Nat Climate Adv Bd. *Mem:* AAAS; Am Phys Soc; Am Chem Soc; Soc Int Develop. *Res:* Science and technology in developing countries; role of development assistance organizations in technological research and technology transfer; interpretation of electronic spectra of porphyrins and other large aromatic rings; primary processes of photosynthesis. *Mailing Add:* Int Bank for Reconstruct & Develop 1818 H St NW Washington DC 20433

WEISS, CHARLES FREDERICK, b Cohoctah, Mich, Apr 2, 21; m 47; c 3. PEDIATRICS, PHARMACOLOGY. *Educ:* Univ Mich, BA, 42; Vanderbilt Univ, MD, 49; Am Bd Pediat, dipl, 60. *Prof Exp:* Pvt pract, 54-58; med coordr clin invest in pediat & virus res, Parke, Davis & Co, Mich, 58-69; from instr to assoc prof pharm & pharmacol & assoc prof pediat, Col Med, Univ Fla, 69-73; chief of staff, Hope Haven Children's Hosp, 73-77; COORDR PROFESSIONAL AFFAIRS & CONSULT PEDIAT TO SURGEON GENERAL, US AIR FORCE, 77- *Concurrent Pos:* Staff physician, Children's Hosp, Mich, 54-69 & Receiving Hosp, Detroit; clin asst prof pediat & commun dis, Univ Hosp, Univ Mich, Ann Arbor; med consult to dir div ment retardation, State of Fla, 69-; consult to Surgeon Gen, US Air Force; med dir & vpres, Fla Spec Olympics. *Mem:* Aerospace Med Asn; AMA; fel Am Acad Pediat; Am Pub Health Asn; Am Fedn Clin Res. *Res:* Virus and infectious diseases; pediatric clinical pharmacology. *Mailing Add:* 1317 4th St SW Washington DC 20024

WEISS, CHARLES MANUEL, b Scranton, Pa, Dec 7, 18; m 42. ENVIRONMENTAL BIOLOGY. *Educ:* Rutgers Univ, BS, 39; Johns Hopkins Univ, PhD(biol), 50. *Prof Exp:* Asst bacteriologist, Woods Hole Oceanog Inst, 40-42, res assoc & biologist in-chg, Miami Beach Sta, 42-46, res assoc marine biol, 46-47; chemist-biologist, Baltimore Harbor Proj, Dept Sanit Eng, Johns Hopkins Univ, 47-50; basin biologist, Div Water Pollution Control, USPHS, 50-52; biologist, Sanit Chem Br, Med Labs, Army Chem Ctr, Edgewood, Md, 52-56; assoc prof sanit sci, 56-62, dep head, Dept Environ Sci & Eng, 67-77, PROF ENVIRON BIOL, SCH PUB HEALTH, UNIV NC, CHAPEL HILL, 62- *Concurrent Pos:* Consult, Pan Am Health Orgn. *Mem:* Fel AAAS; Am Chem Soc; Soc Int Limnol; Am Soc Microbiol; fel Am Pub Health Asn. *Res:* Response of aquatic biota to environmental stress; water quality criteria and indices; limnology of lakes and impoundments; stream pollution. *Mailing Add:* Dept of Environ Sci & Eng Univ of NC Sch of Pub Health Chapel Hill NC 27514

WEISS, DANIEL LEIGH, b Long Branch, NJ, July 27, 23; m 51; c 3. PATHOLOGY, MEDICAL SCIENCE. *Educ:* Columbia Univ, AB, 43, MD, 46. *Prof Exp:* Res asst path & exp med, Beth Israel Hosp, 50-51; res asst path, Mt Sinai Hosp, NY, 51-53; dir inst path & lab med, DC Gen Hosp, 53-63; prof path, Col Med, Univ Ky, 63-77; EXEC SECY DIV MED SCI, NAT RES COUN, NAT ACAD SCI, 77- *Concurrent Pos:* Clin prof, Georgetown Univ, 53-63, George Washington Univ, 53-63 & 79- & Howard Univ, 59-63; consult, NIH, 56-73; US liasion rep, Comt Genetic Experimentation, WHO, 78-; mem biomech adv comn, US Dept Transp, 79-81 & Health Servs Comn, Am Red Cross, 80; rep, Nat Res Coun, Interagency Comn, Handicapped Res, 80-81 & Comn Nat Standards, Medicolegal Invest Death, Nat Inst Justice, US Dept Justice, 80- *Mem:* Am Soc Clin Path; Am Asn Path; Col Am Path; Am Soc Exp Path; Asn Clin Sci. *Res:* Experimental virus infection; primary and secondary vasculitis; lymphoma immunobiology; pathology of infection and immunity; skeletal pathology; paleopathology; science administration; radiation pathobiology. *Mailing Add:* Nat Res Coun Nat Acad of Sci 2101 Constitution Ave NW Washington DC 20418

WEISS, DAVID STEVEN, b Newark, NJ, Mar 3, 44; m 69. ORGANIC CHEMISTRY, PHOTOCHEMISTRY. *Educ:* Lehigh Univ, BS, 65; Columbia Univ, PhD(chem), 69. *Prof Exp:* NIH fel, Iowa State Univ, 69-72; asst prof chem, Univ Mich, Ann Arbor, 72-78; MEM STAFF, RES LABS, EASTMAN KODAK CO, 78- *Mem:* Royal Soc Chem; Inter-Am Photochem Soc; Am Chem Soc. *Mailing Add:* Eastman Kodak Co Res Labs Rochester NY 14650

WEISS, DAVID WALTER, b Vienna, Austria, July 6, 27; nat US; m 51; c 3. MICROBIOLOGY, IMMUNOLOGY. *Educ:* Brooklyn Col, BA, 49; Rutgers Univ, PhD(microbiol), 52; Oxford Univ, DPhil & Med, 57. *Prof Exp:* Asst, Rockefeller Inst 52-55; dir med res coun tuberc unit, Oxford Univ, 56-57; from asst prof to prof bact & immunol, Univ Calif, Berkeley, 57-67, res immunologist, Cancer Res Genetics Lab, 62-67; PROF IMMUNOL & CHMN LAUTENBERG CTR GEN RES & TUMOR IMMUNOL, HADASSAH MED SCH, HEBREW UNIV, JERUSALEM, 68- *Concurrent Pos:* Merck sr fel, Nat Acad Sci, 55-57; Am Cancer Soc scholar, 62-63; res prof, Miller Inst Basic Res Sci, 66-67; lectr, Univ Calif, 64-68; vis prof neoplastic dis, Mt Sinai Med Sch, NY, 77-78; mem, Midwinter Conf Immunologists. *Honors & Awards:* Herbert Abeles Scholar, 74; Ungerman-Lubin Cancer Res Award, 77. *Mem:* Am Asn Cancer Res; Transplantation Soc; Am Asn Immunologists; NY Acad Sci; Path Soc Gt Brit & Ireland. *Res:* Pathogenesis and host-parasite relationships; development of nonliving vaccines; relationship of specific and nonspecific immunogenic activities of microorganisms; tumor immunology; mechanisms of immunological unresponsiveness; oncogenic viruses; antibody formation; endotoxins. *Mailing Add:* 20A Rehov Radak Rehavia Jerusalem Israel

WEISS, DENNIS, b New York, NY, July 2, 40; m 65; c 2. MICROPALEONTOLOGY, ENVIRONMENTAL GEOLOGY. *Educ:* City Col New York, BS, 63; NY Univ, MS, 67, PhD(geol), 71. *Prof Exp:* Lectr geol, 64-71, asst prof, 71-80, ASSOC PROF EARTH & PLANTARY SCI, CITY COL NEW YORK, 80- *Mem:* AAAS; Geol Soc Am; Soc Econ Paleontologists & Mineralogists; Am Asn Stratig Palynologists; Nat Asn Geol Teachers. *Res:* Quaternary paleo-environments. *Mailing Add:* Dept Earth & Planetary Sci City Col of New York New York NY 10031

WEISS, DOUGLAS EUGENE, b Aurora, Ill, July 28, 45. ORGANIC POLYMER CHEMISTRY. *Educ:* Univ Kans, BS, 68; Univ Nebr, PhD(org chem), 72. *Prof Exp:* Sr res assoc polymers, Univ E Anglia, 72-73; res assoc org chem, Univ Nebr, 73-74; chemist, Elastomer Chem Dept, E I du Pont de Nemours & Co, Inc, 74-78; res specialist, 78-81, PROD DEVELOP SUPVR, 3M CO, 81- *Mem:* Am Chem Soc; Sigma Xi. *Res:* Synthesis and development of polyurethane casting systems and carbon-13 nuclear magnetic resonance of polymers. *Mailing Add:* 4401 Bryant Ave S Minneapolis MN 55409

WEISS, EARLE BURTON, b Waltham, Mass, Nov 23, 32; m 63; c 2. PULMONARY PHYSIOLOGY. *Educ:* Northeastern Univ, BS, 55; Mass Inst Technol, MS, 57; Albert Einstein Col Med, MD, 61; Am Bd Internal Med, dipl, 69. *Prof Exp:* Nat Heart Inst fel, Tufts Lung Sta, Boston City Hosp, 64-66; from instr to assoc prof, Sch Med, Tufts Univ, 66-77; assoc prof, 71-77, PROF MED, MED SCH, UNIV MASS, 77- DIR DEPT RESPIRATORY DIS, ST VINCENT HOSP, 71- *Concurrent Pos:* Assoc, Tufts Lung Sta, Boston City Hosp, 66-71, physician chg, Pulmonary Function & Physiol Sect, Hosp, 66-71 & Cent Arterial Blood Gas Lab, 67-71, assisting physician, Tufts Med Serv, 67-70, assoc dir, 69-70, dir respiratory intensive care unit, 70-71; consult physiol, Norfolk County Sanatorium, Mass, 66-69; mem toxicol info prog, Nat Libr Med, 70-; tuberc consult, Mass Dept Pub Health, 72-; lectr med, Med Sch, Tufts Univ, 78; assoc affil prof life sci, Worcester Polytech Inst, 76- *Mem:* AAAS; Am Fedn Clin Res; fel Am Col Physicians; fel Am Col Chest Physicians; Am Soc Internal Med. *Mailing Add:* Dept of Respiratory Dis St Vincent Hosp 25 Winthrop St Worcester MA 01610

WEISS, EDWIN, b Brooklyn, NY, Aug 23, 27; m 52; c 2. ALGEBRA. *Educ:* Brooklyn Col, BS, 48; Mass Inst Technol, PhD, 53. *Prof Exp:* Instr math, Univ Mich, 53-54; NSF fel, Inst Advan Study, 54-55; Benjamin Peirce instr, Harvard Univ, 55-58; asst prof, Univ Calif, Los Angeles, 58-59; mem staff, Lincoln Lab, Mass Inst Technol, 59-65; PROF MATH, BOSTON UNIV, 65- *Mem:* Am Math Soc. *Mailing Add:* 16 Warwick Rd Brookline MA 02146

WEISS, EMILIO, b Pakrac, Yugoslavia, Oct 4, 18; nat US; m 43; c 2. MEDICAL MICROBIOLOGY. *Educ:* Univ Kans, AB, 41; Univ Chicago, MS, 42, PhD(bact), 48. *Prof Exp:* Asst histol, parasitol & bact, Univ Chicago, 42 & 47-48; res assoc, 48-50; instr bact, Loyola Univ, Ill, 47-48; asst prof, Ind Univ, 50-53; chief virol br, Chem Corps Biol Lab, US Dept Army, Ft Detrick, Md, 53-54; asst head virol div, 54-63, dep dir microbiol dept, 63-72, dir, 72-74, chmn microbiol dept, 74-80, CHAIR SCI DEPT, NAVAL MED RES INST, NAT NAVAL MED CTR, 80-; RES PROF PREV MED & BIOMETRICS, UNIFORMED SERV UNIV HEALTH SCI, 77- *Mem:* Am Soc Microbiol; Soc Exp Biol & Med; Am Asn Immunologists; Am Acad Microbiol. *Res:* Microbiol physiology and pathogenesis; rickettsiae, chlamydiae and other bacterial pathogens. *Mailing Add:* Naval Med Res Inst Bethesda MD 20814

WEISS, FRED TOBY, b Oakland, Calif, July 24, 16; m 40; c 3. ANALYTICAL CHEMISTRY, ENVIRONMENTAL CHEMISTRY. *Educ:* Univ Calif, Los Angeles, BS, 38; Harvard Univ, MS, 40, PhD(chem), 41. *Prof Exp:* Res chemist, Shell Oil Co, Ill, 41-43, group leader fuels res, 43-46, res chemist, Shell Develop Co, Calif, 46-52, res supvr, 52-72, staff res chemist, Bellaire Res Ctr, Tex, 72-75, sr staff res chemist, Bellaire Res Ctr, Shell Develop Co, Tex, 75-81, SR STAFF ENVIRON SCIENTIST, SHELL OIL CO, 81- *Concurrent Pos:* Mem adv comt, NSF-Res Appl to Nat Needs Study of Petrol Indust in Del Estuary, 74-77; mem outer continental shelf sci adv comt, US Dept Interior, 79- *Mem:* AAAS; Am Chem Soc; Am Soc Testing & Mat. *Res:* Characterization and analysis of organic structures; analytical methods for process control; combined use of chemical and physical methods for analysis of organic compounds; environmental analysis; development of analytical methods for studying fate and effects of petroleum in marine environments; surveys of impacts of offshore petroleum operations in the environment. *Mailing Add:* Shell Oil Co PO Box 250 San Ramon CA 94583

WEISS, GARY BRUCE, b New York, NY, Oct 5, 44; div. HEMATOLOGY, BIOCHEMISTRY. *Educ:* NY Univ, BA, 65, MD, 71, PhD(biochem), 72. *Prof Exp:* Intern med, Sch Med, Univ Calif, San Francisco, 71-72, resident, 72-73; res assoc hemat, Nat Heart & Lung Inst, Bethesda, Md, 73-76; fel hemat, Univ Wash, 76-77; ASST PROF INT MED, HUMAN BIOL CHEM & GENETICS, UNIV TEX MED BR GALVESTON, 77- *Mem:* Am Fedn Clin Res; Asn Comput Mach; Am Soc Hemat; Am Soc Biol Chemists; Am Statist Asn. *Res:* Mechanism of action of RNA-directed DNA polymerase. *Mailing Add:* Div of Hemat Univ of Tex Med Br Galveston TX 77550

WEISS, GEORGE B, b Plainfield, NJ, Apr 29, 35; m 60; c 2. PHARMACOLOGY. *Educ:* Princeton Univ, AB, 57; Vanderbilt Univ, PhD(pharmacol), 62. *Prof Exp:* USPHS res fels pharmacol, Vanderbilt Univ, 62 & Univ Pa, 62-64; from asst prof to assoc prof pharmacol, Med Col Va, 64-70; assoc prof, 70-74, PROF PHARMACOL, UNIV TEX HEALTH SCI CTR DALLAS, 74- *Mem:* Biophys Soc; Am Soc Pharmacol & Exp Therapeut; Am Physiol Soc. *Res:* Cellular pharmacology; actions of drugs on membrane permeability to ions; excitation-contraction coupling and calcium ion in smooth (especially vascular) and striated muscle; actions of calcium antagonists, especially calcium channel blockers. *Mailing Add:* Dept of Pharmacol Univ of Tex Health Sci Ctr Dallas TX 75235

WEISS, GEORGE HERBERT, b New York, NY, Feb 19, 30; m 61; c 3. APPLIED MATHEMATICS. *Educ:* Columbia Univ, AB, 51; Univ Md, MA, 53, PhD, 58. *Prof Exp:* Physicist, US Naval Ord Lab, 51-54; math asst, Ballistic Res Lab, Aberdeen Proving Ground, US Army, 54-56; asst math, Inst Fluid Dynamics & Appl Math, Univ Md, 56-58, res assoc, 59-60, res asst prof, 60-63; Weizmann fel, Weizmann Inst Sci, 58-59; NIH study grant, Rockefeller Inst, 63-64; study grant, 64-67, CHIEF PHYS SCI LAB, DIV COMPUT RES & TECHNOL, NIH, 67- *Concurrent Pos:* Physicist, US Naval Ord Lab, 56-61; consult, Gen Motors Corp, 60-64; consult, IBM Corp, 64; Fulbright sr fel, Imp Col, Univ London, 68-69; assoc ed, Transp Res, 73- *Honors & Awards:* Wash Acad Sci Award, 66; Superior Serv Award, NIH, 70. *Mem:* Opers Res Soc Am. *Res:* Traffic theory; statistical mechanics; biometry; biochemical separation techniques, stochastic processes. *Mailing Add:* 1105 N Belgrade Rd Silver Spring MD 20902

WEISS, GERALD S, b Boyertown, Pa, July 26, 34; m 58; c 3. INORGANIC CHEMISTRY. *Educ:* Drexel Inst, BS, 57; Univ Pa, PhD(inorg chem, anal chem), 65. *Prof Exp:* Res chemist, Rohm & Haas Co, 57-59; instr chem, Drexel Inst, 59-65, asst prof, 65-67; assoc prof, 67-69, PROF CHEM, MILLERSVILLE STATE COL, 69-, CHMN DEPT, 75- *Mem:* Am Chem Soc. *Res:* Synthesis of volatile hydrides of group IV elements; infrared spectroscopic analysis of small molecules; heavy metal complex ion synthesis and spectroscopic analysis. *Mailing Add:* 306 Ruby Millersville PA 17551

WEISS, GERSON, b New York, NY, Aug 1, 39; m 59; c 4. REPRODUCTIVE ENDOCRINOLOGY. *Educ:* NY Univ, BA, 60, MD, 64; Am Bd Obstet & Gynec, dipl, 71, cert reproductive endocrinol, 74, 81. *Prof Exp:* From instr to asst prof, 69-76, assoc prof, 76-80, PROF OBSTET-GYNEC, SCH MED & DIR DIV REPRODUCTION-ENDOCRINOL, NY UNIV MED CTR, 80- *Concurrent Pos:* Fel reproductive endocrinol, Sch Med, Univ Pittsburgh, 71-73; John Polachek Found Med Res grant, 75; Nat Inst Child Health & Human Develop res grant, 75; United Cerebral Palsy res grant, 77; prin invesr, Mellon Found; res grants, Nat Inst Health; Virus Cancer Prog, Nat Cancer Inst. *Mem:* Soc Gynec Invest; Endocrine Soc; Am Fertil Soc; Soc Study Reproduction; NY Acad Med. *Res:* Control and function of the pregnancy and postpartum corpus luteum; relaxin physiology; control of pituitary gonadotropin secretion. *Mailing Add:* Dept of Obstet-Gynec NY Univ Med Ctr New York NY 10016

WEISS, GUIDO LEOPOLD, b Trieste, Italy, Dec 29, 28; nat US; m 50. MATHEMATICS. *Educ:* Univ Chicago, PhB, 49, MS, 51, PhD, 56. *Prof Exp:* From instr to assoc prof math, DePaul Univ, 55-60; chmn dept, 67-70, PROF MATH, WASH UNIV, 66- *Honors & Awards:* Chauvenet Prize, Math Asn Am, 67. *Mem:* Am Math Soc; Math Asn Am. *Res:* Harmonic analysis; complex and real variables. *Mailing Add:* Dept of Math Wash Univ St Louis MO 63130

WEISS, HAROLD GILBERT, b Perth Amboy, NJ, Feb 6, 23; m 44; c 2. INORGANIC CHEMISTRY, PHYSICAL CHEMISTRY. *Educ:* Univ Calif, Los Angeles, BS, 48. *Prof Exp:* Res chemist, US Naval Ord Test Sta, 48-52; supvr catalysis res, Olin Mathieson Chem Corp, 52-59; lab mgr, Nat Eng Sci Co, 59-61; dir chem, Dynamic Sci Corp, 61-66; PRES, WEST COAST TECH SERV, INC, 66- *Mem:* Am Chem Soc; Am Inst Chemists; Inst Environ Sci. *Res:* Boron hydrides; organoboranes; surface chemistry and catalysis; analytical chemistry; mass and infrared spectrometry; high vacuum technology; combustion-fire research; environmental control; analytical instrumentation. *Mailing Add:* 4016 Montego Dr Huntington Beach CA 92649

WEISS, HAROLD SAMUEL, b New York, NY, Sept 10, 22; m 49; c 4. PHYSIOLOGY. *Educ:* Rutgers Univ, BSc, 47, MSc, 49, PhD(physiol), 50. *Prof Exp:* From instr to assoc prof avian physiol, Rutgers Univ, 50-62; assoc prof, 62-67, PROF PHYSIOL, COL MED, OHIO STATE UNIV, 67- *Mem:* Am Physiol Soc; Poultry Sci Asn; Soc Exp Biol & Med; Aerospace Med Asn; Undersea Med Soc. *Res:* Cardiopulmonary; blood pressure; atherosclerosis; lung mechanics; environmental physiology; acceleration; temperature control; gaseous environment and respiratory disease. *Mailing Add:* Dept of Physiol Ohio State Univ Col of Med Columbus OH 43210

WEISS, HARRY JOSEPH, b Pittsburgh, Pa, Feb 15, 23; m 47; c 3. APPLIED MECHANICS, APPLIED MATHEMATICS. *Educ:* Carnegie Mellon Univ, BS, 47, MS, 49, DSc(appl math), 51. *Prof Exp:* Instr math, Carnegie-Mellon Univ, 49-51; asst prof appl math, Brown Univ, 51-53; from asst prof to prof math, 54-64, PROF ENG MECH & HEAD DEPT, IOWA STATE UNIV, 64- *Concurrent Pos:* Vis scientist, Nat Bur Standards, 61; consult, Gen Dynamics Astronaut, 62-66. *Mem:* Soc Eng Sci (vpres, 77-79); Am Soc Mech Engrs; Sigma Xi. *Res:* Integral transforms; partial differential equations; boundary value problems; elasticity. *Mailing Add:* Dept of Eng Sci & Mech Iowa State Univ Ames IA 50011

WEISS, HARVEY JEROME, b New York, NY, June 30, 29; m 57; c 2. INTERNAL MEDICINE, HEMATOLOGY. *Educ:* Harvard Univ, AB, 51, MD, 55. *Prof Exp:* Intern, Bellevue Hosp, Columbia Univ, 55-56; resident med, Manhattan Vet Admin Hosp, New York, 56-58; Dazian fel hemat, Mt Sinai Hosp, New York, 58-59; instr, Sch Med, NY Univ, 62-64; asst attend hematologist, Mt Sinai Hosp, 65-69; assoc clin prof, 69-71, assoc prof, 72-74, PROF MED, COL PHYSICIANS & SURGEONS, COLUMBIA UNIV, 75- *Concurrent Pos:* Consult, Walter Reed Army Med Ctr, 65-70; asst prof med, Mt Sinai Sch Med, 66-69; dir div hemat, Roosevelt Hosp, New York, 69-; mem hemat speciality comt, Am Bd Internal Med, 81- *Mem:* Soc Exp Biol & Med; Am Physiol Soc; Am Soc Clin Invest; Am Soc Hemat; Asn Am Physicians. *Res:* Hematology; blood coagulation; disorders of hemostasis; platelet physiology. *Mailing Add:* Dept of Med Roosevelt Hosp 428 W 59th St New York NY 10019

WEISS, HARVEY RICHARD, b New York, NY, May 13, 43; m 66; c 2. PHYSIOLOGY, PHARMACOLOGY. *Educ:* City Col New York, BS, 65; Duke Univ, PhD(physiol), 69. *Prof Exp:* Warner-Lambert joint fel pharmacol, Warner-Lambert Res Inst & Col Physicians & Surgeons, Columbia Univ, 69-71; asst prof, 71-76, ASSOC PROF PHYSIOL, RUTGERS MED SCH, COL MED & DENT NJ, 76-, ASSOC PROF BIOPHYSICS, 80- *Mem:* AAAS; Am Physiol Soc. *Res:* Physiologic and pharmacologic control of oxygen transport to tissue; coronary circulation; regional cerebral and myocardial oxygen consumption. *Mailing Add:* Dept of Physiol & Biophysics Rutgers Med Sch Piscataway NJ 08854

WEISS, HERBERT G, b Elizabeth, NJ, Oct 2, 18; m 49; c 3. ELECTRONICS. *Educ:* Mass Inst Technol, SB, 40. *Prof Exp:* Res assoc, Mass Inst Technol, 39-40, mem staff, Radiation Lab, 41-45, Nat Res Coun fel, 45; group leader in charge electronics res sect, Physics Div, Los Alamos Sci Lab, Calif, 45-48; sr engr, Raytheon Mfg Co, 48-52; group leader radar systs, Lincoln Lab, Mass Inst Technol, 52-60, div head, 60-79; VPRES ENG, US WINDPOWER, INC, 80- *Concurrent Pos:* Mem strategic mil panel, President's Sci Adv Panel, 71-; chief engr, Northwest Radio Observ Corp. *Mem:* Am Phys Soc; Inst Elec & Electronics Engrs; fel Am Acad Arts & Sci; Inst Navig. *Res:* Design of radar systems, wide band amplifiers, nuclear instruments and control systems; frequency control for pulsed systems; radio astronomy instrumentation; air traffic control; windpower systems. *Mailing Add:* 28 Barberry Rd Lexington MA 02173

WEISS, HERBERT KLEMM, b Lawrence, Mass, June 22, 17; m 45; c 2. SYSTEMS DESIGN & SYSTEMS SCIENCE. *Educ:* Mass Inst Technol, BS, 37, MS, 38. *Prof Exp:* Mech engr, Coast Artillery Bd, Va, 38-42, Anti-aircraft Artillery Bd, NC, 42-44 & Army Ground Forces Bd, Tex, 44-46; chief, Weapons Effect Br & dep chief, Terminal Ballistics Lab, Aberdeen Proving Ground, US Dept Army, Md, 46-50, chief, Weapon Systs Lab, 50-53; chief, Weapon Systs Anal Dept, Northrop Aircraft Corp, 53-58; mgr, Adv Systs Develop, Aeronutronic Div, Ford Motor Co, 58-60, mgr, Mil Systs Planning, 60-62; dir, Systs Anal & Eval, Aerospace Corp, 62-65; sr scientist, 65-80, SCIENTIST, DATA SYSTS DIV, LITTON INDUSTS, 80- *Concurrent Pos:* Mem tech adv panel ord, Off Asst Secy Defense Res & Develop, 54-64; consult, Weapons Systs Eval Group, Off Asst Secy Defense, 55-56; lectr, Univ Calif, Los Angeles, 57-58; consult, Sci Adv Bd, US Air Force, 58-59, mem, 59-63; summer mem study group, Nat Acad Sci-US Air Force, 58 & Proj Endicott, Opers Eval Group, US Navy, 60; consult, Opers Eval Group, US Navy, 60-62; mem, US Army Sci Adv Panel, 65-76. *Mem:* AAAS; Opers Res Soc Am (vpres, 58-59); assoc fel Am Inst Aeronaut & Astronaut; sr mem Inst Elec & Electronics Engrs. *Res:* Fire control; servo-mechanisms; computing devices; weapon systems research and development; operations research; systems analysis; ballistics; management sciences. *Mailing Add:* PO Box 2668 Palos Verdes Peninsula CA 90274

WEISS, HERBERT V, b Brooklyn, NY, Nov 16, 21; m 55; c 2. CHEMISTRY. *Educ:* NY Univ, BA, 42, MS, 49; Univ Cincinnati, PhD(biochem), 52. *Prof Exp:* Toxicologist, Chief Med Exam Lab, New York, 47-49; fel physiol, Sch Med, Univ Rochester, 52-53; instr indust med, Post-grad Med Sch, NY Univ, 53-56; supvry radiochemist, US Naval Radiol Defense Lab, San Francisco, 56-69; RES CHEMIST, NAVAL OCEANS SYSTS CTR, 69- *Concurrent Pos:* Adj prof, San Diego State Univ. *Mem:* AAAS; Am Chem Soc. *Res:* Nuclear chemistry; analytical chemistry; industrial hygiene and toxicology; environmental chemistry. *Mailing Add:* Naval Ocean Systs Ctr San Diego CA 92152

WEISS, IRA PAUL, b New York, NY, Feb 27, 42; m 67; c 2. NEUROSCIENCES. *Educ:* City Col New York, BS, 65; Syracuse Univ, PhD(physiol, psychol), 69. *Prof Exp:* Instr psychol, Onondaga Community Col, 68; NIH fel neurophysiol, Callier Hearing & Speech Ctr, Dallas, Tex, 69-70, NIH spec fel neurophysiol & consult res design, 70-72; res psychologists neurosci, 72-80, vchmn, Dept Psychol, 75-76, ASSOC DIR, EVOKED RESPONSE LAB, CHILDRENS HOSP NAT MED CTR, 78- *Concurrent Pos:* Asst prof lectr, Sch Med, George Washington Univ, 72-80, assoc prof lectr, 80- *Mem:* Soc Neurosci; Soc Psychophysiol Res; AAAS. *Res:* Relationships of brainstem and cortical sensory evoked potentials to developments, neurological and sensory disorders and to behavior. *Mailing Add:* Childrens Hosp Nat Med Ctr 111 Michigan Ave NW Washington DC 20010

WEISS, IRMA TUCK, b New York, NY, Aug 5, 13; m 38; c 2. BIOCHEMISTRY, ORGANIC CHEMISTRY. *Educ:* NY Univ, BS, 33, MS, 36, PhD, 42. *Prof Exp:* Asst instr chem, Washington Sq Col, 40-42, from instr to assoc prof biochem, Col Dent, 43-76, prof, 76-80, EMER PROF BIOCHEM, COL DENT, NY UNIV, 80- *Mem:* Sigma Xi (secy, Sci Res Soc Am, 59-60, treas, 60-61, vpres, 61-62, pres, 62-63); Am Chem Soc. *Res:* Organic synthesis; application of biochemistry in clinical dentistry; electrophoresis studies of salivary proteins. *Mailing Add:* Dept of Biochem Col of Dent NY Univ New York NY 10010

WEISS, IRVING, b New York, Apr 10, 19; m 44; c 3. MATHEMATICAL STATISTICS. *Educ:* Univ Mich, BS, 41; Columbia Univ, MA, 48; Stanford Univ, PhD(statist), 55. *Prof Exp:* Res asst statist, Stanford Univ, 51-55; instr math, Lehigh Univ, 55-56; tech staff statistician, Bell Tel Labs, 56-59 & Mitre Corp, 59-62; ASSOC PROF MATH, UNIV COLO, BOULDER, 62- *Concurrent Pos:* Consult, State Dept Employ, Colo, 63, Beech Aircraft Corp, 63-64, dept biol, Univ Rochester, 64-65, Nat Ctr Atmospheric Res, 64-72 & 75, Behav Res & Eval Corp, 73-74 & US Environ Protection Agency, 75. *Mem:* Inst Math Statist; Am Statist Asn. *Res:* Probability; applied probability theory; statistical inference; stochastic processes; control charts; tolerance intervals. *Mailing Add:* Dept of Math Univ of Colo Boulder CO 80309

WEISS, JAMES ALLYN, b West Bend, Wis, Apr 16, 43; m 71. ORGANIC CHEMISTRY. *Educ:* Univ Wis-Madison, BS, 65; Pa State Univ, University Park, PhD(chem), 71. *Prof Exp:* ASST PROF CHEM, PA STATE UNIV, WORTHINGTON SCRANTON CAMPUS, 71- *Mem:* AAAS; Am Chem Soc. *Res:* Organic synthesis; isolation and structural elucidation of natural products; stereochemistry of organic molecules. *Mailing Add:* Dept of Chem Pa State Univ Worthington Scranton Campus Dunmore PA 18512

WEISS, JAMES MOSES AARON, b St Paul, Minn, Oct 22, 21; m 46; c 2. PSYCHIATRY. *Educ:* Univ Minn, AB, 41, BS, 47, MB, 49, MD, 50; Yale Univ, MPH, 51; Am Bd Psychiat & Neurol, dipl, 57. *Prof Exp:* Asst psychol, Col St Thomas, 41-42; intern med, USPHS Hosp, Seattle, 49-50; from instr to asst prof psychiat, Sch Med, Wash Univ, 54-60; assoc prof & actg chmn dept, 60-61, PROF PSYCHIAT & CHMN DEPT, SCH MED, UNIV MO-COLUMBIA, 61-, PROF COMMUNITY MEDICINE, 71- *Concurrent Pos:* Res & clin fel psychiat, Sch Med, Yale Univ, 51-53; fac fel, Inter-Univ Coun Inst Social Geront, Univ Conn, 58; dir training, Malcolm Bliss Ment Health Ctr, City of St Louis, 54-60, dir psychiat clin, 54-59, dir div community psychiat serv, 58-59; vis psychiatrist, St Louis City Hosps, Barnes & Affil Hosps & Wash Univ Clins, 54-60; consult to state, fed & nat agencies & orgn, 60-; vis prof, Inst Criminol, Cambridge Univ, 68-69. *Mem:* Fel Royal Col Psychiatrists; fel Am Psychiat Asn; fel Am Pub Health Asn; fel Royal Soc Med; fel Am Col Psychiatrists. *Res:* Social psychiatry and gerontology; psychiatric problems of aging; suicide; homicide; antisocial behavior. *Mailing Add:* Dept of Psychiat Univ of Mo Columbia MO 65201

WEISS, JAMES OWEN, b Memphis, Tenn, Sept 25, 31; m 55; c 3. ORGANIC CHEMISTRY, POLYMER CHEMISTRY. *Educ:* Duke Univ, BS, 52; Univ Va, MS, 54, PhD(org chem), 57. *Prof Exp:* Res chemist, Shell Oil Co, 57-58 & E I du Pont de Nemours & Co, 58-61; res chemist, Chemstrand Res Ctr, 61-66; res mgr fiber develop, Beaunit Fibers, 66-68; group leader fiber develop, Celanese Fibers Co, 68-72; chem develop mgr, 73-78, qual control dir, 78-81, FILAMENT PROD DIR, HOECHST FIBERS INDUSTS, 81- *Mem:* Am Chem Soc. *Res:* Polyester fiber research and development; nylon, high temperature resistant fiber, spandex fiber, polypropylene fiber and vinyl polymer and fiber research and development. *Mailing Add:* Hoechst Fibers Industs PO Box 5887 Spartanburg SC 29304

WEISS, JAY M, b Jersey City, NJ, Mar 20, 41; m 63; c 2. PSYCHOPHYSIOLOGY. *Educ:* Lafayette Col, BA, 62; Yale Univ, PhD(psychol), 67. *Prof Exp:* USPHS fel & guest investr, 67-68, asst prof, 69-73, ASSOC PROF PHYSIOL PSYCHOL, ROCKEFELLER UNIV, 73- *Res:* Psychological factors influencing physiological effects of stress; psychosomatic disorders; motivation. *Mailing Add:* Rockefeller Univ 66th St & York Ave New York NY 10021

WEISS, JEFFREY MARTIN, b Philadelphia, Pa, July 1, 44; m 67; c 2. HIGH ENERGY PHYSICS. *Educ:* Princeton Univ, AB, 66; Harvard Univ, MA, 67, PhD(physics), 72. *Prof Exp:* Vis scientist high energy physics, Europ Orgn Nuclear Res, Geneva, Switz, 72-74; res assoc, Nevis Labs, Columbia Univ, 74-76; res assoc physics, Stanford Linear Accelerator Ctr, Stanford Univ, 76-81; PHYSICIST, ARGONNE NAT LAB, 81- *Concurrent Pos:* NSF fel, Europ Orgn Nuclear Res, 72-73; consult, Dynametrics Co, Philadelphia, Pa, 78-80. *Mem:* Am Phys Soc. *Res:* Electron-positron colliding beam physics; lepton and dilepton production by hadrons; inclusive hadron production; intersecting storage rings; charmed baryons and baryon production. *Mailing Add:* 1572 Peacock Ave Sunnyvale CA 94087

WEISS, JERALD AUBREY, b Cleveland, Ohio, June 9, 22; m 49; c 2. MICROWAVE PHYSICS. *Educ:* Ohio State Univ, PhD(physics), 53. *Prof Exp:* Instr math, Univ Wyo, 49-51; mem tech staff magnetic mat, Bell Tel Labs, Inc, 53-61; vpres, Hyletronics Corp, Mass, 61-62; from asst prof to assoc prof, 62-66, PROF PHYSICS, WORCESTER POLYTECH INST, 66- *Concurrent Pos:* Consult, US Army Natick Res & Develop Ctr, 75 & Lincoln Lab, Mass Inst Technol, 62- *Mem:* Am Phys Soc; sr mem Inst Elec & Electronics Engrs; AAAS; Sigma Xi. *Res:* Theory of atomic and molecular structure; magnetic materials and electromagnetic interactions, theory and applications; magnetic resonance spectroscopy and microwave applications. *Mailing Add:* Dept Physics Worcester Polytech Inst Worcester MA 01609

WEISS, JEROME, b Brooklyn, NY, Aug 27, 22; m 43; c 2. PHYSICAL CHEMISTRY. *Educ:* Cornell Univ, BA, 48; Ind Univ, PhD(phys chem), 51. *Prof Exp:* Asst chem, Ind Univ, 48-50, instr, Exten, 50; chemist, Brookhaven Nat Lab, 51-73; teacher, Smithtown High Sch, 75-77; INSTR CHEM, SUFFOLK COUNTY COMMUNITY COL, 73-; TEACHER, NORTHFORT HIGH SCH, 78- *Concurrent Pos:* Lectr, Hofstra Col, 55; Dewar res fel, Univ Edinburgh, 57; consult, Am Soc Testing & Mat. *Mem:* AAAS; Radiation Res Soc; Royal Soc Chem; NY Acad Sci; fel Am Inst Chemists. *Res:* Organic radiation chemistry; chemical dosimetry; health physics; membrane transport. *Mailing Add:* 17 Locust Ave Stony Brook NY 11790

WEISS, JONAS, b New York, NY, Feb 17, 34; m 59; c 3. POLYMER CHEMISTRY. *Educ:* City Col New York, BS, 55; NY Univ, PhD(phys chem), 62. *Prof Exp:* Chemist, Esso Res & Eng Co, 62-64; supvr org & polymer chem, Am Standard Co, 64-70; group leader polymer chem, Nat Patent Develop Corp, 70-74; group leader polymer applns, 74-80, SR STAFF SCIENTIST, CIBA-GEIGY CORP, 80- *Mem:* Am Chem Soc; Soc Advan Mat & Process Eng. *Res:* Polymers and plastics for composites, coatings, sealants, adhesives and binders; permeability and rate of release of polymers; polymers and plastics for building materials; foam insulation; indicators and controls; semi-permeable membranes; ion-exchange polymers. *Mailing Add:* Ciba-Geigy Corp Saw Mill River Rd Ardsley NY 10502

WEISS, JONATHAN DAVID, experimental solid state physics, see previous edition

WEISS, JOSEPH FRANCIS, b Taylor, Pa, Jan 26, 40; m 68; c 2. BIOCHEMISTRY, RADIOBIOLOGY. *Educ:* Univ Scranton, BS, 61; Ohio State Univ, MS, 63, PhD(physiol chem), 66. *Prof Exp:* NIH fel neurochem, Inst Pharmacol, Univ Milan, Italy, 66-68; instr neurosurg in biochem cancer, Med Ctr, NY Univ, 68-72, asst prof exp neurosurg, 72-74; res chemist biochem & radiobiol, 74-76, CHIEF PHYSIOL CHEM DIV, ARMED FORCES RADIOBIOL RES INST, DEFENSE NUCLEAR AGENCY, 76- *Concurrent Pos:* Adj lectr chem, Hostos Community Col, City Univ New York, 74- *Mem:* Am Chem Soc; assoc Am Asn Neuropathologists; Am Asn Cancer Res; Am Soc Clin Oncol; Radiation Res Soc. *Res:* Biochemical markers of cancer and radiation injury; glycoproteins, lipids, trace metals; radiobiology; immunopharmacology; neurochemistry; carcinogenesis. *Mailing Add:* Dept Biochem Armed Forces Radiobiol Res Inst Bethesda MD 20014

WEISS, JOSEPH FRANKLIN, inorganic & analytical chemistry, see previous edition

WEISS, JOSEPH JACOB, b Detroit, Mich, Mar 22, 34; m 68; c 2. RHEUMATOLOGY. *Educ:* Univ Mich, BA, 55, MD, 61. *Prof Exp:* Asst dir, Rheum Sect, 72, ATTEND PHYSICIAN, WAYNE COUNTY GEN HOSP, 71-; ASST PROF INTERNAL MED, MED SCH, UNIV MICH, 72- *Concurrent Pos:* Rheumatol consult, Vet Admin Hosp, Ann Arbor, Mich, 75- *Mem:* Fel Am Col Physicians; Am Soc Clin Res; Am Fedn Clin Res. *Res:* Investigation of the etiology of frozen shoulder; use of arthrography to delineate the cause and assist the diagnosis of shoulder pain and immobility. *Mailing Add:* Dept of Med Wayne County Gen Hosp Eloise MI 48132

WEISS, KARL H, b Hamburg, Ger, June 21, 26; nat US; m 48; c 2. PHYSICAL CHEMISTRY. *Educ:* Columbia Univ, BS, 51; NY Univ, PhD(chem), 57. *Prof Exp:* Res chemist, Color Res Corp, 47-50, tech adminr, 50-54; instr chem, NY Univ, 56-59, asst prof, 59-61; from asst prof to assoc prof, 61-65, chmn dept, 69-79, PROF CHEM, NORTHEASTERN UNIV, 65-, VPROVOST, RES & GRAD STUDIES, 79- *Concurrent Pos:* NSF sr fel, Quantum Chem Group, Univ Uppsala, 68-69; Fulbright-Hayes scholar, 77-78; vis prof, Univ Konstanz, W Ger, 77-78. *Mem:* Am Chem Soc; NY Acad Sci; Royal Soc Chem; Am Inst Chem; Am Soc Photobiol. *Res:* Photochemistry of complex molecules; laser photochemistry; quantum chemistry; charge transfer interaction. *Mailing Add:* Dept of Chem Northeastern Univ Boston MA 02115

WEISS, KENNETH MONRAD, b Cleveland, Ohio, Nov 29, 41; m 65; c 2. GENETIC EPIDEMIOLOGY, BIOLOGICAL ANTHROPOLOGY. *Educ:* Oberlin Col, BA, 63; Univ Mich, MA, 69, PhD(biol anthrop), 72. *Prof Exp:* Res assoc human genetics, Med Sch, Univ Mich, 72-73; ASSOC PROF DEMOG & POP GENETICS, UNIV TEX GRAD SCH BIOMED SCI, HOUSTON, 73- *Concurrent Pos:* Assoc prof, Univ Tex Sch Pub Health, Houston, 74- *Honors & Awards:* Juan Comas Award, Am Asn Phys Anthropologists, 72. *Mem:* AAAS; Am Asn Phys Anthropologists; Soc Epidemiol Res; Sigma Xi; Am Asn Human Genetics. *Res:* Demographic evolution of human populations; demographic genetic epidemiology of degenerative diseases; human evolution and biological anthropology. *Mailing Add:* Ctr Demog & Pop Genetics PO Box 20334 Houston TX 77025

WEISS, KLAUDIUSZ ROBERT, b Le Mans, France, June 7, 44. NEUROBIOLOGY. *Educ:* Univ Warsaw, MA, 67; State Univ NY Stony Brook, PhD(psychol), 73. *Prof Exp:* Fel, 73-76, ASST PROF, DEPT ANAT & PSYCHIAT, COLUMBIA UNIV COL PHYSICIANS & SURGEONS, 77-; SR RES SCIENTIST, NY STATE PSYCHIAT INST, 76- *Mem:* Soc Neurosci; Am Soc Zool. *Res:* Analysis of the neural basis of behavioral plasticity. *Mailing Add:* Div of Neurobiol & Behav Col of Physicians & Surgeons New York NY 10032

WEISS, LAWRENCE H(EISLER), b Chicago, Ill, May 14, 38; m 62; c 2. CHEMICAL ENGINEERING. *Educ:* Ill Inst Technol, BS, 59; Univ Calif, Berkeley, MS, 62; Johns Hopkins Univ, PhD(chem eng), 68. *Prof Exp:* Assoc develop engr, United Tech Ctr Div, United Aircraft Corp, 61-63; res scientist, Res & Develop Div, Union Camp Corp, NJ, 67-72; chem systs res specialist, Consol Edison Co NY, Inc, 72-75; sr technologist, Chem Systs Inc, 75-77, mgr eng projs, 77-82; MANAGING PARTNER, ENERGY TECHNOL ASSOCS, 82- *Concurrent Pos:* Mem, Interagency Flue Gas Desulfurization Task Force, US Environ Protection Agency. *Mem:* Am Inst Chem Engrs; Am Chem Soc. *Res:* Chemical process research and development; coal conversion and utilization; emissions control; alcohol fuels; industrial microbiology. *Mailing Add:* Energy Technol Assocs 122 E 42nd St New York NY 10168

WEISS, LAWRENCE R, b Brooklyn, NY, Feb 13, 31; m 59; c 2. PHARMACOLOGY, TOXICOLOGY. *Educ:* Univ Fla, BSc, 53; Ohio State Univ, MSc, 59, PhD(pharmacol), 62. *Prof Exp:* Pharmacologist & toxicologist, Pesticide Sect, Div Toxicol Eval, Bur Sci, 63-69, toxicologist, Div Pharmacol & Toxicol, 69-72, PROJ LEADER-GROUP SUPVR DRUG PHARMACOL & TOXICOL, DIV DRUG BIOL, FOOD & DRUG ADMIN, 72- *Mem:* AAAS; NY Acad Sci; Am Soc Pharmacol & Exp Therapeut; Soc Toxicol; Geront Soc. *Res:* Geriatric pharmacology and toxicology; age related adverse drug reactions on central nervous system and heart. *Mailing Add:* Div of Drug Biol Food & Drug Admin Washington DC 20204

WEISS, LEON, b Brooklyn, NY, Oct 4, 25; m 49; c 6. ANATOMY. *Educ:* Long Island Col Med, MD, 48. *Prof Exp:* Intern med, Maimonides Hosp, Brooklyn, NY, 48-49, asst resident, 49-50; instr med, Col Med, State Univ NY Downstate Med Ctr, 52-53; lectr, Grad Sch, Univ Md, 54-55; assoc anat, Harvard Med Sch, 55-57, from asst prof to prof anat, 57-76, Sch Med, Johns Hopkins Univ; PROF CELL BIOL & CHMN DEPT ANIMAL BIOL, UNIV PA SCH VET MED, 76- *Concurrent Pos:* USPHS res fel anat, Harvard Med Sch, 50-52; mem med mission to establish hemat lab, Nat Defense Med Ctr, Formosa, 55. *Mem:* Electron Micros Soc Am; Histochem Soc; Am Asn Anatomists; Tissue Cult Asn. *Res:* Microscopic anatomy; electron microscopy; histochemistry; tissue culture; connective tissues; reticuloendothelial system; histophysiology of the lympho-hematopoietic system. *Mailing Add:* 3800 Spruce St Philadelphia PA 19104

WEISS, LEONARD, b Brooklyn, NY, Mar 14, 34; m 58; c 2. APPLIED MATHEMATICS, ENGINEERING. *Educ:* City Col New York, BEE, 56; Columbia Univ, MSEE, 59; Johns Hopkins Univ, PhD(elec eng), 62. *Prof Exp:* Lectr elec eng, City Col New York, 56-59; staff scientist, Res Inst Adv Studies, 62-64; from asst prof to math & assoc prof appl math & eng, Brown Univ, 64-68; prof elec eng, Inst Fluid Dynamics & Appl Math, Univ Md, College Park, 68-78; STAFF DIR, US SENATE SUBCOMT ON ENERGY, NUCLEAR PROLIFERATION & FED SERV, 77- *Concurrent Pos:* Sloan res fel, 66-68; res mathematician, Naval Res Lab, Washington, DC, 70-77; legis asst to Sen John Glenn, 76-77; Cong sci fel, Inst Elec & Electronics Engrs, 76-77. *Mem:* AAAS; Am Math Soc; Soc Indust & Appl Math; Math Asn Am; Inst Elec & Electronics Engrs. *Res:* System theory; control theory; signal theory; analysis and structure of dynamical systems described by differential equations; nuclear proliferation. *Mailing Add:* Inst for Fluid Dynamics & Appl Math Univ of Md College Park MD 20742

WEISS, LEONARD, b London, Eng, June 15, 28; m 51; c 3. PATHOLOGY, CELL BIOLOGY. *Educ:* Cambridge Univ, BA, 50, MA, MB, BChir, 53, MD, 58, PhD(biol), 63, ScD, 71. *Prof Exp:* House physician, Westminster Hosp, Univ London, 54-55, resident pathologist, Hosp & res assoc & registr morbid anat, Med Sch, Univ, 55-58; mem sci staff, Med Res Coun, Nat Inst Med Res, London, 58-60 & Strangeways Res Lab, Cambridge Univ, 60-64; DIR CANCER RES, DEPT EXP PATH, ROSWELL PARK MEM INST, 64-; RES PROF DERMAT, MED SCH, STATE UNIV NY BUFFALO, 74-

Concurrent Pos: Res prof biophys, State Univ NY Buffalo, 65-74. *Mem:* Fel AAAS; Path Soc Gt Brit & Ireland; fel Royal Col Path; fel Brit Inst Biol; fel Col Am Pathologists. *Res:* Metastasis; biophysics of cell contact phenomena; ultrasound in medicine. *Mailing Add:* Dept of Exp Path Roswell Park Mem Inst Buffalo NY 14263

WEISS, LIONEL EDWARD, b London, Eng, Dec 11, 27; m 64; c 2. GEOLOGY. *Educ:* Univ Birmingham, BSc, 49, PhD, 53; Univ Edinburgh, ScD, 56. *Prof Exp:* Res assoc, 51-53, assoc, 56-57, from asst prof to assoc prof, 57-64, Miller res prof, 65-67, PROF GEOL, UNIV CALIF, BERKELEY, 64- *Concurrent Pos:* Guggenheim fel, 61 & 69. *Res:* Natural and experimental deformation of rocks and minerals; structural geology. *Mailing Add:* Dept of Geol & Geophys Univ of Calif Berkeley CA 94720

WEISS, LIONEL IRA, b New York, NY, Sept 5, 23; m 46; c 3. MATHEMATICAL STATISTICS. *Educ:* Columbia Univ, BA, 43, MA, 45, PhD(math statist), 53. *Prof Exp:* From asst prof to assoc prof statist, Univ Va, 49-56; assoc prof math, Univ Ore, 56-57; assoc prof, 57-61, PROF OPERS RES, CORNELL UNIV, 61- *Concurrent Pos:* Mem, Nat Res Coun, 66-69. *Mem:* Inst Math Statist; NY Acad Sci. *Res:* Statistical decision theory; asymptotic statistical theory. *Mailing Add:* Dept of Opers Res Upson Hall Cornell Univ Ithaca NY 14853

WEISS, LOUIS CHARLES, b New Orleans, La, July 10, 25; m 49; c 4. ELECTRIC FIELDS, TEXTILE PHYSICS. *Educ:* Tulane Univ, BS, 47, MS, 53. *Prof Exp:* Physicist & engr, Waterways Exp Sta, Corps Engrs, US Dept Defense, 47-48; physicist, 48-65, RES PHYSICIST, SOUTHERN REGIONAL RES CTR, USDA, 65- *Concurrent Pos:* Asst, La State Univ, 54-58. *Mem:* AAAS; Sigma Xi; Fiber Soc; Asn Textile Chemists & Colorists. *Res:* Charge and transportation of particulates and fibers by electric fields; electrostatics and mechanics of natural and modified textile fibers, yarns and fabrics; cotton processing; beta decay; strain gages; instrumentation physics. *Mailing Add:* Southern Regional Res Ctr PO Box 19687 New Orleans LA 70179

WEISS, MALCOLM PICKETT, b Washington, DC, June 28, 21; m 43; c 4. GEOLOGY. *Educ:* Univ Minn, PhD(geol), 53. *Prof Exp:* From instr to assoc prof geol, Ohio State Univ, 52-67; chmn dept, 67-72, PROF GEOL, NORTHERN ILL UNIV, 67- *Mem:* Geol Soc Am; Soc Econ Paleontologists & Mineralogists; Am Asn Petrol Geologists. *Res:* Stratigraphy; sedimentary petrography; carbonate petrology. *Mailing Add:* Dept of Geol Northern Ill Univ De Kalb IL 60115

WEISS, MARK LAWRENCE, b Brooklyn, NY, Nov 1, 45; m 69; c 1. PRIMATOLOGY, PHYSICAL ANTHROPOLOGY. *Educ:* State Univ NY Binghamton, BA, 66; Univ Calif, Berkeley, MA, 68, PhD(anthrop), 69. *Prof Exp:* Asst prof, 69-74, ASSOC PROF ANTHROP, WAYNE STATE UNIV, 74- *Concurrent Pos:* Adj anat, Sch Med, Wayne State Univ, 69-; fel, William Beaumont Hosp, 74. *Mem:* AAAS; Am Anthrop Asn; Am Asn Phys Anthropologists; Am Soc Human Genetics; Brit Soc Study Human Biol. *Res:* Biochemical polymorphisms; primate genetics; primate microevolution. *Mailing Add:* Dept of Anthrop Wayne State Univ Detroit MI 48202

WEISS, MARTIN, b New York, NY, Jan 21, 19; m 49; c 3. GEOLOGY. *Educ:* City Col New York, BS, 48; Univ Mich, MS, 51, PhD(geol), 54. *Prof Exp:* Asst geol, Mus Paleont, Univ Mich, 51-53; geologist, US Geol Surv, 53-63; oceanogr, Nat Oceanog Data Ctr, 63-72, marine geologist, Nat Geophys & Solar Terrestrial Data Ctr, Nat Oceanic & Atmospheric Admin, 68-75; MEM STAFF, US GEOL SUR, RESTON, 75- *Mem:* Geol Soc Am; Am Geophys Union; Marine Technol Soc. *Res:* Geological oceanography; military geology; Paleozoic ostracoda; review of environmental import statements. *Mailing Add:* US Geol Sur Nat Ctr Stop 760 Reston VA 22092

WEISS, MARTIN GEORGE, b Muscatine, Iowa, Oct 30, 11; m 38; c 2. PLANT BREEDING. *Educ:* Iowa State Univ, BS, 34, MS, 35, PhD(genetics, plant breeding), 41. *Prof Exp:* Asst geneticist, Div Forage Crops & Dis, Bur Plant Indust, USDA, 36-41; res prof farm crops, Exp Sta, Iowa State Col, 45-49; soybean proj leader, Div Forage Crops & Dis, USDA, 50-53, chief field crops res br, Agr Res Serv, 53-57, assoc dir, Crops Res Div, 57-63, asst to dep adminr farm res, 64-69, asst to assoc adminr, 70-71, dir int progs div, 71-73; agr res adv, Ministry Agr, Govt Iran & Develop & Resources Corp, Tehran, Iran, 74-76; AGR RES CONSULT, OFF TECHNOL ASSESSMENT, US CONGRESS, 76- *Concurrent Pos:* Agr res consult, Campbell Soup Co, Sudan & Food & Agr Orgn, UN, Ethiopia, 77- *Mem:* Fel Am Soc Agron; Genetics Soc Am; Crop Sci Soc Am (pres, 58); hon mem Am Soybean Asn; hon mem Asn Off Seed Certifying Agencies. *Res:* Early generation testing of soybeans, barley and forage crops; plant breeding methods; improvement of birdsfoot trefoil, orchardgrass, bromegrass and soybeans; agricultural research administration. *Mailing Add:* 11122 Emack Rd Beltsville MD 20705

WEISS, MARTIN JOSEPH, b New York, NY, May 4, 23; m 51; c 3. ORGANIC CHEMISTRY. *Educ:* NY Univ, AB, 44; Duke Univ, PhD(chem), 49. *Prof Exp:* Asst, Duke Univ, 44-47; res fel org chem, Hickrill Chem Res Found, 49-50; res chemist, Pharmaceut Res Dept, Calco Chem Div, 50-54, group leader, Lederle Labs, 54-75, DEPT HEAD, LEDERLE LABS, AM CYANAMID CO, 75- *Concurrent Pos:* Asst, Comt Med Res, Off Sci Res & Develop, Duke Univ, 44-45. *Mem:* Am Chem Soc. *Res:* Synthetic medicinal chemistry in prostaglandins, antibiotics, steroids, nucleosides and carbohydrates, indoles and other heterocyclics; chemotherapy; anti-arthritic, anti-allergy, anti-atherosclerotic and hypoglycemic agents. *Mailing Add:* Lederle Labs Am Cyanamid Co Pearl River NY 10965

WEISS, MARVIN, b New York, NY, Feb 6, 14; m 40; c 3. PHARMACEUTICAL CHEMISTRY, SCIENCE ADMINISTRATION. *Educ:* Brooklyn Col, BS, 37; Univ Ill, MS, 38. *Prof Exp:* Dir develop & control labs, Am Pharmaceut Co, 41-57; dir anal lab, Berkeley Chem Corp, 57-66; group leader corp control & anal, Millmaster Onyx Corp, 66, dir anal lab, Berkeley Chem Dept, Millmaster Onyx Group, 66-78, corp tech dir, 66-78, TECH DIR, A GROSS & CO DIV, MILLMASTER ONYX CORP, 78- *Concurrent Pos:* Group consult, Mantrose-Hauser Div, US Printing Ink Div, Onyx Div & Carboquimica SA Div, 65- *Mem:* Am Chem Soc; Am Oil Chemists Soc; NY Acad Sci. *Res:* Urethanes; nitrogen heterocycles; multiple condensations; acetic acid-ammonium acetate reactions with carbonyl compounds; crossed Cannizzaro syntheses; urea reactions; radiation curable inks and coatings; fatty acids and fatty acid derivates; shellac and shellac derivatives. *Mailing Add:* 227 Elkwood Ave New Providence NJ 07974

WEISS, MAX LESLIE, b Salt Lake City, Utah, Aug 12, 33; m; c 4. MATHEMATICS. *Educ:* Yale Univ, BA, 55; Cornell Univ, MS, 58; Univ Wash, PhD(math), 62. *Prof Exp:* Instr math, Reed Col, 58-60 & Univ Wash, 62-63; NSF fel, Inst Advan Study, 63-64; from asst prof to assoc prof, 64-72, PROF MATH, UNIV CALIF, SANTA BARBARA, 72- *Concurrent Pos:* Assoc provost, Col Creative Studies, 71-77. *Mem:* Am Math Soc; Asn Mem Inst Advan Study. *Res:* Function algebras and complex variables. *Mailing Add:* Dept of Math Univ of Calif Santa Barbara CA 93106

WEISS, MAX TIBOR, b Hungary, Dec 29, 22; nat US; m 53; c 4. PHYSICS. *Educ:* Mass Inst Technol, MS, 47, PhD(physics), 51. *Prof Exp:* Engr, Radio Corp Am, 43-44 & US Naval Ord Lab, 45-46; res assoc, Microwave Spectros Lab, Mass Inst Technol, 46-50; mem tech staff, Bel Tel Labs, Inc, 50-59; assoc dept mgr, Appl Physics Dept, Hughes Aircraft Corp, 59-61; dir electronics lab, Aerospace Corp, 61-63, gen mgr labs div, 63-67, asst mgr eng opers, TRW Systs, 67-68; gen mgr, Electronics & Optics Div, 68-78, VPRES & GEN MGR, LAB OPERS, AEROSPACE CORP, 78- *Concurrent Pos:* Lectr, City Col New York, 53. *Mem:* AAAS; fel Inst Elec & Electronics Engrs; fel Am Phys Soc. *Res:* Microwaves; magnetics; quantum electronics; communications; microelectronics. *Mailing Add:* VPres & Gen Mgr Lab Opers Aerospace Corp PO Box 92957 Los Angeles CA 90009

WEISS, MICHAEL DAVID, b Chicago, Ill, Nov 12, 42. ECONOMETRICS, MATHEMATICAL ECONOMICS. *Educ:* Brandeis Univ, BA, 64; Brown Univ, PhD(math), 70. *Prof Exp:* Asst prof math, Wayne State Univ, 69-74; analyst, Ketron Inc, 74-76; MATH STATISTICIAN, ECON RES SERV, USDA, 76- *Mem:* Am Math Soc; Soc Indust & Appl Math; Economet Soc. *Res:* Econometrics and mathematical economics; probability and statistics; ergodic theory; theory of fuzzy sets; applications. *Mailing Add:* 7797 Heatherton Lane Potomac MD 20854

WEISS, MICHAEL KARL, b Hatzfeld, Romania, Nov 11, 28; nat US; m 54; c 3. CHEMISTRY. *Educ:* Western Reserve Univ, MS, 55. *Prof Exp:* Res chemist, Harshaw Chem Co, 52-54; supvr anal chem, Repub Steel Corp Res Ctr, 55-62, chief anal sect, 62-67, head anal div, 67-72, MGR QUAL CONTROL DEPT, BUNKER HILL CO, 72- *Mem:* AAAS; Am Chem Soc; Soc Appl Spectros; Am Soc Testing & Mat. *Mailing Add:* E 5730 Sunnyside Rd Coeur d'Alene ID 83814

WEISS, MICHAEL STEPHEN, b Queens Co, NY, Mar 20, 43; m 65; c 2. SPEECH & HEARING SCIENCES, SPEECH PATHOLOGY. *Educ:* Long Island Univ, BA, 64; Purdue Univ, MS, 68, PhD(speech sci), 70. *Prof Exp:* Coordr res, Cleveland Hearing & Speech Ctr & sr res assoc speech sci, Case Western Reserve Univ, 70-71; asst prof speech, Howard Univ, 71-72; instr laryngol & otol & sci dir, Info Ctr Hearing, Speech & Disorders Human Commun, Sch Med, Johns Hopkins Univ, 72-76; coordr continuing educ media, Boys Town Inst Commun Disorders Children, 76-78; ASSOC PROF DEPT SPEECH PATH & AUDIOL, WEST CHESTER STATE COL, 78- *Concurrent Pos:* Lectr, Gallaudet Col, 74-76; assoc prof otolaryngol, Creighton Univ, 76-78. *Mem:* AAAS; Am Speech & Hearing Asn; Acoust Soc Am. *Res:* Speech science; physiological and acoustical events which underlie speech production and perception. *Mailing Add:* Dept of Speech Path & Audiol West Chester State Col West Chester PA 19380

WEISS, MITCHELL JOSEPH, b Chicago, Ill, Nov 12, 42. INVERTEBRATE ZOOLOGY. *Educ:* Brown Univ, ScB, 64; Univ Mich, PhD(zool), 70. *Prof Exp:* Instr zool, Univ Iowa, 73-74; ASST PROF BIOL, LIVINGSTON COL, RUTGERS UNIV, NEW BRUNSWICK, 74- *Concurrent Pos:* NIH res fel, Univ Wash, 70-73. *Mem:* Am Soc Zoologists; Soc Neuroscience; Am Microscopical Soc; Soc Develop Biol; Int Asn Meiobenthologists. *Res:* Functional and comparative anatomy and development of invertebrate central nervous systems, at both microscopic and ultrastructural levels; biology of Gastrotricha; current emphasis on insect brain centers and sexuality in gastrotrichs. *Mailing Add:* Dept of Biol Livingston Col Rutgers Univ New Brunswick NJ 08903

WEISS, MORRIS J, physical chemistry, see previous edition

WEISS, NOEL SCOTT, b Chicago, Ill, Mar 10, 43. EPIDEMIOLOGY. *Educ:* Stanford Univ, MD, 67; Harvard Univ, MPH, 69, DrPH, 71. *Prof Exp:* Epidemiologist, Nat Ctr Health Statist, 71-73; from asst prof to assoc prof epidemiol, 73-79, PROF EPIDEMIOL, UNIV WASH, 79- *Res:* Endocrinologic determinants of disease. *Mailing Add:* Dept of Epidemiol Univ of Wash SC 36 Seattle WA 98195

WEISS, NORMAN JAY, b Brooklyn, NY, May 28, 42; m 65; c 2. MATHEMATICAL ANALYSIS. *Educ:* Harvard Univ, BA, 63; Princeton Univ, PhD, 66. *Prof Exp:* Instr math, Princeton Univ, 66-68; asst prof, Columbia Univ, 68-71; asst prof, 71-72, ASSOC PROF MATH, QUEENS COL, NY, 73- *Mem:* Am Math Soc. *Res:* Real and Fourier analysis. *Mailing Add:* Dept of Math Queens Col Flushing NY 11367

WEISS, PAUL, b Sagan, Ger, Apr 9, 11; m 42; c 2. PHYSICS. *Educ:* Cambridge Univ, PhD(math), 36. *Prof Exp:* Asst lectr math physics, Queen's Univ, Belfast, 39; lectr appl math, Westfield Col, Univ London, 41-51; math physicist, Electron Lab, Gen Elec Co, 52-57; consult res & develop labs, Avco Corp, 57-58; assoc prof physics & math, 58-62, from assoc prof to prof math, 62-81, EMER PROF MATH, WAYNE STATE UNIV, 81- *Concurrent Pos:* Mem, Inst Advan Study, 50-51. *Mem:* Am Math Soc; Am Phys Soc; London Math Soc. *Res:* Differential equations of mathematical physics. *Mailing Add:* Dept Math Wayne State Univ Detroit MI 48202

WEISS, PAUL ALFRED, b Vienna, Austria, Mar 21, 98; nat US; m 26. BIOLOGY. *Educ:* Univ Vienna, PhD(biol), 22. *Hon Degrees:* MD, Univ Frankfurt, 49; ScD, Univ Giessen, 57; Dr Med & Surg, Univ Helsinki, 66; ScD, Univ Notre Dame, 72. *Prof Exp:* Asst dir biol res inst, Vienna Acad Sci, 22-29; fel, Kaiser Wilhelm Inst, Berlin, 29-31; Sterling fel, Yale Univ, 31-33; from asst prof to prof zool, Univ Chicago, 33-54, chmn div biol, Master's Prog, 47-54; mem prof develop biol & head lab, 54-64, EMER MEM, ROCKEFELLER UNIV, 64-, EMER PROF BIOL, 54- *Concurrent Pos:* Vienna Acad Sci fel, Zool Sta, Naples, 26; Rockefeller Found fel, Oceanog Inst, Monaco & Kaiser Wilhelm Inst, 27-29, Johnson Found, Univ Pa, 35, Univs, Cambridge, Zurich, Amsterdam & Free Univ Brussels, 37; vis prof, Univs, Frankfurt, 48-49, Washington, 49, Stanford, 50, Nebr, 51 & Mass Inst Technol, 56-57; mem inst basic res, Univ Calif, 56-59; distinguished vis prof, NY Univ, 60; vis prof, Indust Univ Santander, 63; assoc neurosci res prog, Mass Inst Technol, 63-; distinguished vis scholar, Pratt Inst, 64; dean & univ prof, Univ Tex, 64-66; distinguished vis lectr, Univ Ga & Tulane Univ, 66; spec lectr, Col de France, 66; distinguished prof, Tex A&M Univ, 66-67; distinguished vis lectr, State Univ NY Buffalo, 67; Spec consult, US Dept State, 51; chief sci adv, Brussels World Fair, 56-58; mem, President's Sci Adv Comt, 58-60; consult, President's Off Sci & Technol, 59-; ed, Quart Rev Biol, Develop Biol, J Theoret Biol, Perspectives in Biol & Med, Annee Biologique, France & Biophysik, Ger; chmn comt neurobiol, Nat Res Coun, 47-53, chmn div biol & agr, 51-55, comt develop biol, Biol Coun, 51-63, comt, Int Union Biol Sci, 53-64, mem-at-large, 55-, chmn comt int biol sta, 63-65; mem, Elliott Medal Comt, Nat Acad Sci, 57-60, Hartley Medal Comt, 59-62, Agassiz Medal Comt, 60-63, adv comt, Off Sci Personnel, 60-, chmn renewable resources, Comt Natural Resources, 61-62, mem, Henry Fund Comt, 62-65, adv comt int opers & prog, 62-, mem coun, 64-67; chmn, Merck Fellowship Bd; mem bd dir, Am Inst Biol Sci, 48-50; mem, Fulbright Comt for Int Exchange of Persons, 49-52; mem res coun, United Cerebral Palsy Asns, 51-53; adv bd, Mass Gen Hosp, 52-55; mem corp, Marine Biol Lab, Woods Hole & Bermuda Biol Sta; mem, Coun Indust Res & Develop to Gov NY State, 60-64; mem sci adv bd, Pac Sci Ctr, 62-; mem adv bd, Mt Sinai Hosp & Sch Med, New York, 63-66; chmn, US nat comt, Int Union Biol Sci, 52-, chmn US deleg, 53, 55, 58 & 61, chmn policy bd, 53-55, mem adv coun, Naples Sta; chmn US deleg, Int Coun Sci Unions, 61. *Honors & Awards:* Cert of Merit, US Off Sci Res & Develop, 45; Citation of Merit, US Depts Army & Navy, 45; Grand Medal Geoffrey St Hilaire, France, 55; Leitz Award, 57; Pub Serv Cert, US Dept State, 58; Eleven Lect Awards, 58-69; Weinstein Award, United Cerebral Palsy Asns, 59; John F Lewis Prize, Am Philos Soc, 71; Semicentennial Doctor's Dipl, Univ Vienna, 72. *Mem:* Nat Acad Sci; AAAS (vpres, 53); Soc Develop Biol; Harvey Soc (pres, 62); Int Soc Develop Biol (vpres, 49). *Res:* Experimental and theoretical analysis of growth and differentiation in animals; tissue culture; nerve development; regeneration and wound healing; electron microscopy; functional adaptation; coordination of nerve centers; biological education and research. *Mailing Add:* New York NY

WEISS, PAUL B, b New York, NY, Mar 14, 38; div; c 3. PHYSICS, COMPUTER SCIENCE. *Educ:* Univ Chicago, SB, 58; Fla State Univ, MS, 61, PhD(physics), 63; Univ NMex, MBA, 79. *Prof Exp:* Staff mem, Lawrence Livermore Lab, 63-73, STAFF MEM PHYSICS, LOS ALAMOS NAT LAB, UNIV CALIF, 73- *Res:* Imaging; both visible and infrared image processing; minicomputer processing of images; neutron physics. *Mailing Add:* Los Alamos Nat Lab MS406 Los Alamos NM 87545

WEISS, PETER JOSEPH, b Vienna, Austria, Nov 23, 18; nat US; m 48; c 2. PHARMACEUTICAL CHEMISTRY. *Educ:* George Washington Univ, BS, 51; Georgetown Univ, MS, 53, PhD(biochem), 56. *Prof Exp:* Chemist, Food & Drug Admin, 47-56, chief chem br, Div Antibiotics, 56-70, dep dir, Nat Ctr Antibiotic Anal, 70-71, dir, 72-79; RETIRED. *Mem:* Am Chem Soc; Acad Pharmaceut Sci; Am Pharmaceut Asn. *Res:* Chemical analysis of antibiotics. *Mailing Add:* 1309 Caddington Ave Silver Spring MD 20901

WEISS, PETER REIFER, b Portland, Maine, May 13, 15; m; c 1. THEORETICAL PHYSICS. *Educ:* Bowdoin Col, AB, 35; Harvard Univ, MA, 36, PhD(physics), 40. *Prof Exp:* Instr, Harvard Univ, 40-42; mem staff, Radiation Lab, Mass Inst Technol, 42-46; from asst prof to assoc prof, 46-57, chmn dept, 64-72, PROF PHYSICS, RUTGERS UNIV, NEW BRUNSWICK, 57- *Mem:* Fel Am Phys Soc. *Res:* Theory of the solid state; magnetism; superconductivity; transport theory. *Mailing Add:* Dept of Physics Rutgers Univ New Brunswick NJ 08903

WEISS, PHILIP, b New York, NY, June 12, 16; m 43; c 2. ORGANIC CHEMISTRY. *Educ:* NY Univ, BS, 39, MSc, 41, PhD(org 48. *Prof Exp:* Res chemist, Lederle Labs, Am Cyanamid Co, 41-46; sr res chemist, Wallace & Tiernan Prod, Inc, 46-52; sr proj chemist, Colgate-Palmolive Co, 52-57; sr res scientist, Electrochem Dept, Res Labs, Gen Motors Corp, 57-58, asst head electrochem & polymers dept, 58-59, head, Polymers Dept, Res Labs, 59-81; ADJ PROF, DEPT CHEM, OAKLAND UNIV, 80- *Concurrent Pos:* Instr, Cooper 49-51; mem, Bd Trustees, Paint Res Inst, 61-63 & Plastics Inst Am, 64-69; ed, J Appl Polymer Sci; mem, Comt Critical & Strategic Mat, Nat Mat Adv Bd, Adv Bd, Col Eng, Univ Detroit & Adv Bd, Polymer Prog, Col Eng, Princeton Univ; US rep, Plastics & High Polymers Sect, Int Union Pure & Appl Chem; proj mgr, Paint Res Inst. *Honors & Awards:* Exner Medal, 69. *Mem:* Am Chem Soc; Soc Plastics Engrs. *Res:* Polymer synthesis, research and development in plastics, rubber, adhesives and surface coatings; graft and block copolymers; mechanisms of finish failure; adhesion and cohesion; mechanical behavior of polymers; polymer flammability, aging, waste disposal and processing. *Mailing Add:* Dept Chem Oakland Univ Rochester MI 48063

WEISS, RAINER, b Berlin, Ger, Sept 29, 32; US citizen; m 59; c 2. PHYSICS. *Educ:* Mass Inst Technol, BS, 55, PhD(physics), 62. *Prof Exp:* Asst prof physics, Tufts Univ, 60-62; res assoc, Princeton Univ, 62-64; from asst prof to assoc prof, 64-74, PROF PHYSICS, MASS INST TECHNOL, 74- *Res:* Experimental relativity, infrared astronomy; atomic physics. *Mailing Add:* Rm 20F001 Mass Inst of Technol Cambridge MA 02139

WEISS, RICHARD GERALD, b Akron, Ohio, Nov 13, 42. PHOTOCHEMISTRY, PHYSICAL ORGANIC CHEMISTRY. *Educ:* Brown Univ, ScB, 65; Univ Conn, MS, 67, PhD(chem), 69. *Prof Exp:* NIH res fel chem, Calif Inst Technol, 69-71; vis prof, Inst Chem, Univ Sao Paulo, 71-74; asst prof chem, 74-80, ASSOC PROF CHEM, GEORGETOWN UNIV, 80- *Concurrent Pos:* Nat Acad Sci overseas fel, 71-74; vis scientist, Max Planck Inst Fur Strahlenchemie, 81-82; vis prof, Ecole Nat Superieure de Chimie, Strasbourg, 82 & Univ Bordeaux, 82. *Mem:* Am Chem Soc; InterAm Photochem Soc; Europ Photochem Asn. *Res:* Mechanisms and rates of organic and photochemical reactions; steric effects in electronic energy transfer and in decay of excited states; mechanistic studies in ordered media. *Mailing Add:* 4604 W Virginia Ave Bethesda MD 20814

WEISS, RICHARD JEROME, b New York, NY, Dec 14, 23; m; c 2. PHYSICS. *Educ:* City Col New York, BS, 44; Univ Calif, MA, 47; NY Univ, PhD(physics), 50. *Prof Exp:* Physicist, US Army Mat Res Ctr, 50-80; PROF, KINGS COL, LONDON, 80-; PROF, UNIV SURREY, ENGLAND, 81- *Concurrent Pos:* Vis fel, Cavendish Labs, Cambridge Univ, 56-57; lectr, Mass Inst Technol, 59; Secy Army fel, Imp Col, Univ London, 62-63; chmn, Comn Electron Distributions, Int Union Crystallog, 72-75. *Honors & Awards:* Rockefeller Pub Serv Award, 56. *Mem:* Am Phys Soc; Am Crystallog Soc. *Res:* Solid state, neutron and x-ray physics; electron structure of solids. *Mailing Add:* 4 Lawson St Avon MA 02322

WEISS, RICHARD LAWRENCE, b New York, NY, Dec 28, 40; m 71; c 2. CELL BIOLOGY, BOTANY. *Educ:* Univ Conn, BA, 64; Calif State Univ, Long Beach, MS, 70; Ind Univ, PhD(microbiol), 72. *Prof Exp:* Res fel bot, Univ Calif, Berkeley, 73-74; res fel cell biol, Harvard Univ, 74-75 & 75-76; res assoc med microbiol, Univ Calif, Irvine, 76-77; asst prof, 77-80, ASSOC PROF BOT, CALIF STATE UNIV, SAN DIEGO, 80- *Concurrent Pos:* Am Cancer Soc fel, Univ Calif, Berkeley, 73-74; NIH fel cell biol, Harvard Univ, 75-76; NIH grant, Calif State Univ, San Diego, 78- *Mem:* Sigma Xi. *Res:* Mechanism of cell fusion; cell-cell interaction; cell differentiation cell structure; biological electron microscopy; autoradiography. *Mailing Add:* Dept of Bot Calif State Univ San Diego CA 92182

WEISS, RICHARD LOUIS, b Evanston, Ill, June 24, 44. BIOCHEMISTRY, GENETICS. *Educ:* Stanford Univ, BS, 66; Univ Wash, PhD(biochem), 71. *Prof Exp:* USPHS fel, Univ Mich, 71-72, Am Cancer Soc fel, 72-73; asst prof, 74-80, ASSOC PROF CHEM, UNIV CALIF, LOS ANGELES, 80- *Mem:* Am Chem Soc; Am Soc Microbiol; Genetics Soc Am. *Res:* Regulation of amino acid metabolism in eucaryotic microorganisms. *Mailing Add:* Dept Chem Univ Calif Los Angeles CA 90024

WEISS, RICHARD RAYMOND, b Takoma Park, Md, Aug 26, 28; m 56; c 2. METEOROLOGY, ELECTRICAL ENGINEERING. *Educ:* Univ Md, BSE, 52; Univ Mich, Ann Arbor, MSE, 55; Univ Wash, PhD(elec eng), 67. *Prof Exp:* Engr, Sperry Gyroscope Co, 52-54; cardiovasc trainee, Univ Wash, 59-60; asst prof elec eng, Seattle Univ, 60-64; lectr, Univ Wash, 64-67, res asst prof, 67-74, sr res assoc atmospheric sci, 74-81; ASSOC PROF ELEC ENG, SEATTLE UNIV, 81- *Mem:* Inst Elec & Electronics Engrs; Am Geophys Union. *Res:* Radar meteorology. *Mailing Add:* 1501 McGilvra Blvd E Seattle WA 98112

WEISS, ROBERT ALAN, b Cleveland, Ohio, Oct 29, 50. POLYMER SCIENCE. *Educ:* Northwestern Univ, BS, 72; Univ Mass, PhD(chem eng), 75. *Prof Exp:* Res engr, Exxon Chem Co, 75-77, staff engr polymer sci, Exxon Res & Eng Co, 77-81; ASSOC PROF, DEPT CHEM ENG, UNIV CONN, 81- *Mem:* Soc Plastics Engrs; Am Chem Soc; Soc Rheol; NAm Thermal Anal Soc. *Res:* Polymer structure; property relationships; ionomers; composite materials. *Mailing Add:* Inst Mat Sci Univ Conn Storrs CT 06268

WEISS, ROBERT F, b New York, NY, Mar 10, 37; m 59; c 4. FLUID MECHANICS. *Educ:* NY Univ, BAeroE, 58, EngScD(aeronaut), 63; Mass Inst Technol, MS, 59. *Prof Exp:* Prin res scientist & chmn aerophysics, Avco Everett Res Lab, 63-72, vpres appl technol, 72-73; PRES & CHMN BD, PHYS SCI, INC, 73- *Mem:* Am Inst Aeronaut & Astronaut. *Res:* Reentry physics; laser-material interactions; laser propulsion; hypervelocity impact. *Mailing Add:* 30 Commerce Way Woburn MA 01801

WEISS, ROBERT JEROME, b West New York, NJ, Dec 9, 17; m 45; c 3. PSYCHIATRY. *Educ:* George Washington Univ, AB, 47; Columbia Univ, MD, 51. *Prof Exp:* Intern, Columbia Div, Bellevue Hosp, 51, asst resident med, 53; resident psychiat, Columbia Psychoanal Clin, 54-59; chief, Mary Hitchcock Mem Hosp, Hanover, NH, 59-70; vis prof, 70-75, assoc dir, Ctr Community Health & Med Care, Harvard Med Sch, 70-75, assoc dean health care progs, 71-75; PROF PSYCHIAT & SOCIAL MED, COL PHYSICIANS & SURGEONS, COLUMBIA UNIV, 75-, DIR, CTR COMMUNITY HEALTH SYSTS, 75-, DELAMAR PROF PUB HEALTH PRACT, 80-, DEAN, SCH PUB HEALTH, 80- *Concurrent Pos:* NIMH career teacher trainee, Columbia Univ, 56-58; resident, NY State Psychiat Inst & Presby Hosp, New York, 57; asst attend, Vanderbilt Clin, 57-58; assoc, Col Physicians & Surgeons, Columbia Univ, 57-59; asst attend, Presby Hosp, 58-59; consult, NH Div Ment Health, 59-70, Vet Admin Hosp, White River Junction, Vt, 60-70 & Bur Health Manpower Educ, 72-; prof psychiat & chmn dept, Dartmouth Med Sch, 59-70; chmn adv comn, NH Dept Health & Welfare, 61; mem exec comt, NH Ment Health Planning Proj, 64-66 & Adv Comn Ment Health Construct NH, 65-70; coordr panel, NIMH, 65-67, chmn subcomt psychiat, 67-68; psychiatrist, Beth Israel Hosp, 70-75; attend, Presby Hosp, New York, 75-; consult, Nat Ctr Health Serv Res, 75-; consult, NIMH, 77- *Honors & Awards:* Bi-Centennial Medal, Columbia Univ Col Physicians & Surgeons, 67. *Mem:* AAAS; fel Am Psychiat Asn; Am Asn Med Cols; Am Acad Psychoanal; NY Acad Sci. *Res:* Epidemiology; health care; preventive psychiatry; community medicine. *Mailing Add:* Columbia Univ Ctr Community Health Systs 21 Audubon Ave New York NY 10032

WEISS, ROBERT JOHN, b Pomona, Calif, Apr 9, 37; m 64; c 2. MATHEMATICS. *Educ:* La Verne Col, BA, 58; Univ Calif, Los Angeles, MA & PhD(math), 62. *Prof Exp:* Assoc prof math, Bridgewater Col, 62-68; assoc prof & head dept, 68-74, PROF MATH, MARY BALDWIN COL, 74- *Mem:* Am Math Soc; Math Asn Am. *Res:* Algebraic topology. *Mailing Add:* Dept of Math Mary Baldwin Col Staunton VA 24401

WEISS, ROBERT MARTIN, b New York, NY. UROLOGY, PHARMACOLOGY. *Educ:* Franklin & Marshall Col, BS, 57; State Univ NY Downstate Med Ctr, MD, 60. *Prof Exp:* Intern med, Second (Cornell) Med Div, Bellevue Hosp, New York, 60-61; resident gen surg, Beth Israel Hosp, New York, 61-62; resident urol, Columbia-Presby Med Ctr, 63-64; fel, Col Physicians & Surgeons, Columbia Univ, 64-65; resident, Columbia-Presby Med Ctr, 65-67; instr surg-urol, 67-68, asst prof urol, 68-71, assoc prof surg-urol, 71-76, PROF SURG-UROL, SCH MED, YALE UNIV, 76- *Concurrent Pos:* Res assoc pharmacol, Col Physicians & Surgeons, Columbia Univ, 67-75, adj assoc prof, 75-77, adj prof, 77-; attend, Yale-New Haven Hosp, 67-; consult, West Haven Vet Admin Hosp, 67- & Waterbury Hosp, 76-; mem obstruction & neuromuscular dis comt, Nat Inst Arthritis, Metab & Digestive Dis, 74-75; fel, Timothy Dwight Col, Yale Univ, 74-; asst ed, J Urol, 75-; mem adv panel, US Pharmacopeia & Nat Formulary, 76-81. *Mem:* Am Physiol Soc; Soc Gen Physiologists; Am Acad Pediat; Am Col Surgeons; Am Urol Asn. *Res:* Mechanical and electrophysiologic properties of ureteral smooth muscle; role of cyclic nucleotides in smooth muscle function. *Mailing Add:* Yale-New Haven Hosp 789 Howard Ave New Haven CT 06510

WEISS, ROGER HARVEY, b New York, NY, July 13, 26; m 53; c 2. ANALYTICAL CHEMISTRY. *Educ:* Col Holy Cross, BNaval Sci, 46; Cornell Univ, AB, 50; Ga Inst Technol, PhD(chem), 68. *Prof Exp:* Instr chem, Univ Toledo, 54-57; from asst prof to assoc prof, 59-, PROF CHEM, HUMBOLDT STATE UNIV, 74- *Concurrent Pos:* Fulbright lectr, Univ Sind, Pakistan, 73-74. *Mem:* Am Chem Soc. *Res:* Titrimetry with solid titrants; trace analysis; chelation; absorption spectrophotometry; photometric titrations. *Mailing Add:* Dept of Chem Humboldt State Univ Arcata CA 95521

WEISS, ROLAND GEORGE, b Milwaukee, Wis, July 11, 49. INDUSTRIAL ENGINEERING. *Educ:* Univ Wis-Milwaukee, BS, 72; Northwestern Univ, MS, 75, PhD(indust eng), 76. *Prof Exp:* Oper res analyst technol policy, Exp Technol Incentives Prog, Ctr Field Methods, Nat Bur Standards, 76-79; SYSTS ENGR, BELL LABS, 79- *Concurrent Pos:* Prof relations vchmn, Col Pub Progs & Processes, Inst Mgt Sci, 77-81. *Mem:* AAAS; Am Inst Indust Engrs; Am Psychol Asn; Inst Elec & Electronics Engrs; Inst Mgt Sci. *Res:* Development of methodology for analyzing complex, unstructured problems, including systems analysis, decision and architectural design and administrative experimentation; systems engineering of large, advanced systems with hardware, software, organizational market components. *Mailing Add:* 142 S St Apt A Red Bank NJ 07701

WEISS, RONALD, b Chicago, Ill, Jan 29, 37; m 67; c 3. FOOD SCIENCE. *Educ:* Ariz State Univ, BS, 58, MS, 59; Mich State Univ, PhD(chem), 64, MBA, 67. *Prof Exp:* Res chemist, 64-67, proj coordr, 67-69, mgr prod develop, 69-73, dir growth & develop, 73-75, DIR PLANNING, MILES LABS, INC, 75- *Mem:* Am Chem Soc; Inst Food Technologists; Soft Drink Technologists Asn. *Mailing Add:* Biotechnol Group Miles Labs PO Box 932 Elkhart IN 46515

WEISS, SAMUEL, b Warsaw, Poland, Sept 26, 20; m 49; c 3. ENVIRONMENTAL ENGINEERING, PROCESS DEVELOPMENT. *Educ:* Va Polytech Inst, BS, 44; Univ Md, MS, 54. *Prof Exp:* Res chemist, Nopco Chem Co, 56-58; pilot plant supvr, Warner-Lambert Res Inst, 58-60; process develop engr, Universal Oil Prod Chem Co, 60-64; chem design consult, Leonard Process Co, 64-65; supvr process develop, Tenneco Chem Co, NJ, 65-71; PRIN ENVIRON ENGR, STAUFFER CHEM CO, 72- *Mem:* Am Chem Soc; Am Inst Chem Eng. *Res:* Design and development of continuous reaction systems for preparation of organic chemicals; design of systems for protection of environment; compliance with air pollution control laws; design of plants for chlorination of organics; simplification and cost reductions; process improvement. *Mailing Add:* 168 Mohawk Dr River Edge NJ 07661

WEISS, SAMUEL BERNARD, b New York, NY, May 18, 26; m 61; c 2. BIOCHEMISTRY. *Educ:* City Col New York, BS, 48; Univ Southern Calif, PhD(biochem), 54. *Prof Exp:* Res assoc biochem, Mass Gen Hosp, Boston, 56-57; asst prof, Rockefeller Inst, 57-58; asst prof, 58-63, PROF BIOCHEM, UNIV CHICAGO, 63- *Concurrent Pos:* Am Heart Asn fel biochem, Univ Chicago, 54-56; Guggenheim fel, Salk Inst, 70-71; res assoc, Argonne Cancer Res Hosp, 58-, assoc dir, 67-74. *Honors & Awards:* Theobold Smith Award, AAAS, 61; Am Chem Soc Award Enzyme Chem, 66. *Mem:* Am Soc Biol Chemists; Am Acad Arts & Sci. *Res:* Enzymology of reactions in the synthesis of lipids, proteins and nucleic acids; viral transfer RNAs; mechanism of action of polycyclic aromatic hydrocarbons. *Mailing Add:* Franklin McLean Mem Res Inst 950 E 59th St Chicago IL 60637

WEISS, SIDNEY, b New York, NY, Dec 16, 20; m 44; c 3. BIOCHEMISTRY. *Educ:* Queens Col, NY, BS, 42; Fordham Univ, MS, 46, PhD(biochem), 49; Rutgers Univ, MS, 66. *Prof Exp:* Res chemist, Food Res Labs, Inc, NY, 42-46; res assoc biochem, Inst Cancer Res, Philadelphia, Pa, 49-58; sr res chemist, 58-59, sect head, 59-63, mgr biol res, 63-74, assoc dir res, 74-79, DIR BASIC RES, COLGATE-PALMOLIVE CO, 79- *Mem:* Am Chem Soc; Am Soc Biol Chem; Am Asn Dent Res; Am Statist Asn. *Res:* Biological oxidations; enzymatic reactions and microbiological transformations. *Mailing Add:* 909 River Rd Piscataway NJ 08854

WEISS, SOL, b Austria, Apr 19, 13; US citizen; m 40; c 2. MATHEMATICS. *Educ:* Brooklyn Col, BS, 34; Columbia Univ, MA, 36. *Prof Exp:* Teacher, Philadelphia Pub Sch Syst, Pa, chmn dept math, 50-64; asst prof math, West Chester State Col, 64-65, assoc prof, 65-78; RETIRED. *Concurrent Pos:* Consult, Wilmington Sch Dist, Del, 64, Philadelphia Pub Sch Syst, 64-65 & 67-, Cecil County Pub Schs, Md, 66, Upward Bound Prog, Franklin & Marshall Col, 67 & Lehigh Univ Social Restoration Prog, Pa State Prisons, 73-74. *Mem:* Math Asn Am. *Res:* Mathematics education for the low achiever. *Mailing Add:* 102 Crosshill Rd Overbrook Hills PA 19151

WEISS, STANLEY, b New York, NY, Apr 9, 29; m 60; c 3. METALLURGY. *Educ:* Polytech Inst Brooklyn, BMetE, 51; Mass Inst Technol, SM, 55, ScD(metall), 64. *Prof Exp:* Engr, Gen Elec Co, 51-54; sr engr, Alco Prod, 55-56; mgr welding eng, Gen Elec Co, Ohio, 56-61; res assoc metall, Mass Inst Technol, 64-68; ASSOC PROF MAT, UNIV WIS-MILWAUKEE, 68- *Concurrent Pos:* Consult, Gen Elec Co, 61-, Standard Thomson Corp, 63-68, Walter Kidde-Fenwal Div, 64-68 & Cryogenics Technol, 65-; corp consult, Snap-On Tools Corp, 71- *Mem:* Am Welding Soc; Soc Mfg Engrs; Am Soc Metals; Am Ceramics Soc. *Res:* Brazing mechanisms; residual stresses in welding; failure analysis; forged powder metals; joining of forged powder metals; corrosion of prosthetic devices. *Mailing Add:* Col of Eng Univ of Wis Milwaukee WI 53201

WEISS, STEPHEN FREDRICK, b Berkeley, Calif, Mar 6, 44; m 68. COMPUTER SCIENCE. *Educ:* Carnegie-Mellon Univ, BS, 66; Cornell Univ, MS, 69, PhD(comput sci), 70. *Prof Exp:* Asst prof, 70-75, ASSOC PROF COMPUT SCI, UNIV NC, CHAPEL HILL, 75- *Concurrent Pos:* Consult, Environ Protection Agency, 75-78, Res Triangle Inst & Lipids Res Clinics. *Mem:* Asn Comput Mach; Asn Computational Ling. *Res:* Natural language analysis; information retrieval; very-large-scale integration design. *Mailing Add:* Dept of Comput Sci Univ of NC Chapel Hill NC 27514

WEISS, THEODORE JOEL, b Rochester, NY, Aug 16, 19; m 41; c 2. LIPID CHEMISTRY. *Educ:* Syracuse Univ, AB, 40, PhD(biochem), 53. *Prof Exp:* Asst chemist feed control, State Inspection & Regulatory Serv, Md, 41-43; res chemist powdered milk, Borden Co, 44-49 & Dairymen's League Coop Asn, 49-52; res chemist & div head, Swift & Co, 52-63; tech dir, Capital City Prod Co, 63-64; sr proj leader, Res & Develop Dept, Hunt-Wesson Foods, Inc, 64-68; res chemist, Southern Utilization Res & Develop Div, Agr Res Serv, USDA, 68-70, Dairy Prod Lab, 70-72; TECH MGR INDUST SALES DEPT, HUNT-WESSON FOODS, INC, 72- *Mem:* AAAS; Am Chem Soc; Inst Food Technologists; Am Oil Chem Soc. *Res:* Edible fats and oils; margarine; peanut butter; mayonnaise. *Mailing Add:* Indust Sales Dept Hunt-Wesson 1645 W Valencia Dr Fullerton CA 92634

WEISS, THOMAS E, b New Orleans, La, June 15, 16; m 50; c 2. MEDICINE. *Educ:* Tulane Univ, MD, 40. *Prof Exp:* From instr to assoc prof med, 47-64, PROF CLIN MED, SCH MED, TULANE UNIV, 64- *Concurrent Pos:* Mem staff, Ochsner Clin; trustee, Alton Ochsner Med Found. *Mem:* Am Rheumatism Asn (past pres). *Res:* Rheumatic diseases; gout, clinical observations and correlating clinical finds with test and treatments; studies of radioisotope joint scanning in patients with arthritis. *Mailing Add:* Ochsner Clin 1514 Jefferson Hwy New Orleans LA 70121

WEISS, ULRICH, b Prague, Czech, Jan 24, 08; nat US; m 37; c 2. ORGANIC CHEMISTRY. *Educ:* Univ Prague, PhD(chem), 30. *Prof Exp:* Res chemist, Norgine, Inc, Czech, 30-39; asst to mgr, Norgan, Inc, France, 39-40; res chemist, Endo Prod, Inc, 41-51; chemist, Tuberc Res Lab, USPHS, 51-53; res assoc, Columbia Univ, 53-54; chemist, New York Bot Garden, 55-57; exec secy, Dent Study Sect, Div Res Grants, NIH, 57-58, chemist, 58-78, EMER SCIENTIST, LAB CHEM PHYSICS, NAT INST ARTHRITIS, DIABETES, & DIGESTIVE & KIDNEY DIS, 78- *Concurrent Pos:* Instr, Brooklyn Col, 52-55. *Mem:* Am Chem Soc; The Chem Soc; NY Acad Sci. *Res:* Chemistry of natural compounds; medicinal chemistry; biosynthesis; morphine derivatives; chiroptical effects; synthesis of cyclopentanoid ring systems. *Mailing Add:* Bldg 2 Room 122 Nat Insts of Health Bethesda MD 20205

WEISS, VIRGIL WAYNE, polymer chemistry, see previous edition

WEISS, VOLKER, b Rottenmann, Austria, Sept 2, 30; nat US; m 57; c 2. METALLURGY. *Educ:* Vienna Tech Univ, dipl, 53; Syracuse Univ, MS, 55, PhD(solid state sci & technol), 57. *Prof Exp:* Asst, Neth Steel Factory, 52; res assoc metall, 54-57, from asst prof to assoc prof, 57-65, prof mat sci, 65-77, assoc chmn metall, 65-72, CHMN SOLID STATE SCI & TECHNOL PROG, SYRACUSE UNIV, 65-, ASSOC DEAN SPONSORED PROGS, L C SMITH COL ENG, 72-, DIR INST ENG, 76-, PROF ENG & VPRES RES & GRAD AFFAIRS, 77- *Concurrent Pos:* Indust consult, US & Ger, 56- *Mem:* Fel Am Soc Metals; Am Soc Testing & Mat; Am Inst Mining, Metall & Petrol Engrs; Brit Inst Metals; Ger Metall Soc. *Res:* Metal physics; fracture mechanics; fatigue; residual stresses; solid state reactions; superplasticity; x-ray diffraction. *Mailing Add:* 304 Admin Bldg Syracuse Univ Syracuse NY 13210

WEISS, WILLIAM, b New York, NY, June 12, 23; m 56; c 4. BIOSTATISTICS, EPIDEMIOLOGY. *Educ:* George Washington Univ, BA, 48. *Prof Exp:* Chief statistician, US Food & Drug Admin, 52-62; asst chief perinatal res br, 62-66, CHIEF, OFF BIOMET & FIELD STUDIES, NAT INST NEUROL & COMMUN DIS & STROKE, NIH, BETHESDA, MD, 66- *Mem:* Biomet Soc; Am Statist Asn; Drug Info Asn. *Res:* Biostatistical applications in neurology; communicative disorders; perinatal research; design and analysis of clinical trials in neurological disease; design and implementation of clinical data banks in stroke and traumatic coma; design and implementation of national probability sample surveys of chronic and debilitating headache and other neurological disorders. *Mailing Add:* 609 Jerry Lane NW Vienna VA 22180

WEISS, WILLIAM, b Philadelphia, Pa, July 29, 19; m 41; c 3. PULMONARY DISEASES, EPIDEMIOLOGY. *Educ:* Univ Pa, BA, 40, MD, 44. *Prof Exp:* Mem staff, Sch Med & Grad Sch Med, Univ Pa & Med Col Pa, 45-66; assoc prof, 66-70, PROF MED, HAHNEMANN MED COL, 70-, DIR DIV OCCUP MED, 75- *Concurrent Pos:* Chief tuberc, Harbor Gen Hosp,

Torrance, Calif, 49-50; clin dir, Pulmonary Dis Serv, Philadelphia Gen Hosp, 50-74; chest consult, Norristown State Hosp, Pa, 51-60; dir, Philadelphia Pulmonary Neoplasm Res Proj, 57-67; Int Agency Res Cancer travel fel, London Mass Radiography Units, 69; ed, Philadelphia Med, 76- *Mem:* AMA; Am Thoracic Soc; Am Col Physicians. *Res:* Pulmonary disease, particularly lung cancer. *Mailing Add:* 3912 Netherfield Rd Philadelphia PA 19129

WEISSBACH, ARTHUR, b New York, NY, Aug 27, 27; m 58; c 2. BIOCHEMISTRY. *Educ:* City Col New York, BS, 47; Columbia Univ, PhD(biochem), 53. *Prof Exp:* Nat Found Infantile Paralysis fel, NIH, 53-55; asst prof biochem, Albany Med Col, Union Univ, NY, 55-56; biochemist, NIH, 56-68; HEAD DEPT CELL BIOL, ROCHE INST MOLECULAR BIOL, 68- *Concurrent Pos:* Prof lectr, Georgetown Univ, 57-58; NSF fel, 59-60; prof lectr, George Washington Univ, 61-66; adj prof, Dept Human Genetics & Develop, Columbia Univ, 69- & Unvi Med & Dent, NJ, 81- *Mem:* Am Soc Biol Chemists; Am Soc Microbiol. *Res:* Biochemistry of animal viruses and cellular nucleic acids. *Mailing Add:* Dept Cell Biol Roche Inst Molec Biol Nutley NJ 07110

WEISSBACH, HERBERT, b New York, NY, Mar 16, 32; c 4. BIOCHEMISTRY, MOLECULAR BIOLOGY. *Educ:* George Washington Univ, MS, 55, PhD, 57. *Prof Exp:* Biochemist, Nat Heart Inst, 53-58; lectr, George Washington Univ, 62-68; head sect enzymes & metab & actg chief lab clin biochem, NIH, 68-69; ASSOC DIR, ROCHE INST MOLECULAR BIOL & DIR DEPT BIOCHEM, 69- *Concurrent Pos:* NSF travel grant, Int Cong Biol Chem Socs, Moscow, 61; ed, Arch Biochem Biophys, 67-72, exec ed, 72-; ed, J Pharmacol & Exp Therapeut, 67-72, Int J Neuropharm, 69- 76 & J Biol Chem, 72-77; adj prof, Dept Human Genetics, Columbia Univ, 69- *Honors & Awards:* Superior Serv Award, Dept Health, Educ & Welfare, 68; Am Chem Soc Enzyme Award. *Mem:* AAAS; Am Soc Biol Chemists; Am Chem Soc; Am Soc Pharmacol & Therapeut; Am Soc Microbiol. *Res:* Protein synthesis; gene expression; mechanism of enzyme & coenzyme action. *Mailing Add:* Dept of Biochem Roche Inst of Molec Biol Nutley NJ 07110

WEISSBERG, ALFRED, b Boston, Mass, Jan 29, 28; wid; c 3. MATHEMATICS, SCIENCE ADMINISTRATION. *Educ:* Northeastern Univ, BS, 52; Univ NH, MS, 54. *Prof Exp:* Prin mathematician, Battelle Mem Inst, 53-60; math statistician, US Food & Drug Admin, 60-64; supvry opers res analyst, Nat Bur Standards, 64-67; head file orgn & statist, Toxicol Info Prog, Nat Libr Med, 67-70; Sci & Technol Commun Off, 70-80, SCI ADMIN, NAT INST NEUROL COMM DIS & STROKE, NIH, 80- *Mem:* AAAS; Am Soc Info Sci; Am Statist Asn. *Res:* Mathematical statistics; information system design and operation; application of computer systems to information retrieval. *Mailing Add:* 1024 Noyes Dr Silver Spring MD 20910

WEISSBERG, ROBERT MURRAY, b Cleveland, Ohio, Mar 3, 40. PHARMACOLOGY, PHYSIOLOGY. *Educ:* Ohio State Univ, PhD(physiol), 72. *Prof Exp:* STAFF RESEARCHER PHARMACOL, SYNTEX RES, 73- *Mem:* Am Soc Pharmacol & Exp Therapeut. *Res:* Respiratory pharmacology. *Mailing Add:* Syntex Res 3401 Hillview Ave Palo Alto CA 94304

WEISSBLUTH, MITCHEL, b Russia, Jan 7, 15; m 40; c 3. PHYSICS. *Educ:* Brooklyn Col, BA, 36; George Washington Univ, MA, 41; Univ Calif, PhD, 50. *Prof Exp:* Metallurgist, US Navy Yard, Washington, DC, 37-41; radio engr, Crosley Radio Corp, Ohio, 42-43; sr res engr, Jet Propulsion Lab, Calif Inst Technol, 43-45; asst physics, Univ Calif, 45-49, lectr, 50; res assoc, 50-51, instr, 51-54, assoc prof appl physics, 67-76, asst prof radiol physics, 54-66, dir, Biophys Lab, 64-67, PROF APPL PHYSICS, STANFORD UNIV, 76- *Concurrent Pos:* Physicist, Western Regional Res Lab, Bur Agr & Indust Chem, USDA, 48; Fulbright grant, Weizmann Inst Sci, Israel, 60-61; liaison scientist, Off Naval Res, London, 67-68, sr liaison scientist, Off Naval Res, Tokyo, 78-79. *Mem:* Am Phys Soc; Int Soc Quantum Biol (pres, 73-75). *Res:* Rocket motors; pion production; light scattering; x-ray microscopy; medical accelerators; electron spin resonance; thermoluminescence; enzyme reactions in magnetic fields; hypochromism; triplet states; Mossbauer resonance; electronic states in hemoglobin; Jahn-Teller effect; synchrotron radiation. *Mailing Add:* Dept Appl Physics Stanford Univ Stanford CA 94305

WEISSE, ALLEN B, b New York, NY, Dec 6, 29; m 67; c 2. CARDIOLOGY, MEDICINE. *Educ:* NY Univ, BA, 50; State Univ NY, MD, 58; Am Bd Internal Med, dipl, 65, cert cardiovasc dis, 67. *Prof Exp:* Res fel cardiol, Sch Med, Univ Utah, 61-63; instr med, Sch Med, Seton Hall Univ, 63-65; from instr to assoc prof, 65-74, PROF MED, NJ MED SCH, COL MED & DENT NJ, 74- *Mem:* Am Fedn Clin Res; Am Physiol Soc; Am Heart Asn; Am Col Physicians; Am Col Cardiol. *Res:* Cardiovascular physiology and disease. *Mailing Add:* NJ Med Sch Col Med & Dent NJ 100 Bergen St Newark NJ 07103

WEISSENBERGER, STEIN, b San Francisco, Calif, July 30, 37; m 59; c 2. SYSTEMS ANALYSIS. *Educ:* Mass Inst Technol, BS & MS, 60; Stanford Univ, PhD(aeronaut & astronaut sci), 65. *Prof Exp:* Dynamics engr, Lockheed Missiles & Space Co, 62-65; from asst prof to assoc prof mech eng, Univ Santa Clara, 65-76; GROUP LEADER, LAWRENCE LIVERMORE LAB, UNIV CALIF, 76- *Concurrent Pos:* Nat Res Coun sr res assoc, NASA-Ames Res Ctr, 73-75. *Mem:* Am Soc Mech Engrs; Inst Elec & Electronics Engrs. *Res:* Control and decision theory; control systems. *Mailing Add:* 315 Chatham Way Mountain View CA 94040

WEISSENBURGER, DON WILLIAM, b New Brunswick, NJ, May 22, 47. MAGNETO DYNAMICS, MAGNETOSTATICS. *Educ:* Colo Col, BS, 69. *Prof Exp:* MEM ENG & SCI STAFF, PLASMA PHYSICS LAB, PRINCETON UNIV, 75- *Res:* Design and analysis of magnetic fields, eddy currents and related phenomena associated with controlled fusion research. *Mailing Add:* Plasma Physics Lab Princeton Univ Princeton NJ 08544

WEISSER, DAVID LEROY, b Carnegie, Okla, Apr 4, 49; m 77. HORTICULTURE, PLANT PHYSIOLOGY. *Educ:* Calif State Univ, Los Angeles, BA, 70; Univ Calif, Davis, MA, 73; Cornell Univ, PhD(floricult), 78. *Prof Exp:* ASST PROF HORT DIV AGR, ARIZ STATE UNIV, 77- *Res:* Flowering, apical dominance and auxin physiology in plants. *Mailing Add:* 513 E Ellis Dr Tempe AZ 85282

WEISSER, EUGENE P, b Pittsburgh, Pa, Feb 12, 22; m 48; c 5. CHEMICAL ENGINEERING. *Educ:* Univ Pittsburgh, BS, 49. *Prof Exp:* Res asst chem eng, Mellon Inst, 49-51; jr chem engr, Res Dept, Koppers Co, Inc, Monroeville, Pa, 51-55, chem engr, 55-60, sr chem engr, 60-61, group mgr res eng, 61-67, sr res group mgr, 67-77; mgr res eng, Arco Polymers, Inc, Atlantic Richfield Co, Philadelphia, 77-81, MGR, PILOT PLANT SERV, ARCO CHEM CO, PHILADELPHIA, 81- *Mem:* Am Inst Chem Engrs. *Res:* The design, construction and operation of pilot plants, particularly concerning polymers. *Mailing Add:* 265 Canterbury Ct West Chester PA 19380

WEISSGERBER, RUDOLPH E, b Ger, June 2, 21; US citizen; m 50; c 1. MEDICINE. *Educ:* Univ Greifswald, MD, 45; Univ Hamburg, dipl trop dis & med parasitol, 48; Emory Univ, cert bus admin, 65. *Prof Exp:* Pres, Nordmark Chem Co, NY, 52-55; med sci dir, E R Squibb & Sons, Inc, Europe, 55-63, dir prod planning & develop, E R Squibb Int Co, NY, 63-64, dir res & develop, Squibb Int Co, 65-66; vpres & sci dir, Int Div, Bristol-Myers Co, 67-68; vpres, Merrell Int & dir, Sci & Com Develop-Europe, Richardson-Merrrell Inc, 69-81, DIR, LICENSING MGT, MERRELL DOW PHARMACEUT, INC, EUROPE, 81- *Mailing Add:* Merrell Dow Pharmaceut GmbH PO Box 1406 D-8032 Graefelfing/Munich West Germany

WEISSHAAR, TERRENCE ALLEN, aeroelasticity, structural mechanics, see previous edition

WEISSKOPF, BERNARD, b Berlin, Ger, Dec 11, 29; US citizen; m 65; c 2. PEDIATRICS, PSYCHIATRY. *Educ:* Syracuse Univ, BA, 51; State Univ Leiden, MD, 55; Am Bd Pediat, dipl, 65. *Prof Exp:* Physician, State Univ Leiden, 58; intern, Meadowbrook Hosp, Hempstead, NY, 58-59, resident pediat, 59-60; asst chief pediat, US Air Force Hosp, Maxwell AFB, 60-62; fel pediat & child psychiat, Hosp & Sch Med, Johns Hopkins Univ, 62-64; asst prof pediat, Univ Ill Col Med, 64-66; assoc prof, 66-72, PROF PEDIAT, SCH MED, UNIV LOUISVILLE, 72-, ASSOC PSYCHIAT, ASSOC OBSTET & GYNEC & DIR CHILD EVAL CTR, 66- *Concurrent Pos:* Clin coordr, Ill State Pediat Inst, 64-66. *Mem:* Fel Am Acad Pediat; Am Asn Ment Deficiency; Am Soc Human Genetics. *Res:* Behavioral aspects of pediatrics, especially learning disorders and mental retardation genetics. *Mailing Add:* Child Eval Ctr 334 E Broadway Louisville KY 40202

WEISSKOPF, MARTIN CHARLES, b Omaha, Nebr, Apr 21, 42; m 62; c 2. X-RAY ASTRONOMY, ASTROPHYSICS. *Educ:* Oberlin Col, AB, 64; Brandeis Univ, PhD(physics), 69. *Prof Exp:* Res assoc physics, Brandeis Univ, 68-69; res assoc, Columbia Univ, 69-71, lectr, 70-71, asst prof, 71-77; SR X-RAY ASTRONOMER ASTROPHYS, MARSHALL SPACE FLIGHT CTR, NASA, 77- *Concurrent Pos:* Co-investr, High Energy Astron Observ-2, NASA, 72- & Columbia Exp NASA's OSO-8, 75-77; guest-investr, NASA's High Energy Astrophys Observ-1, 78- *Mem:* Am Phys Soc; Am Astron Soc. *Res:* X-ray astronomy and high energy astrophysics. *Mailing Add:* Code ES-62 Marshall Space Flight Ctr Marshall Space Flight Center AL 35812

WEISSKOPF, VICTOR FREDERICK, b Vienna, Austria, Sept 19, 08; nat US; m 34; c 2. PHYSICS. *Educ:* Univ Göttingen, PhD(physics), 31. *Hon Degrees:* PhD, sixteen from various US & foreign univs, 61-70. *Prof Exp:* Res assoc, Univ Berlin, 31-32; Rockefeller Found fel, Univs Copenhagen & Cambridge, 32-33; res assoc, Swiss Fed Inst Technol, 33-36 & Univ Copenhagen, 36-37; from instr to asst prof physics, Univ Rochester, 37-43; group leader, Los Alamos Sci Lab, 43-47; prof, 45-74, INST EMER PROF PHYSICS & SR LECTR, MASS INST TECHNOL, 74- *Concurrent Pos:* Dir gen, Europ Ctr Nuclear Res, 61-65. *Honors & Awards:* Planck Medal, 56; Prix Mondial Cino Del Duca, 72. *Mem:* Nat Acad Sci; fel Am Phys Soc (vpres, 59, pres, 60); Fedn Am Sci; cor mem Fr, Austrian, Danish, Scottish & Bavarian Acads Sci. *Res:* Quantum mechanics; electron theory; theory of nuclear phenomena; nuclear physics. *Mailing Add:* 36 Arlington St Cambridge MA 02140

WEISSLER, ARNOLD M, b Brooklyn, NY, May 13, 27; c 4. CARDIOLOGY, INTERNAL MEDICINE. *Educ:* NY Univ, BA, 48; State Univ NY Downstate Med Ctr, MD, 53. *Prof Exp:* Trainee internal med, Maimonides Hosp, 53-54 & Duke Hosp, 54-60, assoc med, Duke Hosp, 59-60; asst prof, Univ Tex Med Br Galveston, 60-61; from asst prof to prof, Ohio State Univ, 61-71, dir div cardiol, 63-71; prof med & chmn dept, 71-81, CHIEF DIV CARDION, WAYNE STATE UNIV, 81- *Concurrent Pos:* Am Heart Asn res fel, Duke Hosp, Durham, NC, 55-57; chief, Dept Med, Harper-Grace Hosps, 71-81; mem cardiovasc bd, Am Bd Internal Med, chmn, 75-77; fel coun clin cardiol, Am Heart Asn, 78, chmn, 78-80. *Mem:* Fel Am Col Physicians; Am Clin & Climat Asn; fel Am Col Cardiol; Am Soc Clin Invest; Am Soc Pharmacol & Exp Therapeut. *Res:* Cardiovascular physiology; congestive heart failure; noninvasive techniques in cardiology; myocardial metabolism. *Mailing Add:* Dept of Internal Med Wayne State Univ Sch of Med Detroit MI 48201

WEISSLER, GERHARD LUDWIG, b Eilenburg, Ger, Feb 20, 18; nat US; m 53; c 2. PHYSICS. *Educ:* Univ Calif, MA, 41, PhD(physics), 42; Am Bd Radiol, dipl, 52. *Prof Exp:* Instr radiol, Med Sch, Univ Calif, 42-44; from asst prof to assoc prof, 44-52, head dept, 51-56, PROF PHYSICS, UNIV SOUTHERN CALIF, 52- *Mem:* Fel Am Phys Soc; fel Optical Soc Am. *Res:* Gaseous electronics; vacuum ultraviolet radiation physics; photo-absorption and photo-ionization cross sections; photoelectric effect; optical constants and solid state physics; upper atmosphere and astrophysical problems; nuclear accelerator physics; vacuum ultraviolet spectroscopy of hot gaseous plasmas. *Mailing Add:* Dept Physics Univ Southern Calif Los Angeles CA 90007

WEISSMAN, ALBERT, b New York, NY, Aug 1, 33; m 57; c 5. PSYCHOPHARMACOLOGY. *Educ:* NY Univ, BA, 54; Columbia Univ, MA, 55, PhD, 58. *Prof Exp:* Instr psychol, Columbia Univ, 57; sr res psychologist, Pfizer Res Labs, 58-61, mgr psychopharmacol, 61-72, ASST DIR PHARMACOL, PFIZER INC, 72- *Mem:* Am Soc Pharmacol & Exp Therapeut. *Res:* Catecholamines and indolylalkylamines; learning and memory; addiction. *Mailing Add:* Med Res Lab Pfizer Inc Groton CT 06340

WEISSMAN, DAVID BRUCE, b New York, NY, Jan 17, 47. POPULATION BIOLOGY, ENTOMOLOGY. *Educ:* Univ Calif, Los Angeles, BA, 69; Stanford Univ, PhD(pop biol & ecol), 75; Univ Calif, Irvine, MD, 79. *Prof Exp:* ASST RES ENTOMOLOGIST, UNIV CALIF, IRVINE, 77- *Concurrent Pos:* Grants, Sigma Xi, 77-, Explorers Club, 77-78 & Am Philos Soc, 77-78; assoc dept entom, Calif Acad Sci, 77- *Mem:* Sigma Xi. *Res:* Bionomics, systematics and zoogeography of the orthoptera of Baja California and the California channel islands; field crickets of the west; trimerotropine grasshoppers. *Mailing Add:* Dept Anesthesia Stanford Univ Stanford CA 94305

WEISSMAN, DAVID E(VERETT), b New York, NY, Sept 18, 37; m 61; c 3. ELECTRICAL ENGINEERING, RADAR REMOTE SENSING. *Educ:* NY Univ, BA & BEE, 60, MEE, 61; Stanford Univ, PhD(elec eng), 68. *Prof Exp:* Asst elec eng, NY Univ, 60-61; elec engr, Dorne & Margolin, Inc, 61-63; res engr, Stanford Res Inst, 63-68; asst prof, 68-75, assoc prof, 75-82, PROF ENG SCI, HOFSTRA UNIV, 82- *Concurrent Pos:* Ed-in-chief, Inst Elec & Electronics Engrs J Oceanic Eng, 79-82. *Mem:* AAAS; Inst Elec & Electronics Engrs; Int Sci Radio Union; Am Geophys Union. *Res:* Development of radar remote sensing techniques for ocean surface observation from aircraft and satellites and other random media probing; demonstrated the usefulness of dual frequency radars to the measurement of ocean wave heights and directional spectrum. *Mailing Add:* Dept Eng Sci Hofstra Univ Hempstead NY 11550

WEISSMAN, EARL BERNARD, b Detroit, Mich, Feb 21, 42; m 67; c 2. CLINICAL CHEMISTRY. *Educ:* Wayne State Univ, BS, 65, PhD(biochem), 72. *Prof Exp:* Fel clin chem, Buffalo Gen Hosp, 72-74; asst mgr lab opers, Lab Procedures, Upjohn Co, 74-77; TECH DIR, AM REFINING LAB, 78- *Concurrent Pos:* Consult, Ventura County Gen Hosp, 74-78; asst prof, Calif State Univ, 75- *Mem:* Am Asn Clin Chemists. *Res:* Porphyrin metabolism; clinical methods development. *Mailing Add:* 10702 Providence Dr Villa Park CA 92667

WEISSMAN, EUGENE Y(EHUDA), b Bucharest, Romania, Sept 23, 31; US citizen; m 58; c 2. TECHNICAL MANAGEMENT, PHYSICAL CHEMISTRY. *Educ:* Israel Inst Technol, BSc, 53, ChemE, 54; Univ Mich, MSc, 59; Case Inst Technol, PhD(chem eng), 63; Univ Chicago, MBA, 72. *Prof Exp:* Chem engr, Israel Atomic Energy Comn, 53-57, actg proj dir separation processes & water isotopes, 57-58; asst, Case Inst Technol, 59-63; chem engr, Res & Develop Ctr, Gen Elec Co, 63-65, sr engr direct energy conversion oper, 65, mgr appl res & tech develop, 65-68; mgr electrochem res dept, Globe-Union, Inc, 68-73; dir inorg-electrol res & develop, 73-76, tech dir chem spec bus, 76-79, DIR RES TECH SUPPORT, BASF, WYANDOTTE CORP, 79- *Concurrent Pos:* Res & develop engr, Hercules Powder Co, 60-61. *Mem:* Am Inst Chem Engrs; Electrochem Soc; Am Mgt Asn. *Res:* Electrochemistry and electrochemical engineering; transport phenomena; surface phenomena; research and development management; materials; formulations chemistry; analytical chemistry; information science. *Mailing Add:* 356 N Clifton Rd Birmingham MI 48010

WEISSMAN, GERARD SELWYN, b Brooklyn, NY, Oct 18, 21; m 55, 79; c 2. PLANT PHYSIOLOGY. *Educ:* Brooklyn Col, BA, 42; Columbia Univ, MA, 48, PhD(bot), 50. *Prof Exp:* Asst plant physiol, Columbia Univ, 46-49, res assoc, 49-50; from instr to assoc prof biol, 50-62, fac fel, 66, PROF BOT, CAMDEN COL ARTS & SCI, RUTGERS UNIV, CAMDEN, 62- *Concurrent Pos:* Vpres acad affairs on leave, Trenton State Col, 70. *Mem:* AAAS; Am Soc Plant Physiologists; Bot Soc Am. *Res:* Enzyme regulation; nitrogen metabolism. *Mailing Add:* Rutgers Univ Camden Col Arts & Sci Camden NJ 08102

WEISSMAN, HERMAN BENJAMIN, b Chicago, Ill, May 16, 20; m 45; c 1. PHYSICS. *Educ:* Univ Chicago, SB, 52; Ill Inst Technol, MS, 54, PhD(physics), 59. *Prof Exp:* Chemist, Qm Corps, US Dept Army, 51-52 & Armour Res Found, Ill Inst Technol, 53-54; instr, Chicago Jr Col, 54; asst prof, Elmhurst Col, 54-56 & Univ Ill, 56-59; sr res physicist, Bell & Howell Co, 59-60; asst prof, 60-63, PROF PHYSICS, UNIV ILL, CHICAGO CIRCLE, 63- *Mem:* Am Asn Physics Teachers. *Res:* Atomic and molecular physics. *Mailing Add:* Dept of Physics Univ of Ill at Chicago Circle Chicago IL 60680

WEISSMAN, IRA, b Chicago, Ill, Feb 23, 23; m 43; c 2. ELECTRICAL ENGINEERING, PHYSICS. *Educ:* Univ Ill, BS, 49, MS, 50, PhD(elec eng), 60. *Prof Exp:* Physicist, Photo Physics Lab, Wright Patterson AFB, 51; res assoc, Coordinated Sci Lab, Univ Ill, 51-60; SR SCIENTIST, VARIAN ASSOCS, 60-, GROUP LEADER NEW MAT & TECHNIQUES, 69- *Mem:* Am Phys Soc. *Res:* Solid state physics of metals and alloys; applications to thermionics and superconductivity; materials technology; synthesis and evaluation. *Mailing Add:* 4228 Pomona Ave Palo Alto CA 94306

WEISSMAN, JOSEPH CHARLES, New York City, NY, Oct 15, 50. BIOCHEMICAL ENGINEERING, BIOENERGETICS. *Educ:* Cornell Univ, BA, 71; Univ Calif, Berkeley, PhD(biophysics), 78, MS, 80. *Prof Exp:* Asst res biophysicist, Univ Calif, Berkeley, 78-79; MGR RES & DEVELOP, ECOENERGETICS, INC, 80- *Concurrent Pos:* Res consult, 78-80; prin investr, Ecoenergetics, Inc, 80- *Mem:* AAAS. *Res:* Kinetics of microbial growth and product formation; development of fermentation systems. *Mailing Add:* 3498 Brehme Lane Vacaville CA 95688

WEISSMAN, MICHAEL BENJAMIN, b St Louis, Mo, Aug 28, 49. FLUCTUATION SPECTROSCOPY. *Educ:* Harvard Univ, AB, 70; Univ Calif, San Diego, MS, 72, PhD(physics), 76. *Prof Exp:* Res fel chem, Harvard Univ, 76-78; ASST PROF PHYSICS, UNIV ILL, URBANA, 78- *Concurrent Pos:* NSF fel, 77-78. *Mem:* Biophys Soc. *Res:* Fluctuation spectroscopy; techniques and applications to biophysics; origins of 1/f noise in electrical systems. *Mailing Add:* Dept Physics Univ Ill Urbana IL 61801

WEISSMAN, MICHAEL HERBERT, b New York, NY, Jan 15, 42; m 67; c 3. PEDIATRICS, BIOMEDICAL ENGINEERING. *Educ:* Cooper Union, BME, 63; Northwestern Univ, Evanston, MS, 65, PhD(civil eng), 67; Washington Univ, MD, 76. *Prof Exp:* Res asst, Northwestern Univ, Evanston, 65-67; asst prof bioeng, Carnegie-Mellon Univ, 67-71, assoc prof bioeng & chem eng, 71-73; pediat resident, Bronx Munic Hosp Ctr, 76-79, pediat chief resident, 79-80; PEDIATRICIAN, MT KISCO MED GROUP, 80- *Concurrent Pos:* NIH grant, Carnegie-Mellon Univ, 69-74. *Mem:* Sigma Xi; Am Soc Mech Engrs; Biomed Eng Soc; AMA. *Res:* Artificial internal organs; biological transport processes; physiological systems analysis; fluid mechanics; physiological simulation; general pediatrics. *Mailing Add:* Dept of Pediat Mt Kisco Med Group Mt Kisco NY 10549

WEISSMAN, MYRNA MILGRAM, b Boston, Mass, Apr 17, 35. EPIDEMIOLOGY, PSYCHIATRY. *Educ:* Brandeis Univ, BA, 56; Univ Pa, MSW, 58; Yale Univ, PhD(chronic dis epidemiol), 74. *Prof Exp:* Psychiat social worker, Inst Juv Res, 58-59 & Dept Psychol Med, Southern Gen Hosp, 59-60; social worker, Clin Ctr, NIH, 60-67; res assoc psychiat, Clin Psychopharmacol Res Unit, 67-71, asst prof psychiat, Conn Ment Health Ctr, 71-74, assoc prof psychiat, 75-77, ASSOC PROF PSYCHIAT & EPIDEMIOL, SCH MED, YALE UNIV, 77-, DIR DEPRESSION RES UNIT, CONN MENT HEALTH CTR, 72- *Concurrent Pos:* Chmn utilization rev proj, Yale Univ Suicide Panel, 69-72; consult, Psychopharmacol Res Br, NIMH, 73-76, Clin Res Br, 77 & Nat Inst Drug Abuse, 77; mem, White House Task Force Epidemiol of Ment Health, 77-78, Nat Adv Comt, NIMH, 78 & Res Study Sect, Nat Inst Alcohol Abuse & Alcoholism, 75-80; consult planning epidemiol res, Alcohol, Drug Abuse & Ment Health Admin, 78; consult, HEW, 78. *Honors & Awards:* Found Fund Prize Res in Psychiat, Am Psychiat Asn, 78. *Mem:* AAAS; Am Asn Suicidology; Am Orthopsychiat Asn; Am Pub Health Asn; Int Epidemiol Asn. *Res:* Effectiveness of pharmacotherapy and psychotherapy in the treatment of depression; development of model methodologies for use in cognate studies in the future. *Mailing Add:* Yale Univ Sch of Med 904 Howard Ave Suite 2A New Haven CT 06519

WEISSMAN, NORMAN, b New York, NY, Sept 12, 14; m 37; c 3. CLINICAL CHEMISTRY, TOXICOLOGY. *Educ:* City Col New York, BS, 35; Columbia Univ, PhD(biochem), 41. *Prof Exp:* Res fel dent med, Harvard Sch Dent Med, 41-43, instr, 43-46; lectr, Johns Hopkins Univ, 46-47, asst prof physiol chem & prev med, Sch Med, 47-51; assoc prof med, Col Med, State Univ NY Downstate Med Ctr, 51-56; assoc prof path & biochem, Col Med, Univ Utah, 56-70; asst dir, Chem Dept, 70-74, sr res scientist, Res Dept, 74-80, RES ASSOC, BIO-SCI LABS, 80- *Concurrent Pos:* Chemist, Maimonides Hosp, New York, 51-56 & Univ Hosp, Univ Utah, 57-65; consult, Vet Admin Hosp, Salt Lake City, Utah, 60-70. *Mem:* Am Soc Biol Chemists; Am Asn Clin Chemists; Am Acad Forensic Sci; Harvey Soc. *Res:* Amino acid metabolism; bacterial chemistry; histochemistry; copper and connective tissue; toxicology methods. *Mailing Add:* Bio-Science Labs 7600 Tyrone Ave Van Nuys CA 91405

WEISSMAN, PAUL MORTON, b New York, NY, Oct 17, 36; m 71; c 2. ORGANOMETALLIC CHEMISTRY, ELECTROCHEMISTRY. *Educ:* City Col New York, BS, 60; Purdue Univ, Lafayette, PhD(chem), 64. *Prof Exp:* Res asst air pollution, NIH, Md, 59-60; res chemist, Gen Aniline & Film, Inc, 64-65; Petrol Res Fund grant, Univ Cincinnati, 65-66; asst prof chem, Brock Univ, 66-68; asst prof, 68-72, ASSOC PROF CHEM & CHMN DEPT, FAIRLEIGH DICKINSON UNIV, 72- *Concurrent Pos:* Nat Res Coun Can grant, Brock Univ, 66-68; NSF fel, Brandeis Univ, 67. *Mem:* NY Acad Sci. *Res:* Organometallic synthesis and reaction mechanisms; voltammetry in non-aqueous solvents; transition metal complexes containing a metal-metal bond; food chemistry and nutrition. *Mailing Add:* Dept of Chem Fairleigh Dickinson Univ Madison NJ 07940

WEISSMAN, PAUL ROBERT, b Brooklyn, NY, Sept 28, 47. ASTRONOMY, COMETS. *Educ:* Cornell Univ, AB, 69; Univ Mass, MS, 71; Univ Calif, Los Angeles, PhD(planetary physics), 78. *Prof Exp:* sr scientist, 74-80, MEM TECH STAFF, ASTRON JET PROPULSION LAB, CALIF INST TECHNOL, 80- *Mem:* Am Astron Soc; Sigma Xi; AAAS; Int Astron Union. *Res:* Physical and dynamical studies of small bodies in the solar system, comets, meteors and asteroids; theories of origin and implications for formation of the solar system; design of spacecraft and trajectories for solar system exploration; celestial mechanics; planetary sciences. *Mailing Add:* Mail Stop 183 301 Jet Propulsion Lab 4800 Oak Grove Dr Pasadena CA 91109

WEISSMAN, ROBERT HENRY, b Chicago, Ill, July 4, 42. SOLID STATE ELECTRONICS. *Educ:* Univ Mich, BS, 64; Stanford Univ, MS, 65, PhD(elec eng), 70. *Prof Exp:* Mem tech staff res & develop light-emitting diode devices, 70-73, proj mgr res & develop mat & processes, 73-80, RES & DEVELOP SECT MGR, HEWLETT PACKARD CO, 80- *Mem:* Electrochem Soc; Int Soc Hybrid Microelectronics. *Res:* Materials and process technology; solid state device physics; optoelectronic devices; optical fiber technology. *Mailing Add:* 250 Del Medio Apt 318A Mountain View CA 94040

WEISSMAN, SAMUEL ISAAC, b South Bend, Ind, June 25, 12; m 43; c 2. PHYSICAL CHEMISTRY. *Educ:* Univ Chicago, BS, 33, PhD(phys chem), 38. *Prof Exp:* Fel, Univ Chicago, 39-41; Nat Res Coun fel, Univ Calif, 41-42; res chemist, Manhattan Proj, Calif, 42-43 & NMex, 43-46; from asst prof to assoc prof, 46-55, prof, 55-80, EMER PROF CHEM, WASHINGTON UNIV, 80- *Mem:* Nat Acad Sci; Am Chem Soc. *Res:* Chemical spectroscopy; fluorescence; electrical conductivity; paramagnetic resonance. *Mailing Add:* Dept of Chem Wash Univ St Louis MO 63130

WEISSMAN, SHERMAN MORTON, b Chicago, Ill, Nov 22, 30; m 59; c 4. PHYSIOLOGY, BIOCHEMISTRY. *Educ:* Northwestern Univ, BS, 50; Univ Chicago, MS, 51; Harvard Univ, MD, 55. *Prof Exp:* Clin assoc cancer, NIH, 56-58; USPHS fel biochem & nucleic acids, Glasgow Univ, 59-60; sr investr, NIH, 60-67; assoc prof med, 67-71, PROF MED & MOLECULAR BIOPHYS & BIOCHEM, SCH MED, YALE UNIV, 71-, PROF HUMAN GENETICS, 72- *Mem:* Am Soc Biol Chemists; Am Soc Clin Invest; Am Asn Physicians; Brit Biochem Soc. *Res:* Nucleic acid metabolism; molecular genetics. *Mailing Add:* 610 Hunter Radiation Yale Univ Sch of Med New Haven CT 06510

WEISSMAN, SIGMUND, b Vienna, Austria, July 1, 17; nat US; m 45; c 2. CRYSTALLOGRAPHY. *Educ:* Polytech Inst Brooklyn, PhD(chem), 52. *Prof Exp:* Res specialist x-ray diffraction, Col Eng, 49-63, PROF MAT ENG & DIR MAT RES LAB, RUTGERS UNIV, NEW BRUNSWICK, 63- *Concurrent Pos:* Consult, Lawrence Livermore Lab & Univ Calif, Savannah River Lab, US Steel Corp, Monroeville, Pa; ed, Metals & Alloys, Joint Comt Powder Diffraction Standards, Int Ctr Diffraction Data. *Honors & Awards:* Howe Medal, Am Soc Metals, 62. *Mem:* Am Crystallog Asn; Am Inst Mining, Metall & Petrol Engrs; Am Soc Metals; Am Soc Testing & Mat; NY Acad Sci. *Res:* X-ray crystallography; crystal imperfections of metals and alloys; irradiation of solids; recrystallization; recovery deformation; creep and fatigue of metals and alloys. *Mailing Add:* Dept of Mech & Mat Sci Col of Eng Rutgers Univ Piscataway NJ 08854

WEISSMAN, SUZANNE HEISLER, b The Dalles, Ore, June 20, 49; m 76. ANALYTICAL CHEMISTRY. *Educ:* Ore State Univ, BS, 71; Univ Ill, MS, 73, PhD(chem), 75. *Prof Exp:* Vis lectr chem, Univ Ill, 75, vis asst prof, 76; chemist, Lovelace Biomed & Environ Res Inst, Inc. 76-80; ANAL CHEMIST, SANDIA NAT LABS, 80- *Mem:* Am Chem Soc; Soc Appl Spectros. *Res:* Determination of trace elements, ultratrace analyses, inductively coupled plasma-atomic emission spectroscopy, and atomic absorption spectroscopy. *Mailing Add:* Anal Chem Div Sandia Nat Labs Albuquerque NM 87185

WEISSMAN, WILLIAM, b New York, NY, Oct 12, 18; m 48; c 2. SURFACE CHEMISTRY. *Educ:* Univ Ala, Tuscaloosa, BA, 39; St John's Univ, NY, dipl chem, 44 & Newark Col Eng, dipl chem, 48. *Hon Degrees:* PhD, Sci Inst Caracas, 52. *Prof Exp:* Head insulation dept, Inslx Co, 39-46; lacquer chemist, Maas & Waldstein Co, Inc, 46-53; chief chemist, Nat Foil Co, Inc, 53-58; res chemist, Metro Adhesives Inc, 58-61; teacher chem, Passaic County Tech & Voc High Sch, 61-69; res chemist, US Rubber Reclaiming Co, Inc, 69-73; adhesive chemist, Cataphote Div, Ferro Inc, 73-74; sr scientist, Vicksburg Chem Co, 74-75; CONSULT, COMPLEX CHEMS, INC, 75- *Concurrent Pos:* Consult, Standard Chem Co, 53-69; Sussex County Bd Educ fel, Sussex County Tech Sch, Newton, NJ, 64-65; Passaic County Bd Educ fel, Montclair State Col, 67-68; environ consult. *Mem:* Am Chem Soc; AAAS; Nat Geog Soc. *Res:* Adhesion and cohesion, organic and inorganic gases, liquids and solids; atomic micro and macro parameters. *Mailing Add:* 108 Katherine Dr Vicksburg MS 39180

WEISSMANN, BERNARD, b New York, NY, Dec 2, 17. BIOCHEMISTRY. *Educ:* City Col New York, BS, 38; Univ Mich, MS, 39, PhD, 51. *Prof Exp:* Res assoc, Col Physicians & Surgeons, Columbia Univ, 50-53 & Mt Sinai Hosp, New York, 53-57; from asst prof to assoc prof, 58-67, PROF BIOL CHEM, UNIV ILL COL MED, 67- *Mem:* Am Soc Biol Chem; Am Chem Soc; Brit Biochem Soc; Soc Complex Carbohydrates. *Res:* Enzymology and structure of acid mucopolysaccharide catabolism; synthetic carbohydrate chemistry. *Mailing Add:* Dept of Biol Chem Univ of Ill Col of Med Chicago IL 60612

WEISSMANN, GERALD, b Vienna, Austria, Aug 7, 30; US citizen; m 53; c 2. CELL BIOLOGY, INTERNAL MEDICINE. *Educ:* Columbia Univ, BA, 50; NY Univ, MD, 54; Am Bd Internal Med, dipl, 63. *Prof Exp:* Res fel biochem, Arthritis & Rheumatism Found, 58-59; from instr to assoc prof, 59-70, PROF MED, SCH MED, NY UNIV, 70-, DIR DIV RHEUMATOLOGY, 74- *Concurrent Pos:* USPHS spec res fel, Strangeways Res Lab, Cambridge Univ, 60-61; sr investr, Arthritis & Rheumatism Found, 61-65; career investr, Health Res Coun, New York, 66-70; consult, US Food & Drug Admin & Nat Heart & Lung Inst, NIH; investr & instr physiol, Marine Biol Lab, Woods Hole, Mass, 70-; Guggenheim fel, Ctr Immunol & Physiol, Paris, 73-74; ed-in-chief, Inflammation, Advan Inflammation Res. *Honors & Awards:* Alessandro Robecchi Prize for Rheumatology, 72; Marine Biol Lab Prize, 74 & 79; Lila Grubin Award, 79. *Mem:* Am Soc Cell Biol; Am Soc Exp Path; Am Soc Clin Invest; Am Rheumatism Asn (pres, 81-82); Soc Exp Biol & Med. *Res:* Study of lysosomes as they relate to cell injury; physiology and pharmacology of lysosomes and of artificial lipid structures; neutrophil activation; prostaglandins; leukotrienes. *Mailing Add:* NY Univ Med Ctr 550 First Ave New York NY 10016

WEISSMANN, GERD FRIEDRICH HORST, b Leipzig, Ger, Nov 26, 23; US citizen; m 54; c 3. MATERIALS & SOIL SCIENCE. *Educ:* Tech Univ, Berlin, Dipl Ing, 50, Dr Ing, 70; Pa State Univ, MS, 53. *Prof Exp:* supvr mech mat, Bell Tel Labs, 53-81; PRES, DAMPING MEASUREMENT SYSTS, 81- *Mem:* Am Soc Civil Engrs; Am Soc Test & Mat; Soc Exp Stress Anal. *Res:* Materials research; classification of metals; soil dynamics; foundation engineering; experimental mechanics. *Mailing Add:* 36 Circle Rd Florham Park NJ 07932

WEIST, WILLIAM GODFREY, JR, b New York, NY, July 6, 31; m 56; c 4. GEOLOGY, HYDROLOGY. *Educ:* Amherst Col, BA, 53; Univ Colo, MS, 56. *Prof Exp:* Geologist, Ground Water Br, US Geol Surv, Colo, 56-67, hydrologist, Water Resources Div, NY, 67-70, supvry hydrologist, Ind, 70-73, asst dist chief, Ind Dist, 72-73, chief, 73-75, staff hydrologist, Hydrol Studies Sect, Ind Dist, 75-79, hydrologist, Environ Affairs Off, Denver, 79-82, HYDROLOGIST, OFF SURFACE MINING, DENVER, US GEOL SURV, 82- *Mem:* Geol Soc Am; Am Inst Prof Geologists; Nat Water Well Asn; AAAS; Fedn Am Scientists. *Res:* Ground-water hydrology. *Mailing Add:* Off Surface Mining 1020 15th St Denver CO 80202

WEISTROP, DONNA ETTA, b New York, NY, June 10, 44. ASTRONOMY. *Educ:* Wellesley Col, BA, 65; Calif Inst Technol, PhD(astron), 71. *Prof Exp:* Vis lectr astron, Tel Aviv Univ, 71-73; univ fel astron, Ohio State Univ, 73-74; asst astronr, Kitt Peak Nat Observ, 74-77; res fel, Univ Ariz, 77-78; ASTROPHYSICIST, GODDARD SPACE FLIGHT CTR, 78- *Concurrent Pos:* Vis scientist, Lunar & Planetary Lab, Univ Ariz, 78-80. *Mem:* Am Astron Soc; Int Astron Union. *Res:* Characteristics of the reulosity associated with BL lac objects and quasi-stellar objects; devlopment of and applications for electronic detectors; luminosity funtions and density distrubutions of intrinsically faint stars; QSO's and BLLac objects. *Mailing Add:* NASA|GSFC Code 681 LASP Greenbelt MD 20771

WEISTROP, JESSIE SYD, b New York, NY, Apr 14, 48. PLANT PHYSIOLOGY, CELL BIOLOGY. *Educ:* State Univ NY Stony Brook, BS, 69; Univ Mass, Amherst, MA, 71, PhD(bot), 75. *Prof Exp:* FEL MEMBRANE BIOSYNTHESIS, RADIATION BIOL LAB, SMITHSONIAN INST, 74- *Mem:* AAAS; Bot Soc Am. *Res:* Biochemical and ultrastructural development of chloroplasts and the biosynthesis of chloroplast membranes; sulfate metabolism in algae. *Mailing Add:* Radiation Biol Lab 12441 Parklawn Dr Rockville MD 20852

WEISZ, JUDITH, b Budapest, Hungary, Aug 6, 26; Brit citizen. REPRODUCTIVE PHYSIOLOGY, NEUROENDOCRINOLOGY. *Educ:* Newnham Col, Eng, BA, 48, MB, BCh, 51. *Prof Exp:* Clin training, London Hosp, Eng, 48-51; intern, Hadassah Med Sch, Hebrew Univ, Jerusalem, 52-54; second asst internal med, Tel Hashomer Govt & Mil Hosp, Israel, 54-56; registr internal med, London Hosp, Eng, 56-57; first asst internal med, Tel Hashomer Govt & Mil Hosp, Israel, 57-59; res fel endocrinol, Mt Sinai Hosp, New York, 60-62; fel, Training Prog Steroid Biochem, Worcester Found Exp Biol, Mass, 62-63, staff scientist, Training Prog Reproductive Physiol, 63-70, assoc dir, Training Prog Physiol of Reproduction, 68-72, sr scientist, Worcester Found Exp Biol, 70-72; PROF, PROF, DIV REPRODUCTIVE BIOL, DEPT OBSTET & GYNEC, MILTON S HERSHEY MED CTR, PA STATE UNIV, 76- HEAD DIV, 75-, SR MEM, GRAD SCH FAC, UNIV, 73- *Mem:* Brit Med Asn; Endocrine Soc; Int Soc Neuroendocrinol; Soc Study Reproduction. *Res:* Neuroendocrine regulation of reproductive function; steroid biochemistry. *Mailing Add:* Div of Reproductive Biol Milton S Hershey Med Ctr Hershey PA 17033

WEISZ, PAUL B, b Vienna, Austria, Nov 3, 21; nat US; m 45; c 3. EMBRYOLOGY. *Educ:* McGill Univ, BSc, 43, MSc, 44, PhD(zool), 46. *Prof Exp:* Demonstr zool, McGill Univ, 43-46, lectr, 46-47, lectr biol, Sir George Williams Col, 43-44, lectr, 44-47; from instr to assoc prof, 47-57, PROF BIOL, BROWN UNIV, 57- *Concurrent Pos:* Mem, Ed Policies Comn & Comn Undergrad Educ Biol Sci. *Mem:* Soc Develop Biol; Am Soc Zool; Nat Asn Biol Teachers; Nat Sci Teachers Asn. *Res:* Embryology and development of amphibians and crustaceans; morphogenesis; cytochemistry and nuclear functions in Protozoa; comparative embryology; science writing. *Mailing Add:* Div of Biol & Med Sci Brown Univ Providence RI 02912

WEISZ, PAUL BURG, b Pilsen, Czech, July 2, 19; m 43; c 2. CHEMISTRY, CHEMICAL ENGINEERING. *Educ:* Ala Polytech Univ, BSc, 40; Swiss Fed Inst Technol, ScD, 66. *Prof Exp:* Asst, Univ Berlin, 38-39 & Bartol Res Found, Pa, 40-46; res assoc, 46-61, sr scientist, 61-67, mgr process res, 67-69, MGR CENT RES DIV, MOBIL RES & DEVELOP CORP, 69- *Concurrent Pos:* Instr, Swarthmore Col, 42-43; vis prof, Princeton Univ, 74-76; agent, US Patent Off. *Honors & Awards:* Murphee Award, Am Chem Soc, 72, Pioneer Award, Am Inst Chemists, 74; Leo Friend Award, Am Chem Soc, 77; Wilhelm Award, Am Inst Chem Eng, 78. *Mem:* Fel Am Phys Soc; Am Chem Soc; Nat Acad Eng; fel Am Inst Chemists; Am Inst Chem Engrs. *Res:* Cosmic rays; Geiger counters; electric discharge phenomena; catalysis; diffusion phenomena; petroleum; petroleum processes; energy technology; basic and interdisciplinary phenomena in the sciences. *Mailing Add:* Mobil Res & Develop Corp PO Box 1025 Princeton NJ 08540

WEISZ, ROBERT STEPHEN, b New York, NY, May 24, 18; m 56; c 3. INORGANIC CHEMISTRY. *Educ:* Cornell Univ, AB, 39, PhD(chem), 42. *Prof Exp:* Asst instr chem, Cornell Univ, 39-41; res fel, Westinghouse Elec & Mfg Co, 42, res engr, 42-46; res engr, Thomas A Edison, Inc, 46-49 & RCA Labs, 49-56; res dir, Telemeter Memories, Inc, 56-60, Ampex Comput Prod Co, 60-61 & Electronics Memories, Inc, 61-69; INDUST CONSULT, 69- *Mem:* Am Chem Soc. *Res:* Reactions in solids; ceramics; electrical properties of inorganic compounds; magnetic materials. *Mailing Add:* 2109 Mt Calvary Rd Santa Barbara CA 93105

WEITKAMP, LOWELL R, b Lincoln, Nebr, June 13, 36; m 73; c 1. BIOCHEMICAL GENETICS. *Educ:* Reed Col, BA, 58; Univ Rochester, MD, 63; Univ Mich, MS, 66. *Prof Exp:* Internship, Univ Wis Hosp, Madison, 63-64; fel, Univ Mich, 64-66, res assoc, 66-69; from asst prof to assoc prof, 69-78, PROF MED, SCH MED, UNIV ROCHESTER, 78- *Concurrent Pos:* NIH res career develop award, 71-76; vis prof, Univ Inst Med Genetics, Univ Copenhagen, 73; vis fel, Dept Human Biol, John Curtin Sch Med Res, Australian Nat Univ, 75-76; NIMH res scientist develop award, 76-81. *Mem:* Am Asn Clin Histocompatibility Testing; Am Soc Human Genetics; Int Soc Animal Blood Group Res. *Res:* Biochemical genetic markers in susceptibility to nonmendelian familial diseases and decreased reproductive performance. *Mailing Add:* Div Genetics Box 641 Med Ctr Univ Rochester 601 Elmwood Ave Rochester NY 14642

WEITKAMP, WILLIAM GEORGE, b Fremont, Nebr, June 22, 34; m 56; c 3. NUCLEAR PHYSICS. *Educ:* St Olaf Col, BA, 56; Univ Wis, MS, 61, PhD(physics), 65. *Prof Exp:* Res asst physics, Univ Wis, 59-64; res asst prof, Univ Wash, Seattle, 64-67; asst prof, Univ Pittsburgh, 67-68; sr res assoc, 68-73, res assoc prof physics, 73-78, RES PROF PHYSICS, UNIV WASH, 78- TECH DIR, NUCLEAR PHYSICS LAB, 68- *Concurrent Pos:* Acad guest, Eignossische Technische Hochschule, Zürich, Switz, 74-75. *Mem:* Am Phys Soc. *Res:* Polarization phenomena in reactions involving light nuclei; time reversal invarience in nuclear reactions; isobaric analog states in heavy nuclei; nuclear instrumentation. *Mailing Add:* Nuclear Physics Lab Univ of Wash Seattle WA 98195

WEITLAUF, HARRY, b Seattle, Wash, July 8, 37; m 64. REPRODUCTIVE PHYSIOLOGY. *Educ:* Univ Wash, BS, 59, MD, 63. *Prof Exp:* Fel reproductive physiol, Med Ctr, Univ Kans, 66-68, from asst prof to assoc prof anat, 68-74; assoc prof, 74-80, PROF ANAT, UNIV ORE MED CTR, 80- *Mem:* Am Asn Anat; Soc Study Reproduction. *Res:* Blastocyst metabolism during the preimplantation phase of development. *Mailing Add:* Dept of Anat Univ of Ore Med Ctr Portland OR 97201

WEITSMAN, ALLEN WILLIAM, b Greenbelt, Md, July 11, 40; div; c 4. MATHEMATICS. *Educ:* Syracuse Univ, BS, 62, MS, 64, PhD(math), 68. *Prof Exp:* From asst prof to assoc prof, 68-74, PROF MATH, PURDUE UNIV, LAFAYETTE, 74- *Concurrent Pos:* NSF grants, 69-81; Sloan Found grant, 72. *Res:* Classical function theory. *Mailing Add:* Dept of Math Purdue Univ Lafayette IN 47907

WEITZ, ERIC, b New York, NY, Sept 18, 47. CHEMICAL PHYSICS, PHYSICAL CHEMISTRY. *Educ:* Mass Inst Technol, BS, 68; Columbia Univ, PhD(chem), 72. *Prof Exp:* Res assoc chem, Univ Calif, Berkeley, 72-74; asst prof, 74-80, ASSOC PROF CHEM, NORTHWESTERN UNIV, EVANSTON, 80- *Concurrent Pos:* Alfred P Sloan fel. *Mem:* Am Phys Soc; Am Chem Soc. *Res:* Vibrational energy transfer in small molecules and the relation of internal energy to chemical reactivity; applications to laser-induced chemistry; isotope separation; studies of matrix isolated molecules; laser induced surface processes. *Mailing Add:* Dept of Chem Northwestern Univ Evanston IL 60201

WEITZ, JOHN HILLS, b Cleveland, Ohio, Sept 20, 16; m 45; c 3. MINERALOGY, ECONOMIC GEOLOGY. *Educ:* Wesleyan Univ, BA, 38; Lehigh Univ, MS, 40; Pa State Univ, PhD(geol), 54. *Prof Exp:* Asst, Johns Hopkins Univ, 40-42; from jr mineral economist to mineral economist, US Bur Mines, Washington, DC, 42-46; coop geologist, State Geol Surv, Pa, 46-52; asst prof geol, Lehigh Univ, 47-52; geologist & secy, 52-61, PRES, INDEPENDENT EXPLOSIVES CO, 61- *Mem:* AAAS; Geol Soc Am; Mineral Soc Am; Am Inst Mining, Metall & Petrol Engrs; Soc Explosive Engrs. *Res:* Economic geology; clay minerals. *Mailing Add:* Independent Explosives Co 20950 Center Ridge Rd Rocky River OH 44116

WEITZ, JOSEPH LEONARD, b Cleveland, Ohio, June 2, 22; m 49; c 3. GEOLOGY. *Educ:* Wesleyan Univ, BA, 44; Yale Univ, MS, 46, PhD(geol), 54. *Prof Exp:* Geologist, Fuels Br, US Geol Surv, 48-55 & Independent Explosives Co, Pa, 55-58; asst prof geol, Wesleyan Univ, 58-60 & Colo State Univ, 60-61; assoc prof, Hanover Col, 61-62; assoc prof, 62-67, PROF GEOL, COLO STATE UNIV, 67- *Concurrent Pos:* Geologist, US Geol Surv, 66-; dir, Earth Sci Curric Proj, Colo, 67-69; mem, Coun Educ Geol Sci, 67-72; ed, J Geol Educ, 71-74. *Mem:* Geol Soc Am; Am Asn Petrol Geologists. *Res:* Geology of mineral fuels; Mesozoic stratigraphy; structural geology; geologic compilation. *Mailing Add:* Dept of Earth Resources Colo State Univ Ft Collins CO 80523

WEITZMAN, ELLIOT D, b Newark, NJ, Feb 4, 29; m; c 2. NEUROLOGY, NEUROPHYSIOLOGY. *Educ:* Univ Iowa, BA, 50; Univ Chicago, MD, 55. *Prof Exp:* Instr neuroanat, Univ Chicago, 51-52; instr med physiol, Univ Ill, 52; asst neurol, Columbia Univ, 58-59; assoc, 61-63, from asst prof to assoc prof, 63-69, PROF NEUROL, ALBERT EINSTEIN COL MED, 69-, CHMN DEPT, 71-, PROF NEUROSCI, 74-; CHIEF DIV NEUROL, MONTEFIORE HOSP & MED CTR, 69- *Concurrent Pos:* Consult, Jacobi Hosp, 61-69, Bronx Vet Admin Hosp, 63-67 & Health Res Coun, New York, 64-69; ed, Sleep Reviews. *Mem:* Am Neurol Asn; Soc Neurosci; Am Acad Neurol; Asn Res Nerv & Ment Dis; Asn Psychophysiol. *Res:* Study of sleep. *Mailing Add:* Dept of Neurol Montefiore Hosp & Med Ctr Bronx NY 10467

WEITZMAN, LEO, b USSR, Dec 15, 43; US citizen; m 70; c 2. CHEMICAL ENGINEERING. *Educ:* Cooper Union, New York, BChE, 66; Purdue Univ, Lafayette, Ind, MS, 69, PhD(chem eng), 72. *Prof Exp:* Environ protection engr air pollution, Ill Environ Protection Agency, 72-74; chem engr org chem, US Environ Protection Agency, 74-80; RES MGR, ACUREX WASTE TECHNOL INC, 80- *Concurrent Pos:* Instr, Eve Col, Univ Cincinnati, 77- *Mem:* Air Pollution Control Asn; Am Inst Chem Engrs. *Res:* Measurement and control of industrial pollution in air, water and solid waste with emphasis on toxic materials and polychlorinated biphenyls. *Mailing Add:* Acurex Waste Technol Inc 8078 Beechmont Ave Cincinnati OH 45230

WEITZMAN, STANLEY HOWARD, b Mill Valley, Calif, Mar 16, 27; m 48; c 2. ICHTHYOLOGY. *Educ:* Univ Calif, AB, 51, AM, 53; Stanford Univ, PhD(biol), 60. *Prof Exp:* Sr lab technician, Univ Calif, 50-56; instr anat, Sch Med, Stanford Univ, 57-62; assoc cur, 63-67, CUR, DIV FISHES, US NAT MUS, SMITHSONIAN INST, 67- *Mem:* Am Soc Ichthyologists & Herpetologists; Am Fisheries Soc; Soc Syst Zool; Soc Study Evolution. *Res:* Evolution, taxonomy and morphology of fishes. *Mailing Add:* Div of Fishes US Nat Mus Smithsonian Inst Washington DC 20560

WEITZNER, HAROLD, b Boston, Mass, May 19, 33; m 62; c 2. APPLIED MATHEMATICS, PLASMA PHYSICS. *Educ:* Univ Calif, AB, 54; Harvard Univ, AM, 55, PhD(physics), 58. *Prof Exp:* NSF fel, 58-59; assoc res scientist, 59-60, res scientist, 60-62, from asst prof to assoc prof, 62-69, PROF MATH, COURANT INST MATH SCI, NY UNIV, 69- *Concurrent Pos:* Consult, Los Alamos Nat Lab, Univ Calif, 62-, Lawrence Livermore Lab, Univ Calif, Livermore, 77- & Oak Ridge Nat Lab, 78- *Mem:* Am Phys Soc. *Res:* Wave propagation problems in magnetohydrodynamics; kinetic theory and plasma oscillation problems; magnetohydrodynamic equilibrium; stability theory. *Mailing Add:* NYU Courant Inst of Math Sci 251 Mercer St New York NY 10012

WEITZNER, STANLEY, b New York, NY, Mar 11, 31; m 61; c 3. PATHOLOGY. *Educ:* NY Univ, BA, 51; Univ Geneva, MD, 56. *Prof Exp:* Intern, Queens Gen Hosp, Jamaica, NY, 57-58; resident path, Vet Admin Hosp, New York, 58-62; assoc pathologist, Southside Hosp, Bay Shore, 63-64; dir lab, Monticello Hosp, 65-66; from instr to assoc prof path, Sch Med, Univ NMex, 67-74; assoc prof, Univ Tex Health Sci Ctr, San Antonio, 74-75; assoc prof path, Univ Miss Med Ctr, Jackson, 75-76, prof path & dir surg path, 75-78; prof path, Northeastern Ohio Univs Col Med, 78-81; dir labs & chief path, Timken Mercy Hosp, 78-81; PROF PATH, MED SCH, UNIV TEX, HOUSTON, 81- *Concurrent Pos:* Instr, Sch Med, NY Univ, 60-61; dep med examr, Suffolk County, NY, 64; assoc, Col Physicians & Surgeons, Columbia Univ, 65-67; asst chief lab, Vet Admin Hosp, Albuquerque, NMex, 66-74; chief anat path, Vet Admin Hosp, San Antonio, 74-75. *Mem:* Int Acad Path; Am Soc Clin Path; Am Acad Oral Path; NY Acad Sci. *Res:* Laboratory medicine with prime interest in surgical and anatomical pathology. *Mailing Add:* Dept Path & Lab Med 6431 Fannin St Univ Tex Med Sch Houston TX 77030

WEIZENBAUM, JOSEPH, b Berlin, Ger, Jan 8, 23; US citizen; m 52; c 4. COMPUTER SCIENCE. *Educ:* Wayne Univ, BS, 48, MS, 50. *Prof Exp:* Syst engr, Comput Develop Lab, Gen Elec Co, 55-63; vis assoc prof elec eng, 63-64, assoc prof, 64-70, PROF COMPUT SCI & ENG, MASS INST TECHNOL, 70- *Concurrent Pos:* Ed, Int J Man-Mach Studies, 70-; mem secy's adv comt automated personel data syst, US Dept Health, Educ & Welfare, 72-; fel, Ctr Advan Study Behav Sci, 72-73; Vinton Hayes sr res fel, Harvard Univ, 73-74. *Mem:* Fel AAAS; Asn Comput Mach. *Res:* Artificial intelligence; natural language understanding by computers; social implications of computers and cybernetics; structure of computer languages. *Mailing Add:* Dept of Comput Sci Mass Inst Technol Cambridge MA 02139

WEJKSNORA, PETER JAMES, b Brooklyn, NY, Jan 12, 50; m 72. BIOLOGY, BIOCHEMISTRY. *Educ:* Brooklyn Col, BS, 72; Brandeis Univ, PhD(biol), 77. *Prof Exp:* Res assoc biochem, Albert Einstein Col Med, 77-81; ASST PROF, DEPT ZOOL, UNIV WIS-MILWAUKEE, 81- *Concurrent Pos:* Fel, Nat Inst Health, 77- *Res:* Ribosomal control in eukaryotic cells. *Mailing Add:* Dept Zool Univ Wis 3201 N Maryland Ave Milwaukee WI 53201

WEKSLER, BABETTE BARBASH, b New York, NY, Jan 18, 37; m 58; c 2. HEMATOLOGY, INTERNAL MEDICINE. *Educ:* Swarthmore Col, BA, 58; Col Physicians & Surgeons Columbia Univ, MD, 63. *Prof Exp:* Intern med, Bronx Munic Hosp, 63-64; resident, Georgetown Univ Hosp, 65-67; USPHS fel microbiol, Wright Fleming Inst St Mary's Hosp Med Sch, London, 67-68; Am Cancer Soc Clin fel hemat, NY Hosp Cornell Med Ctr, 68-69; asst prof, 70-75, assoc prof, 75-80, PROF MED, CORNELL UNIV MED COL, 81- *Concurrent Pos:* Assoc attend physician, NY Hosp Cornell Med Ctr, 75-80, attend physician, 81- *Mem:* Fel NY Acad Sci (gov, 78-80); Am Fedn Clin Res; Am Soc Hemat; Am Physiol Soc; Am Soc Clin Invest. *Res:* Platelet physiology and biochemistry; inflammation and hemostasis; prostaglandins. *Mailing Add:* Cornell Univ Med Col 1300 York Ave New York NY 10021

WEKSLER, MARC EDWARD, b New York, NY, Apr 16, 37; m 58; c 2. MEDICINE, IMMUNOLOGY. *Educ:* Swarthmore Col, BA, 58; Columbia Univ, MD, 62. *Prof Exp:* From asst prof to assoc prof, 70-78, WRIGHT PROF MED, MED COL, CORNELL UNIV, 78-, DIR DIV GERIATRICS & GERONT, 78- *Concurrent Pos:* USPHS fel, Transplantation Unit, St Mary's Hosp, London, Eng, 67-68 & spec fel, New York Hosp, 68-70; asst attend physician, New York Hosp, 70-75, assoc attend physician, 75-78, attend physician, 78 & dir geront & geriat; adj physician, Mem Hosp, New York; law lectr, Cornell Univ, 80. *Mem:* Am Soc Clin Invest; fel Am Col Physicians; Am Asn Immunologists; Geront Soc. *Res:* Gerontology and cellular immunology. *Mailing Add:* Dept of Med Cornell Univ Med Col New York NY 10021

WEKSTEIN, DAVID ROBERT, b Boston, Mass, Feb 26, 37; m 58; c 4. PHYSIOLOGY. *Educ:* Boston Univ, AB, 57, MA, 58; Univ Rochester, PhD(physiol), 62. *Prof Exp:* From instr to asst prof, 62-68, ASSOC PROF PHYSIOL, COL MED, UNIV KY, 68-, ASSOC DIR, MULTIDISCIPLINARY CTR OF GERONT, 79- *Mem:* AAAS; Soc Exp Biol & Med; Geront Soc; Am Soc Zoologists; Am Physiol Soc. *Res:* Developmental physiology; physiology of temperature regulation; biology of aging; circadian rhythms. *Mailing Add:* Dept Physiol & Biophys Univ Ky Col Med Lexington KY 40506

WELBAND, WILBUR A, b Regina, Sask, July 11, 31; m 54; c 4. ANATOMY, NEUROLOGY. *Educ:* George Williams Col, BS, 54, MS, 56; Loyola Univ, Ill, PhD(anat), 61. *Prof Exp:* Instr anat, Stritch Sch Med, Loyola Univ, Ill, 61-63; asst prof anat, 63-69, instr neurol, 66-68, ASST PROF NEUROL, MED COL GA, 68-, ASSOC PROF ANAT, 69- *Concurrent Pos:* Grants, USPHS, 63 & Damon Runyon Mem, 65-; consult physiologist, Vet Admin Hosp, Augusta, Ga, 68- *Mem:* AAAS; Am Asn Anatomists; assoc Am Acad Neurol. *Res:* Clinical and experimental studies in electromyography; myoneural junction anatomy and pathology. *Mailing Add:* 1900 Curtis Dr Augusta GA 29841

WELBY, CHARLES WILLIAM, b Bakersfield, Calif, Oct 9, 26; m 48; c 2. HYDROGEOLOGY, STRATIGRAPHY. *Educ:* Univ Calif, BS, 48, MS, 49; Mass Inst Technol, PhD(geol), 52. *Prof Exp:* Geologist, Calif Co, 52-54; asst prof geol, Middlebury Col, 54-58, Trinity Col, Conn, 58-61 & Rensselaer Polytech Inst, 61-62; assoc prof geol & chmn dept, Southern Miss Univ, 62-65; assoc prof, 65-77, PROF GEOL, NC STATE UNIV, 77- *Concurrent Pos:* Consult groundwater, environ geol, remote sensing, shoreline errosion. *Mem:* Am Asn Petrol Geologists; fel Geol Soc Am; Soc Econ Paleont & Mineral; Asn Eng Geologists; Nat Water Well Asn. *Res:* Occurrence and management of ground water; structure and stratigraphy; occurrence and exploration for petroleum; ground water pollution; environmental geology; remote sensing. *Mailing Add:* Dept Marine Earth Atmospheric Sci NC State Univ PO Box 506B Raleigh NC 27650

WELCH, AARON WADDINGTON, b Georgetown, Md, July 25, 16; m 41; c 3. BOTANY. *Educ:* Univ Md, BS, 37; Iowa State Col, PhD(plant path), 42. *Prof Exp:* Mgr, Southeastern Exp Sta, Iowa, 40-42; assoc pathologist, Div Forage Crops, USDA, 45-47; plant pathologist, Exp Sta, 47-60, mgr res & develop farm, Clayton, 60-73, DIR RES & DEVELOP FARM, CLAYTON, E I DU PONT DE NEMOURS & CO, INC, 73- *Mem:* Am Phytopath Soc. *Res:* Plant pathology; helminthology; herbicides. *Mailing Add:* Res & Develop Farm 3209 Kenly Ct E I du Pont de Nemours & Co Inc Raleigh NC 27607

WELCH, ARNOLD D(EMERRITT), b Nottingham, NH, Nov 7, 08; m 33, 66; c 3. PHARMACOLOGY, CHEMOTHERAPY. *Educ:* Univ Fla, BS, 30, MS, 31; Univ Toronto, PhD(pharmacol), 34; Washington Univ, MD, 39. *Hon Degrees:* DSc, Univ Fla, 73. *Prof Exp:* Asst physiol, Exp Sta, Univ Fla, 29-31; asst pharmacol, Sch Med, Washington Univ, 35-36, instr, 36-40; dir pharmacol res, Sharp & Dohme, Inc, 40-44, asst dir res, 42-43, dir, 43-44; prof pharmacol & dir dept, Sch Med, Western Reserve Univ, 44-53; prof & chmn dept, Sch Med & Grad Sch, Yale Univ, 53-67, Eugene Higgins prof, 57-67; dir, Squibb Inst Med Res, 67-72, pres, 72-74, vpres res & develop, E R Squibb & Sons, Inc, 67-74; chmn, 75-81, EMER MEM, DIV BIOCHEM & CLIN PHARMACOL, ST JUDE CHILDREN'S RES HOSP, 81-; PROF PHARMACOL, UNIV TENN SCH MED, 75- *Concurrent Pos:* Fulbright scholar, Oxford Univ, 52; Commonwealth scholar, Univ Frankfurt, 64-65; mem, Sci Adv Comt, Leonard Wood Mem Found, 48-53; mem comts, Nat Res Coun, 48-56, chmn comt growth, 52-54; consult to Surgeon Gen, USPHS, 52-64; mem, Div Comt Biol & Med Res, NSF, 53-55; mem, Pharmcol & Exp Therapeut Study Sect, NIH, 59-63, chmn, 60-63, chmn chemother study sect, 63-65; mem, Sci Adv Bd, St Jude Hosp, 69-72; mem, Sci Adv Bd Biol Sci, Princeton Univ, 69-75. *Honors & Awards:* Sollmann Award, Am Soc Pharmacol & Exp Therapeut, 66. *Mem:* Asn Am Physicians; Am Soc Hemat; Brit Biochem Soc; Am Soc Clin Pharmacol & Therapeut; Am Asn Cancer Res. *Res:* Cellular localization of pressor amines; sulfonamides; filariasis; structure and action of choline-like compounds; biosynthesis of labile methyl group; biosynthesis and antagonism of utilization of nucleic acid precursors; metabolic approaches to cancer and virus chemotherapy; inhibition of enzyme induction; mechanisms of resistance to cytotoxic nucleosides; biochemical approaches to cancer chemotherapy. *Mailing Add:* St Jude Children's Res Hosp 332 N Lauderdale Memphis TN 38101

WELCH, ASHLEY JAMES, b Ft Worth, Tex, May 3, 33; m 52; c 3. ELECTRICAL & BIOMEDICAL ENGINEERING. *Educ:* Tex Tech Col, BS, 55; Southern Methodist Univ, MS, 59; Rice Univ, PhD(elec eng), 64. *Prof Exp:* Aerophys engr, Gen Dynamics/Ft Worth, 57-60; instr elec eng, Rice Univ, 60-64; from asst prof to assoc prof, 64-74, dir, Eng Comput Facil, 70-71, dir biomed eng prog, 71-75, PROF ELEC ENG & BIOMED ENGR, UNIV TEX, AUSTIN, 75- *Mem:* Inst Elec & Electronics Engrs; Asn Res Vision & Ophthal. *Res:* Analysis of medical data and the application of laser techniques in biomedical research. *Mailing Add:* Dept Elec Eng Univ Tex Austin TX 78712

WELCH, BILLY EDWARD, physiology, biochemistry, see previous edition

WELCH, CHARLES DARREL, b Albright, WVa, Sept 2, 19; m 48; c 3. AGRONOMY. *Educ:* Univ WVa, BS, 42; NC State Univ, MS, 48, PhD(soils), 60. *Prof Exp:* Instr soil fertil, NC State Univ, 48-49; agronomist, NC Dept Agr, 50-63; EXTEN SOIL CHEMIST, TEX A&M UNIV, 63- *Mem:* AAAS; Am Soc Agron; Soil Sci Soc Am. *Res:* Plant nutrient response in field and greenhouse soils; soil tests for nitrogen. *Mailing Add:* Soil Testing Lab Tex A&M Univ College Station TX 77843

WELCH, CLAUDE ALTON, b Flint, Mich, Oct 24, 21; m 49; c 2. ZOOLOGY. *Educ:* Mich State Univ, BS, 48, PhD(zool), S7. *Prof Exp:* From instr to prof natural sci, Mich State Univ, 53-69; prof, 69-73, chmn dept, 69-77, O T WALTER PROF BIOL, MACALESTER COL, 73- *Concurrent Pos:* Supvr blue version writing team, Biol Sci Curriculum Study, 61, consult, Adaptation Comt, Japan, 63-65 & Turkey, 65. *Mem:* AAAS; Nat Asn Biol Teachers (pres, 72); Nat Sci Teachers Asn. *Res:* Cell physiology. *Mailing Add:* Dept of Biol Macalester Col St Paul MN 55101

WELCH, CLETUS NORMAN, b Convoy, Ohio, Feb 2, 37; m 60; c 2. PHYSICAL INORGANIC CHEMISTRY. *Educ:* Bowling Green State Univ, BS, 61; Ohio State Univ, MS, 64, PhD(chem), 66. *Prof Exp:* RES ASSOC, PPG INDUSTS, INC, 66- *Mem:* Am Chem Soc. *Res:* Halogen and halogen-oxygen chemistry; synthesis of electrocatalysts; electrode processes; electrochemical cell design and materials of construction; electroless, electrolytic and vapor deposition of metallic coatings. *Mailing Add:* 690 Yager Rd Clinton OH 44216

WELCH, DAVID O(TIS), b Richmond, Va, Mar 9, 38; m 78; c 2. MATERIALS SCIENCE, SOLID STATE PHYSICS. *Educ:* Univ Tenn, BS, 60; Mass Inst Technol, SM, 62; Univ Pa, PhD(metall), 64. *Prof Exp:* Res assoc metal physics, Res Inst Advan Studies, Martin Co, 62; NATO res fel, Solid State Physics Div, Atomic Energy Res Estab, Harwell, Eng, 64-65; asst prof metal phys, Solid State & Mat Prog, Princeton Univ, 66-72, res fel, 72; assoc physicist, 72-75, physicist, Physics Dept, 75-77, PHYSICIST, METALL & MAT SCI DIV, BROOKHAVEN NAT LAB, 77- *Concurrent Pos:* Consult, Metals & Ceramics Div, Oak Ridge Nat Lab, 66-68; consult & vis scientist, Mat Sci Div, Argonne Nat Lab, 68; vis prof, Univ Sao Paulo, 70; adj prof mat sci, State Univ NY Stony Brook, 80-; mem solid state sci panel, Nat Res Coun, 80- *Mem:* AAAS; Am Phys Soc; Sigma Xi. *Res:* Theoretical materials science; defects and diffusion in crystals; anelasticity; x-ray studies of crystal defects; biological materials; superconducting materials; metal-hydrogen systems. *Mailing Add:* Bldg 480 Brookhaven Nat Lab Upton NY 11973

WELCH, DEAN EARL, b Aledo, Ill, Aug 5, 37; m 58; c 6. ORGANIC CHEMISTRY. *Educ:* Monmouth Col, BA, 59; Mass Inst Technol, PhD(org chem), 63. *Prof Exp:* Chemist, Escambia Chem Corp, 63-64; assoc scientist, 64-66, scientist, 66-68, qual assurance dir, 68-69, chem res dir, 69-71, res dir, 71-72, VPRES RES, SALSBURY LABS, 72- *Mem:* Am Chem Soc. *Res:* Organic synthesis; research and development administration. *Mailing Add:* Salsbury Labs Rockford Rd Charles City IA 50616

WELCH, FRANK JOSEPH, b Fresno, Calif, Aug 5, 29; m 54; c 5. ORGANIC CHEMISTRY. *Educ:* Fresno State Univ, BS, 51; Stanford Univ, PhD(org chem), 54. *Prof Exp:* Res chemist polymers, Union Carbide Chem Co, 54-62, group leader latex polymerization, Res & Develop Dept, Union Carbide Corp, 62-71; DIR RES, AVERY LABEL DIV, AVERY INT, 71- *Mem:* Tech Asn Pulp & Paper Indust; Am Chem Soc. *Res:* Ionic and free radical polymerization kinetics; organo-metallic and organophosphorus chemistry; latex polymerization; coatings and printing inks. *Mailing Add:* Avery Label Co 777 E Foothill Blvd Azusa CA 91702

WELCH, GARTH LARRY, b Brigham City, Utah, Feb 14, 37; m 60; c 6. ACADEMIC ADMINISTRATION, INORGANIC CHEMISTRY. *Educ:* Univ Utah, BS, 59, PhD(inorg chem), 63. *Prof Exp:* Fel, Univ Calif, Los Angeles, 62-64; from asst prof to assoc prof, 64-72, PROF CHEM, WEBER STATE COL, 72-, DEAN, SCH NATURAL SCI, 74- *Concurrent Pos:* Vis prof, Brigham Young Univ, 80. *Mem:* Am Chem Soc; Sigma Xi. *Res:* Kinetics of complex ions; reversion rates of polymers. *Mailing Add:* Sch of Natural Sci Weber State Col Ogden UT 84408

WELCH, GARY ALAN, b Santa Monica, Calif, June 19, 42. ASTRONOMY. *Educ:* Harvey Mudd Col, BSc, 64; Univ Wash, MSc, 67, PhD(astron), 69. *Prof Exp:* Asst prof astron, Wheaton Col, 73-74; asst prof, 74-78, ASSOC PROF ASTRON, SAINT MARY'S UNIV, HALIFAX, 78- *Concurrent Pos:* Hon fel astron, Univ Wis, Madison, 80-81. *Mem:* Int Astron Union; Am Astron Soc; Can Astron Soc; Royal Astron Soc Can; Astron Soc Pac. *Res:* Photometry and spectroscopy of galaxies at ultraviolet wavelengths for the purpose of determining stellar content; structure and evolution of galaxies within clusters; digital imaging devices for astronomy. *Mailing Add:* Dept Astron Saint Mary's Univ Halifax NS B3H 3C3 Can

WELCH, GARY WILLIAM, b Buffalo, NY, Jan 4, 43; m 72; c 5. ANESTHESIOLOGY, CRITICAL CARE MEDICINE. *Educ:* Univ Va, BA,64, MD, 70, PhD(anat), 70. *Prof Exp:* Chief anesthesiol sect, US Army Inst Surg Res, 74-76; asst prof, 77-79, vchmn, 80-81, ASSOC PROF ANESTHESIOL & SURG, UNIV MASS MED CTR, 79-, ACTG CHMN, DEPT ANESTHESIOL, 81- *Concurrent Pos:* Dir, Surg Intensive Care Unit, Univ Mass Med Ctr, 78- *Mem:* Soc Critical Care Med; Am Shock Soc; Am Burn Asn; Am Soc Anesthesiologists. *Res:* High frequency; high pressure; jet ventilation; metabolic changes following major surgery; use of epidural narcotics for pain relief; fluid therapy for treatment of shock. *Mailing Add:* Univ Mass Dept Surg 55 Lake Ave N Worcester MA 01605

WELCH, GEORGE BURNS, b Soso, Miss, Nov 23, 20; m 54; c 1. AGRICULTURAL ENGINEERING. *Educ:* Miss State Univ, BS, 47; Tex Agr & Mech Col, MS, 50; Okla State Univ, PhD(eng), 65. *Prof Exp:* Instr agr, Jones County Jr Col, 47-48; instr agr eng, Miss State Univ, 48-49, assoc agr engr, Miss Agr Exp Sta, 51-62, assoc prof agr eng, 52-62; res asst, Okla State Univ, 62-65; prof agr eng & agr engr, 65-80, PROF AGR & BIOL ENG, MISS STATE UNIV, 80- *Concurrent Pos:* Miss State Univ-US Agency Int Develop seed processing engr, Brazil, 70-72. *Mem:* Am Soc Agr Engrs. *Res:* Design of agricultural machinery and agricultural buildings; design of seed processing and storage facilities for tropical countries. *Mailing Add:* Dept of Biol & Agr Eng Box 5465 Mississippi State MS 39762

WELCH, GEORGE RICKEY, b Rockwood, Tenn, May 29, 47; m 67; c 2. THEORETICAL BIOCHEMISTRY, BIOPHYSICAL CHEMISTRY. *Educ:* Univ Tenn, BS, 70, PhD(biochem), 75. *Prof Exp:* Res fel theoret biophys, Univ Libre Bruxelles, 75-77; res scientist biochem, Univ Tex Med Sch, 77-78; ASST PROF BIOL SCI, UNIV NEW ORLEANS, 78- *Concurrent Pos:* Res fel, Solvay Int Inst Physics & Chem, 75-77. *Mem:* AAAS; Am Phys Soc; Biophys Soc. *Res:* Enzymology and metabolic regulation; theoretical biophysical chemistry; modeling of biochemical processes; bioenergetics. *Mailing Add:* Dept of Biol Sci Univ of New Orleans New Orleans LA 70122

WELCH, GINA CHURCH, b Elkhart, Ind, July 18, 52; m 80. MOLECULAR BIOLOGY. *Educ:* Skidmore Col, BA, 74; Union Univ, PhD(biochem), 79. *Prof Exp:* res fel, Div Neurosurg, Albany Med Col, Union Univ, 76-79; tech coordr, Phys Chem Lab, 79-81, MEM STAFF, ELECTRON & BIOSCI BR, GEN ELEC CORP RES & DEVELOP, 81- *Mem:* NY Acad Sci; AAAS. *Mailing Add:* Gen Elec Corp Res & Develop PO Box 8 Schenectady NY 12301

WELCH, GORDON E, b Sabinal, Tex, Aug 20, 33; m 57; c 3. MICROBIOLOGY. *Educ:* Southwest Tex State Univ, BS, 60, MA, 62; Tex A&M Univ, PhD(microbiol), 66. *Prof Exp:* Chmn dept biol & chem, Southwest Tex Jr Col, 60-62; assoc prof biol, San Antonio Col, 66-67; assoc prof, 67-73, PROF BIOL, ANGELO STATE UNIV, 73-, DEAN COL SCI, 77- *Concurrent Pos:* Consult, Bexar Co Hosp Dist, San Antonio, Tex, 66. *Mem:* AAAS; Am Soc Microbiol; Am Inst Biol Sci. *Res:* Virology, particularly myxoviruses, their nature, properties and pathogenicity. *Mailing Add:* Dept of Biol Angelo State Univ San Angelo TX 76901

WELCH, GRAEME P, b Los Angeles, Calif, Nov 25, 17; m 45; c 4. BIOPHYSICS. *Educ:* Univ Calif, Los Angeles, AB, 40; Univ Calif, Berkeley, MA, 50, PhD(biophys), 57. *Prof Exp:* Assoc physicist, Div War Res, Univ Calif, 41-45, physicist, Donner Lab, 48-59; engr biophys, Saclay Nuclear Res Ctr, France, 59-61; BIOPHYSICIST, DONNER LAB, BERKELEY RADIATION LAB, UNIV CALIF, BERKELEY, 61- *Mem:* Radiation Res Soc. *Res:* Biological effects of radiation; physics and dosimetry of heavy-particle radiations. *Mailing Add:* Lawrence Berkeley Lab Univ Calif Berkeley CA 94720

WELCH, H(OMER) WILLIAM, b Beardstown, Ill, Oct 21, 20; m 42; c 2. ELECTRONIC & ELECTRICAL ENGINEERING. *Educ:* DePauw Univ, BA, 42; Univ Mich, MS, 49, PhD, 52. *Prof Exp:* Asst physics & electronics, Univ Wis, 42-43; res assoc, Radio Res Lab, Harvard Univ, 43-45; instr physics, Purdue Univ, 45-46; res physicist, Eng Res Inst, Univ Mich, 46-50, proj leader, Electronic Defense Group, 51-53, from assoc prof to prof elec eng, 53-57; dir res & develop, Motorola Mil Electronics Div, 57-62, gen mgr control syst div, 62-66, asst to chief tech off, 66-67; asst dean, Col Eng Sci, 68-80, PROF ENG, ARIZ STATE UNIV, 67-, DIR, PROG SOCIETY, VALUES & TECHNOL, 79- *Concurrent Pos:* Mem adv groups, US Dept Defense. *Mem:* Fel Inst Elec & Electronics Engrs; Am Soc Eng Educ; Soc Hist Technol; fel AAAS. *Res:* Microwave tubes and solid state devices; communications systems; integrated microelectronics; remote monitoring and control systems; social impacts of technology. *Mailing Add:* Col Eng & Appl Sci Ariz State Univ Tempe AZ 85281

WELCH, HUGH GORDON, b Memphis, Tenn, Oct 30, 37; m 59; c 2. EXERCISE PHYSIOLOGY, RESPIRATORY PHYSIOLOGY. *Educ:* Lambuth Col, BA, 59; Univ Fla, PhD(physiol), 66. *Prof Exp:* Asst prof, Univ Mich, Ann Arbor, 66-68; assoc prof, 68-76, PROF PHYSIOL, UNIV TENN, KNOXVILLE, 76- *Concurrent Pos:* Guest scientist, Univ Copenhagen, Denmark, 74-75. *Mem:* Am Physiol Soc; Am Col Sports Med. *Res:* Physiology of exercise-in particular in the study of those factors that limit human work capacity in health and in certain disease states. *Mailing Add:* Dept Zool Univ Tenn Knoxville TN 37996

WELCH, J PHILIP, b Macclesfield, Eng, June 18, 33; m 58; c 4. HUMAN GENETICS. *Educ:* Univ Edinburgh, MB & ChB, 58; Johns Hopkins Univ, PhD, 69. *Prof Exp:* Fel med, Johns Hopkins Hosp, 63-67; asst prof, 67-72, ASSOC PROF PEDIAT, DALHOUSIE UNIV, 72- *Concurrent Pos:* Consult, Children's Hosp, Victoria Gen Hosp, Grace Maternity Hosp & Halifax Infirmary, 67- *Mem:* Am Soc Human Genetics; Am Fedn Clin Res; Am Asn Advan Aging Res; Can Genetics Soc; Soc Study Social Biol. *Res:* Biochemical, behavioral and cytogenetic aspect of mental abilities and aberrations. *Mailing Add:* Dept Pediat Dalhousie Univ Halifax NS B3H 3T5 Can

WELCH, JAMES ALEXANDER, b Versailles, Ky, May 25, 24; m 51; c 2. ANIMAL HUSBANDRY, ANIMAL PHYSIOLOGY. *Educ:* Univ Ky, BS, 47; Univ Ill, PhD(animal sci), 52. *Prof Exp:* From asst prof to assoc prof animal husb, 52-60, actg chmn dept animal sci, 62, PROF ANIMAL SCI, UNIV WVA & ANIMAL SCIENTIST, EXP STA, 60- *Concurrent Pos:* From asst animal husbandman to assoc animal husbandman, 52-60; chief party, WVa Univ-AID contract team, Uganda & lectr, Vet Training Inst, Entebbe, 63-66. *Mem:* Fel AAAS; Am Soc Animal Sci. *Mailing Add:* Div Animal & Vet Sci WVa Univ Morgantown WV 26506

WELCH, JAMES EDWARD, b San Rafael, Calif, July 19, 11; m 37; c 3. GENETICS. *Educ:* Univ Calif, BS, 34, MS, 35; Cornell Univ, PhD(genetics), 42. *Prof Exp:* Trainee agron, Soil Conserv Serv, USDA, 35, jr agr aide, 35-36, agr aide, 36; jr olericulturist, Exp Sta, Univ Hawaii, 36-38, asst olericulturist, 38-39; asst, Maize Genetics Coop, Cornell Univ, 40-42; asst horticulturist, Exp Sta, La State Univ, 42-43; assoc horticulturist, Regional Veg Breeding Lab, USDA, SC, 43-47; asst olericulturist, 47-52, assoc olericulturist, 52-79, EMER ASSOC OLERICULTURIST, EXP STA, UNIV CALIF, DAVIS, 79- *Concurrent Pos:* Lectr veg crops, Col Agr, Univ Calif, Davis, 49-59 & 76-79; collabr, Plant Sci Res Div, USDA, 58-74. *Mem:* Fel AAAS; Am Inst Biol Sci; Am Soc Hort Sci; Am Genetic Asn. *Res:* Plant morphological characters associated with earworm resistance in maize; genetic linkage in autotetraploid maize; genetics of male sterility in the carrot; breeding improved varieties of vegetable crops, especially sweet corn, lima beans, carrots, celery, tomatoes and lettuce. *Mailing Add:* Dept of Veg Crops Univ of Calif Davis CA 95616

WELCH, JAMES GRAHAM, b Ithaca, NY, Aug 16, 32; m 56; c 4. ANIMAL NUTRITION. *Educ:* Cornell Univ, BS, 55; Univ Wis, MS, 57, PhD(biochem, animal husb), 59. *Prof Exp:* Asst, Univ Wis, 55-59; asst prof animal husb, Rutgers Univ, 59-63, assoc prof nutrit, 63-68; assoc prof, 68-70, PROF ANIMAL SCI, UNIV VT, 70- *Mem:* AAAS; Am Soc Animal Sci; Am Dairy Sci Asn; Am Inst Nutrit. *Res:* Ruminant nutrition. *Mailing Add:* Dept of Animal Sci Univ of Vt Burlington VT 05401

WELCH, JAMES LEE, b Medford, Ore, June 23, 46. HEALTH SCIENCES. *Educ:* S Ore State Col, BS, 68; Loma Linda Univ, BS, 69, MPH, 72, DHSC, 74. *Prof Exp:* Chief technologist med technol, Park Ave Hosp, 69-70; supvr lab, Hollywood Presbyterian Hosp, 70-72, Temple Hosp, 72-; CHMN & ASSOC PROF MED TECHNOL HEALTH SCI, CALIF STATE UNIV, DOMINGUEZ HILLS, 75- *Concurrent Pos:* Mem, Am Bd Bioanal, 75-; consult exten allied health, Univ Calif, Riverside, 74- *Mem:* AAAS; Am Soc Clin Pathologists; Am Pub Health Asn. *Mailing Add:* Calif State Univ Dominguez Hills Carson CA 90747

WELCH, JANE MARIE, b Springfield, Mass, May 16, 50; m 77. NUCLEAR WASTE FORMS. *Educ:* Univ Mass, BS, 72; Pa State Univ, MS, 74, PhD(geochem & mineral), 78. *Prof Exp:* SCIENTIST, EG&G IDAHO, INC, 80- *Mem:* Am Ceramic Soc; Mat Res Soc. *Res:* Phase equilibria of silicate and titanate systems; development and characterization of nuclear waste forms. *Mailing Add:* 750 Brandon Dr Idaho Falls ID 83402

WELCH, JASPER ARTHUR, JR, b Baton Rouge, La, Jan 5, 1931; m 53; c 3. OPERATIONS RESEARCH. *Educ:* La State Univ, BS, 52; Univ Calif, Berkeley, MA, 54, PhD(physics), 58. *Prof Exp:* US Air Force, 52-, group leader, Lawrence Livermore Lab, 53-57, Weapons Lab, 57-62; sr staff, RAND Corp, 62-64; US Air Force, asst to comdr, systs command, 64-65, tech dir, WCoast Study Facil, 65-68, chief anal, Studies & Analyses, 69-71, asst dir defense, Res & Eng, Off Secy Defense, 71-73, sr asst to Secy Defense for Atomic Energy, 73-74, asst strategic initiatives Hq, 74-75, asst chief of staff, Studies & Analyses, 75-79, coordn, Defense Pol, Nat Security Coun, 79-81, spec asst chief staff, Hq, 81, ASST DEP CHIEF OF STAFF, RES & DEVELOP, HQ US AIR FORCE, 81- *Concurrent Pos:* Mem, NASA Adv Comt Fluid Mech, 64-66; Consult, Presidents Sci Adv Comt, 62-65, NATO Adv Group Aerospace, Res & Develop, 71-80, Defense Sci Bd, 68-, Air Force Sci Adv Bd, 57-, Army Sci Bd, 80- *Mem:* Am Phys Soc; Am Geophys Union; Coun Foreign Rel; Nat Acad Eng. *Res:* Aerospace system requirements, design and program management. *Mailing Add:* 5048 N 37th St Arlington VA 22207

WELCH, JEROME EUGENE, b Portland, Maine, Jan 11, 45; m 66; c 2. SOILS GEOCHEMISTRY. *Educ:* Calif Polytech State Univ, BS, 72; Univ Calif, Riverside, PhD(soil chem), 79. *Prof Exp:* Res assoc, Dept Soil & Environ Sci, Univ Calif, Riverside, 72-78; ASST SCIENTIST, KANS GEOL SURV, UNIV KANS, 78- *Mem:* Soil Sci Soc Am; Soc Environ Geochem & Health; Int Soc Soil Sci. *Res:* Determining the trace element geochemistry of the major agricultural soils of Kansas; determining the trace element geochemistry of Kansas soils that have been disturbed or affected as a result of mineral and coal mining; geochemical and hydrological investigations of solid and hazardous waste disposal sites. *Mailing Add:* Kans Geol Surv 1930 Ave A Campus West Univ Kans Lawrence KS 66044

WELCH, LESTER MARSHALL, petroleum chemistry, see previous edition

WELCH, LIN, b Tahoka, Tex, Dec 9, 27; m 50; c 3. SPEECH PATHOLOGY. *Educ:* WTex State Univ, BS, 48; Baylor Univ, MA, 49; Univ Mo, PhD(speech path), 60. *Prof Exp:* Instr speech, Blue Mountain Col, 52-53; instr, Univ Mo, 53-56; PROF SPEECH PATH & AUDIOL, CENT MO STATE UNIV, 56-, HEAD DEPT, 70- *Concurrent Pos:* Proj dir, Neurol & Sensory Dis Prof grants, 64-66; dir, Cleft Palate Camp, Mo Crippled Children's Serv, 66, 67, 68 & 69; chmn, Continuing Educ Comt, Am Speech & Hearing Asn, 72-73. *Mem:* Am Speech & Hearing Asn. *Res:* Cleft palate; stuttering. *Mailing Add:* Dept of Speech Path & Audiol Cent Mo State Univ Warrensburg MO 64093

WELCH, LLOYD RICHARD, b Detroit, Mich, Sept 28, 27; m 53; c 3. MATHEMATICS. *Educ:* Univ Ill, BS, 51; Calif Inst Technol, PhD(math), 58. *Prof Exp:* Sr res engr, Jet Propulsion Lab, Calif Inst Technol, 57-59; staff mathematician, Inst Defense Anal, 59-65; assoc prof elec eng, 65-68, PROF ELEC ENG, UNIV SOUTHERN CALIF, 68- *Mem:* Am Math Soc; Math Asn Am; Soc Indust & Appl Math. *Res:* Probability theory; combinatorics; communication theory. *Mailing Add:* Dept of Elec Eng Univ of Southern Calif Los Angeles CA 90007

WELCH, MELVIN BRUCE, b Hood River, Ore, Feb 24, 45; m 67; c 2. INORGANIC CHEMISTRY, POLYMER CHEMISTRY. *Educ:* Linfield Col, BA, 67; Univ Utah, PhD(inorg chem), 74. *Prof Exp:* Res chemist, 74-80, SR RES CHEMIST, PHILLIPS PETROL CO, 80- *Mem:* Am Chem Soc. *Res:* Olefin polymerization and organometallic chemistry. *Mailing Add:* 4716 Barlow Dr Bartlesville OK 74003

WELCH, MICHAEL JOHN, b Stoke-on-Trent, Eng, June 28, 39. RADIOCHEMISTRY, NUCLEAR MEDICINE. *Educ:* Cambridge Univ, BA, 61, MA, 64; Univ London, PhD(radiochem), 65. *Prof Exp:* Res assoc chem, Brookhaven Nat Lab, 65-67; from asst prof to assoc prof, 67-74, PROF RADIATION CHEM, SCH MED, WASHINGTON UNIV, 74- *Honors & Awards:* Paul C Aebersold Award, Soc Nuclear Med, 80. *Mem:* The Chem Soc; Am Chem Soc; Soc Nuclear Med; Radiation Res Soc. *Res:* Hot atom chemistry; isotopes in medicine. *Mailing Add:* Dept of Radiol Washington Univ Sch of Med St Louis MO 63110

WELCH, PETER D, b Detroit, Mich, May 19, 28; m 74; c 2. MATHEMATICAL STATISTICS. *Educ:* Univ Wis, MS, 51; NMex State Univ, MS, 56; Columbia Univ, PhD(math statist), 63. *Prof Exp:* Assoc mathematician, Phys Sci Lab, NMex State Univ, 51-56; RES STAFF MEM PROBABILITY & STATIST, IBM RES CTR, 56- *Concurrent Pos:* Adj prof, Columbia Univ, 64-65, 74-75. *Mem:* Inst Elec & Electronics Engrs. *Res:* Queueing theory; time series analysis; signal processing. *Mailing Add:* 85 Croton Ave Mt Kisco NY 10549

WELCH, RAYMOND LEE, b Emporia, Kans, Nov 2, 43; m 64; c 1. ORGANIC CHEMISTRY, ORGANIC COATINGS. *Educ:* Kans State Teachers Col, BA, 65; Iowa State Univ, PhD(org chem), 69. *Prof Exp:* RES CHEMIST, HERCULES RES CTR, WILMINGTON, 69- *Mem:* Am Chem Soc. *Res:* Product development; polyesters; kinetics & mechanism of hydrocarbon autoxidation; organic coatings. *Mailing Add:* Tatnall Estates Rte 2 Box 109 Springhouse Lane Hockessin DE 19707

WELCH, RICHARD MARTIN, b Brooklyn, NY, Nov 4, 33; m 54; c 3. BIOCHEMICAL PHARMACOLOGY. *Educ:* St John's Univ, NY, BS, 57; Jefferson Med Col, MS, 60, PhD(pharmacol), 62. *Prof Exp:* Asst prof pharmacol, Jefferson Med Col, 62-63; GROUP LEADER MEDICINAL BIOCHEM, BURROUGHS WELLCOME RES LABS, 65-, SR PHARMACOLOGIST, 77- *Concurrent Pos:* Fel, Albert Einstein Col Med, 63-65. *Mem:* Am Soc Pharmacol & Exp Therapeut. *Res:* Pharmacodynamics; absorption, distribution and metabolism of drugs. *Mailing Add:* Med Biochem Burroughs Wellcome Res Labs Research Triangle Park NC 27609

WELCH, ROBERT CHARLES WILLIAM, b Strathroy, Ont, June 16, 42; US citizen; m 71. CHEMICAL ENGINEERING. *Educ:* Univ Tex, Austin, BS, 63, PhD(chem eng), 68. *Prof Exp:* Engr, Esso Res Labs, 68-73, researchers & engr, Exxon Co, 73-82, ENGR, ESSO LTD, LONDON, 82- *Mem:* Am Inst Chem Engrs; Nat Soc Prof Engrs. *Res:* Process and catalyst research and development; planning engineering. *Mailing Add:* Exxon Res & Eng Co PO Box 101 Florham Park NJ 07932

WELCH, ROBIN IVOR, b Douglas, Ariz, Mar 13, 30; m 68; c 4. EARTH SCIENCE, ECOLOGY. *Educ:* Univ Calif, Berkeley, BS, 55, MS, 56, PhD(wildland resource sci), 71. *Prof Exp:* Sr eng photo interpretation res, Mark Systs, Inc, 63-66; sr eng syst anal res, Stanford Res Inst, 66-70; res eng remote sensing res & teaching, Earth Satellite Corp, 70-75; assoc res scientist & vis assoc prof, Tex A&M Univ, 75-77; prog mgr & dir training remote sensing res Airview spec corp contract, Ames Res Ctr, NASA, Humboldt State Univ, 77-81; PRES & FOUNDER AERIAL PHOTO RES, AIRVIEW SPECIALISTS CORP, 54-; OPERS RES SPECIALIST, LOCKHEED MISSLES & SPACE CO, 81- *Concurrent Pos:* Consult, State Alaska Dept Econ Develop, 69-72, NASA Johnson Space Ctr, 75-77, CIA, 73-75, Greek Govt, 72-73 & Argentine Govt, 70-71. *Mem:* Am Soc Photogram; Am Forestry Asn. *Res:* Remote sensing of earth agriculture and water resources; data analysis by interactive man and machine systems of remote sensing data; teaching methods and curriculum development in remote sensing applications. *Mailing Add:* 3419 Churin Dr Mountain View CA 94040

WELCH, RODNEY CHANNING, b Ayrshire, Iowa, Dec 16, 04; m 37; c 3. FOOD SCIENCE. *Educ:* State Col Wash, BS, 28, MS, 31; Pa State Col, PhD(dairy husb), 35. *Prof Exp:* Asst county agent, Exten Serv, State Col Wash, 28-30; asst, Pa State Col, 31-34; dir lab, Sylvan Seal Milk, Inc, 34-43; supt, Wilbur Chocolate Co, 43-57, vpres, 55-71, dir, 59-71, tech consult, 71-73; CONSULT, 73- *Concurrent Pos:* Volunteer exec, Int Exec Serv Corps, 75- *Mem:* Am Asn Cereal Chem; NY Acad Sci; Inst Food Technologists; Am Asn Candy Technol. *Res:* Milk and chocolate products. *Mailing Add:* 415 S Cedar St Lititz PA 17543

WELCH, RONALD MAURICE, b Chicago, Ill, Dec 30, 43; m 67. ATMOSPHERIC PHYSICS, METEOROLOGY. *Educ:* Calif State Univ, Long Beach, BS, 65, MA, 67; Univ Utah, PhD(physics), 71, PhD(meteorol), 76. *Prof Exp:* Engr-scientist, Missile & Space Systs Div, Douglas Aircraft Co, Calif, 66; res assoc geophys, Univ Utah, 71-72, res assoc physics, 72, teaching assoc, 72-73, assoc instr, Meteorol Dept, 73-74, res assoc, 74-76; res assoc, Dept Atmospheric Sci, Colo State Univ, 76-80; MEM STAFF, METEOROL INST, UNIV MAINZ, GER, 80- *Concurrent Pos:* Vis scientist, Inst Meterol, Univ Mainz, 78- *Mem:* AAAS; Am Phys Soc; Am Geophys Union; Sigma Xi; Am Meteorol Soc. *Res:* Radiative transfer in planetary atmospheres; climatology; electronic properties of materials. *Mailing Add:* Inst Fur Meteorol Univ Mainz 65 Mainz West Germany

WELCH, ROSS MAYNARD, b Lancaster, Calif, May 8, 43; m 65; c 2. PLANT NUTRITION, PLANT PHYSIOLOGY. *Educ:* Calif State Polytech Univ, San Luis Obispo, 66; Univ Calif, Davis, MS, 69, PhD(soil sci), 71. *Prof Exp:* Res assoc plant mineral nutrit, Dept Agron & US Plant, Soil & Nutrit Lab, 71-72, PLANT PHYSIOLOGIST, SCI & EDUC ADMIN-AGR RES SERV, US PLANT, SOIL & NUTRIT LAB, USDA, CORNELL UNIV, 72- *Concurrent Pos:* Asst prof agron, Cornell Univ, 74-; vis prof, Sch Environ & Life Sci, Murdoch Univ, WAustralia, 80-81. *Mem:* NY Acad Sci; Sigma Xi; Am Soc Plant Physiol; Am Soc Agron; Soc Environ Geochem & Health. *Res:* Plant mineral nutrition; ion transport by plant tissues and cells; trace element physiology; physiological form and bioavailability of mineral elements in plants to animals and humans. *Mailing Add:* US Plant Soil & Nutrit Lab Cornell Univ Tower Rd Ithaca NY 14853

WELCH, ROY ALLEN, b Waukesha, Wis, Nov 14, 39; m 67. GEOGRAPHY, PHOTOGRAMMETRY. *Educ:* Carroll Col, BS, 61; Univ Okla, MA, 65; Univ Glasgow, PhD(geog, photogram), 68. *Prof Exp:* Photo-analyst geog, US Govt, 62-64; mgr earth sci dept, Itek Corp, 68-69; Nat Acad Sci-Nat Res Counc res assoc, US Geol Surv, 69-71; assoc prof geog, 71-77, PROF GEOG, UNIV GA, 77- *Concurrent Pos:* Consult, AID, 72; mem working group image qual & optical transfer function-modulation transfer function, Comn I, Int Soc Photogram, 72-76; mem remote sensing comt, Asn Am Geogrs, 73-75; remote sensing specialist, US Geol Surv, 73- *Honors & Awards:* III Talbert Abrams, Am Soc Photogram, 71, Presidential Citation, 75. *Mem:* Am Soc Photogram; Brit Photogram Soc; Asn Am Geogrs; Brit Cartog Soc; Sigma Xi. *Res:* Analyses of the quality and applications of aircraft and satellite imagery for geographic tasks, with particular reference to land use mapping and cartography. *Mailing Add:* Dept of Geog Univ of Ga Athens GA 30602

WELCH, STEPHEN MELWOOD, b San Diego, Calif, July 1, 49; m 73. ENTOMOLOGY, SYSTEMS SCIENCE. *Educ:* Mich State Univ, BS, 71, PhD(zool), 77. *Prof Exp:* Asst prof, 78-81, ASSOC PROF ENTOM, KANS STATE UNIV, 81- *Mem:* Entom Soc Am; Asn Comput Mach. *Res:* The application of computers, systems science and population biology to the management of agricultural pests. *Mailing Add:* Dept of Entom Kans State Univ Manhattan KS 66506

WELCH, STEVEN CHARLES, b Inglewood, Calif, Feb 18, 40; div; c 2. CHEMISTRY. *Educ:* Univ Calif, Los Angeles, BS, 64; Univ Southern Calif, PhD(chem), 68. *Prof Exp:* NIH fel, Calif Inst Technol, 68-70; asst prof, 70-77, assoc prof, 77-81, PROF CHEM & PHARM, UNIV HOUSTON, 81- *Concurrent Pos:* Nat Inst Gen Med Sci grant, Univ Houston, 71-77, Welch Found grant, 72-81; Nat Cancer Inst contract, 77-80. *Mem:* Am Chem Soc; Royal Soc Chem. *Res:* Synthetic organic chemistry; synthesis of molecules of theoretical and biological interest. *Mailing Add:* Dept of Chem Univ of Houston Houston TX 77004

WELCH, WALTER RAYNES, b Rumford, Maine, Oct 25, 20; m 44; c 3. MARINE BIOLOGY. *Educ:* Univ Maine, BS, 47, MS, 50. *Prof Exp:* Fisheries res biologist, Clam Prog, US Nat Marine Fisheries Serv, 49-58, prog leader, 58-64, proj leader lobster prog, 64-67, prog leader, 67-71, asst lab dir, 71-73, consult div water resources mgt & marine adv serv, 71-73; marine resource scientist & proj leader, 73-78, div chief, 78-81, ASST RES DIR, MAINE DEPT MARINE RESOURCES, 81- *Concurrent Pos:* Pvt consult molluscan & environ probs, 78- *Honors & Awards:* Superior Performance Award, US Bur Com Fisheries, 69; Unit Citation, Nat Oceanic & Atmospheric Admin, 73. *Mem:* Nat Shellfisheries Asn. *Res:* Molluscan and crustacean ecology; environmental measurement and interpretation. *Mailing Add:* Fisheries Res Lab Maine Dept of Marine Resources West Boothbay Harbor ME 04575

WELCH, WILLARD MCKOWAN, JR, b Frankfort, Ky, Mar 1, 44; m 66; c 2. ORGANIC CHEMISTRY. *Educ:* Mass Inst Technol, BS, 65; Rice Univ, PhD(org chem), 69. *Prof Exp:* RES CHEMIST, MED RES LABS, PFIZER, INC, 70- *Res:* Synthetic organic chemistry; central nervous system drugs; heterocyclic chemistry. *Mailing Add:* Med Res Labs Pfizer Inc Groton CT 06340

WELCH, WILLIAM HENRY, JR, b Los Angeles, Calif, Dec 13, 40; m 65; c 4. BIOCHEMISTRY. *Educ:* Univ Calif, Berkeley, BA, 63; Univ Kans, PhD(biochem), 69. *Prof Exp:* NIH fel, Brandeis Univ, 69-70; asst prof, 70-76, ASSOC PROF BIOCHEM, UNIV NEV, RENO, 76- *Mem:* Sigma Xi; AAAS; Am Chem Soc. *Res:* Enzymology; molecular basis of adaptive phenomena; mechanism of small ionic effectors of enzymic activity. *Mailing Add:* Dept of Biochem Univ of Nev Reno NV 89557

WELCH, WILLIAM JOHN, b Chester, Pa, Jan 17, 34; m 55; c 3. RADIO ASTRONOMY. *Educ:* Stanford Univ, BS, 55; Univ Calif, Berkeley, PhD(eng sci), 60. *Hon Degrees:* Dr, Univ Bordeaux I, 79. *Prof Exp:* From asst prof to prof elec eng, 60-72, PROF ELEC ENG & ASTRON & DIR RADIO ASTRON LAB, UNIV CALIF, BERKELEY, 72- *Concurrent Pos:* Mem, NSF Atron Adv Panel, 73-76; trustee at large, Assoc Univ Inc, 74-81; mem, Arecibu Adv Bd, 77-80. *Mem:* Am Astron Soc; Inst Elec & Electronics Eng; Int Sci Radio Union; AAAS; Int Astron Union. *Res:* Radio astronomical studies of the planets, interstellar medium and extragalactic radio sources; instrumenation for radio astronomy at millimeter wave lengths. *Mailing Add:* Radio Astron Lab Univ of Calif Berkeley CA 94720

WELCH, WINONA HAZEL, b Goodland, Ind, May 5, 96. BOTANY. *Educ:* DePauw Univ, AB, 23; Univ Ill, AM, 25; Ind Univ, PhD(bot), 28. *Prof Exp:* Asst bot, Univ Ill, 23-26; head dept biol, Cent Norm Col, Ind, 26-27; instr bot, Ind Univ, 28-30; from asst prof to prof, 30-61, actg head dept bot & bact, 39-40, 46-47, 53, head dept, 56-61, EMER PROF BOT, DePAUW UNIV, 61-, CUR HERBARIUM, 64- *Concurrent Pos:* Res grants, Ind Acad, 37, 41, 51, 54-55, 57-59, 64-78; Am Philos Soc grant, 37, 53; grad coun grant, DePauw Univ, 40-68; NSF grant, 60; Sigma Xi grant, 63-68; lectr-consult, Pigeon Lake Field Sta in Cryptogamic Botany, Wis Field Biol Prog, 64 & Plymouth State Col, 71. *Mem:* AAAS; Bot Soc Am; Am Soc Plant Taxon; Am Bryol & Lichenological Soc (vpres, 36-38, secy-treas, 41-54, pres, 54-56); Torrey Bot Club. *Res:* Plant ecology and taxonomy; bryophytes of Indiana; Fontinalaceae monographs for North America and the World; Hookeriaceae monographs for North America, West Indies and Central America. *Mailing Add:* Dept Bot & Bact 8 Harrison Hall DePauw Univ Greencastle IN 46135

WELCH, ZARA D, b North Manchester, Ind, June 28, 15. ORGANIC CHEMISTRY. *Educ:* Manchester Col, AB, 37; Purdue Univ, MS, 39, PhD(org chem), 42. *Prof Exp:* Asst, Purdue Univ, 37-41; res chemist, Va Smelting Co, 42; res fel chem, 42-49, from instr to asst prof, 49-63, admin asst to head, 49-68, ASSOC PROF CHEM, PURDUE UNIV, 63-, ASST TO HEAD DEPT, 68- *Concurrent Pos:* Off Sci Res & Develop fel, 42-43. *Mem:* Am Chem Soc. *Res:* Dehydrohalogenation; halogenation; fluorine chemistry; recovery of uranium. *Mailing Add:* Dept of Chem Purdue Univ West Lafayette IN 47907

WELCHER, RICHARD PARKE, b Hartford, Conn, July 21, 19; m 50; c 5. CHEMISTRY. *Educ:* Trinity Col, Conn, AB, 41; Mass Inst Technol, BS, 43, PhD(org chem), 47. *Prof Exp:* Control supvr anal dept, Tenn Eastman Corp, Tenn, 44-45; sr res chemist, Am Cyanamid Co, Stamford, 47-81. *Mem:* Am Chem Soc; Sigma Xi. *Res:* Heterocyclic compounds; organophosphorus, nitrogen and sulfur chemistry; nitriles, amides, polyamines, cyanogen, s-triazines, dicyandiamide; biocides, ion and electron exchange resins; surfactants; mining chemicals; chemistry of cationic polymers. *Mailing Add:* 16 Watch Tower Lane Old Greenwich CT 06870

WELD, CHARLES BEECHER, b Vancouver, BC, Feb 3, 99; m 30; c 3. HUMAN PHYSIOLOGY. *Educ:* Univ BC, BA, 22, MA, 24; Univ Toronto, MD, 29; Dalhousie Univ, LLD, 70. *Prof Exp:* Asst, Connaught Labs, Univ Toronto, 24, res assoc & lectr physiol, 30-36; prof, 36-69, EMER PROF PHYSIOL, DALHOUSIE UNIV, 69- *Concurrent Pos:* Physiologist, Hosp Sick Children, Toronto, 31-36; dir, NS Mus, 50- *Honors & Awards:* Starr Gold Medal, 33. *Mem:* Am Physiol Soc; Can Physiol Soc (pres, 46); fel Royal Soc Can. *Res:* Diphtheria toxoid; freezing of fish; parathyroid; acute intestinal obstruction; pneumothorax; aqueous humor; lipemia; intestinal secretion; interstitial fluid pressures. *Mailing Add:* 6550 Waegwoltic Ave Halifax NS B3H 2B4 Can

WELDEN, ARTHUR LUNA, b Birmingham, Ala, Jan 27, 27; m 50; c 2. MYCOLOGY. *Educ:* Birmingham-Southern Col, AB, 50; Univ Tenn, MS, 51; Univ Iowa, PhD(bot), 54. *Prof Exp:* Asst prof biol, Milliken Univ, 54-55; from instr to prof bot, 55-79, IDA RICHARDSON PROF BOT, TULANE UNIV, 80- *Concurrent Pos:* Am Philos Soc grant, 57; NSF grantee, 60- *Mem:* Mycol Soc Am; Sigma Xi; Int Asn Plant Taxon; Asn Trop Biol; Bot Soc Mex. *Res:* Myxomycetes; tropical fungi; Thelephoraceae. *Mailing Add:* Dept Biol Tulane Univ New Orleans LA 70118

WELDER, FRANK A, geomorphology, stratigraphy, see previous edition

WELDON, EDWARD J, JR, b New York, NY, Apr 8, 38; m 65; c 3. INFORMATION SCIENCE. *Educ:* Manhattan Col, BSEE, 58; Univ Fla, MSEE, 60, PhD(elec eng), 63. *Prof Exp:* Engr, Bell Tel Labs, 63-66; assoc prof, 66-71, PROF ELEC ENG, UNIV HAWAII, 71- *Concurrent Pos:* Pres, Adtech, Inc. *Mem:* AAAS; Inst Elec & Electronics Engrs. *Res:* Information theory; coding error control. *Mailing Add:* Dept of Elec Eng 2444 Dole St Honolulu HI 96822

WELDON, HENRY ARTHUR, b Atlanta, Ga, July 11, 47; m 69. UNIFIED GAUGE THEORIES COSMOLOGY. *Educ:* Mass Inst Technol, SB, 69, PhD(physics), 74. *Prof Exp:* Res assoc, Stanford Linear Accelerator Ctr, 74-76; res assoc, 76-79, ASST PROF PHYSICS, UNIV PA, 79- *Res:* Unified gauge theories of strong, weak and electromagnetic interactions; cross polarization violation and baryon generation in the early universe; high temperature field theory and applications to cosmology. *Mailing Add:* Dept Physics Univ Pa Philadelphia PA

WELDON, JOHN WILLIAM, chemistry, deceased

WELDON, VIRGINIA V, b Toronto, Ont, Sept 8, 35; US citizen; m 63; c 2. PEDIATRIC ENDOCRINOLOGY, MEDICAL ADMINISTRATION. *Educ:* Smith Col, AB, 57; State Univ NY Buffalo, MD, 62. *Prof Exp:* Intern, resident & fel, Sch Med, Johns Hopkins Univ & Hosp, 62-67, instr pediat, Univ, 67-68; from instr to assoc prof, 68-79, asst vchancellor med affairs, 75-81, PROF PEDIAT, SCH MED, WASHINGTON UNIV, 79-, ASSOC VCHANCELLOR MED AFFAIRS, 81-; CO-DIR DIV METAB & ENDOCRINOL, ST LOUIS CHILDREN'S HOSP, 73- *Concurrent Pos:*

Consult, Adv Comt Endocrinol & Metab, Food & Drug Admin, 73-76; mem, State of Mo Health Manpower Planning Task Force, 76-; co-dir div metab & endocrinol, St Louis Children's Hosp, 73-77; gen clin res ctr adv comt, NIH, 76-80, nat adv res resources coun, 80-84. *Mem:* AAAS; Sigma Xi; Endocrine Soc; Soc Pediat Res; Am Pediat Soc. *Res:* Aldosterone secretion in children; disorders of growth and growth hormone secretion in children. *Mailing Add:* Box 8106 660 S Euclid Ave Washington Univ Sch Med St Louis MO 63110

WELFORD, NORMAN TRAVISS, b London, Eng, Feb 5, 21; nat US; m 44; c 3. BIOMEDICAL ENGINEERING. *Educ:* Cambridge Univ, BA, 41, MA & MB, BCh, 45. *Prof Exp:* Intern & resident, Addenbrooks Hosp, Cambridge, Eng, 45-46; res assoc biophys, Univ Western Ont, 55-56; assoc prof psychophysiol, Antioch Col & res assoc psychophysiol-neurophysiol, Fels Res Inst, 56-66; dir biomed eng & fac assoc psychiat, Univ Tex Med Br, Galveston, 66-78; MED OFFICER, BUR MED DEVICES, FOOD & DRUG ADMIN, 78- *Concurrent Pos:* USPHS res fel, Univ Western Ont, 55-56. *Mem:* Soc Psychophysiol Res; Inst Elec & Electronics Engrs; Sigma Xi; Asn Advan Med Instrumentation. *Res:* Automation of data gathering and handling and stimulus presentation; psychophysiology of human sensory-motor performance and fetal heart rate behavior. *Mailing Add:* Bur of Med Devices HFK 420 8757 Georgia Ave Silver Spring MD 20910

WELGE, HENRY JOHN, b St Louis, Mo, Aug 15, 07; m 40; c 2. FLUID DYNAMICS. *Educ:* Univ Ill, BSc, 29; Calif Inst Technol, MSc, 32, PhD(phys chem), 36. *Prof Exp:* Anal chemsit, Richfield Oil Co, Calif, 29-31; res chemist, Tex Co, 37; from instr to asst prof chem, Agr & Mech Col, Tex, 37-44; sr res chemist, Exxon Prod Res Co, Houston, Tex, 44-72; CONSULT PETROL PROD, 72- *Mem:* Am Inst Mining, Metall & Petrol Eng. *Res:* Photochemistry; reaction kinetics and equilibria and diffusion; capillarity in petroleum production; single phase and multiphase fluid flow in porous media. *Mailing Add:* 286 St Josephs Long Beach CA 90803

WELHAN, JOHN ANDREW, b Winnipeg, Man, Aug 24, 50; m 78; c 2. ISOTOPE GEOCHEMISTRY, GEOTHERMAL CHEMISTRY. *Educ:* Univ Man, BSc, 72; Univ Waterloo, MSc, 74; Univ Calif, San Diego, PhD(geol sci), 81. *Prof Exp:* Staff res assoc III, 74-81, FEL RES GEOLOGIST VI, SCRIPPS INST OCEANOG, 81- *Concurrent Pos:* Consult, Geothermal Div, Union Oil Co & Harding-Lawson Assocs, 80. *Mem:* Am Geophys Union; Geothermal Resources Coun. *Res:* Origins and geochemical significance of hydrothermal methane in mid-ocean ridges and continental geothermal systems; carbon hydrogen and nitrogen isotopic anomalies in hydro-thermal gases and correlations with gas and helium isotope compositions. *Mailing Add:* Geol Res Div A-020 Scripps Inst Oceanog La Jolla CA 92093

WELIKY, IRVING, b Mt Vernon, NY, Aug 29, 24; m 51; c 4. CLINICAL PHARMACOLOGY. *Educ:* Ill Wesleyan Univ, BS, 48; Columbia Univ, PhD(biochem), 58. *Prof Exp:* Res asst, Sloan-Kettering Inst Cancer Res, 49-52; res fel, Mass Gen Hosp, 57-60, asst biochemist, 60-62; asst prof biochem, Sch Med, Univ Pittsburgh, 62-68; sr res investr, Squibb Inst Med Res, 68-69, res group leader drug metab, 69-73, asst clin pharmacol dir, 73-76, assoc clin pharmacol dir, 76-77; assoc dir, 77-79, DIR CLIN PHARMACOL, WALLACE LABS, 79- *Concurrent Pos:* Res fel biol chem, Harvard Med Sch, 57-60, res assoc, 60-62; asst prof obstet & gynec & mem grad fac, Univ Pittsburgh, 62-68. *Mem:* Am Soc Clin Pharmacol & Therapeut; Am Col Clin Pharmacol; AAAS; NY Acad Sci. *Res:* Intermediary metabolism of purines and pyrimidines; biosynthesis of porphyrins; biosynthesis and metabolism of steroid hormones in tumor and normal tissues; pharmacology; pharmacokinetics. *Mailing Add:* Wallace Labs Half Acre Rd Cranbury NJ 08512

WELIKY, NORMAN, b New York, NY, Nov 1, 19; m 55; c 2. ORGANIC CHEMISTRY, IMMUNOCHEMISTRY. *Educ:* City Col New York, BChE, 39; Polytech Inst Brooklyn, PhD(chem), 57. *Prof Exp:* Chemist, Mineral Pigments Corp, 46-47 & Reichhold Chem, Inc, 50-52; Nuclear Magnetic Resonance res fel chem, Harvard Univ, 56-57; res fel hemoglobins, Dept Chem & Chem Eng, Calif Inst Technol, 57-59, group supvr molecular struct & synthesis, Jet Propulsion Lab, 59-65; mem tech staff, Biosci Dept, TRW Systs, 66-67, asst mgr biosci & electrochem dept, 68-71, sr scientist, 71-75; RES SCIENTIST DIV ALLERGY & IMMUNOL, DEPT PEDIAT, LOS ANGELES COUNTY HARBOR-UNIV CALIF LOS ANGELES MED CTR, 76- *Concurrent Pos:* Consult, seperation techniques, immunochemistry. *Mem:* AAAS; Am Chem Soc; Royal Soc Chem; Sigma Xi. *Res:* Physical chemistry; enzyme chemistry; specific insoluble adsorbents; biological specificity; immunology-allergy; environmental quality criteria; cancer research. *Mailing Add:* 1072 Ridge Crest St Monterey Park CA 91754

WELKER, CAROL, b New York, NY, Jan 28, 37; m 65; c 1. NEUROPHYSIOLOGY. *Educ:* Brooklyn Col, BA, 56; Univ Chicago, MA, 60, PhD(anthrop), 62. *Prof Exp:* NIH fel neurophysiol, Univ Wis-Madison, 62-63; instr physiol, New York Med Col, 64-65; RES SCIENTIST NEUROPHYSIOL, CENT WIS COLONY & TRAINING SCH, WIS DEPT HEALTH & SOCIAL SERV, 65- *Concurrent Pos:* Nat Inst Neurol Dis & Stroke grant neurophysiol, Cent Wis Colony & Training Sch, 67-73. *Mem:* AAAS; Am Asn Anatomists; Animal Behav Soc. *Res:* Neurophysiology and neuroanatomy of the somatic sensory systems in mammals; development of the mammalian brain and behavior. *Mailing Add:* Dept Res Cent Wis Colony Sch Madison WI 53707

WELKER, EVERETT LINUS, b Greenview, Ill, Mar 30, 11; m 33; c 2. MATHMATICAL STATISTICS. *Educ:* Univ Ill, AB, 30, AM, 31, PhD(math statist), 38. *Prof Exp:* Asst math, Univ Ill, 35-38, instr, 38-42, assoc, 42-44, from asst prof to assoc prof, 44-47, assoc math, Bur Med Econ Res, AMA, 47-52; statistician, Dept Defense, 52-57; mgr adv studies dept, ARINC Res Corp, 57-63; mgr syst effectiveness anal prog, Tempo, Gen Elec Ctr Advan Studies, Calif, 63-71; staff scientist, TRW Systs, 71-76; CONSULT, 76- *Mem:* Am Statist Asn; Inst Math Statist; Am Inst Aeronaut & Astronaut. *Res:* Correlation theory; vital and engineering statistics; biometrics; reliability. *Mailing Add:* 365 San Roque Dr Escondido CA 92025

WELKER, GEORGE W, b Cumberland City, Tenn, July 4, 23; m 50; c 3. PARASITOLOGY, BACTERIOLOGY. *Educ:* Mid Tenn State Univ, BS, 44; George Peabody Col, MA, 50; Ohio State Univ, PhD, 62. *Prof Exp:* Teacher high sch, Ohio, 46-49; asst biol, George Peabody Col, 49-50; from asst prof to assoc prof, 50-65, PROF BIOL, BALL STATE UNIV, 65-, CHMN BIOL DEPT, 80- *Concurrent Pos:* Danforth teacher study grant, 57-58. *Mem:* AAAS; Am Sci Affil. *Res:* Helminth parasites and microbial physiology. *Mailing Add:* Dept of Biol Ball State Univ Muncie IN 47306

WELKER, JOHN REED, b Rexburg, Idaho, Dec 1, 36; m 58; c 3. CHEMICAL ENGINEERING. *Educ:* Univ Idaho, BS, 59, MS, 61; Univ Okla, PhD(chem eng), 65. *Prof Exp:* Instr, Univ Idaho, 60-61; group leader, Oil Recovery Corp, 62-63; res engr, Res Inst, Univ Okla, 65-70; vpres, Univ Engrs, Inc, 70-77; PRES, APPL TECHNOL CORP, 77- *Mem:* Am Inst Chem Engrs; Am Chem Soc; Combustion Inst; Am Gas Asn. *Res:* Fire research; fire safety; atmospheric dispersion; liquefied natural gas plant safety; fire extinguishment and control. *Mailing Add:* PO Box FF Norman OK 73070

WELKER, NEIL ERNEST, b Batavia, NY, Apr 21, 32; m 76; c 6. BIOCHEMISTRY. *Educ:* Univ Buffalo, BA, 58; Western Reserve Univ, PhD(microbiol), 63. *Prof Exp:* Fel, Univ Ill, Urbana, 63-64; from asst prof to assoc prof bio sci, 64-74, PROF BIOCHEM, MOLECULAR & CELL BIOL, NORTHWESTERN UNIV, 74- *Mem:* AAAS; Am Soc Microbiol; Brit Soc Gen Microbiol; Am Soc Biol Chemists. *Mailing Add:* Dept Biochem Molecular Biol & Cell Biol Northwestern Univ Evanston IL 60201

WELKER, WALLACE I, b Batavia, NY, Dec 17, 26. NEUROPHYSIOLOGY, NEUROANATOMY. *Educ:* Univ Chicago, PhD(psychol), 54. *Prof Exp:* Asst, Yerkes Labs Primate Biol, 52-54; PROF NEUROPHYSIOL, MED SCH, UNIV WIS-MADISON, 67- *Concurrent Pos:* NIH fel neurophysiol, Univ Wis-Madison, 54-56, Sister Kenny Found scholar, 57-62, NIH career develop fel, 62-67. *Mem:* Am Asn Anatomists; Soc Neurosci. *Res:* Psychology; neural correlates of behavior; comparative physiology. *Mailing Add:* Dept Neurophysiol 283 Med Sci Bldg Med Sch Univ Wis-Madison Madison WI 53706

WELKER, WILLIAM V, JR, b Milwaukee, Wis, Nov 12, 28; m 51; c 4. WEED SCIENCE, HORTICULTURE. *Educ:* Univ Wis, BS, 52, PhD(hort, plant physiol), 62. *Prof Exp:* RES HORTICULTURIST, SCI & EDUC ADMIN-AGR RES, USDA, 59-; RES PROF SOILS & CROPS, RUTGERS UNIV, NEW BRUNSWICK, 59- *Mem:* Weed Sci Soc Am; Am Soc Hort Sci. *Res:* Chemical control of weeds in horticultural crops; influence of long term use of herbicides upon crops; fate of herbicides in soil. *Mailing Add:* Soil Crop Dept of NJ Agr Exp Sta Rutgers Univ New Brunswick NJ 08903

WELKIE, CAROL JEAN, b Pittsburgh, Pa, Aug 21, 51. ENGINEERING GEOPHYSICS. *Educ:* Rensselaer Polytech Inst, BS, 73; Univ Wis, MS, 76, PhD(oceanog), 80. *Prof Exp:* Res asst, Univ Wis-Madison, 74-80; SR RES GEOPHYSICIST, EXXON PROD RES CO, 80- *Concurrent Pos:* Teaching asst, Univ Wis-Madison, 76-77. *Mem:* Soc Explor Geophysicists; Am Geophys Union; Marine Technol Soc; Sigma Xi. *Res:* Evaluation and design of seismic source and receiver arrays for offshore oil exploration; development of exploration techniques and strategies for offshore placer exploration. *Mailing Add:* Exxon Prod Res PO Box 2189 SW-547 Houston TX 77001

WELKIE, GEORGE WILLIAM, b Hazleton, Pa, Apr 11, 32; m 57; c 2. VIROLOGY, PLANT PHYSIOLOGY. *Educ:* Pa State Univ, BS, 52, MS, 54; Univ Wis, PhD(plant path), 57. *Prof Exp:* Asst prof, 57-62, ASSOC PROF BOT & PLANT PATH, UTAH STATE UNIV, 62- *Concurrent Pos:* NSF fel virol, Rothamsted Exp Sta, Eng. *Mem:* Am Phytopath Soc. *Res:* Virus infection and synthesis; effect of virus infection on host metabolism; mineral nutrition of plants with relation to metabolism. *Mailing Add:* Dept of Bot UMC 45 Utah State Univ Logan UT 84322

WELKOWITZ, WALTER, b Brooklyn, NY, Aug 3, 26; m 51; c 3. ELECTRICAL ENGINEERING. *Educ:* Cooper Union, BS, 48; Univ Ill, MS, 49, PhD, 54. *Prof Exp:* Res assoc elec eng, Bioacoustics Lab, Univ Ill, 48-54; lectr acoustics, Grad Sch Eng, Columbia Univ, 54-55; gen mgr, Gulton Industs, Inc, 55-64; PROF ELEC ENG, RUTGERS UNIV, NEW BRUNSWICK, 64-, CHMN DEPT, 72- *Concurrent Pos:* Adj prof, Rutgers Med Sch, Col Med & Dent, NJ, 72- *Mem:* Fel Inst Elec & Electronics Engrs; Am Soc Artificial Internal Organs; Soc Math Biol; NY Acad Sci. *Res:* Biomedical engineering; instrumentation. *Mailing Add:* Dept of Elec Eng Rutgers Univ PO Box 904 Piscataway NJ 08854

WELL, WALTER I, electrical engineering, see previous edition

WELLAND, GRANT VINCENT, b Toronto, Ont, June 25, 40; m 66. MATHEMATICS. *Educ:* Purdue Univ, BS, 63, MS, 65, PhD(math), 66. *Prof Exp:* Teaching asst math, Purdue Univ, 63-65; from asst prof to assoc prof, 66-70; assoc prof, 70-77, PROF MATH & COORDR PROBS & STATIST, UNIV MO-ST LOUIS, 77- *Concurrent Pos:* Dir, NSF undergrad res prog, 67-68; NSF res grant, 68-70; vis prof, Univ Madrid, 70. *Mem:* AAAS; Am Math Soc. *Res:* Harmonic analysis and differentiation. *Mailing Add:* Dept of Math Univ of Mo St Louis MO 63121

WELLAND, ROBERT ROY, b Toronto, Ont, Jan 31, 33; m 57; c 3. MATHEMATICS. *Educ:* Univ Okla, BS, 56, MA, 57; Purdue Univ, PhD, 60. *Prof Exp:* Instr math, Univ Okla, 56-57; NSF asst, Purdue Univ, 57-58, from instr to asst prof, 58-60; asst prof, Ohio State Univ, 60-63; asst prof, 63-74, ASSOC PROF MATH, NORTHWESTERN UNIV, EVANSTON, 74- *Concurrent Pos:* Vis instr, Univ Chicago, 61. *Mem:* Am Math Soc. *Res:* Functional analysis; special spaces; nonlinear analysis. *Mailing Add:* Dept of Math Northwestern Univ Evanston IL 60201

WELLDON, PAUL BURKE, b Nashua, NH, May 10, 16; m 41; c 2. ORGANIC CHEMISTRY. *Educ:* Dartmouth Col, AB, 37, AM, 39; Univ Ill, PhD(org chem), 42. *Prof Exp:* Instr chem, Dartmouth Col, 37-39; res chemist, Hercules Inc, 42-51, mgr, Cellulose Prod Res Div, 52-60, tech asst to dir res, 60-62, mgr, Appln Res Div, 62-65, mgr, Personnel Div, Res Ctr, 67-79; RETIRED. *Mem:* Am Chem Soc. *Res:* Chlorination of organic compounds; chemistry of cellulose derivatives; polyolefins; polymer applications. *Mailing Add:* Harbor Lights Islesboro ME 04848

WELLENREITER, RODGER HENRY, b Bloomington, Ill, Oct 23, 42; m 63; c 2. POULTRY NUTRITION. *Educ:* Ill State Univ, BS, 64; Mich State Univ, MS, 67, PhD(animal husb), 70. *Prof Exp:* Sr scientist, 70-80, RES SCIENTIST POULTRY NUTRIT, LILLY RES LABS, ELI LILLY & CO, 80- *Concurrent Pos:* Sigma Xi res award, 70. *Mem:* Poultry Sci Asn; World Poultry Sci Asn; Sigma Xi. *Res:* Means of improving the efficiency of conversion of animal feedstuffs into products for human comsumption. *Mailing Add:* RR 8 Box 193 Greenfield IN 46140

WELLER, CHARLES STAGG, JR, b Nashville, Tenn, Dec 28, 40; m 66; c 2. PHYSICS. *Educ:* Mass Inst Technol, BS, 62; Univ Pittsburgh, PhD(physics), 67. *Prof Exp:* RES PHYSICIST, NAVAL RES LAB, 67-, SECT HEAD, 74- *Mem:* Am Phys Soc; Am Geophys Union; Am Astron Soc; Int Astron Union. *Res:* Space science; upper atmospheric studies; interplanetary medium; ultraviolet optics. *Mailing Add:* Naval Res Lab Washington DC 20375

WELLER, DAVID LLOYD, b Munfordville, Ky, Sept 28, 38; m 68; c 1. BIOCHEMISTRY, MOLECULAR BIOLOGY. *Educ:* Rochester Inst Technol, BS, 62; Iowa State Univ, PhD(bio-chem), 66. *Prof Exp:* Res fel molecular biol, Children's Cancer Res Found, Boston, Mass, 66-67; asst prof agr biochem, 67-71, chmn biol sci prog, 71-75, chmn cell biol, 72-75, asst dean, Col Agr & assoc dir, Agr Exp Sta, 75-77, assoc prof, 71-77, PROF BIOCHEM & MICROBIOL, UNIV VT, 77- *Mem:* Am Chem Soc; Biophys Soc; NY Acad Sci; Am Inst Chem; Soc Protozoologists. *Res:* Ribosomes and RNAases of Entamoeba; isoeclectric focusing of proteins. *Mailing Add:* Hills Agr Sci Bldg Univ of Vt Burlington VT 05401

WELLER, EDWARD F(RANK), JR, b Baltimore, MD, Nov 30, 1919; m 43; c 3. ELECTRONIC ENGINEERING. *Educ:* Univ Cincinnati, EE, 43. *Prof Exp:* Res engr instrumentation, 46-52, asst head, Physics Dept, 52-62, head, Electronics & Instrumentation Dept, 62-74, HEAD, ELECTRONICS DEPT, GEN MOTORS RES LABS, 74- *Mem:* Fel Inst Elec & Electronics Engrs; Sigma Xi. *Res:* Ferroelectricity. *Mailing Add:* Electronics Dept Gen Motors Res Labs Gen Motors Tech Ctr Warren MI 48090

WELLER, EDWIN MATTHEW, chemical embryology, developmental physiology, deceased

WELLER, GLENN PETER, b New Orleans, La, Dec 7, 43; m 69; c 2. MATHEMATICS. *Educ:* Tulane Univ, BA, 64; Univ Chicago, SM, 65, PhD(math), 68. *Prof Exp:* Asst prof math, Roosevelt Univ, 68-69 & Univ Ill, Chicago Circle, 69-75; ASST PROF, KENNEDY-KING COL, 75- *Mem:* Math Asn Am. *Res:* Geometric topology. *Mailing Add:* 5478 S Woodlawn Ave Chicago IL 60615

WELLER, GUNTER ERNST, b Haifa, June 14, 34; m 63; c 3. METEOROLOGY. *Educ:* Univ Melbourne, BSc, 62, MSc, 65, PhD(meteorol), 67. *Prof Exp:* Meteorologist, Commonwealth Bur Meteorol, 60-61; glaciologist, Australian Nat Antarctic Res Exped, 62-66; NSF res fel, Univ Melbourne, 67; from asst prof to assoc prof geophys, 68-73, prog mgr polar meteorol, Off Polar Progs, NSF, 72-74, prof geophys, Geophys Inst, 73-81, proj mgr, Nat Oceanic & Atmospheric Admin, Outer Continental Shelf, Arctic Proj Off, 75-81, ASSOC DIR PLANNING & PROF GEOPHYS, GEOPHYS INST, UNIV ALASKA, 78- *Concurrent Pos:* US rep, Working Group Meteorol, Sci Comt Antarctic Res, 74-; mem, Polar Res Bd, Nat Acad Sci, 75-79; pres, Int Comn Polar Meteorol, Int Union Geod & Geophys, 80-; mem, Nat Climate Res Climate Res Comt, Nat Acad Sci, 81- *Honors & Awards:* Polar Medal, Commonwealth of Australia; Antarctic Serv Medal, US Govt, 74. *Mem:* Am Meteorol Soc; Am Geophys Union; Arctic Inst NAm; Glaciol Soc. *Res:* Polar meteorology and climatology; micrometeorology; glacio-meteorology; problems of resource recovery in polar regions. *Mailing Add:* Geophys Inst Univ of Alaska Fairbanks AK 99701

WELLER, HARRY, b Philadelphia, Pa, Feb 7, 16; m 42; c 3. ZOOLOGY. *Educ:* Univ Pa, BA, 37, PhD(zool), 55; Univ Del, MA, 51. *Prof Exp:* Res assoc physiol, Sch Med, Univ Va, 54-57; assoc prof, 57-80, PROF ZOOL, MIAMI UNIV, 80- *Mem:* Am Soc Zool; NY Acad Sci; Sigma Xi. *Res:* Cell physiology; comparative endocrinology. *Mailing Add:* Dept of Zool Miami Univ Oxford OH 45056

WELLER, HENRY RICHARD, b East Rutherford, NJ, Mar 15, 41; m 64; c 2. NUCLEAR PHYSICS. *Educ:* Fairleigh Dickinson Univ, BS, 62; Duke Univ, PhD(nuclear physics), 68. *Prof Exp:* Fel physics, Univ Fla, 67-68, from asst prof to assoc prof, 68-78, prof, 78-80; PROF PHYSICS, DUKE UNIV, 80- *Mem:* Am Phys Soc. *Res:* Experimental nuclear structure studies, especially reaction mechanism of helium-3 induced reactions on light nuclei and capture reactions involYing polarized and unpolarized projectiles. *Mailing Add:* Dept Physics Duke Univ Durham NC 27706

WELLER, JOHN MARTIN, b Ann Arbor, Mich, Mar 4, 19; m 79; c 3. INTERNAL MEDICINE, NEPHROLOGY. *Educ:* Univ Mich, AB, 40; Harvard Med Sch, MD, 43; Am Bd Internal Med, dipl, 53. *Prof Exp:* Asst & instr med, Harvard Med Sch, 50-53; from asst prof to assoc prof, 53-63, PROF INTERNAL MED, UNIV MICH, ANN ARBOR, 63- *Concurrent Pos:* Am Col Physicians Stengel res fel, 48-49; res & teaching fel biochem, Harvard Med Sch, 48-50; Nat Res Coun fel med sci, 49-50; asst & jr assoc med, Peter Bent Brigham Hosp, Boston, 50-53. *Mem:* Soc Exp Biol & Med; Am Physiol Soc; Am Fedn Clin Res; fel Am Col Physicians. *Res:* Electrolyte metabolism; renal physiology and diseases. *Mailing Add:* Univ Hosp Box 19 D3238 SACB Ann Arbor MI 48109

WELLER, LAWRENCE ALLENBY, b New York, NY, July 3, 27; m 57; c 2. ELECTROMAGNETIC PULSE, AIRCRAFT ELECTRONICS. *Educ:* City Col New York, BS, 49; Univ Toronto, MA, 52; Ohio State Univ, PhD(physics), 73. *Prof Exp:* Physicist, Warner & Swasey Res Corp, 53-56, Foster Wheller Corp, 56-68; sr res physicist, Monsanto Co, 58-71; res asst & fel, Dept Physics, Ohio State Univ, 71-74; engr, Cincinnati Electronics Corp, 74-75; physicist, Kornylak Corp, 75-76; sr scientist, Pedco Environ, Inc, 76-77; eng technician, Nat Inst Occup Safety & Health, 77-80; SPECIALIST ENGR, BOEING CO, 80- *Concurrent Pos:* Res assoc, Dept Physics, Ohio State Univ, 74-80. *Mem:* Am Phys Soc; Am Nuclear Soc. *Res:* Infrared spectra of molecules; lasers; materials handling machinery; isotope separation; nuclear engineering; protective equipment for workers; electromagnetic pulse effects on electrical and electronic systems. *Mailing Add:* 8612 Chalet Dr Wichita KS 67207

WELLER, LOWELL ERNEST, b Continental, Ohio, Apr 17, 23; m 44; c 2. ORGANIC CHEMISTRY, BIOCHEMISTRY. *Educ:* Bowling Green State Univ, BS, 48; Mich State Univ, MS, 51, PhD(chem), 56. *Prof Exp:* Asst chem, Bowling Green State Univ, 46-48; from instr to asst prof biochem, Mich State Univ, 48-57; assoc prof chem, 57-58, PROF CHEM, UNIV EVANSVILLE, 58-, HEAD DEPT, 57- *Mem:* AAAS; Am Chem Soc; Royal Soc Chem; Sigma Xi. *Res:* Organic synthesis, reaction mechanisms and structure determination especially by spectroscopic methods. *Mailing Add:* Dept of Chem Univ of Evansville Evansville IN 47702

WELLER, MILTON WEBSTER, b St Louis, Mo, May 23, 29; m 47; c 1. ANIMAL ECOLOGY. *Educ:* Univ Mo, AB, 51, MA, 54, PhD(zool), 56. *Prof Exp:* Instr zool, Univ Mo, 56-57; from asst prof to prof, Iowa State Univ, 57-74, chmn fisheries & wildlife sect, 67-74; PROF & HEAD DEPT ENTOM, FISHERIES & WILDLIFE, UNIV MINN, ST PAUL, 74- *Concurrent Pos:* NSF res grants, 64-65, 70-74 & 76-77. *Mem:* Fel AAAS; Ecol Soc Am; Cooper Ornith Soc; Wildlife Soc; fel Am Ornith Union. *Res:* Avian ecology, especially reproductive behavior, productivity, habitat and human relationships of waterfowl with special emphasis on prairie and polar habitats. *Mailing Add:* Dept of Entom Fisheries & Wildlife Univ of Minn St Paul MN 55108

WELLER, PAUL FRANKLIN, b Kankakee, Ill, Aug 30, 35; m 58; c 2. INORGANIC CHEMISTRY. *Educ:* Univ Ill, BS, 57; Cornell Univ, PhD(chem), 62. *Prof Exp:* Res scientist, T J Watson Res Ctr, Int Bus Mach Corp, 61-65; from asst prof to prof chem, State Univ NY Col Fredonia, 65-75, chmn dept, 74-75; prof chem & dean arts & sci, Western Ill Univ, 75-79; ACAD VPRES, CALIF POLYTECH UNIV, POMONA, 79- *Mem:* AAAS; Am Chem Soc; Asn Arts Home Econ. *Res:* Wide band gap semiconductors; defect oxides; solid state materials characterization; crystal growth. *Mailing Add:* Acad VPres Calif State Polytech Univ Pomona CA 91768

WELLER, RICHARD IRWIN, b Newark, NJ, Mar 3, 21; m 53; c 2. PHYSICS, ACADEMIC ADMINISTRATION. *Educ:* City Col New York, BEE, 44; Union Col, BS, 48; Fordham Univ, MS, 50, PhD(physics), 53. *Prof Exp:* Elec engr, NAm Phillips Co, 44, Guy F Atkinson Co, 44-45, NAm Phillips Co, 45-46, Crow, Lewis & Wick, 47, Edward E Ashley, 48, Allied Processes Co, 50, V L Falotico & Assocs, 50-51 & Singmaster & Breyer, 51; instr physics, Brooklyn Col, 52-53; asst prof, State Univ, NY Maritime Col, 53-54; med physicist, Brookhaven Nat Lab, 54-57; prof physics, Franklin & Marshall Col, 57-70, chmn dept, 57-61; PROF PHYSICS & DEAN SCH SCI & MATH, EDINBORO STATE COL, 70- *Concurrent Pos:* Instr, Manhattan Col, 49-50, Fordham Univ, 50-52 & Newark Col Eng, 52-53; consult, Brookhaven Nat Lab, Fairchild Camera & Instrument Corp & Nuclear Sci & Eng Corp; mem Nat Res Coun subcomt, Nat Acad Sci. *Mem:* AAAS; Am Asn Univ Prof; Inst Elec & Electronics Engrs; Sigma Xi; Am Soc Eng Educ; Health Physics Soc. *Res:* Atmospheric electricity; radioactivity; radioisotopes dosimetry and instrumentation; biophysics. *Mailing Add:* Sch of Sci & Math Edinboro State Col Edinboro PA 16444

WELLER, ROBERT ANDREW, b Boston, Mass, July 27, 50; m 72. OCEANOGRAPHY. *Educ:* Havard Univ, BA, 72; Univ Calif, San Diego, PhD(oceanog), 78. *Prof Exp:* Res asst, Harvard Univ, 70-72; Res asst, Scripps Inst Oceanog, 72-78, res oceanographer, 78-79; scholar, 79-80, ASST SCIENTIST, WOODS HOLE OCEANOG INST, 80- *Mem:* Am Geophys Union; Am Meteorol Soc. *Res:* Experimental work in observing and understanding the response of the upper ocean to atmospheric forcing. *Mailing Add:* Clark Lab Woods Hole Oceanog Inst Woods Hole MA 02543

WELLER, S(OL) W(ILLIAM), b Detroit, Mich, July 27, 18; m 43; c 4. PHYSICAL CHEMISTRY, CHEMICAL ENGINEERING. *Educ:* Wayne State Univ, BS, 38; Univ Chicago, PhD(chem), 41. *Prof Exp:* Fel, NY Univ, 41; res assoc, Nat Defense Res Comt, Chicago, 41-43; proj leader, Gen Foods Corp, 43-44; res scientist, Manhattan Proj, Columbia Univ, 44-45; phys chemist, US Bur Mines, Pa, 45-47, asst chief, Coal Hydrogenation Sect, 47-50; chief, Fundamental Res Sect, Houdry Process Corp, 50-58; mgr, Propulsion Dept Aeronutronic Div, Ford Motor Co, 58-60, mem sr staff, 60, mgr chem & mat, 60-63, dir, Chem Lab, 63-65; actg chmn dept chem eng, 68-69, 72-73 & 76-77, PROF CHEM ENG, STATE UNIV NY BUFFALO, AMHERST, 65- *Concurrent Pos:* Civilian, Atomic Energy Comn, 44; vis prof, Univ Calif, Berkeley, 67; UN tech expert, Israel, 71-72; sr Fulbright lectr, Univ Madrid, 75, Istanbul Tech Univ, 81. *Honors & Awards:* H H Storch Award, 81; E V Murphree Award, 82. *Mem:* AAAS; Am Chem Soc; Am Inst Chem Engrs. *Res:* Catalysis; kinetics and mechanisms of catalytic reactions; synthetic liquid fuels. *Mailing Add:* Dept of Chem Eng State Univ of NY at Buffalo Amherst NY 14260

WELLER, THOMAS HUCKLE, b Ann Arbor, Mich, June 15, 15; m 45; c 4. TROPICAL MEDICINE, INFECTIOUS DISEASES. *Educ:* Univ Mich, AB, 36, MS, 37; Harvard Med Sch, MD, 40. *Hon Degrees:* LLD, Univ Mich, 56; ScD, Gustavus Adolphus Col, 75; LHD, Lowell Univ, 77. *Prof Exp:* Res fel comp path & trop med, Harvard Med Sch, 40, teaching fel bact, 40-41, Milton fel pediat, 47-48; USPHS fel, 48; instr comp path & trop med, 48-49, from asst prof to assoc prof trop pub health, 49-54, head dept, 54-81, STRONG PROF TROP PUB HEALTH, SCH PUB HEALTH, HARVARD UNIV, 54-, DIR CTR PREV INFECTIOUS DIS, 66- *Concurrent Pos:* Intern, Children's Hosp, 41-42, asst res, 46, asst dir res, Div Infectious Dis, Children's Med Ctr, 49-56, assoc physician, 49-55; area consult, US Vet Admin, 49-64; consult & mem trop med & parasitol study sect, USPHS, 53-55; dir, Comn Parasitic Dis, Armed Forces Epidemiol Br, 53-59, mem, 59-72. *Honors & Awards:* Nobel Prize Physiol & Med, 54; Mead Johnson Award, Am Acad Pediat, 53; co-winner, Kimble Methodol Award, 54; Ledlie Prize, 63; Weinstein Award, 73; Bristol Award, Infectious Dis Soc Am, 80. *Mem:* Nat Acad Sci; Am Soc Trop Med & Hyg (pres, 64); Am Asn Immunologists; Asn Am Physicians. *Res:* In vitro cultivation of viruses, especially poliomyelitis, mumps and Coxsackie viruses; etiology of epidemic pleurodynia, varicella and Herpes zoster; cytomegalic inclusion and Rubella; helminth infections, especially schistosomiasis and enterobiasis. *Mailing Add:* Dept Trop Pub Health Harvard Sch Pub Health Boston MA 02115

WELLERSON, RALPH, JR, b New York, NY, Dec 12, 24; m 51; c 2. MICROBIOLOGY. *Educ:* Hobart Col, BS, 49; Rutgers Univ, MS, 51; Purdue Univ, PhD(bact), 54. *Prof Exp:* Sr scientist, 54-62, RES FEL MICROBIOL, DIV MICROBIOL, ORTHO RES FOUND, ORTHO PHARMACEUT CORP, RARITAN, NJ, 62- *Mem:* Am Soc Microbiol. *Res:* Metabolism and nutrition of microorganisms; microbial fermentations; chemotherapy of Trichomonas vaginalis; immunological control of fertility. *Mailing Add:* 14 Oxbow Lane Basking Ridge NJ 07920

WELLES, HARRY LESLIE, b Rockville, Conn, Jan 2, 45; m 66; c 1. PHARMACEUTICS. *Educ:* Cent Conn State Col, BS, 67; Univ Conn, MS, 69, PhD(pharmaceut), 74. *Prof Exp:* Res assoc pharmaceut, Sch Pharm, Univ Wis-Madison, 72-74; asst prof pharmaceut, Col Pharm, Dalhousie Univ, 74-80; RES SCIENTIST, NORWICH-EATON PHARMACEUT, NORWICH, NY, 80- *Mem:* Am Pharmaceut Asn; Sigma Xi. *Res:* Parenteral formulations, dissolution, drug-excipient interactions. *Mailing Add:* Norwich-Eaton Pharmaceut Box 191 Norwich NY 13815

WELLES, SAMUEL PAUL, b Gloucester, Mass, Nov 9, 07; m 31; c 3. VERTEBRATE PALEONTOLOGY. *Educ:* Univ Calif, AB, 30, PhD(vert paleont), 40. *Prof Exp:* Field & lab asst, 31-39, asst cur reptiles & amphibians, 39-42, sr mus cur, 42-46, prin mus cur, 46-47, prin mus paleontologist & lectr, 46-76, actg dir, 47-48, RES ASSOC, MUS PALEONT, UNIV CALIF, BERKELEY, 76- *Concurrent Pos:* Mem, US Nat Mus exped, 30 & Univ Calif expeds, 31-42, 45, 47, 49, 56, 58, 64-68, 72, 73, 76, 81; Fulbright scholar, Univ Canterbury, 69-70. *Mem:* Fel Geol Soc Am; Paleont Soc; Soc Vert Paleont. *Res:* Triassic labyrinthodonts; Cretaceous Plesiosaurs; dinosaurs. *Mailing Add:* Mus of Paleont Univ of Calif Berkeley CA 94720

WELLHAUSEN, EDWIN JOHN, b Fairfax, Okla, Sept 10, 07; m 37; c 1. PLANT BREEDING. *Educ:* Univ Idaho, BS, 32; Iowa State Col, PhD(plant genetics), 36. *Hon Degrees:* DSc, San Carlos Univ, Guatemala, 60; DSc, Univ Nebr, 69. *Prof Exp:* Gen Ed Bd fel genetics, Rockefeller Inst & Univ Calif, 36-37; assoc agronomist, Exp Sta, Mont State Col, 37-38; assoc prof agron, Univ WVa & assoc geneticist, Exp Sta, 39-43; geneticist, 43-51, local dir, Mex Agr Prog, 52-58, dir Inter-Am Corn Improv Prog, 59-66, dir int maize & wheat improv ctr, 66-71, assoc dir agr sci, 59-73, SPEC STAFF MEM, ROCKEFELLER FOUND, MEX, 73- *Honors & Awards:* Aztec Eagle Award, Govt of Mex, 69; Int Agron Award, Am Soc Agron, 69; Gran Oficial de Order del Merito Agricola, Govt of Colombia. *Mem:* AAAS; Genetics Soc Am; Am Phytopath Soc; Bot Soc Am; fel Am Soc Agron. *Res:* Genetics of disease resistance; genetic diversification and origin of corn types in Mexico and Central America; corn breeding methods for Latin America; research adminstration. *Mailing Add:* Rockefeller Found Calle Londres 40 Despacho 101 Mexico City DF 06600 Mexico

WELLING, DANIEL J, b Kansas City, Mo, May 1, 37. THEORETICAL PHYSICS, BIOPHYSICS. *Educ:* Rockhurst Col, BS, 58; St Louis Univ, PhD(physics), 63. *Prof Exp:* Asst prof physics, Southern Ill Univ, 64; AEC fel theoret physics, Argonne Nat Lab, 64-66; asst prof & assoc scientist, Univ Wis-Milwaukee, 66-72; vis assoc prof path, 72-73, assoc prof path & physiol, 73-80, ADJ PROF PATH & PHYSIOL, MED CTR, UNIV KANS, 80- *Concurrent Pos:* Assoc scientist, McDonnell Aircraft Corp, 63. *Mem:* Am Phys Soc; Am Soc Nephrology. *Res:* Medical physics; mathematical modeling of transport in the nephron. *Mailing Add:* Dept of Physiol Univ of Kans Med Ctr Kansas City KS 66103

WELLINGTON, GEORGE HARVEY, b Springport, Mich, Sept 19, 15; m 39; c 3. ANIMAL SCIENCE. *Educ:* Mich State Univ, BS, 37, PhD, 54; Kans State Univ, MS, 40. *Prof Exp:* Asst, Kans State Univ, 38-40; agr exten agent, Mich, 45-46; from asst prof to prof animal sci, 47-77, EMER PROF ANIMAL & FOOD SCI, CORNELL UNIV, 78- *Concurrent Pos:* Ford Found consult livestock in Syria, 62; vis prof, Univ Aleppo, Syria, 65-66; consult, Fed Univ Minas Gerias, Brazil, 78. *Honors & Awards:* Signal Serv Award, Am Meat Sci Asn, 66. *Mem:* Am Soc Animal Sci; Am Meat Sci Asn; Inst Food Technol. *Res:* Meat animal development and composition; meat quality factors and processing. *Mailing Add:* Morrison Hall Cornell Univ Ithaca NY 14850

WELLINGTON, JOHN SESSIONS, b Glendale, Calif, Sept 28, 21; m 44; c 2. PATHOLOGY. *Educ:* Univ Calif, Berkeley, AB, 42; Univ Calif, San Francisco, MD, 45. *Prof Exp:* Instr path, Sch Med, Univ Calif, 53-55, lectr, 55-56; vis asst prof, Univ Indonesia, 56-58; assoc prof path, Sch Med, Univ Calif, San Francisco, 58-69, prof, 69-77, assoc dean, 65-77; PROF PATH, JOHN A BURNS SCH MED, UNIV HAWAII, HONOLULU, 77- *Mem:* Fel Col Am Path; Am Soc Exp Path; Int Acad Path. *Res:* Leukemia; injury and repair in hematopoietic tissue. *Mailing Add:* Sch Med Univ Hawaii 1960 East-West Rd Honolulu HI 96822

WELLINGTON, WILLIAM GEORGE, b Vancouver, BC, Aug 16, 20; m 59; c 2. INSECT ECOLOGY, BIOMETEOROLOGY. *Educ:* Univ BC, BA, 41; Univ Toronto, MA, 45, PhD(zool, entom), 47. *Prof Exp:* Meteorol officer, Meteorol Serv, Can Dept Transport, 42-45; forest biologist, Forest Biol Div, Can Dept Agr, 46-60; head bioclimat sect, Can Dept Forestry, 60-64, prin scientist insect ecol, 64-68; prof ecol, Univ Toronto, 68-70; dir, Inst Animal Resource Ecol, 73-79, PROF PLANT SCI & RESOURCE ECOL, UNIV BC, 70- *Concurrent Pos:* Mem, Exec Biol Coun Can, 77-78. *Honors & Awards:* Gold Medal for Outstanding Achievement in Can Entom, Entom Soc Can, 68; Outstanding Achievement Award Bioclimat, Am Meteorol Soc, 69. *Mem:* AAAS; Am Meteorol Soc; Can Soc Zoologists; Entom Soc Am; fel Entom Soc Can (pres, 77-78). *Res:* Micro- and synoptic climatology; interdisciplinary associations of meteorology and the life sciences; population biology; physiological, behavioral and social variations affecting population dynamics; insect behavior; human ecology. *Mailing Add:* Inst Animal Resource Ecol Univ BC Vancouver BC V6T 1W5 Can

WELLIVER, PAUL WESLEY, b Danville, Pa, Mar 28, 31; m 56; c 2. SCIENCE EDUCATION. *Educ:* Western Md Col, BA, 52; Pa State Univ, MEd, 58, PhD(sci educ), 65. *Prof Exp:* Teacher gen sci, Roosevelt Jr High, Pa, 55-58; lectr nuclear energy, Oak Ridge Inst Nuclear Studies, 59-60; TV studio teacher phys sci, NC In-Sch TV, 61-66; consult sci educ, NC Dept Educ, 66-67; dir educ instr TV, Miss Authority Educ TV, 67-69; PROF EDUC SCI EDUC, PA STATE UNIV, 69- *Concurrent Pos:* NSF fel, Pa State Univ, 58-59; consult nat proj improv TV instr, Nat Asn Educ Broadcasters, 64-65 & invest sci proj, Pa Dept Educ, 70-78; dir, Comprehensive Sch Improv ITV Proj, 66-67, Miss ITV Curric Lab, 67-68, instr develop inst proj, Pa State Univ, 73-77 & sci ITV proj, Pa Dept Educ, 72-78; bd dir, Asn Educ Commun & Technol, 78-82. *Mem:* AAAS; Nat Asn Res Sci Teaching; Nat Sci Teachers Asn; Nat Soc Study Educ; Asn Educ Commun & Technol. *Res:* The application of communications media and technology to the development, dissemination, implementation and maintenance of science instruction over a large geographic region. *Mailing Add:* Pa State Univ 320 Rackley Bldg University Park PA 16802

WELLMAN, ANGELA MYRA, b Sudbury, Suffolk, Eng, June 13, 35; m 59. MICROBIAL PHYSIOLOGY. *Educ:* Bristol Univ, BSc, 56, PhD(mycol), 61. *Prof Exp:* Demonstr bot, Bristol Univ, 56-59; Nat Res Coun Can fel, 59-61, instr, 61-62, lectr, 62-64, asst prof, 64-68, asst dean sci, 74-75, ASSOC DEAN SCI, UNIV WESTERN ONT, 75-, ASSOC PROF BOT, 68- *Mem:* Can Soc Microbiol; Brit Mycol Soc; Soc Cryobiol. *Res:* Cryobiology; survival of fungal spores after exposure to low temperature; purine metabolism in Neurospora; hydrocarbon oxidation by micro-organisms. *Mailing Add:* Off Dean Sci Natural Sci Ctr Univ Western Ont London ON N6A 3K7 Can

WELLMAN, DENNIS LEE, b Freeport, Ill, Mar 18, 42; m 68; c 2. ATMOSPHERIC PHYSICS, ATMOSPHERIC CHEMISTRY. *Educ:* Univ Colo, BS, 71. *Prof Exp:* Electronics engr aerospace, Ball Bros Res Corp, 72; ELECTRONICS ENGR ATMOSPHERIC RES, NAT OCEANIC & ATMOSPHERIC ADMIN, 72- *Mem:* Am Geophys Union. *Res:* Inadvertent alterations of precipitation distribution and amount; physical and chemical characteristics of natural and man-made aerosols; chemical reactions of pollutant gases; atmospheric transmissivity. *Mailing Add:* Nat Oceanic & Atmospheric Admin 825 Broadway ERL/OWRM RX8 Boulder CO 80302

WELLMAN, HENRY NELSON, b Kansas City, Kans, Nov 10, 33; m 57; c 6. INTERNAL MEDICINE. *Educ:* Rockhurst Col, BS, 56; Sch Med, St Louis Univ, MD, 60. *Prof Exp:* Intern med, St Louis Univ Hosps, 60-61, postgrad radiol biol & med, 61; resident med, Univ Cincinnati, 63-65, fel, 65-66, asst prof med & radiol, Sch Med, 66-69, assoc prof, 69-71; PROF MED & RADIOL, SCH MED, IND UNIV, 71- *Concurrent Pos:* Asst attend physician, Cincinnati Gen Hosp, 67-70; chief nuclear med sect, Pop Studies Prog, Dept Health, Educ & Welfare, 69-71; sr scientist award, Alexander Von Humboldt Found, 79-80; US tech advisor, Int Electrotech Comt, 77-81; dir nuclear med, Sch Med, Ind Univ, 72- & staff radiol med, Univ Med Ctr, 71-; consult, Bur Drugs, Div Oncol & Radiopharm, 75- & WHO, 77- *Mem:* Am Med Asn; Am Col Physicians; Am Col Radiol; Am Col Nuclear Physicians; Soc Nuclear Med. *Res:* Development of newer diagnostic uses of radiolabelled substances, especially in pulmonary, skeletal and neoplastic processes for clinical nuclear medicine. *Mailing Add:* Sch Med Ind Univ 1100 W Michigan St Indianapolis IN 46223

WELLMAN, RUSSEL ELMER, b New Berlin, NY, July 16, 22; m 48; c 2. PHYSICAL CHEMISTRY. *Educ:* Howard Col, BA, 50; Univ Rochester, PhD(phys chem), 55. *Prof Exp:* Res chemist, Callery Chem Co, 55, group leader appl chem, 56-60; sr chemist, Inorg & Phys Chem Sect, Southern Res Inst, 60-66; unit mgr polymer technol, 66-67, scientist, 67-73, SR CHEMIST, XEROX CORP, ROCHESTER, NY, 73- *Mem:* AAAS; Am Chem Soc; NY Acad Sci; Am Inst Chem. *Res:* Viscometry; physical chemistry of polymers; adhesion of polymers; microencapsulation. *Mailing Add:* 4917 Cory Corners Rd Marion NY 14505

WELLMAN, WILLIAM EDWARD, b Ft Wayne, Ind, Oct 22, 32; m 66; c 2. ORGANIC CHEMISTRY. *Educ:* Col Wooster, BA, 54; Ohio State Univ, PhD(org chem), 60. *Prof Exp:* Chemist, Esso Res & Eng Co, 60-63, sr chemist, 63-64, proj leader, 64-69, res assoc, 68-73, sect head, 69-73, mgr oxygen solvents & lower alcohols, Solvents Technol Div, 73-80, MGR TECHNOL DEVELOP & APPLN, EXXON CHEM CO, 80- *Res:* Petrochemicals, solvents and fiber intermediates; process development. *Mailing Add:* Exxon Chem Co PO Box 536 Linden NJ 07036

WELLMANN, KLAUS FRIEDRICH, b Gerbstedt, Ger, Feb 18, 29; US citizen; m 56. ANATOMIC PATHOLOGY, CLINICAL PATHOLOGY. *Educ:* Heidelberg Col, MD, 54. *Prof Exp:* Intern & resident path, surg & pediat, var Ger hosps, 55-57; intern med & surg, Wheeling Hosp, WVa, 57; resident path, Mem Hosp, Charlotte, NC, 58, County Hosp, Milwaukee, Wis, 58-59, Path Inst, Univ Cologne, 60 & Civic Hosp, Ottawa, Ont, 60-62; resident, Jewish Chronic Dis Hosp, Brooklyn, NY, 62-64, asst pathologist,

63-68; asst dir lab, Kingsbrook Jewish Med Ctr, 68-72, assoc dir lab, 72-77, res assoc, Isaac Albert Res Inst, 64-77; ASSOC DIR LABS, BEEKMAN DOWNTOWN HOSP, NEW YORK, 77- *Concurrent Pos:* From clin asst prof to clin assoc prof path, State Univ NY Downstate Med Ctr, 65-73, clin prof, 73- *Honors & Awards:* Gold Award, Am Soc Clin Pathologists-Col Am Pathologists, 68. *Mem:* Am Soc Clin Pathologists; AMA; Am Asn Pathologists; Fedn Am Socs Exp Biol. *Res:* Ultrastructure of pancreatic pathology; radiation damage; experimental diabetes; fluorescence microscopy; autopsy pathology. *Mailing Add:* Beekman Downtown Hosp 170 William St New York NY 10038

WELLNER, DANIEL, b Antwerp, Belg, June 9, 34; US citizen; m 62; c 1. BIOCHEMISTRY. *Educ:* Harvard Col, AB, 56; Tufts Univ, PhD(biochem), 61. *Prof Exp:* Instr biochem, Sch Med, Tufts Univ, 62-63, sr instr, 63-65, asst prof, 65-67; asst prof, 67-69, ASSOC PROF BIOCHEM, MED COL, CORNELL UNIV, 69- *Concurrent Pos:* NATO fel biochem, Weizmann Inst Sci, 61-62; Lederle med fac award, 64-67. *Mem:* Sigma Xi; Am Chem Soc; NY Acad Sci; Harvey Soc; Am Soc Biol Chemists. *Res:* Ribonuclease; amino acid oxidases; flavoproteins; mechanism of enzyme action; biochemistry of cancer; inborn errors of metabolism. *Mailing Add:* Dept of Biochem Cornell Univ Med Col New York NY 10021

WELLNER, MARCEL, b Antwerp, Belg, Feb 8, 30; US citizen; m 61; c 2. PHYSICS. *Educ:* Mass Inst Technol, BS, 52; Princeton Univ, PhD(physics), 58. *Prof Exp:* Instr physics, Princeton Univ, 56-58 & Brandeis Univ, 58-59; mem, Inst Advan Study, 59-60; res assoc physics, Univ Ind, 60-63; NSF fel, Atomic Energy Res Estab, Eng, 63-64; from asst prof to assoc prof, 64-71, PROF PHYSICS, SYRACUSE UNIV, 71- *Concurrent Pos:* Physicist, Cavendish Lab, Cambridge Univ, Eng, 68-69; vis scientist, Inst Advan Studies, Dublin, Ireland, 80. *Mem:* Am Phys Soc. *Res:* Quantum field theory and mathematical methods. *Mailing Add:* Dept of Physics Syracuse Univ Syracuse NY 13210

WELLNER, VAIRA PAMILJANS, b Aluksne, Latvia, Jan 28, 36; US citizen; m 62; c 1. BIOCHEMISTRY. *Educ:* Boston Univ, AB, 58; Tufts Univ, PhD(biochem), 64. *Prof Exp:* Res assoc biochem, Sch Med, Tufts Univ, 66-67; RES ASSOC BIOCHEM, COL MED, CORNELL UNIV, 72- *Concurrent Pos:* Res fel biochem, Sch Med, Tufts Univ, 63-66 & Col Med, Cornell Univ, 67-72. *Mem:* Am Chem Soc. *Res:* Mechanisms of enzyme action. *Mailing Add:* Dept of Biochem Cornell Univ Med Col New York NY 10021

WELLOCK, LOIS MARGARET, b Harbor Beach, Mich. PHYSICAL MEDICINE. *Educ:* Eastern Mich Univ, BS, 39; Northwestern Univ, cert phys ther, 43; Univ Mich, MS, 48, PhD(educ), 65. *Prof Exp:* Phys therapist, Hosps & Pub Schs, 43-47; asst prof health & phys educ, Bowling Green State Univ, 48-54; asst prof phys ther, Med Sch, Northwestern Univ, 54-65; ASST PROF PHYS THER, UNIV MICH, ANN ARBOR, 65- *Mem:* Am Phys Ther Asn. *Res:* Therapeutic exercise; educational preparation. *Mailing Add:* Curric in Phys Ther Univ of Mich Ann Arbor MI 48104

WELLONS, JESSE DAVIS, III, b Roanoke, Va, Apr 4, 38; m 58; c 4. WOOD TECHNOLOGY, POLYMER SCIENCE. *Educ:* Duke Univ, BS, 60, MF, 63, PhD(wood technol, polymer sci), 66. *Prof Exp:* Res chemist, Res Triangle Inst, NC, 62-65, res assoc wood chem, Iowa State Univ, 65-66, , from asst prof to assoc prof, 66-70; assoc prof forest prod chem, Ore State Univ, 70-77, prof, 77-81; MGR RES & DEVELOP, CHEM DIV, GEORGIA PAC CORP, 81- *Mem:* Forest Prod Res Soc; Soc Wood Sci & Technol. *Res:* Wood adhesives; tannin adhesives; plywood processing; use of plastics to modify properties of wood; sorption and diffusion of monomers in wood. *Mailing Add:* Georgia Pac Corp Chem Div 2175 Park Lake Dr NE Atlanta GA 30345

WELLS, ADONIRAM JUDSON, b Chicago, Ill, Apr 1, 17; m 37; c 6. PHYSICAL CHEMISTRY. *Educ:* Harvard Univ, SB, 38, AM, 40, PhD(phys chem), 41. *Prof Exp:* Res chemist, Ammonia Dept, E I du Pont de Nemours & Co, Del, 41-46, res supvr, 46-48, mgt asst, 48-50, mgr film develop, 50-53, dir, Yerkes Res Lab, NY, 53-55, asst res dir film dept, Del, 55-59, res dir electrochem dept, 59-69, dir indust prod div, 69-77, dir specialty prods div, Fabrics & Finishes Dept, 77-80; CONSULT, AM LUNG ASN, 81- *Mem:* Am Chem Soc. *Res:* Infrared and Raman spectroscopy; thermodynamics; process and market development; polymer chemistry; high temperatures. *Mailing Add:* 102 Kildonan Glen Wilmington DE 19807

WELLS, BARBARA DURYEA, b Birmingham, Ala, Feb 4, 39. SPECTROSCOPY, NUCLEIC ACID CHEMISTRY. *Educ:* Univ Miami, BS, 60; Univ Calif, San Francisco, MS, 69, PhD(biochem & biophysics), 73. *Prof Exp:* Instr chem, Polk Jr Col, 65; technician, Univ Calif, San Francisco, 66-68; fel, Fla State Univ, 73-75, Columbia Univ, 75-78; res scientist, Johns Hopkins Univ, 78-79; ASST PROF BIOCHEM, UNIV WIS-MILWAUKEE, 79- *Mem:* Am Soc Biol Chemists; Biophys Soc; Am Chem Soc; Sigma Xi; AAAS. *Res:* Spectroscopic techniques; fluorescence electron paramagnetic resonance, nuclear magnetic resonance for studying the structure of transfer RNA in order to correlate structural changes with biological functions. *Mailing Add:* Chem Dept Univ Wis Milwaukee WI 53201

WELLS, BENJAMIN B, JR, b Rochester, Minn, May 31, 41; m 67. MATHEMATICAL ANALYSIS. *Educ:* Univ Mich, BS, 61, MS, 62; Univ Calif, Berkeley, PhD(math), 67. *Prof Exp:* From instr to asst prof math, Univ Ore, 67-70; Fulbright lectr, Univ Santiago, Chile, 70-71; assoc prof, 71-76, PROF MATH, UNIV HAWAII, 76- *Mem:* Am Math Soc. *Res:* Measure theory; harmonic analysis. *Mailing Add:* Dept of Math Univ of Hawaii Honolulu HI 96822

WELLS, BOBBY R, b Wickliffe, Ky, July 30, 34; m 60; c 1. SOIL CHEMISTRY, SOIL FERTILITY. *Educ:* Murray State Univ, BS, 59; Univ Ark, MS, 61; Univ Mo, PhD(soil chem), 64. *Prof Exp:* Asst soils, Univ Ark, 59-60; asst county agent, Univ Mo, 60-61, asst soils, 61-64; asst prof agr, Murray State Univ, 64-66; asst prof, Rice Br Exp Sta, 66-70, assoc prof, 70-75, PROF AGRON, RICE EXP STA, UNIV ARK, FAYETTEVILLE, 75- *Mem:* Am Soc Agron; Soil Sci Soc Am. *Res:* Investigations into soil-plant relationships for rice. *Mailing Add:* Rice Br Exp Sta PO Box 351 Stuttgart AR 72610

WELLS, CHARLES EDMON, b Dothan, Ala, May 19, 29; m 62; c 3. PSYCHIATRY, NEUROLOGY. *Educ:* Emory Univ, AB, 48, MD, 53. *Prof Exp:* From intern to asst resident med, New York Hosp, 53-54; clin assoc neurol, NIH, 54-56; resident, New York Hosp, 57-58; assoc prof neurol, 61-75, psychiat, 68-72, PROF NEUROL, SCH MED, VANDERBILT UNIV, 75-, PROF PSYCHIAT & VCHMN DEPT, 72- *Concurrent Pos:* NIH fel neurol, New York Hosp-Cornell Med Ctr, 58-59; mem coun aging, Am Phychiat Asn, 82- *Mem:* Am Psychiat Asn; Am Col Psychiat; Am Neurol Asn; Asn Res Nerv & Ment Dis. *Res:* Dementia; neuropsychiatry; use of literature in teaching of psychiatry. *Mailing Add:* Dept of Psychiat Vanderbilt Univ Sch of Med Nashville TN 37232

WELLS, CHARLES FREDERICK, b Atlanta, Ga, May 4, 37; m 62; c 2. ALGEBRA. *Educ:* Oberlin Col, AB, 62; Duke Univ, PhD(math), 65. *Prof Exp:* Asst prof math, 65-72, ASSOC PROF MATH, CASE WESTERN RESERVE UNIV, 72- *Concurrent Pos:* Prin investr, NSF grants, 65-67; guest, Math Res Inst, Swiss Fed Inst Technol, Zurich, 75-76. *Mem:* Math Asn Am; Am Math Soc. *Res:* Algebraic theory of semigroups and small categories; algebraic cohomology. *Mailing Add:* Dept of Math Case Western Reserve Univ Cleveland OH 44106

WELLS, CHARLES HENRY, b Chicago, Ill, Dec 6, 31; m 56; c 2. PHYSIOLOGY. *Educ:* Randolph-Macon Col, BA, 54; Mich State Univ, MS, 60, PhD(physiol), 63. *Prof Exp:* Instr physiol, Univ Tex Med Br, 62-64; asst prof, Med Col SC, 64-67; asst prof, Univ Tex Med Br, Galveston, 67-73, assoc prof physiol, 73-80; WITH CRITIKON CORP, 80- *Concurrent Pos:* Consult, US Air Force, 69-; chief, Physiol Div, Shriners Burns Inst. *Mem:* Fedn Am Socs Exp Biol; Undersea Med Soc; Am Physiol Soc; Am Burn Asn; Int Soc Burn Injury. *Res:* Blood rheology, microcirculation in stress; thermal injury; decompression sickness; computer aided instructional systems development. *Mailing Add:* Critikon Corp PO Box 19154 Irvine CA 92713

WELLS, CHARLES ROBERT EDWIN, b New Brighton, Pa, Aug 6, 13; m 41; c 4. PEDIATRIC CARDIOLOGY. *Educ:* Grove City Col, BS, 35; Temple Univ, MD, 40, MS, 49. *Prof Exp:* Pvt pract, 49-62; PROF PEDIAT, SCH MED, TEMPLE UNIV, 67- *Concurrent Pos:* Attend pediatrician & attend cardiologist, St Christopher's Hosp for Children, 49-, chief dept cardiol, 62-72, sr consult, Dept Cardiol, 72- *Mailing Add:* Sch Med Temple Univ Philadelphia PA 19122

WELLS, CHARLES VAN, b Summerton, SC, July 1, 37; m 66; c 2. BOTANY. *Educ:* Presby Col, SC, BS, 59; Appalachian State Univ, MA, 63; Univ Ariz, PhD(bot), 69. *Prof Exp:* Teacher & coach, High Sch, SC, 59-62; teaching asst biol, Appalachian State Univ, 62-63; asst prof biol, Newberry Col, 63-64; teaching asst biol, Univ Ariz, 64-69; assoc prof, 64-80, PROF BIOL, LENOIR RHYNE COL, 80- *Res:* Effects of radiation on vegetative morphology of sirogonium. *Mailing Add:* Dept of Biol Lenoir Rhyne Col Box 473 Hickory NC 28601

WELLS, DAN M(OODY), b Graham, Tex, Nov 6, 26; m 51; c 2. CIVIL & SANITARY ENGINEERING. *Educ:* Tex Tech Col, BS, 51; Univ Mo, MS, 54; Univ Tex, PhD(civil eng), 66. *Prof Exp:* Mgt employee, Southwestern Bell Tel Co, Okla, 54-57; partner, Campbell, Wells & Assocs, Engrs, 57-63; assoc prof civil eng, 66-72, PROF CIVIL ENG, TEX TECH UNIV, 72-, DIR WATER RESOURCES DIV, 76- *Mem:* Am Water Works Asn; Am Soc Civil Engrs; Water Pollution Control Fedn. *Res:* Water resources, engineering and management; water quality management. *Mailing Add:* 3516 45 St Lubbock TX 70413

WELLS, DANIEL R, b New York, NY, May 2, 21; m 43; c 2. PHYSICS. *Educ:* Cornell Univ, BME, 42; NY Univ, MS, 55; Stevens Inst Technol, PhD(physics), 63. *Prof Exp:* Res assoc plasma physics, Princton Univ, 55-64; assoc prof physics, 64-67, PROF PHYSICS, UNIV MIAMI, 67- *Concurrent Pos:* Res assoc, Stevens Inst Technol, 61-64; assoc prof, Seton Hall, 62-64; res grants, AEC & Air Force Off Sci Res, 64-74. *Mem:* Am Phys Soc. *Res:* Controlled thermonuclear research. *Mailing Add:* Dept of Physics Univ of Miami Coral Gables FL 33124

WELLS, DARRELL GIBSON, b Pierre, SDak, Feb 21, 17; m 46; c 3. PLANT BREEDING, PLANT PATHOLOGY. *Educ:* SDak State Col, BS, 41; State Col Wash, MS, 43; Univ Wis, PhD, 49. *Prof Exp:* Asst agronomist, State Col Wash, 43-45; asst, Univ Wis, 45-49; from assoc prof to prof agron, Miss State Univ, 49-62; PROF WHEAT BREEDING, S DAK STATE UNIV, 62- *Concurrent Pos:* Mem tech asst mission, Western Region, Nigeria, Int Develop Serv, 58-60. *Mem:* Am Soc Agron. *Res:* Small grain genetics and breeding; cowpea and lima bean breeding. *Mailing Add:* Dept Plant Sci SDak State Univ Brookings SD 57006

WELLS, DARTHON VERNON, b Saline Co, Ark, Oct 11, 29; m 50; c 3. ORGANIC CHEMISTRY. *Educ:* Univ Northern Ala, BS, 54; Univ Miss, MS, 57; Univ SC, PhD(chem), 60. *Prof Exp:* Res assoc chem, Brown Univ, 59-61; from asst prof to assoc prof, 61-72, PROF CHEM, LA STATE UNIV, ALEXANDRIA, 72- *Mem:* Am Chem Soc; Sigma Xi. *Res:* Chemistry of organic peroxide decomposition; nucleophilic displacement of phosphorus; carbanion rearrangement reactions. *Mailing Add:* Dept of Chem La State Univ Alexandria LA 71301

WELLS, EDDIE N, b Mar 13, 40; US citizen. PLANETOLOGY, REMOTE SENSING. *Educ:* Murray State Univ, BS, 62; Univ Pittsburgh, PhD(earth & planets), 77. *Prof Exp:* Res assoc, Lab Planetary Studies, Cornell Univ, 77-79; res assoc, 79-81, RES ASST PROF GEOL & PLANETARY SCI, UNIV PITTSBURGH, 82- *Mem:* Am Geophys Union. *Res:* Remote sensing of the earth; remote sensing observations of moon and planets; laboratory studies of optical properties of rocks, minerals, glasses, and ices. *Mailing Add:* 321 Old Eng Hall Univ Pittsburgh Pittsburgh PA 15260

WELLS, EDWARD C(URTIS), b Boise, Idaho, Aug 26, 10; m 34; c 2. MECHANICAL ENGINEERING. *Educ:* Stanford Univ, BA, 31; Univ Portland, LLD, 46. *Hon Degrees:* DSc, Willamette Univ, 53. *Prof Exp:* Draftsman & engr, Boeing Co, 31-33, group engr, 33-34, asst prof engr, 34-37, chief preliminary design engr, 37-38, chief proj engr, 38-39, asst chief engr, 39-43, chief engr, 43-47, vpres & chief engr, 47-48, vpres eng, 48-58, vpres & gen mgr systs mgt off, 58-59, vpres eng, 59-61, vpres & gen mgr mil aircraft systs div, 61-63, vpres prod develop, 66-67, sr vpres, 67-72, MEM BD DIRS, BOEING CO, 51-, CONSULT, 72- *Concurrent Pos:* Consult, Secy of War, 44-; mem indust & ed adv bd, US Dept Air Force, 53-54; trustee, Willamette Univ, 55-; mem adv bd inst technol, adv bd, Inst Technol, Wash State Univ, 57-60; mem, State Adv Coun Atomic Energy, Wash, 58-60; mem, Air Force Hist Found. *Honors & Awards:* Sperry Award, Inst Aerospace Sci, Am Inst Aeronaut & Astronaut, 42; Fawcett Aviation Award, 44; Presidential Cert of Merit, 48. *Mem:* Nat Acad Eng; AAAS; Am Soc Eng Educ; Am Astronaut Soc; fel Am Inst Aeronaut & Astronaut (pres, 58). *Mailing Add:* Boeing Co PO Box 3707 Seattle WA 98124

WELLS, EDWARD JOSEPH, b Sydney, Australia, Oct 10, 36; m 62; c 2. PHYSICAL CHEMISTRY. *Educ:* Univ Sydney, BSc, 58, MSc, 60; Oxford Univ, DPhil(magnetic resonance), 62. *Prof Exp:* Gowrie travelling scholar, 59-61; fel magnetic resonance, Univ BC, 61-63; instr phys chem, 63-64; res assoc magnetic resonance, Univ Ill, Urbana, 64-65; asst prof chem, 65-67, actg chmn dept, 75-76, chmn dept, 76-79, ASSOC PROF CHEM, SIMON FRASER UNIV, 67-, ASSOC MEM PHYSICS DEPT, 69- *Concurrent Pos:* With Australian Nat Serv, 55-58. *Mem:* Fel Chem Inst Can; fel Royal Soc Chem; Am Inst Physics; fel Royal Soc Arts; Can Asn Physicists. *Res:* Chemical and biological applications of nuclear magnetic resonance. *Mailing Add:* Dept of Chem Simon Fraser Univ Burnaby BC V5A 1S6 Can

WELLS, ELIZABETH FORTSON, b Agnes Scott Col, Ga, BA, 65; Univ NC, Chapel Hill, MA, 70, PhD(bot), 77. PLANT TAXONOMY, FLAVONOID CHEMOTAXONOMY. *Prof Exp:* Instr biol, Univ Richmond, 70-72; fel, Univ BC, 77-79; ASST PROF BOT, GEORGE WASHINGTON UNIV, 79- *Mem:* Am Soc Plant Taxonomists; Bot Soc Am; Int Asn Plant Taxon; Asn Southeastern Biologists. *Res:* Revising the genus heuchera (saxifragaceae) using breeding studies, flavonoid analysis and morphometrics; flavonoids in Aceraceae. *Mailing Add:* Dept Biol Sci George Washington Univ Washington DC 20052

WELLS, EUGENE ERNEST, JR, organic chemistry, electrochemistry, see previous edition

WELLS, FRANK EDWARD, b Granby, Mo, Mar 29, 25; m 47; c 2. RAPID ANALYTICAL METHODOLOGY, ENZYME IMMOBILIZATION. *Educ:* Southwest Mo State Univ, BS, 51; Purdue Univ, MS, 58, PhD(bact), 61. *Prof Exp:* Med technologist, Vets Admin Hosp, Springfield, 51-53; lab dir, Henningsen Foods Inc, 53-56; instr food prods technol, Purdue Univ, 56-61; tech dir, Monarck Egg Corp, 61; sr microbiologist, 61-65, PRIN MICROBIOLOGIST, MIDWEST RES INST, 65- *Mem:* Soc Invert Path; Wildlife Dis Asn. *Res:* Control agents for food spoilage; microbial insect control agents; disease monitoring of laboratory animals; biodegredation of xenobiotics in soil; detection of aerosolized biological agents; industrial fermentations. *Mailing Add:* 3200 NE 64th Terrace Kansas City MO 64119

WELLS, FREDERICK JOSEPH, b Dayton, Ohio, Nov 13, 44. SEISMOLOGY. *Educ:* Univ Dayton, BS, 66; Brown Univ, ScM, 68, PhD(seismol), 72. *Prof Exp:* Res geophysicist, 72-75, advan res geophysicist, Denver Res Ctr, Marathon Oil Co, 75-77, sr geophysicist, 77-80, MGR GEOPHYS PROJ, MARATHON INT OIL CO, 80- *Mem:* Soc Explor Geophysicists; Am Asn Petrol Geologists. *Res:* Empirical and theoretical research of the seismic response of sedimentary rocks as a function of rock type, pore fluid and seismic frequency from the megahertz to the hertz range. *Mailing Add:* Marathon Oil Co 539 S Main St Findlay OH 45840

WELLS, GARLAND RAY, b El Dorado, Ark, Oct 10, 36; m 56; c 1. FORESTRY, ECONOMICS. *Educ:* La Polytech Inst, BS, 58; NC State Univ, MF, 61; Duke Univ, DF, 68. *Prof Exp:* From instr to asst prof forestry, La Polytech Inst, 62-65; asst prof, 65-75, ASSOC PROF FORESTRY, UNIV TENN, KNOXVILLE, 75- *Mem:* Soc Am Foresters; Am Econ Asn. *Res:* Land ownership research especially the practice of forestry by private, non-industrial forest owners. *Mailing Add:* Dept of Forestry Univ of Tenn Knoxville TN 37901

WELLS, GARY NEIL, b Springfield, Ill, Nov 19, 41; m 65; c 2. PLANT PHYSIOLOGY, BIOCHEMISTRY. *Educ:* Western Ill Univ, BA, 65, MS, 67; Univ Ill, PhD(plant biochem), 71. *Prof Exp:* Chem eng tech chem, Ill State Dept, 61-63; res assoc molecular biol, Univ Okla, 71-73; ASSOC PROF BIOL, FLA INST TECHNOL, 73- *Concurrent Pos:* NIH fel, Univ Okla, 72-73; NASA grant, Fla Inst Technol, 77-, NIH grant, 76- *Mem:* AAAS; Am Soc Plant Physiol; Am Soc Photo Biol. *Res:* Molecular biology of development; regulatory mechanisms operating at the level of transcription and translation and their role in plant growth and development. *Mailing Add:* Dept of Biol Sci Fla Inst of Technol Melbourne FL 32901

WELLS, GEORGE SHERMAN, biochemistry, see previous edition

WELLS, HENRY BRADLEY, b Ridgeland, SC; m 47; c 4. BIOSTATISTICS. *Educ:* Emory Univ, BA, 50; Univ NC, MSPH, 53, PhD(biostatist), 59. *Prof Exp:* Chief statistician, Ga State Dept Pub Health, 50-55; statistician, NC State Bd Health, 56-58, consult, 58-64; from instr to assoc prof biostatist, 58-69, prof biostatist, 69-80, EMER PROF, SCH PUB HEALTH, UNIV NC, CHAPEL HILL, 81-; PROF BIOSTATIST, BOWMAN GRAY SCH MED, WAKE FORREST UNIV, 81- *Mem:* Am Statist Asn; Biomet Soc; Am Pub Health Asn; Int Statist Inst; Int Asn Surv Statisticians. *Res:* Design of clinical trials, survivorship analysis; survey methods in demographic research; evaluation of health programs. *Mailing Add:* Bowman Gray Sch Med Winston-Salem NC 27103

WELLS, HERBERT, b New Haven, Conn, July 27, 30; m 59; c 3. PHARMACOLOGY, ORTHODONTICS. *Educ:* Yale Univ, BA, 52; Harvard Univ, DMD, 56. *Prof Exp:* Res assoc orthod, Sch Dent Med, Harvard Univ, 59-60, assoc pharmacol, 60-63, asst prof dent & dir, Dent Clin, 63-68; PROF PHARMACOL, HENRY M GOLDMAN SCH GRAD DENT, BOSTON UNIV, 68-, ASST DEAN, PREDOCTORAL PROG, 80- *Concurrent Pos:* Res fel orthod & pharmacol, Sch Dent Med, Harvard Univ, 56-59; mem, Panel Drugs Dent, Nat Res Coun, 66- & Dent Study Sect, NIH, 74- *Honors & Awards:* Lord-Chaim Res Award, 60; Oral Sci Prize, Int Asn Dent Res, 64. *Mem:* Am Soc Pharmacol & Exp Therapeut; Int Asn Dent Res. *Res:* Growth and secretion of exocrine and endocrine glands; salivary glands; parathyroid glands; experimental teratology; cleft palate formation. *Mailing Add:* Oral Pharmacol Lab Boston Univ Sch of Grad Dent Boston MA 02118

WELLS, HERBERT ARTHUR, b Jersey City, NJ, Aug 4, 21; m 46; c 3. MECHANICAL ENGINEERING. *Educ:* Cooper Union, BME, 47; Newark Col Eng, MSME, 52. *Prof Exp:* Mem tech staff, 47-56, SUPVR, BELL TEL LABS, INC, 56- *Mem:* Am Soc Mech Engrs. *Res:* Ship design and cable laying methods; hardening of structures to resist nuclear blast effects; antenna structural design for arctic and other applications. *Mailing Add:* Underwater Systs Bell Tel Labs Whippany NJ 07981

WELLS, HOMER DOUGLAS, b Blaine, Ky, Nov 11, 23; m 42; c 1. PLANT PATHOLOGY. *Educ:* Univ Ky, BS, 48, MS, 49; NC State Col, PhD(plant path), 54. *Prof Exp:* Tech asst agron agr exp sta, Univ Ky, 48-49, asst, 49-50; asst plant path, NC State Col, 50-52; asst agronomist, 52-53, PATHOLOGIST FORAGE CROPS, GA COASTAL PLAIN EXP STA, USDA, 53- *Mem:* Am Phytopath Soc. *Res:* Turf and forage crop disease problems. *Mailing Add:* Ga Coastal Plain Exp Sta Tifton GA 31794

WELLS, IBERT CLIFTON, b Fayette, Mo, Apr 12, 21; m 48; c 6. BIOCHEMISTRY. *Educ:* Cent Methodist Col, AB, 42; St Louis Univ, PhD(biochem), 48. *Prof Exp:* From instr to assoc prof biochem, Col Med, State Univ NY Upstate Med Ctr, 50-61; chmn dept, 61-76, PROF BIOCHEM, SCH MED, CREIGHTON UNIV, 61-, PROF MED, 76- *Concurrent Pos:* Nat Res Coun fel, Calif Inst Technol, 48-50. *Honors & Awards:* Com Solvents Corp Award, 52. *Mem:* Am Soc Biol Chemists; Soc Exp Biol & Med. *Res:* Cholesterol metabolism; choline and one-carbon metabolism; biochemistry of disease. *Mailing Add:* Dept of Biochem Creighton Univ Sch of Med Omaha NE 68131

WELLS, J GORDON, b Salt Lake City, Utah, Sept 18, 18; m 41; c 1. PHYSIOLOGY. *Educ:* Pepperdine Col, BS, 46; Univ Southern Calif, PhD, 51. *Prof Exp:* Mem fac phys educ, Pepperdine Col, 46-48; asst aviation physiol, Univ Southern Calif, 48-49; aviation physiologist, US Air Force Sch Aviation Med, 49-56; supvr human eng, Norair Div, Northrop Corp, 56-61; asst dir life sci, Appl Sci, Space & Info Systs Div, NAm Aviation, Inc, 61-62, mgr Apollo Crew Systs, Apollo Eng, 62-66, asst to vpres & gen mgr life sci opers, 66-67, dir space progs, Life Sci Opers, 67, mgr life sci & systs, Sci & Technol, Res Eng & Test, Space Div, 67-68, mgr life sci & systs, 68-71, supvr life sci, Systs Eng & Technol, Res & Eng & Test, Space Div, NAm Rockwell Corp, 71-75; ASSOC DEAN ADMIN, GRAD SCH EDUC, PEPPERDINE UNIV, 75- *Mem:* AAAS; Human Factors Soc; Am Astronaut Soc; assoc fel Am Inst Aeronaut & Astronaut; fel Aerospace Med Asn (vpres, 59-60). *Res:* Physiological aspects of aerospace medicine; human factors and bioastronautics. *Mailing Add:* 11 La Vista Verde Dr Rancho Palos Verdes CA 90274

WELLS, JACK E, b Kansas City, Kans, Jan 14, 22; m 42; c 2. PEDODONTICS. *Educ:* Univ Mo-Kansas City, DDS, 51, MSD, 57. *Prof Exp:* From assoc prof to prof dent & chmn dept pedodontics, Sch Med, Univ Mo-Kansas City, 57-73; PROF PEDODONTICS & DEAN COL DENT, UNIV TENN CTR HEALTH SCI, MEMPHIS, 73- *Concurrent Pos:* Dir undergrad pedodontics, Univ Mo-Kansas City, 57-58, coordr chairside dent asst prog, 57-73, asst dean, Sch Dent, 60-63, proj dir chronically ill, Aged & Handicapped Dent Proj & assoc dean, 63-73; chief dent serv, Children's Mercy Hosp, 59-73. *Mem:* Am Col Dent; Am Acad Pedodontics; Int Asn Dent Res. *Res:* Dentistry. *Mailing Add:* Col of Dent Univ Tenn Ctr Health Sci Memphis TN 38103

WELLS, JACK NULK, b McLouth, Kans, May 17, 37; m 60; c 2. MEDICINAL CHEMISTRY, PHARMACOLOGY. *Educ:* Park Col, BA, 59; Univ Mich, MS, 62, PhD(med chem), 63. *Prof Exp:* From asst prof to assoc prof med chem, Purdue Univ, 63-67; vis scholar, 72-73, asst prof physiol, 73-75, asst prof pharmacol, 75-77, ASSOC PROF PHARMACOL, SCH MED, VANDERBILT UNIV, 77- *Concurrent Pos:* Fel, Ohio State Univ, 63. *Mem:* AAAS; Am Soc Pharmacol & Exp Therapeut; Am Chem Soc. *Res:* Phosphodiesterase; smooth muscle physiology. *Mailing Add:* Dept Pharmacol Vanderbilt Univ Sch Med Nashville TN 37232

WELLS, JACQUELINE GAYE, b Pittsburgh, Pa, May 17, 31; m 51; c 2. ALGEBRA. *Educ:* Univ Pittsburgh, BS, 52, MS, 64, PhD(math), 72. *Prof Exp:* ASST PROF MATH, PA STATE UNIV, McKEESPORT, 64- *Mailing Add:* 1005 Faucett McKeesport PA 15132

WELLS, JAMES EDWARD, b Akron, Ohio, Dec 12, 43; m 65. PHYSICAL INORGANIC CHEMISTRY. *Educ:* Univ Cincinnati, BS, 65; Purdue Univ, PhD(chem), 72. *Prof Exp:* Res chemist, Goodyear Atomic Corp, 65-67; res chemist, Houdry Labs, Air Prod & Chem Inc, 73-81; RES CHEMIST, PQ CORP, 81- *Res:* Heterogeneous catalysis, including oxidation catalysts, specialty catalysts, and various petroleum refining catalysts; preparation, properties and applications of such catalysts; silicas; plasma spectroscopy. *Mailing Add:* Houdry Labs Air Prod & Chem Inc PO Box 427 Marcus Hook PA 19061

WELLS, JAMES HOWARD, b Howe, Tex, June 20, 32; m 53; c 2. MATHEMATICS. *Educ:* Tex Tech Col, BS, 52, MS, 54; Univ Tex, PhD(math), 58. *Prof Exp:* Instr math, Univ Tex, 57-58; from instr to asst prof, Univ NC, 58-59; vis asst prof, Univ Calif, Berkeley, 60-61; assoc prof, 62-69, PROF MATH, UNIV KY, 69- *Mem:* Am Math Soc; Math Asn Am. *Res:* Analysis. *Mailing Add:* Dept of Math Univ of Ky Lexington KY 40506

WELLS, JAMES RAY, b Delaware, Ohio, May 28, 32; m 58; c 2. PLANT TAXONOMY. *Educ:* Univ Tenn, BS, 54, MS, 56; Ohio State Univ, PhD(bot), 63. *Prof Exp:* Asst prof biol, ECarolina Col, 63-64 & Old Dominion Col, 64-66; BOTANIST & ASST TO DIR, CRANBROOK INST SCI, 66- *Concurrent Pos:* Vis prof, Stephen F Austin State Col, 64; NSF grant, 67-69; adj assoc prof biol, Oakland Univ, 69- & Wayne State Univ, 73-; chmn, Mich Natural Areas Coun, 70-72. *Mem:* Am Soc Plant Taxon; Bot Soc Am; Am Soc Nat; Int Soc Plant Taxon. *Res:* Plant ecology; biosystematics of the genus Polymnia including chemotaxonomy. *Mailing Add:* Cranbrook Inst of Sci 500 Lone Pine Rd Bloomfield Hills MI 48013

WELLS, JAMES ROBERT, b Moundsville, WVa, Apr 5, 40; m 81; c 2. CHEMISTRY, STRATEGIC PLANNING. *Educ:* Wheeling Col, BS, 62; Univ Pittsburgh, PhD(chem), 67. *Prof Exp:* Chemist plastics dept, Exp Sta, 67-70, sr res chemist, Sabine River Lab, 70-72, res supvr, Polymer Intermediates Dept, 72-74, lab dir, 74-76, prod supt nylon intermediates-methanol-power, Sabine River Works, Plastics Prod & Resins Dept, 76-77, res mgr, Feedstocks Res & Develop Div, Cent Res & Develop Dept, 77-79, prin consult, Corp Plans Dept, Wilmington, 79-81, PRIN CONSULT, CENT RES & DEVELOP DEPT, E I DU PONT DE NEMOURS & CO, INC, 81- *Mem:* Am Chem Soc. *Mailing Add:* Cent Res & Develop Dept E I du Pont de Nemours & Co Inc 1007 Market St Wilmington DE 19898

WELLS, JANE FRANCES, b Davenport, Iowa, Feb 24, 44. MATHEMATICS. *Educ:* Marycrest Col, BA, 66; Univ Iowa, MS, 67, PhD(math), 70. *Prof Exp:* Asst prof math, Purdue Univ, Ft Wayne, 70-74; UNIV PROF, GOVERNORS STATE UNIV, 74- *Concurrent Pos:* Vis appointment, US Environ Protection Agency, 80-81. *Mem:* Am Math Soc; Math Asn Am; Am Statist Asn; Asn Women Math. *Res:* Noether lattices, data analysis, quality control. *Mailing Add:* Col Bus & Pub Serv Governors State Univ Park Forest IL 60466

WELLS, JAY BYRON, b Chicago, Ill, July 3, 26; m 48; c 5. PHYSIOLOGY. *Educ:* Univ Denver, AB, 51, MS, 52; Univ Rochester, PhD(physiol), 64. *Prof Exp:* Res physiologist, Med Neurol Br, 54-59, 63-75, RES PHYSIOLOGIST, LAB BIOPHYS, SECT NEURAL MEMBRANES, NAT INST NEUROL & COMMUN DIS & STROKE, MARINE BIOL LAB, WOODS HOLE, MASS, 76- *Mem:* Biophys Soc. *Res:* Nerve-muscle physiology and pharmacology; muscle mechanics; respiratory physiology; neural membranes. *Mailing Add:* Lab Biophys NINCDS Marine Biol Lab Woods Hole MA 02543

WELLS, JOHN ARTHUR, b Clearwater, Fla, Oct 2, 35. PLANT CHEMISTRY. *Educ:* Univ Fla, BSCh, 58; Auburn Univ, PhD(chem), 70. *Prof Exp:* Chemist, Naval Stores Lab, 58-61, res chemist, 70-73, RES CHEMIST, US VEGETABLE LAB, USDA, 73- *Mem:* Am Chem Soc; Am Soc Hort Sci. *Res:* Chemistry of plant material developed in a vegetable breeding program; biochemical nature of plant host resistance to diseases and insects; nutrients and toxicants in new breeding lines. *Mailing Add:* US Vegetable Lab 2875 Savannah Hwy Charleston SC 29407

WELLS, JOHN CALHOUN, JR, b Tampa, Fla, May 12, 41; m 63; c 2. EXPERIMENTAL NUCLEAR PHYSICS. *Educ:* Fla State Univ, BS, 61; Johns Hopkins Univ, PhD(physics), 68. *Prof Exp:* Nat Acad Sci-Nat Res Coun assoc & res physicist, US Naval Ord Lab, Md, 68-70; from asst prof to assoc prof, 70-80, PROF PHYSICS, TENN TECHNOL UNIV, 80- *Concurrent Pos:* Consult physics div, Oak Ridge Nat Lab, 71- *Mem:* Am Phys Soc; Sigma Xi; NY Acad Sci; Am Asn Univ Prof; Am Asn Physics Teachers. *Res:* Nuclear charged-particle reactions; heavy-ion reactions; gamma-ray spectroscopy; neutron reactions. *Mailing Add:* Dept of Physics Tenn Technol Univ Cookeville TN 38501

WELLS, JOHN CLARENCE, b Philadelphia, Pa, Jan 12, 14; m 44; c 4. PHYSICS. *Educ:* Colgate Univ, AB, 37; Columbia Univ, MA, 40, EdD(sci ed), 52. *Prof Exp:* Teacher, Pleasant Hill Acad, Tenn, 37-39; teacher high sch, NY, 39-42; ballistic supvr, Radford Ord Works, 42-45; teacher high sch, NY, 45-46; asst, Dept Natural Sci, Teachers Col, Columbia Univ, 46-47; assoc prof physics, 47-53, prof physics, 47-79, PLANETARIUM DIR, JAMES MADISON UNIV, VA, 47- *Mem:* Nat Sci Teachers Asn; Int Planetarium Soc. *Res:* Teaching. *Mailing Add:* Dept of Physics James Madison Univ Harrisonburg VA 22801

WELLS, JOHN MORGAN, JR, b Hopewell, Va, Apr 12, 40. MARINE BIOLOGY. *Educ:* Randolph-Macon Col, BS, 62; Univ Calif, San Diego, PhD(marine biol), 69. *Prof Exp:* Res physiologist, Wrightsville Marine Bio-Med Lab, NC, 69-72; asst prof physiol, Sch Med, Univ NC, 70-72; sci coordr marine biol, Manned undersea sci & technol off, 72-78, DIR, NAT OCEANIC & ATMOSPHERIC ADMIN, 78- *Res:* Blood function at high hydrostatic and inert gas pressures; physiological symbiosis between algae and invertebrates; community metabolism of marine benthic communities; diving physiology. *Mailing Add:* Manned Undersea Sci & Technol Off NOAA OE-3 6010 Executive Blvd Rockville MD 20852

WELLS, JOHN WEST, b Philadelphia, Pa, July 15, 07; m 32; c 1. PALEONTOLOGY, MARINE ZOOLOGY. *Educ:* Univ Pittsburgh, BS, 28; Cornell Univ, MA, 30, PhD(paleont), 33. *Prof Exp:* Instr geol, Univ Tex, 29-31; Nat Res Coun fel, Brit Mus, Paris & Berlin, 33-34; asst sci, NY State Norm Sch, 37-38; from instr to prof geol, Ohio State Univ, 38-48; prof geol, 48-74, EMER PROF GEOL, CORNELL UNIV, 74- *Concurrent Pos:* Geologist, US Geol Surv, 46-, Off Strategic Serv, 44-45, Bikini Sci Resurv, 47 & Pac Sci Bd, Arno Atoll Exped, 50; Fulbright lectr, Univ Queensland, 54; pres, Paleont Res Inst, 61-64. *Honors & Awards:* Paleont Medal, Paleont Soc, 74. *Mem:* Nat Acad Sci; fel Geol Soc Am; Paleont Soc (pres, 61-62); Soc Vert Paleont; Paleont Asn. *Res:* Invertebrate paleontology and paleoecology; vertebrate paleontology; stratigraphy; invertebrate zoology. *Mailing Add:* Dept of Geol Sci Cornell Univ Ithaca NY 14853

WELLS, JOSEPH, b Boston, Mass, Oct 6, 34; m 56; c 5. NEUROANATOMY, NEUROBIOLOGY. *Educ:* Univ RI, BS, 56; Duke Univ, PhD(anat), 59. *Prof Exp:* Instr anat, Duke Univ, 59-61 & Yale Univ, 61-63; asst prof, Sch Med, Univ Md, Baltimore, 63-68; ASSOC PROF ANAT, COL MED, UNIV VT, 68- *Concurrent Pos:* NIH fel, 59-61; Nat Inst Neurol Dis & Blindness res grant, 64-67; Lederle Med Fac Award, Univ Md, 68, Sandoz Found fel neurosci, 78-80. *Mem:* Am Asn Anatomists; Soc Neurosci. *Res:* Neuroanatomy using silver stains; systems neurobiology using electron microscopy; neuronal plasticity of somatosensory system. *Mailing Add:* Dept Anat Col Med Univ Vt Burlington VT 05401

WELLS, JOSEPH M(ICHAEL), b Boston, Mass, Oct 16, 40; m 65. PHYSICAL & MECHANICAL METALLURGY. *Educ:* Northeastern Univ, BS, 63, MS, 65; Mass Inst Technol, ScD(phys metall), 70. *Prof Exp:* Sr engr, Res & Develop Ctr, 72-76, MGR POWER GENERATION MAT RES, RES & DEVELOP CTR, WESTINGHOUSE ELEC CORP, 76- *Concurrent Pos:* Partic scientist, US/USSR Sci & Technol Exchange, 78; mem adv bd, Ctr Joining Mat, Carnegie-Mellon Univ, 79-81. *Mem:* Am Soc Metals; Am Welding Soc; Sigma Xi. *Res:* Fracture; fatigue, creep; environmental effects; cryostructural materials. *Mailing Add:* 81 Sequoia Dr Export PA 15632

WELLS, JOSEPH S, b Meade, Kans, Mar 19, 30; m 56; c 4. PHYSICS. *Educ:* Kans State Univ, BS, 56, MS, 58; Univ Colo, PhD(physics), 64. *Prof Exp:* Proj leader microwave noise, Electronics Calibration Ctr, 59-62, physicist, Radio & Microwave Mat Sect, 62-67, res physicist, Quantum Electronics Div, 67-73, RES PHYSICIST, TIME & FREQUENCY DIV, NAT BUR STANDARDS, 74- *Concurrent Pos:* Res assoc, Physics Dept, Univ Colo, 64-66, lectr, 66-73, adj prof, 73-79. *Mem:* Am Phys Soc; Sci Res Soc Am. *Res:* Paramagnetic and antiferromagnetic resonance; microwave measurements; infrared frequency synthesis; laser stabilization and frequency measurements; tunable lasers and spectroscopy; infrared frequency standards and molecular spectroscopy. *Mailing Add:* Time & Frequency Div Nat Bur of Standards Boulder CO 80303

WELLS, KENNETH, b Portsmouth, Ohio, July 24, 27; m 54; c 2. MYCOLOGY. *Educ:* Univ Ky, BS, 50; Univ Iowa, MS & PhD(bot), 57. *Prof Exp:* Asst bot, Univ Iowa, 54-57; instr & jr botanist, 57-58, from asst prof & asst botanist to assoc prof & assoc botanist, 59-72, PROF BOT & BOTANIST, UNIV CALIF, DAVIS, 72-, CHMN DEPT BOT & AGR BOT, 78- *Concurrent Pos:* Fulbright res fel, Inst Bot, Sao Paulo, Brazil, 63-64; Nat Acad Sci exchange scientist, Romania, 71-72; hon res assoc, Dept Bot, Univ BC, 78-79. *Mem:* Mycol Soc Am; Brit Mycol Soc; Mycol Soc Japan. *Res:* Taxonomy of the fungi, especially the Tremellales; ultrastructure of the fungi, especially of the basidium; general mycology. *Mailing Add:* Dept of Bot Univ of Calif Davis CA 95616

WELLS, KENNETH LINCOLN, b Lone Mountain, Tenn, May 28, 35; m 60. SOIL SCIENCE, AGRONOMY. *Educ:* Univ Tenn, BS, 57, MS, 59; Iowa State Univ, PhD(soil sci), 63. *Prof Exp:* Res assoc soils, Iowa State Univ, 59-63; agriculturist, Tenn Valley Authority, 63-65, agronomist, 65-69; from asst prof to assoc prof agron, prof, 69-77, EXTEN PROF AGRON, UNIV KY, 77- *Mem:* Am Soc Agron; Soil Sci Soc Am. *Res:* Soil fertility, crop production, genesis and classification. *Mailing Add:* Dept of Agron Univ of Ky Lexington KY 40506

WELLS, KENTWOOD DAVID, b Alexandria, Va, Mar 23, 48. HERPETOLOGY, ANIMAL BEHAVIOR. *Educ:* Duke Univ, AB, 70; Cornell Univ, PhD(vert zool), 76. *Prof Exp:* ASST PROF BIOL, UNIV CONN, 77- *Concurrent Pos:* Fel, Smithsonian Trop Res Inst, 75-76; res grant, Nat Geog Soc, 78-79. *Mem:* Am Soc Ichthyol & Herpet; Soc Study Amphibians & Reptiles; Ecol Soc Am; Animal Behav Soc. *Res:* Social behavior, mating systems and behavioral ecology of vertebrates, especially amphibians; history of science, especially evolutionary biology and early behavioral studies. *Mailing Add:* Biol Sci Group U-43 Univ of Conn Storrs CT 06268

WELLS, LARRY GENE, b Covington, Ky, July 28, 47; m 71; c 2. AGRICULTURAL ENGINEERING. *Educ:* Univ Ky, BS, 69, MS, 71; NC State Univ, PhD(biol, agr eng & math), 75. *Prof Exp:* Asst prof, 74-79, ASSOC PROF AGR ENG, UNIV KY, 79- *Concurrent Pos:* Prin investr, NSF Res Initiation Grant, 76-78; investr, NSF Res Grant, 76-77; prin investr, Burley Tobacco Coun Grant, 78-81; investr, Sci & Educ Admin Grant, 78-80. *Mem:* Am Soc Agr Eng; Int Soc Terrain Vehicle Systs. *Res:* Application of systems simulation techniques in the selection and management of agricultural machinery systems; characterization of vehicle soil relationships in agriculture and surface mine reclaimation. *Mailing Add:* Dept Agr Eng Univ Ky Lexington KY 40506

WELLS, MARION ALVA, b Mahaska, Kans, Dec 20, 22; m 46; c 6. ELECTRICAL ENGINEERING. *Educ:* Iowa State Univ, BSEE, 46; Univ NMex, MSEE, 54. *Prof Exp:* Engr, Rauland Corp Div, Zenith Corp, Ill, 46-49; mem staff, Sandia Corp, NMex, 49-54; develop engr, Datalab Div, Consol Electrodyn Corp, Bell & Howell Co, 54-57, sr develop engr, 57-59, sr supvry engr, 59-61, eng dept mgr, Data Recorders Div, 61-63, prin supvry engr, electronic instrumentation group, Data Instruments Div, 63-80; SR PRIN ENG TEST INSTRUMENTS, HONEYWELL INC, 80- *Mem:* Inst Elec & Electronics Engrs. *Res:* Electronic circuits and transformer design; development of magnetic tape recording systems for instrumentation systems; servo control system design; electronic systems analysis; proposal writing. *Mailing Add:* Test Instruments Honeywell Inc 4800 E Dry Creek Rd Denver CO 80217

WELLS, MARION ROBERT, b Jackson, Miss, Feb 9, 37; m 59; c 3. CELL PHYSIOLOGY. *Educ:* Memphis State Univ, BS, 60, MA, 63; Miss State Univ, PhD(zool), 71. *Prof Exp:* Instr biol, Troy State Col, 63-64; assoc prof, 64-77, PROF BIOL, MID TENN STATE UNIV, 77- *Mem:* Sigma Xi. *Res:* Binding of insecticides to cell particulate. *Mailing Add:* Dept of Biol Mid Tenn State Univ Murfreesboro TN 37130

WELLS, MARK BRIMHALL, b Pocatello, Idaho, June 10, 29; m 74; c 6. COMPUTER SCIENCE, MATHEMATICS. *Educ:* Denver Univ, BA, 50; Univ Calif, Berkeley, PhD(math), 61. *Prof Exp:* Staff mem prog, Los Alamos Sci Lab, Univ Calif, 51-68; group leader comput sci, 68-73; vis prof math sci, Rice Univ, 70; vis prof math & comput sci, Univ Denver, 77-78; staff mem comput sci, Los Alamos Nat Lab, Univ Calif, 73-80; DEPT HEAD, COMPUT SCI DEPT, NMEX STATE UNIV, 80- *Mem:* Asn Comput Mach; Am Math Soc; Math Asn Am. *Res:* Programming languages; combinatorial algorithm design. *Mailing Add:* Comput Sci Dept NMex State Univ Las Cruces NM 88003

WELLS, MARTIN GODFREY HEADLAM, b Redhill, Surrey, Eng, Mar 18, 35; m 59; c 4. FERROUS PHYSICAL METALLURGY. *Educ:* Royal Sch Mines, Imperial Col Sci & Technol, London Univ, BSc, 57, PhD(phys metall), 61. *Hon Degrees:* ARSM, Royal Sch Mines, Imperial Col Sci & Technol, London Univ, 57 & DIC, 61. *Prof Exp:* Res metallurgist, Jones & Laughlin Steel Corp, 61-63, sr res metallurgist eng, 63-67; mgr, 67-68, assoc dir, 68-70, TECH DIR FERROUS METALL, CRUCIBLE RES CTR, COLT INDUST, 70- *Concurrent Pos:* Fac mem, Carnegie-Mellon Univ, 61-63. *Mem:* Am Soc Metals; Am Inst Mining, Metall & Petrol Engrs; Am Soc Testing & Mat. *Res:* New product/alloy development of specialty steels for a wide diversity of applications, through research in structure-property relationships and processing of these materials. *Mailing Add:* Crucible Res Ctr Col Indust PO Box 88 Pittsburgh PA 15230

WELLS, MICHAEL ARTHUR, b Los Angeles, Calif, Nov 8, 38; m 58; c 3. BIOCHEMISTRY. *Educ:* Univ Southern Calif, BA, 61; Univ Ky, PhD(biochem), 65. *Prof Exp:* Am Cancer Soc fel biochem, Univ Wash, 65-67; asst prof, 67-72, assoc prof, 72-77, PROF BIOCHEM, UNIV ARIZ, 77- *Concurrent Pos:* Macy fac scholar, Josiah Macy Found, 75-76. *Mem:* AAAS; Am Chem Soc; Am Soc Biol Chemists. *Res:* Complex lipids, their synthesis, chemical and physical properties, metabolism and interaction with proteins; fat digestion and absorption in suckling animals. *Mailing Add:* Dept of Biochem Univ of Ariz Tucson AZ 85724

WELLS, MICHAEL BYRON, b Kansas City, Mo, July 3, 22; m 48; c 4. OPTICAL PHYSICS, RADIATION PHYSICS. *Educ:* Univ Mo-Kansas City, BA, 48, MA, 50. *Prof Exp:* Instr, Univ Mo-Kansas City, 50-56; proj nuclear engr, Gen Dynamics, Ft Worth, Tex, 56-63; VPRES, RADIATION RES ASSOCS, INC, 63- *Concurrent Pos:* Instr, Tex Christian Univ, 58-63. *Mem:* Am Nuclear Soc; Optical Soc Am. *Res:* Nuclear radiation transport calculations; radiation shielding; atmospheric optics; ultraviolet, visible and infrared radiation transport in planetary atmospheres; nuclear engineering. *Mailing Add:* Radiations Res Assoc Inc 3550 Hulen St Ft Worth TX 76107

WELLS, MILTON ERNEST, b Calera, Okla, Nov 28, 32; m 55; c 2. ANIMAL BREEDING. *Educ:* Okla State Univ, BS, 55, MS, 59, PhD(animal breeding), 62. *Prof Exp:* Asst prof animal sci, Imp Ethiopian Col Agr, 61-65; asst prof dairy sci, 65-74, assoc prof, 74-77, PROF ANIMAL SCI, OKLA STATE UNIV, 77- *Mem:* Am Soc Animal Sci; Am Dairy Sci Asn. *Res:* Reproductive physiology; vibriosis; international animal agriculture; acrosome of sperm cells. *Mailing Add:* Dept of Animal Sci Okla State Univ Stillwater OK 74074

WELLS, OTHO SYLVESTER, b Burgaw, NC, Sept 15, 38; m 68; c 2. HORTICULTURE. *Educ:* NC State Univ, BS, 61; Mich State Univ, MS, 63; Rutgers Univ, PhD(hort), 66. *Prof Exp:* Asst prof, 66-71, ASSOC PROF PLANT SCI, UNIV NH, 71-, EXTEN HORTICULTURIST, VEGETABLES, 74- *Mem:* Am Soc Hort Sci. *Res:* Crop production under environmentally controlled conditions. *Mailing Add:* Dept of Plant Sci Univ of NH Durham NH 03824

WELLS, OUIDA CAROLYN, b Atlanta, Ga, July 23, 33. ZOOLOGY. *Educ:* Agnes Scott Col, BA, 55; Emory Univ, MS, 56, PhD(genetics), 58. *Prof Exp:* Asst, Emory Univ, 55-57; res assoc, Oak Ridge Nat Lab, 58-60; asst prof biol, 60-65, assoc prof natural sci, 65-68, from asst dean to dean, 69-81, PROF BIOL, LONGWOOD COL, 68- *Mem:* Genetics Soc Am; Soc Protozool. *Res:* Genetics, cytology, physiology and biochemistry of microorganisms; radiation biology of ciliate Tetrahymena pyriformis, especially survival and death of irradiated cells using high levels of ionizing radiation. *Mailing Add:* Longwood Col Farmville VA 23901

WELLS, PATRICK HARRINGTON, b Palo Alto, Calif, June 19, 26; m 51; c 3. BIOLOGY. *Educ:* Univ Calif, AB, 48; Stanford Univ, PhD(biol), 51. *Prof Exp:* Asst prof zool, Univ Mo, 51-57; from asst prof to assoc prof biol, 57-71, PROF BIOL, OCCIDENTAL COL, 71- *Concurrent Pos:* Res assoc, Univ Calif, 67-72; ed, Southern Calif Acad Sci Bull, 72-75. *Mem:* Fel AAAS; Bee Res Asn; Am Soc Zool; Lepidop Soc; Ecol Soc Am. *Res:* Physiology, experimental biology and animal behavior; physiology of learning in invertebrate animals; foraging behavior and recruitment in honey bees; natural history; population biology, ecology and physiology of butterflies and other arthropods. *Mailing Add:* Dept of Biol Occidental Col Los Angeles CA 90041

WELLS, PATRICK ROLAND, b Liberty, Tex, Apr 1, 31. PHARMACOLOGY. *Educ:* Tex Southern Univ, BS, 57; Univ Nebr, MS, 59, PhD(pharmaceut sci), 61. *Prof Exp:* Asst prof pharmacol, Fordham Univ, 61-63; from asst prof to assoc prof & actg chmn dept, Univ Nebr, 63-70; PROF PHARMACOL & DEAN SCH PHARM, TEX SOUTHERN UNIV, 70- *Mem:* Nat Pharmaceut Asn; Sigma Xi; Am Pharmaceut Asn. *Res:* Cardiovascular screening of plant tissue culture. *Mailing Add:* Sch of Pharm Tex Southern Univ Houston TX 77004

WELLS, PAULA PARKER, organic chemistry, see previous edition

WELLS, PHILIP VINCENT, b Brooklyn, NY, Apr 24, 28; m 59; c 4. BOTANY. *Educ:* Brooklyn Col, BA, 51; Univ Wis, MS, 56; Duke Univ, PhD(bot), 59. *Prof Exp:* Asst, Univ Wis, 54-55 & Duke Univ, 55-58; instr bot, Univ Calif, Santa Barbara, 58-59 & Calif Polytech Col, 59-60; res assoc biol, NMex Highlands Univ, 60-62; from asst prof to assoc prof bot, 62-71, PROF BOT & SYST ECOL, UNIV KANS, 71- *Concurrent Pos:* Actg dir, Bot Garden & vis assoc prof, Univ Calif, Berkeley, 66-67. *Mem:* AAAS; Soc Study Evolution; Bot Soc Am; Ecol Soc Am. *Res:* Pleistocene paleobotany; systematics, ecology and evolution in Arctostaphylos; vegetation of North America; physiological ecology. *Mailing Add:* Dept of Bot Univ of Kans Lawrence KS 66044

WELLS, PHILLIP RICHARD, b Northampton, Mass, May 23, 31; m 62; c 3. FOOD SCIENCE, DAIRY SCIENCE. *Educ:* Univ Mass, BS, 57; Pa State Univ, MS, 59; Rutgers Univ, PhD(dairy sci), 62. *Prof Exp:* Proj leader food prod develop, Colgate Palmolive Co, 62-66; sect leader new prod develop, Corn Prod Co, 66-72, asst to dir res, 72-75, asst dir tech serv, 75-78, asst to dir nutrit, 78-79, NUTRIT RES ASSOC, BEST FOODS, CPC INT, 79- *Mem:* Am Dairy Sci Asn; Inst Food Technol. *Res:* Dried and concentrated dairy products; snack products; stabilizers and emulsifiers; protein based foods; dried eggs; research management; food composition and nutrition. *Mailing Add:* Best Foods Res Ctr CPC Int 1120 Commerce Ave Union NJ 07083

WELLS, RALPH GORDON, b Newark, Ohio, Sept 24, 15; m 42. MATERIALS SCIENCE. *Educ:* Muskingum Col, BA, 39; Ohio State Univ, MSc, 47; Univ Mich, PhD(mineral), 51. *Prof Exp:* Res metallurgist, US Steel Corp, 47-51, supvry technologist, 51-55; assoc res engr, Univ Mich, 56-59; SR RES SCIENTIST, RES CTR, COLT INDUSTS CRUCIBLE INC, 59- *Concurrent Pos:* Res assoc minerals, Carnegie Mus Natural Hist, 76- *Mem:* Am Phys Soc; sr mem Inst Elec & Electronics Engrs; Am Inst Mining, Metall & Petrol Eng. *Res:* Application of Tools and techniques of mineralogy and crystallography to metallurgy and ceramics. *Mailing Add:* Res Ctr Colt Industs Crucible Inc Box 88 Pittsburgh PA 15230

WELLS, RAYMOND O'NEIL, JR, b Dallas, Tex, June 12, 40; m 63; c 1. MATHEMATICS. *Educ:* Rice Univ, BS, 62; NY Univ, MS, 64, PhD(math), 65. *Prof Exp:* From asst prof to assoc prof, 65-74, PROF MATH, RICE UNIV, 74- *Concurrent Pos:* Vis asst prof, Brandeis Univ, 67-68; mem, Inst Advan Study, 70-71; mem Regional Conf Bd, Conf Bd Math Sci, 74-77; Guggenheim fel, John Simon Guggenheim Mem Found, 74-75; US sr scientist award, Alexander von Humboldt Found, 74-75; vis prof math, Univ Göttingen, 74-75; ed, Trans Am Math Soc, 79-83. *Mem:* Am Math Soc; Math Asn Am. *Res:* Analytic continuation and approximation theory in several complex variables; theory of complex manifolds and spaces; automorphic functions; algebraic geometry; mathematical physics. *Mailing Add:* Dept of Math Rice Univ Houston TX 77001

WELLS, ROBERT DALE, b Uniontown, Pa, Oct 2, 38; m 60; c 2. BIOCHEMISTRY, MOLECULAR BIOLOGY. *Educ:* Ohio Wesleyan Univ, BS, 60; Univ Pittsburgh, PhD(biochem), 64. *Prof Exp:* NIH fel, Univ Pittsburgh, 64; NIH fel, enzyme Inst, Univ Wis-Madison, 64-66; from asst prof to assoc prof biochem, 66-73, prof biochem, 73-81, PROF & CHMN, DEPT BIOCHEM, SCHS MED & DENT, UNIV ALA, BIRMINGHAM, 82- *Concurrent Pos:* Mem regional coun, Am Inst Biol Sci, 66-68; Guggenheum Award, 76-77; ed, J Biol Chem, 77- *Mem:* AAAS; Am Chem Soc; Am Soc Biol Chem; Sigma Xi; Am Soc Microbiol. *Res:* Polynucleotides synthesis; DNA physical chemistry, synthesis and replication; polypeptide synthesis; tumor virology. *Mailing Add:* Dept Biochem Univ Ala University Sta Birmingham AL 35294

WELLS, ROBERT REID, metallurgy, see previous edition

WELLS, ROE, internal medicine, see previous edition

WELLS, RUSSELL FREDERICK, b Brooklyn, NY, Oct 24, 37; m 75; c 2. EXERCISE PHYSIOLOGY, SPORTS MEDICINE. *Educ:* Lafayette Col, BA, 59; Springfield Col, MS, 62; Univ NC, Chapel Hill, MA, 66; Purdue Univ, PhD(biol educ), 70. *Prof Exp:* Teacher & coach pvt sch, NC, 62-65; NSF acad year fel zool, Univ NC, Chapel Hill, 65-66; asst prof biol, Montclair State Col, 66-68; asst prof biol sci, Purdue Univ, 70-71; asst prof, 71-74, ASSOC PROF BIOL, ST LAWRENCE UNIV, 74-, ASOC DEAN COL, 81- *Concurrent Pos:* Adj prof, San Diego State Univ, 78-79; vis assoc res physiologist, Univ Calif, San Diego, 78-79. *Mem:* Am Inst Biol Sci; Nat Asn Biol Teachers; Am Col Sports Med. *Res:* Development of biological teaching materials for individualized instruction, primarily audio-tutorial; development of time-lapse cine studies of prolonged biological phenomena; physiology of exercise as it pertains to adult fitness and cardiac rehabilitation. *Mailing Add:* Dept of Biol St Lawrence Univ Canton NY 13617

WELLS, STEWART ALDERSON, b Saskatoon, Sask, May 16, 20; wid; c 3. GENETICS. *Educ:* Univ Sask, BSA, 42, MSc, 45; Univ Alta, PhD(genetics), 55. *Prof Exp:* Asst, Univ Sask, 42-45; res officer, Exp Sta, Sask, 45-48 & Alta, 48-66, RES SCIENTIST, BARLEY BREEDING, LETHBRIDGE RES STA, CAN DEPT AGR, ALTA, 66- *Mem:* Can Soc Agron; Genetics Soc Can; Agr Inst Can. *Res:* Cereal breeding. *Mailing Add:* Plant Sci Sect Res Sta Can Dept of Agr Lethbridge AB T1J 4B1 Can

WELLS, THOMAS EARL, b Payette, Idaho, Feb 17, 23; m 75. PHYSICS. *Educ:* Univ Idaho, BS, 48, MS, 49. *Prof Exp:* Prod develop analyst physics, NAm Aviation, Inc, 52; PHYSICIST, NAT BUR STANDARDS, 52- *Mem:* Am Asn Physics Teachers; Inst Elec & Electronics Engrs; AAAS. *Res:* Electrical measurements. *Mailing Add:* B146 MET Nat Bur of Standards Washington DC 20234

WELLS, WARREN F, b Des Moines, Iowa, May 16, 26; m 50; c 3. BIOCHEMISTRY. *Educ:* Univ Northern Iowa, BA, 50, MA, 55; Univ Ill, PhD(biochem), 59. *Prof Exp:* Instr sci, Clear Lake High Sch, Iowa, 50-52; instr chem, Undergrad Div, Univ Ill, 53-54, res asst biochem, Col Med, 54-59; from instr to asst prof, 59-70, ASSOC PROF BIOCHEM, MED & DENT SCHS, NORTHWESTERN UNIV, CHICAGO, 70- *Concurrent Pos:* Consult, Col Am Path, 62-64; biochemist, Vet Admin Hosp, 63-65; consult, Vet Admin Hosps, 64-74; lectr, Dept Ment Health, State of Ill, 67-69. *Mem:* AAAS; Am Chem Soc; NY Acad Sci; Am Asn Dent Schs. *Res:* Nucleic acid and protein metabolism of normal and pathologic nervous tissue; biochemical changes accompanying periodontal disease. *Mailing Add:* Dept of Biochem Northwestern Univ McGaw Med Ctr Chicago IL 60611

WELLS, WILLARD H, b Austin, Tex, Feb 23, 31; m 56; c 2. OPTICAL PHYSICS. *Educ:* Univ Tex, BS, 52; Calif Inst Technol, PhD(physics), 59. *Prof Exp:* Scientist, Jet Propulsion Lab, Calif Inst Technol, 59-62, res group supvr, 62-67; CHIEF SCIENTIST, TETRA TECH, INC, 67- *Mem:* Am Phys Soc. *Res:* Quantum electronics and mechanics; applied mathematics; spacecraft mechanics and space communications; underwater optical systems; optical communications including fiber optics. *Mailing Add:* Tetra Tech Inc 630 N Rosemead Pasadena CA 91107

WELLS, WILLIAM LOCHRIDGE, b Mayfield, Ky, Oct 12, 39. CHEMISTRY, CHEMICAL ENGINEERING. *Educ:* Univ Ky, BSChE, 62; Univ Ill, Urbana, MS, 64, PhD(chem), 67; Univ SC, MSChE, 74. *Prof Exp:* Asst, Univ Ill, 62-67; asst prof, Murray State Univ, 67-69; NSF grant & res assoc, Wayne State Univ, 69-71; asst prof, Southwest Baptist Col, 71-72; res asst chem eng, Univ SC, 72-73; prof, Midlands Tech Col, 73-75; chem engr, 75-77, projs mgr air res, 77-80, PROG MGR, GASEOUS EMISSION CONTROL, TENN VALLEY AUTHORITY, 80- *Mem:* Am Chem Soc; Royal Soc Chem; Am Inst Chem Engrs; Nat Soc Prof Engrs. *Res:* Photochemistry of inorganic compounds; organometallic compounds; separation of lanthanides and actinides by solvent extraction; air pollution control technology research. *Mailing Add:* Tenn Valley Authority 1120 Chestnut Tower II Chattanooga TN 37401

WELLS, WILLIAM RAYMOND, b Winder, Ga, Nov 28, 36; m 56; c 3. AEROSPACE ENGINEERING, APPLIED MATHEMATICS. *Educ:* Ga Inst Technol, BS, 59; Va Polytech Inst, MS, 61, PhD(aerospace eng), 68; Harvard Univ, MA, 64. *Prof Exp:* Aerospace technologist, Langley Res Ctr, NASA, 59-68; from asst prof to prof aerospace eng, Univ Cincinnati, 68-77; PROF ENG & CHMN DEPT, WRIGHT STATE UNIV, 77- *Concurrent Pos:* NASA grant, Langley Res Ctr, 70-; consult, Flight Dynamics Lab, US Air Force, 72- *Mem:* Assoc fel Am Inst Aeronaut & Astronaut; Am Soc Eng Educ; Am Acad Mech; Am Asn Univ Prof. *Res:* Systems identification, flight mechanics and control theory. *Mailing Add:* Wright State Univ Dayton OH 45435

WELLS, WILLIAM T, b Wytheville, Va, Aug 9, 33; m 55; c 3. APPLIED STATISTICS, APPLIED MATHEMATICS. *Educ:* Col William & Mary, BS, 54; NC State Univ, MS, 56, PhD(exp statist), 59. *Prof Exp:* Res asst appl math, NC State Col, 58-59; statistician, Res Triangle Inst, 59-62; engr guided missiles range div, Pan Am World Airways, Inc, 62-65; sr consult appl statist, 65-67, mgr appl sci dept, 67-68, vpres & dir appl sci div, Wolf Res & Develop Corp, 68-77; V PRES ENG, EG&G/WASH ANAL SERV CTR, INC, 77- *Mem:* Inst Math Statist; Am Statist Asn. *Res:* Statistical methods in trajectory determination; geodesy; instrumentation evaluation; biomedical data analysis. *Mailing Add:* EG&G/Wash Anal Serv Ctr Inc 6801 Kenilworth Ave Riverdale MD 20840

WELLS, WILLIAM WOOD, b Traverse City, Mich, June 8, 27; m 50; c 4. BIOCHEMISTRY. *Educ:* Univ Mich, BS, 49, MS, 51; Univ Wis, PhD, 55. *Prof Exp:* Res assoc, Upjohn Co, 51-52; asst biochem, Univ Wis, 52-55; from instr to assoc prof, Univ Pittsburgh, 55-66; PROF BIOCHEM, MICH STATE UNIV, 66- *Concurrent Pos:* Mem, Metab Study Sect, NIH, 66-70. *Mem:* Am Chem Soc; Am Soc Biol Chem; Am Soc Neurochem; Int Soc Neurochem; Am Inst Nutrit. *Res:* Sterol structure and metabolism; relationship of sterol metabolism to experimental atherosclerosis; galactose metabolism and mental retardation; brain energy metabolism; metabolic regulations of lysosomes; microtubule associated enzymes; myoinositol metabolism. *Mailing Add:* Dept of Biochem Mich State Univ East Lansing MI 48824

WELLSO, STANLEY GORDON, b Oshkosh, Wis, Feb 13, 35; m 57; c 3. ENTOMOLOGY. *Educ:* Univ Wis, BS, 57; Tex A&M Univ, MS, 62, PhD(entom), 66. *Prof Exp:* Asst prof entom, Colo State Univ, 65-67; entomologist, 67-73, RES LEADER ENTOM & SMALL GRAINS, SCI & EDUC ADMIN-FED RES, USDA, MICH STATE UNIV, 73- *Concurrent Pos:* Adj prof entom, Mich State Univ, 77- *Mem:* AAAS; Entom Soc Am. *Res:* Diapause induction and termination in insects; influence of photoperiod on insect's growth and development; rearing insects on artificial diets; ecological studies with grasshoppers; taxonomy and ecology of buprestids; small grain insects; insect behavior and feeding during oviposition; buprestid taxonomy. *Mailing Add:* USDA Sci & Educ Admin-Fed Res Dept of Entom Mich State Univ East Lansing MI 48824

WELLWOOD, ARNOLD AUGUSTUS, cytogenetics, plant morphology, see previous edition

WELMERS, EVERETT THOMAS, b Orange City, Iowa, Oct 27, 12; m 38; c 2. MATHEMATICS. *Educ:* Hope Col, AB, 32; Univ Mich, PhD(math), 37. *Hon Degrees:* ScD, Hope Col, 66. *Prof Exp:* From instr to asst prof math, Mich State Col, 37-44; flight res engr, Bell Aircraft Corp, 44, flutter engr, 44-46, group leader dynamic anal, 46-49, chief dynamics, 49-57, dir, L D Bell Res Ctr, 57-60, asst to pres, Corp, 58-60; group dir satellite systs, Aerospace Corp, 60-63, asst for tech oper, Manned Systs Div, 64-67, asst to gen mgr, El Segundo Tech Opers, 67-68, asst to pres, 68-77, aerospace historian, 78-80; DEAN, COL ENG, NORTHROP UNIV, 80- *Concurrent Pos:* Prof, Millard Fillmore Col, 45-59; mem, Air Training Command Adv Bd, 57-68; on leave to Inst Defense Anal & Adv Res Proj Agency, 59-60; comnr, Community Redevelop Agency, City of Los Angeles, 68- *Mem:* Am Math Soc; Math Asn Am; Am Inst Aeronaut & Astronaut; Inst Elec & Electronics Engrs. *Res:* Integration theory; jet propulsion; flutter; applied mathematics; aircraft and helicopter dynamics; operations analysis; computers; system analysis; satellites. *Mailing Add:* 1626 Old Oak Rd Los Angeles CA 90049

WELNA, CECILIA, b New Britain, Conn. MATHEMATICS. *Educ:* St Joseph Col, Conn, BS, 49; Univ Conn, MA, 52, PhD(ed), 60. *Prof Exp:* Instr, Mt St Joseph Acad, 49-50; asst instr math, Univ Conn, 50-55; instr, Univ Mass, 55-56; from asst prof to assoc prof, 56-68, PROF MATH & CHMN DEPT, UNIV HARTFORD, 68- *Mem:* Math Asn Am; Am Math Soc; Sigma Xi; Nat Coun Teachers of Math. *Mailing Add:* Dept Math Physics & Comput Sci 200 Bloomfield Ave West Hartford CT 06117

WELSCH, CLIFFORD WILLIAM, JR, b St Louis, Mo, Sept 10, 35; m 58; c 3. PHYSIOLOGICAL CHEMISTRY, ONCOLOGY. *Educ:* Univ Mo, BS, 57, MS, 62, PhD(physiol chem), 65. *Prof Exp:* Instr physiol chem, Univ Mo, 63-65; asst prof natural sci, 65-66, from asst prof to assoc prof anat, 68-76, PROF ANAT, COL HUMAN MED, MICH STATE UNIV, 76- *Concurrent Pos:* Nat Cancer Inst res fel oncol, Mich State Univ, 66-68; NIH career development award, 71-76; assoc ed, J Cancer Res, 80- *Mem:* AAAS; Am Asn Cancer Res; Soc Exp Biol & Med; Am Physiol Soc. *Res:* Investigations in mammary gland carcinogenesis. *Mailing Add:* 11408 Forest Hill Rd DeWitt MI 48820

WELSCH, FEDERICO, b Sevilla, Spain, Dec 26, 33; US citizen; m 59; c 4. MOLECULAR BIOLOGY, MEDICINE. *Educ:* Univ Barcelona, BA, 50; Univ Valencia. MD, 55, DMedSci, 57; Ctr Res & Advan Study, Mex, MS, 65; Dartmouth Col, PhD(molecular biol), 68. *Prof Exp:* Intern internal med, Univ Hamburg, 54-55; from instr to asst prof physiol chem, Univ Valencia, 55-57; prof physiol, Univ Guadalajara, 58-60; prof biochem, Univ Chihuahua, 60-63; instr, Ctr Advan Res & Study, Mex, 63-65; asst prof, Dartmouth Med Sch, 68-70; assoc dir, 70-74, EXEC DIR, WORCESTER FOUND EXP BIOL, 74-; ASSOC RES PROF BIOCHEM, MED SCH, UNIV MASS, 70- *Concurrent Pos:* USPHS & Am Heart Asn grants, Dartmouth Med Sch & Worcester Found, 68-; hon collabr, Span Res Coun, 58; sr Fulbright scholar, Peru, 75; pub policy scholar, Off Dir, NIH, 77; mem IV prog, health syst mgt, Bus Sch, Harvard Univ, 75; govt affairs liaison, Asn Independent Res Insts. *Mem:* AAAS; Am Chem Soc; Asn Am Med Cols. *Res:* Molecular biology and medicine. *Mailing Add:* Worcester Found for Exp Biol 222 Maple Ave Shrewsbury MA 01545

WELSCH, FRANK, b Berlin, Ger, Apr 14, 41; m 68; c 1. PRENATAL TOXICOLOGY, TERATOGENESIS. *Educ:* Free Univ, Berlin, DVM, 65. *Prof Exp:* From instr pharmacol to prof toxicol, Mich State Univ, East Lansing, 71-82; SR SCIENTIST TOXICOL, CHEM INDUST INST TOXICOL, 82- *Concurrent Pos:* Prin investr, Extramural Prog, NIH, Nat Inst Child Health & Human Develop, 72-80, Nat Found March Dimes, 75-78, Nat Inst Environ Health Sci, NIH, 80. *Mem:* Am Soc Pharmacol & Exp Therpeut; Soc Toxicol; Teratol Soc; Ger Pharmacol Soc. *Res:* Effects of chemicals on structural, biochemical and functional development of mammalian species; placenta function. *Mailing Add:* Chem Indust Inst Toxicol PO Box 12137 Research Triangle Park NC 27709

WELSCH, GERHARD EGON, b Saarland, Ger, Sept 19, 44; m 73; c 2. MATERIALS SCIENCE, METALLURGICAL ENGINEERING. *Educ:* Aachen Tech Univ, dipl ing, 68; Case Western Reserve Univ, MS, 70, PhD(mat sci), 74. *Prof Exp:* Res scientist aircraft mat, Deutsche Forschungs, Versuchsanstalt für Luft, Raumfahrt, Cologne, Ger, 74-76; SR RES ENGR REFRACTORY METALS, GEN ELEC CO, 76- *Mem:* Verein Deutscher Eisenhüttenlente; Deutsche Gesellschaft Metallkunde; Metall Soc Am Inst Mech Engrs; Am Soc Metals. *Res:* Mechanical and electrical properties of refractory metals and of titanium alloys; processing of metals; electron microscopy; ion implantation into metals. *Mailing Add:* Gen Elec Co Nela Park 1363 East Cleveland OH 44112

WELSCH, ROY ELMER, b Kansas City, Mo, July 31, 43. STATISTICS. *Educ:* Princeton Univ, AB, 65; Stanford Univ, MS, 66, PhD(math), 69. *Prof Exp:* Asst prof opers res, 69-73, assoc prof, 73-79, PROF MGT SCI & STATIST, SLOAN SCH MGT, MASS INST TECHNOL, 79- *Concurrent Pos:* Assoc ed, J Am Statist Asn. *Mem:* Fel Am Statist Asn; Inst Math Statist. *Res:* Data analysis; robust statistics; multiple comparisons; graphics. *Mailing Add:* Sloan Sch Mgt Mass Inst Technol Cambridge MA 02139

WELSH, BARBARA LATHROP, b New London, Conn. MARINE ECOLOGY. *Educ:* Mt Holyoke Col, BA, 57; Univ Md, MS, 70; Univ RI, PhD(oceanog), 73. *Prof Exp:* Instr zool, Univ Md, 68-69; sr ecologist marine systs, Vast, Inc, 72-73; asst prof biol sci, 73, ASSOC PROF MARINE SCI & BIOL SCI, UNIV CONN, 73- *Concurrent Pos:* Appointment, comt hazardous mat, Nat Res Coun, Nat Acad Sci, 73-76; consult, Normandean Assocs, 75- & Environ Qual Bd, Commonwealth Puerto Rico, 76-77. *Mem:* Estuarine Res Fedn (pres, 81-83); Am Soc Limnol & Oceanog; Ecol Soc Am; Sigma Xi; New Eng Estuarine Res Soc. *Res:* Ecology of marine coastal systems, particularly detrital based systems with tidal interaction. *Mailing Add:* Marine Sci Inst Avery Pt Groton CT 06340

WELSH, DAVID ALBERT, b Pittsburgh, Pa, Oct 25, 42; m 64; c 3. ORGANIC CHEMISTRY, POLYMER CHEMISTRY. *Educ:* Carnegie Mellon Univ, BS, 64, MS, 68, PhD(org chem), 69. *Prof Exp:* Res chemist, Kippers Co Res Labs, 68-69, Edgewood Arsenal, 69-71 & Koppers Co Res Labs, 71-74; SR RES SCIENTIST, RES DEPT, ARCO/POLYMERS INC, 74- *Mem:* Am Chem Soc. *Res:* Free radical polymerization and copolymerization; polymer properties; organic synthesis. *Mailing Add:* 1042 Harvard Rd Monroeville PA 15146

WELSH, GEORGE W, III, b New York, NY, Aug 7, 20; m 50; c 2. INTERNAL MEDICINE, ENDOCRINOLOGY. *Educ:* Yale Univ, BA, 42; Univ Rochester, MD, 50; Am Bd Internal Med, dipl, 57. *Prof Exp:* Asst med, Med Col, Cornell Univ, 51-52, Dartmouth Med Sch, 52-54 & Sch Med, Univ Wash, 54-55; from instr to asst prof med, 56-64, dir continuing med educ, 65-68, dir off continuing educ health sci, 68-74, ASSOC PROF MED, COL MED, UNIV VT, 64- *Concurrent Pos:* Fel med, Mary Hitchcock Hosp, Hanover, NH, 52-53; Nat Inst Arthritis & Metab Dis trainee, Sch Med, Univ Wash, 54-55, USPHS res fel, 55; USPHS grants, 62-66; chmn interdept coun aging, State of Vt, 63-69; mem adv comt, Northeast Regional Med Libr Serv, 70-74, chmn, 72; adv coun, Off Health Care Educ, Northeast Ctr Continuing Educ, 71- *Mem:* Fel Am Col Physicians; Am Diabetes Asn; Endocrine Soc; Am Fedn Clin Res; Am Soc Internal Med. *Mailing Add:* Univ Assocs in Med Univ of St Burlington VT 05401

WELSH, HARRY L, b Aurora, Ont, Mar 23, 10; m 42. ATOMIC PHYSICS, MOLECULAR PHYSICS. *Educ:* Univ Toronto, BA, 30, MA, 31, PhD(physics), 36. *Hon Degrees:* DSc, Univ Windsor, 64 & Mem Univ Nfld, 68. *Prof Exp:* From asst prof to assoc prof, 42-54, prof, 54-78, chmn dept, 62-68, EMER PROF PHYSICS, UNIV TORONTO, 78- *Honors & Awards:* Gold Medal, Can Asn Physicists, 61; Tory Medal, Royal Soc Can, 63; Officer, Order of Can, 72; Meggers Medal, Optical Soc Am, 74. *Mem:* Fel Am Phys Soc; fel Royal Soc Can; Royal Astron Soc; Can Asn Physicists (pres, 73-74); fel Optical Soc Am. *Res:* Infrared and Raman spectra, low temperature and high pressure spectroscopy. *Mailing Add:* Dept Physics Univ Toronto Toronto ON M5S 1A7 Can

WELSH, JAMES FRANCIS, b Pittsburgh, Pa, June 21, 30; m 55; c 5. ZOOLOGY. *Educ:* State Univ NY, BA, 53; Univ Calif, Los Angeles, PhD, 59. *Prof Exp:* Instr biol, St Mary's Col, 57-58; instr zool & human anat, Univ Calif, Los Angeles, 58-59; asst prof anat & physiol, 59-67, assoc prof physiol, 67-70, PROF ZOOL, HUMBOLDT STATE UNIV, 70- *Mem:* AAAS; Am Soc Parasitol; Wildlife Dis Asn. *Res:* Immunological research on Hymenolepis nana; enzyme systems of trematodes. *Mailing Add:* Dept of Zool Humboldt State Univ Arcata CA 95521

WELSH, JAMES RALPH, b Langdon, NDak, Sept 4, 33; m 52; c 4. PLANT BREEDING, PLANT GENETICS. *Educ:* NDak State Univ, BS, 56; Mont State Univ, PhD(plant genetics), 63. *Prof Exp:* Exten agt agron, NDak Exten Serv, 56-60; from asst prof to assoc prof, Mont State Univ, 63-68; assoc prof, Colo State Univ, 68-72, prof agron, 72-80; DEAN AGR & DIR, AGR EXP STA, MONT STATE UNIV, 80- *Mem:* Fel Am Soc Agron; Crop Sci Soc Am; Sigma Xi. *Res:* Wheat breeding and genetics; drought tolerance in winter wheat; high yielding cultivars. *Mailing Add:* Dean Agr Mont State Univ Bozeman MT 59717

WELSH, JOHN ELLIOTT, SR, b Berea, Ky, Nov 4, 27; m 65; c 3. GEOLOGY. *Educ:* Berea Col, AB, 50; Univ Wyo, MA, 51; Univ Utah, PhD(geol), 59. *Prof Exp:* Jr geologist, Magnolia Petrol Corp, 51; geologist, Shell Oil Co, 53-56; asst prof geol, Western State Col Colo, 56-61 & Colo State Univ, 61-62; res geologist, Kennecott Explor Inc, Salt Lake City, 70-79; CONSULT GEOLOGIST, 56-70 & 79- *Mem:* Am Asn Petrol Geol; Soc Econ Geol. *Res:* Structural and stratigraphic analysis of mining districts; stratigraphy of the overthrust belt in the western United States; nonmetallic geology. *Mailing Add:* 4780 Bonair St Holladay UT 84117

WELSH, LAWRENCE B, b Santa Barbara, Calif, Oct 21, 39; m 61; c 1. SOLID STATE PHYSICS. *Educ:* Pomona Col, BA, 61; Univ Calif, Berkeley, PhD(physics), 66. *Prof Exp:* Fel physics, Univ Pa, 66-68; asst prof, Northwestern Univ, Evanston, 68-74; group leader mat sci, 74-81, RES MGR, VOP, INC, 81- *Concurrent Pos:* Vis asst prof physics, Northwestern Univ, 74-75. *Mem:* Am Phys Soc; Am Vac Soc; Electrochem Soc; AAAS. *Res:* Ceramics; thin film depositions; fuel cell technology; nuclear magnetic resonance in metals. *Mailing Add:* Corp Res Ctr UOP Inc Des Plaines IL 60016

WELSH, MAURICE FITZWILLIAM, horticulture, see previous edition

WELSH, RICHARD STANLEY, b Philadelphia, Pa, Nov 15, 21; m 56; c 2. BIOCHEMISTRY. *Educ:* Harvard Col, SB, 43; Univ Pa, MS, 46; Stanford Univ, PhD(biochem, phys chem), 52. *Prof Exp:* Asst instr inorg anal, Univ Pa, 44-45; technician virus res, Rockefeller Inst, 46-47; res asst, Stanford Univ, 57-59; Am Heart Asn advan res fel, Univ Redlands, 59-61, Am Heart Asn estab investr, 61-64; Am Heart Asn estab investr, Univ Calif, Riverside, 64-65, Lab Molecular Biol, NIH, 65-66 & Brookhaven Nat Lab, 66-67; assoc scientist, Div Microbiol, Brookhaven Nat Lab, 67-68; RES ASSOC, INST MED, ATOMIC RES INST, W GER, 68- *Concurrent Pos:* Am Heart Asn res fel virus res, Univ Redlands, 57-59. *Mem:* Biophys Soc; NY Acad Sci. *Res:* Molecular characterization of DNA subunit fractions isolated nondegradatively from calf thymus, liver and other sources; polymerization reactions of the subunits with specific phosphopeptides, enzymes, adenosinetriphosphate and their biological significance; characterization of the phosphopeptides split out of DNA during its cleavage into subunits by reaction with chelating reagents and mechanism of the reaction. *Mailing Add:* Inst for Med Atomic Res Inst 517 Julich West Germany

WELSH, ROBERT EDWARD, b Pittsburgh, Pa, Oct 1, 32; m 56; c 3. PHYSICS. *Educ:* Georgetown Univ, BS, 54; Pa State Univ, PhD(physics), 60. *Prof Exp:* Res physicist, Carnegie Inst Technol, 60-63, asst dir nuclear res ctr, 62-63; assoc prof physics, 63-68, asst dir, Space Radiation Effects Lab, 67-72, PROF PHYSICS, COL WILLIAM & MARY, 68- *Concurrent Pos:* Consult, Langley Res Ctr, NASA, 64-66; guest scientist, Argonne Nat Lab & Brookhaven Nat Lab, 71-; res assoc, Rutherford Lab, Eng, 72-73. *Mem:* Fel Am Phys Soc; Am Asn Univ Prof. *Res:* Experimental nuclear physics; muon physics; exotic atoms. *Mailing Add:* Dept Physics Col William & Mary Williamsburg VA 23185

WELSH, RONALD, b Houston, Tex, Oct 13, 26; m 50; c 3. PATHOLOGY. *Educ:* Univ Tex, BA, 47, MD, 50; Am Bd Path, dipl, 55. *Prof Exp:* Asst prof path, Univ Tex Med Br Galveston, 55-57; from asst prof to assoc prof, 57-63, PROF PATH, SCH MED, LA STATE UNIV NEW ORLEANS, 63- *Concurrent Pos:* Pathologist, Univ Tex Med Br Hosps, Galveston, 55-57; sr vis pathologist, Charity Hosp, New Orleans, 57-, sect dir surg path; pathologist, Coroner's Off, Orleans Parish; path consult, Vet Admin Hosp, New Orleans. *Mem:* Am Soc Clin Path; Am Soc Exp Path; Am Asn Pathologists; Col Am Path; Int Acad Path. *Res:* Thyroid disease; electron microscopy, particularly of basic activities of inflammatory cells; oncology; surgical pathology. *Mailing Add:* Dept of Path La State Univ Med Ctr New Orleans LA 70112

WELSH, THOMAS LAURENCE, b Chicago, Ill, Nov 8, 32; m 60; c 3. FOOD SCIENCE, PHARMACEUTICAL CHEMISTRY. *Educ:* Univ Ill, BS, 59, PhD(pharmaceut chem), 63. *Prof Exp:* Res pharmacist, Miles Labs, Inc, 62-67; tech dir, Xttrium Labs, 67-69; V PRES RES & DEVELOP, MILES LABS, INC, 69- *Mem:* Soap & Detergent Asn. *Res:* Protein food products; effervescent pharmaceutical products; micronutrient delivery systems; human nutrition. *Mailing Add:* Miles Labs Inc 7123 W 65th St Chicago IL 60638

WELSH, WILLIAM JAMES, b Philadelphia, Pa, Dec 24, 47. THEORETICAL & PHYSICAL CHEMISTRY. *Educ:* St Joseph Col, BS, 69; Univ Pa, PhD(theoret phys chem), 75. *Prof Exp:* Instr chem, Univ Pa, 69-74; chemist, Procter & Gamble Co, 75-78; ASST PROF DEPT CHEM & PHYSICS, EDGECLIFF COL, 78- *Concurrent Pos:* Fel theoret polymer chem, Univ Cincinnati, 78- *Res:* Configuration, dependent properties and conformational energies of long chain molecules; statistical mechanics; intermolecular forces; theory of liquids; physical adsorption. *Mailing Add:* Dept of Chem & Physics 2220 Victory Pkwy Cincinnati OH 45206

WELSHIMER, HERBERT JEFFERSON, b West Mansfield, Ohio, Feb 23, 20; m 46; c 3. BACTERIOLOGY. *Educ:* Ohio State Univ, BSc, 43, PhD(bact), 47. *Prof Exp:* Asst med bact, Ohio State Univ, 44-46; instr bact, Ind Univ, 47-49; from asst prof to assoc prof, 49-68, PROF BACT, MED COL VA, VA COMMONWEALTH UNIV, 68- *Concurrent Pos:* USPHS fel, Ohio State Univ, 47; attend bacteriologist, Johnston-Willis Hosp, 54-; chmn subcomt listeria & related organisms, Int Comt Syst Bact, 74- *Mem:* AAAS; Am Soc Microbiol; fel Am Acad Microbiol; NY Acad Sci. *Res:* Clinical bacteriology; immunology; lysozyme; bacteriophage; bacterial cytology; listeriosis. *Mailing Add:* 7400 Biscayne Rd Richmond VA 23229

WELSHONS, WILLIAM JOHN, b Pitcairn, Pa, July 18, 22; m 49; c 4. GENETICS. *Educ:* Univ Calif, BA, 49, MA, 52, PhD(zool), 54. *Prof Exp:* Res assoc, Biol Div, Oak Ridge Nat Lab, 54-55, mem staff, 55-65; prof genetics & head dept, 65-75, PROF GENETICS, IOWA STATE UNIV, 75- *Concurrent Pos:* NSF sr fel, Santiago, Chile, 63-64; mem adv comt, Chem Rev Bd, State Iowa, 70-71. *Mem:* Genetics Soc Am; Am Inst Biol Sci; Sigma Xi; Am Soc Naturalists. *Res:* Gene structure recombination and cytogenetic analysis in Drosophila; mammalian sex determination and cytogenetics. *Mailing Add:* Dept of Genetics Iowa State Univ Ames IA 50011

WELSTEAD, WILLIAM JOHN, JR, b Newport News, Va, July 17, 35; m 57; c 3. ORGANIC CHEMISTRY. *Educ:* Univ Richmond, BS, 57; Univ Va, PhD(chem), 62. *Prof Exp:* Org chemist, Army Chem Ctr, Md, 62; NSF grant, Iowa State Univ, 63; res chemist, 64-72, assoc dir chem res, 72-73, DIR CHEM RES, A H ROBINS CO, 73- *Mem:* AAAS; Am Chem Soc. *Res:* Synthetic organic and medicinal chemistry; heterocyclics. *Mailing Add:* 1211 Sherwood Ave Richmond VA 23220

WELSTED, JOHN EDWARD, b Norwich, Eng, Dec 6, 35; m 62; c 2. PHYSICAL GEOGRAPHY. *Educ:* Bristol Univ, BSc, 58, cert educ, 61, PhD(geog), 71; McGill Univ, MSc, 60. *Prof Exp:* Asst master geog, Maidenhead Grammar Sch, Eng, 61-62; teacher, Oromocto High Sch, NB, 62-64; demonstr geog, Bristol Univ, 64-65; from asst prof to assoc prof, 65-78, PROF GEOG, BRANDON UNIV, 78- *Mem:* Can Asn Geog; Can Water Resources Asn; Asn Am Geog; Brit Geog Asn. *Res:* Glacial deposition in southwest Manitoba; rate of meander migration on rivers in southwest Manitoba; flooding by the rivers of southwest Manitoba. *Mailing Add:* Dept of Geog Brandon Univ Brandon MB R7A 6A9 Can

WELT, ISAAC DAVIDSON, b Montreal, Que, May 13, 22; nat US; m 45; c 3. INFORMATION SCIENCE, DOCUMENTATION. *Educ:* McGill Univ, BSc, 44, MSc, 45; Yale Univ, PhD(physiol chem), 49. *Prof Exp:* Instr chem, Sir George Williams Col, 46; lab asst anat, Yale Univ, 46-47, asst, Nutrit Lab, 47-48; instr chem, New Haven YMCA Jr Col, Conn, 48-49; asst, Div Physiol & Nutrit, Pub Health Res Inst New York, Inc, 49-51; asst prof biochem, Col Med, Baylor Univ, 51-53; res assoc pharmacol, Chem-Biol Coord Ctr, Nat Res Coun, Washington, DC, 53-55, dir cardiovasc lit proj, Div Med Sci, Nat Acad Sci-Nat Res Coun, 55-61; assoc dir & chief, Wash Br, Inst Advan Med Commun, 61-64; prog dir sci & tech info systs, 64-67, PROF INFO SCI, CTR TECHNOL & ADMIN, AM UNIV, 64- *Concurrent Pos:* Asst dir radioisotope unit, Vet Admin Hosp, Tex, 51-53; prof lectr chem, Am Univ, 56-61. *Mem:* AAAS; Am Chem Soc; Am Soc Info Sci. *Res:* Endocrine influences and isotopes in intermediary; metabolism; nutrition; medical and biological literature research; chemical-biological correlations; research administration; education in information science and documentation; information storage and retrieval systems. *Mailing Add:* Ctr Technol & Admin Am Univ Washington DC 20016

WELT, MARTIN A, b Brooklyn, NY, Oct 7, 32; m 62; c 3. NUCLEONICS. *Educ:* Clarkson Col, BChE, 54; Iowa State Univ, MS, 55; Mass Inst Technol, SM, 57; NC State Univ, PhD(physics), 64. *Prof Exp:* Reactor physicist, US AEC, Washington, DC, 57-58; supvr energy conversion sect, Chance Vought Corp, 59-61; pres, Int Sci Corp, NC, 61-67; PRES, RADIATION TECHNOL, INC, 68- *Concurrent Pos:* Lectr, George Washington Univ, 58; adj prof, Southern Methodist Univ, 60-62; asst prof, NC State Univ, 64-67; mem, Ames Lab, US AEC, 54-55; aeronaut res scientist, Lewis Lab, Nat Adv

Comt Aeronaut, 56; aeronaut res scientist, Union Carbide Co, Tenn, 56-66; dir, Adv Res Assocs, 62-63; mem, Working Comt, Proj Starfire, Southern Interstates Nuclear Bd, 64-65; dir, Nuclear Reactor Proj, NC State Univ, 64-66. *Mem:* AAAS; Am Nuclear Soc; Am Chem Soc; Am Phys Soc; Nat Soc Prof Eng. *Res:* Saline water conversion; radioisotope and radiation physics; plasma oscillations; radiation processing; design and analysis of nuclear facilities; hazards evaluation; thermoelectric energy conversion; nuclear research administration. *Mailing Add:* Radiation Technol Inc Lake Denmark Rd Rockaway NJ 07866

WELTER, ALPHONSE NICHOLAS, b Dudelange, Luxembourg, Apr 8, 25; US citizen; m 54; c 5. ANATOMY, HYDROBIOLOGY. *Educ:* Loras Col, AB, 52; Univ Ill, MS, 57, PhD(physiol), 59. *Prof Exp:* Instr physiol, Sch Med, Marquette Univ, 59-62; res physiologist, Lederle Div, Am Cyanamid Co, 62-67; RES SPECIALIST, 3M CO, 67- *Concurrent Pos:* USPHS fel, 59-61; Nat Heart Inst res fel, 61-62; grants, Wis Heart Asn, 60-61 & Am Heart Asn, 60-62. *Mem:* AAAS; assoc mem Am Physiol Soc; NY Acad Sci; Soc Environ Toxicol & Chem. *Res:* Cardiovascular physiology and pharmacology, specifically pulmonary circulation; respiratory and renal physiology. *Mailing Add:* Bldg 21- 2W(58) 3M Co Box 33331 St Paul MN 55133

WELTER, C JOSEPH, b Tiffin, Ohio, June 11, 32; m 55; c 3. MICROBIOLOGY, IMMUNOLOGY. *Educ:* King's Col, BS, 54; Univ Notre Dame, MS, 56; Mich State Univ, PhD, 59. *Prof Exp:* Asst zool, Univ Notre Dame, 54-56; asst parasitol, Mich State Univ, 56-59; dir res, Diamond Labs, Inc, 59-69, vpres res, 69-74; pres, Ambico, Inc, 74-77; MEM STAFF, DIAMOND LABS, 77- *Mem:* AAAS; Am Soc Parasitol; US Animal Health Asn; Am Soc Trop Med & Hyg; Am Soc Microbiol. *Res:* Protozoology; parasitology; virology. *Mailing Add:* Diamond Labs 2538 SE 43rd St Des Moines IA 50317

WELTER, DAVE ALLEN, b Lorain, Ohio, Aug 7, 36; m 64; c 2. CYTOGENETICS, CHROMOSOME STRUCTURE. *Educ:* Univ Ga, BS, 61; Med Col Ga, MS, 62, PhD(anat), 70. *Prof Exp:* Dir cytogenetics lab, Gracewood Hosp, 62-69; instr, 70-72, asst prof, 72-79, ASSOC PROF ANAT, MED COL GA, 79- *Concurrent Pos:* Cytogenetic consult, Ft Gordon Hosp, 65 & Gracewood Hosp, Ga, 69- *Res:* Birth defects; neuroanatomy; gross anatomy; embryology. *Mailing Add:* Dept of Anat Med Col of Ga Augusta GA 30902

WELTMAN, A STANLEY, physiology, endocrinology, see previous edition

WELTMAN, CLARENCE A, b New York, NY, Mar 17, 19; m 43; c 2. PHYSICAL CHEMISTRY, ORGANIC CHEMISTRY. *Educ:* NY Univ, BA, 40. *Prof Exp:* Assoc chemist, Explosives Res Lab, Nat Defense Res Comt, 41-45; res chemist, 45-49, chief chemist, 49-54, exec vpres & tech dir, 54-60, PRES, ALOX CORP, 60- *Concurrent Pos:* Vpres, RPM Inc, 80-, corp dir res & develop, 81- *Mem:* AAAS; Am Chem Soc; Am Soc Testing & Mat; Am Soc Lubrication Eng; Nat Asn Corrosion Eng. *Res:* Development of organic surface active agents and their application to problems of lubrication and corrosion prevention. *Mailing Add:* Alox Corp Buffalo Ave & Iroquois St Niagara Falls NY 14302

WELTMAN, JOEL KENNETH, b New York, NY, May 22, 33; m 56; c 2. IMMUNOLOGY, BIOCHEMISTRY. *Educ:* State Univ NY, MD, 58; Univ Colo, PhD(microbiol), 63; Brown Univ, MA, 72. *Prof Exp:* Intern, Ind Univ, 58-59; instr microbiol, Univ Colo, 63; asst prof, 66-70, ASSOC PROF MED, BROWN UNIV, 70- *Mem:* Am Chem Soc; Biophys Soc; Am Soc Biol Chemists; Am Soc Microbiol. *Res:* Immunology and protein chemistry. *Mailing Add:* Div of Biomed Sci Brown Univ Providence RI 02912

WELTNER, WILLIAM, JR, b Baltimore, Md, Dec 8, 22; m 47; c 3. PHYSICAL CHEMISTRY. *Educ:* Johns Hopkins Univ, BE, 43; Univ Calif, PhD(chem), 50. *Prof Exp:* Res asst, Hercules Powder Co, Del, 43-44 & Manhattan Proj, Columbia Univ, 44-46; fel, Univ Minn, 50; instr chem, Johns Hopkins Univ, 50-54; fel, Harvard Univ, 54-56; res chemist, Union Carbide Res Inst, Tarrytown, NY, 56-66; PROF CHEM, UNIV FLA, 66- *Concurrent Pos:* Mem opers res group, US Army Chem Ctr, 51-52; consult, Nat Bur Stand, 54. *Mem:* Am Chem Soc; Am Phys Soc. *Res:* Adsorption; thermodynamics; quantum and high temperature chemistry; spectroscopy. *Mailing Add:* Dept of Chem Univ of Fla Gainesville FL 32601

WELTON, ANN FRANCES, b Evanston, Ill, Oct 6, 47. PHARMACOLOGY, BIOCHEMISTRY. *Educ:* Lake Forest Col, BA, 69; Mich State Univ, PhD(biochem), 74. *Prof Exp:* Asst biochem dept, Mich State Univ, 69-74; fel lab nutrit & endocrinol, Nat Inst Health, 74-77; sr scientist pharmacol, 77-79, RES GROUP CHIEF, HOFFMANN-LA ROCHE, INC, 79- *Concurrent Pos:* NIH fel, Nat Res Serv Award, 74-77. *Mem:* AAAS; Biophys Soc; NY Acad Sci; Am Soc Pharm & Exp Therapeuts; Am Women Sci. *Res:* Membrane biochemistry; cyclic nucleotide metabolism; development of antiallergy agents; immunology; therapeutics for pulmonary and allergic diseases; arichidlonic acid metabolism; cyclic nucleotide metabolism; membrane biochemistry. *Mailing Add:* Dept of Pharmacol Hoffmann-La Roche Inc Nutley NJ 07110

WELTON, THEODORE ALLEN, b Saratoga Springs, NY, July 4, 18; m 43; c 4. THEORETICAL PHYSICS. *Educ:* Mass Inst Technol, BS, 39; Univ Ill, PhD(physics), 43. *Prof Exp:* Instr physics, Univ Ill, 43-44; jr scientist theoret physics, Los Alamos Sci Lab, 44-45; res assoc, Mass Inst Technol, 46-48; asst prof, Univ Pa, 48-50; prin physicist, 50-59, SR PHYSICIST, OAK RIDGE NAT LAB, 59-; FORD FOUND PROF PHYSICS, UNIV TENN, 63- *Mem:* Fel AAAS; fel Am Phys Soc; Electron Micros Soc Am. *Res:* Quantum theory of fields; theoretical nuclear physics; quantum theory of irreversible processes; theory of nuclear reactors and shielding; theory of particle accelerators; theory of lasers; theory of electron microscopy. *Mailing Add:* 121 Clark Lane Oak Ridge TN 37830

WELTON, WILLIAM ARCH, b Fairmont, WVa, June 21, 28; m 56; c 2. DERMATOLOGY. *Educ:* Harvard Univ, AB, 50; Univ Md, MD, 54. *Prof Exp:* CHMN DIV DERMAT, SCH MED, W VA UNIV, 61- *Concurrent Pos:* Osborne fel dermal path, 59-60. *Mem:* Am Acad Dermat. *Res:* Skin pathology. *Mailing Add:* Dept of Med WVa Univ Sch of Med Morgantown WV 26506

WELTY, JAMES RICHARD, b Garden City, Kans, Oct 23, 33; m 53; c 5. MECHANICAL ENGINEERING, CHEMICAL ENGINEERING. *Educ:* Ore State Univ, BS, 54, MS, 59, PhD(chem eng), 62. *Prof Exp:* Test engr, Pratt & Whitney Aircraft, 54; instr mech eng, 58-61, from asst prof to assoc prof, 62-67, PROF MECH ENG, ORE STATE UNIV, 67-, HEAD DEPT, 70- *Concurrent Pos:* Res engr, US Bur Mines, Ore, 62-64; mem tech staff, Bell Tel Labs, Pa, 64; vis prof, Thayer Sch Eng, Dartmouth Col, 67; res grants, US Environ Protection Agency, 68-71, US AEC, US Dept Energy & NSF, 69- *Mem:* Am Soc Mech Engrs. *Res:* Heat transfer; natural convection in liquid metals; non-Newtonian fluids in natural and forced flows; numerical modeling of thermal plumes; fluidized bed heat transfer. *Mailing Add:* Dept of Mech Eng Ore State Univ Corvallis OR 97331

WELTY, JOSEPH D, b Marion, Ind, Nov 22, 31; m 76; c 4. PHARMACOLOGY, PHYSIOLOGY. *Educ:* Purdue Univ, BS, 58; Univ SDak, MA, 62, PhD(pharmacol), 63. *Prof Exp:* Asst scientist, Dr Salisbury Labs, 58-61; instr pharmacol, 63-64, from asst prof to assoc prof physiol, 64-72, PROF PHYSIOL, SCH MED, UNIV SDAK, VERMILLION, 72- *Concurrent Pos:* Consult staff, Sacred Heart Hosp, Yankton, SDak, 67-; mem, Int Study Group Res Cardiac Metab. *Mem:* Soc Exp Biol & Med; Am Physiol Soc. *Res:* Cardiovascular physiology, contractile proteins in congestive heart failure and antiarrhythmias. *Mailing Add:* Dept Physiol Univ SDak Sch Med Vermillion SD 57069

WELTY, RONALD EARLE, b Winona, Minn, Dec 7, 34; m 62; c 2. PLANT PATHOLOGY. *Educ:* Winona State Univ, BS, 56; Univ Minn, MS, 61, PhD(plant path), 65. *Prof Exp:* Teacher high sch, Minn, 56-57 & 58-59; res asst plant path, Univ Minn, 59-61 & 62-65; instr bot & plant path, La State Univ, 62; res assoc, 65-66, asst prof, 66-70, assoc prof, 70-76, PROF PLANT PATH, NC STATE UNIV, 76-; PLANT PATHOLOGIST, SCI & EDUC ADMIN-AGR RES, USDA, 66- *Mem:* Sigma Xi; Mycol Soc Am; Am Phytopath Soc; Am Forage & Grassland Coun. *Res:* Diseases of forage crops; soil-borne fungus diseases; general phytopathology. *Mailing Add:* USDA Dept of Plant Path NC State Univ Raleigh NC 27607

WEMMER, DAVID EARL, b Sacramento, Calif, Aug 27, 51; m 75; c 2. MAGNETIC RESONANCE. *Educ:* Univ Calif, Davis, BS, 73, Berkeley, PhD(chem), 79. *Prof Exp:* Fel physics, Univ Dortmund, Fed Rep Ger, 78-79; RES ASSOC BIOPHYSICS, STANFORD MAGNETIC RESONANCE LAB, STANFORD UNIV, 79- *Mem:* Am Chem Soc. *Res:* Applications of magnetic resonance in biophysics; problems ofmolecular structure and dynamics. *Mailing Add:* Stanford Magnetic Resonance Lab 119 Org Chem Stanford Univ Stanford CA 84305

WEMPE, LAWRENCE KYRAN, organic chemistry, see previous edition

WEMPLE, STUART H(ARRY), b Rockford, Ill, July 27, 30; m 67; c 3. SOLID STATE PHYSICS, ELECTRICAL ENGINEERING. *Educ:* Northwestern Univ, BS, 53; Calif Inst Technol, MS, 54; Mass Inst Technol, PhD(elec eng), 63. *Prof Exp:* MEM TECH STAFF, BELL LABS, 54- *Mem:* Am Phys Soc; Inst Elec & Electronics Engrs. *Res:* Transport and optical properties of wide band gap semiconductors, including the effects of phase transition; gallium arsenide field-effect transistors and integrated circuits. *Mailing Add:* Bell Labs Rm 2D 421 PO Box 262 Murray Hill NJ 07974

WEMYSS, COURTNEY TITUS, JR, b Arlington, NJ, Dec 30, 22; m 51; c 3. ZOOLOGY. *Educ:* Swarthmore Col, AB, 47; Rutgers Univ, PhD, 51. *Prof Exp:* Asst zool, Rutgers Univ, 47-51; res fel bact & immunol, Harvard Med Sch, 51-52; asst prof biol, Loyola Univ, 53-54; instr physiol, NY Med Col, 54-60; assoc prof, 60-70, PROF BIOL, HOFSTRA UNIV, 70- *Concurrent Pos:* Guest investr, Rockefeller Inst, 60- *Mem:* NY Acad Sci. *Res:* Invertebrate immunity; comparative serology; tissue specificity. *Mailing Add:* Dept of Biol Hofstra Univ Hempstead NY 11550

WEN, CHIN-YUNG, b Taiwan, Dec 5, 28. CHEMICAL ENGINEERING. *Educ:* Nat Taiwan Univ, BS, 51, WVa Univ, MSChE, 53, PhD, 56. *Prof Exp:* From instr to assoc prof, 54-63, chmn dept, 69-81, PROF CHEM ENG, WVA UNIV, 63- *Concurrent Pos:* Ad hoc panelist direct combustion of coal, Nat Res Coun, 76-77. *Honors & Awards:* Alcoa Award, Alcoa Found, 76, 77 & 78. *Mem:* Am Chem Soc; Am Inst Chem Engrs; Chem Eng Soc Japan. *Res:* Heat and mass transfer; solid-gas and solid-liquid contacting; reaction engineering; optimization; coal conversion technologies. *Mailing Add:* Dept of Chem Eng WVa Univ Morgantown WV 26506

WEN, HENRY L, b Nanking, China, Feb 2, 17; US citizen; m 45; c 2. MECHANICAL ENGINEERING. *Educ:* St John's Univ China, AB, 38; Univ Ind, MA, 40, PhD, 43; Harvard Univ, MBA, 42; Cath Univ, BME, 60; Newark Col Eng, MSME, 65. *Prof Exp:* Vpres, Yung Heng Mach Work, 36-39; pres, Yuen Neng Chem Works, 48-49; tech expert, Dept Agr & Labor, Formosa, 50-53; asst proj engr, Wright Aeronaut Div, Curtiss-Wright Corp, 60-66; proj engr, Stravos Div, Fairchild-Hiller Corp, 66-67; SR STAFF ENGR IN CHG APPLNS RES, SINGER-KEARFOTT AEROSPACE DIV, LITTLE FALLS, 67- *Concurrent Pos:* Pres, Kin Foong Enamel Ware Mfr, 47-50; adj prof indust eng, Fairleigh Dickinson Univ & adj prof mech technol, NY Inst Technol, 64-80. *Honors & Awards:* Incentive Awards, Curtiss-Wright Corp, 63 & 64. *Mem:* Nat Soc Prof Engrs; Am Ord Asn; Am Mgt Asn. *Res:* High precision and nontraditional machining processes. *Mailing Add:* 241 River Rd Bogata NJ 07603

WEN, RICHARD YUTZE, b Shanghai, China, Mar 17, 30; m 62; c 2. ORGANIC POLYMER CHEMISTRY. *Educ:* Wesleyan Univ, BA, 51; Univ Mich, MS, 53; Ind Univ, PhD(org chem), 62. *Prof Exp:* Chemist, Nalco Chem Co, 53-56; res chemist, Dow Chem Co, Mich, 62-69; sr chemist, 69-74, res specialist, Cent Res Labs, 74-78, RES SPECIALIST, MAGNETIC TAPE DIV, 3M CO, 78- *Mem:* AAAS; Am Chem Soc. *Res:* Coating technology. *Mailing Add:* Bldg 236-2C 3M Ctr 3M Co St Paul MN 55101

WEN, SUNG-FENG, b Hsinchu, Taiwan, Mar 3, 33; US citizen; m 66; c 2. MEDICINE. *Educ:* Nat Taiwan Univ, MB, 58. *Prof Exp:* Intern med, Univ Louisville, 62-63; resident, Chicago Med Sch, 63-64; res fel nephrol, Univ Wis-Madison, 64-66, instr, 66-67; res fel renal physiol, McGill Univ, 67-70; asst prof med, 70-74, assoc prof, 74-79, Rennebohm Prof, 75-80, PROF MED, UNIV WIS-MADISON, 79- *Concurrent Pos:* Mem coun kidney cardiovasc dis, Am Heart Asn. *Mem:* Am Fedn Clin Res; Am Soc Nephrol; Int Soc Nephrol; Nat Kidney Found. *Res:* Renal physiology and pathophysiology, especially related to renal transport of sodium, potassium, phosphate and glucose under normal and abnormal conditions using micropuncture techniques. *Mailing Add:* 600 Highland Ave Madison WI 53792

WEN, WEN-YANG, b Hsin-tsu, Taiwan, Mar 7, 31; m 59; c 2. PHYSICAL CHEMISTRY. *Educ:* Nat Taiwan Univ, BS, 53; Univ Pittsburgh, PhD(chem), 57. *Prof Exp:* Res assoc, Univ Pittsburgh, 57-58; res fel, Northwestern Univ, 58-60; asst prof chem, DePaul Univ, 60-62; from asst prof to assoc prof, 62-73, PROF CHEM, CLARK UNIV, 73- *Concurrent Pos:* Humboldt scholar, Univ Karlsruhe, 70-71 & 73, Univ Goettingen, 76 & Morgantown Energy Technol Ctr, DOE, 78-79. *Mem:* Am Chem Soc; Am Asn Univ Prof; AAAS; Sigma Xi; NY Acad Sci. *Res:* Structure of water; themodynamic properties of large ions in solutions; tetraalkylammonium salts and hydrophobic bonds; nuclear magnetic resonance; alkali metal catalysis on coal gasification; thermal and catalytic cracking of coal tars. *Mailing Add:* Dept of Chem Clark Univ Worcester MA 01610

WEND, DAVID VAN VRANKEN, b Poughkeepsie, NY, Oct 18, 23; m 53; c 3. MATHEMATICS. *Educ:* Univ Mich, BS, 45, MA, 46, PhD(math), 55. *Prof Exp:* Instr math, Reed Col, 49-51 & Iowa State Univ, 52-55; from asst prof to assoc prof, Univ Utah, 55-66; assoc prof, 66-67, PROF MATH, MONT STATE UNIV, 67- *Mem:* Am Math Soc. *Res:* Functions of a complex variable; differential equations. *Mailing Add:* Dept Math Mont State Univ Bozeman MT 59717

WENDE, CHARLES DAVID, b Wilmington, Del, Dec 4, 41; m 65; c 1. SPACE PHYSICS. *Educ:* Mass Inst Technol, BS, 63; Univ Iowa, MS, 66, PhD(physics), 68. *Prof Exp:* Res assoc space physics, Univ Iowa, 68-69; ASTROPHYSICIST, GODDARD SPACE FLIGHT CTR, NASA, 69- *Mem:* AAAS; Am Geophys Union; Int Union Radio Sci. *Res:* Solar x-ray and radio astronomy; x-ray astronomy; application of interactive computing to modeling experiment hardware and to data reduction and analysis. *Mailing Add:* 8700 Nightingale Dr Seabrook MD 20801

WENDEL, CARLTON TYRUS, b Fredericksburg, Tex, Oct 6, 39; m 63; c 2. ANALYTICAL CHEMISTRY. *Educ:* Tex Lutheran Col, BS, 62; Tex Tech Col, MS, 65, PhD(chem), 67. *Prof Exp:* Instr, 67-69, asst prof, 69-80, ASSOC PROF CHEM, TEX WOMAN'S UNIV, 80- *Mem:* Am Chem Soc; Sigma Xi. *Res:* Chemical aspects of water pollution. *Mailing Add:* Dept of Chem Tex Woman's Univ Denton TX 76204

WENDEL, HERBERT A, b Ludwigshafen, Ger, Feb 17, 14; nat US; m 44; c 3. PHARMACOLOGY, INTERNAL MEDICINE. *Educ:* Univ Berlin, DrMed, 39. *Prof Exp:* Res asst pharmacol, Univ Berlin, 46-49; lectr, Univ Mainz, 50-51; res assoc, Univ Pa, 52-56; asst sect head, Smith Kline & French Labs, 56-60; consult, Farbenfabriken Bayer, Ger, 60-61; mgr clin eval, E I du Pont de Nemours & Co, 61-64; dir res, Warren-Teed Pharmaceut Inc, Ohio, 64-68; assoc prof pharmacol, 68-76, prof, 76-79, EMER PROF PHARMACOL, MED SCH, UNIV ORE, 79- *Mem:* AAAS; Am Soc Pharmacol & Exp Therapeut; Am Soc Clin Pharmacol & Therapeut; Ger Pharmacol Soc. *Res:* Drug research; clinical drug investigation. *Mailing Add:* Dept of Pharm Univ of Ore Med Sch Portland OR 97201

WENDEL, JAMES GUTWILLIG, b Portland, Ore, Apr, 18, 22; m 44; c 6. MATHEMATICS. *Educ:* Reed Col, BA, 43; Calif Inst Technol, PhD(math), 48. *Prof Exp:* Asst Nat Defense Res Comt, Calif Inst Technol, 42-45, instr, 45-48; instr math, Yale Univ, 48-51; assoc mathematician, Rand Corp, 51-52; from asst prof to assoc prof math, La State Univ, 52-55; from asst prof to assoc prof, 55-61, assoc chmn dept, 68-70 & 79-, PROF MATH, UNIV MICH, ANN ARBOR, 61- *Concurrent Pos:* Vis prof, Aarhus Univ, 62-64, Univ London, 70-71, Univ WAustralia, 78 & Calif Inst Technol, 79. *Mem:* Am Math Soc; Math Asn Am; Inst Math Statist. *Res:* Probability theory. *Mailing Add:* Dept of Math Univ of Mich Ann Arbor MI 48109

WENDEL, MARTIN M(AURICE), chemical engineering, see previous edition

WENDEL, OTTO THEODORE, JR, b Philadelphia, Pa, Mar 21, 48; m 69; c 1. NEUROPHARMACOLOGY, CARDIOVASCULAR PHARMACOLOGY. *Educ:* St Andrews Col, BA, 69; Wake Forest Univ, MS, 73, PhD(pharmacol), 74. *Prof Exp:* Instr neuropharmacol, Dept Neurol, Bowman Gray Sch Med, 74-76, instr pharmacol, 76-78, asst prof, 78-79; ASST PROF PHARMACOL, DEPT PHARMACOL, KIRKSVILLE COL OSTEOP MED, 79- *Concurrent Pos:* Assoc community med, Bowman Gray Sch Med, 74-79. *Mem:* Sigma Xi; Soc Neurosci. *Res:* The relationship between endogneous opioid activity and the genesis and or maintenance of hypertension. *Mailing Add:* Dept Pharmacol Kirksville Col Osteop Med Kirksville MO 63501

WENDEL, SAMUEL REECE, b Charleston, Ill, Sept 1, 44; m 67; c 3. BIOINORGANIC CHEMISTRY, ORGANOMETALLIC CHEMISTRY. *Educ:* Univ Ill, Urbana, BS, 66; Univ Mont, PhD(org chem), 73. *Prof Exp:* Chemist, 66-69, SR PROJ CHEMIST ORGANOSILICON CHEM, DOW CORNING CORP, 73- *Mem:* AAAS; Am Chem Soc. *Res:* Design and synthesis of bioactive organosilicon compounds; silicone biomaterials. *Mailing Add:* Dow Corning Corp Midland MI 48640

WENDELKEN, JOHN FRANKLIN, b Lexington, Ky, Nov 12, 45; m 68; c 2. SURFACE & SOLID STATE PHYSICS. *Educ:* Univ Ill, BS, 68, MS, 70, PhD(physics), 75. *Prof Exp:* PHYSICIST SURFACE PHYSICS, OAK RIDGE NAT LAB, 74- *Mem:* Am Phys Soc; Am Vacuum Soc; Am Chem Soc. *Res:* Geometric, electronic and ribrational properties of clean and absorbate covered single crystal surfaces. *Mailing Add:* Solid State Div Oak Ridge Nat Lab PO Box X Oak Ridge TN 37830

WENDEN, HENRY EDWARD, b New York, NY, Nov 24, 16; m 43; c 4. MINERALOGY. *Educ:* Yale Univ, BS, 38; Harvard Univ, MA, 50, PhD, 58. *Prof Exp:* Instr physics & geol, Boston Univ, 49-53; asst prof mineral & geol, Tufts Univ, 53-57; from asst prof to assoc prof mineral, 57-63, PROF MINERAL, OHIO STATE UNIV, 63- *Concurrent Pos:* Res assoc, Harvard Univ, 58. *Honors & Awards:* Neil Miner Award, Nat Asn Geol Teachers, 61. *Mem:* Fel Mineral Soc Am; Nat Asn Geol Teachers; Mineral Asn Can. *Res:* Crystal chemistry; history of mineralogy and crystallography; x-ray crystallography; crystal morphology; physical and electrical properties of crystals. *Mailing Add:* Dept Geol & Mineral Ohio State Univ 104 W 19th Ave Columbus OH 43210

WENDER, IRVING, b New York, NY, June 19, 15; m 42; c 3. FUEL SCIENCE, ORGANOMETALLIC CHEMISTRY. *Educ:* City Col New York, BS, 36; Columbia Univ, MA, 45; Univ Pittsburgh, PhD(chem), 50. *Prof Exp:* Chemist & res assoc, Manhattan Proj, Univ Chicago, 44-46; org chemist, Pittsburgh Coal Res Ctr, US Bur Mines, 46-53, chief chem sect, 53-71, res dir, Pittsburgh Energy Res Ctr, Energy Res & Develop Admin, 71-75, dir, 75-77, dir, Pittsburgh Energy Technol Ctr, Dept Energy, 77-78, spec adv to prog dir fossil energy, 78-79, dir, Off Advan Res & Technol, Off Fossil Energy, 79-81; RES PROF, DETP CHEM/PETROL ENG, UNIV PITTSBURGH, 81- *Concurrent Pos:* Lectr, Univ Pittsburgh, 63-69, adj prof, 69-78. *Honors & Awards:* Bituminuous Coal Res Award, 56, 60; H H Storch Award, 64; Pittsburgh Award, Am Chem Soc, 68; K K Kelley Award, 69; Career Serv Award, Nat Civil Serv League, 76; Award, Am Chem Soc, 82. *Mem:* Am Chem Soc; The Chem Soc. *Res:* Chemistry of carbon monoxide, metal carbonyls, coal conversion; catalysis; reactions at high pressures; synthetic fuels from coal; carbon monoxide chemistry. *Mailing Add:* Dept Chem/Petrol Eng 1249 Benedum Hall Univ Pittsburgh Pittsburgh PA 15261

WENDER, PAUL H, b New York, NY, May 12, 34; m 70; c 3. PSYCHIATRY, CHILD PSYCHIATRY. *Educ:* Harvard Univ, AB, 55; Columbia Univ, MD, 59. *Prof Exp:* Intern, Barnes Hosp, St Louis, 59-60; resident adult psychiat, Mass Ment Health Ctr, 60-62; resident, St Elizabeth's Hosp, 62-63; resident child psychiat, Johns Hopkins Univ, 64-67, asst prof pediat & psychiat, 67-73; PROF PSYCHIAT, COL MED, UNIV UTAH, 73- *Concurrent Pos:* NIMH fel, NIH, Bethesda, Md, 64-66, res psychiatrist, 67-73. *Honors & Awards:* Hofheimer Award, Am Psychiat Asn, 74. *Mem:* Am Psychiat Asn; Am Acad Child Psychiat; Psychiat Res Soc. *Res:* Genetics and schizophrenia; minimal brain dysfunction in children. *Mailing Add:* Dept of Psychiat Univ of Utah Col of Med Salt Lake City UT 84132

WENDER, SIMON HAROLD, b Dalton, Ga, Sept 4, 13; m 42; c 3. BIOCHEMISTRY. *Educ:* Emory Univ, AB, 34, MS, 35; Univ Minn, PhD(agr biochem), 38. *Prof Exp:* Res assoc, Med Sch, Emory Univ, 38-39; assoc chemist, Exp Sta, Agr & Mech Col, Tex, 39-41; from instr to asst prof chem, Univ Ky, 41-46; assoc prof biochem, 46-49, prof, 49-53, RES PROF BIOCHEM, UNIV OKLA, 53- *Concurrent Pos:* Former mem bd dirs, Oak Ridge Assoc Univs; past chmn coun, Oak Ridge Inst Nuclear Studies, Okla, rep to coun, 52-64 & 71-80; vis res assoc, Argonne Nat Lab, 54-64; vis prof, Univ Wis, 66. *Mem:* Fel AAAS; Am Chem Soc; Am Soc Biol Chem; Soc Exp Biol & Med; Am Soc Plant Physiol. *Res:* Chromatography; plant phenolics and plant and animal oxidoreductases. *Mailing Add:* Dept Chem 620 Parrington Oval Univ Okla Norman OK 73019

WENDLAND, RAY THEODORE, b Minneapolis, Minn, July 11, 11; m 46; c 1. ORGANIC CHEMISTRY. *Educ:* Carleton Col, BA, 33; Iowa State Univ, PhD(chem), 37. *Prof Exp:* Res chemist, Universal Oil Prod Co, 38-39; instr org chem & biochem, Coe Col, 39-42; asst prof, Middlebury Col, 42-43; res chemist synthetic rubber, War Prod Bd, Univ Minn, 43-44; asst prof org & biol chem, Lehigh Univ, 44-47; prof org chem, NDak State Univ, 47-55; res fel petrol chem, Mellon Inst, 55-58; prof chem & chmn div sci & math, Winona State Col, 58-63; prof chem, 63-76, EMER PROF CHEM, CARROLL COL, WIS, 76- *Concurrent Pos:* Consult. *Mem:* AAAS; Am Chem Soc; Sigma Xi. *Res:* Organic synthesis; polymer and petroleum chemistry. *Mailing Add:* W230S2354 Morningside Dr Waukesha WI 53186

WENDLAND, WAYNE MARCEL, b Beaver Dam, Wis, Aug 9, 34; m 56; c 4. METEOROLOGY, PALEOCLIMATOLOGY. *Educ:* Lawrence Col, BA, 56; Univ Wis-Madison, MS, 65, PhD(meteorol), 72. *Prof Exp:* Proj supvr meteorol, Univ Wis-Madison, 66-70, instr climat, 70, asst prof geog & meteor, 70-76; assoc prof geog, Univ Ill, Urbana, 76-80; HEAD, CLIMAT SECT, ILL STATE WATER SURV, 80- *Concurrent Pos:* Adj assoc prof geog, Univ Ill, Urbana. *Mem:* AAAS; Am Meteorol Soc; Am Quaternary Asn; Sigma Xi; Tree Ring Soc (vpres, 74-). *Res:* Past climatic circulation patterns; climatic episodes of the Holocene; climatic reconstructions from tree rings; climatic variability. *Mailing Add:* Ill State Water Surv Box 5050 Sta A Champaign IL 61820

WENDLAND, WOLFGANG LEOPOLD, b Poznan, Poland, Sept 20, 36; Ger citizen; m 64; c 2. MATHEMATICS, MECHANICAL ENGINEERING. *Educ:* Tech Univ, Berlin, BS(mech eng), 58, BS(math), 58, dipl ing, 61, Dr Ing, 65, Habilitation, 69. *Prof Exp:* Sci collabr, Tech Univ Berlin, 61-63, sci asst, 63-64; sci asst dept numerical math, Hahn Meitner Inst, Berlin, 64-69, prof, 69-70; PROF, TECH UNIV DARMSTADT, 70- *Concurrent Pos:* Vis unidel chair prof, Univ Del, 73-74; chmn math dept, Tech Univ Darmstadt, 74-75; Fulbright Stipendium, Univ Del, 77-; vis prof, Ore State Univ, 77-, Univ Md, 81, Univ Del, 81, Univ Concepcion, Chile, 81. *Mem:* Am Math Soc; Ger Asn Appl Math Mech; Soc Appl Math Mech; Int Soc Interaction Mech Math; Int Soc Comp Mech Eng. *Res:* Applied mathematics; partial differential equations; mathematical physics. *Mailing Add:* Dieburger St 34 6104 Seeheim Malchen West Germany

WENDLANDT, WESLEY W, b Galesville, Wis, Nov 20, 27. INORGANIC CHEMISTRY, ANALYTICAL CHEMISTRY. *Educ:* Wis State Col, River Falls, BS, 50; Univ Iowa, MS, 52, PhD(chem), 54. *Prof Exp:* From asst prof to prof chem, Tex Tech Col, 54-66; chmn dept, 66-72, PROF CHEM, UNIV HOUSTON, 66- *Concurrent Pos:* Vis prof, NMex Highlands Univ, 61; ed-in-chief, Thermochimica Acta. *Honors & Awards:* Mettler Award, 70. *Mem:* AAAS; Am Chem Soc; The Chem Soc; NAm Thermal Anal Soc; Int Confedn Thermal Anal. *Res:* Coordination compounds; metal chelates; thermogravimetry; differential thermal analysis; solid state chemistry; reflectance spectroscopy. *Mailing Add:* Dept of Chem Univ of Houston Houston TX 77004

WENDLER, GERD DIERK, b Hamburg, WGer, June 16, 39; m 69; c 2. METEOROLOGY. *Educ:* Innsbruck Univ, PhD(meteorol), 64. *Prof Exp:* Data process asst meteorol, Inst Meteorol, Innsbruck Univ, 60-64, res asst, 65-66; asst geophysicist, 66-67, asst prof meteorol, 67-70, ASSOC PROF METEOROL, GEOPHYS INST, UNIV ALASKA, FAIRBANKS, 70- *Concurrent Pos:* NSF grant, McCall Glacier, Geophys Inst, Univ Alaska, Fairbanks, 69-, Sea grant Arctic Ocean, 71- & NASA satellite grant cent Alaska, 72- *Mem:* Am Meteorol Soc; Am Geophys Union; Glaciol Soc; Arctic Inst NAm; Ger Soc Polar Res. *Res:* Meteorology in the arctic, especially of Alaska. *Mailing Add:* Geophys Inst Univ of Alaska Fairbanks AK 99701

WENDLER, HENRY O, b Red Bluff, Calif, Apr 30, 24; div; c 4. FISH BIOLOGY, FISHERIES MANAGEMENT. *Educ:* Univ Wash, BS, 51. *Prof Exp:* Aquatic biologist, Wash Dept Fisheries, 51-64, sr biologist, 64-75, mgr, Off Intergovt Opers, 75-77, asst dir intergovt opers, 78-79; FISHERY CONSULT, 79- *Concurrent Pos:* Lectr, Univ Wash, 68-78. *Mem:* Fel Am Inst Fishery Res Biol; Pac Fishery Biologists. *Res:* Fisheries development. *Mailing Add:* Pac Marine Fisheries Comn 528 SW Mill St Portland OR 97201

WENDLER, NORMAN LORD, b Stockton, Calif, Dec 18, 15; m 47; c 2. ORGANIC CHEMISTRY. *Educ:* Middlebury Col, AB, 37; Rutgers Univ, MSc, 39; Univ Mich, PhD(org chem), 44. *Prof Exp:* Res chemist, Merck & Co, Inc, 39-41; Lilly fel, Harvard Univ, 45-46; Swiss-Am exchange fel, Univ Basel, 46-47; res chemist, 47-69, sr investr, Res Labs, 69-74, SR SCIENTIST, MERCK SHARP & DOHME RES LABS, MERCK & CO, INC, 74- *Honors & Awards:* Buck Whitney Medal, Am Chem Soc, 77. *Res:* Synthesis in the field of natural products. *Mailing Add:* Merck Sharp & Dohme Res Labs PO Box 2000 Rahway NJ 07065

WENDRICKS, ROLAND N, b Casco, Wis, July 26, 30; m 52; c 4. PHYSICAL CHEMISTRY. *Educ:* St Norbert Col, BS, 52; Northwestern Univ, MS, 61. *Prof Exp:* Group supvr blow molding process, 52-67, supvr blow molding plastics res & develop, 67-70, MGR PLASTICS EQUIP ENG, AM CAN CO, 70- *Mem:* Soc Plastics Eng. *Res:* Processing of thermoplastic polymers. *Mailing Add:* Am Can Co 1350 S River Rd Batavia IL 60510

WENDROFF, BURTON, b New York, NY, Mar 10, 30. MATHEMATICS. *Educ:* NY Univ, BA, 51, PhD(math), 58; Mass Inst Technol, SM, 52. *Prof Exp:* Staff mem, Los Alamos Sci Lab, 52-66; from assoc prof to prof math, Univ Denver, 66-74; GROUP LEADER & STAFF MEM, LOS ALAMOS SCI LAB, 73- *Mem:* Am Math Soc; Soc Indust & Appl Math. *Res:* Applied mathematics; numerical analysis. *Mailing Add:* Los Alamos Sci Lab Group T-7 MS 233 Los Alamos NM 87545

WENDT, ARNOLD, b Red Bud, Ill, Jan 14, 22; m 43; c 1. MATHEMATICS. *Educ:* Univ Wis, PhD(math), 52. *Prof Exp:* PROF MATH, WESTERN ILL UNIV, 52- *Mem:* AAAS; Am Math Soc; Math Asn Am. *Res:* Analysis and applied mathematics. *Mailing Add:* Dept of Math Western Ill Univ Macomb IL 61455

WENDT, CHARLES WILLIAM, b Plainview, Tex, July 12, 31; m 55; c 4. SOIL PHYSICS. *Educ:* Tex A&M Univ, BS, 51, PhD(soil physics), 66; Tex Tech Col, MS, 57. *Prof Exp:* Res asst agron, Tex Tech Col, 53-55, from instr to asst prof, 57-63; res asst soil physics, 63-65, res assoc, 65-66, from asst prof to assoc prof, 66-74, PROF SOIL PHYSICS, TEX A&M UNIV, 74- *Concurrent Pos:* Off Water Resources Res US Dept Interior res grant, Agr Res & Exten Ctr, Tex A&M Univ, 67-70 & Environ Protection Agency res grant, Veg Res Sta, 70-76; mem, Brit Plant Growth Regulator Group, 81. *Mem:* AAAS; Am Soc Agron; Soil Sci Soc Am; Am Soc Plant Physiol. *Res:* Efficient utilization of rainfall and irrigation water for crop production; plant modification for more efficient water use. *Mailing Add:* Tex Agr Exp Sta Tex A&M Univ Agr Res & Exten Ctr Rt 3 Lubbock TX 79401

WENDT, JOST O L, b Berlin, Ger, July 2, 41; m 61; c 2. CHEMICAL ENGINEERING, COMBUSTION. *Educ:* Glasgow Univ, BSc, 63; Johns Hopkins Univ, MSE, 66, PhD(chem eng), 68. *Prof Exp:* Instr thermodyn, Johns Hopkins Univ, 66-67; engr, Emeryville Res Ctr, Shell Develop Co, Calif, 68-72; asst prof, 72-75, assoc prof, 75-79, PROF CHEM ENG, UNIV ARIZ, 79- *Concurrent Pos:* Consult in combustion appln. *Mem:* Am Inst Chem Engrs; Combustion Inst; Int Flame Res Found. *Res:* Combustion generated air pollution; pollution aspects of burner design; coal combustion; kinetics; combustion science. *Mailing Add:* Dept of Chem Eng Univ of Ariz Tucson AZ 85721

WENDT, RICHARD P, b St Louis, Mo, Oct 6, 32; m 70; c 2. PHYSICAL CHEMISTRY, TRANSPORT PROCESSES. *Educ:* Washington Univ, AB, 54; Univ Wis, PhD(phys chem), 61. *Prof Exp:* Asst prof chem, La State Univ, 62-66; assoc prof, 66-73, PROF CHEM, LOYOLA UNIV, NEW ORLEANS, 73- *Concurrent Pos:* Consult res div, Vet Admin Hosp, New Orleans, 66-, NIH res fel, 71; consult, Gulf South Res Inst, 73- *Mem:* AAAS. *Res:* Diffusion in liquids; nonequilibrium thermodynamics; mass transfer across synthetic membranes. *Mailing Add:* 7312 Windsor New Orleans LA 70123

WENDT, ROBERT CHARLES, b Aurora, Ill, July 5, 29; m 53; c 4. SURFACE & POLYMER CHEMISTRY. *Educ:* NCent Col, Ill, BA, 51; Univ Ill, PhD(phys chem), 55. *Prof Exp:* Res chemist, Yerkes Lab, Film Dept, 55-64, staff scientist, 64-69, staff scientist, Exp Sta Lab, Film Dept, 69-75, sr res chemist, 76-81, RES ASSOC, EXP STA LAB, PLASTICS, PROD & RESINS DEPT, E I DU PONT DE NEMOURS & CO, INC, 81- *Mem:* Am Chem Soc; Am Vacuum Soc; Elec Micros Soc Am. *Res:* Diffusion phenomena; polymer physical properties; adhesion; polymer surface chemistry and physics; electron spectroscopy. *Mailing Add:* 3316 Coachman Rd Wilmington DE 19803

WENDT, ROBERT L(OUIS), b Chicago, Ill, July 10, 20; m 46. ENGINEERING. *Educ:* Harvard Univ, AB, 40. *Prof Exp:* Eng, Sperry Gyroscope Co, 40-52, mgr eng, 52-57, mgr sales & subcontracts, 57-62, mgr B-58 bomb navig syst prog, 62-63, dir prog control, 63-64, mgr, Polaris/Poseidon, 64-69, group mgr ship & mil systs, 69-71, vpres & gen mgr, Systs Mgt, 71-75, vpres & gen mgr, Gyroscope, 75-80, PRES, SPERRY DIV, SPERRY CORP, 80- *Mem:* Sr mem Inst Elec & Electronics Engrs; Inst Navig; Am Soc Naval Engrs. *Res:* Management of major programs, especially development and production of complex electronic systems. *Mailing Add:* Sperry Div Hq Sperry Corp Great Neck NY 11020

WENDT, THEODORE MIL, b Ft Collins, Colo, Sept 14, 40; m 63; c 2. MICROBIOLOGY, CHEMISTRY. *Educ:* Colo State Univ, BS, 64, MS, 66, PhD(microbiol), 68. *Prof Exp:* Res microbiologist, US Army Natick Labs, Res & Develop Command, 68-78; mgr microbiol, Arbook, Inc, 78-80; MGR MICROBIOL, SURGIKOS, INC, 81- *Mem:* Am Soc Microbiol; Sigma Xi; AAAS; Soc Indust Microbiol. *Res:* Microbiological deterioration of materials, especially polymers; water pollution abatement through biological activity; relationship of chemical structure to biological susceptibility; aquatic microbial ecology; disinfectants; biocides in health care; clinical environments; clinical research and toxicology. *Mailing Add:* 5400 Overridge Dr Arlington TX 76017

WENESER, JOSEPH, b New York, NY, Nov 23, 22; m 56. THEORETICAL PHYSICS. *Educ:* City Col, BS, 42; Columbia Univ, MA, 48, PhD(physics), 52. *Prof Exp:* Asst physics, Manhattan Proj, Columbia Univ, 42-46; assoc physicist, Brookhaven Nat Lab, 52-55; asst prof, Univ Ill, 55-57; chmn dept physics, 70-75, SR PHYSICIST, BROOKHAVEN NAT LAB, 57- *Mem:* Fel Am Phys Soc. *Res:* Theoretical nuclear physics. *Mailing Add:* Dept of Physics Bldg 510A Brookhaven Nat Lab Upton NY 11973

WENG, LIH-JYH, b Fukien, China, Dec 3, 37; m 66; c 2. ELECTRICAL ENGINEERING, COMPUTER SCIENCE. *Educ:* Cheng Kung Univ, Taiwan, BS, 59; Northeastern Univ, MSEE, 63, PhD(elec eng), 66. *Prof Exp:* Res engr, Adcom, Inc, 65-66; sr res assoc coding theory, Northeastern Univ, 66-67, from asst prof to assoc prof elec eng, 67-73; sr eng specialist, CNR, Inc, 73-78; CONSULT ENGR, DIGITAL EQUIP CORP, 78- *Concurrent Pos:* NSF initiation grant, 68-69; consult, Honeywell Info Systs Inc, Mass, 70-71; lectr, Northeastern Univ, 73- *Mem:* Inst Elec & Electronics Engrs. *Res:* Algebraic coding theory; digital communications; mass storage techniques in computers; error-control; communication theory. *Mailing Add:* Digital Equip Corp 146 Main St Maynard MA 01754

WENG, SHU-HAUN, b Taiwan, Oct 27, 50; m 80. ANALYTICAL CHEMISTRY. *Educ:* Nat Taiwan Univ, BSChE, 72; Oberlin Col, MA, 74; Ohio State Univ, Columbus, PhD(anal chem), 79. *Prof Exp:* Fel chem, 79-80, SR RES ASSOC, DEPT CHEM ENG, OHIO STATE UNIV, 80- *Mem:* Am Chem Soc; Am Inst Chem Engrs. *Res:* Rheological properties of viscoelastic fluids including polymer solutions and carbon slurries; kinetic studies on the vedox reaction of tetramethylpyridyliron porphyrin and oxygen molecule in the aqueous solution; methods of the kinetic and equilibrium studies in the solution system; computer applications. *Mailing Add:* 1286 Castleton Rd N Columbus OH 43220

WENG, TU-LUNG, b Tainan, Taiwan, Jan 14, 31; m 57; c 3. ENGINEERING MECHANICS, MECHANICAL ENGINEERING. *Educ:* Purdue Univ, BSME, 55; Carnegie Inst Technol, MS, 56; Pa State Univ, PhD(eng mech), 61. *Prof Exp:* Res engr, Chem Div, Union Carbide Corp, 55-58; instr eng mech, Pa State Univ, 60-61; staff res engr, Carbon Prod Div, Union Carbide Corp, 61-78; SR STAFF RES SCIENTIST, REDUCTION RES DIV, KAISER ALUMINUM & CHEM CORP, 78- *Res:* Thermal stresses in anisotropic materials; mechanical properties, fracture criteria and multiaxial stress tests of graphites and composites; physical properties of carbon cathodes; aluminum reduction cell design. *Mailing Add:* Reduction Res Div Kaiser Aluminum & Chem Corp 23333 Stevens Creek Blvd Cupertino CA 95014

WENG, TUNG HSIANG, b Fukien, China, Jan 16, 33; m 61; c 3. ELECTRICAL ENGINEERING. *Educ:* Nat Taiwan Univ, BS, 56; Univ Iowa, MS, 59; Univ Mo-Columbia, PhD(elec eng), 67. *Prof Exp:* Design engr, Oak Mfg Co, 60-61; proj engr, Sula Elec Co, 61-63 & Simpson Elec Co, 63-64; asst prof elec eng, Univ Mo-Columbia, 67-69; asst prof, 69-71, ASSOC PROF ELEC ENG, OAKLAND UNIV, 71- *Mem:* Inst Elec & Electronics Engrs; Sigma Xi. *Res:* Solid state theory, particularly thin film properties and devices. *Mailing Add:* Sch of Eng Oakland Univ Rochester MI 48063

WENG, (FRANK) TZONG-RUEY, b Jakarta, Indonesia, Jan 5, 34; US citizen; m 72. MEDICINE, PEDIATRICS. *Educ:* Nat Taiwan Univ, MD, 60. *Prof Exp:* Asst prof pediat, Sch Med, NY Univ, 70-75; assoc prof pediat, Sch Med, Wayne State Univ, 75-80; MEM STAFF, CHILDREN'S HOSP PITTSBURGH, 80- *Mem:* Fel Am Acad Pediat; fel Am Col Chest Physicians; Am Thoracic Soc. *Res:* Pulmonary diseases in children. *Mailing Add:* Children's Hosp Pittsburgh 125 DeSoto St Pittsburgh PA 15213

WENG, WU-TSUNG WILLIAM, b Taiwan, China, Aug 11, 44; m 67; c 1. ACCELERATOR & NUCLEAR PHYSICS. *Educ:* Nat Taiwan Univ, BSEE, 66; Nat Tsing-Hua Univ, MS, 68; State Univ NY Stony Brook, PhD(physics), 74. *Prof Exp:* Res assoc nuclear physics, Univ Ariz, 74-76; ASST PHYSICIST ACCELERATOR, BROOKHAVEN NAT LAB, 77- *Mem:* Am Phys Soc. *Res:* Particle dynamics in proton synchrotron and colliding beam machine; focusing and transport of high energy charged particles. *Mailing Add:* Accelerator Dept Brookhaven Nat Lab Upton NY 11973

WENGER, BYRON SYLVESTER, b Russell, Kans, Oct 13, 19; m 47; c 4. DEVELOPMENTAL BIOLOGY. *Educ:* Univ Wyo, BS, 40, MS, 41; Washington Univ, PhD(zool), 49. *Prof Exp:* NIH fel pharmacol, Washington Univ, 49-51; from asst prof to assoc prof anat, Univ Kans, 51-62, from assoc prof comp biochem & physiol to prof biochem, 62-69; PROF ANAT, UNIV SASK, 69- *Concurrent Pos:* Vis assoc prof, Washington Univ, 64-66; res assoc, Univ Calif, Davis, 79-80. *Mem:* Am Asn Anatomists; Am Soc Zoologists; Soc Develop Biol; Am Soc Neurochemists; Am Soc Cell Biol. *Res:* Experimental and biochemical studies of differentiation in normal chick and mouse embryos and during genetic and drug induced teratogenesis. *Mailing Add:* Dept of Anat Univ of Sask Saskatoon SK S7N 0V3 Can

WENGER, CHRISTIAN BRUCE, b Philadelphia, Pa, July 24, 42. THERMOREGULATION, CIRCULATION. *Educ:* Col Wooster, AB, 64; Yale Univ, MD, 70, PhD(environ physiol), 73. *Prof Exp:* Instr physics, Col Wooster, 67-68; vis asst fel, 74-75, ASST FEL PHYSIOL, JOHN B PIERCE FOUND LAB, 75- *Concurrent Pos:* Guest referee ed, Am Physiol Soc, 73-; post-doc fel, Dept Epidemiol & Pub Health, Yale Univ, 74-76, asst prof, 76- *Mem:* Am Physiol Soc; Sigma Xi. *Res:* Thermoregulatory physiology; circulatory effects of thermal stress and exercise. *Mailing Add:* John B Pierce Found Lab 290 Congress Ave New Haven CT 06519

WENGER, DAVID ARTHUR, b Philadelphia, Pa, June 3, 42; m 66; c 1. BIOCHEMICAL GENETICS, PEDIATRICS. *Educ:* Temple Univ, BS, 64, PhD(biochem), 68. *Prof Exp:* Asst prof pediat & neurol, 71-76, assoc prof pediat, 76-77, ASSOC PROF PEDIAT, BIOPHYS & GENETICS, B F STOLINSKY RES LABS, MED CTR, UNIV COLO, DENVER, 77- *Concurrent Pos:* Fel, Weizmann Inst Sci, Rehovot, Israel, 68-69; Multiple Sclerosis fel, Sch Med, Univ Calif, San Diego, 69-71. *Mem:* AAAS; Soc Pediat Res; Am Soc Neurochem; Soc Carbohydrate Res; Int Soc Neurochem. *Res:* Lipid biochemistry; sphingolipidoses; genetic disease of children; lysosomal enzymes. *Mailing Add:* Dept of Pediat Univ of Colo Med Ctr Denver CO 80220

WENGER, FRANZ, b Bern, Switz, Nov 28, 25; nat US; m 55. PHYSICAL CHEMISTRY. *Educ:* Univ Bern, Lic phil nat, 53, PhD(chem), 54. *Prof Exp:* Chemist, Lonza, Inc, Switz, 55; fel photochem, Nat Res Coun Can, 55-57; fel polymer sci, Mellon Inst, 58-63; sr staff assoc, Cent Res Lab, Celanese Corp, NJ, 63-66; mgr spec prod res, Polaroid Corp, Mass, 66-69; GROUP V PRES-IN-CHG RES & DEVELOP & ENG, ENGELHARD INDUSTS DIV, ENGELHARD MINERALS & CHEM CORP, NEWARK, 69- *Mem:* Am Chem Soc. *Res:* Reaction kinetics; structure-properties relationship of polymeric materials; photographic technology; process research and development. *Mailing Add:* 363 Cherry Hill Rd Mountainside NJ 07092

WENGER, HERBERT CHARLES, b Silverdale, Pa, May 17, 26; m 48; c 4. PHARMACOLOGY, PHYSIOLOGY. *Educ:* Goshen Col, BA, 52. *Prof Exp:* Res asst pharmacol, Sharp & Dohme Med Res Labs, 54-55; res assoc, 56-65, res pharmacologist, 66-81, SR RES PHARMACOLOGIST, MERCK INST THERAPEUT RES, 81- *Res:* Pharmacodyamics of cardiovascular drugs including antiarrhythmic and antifibrillatory drugs, compounds and calcium channel blockers affectiing the renin-angiotensin system; serotonin antagonists; antihistaminics. *Mailing Add:* Dept of Pharmacol Merck Inst for Therapeut Res West Point PA 19486

WENGER, JOHN C, b Manhattan, NY, Jan 13, 41; m 63; c 2. MEASURE THEORY. *Educ:* Univ Mich, BS, 63; Univ Chicago, SM, 66; Ill Inst Technol, PhD(math), 79. *Prof Exp:* ASSOC PROF MATH, LOOP COL, 68- *Concurrent Pos:* Teaching asst, Ill Inst Technol, 77-79, instr, 79- *Mem:* Math Asn Am; Am Math Soc; Nat Coun Teachers Math. *Res:* Generalizations of the Riesz-Markov representation theorem in both topological and more abstract settings. *Mailing Add:* 198 Bloom St Highland Park IL 60035

WENGER, LOWELL EDWARD, b Middlebury, Ind, Nov 17, 48; m 76; c 2. PHYSICS. *Educ:* Purdue Univ, BS, 71, MS, 73, PhD(physics), 75. *Prof Exp:* Res assoc physics, Purdue Univ, 75-76; asst prof, 76-81, ASSOC PROF PHYSICS, WAYNE STATE UNIV, 81- *Concurrent Pos:* Grants, Cottrell Res Corp, 77-79 & Wayne State Fac Res Award, 77-78; fel, Alfred P Sloan Res Found, 78-82. *Mem:* Am Phys Soc; Sigma Xi. *Res:* Study of magnetic properties of magnetic alloys; heat capacity and magnetic susceptibilities of solids at very low temperatures. *Mailing Add:* Dept Physics Wayne State Univ Detroit MI 48202

WENGER, NANETTE KASS, b New York, NY, Sept 3, 30. MEDICINE, CARDIOLOGY. *Educ:* Hunter Col, BA, 51; Harvard Med Sch, 54. *Prof Exp:* Intern, Mt Sinai Hosp, New York, 54-55, resident med, 55-56, chief resident cardiol, 56-57; sr asst resident med, Grady Mem Hosp, Atlanta, 58; instr med, 59-62, assoc, 62-64, from asst prof to assoc prof, 64-71, PROF MED, SCH MED, EMORY UNIV, 71-, DIR, CARDIAC CLINS, GRADY MEM HOSP, ATLANTA, 60- *Concurrent Pos:* Fel cardiol, Sch Med, Grady Mem Hosp, Emory Univ, 58-59; fel coun clin cardiol, Am Heart Asn, 70; dir, Proj Cardiac Eval & Med & Voc Rehab, 66-; mem, Rehab Comt, Inter-Soc Comn Heart Disease Resources, 69-75; mem, Nat Thrombosis Adv Comt, 71-74 & Heart Panel, Heart, Lung & Blood Vessel Dis Act, 72; consult, Int Div Social & Rehab Serv, Dept Health, Educ & Welfare, 70- & J Chest, 70-; chmn, Prog Comt, Am Heart Asn, 75-76; mem, Clin Trials Comn, Nat Heart, Lung & Blood Inst, 78-81. *Mem:* AMA; fel Am Col Cardiol; Am Heart Asn (past vpres); Am Fedn Clin Res; Am Thoracic Asn (vpres, 75-). *Res:* Urokinase pulmonary embolism trial; ischemic heart disease in young adults; clinical evaluation of myocardial infarction patients; evaluation of patient education programs. *Mailing Add:* Dept of Med Emory Univ Sch of Med Atlanta GA 30322

WENGER, RONALD HAROLD, b Dayton, Ohio, Nov 30, 37; m 63. MATHEMATICS. *Educ:* Miami Univ, Ohio, AB, 59; Mich State Univ, MS, 61, PhD(math), 65. *Prof Exp:* ASST PROF MATH, UNIV DEL, 65-, ASST TO PROVOST FOR ACAD PLANNING, 69-, ASSOC DEAN, COL ARTS & SCI, 72- *Concurrent Pos:* Asst dean, Col Arts & Sci, 68-69; Am Coun Educ fel acad admin, 70-71. *Mem:* Am Math Soc; Math Asn Am. *Res:* Semigroup rings. *Mailing Add:* Dean's Off Col of Arts & Sci Univ of Del Newark DE 19711

WENGER, THOMAS LEE, b New York, NY, Feb 20, 45; m 67; c 2. MEDICINE. *Educ:* Princeton Univ, AB, 66; Boston Univ, MD, 71. *Prof Exp:* House officer, Harlem Hosp Med Ctr, 71-75; res assoc, Columbia Presby Med Ctr, 74-75; cardiol fel, Duke Univ Med Ctr, 75-78; SR CLIN RES SCIENTIST, BURROUGHS WELLCOME CO, 78- *Concurrent Pos:* Adj asst prof med, Duke Univ Med Ctr, 78- *Res:* Cardiovascular electrophysiology and pharmacology. *Mailing Add:* Burroughs Wellcome Co 3030 Cornwallis Rd Research Triangle Park NC 27709

WENGERT, PAUL R, b Schenectady, NY, Apr 23, 43; m 65; c 3. MATERIALS ENGINEERING, THERMODYNAMICS. *Educ:* Purdue Univ, BS, 65; Univ Calif, Berkeley, PhD(chem), 69. *Prof Exp:* Teaching asst chem, Univ Calif, Berkeley, 65-67, res asst, 67-69; res engr, 69-74, corp planning operations analyst, 74-78, mgr bus planning, Energy Prod Group, 77-79, bus planning analyst, Closure Div, 79-80, marketing mgr, 80-81, MGR BUS DEVELOP, OWENS-ILL, INC, 81- *Concurrent Pos:* Res engr, Prog Mgt Develop, Harvard Univ, 74. *Res:* Materials and process engineering of glass and ceramics ; metals product development; chemical engineering. *Mailing Add:* World Headquarters/24 Owens-Ill Inc One Seagate Toledo OH 43666

WENIG, HAROLD G(EORGE), b New York, NY, Sept 24, 24; m 49; c 2. MECHANICAL ENGINEERING, ELECTROMAGNETISM. *Educ:* City Col New York, BME, 45; Yale Univ, ME, 48; NY Univ, ScD(mech eng), 52. *Prof Exp:* Stress analyst, Otis Elevator Co, 45; mech designer, H K Ferguson Co, 47; mech engr, Sanderson & Porter Co, 48-49; dir eng projs, Bulova Res & Develop Labs, Inc, 51-58; consult engr, 58-59; PRES, WRIGHT INDUSTS, INC, 59- *Concurrent Pos:* Dir, Dynamic Instrument Corp & Krystinel Corp. *Honors & Awards:* I B Laskowitz Gold Medal, NY Acad Sci, 68. *Mem:* Nat Soc Prof Engrs; fel NY Acad Sci; Tech Asn Pulp & Paper Indust; Inst Elec & Electronics Engrs; Soc Photog Scientists & Engrs. *Res:* Aerothermodynamics; dynamics of rigid bodies in extreme force fields; hydrology; research and development management; magnetism and magnetic materials. *Mailing Add:* 2675 Ocean Ave Brooklyn NY 11229

WENIG, JEFFREY, pharmacology, physiology, see previous edition

WENIS, EDWARD, b Linden, NJ, May 22, 19; m 42; c 2. CHEMICAL ENGINEERING. *Educ:* Newark Col Eng, BS, 40; Stevens Inst Technol, MS, 42. *Prof Exp:* Salesman, Sun Oil Co, 38-39; chemist & county supvr Dutch elm disease, USDA, Pa, 39-42; org chemist, 42-66, MGR, THIN LAYER CHROMATOGRAM LABS & CHEM SERV, HOFFMANN-LA ROCHE, INC, 66- *Mem:* Am Chem Soc; fel Am Inst Chemists. *Res:* Synthesis of new drugs; development of riboflavin, lyxoflavin, folic acid and khellin; antituberculosis, hypoglycemic agents and psychoenergizers. *Mailing Add:* 104 Hillcrest Ave Leonia NJ 07605

WENK, EDWARD, JR, b Baltimore, Md, Jan 24, 20; m 41; c 3. SCIENCE POLICY, CIVIL ENGINEERING. *Educ:* Johns Hopkins Univ, BE, 40, DEng, 50; Harvard Univ, MSc, 47. *Hon Degrees:* DSc, Univ RI, 68. *Prof Exp:* Ship struct designer, Boston Navy Shipyard, Mass, 41-42; supvr turret test sect, David Taylor Model Basin, US Naval Dept, 42-45, supt struct dynamics sect, 45-48, head submarine struct br, 48-50, chief struct div, 50-56; chmn dept eng mech, Southwest Res Inst, 56-59; sr specialist sci & technol, Legis Reference Serv, Libr Cong, 59-61; tech asst to President's Sci Adv, White House, 61-62; tech asst to dir, Off Sci & Technol & exec secy, Fed Coun Sci & Technol, 62-64, chief, Sci Policy Res Div & spec adv to librn, Libr Cong, 64-66; exec secy, Nat Coun Marine Resources & Eng Develop, Exec Off of President, 66-70; dir, prog social mgt technol, 73-78, PROF ENG & PUB AFFAIRS, UNIV WASH, 70- *Concurrent Pos:* Mem pressure vessel res comt & chmn, Design Div, Welding Res Coun, 53-59; lectr, Univ Md, 52 & 54-56; consult comt undersea warfare, Nat Acad Sci, 57-58, mem panel naval vehicles, 60-71; chmn comt pub eng policy, Nat Acad Eng, 69-75; vis scholar, Woodrow Wilson Int Ctr Scholars, 70-71; Ford Found fel, 70-72; mem bd dirs, URS Systs Corp, 71-; mem, Nat Adv Comt Oceans & Atmosphere, 71-72; vchmn, US Cong Technol Assessment Adv Coun, 74-79; consult to White House, US Cong, Nat Oceanic & Atmospheric Admin & UN Secretariat, UK, Sweden, Australia & Philippines. *Mem:* Nat Acad Eng; Am Soc Civil Engrs; Soc Exp Stress Anal (pres, 57-58); fel Am Soc Mech Engrs; Sigma Xi. *Res:* Applied mechanics; strength of ships and deep-diving submarines; experimental stress analysis; thin shell structures; ocean engineering; marine affairs; technology assessment; science policy research; public administration; futures; decision theory. *Mailing Add:* 316 Guggenheim Hall FS-15 Univ Wash Seattle WA 98195

WENK, EUGENE J, b New York, NY, Oct 21, 27; m 54; c 3. HORMONE RECEPTORS, OCULAR TISSUE. *Educ:* Columbia Univ, AB, 50, AM, 51; New York Med Col, PhD(anat), 72. *Prof Exp:* From instr to asst prof, 72-79, ASSOC PROF ANAT, NEW YORK MED COL, 79- *Mem:* AAAS; Am Asn Anatomists; Electron Microscope Soc Am; Asn Res Vision & Ophthalmol. *Res:* Ultrastructure and function of ocular tissue. *Mailing Add:* Dept of Anat New York Med Col Valhalla NY 10595

WENK, HANS-RUDOLF, b Zurich, Switz, Oct 25, 41; m 70. CRYSTALLOGRAPHY, STRUCTURAL GEOLOGY. *Educ:* Univ Basel, BA, 63; Univ Zurich, PhD(crystallog), 65. *Prof Exp:* NSF fel, Inst Geophys, Univ Calif, Los Angeles, 66-67; from asst prof to assoc prof geol, 67-73, PROF GEOL & GEOPHYS, UNIV CALIF, BERKELEY, 73- *Concurrent Pos:* Co-worker, Swiss Geol Comn, 66-; Miller prof, Miller Inst Basic Res, 71-72. *Mem:* Mineral Soc Am; Swiss Mineral & Petrog Soc; Swiss Soc Natural Hist; Am Geophys Union; Am Crystallog Asn. *Res:* Structural geology of metamorphic belts; experimental rock deformation; preferred orientation; crystal chemistry of silicates, plagioclase, crystal structures and refinements; electron microscopy; x-ray diffraction. *Mailing Add:* Dept of Geol & Geophys Univ of Calif 497 Earth Sci Bldg Berkeley CA 94720

WENK, SAMUEL AUGUSTINE, b Vineland, NJ, Dec 25, 14. NONDESTRUCTIVE TESTING. *Educ:* Va Polytech Inst, BS, 36. *Prof Exp:* Head eng test sect, Lawrence Radiation Lab, 57-59; mgr radiographic prod, Appl Radiation Corp, 59-60; mgr accelerators, Varian Assocs, 60-67; asst chief nondestructive evaluation sect, Avco Space Syst, 67-69; mgr radiography, High Voltage Eng, 69-70; INST ENG NONDESTRUCTIVE TESTING, SOUTHWEST RES INST, 70- *Concurrent Pos:* Bd dirs, Am Soc Testing & Mats, 65-68; Lester honor lectr, Am Soc Nondestructive Testing, 68; consult mem, Am Soc Mech Eng, 68-70, nuclear adv bd, Am Nat Standards Inst, 68-70; chmn comt nondestructive eval , Nat Mat Adv Bd, 67-69. *Mem:* Fel Am Soc Nondestructive Testing (pres, 77-78); Am Soc Testing & Mat; Sigma Xi; Am Men Sci. *Res:* Nondestructive testing, primarily in the field of radiography; development of a lightweight, high-energy x-ray source; studies on the feasibility of utilizing real-time imaging systems for nuclear power plant applications. *Mailing Add:* Southwest Res Inst 6220 Culebra Rd San Antonio TX 78284

WENKERT, ERNEST, b Vienna, Austria, Oct 16, 25; nat US; m 48; c 4. ORGANIC CHEMISTRY. *Educ:* Univ Wash, BS, 45, MS, 47; Harvard Univ, PhD(chem), 51. *Hon Degrees:* Dr, Univ Paris-Sud, 78. *Prof Exp:* Instr chem, Lower Columbia Jr Col, 47-48; from asst prof to prof org chem, Iowa State Univ, 51-61; prof, Ind Univ, Bloomington, 61-69, Herman T Briscoe prof, 69-73; E D Butcher prof chem, Rice Univ, 73-80, chmn dept, 76-80; PROF CHEM, UNIV CALIF, SAN DIEGO, 80- *Concurrent Pos:* Lectr & vis prof, var US & foreign orgn & acad insts, 51-; actg head dept org chem, Weizmann Inst, 64-65; Guggenheim fel, 65-66; mem NIH med chem B study sect, 71-72, chmn, 72-75; chmn, Gordon Conf Steroids & Other Natural Prod, 64 & 65; mem, NIH med chem B fel rev comn, 67-70; mem, Comt Direction, Inst Chem Substances Naturelles, France, 74-77; mem, Oak Ridge Nat Lab Chem Div Adv Comn, 75-; chief tech adv, UNESCO, 78. *Honors & Awards:* Ernest Guenther Award, Am Chem Soc. *Mem:* Am Chem Soc; Royal Soc Chem; corresp mem Acad Brazileira Ciencias; Swiss Chem Soc. *Mailing Add:* Chem Dept D-006 Univ Calif San Diego La Jolla CA 92093

WENNER, ADRIAN MANLEY, b Roseau, Minn, May 24, 28; m 57; c 2. ZOOLOGY. *Educ:* Gustavus Adolphus Col, BS, 51; Chico State Col, MA, 55; Univ Mich, MS, 58, PhD(zool), 61. *Prof Exp:* Prin elem sch, Ore, 54-55; teacher high sch, Calif, 55-56; fel zool, Univ Mich, 56-60; from asst prof biol sci to assoc prof biol, 60-73, PROF NATURAL HIST, UNIV CALIF, SANTA BARBARA, 73- *Concurrent Pos:* Consult, Teledyne, Inc, 62-64 & Autonetics Div, NAm Aviation, Inc, 64-65. *Mem:* AAAS; Am Soc Zoologists; Sigma Xi; Am Soc Naturalists. *Res:* Problems of growth in marine crustaceans as it occurs in nature; natural history of marine crustacea; animal communication. *Mailing Add:* Marine Sci Inst Univ Calif Santa Barbara CA 93106

WENNER, BRUCE RICHARD, b Lancaster, Pa, Apr 25, 38; m 65; c 3. TOPOLOGY. *Educ:* Col Wooster, BA, 60; Duke Univ, PhD(math), 64. *Prof Exp:* Asst prof math, Univ Vt, 64-68; from asst prof to assoc prof, 68-76, PROF MATH, UNIV MO-KANSAS CITY, 76- *Concurrent Pos:* NASA res grant, 65-66. *Mem:* Am Math Soc; Math Asn Am. *Res:* Dimension theory with regard to topological dimension functions, especially metrizable spaces. *Mailing Add:* Dept of Math Univ of Mo Kansas City MO 64110

WENNER, CHARLES EARL, b Lattimer, Pa, May 2, 24; m 48; c 2. BIOCHEMISTRY. *Educ:* Temple Univ, BA, 48, PhD(chem), 53. *Prof Exp:* Res fel, Lankenau Hosp Res Inst & Inst Cancer Res, 50-54, res assoc, 54-55; sr scientist, Dept Exp Biol, 56-61, assoc scientist, 61-65, ASSOC CHIEF SCIENTIST, DEPT EXP BIOL, ROSWELL PARK MEM INST, 65-; RES PROF BIOCHEM, GRAD SCH, STATE UNIV NY BUFFALO, 70-, CHMN, DEPT BIOCHEM, ROSWELL PARK DIV, 80- *Concurrent Pos:* Runyon fel, Inst Cancer Res, 52-54; from asst prof to assoc prof biochem, Grad Sch, State Univ NY Buffalo, 58-70; Johnson Res Found vis res prof, Univ Pa, 65-66. *Mem:* Am Chem Soc; Am Asn Cancer Res; Biophys Soc; Fedn Am Soc Exp Biol. *Res:* Energy control mechanisms; membrane biochemistry; mechanism of action of cocarcinogens; membrane transport and cell proliferation. *Mailing Add:* Dept of Exp Biol 666 Elm St Roswell Park Mem Inst Buffalo NY 14263

WENNER, DAVID BRUCE, b Flint, Mich, May 28, 41; m 68. GEOCHEMISTRY, GEOLOGY. *Educ:* Univ Cincinnati, BS, 63; Calif Inst Technol, MS, 66, PhD(geochem), 71. *Prof Exp:* Vis asst prof, 71, asst prof, 71-80, ASSOC PROF GEOL, UNIV GA, 80- *Mem:* AAAS; Geol Soc Am; Am Geophys Union. *Res:* Stable isotope geochemistry with applications to igneous and metamorphic rocks. *Mailing Add:* Dept of Geol Univ of Ga Athens GA 30602

WENNER, HERBERT ALLAN, b Drums, Pa, Nov 14, 12; m 42; c 4. MEDICINE. *Educ:* Bucknell Univ, BSc, 33; Univ Rochester, MD, 39; Am Bd Microbiol, dipl, 62; Am Bd Pediat, 49. *Prof Exp:* Instr prev med, Sch Med, Yale Univ, 44-46; from asst prof to assoc prof pediat & bact, Univ Kans, 46-51, res prof pediat, 51-69; distinguished prof pediat, 69-81, CLIN PROF, SCH DENT, UNIV MO-KANSAS CITY, 70- *Concurrent Pos:* Babbott fel, Sch Med, Yale Univ, 41-42; Nat Res Coun fel, Yale Univ & Johns Hopkins Univ, 43-44; NIH res career award, 62-69; assoc physician, Dept Internal Med, New Haven Hosp, Conn, 44-46; consult, Mo State Bd Health & Nat Commun Dis Ctr; mem, Echovirus Subcomt, Picornavirus Study Group, NIH; clin prof pediat, Univ Kans Med Ctr, Kansas City, 73- *Honors & Awards:* Presidential & Distinguished Serv Awards, Nat Found Infantile Paralysis; Cert Serv Award, Panel Picornaviruses, NIH. *Mem:* Fel AAAS; fel Am Acad Pediat; fel Am Pub Health Asn; Soc Pediat Res; Am Pediat Soc. *Res:* Etiology, pathogenesis and epidemiology of infectious diseases. *Mailing Add:* Children's Mercy Hosp Univ Mo Kansas City MO 64108

WENNERBERG, A(LLAN) L(ORENS), b Chicago, Ill, Jan 20, 32; m 53; c 2. ELECTRONIC ENGINEERING. *Educ:* Ind Inst Technol, BSEE, 56; Univ Notre Dame, MSEE, 61. *Prof Exp:* Res engr, Sylvania Microwave Res Lab, 56-57; res engr, 57-65, mgr electronics res, 65-67, dir electronics res, 67-69, DIR RES, WHIRLPOOL CORP, 69- *Mem:* Inst Elec & Electronics Engrs; Sci Res Soc Am. *Res:* Precision control systems involving digital techniques implemented with microcircuitry. *Mailing Add:* Res & Eng Ctr Monte Rd Benton Harbor MI 49022

WENNERSTROM, ARTHUR J(OHN), b New York, NY, Jan 11, 35. FLUID MECHANICS. *Educ:* Duke Univ, BS, 56; Mass Inst Technol, MS, 58; Swiss Fed Inst Technol, DScTech(compressor aerodyn), 65. *Prof Exp:* Sr engr, Aircraft Armaments, Inc, 58-59; res engr, Sulzer Bros, Ltd, Switz, 60-62; proj engr, Northern Res & Eng Corp, 65-67; group leader, 67-75, CHIEF, COMPRESSOR RES GROUP, AIR FORCE AERO PROPULSION LAB, 75- *Concurrent Pos:* US coordr, Propulsion & Energetics Panel, Adv Group Aerospace Res & Develop, NATO, 77. *Mem:* Fel Am Soc Mech Engrs; fel Am Inst Aeronaut & Astronaut. *Res:* Gas turbines; aerodynamics of transonic and supersonic axial compressors; experimental aerodynamics; aerodynamic instrumentation and measurement techniques. *Mailing Add:* Air Force Aero Propulsion Lab AFWAL/POTX Wright-Patterson AFB OH 45433

WENNERSTROM, DAVID E, b Glendale, Calif, June 19, 45; m 73; c 2. MICROBIAL PHYSIOLOGY, MICROBIAL PATHOGENESIS. *Educ:* Univ Ark, BS, 68, MS, 70; Univ Tenn, PhD(microbiol), 73. *Prof Exp:* Fel lipid biochem, Hormel Inst, Univ Minn, 73-76; ASST PROF MICROBIAL PHYSIOL, DEPT MICROBIOL & IMMUNOL, UNIV ARK MED SCI, 76- *Concurrent Pos:* Prin invest, Inst Allergy & Infectious Dis, NIH, Univ Ark Med Sci, 80-83. *Mem:* Am Soc Microbiol; AAAS; Sigma Xi. *Res:* Pathogenesis of group B streptococci in lung tissue is studied using mice which have been shown to be an appropriate model of early-onset group B streptococcal disease of the human newborn. *Mailing Add:* Dept Microbiol & Immunol Univ Ark Med Sci 4301 W Markham Little Rock AK 72205

WENRICH, KAREN JANE, b Lebanon, Pa, Apr 9, 47; m 69. GEOLOGY. *Educ:* Pa State Univ, BS, 69, MS, 71, PhD(geol), 75. *Prof Exp:* Geologist, Molybdenum Corp Am, 69; instr geol, Bucknell Univ, 73-74; GEOLOGIST, US GEOL SURV, 74- *Concurrent Pos:* US Geol Surv adv, Energy Res & Develop Admin Nat Uranium Resource Eval Prog, 75-78. *Mem:* Geol Soc Am; Sigma Xi; Am Geophys Union. *Res:* Uranium exploration, specifically developing exploration guides for uranium silicic volcanic rocks and the use of uranium in water, stream sediments, soils and modern decaying plant materials as a tool for exploration; trace element geochemistry in volcanic rocks. *Mailing Add:* Mail Stop 916 Fed Ctr US Geol Surv Denver CO 80225

WENSCH, GLEN W(ILLIAM), b Chicago, Ill, Nov 15, 17; m 42; c 2. PHYSICAL METALLURGY. *Educ:* Univ Ill, BS, 46, MS, 47, PhD(metall eng), 49. *Prof Exp:* Staff metall engr, Los Alamos Sci Lab, 49-51; sr res metallurgist, Fansteel Metall Co, 51-52; chief reactor mat br, Savannah River Proj, US Atomic Energy Comn, 52-54; sr metall engr, Vitro Corp, 54-55; chief liquid metal projs br, US AEC, 55-70, spec asst to dir reactor develop, 70-76, staff asst to asst adminr, ERDA, 76-78; CONSULT ENGR, 78- *Concurrent Pos:* Chief, Fast Reactor Team, Europe, 55, 57, 59, 60 & 63; pres, Int Plutonium Conf, France, 60; mem & leader, Power Reactor Deleg, USSR, 64 & 70; US mem, Int Working Group Fast Reactors, Int Atomic Energy Agency. *Mem:* AAAS; Am Soc Metals; Am Nuclear Soc; fel NY Acad Sci; fel Am Inst Chemists. *Res:* Plutonium; sodium components and technology; fast breeder reactors. *Mailing Add:* 2207 Noel Dr Champaign IL 61820

WENSKA, TOM MARION, mathematics, see previous edition

WENSLEY, CHARLES GELEN, b Niagara Falls, NY, Feb 19, 49; m 77; c 2. POLYMER PHYSICAL CHEMISTRY, FORMULATIONS DEVELOPMENT. *Educ:* Univ Calif, San Diego, BA, 71; Univ Wis, Madison PhD(chem), 77. *Prof Exp:* MGR SPEC MEMBRANE DEVELOP, ENVIROGENICS SYSTS CO, 78- *Res:* Develop synthetic semi-permeable membranes that have the capacity to separate mixtures of gases, or salts from water, or components of an azeotrope using pressure as the driving force. *Mailing Add:* 1132 Overden Pl Pomona CA 91766

WENT, FRITS WARMOLT, b Utrecht, Neth, May 18, 03; nat US; m 27; c 2. BOTANY. *Educ:* Univ Utrecht, AB, 22, MA, 25, PhD(bot), 27. *Hon Degrees:* PhD, Univ Paris, 56, Methodist Cent Col, 63 & Univ Upsala, 68; DSc, McGill Univ, 59; LLD, Univ Edmonton, 71. *Prof Exp:* Asst, Univ Utrecht, 22-27; plant physiologist, Bot Gardens, Java, 28-30, head foreigners lab, 30-32; instr bot, Med Col, Batavia, Java, 30-31; from asst prof to prof plant physiol, Calif Inst Technol, 33-58; dir, Mo Bot Garden, 58-63; prof bot, Washington Univ, 63-65; distinguished prof, 65-75, EMER RES PROF BOT, DESERT RES INST, UNIV NEV, RENO, 75- *Concurrent Pos:* With USDA; trustee, Calif Arboretum Found, 47-58; pres, Am Inst Biol Sci, 62. *Honors & Awards:*

Hodgkins Award, Smithsonian Inst, 67. *Mem:* Nat Acad Sci; AAAS; Am Soc Plant Physiol (pres, 47); Bot Soc Am (pres, 58); Ecol Soc Am. *Res:* Plant physiology; growth, climatic responses, translocation and water relationships; hormones; relation between climate and vegetation; physiology of crop plants; volatile substances of plant origin in atmosphere. *Mailing Add:* Desert Res Inst Univ of Nev Reno NV 89507

WENT, HANS ADRIAAN, b Bogor, Indonesia, Dec 3, 29; nat US; m 51; c 2. PHYSIOLOGY. *Educ:* Univ Calif, AB, 51, MA, 53, PhD(zool), 58. *Prof Exp:* From instr to asst prof, 59-69, ASSOC PROF ZOOL, WASH STATE UNIV, 69- *Mem:* Am Soc Zool. *Res:* Cell division, especially molecular origin of mitotic apparatus; cell physiology. *Mailing Add:* Dept of Zool & Zoophysiology Wash State Univ Pullman WA 91663

WENTE, HENRY CHRISTIAN, b New York, NY, Aug 18, 36. MATHEMATICS. *Educ:* Harvard Univ, BA, 58, MA, 59, PhD(math), 66. *Prof Exp:* From instr to asst prof, Tufts Univ, 63-70, lectr, 70-71; from asst prof to assoc prof math, 71-77, PROF MATH, UNIV TOLEDO, 77- *Concurrent Pos:* Univ grant & res assoc, Math Inst, Univ Bonn, 72-73. *Mem:* AAAS; Am Math Soc. *Res:* Existence theorems in the calculus of variations, especially those arising from two-dimensional parametric surfaces immersed in Euclidean space; surfaces minimizing area subject to a volume constraint. *Mailing Add:* Dept of Math Univ of Toledo Toledo OH 43606

WENTINK, TUNIS, JR, b Paterson, NJ, Feb 3, 20; m 46, 68. PHYSICAL CHEMISTRY. *Educ:* Rutgers Univ, BS, 41; Cornell Univ, PhD(chem), 54. *Prof Exp:* Res chemist, Photoprods Div, E I du Pont de Nemours & Co, 41-43; from res assoc to mem staff, Div Indust Co-op, Mass Inst Technol, 47-48; from res assoc to specialist microwave spectros, Brookhaven Nat Lab, 48-50; asst, Cornell Univ, 50-54; physicist, Gen Elec Co, 53-55; prin res scientist & supvr, Chem Lab, Avco-Everett Res Lab, Avco Corp, 55-59, from prin scientist to sr consult scientist, Adv Res & Develop Div, 59-67; prin scientist, GCA Corp, 67-68; head exp physics dept, Panametrics, Inc, 68-70; assoc dir, dir Inst Arctic Environ Eng, 72-73, 72-, PROF PHYSICS, GEOPHYS INST, UNIV ALASKA, 70- *Concurrent Pos:* NSF vis prof, Geophys Inst, Univ Alaska, 68; consult. *Mem:* hom mem Sigma Xi. *Res:* Spectroscopy; radiation chemistry of high temperature gases and solids; ultraviolet to microwave regions and instrumentation; molecular absolute intensities and radiative lifetimes; wind energy; energy systems; re-entry physics and signatures; ablation; arctic environmental technology. *Mailing Add:* Geophys Inst Univ of Alaska Fairbanks AK 99701

WENTLAND, MARK PHILIP, b New Britain, Conn, Jan 22, 45; m 70. ORGANIC CHEMISTRY, MEDICINAL CHEMISTRY. *Educ:* Cent Conn State Col, BS, 66; Rice Univ, PhD(chem), 70. *Prof Exp:* SR CHEMIST, STERLING-WINTHROP RES INST, 70- *Concurrent Pos:* Adj assoc prof, Rensselaer Polytech Inst, 71- *Mem:* Am Chem Soc. *Res:* The design and synthesis of potentially useful medicinal agents. *Mailing Add:* Sterling-Winthrop Res Inst Rensselaer NY 12144

WENTLAND, STEPHEN HENRY, b New Britain, Conn, May 1, 40; m 65; c 2. BIOCHEMISTRY, ORGANIC CHEMISTRY. *Educ:* Rensselaer Polytech Inst, BS, 62; Yale Univ, MS, 64, PhD(chem), 68. *Prof Exp:* NIH fel chem, Ind Univ, Bloomington, 68-70; sr org chemist, Smith Kline & French, Inc, 70-72; res assoc biochemist, Univ Colo Med Ctr, DenVer, 72-74, instr med, 74-77; PROF CHEM, HOUSTON BAPTIST UNIV, 77- *Mem:* Am Chem Soc. *Res:* Synthesis and assay of biochemical and organic compounds. *Mailing Add:* 11426 Carvel Lane Houston TX 77072

WENTORF, ROBERT H, JR, b Wis, May 28, 26; m 49; c 3. PHYSICAL CHEMISTRY. *Educ:* Univ Wis, BSChE, 48, PhD(chem), 52. *Prof Exp:* Asst chem, Univ Wis, 46; RES ASSOC CHEM, CORP RES & DEVELOP CTR, GEN ELEC CO, 52- *Concurrent Pos:* Brittingham vis prof, Univ Wis, 67-68. *Honors & Awards:* Ipatieff Prize, 65. *Mem:* Nat Acad Eng; Am Chem Soc. *Res:* High pressure chemistry and physics, diamond synthesis, energy systems, solar energy utilization. *Mailing Add:* Gen Elec Res & Develop PO Box 8 Schenectady NY 12345

WENTWORTH, BERNARD C, b Freedom, Maine, Feb 16, 35; m 60; c 4. AVIAN PHYSIOLOGY. *Educ:* Univ Maine, Orono, BS, 57; Univ Mass, MS, 60, PhD(avian physiol), 63. *Prof Exp:* Physiologist, US Dept Interior, 63-69; assoc prof, 69-73, PROF POULTRY SCI, UNIV WIS-MADISON, 73- *Mem:* AAAS; Poultry Sci Asn; Soc Study Reproduction; Endocrine Soc. *Res:* Basic physiology of birds and comparative endocrinology of animals as related to applied benefits to biomedicine and agriculture. *Mailing Add:* Dept of Poultry Sci Animal Sci Bldg Univ of Wis Madison WI 53706

WENTWORTH, BERTTINA BROWN, b Rockfort, Ill, Aug 9, 19. MICROBIOLOGY. *Educ:* Univ Ky, BS, 41; Ohio State Univ, MS, 58; Univ Calif, Los Angeles, PhD(microbiol), 64. *Prof Exp:* Microbiologist, Ohio Dept Health, Columbus, 49-59; NIH fel, Australian Nat Univ, 64-66; assoc prof pathobiol, Sch Pub Health, Univ Wash, 67-73; DEP LAB DIR, BUR DIS CONTROL & LAB SERV, MICH DEPT PUB HEALTH, 73- *Concurrent Pos:* Adj assoc prof, Mich State Univ, 73- *Mem:* Am Soc Microbiol; Am Pub Health Asn; Am Asn Immunol. *Res:* Virology; immunology. *Mailing Add:* Bur Lab Mich Dept Pub Health 3500 N Logan Lansing MI 48909

WENTWORTH, CARL M, JR, b New York, NY, Feb 8, 36; m 68; c 2. TECTONICS, ENVIRONMENTAL GEOLOGY. *Educ:* Dartmouth Col, AB, 58; Stanford Univ, MS, 60, PhD(geol), 67. *Prof Exp:* GEOLOGIST, US GEOL SURV, 63- *Mem:* Geol Soc Am; Soc Econ Paleontologists & Mineralogists; Seismol Soc Am. *Res:* Neotectonics; major geologic hazards of United States; active faults and movement histories; landslides and slope stability; engineering character of geologic materials; geology of California Coast Ranges. *Mailing Add:* US Geol Surv 345 Middlefield Rd Menlo Park CA 94025

WENTWORTH, GARY, b Orange, Mass, Aug 3, 39; m 61; c 2. ORGANIC CHEMISTRY, POLYMER CHEMISTRY. *Educ:* Rensselaer Polytech Inst, BS, 61; Ga Inst Technol, PhD(org chem), 66. *Prof Exp:* Res chemist, Union Carbide Corp, 66-68; sr res chemist, Monsanto Develop Ctr, 68-73, res specialist, 73-76; RES GROUP LEADER, MONSANTO POLYMERS & RESINS CO, 76- *Mem:* Am Chem Soc; The Chem Soc. *Res:* Fiber chemistry; free radical polymerization; alternating copolymerization; polymer structure/property relationships. *Mailing Add:* Monsanto Polymers & Resins Co 730 Worcester St Indian Orchard MA 01151

WENTWORTH, RUPERT A D, b Hattiesburg, Miss, Nov S, 34; m 56, 72; c 3. INORGANIC CHEMISTRY. *Educ:* Fordham Univ, BS, 55; Mich State Univ, PhD(inorg chem), 63. *Prof Exp:* Fel with Prof T S Piper, Univ Ill, 63-65; from asst prof to assoc prof, 65-74, PROF CHEM, COL ARTS & SCI, GRAD SCH, IND UNIV, BLOOMINGTON, 74- *Mem:* Am Chem Soc. *Res:* The chemistry of simple molybdenum complexes with substrates for molybdoenzymes. *Mailing Add:* Dept of Chem Ind Univ Grad Sch Col of Arts & Sci Bloomington IN 47401

WENTWORTH, STANLEY EARL, b Natick, Mass, July 13, 40; m 67; c 2. ORGANIC POLYMER CHEMISTRY. *Educ:* Northeastern Univ, BS, 63, PhD(org chem), 67. *Prof Exp:* Res chemist, Army Natick Labs, 67-68, RES CHEMIST, ORG MAT LAB, ARMY MAT & MECH RES CTR, 70- *Mem:* Am Chem Soc. *Res:* Organic synthesis in the areas of organofluorine compounds, diazoalkanes and monomers for high temperature resins; thermal analysis of organic materials; synthesis of polyphenylquinoxalines and polyurethanes; studies of adhesives and adhesive bonding synthesis of semiconductive polymers. *Mailing Add:* Org Mat Lab Army Mat & Mech Res Ctr Watertown MA 02172

WENTWORTH, THOMAS RALPH, b Boston, Mass, Sept 4, 48. PLANT ECOLOGY. *Educ:* Dartmouth Col, AB, 70; Cornell Univ, PhD(plant ecol), 76. *Prof Exp:* ASST PROF BOT, NC STATE UNIV, 76- *Mem:* Ecol Soc Am; Brit Ecol Soc; Sigma Xi. *Res:* Plant community ecology. *Mailing Add:* Dept Bot NC State Univ Raleigh NC 27650

WENTWORTH, WAYNE, b Rochester, Minn, May 29, 30; m 54; c 4. ANALYTICAL CHEMISTRY, PHYSICAL CHEMISTRY. *Educ:* St Olaf Col, BA, 52; Fla State Univ, PhD(chem), 57. *Prof Exp:* Res mathematician, Radio Corp Am, 56-59; from asst prof to assoc prof, 59-68, PROF CHEM, UNIV HOUSTON, 68- *Mem:* Am Chem Soc. *Res:* Electron attachment to molecules; molecular complexes; molecular spectroscopy. *Mailing Add:* Dept of Chem Univ of Houston 4800 Calhoun St Houston TX 77004

WENTZ, WILLIAM ALAN, b Kenton, Ohio, Nov 10, 46; m 69. WILDLIFE MANAGEMENT. *Educ:* Ohio State Univ, BSc, 69; Ore State Univ, MSc, 71; Univ Mich, PhD(wildlife mgt), 76. *Prof Exp:* Asst cur bot, Ohio State Univ, 71-72; res assoc wetlands, Univ Mich, 74-75; asst prof & exten wildlife specialist, 75-80, assoc prof & asst leader, SDak Coop Wildlife Res Unit, SDak State Univ, 80-81; DIR, FISHERIES & WILDLIFE PROGS, NAT WILDLIFE FEDN, WASHINGON, DC, 81- *Concurrent Pos:* Consult, Mo River Basin Comn, 78- *Mem:* AAAS; Wildlife Soc; Sigma Xi; Ecol Soc Am. *Res:* Wetlands ecology and management; wildlife and natural resources administration. *Mailing Add:* Dept of Wildlife & Fisheries Sci SDak State Univ Brookings SD 57007

WENTZ, WILLIAM BUDD, b Philadelphia, Pa, Aug 9, 24; m 45; c 3. OBSTETRICS & GYNECOLOGY, ONCOLOGY. *Educ:* Univ Pa, BA, 51, MA, 53; Western Reserve Univ, MD, 58; Am Bd Obstet & Gynec, dipl, 66. *Prof Exp:* Prin investr physiol, US Naval Aviation Med Acceleration Lab, 53-54; intern med, Lankenau Hosp, Philadelphia, Pa, 48-49, prin investr gynec & oncol, 59-63; asst prof obstet & gynec, Hahnemann Med Col, 63-66; assoc prof obstet & gynec, 66-71, PROF REPRODUCTIVE BIOL, SCH MED, CASE WESTERN RESERVE UNIV, 71- *Concurrent Pos:* Am Cancer Soc grants, Lankenau Hosp, Philadelphia, 59-63; Nat Cancer Inst gramts, 64- *Mem:* Am Col Obstet & Gynec; Soc Gynec Oncol; Am Soc Cytol. *Res:* Experimental gynecological pathology; carcinogenesis; cancer research treatment of malignant and premalignant disease. *Mailing Add:* Dept of Reproductive Biol Case Western Reserve Univ Cleveland OH 44106

WENTZ, WILLIAM HENRY, (JR), b Wichita, Kans, Dec 18, 33; m 55; c 2. AERONAUTICAL ENGINEERING, MECHANICAL ENGINEERING. *Educ:* Univ Wichita, BS, 55, MS, 61; Univ Kans, PhD(eng mech), 69. *Prof Exp:* Instr mech eng, Univ Wichita, 57-58; res engr, Boeing Co, 58-63; from asst prof to assoc prof aeronaut eng, 63-75, PROF AERONAUT ENG, WICHITA STATE UNIV, 75- *Concurrent Pos:* NSF sci fac fel, 67-68; prin investr NASA res grants, Wichita State Univ, 70- *Mem:* Assoc fel Am Inst Aeronaut & Astronaut; Am Soc Eng Educ; Soc Automotive Engrs. *Res:* Aerodynamics of wings and bodies; low speed delta wing vortex flows; trailing vortices and wake turbulence; computer analysis of airfoil sections; airfoil, flap and control surface design; separated flows; wind tunnel testing techniques and instrumentation; wind turbine blade and control system design. *Mailing Add:* Dept Aeronaut Eng Wichita State Univ Box 44 Wichita KS 67208

WENTZEL, DONAT GOTTHARD, b Zürich, Switz, June 25, 34; US citizen; m 59; c 1. ASTROPHYSICS. *Educ:* Univ Chicago, BA, 54, BS, 55, MS, 56, PhD(physics), 60. *Prof Exp:* From instr to assoc prof astron, Univ Mich, 60-66; assoc prof, 67-74, PROF ASTRON, UNIV MD, COLLEGE PARK, 74- *Concurrent Pos:* Alfred P Sloan res fel, 62-66; vis lectr, Princeton Univ, 64; vis prof, Tata Inst Fundamental Res, Bombay, 73; acad guest, Fed Inst Technol, Zurich, 78; mem, President's Comn on Teaching Astron, Int Astron Union, 79-82. *Mem:* Fel AAAS; Am Astron Soc; Int Astron Union. *Res:* Effects of magnetic fields on fluid dynamics and charged particles on the sun and in interplanetary and interstellar space; astronomy education. *Mailing Add:* Astron Prog Univ of Md College Park MD 20742

WENZEL, ALAN RICHARD, b Port Chester, NY, Feb 8, 38. APPLIED MATHEMATICS. *Educ:* NY Univ, BAE, 60, MS, 62, PhD(math), 70. *Prof Exp:* Mem res staff, Wyle Labs, 65-68; res assoc, Univ Miami, 70-73; Nat Res Coun assoc, Ames Res Ctr, NASA, 73-75, vis scientist, Inst Comput Appln Sci & Eng, Langley Res Ctr, 75-80; WITH NAVAL OCEAN RES & DEVELOP ACTIV, 80- *Mem:* Acoust Soc Am. *Res:* Theoretical research in fluid dynamics and wave propagation. *Mailing Add:* Naval Ocean Res & Develop Activ Code 340 NSTL Station MS 39529

WENZEL, ALEXANDER B, b Mexico City, Mex, Aug 12, 36; US citizen; m 60; c 3. MECHANICAL ENGINEERING, PHYSICS. *Educ:* NMex Mil Inst, BS, 56; NMex State Univ, MS, 59; St Mary's Univ, MBA, 72. *Prof Exp:* Instr physics & math, NMex State Univ, 56-57, Univ Md, 57-60 & Univ Del, 60-62; head terminal ballistics, Lab Ballistics & Explosives, Gen Motors Defense Labs, 62-66; mgr mat dynamics, Lab Ballistics & Shock Physics, Cleveland Army Tank-Auto Comn, 66-68; sr engr ballistics & explosives, 68-71, group leader, 71-73, mgr, 73-77, DIR BALLISTICS & EXPLOSIVES, SOUTHWEST RES INST, 77- *Concurrent Pos:* Sci adv, Phys Sci Lab, NMex, 56-57. *Mem:* Am Defense Preparedness Asn; Instrument Soc Am; Am Inst Aeronaut & Astronaut. *Res:* Explosive and ballistic technology; impulsive loading of structures; vulnerability and survivability analyses; hazards and safety analysis; response of materials to high strains and pressures; weapons effects; penetration mechanics; shaped charge technology. *Mailing Add:* 3211 Hitching Post San Antonio TX 78218

WENZEL, BERNICE MARTHA, b Bridgeport, Conn, June 22, 21; m 52. NEUROBEHAVIOR, MEDICAL EDUCATION. *Educ:* Beaver Col, AB, 42; Columbia Univ, AM, 43, PhD(psychol), 48. *Prof Exp:* Instr psychol, Newcomb Col, Tulane Univ, 45-46; from instr to asst prof, Barnard Col, Columbia Univ, 46-55; from asst prof to assoc prof physiol, 59-69, vchmn dept, 71-73, PROF PHYSIOL, SCH MED, UNIV CALIF, LOS ANGELES, 69-, PROF PSYCHIAT, 71-, ASST DEAN, 74-; MED EPIDEMIOLOGIST INFECTIOUS DIS CONTROL, CALIF DEPT HEALTH SERV, 70- *Concurrent Pos:* Fel, Ment Health Training Prog, Sch Med, Univ Calif, Los Angeles, 57-59. *Mem:* Fel AAAS; Bay Area Infectious Dis Soc; Am Physiol Soc; Int Brain Res Orgn; Soc Neurosci. *Res:* Behavioral physiology; olfaction. *Mailing Add:* Dept Physiol Univ Calif Sch Med Los Angeles CA 90024

WENZEL, BRUCE ERICKSON, b New Orleans, La, Jan 14, 38; m 64; c 2. PHYSICAL & ANALYTICAL CHEMISTRY. *Educ:* Tulane Univ, BS, 59; Mich State Univ, PhD(chem), 69. *Prof Exp:* Instrument analyst chem, Univ Mich, 61-63; proj chemist, Standard Oil Co, 68-70, anal chemist, 70-76; group leader anal, Ashland Petrol Co, 76-80; WITH, LAGO OIL & TRANSPORTATION, 80- *Concurrent Pos:* Indust adv comt dept chem, Marshall Univ, 77-; adv comt mat anal dept, Inst Mining & Minerals Res, Ky Ctr Energy Res, 78- *Mem:* Sigma Xi; Am Chem Soc. *Res:* Sulfur specific detectors in gas chromatography; gas chromatographic analysis of petroleum, shale oil and coal liquifaction products; general analysis of petroleum, shale oil and coal liquifaction fractions. *Mailing Add:* Lago Oil & Transportation 396 Alhambra Circle Esso Inter Am Coral Gables FL 33134

WENZEL, DUANE GREVE, b Wausau, Wis, Sept 18, 20; m 43; c 4. PHARMACOLOGY. *Educ:* Univ Wis, BS, 45, PhD, 48. *Prof Exp:* From asst prof to assoc prof, 48-56, PROF PHARMACOL, SCH PHARM, UNIV KANS, 56- *Mem:* Tissue Cult Asn; Am Pharmaceut Asn; Soc Toxicol. *Res:* Cause, treatment and prophylaxis of cardiovascular disease; pharmacology and toxicology of environmental agents in cultured cells. *Mailing Add:* Dept of Pharmacol & Toxicol Univ of Kans Sch of Pharm Lawrence KS 66044

WENZEL, FREDERICK J, b Marshfield, Wis, Aug 5, 30; m 52; c 6. BIOCHEMISTRY, BIOLOGY. *Educ:* Univ Wis-Stevens Point, BS, 56; Univ Chicago, MBA, 79. *Prof Exp:* Res asst, St Joseph's Hosp, Marshfield, 50-53; dir labs, Marshfield Clin, 53-65, secy found, 58-64, exec dir, Marshfield Med Found, 65-76, EXEC DIR, MARSHFIELD CLIN, 76- *Mem:* Am Pub Health Asn; NY Acad Sci; Am Fedn Clin Res. *Res:* Hypersensitivity phenomenon in the lung, such as farmer's lung and maple bark disease; health services; natural history of pulmonary thromboembolism, especially diagnosis and treatment and studies of the fibrinolytic process in this disease. *Mailing Add:* Marshfield Clin 1000 N Oak Ave Marshfield WI 54449

WENZEL, HARRY G, JR, b Pittsburgh, Pa, Sept 4, 37; m 63; c 1. CIVIL ENGINEERING. *Educ:* Carnegie Inst Technol, BS, 59, MS, 61, PhD(civil eng), 64. *Prof Exp:* Instr civil eng, Carnegie Inst Technol, 62-64; asst prof, 64-71, ASSOC PROF CIVIL ENG, UNIV ILL, URBANA, 71- *Honors & Awards:* Walter L Huber Res Prize, Am Soc Civil Engrs, 77. *Mem:* Am Soc Civil Engrs; Am Geophys Union. *Res:* Hydrology; hydraulic engineering; urban water resources. *Mailing Add:* Dept Civil Eng Univ Ill 208 N Romine St Urbana IL 61801

WENZEL, JAMES GOTTLIEB, b Springfield, Minn, Oct 16, 26; m 50; c 4. OCEAN ENGINEERING. *Educ:* Univ Minn, BAeroEng, 48, MS, 50. *Prof Exp:* Aerodynamic engr, Convair, San Diego, 48-55, proj mgr anti-submarine warfare & ocean systs, 56-57, asst to vpres eng, 58-59; asst to sr vpres eng, Gen Dynamics, San Diego, 59-61; mgr govt planning, US Navy, 61-62; mgr cruise missiles systs, 62-63, mgr ocean systs, 63-70, asst gen mgr res & develop div & dir ocean systs, 70-72, V PRES OCEAN SYSTS, LOCKHEED MISSILES & SPACE CO, INC, 72- *Concurrent Pos:* Instr, Univ Minn, 49-50; lectr eng, Univ Calif, Los Angeles, 50-57, lectr ocean syst develop planning, 66, lectr deep submergence systs develop, 68; vpres, Lockheed Petrol Systs Ltd, Vancouver, BC, 70- *Mem:* Nat Acad Eng; fel & assoc mem Am Inst Aeronaut & Astronaut; assoc mem Royal Aeronaut Soc; Soc Naval Architects & Marine Engrs; Marine Tech Soc. *Res:* Pioneer in development of Deep Quest research submarine system, 8,000 feet, deep submergence rescues system, 5,000 feet, deep sybmergence search vehicle, 20,000 feet, offshore petroleum system and deep ocean mining system. *Mailing Add:* Orgn 57-01 Bldg 150 PO Box 504 Sunnyvale CA 94088

WENZEL, LEONARD A(NDREW), b Palo Alto, Calif, Jan 21, 23; m 44; c 4. CHEMICAL ENGINEERING. *Educ:* Pa State Col, BS, 43; Univ Mich, MS, 48, PhD(chem eng), 49. *Prof Exp:* Develop engr, Colgate-Palmolive-Peet Co, 49-51; from asst prof to assoc prof chem eng, 51-61, PROF CHEM ENG, LEHIGH UNIV, 61-, CHMN DEPT, 62- *Concurrent Pos:* Mem exec comt, Cryogenic Eng Conf, 64-67; lectr, Univ Ala, Huntsville, 64- & Esso Res & Eng Co, 65-66; expert chem eng & proj coord, Proj COL-5, UNESCO, Bucaramanga, Colombia, 69-70; consult, Air Prod & Chem, Pearsall Chem Co & United Aircraft Corp. *Mem:* Am Chem Soc; Am Inst Chem Engrs; Am Soc Eng Educ. *Res:* Low temperature processing; heat transfer; thermodynamics. *Mailing Add:* Dept of Chem Eng Lehigh Univ Bethlehem PA 18015

WENZEL, RICHARD LOUIS, b Marietta, Ohio, Sept 4, 21; m 47; c 3. PUBLIC HEALTH ADMINISTRATION, PREVENTIVE MEDICINE. *Educ:* Marietta Col, AB, 43; Ohio State Univ, MD, 46; Univ Mich, MPH, 47; Am Bd Prev Med, cert pub health, 63. *Prof Exp:* Intern, Jersey City Med Ctr, 46-47; resident obstet & gynec, St Ann's Maternity Hosp, Columbus, Ohio, 47; chief commun dis & dep health off, Columbus Dept Health, 53-58; health officer, Marietta & Washington County, 58-60; assoc prof pub health admin, Sch Pub Health, Univ Mich, Ann Arbor, 60-70; HEALTH COMNR, TOLEDO & LUCAS COUNTY HEALTH DEPTS, 70- *Concurrent Pos:* Asst prof, Col Med, Ohio State Univ, 54-57; consult, Div Health Mobilization, USPHS, 61-72, Div Indian Health, 64-67 & Bur Med Serv, 66-67; mem, Emergency Health Preparedness Adv Comt, 67-72; consult, Nat Comn Community Health Serv, 64-66; assoc clin prof, Dept Social Med, Med Col Ohio; adj prof pub health admin, Sch Pub Health, Univ Mich, Ann Arbor, 70- *Mem:* Fel Am Pub Health Asn; fel Am Col Prev Med; US Conf City Health Offs. *Res:* Survey, assessment, and evaluation of community health services. *Mailing Add:* Toledo Health Dept 635 N Erie St Toledo OH 43624

WENZEL, ROBERT GALE, b Terra Bella, Calif, June 23, 32; m 73; c 2. PHYSICS, OPTICS. *Educ:* Univ Calif, Berkeley, BA, 59; Univ NMex, MS, 66, PhD(physics), 79. *Prof Exp:* STAFF MEM PHYSICS, LOS ALAMOS NAT LAB, 59- *Concurrent Pos:* Int Atomic Energy Agency vis scientist, Inst Atomic Energy, Sao Paulo, Brazil, 66-67; sr vis fel, UK Sci Res Coun, Heriot-Watt Univ, 81. *Res:* Tunable lasers, nonlinear optics and picosecond optical devices. *Mailing Add:* AP-2 MS-J564 Los Alamos Nat Lab Los Alamos NM 87545

WENZEL, RUPERT LEON, b Owen, Wis, Oct 16, 15; m 40; c 3. ZOOLOGY. *Educ:* Cent YMCA Col, AB, 38, Univ Chicago, PhD(zool), 62. *Prof Exp:* Asst zool, Cent YMCA Col, 36-38; res asst, Univ Chicago, 37-40; asst cur, 40-50, chmn, Dept Zool, 70-77, cur, 51-80, EMER CUR INSECTS, FIELD MUS NATURAL HIST, 81- *Concurrent Pos:* Lectr, Roosevelt Col, 46-47 & Univ Chicago, 62-80; res assoc biol, Northwestern Univ, 59-80, vis prof, 63. *Honors & Awards:* Order of Vasco Nunez de Balboa, Panama, 67. *Mem:* AAAS; Entom Soc Am; Soc Study Evolution; Soc Syst Zool; Asn Trop Biol. *Res:* Taxonomy of streblid and nycteribiid batflies and histerid beetles; zoogeography; evolution of ectoparasites of terrestrial vertebrates. *Mailing Add:* Dept of Zool Field Mus of Natural Hist Chicago IL 60605

WENZEL, WILLIAM ALFRED, b Cincinnati, Ohio, Apr 30, 24; m 55; c 2. ELEMENTARY PARTICLE PHYSICS. *Educ:* Williams Col, AB, 44; Calif Inst Technol, MS, 48, PhD(physics), 52. *Prof Exp:* Res fel physics, Calif Inst Technol, 52-53; assoc dir physics, 70-73, RES PHYSICIST, LAWRENCE BERKELEY LAB, UNIV CALIF, 53- *Mem:* Fel Am Phys Soc; AAAS. *Res:* Experimentation in elementary particle physics; study of weak and electromagnetic interactions and of hadron phenomena at high transverse momenta; development of electronic instrumentation and accelerator facilities. *Mailing Add:* Physics Div Lawrence Berkeley Lab Univ Calif Berkeley CA 94720

WENZEL, ZITA MARTA, b New York, NY, Sept 16, 53. BIOLOGICAL RHYTHMS, AGING. *Educ:* Adelphi Univ, BA, 75; State Univ NY Binghamton, MA, 78, PhD(psychobiol), 80. *Prof Exp:* FEL AGING, ANDRUS GERONT CTR, UNIV SOUTHERN CALIF, 80- *Concurrent Pos:* Inst psychol, Pepperdine Univ, Mt St Mary's Col, & Univ Calif, Los Angels, 81-82; consult comput statist, Univ Southern Calif, 81- *Mem:* Int Soc Chronobiol; AAAS; NY Acad Sci; Soc Neurosci. *Res:* Neural control of behavioral and physiological rhythms in the organisms expression of dynamic homeostasis, and the changes in these rhythmic relationships with ontogeny, aging and psychopathology. *Mailing Add:* Andrus Geront Ctr Res Inst Univ Southern Calif Los Angeles CA 90089

WENZINGER, GEORGE ROBERT, b Newport News, Va, July 24, 33. CHEMISTRY. *Educ:* Washington Univ, AB, 55; Univ Rochester, PhD(chem), 60. *Prof Exp:* NSF fel, Yale Univ, 62-63; asst prof, 63-76, ASSOC PROF ORG CHEM, UNIV S FLA, 76- *Mem:* AAAS; Am Chem Soc. *Res:* Conjugate elimination reactions; synthesis. *Mailing Add:* Dept of Chem Univ of SFla Tampa FL 33620

WENZL, JAMES E, b Greenleaf, Kans, Mar 24, 35; c 4. PEDIATRIC NEPHROLOGY. *Educ:* Creighton Univ, MD, 59; Univ Minn, Minneapolis, MS, 63. *Prof Exp:* Asst prof, 67-71, assoc prof, 71-75, PROF PEDIATRICS, UNIV OKLA HEALTH SCI CTR, OKLAHOMA CITY, 75- *Concurrent Pos:* Chief pediat, Nephrology Serv, Okla Children's Mem Hosp, Olkahoma City, 73-; interim chmn pediatrics, Health Sci Ctr, Univ Okla, Oklahoma City, 76-77, vchmn, 77-,; J Pediat Prof, Eastern Va Med Sch, Norfolk & Med Col Va, Richmond, 76; vis prof, Hosp Nat DeNinos, Sch Med, Univ Costa Rica, San Jose, 77; assoc ed, Contemporary Dialysis, 81- *Mem:* Am Soc Nephrology; Am Soc Pediat Nephrology; Int Soc Nephrology; AMA. *Mailing Add:* Dept Pediat PO Box 26901 Oklahoma City OK 73190

WEPPELMAN, ROGER MICHAEL, b Pittsburgh, Pa, Nov 4, 44; m 71. BIOCHEMISTRY, ENDOCRINOLOGY. *Educ:* Univ Pittsburgh, BS, 65, PhD(microbiol), 70. *Prof Exp:* Instr microbiol, Univ Pittsburgh, 70-71; Am Cancer Soc fel biochem, Univ Calif, Berkeley, 71-73; sr res biochemist, Dept Basic Animal Sci Res, 73-77, res fel, 77-80, SR RES FEL, DEPT BASIC

ANIMAL SCI RES, MERCK & CO, 80- *Mem:* Sigma Xi; Soc Study Reproduction. *Res:* Endocrinology of Avian growth and reproduction; genetics of drug resistance of parasitic protozoa. *Mailing Add:* 1232 Sunnyfield Lane Scotch Plains NJ 07076

WERBEL, LESLIE MORTON, b New York, NY, Mar 31, 31; m 58; c 3. ORGANIC CHEMISTRY. *Educ:* Queens Col, NY, BS, 51; Columbia Univ, AM, 52; Univ Ill, PhD(chem), 57. *Prof Exp:* Res chemist, 57-67, sr res chemist, 67-75, sr res scientist, 75-76, sr res assoc, 76-77, dir chem prod contract res, Parke, Davis & Co, 77-80, DIR CHEM CONTRACT RES, PARKE-DAVIS PHARMACEUTICAL RES DIV, WARNER-LAMBERT CO, 80- *Concurrent Pos:* Lectr col pharm, Univ Mich, 67, adj prof, 71. *Mem:* Am Chem Soc; Royal Soc Chem; Int Soc Heterocyclic Chem. *Res:* Medicinal chemistry; chemotherapy of parasitic infections; cancer chemotherapy; relation of intermediary metabolism of host and invading organism to drug action; novel heterocyclic ring systems. *Mailing Add:* Parke Davis & Co 2800 Plymouth Rd Ann Arbor MI 48106

WERBER, ERNA ALTURE, b Vienna, Austria, Dec 9, 09; nat US. VIROLOGY. *Educ:* Univ Vienna, PhD, 29. *Prof Exp:* Mem staff, Rudolf & Child Hosp, Vienna, Austria, 30-36 & Beth Israel Hosp, Boston, 37-39; asst microbiologist, Squibb Inst, NJ, 40-42; microbiologist, Wallace Labs, 43-44; chief microbiologist, Loewe Res Labs, 44-58; virologist & dir, Virus Lab, Delaware, Inc, 59-61; res assoc infectious dis, Med Sch, Cornell Univ & Bellevue Hosp, 61-68; res assoc pediat microbiol, Med Sch, NY Univ & Bellevue Hosp, 68-71; MYCOLOGIST, MONTEFIORE HOSP MED CTR, 71-, DIR MYCOL LAB, 81- *Mem:* Soc Exp Biol & Med; Am Soc Microbiol; Am Asn Immunol; Mycol Soc Am; Am Thoracic Soc. *Res:* Chemotherapy; antibiotics; tissue culture; bacteriology; serology; granulomous diseases; mutation of Cryptococci neoformans. *Mailing Add:* Apt 3D 170 W 73rd St New York NY 10023

WERBER, FRANK XAVIER, b Vienna, Austria, Apr 8, 24; nat US; m 50; c 2. ORGANIC CHEMISTRY, POLYMER CHEMISTRY. *Educ:* Queens Col, NY, BS, 44; Univ Ill, MS, 47, PhD(chem), 49. *Prof Exp:* Asst, Queens Col, NY, 46; res chemist, Org Res Dept, Res Ctr, B F Goodrich Co, 49-55, sr res chemist, 55-56; dir polymer res, Res Div, W R Grace & Co, 57-63, vpres org & polymer res, 63-67; V PRES RES & DEVELOP, J P STEVENS & CO, INC, 67- *Concurrent Pos:* Chmn bd, Textile Res Inst, 73-75; mem bd, Indust Res Inst, 76-79. *Mem:* AAAS; Am Chem Soc; NY Acad Sci; Am Asn Textile Technol; Am Asn Textile Chemists & Colorists. *Res:* Industrial organic chemistry; modification of polymers; adhesives; condensation polymers; textile chemistry, technology, machinery and engineering. *Mailing Add:* J P Stevens & Co Inc PO Box 2850 Greenville SC 29602

WERBIN, HAROLD, b New York, NY, Oct 2, 22; m 77. BIOLOGICAL CHEMISTRY, CANCER. *Educ:* Brooklyn Col, BS, 44; Polytech Inst Brooklyn, MS, 47, PhD(chem), 50. *Prof Exp:* Asst, Brooklyn Jewish Hosp, 44-46; res assoc, Polytech Inst Brooklyn, 47-48; dir labs, Hillside Hosp, 50-53; res assoc biochem, Argonne Cancer Res Hosp, Chicago, 53-56; res biochemist dept physiol & soils & plant nutrit, Univ Calif, Berkeley, 57-66; ASSOC PROF BIOL, UNIV TEX, DALLAS, 66- *Concurrent Pos:* AEC contract, 67-, Energy Res & Develop Admin contract, 75-76; NSF grant, 67-71 & 78-80; Robert A Welch Found grant, 71- *Mem:* Am Soc Biol Chem; Am Chem Soc; Inst Soc Ethics & Life Sci. *Res:* Interactions of chemical carcinogens with chromatin. *Mailing Add:* Prog in Biol Univ of Tex Dallas PO Box 688 Richardson TX 75080

WERBLIN, FRANK SIMON, b New York, NY, Jan 24, 37; c 1. BIOENGINEERING. *Educ:* Mass Inst Technol, BS, 58, MS, 62; Johns Hopkins Univ, PhD(bioeng), 68. *Prof Exp:* From asst prof to assoc prof, 70-75, PROF ELEC ENG, UNIV CALIF, BERKELEY, 75- *Concurrent Pos:* Guggenheim fel, 74; Miller Professorship, Miller Found, 76. *Res:* Neurophysiological and biochemical basis for function of the vertebrate retina; mechanisms of light transduction, contrast detection, gain control studied in terms of molecular events in photoreceptors, ionic events at synapses, membrane events in neurons. *Mailing Add:* Dept of Elec Eng Univ of Calif Berkeley CA 94720

WERDEGAR, DAVID, b New York, NY, Sept 16, 30; m 61; c 2. COMMUNITY HEALTH. *Educ:* Cornell Univ, AB, 51, MA, 52; New York Med Col, MD, 56; Univ Calif, Berkeley, MPH, 70. *Prof Exp:* Consult, Calif State Dept Pub Health, 64-65; asst prof family & community med, 65-69, assoc prof, 69-75, PROF MED, DIV AMBULATORY COMMUNITY MED & ACTG DEAN, SCH MED, UNIV CALIF, FRESNO, 75- *Concurrent Pos:* NIMH spec fel, Univ Calif, San Francisco, 63-64, Dept Health, Educ & Welfare Div Chronic Dis fel, 64-67; co-dir, Regional Med Prog Cardiovasc Dis Prev Northwest Calif, 67-70; planning officer, Regional Med Prog, Calif; med dir, Univ Calif Home Care Serv, 65- *Mem:* AAAS; Am Pub Health Asn; Asn Teachers Prev Med; Am Fedn Clin Res; Am Col Physicians. *Res:* Family medicine; health policy; social aspects of health care; organization of health care services; evaluation of quality of health care. *Mailing Add:* Univ Calif Fresno CA 93703

WERDEL, JUDITH ANN, b Lackawanna, NY, June 22, 37. INFORMATION SCIENCE, SCIENCE POLICY. *Educ:* State Univ NY Buffalo, BA, 58; Mt Holyoke Col, MA, 59. *Prof Exp:* Sci info specialist, Shell Develop Co, Calif, 59-63; prof asst info sci, Off Doc, 63-70, prof assoc, Bd Int Orgn & Progs & Bd Sci & Technol for Int Develop, 70-74, staff officer, Comt Int Sci & Tech Info Progs, 74-81, PROF ASSOC, BD SCI & TECHNOL, INT DEVELOP, COMN INT RELS, NAT ACAD SCI, 81- *Concurrent Pos:* Secy bd dirs, Doc Abstr, Inc, 66-68. *Mem:* Am Soc Info Sci. *Res:* National and international policies and programs for the development of scientific and technical information systems; technical assistance in scientific and technical information systems; promotion and development of the field of information science and technology. *Mailing Add:* Comn on Int Rels Nat Acad of Sci Washington DC 20418

WERDER, ALVAR ARVID, b Sweden, Mar 12, 17; nat US; m 44; c 2. MICROBIOLOGY. *Educ:* Univ Minn, BA, 45, MS, 47, PhD, 49. *Prof Exp:* From instr to asst prof bact, Univ Minn, 49-52; assoc prof, 52-55, chmn dept, 61-82, PROF MICROBIOL, SCH MED, UNIV KANS, 55- *Mem:* Am Soc Microbiol; Am Asn Pathologists. *Res:* Oncogenic viruses; studies on germfree animals. *Mailing Add:* Dept of Microbiol Univ of Kans Sch of Med Kansas City KS 66103

WERESUB, LUELLA KAYLA, mycology, deceased

WERGEDAL, JON E, b Eau Claire, Wis, Feb 19, 36. BIOCHEMISTRY. *Educ:* St Olaf Col, BA, 58; Univ Wis, MS, 60, PhD(biochem), 63. *Prof Exp:* BIOCHEMIST, VET ADMIN HOSP, SEATTLE, 62- *Concurrent Pos:* Res instr med, Sch Med, Univ Wash, 63-71, res asst prof, 71-76. *Mem:* AAAS. *Res:* Bone metabolism. *Mailing Add:* Dept of Biochem Vet Admin Hosp American Lake WA 98493

WERGIN, WILLIAM PETER, b Manitowoc, Wis, Apr 20, 42; m 62; c 2. CYTOLOGY. *Educ:* Univ Wis-Madison, BS, 64, PhD(bot), 70. *Prof Exp:* Res cytologist plant path, 70-72, res cytologist weed sci, 72-74, res cytologist nematol & proj leader animal reproduction, Agr Res Serv, 74-79, LAB CHIEF, PLANT STRESS LAB, USDA, 79- *Honors & Awards:* Diamond Award, Bot Soc Am, 75; prin investr, Agr Competitive Grants Prog, 78 & co-prin investr, US-Israel Agr Res & Develop Fund, 79. *Mem:* Am Soc Cell Biol; Bot Soc Am; Electron Micros Soc Am; Am Soc Plant Physiologists; Soc Nematologists. *Res:* Current transmission and scanning electron microscopic examinations include host-parasite interactions between higher plants and nematodes and effects of environmental stress on crop plants; environmental stress effects caused by air pollutants, mineral deficiencies or toxicities and temperature, water and light extremes in plants. *Mailing Add:* Beltsville Agr Res Ctr-E Agr Res Serv USDA Beltsville MD 20705

WERKEMA, GEORGE JAN, b Vancouver, Wash, Nov 24, 36; m 69. PHYSICAL CHEMISTRY, HEALTH PHYSICS. *Educ:* Calvin Col, BS, 58; Univ Colo, PhD(chem), 65. *Prof Exp:* From res chemist to sr res chemist, Dow Chem Co, 63-72, res mgr, Rocky Flats Div, 72-75; health physicist, US Energy Res & Develop Admin, 75-81; CHIEF HEALTH PROTECTION BR, US DEPT ENERGY, ALBUQUERQUE, 81- *Mem:* Am Chem Soc; Sigma Xi; Health Physics Soc. *Res:* X-ray crystallography; computer programming; instrument development; health physics; environmental control and monitoring; industrial hygiene. *Mailing Add:* 3504 Embudito Dr NE Albuquerque NM 87111

WERKEMA, MARILYN VERYL, environmental sciences, nuclear materials, see previous edition

WERKHEISER, ARTHUR H, JR, b Easton, Pa, May 2, 35; m 62; c 2. LASERS. *Educ:* Lafayette Col, BS, 57; Univ Tenn, MS, 59, PhD(physics), 65. *Prof Exp:* Instr physics, Univ Tenn, 64; physicist, Res & Develop Directorate, 65-75, BR CHIEF, MODELING & ANAL DIV, ARMY HIGH ENERGY LASERS RES & ENG DIRECTORATE, US ARMY MISSILE COMMAND, REDSTONE ARSENAL, ALA, 75- *Mem:* Am Phys Soc. *Res:* Isomer shifts of solid solutions; conduction electron polarization; Mössbauer effect physics; mathematical modeling of high energy laser systems. *Mailing Add:* 1602 Drake Ave Huntsville AL 35802

WERKING, ROBERT JUNIOR, b Richmond, Ind, Jan 21, 30; m 51; c 2. SCIENCE EDUCATION. *Educ:* Hillsdale Col, BS, 61; Syracuse Univ, MS, 65; Ind Univ, Bloomington, EdD(sci educ), 71. *Prof Exp:* Asst prof physics, 65-69, asst prof sci educ, 71-73, CHMN DIV NATURAL SCI & MATH, MARION COL, 73- *Mem:* Am Asn Physics Teachers; Nat Sci Teachers Asn; Am Sci Affil. *Res:* Science instruction; instructional objectives; teaching effectiveness; instructional methods. *Mailing Add:* Div of Natural Sci & Math Marion Col Marion IN 46952

WERKMAN, SIDNEY LEE, b Washington, DC, May 3, 27; c 1. MEDICINE. *Educ:* Williams Col, AB, 48; Cornell Univ, MD, 52. *Prof Exp:* Assoc prof psychiat, Med Sch, George Washington Univ, 61-69; assoc prof, 69-72, PROF PSYCHIAT, UNIV COLO MED CTR, DENVER, 72- *Concurrent Pos:* Commonwealth Fund fel, Florence, Italy, 63-64; res consult, USPHS, 60-68; assoc dir, Joint Comn Ment Health Children, 67-68; consult, NIMH, 74- *Mem:* AAAS; Am Psychiat Asn; Am Acad Child Psychiat; Am Orthopsychiat Asn; Group Advan Psychiat. *Res:* Psychological factors in nutrition and development; brain dysfunction in children; attitude studies; psychological adjustment of Americans overseas. *Mailing Add:* Dept of Psychiat Univ of Colo Med Ctr Denver CO 80220

WERLE, MICHAEL JOSEPH, aerospace engineering, see previous edition

WERMAN, ROBERT, b Brooklyn, NY, May 2, 29; m 54; c 4. NEUROPHYSIOLOGY. *Educ:* NY Univ, AB, 48, MD, 52. *Prof Exp:* Intern, Montefiore Hosp, New York, 52-53; resident neurol, Mt Sinai Hosp, 53-54 & 56-58; asst prof, Col Physicians & Surgeons, Columbia Univ, 60-61; prof psychiat, Sch Med, Ind Univ, Indianapolis, 61-69, prof anat & physiol, Ind Univ Bloomington, 64-69; PROF NEUROPHYSIOL, HEBREW UNIV, JERUSALEM, 69- *Concurrent Pos:* Nat Inst Neurol Dis & Blindness trainee neurophysiol, Columbia Univ, 58-60; vis scientist, Cambridge Univ, 60-61. *Mem:* AAAS; Soc Gen Physiologists; Am Physiol Soc. *Res:* Electrophysiology; neuromuscular junction; membrane properties and ionic movements; synaptic physiology; spinal cord. *Mailing Add:* Hebrew Univ of Jerusalem Jerusalem Israel

WERMUND, EDMUND GERALD, JR, b Arlington, NJ, Apr 15, 26; m 76; c 2. GEOLOGY. *Educ:* Franklin & Marshall Col, BS, 48; La State Univ, PhD(geol), 61. *Prof Exp:* Instr geol, La State Univ, 52-57; sr res technologist, Field Res Lab, Mobil Oil Corp, 57-68, res assoc, Mobil Res & Develop Corp, 68-70; tech mgr, Remote Sensing, Inc, 70-71; res scientist, Bur Econ Geol, 71-73, ASSOC DIR, BUR ECON GEOL, UNIV TEX, AUSTIN, 73- *Mem:* AAAS; Am Asn Petrol Geologists; fel Geol Soc Am; Am Soc Photogram; Sigma Xi. *Res:* Petroleum geology, environmental geology; regional geology. *Mailing Add:* Box X Bur of Econ Geol Univ of Tex Austin TX 78712

WERMUS, GERALD R, b St Paul, Minn, May 8, 38; m 65; c 2. BIOCHEMISTRY, CLINICAL CHEMISTRY. *Educ:* Col St Thomas, BS, 60; Ariz State Univ, MS, 63; Iowa State Univ, PhD(biochem), 66. *Prof Exp:* Formulation chemist, Econ Lab, Inc, 60-61; res chemist, Photo Prod Dept, 61-72, res supvr, 72-74, res mgr, 74-78, tech serv mgr, Instrument Prod Div, 78-81, MGR, NEW METHODS, PHOTO PROD DEPT, CLIN SYSTS DIV, E I DU PONT DE NEMOURS & CO, INC, 81- *Concurrent Pos:* Mem, Nat Comt Clin Lab Standards. *Mem:* Am Asn Clin Chem; Am Chem Soc; Asn Advan Med Instrumentation. *Res:* Development of clinical laboratory methodology; bacterial metabolism; lipid peroxidation; laboratory administration. *Mailing Add:* 114 Venus Dr Newark DE 19711

WERMUTH, JEROME FRANCIS, b Madison, Wis, Oct 19, 36; m 64; c 5. DEVELOPMENTAL BIOLOGY. *Educ:* Univ Wis-Madison, BS, 57, MS, 60; Ind Univ, PhD(zool), 68. *Prof Exp:* Instr biol, Rockhurst Col, 61-64; asst prof, St Joseph's Col, Ind, 65-66; res assoc, Univ Notre Dame, 68-69; asst prof, 69-78, ASSOC PROF BIOL, PURDUE UNIV, CALUMET CAMPUS, 78- *Concurrent Pos:* Vis asst prof & Nat Cancer Inst spec res fel life sci, Ind State Univ, Terre Haute, 72-73; vis asst prof zool, Ind Univ, Bloomington, 75-76. *Mem:* NY Acad Sci. *Res:* Effects of x-irradiation on the developmental physiology of colonial marine cnidarians. *Mailing Add:* Dept of Biol Purdue Univ Calumet Hammond IN 46323

WERNAU, WILLIAM CHARLES, b Flushing, NY, Jan 22, 47; m 68; c 4. BIOCHEMICAL ENGINEERING, FERMENTATION. *Educ:* Cooper Union, BS, 68; Univ Calif, Berkeley, PhD(chem eng), 72. *Prof Exp:* MGR FERMENTATION RES & DEVELOP, PFIZER, INC, 72- *Mem:* Am Inst Chem Eng; Am Chem Soc. *Res:* Continuous fermentation, organic acid biosynthesis, biopolymer synthesis (patents), enzyme production, pilot plant scale-up, fermentor design, fermentation and recovery process development; mass transfer in aerobic systems. *Mailing Add:* 58 Latham St Groton CT 06340

WERNEKE, MICHAEL FRANCIS, inorganic chemistry, see previous edition

WERNER, ARNOLD, b Brooklyn, NY, June 8, 38; m 69; c 2. PSYCHOSOMATIC MEDICINE, MEDICAL EDUCATION. *Educ:* Brooklyn Col, BS, 59; Univ Rochester, MD, 63. *Prof Exp:* Instr psychiat, Sch Med, Univ Rochester, 66-67, Temple Univ, 67-69; asst prof, 69-72, assoc prof, 72-78, PROF PSYCHIAT, MICH STATE UNIV, 78- *Mem:* Fel Am Psychiat Asn; Am Psychosomatic Soc. *Mailing Add:* A228 E Fee Hall Dept Psychiat Mich State Univ East Lansing MI 48824

WERNER, DANIEL PAUL, b Philadelphia, Pa, Dec 12, 38; m 63; c 2. MECHANICAL ENGINEERING. *Educ:* Drexel Univ, BSME, 61; Univ Denver, MSME, 63; Univ Mich, Ann Arbor, PhD(mech eng), 68. *Prof Exp:* Asst prof mech eng, Duke Univ, 68-71; chief compressor engr, Freezing Equip Sales, Inc, 71-77; MGR RES & DEVELOP ENG, AIRCONDITIONING PROD, BOHN HEAT TRANSFER DIV, GULF & WESTERN IND, INC, 77- *Mem:* Am Soc Mech Engrs; Am Soc Heating, Refrig & Air-Conditioning Eng. *Res:* Pressure drop and heat transfer in two phase liquid-gas flows; thermal stresses in thick walled heat exchanger tubing; mechanical refrigeration systems development. *Mailing Add:* 1710 Crestview Dr Danville IL 61832

WERNER, EARL EDWARD, b Aliquippa, Pa, July 11, 44; m 71. ECOLOGY, ZOOLOGY. *Educ:* Columbia Univ, AB, 66; Mich State Univ, PhD(ecol), 72. *Prof Exp:* Asst prof, Univ Iowa, 72-73; ASSOC PROF ZOOL, MICH STATE UNIV KELLOGG BIOL STA, 78- *Concurrent Pos:* Ed, Ecol & Ecological Monographs, 79- *Honors & Awards:* Mercer Award, Ecol Soc Am, 78. *Mem:* AAAS; Ecol Soc Am; Brit Ecol Soc; Int Soc Theoret & Appl Limnol. *Res:* Community ecology; population biology; competition; foraging strategies. *Mailing Add:* Kellogg Biol Sta Mich State Univ Hickory Corners MI 49060

WERNER, ERVIN ROBERT, JR, b Philadelphia, Pa, May 2, 32; m 53; c 5. ORGANIC CHEMISTRY. *Educ:* Haverford Col, BS, 54; Univ Md, MS, 58; Univ Pa, PhD(org chem), 60. *Prof Exp:* Chemist, Rohm & Haas Co, 57-60; res chemist, 60-69, staff chemist, 69-72, RES ASSOC, E I DU PONT DE NEMOURS & CO, INC, 72- *Mem:* Am Chem Soc; Fedn Soc Paint Technol. *Res:* Organic synthesis; flame retardant polyesters; organophosphorus chemistry; water solution polymers; aqueous wire enamels; emulsion systems and house paints; interior emulsion paints. *Mailing Add:* E I du Pont de Nemours & Co Inc 3500 Grays Ferry Ave Philadelphia PA 19146

WERNER, F(RED) E(UGENE), b Mansfield, Ohio, Sept 22, 27; m 51; c 3. PHYSICAL METALLURGY, MAGNETIC MATERIALS. *Educ:* Mass Inst Technol, SB, 50, ScD(metall), 55. *Prof Exp:* Instr metall, Mass Inst Technol, 50-53, asst, 53-55; res engr, Res Labs, 55-60, sect mgr alloy studies, 60-62, mgr metall dept, 62-68, mat consult, 69, MGR MAGNETICS DEPT, RES LABS, WESTINGHOUSE ELEC CORP, 70- *Mem:* Soc Metals; Inst Mining, Metall & Petrol Engrs; Inst Elec & Electronics Engrs; fel Am Soc Metals. *Res:* Metallic alloys; application of metals and alloys to practical uses; metals processing, research and development in physical and mechanical metallurgy; metals joining; soft and permanent magnetic materials. *Mailing Add:* Res Labs Westinghouse Elec Corp Pittsburgh PA 15235

WERNER, FLOYD GERALD, b Ottawa, Ill, June 1, 21; m 52; c 3. ENTOMOLOGY. *Educ:* Harvard Univ, SB, 43, PhD(biol), 50. *Prof Exp:* From asst prof to assoc prof zool, Univ Vt, 50-54; inchg econ insect surv, 54, asst prof, 54-58, assoc prof, 58-60, PROF ENTOM & RES SCIENTIST, EXP STA, UNIV ARIZ, 60- *Mem:* AAAS; Entom Soc Am; Soc Syst Zool. *Res:* Taxonomy of Coleoptera, Meloidae and Anthicidae; monitoring insect parasitoids in crop plants. *Mailing Add:* Dept Entom Univ Ariz Tucson AZ 85721

WERNER, FRANK D(AVID), b Junction City, Kans, Mar 14, 22; m 46; c 3. AERONAUTICAL ENGINEERING. *Educ:* Kans State Col, BS, 43; Univ Minn, MS, 48, PhD(aeronaut eng), 55. *Prof Exp:* Jr physicist, Appl Physics Lab, Johns Hopkins Univ, 43-47; res assoc, Rosemount Aeronaut Lab, Univ Minn, 47-56; pres, Rosemount, Inc, 56-58; pres & dir, Origin Inc, 68-76; PRES, PARK ENERGY CO, 76- *Concurrent Pos:* Consult, 48-57. *Mem:* Am Phys Soc; Instrument Soc Am; Am Inst Aeronaut & Astronaut. *Res:* Instrumentation, particularly temperature and pressure measurement; platinum resistance thermometry and measurement of air data parameters for airplane flights; solar heat collectors. *Mailing Add:* Park Energy Co Star Rte Box 9 Jackson WY 83001

WERNER, GERHARD, b Vienna, Austria, Sept 28, 21; m 58. PHARMACOLOGY, PSYCHIATRY. *Educ:* Univ Vienna, MD, 45. *Prof Exp:* From instr to asst prof pharmacol, Univ Vienna, 43-52; prof, Univ Calcutta, 52-54 & Med Sch, Univ Sao Paulo, 55-57; assoc prof, Med Col, Cornell Univ, 57-61 & Med Sch, Johns Hopkins Univ, 61-65; chmn dept, 65-75, dean, Sch Med, 74-78, PROF PHARMACOL, SCH MED, UNIV PITTSBURGH, 65-, PROF PSYCHOL, 70-, PROF PSYCHIAT, 78-, F S CHEEVER DISTINGUISHED PROF, 80- *Concurrent Pos:* Mem adv bd, Indian Coun Med Res, 52-54; mem pharmacol study sect, NIH, 65-69, mem chem-biol info handling prog, 68-71; NSF consult, 69-71. *Mem:* Am Soc Pharmacol & Exp Therapeut; Soc Exp Biol & Med; Am Physiol Soc; Int Brain Res Orgn; Asn Res Nerve & Ment Dis. *Res:* Neuropharmacology; psychoanalysis; neurophysiology; computer applications. *Mailing Add:* Dept of Psychiat Univ of Pittsburgh Sch of Med Pittsburgh PA 15261

WERNER, HARRY JAY, b Brooklyn, NY, June 7, 21; m 43; c 3. GEOLOGY. *Educ:* Syracuse Univ, AB, 47, PhD(geol), 56; Wash Univ, AM, 49. *Prof Exp:* Field geologist, State Geol Surv, Va, 48-51; asst prof geol, St Lawrence Univ, 51-55; res geologist, Pan Am Petrol Corp, 55-60, res sect supvr, 60-63; assoc prof geol, Univ Pittsburgh, 63-80; WITH SEMINOLE ENERGY, 80- *Mem:* Geol Soc Am; Am Asn Petrol Geologists. *Res:* Stratigraphy; petrology; structural geology; carbonate sedimentation; underwater drilling techniques. *Mailing Add:* Suite 205 Seminole Energy 239 E Commercial Blvd Lauderdale-by-the-Sea FL 33308

WERNER, HENRY JAMES, b Hartford, Wis, Oct 9, 14; m 47. HISTOLOGY, CYTOLOGY. *Educ:* Marquette Univ, BS, 39, MS, 41; Univ Md, PhD(histol, cytol), 48. *Prof Exp:* Lab asst, Marquette Univ, 39-41; head dept sci, Shenandoah Col, 41-43; Harvard biol teaching fel, 44-45; instr histol & cytol, Univ Md, 46-48; assoc prof, Otterbein Col, 48-49; assoc prof zool, 49-67, prof, 67-80, EMER PROF ZOOL, LA STATE UNIV, BATON ROUGE, 80- *Mem:* Am Soc Cell Biol; Electron Micros Soc Am. *Res:* Electron microscopy; human fungi. *Mailing Add:* Dept of Zool La State Univ Baton Rouge LA 70803

WERNER, JOAN KATHLEEN, b Adams, Wis, Aug 13, 32. NEUROANATOMY, GROSS ANATOMY. *Educ:* Univ Wis, BS, 54, PhD(anat), 72. *Prof Exp:* Staff phys therapist, St Luke's Hosp, Milwaukee, Wis, 54-55; staff phys therapist, Vet Admin Hosp, Iron Mountain, 55-58; teaching asst anat, Med Sch, Univ Wis, 58-60; asst chief phys ther, Vet Admin Hosp, Madison, 60-65; chief phys ther, Vis Nurse Serv, Madison, 65-66; instr phys ther, 66-68, asst prof, 72-78, ASSOC PROF ANAT & DIR, PROG PHYS THERAPY, MED SCH, UNIV WIS-MADISON, 78- *Concurrent Pos:* NIH fel, Univ Wis, 74-76; examr, State Wis Phys Ther Exam Coun, 74-77. *Mem:* AAAS; Am Asn Anatomists; Soc Neurosci; Am Phys Ther Asn. *Res:* Dependency of the somatosensory receptors upon normal innervation during development. *Mailing Add:* Prog in Phys Therapy Univ of Wis 1308 W Dayton St Madison WI 53706

WERNER, JOHN ELLIS, b Erie, Pa, Oct 25, 32; m 57; c 4. METALLURGY, CHEMICAL ENGINEERING. *Educ:* Pa State Univ, BS, 54, MS, 60. *Prof Exp:* Metall engr, Lackawanna Plant, 54-58, res engr, Res Dept, 60-65, supvr steelmaking processes, Steelmaking Sect, 65-66, asst sect mgr, 66-69, sect mgr phys metall, Homer Res Labs, 69-74, asst div mgr prod res, 74-76, asst div mgr primary processes, 76-78, DIV MGR RAW MAT & CHEM PROCESSES, RES DEPT, BETHLEHEM STEEL CORP, 78- *Mem:* Am Inst Mining, Metall & Petrol Engrs; Am Soc Metals. *Res:* Steelmaking processes; microstructural control to enhance properties; research management; technical forecasting. *Mailing Add:* Res Dept Bethlehem Steel Corp Bethlehem PA 18016

WERNER, JOHN KIRWIN, b Conrad, Mont, Sept 14, 41; m 67; c 2. HERPETOLOGY, PARASITOLOGY. *Educ:* Carroll Col, Mont, BA, 63; Univ Notre Dame, PhD(biol), 68. *Prof Exp:* Chief dept med zool, 406th Med Lab, US Med Command, Japan, 68-71; asst prof biol, 71-75, head dept, 75-78, ASSOC PROF BIOL, NORTHERN MICH UNIV, 75- *Concurrent Pos:* Assoc investr, US Army Res & Develop Protocol, 68-71; US Forest Serv grants amphibian ecol, 71-75; scientist, Int Ctr Med Res, Cali, Colombia, 78-81. *Mem:* Herpetologists League; Am Soc Parasitologists; Am Soc Ichthyologists & Herpetologists. *Res:* Ecology and reproduction of amphibians and reptiles; blood parasites of lower vertebrates. *Mailing Add:* Dept Biol Northern Mich Univ Marquette MI 49855

WERNER, LINCOLN HARVEY, b New York, NY, Feb 19, 18; m 44; c 2. ORGANIC CHEMISTRY. *Educ:* Swiss Fed Inst Technol, dipl, 41, DrTechSci, 44. *Prof Exp:* Asst, Swiss Fed Inst Technol, 44-46; res chemist, Ciba Basle, Ltd, 46-47, res chemist, Ciba Pharmaceut Prods, Inc, NJ, 47-68, MGR CHEM RES ADMIN, CIBA PHARMACEUT CO, 68- *Mem:* Am Chem Soc. *Res:* Pharmaceuticals; cardiovascular drugs; diuretics. *Mailing Add:* Pharmaceut Div Ciba-Geigy Corp 556 Morris Ave Summit NJ 07901

WERNER, MARIO, b Zurich, Switz, Aug 21, 31; US citizen; m 68. LABORATORY MEDICINE. *Educ:* Univ Zurich, MD, 56, DrMed, 60. *Prof Exp:* Asst physician, Kantonsspital St Gallen, Switz, 57-58 & Univ Basel, 58-61; NIH res fel metab, Swiss Acad Med Sci, 61-62; NIH res fel physiol, Rockefeller Univ, 62-64; head physician, Med Sch Essen, WGer, 64-66; asst prof lab med, Univ Calif, San Francisco, 67-70; assoc prof med path, Wash Univ, 70-72; PROF LAB MED, GEORGE WASHINGTON UNIV, 72- *Concurrent Pos:* Consult, Univ Tex M D Anderson Hosp & Tumor Inst, 70-80 & Nat Heart & Lung Inst, 73-; chmn health care delivery comt, Bi-State Regional Med Prog, 71-72; trustee, Found Interdisciplinary Biocharacterizations Pop, 71-75; mem, Path A Study Sect, NIH, 75-80; mem clin chem device classification panel, Food & Drug Admin, 77-79; dir, Am Bd Clin Chem. *Mem:* Am Soc Clin Path; Col Am Path; Acad Clin Lab Physicians & Sci; Am Asn Clin Chem; Am Fedn Clin Res. *Res:* Laboratory data processing and diagnostic discrimination by computer; blood protein and lipoprotein metabolism. *Mailing Add:* Div of Lab Med George Washington Univ Med Ctr Washington DC 20037

WERNER, MICHAEL WOLOCK, b Chicago, Ill, Oct 9, 42; m 67; c 2. ASTROPHYSICS, INFRARED ASTRONOMY. *Educ:* Haverford Col, BA, 63; Cornell Univ, PhD(astron), 68. *Prof Exp:* Res physicist, US Naval Res Lab, 63-64; vis fel, Inst Theoret Astron, Cambridge, Eng, 68-69; lectr physics, Univ Calif, Berkeley, 69-72; asst prof physics, Calif Inst Technol, 72-79, staff assoc, Hale Observ, 72-79; RES SCIENTIST, AMES RES CTR, NASA, 79- *Mem:* AAAS; Am Astron Soc. *Res:* Observational infrared astronomy; astrophysics of the interstellar medium; development of telescopes and systems for infrared space astronomy. *Mailing Add:* Space Sci Div NASA Ames Res Ctr Moffett Field CA 94035

WERNER, PATRICIA ANN SNYDER, b Flint, Mich, July 7, 41; m 71. ECOLOGY, BOTANY. *Educ:* Mich State Univ, MS, 68, PhD(plant ecol), 72. *Prof Exp:* Res assoc ecol, Univ Iowa, 72-73; asst prof, 73-78, assoc prof terrestrial ecol, 78-80, ASSOC PROF BOT & ZOOL, MICH STATE UNIV, 80- *Concurrent Pos:* Prin investr grants, NSF, 73-; vis prof, Univ Dtago, Dunedin, New Zealand, 81. *Mem:* Ecol Soc Am; Bot Soc Am; Brit Ecol Soc; Int Soc Plant Pop Biol (secy/treas, 77-). *Res:* Plant population ecology; evolutionary ecology; life histories and competition among herbaceous plants; weeds; goldenrods; community structure; niche theory and empirical quantification; species relationships in disturbed communities; succession; seeds. *Mailing Add:* Kellogg Biol Sta Mich State Univ Hickory Corners MI 49060

WERNER, RAYMOND EDMUND, b Cincinnati, Ohio, Apr 18, 19; m 41; c 2. ORGANIC CHEMISTRY. *Educ:* Univ Cincinnati, ChE, 41, MS, 43, ScD(org chem), 45; Xavier Univ, Ohio, MBA, 69. *Prof Exp:* Res chemist, Interchem Corp, Ohio, 45-46; develop chemist, Sterling Drug, Inc, 46-55, dir develop, 55-75, vpres res & develop, Tech Ctr, Hilton Davis Div, 75-80. *Mem:* Am Chem Soc. *Res:* Administration of research and development in areas of fine organics, dyes, pharmaceuticals, pigments and graphic arts materials. *Mailing Add:* 9400 Southgate Dr Cincinnati OH 45241

WERNER, RICHARD ALLEN, b Reading, Pa, Feb 20, 36. ENTOMOLOGY. *Educ:* Pa State Univ, BS, 58 & 60; Univ Md, MS, 66; NC State Univ, PhD(entom), 71. *Prof Exp:* Forester, 57-59, res entomologist, Forestry Sci Lab, NC, 60-74, RES ENTOMOLOGIST, INST NORTHERN FORESTRY, US FOREST SERV, USDA, 74- *Concurrent Pos:* NIH res grant, Univ Md, 64-65; affil prof forestry, Univ Alaska, 76- *Mem:* Soc Am Foresters; Entom Soc Can; Entom Soc Am. *Res:* Aggregation behavior of bark beetles to host and insect produced chemicals; bark beetle biology and behavior in white spruce ecosystems; hardwood defoliators biology and behavior in Taiga ecosystems. *Mailing Add:* USDA Forest Serv Inst of Northern Forestry Fairbanks AK 99701

WERNER, ROBERT GEORGE, b Plymouth, Ind, Mar 6, 36; m 58; c 2. ZOOLOGY. *Educ:* Purdue Univ, BS, 58; Univ Calif, Los Angeles, MA, 63; Ind Univ, PhD(zool), 66. *Prof Exp:* Asst prof zool, State Univ NY Col Forestry, Syracuse, 66-69; asst prof fisheries, Cornell Univ, 69-70; assoc prof, 70-76, PROF ZOOL, STATE UNIV NY COL ENVIRON SCI & FORESTRY, 76- *Concurrent Pos:* Vis scientist, Scottish Marine Biol Asn, 78. *Mem:* Am Fisheries Soc; Am Soc Limnol & Oceanog; Ecol Soc Am. *Res:* Ecology of larval freshwater fish. *Mailing Add:* Dept Forest Zool State Univ NY Col Environ Sci & Forestry Syracuse NY 13210

WERNER, RUDOLF, b Königsberg, Ger, Dec 17, 34; m 61; c 2. CHEMISTRY. *Educ:* Univ Freiburg, Dipl(chem), 60, Dr rer nat(chem), 63. *Prof Exp:* Res asst, Inst Macromolecular Chem, Univ Freiburg, 61-65; res assoc, Carnegie Inst Genetics Res Unit, 65-67; sr staff investr, Cold Spring Harbor Lab Quant Biol, 68-70; assoc prof, 70-77, PROF BIOCHEM, SCH MED, UNIV MIAMI, 77- *Concurrent Pos:* Estab investr, Am Heart Asn, 69-74. *Mem:* AAAS; Am Soc Biol Chemists. *Res:* Molecular biology; DNA replication. *Mailing Add:* Dept Biochem Rosenstiel Sch Med Univ Miami Miami FL 33136

WERNER, SAMUEL ALFRED, b Elgin, Ill, Jan 5, 37; m 61; c 1. SOLID STATE PHYSICS, NUCLEAR ENGINEERING. *Educ:* Dartmouth Col, AB, 59, MS, 61; Univ Mich, Ann Arbor, PhD(nuclear eng), 65. *Prof Exp:* Instr solid state physics & mat, Thayer Sch Eng, Dartmouth Col, 60-61; staff scientist, Physics Dept, Sci Lab, Ford Motor Co, 65-70, sr scientist, 70-75; PROF PHYSICS, UNIV MO-COLUMBIA, 75- *Concurrent Pos:* Consult, Argonne Nat Lab, 68-; adj assoc prof, Univ Mich, 69-74; guest scientist, Aktiebolaget Atomenergi, Sweden, 70. *Mem:* AAAS; fel Am Phys Soc. *Res:* Neutron scattering; magnetism; physics of metals and alloys. *Mailing Add:* Dept Physics Univ Mo Columbia MO 65211

WERNER, SANFORD BENSON, b Newark, NJ, Jan 5, 39; m 68; c 2. PREVENTIVE MEDICINE. *Educ:* Rutgers Univ, BA, 60; Wash Univ, MD, 64; Univ Calif, MPH, 70. *Prof Exp:* Intern internal med, Vanderbilt Univ Hosp, Nashville, Tenn, 64-65; med epidemiologist, Epidemic Intel Serv, Ctr Dis Control, Ga, 65-67; resident internal med, Univ Wash Hosps, Seattle, 67-69; internist, Alaska Clin, Anchorage, 69; MED EPIDEMIOLOGIST INFECTIOUS DIS CONTROL, CALIF STATE DEPT HEALTH, 70- *Concurrent Pos:* Resident prev med, Sch Pub Health, Univ Calif, Berkeley, 70-71, lectr infectious dis epidemiol, 70- *Mem:* Fel Am Col Prev Med. *Res:* Epidemiology of botulism, typhoid, salmonellosis and other enteric diseases. *Mailing Add:* 2151 Berkeley Way Berkeley CA 94704

WERNER, SIDNEY CHARLES, b New York, NY, June 29, 09; m 47; c 4. THYROID, MEDICINE. *Educ:* Columbia Univ, AB, 29, MD, 32, ScD(med), 37. *Prof Exp:* Asst med, Col Physicians & Surgeons, Columbia Univ, 34-78, prof, 74-78, EMER PROF CLIN MED, 78- *Concurrent Pos:* From intern to attend physician, Presby Hosp, New York, 32-74, consult med, 74-; spec consult, Endocrine Study Sect, NIH, 52-55, endocrine panel, Nat Cancer Inst, 55-58, Cancer Chemother Serv Ctr, 58-62; Jacobaeus lectr, Finland, 68; consult, Var Hosps, NY & Conn; vis prof, Univ Ariz, 78- *Honors & Awards:* Wilson Award, 60; Stevens Triennial Award, 66; Distinguished Serv Award, Am Thyroid Asn, 69; Distinguished Thyroid Scientist, Int Thyroid Cong, 75. *Mem:* Fel AAAS; Am Thyroid Asn (pres, 72-73); Am Soc Clin Invest; Endocrine Soc; Asn Am Physicians. *Res:* Thyroid physiology and disease. *Mailing Add:* Univ of Ariz Health Sci Ctr Tucson AZ 85724

WERNER, THOMAS CLYDE, b York, Pa, June 19, 42; m 65; c 2. ANALYTICAL CHEMISTRY. *Educ:* Juniata Col, BS, 64; Mass Inst Technol, PhD(anal chem), 69. *Prof Exp:* Fel chem, Harvard Med Sch & Mass Gen Hosp, Boston, 69-70; fel med sch, Tufts Univ, 70-71; asst prof, 71-76, ASSOC PROF CHEM, UNION COL, NY, 76- *Mem:* Am Chem Soc. *Res:* Application of absorption and luminescence spectroscopy to the study of molecular structure. *Mailing Add:* Dept of Chem Union Col Schenectady NY 12308

WERNER, WILLIAM ERNEST, JR, b Mt Marion, NY, June 30, 25; m 47; c 2. ECOLOGY. *Educ:* State Univ NY, BA, 50, MA, 51; Cornell Univ, PhD(mammal), 54. *Prof Exp:* Instr biol, State Univ NY Col Teachers, Albany, 51-52; PROF BIOL, BLACKBURN COL, 54- *Concurrent Pos:* Nat Heart Inst fel, Marine Inst, Miami, 63-64. *Mem:* AAAS; Am Soc Mammalogists; Am Soc Ichthyologists & Herpetologists; Ecol Soc Am; Sigma Xi. *Res:* Ecology of mammals, reptiles, amphibians and marine invertebrates. *Mailing Add:* Dept of Biol Blackburn Col Carlinville IL 62626

WERNICK, JACK H(ARRY), b St Paul, Minn, May 19, 23; m 47; c 2. PHYSICAL METALLURGY, SOLID STATE CHEMISTRY. *Educ:* Univ Minn, BS, 47, MS, 48; Pa State Univ, PhD(metall, chem), 54. *Prof Exp:* Metallurgist, Manhattan Proj, Los Alamos Sci Lab, Calif, 44-46; instr metall, Pa State Univ, 49-54; mem tech staff, 54-64, head, Physical Metall Res Dept, 64-73, head, Solid State Chem Res Dept, 73-81, HEAD, DEVICE MAT RES DEPT, BELL LABS, 81- *Mem:* Nat Acad Eng; Am Soc Metals; fel Am Inst Mining, Metall & Petrol Engrs; fel Am Phys Soc; fel NY Acad Sci. *Res:* Constitution and physical chemistry of materials, particularly thermodynamic, magnetic and semiconducting properties. *Mailing Add:* Bell Tel Labs Inc Mountain Ave Murray Hill NJ 07971

WERNICK, ROBERT J, b New York, NY, June 19, 28; m 54; c 3. MATHEMATICS. *Educ:* Univ Mich, Ann Arbor, BSE, 49; Stevens Inst Technol, MS, 52; Rensselaer Polytech Inst, PhD(math), 69. *Prof Exp:* Res engr, Stevens Inst Technol, 51-53; tech asst, Panel Hydrodyn Submerged Bodies, Comt Undersea Warfare, Nat Res Coun, Washington, DC, 54; mathematician, Gen Eng Labs, Gen Elec Co, NY, 59-62 & Mech Technol, Inc, 62-64; asst prof math, State Univ NY Albany, 64-68; ASSOC PROF MATH, STATE UNIV NY OSWEGO, 69- *Concurrent Pos:* Consult, Advan Technol Labs, Gen Elec Co, NY, 63-66 & Mech Technol, Inc, 65; referee, J Appl Mech, 69- *Mem:* Am Math Soc; Soc Indust & Appl Math; Math Asn Am. *Res:* Numerical analysis; game theory applied to determining the spectra of linear operators. *Mailing Add:* Dept of Math State Univ of NY Oswego NY 13126

WERNICK, WILLIAM, b New York, NY, Dec 18, 10; m 33; c 2. MATHEMATICS. *Educ:* NY Univ, BS, 33, MS, 34, PhD(math), 41. *Prof Exp:* Teacher, New York Bd Educ, 37-46, chmn dept math, 46-65; assoc prof math, City Col New York, 65-77; RETIRED. *Concurrent Pos:* Lectr, Hunter Col, 46-50; assoc, Columbia Univ, 50-65. *Mem:* Am Math Soc; Math Asn Am; Asn Symbolic Logic. *Res:* Symbolic logic; general topology; calculus of operators; complete sets of logical functions; functional dependence in the calculus of propositions; distributive properties of set operators. *Mailing Add:* 3986 Hillman Ave New York NY 10463

WERNIMONT, GRANT (THEODORE), b Geneva, Nebr, Nov 30, 04; m 34; c 1. ANALYTICAL CHEMISTRY, APPLIED STATISTICS. *Educ:* Nebr Wesleyan Univ, AB, 27; Univ Utah, AM, 29; Purdue Univ, PhD(anal & inorg chem), 34. *Prof Exp:* Asst chem, Univ Utah, 27-29; asst, Purdue Univ, 29-34, instr, 34-35; anal & res chemist, Eastman Kodak Co, 35-69; vis prof chem, Purdue Univ, Lafayette, 69-71; CONSULT TO MANAGING DIR, AM SOC TESTING & MAT, 74- *Concurrent Pos:* Mem adv comt, Bur Med Devises & Diag Prod, Food & Drug Admin, 73-76. *Honors & Awards:* H F Dodge Award, Am Soc Testing & Mat, 80. *Mem:* Am Chem Soc; Am Soc Qual Control; AAAS. *Res:* Physical properties of liquid nitrous oxide; determination of the zirconium-hafnium ratio; chemical determination of water; determination of selenium in urine; electrometric titrations by the deadstop end point method; statistical quality control; electronic data processing; multivariate principle component analysis. *Mailing Add:* 400 N River Rd Apt 1111 West Lafayette IN 47906

WERNSMAN, EARL ALLEN, b Vernon, Ill, Nov 4, 35; m 59; c 1. CROP BREEDING. *Educ:* Univ Ill, Urbana, BS, 58, MS, 60; Purdue Univ, PhD(genetics), 63. *Prof Exp:* Res assoc genetics, Iowa State Univ, 63-64; from asst prof to assoc prof, 64-72, PROF GENETICS, NC STATE UNIV, 72- *Mem:* Am Soc Agron; Am Genetic Asn; Genetics Soc Can; AAAS. *Res:* Genetics of Nicotiana and alkaloid production; physiology of cytoplasmic male-sterility in Nicotiana; interspecific hybridization in Nicotiana, tissue and anther culture. *Mailing Add:* Dept of Crop Sci NC State Univ Raleigh NC 27607

WERNTZ, CARL W, b Washington, DC, Aug 7, 31; m 58; c 2. THEORETICAL NUCLEAR PHYSICS, ASTROPHYSICS. *Educ:* George Washington Univ, BS, 53; Univ Minn, MS, 55, PhD(physics), 60. *Prof Exp:* Res assoc physics, Univ Wis, 60-62; assoc prof, 62-70, chmn dept, 75-78,

PROF PHYSICS, CATH UNIV AM, 70- *Mem:* Am Phys Soc; Am Asn Physics Teachers. *Res:* Theory of interaction of pions with nuclei; study of solar nuclear reactions; three body problem. *Mailing Add:* Dept of Physics Cath Univ of Am Washington DC 20064

WERNTZ, HENRY OSCAR, b Atlantic City, NJ, Jan 19, 30; m 57; c 3. ZOOLOGY. *Educ:* Rutgers Univ, BS, 52; Yale Univ, PhD(zool), 58. *Prof Exp:* Instr biol, Harvard Univ, 57-60; asst prof biol, 60-64, actg chmn dept, 66-67, ASSOC PROF BIOL, NORTHEASTERN UNIV, 64-, CHMN DEPT, 75- *Mem:* AAAS; Am Soc Zoologists. *Res:* Osmotic and ionic regulation in invertebrates; environmental physiology. *Mailing Add:* Dept of Biol Northeastern Univ Boston MA 02115

WERNTZ, JAMES HERBERT, JR, b Wilmington, Del, Sept 3, 28; m 55; c 4. EDUCATIONAL ADMINISTRATION, PHYSICS. *Educ:* Oberlin Col, BA, 50; Univ Wis, MS, 52, PhD(physics), 57. *Prof Exp:* From asst prof to assoc prof physics, Univ Minn, Minneapolis, 56-68, prof, 68-81, dir, Ctr Educ Develop, 67-81, dir, Univ Col, 78-81; VCHANCELLOR ACAD AFFAIRS & PROF PHYSICS, UNIV NC, CHARLOTTE, 81- *Mem:* AAAS; Am Asn Higher Educ; Am Phys Soc; Am Asn Physics Teachers. *Res:* Physics of very low temperatures, especially liquid helium phenomena; science education. *Mailing Add:* 127 Cabell Way Charlotte NC 28211

WERNY, FRANK, b Ger, June 6, 36; US citizen; m; c 5. NATURAL PRODUCTS CHEMISTRY, TEXTILE TECHNOLOGY. *Educ:* Univ Puget Sound, BS, 58; Univ Hawaii, PhD(org chem), 63. *Prof Exp:* Ford Found fel, Free Univ Berlin, 62-63; res chemist, Carothers Res Lab, 63-67, sr res chemist, Textile Res Lab, 67-72, sr res chemist, Christina Labs, 72-76, SR RES CHEMIST, CHESTNUT RUN TEXTILE RES LAB, E I DU PONT DE NEMOURS & CO, INC, 76- *Mem:* Am Chem Soc. *Res:* Polyamide polymers and fibers; flammability of polymers and textiles; irradiation grafting and melt blending of polymers; polymer rheology; carpet yarns and carpets; nonwoven fabric research and development. *Mailing Add:* 13 Durboraw Rd Sherwood Green Wilmington DE 19810

WERSHAW, ROBERT LAWRENCE, b Norwalk, Conn, Sept 17, 35; m 63; c 2. HYDROLOGY, GEOCHEMISTRY. *Educ:* Tex Western Col, BS, 57; Calif Inst Technol, MS, 59; Univ Tex, PhD(geol), 63. *Prof Exp:* HYDROLOGIST, US GEOL SURV, 63- *Mem:* Geochem Soc; Am Chem Soc. *Res:* Geochemistry of naturally occurring polyelectrolytes and their interaction with water pollutants. *Mailing Add:* 1566 Winona Ct Denver CO 80204

WERT, CHARLES ALLEN, b Battle Creek, Iowa, Dec 31, 19; m 42; c 2. MATERIALS SCIENCE ENGINEERING. *Educ:* Morningside Col, BA, 41; Univ Iowa, MS, 43, PhD(physics), 48. *Prof Exp:* Mem staff radiation lab, Mass Inst Technol, 43-45; asst, Univ Iowa, 46-48; instr inst study metals, Univ Chicago, 48-50; from assoc prof to prof mining & metall eng, 50-56, PROF METALL & MINING ENG, UNIV ILL, URBANA, 56-, HEAD DEPT, 66- *Concurrent Pos:* Alexander von Humboldt Found sr scientist award, WGer, 81. *Mem:* Am Phys Soc; Am Inst Mining, Metall & Petrol Engrs; fel Am Soc Metals; AAAS. *Res:* Internal friction of metals; diffusion in solids; electron microscopy of solids; alloying behavior of metals with carbon, nitrogen, oxygen and carbon; chemistry and physical structure of coal. *Mailing Add:* Dept Metall & Mining Eng Univ Ill Urbana IL 61801

WERT, JAMES J, b Barron County, Wis, Jan 9, 33; m 58; c 2. ENGINEERING, MATERIALS SCIENCE. *Educ:* Univ Wis, BS, 57, MS, 58, PhD(metall eng), 61. *Prof Exp:* Asst engr, Bettis Atomic Power Lab, 58-59; res scientist, A O Smith Corp, 61; from asst prof to prof metall eng, 61-72, dir mat sci & eng div, 67-69, chmn dept mat sci & eng, 69-72, chmn mat, mech & struct div, 72-76, GEORGE A SLOAN PROF METALL, VANDERBILT UNIV, 72-, CHMN DEPT MECH ENG & MAT SCI, 76- *Concurrent Pos:* Westinghouse fel, Carnegie Inst Technol; consult, Nat Acad Sci; vis prof, Cambridge Univ, 74-75. *Mem:* Am Soc Eng Educ; Brit Inst Metals; Am Inst Mining, Metall & Petrol Engrs; Am Welding Soc; Royal Micros Soc. *Res:* X-ray diffraction studies of the effects of deformation on superlattice structures; kinetics of antiphase domain growth; residual stresses in metals, friction and wear. *Mailing Add:* 2510 Ridgewood Dr Nashville TN 37215

WERT, JOHN ARTHUR, physical metallurgy, see previous edition

WERT, JONATHAN MAXWELL, JR, b Port Royal, Pa, Nov 8, 39; m 62; c 3. ENVIRONMENTAL SCIENCES. *Educ:* Austin Peay State Univ, BS, 66, MS, 68; Univ Ala, PhD(educ planning), 74. *Prof Exp:* Chief naturalist, Pa Dept Environ Resources, 68-69; chief naturalist, Bays Mountain Park, 69-71; supvr environ educ sect, Tenn Valley Authority, 71-75; consult energy conserv, environ ctr, Univ Tenn, Knoxville, 75-77; sr prof assoc, Energy Exten Serv, Pa State Univ, 77-81; CHIEF DIV ENERGY PROG DEVELOP, PA DEPT COMMUNITY AFFAIRS, 81- *Concurrent Pos:* Mem adv bd, Environ Educ Report, Inc, 74-; mem nat adv coun environ educ, Dept Health, Educ & Welfare, 75-78. *Mem:* Conserv Educ Asn; Am Soc Ecol Educ; Nat Audubon Soc; Nat Educ Asn. *Res:* Development of methodologies for carrying out comprehensive environmental planning, including technological assessment, cost-benefit analysis and environmental impact assessment; energy conservation; systems planning. *Mailing Add:* 42 First St Port Royal PA 17082

WERTH, GLENN CONRAD, b Denver, Colo, July 21, 26; m 50; c 3. GEOPHYSICS. *Educ:* Univ Colo, BS, 49; Univ Calif, Los Angeles, MS, 50, PhD(physics, acoustics), 53. *Prof Exp:* Physicist, Arthur D Little, Inc, 53-54 & Calif Res Corp, 54-59; physicist, 59-66, assoc dir, Lawrence Livermore Lab, Univ Calif, 66-81; DIR NEW PROG DEVELOP, WOODWARD CLYDE CONSULTS, 81- *Mem:* Seismol Soc; Am Nuclear Soc; Am Geophys Union; Corporate Planning Asn. *Res:* Seismology; geophysical exploration for oil; use of nuclear explosives in industry and commerce; development of alternate energy supplies; analysis of energy issues and role for research and development; corporate planning. *Mailing Add:* Woodward Clyde Consults 600 Montgomery St San Francisco CA 94111

WERTH, JEAN MARIE, b Rochester, NY, Jan 21, 43. MICROBIAL PHYSIOLOGY. *Educ:* Nazareth Col Rochester, BS, 64; Syracuse Univ, MS, 69, PhD(microbiol), 73. *Prof Exp:* Asst prof, 72-77, ASSOC PROF BIOL, WILLIAM PATERSON COL, 77- *Concurrent Pos:* Vis scientist, Roche Inst Molecular Biol, 80-81. *Mem:* AAAS; Am Soc Microbiol; Sigma Xi; NY Acad Sci. *Res:* Effects of antibiotics and hormones on growth and extracellular lysin production in strains of Streptococcus zymogenes and various soil bacteria; isolation and characterization of protein-bound methionine sulfoxide reductase. *Mailing Add:* Dept Biol William Paterson Col Wayne NJ 07470

WERTH, JOHN, b Sarrebruck, France, Apr 11, 27; US citizen; m 51; c 2. ELECTROCHEMICAL & ELECTRICAL ENGINEERING. *Educ:* Manhattan Col, BSEE, 51; Columbia Univ, MS, 61. *Prof Exp:* Res engr, Am Bosch-Arma Corp, 51-55; res consult, ACF Electronics, 55-59, lab dir, 59-60; sect head power & energy conversion, Gen Motors Res Labs, Calif, 60-70; SR RES ASSOC, ESB TECHNOL CO, 70- *Concurrent Pos:* Assoc ed, Energy Conversion J, 66-; mem, Morse Comt Elec Vehicles, Com Dept, 67. *Mem:* Sr mem Inst Elec & Electronics Engrs; Electrochem Soc. *Res:* Batteries; electromagnetic components; instrumentation; electric motor, high energy battery and electric vehicle. *Mailing Add:* ESB Technol Co 19 W College Ave Yardley PA 19067

WERTH, JOHN ST CLAIR, JR, b Bluefield, WVa, Nov 22, 40; m 61; c 2. MATHEMATICS. *Educ:* Emory Univ, BS, 62, MS, 63; Univ Wash, PhD(math), 68. *Prof Exp:* Lectr math, Emory Univ, 62-63; res instr, NMex State Univ, 68-69, asst prof, 69-74; asst prof, 74-77, ASSOC PROF MATH, UNIV NEV, LAS VEGAS, 77- *Concurrent Pos:* Reviewer, Math Rev, 71-72. *Mem:* Am Math Soc. *Res:* Abelian groups; ring theory. *Mailing Add:* Dept of Math Univ of Nev Las Vegas NV 89109

WERTH, RICHARD GEORGE, b Markesan, Wis, Feb 5, 20; m 43; c 1. ORGANIC CHEMISTRY. *Educ:* Wartburg Col, BA, 42; Univ Wis, MS, 48, PhD, 50. *Prof Exp:* Jr chemist, Electrochem Dept, E I du Pont de Nemours & Co, 42-44 & 46; Alumni Res Found asst, Univ Wis, 48-50; assoc prof chem, 50-53, head dept, 61-69, chmn dept, 74-77, PROF CHEM, CONCORDIA COL, MOORHEAD, MINN, 53- CHMN DEPT. *Concurrent Pos:* Res partic, Oak Ridge Nat Lab, 62-63; vis fel, Cornell Univ, 70-71. *Mem:* AAAS; Am Chem Soc; Am Inst Chemists; Soc Appl Spectros. *Res:* Methods of organic synthesis of polycyclic compounds; formaldehyde products; reaction mechanism for dehydration of bicycloheptanediols; mass spectra of vinylogous imides. *Mailing Add:* 1207 S Seventh St Moorhead MN 56560

WERTH, ROBERT JOSEPH, b Hays, Kans, Apr 4, 40; c 1. ZOOLOGY. *Educ:* St Benedict's Col, Kans, BS, 61; Univ Mo-Kansas City, MS, 65; Univ Colo, Boulder, PhD(zool), 69. *Prof Exp:* Asst prof, 69-76, ASSOC PROF BIOL, PURDUE UNIV, CALUMET CAMPUS, 76- *Mem:* AAAS; Am Soc Ichthyologists & Herpetologists. *Res:* Reptilian ecology and physiology; correlation of environmental requirement with physiological adaptation. *Mailing Add:* Dept of Biol Purdue Univ Calumet Campus Hammond IN 46323

WERTHEIM, ARTHUR ROBERT, b Newark, NJ, July 5, 15; m 47. MEDICINE. *Educ:* Dartmouth Col, AB, 35; Jefferson Med Col, MD, 39; Am Bd Internal Med, dipl, 50, recertification, 74. *Prof Exp:* Intern, Philadelphia Gen Hosp, 39-41, resident, 41-43; resident, Goldwater Mem Hosp, 46-47; asst, Long Island Col Med, 48; instr, Col Med, State Univ NY Downstate Med Ctr, 49-51; from asst prof to assoc prof, 51-69, prof, 69-81, EMER PROF MED, COL PHYSICIANS & SURGEONS, COLUMBIA UNIV, 81- *Concurrent Pos:* Res fel, Goldwater Mem Hosp, 47; asst med, Col Physicians & Surgeons, Columbia Univ, 47; from clin assoc to dir med serv, Maimonides Hosp, Brooklyn, 48-51; res assoc, Goldwater Mem Hosp, 51-54, vis physician, 54-68; actg chief, Med Serv, Francis Delafield Hosp, New York, 71-74, chief, 74-75; attending physician, Presby Hosp, NY, 81, consult med serv, 81- *Mem:* Harvey Soc; AMA; fel Am Col Physicians. *Res:* Clinical and laboratory research in chronic diseases; metabolic aspects of hypertension and atherosclerosis. *Mailing Add:* 52-47 241 St Douglaston NY 11362

WERTHEIM, GUNTHER KLAUS, b Berlin, Ger, Feb 26, 27; nat US; m 56; c 3. SOLID STATE PHYSICS. *Educ:* Stevens Inst Technol, ME, 51; Harvard Univ, AM, 52, PhD(physics), 55. *Prof Exp:* Assoc phys oceanog, Woods Hole Oceanog Inst, 54; mem tech staff, Bell Tel Labs, Inc, 55-62, HEAD CRYSTAL PHYSICS RES DEPT, BELL LABS, 62- *Concurrent Pos:* Adj prof, Stevens Inst Technol, 66-68; mem vis comts physics, Harvard Univ, 69-75 & Bartol Res Found, 72- *Mem:* Am Phys Soc; Sigma Xi. *Res:* X-ray photoelectron spectroscopy; Mössbauer effect; angular correlations; magnetism; semiconductors. *Mailing Add:* Bell Labs Murray Hill NJ 07974

WERTHEIM, ROBERT HALLEY, b Carlsbad, NMex, Nov 9, 22; m 46; c 2. NUCLEAR PHYSICS. *Educ:* US Naval Acad, BS, 45; Mass Inst Technol, SM, 54. *Prof Exp:* Staff officer, Armed Forces Spec Weapons Proj, US Navy, 48-49, spec asst nuclear applns, Spec Projs Off, 56, head re-entry body sect, 56-61, weapons develop dept, Naval Ord Test Sta, 61-62, mem staff, Dir of Defense Res & Eng, 62-65, head missile br, Spec Projs Off, 65-67, dep tech dir, 67-68, tech dir, 68-77, dir Spec Projs Off, 77-80; SR VPRES, SCI & ENG, LOCKHEED CORP, 81- *Concurrent Pos:* Consult, Off Secy Defense; mem, Sci Adv Group on Effects, Defense Nuclear Agency; mem, Nat Security Adv Group, Los Alamos Nat Lab. *Honors & Awards:* William S Parsons Award, 71, Legion of Merit, 72; Gold Medal, Am Soc Naval Engrs, 73. *Mem:* Nat Acad Eng; Sigma Xi; Am Soc Naval Engrs; assoc fel Am Inst Aeronaut & Astronaut. *Res:* Weapons systems research, development and testing, especially ballistic missiles and nuclear applications. *Mailing Add:* Sci & Eng Lockheed Corp PO Box 551 Burbank CA 91520

WERTHEIMER, ALAN LEE, b Cleveland, Ohio, Dec 22, 46; m 69; c 2. OPTICAL ENGINEERING, MICROPROCESSORS. *Educ:* Univ Rochester, BS, 68, PhD(optics), 74. *Prof Exp:* Optical system and lens design, Itek Corp, 68-69; SR SCIENTIST OPTICS RES, LEEDS & NORTHRUP CO, 74- *Mem:* Optical Soc Am; Soc Photo-Optical Instrumentation Eng. *Res:*

Light scattering to analyze particle size distributions in air and liquid media; engineering and project management of optically based, microprocessor controlled measuring and recording instruments; optical processing of photographic images; fiber optics communications. *Mailing Add:* Leeds & Northrup Co Tech Ctr North Wales PA 19454

WERTHEIMER, ALBERT I, b Buffalo, NY, Sept 14, 42; m 65; c 2. PUBLIC HEALTH ADMINISTRATION. *Educ:* Univ Buffalo, BS, 65; State Univ NY Buffalo, MBA, 67; Purdue Univ, PhD(med sociol, pharm), 69. *Prof Exp:* Asst prof pharm, Sch Pharm, State Univ NY Buffalo, 69-71, asst prof mkt, Sch Mgt, 70-71; researcher med care, Social Security Admin, Dept Health, Educ & Welfare, 72 & USPHS 72-73; ASSOC PROF PHARM ADMIN & DIR GRAD PROG, UNIV MINN, MINNEAPOLIS, 73- *Concurrent Pos:* WHO fel, 75. *Mem:* Am Pub Health Asn; Am Pharmaceut Asn; Am Sociol Asn; AMA. *Res:* Drug use process; drug ecology studies. *Mailing Add:* Col of Pharm Univ of Minn Minneapolis MN 55455

WERTHEIMER, FREDERICK WILLIAM, b Saginaw, Mich, May 21, 25; m 56; c 3. PERIODONTOLOGY, ORAL PATHOLOGY. *Educ:* Univ Mich, DDS, 49; Northwestern Univ, MSD, 54; Georgetown Univ, MS, 60; Am Bd Periodont, dipl; Am Bd Oral Pathol, dipl. *Prof Exp:* Pvt practr, 52-53 & 54-58; investr dent, Nat Inst Dent Res, 60-61; sr assoc periodont, Henry Ford Hosp, Detroit, 62-68; assoc prof path, 65-68, PROF PATH & CHMN DEPT, DENT SCH, UNIV DETROIT, 68- *Concurrent Pos:* NIH res & training grants, 65-; adj assoc prof, Med Sch, Wayne State Univ; consult, Vet Admin Hosp & Detroit Gen Hosp, Detroit. *Mem:* Fel AAAS; fel Am Acad Oral Path; fel Am Col Dent; fel Int Col Dent; Am Acad Periodont. *Res:* Histochemistry of periodontal disease and oral neoplasia. *Mailing Add:* Dept Path Dent Sch Univ Detroit 2985 E Jefferson Ave Detroit MI 48207

WERTHEIMER, MICHAEL ROBERT, b Capetown, SAfrica, Jan 22, 40; Can citizen; m 73; c 2. SOLID STATE PHYSICS, MATERIALS SCIENCE. *Educ:* Univ Toronto, BASc, 62, MA, 63; Univ Grenoble, Dr es Sc, 67. *Prof Exp:* Process engr thermodyn, Can Liquid Air Ltd, 63-64, res engr cryog, 67-72; PROF ENG PHYSICS, ECOLE POLYTECH, MONTREAL, 73- *Concurrent Pos:* Consult, Montreal Transport Comn, 75-77, IBM Corp, 77- & Leybold-Heraeus Ges Beschranker Haftung, 80-; pres, Polyplasma Inc, 82- *Mem:* Inst Elec & Electronics Engrs; Elec Insulation Soc; Am Phys Soc; Can Asn Physicists. *Res:* Electrical insulation; dielectrics; polymers; plasma chemistry; materials science; surface science. *Mailing Add:* Dept Eng Physics Box 6079 Sta A Montreal PQ H3C 3A7 Can

WERTHESSEN, NICHOLAS THEODORE, endocrinology, deceased

WERTMAN, LOUIS, b New York, NY, Oct 2, 25; m 47; c 3. BIOMEDICAL ENGINEERING. *Educ:* City Col New York, BME, 50. *Prof Exp:* Assoc prof, 51-65, PROF MECH TECHNOL, NEW YORK CITY COMMUNITY COL, 65-, ADMINR ELECTROMECH, 66- *Concurrent Pos:* Consult engr, 60- *Mem:* AAAS; Am Soc Eng Educ; Soc Mfg Engrs; Nat Soc Prof Engrs. *Res:* Automated biomedical engineering utilizing electromechanical components and systems; educational research in new program development. *Mailing Add:* 57 Montague Brooklyn NY 11201

WERTMAN, WILLIAM THOMAS, b Franklin, Pa, Dec 25, 20; m 42; c 3. PETROLEUM ENGINEERING, CHEMICAL ENGINEERING. *Educ:* Grove City Col, BS, 42. *Prof Exp:* Chem engr, Joseph E Seagram & Sons, Inc, Md, 42-45 & Bradford Labs, Inc, Pa, 46-48; chem engr, Petrol & Natural Gas Div, US Bur Mines, Pa, 48-54, proj leader, Morgantown Petrol Res Lab, WVa, 54-63, proj cooodr, 63-65, actg chief lab, 65-66, chief lab, 66-70, dep res dir, Morgantown Energy Res Ctr, 70-75, sr staff specialist, Morgantown Energy Technol Ctr, US Dept Energy, 75-81; SR PETROL ENGR, SCI APPLICATIONS, INC, MORGANTOWN, WVA, 81- *Mem:* Am Chem Soc; Soc Petrol Engrs; Am Petrol Inst; Am Gas Asn. *Res:* Petroleum and natural gas production; reservoir engineering and rock analysis; subsurface formation temperatures; fluid flow through porous media; water analysis and treatment; coal chemistry and gasification research. *Mailing Add:* 433 Washington St Morgantown WV 26505

WERTZ, DAVID HUNTINGTON, b Johnstown, Pa, May 18, 45; m 74. POLYMER CHEMISTRY. *Educ:* Hamilton Col, BA, 67; Univ Ga, PhD(phys org chem), 74. *Prof Exp:* Fel biophys chem, Cornell Univ, 74-77; RES CHEMIST POLYMER CHEM, ALLIED CORP, 77- *Mem:* Am Chem Soc. *Mailing Add:* Allied Corp PO Box 1021R Morristown NJ 07960

WERTZ, DAVID LEE, b Hammond, Ind, Feb 3, 40; m 61; c 2. INORGANIC CHEMISTRY, PHYSICAL CHEMISTRY. *Educ:* Ark State Univ, BS, 62; Univ Ark, PhD(chem), 66. *Prof Exp:* From asst prof to assoc prof, 66-74, PROF CHEM, UNIV SOUTHERN MISS, 74- *Mem:* Am Chem Soc. *Res:* X-ray diffraction and spectral studies of solute-solvent interactions in concentrated solutions; x-ray diffraction studies of liquid structure. *Mailing Add:* Box 5043 Southern Sta Hattiesburg MS 39401

WERTZ, DENNIS WILLIAM, b Reading, Pa, Mar 21, 42; m 62; c 2. PHYSICAL CHEMISTRY. *Educ:* Univ Md, BS, 64; Univ SC, PhD(chem), 68. *Prof Exp:* Res assoc spectros, Mass Inst Technol, 68-69; asst prof, 69-74, ASSOC PROF CHEM, NC STATE UNIV, 74- *Mem:* AAAS. *Res:* Spectroscopic investigations of small ring molecules; infrared and Raman investigations of organometallic compounds. *Mailing Add:* Dept of Chem NC State Univ Raleigh NC 27607

WERTZ, GAIL T WILLIAMS, b Washington, DC, Oct 31, 43; m 66. VIROLOGY. *Educ:* Col William & Mary, BS, 66; Univ Pittsburgh, PhD(microbiol), 70. *Prof Exp:* NIH fel, Med Sch, Univ Mich, Ann Arbor, 70-71, sr res assoc virol, 71-73; ASST PROF BACT & IMMUNOL, MED SCH, UNIV NC, CHAPEL HILL, 73- *Concurrent Pos:* NSF & NIH res grants. *Mem:* AAAS; Am Soc Microbiol; Am Tissue Cult Asn; Sigma Xi. *Res:* Virus-host interactions; viral replication; mechanism of viral nucleic acid synthesis and replication; effect of virus on host macromolecular synthesis and host response to infection-interference phenomenon. *Mailing Add:* 608 Laurel Hill Rd Chapel Hill NC 27514

WERTZ, HARVEY J, b Muskogee, Okla, May 1, 36. ELECTRICAL ENGINEERING, APPLIED MATHEMATICS. *Educ:* Univ Kans, BSEE, 58, MSEE, 59; Univ Wis, PhD(elec eng), 62. *Prof Exp:* Instr elec eng, Univ Kans, 58-59; from asst prof to assoc prof, Univ Wis-Madison, 62-69; consult, 64-65, 68-69, mem tech staff, 66-68, 69-73, head, Orbital Systs Prog Dept, 73-79, PRIN DIR MATH & PROG SUBDIV & SIGNAL ANAL & COMPUT DEVELOP SUBDIV, AEROSPACE CORP, 80- *Concurrent Pos:* Asst prof, Math Res Ctr, US Army. *Mem:* Soc Indust & Appl Math; Asn Comput Mach; Inst Elec & Electronics Engrs. *Res:* Application of mathematics and computing to the analysis and synthesis of physical systems; development of user-oriented software, especially library quality subroutines and precompilers. *Mailing Add:* Aerospace Corp PO Box 92957 Los Angeles CA 90009

WERTZ, JAMES RICHARD, b Kingman, Ariz, Feb 20, 44; m 67; c 1. THEORETICAL ASTROPHYSICS, ASTRONAUTICS. *Educ:* Mass Inst Technol, SB, 66; Univ Tex, Austin, PhD(physics), 70. *Prof Exp:* Asst prof physics & astron, Moorhead State Col, 70-73, NSF inst grant, 71-73; sr analyst, Comput Sci Corp, 73-78; dir spacecraft eng, Western Union Space Comt, 78-80, SR SYSTS ENGR, TRW, 80- *Concurrent Pos:* Mem task group educ astron, Am Astron Soc, 74- *Mem:* AAAS; Brit Interplanetary Soc; Am Phys Soc; Am Astron Soc; Am Inst Aeronaut & Astronaut. *Res:* Spacecraft attitude determination, interstellar travel and navigation; hierarchical cosmology. *Mailing Add:* TRW Space Systs One Space Park Redondo Beach CA 90278

WERTZ, JOHN EDWARD, b Denver, Colo, Dec 4, 16; m 43; c 3. CHEMISTRY. *Educ:* Univ Denver, BS, 37, MS, 38; Univ Chicago, PhD(chem), 48. *Prof Exp:* Asst prof chem, Augustana Col, 41-44; instr physics, Gustavus Adolphus Col, 44-45; instr mech eng, 45-47, from asst prof to prof phys chem, 48-74, PROF CHEM, UNIV MINN, MINNEAPOLIS, 74- *Concurrent Pos:* Fulbright res scholar & Guggenheim fel, Clarendon Lab, Oxford Univ, 57-58. *Mem:* Fel Am Phys Soc; Brit Inst Physics; Am Chem Soc; The Chem Soc. *Res:* Fluorescence of crystals; surface energy of solids; adsorption of vapors on solids; magnetic susceptibility of adsorbed layers; nuclear and paramagnetic resonance; structure and electronic properties of defects in solids; infrared detectors. *Mailing Add:* Dept of Chem Univ of Minn Minneapolis MN 55455

WESCHLER, CHARLES JOHN, b Youngstown, Ohio, Jan 29, 48; m 71. ATMOSPHERIC CHEMISTRY. *Educ:* Boston Col, BS, 69; Univ Chicago, MS, 72, PhD(chem), 74. *Prof Exp:* Fel phys inorg chem, Northwestern Univ, 74-75; MEM TECH STAFF CHEM, BELL LABS, 75- *Concurrent Pos:* Lab grad partic, Argonne Nat Lab, 72-73. *Mem:* AAAS; Am Chem Soc. *Res:* Indoor aerosols; elemental and chemical composition of aerosols as a function of particle size; chemistry occuring within atmospheric aerosols; comparisons between indoor and outdoor aerosols. *Mailing Add:* Bell Labs Crawfords Corner Rd Holmdel NJ 07733

WESCHLER, JOSEPH ROBERT, organic chemistry, see previous edition

WESCOTT, EUGENE MICHAEL, b Hampton, Iowa, Feb 15, 32; m 60; c 4. SPACE PHYSICS, EXPLORATION GEOPHYSICS. *Educ:* Univ Calif, Los Angeles, AB, 55; Univ Alaska, MS, 60, PhD(geophys), 64. *Prof Exp:* Geophysicist, Geophys Res & Develop Br, US Atomic Energy Comn, 55-58; sr res asst, 58-64, from asst prof to assoc prof, 64-74, PROF RES GEOPHYS, GEOPHYS INST UNIV ALASKA, 74- *Concurrent Pos:* Resident res assoc nat acad sci, NASA Goddard Space Flight Ctr, 66-69; vis prof inst geophys & planetary physics, Univ Calif, Los Angeles, 76-77. *Mem:* Am Geophys Union; Int Asn Geomagnetism & Aeronomy; Soc Explor Geophys. *Res:* Electric and magnetic fields of the upper atmosphere and of magnetospheric plasmas; auroral mechanisms earthquake prediction. *Mailing Add:* Geophys Inst Univ of Alaska Fairbanks AK 99701

WESCOTT, LYLE DUMOND, JR, b Hackensack, NJ, Jan 27, 37; div; c 2. ORGANIC CHEMISTRY. *Educ:* Ga Inst Technol, BS, 59; Pa State Univ, PhD(chem), 63. *Prof Exp:* Res fel, Pa State Univ, 63-64; res chemist, Baytown Labs, Esso Res & Eng Co, Tex, 64-68; asst prof chem, 68-71, assoc prof, 71-77, PROF CHEM, CHRISTIAN BROS COL, 77-, HEAD DEPT, 74- *Mem:* Am Chem Soc; Royal Soc Chem. *Res:* Low temperature reactions of vapor species of refractory materials; stabilization of polymeric materials; flame and smoke suppressants for polymeric materials adhesives. *Mailing Add:* Dept Chem Christian Bros Col 650 E Pkwy S Memphis TN 38104

WESCOTT, RICHARD BRESLICH, b Chicago, Ill, July 8, 32; m 54; c 3. VETERINARY PARASITOLOGY. *Educ:* Univ Wis, BS, 54, MS, 64, PhD(vet med), 65; Univ Minn, DVM, 58; Am Col Lab Animal Med, dipl, 67. *Prof Exp:* USPHS fel parasitol, Univ Wis, 62-65; assoc prof vet microbiol, Sch Vet Med, Univ Mo-Columbia, 65-71; PROF VET PATH, WASH STATE UNIV, 71- *Concurrent Pos:* Actg chmn dept vet path, Wash State Univ, 75-77. *Mem:* Am Vet Med Asn. *Res:* Laboratory animal medicine; nematode-virus interactions in gnotobiotic host animals. *Mailing Add:* Dept of Vet Path Wash State Univ Pullman WA 99163

WESCOTT, WILLIAM B, b Pendleton, Ore, Nov 10, 22; m 69; c 2. ORAL PATHOLOGY. *Educ:* Univ Ore, DMD, 51, MS, 62. *Prof Exp:* Dir oral tumor registry, Dent Sch, Univ Ore, 53-54; pvt practr gen dent, Ore, 53-59; asst gen path, Dent Sch, Univ Ore, 59-60; from asst prof to assoc prof path, 62-69, prof path & assoc dean admin affairs, 69-72; co-dir res & educ training prog, Oral Dis Res Lab, Vet Admin Hosp, Houston, 72-75; chief dent serv, Vet Admin Hosp, Durham, NC, 75-78; co-dir, Southeastern Regional Med Educ Ctr, Birmingham, 78-79; PROF ORAL DIAGNOSTIC RADIOL PATH, DENT SCH, LOMA LINDA UNIV, 79- *Concurrent Pos:* Am Cancer Soc fel, 59-61; USPHS fel, 61-63; clin assoc oral & dent med, Med Sch, Univ Ore, sr clin instr, 67-69; prof path, Univ Tex Dent Br, Houston, 72-75 & Duke Univ Med Sch, 76-78; prof dent, Univ NC, 75-78; consult, US Naval Regional Dent Ctr, 82- *Mem:* Am Dent Asn; Int Asn Dent Res; fel Am Acad Oral Path; Int Asn Microbiol; fel Am Col Dent. *Res:* Correlation of clinical and histopathologic findings; fluorescent antibody technic; foreign body reaction; bacteriologic and fungal changes under bizarre atmospheres and increased pressures; immunology; salivary glands. *Mailing Add:* Dent Educ Ctr Vet Admin Wadsworth Med Ctr Los Angeles CA 90073

WESELI, DONALD FENTON, immunology, see previous edition

WESELOH, RONALD MACK, b Los Angeles, Calif, June 30, 44. ENTOMOLOGY. *Educ:* Brigham Young Univ, BS, 66; Univ Calif, Riverside, PhD(entom), 70. *Prof Exp:* Asst agr scientist, 70-75, assoc agr scientist, 75-81, AGR SCIENTIST, CONN AGR EXP STA, 81- *Mem:* Entom Soc Am; Entom Soc Can; Sigma Xi; Int Orgn Biol Control. *Res:* Control of insect pests by means of parasites; insect behavior and ecology. *Mailing Add:* Dept of Entom Conn Agr Exp Sta New Haven CT 06504

WESELY, MARVIN LARRY, b Cedar Bluffs, Nebr, May 5, 44; m 68; c 2. AGRICULTURAL METEOROLOGY. *Educ:* Univ Nebr, Lincoln, BS, 65; Univ Wis-Madison, MS, 68, PhD(soil sci), 70. *Prof Exp:* Physicist, US Army Ballistic Res Labs, 70-73; asst meteorologist, 73-76, METEOROLOGIST, ARGONNE NAT LAB, 76-, SECT HEAD, ATMOSPHERIC PHYSICS SECT, RADIOL & ENVIRON RES DIV, 81- *Mem:* Am Meteorol Soc; Am Soc Agron; Am Geophys Union; Royal Meteorol Soc; AAAS. *Res:* Studies of turbulent transfer of heat, momentum and pollutants in the lower atmosphere; remote sensing of turbulence using line-of-sight optical techniques; nonspectral measurements of solar radiation components. *Mailing Add:* Argonne Nat Lab Bldg 181 Argonne IL 60439

WESENBERG, CLARENCE L, b Bradley, SDak, May 15, 20; m 42; c 6. ELECTRONIC ENGINEERING. *Educ:* SDak State Univ, BS, 43. *Prof Exp:* Radial-physics surveyor, Argonne Nat Lab, 44-46, electronics designer, 46-53; electronics engr, Stromberg-Carlson Co, 53-58, reliability engr, Gen Dynamics/Electronics, 58-62; prof reliability engr, Honeywell, Inc, 62-67; SR RELIABILITY ENGR, 3M CO, 67- *Mem:* Inst Elec & Electronics Engrs. *Res:* Metrology engineering involving calibration and measurements via mechanical and electromechanical instruments; maintaining accurate parameter measurement control for all magnetic tape parameters affecting performance and usage. *Mailing Add:* 8617 W River Rd N Minneapolis MN 55444

WESENBERG, DARRELL, b Madison, Wis, Dec 6, 39; m 68; c 3. AGRONOMY, GENETICS. *Educ:* Univ Wis-Madison, BS, 62, MS, 65, PhD(agron), 68. *Prof Exp:* RES AGRONOMIST, RES & EXTEN CTR, AGR RES SERV, USDA, 68- *Mem:* Crops Sci Soc Am; Am Soc Agron; AAAS; Am Genetic Asn; Sigma Xi. *Res:* Plant breeding and plant genetics in cereal crops. *Mailing Add:* Res & Exten Ctr Agr Res Serv USDA Aberdeen ID 83210

WESER, ELLIOT, b New York, NY, Jan 12, 32; m 55; c 1. MEDICINE, GASTROENTEROLOGY. *Educ:* Columbia Univ, AB, 53, MD, 57; Am Bd Internal Med, dipl, 64; Am Bd Nutrit, cert, 71. *Prof Exp:* Med intern & asst resident, Sch Med & King County Hosp, Univ Wash, 57-59; sr resident med, Bronx Munic Hosp Ctr, Albert Einstein Col of Med, 59-60; clin assoc gastroenterol, Nat Inst Arthritis & Metab Dis, 61-63; from instr to asst prof med, Med Col, Cornell Univ, 63-67; prof physiol & med, Univ Tex Med Sch, San Antonio, 67-76, dep chmn dept, 69-76, head sect gastroenterol, 67-76; CHIEF MED SERV, AUDIE L MURPHY VET ADMIN HOSP, SAN ANTONIO, 76- *Concurrent Pos:* Res fel med, New York Hosp-Cornell Med Ctr, 60-61; New York Res Coun career scientist award, 63-67; asst attend physician, New York Hosp, 64-67; asst vis physician, Bellevue Hosp, 64-67; attend physician, Bexar County Hosps, 67- *Mem:* AAAS; fel Am Col Physicians; Am Fedn Clin Res; Am Gastroenterol Asn; AMA. *Mailing Add:* Univ Tex Health Sci Ctr 7703 Floyd Curl Dr San Antonio TX 78284

WESLER, OSCAR, b Brooklyn, NY, July 12, 21. MATHEMATICS, STATISTICS. *Educ:* City Col New York, BS, 42; NY Univ, MS, 43; Stanford Univ, PhD(math statist), 55. *Prof Exp:* Asst math, NY Univ, 42-43; asst & instr, Princeton Univ, 43-46; res assoc math statist, Stanford Univ, 52-55, actg asst prof statist, 55-56; from asst prof to assoc prof math, Univ Mich, 56-64; PROF STATIST & MATH, NC STATE UNIV, 64- *Concurrent Pos:* Consult inst sci & technnol, Univ Mich, 56-64; vis assoc prof, Stanford Univ, 60, vis prof, 62-63, 73, 74 & 78; NSF nat lectr, 63-; prof on-site studies prog, Int Bus Mach Corp, 66-; vis scholar, Univ Calif, Berkeley, 72-73. *Mem:* Am Math Soc; Inst Math Statist. *Res:* Probability and statistics; stochastic processes; statistical decision theory; functional analysis. *Mailing Add:* Dept of Statist NC State Univ Raleigh NC 27607

WESLEY, DEAN E, b Flint, Mich, Feb 26, 37; m 59; c 4. SOIL FERTILITY. *Educ:* Mich State Univ, BS, 61; SDak State Univ, PhD(soil fertil), 65. *Prof Exp:* Exten soil specialist & asst SCI & EDUC ADMIN-AGR RES, Univ Nebr, 65-66; from asst prof to assoc prof agron, 66-74, assoc prof, 74-80, PROF AGR, WESTERN ILL UNIV, 80- *Mem:* Am Soc Agron; Soil Sci Soc Am; Soil Conserv Soc Am. *Res:* Plant nutrition; nutrients such as phosphorus, zinc, iron and sulfur. *Mailing Add:* Indian Trail Macomb IL 61455

WESLEY, ROBERT COOK, b Jamestown, Ky, Aug 19, 26; m 53; c 2. DENTISTRY. *Educ:* Berea Col, AB, 50; Univ Louisville, DMD, 54. *Prof Exp:* Pvt practr, 54-67; asst prof prosthodont, 67-72, actg dir, Gen Pract Residency Dent, 80-80, ASSOC PROF PROSTHODONT, COL DENT, UNIV KY, 72-, ASSOC PROF FAMILY PRACT & DIR DIV ORAL HEALTH, DEPT FAMILY PRACT, COL MED, 75-, DIR, GEN PRACT RESIDENCY DENT, 78- *Concurrent Pos:* Consult, Vet Admin Hosp, Lexington, Ky, 72; ed, Southeastern Acad Newslett, 73- *Mem:* Int Asn Dent Res; Am Dent Asn. *Res:* Complete dentures especially related to geriatric patients. *Mailing Add:* Col of Dent Univ of Ky Med Ctr Lexington KY 40506

WESLEY, ROY LEWIS, b Liberty, Ky, May 1, 29; m 54; c 5. FOOD SCIENCE. *Educ:* Berea Col, BS, 55; Purdue Univ, MS, 58, PhD, 66. *Prof Exp:* From asst prof to assoc prof poultry sci, 58-74, PROF POULTRY SCI, VA POLYTECH INST & STATE UNIV, 74- *Mem:* Poultry Sci Asn; Inst Food Technol. *Res:* Physiology. *Mailing Add:* Dept of Food Sci Va Polytech Inst & State Univ Blacksburg VA 24061

WESLEY, WALTER GLEN, b Ft Worth, Tex, Oct 12, 38; m 68; c 5. THEORETICAL PHYSICS. *Educ:* Tex Christian Univ, BA, 61; Univ NC, PhD(physics), 70. *Prof Exp:* From asst prof to assoc prof physics, 66-75, PROF PHYSICS, MOORHEAD STATE UNIV, 75- *Mem:* Hist Sci Soc; Royal Astron Soc Can; Am Asn Physics Teachers. *Res:* Gravitational theory and quantum gravitation; interaction of science and society; history of astronomy and physics: 17-19th century. *Mailing Add:* Dept of Physics Moorhead State Univ Moorhead MN 56560

WESLEY, WILLIAM KEITH, agronomy, see previous edition

WESNER, JOHN WILLIAM, b Newark, NJ, July 14, 36; m 65; c 2. PHYSICAL DESIGN, CONSUMER PRODUCT DESIGN. *Educ:* Carnegie Inst Technol, BS, 58; Calif Inst Technol, MS, 59; Carnegie-Mellon Univ, PhD(mech eng), 68. *Prof Exp:* Sr engr, Atomic Power Div, Westinghouse Elec Corp, 64-68; mem tech staff, 68-76, SUPVR, BELL TEL LABS, 76- *Mem:* Am Soc Mech Engrs; Nat Soc Prof Engrs; Sigma Xi. *Res:* Physical design (mechanical development and design) of new business telecommunications terminals. *Mailing Add:* Bell Tel Labs Crawfords Corners Rd Holmdel NJ 07733

WESOLOSKI, GEORGE D, animal nutrition, see previous edition

WESOLOWSKI, WAYNE EDWARD, b Cicero, Ill, July 25, 45; m 68; c 2. PHYSICAL & ENVIRONMENTAL CHEMISTRY. *Educ:* St Procopius Col, BS, 67; Univ Ariz, PhD(chem), 71. *Prof Exp:* Res scientist, Freeman Lab, Inc, 71-73; vpres, Chicago Sci, Inc, 73-74; ASSOC PROF, ILL BENEDICTINE COL, 74- *Concurrent Pos:* Fel, Res Corp, 74-75. *Mem:* Am Chem Soc; Air Pollution Control Asn. *Res:* Paramagnetic behavior of transition metals in anisotropic ligand fields; isokinetic particulate sampling of stationary environmental pollution sources. *Mailing Add:* 418 E Washington St Marengo IL 60152

WESSEL, GUNTER KURT, b Berlin, Ger, Mar 29, 20; US citizen; m 53; c 3. PHYSICS. *Educ:* Tech Hochsch, Berlin, BS, 40; Univ Göttingen, dipl, 47, PhD(physics), 48. *Prof Exp:* Physicist, Lorenz Radio AG, Berlin, 43-45; fel, Nat Res Coun Can, 51-53; consult physics, Gen Elec Co, NY, 53-61; PROF PHYSICS, SYRACUSE UNIV, 61- *Res:* Atomic physics; spectroscopy; masers; lasers; magnetic resonance. *Mailing Add:* Dept of Physics Syracuse Univ Syracuse NY 13210

WESSEL, HANS U, b Duisburg, Ger, Apr 18, 27; US citizen; m 55; c 5. CARDIOLOGY, PHYSIOLOGY. *Educ:* Univ Freiburg, MD, 53. *Prof Exp:* Instr med, 60-63, assoc, 63-65, asst prof, 65-67, asst prof pediat, 67-71, assoc prof eng sci, 73-76, PROF PEDIAT, MED SCH, NORTHWESTERN UNIV, CHICAGO, 76-, PROF ENG SCI, 76- *Concurrent Pos:* NIH cardiovasc res trainee, Med Sch, Northwestern Univ, Chicago, 61-63; Am Heart Asn estab investr, 65-70, fel coun circulation, 65- *Mem:* AAAS; assoc fel Am Col Cardiol; assoc mem Inst Elec & Electronics Engrs; sr mem Instrument Soc Am; Biomed Eng Soc. *Res:* Bioengineering; effect of pulmonary vascular disease on pulmonary gas exchange; instrumentation; indicator dilution techniques; thermal velocity probes; patient monitoring system; exercise physiology in children. *Mailing Add:* 63 Mulberry Rd Deerfield IL 60015

WESSEL, JOHN EMMIT, b Los Angeles, Calif, Mar 8, 42. CHEMICAL PHYSICS. *Educ:* Univ Calif, Los Angeles, BS, 65; Univ Chicago, PhD(chem), 70. *Prof Exp:* Fel chem, Univ Pa, 69-72, instr, 72-74; mem tech staff, 74-78, res scientist, 78-80, SR SCIENTIST, CHEM & PHYSICS LAB, AEROSPACE CORP, 80- *Mem:* Am Phys Soc; Sigma Xi; AAAS; Am Chem Soc. *Res:* Laser spectroscopy applied to atomic and molecular detection, laser communications, and infrared detection. *Mailing Add:* 544 1st St Manhattan Beach CA 90266

WESSEL, PAUL ROGER, b Cape Girardeau, Mo, Aug 27, 38; m 58. OCEAN ACOUSTICS, SOLID STATE PHYSICS. *Educ:* Southeast Mo State Univ, BS, 58; Univ Md, MS, 62. *Prof Exp:* Res physicist, 58-75, br head electromagnetics, 75-77, div head radiation, 77-79, syst eng, 79-80, DEPT HEAD RES & TECHNOL, NAVAL SURFACE WEAPONS CTR, MO, 80- *Res:* Optical properties of semiconductors; electromagnetic propagation in conducting media; ocean acoustics and interaction of sound with the ocean floor. *Mailing Add:* Res & Technol Dept Naval Surface Weapons Ctr Silver Spring MD 20910

WESSELLS, NORMAN KEITH, b Jersey City, NJ, May 11, 32; c 3. DEVELOPMENTAL BIOLOGY. *Educ:* Yale Univ, BS, 54, PhD(zool), 60. *Prof Exp:* Am Cancer Soc fel, 60-62; from asst prof to assoc prof biol sci, 62-70, chmn dept, 72-78, actg dir, Hopkins Marine Sta, 72-76, assoc dean humanities & sci, 77-81, PROF BIOL SCI, STANFORD UNIV, 71-, DEAN HUMANITIES & SCI, 81- *Concurrent Pos:* Am Cancer Soc scholar cancer res, Dept Biochem, Univ Wash, 68-69; Guggenheim Found fel, 75-76; chmn, Yale Coun Comt Biol Sci. *Honors & Awards:* Herman Beerman Award, Soc Investigative Dermatol, 71. *Mem:* Am Soc Zoologists; Soc Develop Biol (pres, 78). *Res:* Embryonic induction; cytodifferentiation; chemistry, ultrastructure of skin, pancreas development; development of nerve cells, axons. *Mailing Add:* Dept of Biol Sci Stanford Univ Stanford CA 94305

WESSELS, BRUCE WARREN, b New York, NY, Oct 18, 46; m 68; c 1. MATERIALS SCIENCE. *Educ:* Univ Pa, BS, 68; Mass Inst Technol, PhD(mat sci), 73. *Prof Exp:* Mem tech staff, Gen Elec Res Ctr, 72-77; asst prof, 77-80, ASSOC PROF MAT SCI, NORTHWESTERN UNIV, 80- *Concurrent Pos:* Prin investr, NSF grant. *Mem:* Electrochem Soc; Am Inst Mining, Metall & Petrol Eng. *Res:* Semiconductor physics; defects in semiconductors; thin films. *Mailing Add:* Dept Mat Sci Northwestern Univ Evanston IL 60201

WESSENAUER, GABRIEL OTTO, b Sewickley, Pa, Oct 21, 06; m 34; c 2. ELECTRICAL ENGINEERING. *Educ:* Carnegie Inst Technol, BS, 27. *Prof Exp:* Asst engr, WVa Power & Transmission Co, 27-31; develop engr, WPa Elec Co, 31-34; asst elec engr, WPa Power Co, 35; hydraul engr, TVA, 35-37, power supply engr, 37-39, asst to mgr power, 40-41, actg mgr, 41-44, asst mgr, 42-44, mgr, 44-70; ELEC POWER CONSULT, 70- *Concurrent Pos:* Mem bd dirs, Atomic Indust Forum, 67-70. *Honors & Awards:* Rockefeller Pub Serv Award, 63. *Mem:* Nat Acad Eng; fel Am Soc Civil Engrs. *Mailing Add:* 2931 Nurick Dr NW Chattanooga TN 37415

WESSLER, MAX ALDEN, b Jacksonville, Ill, Jan 16, 31; m 53; c 3. THERMODYNAMICS. *Educ:* Bradley Univ, BSME, 52; Univ Southern Calif, MSME, 54; Purdue Univ, PhD, 66. *Prof Exp:* Mech engr, Guided Missiles Labs, Hughes Aircraft Co, Calif, 52-54; assoc prof mech eng, 56-71, PROF MECH ENG, BRADLEY UNIV, 71-, CHMN DEPT, 74- *Concurrent Pos:* Mem tech staff, Electron Dynamics Dept, Hughes Res Labs, 60-62; mem bd dir, Accrediation Bd Eng & Technol, 77- *Mem:* Soc Automotive Engrs; Combustion Inst; Am Soc Eng Educ; Am Soc Mech Engrs. *Res:* Thermodynamics and combustion; fluid mechanics. *Mailing Add:* 923 N Maplewood Ave Peoria IL 61606

WESSLER, STANFORD, b New York, NY, Apr 20, 17; m 42; c 3. MEDICINE. *Educ:* Harvard Univ, BA, 38; NY Univ, MD, 42; Am Bd Internal Med, dipl. *Prof Exp:* Asst med, Harvard Med Sch, 49-51, instr, 51-54, assoc, 54-57, asst prof & tutor, 57-64; prof med, Sch Med, Washington Univ, 64-74, John E & Adeline Simon prof, 66-74; PROF MED, SCH MED & ASSOC DEAN POST-GRAD SCH MED, NY UNIV, 74- *Concurrent Pos:* Res fel med, Harvard Med Sch, 46-49; Nat Heart Inst trainee, 49-51; Am Heart Asn estab investr, 54-59; James F Mitchell Award heart & vascular res, 72-; asst, Beth Israel Hosp, Boston, 46-49, assoc, 49-56, physician, Vasc Clin, 54-64, assoc vis physician, 57-58, vis physician, 59-64, head, Anticoagulation Clin, 60-64, dir, Clin Res Ctr Thrombosis & Atherosclerosis, 61-64, assoc dir, 64-; mem, Comt Thrombosis & Hemorrhage, Nat Res Coun, 60-64; physician-in-chief, Jewish Hosp, St Louis & assoc physician, Barnes Hosp, 64-75; mem, Med Adv Bd, Coun Circulation, Am Heart Asn, 64- & Coun Stroke, 67-76, vchmn, Coun Thrombosis, 71-74, chmn, 74-76, chmn, Publ Comt, 72-77, vpres coun, 74-76; vchmn heart training comt, Nat Heart Inst, 65-67 & mem, Thrombosis Adv Comt, 67-71; chmn, Subgroup Thromboembolism, Inter-Soc Comn Heart Dis Resources, 69-72; dir, Nat Heart & Lung Inst Thrombosis Ctr, Washington Univ Sch Med, 71-74; mem, Comn Stroke, Nat Inst Neurol Dis & Stroke, 72-74; attend physician, NY Univ Med Ctr, Univ Hosp, New York, 74- & Bellevue Hosp Ctr, 74- *Honors & Awards:* James F Mitchell Award, Heart & Vascular Res, 72. *Mem:* Am Fedn Clin; Am Soc Hematol; Int Soc Internal Med. *Res:* Am Physiol Soc; Am Soc Clin Invest; fel Am Col Physicians; Asn Am Physicians. Res: Blood coagulation; peripheral vascular disease. *Mailing Add:* NY Univ Sch of Med First Ave New York NY 10016

WESSLING, FRANCIS CHRISTOPHER, JR, mechanical engineering, solar energy, see previous edition

WESSLING, RITCHIE A, b Iowa, Sept 15, 32; m 61; c 5. PHYSICAL CHEMISTRY, POLYMER SCIENCE. *Educ:* Mich State Univ, BS, 57, MS, 59; Univ Pa, PhD(phys chem), 62. *Prof Exp:* Chemist, Wyandotte Chem Co, 59; chemist, Polymer Res Lab, Dow Chem Co, 62, assoc scientist, polymer sci group, 68-78, res scientist, Cent Res, Phys Res Lab, 78-80, RES SCIENTIST, AG PROD DEPT, DOW CHEM USA, 80- *Mem:* Am Chem Soc; AAAS. *Res:* Relationship between physical properties of polymeric materials and their chemical structure; cathodic electrodeposition; synthesis and applications of cationic latexes. *Mailing Add:* AG Prod Dept Dow Chem USA 9001 Bldg Midland MI 48640

WESSLING, WOLFGANG HEINRICH, b Hakeborn, Ger, Nov 27, 28; US citizen; m 58. GENETICS, PLANT PATHOLOGY. *Educ:* Hannover Tech Univ, dipl Gartner, 53; Cornell Univ, MS, 55; NC State Univ, PhD(genetics), 57. *Prof Exp:* Foreign aid adv plant breeding, Ger Govt, 57-58; dir exp sta, Anderson Clayton Co, Brazil, 59-63; plant breeder, Farmers Forage Res, Ind, 63-65 & Delta & Pine Land Co, Courtaulds, Ltd, Miss, 65-71; mgr, 71-73, ASSOC DIR, COTTON, INC, 73- *Concurrent Pos:* Adj prof crop sci dept, NC State Univ; mem res comt, Plains Cotton Growers, Inc. *Mem:* Am Soc Agron; Am Genetics Asn. *Res:* Insect resistance; cotton genetics and pathology. *Mailing Add:* 8616 Valley Brook Dr Raleigh NC 27612

WESSMAN, GARNER ELMER, b Cokato, Minn, Sept 14, 20; m 43, 69; c 5. BACTERIOLOGY. *Educ:* Buena Vista Col, BS, 42; Iowa State Univ, PhD(physiol bact), 52. *Prof Exp:* Instr bact, Iowa State Univ, 49-52; med bacteriologist, Safety Div, Ft Detrick, 52-53, med bact div, 54-61; bacteriologist, Inst Paper Chem, 53-54; RES BACTERIOLOGIST, NAT ANIMAL DIS CTR, USDA, 61- *Mem:* Am Acad Microbiol; Am Soc Microbiol; Conf Res Workers Animal Dis. *Res:* Nutrition and physiology of Pasteurella; immunochemistry of streptococci. *Mailing Add:* Nat Animal Dis Ctr Ames IA 50010

WESSON, JAMES ROBERT, b Jackson Gap, Ala, Nov 1, 21; m 43; c 4. MATHEMATICS. *Educ:* Birmingham-Southern Col, BS, 49; Vanderbilt Univ, MA, 49, PhD(math), 53. *Prof Exp:* Instr math, Univ Tenn, 49-50; from asst prof to assoc prof, Birmingham-Southern Col, 51-57; from asst prof to assoc prof, 57-66, PROF MATH, VANDERBILT UNIV, 61-, ASSOC DEAN, 80- *Concurrent Pos:* Dir undergrad studies, Vanderbilt Univ, 70-77. *Mem:* Am Math Soc; Math Asn Am. *Res:* Projective planes; abstract algebra; numerical solutions of differential equations. *Mailing Add:* Dept of Math Vanderbilt Univ Box 1595 Sta B Nashville TN 37235

WESSON, LAURENCE GODDARD, JR, b Midland, Mich, Oct 18, 17; m 48; c 4. PHYSIOLOGY, INTERNAL MEDICINE. *Educ:* Haverford Col, AB, 38; Harvard Univ, MD, 42. *Prof Exp:* From instr to asst prof physiol, Col Med, NY Univ, 46-50, from instr to assoc prof med, Postgrad Med Sch, 50-62; PROF MED, JEFFERSON MED COL, 62- *Mem:* Am Physiol Soc; Am Fedn Clin. *Res:* Am Soc Nephrology. Res: Renal and cellular physiology; renal diseases. *Mailing Add:* Dept of Med Jefferson Med Col Philadelphia PA 19107

WESSON, ROBERT LAUGHLIN, b San Francisco, Calif, Feb 26, 44; m 66; c 2. SEISMOLOGY, TECTONOPHYSICS. *Educ:* Mass Inst Technol, SB, 66; Stanford Univ, MS, 68, PhD(geophysics), 70. *Prof Exp:* Res assoc, 70-72, chief, Off Earthquake Studies, 78-80, asst dir res, 80-81, GEOPHYSICIST, US GEOL SURV, 72-, ASST DIR RES PROGS, 81- *Concurrent Pos:* US chmn, US-USSR Working Group Earthquake Prediction, 78-82. *Mem:* Am Geophys Union; Seismol Soc Am; Geol Soc Am; Earthquake Engr Res Inst; AAAS. *Res:* Earthquake prediction; seismology; tectonophysics. *Mailing Add:* 171 Nat Ctr US Geol Surv Reston VA 22092

WEST, A(RNOLD) SUMNER, b Philadelphia, Pa, Jan 12, 22; m 46; c 2. CHEMICAL ENGINEERING. *Educ:* Univ Pa, BS, 43; Pa State Univ, MS, 46. *Prof Exp:* Asst, Pa State Univ, 43-46; process engr, 46-52, process group leader, 52-62, semi-works supt & head res comput lab, 62-72, mgr petrol chem res, 72-77, SR TECH SPECIALIST GOVT & REGULATORY AFFAIRS, ROHM AND HAAS CO, 78- *Honors & Awards:* Founders Award, Am Inst Chem Engrs, 79. *Mem:* Am Chem Soc; Nat Soc Prof Engrs; Am Inst Chem Engrs (pres, 77); Soc Automotive Engrs; Water Pollution Control Fedn. *Mailing Add:* Rohm and Haas Co Independence Mall W Philadelphia PA 19105

WEST, ARTHUR JAMES, II, b Boston, Mass, Dec 14, 27; div; c 3. PARASITOLOGY, MARINE BIOLOGY. *Educ:* Suffolk Univ, BS, 51, MA, 56; Univ NH, MS, 62, PhD(zool), 64. *Prof Exp:* From instr to assoc prof biol, Suffolk Univ, 52-65, prof & co-chmn dept, 65-68; dean div natural sci, New Eng Col, 68-70; chmn dept biol, 70-73, prog dir, Pre-Col Educ in Sci, NSF, 72-73, PROF BIOL, SUFFOLK UNIV, 70-, CHMN DEPT, 78-, DIR, ROBERT S FRIEDMAN COBSCOOK BAY LAB, 75- *Concurrent Pos:* Instr sci & chmn dept, Emerson Col, 56-59; asst prof biol & chmn dept, Mass Col Optom, 57-60; mem, Gov Comn Ocean Mgt, Mass; NSF dir var prog, NH Col & Univ Coun, 68-78 & 78- *Mem:* Am Soc Parasitol; Am Inst Biol Scientists. *Res:* Embryology and histochemistry of larval forms of Acanthocephala; morphology of priapulids; life cycle studies of marine parasites. *Mailing Add:* Suffolk Univ 41 Temple St Boston MA 02114

WEST, BRUCE DAVID, b Madison, Wis, July 10, 35; m 57; c 2. BIOCHEMISTRY. *Educ:* Univ Wis, BS, 57, MS, 61, PhD(biochem), 62. *Prof Exp:* Fel biochem, Univ Wis, 62-63; asst prof chem, Univ NMex, 63-69; asst prof, 69-74, ASSOC PROF CHEM, EASTERN MICH UNIV, 74- *Mem:* Am Chem Soc; The Chem Soc. *Res:* Coumarin anticoagulants; structure-activity relationship, synthesis, biodegradation. *Mailing Add:* Dept of Chem Eastern Mich Univ Ypsilanti MI 48197

WEST, C(HARLES) TYRRELL, b Crestline, Ohio, July 1, 15; m 47; c 2. ENGINEERING MECHANICS. *Educ:* Ohio State Univ, BCE, 39, MSc, 46; Cornell Univ, PhD(eng mech), 51. *Prof Exp:* Bridge test analyst, Asn Am RR, 40-41 & 46; instr eng mech, 46-48, asst prof, 48-51, assoc prof, 51-52, prof, 53-77, chmn dept, 53-72, EMER PROF ENG MECH, OHIO STATE UNIV, 77- *Concurrent Pos:* Res scientist, Autometric Corp, 60; vis prof, Indian Inst Technol, Kanpur, 69-71. *Mem:* Am Soc Civil Engrs; Am Soc Mech Engrs. *Res:* Classical and vehicle dynamics; linear and nonlinear vibrations. *Mailing Add:* 7704 Lincoln Hwy Crestline OH 44827

WEST, CHARLES ALLEN, b Greencastle, Ind, Nov 4, 27; m 52; c 2. BIOCHEMISTRY. *Educ:* DePauw Univ, AB, 49; Univ Ill, PhD(chem), 52. *Hon Degrees:* DSc, DePauw Univ, 81. *Prof Exp:* Instr chem, 52 & 55, from asst prof to assoc prof, 56-67, vchmn dept, 70-75, PROF CHEM, UNIV CALIF, LOS ANGELES, 67-, CHMN DEPT, 81- *Concurrent Pos:* Guggenheim fel, 61-62. *Mem:* Am Chem Soc; Am Soc Biol Chemists; Am Soc Plant Physiol. *Res:* Chemistry and biosynthesis of natural products of physiological importance, including gibberellins and other plant growth regulators; metabolic regulation; molecular basis of plant disease resistance. *Mailing Add:* Dept Chem & Biochem Univ Calif Los Angeles CA 90024

WEST, CHARLES DAVID, b Riverside, Calif, July 25, 37; m 63; c 1. ANALYTICAL CHEMISTRY. *Educ:* Pomona Col, BA, 59; Mass Inst Technol, PhD(anal chem), 64. *Prof Exp:* From res chemist to sr res chemist, Beckman Instruments, Inc, 64-67; asst prof, 67-74, ASSOC PROF CHEM, OCCIDENTAL COL, 74- *Mem:* AAAS; Am Chem Soc; Optical Soc Am; Soc Appl Spectros. *Res:* Emission spectroscopy; flame photometry; atomic absorption instrument design; atomic and molecular fluorescence instrumentation. *Mailing Add:* Dept of Chem Occidental Col 1600 Campus Rd Los Angeles CA 90041

WEST, CHARLES DONALD, b Ogden, Utah, Oct 25, 20; m 46; c 4. BIOCHEMISTRY. *Educ:* Univ Utah, BA, 41, MD, 44, PhD, 50. *Prof Exp:* Instr med, Med Col, Cornell Univ, 50-54, res assoc, Sloan-Kettering Div, 52-53, asst prof, 53-57; from asst res prof to assoc res prof biochem, 57-71, assoc prof med, 65-69, PROF MED, MED CTR, UNIV UTAH, 69-, PROF BIOCHEM, 71-, CO-DIR, CLIN RES CTR, 66- *Concurrent Pos:* From asst to assoc, Sloan-Kettering Inst Cancer Res. 50-57; asst dir prof serv res & assoc chief staff, Vet Admin Hosp, Salt Lake City, 57-65. *Mem:* AAAS; Endocrine Soc; Asn Cancer Res; Fedn Clin. *Res:* Harvey Soc. Res: Endocrinology. *Mailing Add:* Univ of Utah Med Ctr 50 N Medical Dr Salt Lake City UT 84132

WEST, CHARLES HUTCHISON KEESOR, b Wheeling, WVa, Aug 9, 48; m 72; c 2. PHYSIOLOGY, NEUROPHYSIOLOGY. *Educ:* Ohio Univ, BS, 70, MS, 72; Mich State Univ, PhD(physiol), 77. *Prof Exp:* Res asst zool, Ohio Univ, 71, teaching asst, 71-72; res asst physiol, Mich State Univ, 72-77; fel neurophysiol, Univ Wis, 77-80; RES SSCIENTIST, GA MENTAL HEALTH INST, 80-; ASST PROF, DEPT PHYCHIATRY, EMORY UNIV, 80- *Mem:* AAAS; Am Soc Zool; Soc Neurosci. *Res:* Basic motivation and attention controlling brain mechanisms and their relationship to mental illness; principle techniques utilized are electrophysiology and intracranial self-stimulation paradigm with various physiological, pharmacological and behavioral manipulations. *Mailing Add:* Ga Mental Health Inst 1256 Briarcliff Rd NE Atlanta GA 30306

WEST, CHARLES P, b New York, NY, Aug 28, 16; m 42; c 4. ORGANIC CHEMISTRY. *Educ:* City Col New York, BS, 36; Univ Chicago, PhD(org chem), 39. *Prof Exp:* Dir res, Neo Metal & Chem Co, 39-41; vpres, Nat Chem & Color Co, 46-54; PRES & DIR, RESIN RES LABS, INC, NEWARK, NJ, 54- *Concurrent Pos:* Guest lectr, Newark Col Eng, 59-60. *Mem:* AAAS; Am Chem Soc; Soc Plastics Eng; Nat Asn Corrosion Eng; fel Am Inst Chem. *Res:* Resins and polymers, particularly emulsion and dispersion polymers. *Mailing Add:* 60 Sharon Ct Metuchen NJ 08840

WEST, CHRISTOPHER DRANE, b Norfolk, Va, April 29, 43; m 65; c 3. NEUROANATOMY. *Educ:* Brown Univ, AB, 64; Boston Univ, AM, 66, PhD(exp & physiol psychol), 73. *Prof Exp:* NIMH trainee exp biol, Worcester Found, 72-75; RESEARCHER PSYCHOL, VET ADMIN HOSP, MASS, 75-; ASST PROF ANAT & NEUROSCI, SCH MED, BOSTON UNIV, 78- *Concurrent Pos:* NIH prin investr, Div Dept Neurol, Harvard Med Sch, 76-77; lectr neurol, Harvard Neurol Unit, Beth Israel Hosp, 75- *Mem:* Am Asn Anatomists; AAAS; Am Psychol Asn; NY Acad Sci. *Res:* Comparative neuromorphology of the auditory system and auditory behavior; changes in neuron morphology and synaptic sites with age; accumuation of lipofuscin pigment in neurons; relation to aging, neuron functioning and morphology. *Mailing Add:* 10 Remington St Cambridge MA 02138

WEST, CLARK DARWIN, b Jamestown, NY, July 4, 18; m 44; c 3. IMMUNOLOGY, NEPHROLOGY. *Educ:* Col Wooster, AB, 40; Univ Mich, MD, 43. *Prof Exp:* Intern surg, Univ Mich Hosp, 43-44, resident pediat, 44-46; from asst prof to assoc prof, 51-62, PROF PEDIAT, COL MED, UNIV CINCINNATI, 62- *Concurrent Pos:* Children's Hosp Res Found scholar, 48-49, fel, 53-; Nat Res Coun sr fel pediat, Children's Hosp Res Found, 49-50 & Cardiopulmonary Lab, Bellevue Hosp, New York, 50-51; res assoc, Children's Hosp Res Found, 51-53, assoc dir, 63-, supv biochemist, Hosp, 51-65, attend pediatrician, 51-; attend pediatrician, Cincinnati Gen Hosp, 53-; mem, Gen Clin Res Ctr Comt, Div Res Facilities & resources, NIH, 65-69; mem, Urol & Renal Dis Training Comt, Nat Inst Arthritis, Metab & Digestive Dis, 72-73. *Mem:* Am Physiol Soc; Soc Pediat Res (secy-treas, 58-62, pres, 63-64); Am Soc Nephrology; Am Asn Immunologists; Am Pediat Soc. *Res:* Abnormalities of the immune system related to the pathogenesis of glomerulonephritis. *Mailing Add:* Children's Hosp Res Found Elland Ave & Bethesda Cincinnati OH 45229

WEST, COLIN DOUGLAS, b Rochdale, Eng, June 21, 41; m 65; c 1. CLASSICAL PHYSICS. *Educ:* Univ Liverpool, BSc, 61, MSc, 64, PhD(physics), 65. *Prof Exp:* Res fel, Res Lab, Harwell, 65-68; sci officer, United Kingdom Atomic Energy Authority, 68-73; vis scientist, Oak Ridge Nat Lab, 73-74; proj mgr physics, UK Atomic Energy Res Lab, 74-77; res assoc planning, 77-80, MGR & SYSTS TECHNOL GROUP, OAK RIDGE NAT LAB, 81- *Concurrent Pos:* Nuclear physics res fel, Univ Liverpool, 63-65. *Res:* Application of long range planning techniques to laboratory and research organizations; small scale heat engines for irrigation and other applications; irradiation engineering. *Mailing Add:* Oak Ridge Nat Lab PO Box Y Oak Ridge TN 37830

WEST, DAVID ARMSTRONG, b Beirut, Lebanon, Apr 9, 33; US citizen; m 58; c 3. GENETICS. *Educ:* Cornell Univ, BA, 55, PhD(vert zool), 59. *Prof Exp:* Asst prof zool, Cornell Univ, 59-60; NATO fel, 60-61; USPHS fel, 61-62; asst prof zool, 62-68, ASSOC PROF ZOOL, VA POLYTECH INST & STATE UNIV, 68- *Concurrent Pos:* Sci Res Coun sr vis fel, 66; ed, Va J Sci, 74-76. *Mem:* Lepidopterist Soc; AAAS; Soc Study Evolution; Genetic Soc Am; Am Soc Naturalists. *Res:* Ecological genetics; genetics of natural populations of isopods and butterflies; polymorphisms. *Mailing Add:* Dept of Biol Va Polytech Inst & State Univ Blacksburg VA 24061

WEST, DENNIS R, b Kennett, Mo, Nov 22, 46; m 69; c 1. CROP BREEDING, QUANTITATIVE GENETICS. *Educ:* Miss State Univ, BS, 69, MS, 75; Univ Nebr, PhD(agron), 78. *Prof Exp:* Res assoc, NC State Univ, 78-79; ASST PROF GENETICS, UNIV TENN, 79- *Mem:* Am Soc Agron; Crop Sci Soc Am; AAAS; Coun Agr Sci & Technol. *Res:* Basic and applied research in plant breeding and genetics; quantitative genetics; maize breeding; host plant resistance; development of maize germplasm. *Mailing Add:* Plant & Soil Sci Dept Univ Tenn PO Box 1071 Knoxville TN 37996

WEST, DONALD COREY, b Harrington Harbour, Que, Jan 19, 18; m 44; c 3. COMPUTER SCIENCE. *Educ:* Acadia Univ, BSc, 39, BA, 40; Univ Toronto, MA, 41, PhD(physics), 52. *Prof Exp:* Instr physics, Acadia Univ, 45-47; physicist, NS Res Found, 48-53 & Cent Res Lab, Can Industs, Ltd, Que, 53-70; assoc prof comput sci & dir comput ctr, Loyola Campus, 70-75, chmn dept comput sci, 71-76, CHMN QUANTITATIVE METHODS, CONCORDIA UNIV, 76-78, 81-; RETIRED. *Mem:* Asn Comput Mach; Can Info Processing Soc. *Res:* Naval radar; photoelectricity; high polymer plastics, especially molecular weight determinations and rheology; electrical digital and analog computers; operations research. *Mailing Add:* Dept Quantitative Methods Concordia Univ 7141 Sherbrooke St W Montreal PQ H4B 1R6 Can

WEST, DONALD K, b Providence, RI, May 14, 29; m 57; c 3. ASTROPHYSICS. *Educ:* Univ RI, BS, 57; Rutgers Univ, MS, 60; Univ Wis, PhD(astron), 64. *Prof Exp:* ASTROPHYSICIST, GODDARD SPACE FLIGHT CTR, NASA, 64- & OBS ADMINR, 78- *Mem:* Am Astron Soc. *Res:* Physics of emission line stars; astronomical observations from space telescopes. *Mailing Add:* Code 672 Goddard Space Flight Ctr Greenbelt MD 20715

WEST, DONALD MARKHAM, b Pasadena, Calif, Apr 22, 25; m 48. ANALYTICAL CHEMISTRY. *Educ:* Stanford Univ, BS, 49, PhD(chem), 58. *Prof Exp:* Actg instr chem, Stanford Univ, 54-55; from asst prof to assoc prof, 56-65, PROF CHEM, SAN JOSE STATE UNIV, 65- *Mem:* Am Chem Soc. *Res:* Analysis of organic compounds. *Mailing Add:* Dept of Chem San Jose State Univ 125 S Seventh St San Jose CA 95192

WEST, DOUGLAS XAVIER, b Tacoma, Wash, June 11, 37; m 64; c 2. INORGANIC CHEMISTRY. *Educ:* Whitman Col, AB, 59; Wash State Univ, PhD(chem), 64. *Prof Exp:* Instr chem, Upsala Col, 64-65; from asst prof to prof, Cent Mich Univ, 65-75, dir univ honors progs, 70-72; PROF INORG CHEM & CHMN DEPT, ILL STATE UNIV, 75- *Mem:* Am Chem Soc; Sigma Xi; Royal Soc Chem. *Res:* Chemistry of pentacyanometallates, kinetics and mechanisms; transition metal complexes of n-oxides and sulfoxides; electron spin resonance. *Mailing Add:* Dept of Chem Ill State Univ Normal IL 61761

WEST, EDMUND CARY, b Santa Ana, Calif, Mar 18, 36. EXPERIMENTAL HIGH ENERGY PHYSICS. *Educ:* Stanford Univ, BS, 58; Univ Wis, MS, 60, PhD(physics), 66. *Prof Exp:* Lectr physics & res asst, 65-66, asst prof, 67-72, syst mgr, Polly proj anal sci photographs, 72-77, ADMINR, DIGITAL EVAL COMPUT SYST-10, COMPUT SERV, UNIV TORONTO, 77- *Res:* Bubble chamber physics; use of computers in measurement of various types of scientific photographs. *Mailing Add:* Comput Serv Univ Toronto Toronto ON M5S 1A1 Can

WEST, EDWARD STAUNTON, b Stuart, Va, Sept 9, 96; m 20. BIOCHEMISTRY. *Educ:* Randolph-Macon Col, AB, 17; Kans State Col, MS, 20; Univ Chicago, PhD(org chem), 23. *Hon Degrees:* LLD, Randolph-Macon Col, 65; DSc, Univ Portland, 69. *Prof Exp:* From asst to instr chem, Kans State Col, 17-22; asst org chem, Univ Chicago, 22-23; from instr to assoc prof biochem, Sch Med, Wash Univ, 23-34; prof biochem & head dept, Sch Med, 34-66, EMER PROF BIOCHEM, SCH MED, UNIV ORE, 66-; ASST TO DIR, ORE REGIONAL PRIMATE RES CTR, 66- *Concurrent Pos:* Shaffer lectr med sch, Washington Univ, 56; mem adv coun, Life Ins Med Res Fund, 56-59, chmn, 59-60; mem biochem test comt, Nat Bd Med Examr, 57-58, chmn, 58-61, mem bd, 58-61; sr scientist, Ore Regional Primate Res Ctr, 60-66. *Mem:* AAAS; Am Chem Soc; Am Soc Biol Chemists; Soc Exp Biol & Med. *Res:* Carbohydrate chemistry and metabolism; chemistry and metabolism of ascorbic acid; lipid metabolism; ketosis; tissue phosphates. *Mailing Add:* Ore Regional Primate Res Ctr 505 NW 185th Ave Beaverton OR 97005

WEST, ERIC NEIL, b Montreal, Que, Mar 28, 41; m 65; c 2. STATISTICS, COMPUTER SCIENCE. *Educ:* Royal Mil Col Can, BSc, 63; Iowa State Univ, MS, 67, PhD(statist), 70. *Prof Exp:* Res assoc statist & comput, Iowa State Univ, 67-70; asst prof comput sci, Univ Alta, 70-72; assoc prof statist & comput sci, 72-73, ASSOC PROF QUANT METHODS, SIR GEORGE WILLIAMS CAMPUS, CONCORDIA UNIV, 73- *Concurrent Pos:* Consult, Pro Data Serv, 70-; pvt consult, 70- *Mem:* Am Statist Asn; Inst Math Statist; Sigma Xi. *Res:* Statistical inference; computation systems analysis; business decision making; forecasting. *Mailing Add:* 5728 Hamilton Montreal PQ H4E 3B9 Can

WEST, FELICIA EMMINGER, b Chicora, Pa, Sept 14, 26; m 48; c 2. SCIENCE EDUCATION. *Educ:* J B Stetson Univ, BS, 48; Univ Fla, MEd, 65, EdD(sci educ), geol), 71. *Prof Exp:* Teacher high sch, Fla, 60-64; instr physics & earth sci, Miami Dade Jr Col, 65-66; instr earth sci & phys sci, St Johns River Jr Col, 66-67; teacher & student gen sci, Lab Sch, Univ Fla, 67-69, teacher & asst prof gen sci & earth sci, 69-72; staff assoc, AAAS, 72-75; CHMN DIV NATURAL SCI, MATH & PHYS EDUC, FLA JR COL, S CAMPUS, 75- *Concurrent Pos:* Coord ed, Fla Asn Sci Teachers J, 75-; mem bd dirs, Fedn Unified Sci Educ. *Res:* Development of unified science curriculum materials for use at community college level; development of field guides to specific sites in Florida for use by secondary and community college instructors. *Mailing Add:* 424 Oceanwood Dr Neptune Beach FL 32233

WEST, FRED RALPH, JR, b Pittsburgh, Pa, June 7, 25. PHARMACOLOGY. *Educ:* Hampton Inst, BS, 47; Tuskegee Inst, MS, 48; Univ Chicago, PhD(pharmacol), 56; Howard Univ, MD, 63. *Prof Exp:* Instr chem, St Augustine's Col, 48-50; asst, George W Carver Found, 50-53; instr pharmacol, 56-65, ASST PROF PHARMACOL, SCH MED, HOWARD UNIV, 65- *Mem:* AAAS. *Res:* Cultivation of animal and plant cells in vitro. *Mailing Add:* Dept of Pharmacol Howard Univ Sch of Med Washington DC 20001

WEST, GEORGE CURTISS, b Newton, Mass, May 13, 31; c 4. PHYSIOLOGICAL ECOLOGY, ORNITHOLOGY. *Educ:* Middlebury Col, BA, 53; Univ Ill, Urbana, MS, 56, PhD(physiol ecol), 58. *Prof Exp:* Fel div biosci, Nat Res Coun Can, 59-60; asst prof zool, Univ RI, 60-63; from asst prof to prof zoophysiol, Inst Arctic Biol, 63-, actg dean, Col Biol Sci & Renewable Resources, 74-75, actg dir, Div Life Sci & Inst Arctic Biol, 74-77, dir, Biomed Ctr, 72-80, PROF ZOOPHYSIOL, UNIV ALASKA, 80- *Concurrent Pos:* Alexander von Humboldt Found fel, Aschoff Div, Max Planck Inst Physiol of Behav, 71-72; mem US-USSR bilateral exchange working group protection northern ecosysts, 75- *Mem:* Am Ornith Union; Am Physiol Soc; Ecol Soc Am; Wildlife Soc; Wilson Ornith Soc. *Res:* Bioenergetics and temperature regulation of birds; migration, fat deposition, food habits of birds; fatty acid analysis of plant and animal lipids. *Mailing Add:* Inst of Arctic Biol Univ of Alaska Fairbanks AK 99701

WEST, GORDON FOX, b Toronto, Ont, Apr 21, 33. GEOPHYSICS. *Educ:* Univ Toronto, BASc, 55, MA, 57, PhD(geophys), 60. *Prof Exp:* Geophysicist, Dom Gulf Co, 55-56; lectr geophys, 58-66, assoc prof, 66-72, PROF PHYSICS, UNIV TORONTO, 72- *Mem:* Soc Explor Geophysicists; Am Geophys Union; Geol Asn Can; Can Asn Physicists. *Res:* Electromagnetic geophysical methods; geophysical studies of precambrian shields. *Mailing Add:* Geophys Lab Dept of Physics Univ of Toronto Toronto Can

WEST, GREGORY JOHN, b Salt Lake City, Utah, Apr 28, 49; m 78; c 1. RADIATION BIOLOGY, NEUROCHEMISTRY. *Educ:* Princeton Univ, AB, 71; Univ Calif, Los Angeles, PhD(biol chem), 78. *Prof Exp:* Sr fel neurochem, Dept Pharmacol, Univ Washington, 78-79; researcher radiation biol, Lab Nuclear Med & Radiation Biol, Univ Calif, Los Angeles, 79; ASST RES BIOCHEMIST RADIATION BIOL, DEPT RADIOL, UNIV CALIF,

SAN DIEGO, 79- *Mem:* Radiation Res Soc; Tissue Cult Asn. *Res:* Radioimmunoassay used to follow the production and repair of damaged bases in DNA in vitro and in cell culture models. *Mailing Add:* Dept Radiol Univ Calif San Diego CA 92093

WEST, HARRY IRWIN, JR, b Foley, Ala, Dec 3, 25; m 56; c 4. SPACE PHYSICS, NUCLEAR PHYSICS. *Educ:* Auburn Univ, BS, 46, MS, 47; Stanford Univ, PhD(physics), 55. *Prof Exp:* PHYSICIST, LAWRENCE LIVERMORE NAT LAB, UNIV CALIF, 55- *Mem:* Fel Am Phys Soc; Am Geophys Union. *Res:* Nuclear spectroscopy and measurements of charged particles in the earth's radiation belts. *Mailing Add:* L-232 Lawrence Livermore Nat Lab Univ of Calif Livermore CA 94550

WEST, JAMES EDWARD, b Grinnell, Iowa, May 1, 44; m 65; c 2. MATHEMATICS. *Educ:* La State Univ, BS, 64, PhD(math), 67. *Prof Exp:* Mem, Inst Advan Study, 67-68, 77-78; asst prof math, Univ Ky, 68-69; asst prof, 69-72, assoc prof, 72-76, PROF MATH, CORNELL UNIV, 76- *Concurrent Pos:* Vis prof, La State Univ, 72 & Univ KY, 80; vis prof La State Univ, 72, Univ KY, 80; lectr, Stefan Bunach Inst, Warsaw, 74; exchange scientist, Nat Acad Sci, USSR & Poland, 78; NSF res grant, 70-81. *Mem:* Am Math Soc; NY Acad Sci; AAAS. *Res:* Topology of infinite-dimensional spaces and manifolds; geometric and point-set topology. *Mailing Add:* Dept of Math Cornell Univ Ithaca NY 14853

WEST, JERRY LEE, b North Wilkesboro, NC, Nov 1, 40; m 65; c 2. FISH BIOLOGY, ZOOLOGY. *Educ:* Appalachian State Univ, BS, 62; NC State Univ, MS, 65, PhD(zool), 68. *Prof Exp:* Asst prof biol, 67-73, actg head dept, 74-77, ASSOC PROF BIOL, WESTERN CAROLINA UNIV, 73- *Mem:* Am Fisheries Soc; Am Inst Fishery Res Biologists. *Res:* Effects of sediment on trout streams. *Mailing Add:* Dept of Biol Western Carolina Univ Cullowhee NC 28723

WEST, JOHN B(ERNARD), b Elliott, Iowa, Feb 23, 25; m 47; c 4. CHEMICAL ENGINEERING, NUCLEAR ENGINEERING. *Educ:* Iowa State Univ, BS, 48, PhD, 54. *Prof Exp:* Jr engr, Gen Elec Co, NY, 48-50; from asst prof to prof, Sch Chem Eng, Okla State Univ, 54-76; MGR, BLACK FOX STA ENG, PUB SERV CO OKLA, 76-, ACTG MGR, BLACK FOX STA PROJ, 81- *Mem:* Am Inst Chem Engrs. *Res:* Water treatment; radioactive waste management; radiation protection; project management. *Mailing Add:* Pub Serv Co Okla PO Box 201 Tulsa OK 74102

WEST, JOHN B, b Adelaide, SAustralia, Dec 27, 28. PHYSIOLOGY, MEDICINE. *Educ:* Univ Adelaide, MB, BS, 52, MD, 58, DSc, 80; Univ London, PhD(appl physiol), 60. *Prof Exp:* Res assoc respiratory physiol, Royal Postgrad Med Sch, London, 54-60; physiologist, Himalayan Sci & Mountaineering Exped, 60-61; asst prof physiol, Univ Buffalo, 61-62; lectr med, Royal Postgrad Sch, London, 63-68; PROF MED, UNIV CALIF, SAN DIEGO, 69- *Concurrent Pos:* Mem, Cardiovasc Study Sect, NIH, 71-75. *Mem:* Am Physiol Soc; Am Soc Clin Invest; Am Thoracic Soc; Brit Physiol Soc; Royal Col Physicians. *Res:* Respiratory function in health and disease. *Mailing Add:* Dept Med Univ Calif San Diego La Jolla CA 92093

WEST, JOHN M(AURICE), b Long Branch, NJ, June 10, 27; m 51; c 2. FERMENTATION, BIOCHEMICAL ENGINEERING. *Educ:* Columbia Univ, BA, 50, BS, 51, MS, 54. *Prof Exp:* Res chem engr, E R Squibb Div, Olin Mathieson Chem Corp, 53-60; prod mgr enzymes, Nopco Chem Co, 60-63; group leader, 63-77, dir fermentation process develop, 77-80, DIR BIOTECHNOLOGY, HOFFMANN-LA ROCHE, INC, 80- *Mem:* Am Soc Microbiol; Am Inst Chem Engrs; Am Chem Soc. *Res:* Fermentation process development and engineering; continuous sterilization automatic foam control; automatic chemical analysis and control; pH control; deeptank and semi-solid fermentations; isolation recovery, purification of fermentation and natural products; biotechnology process evaluations. *Mailing Add:* 87 Cooper Ave Montclair NJ 07043

WEST, JOHN WYATT, b Decaturville, Tenn, Oct 18, 23; m 47; c 3. POULTRY NUTRITION. *Educ:* Univ Tenn, BSA, 47, MS, 48; Purdue Univ, PhD(poultry nutrit), 51. *Prof Exp:* Asst dir feeds res, Security Mills, Inc, Tenn, 51; from assoc prof to prof poultry husb, Miss State Univ, 52-56; prof poultry sci & head dept, Okla State Univ, 56-68; ASSOC DEAN, SCH AGR & NATURAL RESOURCES, CALIF POLYTECH STATE UNIV, SAN LUIS OBISPO, 68- *Mem:* Poultry Sci Asn. *Res:* Arsenic compounds and vitamin-amino acid interrelationships in poultry nutrition; nutritional value of cottonseed meal in broiler and turkey rations; antibiotic-protein interrelationships in broiler rations. *Mailing Add:* Sch of Agr & Natural Resources Calif Polytech State Univ San Luis Obispo CA 93407

WEST, KEITH P, b Simla, Colo, Aug 20, 20; m 46; c 3. ZOOLOGY, RADIATION BIOLOGY. *Educ:* Chico State Col, AB, 42; Stanford Univ, MA, 48. *Prof Exp:* Instr biol & chem, Vallejo Col, 47-48; from instr to PROF BIOL SCI, DREXEL UNIV, 48- *Concurrent Pos:* Asst dean col eng & sci, Drexel Univ, 67-68, actg head dept biol sci, 71-72. *Mem:* AAAS; Health Physics Soc. *Res:* Biological effects of radiation; sanitary quality control of food products. *Mailing Add:* Dept of Biol Sci Drexel Univ Philadelphia PA 19104

WEST, KELLY M, b Oklahoma City, Okla, May 31, 25. MEDICINE. *Educ:* Univ Okla, MD, 48; Am Bd Internal Med, dipl, 54. *Prof Exp:* Clin asst, 52, from instr to prof, 53-75, PROF BIOSTATIST & EPIDEMIOL & CLIN PROF MED, UNIV OKLA HEALTH SCI CTR, 75- *Concurrent Pos:* Consult, Nat Libr Med, NIH & WHO. *Mem:* Fel Am Col Physicians. *Res:* Diabetes; nutrition; epidemiology of diabetes and obesity. *Mailing Add:* Univ of Okla Health Sci Ctr 800 NE 13th St Oklahoma City OK 73104

WEST, KENNETH CALVIN, b Broken Bow, Nebr, Apr 1, 35; m 60; c 3. ANALYTICAL CHEMISTRY. *Educ:* Wheaton Col, Ill, BS, 56; Ind Univ, PhD(anal chem), 67. *Prof Exp:* Asst prof chem, 67-75, ASSOC PROF CHEM, ST LAWRENCE UNIV, 75- *Mem:* Am Chem Soc. *Res:* Instrumentation. *Mailing Add:* Dept Chem St Lawrence Univ Canton NY 13617

WEST, LOUIS JOLYON, b New York, NY, Oct 6, 24; m 44; c 3. PSYCHIATRY, NEUROLOGY. *Educ:* Univ Minn, BS, 46, MB, 48, MD, 49; Am Bd Psychiat & Neurol, dipl, 54. *Prof Exp:* Intern med, Univ Hosps, Univ Minn, 48-49; asst psychiat, Med Col, Cornell Univ, 49-52; prof psychiat & head dept psychiat, neurol & behav sci, Sch Med, Univ Okla, 54-69; PROF PSYCHIAT & CHMN DEPT, SCH MED, UNIV CALIF, LOS ANGELES, 69-, MED DIR, NEUROPSYCHIAT INST, 69-, PSYCHIATRIST IN CHIEF, UNIV CALIF HOSPS & CLINS, 69- *Concurrent Pos:* Resident, Payne Whitney Clin, New York Hosp, 49-52; res coordr, Okla Alcoholism Asn & chief behav sci, Okla Med Res Found, 56-69; consult, Oklahoma City Vet Admin Hosp, 56-69, US Air Force Hosp, Tinker AFB, Okla, 56-66, US Air Force Aero-Space Med Ctr, 61-66 & Peace Corps, 62-63; nat consult, Surgeon Gen, US Air Force, 57-62, mem adv coun, Behav Sci Div, Air Force Off Sci Res, 56-58; mem prof adv coun, Nat Asn Ment Health, 59-64; consult, US Info Agency, 60-61; mem exec coun adv comt behav res, Nat Acad Sci-Nat Res Coun, 61-63; mem nat adv comt psychiat, neurol & psychol, Spec Med Adv Group, US Vet Admin; mem, Nat Adv Ment Health Coun, NIMH, 65-69, White House Conf Civil Rights, 66 & Nat Adv Comt Alcoholism, Dept Health, Educ & Welfare; consult ed, Med Aspects Human Sexuality, 67-; mem bd dir, Kittay Found, 72-; mem residency rev comt psychiat & neurol, AMA, 73-; mem adv panel res & develop, US Army, 74- *Mem:* Fel Am Col Neuropsychopharmacol; fel Am Col Psychiat; fel Am Psychiat Asn; Pavlovian Soc NAm (pres, 74-75); Soc Biol Psychiat. *Res:* Experimental psychopathology, especially relating to disturbances of perception and altered states of consciousness; psychophysiological correlates in clinical practice; alcohol and drug abuse; life-threatening behavior; interaction of biological, psychological and sociocultural factors in personality development and function. *Mailing Add:* 760 Westwood Plaza Los Angeles CA 90024

WEST, MARTIN LUTHER, b Waco, Tex, Dec 25, 36; m 68; c 2. RADIATION CHEMISTRY, RADIATION PHYSICS. *Educ:* Univ Tex, BS, 60, MA, 62, PhD(physics), 67. *Prof Exp:* SR RES SCIENTIST PHYSICS, PAC NORTHWEST LAB BATTELLE NORTHWEST, 67- *Mem:* AAAS; Radiation Res Soc. *Res:* Reaction mechanisms and fast kinetic measurements for charged particle impact; pulsed radioluminescence and UV spectroscopy instrumentation. *Mailing Add:* Pac Northwest Lab PO Box 999 Richland WA 99352

WEST, MIKE HAROLD, b Lewiston, Idaho, Feb 29, 48; m 73; c 1. ANALYTICAL CHEMISTRY. *Educ:* Western Wash State Col, BA, 70; Wash State Univ, PhD(chem), 76. *Prof Exp:* Res assoc, Univ New Orleans, 75-76; asst prof chem, Tougaloo Col, 76-77; res assoc, Tex A&M Univ, 77-78; sr chemist, Coors Spectro Chem Lab, Coors Porcelain Co, 78-81; SR CHEMIST, ENERGY SYSTS GROUP, ROCKWELL HANFORD OPERS, 81- *Mem:* Am Chem Soc; Soc Appl Spectroscopy. *Res:* Analysis and characterization of geological materials by atomic spectroscopy and ion chromatography; atomizers for flame and nonflame (electrothermal) atomic absorption and emission spectroscopy. *Mailing Add:* Rockwell Hanford Opers PO Box 800 Richland WA 99352

WEST, NEIL ELLIOTT, b Portland, Ore, Dec 17, 37; m 63; c 1. ECOLOGY. *Educ:* Ore State Univ, BS, 60, PhD(plant ecol), 64. *Prof Exp:* From asst prof to assoc prof plant ecol, Dept Range Sci & Ecol Ctr, 64-75, PROF RANGE SCI, UTAH STATE UNIV, 75- *Concurrent Pos:* Forest ecologist, Ore Forest Res Lab, Ore State Univ, 63; NSF fel & vis prof, Inst Ecol, Univ Ga, 70-71; Mellon vis lectr, Yale Sch Forestry & Envir Studies, 78-79; consult, Nat Park Serv, Occidental Petrol, Argonne Nat Lab & Environ Protection Agency. *Mem:* Int Asn Ecol; Ecol Soc Am; Brit Ecol Soc; Int Soc Plant Geog & Ecol. *Res:* Plant ecology theory and its application to wildland resource management, particularly synecology and soil-vegetation relationships; systems ecology; community structure succession, productivity, nutrient cycling in arid, semi-arid, riparian and woodland ecosystems. *Mailing Add:* Dept of Range Sci Utah State Univ UMC 52 Logan UT 84322

WEST, NORMAN REED, b Oak Park, Ill, Aug 13, 43; m 68; c 3. NEUROBIOLOGY, PSYCHOPHARMACOLOGY. *Educ:* Judson Col, BA, 67; Thomas Jefferson Univ, PhD(pharmacol), 74. *Prof Exp:* ASST PROF ANAT & PHARMACOL, STATE UNIV NY, UPSTATE MED CTR, SYRACUSE, NY, 77- *Concurrent Pos:* PMAF fel, Dept Anat & Neurobiol, Sch Med, Wash Univ, Mo, 73-75, NIH fel, 75-77. *Mem:* Soc Neurosci; Am Asn Anat; Am Soc Pharmacol & Exp Therapeut. *Res:* Beneficial and toxic cytological effects of endogenous and exogenous agents administered either in vivo or in tissue culture to healthy, injured, diseased, developing or regenerating nerve tissues. *Mailing Add:* Dept of Anat 766 Irving Ave Syracuse NY 13210

WEST, PHILIP WILLIAM, b Crookston, Minn, Apr 12, 13; m 35, 64; c 3. CHEMISTRY. *Educ:* Univ NDak, BS & MS, 35; Univ Iowa, PhD(chem), 39. *Hon Degrees:* DSc, Univ NDak, 58. *Prof Exp:* Asst chemist, State Geol Surv, NDak, 35-36; asst sanit chem, Univ Iowa, 36-37; asst chemist, State Dept Health, Iowa, 37-40; res chemist & microchemist, Econ Lab, Inc, Minn, 40; from instr to prof, 40-53, Boyd prof, 53-80, EMER BOYD PROF CHEM, LA STATE UNIV, BATON ROUGE, 80-; CHMMN & DIR, WEST-PAINE LABS, BATON ROUGE, 80- *Concurrent Pos:* Smith lectr, 55; consult, Ethyl Corp, A D Little Co & USPHS; consult, Kem-Tech Labs, Inc & chmn bd, 66-73; ed, Analytica Chimica Acta, 58-77; co-ed, Sci Total Environ, 73-77; mem working party 1, Sci Comt Probs Environ; adj prof, Environ Protection Agency; mem chem panel, NSF; pres comt new reactions, Int Union Pure & Appl Chem & pres anal chem div, 66-70, mem sect toxicol & indust hyg; mem study sect, USPHS, 60-65. *Honors & Awards:* Southwest Award, Am Chem Soc, 54; Coates Award, 67; Fisher Award, 74 & Creative Advances Environ Sci & Technol Award, Am Chem Soc, 81. *Mem:* Am Chem Soc; hon mem Brit Soc Anal Chem; hon mem Austrian Asn Microchem & Anal Chem; hon men Japanese Soc Anal Chem. *Res:* Water treatment and analysis; polarized light microscopy; spot tests; organic reagents; complex ions; analysis of petroleum; polarography; chromatography; high frequency titrations; inorganic extractions; catalyzed and induced reactions; air pollution; industrial hygiene; personal monitors. *Mailing Add:* Dept of Chem La State Univ Baton Rouge LA 70803

WEST, RICHARD FUSSELL, b Rockland, Maine, Aug 27, 17; m 42; c 2. FORESTRY, WOOD TECHNOLOGY. *Educ:* Rutgers Univ, BS, 40; Yale Univ, MF, 42. *Prof Exp:* Wood technologist, Chance Vought Aircraft Corp, 43-44; chemist, Crocker-Burbank & Co, 44-46; asst prof wood technol, Sch Forestry, La State Univ, 46-53; assoc prof & head dept, Col Agr, Rutgers Univ, New Brunswick, 53-60, prof forestry, Cook Col, 60-81; RETIRED. *Concurrent Pos:* Consult wood technologist, 53- *Mem:* Soc Wood Sci & Technol; Soc Am Foresters; Forest Prod Res Soc. *Res:* Wood properties, treatment and use; forest policy and forest land management and use. *Mailing Add:* Forestry Sect Cook Col Rutgers Univ New Brunswick NJ 08903

WEST, RICHARD LOWELL, b Quincy, Fla, Mar 20, 34; m 56; c 4. ORGANIC CHEMISTRY. *Educ:* Univ of the South, BS, 55; Univ Rochester, PhD(chem), 61; Univ Del, MBA, 73. *Prof Exp:* Sr chemist, Atlas Chem Ind, Inc, 59-66, res chemist, 66-70, res supvr chem, ICI Am Inc, 70-74, MGR CHEM & POLYMER RES, ICI AMERICAS INC, 75- *Mem:* Am Chem Soc; Am Asn Textile Chemists & Colorists; Am Oil Chemists Soc; NY Acad Sci. *Res:* Organic polymer synthesis; organic synthesis; surfactants; textile adjuncts; industrial chemical development. *Mailing Add:* ICI Americas Inc Wilmington DE 19897

WEST, ROBERT A, b Valparaiso, Ind, June 14, 51. PLANETARY ATMOSPHERES, RADIATIVE TRANSFER. *Educ:* Calif Inst Technol, BS, 73; Univ Ariz, PhD(planetary sci), 77. *Prof Exp:* Res asst, Calif Inst Technol, 69-73; RES ASSOC, UNIV COLO, BOULDER, 78-, LECTR ASTRON, 79- *Concurrent Pos:* Co-invest, Voyager Target Selection Working Group, 79-80, Voyager Photopolarimeter Exp, 80- *Mem:* Am Astron Soc; Am Geophys Union. *Res:* Radiative transfer in planetary atmospheres including observation and interpretation of multiply-scattered light observed by spacecraft and ground-based instruments. *Mailing Add:* Lab Atmospheric & Space Physics Univ Colo Campus Box 392 Boulder CO 80309

WEST, ROBERT ELMER, b Blackfoot, Idaho, Apr 2, 38; div; c 3. EXPLORATION GEOPHYSICS. *Educ:* Univ Idaho, BS, 61; Univ Ariz, MS, 70, PhD(geosci), 72. *Prof Exp:* Physicist, Phillips Petrol Co, 61-62, 65; res assoc geophys, Univ Ariz, 68-69, 71-72; geophysicist, Humble Oil & Refining Co, 72-74; GEOPHYSICIST, MINING GEOPHYS SURV, 74- *Mem:* Soc Explor Geophys. *Res:* Application of gravity, magnetics and electrical methods to engineering studies and to exploration for ore deposits, petroleum, ground water and geothermal energy sources. *Mailing Add:* Mining Geophys Surv 2400 E Grant Rd Tucson AZ 85719

WEST, ROBERT MACLELLAN, b Appleton, Wis, Sept 1, 42; m 65; c 1. VERTEBRATE PALEONTOLOGY. *Educ:* Lawrence Col, BA, 63; Univ Chicago, SM, 64, PhD(evolutionary biol), 68. *Prof Exp:* Res assoc geol & geophys sci, Princeton Univ, 68-69; asst prof biol, Adelphi Univ, 69-74; CUR GEOL, MILWAUKEE PUB MUS, 74- *Concurrent Pos:* Adj assoc prof, Dept Geol Sci, Univ Wis-Milwaukee, 74- *Honors & Awards:* Guyot Award, Nat Geog Soc, 81. *Mem:* Geol Soc Am; Soc Study Evolution; Am Soc Mammal. *Res:* Asiatic mammalian evolution; paleontologic aspects of plate tectonics; evolution of early Tertiary mammals and mammalian communities; biostratigraphy of Tertiary deposits of intermontane basins in North America. *Mailing Add:* Dept of Geol Milwaukee Pub Mus 800 W Wells St Milwaukee WI 53233

WEST, RONALD E(MMETT), b Rosebush, Mich, Sept 7, 33; m 55; c 3. CHEMICAL ENGINEERING. *Educ:* Univ Mich, BSE, 54, MSE, 55, PhD(chem eng), 58. *Prof Exp:* From asst prof to assoc prof, 57-74, PROF CHEM ENG, UNIV COLO, BOULDER, 74- *Mem:* Am Inst Chem Engrs; Water Pollution Control Fedn. *Res:* Water pollution control. *Mailing Add:* Dept Chem Eng Univ Colo Boulder CO 80309

WEST, RONALD ROBERT, b Centralia, Ill, Nov 14, 35; m 58, 78; c 2. PALEOBIOLOGY, PALEOECOLOGY. *Educ:* Univ Mo-Rolla, BS, 58; Univ Kans, MS, 62; Univ Okla, PhD(paleoecol geol), 70. *Prof Exp:* Stratigrapher, Shell Oil Co, Okla, 56, micropaleontologist, La, 58-59; invertebrate paleontologist, Kans Geol Surv, 60, geologist, 61; paleobiologist & paleoecologist, Humble Oil & Refining Co, Tex & Okla, 61-67; instr geol, Univ Okla, 67-68; asst prof paleobiol, 69-74, ASSOC PROF PALAEOBIOL, DEPT GEOL, KANS STATE UNIV, 74-, ANCILLARY PROF BIOL DIV, 74- *Concurrent Pos:* Am Chem Soc-Petrol Res Fund grant paleobiol; mem adv coun, Friends of Woodrow Wilson Nat Fel Found; consult res lab, Amoco Prod Co, Okla, 74-; NSF grant, Nat Mus Natural Hist, 77-78. *Honors & Awards:* Geol Soc Am Award, 72. *Mem:* Int Paleont Asn; Paleont Soc; Soc Econ Mineralogists & Paleontologists; Paleont Asn; Geol Soc Am. *Res:* Paleoecology and paleobiology of upper paleozoic invertebrates; structure and dynamics of benthic fossil communities; population studies and ecology of modern and fossil brachiopods and bivalves; carbonate sedimentation reefs; recent marine invertebrate ecology; organism/substitute relationships and functional morphology of marine invertebrates Cbrachiopods & bivalves. *Mailing Add:* Palaeobiol Lab Dept of Geol Kans State Univ Manhattan KS 66506

WEST, ROSE GAYLE, b Pascagoula, Miss, Oct 31, 43; m 62; c 1. PHYSICAL CHEMISTRY. *Educ:* Univ Southern Miss, BA, 65, PhD(phys chem), 69. *Prof Exp:* Asst prof chem, 68-73, actg chmn dept, 72-74, ASSOC PROF CHEM, WILLIAM CAREY COL, 73-, CHMN DEPT, 74- *Mem:* Am Chem Soc. *Res:* Thermo chemistry, heats of combustion and resonance energies of aromatic hydrocarbons and 5- and 6-membered aromatic nitrogen heterocyclic compounds; special projects for undergraduate physical chemistry laboratories. *Mailing Add:* RFD 3 Box 248 William Carey Col Sumrall MS 39482

WEST, SEYMOUR S, b New York, NY, Apr 19, 20; m 47; c 3. BIOPHYSICS, ANATOMY. *Educ:* City Col New York, BEE, 50; Western Reserve Univ, PhD(biophys, anat), 63. *Prof Exp:* Sr engr, A B Dumont Labs, Inc, 54-57; asst prof biomed eng, Western Reserve Univ, 62-64; sr scientist & head dept phys biol, Melpar, Inc, 64-66; assoc prof biomed eng & actg head dept, 66-67, assoc prof eng biophys & actg chmn dept, 67-69, PROF ENG BIOPHYS & CHMN DEPT, MED CTR, UNIV ALA, 69- *Concurrent Pos:* Mem, Automation in Med Lab Sci Rev Comt, NIH. *Mem:* Fel Royal Micros Soc; Biophys Soc; Inst Elec & Electronics Engrs; Biomed Eng Soc; Int Asn Dent Res. *Res:* Relation of physical optical properties of living cells and their morphological components to cytochemistry and physical chemistry; television fluorescence spectrophotometry and microspectropolarimetry. *Mailing Add:* Dept of Eng Biophys Univ of Ala Med Ctr Univ Sta Birmingham AL 35294

WEST, SHERLIE HILL, b Forbus, Tenn, Feb 18, 27; m 49; c 2. PLANT PHYSIOLOGY, AGRONOMY. *Educ:* Tenn Polytech Univ, BS, 49; Univ Ky, MS, 54; Univ Ill, PhD(agron, bot), 58. *Prof Exp:* Asst agronomist, Univ Ky, 54-55; res agronomist, USDA, 58-60; from asst agronomist to assoc agronomist, 58-70, asst dean res, Inst Food & Agr Sci, 72-79, AGRONOMIST, UNIV FLA, 70-, PROF SEED TECHNOL, 79- *Concurrent Pos:* Consult, O M Scott & Sons, Ohio, 59-64; plant physiologist, USDA, 60-72. *Mem:* Am Chem Soc; Am Soc Plant Physiol; Am Soc Agron. *Res:* Nucleic acid metabolism and growth due to environmental factors; mechanism of hormone action; drought and cold tolerance; genetic criteria of selection of superior plants; cool temperature effects on carbohydrate metabolism; mechanisms of cool temperature dormancy in tropical grasses; seed quality and deterioration. *Mailing Add:* Agron Dept Seed Lab Univ Fla Bldg 661 Gainesville FL 32611

WEST, TERRY RONALD, b St Louis, Mo, Aug 15, 36; m 57; c 2. ENGINEERING GEOLOGY, CIVIL ENGINEERING. *Educ:* Wash Univ, AB & BS, 59, MA, 62; Purdue Univ, Lafayette, MSCE, 64, PhD(eng geol), 66. *Prof Exp:* Teaching asst geol, Wash Univ, 59-61; staff engr, H M Reitz Consult Engr, Mo, 61; from instr to asst prof eng geol, 61-71, ASSOC PROF ENG GEOL, PURDUE UNIV, WEST LAFAYETTE, 71-, TEAM LEADER ENG SOILS GROUP, LAB APPL REMOTE SENSING, 69- *Concurrent Pos:* Consult, ATEC Assoc Inc, 69- *Mem:* Geol Soc Am; Am Soc Civil Engrs; Asn Eng Geol; Am Soc Testing & Mat. *Res:* Evaluation of geological materials for engineering uses; remote sensing of earth materials; subsurface geology and ground water. *Mailing Add:* Dept of Geosci Purdue Univ West Lafayette IN 47907

WEST, THEODORE CLINTON, b Central, SC, May 17, 19; m 42; c 3. PHARMACOLOGY. *Educ:* Univ Wash, BS, 48, MS, 49, PhD(pharmacol), 52. *Prof Exp:* From instr to prof pharmacol, Univ Wash, 49-68, asst chmn dept, 63-68, asst dean planning, 66-68; prof med educ & pharmacol & dir off med educ, 68-77, PROF MED, SCH MED, UNIV CALIF, DAVIS, 78- *Mem:* Am Soc Pharmacol & Exp Therapeut. *Res:* Pharmacology of cardiac and smooth muscle; medical education. *Mailing Add:* Off of Med Educ Univ of Calif Sch of Med Davis CA 95616

WEST, WALTER SCOTT, b Fayette, Wis, Mar 12, 12; m 40; c 3. ECONOMIC GEOLOGY, GEOCHEMISTRY. *Educ:* Cornell Col, AB, 34; Univ Wis-Platteville, BE, 35; Univ Tenn, MS, 37. *Prof Exp:* Prin high sch, Mo, 37-38; instr geol, Univ NC, 40-42; eng aide & cartographer, Alaskan Geol Br, 42-46, geologist, 46-54, secy geol names comt, Geol Div, 54-67, CHIEF, WIS LEAD-ZINC PROJ, EASTERN MINERAL RESOURCES BR, GEOL DIV, US GEOL SURV, 66- *Mem:* Am Inst Mining, Metall & Petrol Eng; Arctic Inst NAm; Soc Econ Geologists. *Res:* Radioactive deposits, pumice and riprap in Alaska; trace element and lead isotope studies; mineralogy and genesis of lead and zinc deposits in Wisconsin and Tennessee; geologic and geochemical mapping and topical studies in Upper Mississippi Valley zinc-lead district, Wisconsin, Illinois, Iowa and Minnesota; stratigraphy. *Mailing Add:* US Geol Surv Royce Hall Univ Wis Platteville WI 53818

WEST, WARWICK REED, JR, b Evington, Va, Feb 9, 22; m 46; c 3. INVERTEBRATE ZOOLOGY. *Educ:* Lynchburg Col, BS, 43; Univ Va, PhD(biol), 52. *Prof Exp:* Instr biol, Lynchburg Col, 46-49 & 52; from asst prof to assoc prof, 52-66, PROF BIOL, UNIV RICHMOND, 66-, CHMN DEPT, 65- *Mem:* AAAS. *Res:* Milipede anatomy. *Mailing Add:* Dept of Biol Univ of Richmond Richmond VA 23173

WEST, WILLIAM LIONEL, b Charlotte, NC, Nov 30, 23; m 72. ZOOLOGY, PHARMACOLOGY. *Educ:* J C Smith Univ, BS, 47; Univ Iowa, PhD, 55. *Prof Exp:* Asst zool, Univ Iowa, 49-55, res assoc radiation, Col Med, 55-56; from instr to assoc prof pharmacol, 56-73, PROF PHARMACOL & RADIOL & CHMN DEPT PHARMACOL, COL MED, HOWARD UNIV, 73- *Mem:* Am Soc Zool; Am Soc Pharmacol & Exp Therapeut; Am Physiol Soc; Am Nuclear Soc; NY Acad Sci. *Res:* Biochemical and endocrine pharmacology; cellular physiology. *Mailing Add:* Dept of Pharmacol Howard Univ Col of Med Washington DC 20001

WEST, WILLIAM T, b Holyoke, Mass, June 26, 25; m 50; c 2. HISTOLOGY, ANATOMY. *Educ:* Am Inst Col, BA, 49; Univ Rochester, PhD(anat), 56. *Prof Exp:* Fel anat, Univ Rochester, 56-57, instr, 57-58; assoc staff scientist, Jackson Mem Lab, 58-62; asst prof, 62-69, ASSOC PROF ANAT, STATE UNIV NY DOWNSTATE MED CTR, 69- *Res:* Histopathology; human anatomy; pathology; endocrinology. *Mailing Add:* Dept of Anat State Univ NY Downstate Med Ctr Brooklyn NY 11203

WESTALL, FREDERICK CHARLES, b Pasadena, Calif, Nov 6, 43; m 68. BIOCHEMISTRY. *Educ:* Univ Calif, Los Angeles, BS, 64; San Diego State Col, MS, 66; Univ Calif, San Diego, PhD(chem), 70. *Prof Exp:* Multiple Sclerosis Soc res fel biochem, 70-72, res assoc, 72-73, ASST RES PROF BIOCHEM, SALK INST, 73-; ASSOC RES PROF, LINUS PAULING INST SCI & MED, MENLO PARK, CALIF, 75-; ASSOC RES PROF, SALK INST, 79- *Mem:* Am Chem Soc; Tissue Cult Soc; NY Acad Sci; Soc Neurosci; Am Acad Neurol. *Res:* Biochemistry of neurological diseases; solid phase peptide synthesis; chromatographic techniques of disease identification; aging; immunological effects of adjuvants. *Mailing Add:* 10010 N Torrey Pine Rd La Jolla CA 92037

WESTAWAY, KENNETH C, b Hamilton, Ont, Aug 14, 38; m 62; c 3. PHYSICAL ORGANIC CHEMISTRY. *Educ:* McMaster Univ, BSc, 62, PhD(phys org chem), 68. *Prof Exp:* Asst prof chem, 68-75, chmn dept, 74-76, ASSOC PROF CHEM, LAURENTIAN UNIV, 75- *Concurrent Pos:* Vis prof, Univ Wis-Madison, 76-77. *Mem:* Fel Chem Inst Can; Am Chem Soc. *Res:* Mechanisms of organic reactions; nucleophilic substitution reactions and elimination reactions; kinetic isotope effects are used to determine how solvents affect the transition state of SN reactions. identification and analysis of organic compounds; detection and analysis of PAH; acid mists and gaseous pollutants in dieselized underground mines. *Mailing Add:* Dept of Chem Laurentian Univ Sudbury ON P3E 2C6 Can

WESTBERG, KARL ROGERS, b Norwalk, Conn, Dec 17, 39; m 71; c 3. CHEMISTRY, PHYSICS. *Educ:* Bowdoin Col, BA, 61; Brown Univ, PhD(chem), 69. *Prof Exp:* Engr, Perkin-Elmer Corp, 61; MEM TECH STAFF, AEROSPACE CORP, 68- *Mem:* Am Chem Soc; Am Phys Soc. *Res:* Chemical kinetics; electron attachment; aerospace sciences; air-pollution chemistry. *Mailing Add:* Aerospace Corp PO Box 92957 Los Angeles CA 90009

WESTBROOK, DAVID REX, b London, Eng, May 12, 37; m 60; c 2. APPLIED MATHEMATICS. *Educ:* Univ London, BSc, 58, PhD, 61. *Prof Exp:* Lectr math, Univ Singapore, 61-64; sr lectr, Univ Melbourne, 64; lectr, Univ Nottingham, 64-65; vis mem, NY Univ, 65-66; asst prof, 66-71, ASSOC PROF MATH, UNIV CALGARY, 71- *Concurrent Pos:* Nat Res Coun Can res grant, 67-68. *Mem:* Am Math Soc; Soc Indust & Appl Math. *Res:* Theory of elastic plates and shells. *Mailing Add:* Dept Math Statist & Comput Sci Univ of Calgary Calgary AB T2N 1N4 Can

WESTBROOK, GEORGE FRANKLIN, food chemistry, deceased

WESTBROOK, J(ACK) H(ALL), b Troy, NY, Aug 19, 24; m 47; c 5. PHYSICAL METALLURGY, CERAMICS. *Educ:* Rensselaer Polytech Inst, BMetE, 44, MMetE, 47; Mass Inst Technol, ScD(metall), 49. *Prof Exp:* Asst metall, Rensselaer Polytech Inst, 44, 46-47 & Mass Inst Technol, 47-49; res assoc, Res & Develop Ctr, 49-71, mgr eng mat & processes info oper, 71-74, mgr, Mat Info Serv, Corp Res & Develop, 74-81, MGR SPEC PROJS, MAT INFO SERV, GEN ELEC CO, 81- *Concurrent Pos:* Adj assoc prof, Rensselaer Polytech Inst, 57-59; mem subcomts nat mat adv bd, Nat Acad Sci, 59-63, 68, 75-77 & 79-82; chmn, Gordon Conf Solid State Studies in Ceramics, 60; Nat Acad Sci US-USSR exchange fel, 71; trustee, Eng Index, Inc, 71-80; consult, US Air Force, US Army, Nat Sci Fedn, NASA & Advan Res Proj Agency, Dept Defense; chmn, Mat Info Comn, Fedn Mat, 74-; mem mat adv panel, Off Technol Assessment, US Cong, 75-77; chmn adv panel on data for indust needs, CODATA, 76- *Honors & Awards:* Turner Award, Electrochem Soc, 57; Templin Award, Am Soc Testing & Mat, 59; Geisler Award, Am Soc Metals, 59, Campbell Mem Lectr, 76; Award, Am Inst Mining, Metall & Petrol Engrs, 63; Award, Am Ceramic Soc, 67; Hofmann Prize, Lead Develop Asn, 71; Jaffries Mem lectr, Am Soc Metals, 79. *Mem:* Am Soc Metals; Am Inst Mining, Metall & Petrol Engrs; fel Am Ceramic Soc; Electrochem Soc; fel AAAS. *Res:* Intermetallic compounds; mechanical properties of refractory materials; hardness measurement techniques; grain boundaries; materials information; research and development planning; technological forecasting and assessment; history of metallurgy. *Mailing Add:* Gen Elec Co FNB/120 Erie Blvd Schenectady NY 12305

WESTBROOK, RUSSELL DAVID, b Cleveland, Ohio, Mar 21, 21; m 49; c 3. SOLID STATE PHYSICS. *Educ:* Col Wooster, BA, 42; Ohio State Univ, MS, 48. *Prof Exp:* Mem staff, US Naval Res Lab, 42-43; technician, Brush Develop Co, 46; group leader res labs, Union Carbide Corp, 48-66; PHYSICIST, SOLID STATE DIV, OAK RIDGE NAT LAB, 66- *Mem:* Inst Elec & Electronics Engrs. *Res:* Physics of carbon and graphite; intermetallic compounds; silicon; germanium; growth and analysis of semiconductor single crystals; photovaltaic conversion; laser annealing of semiconductors. *Mailing Add:* Solid State Div Bldg 2000 Oak Ridge Nat Lab PO Box X Oak Ridge TN 37830

WESTBY, CARL A, b Los Angeles, Calif, Feb 8, 36; m 58; c 6. MICROBIAL PHYSIOLOGY. *Educ:* Univ Calif, Riverside, AB, 58; Univ Calif, Davis, PhD(bact), 64. *Prof Exp:* Fel bact physiol, Sch Med, Univ Pa, 64-67; asst prof bact, Utah State Univ, 67-73; assoc prof, 73-80, PROF MICROBIOL, SDAK STATE UNIV, 80- *Concurrent Pos:* Med prod consult, Med Prod Div, 3M Co, 74- *Mem:* Am Soc Microbiol; Sigma Xi. *Res:* Bacterial physiology and genetics. *Mailing Add:* Dept of Microbiol SDak State Univ Brookings SD 57006

WESTCOTT, DONALD ELVIN, food technology, see previous edition

WESTCOTT, PETER WALTER, b Mt Vernon, NY, Nov 5, 38; m 64. ECOLOGY, ZOOLOGY. *Educ:* Amherst Col, BA, 60; Univ Ariz, MS, 62; Univ Fla, PhD(zool), 70. *Prof Exp:* Asst prof zool, Univ Nebr, Lincoln, 70-71; PROF ECOL, BIOL SCI CTR, LONDRINA STATE UNIV, BRAZIL, 72- *Mem:* Am Ornith Union; Sociadade Brasilero para o Progresso da Cienca; Cooper Ornith Soc. *Res:* Field studies of avian social and breeding behavior and ecology; field studies of tropical avian social structures. *Mailing Add:* Biol Sci Ctr Londrina State Univ Univ Campus PO Box 1530 Londrina 86-100 Parana Brazil

WESTCOTT, WAYNE LESLIE, b Blue Hill, Nebr, Sept 22, 18; m 41; c 2. BIOCHEMISTRY. *Educ:* Univ Nebr, BSc, 47; Univ Utah, MS, 49, PhD(biochem), 53. *Prof Exp:* Tech asst to supt biol & biochem mfg, E R Squibb & Sons, 53-55, head dept biol & biochem mfg, 55-59, sr res scientist, Squibb Inst Med Res Div, Olin Mathieson Chem Corp, 59-64, res supvr, Biol Dept, 64-68; head natural prod develop, Armour Pharmaceut Co, Ill, 68-72, dir mfg processes, 72-75; mgr prod & process improv, Sci Prod Div, Abbott Labs, 75-78; DIR TECH OPERS, ALPHA THERAPEUT CORP, 78- *Mem:* Am Chem Soc; AAAS; Int Asn Biol Standardization; NY Acad Sci. *Res:* Isolation of natural products from tissues of animal origin; protein isolation; blood fractionation. *Mailing Add:* Alpha Therapeut Corp 5555 Valley Blvd Los Angeles CA 90023

WESTDAL, PAUL HAROLD, b Wynyard, Sask, Nov 5, 21; m 47; c 3. ENTOMOLOGY, VIROLOGY. *Educ:* Univ Man, BSc, 47, MSc, 50, PhD(entom), 69. *Prof Exp:* Res entomologist, 46-74, SR RES ENTOMOLOGIST ECON ENTOM, AGR CAN, 75- *Concurrent Pos:* Adj prof, Univ Man, 71-; ed, The Man Entomologist, 77-81. *Mem:* Entom Soc Can; Entom Soc NZ. *Res:* Biology and control of insect pests of sunflowers and rapeseed. *Mailing Add:* Res Sta 195 Dafoe Rd Winnipeg MB R3T 2M9 Can

WESTDORP, WOLFGANG ALFRED, solid state physics, physical metallurgy, see previous edition

WESTENBARGER, GENE ARLAN, b Lancaster, Ohio, July 25, 35; m 58; c 4. PHYSICAL CHEMISTRY. *Educ:* Ohio Univ, BS, 57; Univ Calif, Berkeley, PhD(phys chem), 63. *Prof Exp:* Chemist, Battelle Mem Inst, 57; res & develop coordr, Qm Food & Container Inst, 58-59; asst prof, 63-67, ASSOC PROF PHYS CHEM, OHIO UNIV, 67- *Mem:* AAAS; Am Phys Soc; Am Chem Soc. *Res:* Thermodynamic and magnetic studies at low temperature. *Mailing Add:* Dept of Chem Ohio Univ Athens OH 45701

WESTENBERG, ARTHUR AYER, b Menomonie, Wis, Mar 1, 22; m 45; c 1. CHEMICAL PHYSICS. *Educ:* Carleton Col, AB, 43; Harvard Univ, AM, 48, PhD(chem), 50. *Prof Exp:* Chemist, Mayo Clin, 50; asst prof chem, Lafayette Col, 50-52; sr staff mem, Appl Physics Lab, Johns Hopkins Univ, 52-58, prin staff mem, 58-77, supvr chem physics res, 63-77; RETIRED. *Concurrent Pos:* Consult, Proj Squid, Off Naval Res, 60-65; mem adv comt, Army Res Off, 66-71; mem comt assess environ effects of supersonic transport, US Dept Com, 71. *Honors & Awards:* Hillebrand Award, Am Chem Soc, 66; Silver Medal, Combustion Inst, 66. *Res:* Chemical kinetics; high temperature gas properties; combustion; air pollution chemistry; electron spin resonance spectroscopy. *Mailing Add:* West Road Manchester VT 05254

WESTER, JOHN WALTER, JR, b Youngstown, Ohio, Sept 30, 20; m 43; c 7. APPLIED MATHEMATICS. *Educ:* Dartmouth Col, AB, 42. *Prof Exp:* Res asst elec eng, Mass Inst Technol, 46-47; mathematician & assoc dir, Lab Appl Sci, Univ Chicago, 47-62; exec dir, 62-69, res dir, 69-73, trustee, 61-81, EXEC DIR, ACAD INTERSCI METHODOLOGY, 81- *Concurrent Pos:* Chmn bd, Wester Fuel & Supply Co; pres, Indianola Realty Inc, Burnkey Inc & Wholesale Distrib Co, Youngstown, Ohio, 67-81. *Mem:* Opers Res Soc Am; Soc Indust & Appl Math. *Res:* Planning and analysis of governmental and business operations management; solar energy research; management information systems. *Mailing Add:* 18456 Dundee Ave Homewood IL 60430

WESTER, RONALD CLARENCE, b Gardner, Mass, Aug 26, 40; m 67; c 2. DRUG METABOLISM, PHARMACOKINETICS. *Educ:* Clark Univ, AB, 62; Univ Ill, Urbana, MS, 69, PhD(physiol), 70. *Prof Exp:* Res asst metab, Univ Rochester Sch Med, 64-66, res asst, Worcester Fedn Exp Biol, 62-64; res investr, G D Searle & Co, 72-76, res scientist drug metab, 76-81; PROF PHARM, SCH PHARM & RES DERMATOLOGIST, SCH MED, UNIV CALIF, SAN FRANCISCO, 81- *Concurrent Pos:* Fel, Univ Ill, 66-70, Cornell Univ, 70-72; vis scientist, Ore Regional Primate Ctr, 72. *Mem:* Am Soc Clin Pharmacol & Therapeut. *Res:* Bioavailability and drug metabolism in experimental animals and man; percutaneous absorption in experimental animals and man; clinical dermatology and pharmaceutical sciences. *Mailing Add:* 837 Butternut Dr San Rafael CA 94903

WESTERBERG, ARTHUR WILLIAM, b St Paul, Minn, Oct 9, 38; m 63; c 2. CHEMICAL ENGINEERING. *Educ:* Univ Minn, Minneapolis, BSc, 60; Princeton Univ, MSc, 61; Univ London, PhD(chem eng) & Imp Col, dipl, 64. *Prof Exp:* Sr analyst software eng, Control Data Corp, 65-67; from asst prof to prof chem eng, Univ Fla, 67-76; dir, Design Res Ctr, 78-80, PROF CHEM ENG, CARNEGIE-MELLON UNIV, 76-, DEPT HEAD CHEM ENG, 80- *Mem:* Am Inst Chem Engrs; Comput Aides Chem Eng Educ (secy, 71-72); Am Soc Eng Educ. *Res:* Developing computer software systems to aid in process design and optimization; start-up control of processes. *Mailing Add:* Dept of Chem Eng Carnegie-Mellon Univ Pittsburgh PA 15213

WESTERDAHL, CAROLYN ANN LOVEJOY, b Oklahoma City, Okla, Apr 16, 35; m 61. SURFACE SCIENCE. *Educ:* Univ Chicago, BA, 55, BS, 57; Univ Calif, Berkeley, PhD(chem), 61. *Prof Exp:* CHEMIST, PICATINNY ARSENAL, 67- *Mem:* Sigma Xi; Am Chem Soc. *Res:* Surface studies. *Mailing Add:* 7 Comanche Trail Denville NJ 07834

WESTERDAHL, RAYMOND P, b Chicago, Ill, Mar 22, 29; m 61. PHYSICAL CHEMISTRY. *Educ:* Univ Ill, BS, 51; Univ Chicago, MS, 59, PhD(phys chem), 62. *Prof Exp:* Res chemist, Esso Res & Eng Co, Standard Oil Co, NJ, 62-67; res chemist, Feltman Res Lab, Picatinny Arsenal, 67-77, CHEM ENGR, US ARMY ARMAMENT RES & DEVELOP COMMAND, 77- *Mem:* AAAS; fel Am Inst Chemists; Am Chem Soc; Soc Appl Spectros. *Res:* Mechanisms of pyrotechnic reactions; Raman spectroscopy; chemiluminescent reactions; reactions in fused salts; analysis and control of air and water pollutants. *Mailing Add:* 7 Comanche Trail Denville NJ 07834

WESTERFIELD, CLIFFORD, b Ohio Co, Ky, Apr 7, 08; m 36; c 4. VETERINARY ANATOMY. *Educ:* Western Ky State Teachers Col, BS, 30; Univ Ky, MS, 32; Mich State Col, DVM, 38. *Prof Exp:* Instr sci, Western Ky State Teachers Col, 30-31; high sch teacher, 33-35; jr vet, Bur Animal Indust, USDA, Washington, DC, 38-39; asst vet, Exp Sta, Univ Ky, 39-40, assoc animal pathologist, 45-46; asst prof vet anat, Ohio State Univ, 40-44; prof vet anat & histol & head dept, Univ Ga, 46-53; asst prof, Iowa State Col, 53-54; prof vet anat & histol & head dept, 54-62, prof vet anat, 62-75, EMER PROF VET ANAT, COL VET MED, UNIV GA, 75- *Mem:* AAAS; Am Asn Vet Anat (secy, 58, pres, 60); Am Vet Med Asn; World Asn Vet Anat. *Res:* Equine diseases; histopathology; veterinary histology. *Mailing Add:* 116 Whitehead Rd Athens GA 30601

WESTERHOUT, GART, b The Hague, Neth, June 15, 27; m 56; c 5. ASTRONOMY. *Educ:* State Univ Leiden, Drs, 54, PhD(astron), 58. *Prof Exp:* Res asst astron, Univ Observ, State Univ Leiden, 52-54, sci officer, 54-59, chief sci officer, 59-62; dir astron prog, 62-73, chmn div math, phys & eng sci, 72-73, prof astron, Univ Md, College Park, 62-77; SCI DIR, US NAVAL OBSERV, 77- *Concurrent Pos:* NATO fel, 59; mem user's comt, Nat Radio Astron Observ, 65-; mem US nat comt, Int Astron Union, 71-74; trustee-at-large, Assoc Univs Inc, 71-74; mem comt radio frequencies, Nat Res Coun, 72-; mem US nat comt, Int Sci Radio Union, 72-78, chmn comn radio-astron, 75-78; Humboldt Found award, Ger, 73; mem, Inter-Union Comn for Allocation of Frequencies, 75- *Mem:* Am Astron Soc; Royal Astron Soc; Int Astron Union. *Res:* Radio astronomy; 21-centimeter line research; fundamental astronomy; galactic structure. *Mailing Add:* Off of Sci Dir US Naval Observ Washington DC 20390

WESTERMAN, ARTHUR B(AER), b Pittsburgh, Pa, June 29, 19; m 42; c 3. METALLURGY. *Educ:* Carnegie Inst Technol, BS, 39. *Prof Exp:* Asst metallurgist, Crucible Steel Co Am, Pa, 39-42; res metallurgist, Metals Res Lab, Carnegie Inst Technol, 42-43; res engr, 43-50, asst div chief, 50-58, proj coordr, 58-62, asst res mgr, 62-75, coordr large proj, 75-80, MEM STAFF, BATTELLE MEM INST, BATTELLE DEVELOP CORP, 80- *Mem:* Am Soc Metals; AAAS. *Res:* Scientific and technical information. *Mailing Add:* 71 N Merkle Rd Columbus OH 43209

WESTERMAN, EDWIN J(AMES), b USA, Jan 18, 35; m 59; c 5. METALLURGICAL ENGINEERING, METALLURGY. *Educ:* Mont Sch Mineral Sci & Technol, BS, 56; Rensselaer Polytech Inst, PhD(metall), 59. *Prof Exp:* Metallurgist, Res Lab, Gen Elec Co, 59-61; metallurgist, Wash, 61-69, head alloy metall sect, 70-73, mgr, Alloy & Properties Res Dept, 73-79, METALLURGIST, CTR FOR TECHNOL, KAISER ALUMINUM & CHEM CORP, 69-, MGR, REDUCTION RES DEPT, 80- *Mem:* Am Soc Metals; Am Inst Mining, Metall & Petrol Engrs. *Res:* Powder metallurgy; aluminum alloy development; x-ray diffraction; electron and ion microprobes; nondestructive testing of metals. *Mailing Add:* 164 Woodview Terr Dr San Ramon CA 94583

WESTERMAN, HOWARD ROBERT, b Jersey City, NJ, Feb 17, 26; m 50; c 2. SYSTEMS ENGINEERING. *Educ:* St Peter's Col, BS, 48; Univ Chicago, SM, 49; Columbia Univ, PhD(chem physics), 52. *Prof Exp:* Analyst oper res, Off Chief Naval Oper, 52-54; mem tech staff, 54-66, DEPT HEAD SYST ENG, BELL TEL LABS, INC, 66- *Concurrent Pos:* Allied Chem Co fel, Columbia Univ, 52-53. *Res:* Quantum mechanics; operations research; orbital mechanics. *Mailing Add:* Bell Tel Lab Inc 185 Monmouth Pkwy West Long Branch NJ 07764

WESTERMAN, IRA JOHN, b Louisville, Ky, Oct 10, 45; m 79. ORGANIC CHEMISTRY, POLYMER CHEMISTRY. *Educ:* Univ Ky, BS, 67; Duke Univ, MS, 69, PhD(org chem), 73. *Prof Exp:* Res fel, Univ Ariz, 73-74; sr res chemist polymer chem, B F Goodrich Chem Div, 74-80; SR RES CHEMIST POLYMER CHEM, PHILLIPS PETROL CO, 80- *Mem:* Am Chem Soc; Soc Plastics Engrs. *Res:* Polyelectrolytes; water-soluble polymers; heterocyclic chemistry; polar cycloadditions; oil recovery chemicals. *Mailing Add:* Phillips Res Ctr RB-6 Phillips Petrol Co Bartlesville OK 74004

WESTERMAN, RICHARD EARL, b Great Falls, Mont, Jan 18, 35; m 58; c 4. METALLURGY. *Educ:* Mont Col Mineral Sci & Technol, BS, 56; Rensselaer Polytech Inst, PhD(metall), 60. *Prof Exp:* Engr, Hanford Labs, Gen Elec Co, 56-62, sr scientist, 62-64; res assoc corrosion res, 64-66, mgr, 66-69, res assoc, Metall Sect, 69-80, TECH LEADER ENVIRON MECH PROPERTIES, PAC NORTHWEST LAB, BATTELLE MEM INST, 80- *Concurrent Pos:* Lectr, Richland Joint Ctr Grad Study. *Mem:* Am Soc Metals. *Res:* Kinetics of high temperature oxidation and evaporation of superalloys; diffusion and solubility of hydrogen in iron, zirconium and titanium alloys; gas-metal reactions; aqueous corrosion; thermodynamics; powder metallurgy; dental implant development; nuclear waste disposal. *Mailing Add:* Pac Northwest Lab Battelle Mem Inst PO Box 999 Richland WA 99352

WESTERMAN, WILLIAM JOSEPH, b St Louis, Mo, June 27, 37; m 63; c 3. MECHANICAL ENGINEERING, PHYSICS. *Educ:* Vanderbilt Univ, BSME, 59, MS, 61; Washington Univ, DSc, 64. *Prof Exp:* Lectr elec eng, Washington Univ, 60-63; res scientist mech eng, Martin Co, 64-67; mgr special eng prog, McDonnell Douglas, 67-74; gen mgr res & develop, Chamberlain Mfg Co, 74-80; PRES, COGSDILL TOOL PROD CORP, 80- *Concurrent Pos:* Adj assoc prof, Univ Fla, 64-73; fel, NSF, 62-63. *Mem:* Am Soc Mech Eng; Soc Mfg Engr; Soc Auto Engrs. *Res:* Fluidics; automatic controls; fluid systems contamination. *Mailing Add:* 207 East Springs Rd Columbia SC 27204

WESTERMANN, D(ONALD) H(ERBERT), chemical engineering, bioengineering, see previous edition

WESTERMANN, D T, b July 4, 41; US citizen. SOIL SCIENCE, SOIL CHEMISTRY. *Educ:* Colo State Univ, BS, 63; Ore State Univ, MS, 65, PhD, 68. *Prof Exp:* SOIL SCIENTIST, SNAKE RIVER CONSERV RES CTR, SCI & EDUC ADMIN-AGR RES, USDA, 68- *Concurrent Pos:* Affil prof, Univ Idaho, 71- *Res:* Plant nutrition. *Mailing Add:* Snake River Conserv Res Ctr USDA Rte 1 Box 186 Kimberly ID 83341

WESTERMANN, FRED ERNST, b Cincinnati, Ohio, Mar 14, 21; m 49; c 3. METALLURGICAL & MATERIALS ENGINEERING. *Educ:* Univ Cincinnati, ChE, 43, MS, 47, PhD(metall eng), 57. *Prof Exp:* Jr engr develop elastomers, Inland Mfg Div Gen Motors Corp, 43-44; FAC METALL ENG, COL ENG UNIV CINCINNATI, 48- *Concurrent Pos:* Consult, Gen Elec Aircraft Nuclear Propulsion, 57-61, Metcut Res Assoc, Inc, 65-74 & Delhi Foundry Sand Co, 75-78; co investr grant, NSF, 73-76, mem mat adv team educ modules mat sci & eng, 76- *Mem:* Fel Am Soc Metals; Am Soc Eng Educ; Am Foundrymen's Soc; Sigma Xi. *Res:* Powder metallurgy; powder characterization, compaction and sintering; foundry engineering; molding materials; cast iron structure property relationships; welding metallurgy. *Mailing Add:* Dept of Mat Sci & Metall Eng Mail Loc 12 Univ Cincinnati Cincinnati OH 45221

WESTERMANN, GERD ERNST GEROLD, b Berlin, Ger, May 11, 27; m 56; c 3. GEOLOGY. *Educ:* Brunswick Tech Univ, BSc, 50; Univ Tübingen, MSc & PhD(geol, paleont), 53. *Prof Exp:* Paleontologist, Geol Surv Ger, 53-57; from lectr to assoc prof, 57-69, PROF GEOL, McMASTER UNIV, 69- *Concurrent Pos:* Consult, 58-62; mem, Chilean Jurassic Comt. *Mem:* Paleont Res Inst; Am Paleont Soc; Soc Econ Paleont & Mineral; Can Palaeont Asn; Int Paleont Asn (secy-gen). *Res:* Mesozoic Mollusca, especially Jurassic Ammonoidea and Triassic Pectinacea; functional morphology; taxonomy; intercontinental biochronology and biogeography. *Mailing Add:* Dept of Geol McMaster Univ Hamilton ON L8S 4L8 Can

WESTERN, DONALD WARD, b Poland, NY, May 7, 15; m 43; c 5. MATHEMATICS. *Educ:* Denison Univ, BA, 37; Mich State Col, MA, 39; Brown Univ, PhD(math), 46. *Prof Exp:* Instr math, Mich State Col, 37-39; from assoc prof to prof math, 48-74, chmn, Dept Math & Astron, 52-72, Charles A Dana prof, 74-80, EMER PROF MATH, FRANKLIN & MARSHALL COL, 80- *Concurrent Pos:* NSF fac fel, 60. *Mem:* Am Math Soc; Math Asn Am. *Res:* Inequalities in the complex plane. *Mailing Add:* Dept of Math & Astron Franklin & Marshall Col Lancaster PA 17604

WESTERVELT, CLINTON ALBERT, JR, b Portland, Ore, June 15, 36; m 65. INVERTEBRATE ZOOLOGY, PARASITOLOGY. *Educ:* Lewis & Clark Col, BA, 58; Univ Ariz, MS, 61, PhD(zool), 66. *Prof Exp:* Asst prof, 65-69, ASSOC PROF BIOL, CHAPMAN COL, 69- *Mem:* Am Soc Parasitologists. *Res:* Biology and systematics of decapod crustaceans, primarily Anomurans; biology and systematics of rhabdocoel turbellarians. *Mailing Add:* Dept of Biol Chapman Col Orange CA 92666

WESTERVELT, FRANKLIN HERBERT, b Benton Harbor, Mich, Mar 26, 30; m 48; c 2. ENGINEERING, COMPUTER SCIENCE. *Educ:* Univ Mich, Ann Arbor, BSE(mech eng) & BSE(math), 52, MSE, 53, PhD(mech eng), 61. *Prof Exp:* Instr eng graphics, Univ Mich, Ann Arbor, 53-56, res assoc comput ctr, 61-66, assoc dir ctr, 66-71, from asst prof to prof mech eng, 61-71; PROF ENG & COMPUT SCI & DIR COMPUT SERV CTR, WAYNE STATE UNIV, 71- *Concurrent Pos:* Proj dir conversational use of comput, Advan Res Projs Agency-US Dept Defense, 65-70; trustee, Argonne Univs Asn, 71- *Mem:* Asn Comput Mach; Nat Soc Prof Engrs. *Res:* Computing systems; computer graphics; interactive computing; systems architecture; micro-programming; information management systems. *Mailing Add:* Comput Serv Ctr 5925 Woodward Ave Detroit MI 48202

WESTERVELT, FREDERIC RALLARD, JR, b Washington, DC, June 11, 31; m; c 2. NEPHROLOGY. *Educ:* Univ Va, MD, 55. *Prof Exp:* HEAD, RENAL DIV, DEPT MED, UNIV VA, 64-, DIR, DEPT RENAL SERV, 65-, PROF MED, 78- *Mem:* Am Col Physicians; Am Soc Artificial Internal Organs. *Res:* Hermodialysis; uremia. *Mailing Add:* Box 133 Renal Div Dept Med Sch Med Univ Va Charlottesville VA 22901

WESTERVELT, PETER JOCELYN, b Albany, NY, Dec 16, 19. THEORETICAL PHYSICS. *Educ:* Mass Inst Technol, BS, 47, MS, 49, PhD(physics), 51. *Prof Exp:* Mem staff, Radiation Lab, Mass Inst Technol, 40-41 & Underwater Sound Lab, 41-45, asst physics, 46-47, res assoc, 48-50; from asst prof to assoc prof, 51-70, PROF PHYSICS, BROWN UNIV, 70- *Concurrent Pos:* Consult to asst attache for res, US Navy, Am Embassy, London, 51-52, Bolt, Beranek & Newman, Inc & Appl Res Labs, Univ Tex, Austin, 71- Mem subcomt aircraft noise, NASA, 54-59; mem comt hearing & bio-acoust, Armed Forces-Nat Res Coun, 57-, mem exec coun, 60-61, chmn, 67-68; mem sonic boom comt, Nat Acad Sci, 68-71. *Mem:* Fel Acoust Soc Am; fel Am Phys Soc; Am Astron Soc. *Res:* Physical effects of high amplitude sound waves; air acoustics; underwater sound; general relativity. *Mailing Add:* Dept of Physics Brown Univ Providence RI 02912

WESTFAHL, JEROME CLARENCE, b Milwaukee, Wis, Jan 10, 20; m 42; c 3. ORGANIC CHEMISTRY. *Educ:* Univ Wis, BS, 42; Cornell Univ, PhD(chem), 50. *Prof Exp:* Chemist, B F Goodrich Co, 42-47; asst, Baker Lab, Cornell Univ, 47-50; res chemist, Res & Develop Ctr, B F Goodrich Co, 50-60, res assoc, 60-68, sr res assoc, 68-82; RETIRED. *Mem:* Am Chem Soc. *Res:* Synthesis of substituted 1,3-butadienes; chemistry of vinylidene cyanide; nuclear magnetic resonance and electron paramagnetic resonance spectroscopy; computer applications in chemistry. *Mailing Add:* B F Goodrich Res & Develop Ctr Brecksville OH 44141

WESTFAHL, PAMELA KAY, b Miami, Okla. REPRODUCTIVE PHYSIOLOGY. *Educ:* Wash State Univ, BSc, 72; Univ Okla, PhD(physiol), 80. *Prof Exp:* FEL, ORE REGIONAL PRIMATE RES CTR, 80- *Mem:* Soc Study Reprod. *Res:* Factors involved in regulation of the primate corpus luteum during the menstrual cycle and pregnancy; feedback relationships of gonadal hormones on hypothalamic-pituitary function. *Mailing Add:* Ore Regional Primate Res Ctr 505 NW 185th Ave Beaverton OR 97006

WESTFALL, DAVID PATRICK, b Harrisburg, WVa, June 9, 42; m 65; c 2. PHARMACOLOGY. *Educ:* Brown Univ, BA, 64; WVa Univ, MS, 66, PhD(pharmacol), 68. *Prof Exp:* Demonstr pharmacol, Oxford Univ, 68-70; asst prof, 70-73, assoc prof, 73-77, PROF PHARMACOL, MED SCH, WVA UNIV, 77- *Concurrent Pos:* J H Burn fel pharmacol, Oxford Univ, 68-70. *Mem:* AAAS; Am Soc Pharmacol & Exp Therapeut; Soc Neurosci. *Res:* Pharmacology and physiology of smooth and cardiac muscle; factors governing the sensitivity of muscle to drugs. *Mailing Add:* Dept of Pharmacol WVa Univ Med Sch Morgantown WV 26506

WESTFALL, DWAYNE GENE, b Aberdeen, Idaho, Nov 21, 38; m 61; c 2. SOIL CHEMISTRY, AGRONOMY. *Educ:* Univ Idaho, BS, 61; Wash State Univ, PhD(soils), 68. *Prof Exp:* Res asst soils, Wash State Univ, 66-67; from asst prof to assoc prof soil chem, Tex A&M Univ, 67-74, assoc prof soil & crop sci, Agr Res & Exten Ctr, 74-78; SR PLANT NUTRITIONIST, GREAT WESTERN SUGAR CO AGR RES CTR, LONGMONT, 78- *Concurrent Pos:* Prof, Dept Agron, Colo State Univ, Ft Collins, 78-80; mem staff soil fertility, Colo State Univ Water Mgt Res Prog, Lahore, Pakistan, 78-80. *Mem:*

Sigma Xi; Am Soc Agron; Soil Sci Soc Am. *Res:* Soil chemistry of submerged soils; fertility of rice, pasture, sugarbeets and other agramomic crops; micronutrients and nitrogen efficiency and utilization; research and training programs in developing countries; pollution and quality of irrigation waters. *Mailing Add:* Dept of Agron Colo State Univ Ft Collins CO 80523

WESTFALL, HELEN NAOMI, b Grafton, WVa, June 23, 33; m 52; c 3. BACTERIAL PHYSIOLOGY, PATHOGENICITY. *Educ:* Old Dominion Univ, BS, 71, MS, 74; WVa Univ, PhD(med microbiol), 80. *Prof Exp:* Res asst, Old Dominion Univ, 71-72, asst, Gen Biol & Life Sci Labs, 73-74; sci instr, Portsmouth Catholic High Sch, 74-75; instr biol, Alderson-Broaddus Col, 75-77; Benedum fel, WVa Univ, 77-80; NAT RES COUN ASSOC, NAVAL MED RES INST, 80- *Mem:* Am Soc Microbiol; Sigma Xi; Am Soc Rickettsiology & Richettsial Dis; Am Women Sci. *Res:* Techniques to isolate, identify and determine virulence and physiology of Legionella; electron-capture gas chromatography studies of fatty acids of Rochalimaea; radioisotope investigations of isoleucine biosynthesis in Leptospira; determination of ability of motor neurons to repair damage to their deoxyribonucleic acid. *Mailing Add:* Nat Naval Med Ctr Naval Med Res Inst Bethesda MD 20814

WESTFALL, JANE ANNE, b Berkeley, Calif, June 21, 28. NEUROCYTOLOGY. *Educ:* Col Pac, AB, 50; Mills Col, MA, 52; Univ Calif, Berkeley, PhD(zool), 65. *Prof Exp:* Res asst zool, Univ NC, 52-53 & Univ Calif, Berkeley, 55-56; lab technician cancer res, Univ Calif, Berkeley, 57-58, lab technician zool, 58-65, asst res zoologist, 65-67; asst prof anat, 67-70, assoc prof physiol sci & dir ultrastruct res lab, 70-76, PROF ANAT & PHYSIOL, KANS STATE UNIV, 76- *Concurrent Pos:* Vis prof molecular, cellular & develop biol, Univ Colo, Boulder, 74-75. *Mem:* Electron Micros Soc Am; Am Soc Cell Biol; Am Soc Zoologists; Soc Neurosci; Am Asn Anat. *Res:* Electron microscopy, scanning, conventional and high voltage, of sensory receptors, synapses and neuromuscular junctions in simple nervous systems. *Mailing Add:* Dept of Anat & Physiol Kans State Univ Manhattan KS 66506

WESTFALL, MINTER JACKSON, JR, b Orlando, Fla, Jan 28, 16; m 45; c 3. BIOLOGY. *Educ:* Rollins Col, BS, 41; Cornell Univ, PhD(nature study), 47. *Prof Exp:* Wildlife technician, Ala Coop Wildlife Res Unit, 37; asst dir mus, Rollins Col, 37-40; from asst to sr asst biol, Cornell Univ, 42-47; from asst prof to assoc prof, 47-69, PROF ZOOL & ENTOM, UNIV FLA, 69- *Concurrent Pos:* US dep game warden, 36-70; Howell fel, Highlands Biol Sta, NC, 53. *Mem:* Entom Soc Am. *Res:* Wildlife management of mourning dove; bird migration and movement; taxonomy, ecology, zoogeography, life histories of the Odonata. *Mailing Add:* Dept of Zool Univ of Fla Gainesville FL 32611

WESTFALL, THOMAS CREED, b Latrobe, Pa, Oct 31, 37; m 61; c 1. PHARMACOLOGY. *Educ:* WVa Univ, AB, 59, MS, 61, PhD(pharmacol), 62. *Prof Exp:* From instr to asst prof pharmacol, WVa Univ, 62-65; from asst prof to assoc prof pharmacol, Sch Med, Univ Va, prof, 69-80; MEM FAC, DEPT PHARMACOL, SCH MED, ST LOUIS UNIV, 80- *Concurrent Pos:* Nat Heart Inst fel physiol, Karolinska Inst, Sweden, 63-64; dir grad studies, Dept Pharmacol, Sch Med, Univ Va, 68-; IUPHAR int fel, 74; vis fac scholar, Group Biochem Neuropharmacol, Lab Molecular Biol, Col France, Paris, 74-75. *Mem:* AAAS; Am Soc Pharmacol & Exp Therapeut; Soc Exp Biol & Med; Soc Neurosci; Am Heart Asn. *Res:* Autonomic, cardiovascular, biochemical and neuropharmacology; influence of drugs on the syntheses, uptake, storage, metabolism and receptor interaction of biogenic amines, particularly catecholamines; cardiovascular and autonomic actions of nicotine; neurotransmitter physiology and pharmacology. *Mailing Add:* Dept Pharmacol Sch Med St Louis Univ St Louis MO 63104

WESTFIELD, JAMES DELON, b Nov 21, 37; US citizen; m 61; c 4. ENVIRONMENTAL ENGINEERING, TECHNOLOGY ASSESSMENT. *Educ:* Univ Nev, Reno, BS, 61; Univ Mich, Ann Arbor, MPH, 64, PhD(environ sci), 66. *Prof Exp:* Chemist, Nev State Health Dept, 61-62; consult engr sanit eng, Industs, 62-66; asst prof civil eng, Ga Inst Technol, 66-68; sr sanit engr & off mgr, Eng Sci Inc, Calif, 68-72; dir environ eng group, Tetra Tech Inc, 72-73; VPRES, DEVELOP SCI INC, SAGAMORE, 73- *Concurrent Pos:* Dir solid waste training prog, Ga Inst Technol; consult, Agua Tech Inc & prin, Eco Sci Labs, 67-68; Ford Found residency in eng pract grant, 68-69. *Mem:* Am Soc Civil Engrs; Am Chem Soc; Sigma Xi. *Res:* Energy systems design; chemical and physical water and wastewater treatment; resource management; technology assessment. *Mailing Add:* Box 144 Sagamore MA 02561

WESTGARD, JAMES BLAKE, b Billings, Mont, Feb 12, 35; m 66; c 2. ELEMENTARY PARTICLE PHYSICS. *Educ:* Reed Col, BA, 57; Syracuse Univ, PhD(physics), 63. *Prof Exp:* Res fel physics, Carnegie Inst Technol, 63-66; asst prof, 66-73, assoc prof, 66-80, PROF PHYSICS, IND STATE UNIV, TERRE HAUTE, 80- *Mem:* Am Phys Soc. *Res:* Particle physics. *Mailing Add:* Dept of Physics Ind State Univ Terre Haute IN 47809

WESTHAUS, PAUL ANTHONY, b St Louis, Mo, Dec 10, 38. ATOMIC PHYSICS, MOLECULAR PHYSICS. *Educ:* St Louis Univ, BS, 61; Washington Univ, PhD(physics), 66. *Prof Exp:* Proj assoc, Theoret Chem Inst, Univ Wis, 66-67; ASSOC PROF PHYSICS, OKLA STATE UNIV, 68- *Concurrent Pos:* Res staff scientist, Yale Univ, 69; NIH career develop award, 72-77. *Mem:* Am Phys Soc. *Res:* Atomic structure and radiative transitions; electronic structure of molecules and intermolecular forces; quantum biology; many-electron problem. *Mailing Add:* Dept of Physics Okla State Univ Stillwater OK 74074

WESTHEAD, EDWARD WILLIAM, JR, b Philadelphia, Pa, June 19, 30; m; c 2. BIOCHEMISTRY. *Educ:* Haverford Col, BA, 51, MA, 52; Polytech Inst Brooklyn, PhD(polymer & phys chem), 55. *Prof Exp:* Am Scand Found res fel, Biochem Inst, Univ Uppsala, 55-56, NSF res fel, 56-57; res assoc physiol chem, Univ Minn, 58-60; asst prof biochem, Dartmouth Med Sch, 61-66; assoc prof & actg head dept, 66-71, PROF BIOCHEM, UNIV MASS, AMHERST, 71- *Concurrent Pos:* NIH career develop award, 61-66; NIH spec fel, Oxford Univ, 72-73. *Mem:* Am Chem Soc; Am Soc Biol Chemists. *Res:* Enzyme mechanisms and control; biochemistry of catecholamine secretion. *Mailing Add:* Dept of Biochem Univ of Mass Amherst MA 01002

WESTHEIMER, FRANK HENRY, b Baltimore, Md, Jan 15, 12; m 37; c 2. ORGANIC CHEMISTRY, ENZYMOLOGY. *Educ:* Dartmouth Col, AB, 32; Harvard Univ, MA, 33, PhD(chem), 35. *Hon Degrees:* DSc, Dartmouth Col, 61, Univ Chicago, 73, Univ Cincinnati, 76 & Tufts Univ, 78. *Prof Exp:* Nat Res Coun fel chem, Columbia Univ, 35-36; res assoc org chem, Univ Chicago, 36-37, from instr to asst prof chem, 37-44; res supvr, Explosives Res Lab, Nat Defense Res Comt, Pa, 44-45; from assoc prof to prof chem, Univ Chicago, 46-54; prof chem, 54-60, chmn dept, 59-62, LOEB PROF CHEM, HARVARD UNIV, 60- *Concurrent Pos:* Vis prof chem, Harvard Univ, 53-54; chmn comt surv chem, Nat Acad Sci, 64-65, mem coun, 72-75 & 76-79; mem, President's Sci Adv Comt, 67-70. *Honors & Awards:* Willard Gibbs Medal, 70; James Flack Norris Award, Am Chem Soc, 70; Theodore William Richards Medal, 76; Richard Kokes Award, Nat Acad Sci, 80; Chas Frederick Chandler Award, 80; Lewis C Roseustiel Award, 81. *Mem:* Nat Acad Sci; Am Philos Soc; Am Chem Soc; fel AAAS. *Res:* Electrostatic effects in organic chemistry; mechanism of nitration; chemical and biochemical oxidation; theory of steric effects; enzymic and chemical decarboxylation; phosphate esters; photoaffinity labeling. *Mailing Add:* Conant Lab Harvard Univ Cambridge MA 02138

WESTHEIMER, GERALD, b Berlin, Ger, May 13, 24. PHYSIOLOGICAL OPTICS. *Educ:* Univ Sydney, BSc, 47; Ohio State Univ, PhD(physics), 53. *Prof Exp:* Optometrist, Australia, 45-51; assoc optom, Ohio State Univ, 51-52; from asst prof to assoc prof physiol optics, 54-60; prof, Univ Houston, 53-54; assoc prof physiol optics & optom, 60-63, prof physiol optics, 63-68, chmn physiol optics group, 64-67, PROF PHYSIOL, UNIV CALIF, BERKELEY, 68- *Concurrent Pos:* Vis researcher, Physiol Lab, Cambridge Univ, 58-59; mem, Nat Acad Sci-Nat Res Coun Comt Vision, 57-72, mem exec coun, 69-72; mem visual sci study sect, NIH, 66-70, mem vision res training comt, Nat Eye Inst, 70-74; ed, Vision Res, 72-79; assoc ed, Invest Ophthalmol, 73-77, Exp Brain Res, 73, Optics Lett, 77-79, J Optical Soc Am, 80- & Human Neurobiol, 81-; mem commun sci cluster, President's Biomed Res Panel, 75; chmn, Visual Sci B Study Sect, NIH, 77-79; chmn, Bd Sci Counrs, Nat Eye Inst, NIH, 80- *Honors & Awards:* Tillyer Medal, Optical Soc Am, 78; Proctor Medal, Asn Res Vision & Ophthalmol, 79. *Mem:* Fel AAAS; Sigma Xi; Optical Soc Am; Soc Neurosci; assoc Brit Physiol Soc. *Res:* Biophysics and physiology of visual system; neurophysiology. *Mailing Add:* Dept of Physiol-Anat Univ of Calif Berkeley CA 94720

WESTHOFF, DENNIS CHARLES, b Jersey City, NJ, Nov 20, 42; m 63, 78; c 1. FOOD MICROBIOLOGY. *Educ:* Univ Ga, BSA, 66; NC State Univ, MS, 68, PhD(food sci), 71. *Prof Exp:* Asst prof, 70-74, assoc prof, 74-79, PROF DAIRY SCI, UNIV MD, COLLEGE PARK, 79-, CHMN DEPT, 81- *Concurrent Pos:* Sci adv, Food & Drug Admin, 76- *Mem:* Am Soc Microbiol; Am Dairy Sci Asn; NY Acad Sci. *Res:* Bioprocessing of foods; food safety. *Mailing Add:* Dept of Dairy Sci Univ of Md College Park MD 20740

WESTINE, PETER SVEN, b Boston, Mass, April 8, 40; m 62; c 2. DYNAMIC MODELING, EFFECTS OF EXPLOSIONS. *Educ:* Swarthmore Col, Pa, BS, 62; Cornell Univ, MCE, 64. *Prof Exp:* Res engr, 64-71, sr engr, 71-79, STAFF ENGR, SOUTHWEST RES INST, 79- *Mem:* Am Soc Civil Engrs. *Res:* The effects of explosion (ground shock, air blast, fragments, and thermal fireballs) on shelters, buildings, people, aircraft and vehicles. *Mailing Add:* 15511 Oak Grove San Antonio TX 78255

WESTING, ARTHUR HERBERT, b New York, NY, July 18, 28; m 56; c 2. ECOLOGY. *Educ:* Columbia Univ, AB, 50, Yale Univ, MF, 54, PhD, 59. *Hon Degrees:* DSc, Windlam Col, 73. *Prof Exp:* Res forester, US Forest Serv, 54-55; asst prof forestry, Purdue Univ, 59-64; assoc prof tree physiol, Univ Mass, 64-65; assoc prof biol, Middlebury Col, 65-66; assoc prof bot, Windham Col, 66-71, chmn dept biol, 66-74, prof bot, 71-76; sr res fel, Stockholm Int Peace Res Inst, 76-78; PROF ECOL & DEAN, SCH NATURAL SCI, HAMPSHIRE COL, 78- *Concurrent Pos:* Fel forest biol, NC State Col, 60; Bullard fel, Harvard Univ, 63-64, res fel, 70; fel bot, Univ Mass, 66; trustee, Vt Wild Land Found, 66-75, Vt Acad Arts & Sci, 67-71 & Rachel Carson Coun, 79; fel nuclear sci, St Augustine's Col, 68; vis scholar, Stockholm Int Peace Res Inst, 75. *Mem:* Fel AAAS; Soc Am Foresters; fel Scientists' Inst Pub Info; Int Peace Res Asn. *Res:* Forest ecology; environmental effects of war. *Mailing Add:* Sch Natural Sci Hampshire Col Amherst MA 01002

WESTKAEMPER, JOHN C(ONRAD), b San Antonio, Tex, Dec 5, 23; m 47; c 2. AERONAUTICAL ENGINEERING, MECHANICAL ENGINEERING. *Educ:* Univ Tex, BS, 47, MS, 59, PhD, 67. *Prof Exp:* Aerodynamicist, Consol Vultee Aircraft Corp, 47-50; from sr engr to asst proj engr, Sverdrup & Parcel, Inc, 50-52; sr res engr, Convair Div, Gen Dynamics Corp, 52-55; res engr, Defense Res Lab, Univ Tex, 55-60; res engr, Res Br, Engine Test Facil, ARO, Inc, 60; spec instr, Appl Res Lab, 57-60, asst prof aerospace eng, 60-67, ASSOC PROF AEROSPACE ENG, UNIV TEX, AUSTIN, 67-, RES ENGR, APPL RES LAB, 60- *Mem:* Am Inst Acronaut & Astronaut; Sigma Xi; Am Soc Eng Educ. *Res:* Fluid mechanics and heat transfer, including testing and test facility design. *Mailing Add:* Col of Eng Univ of Tex Austin TX 78712

WESTKAEMPER, REMBERTA, b Spring Hill, Minn, Jan 2, 90. BOTANY. *Educ:* Col St Benedict, Minn, BA, 19; Univ Minn, MS, 22, PhD(bot), 29. *Prof Exp:* Asst prof bot, 17-22, prof biol, 22-57, head dept, 29-57, pres, 57-61, prof biol, 61-73, EMER PROF BIOL, COL ST BENEDICT, MINN, 73- *Mem:* Sigma Xi; AAAS. *Res:* Vitamin content of marine algae; flora of Stearns County. *Mailing Add:* Col of St Benedict St Joseph MN 56374

WESTLAKE, DONALD G(ILBERT), b Aurora, Ill, July 9, 28; m 50; c 1. METALLURGY. *Educ:* Northern Ill Univ, BS, 50; Iowa State Univ, PhD(metall), 59. *Prof Exp:* Teacher high sch, Ill, 50-51; jr chemist, Argonne Nat Lab, 51-52; asst, Iowa State Univ, 54-59; asst metallurgist, 59-64, assoc metallurgist, Mat Sci Div, 64-72, METALLURGIST, MAT SCI DIV, ARGONNE NAT LAB, 72- *Mem:* Am Inst Mining, Metall & Petrol Engrs; Sigma Xi. *Res:* Metal-hydrogen alloys; structure and properties of metal hydrides; reaction rates and diffusion; hydrogen embrittlement of metals; interstitial occupancy in hydrides of intermetallic compounds; deformation twinning. *Mailing Add:* Mat Sci Div Argonne Nat Lab Bldg 212-C 228 Argonne IL 60439

WESTLAKE, DONALD WILLIAM SPECK, b Woodstock, Ont, Feb 27, 31; m 54. MICROBIOLOGY. *Educ:* Univ BC, BS, 53, MS, 55; Univ Wis, PhD, 58. *Prof Exp:* From asst res officer to assoc res officer, Nat Res Coun Can, 58-66; assoc prof microbiol, 66-69, PROF MICROBIOL & CHMN DEPT, UNIV ALTA, 69- *Mem:* Can Soc Microbiol; Chem Inst Can; Can Soc Biochem; Brit Soc Gen Microbiol. *Res:* Microbial biochemistry; environmental microbiology; metabolic pathways; fermentations. *Mailing Add:* Dept of Microbiol Fac of Sci Univ of Alta Edmonton AB T6G 2E1 Can

WESTLAKE, HARRY EDWARD, JR, b Jersey City, NJ, Oct 13, 15; m 43; c 2. ORGANIC CHEMISTRY. *Educ:* Princeton Univ, AB, 37, AM, 39, PhD(chem), 40; NY Univ, JD, 58. *Prof Exp:* Fel, Mellon Inst Indust Res, 40-44, sr fel, 44-46; chemist, Am Cyanamid Co, NJ, 46-52, tech patent supvr, 52-54, patent agt, Conn, 54-58, patent attorney, 58-60; patent sect chief, Merck & Co, Inc, 60-66, asst patent counsel, 66-69, patent counsel, 69-72, asst dir patents, 72-80; RETIRED. *Mem:* Am Chem Soc; The Chem Soc. *Res:* Organic sulfur compounds; sulfur containing resins; vat dyestuffs; sulfur dyes; patent law. *Mailing Add:* Patent Dept Merck & Co Rahway NJ 07065

WESTLAKE, ROBERT ELMER, b Jersey City, NJ, Oct 2, 18; m 44; c 3. INTERNAL MEDICINE, CARDIOLOGY. *Educ:* Princeton Univ, AB, 40; Columbia Univ, MD, 43. *Prof Exp:* From instr to asst prof med, Col Med, State Univ NY Upstate Med Ctr, 49-52, from clin asst prof to clin prof, 52-67; dir prof serv, Community-Gen Hosp, 67-81; EMER CLIN PROF, STATE UNIV NY UPSTATE MED CTR, 81- *Concurrent Pos:* Mem, Adv Comt Heart, Cancer & Stroke, Surgeon Gen, 66-67; mem, Adv Coun, US Dept Defense, 69-74; electrocardiographer, Syracuse Med Ctr; pres, PSRO of Cent NY; chmn, Bd Dirs, Blue Shield Cent NY. *Mem:* AAAS; Am Col Physicians; Am Fedn Clin. *Res:* Am Soc Internal Med (pres, 65-66); fel Soc Advan Med Systs. Res: Electrocardiography. *Mailing Add:* Box 413 Harmes Way North Eastham MA 02651

WESTLAKE, WILFRED JAMES, b Weston-super-Mare, Eng, Mar 21, 29; US citizen; m 69. MATHEMATICS, STATISTICS. *Educ:* Univ London, BSc, 50, PhD(math), 53. *Prof Exp:* Sci officer, Govt Commun Hq, UK, 52-56, sr sci officer, 56-60; sr statistician, E I du Pont de Nemours & Co, 60-63; staff specialist, Control Data Corp, 63-66; prin scientist, Booz-Allen Appl Res, Inc, Calif, 66, res dir, 66-68; asst dir biostatist, 68-70, assoc dir, 70-73, dir biostatist, 73-81, DIR CLIN DATA MGT, SMITH KLINE & FRENCH LABS, 81- *Concurrent Pos:* Adj assoc prof biomet, Sch Med, Temple Univ, 69-; assoc ed, Biometrics, 75- *Mem:* Fel Am Statist Asn; Biomet Soc; Soc Clin Trials; Acad Pharmaceut Sci. *Res:* Design of experiments; analysis of variance; regression analysis. *Mailing Add:* Dept Clin Data Mgt Smith Kline & French Labs Philadelphia PA 19101

WESTLAND, ALAN DUANE, b Toledo, Ohio, Dec 29, 29; m 56. INORGANIC CHEMISTRY. *Educ:* Univ Toronto, BA, 53, MA, 54, PhD(chem), 56. *Prof Exp:* Fel, Univ Münster, 56-58; from asst prof to assoc prof, 58-69, PROF INORG CHEM, UNIV OTTAWA, 69- *Mem:* Am Chem Soc; Chem Inst Can; Royal Soc Chem; Can Inst Mining & Metall. *Res:* Preparative and physical inorganic chemistry of the transition elements. *Mailing Add:* Dept of Chem Univ of Ottawa Ottawa ON K1N 9B4 Can

WESTLAND, ROGER D(EAN), b Winnebago Co, Iowa, June 26, 28; m 56; c 2. PHARMACEUTICAL CHEMISTRY, ORGANIC CHEMISTRY. *Educ:* St Olaf Col, AB, 50; Univ Kans, MS, 52; Univ Mich, PhD(chem), 59. *Prof Exp:* Asst res chemist, Parke, Davis & Co, 52-55; asst, Univ Mich, 57-58; assoc res chemist, 59-62, res chemist, 62-67, sr res chemist, 67-71, res scientist, 71-73, MGR CHEM-BIOL INFO, WARNER-LAMBERT/PARKE-DAVIS PHARMACEUT RES DIV, 73- *Mem:* Am Chem Soc; Sigma Xi. *Res:* Medicinal chemistry and information science. *Mailing Add:* Warner-Lambert/Parke-Davis 2800 Plymouth Rd Ann Arbor MI 48106

WESTLER, WILLIAM MILO, b Grove City, Pa, Dec 28, 50; m 80. PHYSICAL BIOCHEMISTRY. *Educ:* Grove City Col, BS, 72; John Carroll Univ, MS, 74; Purdue Univ, PhD(chem), 80. *Prof Exp:* OPERS DIR, BIOCHEM MAGNETIC RESONANCE LAB, PURDUE UNIV, 79- *Mem:* Am Chem Soc. *Res:* One dimensional and two dimensional nuclear magnetic resonance spectroscopic techniques applied to the investigation of the structural and the dynamic properties of biological macromolecules. *Mailing Add:* Dept Chem Purdue Univ West Lafayette IN 47907

WESTLEY, JOHN LEONARD, b Wilsonville, Nebr, Aug 29, 27; m 56; c 3. ENZYMOLOGY, SULFUR BIOCHEMISTRY. *Educ:* Univ Chicago, PhB, 48, PhD(biochem), 54. *Prof Exp:* NSF fel biochem, Calif Inst Technol, 54-55, res fel, 55-56; from instr to assoc prof, 56-64, PROF BIOCHEM, UNIV CHICAGO, 64- *Concurrent Pos:* USPHS res career develop award, 62-72. *Mem:* Am Soc Biol Chemists. *Res:* Mechanisms of enzyme action; prebiotic catalysis; sulfur metabolism; kinetic analysis; enzyme regulation; cyanide detoxication. *Mailing Add:* Dept of Biochem 920 E 58th St Chicago IL 60637

WESTLEY, JOHN WILLIAM, b Cambridge, Eng, Feb 5, 36; m 59; c 2. ORGANIC CHEMISTRY, BIOCHEMISTRY. *Educ:* Univ Nottingham, BSc, 58, PhD(org chem), 61. *Prof Exp:* Res assoc org chem, Stanford Univ, 61-62 & Med Ctr, Univ Calif, San Francisco, 62-63; res assoc org chem & biochem, Sch Med, Stanford Univ, 63-68; sr chemist, 68-71, res fel, Dept Microbiol, 71-80, ASST DIR MICROBIOL, CHEM RES DEPT, HOFFMAN-LA ROCHE INC, 80- *Concurrent Pos:* Squibb Inst Med Res & NIH fels, 61-62; NIH fel, 62-63; NASA grant, 63-68. *Mem:* Am Chem Soc; Royal Soc Chem; NY Acad Sci; Sigma Xi. *Res:* Structure determination, chemistry and biosynthesis of antibiotics; optical resolution of asymmetric compounds by gas chromatography; the polyether antibiotics; ionophores. *Mailing Add:* Chem Res Dept Hoffmann-La Roche Inc Nutley NJ 07110

WESTMACOTT, KENNETH HARRY, b Wantage, Eng, Nov 22, 29; m 64; c 2. PHYSICAL METALLURGY, MATERIALS SCIENCE. *Educ:* Univ Birmingham, PhD(phys metall, mat sci), 69. *Prof Exp:* Exp officer metall, Atomic Energy Res Estab, Eng, 51-62; res assoc mat sci, Stanford Univ, 63; res physicist metal physics, Michelson Lab, US Naval Weapons Ctr, 64-76; PRIN INVESTR, LAWRENCE BERKELEY LAB, 76- *Mem:* Assoc Brit Inst Metall; Am Inst Mining, Metall & Petrol Engrs. *Res:* Structure of metals; crystal lattice defects; mechanical properties; relation of microstructure to properties; quench and irradiation damage; dislocation theory; transmission electron microscopy. *Mailing Add:* Mat & Molecular Res Div Lawrence Berkeley Lab Berkeley CA 94720

WESTMAN, ALBERT ERNEST ROBERTS, b Ottawa, Ont, May 31, 00; m 25; c 3. PHYSICAL INORGANIC CHEMISTRY. *Educ:* Univ Toronto, BA, 21, MA, 22, PhD(electrochem), 24. *Prof Exp:* Res assoc ceramics, Eng Exp Sta, Univ Ill, 24-28; assoc prof, Rutgers Univ, 28-29; dir chem dept, Ont Res Found, 29-58, dir res, 58-65; appl res consult, 65-76; RETIRED. *Concurrent Pos:* Researcher, Carborundum Co & Dept Mines, Ont; asst, Univ Toronto. *Honors & Awards:* Forrest Award, Am Ceramic Soc, 54. *Mem:* fel Royal Soc Can; fel Am Ceramic Soc; fel Am Soc Qual Control; fel Brit Soc Glass Technol; fel Am Statist Asn. *Res:* Physical and industrial chemistry; refractories; electric furnace arcs; statistics; plating; corrosion; phosphates; glass. *Mailing Add:* 35 Glenayr Rd Toronto ON M5P 3B9 Can

WESTMAN, JACK CONRAD, b Cadillac, Mich, Oct 28, 27; m 53; c 3. CHILD PSYCHIATRY. *Educ:* Univ Mich, BS, 49, MD, 52, MS, 59. *Prof Exp:* Intern, Duke Univ Hosp, 52-53; resident psychiat, Univ Mich, 56-57; from instr to assoc prof, Med Sch, Univ Mich, 58-65; coordr diag & treat unit, Ctr Ment Retardation & Human Develop, 66-74, PROF PSYCHIAT, MED SCH, UNIV WIS-MADISON, 65-, DIR CHILD PSYCHIAT DIV, UNIV HOSPS, 65- *Concurrent Pos:* Fel child psychiat, Univ Mich, 57-59; lectr, Sch Social Work, Univ Mich, 59-64; mem, Sr Staff, Children's Psychiat Hosp, Ann Arbor, Mich, 59-65, dir outpatient serv, 61-62, dir outpatient & day care serv, 62-65. *Mem:* Fel Am Orthopsychiat Asn; Asn Am Med Cols; fel Am Acad Child Psychiat; Am Asn Ment Deficiency; Soc Prof Child Psychiatrists. *Res:* Efficacy of medication of hyperkinetic system; psychiatric aspects of learning disabilities and mental retardation; the role of child psychiatry in divorce; predicting later adjustment from nursery school behavior; individual differences in children; child advocacy. *Mailing Add:* 600 Highland Ave Madison WI 53706

WESTMAN, WALTER EMIL, b New York, NY, Nov 5, 45. PLANT ECOLOGY, ENVIRONMENTAL POLICY. *Educ:* Swarthmore Col, BA, 66; Macquarie Univ, MSc, 69; Cornell Univ, PhD(ecol), 71. *Prof Exp:* Congressional fel ecol, US Senate Subcomt Air & Water Pollution, 71; lectr bot, Univ Queensland, 72-74; vis prof environ planning, 75-76, PROF GEOG, UNIV CALIF, LOS ANGELES, 76- *Concurrent Pos:* Consult, Off Technol Assessment, 76-79; prin investr, NSF, 77- *Mem:* Ecol Soc Am; Brit Ecol Soc. *Res:* Synecology of terrestrial vegetation; water quality management; environmental impact assessment; general environmental sciences. *Mailing Add:* Dept of Geog Univ of Calif Los Angeles CA 90024

WESTMANN, RUSSELL A, b Fresno, Calif, May 20, 36; m 58; c 2. CIVIL ENGINEERING, APPLIED MECHANICS. *Educ:* Univ Calif, Berkeley, BS, 59, MS, 60, PhD(civil eng), 62. *Prof Exp:* Actg asst prof civil eng, Univ Calif, Berkeley, 62; NSF fel math, 62-63; res fel aeronaut, Calif Inst Technol, 63-65, asst prof civil eng, 65-66; from asst prof to assoc prof mech & struct, 66-73, actg chmn dept, Sch Eng & Appl Sci, 69-70, assoc dean, 76-81, PROF MECH & STRUCT, SCH ENG & APPL SCI, UNIV CALIF, LOS ANGELES, 73- *Concurrent Pos:* Mem transp res bd, Nat Res Coun, 65-75; sr vis fel, Sci Res Coun, Eng, 74. *Mem:* Am Soc Civil Engrs. *Res:* Solid mechanics; engineering mathematics; fracture mechanics. *Mailing Add:* Sch of Eng & Appl Sci 5732E Boelter Hall Univ of Calif Los Angeles CA 90024

WESTMEYER, PAUL, b Dillsboro, Ind, Dec 9, 25; m 47; c 6. SCIENCE EDUCATION. *Educ:* Ball State Univ, BS, 49, MS, 53; Univ Ill, EdD, 60. *Prof Exp:* Pub sch teacher, Ind, 49-54; instr chem & sci, Univ Ill High Sch, 54-61; from asst prof to assoc prof sci educ, Univ Ill, 60-63; assoc prof, Univ Tex, 63-66; prof, Fla State Univ, 66-73; PROF EDUC, UNIV TEX, SAN ANTONIO, 73- *Concurrent Pos:* Instr, Exten, Purdue Univ, 51-54; consult, Chicago Sch Bd, Ill, 54; proj assoc, Earlham Col, 59-62; partic, Int Seminar Chem, Dublin, Ireland, 60; consult, CBA Insts, 61-63; NSF in-serv grant, 64-65, coop col-sch sci grants, 64-66, summer inst grants & in-serv grants, 67-73. *Mem:* AAAS; Am Chem Soc; Nat Asn Res Sci Teaching; Nat Sci Teachers Asn; Asn Educ Teachers Sci (pres, 71-72). *Res:* Course development and evaluation; computer-assisted-instruction in chemistry; development of laboratory materials, tests and instructional procedures in chemistry; better utilization of staff in science teaching. *Mailing Add:* 6700 North FM 1604 W San Antonio TX 78285

WESTMORE, JOHN BRIAN, b Welling, Eng, Apr 23, 37; m 61; c 2. PHYSICAL CHEMISTRY, INORGANIC CHEMISTRY. *Educ:* Univ London, BSc, 58, PhD(phys chem), 61. *Prof Exp:* Fel chem, Nat Res Coun Can, 61-63; asst prof, 63-69, assoc prof, 69-76, PROF CHEM, UNIV MAN, 76- *Mem:* Chem Inst Can; The Chem Soc; Am Soc Mass Spectrometry. *Res:* Ionization and dissociation of molecules; chromatography and mass spectrometry of metal chelates, nucleosides and nucleotides; analytical chemistry; thermodynamics of metal chelation. *Mailing Add:* Dept of Chem Univ of Man Winnipeg MB R3T 2N2 Can

WESTMORELAND, DAVID GRAY, b Mooresville, NC, Aug 5, 46; m 80; c 1. ANALYTICAL & PHYSICAL CHEMISTRY. *Educ:* Univ NC, Chapel Hill, BS, 68; Stanford Univ, PhD(chem), 73. *Prof Exp:* SR SCIENTIST CHEM, ROHM & HAAS CO, 73- *Mem:* Am Chem Soc; Am Soc Mass Spectrometry. *Res:* Structure determination of unknown compounds; trace analysis for environmental pollutants. *Mailing Add:* Rohm & Haas Co Norristown & McKean Rds Spring House PA 19477

WESTMORELAND, THOMAS DELBERT, JR, b Vivian, La, June 2, 40; m 66; c 2. CHEMICAL ENGINEERING. *Educ:* NTex State Univ, BS, 63, MS, 65; La State Univ, PhD(inorg chem), 71. *Prof Exp:* Instr & res dir chem, Lewisville High Sch, Tex, 64; grad teaching asst, NTex, State Univ, 63-65; grad teaching asst, La State Univ, 66-69, res fel, 71-72; sr exp anal engr, United Technol Corp, 72-76; SR RES CHEMIST, PENNZOIL CO, 76- *Concurrent Pos:* Consult, Dixilyn Corp, 69. *Mem:* Am Chem Soc; Sigma Xi. *Res:* Conversion of low-grade phosphatic ores to fertilizer grade phosphate products; hydrometallurgical refining of copper; ion-ion and ion-solvent interaction studies by nuclear magnetic resonance. *Mailing Add:* 9319 Midvale Dr Shreveport LA 71118

WESTMORELAND, WINFRED WILLIAM, b Santa Maria, Calif, Feb 7, 19; m 42; c 3. DENTISTRY. *Educ:* Col Physicians & Surgeons San Francisco, DDS, 42; Univ Calif, MPH, 57; Am Bd Dent Pub Health, dipl. *Prof Exp:* Extern oral surg, San Francisco Hosp, 46-47; clin instr oper dent, Col Physicians & Surgeons, Univ of Pac, 49-53, asst clin prof prosthetic dent & lectr dent mat, 53-58, lectr pub health dent, 58-69, asst clin prof dent pub health, 66-69; sr dent consult, Calif Dept Health, Oakland, 67-81; DENT HEALTH PROG CONSULT, 81- *Concurrent Pos:* Pub health dent officer, Calif State Dept Health, 55-67; consult, Resident Training Prog, US Army, Ft Ord, Calif, 67-72; pvt practr. *Mem:* Am Dent Asn; Am Pub Health Asn; Int Asn Dent Res. *Res:* Epidemiology of dental caries; periodontal disease; cleft lip and palate; radiation exposure; dental fluorosis; dental health administration and education. *Mailing Add:* 644 S N St Livermore CA 94550

WESTNEAT, DAVID FRENCH, b Oradell, NJ, June 18, 29; m 58; c 3. ANALYTICAL CHEMISTRY. *Educ:* Allegheny Col, BS, 50; Univ Pittsburgh, PhD(chem), 56. *Prof Exp:* Res chemist, E I du Pont de Nemours & Co, 56-60; asst prof chem, Akron Univ, 60-65; chmn dept, 68-72, assoc prof, 65-77, PROF CHEM, WITTENBERG UNIV, 77- *Concurrent Pos:* Vis prof, Sci & Soc Prog, Cornell Univ, 72-73; vis scientist, Univ Hyg Lab, Univ Iowa, 80-81. *Mem:* AAAS; Am Chem Soc. *Res:* Instrumental analysis, especially absorption spectroscopy and gas chromatography. *Mailing Add:* Dept of Chem Wittenberg Univ Springfield OH 45501

WESTON, ARTHUR WALTER, b Smiths Falls, Ont, Feb 13, 14; nat US; m 40; c 4. ORGANIC CHEMISTRY. *Educ:* Queen's Univ, Ont, BA, 34, MA, 35; Northwestern Univ, PhD(org chem), 38. *Prof Exp:* Asst chem, Northwestern Univ, 35-37, res assoc, 38-40; from res chemist to asst head org res, 40-54, asst to dir develop, 54-55, asst dir, 55-57, dir res, 57-59, dir res & develop, 59-61, dir co, 59-69, vpres res & develop, 61-68, vpres sci affairs, 68-78, vpres corp licensing, 78-79, CONSULT, ABBOTT LABS, 79-; PRES, ARTHUR W WESTON & ASSOCS, INC, 79- *Concurrent Pos:* Mem war manpower comn, Off Sci Res & Develop, 42-45; mem exec comt, Div Chem & Chem Technol, Nat Res Coun, 61-65; mem ad hoc comt chem agts, Dept of Defense, 61-65; mem, Indust Res Inst & Dirs Indust Res; mem indust panel sci & technol, NSF, 74- *Mem:* Am Chem Soc; Pharmaceut Mfrs Asn; Chem Inst Can; Sigma Xi. *Res:* Organic medicinals; antibiotics; plant processes. *Mailing Add:* 349 E Hilldale Pl Lake Forest IL 60045

WESTON, CHARLES RICHARD, b South Gate, Calif, Apr 24, 33; m 53; c 4. DEVELOPMENTAL BIOLOGY, MICROBIAL ECOLOGY. *Educ:* Univ Calif, Santa Barbara, BA, 57; Princeton Univ, PhD(biol), 65. *Prof Exp:* Res scientist, E R Squibb Inst Med Res, 60-61; res assoc & asst prof, Univ Rochester, 62-66; Nat Acad Sci-Nat Res Coun resident res assoc, Jet Propulsion Lab, Calif Inst Technol, 66-68; lectr, 68-69, ASSOC PROF BIOL, CALIF STATE UNIV, NORTHRIDGE, 70- *Mem:* AAAS; Bot Soc Am; Am Soc Microbiol. *Res:* Morphogenesis of fungal mycelium; development of instrumentation for remote life detection; interactions and distribution of soil microorganisms. *Mailing Add:* Dept of Biol Calif State Univ Northridge CA 91324

WESTON, HENRY GRIGGS, JR, b Hemet, Calif, Apr 7, 22; m 47; c 3. ECOLOGY, VERTEBRATE ZOOLOGY. *Educ:* San Diego State Col, BA, 43; Univ Calif, Berkeley, MA, 47; Iowa State Col, PhD(zool), 50. *Prof Exp:* Asst prof biol, Grinnell Col, 50-55; PROF BIOL, SAN JOSE STATE UNIV, 55- *Mem:* Wildlife Soc; Cooper Ornith Soc; Am Ornith Union; Am Soc Mammal. *Res:* Birds of California; bird-banding; field ecology. *Mailing Add:* Dept of Biol San Jose St Univ 125 S Seventh St San Jose CA 95192

WESTON, JAMES A, b Washington, DC, June 20, 36; m 58; c 2. DEVELOPMENTAL BIOLOGY, CELL BIOLOGY. *Educ:* Cornell Univ, AB, 58; Yale Univ, PhD(biol), 62. *Prof Exp:* USPHS fel zool, Univ Col, Univ London, 62-64; from asst prof to assoc prof biol, Case Western Reserve Univ, 64-70; assoc prof, 70-74, PROF BIOL, UNIV ORE, 74- *Mem:* AAAS; Am Soc Zoologists; Soc Develop Biol (secy, 73-76); Int Soc Develop Biol; Am Soc Cell Biol. *Res:* Cellular control of morphogenetic movements in vertebrate development; regulation of cellular phenotypic expression of neural crest cells in vivo and in vitro; properties of cell surfaces in normal and transformed states. *Mailing Add:* Dept of Biol Univ of Ore Eugene OR 97403

WESTON, JAMES T, b Newark, NJ, May 16, 24; m 52; c 2. MEDICINE, PATHOLOGY. *Educ:* Cornell Univ, MD, 48; Am Bd Path, dipl, cert anat path, 67, forensic path, 68. *Prof Exp:* Intern path, Children's Hosp, Boston, 48-49; pathologist, Off Coroner, San Diego, 52-53, chief med dept, 54-61; asst med examr, Off Med Examr, Pa, 61-67; from asst prof to assoc prof path, Col Med, Univ Utah, 70-73; PROF PATH, SCH MED, UNIV N MEX, 73-; CHIEF MED INVESTR, STATE N MEX, 73- *Concurrent Pos:* Fel path, Mem Hosp Cancer, New York, 53-54; assoc pathologist, San Diego County Hosp & Community Hosp, Chula Vista, Calif, 56-61; vis lectr, Jefferson Med Col, 62-67; chief med examr, Utah State Dept Health, 67-73; consult & mem, Sci Adv Bd Consult, Armed Forces Inst Path, 71-75. *Mem:* Fel Am Acad Forensic Sci (secy-treas, 71-75, pres, 75); Am Soc Clin Path; Col Am Pathologists; Am Asn Pathologists; Int Acad Path. *Res:* Child abuse patterns; sociologic and pathologic correlations; environmental pathology; iatrogenic disease; automobile accident injury patterns; forensic pathology. *Mailing Add:* Dept Path Univ NMex Albuquerque NM 87131

WESTON, JOHN COLBY, b Dover-Foxcroft, Maine, Dec 31, 26; m 51; c 2. HISTOLOGY, EMBRYOLOGY. *Educ:* Bowdoin Col, AB, 51; Syracuse Univ, MS, 54, PhD(zool), 56. *Prof Exp:* From instr to assoc prof anat, Col Med, Ohio State Univ, 55-67; assoc prof, 67-69, PROF BIOL, MUHLENBURG COL, 69-, CHIEF HEALTH PROF ADV, 76- *Mem:* Am Asn Anat; Electron Micros Soc Am; Soc Develop Biol. *Res:* Biochemical, histochemical and electron microscopic analyses of development; cytology. *Mailing Add:* Dept of Biol Muhlenburg Col Allentown PA 18104

WESTON, KENNETH CLAYTON, b Buffalo, NY, Jan 8, 32; m 63; c 3. COMPUTER AIDED ENGINEERING. *Educ:* Cornell Univ, BME, 55; Rice Univ, MS, 65, PhD(mech eng), 69. *Prof Exp:* Res scientist aerodyn & thermodyn, NASA Lewis Res Ctr, Ohio, 55-58, res engr, Space Task Group, Va, 58-60, sect head aerothermodyn, Manned Spacecraft Ctr, Tex, 60-68; assoc prof mech & aerospace eng, 68-80, PROF MECH ENG, UNIV TULSA, 80- *Concurrent Pos:* NASA res grant, Univ Tulsa, 72-74 & NSF grant, 77-79. *Honors & Awards:* Teetor Award, Soc Automotive Engrs, 78. *Mem:* Am Soc Eng Educ; Am Soc Heating, Refrig & Air-Conditioning Engrs; Am Inst Aeronaut & Astronaut; Am Soc Mech Engrs; Soc Automotive Engrs. *Res:* Combined radiative and conductive energy transfer; thermodynamics; mechanics of continua; fluid mechanics; energy conversion; computer aided design and graphics; gas turbines; computer data acquisition; air conditioning systems. *Mailing Add:* Dept Mech Eng Univ Tulsa Tulsa OK 74104

WESTON, KENNETH W, b Milwaukee, Wis, Feb 1, 29; m 66; c 2. ALGEBRA. *Educ:* Univ Wis, BS, 53, MS, 55, PhD(math), 63. *Prof Exp:* Instr math, Univ Wis-Milwaukee, 61-63; asst prof, Univ Notre Dame, 63-69; assoc prof, Marquette Univ, 69-71; ASSOC PROF MATH, UNIV WIS-PARKSIDE, 71- *Mem:* Am Math Soc; Math Asn Am. *Res:* Groups satisfying Engel condition and connections between ring and group theory; model theory. *Mailing Add:* Div of Sci Univ of Wis-Parkside Kenosha WI 53140

WESTON, RALPH E, JR, b San Francisco, Calif, Nov 9, 23; m 51; c 3. CHEMICAL KINETICS. *Educ:* Univ Calif, BS, 46; Stanford Univ, PhD(chem), 50. *Prof Exp:* Asst, Stanford Univ, 47-49; from assoc chemist to chemist, 51-65, SR CHEMIST, BROOKHAVEN NAT LAB, 65- *Concurrent Pos:* Vis scientist, Saclay Nuclear Res Ctr, France, 60-61; vis lectr, Univ Calif, Berkeley, 68-69; lectr, Columbia Univ, 71-72; mem comt chem kinetics, Nat Res Coun, 75-77, Army Basic Res Comt, 75-81, Adv Bd, Off Chem & Chem Technol, 80-81. *Mem:* AAAS; Am Chem Soc; Sigma Xi. *Res:* Kinetics of gas phase reactions; isotope effects in reaction kinetics and equilibria; photochemistry; application of lasers to chemical problems. *Mailing Add:* Chem Dept Brookhaven Nat Lab Upton NY 11973

WESTON, ROY FRANCIS, b Reedsburg, Wis, June 25, 11; m 34; c 2. ENVIRONMENTAL ENGINEERING. *Educ:* Univ Wis, BCE, 33; NY Univ, MCE, 39; Environ Eng Intersoc, dipl. *Hon Degrees:* DEng, Drexel Univ, 81. *Prof Exp:* Jr hwy engr, Wis Hwy Dept, 34-36; dist engr, Wis Dept Health, 36-37; sanit eng res fel, NY Univ, 37-39; sanit engr, Atlantic Refining Co, Philadelphia, 39-55; PRES & CHMN BD, ROY F WESTON, INC, ENVIRON CONSULTS, 55- *Concurrent Pos:* Mem vis comt, Dept Civil & Urban Eng, Univ Pa & Ctr Marine & Environ Studies, Lehigh Univ; pres, Am Acad Environ Engrs, 73-74; mem, US Environ Control Seminar, Netherlands & Eastern Europe, 72; mem, Comt Environ, US Chamber Commerce, 75; mem, Indust & Prof Adv Comt, Pa State Univ, 75. *Honors & Awards:* Indust Wastes Medal, Water Pollution Control Fedn, 50, Arthur Sidney Bedell Award, 59; Gordon Maskew Fair Award, Am Acad Environ Engrs, 77. *Mem:* Nat Acad Eng; fel Am Soc Civil Engrs; Am Pub Health Asn; Am Chem Soc; Am Inst Chem Engrs. *Res:* Environmental control. *Mailing Add:* Roy F Weston Inc Weston Way West Chester PA 19380

WESTON, VAUGHAN HATHERLEY, b Parry Sound, Ont, May 1, 31; m 54; c 4. APPLIED MATHEMATICS, THEORETICAL PHYSICS. *Educ:* Univ Toronto, BA, 53, MA, 54, PhD, 56. *Prof Exp:* Lectr math, Univ Toronto, 57-58; res assoc, Radiation Lab, Univ Mich, 58-59, from assoc res mathematician to res mathematician, 59-69; PROF MATH, PURDUE UNIV, WEST LAFAYETTE, 69- *Mem:* Am Math Soc; Soc Indust & Appl Math; Am Phys Soc. *Res:* Electromagnetic theory; diffraction; plasmas; inverse scattering. *Mailing Add:* Div of Math Sci Purdue Univ West Lafayette IN 47907

WESTOVER, JAMES DONALD, b Clarkdale, Ariz, Sept 22, 34; m 59; c 4. ORGANIC CHEMISTRY. *Educ:* Ariz State Univ, BS, 50, MS, 62; Brigham Young Univ, PhD(chem), 66. *Prof Exp:* Res chemist, Dacron Res Lab, E I du Pont de Nemours & Co, Inc, NC, 65-70; asst prof, 70-76, ASSOC PROF CHEM, CALIF POLYTECH STATE UNIV, SAN LUIS OBISPO, 77- *Res:* Synthetic organic chemistry in area of nitrogen heterocyclic compounds; polyester fibers. *Mailing Add:* Dept of Chem Calif Polytech State Univ San Luis Obispo CA 93407

WESTOVER, LEMOYNE BYRON, b Curwensville, Pa, Aug 12, 28; m 52; c 3. ANALYTICAL CHEMISTRY. *Educ:* Dickinson Col, BS, 50; Pa State Univ, MS, 52. *Prof Exp:* Chemist anal chem, Hercules, 52-54, US Army, 54-56; chemist anal chem, 56-59, group leader, mass spectros, 59-70, RES MGR ANAL CHEM, DOW CHEMICAL CO, 70- *Mem:* Am Chem Soc; Sigma Xi. *Res:* Mass spectrometry; liquid chromatography; gas chromatography; infrared spectroscopy. *Mailing Add:* 4911 Barto Midland MI 48640

WESTOVER, THOMAS A(RCHIE), b Westover, Pa, June 1, 09; m 40; c 3. ELECTRICAL ENGINEERING. *Educ:* Carnegie Inst Technol, BSc, 36; Stevens Inst Technol, MSc, 45. *Prof Exp:* Tester & inspector, Allis Chalmers Mfg Co, Pa, 36-40; tester, Pub Serv Elec & Gas Co, NJ, 40-42; sr engr, Fairchild Camera & Instrument Corp, 42-46, proj engr, 46-47; staff engr, Servo Corp Am, 47-54, engr in charge control systs, Eng Dept, 54-61; asst chief electronics engr, Missile Systs Div, Repub Aviation Corp, 61-63; asst chief engr, Electronic Prod Div, Fairchild Hiller Corp, 63-65; eng mgr, Railroad Prods Div, 65-70, SR CONSULT ENGR, ADVAN ENG DEPT, SERVO CORP AM, 70- *Concurrent Pos:* Instr, State Univ NY Agr & Tech Inst, Long Island, 50-60. *Mem:* Sr mem Inst Elec & Electronics Engrs. *Res:* Servomechanisms; electricity and magnetism; instruments and equipment; electronic and infrared systems; meteorological measurement systems. *Mailing Add:* Eng Dept Servo Corp of Am 111 New South Rd Hicksville NY 11802

WESTPHAL, JAMES ADOLPH, b Dubuque, Iowa, June 13, 30. PLANETARY SCIENCES. *Educ:* Univ Tulsa, BS, 53. *Prof Exp:* Sr res fel, 66-71, assoc prof planetary sci, Calif Inst Technol, 71-77; PROF PLANETARY SCI, CALIF INST TECHNOL, 78- *Mem:* Am Astron Soc. *Res:* Infrared astronomy; infrared atmospheric properties; planetary astronomy; astronomical instrumentation; space astronomy. *Mailing Add:* MS 170-25 Calif Inst Technol Pasadena CA 91125

WESTPHAL, MILTON C, JR, b Philadelphia, Pa, June 2, 26; m 78; c 6. PEDIATRICS, GASTROENTEROLOGY. *Educ:* Yale Univ, BS, 47; Univ Pa, MD, 51; Am Bd Pediat, dipl, 57. *Prof Exp:* Intern, Univ Pa Hosp, 51-52; resident, Children's Hosp Philadelphia, 54-56; asst instr pediat, Sch Med, Univ Pa, 56-57, instr, 57-61, assoc prof, 65-67; chmn dept, 67-76, PROF PEDIAT, COL MED, MED UNIV SC, 67-, CHIEF, SECT GASTROENTEROL, 76- *Concurrent Pos:* Chief resident, Children's Hosp Philadelphia, 56-57, from asst physician to assoc physician, 57-61, mem, Res Dept, 57-61; asst pediatrician to outpatients, Pa Hosp, 57-58, hosp, 58-59, assoc pediatrician, 59-61; asst attend, Children's Hosp Buffalo, 61-64, assoc attend, 64-; dir, Buffalo Poison Control Ctr, 61-67; proj dir & chmn, Comt Prin Investrs, Collab Study Cerebral Palsy, Ment Retardation & Other Neurol & Sensory Dis Infancy & Childhood, 63-64. *Mem:* Am Pediat Soc. *Res:* Gastroenterology; medical application of decision theory. *Mailing Add:* Dept of Pediat Med Univ of SC Col of Med Charleston SC 29401

WESTPHAL, WARREN HENRY, b Easton, Pa, Feb 19, 25; m 46; c 3. ENERGY MINERAL DEVELOPMENT. *Educ:* Columbia Univ, AB, 47. *Prof Exp:* Jr mining engr, NJ Zinc Co, NJ, 47-48, geologist, 48-49, res geologist, Pa, 49-50, geophysicist, Colo, 50-55; sr geologist, Tidewater Assoc Oil Co, NMex, 55; chief geophysicist, Utah Construct & Mining Co, 56-59; sr geophysicist, Stanford Res Inst, 59-66, chmn earth sci dept, 66-69; vpres mining, Intercontinental Energy Corp, 69-79; PRES, WESTPHAL ASSOCS INC, 79- *Mem:* AAAS; Am Inst Prof Geologists; Am Asn Petrol Geologists; Am Inst Mining, Metall & Petrol Engrs; Soc Economic Geologists. *Res:* Earthquake seismology; uranium geology; in-sito mining. *Mailing Add:* 4398 S Akron Englewood CO 80111

WESTRUM, EDGAR FRANCIS, JR, b Albert Lea, Minn, Mar 16, 19; m 43; c 4. PHYSICAL CHEMISTRY, THERMODYNAMICS. *Educ:* Univ Minn, BChem, 40; Univ Calif, PhD(phys chem), 44. *Prof Exp:* Res chemist, Metall Lab, Univ Chicago, 44-46 & Radiation Lab, Univ Calif, 46; from asst prof to assoc prof, 46-57, PROF PHYS CHEM, UNIV MICH, ANN ARBOR, 58- *Concurrent Pos:* Chmn comt data for sci & technol, Nat Acad Sci, 73; chmn comn & phys chem div, Int Union Pure & Appl Chem, 73-77; ed, J Chem Thermodyn, 68-79 & Bull Thermodyn & Thermochem, 55-75; assoc ed, Comt on Data for Sci & Technol Bull, 74- *Mem:* Fel AAAS; fel Am Inst Chemists; Am Chem Soc; The Chem Soc; fel Am Phys Soc. *Res:* Thermodynamics, actinide, lanthanide, and transition compounds; thermochemistry; cryogenic calorimetry; molecular dynamics plastic crystals; thermophysics of phase ordering, Schottky, transitions. *Mailing Add:* Dept of Chem Univ of Mich Ann Arbor MI 48109

WESTRUM, LESNICK EDWARD, b Tacoma, Wash, Oct 19, 34. NEUROSURGERY, BIOLOGICAL STRUCTURE. *Educ:* Wash State Univ, BS, 58; Univ Wash, MD, 63; Univ London, PhD(anat), 66. *Prof Exp:* NIH fel, Univ London, 63-66, hon res asst anat, Univ Col, 64-66; res asst prof, 66-67, asst prof, 67-77, ASSOC PROF SURG & BIOL STRUCT, SCH MED, UNIV WASH, 77- *Mem:* AAAS; Am Asn Anatomists; Soc Neurosci. *Res:* Studies of synapses in normal and experimental conditions; emphasis on trigeminal and limbic systems. *Mailing Add:* Dept of Neurol Surg Univ of Wash Sch of Med Seattle WA 98195

WESTWATER, EDGEWORTH RUPERT, b Denver, Colo, Oct 29, 37; m 61; c 3. ATMOSPHERIC PHYSICS. *Educ:* Western State Col Colo, BA, 59; Colo Univ, MS, 62, PhD(physics), 70. *Prof Exp:* Chemist cement chem, Ideal Cement Co, 59-60; physicist atmospheric physics, Nat Bur Standards, 60-65 & Environ Sci Serv Admin, 65-70; PHYSICIST ATMOSPHERIC PHYSICS, NAT OCEANIC & ATMOSPHERIC ADMIN, 70- *Concurrent Pos:* Mem ad hoc working group inversion methods, Radiation Comn, Int Asn Meteorol & Atmospheric Physics, 66- *Mem:* Am Meteorol Soc; Optical Soc Am; Soc Indust & Appl Math; Math Asn Am; Sigma Xi. *Res:* Remote sensing of the atmosphere; radiative transfer in the atmosphere; mathematics of ill-posed problems. *Mailing Add:* R45x4 Wave Propagation Lab 325 Broadway Boulder CO 80303

WESTWATER, J(AMES) W(ILLIAM), b Danville, Ill, Nov 24, 19; m 42; c 4. CHEMICAL ENGINEERING. *Educ:* Univ Ill, BS, 41; Univ Del, MChE, 43, PhD(chem eng), 48. *Prof Exp:* From asst prof to assoc prof, 48-59, head dept, 62-80, PROF CHEM ENG, UNIV ILL, 59- *Concurrent Pos:* Lectr, Am Inst Chem Engrs, 64; Donald L Katz lectureship, Univ Mich, 78. *Honors & Awards:* William H Walker Award, Am Inst Chem Engrs, 66; Max Jakob Award, Am Soc Mech Engrs, 72; Vincent Bendix Award, Am Soc Eng Educ, 74. *Mem:* Nat Acad Eng; Am Chem Soc; Am Soc Eng Educ; Am Inst Chem Engrs; Am Soc Mech Engrs. *Res:* Heat transfer; phase changes; boiling; condensation. *Mailing Add:* Dept of Chem Eng Univ of Ill Urbana IL 61801

WESTWICK, ROY, b Vancouver, BC, May 23, 33; m 59; c 2. MATHEMATICS. *Educ:* Univ BC, BA, 56, MA, 57, PhD(math), 60. *Prof Exp:* Nat Res coun Can overseas fel, math, Univ Col, London, 60-62; from asst prof to assoc prof, 62-70, PROF MATH, UNIV BC, 70- *Concurrent Pos:* Can Coun sr fel, 67-68. *Mem:* Can Math Cong. *Res:* Linear and multilinear algebra; measure theory. *Mailing Add:* Dept of Math Univ of BC Vancouver BC V6T 1W5 Can

WESTWOOD, ALBERT RONALD CLIFTON, b Birmingham, Eng, June 9, 32; nat US; m 56; c 2. RESEARCH MANAGEMENT, MATERIALS SCIENCE. *Educ:* Univ Birmingham, BSc, 53, PhD(phys metall), 56, DSc(mat sci), 68; Coun Eng Inst, UK, CEng, 78. *Prof Exp:* Tech officer, Imp Chem Industs, Eng, 56-58; scientist, Res Inst Advan Studies, Martin Marietta Corp, Baltimore, 58-61, sr scientist, 61-64, assoc dir & head, Mat Sci Dept, 64-69, dep dir, 69-74, DIR, MARTIN MARIETTA LABS, BALTIMORE, 74- *Concurrent Pos:* Lectr, Chance Tech Col, Eng, 54 & Handsworth Tech Col, 54-56; fel, Johns Hopkins Univ, 65-; guest lectr, Acad Sci, USSR, 69, 76, 78 & 81; mem adv comt, Inorg Mat Div, Nat Bur Standards, 72-75; mem adv bd, Jour Mat Sci, UK, 74-, Colloids & Surfaces & Mech & Physics of Surfaces, 79-; mem rev comt, Mat Sci Div, Argonne Nat Labs, 76-82; mem, Nat Mat Adv Bd, Nat Res Coun, 80-; mem mat res adv comn, NSF, 80- *Honors & Awards:* Beilby Medal & Prize, Royal Inst Chem-Brit Inst Metals-Soc Chem Indust, 70; Tewksbury lectr, Univ Melbourne, Australia, 74. *Mem:* Nat Acad Eng; fel Am Soc Metals; fel Brit Inst Metall; fel Brit Inst Physics; Am Inst Mining, Metall & Petrol Engrs. *Res:* Management theory; mechanical behavior, chemomechanical effects, surface and environmental effects; surface physics and chemistry, adsorption phenomena; metals, ceramics, refractories, biotechnology, cement, minerals and dyestuffs; aluminum extraction, smelting and processing. *Mailing Add:* 908 E Joppa Rd Towson MD 21204

WESTWOOD, MELVIN (NEIL), b Hiawatha, Utah, Mar 25, 23; m 46; c 4. POMOLOGY, PLANT PHYSIOLOGY. *Educ:* Utah State Univ, BS, 53; Wash State Univ, PhD(pomol, plant physiol), 56. *Prof Exp:* Asst field botanist, Utah State Univ, 51-52, supt, Hort Res Field Sta, 52-53; asst, Wash State Univ, 53-55; from asst res horticulturist to res horticulturist, USDA, 55-60; assoc prof, 60-67, PROF HORT, ORE STATE UNIV, 67- *Honors & Awards:* Gourley Award, Am Soc Hort Sci, 58 & 77 & Stark Award, 69 & 77; Paul Howe Shepard Award, Am Pomol Soc, 68; Wilder Medal Award, Am Pomol Soc, 81. *Mem:* AAAS; fel Am Soc Hort Sci (pres, 74-75); Am Soc Plant Physiologists; Scand Soc Plant Physiol. *Res:* Deciduous fruit tree and rootstock physiology; growth dynamics; plant hormones; chemical thinning; high density orchard systems. *Mailing Add:* Dept of Hort Ore State Univ Corvallis OR 97331

WESTWOOD, WILLIAM DICKSON, b Kirkcaldy, Scotland, Jan 4, 37; m 61; c 1. PHYSICS. *Educ:* Univ Aberdeen, BSc, 59, PhD(physics), 62. *Hon Degrees:* PhD(physics), Univ Adelaide, 66. *Prof Exp:* Scientist, Northern Elec Co Ltd, 62-65; lectr physics, Flinders Univ, Australia, 66-69; scientist, Northern Elec Co Ltd, 69-70; mgr thin film physics, 71-79, MGR MAT & DEVICE RES, BELL-NORTHERN RES LTD, 79- *Mem:* Fel Brit Inst Physics; Can Asn Physicists; Am Vacuum Soc. *Res:* Thin film physics; sputtering; spectroscopy of gas discharges; integrated optics; surface analysis; optical recording devices. *Mailing Add:* Dept 5C11 Bell-Northern Res Ltd Box 3511 Sta C Ottawa ON K1X 4H7 Can

WESWIG, PAUL HENRY, b St Paul, Minn, July 13, 13; m 40; c 2. ANIMAL NUTRITION. *Educ:* St Olaf Col, BA, 35; Univ Minn, MS, 39, PhD(biochem), 41. *Prof Exp:* Instr chem, St Olaf Col, 36-37; asst biochem, Univ Minn, 38-41; asst prof biochem, Univ & asst chemist, Exp Sta, 41-42, assoc prof biochem, 46-47, PROF BIOCHEM, ORE STATE UNIV, 57- *Mem:* Am Chem Soc; Am Inst Nutrit; Am Dairy Sci Asn; Am Soc Animal Sci. *Res:* Trace mineral metabolism in ruminants and laboratory animals including requirement, interrelationship, toxicity, tissue enzyme activity and element concentration including selenium, copper and heavy metals. *Mailing Add:* Dept of Agr Chem Ore State Univ Corvallis OR 97331

WETEGROVE, ROBERT LLOYD, b San Diego, Calif, Jan 25, 48; m 71. MICROBIOLOGY, INDUSTRIAL WATER TREATMENT. *Educ:* Univ Tex, Austin, BA, 70, MA, 72, PhD(microbiol), 78. *Prof Exp:* Res scientist microbiol, 78-81, RES GROUP LEADER, WASTE TREAT CHEMICALS, NALCO CHEM CO, 81- *Concurrent Pos:* Consult, Microbiol Consult, Inc, 78- *Mem:* AAAS; Am Soc Microbiol; Soc Indust Microbiol; Water Pollution Control Fedn; Am Water Works Asn. *Res:* Microbial physiology and organic polymer chemistry relating to industrial water treatment . *Mailing Add:* 1801 Diehl Rd Nalco Tech Ctr Naperville IL 60566

WETENKAMP, HARRY R, b Forest Park, Ill, Jan 25, 19; m 42; c 2. MECHANICS. *Educ:* Univ Ill, BS, 42, MS, 50. *Prof Exp:* Ord inspector, Rochester Ord Dist, 42-43; res asst, 46-47, res assoc, 47-50, from asst prof to assoc prof, 50-59, PROF THEORET & APPL MECH, UNIV ILL, URBANA, 59- *Mem:* Am Soc Eng Educ; Am Soc Metals. *Res:* Thermal damage of railway car wheel material. *Mailing Add:* Dept of Theoret Appl Mech Univ of Ill Urbana IL 61801

WETHERELL, DONALD FRANCIS, b Manchester, Conn, Nov 25, 27; m 49; c 4. PLANT PHYSIOLOGY. *Educ:* Univ Conn, BA, 51; Univ Md, MS, 53, PhD(plant physiol), 56. *Prof Exp:* Res assoc & lectr plant physiol, Univ Md, 56-58; from asst prof to assoc prof plant physiol, 58-67, actg chmn dept bot, 61-64, chmn regulatory biol sect, 67-68, PROF PLANT PHYSIOL, UNIV CONN, 67- *Concurrent Pos:* Guggenheim fel, 65-66. *Mem:* Am Soc Plant Physiologists; Int Asn Plant Tissue Cult. *Res:* Regulatory mechanisms of growth and development in plants. *Mailing Add:* Biol Sci Group Univ Conn Storrs CT 06268

WETHERELL, HERBERT RANSON, JR, b Chicago, Ill, Jan 25, 27; m 62; c 1. PHARMACOLOGY, TOXICOLOGY. *Educ:* Yale Univ, BS, 49, PhD(pharmacol), 54. *Prof Exp:* Asst prof physiol & pharmacol, Med Col, Univ Nebr, 53-61; toxicologist, Wayne County Med Examr Off, 61-72; toxicologist, Crime Lab, Mich Dept Pub Health, 72-77; TOXICOLOGIST, CRIME LAB, MICH STATE POLICE, 77- *Mem:* Am Chem Soc; Am Acad Forensic Sci; Royal Soc Chem London. *Res:* Relationship between chemical structure and pharmacologic activity; toxicology and drug metabolism; chlorophyll chemistry; infrared spectrophotometry. *Mailing Add:* Toxicol Lab Forensic Sci Div 714 S Harrison Rd East Lansing MI 48823

WETHERILL, GEORGE WEST, b Philadelphia, Pa, Aug 12, 25; m 50. GEOPHYSICS. *Educ:* Univ Chicago, PhB, 48, SB, 49, MS, 51, PhD(physics), 53. *Prof Exp:* Mem staff, Carnegie Inst, Washington Dept Terrestrial Magnetism, 53-60; prof geophys & geol, Univ Calif, Los Angeles, 60-75, chmn dept planetary & space sci, 68-72; DIR DEPT TERRESTRIAL MAGNETISM, CARNEGIE INST WASHINGTON, 75- *Concurrent Pos:* Vis prof, Calif Inst Technol, 59. *Honors & Awards:* Leonard Medal, Meteoritical Soc, 81. *Mem:* Nat Acad Sci; fel Am Acad Arts & Sci; fel Am Geophys Union; Meteoritical Soc (vpres, 72-74 & 80-82); Geochem Soc (vpres, 73-74, pres, 74-75). *Res:* Planetology; geochronology; meteorites; origin and evolution of solar system; lunar history; Precambrian geology; kinetics of human lead metabolism. *Mailing Add:* Dept of Terrestrial Magnetism Carnegie Inst Washington DC 20015

WETHERINGTON, RONALD K, b St Petersburg, Fla, Nov 27, 35; m 72; c 3. BIOLOGICAL ANTHROPOLOGY. *Educ:* Tex Tech Univ, BA, 58; Univ Mich, MA, 60, PhD(anthrop), 64. *Prof Exp:* PROF ANTHROP, SOUTHERN METHODIST UNIV, 64- *Mem:* Sigma Xi; Soc Med Anthrop; AAAS; Am Asn Phys Anthrop. *Res:* Skeletal growth and development in man; human ecology and evolutionary theory; adaptive aspects of human demography. *Mailing Add:* Dept of Anthrop Southern Methodist Univ Dallas TX 75222

WETHERN, JAMES DOUGLAS, b Minneapolis, Minn, July 12, 26; m 48; c 4. CHEMICAL ENGINEERING. *Educ:* Univ Wis, BS, 47; Inst Paper Chem, MS, 49, PhD(paper chem, eng), 52. *Prof Exp:* Sr engr, Crown Zellerbach Corp, 51-53, chief pulping sect, 53-55, chief paper sect, 55-56, coordr appl res, 56-59; tech dir, Pulp & Paperboard Div, Riegel Paper Co, 59, mgr mfg serv, 59-65, vpres & res mgr, La Opers, 65-68, vpres mfg, Paper Div, 68-72; vpres, mfg, 72-80, PRES MFG, BRUNSWICK PULP & PAPER CO, 80- *Mem:* Tech Asn Pulp & Paper Indust; Am Mgt Asn. *Res:* Pulp and paper. *Mailing Add:* Brunswick Pulp & Paper Co PO Box 1438 Brunswick GA 31520

WETHINGTON, JOHN A(BNER), JR, b Tallahassee, Fla, Apr 18, 21; m 43; c 1. NUCLEAR ENGINEERING, CHEMISTRY. *Educ:* Emory Univ, AB, 42, MS, 43; Northwestern Univ, Evanston, PhD(chem & physics), 49. *Prof Exp:* Vis res asst chem, Princeton Univ, 43-44; scientist, Fercleve Corp, Tenn, 44-45; assoc scientist, Oak Ridge Nat Lab, 45-46, sr scientist, 49-53; asst prof chem eng, 53-56, assoc prof nuclear eng, 56-60, PROF NUCLEAR ENG, UNIV FLA, 60- *Concurrent Pos:* Spec lectr, Univ Tenn, 50-52; US del, Geneva Atomic Energy Conf, Switz, 58; consult, PR Nuclear Ctr, 61-63; vis scientist, Oak Ridge Nat Lab, 58, 79-80 & Lawrence Livermore Lab, 71-72. *Honors & Awards:* Award, Southern Sect, Am Soc Eng Educ, 57. *Mem:* AAAS; Am Chem Soc; Am Nuclear Soc. *Res:* Surface physics; exchange reactions; use of nuclear explosions; processing of nuclear reactor fuel; isotope separation; effect of ionizing radiation on fluorocarbons; radioactive waste disposal; tehnologically enhanced natural radiation. *Mailing Add:* Dept of Nuclear Eng Univ of Fla Gainesville FL 32601

WETLAUFER, DONALD BURTON, b New Berlin, Apr 4, 25; m 50; c 2. BIOCHEMISTRY. *Educ:* Univ Wis, BS, 46, PhD(biochem), 54. *Prof Exp:* Jr chemist, Argonne Nat Lab, 44 & 46-47; res chemist, Bjorksten Res Labs, Inc, 48-50; asst anal chem, Univ Wis, 44-46, asst biochem, 50-52, res assoc enzymol, Inst Enzyme Res, 54; res assoc, Children's Cancer Res Found & Dept Biol Chem, Harvard Med Sch, 58-61; asst prof biochem, Sch Med, Ind Univ, Indianapolis, 61-62; from assoc prof to prof biochem, Med Sch, Univ Minn, Minneapolis, 62-75; DUPONT PROF CHEM & CHMN DEPT, UNIV DEL, 75- *Concurrent Pos:* Nat Found Infantile Paralysis fel protein chem, Carlsberg Lab, Denmark, 55-56; Am Heart Asn fel, Biol Labs, Harvard Univ, 56-58; tutor, Harvard Univ, 58-61; prin investr, USPHS, 61-; consult, Nat Inst Gen Med Sci, 64-e; investr, Max Planck Inst Ernahrungsphysiologie, 74-78; consult, NSF, 80- *Mem:* Am Chem Soc; Am Soc Biol Chemists; Biophys Soc; fel Am Inst Chemists. *Res:* Chemical and physical basis of structure, stability and reactivity of proteins; acquisition of three-dimensional structure of macromolecules; mechanisms of enzyme action. *Mailing Add:* Dept of Chem Univ of Del Newark DE 19711

WETLAUFER, PAMELA HEALD, b New York, NY, June 15, 50; m 72. ECONOMIC GEOLOGY, REMOTE SENSING. *Educ:* Vassar Col, BA, 71; George Washington Univ, MS, 77. *Prof Exp:* Res asst radioactive nuclides, Yale Univ, 71-72; res geologist remote sensing metalliferous ore deposits, 72-74, RES GEOLOGIST ENVIRON ORE DEPOSITION, US GEOL SURV, 74- *Mem:* Soc Econ Geol; Mineral Soc Am; Geochem Soc; Geol Soc Am; Int Asn Genesis Ore Deposits. *Res:* Study of physical and chemical parameters involved in ore formation and integration with geologic factors to deduce models of ore genesis; geologic analysis and interpretation of satellite imagery and aerial photography for delineation of patterns of ore deposit distribution. *Mailing Add:* US Geol Surv Nat Ctr MS 959 Reston VA 22092

WETMORE, CLIFFORD MAJOR, b Akron, Ohio, June 18, 34; m 59; c 2. LICHENOLOGY. *Educ:* Mich State Univ, BS, 56, MS, 59, PhD(bot), 65. *Prof Exp:* From instr to assoc prof biol, Wartburg Col, 64-70; asst prof, 70-72, ASSOC PROF BOT, UNIV MINN, ST PAUL, 72- *Concurrent Pos:* NSF res grants, 66-68 & 71-73, fel, 70. *Mem:* AAAS; Am Bryol & Lichenological Soc; Int Asn Plant Taxonomists; Brit Lichen Soc; Sigma Xi. *Res:* Lichens of the Black Hills, South Dakota, and Minnesota; desert lichens; ultrastructure of lichens; lichen genera; distributions of lichens; herbarium computer techniques; lichens and air pollution. *Mailing Add:* Dept of Bot Univ of Minn St Paul MN 55108

WETMORE, DAVID EUGENE, b Stella, Nebr, Dec 18, 35; m 59; c 2. ORGANIC CHEMISTRY, COMPUTER LITERACY. *Educ:* Park Col, BA, 58; Univ Kans, MA, 62; Tex A&M Univ, PhD(org chem), 65. *Prof Exp:* Res chemist, Sun Oil Co, 65-67; asst prof, 67-70, chmn chem prog, 68-77, ASSOC PROF CHEM, ST ANDREWS PRESBY COL, 70-, CHMN SCI DIV, 77- *Concurrent Pos:* Consult, Coun Independent Cols. *Mem:* Am Chem Soc. *Res:* Computer education; nitrogen compounds in shale oil; beta-lactone syntheses and reactions. *Mailing Add:* Dept of Chem St Andrews Presby Col Laurinburg NC 28352

WETMORE, RALPH HARTLEY, b Yarmouth, NS, Apr 27, 92; nat US; m 23, 40; c 2. BOTANY, MORPHOLOGY. *Educ:* Acadia Univ, BSc, 21; Harvard Univ, AM, 22, PhD(bot), 24. *Hon Degrees:* DSc, Acadia Univ, 48. *Prof Exp:* Nat Res Coun fel bot, 24-25, asst prof, 25-26, from asst prof to prof bot, 26-62, chmn dept, 32-34, dir bot labs, 33-34, chmn dept biol, 46-47, dir biol labs, 52-56, EMER PROF, HARVARD UNIV 62- *Concurrent Pos:* Grants, Milton Fund, Harvard Univ, Am Cancer Soc, 48-58 & NSF, 52-66; vis res prof, Dartmouth Col, 66-67 & Simon Fraser Univ, 72; asst prof, Acadia Univ, 25-26. *Honors & Awards:* Jeanette S Pelton Award in Exp Plant Morphol, 69. *Mem:* Nat Acad Sci; fel Am Acad Arts & Sci; fel AAAS; Bot Soc Am (pres, 53); Am Soc Plant Physiologists. *Res:* Plant antomy; morphogenesis; development of vascular plants. *Mailing Add:* 19 Garden St 43 Cambridge MA 02138

WETMORE, STANLEY IRWIN, JR, b Queens, NY, June 1, 39; m 61; c 2. ORGANIC CHEMISTRY. *Educ:* Rensselaer Polytech Inst, BS, 60, MS, 62; State Univ NY Buffalo, PhD(org chem), 73. *Prof Exp:* Chemist, Mobil Oil Corp, 62-63; from instr to asst prof, 64-71, assoc prof, 75-79, PROF CHEM, VA MIL INST, 79- *Concurrent Pos:* NSF sci fac fel, 70-71. *Mem:* Am Chem Soc; Sigma Xi. *Res:* Synthesis and properties of unique carbenes; photochemistry of small ring heterocyclic compounds; development of ethanol as farm fuel. *Mailing Add:* Dept of Chem Va Mil Inst Lexington VA 24450

WETMUR, JAMES GERARD, b New Castle, Pa, July 1, 41; m 65; c 3. BIOPHYSICAL CHEMISTRY. *Educ:* Yale Univ, BS, 63; Calif Inst Technol, PhD(chem), 67. *Prof Exp:* Asst prof chem & biochem, Univ Ill, Urbana, 69-74; ASSOC PROF MICROBIOL, MT SINAI SCH MED, CITY UNIV NEW YORK, 74- *Mem:* Am Chem Soc; Biophys Soc; Am Soc Biol Chemists; Am Soc Microbiol. *Res:* Kinetics of renaturation of DNA; DNA-protein interactions. *Mailing Add:* Dept Microbiol Mt Sinai Sch Med City Univ New York New York NY 10029

WETS, ROGER J B, b Uccle, Belgium, Feb 20, 37; m 61; c 2. MATHEMATICS. *Educ:* Free Univ Brussels, BA, 59; Univ Calif, Berkeley, PhD(appl math), 64. *Prof Exp:* Staff mem, Boeing Sci Res Lab, Wash, 64-70; prof math, Univ Chicago, 70-71; PROF MATH, UNIV KY, 71- *Concurrent Pos:* Vis lectr, Univ Wash, 66, Univ Calif, Berkeley, 67 & Inst Info & Automation Res, Paris, 69; vis res, Math Ctr, Montreal, 70; Guggenheim fel, 81-82. *Mem:* Am Math Soc; Soc Indust & Appl Math. *Res:* Mathematical programming; stochastic optimization. *Mailing Add:* Dept Math Univ Ky Lexington KY 40506

WETSTONE, HOWARD J, b Hartford, Conn, Apr 27, 26; m 47. INTERNAL MEDICINE, BIOCHEMISTRY. *Educ:* Wesleyan Univ, BA, 47; Tufts Univ, MD, 51. *Prof Exp:* Intern med, New Eng Ctr Hosp, 51-52, jr asst resident, 52-53; asst resident, 53-54, resident, 54-55, dir liver enzyme lab, 58-60, dir biochem res lab, 60-63, dir med res, 63-66, asst dir dept med, 66-70, dir outpatient dept, 70-72, DIR AMBULATORY SERV, HARTFORD HOSP, 72-, SR PHYSICIAN INTERNAL MED, 70- *Concurrent Pos:* Assoc prof med & community med & health care, Med Sch, Univ Conn, 71- *Mem:* Sigma Xi; Am Col Physicians. *Res:* Pharmacogenetics; hypertension; enzymology; community health systems; primary care. *Mailing Add:* Hartford Hosp Hartford CT 06105

WETTACH, WILLIAM, b Pittsburgh, Pa, Mar 13, 10; m 40; c 3. CHEMICAL ENGINEERING. *Educ:* Princeton Univ, BS, 32, ChE, 33; Univ Pittsburgh, PhD(chem eng), 41. *Prof Exp:* Vpres, W W Lawrence & Co, 33-35 & Wettach Paint & Chem Co, 35-38; chemist, Peerless Paint & Chem Co, 38-40; managing dir, Indust Paint Co, 40-53, pres, 53-69; vpres & tech dir, Sterling Div, Reichhold Chem Inc, 69-80; RETIRED. *Concurrent Pos:* Vpres, Sterling Varnish Co, 41-69, Mercury Varnish & Sterling Varnish of Can, 67-75. *Mem:* AAAS; Am Chem Soc; Am Inst Chem Engrs; fel Am Inst Chem; Sigma Xi. *Res:* Developmennt of water soluble alkyd resins; formulation of industrial coatings for metallic substances. *Mailing Add:* 659 Grove St Sewickley PA 15143

WETTACK, F SHELDON, b Coffeyville, Kans, Dec 5, 38; m 56; c 4. PHYSICAL CHEMISTRY. *Educ:* San Jose State Col, AB, 60, MA, 62; Univ Tex, Austin, PhD(chem), 68. *Prof Exp:* High sch teacher, Calif, 61-64; from asst prof to assoc prof, 67-72, PROF CHEM, HOPE COL, 72-, DEAN NATURAL SCI, 74- *Concurrent Pos:* Camille & Henry Dreyfus Found Teacher-Scholar Award, 70-75. *Mem:* Am Chem Soc. *Res:* Photochemistry; energy transfer; fluorescence spectroscopy. *Mailing Add:* Dept of Chem Hope Col Holland MI 49423

WETTE, REIMUT, b Mannheim, Ger, May 12, 27; US citizen; m 51; c 5. BIOSTATISTICS, BIOMATHEMATICS. *Educ:* Univ Heidelberg, MS, 52, DSc(natural sci), 55. *Prof Exp:* Sci asst biomet, Zool Inst, Univ Heidelberg, 52-61; asst biometrician, Univ Tex, 61-64, mem grad fac, 65-66, assoc prof biomath, Univ Tex M D Anderson Hosp & Tumor Inst, 64-66; PROF BIOSTATIST, SCH MED, WASHINGTON UNIV, 66- *Mem:* Am Statist Asn; Biomet Soc; Inst Math Statist. *Res:* Mathematical approaches to basic science and medical aspects of neoplasia; application and problem-oriented development of mathematical-statistical methodology in biomedical research; methods of mathematical-genetical epidemiology. *Mailing Add:* Div of Biostatist Dept of Prev Med Box 8067 Washington Univ Sch of Med St Louis MO 63110

WETTEMANN, ROBERT PAUL, b New Haven, Conn, Nov 12, 44; m 68; c 3. REPRODUCTIVE PHYSIOLOGY. *Educ:* Univ Conn, BS, 66; Mich State Univ, MS, 68, PhD(dairy), 72. *Prof Exp:* Asst prof, 72-75, assoc prof, 75-80, PROF ANIMAL SCI, OKLA STATE UNIV, 80- *Honors & Awards:* Richard Hoyt Award, Am Dairy Sci Asn, 71. *Mem:* Am Soc Animal Sci; Am Dairy Sci Asn; Soc Study Fertil; Soc Study Reproduction. *Res:* Influence of the environment on endocrine and reproductive function in animals. *Mailing Add:* Dept of Animal Sci Okla State Univ Stillwater OK 74074

WETTER, LESLIE ROBERT, b Millet, Alta, Apr 17, 17; m 42; c 1. BIOCHEMISTRY. *Educ:* Univ Alta, BSc, 44, MSc, 46; Univ Wis, PhD(biochem), 50. *Prof Exp:* Asst plant biochem, Univ Alta, 46; from asst res officer to sr res officer, Prairie Regional Lab, Nat Res Coun Can, 50-70, assoc mem coun, 72-73, prin res officer, 70-81; RETIRED. *Mem:* Am Soc Plant Physiologists; Can Soc Plant Physiologists; Chem Inst Can. *Res:* Biosynthesis of thioglucosides in higher plants; enzymes in higher plants, particularly those related to thioglucosides; utilization of isotopes in plant metabolism; toxic properties in rape meal; plant cell cultures and their isoenzyme systems. *Mailing Add:* Prairie Regional Lab Nat Res Coun Saskatoon SK S7N 0W9 Can

WETTERHAHN, KAREN E, b Plattsburgh, NY, Oct 16, 48. INORGANIC BIOCHEMISTRY, PHYSICAL BIOCHEMISTRY. *Educ:* St Lawrence Univ, BS, 70; Columbia Univ, PhD(chem), 75. *Prof Exp:* Chemist formulations, Mearl Corp, 70-71; res fel chem, Columbia Univ, 71-75; fel biochem, Inst Cancer Res, 75-76; ASST PROF, DEPT CHEM, DARTMOUTH COL, 76-, ASST PROF BIOCHEM PROG, 78- *Concurrent Pos:* Alfred P Sloan fel, 81-83. *Mem:* AAAS; Am Chem Soc; Int Asn Bioinorg Scientists. *Res:* Mechanisms of chemical carcinogenesis; metabolism and nucleic acid interactions of carcinogens; inorganic (metal) carcinogenesis; structure-function relationships of modified nucleic acids. *Mailing Add:* Dept Chem Dartmouth Col Hanover NH 03755

WETTERSTROM, WILMA ELAINE, b Hayward, Calif, Dec 20, 45. ARCHAEOLOGICAL BOTONY, PALEO-NUTRITION. *Educ:* Univ Mich, BA, 68, MA, 69, PhD(anthropol), 76. *Prof Exp:* Instr, 74-76, asst prof, 76-82, ASSOC PROF, ANTHROP & ARCHAEOL PROG, MASS INST TECHNOL, 82- *Mem:* Am Anthrop Asn; Soc Am Archaeol; Soc Econ Bot; Soc Archeol Sci; AAAS. *Res:* The orgins and development of agriculture and the effect on human diet and health; collection and analysis of archaeological plant remains in Egypt and the American southwest. *Mailing Add:* 20B-138 Mass Inst Technol Cambridge MA 02139

WETTSTEIN, FELIX O, b Uerikon, Switz, Jan 1, 32; m 60; c 3. MOLECULAR BIOLOGY. *Educ:* Swiss Fed Inst Technol, BS, 56, PhD(agr chem), 60. *Prof Exp:* Fel, Univ Pittsburgh, 60-64; asst res biochemist, Univ Calif, Berkeley, 64-67; assoc prof, 67-74, PROF MOLECULAR BIOL, MED MICROBIOL & IMMUNOL, UNIV CALIF, LOS ANGELES, 74-, V CHMN DEPT, 77- *Mem:* AAAS; Am Soc Microbiol. *Res:* Regulation of RNA and protein biosynthesis in differentiating and transformed animal cells. *Mailing Add:* Dept of Med Microbiol & Immunol Univ of Calif Los Angeles CA 90024

WETZEL, ALLAN BROOKE, b Dayton, Ohio, May 29, 33; m 59; c 3. NEUROPSYCHOLOGY. *Educ:* Univ Ky, BS, 54; Ohio State Univ, MA, 63, PhD(psychol), 65. *Prof Exp:* Trainee biosci, Stanford Univ, 65-67; trainee neurophysiol, Univ Wis-Madison, 67-69, Nat Inst Neurol Dis & Stroke spec fel, 68-69; instr surg, 70-74, ASST PROF SURG & OTO-MAXILLOFACIAL SURG, MED SCH, NORTHWESTERN UNIV, CHICAGO, 74- *Concurrent Pos:* Res investr neuropsychol, Neurosurg Res Lab, Northwestern Mem Hosp, 70-74. *Mem:* AAAS; Am Psychol Asn; Soc Neurosci. *Res:* Brain function; neurophysiology; neuroendocrinology. *Mailing Add:* Dept Surg & Oto-Maxillofacial Surg Northwestern Univ Chicago IL 60611

WETZEL, JOHN EDWIN, b Hammond, Ind, Mar 6, 32; m 62. MATHEMATICS. *Educ:* Purdue Univ, Lafayette, BS, 54; Stanford Univ, PhD(math), 64. *Prof Exp:* From instr to asst prof, 61-68, ASSOC PROF MATH, UNIV ILL, URBANA-CHAMPAIGN, 68- *Mem:* Am Math Soc; Math Asn Am. *Res:* Combinational geometry. *Mailing Add:* Dept of Math Univ Ill Urbana-Champaign 1409 W Green St Urbana IL 61801

WETZEL, KARL JOSEPH, b Waynesboro, Va, May 29, 37; m 68. EXPERIMENTAL NUCLEAR PHYSICS. *Educ:* Georgetown Univ, BS, 59; Yale Univ, MS, 60, PhD(physics), 65. *Prof Exp:* NSF fel, Inst Tech Nuclear Physics, Darmstadt, Ger, 65-66, Ger Govt guest res fel, 66-67; fel, Argonne Nat Lab, 67-69; from asst prof to assoc prof physics, 72-81, PROF PHYSICS, UNIV PORTLAND, 81- *Concurrent Pos:* Vis assoc prof neurol, Univ Ore, Health Sci Ctr, 76-77, chmn physical life sci, 80-; NSF fac fel, 76-77. *Mem:* Am Phys Soc. *Res:* Neutron capture gamma rays; electron and photon scattering; photonuclear processes; electroneurological measurements; pionic atoms. *Mailing Add:* Dept of Physics Univ of Portland Portland OR 97203

WETZEL, LEWIS BERNARD, applied physics, see previous edition

WETZEL, NICHOLAS, b Jacksonville, Fla, July 17, 20; m 45; c 6. NEUROSURGERY. *Educ:* Princeton Univ, AB, 42; Northwestern Univ, MD, 46, MS, 50, PhD, 58. *Prof Exp:* Clin asst, 52-54, instr, 54-55, assoc, 55-57, asst prof, 57-63, ASSOC PROF SURG, MED SCH, NORTHWESTERN UNIV, CHICAGO, 63- *Mem:* AAAS; Am Asn Neurol Surg; AMA; Am Col Surgeons. *Res:* Human stereotaxic surgery for movement disorders; intractable pain; human olfactory system. *Mailing Add:* 1625 Judson Evanston IL 60201

WETZEL, RALPH MARTIN, b Macomb, Ill, June 30, 17; m 47; c 3. MAMMALOGY. *Educ:* Western Ill Univ, BE, 38; Univ Ill, MS, 39, PhD, 49. *Prof Exp:* Spec asst conserv educ, Univ Ill, 39-40, asst zool, 46-49; from instr to assoc prof, 49-66, PROF ZOOL, UNIV CONN, 66- *Concurrent Pos:* Sr clerk, Ord Dept, US War Dept, 41; scientist in residence, US Nat Mus, Smithsonian Inst, 68-71, field work in Chaco Paraguay, 72-78; res assoc, Dept Vert Zool, Smithsonian Inst, 73-83. *Mem:* Am Soc Mammalogists; Soc Syst Zool; Ecol Soc Am; Sigma Xi; Asn Trop Biol. *Res:* Neotropical mammals; speciation and zoogeography; evolution of South American Tayassuidae. *Mailing Add:* Dept Syst & Evolutionary Biol Biol Sci Group Univ Conn Storrs CT 06268

WETZEL, ROBERT GEORGE, b Ann Arbor, Mich, Aug 16, 36; m 59; c 4. LIMNOLOGY. *Educ:* Univ Mich, BSc, 58, MSc, 59; Univ Calif, Davis, PhD(limnol), 62. *Prof Exp:* Tech asst, Univ Mich, 58-59; res technician, US Fish & Wildlife Serv, Mich, 59; res & tech asst, Univ Calif, 59-62; res assoc, Ind Univ, 62-65; from asst prof to assoc prof, 65-71, PROF BOT, MICH STATE UNIV, 71- *Concurrent Pos:* Res fel, Aquatic Res Unit, Ind Dept Natural Resources, 63-64; NSF res fel, 63-65 & 67-69, travel award, Int Asn Limnol Cong, 65 & 68; partic, AEC Contract, 65-; co-ed, Communications, 65-; Off Water Resources Res res fel, 69-71; int consult, Int Biol Prog, Int Coun Sci Unions, 69-; NSF grant, 72-73. *Mem:* Fel AAAS; Am Inst Biol Sci; Am Soc Limnol & Oceanog; Ecol Soc Am; Int Asn Theoret & Appl Limnol (gen secy & treas, 68-). *Res:* Biological productivity of California, Indiana and Michigan lakes; physiological ecology of algae and aquatic macrophytes. *Mailing Add:* W K Kellogg Biol Sta Mich State Univ Hickory Corners MI 49060

WETZEL, ROLAND H(ERMAN), b Wis, Apr 29, 23; m 45; c 2. CHEMICAL ENGINEERING. *Educ:* Univ Wis, BS, 45, PhD(chem eng), 51. *Prof Exp:* Asst chem eng, Univ Wis, 46-50; res engr process develop, E I du Pont de Nemours & Co, Inc, 51-53, res supvr, 54-66, res mgr, 67-69, asst lab dir, Pigments Dept, 69-73, tech supt, 73-75, eng assoc, 76-77; RETIRED. *Mem:* Am Chem Soc; Am Inst Chem Engrs; Am Inst Chemists; Sigma Xi. *Res:* Unit operations; process development. *Mailing Add:* RD 2 Box 253 Landenberg PA 19350

WETZEL, RONALD BURNELL, b Hanover, Pa, May 26, 46; m 76; c 1. PROTEIN CHEMISTRY. *Educ:* Drexel Univ, BS, 69; Univ Calif, Berkely, PhD(org chem), 73. *Prof Exp:* Fel, Max Planck Inst Exp Med, 73-75 & Dept Molecular Biophys & Biochem, Yale Univ, 75-78; SR SCIENTIST, DEPT PROTEIN BIOCHEM, GENENTECH, INC, 78- *Mem:* Am Chem Soc; AAAS. *Res:* Relationship between protein structure and function in effector molecules such as interferon and how recombinant DNA methods can be used to prove these relationships. *Mailing Add:* Dept Protein Biochem Genentech Inc 460 Point San Bruno Blvd San Francisco CA 94080

WETZSTEIN, H(ANNS) J(UERGEN), b Wuppertal-E, Ger, June, 1920; nat US; m 54; c 2. ELECTRICAL ENGINEERING. *Educ:* Univ Cape Town, BSc, 47; Harvard Univ, MS, 49, DSc(elec eng), 52. *Prof Exp:* Dir res, Sci Specialties Corp, 53-55; sr eng scientist, Missile Electronics & Controls Dept, Radio Corp Am, 55-61; mem staff, Inst Naval Studies, Inst Defence Anal, 61-65; mem sr staff, Arthur D Little, Inc, Mass, 65-67; sr eng scientist, Aerospace Syst Div, RCA Corp, 67-71; prin elec engr, Optical Syst Div, ITEK Corp, Lexington, 71-77; SR STAFF ENGR, W J SCHAFER ASSOCS INC, 77- *Res:* Servomechanism; system analysis; transistor measurements; analog-digital conversion and computers; passive detection physics and techniques; submarine and antisubmarine warfare; laser systems; active optics; military detection systems. *Mailing Add:* 33 Bayfield Rd Wayland MA 01778

WEWERKA, EUGENE MICHAEL, b St Paul, Minn, Nov 7, 38; m 59; c 4. PHYSICAL ORGANIC CHEMISTRY. *Educ:* Univ Minn, BA, 62, PhD(org chem), 65. *Prof Exp:* STAFF MEM, LOS ALAMOS SCI LAB, 65- *Concurrent Pos:* Adj prof, Univ NMex, 72- *Mem:* Fel Am Inst Chemists; Am Chem Soc. *Res:* Chemical kinetics; mechanism studies; polymer characterization; analytical methods; physical chemistry of polymers; chemistry of coal and oil shale conversion processes; fossil fuels environmental studies; environmental chemistry. *Mailing Add:* Los Alamos Sci Lab Univ of Calif Los Alamos NM 87544

WEXELL, DALE RICHARD, b Corning, NY, Apr 10, 43; m 78. INORGANIC CHEMISTRY, GLASS & CERAMICS. *Educ:* Fordham Univ, BS, 64; Georgetown Univ, MS, 69, PhD(inorg chem), 71. *Prof Exp:* Instr chem, Georgetown Univ, 64-70; pres, Premium Enterprises, Inc, 65-70; fel, 71-72, res scientist glass chem, 72-80, RES SUPVR, CORNING GLASS WORKS, 81- *Concurrent Pos:* Mem, Nat Mat Res Coun, 81- *Mem:* AAAS; Am Chem Soc; Royal Soc Chem; Am Ceramic Soc; Sigma Xi. *Res:* Aqueous silicates; heteropoly electrolytes; high-temperature materials; surface chemistry of glass; inorganic coatings technology; opal glasses; microwave processing; photochromism; electrical, magnetic and optical behavior in glass and ceramics. *Mailing Add:* Sullivan Park Corning Glass Works Corning NY 14831

WEXLER, ARTHUR SAMUEL, b New York, NY, Oct 27, 18; m 47; c 3. ANALYTICAL CHEMISTRY. *Educ:* Kans State Col, BS, 40; Polytech Inst Brooklyn, PhD(chem), 51. *Prof Exp:* Chemist, C F Kirk & Co, 47-49 & Nopco Chem Co, 49-51; sr chemist, Pepsi-Cola Co, 51-60; MGR ANAL LAB, DEWEY & ALMY CHEM DIV, W R GRACE & CO, CAMBRIDGE, 60- *Mem:* Am Chem Soc. *Res:* Analytical methods for monomers and polymers; physical organic chemistry; biochemistry; infrared spectroscopy. *Mailing Add:* Dewey & Almy Chem Div W R Grace & Co 55 Hayden Ave Lexington MA 02173

WEXLER, BERNARD CARL, b Boston, Mass, May 1, 23; m 46; c 3. EXPERIMENTAL MEDICINE. *Educ:* Univ Ore, BS, 47; Univ Calif, MA, 48; Stanford Univ, PhD(anat, biochem), 52. *Prof Exp:* Asst anat, Sch Med, Stanford Univ, 49-52; mem res staff, Baxter Labs, 52-55; res assoc, May Inst Med Res, 55-61, asst dir, 61-64; from asst prof to assoc prof exp path, 55-71, exp med, 71-75, PROF EXP MED & PATH, COL MED, UNIV CINCINNATI, 75-; DIR, MAY INST MED RES, 64- *Concurrent Pos:* Am Heart Asn advan res fel, 60-62; Nat Heart Inst res career develop award,

62-72; lectr, Dominican Col, 50-52; res assoc, Stanford Res Inst, 51-52; mem, Coun Arteriosclerosis & Coun Basic Sci, Am Heart Asn, 62-, Coun Stroke & Coun High Blood Pressure Res; mem, Coun Arteriosclerosis & Ischemic Heart Dis, Int Soc Cardiol; mem med staff, Jewish Hosp, Cincinnati. *Mem:* Am Soc Physiologists; AAAS; Am Diabetes Asn; Asn Am Med Cols; Endocrine Soc. *Res:* Pituitary-adrenal physiology; experimental pathology. *Mailing Add:* May Inst for Med Res 421 Ridgeway Ave Cincinnati OH 45229

WEXLER, JONATHAN DAVID, b Phoenix, Ariz, Dec 12, 37. COMPUTER SCIENCE. *Educ:* Ariz State Univ, BS, 59; Univ Wis-Madison, MS, 65, PhD(comput sci), 70. *Prof Exp:* Asst mathematician, Ill Inst Technol Res Inst, 61-64; asst prof, Comput Sci Dept, State Univ NY Buffalo, 70-75; software eng specialist, Western Develop Labs, Ford Aerospace & Commun Corp, Palo Alto, 76-79; SOFTWARE DEVELOP ENGR, BTI COMPUT SYSTS, SUNNYVALE, CALIF, 79- *Mem:* Asn Comput Mach. *Res:* Data structure representations of knowledge; software engineering methodologies; artificial intelligence; computer based interactive teaching systems; knowledge-based remote diagnostic systems for computers. *Mailing Add:* 986 Starflower Ct Sunnyvale CA 94086

WEXLER, SOLOMON, b Milwaukee, Wis, June 16, 19; m 51; c 2. CHEMICAL PHYSICS. *Educ:* Univ Chicago, BS, 41, PhD(chem), 48. *Prof Exp:* Jr chemist, Metall Lab, Univ Chicago, 42-44; jr scientist, Los Alamos Sci Lab, 44-46; assoc chemist, Oak Ridge Nat Lab, 46; SR CHEMIST, ARGONNE NAT LAB, 48- *Concurrent Pos:* Mem panel molecular beam exp for space shuttle, NASA, 74-75. *Mem:* AAAS; Am Chem Soc; Am Phys Soc. *Res:* High-pressure mass spectrometry; interactions of ions with molecules; molecular beam-magnetic resonance spectroscopy; analytical chemistry of uranium and plutonium; chemical accelerators; ion cyclotron resonance spectroscopy; chemi-ionization reactions in accelerated crossed-molecular beams; molecular beam studies of metal atom clusters. *Mailing Add:* Argonne Nat Lab 9700 S Cass Ave Argonne IL 60439

WEY, JONG-SHINN, b Taiwan, Oct 26, 44; m 66; c 2. CHEMICAL ENGINEERING, CRYSTALLIZATION PERCIPITATION. *Educ:* Nat Taiwan Univ, BS, 67; Clarkson Col Technol, MS, 70, PhD(chem eng), 73. *Prof Exp:* Res asst chem eng, Clarkson Col Technol, 68-73; sr res chemist crystallization precipitation, 73-78, RES ASSOC, RES LABS, EASTMAN KODAK, CO, 78- *Concurrent Pos:* Nat crystallization comt, Am Inst Chem Eng, 77- *Mem:* Am Inst Chem Eng; Sigma Xi; Soc Photog Sci & Eng. *Res:* Crystallization; precipitation; nucleation; growth; size-distribution control; solid liquid separation. *Mailing Add:* Res Labs Eastman Kodak Co Rochester NY 14650

WEYAND, JOHN DAVID, b Faulkton, SDak, Aug 13, 39; m 63; c 5. CERAMIC ENGINEERING, GEOLOGICAL ENGINEERING. *Educ:* SDak Sch Mines & Technol, BS, 61; Univ Mo, Rolla, MS, 64, PhD(ceramic eng), 71. *Prof Exp:* Jr geologist field geol, Shell Oil Co, 61; ceramic engr, Minn Mining & Mfg Co, 62-66 & Battelle Mem Inst, 66-68; supvr refractories, Interpace Corp, 71-73; SR ENGR CERAMICS, ALUMINUM CO AM, 73- *Mem:* Am Ceramic Soc; Nat Inst Ceramic Eng. *Res:* Boride, nitride and oxide ceramic development for place- ment in chloride and fluoride electroylsis cells as corrosion resistant refractories or electrodes; refractories, substrate, infrared and light transmitting ceramics and elements. *Mailing Add:* Alcoa Tech Ctr Alcoa Center PA 15069

WEYBREW, JOSEPH ARTHUR, b Wamego, Kans, July 13, 15; m 42; c 2. PLANT CHEMISTRY. *Educ:* Kans State Col, BS, 38, MS, 39; Univ Wis, PhD(plant physiol), 42. *Prof Exp:* Res dir, W J Small Co, 42; asst nutritionist, Exp Sta, Kans State Col, 42-43; chief chemist, Indust Hyg Div, State Bd Health, Kans, 43; assoc res prof animal nutrit, 46-49, assoc res prof agron, 49-51, res prof, 51-56, res prof chem, 56-60, actg head chem res, 57-60, WILLIAM NEALS REYNOLDS DISTINGUISHED PROF AGR, NC STATE UNIV, 57- *Concurrent Pos:* Res prof field crops, 60-76. *Mem:* AAAS; Am Chem Soc. *Res:* Tobacco biochemistry, especially fluecuring and quality evaluation; tobacco biogenetics. *Mailing Add:* 112 Pineland Circle Raleigh NC 27607

WEYH, JOHN ARTHUR, b Havre, Mont, Sept 9, 42; m 62; c 4. ANALYTICAL CHEMISTRY, INORGANIC CHEMISTRY. *Educ:* Col Great Falls, BA, 64; Wash State Univ, MS, 66, PhD(chem), 68. *Prof Exp:* Instr chem, Wash State Univ, 66-67; from asst prof to assoc prof, 68-78, PROF CHEM, WESTERN WASHINGTON UNIV, 78- *Mem:* Am Chem Soc. *Res:* Synthesis, characterization and kinetic studies on coordination compounds. *Mailing Add:* Dept of Chem Western Wash Univ Bellingham WA 98225

WEYHENMEYER, JAMES ALAN, b Hazelton, Pa, Feb 12, 51; m 73; c 1. NEUROCHEMISTRY, NEUROANATOMY. *Educ:* Knox Col, BA, 73; Ind Univ, PhD(anat), 77. *Prof Exp:* Assoc instr anat, Sch Med, Ind univ, 73-77; fel, Col Med, Univ Iowa, 77-79; ASST PROF NEUROSCI, COL MED, UNIV ILL, 79- *Mem:* Soc Neurosci. *Res:* Chemical and functional anatomy of neuropeptides and their receptors in the mammalian central nervous system; localization, characterization and interactions of angiotensin II, its receptor and norepinephrine in the central nervous system as they relate to pathophysiology of hypertension. *Mailing Add:* Col Med Univ Ill 506 S Mathews Urbana IL 61801

WEYHMANN, WALTER VICTOR, b Roanoke, Va, Nov 27, 35; m 57; c 1. SOLID STATE PHYSICS, LOW TEMPERATURE PHYSICS. *Educ:* Duke Univ, BS, 57; Harvard Univ, AM, 58, PhD(physics), 63. *Prof Exp:* Res fel physics, Harvard Univ, 63-64; from asst prof to assoc prof 64-75, PROF PHYSICS & HEAD SCH PHYSICS & ASTRON, UNIV MINN, MINNEAPOLIS, 75- *Mem:* Am Phys Soc. *Res:* Nuclear magnetic resonance measurement of sublattice magnetizations; weak magnetic phenomena and nuclear ordering at very low temperatures; production of very low temperatures. *Mailing Add:* Sch of Physics & Astron Univ of Minn Minneapolis MN 55455

WEYL, PETER K, b Ger, May 6, 24; nat US; m 47; c 3. ENVIRONMENTAL MANAGEMENT. *Educ:* Univ Chicago, ScM, 51, PhD(physics), 53. *Prof Exp:* Lectr physics, Roosevelt Col, 51-53; asst prof, Brazilian Ctr Phys Res, 53-54; physicist, Explor & Prod Res Labs, Shell Develop Co, 54-59, sr physicist, 59-63; prof oceanog, Ore State Univ, 63-66; PROF OCEANOG, STATE UNIV NY STONY BROOK, 66- *Concurrent Pos:* Lectr, Univ Houston, 55-62; vis prof, Hebrew Univ Jerusalem, 72-73 & Univ Concepcion, Chile, 79. *Mem:* AAAS; Am Geophys Union; Am Soc Limnol & Oceanog. *Res:* Chemical and physical oceanography; ocean-climate interaction; environmental stability; coastal zone management. *Mailing Add:* 90 Christian Ave Stony Brook NY 11790

WEYLAND, JACK ARNOLD, b Butte, Mont, June 12, 40; m 65; c 3. PHYSICS, SCIENCE COMMUNICATIONS. *Educ:* Mont State Univ, BS, 62, PhD(solid state physics), 69. *Prof Exp:* Asst prof, 68-77, ASSOC PROF PHYSICS, SDAK SCH MINES & TECHNOL, 78- *Concurrent Pos:* Res corp res grant, 70-77. *Mem:* AAAS; Am Phys Soc; Am Asn Physics Teachers. *Res:* High pressure diffusion and magnetic susceptibility studies. *Mailing Add:* Dept of Physics SDak Sch of Mines & Technol Rapid City SD 57701

WEYLER, MICHAEL E, b Boston, Mass, 40; m 62; c 3. OCEAN ENGINEERING, OFFSHORE CONSTRUCTION. *Educ:* Tufts Univ, BSME, 62; Univ Mich Ann Arbor, MSE, 63, PhD(mech eng), 69. *Prof Exp:* Asst prof, Univ Mich, Dearborn, 63-69; construct officer, US Navy, 70-71, ocean engr, 71-78, pub works officer, 78-80; instr mech eng, US Naval Acad, Annapolis, 80-82; SR RES SPECIALIST, EXXON PROD RES, HOUSTON, 82- *Mem:* Nat Soc Prof Engrs; Soc Am Military Engrs. *Res:* Application of field experience in ocean construction to advances in the state-of-the-art of offshore structure engineering, with emphasis on the development of procedures for the installation of such structures. *Mailing Add:* Exxon Prod Res PO Box 2189 Houston TX 77001

WEYMANN, HELMUT DIETRICH, b Duisburg, Ger, Aug 2, 27; nat US; m 54; c 3. RHEOLOGY. *Educ:* Aachen Tech Univ, DSc(physics), 54. *Prof Exp:* Res assoc fluid dynamics, Univ Md, 54-55; privat docent appl mech, Aachen Tech Univ, 56-57; asst res prof fluid dynamics, Univ Md, 57-60; assoc prof mech eng, 60-65, PROF MECH & AEROSPACE SCI, UNIV ROCHESTER, 65- *Concurrent Pos:* Consult, Nat Bur Standards, Washington, DC, 59-61; vis prof, Univ Md, 67-68 & Aachen Tech Univ, 75-76. *Mem:* Am Phys Soc; Soc Rheol; Ger Phys Soc; Ger Soc Appl Math & Mech. *Res:* Rheology; biorheology. *Mailing Add:* Dept Mech & Aerospace Sci Univ Rochester Rochester NY 14627

WEYMANN, RAY J, b Los Angeles, Calif, Dec 2, 34; m 56; c 3. ASTRONOMY. *Educ:* Calif Inst Technol, BS, 56; Princeton Univ, PhD(astron), 59. *Prof Exp:* Res fel astron, Calif Inst Technol, 59-61; from asst prof to assoc prof, 61-67, PROF ASTRON, UNIV ARIZ, 67-, HEAD DEPT ASTRON & DIR & ASTRONR, ASTRONOMER STEWARD OBSERV, 70- *Mem:* Am Astron Soc; Royal Astron Soc. *Res:* Theoretical astrophysics; stellar spectroscopy. *Mailing Add:* Steward Observ Univ of Ariz Tucson AZ 85721

WEYMOUTH, JOHN WALTER, b Palo Alto, Calif, Jan 14, 22; m 66; c 3. SOLID STATE PHYSICS, ARCHAEOMETRY. *Educ:* Univ Calif, AB, 43, MA, 50, PhD(physics), 51. *Prof Exp:* Instr physics, Vassar Col, 52-54; from asst prof to assoc prof, Clarkson Col Technol, 54-58; from asst prof to assoc prof, 58-64, PROF PHYSICS, UNIV NEBR-LINCOLN, 64- *Mem:* Am Phys Soc; Soc Am Archaeol; Am Crystallog Asn; Soc Historical Archaeol; Soc Archaeol Sci (vpres, 81-82). *Res:* Solid state physics; x-ray diffraction; lattice dynamics; physical methods in archaeology; geophysical surveying of archaelogical sites. *Mailing Add:* Dept Physics Univ Nebr Lincoln NE 68588

WEYMOUTH, PATRICIA PERKINS, b Birmingham, Mich, Dec 31, 18; div; c 3. NATURAL SCIENCE, HISTORY OF SCIENCE. *Educ:* Russell Sage Col, AB, 40; Univ Cincinnati, PhD(biochem), 44. *Prof Exp:* Asst biochem, Armored Med Res Lab, Ft Knox, 44-46; res assoc med physics, Univ Calif, 46-49; res assoc radio, Stanford-Lane Hosp, San Francisco, 49-52, Vassar Col, 52-54 & Clarkson Col Technol, 54-58; res assoc biochem & nutrit, Univ Nebr, 58-67; res assoc, 67-69, assoc prof, 69-75, PROF NATURAL SCI, MICH STATE UNIV, 75- *Mem:* Fel AAAS; NY Acad Sci; Sigma Xi. *Res:* Bacteriological and cancer biochemistry; nucleic acid and enzyme studies; interpenetrance of science and other disciplines. *Mailing Add:* Dept of Natural Sci Mich State Univ East Lansing MI 48823

WEYMOUTH, RICHARD J, b Brewer, Maine, July 19, 28; m; c 1. ANATOMY, ENDOCRINOLOGY. *Educ:* Univ Maine, BS, 50; Univ Mich, MS & PhD, 55; Marquette Univ, MD, 63. *Prof Exp:* Instr anat, Miami Univ, 55-59; asst prof, Sch Med, Marquette Univ, 59-61; intern, Univ Mich Hosps, 63-64; from assoc prof to prof anat, Med Col Va, 64-75; PROF ANAT & CHMN DEPT, SCH MED, UNIV SC, 75- & ASSOC DEAN STUDENT AFFAIRS & ADMIS, 76- *Concurrent Pos:* Lectr med, Med Col Va, 64-75. *Res:* Electron microscopy, endocrine glands and kidney. *Mailing Add:* Dept of Anat Sch of Med Univ of SC Columbia SC 29208

WEYNA, PHILIP LEO, b Chicago, Ill, May 11, 32; m 54; c 4. ORGANIC CHEMISTRY, POLYMER CHEMISTRY. *Educ:* Loyola Univ, Ill, BS, 54; Univ Wis, PhD(org chem), 58. *Prof Exp:* Res chemist, Morton Chem Co, 58-64, supvr polymer res, 64-66, dir, 66-73, mgr chem specialties bus group, 73-76, dir com develop, 76-82. *Mem:* Am Chem Soc; Tech Asn Pulp & Paper Indust. *Res:* Polymeric coatings and adhesives. *Mailing Add:* 6604 Rhode Island Trail Crystal Lake IL 60014

WEYNAND, EDMUND E, b San Antonio, Tex, Nov 21, 20; m 50; c 4. MECHANICAL ENGINEERING, AERODYNAMICS. *Educ:* Univ Tex, BS, 49; Mass Inst Technol, SM, 50, MechE, 51, ScD(mech eng), 53. *Prof Exp:* Asst eng & draftsman, San Antonio Air Depot, 42; asst, Proj Squid, Mass Inst Technol, 52-53; sr & proj propulsion engr, Convair Div, Gen Dynamics Corp, Tex, 53-56; assoc prof mech eng, 56-62, PROF MECH ENG, SOUTHERN

METHODIST UNIV, 62- *Concurrent Pos:* Consult, Convair Div, Gen Dynamics Corp, 57-59 & Ling-Tempco-Vought, Vought Aeronautics. *Mem:* Am Inst Aeronaut & Astronaut; Am Soc Eng Educ. *Res:* Internal aerodynamics; nozzles; jet mixing; base drag; inlets; wind tunnel testing; ejectors; optical instrumentation; thermodynamics; heat transfer; fluid mechanics. *Mailing Add:* Inst of Technol Southern Methodist Univ Dallas TX 75275

WEYTER, FREDERICK WILLIAM, b Philadelphia, Pa, Oct 7, 34; m 65; c 2. BIOCHEMICAL GENETICS. *Educ:* Univ Pa, AB, 56; Amherst Col, MA, 58; Univ Ill, PhD(biochem), 62. *Prof Exp:* From instr to asst prof, 62-73, ASSOC PROF BIOL, COLGATE UNIV, 73- *Concurrent Pos:* Fulbright lectr, Afghanistan, 65-66. *Mem:* Am Chem Soc. *Res:* Drug metabolism in microorganisms; regulation of arginine biosynthesis in E coli. *Mailing Add:* Dept of Biol Colgate Univ Hamilton NY 13346

WHALEN, JAMES JOSEPH, b Meriden, Conn, Feb 16, 35; m 59; c 3. ELECTRICAL ENGINEERING. *Educ:* Cornell Univ, BEE, 58; Johns Hopkins Univ, MSE, 62, PhD(elec eng), 69. *Prof Exp:* Res staff asst, Carlyle Barton Lab, Johns Hopkins Univ, 62-69, assoc res scientist, 69-70; res scientist, Nat Oceanic & Atmospheric Admin, 70; asst prof, 70-77, assoc prof, 77-81, PROF ELEC ENG, STATE UNIV NY, BUFFALO, 81- *Concurrent Pos:* Consult, McDonnell Douglas Corp, St Louis, Mo, 76-78, Southeast Ctr Elec Eng Educ, 77-79 & Universal Energy Systs, 79-82. *Mem:* Inst Elec & Electronics Engrs; Am Soc Eng Educ. *Res:* Semiconductor devices; microelectronics, metal-semiconductor field-effect transistor technology; electronic circuits; electronic circuit analysis program applications; electromagnetic compatibility, RFI effects in integrated circuits; microwaves; millimeter waves; cryogenics electronics; instrumentation; measurements. *Mailing Add:* Dept of Elec Eng Rm 1 4232 Ridge Lea Rd Amherst NY 14226

WHALEN, JAMES WILLIAM, b Enid, Okla, Mar 16, 23; m 46; c 2. SURFACE CHEMISTRY. *Educ:* Univ Okla, BS, 46, MS, 47, PhD(chem), 51. *Prof Exp:* Res assoc, Mobil Oil Corp, 50-68; chmn dept chem, 68-72, dean col sci, 72-75, PROF CHEM, UNIV TEX, EL PASO, 68- *Res:* Surface phenomena; adsorption; calorimetry. *Mailing Add:* Dept of Chem Univ of Tex El Paso TX 79968

WHALEN, JOSEPH WILSON, b Battle Creek, Mich, May 27, 23; m 54; c 2. MICROBIOLOGY. *Educ:* Mich State Univ, BS, 49, MS, 51, PhD(microbiol), 55. *Prof Exp:* Bacteriologist, Arthur S Kimball Sanatorium, Battle Creek, 48-50, lab dir, 54-55; bacteriologist, Calhoun County Health Dept, Mich, 50-52; bacteriologist, Biol Labs, Pitman-Moore Co, 55-56, head bact dept, 56-64, mgr bact & immunochem depts, 64-71; asst to dir, Biol Labs, 72-73, res specialist, 73-76, SR RES SPECIALIST, DOW CHEM CO, 76- *Mem:* Sigma Xi; Am Soc Microbiol. *Res:* Bacteriological and immunochemical investigations in tuberculosis; bacterins and vaccines; antimicrobial agents; antibiotics; chemotherapy. *Mailing Add:* 6014 Sturgeon Creek Pkwy Midland MI 48640

WHALEN, THOMAS J(OHN), b Rochester, NY, Sept 1, 31; m 53; c 8. PHYSICAL METALLURGY, CERAMICS. *Educ:* Alfred Univ, BS, 53; Pa State Univ, MS, 55, PhD(metall), 57. *Prof Exp:* Asst, Pa State Univ, 53-55; PRIN RES SCIENTIST, SCI RES STAFF, FORD MOTOR CO, 57- *Mem:* Fel Am Ceramic Soc; Am Soc Metals. *Res:* Powder metallurgy; surface energies of solids, liquids and glasses; mechanical strength of ceramics; processing and mechanical properties of ceramics. *Mailing Add:* Ford Motor Co 20000 Rotunda Dr Dearborn MI 48121

WHALEN, WILLIAM JAMES, b Ft Dodge, Iowa, July 9, 15; m 46; c 3. PHYSIOLOGY. *Educ:* Stanford Univ, BA, 48, MA, 49, PhD(physiol), 51. *Prof Exp:* Asst physiol, Stanford Univ, 48-49, res assoc, 49-51, instr, 50-51; from instr to asst prof, Univ Calif, Los Angeles, 51-60; assoc prof, Col Med, Univ Iowa, 60-67; DIR RES, ST VINCENT CHARITY HOSP, 67- *Concurrent Pos:* Fulbright scholar, 58-59; adj prof, Case Western Reserve Univ, 67-80, emer prof, 80- *Mem:* AAAS; Microcirc Soc; Am Physiol Soc; Cardiac Muscle Soc (pres, 66-68); NY Acad Sci. *Res:* Cardiovascular research; cardiac function in isolated preparations; respiratory control mechanisms; autonomic pharmacology; tissue oxygen tension and cell metabolism; chemoreceptors. *Mailing Add:* 2805 Bellamah Dr Santa Fe NM 87501

WHALEY, HOWARD ARNOLD, b Iroquois, Ill, Sept 1, 34; m 54; c 4. ORGANIC CHEMISTRY. *Educ:* Univ Ill, Urbana, BS, 56; Univ Wis-Madison, PhD(org chem), 61. *Prof Exp:* Res chemist, Lederle Labs, Am Cyanamid Co, 61-66; RES CHEMIST, UPJOHN CO, 66- *Mem:* Am Chem Soc. *Res:* Finding, isolating and studying new antibiotics and modifying known antibiotics. *Mailing Add:* Infectious Dis Dept Upjohn Co Kalamazoo MI 49002

WHALEY, JULIAN WENDELL, b Parkersburg, WVa, Aug 12, 37; m 61; c 3. PLANT PATHOLOGY, PLANT SCIENCE. *Educ:* West Liberty State Col, BS, 59; WVa Univ, MS, 61; Univ Ariz, PhD(plant path), 64. *Prof Exp:* Sr plant pathologist, Eli Lilly & Co, 64-70; PROF PLANT SCI, CALIF STATE UNIV, FRESNO, 70- *Mem:* Am Phytopath Soc. *Res:* Plant protection; pesticides; soil fungi; grape diseases. *Mailing Add:* Dept of Plant Sci Calif State Univ Fresno CA 93740

WHALEY, PETER WALTER, b Baltimore, Md, June 27, 37; m 60; c 3. GEOLOGY. *Educ:* Ohio Wesleyan Univ, BA, 59; Univ Ky, MS, 64; La State Univ, PhD(geol), 69. *Prof Exp:* From asst prof to assoc prof, 68-77, PROF GEOL, MURRAY STATE UNIV, 77- *Mem:* Soc Econ Paleontologists & Mineralogists; Geol Soc Am; Sigma Xi. *Res:* Modern depositional environments; carboniferous system of the Eastern United States. *Mailing Add:* Box 2560 Murray State Univ Murray KY 42071

WHALEY, RANDALL MCVAY, b Hastings, Nebr, Aug 21, 15; m 39; c 3. PHYSICS. *Educ:* Univ Colo, BA, 38, MA, 40; Purdue Univ, PhD(physics), 47. *Hon Degrees:* DSc, Philadelphia Col Pharm & Sci, 72; DHL, Pa Col Pediat Med, 81. *Prof Exp:* Asst, Univ Colo, 38-40; tech asst to sales mgr, G-M Labs, Inc, Ill, 40-41; from instr to prof physics, Purdue Univ, 45-59, exec asst head dept, 54-59, assoc dean sch sci, educ & humanities & actg dir res found, 59-60; vpres grad studies & res, Wayne State Univ, 60-65; chancellor, Univ Mo-Kansas City, 65-67; consult, Am Coun Educ, Washington, DC, 67-68; prin, Cresap, McCormick & Paget Inc, NY, 68-70; PRES, UNIVERSITY CITY SCI CTR, 70- *Concurrent Pos:* Exec dir adv bd educ, Nat Acad Sci, 57-59; pres, Uni-Coll Corp, 71-74, vchmn, 74-80. *Mem:* Fel AAAS; Am Soc Eng Educ; Am Asn Physics Teachers; Am Sci Film Asn (pres, 63-80); Int Sci Film Asn (pres, 64-). *Res:* Cosmic rays; semiconductors; electron synchrotron; educational administration; solid state physics; high energy nuclear physics; applied communications. *Mailing Add:* University City Sci Ctr 3624 Science Center Philadelphia PA 19104

WHALEY, ROSS SAMUEL, b Detroit, Mich, Nov 7, 37; c 3. FOREST ECONOMICS. *Educ:* Univ Mich, BS, 59; Colo State Univ, MS, 61; Univ Mich, PhD(natural resource econ), 69. *Prof Exp:* Instr forestry, Colo State Univ, 60-61; res forester, Southern Forest Exp Sta, US Forest Serv, 61-63; asst prof natural resource econ, Utah State Univ, 65-67, prof forest sci & head dept, 67-69; assoc dean col forestry & natural resources, Colo State Univ, 70-73; head dept landscape archit & regional planning, Univ Mass, 73-76, dean, Col Food & Natural Resources, 76-78; DIR FOREST ECON, FOREST SERV, USDA, 78- *Concurrent Pos:* Consult, Intermountain Forest & Range Exp Sta, USD Forest Serv, 66-67, Rocky Mountain Forest & Range Exp Sta, 67, Pub Land Law Rev Comn, 70, Wallace, McHarg, Roberts & Todd, Joe Meheen Eng & Geddes, Brecher, Qualls, Cunningham, Architects. *Mem:* Soc Am Foresters; Sigma Xi; Am Econ Asn. *Res:* Application of economic theory to problems of natural resources policy and regional planning. *Mailing Add:* Forest Serv USDA PO Box 2417 Washington DC 20013

WHALEY, THOMAS PATRICK, b Atchison, Kans, Jan 13, 23. APPLIED SOLAR THERMAL ENERGY. *Educ:* St Benedicts Col, BS, 42; Univ Kans, PhD(chem), 50. *Prof Exp:* Proj leader, Res Lab, Ethyl Corp, 50-55, res supvr, Develop Lab, 55-58, sr res assoc, 58-62; mgr inorg & phys chem, Int Minerals & Chem Corp, 62-69, dir, Anal & Tech Serv, 69-74; tech dir, Sipi Metals Corp, 74-76; assoc dir solar energy, 76-81, SR ADVISOR, INST GAS TECHNOL, 81- *Concurrent Pos:* Consult, Dearborn Chem Co, 74; instr, Oakton Community Col, 74; ed, Chem Bull, 76-81. *Mem:* Am Chem Soc; Int Solar Energy Soc; Solar Thermal Energy Soc; AAAS. *Res:* Alkali metals; organometallics; inorganic compounds of alkali and alkaline earth metals; refractory metals; metal plating; inorganic phosphates; non-ferrous metals; precious metals; solar energy; fossil fuels; solar production of chemicals; energy planning and systems analysis. *Mailing Add:* Inst Gas Technol IIT Ctr 3424 S State St Chicago IL 60616

WHALEY, THOMAS WILLIAMS, b Albuquerque, NMex, June 13, 42. ORGANIC CHEMISTRY. *Educ:* Univ NMex, BS, 67, MS, 69, PhD(chem), 71. *Prof Exp:* MEM STAFF CHEM, LOS ALAMOS SCI LAB, UNIV CALIF, 71- *Concurrent Pos:* Adj asst prof chem, Univ NMex, Los Alamos Grad Ctr, 73-; ed, J Labelled Compounds & Radiopharmaceut, 74- *Mem:* Am Chem Soc; Sigma Xi; AAAS. *Res:* Organic synthesis with stable isotopes. *Mailing Add:* Los Alamos Sci Lab PO Box 1663 MS 890 Los Alamos NM 87545

WHALEY, WILLIAM GORDON, b New York, NY, Jan 16, 14; m 38; c 1. BIOLOGY. *Educ:* Univ Mass, BS, 36; Columbia Univ, PhD(biol sci), 39. *Prof Exp:* Chemist, Arbuckle Bros, NY, 36-38; lectr bot, Barnard Col, Columbia, 39-40, instr, 40-43; sr geneticist, USDA, 43-46; assoc prof, 46-48, chmn dept, 49-62, assoc dean grad sch, 54-57 & dean, 57-72, dir, Univ Res Inst, 57-72, PROF BOT, UNIV TEX, AUSTIN, 48-, DIR CELL RES INST, 47-, ASHBEL SMITH PROF CELL BIOL, 72- *Concurrent Pos:* Mem adv comt educ, NSF, 64-69, chmn, 67-69; vis prof, Rockefeller Univ, 64-72; Univ Leningrad, 78. *Honors & Awards:* Merit Award, Bot Soc Am, 78. *Mem:* Am Soc Cell Biol; Bot Soc Am; Genetics Soc Am; Soc Develop Biol; Am Soc Plant Physiol; Torrey Bot Club (treas, 41-43). *Res:* Growth and development; Golgi apparatus function; developmental ultrastructure. *Mailing Add:* Biol Labs 220 Univ of Tex Austin TX 78712

WHALEY, WILSON MONROE, b Baltimore, Md, July 21, 20; m 56; c 3. TEXTILE CHEMISTRY. *Educ:* Univ Md, BS, 42, MS, 44, PhD(chem), 47. *Prof Exp:* Org chemist, Naval Res Lab, 44-47; fel chem, Univ Ill, 47-49; asst prof, Univ Tenn, 49-53; asst dir res labs, Pabst Brewing Co, 53-55; sect head chem, Res Ctr, Gen Foods Corp, 55-59; asst tech dir, Midwest Div, Arthur D Little, Inc, 59-62; mgr indust develop, IIT Res Inst, 62-65, mgr org chem, 63-65; dir res & planning, Burlington Industs, Inc, 65-71; pres, Whaley Assocs, NY, 71-75; PROF TEXTILE CHEM & HEAD DEPT, NC STATE UNIV, 75- *Concurrent Pos:* Consult, Oak Ridge Nat Lab, 51-55; adj assoc prof, Cornell Univ, 74-75. *Mem:* Am Asn Textile Chemists & Colorists; Am Chem Soc; Am Inst Chemists. *Res:* Synthesis and chemistry of dyes; heterocyclic and organophosphorus compounds; proteins; carbohydrates; polymer syntheses; textile fibers, finishes and processes; plastics, resins and composite structures; textile chemicals, polymers and processes. *Mailing Add:* Sch of Textiles Box 5666 Raleigh NC 27650

WHALIN, EDWIN ANSIL, JR, b Barlow, Ky, Mar 6, 24; m 48; c 4. PHYSICS. *Educ:* Univ Ill, BS, 45, MS, 47, PhD(physics), 54. *Prof Exp:* From asst prof to prof physics, Univ NDak, 54-66; assoc prof, 66-70, PROF PHYSICS, EASTERN ILL UNIV, 70- *Mem:* Am Phys Soc. *Res:* Nuclear physics. *Mailing Add:* Dept of Physics Eastern Ill Univ Charleston IL 61920

WHALING, WARD, b Dallas, Tex, Sept 29, 23. ATOMIC PHYSICS. *Educ:* Rice Inst, BA, 44, MA, 47, PhD(physics), 49. *Prof Exp:* Fel, 49-52, from asst prof to assoc prof, 52-62, PROF PHYSICS, CALIF INST TECHNOL, 62- *Mem:* Am Phys Soc. *Res:* Penetration of charged particles through matter; atomic spectroscopy. *Mailing Add:* Dept of Physics 106-38 Calif Inst of Technol Pasadena CA 91125

WHALLEY, EDWARD, b Darwen, Eng, June 20, 25; m 56; c 3. PHYSICAL CHEMISTRY. *Educ:* Univ London, BSc & ARCS, 45, PhD(phys chem), 49, DSc, 63; Imp Col, dipl, 49. *Prof Exp:* Lectr chem, Royal Tech Col, Salford, Eng, 48-50; fel, 50-52, asst res officer, Pure Chem Div, 52-53, from asst res officer to sr res officer, Appl Chem Div, 53-61, PRIN RES OFFICER, CHEM DIV, NAT RES COUN CAN, 62-, HEAD HIGH PRESSURE SECT, 62- *Concurrent Pos:* Vis prof, Univ Western Ont, 67 & Kyoto Univ, Japan, 74-75; assoc mem comn thermodyn & thermochem, Int Union Pure & Appl Chem, 73-78; chmn, Can Nat Comt for Int Asn Properties of Steam, 74-; treas, Int Asn Advan High Pressure Sci & Technol, 75- *Mem:* Am Phys Soc; Chem Inst Can; fel Royal Soc Can (assoc hon treas, 69-71, assoc hon secy, 71-74, hon secy, 74-77); Int Glacial Soc. *Res:* High pressure physical chemistry; far infrared and Raman spectroscopy. *Mailing Add:* Div of Chem Nat Res Coun Ottawa ON K1A 0R9 Can

WHALLEY, LAWRENCE ROBERT, b Los Angeles, Calif, Dec 13, 43. PHYSICS. *Educ:* Univ Southern Calif, BS, 66, MS, 70; Univ Ill, PhD(physics), 74. *Prof Exp:* Res assoc physics, Univ Maine, 75-77, vis asst prof, 77-80. *Mem:* Sigma Xi. *Res:* Dynamic properties of liquid crystals. *Mailing Add:* 93 N Main St Orono ME 04473

WHAN, GLENN A(LAN), b North Lima, Ohio, Aug 8, 30; m 55; c 3. CHEMICAL & NUCLEAR ENGINEERING. *Educ:* Ind Inst Technol, BSChE, 51; Mont State Univ, MSChE, 53; Carnegie Inst Technol, PhD(chem eng), 57. *Prof Exp:* Asst prof chem eng, Univ NMex, 57-59; mem staff, Nuclear Propulsion Div, Los Alamos Sci Lab, Univ Calif, 59-60; from asst prof to assoc prof, 60-66, prof nuclear eng & chmn dept, 66-71, chmn dept chem & nuclear eng, 71-75, PROF CHEM & NUCLEAR ENG, UNIV N MEX, 71-, ASSOC DEAN, COL ENG, 76- *Concurrent Pos:* Consult, ACF Indust, Inc, 58-63, Sandia Lab, 63-68, US AEC Int Div, Lisbon, Portugal, 68, Western Interstate Nuclear Bd, Denver, Colo, 71, Los Alamos Sci Lab, 75 & State of NMex, 78; vis staff mem, Eng Div, Los Alamos Sci Lab, 74-75. *Mem:* Fel Am Nuclear Soc; Am Inst Chem Engrs; Am Soc Eng Educ; Sigma Xi; Nat Soc Prof Engrs. *Res:* Energy resources and systems analysis; nuclear energy systems and safety; nuclear fuel cycles; radioactive waste management; benefit-risk-cost analysis; technology assessment. *Mailing Add:* Dept of Chem & Nuclear Eng Univ of NMex Albuquerque NM 87131

WHAN, RUTH ELAINE, b Brownsville, Pa, Oct 28, 31; m 55; c 3. PHYSICAL CHEMISTRY. *Educ:* Allegheny Col, BS, 52; Carnegie Inst Technol, MS, 54; Univ NMex, PhD(phys chem), 61. *Prof Exp:* Res assoc phys chem, Callery Chem Co Div, Mine Safety Appliances Co, 54-57; fel, NSF grant chem to Dr Glenn Crosby, Univ NMex, 61-62; staff mem, 62-72, div supvr, Mat Anal Div II, 62-77, div supvr, Explosive Mat Div, 77-78, DEPT MGR, CHEM & MAT CHARACTERIZATION DEPT, SANDIA LABS DIV, WESTERN ELEC CORP, 78- *Mem:* Am Chem Soc; Asn Women Sci. *Res:* Explosive and pyrotechnic materials, compatibility; corrosion; molecular spectroscopy; luminescence of rare earth chelates; optical studies of radiation damage in semiconductors; effect of ion implantation in semiconductors; scanning electron microscopy; carbon composite analysis. *Mailing Add:* Dept 5820 Sandia Labs Albuquerque NM 87185

WHANG, ROBERT, b Honolulu, Hawaii, Mar 7, 28; m 56; c 4. INTERNAL MEDICINE, NEPHROLOGY. *Educ:* St Louis Univ, BS, 52, MD, 56; Am Bd Internal Med, dipl, 65, 74, cert nephrol, 72; Am Bd Nutrit, cert, 81. *Prof Exp:* Intern med, Johns Hopkins Univ Hosp, 56-57; asst resident, Baltimore City Hosps, 57-59, resident, 59-60; from instr to assoc prof med, Sch Med, Univ NMex, 63-71; prof, Sch Med, Univ Conn, 71-73, assoc dean, Vet Admin Hosp Affairs, 72-73; prof med, Sch Med, Ind Univ, Indianapolis, 73-78; PROF MED & VHEAD DEPT MED, COL MED, UNIV OKLA, OKLAHOMA CITY, 78-; CHIEF, MED SERV, VET ADMIN HOSP, 78- *Concurrent Pos:* Life Ins Med res fel, Univ NC, 60-62, USPHS trainee renal dis, 62-63; chief metab, Vet Admin Hosp, Albuquerque, 66-71; chief staff, Vet Admin Hosp, Newington, Conn, 71-73 & Indianapolis, Ind, 73-78. *Mem:* Fel Am Col Physicians; Am Fedn Clin Res; Int Soc Nephrology; Am Soc Nephrology; Am Col Nutrit. *Res:* Magnesium deficiency, interrelationship of magnesium and potassium, electrolyte changes in uremia. *Mailing Add:* Vet Admin Hosp 921 NE 13th St Oklahoma City OK 73104

WHANG, SUKOO JACK, b Seoul, Korea, Feb 3, 34; US citizen; m 63; c 3. MEDICAL MICROBIOLOGY, IMMUNOLOGY. *Educ:* Univ Calif, Los Angeles, MS, 60, PhD(med microbiol, immunol), 63, MD, 72; Am Bd Med Microbiol, dipl, 75; Am Bd Path, dipl, 77. *Prof Exp:* Asst prof microbiol, Calif State Polytech Univ, 63-64; chief microbiol & serol dept, Providence Hosp, Southfield, Mich, 64-65; chief microbiol & immunol dept, Ref Lab, Div Abbott Labs, Calif, 65-69; CHIEF MICROBIOL & IMMUNOL DIV, CLIN LAB, CHMN INFECTION CONTROL COMT & PROG DIR SCH MED TECHNOL, WHITE MEM MED CTR, LOS ANGELES, 72- *Concurrent Pos:* Chief microbiol & Immunol Div, Clin Lab, White Mem Med Ctr, 69-70; adj prof, Pacific Union Col, Angwin, 77- *Mem:* NY Acad Sci; Am Soc Microbiol; Sigma Xi; Am Col Physicians; fel Am Soc Clin Pathologists. *Res:* Clinical microbiology, pathology and serology; syphilis serology; diagnostic tests for the detection of inborn errors of metabolism; fluorescent antibody testing. *Mailing Add:* 1325 Via Del Ray South Pasadena CA 91030

WHANG, YUN CHOW, b Foochow, China, Dec 13, 33; m 59; c 3. SPACE SCIENCE, FLUID MECHANICS. *Educ:* Taiwan Col Eng, BS, 54; Univ Minn, Minneapolis, PhD(fluid mech), 61. *Prof Exp:* Asst prof aerospace eng, Univ Fla, 61-62; from asst prof to assoc prof space sci, 62-67, PROF MECH ENG, CATH UNIV AM, 67-, CHMN DEPT, 71- *Concurrent Pos:* NASA grant, Cath Univ Am, 69-, NSF grant, 71- *Mem:* Assoc fel Am Inst Aeronaut & Astronaut; Am Geophys Union; Am Soc Mech Engrs; Am Soc Eng Educ. *Res:* Solar wind and its interaction with the earth, the moon and other planets. *Mailing Add:* Dept of Mech Eng Cath Univ of Am Washington DC 20064

WHANGBO, MYUNG HWAN, b Korea, Oct 21, 45; Can citizen; c 1. ORGANIC CHEMISTRY, SOLID STATE CHEMISTRY. *Educ:* Seoul Univ, BSc, 68, MSc, 70; Queens Univ, PhD(chem), 74. *Prof Exp:* Fel, Queens Univ, 75-76; assoc chem, Cornell Univ, 76-77; asst prof, 78-81, ASSOC PROF CHEM, NC STATE UNIV, 81- *Concurrent Pos:* Camille & Henry Dreyfus teacher-scholar, 80-85; vis prof, Bell Labs, Murray Hill, 81. *Mem:* Am Chem Soc; Sigma Xi; NY Acad Sci. *Res:* Molecular orbital interpretation of structures and reactivities of organic and organometallic systems; structure property relationships of crystalline materials; theoretical chemistry. *Mailing Add:* Dept Chem NC State Univ Raleigh NC 27650

WHANGER, PHILIP DANIEL, b Lewisburg, WVa, Aug 30, 36; m 64; c 2. NUTRITIONAL BIOCHEMISTRY. *Educ:* Berry Col, BS, 59; WVa Univ, MS, 61; NC State Univ, PhD(nutrit), 65. *Prof Exp:* Res assoc biochem, Mich State Univ, 65-66; from asst prof to assoc prof, 66-78, PROF NUTRIT & BIOCHEM, ORE STATE UNIV, 78- *Concurrent Pos:* NIH res fel, Mich State Univ, 66-67, res grants selenium & myopathies, Ore State Univ, 68-; NIH spec fel, 72; assoc staff, Harvard Med Sch, 72-73; zinc & metallothionein metabolism, 76-; selenium dificiencies in primates, 78-; NSF Int fel, 80-81; Vis Sci, Commonwealth Sci & Indust Res Orgn, Wembley, Western Australia. *Mem:* Am Inst Nutrit; Am Soc Animal Sci; Int Bioinorganic Scientists; Soc Environ Geochem & Health. *Res:* Altered metabolic pathways under sulfur deficiency; relationships of vitamin E and selenium in myopathies, biochemical properties of selenium and cadmium metallo-proteins, metabolic pathways in rumen microbes. *Mailing Add:* Dept Agr Chem Ore State Univ Corvallis OR 97331

WHAPLES, GEORGE WILLIAM, mathematics, deceased

WHARTON, CHARLES BENJAMIN, b Gold Hill, Ore, Mar 29, 26; m 53; c 3. PLASMA PHYSICS, MICROWAVE TECHNOLOGY. *Educ:* Univ Calif, Berkeley, BSEE, 50, MS, 52. *Prof Exp:* Proj engr, Lawrence Radiation Lab, Univ Calif, 50-62; staff mem exp physics, Gen Atomic Div, Gen Dynamics Corp, Calif, 62-67; dir lab plasma studies, 72-73, PROF PLASMA PHYSICS, CORNELL UNIV, 67- *Concurrent Pos:* Tech advisor, UN Conf on Peaceful Uses of Atomic Energy, Geneva, Switz, 58; sci engr, Max Planck Inst Physics & Astrophys, Ger, 59-60; consult, Aerojet-Gen Nucleonics Div, Gen Tire & Rubber Co, 60-62, US Naval Res Lab, Washington, DC, 70-, Power Conversion Technol, Inc, 79-81 & Occidental Res Corp, 79-; controlled fusion res mem eval panel on quantum electronics & plasma physics, Nat Res Coun, 70-73; vis scientist, Max Planck Inst Plasma Physics, Munich, Ger, 73-74; consult, Lawrence Livermore Lab, 75-77; dir courses, Int Sch Plasma Physics, Varenna, Italy, 78 & 82; vis prof, Univ Calif, Irvine, 79-80 & Occidental Res Corp, 80-81; US participating scientist, Joint Prog Plasma Physics, Cornell Univ & Physical Res Lab, Ahmedabad, India, 81-84. *Honors & Awards:* Alexander von Humboldt sr scientist award, 73. *Mem:* Fel Am Phys Soc; fel Inst Elec & Electronics Engrs; Nuclear & Plasma Sci Soc (vpres, 75). *Res:* Plasma diagnostics; waves in plasmas; plasma instabilities; microwave technology; electronic circuitry; nonlinear waves; relativistic electron beams; plasma heating; controlled fusion research; intense ion beams. *Mailing Add:* Phillips Hall Cornell Univ Ithaca NY 14853

WHARTON, CHARLES HEIZER, b Minneapolis, Minn, July 28, 23. VERTEBRATE ZOOLOGY, ECOLOGY. *Educ:* Emory Univ, AB, 51; Cornell Univ, MS, 54; Univ Fla, PhD, 58. *Prof Exp:* Pvt zoologist, Philippines, 46-47; spec consult, Int Div, USPHS, 50; mem scrub-typhus team, US Dept Army, Borneo, 51; dir, Forest Cattle Surv Exped Southeast Asia, Coolidge Found, 51-52; asst prof, 58-66, PROF BIOL, GA STATE UNIV, 66- *Concurrent Pos:* Prin investr, Joint Kouprey Venture, Nat Acad Sci, 63-64; chmn, Ga Coun for Preservation of Natural Areas, 66-68. *Mem:* Am Soc Mammal; Am Soc Ichthyol & Herpet; Ecol Soc Am. *Res:* Mammalogy; herpetology; international and natural area conservation; vertebrate epidemiology; biology of vertebrates; Southern River swamp ecosystems. *Mailing Add:* Inst Ecol Univ Ga Athens GA 30602

WHARTON, DAVID CARRIE, b Avoca, Pa, Nov 3, 30; m 61; c 2. BIOCHEMISTRY. *Educ:* Pa State Univ, BS, 52, MS, 54, PhD(bot), 56. *Prof Exp:* Asst plant path, Pa State Univ, 52-56; fel enzyme chem, Enzyme Inst, Univ Wis, 59-61; res scientist, E I du Pont de Nemours & Co, 61-62; asst prof biochem, Univ Wis, 62-64 & Sch Med, Univ Va, 64-66; from asst prof to assoc prof, Cornell Univ, 66-73; PROF BIOCHEM, UNIV TEX HEALTH SCI CTR, SAN ANTONIO, 73- *Mem:* Am Soc Biol Chemists; Am Chem Soc; Brit Soc Gen Microbiol. *Res:* Electron transport; metalloenzymes. *Mailing Add:* Dept of Biochem Univ of Tex Health Sci Ctr San Antonio TX 78284

WHARTON, H(ARRY) WHITNEY, b Watertown, NY, May 4, 31; m 55; c 2. ANALYTICAL CHEMISTRY. *Educ:* Iowa State Univ, BS, 53, MS, 58, PhD(anal chem), 60. *Prof Exp:* Res chemist, Rath Packing Co, 56; asst anal chem, Iowa State Univ, 56-60; res chemist, 60-61, group leader anal chem, 61-64, group leader, Soap Prod Div, 65, sect head anal chem, Food Prod Div, 65-70, sect head new prod res, 70-74, SECT HEAD FOODS ANAL, FOOD PROD DIV, PROCTER & GAMBLE CO, 74- *Mem:* AAAS; Am Chem Soc; Am Oil Chem Soc. *Res:* Micro methods of analysis involving spectrophotometry, microdiffusion, spectrophotometric and nonaqueous titrations, polarography and inorganic oxidation-reduction reactions; development of analytical methods for food products; development of new food products. *Mailing Add:* Procter & Gamble Co Food Prod Div 6071 Ctr Hill Rd Cincinnati OH 45224

WHARTON, JAMES HENRY, b Mangum, Okla, July 23, 37; m 56; c 2. PHYSICAL CHEMISTRY. *Educ:* Northeast La Univ, BS, 59; La State Univ, PhD(phys chem), 62. *Prof Exp:* Asst prof, 62-63 & 65-69, assoc dean, Col Chem & Physics, 69-71, assoc prof, 69-80, PROF CHEM, LA STATE UNIV, BATON ROUGE, 80-, DEAN, GEN COL, 71- *Concurrent Pos:* Consult, Univ Tex, San Antonio, 70-71. *Mem:* Am Chem Soc. *Res:* Molecular spectroscopy; electron spin resonance. *Mailing Add:* Box 12 Dept of Chem La State Univ Baton Rouge LA 70803

WHARTON, LENNARD, b Boston, Mass, Dec 10, 33; m 57; c 3. PHYSICAL CHEMISTRY. *Educ:* Mass Inst Technol, BS, 55; Univ Cambridge, MA, 57; Harvard Univ, PhD(chem), 63. *Prof Exp:* From asst prof to assoc prof chem, Univ Chicago, 63-78, prof chem, 78; VPRES ENG & TECHNOL, WORTHINGTON GROUP, MCGRAW EDISON CO, 78- *Concurrent Pos:* Alfred P Sloan res fel, 64-66; res assoc prof, Univ Chicago, 78-83; consult, Northrop Electronics Div, 77-78; vpres technol, Studebaker Worthington Corp, 78- *Mem:* Am Phys Soc; sr mem Inst Elec & Electronics Engrs; Am Inst Ehem Engrs; AAAS; Am Soc Mech Engrs. *Res:* Molecular beams and structure; spectroscopy; chemical kinetics; experimental physical chemistry; scattering phenomena; surface sciences; solar energy conversion; electrical power transmission and distribution. *Mailing Add:* Worthington Group McGraw-Edison Co 1701 Golf Road Rolling Meadows IL 60008

WHARTON, MARION AGNES, b Cayuga, Ont, Nov 17, 10; nat US. NUTRITION. *Educ:* Univ Toronto, BA, 33; Univ Western Ont, MS, 34; Mich State Univ, PhD(nutrit), 47; Am Bd Nutrit, dipl. *Prof Exp:* Instr, Univ Toronto, 36-37; dietician, Prov Dept Health, Ont, 37-39; asst, Mich State Univ, 40-46; res nutritionist, Univ WVa, 46-48; asst prof foods & nutrit, Ohio State Univ, 48-52; from asst prof to assoc prof, NDak Agr Col, 52-55; prof, Univ Southern Ill, 55-61 & Univ RI, 61-63; assoc prof, Iowa State Univ, 63-65; from assoc prof to prof, 65-78, EMER PROF FOODS & NUTRIT, CALIF STATE UNIV, LONG BEACH, 78- *Mem:* Soc Nutrit Educ; Am Dietetic Asn; Am Home Econ Asn; Sigma Xi. *Mailing Add:* 10074 Bloomfield St Cypress CA 90630

WHARTON, PETER STANLEY, b Oxford, Eng, May 9, 31; m 55; c 4. ORGANIC CHEMISTRY. *Educ:* Cambridge Univ, BA, 52, MA, 57; Yale Univ, MS, 57, PhD, 59. *Prof Exp:* Fel, Columbia Univ, 58-60; from instr to prof org chem, Univ Wis-Madison, 60-68; PROF CHEM, WESLEYAN UNIV, 68- *Honors & Awards:* Frederick Gardner Cottrell Award, 61. *Mem:* Am Chem Soc; The Chem Soc. *Res:* Synthetic and mechanistic alicyclic chemistry. *Mailing Add:* Dept of Chem Wesleyan Univ Middletown CT 06457

WHARTON, RUSSELL PERRY, b Memphis, Tenn, Sept 11, 41; m 63; c 2. ELECTRICAL ENGINEERING, ENGINEERING MANAGEMENT. *Educ:* Ga Inst Technol, BEE, 63, MSEE, 66, PhD(elec eng), 70. *Prof Exp:* Elec engr, Gen Dynamics, Pomona, 63-64; instr, Ga Inst Technol, 64-70; proj engr, 70-73, eng mgr, 74-80, TECH ELEC MGR, SCHLUMBERGER, 80- *Concurrent Pos:* Consult, Sperry Microwave Electronics Co, 68-70 & Univ Houston, 80-; co-founder, Drug/Alcohol Abuse Halfway House, Houston, 79-; presented papers & lectures, NAm, SAm, Europe, Mid East & Far East. *Mem:* Inst Elec & Electronic Eng; Am Phys Soc; Soc Explor Geophys; Sigma Xi; Soc Prof Well Log Analysts. *Res:* Research and development of very high temperature electrical and microwave instrumentation for determining electromagnetic characteristics of deep subsurface formations adjacent to the borehole wall in oil and gas wells. *Mailing Add:* 12431 Stafford Springs Dr Houston TX 77077

WHARTON, WALTER WASHINGTON, b Boone, Ky, Mar 25, 26; m 47; c 5. PHYSICAL CHEMISTRY. *Educ:* Georgetown Col, AB, 50; Univ Ky, MS, 52, PhD, 55. *Prof Exp:* Res chemist, 54-59, SUPVR RES CHEM & CHIEF ADV TECHNOL BR, PROPULSION DIR, US ARMY MISSILE RES & DEVELOP COMMAND, REDSTONE ARSENAL, 59- *Concurrent Pos:* Instr, Exten Ctr, Univ Ala, 56- *Mem:* Am Chem Soc. *Res:* Propulsion technology; propellant chemistry; combustion kinetics; laser technology. *Mailing Add:* 2811 Barcody Rd SE Huntsville AL 35801

WHARTON, WILLIAM RAYMOND, b Knoxville, Tenn, Mar 30, 43; m 67; c 3. EXPERIMENTAL NUCLEAR PHYSICS. *Educ:* Stanford Univ, BS, 65; Univ Wash, PhD(nuclear physics), 72. *Prof Exp:* Res assoc exp nuclear physics, Argonne Nat Lab, 72-74 & Rutgers Univ, 74-75; asst prof, 75-80, ASSOC PROF PHYSICS, CARNEGIE-MELLON UNIV, 80- *Mem:* Am Phys Soc. *Res:* Experimental medium energy nuclear physics involving the study of nuclei or nucleons interacting with pions, kaons and antiprotons. *Mailing Add:* Dept of Physics Carnegie-Mellon Univ Pittsburgh PA 15213

WHATLEY, ALFRED T, b Denver, Colo, Apr 20, 22; div; c 4. PHYSICAL CHEMISTRY. *Educ:* Princeton Univ, AB, 48, AM, 50, PhD(chem), 52. *Prof Exp:* Chemist, Hanford Works, Gen Elec Co, 52-55, eng consult, Aircraft Nuclear Propulsion, 55-57, physicist, Vallecitos Atomic Lab, 57-61; staff engr, Martin Co, 61-62; sr sci specialist, EG&G, 62-70; exec dir, Western Interstate Nuclear Bd, Lakewood, Colo, 70-76; RETIRED. *Concurrent Pos:* Mem, Colo Air Pollution Control Comn, chmn, 78- *Mem:* Am Nuclear Soc. *Res:* Nuclear science. *Mailing Add:* PO Box 540 Breckenridge CO 80424

WHATLEY, BOOKER TILLMAN, b Alexandria, Ala, Nov 5, 15; m 43. HORTICULTURE, PLANT PHYSIOLOGY. *Educ:* Ala Agr & Mech Col, BS, 41; Rutgers Univ, PhD, 57. *Prof Exp:* Agr exten agent, Butler County, Ala, 46-47; prin high sch, Ala, 47-50; tech oper officer, Chofu Hydroponic Farm, Japan, 50-54; assoc prof & head dept hort, Southern Univ, 57-60; adv hort, US Opers Mission, Ministry Agr, Ghana, 60-62; prof hort, Southern Univ, 62-68; prof plant & soil sci, Tuskegee Inst, 68-81; PRES, WHATLEY FARMS, INC, 81- *Mem:* AAAS; Am Soc Hort Sci; Am Soc Plant Physiol. *Res:* The effect of budding methods, wrapping materials and hormones on Myristica fragrans and its vegetative propagation. *Mailing Add:* Dept Plant & Soil Sci Tuskegee Institute AL 36088

WHATLEY, JAMES ARNOLD, b Calvert, Tex, Feb 26, 16; m 39; c 2. ANIMAL BREEDING. *Educ:* Agr & Mech Col, Tex, BS, 36; Iowa State Col, MS, 37, PhD(animal breeding), 39. *Prof Exp:* From asst prof to prof animal husb, Okla State Univ, 39-64, from assoc dir to dir, Agr Exp Sta, 64-74, dir agr res, 66-68, dean agr, 68-74, assoc dir, Agr Exp Sta, 74-81; RETIRED. *Concurrent Pos:* With bur animal indust, USDA, 44. *Mem:* Sigma Xi; Am Soc Animal Sci. *Res:* Swine breeding. *Mailing Add:* 2221 W Eighth Stillwater OK 74074

WHATLEY, MARVIN E, b New Orleans, La, May 31, 26; m 61; c 5. CHEMICAL ENGINEERING. *Educ:* La State Univ, BS, 48; Iowa State Univ, MS, 50, PhD(chem eng), 53. *Prof Exp:* Res asst thorium processing, Ames Lab, 48-53; develop engr, Oak Ridge Nat Lab, 53-55, teacher chem tech, Oak Ridge Sch Reactor Technol, 55-57, group leader reactor processing develop, chem tech div, 57-59, sect chief radio chem processing, 60-70; prof chem eng, Univ Tenn, 63-70; PROJ ENGR, UNION CARBIDE CORP, 70- *Mem:* Am Chem Soc; Am Inst Chem Engrs. *Res:* Radio chemical processing; diffusional operations, including solvent extraction, ion exchange, high temperature distillation and foam separation. *Mailing Add:* Union Carbide Corp Oak Ridge TN 37705

WHATLEY, THOMAS ALVAH, b Midland, Ark, Aug 23, 32; m 54; c 4. PHYSICAL CHEMISTRY, INSTRUMENTATION. *Educ:* Fresno State Col, BS, 53; Univ Ore, PhD(phys chem), 61. *Prof Exp:* Sr scientist, Lockheed Aircraft Corp, 58-61; inorg res group head, United Tech Div, United Aircraft Corp, 61-65; sr res chemist, F&M Div, Hewlett-Packard Co, Pa, 65-68; eng specialist, Appl Res Labs, 68-74, mgr appln, 74-78; CONSULT MEM ENG STAFF, XEROX CORP, 78- *Mem:* Am Chem Soc; Am Soc Mass Spectrometry; Microbeam Anal Soc; Am Vacuum Soc. *Res:* Ion probe mass spectrometry; analytical instrumentation development; material science; solid state device structure analysis; ion-solid interactions. *Mailing Add:* Xerox Corp M2-19 701 S Aviation Blvd El Segundo CA 90245

WHAYNE, TOM FRENCH, b Columbus, Ky, Dec 26, 05; m 34; c 2. MEDICINE. *Educ:* Univ Ky, AB, 27; Washington Univ, MD, 31; Harvard Univ, MPH, 49, DrPH, 50; Am Bd Prev Med, dipl, 49. *Prof Exp:* Intern, Mo Baptist Hosp, St Louis, 31-32; house physician, Mo Pac Hosp, 32-33; surgeon, Civilian Conserv Corps, 33-34; physician, Fitzsimons Gen Hosp, Denver, 34; physician, CZ, Med Corps, US Army, 38-41, physician, Off Surgeon Gen, 41-43, asst mil attache med, US Embassy, London, 43-44, chief prev med sect, 12th Army Group, 44-45; chief prev med sect, Off Chief Surgeon, Europe, 45-46, dep chief prev med div, Off Surgeon Gen, Washington, DC, 46-47, chief, 47-48, chief dept training doctrines, Army Med Serv Grad Sch, Walter Reed Army Med Ctr, 50-51, chief prev med div, Off Surgeon Gen, DC, 51-55; prof prev med & pub health, Sch Med, Univ Pa, 55-63, assoc dean, 58-63; asst vpres med ctr, 63-67, actg dean col med, 66-67, prof community med & assoc dean col med, 63-72, EMER PROF COMMUNITY MED, UNIV KY, 74- *Concurrent Pos:* Consult, Surgeon Gen, US Army, 55-75; adv, US Deleg, World Health Assembly, Geneva, 48 & 53; mem, Bd Dirs, Gorgas Mem Inst Trop & Prev Med. *Mem:* Fel Am Soc Trop Med & Hyg; Am Epidemiol Soc; fel Am Pub Health Asn; fel NY Acad Med; fel Am Col Prev Med. *Res:* Epidemiology. *Mailing Add:* 623 Tateswood Dr Lexington KY 40502

WHEALTON, JOHN HOBSON, b Brooklyn, NY, Apr 27, 43; m 72. PLASMA PHYSICS. *Educ:* Univ Lowell, BS, 66; Univ Del, MS, 68, PhD(physics), 71. *Prof Exp:* Res assoc Div Eng, Brown Univ, 71-72, res assoc, Dept Chem, 72-73; res assoc, Joint Inst Lab Astrophys, Univ Colo-Nat Bur Stand, 73-75, MEM STAFF, THERMONUCLEAR DIV, OAK RIDGE NAT LABS, 75- *Mem:* Am Phys Soc. *Res:* Analysis of drift tube swarm experiments; kinetic theory of diffusion and mobility in collision-dominated weakly ionized gases in presence of strong fields; space charge ion optics and steering relevent to neutral beam plasma heating; numerical methods for convergence of Poisson-Vlasov equations; double plasma direct recovery devices; neutralizer transport. *Mailing Add:* Thermonuclear Div Oak Ridge Nat Labs Oak Ridge TN 37830

WHEASLER, ROBERT, b Indianapolis, Ind, Dec 26, 24; m 46; c 2. AERONAUTICAL ENGINEERING, AERODYNAMICS. *Educ:* Purdue Univ, BS, 53, MS, 54, Univ Okla, PhD(eng sci), 64. *Prof Exp:* Res engr, Boeing Airplane Co, 54-55; res engr, Aircraft Gas Turbine Div, Gen Elec Co, 55; instr aeronaut eng, Purdue Univ, 55-58; asst prof, 58-65, PROF AERONAUT & MECH ENG, UNIV WYO, 65- *Concurrent Pos:* Instr, Univ Okla, 60. *Mem:* Am Soc Eng Educ; Am Inst Aeronaut & Astronaut; Sigma Xi. *Res:* Thermodynamics; heat transfer; aircraft and missile propulsion; gas dynamics. *Mailing Add:* Dept of Mech Eng Univ of Wyo Laramie WY 82070

WHEAT, JOHN DAVID, b Ranger, Tex, July 12, 21; m 50; c 3. ANIMAL GENETICS. *Educ:* Agr & Mech Col, Tex, BS, 42, MS, 51; Iowa State Col, PhD(animal breeding, genetics), 54. *Prof Exp:* From asst prof to assoc prof, 54-69, PROF ANIMAL SCI & INDUST, KANS STATE UNIV, 69- *Concurrent Pos:* Beef cattle breeding adv, Ministry of Animal & Forest Resources, US Agency Int Develop-Kans State Univ Contract Team, Northern Nigeria, 66-68; mem fac, Ahmadu Bello Univ, Nigeria, 66-68, livestock breeding consult, Taiwan, 72 & 75. *Mem:* Am Soc Animal Sci; Am Genetic Asn. *Res:* Population genetics; muscling selection research in swine. *Mailing Add:* Dept of Animal Sci & Indust Kans State Univ Manhattan KS 66506

WHEAT, JOSEPH ALLEN, b Charlottesville, Va, Mar 31, 13; m 42; c 1. CHEMISTRY. *Educ:* Univ Va, BS, 34; Cornell Univ, MS, 36, PhD(inorg chem), 39. *Prof Exp:* Instr chem, Trinity Col, Conn, 39-40; microchemist, Biochem Res Found, Del, 40-41; chemist, Celanese Corp Am, NJ, 41-49; spectroscopist, Air Reduction Co, 49-53; chemist, Savannah River Lab, Atomic Energy Div, E I du Pont de Nemours & Co, Inc, 53-78; PROF COMPUT SCI, VOORHEES COL, 67-, TRUSTEE, 74- *Mem:* Am Chem Soc; Soc Appl Spectros; Am Inst Chemists. *Res:* instrumental analysis; infrared, emission and atomic absorption spectroscopy; application of computers and programmable calculators to reduction of spectroscopic data; programming of computer to interact simultaneously with from one to four data gathering instruments, such as 4K channel pulse height analyzer, infrared spectrophotometer, atomic absorption spectrometer. *Mailing Add:* 1478 Canterbury Ct SE Aiken SC 29801

WHEAT, PERCY WAYNE, b Bogalusa, La, Apr 18, 40; m 63; c 2. INDUSTRIAL ORGANIC CHEMISTRY. *Educ:* Miss Col, BS, 62; Univ Ala, Tuscaloosa, PhD(org chem), 70. *Prof Exp:* Chemist, Liggett & Myers Tobacco Co, NC, 63-65; instr org chem, Univ Ala, Tuscaloosa, 68-69; sr develop chemist, Ciba-Geigy Corp, 70-76; plant mgr, Vega Chem, Inc, 77-78; tech dir, Kalama Specialty Chem, Inc, 79-80. *Mem:* Am Chem Soc. *Res:* Reaction mechanisms; organic synthesis and process development for textile auxiliaries; specialty and agricultural chemicals. *Mailing Add:* 4018 Coapites Pasadena TX 77504

WHEAT, ROBERT WAYNE, b Springfield, Mo, Nov 10, 26; m 48; c 3. MICROBIOLOGY, BIOCHEMISTRY. *Educ:* Wash Univ, PhD(microbiol), 55. *Prof Exp:* USPHS fel biochem, NIH, Md, 55-56; instr biochem, 56-58, assoc, 58-60, assoc prof microbiol, 66-74, ASST PROF BIOCHEM, SCH MED, DUKE UNIV, 60-, PROF MICROBIOL, 74- *Concurrent Pos:* NIH consult, 69-72. *Mem:* Am Chem Soc; Am Soc Biol Chem; Am Soc Microbiol. *Res:* Biochemistry of microorganisms, amino sugars and polysaccharides; cell surface antigens. *Mailing Add:* Dept of Microbiol & Biochem Duke Univ Med Ctr Durham NC 27710

WHEATCROFT, MERRILL GORDON, b Utica, Kans, Oct 20, 14; m 39; c 4. DENTAL PATHOLOGY. *Educ:* Univ Kansas City, DDS, 39. *Prof Exp:* Dent res officer, Naval Med Res Inst, Md, 49-52, head dent res, Naval Med Res Unit, Egypt, 52-55, head res & sci, Naval Dent Sch, 55-60; assoc prof dent res, 60-67, PROF PATH, UNIV TEX DENT BR, HOUSTON, 67- *Mem:* AAAS; Am Dent Asn; fel Am Col Dent; Int Asn Dent Res. *Res:* Changes in the contents of the gingival crevice and associated tissues in periodontal disease. *Mailing Add:* PO Box 20068 Houston TX 77025

WHEATLAND, DAVID ALAN, b Boston, Mass, Aug 27, 40; m 65; c 1. INORGANIC CHEMISTRY. *Educ:* Brown Univ, ScB, 63; Univ Md, PhD(inorg chem), 67. *Prof Exp:* Asst prof chem, Bowdoin Col, 67-73; RES CHEMIST, S D WARREN RES LAB, 73- *Concurrent Pos:* Petrol Res Fund grant, 68-70. *Res:* Reprographic research and development. *Mailing Add:* Stornway Rd Portland ME 04110

WHEATLEY, JOHN CHARLES, b Tucson, Ariz, Feb 17, 27; m 49; c 2. PHYSICS. *Educ:* Univ Pittsburgh, PhD(physics), 52. *Hon Degrees:* DSc, Leiden Univ, Neth, 75. *Prof Exp:* From instr to prof, Univ Ill, 52-67; PROF PHYSICS, UNIV CALIF, SAN DIEGO, 67- *Concurrent Pos:* Guggenheim fel, Univ Leiden, 54-55. *Honors & Awards:* Simon Prize, 66; Ninth Fritz London Award, 75. *Mem:* Nat Acad Sci. *Res:* Cryogenics; low temperature physics; experimental research at millikelvin temperatures with emphasis on properties of helium. *Mailing Add:* Dept of Physics B-019 Univ of Calif La Jolla CA 92093

WHEATLEY, VICTOR RICHARD, b London, Eng, Nov 4, 18; m 43; c 2. BIOCHEMISTRY. *Educ:* Univ London, BSc, 47, PhD(org chem), 50, DSc(chem, biochem), 68. *Prof Exp:* Biochemist, St Bartholomew's Hosp Med Col, London, 48-57; res assoc dermat, Univ Chicago, 57-59; sr res assoc, Stanford Univ, 59-62; ASSOC PROF DERMAT, MED CTR, NY UNIV, 62- *Concurrent Pos:* NIH fels, Med Ctr, NY Univ, 62-68. *Honors & Awards:* Bronze Medal, Am Acad Dermat, 58; Spec Award, Soc Cosmetic Chem, 62. *Mem:* Am Soc Biol Chemists; NY Zoological Soc; NY Acad Sci; Am Inst Chemists. *Res:* Biochemistry of skin, especially the lipid metabolism of skin. *Mailing Add:* Dept of Dermat NY Univ Med Ctr New York NY 10016

WHEATLEY, W(ILLIAM) A(RTHUR), b Deming, NMex, Nov 9, 23; m 45; c 4. ELECTRONICS. *Educ:* Univ Mich, BS, 47, MS, 48. *Prof Exp:* Res assoc electronics, Willow Run Res Ctr, Univ Mich, 48-50, res engr res admin, 50-55; vpres, Strand Eng Co, 55-60; vpres, Electronic Assistance Corp, 60-64, mgt consult, 64-68; mkt mgr, United Telecontrol Electronics, 68-70; gen mgr, Wave Energy Systs, Inc, Newtown, Pa, 70-72; COMMUN CONSULT, HARVEY J KRASNER ASSOCS INC, 72- *Mem:* Inst Elec & Electronics Engrs. *Res:* Analog computers; complex military system design; electronic equipment prototype design; field test; research administration; engineering management; management consulting. *Mailing Add:* 25 Bamm Hollow Rd Middletown NJ 07748

WHEATON, BURDETTE CARL, b Mankato, Minn, July 3, 38; m 68; c 3. ALGEBRA. *Educ:* Mankato State Col, BS, 59; Univ Iowa, MS, 61, PhD(math), 65. *Prof Exp:* Instr math, Univ Iowa, 59-63; asst prof, Western Ill Univ, 63-65; asst prof, 65-72, PROF MATH, MANKATO STATE UNIV, 72- *Mem:* Am Math Soc; Math Asn Am; Sigma Xi. *Res:* Abstract algebra, particularly group theory and group representations. *Mailing Add:* Dept of Math Mankato State Univ Mankato MN 56001

WHEATON, ELMER PAUL, b Elyria, Ohio, Aug 15, 09; m 33; c 2. PHYSICS, ENGINEERING. *Educ:* Pomona Col, BA, 33. *Prof Exp:* Sound technician, Columbia Motion Picture Studios, 33; riveter & assembler, Douglas Aircraft Co, 34-36, res engr, 36-40, asst chief res sect, 40-43 & eng labs, 43, spec asst to vpres eng, 43-44, on loan to radiation lab, Mass Inst Technol, 44, on loan to Rand Corp, 45, mgr appl physics lab, 45, chief dynamics & sound control, Missile Projs, 45-55, chief missiles engr, 55-58, dir missiles & space systs, 58, vpres eng, 58-60, vpres eng technol, 60-61, vpres eng & corp vpres, 61, dir, Astropower, Inc, 61; asst to pres, Lockheed Missiles & Space Co, Lockheed Aircraft Corp, 62, vpres & gen mgr, Space Prog Div, 62-63, vpres & gen mgr, Res & Develop Div, 63-74, vpres, Corp, 62-74, pres, Lockheed Petrol Serv Ltd, 72-74; CONSULT, 74- *Concurrent Pos:* Lectr, Guggenheim Aeronaut Lab, Calif Inst Technol, 41-54; mem spec indust comt missiles for res & develop, Off Secy Air Force, 54; consult, Adv Panel Aeronaut Res & Eng, Off Dir Defense, 57-59; mem comt ocean eng, Nat Acad Eng, 67-; consult & mem panel ocean eng, Nat Coun Marine Resources & Eng Develop, 68-69; mem, Calif State Marine Res Comt, 72-78, marine bd, Mat Acad Sci-Nat Acad Eng, adv panel, Int Decade Ocean Explor, NSF, 70-71 & Sea Grant Coord Coun, Univ Calif, 70- *Honors & Awards:* Cert Merit, Depts War & Navy, 47 & Off Sci Res & Develop; Robert M Thompson Award for outstanding civilian leadership, Navy League US, 71; Aerospaces Contrib to Soc Award, Am Inst Aeronaut & Astronaut, 78. *Mem:* AAAS; fel Am Inst Aeronaut & Astronaut; fel Am Astronaut Soc; fel Royal Aeronaut Soc; fel Marine Technol Soc (past pres). *Res:* Acoustics; electronics; aeronautical and systems engineering; flutter and vibration; missile and space systems engineering; aerospace management; ocean systems engineering and management; research and development management. *Mailing Add:* 127 Solana Rd Portola Valley CA 94205

WHEATON, GREGORY ALAN, b Muskegon, Mich, July 18, 47; m 73. ORGANIC CHEMISTRY. *Educ:* State Univ Iowa, BS, 69, MS, 73, PhD(org chem), 76. *Prof Exp:* Res chemist org chem, Atlantic Richfield Co, 76-81; RES SCIENTIST, PENNWALT CORP, 81- *Mem:* Am Chem Soc; Sigma Xi. *Res:* Homogeneous and heterogeneous catalysis in the conversion of petrochemical feedstocks to chemical intermediates, particularly partial oxidation of 2, 3 and 4 carbon olefins. *Mailing Add:* Pennwalt Corp 900 First Ave King of Prussia PA 19406

WHEATON, JONATHAN EDWARD, b Fullerton, Calif, Jan 22, 47; m 67; c 2. NEUROENDOCRINOLOGY. *Educ:* Univ Calif, Davis, BS, 69; Ore State Univ, MS, 70, PhD(animal physiol), 73. *Prof Exp:* Fel neuroendocrinol, Southwestern Med Sch, 73-75; asst prof, 75-80, ASSOC PROF PHYSIOL, UNIV MINN, ST PAUL, 80- *Mem:* Am Soc Animal Sci; Sigma Xi; Soc Study Reprod. *Res:* Control and effects of neurohormones; reproductive endocrinology. *Mailing Add:* Dept of Animal Sci Univ of Minn St Paul MN 55108

WHEATON, ROBERT MILLER, b Danbury, Ohio, Oct 11, 19; m 43, 67; c 5. INDUSTRIAL CHEMISTRY. *Educ:* Oberlin Col, AB, 41. *Prof Exp:* Chemist, Celotex Corp, 41; chemist & process specialist, Trojan Powder Co, 42-43, head process specialists, 44-45; chemist, 46-49, group leader res, 50-55, div leader, 56-71, ASSOC SCIENTIST, WESTERN DIV RES, DOW CHEM CO, 72- *Concurrent Pos:* Chmn, Gordon Res Conf Ion Exchange, 63. *Mem:* Am Chem Soc; Sigma Xi. *Res:* Synthesis, applications and properties of ion exchange resins. *Mailing Add:* 156 Warwick Dr Walnut Creek CA 94598

WHEATON, THOMAS ADAIR, b Orlando, Fla, Apr 5, 36; m 61; c 2. PLANT PHYSIOLOGY, HORTICULTURE. *Educ:* Univ Fla, BS, 58, MS, 60; Univ Calif, Davis, PhD(plant physiol), 63. *Prof Exp:* Asst horticulturist, 63-70, assoc prof hort & assoc horticulturist, 70-79, PROF & HORTICULTURIST, INST FOOD & AGR SCI, AGR RES & EDUC CTR, UNIV FLA, LAKE ALFRED, 79- *Mem:* Am Soc Plant Physiol; Am Soc Hort Sci. *Res:* Chilling injury in plants; nitrogen metabolism and growth regulation in citrus. *Mailing Add:* Univ Fla 700 Exp Sta Rd Lake Alfred FL 33850

WHEBY, MUNSEY S, b Roanoke, Va, Nov 19, 30; m 55; c 3. INTERNAL MEDICINE. *Educ:* Roanoke Col, BS, 51; Univ Va, MD, 55. *Prof Exp:* Asst chief hemat, Walter Reed Army Inst Res & Walter Reed Gen Hosp, 59-61, chief gastroenterol, Walter Reed Army Inst Res, 61-62, chief med div, US Army Trop Res Med Lab, 62-65; assoc prof med, Rutgers Med Sch, 65-66; assoc prof, 66-72, PROF MED, SCH MED, UNIV VA, 72- *Mem:* Am Fedn Clin Res; AMA; Am Soc Hemat. *Res:* Gastrointestinal absorption of iron; folic acid and B-12 metabolism. *Mailing Add:* Dept of Internal Med Univ of Va Sch of Med Charlottesville VA 22908

WHEDON, GEORGE DONALD, b Geneva, NY, July 4, 15; m 42; c 2. MEDICAL RESEARCH ADMINISTRATION, AEROSPACE MEDICINE. *Educ:* Hobart Col, AB, 36; Univ Rochester, MD, 41; Am Bd Internal Med, dipl, 50; Am Bd Nutrit, cert, 68. *Hon Degrees:* ScD, Hobart Col, 67 & Univ Rochester, 78. *Prof Exp:* Intern med, Mary Imogene Bassett Hosp, Cooperstown, NY, 41-42; asst, Sch Med & asst resident, Strong Mem Hosp, Univ Rochester, 42-44; from instr to asst prof, Cornell Univ, 44-52; chief metab dis br, 52-65, asst dir inst, 56-62, dir, 62-81, SR SCI ADVR, NAT INST ARTHRITIS, DIABETES, DIGESTIVE & KIDNEY DIS, 81- *Concurrent Pos:* USPHS fel, NY Hosp-Cornell Med Ctr, 51; from asst physician to physician, Outpatient Dept, NY Hosp-Cornell Med Ctr, 44-52; mem, Subcomt Calcium Comt Dietary Allowances, Food & Nutrit Bd, Nat Res Coun, 59-64; consult space med div, NASA, 63-; mem, Med Alumni Coun, Sch Med, Univ Rochester, 71-76, Trustees Coun, 71-76, vchmn, 73, chmn, 74-75; chmn, Adv Panel Med Prog to NASA, Am Inst Biol Sci, 71-76; chmn, Life Sci Comt, NASA, 74-78, mem, Space Prog Adv Coun, 74-78. *Honors & Awards:* Ayerst Award, Endocrine Soc, 74; Arnold D Tuttle Mem Award, Aerospace Med Asn, 78. *Mem:* AAAS; Am Rheumatism Asn; Am Gastroenterol Asn; Orthop Res Soc; Am Inst Nutrit. *Res:* Metabolic and physiological aspects of convalescence and immobilization; metabolic and kinetic studies of disorders of bone; space medicine, particularly musculoskeletal metabolism. *Mailing Add:* Nat Inst of Arthritis Metab & Digestive Dis Bethesda MD 20014

WHEEDEN, RICHARD LEE, b Baltimore, Md, Nov 29, 40; m 62; c 2. MATHEMATICS. *Educ:* Johns Hopkins Univ, AB, 61; Univ Chicago, MS, 62, PhD(math), 65. *Prof Exp:* Instr math, Univ Chicago, 65-66; mem, Inst Adv Study, 66-67; from asst prof to assoc prof, 67-74, PROF MATH, RUTGERS UNIV, NEW BRUNSWICK, 74- *Concurrent Pos:* NSF fel, 66-67. *Mem:* Am Math Soc. *Res:* Harmonic analysis. *Mailing Add:* Dept of Math Rutgers Univ New Brunswick NJ 08903

WHEELER, ALBERT HAROLD, b St Louis, Mo, Dec 11, 15; m 38; c 3. BACTERIOLOGY. *Educ:* Lincoln Univ, AB, 36; Iowa State Col, MS, 37; Univ Mich, MSPH, 38, DrPH, 44. *Prof Exp:* Clin technician, Col Med, Howard Univ, 38-40; asst, 41-44, res assoc, Univ Hosp, 44-52, asst prof bact, 52-58, ASSOC PROF BACT, MED SCH, UNIV MICH, ANN ARBOR, 59-, ASSOC PROF MICROBIOL, 74- *Concurrent Pos:* Consult, Serol Lab, Univ Hosp, Univ Mich. *Mem:* Am Asn Immunol. *Res:* Active and passive immunity in experimental syphilis; serodiagnosis of syphilis; serology of biologic false positive reactions in syphilis; treponemicidal activity of various animal sera and complements. *Mailing Add:* 234 Eighth St Ann Arbor MI 48103

WHEELER, ALFRED GEORGE, JR, b Nebraska City, Nebr, Apr 11, 44. ENTOMOLOGY. *Educ:* Grinnell Col, BA, 66; Cornell Univ, PhD(insect ecol), 71. *Prof Exp:* ENTOMOLOGIST, BUR PLANT INDUST, PA DEPT AGR, 71- *Concurrent Pos:* Consult, Dames & Moore, 74-; adj asst prof, Pa State Univ, 73-81, adj assoc prof, 81- *Mem:* Entom Soc Am. *Res:* Life history studies of Hemiptera-Heteroptera, especially Miridae; biology of insects affecting ornamental plants; study of insect-plant associations. *Mailing Add:* Bur Plant Indust Pa Dept Agr 2301 N Cameron St Harrisburg PA 17110

WHEELER, ALFRED PORTIUS, b Brooklyn, NY, Sept 16, 47; m 69; c 3. PHYSIOLOGY, CELL BIOLOGY. *Educ:* Butler Univ, BS, 69; Duke Univ, PhD(zool), 75. *Prof Exp:* Instr, Duke Univ, 74-76; ASST PROF ZOOL, CLEMSON UNIV, 76- *Concurrent Pos:* Vis prof, Duke Univ, 77- *Mem:* Sigma Xi; Am Soc Zoologists. *Res:* Physiology of biomineralization, especially in molluscs; physiology and subcellular localization of carbonic anhydrase. *Mailing Add:* Dept Zool Clemson Univ Clemson SC 29631

WHEELER, ALLAN GORDON, b Gary, Ind, July 12, 23; m 49; c 4. PHARMACOLOGY, PHYSIOLOGY. *Educ:* Valparaiso Univ, BA, 48; Univ Wis, MA, 50. *Prof Exp:* Asst pharmacol & anesthesiol, Univ Wis, 50-54; assoc pharmacologist, Res Ctr, Mead Johnson & Co, Ind, 54-58, sr pharmacologist, 54-59, group leader toxicol, 59-68; SUPVR INDUST TOXICOL, BIO-MED RES LAB, ICI US, INC, 68- *Mem:* Am Indust Hyg Asn; Drug Info Asn; Environ Mutagen Soc; Sigma Xi; Am Asn Lab Animal Sci. *Res:* Anesthesiology; toxicology. *Mailing Add:* Bio-Med Res Lab ICI US Inc Concord Pike & New Murphy Rd Wilmington DE 19897

WHEELER, BERNICE MARION, b Winsted, Conn, June 30, 15. ZOOLOGY. *Educ:* Conn Col, AB, 37; Smith Col, MA, 39; Yale Univ, PhD(zool), 48. *Prof Exp:* Asst zool, Smith Col, 37-39; instr, Westbrook Jr Col, 39-42; asst, Yale Univ, 42-47; from instr to assoc prof, 47-66, prof, 66-80, EMER PROF ZOOL, CONN COL, 80- *Concurrent Pos:* Ford Found fel, 54-55. *Mem:* Am Genetic Asn. *Res:* Genetics; ecology; evolution. *Mailing Add:* Dept of Zool Conn Col PO Box 1553 New London CT 06320

WHEELER, CHARLES MERVYN, JR, b Moundsville, WVa, Oct 29, 21; m 43; c 6. PHYSICAL CHEMISTRY. *Educ:* WVa Univ, BS, 47, MS, 49, PhD(chem), 51. *Prof Exp:* Asst prof, 50-55, dean students, 60-61, assoc prof, 55-80, PROF CHEM, UNIV NH, 80- *Concurrent Pos:* Consult, Lima, 57, 59 & 60; chmn postgrad chem dept, Am Col, Madurai, India, 68-69. *Mem:* Am Chem Soc. *Res:* Metal-ion complexes. *Mailing Add:* Parsons Hall Univ of NH Durham NH 03824

WHEELER, CLAYTON EUGENE, JR, b Viroqua, Wis, June 30, 17; m 52; c 3. DERMATOLOGY. *Educ:* Univ Wis, BA, 38, MD, 41; Am Bd Dermat, dipl, 51. *Prof Exp:* Resident & instr internal med, Med Sch, Univ Mich, 42-44, resident & instr dermat, 49-51; from asst prof to prof, Sch Med, Univ Va, 51-62; chief div, 62-72, PROF DERMAT, SCH MED, UNIV NC, CHAPEL HILL, 62-, CHMN DEPT, 72- *Concurrent Pos:* Res fel endocrinol & metab, Univ Mich, 47-48; chmn, Residency Rev Comt Dermat; rep, Am Bd Med Specialties; pres, Am Bd Dermat. *Honors & Awards:* Rothman Award, 79. *Mem:* Soc Invest Dermat (pres, 73-74); AMA; Am Acad Dermat; Asn Prof Dermat (pres, 75-76). *Res:* Viral diseases of skin, especially Herpes simplex; tissue culture of skin and contact sensitivity. *Mailing Add:* Dept of Dermat NC Mem Hosp Chapel Hill NC 27514

WHEELER, DARRELL DEANE, b West Liberty, Ky, Feb 24, 39; m 63; c 2. PHYSIOLOGY. *Educ:* Transylvania Col, AB, 62; Univ Ky, PhD(physiol), 67. *Prof Exp:* Asst prof, 68-75, assoc prof, 75-81, PROF PHYSIOL, MED UNIV SC, 81- *Concurrent Pos:* NIH fel physiol & biophys, Univ Ky, 67-68; NIH res grants, 69-72 & 75- *Mem:* Am Physiol Soc; AAAS. *Res:* Cell physiology; aging and membrane transport in the nervous system. *Mailing Add:* Dept of Physiol Med Univ of SC Charleston SC 29403

WHEELER, DESMOND MICHAEL SHERLOCK, b Northwich, Cheshire, Eng, Apr 18, 29; m 53. ORGANIC CHEMISTRY. *Educ:* Nat Univ Ireland, BSc, 50, PhD(chem), 55, DSc, 77; DSc, 77; Univ Dublin, MA, 54. *Prof Exp:* Dep lectr phys chem, Trinity Col, Dublin, 52-53, asst lectr org chem, 53-55; res fel chem, Harvard Univ, 55-58; asst prof chem, Univ Nebr, 58-59 & Univ SC, 59-61; from asst prof to assoc prof, 61-66, PROF CHEM, UNIV NEBR, LINCOLN, 66- *Concurrent Pos:* Res fel, Univ Sussex, 67-68; NATO sr fel, Sch Pharm, Univ London, 70; vis scholar, Columbia Univ, 78. *Mem:* Am Chem Soc; Royal Soc Chem; Inst Chem Ireland. *Res:* Chemistry of natural products; synthesis of diterpenoid acids; stereochemistry of reductions; structures of plant extractives; naturally occurring quinones; photochemistry. *Mailing Add:* Dept of Chem Univ of Nebr Lincoln NE 68588

WHEELER, DONALD ALSOP, b Philadlephia, Pa, Aug 16, 31; m 53; c 4. HUMAN GENETICS, EVOLUTION. *Educ:* Mich State Univ, BS, 53, MS, 56; Cornell Univ, PhD(plant breeding), 61. *Prof Exp:* Instr biol, Delta Col, 61-65, head dept, 63-65; assoc prof, 65-73, asst head dept, 71-73, PROF BIOL, EDINBORO STATE COL, 73- *Mem:* Sigma Xi; AAAS. *Mailing Add:* Sherrod Hill Rd RD 2 Edinboro PA 16412

WHEELER, DONALD BINGHAM, JR, b Cleveland, Ohio, May 24, 17. PHYSICS. *Educ:* Lehigh Univ, BS, 38; Calif Inst Technol, PhD(physics), 47. *Prof Exp:* Instr physics, Occidental Col, 41-42; asst prof, 47-57, ASSOC PROF PHYSICS, LEHIGH UNIV, 57- *Mem:* Am Phys Soc. *Res:* Electric dipole moment determinations; microwave propagation; dispersion and absorption of electromagnetic waves in fatty acids. *Mailing Add:* Dept of Physics Lehigh Univ Bethlehem PA 18015

WHEELER, DONALD JEFFERSON, b Oklahoma City, Okla, Sept 30, 44; m 66; c 2. APPLIED STATISTICS, MATHEMATICAL STATISTICS. *Educ:* Univ Tex, BA, 66; Southern Methodist Univ, MS, 68, PhD(statist), 70. *Prof Exp:* ASSOC PROF STATIST, UNIV TENN, KNOXVILLE, 70- *Concurrent Pos:* Consult, US Steel. *Mem:* Am Statist Asn; Am Soc Qual Control. *Res:* Applications of statistics in marketing and behavioral science. *Mailing Add:* Dept Statist Univ Tenn Knoxville TN 37916

WHEELER, EDWARD NORWOOD, b Yancey, Tex, Oct 11, 27; m 50; c 5. ORGANIC CHEMISTRY. *Educ:* Tex Col Arts & Indust, BS, 47, BSCE, 49; Univ Tex, MA, 51, PhD(org chem), 53. *Prof Exp:* Res chemist, 53-55, group leader, 55-62, sect head, 62-67, dir chem res, 67-69, dir res, Tech Ctr, 69-72, dir develop, 72-74, dir planning, 74-75, dir res, develop & planning, 75-76, vpres res, develop & planning, 76-79, VPRES RES & DEVELOP, CELANESE CHEM CO, 79- *Mem:* AAAS; Am Chem Soc; NY Acad Sci; Am Inst Chem Engrs. *Res:* Acrylic acid; vinyl monomers; propiolactone reactions; palladium-olefin reactions; liquid phase oxidation of carbonyl compounds and olefins; process development and synthesis of petrochemicals. *Mailing Add:* 9238 Moss Haven Dallas TX 75231

WHEELER, EDWARD STUBBS, b Philadelphia, Pa, June 3, 27; m 52; c 4. RESEARCH ADMINISTRATION. *Educ:* Haverford Col, AB, 48; Cornell Univ, PhD(chem), 52. *Prof Exp:* Asst chem, Cornell Univ, 48-51; assoc chemist org chem res, Atlantic Ref Co, 52-53, supv chemist, 53-59; mgr adhesives div, Amchem Prods, Inc, 59-62; mgr thermosetting polymer develop, Insulating Mat Dept, Gen Elec Co, 63-66, mgr-engr, Insulator Dept, 66-71, consult, Corp Exec Staff, 71-75; VPRES TECHNOL, LAPP DIV, INTERPACE CORP, 75- *Concurrent Pos:* Mem bd dirs, Am Nat Metric Coun, 74-75. *Mem:* AAAS; Am Chem Soc; Soc Plastics Eng; Inst Elec & Electronics Engrs; Am Soc Testing & Mat. *Res:* Synthetic organic chemistry; polymers; electrical insulation; insulators; engineering standards; metric conversion. *Mailing Add:* Lapp Div Interpace Corp Gilbert St LeRoy NY 14482

WHEELER, FRANK CARLISLE, b Millinocket, Maine, Jan 26, 17; m 46; c 2. PHARMACEUTICAL CHEMISTRY. *Educ:* Mass Col Pharm, BS, 40, MS, 42; Purdue Univ, PhD(pharmaceut chem), 49. *Prof Exp:* Anal chemist, Burroughs Wellcome & Co, 42-43; pharmaceut chemist, 49-58, chief ampoule pilot plant, 58-65, head, 65-66, dir, Parenteral Opers Div, 66-75, DIR QUAL CONTROL & TECH SERV, ELI LILLY & CO, 75- *Mem:* Am Chem Soc; Am Pharmaceut Asn; Pharmaceut Mfrs Asn; Parenteral Drug Asn. *Res:* Pharmaceutical development; manufacture and control of chiefly parenteral products. *Mailing Add:* 6815 Farmleigh Dr Indianapolis IN 46220

WHEELER, GEORGE LAWRENCE, b Rockville Center, NY, June 16, 44; m 68; c 1. PHYSICAL CHEMISTRY, BIOCHEMISTRY. *Educ:* Cath Univ Am, AB, 67; Univ Md, PhD(phys chem), 73. *Prof Exp:* Grad res asst phys chem, Univ Md, 69-73; res assoc phys chem, Yale Univ, 73-75, res assoc biochem, Med Sch, 75-77; asst prof, 77-80, ASSOC PROF CHEM, UNIV NEW HAVEN, 80- *Concurrent Pos:* NSF/Inst Sci Equip Prog grant, Univ New Haven, 77- *Mem:* Am Chem Soc; Am Crystallog Asn. *Res:* Biochemistry of light activated enzymes in the retina; intermolecular interactions in molecular crystals. *Mailing Add:* Dept of Chem 300 Orange Ave West Haven CT 06516

WHEELER, GEORGE WILLIS, b Mantorville, Minn, Sept 16, 22; m 44; c 2. PHYSICS. *Educ:* Macalester Col, BA, 44; Harvard Univ, SM, 48, PhD, 50. *Hon Degrees:* ScD, Macalester Col, 65. *Prof Exp:* Asst appl physics, Harvard Univ, 49-50; mem tech staff, 50-53, spec systs engr, 53-55, dir transmission systs develop, 55-59, dir mil commun systs eng, 59-64, dir spec defense studies, Madison, 64-74, MEM STAFF, BELL TEL LABS, ILL, 74- *Mem:* Sr mem Inst Elec & Electronics Eng; Am Phys Soc; Sigma Xi. *Res:* Microwaves and antenna; communications and radar systems. *Mailing Add:* Bell Tel Labs Naperville Rd Naperville IL 60540

WHEELER, GILBERT VERNON, b Sour Lake, Tex, July 5, 22; m 42; c 2. CHEMISTRY. *Educ:* Millikin Univ, BS, 44; Univ Ill, MS, 47. *Prof Exp:* Instr physics, Millikin Univ, 43-44; physicist, Res & Develop Dept, Phillips Petrol Co, 48-51, physicist, Atomic Energy Div, 52-53, reactor engr, 51-52, supvr spectrochem lab, 53-63, supvr spectros sect, 63-65; supvr spectros sect, Allied Chem Corp, 65-78; staff scientist, Exxon Nuclear Idaho, 78-81; RETIRED. *Concurrent Pos:* Int del, Soc Appl Spectros, 75, 77 & 79. *Mem:* Soc Appl Spectros (pres, 73); Am Soc Mass Spectrometry. *Res:* Graphite furnaces; inductive coupled plasmas and sputter sources for spectroscopy; isotopic and isotope dilution mass spectrometry. *Mailing Add:* Box 235 A Salmon ID 83467

WHEELER, GLYNN PEARCE, b Milan, Tenn, Oct 13, 19; m 43; c 2. BIOCHEMISTRY. *Educ:* Vanderbilt Univ, AB, 41; Univ Akron, MS, 47; Vanderbilt Univ, PhD(org chem), 50. *Prof Exp:* Anal chemist, Tenn Coal, Iron & RR Co, Ala, 41; shift supvr, Ala Ord Works, 42; res chemist, B F Goodrich Co, Ohio, 42-46; chemist, 46-48, biochemist, 50-56, head intermediary metab sect, 56-66, HEAD CANCER BIOCHEM DIV, SOUTHERN RES INST, 66- *Mem:* AAAS; Am Chem Soc; Cell Kinetics Soc; Am Asn Cancer Res; Am Soc Biol Chem. *Res:* Cancer biochemistry; chemotherapy of cancer; nucleic acids. *Mailing Add:* Southern Res Inst Biochem Dept 2000 Ninth Ave S Birmingham AL 35205

WHEELER, HAROLD A(LDEN), b St Paul, Minn, May 10, 03; m 26; c 3. RADIO ENGINEERING. *Educ:* George Washington Univ, BS, 25. *Hon Degrees:* DSc, George Washington Univ, 72; DEng, Stevens Inst Technol, 78. *Prof Exp:* Engr, Hazeltine Corp, NJ, 24-29, engr, Hazeltine Serv Corp, NY, 29-39, vpres & chief consult engr, Hazeltine Electronics Corp, 39-46; pres, Wheeler Labs, Inc, 47-68; vpres & dir, 59-65, chmn bd, 65-77, chief scientist, 68-77, EMER DIR & CHMN BD, HAZELTINE CORP, 77- *Concurrent Pos:* Consult, Off Secy Defense, 50-64 & Defense Sci Bd, 63-64. *Honors & Awards:* Modern Pioneer Award, Nat Asn Mfrs, 40; Liebmann Prize, Inst Radio Engrs, 40, Medal of Honor, 64; Armstrong Medal, Radio Club Am, 64. *Mem:* Fel Inst Elec & Electronics Engrs; assoc mem Brit Inst Elec Engrs. *Res:* Radio receivers and transmitters; television; radar; antennas; microwaves; communication network theory; conformal mapping of fields; tracking radar for guided missile systems; submarine and subsurface radio communication; radio guidance of aircraft. *Mailing Add:* 59 Derby Pl Smithtown NY 11787

WHEELER, HARRY ERNEST, b WCharleston, Vt, Jan 25, 19; m 44. PHYTOPATHOLOGY. *Educ:* Univ Vt, BS, 41; La State Univ, MS, 47, PhD(bot), 49. *Prof Exp:* Lab asst bot & bact, Univ Vt, 39-41; asst bot & plant path, La State Univ, 46-49, from asst prof to prof bot & plant path, 49-67; PROF PLANT PATH, UNIV KY, 67- *Concurrent Pos:* Vis investr & res partic, Biol Div, Oak Ridge Nat Lab, 49-50; Guggenheim fel, Biol Labs, Harvard Univ, 58. *Mem:* AAAS; Bot Soc Am; Am Phytopath Soc; Mycol Soc Am. *Res:* Genetics and cytology of fungi; host relations of plant path- ogens; electron microscopy. *Mailing Add:* Dept of Plant Path Univ of Ky Lexington KY 40506

WHEELER, HARRY OGDEN, microbiology, immunology, see previous edition

WHEELER, HENRY ORSON, b Los Angeles, Calif, Apr 7, 24; m 47; c 2. MEDICINE. *Educ:* Harvard Med Sch, MD, 51. *Prof Exp:* Assoc prof med, Col Physicians & Surgeons, Columbia Univ, 62-68; PROF MED, SCH MED, UNIV CALIF, SAN DIEGO, 68- *Mem:* Fedn Am Socs Exp Biol; AAAS; Am Soc Clin Invest; Am Physiol Soc. *Res:* Hepatic physiology; bile formation; gallbladder; ion transport. *Mailing Add:* Dept of Med Sch of Med Univ of Calif at San Diego La Jolla CA 92037

WHEELER, JAMES DONLAN, b St Louis, Mo, July 19, 23. PHARMACEUTICAL CHEMISTRY, BIOCHEMISTRY. *Educ:* St Louis Univ, AB, 47, PhL, 48, MS, 52, STL, 56; Univ Mo-Kansas City, PhD(pharmaceut chem), 65. *Prof Exp:* Instr chem high sch, St Louis Univ, 50-51; from instr to assoc prof, 56-74, head dept, 67-74, PROF CHEM, ROCKHURST COL, 74- *Mem:* AAAS; Am Chem Soc; NY Acad Sci; Nat Sci Teachers Asn. *Res:* Biochemistry and physiology of the effects of training and exercise; learning theory as applied to freshman chemistry students. *Mailing Add:* Rockhurst Col 5225 Troost Kansas City MO 64110

WHEELER, JAMES ENGLISH, b Durham, NC, May 5, 38; m 66; c 3. PATHOLOGY. *Educ:* Harvard Univ, AB, 58; Johns Hopkins Univ, MD, 62. *Prof Exp:* Intern med, Johns Hopkins Univ, 62-63, resident path, 63-66; resident path, State Univ NY Upstate Med Ctr, 69-70; assoc, 70-72, asst prof path, 72-76, ASSOC PROF PATH & OBSTET & GYNEC, SCH MED, UNIV PA, 76- *Concurrent Pos:* USPHS cancer control sr clin trainee, Mem Hosp Cancer & Allied Dis, New York, 66-67. *Mem:* Fel Int Acad Path; AAAS; Int Soc Gynec Pathologists. *Res:* Surgical and gynecological pathology. *Mailing Add:* Dept of Path Hosp of the Univ of Pa Philadelphia PA 19104

WHEELER, JAMES WILLIAM, JR, b Clarksburg, WVa, Oct 2, 34; m 57; c 1. ORGANIC CHEMISTRY. *Educ:* Antioch Col, BS, 57; Stanford Univ, MS, 59, PhD(chem), 62. *Prof Exp:* NSF fel chem, Cornell Univ, 63-64, NIH trainee, 64; from asst prof to assoc prof, 64-71, NIH spec fel, 71-72, PROF CHEM, HOWARD UNIV, 71- *Mem:* AAAS; Am Chem Soc; Am Soc Mass Spectros. *Res:* Chemistry of arthropod and mammalian pheromones, small ring compounds and monoterpenes. *Mailing Add:* Dept of Chem Howard Univ Washington DC 20059

WHEELER, JEANETTE NORRIS, b Newton, Iowa, May 21, 18; m 41; c 1. ENTOMOLOGY. *Educ:* Univ NDak, BA, 39, MS, 56, PhD, 62. *Prof Exp:* From instr biol to asst prof, Univ NDak, 46-65, res assoc, 65-67; RES ASSOC, DESERT RES INST, UNIV NEV SYST, RENO, 67- *Concurrent Pos:* Res assoc entom, Natural Hist Mus, Los Angeles County, 76- *Mem:* Entom Soc Am. *Res:* Taxonomy and morphology of the ant larvae; desert ants; ants of Nevada. *Mailing Add:* Desert Res Inst Univ of Nev Syst Reno NV 89506

WHEELER, JOE DARR, b Dallas, Tex, Dec 29, 30; m 55; c 2. CHEMICAL ENGINEERING, THERMODYNAMICS. *Educ:* Rice Univ, BA, 52, BS, 53; Purdue Univ, PhD(chem eng), 64. *Prof Exp:* Foreman chem eng, Am Cyanamid Co, 53; salesman houses, S R Franck & Co, 54; chem engr, Humble Oil & Refining Co, 57-59; SR RES ENGR, EXXON PROD RES CO, 63- *Res:* Thermodynamics of non-ideal mixtures; applied statistics; fluid mechanics; permafrost drilling. *Mailing Add:* 1964 Winrock Houston TX 77057

WHEELER, JOHN ARCHIBALD, b Jacksonville, Fla, July 9, 11; m 35; c 3. THEORETICAL PHYSICS. *Educ:* Johns Hopkins Univ, PhD(physics), 33. *Hon Degrees:* ScD, Univ NC, 59, Yale Univ, 74; PhD, Univ Uppsala, 75. *Prof Exp:* Nat Res Coun fel, NY Univ & Copenhagen Univ, 33-35; from asst prof to assoc prof physics, Univ NC, 35-38; asst prof, Princeton Univ, 38-42, physicist atomic energy proj, 39-42; physicist, Metall Lab, Univ Chicago, 42-43, E I du Pont de Nemours & Co, Del, 43-44, Hanford Eng Works, Wash, 44-45 & Los Alamos Sci Lab, 50-53; from assoc prof to prof, 45-66, Joseph Henry prof, 66-76, EMER PROF PHYSICS, PRINCETON UNIV, 76-; DIR CTR THEORET PHYSICS, UNIV TEX, AUSTIN, 76-, JANE & ROLAND BLUMBERG PROF PHYSICS, 80- *Concurrent Pos:* US rep cosmic ray comn, Int Union Pure & Appl Physics, Poland, 47, vpres, Union, 51-54; Guggenheim fel, Univ Paris & Copenhagen Univ, 49-50; dir proj Matterhorn, Princeton Univ, 51-53; Lorentz prof, Univ Leiden, 56; mem adv comt, Oak Ridge Nat Lab, 57-67; sci adv, US Senate Del, Conf NATO Parliamentarians, France, 57; mem, Joint Congressional Comt Atomic Energy, 58; proj chmn, Dept Defense Advan, Res Proj Agency, 58; consult, AEC; trustee, Battelle Mem Inst, 60-; Fulbright prof, Kyoto Univ, 62; chmn joint comt on hist theoret physics in 20th century, Am Phys Soc-Am Philos Soc, 62-; vis fel, Clare Col, Cambridge Univ, 64; chmn, US Gen Adv Comt Arms Control & Disarmament, 69-76; Battelle Mem prof, Univ Wash, 75. *Honors & Awards:* Morrison Prize, NY Acad Sci, 46; Einstein Prize, Strauss Found, 66; Enrico Fermi Award, AEC, 68; Franklin Medal, Franklin Inst, 69; Nat Medal Sci, 71. *Mem:* Nat Acad Sci; fel Am Phys Soc (pres, 66); Am Philos Soc (vpres, 71-73); Am Math Soc; Am Acad Arts & Sci. *Res:* Atomic and nuclear physics; scattering theory; fission; nuclear chain reactors; direct electromagnetic interaction between particles; mathematics of semiclassical analysis of physical processes; mu-meson; relativity; space-time and geometrodynamics. *Mailing Add:* Dept of Physics Univ of Tex Austin TX 79712

WHEELER, JOHN C, b Urbana, Ill, Mar 26, 41; m 63; c 1. THEORETICAL CHEMISTRY, CHEMICAL PHYSICS. *Educ:* Oberlin Col, BA, 63; Cornell Univ, PhD(theoret chem), 68. *Prof Exp:* NSF fel chem, Harvard Univ, 67-69; from asst prof to assoc prof 69-81, PROF CHEM, UNIV CALIF, SAN DIEGO, 81- *Concurrent Pos:* Alfred P Sloan Found fel, 72-76. *Mem:* Sigma Xi; Am Phys Soc; Am Chem Soc. *Res:* Statistical mechanics and thermodynamics of single and multi component systems, phase transitions and critical phenomena; rigorous bounds in statistical mechanics and thermodynamics; equilibrium polymerization and polymer solutions; reconstruction of densities from modified moments; surface properties of solids from modified moments. *Mailing Add:* Dept Chem B014 Univ Calif La Jolla CA 92093

WHEELER, JOHN CRAIG, b Glendale, Calif, Apr 5, 43; m 66; c 2. THEORETICAL ASTROPHYSICS. *Educ:* Mass Inst Technol, BS, 65; Univ Colo, PhD(physics), 69. *Prof Exp:* Res fel, Calif Inst Technol, 69-71; asst prof astron, Harvard Univ, 71-74; assoc prof, 74-80, PROF ASTRON & DIR, CTR THEORET PHYSICS, UNIV TEX, AUSTIN, 80- *Mem:* Am Astron Soc; Sigma Xi; Int Astron Union. *Res:* High energy and relativistic astrophysics; supernova hydrodynamics; black hole physics; active nuclei of galaxies; compact objects in binary systems. *Mailing Add:* Dept of Astron Univ of Tex Austin TX 78712

WHEELER, JOHN OLIVER, b Mussoorie, India, Dec 19, 24; m 52; c 2. GEOLOGY. *Educ:* Univ BC, BASc, 47; Columbia Univ, PhD(geol), 56. *Prof Exp:* Asst geol, Columbia Univ, 49-51; tech officer, 52-55, geologist, 56-67, head cordilleran & Pac margins sect, 67-70, chief regional & econ geol div, 70-73, dep dir, 73-79, RES SCIENTIST, GEOL SURV CAN, 79- *Concurrent Pos:* Vis prof, Univ Toronto, 72. *Mem:* Fel Royal Soc Can; fel Geol Soc Am; Geol Asn Can (pres, 70-71); Can Inst Mining & Metall; Can Geosci Coun (pres, 81). *Res:* Geological mapping in Central and Southern Yukon and Southeastern British Columbia; glacial geology in Southern Yukon; tectonics and structure of southern part of Western Canadian cordillera; recent glacier fluctuations of Selkirk Mountains; tectonics of Canadian cordillera and Canada. *Mailing Add:* Cordilleran Div Geol Surv Can 1001 W Pender St Vancouver BC V6B 1R8 Can

WHEELER, KEITH WILSON, b Iowa City, Iowa, Jan 9, 18; m 40; c 2. INFORMATION SCIENCE. *Educ:* Knox Col, AB, 38; Purdue Univ, MS, 40, PhD(org chem), 44. *Prof Exp:* Asst, Purdue Univ, 39-43; res chemist, William S Merrell Co, Ohio, 43-56, head records off, 57-64, head sci info dept, 64-71; sr prin investr, Tech Info Serv Dept, 71-80, SR RES ASSOC, PLANNING DEPT, MEAD JOHNSON RES CTR, 80- *Mem:* Fel AAAS; fel Am Inst Chemists; Sigma Xi; Am Chem Soc; Drug Info Asn. *Res:* Documentation. *Mailing Add:* Res Admin Dept Mead Johnson Res Ctr Evansville IN 47721

WHEELER, KENNETH THEODORE, JR, b Dover, NH, Sept 11, 40; m 80. BIOPHYSICS, RADIATION BIOLOGY. *Educ:* Harvard Univ, BA, 62; Wesleyan Univ, MAT, 63; Univ Kans, PhD(radiation biophys), 70. *Prof Exp:* Asst radiation biologist, Colo State Univ, 70-72, asst prof radiation biol, 72; from asst prof to assoc prof neurol surg & radiol, Med Sch, Univ Calif, San Francisco, 72-76; assoc prof radiation oncol, Univ Rochester, 76-81; ASSOC PROF RADIATION MED, RI HOSP, BROWN UNIV, 81- *Mem:* Radiation Res Soc; Biophys Soc; Am Asn Cancer Res; Sigma Xi. *Res:* In vivo DNA damage and repair in normal nondividing tissue and tumor tissue; development of combined modality therapy for brain tumors; radiation oncology in radiology and radiation biology and biophysics; molecular mechanisms of tumor cell heterogeneity. *Mailing Add:* Dept Radiation Onclo 593 Eddy St Rhode Island Hosp Providence RI 02828

WHEELER, LARRY MEADE, pharmaceutical chemistry, deceased

WHEELER, LAWRENCE, b Indianapolis, Ind, Apr 4, 23; m 46; c 2. ENVIRONMENTAL PSYCHOLOGY, PSYCHOPHYSICS. *Educ:* Ind Univ, AB, 48, MA, 50, PhD(psychol), 62. *Prof Exp:* From res asst to teaching asst psychol, Ind Univ, 45-50; indust engr electronics, Sarkes Tarzian Inc, 53-58; from res assoc to instr psychol, Ind Univ, 58-63; from asst prof to assoc prof psychol, Calif State Col Hayward, 64-69; PROF PSYCHOL & OPTICAL SCI, UNIV ARIZ, 69-, CHMN DEPT PSYCHOL, 75- *Concurrent Pos:* Dir behav res, Archonics Corp, 58-80; fel life sci, Carnegie Inst Wash, Nat Phys Lab, Teddington, Eng, 63-64. *Mem:* Am Psychol Asn; Sigma Xi; AAAS. *Res:* Visual psychophysics for evaluation of image quality and information retrieval; environmental psychology; assessment of user responses to constructed environments. *Mailing Add:* Dept of Psychol Col of Lib Arts Univ of Ariz Tucson AZ 85721

WHEELER, LEWIS TURNER, b Houston, Tex, Sept 28, 40. MECHANICS. *Educ:* Univ Houston, BS, 63, MS, 64; Calif Inst Technol, PhD, 69. *Prof Exp:* From asst prof to assoc prof, 68-76, PROF MECH ENG & MATH, UNIV HOUSTON, 76- *Concurrent Pos:* NSF grants, 69-71 & 72- *Mem:* Assoc Am Soc Mech Engrs; Soc Indust & Appl Math; Soc Natural Philos; Am Acad Mech. *Res:* Mathematical theory of elasticity; wave propagation in solids. *Mailing Add:* Dept of Mech Eng Univ of Houston Houston TX 77004

WHEELER, MARSHALL RALPH, b Carlinville, Ill, Apr 7, 17; m 44, 66; c 3. ZOOLOGY, GENETICS. *Educ:* Baylor Univ, BA, 39; Univ Tex, PhD(genetics), 47. *Prof Exp:* From instr to prof, 47-77, EMER PROF ZOOL, UNIV TEX, AUSTIN, 77- *Concurrent Pos:* Gosney fel, Calif Inst Technol, 49-50. *Mem:* Genetics Soc Am; Am Soc Nat; Soc Study Evolution; Soc Syst Zool; Entom Soc Am. *Res:* Speciation and taxonomy in Drosophila; biology of acalyptrate Diptera; insect cytogenetics. *Mailing Add:* Dept of Zool Univ of Tex Austin TX 78712

WHEELER, MARY FANETT, b Cuero, Tex, Dec 21, 38; m 63; c 1. NUMERICAL ANALYSIS. *Educ:* Univ Tex, BA, 60, MA, 63, PhD(math), 71. *Prof Exp:* Programmer math, Univ Tex Comput Ctr, 61-65; from programmer to instr, 65-73, from asst prof to assoc prof, 73-81, PROF MATH SCI, RICE UNIV, 81- *Mem:* Am Math Soc; Soc Indust & Appl Math. *Res:* Numerical solution of partial and ordinary differential equations. *Mailing Add:* Dept of Math Sci Rice Univ Houston TX 77001

WHEELER, MICHAEL HUGH, b Rolla, Mo, Nov 13, 40; m 69; c 1. BIOCHEMISTRY, BIOLOGY. *Educ:* Tex A&M Univ, BS, 65, MS, 70. *Prof Exp:* Microbiologist, Wadley Inst Molecular Biol, 71-72; RES CHEMIST, NAT COTTON PATH RES LAB, SCI & EDUC ADMIN, USDA, 72- *Mem:* Electron Microscope Soc Am; Am Chem Soc; Am Phytopath Soc. *Res:* Biochemical and utrastructural aspects of fungal physiology and morphogenesis; melanogenesis; cell wall composition; nuclear behavior and host-plant, fungal-parasite interactions. *Mailing Add:* 1003 Timm Dr College Station TX 77840

WHEELER, NICHOLAS ALLAN, b The Dalles, Ore, May 24, 33; m 62; c 2. MATHEMATICAL PHYSICS. *Educ:* Reed Col, BA, 55; Brandeis Univ, PhD(physics), 60. *Prof Exp:* NSF fel, State Univ Utrecht & Europ Orgn Nuclear Res, 60-62; res assoc physics, Brandeis Univ, 62-63; asst prof, 63-65, assoc prof, 65-77, PROF PHYSICS, REED COL, 77- *Res:* Structure and interconnections among physical theories, especially classical and quantum dynamics, classical field theories, statistical mechanics and thermodynamics. *Mailing Add:* Dept of Physics Reed Col Portland OR 97202

WHEELER, PHILIP RIDGLY, b Grand Rapids, Mich, July 21, 07; m 34. FORESTRY. *Educ:* Univ Mich, BSF, 29, MF, 30. *Prof Exp:* Aide to organizer, Brazilian Forest Serv, 30-31; jr forester, Southern Forest Exp Sta, US Forest Serv, 31-34, asst forest economist, 34-35, assoc forest economist & comput chief, Southern Forest Surv, 35-39, forest economist in chg mensurational anal, 39-42, prog leader, Ozark Br Sta, 45-47, chief div forest mgt res, 47-51, chief div forest econ res, 51-62; consult, 62-66; forest resource economist & consult, Food & Agr Orgn UN, 66; resource analyst, Southern Forest Resource Anal Comt, 67-69; CONSULT, 69- *Honors & Awards:* Superior Service Award, Secy Agr, 62; Sir William Schlich Mem Award, Soc Am Foresters, 70. *Mem:* Fel Soc Am Foresters. *Res:* Regional forest resources and growth, forest survey mensurational methods, procedures and instruments and wood, using plant location studies. *Mailing Add:* 2616 Jefferson Ave New Orleans LA 70115

WHEELER, RALPH JOHN, b Devine, Tex, Sept 14, 29; m 57; c 1. ANALYTICAL CHEMISTRY. *Educ:* Trinity Univ, San Antonio, Tex, BS, 63. *Prof Exp:* Res chemist, Southwest Res Inst, 63-68; anal chemist, 68-73, mgr anal chem, 73-74, ASSOC DIR, LIFE SCI DIV, GULF SOUTH RES INST, 74- *Mem:* Am Chem Soc; Am Col Toxicol. *Res:* Carcinogenesis bioassay of pesticides and other environmental chemicals; development of new chromatographic instrumentation and methodology for the analysis of airborne polynuclear arenes. *Mailing Add:* Gulf South Res Inst PO Box 1177 New Iberia LA 70560

WHEELER, RICHARD HUNTING, b Brooklyn, NY, Jan 30, 31; m 54; c 3. FOREST HYDROLOGY. *Educ:* Univ Maine, Orono, BS, 53; Colo State Univ, MF, 69. *Prof Exp:* Forester, Savannah River Proj, US Forest Serv-AEC, SC, 57-59; forester, Ouachita Nat Forest, US Forest Serv, 59-62, forester & staff consult water resources, Roosevelt Nat Forest, 62-64 & Arapaho Nat Forest, 64-66, hydrologist & staff consult, Northern Region, Div Soil, Air & Water Mgt, 66-74; forest hydrologist & consult, Food & Agr Orgn UN, Mae Sa Watershed Proj, Chiang Mai, Thailand, 74-77; hydrologist & staff consult, Northern Region, USDA Forest Serv, Missoula, Mont, 77-79; hydrologist & staff consult, Mt Hood Nat Forest, 79-80. *Concurrent Pos:* Consult to UN Environ Prog, Asia & Pac Region, Bangkok, Thailand. *Mem:* Soc Am Foresters; Am Forestry Asn; Am Geophys Union. *Res:* Wildlife water quality and water resource management; general forest management. *Mailing Add:* 19559 SE Div Gresham OR 97030

WHEELER, ROBERT FRANCIS, b Austin, Tex, Nov 3, 43; m 76. FUNCTIONAL ANALYSIS, GENERAL TOPOLOGY. *Educ:* Rice Univ, BS, 65; Univ Mo, Columbia, MA, 68, PhD(math), 70. *Prof Exp:* Vis asst prof math, La State Univ, 71-72; asst prof, 72-76, ASSOC PROF MATH, NORTHERN ILL UNIV, 76- *Concurrent Pos:* Math res grants, NSF, 77-78 & 80-81. *Mem:* Am Math Soc; Math Asn Am; Sigma Xi. *Res:* Measures on topological spaces; the strict topology on spaces of continuous functions. *Mailing Add:* Dept of Math Sci Northern Ill Univ De Kalb IL 60115

WHEELER, ROBERT LEE, b Minneapolis, Minn, Jan 17, 44; m 67; c 3. MATHEMATICS. *Educ:* Univ Minn, BS, 66; Univ Wis-Madison, MA, 69, PhD(math), 71. *Prof Exp:* From asst prof to assoc prof math, Univ Mo, Columbia, 71-80; ASSOC PROF MATH, VA POLYTECH INST & STATE UNIV, 80- *Concurrent Pos:* Vis asst prof math, Iowa State Univ, 74-75. *Mem:* Am Math Soc; Soc Indust & Appl Math; Math Asn Am. *Res:* Volterra integral equations; tauberian theory; functions of one complex variable. *Mailing Add:* Dept Math Va Polytech Inst & State Univ Blacksburg VA 24061

WHEELER, ROBERT STEVENSON, avian physiology, deceased

WHEELER, RURIC E, b Grayson Co, Ky, Nov 30, 23; m 46; c 2. MATHEMATICAL STATISTICS. *Educ:* Western Ky State Col, AB, 47; Univ Ky, MS, 48, PhD(math, statist), 52. *Prof Exp:* Instr math & statist, Univ Ky, 48-52; asst prof, Fla State Univ, 52-53; assoc prof, 53-55, head dept math & eng, 56-65, chmn div natural sci, 65-70, asst to acad dean, 67-68, dean, Howard Col Arts & Sci, 68-70, PROF MATH, SAMFORD UNIV, 56-, VPRES ACAD AFFAIRS, 70- *Concurrent Pos:* Consult, Dynamics Dept, Hayes Int Corp, 56-67; trustee, Mid-South Technol Inst, 58-67; dir, NSF vis sci prog, 63-67 & coop prog, 65-67; trustee, Gorgas Found, 68-; mem, Am Conf Acad Deans. *Mem:* Am Math Soc; Math Asn Am; Am Statist Asn; Inst Math Statist. *Res:* Statistical distributions; stochastic processes. *Mailing Add:* Dept of Math Samford Univ Birmingham AL 35209

WHEELER, RUSSELL LEONARD, b Freeport, NY, June 12, 43. STRUCTURAL GEOLOGY, TECTONICS. *Educ:* Yale Univ, BS, 66; Princeton Univ, PhD(geol), 73. *Prof Exp:* Asst prof geol, WVa Univ, 71-77, assoc prof, 77-80; WITH US GEOLOGICAL SURVEY, 80- *Concurrent Pos:* Grants, WVa Univ Fac Senate, 74 & Petrol Res Fund, Am Chem Soc, 74-77; mem fac, US Geol Surv, 75-77; contract, US Dept Energy, 78. *Mem:* AAAS; Geol Soc Am; Am Geophys Union. *Res:* Structural analysis of fold and thrust belts; applications of robust statistical methods to structural geology and tectonics and economic applications thereof. *Mailing Add:* US Geological Survey Fed Ctr Mail Stop 966 Box 25046 Denver CO 80225

WHEELER, SAMUEL CRANE, JR, b Montclair, NJ, June 3, 13; m 42; c 6. PHYSICS. *Educ:* Miami Univ, AB, 42; Univ Ill, MS, 43; Ohio State Univ, PhD(physics), 60. *Prof Exp:* Asst, Miami Univ, 39-42, instr physics, 43-44; asst, Univ Ill, 42-43; asst physicist, Div War Res, Univ Calif, San Diego, 44-46; physicist, US Navy Electronics Lab, 46-48; from instr to prof, 48-78, chmn dept physics & astron, 60-70, EMER PROF PHYSICS, DENISON UNIV, 78- *Concurrent Pos:* NSF fac fel, 59-60 & prog dir, Div Instnl Progs, 63-64, consult, Div Undergrad Educ Sci, 66-; mem exam bd, NCent Asn Cols & Sec Schs, Comn Higher Educ, 70- *Mem:* Am Phys Soc; Am Asn Physics Teachers; Am Astron Soc. *Res:* Underwater sound calibration techniques; sonic properties of materials; theory of infrared spectra of polyatomic molecules; theoretical molecular physics. *Mailing Add:* 2342 Silver St SW Granville OH 43023

WHEELER, THOMAS NEIL, b Ocala, Fla, Feb 6, 43; m 67. PESTICIDES, SYNTHETIC ORGANIC CHEMISTRY. *Educ:* Univ Fla, BS, 64; Cornell Univ, PhD(org chem), 69. *Prof Exp:* From asst prof to assoc prof chem, Fla Technol Univ, 69-75; res chemist, 75-80, RES SCIENTIST/GROUP LEADER, UNION CARBIDE CORP, 80- *Concurrent Pos:* Petrol res fund type B grant, Fla Technol Univ, 70-72. *Mem:* Am Chem Soc. *Res:* Exploratory synthesis of pesticides. *Mailing Add:* Union Carbide Agr Prod PO Box 12014 Research Triangle Park NC 27709

WHEELER, WALTER HALL, b Syracuse, NY, Dec 21, 23; m 45; c 2. VERTEBRATE PALEONTOLOGY. *Educ:* Univ Mich, BS, 45, MS, 48; Yale Univ, PhD(geol), 51. *Prof Exp:* From instr to assoc prof, 51-68, PROF GEOL, UNIV NC, CHAPEL HILL, 68- *Concurrent Pos:* Vis scholar, Univ Calif, Berkeley, 66-67. *Mem:* Geol Soc Am; Am Inst Prof Geologists; Soc Vert Paleont; Am Asn Petrol Geol; Paleont Soc. *Res:* Large early Tertiary mammals; stratigraphy and paleontology of the North Carolina coastal plain; the Triassic of North Carolina. *Mailing Add:* Dept Geol Univ NC Chapel Hill NC 27514

WHEELER, WARREN R(AY), b Gaines, NY, Apr 24, 12; m 35; c 3. ELECTRICAL ENGINEERING. *Educ:* Rensselaer Polytech Inst, EE, 34; Univ Colo, MS, 57, PhD, 63. *Prof Exp:* Instr elec eng, Univ Rochester, 44-47, asst prof, 47-50; sr engr, Stromberg Carlson Co, 51-53; asst prof, 53-57, assoc prof, 57-62, prof, 62-77, assoc dean grad div, 66-70, dean eng, 74-77, EMER PROF ELEC ENG, UNIV DENVER, 77- *Concurrent Pos:* Owner, Ont Radio & Elec Co, 44-51; transmitter engr, Sta WHAM, Stromberg Carlson Co, 35-44. *Mem:* Inst Elec & Electronics Engrs; Sigma Xi. *Res:* Theoretical and experimental evaluation of communication and direction finding antennas; analysis and synthesis of active networks. *Mailing Add:* 5242 E Maplewood Pl Littleton CO 80121

WHEELER, WILLIAM HOLLIS, b Akron, Ohio, Feb 10, 46; m 68. MATHEMATICAL LOGIC. *Educ:* Vanderbilt Univ, BA, 68; Yale Univ, PhD(math), 72. *Prof Exp:* Asst prof, 72-80, ASSOC PROF MATH, IND UNIV, BLOOMINGTON, 80- *Concurrent Pos:* Vis lectr math, Bedford Col, Univ London, 73-74. *Mem:* Am Math Soc; Asn Symbolic Logic. *Res:* Model theory; metamathematics of algebra; applications of logic to algebra. *Mailing Add:* Dept Math Ind Univ Bloomington IN 47401

WHEELER, WILLIAM JOE, b Flora, Ind, Oct 14, 40; m 62; c 2. MEDICINAL CHEMISTRY. *Educ:* Purdue Univ, BS, 62; Butler Univ, MS, 66; Purdue Univ, PhD(med chem), 70. *Prof Exp:* Teacher math & sci, Northwestern Sch Corp, Henry County, Ind, 62-63; anal chemist, Allison Div, Gen Motors Corp, Ind, 63-65; org chemist, Eli Lilly & Co, 65-67; asst, Purdue Univ, Lafayette, 67-68, fel, 68-70; sr pharmaceut chemist, 70-80, RES SCIENTIST, ELI LILLY & CO, 80- *Mem:* Am Chem Soc; Am Soc Microbiol; Sigma Xi. *Res:* Beta-lactam antibiotics, anti-inflammatory compounds. *Mailing Add:* 1555 N Huber St Indianapolis IN 46219

WHEELER, WILLIAM RALEIGH, b Indianapolis, Ind, Jan 10, 16; m 44; c 2. ORGANIC CHEMISTRY, CHEMICAL ENGINEERING. *Educ:* Univ Ill, BS, 36; Pa State Col, MS, 37, PhD, 41. *Prof Exp:* Res & develop chemist, Reilly Tar & Chem Corp, 39-42, 45-47; res chemist, Cincinnati Milling Mach Co, 47-49; res & develop chemist, 49-74, Reilly Tar & Chem Corp, 49-74, dir, Reilly Labs, 74-77, vpres res, 77-81; RETIRED. *Mem:* AAAS; Am Inst Chem Eng; Am Chem Soc; Royal Soc Chem. *Res:* Heterogeneous catalytic reactions; process development and plant design. *Mailing Add:* 502 W 77th St Indianapolis IN 46260

WHEELER, WILLIS BOLY, b Oakland, Calif, June 13, 38; m 64; c 2. BIOCHEMISTRY. *Educ:* George Washington Univ, BS, 61, MS, 63; Pa State Univ, PhD(biochem), 66. *Prof Exp:* Res asst cancer, George Washington Univ, 61-63; instr chem pesticides, Pa State Univ, 64-66; asst prof 66-72, assoc prof, 72-78, PROF PESTICIDES, UNIV FLA, 78- *Mem:* AAAS; Am Chem Soc. *Res:* Disappearance of chemical from plant and plant environment; behavior of pesticides in soil ecosystems; movement through soils; effects on soil microbial populations; metabolism; residue detection methodology. *Mailing Add:* Pesticide Res Lab Dept Food Sci Univ of Fla Gainesville FL 32611

WHEELESS, LEON LUM, JR, b Jackson, Miss, Nov 6, 35; m 57; c 3. ANALYTICAL CYTOLOGY, BIOMEDICAL ENGINEERING. *Educ:* Mass Inst Technol, SB, 58; Univ Rochester, MS, 62, PhD(elec eng), 65. *Prof Exp:* Sect head, Electronics Dept, Bausch & Lomb, Inc, 58-61, tech specialist, Biophys Dept, 61-65, res scientist, Cent Res Lab, 65-68, sr res scientist, Biomed Res Dept, Anal Systs Div, 68-69, dir biomed res, 69-71; assoc prof, 71-81, PROF PATH & ELEC ENG, MED CTR, UNIV ROCHESTER, 81-, DIR, ANAL CYTOL DIV, DEPT PATH, 75- *Mem:* Inst Elec & Electronics Engrs; Am Soc Cytol; Soc Anal Cytol. *Res:* Biomedical instrumentation; computerized systems for automatic recognition of abnormal cells; automated cytopathology instrumentation; pattern recognition. *Mailing Add:* Dept of Path Univ of Rochester Med Ctr Rochester NY 14642

WHEELIS, MARK LEWIS, b Chelsea, Mass, Jan 8, 44; m 65; c 2. MICROBIOLOGY, GENETICS. *Educ:* Univ Calif, Berkeley, AB, 65, MA, 67, PhD(bacteriol), 69. *Prof Exp:* Lab technician bacteriol, Univ Calif, Berkeley, 65-66; res assoc, Univ Ill, Urbana-Champaign, 69-70; asstprof, 70-76, ASSOC PROF BACTERIOL, COL LETTERS & SCI, UNIV CALIF, DAVIS, 76- *Concurrent Pos:* USPHS res grant, Univ Calif, Davis, 72-73. *Mem:* Am Soc Microbiol; Genetics Soc Am; Brit Soc Gen Microbiol; Am Soc Biol Chemists. *Res:* bacterial metabolism; dissimilation of aromatic acids. *Mailing Add:* Dept of Bacteriol Univ Calif Col Letters & Sci Davis CA 95616

WHEELOCK, EARLE FREDERICK, b New York, NY, Feb 19, 27; m 55; c 3. ONCOLOGY. *Educ:* Mass Inst Technol, BS, 50; Columbia Univ, MD, 55; Rockefeller Inst, PhD(biol), 61. *Prof Exp:* Intern med, Clins, Univ Chicago, 55-56; resident, Strong Mem Hosp, Rochester, NY, 56-57; fel biol & virol, Rockefeller Inst, 57-61; from asst prof to assoc prof prev med, Sch Med, Western Reserve Univ, 61-71; prof microbiol, Jefferson Med Col, 71-81; PROF PATH, HAHNEMANN MED COL, 81- *Concurrent Pos:* USPHS res career develop award, 66-71. *Mem:* Am Soc Clin Invest; Am Asn Immunol; Soc Exp Biol & Med; Am Soc Microbiol; Am Asn Cancer Res. *Res:* Animal virology; mechanism of host resistance to viral infections; role of leucocytes and interferon in human viral infections; effect of nontumor viruses on virus-induced leukemia in mice; suppression of leukemia viral infections; tumor dormant states in animals and man. *Mailing Add:* Dept Path Hahnemann Med Col 216 W Broad St Philadelphia PA 19102

WHEELOCK, KENNETH STEVEN, b Kansas City, Mo, Sept 18, 43; m 72; c 1. PETROLEUM CHEMISTRY, INORGANIC CHEMISTRY. *Educ:* Univ Mo-Kansas City, BS, 65; Tulane Univ, PhD(chem), 70. *Prof Exp:* Chemist, 69-72, res chemist, 72-77, STAFF CHEMIST, EXXON RES & DEVELOP LABS, 77- *Concurrent Pos:* Consult, Dept Chem, Tulane Univ, 70- *Honors & Awards:* Award, Am Chem Soc, 65. *Mem:* Am Chem Soc; AAAS; NY Acad Sci; Sigma Xi. *Res:* Theoretical aspects of transition metal chemistry and catalysis; low valent complexes of transition metals with unsaturated ligands; quantum chemistry of catalysis; theory of finely divided metals; peruvskite catalysts. *Mailing Add:* Exxon Res & Develop Labs PO Box 2226 Baton Rouge LA 70821

WHEELOCK, THOMAS DAVID, b Chihuahua, Mex, May 15, 25; m 52; c 2. CHEMICAL ENGINEERING. *Educ:* Iowa State Univ, BS, 49, PhD(chem eng), 58. *Prof Exp:* Sales engr, Chem Equip Co Calif, 49-51; chem engr, Westvaco Chlor-Alkali Div, Food Mach & Chem Corp, 51-54; from instr to assoc prof, 57-64, PROF CHEM ENG, IOWA STATE UNIV, 64- *Concurrent Pos:* Masua hon lectr, 80-81. *Mem:* Am Chem Soc; Am Soc Eng Educ; Soc Mining Engrs, Am Inst Chem Engrs. *Res:* Process thermodynamics and kinetics; fluidized bed reactors; coal and other mineral utilization processes. *Mailing Add:* Dept of Chem Eng Iowa State Univ Ames IA 50011

WHEELON, ALBERT DEWELL, b Moline, Ill, Jan 18, 29; m 53; c 2. THEORETICAL PHYSICS. *Educ:* Stanford Univ, BSc, 49; Mass Inst Technol, PhD(physics), 52. *Prof Exp:* Asst, Res Lab Electronics, Mass Inst Technol, 51-52; sr mem tech staff, Ramo-Wooldridge Corp, 53-62; with US Govt, 62-66; vpres & group exec, 66-80, SR VPRES & PRES SPACE & COMMUN GROUP, HUGHES AIRCRAFT CO, 80- *Mem:* Nat Acad Eng; Int Union Radio Sci; Am Phys Soc; fel Inst Elec & Electronics Engrs. *Res:* Meson theory; general relativity; turbulence theory; analysis of ballistic missile and space systems; electromagnetic propagation and radio signal statistics. *Mailing Add:* 320 S Canyon View Dr Los Angeles CA 90049

WHEELWRIGHT, EARL J, b Rexburg, Idaho, Mar 26, 28; m 47; c 6. NUCLEAR CHEMISTRY. *Educ:* Brigham Young Univ, BS, 50; Iowa State Univ, PhD, 55. *Prof Exp:* Chemist, Hanford Atomic Prod Oper, Gen Elec Co, 55-60, sr scientist, 60-64; res assoc, 65-77, SR STAFF SCIENTIST, PAC NORTHWEST LABS, BATTELLE MEM INST, 77- *Mem:* Am Nuclear Soc. *Res:* Separation chemistry, ion exchange and chelation chemistry as applied to lanthanides, actinides and fission products. *Mailing Add:* 1416 Sunset Richland WA 99352

WHEILDON, W(ILLIAM) M(AXWELL), JR, b Ashland, Mass, June 16, 08; m 51; c 3. MECHANICAL ENGINEERING. *Educ:* Mass Inst Technol, BS, 30, MS, 31. *Prof Exp:* Res engr, Norton Co, 37-66, chief protective prod, Div Res & Develop, 66-67, res assoc indust ceramics, 67-73; RETIRED. *Concurrent Pos:* Mech engr consult, 73- *Mem:* Assoc fel Am Inst Aeronaut & Astronaut; Am Chem Soc; Am Welding Soc; Am Soc Testing & Mat. *Res:* Abrasion and corrosion resistant ceramic materials beyond the range of metals; high temperature ceramic protective and insulating coatings; flame-sprayed ceramic coatings; ceramic cutting tools; ceramic armor and hot pressed industrial ceramics. *Mailing Add:* 84 Gates St Framingham MA 01701

WHELAN, BARBARA JEAN KING, b Reno, Nev, Nov 12, 39; m 70. ORGANIC CHEMISTRY. *Educ:* Univ Calif, Davis, BS, 61; Mass Inst Technol, PhD(org chem), 65. *Prof Exp:* NIH fel chem, Brandeis Univ, 65-67; from asst prof to assoc prof, Fairleigh Dickinson Univ, 67-75; res assoc, 75-78, RES SPECIALIST, WOODS HOLE OCEANOG INST, 78- *Mem:* Am Asn Petrol Geologists; Geol Soc Am; AAAS; Am Chem Soc. *Res:* Organic geochemistry; petroleum genesis; chemical and microbiological transformations of organic compounds in marine sediments. *Mailing Add:* Dept of Chem Woods Hole Oceanog Inst Woods Hole MA 02543

WHELAN, ELIZABETH M, b New York, NY, Dec 4, 43; m 71; c 1. EPIDEMIOLOGY, PUBLIC HEALTH. *Educ:* Conn Col, AB, 65; Yale Univ, MPH, 67; Harvard Univ, MS, 68, ScD, 71. *Prof Exp:* EXEC DIR AM COUN SCI & HEALTH, 72- *Concurrent Pos:* Res assoc, Sch Pub Health, Harvard Univ, 74- *Mem:* Am Pub Health Asn; Nutrit Today Asn. *Res:* Author or coauthor of over 100 publications. *Mailing Add:* 1995 Broadway New York NY 10023

WHELAN, JAMES ARTHUR, b Steele Co, Minn, Sept 25, 28; m 50; c 3. ECONOMIC GEOLOGY. *Educ:* Univ Minn, BMinE, 49, MS, 56, PhD, 59. *Prof Exp:* Instr mining eng, Univ Minn, 57-59; from asst prof to prof mineral, Univ Utah, 59-68, prof mining & geol eng, 68-69; dep off in chg construct, US Navy, Marianas, 69-71; PROF GEOL & GEOPHYS SCI, UNIV UTAH, 71- *Mem:* Geol Soc Am. *Res:* Geochemistry; mineralogy. *Mailing Add:* Dept of Geol Univ of Utah Salt Lake City UT 84112

WHELAN, JOHN MICHAEL, b Lyndhurst, NJ, Sept 12, 21; m 43; c 3. POLYMER CHEMISTRY. *Educ:* Stevens Inst Technol, ME, 41, MS, 43; Polytech Inst Brooklyn, PhD(org chem), 59. *Prof Exp:* Res chemist, 41-53, group leader, 53-55, sect head, 55-63, asst dir res & develop, 63-72, RES ASSOC, UNION CARBIDE CORP, 72- *Mem:* Am Chem Soc. *Res:* Synthetic polymers. *Mailing Add:* Union Carbide Res & Develop Labs 1 River Rd Bound Brook NJ 08805

WHELAN, THOMAS, III, b Houston, Tex, Dec 21, 44; m 68; c 1. MARINE GEOCHEMISTRY. *Educ:* Austin Col, BA, 66; Univ Tex, Austin, MA, 68; Tex A&M Univ, PhD(chem oceanog), 71. *Prof Exp:* Asst prof marine sci, Coastal Studies Inst, La State Univ, Baton Rouge, 71-75, assoc prof marine sci, 75-79; PRES, CARBON SYSTS, INC, 79- *Mem:* Geochem Soc; AAAS; Am Asn Plant Physiologists. *Res:* Organic geochemistry of marine environments; geochemistry of natural gases; effects of oil in coastal environment. *Mailing Add:* 1287 Main St Baton Rouge LA 70802

WHELAN, WILLIAM JOSEPH, b Salford, UK, Nov 14, 24; m 51. BIOCHEMISTRY. *Educ:* Univ Birmingham, BSc, 45, PhD, 48, DSc(org chem), 55. *Prof Exp:* Sr lectr, Univ Col NWales, 48-55; sr mem, Lister Inst Prev Med, London, Eng, 56-64; prof biochem, Royal Free Hosp Sch Med, Univ London, 64-67; PROF BIOCHEM & CHMN DEPT, SCH MED, UNIV MIAMI, 67- *Concurrent Pos:* Secy-gen, Fedn Europ Biochem Socs, 65-67 & Pan-Am Asn Biochem Socs, 69-72; mem physiol chem study sect, NIH, 71-75, chmn, 73-75; gen-secy, Int Union Biochem, 73-; ed-in-chief, Trends Biochem Sci, 76-78; chmn, Comt Genetic Exp, 77-81; mem exec bd, Int Coun Sci Unions, 78-80. *Honors & Awards:* Carl Lucas Alsberg Lectr, 67; Ciba Medal & Lectr, 69; Diplome d'Honneur, Fedn Europ Biochem Socs, 74; Saare Medal, Asn Cereal Res, 79. *Mem:* Brit Biochem Soc; Am Soc Biol Chem; Am Chem Soc. *Res:* Glycogen and starch, structure and metabolism. *Mailing Add:* Dept Biochem Sch Med Univ Miami PO Box 016129 Miami FL 33101

WHELAN, WILLIAM PAUL, JR, b Brooklyn, NY, Sept 22, 23; m 55; c 3. ORGANIC POLYMER CHEMISTRY. *Educ:* Holy Cross Col, AB, 43, MS, 47; Columbia Univ, PhD(chem), 52. *Prof Exp:* Res scientist, 52-66, SR RES SCIENTIST, CORP RES & DEVELOP, UNIROYAL INC, WORLD HQ, MIDDLEBURY, 66- *Mem:* Am Chem Soc; Sigma Xi. *Res:* Flame and smoke inhibition in polymers; rocket motor insulators; rubber and plastic product formulation; cellular products; polyurethane synthesis; vinyl polymerization; blowing agents; ablatives; organic synthesis; reaction mechanisms; solvolysis theory; crystallization kinetics; photopolymers. *Mailing Add:* Orchard Lane Woodbury CT 06798

WHELLY, SANDRA MARIE, b Fall River, Mass, Aug 8, 45. BIOCHEMISTRY. *Educ:* Salve Regina Col, BA, 68; Univ Nebr, PhD(biochem), 73. *Prof Exp:* Res asst chem, Salve Regina Col, 67-68; res asst microbiol, Peter Bent Brigham Hosp, 68-69; NIH trainee biochem, Eppley Inst, Col Med, Univ Nebr, 69-72, grad res asst, 72- 73; fel, Temple Univ, Sch Med, 74-76, res assoc 76-77; res asst prof, 77-81, ASST PROF BIOCHEM, TEXAS TECH UNIV HEALTH SCI CTR, 81- *Concurrent Pos:* Res assoc grant, Am Cancer Soc, 74-75; NIH res grant, Child Health & Develop, 81-84. *Res:* Transcriptional and translational control mechanisms of cellular proliferation; biochemistry of hormone action. *Mailing Add:* Tex Tech Univ Health Sci Ctr Lubbock TX 79430

WHELTON, ANDREW, b Cork, Ireland, Oct 6, 40; m 74. MEDICINE. *Educ:* Nat Univ Ireland, MB & MD, 63. *Prof Exp:* Mem staff, Renal Metal Unit, Walter Reed Army Inst Res, 67-68; ASSOC PROF MED, SCH MED, JOHNS HOPKINS UNIV, 76- *Concurrent Pos:* Consult renal dis, USPHS Hosp, Baltimore, 71- & Union Mem Hosp, 73-; consult renal dis to Surgeon Gen US Air Force, Washington, DC, 71-; consult med, Dept Obstetrics & Gynec, Johns Hopkins Univ, 75- *Mem:* Int Soc Nephrology; AMA; Am Soc Nephrology; Am Fedn Clin Res; fel Am Col Clin Pharmacol. *Res:* Drug metabolism in renal failure; drug nephrotoxicity; acute renal failure. *Mailing Add:* Nephrology Div Johns Hopkins Univ Sch of Med Baltimore MD 21205

WHELTON, BARTLETT DAVID, b San Francisco, Calif, Dec 2, 41. MEDICINAL CHEMISTRY. *Educ:* Univ San Francisco, BS, 63; Univ Wash, PhD(med chem), 69. *Prof Exp:* Fel med chem, Univ Alta, 69-71; asst prof, Univ of the Pac, 71-74; asst prof, 74-80, ASSOC PROF MED CHEM, EASTERN WASH UNIV, 80- *Mem:* Am Chem Soc; Sigma Xi. *Res:* Synthesis of antineoplastic agents; heavy metal toxicology. *Mailing Add:* Dept of Chem Eastern Wash Univ Cheney WA 99004

WHEREAT, ARTHUR FINCH, b New York, NY, June 30, 27; m 53; c 3. CARDIOVASCULAR DISEASES. *Educ:* Williams Col, BA, 47; Univ Pa, MD, 51. *Prof Exp:* Intern & med resident internal med, Hosp Univ Pa, 51-54, fel cardiol, 54-56; assoc in biochem, 56-60, asst prof med, 60-68, ASSOC PROF MED, SCH MED, UNIV PA, 68-; CHIEF OF STAFF, VET ADMIN HOSP, PHILADELPHIA, 76- *Concurrent Pos:* Mem coun arteriosclerosis, Am Heart Asn, 64 & coun clin cardiol, 69. *Mem:* Fel Am Col Physicians; fel Am Col Cardiol; Am Soc Biol Chemists; Am Physiol Soc; Am Heart Asn. *Res:* Biochemical changes in arterial wall associated with atherogenesis; biochemical changes in heart muscle during hypoxia and ischemia. *Mailing Add:* Vet Admin Hosp 38th & University Ave Philadelphia PA 19104

WHERRETT, JOHN ROSS, b Regina, Saskatchewan, Nov 28, 30; m 58; c 2. NEUROLOGY, NEUROCHEMISTRY. *Educ:* Queen's Univ, MDCM, 55; Royal Col Physicians & Surgeons, FRCP, 63; Univ London, PhD(biochem), 66. *Prof Exp:* Clin teacher, 63-65, assoc 65-68, from asst prof to assoc prof, 68-75, PROF & DIR NEUROL PROG MED, UNIV TORONTO, 75- *Concurrent Pos:* Travelling fel, R S McLaughlin Found, 58-60; scholar acad med, Markle Found, 63-68; res fel, Am Col Physicians, 63-66; staff physician, Toronto Gen Hosp, 63-; consult neurol, Clarke Inst Psychiat, Univ Toronto, 69-75; mem & chmn grant comt neurosciences, Med Res Coun Can, 67-72; mem, Inst Med Sci, Univ Toronto, 69-; mem & chmn comt fel review, Ont Ministry Health, 71-77; mem, Bd & Med Res Comt, Ont Heart Found, 77-

Mem: Am Acad Neurol; Am Neurol Asn; Am Soc Neurochem; Can Neurol Soc (pres, 78-79); Can Soc Clin Invest. *Res:* Investigation of the structure and metabolism of glycosphingolipids and phospholipids and of the disturbances occurring in inherited degenerative diseases of the nervous system. *Mailing Add:* Toronto Gen Hosp 221 11 Eaton N Toronto ON M5G 1L7 Can

WHETSEL, KERMIT BAZIL, b Tenn, Dec 9, 23; m 49; c 4. ANALYTICAL CHEMISTRY. *Educ:* East Tenn State Univ, BS, 43; Univ Tenn, MS, 47, PhD(chem), 50. *Prof Exp:* From chemist to sr chemist, 50-66, develop assoc, 66-73, sr develop assoc, 73-81, DEVELOP FEL, TENN EASTMAN CO DIV, EASTMAN KODAK CO, 81- *Concurrent Pos:* Nat Acad Sci-Nat Res Coun resident res assoc, US Naval Res Lab, 60-61. *Mem:* Am Chem Soc; Soc Appl Spectros; Coblentz Soc; Am Soc Testing & Mat. *Res:* Instrumental analysis of organic compounds; correlation of absorption spectra with structure; solvent effects on infrared spectra; spectroscopic study of hydrogen bonded complexes. *Mailing Add:* Tenn Eastman Co Kingsport TN 37662

WHETSTONE, JAMES ROBERT, physics, see previous edition

WHETSTONE, STANLEY L, JR, b Newark, NJ, Aug 30, 25; m 52; c 4. EXPERIMENTAL NUCLEAR PHYSICS. *Educ:* Williams Col, BA, 49; Univ Calif, Berkeley, PhD(physics), 55. *Prof Exp:* Staff mem & physicist, Los Alamos Sci Lab, 55-70 & 75-76; physics sect head, Int Atomic Energy Agency, Vienna, Austria, 70-75; NUCLEAR PHYSICIST, US DEPT ENERGY, 76- *Concurrent Pos:* Vis lectr, Univ Wash, 67-68. *Mem:* Am Phys Soc. *Mailing Add:* ER-23/GTN US Dept of Energy Washington DC 20545

WHETTEN, JOHN T, b Willimantic, Conn, Mar 16, 35; m 60; c 3. GEOLOGY, OCEANOGRAPHY. *Educ:* Princeton Univ, AB, 57; Univ Calif, Berkeley, MA, 59; Princeton Univ, PhD(geol), 62. *Prof Exp:* Fulbright fel, Australia & NZ, 62-63; res instr oceanog, 63-64, res asst prof, 64-65, from asst prof to assoc prof, 65-72, assoc dean grad sch, 68-69, chmn dept, 69-74, PROF GEOL SCI, UNIV WASH, 72-; GEOLOGIST, US GEOL SURV, SEATTLE, 75- *Mem:* AAAS; Geol Soc Am; Soc Econ Paleontologists & Mineralogists. *Res:* Sedimentology; sedimentary petrology; marine geology. *Mailing Add:* Dept of Geol Sci Univ of Wash Seattle WA 98195

WHETTEN, NATHAN REY, b Provo, Utah, Aug 11, 28; m 53; c 3. PHYSICS. *Educ:* Yale Univ, BS, 49, MS, 50, PhD(physics), 53. *Prof Exp:* PHYSICIST, RES LAB, GEN ELEC CO, 53- *Concurrent Pos:* Vis lectr, Union Col, 64-65, adj prof, 67- *Mem:* Am Phys Soc; hon life mem Am Vacuum Soc (pres-elect, 75, pres, 76). *Res:* Cosmic rays; secondary electron emission; surface physics; high vacuum; mass spectrometry; electron physics; medical physics. *Mailing Add:* Res & Develop Ctr Gen Elec Co PO Box 8 Schenectady NY 12305

WHICKER, DONALD, b Noblesville, Ind, Nov 23, 44. STRUCTURAL ANALYSIS. *Educ:* Purdue Univ, BS, 67, MS, 68, PhD(eng), 73. *Prof Exp:* Assoc sr res engr, 73-79, sr res engr, 79-80, STAFF RES ENGR, GEN MOTORS RES LABS, 80- *Mem:* Am Soc Mech Engrs; Soc Automotive Engrs. *Res:* Lubrication; tire traction; tire rolling resistance; development and application of analytical techniques for engine structural analysis and design. *Mailing Add:* Eng Mech Dept Gen Motors Res Labs Warren MI 48098

WHICKER, FLOYD WARD, b Cedar City, Utah, July 24, 37; m 57; c 3. RADIATION BIOLOGY, ECOLOGY. *Educ:* Colo State Univ, BS, 62, PhD(radiation biol), 65. *Prof Exp:* Asst prof, 65-72, assoc prof radiation biol, 72-80, PROF RADIOL, COLO STATE UNIV, 74-, PROF RADIATION BIOL, 80- *Concurrent Pos:* Consult, Western Rad Consult, Inc & Rockwell Int. *Mem:* AAAS; Ecol Soc Am; Wildlife Soc; Health Physics Soc. *Res:* Radiation ecology; radionuclide behavior in natural ecosystems and radiation effects on plant and animal populations. *Mailing Add:* Dept of Radiol & Radiation Biol Colo State Univ Ft Collins CO 80523

WHICKER, LAWRENCE R, b Bristol, Va, Oct 3, 34; m 58; c 1. MICROWAVE PHYSICS, ELECTROMAGNETISM. *Educ:* Univ Tenn, BS, 57, MS, 58; Purdue Univ, PhD(elec eng), 64. *Prof Exp:* Teaching asst, Univ Tenn, 58; sr engr, Microwave Electronics Div, Sperry Rand Corp, 58-61; fel engr, Surface Div, Westinghouse Elec Corp, 64-65, assoc dir appl physics, 65-66, mgr microwave physics group, Aerospace Div, 66-68, adv engr microwave & antenna group, 68-69; HEAD MICROWAVE TECHNIQUES BR, ELECTRONICS DIV, NAVAL RES LAB, 69- *Concurrent Pos:* Lectr, Univ Md, 64-; vpres res & develop, I-Tel, Inc, 67-68. *Mem:* Sr mem Inst Elec & Electronics Engrs. *Res:* Millimeter-coupled mode techniques; microwave filters; electromagnetic propagation studies; microwave solid state techniques, including microwave latching phasers, acoustics and integrated circuits. *Mailing Add:* US Naval Res Lab 4555 Overlook Ave Washington DC 20375

WHIDBY, JERRY FRANK, b Baltimore, Md, Oct 29, 43; m 67; c 2. ANALYTICAL CHEMISTRY, PHYSICAL CHEMISTRY. *Educ:* NGa Col, BS, 65; Univ Ga, PhD(anal chem), 70. *Prof Exp:* Res chemist, Gen Elec Co, Mo, 71-72; res assoc anal chem, 72-75, res chemist, 75-80, sr scientist, 80-81, MGR RES & DEVELOP, PHILIP MORRIS INC, 81- *Mem:* Am Chem Soc. *Res:* Proton exchange kinetics; environmental research-sensors; kinetics of filter action. *Mailing Add:* Philip Morris USA Res Ctr PO Box 26583 Richmond VA 23261

WHIFFEN, JAMES DOUGLASS, b New York, NY, Jan 16, 31; m 60; c 1. SURGERY, BIOENGINEERING. *Educ:* Univ Wis, BS, 52, MD, 55; Am Bd Surg, dipl, 63. *Prof Exp:* Intern, Ohio State Univ, 55-56; resident, 56-57 & 59-62, from instr to assoc prof, 62-71, actg chmn dept, 72-74, PROF SURG, MED SCH, UNIV WIS-MADISON, 71-, ASST DEAN MED SCH, 75- *Concurrent Pos:* Nat Heart Inst res fel, 62-64; res career develop award, 65-75; Markle Scholar, 66- *Mem:* Am Col Surg; Am Soc Artificial Internal Organs; Am Soc Test & Mat. *Res:* Cardiovascular prostheses; cardiopulmonary support devices; biomaterials. *Mailing Add:* Univ Hosps 1300 University Ave Madison WI 53706

WHIGHAM, DAVID KEITH, b Blanchard, Iowa, Aug 15, 38; m 64; c 3. AGRONOMY. *Educ:* Iowa State Univ, BS, 66, MS, 69, PhD(crop prod), 71. *Prof Exp:* Instr agron, Iowa State Univ, 68-71; agronomist, USDA, 71-73; asst prof agron, Univ Ill, Urbana, 73-77; asst prof, 77-78, ASSOC PROF AGRON, IOWA STATE UNIV, 78- *Mem:* Am Soc Agron; Crop Sci Soc Am; Nat Asn Col & Teachers Agr. *Res:* Crop production of economic crops; international soybean research. *Mailing Add:* Dept of Agron Iowa State Univ Ames IA 50011

WHIKEHART, DAVID RALPH, b Pittsburgh, Pa, Aug 21, 39; m 69; c 2. PLASMA MEMBRANES, TRANSPORT ENZYMES. *Educ:* WVa Univ, PhD(biochem), 69. *Prof Exp:* Res assoc, Harvard Med Sch, 71-72; asst biochemist, McLean Hosp, Belmont, Mass, 71-72; spec fel, Nat Eye Inst, 72-74, sr staff fel ophthalmic biochem, 74-78; asst prof, 78-81, ASSOC PROF, SCH OPTOM, UNIV ALA, BIRMINGHAM, 81- *Concurrent Pos:* Res fel neurochem, Harvard Med Sch, 69-71, fel neurochem, McLean Hosp, Belmont, Mass, 69-71; asst prof, dept biochem, Sch Med, Univ Ala, Birmingham, 79- *Mem:* Asn Res Vision & Ophthal. *Res:* Metabolism and transport in the cornea; biochemistry of alkali burned corneas; biochemistry of corneal tissue cultures. *Mailing Add:* Dept of Physiol Optics Univ Ala Med Ctr Sch Optom Birmingham AL 35294

WHILLANS, IAN MORLEY, b Toronto, Ont, Feb 25, 44; m 74. GLACIOLOGY, GLACIAL GEOLOGY. *Educ:* Univ Bristol, BSc, 66; Ohio State Univ, PhD(geol), 75. *Prof Exp:* Vis scientist glaciol, Geophys Isotope Lab, Univ Copen- hagen, 75-76; res assoc, Inst Polar Studies, 76-77; ASST PROF GEOL, OHIO STATE UNIV, 77- *Concurrent Pos:* Mem, comt snow & ice, Am Geophys Union, 76-77 & comt glaciol, Polar Res Bd, Nat Acad Sci, 78- *Mem:* Int Glaciol Soc; Am Geophys Union. *Res:* Dynamics of polar ice sheets; mechanics of quaternary ice sheets. *Mailing Add:* Dept of Geol & Mineral Ohio State Univ Columbus OH 43210

WHINNERY, JOHN R(OY), b Read, Colo, July 26, 16; m 44; c 3. ELECTRICAL ENGINEERING. *Educ:* Univ Calif, BS, 37, PhD(elec eng), 48. *Prof Exp:* Test engr, Gen Elec Co, NY, 37-38, asst engr, 38-40, supvr, High Frequency Sect, 40-42, develop engr, 42-45, res engr, 45-46; from lectr to assoc prof elec eng, 46-52, head dept, 56-59, dean col eng, 59-63, PROF ELEC ENG, UNIV CALIF, BERKELEY, 52- *Concurrent Pos:* Head microwave tube res, Hughes Aircraft Co, 51-52, Guggenheim fel, 59; mem adv group electron tubes, US Dept Defense, 56-66; vis mem tech staff, Bell Tel Labs, 63-64; mem sci & technol comt manned space flight, NASA, 64-70; mem standing comt controlled thermonuclear res, Atomic Energy Comn, 70-; mem, President's Comt Nat Medal Sci, 70-72 & 79-81. *Honors & Awards:* Educ Medal, Inst Elec & Electronics Engrs, 67. *Mem:* Nat Acad Sci; Nat Acad Eng; Am Phys Soc; fel Inst Elec & Electronics Engrs; Optical Soc Am. *Res:* Microwave and quantum electronics, including microwave electron devices, wave guiding systems, optical guiding systems and lasers for communication purposes. *Mailing Add:* Dept of Elec Eng & Comput Sci Univ of Calif Berkeley CA 94720

WHIPKEY, KENNETH LEE, b Cortland, Ohio, June 5, 32; m 62. MATHEMATICS, STATISTICS. *Educ:* Kent State Univ, AB, 53, MA, 58; Case Western Reserve Univ, PhD(educ statist), 69. *Prof Exp:* Instr high sch, 54-57; asst math, Kent State Univ, 57-58; instr high sch, 58-59; asst prof, Youngstown Univ, 59-67; assoc prof, 68-76, PROF MATH, WESTMINSTER COL, PA, 76- *Concurrent Pos:* Instr, In-Serv Insts Teachers, NSF, 64-67; lectr & vis scientist, Ohio Acad Sci, 64-66; lectr, Holt, Rinehart & Winston, 65. *Mem:* Math Asn Am. *Res:* Factor analysis; calculus. *Mailing Add:* 456 Bradley Lane Youngstown OH 44504

WHIPP, ARTHUR ANDREW, entomology, see previous edition

WHIPP, SHANNON CARL, b Jacksonville, Fla, May 3, 31; m 56; c 5. VETERINARY PHYSIOLOGY, VETERINARY SURGERY. *Educ:* Univ Minn, BS, 57, DVM, 59, PhD(physiol), 65. *Prof Exp:* Field vet, Minn Livestock Bd, 59-60; instr physiol, Univ Minn, 60-65; res vet, 65-77, res leader, 77-80, CHIEF PHYSIOPATH DIV, NAT ANIMAL DIS CTR, AGR RES SERV, USDA, 80- *Concurrent Pos:* NIH fel, 62-65. *Mem:* Am Soc Vet Physiol & Pharmacol; Am Vet Med Asn; Comp Gastroenterol Soc; Conf Res Workers Animal Dis; NY Acad Sci. *Res:* Mechanisms of diarrhea; adrenal function in domestic animals; secretory diarrhea; enteric colibacillosis. *Mailing Add:* Nat Animal Dis Ctr PO Box 70 Ames IA 50010

WHIPPEY, PATRICK WILLIAM, b Reading, UK, Feb 18, 40. IMAGE PROCESSING. *Educ:* Univ Reading, BSc, 62, PhD(physics), 66. *Prof Exp:* Asst lectr physics, Univ Reading, 65-66; lectr, 66-67, asst prof, 67-72, ASSOC PROF PHYSICS, UNIV WESTERN ONT, 72- *Mem:* Can Asn Physicists. *Res:* Electron spin resonance in diamond; optical properties of rare earth doped calcium fluoride. *Mailing Add:* Dept of Physics Univ of Western Ont London ON N6A 5B8 Can

WHIPPLE, CHRISTOPHER GEORGE, b Columbus, Ohio, Feb 17, 49; m 70; c 2. RISK ANALYSIS, ENERGY ECONOMICS. *Educ:* Purdue Univ, BS, 70; Calif Inst Technol, MS, 71, PhD(eng sci), 74. *Prof Exp:* Mem tech staff, Planning Div, 74-77, mgr special studies, 77-78, TECH MGR, ELEC POWER RES INST ENERGY STUDY CTR, 78- *Concurrent Pos:* Lectr mech eng, Stanford Univ, 78-79; course dir, Chautauqua-Type Short Course, Col Teachers, NSF-AAAS, 78-81, Adv Study Inst Technol Risk Assessment, NATO, 81; contractor, Off Air Qual Planning & Standards, Environ Protection Agency, 80; mem Adv Comt, NSF Proj Risk Assessment, 78, 81-82. *Mem:* Soc Risk Anal; AAAS; Sigma Xi. *Res:* Analysis and management of technological risks; projection of energy supply and demand; analysis of new energy technology integration. *Mailing Add:* Elec Power Res Inst 3412 Hillview Ave Palo Alto CA 94303

WHIPPLE, EARL BENNETT, b Thomson, Ga, Apr 9, 30; m 51; c 4. PHYSICAL CHEMISTRY. *Educ:* Emory Univ, BS, 51, PhD(phys chem), 59. *Prof Exp:* Chemist, Va-Carolina Chem Corp, Va, 52-53; res scientist chem, Union Carbide Res Inst, 59-66, group leader chem, 66-70, mgr res, Cent Sci Lab, Tarrytown Tech Ctr, Union Carbide Corp, 70-74; RES ADV, CENT RES, PFIZER, INC, 74- *Concurrent Pos:* Adj prof, Rockefeller Univ, 69-74. *Mem:* NY Acad Sci; Am Chem Soc. *Res:* Chemical applications of nuclear and electron spin resonance; structure and electronic properties of molecules. *Mailing Add:* 4 Dwayne Rd Old Saybrook CT 06475

WHIPPLE, FRED LAWRENCE, b Red Oak, Iowa, Nov 5, 06; m 46; c 3. ASTRONOMY, SPACE PHYSICS. *Educ:* Univ Calif, Los Angeles, AB, 27; Univ Calif, Berkeley, PhD(astron), 31. *Hon Degrees:* MA, Harvard Univ, 45; DSc, Am Int Col, 48 & Temple Univ, 61; DLitt, Northeastern Univ, 61. *Prof Exp:* Instr, Univ, 32-38, lectr, 38-45, from assoc prof to prof, 45-70, chmn dept, 49-56, Phillips prof, 70-77, EMER PHILLIPS PROF ASTRON, HARVARD UNIV, 77-, MEM STAFF, OBSERV, 31- *Concurrent Pos:* Res assoc radio res lab, Off Sci Res & Develop, 42-45; leader, Harvard proj upper atmospheric & meteor res, Bur Ord, US Navy, 46-51, Air Res & Develop Command, US Air Force, 48-62, Off Naval Res, 51-57, Off Ord Res, US Army, 53-57, dir, Harvard Radio Meteor Proj, Nat Bur Standards, 57-61, NSF, 60-63 & NASA, 63-; Lowell lectr, Lowell Technol Inst, 47; dir, Astrophys Observ, Smithsonian Inst, 55-73,sr scientist, Astrophys Observ, 73-77; ed, Smithsonian Contrib Astrophys, 56-; regional ed, Planetary & Space Sci, 58-, mem, US Rocket & Satellite Res Panel, 46-; mem subcomt, Nat Adv Comt Aeronaut, 46-52; mem panel upper atmosphere, US Res & Develop Bd, 47-52; adv panel astron, NSF, 52-55, chmn, 54-55, mem div comt math & phys sci, 64-; mem sci adv bd, US Air Force, 53-62, assoc adv, 63-67, mem geophys & space tech panels; mem comts meteorol & atmospheric sci, Nat Acad Sci-Nat Res Coun, 58-, space sci bd, 58- & subcomt potential contamination & interference from space exp, 63-; dir optical satellite tracking proj & proj dir orbiting astron observ, NASA, 58-72, mem space sci working group orbiting astron observ, 59-69, consult aeronomy subcomt, 61-63, comt planetary atmospheres, 62-63, dir meteorite photog & recovery prog, 62-73, mem working group geod satellite prog, 63- & mem comet & asteroid sci adv comt, 71-72, chmn, 73-74; mem joint bio-astronaut comt, Armed Forces-Nat Res Coun, 59-61; spec consult comt sci & astronaut, US House Rep, 60-73; mem working groups geod satellites & tracking, telemetry & dynamics, Comt Space Res, 60-, chmn sci coun geod uses artificial satellites, 65-; chmn, Gordon Res Conf Chem & Physics Space, 63; trustee-at-large, Univ Corp Atmospheric Res, Colo, 64-68 & mem, Comt Nat Ctr Atmospheric Res Staff-Univ rels, 65-68. Mem, vpres & pres comns, Int Astron Union, 32-, voting rep, 52 & 55; deleg, Inter-Am Astrophys Cong, Mex, 42; mem comn 3, U S nat comt, Int Sci Radio Union, 49-61; Int Astron Fedn, 55-; mem working group satellite tracking & comput & chief investr proj optical tracking artificial earth satellites, Int Geophys Yr, 55-58, mem tech panel earth satellite prog & tech panel rocketry, 55-59. *Honors & Awards:* Donohue Medals; President's Cert Merit; Smith Medal, Nat Acad Sci, 49; Except Serv Award, US Air Force, 60; Medal, Univ Liege, 60; Award, Am Astronaut Soc, 61; Comdr, Order of Merit Res & Invention, France, 62; President's Distinguished Fed Civilian Serv Award, 63; Space Pioneers Medallion, 68; Pub Serv Award, NASA, 69; Leonard Medal, Meteoritical Soc, 70; Kepler Medal, AAAS, 71; Career Serv Award, Nat Civil Serv League, 72; Henry Medal, Bd Regents, Smithsonian Inst, 73. *Mem:* Nat Acad Sci; fel Am Astron Soc (vpres, 48-50); fel Am Astronaut Soc (vpres, 62-64); fel Am Geophys Union; fel Am Inst Aeronaut & Astronaut. *Res:* Photometry; computation of comet discoveries; colors of external galaxies; novae; meteor orbits; earth's upper atmosphere; stellar and pla. *Mailing Add:* Belmont MA

WHIPPLE, GERALD HOWARD, b Calif, Feb 6, 23; m 47; c 5. MEDICINE. *Educ:* Harvard Univ, SB, 43; Univ Calif, MD, 46; Am Bd Internal Med, dipl, 60. *Prof Exp:* Instr, Sch Med, Boston Univ, 56-57, assoc, 57-60, from asst prof to assoc prof, 60-68; from assoc prof to prof med, Col Med, Univ Calif, Irvine, 71-78, chief cardiol div, 74-78; PROF CARDIOL MED & DIR, DIV CARDIOL, UNIV RENO, 78- *Concurrent Pos:* Res fel med, Harvard Univ, 53-56; vol asst med, Congenital Heart Clin, Children's Med Ctr, Boston, 54-56; physician in chg, EKG Lab, Univ Hosp, Boston Univ, 56-58, physician, Cardiac Care Univ, 65-68, assoc vis physician, 56-68, assoc mem, Evans Mem Res Found, 56-68, sect head clin cardiol res; consult cardiol, Congenital Heart Clin, Boston City Hosp, 58-59; res consult, Providence Vet Admin Hosp, RI, 60-68; res assoc, Mass Inst Technol, 63-66; fel coun clin cardiol, Am Heart Asn; heart coordr area VIII, Regional Med Prog Cancer, Heart & Stroke, 68-; physician & dir intensive cardiac care unit, Orange County Med Ctr, 69-70; chief med serv, Vet Admin Hosp, Long Beach, 70-74 & Reno, 81- *Mem:* Fel Am Col Physicians; fel Am Col Cardiol. *Res:* Academic cardiology; cardiology; cardiac arrhythmias; epidemiologic evaluation of acute ischemic heart disease and sudden death. *Mailing Add:* Div Cardiol Univ Reno Reno NV 89507

WHIPPLE, JEANNETTE ADAIR, fish biology, environmental physiology, see previous edition

WHIPPLE, ROYSON NEWTON, b Buffalo, NY, May 28, 12; m 35; c 2. FOOD TECHNOLOGY. *Educ:* Univ Mich, BS, 35; Cornell Univ, MS, 39. *Prof Exp:* Instr high sch, NY, 35-45; prof & head div food technol, 45-57, PRES, STATE UNIV NY AGR & TECH COL, MORRISVILLE, 57- *Mem:* Inst Food Technologists. *Res:* Background needs for food technologists engaged in fruit and vegetable processing. *Mailing Add:* Box 206 Morrisville NY 13408

WHIRLOW, DONALD KENT, b Pittsburgh, Pa, May 2, 38; m 62; c 3. FLUID DYNAMICS, AERODYNAMICS. *Educ:* Carnegie Inst Technol, BS, 60, MS, 61, PhD(mech eng), 64. *Prof Exp:* Sr engr, 66-71, mgr fluid dynamics, 71-76, ADV ENGR, FLUID DYNAMICS RES, WESTINGHOUSE RES & DEVELOP CTR, 76- *Mem:* Am Soc Mech Engrs; Sigma Xi. *Res:* Fluid dynamics and heat transfer; turbomachinery; acoustic flowmetering; transformers; transonic flow; unsteady aerodynamics; two-phase steam flow; finite element analysis. *Mailing Add:* Westinghouse Elec Corp 1310 Beulah Rd Pittsburgh PA 15235

WHISLER, FRANK DUANE, b Burton, WVa, Nov 20, 34; m 56; c 4. SOIL PHYSICS. *Educ:* Univ WVa, BS, 57, MS, 58; Univ Ill, PhD(soil physics), 64. *Prof Exp:* Soil scientist, Agr Res Serv, USDA, Ill, 58-69, soil scientist, Water Conserv Lab, 69-73; PROF AGRON & AGRONOMIST, MISS STATE UNIV, 73- *Honors & Awards:* Award, Soil Sci Soc Am, 63. *Mem:* Am Soc Agron; Soil Sci Soc Am. *Res:* Water movement into and through soils or other porous material from both a theoretical and experimental point of view. *Mailing Add:* Dept of Agron Miss State Univ Box 5248 Mississippi State MS 39759

WHISLER, HOWARD CLINTON, b Oakland, Calif, Feb 4, 31; m 53; c 2. BOTANY, MICROBIOLOGY. *Educ:* Univ Calif, Berkeley, BSc, 54, PhD(bot), 61. *Prof Exp:* NATO fel, Univ Montpellier, 60-61; asst prof bot, McGill Univ, 61-63; from asst prof to assoc prof, 63-73, PROF BOT, UNIV WASH, 73- *Concurrent Pos:* NSF fel, Univ Geneva, 68-69. *Mem:* Mycol Soc Am; Soc Invert Path. *Res:* Development of the aquatic phycomycetes; insect microbiology. *Mailing Add:* Dept of Bot Univ of Wash Seattle WA 98195

WHISLER, KENNETH EUGENE, physiology, clinical chemistry, see previous edition

WHISLER, WALTER WILLIAM, b Davenport, Iowa, Feb 9, 34; m 59; c 2. BIOCHEMISTRY, NEUROSURGERY. *Educ:* Augustana Col, AB, 55; Univ Ill, MD, 59, PhD(biochem), 69; Am Bd Neurol Surg, dipl, 67. *Prof Exp:* USPHS fel, 64-65; PROF BIOCHEM & NEUROSURG & CHMN DEPT NEUROSURG, RUSH MED COL, 70- *Concurrent Pos:* Attend neurosurgeon & chmn dept neurosurg, Presby-St Luke's Hosp, 70-; clin assoc prof, Univ Ill Col Med, 70- *Mem:* AMA; Am Asn Neurol Surg; Cong Neurol Surg; Int Soc Res Stereoencephalotomy. *Res:* Mechanisms of catecholomine oxidation; metabolism of the psychotomimetic amines; biochemistry of brain tumors. *Mailing Add:* Dept of Neurosurg Presby-St Luke's Hosp Chicago IL 60612

WHISNANT, JACK PAGE, b Little Rock, Ark, Oct 26, 24; m 44; c 3. MEDICINE, NEUROLOGY. *Educ:* Univ Ark, BS, 48, MD, 51. *Prof Exp:* From instr to assoc prof, 56-69, PROF NEUROL, MAYO MED SCH, UNIV MINN, 69-, CHMN DEPT, 71- *Concurrent Pos:* Consult, Mayo Clin, 55-, head sect neurol, 63-71. *Mem:* Am Acad Neurol; Am Neurol Asn. *Res:* Clinical neurology, especially vascular diseases of the nervous system. *Mailing Add:* Dept Neurol Mayo Med Sch Univ of Minn Rochester MN 55901

WHISONANT, ROBERT CLYDE, b Columbia, SC, Apr 20, 41; m 63; c 2. STRATIGRAPHY, SEDIMENTOLOGY. *Educ:* Clemson Univ, BS, 63; Fla State Univ, MS, 65, PhD(geol), 67. *Prof Exp:* Petrol geologist, Humble Oil & Ref Co, 67-71; asst prof, 71-72, assoc prof geol, 72-81, PROF & CHMN GEOL, RADFORD UNIV, 81- *Mem:* Geol Soc Am; Am Asn Petrol Geol; Soc Econ Paleontologists & Mineralogists; Sigma Xi. *Res:* Paleozoic rocks of the southern Appalachians, specifically, sedimentary petrography and paleocurrent features; paleoenvironmental determinations; stratigraphic analysis. *Mailing Add:* Dept of Geol Radford Univ Radford VA 24142

WHISSELL-BUECHY, DOROTHY Y E, b St Louis, Mo, Apr 12, 26; m 56; c 3. HUMAN GENETICS. *Educ:* Wellesley Col, AB, 48; Univ Tex Southwestern Med Sch Dallas, MD, 56; Univ Calif, Berkeley, PhD(genetics), 68. *Prof Exp:* INSTR GENETICS IN GENETICS, UNIV CALIF, BERKELEY, 64-, ASST RES GENETICIST, INST HUMAN DEVELOP, 69- *Concurrent Pos:* Instr, Univ Exten, 71- *Mem:* Behav Genetics Asn. *Res:* assessment of health at various stages of development, especially middle age; genetics of olfaction; genetics of personality. *Mailing Add:* 1203 Tolman Hall Univ Calif Inst Human Develop Berkeley CA 94720

WHISTLER, DAVID PAUL, b Summit, NJ, June 15, 40; m 64; c 2. VERTEBRATE PALEONTOLOGY. *Educ:* Univ Calif, Riverside, BA, 63, MA, 65; Univ Calif, Berkeley, PhD(paleont), 69. *Prof Exp:* Mus scientist paleont, Univ Calif Mus Paleont, 67-69; asst prof geol, Tex Tech Univ, 69-70; CUR VERT PALEONT, NATURAL HIST MUS, LOS ANGELES COUNTY, 69- *Mem:* Soc Vert Paleont; Paleont Soc; Geol Soc Am; Am Soc Mammalogists. *Res:* Evolution, taxonomy and biostratigraphy of smaller vertebrates, amphibians, reptiles rodents and insectivores in later Tertiary. *Mailing Add:* 900 Expos Blvd Los Angeles CA 90007

WHISTLER, ROY LESTER, b Morgantown, WVa, Mar 21, 12; m 35; c 1. CHEMISTRY. *Educ:* Heidelberg Col, BS, 34; Ohio State Univ, MS, 35; Iowa State Univ, PhD, 38. *Prof Exp:* Instr chem, Iowa State Col, 35-38; fel, Nat Bur Stand, 38-40; head starch struct sect, USDA, 40-45 & Northern Regional Res Lab, Bur Agr Chem & Eng, 45-46; asst head dept, 48-60, chmn inst agr utilization res, 61-78, prof biochem, 46-75, HILLENBRAND DISTINGUISHED PROF BIOCHEM, PURDUE UNIV, WEST LAFAYETTE, 75- *Concurrent Pos:* Vis lectr, Univ Witwatersrand, 61, Cape Town, 65, NZ & Australia, 67 & 74, Czech Acad Sci & Hungarian Acad Sci, 68, Taiwan, 70 & France & Poland, 75; Far East, Vladivostok Acad Sci lectr to USSR, 76; Nat Res Coun lectr, Brazil, 77; Welsh Found lectr, Tex, 77; guest lectr, Repub SAfrica, 77; guest, Polish Acad Sci, 78. *Honors & Awards:* Hudson Award, Am Chem Soc, 60, Payen Award, 67; Annual Res Award, Japanese Tech Soc Starch, 67; Alsberg Schoch Award, Am Asn Cereal Chem, 70, Osborn Medal, 74; German Saare Medal, 74. *Mem:* AAAS; Am Chem Soc; Am Soc Biol Chemists; Am Asn Cereal Chem (pres, 72-73); Am Inst Chemists (pres, 80-81). *Res:* Chemistry and biochemistry of carbohydrates, particularly polysaccharides; polysaccharide chemistry. *Mailing Add:* Dept Biochem Purdue Univ West Lafayette IN 47907

WHITACRE, DAVID MARTIN, b Mariemont, Ohio, Dec 4, 43; m 66; c 2. ENVIRONMENTAL SCIENCES. *Educ:* Wilmington Col, Ohio, AB, 65; Ohio State Univ, MSc, 66; Univ Ariz, PhD(entom, zool), 69. *Prof Exp:* Asst prof biol, Univ PR, Mayaguez, 69-71; State of Ariz res grant entom, Univ Ariz, 71-72; proj mgr entom toxicol, 72-73, DIR ENVIRON RES, VELSICOL CHEM CORP, 73- *Mem:* Entom Soc Am; Am Chem Soc. *Res:* Metabolism of pesticides in plants and animals. *Mailing Add:* Velsicol Chem Corp 341 E Ohio St Chicago IL 60611

WHITACRE, GALE R(OBERT), b Salem, Ohio, June 23, 33; m 57; c 3. MECHANICAL ENGINEERING. *Educ:* Univ Cincinnati, BS, 56; Purdue Univ, MS, 58. *Prof Exp:* Res mech engr, 57-65, sr mech engr, 65-71, fel, 71-77, PRIN RESEARCHER, BATTELLE MEM INST, 77- *Mem:* Am Soc Mech Engrs. *Res:* Heat transfer; boundary layer flow; ablation; re-entry thermal analysis. *Mailing Add:* 3042 Midgard Ave Columbus OH 43202

WHITAKER, CLAY WESTERFIELD, b Greenville, Ky, Apr 17, 24; m; c 4. OTOLARYNGOLOGY. *Educ:* Berea Col, BA, 48; Western Reserve Univ, MD, 52; Am Bd Otolaryngol, dipl, 58. *Prof Exp:* Asst otolaryngologist, Highland View Hosp, Cleveland, Ohio, 52; asst to dir ear, nose & throat dept, St Luke's Hosp, Cleveland, 56; asst otolaryngologist, Univ Hosp & demonstr & clin instr otolaryngol, Med Sch, Western Reserve Univ, 56-61; from asst prof to assoc prof, 64-70, PROF SURG, SCH MED, UNIV SOUTHERN CALIF, 70-; PROF & DIR EAR, NOSE & THROAT RES TRAINING, LOS ANGELES COUNTY-UNIV SOUTHERN CALIF MED CTR, 64-, CHIEF PHYSICIAN & DIR DEPT OTOLARYNGOL, 65- *Concurrent Pos:* Consult, Highland View Hosp, Cleveland, 56-61, Dept Pub Social Serv-Med Sci Div Hearing Aid Prog, Los Angeles County, 65-, Porterville State Hosp, Calif, 66-, tech adv comt on hearing aids, Dept Health Care Serv, State of Calif, 67-, Children's Hosp, Los Angeles, 67- & Hollywood Presby Hosp, Los Angeles, 67- *Mem:* AMA; Am Acad Ophthal & Otolaryngol. *Res:* Otorhinolaryngology; experimental surgery for device as practical prosthetic larynx; etiologic factors influencing Bell's Palsy. *Mailing Add:* Dept of Otolaryngol LAC-USC Med Ctr Box 795 Los Angeles CA 90033

WHITAKER, ELLIS HOBART, b Salem, Mass, Dec 2, 08; m 35, 66; c 2. PLANT PHYSIOLOGY. *Educ:* Worcester Polytech Inst, BS, 30; Cornell Univ, MS, 36, PhD(plant physiol), 49. *Prof Exp:* Engr, Gilbert & Barker Mfg, Mass, 30-31; teacher, Monson Acad, 33-35 & Westover Sch, Conn, 36-39; asst gen bot, Cornell Univ, 40-41; instr phys sci & gen biol, State Univ NY Col Oneonta, 41-48, asst prof chem, 48-54, assoc prof biol, 54-64; from assoc prof to prof biol, 64-76, EMER PROF BIOL, SOUTHEASTERN MASS UNIV, 76- *Concurrent Pos:* Consult, W W Norton Co, 79-80. *Mem:* Fel AAAS. *Res:* General biology; enzymes in insectivorous plants. *Mailing Add:* 32 Prospect St South Dartmouth MA 02748

WHITAKER, EWEN A, b London, Eng, June 22, 22; m 46; c 3. PLANETARY SCIENCES, HISTORY OF SELENOGRAPHY. *Educ:* Brit Inst Mech Eng, cert, 42. *Prof Exp:* Lab asst chem anal & phys testing, Siemens Bros & Co Ltd, 40-41, lab asst spectrochem anal, 41-49; sci asst, Royal Greenwich Observ, 49-53, from asst exp officer to exp officer, 53-58; res assoc, Yerkes Observ, Univ Chicago, 58-60; RES ASSOC, LUNAR & PLANETARY LAB, UNIV ARIZ, 60-, RES FEL, 76- *Concurrent Pos:* Co-experimenter, Ranger moonshots, 62-66; mem TV exp team, Surveyor Spacecraft, 64-68; mem site selection team, Orbiter 5, 67-68; mem, Apollo Orbital Sci Photo Team, 69-73. *Mem:* Int Astron Union; Am Astron Soc; fel Royal Astron Soc. *Res:* Study of moon, particularly of surface features and properties by earthbased telescopic observations and research and spacecraft; history of selenography; standardization of lunar nomenclature. *Mailing Add:* Lunar & Planetary Lab Univ of Ariz Tucson AZ 85721

WHITAKER, H(ENRY) PHILIP, b Penn Yan, NY, June 24, 21; m 52; c 3. AERONAUTICAL ENGINEERING. *Educ:* Mass Inst Technol, SB, 44, SM, 59. *Prof Exp:* Dynamicist, Convair Div, Gen Dynamics Corp, 44-47; mem staff, Instrumentation Lab, 47-57, lectr aeronaut, 56-59, dep assoc dir, Draper Lab, 57-64, assoc prof aeronaut, 59-65, PROF AERONAUT & ASTRONAUT, MASS INST TECHNOL, 65-, CONSULT, DRAPER LAB, 64- *Mem:* Soc Automotive Engrs; Am Inst Aeronaut & Astronaut. *Res:* Guidance and control of flight vehicles; automatic control; flight transportation. *Mailing Add:* Dept of Aeronaut & Astronaut Mass Inst of Technol Cambridge MA 02139

WHITAKER, JOHN O, JR, b Oneonta, NY, Apr 22, 35; m 57; c 3. VERTEBRATE ECOLOGY, MAMMALOGY. *Educ:* Cornell Univ, BS, 57, PhD(vert zool), 62. *Prof Exp:* From asst prof to assoc prof, 62-71, PROF LIFE SCI, IND STATE UNIV, TERRE HAUTE, 71- *Mem:* Fel AAAS; Am Soc Mammal; Ecol Soc Am; Soc Study Amphibians & Reptiles; Am Inst Biol Sci. *Res:* Food habits, parasites, habitats and interrelations of species. *Mailing Add:* Dept of Life Sci Ind State Univ Terre Haute IN 47809

WHITAKER, JOHN ROBERT, b Lubbock, Tex, Sept 13, 29; m 52; c 4. BIOCHEMISTRY. *Educ:* Berea Col, AB, 51; Ohio State Univ, PhD(agr biochem), 54. *Prof Exp:* Lab asst chem, Berea Col, 50-51; asst agr biochem, Ohio State Univ, 51-52, asst instr, 53-54, fel, 54; from instr to assoc prof, 56-67, PROF FOOD SCI & TECHNOL, UNIV CALIF, DAVIS, 67-, ASSOC DEAN, COL AGR & ENVIRON SCI, 75- *Concurrent Pos:* NIH spec fel, Northwestern Univ, 63-64; vis prof, Vet Col, Norway, 72 & Univ Bristol, Eng, 72-73, Norwegin Food Res Inst, 79, Instituto Pulitecno Nacional, Mexico, 80, Univ Campina, Brizil, 80, Metropolitana Univ, Mexico, 80. *Honors & Awards:* Centennial Achievement Award, Ohio State Univ, 70; William V Cruess Award, Inst Food Technologists, 73. *Mem:* Am Chem Soc; Inst Food Technologists; Am Soc Biol Chemists. *Res:* Relationship between structure and function in enzymes; chemical improvement of proteins for food use. *Mailing Add:* Dept of Food Sci & Technol Univ of Calif Davis CA 95616

WHITAKER, LESLIE A, b Denver, Colo, Sept 25, 23; m 51; c 3. ANALYTICAL CHEMISTRY. *Educ:* Univ Denver, BS, 49, MA, 56; Univ of the Pac, PhD(anal chem), 68. *Prof Exp:* Teacher chem & physics, Littleton High Sch, 52-54; instr chem, Scottsbluff Col, 56-57; asst prof & dean of fac, Cottey Col, 57-61; instr, Col of Desert, 62-64; assoc prof, Calif Polytech State Univ, San Luis Obispo, 67-72; teacher & bus mgr, Desert Sun Sch, 72-75; DIR LABS CHEM, UNIV SOUTHERN CALIF, 75- *Mem:* Am Chem Soc. *Mailing Add:* Dept of Chem Univ of Southern Calif Los Angeles CA 90007

WHITAKER, MACK LEE, b Forest City, NC, Dec 2, 31; m 56; c 2. MATHEMATICS. *Educ:* Appalachian State Teachers Col, BS, 53, MA, 56; Fla State Univ, EdD, 61. *Prof Exp:* Teacher, Piedmont High Sch, 56-58; from assoc prof to prof math, Radford Col, 60-68, chmn dept, 62-66; assoc prof math educ, Auburn Univ, 68-69; PROF MATH, RADFORD UNIV, 69- *Mem:* Math Asn Am. *Res:* Mathematics education; abstract algebra; foundations of mathematics. *Mailing Add:* Dept of Math Radford Col Radford VA 24141

WHITAKER, ROBERT DALLAS, b Tampa, Fla, Mar 5, 33; m 60; c 3. INORGANIC CHEMISTRY. *Educ:* Univ Washington & Lee, BS, 55; Univ Fla, PhD(inorg chem), 59. *Prof Exp:* Asst prof chem, Washington & Lee Univ, 59-62; from asst prof to assoc prof, 62-74, PROF CHEM, UNIV SOUTH FLA, TAMPA, 74- *Mem:* Am Chem Soc. *Res:* Molecular addition compounds. *Mailing Add:* Dept Chem Univ SFla Tampa FL 33620

WHITAKER, SIDNEY HOPKINS, b Spring Valley, Ill, Apr 7, 40. GEOLOGY. *Educ:* Oberlin Col, BA, 62; Univ Ill, PhD(geol), 65. *Prof Exp:* Fel, Sask Res Coun, 65-67, asst res officer, 67-71, assoc res officer geol, 71-75, sr res scientist geol, 75-77; pres, Silverspoon Res & Consult Ltd, 77-81; SR RES OFFICER HYDROGEOL, ATOMIC ENERGY CAN LTD, 81- *Concurrent Pos:* Mem geosci working group, Can Adv Comt Remote Sensing, Can Ctr Remote Sensing. *Mem:* Glaciol Soc; Geol Asn Can; Geol Soc Am. *Res:* Review Canadian geoscience programs for deep disposal of radioactive waste; techniques of groundwater exploration; hydrogeology; field geology; mapping; subsurface exploration and stratigraphy; lignite exploration. *Mailing Add:* Box 3044 Saskatoon SK S7K 3S9 Can

WHITAKER, THOMAS BURTON, b Asheville, NC, May 16, 39; m 60; c 1. AGRICULTURAL ENGINEERING. *Educ:* NC State Univ, BS, 62, MS, 64; Ohio State Univ, PhD(agr eng), 67. *Prof Exp:* From asst prof to assoc prof, 67-76, PROF BIOL & AGR ENG, NC STATE UNIV, 76-, AGR ENGR, AGR RES SERV, USDA, 67- *Honors & Awards:* Bailey Award, Am Peanut Res & Educ Asn, 76; Golden Peanut Res Award, Nat Peanut Coun, 80. *Mem:* Am Soc Agr Engrs; Am Peanut Res & Educ Soc; Sigma Xi. *Res:* Quality control of agricultural commodities with main emphasis concerning the detection, control, and elimination of mycotoxins in food products. *Mailing Add:* Sci & Educ Admin Agr Res USDA NC State Univ Raleigh NC 27650

WHITAKER, THOMAS WALLACE, b Monrovia, Calif, Aug 13, 05; m 31; c 2. GENETICS. *Educ:* Univ Calif, BS, 27; Univ Va, MS, 29, PhD(genetics, cytol), 31. *Prof Exp:* Asst bot, Bussey Inst & Arnold Arboretum fel, Harvard Univ, 31-34; assoc prof bot, Agnes Scott Col, 34-36; from assoc geneticist to geneticist, Bur Plant Indust, 36-52, sr geneticist, Hort Crops Res Br, 52-56, prin geneticist & invest leader, Crops Res Div, 56-61, res geneticist & invest leader, 61-73, COLLABR CROPS, SCI & EDUC ADMIN-FED RES, WESTERN REGION, USDA, 73- *Concurrent Pos:* Guggenheim Mem Found fel, Wash Univ, 46-47 & Univ Calif, Davis, 59; consult, Peabody Archaeol Proj, Tehuacan, Mex, 62; lectr, Tulane Univ, 67, Univ Ariz, 71, Univ Ragistan, 72, Purdue Univ, 72 & Univ Ill, 73, Univ Nacional de la Plata, 80-81; ed, Hortsci, 69, Jour, 69-75; mem comt genetic vulnerability of major crops, Nat Res Coun, 71; res assoc, Univ Calif, San Diego, 73- *Mem:* Fel Am Soc Hort Sci (pres, 74); hon life mem Can Soc Hort Sci; fel Torrey Bot Club; Soc Econ Bot (pres, 69); Am Plant Life Soc (exec secy, 55-). *Res:* Plant breeding; vegetable crops; genetics and cytology of Lactuca and the Cucurbitaceae; origin and domestication of cucurbits as related to cultural history; development of lettuce cultivars. *Mailing Add:* PO Box 150 La Jolla CA 92038

WHITAKER, WILLIAM ARMSTRONG, b Little Rock, Ark, Jan 10, 36; m 57; c 2. COMPUTER SCIENCE, NATURAL SCIENCE. *Educ:* Tulane Univ, BS, 55, MS, 56; Univ Chicago, PhD(physics), 63. *Prof Exp:* Asst physics, Tulane Univ, 54-56; US Air Force, 56-, prof off res & develop, 57-68, chief high altitude group, Weapons Lab, 68-70, chief scientist, 70-72, mil asst res, Off Dir Defense Res & Eng, 73-75, spec asst to dir defense advan res proj agency, 75-80, TECH DIR FOR DIGITAL APPLICATIONS, AIR FORCE ARMAMENT DEVELOP LAB, ELGIN AFB, 80- *Mem:* Am Phys Soc; Am Astron Soc; Am Geophys Union; Am Meteorol Soc; Inst Elec & Electronics Engrs. *Res:* Direction of advanced research, defense software management, common high order computer programming languages. *Mailing Add:* Box 458 Valparaiso FL 32580

WHITBY, KENNETH T(HOMAS), b Fond du Lac, Wis, Feb 6, 25; m 48; c 4. MECHANICAL ENGINEERING. *Educ:* Univ Minn, BS, 46, BME, 48, PhD(mech eng, biol chem), 54. *Prof Exp:* Instr, 46-52, res assoc, 54-57, from asst prof to assoc prof, 58-66, PROF MECH ENG, UNIV MINN, MINNEAPOLIS, 66-, DIR ENVIRON DIV, 75- *Concurrent Pos:* Consult, 3M Co; USPHS fel, Ger, 67-68; mem panel on abatement of particulate emissions from stationary sources, Nat Res Coun, 71-; mem panel on air pollution, Chem & Physics Adv Comt, Environ Protection Agency. *Mem:* Nat Acad Eng; AAAS; Am Soc Mech Engrs; NY Acad Sci; Air Pollution Control Asn. *Res:* Small particle technology, particularly particle size analysis; particle processing; air cleaning; aerosol physics; thermodynamics; combustion; air pollution. *Mailing Add:* Dept of Mech Eng Univ of Minn Minneapolis MN 55455

WHITBY, OWEN, b Luton, Eng, Feb 24, 42; Can & UK citizen; m 70. STATISTICS. *Educ:* McMaster Univ, BSc Hons, 64; Stanford Univ, MS, 66, PhD(statist), 72. *Prof Exp:* From asst prof to assoc prof statist, Teachers Col, Columbia Univ, 71-78; MATHEMATICAL STATISTICIAN, 78- *Mem:* AAAS; Am Statist Asn; Asn Comput Mach; Biomet Soc; Inst Math Statist. *Res:* Biostatistics; mathematical statistics; actuarial methods. *Mailing Add:* 106 Morningside Dr New York NY 10027

WHITCOMB, CARL ERWIN, b Independence, Kans, Oct 26, 39; m 63; c 2. HORTICULTURE, PLANT ECOLOGY. *Educ:* Kans State Univ, BSA, 64; Iowa State Univ, MS, 66, PhD(hort, plant ecol), 69. *Prof Exp:* Asst prof ornamental hort, Univ Fla, 67-72; PROF HORT, OKLA STATE UNIV, 72-

Mem: Am Soc Hort Sci; Ecol Soc Am; Am Soc Agron; Soc Am Foresters. *Res:* Plant interactions in man-made or man-managed landscapes; production, establishment and maintenance of landscape plants. *Mailing Add:* Dept of Hort Okla State Univ Stillwater OK 74074

WHITCOMB, DONALD LEROY, b Ilion, NY, Feb 1, 25; m 48; c 4. ANALYTICAL CHEMISTRY. *Educ:* Univ Rochester, BS, 52, PhD(phys chem), 56. *Prof Exp:* Res chemist, Res Labs, Eastman Kodak Co, NY, 46-53; mem tech staff, Bell Tel Labs, Pa, 56-63; mem tech staff, Microwave Tube Div, Hughes Aircraft Co, 63-64 & Space Systs Div, 64-66; chemist, Motorola Semiconductor Prod Inc, 66-70; chief chemist, Ariz State Dept Health, 70-81; CHEM SUPVR, WRF OPERS, ARIZ PUB SERV CO, 81- *Mem:* Am Chem Soc; Am Phys Soc. *Mailing Add:* 4414 N Dromedary Rd Phoenix AZ 85018

WHITCOMB, STANLEY E, b Denver, Colo, Jan 23, 51; m 77. ASTROPHYSICS. *Educ:* Calif Inst Technol, BS, 73; Univ Chicago, PhD(physics), 80. *Prof Exp:* Nat Needs fel, Univ Chicago, 80; ASST PROF PHYSICS, CALIF INST TECHNOL, 80- *Mem:* Am Phys Soc; Am Astron Soc. *Res:* Experimental gravitation primarily involving the development of laser interferometric gravitational wave detectors for the study of astrophysical sources. *Mailing Add:* Calif Inst Technol 130-33 Pasadena CA 91125

WHITCOMB, STUART ESTES, physics, deceased

WHITCOMB, WALTER HENRY, b Enid, Okla, Jan 26, 28; m 46; c 3. INTERNAL MEDICINE, NUCLEAR MEDICINE. *Educ:* Univ Okla, BA, 50, MD, 53; Am Bd Nuclear Med, dipl, 72. *Prof Exp:* Clin asst, Sch Med & chief res med, Med Ctr, Univ Okla, 56-57, chief exp med group, Radiobiol Lab, Univ Tex-US Air Force, 58-60; investr & instr radiobiol, Bionucleonics Dept, US Air Force Sch Aerospace Med, 60-62; from asst prof to assoc prof, 62-79, PROF MED, SCH MED, UNIV OKLA, 79-; DIR, VET ADMIN MED CTR, 81- *Concurrent Pos:* Res fel hemat, Univ Okla, 57-58; clin investr, Southwest Cancer Chemother Study Group, Vet Admin Hosp, 62-66, chief radioisotopes serv & hemat sect, 62-70, assoc chief staff res & educ, 63-67; from asst prof to assoc prof radiol, Sch Med, Univ Okla, 64-79, asst dean vet affairs, 70-79; chief staff, Vet Admin Hosp, 70-79; mgt support staff, Dept Med & Surg, Vet Admin Cent Off, 79-81. *Mem:* Am Col Physicians; Cent Soc Clin Res; Am Soc Hemat. *Res:* Biological effects of radiation; control of erythropoiesis; physiology of erythropoietin and erythropoietin inhibitor factors; operations research. *Mailing Add:* Vet Admin Med Ctr Oklahoma City OK 73104

WHITCOMB, WILLARD HALL, b Manchester, NH, July 2, 15; m 43. ENTOMOLOGY. *Educ:* Bates Col, BS, 38; Agr & Mech Col, Tex, MS, 42; Cornell Univ, PhD(entom), 47. *Prof Exp:* Entomologist, Ministry Agr, Venezuela, 47-52 & Shell Co, Venezuela, 52-56; prof entom, Univ Ark, 56-57; prof entom, Big Bend Hort Lab, Univ Fla, 67-69, PROF ENTOM, UNIV FLA, 69- *Mem:* Entom Soc Am; Entom Soc Can; Int Orgn Biol Control. *Res:* Biological control of arthropods; ecology and population dynamics; pest management; tropical entomology. *Mailing Add:* Dept of Entom Univ of Fla Gainesville FL 32611

WHITE, ABRAHAM, b Cleveland, Ohio, Mar 8, 08; m 37. BIOCHEMISTRY. *Educ:* Univ Denver, AB, 27, MA, 28; Univ Mich, PhD(physiol chem), 31. *Hon Degrees:* LHD, Yeshiva Univ, 59; DSc, Univ Denver, 75. *Prof Exp:* Asst chem, Univ Denver, 27-28; asst physiol chem, Univ Mich, 28-30; Sterling fel, Yale Univ, 31-32, Am Physiol Soc Porter fel, 32-33, instr sch med, 33-37, from asst prof to assoc prof, 37-48, exec officer dept, 47-48; prof & chmn dept, Sch Med, Univ Calif, Los Angeles, 48-51; vpres & dir res, Chem Specialties Co, Inc, NY, 51-53; prof biochem, chmn dept & assoc dean, Albert Einstein Col Med, Yeshiva Univ, 53-72; sr scientist, 72-73, distinguished scientist, Syntex Res, 73-77; EMER PROF BIOCHEM, ALBERT EINSTEIN COL MED, YESHIVA UNIV, 77- *Concurrent Pos:* Am Physiol Soc fel, Int Physiol Cong, USSR, 35; consult, US Vet Admin, Calif, 49-51; vis prof biochem, Med Sch, Stanford Univ, 72-73, consult prof biochem, 73-; vis prof biochem, Albert Einstein Col Med, Yeshiva Univ, 72- *Honors & Awards:* Lilly Prize, Am Chem Soc, 38. *Mem:* Nat Acad Sci; Am Chem Soc; Soc Exp Biol & Med; fel NY Acad Sci; Am Soc Cell Biol. *Res:* Chemistry and metabolism of amino acids, functions of lymphoid tissue; biochemistry of hormones. *Mailing Add:* 580 Arastradero Rd Apt 507 Palo Alto CA 94306

WHITE, ALAN GEORGE CASTLE, b Boston, Eng, Aug 12, 16; nat US; m 45; c 2. BACTERIOLOGY. *Educ:* RI State Col, BS, 38; Pa State Col, MS, 40; Iowa State Col, PhD(bact), 47. *Prof Exp:* Technician, State Dept Health, RI, 38; res bacteriologist, J E Seagram & Sons, Inc, Ky, 39-40; tech asst, Rockefeller Inst, 40-43; instr bact, Iowa State Univ, 46-47; from asst prof to prof biochem, Sch Med, Tulane Univ, 47-67; PROF BIOL & HEAD DEPT, VA MIL INST, 67- *Mem:* Am Soc Biol Chemists; Am Soc Microbiol; Soc Exp Biol & Med; Sigma Xi. *Res:* Microbial fermentations; tracer studies in metabolism; microbial metabolism of arginine. *Mailing Add:* Dept of Biol Va Mil Inst Lexington VA 24450

WHITE, ALAN JONATHON, inorganic chemistry, organometallic chemistry, see previous edition

WHITE, ALAN WHITCOMB, b Norwood, Mass, March 15, 45; m 71; c 3. PHYTOPLANKTON ECOLOGY & PHYSIOLOGY. *Educ:* Col William & Mary, BS, 66; Harvard Univ, MA, 69, PhD(biol), 72. *Prof Exp:* Fel, Dept Microbiol & Chem, Hadassan Med Sch, Jerusalem, 72-73; RES SCIENTIST, CAN DEPT FISHERIES & OCEANS, 73- *Concurrent Pos:* Asst ed, J Fisheries Res Bd, Can, 78; vis scientist, Nansei Regional Fisheries Res Lab, Hiroshima, Japan, 82-83. *Mem:* Phycol Soc Am; Am Soc Limnol & Oceanog. *Res:* Ecology, physiology and toxicology of toxic dinoflagellate blooms and red tides; the fate of dinoflagellate toxins in the marine food web; consequences of the toxins for fisheries resources. *Mailing Add:* Fisheries Environ Sci Div Dept Fisheries Biol Sta St Andrews NB EOG 2XO Can

WHITE, ALBERT CORNELIUS, b Clearwater, Fla, July 17, 27; m 49; c 3. ENTOMOLOGY. *Educ:* Clemson Col, BS, 51; Univ Wis, MS, 53. *Prof Exp:* Res entomologist, Ortho Div, Chevron Chem Co, 53-69, int res specialist, 69-76; INDEPENDENT CONSULT, 78- *Concurrent Pos:* Entomologist, W Fla Arthroprod Res Lab, 77-78. *Mem:* Entom Soc Am; Mex Entom Soc; Am Register Prof Entomologists. *Res:* Contract research and development on all pesticides, citrus production and pest control consultation; investigations of pesticide damage and loss claims. *Mailing Add:* White Consult Serv 817 W Fairbanks Ave Orlando FL 32804

WHITE, ALBERT GEORGE, JR, b Centralia, Ill, July 16, 40; m 67; c 4. MATHEMATICS. *Educ:* Southern Ill Univ, Edwardsville, BA, 62; Univ Mo-Columbia, MA, 64; St Louis Univ, PhD(math), 68. *Prof Exp:* Asst prof math, Ill State Univ, 67-69; assoc prof, 69-77, PROF MATH, ST BONAVENTURE UNIV, 77-, CHMN DEPT, 70- *Mem:* Am Math Soc; Math Asn Am. *Mailing Add:* Dept of Math St Bonaventure Univ St Bonaventure NY 14778

WHITE, ALBERT M, b Derby, Conn, June 12, 26; m 55; c 6. CLINICAL PHARMACY. *Educ:* Univ Conn, BS, 48, MS, 52. *Prof Exp:* Asst chem & pharm, Univ Conn, 50-52; from instr to assoc prof, 56-72, PROF PHARM, ALBANY COL PHARM, 72-, ASST DEAN, 74-, DIR PHARM SERV TERESIAN HOUSE, 75- *Concurrent Pos:* Clin assoc prof admin med, State Univ NY Upstate Med Ctr; assoc clin prof, Albany Vet Admin Hosp; consult, Whitney M Young Health Ctr & Villa Mary Immaculate Nursing Home & NY Dept Health; state dir, Am Bd Dipl in Pharm. *Mem:* Am Pharmaceut Asn; Am Soc Hosp Pharmacists; Am Soc Consult Pharmacists; Am Asn Cols Pharm. *Res:* Delivery of clinical pharmaceutical services to institutionalized and health center patients; practice of clinical pharmacy by community pharmacists; evaluation of practice experience programs. *Mailing Add:* Albany Col Pharm Albany NY 12208

WHITE, ALLEN INGOLF, b Silverton, Ore, July 10, 14; m 38; c 3. PHARMACEUTICAL CHEMISTRY. *Educ:* Univ Minn, BS,37, MS, 38, PhD(pharmaceut chem), 40. *Prof Exp:* With bur plant indust, USDA, 38-40; from instr to assoc prof pharm, Wash State Univ, 40-48, prof, 48-80, dean, Col Pharm, 60-80. *Concurrent Pos:* Dir, Am Found Pharmaceut Educ, 75-; mem governing body, E Wash Health Systs Agency, 76- & Wash State Health Coord Coun, 78- *Mem:* AAAS; Am Chem Soc; Am Pharmaceut Asn; Am Asn Cols Pharm (pres, 74-75); Sigma Xi. *Res:* Organic synthesis of medicinal products. *Mailing Add:* 1040 Indiana Pullman WA 99163

WHITE, ALVIN MURRAY, b New York, NY, June 21, 25; m 46; c 2. MATHEMATICS, SCIENCE EDUCATION. *Educ:* Columbia Univ, AB, 49; Univ Calif, Los Angeles, MA, 51; Stanford Univ, PhD, 61. *Prof Exp:* Asst prof math, Univ Santa Clara, 54-61; mem math res ctr, US Army, Wis, 61-62; assoc prof, 62-80, PROF MATH, HARVEY MUDD COL, 80- *Concurrent Pos:* Fac fel, Danforth Found, 75-76; vis scientist, Div Study & Res in Educ, Mass Inst Technol, 76; mem blue ribbon comt on writing standards, Calif Comn Post Sec Educ, 80; initiator & proj dir, New Interdisciplinary Holistic Approaches to Teaching/Learning, Fund Improv Post Sec Educ, 77-81. *Mem:* Am Math Soc; Math Asn Am; Fedn Am Scientists; AAAS; Am Asn Univ Profs. *Res:* Function theoretical aspects of partial differential equations; quasiconformal mapping; nature of scientific creativity; nurture of scientific creativity; interdisciplinary teaching. *Mailing Add:* Dept of Math Harvey Mudd Col Claremont CA 91711

WHITE, ANDREW MICHAEL, b Elyria, Ohio, Mar 17, 42; m 65; c 2. ICHTHYOLOGY, LIMNOLOGY. *Educ:* Ohio State Univ, BS, 66, PhD(zool), 73. *Prof Exp:* Res assoc parasitol, US Dept Interior Dis Invest Lab, 63-64; teaching assoc zool, Ohio State Univ, 65-70; trustee ecol, Cleveland Environ Res, 73-77; PROF BIOL, JOHN CARROLL UNIV, 70- *Concurrent Pos:* Res dir grant, USEPA Study Lake Erie Fisheries, 72-75; assoc cur fishes, Cleveland Mus Natural Hist, 75-; mem endangered species comt, Ohio Biol Surv, 76-; consult, Nat Comn Water Quality, 76-77; vpres ecologist, Environ Resource Asn, 77-; res dir grant, NOACA Fish Degredation NE Ohio Streams, 77-78. *Mem:* Am Asn Parasitol; Am Fisheries Soc; Am Micros Soc. *Res:* Freshwater fisheries research, especially concerned with the Great Lakes ecosystem; major emphasis of ecology of non-game species in relation to spawning, growth zoogeography, subspeciation and niche utilization. *Mailing Add:* Dept of Biol 20700 N Park Blvd Cleveland OH 44118

WHITE, ANDREW WILSON, JR, b Thomaston, Ga, Aug 1, 27; m 50; c 2. SOIL CONSERVATION, SOIL FERTILITY. *Educ:* Univ Ga, BS, 49, MS, 58, PhD, 69. *Prof Exp:* Soil scientist, Soil & Water Conserv Res Div, 51-61, res soil scientist, Southern Piedmont Conserv Res Ctr, 61-75, SOIL SCIENTIST, SOUTHEASTERN FRUIT & NUT TREE LAB, SCI & EDUC ADMIN-AGR RES, USDA, 75- *Mem:* Am Soc Agron; Soil Sci Soc Am; Soil Conserv Soc Am; Southeast Pecan Growers Asn. *Res:* Soil management problems related to pesticides and soil and water conservation; soil fertility and management problems related to pecan production. *Mailing Add:* Southeast Fruit & Nut Tree Lab Sci & Educ Admin-Agr Res USDA Byron GA 31008

WHITE, ARDIS H, b Josephine, Tex, Sept 30, 21; m 42; c 2. CIVIL ENGINEERING. *Educ:* Southern Methodist Univ, BSCE, 43; Univ Tex, MSCE, 48; Univ Calif, Los Angeles, PhD(eng), 53. *Prof Exp:* Instr civil eng, Southern Methodist Univ, 46-47 & Univ Tex, 48-49; asst prof, Univ Ark, 49-50, Univ Southern Calif, 50-53 & Rice Univ, 53-55; from asst prof to assoc prof, 55-66, chmn dept, 67-76, PROF CIVIL ENG, UNIV HOUSTON, 67- *Mem:* Am Soc Civil Engrs; Am Soc Eng Educ; Nat Soc Prof Engrs; Soc Exp Stress Anal; Am Concrete Inst. *Res:* Structural analysis and design; experimental stress analysis. *Mailing Add:* Dept of Civil Eng 3801 Cullen Blvd Houston TX 77004

WHITE, ARLYNN QUINTON, JR, b Norfolk, Va, Jan 17, 46. INVERTEBRATE PHYSIOLOGY, MARINE ECOLOGY. *Educ:* NC Wesleyan Col, BS, 68; Univ Va, MS, 72; Univ SC, PhD(biol), 76. *Prof Exp:* Instr biol, Univ SC, 76; vis asst prof, 76-78, ASST PROF BIOL & ASSOC DIR ENVIRON CTR, JACKSONVILLE UNIV, 78- *Mem:* AAAS; Am Soc Zoologists; Sigma Xi; Am Inst Biol Sci. *Res:* Behavioral physiology; locomotion in decapods; rhythmicity in marine invertebrates; effects of pollutants on behavior and physiology. *Mailing Add:* Dept of Biol Jacksonville Univ Jacksonville FL 32211

WHITE, ARNOLD ALLEN, b New York, NY, Oct 13, 23; m 53; c 5. BIOCHEMISTRY. *Educ:* Univ Iowa, AB, 47, MS, 49; Georgetown Univ, PhD(biochem), 54. *Prof Exp:* From instr to asst prof biochem, Georgetown Univ, 52-56; from asst prof to assoc prof, 56-77, PROF BIOCHEM, UNIV MO-COLUMBIA, 77-, INVESTR, DALTON RES CTR, 66- *Mem:* AAAS; Am Soc Biol Chemists; Sigma Xi. *Res:* Mechanism of hormone action; cyclic nucleotide research. *Mailing Add:* Dalton Res Ctr Univ of Mo Columbia MO 65211

WHITE, ARTHUR C, b Williamsburg, Ky, Aug 1, 25; m 49; c 3. INTERNAL MEDICINE, INFECTIOUS DISEASES. *Educ:* Univ Ky, BS; Harvard Univ, MD, 52. *Prof Exp:* Instr med, Vanderbilt Univ, 53-58; from instr to asst prof, Univ Louisville, 58-63; assoc prof, Med Col Ga, 63-67; PROF MED, SCH MED, IND UNIV, INDIANAPOLIS, 67- *Concurrent Pos:* Consult, Vet Admin Hosps, Louisville, Ky, 59-63 & Augusta, Ga, 63-67; drug efficacy study, Nat Acad Sci, 66. *Mem:* Am Soc Microbiol; Am Fedn Clin Res; Am Col Physicians; Infectious Dis Soc Am. *Res:* Staphylococcal epidemiology and immunology; immunoglobulins and their activity; immunology of gram negative infections; histamine release. *Mailing Add:* Infectious Dis Div Ind Univ Sch of Med Indianapolis IN 46223

WHITE, ARTHUR THOMAS, II, b Orange, NJ, Oct 7, 39; m 61; c 2. MATHEMATICS. *Educ:* Oberlin Col, AB, 61; Mich State Univ, MS, 66, PhD(math), 69. *Prof Exp:* Actuarial trainee, Home Life Ins Co, 61-62; asst prof, 69-73, assoc prof, 73-79, PROF MATH, WESTERN MICH UNIV, 79- *Concurrent Pos:* Asst & fel, Mich State Univ, 65-69; NSF grant, 73-74; managing ed, J Graph Theory, 78-80. *Mem:* Am Math Soc; London Math Soc; Math Asn Am; Sigma Xi; Nat Coun Teachers Math. *Res:* Topological graph theory. *Mailing Add:* 2502 Law Ave Kalamazoo MI 49008

WHITE, AUGUSTUS AARON, III, b Memphis, Tenn, June 4, 36; m 74; c 3. ORTHOPEDIC SURGERY, BIOMEDICAL ENGINEERING. *Educ:* Brown Univ, BA, 57; Stanford Univ, MD, 61; Karolinska Inst, Sweden, DrMedSc, 69. *Prof Exp:* Intern, Univ Hosp, Ann Arbor, Mich, 61-62; from instr to assoc prof orthop surg, Sch Med, Yale Univ, 65-78, dir biomech res, Sect Orthop Surg, 73-78; PROF ORTHOP SURG, HARVARD MED SCH, 78-; ORTHOP SURGEON-IN-CHIEF, BETH ISRAEL HOSP, 78- *Concurrent Pos:* Chief resident orthop surg, Vet Admin Hosp, West Haven, Conn, 66; attend orthop surgeon, Yale-New Haven Hosp, 69-78; consult, Vet Admin Hosp, West Haven & Hill Health Ctr, New Haven, 69-78; mem bioeng res comt, Int Coun Sports & Phys Educ, 74; Am Brit Can traveling fel award, Am Orthop Asn, 75; vpres health affairs, Soulville Found, 76; mem adv coun, Nat Arthritis, Metab & Digestive Dis, 79-82; bd fel, Brown Univ, 81-82. *Mem:* Orthop Res Soc; Cervical Spine Res Soc; Int Soc Study Lumbar Spine; Am Acad Orthop Surgeons; Nat Med Asn. *Res:* Mechanical studies on the entire human spine designed to provide knowledge and technology applicable to clinical problems; development of an engineering system which will accelerate fracture healing. *Mailing Add:* Beth Israel Hosp 330 Brookline Ave Boston MA 02215

WHITE, BERNARD HENRY, b Chicago, Ill, Oct 15, 47; m 68; c 3. PHYSICAL CHEMISTRY, CHEMICAL ENGINEERING. *Educ:* Univ Cincinnati, BS, 69; Univ Wash, MS, 71; Univ Houston, PhD(phys chem), 76. *Prof Exp:* Chemist, 76-77, res chemist, 77-78, sr chemist, 78-81, OPERS SECT HEAD, EXXON RES & ENG CO, 81- *Concurrent Pos:* Robert A Welch Res Fel, Dept Chem, Univ Houston, 73-76. *Mem:* Am Chem Soc; Am Phys Soc. *Res:* Synthetic fuels, both liquids and gases, derived from coal; basic investigations covering the chemistry of coal liquefaction and gasification; applied investigations covering appropriate process designs. *Mailing Add:* Exxon Res & Eng Co PO Box 4255 Baytown TX 77520

WHITE, BERNARD J, b Portland, Ore, Jan 8, 37; m 63; c 5. BIOCHEMISTRY. *Educ:* Univ Portland, BS, 58; Univ Ore, MA, 61, PhD(biochem), 63. *Prof Exp:* Asst prof chem, Loras Col, 63-68; asst prof, 68-74, ASSOC PROF BIOCHEM, IOWA STATE UNIV, 74- *Mem:* AAAS; Am Chem Soc. *Res:* Protein structure; biochemical evolution; enzymology. *Mailing Add:* Dept of Biochem & Biophys Iowa State Univ Ames IA 50010

WHITE, BLANCHE BABETTE, b Cumberland, Md, July 25, 05. CHEMISTRY. *Educ:* Goucher Col, AB, 25; Univ Chicago, MS, 27. *Prof Exp:* Asst chem, Goucher Col, 25-26; chemist, Celanese Corp Am, 27-45, sect head cellulose derivatives, 46-56; head tech info, Charlotte Develop Labs, NC, 56-59; asst librn, Res Div, W R Grace & Co, 59-63, lit scientist, 63-70; chem lit consult, 70-80. *Mem:* Am Chem Soc. *Res:* Scientific information retrieval; cellulose chemistry. *Mailing Add:* 4450 S Park Ave Apt 309 Chevy Chase MD 20815

WHITE, BRIAN, b Brigg, Eng, Feb 19, 36; m 62; c 2. GEOLOGY. *Educ:* Univ Wales, BSc, 63, PhD(geol), 66. *Prof Exp:* Fel, Dalhousie Univ, 66-68; from instr to asst prof, 68-73, ASSOC PROF GEOL & CHMN DEPT, SMITH COL, 73- *Mem:* Soc Econ Paleontologists & Mineralogists; Geol Soc Am. *Res:* Stratigraphy, sedimentary petrology and micropaleobotany of precambrian sedimentary rocks; impact of urban development on the hydrogeology of small river basins. *Mailing Add:* Dept of Geol Smith Col Northampton MA 01063

WHITE, BRUCE LANGTON, b Wellington, NZ, Mar 2, 31; m 54; c 2. PHYSICS. *Educ:* New Zealand, BSc, 52; Univ London, DIC & PhD, 56. *Prof Exp:* Res fel, 56-59, res assoc, 59-60, from asst prof to assoc prof, 60-70, PROF PHYSICS, UNIV BC, 70- *Mem:* Am Phys Soc. *Res:* Experimental low energy nuclear physics; experimental cosmology and gravitation; Mössbauer effect. *Mailing Add:* Dept of Physics Univ BC 6224 Agr Rd Vancouver BC V6T 1W5 Can

WHITE, CHARLES A, JR, b San Diego, Calif, Aug 1, 22; m 60; c 3. OBSTETRICS & GYNECOLOGY. *Educ:* Colo Agr & Mech Col, DVM, 45; Univ Utah, MD, 55; Am Bd Obstet & Gynec, dipl, 64. *Prof Exp:* Pvt pract vet med, 45-51; intern, Salt Lake County Gen Hosp, 55-56; resident obstet & gynec, Dee Mem Hosp, Ogden, Utah, 56-57; resident, Univ Hosp, Univ Iowa, 59-61, assoc, Col Med, 61-62, from asst prof to prof, 62-74; prof obstet & gynec & chmn dept, WVa Univ, 74-80; PROF OBSTET & GYNEC & HEAD DEPT, SCH MED, LA STATE UNIV, 80- *Concurrent Pos:* Examr, Am Bd Obstet & Gynec, 71- *Mem:* AMA; Am Asn Obstetricians & Gynecologists; Am Col Obstet & Gynec; NY Acad Sci. *Mailing Add:* La State Univ Med Sch 1542 Tulane Ave New Orleans LA 70112

WHITE, CHARLES F(LOYD), b Columbus, NMex, Aug 4, 13; m 51; c 3. ELECTRONICS, SYSTEMS ENGINEERING. *Educ:* Univ Calif, BS, 35, MS, 38. *Prof Exp:* Electronics lab asst, Farnsworth TV Lab, Calif, 38; instr elec eng, Univ Calif, 38-39 & Yale Univ, 39-40; from physicist to elec engr, US Dept Navy, DC & Calif, 40-43, sect head spec electronic instrumentation develop, US Naval Res Lab, 46-53, consult & coordr radar systs res, 53-59, consult electronic eng, res & develop, 59-66, systs analyst naval anal staff, 66-68, electronics scientist, Satellite Commun Br, 69-75; CONSULT, 75- *Mem:* Sigma Xi; Inst Elec & Electronics Engrs. *Res:* Signal and data processing; electrical networks; technical writing. *Mailing Add:* 4216 Dorris Rd Irving TX 75062

WHITE, CHARLES HENRY, b Birmingham, Ala, Mar 15, 43; m 65; c 1. DAIRY MICROBIOLOGY. *Educ:* Miss State Univ, BS, 65, MS, 69; Univ Mo, PhD(dairy microbiol), 71. *Prof Exp:* Sr food scientist, Archer Daniels Midland Co, 71-72; asst prof dairy microbiol, Univ Ga, 72-76; dir, qaul assurance, Dean Foods Co, 76-80; ASSOC PROF DAIRY SCI, LA STATE UNIV, 80- *Concurrent Pos:* Consult, Long Life Dairy Prod, 73-; partic, Comt to Revise Stand Methods for Exam Dairy Prod, 74- *Mem:* Am Dairy Sci Asn; Inst Food Technol; Int Asn Milk & Food Sanitarians; Nat Environ Health Asn; Cult Dairy Prod Inst. *Res:* Psychrotrophic bacteria and relationship with shelf-life of dairy products, including measurement of proteolytic activity of raw milk as well as determination of heat-stable protease from the psychrotrophs; diacetyl reductases. *Mailing Add:* Dairy Sci Dept La State Univ Baton Rouge LA 70803

WHITE, CHARLES RAYMOND, b Wabash, Ind, Dec 23, 33; m; c 1. OPERATIONS RESEARCH, INDUSTRIAL ENGINEERING. *Educ:* Purdue Univ, BSME, 55, MSIE, 57, PhD(opers res), 63. *Prof Exp:* Opers res analyst, Armour & Co, 63-66; ASSOC PROF INDUST ENG, AUBURN UNIV, 66- *Mem:* Inst Mgt Sci; Am Inst Indust Engrs. *Res:* Maintenance engineering and energy conservation. *Mailing Add:* Dept of Indust Eng Auburn Univ Auburn AL 36830

WHITE, CHARLEY MONROE, b Rose Hill, Ill, Dec 9, 32; m 60; c 3. ECOLOGY, WILDLIFE BIOLOGY. *Educ:* Eastern Ill Univ, BS, 60; Purdue Univ, MS, 62, PhD(ecol), 68. *Prof Exp:* Asst prof, 66-71, assoc prof, 71-78, PROF BIOL, UNIV WIS-STEVENS POINT, 78- *Mem:* Wildlife Soc; Am Soc Mammal. *Res:* Productivity of White-tailed deer; population dynamics. *Mailing Add:* Dept of Biol Univ of Wis Stevens Point WI 54481

WHITE, CHRISTOPHER CLARKE, b Haverhill, Mass, June 24, 37. MATHEMATICS. *Educ:* Bowdoin Col, AB, 59; Miami Univ, MA, 63; Univ Ore, PhD(math), 67. *Prof Exp:* Asst prof math, Univ NH, 67-70; ASSOC PROF MATH, CASTLETON STATE COL, 70-, CHMN DEPT, 74- *Res:* Banach algebras; harmonic analysis. *Mailing Add:* Dept Math Castleton State Col Castleton VT 05735

WHITE, CLARK WOODY, b Rome, Ga, May 4, 40; m 70; c 2. PHYSICS. *Educ:* Mass Inst Technol, BS, 62; Duke Univ, PhD(physics), 67. *Prof Exp:* Mem tech staff physics, Bell Labs, 67-75; MEM RES STAFF PHYSICS, OAK RIDGE NAT LAB, 75- *Res:* Solid state physics; ion-solid collisions; surface physics; ion implantation; laser annealing. *Mailing Add:* Solid State Div Oak Ridge Nat Lab Oak Ridge TN 37830

WHITE, CLAYTON M, b Afton, Wyo, Apr 19, 36; m 59; c 5. VERTEBRATE ZOOLOGY, ECOLOGY. *Educ:* Univ Utah, AB, 61, PhD(zool), 68. *Prof Exp:* Instr zool & cur birds, Univ Kans, 65-66; instr zool & res fel, Cornell Univ, 68-70; asst prof, 70-74, assoc prof zool, 74-78, PROF BRIGHAM YOUNG UNIV, 78- *Concurrent Pos:* Consult, Columbus Labs, Battelle Mem Inst, 72- *Honors & Awards:* Francis B Roberts Award, 68. *Mem:* AAAS; Am Ornith Union; Soc Syst Zool; Cooper Ornith Union; Wilson Ornith Soc. *Res:* Avian evolution and systematics; ecology of raptorial birds; impact of environmental pollution in avian populations. *Mailing Add:* Dept Zool Brigham Young Univ Provo UT 84601

WHITE, COLIN, b Australia, Aug 25, 13; m 43; c 2. BIOMETRY. *Educ:* Univ Sydney, BSc, 35, MSc, 36, MB & BS, 40. *Prof Exp:* Intern, Sydney Hosp, Australia, 41; lectr physiol, Univ Sydney, 42; med officer, Australian Inst Anat, 43-46; lectr physiol, Univ Birmingham, 46-48; asst prof, Univ Pa, 48-50; lectr physiol, Univ Birmingham, 50-53; from asst prof to assoc prof, 53-62, PROF PUB HEALTH, SCH MED, YALE UNIV, 62- *Mem:* Am Statist Asn; Biomet Soc; Royal Statist Soc; fel Int Statist Inst. *Res:* Epidemiology of chronic diseases; vital statistics. *Mailing Add:* 107 Thornton St Hamden CT 06517

WHITE, DABNEY KATHERINE, b Rochester, NY, Aug 2, 49. PHYSICAL ORGANIC CHEMISTRY. *Educ:* Brown Univ, AB, 71; Mass Inst Technol, PhD(chem), 76. *Prof Exp:* Fel, Univ Calif, San Diego, 76-79; ASST PROF CHEM, WASHINGTON UNIV, 79- *Mem:* Am Chem Soc. *Res:* Mechanisms of organic and bioorganic reactions; chemiluminescence; excited states of radicals; electron transfer in heme proteins. *Mailing Add:* Dept Chem Washington Univ St Louis MO 63130

WHITE, DAVID, b Russia, Jan 14, 25; nat US; m 45; c 3. PHYSICAL CHEMISTRY. *Educ:* McGill Univ, BSc, 44; Univ Toronto, PhD(chem), 47. *Prof Exp:* Asst, Univ Toronto, 44-47; fel, Ohio State Univ, 48-50, asst dir cryogenic lab, 50-53; asst prof chem, Syracuse Univ, 53-54; from asst prof to prof, Ohio State Univ, 54-66; PROF CHEM & CHMN DEPT, UNIV PA, 66- *Concurrent Pos:* Vis prof, Technion & Weizmann Insts, Israel, 63-64; Fulbright fel & vis prof, Univ Kyoto & Univ Tokyo, Japan, 65; Nat Ctr Sci Res fel & vis prof, Inst Appl Quantum Mech, France, 74-75. *Mem:* Am Chem Soc; Sigma Xi; Am Phys Soc. *Res:* Low temperature thermodynamics and solid state nuclear magnetic resonance; molecular structure from NMR studies of matrix isolated spectra; optical coherence and relaxation studies of solids at low temperatures. *Mailing Add:* Dept of Chem Univ of Pa Philadelphia PA 19104

WHITE, DAVID, b Boston, Mass, Apr 26, 36; m 59; c 3. MICROBIOLOGY. *Educ:* Brandeis Univ, AB, 58, PhD(biol), 65. *Prof Exp:* Res scientist, Exobiol Div, Ames Res Ctr, NASA, 63-65; res assoc microbial physiol, Med Sch, Univ Minn, 65-67; asst prof, 67-74, ASSOC PROF MICROBIOL, IND UNIV, BLOOMINGTON, 74-, ASSOC PROF GEOL, 80- *Concurrent Pos:* Res grants, Am Cancer Soc, 68-70, NSF, 68-70, 70-72. *Mem:* Am Soc Microbiol. *Res:* Microbial physiology; microbial development; myxobacteria. *Mailing Add:* Dept of Microbiol Ind Univ Bloomington IN 47401

WHITE, DAVID ARCHER, b Philadelphia, Pa, Jan 22, 27; m 52; c 3. GEOLOGY. *Educ:* Dartmouth Col, BA, 50; Univ Minn, MS, 51, PhD(geol), 54. *Prof Exp:* RES ADV, EXXON PROD RES CO, 54- *Mem:* Geol Soc Am; Am Asn Petrol Geol. *Res:* Geology of the Mesabi range, Minnesota; geochemistry; stratigraphy; hydrocarbon assessment. *Mailing Add:* Box 2189 Houston TX 77001

WHITE, DAVID CALVIN, b Sunnyside, Wash, Feb 18, 22; m; c 49, 66; c 2. ELECTRICAL ENGINEERING. *Educ:* Stanford Univ, BS, 46, MS, 47, PhD, 49. *Prof Exp:* Elec engr, Kaiser Co, Inc, 42-45; assoc prof elec eng, Univ Fla, 49-52; from asst prof to prof, 52-62, Ford prof, 62-70, DIR ENERGY LAB, MASS INST TECHNOL, 70- *Concurrent Pos:* Lectr, Univ London, 61; vis prof & consult, Purdue Univ, 64-68; sr adv & vis prof, Birla Inst Technol & Sci, Pilani, India, 68-70; coun mem, Univ Benin, Nigeria, 70-; trustee, Lowell Technol Inst, 72- *Honors & Awards:* Westinghouse Award, Am Soc Eng Educ, 61. *Mem:* Fel Inst Elec & Electronics Engrs; fel Am Acad Arts & Sci; Am Inst Aeronaut & Astronaut; Am Soc Eng Educ; Nat Acad Engrs. *Res:* Energy supply and demand analysis; energy conversion devices and systems; semiconductor and magnetic devices. *Mailing Add:* Mass Inst of Technol Energy Lab 1-23 Amherst St Bldg E40 Cambridge MA 02139

WHITE, DAVID CLEAVELAND, b Moline, Ill, May 18, 29; m 56; c 3. BIOCHEMISTRY. *Educ:* Dartmouth Col, AB, 51; Tufts Univ, MD, 55; Rockefeller Univ, PhD(biochem), 62. *Prof Exp:* Intern, Univ Hosp, Univ Pa, 55-56, instr physiol, 56-58, res assoc med, 58; from asst prof to prof biochem, Univ Ky, 62-72; PROF BIOL & ASSOC DIR, PROG MED SCI, FLA STATE UNIV, 72- *Concurrent Pos:* Prof community health & family med, Med Sch, Univ Fla, Gainesville, 75-; adj prof, Interdept Toxicol Prog, Med Ctr, Univ Ark, Little Rock & Nat Ctr Toxicol Res, Jefferson, 81- *Mem:* Am Soc Biol Chem; Am Soc Limnol & Oceanog; Am Diabetic Asn; Gulf Estuarine Res Soc. *Res:* Microbial ecology of estuarine and marine benthus. *Mailing Add:* 310 Nuclear Res Fla State Univ Tallahassee FL 32306

WHITE, DAVID EVANS, b Syracuse, NY, Dec 13, 32; m 52; c 4. FOREST ECONOMICS. *Educ:* State Univ NY Col Forestry, Syracuse Univ, BS, 59, MS, 60, PhD(econ), 65. *Prof Exp:* Forester, Crown-Zellerbach Corp, 60-61; instr forest econ, State Univ NY Col Forestry, Syracuse Univ, 61-64; from asst prof to assoc prof, 64-71, dir div forestry, 66-76, PROF FOREST ECON & POLICY, WEST VA UNIV, 71- *Mem:* Soc Am Foresters. *Res:* Forest resources policy and administration; multi-disciplinary studies in environmental decision-making; natural resources economics; land use planning. *Mailing Add:* Div of Forestry WVa Univ Morgantown WV 26506

WHITE, DAVID GOVER, b Woodbury, NJ, Sept 21, 27; m 59. INORGANIC CHEMISTRY. *Educ:* Cornell Univ, BChE, 50; Harvard Univ, PhD(chem), 54. *Prof Exp:* From asst prof to assoc prof, 53-62, PROF CHEM, GEORGE WASHINGTON UNIV, 62- *Concurrent Pos:* NSF fel, 60. *Mem:* AAAS; Am Chem Soc; Royal Soc Chem. *Res:* Organometallic chemistry; boron-nitrogen compounds; metal complexes. *Mailing Add:* Dept of Chem George Washington Univ Washington DC 20052

WHITE, DAVID HALBERT, b Midland, Mich, Jan 25, 45. PHYSICAL ORGANIC CHEMISTRY, CHEMICAL EVOLUTION. *Educ:* Mich State Univ, BS, 67; Calif Inst Technol, PhD(chem), 72. *Prof Exp:* Asst prof chem, Lawrence Univ, 73-75; asst prof, 75-80, ASSOC PROF CHEM, UNIV SANTA CLARA, 80- *Mem:* AAAS; Am Chem Soc; Fedn Am Scientists; Sigma Xi. *Res:* Origin of genetic processes and self-reproducing molecules; carbene and diradical intermediates; homoaromaticity. *Mailing Add:* Dept of Chem Univ of Santa Clara Santa Clara CA 95053

WHITE, DAVID HYWEL, b Cardiff, Wales, June 4, 31; m 54; c 2. EXPERIMENTAL HIGH ENERGY PHYSICS. *Educ:* Univ Wales, BSc, 53; Univ Birmingham, PhD(physics), 56. *Prof Exp:* Res fel physics, Univ Birmingham, 56-58, asst lectr, 58-59; res assoc, Univ Pa, 59-62, asst prof, 62-65; assoc prof, 65-69, prof physics, Cornell Univ, 69-78; SR PHYSICIST, BROOKHAVEN NAT LAB, 78- *Mem:* Am Phys Soc; AAAS. *Res:* Experimental high energy physics; weak interactions; strong interactions; electromagnetic interactions. *Mailing Add:* Isabelle Proj Brookhaven Nat Lab Upton NY 11973

WHITE, DAVID RAYMOND, b Oak Park, Ill, Sept 20, 40; m 64; c 1. ORGANIC CHEMISTRY. *Educ:* St John's Univ, BA, 62; Univ Wis, PhD(org chem), 66. *Prof Exp:* Grant, NIH, 66-68; MEM STAFF, UPJOHN CO, 68- *Mem:* Am Chem Soc; The Chem Soc. *Res:* Biogenetic type synthesis; steroid reactions; new synthetic methods; prostaglandin synthesis. *Mailing Add:* Up John Co 7000 Portage Rd Kalamazoo MI 49001

WHITE, DAVID SANFORD, b Ashburnham, Mass, Sept 16, 45; m 66; c 1. LIMNOLOGY, AQUATIC ENTOMOLOGY. *Educ:* DePauw Univ, AB & MS, 70; Univ Louisville, PhD (biol), 74. *Prof Exp:* Res biol ecol, Univ Okla, Biol Sta, 74-77; res scientist limnol, 77-80, ASSOC RES LIMINOLOGIST, GREAT LAKES RES DIV & ASST PROF NATURAL RESOURCES, UNIV MICH, 80- *Concurrent Pos:* Vis scientist, Ill Natural Hist Surv, 77. *Mem:* Entom Soc Am; Am Entom Soc; Ecol Soc Am. *Res:* Benthic ecology, the distribution and abundance of aquatic invertebrates in relation to sediment and water quality; ecology and systematics of riffle beetles. *Mailing Add:* Great Lakes Res Div Univ of Mich Ann Arbor MI 48109

WHITE, DEAN KINCAID, b Tulsa, Okla, Aug 27, 44; m 67; c 1. DENTAL PATHOLOGY. *Educ:* Univ Okla, BS, 66; Univ Mo-Kansas City, DDS, 70; Ind Univ, MSD, 72; Am Bd Oral Path, dipl, 75. *Prof Exp:* Asst prof path, Sch Dent, Temple Univ, 72-77; ASSOC PROF ORAL PATH & CHMN DEPT, COL DENT, UNIV KY, 77- *Mem:* Am Dent Asn; Am Acad Oral Pathologists. *Res:* Clinical research in oral neoplasia. *Mailing Add:* Dept of Oral Path Univ of Ky Col of Dent Lexington KY 40506

WHITE, DENIS NALDRETT, b Bristol, Eng, June 10, 16; m 38; c 4. MEDICINE. *Educ:* Cambridge Univ, BA, 37, MA, MB & BCh, 40, MD, 56; FRCP, FACP. *Prof Exp:* First asst med, London Hosp, 43-46; sr registr, Univ London, 46-48; from asst prof assoc prof, 48-60, prof, 60-81, EMER PROF, QUEEN'S UNIV, ONT, 81-, ASST PROF DIAG RADIOL, 77- *Mem:* Fel Am Col Physicians; Am Electroencephalog Soc; Am Acad Neurol; Can Soc Electroencephalog; Am Inst Ultrasonics in Med (past pres). *Res:* Neurology; medical ultrasonics; ultrasonic doppler techniques. *Mailing Add:* 230 Alwington Place Kingston ON K7L 4P8 Can

WHITE, DONALD BENJAMIN, b Framingham, Mass, Feb 15, 30; m 53; c 6. ORNAMENTAL HORTICULTURE, GENETICS. *Educ:* Univ Mass, BS, 56; Iowa State Univ, PhD(hort genetics, breeding), 61. *Prof Exp:* Res assoc hort, Iowa State Univ, 56-59, res asst, 59-61; from asst prof to assoc prof, 61-69, PROF HORT, UNIV MINN, ST PAUL, 69-, PROF LANDSCAPE ARCHIT, 74- *Mem:* Am Soc Hort Sci; Am Soc Agron; Soil Sci Soc Am. *Res:* Physiology of cold acclimation and dwarfing of woody plants; breeding and genetics of grasses; physiology of chemical growth regulation of monocots. *Mailing Add:* Dept of Hort Sci Univ of Minn St Paul MN 55101

WHITE, DONALD EDWARD, b Dinuba, Calif, May 7, 14; m 41; c 3. GEOLOGY. *Educ:* Stanford Univ, AB, 36; Princeton Univ, PhD(econ geol, petrol), 39. *Prof Exp:* Assoc geologist, Geol Surv Nfld, Can, 37-38; geologist, 39-63, RES GEOLOGIST, US GEOL SURV, 63- *Concurrent Pos:* Asst chief mineral deposits br, US Geol Surv, DC, 58-60. *Honors & Awards:* Distinguished Serv Award, US Dept Interior, 71. *Mem:* Nat Acad Sci; fel Geol Soc Am; Fel Soc Econ Geologists; fel Mineral Soc Am; Geochem Soc. *Res:* Origin and geochemistry of thermal and mineral springs and their relations to volcanism and ore deposits; geothermal energy; origin and nature of ore-forming fluids; origin and characteristics of geysers; isotope geology of waters; rock alteration; abnormal geothermal gradients. *Mailing Add:* US Geol Surv 345 Middlefield Rd Menlo Park CA 94025

WHITE, DONALD GLENN, b Charleston, WVa, Mar 16, 46; m 68; c 1. PLANT PATHOLOGY. *Educ:* Marshall Univ, BA, 68, MS, 70; Ohio State Univ, PhD(plant path), 73. *Prof Exp:* Lectr plant path, Ohio State Univ, 73-74; ASST PROF PLANT PATH, UNIV ILL, URBANA, 74- *Mem:* Am Phytopath Soc; Crop Sci Soc Am; Am Soc Agron. *Res:* Fungal diseases of field crops; stalk rot, ear rot, storage molds of corn; mycotoxins. *Mailing Add:* S518 Turner Hall Univ Ill Urbana IL 61801

WHITE, DONALD HARVEY, b Berkeley, Calif, Apr 30, 31; m 53; c 5. NUCLEAR PHYSICS, PARTICLE PHYSICS. *Educ:* Univ Calif, Berkeley, BA, 53; Cornell Univ, PhD(physics), 60. *Prof Exp:* Asst Cornell Univ, 53-57, part-time instr, 57-58, asst, 59-60; res physicist, Lawrence Livermore Lab, Univ Calif, 60-71; PROF PHYSICS, WESTERN ORE STATE COL, 71- *Concurrent Pos:* Lectr, Univ Calif, Berkeley, 70; consult, Lawrence Livermore Lab, 71-; vis res physicist, Inst Lave-Langevin, Grenoble, France, 77-78; fel, Minna-Heineman, 77-78. *Mem:* Am Phys Soc; Am Asn Physics Teachers. *Res:* Experimental nuclear physics; bubble chamber; thermal-neutron capture processes; nuclear spectroscopy. *Mailing Add:* Dept Natural Sci & Math Wesern Ore State Col Monmouth OR 97361

WHITE, DONALD PERRY, b New York, NY, May 19, 16; m 46; c 3. FORESTRY, SOIL SCIENCE. *Educ:* State Univ NY, BS, 37; Univ Wis, MS, 40, PhD(forest soils), 51. *Prof Exp:* Asst soils, Univ Wis, 38-40; forester, US Indian Serv, 40-42 & 46-47; asst soils, Univ Wis, 47-48; from instr to asst prof silvicult, State Univ NY Col Forestry, Syracuse Univ, 48-56; assoc prof forestry, Mich State Univ, 57-64, mem adv bd forest sci, 59-65, prof, 65-80. *Concurrent Pos:* Collabr, US Forest Serv, 59-64; comnr, NAm Foreign Soils Conf, 68-78. *Mem:* Soc Am Foresters; Soil Sci Soc Am. *Res:* Forest soils and fertilization; forest hydrology; watershed management; herbicides; reforestation techniques; Christmas trees. *Mailing Add:* 2870 College Rd Halt MI 48842

WHITE, DONALD ROBERTSON, b Schenectady, NY, Sept 27, 24; m 47; c 4. OPTICAL PHYSICS. *Educ:* Union Col, BS, 48; Princeton Univ, MA, 50, PhD(physics), 51. *Prof Exp:* Res asst physics, Princeton Univ, 51-52; physicist, 52-68, mgr optical physics br, 68-79, TECH ADMINR, CORP RES & DEVELOP CTR, GEN ELEC CO, 79- *Concurrent Pos:* Adj prof, Rensselaer Polytech Inst, 60-65. *Mem:* Fel Am Phys Soc; Combustion Inst. *Res:* Shock tubes and shock wave phenomena; gaseous detonation; optically pumped lasers; light scattering sensors. *Mailing Add:* RD1 Box 340A Garnsey Rd Rexford NY 12148

WHITE, DONALD WILMOT, JR, b Syracuse, NY, Aug 16, 17; m 44; c 3. METALLURGY. *Educ:* Columbia Univ, AB, 38, BS, 39, MS, 40. *Prof Exp:* Metallurgist, Crucible Steel Co Am, NY, 40-42 & Sylvania Elec Prod, Inc, Pa & NY, 42-47; mgr adv mat develop, Knolls Atomic Power Lab, 47-58; chief, Dept Metall, Ctr Study Nuclear Energy, Belg, 58-60; mgr high temperature electrochem, Gen Elec Co, 60-69, liaison scientist, Res & Develop Ctr, 69-81; RETIRED. *Mem:* Am Soc Metals. *Res:* High temperature electrochemistry; fuel cells; nuclear materials; general metallurgy and ceramics. *Mailing Add:* 9 Parkwood Dr Burnt Hills NY 12027

WHITE, DWAIN MONTGOMERY, b Minneapolis, Minn, Feb 16, 31; m 56; c 4. ORGANIC CHEMISTRY, POLYMER CHEMISTRY. *Educ:* Univ Wis, BS, 53, PhD(chem), 56. *Prof Exp:* RES CHEMIST, RES & DEVELOP CTR, GEN ELEC CO, 56- *Mem:* Am Chem Soc; Sigma Xi. *Res:* Organic synthesis and structure determination; oxidative coupling reactions; heterocyclics; synthesis and reactions of polyphenylene oxides. *Mailing Add:* Gen Elec Res & Develop Ctr PO Box 8 Schenectady NY 12345

WHITE, EDGAR C, b Fielden, Ky, Dec 14, 12; m 40; c 2. SURGERY. *Educ:* Univ Louisville, MD, 37. *Prof Exp:* Asst instr clin surg, Sch Med, Univ Louisville, 39-41, instr, 46-48; asst chief surg serv, Vet Admin Hosp, Louisville, 48-49; HEAD DEPT SURG & CHIEF SECT GEN SURG, UNIV TEX M D ANDERSON HOSP & TUMOR INST, HOUSTON, 49-, PROF SURG, UNIV TEX MED SCH, HOUSTON, 63- *Concurrent Pos:* Clin asst prof, Col Med, Baylor Univ, 50-66, clin assoc prof, 66-; from assoc prof to prof, Postgrad Sch Med, Univ Tex, 50-63; consult, Tex Children's & St Luke's Hosps, Houston, 55- *Mem:* Am Cancer Soc; Am Col Surg; AMA. *Res:* Clinical oncology; surgical physiology and pathology. *Mailing Add:* 6723 Bertner Ave Houston TX 77025

WHITE, EDMUND W(ILLIAM), b Philadelphia, Pa, July 8, 20; m 48; c 4. CHEMICAL ENGINEERING, FUELS CHEMISTRY. *Educ:* Columbia Univ, AB, 40, BS, 41, ChE, 42; Lehigh Univ, PhD(chem eng), 52; Am Univ, cert opers res, 71. *Prof Exp:* Chem engr, Westvaco Chlorine Prods Corp, 42-44; design engr, C L Mantell, 46-47; tech staff engr, Diamond Alkali Co, 47-49; asst chem eng, Inst Res, Lehigh Univ, 49-50 & univ, 50-51; pilot plant engr & proj leader, Cities Serv Res & Develop Co, NJ, 51-56, staff engr, New York, 56-60, staff engr & budget officer, Cities Serv Athabasca, Inc, 60-65; oper res analyst, Naval Supply Systs Command, 65-66, FUEL RES ENGR, DAVID TAYLOR NAVAL SHIP RES & DEVELOP CTR, ANNAPOLIS LAB, 66- *Mem:* Am Chem Soc; Am Inst Chem Engrs; Sigma Xi; Am Petrol Inst; Am Soc Testing & Mat. *Res:* Synfuels properties and composition; ship fuels and fuel systems; fuel purification; liquid-solid and liquid-liquid separations; filters and filter/separators; fuel storage and stability; fuels at low temperatures. *Mailing Add:* 908 Crest Park Dr Silver Spring MD 20903

WHITE, EDWARD, b Florence, SC, Nov 23, 33; m 55; c 5. IMMUNOLOGY, ENDODONTICS. *Educ:* Emory Univ, DDS, 58; Med Univ SC, MS, 66; Univ Calif, Los Angeles, PhD(microbiol, immunol), 69. *Prof Exp:* Asst prof microbiol & immunol, Sch Dent, Univ Southern Calif, 69-72; chmn dept, 72-77, PROF ENDODONTICS, COL DENT MED, MED UNIV SC, 72- *Mem:* Transplantation Soc; Am Soc Microbiol. *Res:* Immunology of transplantation; etiology of dental pulpal disease. *Mailing Add:* 707 Ventura Pl Mount Pleasant SC 29464

WHITE, EDWARD AUSTIN, b Brooklyn, NY, Nov 28, 15; m 48; c 2. BIOCHEMISTRY, NUTRITION. *Educ:* Fordham Univ, BS, 37, MS, 40, PhD(biochem), 46. *Prof Exp:* Instr anal chem, Fordham Univ, 37-40; anal res chemist, Calco Chem Co, NJ, 40-42 & Winthrop Chem Co, NY & DC, 42-43; prof biochem, Col Mt St Vincent, 43-46; actg head dept chem, Inst Appl Arts & Sci, NY, 46-47; chief chem gen lab, Japan, 47-50, ADV MED SCI, US DEPT ARMY, WASHINGTON, DC, 50- *Mem:* Fel AAAS; Am Chem Soc; fel Am Inst Chem. *Res:* Nutrition in animals; analytical methods; pharmaceuticals; scientific translation. *Mailing Add:* 5307 Sangamore Rd Bethesda MD 20816

WHITE, EDWARD JOHN, b Haverhill, Iowa, Jan 26, 32; m 59; c 5. ELECTRICAL ENGINEERING. *Educ:* Iowa State Univ, BS, 58; Univ Va, MEE, 62, DSc(elec eng), 66. *Prof Exp:* Electronic engr, US Govt, 58-59; instr, 59-65, lectr, 65-66, asst prof, 66-69, asst to dean, Sch Eng & Appl Sci, 74-77, actg asst dean, 76-77, asst dean, 77-79, ASSOC PROF ELEC ENG, SCH ENG & APPL SCI, UNIV VA, 69-, ASST CHMN, DEPT ELEC ENG, 80- *Mem:* Inst Elec & Electronics Engrs. *Res:* Computer graphics; computer aided circuit design. *Mailing Add:* 208 Bennington Rd Charlottesville VA 22901

WHITE, EDWARD LEWIS, b Boston, Mass, Jan 8, 47; m 70. NEUROANATOMY. *Educ:* Clark Univ, AB, 68; Georgetown Univ, PhD(anat), 72. *Prof Exp:* Premier asst anat, Inst Anat Normale, Switz, 73-75; asst prof, 75-81, ASSOC PROF ANAT, SCH MED, BOSTON UNIV, 81- *Mem:* Am Asn Anatomists. *Res:* Ultrastructure and synaptic organization in mammalian central nervous systems. *Mailing Add:* Boston Univ Sch of Med 80 E Concord St Boston MA 02118

WHITE, EDWARD RODERICK, b Richwood, WVa, Nov 1, 31; m 54; c 3. PHYSICAL CHEMISTRY. *Educ:* Marietta Col, BS, 53; Ohio State Univ, PhD(phys chem), 57. *Prof Exp:* Res chemist, Union Carbide Olefins Corp, WVa, 58-62; res physicist, IIT Res Inst, 62-64; sr scientist, Nuclear Sci & Eng Corp, Pa, 64-65; res assoc radiation chem & biol, Grad Sch Pub Health, Univ Pittsburgh, 65-67, asst res prof, 67-69; sr anal chemist, 69-72, sr res investr, 72-79, ASST DIR ANAL & PHYS CHEM DEPT, SMITH KLINE & FRENCH LABS, 79- *Mem:* Sigma Xi; AAAS; Am Chem Soc. *Res:* Gas, high pressure liquid and thin layer chromatography; pharmaceutical analysis; radiation chemistry; electron impact phenomena; kinetics; tracer and vacuum techniques; spectroscopy. *Mailing Add:* Smith Kline & French Labs 1500 Spring Garden St Philadelphia PA 19101

WHITE, EDWIN HENRY, b Gouverneur, NY, Dec 22, 37; m 61; c 3. FORESTRY, SOIL SCIENCE. *Educ:* State Univ NY Col Forestry, Syracuse Univ, BS, 62, MS, 64; Auburn Univ, PhD(soils), 69. *Prof Exp:* Technician forest soils, State Univ NY Col Forestry, Syracuse Univ, 61-62; instr forestry, Auburn Univ, 64-65, res asst, 65-68; fel forestry & soils, Univ Fla, 68-69; res soil scientist, US Forest Serv, Miss, 69-70; asst prof forestry, Univ Ky, 70-74; assoc prof forest resources, Univ Minn, 74-78, prof, 78-80; PROF FOREST RESOURCES, STATE UNIV NY, SYRACUSE, COL ENVIRON SCI & FORESTRY, SCH FORESTRY, 80- *Mem:* Soil Sci Soc Am; Soil Conserv Soc Am; Soc Am Foresters. *Res:* Forest soils and silviculture; soil-site-species relationships; tree planting research. *Mailing Add:* 346 Illick Hall State Univ NY Col Environ Sci & Forestry Syracuse NY 13210

WHITE, ELIZABETH LLOYD, b Norfolk, Va, Sept 28, 16. EXPERIMENTAL EMBRYOLOGY, MOLECULAR BIOLOGY. *Educ:* Goucher Col, AB, 37; Bryn Mawr Col, MA, 38, PhD(embryol), 47. *Prof Exp:* Researcher, Wistar Inst, Univ Pa, 40-42; chemist, Res Dept, Gen Refractories Co, 42-46; instr zool, Wash Univ, 47-49; from asst prof to assoc prof zool, 49-61, prof biol, 61-78, EMER PROF BIOL, WHEATON COL, MASS, 78- *Concurrent Pos:* NSF fel hist of sci, Johns Hopkins Univ & Cambridge Univ, 58-59; NSF fel & vis prof biol, Johns Hopkins Univ, 66-67, sr res assoc, 73-74. *Mem:* Fel AAAS; Soc Develop Biol; Am Asn Anat. *Res:* Experimental embryology of teleosts; history of science; specialized nuclear RNA in chick limb-bud differentiation. *Mailing Add:* 221 Stony Run Lane Baltimore MD 21210

WHITE, ELIZABETH LOCZI, b McKees Rocks, Pa, Mar 9, 36; m 59; c 2. CIVIL ENGINEERING. *Educ:* Univ Pittsburgh, BS, 58; Pa State Univ, MS, 69, PhD(civil eng), 75. *Prof Exp:* Civil engr II highway design, Pa Dept Transp, 57, civil engr IV bridge design, 58-59; RES ASSOC CEMENT & SEDIMENT RES, PA STATE UNIV, 75- *Concurrent Pos:* Fel, Am Asn Univ Women, 74-75. *Mem:* Am Soc Civil Eng. *Res:* Surface water hydrology; sediment transport, soil properties and flood frequency statistics; chemistry and properties of high temperature cements; geothermal wells and nuclear waste disposal; engineering problems in carbonate rock terrains; computer application to civil engineering. *Mailing Add:* Dept of Civil Eng 212 Sackett Bldg University Park PA 16802

WHITE, EMIL HENRY, b Akron, Ohio, Aug 17, 26. ORGANIC CHEMISTRY. *Educ:* Univ Akron, BS, 47; Purdue Univ, MS, 48, PhD(chem), 50. *Prof Exp:* Fel, Univ Chicago, 50-51 & Harvard Univ, 51-52; instr org chem, Yale Univ, 52-56; from asst prof to assoc prof, 57-64, prof org chem, 64-80, D MEAD JOHNSON PROF CHEM, JOHNS HOPKINS UNIV, 80- *Concurrent Pos:* Guggenheim fel, 58-59; NIH sr fel, 65-66 & 72-73. *Mem:* AAAS; Am Chem Soc. *Res:* Mechanism of reaction in organic chemistry; active site mapping of enzymes; chemiluminescence and bioluminescence; deamination reactions. *Mailing Add:* Dept of Chem Dunning Hall Johns Hopkins Univ Baltimore MD 21218

WHITE, EUGENE WILBERT, b Indiana, Pa, Jan 23, 33; m 52; c 3. INSTRUMENTATION, MINERALOGY. *Educ:* Pa State Univ, BS, 55, MS, 58, PhD(solid state tech), 65. *Prof Exp:* Res asst mineral, Pa State Univ, 55-59; head, X-ray Diffraction Applns Lab, Picker X-ray Co, Ohio, 59-61; design engr, Tem-Pres Res, Inc, Pa, 61; res asst electron microprobe, 62-65, from asst prof to assoc prof solid state sci, 65-74, PROF SOLID STATE SCI, MAT RES LAB, PA STATE UNIV, 74- *Mem:* Am Crystallog Asn. *Res:* Electron microprobe research; x-ray spectroscopy. *Mailing Add:* Mat Res Lab Res Bldg No 1 Pa State Univ University Park PA 16802

WHITE, FLORENCE ROY, b Newcastle, Pa, Mar 6, 09; m 32; c 4. BIOCHEMISTRY. *Educ:* Univ Ill, AB, 30, AM, 31; Univ Mich, PhD(chem), 35. *Prof Exp:* Asst physiol, Sch Med, Univ Mich, 35-36; res asst, Sch Med, Yale Univ, 38-39; asst chemist, Bur Home Econ, USDA, 42; chemist, NIH, 42-45; res asst, Nat Acad Sci, 56-58; chemist, Cancer Chemo Nat Serv Ctr, Nat Cancer Inst, 58-66, head biochem sect, Drug Eval Br, 66-77; RETIRED. *Concurrent Pos:* Res fel, Univ Mich, 36-38. *Mem:* Am Soc Biol Chem; Am Asn Cancer Res. *Res:* Biochemistry of cancer. *Mailing Add:* 24728 Ridge Rd Damascus MD 20872

WHITE, FRANCIS MICHAEL, b Indianapolis, Ind, Aug 6, 18; m 41; c 5. ZOOLOGY, PARASITOLOGY. *Educ:* Earlham Col, AB, 39; Purdue Univ, MS, 41. *Prof Exp:* Asst biol, Purdue Univ, 39-41; instr biol, 41-44 & 46-47, from asst prof to assoc prof zool, 47-64, PROF BIOL, PHILADELPHIA COL PHARM & SCI, 64-, DIR, DEPT BIOL SCI, 81- *Concurrent Pos:* Lectr, Wagner Free Inst Sci, 67- *Mem:* Am Soc Parasitol; Am Inst Biol Sci. *Res:* Nematode parasites of fish; interrelationships of parasites as determined by chromatographic tests; drug testing on rats. *Mailing Add:* Dept Biol Sci Philadelphia Col of Pharm & Sci Philadelphia PA 19104

WHITE, FRANKLIN ESTABROOK, b Denver, Colo, Mar 26, 22; m 44; c 2. INSTRUMENTATION. *Educ:* Univ Denver, BS, 48, MA, 51; Univ Mich, MS, 55. *Prof Exp:* Res assoc atmospheric infrared studies, Univ Denver, 49-51; infrared instrumentation, Univ Mich, 51-55; teacher, 59-62, RES PHYSICIST, UNIV DENVER, 55- *Concurrent Pos:* Consult, Air Force Opers Anal Off, 56-71. *Mem:* Am Phys Soc; Sigma Xi. *Res:* Atmospheric infrared absorption; balloon and rocket instrumentation; radio propagation and telemetry; operations analysis; electronics. *Mailing Add:* Dept of Physics Univ of Denver Denver CO 80208

WHITE, FRANKLIN HENRY, b Alton, Ill, Feb 11, 19; m 47; c 2. VETERINARY MICROBIOLOGY. *Educ:* Shurtleff Col, BS, 42; Univ Ill, MS, 48, PhD(bact), 55; Am Bd Med Microbiol, cert pub health & med lab microbiol, 74. *Prof Exp:* Bacteriologist, State Dept Pub Health, Ill, 46-49; instr bact, Col Vet Med, Univ Ill, 49-55; from asst bacteriologist to assoc bacteriologist, 55-67, assoc prof bact, 61-67, PROF BACT & BACTERIOLOGIST, UNIV FLA, 67- *Mem:* Am Soc Microbiol; Conf Res Workers Animal Dis; Wildlife Dis Asn; US Animal Health Asn. *Res:* Pathogenic microbiology and immunology; leptospirosis; vibriosis; wildlife diseases; epizootiology. *Mailing Add:* Col of Vet Med Univ of Fla Gainesville FL 32610

WHITE, FRED D(ONALD), b Charleroi, Pa, Oct 11, 18; m 43; c 3. METEOROLOGY. *Educ:* Miami Univ, Ohio, AB, 41; Univ Wis, PhD(meteorol), 63. *Prof Exp:* Meteorologist, US Weather Bur, 46-58; prog dir meteorol, NSF, 58-66, head atmospheric sci, 66-76; CONSULT, 76- *Concurrent Pos:* Staff officer, Nat Res Coun, Nat Acad Sci, 78-; ed, Newsletter, Am Meteorol Soc, 80- *Mem:* Fel Am Meteorol Soc; fel Am Geophys Union; fel AAAS. *Res:* Research and administration in all fields of atmospheric sciences. *Mailing Add:* 3631 N Harrison St Arlington VA 22207

WHITE, FRED G, b Spanish Fork, Utah, Jan 19, 28; m 54; c 7. PLANT BIOCHEMISTRY. *Educ:* Brigham Young Univ, BS, 52, MS, 56; Univ Calif, PhD(biochem), 61. *Prof Exp:* From asst prof to assoc prof, 61-72, PROF CHEM, BRIGHAM YOUNG UNIV, 72- *Concurrent Pos:* Estab investr, Am Heart Asn, 65-70. *Mem:* AAAS; Am Chem Soc; Am Inst Biol Sci; NY Acad Sci; Sigma Xi. *Res:* Mechanisms of enzymes and co-enzymes; biological nitrogen fixation; plant growth regulators; plant biochemistry; plant genetic engineering. *Mailing Add:* Grad Sect Biochem Brigham Young Univ Provo UT 84602

WHITE, FRED NEWTON, b Yelgar, La, June 17, 27; m 51. CARDIOVASCULAR PHYSIOLOGY, COMPARATIVE PHYSIOLOGY. *Educ:* Univ Houston, BS, 50, MS, 51; Univ Ill, PhD(zool), 55. *Prof Exp:* Asst prof biol, Univ Houston, 55-57; asst prof exp med, Southwestern Med Sch, Univ Tex, 58-59 & 62-63; assoc prof physiol, Am Univ Beirut, 59-62; prof physiol, Sch Med, Univ Calif, Los Angeles, 63-76; PROF PHYSIOL & DIR PHYSIOL RES LAB, SCRIPPS INST OCEANOG, UNIV CALIF, SAN DIEGO, 76- *Concurrent Pos:* Am Physiol Soc cardiovasc training fels, 57 & 58. *Mem:* Am Physiol Soc; Fedn Am Socs Exp Biol; Soc Exp Biol & Med. *Res:* Control of renin secretion; peripheral circulation; comparative aspects of vertebrate circulation; environmental physiology. *Mailing Add:* Physiol Res Lab A-004 Univ of Calif San Diego La Jolla CA 92037

WHITE, FREDERICK ANDREW, b Detroit, Mich, Mar 11, 18; m 42; c 4. PHYSICS. *Educ:* Wayne Univ, BS, 40; Univ Mich, MS, 41; Univ Wis, PhD, 59. *Prof Exp:* Sr inspector, Rochester Army Ord Plant, NY, 41-43; asst physicist, Manhattan Proj, Univ Rochester, 43-45, grad instr, Univ, 45-46; asst physics, Knolls Atomic Power Lab, Gen Elec Co, 47-48, res assoc, 48-57, consult physicist, 59-62; PROF NUCLEAR ENG & INDUST LIAISON SCIENTIST, RENSSELAER POLYTECH INST, 62- *Concurrent Pos:* Consult, Bell Tel Labs, 69. *Mem:* AAAS; Am Inst Aeronaut & Astronaut; Am Nuclear Soc; Am Phys Soc; Am Soc Eng Educ. *Res:* Mass spectrometry and isotopic abundance measurements; acoustics; diffusion in metals; semiconductor devices; interaction of ions with matter; plasma diagnostics. *Mailing Add:* Dept of Nuclear Eng Rensselaer Polytech Inst Troy NY 12181

WHITE, FREDERICK HOWARD, JR, b Washington, DC, Jan 19, 26. PROTEIN CHEMISTRY. *Educ:* Univ Va, BS, 49; Univ Md, MS, 52; Univ Wis, PhD(biochem), 57. *Prof Exp:* Asst chem, Univ Md, 51-52; chemist, Nat Heart Inst, 52-53; asst biochem, Univ Wis, 53-56; chemist, Lab Biochem, 56-75, CHEMIST, LAB CELL BIOL, NAT HEART, LUNG & BLOOD INST, 75- *Mem:* AAAS; NY Acad Sci; Am Chem Soc; Am Soc Biol Chem; Radiation Res Soc. *Res:* Chemistry of sulfur in proteins; protein conformation; radiolysis of proteins. *Mailing Add:* Lab of Cell Biol Nat Heart Lung & Blood Inst Bethesda MD 20205

WHITE, FREDRIC PAUL, b New York, NY, July 24, 42; m 64; c 1. BIOCHEMISTRY, NEUROSCIENCES. *Educ:* Purdue Univ, BChE, 64; Ind Univ, PhD(biol chem), 71. *Prof Exp:* Chem engr, E I du Pont de Nemours & Co, Inc, 64-66; biochem trainee, NIH, 67-71; res scientist neurochem, Med Sch, Univ Colo, 72-73; vis asst prof neurophys, Ind State Univ, 73-74; asst prof, 74-77, ASSOC PROF BIOCHEM, MEM UNIV NFLD, 78- *Concurrent Pos:* Vis scientist, Med Res Coun, 81-82. *Mem:* Am Soc Neurochem; Soc Neurosci. *Res:* Cellular physiology of cerebral endothelial cells and pericytes; synthesis of the stress protein traumin by cells in response to trauma. *Mailing Add:* Fac Med Mem Univ Nfld St John's NF A1C 5S7 Can

WHITE, GEOFFREY OTIS, solid state physics, magnetic materials, see previous edition

WHITE, GEORGE ALBERT, agronomy, botany, see previous edition

WHITE, GEORGE CHARLES, JR, b Coatesville, Pa, Sept 14, 18; m 43; c 2. PHYSICS. *Educ:* Villanova Univ, BS, 39. *Prof Exp:* Physicist, Physics & Math Br, Pitman-Dunn Res Labs, 46-52, chief, 53-57, asst dir, Physics Res Lab, 57-58, asst spec missions off, 59-60, tech asst, Inst Res, 60-64, tech asst, Off of Dir, Pitman-Dunn Res Labs, 65-71, dep dir, Pitman-Dunn Res Labs, Frankford Arsenal, US Dept Army, 72-77; CONSULT, PHYS SCI & ADMIN RES, 77- *Mem:* Am Phys Soc; Am Nuclear Soc; Sigma Xi. *Res:* Nuclear, radiation and solid state physics; materials research. *Mailing Add:* 705 Avondale Rd Erdenheim PA 19118

WHITE, GEORGE MATTHEWS, b Salt Lake City, Utah, Dec 7, 41. COMMUNICATION SCIENCE. *Educ:* Mich State Univ, BS, 64; Univ Ore, PhD(chem phys), 68. *Prof Exp:* NIH res fel, Dept Comput Sci, Stanford Univ, 68-70; res scientist comput sci, Xerox Palo Alto Res Ctr, 70-77; res scientist, ITT Defence Commun Div, 77-80; mgr, Speech Recognition Unit, Auricle Inc, 80-81; PRES & CHMN BD, TEXTICON, INC, 81- *Mem:* Inst Elec & Electronic Engrs; Asn Comput Mach; Acoust Soc Am; Pattern Recognition Soc. *Res:* Pattern recognition, machine perception, artificial intelligence, automatic speech recognition, signal processing and perceptual psychology. *Mailing Add:* TEXTICON 253 Martens Ave Mountain View CA 94040

WHITE, GEORGE MICHAEL, b Toronto, Ont, June 14, 39; m 64; c 3. COMPUTER SCIENCE. *Educ:* Univ Toronto, BASc, 61; Univ Alta, MSc, 65; Univ Calgary, PhD, 68. *Prof Exp:* Systs engr, CAE Electronics, 61-62; Irish Govt fel, Univ Col, Dublin, 68-70; ASST PROF COMPUT SCI, UNIV OTTAWA, 70- *Mem:* Asn Comput Mach; Can Info Processing Soc. *Mailing Add:* Dept of Comput Sci Univ of Ottawa Ottawa ON K1N 6N5 Can

WHITE, GEORGE NICHOLS, JR, b Concord, Mass, July 1, 19; m 48; c 3. APPLIED MATHEMATICS. *Educ:* Harvard Univ, BS, 41; Brown Univ, MS, 48, PhD(appl math), 50. *Prof Exp:* Trainee, Phys Test Lab, T Mason Co, 41-42; technician radar, US Civil Serv, 42-45; technician electronics, Oceanog Inst, Woods Hole, 45-46; res assoc appl math, Brown Univ, 48-50; MEM STAFF APPL MATH, LOS ALAMOS NAT LAB, 50- *Concurrent Pos:* Prof, Univ NMex, 57-60. *Mem:* Am Math Soc; Soc Indust Appl Math. *Res:* Mathematics theory of plasticity; hydrodynamics; elasticity. *Mailing Add:* 119 Tunyo Los Alamos NM 87544

WHITE, GEORGE ROWLAND, b Niagara Falls, NY, Feb 22, 29; m 57. HIGH TECHNOLOGY, IMAGING SYSTEMS. *Educ:* Wesleyan Univ, BA, 50; Iowa State Univ, PhD(physics), 55; Univ Calif, Los Angeles, MS, 67. *Prof Exp:* From engr to dept mgr, Sperry Gyroscope Co, 55-64; from div mgr to chief scientist, 64-67, eng dept mgr, 67-68, div vpres, 68-72, staff vpres, 72-73, vpres prod planning, 74-76, vpres advan develop, 77-79, VPRES RES & DEVELOP & ENG, XEROX CORP, 79- *Concurrent Pos:* Carroll-Ford Found vis prof bus admin, Grad Sch Bus Admin, Harvard Univ, 76-77; chmn, Human Relations Comn, Monroe Co, 77-79; chmn planning bd, Polytech Inst NY, Inst Imaging Sci, 79- *Mem:* Optical Soc Am; Am Phys Soc; Inst Elec & Electronics Engrs; Indust Res Inst. *Res:* Management of technological innovation; development of xerographic and electronic imaging systems; lasers; microwave tubes; particle physics. *Mailing Add:* Xerox Corp 800 Long Ridge Rd Stamford CT 06904

WHITE, GEORGE V S, b Opelousas, La, Dec 15, 23; m 48; c 3. VERTEBRATE ZOOLOGY. *Educ:* Univ Southwestern La, BS, 44; La State Univ, MS, 47, PhD, 54. *Prof Exp:* Instr zool, Westminster Col, Mo, 50-53; asst prof, Memphis State Univ, 54-55; PROF BIOL, McNEESE STATE UNIV, 55-, HEAD DEPT, 70- *Res:* Comparative anatomy; mammalian histology. *Mailing Add:* Dept of Biol McNeese State Univ Lake Charles LA 70609

WHITE, GEORGE WILLARD, b North Lawrence, Ohio, July 8, 03; m 28. GEOLOGY. *Educ:* Otterbein Col, AB, 21; Ohio State Univ, MA, 25, PhD(geol), 33. *Hon Degrees:* ScD, Otterbein Col, 49, Univ NH, 55, Bowling Green State Univ, 63. *Prof Exp:* Instr geol, Univ Tenn, 25-26; from instr to prof, Univ NH, 26-41, actg dean grad sch, 40; prof geol, Ohio State Univ, 41-47; prof & head dept, 47-54, res prof, 65-71, EMER RES PROF GEOL, UNIV ILL, URBANA, 71- *Concurrent Pos:* Geologist, Water Resources Br, US Geol Surv, 42-46 & 49-69; state geologist, Ohio, 46-47; consult, State Geol Surv, Ill, 48-; Gurley lectr, Cornell Univ, 55; vpres NAm, Int Comn Hist Geol, 65-77; chmn, US Nat Comt Hist Geol, 74-77; consult, Geol Surv Ohio, 73-80. *Honors & Awards:* Orton Award, Ohio State Univ, 61. *Mem:* AAAS (vpres, 51); fel Geol Soc Am; Am Asn Petrol Geol; Am Inst Mining, Metall & Petrol Eng; Hist Sci Soc. *Res:* Ground water and glacial geology; history of American geology. *Mailing Add:* 254 Natural Hist Bldg Univ of Ill Urbana IL 61801

WHITE, GERALD M(ILTON), b Detroit, Mich, Dec 6, 29; m 56; c 4. COMPUTER SCIENCE. *Educ:* Univ Mich, BS, 51; Harvard Univ, MS, 53, PhD(appl physics), 58. *Prof Exp:* Res assoc, Res Lab, 57-64, mgr comput oper, Res & Develop Ctr, 64-69, res assoc info systs, 69-77, INFO SYSTS ENGR, RES & DEVELOP CTR, GEN ELEC CO, 77- *Mem:* Inst Elec & Electronics Engrs. *Res:* Information processing; computer systems and languages. *Mailing Add:* 1274 Hawthorne Rd Schenectady NY 12309

WHITE, GIFFORD, b San Saba, Tex, Feb 17, 12; m 35; c 2. PHYSICS. *Educ:* Univ Tex, BA & MA, 39. *Prof Exp:* Geophysicist, Humble Oil & Refining Co, 34-38; res engr, Sperry Gyroscope Co, 41-47; vpres, Statham Instruments, Inc, 47-52; pres, 53-79, CHMN BD, WHITE INSTRUMENTS, INC, 79- *Honors & Awards:* Cert of Appreciation, US War Dept, 45. *Mem:* Am Phys Soc; Soc Explor Geophys; fel Inst Elec & Electronics Eng. *Res:* Instrumentation for physical measurements; circuit theory. *Mailing Add:* White Instruments Inc Box 698 Austin TX 78767

WHITE, GILBERT FOWLER, b Chicago, Ill, Nov 26, 11; m 44; c 3. WATER RESOURCES, NATURAL HAZARDS. *Educ:* Univ Chicago, SB, 32, SM, 34, PhD(geog), 42. *Prof Exp:* Geographer, Miss Valley Comt, Public Work Admin, 34-35, Nat Resources Planning Bd, 35-40, Bur Budget, 40-42; volunteer, Am Friends Serv Comt, 42-46; pres, Haverford Col, 46-55; prof geog, Univ Chicago, 56-69, Univ Colo, 70-78; DIR, NATURAL HAZARDS INFO CTR, 76-; EMER DISTINGUISHED PROF & EMER DIR, INST BEHAV SCI, 78- *Concurrent Pos:* VChmn, Pres Water Resources Policy Comn, 50-51; vis prof, Univ Oxford, 62-63; chmn, Bur Budget Task Force Fed Flood Policy, 65-66; chmn bd, Resources Future, 74-79; chmn, Comn Natural Resources, Nat Res Coun, 77-80, pres, Sci Comt on Problems Environ, 76-82. *Honors & Awards:* Daly Medal, Am Geog Soc, 71; Eben Award, Am Water Resources Asn, 72; Environ Award, Nat Acad Sci, 80. *Mem:* Nat Acad Sci; Asn Am Geographers (pres, 61-62); Am Geophys Union; hon mem Am Planning Asn. *Res:* Natural resources management; environmental policy; natural hazards. *Mailing Add:* Inst Behav Sci Campus Box 482 Univ Colo Boulder CO 80309

WHITE, GORDON ALLAN, b Vancouver, BC, Nov 8, 32; m 59. PLANT PHYSIOLOGY, BIOCHEMISTRY. *Educ:* Univ BC, BA, 54, MA, 55; Iowa State Univ, PhD, 59. *Prof Exp:* Fel plant biochem, Prairie Regional Lab, Nat Res Coun Can, 59-60; asst prof chem, Ore State Univ, 60-62; Plant biochemist, 62-77, RES SCIENTIST, LONDON RES INST, CAN DEPT AGR, 77- *Mem:* Am Soc Plant Physiologists. *Res:* Oxidative enzymes and their role in metabolism; biochemistry of fungi, including obligate parasites; carbohydrate catabolism in microorganisms. *Mailing Add:* London Res Inst Can Dept of Agr University Sub Post Off London ON N6A 5B7 Can

WHITE, GORDON JUSTICE, b Elgin, Ill, May 3, 31; m 53; c 4. IMMUNOCHEMISTRY, BIOCHEMISTRY. *Educ:* Univ Ill, BS, 53; Northwestern Univ, MS, 58; Brandeis Univ, PhD(biol), 62. *Prof Exp:* Res assoc virol, 62-68, RES ASSOC IMMUNOL, UPJOHN CO, 68- *Res:*

Pathogenesis of upper respiratory virus disease; enzyme modification of biological activity of gamma globulin; studies of inhibitors of serum complement and of production and detection of reagin-like antibodies in the rat; modulation of immediate hypersensitivity reactions by control of intracellular cyclic nucleotide levels. *Mailing Add:* Dept 7244 The Upjohn Co Kalamazoo MI 49006

WHITE, HAROLD BANCROFT, III, b Hartford, Conn, Feb 26, 43; m 66; c 3. BIOCHEMISTRY. *Educ:* Pa State Univ, BS, 65; Brandeis Univ, PhD(biochem), 70. *Prof Exp:* Res fel chem, Harvard Univ, 70-71; asst prof, 71-77, ASSOC PROF CHEM, UNIV DEL, 77- *Concurrent Pos:* Res career develop award, NIH, 77-81; ed bd, J Molecular Evolution, 77-82; vis res scientist genetics, Univ Calif, Davis, 77-78. *Mem:* AAAS; Am Soc Biol Chemists; Am Entom Soc; Soc Study Evolution. *Res:* Molecular evolution; protein polymorphism; isozymes; vitamin binding proteins; glycerol 3-phosphate dehydrogenase structure and function; odonata; glycoproteins; egg yolk deposition. *Mailing Add:* Dept Chem Univ Del Newark DE 19711

WHITE, HAROLD BIRTS, JR, b Little Rock, Ark, Mar 13, 29; m 58; c 2. BIOCHEMISTRY. *Educ:* Columbia Univ, AB, 51, MA, 53, PhD(physiol), 57. *Prof Exp:* Fel, Purdue Univ, 57-59, asst prof biochem, 59-61; from asst prof to assoc prof, 61-68, PROF BIOCHEM, SCH MED, UNIV MISS, 68- *Concurrent Pos:* Vis scientist, Univ Milan, 68-69. *Mem:* Am Chem Soc; Am Soc Biol Chem. *Res:* Brain lipid modification; poxvirus influence on lipid metabolism. *Mailing Add:* Dept of Biochem Univ of Miss Sch of Med Jackson MS 39216

WHITE, HAROLD D(OUGLAS), b Sugar Valley, Ga, Aug 29, 10; m 35; c 2. AGRICULTURAL ENGINEERING. *Educ:* Univ Ga, BS, 34; Iowa State Col, MS, 38. *Prof Exp:* Agr engr, Abraham Baldwin Agr Col, 34-37; asst, Exp Sta, Univ Iowa, 37; instr agr eng, Iowa State Col, 38-41; asst agr engr, Univ Ga, 41-43; spec supvr, State Dept Educ, Ga, 43-45; from assoc prof to prof, 45-74, EMER PROF AGR ENG, UNIV GA, 74- *Concurrent Pos:* Pres, Prof Engrs & Assocs P C, 76-; vpres, Econo Eng, 77- *Mem:* Sigma Xi; fel Am Soc Agr Engrs; Nat Soc Prof Engrs; Poultry Sci Asn. *Res:* Food and feed processing facilities and equipment; materials handling; dairy and poultry engineering. *Mailing Add:* 561 University Dr Athens GA 30605

WHITE, HAROLD J, b New York, NY, Jan 4, 20. PATHOLOGY. *Educ:* Harvard Univ, BS, 41; Univ Geneva, MD, 52. *Prof Exp:* Instr path, Sch Med, Yale Univ, 57-58; asst prof, 58-61, PROF PATH, SCH MED, UNIV ARK, LITTLE ROCK, 66- *Concurrent Pos:* Mem staff, Vet Admin Hosp, 60- *Mem:* NY Acad Med; Int Acad Path. *Res:* Role of mucopolysaccharides and collagen in pathologic conditions. *Mailing Add:* Dept of Path Univ of Ark Little Rock AR 72201

WHITE, HAROLD KEITH, b Straughn, Ind, July 11, 23; m 47; c 3. ORGANIC CHEMISTRY, BIOCHEMISTRY. *Educ:* Butler Univ, BS, 47; Purdue Univ, MS, 50; Ind Univ, PhD(org chem), 54. *Prof Exp:* Asst chemist, State Chem Off Ind, 47-49; res chemist, Mead Johnson & Co, 53-55; assoc prof, 55-57, PROF CHEM, HANOVER COL, 57- *Mem:* Am Chem Soc. *Res:* Stereochemistry; synthesis of polycyclics; medicinal chemistry. *Mailing Add:* Dept of Chem Hanover Col Hanover IN 47243

WHITE, HAROLD MCCOY, b Camden, SC, Feb 1, 32; m 55; c 3. ORGANIC CHEMISTRY. *Educ:* Clemson Univ, BS, 54, PhD(org chem), 62. *Prof Exp:* Chemist, SC Agr Res Sta, 54-55; fel ozone chem, Univ Tex, 62-64; from asst prof to assoc prof chem, 64-71, PROF CHEM, SOUTHWESTERN STATE COL, 71- *Concurrent Pos:* Welch Found fel, 63-64. *Mem:* Am Chem Soc; Sigma Xi. *Res:* Reactions of ozone with organic compounds; mechanism of the ozonation of hydrocarbons and reactions of ozone in basic media. *Mailing Add:* Dept of Chem Southwestern Okla State Univ Weatherford OK 73096

WHITE, HARRIS HERMAN, b Ft Worth, Tex, June 24, 49; m 73; c 4. BIOLOGICAL OCEANOGRAPHY. *Educ:* Univ Wash, BS(oceanog) & BS(zool), 71; Univ RI, PhD (oceanog), 76. *Prof Exp:* Asst prof oceanog, Old Dominion Univ, 76-79; ECOLOGIST, NAT OCEANIC & ATMOSPHERIC ADMIN, 80- *Res:* Marine pollution. *Mailing Add:* NOAA/Nat Ocean Surv 6001 Executive Blvd Rm 324 Rockville MD 20852

WHITE, HARRY JOSEPH, b Philadelphia, Pa, Feb 19, 31; m 56; c 4. ORGANIC CHEMISTRY. *Educ:* LaSalle Col, BA, 54; Univ Notre Dame, PhD(org chem), 58. *Prof Exp:* Res chemist, 58-67, coordr PhD recruiting, 67-68, asst mgr manpower & employment, 68-72, MGR RECRUITING & PLACEMENT, ROHM AND HAAS CO, 72- *Mem:* Am Chem Soc. *Res:* Technical recruiting, placement and manpower planning; petroleum additives; polymer chemistry. *Mailing Add:* Rohm and Haas Co Independence Mall W Philadelphia PA 19105

WHITE, HELEN LYNG, b Oceanside, NY, Oct 25, 30; m 55; c 2. BIOCHEMISTRY, ENZYMOLOGY. *Educ:* Russell Sage Col, BA, 52; Univ Del, MS, 63; Univ NC, Chapel Hill, PhD(biochem), 67. *Prof Exp:* Chemist, E I du Pont de Nemours & Co, Inc, 52-56; res assoc med chem, Univ NC, 67-70; SR RES PHARMACOLOGIST, WELLCOME RES LABS, 70- *Mem:* Am Soc Pharmacol & Exp Therapeut; Am Soc Biol Chemists; Am Chem Soc. *Res:* Enzyme mechanisms and inhibitors; neurochemistry. *Mailing Add:* Dept of Pharmacol Wellcome Res Labs Research Triangle Park NC 27709

WHITE, HENRY W, b Blytheville, Ark, Dec 20, 41; m 62; c 2. PHYSICS. *Educ:* Pepperdine Col, BA, 63; Univ Calif, Riverside, MS, 65, PhD(physics), 69. *Prof Exp:* ASSOC PROF PHYSICS, UNIV MO-COLUMBIA, 69- *Mem:* Am Phys Soc; Am Asn Physics Teachers. *Res:* Low temperature thermal properties; inelastic electron tunneling spectroscopy. *Mailing Add:* Dept Physics Univ Mo Columbia MO 65211

WHITE, HERMAN BRENNER, JR, b Tuskegee, Ala, Sept 28, 48; m 76. PARTICLE PHYSICS. *Educ:* Earlham Col, BA, 70; Mich State Univ, MS, 74. *Prof Exp:* Resident res assoc nuclear physics, Argonne Nat Lab, 71; Alfred P Sloan Found fel accelerator & particle physics, Europ Orgn Nuclear Res, Geneva, Switz, 72; staff physicist particle physics, Univs Res Asn, Fermi Nat Accelerator Lab, 74-76; teaching fel physics, Yale Univ, 76-78; STAFF PHYSICIST PARTICLE PHYSICS, FERMI NAT ACCELERATOR LAB, 78- *Mem:* Am Inst Physics. *Res:* Study of high energy hadrons production and neutrino production; development of neutrino distribution formulas. *Mailing Add:* Neutrino Dept Res Div Fermilab PO Box 500 Batavia IL 60510

WHITE, HORACE FREDERICK, b Fresno, Calif, Apr 25, 25; m 52; c 3. PHYSICAL CHEMISTRY. *Educ:* Fresno State Col, AB, 47; Ore State Col, MS, 50; Brown Univ, PhD(phys chem), 53. *Prof Exp:* Fel, Univ Minn, 52-54; spectroscopist, Res Dept, M W Kellogg Co Div, Pullman, Inc, 54-56, instrumental methods supvr, 56-57; spectroscopist, Res Dept, Union Carbide Chem Co, 57-65; from asst prof to assoc prof chem, 65-75, actg chmn dept, 66-68, PROF CHEM, PORTLAND STATE UNIV, 75- *Mem:* Am Chem Soc. *Res:* Molecular structure using infrared spectroscopy and nuclear magnetic resonance spectrometry techniques; mass spectrometry; x-ray crystallography for structural determinations. *Mailing Add:* Portland State Univ Dept Chem PO Box 751 Portland OR 97207

WHITE, HOWARD DWAINE, b Des Moines, Iowa, Oct 24, 46. BIOCHEMISTRY. *Educ:* Univ Colo, BA, 69; Brandeis Univ, PhD(biochem), 73. *Prof Exp:* Fel biophysics, Med Res Coun, London, 73-76, mem sci staff, 76-78; ASST PROF BIOCHEM, UNIV ARIZ, 78- *Mem:* Biophys Soc; Brit Biophys Soc. *Res:* The mechanism by which ATP hydrolysis is coupled to the production of mechanical work in muscle and other contractile systems. *Mailing Add:* Dept of Biochem Univ of Ariz Tucson AZ 85712

WHITE, HOWARD JULIAN, JR, b Batavia, NY, Nov 20, 20; m 49; c 2. SCIENCE ADMINISTRATION. *Educ:* Princeton Univ, AB, 42, PhD(chem), 47; Univ Wis, MS, 44. *Prof Exp:* Asst chem, Univ Wis, 42-44; from res chemist to assoc dir res, Textile Res Inst, NJ, 47-57, dir, 57-60; sr phys chemist, Stanford Res Inst, 60-61; spec asst res to Asst Secy Navy, Res & Develop, 61-64; asst chief phys chem div, 64-66, PROG MGR, OFF STANDARD REFERENCE DATA, NAT BUR STANDARDS, 66- *Mem:* AAAS; Am Chem Soc; Fiber Soc; Calorimetry Conf. *Res:* Surface chemistry; solutions, swelling, adsorption and dyeing of fibers; reference data on thermodynamics and transport properties and colloid and surface properties. *Mailing Add:* 8028 Park Overlook Dr Bethesda MD 20817

WHITE, HOWARD SORREL, b Philadelphia, Pa, Oct 11, 34; m 59; c 2. ORGANIC CHEMISTRY. *Educ:* Philadelphia Col Pharm & Sci, BSc, 56; Temple Univ, MA, 58, PhD(org chem), 63. *Prof Exp:* Res chemist, Archer-Daniels-Midland Co, 63-67; res chemist, Gillette Co, 67-70; res chemist, Armstrong Cork Co, 70-77; SUPVR, POLYMERS MAT ENG DEPT, AMP INC, 78- *Mem:* AAAS; Am Chem Soc. *Res:* Structure-property relationships in polymers; polyurethanes; high temperature polymers of interest to electronics industry; film and coatings technology. *Mailing Add:* 243 Beacon Dr Harrisburg PA 17112

WHITE, JACK EDWARD, b Stuart, Fla, July 24, 21; m 45; c 5. MEDICINE. *Educ:* Fla Agr & Mech Univ, BS, 41; Howard Univ, MD, 44; Am Bd Surg, dipl, 51. *Prof Exp:* Intern med & surg, Freedmen's Hosp, 45, asst resident surgeon surg, 45-46, chief resident surgeon chest surg, 47-48, chief resident gen surg, 48-49; asst resident surgeon, Mem Ctr, New York, 49-50, resident surgeon, 50-51; from asst prof to assoc prof, 51-63, PROF SURG, MED SCH, HOWARD UNIV, 63-, DIR CANCER TEACHING PROJ, 51-, DIR, CANCER RES CTR, 72-, PROF ONCOL, 74- *Concurrent Pos:* Consult, Nat Cancer Inst, 53-56; surgeon, Freedmen's Hosp, 51-, chmn dept oncol, 73-; attend surgeon, Washington Hosp Ctr, 63-; mem rev comt, Support Serv, Div Cancer Control, Nat Cancer Inst, 74-77. *Mem:* Inst Med-Nat Acad Sci; fel Am Col Surg; Am Radium Soc; Soc Surg Alimentary Tract; Soc Head & Neck Surg. *Res:* Cancer of tongue, breast, mesentery, soft parts and lymphatic organs; penetrating trauma of abdomen; cancer epidemiology; retroperitonitis; cancer chemotherapy; peptic ulcer; pheochromocytoma. *Mailing Add:* 1610 Jackson NE Washington DC 20018

WHITE, JACK LEE, b Los Angeles, Calif, Oct 29, 25; m 50; c 1. MATERIALS SCIENCE, CARBON & GRAPHITE. *Educ:* Calif Inst Technol, BS, 49; Carnegie Inst Technol, BS, 50; Imp Col Univ London, dipl, 55; Univ Calif, PhD(metall), 55. *Prof Exp:* Res engr, Univ Calif, 55; Nat Acad Sci res assoc, US Naval Res Lab, 55-57; mem staff, Gen Atomic Atomic, 58-67; res off, Petten Ctr, Europ Atomic Energy Comn, 67-69; vis scientist, Gulf Gen Atomic, 69-70; assoc prof mat sci, Univ Calif, Davis, 71-72; STAFF SCIENTIST, AEROSPACE CORP, 73- *Concurrent Pos:* Consult, Gulf Gen Atomic, Europe Atomic Energy Comn, 70-73. *Mem:* AAAS; Am Chem Soc; Am Ceramic Soc; Am Inst Mining, Metall & Petrol Eng; Brit Inst Metals. *Res:* Carbonaceous and graphitic materials; high-temperature materials; high-temperature physical chemistry; metallurgical thermodynamics. *Mailing Add:* 690 Rimini Rd Del Mar CA 92014

WHITE, JAMES CARL, b Ft Wayne, Ind, Mar 1, 22; m 46; c 4. ANALYTICAL CHEMISTRY. *Educ:* Ind Univ, BS, 43; Ohio State Univ, MS, 48, PhD(chem), 50. *Prof Exp:* Chemist, Joslyn Mfg Co, 46; asst, Ohio State Univ, 46-50; asst div dir, Oak Ridge Nat Lab, 50-67, assoc dir, Anal Chem Div, 67-72, dir, 72-76; TECH SERV MGR, NUCLEAR DIV, UNION CARBIDE CORP, 76- *Mem:* AAAS; Am Chem Soc; Int Union Pure & Appl Chem; Fedn Anal Chem & Spectros. *Res:* Research administration; molten salts; separations; reference materials. *Mailing Add:* 5425 Shenandoah Trail Knoxville TN 37919

WHITE, JAMES CARRICK, b Scobey, Mont, Oct 29, 16; m 41; c 3. FOOD MICROBIOLOGY. *Educ:* Cornell Univ, PhD(bact), 44. *Prof Exp:* Dir res, Borden Cheese Co, 44-46; assoc prof dairy indust, 46-51, prof food sci, 77-80, PROF DAIRY INDUST, CORNELL UNIV, 51-, PROF HOTEL ADMIN,

72-, ASST DEAN HOTAL ADMIN, 79- *Mem:* Inst Food Technol; Int Asn Milk, Food & Environ Sanitarians. *Res:* Food poisoning; waste technology; food sanitation. *Mailing Add:* Sch Hotel Admin Cornell Univ Ithaca NY 14850

WHITE, JAMES CLARENCE, b Hodge, La, July 7, 36; m 57; c 2. PLANT PATHOLOGY. *Educ:* La Polytech Inst, BS, 59; La State Univ, MS, 61, PhD(plant path), 63. *Prof Exp:* Asst prof bot, Southeastern La Col, 63-65; asst prof, 65-70, PROF BOT, LA TECH UNIV, 70-, PROF BACTERIOL, 77- *Mem:* Am Phytopath Soc. *Res:* Pathological histology and studies of Tabasco pepper plants infected with tobacco etch virus. *Mailing Add:* Dept of Bot & Bacteriol La Tech Univ Ruston LA 71270

WHITE, JAMES DAVID, b Bristol, Eng, June 14, 35; m 60; c 2. ORGANIC CHEMISTRY. *Educ:* Cambridge Univ, BA, 59; Univ BC, MSc, 61; Mass Inst Technol, PhD(org chem), 65. *Prof Exp:* From instr to asst prof chem, Harvard Univ, 65-71; assoc prof, 71-76, PROF CHEM, ORE STATE UNIV, 76- *Concurrent Pos:* Consult med chem, NIH. *Mem:* Am Chem Soc; Royal Soc Chem. *Res:* Organic synthesis and photochemistry; chemistry of natural products; heterocyclic compounds. *Mailing Add:* Dept of Chem Ore State Univ Corvallis OR 97331

WHITE, JAMES EDWARD, b Cherokee, Tex, May 10, 18; m 41; c 4. ACOUSTICS. *Educ:* Univ Tex, BS, 40, MA, 46; Mass Inst Technol, PhD(phsycis), 49. *Prof Exp:* Physicist, Underwater Sound Lab, Mass Inst Technol, 41-45, Defense Res Lab, Univ Tex, 45-46, Mobil Oil Co, 49-55, Marathon Oil Co, 55-69 & Globe Universal Sci, Inc, 69-72; mem faculty, Colo Sch Mines, 72-73; L A Nelson prof geol sci, Univ Tex, El Paso, 73-76; CHARLES HENRY GREEN PROF EXPLOR GEOPHYS, COLO SCH MINES, 76- *Concurrent Pos:* Nat Acad Sci exchange scientist, USSR & Yugoslavia, 73-74; mem space appl bd, Nat Acad Eng, 73-78; Esso vis prof, Univ Sydney, Australia, 75; delegate, Soc Explor Geophys Conf, China Geophys Soc, 81. *Mem:* Fel Acoust Soc Am; Europ Asn Explor Geophys; Seismol Soc Am; hon mem Soc Explor Geophys (past pres); Am Geophys Union. *Res:* Seismic prospecting; waves in solids; engineering geophysics; earthquake dynamics. *Mailing Add:* Dept of Geophys Colo Sch of Mines Golden CO 80401

WHITE, JAMES EDWIN, b Pittsburgh, Pa, June 4, 35; m 60; c 2. BIOLOGY, ECOLOGY. *Educ:* Dartmouth Col, AB, 57; Rutgers Univ, PhD(zool), 61. *Prof Exp:* Asst prof biol, Parsons Col, 61-62; from instr to assoc prof, 62-74, PROF BIOL, KEUKA COL, 74-, CHMN DEPT, 69- *Concurrent Pos:* Consult, NY State Scholar Exam, 64-65; actg acad dean, Keuka Col, 77-78. *Mem:* AAAS; Am Soc Mammal; Ecol Soc Am. *Res:* Mammal population ecology; animal behavior; small mammal parasites. *Mailing Add:* Div Natural Sci & Math Keuka Col Keuka Park NY 14478

WHITE, JAMES L(INDSAY), b Brooklyn, NY, Jan 3, 38; m 66. POLYMER ENGINEERING. *Educ:* Polytech Inst Brooklyn, BChE, 59; Univ Del, MChE, 62, PhD(chem eng), 65. *Prof Exp:* Res engr, Res Ctr, US Rubber Co, NJ, 63-66, Mich, 66-67; from assoc prof to prof, 67-70, ALUMNI DISTINGUISHED SERV PROF ENG, UNIV TENN, KNOXVILLE, 74-, PROF-IN-CHARGE POLYMER ENG, 76- *Honors & Awards:* Bincham Medal, Soc Rehol, 81. *Mem:* Am Chem Soc; Soc Rheol; Soc Plastics Engrs; Brit Soc Rheol; Soc Fiber Sci & Technol of Japan. *Res:* Rheology of polymer systems; characterization of structure and orientation in solid polymers; polymer processing; fibers and films; filled polymer systems and composites; rubber technology; history of the polymer industry. *Mailing Add:* Polymer Eng Prog Univ Tenn Knoxville TN 37916

WHITE, JAMES PATRICK, b Indianapolis, Ind, Sept 13, 39; m 62; c 4. MICROBIAL PHYSIOLOGY. *Educ:* Marian Col, Ind, BS, 62; Univ Ark, MS, 65, PhD(microbiol), 67. *Prof Exp:* From asst prof to assoc prof microbiol, 70-77, assoc prof biol, 74-77, PROF BIOL, ST BONAVENTURE UNIV, 77-74- *Mem:* AAAS; Am Soc Microbiol; Mycol Soc Am. *Res:* Physiology and nutrition of pigment formation in Helminthosporium species; effects of trace elements in nitrogen metabolism of microorganisms. *Mailing Add:* Dept of Biol St Bonaventure Univ St Bonaventure NY 14778

WHITE, JAMES RUSHTON, b Ft Benning, Ga, July 28, 23; m 55; c 2. BIOCHEMISTRY. *Educ:* Stanford Univ, BS, 48, PhD(chem), 53. *Prof Exp:* Res chemist, Pioneering Res Lab, E I du Pont de Nemours & Co, Inc, 53-59; res assoc biochem, Univ Pa, 59-62; from asst prof to assoc prof, 62-71, PROF BIOCHEM, SCH MED, UNIV NC, CHAPEL HILL, 71- *Concurrent Pos:* NSF fel, 60-62. *Mem:* AAAS; Am Soc Biol Chem; Am Chem Soc; Biophys Soc; Am Soc Microbiol. *Res:* Macromolecular metabolism in bacteria; antibacterial action of antibiotics and other inhibitors; complexes of nucleic acids with low molecular weight ligands. *Mailing Add:* Dept of Biochem Univ of NC Med Sch Chapel Hill NC 27514

WHITE, JAMES RUSSELL, b Elgin, Ill, July 13, 19; m 44; c 1. PHYSICAL CHEMISTRY. *Educ:* Ind Univ, BS, 42; Yale Univ, PhD(phys chem), 44. *Prof Exp:* Phys chemist, Tenn Eastman Corp, 44-47; res assoc physics, Socony-Vacuum Oil Co, 47-59, supvr nuclear res group, Mobil Res & Develop Corp, 59-69, MGR RESOURCES & PROD RES SECT, MOBIL RES & DEVELOP CORP, 69- *Mem:* AAAS; Am Chem Soc; Am Nuclear Soc. *Res:* Mass spectrometry; radio chemical tracers; phycial chemistry of solutions; ionization potentials; lubricants and lubrication; thermal diffusion; radiation chemistry. *Mailing Add:* Mobil Res & Develop Corp Box 1025 Princeton NJ 08540

WHITE, JAMES VICTOR, b Hammond, Ind, May 20, 41; m 66. ACOUSTICS, DYNAMICS. *Educ:* Northwestern Univ, Evanston, BS, 64; Harvard Univ, SM, 65, PhD(acoust), 70. *Prof Exp:* Engr, Jensen Mfg Co, 63-64; asst prof mech eng, Stevens Inst Technol, 70-74; staff scientist, Sound Reprod Dept, CBS Tech Ctr, 74-80; MEM TECH STAFF, ANAL SCI CORP, 80- *Concurrent Pos:* Fel, Harvard Univ, 70. *Mem:* Inst Elec & Electronics Engrs; Am Soc Mech Engrs; Acoust Soc Am; Audio Eng Soc. *Res:* Stylus-groove interaction in phonographs; noise control; modeling and identification of dynamic systems. *Mailing Add:* Anal Sci Corp 6 Jacob Way Reading MA 01867

WHITE, JAMES WILSON, b Salisbury, NC, May 29, 14; m 42; c 3. PHYSICS. *Educ:* Davidson Col, BS, 34; Univ NC, MS, 36, PhD(physics), 38. *Hon Degrees:* DSc, King Col, 65. *Prof Exp:* Instr physics, Emory Jr Col, 38-39; prof, King Col, 39-42; instr, Univ Tenn, 42-44; res physicist, Fulton Sylphon Co, 44-45; from asst prof to assoc prof, 45-58, PROF PHYSICS, UNIV TENN, KNOXVILLE, 58- *Mem:* Am Phys Soc; Am Asn Physics Teachers. *Res:* Instrumentation. *Mailing Add:* Dept of Physics-Astron Univ of Tenn Knoxville TN 37996

WHITE, JANE VICKNAIR, b Houma, La, Feb 10, 47; m 68; c 2. NUTRITION. *Educ:* St Mary's Diminican Col, BS, 68; Univ Tenn, Knoxville, PhD(nutrit), 75. *Prof Exp:* Asst prof, 75-80, ASSOC PROF NUTRIT, DEPT FAMILY PRACT MED, UNIV TENN, KNOXVILLE, 75- *Concurrent Pos:* Clin nutrit consult, Vet Admin Cent Off, Washington, DC, 79- *Mem:* Am Dietetic Asn; Am Home Econ Asn; Nat Educ Asn. *Res:* Effect of sulfur nutrition on the enzymes of carbohydrate and fat metabolism; nutrition education in family practice residency programs. *Mailing Add:* Dept Family Pract Med Univ Tenn Ctr Health Sci Knoxville TN 37916

WHITE, JERRY EUGENE, b Mt Vernon, Ill, Oct 6, 46; m 68. ORGANIC CHEMISTRY. *Educ:* Southern Ill Univ, Carbondale, BA, 68; Vanderbilt Univ, PhD(chem), 72. *Prof Exp:* Res chemist polymer synthesis, Army Mat & Mech Res Ctr, 73-76; sr res chemist, New Prod Lab, Granville Res & Develop Ctr, Dow Chem USA, 76-81, PROJ LEADER, CENT RES-PLASTICS LAB, DOW CHEM CO, MIDLAND, MICH, 81- *Mem:* AAAS; Am Chem Soc; Sigma Xi. *Res:* Synthetic, structural and mechanistic studies in the chemistry of novel organic sulfur compounds; preparation and characterization of high molecular weight, special service polymers; nuclear magnetic resonance spectroscopy of macromolecules; polymer modification reactions. *Mailing Add:* Cent Res-Plastics Lab Bldg 1702 Dow Chem Co Midland MI 48640

WHITE, JERRY EUGENE, b Garden City, Iowa, June 11, 37; m 58; c 4. ASTRODYNAMICS. *Educ:* Univ Wash, BS, 59; US Air Force Inst Technol, MS, 64; Purdue Univ, PhD(astronaut), 70. *Prof Exp:* Mission controller, Air Force Missile Test Ctr, US Air Force, 60-62, assoc prof astronaut, US Air Force Acad, 64-66 & 68-72, astronaut engr, Aerospace Defense Command, Colo, 72-73; astronaut engr, Aerospace Defense Command, 73-78, ASTRONAUT ENGR, SECURITY COMMAND, US AIR FORCE RESERVE, 79- *Concurrent Pos:* Regional dir, Navigators, 73- *Mem:* Am Inst Aeronaut & Astronaut. *Res:* Orbit determination; optimization. *Mailing Add:* 32230 23rd Ave SW Federal Way WA 98003

WHITE, JESSE EDMUND, b Indianapolis, Ind, June 9, 27; m 50; c 3. HISTORY OF CHEMISTRY. *Educ:* Va Mil Inst, BS, 49; Ind Univ, PhD(chem), 58. *Prof Exp:* Asst prof chem, Lafayette Col, 55-59; from asst prof to assoc prof, 59-71, PROF CHEM, SOUTHERN ILL UNIV, EDWARDSVILLE, 71- *Concurrent Pos:* Petrol Res Fund fac award advan sci study, Mass Inst Technol, 63-64. *Mem:* Am Chem Soc; Nat Sci Teachers Asn; Asn Univ Prof. *Res:* Transition metal complexes; history of chemistry. *Mailing Add:* Dept of Chem Southern Ill Univ Edwardsville IL 62026

WHITE, JESSE STEVEN, b Cleveland, Miss, May 9, 17; m. PARASITOLOGY. *Educ:* Delta State Col, BS, 40; Miss State Col, MS, 49; Univ Ala, PhD, 59. *Prof Exp:* Asst prof, 46-59, head div sci, 59-70, prof, 59-80, EMER PROF BIOL, DELTA STATE UNIV, 80- *Concurrent Pos:* NSF fel, 58-59. *Res:* Medical entomology. *Mailing Add:* Dept of Biol Delta State Univ Cleveland MS 38733

WHITE, JOE LLOYD, b Pierce, Okla, Nov 8, 21; m 45; c 5. SOIL MINERALOGY, SOIL CHEMISTRY. *Educ:* Okla State Univ, BS, 44, MS, 45; Univ Wis, PhD(soil chem), 47. *Prof Exp:* From asst prof to assoc prof, 47-60, PROF AGRON, PURDUE UNIV, WEST LAFAYETTE, 60- *Concurrent Pos:* Rockefeller fel natural sci, Nat Res Coun, 53-54; NSF sr fel, Louvain, 65-66; Soil Sci Soc Am Rep, Earth Sci Div, Nat Res Coun, 70-73; Fulbright res scholar, Athens, 72-73; Guggenheim fel, Versailles, 72-73; consult, William H Rorer Co, Pa, 78-; Alexander von Humboldt Found fel, Munich Tech Univ, 80-81. *Honors & Awards:* Charles Medal, Charles Univ, Prague, 61; Soil Sci Award, Am Soc Agron, 69; Sr US Scientist Award, Alexander von Humboldt Found, 80. *Mem:* AAAS; Am Chem Soc; fel Am Soc Agron; fel Mineral Soc Am; Clay Minerals Soc (treas, 69-72). *Res:* Weathering of micaceous minerals; pesticide-soil colloid interactions; application of infrared spectroscopy to study of aluminosilicates; structure and properties of aluminum hydroxide gels and aluminum chlorohydrates; clay-drug interactions. *Mailing Add:* Dept of Agron Purdue Univ West Lafayette IN 47906

WHITE, JOE WADE, b Dill City, Okla, Aug 22, 40; m 62; c 2. PHYSICAL ORGANIC CHEMISTRY. *Educ:* Okla State Univ, BS, 63; Univ Ariz, PhD(chem), 67. *Prof Exp:* Sr chemist, 67-71, res specialist chem, Indust Tape Lab, 71-72, res supvr, Indust Specialties Lab, 72-73, RES MGR, INDUST SPECIALTIES LAB, 3M CO, 73- *Mem:* Am Chem Soc; Soc Plastics Eng. *Res:* Kinetics and rheology of gelling polymerizations. *Mailing Add:* Indust Specialties Lab 3M Co St Paul MN 55101

WHITE, JOHN ANDERSON, b Bahia, Brazil, Oct 18, 19; m 76; c 1. VERTEBRATE ZOOLOGY, PALEONTOLOGY. *Educ:* William Jewell Col, AB, 42; Univ Kans, PhD(zool), 53. *Prof Exp:* Instr biol, William Jewell Col, 46-47 & Univ Ill, 53-55; prof, Calif State Col Long Beach, 55-66; CUR VERT PALEONT, IDAHO MUS NATURAL HIST & PROF BIOL, IDAHO STATE UNIV, 66- *Mem:* Fel AAAS; Am Soc Mammal; Soc Syst Zool; Soc Vert Paleont; Paleont Soc. *Res:* Systematics, evolution and ecology of late Tertiary and Quaternary rodents and logomorphs. *Mailing Add:* Idaho Mus Natural Hist Idaho State Univ Pocatello ID 83209

WHITE, JOHN ARNOLD, b Chicago, Ill, Jan 30, 33; m 64; c 3. CRITICAL PHENOMENA. *Educ:* Oberlin Col, BA, 54; Yale Univ, MS, 55, PhD(physics), 59. *Prof Exp:* Instr physics, Yale Univ, 58-59; instr, Harvard Univ, 59-62; res assoc, Yale Univ, 62-63; physicist, Nat Bur Standards, 63-64; res assoc physics, Univ Md, 65-66; assoc prof, 66-68, PROF PHYSICS, AM UNIV, 68- *Concurrent Pos:* Consult, Nat Bur Standards, 66-72 & 81; NSF grants, Am Univ, 66, 67, 69 & 71; vis scientist, Mass Inst Technol, 72; res contracts, Off Naval Res, 73 & 74. *Mem:* AAAS; Sigma Xi; fel Am Phys Soc. *Res:* Atomic beams; magnetism of rare earth ions in solids; lasers; spontaneous emission in external fields; speed of light; unified time-length standardization; laser light scattering; critical point phenomena in fluids. *Mailing Add:* Dept Physics Am Univ Washington DC 20016

WHITE, JOHN AUSTIN, JR, b Portland, Ark, Dec 5, 39; m 63; c 2. INDUSTRIAL ENGINEERING, OPERATIONS RESEARCH. *Educ:* Univ Ark, Fayetteville, BS, 62; Va Polytech Inst, MS, 66; Ohio State Univ, PhD(indust eng), 70. *Prof Exp:* Indust engr, Tenn Eastman Co, 61-63; instr indust eng, Va Polytech Inst, 63-66; teaching assoc, Ohio State Univ, 66-69; from asst prof to assoc prof indust eng & opers res, Va Polytech Inst & State Univ, 70-74; assoc prof indust & systs eng, 75-77, PROF INDUST & SYSTS ENG, GA INST TECHNOL, 77- *Concurrent Pos:* Mem bd dir, Mat Handling Educ Found, 77-81. *Mem:* Am Inst Indust Engrs; Opers Res Soc Am; Am Soc Eng Educ; Inst Mgt Sci; Int Mat Mgt Soc. *Res:* Development of optimum solutions to facilities layout and location problems, including material handling and warehousing systems. *Mailing Add:* Sch of Indust & Systs Eng Ga Inst of Technol Atlanta GA 30332

WHITE, JOHN DAVID, b Newark, NJ, Feb 14, 28; m 51; c 1. PATHOGENESIS, INFECTIOUS DISEASES. *Educ:* Univ Buffalo, BA, 48, MA, 50; Vanderbilt Univ, PhD(bact), 53. *Prof Exp:* Asst bact, Univ Buffalo, 48-50; asst bot, Vanderbilt Univ, 50-53; res bacteriologist, US Army Hosp, Camp Kilmer, 54-55; bacteriologist, Armed Forces Inst Path, 55-56; bacteriologist, Path Div, US Dept Army, Ft Detrick, 56-59, chief clin path br, 59-68, actg chief path div, 68-71; MICROBIOLOGIST, PATH DIV, US ARMY MED RES INST INFECTIOUS DIS, 71- *Mem:* Am Soc Microbiol; Sigma Xi; Am Asn Pathologists; NY Acad Sci; Electron Micros Soc Am. *Res:* Immunology; fluorescent antibody methods; electron microscopy. *Mailing Add:* US Army Med Res Inst Infect Dis Path Div Ft Detrick Frederick MD 21701

WHITE, JOHN FRANCIS, b New Orleans, La, Feb 9, 21; m 50; c 4. GEOLOGY. *Educ:* Univ Calif, BS, 47, PhD, 55. *Prof Exp:* Geologist, Mining Co Guatemala, 47-48 & Consol Coppermines Corp, 48-51; consult, Hydrothermal Res Proj, 55-59, from asst prof to assoc prof, 55-71, PROF GEOL, ANTIOCH UNIV, 71- *Mem:* Geol Soc Am; Geochem Soc. *Res:* Economic geology; geomorphology; petrology. *Mailing Add:* Dept of Geol Antioch Col Yellow Springs OH 45387

WHITE, JOHN FRANCIS, b Indianapolis, Ind, July 21, 44; m; c 3. PHYSIOLOGY. *Educ:* Marian Col, BS, 66; Ind Univ, PhD(physiol), 70. *Prof Exp:* asst prof, 73-80, ASSOC PROF PHYSIOL, EMORY UNIV, 80- *Concurrent Pos:* NSF training fel, Univ Rochester, 71-72; NIH fel, Univ BC, 72-73. *Mem:* Biophys Soc; Am Physiol Soc. *Res:* Mechanisms of intestinal cotransport of sugars and amino acids with ions by absorptive cells; intracellular ionic activities and compartmentalization of ions. *Mailing Add:* Dept Physiol Div Basic Health Sci Emory Univ Atlanta GA 30322

WHITE, JOHN FRANCIS, b Madison, Wis, Dec 2, 29; m 55; c 1. FOOD & DAIRY SCIENCE. *Educ:* Univ Wis, BS, 51; Harvard Bus Sch, AMP, 74. *Prof Exp:* Food scientist, 54-66, div res coordr, 66-68, tech asst, 68-74, V PRES & DIR RES & DEVELOP, KRAFT INC, 74- *Mem:* AAAS; Inst Food Technol; Am Chem Soc. *Mailing Add:* Kraft Inc 801 Waukegan Rd Glenview IL 60025

WHITE, JOHN FRANCIS, b Boston, Mass, Oct 31, 45; m 70; c 1. CHEMISTRY, CATALYSIS. *Educ:* Amherst Col, BA, 67; Mass Inst Technol, PhD(inorg chem), 72. *Prof Exp:* Group leader res & develop, Emery Industs, 72-76; sr res chemist res & develop, Halcon Res & Develop, 76-78; mgr new ventures res, Oxirane Int, 78-81; MGR PROCESS RES, ARCO CHEM RES & DEVELOP, 81- *Mem:* Am Chem Soc; Sigma Xi. *Res:* Petrochemical process development; homogeous and heterogeneous catalysis; aroma chemical process development. *Mailing Add:* Arco Chem Res & Develop 3801 West Chester Pike Newtown Square PA 19073

WHITE, JOHN GREVILLE, b Saltcoats, Scotland, Mar 27, 22; nat US; m 53; c 3. CHEMISTRY. *Educ:* Glasgow Univ, BSc, 44, PhD(chem), 47. *Prof Exp:* Asst chem, Glasgow Univ, 45-47; from instr to asst prof, Princeton Univ, 47-55; mem tech staff, Radio Corp Am, 56-66; PROF PHYS CHEM, FORDHAM UNIV, 66- *Mem:* Am Chem Soc; Am Crystallog Asn; NY Acad Sci. *Res:* X-ray crystal structure analysis; complex organic structures; accurate small organic structures; inorganic structures. *Mailing Add:* Dept of Chem Fordham Univ Rose Hill Campus Bronx NY 10458

WHITE, JOHN JOSEPH, III, b Arlington, Mass, Apr 24, 39; m 68; c 2. SOLID STATE PHYSICS, MECHANICAL ENGINEERING. *Educ:* Col William & Mary, BS, 60; Univ NC, PhD(physics), 65. *Prof Exp:* Res assoc physics, Univ NC, 65; asst prof physics, Univ Ga, 67-73; sr engr, BDM Corp, 73-74; res scientist, 74-78, prin res scientist, 78-81, GROUP LEADER, COLUMBUS LABS, BATTELLE MEM INST, 81- *Concurrent Pos:* Consult, Oak Ridge Nat Lab, 72-73; dir, Ga State Sci Fair, 73; mem, Landing Vehicle Assault Design Review Panel, 76; mem physics res eval group, Air Force Off Sci Res, 78-; mem pub rels comt, Nat Soc Prof Engrs, 78. *Honors & Awards:* Order of the Engr, Sigma Xi. *Mem:* Am Phys Soc; Am Soc Mech Engrs; Am Defense Preparedness Asn. *Res:* Applied mechanics; impact phenomena; explosion containment; assessment of advanced defense technology; optical properties of silver halides, high resolution specific heat measurements in antiferromagnets; superconductivity in quenched alloys; methods of data analysis. *Mailing Add:* Battelle Columbus Labs 505 King Ave Columbus OH 43201

WHITE, JOHN MARVIN, b Martin, Tenn, June 9, 37; m 56; c 2. GENETICS, ANIMAL BREEDING. *Educ:* Univ Tenn, BS, 59; Pa State Univ, MS, 64; NC State Univ, PhD(animal breeding), 67. *Prof Exp:* From asst prof to prof dairy sci, 67-78, HEAD, DEPT DAIRY SCI, VA POLYTECH INST & STATE UNIV, 78- *Mem:* Biomet Soc; Am Dairy Sci Asn; Am Soc Animal Sci. *Res:* Quantitative genetics; measurement of response to single and multiple trait selection and correlated responses in mice and dairy cattle. *Mailing Add:* Dept of Dairy Sci Va Polytech Inst & State Univ Blacksburg VA 24061

WHITE, JOHN MICHAEL, b Danville, Ill, Nov 26, 38; m 60; c 3. CHEMICAL PHYSICS. *Educ:* Harding Col, BS, 60; Univ Ill, MS, 62, PhD(chem), 66. *Prof Exp:* From asst prof to assoc prof, 66-77, PROF CHEM, UNIV TEX, AUSTIN, 77- *Concurrent Pos:* Vis staff mem, Los Alamos Sci Lab. *Mem:* Am Chem Soc; Am Phys Soc. *Res:* surface chemistry. *Mailing Add:* Dept Chem Univ Tex Austin TX 78712

WHITE, JOHN RILEY, chemical physics, nuclear chemistry, see previous edition

WHITE, JOHN ROBERT, computer sciences, information sciences, see previous edition

WHITE, JOHN S(PENCER), b River Falls, Wis, Mar 7, 26; m 46; c 2. INDUSTRIAL ENGINEERING, QUALITY CONTROL. *Educ:* Univ Minn, PhD(statist), 55. *Prof Exp:* Instr math, Wis State Col, Superior, 47-50; asst prof statist, Univ Manitoba, 53-56; opers res analyst, Ball Res Corp, Ind, 56-57; statistician, Minneapolis-Honeywell Regulator Co, 57-60; sr res mathematician, Res Labs, Gen Motors Corp, 60-68; PROF MECH ENG, UNIV MINN, MINNEAPOLIS, 68- *Concurrent Pos:* Dir, Grad Studies Opers Res, Univ Minn. *Honors & Awards:* Craig Award, Am Soc Quality Control, 79. *Mem:* Am Math Soc; Am Soc Qual Control; Opers Res Soc Am; Am Statist Asn; Math Asn Am. *Res:* Stochastic processes; serial correlation; continuous sampling plans; quality control; nonparametric statistics; Weibull distribution; reliability. *Mailing Add:* 125 Mech Eng Bldg Dept Mech Eng Univ of Minn Minneapolis MN 55455

WHITE, JOHN THOMAS, b El Paso, Tex, Aug 23, 31; m 58; c 3. MATHEMATICS. *Educ:* Univ Tex, BA, 52, MA, 53, PhD(math), 62. *Prof Exp:* Spec instr math, Univ Tex, 59-62; asst prof, Univ Kans, 62-65; ASSOC PROF MATH, TEX TECH UNIV, 65-, CHMN DEPT, 79- *Concurrent Pos:* Fel, Tex Ctr Res, 66-; assoc dir, Comt Undergrad prog math, Univ Calif, Berkeley, 70-71. *Mem:* Math Asn Am; Am Math Soc; Soc Indust & Appl Math; Sigma Xi. *Res:* Distribution theory and transform analysis; integral transform theory. *Mailing Add:* Dept of Math Tex Tech Univ Lubbock TX 79409

WHITE, JOHN W, b Ardmore, Okla, Aug 9, 33; m 54; c 3. GREENHOUSE STRUCTURES, ENERGY CONSERVATION. *Educ:* Okla State Univ, BS, 55; Colo State Univ, MS, 57; Pa State Univ, PhD(hort), 64. *Prof Exp:* From asst prof to assoc prof 64-75, PROF FLORICULT & ASSOC DIR UNIV OFF INDUST RES & INNOVATION, PA STATE UNIV, UNIVERSITY PARK, 75- *Concurrent Pos:* Rev ed, J Am Soc Hort Sci, 71-; consult, Gulf Res Corp, Fafard Peat Co, Lombardo Assocs, Gen Mills Corp & Gov's Waste Heat Energy Coun. *Honors & Awards:* Garland Award, Am Carnation Soc; Alex Laurie Award Educ & Res. *Mem:* Am Soc Hort Sci; Soil Sci Soc Am; Int Solar Energy Soc; Soc Am Floricult. *Res:* Physical and chemical properties of soil; experimental designs and glazings for greenhouse structures; effects of the environment on plant growth; energy conservation for greenhouses; passive solar heating systems. *Mailing Add:* Dept of Hort 101 Tyson Bldg Pa State Univ University Park PA 16802

WHITE, JUNE BROUSSARD, b Elizabeth, La, Aug 27, 24; div; c 2. INORGANIC CHEMISTRY, ANALYTICAL CHEMISTRY. *Educ:* La Polytech Univ, BS, 44; Univ Southwestern La, BS, 59, MS, 61; La State Univ, Baton Rouge, PhD(inorg chem), 70. *Prof Exp:* Anal chemist, Cities Serv Refining Corp, La, 44-45; chemist, Esso Lab, Standard Oil Co, NJ, La, 45-48; teacher, Parish Sch Bd, La, 53-59; asst prof chem, Univ Southwestern La, 61-66; NSF res partic, La State Univ, Baton Rouge, 64 & 66, instr, 66-68; chmn div natural sci, 69-71, PROF CHEM & PHYSICS & CHMN DEPT, UNION UNIV, TENN, 68- *Mem:* Am Chem Soc. *Res:* Transition metal complexes which have d-2 electronic system; electron spin resonance; electronic transitions; magnetic properties. *Mailing Add:* Dept of Chem Union Univ Jackson TN 38301

WHITE, KERR LACHLAN, b Winnipeg, Man, Jan 23, 17; nat US; m; c 2. EPIDEMIOLOGY. *Educ:* McGill Univ, BA, 40, MD & CM, 49; Am Bd Internal Med, dipl, 57. *Hon Degrees:* Dr Med, Univ Peuven, 78. *Prof Exp:* Personnel asst, RCA Victor Co, Can, 41-42; intern & resident med, Mary Hitchcock Mem Hosp, Hanover, NH, 49-52; from asst prof to assoc prof med & prev med, Sch Med, Univ NC, 53-62; prof epidemiol & community med & chmn dept, Col Med, Univ Vt, 62-64; chmn dept, 64-72, prof health care orgn, Sch Hyg & Pub Health, Johns Hopkins Univ, 64-76; dir, Inst Health Care Studies, United Hosp Fund, 76-78; DEP DIR HEALTH SCI, ROCKEFELLER FOUND, NEW YORK, 78- *Concurrent Pos:* Hosmer fel med & psychiat, Royal Victoria Hosp, McGill Univ, 52-53; Commonwealth Fund advan fel, Med Res Coun Gt Brit & Sch Hyg & Trop Med, Univ London, 59-60; consult, Nat Ctr Health Statist & Health Resources Admin, Dept Health, Educ & Welfare, 66-; chmn, US Nat Comn Vital & Health Statist, 75-80; mem expert panel orgn med care, WHO, 67-; mem bd dirs, Found Child Develop, NY, 69-; trustee, Case Western Reserve Univ, 74-78; mem health adv panel, Off Technol Assessment, US Cong, 75- *Mem:* Inst of Med of Nat Acad Sci; AAAS; AMA; fel Am Pub Health Asn; fel Am Col Physicians. *Res:* Medical care, education and epidemiology. *Mailing Add:* Div of Health Sci 1133 Ave of the Americas New York NY 10036

WHITE, KEVIN JOSEPH, b Queens, NY, Aug 28, 36; m 66. MOLECULAR PHYSICS. *Educ:* Georgetown Univ, BS, 58; Duke Univ, PhD(physics), 65. *Prof Exp:* Physicist, Naval Ord Lab, 58; res assoc physics, Duke Univ, 65; PHYSICIST, BALLISTIC RES LABS, 65- *Mem:* Am Phys Soc. *Res:* Millimeter wave microwave spectroscopy; Stark effect in rotational spectra; electron spin resonance; radiation damage in oxidizers; radical formation by atom addition and abstraction reactions; supersonic molecular beams for studying high pressure chemical reactions; combustion of propellants. *Mailing Add:* Armament Res & Develop Command Aberdeen Proving Ground Aberdeen MD 21005

WHITE, LARRY DALE, b Sayre, Okla, Nov 24, 40; m 64; c 2. RANGE MANAGEMENT. *Educ:* Northern Ariz Univ, BS, 63; Univ Ariz, MS, 65, PhD(range ecol), 68. *Prof Exp:* Asst forester, US Forest Serv, 63; range adv, Near East Found, Kenya Govt, 67-69; asst prof range ecosyst mgt, Univ Fla, 70-75, assoc prof, 75-78; RANGE EXTEN SPECIALIST, TEX A&M UNIV, 78- *Mem:* Australian Rangeland Soc; Soc Range Mgt. *Res:* Educational programs for county range needs; total range planning; grazing systems; use of prescribed fire; producer training and demonstration; brush control; range seeding; livestock-wildlife habitat relationships; effects of forestry practices on understory vegetation; manipulation of range ecosystems. *Mailing Add:* Tex A&M Res & Exten Ctr PO Drawer 1849 Uvalde TX 78801

WHITE, LARRY MELVIN, b Duchesne, Utah, May 6, 39; m 59; c 5. RANGE SCIENCE. *Educ:* Utah State Univ, BS, 61; Mont State Univ, MS, 71, PhD(crop & soil sci), 72. *Prof Exp:* Range conservationist, 61-66, RANGE SCIENTIST, AGR RES SERV, USDA, 66- *Mem:* Soc Range Mgt; Am Soc Agron; Crop Sci Soc Am; Am Soc Animal Sci. *Res:* Develop species management and selection inconjunction with chemical curing to extend periods of high quality forage in the northern Great Plains in relationship to range management practices. *Mailing Add:* North Plains Soil & Water Res Ctr PO Box 1109 Sidney MT 59270

WHITE, LAWRENCE KEITH, b Lafayette, Ind, Sept 16, 48; m 77. PHYSICAL CHEMISTRY, INORGANIC CHEMISTRY. *Educ:* Earlham Col, AB, 70; Univ Ill, Urbana, PhD(phys chem), 75. *Prof Exp:* Res assoc bio-inorg chem, Univ NH, 75-76; res scientist pulp & paper chem, Union Camp Corp, 77-78; MEM TECH STAFF, LITHOGRAPHY & IC PROCESSING, DAVID SARNOFF RES CTR, RCA LABS, 78- *Mem:* Am Chem Soc; Sigma Xi; Electrochem Soc. *Res:* Solid state science and technology; reliability and reliability testing; magnetic resonance; metalloproteins; transition metal chemistry; resist technology; lithography. *Mailing Add:* David Sarnoff Res Ctr RCA Labs Princeton NJ 08540

WHITE, LAWRENCE S, b Chelsea, Mass, Mar 9, 23; m 46; c 2. PHYSICS. *Educ:* Mass Inst Technol, BS, 47. *Prof Exp:* Physicist, Res Lab, Titanium Div, Nat Lead Co, South Amboy, 48-62, sr technologist, 62-70; assoc physicist, 70-73, sr scientist, 74-80, GROUP LEADER & MGR, HOFFMANN-LA ROCHE INC, NUTLEY, 80- *Mem:* Am Chem Soc; AAAS; Acad Pharmaceut Sci; Sigma Xi. *Res:* Physical properties and colorimetry of titania pigments; electron microscopy and diffraction; light scattering; surface properties of pharmaceutical solids; scanning electron microscopy. *Mailing Add:* 448 Shadyside Rd Ramsey NJ 07446

WHITE, LEE JAMES, b Saginaw, Mich, Apr 9, 39; m 65; c 1. COMPUTER SCIENCE, ELECTRICAL ENGINEERING. *Educ:* Univ Cincinnati, BSEE, 62; Univ Mich, MSEE, 63, PhD(elec eng), 67. *Prof Exp:* Coop engr, Dow Chem Co, 57-61; asst prof eng, Wright State Univ, 67-68; from asst prof to assoc prof, 68-77, PROF COMPUT & INFO SCI, OHIO STATE UNIV, 77-, CHMN DEPT, 80- *Concurrent Pos:* Consult, Rockwell Int, 73-74 & Monsanto Res Corp, 77- *Mem:* Inst Elec & Electronics Engrs; Soc Indust & Appl Math; Asn Comput Mach; Sigma Xi. *Res:* Analysis of algorithms and software analysis and testing; pattern recognition, automatic document classification, combinational computing and graph theory. *Mailing Add:* Dept of Comput & Info Sci Ohio State Univ 2036 Neil Ave Columbus OH 43210

WHITE, LELAND DARRELL, entomology, botany, see previous edition

WHITE, LENDELL AARON, b Sabetha, Kans, Nov 10, 26; m 48; c 2. BACTERIOLOGY. *Educ:* Univ Kans, BA, 51, MA, 55. *Prof Exp:* Bacteriologist, State Pub Health Lab, Kans, 51-53; asst, Virol Lab, Univ Kans, 53-54; bacteriologist, Spec Res Unit, Lab Br, 55-57, virus diag unit, 57-59, encephalitis sect, Tech Br, 59-60, venereal dis res lab, 60-63 & viral reagents unit, 63-71, SUPVRY RES MICROBIOLOGIST, CTR DIS CONTROL, USPHS, 71- *Mem:* AAAS; Am Soc Microbiol; Sigma Xi. *Res:* Virology; isolation, identification, typing and determination of antigenic relationships of viruses with established strains; serologic and antigenic relationships among the arthropod-borne encephalitides; infectivity and fluorescent antibody studies with Neisseria gonorrhoeae; production of viral reagents; immunization procedures for reference antisera. *Mailing Add:* 2534 Wilson Woods Dr Decatur GA 30033

WHITE, LEROY ALBERT, b New York, NY, June 24, 29; m 58; c 2. PHYSICAL CHEMISTRY. *Educ:* Mass Inst Technol, BS, 50; Columbia Univ, MS, 51. *Prof Exp:* Res chemist, Monsanto Chem Co, 51-55; PROJ LEADER, SPRINGBORN LAB, CONSULTS, HAZARDVILLE, 55- *Mem:* Am Chem Soc. *Res:* Organic synthesis; vinyl polymerization; nylon and epoxy reactions; general polymer development; coatings; membrane technology; photodegradable plastics; adhesives. *Mailing Add:* 78 Root Rd Somers CT 06071

WHITE, LEWIS L, b DeRidder, La, Oct 25, 24; m 48; c 3. EMBRYOLOGY. *Educ:* Southern Univ, BS, 48; Duquesne Univ, MS, 50; Univ Iowa, PhD(zool), 57. *Prof Exp:* Assoc prof embryol, 50-60, head dept biol, 60-70, PROF BIOL, SOUTHERN UNIV, BATON ROUGE, 60-, DEAN COL SCI, 70- *Res:* Development and differentiation of sex. *Mailing Add:* 7920 Nottingham Baton Rouge LA 70807

WHITE, LOCKE, JR, b South Boston, Va, Mar 5, 19. CHEMICAL PHYSICS. *Educ:* Davidson Col, BS, 39; Univ NC, PhD(phys chem), 43. *Prof Exp:* Asst anal chem, Davidson Col, 38-39; lab asst, Univ NC, 39-42; chemist, Naval Res Lab, DC, 42-45; chemist & head phys div, Southern Res Inst, 45-48, asst dir, 48-61; PROF PHYSICS, DAVIDSON COL, 61- *Concurrent Pos:* Lectr, Howard Col, 48; vis prof, Birmingham-Southern Col, 53-54 & 59; vis scientist, Univ Reading, 70-71. *Mem:* AAAS; Am Phys Soc; Am Asn Physics Teachers. *Res:* Properties of aerosols; electronic instrumentation; adsorption; solid state physics. *Mailing Add:* Dept of Physics Davidson Col Davidson NC 28036

WHITE, LOWELL DEANE, b New York, NY, Apr 18, 25; m 48; c 3. PHYSICS. *Educ:* Princeton Univ, AB, 49, MA, 51, PhD(phys), 56. *Prof Exp:* Instr physics, Princeton Univ, 53-55; MEM TECH STAFF, BELL TEL LABS, INC, 55- *Mem:* Am Phys Soc. *Res:* Communications; impedance measurements. *Mailing Add:* Bell Labs 3F 226 Holmdel NJ 07733

WHITE, LOWELL ELMOND, JR, b Tacoma, Wash, Jan 16, 28; m 47; c 3. NEUROSURGERY, MEDICAL EDUCATION. *Educ:* Univ Wash, BS, 51, MD, 53. *Prof Exp:* Asst neurosurg, Sch Med, Univ Wash, 54-57, from instr to assoc prof, 57-70, assoc dean, 65-68; prof neurol surg & chief div, Univ Fla, 70-72; chmn dept, 72-80, PROF NEUROSCI, UNIV SOUTH ALA, 72- *Concurrent Pos:* Guggenheim Found fel, Univ Oslo, 57-58; consult, Div Res Resources & chmn nat adv comt animal resources, NIH, 65-69; consult, USPHS, 65-, grants admin adv comt, Dept of Health Educ & Welfare, 66-70. *Mem:* Am Asn Neuropath; Am Asn Anat; Am Asn Neurol Surg; AMA; Asn Am Med Cols. *Res:* Neuroanatomy and neurological surgery. *Mailing Add:* Mobile AL

WHITE, MALCOLM LUNT, b Schenectady, NY, Aug 16, 27; m 51; c 3. PHYSICAL CHEMISTRY. *Educ:* Colgate Univ, BA, 49; Northwestern Univ, PhD(chem), 53. *Prof Exp:* Investr geochem, NJ Zinc Co, 53-59; res chemist, Am Cyanamid Co, 59-61; MEM TECH STAFF, BELL TEL LABS, 61- *Mem:* Am Chem Soc. *Res:* Nucleation; geochemistry; physical chemistry of colloid systems; surface chemistry; materials for electron device technology; coating and encapsulation of solid state devices; integrated circuit processing development. *Mailing Add:* Bell Tel Labs 555 Union Blvd Allentown PA 18103

WHITE, MARK GILMORE, b Galveston, Tex, Jan 15, 49. CHEMICAL ENGINEERING. *Educ:* Univ Tex, Austin, BSChE, 71; Purdue Univ, MSChE, 73; Rice Univ, PhD(chem eng), 78. *Prof Exp:* Res engr, Amoco Oil Co, 73-74; ASST PROF CHEM, GA INST TECHNOL, 77- *Mem:* Am Inst Chem Eng; Sigma Xi. *Res:* Heterogeneous catalysis, kinetics and reactor design; research with the elucidation of reaction mechanisms over catalysts by a study of the kinetics; characterization of the catalysts and the use of isotopic compounds. *Mailing Add:* Sch of Chem Eng Ga Inst of Technol Atlanta GA 30332

WHITE, MARK W, b Lincoln, Nebr, Nov 9, 47. SIGNAL PROCESSING, ARTIFICIAL INTELLIGENCE. *Educ:* Univ Nebr, BSEE, 71; Univ Calif, Berkeley, PhD(elec eng), 77. *Prof Exp:* ASST PROF PSYCHOPHYSICS, UNIV CALIF, SAN FRANCISCO, 78- *Mem:* Acoust Soc Am; Inst Elec & Electronics Engrs; Int Soc Artifical Organs. *Res:* Psychoacoustics and auditory coding; electrical stimulation of auditory nerve as an aide to the profoundly deaf. *Mailing Add:* 863-HSE Univ Calif 3rd & Parnassus Ave San Francisco CA 94143

WHITE, MARVIN HART, b Bronx, NY, Sept 6, 37; m 65; c 1. SOLID STATE ELECTRONICS & PHYSICS. *Educ:* Univ Mich, Ann Arbor, BSE(physics) & BSE(math), 60, MS, 61; Ohio State Univ, PhD(elec eng), 69. *Prof Exp:* Adv engr, Advan Technol Labs, Westinghouse Elec Corp, 61-81; SHERMAN FAIRCHILD PROF SOLID STATE STUDIES, ELEC & COMPUT ENG DEPT, LEHIGH UNIV, 81- *Concurrent Pos:* Fulbright res vis prof, Catholique Universite, Louvain-la-Nueve, Belgium, 70-79; ed, Electron Device Nat Newsletter, 73-76. *Honors & Awards:* Electron Device Nat lectr, Inst Elec & Electronics Engrs, 82. *Mem:* Fel Inst Elec & Electronics Engrs. *Res:* Solid state electron devices and systems; semiconductor surfaces; integrated circuits; solid state electron device modeling and characterization. *Mailing Add:* Sherman Fairchild Lab #161 LeHigh Univ Bethlehem PA 18015

WHITE, MATTHEW BERTISS, b San Diego, Calif, Oct 28, 34; m; c 3. ATOMIC NUCLEAR PHYSICS. *Educ:* Univ Calif, Berkeley, BA, 56, PhD(atomic & nuclear physics) 62. *Prof Exp:* Math anal, Lawrence Radiation Lab, Berkeley, 57-59; res assoc, Univ Calif, Berkeley, 57-62, fel, 62-63; prin scientist, Philco-Ford Corp, Calif, 63-72; SR ELECTROOPTICAL PHYSICIST, OFF NAVAL RES, EASTERN-CENT REGIONAL OFF, BOSTON, 72-, DIR SCI, 81- *Concurrent Pos:* mem, Adv Group Aerospace Res & Develop, Electro-Magnetic Wave Propagation Panel. *Res:* Gas laser physics and systems applications; author of 18 journal articles. *Mailing Add:* Off Naval Res 666 Summer St Boston MA 02210

WHITE, MAURICE LEOPOLD, b New York, NY, Sept 30, 28; m 51; c 2. MICROBIOLOGY. *Educ:* Univ Calif, Los Angeles, BA, 51, PhD, 57; Am Bd Microbiol, dipl, 66. *Prof Exp:* Chief dept bact, Cedars of Lebanon Hosp, Los Angeles, Calif, 57-63; instr, med microbiol & immunol, Sch Med, Univ Calif, Los Angeles, 63-73; CHIEF, MICROBIOLOGIST UNIT, LAB SERV, WADSWORTH VET ADMIN MED CTR, LOS ANGELES, 63-; LECTR MED MICROBIOL & IMMUNOL, SCH MED, UNIV CALIF, LOS ANGELES, 73- *Mem:* AAAS; Am Soc Microbiol. *Res:* Staphylococcal phosphatase; nutrition and bacteriophage studies of Bordetella pertussis; taxonomy of Brucellaceae and Enterobacteriaceae; clinical microbiology. *Mailing Add:* Lab Serv Vet Admin Wadsworth Med Ctr Los Angeles CA 90073

WHITE, MERIT P(ENNIMAN), b Whately, Mass, Oct 25, 08. CIVIL ENGINEERING. *Educ:* Dartmouth Col, AB, 30, CE, 31; Calif Inst Technol, MS, 32, PhD(civil eng), 35. *Prof Exp:* Engr, Soil Conserv Serv, USDA, 35-37; res assoc, Grad Sch Eng, Harvard Univ, 37-38 & Calif Inst Technol, 38-39; asst prof, Ill Inst Technol, 39-42; sr tech aide, Nat Defense Res Comt, Princeton & London, 42-45; bomb damage analyst, US War Dept, 45, sci consult & supvr prep physics rev, Field Info Agencies Technol, 46-47; sci consult, US Navy Dept, 47; prof, 48-61, head dept, 50-77, COMMONWEALTH PROF CIVIL ENG, UNIV MASS, AMHERST, 61- *Concurrent Pos:* NSF fel, Polish Acad Sci, 64-65. *Honors & Awards:* President's Cert Merit, 48. *Mem:* Am Soc Civil Engrs; Am Soc Mech Engrs; Seismol Soc Am; Inst Mech Engrs; Earthquake Eng Res Inst. *Res:* Structural dynamics. *Mailing Add:* Dept Civil Eng Univ Mass Amherst MA 01003

WHITE, MYRON EDWARD, b Boston, Mass, May 1, 20; m 48; c 4. MATHEMATICS, COMPUTER SCIENCE. *Educ:* Wesleyan Univ, AB, 41; Columbia Univ, AM, 50, PhD(math), 62. *Prof Exp:* From instr to assoc prof math, 53-73, dir sci training progs, 63-73, PROF MATH, STEVENS INST TECHNOL, 73-, DIR MOVE AHEAD PROG, 74- *Concurrent Pos:* Teacher, NSF Math Insts. *Mem:* Am Math Soc; Math Asn Am. *Res:* Computer programming languages. *Mailing Add:* Dept of Math Stevens Inst Technol Hoboken NJ 07030

WHITE, N(IKOLAS) F(REDERICK), b Seattle, Wash, Oct 25, 39; m 61; c 3. PETROLEUM ENGINEERING, CIVIL ENGINEERING. *Educ:* Colo Sch Mines, GeolE, 61; Univ Wyoming, MS, 64; Colo State Univ, PhD(civil eng), 68. *Prof Exp:* Assoc petrol engr, 64-65, res civil engr, 68-74, sr res civil eng, 74-79, supvr, 79-80, SR COORDR, ENG TECH SERV, TEXACO, INC, BELLAIRE, 80- *Mem:* Soc Petrol Engrs. *Res:* Porous media flow; well test design; pressure transient techniques in performance and analysis; petroleum reserve evaluation; enhanced recovery techniques; resevior simulation. *Mailing Add:* 322 Wilchester Blvd Houston TX 77024

WHITE, NATHANIEL MILLER, b Providence, RI, Feb 28, 41; m 67; c 3. ASTRONOMY. *Educ:* Earlham Col, AB, 64; Ohio State Univ, MSc, 67, PhD(astron), 71. *Prof Exp:* Res assoc astron, 69-71, astronomer, 72-78, SR ASTRONOMER, LOWELL OBSERV, 78- *Concurrent Pos:* Rac astron, Yavapai Community Col, 77-78; prin investr, NSF, 72-81. *Mem:* Am Astron Soc; Int Astron Union; Inst Elec & Electronics Engrs. *Res:* Basic data on the atmospheres of cool stars; lunar occultation observations; absolute flux measurements of stars; instrumentation. *Mailing Add:* Lowell Observ Box 1269 Flagstaff AZ 86002

WHITE, NILES C, b Saragossa, Ala, Feb 14, 22; m 52; c 2. CHEMICAL ENGINEERING. *Educ:* Univ Ala, BS, 50. *Prof Exp:* Chem engr, US Naval Ord Sta, 50-51 & Redstone Arsenal, 51-56; supv chemist, Army Rocket & Guided Missile Agency, US Army Missile Command, 56-62, supv res chemist, 62-64, chief, Solid Propellant Chem Br, 64-69; TECH ADV & DIR ENG, PROP DIV, ATLANTIC RES CORP, 79- *Honors & Awards:* Res & Develop Achievement Award, Dept Army, 61. *Mem:* AAAS; Am Chem Soc; Am Inst Chem Engrs; Am Inst Aeronaut & Astronaut. *Res:* Rocket propulsion; propellants; combustion; polymer crystalinity; physical properties of elastomers. *Mailing Add:* 823 Watts Dr SE Huntsville AL 35801

WHITE, NORMAN EDWARD, b Springfield, Ohio, Jan 20, 17; m 54; c 1. PHYSICAL CHEMISTRY. *Educ:* Wittenberg Univ, AB, 38; Univ Pa, MS, 41, PhD(phys chem), 54. *Prof Exp:* From instr to prof chem, Drexel Univ, 47-65; chmn dept, 65-71, PROF CHEM, BLOOMSBURG STATE COL, 65- *Mem:* AAAS; Am Chem Soc. *Res:* Hydrogen bond association; molecular weights in solution. *Mailing Add:* 6 Kent Rd Bloomsburg PA 17815

WHITE, PAUL A, b Hollywood, Calif, Aug 21, 15; m 39; c 4. MATHEMATICS. *Educ:* Univ Calif, Los Angeles, AB, 37, MA, 39; Univ Va, PhD(math), 42. *Prof Exp:* Asst math, Univ Calif, Los Angeles, 37-39; instr, Univ Va, 39-42; asst prof, La State Univ, 42-46; from asst prof to assoc prof, 46-53, PROF MATH, UNIV SOUTHERN CALIF, 53- *Concurrent Pos:* Asst prof, Tulane Univ, 44; mathematician, Ballistics Res Lab, Aberdeen Proving Ground, 45; vis prof, Univ Innsbruck, 60-61; writer & lectr, African Ed Proj, 66-68; NSF lectr, India, 67; writer, UNESCO Arab Math Proj, 69-70; writer & adv bd mem, Sec Sch Math Curriculum Improv Study, 70-72; mem adv bd, Sch Math Study Group, 70-72. *Mem:* Am Math Soc. *Res:* Topology; R-regular convergence spaces. *Mailing Add:* Dept of Math Univ of Southern Calif Los Angeles CA 90008

WHITE, PAUL CHAPIN, b Boston, Mass, Oct 2, 41; m 64; c 2. PHYSICS. *Educ:* Harpur Col, BA, 63; State Univ NY Binghamton, MA, 66; Univ Tex, Austin, PhD(physics), 70. *Prof Exp:* Asst prof physics, St Edward's Univ, 69-75, chmn div phys & biol sci, 72-74; mem staff, 75-80, GROUP LEADER, THERMONUCLEAR APPLN GROUP, LOS ALAMOS NAT LAB, 80- *Mem:* AAAS; Am Asn Physics Teachers. *Res:* General relativistic astrophysics; inhomogeneous cosmologies; relativistic transport theory; radiation biophysics. *Mailing Add:* Los Alamos Nat Lab PO Box 1663 Los Alamos NM 87545

WHITE, PETER, b Philadelphia, Pa, June 12, 30; m 53; c 4. HEMATOLOGY. *Educ:* Yale Univ, BA, 51; Univ Pa, MD, 55. *Prof Exp:* From assoc to asst prof med, Sch Med, Univ Pa, 63-69, assoc dir clin res ctr, 67-69; assoc prof med, Med Col Ohio, 69-72, prof med & chief div hemat, 72-77, dep chmn dept med, 69-75; DIR MED & PROF MED, PRESBY UNIV PA MED CTR, 77- *Concurrent Pos:* USPHS res fel hemat, Sch Med, Univ Pa, 63-65; mem res in nursing in patient care rev comt, Bur Health Prof Educ & Manpower Training, NIH, 70-75; mem coun thromabosis, Am Heart Asn. *Mem:* Am Col Physicians; AAAS; Am Soc Hemat; Am Fedn Clin Res. *Res:* Hemoglobin metabolism. *Mailing Add:* Dept of Med 51 N 39th St Philadelphia PA 19104

WHITE, PHILIP CLEAVER, b Chicago, Ill, May 10, 13; m 39; c 3. CHEMISTRY, FOSSIL FUEL TECHNOLOGY. *Educ:* Univ Chicago, BS, 35, PhD(org chem), 38. *Prof Exp:* Res chemist, Stand Oil Co, Ind, 38-45, group leader, 45, chief chemist, 46-50, div dir, 50-51, mgr res, 56-58, gen mgr res & develop, 58-60; mgr res & develop, Pan Am Refining Corp, 51-56, gen mgr res & develop, Am Oil Co, 61-65, vpres res & develop, 66-69; gen mgr res, Amoco Res Ctr, Standard Oil Co, Ind, 69-75; asst adminr, ERDA, US Govt, 75-77; sr tech adv, Dept Energy, 77-78; CONSULT, 78- *Concurrent Pos:* Pres, Indust Res Inst, 71-72, pres coord res coun, 73-75; emer dir, 75- *Mem:* Am Chem Soc; fel Am Inst Chem Engrs. *Res:* Petroleum products, processes and analysis; research administration. *Mailing Add:* 1812 Klovama Square Washington DC 20008

WHITE, PHILIP TAYLOR, neurology, see previous edition

WHITE, R MILFORD, b Stewartsville, Mo, Jan 14, 32. PHYSICAL CHEMISTRY. *Educ:* Baker Univ, BA, 55; Univ Kans, PhD(phys chem), 60. *Prof Exp:* Asst prof chem, Jacksonville Univ, 60-62; from asst prof to assoc prof, 62-65, PROF CHEM, BAKER UNIV, 65- *Mem:* Am Chem Soc. *Res:* Hot-atom chemistry; radiochemistry; mass spectrometry; nuclear chemistry; photoelectron spectroscopy. *Mailing Add:* Dept of Chem Baker Univ Baldwin KS 66006

WHITE, RALPH LAWRENCE, JR, b Troy, NC, June 19, 41; m 68. SYNTHETIC ORGANIC CHEMISTRY. *Educ:* Univ NC, Chapel Hill, BS, 63; Ind Univ, Bloomington, PhD(org chem), 67. *Prof Exp:* Fel, 67-68; instr med chem, Sch Pharm, Univ NC, Chapel Hill, 68-69; sr res chemist, 69-80, RES ASSOC, NORWICH-EATON PHARMACEUT, 80- *Mem:* Am Chem Soc. *Res:* Chemistry and synthesis of thiophene compounds; synthesis of potential biologically active compounds. *Mailing Add:* Norwich-Eaton Pharmaceut 17 Easton Ave Norwich NY 13815

WHITE, RAY HENRY, b Lakewood, Ohio, Apr 28, 36; m 62; c 3. SOLID STATE PHYSICS. *Educ:* Calif Inst Technol, BS, 57; Univ Calif, Berkeley, PhD(physics), 64. *Prof Exp:* Res asst physics, Univ Calif, 58-63; lectr, Univ Singapore, 63-67; asst prof, Calif State Polytech Col, 67-68; asst prof physics, 68-70, chmn dept, 70-72, chmn dept sci & math, 72-75 & 76-78, assoc prof, 70-81, PROF PHYSICS, UNIV SAN DIEGO, 81- *Concurrent Pos:* Vis fel, Univ Singapore, 75-76. *Mem:* Am Phys Soc. *Res:* Superconductivity; physics of music. *Mailing Add:* Dept of Physics Univ of San Diego San Diego CA 92110

WHITE, RAYMOND E, b Freeport, Ill, May 6, 33; m 56; c 3. ASTRONOMY. *Educ:* Univ Ill, Urbana, BS, 55, PhD(astron), 67. *Prof Exp:* F ASTRONrom instr to asst prof astron, 64-72, asst dir, Steward Observ, 72-74, res assoc & lectr, 74-81, ASSOC PROF & ASSOC ASTRONR, STEWARD OBSERV, UNIV ARIZ, 81- *Mem:* AAAS; Am Astron Soc; Royal Astron Soc; Int Astron Union; Sigma Xi. *Res:* Observational astronomy; structure of the Milky Way Galaxy, particularly with respect to the identification and distribution of Population II stellar component. *Mailing Add:* Steward Observ Univ of Ariz Tucson AZ 85721

WHITE, RAYMOND GENE, b Elana, WVa, Oct 10, 30; m 52; c 2. VETERINARY SCIENCE. *Educ:* Okla State Univ, BS, 58, DVM, 60; Univ Nebr, MS, 71. *Prof Exp:* Res vet, Chemagro Corp, 64-69; field res vet, Univ Nebr, 69-72, exten & res vet, North Platte Sta, 72-80; MEM FAC, COL VET MED, MISS STATE UNIV, 80- *Mem:* Am Vet Med Asn; Am Asn Exten Vet; Am Asn Bovine Practitioners; Am Asn Swine Practitioners; Am Soc Animal Sci. *Res:* Initiating and supervising field research activities involving animal health products, pesticides and anthelmintics. *Mailing Add:* Col Vet Med Drawer V Miss State Univ Mississippi State MS 39762

WHITE, RAYMOND PETRIE, JR, b New York, NY, Feb 13, 37; m 61; c 2. ANATOMY, ORAL SURGERY. *Educ:* Med Col Va, DDS, 62, PhD(anat), 67; Am Bd Oral Surg, dipl, 74. *Prof Exp:* Intern oral surg, Med Col Va, 64-65, from asst resident to resident, 65-67; from asst prof to assoc prof, Col Dent, Univ Ky, 67-71, chmn dept, 69-71; asst dean admin affairs & prof oral surg, Va Commonwealth Univ, 71-74; dean sch dent, 74-81, PROF ORAL & MAXILLOFACIAL SURG, UNIV NC, CHAPEL HILL, 74-81. *Concurrent Pos:* Consult, NIMH, 67-71, Vet Admin Hosp, Lexington, 67-71 & Huntington, 68-71 & McGuire Vet Admin Hosp, Richmond, Va, 71-74; mem adv comt, Am Bd Oral Surg, 74-77, Fayetteville Vet Admin Hosp, NC, 74-; assoc chief staff, NC Mem Hosp, 81- *Mem:* Inst Med-Nat Acad Sci; Am Acad Oral Path; Int Asn Dent Res; Am Asn Oral & Maxillofacial Surg; Sigma Xi. *Res:* Premalignant and malignant oral mucosa; correction facial deformity with surgery-orthodontic therapy; dental health policy & health care delivery. *Mailing Add:* Dept Oral Maxillofacial Surg Univ NC Sch Dent Chapel Hill NC 27514

WHITE, RICHARD ALAN, b Philadelphia, Pa, Oct 25, 35; m 65. DEVELOPMENTAL ANATOMY, MORPHOLOGY. *Educ:* Temple Univ, BS & MEd, 57; Univ Mich, MA, 59, PhD(bot), 62. *Prof Exp:* NSF fel, Univ Manchester, 62-63; from asst prof to assoc prof, 63-73, PROF PLANT ANAT, DUKE UNIV, 73-, CHMN DEPT, 76- *Mem:* AAAS; Bot Soc Am; Torrey Bot Club; Am Fern Soc; Int Soc Plant Morphol. *Res:* Comparative morphology of tracheary cells of ferns; developmental studies of fern stelar patterns; comparative and developmental studies of lower vascular plants. *Mailing Add:* Dept of Bot Duke Univ Durham NC 27706

WHITE, RICHARD ALLAN, b Boston, Mass, June 9, 46. ASTROPHYSICS. *Educ:* Univ Calif, Berkeley, AB, 68; Univ Chicago, MS, 71, PhD(astron), 78. *Prof Exp:* Res asst astron, Univ Chicago, 69-74; res assoc radio astron, Nat Radio Astron Observ, 77-80; NAT ACAD SCI & NAT RES COUN ASSOC, GODDARD SPACE FLIGHT CTR, NASA, 80- *Mem:* Am Astron Soc. *Res:* Galaxies; clusters of galaxies. *Mailing Add:* Goddard Space Flight Ctr NASA Code 661 Greenbelt MD 20771

WHITE, RICHARD EARL, b Akron, Ohio, Aug 23, 33. SYSTEMATIC ENTOMOLOGY. *Educ:* Univ Akron, BS, 57; Ohio State Univ, MSc, 59, PhD(entom), 63. *Prof Exp:* Asst prof zool, Union Col, Ky, 64-65; RES ENTOMOLOGIST, USDA, 65- *Mem:* AAAS; Entom Soc Am. *Res:* Taxonomy of Coleoptera, especially the families Anobiidae and Chrysomelidae. *Mailing Add:* Syst Entom Lab c/o US Nat Mus Natural Hist Washington DC 20560

WHITE, RICHARD JOHN, b Apr 21, 42; Brit citizen; c 4. BIOCHEMISTRY, MICROBIOLOGY. *Educ:* Manchester Univ, BSc, 63; Oxford Univ, PhD (biochem), 66. *Prof Exp:* Scientist bacteriol, Unilever Res Labs, 66-67; lectr biochem, Oxford Univ, 67-69; res scientist microbiol, Lepetit Res Labs, Italy, 69-74; sr scientist, Glaxo Res Labs, 74-76; chief chemotherapy cancer, Frederick Cancer Res Ctr, Litton Bionetics Inc, 76-80; DIR INFECTIOUS DIS RES, LEDERLE LABS, AM CYANAMID CO, 80- *Mem:* AAAS; Am Soc Microbiol; Soc Gen Microbiol. *Res:* Fermentation; biosynthesis and mechanism of action antibiotics. *Mailing Add:* Am Cyanamid Co Med Res Div Lederle Labs Pearle River NY 10965

WHITE, RICHARD MANNING, b Denver, Colo, Apr 25, 30; div; c 2. APPLIED PHYSICS, ELECTRICAL ENGINEERING. *Educ:* Harvard Col, BA, 51; Harvard Univ, AM, 52, PhD(appl physics), 56. *Prof Exp:* Mem tech staff microwave electronics, Gen Elec Microwave Lab, 56-62; PROF ELEC ENG & COMPUT SCI, UNIV CALIF, BERKELEY, 62- *Concurrent Pos:* Guggenheim fel, John Simon Guggenheim Found, 68-69. *Mem:* fel Inst Electronics & Elec Engrs; Am Inst Physics; AAAS. *Res:* Ultrasonics, chiefly surface acoustic waves; solar energy. *Mailing Add:* Dept Elec Eng & Comput Sci Univ Calif Berkeley CA 94720

WHITE, RICHARD NORMAN, b Chetek, Wis, Dec 21, 33; m 57; c 2. STRUCTURAL ENGINEERING. *Educ:* Univ Wis, BS, 56, MS, 57, PhD(plate stability), 61. *Prof Exp:* Engr, John A Strand, 58-59; instr struct, Univ Wis, 58-61; from asst prof to assoc prof, 61-72, PROF STRUCT ENG, CORNELL UNIV, 72-, DIR, SCH CIVIL & ENVIRON ENG, 78- *Concurrent Pos:* Consult, Oak Ridge Nat Labs, 66-68; staff assoc, Gen Atomic Div, Gen Dynamics Corp, Calif, 67-68; vis prof, Univ Calif, Berkeley, 74-75. *Honors & Awards:* Collingwood Prize, Am Soc Civil Engrs, 67. *Mem:* Am Soc Civil Engrs; Am Concrete Inst; Am Soc Eng Educ; Nat Soc Prof Engrs; Am Acad Mech. *Res:* Structural engineering and model analysis; nuclear power plant structures; behavior of reinforced concrete frames and shells. *Mailing Add:* 54 Sunnyslope Rd Ithaca NY 14850

WHITE, RICHARD PAUL, b Gary, Ind, May 27, 25; m 47; c 2. PHARMACOLOGY. *Educ:* Ind State Univ, BS, 47; Univ Kans, MS, 49, PhD(physiol), 54. *Prof Exp:* Instr physiol, Univ Kans, 49-54; psychophysiologist, Galesburg State Res Hosp, Ill, 54-56; from instr to assoc prof, 56-70, PROF PHARMACOL, MED UNITS, UNIV TENN, MEMPHIS, 70- *Concurrent Pos:* NIH career develop award, 59-69. *Mem:* Soc Biol Psychiat; Int Col Neuropsychopharmacol; Soc Neurosci; Int Soc Biochem Pharmacol. *Res:* Neuropharmacology. *Mailing Add:* Dept of Pharmacol Univ of Tenn Med Units Memphis TN 38163

WHITE, RICHARD WALLACE, b Buffalo, NY, June 6, 30; m 60; c 1. UNDERWATER ACOUSTICS. *Educ:* Univ Idaho, BS, 53; Wash State Univ, PhD(physics), 70. *Prof Exp:* Physicist, Atomic Energy Div, Phillips Petrol Corp, Idaho, 60-61 & Stanford Res Inst, 61-63; PHYSICIST, NAVAL OCEAN SYSTS CTR, 68- *Res:* Wave propagation and shock phenomena; acoustic ray tracing in inhomogeneous moving media. *Mailing Add:* Naval Ocean Systs Ctr San Diego CA 92155

WHITE, RICHARD WILLIAM, geology, see previous edition

WHITE, ROBERT ALLAN, b Chicago, Ill, Dec 16, 34; m 57; c 2. AERODYNAMICS, HEAT TRANSFER. *Educ:* Univ Ill, Urbana, BS, 57, MS, 59, PhD(mech eng), 63. *Prof Exp:* Instr mech eng, Univ Ill, 59-63; aeronaut engr, Aeronaut Res Inst Sweden, 60-61, sr res scientist, 63-65; from asst prof to assoc prof, 65-72, PROF MECH ENG, UNIV ILL, URBANA, 72- & DIR AUTOMOTIVE SYSTS LAB, 79- *Concurrent Pos:* NATO sr fel & Thord-Gray fel, Aeronaut Res Inst Sweden, 68, consult, 69. *Res:* Aerodynamics of propulsion systems and vehicle integration; separated flows at subsonic and supersonic mach numbers; dynamics and aerodynamics of automotive systems. *Mailing Add:* Dept of Mech Eng Univ Ill Urbana-Champaign Urbana IL 61801

WHITE, ROBERT ALLEN, b Las Cruces, NMex, Nov 19, 44; m 71; c 2. BIOMATHEMATICS, CHEMICAL PHYSICS. *Educ:* NMex State Univ, BS, 66; Univ Chicago, PhD (chem physics), 70. *Prof Exp:* Fel chem, Rice Univ, 70-75; proj investr, 75-76, asst prof, 76-81, ASSOC PROF BIOMATH, M D ANDERSON HOSP & TUMOR INST, 81- *Mem:* Am Phys Soc. *Res:* Mathematical biology; estimation of cell kinetics parameters, demography and the statistical mechanics of DNA denaturation. *Mailing Add:* M D Anderson Hosp & Tumor Inst 6723 Bertner Ave Houston TX 77030

WHITE, ROBERT B, b Ennis, Tex, Jan 5, 21; m 42; c 3. PSYCHIATRY. *Educ:* Tex A&M Univ, BS, 41; Univ Tex, MD, 44; Western New Eng Inst Psychoanal, cert, 59. *Prof Exp:* From asst psychiatrist to sr psychiatrist, Austen Riggs Ctr, Inc, 51-62; assoc prof psychiat, 62-67, PROF PSYCHIAT, UNIV TEX MED BR GALVESTON, 67- *Concurrent Pos:* Teaching analyst, New Orleans Psychoanal Inst, 62-66, training analyst psychoanal, 66-; consult, Alcoholism Res Proj, Col Med, Baylor Univ, 63-65 & Hedgecroft Hosp, Houston, 63-65; mem gen planning comt comprehensive statewide ment health prog planning, Tex State Dept Health, Austin, 63-65; mem, Residency Review Comt for Psychiatry & Neurology, 71-77; training analyst, Houston-Galveston Psychoanalytic Sch, 74- *Honors & Awards:* David Rapaport Prize, Western New Eng Inst Psychoanal, 59. *Mem:* AAAS; Am Psychoanalytic Asn; fel Am Psychiatric Asn; fel Am Col Psychiatrists; fel Am Col Psychoanal. *Res:* Psychoanalysis. *Mailing Add:* Dept of Psychiat Univ of Tex Med Br Galveston TX 77550

WHITE, ROBERT E(DWARD), b Jersey City, NJ, Aug 31, 17; m 43; c 5. CHEMICAL ENGINEERING. *Educ:* Polytech Inst Brooklyn, BChE, 38, MChE, 40, DChE, 42. *Prof Exp:* Asst chem eng, Polytech Inst Brooklyn, 38-42; jr engr, Vulcan Copper & Supply Co, Ohio, 39-40; res engr, York Corp, Pa, 42-47; asst prof chem eng, Bucknell Univ, 47-49; assoc prof, 49-51, PROF CHEM ENG, VILLANOVA UNIV, 51-, HEAD DEPT, 49- *Concurrent Pos:* Indust consult, 51- *Mem:* Am Soc Eng Educ; fel Am Inst Chem Engrs. *Res:* Drying, pressing and formation in papermaking; high temperature reactions; heat and mass transfer; waste treatment. *Mailing Add:* 201 Bryn Mawr Ave Newtown Square PA 19073

WHITE, ROBERT J, b Duluth, Minn, Jan 21, 26; m 50; c 10. SURGERY, NEUROPHYSIOLOGY. *Educ:* Univ Minn, BS, 51, PhD(neurosurg physiol), 62; Harvard Univ, MD, 53. *Hon Degrees:* DSc, John Carroll Univ, 79 & Cleveland State Univ, 80. *Prof Exp:* Intern surg, Peter Bent Brigham Hosp, 53-54; resident, Boston Children's Hosp & Peter Bent Brigham Hosp, 54-55; asst to staff, Mayo Clin, 58-59, res assoc neurophysiol, 59-61; from asst prof to assoc prof, 61-66, PROF NEUROSURG, SCH MED, CASE WESTERN RESERVE UNIV, 66-, CO-CHMN DEPT, 72-; DIR NEUROSURG & BRAIN RES LAB, CLEVELAND METROP GEN HOSP, 61- *Concurrent Pos:* Fel neurosurg, Mayo Clin, 55-58; assoc neurosurgeon, Univ Hosps & sr attend neurosurgeon, Vet Admin Hosp, 61-; vis prof various univ; consult, Burdenko Neurosurg Inst, Moscow, Polenov Inst, Leningrad, Neurosurg Inst, Kiev & Univs, Rome, Naples, Milan & Palermo; fifteen lectrships, USSR, 61-81 & People's Repub China, 77-81; mem bd dirs, Allen Mem Med Library & Int Ctr Artificial Organs & Transplantation. *Honors & Awards:* L W Freeman Award, Nat Paraplegia Found, 77; Svien lectr, Mayo Clin, 77. *Mem:* Int Soc Transplantation; Am Physiol Soc; Soc Univ Surgeons (past pres); Soc Univ Neurosurg (pres, 77); Am Col Surg. *Res:* Special neurosurgical techniques for vascular disease and tumors of the brain utilizing low temperature and extracorporeal perfusion systems; treatment for spinal cord and head injury involving chemotherapy and low temperature; isolation of the subhuman primate brain and perfect brain isolation; neurochemical and circulatory studies; mind/brain relationship, bioethics and dynamics in health care delivery in the United States and communist countries. *Mailing Add:* Dept of Neurosurg Cleveland Metrop Gen Hosp Cleveland OH 44109

WHITE, ROBERT KELLER, b Greeneville, Tenn, Mar 3, 30; m 52; c 2. PSYCHOPHYSIOLOGY, RADIOBIOLOGY. *Educ:* Milligan Col, BA, 52; Univ Tex, PhD(psychol), 62. *Prof Exp:* Res scientist, Radiobiol Lab, Balcones Res Ctr, Univ Tex, 56-61; asst prof psychol, Tex Tech Col, 61-65; proj dir, Armed Forces Radiobiol Res Lab, Defense Atomic Support Agency, 65-67; mem tech staff space res, Bellcomm, Inc, 67-70; chmn dept, 70-71, PROF PSYCHOL, WILLIAM PATERSON COL NJ, 70- *Concurrent Pos:* Lectr, USDA Grad Sch, 65- & Col Gen Studies, George Washington Univ, 66-67. *Mem:* Am Psychol Asn; Simulation Coun; Am Soc Cybernet. *Res:* Effects of whole body irradiation upon the physiology and behavior of various species; in uterine irradiation of rats; gamma neutron pulse irradiation upon the psychophysiology of monkeys. *Mailing Add:* Dept of Psychol William Paterson Col of NJ Wayne NJ 07470

WHITE, ROBERT LEE, b Plainfield, NJ, Feb 14, 27; m 52; c 4. ELECTRICAL ENGINEERING. *Educ:* Columbia Univ, BA, 49, MA, 51, PhD(physics), 54. *Prof Exp:* Asst geophys, Columbia Univ, 49, asst physics, 49-51, lectr physics & asst chem, 51-52, asst physics, 52-54; res physicist, Res Labs, Hughes Aircraft Co, 54-61; head magnetics dept, Labs, Gen Tel & Electronics Corp, 61-63; PROF ELEC ENG & MAT SCI, STANFORD UNIV, 63-, DIR, INST ELECTRONICS IN MED, 73-, CHMN DEPT ELEC ENG, 81- *Concurrent Pos:* Indust consult, 63-; Guggenheim fel, Oxford Univ, 69-70; vis prof, Tokyo Univ, 75; Guggenheim fel, Swiss Fed Inst Technol, Zurich, 78. *Mem:* Fel Am Phys Soc; fel Inst Elec & Electronics Engrs. *Res:* Microwave spectroscopy; solid state physics, especially magnetics; neurophysiology; neural prostheses, especially auditory. *Mailing Add:* 450 El Escarpado Wy Stanford CA 94035

WHITE, ROBERT M, b Boston, Mass, Feb 13, 23; m 48; c 2. METEOROLOGY. *Educ:* Harvard Univ, BA, 44; Mass Inst Technol, MS, 49, PhD, 50. *Hon Degrees:* DSc, Long Island Univ, 76, Rensselaer Polytech Inst, 77 & Univ Wis, 78. *Prof Exp:* Asst meteorol, Mass Inst Technol, 48-50; chief large scale processes sect, Air Force Cambridge Res Ctr, 52-58 & meteorol develop lab, 58-59; res assoc, Mass Inst Technol, 59; assoc dir res, Travelers Ins Co, 59-60, pres, Travelers Res Ctr, Inc, 60-63; chief weather bur, 63-65 & Environ Sci Serv Admin, 65-70, adminr, Nat Oceanic & Atmospheric Admin, US Dept Com, 71-77; chmn climate res bd, 77-79, ADMINR NAT RES COUN & EXEC OFFICER, NAT ACAD SCI, 79- *Concurrent Pos:* US permanent rep, World Meteorol Orgn, 63-78, mem exec comt, 63-78; fed coordr, Meteorol Serv & Supporting Res, 64-70; co-chmn, Dept Com Meteorol Satellite Prog Rev Bd, NASA, 64-73; mem, President's Comn Marine Sci Eng & Resources, 67-68; mem comt water resources res, Fed Coun Sci & Technol, 67-75; chmn, Interagency Comt Marine Sci & Eng, 70-76; chmn fed comt, Meteorol Serv & Supporting Res, 70-77; chmn, Nat Marine Fisheries Adv Comt, 70-77; mem US deleg, UN Conf Human Environ, Stockholm, 71; chief US deleg, Intergovt Oceanog Comn, UNESCO, Paris, 72-73; mem US deleg, Gov Coun, UN Environ Prog, Nairobi, 73-74; US comnr, Int Whaling Comn, London, 73-77; US chmn, US/France Coop Prog Oceanog, 73-77; chief US deleg, Conf Global Environ Monitoring Systs, UN Environ Prog, 74; US chmn, US/USSR Joint Comn Explor World Oceans, 74-77; chmn comt climate change, White House Domestic Coun, 75, chmn comt weather modification, 76; mem US deleg, UN Conf Desertification, Nairobi, 77; mem coun, Nat Acad Eng, 77-; chmn comt atmosphere & oceans, Fed Coord Coun Sci, Eng & Technol, 77; mem comt atmospheric sci, Nat Res Coun, 78-, mem space appln bd, 78-; mem US deleg, ICSU Gen Assembly, Athens, 78. *Honors & Awards:* Cleveland Abbe Award, Am Meteorol Soc, 69, Fiftieth Anniversary Medal, 70; Rockefeller Pub Serv Award, 74; Matthew Fontaine Maury Award, Smithsonian Inst, 76; Int Conserv Award, Nat Wildlife Fedn, 77; Neptune Award, Am Oceanic Orgn, 77; Spec Award, Marine Technol Soc, 77. *Mem:* Nat Acad Eng; Am Geophys Union; Am Meteorol Soc; AAAS; Marine Technol Soc (vpres, 75-77); Royal Meteorol Soc. *Res:* Atmospheric and ocean sciences; environmental science. *Mailing Add:* Nat Acad of Sci 2101 Constitution Ave NW Washington DC 20418

WHITE, ROBERT MANSON, anthropometrics, physical anthropology, deceased

WHITE, ROBERT MARSHALL, b Reading, Pa, Oct 2, 38. SOLID STATE PHYSICS. *Educ:* Mass Inst Technol, BS, 60; Stanford Univ, PhD(physics), 64. *Prof Exp:* Res physicist, Lincoln Lab, Mass Inst Technol, 60; res assoc, Microwave Lab, Stanford Univ, 63-64; NSF fel, Univ Calif, Berkeley, 65-66; asst prof physics, Stanford Univ, 66-71; NSF sr fel, Cambridge Univ, 71-72; PRIN SCIENTIST, XEROX CORP, 72- *Concurrent Pos:* Lectr, Dept Appl Physics, Stanford Univ, 72-; vis scientist, Ecole Polytech, Paris, 76; distinguished lectr, Magnetics Soc, Inst Elec & Electronics Engrs, 80; Humboldt fel, Max Planck Inst, Stuttgart, 81; Alexander von Humboldt prize, 81. *Mem:* Inst Elec & Electronics Engrs; fel Am Phys Soc. *Res:* Theory of nonlinear phenomena in ferrites; spinwave theory; magneto-optical phenomena; magnetic properties of amorphous materials; disk storage technology. *Mailing Add:* Xerox Palo Alto Res Ctr 3333 Coyote Hill Palo Alto CA 94304

WHITE, ROBERT R(OY), chemical engineering, management, see previous edition

WHITE, ROBERT STEPHEN, b Elsworth, Kans, Dec 28, 20; m 42; c 4. ASTROPHYSICS, SPACE PHYSICS. *Educ:* Southwestern Col, Kans, AB, 42; Univ Ill, MS, 43; Univ Calif, PhD(physics), 51. *Hon Degrees:* DSc, Southwestern Col, Kans, 71. *Prof Exp:* Asst physics, Univ Ill, 42-44; asst, Univ Calif, 46-48; physicist, Lawrence Radiation Lab, Univ Calif, 48-61; physicist & head particles & fields dept, Space Physics Lab, Aerospace Corp, 61-67; chmn dept physics, 70-73, PROF PHYSICS, UNIV CALIF, RIVERSIDE, 67-, ASSOC DIR, INST GEOPHYS & PLANETARY PHYSICS, 67- *Concurrent Pos:* Lectr, Univ Calif, 53-54 & 57-59; NSF sr fel, 61-62. *Mem:* AAAS; fel Am Phys Soc; Am Geophys Union; Am Astron Soc. *Res:* Space physics and astrophysics; radiation belts of Earth and Jupiter; albedo neutrons from Earth; solar neutrons and gamma-rays; gamma-rays from astrophysical sources. *Mailing Add:* Dept of Physics Univ of Calif Riverside CA 92502

WHITE, ROBERT WINSLOW, b Somerville, Mass, Mar 28, 34; m 59; c 2. ORGANIC CHEMISTRY, POLYMER CHEMISTRY. *Educ:* Mass Inst Technol, SB, 55; Univ Ill, PhD(chem), 59. *Prof Exp:* Chemist, Rohm and Haas Co, Pa, 58-69; dept head, Nat Lead Co, NY, 69-72; tech dir, Baker Castor Oil Co, 72-74; bus mgr, Indust Chem Div, 74-79, DIR PROD STRATEGY/TECHNOL, NL CHEM, 80- *Mem:* Am Chem Soc; Royal Soc Chem; Swiss Chem Soc. *Res:* Organic synthesis; process and product development; coatings technology, urethanes, waxes, surface active agents. *Mailing Add:* NL Chem PO Box 700 Hightstown NJ 08520

WHITE, ROBERTA JEAN, b Loup City, Nebr, Dec 8, 26. VIROLOGY. *Educ:* Univ Nebr, AB, 48, MS, 54; Univ Calif, PhD(bact), 61. *Prof Exp:* Technician, Mayo Clin, 48-51; technician, Col Med, Univ Nebr, 51-52, instr microbiol, 54-56; asst bact, Univ Calif, 56-60; asst prof, 61-68, ASSOC PROF VIROL, COL MED, UNIV NEBR, OMAHA, 68- *Mem:* AAAS; Am Soc Microbiol. *Res:* Pathogenesis of virus diseases and multiplication. *Mailing Add:* Dept of Med Microbiol Univ of Nebr Med Ctr Omaha NE 68105

WHITE, RONALD, b Talladega, Ala, Feb 10, 43; m 67; c 2. COMPUTER SCIENCE, ELECTRONICS. *Educ:* Auburn Univ, BEE, 65, MSEE, 66, PhD(elec eng), 71. *Prof Exp:* Res asst digital res, Auburn Univ, 65-66; sr engr eng design, Sperry Rand Space Support Div, Sperry Rand Corp, 67-69; res assoc digital res, Auburn Univ, 69-71; engr mgr data process, US Air Force, Eglin AFB, 71-78; ASSOC PROF COMPUT SCI, JACKSONVILLE STATE UNIV, 78- *Res:* Application of mini computers and microprocessors. *Mailing Add:* Dept of Comput Sci & Eng Jacksonville State Univ Jacksonville AL 36265

WHITE, RONALD JEROME, b Wibaux, Mont, Oct 31, 36; m 61; c 2. ZOOLOGY, PHYSIOLOGY. *Educ:* Calif State Polytech Col, BS, 59; Ore State Univ, MS, 61, PhD(physiol), 68. *Prof Exp:* From asst prof to assoc prof, 69-76, PROF BIOL, EASTERN WASH UNIV, 76- *Concurrent Pos:* Chmn, Dept Biol, Eastern Wash Univ, 80-82. *Mem:* AAAS; Am Soc Zool; Sigma Xi. *Res:* Physiology of reproduction in the pigtail macaque. *Mailing Add:* Dept of Biol Eastern Wash Univ Cheney WA 99004

WHITE, RONALD JOSEPH, b Opelousas, La, Dec 4, 40; m 63; c 3. THEORETICAL CHEMISTRY, APPLIED MATHEMATICS. *Educ:* Univ Southwestern La, BS, 63; Univ Wis, PhD(phys chem), 68. *Prof Exp:* NSF fel, Oxford Univ, 67-68; assoc, Bell Tel Labs, 68-70; asst prof math, Univ Southwestern La, 70-73; res assoc physiol & biophys, Med Ctr, Univ Miss, 73-75; assoc prof math, Univ Southwestern La, 75-77, prof, 77-81, dir univ honors prog, 75-80; MGR SYSTS ANAL, MGT & TECH SERV CO DIV, GEN ELEC CO, HOUSTON, 80- *Mem:* Am Phys Soc; Sigma Xi; Soc Indust Appl Math; Asn Gifted/Talented Students. *Res:* Perturbation theory; quantum mechanics of small atoms and molecules; mathematical models of physical systems; physiological models. *Mailing Add:* Mgt & Tech Serv Gen Elec Co 1050 Bay Area Blvd Houston TX 77058

WHITE, RONALD PAUL, SR, b Coral Gables, Fla, Mar 1, 35; m 60; c 4. SOIL CHEMISTRY, SOIL FERTILITY. *Educ:* Mass State Col Bridgewater, BS, 61; Univ Mass, MS, 63; Mich State Univ, PhD(soil sci), 68. *Prof Exp:* Instr soil sci, Mich State Univ, 65-66; RES SCIENTIST, RES STA, CAN DEPT AGR, 68- *Mem:* Am Soc Agron; Soil Sci Soc Am; Agr Inst Can; Can Soc Agron. *Res:* Soil fertility requirements and crop management practices of corn and potatoes; soil manganese levels and plant manganese toxicity; soil phosphorus; plant root cation exchange capacity; agronomy. *Mailing Add:* Cereal Sect Res Sta Can Dept of Agr PO Box 1210 Charlottetown PE C1A 7M8 Can

WHITE, ROSCOE BERYL, b Freeport, Ill, Dec 20, 37; m 66. PLASMA PHYSICS. *Educ:* Univ Minn, BS, 59; Princeton Univ, PhD(physics), 63. *Prof Exp:* Res asst, Princeton Univ, 62, instr, 62-63; res assoc, Univ Minn, 63; US Acad Sci exchange scientist, Lebedev Inst, Moscow, 63-64; vis scientist, Int Ctr Theoret Physics, Italy, 64-66; asst prof physics, Univ Calif, Los Angeles, 66-72; mem, Inst Advan Study, 72-74; RES PHYSICIST, PRINCETON UNIV, 74- *Res:* Theoretical plasma physics. *Mailing Add:* Plasma Physics Lab Princeton Univ Princeton NJ 08540

WHITE, ROSEANN SPICOLA, b Tampa, Fla, Aug 4, 43; m 65. BIOCHEMISTRY, MICROBIOLOGY. *Educ:* Univ Fla, BS, 65; Univ Tex Southwestern Med Sch, Dallas, PhD(biochem), 70. *Prof Exp:* Asst prof, 69-72, ASSOC PROF MICROBIOL, UNIV CENT FLA, 73- *Concurrent Pos:* Clin chemist, Orange Mem Hosp, 69-72; Sigma Xi grant. *Mem:* AAAS; Am Soc Microbiol; Sigma Xi. *Res:* Control vitamin B-6 biosynthesis; vitamin B-6 regulation of apoenzyme levels; methanogenesis from solid wastes; chemical characterization of H capsulatum antigens. *Mailing Add:* Dept of Biol Sci Univ Cent Fla Orlando FL 32816

WHITE, SAMUEL, JR, b Washington, DC, Aug 23, 26; m 48; c 1. AERONAUTICAL ENGINEERING. *Educ:* US Mil Acad, BS, 48; Purdue Univ, MS, 53. *Prof Exp:* Jet fighter pilot aircraft oper, US Air Force, 48-50, instr aircraft control, Aircraft Controller Sch, 50-52; asst prof mechanics, US Mil Acad, 53-56; engr aeronaut eng, Sikorsky Aircraft, 56-71, proj mgr, 72-73, dept mgr qual assurance, 73-74; proj mgr aeronaut eng, Langley Res Ctr, Va, 74-77; div mgr aeronaut eng, Rotocraft Tech Div, 77-80, DIR RES SUPPORT, AMES RES CTR, NASA, 80- *Honors & Awards:* NASA Except Serv Medal, 78. *Mem:* Am Helicopter Soc. *Res:* Rotorcraft technology; flight research in aircraft stability and control; structural dynamics; noise; vibration; aerodynamic performance; aircraft systems. *Mailing Add:* 200-5 Ames Res Ctr NASA Moffett Field CA 94035

WHITE, SIDNEY EDWARD, b Manchester, NH, Mar 14, 16; m 46; c 1. GEOLOGY. *Educ:* Tufts Col, BS, 39; Harvard Univ, MA, 42; Syracuse Univ, PhD(geol), 51. *Prof Exp:* Lab asst, Tufts Col, 37-40, lab instr, 41-42, instr geol, 47-48; lab instr, Harvard Univ, 42; asst instr geol, Syracuse Univ, 48-51; from asst prof to assoc prof, 51-67, PROF GEOL, OHIO STATE UNIV, 67- *Concurrent Pos:* Recorder, US Geol Surv, 41-42, geologist, US Geol Surv, 46-48; ed, Geol Soc Am, Geomorph Div, 62-71; geologist, NSF Projs, Univ Colo, 64-66, assoc prof, 65-66; Univ Colo Men & Women Scholastic Honoraries award, 65-66. *Mem:* Geol Soc Am; Am Quaternary Asn; Mex Geol Soc. *Res:* Glacial and Pleistocene geology; volcanology; alpine and periglacial mass movement studies. *Mailing Add:* Dept of Geol & Mineral Ohio State Univ Columbus OH 43210

WHITE, STANLEY A, US citizen; m 56; c 4. ELECTRICAL ENGINEERING, SIGNAL PROCESSING. *Educ:* Purdue Univ, BS, 57, MS, 59, PhD(elec eng), 65. *Prof Exp:* Electronics technician, Allison Div, Gen Motors Corp, 56, circuit designer, 57; mem staff, Autonetics Navig Systs Div, NAm Rockwell Corp, 59-61, staff to mgr advan technol, 65-67, group scientist digital systs group, Info Sci Br, 67-70, supvr advan inertial instrument res, Navig & Comput Div, 70, mem tech staff prod eng group, NAm Rockwell Microelectronic Co, 70-72, group leader digital systs group, Info Sci Br, Advan Technol Dept, Res & Technol Div, 72-77, MGR DIGITAL SYSTS & SIGNAL PROCESSING, ELECTRONICS RES CTR, ROCKWELL INT, 78- *Concurrent Pos:* Mem fac, Purdue Univ, Univ Calif, Los Angeles, Irvine & Davis & Univ Southern Calif; univ lectr; chmn & fac mem, Nat Electronics Conf. *Mem:* AAAS; Sigma Xi; fel Inst Elec & Electronics Engrs. *Res:* Applied control theory; systems engineering; microelectronics; digital filtering; digital signal processing; author or coauthor of over 60 publications. *Mailing Add:* 1541 Amberwood Dr Santa Ana CA 92705

WHITE, STANLEY C, b Lebanon, Ohio, Jan 13, 26; m 48; c 5. PREVENTIVE MEDICINE. *Educ:* Miami Univ, AB, 45; Univ Cincinnati, MD, 49; Johns Hopkins Univ, MPH, 53. *Prof Exp:* Asst flight surgeon, Eglin Air Force Base, Fla, 50-51; resident aviation med, Sch Aviation Med, Tex, 51-52, Sch Pub Health & Hyg, Johns Hopkins Univ, 52-53 & Hq Tactical Air Command, Langley Air Force Base, 53-54; chief respiration sect, Physiol Br, Aeromed Lab, Wright Air Develop Ctr, Ohio, 54-58; chief life systs div space task group & Manned Spacecraft Ctr, NASA, Langley Air Force Base & Houston, Tex, 58-63, dir bioastronaut & systs support, Aerospace Med Div, Brooks Air Force Base, 63-64, asst dep res & develop, 64-66, asst bioastronaut to prog dir, Manned Orbiting Lab Prog, DC, 66-69, dir biomed res, Hq Air Force Systs Command, Andrews Air Force Base, Md, 69-70, Skylab med opers officer, Hq NASA, DC, 70-71, asst dir life sci for sci activities, Hq, NASA, 71-74, mil asst med & life sci & asst dir environ & life sci, Off Dir Defense Res & Eng, Pentagon, 74-77; corp dir res & develop, Travenol Labs, 77-82. *Concurrent Pos:* Med Corps, US Air Force, 51-77; mem bioastronaut comt, Nat Res Coun, 59-60; space surgeon, US Dept Defense, 60. *Honors & Awards:* Boyington Award, Am Astronaut Soc, 60; Louis G Bauer Award, Aerospace Med Asn, 62, Theodore C Lyster Award, 74 & Hubertus Strughold Award, Space Med Br, 69; Laureate Award, Int Acad Aviation & Space Med, 62. *Mem:* Fel Am Col Prev Med; fel Aerospace Med Asn; Int Acad Astronaut; Int Acad Aviation & Space Med. *Res:* Aviation medicine leading to manned aerospace flight; vehicle design and operational flight support. *Mailing Add:* 1335 Carol Lane Deerfield IL 60015

WHITE, STANTON M, b Gardner, Mass, Mar 10, 35; m 58; c 2. SEDIMENTARY PETROLOGY, MARINE GEOLOGY. *Educ:* Univ Mass, Amherst, BS, 56; Univ Rochester, MS, 60; Univ Wash, PhD(marine geol), 67. *Prof Exp:* Instr geol, Columbia Basin Col, 60-64; instr oceanog, Univ Wash, 65-67; from asst prof to prof geol, Calif State Univ, Fresno, 67-76; assoc chief scientist, Deep Sea Drilling Proj, Scripps Inst Oceanog, 76-80; MEM STAFF, ROBERTSON RES INC, HOUSTON, 80- *Mem:* AAAS; Geol Soc Am; Soc Econ Paleont & Mineral. *Res:* Mineralogy, petrology and geochemistry of continental shelf sediments; marine sediments. *Mailing Add:* Robertson Res Inc 16730 Hedgecroft Suite 306 Houston TX 77060

WHITE, STEPHEN HALLEY, b Wewoka, Okla, May 14, 40; m 61; c 6. BIOPHYSICS, PHYSIOLOGY. *Educ:* Univ Colo, BA, 63; Univ Wash, MS, 65, PhD(physiol, biophys), 69. *Prof Exp:* Asst prof, 72-75, vchmn dept, 74-75, assoc prof physiol, 75-78, PROF PHYSIOL & BIOPHYS, UNIV CALIF, IRVINE, 78-, CHMN DEPT PHYSIOL & BIOPHYS, 77- *Concurrent Pos:* USPHS grant biochem, Univ Va, 71-72; res grants, NSF & NIH; spec comn cell & membrane biophysics, 78- *Mem:* AAAS; Biophys Soc; Int Union Pure & Appl Biophysics; NY Acad Sci; Am Physiol Soc. *Res:* Structure of biological membranes and the physical chemistry of lipid bilayer membranes. *Mailing Add:* Dept of Physiol Col of Med Univ of Calif Irvine CA 92717

WHITE, STUART COSSITT, b Pasadena, Calif, July 20, 42; m 68; c 2. DENTAL RADIOLOGY. *Educ:* Univ Calif, Berkeley, AB, 64; Univ Calif, Los Angeles, DDS, 68; Univ Rochester, PhD(radiation biol), 73. *Prof Exp:* Asst prof, 73-75, assoc prof, 75-80, PROF DENT, UNIV CALIF, LOS ANGELES, 80- *Concurrent Pos:* USPHS trainee, Univ Rochester, 68-73; prin investr NIH grant, 77-80; co-investr clin cancer educ prog, Univ Calif, Los Angeles, 76-79; prin investr grant, Am Fund Dent Health, 77-78; consult, Xerox Corp, 77-; fel, Am Acad Dent Radiol, 78-; mem bd dirs, Am Bd Oral & Maxillofacial Radiol, 80- *Honors & Awards:* Edward H Hattan Award, Int Asn Dent Res, 67. *Mem:* Radiation Res Soc; Am Acad Dent Radiol. *Res:* Radiation dosimetry; radiographic imaging technique; utility of radiographic examinations. *Mailing Add:* Sch of Dent Univ of Calif Los Angeles CA 90024

WHITE, SUSAN RUTH, b Ft Wayne, Ind, Oct 13, 42; m 64; c 1. NEUROSCIENCES. *Educ:* Purdue Univ, BS, 64; Ind Univ, PhD(psychopharmacol), 71. *Prof Exp:* Fel neurophysiol, Ind State Univ, 72-74; res scientist, 74-75, asst prof, 75-79, ASSOC PROF NEUROSCI, MEM UNIV NFLD, 79- *Mem:* Soc Neurosci; Sigma Xi. *Res:* Neurotransmitters and neuromodulators in the central nervous system. *Mailing Add:* Fac Med Mem Univ Nfld St John's NF A1B 3V6 Can

WHITE, THOMAS DAVID, b Sarnia, Ont, Apr 8, 43; m 65; c 3. NEUROCHEMISTRY, NEUROPHARMACOLOGY. *Educ:* Univ Western Ont, BSc, 65, MSc, 67; Bristol Univ, PhD(pharmacol), 70. *Prof Exp:* asst prof, 71-77, ASSOC PROF PHARMACOL, FAC MED, DALHOUSIE UNIV, 77- *Concurrent Pos:* Med Res Coun Can fel, Univ Alta, 70-71. *Mem:* Can Pharmacol Soc; Int Soc Neurochem; Soc Neurosci. *Res:* Physiology and pharmacology of brain synapses. *Mailing Add:* Dept of Pharmacol Dalhousie Univ Fac of Med Halifax NS B3H 4H7 Can

WHITE, THOMAS GAILAND, b Artesia, NMex, Oct 12, 32; m 58; c 2. PLANT BREEDING. *Educ:* NMex State Univ, BS, 54; Tex A&M Univ, MS, 58, PhD(plant breeding), 62. *Prof Exp:* From instr to asst prof cotton genetics, Tex A&M Univ, 60-65; res geneticist, USDA, 65-67; dir biol res, Occidental Petrol Corp, 67-71; crops develop mgr, 71-74, planning coordr, 74-76, mgr agr res & develop, 76-79, DIR TECH SERV, GILROY FOODS, INC, 79- *Concurrent Pos:* Leader monosomic res proj, Nat Cotton Coun Grant, Found Cotton Res & Educ, 63-66; mem, Agr Res Inst. *Mem:* Am Soc Hort Sci; Am Mgt Asn. *Res:* Basic genetic and cytogenetic research in cotton; applied research in controlled atmosphere use in transport of perishable commodities; genetics and improvement of onions; management, research and development. *Mailing Add:* Gilroy Foods Inc PO Box 1088 Gilroy CA 95020

WHITE, THOMAS JAMES, b Stamford, Conn, Oct 5, 45. BIOCHEMISTRY, MICROBIOLOGY. *Educ:* Johns Hopkins Univ, BA, 67; Univ Calif, Berkeley, PhD(biochem), 76. *Prof Exp:* Fel biochem, G W Hooper Found, Univ Calif, San Francisco, 76-77 & Univ Wis-Madison, 77-78; scientist biochem, 78-81, DIR, RECOMBINANT MOLECULAR RES, CETUS CORP, 81- *Concurrent Pos:* Fel, NIH, 77-78. *Mem:* Am Soc Microbiol; Soc Study Evolution. *Res:* Molecular evolution; antibiotic biosynthesis and resistance; immunochemistry. *Mailing Add:* Cetus Corp 600 Bancroft Way Berkeley CA 94710

WHITE, THOMAS TAYLOR, b New York, NY, 20. SURGERY, PHYSIOLOGY. *Educ:* Harvard Univ, BS, 42; NY Univ, MD, 45; Am Bd Surg, dipl, 53. *Prof Exp:* Instr surg, NY Univ, 50-52; from instr to assoc prof, 53-67, PROF SURG, SCH MED, UNIV WASH, 67- *Concurrent Pos:* Columbia Univ Lambert traveling fel, Europe, 52-53; Am Cancer Soc res grant, 59-60; USPHS grant, 59-; from Guggenheim Found fel, Univ Lyon, 64-65. *Honors & Awards:* Mott Medal, NY Univ, 45. *Mem:* AAAS; Soc Univ Surg; Am Col Surg; Soc Exp Biol & Med; Am Gastroenterol Asn. *Res:* Gastrointestinal physiology; breast cancer; surgical infections; burns; surgery and physiology of the stomach, bile ducts, liver and pancreas; hernia. *Mailing Add:* 1221 Madison St #1411 Seattle WA 98104

WHITE, THOMAS WAYNE, b Caldwell Co, Ky, Dec 9, 34; m 60; c 4. RUMINANT NUTRITION. *Educ:* Univ Ky, BS, 56, MS, 57; Univ Mo-Columbia, PhD(animal nutrit), 60. *Prof Exp:* Asst dist salesman, Nat Oats Co, 61-62; assoc prof, 62-72, PROF ANIMAL SCI, LA STATE UNIV RICE EXP STA, 72- *Concurrent Pos:* On leave, Purdue Univ, 71. *Mem:* Am Soc Animal Sci; Am Dairy Sci Asn. *Res:* Level and source of roughage in ruminant rations as measured by digestibility and feedlot performance; whole shelled corn with various protein supplement for finishing cattle; influence of type and variety of sorghum grain on ration digestibility; forage evaluation and influence of age, breed of cattle and shade on forage utilization. *Mailing Add:* La State Univ Rice Exp Sta PO Box 1429 Crowley LA 70526

WHITE, TIMOTHY LEE, b San Diego, Calif, May 5, 51; m 79; c 1. QUANTITATIVE FOREST GENETICS, FOREST POPULATION BIOLOGY. *Educ:* Univ Calif, Berkeley, BS, 73; NC State Univ, Raleigh, MS, 75; Ore State Univ, PhD(forest genetics), 80. *Prof Exp:* RES FORESTER GENETICS & BIOMET, INT PAPER CO, 79- *Mem:* Sigma Xi. *Res:* Population dynamics and genetics of forest ecosystems. *Mailing Add:* Western Forest Res Ctr 34937 Tennessee Rd Lebanon OR 97355

WHITE, WALTER STANLEY, b Cambridge, Mass, Apr 13, 15; m 41; c 2. ECONOMIC GEOLOGY. *Educ:* Harvard Univ, AB, 36, PhD(struct geol), 46; Calif Inst Technol, MS, 37. *Prof Exp:* Asst, Harvard Univ, 37-40; geologist, US Geol Surv, 39-78, asst chief mineral deposits br, 54-56, asst chief geologist, 60-63; RETIRED. *Concurrent Pos:* Mem, Nat Res Coun, 58-68, mem exec comt earth sci div, 59-61 & 65-68. *Mem:* Fel Geol Soc Am; Soc Econ Geol (vpres, 76). *Res:* Structural geology; structural geology of ore deposits. *Mailing Add:* 3514 Hamlet Pl Chevy Chase MD 20015

WHITE, WARREN D, b Springfield, Mo, July 7, 15; m 40; c 2. MATHEMATICS, ELECTRICAL ENGINEERING. *Educ:* Drury Col, BS, 36; Univ Mo, BSEE, 38. *Prof Exp:* Consult radio engr, DC, 39-41; engr in charge radio frequency div, Columbia Broadcasting Syst, 41-46; eng consult, Airborne Instruments Lab, Cutler-Hammer Inc, 46-65; staff mem, Inst Defense Anal, 65-67; eng consult, Cutler Hammer Inc, 67-74, tech asst to pres, Airborne Instrument Lab, 74-80; CONSULT, 80- *Concurrent Pos:* Spec res assoc, Radio Res Lab, Harvard Univ, 42-45. *Mem:* Fel Inst Elec & Electronics Engrs. *Mailing Add:* 108 Sea Cove Rd Northport NY 11768

WHITE, WILLARD WORSTER, III, b Perth Amboy, NJ, July 6, 44; m 72. MAGNETOHYDRODYNAMICS, PLASMA PHYSICS. *Educ:* Univ Del, BS, 66; Rensselaer Polytech Inst, PhD(physics), 70. *Prof Exp:* Res physicist, 72-77, SR SCIENTIST & ASST ATMOSPHERIC PHENOMENOLOGY DIV LEADER, MISSION RES CORP, 77- *Concurrent Pos:* Res assoc, Rensselaer Polytech Inst, 70-72. *Mem:* Am Phys Soc. *Res:* Electromagnetic phenomena in the ionosphere; surface physics of materials; radiation damage in solids; laser propagation phenomena. *Mailing Add:* 926 Mission Ridge Rd Santa Barbara CA 93103

WHITE, WILLIAM, b Millbrook, Ont, Apr 1, 28; m 60; c 3. MEDICAL PHYSICS, RESEARCH ADMINISTRATION. *Educ:* Queen's Univ, Ont, BSc, 50; McGill Univ, PhD(physics), 61. *Prof Exp:* Res physicist, Bldg Prod Ltd, Montreal, Can, 51-56 & Am Radiator & Standard Sanit Res Lab, NJ, 61-63; dir res, Searle Med Instrumentation Group, Searle Anal, Inc Div, G D Searle & Co, 63-79; PRIN, RES & DEVELOP, WHITE CONSULTS, 79-; DIR RES, SIEMENS GAMMASONICS, INC, 81- *Concurrent Pos:* Consult res & develop mgt, 80- *Mem:* Am Phys Soc; Soc Nuclear Med. *Res:* Nuclear spectroscopy and instrumentation in the physical and biological sciences; penetration of charged particles; blocking and channeling of atomic particles in crystals; automated clinical chemistry apparatus; nuclear medical gamma-ray cameras; methods for the organization of research and development. *Mailing Add:* Siemens Gammasonics Inc 2000 Nuclear Dr Des Plaines IL 60018

WHITE, WILLIAM ALEXANDER, b Paterson, NJ, June 15, 06; m; c 2. GEOLOGY. *Educ:* Duke Univ, AB, 30; Univ NC, MA, 31, PhD(geol), 38; Mont Sch Mines, MS, 34. *Prof Exp:* Petrogr, Lago Petrol Corp, Venezuela, 38-40; assoc geologist, Soil Conserv Serv, USDA, 40-42; asst state geologist, Dept Conserv & Develop, NC, 42-44; assoc prof geol, 44-50, PROF GEOL, UNIV NC, CHAPEL HILL, 50- *Mem:* Fel Am Geol Soc. *Res:* Geomorphology; glacial geology. *Mailing Add:* Dept of Geol Univ of NC Chapel Hill NC 27514

WHITE, WILLIAM ARTHUR, b Sumner, Ill, Dec 9, 16; m 41. MINERALOGY, PETROLOGY. *Educ:* Univ Ill, BS, 40, MS, 47, PhD(geol), 55. *Prof Exp:* Spec asst chem, Ill State Geol Surv, 43-44, asst geol, 44-47, from asst geologist to assoc geologist, 47-54, head clay resources & clay mineral tech sect, 58-73, geologist, 54-79. *Mem:* Fel AAAS; fel Mineral Soc Am; Am Chem Soc; fel Am Geol Soc; Geochem Soc. *Res:* Physical properties of clays as related to soil mechanics; ceramic properties of clays and sediments; clay mineralogy of sediments and the environments in which they were accumulated; the role of clay minerals in environmental geology. *Mailing Add:* 603 Colorado Ave Urbana IL 61801

WHITE, WILLIAM BLAINE, b Huntingdon, Pa, Jan 5, 34; m 59; c 2. GEOCHEMISTRY, MATERIALS SCIENCE. *Educ:* Juniata Col, BS, 54; Pa State Univ, PhD(geochem), 62. *Prof Exp:* Res assoc chem physics, Mellon Inst, 54-58; res assoc geochem, 62-63, from asst prof to assoc prof, 63-72, PROF GEOCHEM, PA STATE UNIV, 72- *Mem:* AAAS; Am Geophys Union; Am Ceramic Soc; Am Mineral Soc; Nat Speleol Soc (exec vpres, 65-67). *Res:* High temperature chemistry; infrared and optical spectroscopy of solids; mineralogy; ground water hydrogeology; solid state chemistry; glass science; infrared, optical and luminescence spectroscopy; geomorphology. *Mailing Add:* 210 Mat Res Lab Pa State Univ University Park PA 16802

WHITE, WILLIAM CHARLES, b Jacksonville, Fla, May 12, 22; m 52. PHYSICS, ASTRONOMY. *Educ:* Ohio Wesleyan Univ, BA, 48; Ohio State Univ, MS, 50. *Prof Exp:* Physicist, 50-73, opers res analyst, 73-78, CONSULT, NAVAL WEAPONS CTR, 78- *Concurrent Pos:* Consult, Astrophys Observ, Smithsonian Inst, 59-60 & Dearborn Observ, Northwestern Univ, 60-62, Ketron, 79-80; sci observer, Stargazer Balloon Flight, 61; partic, Aerial Photog Eclipse of Quiet Sun, 62, NASA Mobile Launch Exped, 65, Sandia Eclipse Exped, 65 & Oceanog & Geophys Exped, SAm, 67. *Mem:* Am Astron Soc; NY Acad Sci; Sigma Xi. *Res:* Astrophysical research with infrared detectors and balloon-bourne observatories; atmospheric physics research with high altitude balloons; ozone as a function of latitude; electronic warfare. *Mailing Add:* Naval Weapons Ctr Code 127 China Lake CA 93555

WHITE, WILLIAM MICHAEL, b Allentown, Pa, Aug 10, 48; m 70; c 3. GEOCHEMISTRY. *Educ:* Univ Calif, Berkeley, BA, 71; Univ RI, PhD(oceanog), 77. *Prof Exp:* Fel geochem, Dept Terrestrial Magnetism, Carnegie Inst, Washington, 77-80; VIS MEM, MAX-PLANK INST CHEM, 80- *Mem:* Geol Soc Am; Am Geophys Union; Geochem Soc. *Res:* Sr and Nd isotope geochemistry of igneous rocks; composition and chemical evolution of earth's mantle. *Mailing Add:* Max Planck Inst Chem Soarstr 23 Postfach 3060 6500 Mainz West Germany

WHITE, WILLIAM NORTH, b Walton, NY, Sept 16, 25; m 51; c 2. PHYSICAL ORGANIC CHEMISTRY. *Educ:* Cornell Univ, AB, 50; Harvard Univ, MA, 51; PhD(org chem), 53. *Prof Exp:* Nat Res Coun fel, Crellin Labs, Calif Inst Technol, 53-54; from asst prof to assoc prof chem, Ohio State Univ, 54-63; chmn dept, 63-71 & 75-76, prof chem, Univ Vt, 63-76, prof and chmn dept chem, Univ Tex, Arlington, 76-77; PROF CHEM, UNIV VT, 77- *Concurrent Pos:* NSF sr fel biol, Brookhaven Nat Labs, 63-64; NSF sr fel chem, Harvard Univ, 65; vis scholar biochem, Brandeis Univ, 74-75. *Mem:* AAAS; Am Chem Soc; The Chem Soc. *Res:* Reaction mechanisms; rearrangements; structure reactivity correlations; electrophilic and nucleophilic substitution mechanisms; carbanion and carbonyl group chemistry. *Mailing Add:* Dept of Chem Univ of Vt Burlington VT 05401

WHITE, WILLIAM WALLACE, b Cleveland, Ohio, Sept 7, 39; m 64; c 2. OPERATIONS RESEARCH, COMPUTER SCIENCE. *Educ:* Princeton Univ, AB, 61; Univ Calif, Berkeley, MS, 63, PhD(eng sci), 66. *Prof Exp:* Staff mem mgt sci, Philadelphia Sci Ctr, 66-74, advan appl adv, Advan Syst Develop Div, 74-75, sr systs anal, syst prod div, 75-77, RES STAFF MEM, T J WATSON RES CTR, IBM CORP, 77- *Concurrent Pos:* Adj assoc prof math, Columbia Univ, 74-79. *Mem:* Opers Res Soc Am; Asn Comput Mach; Math Prog Soc; Inst Elec & Electronics Engrs Comput Soc. *Res:* Computer measurement evaluation; mathematical programming and computer performance; analysis, applied to computer design. *Mailing Add:* IBM T J Watson Res Ctr PO Box 218 Yorktown Heights NY 10598

WHITE, ZEBULON WATERS, b Baltimore, Md, Oct 3, 15; m 39; c 4. FORESTRY. *Educ:* Dartmouth Col, AB, 36; Yale Univ, MF, 38. *Prof Exp:* Consult forester, Pomeroy & McGowin, Ark, 40-58; prof indust forestry, Yale Univ, 58-72, assoc dean sch forestry, 65-71; PRES, ZEBULON WHITE & CO, 72- *Mem:* Soc Am Foresters. *Res:* Industrial forest management. *Mailing Add:* Zebulon White & Co 207 S Holly St Hammond LA 70401

WHITED, DEAN ALLEN, b Nebraska City, Nebr, Mar 28, 40; m 64; c 2. GENETICS, AGRONOMY. *Educ:* Univ Nebr, Lincoln, BS, 62, MS, 64; NDak State Univ, PhD(agron), 67. *Prof Exp:* Agency Int Develop grant & res assoc wheat qual, Univ Nebr, Lincoln, 67-68; asst prof, 68-73, assoc prof, 73-80, PROF AGRON, NDAK STATE UNIV, 80-, CHMN, GENETICS INST, 71- *Mem:* Am Soc Agron; Am Genetic Asn. *Res:* Genetics; genetic counseling at Muscular Dystrophy Clinic; soybean genetics and soybean production. *Mailing Add:* Dept of Agron NDak State Univ Fargo ND 58102

WHITEFIELD, RODNEY JOE, b Lewiston, Idaho, Jan 21, 36. OPTICS, SURFACE PHYSICS. *Educ:* Wash State Univ, BS, 57; San Diego State Univ, MS, 59; Ore State Univ, PhD(physics), 70. *Prof Exp:* Mem staff exp physics, General Atomics, 59-60; STAFF ENGR, IBM CORP, 60- *Mem:* Optical Soc Am. *Res:* Surface measurement and characterization; photo electric effect; ultra high vacuum. *Mailing Add:* 15260 Dickens Ave San Jose CA 95124

WHITEFORD, ROBERT DANIEL, b Atlanta, Ga, Sept 23, 22; m 56; c 1. VETERINARY MEDICINE. *Educ:* Univ Ga, DVM, 51; Iowa State Univ, MS, 56, PhD, 64. *Prof Exp:* Clinician, Ont Vet Col, 51-52; vet, Brunswick Animal Hosp, Ga, 52-54; instr vet anat, Iowa State Univ, 54-57; fel comp ophthal, Col Med, Univ Iowa, 57-59; assoc prof vet anat, Sch Vet Med, Auburn Univ, 59-64, prof anat, 64-69; assoc prof biomed sci, 69-72, PROF BIOMED SCI, UNIV GUELPH, 72- *Mem:* Asn Res Vision & Ophthal; Am Asn Vet Anat. *Res:* Veterinary histology; comparative neuroanatomy; neurophysiology; neuro-ophthalmology; clinical neurology. *Mailing Add:* Dept of Biomed Sci Ont Vet Col Univ Guelph Guelph ON N1G 2W1 Can

WHITEHAIR, CHARLES KENNETH, b Abilene, Kans, Mar 3, 16; m 58; c 2. NUTRITION, PATHOLOGY. *Educ:* Kans State Col, DVM, 40; Univ Wis, MS, 43, PhD(nutrit), 47. *Prof Exp:* Instr animal dis, Univ Wis, 40-47; from asst prof to prof animal nutrit, Okla State Univ, 47-53, head vet res & prof physiol & nutrit, 54-56; PROF PATH, MICH STATE UNIV, 56- *Concurrent Pos:* Assoc prof, Univ Ill, 52-53. *Mem:* Am Asn Path; Soc Exp Biol & Med; Am Inst Nutrit; Conf Res Workers Animal Dis (vpres, 64, pres, 65); Am Vet Med Asn. *Res:* Nutritional pathology; swine nutrition and diseases; metabolic diseases of livestock; relation of nutrition to diseases. *Mailing Add:* Dept of Path Mich State Univ East Lansing MI 48824

WHITEHAIR, LEO A, b Abilene, Kans, June 13, 29; m 58; c 3. VETERINARY MEDICINE, FOOD SCIENCE. *Educ:* Kans State Univ, BS & DVM, 53; Univ Wis, MS, 54, PhD(food sci), 62; Am Col Vet Preventive Med, dipl. *Prof Exp:* Vet off nutrit br, Aeromed Lab, Wright-Patterson AFB, Ohio, 54-58; lab vet nutrit br, Food Inst Armed Forces, Ill, 61-62; vet food technologist, Biol Br, Div Biol & Med, US AEC, 62-67; health scientist adminr, 68-75, DIR PRIMATE RES CTR PROG, ANIMAL RESOURCES BR, DIV RES RESOURCES, NIH, 75- *Concurrent Pos:* Consult advisor, Food & Agr Orgn-UN-WHO-Int Atomic Energy Agency joint expert comt meeting, Rome, 64; tech adv int prog irradiation fruit & fruit juices, Inst Biol & Agr, Seibersdorf Reactor Ctr, Austria, 65; vet off dir, US Pub Health Serv. *Honors & Awards:* Helwig-Jennings Award, 81. *Mem:* Am Vet Med Asn; Am Bd Vet Pub Health (secy-treas, 75-); Am Soc Animal Sci; Inst Food Technologists; Am Asn Vet Nutritionists. *Res:* Animal nutrition; wholesomeness and public health safety aspects of irradiated foods; laboratory animal resources; animal models for biomedical research. *Mailing Add:* Animal Resources Br Div Res Resources Bldg 31 5B-55 NIH Bethesda MD 20205

WHITEHEAD, ANDREW BRUCE, b Quebec, Que, Oct 18, 32; m 62; c 3. PLANETOLOGY, PHYSICS. *Educ:* Univ NB, BSc, 53; McGill Univ, MSc, 55, PhD(physics), 57. *Prof Exp:* Res fel nuclear physics, Atomic Energy Res Estab, Harwell, Eng, 57-60; res fel nuclear physics, 61-62, res specialist, 63-65, group supvr physics, 65-67, sect mgr physics, 67-69, mgr lunar & planetary sci sect, 69-71, asst proj scientist, Mariner 9, 71-73, actg asst mgr, Space Sci Div, 73-75, staff scientist, Space Sci Div, Jet Propulsion Lab, 75-78; mgr progs, 78-79, MGR SENSORS & CONTROLS DEPT, HONEYWELL CORP PHYSICAL SCI CTR, 80-81. *Mem:* Am Phys Soc. *Res:* Nuclear structure; particle detection; secondary electron emission; atomic stopping; photovoltaics; computer science; sensors; controls. *Mailing Add:* Honeywell Corp Mat Sci Ctr 10701 Lyndale Ave S Bloomington MN 55420

WHITEHEAD, ARMAND T, b Reno, Nev, May 19, 36; m 54; c 5. ENTOMOLOGY. *Educ:* Brigham Young Univ, BS, 65; Univ Calif, Berkeley, PhD(entom), 69. *Prof Exp:* asst prof, 69-78, ASSOC PROF ZOOL, BRIGHAM YOUNG UNIV, 78- *Concurrent Pos:* Vis asst prof, Univ Ill, 75-76. *Mem:* Entom Soc Am. *Res:* Neurophysiology and morphology of insect sensory receptors. *Mailing Add:* Dept of Zool Brigham Young Univ Provo UT 84602

WHITEHEAD, DANIEL L(EE), b Walland, Tenn, Dec 25, 15; m 37; c 3. ELECTRICAL ENGINEERING. *Educ:* Univ Tenn, BS, 39; Cornell Univ, MS, 40. *Prof Exp:* Elec engr, Aluminum Co Am, 34-39; engr, Cent Sta, Westinghouse Elec Corp, 41-47, supvr analog comput, 47-51, mgr, High Voltage Labs, 51-68, mgr eng labs, 68-81; CONSULT HIGH VOLTAGE MEASURING TECHNOL, 81- *Concurrent Pos:* Lectr, Univ Pittsburgh, 44- & Carnegie-Mellon Univ, 57-58; lectr high voltahe test tech, Inst Elec & Electronics Engrs, 81- *Mem:* Fel Inst Elec & Electronics Engrs; Am Nat Standards Inst. *Res:* High voltage and high power phenomena and measuring techniques. *Mailing Add:* RD 3 Roundtop Rd Export PA 15632

WHITEHEAD, DONALD REED, botany paleoecology, see previous edition

WHITEHEAD, EUGENE IRVING, b Canton, SDak, Mar 4, 18; m 55; c 2. PLANT BIOCHEMISTRY. *Educ:* SDak State Col, BS, 39, MS, 41. *Prof Exp:* Lab asst, 40-42, sta analyst, 42-43, asst agr chemist, 43-46, assoc chemist, 46-60, assoc prof sta biochem, Grad Fac, 60-67, PROF STA BIOCHEM, GRAD FAC, SDAK STATE UNIV, 67- *Mem:* Am Soc Plant Physiol; Am Chem Soc. *Res:* Nitrogen metabolism of cereal crops; winter hardiness of cereal plants. *Mailing Add:* Dept Chem Sect Exp Sta Biochem SDak State Univ Brookings SD 57006

WHITEHEAD, FLOY EUGENIA, b Athens, Ga, Feb 10, 13. NUTRITION. *Educ:* Univ Ga, BS, 36, MS, 42; Harvard Univ, DSc, 51; Am Bd Nutrit, dipl, 52. *Prof Exp:* Teacher, High Schs, Ga, 36-40; asst prof home econ, WGa Col, 40-42; assoc dir health educ, State Dept Pub Health, Ga, 42-43; assoc prof home econ, La State Univ, 44-48 & Miss State Col, 48-49; fel, Sch Pub Health, Harvard Univ, 49-52; dir nutrit, Wheat Flour Inst, Ill, 52-53; dir nutrit educ, Nat Dairy Coun, 53-55; chmn dept home econ, 55-71, prof, 55-78, EMER PROF HOME ECON, UNIV IOWA, 78- *Concurrent Pos:* Vis lectr, Harvard Univ, 52-54; co-dir nutrit educ res, Pub Schs, Mo, 52-55; pres elect, Nat Coun Adminr Home Econ, 66-67, pres, 67-68; res grant off nutrit, AID, US Dept State. *Honors & Awards:* Roberts Award, Am Dietetic Asn, 56. *Mem:* AAAS; Am Pub Health Asn; Am Home Econ Asn; Am Dietetic Asn; Soc Nutrit Educ. *Res:* Dietary surveys; nutrition education; analysis of nutrition education research, 1900-1970. *Mailing Add:* 306 Ferson Ave Iowa City IA 52240

WHITEHEAD, FRED, b Walland, Tenn, Aug 24, 05; m 35; c 2. CHEMISTRY. *Educ:* Ky Wesleyan Col, AB, 31; Univ Tenn, MS, 33; Univ Mich, PhD(chem), 45. *Prof Exp:* Prof chem, Ky Wesleyan Col, 32-50, dean & registr, 44-50; prof chem, Huntingdon Col, 50-75; RETIRED. *Mem:* Am Chem Soc. *Res:* Rate of dissociation of pentaarylethanes; physics; mathematics. *Mailing Add:* 3496 Cloverdale Rd Montgomery AL 36111

WHITEHEAD, GEORGE WILLIAM, b Bloomington, Ill, Aug 2, 18; m 47. MATHEMATICS. *Educ:* Univ Chicago, SB, 37, SM, 38, PhD(math), 41. *Prof Exp:* Instr math, Univ Tenn, 39, Purdue Univ, 41-45 & Princeton Univ, 45-47; from asst prof to assoc prof, Brown Univ, 47-49; from asst prof to assoc prof, 49-57, PROF MATH, MASS INST TECHNOL, 57- *Concurrent Pos:* Guggenheim fel & Fulbright res scholar, 55-56; vis prof, Princeton Univ, 58-59; NSF sr fel, 65-66; vis res fel, Birkbeck Col, Univ London, 73. *Mem:* Nat Acad Sci; fel Am Acad Arts & Sci; Am Math Soc; Math Asn Am; London Math Soc. *Res:* Algebraic topology, especially homotopy theory. *Mailing Add:* Dept of Math Rm 2-284 Mass Inst of Technol Cambridge MA 02139

WHITEHEAD, HOWARD ALLAN, b Toronto, Ont, Apr 17, 27; m 52; c 4. BACTERIOLOGY. *Educ:* Mt Allison Univ, BSc, 49; McGill Univ, MSc & PhD(bact), 53. *Prof Exp:* RES MGR, KIMBERLY-CLARK CORP, 53- *Mem:* Tech Asn Pulp & Paper Indust; Soc Cosmetic Chem; Can Soc Microbiol; Can Pub Health Asn. *Res:* Lethal and mutagenic effects of ultraviolet irradiation of bacterial microorganisms; menstruation, physiology and feminine hygiene. *Mailing Add:* Kimberly-Clark Corp 2100 N Winchester Rd Neenah WI 54956

WHITEHEAD, JAMES RENNIE, b Clitheroe, Eng, Aug 4, 17; m 44; c 2. PHYSICS. *Educ:* Univ Manchester, BSc, 39; Cambridge Univ, PhD(physics), 49. *Prof Exp:* Scientist, Telecommun Res Estab, Eng, 39-51; assoc prof physics, McGill Univ, 51-55; dir res, RCA Victor Co, Ltd, 55-65; dep dir sci secretariat, Govt Can, 65-67, prin sci adv, 67-71, asst secy int affairs, Ministry of State for Sci & Technol, 71-73, spec adv, 73-75; sr adv, Int Develop Res Ctr, Govt Can, 75-76; SR VPRES, PHILIP A LAPP LTD, 76- *Concurrent Pos:* Sr sci officer, Brit Air Comn, Washington, DC, 44-45 & Cambridge Univ, 46-49; consult, Defence Res Bd Can, 52-54; consult sci policy in Venezuela and Guyana, UNESCO, 70-75; Can deleg to sci & technol policy comt, Orgn Econ Coop & Develop, vchmn comt sci policy, 73-75; mem sci comt, NATO. *Mem:* Fel Royal Soc Can; sr mem Inst Elec & Electronics Engrs; fel Brit Inst Elec Eng; fel Brit Inst Physics; fel Can Aeronaut & Space Inst. *Res:* Physical electronics; circuits; systems propagation; electron microscopy; friction; science policy. *Mailing Add:* 1368 Chattaway Ave Ottawa ON K1H 7S3 Can

WHITEHEAD, JOHN ANDREWS, JR, b Amesbury, Mass, Apr 21, 41; m 64; c 3. OCEANOGRAPHY, GEOPHYSICS. *Educ:* Tufts Univ, BS, 63; Yale Univ, MS, 65, PhD(appl sci), 68. *Prof Exp:* Fel, Inst Geophys & Planetary Physics, Univ Calif, Los Angeles, 68-69, asst res geophysicist, 69-71; asst scientist, 71-73, ASSOC SCIENTIST, WOODS HOLE OCEANOG INST, 73- *Concurrent Pos:* Mem comt geodesy, NAS-Nat Res Coun, 76-; sr fel, Nat Ctr Atmospheric Res, 77-78; mem space & terrestrial applications comt, NASA, 78-81. *Mem:* Am Phys Soc; Am Geophys Union; NY Acad Sci. *Res:* Fluid mechanics of oceans, atmospheres and planetary interiors. *Mailing Add:* Dept Phys Oceanog Woods Hole Oceanog Inst Woods Hole MA 02543

WHITEHEAD, KENNETH E, b Niagara Falls, Ont; US citizen. CHEMICAL ENGINEERING. *Educ:* Univ Toronto, BASc, 52; Ohio State Univ, MSc, 53. *Prof Exp:* Supvr process eng, Atlantic Richfield Co, 62-69; supvr, 72-75, MGR PROCESS ENG RES DEPT, UNION OIL CO CALIF, 75- *Concurrent Pos:* Chmn subcomt liquid wastes, Am Petrol Inst, 76-77. *Mem:* Am Inst Chem Eng. *Res:* Process development and design in petrochemicals and petroleum refining. *Mailing Add:* 566 N Lincoln Ave Fullerton CA 92631

WHITEHEAD, MARIAN NEDRA, b Calif, Sept 5, 22. NUCLEAR PHYSICS, PARTICLE PHYSICS. *Educ:* Reed Col, AB, 44; Columbia Univ, MS, 45; Univ Calif, PhD(physics), 52. *Prof Exp:* Physicist, US Naval Ord Test Sta, 45-46 & Radiation Lab, Univ Calif, 49-60; Fulbright sr res fel, Inst Physics, Bologna, Italy, 61-62; physicist, Stanford Linear Accelerator Ctr, Stanford Univ, 62-64; assoc prof, 64-67, chmn dept, 69-75, PROF PHYSICS, CALIF STATE UNIV, HAYWARD, 67- *Mem:* Fel Am Phys Soc; Am Asn Physics Teachers (treas, 74-78). *Res:* Meson and cosmic physics. *Mailing Add:* Dept of Physics Calif State Univ Hayward CA 94542

WHITEHEAD, MARVIN DELBERT, b Paoli, Okla, Dec 18, 17; m 40; c 1. PHYTOPATHOLOGY, MYCOLOGY. *Educ:* Okla State Univ, BS, 39, MS, 46; Univ Wis, PhD(plant path, mycol), 49. *Prof Exp:* Asst agr aide, Soil Conserv Serv, USDA, Okla, 36-38; asst agron, Okla State Univ, 39-40; sr seed analyst, Fed State Seed Lab, Ala, 40-42; asst plant path, Univ Wis, 46-48; asst prof, Tex A&M Univ, 49-55; assoc prof, Univ Mo, 55-60; prof bot, Edinboro State Col, 60-63; prof plant path, Ga Southern Col, 63-68; PROF BOT & PLANT PATH, GA STATE UNIV, 68- *Concurrent Pos:* Consulting plant pathologist, US Army, Ft McPherson, Ga, 74-, Ft Riley, Kans, 75- & Ft Campbell, Ky, 78- *Mem:* AAAS; Am Phytopath Soc; Mycol Soc Am; Bot Soc Am; Am Inst Biol Sci. *Res:* Field crop disease pathology; soil borne and seed borne diseases; phytopathological histology and techniques; fungus and smut taxonomy; yield loss from plant disease; disease resistance; antibiotics and fungicides in control of Dutch elm disease, oak wilt, verticillium wilt of maple, decline of oak, and hackberry. *Mailing Add:* Dept of Bot Ga State Univ Atlanta GA 30303

WHITEHEAD, MICHAEL ANTHONY, b London, Eng, June 30, 35; m 77. THEORETICAL CHEMISTRY, QUANTUM CHEMISTRY. *Educ:* Univ London, BSc, 56, PhD(phys chem), 60, DSc(theoret & phys chem, 74. *Prof Exp:* Asst lectr chem, Queen Mary Col, Univ London, 58-60; Fulbright scholar, Univ Cincinnati, 60-62, fel, 60-61, asst prof, 61-62; from asst prof to assoc prof, 62-75, PROF CHEM, MCGILL UNIV, 75- *Concurrent Pos:* Nat Res Coun Can travel fel & vis prof, Cambridge Univ, 71-72; vis prof theoret chem, Oxford Univ, 72-74. *Mem:* Am Phys Soc; Am Chem Soc; Can Inst Chem; Royal Soc Chem. *Res:* Nuclear quadrupole resonance; electronegativity theory; molecular orbital calculations; beyond Hartree-Fock calculations; surface absorption; chemical absorption; theoretical chemistry. *Mailing Add:* Dept Chem McGill Univ 801 Sherbrooke St W Montreal PQ H3A 2K6 Can

WHITEHEAD, THOMAS HILLYER, b Maysville, Ga, Sept 5, 04; m 31; c 2. ANALYTICAL CHEMISTRY. *Educ:* Univ Ga, BS, 25; Columbia Univ, AM, 28, PhD(colloid chem), 30. *Prof Exp:* Teacher, High Sch, Ga, 25-27; asst chem, Columbia Univ, 27-30; adj prof, 30-35, prof, 39-72, asst head dept, 46-60, coord instr insts, 60-68, actg dean grad sch, 68-69, dean, 69-72, EMER PROF CHEM, UNIV GA, 72- *Concurrent Pos:* Consult & mem adv coun, Chem Corps, US Dept Army, 48-65, AEC, 52-, US Off Educ, Washington, DC, 65- & F W Dodge Div, McGraw-Hill Inc, 65- *Mem:* AAAS; Am Chem Soc; Sigma Xi. *Res:* Colloid chemistry; oxidation-reduction indicators; inorganic colloidal systems; complex inorganic compounds; indicators in analytical chemistry; iodometric method for copper. *Mailing Add:* 236 Henderson Ave Athens GA 30601

WHITEHEAD, WALTER DEXTER, JR, b San Diego, Calif, Nov 30, 22; m 49; c 2. NUCLEAR PHYSICS, ATOMIC PHYSICS. *Educ:* Univ Va, BS, 44, MS, 46, PhD(physics), 49. *Prof Exp:* Asst, Univ Va, 43-45; physicist, Bartol Res Found, 49-53; from asst prof to assoc prof physics, NC State Col, 53-56; from asst prof to assoc prof, 56-61, chmn dept, 68-69, dean fac arts & sci, 71-72, PROF PHYSICS, UNIV VA, 61-, DIR CTR ADVAN STUDIES, 65-, DEAN GRAD SCH ARTS & SCI, 69- *Concurrent Pos:* Vis scientist, Inst Nuclear Physics, 59-60; mem bd admin, Va Inst Marine Sci, 71-78; mem Nat Res Coun eval panel, Ctr Radiation Res, Inst Basic Standards, 71-74. *Mem:* AAAS; fel Am Phys Soc; Am Asn Physics Teachers; Sigma Xi. *Res:* Nuclear spectroscopy; neutron scattering; photonuclear reactions; x-ray interactions. *Mailing Add:* 444 Cabell Hall Univ of Va Charlottesville VA 22901

WHITEHEAD, WILLIAM EARL, b Martin, Tenn, May 24, 45; m 68; c 1. PSYCHOPHYSIOLOGY. *Educ:* Ariz State Univ, BA, 67; Univ Chicago, PhD(psychol), 73. *Prof Exp:* asst prof, 73-77, ASSOC PROF PSYCHIAT & PHYS MED, COL MED, UNIV CINCINNATI, 77- *Concurrent Pos:* Adj asst prof psychol, Univ Cincinnati, 75- *Mem:* AAAS; Soc Psychophysiol Res; Am Psychosom Soc; Am Biofeedback Soc. *Res:* Biofeedback treatment of psychophysiologic disorders; etiology of psychosomatic disorders; psychotropic drug evaluation. *Mailing Add:* Univ Cincinnati Col of Med 231 Bethesda Ave Cincinnati OH 45267

WHITEHILL, JULES LEONARD, b New York, NY, Mar 7, 12; m 43; c 3. SURGERY, MEDICAL EDUCATION. *Educ:* City Col New York, BSc, 32; NY Univ, MD, 35; Am Bd Surg, dipl, 43. *Prof Exp:* Resident surg, Mt Sinai Hosp, New York, 35-39; chief surg, Cent Manhattan Med Group, 46-48; pvt pract, Ariz, 48-63; from assoc prof to prof surg, 63-70, asst dean clin progs, 63-67, assoc dean, 67-69, chmn dept surg, 68-70, EMER PROF SURG, CHICAGO MED SCH, 70- *Concurrent Pos:* Fel exp surg, Mt Sinai Hosp, New York, 40-42; consult, Vet Admin Hosp, Tucson, Ariz, 48-63, West Side Vet Admin, 68-70, Elgin State Hosp, Ill, 65- & Strategic Air Command, US Air Force, 66-; med dir, dir med educ & attend surgeon, Mt Sinai Hosp Med Ctr, Chicago, 63-68; mem fac, Medcom; ed consult, Excerpta Medica; former co-chmn bd regents & int bd gov, Int Col Surg; vis prof surg, Univ Zagreb; mem sci adv comt & mem bd trustees, Chapman Col, Orange, Calif; Albert Gallatin fel, NY Univ, 77; chmn bd dir, Int Asn Shipboard Educ. *Mem:* Fel Am Col Surg; AMA; fel Royal Soc Med; Int Col Surg; Sigma Xi. *Res:* Electromagnetic measurement of blood flow; prophylaxis of surgical keloids with steroids; automatic device for intestinal anastomosis; medical historian; ethics and philosophy of medicine. *Mailing Add:* 1716 El Camino del Teatro La Jolla CA 92037

WHITEHORN, DAVID, b Ann Arbor, Mich, Nov 17, 41. NEUROPHYSIOLOGY. *Educ:* Univ Mich, BA, 63; Univ Wash, PhD(physiol), 68. *Prof Exp:* USPHS fel, Univ Utah, 68-70; asst prof, 70-77, ASSOC PROF PHYSIOL, COL MED, UNIV VT, 77- *Mem:* Am Physiol Soc; AAAS; Soc Neurosci; Int Asn Study Pain. *Res:* Central nervous system; organization and information processing; nervous system in hypertension. *Mailing Add:* Dept of Physiol Univ of Vt Burlington VT 05401

WHITEHORN, WILLIAM VICTOR, b Detroit, Mich, Oct 3, 15; m 38; c 2. PHYSIOLOGY, MEDICINE. *Educ:* Univ Mich, AB, 36, MD, 39. *Prof Exp:* Asst physiol, Univ Mich, 40-42; res assoc, Ohio State Univ, 42-44, from instr to asst prof physiol & med, 44-47; asst prof physiol, Col Med, Univ Ill, Chicago, 47-50, prof, 54-70; dir div health sci & spec asst to pres for med affairs, Univ Del, 70-74; asst comnr prof & consumer prog, Food & Drug Admin, 74-80. *Concurrent Pos:* Adj prof physiol, Uniformed Serv Univ Health Sci, 80- *Mem:* AAAS; Am Physiol Soc; Soc Exp Biol & Med; Am Heart Asn. *Res:* Cardiac metabolism and function; applied physiology of respiration and circulation. *Mailing Add:* Uniformed Serv Univ Health Sci 4301 Jones Bridge Rd Bethesda MD 20014

WHITEHOUSE, BRUCE ALAN, b Henderson, Ky, Sept 6, 39; m 61; c 2. POLYMER CHEMISTRY, TEXTILE CHEMISTRY. *Educ:* Col Charleston, BS, 63; Ga Inst Technol, PhD(phys chem), 67. *Prof Exp:* Res chemist, Plastics Dept, Polyolefins Div, Orange Tex, 67-72, res chemist, Textile Fibers Dept, Nylon Tech Div, Chattanooga, Tenn, 72-73, sr res chemist, 73, res supvr, Dacron Res Lab, 73-76, res supvr, Textile Res Lab, 76-78, mgr prod strategy, Indust Fibers Div, 78-79, RES MGR, TEXTILE RES LAB, TEXTILE FIBERS DEPT, E I DU PONT DE NEMOURS & CO, INC, 79- *Mem:* Am Chem Soc. *Res:* Solid state structure and properties; solid state nuclear magnetic and quadrupole resonance; structure and properties of polymers; chromatography; polymer synthesis. *Mailing Add:* 10 Kings Grant Rd Hockessin DE 19707

WHITEHOUSE, DAVID R(EMPFER), b Evanston, Ill, Nov 13, 29; m 56; c 3. ELECTRICAL ENGINEERING. *Educ:* Northwestern Univ, BS, 52; Mass Inst Technol, SM, 54, ScD, 58. *Prof Exp:* From asst prof to assoc prof elec eng, Mass Inst Technol, 58-65; prin res scientist, Res Div, 65-67, MGR LASER ADVAN DEVELOP CTR, RAYTHEON CO, 67- *Concurrent Pos:* Consult, 59-65. *Mem:* Am Phys Soc; Inst Elec & Electronics Engrs; Laser Inst Am (pres, 81). *Res:* Lasers; laser and plasma physics. *Mailing Add:* Laser Ctr Raytheon Co Fourth Ave Burlington MA 01803

WHITEHOUSE, FRANK, JR, b Ann Arbor, Mich, Nov 20, 24; m 51; c 4. MICROBIOLOGY, IMMUNOLOGY. *Educ:* Univ Mich, BA & MD, 53. *Prof Exp:* Intern, Blodgett Mem Hosp, Grand Rapids, Mich, 53-54; from instr to asst prof, 54-67, ASSOC PROF MICROBIOL, UNIV MICH, ANN ARBOR, 67- *Concurrent Pos:* Lectr, Ohio State Univ, 59; preprof counsr, Univ Mich, 60-; exec dir, Nat Asn Adv Health Professions. *Honors & Awards:* Sr Fulbright lectr microbiol, 79-80. *Mem:* NY Acad Sci; Soc Exp Biol & Med; Am Inst Biol Sci; Am Soc Microbiol; Asn Am Med Cols. *Res:* Enzymatic degradation of antibodies; tumor immunology; chemotherapy. *Mailing Add:* Dept Microbiol Med Sch Bldg II Univ of Mich Ann Arbor MI 48109

WHITEHOUSE, GARY E, b Trenton, NJ, Aug 13, 38; m 63; c 2. INDUSTRIAL ENGINEERING, OPERATIONS RESEARCH. *Educ:* Lehigh Univ, BS, 60, MS, 62; Ariz State Univ, PhD(indust eng), 66. *Prof Exp:* Instr indust eng, Lehigh Univ, 62-63 & Ariz State Univ, 63-65; from asst prof to prof, Lehigh Univ, 65-78; PROF INDUST ENG & MGT SYSTS & CHMN DEPT, FLA TECHNOL UNIV, 78- *Concurrent Pos:* Consult, Air Prod & Chem Inc, 65- *Mem:* Am Inst Indust Engrs; Inst Mgt Sci; Opers Res Soc Am; Am Soc Eng Educ. *Res:* Theory and applications of networks; mathematical programming; decision theory; production and inventory control. *Mailing Add:* Dept of Indust Eng & Mgt Systs Fla Technol Univ Box 25000 Orlando FL 32816

WHITEHOUSE, GERALD D(EAN), b Sapulpa, Okla, May 17, 36; m 58; c 3. MECHANICAL ENGINEERING. *Educ:* Univ Mo-Rolla, BS, 58; Okla State Univ, MS, 64, PhD(mech eng), 67. *Prof Exp:* Vibration engr, Douglas Aircraft Co, 58-59; from asst prof to assoc prof, 66-77, PROF MECH ENG & CHMN DEPT, LA STATE UNIV, BATON ROUGE, 77- *Mem:* Acoust Soc Am; Am Soc Mech Engrs. *Res:* Research activity in the mechanical design area, particularly in stress analysis and vibrations. *Mailing Add:* Dept of Mech Eng La State Univ Baton Rouge LA 70803

WHITEHOUSE, RONALD LESLIE S, b Birmingham, Eng, Aug 9, 37; Can citizen; div; c 2. ELECTRON MICROSCOPY, MICROBIOLOGY. *Educ:* Univ Nottingham, BSc, 59; Univ Alta, MSc, 61, PhD(plant physiol, biochem), 65. *Prof Exp:* Nat Res Coun Can overseas fel, Bot Lab, Univ Bergen, 66; prof assoc food microbiol, 67-68, asst prof med bact & electron micros, 68-74, ASSOC PROF BACT, UNIV ALTA, 74- *Concurrent Pos:* Sabbatical leave, Dept Molecular Biol, Pasteur Inst, Paris. *Mem:* Micros Soc Can; Am Soc Microbiol; NY Acad Sci. *Res:* Electron microscopic methods for biological materials; electron microscopic investigation of chromosomal activity during sporulation in Bacillus Subtilis; development of preparative techniques; bacterial ultrastructure. *Mailing Add:* Dept Med Microbiol Univ of Alta Edmonton AB T6G 2H7 Can

WHITEHOUSE, WALTER MACINTIRE, SR, b Millersburg, Ohio, Jan 28, 16; m 45, 76; c 3. RADIOLOGY. *Educ:* Eastern Mich Univ, AB, 36; Univ Mich, MS, 37, MD, 41. *Prof Exp:* From instr to assoc prof, 51-63, chmn dept, 65-79, PROF RADIOL, MED SCH, UNIV MICH, ANN ARBOR, 63- *Mem:* Roentgen Ray Soc; Am Thoracic Soc; Am Col Radiol; Radiol Soc NAm. *Res:* Diagnostic radiology with emphasis on thoracic, gastrointestinal and obstetric areas; development and evaluation of radiologic and pararadiologic diagnostic equipment; evaluation of teaching methods in radiology. *Mailing Add:* Dept Radiol Univ Hosp Ann Arbor MI 48104

WHITEHURST, BROOKS M, b Reading, Pa, Apr 9, 30; m 51; c 3. CHEMICAL ENGINEERING. *Educ:* Va Polytech Inst, BS, 51. *Prof Exp:* Sr tech asst, Am Enka Corp, 51-56; sr engr, Ind Chem Div, Mobil Chem Co, 56-63; proj engr, Texaco Exp, Inc, 63-66; process engr, Tex Gulf Sulphur Co, 67-70; supt tech serv, 70-75, mgr eng serv, Tex Gulf, Inc, Aurora, 75-81, PRES, BROOKS WHITEHURST ASSOC, INC, 81- *Mem:* Am Inst Chem Engrs; fel Am Inst Chem; Int Solar Energy Soc; Nat Soc Prof Engrs. *Res:* Rayon yarns; phosphate, fertilizer, fluorine and environmental processes in air and water; alternate energy systems (solar, wood, alcohol), peat-oil slurry fuels and industrial products from sweet potatoes. *Mailing Add:* 1983 Hoods Creek Dr New Bern NC 28560

WHITEHURST, CHARLES A(UGUSTUS), b Cottondale, Fla, June 27, 29; m 56; c 3. MECHANICAL ENGINEERING, ENVIRONMENTAL ENGINEERING. *Educ:* La State Univ, BS, 56; Southern Methodist Univ, MS, 59; Tex A&M Univ, PhD(mech eng), 62. *Prof Exp:* Aerodyn engr, Gen Dynamics /Ft Worth, 56, propulsion engr, 56-59; assoc prof, La Polytech Inst, 62-63; assoc prof mech & aerospace eng, 63-66, from assoc prof to prof, Div Eng Res, 66-77, PROF COASTAL ENG & ASSOC DEAN FOR RES & GRAD ACTIV, LA STATE UNIV, BATON ROUGE, 77- *Concurrent Pos:* Dir & prin investr, Heat, Mass & Momentum Transfer Studies at Low Temperatures Proj, NSF, 62-63; lectr, Manned Spacecraft Ctr, Tex, 65-66; prin investr, Flow Losses in Flexible Hose Proj, NASA, 65-66, prin investr, Jet Shock Interactions Proj, 66-67, prog mgr & prin investr sustaining univ grant, 66-, prin investr related multidiscipline res, NASA Ctr, 69-, prin investr remote sensing studies La Delta, 72-; consult, La Joint Legis Comt Environ Qual, 71-72, prog mgr La environ mgt syst, 72; prog mgr & prin investr res, Off Water Resources Res, 72- *Mem:* Am Soc Mech Engrs; Am Soc Eng Educ. *Res:* Thermodynamics; fluid mechanics; heat transfer; environmental engineering, water resource management and environmental impact assessments. *Mailing Add:* Div of Eng Res La State Univ Baton Rouge LA 70803

WHITEHURST, DARRELL DUAYNE, b Vernon, Ill, July 8, 38; m 67; c 2. ORGANIC CHEMISTRY. *Educ:* Bradley Univ, AB, 60; Univ Iowa, MS, 63, PhD(org chem), 64. *Prof Exp:* Res chemist, 64-65, sr res chemist, 65-68, group leader catalysis, 68-73, res assoc, 74-75, PRIN INVESTR THREE EPRI CONTRACTS, MOBIL RES & DEVELOP CORP, 75-, GROUP MGR COAL & HEAVY LIQUIDS RES, 80- *Concurrent Pos:* Mem comt task force motor fuel & photochem smog, Am Petrol Inst; res assoc, BPRI, 73, prin investr fundamental coal chem study, 75. *Honors & Awards:* Richard A Glen Award & Henry H Storch Award, Am Chem Soc. *Mem:* AAAS; Am Chem Soc. *Res:* Organic syntheses; acetylene oxidations and coordination compounds of platinum; catalysis by ion exchange resins; catalysis by transition metals and compounds thereof; catalysis by zeolites; homogeneous-heterogeneous catalysts interconversion; metal plating; petrochemicals. *Mailing Add:* Mobil Res & Develop Corp Princeton NJ 08540

WHITEHURST, ELDRIDGE AUGUSTUS, b Norfolk, Va, May 26, 23; m 69; c 5. CIVIL ENGINEERING. *Educ:* Va Mil Inst, BSCE, 47; Purdue Univ, MSCE, 51. *Prof Exp:* Assoc res engr, Portland Cement Asn, 47-49; res asst, Joint Hwy Res Proj, Purdue Univ, 50-51, res engr, 51-52; res engr, Tenn Hwy Res Prog, Univ Tenn, Knoxville, 52-62, dir, 52-72, assoc dir, Eng Exp Sta, 54-72, res prof, 62-72; assoc dir, Transp Res Ctr, 72-80, PROF CIVIL ENG, OHIO STATE UNIV, 72-, DIR, TRANSPLEX, 80- *Concurrent Pos:* Consult var firms; mem, Hwy Res Bd, Nat Acad Sci-Nat Res Coun. *Mem:* fel Am Soc Testing & Mat; Am Rd Builders. *Res:* Highway materials; nondestructive testing of concrete, particularly by pulse velocity techniques; slipperiness of pavements, stabilization of pavement base courses; durability of concrete; performance of aggregates; bituminous materials and mixes. *Mailing Add:* Dept of Civil Eng Ohio State Univ Col of Eng Columbus OH 43210

WHITEHURST, HARRY BERNARD, b Dallas, Tex, Sept 13, 22; m 48; c 2. PHYSICAL CHEMISTRY. *Educ:* Rice Inst, BA, 44, MA, 48, PhD(chem), 50. *Prof Exp:* Fel, Univ Minn, 50-51; res chemist, Owens-Corning Fiberglas Corp, 51-59; assoc prof, 59-71, PROF CHEM, ARIZ STATE UNIV, 71- *Mem:* Fel AAAS; Am Chem Soc; fel Am Inst Chemists. *Res:* Radiochemistry; adsorption; surface chemistry of glass; electrical properties of oxides. *Mailing Add:* Dept Chem Ariz State Univ Tempe AZ 85281

WHITEHURST, ROBERT NEAL, b Edwin, Ala, Oct 24, 22; m 50; c 4. PHYSICS, ELECRTOMAGNETISM. *Educ:* Univ Ala, BS, 43, MS, 48; Stanford Univ, PhD(physics), 58. *Prof Exp:* Instr physics, Univ Ala, 48-49; asst microwave, Stanford Univ, 52-54; from asst prof to assoc prof, Univ Ala, 54-61, actg chmn dept, 58-59, prof physics, 61-81; RETIRED. *Concurrent Pos:* Consult, Redstone Arsenal, US Army Rocket & Guided Missile Agency, 54-64; vis scientist, Nat Radio Astron Observ, 70 & 76-77. *Mem:* Am Phys Soc; Am Asn Physics Teachers; Am Astron Soc. *Res:* Radio astronomy. *Mailing Add:* 25 Arcadia Tuscaloosa AL 35404

WHITEHURST, VIRGIL EDWARDS, b Dankurk, Ind; m 55; c 1. PHARMACOLOGY. *Educ:* Anderson Col, BA, 53; Butler Univ, MS, 62; Ind Univ, PhD(biochem), 68. *Prof Exp:* Asst nutrit fluoride chem & preventive dent, Ind Univ, 67-68; assoc prof microbiol & biochem, Howard Univ, 68-73; PHARMACOLOGIST & TOXICOLOGIST, FOOD & DRUG ADMIN, WASHINGTON, DC, 73- *Concurrent Pos:* Vis prof, Howard Univ, 73-78; consult, Commun Progress, Inc, New Haven, Ct, 75-77, Murtis H Taylor Multi-Serv Ctr, Cleveland, Ohio, 78-80. *Mem:* Sigma Xi; Soc Black Scientists. *Res:* Investigate the cardiotoxic effects of beta adrenergic agonists methylxanthenes when used separately and concurrently; cardiotoxic effects of the compound use of sterold and methylxanthenes. *Mailing Add:* 5600 Fishers Lane Rockville MD 20857

WHITEKER, MCELWYN D, b Harrison Co, Ky, Aug 4, 29; m 50; c 3. ANIMAL SCIENCE. *Educ:* Univ Ky, BS, 51, MS, 57, PhD(nutrit, biochem), 61. *Prof Exp:* From asst prof to assoc prof animal sci, Iowa State Univ, 61-67; LIVESTOCK EXTEN SPECIALIST, UNIV KY, 67-, PROF ANIMAL SCI, 69- *Mem:* Am Soc Animal Sci. *Res:* Nutrition; animal breeding. *Mailing Add:* Dept of Animal Sci Univ of Ky Col of Agr Lexington KY 40506

WHITEKER, ROY ARCHIE, b Long Beach, Calif, Aug 22, 27; m 60; c 1. ANALYTICAL CHEMISTRY. *Educ:* Univ Calif, Los Angeles, BS, 50, MS, 52; Calif Inst Technol, PhD(chem), 56. *Prof Exp:* Instr chem, Mass Inst Technol, 55-57; from asst prof to prof, Harvey Mudd Col, 57-74, actg chmn dept, 69-71; dep exec secy, Coun Int Exchange Scholars, 71-72, exec secy, 72-75, dir, 75-76; PROF & DEAN, UNIV PAC, 76- *Concurrent Pos:* NSF sci fac fel, Royal Inst Technol, Sweden, 63-64; vis assoc prof, Univ Calif, Riverside, 67; assoc dir fel off, Nat Res Coun, 67-68; dir summer session, Claremont Grad Sch, 69-70. *Mem:* Am Chem Soc. *Res:* Electroanalytical chemistry; complex ions. *Mailing Add:* 3734 Portsmouth Circle N Stockton CA 95209

WHITELAW, R(OBERT) L(ESLIE), b Tungjen, China, Apr 24, 17; nat US; m 42; c 3. MECHANICAL ENGINEERING. *Educ:* Univ Toronto, MSc, 40. *Prof Exp:* Liaison officer, Brit Air Comn, DC, 40-43; sr tech officer, Winnipeg Test Sta, Nat Res Coun Can, 43-45; sr designer, A V Roe Can Ltd, 45-46; chief gas turbine res & develop, De Laval Co, NJ, 46-48; staff engr, Res Ctr, Babcock & Wilcox Co, 48-55, proj engr, NS Savannah, 55-60; spec asst to dir res, Allison Div, Gen Motors Corp, 60-66; PROF MECH & NUCLEAR ENG, VA POLYTECH INST & STATE UNIV, 66- *Concurrent Pos:* Assoc prof, US Naval Postgrad Sch, 63-64. *Mem:* Am Soc Mech Engrs; Am Nuclear Soc; Am Soc Heating, Refrig & Air-Conditioning Engrs. *Res:* Thermodynamics; power cycles; cable-suspended transportation systems; geothermal power; underwater vehicles; advanced reactor design; flywheel energy storage; liquified natural gas technology; windpower generation; energy-conserving environmental systems. *Mailing Add:* Dept of Mech Eng Va Polytech Inst & State Univ Blacksburg VA 24061

WHITELEY, ARTHUR HENRY, b Dowagiac, Mich, Dec 17, 16; m 44. ZOOLOGY. *Educ:* Kalamazoo Col, BA, 38; Univ Wis, MA, 39; Princeton Univ, PhD(biol), 45. *Prof Exp:* Asst zool, Univ Calif, 39-42; asst biol, Off Sci Res & Develop, Princeton Univ, 42-45, res assoc, Nat Defense Res Comt, 45-46; res assoc zool, Sch Med, Univ Tex, 46; Nat Res Coun fel, Calif Inst Technol, 46-47; from asst prof to assoc prof, 47-57, PROF ZOOL, UNIV WASH, 57- *Concurrent Pos:* Guggenheim fel, Europe, 55-56. *Mem:* Am Soc Zool; Soc Gen Physiol; Soc Develop Biol; Int Soc Develop Biol; Int Soc Cell Biol. *Res:* Physiology of fertilization of marine invertebrates; active transport in eggs; genetic expression in developing invertebrate embryos and regenerating stentors; physiology of interspecies hybrids of sea urchins. *Mailing Add:* Dept of Zool Univ of Wash Seattle WA 98195

WHITELEY, ELI LAMAR, b Florence, Tex, Dec 10, 13; m 49; c 5. SOIL PHYSICS. *Educ:* Tex A&M Univ, BS, 41, PhD(soil physics), 59; NC State Univ, MS, 49. *Prof Exp:* Instr, 46-59, assoc prof, 59-80, EMER ASSOC PROF AGRON, TEX A&M UNIV, 80- *Concurrent Pos:* Mem, Nat Coord Comt New Crops, 65- *Mem:* Am Soc Agron; Soil Sci Soc Am; Crop Sci Soc Am; Int Soc Soil Sci. *Res:* Soil and crop management; new crops, development of new crops for the production of oils, gums and paper pulp. *Mailing Add:* Dept of Soil & Crop Sci Tex A&M Univ College Station TX 77843

WHITELEY, HELEN RIABOFF, b Harbin, China, June 8, 22; nat US; m 44. MICROBIAL PHYSIOLOGY. *Educ:* Univ Calif, Berkeley, BA, 42; Univ Tex, MA, 46; Univ Wash, PhD, 51. *Prof Exp:* AEC fel, 51-53, res assoc microbiol, 53-57, from res asst prof to res assoc prof, 57-64, PROF MICROBIOL, UNIV WASH, 64- *Concurrent Pos:* Mem panel, NIH, 65-70 & 75-78. *Mem:* Am Soc Microbiol (vpres, 74-75, pres, 75-76); Am Acad Microbiol; Am Soc Biol Chem. *Res:* Control of viral transcription in B Subtilis phages; properties of RNA polymerase; echinoderm development. *Mailing Add:* Dept of Microbiol Univ of Wash Seattle WA 98195

WHITELEY, NORMAN MCKEE, clinical biochemistry, see previous edition

WHITELEY, ROGER L, b Trenton, NJ, Jan 30, 30. MECHANICAL METALLURGY. *Educ:* Rensselaer Polytech Inst, BS, 52, MS, 53. *Prof Exp:* Engr, supvr & asst sect mgr, 53-64, sect mgr mech processing, 64-68, asst mgr forming & finishing res, 68-69, MGR CONTROL SYSTS RES, BETHLEHEM STEEL CORP, 69- *Honors & Awards:* Grossman Award, Am Soc Metals, 60. *Mem:* Am Soc Metals; Am Inst Mining & Metall Engrs; Am Iron & Steel Engrs; Am Iron & Steel Inst; Am Inst Physics. *Res:* Sheet steel metallurgy, forming and fabrication of metals, fracture and fatigue; instrumentation and automation of steel processes, rolling and rolling mill analysis, systems analysis. *Mailing Add:* Homer Res Labs Bethlehem Steel Corp Bethlehem PA 18016

WHITELEY, THOMAS EDWARD, b Dunsmuir, Calif, Oct 14, 32; m 53; c 3. ORGANIC CHEMISTRY. *Educ:* Univ Colo, BA, 54; Univ SC, MS, 56; Ohio State Univ, PhD(carbohydrate chem), 60. *Prof Exp:* Res chemist, Eastman Kodak Co, 56-57; res asst carbohydrate chem, Ohio State Univ, 57-59; sr res chemist, 60-63, res assoc photog chem, 63-69, asst div head, 69-76, DIV DIR, EMULSION RES DIV, EASTMAN KODAK CO, 76- *Mem:* Soc Photog Sci & Eng; Sigma Xi. *Res:* Polymer science and technology; photgraphic chemistry related to the silver halide emulsion. *Mailing Add:* Kodak Park Res Labs Eastman Kodak Co Rochester NY 14650

WHITEMAN, ALBERT LEON, b Philadelphia, Pa, Feb 15, 15; m 45. MATHEMATICS. *Educ:* Univ Pa, AB, 36, AM, 37, PhD(math), 40. *Prof Exp:* Asst instr math, Univ Pa, 38-40; Benjamin Peirce instr, Harvard Univ, 40-42; instr, Purdue Univ, 46; res mathematician, US Dept Navy, 46-48; from asst prof to assoc prof, 48-56, PROF MATH, UNIV SOUTHERN CALIF, 56- *Concurrent Pos:* Mem, Inst Advan Study, 52-54, 59-60 & 67-68; chmn res conf theory numbers, NSF, 55 & 63; ed, Pac J Math, 57-62; res mathematician, Inst Defense Anal, 60-61. *Mem:* Am Math Soc; Math Asn Am. *Res:* Theory of numbers; combinatorial analysis. *Mailing Add:* Dept of Math Univ of Southern Calif Los Angeles CA 90007

WHITEMAN, CHARLES E, b Eldred, Ill, Sept 28, 18; m 43; c 3. VETERINARY PATHOLOGY. *Educ:* Kans State Col, DVM, 43; Iowa State Univ, PhD(vet path), 60; Am Col Vet Pathologists, dipl. *Prof Exp:* Assoc prof vet path, Mich State Univ, 60-61; assoc prof, 61-71, PROF VET PATH, COLO STATE UNIV, 71- *Mem:* Am Vet Med Asn; Am Asn Avian Pathologists. *Res:* Placental pathology; respiratory diseases; poultry diseases. *Mailing Add:* Dept of Path Colo State Univ Ft Collins CO 80521

WHITEMAN, ELDON EUGENE, b Tarentum, Pa, May 5, 13; m 39; c 3. ZOOLOGY. *Educ:* Greenville Col, BS, 36; Mich State Univ, MS, 41, PhD(zool), 65. *Prof Exp:* Asst dir, Kellogg Bird Sanctuary, 39-41; prof biol, 46-80, chmn, Natural Sci Div, 63-71, dir environ studies, 72-80, EMER PROF BIOL, SPRING ARBOR COL, 80- *Mem:* Nat Audubon Soc; Nat Wildlife Soc. *Res:* Development of a summer travel course for the college student in the area of environmental studies. *Mailing Add:* Spring Arbor Col Spring Arbor MI 49283

WHITEMAN, JOE V, b Walkerville, Ill, July 13, 19; m 45; c 1. ANIMAL BREEDING. *Educ:* NMex State Univ, BS, 43; Okla State Univ, MS, 51, PhD, 52. *Prof Exp:* From asst prof to assoc prof, 52-63, PROF ANIMAL SCI, OKLA STATE UNIV, 63- *Mem:* AAAS; Am Soc Animal Sci; Biomet Soc. *Res:* Genetic and environmental factors governing the growth and development of meat animals. *Mailing Add:* Dept of Animal Sci Okla State Univ Stillwater OK 74074

WHITEMAN, JOHN DAVID, b Darby, Pa, May 24, 43; m 69; c 2. COATINGS RESEARCH & DEVELOPMENT. *Educ:* LaSalle Col, BA, 65; Univ Pa, PhD(phys chem), 71. *Prof Exp:* Sr res chemist anal chem, 72-75, sr res chemist pharmaceut, 75-76, sr res chemist pioneering coatings, 77-79, RES SECT MGR INDUST COATINGS, ROHM AND HAAS CO, 80- *Concurrent Pos:* Fel, Dept Chem, Univ Pa, 71-72. *Mem:* Am Phys Soc; Am Chem Soc. *Res:* Energy band structure of molecular crystals; polymer physics; structure activity relationships in agricultural and pharmaceutical chemicals; organic coatings; analytical chemistry; high solids coatings. *Mailing Add:* Rohm and Haas Res Labs Norristown & McKean Rds Spring House PA 19477

WHITENBERG, DAVID CALVIN, b Duffau, Tex, Feb 6, 31; m 51; c 1. PLANT PHYSIOLOGY, BIOCHEMISTRY. *Educ:* Tex A&M Univ, BS, 57, MS, 59, PhD(plant physiol, biochem), 62. *Prof Exp:* Res plant physiologist, USDA, 61-65; asst prof, 65-67, assoc prof, 67-80, PROF BIOL, SOUTHWEST TEX STATE UNIV, 80- *Mem:* Am Soc Plant Physiologists; fel Am Inst Chemists. *Res:* Seed physiology and biochemistry. *Mailing Add:* Dept of Biol Southwest Tex State Univ San Marcos TX 78666

WHITER, PAUL FRANCIS, b London, Eng, Aug 28, 34; m 58; c 4. RESEARCH ADMINISTRATION. *Educ:* Univ London, BSc, 60, PhD(org chem), 65. *Prof Exp:* From res scientist to prin scientist, Wilkinson Sword Res Ltd, 63-68, chem proj mgr, Wilkinson Sword, Inc, 68-70, res mgr NAm, 70-73, SPEC PROD MGR, WILKINSON SWORD, INC, 73- *Concurrent Pos:* Asst lectr, Northwest Kent Col Technol, 62-63. *Mem:* AAAS; Am Chem Soc; Royal Soc Chem; Soc Cosmetic Chem. *Res:* Commercialization and management. *Mailing Add:* 80 Hillcrest Ave Summit NJ 07901

WHITESCARVER, JACK EDWARD, b Palestine, Tex, May 16, 37. MEDICAL MICROBIOLOGY. *Educ:* Sam Houston State Univ, Huntsville, BS, 59; Col Med & Dent NJ, PhD(microbiol), 74. *Prof Exp:* Teaching fel biol, Sam Houston Univ, 62-64; res assoc oncol, Univ Tex, M D Anderson Hosp & Tumor Inst, 64-66; res assoc oncol, Southern Calif Cancer Ctr, Los Angeles, 66-71; teaching fel microbiol, Col Med & Dent NJ, 71-74; res fel microbiol, Harvard Univ Sch Pub Health, 74-78; ADMINR HEALTH SCI, NIH & SPEC ASST TO DIR, NAT INST ALLERGY & INFECTIOUS DIS, 78- *Concurrent Pos:* Fel, Albert Soiland Cancer Found, 67-70. *Mem:* Am Soc Microbiol; Am Acad Allergy; Infectious Dis Soc Am. *Res:* Morphology and ultrastructural immunology of Rickettsiae; cell culture studies and host-parasite relationship. *Mailing Add:* Nat Inst Allergy & Infectious Dis NIH Bldg 31 Rm 7A04 Bethesda MD 20205

WHITESELL, JAMES JUDD, b Philadelphia, Pa, Oct 14, 39; m 65; c 1. ENTOMOLOGY. *Educ:* Dickinson Col, BS, 62; Univ Fla, MEd, 67, MS, 69, PhD(entom), 74. *Prof Exp:* Teacher sci, James S Rickards Jr High Sch, 63-67; res assoc lovebug res, Dept Entom, Univ Fla, 73-74; teacher biol & zool, Snead State Jr Col, Ala, 74-76, chmn sci & math div, 75-76; assoc prof entom & zool, dept biol, 76-80, ASSOC PROF SCI EDUC & BIOL, SEC EDUC DEPT, VALDOSTA STATE COL, 81- *Mem:* Sigma Xi; Entom Soc Am. *Res:* Systematics and ecology of sound producing insects. *Mailing Add:* Educ Ctr Valdosta State Col Valdosta GA 31698

WHITESELL, JAMES KELLER, b Philadelphia, Pa, Nov 2, 44; m 66; c 2. SYNTHETIC ORGANIC CHEMISTRY. *Educ:* Pa State Univ, BS, 66; Harvard Univ, PhD(chem), 71. *Prof Exp:* Fel chem, Woodward Res Inst, 70-73; asst prof, 73-79, ASSOC PROF CHEM, UNIV TEX, AUSTIN, 79- *Mem:* Am Chem Soc; Royal Soc Chem. *Res:* Total synthesis of naturally occurring and theoretically interesting molecules; asymmetric induction. *Mailing Add:* Dept of Chem Univ of Tex Austin TX 78712

WHITESELL, WILLIAM JAMES, b Newnan, Ga, Dec 23, 27; m 60; c 5. THEORETICAL PHYSICS. *Educ:* Univ SC, BS, 48; Purdue Univ, MS, 51, PhD(physics), 59. *Prof Exp:* From instr to asst prof physics, Brooklyn Col, 58-63; asst prof, 63-69, assoc prof, 69-81, PROF PHYSICS, ANTIOCH COL, 81- *Concurrent Pos:* Sr lectr, Victoria Univ, Wellington, 70-72. *Mem:* Am Asn Physics Teachers. *Mailing Add:* Dept of Physics Antioch Col Yellow Springs OH 45387

WHITESIDE, BOBBY GENE, b Keota, Okla, June 16, 40; m 64; c 2. FISHERIES. *Educ:* Okla State Univ, BS, 62, MS, 64, PhD(fisheries), 67. *Prof Exp:* Assoc prof, 67-77, PROF BIOL, SOUTHWESTERN TEX STATE UNIV, 77- *Concurrent Pos:* Tex Water Develop Bd grant, 72-73; Soil Conserv Serv grant, 74; US Fish & Wildlife Serv grants, 76; Am Fishing Tackle Mfrs Asn grant, 77; Pro Bass Mag grant, 77; TERA Corp grant, 78. *Mem:* Am Fisheries Soc. *Res:* Fisheries management; population dynamics; ecology. *Mailing Add:* Dept of Biol Southwest Tex State Univ San Marcos TX 78666

WHITESIDE, CHARLES HUGH, b Grapevine, Tex, June 25, 32; m 56; c 2. ANALYTICAL CHEMISTRY, ENVIRONMENTAL SCIENCES. *Educ:* Tex A&M Univ, BS, 53, MS, 58, PhD(biochem), 60. *Prof Exp:* Robert A Welch Found res fel, Dept Biochem & Nutrit, Tex A&M Univ, 60-61; sr scientist, Mead Johnson & Co, 61-64; teacher chem, Kilgore Col, 64-67, chmn dept, 67-71; PRES, ANA-LAB CORP, 67- *Mem:* Am Chem Soc; Am Oil Chemists' Soc. *Res:* Water quality and waste water technology; animal nutrition; solar energy. *Mailing Add:* 2600 Dudley Rd Kilgore TX 75662

WHITESIDE, EUGENE PERRY, b Champaign, Ill, Oct 18, 12; m 36; c 3. SOIL SCIENCE. *Educ:* Univ Ill, BS, 34; Univ Mo, PhD(soils), 44. *Prof Exp:* Asst soil physics & soil surv, Exp Sta, Univ Ill, 34-38; asst soils, Univ Mo, 38-39; assoc soil surv, Exp Sta, Univ Ill, 39-43; assoc soils, Univ Tenn, 43-44; asst chief soil surv & asst prof soil physics, Exp Sta, Univ Ill, 44-49; from assoc prof to prof, 49-78, EMER PROF SOIL SCI, MICH STATE UNIV, 78- *Concurrent Pos:* Assoc soil surv, Emergency Rubber Proj, US Forest Serv, Calif, 43; consult, Natural Resources Sect, Agr Div, Gen Hqs, Supreme Comdr Allied Powers, Japan, 46-47, Rockefeller Found, Mex, 61, Agency Int Develop, Taiwan, 62-63, Arg, 72 & Food & Agr Orgn, UN, 80-81. *Mem:* Fel Soil Sci Soc Am; Int Soil Sci Soc; Soil Conserv Soc Am; fel Am Soc Agron. *Res:* Soil mineralogy, chemistry, geography, classification and genesis. *Mailing Add:* 848 Huntington East Lansing MI 48823

WHITESIDE, JACK OLIVER, b Barnstaple, Eng, June 5, 28; m 51; c 2. PLANT PATHOLOGY. *Educ:* Univ London, BSc, 48, PhD(plant physiol), 53. *Prof Exp:* Plant physiologist, Ministry Agr, Rhodesia, Africa, 48-53, from plant pathologist to chief plant pathologist, 53-67; assoc plant pathologist, Citrus Exp Sta, 68-73, PROF PLANT PATH, UNIV FLA, 73- *Mem:* Int Soc Citricult; Am Phytopath Soc. *Res:* Identification and control of plant diseases present in Rhodesia; behavior and control of fungus diseases of citrus. *Mailing Add:* Agr Res & Educ Ctr Univ of Fla Lake Alfred FL 33850

WHITESIDE, JAMES BROOKS, b Tyler, Tex, Jan 5, 42; m 66; c 3. COMPOSITE MATERIALS, STRUCTURAL MECHANICS. *Educ:* Tulane Univ, BS, 64; Sheffield Univ, PhD(mech eng), 68. *Prof Exp:* Sr engr structural mech, 68-74, group leader composite structures, 74-79, RES LAB HEAD APPL MATH, GRUMMAN AEROSPACE CORP, 79- *Concurrent Pos:* Mem, Fed Aviation Admin Panel Independent Experts Structures, 81-; prof engr, 73- *Res:* Design allowables and stress analysis of composites; moisture diffusion in polymers; fatigue and fracture; experimental stress analysis; mechanical and environmental behavior of composite materials. *Mailing Add:* A08-035 Grumman Aerospace Corp Bethpage NY 11714

WHITESIDE, MELBOURNE C, b Washington, DC, Dec 16, 37; m 61; c 2. AQUATIC ECOLOGY. *Educ:* Willamette Univ, BA, 62; Ariz State Univ, MS, 64; Ind Univ, Bloomington, PhD(zool), 68. *Prof Exp:* Res fel limnol, Univ Minn, 68-69; asst prof ecol & limnol, Calif State Univ, Fullerton, 69-72; from asst prof to assoc prof, 72-80, PROF ZOOL, UNIV TENN, KNOXVILLE, 80- *Mem:* Am Soc Limnol & Oceanog; Ecol Soc Am. *Res:* Paleolimnology; community ecology and population dynamics of aquatic organisms; sampling problems in aquatic environments. *Mailing Add:* Dept of Zool Univ of Tenn Knoxville TN 37916

WHITESIDE, ROBERTA EMERSON, immunology, see previous edition

WHITESIDE, THERESA L, b Katowice, Poland, Mar 10, 39; US citizen; m 61; c 1. IMMUNOLOGY, IMMUNOPATHOLOGY. *Educ:* Columbia Univ, BS, 62, MA, 64, PhD(microbiol), 67; Am Bd Med Lab Immunol, dipl, 79. *Prof Exp:* NIH fel, Sch Med, NY Univ, 67-69, lectr microbiol & assoc res scientist, 69-70; res assoc ophthal, Col Physicians & Surgeons, Columbia Univ, 70-73; asst prof, 73-79, ASSOC PROF PATH, MED SCH, UNIV PITTSBURGH, 79-, ASSOC DIR CLIN IMMUNOPATH, 73- *Concurrent Pos:* NIH spec fel ophthal, Col Physicians & Surgeons, Columbia Univ, 72-73. *Mem:* AAAS; Am Asn Immunologists; Am Asn Pathologists; Am Soc Microbiol. *Res:* Immunology of surface-associated antigens; surface antigens in human lymphomas and leukemias; clinical immunopathology; lymphocyte membrane receptors. *Mailing Add:* Med Sch Dept Path Univ Pittsburgh Pittsburgh PA 15261

WHITESIDE, WESLEY C, b Milan, Ill, Aug 22, 27. BOTANY. *Educ:* Augustana Col, BA, 51; Univ Ill, MS, 56; Fla State Univ, PhD, 59. *Prof Exp:* Instr bot & gen biol, Montgomery Jr Col, 59-60; from asst prof to assoc prof, 60-70, PROF BOT, EASTERN ILL UNIV, 70- *Concurrent Pos:* Res grant, Highlands Biol Sta, 59. *Mem:* Mycol Soc Am. *Res:* Morphology; cytology and taxonomy of the ascomycete fungi, especially the Pyrenomycetes; taxonomy of lichens. *Mailing Add:* Dept of Bot Eastern Ill Univ Charleston IL 61920

WHITESIDES, GEORGE MCCLELLAND, b Louisville, Ky, Aug 3, 39. ORGANIC CHEMISTRY. *Educ:* Harvard Univ, AB, 60; Calif Inst Technol, PhD(chem), 64. *Prof Exp:* From asst prof to assoc prof, 63-74, PROF CHEM, MASS INST TECHNOL, 74- *Mem:* Nat Acad Sci; Am Chem Soc; Am Acad Arts & Sci. *Res:* Mechanisms and structure. *Mailing Add:* Rm 18-298 Dept of Chem Mass Inst of Technol Cambridge MA 02139

WHITESIDES, JOHN LINDSEY, JR, b San Antonio, Tex, Feb 27, 43; m 64; c 2. FLUID MECHANICS, AERONAUTICS. *Educ:* Univ Tex, Austin, BS, 65, PhD(aerospace eng), 68. *Prof Exp:* Asst res prof mech eng, 68-74, assoc prof, 74-80, PROF ENG & APPL SCI, GEORGE WASHINGTON UNIV, 80-, ASST DIR, JOINT INST FOR ADVAN FLIGHT SCI, LANGLEY RES CTR, NASA, 75- *Concurrent Pos:* Coordr, George Washington Univ-NASA Prog, Langley Res Ctr, NASA, 68-75. *Mem:* Assoc fel Am Inst Aeronaut & Astronaut; Soc Eng Sci; Am Soc Eng Educ. *Res:* Analytical methods in fluid mechanics and aeronautics. *Mailing Add:* George Washington Univ JIAFS MS169 Langley Res Ctr NASA Hampton VA 23665

WHITESITT, JOHN ELDON, b Stevensville, Mont, Jan 15, 22; m 44; c 3. MATHEMATICS. *Educ:* Mont State Univ, AB, 43; Univ Ill, AM, 49, PhD(math), 54. *Prof Exp:* From instr to assoc prof, 46-61, head dept, 61-66, PROF MATH, MONT STATE UNIV, 61- *Mem:* Am Math Soc; Math Asn Am. *Res:* Ring theory; linear algebra; Boolean algebra. *Mailing Add:* Dept of Math Mont State Univ Bozeman MT 59715

WHITEWAY, STIRLING GIDDINGS, b Stellarton, NS, May 17, 27; m 52; c 2. PHYSICAL CHEMISTRY, INORGANIC CHEMISTRY. *Educ:* Dalhousie Univ, BSc, 47, dipl, 48, MSc, 49; McGill Univ, PhD(phys chem), 53. *Prof Exp:* Fel photochem, Pure Chem Div, 52-53, from asst res officer to assoc res officer, 53-68, SR RES OFFICER, ATLANTIC REGIONAL LAB, NAT RES COUN CAN, 68- *Concurrent Pos:* Spec lectr, Dalhousie Univ, 54-55. *Mem:* Chem Inst Can; Can Inst Mining & Metall. *Res:* Chemistry of high temperature reactions; chemistry of coal. *Mailing Add:* Nat Res Coun of Can 1411 Oxford St Halifax NS B3H 3Z1 Can

WHITFIELD, CAROL FAYE, b Altoona, Pa, May 14, 39. PHYSIOLOGY, BIOCHEMISTRY. *Educ:* Juniata Col, BS, 61; Syracuse Univ, MS, 64; George Washington Univ, PhD(physiol), 68. *Prof Exp:* Teaching asst zool, Syracuse Univ, 61-63; res assoc, 68-70, ASST PROF PHYSIOL, MILTON S HERSHEY MED CTR, COL MED, PA STATE UNIV, HERSHEY, 70- *Mem:* AAAS; Biophys Soc; Am Physiol Soc. *Res:* Metabolic and hormonal regulation of carrier-mediated sugar transport in erythrocytes and muscle; regulation of membrane permeability; membrane structure; cardiac muscle metabolism; mechanisms of hormone action. *Mailing Add:* Dept of Physiol Milton S Hershey Pa State Univ Hershey PA 17033

WHITFIELD, CAROLYN DICKSON, b Indianapolis, Ind, Aug 21, 41; m 65. BIOCHEMISTRY. *Educ:* Wellesley Col, AB, 63; Univ Chicago, MS, 65; George Washington Univ, PhD(biochem), 69. *Prof Exp:* Wellcome Found fel, Univ Edinburgh, 69-70; Am Cancer Soc fel, 70-72, asst res biol chemist, 72-74, scholar human genetics, 74-76, ASST PROF, DEPT BIOL CHEM, MED SCH, UNIV MICH, ANN ARBOR, 76- *Concurrent Pos:* Estab investr, Am Heart Asn, 77-82. *Res:* Mechanism of action of flavoproteins; isolation and biochemical characterization of Chinese hamster cell mutants in tissue culture; methionine biosynthesis. *Mailing Add:* Dept of Biol Chem Univ of Mich Med Sch Ann Arbor MI 48109

WHITFIELD, DAVID LAWRENCE, aerospace engineering, see previous edition

WHITFIELD, GEORGE BUCKMASTER, JR, b Newark, NJ, Dec 4, 23; m 44; c 3. BIOCHEMISTRY. *Educ:* Cornell Col, BA, 46; Univ Ill, MS, 51, PhD(chem), 53. *Prof Exp:* Jr res scientist, 47-51, sr res scientist, 53-59, sect head microbiol, 59-66, mgr, 66-68, infectious dis res mgr, 68-78, CORP PROD GROUP ADMINR, INFECTIOUS DIS & CARDIOVASC DIS, UPJOHN CO, 78- *Mem:* Am Chem Soc; Am Soc Microbiol; NY Acad Sci. *Res:* Isolation and characterization of new antibiotics and antitumor agents; paper chromatography; microbiological assay; tissue culture; in vitro, in vivo and clinical evaluation of new antibiotics, antifungal and antiparasitic agents. *Mailing Add:* Upjohn Co Kalamazoo MI 49001

WHITFIELD, GEORGE DANLEY, physics, deceased

WHITFIELD, H(AROLD) B(ARNARD), JR, chemical engineering, polymer science, see previous edition

WHITFIELD, HARVEY JAMES, JR, b Chicago, Ill, Apr 10, 40; m 65. MOLECULAR BIOLOGY. *Educ:* Univ Ill, Urbana, BS, 61; Univ Ill Col Med, MD, 64. *Prof Exp:* Intern, Res & Educ Hosp, Chicago, 64-65; staff asst molecular biol, NIH, 65-69; USPHS spec fel, Med Res Coun Microbial Genetics Unit, Univ Edinburgh, 69-70; asst prof, 70-75, ASSOC PROF BIOCHEM, MED SCH, UNIV MICH, 75- *Concurrent Pos:* USPHS grant, Univ Mich, Ann Arbor, 71- *Mem:* AAAS; Am Soc Biol Chemists; Am Soc Microbiol; Genetics Soc Am. *Res:* Replication and segregation of episomal DNA; microbial genetics. *Mailing Add:* Dept of Biol Chem Univ of Mich Ann Arbor MI 48109

WHITFIELD, JACK D, b Paoli, Okla, May 16, 28; m 49; c 3. AERONAUTICAL ENGINEERING, GAS DYNAMICS. *Educ:* Univ Okla, BS, 51; Univ Tenn, MS, 60; Royal Inst Technol, Sweden, DSc, 72. *Prof Exp:* Test engr, Gen Dynamics-Convair, 51-54; engr, Von Karman Gas Dynamics Facil, 54-60, asst mgr hypervelocity br, 60-64, mgr, 64-68, dir, 68-75, dir, Engine Test Facil, 75-76, corp vpres & corp prin advan technol, 76-80, PRES, SVERDRUP CORP, 80- *Concurrent Pos:* Consult, Off Nat Studies & Aeronaut Res, sponsored by adv group for Aeronaut Res & Develop, Paris, 60; consult arc-driven shock tubes, Vitro/Smith Corp, New York, 63; prof aerospace eng, Univ Tenn, 76- *Honors & Awards:* Gen H H Arnold Award, Am Inst Aeronaut & Astronaut, 68. *Mem:* Am Inst Aeronaut & Astronaut; Nat Soc Prof Engrs. *Res:* Experimental and theoretical supersonic and hypersonic aerodynamics, especially studies of viscous flow phenomena; development and advancement of supersonic and hypersonic gas dynamic test facilities; technical and administrative research management. *Mailing Add:* ARO Inc Arnold Air Force Station TN 37389

WHITFIELD, JAMES F, b Sarnia, Ont, July 1, 31; m 51; c 4. CELL PHYSIOLOGY, CANCER. *Educ:* McGill Univ, BSc, 51; Univ Western Ont, MSc, 52, PhD(bact, immunol), 55. *Prof Exp:* Res officer bact & viral genetics, Atomic Energy Can Ltd, 55-58, res officer cellular radiobiol, 58-62; sect chief, Europ Joint Res Ctr, Europ Atomic Energy Comn, Italy, 62-65; head cell physiol sect, Radiation Biol Div, 65-72, HEAD ANIMAL & CELL PHYSIOL SECT, BIOL SCI DIV, NAT RES COUN CAN, 72- *Mem:* Tissue Cult Asn; Am Soc Cell Biol. *Res:* Control of cell proliferation; in vivo and in vitro effects of calcium, hormones and cyclic nucleotides. *Mailing Add:* Biol Sci Div Nat Res Coun of Can Ottawa ON K1A 0R6 Can

WHITFIELD, JOHN HOWARD MERVYN, b Thessalon, Ont, Sept 11, 39; m 60; c 4. MATHEMATICS. *Educ:* Abilene Christian Col, BA, 61; Tex Christian Univ, MA, 62; Case Inst Technol, PhD(math), 66. *Prof Exp:* Asst prof, 65-70, chmn dept, 72-75, ASSOC PROF MATH, LAKEHEAD UNIV, 70- *Concurrent Pos:* Vis scholar, Univ Wash, 71-72; vis prof, Univ Waterloo, 78-79. *Mem:* Am Math Soc; Math Asn Am; Can Math Cong. *Res:* Functional analysis; differentiable functions and norms; geometry of Banach spaces. *Mailing Add:* Dept of Math Sci Lakehead Univ Thunder Bay ON P7B 5E1 Can

WHITFIELD, RICHARD GEORGE, b Philadelphia, Pa, Nov 11, 51; m 73; c 1. PHYSICAL & ANALYTICAL CHEMISTRY. *Educ:* Glassboro State Col, BA, 73; Mich State Univ, PhD(chem), 77. *Prof Exp:* SR RES CHEMIST ANAL, OLIN CHEM GROUP, 78- *Mem:* Am Chem Soc; Sigma Xi. *Res:* Analytical applications of infrared, raman, ultraviolet and visible spectroscopy; instrumental and method development; investigations of the solid state via vibrational spectroscopy; office systems; analytical chemistry as well as materials support. *Mailing Add:* 1112 Fed Rd Exxon Off Systs Co Brookfield CT 96804

WHITFIELD, ROBERT EDWARD, b Waverly, Tenn, Aug 11, 21; m 43; c 4. CHEMISTRY. *Educ:* Univ Tenn, BS, 43; Harvard Univ, AM, 48, PhD(org chem), 49. *Prof Exp:* Res chemist, Shell Develop Co, 43-46, Am Cyanamid Co, 49-51 & Dow Chem Co, 51-58; SR RES CHEMIST, WESTERN REGIONAL RES LAB, USDA, ALBANY, 58- *Mem:* AAAS; Am Chem Soc. *Res:* Organic reaction mechanisms; spectra and structure of molecules; chelates; petrochemicals; physical organic, polymer, fiber and protein chemistry. *Mailing Add:* 1841 Pleasant Hill Rd Pleasant Hill CA 94523

WHITFILL, DONALD LEE, b Madill, Okla, Mar 13, 39; m 60; c 2. PHYSICAL INORGANIC CHEMISTRY. *Educ:* Southeastern State Col, BS, 61; Univ Okla, PhD(chem), 66. *Prof Exp:* Instr chem, Univ Okla, 66-67; res scientist, Plant Foods Res Div, Continental Oil Co, 67-70, res scientist, 70-78, sr res scientist, 78-79; RES GROUP LEADER, PROD RES DIV, CONOCO, INC, 79- *Mem:* Am Chem Soc; Soc Petrol Engrs. *Res:* Transition metal chemistry; electrochemistry; drilling fluid and cement technology. *Mailing Add:* 1700 Cedar Lane Ponca City OK 74601

WHITFORD, ALBERT EDWARD, b Milton, Wis, Oct 22, 05; m 37; c 3. ASTROPHYSICS. *Educ:* Milton Col, BA, 26; Univ Wis, MA, 28, PhD(physics), 32. *Prof Exp:* Asst, Washburn Observ, Univ Wis, 32-33; Nat Res Coun fel, Mt Wilson Observ & Calif Inst Technol, 33-35; res assoc astron, Washburn Observ, Univ Wis, 35-38, asst prof astrophys, 38-46, assoc prof astron, 46-48, prof & dir observ, 48-58; astronomer & dir, 58-68, astronomer & prof, 68-73, EMER PROF ASTRON, LICK OBSERV, UNIV CALIF, SANTA CRUZ, 73- *Concurrent Pos:* Mem staff, Radiation Lab, Mass Inst Technol, 41-46. *Mem:* Nat Acad Sci; Am Astron Soc (vpres, 65-67, pres, 67-70); Am Acad Arts & Sci. *Res:* Photoelectric instrumentation; interstellar absorption; spectrophotometry of stars and galaxies; stellar population of galaxies. *Mailing Add:* 220 Morrissey Blvd Santa Cruz CA 95062

WHITFORD, GARY M, b Gouveneur, NY, Mar 9, 37; m 65; c 2. TOXICOLOGY, PHYSIOLOGY. *Educ:* Univ Rochester, BS, 65, MS, 69, PhD(toxicol), 72; Med Col Ga, DMD, 75. *Prof Exp:* Instr oral biol, NJ Dent Sch, 71-72; asst prof, 72-78, ASSOC PROF ORAL BIOL, MED COL GA, 78- *Mem:* Sigma Xi; Soc Exp Biol Med; Int Asn Dent Res. *Res:* Metabolism, biological effects and toxicology of fluoride. *Mailing Add:* Dept of Oral Biol Med Col of Ga Augusta GA 30902

WHITFORD, HOWARD WAYNE, b Benavides, Tex, Apr 6, 40; m 65; c 2. VETERINARY MICROBIOLOGY. *Educ:* Tex A&M Univ, BS, 63, DVM, 64, PhD(vet microbiol), 76; Am Col Vet Microbiologists, dipl, 73. *Prof Exp:* Vet lab officer res, US Army Med Unit, Frederick, Md, 65-68; vet officer, Rocky Mountain Lab, Nat Inst Allergy & Infectious Dis, USPHS, 68-70; NIH fel vet microbiol, Sch Vet Med, Tex A&M Univ, 70-71, from grad asst to instr, 71-74; BACTERIOLOGIST, DIAG SERV, TEX VET MED DIAG LAB, 74- *Mem:* Am Col Vet Microbiologists; Am Asn Vet Lab Diagnosticians; Am Vet Med Asn; US Animal Health Asn. *Res:* Bacteriologic diagnostic techniques; infectious diseases of sheep and goats; pathogenic bacteriology, immunology of infectious diseases. *Mailing Add:* Drawer 3040 College Station TX 77840

WHITFORD, LARRY ALSTON, b Ernul, NC, Apr 11, 02; m 28; c 4. BOTANY. *Educ:* NC State Col, BS, 25, MS, 29; Ohio State Univ, PhD(bot), 41. *Prof Exp:* High sch teacher, 25-26; from instr to prof, 26-68, EMER PROF BOT, NC STATE UNIV, 68- *Concurrent Pos:* Vis prof, Univ Va, 52 & Univ Fla, 53; consult, Duke Power Co Environ Labs, 73-81 & Aquatic Control, 75-81. *Mem:* AAAS; Phycol Soc Am (vpres, 56, pres, 57); Int Phycol Soc. *Res:* Floristics of fresh-water algae. *Mailing Add:* Dept of Bot NC State Univ Raleigh NC 27607

WHITFORD, PHILIP BURTON, b Argyle, Minn, Jan 9, 20; m 46; c 2. PLANT ECOLOGY. *Educ:* Northern Ill State Teachers Col, BEd, 41; Univ Ill, MS, 42; Univ Wis, PhD(bot), 48. *Prof Exp:* Asst bot, Univ Wis, 46-48; ed asst conserv, State Bd Natural Resources, Md, 48-49; from asst prof to assoc prof, 49-61, chmn dept, 66-69, PROF BOT, UNIV WIS-MILWAUKEE, 61- *Mem:* Fel AAAS; Ecol Soc Am; Am Inst Biol Sci. *Res:* Population and distribution of plants of the prairie-forest border; successions of native plants; resource management; applied ecology and conservation. *Mailing Add:* Dept of Bot Univ of Wis Milwaukee WI 53201

WHITFORD, WALTER GEORGE, b Providence, RI, June 12, 36; m 59, 69; c 3. ECOLOGY. *Educ:* Univ RI, BA, 61, PhD(zool), 64. *Prof Exp:* From asst prof to assoc prof, 64-72, PROF BIOL, N MEX STATE UNIV, 72- *Concurrent Pos:* Coordr Joranada Site & mem desert biome sect, Int Biol Prog, Nat Res Coun; ecol consult, Pub Serv Co NMex, 71- & Union Oil Co Calif, 74-; ed, Ecol Soc Am, 75- *Mem:* AAAS; Am Soc Ichthyologists & Herpetologists; Am Soc Naturalists; Ecol Soc Am; Entom Soc Am. *Res:* Desert ecology; ecology of social insects; arthropod physiological ecology. *Mailing Add:* Dept of Biol NMex State Univ Las Cruces NM 88001

WHITHAM, GERALD BERESFORD, b Halifax, Eng, Dec 13, 27; m 51; c 3. APPLIED MATHEMATICS. *Educ:* Univ Manchester, BSc, 48, MSc, 49, PhD, 53. *Prof Exp:* Res assoc, Inst Math Sci, NY Univ, 51-53; lectr math, Univ Manchester, 53-56; assoc prof, Inst Math Sci, NY Univ, 56-59; prof, Mass Inst Technol, 59-62; PROF MATH, CALIF INST TECHNOL, 62- *Mem:* Fel Am Acad Arts & Sci; fel Royal Soc. *Res:* Fluid dynamics. *Mailing Add:* Dept of Appl Math Calif Inst of Technol Pasadena CA 91125

WHITHAM, KENNETH, b Chesterfield, Eng, Nov 6, 27; m 53; c 3. GEOPHYSICS. *Educ:* Cambridge Univ, BA, 48, MA, 52; Univ Toronto, MA, 49, PhD(geophys), 51. *Prof Exp:* Geophysicist, Dom Observ, Ottawa, 51-64; chief div seismol, 64-73, DIR GEN, EARTH PHYSICS BR, CAN DEPT ENERGY, MINES & RESOURCES, 73- *Mem:* Fel Royal Soc Can. *Res:* Seismology; physics of the earth's interior, including geothermal studies; geomagnetism. *Mailing Add:* 580 Booth St Ottawa ON K2A 3S6 Can

WHITING, ALLEN R, US citizen. NONDESTRUCTIVE TESTING. *Educ:* Univ Tex, BS, 61. *Prof Exp:* X-ray lab technician, Univ Tex, 61; spray dept supvr, Aztec Tile Co, 61-62; asst res engr, Dept Mat Eng, 62-64, res engr, 64-67, sr res engr, 67-69, mgr appl eng, 69-70, mgr appl eng, Dept Spec Eng Serv, 70-72, asst dir, 72-74, dir, Dept Res & Eng, 74-75, dir, Dept Energy Serv, 75-78, EXEC DIR, QUAL ASSURANCE SYSTS & ENG DIV, SOUTHWEST RES INST, 78- *Mem:* Am Soc Nondestructive Testing; Am Soc Testing & Mat; Am Soc Mech Engrs. *Res:* Nondestructive testing including X- and gamma-radiography, ultrasonics, magnetic particle and penetrants as they are applied to solve industry problems and also in the research and development area. *Mailing Add:* Dept of Res & Eng PO Drawer 28510 San Antonio TX 78284

WHITING, ANNE MARGARET, b Morrisville, Vt, May 17, 41. VERTEBRATE ANATOMY, EMBRYOLOGY. *Educ:* Eastern Nazarene Col, AB, 63; Univ Ill, Urbana, MS, 65; Pa State Univ, PhD(zool), 69. *Prof Exp:* From asst prof to assoc prof, 68-73, PROF BIOL, HOUGHTON COL, 73- *Mem:* Sigma Xi; Am Soc Zoologists; Am Inst Biol Sci; Am Sci Affil. *Res:* Morphology, histology and histochemistry of squamate cloacal glands. *Mailing Add:* Dept of Biol Houghton Col Houghton NY 14744

WHITING, FRANK M, b Tucson, Ariz, Dec 5, 32; m 58; c 2. NUTRITION, BIOCHEMISTRY. *Educ:* Univ Ariz, BS, 56, MS, 68, PhD(agr biochem, nutrit), 71. *Prof Exp:* Field man qual control, United Dairymen Ariz, 56-60, res technician pesticide residues, 60-65; res asst, 65-71, asst prof & asst animal scientist, 71-76, assoc prof & assoc animal scientist, 76-81, PROF ANIMAL SCI & ANIMAL SCIENTIST, UNIV ARIZ, 81- *Mem:* Am Dairy Sci Asn. *Res:* Pesticide chemistry; ruminant nutrition; lipid metabolism; pesticide residues in feeds and animal products. *Mailing Add:* Dept Animal Sci Col Agr Univ Ariz Tucson AZ 85721

WHITING, JOHN DALE, JR, b New Castle, Pa, Mar 23, 47. FORENSIC TOXICOLOGY. *Educ:* Westminister Col, BS, 69; Duke Univ, PhD(biochem), 74. *Prof Exp:* Res assoc biol, Princeton Univ, 74-77; res assoc biochem, George Washington Univ, 77-79; RES CHEMIST TOXICOL, ARMED FORCES INST PATH, 79- *Concurrent Pos:* Mem, Subcomt Chromatographic Methods, Nat Comn Clin Lab Studies, 82- *Mem:* AAAS; Am Chem Soc; Am Acad Forensic Sci. *Res:* Isolation and identification of drugs and drug metabolites from tissues using high performance liquid chromatography, gas chromatography, gel chromatography and mass spectrometry and fourier transform infrared; development of analytical procedures to detect tetrahydrocannabinol and its metabolites in biological fluids and tissues. *Mailing Add:* 14002 Eagle Ct Rockville MD 20853

WHITING, R(OBERT) L(OUIS), b San Antonio, Tex, Feb 25, 18; m 44; c 3. PETROLEUM ENGINEERING. *Educ:* Univ Tex, BS, 39, MS, 42. *Prof Exp:* Instr petrol eng, Univ Tex, 39-43; assoc prof, Mo Sch Mines, 45-46; assoc prof, 46-50, head dept, 46-76, PROF PETROL ENG, TEX A&M UNIV, 50- *Concurrent Pos:* Int consult, US Fed Govt, FTC, var petrol co & foreign govts, 46-; dir, Tex Petrol Res Comt, 51-76. *Honors & Awards:* Mineral Indust Educ Award, Am Inst Mech Engrs, 73. *Mem:* Am Inst Mining, Metall & Petrol Engrs; Am Asn Univ Prof; Am Petrol Inst; Am Asn Eng Educ. *Res:* Drilling, production, transportation and marketing in petroleum and natural gas. *Mailing Add:* Dept of Petrol Eng Tex A&M Univ College Station TX 77843

WHITLA, WILLIAM ALEXANDER, b Galt, Ont, Oct 16, 38; m 64; c 3. STRUCTURAL CHEMISTRY. *Educ:* McMaster Univ, BSc, 60, PhD(inorg chem), 65. *Prof Exp:* Nat Res Coun overseas fel x-ray crystallog, Oxford Univ, 65-66; teaching fel, Univ BC, 66-67; asst prof, 67-75, ASSOC PROF CHEM, MT ALLISON UNIV, 75- *Mem:* Am Crystallog Asn; Chem Inst Can; The Chem Soc. *Res:* Bonding in inorganic adducts using x-ray crystallography. *Mailing Add:* Dept of Chem Mt Allison Univ Sackville NB E0A 3C0 Can

WHITLATCH, ROBERT BRUCE, b Boise, Idaho, July 18, 48. MARINE & POPULATION ECOLOGY. *Educ:* Univ Utah, BS, 70; Univ of the Pac, MS, 72; Univ Chicago, PhD(evolutionary biol), 76. *Prof Exp:* Scholar biol, Woods Hole Oceanog Inst, 76-77; ASST PROF BIOL, UNIV CONN, 77- *Mem:* AAAS; Am Inst Biol Sci. *Res:* Population community ecology of marine benthic systems; role of disturbance agents on community structure; resource partitioning in deposit feeding organisms. *Mailing Add:* Marine Res Lab PO Box 278 Noank CT 06340

WHITLEY, JAMES HEYWARD, b Goldsboro, NC, July 6, 26; m 59; c 3. ELECTRIC CONTACT THEORY. *Educ:* Antioch Col, BS, 51; Mass Inst Technol, MS, 54. *Prof Exp:* Res engr, 54-81, ASSOC RES DIR, AMP INC, 81- *Mem:* Inst Elec & Electronics Engrs; AAAS; Electrochem Soc; Am Phys Soc. *Res:* Electronic circuits; ferrite core memory devices; dielectric properties of materials; electric contact phenomena. *Mailing Add:* Bldg 21-01 Box 3608 AMP Inc Harrisburg PA 17105

WHITLEY, JAMES R, b Jamesport, Mo, Apr 21, 21; m 42. BIOCHEMISTRY, NUTRITION. *Educ:* Univ Mo, AB, 42, MS, 47, PhD(agr chem), 52. *Prof Exp:* Pvt herbicide bus, 52-62; SUPT FISHERIES RES, MO DEPT CONSERV, 62- *Mem:* Am Fisheries Soc; Weed Sci Soc Am; Water Pollution Control Fedn. *Res:* Ecology of fish and other aquatic organisms. *Mailing Add:* Mo Dept of Conserv 1110 College Ave Columbia MO 65201

WHITLEY, JOSEPH EFIRD, b Albemarle, NC, Mar 22, 31; m 58; c 2. RADIOLOGY. *Educ:* Wake Forest Col, BS, 51; Bowman Gray Sch Med, MD, 55; Am Bd Radiol, dipl, 60, cert nuclear med, 72. *Prof Exp:* Intern, Pa Hosp, Philadelphia, 55-56; resident radiol, NC Baptist Hosp, Winston-Salem, 56-69; from asst prof to prof radiol, Bowman Gray Sch Med, 62-78; PROF DIAG RADIOL & CHMN DEPT, UNIV MD SCH MED, 78- *Concurrent Pos:* James Picker Found scholar radiol res, Bowman Gray Sch Med, 59-61, advan fel acad radiol, Karolinska Inst, Sweden & Mass Inst Technol, 61-62; consult, Epilepsy Prog, Nat Inst Neurol Dis & Blindness, 67- *Mem:* Am Fedn Clin Res; Asn Univ Radiol; Radiol Soc NAm; Soc Nuclear Med; Am Roentgen Ray Soc. *Res:* Description and evaluation of cardiovascular phenomena by angiographic and radioisotopic techniques, particularly renovascular hypertension and pulmonary embolism; evaluation of modes of medical education. *Mailing Add:* Dept of Diag Radiol 22 Greene St Baltimore MD 21201

WHITLEY, LARRY STEPHEN, b Mattoon, Ill, Jan 30, 37; m 58; c 3. ENVIRONMENTAL BIOLOGY. *Educ:* Eastern Ill Univ, BS, 58; Purdue Univ, MS, 60, PhD(ecol), 63. *Prof Exp:* Instr environ biol, Purdue Univ, 63; from asst prof to assoc prof, 63-71, PROF ZOOL, EASTERN ILL UNIV, 71- *Concurrent Pos:* NIH res grants, 65-67; Fed Water Qual Admin grant, Dept Interior, 69-71. *Mem:* AAAS; Ecol Soc Am; Soc Syst Zool. *Res:* Physiology and systematics of tubificid worms; biology of polluted aquatic ecosystems and the tolerance mechanisms of aquatic organisms. *Mailing Add:* Dept of Zool Eastern Ill Univ Charleston IL 61920

WHITLEY, NANCY O'NEIL, b Winston-Salem, NC, Feb 21, 32; m 58; c 2. RADIOLOGY. *Educ:* Bowman Gray Sch Med, MD, 57. *Prof Exp:* Intern, Jefferson Davis Hosp, Houston, Tex, 57-58; cardiovasc trainee, Bowman Gray Sch Med, 59-61; physician, Med Dept, Western Elec Co, 63-66; resident radiol, Bowman Gray Sch Med, 66-69, from instr to assoc prof, 69-78; PROF RADIOL, UNIV MD SCH MED, 78- *Concurrent Pos:* Fel cardiol, Bowman Gray Sch Med, 58-59. *Mem:* Am Col Radiol; AMA; Asn Univ Radiologists; Radiol Soc NAm. *Res:* Techniques and procedures of angiography. *Mailing Add:* Dept of Radiol 22 Greene St Baltimore MD 21201

WHITLEY, WILLIAM THURMON, b Deland, Fla, Oct 24, 41; m 68. MATHEMATICS. *Educ:* Stetson Univ, BS, 63; Univ NC, Chapel Hill, MA, 66; Va Polytech Inst & State Univ, PhD(math), 69. *Prof Exp:* Instr math, Va Polytech Inst & State Univ, 69-70; assoc prof math, Marshall Univ, 70-79; ASSOC PROF, UNIV NEW HAVEN, 79- *Mem:* Am Math Soc; Math Asn Am. *Res:* Deleted products of topological spaces; rings of continuous real-valued functions. *Mailing Add:* Dept of Math Univ New Haven West Haven CT 06516

WHITLOCK, CHARLES HENRY, b Richmond, Va, Mar 24, 39; m 62; c 2. CIVIL & AERONAUTICAL ENGINEERING. *Educ:* Univ Va, BAE, 61, MAE, 65; Col William & Mary, MBA, 70; Old Dominion Univ, PhD(civil eng), 77. *Prof Exp:* Aerospace res engr, flight mechanics, 61-70, head syst dynamics sect, 70-72, asst head marine anal sect, 72-74, head data anal sect, 74-76, head wave modeling group, 74-77, HEAD SPECTRAL SIGNATURE & OPTICAL MODELING GROUP, MARINE ENVIRON, NASA LANGLEY RES CTR, 76- *Concurrent Pos:* Instr math, Hampton Inst, 66-67. *Mem:* Am Soc Civil Eng; Am Soc Photogram. *Res:* Remote sensing including optical modeling of spectral signals. *Mailing Add:* NASA Langley Res Ctr Mail Stop 272 Hampton VA 23665

WHITLOCK, DAVID GRAHAM, b Portland, Ore, Aug 26, 24; m 48; c 3. NEUROANATOMY, NEUROPHYSIOLOGY. *Educ:* Ore State Col, BS, 46; Univ Ore, MD, 49, PhD, 51. *Prof Exp:* Instr anat, Med Sch, Univ Ore, 50-51; asst prof, Univ Calif, Los Angeles, 51-54; from asst prof to prof, State Univ NY Upstate Med Ctr, 55-67, chmn dept, 66-67; PROF ANAT & CHMN DEPT, UNIV COLO MED CTR, DENVER, 67- *Concurrent Pos:* Fulbright res scholar, Inst Physiol, Pisa, Italy, 51-52; consult, US Sci Exhibit, 61 & Neurol Study Sect, USPHS, 60-64; chmn, Neurol B Study Sect, Nat Inst Neurol Dis & Blindness, 66-67. *Mem:* Am Asn Anatomists; Int Brain Res Orgn. *Res:* Anatomy and physiology of peripheral and central nervous system pathways. *Mailing Add:* 4200 E 9th Ave Denver CO 80220

WHITLOCK, GAYLORD PURCELL, b Mt Vernon, Ill, July 7, 17; m 41; c 2. AGRICULTURE, BIOCHEMISTRY. *Educ:* Southern Ill Univ, BEd, 39; Pa State Col, MS, 41, PhD(agr, biochem), 42. *Prof Exp:* Res asst, Iowa State Col, 43-46, asst prof, 46-47; specialist nutrit serv, Merck & Co, Inc, 47-56; dir health ed, Nat Dairy Coun, 56-61; prog leader family & consumer sci, Agr Exten Serv, 61-74, agriculturist coop exten & vpres agr sci, 73-74, exten nutritionist, 74-80, EMER EXTEN NUTRITIONIST, UNIV CALIF, BERKELEY, 80- *Mem:* Am Chem Soc; Inst Food Technol; Soc Nutrtit Educ; Am Inst Chemists; NY Acad Sci. *Res:* Vitamins; human and animal nutrition; foods. *Mailing Add:* 3980 Rockville Rd Suisun CA 94585

WHITLOCK, HAROLD E(ARL), chemical engineering, see previous edition

WHITLOCK, JOHN HENDRICK, b Medicine Hat, Alta, Sept 10, 13; US citizen; m 35; c 2. VETERINARY PARASITOLOGY, PARASITOLOGY. *Educ:* Iowa State Univ, DVM, 34; Kans State Univ, MS, 35. *Prof Exp:* Asst zool, Kans State Univ, 34-35, from instr to asst prof path, 35-44; from asst prof to assoc prof, 44-51, prof, 51-79, EMER PROF PARASITOL, NY STATE COL VET MED & DIV BIOL SCI, CORNELL UNIV, 79- *Concurrent Pos:* Mem bd trustees, Cornell Univ, 71-76. *Mem:* Fel AAAS; Am Soc Parasitologists; Am Vet Med Asn; Biomet Soc. *Res:* Population biology of parasitisms and disease; experimental epidemiology. *Mailing Add:* Prev Med NY State Vet Col Cornell Univ Ithaca NY 14853

WHITLOCK, L RONALD, b Canton, Pa, July 6, 44; m 68; c 2. ANALYTICAL CHEMISTRY, POLYMER CHEMISTRY. *Educ:* Pa State Univ, BS, 66; Univ Mass, PhD(anal chem), 71. *Prof Exp:* Fel polymer sci, Univ Mass, 70-72; RES ASSOC, EASTMAN KODAK CO RES LABS, 72- *Mem:* Am Chem Soc; Sigma Xi. *Res:* Development of new methods for chemical analysis of polymers and chemicals using modern analytical instruments. *Mailing Add:* Eastman Kodak Co Res Labs 1669 Lake Ave Rochester NY 14650

WHITLOCK, LAPSLEY CRAIG, b Lebanon, Ky, Aug 31, 42; m 62; c 3. EXPERIMENTAL NUCLEAR PHYSICS, SPECTROSCOPY. *Educ:* Georgetown Col, BS, 64; Vanderbilt Univ, PhD, 69. *Prof Exp:* Asst prof, 69-75, assoc prof, 75-81, PROF PHYSICS, MISS COL, 81-, HEAD DEPT, 70- *Mem:* Am Phys Soc; Am Asn Physics Teachers. *Res:* Gamma ray spectroscopy in decay of radioactive nuclides. *Mailing Add:* Dept of Physics Miss Col Clinton MS 39058

WHITLOCK, RICHARD T, b Columbus, Ohio, July 8, 31; m 60; c 1. THEORETICAL PHYSICS. *Educ:* Capital Univ, BS, 58; Western Reserve Univ, MS, 61, PhD(physics), 63. *Prof Exp:* Asst physics, Western Reserve Univ, 58-60, instr, 62-63; from asst prof to assoc prof, Thiel Col, 63-67; ASSOC PROF PHYSICS, UNIV NC, GREENSBORO, 67-, DIR RESIDENTIAL COL, 77- *Mem:* Am Asn Physics Teachers. *Res:* Many-body boson problem with applications to the theory of liquid helium; two-fluid hydrodynamics with applications to the theory of liquid helium; light and sound interactions. *Mailing Add:* Dept of Physics Univ of NC Greensboro NC 27412

WHITLOCK, ROBERT HENRY, b Canton, Pa, July 28, 41; m 63; c 3. VETERINARY MEDICINE, PATHOLOGY. *Educ:* Cornell Univ, DVM, 65, PhD(nutrit path), 70. *Prof Exp:* Intern vet med, NY State Vet Col, Cornell Univ, 65-67, NIH spec fel, 69-70, asst prof, 70-76; assoc prof vet med, Col Vet Med, Univ Ga, 76-78; CHIEF LARGE ANIMAL MED, UNIV PA VET COL, 78- *Mem:* Comp Gastroenterol Soc; Am Soc Vet Clin Path; Am Vet Med Asn. *Res:* Pathogenesis of metabolic diseases in domestic animals. *Mailing Add:* New Boltan Ctr Univ of Pa Vet Col Kennett Square PA 19348

WHITLOW, GRAHAM ANTHONY, b Cardiff, Wales, May 12, 38; m 62; c 2. METALLURGY. *Educ:* Univ Manchester, BScTech, 59; Univ Wales, PhD(metall), 62. *Prof Exp:* Sci officer metall, Atomic Weapons Res Estab, UK Atomic Energy Authority, 62-67; fel engr, Advan Reactors Div, 67-79, FEL ENGR, METALL DEPT RES & DEVELOP CTR, WESTINGHOUSE ELEC CORP, 79- *Mem:* Am Inst Mining, Metall & Petrol Engrs; Metall Soc; Am Inst Mech Engrs; Nat Asn Corrosion Engrs. *Res:* Energy materials development; effects of corrosive environments on high temperature materials; turbine materials development. *Mailing Add:* Westinghouse Res & Develop Ctr 1310 Beulah Rd Pittsburgh PA 15235

WHITLOW, LON WEIDNER, b Scottsville, Ky, Aug 26, 50; m 75; c 1. ANIMAL SCIENCE & NUTRITION. *Educ:* Univ Ky, BS, 72; Univ Fla, MS, 74; Univ Wis, PhD(dairy sci), 79. *Prof Exp:* Res asst, Univ Fla, 72-74, asst exten dairyman, 74-75; res asst, Univ Wis, 74-79; EXTEN DAIRY HUSBANDRY SPECIALIST, NC STATE UNIV, RALEIGH, 79- *Mem:* Am Dairy Sci Asn; Am Soc Animal Sci; Sigma Xi. *Res:* The optimum feeding and nutrition of dairy cattle. *Mailing Add:* Dept Animal Sci 105 Polk Hall NC State Univ Raleigh NC 27650

WHITMAN, ALAN B, b Joliet, Ill, Apr 7, 41. CONTINUUM MECHANICS, MECHANICS. *Educ:* Univ Ill, Urbana, BS, 63; Univ Minn, Minneapolis, MS, 66, PhD(eng mech), 68. *Prof Exp:* Res asst mech, Univ Minn, 63-64; engr, Honeywell, Inc, 64-65; res asst mech, Univ Minn, 65-66; res asst biomech, 66-68, asst prof mech, 68-71, assoc prof, 71-79, PROF MECH, WAYNE STATE UNIV, 79- *Concurrent Pos:* NSF initiation grant, Wayne State Univ, 69-70, res grants, 71-73 & 74-77; res fel, Univ Manitoba, 78-79. *Mem:* Soc Eng Sci; Am Acad Mech. *Res:* Theories of rods and shells, stability theory of continuous systems. *Mailing Add:* Dept Mech Eng Wayne State Univ Detroit MI 48202

WHITMAN, ALAN M, b Philadelphia, Pa, Jan 26, 37; m 59; c 2. MECHANICAL ENGINEERING. *Educ:* Univ Pa, BSME, 58, MSME, 59, PhD(mech eng), 66. *Prof Exp:* Sr res engr, Power Transmission Div, Gen Elec Co, 65-67; asst prof mech eng, Univ Pa, 67-72, assoc prof, 72-80; ASSOC PROF INTERDISCIPLINARY STUDIES, SCH ENG, TEL AVIV UNIV, 80- *Mem:* Am Phys Soc; Am Soc Mech Engrs; Am Inst Aeronaut & Astronaut. *Res:* Plasma physics; gaseous electronics; gas discharges; hydrodynamic impact. *Mailing Add:* Sch Eng Tel Aviv Univ Tel Aviv Israel

WHITMAN, ANDREW PETER, b Detroit, Mich, Feb 28, 26. MATHEMATICS. *Educ:* Tulane Univ, BS, 45; Cath Univ, MS, 58, PhD(math), 61; Woodstock Col, Md, STL, 64. *Prof Exp:* Instr civil eng, Tulane Univ, 46-51; asst prof math, Loyola Univ, La, 65-66, actg chmn dept, 66-67; from asst prof to assoc prof math, Univ Houston, 67-74; ASSOC PROF MATH, CATH UNIV RIO DE JANEIRO SUL, BRAZIL, 74- *Concurrent Pos:* NSF res grant, 66-68. *Mem:* Am Math Soc; Math Asn Am; Soc Brasileria Math. *Res:* Differential topology and geometry. *Mailing Add:* Rua Marques de S Vicente 293 Rio de Janeiro 22.451 Brazil

WHITMAN, CHARLES INKLEY, b New York, NY, Mar 17, 25; m 50; c 5. PHYSICAL CHEMISTRY. *Educ:* Yale Univ, BS, 44, PhD(phys chem), 49. *Prof Exp:* From instr to asst prof chem, NY Univ, 49-53; sr engr, Atomic Energy Div, Sylvania Elec Prod, Inc, 52-54, adv res engr, 54-55, sect head, 55-57, mgr mkt, Sylvania-Corning Nuclear Corp, 57-60, eng specialist, Gen Tel & Electronics Labs, 60-61; asst tech dir, Int Copper Res Asn, Inc, NY, 61-64, tech dir chem, 64-70; dir res & develop, Phelps Dodge Industs, Inc, 70-75; DIR RES & DEVELOP, GLIDDEN METALS GROUP, SCM CORP, 75- *Mem:* Am Powder Metall Inst; Am Soc Metals; Am Inst Mining, Metall & Petrol Engrs. *Res:* Metal fabrication; powder metallurgy; electrical conductors. *Mailing Add:* SCM Corp-Glidden Metals Group 11000 Cedar Ave Cleveland OH 44106

WHITMAN, DONALD RAY, b Ft Wayne, Ind, Nov 7, 31; div; 75; c 2. THEORETICAL CHEMISTRY, PHYSICAL CHEMISTRY. *Educ:* Case Western Reserve Univ, BS, 53; Yale Univ, PhD(phys chem), 57. *Prof Exp:* From asst prof to assoc prof phys chem, 57-70, assoc vpres, 72-74, V PRES, CASE WESTERN RESERVE UNIV, 74-, PROF PHYS CHEM, 70- *Mem:* Am Phys Soc; AAAS. *Res:* Molecular quantum mechanics. *Mailing Add:* Adelbert Hall Case Western Reserve Univ Cleveland OH 44106

WHITMAN, ERWIN N, medical research administration, see previous edition

WHITMAN, GERALD MARTIN, b New York, NY, Jan 18, 41; m 63; c 2. ANTENNAS, MILLIMETER WAVES. *Educ:* Queens Col, BS, 63; Columbia Univ, BSEE, 63; Polytech Inst NY, MS, 67, PhD(electrophysics), 69. *Prof Exp:* Fel electrophysics, Dept Elec Eng, Polytech Inst NY, 69-70; asst prof, 70-78, ASSOC PROF ELEC ENG, NJ INST TECHNOL, 78- *Concurrent Pos:* Consult, Antenna Team, US Army, Ft Monmouth, 73-76, Millimeter Wave Team, 80- & Microwave Res Inst, Polytech Inst NY, 79; delegate, NATO Advan Study Inst, Univ East Anglia, Eng, 79; vis prof, Dept Elec Eng, Polytech Inst NY, 80-81. *Mem:* Inst Elec & Electronics Engrs; Sigma Xi. *Res:* Electromagnetics: scattering from periodic surfaces, radiation by integrated dielectric waveguides and antenna devices, transmission and compression of signals in plasma media and scattering in random media using transport theory. *Mailing Add:* Dept Elec Eng NJ Inst Technol Newark NJ 07102

WHITMAN, PHILIP MARTIN, b Pittsburgh, Pa, Dec 23, 16. MATHEMATICS. *Educ:* Haverford Col, BS, 37; Harvard Univ, AM, 38, PhD(math), 41. *Prof Exp:* Instr math, Harvard Univ, 38-41 & Univ Pa, 41-44; scientist, Los Alamos Sci Lab, Univ Calif, 44-46; asst prof math, Tufts Col, 46-48; mathematician, Appl Physics Lab, Johns Hopkins Univ, 48-61; chmn dept, 61-67, PROF MATH, RI COL, 61- *Concurrent Pos:* Consult, Weapons Systs Eval Group, Off Secy Defense, 51-55; Parsons fel, Johns Hopkins Univ, 58-59; consult, Opers Eval Group, Off Chief Naval Opers, 60-61. *Mem:* AAAS; Am Math Soc; Opers Res Soc Am; Math Asn Am. *Res:* Lattice theory; operations research; authored college algebra and trigonometry texts. *Mailing Add:* Dept of Math RI Col Providence RI 02908

WHITMAN, ROBERT V(AN DUYNE), b Pittsburgh, Pa, Feb 2, 28; m 54; c 2. CIVIL & EARTHQUAKE ENGINEERING. *Educ:* Swarthmore Col, BS, 48; Mass Inst Technol, SM, 49, ScD(civil eng), 51. *Prof Exp:* Res engr, 51-53, from asst prof to assoc prof civil eng, 53-63, PROF CIVIL ENG, MASS INST TECHNOL, 63- *Concurrent Pos:* Consult, govt & indust, 54-; engr, Stanford Res Inst, 63-64; vis scholar, Cambridge Univ, Eng, 76-77; mem Earthquake Eng Res Inst (dir 78-81, vpres 79-81). *Honors & Awards:* Prize, Am Soc Civil Engrs, 62; Terzaghi lectr, Am Soc Civil Engrs, 81. *Mem:* Nat Acad Eng; Am Soc Civil Engrs; Seismol Soc Am; Int Soc Soil Mech & Found Engrs. *Res:* Soil mechanics, especially dynamic problems. *Mailing Add:* Dept of Civil Eng Mass Inst of Technol Cambridge MA 02139

WHITMAN, ROLLIN LAWRENCE, b Pittsfield, Mass, Aug 25, 47; m 70; c 2. ELECTRICAL ENGINEERING, COMPUTER SCIENCE. *Educ:* Univ Wis, BSEE, 70; Univ Colo, MSEE, 74. *Prof Exp:* Engr sci programmer, Martin Marietta Co, 70-76; STAFF MEM SIGNAL PROCESS & IMAGE ANAL, LOS ALAMOS SCI LAB, 76- *Mem:* Inst Elect & Electronic Engrs; Optical Soc Am; Am Vacuum Soc. *Res:* Computer image processing and signal analysis in laser fusion target inspection, modeling reactor safety coolant problems; two-dimensional digital filtering on both large scale computers and interactive- minicomputer systems. *Mailing Add:* Los Alamos Sci Lab Box 1663 Los Alamos NM 87545

WHITMAN, ROY MILTON, b New York, NY, June 16, 25; m 68; c 4. PSYCHIATRY. *Educ:* Ind Univ, BS, 44, MD, 46. *Prof Exp:* Intern, Kings County Hosp, 46-47; resident psychiat, Duke Hosp, 47-48; from instr to asst prof, Univ Chicago, 52-54; from asst prof to assoc prof neurol & psychiat, Med Sch, Northwestern Univ, 54-57, assoc prof, 57; assoc prof, 57-67, PROF PSYCHIAT, COL MED, UNIV CINCINNATI, 67-, ACTG CHMN DEPT, 80- *Concurrent Pos:* USPHS fel, Clins, Univ Chicago, 50-52; chief neurol & psychiat, Vet Admin Res Hosp, Chicago, Ill, 54-57; consult, Vet Admin Hosp, Cincinnati, Ohio, 57-, Ill State Psychiat Inst, 63-68, Cent Clin, Cincinnati, Ohio & Vet Admin Res Hosp, Chicago; clinician, Cincinnati Gen Hosp. *Mem:* Soc Personality Assessment; Am Psychiat Asn; Am Psychoanal Asn; Int Psychoanal Asn. *Res:* Psychophysiology of dreaming; sex research; psychoanalytic methods; techniques in psychoanalysis; psychosomatic medicine. *Mailing Add:* Dept Psychiat Cincinnati Gen Hosp Cincinnati OH 45267

WHITMARSH, CLIFFORD JOHN, b San Diego, Calif, Apr 11, 46; m 80; c 4. BIOPHYSICS. *Educ:* Harvard Univ, MA, 70, PhD(physics), 75. *Prof Exp:* Fel biophysics, Ctr Nuclear Studies Saclay, France, 74-75; fel biophysics, Purdue Univ, 75-79; asst prof, Queens's Univ, Can, 80; ASST PROF, UNIV ILL, 81- *Concurrent Pos:* NSF fel. *Mem:* Biophys Soc; Am Soc Photobiol; Am Soc Plant Physiol. *Res:* Investigation of charge transfer reactions in photosynthetic membranes. *Mailing Add:* Dept Bot Univ Ill 505 S Goodwin St Urbana IL 61801

WHITMER, JOHN CHARLES, b Kingfisher, Okla, Jan 28, 39. PHYSICAL CHEMISTRY. *Educ:* Univ Rochester, BS, 60; Univ Mich, MS, 62, PhD(chem), 65. *Prof Exp:* Asst prof chem, Western Wash Univ, 65-66; lectr, Univ E Africa, 67-69; from asst prof to assoc prof, 69-76, PROF CHEM, WESTERN WASH UNIV, 76- *Mem:* AAAS; Am Chem Soc. *Res:* Molecular spectroscopy. *Mailing Add:* Dept of Chem Western Wash Univ Bellingham WA 98225

WHITMER, ROBERT MOREHOUSE, b Battle Creek, Mich, June 14, 08; m 36, 51; c 2. PHYSICS, ELECTRICAL ENGINEERING. *Educ:* Univ Mich, BA, 28, MA, 34, PhD(physics), 38. *Prof Exp:* Mem staff, Bell Tel Labs, Inc, 28-32; mem fac, Amherst Col, 32-33; engr, Philco Radio & TV Corp, Pa, 35-36; physicist, Hercules Powder Co, 36; instr physics, Purdue Univ, 37-41; mem staff, Radiation Lab, Mass Inst Technol, 41-46; prof physics, Rensselaer Polytech Inst, 46-56; sr staff physicist, TRW Systs, 56-73; CONSULT, 73- *Concurrent Pos:* Consult, US Air Force, 52-53; mem, Security Resources Panel, Off Defense Mobilization, 57; mem, Reentry Body Identification Group, Off Secy Defense, 58. *Mem:* AAAS; Am Phys Soc; sr mem Inst Elec & Electronics Engrs. *Res:* Electromagnetics; wave propagation; electromagnetic shielding; operations analyses. *Mailing Add:* 724 Tenth St Manhattan Beach CA 90266

WHITMER, ROMAYNE FLEMMING, b Chicago, Ill, Sept 5, 25; m 48; c 3. ELECTRO-OPTICS. *Educ:* Univ NMex, BS, 46, Univ Wash, MS, 48; Polytech Inst Brooklyn, PhD(elec eng), 55. *Prof Exp:* Res engr, Sylvania Elec Prod, NY, 48-51; res scientist, Hazeltine Electronics Corp, 51; staff mem, Los Alamos Sci Lab, 52-56; head plasma physics dept, Microwave Physics Lab, Gen Tel & Electronics Labs, Calif, 56-60, lab mgr & res dir, 60-63; asst mgr, Electronic Sci Lab, 63-65, mgr & res dir, 65-72, dir commun & info sci, 72-75, prog mgr, Air Force Laser Progs, 75-77, proposal mgr, Army Homing Overlay Exp, 77-78, PROPOSAL MGR, ARMY RPV SYST, LOCKHEED MISSILES & SPACE CO, 78- *Concurrent Pos:* Mem US Nat Comt, Comn VI, Int Sci Radio Union, 66- *Mem:* Fel Am Phys Soc; Inst Elec & Electronics Engrs; fel Am Phys Soc. *Res:* Electromagnetics; network theory; traveling wave tubes; plasma physics; interaction of electromagnetic waves with ionized gases; laser and optical communications. *Mailing Add:* Lockheed Missiles & Space Co Po Box 504 Dept 90-03 Bldg 150 Sunnyvale CA 94086

WHITMIRE, CARRIE ELLA, b Electra, Tex, Oct 17, 26. BACTERIOLOGY. *Educ:* Univ Tex, BA, 46; Univ Kans, MA, 53, PhD(bact), 55. *Prof Exp:* Bacteriologist, Parkland Hosp, Dallas, Tex, 46-47, Vet Admin Hosp, 47-48 & US Army Chem Ctr, Ft Detrick, Md, 48-52; asst virologist, Univ Kans, 52-55; assoc scientist, Ortho Res Found, NJ, 55-61; proj supvr, Merck Sharp & Dohme Biol Div, Pa, 61-64; tech asst, Winthrop Labs, Biol, NY, 64-67; proj dir & vinaloncologist, Microbiol Assocs, Inc, 67-75, dir dept exp oncol, 75-78; toxicologist, Nat Cancer Inst, 79-81; TOXICOLOGIST, HEAD QUAL ASSURANCE SECT, PROG OPERATION BR, NAT TOXICOL PROG, NAT INST ENVIRON HEALTH SCI, 81- *Mem:* Am Soc Microbiol; Tissue Cult Asn; Soc Exp Biol & Med; Soc Toxicol. *Res:* Medical virology and bacteriology; cancer research. *Mailing Add:* Nat Toxicol Prog Environ Health Sci 7910 Woodmont Ave Bethesda MD 20014

WHITMORE, BRADLEY CHARLES, b Minneapolis, Minn, Jan 14, 53; m 77; c 2. GALACTIC STRUCTURE, GALACTIC DYNAMICS. *Educ:* Univ Mich, BS, 75, MS, 77, PhD(astron), 80. *Prof Exp:* Instr, Univ Mich, 80; CARNEGIE FEL ASTRON, DEPT TERRESTRIAL MAGNETISM, CARNEGIE INST WASHINGTON, 80- *Mem:* Am Astron Soc. *Res:* Structure, dynamics, and evolution of galaxies; comparison of the dynamics of ellipticle galaxies with the spheroidal component of spiral galaxies. *Mailing Add:* Dept Terrestrial Magnetism Carnegie Inst 5241 Broad Br Rd NW Washington DC 20015

WHITMORE, D(ONALD) H(ERBERT), metallurgy, ceramics, see previous edition

WHITMORE, DONALD HERBERT, JR, b Buffalo, NY, May 6, 44; m 70. COMPARATIVE PHYSIOLOGY. *Educ:* Ind Univ, BA, 66; Northwestern Univ, PhD(biol sci), 71. *Prof Exp:* NIH fel insect physiol, Northwestern Univ, 71-73; ASST PROF BIOL, UNIV TEX, ARLINGTON, 73- *Mem:* Sigma Xi; Am Fisheries Soc; Am Soc Zoologists. *Res:* The role of environmental influences on the physiology and biochemistry of animals, particularly how animals adapt to environmental stress. *Mailing Add:* Dept of Biol Univ of Tex Arlington TX 76019

WHITMORE, EDWARD HUGH, b Ottawa, Ill, Feb 26, 26; m 49; c 2. GEOMETRY. *Educ:* Ill State Univ, BS, 48, MS, 51; Ohio State Univ, PhD(math ed, math), 56. *Prof Exp:* Instr high sch, Ill, 48-51; asst prof math, Northern Ill Univ, 55-56; from asst prof to assoc prof, San Francisco State Col, 56-6S; chmn dept, 65-74, PROF MATH, CENT MICH UNIV, 65-, CHMN DEPT, 76- *Mem:* Math Asn Am. *Res:* Mathematics education; sequences in elementary geometry and their history. *Mailing Add:* Dept of Math Cent Mich Univ Mt Pleasant MI 48858

WHITMORE, FRANK WILLIAM, b Ponca City, Okla, May 15, 32; m 55; c 3. PLANT PHYSIOLOGY, BIOCHEMISTRY. *Educ:* Okla State Univ, BS, 54; Univ Mich, MF, 56, PhD(forestry), 64. *Prof Exp:* Res forester, US Forest Serv, 57-61, plant physiologist, 64-65; res assoc forestry, Univ Mich, 65-67; from asst prof to assoc prof, 67-76, PROF FORESTRY, OHIO AGR RES & DEVELOP CTR, OHIO STATE UNIV, 76- *Mem:* AAAS; Soc Am Foresters; Am Soc Plant Physiologists. *Res:* Protoplast technology; lignin biochemistry; tissue culture; physiology of wood formation. *Mailing Add:* Dept of Forestry Ohio Agr Res & Develop Ctr Wooster OH 44691

WHITMORE, GORDON FRANCIS, b Saskatoon, Sask, June 29, 31; m 54; c 2. RADIOBIOLOGY, CANCER. *Educ:* Univ Sask, BA, 53, MA, 54; Yale Univ, PhD(biophys), 57. *Prof Exp:* From asst prof to assoc prof, 60-65, PROF BIOPHYS, UNIV TORONTO, 65-, HEAD DEPT, 71-, ASSOC DEAN FAC MED, 74-; PHYSICIST, ONT CANCER INST, 56-, ASSOC DIR PHYS DIV, 57-, CHMN DEPT MED BIOPHYSICS, 80- *Concurrent Pos:* Vis prof, Pa State Univ, 63; mem, Nat Cancer Inst Grants Panel, 63- & Nat Res Coun Assoc Comt Radiobiol, 64-; mem radiation study sect, NIH, 65- *Honors & Awards:* Ernest Berry-Anderson Prize, Royal Soc Edinburgh, 66. *Mem:* Biophys Soc; Radiation Res Soc; Can Soc Cell Biol; Can Asn Physicists; Royal Soc Can. *Res:* Radiation physics; radiobiology of mammalian cells in vitro; action of chemotherapeutic agents; mammalian cell genetics. *Mailing Add:* Ont Cancer Inst 500 Sherbourne St Toronto ON M4X 1K9 Can

WHITMORE, HARRY E, b Denison, Tex, Dec 7, 20; m 42; c 2. MECHANICAL ENGINEERING. *Educ:* Tex A&M Univ, BS, 42; Purdue Univ, MS, 54. *Prof Exp:* Engr, Astronaut Div, Gen Dynamics, 63-64; RES ENGR, TEX ENG EXP STA, TEX A&M UNIV, 64- *Res:* Propulsion; space research. *Mailing Add:* Tex Eng Exp Sta Tex A&M Univ College Station TX 77843

WHITMORE, HOWARD LLOYD, b Dallas, Wis, Dec 3, 35; m 62; c 2. VETERINARY MEDICINE. *Educ:* Okla State Univ, BS, 58, DVM, 60; Univ Wis, PhD(vet sci), 73; Am Col Theriogenologists, dipl. *Prof Exp:* Vet pvt pract, 60-69; assoc prof, Col Vet Med, Univ Minn, St Paul, 74-80; MEM FAC, DEPT VET CLIN MED, COL VET MED, UNIV ILL, 80- *Honors & Awards:* Burr Beach Award, Dept Vet Sci, Univ Wis, 73. *Mem:* Am Vet Med Asn. *Res:* Fertility; abortion and pregnancy diagnosis in dairy cattle. *Mailing Add:* Dept Vet Clin Col Vet Med Univ Ill Urbana IL 61801

WHITMORE, MARY (ELIZABETH) ROWE, b Oakland, Calif, Oct 26, 36; m 61; c 3. ANATOMY, ZOOLOGY. *Educ:* Univ Calif, Berkeley, BA, 59; Smith Col, MA, 61; Univ Minn, Minneapolis, PhD(anat), 69. *Prof Exp:* Teaching asst zool, Smith Col, 59-61; teaching asst anat, Univ Minn, Minneapolis, 61-66; vis asst prof, 70-71, ASST PROF ZOOL, UNIV OKLA, 72- *Mem:* AAAS; Am Soc Zool; Electron Microscopy Soc Am. *Res:* Comparative morphology and histology of endocrine glands in the lower vertebrates; biology of cyclostomes. *Mailing Add:* Dept of Zool Univ of Okla Norman OK 73019

WHITMORE, RALPH M, b Medina, Tex, Oct 22, 17; m 42; c 2. MATHEMATICS, PROBABILITY. *Educ:* Trinity Univ, BA, 38; Univ Tex, Austin, MA, 41, PhD(math), 64. *Prof Exp:* Instr math, Peacock Acad, 38-39; statistician electronics, City San Antonio, 39-40; instr math statist, Trinity Univ, 40-41; chief instr electronics math, Air Force Tech Sch, 42-44; PROF MATH, PHYSICS & COMPUT SCI & CHMN DEPT MATH, SOUTHWESTERN UNIV, 44- *Concurrent Pos:* Statistician & consult, Sandia Corp, 53-61; NSF fel, Univ Okla, 64. *Mem:* Math Asn Am; Soc Indust & Appl Math. *Mailing Add:* Dept of Math Southwestern Univ Georgetown TX 78626

WHITMORE, ROY ALVIN, JR, b Baltimore, Md, Aug 14, 28; m 53; c 3. FORESTRY. *Educ:* Univ Mich, BSF, 52, MF, 54. *Prof Exp:* Forest economist, Cent States Forest Exp Sta, USDA, 52-58; PROF FORESTRY, UNIV VT, 58- *Mem:* Soc Am Foresters; Forest Prod Res Soc. *Res:* Forest products utilization and marketing. *Mailing Add:* Dept of Forestry Univ of Vt Burlington VT 05401

WHITMORE, ROY WALTER, b San Antonio, Tex, Jan 21, 47; m 69; c 2. STATISTICS. *Educ:* Tex Tech Univ, BS, 69, MS, 71; PhD(statist), 78. *Prof Exp:* Instr math, Stephen F Austin State Univ, 69-71; lectr statist, Tex A&M Univ, 77-78; asst prof math, Univ NC, Greensboro, 78-80; STATISTICIAN, RES TRIANGLE INST, 80- *Mem:* Am Statist Asn; Biomet Soc. *Res:* Compartmental analysis; biological, medical and ecological modeling; general data analysis; linear models; nonlinear regression. *Mailing Add:* Surv Res & Design Ctr Res Triangle Inst Research Triangle Park NC 27713

WHITMORE, STEPHEN CARR, b Holyoke, Mass, Oct 17, 31; m 61; c 3. PHYSICS. *Educ:* Amherst Col, BA, 54; Univ Minn, PhD(liquid helium), 66. *Prof Exp:* Res assoc physics, Univ Mish, 66-69; asst prof, 69-82, ASSOC PROF PHYSICS, UNIV CALIF, 82- *Mem:* Am Phys Soc. *Res:* Low temperature physics; liquid helium; superconducters; semiconductors. *Mailing Add:* Dept Physics Univ Okla Norman OK 73019

WHITMORE, WILLIAM FRANCIS, b Boston, Mass, Jan 6, 17; m 46; c 4. MATHEMATICS, OCEANOGRAPHY. *Educ:* Mass Inst Technol, SB, 38; Univ Calif, PhD(math), 41. *Prof Exp:* With US Naval Ord Lab, Washington, DC, 41-42; instr physics, Mass Inst Technol, 42-46; opers analyst, Opers Eval Group, US Dept Navy, 46-57, chief scientist, Spec Projs Off, Bur Ord, 57-59; consult scientist, Chief Scientist's Staff, Lockheed Aircraft Corp, 59-62, dep chief scientist, 62-64, asst to pres, 64-69, sr consult scientist, 69-74, CHIEF SCIENTIST OCEAN SYSTS, LOCKHEED MISSILES & SPACE CO, 74- *Concurrent Pos:* Spec consult, Air Forces Eval Bd, 45; sci analyst, Commanding Gen, 1st Marine Air Wing, Korea, 53; consult, Defense Sci Bd, 66-68 & Marine Bd, Nat Acad Eng, 72-; chmn, Navy Lab Adv Bd, Ord, 67-75; vis comt dept math, Mass Inst Technol, 71-78. *Honors & Awards:* Meritorious Pub Serv Citation, US Dept Navy, 61. *Mem:* Am Math Soc; Optical Soc Am; Opers Res Soc Am; Math Asn Am; assoc fel Am Inst Aeronaut & Astronaut. *Res:* Classical boundary value problems in physics; weapon systems analysis; oceanography. *Mailing Add:* 14120 Miranda Ave Los Altos Hills CA 94022

WHITNEY, ARTHUR EDWIN, JR, b St Louis, Mo, Apr 21, 38. HEAT TRANSFER, THERMODYNAMICS. *Educ:* Wash Univ, BSME, 59, MS, 60, DSc(eng), 64. *Prof Exp:* Asst prof mech eng, Wash Univ, 64-65; SR GROUP ENGR, McDONNELL DOUGLAS CORP, 65- *Mem:* Am Soc Mech Engrs; Am Inst Aeronaut & Astronaut. *Res:* Heat transfer methods and computer applications applied to aircraft, missiles and spacecraft. *Mailing Add:* Thermodyn Div Lambert Field McDonnell Douglas Corp St Louis MO 63166

WHITNEY, ARTHUR SHELDON, b Oberlin, Ohio, Oct 31, 33; m 64; c 2. AGRONOMY. *Educ:* Ohio State Univ, BS, 55; Cornell Univ, MS, 58; Univ Hawaii, PhD(soil sci), 66. *Prof Exp:* Res instr agron, Univ Philippines, 59-60; from asst agronomist to assoc agronomist, 65-76, AGRONOMIST, HAWAII AGR EXP STA, 76- *Concurrent Pos:* Prin investr, Nitrogen Fixation by Legumes Prog, AID, 75-79. *Mem:* Crop Sci Soc Am; Am Soc Agron; Trop Grassland Soc Australia. *Res:* Pasture management; legume agronomy; plant nutrition. *Mailing Add:* Maui Res Ctr Hawaii Agr Exp Sta PO Box 187 Kula Maui HI 96790

WHITNEY, CHARLES ALLEN, b Milwaukee, Wis, Jan 31, 29; m 51; c 5. ASTROPHYSICS. *Educ:* Mass Inst Technol, BS, 51; Harvard Univ, AM, 53, PhD(astron), 55. *Prof Exp:* Assoc prof, 63-68, PROF ASTRON, HARVARD UNIV, 68-; PHYSICIST, SMITHSONIAN ASTROPHYS OBSERV, 56- *Concurrent Pos:* Guggenheim Found fel, 71. *Mem:* Int Astron Union; Am Astron Soc; Am Acad Arts & Sci. *Res:* History of astronomy; theory of variable stars and associated problems of gas dynamics. *Mailing Add:* Smithsonian Astrophys Observ Cambridge MA 02138

WHITNEY, CHARLES CANDEE, JR, b Newfane, Vt, Oct 12, 39; m 62; c 2. DRUG METABOLISM, PHARMACOKINETICS. *Educ:* Northeastern Univ, AB, 62; Middlebury Col, MS, 64; Univ Calif, Davis, PhD(org chem), 68. *Prof Exp:* Res chemist, E I du Pont de Nemours & Co, Inc, 68; asst chief clin chem, 3rd US Army Med Lab, 68-70; sr res biochemist, 70-80, RES ASSOC, STINE LAB, E I DU PONT DE NEMOURS & CO, INC, 80- *Concurrent Pos:* Mem, Drug Metabol Discussion Group. *Mem:* Am Chem Soc; Sigma Xi. *Res:* Pharmacokinetics, bioavailability and metabolic fate of drugs in the body; analytical methods for the determination of drugs and their metabolites. *Mailing Add:* 130 Timberline Dr Newark DE 19711

WHITNEY, COLIN GORDON, electrooptics, see previous edition

WHITNEY, CYNTHIA KOLB, b Cumberland, Md, July 11, 41; m 63; c 2. ATMOSPHERIC PHYSICS, MATHEMATICAL PHYSICS. *Educ:* Mass Inst Technol, SB, 63, SM, 65, PhD(physics), 68. *Prof Exp:* Staff physicist, 67-80, ASSOC DIV LEADER, CHARLES STARK DRAPER LAB, INC, 80- *Concurrent Pos:* Consult, Advan Appln Flight Exp Prog, NASA, 75. *Honors & Awards:* David Rist Prize, Military Opers Res Soc. *Mem:* AAAS; Am Meteorol Soc; Optical Soc Am; Am Inst Physics; Sigma Xi. *Res:* Statistical description of complex physical systems; decision analysis for flexible manufacturing systems and nuclear power generation systems; mathematical formalisms in fundamental physics. *Mailing Add:* Charles Stark Draper Lab Inc Cambridge MA 02139

WHITNEY, DANIEL EUGENE, b Chicago, Ill, June 8, 38; m 63; c 2. MECHANICAL ENGINEERING. *Educ:* Mass Inst Technol, SB, 60 & 61, MS, 65, PhD(mech eng), 68. *Prof Exp:* From asst prof to assoc prof mech eng, Mass Inst Technol, 68-74; SECT CHIEF, CHARLES STARK DRAPER LAB, 74- *Concurrent Pos:* Consult, Charles Stark Draper Lab, 68-74; mem, Automation Res Coun, 71-78; NSF grant, Mass Inst Technol, 72-73 & Charles Stark Draper Lab, 78-80 & 79-81. *Mem:* Inst Elec & Electronics Engrs; Am Soc Mech Engrs; Robotics Inst Am. *Res:* Application of computers to control systems and to engineering design and manufacturing; robotics. *Mailing Add:* C S Draper Lab 555 Technol Sq Cambridge MA 02139

WHITNEY, DAVID EARLE, b Springfield, Vt, June 18, 40; m 66; c 2. MARINE ECOLOGY. *Educ:* Univ Vt, BA, 63, MS, 65; Univ Del, PhD(biol), 73. *Prof Exp:* Res assoc biol, Brookhaven Nat Lab, 72-75; RES ASSOC BIOL, MARINE INST, UNIV GA, 75- *Mem:* AAAS; Am Soc Limnol & Oceanog; Sigma Xi; Ecol Soc Am. *Res:* Algal primary productivity and nutrient cycling in estuarine and coastal ecosystems. *Mailing Add:* Univ of Ga Marine Inst Sapelo Island GA 31327

WHITNEY, DONALD RANSOM, b Cleveland Heights, Ohio, Nov 27, 15; m 39; c 4. STATISTICS, MATHEMATICAL STATISTICS. *Educ:* Oberlin Col, BA, 36; Princeton Univ, MA, 39; Ohio State Univ, PhD(math), 48. *Prof Exp:* Instr math, Mary Washington Col, 39-42; prof math, 48-70, chmn dept, 70-80, PROF STATIST, OHIO STATE UNIV, 70- *Concurrent Pos:* Consult, Burgess & Niple Ltd, Ohio Bell Tel Co, Pub Utilities Comn, Cincinnati Bell Tel Co, NAm Aviation & Goodyear Atomic Corp. *Mem:* Fel AAAS; fel Am Statist Asn; Inst Math Statist; Biomet Soc; Am Math Soc. *Res:* Non-parametric statistics; general statistical methodology. *Mailing Add:* Dept of Statist Ohio State Univ Columbus OH 43210

WHITNEY, ELEANOR NOSS, b Plainfield, NJ, Oct 5, 38; div; c 3. NUTRITION, HEALTH. *Educ:* Harvard Univ, BA, 60; Washington Univ, PhD(biol), 70. *Prof Exp:* Instr biol, Fla A&M Univ, 70-72; from instr to asst prof, 72-76, ASSOC PROF NUTRIT, FLA STATE UNIV, 76- *Concurrent Pos:* Res assoc chem, Fla State Univ, 70-72. *Mem:* NY Acad Sci; Am Dietetic Asn; Nutrit Today Soc; Soc Nutrit Educ; Am Public Health Asn. *Res:* Obesity; nutrition and mental health; breastfeeding; hyperactivity; nutrition and cancer therapy. *Mailing Add:* Dept of Food & Nutrit Fla State Univ Col of Home Econ Tallahassee FL 32306

WHITNEY, ELLSWORTH DOW, b Buffalo, NY, Sept 17, 28; m 54; c 2. PHYSICAL CHEMISTRY. *Educ:* Univ Buffalo, BA, 50; NY Univ, PhD(phys chem), 54. *Prof Exp:* Chemist, Charles C Kawin Co, 46-50; res chemist, Olin Mathieson Chem Corp, 54-57, chem res proj specialist, 57-59; sr res chemist, Carborundum Co, 59-62, sr res assoc, 62-70; assoc prof, 70-75, dir, Ctr Res Mining & Mineral Resources, 72-82, PROF MAT SCI & ENG, CERAMICS DIV, UNIV FLA, 75-, AFFIL PROF, DEPT NUCLEAR ENG SCI, 76- *Concurrent Pos:* Asst prof, Erie County Technol Inst, 63-68; lectr, Eve Sch, State Univ NY Buffalo, 66-69; partner, Whitney & Onoda, Consult, 74- *Mem:* Am Ceramic Soc; Am Chem Soc; Am Inst Mining, Metall & Petrol Engrs; Soc Mfg Engrs; Am Asn Univ Professors. *Res:* Crystal growth; kinetics of surface exchange; heterogeneous catalysis; boron and metal hydrides; borohydrides; fluorine oxidizers; high energy propellants; ultrahigh pressure solid state phenomena; phase transformations in solids; ceramic cutting tools and abrasives; solid state reaction kinetics, hard materials; mining and mineral research. *Mailing Add:* Ceramic Div Dept Mat Sci & Eng Univ of Fla Gainesville FL 32611

WHITNEY, ELVIN DALE, b West Bountiful, Utah, Mar 23, 28; m 58; c 3. PLANT PATHOLOGY, PLANT BREEDING. *Educ:* Utah State Univ, BS, 50; Cornell Univ, PhD(plant path), 65. *Prof Exp:* PLANT PATHOLOGIST, AGR RES SERV, USDA, 65- *Mem:* Am Phytopath Soc; Int Soc Plant Pathologists; Am Soc Sugar Beet Technologists; Sigma Xi. *Res:* Fungal, bacterial and nematode diseases of sugar beet; breeding for disease resistance. *Mailing Add:* Agr Res Serv US Dept of Agr PO Box 5098 Salinas CA 93915

WHITNEY, GEORGE STEPHEN, b Wheatland, Wyo, Feb 5, 34; m 59; c 3. ORGANIC CHEMISTRY, BIOCHEMISTRY. *Educ:* Univ Colo, BA, 55; Northwestern Univ, PhD(org chem), 62. *Prof Exp:* Asst prof org chem, Wabash Col, 61-62; from asst prof to assoc prof, 62-68, PROF ORG CHEM, WASHINGTON & LEE UNIV, 73- *Concurrent Pos:* Swiss-Am Found fel, Univ Basel, 64-65; Sloan-Washington & Lee fel, Univ Bristol, 70-71. *Res:* Physical organic chemistry and mechanisms; free-radical additions of organic sulfur compounds; cycloalkenes; bicyclic compounds; stereochemistry; organic synthesis. *Mailing Add:* 823 Thorn Hill Rd Lexington VA 24450

WHITNEY, HARVEY STUART, b Langdon, Alta, Oct 14, 35; m 62; c 2. PHYTOPATHOLOGY, MYCOLOGY. *Educ:* Univ Sask, BSA, 56, MSc, 58; Univ Calif, Berkeley, PhD(plant path), 63. *Prof Exp:* Res officer seedling dis, Forest Biol Div, Can Dept Agr, 58-61; RES SCIENTIST, CAN FOREST SERV, CAN DEPT ENVIRON, 61- *Concurrent Pos:* Can Forest Serv fel, Univ Calif, Berkeley, 70-71. *Mem:* AAAS; Soc Invertebrate Path; Mycol Soc Am; Can Phytopath Soc; Can Inst Foresters. *Res:* Taxonomy and heterokaryosis in Rhizoctonia; insect-fungus-tree relationships in conifers attacked by bark beetles; tree resistance and predisposition; symbiology; insect pathology; biological control. *Mailing Add:* 1925 Casa Marcia Victoria BC V8N 2V4 Can

WHITNEY, HASSLER, b New York, NY, Mar 23, 07; m 30, 55; c 2. MATHEMATICS. *Educ:* Yale Univ, PhB, 28, MusB, 29; Harvard Univ, PhD, 32. *Hon Degrees:* ScD, Yale Univ, 47. *Prof Exp:* Instr math, Harvard Univ, 30-31, Nat Res Coun fel & lectr, 31-33, from instr to prof, 33-52; prof, 52-77, EMER PROF MATH, INST ADVAN STUDY, 77- *Concurrent Pos:* Mem math panel, Nat Defense Res Comt, 43-45. *Honors & Awards:* Nat Medal Sci, 76. *Mem:* Nat Acad Sci; Am Math Soc (vpres, 48-50); Am Philos Soc. *Res:* Topology; manifolds; integration theory; analytic varieties. *Mailing Add:* Sch of Math Inst for Advan Study Princeton NJ 08540

WHITNEY, JAMES MARTIN, b Owosso, Mich, Sept 6, 36; m 63; c 3. MATERIALS SCIENCE ENGINEERING. *Educ:* Ill Col, BA, 59; Ga Inst Technol, BSTE, 59, MSTE, 61; Ohio State Univ, MS, 64, PhD(eng mech), 68. *Prof Exp:* Mat engr, 61-66, MAT RES ENGR, NONMETALLIC MAT DIV, US AIR FORCE MAT LAB, 66- *Concurrent Pos:* Air Force liaison rep to ad hoc comt micromech fibrous composites, Mat Adv Bd, 63-64. *Mem:* Fiber Soc; Am Soc Mech Engrs; assoc fel Am Inst Aeronaut & Astronaut; Am Acad Mech; Am Soc Testing & Mat. *Res:* Determination of the mechanical behavior of fibrous composites as a function of constituent properties and geometry, using principles of mechanics and applied mathematics; authored or coauthored over 60 publications including two texts. *Mailing Add:* 4371 Roundtree Dr Dayton OH 45432

WHITNEY, JODIE DOYLE, b Bosque County, Tex, Oct 14, 37; m 60; c 2. AGRICULTURAL ENGINEERING. *Educ:* Tex A&M Univ, BS, 59; Pa State Univ, MS, 62; Okla State Univ, PhD(agr eng), 66. *Prof Exp:* Asst agr engr, 65-72, assoc agr engr, 72-79, AGR ENGR, AGR RES & EDUC CTR, UNIV FLA, 79- *Mem:* Am Soc Agr Engrs. *Res:* Mechanization of low volume spraying and citrus harvesting; management of close spaced citrus plantings. *Mailing Add:* Agr Res & Educ Ctr Univ Fla 700 Exp Sta Rd Lake Alfred FL 33850

WHITNEY, JOEL GAYTON, b Cambridge, Mass, Oct 13, 37; m 71. ORGANIC CHEMISTRY. *Educ:* Harvard Univ, AB, 59; Mass Inst Technol, PhD(org chem), 63. *Prof Exp:* sr res chemist, 63-80, RES SUPVR, BIOCHEM DEPT, E I DU PONT DE NEMOURS & CO INC, 80- *Mem:* Am Chem Soc. *Res:* Amino acid syntheses; medicinal chemistry, especially heterocyclic chemistry; synthesis of central nervous system agents. *Mailing Add:* 16 Beverly Dr Kennett Square PA 19348

WHITNEY, JOHN BARRY, JR, b Augusta, Ga, June 25, 16; m 41; c 3. PLANT PHYSIOLOGY. *Educ:* Univ Ga, BS, 35; NC State Col, MS, 38; Ohio State Univ, PhD(plant physiol), 41. *Prof Exp:* Tutor, Univ Ga, 35-36; asst, Ohio State Univ, 38-41; plant physiologist, Cent Fibre Corp, 41-43 & 46; from asst prof to prof bot, Clemson Univ, 55-80, head dept, 77-80. *Concurrent Pos:* Oak Ridge Inst Nuclear Studies fel, Univ Tenn AEC Agr Res Prog, 52-53; area consult, Biol Sci Curric Study SC, 69-72. *Mem:* Am Soc Plant Physiol. *Res:* Water relations of plants; structure and microchemistry of plant cell walls; plant microchemistry; nutrition of microorganisms; radioisotope tracer applications. *Mailing Add:* 215 Wyatt Ave Clemson SC 29631

WHITNEY, JOHN EDWARD, b Casper, Wyo, July 6, 26; m 49; c 5. PHYSIOLOGY. *Educ:* Univ Calif, Berkeley, AB, 47, MA, 48, PhD(physiol), 51; Cambridge Univ, PhD(biochem), 56. *Prof Exp:* Res assoc physiol, Cedars of Lebanon Hosp, 51-52; res assoc biochem, Univ Calif, Los Angeles, 52-54; from asst prof to assoc prof, 56-62, actg head dept, 59-62, head dept, 62-79, PROF PHYSIOL, SCH MED, UNIV ARK, LITTLE ROCK, 62- *Concurrent Pos:* USPHS fel, Univ Calif, Los Angeles, 52-53; Am Cancer Soc fel, Cambridge Univ, 54-56; fel biochem, Univ Calif, Los Angeles, 52-54. *Mem:* AAAS; Am Physiol Soc; Endocrine Soc; Soc Exp Biol & Med; Am Diabetes Asn. *Res:* Endocrinology and metabolism, especially pancreatic-pituitary hormone interrelationships. *Mailing Add:* Dept of Physiol Univ of Ark Sch of Med Little Rock AR 72201

WHITNEY, JOHN GLEN, b Ponca City, Okla, June 4, 39; m 58; c 4. MICROBIOLOGY. *Educ:* Okla State Univ, BS, 61, PhD(microbiol), 67. *Prof Exp:* Sr microbiologist, 67-72, head fermentation prod res & microbiol res depts, 73-77, dir microbiol & fermentation prod res, Eli Lilly & Co, 77-78,

EXEC DIR & PRES, LILLY RES LABS, 79- *Mem:* Soc Indust Microbiol; Am Soc Microbiol. *Res:* Discovery, isolation and evaluation of fermentation products; control and regulation of secondary metabolism. *Mailing Add:* Fermentation Prod Res Eli Lilly & Co Indianapolis IN 46206

WHITNEY, LESTER F(RANK), b New Bedford, Mass, Mar 21, 28; m 50; c 7. FOOD ENGINEERING, MACHINE DESIGN. *Educ:* Univ Maine, BS, 49; Mich State Univ, MSAE, 51, PhD(agr eng), 64. *Prof Exp:* Design & develop engr, Ariens Co, Wis, 51-53 & Maine Potato Growers, Inc, 53-54; develop engr, Wirthmore Feed Div, Corn Prod, Inc, 54-56, asst chief engr, Mass, 56-59; asst prof agr eng, Univ Mass, 59-62; NSF fel, Mich State Univ, 62-63; PROF FOOD ENG, UNIV MASS, AMHERST, 63- *Concurrent Pos:* Consult engr food mach processing. *Mem:* Am Soc Agr Engrs; Int Food Technologists. *Res:* Agricultural processes; stress analysis; systems analysis; water resources; forage dehydration; fish processing. *Mailing Add:* Dept Food Eng Univ Mass Amherst MA 01002

WHITNEY, MARION ISABELLE, b Austin, Tex, Apr 23, 11. GEOLOGY. *Educ:* Univ Tex, BA, 30, MA, 31, PhD(geol, paleont), 37. *Prof Exp:* Teacher pub sch, 33-36; asst prof geol, Kans State Teachers Col, 37-42; teacher geol & biol, Kilgore Col, 42-46; asst prof geol, Tex Christian Univ, 46-51 & Sul Ross State Col, 51-52; prof geol & biol, Ark Polytech Col, 52-54; assoc prof geol, Tulane Univ, 54-55; assoc prof, La Tech Inst, 55-60; teacher biol, Texarkana Col, 60-61; assoc prof biol, Cent Mich Univ, 61-69, prof, 69-81; RETIRED. *Mem:* Am Asn Petrol Geol; Soc Econ Paleont & Mineral; Geol Soc Am. *Res:* Description of the fauna of the Glen Rose formation of Texas; development of new data concerning the method of aerodynamic erosion of rock, dunes and snow. *Mailing Add:* Dept of Biol Cent Mich Univ Mt Pleasant MI 48858

WHITNEY, NORMAN JOHN, b Langdon, Alta, July 24, 25; m 51; c 4. MYCOLOGY, PLANT PATHOLOGY. *Educ:* Univ Alta, BSc, 47; Univ Western Ont, MSc, 49; Univ Toronto, PhD(mycol, plant path), 53; McGill Univ, BD, 64. *Prof Exp:* Lectr bot, Univ Toronto, 50-52; plant pathologist, Res Sta, Can Dept Agr, 52-61; lectr bot, McGill Univ, 61-64; lectr biol, 65-73, student counr, 66-73, assoc prof, 73-80, PROF BIOL & COUNR STUDENT SERV, UNIV NB, 80- *Mem:* AAAS; Can Phytopath Soc. *Res:* Soil-borne diseases of plants; marine mycology; science and religion; spore germination in the phyllosphere. *Mailing Add:* Dept of Biol Univ of NB Fredericton NB E3B 5A3 Can

WHITNEY, PHILIP LAWRENCE, biochemistry, see previous edition

WHITNEY, PHILIP ROY, b Providence, RI, Nov 10, 35; m 59; c 4. GEOCHEMISTRY, PETROLOGY. *Educ:* Mass Inst Technol, BS, 56, PhD(geol), 62. *Prof Exp:* Asst prof geochem, State Univ NY Col Ceramics, Alfred Univ, 62-67; asst prof geol, Rensselaer Polytech Inst, 67-70; ASSOC SCIENTIST GEOCHEM, NY STATE MUS & SCI SERV, 70- *Concurrent Pos:* Adj assoc prof, Rensselaer Polytech Inst, 75- *Mem:* Geol Soc Am; Geochem Soc. *Res:* Geochemistry and petrology of anorthosite; geology of the Adirondack area; geochemistry of freshwater manganese oxides. *Mailing Add:* Geol Surv NY State Mus & Sci Serv Albany NY 12234

WHITNEY, RICHARD RALPH, b Salt Lake City, Utah, June 29, 27; m 50; c 4. FISHERY BIOLOGY. *Educ:* Univ Utah, MS, 51; Iowa State Col, PhD(fisheries mgt), 55. *Prof Exp:* Res biologist, Salton Sea Invest, Univ Calif, 54-57; proj leader, Susquehanna Fishery Study, State Dept Res & Educ, Md, 58-60; chief tuna behav invests, Tuna Resources Lab, US Bur Com Fisheries, 61-67; UNIT LEADER, WASH COOP FISHERY RES UNIT, 67- *Concurrent Pos:* Tech adv & medium commun, George H Boldt, Sr Judge US Dist Court, Tacoma, 74-79; consult, Conn Yankee Atomic Power Co, 65-74. *Mem:* Fel Am Inst Fishery Res Biol; Ecol Soc Am; Am Fisheries Soc. *Res:* Aquatic ecology; fisheries. *Mailing Add:* Col Fisheries Univ Wash Seattle WA 98195

WHITNEY, RICHARD WILBUR, b Osawatomie, Kans, Nov 1, 38; m 59; c 4. AGRICULTURAL ENGINEERING. *Educ:* Kans State Univ, BS, 61; Okla State Univ, MS, 67, PhD(agr eng), 72. *Prof Exp:* Instr, Kans State Univ, 61-62; asst prof, La State Univ, Baton Rouge, 72-77; instr, 62-69, asst prof, 77-80, ASSOC PROF AGR ENG, OKLA STATE UNIV, 80- *Concurrent Pos:* Consult, Charles Machine Works, Perry Okla, 75, Kincaid Equip Co, Haven, Kans, 77-79, US Pollution Control, Okla City, 80, Kahrs, Nelson, Fanning, Hite & Kellogg, 80 & Eagle Aircraft Co, Boise, Idaho, 81. *Mem:* Am Soc Agr Engrs; Sigma Xi. *Res:* Mechanization of food and fiber production of cotton and horticultural crops; low volume pesticide application equipment and delivery techniques for tick control; development of improved production equipment for forage grasses; determination of potential human inhalation exposure to airborne pentachlorophenol within treated structures. *Mailing Add:* Dept of Agr Eng Okla State Univ Sillwater OK 74074

WHITNEY, ROBERT ARTHUR, JR, b Oklahoma City, Okla, July 27, 35; m 58; c 5. LABORATORY ANIMAL MEDICINE, COMPARATIVE MEDICINE. *Educ:* Okla State Univ, BS, 57, DVM, 59; Ohio State Univ, MS, 65. *Prof Exp:* US Army fel & resident lab animal med, Ohio State Univ, 63-65, chief animal resources br, US Army Edgewood Arsenal, 65-70, dir lab animal training prog, US Army Vet Corps, 68-70, commanding officer, 4th Med Detachment, Viet Nam, 70-71; proj officer, Animal Resources Br, 71-72, CHIEF, VET RESOURCES BR, DIV RES SERV, NIH, 72- *Concurrent Pos:* Consult lab animal med, US Army Surgeon Gen Off, 67-70; exec dir, US Govt Interagency Primate Steering Comt, 80-81. *Mem:* Am Col Lab Animal Med; Am Vet Med Asn; Am Asn Lab Animal Sci; Am Asn Lab Animal Practitioners; Sigma Xi. *Res:* Diseases of laboratory animals; primatology. *Mailing Add:* Vet Resources Br Bldg 14G Rm 102 NIH Bethesda MD 20014

WHITNEY, ROBERT C, b Seattle, Wash, July 20, 19; m 42; c 2. SCIENCE EDUCATION, PHYSICS. *Educ:* Univ Wash, BS, 47; Cornell Univ, MS, 58, PhD(sci educ, physics), 63. *Prof Exp:* Teacher, Wash High Sch, 47-55, 56-57 & 58-59; assoc dir shell merit fels, Shell Found, Cornell Univ, 59-61, assoc dir acad year inst, NSF, 61-63; assoc prof, 63-66, PROF PHYS SCI, CALIF STATE UNIV, HAYWARD, 66- *Concurrent Pos:* Consult, Murray, Fremont & Palo Alto Sch Dist, Calif, 65-66 & Livermore Sch Dist, 67; NSF fel, Univ Wash, 71-72. *Mem:* AAAS; Am Asn Physics Teachers; Nat Sci Teachers Asn. *Res:* Improvement of high school physics facilities; improvement in the teaching of high school physics and elementary science. *Mailing Add:* Dept of Earth Sci Calif State Univ Hayward CA 94542

WHITNEY, ROBERT MCLAUGHLIN, b St Paul, Minn, Sept 28, 11; m 34, 67; c 2. FOOD CHEMISTRY. *Educ:* Augustana Col, SDak, AB, 36; Univ Ill, PhD(phys chem), 44. *Prof Exp:* Instr math, Augustana Col, SDak, 36-37; high sch teacher, NDak, 37-38 & Ill, 38-40; asst chemist, Ill State Water Surv, 40-42; instr chem, Univ Ill, 42-44; res chemist, Dean Milk Co, 44-46; assoc prof dairy mfg res, 46-50, assoc prof dairy technol, 50-59, prof dairy technol, 59-73, PROF FOOD CHEM, UNIV ILL, URBANA, 73- *Concurrent Pos:* Vis prof, Univ PR, Mayaguez, 73-74 & Univ Baghdad, Iraq, 79. *Honors & Awards:* Borden Co Found Res Award, Am Dairy Sci Asn, 61. *Mem:* Am Chem Soc; Am Dairy Sci Asn; fel Am Inst Chemists; Inst Food Technologists. *Res:* Chemical analysis of dairy products; investigation of flavors in dairy products; ultrasonic bactericidal effects; physical-chemical state of milk proteins; investigation of the proteins in the milk fat-globule membrane. *Mailing Add:* Dept of Food Sci Univ of Ill Urbana IL 61801

WHITNEY, ROY DAVIDSON, b Langdon, Alta, Dec 30, 27; m 53; c 4. FOREST PATHOLOGY. *Educ:* Univ BC, BSF, 51; Yale Univ, MF, 54; Queen's Univ, Ont, PhD(forest path), 60. *Prof Exp:* RES SCIENTIST, CAN FORESTRY SERV, 51- *Mem:* Am Phytopath Soc; Can Phytopath Soc. *Res:* Investigations of root rots of conifers, including identification of causal fungi, symptomatology, infection courts, damage appraisal and spore germination; determination of pathogenic potentials by inoculations. *Mailing Add:* Can Forestry Serv Box 490 Sault Ste Marie ON P6A 5M7 Can

WHITNEY, ROY P(OWELL), b Milo, Maine, May 30, 13; m 41; c 2. CHEMICAL ENGINEERING. *Educ:* Mass Inst Technol, SB, 35, SM, 37, ScD(chem eng), 45. *Prof Exp:* Asst, Mass Inst Technol, 35-36, asst dir sch chem eng practice, Bangor Sta, 36-38, dir, 38-42, asst prof chem eng, Univ, 39-45; dir dept indust coop, Univ Maine, 45-47, prof chem eng & actg head dept, 46-47; prof chem eng, 47-79, assoc & group leader, 47-57, dean, 56-76, vpres, 58-78, asst to pres, 76-79, EMER PROF CHEM ENG, INST PAPER CHEM, 79- *Concurrent Pos:* Tech adv, Chem Warfare Serv Develop Lab, US Dept Army, 42-45, consult, Chem Corps, 50-52; chmn, Comt Paper Base Mat, Nat Acad Sci-Nat Res Coun, 60-66. *Honors & Awards:* Colburn Award, Am Inst Chem Engrs, 48; Award, Tech Asn Pulp & Paper Indust, 69, Gold Medal, 80; Pro Bono Labore Award, Finnish Paper Engrs Asn, 78. *Mem:* Am Chem Soc; Am Soc Eng Educ; Tech Asn Pulp & Paper Indust; Am Inst Chem Engrs; Am Inst Chemists. *Res:* Heat and mass transfer, particularly gas absorption and drying; pulp and paper technology. *Mailing Add:* 1709 S Douglas St Appleton WI 54911

WHITNEY, THOMAS ALLEN, b Toledo, Ohio, June 22, 40; m 62; c 3. ORGANIC CHEMISTRY. *Educ:* Northwestern Univ, Evanston, BA, 62; Univ Calif, Los Angeles, PhD(chem), 67. *Prof Exp:* sr staff chemist, 67-80, RES ASSOC, CORP RES LAB, EXXON RES & ENG CO, 80- *Mem:* Am Chem Soc. *Res:* Homogeneous catalysis; asymmetric synthesis; organic reactions. *Mailing Add:* Exxon Res & Eng Co Corp Res Lab PO Box 45 Linden NJ 07036

WHITNEY, WENDELL KEITH, b Miltonvale, Kans, Nov 27, 27; m 45; c 2. ENTOMOLOGY, AGRICULTURE. *Educ:* Kans State Univ, BS, 56, MS, 58, PhD(entom, zool), 62. *Prof Exp:* Biol aide, Stored Prod Insect Br, USDA, Kans, 51-56, entomologist, 56-58; instr entom, Kans State Univ, 58-62; entomologist, Bioprod Dept, Dow Chem Co, 62-68; Ford Found entomologist, Int Inst Trop Agr, Nigeria, 68-73; CHIEF ENTOMOLOGIST, PLANT PROD RES & DEVELOP, CYANAMID INT, 74- *Concurrent Pos:* Res grants, 58-62; consult, Industs & USDA, 59-62. *Mem:* Entom Soc Am; Asn Advan Agr Sci Africa; Entom Soc Nigeria; Nigerian Soc Plant Protection; Am Mosquito Control Asn. *Res:* Plant pest and disease control; control of stored products pests. *Mailing Add:* 121 Sycamore Rd Princeton NJ 08540

WHITNEY, WILLIAM MERRILL, b Coeur d'Alene, Idaho, Dec 5, 29; m 50, 78; c 2. PHYSICS. *Educ:* Calif Inst Technol, BS, 51; Mass Inst Technol, PhD(physics), 56. *Prof Exp:* From instr to asst prof physics, Mass Int Technol, 56-63; mem tech staff, 63-67, mgr guid & control res sect, 67-70, tech leader, Robot Res Prog, 71-78, MGR INFO SYSTS RES SECT, JET PROPULSION LAB, 70- *Mem:* AAAS; Am Phys Soc. *Res:* Low temperature and semiconductor physics; computer science. *Mailing Add:* Info Systs Res Sect 198-229 Jet Propulsion Lab Pasadena CA 91103

WHITSEL, BARRY L, b Mt Union, Pa, Aug 26, 37; m 60; c 2. NEUROPHYSIOLOGY, NEUROPHARMACOLOGY. *Educ:* Gettysburg Col, AB, 59; Univ Pa, MS, 63; Univ Ill, PhD(pharmacol), 66. *Prof Exp:* Res asst psychopharmacol, Wyeth Inst, 59-61; res assoc pharmacol, Sch Med, Univ Pittsburgh, 65-66, from instr to asst prof, 66-74; ASSOC PROF DENT RES & PHYSIOL, SCH MED, UNIV NC, CHAPEL HILL, 74- *Concurrent Pos:* Res scientist develop award, NIMH, 68-73. *Res:* Pharmacology. *Mailing Add:* Dept Physiol Sch Med Univ NC Chapel Hill NC 27514

WHITSELL, JOHN CRAWFORD, II, b St Joseph, Mo, Dec 21, 29; m 65. SURGERY. *Educ:* Grinnell Col, AB, 50; Wash Univ, MD, 54; Am Bd Surg, dipl, 62; Am Bd Thoracic Surg, dipl, 64. *Prof Exp:* Instr surg, Med Col, Cornell Univ, 63-66, asst attend surgeon, New York Hosp, 63-68, from asst prof to assoc prof, 66-70, surg dir, Renal Transplant Unit, 68-75, PROF SURG, MED COL, CORNELL UNIV, 70-, SURG CONSULT RENAL TRANSPLANT UNIT, NEW YORK HOSP-CORNELL MED CTR, 75- *Concurrent Pos:* Assoc attend surgeon, New York Hosp, 68-70, attend surgeon, 70- *Mem:* AMA; Am Col Surg; Transplantation Soc; NY Acad Sci; Harvey Soc. *Res:* Renal transplantation. *Mailing Add:* 517 E 71st St New York NY 10021

WHITSETT, CAROLYN F, b Portsmouth, Va, Nov 21, 45. PATHOLOGY, MEDICINE. *Educ:* Howard Univ, BS, 66, MD, 70. *Prof Exp:* Med internship, 70-71; jr asst resident, Downstate Med Ctr, 71-72; sr asst resident, New York Hisp, 72-73; fel hemat, Montefiore Hosp & Med Ctr, 73-74; fel immunohemat, New York Blood Ctr, 74-75; fel med hemat div, Mem Hosp, 74-75; asst prof med, Cornell Univ, Med Col, 75-77; ASST PROF PATH & MED, EMORY UNIV, SCH MED, 77- *Concurrent Pos:* Res assoc tissue typing lab, Mem Sloan Kettering Cancer Ctr, 75-77; asst attending physician hemat serv, Mem Hosp, 75-77; asst med dir, Mem Hosp Blood Bank, 76-77; med dir, Emory Univ Hosp Blood Bank & Sch Blood Banking, 77- *Mem:* Am Asn Blood Banks; Am Asn Clin Histocompatibility Testing. *Mailing Add:* Emory Univ Hosp 1364 Clifton Rd NE Atlanta GA 30322

WHITSETT, JOHNSON MALLORY, II, b San Antonio, Tex, Jan 26, 41; m 64; c 1. ANIMAL BEHAVIOR, REPRODUCTIVE PHYSIOLOGY. *Educ:* Univ Tex, Austin, BA, 63, PhD(psychol), 70; New Sch Social Res, MA, 66. *Prof Exp:* Fel zool, Univ Tex, Austin, 69-71; from asst prof to assoc prof, 71-81, PROF ZOOL, NC STATE UNIV, 81- *Concurrent Pos:* Res assoc, NC Dept Ment Health, 71-73; mem physiol fac, NC State Univ, 74-; NSF res grant, 78. *Mem:* AAAS; Animal Behav Soc; Am Ornithol Union; Soc Study Reproduction. *Res:* Hormonal and stimulus control of sexual and aggressive behavior in birds and mammals; environmental influence on reproduction; behavioral aspects of sexual development; photoperiodism. *Mailing Add:* Dept of Zool NC State Univ Raleigh NC 27650

WHITSETT, THOMAS L, b Tulsa, Okla, July 14, 36; m 59; c 2. INTERNAL MEDICINE, CLINICAL PHARMACOLOGY. *Educ:* Pasadena Col, BA, 58; Univ Okla, MD, 62. *Prof Exp:* Clin asst, Med Ctr, Univ Okla, 67-68; vis asst prof med, Sch Med, Emory Univ, 69-70; from asst prof med to assoc prof, 70-78, asst prof pharmacol, 70-77, PROF MED, MED CTR, UNIV OKLA, 78-, ASSOC PROF PHARMACOL, 77- *Concurrent Pos:* Found fac develop award, Pharmaceut Mfr Asn, 71; trainee clin pharmacol, Med Ctr, Univ Okla, 67-68 & Sch Med, Emory Univ, 68-70. *Mem:* Am Heart Asn; Am Fedn Clin Res; Am Soc Pharmacol & Exp Therapeut. *Res:* Early phases of new drug investigation, especially cardiovascular and respiratory agents. *Mailing Add:* Univ of Okla Health Sci Ctr Oklahoma City OK 73104

WHITSON, PAUL DAVID, b Gravette, Ark, Mar 20, 40; m 78. BOTANY, PLANT ECOLOGY. *Educ:* Baylor Univ, BS, 62, MS, 65; Univ Okla, PhD(bot), 71. *Prof Exp:* Grad asst biol, Baylor Univ, 63-65; grad asst bot, Univ Okla, 65-71; asst prof biol, Baylor Univ, 70-71; from asst prof to assoc prof, 72-81, PROF BIOL, UNIV NORTHERN IOWA, 81- *Concurrent Pos:* Res consult, Nat Park Serv Univ Okla Res Inst, 69-70; Int Biol Prog fel biol, NMex State Univ, 71-72; prin investr desert biome, Int Biol Prog, 72-75; staff assoc environ, NSF, 76-77; exec secy biol, Fed Comt Ecol Reserves, 76-77; investr endangered species, US Fish & Wildlife Serv, 78- *Mem:* Ecol Soc Am; Brit Ecol Soc; AAAS; Sigma Xi. *Res:* Structure, dynamics and human influences upon woodland and desert vegetation; phenology and productivity of desert annuals; species biology, Southern Appalachian and Midwestern endangered plants; decide forest and prairie reconstruction. *Mailing Add:* Dept of Biol Univ of Northern Iowa Cedar Falls IA 50614

WHITSON, ROBERT EDD, b Spearman, Tex, Apr 30, 42; m 63; c 2. AGRICULTURAL ECONOMICS, RANGE MANAGEMENT. *Educ:* Tex Tech Univ, BS, 65, MS, 67, PhD(agr econ), 74. *Prof Exp:* Area economist, 69-71, asst prof, 74-77, ASSOC PROF RANGE ECON, TEX AGR EXP STA, TEX A&M UNIV, 77- *Mem:* Am Soc Agr Econ; Soc Range Mgt. *Res:* Examination of risk management alternatives for ranchers and an evaluation of changing feed price relationships on efficient ranch organizations. *Mailing Add:* Dept Range Sci Tex A&M Univ College Station TX 77843

WHITT, CARLTON DENNIS, b Elkmont, Ala, July 4, 19; m 42; c 5. INDUSTRIAL CHEMISTRY, ORGANIC POLYMER CHEMISTRY. *Educ:* Univ Ala, AB, 41, MS, 42, PhD(inorg chem), 71. *Prof Exp:* High sch teacher, 40-41; instr org chem, Exten, Univ Ala, 43-45; from asst res chemist to asst assoc res chemist, Tenn Valley Auth, 45-52; chem engr, Chemstrand Corp, 52-64; chem engr, Monsanto Co, 64-78; teaching, Univ Wis Syst, Manitowoc, 78-80; instr, Bethany Col, Kans, 80-82; INSTR, BRADLEY UNIV, ILL, 82- *Mem:* Am Chem Soc. *Res:* Chemical warfare agents; vapor pressures and fundamental data on phosphoric acids; fixation of fertilizers on soils and clays; crystal structure determination by x-ray methods. *Mailing Add:* Chem Dept Bradley Univ Peoria IL 61625

WHITT, DARNELL MOSES, b Greensboro, NC, Apr 30, 13; m 36; c 1. SOIL PHYSICS, FIELD CROPS. *Educ:* NC State Univ, BS, 34; Univ Mo, AM, 35, PhD(crops), 52. *Prof Exp:* Soil surveyor, Soil Conserv Serv, USDA, 35-36, res agronomist, 36-42 & 46-52, res soil conservationist, Agr Res Serv, 52-55, regional liaison officer, Agr Res Serv & Soil Conserv Serv, 55-56, nat liaison officer, 56-59, dir conserv planning, Soil Conserv Serv, 59-63, dir plant sci div, 63-72, dep adminr, 72-75; coordr river basin studies, Int Joint Comn, 75-78; CONSULT, NATURAL RESOURCE CONSERV, 78- *Concurrent Pos:* Mem, Nat Comt Res Needs in Soil & Water Conserv, 58-59; consult, Repub of Nauru & SPac Comn, New Caledonia. *Mem:* Am Soc Agron; Soil Sci Soc Am; Soc Range Mgt; Soil Conserv Soc Am; Int Soc Soil Sci. *Res:* Water pollution. *Mailing Add:* PO Box 82 Green Valley AZ 85614

WHITT, DIXIE DAILEY, b Longmont, Colo, Mar 9, 39; m 63. MICROBIAL ECOLOGY, MICROBIAL PHYSIOLOGY. *Educ:* Colo State Univ, BS, 61, PhD(zool), 65. *Prof Exp:* USPHS fel biochem genetics, Yale Univ, 65-69; RES ASSOC MICROBIOL, UNIV ILL, URBANA, 69- *Mem:* Am Genetics Asn; Asn Gnotobiotics; AAAS; Genetics Soc Am; Am Soc Microbiol. *Res:* Host-parasite interactions; biochemical genetics of microorganisms; host-parasite relationships as an expression of the host's environmental conditions; host-intestinal microflora interactions. *Mailing Add:* Dept Microbiol Univ Ill Urbana IL 61801

WHITT, GREGORY SIDNEY, b Detroit, Mich, June 13, 38; m 63. DEVELOPMENTAL GENETICS, BIOCHEMICAL GENETICS. *Educ:* Colo State Univ, BS, 62, MS, 65; Yale Univ, PhD(biol), 70. *Prof Exp:* From asst prof zool to assoc prof, 69-77, PROF GENETICS & DEVELOP, UNIV ILL, URBANA, 77- *Concurrent Pos:* Assoc ed, J Exp Zool, 74-78 & Develop Genetics, 78-; co-ed, Isozymes: Current Topics Biol & Med Res; ed, Isozyme Bulletin, 78-81; mem adv bd, Biochem Genetics, 75-; mem ed bds, J Molecular Evolution, 79-, J Heredity, 80-; affil aquatic biol sect, Ill Natural Hist Surv, Urbana, 81- *Mem:* Am Genetic Asn; Soc Study Evolution; Am Soc Zoologists; Am Soc Ichthyologists & Herpetologists; Am Soc Naturalists. *Res:* Isozymes as probes of gene structure, function, and evolution; biochemical, developmental, and evolutionary genetics of fishes; genetic and epigenetic regulation of gene expression during development; evolutionary and systematic analyses using duplicate gene structure and regulation. *Mailing Add:* Dept of Genetics & Develop Univ Ill 505 S Goodwin Ave Urbana IL 61801

WHITT, LEE BARLOW, b Vallejo, Calif, Apr 4, 49; c 1. DIFFERENTIAL GEOMETRY, OPERATIONS RESEARCH. *Educ:* Univ Calif, Berkeley, AB, 71; Yale Univ, PhD(math), 75. *Prof Exp:* Asst prof, Cornell Univ, 75-77; asst prof math, Tex A&M Univ, 77-81; ASSOC, D H WAGNER, ASSOCS, 81- *Mem:* Am Math Soc; Math Asn Am. *Res:* The differential geometric properties of manifolds and submanifolds, and the statistical and game theoretic aspects of antisubmarine warfare. *Mailing Add:* Daniel H Wagner, Assocs 1120 W Mercury Blvd Hampton VA 23666

WHITT, WARD, b Buffalo, NY, Jan 29, 42. OPERATIONS RESEARCH, PROBABILITY THEORY MATHEMATICS. *Educ:* Dartmouth Col, AB, 64; Cornell Univ, PhD(opers res), 69. *Prof Exp:* Vis asst prof opers res, Stanford Univ, 68-69; asst prof admin sci, Sch Orgn & Mgt, Yale Univ, 69-73, assoc prof admin sci & statist, 73-77; MEM TECH STAFF, BELL LABS, 77- *Concurrent Pos:* NSF res initiation grant admin sci, Yale Univ, 71-73, jr fac fel, 72-73, res grant, 73-75. *Res:* Probability theory and its applications; mathematical models in the social sciences; queuing theory; stochastic processes. *Mailing Add:* Bell Labs Holmdel NJ 07733

WHITTAKER, FREDERICK HORACE, b Columbus, Ohio, Mar 9, 28; m 52; c 2. PARASITOLOGY. *Educ:* Otterbein Col, BA, 51; Univ Ga, MSc, 56; Univ Ill, PhD(zool, parasitol), 63. *Prof Exp:* Instr biol & chem, Spartanburg Jr Col, 57-58; res biologist, Abbott Labs, Ill, 63-64; from asst prof to assoc prof, 64-72, PROF ZOOL, UNIV LOUISVILLE, 72- *Concurrent Pos:* Consult, Abbott Labs, 64-65. *Mem:* Sigma Xi; Am Soc Parasitologists. *Res:* Effects of fermentation liquors on invertebrates; taxonomy and life cycles of trematodes and cestodes; electron microscopy and scanning electron microscopy of cestodes and trematodes; systematics and ecology of helminths of cavefishes. *Mailing Add:* 401 Deerfield Lane Louisville KY 40207

WHITTAKER, J RICHARD, b Cornwall, Ont, Aug 19, 34; m 62. EMBRYOLOGY, MARINE BIOLOGY. *Educ:* Queen's Univ, Ont, BA, 58, MSc, 59; Yale Univ, PhD(develop biol), 62. *Prof Exp:* Asst prof zool, Univ Calif, Los Angeles, 62-67; assoc prof, Wistar Inst Anat & Biol, 67-81; PROF BIOL & DIR MARINE PROG, BOSTON UNIV, 81- *Concurrent Pos:* Investr, Marine Biol Lab, Woods Hole, 69-, trustee, 78-; assoc prof anat, Sch Med, Univ Pa, 71-81; mem, Alpha Helix Philippine Expedition, 79; vis prof, Kewalo Marine Lab, Univ Hawaii, 81. *Honors & Awards:* MBL Award, Marine Biol Lab, Woods Hole, 71. *Mem:* Am Soc Zool; Soc Develop Biol; Int Soc Develop Biol. *Res:* Egg cytoplasmic determinants of histodifferentiation in marine invertebrate embryos; melanocyte differentiation; melanin biochemistry; ascidian embryology; developmental mechanisms in tunicate evolution; larval settling and marine fouling; developmental resistance to marine pollutants. *Mailing Add:* Marine Prog Marine Biol Lab Boston Univ Woods Hole MA 02543

WHITTAKER, JAMES VICTOR, b Los Angeles, Calif, Aug 1, 31. MATHEMATICS. *Educ:* Univ Calif, Los Angeles, BA, 53, MA, 54, PhD, 58. *Prof Exp:* Assoc math, Univ Calif, Los Angeles, 57-58; from instr to assoc prof, 58-69, PROF MATH, UNIV BC, 69- *Mem:* Am Math Soc; Math Asn Am; Can Math Cong. *Res:* Geometric topology; probability. *Mailing Add:* Dept of Math Univ of BC Vancouver BC V6T 1W5 Can

WHITTAKER, MACK PAGE, b Richfield, Utah, Aug 13, 40; m 60; c 3. INORGANIC CHEMISTRY. *Educ:* Brigham Young Univ, BS, 62; Univ Utah, PhD(inorg chem), 66. *Prof Exp:* Res chemist, Great Lakes Res Corp, Tenn, 66-67, sect head, 67-72, asst tech dir, Great Lakes Carbon Corp, 72-73, tech dir, 73-81, VPRES, TECH, GREAT LAKES CARBON CORP, 81- *Mem:* Am Chem Soc; Am Inst Mining, Metall & Petrol Engrs. *Res:* Fast reaction kinetics; kinetics of inorganic polymerization systems; crystal structure evaluation; x-ray diffraction; high temperature chemistry; carbon and graphite technology. *Mailing Add:* Great Lakes Carbon Corp 299 Park Ave New York NY 10017

WHITTAKER, ROBERT HARDING, ecology, deceased

WHITTAM, JAMES HENRY, b New York, NY, Apr 23, 49. PHYSICAL CHEMISTRY, CHEMICAL ENGINEERING. *Educ:* City Col New York, BS, 72, PhD(phys chem), 75; Boston Univ, MBA, 78. *Prof Exp:* Instr chem, City Col New York, 72-75; proj chemist, Gillette Co, 75-78; mgr res chem & chem eng, 78-80, DIR HEALTH SCI, SHAKLEE CORP RES LAB, 80- *Concurrent Pos:* Consult, Gen Foods Corp, 73-74; adv ed, Cosmetic Tech, 78- *Mem:* Am Chem Soc; Soc Cosmetic Chem; Inst Food Technol; Am Oil Chem Soc. *Res:* Surface and colloid science pertaining to the fields of hair and skin cosmetology and food science, nutrition and engineering. *Mailing Add:* Shaklee Corp Res Lab PO Box 3625 Hayward CA 94545

WHITTEMBURY, GUILLERMO, b Trujillo, Peru, Nov 17, 29; m 61; c 3. BIOPHYSICS. *Educ:* San Marcos Univ, Lima, BM, 55; Univ Cayetano Heredia, Peru, MD, 65. *Prof Exp:* Instr anat, San Marcos Univ, Lima, 49-50, asst prof med, 55-57, asst prof biophys, 60-62; sr scientist, 62-67, head dept gen physiol, 67-70, MEM STAFF, VENEZUELAN INST SCI RES, 70- *Concurrent Pos:* Res fel, Biophys Lab, Harvard Med Sch, 57-60; Rockefeller Found fel, 57-59; Helen Hay Whitney Found fel, 59-60; Daniel Carrion Price fel, Peru, 65; vis prof, Yale Univ, 70; mem, Int Union Pure & Appl Biophysics, 63; dir, Latin Am Ctr Biol, 73; fel, Churchill Col, Cambridge, 76- *Mem:* Am Soc Nephrology; Biophys Soc; Peruvian Nephrology Soc; Int Soc Nephol; Soc Gen Physiologists. *Res:* Transport processes across membranes; kidney physiology. *Mailing Add:* Venezuelan Inst Sci Res PO Box 1827 Caracas Venezuela

WHITTEMORE, ALICE S, b New York, NY, July 5, 36; m 58; c 2. BIOMATHEMATICS, BIOSTATISTICS. *Educ:* Marymount Manhattan Col, BS, 58; Hunter Col, MA, 64; City Univ New York, PhD(math), 67. *Prof Exp:* From asst prof to assoc prof math, Hunter Col, 67-74; adj assoc prof environ med, Med Ctr, NY Univ, 74-76; FAC MEM, DEPT STATIST, STANFORD UNIV, 76- *Concurrent Pos:* City Univ New York res grants, 69 & 70; Sloan Found res grant, Soc Indust & Appl Math Inst Math & Soc, 74-76; Rockefeller Found res grant, 76-77. *Mem:* AAAS; Soc Indust & Appl Math; Sigma Xi; Am Math Soc; Math Asn Am. *Res:* Environmental carcinogenesis. *Mailing Add:* 820 Sonoma Terrace Stanford CA 94305

WHITTEMORE, CHARLES ALAN, b Grand Junction, Colo, Dec 14, 35; m 63; c 2. ORGANIC CHEMISTRY. *Educ:* Stanford Univ, BSc, 57; Univ Colo, PhD(org chem), 63. *Prof Exp:* Sr chemist, Cent Res Labs, Minn Mining & Mfg Co, 63-69; from asst prof to assoc prof chem, Colo Women's Col, 69-77; MEM STAFF, GEORGIA-PACIFIC, 77- *Mem:* Am Chem Soc. *Res:* Organic reaction mechanisms; Friedel-Crafts reactions; phenolic resins; organic synthesis. *Mailing Add:* Georgia-Pacific Corp 2883 Miller Rd Decatur GA 30035

WHITTEMORE, DONALD OSGOOD, b Pittsburgh, Pa, May 4, 44; m 71; c 1. GEOCHEMISTRY, HYDROGEOLOGY. *Educ:* Univ NH, BS, 66; Pa State Univ, University Park, PhD(geochem), 73. *Prof Exp:* Asst prof geol, Kans State Univ, 72-78; ASSOC SCIENTIST, KANS GEOL SURV, 78- *Mem:* AAAS; Am Water Resources Asn; Soil Sci Soc Am; Geochem Soc; Am Geophys Union. *Res:* Low temperature, pressure aqueous geochemistry, especially water resource and pollution geochemistry; chemistry and mineralogy of ferric oxyhydroxides. *Mailing Add:* Kans Geol Surv Univ of Kans Lawrence KS 66044

WHITTEMORE, FREDERICK WINSOR, b Boston, Mass, Apr 8, 16; m 41; c 3. ENTOMOLOGY. *Educ:* Mass State Col, BS, 37, MS, 38, PhD(entom), 41; Johns Hopkins Univ, MPH, 48. *Prof Exp:* Res entomologist, E L Bruce Co, 39-41; entomologist, US Army, 41-62; sr scientist, Pan Am Health Orgn, 62-64; pesticides specialist, Food & Agr Orgn, 64-69, chief, Crop Protection Br, 69-71, sr officer, Plant Protection Serv, 71-73; dep dir opers div, Off Pesticide Progs, US Environ Protection Agency, 73-76; PEST MGT SPECIALIST & ENVIRON COORDR, OFF AGR, DEVELOP SUPPORT BUR, AID, DEPT STATE, 76- *Mem:* Entom Soc Am; Am Mosquito Control Asn. *Res:* Promotion of international agreement on pesticide tolerances and specifications; establishment of laboratory and field test facilities for pesticides in developing countries. *Mailing Add:* Off of Agr Sci/Tech Bur AID Dept of State Washington DC 20523

WHITTEMORE, IRVILLE MERRILL, b Berkeley, Calif, June 12, 28; m 51; c 2. PETROLEUM CHEMISTRY. *Educ:* Univ Calif, Berkeley, BS, 52; Syracuse Univ, PhD(chem), 64. *Prof Exp:* Chemist, Arthur D Little, Inc, 52-55 & Lawrence Radiation Lab, 55-61; res assoc, Syracuse Univ, 61-63; res chemist, 63-69, sr res chemist, 69-77, SR RES ASSOC, CHEVRON RES CO, 77- *Mem:* Am Chem Soc. *Res:* Radiochemistry; kinetics; gas chromatography; photochemistry; environmental chemistry. *Mailing Add:* Chevron Res Co 576 Standard Ave Richmond CA 94802

WHITTEMORE, O(SGOOD) J(AMES), JR, b Clear Lake, Iowa, Jan 24, 19; m 41; c 3. CERAMIC ENGINEERING. *Educ:* Iowa State Univ, BS, 40, CE, 50; Univ Wash, Seattle, MS, 41. *Prof Exp:* Fel refractories, Mellon Inst, 41-44; group leader Manhattan Proj, Mass Inst Technol, 44-46; sr engr, Norton Co, 46-56, chief ceramic engr, 56-59, res assoc explor res, 59-64; assoc prof ceramic eng, 64-69, PROF CERAMIC ENG, UNIV WASH, 69- *Concurrent Pos:* Mem ad hoc comt, Mat Adv Bd, 56 & 58; NASA ceramic mat res grant, 64-; prof, Univ Fed de Sao Carlos, Brazil, 76; NSF sintering grant, 79-; dir, Wash State Mining & Mineral Res Inst, 82- *Honors & Awards:* Worcester Eng Soc Admiral Earle Award, 49; Trinks Indust Heating Award, 55; Azeredo Prize, Brazil, 79. *Mem:* Nat Inst Ceramic Engrs; fel Am Ceramic Soc (vpres, 75-76); Brit Ceramic Soc; Assoc Brasileira de Ceramica; Am Inst Mining & Metall Engrs. *Res:* Refractories; processing; minerals. *Mailing Add:* Ceramic Eng Div FB10 Univ of Wash Seattle WA 98195

WHITTEMORE, RUTH, b Cambridge, Mass, June 11, 17. PEDIATRICS, CARDIOLOGY. *Educ:* Mt Holyoke Col, BA, 38; Johns Hopkins Univ, MD, 42; Am Bd Pediat, dipl, 53, cert pediat cardiol, 61. *Prof Exp:* Intern & resident pediat, New Haven Hosp, 42-44; resident, Johns Hopkins Hosp, 44-45, asst physician, Harriet Lane Cardiac Clin, 45-47; physician, Div Crippled Children, 47-59; dir, New Haven Rheumatic Fever & Cardiac prog, 47-60, sr pediatrician, New Haven Pediat Cardiac Res Prog, 59-66, PEDIAT CARDIOLOGIST & DIR NEW HAVEN PEDIAT CARDIAC RES PROG, STATE DEPT HEALTH, CONN, 66- *Concurrent Pos:* From asst clin prof to assoc clin prof, Sch Med, Yale Univ, 47-66, clin prof pediat, 66-; vchmn, Coun Am Heart Dis Youth, Am Heart Asn, 56-60, chmn, Comt Congential Heart Dis, 56-60; chmn task force heart dis & youth, Conn Heart Asn, 75-77. *Mem:* Fel Am Acad Pediat; fel Am Col Cardiol; NY Acad Sci; Sigma Xi; Am Pediat Soc. *Res:* Rheumatic fever; etiology and prevention of congenital heart defects; diagnostic services and care of the pediatric cardiac patient; pregnancy in the congenital cardiac, growth and development of offspring; hyperlipemia; thirty year follow-up of blood pressure in childhood. *Mailing Add:* Dept of Pediat Yale Univ Sch of Med New Haven CT 06510

WHITTEMORE, WILLIAM LESLIE, b Skowhegan, Maine, Sept 25, 24; m 50. PHYSICS. *Educ:* Colby Col, AB, 45; Harvard Univ, MA, 47, PhD(physics), 49. *Prof Exp:* Assoc scientist, Brookhaven Nat Lab, 48-50, physicist, 50-56; physicist, Gen Atomic Div, Gen Dynamics Corp, 57-67, STAFF PHYSICIST, TRIGA REACTORS FACIL, GEN ATOMIC CO, 67-, SR SCI ADV, 78- *Concurrent Pos:* Vis lectr, Harvard Univ, 50-51; sci consult, Korean Atomic Energy Res Inst, 60-, Indonesian Atomic Agency, 65 & NSF, 70 & 75. *Mem:* Am Phys Soc; Am Nuclear Soc; Archaeol Inst Am. *Res:* Utilization of research reactors; neutron research; neutron radiography, isotopes for nuclear medicine. *Mailing Add:* 2365 Via Siena La Jolla CA 92037

WHITTEN, BARBARA L, b Minneapolis, Minn, Sept 26, 46; m 82. ATOMIC & MOLECULAR PHYSICS, MATHEMATICAL PHYSICS. *Educ:* Carleton Col, BA, 68; Univ Rochester, MA, 71, PhD(physics), 76. *Prof Exp:* Instr, Western Col, Miami Univ, 74-76, asst prof interdisciplinary studies, 76-80; res assoc, Physics Dept, Rice Univ, 80-81; PHYSICIST, LAWRENCE LIVERMORE NAT LAB, 81- *Mem:* Sigma Xi; Am Phys Soc; Am Asn Physics Teachers; Am Math Asn. *Res:* Algebraic statistical mechanics to the measurement problem in quantum mechanics; theoretical and computational studies of atomic and molecular processes in plasmas. *Mailing Add:* Lawrence Livermore Nat Lab L 355 Box 808 Livermore CA 94550

WHITTEN, BERTWELL KNEELAND, b Boston, Mass, Apr 1, 41; m 62; c 3. ENVIRONMENTAL PHYSIOLOGY, COMPARATIVE PHYSIOLOGY. *Educ:* Middlebury Col, AB, 62; Purdue Univ, MS, 64, PhD(environ physiol), 66. *Prof Exp:* Res physiologist, US Army Med Res & Nutrit Lab, Fitzsimons Gen Hosp, 66-68, res physiologist, Res Inst Environ Med, Army Natick Labs, 68-72; assoc prof, 72-74, PROF BIOL SCI, MICH TECHNOL UNIV, 74-, DEPT HEAD, 81- *Mem:* AAAS; Am Soc Zoologists; Am Physiol Soc. *Res:* Cardiovascular adaptations to hypoxia; exercise physiology; effect of hypoxia on intermediary metabolism in animals and man. *Mailing Add:* Dept Biol Sci Mich Technol Univ Houghton MI 49931

WHITTEN, CHARLES A, JR, b Harrisburg, Pa, Jan 20, 40; m 65. NUCLEAR PHYSICS, INTERMEDIATE ENERGY PHYSICS. *Educ:* Yale Univ, BS, 61; Princeton Univ, MA, 63, PhD(physics), 66. *Prof Exp:* Res physicist, A W Wright Nuclear Struct Lab, Yale Univ, 65-68; asst prof nuclear physics, 68-74, assoc prof, 74-80, PROF PHYSICS, UNIV CALIF, LOS ANGELES, 80- *Concurrent Pos:* Vis scientist, Ctr Nuclear Studies, Saclay France, 80-81. *Mem:* Am Phys Soc. *Res:* Direct reaction spectroscopy; isobaric analogue studies; nuclear structure studies with intermediate energy probes; nucleon-nucleon scattering at intermediate energies. *Mailing Add:* Dept of Physics Univ of Calif Los Angeles CA 90024

WHITTEN, DAVID G, b Washington, DC, Jan 25, 38; m 60; c 2. PHYSICAL ORGANIC CHEMISTRY, BIOPHYSICAL CHEMISTRY. *Educ:* Johns Hopkins Univ, BA, 59, MA, 61, PhD(org chem), 63. *Prof Exp:* Sr scientist, Jet Propulsion Lab, Calif Inst Technol, 63-65, NIH fel chem, Inst, 65-66; from asst prof to assoc prof, 66-73, prof chem, 73-80, M A SMITH PROF CHEM, UNIV NC, CHAPEL HILL, 80- *Concurrent Pos:* Consult, Sci Data Systs, Inc, 66, Tenn Eastman Co, 66-79 & Polaroid Corp, 81-; Alfred P Sloan Found fel, 70-; Alexander von Humboldt fel, Max Planck Inst Biophys Chem, 72-73; Alexander von Humboldt sr scientist award, 74-75. *Mem:* Am Chem Soc; Royal Soc Chem; Am Soc Photobiol; Japan Soc Promotion Sci Fel. *Res:* Photobiology; photochemistry in organized monolayer assemblies; solid state and surface chemistry; chemistry of N-heterocyclic compounds; porphyrins and organometallic compounds; chemistry of surfactant assemblies in aqueous solution. *Mailing Add:* Dept of Chem Univ of NC Chapel Hill NC 27514

WHITTEN, ELMER HAMMOND, b Stoughton, Mass, Feb 18, 27; m 50; c 2. MEDICAL PHYSIOLOGY, HEALTH SCIENCES ADMINISTRATION. *Educ:* Northeastern Univ, BS, 52; Mass State Col, Bridgewater, MEd, 67; Colo State Univ, PhD(physiol), 70. *Prof Exp:* Med serv rep drug sales, Pitman-Moore Co, Dow Chem Co, 54-56; admin asst sales, Metals & Controls, Inc, 56-58; head customer serv, Tex Instruments Inc, 58-66; instr human physiol, Colo State Univ, 70; from asst prof med physiol to assoc prof physiol & pharmacol, 70-72, prof physiol, 79, ASSOC DEAN ACAD AFFAIRS, UNIV HEALTH SCI, 72-, CHMN DEPT PHYSIOL, 71- *Mem:* NY Acad Sci; Sigma Xi. *Res:* Neonatal enteritis; transport phenomena across the intestinal wall during stages in the progress of enteritis as it affects electrolytes and water. *Mailing Add:* Chmn Dept of Physiol Univ Health Sci Kansas City MO 64124

WHITTEN, ERIC HAROLD TIMOTHY, b Ilford, Eng, July 26, 27; m 53, 76; c 6. GEOLOGY. *Educ:* Univ London, BSc, 48, PhD(geol), 52, DSc, 68. *Prof Exp:* Managerial chief clerk, Rex Thomas, Ltd, 43-45; lectr geol, Queen Mary Col, Univ London, 48-58; assoc prof geol, Northwestern Univ, Evanston, 58-62, prof, 62-81; VPRES ACAD AFFAIRS & PROF GEOL, MICH TECH UNIV, HOUGHTON, 81. *Concurrent Pos:* Vis assoc prof, Univ Calif, Berkeley, 57 & 60, Univ Calif, Santa Barbara, 59 & Univ Colo, 61 & 63. *Mem:* Fel AAAS; fel Geol Soc Am (pres, 80-); fel Geol Soc London; Brit Geol Asn; Int Asn Math Geol. *Res:* Structural geology and petrology of granitic and deformed rocks; application of statistical analysis to quantitative geology problems. *Mailing Add:* Admin Bldg Mich Technol Univ Houghton MI 49931

WHITTEN, HARRELL DAVID, immunology, see previous edition

WHITTEN, JERRY LYNN, b Bartow, Fla, Aug 13, 37; m 80; c 1. THEORETICAL CHEMISTRY. *Educ:* Ga Inst Technol, BS, 60, PhD(chem), 64. *Prof Exp:* Res assoc chem, Princeton Univ, 63-65, instr, 65; asst prof, Mich State Univ, 65-67; from asst prof to assoc prof, 67-73, PROF CHEM, STATE UNIV NY STONY BROOK, 73- *Concurrent Pos:* Res grants, Petrol Res Fund, 66-67, 74-76 & 77-81 & NSF, 67-72; Alfred P Sloan fel, 69-71; Dept Energy res grants, 77-81; Alexander von Humboldt sr scientist award, 79; vis prof, Univ Bonn & Wuppertal, 79. *Mem:* Am Phys Soc; Am Chem Soc; Sigma Xi. *Res:* Theoretical studies of molecular structure and bonding; ab initio many-electron theory; theory of excited electronic states, metallic surfaces and chemisorption. *Mailing Add:* Dept of Chem State Univ of NY Stony Brook NY 11790

WHITTEN, KENNETH WAYNE, b Collinsville, Ala, Feb 4, 32. INORGANIC CHEMISTRY. *Educ:* Berry Col, AB, 53; Univ Miss, MS, 58; Univ Ill, PhD(inorg chem), 65. *Prof Exp:* Instr chem, Univ Miss, 55-56; asst prof, Berry Col, 56-58; instr, Univ Southwestern La, 58-59; asst prof, Miss State Col Women, 59-60 & Univ Ala, 63-66; asst prof chem & coord gen chem, 67-70, ASSOC PROF CHEM, UNIV GA, 70- *Mem:* Am Chem Soc. *Res:* Synthesis in fused salt media; chemical education; theories of testing. *Mailing Add:* 145 Broom Sedge Trail Athens GA 30605

WHITTEN, MAURICE MASON, b Providence, RI, Oct 1, 23. ANALYTICAL CHEMISTRY, HISTORY OF SCIENCE. *Educ:* Colby Col, AB, 45; Columbia Univ, MA, 49; Ohio State Univ, PhD, 71. *Prof Exp:* Sci teacher, Wilton Acad, 45-48 & Lewiston Maine High Sch, 48-55; instr phys sci, Gorham State Teachers Col, 55-59; TV sci teacher, State Dept Educ, Maine, 59-60; asst prof, Univ Maine, Portland-Gorham, 61-63, assoc prof phys sci & chem, 64-71, prof, 71-77; PROF CHEM, UNIV SOUTHERN MAINE, 78- *Concurrent Pos:* Lectr, Cent Maine Gen Hosp, Lewiston, 52-53. *Honors & Awards:* Elizabeth Thompson Award, Am Acad Arts & Sci, 54. *Mem:* AAAS; Am Chem Soc; Nat Sci Teachers Asn; fel Am Inst Chemists; Hist Sci Soc. *Res:* Science education at the college level, especially critical thinking and scientific literacy; water pollution; history of gun powder mills of Maine. *Mailing Add:* Dept of Chem Univ of Southern Maine Gorham ME 04038

WHITTEN, ROBERT CRAIG, JR, b Bristol, Va, Dec 6, 26; m 53; c 2. AERONOMY. *Educ:* US Merchant Marine Acad, BS, 47; Univ Buffalo, BA, 55; Duke Univ, MA, 58, PhD(theoret physics), 59; San Jose State Univ, MS, 71. *Prof Exp:* Asst, Duke Univ, 55-57, instr, 57-58, asst, 58-59; from physicist to sr physicist, Stanford Res Inst, 59-67; RES SCIENTIST, NASA-AMES RES CTR, 67- *Concurrent Pos:* Lectr, Stanford Univ, 61-62 & 64-66, Univ Santa Clara, 64 & 69 & San Jose State Univ, 72 & 79. *Mem:* Am Geophys Union. *Res:* Structure, chemistry and dynamics of planetary atmospheres and ionospheres; chemistry and meteorology of the stratosphere; the quantum mechanical three body problem; atomic theory. *Mailing Add:* Mail Stop 245-3 Space Sci Div NASA-Ames Res Ctr Moffett Field CA 94035

WHITTENBERGER, JAMES LAVERRE, b Dahinda, Ill, Feb 12, 14; m 43; c 3. PHYSIOLOGY. *Educ:* Univ Chicago, SB, 37, MD, 38. *Hon Degrees:* AM, Harvard Univ, 51. *Prof Exp:* Intern, Cincinnati Gen Hosp, 38-39; Smith fel surg, Univ Chicago, 39-40; asst resident, Thorndike Mem Lab, Boston City Hosp, 40-42, house physician, 4th Med Serv, 42-43; assoc physiol, 46-47, from asst prof to assoc prof, 47-50, PROF PHYSIOL, SCH PUB HEALTH, HARVARD UNIV, 51-, HEAD DEPT, 48-, JAMES STEVENS SIMMONS PROF PUB HEALTH, 58-, ASSOC DEAN, 66- *Concurrent Pos:* Res fel med, Harvard Med Sch, 40-42; Commonwealth Fund fel med & physiol, Sch Med, NY Univ, 43; asst, Peter Bent Brigham Hosp, 46-; consult, Children's Hosp, 48- *Mem:* AAAS; Am Physiol Soc; Am Soc Clin Invest; Soc Toxicol; Am Indust Hyg Asn. *Res:* Respiratory physiology; occupational medicine; environmental health. *Mailing Add:* Physiol Dept Harvard Univ 677 Huntington Ave Weston MA 02115

WHITTIER, ANGUS CHARLES, b Ottawa, Ont, Oct 17, 21; m 48; c 4. PHYSICS. *Educ:* Queen's Univ, Ont, BSc, 48; McGill Univ, MSc & PhD(physics), 52. *Prof Exp:* Asst res officer, Atomic Energy Can, Ltd, 52-55; supv physicist, Atomic Power Dept, Can Gen Elec, 55-67, mgr reactor anal, 67-72; supt shielding & comput br power projs, 72-75, MGR SHIELDING & REACTOR PHYSICS A, ATOMIC ENERGY CAN LTD, ENG CO, SHERIDAN PARK, 77- *Mem:* Am Nuclear Soc; Can Nuclear Soc. *Res:* Nuclear physics, particularly reactor physics. *Mailing Add:* 2493 Vineland Rd Mississauga ON L5K 2A3 Can

WHITTIER, DEAN PAGE, b Worcester, Mass, July 2, 35; m 58; c 2. PLANT MORPHOLOGY. *Educ:* Univ Mass, BS, 57; Harvard Univ, AM, 59, PhD(biol), 61. *Prof Exp:* Asst prof bot, Va Polytech Inst, 61-64; NIH fel biol, Harvard Univ, 64-65; asst prof, 65-68, assoc prof, 68-77, chmn dept gen biol, 75-78, PROF BIOL, VANDERBILT UNIV, 77- *Mem:* Bot Soc Am; Am Fern Soc (treas, 74-75, vpres, 80-81); Int Soc Plant Morphologists. *Res:* Morphogenesis; apomixis in lower vascular plants. *Mailing Add:* Dept of Gen Biol Vanderbilt Univ Nashville TN 37235

WHITTIER, HENRY O, b Schenectady, NY, Sept 1, 37; m 59; c 1. BOTANY, BRYOLOGY. *Educ:* Miami Univ, BS, 59, MA, 61; Columbia Univ, PhD(biol), 68. *Prof Exp:* Res asst bot, Miami Univ Schooner Col Rebel Exped to SPac, 60; instr, Univ Hawaii, 62-64; res asst bryol, NY Bot Garden, 64-68; from asst prof to assoc prof biol sci, Fla Technol Univ, 68-79; PROF BIOL SCI, FLA TECH UNIV, 79- *Mem:* Am Bryol & Lichenological Soc; Am Inst Biol Sci; Sigma Xi; Am Bot Soc; Brit Bryol Soc. *Res:* Tropical botany, taxonomy, ethnobotany, ecology and biogeography, especially Pacific islands Bryophyta. *Mailing Add:* Dept of Biol Sci Fla Tech Univ Orlando FL 32816

WHITTIER, JAMES S(PENCER), b Farmington, Minn, June 19, 35; m 61; c 1. LASERS, MECHANICS. *Educ:* Univ Minn, BS, 57, MS, 58, PhD(mech, mat), 61. *Prof Exp:* Mem tech staff, 61-65, sect mgr, 65-67, HEAD, MECH RES DEPT, LAB OPERS, AEROSPACE CORP, 67- *Concurrent Pos:* Sr res fel, Appl Phys Dept, Cornell Univ, 74-75. *Mem:* Optical Soc Am; Am Inst Aeronaut & Astronaut; Soc Exp Stress Anal. *Res:* Chemical lasers; laser effects; remote sensing of motions; stress wave propagation. *Mailing Add:* Aerophys Lab Aerospace Corp PO Box 92957 Los Angeles CA 90009

WHITTIER, JOHN RENSSELAER, b Washington, DC, Aug 7, 19; m 50; c 2. NEUROLOGY, PSYCHIATRY. *Educ:* Harvard Univ, BA, 39; Columbia Univ, MD, 43; Am Bd Psychiat & Neurol, dipl. *Prof Exp:* Intern, Gorgas Hosp, CZ, 43-44; asst neurol, Col Physicians & Surgeons, Columbia Univ, 46-48, asst resident, Neurol Inst, 48-49; resident psychiatrist, Vet Admin Hosp, Bronx, 49-51; dir psychiat res, Creedmoor Inst Psychobiol Studies, Creedmoor Psychiat Ctr, 54-76; dir div VII psychobiol, Long Island Res Inst, 76-77. *Concurrent Pos:* Asst clin prof neurol, Col Physicians & Surgeons, Columbia Univ, 54-55, asst clin prof psychiat, 55- *Mem:* AAAS; Am Psychiat Asn; Am Asn Anat; Am Acad Neurol. *Res:* Aging; degenerative diseases; neural systems; heredity; research administration. *Mailing Add:* One Mulberry Ave Garden City NY 11530

WHITTIG, LYNN D, b Meridian, Idaho, Jan 16, 22; m 45; c 3. SOIL CHEMISTRY, SOIL MINERALOGY. *Educ:* Univ Wis, BS, 49, MS, 50, PhD(soil sci), 54. *Prof Exp:* Soil scientist, Soil Conserv Serv, USDA, 54-56; from asst prof to assoc prof, 57-70, res assoc, 63-64, vchmn Dept Land, Air & Water Resources, 75-79, PROF SOIL SCI, UNIV CALIF, DAVIS, 70-, ASSOC DIR, INST ECOL, 79- *Mem:* Fel Am Soc Agron; Soil Sci Soc Am; Clay Minerals Soc. *Res:* Clay mineralogy and mineral weathering processes; chemistry, morphology and genesis of salt-affected soils; x-ray diffraction and fluorescence methods of analysis. *Mailing Add:* Dept Land, Air & Water Resources Univ of Calif Davis CA 95616

WHITTINGHAM, MICHAEL STANLEY, b Nottingham, Eng, Dec 22, 41; m 69; c 2. SOLID STATE CHEMISTRY. *Educ:* Oxford Univ, BA, 64, MA, 67, DPhil(chem), 68. *Prof Exp:* Res assoc mat sci, Stanford Univ, 68-72; mem sci staff, 72-75, head chem physics group, 75-78, dir, Solid State & Catalytic Sci Lab, Corp Res Labs, 78-80, MGR CHEM ENG, TECHNOL DIV, EXXON RES & ENG CO, 80- *Concurrent Pos:* Demonstr, Dept Inorg Chem, Oxford Univ, 65-67; prin ed, J Solid State Ionics & assoc ed, J Appl Electrochem. *Mem:* Am Chem Soc; Electrochem Soc; Am Phys Soc; AAAS; Am Inst Chem Engrs. *Res:* Chemical properties of highly non-stoichiometric materials; fast ion transport in solids; electrochemical control of the properties of materials; solid state electrochemistry; high energy-density batteries; synthetic fuels technology. *Mailing Add:* 32 Arlene Ct Fanwood NJ 07023

WHITTINGHAM, WILLIAM FRANCIS, b Beaver Dam, Wis, Feb 23, 26; m 49; c 2. MYCOLOGY. *Educ:* Univ Wis, BS, 50, MS, 52, PhD(bot), 54. *Prof Exp:* Res assoc bact, 54-56, from instr to assoc prof, 56-69, PROF BOT, UNIV WIS-MADISON, 69- *Mem:* Bot Soc Am; Brit Soc Gen Microbiol; Brit Mycol Soc. *Res:* Physiology of fungi; ecology of soil fungi; fungal parasite-host relationships. *Mailing Add:* Dept of Bot Univ of Wis Madison WI 53706

WHITTINGHILL, MAURICE, b St Joseph, Mo, May 15, 09; m 32, 55; c 2. GENETICS. *Educ:* Dartmouth Col, AB, 31; Univ Mich, PhD(zool), 37. *Prof Exp:* Instr, Dartmouth Col, 31-33; asst, Univ Mich, 35; Nat Res Coun fel biol sci, Calif Inst Technol, 36-37; fel biol, Bennington Col, 37-42; assoc prof zool, 42-52, prof, 52-74, vis prof, 74, EMER PROF ZOOL, UNIV NC, CHAPEL HILL, 74- . *Concurrent Pos:* Prof, Univ Mich, 46; sr biologist, Oak Ridge Nat Lab, 49; Wachtmeister vis prof biol, Va Mil Inst, 76; vis prof biol, Univ NC, Wilmington, 77; T E Power Jr prof biol, Elon Col, 79-81. *Mem:* Genetics Soc Am; Am Soc Zool; Am Soc Nat; Am Soc Human Genetics; Am Genetic Asn (vpres, 72, pres, 73). *Res:* Genetics of Drosophila; irradiation and temperature effects; mutation and crossing over; spondylitis. *Mailing Add:* 1905 S Lake Shore Dr Chapel Hill NC 27514

WHITTINGTON, STUART GORDON, b Chesterfield, Eng, Apr 16, 42; Can & UK citizen; m 64; c 2. THEORETICAL CHEMISTRY. *Educ:* Cambridge Univ, BA, 63, PhD(chem), 72. *Prof Exp:* Scientist chem, Unilever Res Lab, UK, 63-66; res fel, Univ Calif, San Diego, 66-67; res fel, Univ Toronto, 67-68; scientist, Unilever Res Lab, UK, 68-70; asst prof, 70-75, assoc prof, 75-80, PROF CHEM, UNIV TORONTO, 80- *Res:* Statistical mechanics; Monte Carlo methods; excluded volume effect in polymers; polymer adsorption and colloid stability; percolation theory; phase transitions and critical phenomena. *Mailing Add:* Dept of Chem Univ of Toronto Toronto ON M5S 1A1 Can

WHITTLE, BETTY ANN, see Kozlowski, Betty Ann

WHITTLE, CHARLES EDWARD, JR, b Brownsville, Ky, Mar 8, 31; m 52; c 10. PHYSICS, APPLIED MATHEMATICS. *Educ:* Centre Col, AB, 49; Washington Univ, PhD(nuclear physics), 53. *Prof Exp:* Fulbright & Res Corp grants, State Univ Leiden, 53-54; res scientist, Union Carbide Corp, 54-56; asst & assoc prof physics, Western Ky Univ, 56-60, prof & chmn dept, 60-62; coordr res, Centre Col Ky, 62-64, from assoc dean to dean, 64-72, prof physics, 62-74, Matton chair appl math, 72-74; ASST DIR, INST ENERGY ANAL, OAK RIDGE ASSOC UNIVS, 74- *Mem:* Am Asn Physics Teachers; Sigma Xi; Phys Soc. *Res:* Nuclear and optical spectroscopy; applied mathematics and geophysics; energy policy analysis and modeling; energy data analysis and validation; geothermal energy assessment; geophysics. *Mailing Add:* Inst for Energy Anal PO Box 117 Oak Ridge TN 37830

WHITTLE, GEORGE PATTERSON, b Eufaula, Ala, July 1, 25; m 63; c 1. WATER TREATMENT ANALYTICAL CHEMISTRY. *Educ:* Ga Inst Technol, BChE, 46, BIE, 47; Univ Fla, MS, 64, PhD(chem), 66. *Prof Exp:* Chem engr, Hercules Powder Co, 47-49; self-employed, Whittle Lumber Co, 50-53; chemist, Swift & Co, 53-55; chief chemist, Allied Chem Co, 55-57; res engr, Tenn Corp, 57-63; PROF CIVIL ENG, UNIV ALA, 67- *Honors & Awards:* Bedell Award, Water Pollution Control Fedn, 77. *Mem:* Am Water Works Asn; Am Soc Civil Eng. *Res:* Water quality modeling, hydrology; water treatment and chemistry, pollution control; colloids; analytical chemistry of water and wastewater; reaction kinetics of halogen residuals in water. *Mailing Add:* Dept of Civil Eng Univ of Ala PO Box 1468 University AL 35486

WHITTLE, JOHN ANTONY, b Settle, Yorks, Eng, Mar 13, 42; m 68. ORGANIC CHEMISTRY, BIOCHEMISTRY. *Educ:* Univ Glasgow, BSc, 64; Imp Col, dipl, & Univ London, PhD(org chem), 67. *Prof Exp:* Fel, Rutgers Univ, NJ, 67-69; asst prof, 69-77, ASSOC PROF CHEM, LAMAR UNIV, 77- *Mem:* Am Chem Soc. *Res:* Biosynthesis of sesquiterpenoids and other natural products; synthesis of sesquiterpenoid ring systems. *Mailing Add:* Dept of Chem Lamar Univ PO Box 10022 Lamar Univ Sta Beaumont TX 77710

WHITTLE, PHILIP RODGER, b Russell Springs, Ky, July 11, 43; m 67; c 2. ORGANIC CHEMISTRY, FORENSIC CHEMISTRY. *Educ:* Univ Ky, BS, 65; Iowa State Univ, PhD(org chem), 69. *Prof Exp:* NIH fel, Univ Colo, Boulder, 69-70; assoc prof, 70-80, PROF CHEM, MO SOUTHERN STATE COL, 80-, DIR, REGIONAL CRIMINALISTICS LAB, 72- *Mem:* Am Chem Soc (secy-treas, 66-); Am Soc Crime Lab Dirs; Am Acad Forensic Scientists. *Res:* Electrocyclic cyclopropane ring openings; toxicology; modern drug analysis; trace evidence; forensic applications. *Mailing Add:* Dept of Chem Mo Southern State Col Joplin MO 64801

WHITTLESEY, EMMET FINLAY, b Winchester, Mass, Oct 9, 23; m 66; c 3. MATHEMATICS. *Educ:* Princeton Univ, AB, 48, MA, 55, PhD(math), 56. *Prof Exp:* Instr math, Pa State Univ, 50-51 & Bates Col, 51-54; from instr to assoc prof, 54-65, PROF MATH, TRINITY COL, CONN, 65- *Concurrent Pos:* NSF fel, 62-63. *Mem:* Am Math Soc; Math Asn Am. *Res:* Combinatorial topology; functional analysis. *Mailing Add:* Dept of Math Trinity Col Hartford CT 06106

WHITTLESEY, JOHN R B, b Los Angeles, Calif, July 21, 27; m 66; c 2. EXPLORATION GEOPHYSICS, MATHEMATICAL STATISTICS. *Educ:* Calif Inst Technol, BS, 48, MS, 50. *Prof Exp:* Instr physics & astron, Univ Nev, 50; Ford Found behav sci grant & res asst, Univ NC, 52-54; res mathematician res clin neuropsychiat inst, Med Ctr, Univ Calif, Los Angeles, 57-62, data processing analyst brain res inst, 62-64; mem res staff seismic explor data processing, Ampex Corp, Calif & Ray Geophys Div, Mandral Industs, 64-73, res scientist seismic data processing, 72-73, SR RES SCIENTIST, MARINE SEISMIC DATA ACQUISITION & PROCESSING PETTY-RAY GEOPHYS GROUP, GEOSOURCE INC, 73- *Concurrent Pos:* Statist consult numerous behav scientists, Calif, 58-71; NIMH spec res fel brain res inst, Univ Calif, Los Angeles, 63-64. *Honors & Awards:* Award, Soc Explor Geophys, 65. *Mem:* Fel AAAS; Soc Explor Geophys. *Res:* Mathematics and digital computers applied to psychiatry, brain research, field 3D signal exploration geophysics; data processing; time-series analysis; seismic processing; laser fusion. *Mailing Add:* Geosource Inc 6909 Southwest Freeway Houston TX 77036

WHITTON, LESLIE, b New Bedford, Mass, Sept 1, 23; m 47; c 4. PLANT CYTOLOGY, PLANT GENETICS. *Educ:* Utah State Univ, BS, 49; Univ Calif, MS, 53; Cornell Univ, PhD, 64. *Prof Exp:* Asst prof hort, Univ Maine, Orono, 56-62; asst prof, 62-64, asst prof bot, 64-68, ASSOC PROF BOT, BRIGHAM YOUNG UNIV, 68- *Mem:* Bot Soc Am; Sigma Xi. *Res:* Cytology, genetics and breeding of small fruit species and native shrub species of the Rocky Mountain region. *Mailing Add:* Dept of Bot & Range Sci Brigham Young Univ Provo UT 84601

WHITTOW, GEORGE CAUSEY, b Milford Haven, UK, Feb 28, 30; m 55; c 1. PHYSIOLOGY. *Educ:* Univ London, BSc, 52; Univ Malaya, PhD(physiol), 57. *Prof Exp:* Asst lectr physiol, Univ Malaya, 52-54, lectr, 54-59; sr sci officer, Hannah Res Inst, Ayr, Scotland, 59-65; assoc prof physiol, Rutgers Univ, New Brunswick, 65-68; PROF PHYSIOL, SCH MED, UNIV HAWAII, 68- *Mem:* Am Physiol Soc; Am Soc Zool; Ecol Soc Am; Brit Inst Biol; Am Ornith Union. *Res:* Physiology of thermoregulation; thermal ecology. *Mailing Add:* Sch of Med Univ of Hawaii Honolulu HI 96822

WHITTY, ELMO BENJAMIN, b Lee, Fla, Mar 6, 37. AGRONOMY. *Educ:* Univ Fla, BSA, 59, MSA, 61; NC State Univ, PhD(soil sci), 65. *Prof Exp:* Asst prof, 66-71, assoc prof, 71-77, PROF AGRON, UNIV FLA, 77- *Mem:* Am Soc Agron; Plant Growth Regulator Soc Am; Am Peanut Res & Educ Soc. *Res:* Tobacco production; cultural practices; plant growth regulators; plant nutrition. *Mailing Add:* Dept Agron Univ Fla Gainesville FL 32611

WHITWELL, JOHN C(OLMAN), b Washington, DC, Nov 17, 09; m 33. CHEMICAL ENGINEERING. *Educ:* Princeton Univ, BSE, 31, ChE, 32. *Prof Exp:* From instr to prof, 32-74, acting chmn dept, 43-46, EMER PROF CHEM ENG, PRINCETON UNIV, 74- *Concurrent Pos:* Off investr, Nat Defense Res Comt, 41-43; dir proj, Rubber Reserve Co, 43-44; engr, Textile Res Inst, 44-46, assoc dir res, 46-49, res assoc, 49-; consult, Union Carbide Chem Co, 53-63, Am Cyanamid Co, 55-74, FMC Corp, 66-68 & Personal Prod Div, Johnson & Johnson, 66-; treas & trustee, Princeton Hosp, 62-71, bd dirs, Med Ctr, Princeton Found, 78-; mem adv budget res comt hosp costs, NJ Comnr Ins, 68-74 & Presidential health serv indust comn, Adv to Cost of Living Coun, 71-72. *Honors & Awards:* Award excellence instr eng studies, Western Elec Corp, 72. *Mem:* Hon fel Textile Res Inst; fel Am Inst Chem Engrs; Am Chem Soc; Am Statist Asn. *Res:* Health industries; physical properties and processing of textile fibers; thermal degradation and properties of polymers; staged operations; design of experiments; mass and energy balances and engineering statistics; process design problems. *Mailing Add:* A223 Eng Quadrangle Princeton Univ Princeton NJ 08540

WHITWORTH, CLYDE W, b Paulding Co, Ga, Oct 9, 26; m 51; c 3. PHARMACY. *Educ:* Univ Ga, BS, 50, MS, 56; Univ Fla, PhD(pharm), 63. *Prof Exp:* From instr to asst prof pharm, Univ Ga, 54-60; asst prof, Northeast La State Col, 63-66; assoc prof, 66-80, PROF PHARM, UNIV GA, 80- *Concurrent Pos:* Mead Johnson res award, 65-66; William A Webster Co grant prod stability, 72- *Mem:* Am Pharmaceut Asn. *Res:* Factors influencing drug absorption and drug release from external preparations. *Mailing Add:* Univ of Ga Sch of Pharm Athens GA 30602

WHITWORTH, WALTER RICHARD, b La Crosse, Wis, Feb 22, 34; m 57; c 4. AQUATIC BIOLOGY. *Educ:* Wis State Col, Stevens Point, BS, 58; Okla State Univ, MS, 61, PhD(zool), 63. *Prof Exp:* Fish biologist, Southeastern Fish Control Lab, 63-64; asst prof fisheries, 64-69, assoc prof, 69-76, PROF FISHERIES, UNIV CONN, 76- *Mem:* Am Fisheries Soc; Am Soc Ichthyol & Herpet; Ecol Soc Am; Am Soc Limnol & Oceanog. *Res:* Effects of the environment on fish; primary productivity; fish taxonomy and toxicology. *Mailing Add:* U-87 Col of Agr & Natural Res Univ of Conn Storrs CT 06268

WHORTON, ELBERT BENJAMIN, b Stamford, Tex, Nov 10, 38; m 62; c 2. RESEARCH DESIGN & ANALYSIS. *Educ:* Baylor Univ, BS(math) & BS(physics), 62; Tulane Univ, MS, 64; Okla Univ, PhD(biostatist & med comput), 68. *Prof Exp:* Surv statistician dir, La State Health Dept, 64-65; from asst prof to assoc prof & dir biomet, Univ Vt, 68-72, asst prof math, 69-72; assoc prof & dir biostatist, Univ Tex Med Br Galveston, 72-82; RES COLLABR, BROOK HAVEN NAT LAB, 82- *Concurrent Pos:* Statist consult, Bur Manpower Intel, NIH, 68-73, Nat Cancer Inst, 73-, Dow Chem Co, 73-80 & Ethyl Corp, 81-82; dir, Educ & Res Comput Ctr, Univ Tex Med Br Galveston, 75-81, assoc dean, Grad Sch Biomed Sci, 76-81; vis prof, Med Sch, Univ Vt, 81. *Mem:* Am Statist Asn; Environ Mutagen Soc; Biomet Soc; Sigma Xi. *Res:* Development and evaluation of experimental and non-experimental designs in environmental toxicology mutagenesis research; development of improved methods for statistical evaluation of research results, particularly in genetic toxicology. *Mailing Add:* 20 Colony Park Circle Galveston TX 77551

WHORTON, RAYBURN HARLEN, b London, Ark, Apr 28, 31; m 56; c 3. PAPER CHEMISTRY. *Educ:* Ark Polytech Col, BS, 53; Univ Ark, MS, 56. *Prof Exp:* Instr chem, Ark Polytech Col, 55-56; res chemist, Crossett Co, 57-62; proj supvr, Ga-Pac Corp, 62-63; sr proj chemist, 64-69, sect leader paper develop, 69-77, GROUP MGR PAPER STRUCTURE & CHEM, ERLING RIIS RES, INT PAPER CO, 77- *Mem:* Tech Asn Pulp & Paper Indust. *Res:* Papermaking; surface and internal sizing; printability coatings; paper-plastic combinations; converting processes. *Mailing Add:* Erling Riis Res Int Paper Co Mobile AL 36652

WHYBROW, PETER CHARLES, b Hertfordshire, Eng, June 13, 39; nat US; m 63; c 2. PSYCHIATRY. *Educ:* Univ London, MB & BS, 62; Royal Col Physicians, dipl, 62; Conjoint Bd Physicians & Surgeons Eng, dipl psychol med, 68. *Hon Degrees:* MA, Dartmouth Col, 74. *Prof Exp:* House physician, Med Res Coun-Univ Col Hosp, London, 62; house surgeon, St Helier Hosp, Surrey, Eng, 63; sr house physician, Univ Col Hosp, London, 63-64; house physician, Prince of Wales Hosp, London, 64; resident psychiat, Univ NC, 65-67, instr, 67-68; sci officer, Med Res Coun, Eng, 68-69; from asst prof to assoc prof, 69-71, chmn dept, 71-78, prof psychiat, 71-79, EXEC DEAN & DEAN, DARTMOUTH MED SCH, 80- *Concurrent Pos:* NIMH res fel, Univ NC, 67-68; lectr, Univ Col Hosp Med Sch, London, 68-69; dir res training, Dartmouth Hitchcock Affil Hosps, 69-71, dir psychiat, 70-; consult, Vet Admin Hosp, 70-; Joshia Macy Jr fac scholar, 78-79; vis scientist div psychobiol, NIMH; chmn psychiat test comt, Nat Bd Med Examrs, 78- *Mem:* Brit Med Asn; fel Royal Col Psychiat; Am Asn Chmn Depts Psychiat (pres, 77-78); Brit Soc Psychosom Res; fel Am Psychiat Asn. *Res:* Psychobiology of affective disorders, particularly pharmacologic and endocrinologic aspects. *Mailing Add:* Dept of Psychiat Dartmouth Med Sch Hanover NH 03755

WHYBURN, LUCILLE ENID, b Lewisville, Tex, July 31, 05; m 25; c 1. MATHEMATICS. *Educ:* Univ Tex, BA, 27, MA, 36. *Prof Exp:* Res assoc math, Johns Hopkins Univ, 31-34; lectr, Univ Va, 44-45, asst prof, 46-47; assoc prof, Sweet Briar Col, 60-62; asst prof, 62-67, ASSOC PROF MATH, UNIV VA, 67- *Concurrent Pos:* Lectr, Univ Tex, 75-76, consult to pres, 77-; mem adv comt or arch, Am Math Humanities Res Ctr, Univ Tex, 79- *Mem:* Am Math Soc; Math Asn Am. *Res:* Rotation groups about a set of fixed points; biographical research into the R L Moore Collection at the University of Texas. *Mailing Add:* 133 Bollingwood Rd Charlottesville VA 22903

WHYTE, DONALD EDWARD, b Regina, Sask, Jan 22; m 18; nat US; m 43; c 4. ORGANIC CHEMISTRY. *Educ:* Univ Sask, BA, 39, MA, 41; Columbia Univ, PhD(chem), 43. *Prof Exp:* Chemist naval stores, Hercules Powder Co, 43-46; head org res sect, 46-52, res serv mgr, 52-57, tech serv mgr, 57-59, dir serv prod develop, 59-61, appl res dir, 61-64, res mgr, 65-71, prod res mgr int opers, dir res & develop int opers, 74-77, VPRES INT RES & DEVELOP, S C JOHNSON & SON, INC, 77- *Concurrent Pos:* Fel, Columbia Univ. *Mem:* Am Chem Soc; Am Oil Chem Soc. Am Soc Qual Control. *Res:* Analytical and market research; new product evaluation; new product development of polishes, coating and porelon; polymers; insecticides; insect repellants; synergists and microbiology; development of new consumer and industrial products for overseas introduction; developing overseas research and development laboratories. *Mailing Add:* S C Johnson & Son Inc Racine WI 53403

WHYTE, MICHAEL PETER, b New York, NY, Dec 19, 46; m 74. INTERNAL MEDICINE. *Educ:* Washington Square Col, NY Univ, BA, 68; State Univ NY, MD, 72. *Prof Exp:* From intern to resident internal med, Dept Med, Bellevue Hosp, New York, 72-74; clin assoc metab neurol, Nat Inst Neurol & Commun Dis & Stroke, NIH, 74-76; fel endocrinol, 76-79, ASST PROF MED, SCH MED, WASHINGTON UNIV, 79- *Res:* Calcium metabolism and metabolic bone disease; alkaline phosphatose; bone dysplasias. *Mailing Add:* Dept Med Jewish Hosp 216 S Kingshighway St Louis MO 63110

WHYTE, THADDEUS EVERETT, JR, b Washington, DC, Dec 8, 37; m 59; c 2. PHYSICAL CHEMISTRY. *Educ:* Georgetown Univ, BS, 60; Howard Univ, MS, 62, PhD(phys chem), 65. *Prof Exp:* Phys chemist, Nat Bur Standards, 62-63; res chemist, Howard Univ, 63-64; lectr chem, Sacramento State Col, 65-67; sr res chemist, Mobil Res & Develop Corp, 67-73, group leader, 69-72, proj leader, Reforming & Spec Process Group, 73-75 & Res Planning & Econ, Res Planning Group, 75-76; mgr, Amines Prod Sect & dir indust chem res & develop, Chem Group, 76-79; DIR SPEC PROJ, CATALYTIC ASSOC, INC, 79- *Concurrent Pos:* Lectr, Dept Sci & Math, Gloucester County Col, NJ, 69-70. *Mem:* Am Chem Soc; Am Inst Chemists; Am Inst Chem Eng. *Res:* Heterogeneous catalysis; structure determination of heterogeneous catalysts; small angle x-ray scattering; industrial chemicals intermediates; petroleum catalysis. *Mailing Add:* Catalytica Assocs Inc Santa Clara CA 95051

WIANT, HARRY VERNON, JR, b Burnsville, WVa, Nov 4, 32; m 54; c 2. FORESTRY. *Educ:* Univ WVa, BSF, 54; Univ Ga, MF, 59; Yale Univ, PhD(forestry), 63. *Prof Exp:* Jr forester, US Forest Serv, 57; asst prof forestry, Humboldt State Col, 61-65; prof & asst to dean, Stephen F Austin State Col, 65-72; PROF FORESTRY, WVA UNIV, 72- *Mem:* Soc Am Foresters. *Res:* Concentration of carbon dioxide near forest floor; ecology and silviculture of redwood; chemical and mechanical control of undesirable hardwoods; prediction of site quality; volume determinations; silviculture of southern forest trees; dendrological techniques. *Mailing Add:* Div Forestry WVa Univ Morgantown WV 26506

WIATROWSKI, CLAUDE ALLAN, b Chicago, Ill, Dec 27, 46. ELECTRICAL ENGINEERING, COMPUTER SCIENCE. *Educ:* Ill Inst Technol, BS, 68; Univ Ariz, MS, 70, PhD(elec eng), 73. *Prof Exp:* Consult geophys, Independent Consult, 71-73; design engr microcomput, Burr Brown Res Corp, 73-75; asst prof elec eng, Univ Colo, 75-81; MEM STAFF, MT AUTOMATION CORP, 81- *Concurrent Pos:* Res asst, Dept Physics, Ill Inst Technol, 67-; res asst, Dept Elec Eng, Univ Ariz, 68-73; pres, Mountain Automation Corp, 76- *Mem:* Inst Elec & Electronics Engrs; Asn Comput Mach; Instrument Soc Am; Am Soc Eng Educ. *Res:* Microcomputer applications, especially industrial control; development techniques for microcomputer systems. *Mailing Add:* PO Box 7037 Mt Automation Corp Colorado Springs CO 80907

WIBERG, DONALD M, b Battle Creek, Mich, Sept, 20, 36; div 79; c 5. CONTROL & BIOMEDICAL ENGINEERING. *Educ:* Calif Inst Technol, BS, 59, MS, 60, PhD(eng), 65. *Prof Exp:* Sr design engr, Gen Dynamics/ Convair, 64-65; asst prof, 65-72, assoc prof, 72-79, PROF ENG, UNIV CALIF, LOS ANGELES, 79-, PROF ANESTHESIA, 80- *Concurrent Pos:* Consult, Douglas Aircraft Co, 66-69 & R & D Assocs, 72-74; Fulbright scholar, 77; consult, Aerospace Corp, 81- *Mem:* Inst Elec & Electronics Engrs; Soc Indust & Appl Math. *Res:* System modelling and parameter identification; biomedical systems, especially respiratory and cardiovascular modelling; optimum control of distributed parameter systems; nuclear reactor kinetics and control; aerospace control. *Mailing Add:* 4532 Boelter Hall Univ of Calif Los Angeles CA 90024

WIBERG, GEORGE STUART, b Winnipeg, Man, Apr 1, 20; m 55; c 2. TOXICOLOGY. *Educ:* Univ Man, BSc, 50, MSc, 51; Univ Alta, PhD(biochem), 55. *Prof Exp:* Chemist physiol & hormone sect food & drug labs, 55-62, res scientist path & toxicol sect, Food & Drug Dir, 62-70, sci adv & actg head hazardous prod sect, Div Toxicol, Food Adv Bur, Health Protection Br, 70-73, HEAD TOXICOL EVAL ENVIRON TOXICOL DIV, ENVIRON HEALTH DIRECTORATE, HEALTH PROTECTION BR, CAN DEPT NAT HEALTH & WELFARE, 73- *Concurrent Pos:* Consult comt experts transport dangerous goods, UN, 74. *Mem:* Can Biochem Soc; Soc Toxicol; Can Soc Res Toxicol. *Res:* Toxicology of household products including dermal, cutaneous and ocular toxicity and inhalation toxicology of household aerosols and solvents. *Mailing Add:* 917 Fairlawn Ottawa ON K2A 3S6 Can

WIBERG, JOHN SAMUEL, b Plaistow, NH, Dec 4, 30; m 52; c 3. BIOCHEMISTRY, GENETICS. *Educ:* Trinity Col, Conn, BS, 52; Univ Rochester, PhD(pharmacol), 56. *Prof Exp:* Clin lab officer, Wright-Patterson Air Force Base, Ohio, 57-58; res assoc biochem, Mass Inst Technol, 59-63; asst prof, 63-70, ASSOC PROF RADIATION BIOL & BIOPHYS, SCH MED & DENT, UNIV ROCHESTER, 70- *Concurrent Pos:* NIH res fel, Mass Inst Technol, 59-60. *Mem:* AAAS; Am Soc Biol Chem; Genetic Soc Am; Am Soc Microbiol; Am Chem Soc. *Res:* Metal ion interactions with nucleic acids and enzymes; biochemical genetics of bacterial viruses; nucleic acid function and metabolism; regulation of protein synthesis. *Mailing Add:* Dept Radiation Biol & Biophys Univ Rochester Sch Med & Dent Rochester NY 14642

WIBERG, KENNETH BERLE, b Brooklyn, NY, Sept 22, 27; m 51; c 3. ORGANIC CHEMISTRY. *Educ:* Mass Inst Technol, BS, 48; Columbia Univ, PhD(chem), 50. *Prof Exp:* Instr chem, Univ Wash, Seattle, 50-52, from asst prof to assoc prof, 52-57; vis prof, Harvard Univ, 57-58; prof, Univ Wash, Seattle, 58-60; prof, 60-68, chmn dept, 68-71, WHITEHEAD PROF CHEM, YALE UNIV, 68- *Concurrent Pos:* Sloan fel, 58-62; Boomer Mem lectr, Univ Alta, 59; Guggenheim fel, 61-62. *Honors & Awards:* Award, Am Chem Soc, 62, J F Norris Award Phys Org Chem, 73. *Mem:* Nat Acad Sci; AAAS; Am Chem Soc; Royal Soc Chem. *Res:* Stereochemistry and kinetics of organic reactions, particularly oxidation reactions and molecular rearrangements; synthesis and reactions of highly strained compounds. *Mailing Add:* Dept Chem Yale Univ 225 Prospect St New Haven CT 06520

WIBERLEY, STEPHEN EDWARD, b Troy, NY, May 31, 19; m 42; c 2. ANALYTICAL CHEMISTRY. *Educ:* Williams Col, AB, 41; Rensselaer Polytech Inst, MS, 48, PhD(chem), 50. *Prof Exp:* Sr chemist, Congoleum Nairn, Inc, 41-44; anal chemist, Gen Elec Corp, 46-48; instr chem, 46-48, res assoc, US AEC contract, 48-50, from asst prof to assoc prof anal chem, 50-57, assoc dean, Grad Sch, 64-65, dean, Grad Sch, 65-79, vprovost grad prog & res, 69-79, PROF ANAL CHEM, RENSSELAER POLYTECH INST, 57- *Concurrent Pos:* Vis physicist, Brookhaven Nat Labs, 50; consult, Imp Color Chem & Paper Corp, Socony-Mobil Oil Co, Inc, Huyck Felt Co, Schenectady Chem, Inc & Nat Gypsum Co. *Mem:* AAAS; Am Chem Soc. *Res:* Instrumental analysis; infrared and Raman spectroscopy; analysis of radioactive elements. *Mailing Add:* Dept Chem Rensselaer Polytech Inst Troy NY 12180

WICANDER, EDWIN REED, b San Francisco, Calif, July 15, 46; m 75. PALEONTOLOGY, GEOLOGY. *Educ:* San Diego State Univ, BS, 69; Univ Calif, Los Angeles, PhD(geol), 73. *Prof Exp:* ASST PROF GEOL, CENT MICH UNIV, 76- *Mem:* Soc Econ Paleontologists & Mineralogists; Paleont Soc; Palaeont Asn; Sigma Xi; Am Asn Stratig Palynologists. *Res:* Micropaleontology. *Mailing Add:* Dept of Geol Cent Mich Univ Mt Pleasant MI 48859

WICHERN, DEAN WILLIAM, b Medford, Wis, Apr 29, 42; m 68; c 2. STATISTICS. *Educ:* Univ Wis-Madison, BS, 64, MS, 65, PhD(statist), 69. *Prof Exp:* From asst to assoc prof bus, 69-76, chmn, Dept Quant Anal, 75-78, PROF BUS, UNIV WIS-MADISON, 76- *Concurrent Pos:* Vis mem, US Army Math Res Ctr, Madison, Wis, 78-79. *Mem:* AAAS; Am Statist Asn; Inst Mgt Sci; Royal Statist Soc. *Res:* Time series analysis; experimental design; applications of statistical methods in business. *Mailing Add:* Sch of Bus 1155 Observatory Dr Madison WI 53706

WICHMANN, EYVIND HUGO, b Stockholm, Sweden, May 30, 28; nat US; m 51; c 2. THEORETICAL PHYSICS. *Educ:* Inst Tech, Finland, AB, 50; Columbia Univ, AM, 53, PhD, 56. *Prof Exp:* Mem staff physics, Inst Advan Study, 55-57; from asst prof to assoc prof, 57-67, PROF PHYSICS, UNIV CALIF, BERKELEY, 67- *Mem:* Am Phys Soc. *Res:* Quantum field theory and quantum electrodynamics. *Mailing Add:* Dept of Physics Univ of Calif Berkeley CA 94720

WICHNER, ROBERT PAUL, b Pecs, Hungary, Apr 29, 33; US citizen; m 54; c 2. ENGINEERING SCIENCE. *Educ:* City Col New York, BS, 54; Univ Cincinnati, MS, 55; Univ Tenn, PhD(eng sci), 64. *Prof Exp:* DEVELOP RES ENGR, OAK RIDGE NAT LAB, 55- *Res:* Experimental and theoretical turbulence research; two-phase flow fluid dynamics and heat transfer; thermal-hydraulic analysis of nuclear reactors; analysis and modeling of thermal discharges. *Mailing Add:* 104 Burgess Lane Oak Ridge TN 37830

WICHOLAS, MARK L, b Lawrence, Mass, June 11, 40; m 65; c 2. INORGANIC CHEMISTRY. *Educ:* Boston Univ, AB, 61; Mich State Univ, MS, 64; Univ Ill, PhD(chem), 67. *Prof Exp:* Asst prof chem, 67-72, ASSOC PROF CHEM, WESTERN WASH UNIV, 72- *Mem:* Am Chem Soc. *Res:* Physical inorganic chemistry; coordination chemistry of transition metals; bioinorganic chemistry. *Mailing Add:* Dept of Chem Western Wash Univ Bellingham WA 98225

WICHT, MARION CAMMACK, b Eastabutchie, Miss, Mar 5, 14; m 40; c 3. MATHEMATICS. *Educ:* Miss Southern Col, BS, 35; Vanderbilt Univ, MA, 36; Auburn Univ, PhD, 57. *Prof Exp:* Master math, Montgomery Bell Acad, 36-38; actuary, Liberty Mutual Ins Co, 38-40; master, Montgomery Bell Acad, 40-42; instr airplane mechs, US Army Air Forces, 42-43; instr math, La State Univ, 46-50; prof math & head dept, N Ga Col, 50-77; RETIRED. *Concurrent Pos:* Exchange scholar, Univ Berlin, 39-40; instr, Vanderbilt Univ, 40-42; vis prof, US Naval Postgrad Sch, 63-64; vis prof, Univ Ariz, 71. *Mem:* Math Asn Am; Am Math Soc; Asn Comput Mach; Soc Indust & Appl Math. *Res:* Poles and polars; foundations of Riemannian geometry; polyharmonics of polynomials. *Mailing Add:* PO Box 343 Dahlonega GA 30533

WICHT, ROBERT JOSEPH, b Omaha, Nebr, Oct 11, 51; m 70; c 2. BIOLOGY. *Educ:* US Army Signal Sch, Diplom, 70; Kearney State Col, BSc, 76. *Prof Exp:* Prog dir electronics, Telesis Corp, 68-69; sta controller, US Army, 69-71; MGR REFUGE, NAT AUDUBON SOC, 74- *Concurrent Pos:* Consult, Univ Colo Med Ctr, Denver, 71; consult, US Fish & Wildlife Serv, 74-, res biologist, 78-; comt mem, US Dept Interior Platte River Nat Wildlife Study, 77-; sci resource group, AAAS, 77-; consult, House Rep US Congress Comt Sci & Technol, 78- *Mem:* AAAS; Wildlife Dis Asn; Wildlife Soc; Am Inst Biol Sci. *Res:* Regeneration; wildlife disease; habitat management; microbiology; bacteriology; parasitology; ecology. *Mailing Add:* PO Box 387 Grand Island NE 68801

WICHTERMAN, RALPH, b Philadelphia, Pa, Sept 8, 07; m 33; c 2. ZOOLOGY. *Educ:* Temple Univ, BS, 30; Univ Pa, MA, 32, PhD(zool), 36. *Prof Exp:* Asst instr, 29-32, instr biol, 32-39, from asst prof to assoc prof, 39-49, prof, 50-74, EMER PROF BIOL, TEMPLE UNIV, 75- *Concurrent Pos:* Guest investr, Dry Tortugas Lab, 39; vis prof, Univ Pa, 51; AEC protozoologist, Acad Natural Sci, Philadephia, 52; lectr, Nenski Inst Exp Biol, Warsaw, Poland, 62; Am Philos Soc-NSF award, Zool Sta, Naples, Italy, 62 & 69; mem corp, Marine Biol Lab, Woods Hole. *Mem:* Fel AAAS; Am Soc Zool; Am Soc Parasitol; Micros Soc Am; Soc Protozool. *Res:* Protozoology; parasitology; cytology; histology; parasitic protozoa; sexual processes in ciliates; biology of Paramecium; gamma and x-radiation of protozoa. *Mailing Add:* 31 Buzzards Bay Ave Woods Hole MA 02543

WICK, EMILY LIPPINCOTT, b Youngstown, Ohio, Dec 9, 21. ORGANIC CHEMISTRY, ACADEMIC ADMINISTRATION. *Educ:* Mt Holyoke Col, AB, 43, MA, 45; Mass Inst Technol, PhD(org chem), 51. *Hon Degrees:* ScD, Mt Holyoke Col, 72. *Prof Exp:* Instr chem, Mt Holyoke Col, 45-46; res assoc org chem, Mass Inst Technol, 51-53; org chemist flavor lab, Arthur D Little, Inc, 53-57; res assoc food sci, Mass Inst Technol, 57-59, asst prof food chem, 59-63, from assoc prof to prof, 63-73, assoc dean student affairs, 65-72; prof chem & dean fac, 73-80, ASST TO THE PRES, LONG RANGE PLANNING, MT HOLYOKE COL, 81- *Mem:* AAAS; Am Chem Soc; Inst Food Technol. *Res:* Chemistry of food and natural products. *Mailing Add:* Mary Lyon Hall Mt Holyoke Col South Hadley MA 01075

WICK, GIAN CARLO, b Torino, Italy, Oct 15, 09; nat US; m 43; c 2. PHYSICS. *Educ:* Univ Torino, PhD(physics), 30. *Prof Exp:* Asst prof theoret physics, Univ Palermo, 37-38; assoc prof, Univ Padova, 38-40; prof, Univ Rome, 40-45; prof, Univ Notre Dame, 46-48; prof, Univ Calif, 48-50; prof, Carnegie Inst Technol, 51-57; sr physicist, Brookhaven Nat Lab, 57-65; prof physics, 65-77, EMER PROF PHYSICS, COLUMBIA UNIV, 77- *Mem:* Nat Acad Sci; fel Am Phys Soc; Am Acad Arts & Sci. *Res:* Nuclear physics; elementary physics. *Mailing Add:* Scuola Normale Superiore Piazza Del Cavalleri 56100 Pisa Italy

WICK, JAMES ROY, b Henry Co, Iowa, Dec 17, 12; m 42; c 2. ENTOMOLOGY. *Educ:* Iowa Wesleyan Col, BS, 48; Kans State Col, MS, 50; Iowa State Col, PhD(entom), 54. *Prof Exp:* Instr biol, Iowa State Col, 52-54, asst prof, 54-59; assoc prof, 59-64, PROF ZOOL & CHMN DEPT BIOL SCI, NORTHERN ARIZ UNIV, 64- *Mem:* AAAS; Am Inst Biol Sci; Am Entom Soc. *Res:* Insect histology and developmental anatomy. *Mailing Add:* Dept of Biol Sci Box 5640 Northern Ariz Univ Flagstaff AZ 86001

WICK, LAWRENCE BERNARD, b Abbey, Sask, Can, May 2, 17; US citizen; m 46; c 2. ORGANIC CHEMISTRY. *Educ:* Univ Mich, BS, 40, MS, 43, PhD, 48. *Prof Exp:* Res chemist, Gen Motors Corp, 41-42 & Manhattan Proj, Tenn, 44-45; asst prof chem, Northern Ill State Col, 47-49, Coe Col, 49-51 & Kans State Col, 51-52; res chemist, Glidden Co, 52-58; assoc prof chem, Drury Col, 58-60; assoc prof, 60-72, prof, 72-81, EMER PROF, OHIO WESLEYAN UNIV, 81- *Concurrent Pos:* Res assoc, Kings Col, Univ London, 71. *Mem:* Am Chem Soc; The Chem Soc; Swiss Chem Soc. *Res:* Synthesis and reactions of cyclic ketones; synthesis of steroids; organo-phosphorus chemistry. *Mailing Add:* Dept of Chem Ohio Wesleyan Univ Delaware OH 43015

WICK, O(SWALD) J, b Fargo, NDak, July 15, 14; m 41; c 3. METALLURGICAL & MINING ENGINEERING. *Educ:* Mont Sch Mines, BS, 36, MS, 37. *Prof Exp:* Assoc metall, Col Mines, Univ Wash, Seattle, 37-42; gen supt mercury mine, Pac Mining Co, Wash, 42; metallurgist, Metall Lab, Puget Sound Naval Shipyard, 42-50; metallurgist pile technol, Gen Elec Co, 50-54, sr engr, 54-56, head prod metall, 56, mgr plutonium metall, Hanford Labs, 56-62, mgr metall develop, 62-65; mgr, 65-66, dep mgr metall dept, 66-68, assoc mgr chem & metall div, 68-71, STAFF ENGR, CHEM TECHNOL DEPT, PAC NORTHWEST LAB, BATTELLE MEM INST, 71- *Concurrent Pos:* Tech adv, US Deleg Second Int Conf Peaceful Uses Atomic Energy, Geneva, 58. *Mem:* Am Inst Mining, Metall & Petrol Engrs; Am Soc Metals. *Res:* Plutonium metallurgy; metal fabrication; nuclear fuel; mineral dressing. *Mailing Add:* Chem Technol Dept PO Box 999 Battelle Mem Inst Richland WA 99352

WICK, ROBERT S(ENTERS), b Port Washington, NY, Dec 4, 25; m 47; c 5. MECHANICAL ENGINEERING. *Educ:* Rensselaer Polytech Inst, BME, 46; Stevens Inst Technol, MS, 48; Univ Ill, PhD(mech eng), 52. *Prof Exp:* Res engr, Standard Oil Develop Co, 46-47; instr mech eng, Syracuse Univ, 48-50; sr res engr, Jet Propulsion Lab, Calif Inst Technol, 52-55, res group supvr, 55; sr engr, Bettis Atomic Power Lab, Westinghouse Elec Corp, 55-57, supvr, 57-59, mgr adv core nuclear design, 59-62, mgr power physics dept & power reactor eng, 62-66; PROF NUCLEAR & AEROSPACE ENG, TEX A&M UNIV, 66- *Mem:* AAAS; Am Nuclear Soc; Am Soc Mech Engrs; Am Inst Aeronaut & Astronaut. *Res:* Nuclear reactor technology; rocket propulsion and combustion; applied and fluid mechanics; thermodynamics. *Mailing Add:* 1204 Neal Pickett College Station TX 77840

WICKE, BRIAN GARFIELD, b Berea, Ohio, July 24, 44; m 67; c 2. PHYSICAL CHEMISTRY. *Educ:* DePauw Univ, BA, 66; Harvard Univ, MA, 71, PhD(phys chem), 71. *Prof Exp:* Res assoc chem, Quantum Inst, Univ Calif, Santa Barbara, 74-75, vis scholar, 75-76; scientist, TRW Systs Group, Redondo Beach, Calif, 76-78; assoc sr res scientist, 78-80, SR STAFF SCIENTIST, GEN MOTORS LAB, 80- *Mem:* InterAm Photochem Soc. *Res:* Chemical kinetics, with particular emphasis on spectroscopic diagnostics, including chemiluminescence, laser induced fluorescence, and laser spectroscopy. *Mailing Add:* Phys Chem Dept Gen Motors Res Lab Warren MI 48090

WICKE, HOWARD HENRY, b Chicago, Ill, Aug 29, 24; m 45; c 4. TOPOLOGY. *Educ:* Univ Iowa, PhD(math), 52. *Prof Exp:* Instr math, Lehigh Univ, 52-54; mem staff, Sandia Corp, 54-61, supvr, 61-70; PROF MATH, OHIO UNIV, 70- *Mem:* Am Math Soc; Math Asn Am. *Res:* General topology; point-set topology; set theory; applied mathematics. *Mailing Add:* Dept of Math Ohio Univ Athens OH 45701

WICKELGREN, WARREN OTIS, b Munster, Ind, Oct 15, 41; m 65; c 2. NEUROPHYSIOLOGY. *Educ:* Univ Mich, Ann Arbor, AB, 63; Yale Univ, PhD(psychol), 67. *Prof Exp:* NIH trainee, Yale Univ, 67-69, asst prof physiol, 69-70; asst prof, 70-76, ASSOC PROF PHYSIOL, UNIV COLO MED CTR, DENVER, 76- *Concurrent Pos:* NIH res career develop award, Univ Colo Med Ctr, Denver, 71. *Mem:* Soc Neurosci; Am Physiol Soc. *Res:* Organization of simple vertebrate nervous systems; neurophysiology of learning. *Mailing Add:* Dept Physiol Univ Colo Med Ctr Denver CO 80262

WICKER, ED FRANKLIN, plant pathology, forestry, see previous edition

WICKER, EVERETT E, b Lockport, NY, Apr 6, 19; m 43; c 2. NUCLEAR SCIENCE. *Educ:* Univ Pittsburgh, BS, 41; Carnegie-Mellon Univ, MS, 57. *Prof Exp:* Physicist, Kennametal, Inc, 41-42 & 46-47; from asst technologist to technologist, 47-54, from supvry technologist to res technologist, 54-64, ASSOC RES CONSULT, RES LAB, US STEEL CORP, 64- *Mem:* Am Phys Soc; Am Nuclear Soc. *Res:* Neutron and charged particle activation analysis; nuclear reactor materials; nuclear and reactor physics; industrial and research uses of radioisotopes and radiation. *Mailing Add:* US Steel Corp Res Lab MS 73 125 Jamison Lane Monroeville PA 15146

WICKER, ROBERT KIRK, b Altoona, Pa, Mar 4, 38; m 61; c 3. PHYSICAL INORGANIC CHEMISTRY. *Educ:* Juniata Col, BS, 60; Univ Del, MS, 63, PhD(phys chem), 66. *Prof Exp:* Asst prof chem, Davis & Elkins Col, 65-67; asst prof, 67-70, ASSOC PROF CHEM, WASHINGTON & JEFFERSON COL, 70- *Mem:* AAAS; Am Chem Soc. *Res:* Thermodynamic properties of nonaqueous electrolyte solutions; preparation and structure determinations of copper complexes. *Mailing Add:* Dept of Chem Washington & Jefferson Col Washington PA 15301

WICKER, THOMAS HAMILTON, JR, b Orlando, Fla, Nov 19, 23; m 49; c 3. ORGANIC CHEMISTRY, POLYMER CHEMISTRY. *Educ:* Univ Fla, BS, 44, MS, 48, PhD(org chem), 51. *Prof Exp:* From assoc res chemist to res chemist, 51-58, sr res chemist, 58-76, RES ASSOC, TENN EASTMAN CO, 77- *Mem:* Am Chem Soc; Sigma Xi. *Res:* 2-cyanoacrylate adhesives; condensation polymers; organic chemistry. *Mailing Add:* 4619 Mitchell Rd Kingsport TN 37664

WICKERHAUSER, MILAN, b Zemun, Yugoslavia, Aug 28, 22; m 56; c 2. BIOCHEMISTRY. *Educ:* Chem engr, Univ Zagreb, 46, PhD, 61. *Prof Exp:* Develop chemist, Inst Immunol, Yugoslavia, 46-53, head dept serum & toxoid purification, 53-57, head dept human plasma fractionation, 57-62; immunochemist, Immunol, Inc, Ill, 63; res assoc fractionation plasma protein & blood coagulation studies, Hyland Labs, Calif, 64-66; dir, Am Red Cross Nat Fractionation Ctr, Blood Res Lab, 70-79, SR RES SCIENTIST, AM RED CROSS, 66-, HEAD PLASMA FRACTIONATION SECT, 68- *Concurrent Pos:* WHO fel, Wellcome Physiol Res Lab, Eng, Lister Inst Prev Med, London & State Serum Inst, Copenhagen, 50. *Mem:* Am Asn Blood Banks; Int Soc Blood Transfusion; Int Soc Thrombosis and Haemostasis. *Res:* Isolation and characterization of plasma proteins with special emphasis on the large scale methodology; blood coagulation; immunoglobulins; development of large-scale plasma fractionation methods. *Mailing Add:* Am Red Cross Blood Serv Labs 9312 Old Georgetown Rd Bethesda MD 20814

WICKERSHAM, EDWARD WALKER, b Kelton, Pa, Apr 26, 32; m 59; c 3. REPRODUCTIVE PHYSIOLOGY, HUMAN SEXUALITY. *Educ:* Pa State Univ, BS, 57, MS, 59; Univ Wis, PhD(dairy physiol), 62. *Prof Exp:* NIH trainee endocrinol, Univ Wis, 62-63; asst prof biol, WVa Univ, 63-64; asst prof zool, 64-68, ASSOC PROF BIOL, PA STATE UNIV, 68- *Mem:* Am Pub Health Asn; Brit Soc Study Fertil; Soc Study Reproduction; Am Asn Sex Educators, Counselors & Therapists. *Res:* Mammalian reproductive physiology and endocrinology; physiology of fertility regulation; biological and health aspects of human sexuality. *Mailing Add:* Dept of Biol 417 Mueller Lab Pa State Univ University Park PA 16802

WICKERSHEIM, KENNETH ALAN, b Fullerton, Calif, Mar 4, 28; m 52, 67; c 2. SOLID STATE PHYSICS, SPECTROSCOPY. *Educ:* Univ Calif, Los Angeles, AB, 50, MA, 56, PhD(physics), 59. *Prof Exp:* Mem staff, Los Alamos Sci Lab, 53-55; asst physics, Univ Calif, Los Angeles, 55-58; mem staff res labs, Hughes Aircraft Co, 58-61; res physicist, Palo Alto Labs, Gen Tel & Electronics Lab, Inc, 61-63; assoc prof mat sci, Stanford Univ, 63-64; staff scientist solid state physics, Lockheed Palo Alto Res Labs, 64-65, sr mem, 65-66, head adv electronics, 66-70; pres, Spectrotherm Corp, 70-75; vpres res & develop, UTI Corp, 75-77; vpres & gen mgr, Quantex Corp, 77-78; PRES, LUXTRON CORP, 78- *Concurrent Pos:* Res assoc sch earth sci, Stanford Univ, 64-; consult, Appl Physics Corp, 63-64, Quantic Industs, 77-, AGA Corp, 78-79. *Mem:* AAAS; fel Am Phys Soc. *Res:* Optical properties of materials; spectra of rare earth ions in solids; infrared spectra of crystals; optical and infrared instrumentation; medical and industrial thermography; optoelectronic instrumentation. *Mailing Add:* 3895 Middlefield Rd Palo Alto CA 94303

WICKES, GLENN FRENCH, b Cleveland, Ohio, May 8, 18; m 42; c 3. ZOOLOGY, CHEMISTRY. *Educ:* Baldwin-Wallace Col, BS, 41. *Prof Exp:* Lab asst, Gen Elec Co, 36-37; shift foreman, 41-42, supvr natural estrone, 45-47, assoc pharmaceut develop, 47-50, mgr sterile prod, 50-55, dir sterile prod mgr, 55-60, prod mgr, 60-64, V PRES PROD & DEVELOP, BEN VENUE LABS, INC, 64- *Mem:* Soc Cryobiol; Parenteral Drug Asn; Health Indust Mfrs Asn. *Res:* Development of lyophilized dosage forms of special drugs to be used in cancer chemotherapy. *Mailing Add:* Ben Venue Labs Inc 270 Northfield Rd Bedford OH 44146

WICKES, HARRY E, b Portland, Ore, June 24, 25; m 49; c 3. MATHEMATICS. *Educ:* Brigham Young Univ, BS, 50, MEd, 54; Harvard Univ, MEd, 62; Colo State Col, EdD, 67. *Prof Exp:* Teacher high sch, Mont, 50-51, Idaho, 51-54, prin elem & high sch, 54-57; instr math, 57-63, form asst prof to assoc prof, 64-75, PROF MATH, BRIGHAM YOUNG UNIV, 75- *Mem:* Math Asn Am; Nat Coun Teachers Math. *Res:* Mathematics education. *Mailing Add:* Dept Math Brigham Young Univ Provo UT 84602

WICKES, WILLIAM CASTLES, b Lynwood, Calif, Nov 25, 46; m 71; c 2. COSMOLOGY. *Educ:* Univ Calif, Los Angeles, BS, 67; Princeton Univ, MA, 69, PhD(physics), 72. *Prof Exp:* From res assoc to instr physics, Princeton Univ, asst prof, 75-78; asst prof physics, Univ Md, 78-81; TECH STAFF, CORVALLIS DIV, HEWLETT-PACKARD CO, 81- *Mem:* Am Astron Soc; Sigma Xi. *Res:* Double star interforometry; experimental and theoretical cosmology; computer science. *Mailing Add:* Hewlett-Packard 1000 NE Circle Blvd Corvallis OR 97330

WICKHAM, DONALD G, b Beaverton, Ore, Feb 24, 22; m 54; c 2. INORGANIC CHEMISTRY. *Educ:* Univ Denver, BS, 47, MS, 50; Mass Inst Technol, PhD(inorg chem), 54. *Prof Exp:* Chemist, Lincoln Lab, Mass Inst Technol, 54-57, sect leader, 57-60; mem staff, Res Labs, Hughes Aircraft Co, 60-61; mgr mat res & develop, Components Div, 61-65, MGR FERRITE MEMORY-CORE DEVELOP, AMPEX COMPUT PROD CO, 65- *Mem:* Am Crystallog Asn; Am Phys Soc. *Res:* Inorganic solid state chemistry; magnetic materials; inorganic syntheses. *Mailing Add:* Ampex Memory Prods Div 200 N Nash St El Segundo CA 90245

WICKHAM, JAMES EDGAR, JR, b Glen Allen, Va, Apr 7, 33; m 53; c 2. ANALYTICAL CHEMISTRY, INORGANIC CHEMISTRY. *Educ:* Randolph-Macon Col, BS, 57. *Prof Exp:* Asst chemist, Philip Morris, Inc, 57-59, group leader, 59-62, supvr, 62-69, head cigarette testing, 69-71, sr scientist, 71-74, MGR CIGARETTE TESTING SERV, PHILIP MORRIS USA, 74- *Mem:* AAAS; Am Chem Soc. *Res:* Wet and instrumental methods development; gas-liquid chromatography tobacco and smoke chemistry; quality control operations; smoking technology; air flow; research and development management. *Mailing Add:* Philip Morris USA Develop Div PO Box 26583 Richmond VA 23261

WICKHAM, WILLIAM TERRY, JR, b Cleveland, Ohio, May 28, 29; m 52; c 3. POLYMER CHEMISTRY, POLYMER PHYSICS. *Educ:* Heidelberg Col, AB, 51; Case Inst Technol, MS, 54, PhD(org chem), 56. *Prof Exp:* Instr, Case Inst Technol, 55-56; res chemist, Owens-Ill Glass Co, 56-58; group leader, Dow Chem Co, 58-62; tech mgr, Celanese Plastics Co, 62-67; dir res, Southern Div, Dayco Corp, 67-72, vpres res & develop, 72-76; tech dir,

Crosby Chem Inc, Picaynne, 76-77; ASSOC PROF, HEIDELBERG COL, TIFFIN, OHIO, 77- *Mem:* Am Chem Soc; Am Phys Soc; Am Inst Chemists. *Res:* Polymer morphology; synthesis; stability; structure; manufacture; research managment. *Mailing Add:* Heidelberg Col Tiffin OH 44883

WICKLER, STEVEN JOHN, b Volga, SDak, May 17, 52. ENERGETICS, THERMOGENESIS. *Educ:* Univ Calif, Riverside, BA, 74; Univ Mich, MS, 77, PhD(zool), 79. *Prof Exp:* VIS ASST PROF, DEPT ANIMAL PHYSIOL, UNIV CALIF, DAVIS, 79- *Mem:* Am Physiol Soc; Am Soc Zoologists. *Res:* Examine whole animal, tissue, and biochemical adaptations with particular emphasis on energetics and thermogenesis. *Mailing Add:* Dept Animal Physiol Univ Calif Davis CA 95616

WICKLIFF, JAMES LEROY, b Knoxville, Iowa, Nov 14, 31; m 56; c 3. PLANT PHYSIOLOGY, PHOTOBIOLOGY. *Educ:* Iowa State Univ, BS, 55, PhD(plant physiol), 62. *Prof Exp:* Assoc bot & plant path, Iowa State Univ, 62-65; asst prof bot & bact, 65-69, ASSOC PROF BOT & BACT, UNIV ARK, FAYETTEVILLE, 69- *Mem:* AAAS; Am Soc Plant Physiol; Am Inst Biol Sci; Am Soc Photobiol. *Res:* Chlorophyll biochemistry; photosynthesis; photophysiology of higher plants. *Mailing Add:* Dept Bot & Bact Univ Ark Fayetteville AR 72701

WICKLOW, DONALD THOMAS, b San Francisco, Calif, June 22, 40; m 70; c 1. MYCOLOGY, ECOLOGY. *Educ:* San Francisco State Col, BA, 62, MA, 64; Univ Wis, PhD(bot), 71. *Prof Exp:* Instr biol, Univ Wis Ctr-Waukesha, 69-70; asst prof, Univ Pittsburgh, 70-76; RES SCIENTIST MYCOL, NORTHERN REGIONAL RES CTR, US DEPT AGR, 77- *Concurrent Pos:* Consult, Natural Resource Ecol Lab, Ft Collins, Colo, 74-76; chmn steering comt microbiol & ecol, Argonne Nat Labs, 78-80; mem adv panel ecol & ecosysts studies, NSF, 78-81. *Honors & Awards:* Alexopoulous Prize, Mycol Soc Am, 80. *Mem:* Brit Mycol Soc; Mycol Soc Am; Ecol Soc Am; Mycol Soc Am; Am Soc Microbiol. *Res:* Ecology of fungal communities, their organization and role in both native and man-managed ecosystems. *Mailing Add:* Northern Regional Res Ctr 1815 N University St Peoria IL 61604

WICKLUND, ARTHUR BARRY, b Dec 8, 42; US citizen; m 74. EXPERIMENTAL HIGH ENERGY PHYSICS. *Educ:* Harvard Univ, BA, 64; Univ Calif, Berkeley, PhD(physics), 70. *Prof Exp:* Res asst high energy physics, Univ Calif, Berkeley, 65-70; fel, 70-73, asst physicist, 73-76, PHYSICIST, ARGONNE NAT LAB, 76- *Mem:* Am Phys Soc. *Res:* Strong interaction phenomenology; production mechanisms in few body reactions. *Mailing Add:* Argonne Nat Lab Bldg 362 9700 S Cass Ave Argonne IL 60439

WICKMAN, HERBERT HOLLIS, b Omaha, Nebr, Sept 30, 36; m 57; c 2. PHYSICAL CHEMISTRY, BIOPHYSICS. *Educ:* Univ Omaha, AB, 59; Univ Calif, Berkeley, PhD(chem), 64. *Prof Exp:* Mem tech staff chem physics res lab, Bell Tel Labs, NJ, 64-70; vis scientist, Demokritos Nuclear Res Ctr, Greece, 69-70; ASSOC PROF CHEM, ORE STATE UNIV, 70- *Mem:* Am Chem Soc; Am Phys Soc; Biophysics Soc; Sigma Xi. *Res:* Magnetic and structural cooperative phenomena; metalloenzyme biophysics. *Mailing Add:* Dept of Chem Ore State Univ Corvallis OR 97331

WICKREMA SINHA, ASOKA J, b Colombo, Ceylon, Sept 8, 37; US citizen. BIOCHEMISTRY, ORGANIC CHEMISTRY. *Educ:* Univ London, BSc, 61; Univ Birmingham, MSc, 64, PhD(org chem), 66. *Prof Exp:* Fel biochem, Univ Birmingham, 66-67; staff scientist, Worcester Found Exp Biol, 67-69; res scientist chem & biochem, 69-75, SR RES SCIENTIST, RES DIV, UPJOHN CO, 75- *Mem:* Am Chem Soc; The Chem Soc; Brit Biochem Soc. *Res:* Chemical synthesis; carbonium ion chemistry; biosynthesis and metabolism of steroids; in vivo and in vitro metabolism; analytical methods and assay development; metabolism absorption, distribution and excretion of drugs; isolation and structure elucidation; radiotracer techniques. *Mailing Add:* Res Div Upjohn Co Kalamazoo MI 49001

WICKS, CHARLES E(DWARD), b Prineville, Ore, July 9, 25; m 48; c 3. CHEMICAL ENGINEERING. *Educ:* Ore State Col, BS, 50; Carnegie Inst Technol, MS, 52, PhD, 54. *Prof Exp:* From asst prof to assoc prof, 54-60, PROF CHEM ENG, ORE STATE UNIV, 60-, HEAD DEPT, 70- *Concurrent Pos:* Chem engr, US Bur Mines, 56-58, proj leader, 58-; consult, US Bur Mines, 56-, Pac Power & Light Co, 58-60, Year-in-Indust, E I du Pont de Nemours & Co, 64-65 & Ore Metall Corp, 66-; NSF fel, Univ Wis, 60-61; expert witness prod reliability, various law firms. *Mem:* Am Inst Chem Engrs; Am Soc Eng Educ. *Res:* Waste water treatment; vapor-liquid equilibria; simultaneous heat and mass transfer phenomena. *Mailing Add:* Dept Chem Eng Ore State Univ Corvallis OR 97331

WICKS, FREDERICK JOHN, b Winnipeg, Man, Nov 22, 37; m 67. MINERALOGY. *Educ:* Univ Man, BSc, 60, MSc, 65; Oxford Univ, DPhil(mineral), 69. *Prof Exp:* Geologist, Giant Yellowknife Mines Ltd, 60 & 61; consult mineralogist, Govt & Indust, 62; mineralogist, Man Hwys Br, 63-65 & Geol Surv Can, 67; asst cur, 70-75, assoc cur, 75-80, CUR MINERAL, ROYAL ONT MUS, 80- *Concurrent Pos:* Adj prof, Dept Earth Sci, Univ Man, Winnipeg; assoc prof, Dept Geol, Univ Toronto, 80- *Honors & Awards:* Hawley Award, Mineral Asn Can, 77 & 78. *Mem:* Mineral Asn Can (secy, 73-75); fel Geol Asn Can; fel Mineral Soc Am; Clay Minerals Soc. *Res:* Structure, chemistry and paragenesis of the serpentine minerals; asbestos deposites; geochemistry and paragenesis of Columbian emerald deposits. *Mailing Add:* Dept of Mineral & Geol Royal Ont Mus 100 Queen's Park Toronto ON M5S 2C6 Can

WICKS, GEORGE GARY, b Copaigue, NY, June 26, 45; m 69; c 1. MATERIALS SCIENCE. *Educ:* Fla State Univ, BS, 67, MS, 69; Harvard Univ, SM, 71; Mass Inst Technol, PhD(eng mat), 75. *Prof Exp:* Engr, 69-70, RES METALLURGIST, SAVANNAH RIVER LAB, E I DU PONT DE NEMOURS & CO, INC, 75- *Res:* Structure and science of glass and amorphous materials; immobilization of radioactive waste in glass matrices. *Mailing Add:* Savannah River Lab Bldg 773-A F148 Aiken SC 29801

WICKS, THOMAS CHARLES, b Birmingham, Ala, May 20, 47; div. PHARMACOLOGY, PHYSIOLOGY. *Educ:* Univ Maine, BS, 69; Georgetown Univ, PhD(physiol), 74. *Prof Exp:* Fel physiol, Georgetown Univ Med Ctr, 74-76, res assoc, 76-77; sr pharmacologist, Wyeth Labs, Inc, 77-81; SR INVESTR, SMITH KLINE CORP, 82- *Res:* Physiology and pharmacology of hypertension; cardiovascular physiology of prostaglandins. *Mailing Add:* Smith Kline Corp PO Box 7929 Philadelphia PA 19101

WICKS, WESLEY DOANE, b Providence, RI, Feb 13, 36; m 59; c 3. BIOCHEMISTRY, PHARMACOLOGY. *Educ:* Bates Col, BS, 57; Harvard Univ, MA, 59, PhD(med sci), 64. *Prof Exp:* Staff mem biochem, Biol Div, Oak Ridge Nat Lab, Tenn, 65-69; staff mem, Div Res, Nat Jewish Hosp, Denver, 69-72; assoc prof, 72-78, PROF PHARMACOL, MED CTR, UNIV COLO, DENVER, 78- *Concurrent Pos:* Am Cancer Soc fel, Biol Div, Oak Ridge Nat Lab, Tenn, 63-65; hon fac mem, Dept Biosci, Fed Univ Pernambuco, Recife, Brazil, 68- *Mem:* AAAS; Am Soc Biol Chem; Am Soc Pharmacol & Exp Therapeut; Am Chem Soc; Endocrine Soc. *Res:* Regulation of specific protein synthesis by hormones and cyclic adenosine phosphate; use of cultured cells for studies of biochemical regulatory mechanisms. *Mailing Add:* Dept of Pharmacol Univ of Colo Med Ctr Denver CO 80220

WICKS, ZENO W, JR, b Port Jervis, NY, July 24, 20; m 41; c 6. POLYMER CHEMISTRY. *Educ:* Oberlin Col, AB, 41; Univ Ill, PhD(org chem), 44. *Prof Exp:* Res chemist, Interchem Corp, 44-47, dist tech dir finishes div, 48-49, res dir textile colors div, 49-51, assoc dir cent res labs, 51-54, dir, 54-59, mgr com develop, 59-61, vpres planning, 62-63, vpres & dir corp, 64-69; mem staff, Inmont Corp, NY, 69-72; prof, 72-80, DISTINGUISHED PROF, DEPT POLYMERS & COATINGS, NDAK STATE UNIV, 81-, CHMN DEPT, 72- *Mem:* Am Chem Soc; Soc Coatings Technol; Oil & Colour Chemists Asn. *Res:* Organic surface coatings and related polymer research. *Mailing Add:* Dept of Polymers & Coatings NDak State Univ Fargo ND 58105

WICKSON, EDWARD JAMES, b New York, NY, Jan 25, 20; m 52; c 5. PLASTICS CHEMISTRY. *Educ:* Univ Calif, Berkeley, BS, 42. *Prof Exp:* Anal chemist, Gen Chem Co, Calif, 42-43; chemist, Celanese Corp Am, NJ, 46-50; admin asst to lab dir, Vitro Corp Am, 51-54; sr chemist, Chicopee Mfg Co, 54-55; sr chemist, Enjay Labs, Esso Res & Eng Co, 55-56, group leader, 56-60, res assoc, 60-61, head chem sect, 61-69, vinyl indust assoc, Enjay Chem Co, 69-71, sr res assoc, Enjay Chem Lab, 71-75, chief scientist plasticizers, Esso Chem Europe, 75-78, CHIEF PROD APPLNS, EXXON CHEM CO, 78- *Mem:* Am Chem Soc; sr mem Soc Plastics Eng. *Res:* Plasticizers; chemical specialties; oxo alcohols; trialkylacetic acids; propylene polymers. *Mailing Add:* 7973 Walden Rd Baton Rouge LA 70808

WICKSTEN, MARY KATHERINE, b San Francisco, Calif, Mar 17, 48. BIOLOGY, INVERTEBRATE ZOOLOGY. *Educ:* Humboldt State Col, BA, 70, MA, 72; Univ Southern Calif, PhD(biol), 77. *Prof Exp:* Teaching asst biol, Humboldt State Col, 72 & Univ Southern Calif, 73-75 & 76-77; scientist marine biol, Bur Land Mgt Southern Calif Benthic Studies & Anal, 75-76; res assoc marine biol, Los Angeles Harbor Proj, 77-80. *Concurrent Pos:* Consult systematist, King Harbor Proj, 74-, Gulf Alaska Offshore Surv, 76-77, Bur Land Mgt Southern Calif Benthic Studies & Anal Seasonal Study, 76- & Bur Land Mgt Southern Calif Mussel Bed Surv, 77-; vis asst prof, Tex A&M Univ, 80-82. *Mem:* Am Micros Soc; Am Soc Zoologists; Pac Sci Asn. *Res:* Behavior, systematics, and zoogeography of decapod crustaceans of the eastern Pacific Ocean. *Mailing Add:* Dept Biol Tex A&M Univ College Station TX 77843

WICKSTROM, CONRAD EUGENE, b Modesto, Calif, Sept 3, 43; m 77. MICROBIAL ECOLOGY, PHYCOLOGY. *Educ:* Calif State Univ, Chico, BA, 65, MA, 68; Univ Ore, PhD(biol), 74. *Prof Exp:* Instr, 73-74, ASST PROF BIOL, EMORY UNIV, 74- *Concurrent Pos:* Prin investr NSF grant, 78-80. *Mem:* AAAS; Am Soc Microbiol; Am Soc Limnol & Oceanog; Ecol Soc Am; Phycological Soc Am. *Res:* Algal autecology; biotic components of nitrogen cycle, especially asymbiotic nitrogen fixation; biotic and abiotic control of microbial community structure and function; natural thermal systems and thermal enrichments. *Mailing Add:* Dept of Biol Emory Univ Atlanta GA 30322

WICKSTROM, ERIC, b Chicago, Ill, Dec 21, 46; m 67; c 2. BIOPHYSICAL CHEMISTRY. *Educ:* Calif Inst Technol, BS, 68; Univ Calif, Berkeley, PhD(chem), 72. *Prof Exp:* Res asst chem, Univ Calif, Berkeley, 68-72; res assoc molecular, cellular & develop biol, Univ Colo, Boulder, 73-74; ASST PROF CHEM, UNIV DENVER, 74- *Mem:* Am Chem Soc. *Res:* Tertiary structure of transfer RNA; protein synthesis initiation; thylakoid membrane organization. *Mailing Add:* Dept of Chem Univ of Denver Denver CO 80208

WICKSTROM, JACK, b Omaha, Nebr, Aug 7, 13; m 40; c 3. MEDICINE. *Educ:* Univ Nebr, AB, 35, MD, 39. *Prof Exp:* Assoc prof orthop, 46-56, prof & chmn dept, 56-79, EMER PROF ORTHOP, SCH MED, TULANE UNIV, 79- *Concurrent Pos:* Fel path, Univ Nebr, 44; fel orthop surg, Sch Med, Tulane Univ, 44-46. *Honors & Awards:* Gold Medal, Am Acad Orthop Surg, 51; Scudder Orator, Am Col Surg, 74. *Mem:* AAAS. *Res:* Bone metabolism and growth; biomechanics; surgical implants and injury control. *Mailing Add:* 1430 Tulane Ave New Orleans LA 70112

WIDDEN, PAUL RODNEY, b London, Eng, Sept 23, 43; m 67; c 3. SOIL MICROBIOLOGY. *Educ:* Univ Liverpool, BSc Hons, 65; Univ Calgary, PhD(mycol), 71. *Prof Exp:* Asst prof, 73-76, ASSOC PROF MICROBIAL ECOL, CONCORDIA UNIV, LOYOLA CAMPUS, 76- *Concurrent Pos:* Nat Res Coun Can operating grant, 75-84; Univ res grant, Imperial Oil Ltd, 78-81. *Mem:* Can Soc Microbiologists. *Res:* The distribution of fungi in tundra and temperate forest soils; effects of environment on the distribution of soil fungi; crude oil degradation by arctic soil fungi. *Mailing Add:* Dept of Biol Loyola Campus Concordia Univ 7141 Sherbrooke W Montreal PQ H4B 1R6 Can

WIDDER, JAMES STONE, b Cleveland, Ohio, Feb 28, 35; m 60; c 1. IMMUNOLOGY, BIOCHEMISTRY. *Educ:* Ohio State Univ, BS, 57, MS, 59, PhD(immunol), 62. *Prof Exp:* Res microbiologist, Miami Valley Lab, 62-64, prod researcher, Winton Hill Tech Ctr, 64-74, sect head basic skin res & proj, 74-76, ASSOC DIR, MIAMI VALLEY LAB, PROCTER & GAMBLE CO, 76- *Concurrent Pos:* Lectr, Univ Cincinnati, 62- *Mem:* AAAS; Am Soc Microbiol; Int Asn Dent Res (secy, 66-67). *Res:* Product development of biologically oriented products and associated governmental problems. *Mailing Add:* Miami Valley Lab Procter & Gamble Co Cincinnati OH 45224

WIDEBURG, NORMAN EARL, b Chicago, Ill, Mar 8, 33; m 58; c 4. INDUSTRIAL MICROBIOLOGY. *Educ:* Ill Inst Technol, BS, 54; Univ Wis, MS, 56. *Prof Exp:* BIOCHEMIST, ABBOTT LABS, 58- *Mem:* AAAS; Am Chem Soc; Am Soc Microbiol. *Res:* Microbial transformations; fermentation; enzymes; antibiotics. *Mailing Add:* Abbott Labs North Chicago IL 60064

WIDEMAN, CHARLES JAMES, b Walkermine, Calif, Feb 7, 36; m 63; c 2. GEOPHYSICS. *Educ:* Colo Sch Mines, BSc, 58, MSc, 67, PhD(geophys), 75. *Prof Exp:* Sr geophysicist, Westinghouse Elec Corp, 67-68; asst prof, 68-73, ASSOC PROF GEOPHYS & CHMN DEPT, MONT COL MINERAL SCI & TECHNOL, 73- *Mem:* Seismol Soc Am. *Res:* Local seismicity; seismic risk analysis and earth strain studies; gravity investigations over and near the Boulder Batholith of Southwestern Montana. *Mailing Add:* Mont Col Mineral Sci & Technol Butte MT 59701

WIDEMAN, CYRILLA HELEN, b Toledo, Ohio, Nov 26, 26. PHYSIOLOGY, BIOCHEMISTRY. *Educ:* Notre Dame Col, Ohio, BS, 49; Univ Notre Dame, MS, 60; Ill Inst Technol, PhD(biol), 70. *Prof Exp:* High sch teacher natural sci, Notre Dame Acad, Elyria Cath High Sch, 49-56; instr biol & chem, Notre Dame Col, 56-61, asst prof biol, 61-67; grad asst, Ill Inst Technol, 67-70; fel biochem & physiol, Cleveland Clin, 70-72; assoc prof biol, 72-77, PROF BIOL, JOHN CARROLL UNIV, 77- *Concurrent Pos:* NIH fel, 70-72; NSF & John Carroll Univ grant, 74. *Mem:* AAAS; Am Inst Biol Sci; NY Acad Sci; Soc Neurosci. *Res:* Neuroendocrinological and biochemical relationships underlying brain behavior patterns with special emphasis on the limbic system, especially hippocampal formation. *Mailing Add:* Dept of Biol John Carroll Univ Cleveland OH 44118

WIDEMAN, LAWSON GIBSON, b Morrelton, Mo, July 17, 43; m 65; c 3. ORGANIC CHEMISTRY. *Educ:* Univ Mo-Rolla, BS, 66, MS, 67; Univ Akron, PhD(chem), 71. *Prof Exp:* Staff res chemist, 67-71, SR RES CHEMIST, RES DIV, GOODYEAR TIRE & RUBBER CO, 71- *Concurrent Pos:* Part-time mem fac, Univ Akron, 81- *Mem:* Am Chem Soc; Sigma Xi. *Res:* Homogeneous and heterogeneous catalysis; chemistry of carbanions in solution; selective reactions of organoboranes; homo- and heterogeneous hydrogenation reactions. *Mailing Add:* Goodyear Tire & Rubber Co 142 Goodyear Blvd Akron OH 44316

WIDEMAN, ROBERT FREDERICK, JR, b Dallas, Tex, June 16, 49; m 71; c 1. AVIAN PHYSIOLOGY, RENAL PHYSIOLOGY. *Educ:* Univ Del, BA, 71; Univ Conn, MS, 74, PhD(physiol), 78. *Prof Exp:* Fel physiol, Col Med, Univ Ariz, 78-81; ASST PROF AVIAN PHYSIOL, POULTRY SCI DEPT, PA STATE UNIV, 81- *Mem:* AAAS; Am Soc Zoologists; Am Physiol Soc; Poultry Sci Asn. *Res:* Avian renal and endocrine physiology; endocrinological regulation of renal calcium and phosphate transport; renal and endocrine microanatomy. *Mailing Add:* 206 Animal Indust Bldg Pa State Univ University Park PA 16802

WIDENER, MAURICE WARD, b Corpus Christi, Tex, Aug 12, 26; m 55; c 2. ELECTRICAL ENGINEERING, ACOUSTICS. *Educ:* Univ Tex, BS, 48, MS, 56. *Prof Exp:* Test engr, Gen Elec Co, 48-50; elec engr, Convair, Tex, 50-52; res engr, Defense Res Lab, Univ Tex, 52-56; assoc engr, Int Bus Mach Corp, Calif, 56-57; staff engr, Ampex Corp, 57-61; res engr, Philco Corp, 61-62; RES ENGR, APPL RES LAB, UNIV TEX, AUSTIN, 62- *Mem:* Acoust Soc Am; Audio Eng Soc. *Res:* Signal theory and signal techniques for sonar detection systems; acoustic transducers for air and sonar; defense systems design. *Mailing Add:* 203 Westbrook Dr Austin TX 78746

WIDERA, GEORG ERNST OTTO, b Dortmund, W Ger, Feb 16, 38; US citizen. ENGINEERING MECHANICS. *Educ:* Univ Wis-Madison, BS, 60, MS, 62, PhD(eng mech), 65. *Prof Exp:* From asst prof to assoc prof, 65-73, PROF ENG MECH, UNIV ILL, CHICAGO CIRCLE, 73- *Concurrent Pos:* Alexander von Humboldt fel, Univ Stuttgart, 68-69, vis prof, 68; vis scientist, Argonne Nat Lab, 68; vis prof, Univ Wis, Milwaukee, 73-74 & Marquette Univ, 78-79; assoc ed, J Pressure Vessel Technol, 77-81; consult various indust orgn. *Mem:* Am Acad Mech; Am Soc Mech Engrs; Ger Soc Appl Math & Mech; Am Soc Civil Engrs. *Res:* Plates and shells; composite materials; mechanics of deformation processing; noise control. *Mailing Add:* Dept of Mat Eng Box 4348 Univ of Ill Chicago Circle Chicago IL 60680

WIDERQUIST, V(ERNON) R(OBERTS), b Ft Myers, Fla, Sept 21, 22; m 49; c 3. ELECTRICAL ENGINEERING. *Educ:* Ga Inst Technol, BS, 43, MS, 48. *Prof Exp:* Res prof, Eng Exp Sta, Ga Inst Technol, 46-56; PROJ MGR, TRW DEFENSE & SPACE SYSTS GROUP, TRW INC, 56- *Mem:* Inst Elec & Electronics Engrs; Sigma Xi; AAAS. *Res:* Program and general management. *Mailing Add:* PO Box 58333 Houston TX 77058

WIDESS, MOSES B, b Sverdlovsk, Russia, Sept 21, 11; nat US; m 35; c 2. GEOPHYSICS. *Educ:* Calif Inst Technol, BS, 33, MS, 34, PhD(elec eng), 36. *Prof Exp:* Party chief, Western Geophys Co, Calif, 36-42; consult geophysicist, Amoco Prod Co, 42-73; CONSULT, 73- *Mem:* Soc Explor Geophys; Am Geophys Union; Europ Asn Explor Geophys. *Res:* Geophysical interpretation and methods. *Mailing Add:* 11617 Monica Lane Houston TX 77024

WIDGOFF, MILDRED, b Buffalo, NY, Aug 24, 24; m 45; c 2. ELEMENTARY PARTICLE PHYSICS. *Educ:* Univ Buffalo, BA, 44; Cornell Univ, PhD(physics), 52. *Prof Exp:* Asst physics, Manhattan Proj, 44-45; assoc physics, Brookhaven Nat Lab, 52-54; res fel, Harvard Univ, 55-58; res asst prof physics, 58-66, res assoc prof, 66-74, exec officer dep, 68-81, PROF PHYSICS, BROWN UNIV, 74- *Mem:* Fel Am Phys Soc. *Res:* Cosmic rays; medium and high energy particle physics; studies of interactions of elementary experimental particles at medium and high energies. *Mailing Add:* Dept Physics Brown Univ Box 1843 Providence RI 02912

WIDHOLM, JACK MILTON, b Watseka, Ill, Mar 11, 39; m 64; c 3. PLANT PHYSIOLOGY, GENETICS. *Educ:* Univ Ill, BS, 61; Calif Inst Technol, PhD(biochem), 66. *Prof Exp:* Res chemist, Int Minerals & Chem Corp, 65-68; asst prof physiol dept agron, 68-73, assoc prof, 73-77, PROF PLANT PHYSIOL DEPT AGRON, UNIV ILL, URBANA, 77- *Mem:* Am Soc Plant Physiol; Tissue Cult Asn; Scand Soc Plant Physiol; Am Soc Agron. *Res:* Plant biochemistry and genetics, especially genetic manipulation, control of amino acid biosynthesis and photorespiration. *Mailing Add:* Dept of Agron Univ of Ill Urbana IL 61801

WIDIN, KATHARINE DOUGLAS, b Cleveland, Ohio, Oct 1, 52; m 74. BIOLOGY. *Educ:* Kenyon Col, AB, 74; Univ Minn, MS, 77, PhD(phytopath), 80. *Prof Exp:* Lectr biol & microbiol, 80-81, ASST PROF BIOL, MICROBIOL & BOT, CURRY COL, MILTON, MASS, 81- *Concurrent Pos:* Lectr entom & plant dis, Mass Bay Community Col, 80-82; consult, Plant Insect & Dis Clinics, Regional Garden Ctrs, 81- *Mem:* Am Phytopath Soc; Mycol Soc Am; Sigma Xi. *Mailing Add:* Sci Div Curry Col Brush Hill Rd Milton MA 02186

WIDMAIER, ROBERT GEORGE, b Riverside, NJ, June 18, 48; m 77. BIOCHEMISTRY, PHARMACEUTICAL CHEMISTRY. *Educ:* ECarolina Univ, BS, 70; Purdue Univ, PhD(biochem), 76. *Prof Exp:* Res asst biochem, Purdue Univ, 71-74, teaching asst, 74-76; res biochemist basic food sci, Res & Develop, Kraft Inc, 76-79; MEM STAFF, KURTH MALTING CORP, 79- *Mem:* Am Chem Soc; Inst Food Technologists. *Res:* Flavor development in cultured food products; enzyme analysis; clinical diagnosis; drug metabolism; immunology. *Mailing Add:* Kurth Malting Corp 2100 S 43rd St Milwaukee WI 53219

WIDMANN, FRANCES KING, b Boston, Mass, July 23, 35; div; c 2. PATHOLOGY. *Educ:* Swarthmore Col, BA, 56; Western Reserve Univ, MD, 60; Am Bd Path, dipl & cert anat & clin path, 65, cert immunohemat, 73. *Prof Exp:* Intern, Cleveland Metrop Gen Hosp, Ohio, 60-61; resident anat & clin path, Sch Med, Univ NC, Chapel Hill, 61-64; resident clin path, Norfolk Gen Hosp, Va, 64-65, staff pathologist, 65-66; from instr to asst prof path, Sch Med, Univ NC, Chapel Hill, 66-70; asst prof, 71-73, assoc dir, 71-73, DIR, SCH MED TECHNOL, DUKE UNIV, 73-, ASSOC PROF PATH, SCH MED, 73-; ASST CHIEF LAB SERV, VET ADMIN HOSP, 72- *Concurrent Pos:* Ed, Tech Manual, Am Asn Blood Banks. *Mem:* Am Asn Blood Banks. *Res:* Blood banking and medical education, especially in clinical pathology and medical technology training. *Mailing Add:* Vet Admin Hosp 508 Fulton St Durham NC 27710

WIDMARK, RUDOLPH M, b Horn, Austria, July 18, 25; m 55; c 1. IMMUNOLOGY, MEDICAL MICROBIOLOGY. *Educ:* Univ Timisoara, Romania, MD, 52; Univ Bucharest, PhD(immunol, microbiol), 56. *Prof Exp:* Instr path, Sch Med, Univ Timisoara, 49-52, asst prof virol, 52; asst prof microbiol, Sch Med, Univ Bucharest, 53-55; assoc prof, Cantacuzino Inst, Bucharest, 56-62; dep dir clin lab, Hanusch Hosp, Vienna, 62-63; trainee med & arthritis, State Univ NY Downstate Med Ctr, 64, asst prof microbiol & immunol, 64-67; dir immunol, Denver Chem Mfg Co, 67-68; staff consult life sci, Technicon Corp, 68-71; dir biol res, BioQuest, 71; asst dir clin res, Ayerst Labs, 71-75; med dir, Behringwerke Ag, 75-79; ASSOC DIR CLIN RES, IVES LABS, 79- *Res:* Antigen-antibody reactions; passive hemagglutination; heterophil antibodies; preservation of erythrocytes for antigen-antibody reactions. *Mailing Add:* Ives Labs 685 Third Ave New York NY 10017

WIDMAYER, DOROTHEA JANE, b Washington, DC, Oct 10, 30. ZOOLOGY, MICROBIAL GENETICS. *Educ:* Wellesley Col, BA, 53, MA, 55; Ind Univ, PhD(zool), 62. *Prof Exp:* Instr biol, Simmons Col, 55-57; instr zool, 61-63, from asst prof to assoc prof biol, 63-74, prof, 74-75, KENAN PROF BIOL, WELLESLEY COL, 75-, CHMN DEPT BIOL SCI, 72- *Concurrent Pos:* NSF sci fac fel inst animal genetics, Univ Edinburgh, 67-68; grant, Ascent of Man, Res Corp, 74. *Mem:* AAAS; Genetics Soc Am; Am Soc Zool; Soc Protozool. *Res:* Gene action and cytoplasmic inheritance in Paramecium aurelia. *Mailing Add:* Dept of Biol Sci Wellesley Col Wellesley MA 02181

WIDMER, CARL, b Kingston, Pa, Mar 3, 24; m 59; c 2. BIOCHEMISTRY. *Educ:* Pa State Univ, BS, 48; Agr & Mech Col, Tex, MS, 49; Univ Rochester, PhD(biochem), 52. *Prof Exp:* USPHS fel, Ore State Col, 54-56; fel inst enzyme res, Univ Wis, 56-57; asst prof chem, Humboldt State Col, 57-61; assoc prof, Agrarian Univ, Peru, 62-64; asst prof biochem & nutrit, Tex A&M Univ, 65-66; ASSOC PROF CHEM, ELBERT COVELL COL, UNIV OF PAC, 66- *Mem:* AAAS. *Res:* Human nutrition; limnology. *Mailing Add:* Elbert Covell Col Univ of the Pac Stockton CA 95211

WIDMER, ELMER ANDREAS, b Dodge, NDak, Apr 27, 25; m; c 2. HELMINTHOLOGY, MEDICAL PARASITOLOGY. *Educ:* Union Col, Nebr, BA, 51; Univ Colo, MA, 56; Colo State Univ, PhD(zool), 65; Univ NC, MPH, 74. *Prof Exp:* Teacher, High Sch, 52-53; instr biol, La Sierra Col, 53-58, from asst prof to assoc prof, 58-67; assoc prof environ & trop health, 67-71, chmn dept, 67-78, interim assoc dean, 78-80 PROF ENVIRON & TROP HEALTH, LOMA LINDA UNIV, 71-, ASSOC DEAN, ACAD AFFAIRS, SCH HEALTH, 80- *Concurrent Pos:* Fel sch med, La State Univ, 66; WHO fel, Africa, 71. *Mem:* Am Pub Health Asn; Royal Soc Trop Med & Hyg; Am Soc Parasitol; Am Soc Trop Med & Hyg; Wildlife Dis Asn. *Res:* Reptilian parasitology; tropical helminthology; host-parasite interactions between cestodes. *Mailing Add:* Dept of Environ & Trop Health Sch of Health Loma Linda Univ Loma Linda CA 92350

WIDMER, KEMBLE, b New Rochelle, NY, Feb 26, 13; m 39; c 2. GEOLOGY. *Educ:* Lehigh Univ, AB, 37; Princeton Univ, MA, 47, PhD(geol), 50. *Prof Exp:* From instr to asst prof geol, Rutgers Univ, 48-50; assoc prof & chmn dept, Champlain Col, NY, 50-53; prin geologist, Div Sci, Bur Geol & Topog, NJ Dept Environ Protection, 53-58, nuclear indust coordr, 63-68, state geologist, 58-80, nuclear indust coordr, 63-74; RETIRED. *Concurrent Pos:* Tech consult, US Mil Acad, 63-81; seminar assoc, Columbia Univ; mem adv comt on water data for pub use, US Geol Survey, 76-80. *Mem:* AAAS; Geol Soc Am; Am Inst Mining, Metall & Petrol Eng. *Res:* Areal, economic, Pleistocene and engineering geology. *Mailing Add:* 228 King George Rd Pennington NJ 08534

WIDMER, RICHARD ERNEST, b West New York, NJ, June 19, 22; m 56; c 3. HORTICULTURE. *Educ:* Rutgers Univ, BS, 43, MS, 49; Univ Minn, PhD(hort), 55. *Prof Exp:* Instr hort, 49-55, from asst prof to assoc prof, 55-64, PROF HORT, UNIV MINN, ST PAUL, 64- *Concurrent Pos:* Fulbright study grant, Agr Inst, Ireland, 68-69; AID consult, Hassan II Inst Agron & Vet Med, Rabat, Morocco, 73; sr res fel, New Zealand Nat Res Adv Coun, Levin Hort Res Ctr, 80-81. *Honors & Awards:* Alex Laurie Award, Soc Am Florists, 77. *Mem:* Fel Am Soc Hort Sci; Int Hort Soc. *Res:* Physiological studies of commercial greenhouse crops; breeding of garden chrysanthemums; ornamental horticulture. *Mailing Add:* Dept of Hort Sci &Landscape Archit 1970 Folwell Ave St Paul MN 55108

WIDMER, ROBERT H, b Hawthorne, NJ, May 17, 16; m 45; c 2. AERONAUTICAL ENGINEERING, SYSTEMS ENGINEERING. *Educ:* Rensselaer Polytech Inst, BS, 38; Calif Inst Technol, MS, 39. *Hon Degrees:* ScD, Tex Christian Univ, 67. *Prof Exp:* Chief aerodyn, Ft Worth Div, 49-51, asst chief engr tech design, 51-59, chief engr, 59-61, vpres res & eng, 61-71, vpres res & eng, Convair Div, Ft Worth & San Diego, 71-74, V PRES SCI & ENG, CORP OFF, GEN DYNAMICS CORP, ST LOUIS, 74- *Concurrent Pos:* Mem comts aerodyn & propulsion, Nat Adv Comt Aeronaut, 48-58; consult res & eng, Off Asst Secy Defense, 58-64 & US Air Force Sci Adv Bd, 54-58; mem bd dirs, Univ Tex Eng Found, 56-68, Tex Christian Univ Res Found, 73-77 & Southern Methodist Univ Found Sci & Eng, 73- *Honors & Awards:* Field of Sci Award, Air Force Asn, 49; Spirit of St Louis Medal, Am Soc Mech Engrs, 63. *Mem:* Nat Acad Eng; fel Am Inst Aeronaut & Astronaut; Nat Soc Prof Engrs; Air Force Asn. *Mailing Add:* Gen Dynamic Corp Pierre Laclede Ctr St Louis MO 63105

WIDMER, WILBUR JAMES, b West New York, NJ, Oct 20, 18; m 50; c 3. ENVIRONMENTAL ENGINEERING, LIMNOLOGY. *Educ:* Cooper Union, BCE, 46; Mass Inst Technol, SM, 48. *Prof Exp:* Technician, Gibbs & Cox, Inc, NY, 43-47; from instr to assoc prof, 48-73, PROF CIVIL ENG, UNIV CONN, 73- *Concurrent Pos:* Consult, Conn State Water Resources Comn, 50-52, C W Riva Co, RI, 50-63 & J M Minges Assocs, Conn, 59-63; res asst, Mass Inst Technol, 56-57; NSF sci fac fel biol oceanog, Narragansett Marine Lab, RI, 64-66; WHO assignment as prof sanit eng, W Pakistan Univ Eng & Technol, Lahore & sanit eng adv, Govt Pakistan, 68-70; sanit eng consult in Brazil, Pan-Am Health Orgn, 72; sanitary eng consult, WHO, Egypt, Saudia Arabia & Sudan, 79. *Honors & Awards:* Bedell Award Water Pollution Control, Water Pollution Control Fedn, 72. *Mem:* Fel Royal Soc Health; fel Am Soc Civil Engrs; Am Soc Limnol & Oceanog; Am Water Works Asn; Am Acad Environ Engrs. *Res:* Eutrophication and pollution ecology of fresh and marine waters; waste water treatment systems. *Mailing Add:* Dept of Civil Eng Box U-37 Univ of Conn Storrs CT 06268

WIDMOYER, FRED BIXLER, b Grandfield, Okla, Nov 25, 20; m 61; c 3. HORTICULTURE. *Educ:* Tex Tech Col, BA, 42, MS, 50; Mich State Univ, PhD(ornamental hort), 54. *Prof Exp:* Instr bot, Tex Tech Col, 46-50; asst prof & exten specialist hort, Mich State Univ, 54-60; assoc prof landscape design & nursery mgt, Univ Conn, 60-63; prin horticulturist, Sci & Educ Admin-Coop Res, USDA, 77-78, PROF HORT & HEAD DEPT, N MEX STATE UNIV, 63-77 & 78- *Concurrent Pos:* Mem adv comt, Nat Arboretum; mem rev team hort, Coop State Res Serv, USDA. *Honors & Awards:* Esther Longyear Murphy Medal, 61. *Mem:* Am Asn Bot Gardens & Arboretums (pres, 82-83); fel Am Soc Hort Sci. *Res:* Ornamental horticulture; plant anatomy; growth regulators and plant propagation; developmental morphology. *Mailing Add:* Dept Hort NMex State Univ Box 3530 Las Cruces NM 88003

WIDNALL, SHEILA EVANS, b Tacoma, Wash, July 13, 38; m 60; c 2. AERONAUTICAL ENGINEERING, FLUID MECHANICS. *Educ:* Mass Inst Technol, BS & MS, 61, ScD(aeronaut eng), 64. *Prof Exp:* Res asst aerodyn, 61-64, Ford fel, 64-66, asst prof, 64-70, assoc prof, 70-74, chairperson, women fac, 76-77, head, Dynamics Div, Dept Aeronaut & Astronaut, 78-79, PROF AERODYN, MASS INST TECHNOL, 74- *Concurrent Pos:* Consult several industs; dir univ res, US Dept Transp, DC, 74-75; mem space & aeronaut bd, Nat Acad Eng, 75-78; mem adv comt, NSF, US Air Force & US Dept Transp; mem bd gov, US Air Force Acad, 78- *Honors & Awards:* Lawrence Sperry Award, Am Inst Aeronaut & Astronaut, 72; Outstanding Achievement Award, Soc Women Engrs. *Mem:* Am Inst Aeronaut & Astronaut; Am Phys Soc; Soc Women Engrs; AAAS. *Res:* Unsteady aerodynamics; aeroelasticity; aerodynamic noise; turbulence; applied mathematics; vortex flows; numerical analysis; university administration; research and development management; aerospace; transportation; aerodynamics and fluid mechanics; acoustics; noise and vibration. *Mailing Add:* Dept Aeronaut & Astronaut Mass Inst Technol Cambridge MA 02139

WIDNELL, CHRISTOPHER COURTENAY, b London, Eng, May 19, 40; m 65; c 2. CELL BIOLOGY, BIOCHEMISTRY. *Educ:* Cambridge Univ, BA, 62; Univ London, PhD(biochem), 65. *Prof Exp:* Res assoc cell biol, Rockefeller Univ, 66-68; staff mem biochem, Nat Inst Med Res, London, Eng, 68-69; assoc prof, 69-77, PROF ANAT & CELL BIOL, SCH MED, UNIV PITTSBURGH, 77- *Concurrent Pos:* Jane Coffin Childs fel, Univ Chicago, 65-66; ed, Arch Biochem & Biophys, 72-; sr Fogarty int fel, Int Inst Cellular & Molecular Path, Brussels, 78-79. *Mem:* Am Soc Biol Chem; Am Soc Cell Biol; Brit Biochem Soc. *Res:* Membrane structure and function; cytochemical localization of membrane proteins; synthesis and assembly of membrane components; cellular aging; endocytosis and membrane recycling. *Mailing Add:* Dept Anat & Cell Biol Univ Pittsburgh Sch Med Pittsburgh PA 15261

WIDNER, JIMMY NEWTON, b Clovis, NMex, Feb 10, 42; m 64; c 2. CROP BREEDING. *Educ:* NMex State Univ, BS, 64; NDak State Univ, PhD(agron), 68. *Prof Exp:* Plant breeder, Great Western Sugar Co, Colo, 68-72; res mgr, Northern Ohio Sugar Co, 72-75; SR PLANT BREEDER, GREAT WESTERN SUGAR CO, 75- *Mem:* Am Soc Agron; Crop Sci Soc Am; Am Soc Sugar Beet Technol. *Res:* Development of improved varieties and hybrids of sugar beets. *Mailing Add:* Agr Res Ctr Great Western Sugar Co Longmont CO 80501

WIDNER, WILLIAM RICHARD, b Baxter Co, Ark, Apr 24, 20; m 43; c 1. PHYSIOLOGY, BACTERIOLOGY. *Educ:* Eastern NMex Univ, AB, 42; Univ NMex, MS, 48, PhD, 52. *Prof Exp:* Lab asst biol, Eastern NMex Univ, 42; asst, Univ NMex, 46-48; biomed researcher, Los Alamos Sci Lab, 48-50; asst, Univ NMex, 50-52; indust hygienist, Sandia Corp, 52-55; teacher, Albuquerque Indian Sch, NMex, 55-56; prof biol & head dept, Howard Payne Col, 56-59; asst prof biol & bact, 59-64, PROF BIOL, BAYLOR UNIV, 64- *Mem:* AAAS; Am Soc Microbiol; Sigma Xi (treas, 73-74). *Res:* Cell mitoses and growth of normal and malignant tissues; effects of ionizing radiations on living cells; radiation produced cataracts; bacterial metabolism. *Mailing Add:* 111 Turtle Creek Dr Waco TX 76710

WIDOM, BENJAMIN, b Newark, NJ, Oct 13, 27; m 53; c 3. PHYSICAL CHEMISTRY. *Educ:* Columbia Univ, AB, 49; Cornell Univ, PhD(chem), 53. *Prof Exp:* Res assoc chem, Univ NC, 52-54; instr, 54-55, from asst prof to assoc prof, 55-63, PROF CHEM, CORNELL UNIV, 63- *Concurrent Pos:* Guggenheim & Fulbright fels, 61-62; NSF sr fel, 65; Guggenheim fel, 69; van der Waals prof, Univ Amsterdam, 72; IBM prof, Oxford Univ, 78. *Mem:* Nat Acad Sci; Am Phys Soc; Am Chem Soc. *Res:* phase transitions; statistical mechanics. *Mailing Add:* Dept of Chem Cornell Univ Ithaca NY 14853

WIDOM, HAROLD, b Newark, NJ, Sept 23, 32; m 55; c 3. MATHEMATICS. *Educ:* Univ Chicago, SM, 52, PhD(math), 55. *Prof Exp:* From instr to prof math, Cornell Univ, 55-68; PROF MATH, UNIV CALIF, SANTA CRUZ, 68- *Concurrent Pos:* Res fels, NSF, 59-60 & Sloan Found, 61-63; Guggenheim res fel, 67-68 & 72-73. *Mem:* Am Math Soc. *Res:* operator theory. *Mailing Add:* Dept of Math Univ of Calif Santa Cruz CA 95060

WIDOW, BERNARD, b Norwich, Conn, Dec 24, 29; m 59; c 2. ELECTRICAL ENGINEERING. *Educ:* Mass Inst Technol, SB, 51, SM, 53, ScD, 56. *Prof Exp:* Mem staff elec eng, Lincoln Lab, Mass Inst Technol, 51-56, asst prof, 56-59; assoc prof, 59-68, PROF ELEC ENG, STANFORD UNIV, 68- *Concurrent Pos:* Francqui chair, Cath Univ Louvain, 66-67. *Mem:* Fel AAAS; fel Inst Elec & Electronics Engrs. *Res:* Systems theory; theory of control systems; sampled and quantized data systems; adaptive logic automata; pattern recognition; biomedical engineering. *Mailing Add:* Dept of Elec Eng Durand 139 Stanford Univ Stanford CA 94305

WIDRA, ABE, b Philadelphia, Pa, Jan 17, 24; m 52; c 4. MICROBIOLOGY. *Educ:* Brooklyn Col, BA, 48; Univ Fla, MS, 52; Univ Pa, PhD(med microbiol), 54; Am Bd Med Microbiol, dipl, 69. *Prof Exp:* Tech asst bact & serol, Philadelphia Gen Hosp, 49-50; res assoc cytol & cytogenetics, Univ Pa, 54-55; instr bact & immunol, Univ NC, 55-59, asst prof, 59-64; ASSOC PROF MICROBIOL, MED CTR, UNIV ILL, CHICAGO, 64- *Concurrent Pos:* Consult, Presby-St Luke's Hosp, Chicago, 66-80. *Mem:* Am Soc Microbiol. *Res:* Medical mycology. *Mailing Add:* 307 Keystone Ave River Forest IL 60305

WIDSTROM, NEIL WAYNE, b Hecla, SDak, Nov 11, 33; m 60; c 2. GENETICS, PLANT BREEDING. *Educ:* SDak State Univ, BS, 59, PhD(plant breeding), 62. *Prof Exp:* Fel genetics, NC State Univ, 63-64; RES GENETICIST PLANTS, AGR RES SERV, USDA, 64- *Mem:* AAAS; Am Soc Agron; Crop Sci Soc Am; Genetics Soc Am; Am Genetic Asn. *Res:* Plant genetics; genetics of resistance to insects by plants; resistance in corn to aflatoxin contamination; sweetstalk corn for alcohol and biomass production. *Mailing Add:* Southern Grain Insects Res Lab Coastal Plain Exp Sta Tifton GA 31794

WIEBE, DONALD, b Indicott, Nebr, June 30, 23; m; c 2. ENGINEERING. *Educ:* WVa Univ, BS, 49, MS, 59. *Prof Exp:* Res engr, Joy Mfg Co, 49-51; asst prof mining eng, WVa Univ, 51-53; mgr exp sta, Joy Mfg Co, 53-63; mgr eng mech, Astronuclear Lab, Westinghouse Elec Corp, 63-64; mgr, 64-76, VPRES RES & ENG, A STUCKI CO, 76- *Mem:* Soc Exp Stress Anal; Air Pollution Control Asn; Am Inst Mining, Metall & Petrol Engrs; fel Am Soc Mech Engrs; Instrument Soc. *Res:* Product engineering and development; mining, industrial-dust collection; applied research; experimental mechanics, heat transfer-cryogenics; fluid flow. *Mailing Add:* Res & Eng 2600 Neville Rd Pittsburgh PA 15225

WIEBE, H ALLAN, b Alta, Can, May 7, 40. PRECIPITATION SCAVENGING, ANALYTICAL METHODS. *Educ:* Univ Alta, BSc, 62, PhD(chem), 67. *Prof Exp:* Res assoc, Pa State Univ, 67-70; res fel, Nat Res Coun Can, 71-72; RES SCIENTIST ATMOSPHERIC CHEM, ATMOSPHERIC ENVIRON SERV, 72- *Res:* Scavenging of atmospheric gases and aeronols by clouds and precipitation; long range transport of air pollutants; analytical methodology development; far measurement of atmospheric gas and aerosols. *Mailing Add:* Atmospheric Envirn Serv 4905 Dufferin St Downsview ON M3H 5T4 Can

WIEBE, HERMAN HENRY, b Newton, Kans, May 30, 21; m 51; c 2. BOTANY, PLANT PHYSIOLOGY. *Educ:* Goshen Col, BA, 47; Univ Iowa, MS, 49; Duke Univ, PhD(bot), 53. *Prof Exp:* Instr bot, NC State Col, 49-50 & 52-53; res partic, Oak Ridge Inst Nuclear Studies, 53-54; assoc prof bot, 54-62, prof bot, 62-80, PROF BIOL, UTAH STATE UNIV, 80- *Concurrent Pos:* NSF fel, Bot Inst, Stuttgart-Hohenheim, Ger, 64-65; Fulbright Hays vis prof, Trinity Col, Dublin, 73-74. *Mem:* AAAS; Am Soc Plant Physiol; Scand Soc Plant Physiol. *Res:* Plant water relations; air pollution injury; mineral nutrition. *Mailing Add:* Dept of Bot Utah State Univ Logan UT 84322

WIEBE, JOHN, b Sask, June 3, 26; m 47; c 6. HORTICULTURE. *Educ:* Ont Agr Col, BSA, 51; Cornell Univ, MS, 53, PhD, 55. *Prof Exp:* Res scientist, Hort Res Inst, Ont Dept Agr, 55-76; DIR ALTA HORT RES CTR, ALTA DEPT AGR, BROOKS, 76- *Res:* Viticulture and physiology. *Mailing Add:* Alta Hort Res Ctr Bag Serv 200 Brooks AB T0J 0J0 Can

WIEBE, JOHN PETER, b Neu-Schönsee, Ukraine, Aug 28, 38; Can citizen; m 64; c 2. PHYSIOLOGY, ENDOCRINOLOGY. *Educ:* Univ BC, BSc, 63, PhD(physiol), 67. *Prof Exp:* Nat Res Coun Can res fel zool, Univ Leeds, 68-69; asst prof endocrinol, Tex A&M Univ, 70-72; asst prof physiol, 72-77, asst prof zool, 74-77, ASSOC PROF ZOOL, UNIV WESTERN ONT, 77- *Mem:* AAAS; Am Soc Zool; Can Soc Zool. *Res:* Mechanisms of hormone action; environmental endocrinology; reproductive physiology; photic effects on cellular components. *Mailing Add:* Dept of Zool Univ of Western Ont London ON N6A 5B8 Can

WIEBE, LEONARD IRVING, b Swift Current, Sask, Oct 14, 41; c 3. BIONUCLEONICS. *Educ:* Univ Sask, BSP, 63, MSc, 66; Univ Sydney, PhD(drug metab), 69. *Prof Exp:* Asst prof pharmaceut chem bionucleonics, 70-73, chmn bionucleonics div, 74-75, assoc prof, 73-78, PROF BIONUCLEONICS, UNIV ALTA, 78-, CHMN RES REACTOR COMT, 74- *Concurrent Pos:* Sessional lectr, Univ Sask, 65-66; fel, Univ Alta, 69-70; sessional lectr, Univ Sydney, 73; von Humboldt fel, Ger Cancer Res Ctr, 76-77. *Res:* Production of short-lived radionuclides for incorporation into radiopharmaceuticals for use in diagnostic nuclear medicine. *Mailing Add:* Div Bionucleonics & Radiopharm Univ Alta Edmonton AB T5H 0Z8 Can

WIEBE, MICHAEL EUGENE, b Newton, Kans, Oct 1, 42; m 65. MICROBIOLOGY. *Educ:* Sterling Col, BS, 65; Univ Kans, PhD(microbiol), 71. *Prof Exp:* Fel microbiol, Duke Univ Med Ctr, 71-73; asst prof, Med Col, Cornell Univ, 73-81; ASSOC DIR BLOOD DERIVATIVE RES & DEVELOP, NEW YORK BLOOD CTR, 80-, ASSOC INVESTR, LINDSLEY F KIMBALL RES INST, 80- *Concurrent Pos:* Mem, Subcomt Interrelationships among Catalogued Arboviruses, Am Comt Arthropod-born Viruses, 77-80; prin investr contracts, US Army Med Res & Develop Command, 77-81; adj assoc prof, Med Col, Cornell Univ, 81-; mem, Critical Reviews in Microbiol Adv Bd, Can Res Coun, 82- *Mem:* Am Soc Microbiol; Am Soc Virol; Am Soc Trop Med & Hyg; AAAS; Soc Exp Biol & Med. *Res:* Molecular virology and cell biology; mechanisms of induction, synthesis and regulation of human interferons and lymphokines; mechanisms of virus replication, host cell response, and viral virulence. *Mailing Add:* Blood Derivatives Prog New York Blood Ctr 310 E 67th St New York NY 10021

WIEBE, PETER HOWARD, b Salinas, Calif, Oct 2, 40; m 68; c 2. BIOLOGICAL OCEANOGRAPHY, MARINE BIOLOGY. *Educ:* Ariz State Col, Flagstaff, BS, 62; Scripps Inst Oceanog, Univ Calif, San Diego, PhD(biol oceanog), 68. *Prof Exp:* Fel biol oceanog, Hopkins Marine Sta, Stanford Univ, 68-69; asst scientist, 69-74, ASSOC SCIENTIST BIOL OCEANOG, WOODS HOLE OCEANOG INS INST, 74- *Concurrent Pos:* Numerous NSF grants & Off of Naval Res contracts. *Mem:* Am Soc Limnol & Oceanog; AAAS. *Res:* Quantitative ecology of zooplankton with emphasis on the biological and physical-chemical factors which act to regulate the distribution and abundance of oceanic populations and communities. *Mailing Add:* Woods Hole Oceanog Inst Woods Hole MA 02543

WIEBE, RICHARD PENNER, b Pittsburgh, Pa, Jan 5, 28; m 56; c 2. MATHEMATICAL LOGIC. *Educ:* Univ Ill, Urbana, BS, 49, MS, 51; Univ Calif, Berkeley, PhD(philos), 64. *Prof Exp:* Instr philos, Johns Hopkins Univ, 60-62; ASST PROF MATH, ST MARY'S COL, CALIF, 63- *Res:* Foundations of mathematics; semantics; philosophy of science and mathematics. *Mailing Add:* Dept of Math St Mary's Col of Calif Moraga CA 94575

WIEBE, ROBERT A, b San Meteo, Calif, Nov 2, 39; m 65. PETROLOGY. *Educ:* Stanford Univ, BS, 61; Univ Wash, Seattle, MS, 63; Stanford Univ, PhD, 66. *Prof Exp:* Asst prof geol, 66-73, ASSOC PROF GEOL, FRANKLIN & MARSHALL COL, 73-, CHMN DEPT, 76- *Concurrent Pos:* NATO fel, Univ Edinburgh, 72-73. *Mem:* Geol Soc Am; Mineral Soc Am. *Res:* Igneous and metamorphic petrology; mineralogy; plutonic igneious rocks of the Northern Appalachians; the Nain Anorthosite-Adamellite complex. *Mailing Add:* Dept of Geol Franklin & Marshall Col Lancaster PA 17604

WIEBE, WILLIAM JOHN, b San Mateo, Calif, Mar, 14, 35; m 60; c 3. MICROBIAL ECOLOGY, ANAEROBIC METABOLISM. *Educ:* Stanford Univ, BA, 57; Univ Wash, PhD(fisheries), 65. *Prof Exp:* Fel microbiol & electron micros, Georgetown Univ, 65-67; asst prof, 67-72, assoc prof, 72-77, PROF MICROBIOL, UNIV GA, 77- *Concurrent Pos:* Vis prof, Div Fisheries & Oceanog, Commonwealth Sci & Indust Res Orgn, 75, officer-in-chg, 79-82; mem, Panel Adv Comt Ecol & Ecosyst, NSF, 78, Sci Comt Coral Reefs, Pac Sci Asn, 79. *Mem:* Am Soc Microbiol; Am Soc Limnol & Oceanog; Australian Soc Microbiol; Western Naturalist Asn; Int Soc Coral Reefs. *Res:* Marine microbial ecology in nearshore coastal and estuarine environments; salt marsh sediment fermentation; sulfate reduction and methanogenesis, in coastal zones and coral reefs; macrophyte decomposition and nitrogen fixation. *Mailing Add:* Dept Microbiol Univ Ga Athens GA 30602

WIEBELHAUS, VIRGIL D, b Fairfax, SDak, Feb 19, 16; m 51; c 1. BIOCHEMISTRY, PHARMACOLOGY. *Educ:* SDak State Col, BS, 39; Purdue Univ, MS, 41; Univ Wis, PhD(biochem), 48. *Prof Exp:* Res assoc, Sharp & Dohme, 49-56; sr scientist, 56-61, group leader, 61-67, asst dir, 67-71, ASSOC DIR BIOCHEM & RES MICROBIOL, SMITH KLINE & FRENCH LABS, 71- *Mem:* Am Soc Nephrology; Am Soc Pharmacol & Exp Therapeut; Biophys Soc; Brit Biochem Soc; Int Soc Biochem Pharmacol. *Res:* Oxidative phosphorylation; carbohydrate metabolism; thyroxine toxicity; renal transport mechanisms; diuretic pharmacology; catecholamine metabolism; anti-inflammatory physiology; gastric acid biochemistry. *Mailing Add:* Smith Kline & French Labs 1500 Spring Garden St Philadelphia PA 19101

WIEBELT, JOHN ALBERT, b Akron, Ohio, June 7, 27; m 50; c 2. MECHANICAL ENGINEERING. *Educ:* Tex Technol Col, BS, 50; Southern Methodist Univ, MS, 56; Okla State Univ, PhD(eng), 60. *Prof Exp:* Jr engr, Southwestern Bell Tel Co, 50-52; from instr to asst prof mech eng, Southern Methodist Univ, 52-58; from asst prof to assoc prof, 58-65, PROF MECH ENG, OKLA STATE UNIV, 65- *Mem:* Soc Mech Engrs; Int Solar Energy Soc. *Res:* Radiation heat transfer. *Mailing Add:* Sch of Mech Eng Okla State Univ Stillwater OK 74074

WIEBERS, JOYCE ADAMS, b Lancaster, Ohio, Nov 16, 26; m 57; c 2. ANALYTICAL BIOCHEMISTRY. *Educ:* Col Mt St Joseph, BS, 47; Univ Cincinnati, MS, 50; Purdue Univ, PhD(bact), 58. *Prof Exp:* Asst bact, 54, res assoc, 58-65, asst prof org chem, 66-70, res biochemist, Dept Biol Sci, 70-74, ASSOC PROF BIOL CHEM, PURDUE UNIV, LAFAYETTE, 74- *Mem:* Am Chem Soc; Am Soc Biol Chem; Am Soc Mass Spectrometry. *Res:* Mass spectrometry of nucleic acids; synthesis of defined oligoribonucleotides; enzymology; DNA sequence by mass spectrometry. *Mailing Add:* Dept of Biol Sci Purdue Univ West Lafayette IN 47907

WIEBOLD, WILLIAM JOHN, b Vinton, Iowa, Oct 27, 49; m 73; c 1. AGRONOMY, CROP PHYSIOLOGY. *Educ:* Iowa State Univ, BS, 71, MS, 74; Univ Ga, PhD(agron), 78. *Prof Exp:* Res asst soybean breeding, Iowa State Univ, 69-71, teaching asst, 71, res asst soybean physiol, 72-74; res asst, Univ Ga, 74-78, instr crop sci, 77; ASST PROF SOYBEAN PHYSIOL, UNIV MD, 78- *Mem:* Am Soc Agron; Crop Sci Soc Am. *Res:* Physiological and morphological limitations to soybean yield. *Mailing Add:* Dept of Agron Univ of Md College Park MD 20742

WIEBUSCH, F B, b Brenham, Tex, Aug 26, 23. PERIODONTOLOGY. *Educ:* Univ Tex, BBA, 43, DDS, 47; Am Bd Periodont, dipl. *Prof Exp:* Pub health dent consult, State Health Dept, Tex, 47-51; prof oral diag & therapeut & chmn dept, 54-71, PROF PERIODONT & ASST DEAN CONTINUING EDUC, MED COL VA, 71- *Concurrent Pos:* Consult, Vet Admin Hosps, Richmond & Salem, Va. *Mem:* Am Dent Asn; Am Acad Periodont; fel Int Col Dent; fel Am Col Dent; Am Acad Dent Med. *Res:* Periodontics. *Mailing Add:* MCV Box 566 Richmond VA 23298

WIEBUSH, JOSEPH ROY, b Lancaster, Pa, Oct 18, 20; m 43; c 1. ANALYTICAL CHEMISTRY, MARINE CHEMISTRY. *Educ:* Franklin & Marshall Col, BS, 41; Univ Md, MS, 51, PhD(chem), 55. *Prof Exp:* Supvr explosives dept, Hercules Powder Co, 41-43, chemist, 46-48; asst chem, Univ Md, 48-51; res chemist, Mead Corp, Ohio, 55-56; dir res, Nat Inst Drycleaning, 56-60; from assoc prof to prof chem, US Naval Acad, 60-81, chmn dept, 66-77. *Concurrent Pos:* Adj prof, Univ Cent Fla, 81- *Mem:* Am Chem Soc; Sigma Xi. *Res:* Fluorescence analysis; toxicity of organic solvents; analytical techniques for trace elements; marine corrosion and fouling; oceanographic applications; environmental pollution; general chemistry texts. *Mailing Add:* 1830 Ramie Rd Clermont FL 32711

WIECH, NORBERT LEONARD, b Chicago, Ill, Mar 13, 39; m 61; c 3. BIOCHEMICAL, PHARMACOLOGY. *Educ:* Univ Notre Dame, BS, 60, MS, 63; Tulane Univ, PhD(biochem), 66. *Prof Exp:* Res assoc nutrit, Sch Pub Health, Harvard Univ, 66-67; sect head biochem pharm, Merrell Int, Strasbourg, France, 72-74, SECT HEAD BIOCHEM PHARMACOL, MERRELL RES CTR, MERRELL-DOW, CINCINNATI, 67- *Concurrent Pos:* Adj assoc prof exp med, Univ Cincinnati, 78- *Mem:* AAAS; Am Oil Chemists Soc; Am Chem Soc; NY Acad Sci; Am Diabetes Asn. *Res:* Membrane receptors; neuropharmacology; carbohydrate-lipid metabolism in health and disease. *Mailing Add:* Merrell Nat Labs Dept Biochem Merrell Research Dr Cincinnati OH 45215

WIECHELMAN, KAREN JANICE, b Central City, Nebr, Apr 30, 47; m 70. BIOPHYSICAL CHEMISTRY. *Educ:* Univ Nebr, BS, 69, PhD(biochem), 73. *Prof Exp:* Res assoc biophys, Univ Pittsburgh, 73-76; ASST PROF CHEM, UNIV SOUTHWESTERN LA, 76- *Res:* Use of fluorescence techniques to investigate various biological systems. *Mailing Add:* Dept of Chem Univ of Southwestern La Lafayette LA 70504

WIECZOROWSKI, ELSIE, b Chicago, Ill, July 4, 06. PEDIATRICS. *Educ:* Northwestern Univ, BS, 29, MS, 31, PhD(path), 37, MD, 45. *Prof Exp:* Asst, Med Sch, Northwestern Univ, 38-42; fel, Mayo Clin, 44-46; instr & Abt fel, 46-49, assoc, 49-59, ASST PROF PEDIAT, MED SCH, NORTHWESTERN UNIV, CHICAGO, 59- *Mem:* Fel AMA; fel Am Acad Pediat; Sigma Xi. *Mailing Add:* 932 Wolfram St Chicago IL 60657

WIED, GEORGE LUDWIG, b Carlsbad, Czech, Feb 7, 21; wid. OBSTETRICS & GYNECOLOGY. *Educ:* Charles Univ, Prague, MD, 44. *Prof Exp:* Intern, County Hosp, Carlsbad, Czech, 45; resident obstet & gynec, Univ Munich, 46-48; asst, Univ Berlin, 48-52, co-chmn dept, 53; from asst prof to assoc prof, 54-65, actg chmn dept, 74-75, PROF OBSTET & GYNEC, SCH MED, UNIV CHICAGO, 65-, PROF PATH, 67-, DIR SCHS CYTOTECHNOL & CYTOCYBERNET, 59- *Concurrent Pos:* Ed-in-chief, Acta Cytologica, 57-; ed, Monogr Clin Cytol, 64-; ed-in-chief, J Reproductive Med, 67-; ed-in-chief, Anal & Quantitative Cytol, 79- *Honors & Awards:* Surgeon Gen Cert Merit, 52; Goldblatt Cytol Award, 61; George N

Papanicolaou Cytol Award, 70. *Mem:* Am Soc Cytol (pres, 65-66); Am Soc Cell Biol; Int Acad Cytol (pres elect, 74-77, pres, 77-80); Ger Soc Obstet & Gynec; Ger Soc Cytol. *Res:* Cytopathology; exfoliative cytology; biological image processing. *Mailing Add:* Dept Obstet & Gynec Sch Med Univ Chicago Chicago IL 60637

WIEDEMAN, MARY PURCELL, b Lexington, Ky, June 21, 19. PHYSIOLOGY. *Educ:* Univ Ky, MS, 43; Ind Univ, PhD(physiol), 53. *Prof Exp:* Assoc physiol, Woman's Med Col Pa, 53-56; from asst prof to assoc prof, 56-67, PROF PHYSIOL, SCH MED, TEMPLE UNIV, 67- *Honors & Awards:* Honor Achievement Award, Angiol Res Found, 65. *Mem:* Am Physiol Soc; Microcirc Soc; Am Asn Anat; NY Acad Sci. *Res:* Microcirculatory physiology. *Mailing Add:* Dept of Physiol Temple Univ Sch of Med Philadelphia PA 19140

WIEDEMAN, VARLEY EARL, b Oklahoma City, Okla, Mar 14, 33; m 63; c 2. BOTANY, ECOLOGY. *Educ:* Univ Okla, BS, 57, MS, 60; Univ Tex, PhD(bot), 64. *Prof Exp:* Chemist-biologist, USPHS, 59-61; from asst prof to assoc prof, 64-74, PROF PLANT ECOL, UNIV LOUISVILLE, 74- *Mem:* Bot Soc Am; Am Phycol Soc; Am Water Resources Asn; Int Phycol Soc. *Res:* Ecology of algae with relation to water pollution, water treatment and sewage treatment; physiological ecology of spring herbaceous perennials. *Mailing Add:* Dept of Biol Univ of Louisville Louisville KY 40208

WIEDEMANN, ALFRED MAX, b Chicago, Ill, Nov 24, 31; c 2. PLANT ECOLOGY. *Educ:* Utah State Univ, BS, 60, MS, 62; Ore State Univ, PhD(bot), 66. *Prof Exp:* Asst prof bot, Ore State Univ, 65-67, asst prof range mgt, 70; sci fac gen sci, N Geelong High Sch, Victoria, Australia, 69-70; MEM FAC BIOL, EVERGREEN STATE UNIV, 70- *Concurrent Pos:* Lectr bot, Univ Malaya, 67-68; fel, Commonwealth Sci & Indust Res Orgn, Australia-NSF, 68-69. *Mem:* Ecol Soc Am; Brit Ecol Soc. *Res:* Vegatation of interior and coastal sand dunes; identification and description of natural areas. *Mailing Add:* Dept of Biol Evergreen State Col Olympia WA 08505

WIEDEMEIER, HERIBERT, b Steinheim, WGer, Aug 4, 28; nat US. INORGANIC CHEMISTRY. *Educ:* Univ Muenster, BS, 54, MSc, 57, DSc, 60. *Prof Exp:* Asst inorg & phys chem, Univ Muenster, 56-58, instr, 58-60; res assoc chem, Univ Kans, 60-62; res assoc, Univ Muenster, 62-63; res assoc, Univ Kans, 63-64; asst prof, 64-67, assoc prof phys chem, 67-72, PROF CHEM, RENSSELAER POLYTECH INST, 72- *Honors & Awards:* Medal Exceptional Sci Achievement, NASA, 74. *Mem:* AAAS; Am Chem Soc; Ger Chem Soc. *Res:* Growth of single crystals of metal chalcogenides; crystal growth mechanism and morphology; thermodynamic and kinetic studies of condensation and vaporization processes of inorganic materials at elevated temperatures; crystal growth in zero-gravity. *Mailing Add:* Dept of Chem Rensselaer Polytech Inst Troy NY 12181

WIEDENBECK, MARCELLUS LEE, b Lancaster, NY, Oct 11, 19; m 46; c 6. NUCLEAR PHYSICS. *Educ:* Canisius Col, BS, 41; Univ Notre Dame, MS, 42, PhD(physics), 45. *Prof Exp:* Instr physics, Univ Notre Dame, 44-46; from asst prof to assoc prof, 46-55, PROF PHYSICS, UNIV MICH, ANN ARBOR, 55- *Mem:* Am Phys Soc. *Res:* Nuclear spectroscopy; beta ray and alpha ray spectra; coincidence methods; spectroscopy of some heavy nuclei. *Mailing Add:* Dept of Physics Univ of Mich Ann Arbor MI 48109

WIEDENHEFT, CHARLES JOHN, b Sandusky, Ohio, Oct 23, 41. CHEMISTRY. *Educ:* Capital Univ, BS, 63; Case Western Reserve Univ, MS, 65, PhD(chem), 67. *Prof Exp:* RES SPECIALIST, MONSANTO RES CORP, 67- *Mem:* AAAS; Am Chem Soc. *Res:* Coordination compounds of the actinide ions. *Mailing Add:* Monsanto Res Corp Mound Lab Miamisburg OH 45342

WIEDENMANN, LYNN G, b Moline, Ill, Apr 21, 28; m 56; c 4. POLYMER CHEMISTRY, ORGANIC CHEMISTRY. *Educ:* Ill Wesleyan Univ, BS, 50; Univ Iowa, MS, 52, PhD(org chem), 55. *Prof Exp:* Asst chemist, Rocky Mountain Arsenal, 55-57; res chemist, Tex-US Chem Corp, 57-60; res chemist, Rock Island Arsenal, 60-69; PROF CHEM & HEAD DEPT, BLACK HAWK COL, 69- *Mem:* Am Chem Soc. *Res:* Polymer synthesis; high temperature resistant elastomers; boron and stereoregular butadiene polymers; butadiene derivatives; antioxidants; organic phosphorus compounds; dibenzopyrylium compounds. *Mailing Add:* Dept of Chem Black Hawk Col Moline IL 61265

WIEDER, GRACE MARILYN, b New York, NY, May 10, 28. INFRARED & RAMAN SPECTROSCOPY. *Educ:* Univ Vt, BA, 49; Mt Holyoke Col, AM, 51; Polytech Inst Brooklyn, PhD(phys chem), 61. *Prof Exp:* Res assoc chem, Univ Southern Calif, 60-62; instr, 62-65, asst prof, 66-77, ASSOC PROF CHEM, BROOKLYN COL, 78- *Concurrent Pos:* Vis scientist, Univ Wash, 70-71. *Mem:* Am Chem Soc; Am Phys Soc; Sigma Xi. *Res:* Stability constants and spectra of donor-acceptor complexes; Raman and infrared spectra of crystals. *Mailing Add:* Dept of Chem Brooklyn Col Brooklyn NY 11210

WIEDER, HAROLD, b Cleveland, Ohio, July 18, 27; m 63; c 3. OPTICAL PHYSICS. *Educ:* Univ Rochester, BS, 50, MA, 57, MS, 58; Case Inst Technol, PhD(physics), 64. *Prof Exp:* Engr, Sarnoff Res Ctr, RCA Labs, 50-54; physicist, Parma Res Ctr, Union Carbide Corp, 57-61; physicist, Watson Res Ctr, 63-68, PHYSICIST, IBM CORP, 63- & SAN JOSE LAB, 68- *Mem:* Am Phys Soc. *Res:* Optical, magneto-optic, photoconductive, and structural properties of ordered and disordered films; transient thermal and thermomagnetic techniques; mode coupling and intra-cavity laser effects; level crossing and anticrossing spectroscopy. *Mailing Add:* 20175 Knollwood Dr Saratoga CA 95070

WIEDER, IRWIN, b Cleveland, Ohio, Sept 26, 25; m 53; c 4. MOLECULAR BIOPHYSICS, SPECTROSCOPY. *Educ:* Case Inst Technol, BS, 50; Stanford Univ, PhD(physics), 56. *Prof Exp:* Asst, Stanford Univ, 51-56; res physicist, Westinghouse Elec Corp, 56-60 & Varian Assocs, 60-61; dir res, Interphase Corp, 61-66; prin scientist, Carver Corp, 66-69; NIH spec fel, Dept Biol Sci, Stanford Univ, 70-71; vis prof, dept electronics, Weizmann Inst Sci, Israel, 71-73; PRES & TECH DIR, ANAL RADIATION CORP, 74- *Mem:* Am Phys Soc; Inst Elec & Electronics Engrs. *Res:* Magnetic resonance; microwave-optical effects; optical pumping in gases, liquids and solids; masers and lasers; energy transfer in biological systems; cellular communication; cell membranes and surfaces; immunofluorescent, laser induced fluorescent and fluorescent antibody spectroscopy. *Mailing Add:* 459 Panchita Way Los Altos CA 94022

WIEDER, SOL, b Bronx, NY, Jan 6, 40; m 63; c 3. PHYSICS. *Educ:* City Col New York, BS, 61; NY Univ, MS, 62, PhD(physics), 66. *Prof Exp:* Lectr physics, City Col New York, 62-64; instr, NY Univ, 64-65; instr, Bronx Community Col, 65-66; mem tech staff, Bell Tel Labs, Inc, 66-67; asst prof, NY Univ, 67; assoc prof, 67-75, PROF PHYSICS, FAIRLEIGH DICKINSON UNIV, 75- *Mem:* Am Phys Soc; Am Geophys Union; Am Asn Physics Teachers. *Res:* Many-particle physics; geophysics; solar energy. *Mailing Add:* Dept of Physics Fairleigh Dickinson Univ Teaneck NJ 07666

WIEDERHIELM, CURT ARNE, b Motala, Sweden, Dec 11, 23; US citizen; div; c 2. CARDIOVASCULAR PHYSIOLOGY. *Educ:* Univ Wash, PhD(physiol), 61. *Prof Exp:* Res asst, 48-50, chief lab asst surg, 51-53, chief lab asst cardiol, 53-57, asst dir cardiovasc training prog, 56-66, from instr to assoc prof, 61-70, PROF PHYSIOL & BIOPHYS, SCH MED, UNIV WASH, 70- *Concurrent Pos:* USPHS career res develop award, 64-74. *Mem:* Microcirc Soc; Am Physiol Soc; Int Soc Biorheol; Int Soc Hemorheol; Simulation Coun. *Res:* Physiology and biophysics of the microcirculation; viscoelastic wall properties of microscopic blood vessels; transcapillary and interstitial transport phenomena; peripheral control of blood flow and exchange processes; blood rheology. *Mailing Add:* Dept of Physiol & Biophys SJ-40 Univ of Wash Seattle WA 98195

WIEDERHOLD, EDWARD W(ILLIAM), b Clermont Co, Ohio, Nov 4, 21. CHEMICAL & NUCLEAR ENGINEERING. *Educ:* Ohio State Univ, BChE, 49. *Prof Exp:* Chem engr, Atomic Energy Comn, 50-52; chem engr, Mound Lab, Monsanto Co, 52-58, res chemist, 58-59, sr res chemist, 59-68; first officer, Div Nuclear Safety & Environ Protection, Int Atomic Energy Agency, Vienna, Austria, 68-78; CONTRACT ENGR & SYSTS DEVELOP ENGR, GEN DEVICES INC, 78- *Mem:* Am Chem Soc; Am Soc Testing & Mat; Nat Soc Prof Engrs. *Res:* Industrial waste disposal; reactor coolants; cryogenics. *Mailing Add:* Rte 1 Milford OH 45150

WIEDERHOLD, PIETER RIJK, b Malang, Indonesia, Jan 24, 28; US citizen; m 56; c 3. PHYSICS, ELECTRICAL ENGINEERING. *Educ:* Delft Univ Technol, Ir, 53. *Prof Exp:* Sr proj engr, Sylvania Elec Prod, Inc, 53-61; mgr energy conversion, Ion Physics Corp, Inc, 61-64; mgr cryogenics, Magnion, Inc, 64-66; div mgr space physics, Comstock & Wescott, Inc, 66-74; PRES, GEN EASTERN CORP, 74- *Mem:* Inst Elec & Electronics Engrs; Am Meteorol Soc; Instrument Soc Am. *Res:* Superconductivity; magnetics; energy conversion; humidity instruments. *Mailing Add:* Gen Eastern Corp 36 Maple St Watertown MA 02172

WIEDERHOLT, WIGBERT C, b Warmbrunn, Ger, Apr 22, 31; US citizen; m 60; c 3. NEUROLOGY, NEUROPHYSIOLOGY. *Educ:* Univ Freiburg, MD, 56. *Prof Exp:* Asst to staff neurol, Mayo Clin, 65; from asst prof to assoc prof med, Ohio State Univ, 66-72, chief clin neurophysiol, 69-72; neurologist-in-chief, Dept Neurosci, 73-78, PROF NEUROSCI, UNIV CALIF, SAN DIEGO, 72-, CHMN DEPT NEUROSCI, 78- *Honors & Awards:* S Weir Mitchel Award, Am Acad Neurol, 65. *Mem:* AAAS; fel Am Acad Neurol; Am Neurol Asn; Am Electroencephalog Soc; Am Asn Electromyog & Electrodiag (secy-treas, 71-). *Res:* Far-yield evoked Potentials. *Mailing Add:* Dept of Neurosci M-008 Univ of Calif San Diego La Jolla CA 92093

WIEDERICK, HARVEY DALE, b Wetaskiwin, Can, May 10, 37; m 63; c 3. PHYSICS. *Educ:* Royal Mil Col Can, BSc, 59; Johns Hopkins Univ, MAT, 64; Queen's Univ, Ont, PhD(physics), 68. *Prof Exp:* Fel physics, Univ Tronoto, 68-69; lectr, Royal Mil Col Can, 69-73, asst prof, 74-77; exchange teacher, Royal Mil Col Sci, Eng, 73-74; Nuffield Found res fel, Univ Kent, Canterbury, Eng, 77-78; ASSOC PROF PHYSICS, ROYAL MIL COL CAN, 78- *Concurrent Pos:* Defence Res Bd Can grant, 70- *Res:* Electrical impedance and transient effects in the intermediate state in pure and impure type I superconductors and in type II superconductors. *Mailing Add:* Dept of Physics Royal Mil Col Kingston ON K7L 2M3 Can

WIEDERSICH, H(ARTMUT), materials science, solid state physics, see previous edition

WIEDMAN, HAROLD W, b Palermo, Calif, Jan 11, 30. PHYTOPATHOLOGY. *Educ:* Chico State Col, AB, 52; Ore State Col, PhD(bot), 56. *Prof Exp:* Asst, Ore State Col, 53-56; asst plant pathologist, NMex State Univ, 56-58 & State Dept Agr, Calif, 58-59; asst prof bot, Humboldt State Col, 59-61; from asst prof to assoc prof, 61-69, PROF BIOL SCI, CALIF STATE UNIV, SACRAMENTO, 69- *Mem:* Am Phytopath Soc; Bot Soc Am. *Res:* Soil-borne diseases; biological control; diseases of vegetables and cotton. *Mailing Add:* Dept of Biol Sci Calif State Univ Sacramento CA 95819

WIEDMEIER, VERNON THOMAS, b Harvey, NDak, Jan 10, 35; m 57; c 4. PHYSIOLOGY. *Educ:* NDak State Teachers Col, Valley City, BS, 59; NDak State Univ, MS, 61; Marquette Univ, PhD(physiol), 68. *Prof Exp:* Instr biol, NPark Col, 60-61; asst prof, St Ambrose Col, 61-64; asst prof, 71-75, ASSOC PROF PHYSIOL, MED COL GA, 75- *Concurrent Pos:* NIH trainee, Univ Va, 69-70 & fel, 70-71. *Mem:* Am Physiol Soc. *Res:* Myocardial metabolism and the regulation of coronary blood flow. *Mailing Add:* Dept of Physiol Med Col of Ga Augusta GA 30902

WIEGAND, CLYDE EDWARD, experimental physics, see previous edition

WIEGAND, CRAIG LOREN, b Santa Rosa, Tex, Jan 11, 33; m 62; c 2. IRRIGATION SALINITY, REMOTE SENSING. *Educ:* Agr & Mech Col, Tex, BS, 55, MS, 56; Utah State Univ, PhD(soil physics), 60. *Prof Exp:* Res soil scientist, 60-78, tech adv, Sci & Educ Admin-Agr Res, 73-80, MEM STAFF, AGR RES SERV, USDA, 80- *Concurrent Pos:* Mid-career fel, Woodrow Wilson Sch Pub & Int Affairs, 74-75. *Honors & Awards:* Superior Performance Award, 70. *Mem:* Fel AAAS; fel Soil Sci Soc Am; Am Soc Hort Sci; Am Soc Agron; Int Soil Sci Soc. *Res:* Remote sensing hydrology; plant physiology; micrometeorology; plant-water relations; crop modeling; principal investigator on NASA contracts dealing with earth observation satellite data applications to agriculture. *Mailing Add:* Soil & Water Conserv Res Agr Res Sta USDA Box 267 Weslaco TX 78596

WIEGAND, DONALD ARTHUR, b Rochester, NY, July 21, 27; m 59; c 2. SOLID STATE PHYSICS. *Educ:* Cornell Univ, BEE, 52, MEE, 53, PhD(eng physics), 56. *Prof Exp:* Asst & assoc physics, Cornell Univ, 55-56; res physicist, Carnegie-Mellon Univ, 56-59, from asst prof to assoc prof physics, 59-68; res physicist, Feldman Res Lab, Picatinny Arsenal, 68-; SUPVR RES PHYSICIST, ENERGETIC MAT DIV, ARRADGOM, 79- *Concurrent Pos:* Fulbright grant, Darmstadt Tech Univ, WGer, 60-61. *Mem:* Am Phys Soc. *Res:* Imperfections in solids; luminescence; photo-conductive processes; optical absorption; x-ray diffraction; x-ray photoelectron spectroscopy; metastable solids; mechanical properties of solids. *Mailing Add:* Energetic Mats Div LCWSL ARRADGOM Dover NJ 07801

WIEGAND, GAYL, b Estherville, Iowa, July 18, 39. ORGANIC CHEMISTRY. *Educ:* Univ Iowa, BS, 61; Univ Mass, PhD(org chem), 65. *Prof Exp:* Asst prof, 65-72, assoc prof, 72-77, PROF CHEM, IDAHO STATE UNIV, 77- *Mem:* Am Chem Soc; Sigma Xi. *Res:* Mechanisms of organic like reactions occurring at elements other than carbon; organosulfur chemistry; kinetics of slow chemical reactions. *Mailing Add:* Dept of Chem Idaho State Univ Pocatello ID 83209

WIEGAND, OSCAR FERNANDO, b Mex, Nov 3, 21; US citizen; m 49; c 5. PLANT PHYSIOLOGY. *Educ:* Univ Tex, BA, 50, MA, 52, PhD(cell physiol, chem), 56. *Hon Degrees:* Dr, Univ Guadalajara, 65. *Prof Exp:* Asst prof biol, ETex State Col, 56-57; asst prof pharmacol, Univ Tex Southwest Med Sch, 57-60, vis lectr, Univ Tex, Austin, 60-62, asst prof zool, 62-77, ASSOC PROF ZOOL, UNIV TEX, AUSTIN, 77- *Concurrent Pos:* Smith-Mundt fel & vis prof, Univ Guadalajara, 61-62, Distinguished prof, 62, gen coord model univ develop prog, 63-67; mem study group for reform & improv educ, Latin Am Univ, 65-; head consult, Univ Reform Model, Cath Univ Rio de Janeiro, 66-; consult univ reform prog, Agency Int Develop-Govt Brazil, 66- *Mem:* Am Soc Pharmacol & Exp Therapeut; Soc Gen Physiol. *Res:* Photomorphogenesis, growth physiology and tropisms; water and electrolyte equilibria in tissues; histamine reactions; tracer technique; respiromtery; growth methods for plant tissues. *Mailing Add:* Dept of Zool Univ of Tex Austin TX 78712

WIEGAND, RONALD GAY, b Chicago, Ill, Dec 28, 29; m 56; c 4. PHARMACOLOGY, BIOCHEMISTRY. *Educ:* Mass Inst Technol, BS, 52, MS, 53; Emory Univ, PhD(pharmacol), 56; Univ Chicago, MBA, 71. *Prof Exp:* Assoc histochemist, Armed Forces Inst Path, Walter Reed Army Med Ctr, 57-58; asst pathologist, Med Res & Nutrit Labs, Fitzsimons Army Hosp, Denver, 58; res pharmacologist, 58-61, group leader, 61-63, head chem pharmacol sect, 63-70, mgr chem pharmacol, 70-73, dir prod planning, 73-75, dir res & develop, Agr & Vet Prod Div, 75-78, dir antibiotics & natural prod res, 79-81, MGR INFO SERV, ABBOTT LABS, 81- *Mem:* Am Soc Pharmacol. *Res:* Drug absorption, distribution, excretion and metabolism; pharmacokinetics; biopharmaceutics; mechanism of drug action. *Mailing Add:* Abbott Labs Abbott Park North Chicago IL 60064

WIEGAND, SYLVIA MARGARET, b Cape Town, SAfrica, Mar 8, 45; US citizen; m 66; c 1. ALGEBRA. *Educ:* Bryn Mawr Col, AB, 66; Univ Wash, MA, 67; Univ Wis, PhD(algebra), 72. *Prof Exp:* Comput programmer, Univ Wis, 65 & Bryn Mawr Col, 65-66; teaching asst math, Univ Wis, 67-72; from instr to asst prof, 72-76, ASSOC PROF MATH, UNIV NEBR, LINCOLN, 76- *Mem:* Am Math Soc; Math Asn Am; Asn Women Math. *Res:* Commutative algebra. *Mailing Add:* Dept of Math Univ of Nebr Lincoln NE 68588

WIEGANDT, HERBERT F(REDERICK), b Newaygo, Mich, Jan 4, 17; m 44; c 2. CHEMICAL ENGINEERING. *Educ:* Purdue Univ, BSChE, 38, MSE, 39, PhD(chem eng), 41. *Prof Exp:* Asst process develop, Eng Exp Sta, Purdue Univ, 38-41; chem engr, Standard Oil Co, Ind, 41-44 & Armour Res Found, Ill Inst Technol, 44-47; from asst prof to assoc prof chem eng, 47-60, PROF CHEM ENG, CORNELL UNIV, 60- *Concurrent Pos:* With Monsanto Chem Co, 52 & French Petrol Inst, 61, 64; tech adv, Compagnie Francaise Raffinage, Paris, 72-82. *Mem:* AAAS; Am Chem Soc; Am Inst Chem Engrs. *Res:* Desalination; petroleum processes; extractions; distillation; crystallization. *Mailing Add:* Dept of Chem Eng Cornell Univ Ithaca NY 14853

WIEGEL, ROBERT L, b San Francisco, Calif, Oct 17, 22; m 48; c 3. OCEAN ENGINEERING. *Educ:* Univ Calif, BS, 43, MS, 49. *Prof Exp:* Jr res engr, 46-52, lectr civil eng, 56-60, assoc prof, 60-63, asst dean, 63-72, assoc res engr, 52-60, actg dean, 72-73, PROF CIVIL ENG, UNIV CALIF, BERKELEY, 63- *Concurrent Pos:* Dir, Calif State Tech Serv Prog, 65-68; mem comt earthquake eng res, Nat Acad Eng, mem, Marine Bd; pres, Int Comt Oceanic Resources, 72-75; consult. *Honors & Awards:* Prize, Am Soc Civil Engrs, 62. *Mem:* Nat Acad Eng; fel Am Soc Civil Engrs; fel AAAS; Int Asn Hydraul Res. *Res:* Ocean and coastal engineering; technology transfer. *Mailing Add:* 412 O'Brien Hall Univ of Calif Berkeley CA 94720

WIEGERT, PHILIP E, b Antigo, Wis, Apr 7, 27; m 59; c 6. ORGANIC CHEMISTRY, PHYSICAL CHEMISTRY. *Educ:* Univ Wis, BS, 50; Univ Ill, MS, 51, PhD, 54. *Prof Exp:* Chemist, Mallinckrodt Chem Works, 54-61, group leader, 61-66, asst dir pharmaceut chem, 66-74, plant mgr, 74-77, DIR RES & DEVELOP, NAT CATHETER CORP DIV, MALLINCKRODT INC, 77- *Mem:* Am Chem Soc; The Chem Soc; Am Soc Testing & Mat; Asn Advan Med Instrumentation. *Res:* X-ray contrast media; opium alkaloids; pharmaceutical chemicals; medical devices; standards development. *Mailing Add:* NCC Div Mallinckrodt Inc Hook Rd Argyle NY 12809

WIEGERT, RICHARD G, b Toledo, Ohio, Sept 9, 32; m 55; c 2. ECOLOGY. *Educ:* Adrian Col, BS, 54; Mich State Univ, MS, 58; Univ Mich, PhD(zool), 62. *Prof Exp:* Instr zool, Univ Mich, 61-62; from asst prof to assoc prof, 62-71, PROF ZOOL, UNIV GA, 71- Prof Exp: NSF grants, Yellowstone Nat Park, 68-78, Sapelo Island Salt Marsh, 75-78; EPRF grant, microcosms, 78- *Mem:* AAAS; Am Soc Mammal; Ecol Soc Am; Brit Ecol Soc; Am Soc Naturalists. *Res:* Plant and animal ecolog, particularly problems of population and community energy utilization; population density regulation; interspecies competition; systems ecology and modeling the dynamics of thermal spring and estuarine communities. *Mailing Add:* Dept of Zool Univ of Ga Athens GA 30602

WIEGMANN, NORMAN ARTHUR, b Los Angeles, Calif, Apr 13, 20. ALGEBRA. *Educ:* Univ Southern Calif, AB, 41; Univ Wis, MA, 43, PhD(math), 47. *Prof Exp:* Asst math, Univ Wis, 41-47; instr, Univ Mich, 47-51; mem staff, Nat Bur Stand, 51-53; from assoc prof to prof, Cath Univ Am, 53-60; prof, George Washington Univ, 60-66; PROF MATH, CALIF STATE UNIV DOMINGUEZ HILLS, 66- *Mem:* Am Math Soc. *Res:* Abstract algebra; matrix theory. *Mailing Add:* Dept of Math Calif State Univ 1000 E Victoria St Dominguez Hills CA 90747

WIEHE, IRWIN ANDREW, b Cincinnati, Ohio, Oct 26, 39; m 67; c 3. CHEMICAL ENGINEERING. *Educ:* Univ Cincinnati, ChE, 62; Va Polytech Inst, MS, 65; Wash Univ, DSc(chem eng), 67. *Prof Exp:* Asst prof chem eng, Univ Rochester, 66-72; res scientist, Xerox Corp, 72-77, sr scientist, 72-77; RES ASSOC, EXXON CORP, 77- *Concurrent Pos:* Petrol Res Found grant, Univ Rochester, 68-71. *Mem:* Am Inst Chem Engrs; Am Chem Soc; Sigma Xi. *Res:* Polymer processing; thermodynamics of gas and liquid mixtures; conversion of heavy oils. *Mailing Add:* 5 Pembrooke Rd Chatham NJ 07928

WIELAND, BRUCE WENDELL, b Carroll, Iowa, Apr 15, 37. MECHANICAL ENGINEERING. *Educ:* Iowa State Univ, BS, 60; Ohio State Univ, PhD(nuclear eng), 73. *Prof Exp:* Engr, Oak Ridge Nat Lab, 60-66; res engr, Battelle Mem Inst, 67-68; NIH spec res fel, Ohio State Univ, 69-73; scientist med radioisotopes, Oak Ridge Assoc Univs, 74-80; SCIENTIST, POSITRON RADIOPHARMACEUT, BROOKHAVEN NAT LAB, 81- *Concurrent Pos:* Res assoc, Sch Med, Washington Univ, 71-73; consult, Oak Ridge Assoc Univs, 72-73; assoc prof, Univ Calif, Los Angeles, 81. *Mem:* Soc Nuclear Med. *Res:* Applications of accelerator-produced radioisotopes in nuclear medicine. *Mailing Add:* Dept Chem 555 Brookhaven Nat Lab Upton NY 11973

WIELAND, DENTON R, b Yorktown, Tex, Oct 28, 27; m 54; c 2. PETROLEUM ENGINEERING. *Educ:* Agr & Mech Col, Tex, BS, 53, MS, 56, PhD, 58. *Prof Exp:* Asst prof petrol eng, Univ Tulsa, 57-61, assoc prof & actg head dept, 61-64; dir tech develop, Dowell Div, Dow Chem Co, 64-68, supvr customer serv, 68-69, mgr sales develop dept, 69-72, mgr eng, 72-76; consult, 76-78; proj leader well completions, Osco, 78-79; sr prod mgr, 79-80, GEN SUPVR, CHEVRON, 80- *Mem:* Am Inst Mining, Metall & Petrol Egnrs. *Res:* Physical chemistry of petroleum engineering. *Mailing Add:* PO Box 679 Calvert TX 77837

WIEMER, DAVID F, b Burlington, Wis, Mar 17, 50; m 72; c 3. CHEMICAL ECOLOGY. *Educ:* Marquette Univ, BS, 72; Univ Ill, PhD(org chem), 76. *Prof Exp:* NIH fel, Cornell Univ, 76-78; ASST PROF CHEM, UNIV IOWA, 78- *Mem:* Am Chem Soc; Sigma Xi; AAAS. *Res:* Isolation, characterization, and synthesis of biologically active natural products; insect pheromones and defensive substances. *Mailing Add:* Dept Chem Univ Iowa Iowa City IA 52242

WIEN, RICHARD W, JR, b Bay County, Fla, May 17, 45; m 68; c 2. PHYSICAL CHEMISTRY, PHOTOGRAPHIC SCIENCE. *Educ:* Purdue Univ, BS, 67; Stanford Univ, PhD(phys chem), 71. *Prof Exp:* NSF fel phys chem, Stanford Univ, 67-71; sr res chemist photog sci, 71-79, PROJ LEADER PHOTOG TECHNOL DIV, EASTMAN KODAK RES LAB, 79- *Concurrent Pos:* Nat tour speaker, Am Chem Soc, 78- *Mem:* Am Chem Soc; AAAS. *Res:* Improvement of photographic speed of color reversal films; development of reversal color papers; development of new high speed color photographic systems. *Mailing Add:* Eastman Kodak Co Bldg 69 Kodak Park Rochester NY 14650

WIENER, EARL LOUIS, b Shreveport, La, May 30, 33; m 55; c 2. INDUSTRIAL ENGINEERING, PSYCHOLOGY. *Educ:* Duke Univ, BA, 55; Ohio State Univ, MA, 59, PhD(psychol, indust eng), 61. *Prof Exp:* Asst, Aviation Psychol Lab, Ohio State Univ, 58-59, opers res group, 59-60, res assoc systs res group, 60-61; asst prof psychol & indust eng, 62-66, PROF MGT SCI & ADJ PROF PSYCHOL, UNIV MIAMI, 66- *Mem:* Human Factors Soc; Am Psychol Asn; Soc Eng Psychol; Am Inst Indust Engrs. *Res:* Human factors; aviation safety; human vigilance and monitoring; effect of human performance on systems performance; traffic safety. *Mailing Add:* Dept Mgt Sci Univ Miami Box 248237 Coral Gables FL 33124

WIENER, GEORGE W, b Providence, RI, Jan 4, 22; m 43; c 1. PHYSICAL METALLURGY. *Educ:* Univ Wis, BA, 43; Univ Pittsburgh, MS, 49, PhD(metall), 53. *Prof Exp:* Spectroscopist, Ladish Forge Co, 43-46; spectroscopist, 46-49, from res metallurgist to mgr, Magnetics Dept, Res Labs, 46-69, res dir, Res Labs, 69-76, mgr, Energy Systs Div, 76-81, MGR, MAT SCI DIV, RES LABS, WESTINGHOUSE ELEC CORP, 81- *Concurrent Pos:* Lectr, Univ Pittsburgh, 52-54, adj prof, 63-68. *Mem:* Fel Am Soc Metals; Am Inst Mining, Metall & Petrol Engrs; Metall Soc. *Res:* Physical metallurgical investigations relating structure of metals to ferromagnetism; electric power generation and transmission. *Mailing Add:* 2348 Marbury Rd Pittsburgh PA 15221

WIENER, HOWARD LAWRENCE, b Portland, Ore, Mar 16, 37; m 62; c 1. STATISTICS, OPERATIONS RESEARCH. *Educ:* Univ Ore, BS, 59; Northwestern Univ, Evanston, MS, 61; Cath Univ Am, PhD(math), 71. *Prof Exp:* Sci analyst opers eval group, Ctr Naval Anal, Va, 61-63, opers res analyst-mathematician, Naval Ord Lab, MD, 63-71, opers res analyst, 71-75, head opers anal & planning sect, 75-81, SUPVRY OPERS RES ANALYST, COMBAT MGT BR, NAVAL RES LAB, WASHINGTON, DC, 81- *Mem:* Am Statist Asn; Opers Res Soc Am. *Res:* Applications of statistics and probability to operational problems; data analysis; time series analysis. *Mailing Add:* Combat Mgt Br Code 7575 4555 Overlook Ave SW Washington DC 20375

WIENER, JOSEPH, b Toronto, Ont, Sept 21, 27; m 54; c 2. PATHOLOGY, CELL BIOLOGY. *Educ:* Univ Toronto, MD, 53. *Prof Exp:* Assoc path, Col Physicians & Surgeons, Columbia Univ, 60-63, asst prof, 63-68; prof path & attend pathologist, NY Med Col, 68-78; PROF & CHMN DEPT PATH, SCH MED, WAYNE STATE UNIV, 78-; CHMN DEPT PATH, DETROIT GEN HOSP, 78- *Mem:* Am Soc Cell Biol; Am Soc Exp Path; Am Asn Path & Bact. *Res:* Experimental pathology. *Mailing Add:* Dept of Path NY Med Col Basic Sci Bldg Valhalla NY 10595

WIENER, L(UDWIG) D(AVID), b Nashville, Tenn, Aug 10, 26; m 51; c 2. CHEMICAL ENGINEERING. *Educ:* Vanderbilt Univ, BE, 45, MS, 46; Univ Cincinnati, PhD(chem eng), 49. *Prof Exp:* ENG ASSOC, MOBIL RES & DEVELOP CORP, 49- *Mem:* Soc Petrol Engrs. *Res:* Hydrotropic solutions; drilling fluids; thermodynamic properties of hydrocarbon systems. *Mailing Add:* Field Res Lab PO Box 900 Mobil Res & Develop Corp Dallas TX 75221

WIENER, ROBERT NEWMAN, b New York, NY, Aug 27, 30; m 54; c 3. CHEMISTRY. *Educ:* Harvard Univ, AB, 51; Univ Pa, MS, 53, PhD, 56. *Prof Exp:* Asst instr chem, Univ Pa, 51-54; instr, Rutgers Univ, 55-58; asst prof, 58-62, ASSOC PROF CHEM, NORTHEASTERN UNIV, 62- *Mem:* Am Phys Soc. *Res:* Physical chemistry; molecular spectroscopy. *Mailing Add:* Dept of Chem Northeastern Univ Boston MA 02115

WIENER, SIDNEY, b New York, NY, Nov 17, 22; m 44; c 2. MATERIALS SCIENCE. *Educ:* Univ Calif, Los Angeles, BS, 47; Univ Calif, Berkeley, PhD(biochem), 52. *Prof Exp:* Exploitation engr, Prod Lab, Shell Oil Co, 52-56; mem tech staff, Airborne Systs Labs, 57-60, group head org mat, Res & Develop Div, 60-62, sect head, 62-65, asst dept mgr mat tech, 65-70, mgr space & common group support activity, 70-73, mgr proj control, 74-78, sr staff engr, Components & Mat Labs, 78-81, SR STAFF ENGR, PROD ASSURANCE ENG, SPACE & COMMUNICATION GROUP, HUGHES AIRCRAFT CO, 81- *Mem:* AAAS; Am Chem Soc; Sigma Xi. *Res:* Physical chemistry and elucidation of structure of nucleic acid using enzymatic reactions and acid-base relations; technical administration in materials. *Mailing Add:* 5609 Edgemere Dr Torrance CA 90503

WIENER, STANLEY L, b New York, NY, Nov 5, 30; m 53; c 3. INTERNAL MEDICINE, EXPERIMENTAL PATHOLOGY. *Educ:* Univ Rochester, AB, 52; Sch Med, Univ Rochester, MD, 56. *Prof Exp:* From asst prof to assoc prof med, State Univ NY Stony Brook, 71-72; assoc dir res & educ, Long Island Jewish-Hillside Med Ctr, 72-73, assoc dir med, 73-80; MEM FAC, COL MED, ETENN STATE UNIV, 80- *Concurrent Pos:* Chmn res comt, Am Heart Asn, NY State Affil, 7375. *Mem:* Am Soc Exp Path; Am Soc Exp Biol & Med; Am Fedn Clin Res; Am Rheumatism Asn. *Res:* In vivo studies of fibroblast activation and studies of neutrophil chemotaxis and enzyme release into inflammatory liquid. *Mailing Add:* Col Med ETenn State Univ Johnson City TN 37601

WIENKE, BRUCE RAY, b Chicago, Ill, Sept 21, 40; m 81. THEORETICAL PHYSICS, COMPUTATIONAL PHYSICS. *Educ:* Univ Wis, BS, 63; Marquette Univ, MS, 65; Northwestern Univ, PhD(physics), 71. *Prof Exp:* Teaching asst physics, Northwestern Univ & Marquette Univ, 63-67; res asst theoret physics, Northwestern Univ, 70-71; staff mem, 71-72, staff mem comput physics, 72-78, staff mem comput math, Los Alamos Sci Lab, 79, physicist, Mission Res Corp, 80, SECT LEADER COMPUT PHYSICS, LOS ALAMOS NAT LAB, 81- *Concurrent Pos:* Staff mem, Argonne Nat Lab, 66-68; consult, Square D Co, Milwaukee, 66-72 & Prof Asn Diving Instrs, 77-; instr, Col Santa Fe, 76- *Honors & Awards:* Bausch & Lomb Sci Award, 58. *Mem:* Am Phys Soc; Am Nuclear Soc; Soc Indust & Appl Math; Am Acad Mech; Int Oceanog Soc. *Res:* Theoretical particle and nuclear physics; transport theory and applications for neutral and charged particles; computational physics and numerical methodology; mathematical physics and computing science. *Mailing Add:* Los Alamos Sci Lab PO Box 1663 MS-265 Los Alamos NM 87545

WIENKER, CURTIS WAKEFIELD, b Seattle, Wash, Feb 3, 45; m 66; c 1. PHYSICAL ANTHROPOLOGY. *Educ:* Univ Wash, BA, 67; Univ Ariz, MA, 70, PhD(anthrop), 75. *Prof Exp:* From lectr to asst prof, 72-78, ASSOC PROF ANTHROP, UNIV S FLA, 78- *Mem:* Am Asn Phys Anthrop; Sigma Xi; Human Biol Coun. *Res:* Living human biological variation; human evolution; Black population biology; cultural influences on human biology. *Mailing Add:* Dept of Anthrop Univ of SFla Tampa FL 33620

WIENS, DELBERT, b Munich, NDak, July 9, 32; m 55; c 3. SYSTEMATIC BIOLOGY, EVOLUTIONARY BIOLOGY. *Educ:* Pomona Col, BA, 55; Univ Utah, MS, 57; Claremont Grad Sch, PhD(bot), 61. *Prof Exp:* Instr biol, Univ Colo, 60-62, asst prof, 62-64; asst prof bot, 64-66, assoc prof biol, 67-74, PROF BIOL, UNIV UTAH, 74- *Concurrent Pos:* Fulbright lectr & hon prof, Univ Guayaquil, 64-65; mem, Flora of Ceylon Proj, 68; vis lectr, Flinders Univ SAustralia, 72. *Mem:* AAAS; Am Soc Plant Taxon; Bot Soc Am; Int Asn Plant Taxon; Soc Study Evolution. *Res:* Systematics, biogeography, chromosome systems and pollination ecology of flowering plants, particularly the mistletoe family. *Mailing Add:* Dept of Biol Univ of Utah Salt Lake City UT 84112

WIENS, JOHN ANTHONY, b Moscow, Idaho, Sept 29, 39; div; c 2. ECOLOGY, ANIMAL BEHAVIOR. *Educ:* Univ Okla, BS, 61; Univ Wis, MS, 63, PhD(zool), 66. *Prof Exp:* From asst prof to assoc prof zool, 66-75, prof zool, Ore State Univ, 75-78; PROF UNIV NMEX, 78- *Concurrent Pos:* NSF res grant, 67-69 & 74-; Am Philos Soc res grant, 72-75; vis prof, Colo State Univ, 73-77; Nat Oceanic Atmospheric Admin res contract, 75-81; US Forest Serv res contract, 76-81; ed, The Auk, 76- *Mem:* Am Soc Naturalists; fel Am Ornith Union (treas, 74-); Ecol Soc Am; Animal Behav Soc; Brit Ecol Soc. *Res:* Vertebrate community structure and function; population modeling and analysis; vertebrate behavioral ecology; methods of habitat description and analysis. *Mailing Add:* Dept Biol Univ NMex Albuquerque NM 87131

WIER, CHARLES EUGENE, b Jasonville, Ind, May 15, 21; m 49; c 3. ECONOMIC GEOLOGY. *Educ:* Ind Univ, AB, 43, AM, 50, PhD(econ geol), 55. *Prof Exp:* Geologist & head coal sect, Ind Geol Surv, 49-75; assoc prof geol, Ind Univ, Bloomington, 65-75; MGR COAL EXPLOR, AMAX COAL CO, 75- *Mem:* Geol Soc Am; Soc Econ Geol; Am Asn Petrol Geol; Am Inst Mining, Metall & Petrol Engrs. *Res:* Pennsylvanian stratigraphy; coal resources and coal petrology; environmental geology. *Mailing Add:* AMAX Coal Co Indianapolis IN 46225

WIER, DAVID DEWEY, b Sidon, Miss, Sept 3, 23; m 44; c 2. ELECTRICAL ENGINEERING. *Educ:* Miss State Univ, BS, 44; La Polytech Inst, MS, 64. *Prof Exp:* Design engr, Reliance Elec & Eng Co, 44-46; distribution engr, Miss Power Co, 46-52; self employed, 52-57; from instr to asst prof elec eng, 57-64, ASSOC PROF ELEC ENG, MISS STATE UNIV, 64- *Mem:* Nat Soc Prof Engrs; Inst Elec & Electronics Engrs. *Res:* Magnetomotive forming of metals for use in construction of space vehicles. *Mailing Add:* Dept of Elec Eng PO Drawer EE Mississippi State MS 39762

WIER, JACK KNIGHT, b Cairo, Nebr, Aug 31, 23; m 47. PHARMACOGNOSY. *Educ:* Univ Wis, PhB, 45; Univ Nebr, BS, 56; Univ Wash, Seattle, MS, 59, PhD(pharmacog), 61. *Prof Exp:* Asst prof pharmacog, 61-67, ASSOC PROF PHARMACOG, UNIV NC, CHAPEL HILL, 67- *Concurrent Pos:* Consult, F W Dodge Co Div, McGraw-Hill, Inc, 65-69. *Mem:* Am Soc Pharmacog (secy, 70-79, pres, 79-81); Am Pharmaceut Asn; Acad Pharmaceut Sci. *Res:* Metabolic products of macrofungi; biosynthesis of indole alkaloids in higher plants. *Mailing Add:* Beard Hall Univ of NC Chapel Hill NC 27514

WIER, JOSEPH M(ARION), b Amsterdam, Mo, Mar 2, 24; m 48; c 2. ELECTRICAL ENGINEERING. *Educ:* Iowa State Col, BS, 49, MS, 50; Univ Ill, PhD(elec eng), 56. *Prof Exp:* Instr elec eng, Iowa State Col, 50; asst digital comput lab, Univ Ill, 50-51, res assoc, 51-56; mem tech staff, 56-59, head switching systs study dept, 59-72, head data mgt systs dept, 72-77, head qual theory & systs dept, 77-80, HEAD, CUSTOMER EQUIP QUAL DEPT, BELL TEL LABS, 80- *Mem:* AAAS; Inst Elec & Electronics Engrs. *Res:* Electronic digital computers; data communications; data management systems; systems theory. *Mailing Add:* 41 E Larchmont Dr Colts Neck NJ 07722

WIER, KAREN, b Eau Claire, Wis, Dec 31, 37; div 74. GEOLOGY. *Educ:* Univ Wash, Seattle, BS, 59; Bryn Mawr Col, PhD(geol), 63. *Prof Exp:* Teaching asst, Bryn Mawr Col, 59-61; GEOLOGIST, US GEOL SURV, 65- *Res:* Petrology; petrography; structure of metamorphic rocks. *Mailing Add:* US Geol Surv Nat Ctr Stop 928 Reston VA 22092

WIERBICKI, EUGEN, b Krasnae, Byelorussia, Jan 4, 22; nat US; m 49; c 2. BIOCHEMISTRY, AGRICULTURAL CHEMISTRY. *Educ:* Munich Tech Univ, DrAgr Sci, 49; Ohio State Univ, PhD(biochem), 53. *Prof Exp:* Asst, Ohio State Univ, 50-51, res assoc meat biochem, Res Found, 54-56; res scientist & proj leader, Rath Packing Co, 56-60, mgr meat res, 61-62; chief irradiated food prod div, Food Lab, US Army Natick Develop Ctr, 62-74, head irradiated food prod group, Radiation Preserv Food Div, Food Eng Lab, 74-80; RES LEADER FOOD IRRADIATION RES, FOOD SAFETY LAB, USDA, PHILADELPHIA, 81- *Concurrent Pos:* Abstr, Chem Abstracts, 54-64; mem USDA indust food res team, USSR, 60; tour dir, USSR Food Processing Del to US, 64. *Mem:* Fel AAAS; Am Chem Soc; Inst Food Technol; NY Acad Sci; Am Meat Sci Asn. *Res:* Radiation preservation of foods; product technology, radiation processing, process specifications and quality control of irradiated foods; meat science and technology. *Mailing Add:* Food Irradiation Res Eastern Regional Res Lab USDA Philadelphia PA 19118

WIERCINSKI, FLOYD JOSEPH, b Cicero, Ill, Dec 8, 12; m 40; c 3. CELL PHYSIOLOGY. *Educ:* Univ Chicago, BS, 36, MS, 38; Univ Pa, PhD(gen physiol), 43. *Prof Exp:* Asst physiol, Univ Pa, 40-42, instr, 42-43; instr biol, Cath Univ, 43-44; assoc pharmacol, Stritch Sch Med, Loyola, Ill, 44-46; chmn dept biol, Lewis Col, 45-47; instr physiol, Ill Inst Technol, 47-48; asst prof, Hahnemann Med Col, 48-57; assoc prof biol sci & in-chg radiation biol, Drexel Inst, 57-63; PROF BIOL, NORTHEASTERN ILL UNIV, 64- *Concurrent Pos:* Partic radioisotope methodology, Hahnemann Med Col, 56; res fel, Lankenau Hosp, Philadelphia, 58-59; partic radiation biol, Univ Rochester, 61; partic AEC prog phys chem, Univ Minn, 63-64; assoc prof biol sci eve div, Northwestern Univ, 65-67, prof, 67-; mem corp, Marine Biol Lab, Woods Hole, 56. *Honors & Awards:* Recognition Award, Am Inst Ultrasonics Med, 64. *Mem:* Am Physiol Soc; Soc Gen Physiol. *Res:* Supersonic effects in living organisms; contraction nodes in muscle fibers; effect of trypsin on muscle protoplasm; pH of animal cells; adenosine triphosphate and cations in muscle fiber; intracellular pH; contraction sites in muscle fiber; mechanisms in muscle contraction; concepts in muscle contractions. *Mailing Add:* Dept of Biol Northeastern Ill Univ Chicago IL 60625

WIERENGA, PETER J, b Uithuizen, Neth, June 27, 34; m 63; c 3. SOIL PHYSICS, AGRONOMY. *Educ:* State Agr Univ, Wageningen, BS, 61, MS, 63; Univ Calif, Davis, PhD(soil sci), 68. *Prof Exp:* Res water scientist, Univ Calif, Davis, 65-68; asst prof agron, 68-72, assoc prof, 72-75, PROF AGRON, N MEX STATE UNIV, 75- *Concurrent Pos:* Consult, Battelle Northwest,

Los Alamos Sci Lab, Sandia Labs, EGG & Off Technol Assessment US Congress; assoc ed, Soil Sci Soc Am; vis scientist, Centre Nat Rech Sci, Inst Mecanique, Grenoble, France, 75- *Mem:* Fel Am Soc Agron; fel Soil Sci Soc Am; Am Geophys Union; Neth Royal Soc Agr Sci; AAAS. *Res:* Simulation of transfer processes in soils, such as movement of water, heat and salts; quality of irrigation return flow; irrigation management; trickle irrigation. *Mailing Add:* Dept of Agron NMex State Univ PO Box 3Q Las Cruces NM 88003

WIERENGA, WENDELL, b Hudsonville, Mich, Feb 5, 48; m 68; c 1. ORGANIC CHEMISTRY. *Educ:* Hope Col, BA, 70; Stanford Univ, PhD(org chem), 73. *Prof Exp:* Res scientist org chem, Exp Chem Res, 74-78, HEAD CANCER RES, UPJOHN CO, 81- *Concurrent Pos:* Fel, Am Cancer Soc, Dept Chem, Stanford Univ, 73-74. *Mem:* Am Chem Soc; Royal Soc Chem; Royal Inst Chem. *Res:* Design and synthesis of biologically and medicinally important organic compounds. *Mailing Add:* Cancer Res Upjohn Co Kalamazoo MI 49001

WIERENGO, CYRIL JOHN, JR, b Picayune, Miss, Mar 7, 40; m 62; c 2. ORGANIC CHEMISTRY. *Educ:* Univ Southern Miss, BA, 62, MS, 64; Miss State Univ, PhD(chem), 74. *Prof Exp:* Res chemist, Dow Chem Co, 64-67; PROF CHEM, MISS UNIV FOR WOMEN, 67- *Mem:* Am Chem Soc; Sigma Xi. *Res:* The synthesis and chemistry of bis-heterocyclic compounds. *Mailing Add:* Miss Univ of Women Box W119 Columbus MS 39701

WIERSEMA, RICHARD JOSEPH, b St Louis, Mo, Aug 9, 41. INORGANIC CHEMISTRY. *Educ:* St Louis Univ, BS, 65; Univ Kans, PhD(inorg chem), 69. *Prof Exp:* Fel inorg chem, Univ Calif, Los Angeles, 69-74; sr chemist, Res Div, Rohm and Haas Co, 74-80. *Mem:* Am Chem Soc. *Res:* Basic development and evaluation of materials to be used in the context of industrial coatings. *Mailing Add:* 2516 Toltec Circle San Ramon CA 94583

WIERSMA, DANIEL, b Volga, SDak, Nov 4, 16; m 43; c 2. SOIL SCIENCE. *Educ:* SDak State Univ, BS, 42; Univ Wyo, MS, 52; Univ Calif, PhD, 56. *Prof Exp:* County agr exten agent, Butte County, SDak, 46-52; asst, Univ Calif, 52-55; from asst prof to assoc prof agron, 56-64, PROF AGRON, PURDUE UNIV, 64-, DIR WATER RESOURCES RES CTR, 65- *Concurrent Pos:* Consult Rockefeller agr prog, Colombia, SAm, 63 & 65. *Mem:* Am Soc Agron; Soil Sci Soc Am; Soil Conserv Soc Am. *Res:* Water resources development; plant, soil and water relations; response of plants to water conditions; use of water by plants as affected by soil, water and climate. *Mailing Add:* Dept Agron Agr Exp Sta Purdue Univ West Lafayette IN 47906

WIERSMA, JAMES H, b Beaver Dam, Wis, Jan 4, 40; m 61; c 1. ANALYTICAL CHEMISTRY. *Educ:* Wis State Univ, Oshkosh, BS, 61; Univ Mo, Kansas City, MS, 65, PhD(chem), 68. *Prof Exp:* Clin chemist, Mercy Hosp, Oshkosh, 61-62; USPHS traineeship water chem, 67-68; asst prof chem, 68-72, ASSOC PROF CHEM, UNIV WIS-GREEN BAY, 72- *Mem:* AAAS; Sigma Xi; Am Chem Soc. *Res:* Environmental sciences especially related chemistry and development of analytical methods. *Mailing Add:* Sci & Environ Change Univ of Wis 120 S University Circle Dr Green Bay WI 54301

WIERWILLE, WALTER W(ERNER), b Cincinnati, Ohio, July 3, 36; m 61; c 2. HUMAN FACTORS & INDUSTRIAL ENGINEERING. *Educ:* Univ Ill, Urbana, BSEE, 58; Cornell Univ, PhD(elec eng), 61. *Prof Exp:* Res asst comput ctr, Cornell Univ, 60-61, assoc electronics engr, Avionics Dept, Physics Div, Cornell Aeronaut Lab, 61-63, res electronics engr, 63-65, prin electronics engr, 65-67, head dynamic systs sect, 67-69; supvry scientist, Sanders Assocs, 69-70, mgr, Electronic Counter-Measures Systs Group, 70-71; assoc prof elec & indust eng & opers res, 71-73, PROF ELEC & INDUST ENG & OPERS RES, VA POLYTECH INST & STATE UNIV, 73- *Concurrent Pos:* Consult, NY Transit Authority, Gen Motors Corp, 74- & US Navy, 77- *Mem:* Sr mem Inst Elec & Electronics Engrs; fel Human Factors Soc; Soc Indust & Appl Math; sr mem Am Inst Indust Engrs. *Res:* Command and control; workspace layout; human performance modeling; man-machine system simulation; human operator workload; vehicle handling; operator/system interface design. *Mailing Add:* Dept of Indust & Elec Eng & Va Polytech Inst & State Univ Blacksburg VA 24061

WIESBOECK, ROBERT A, b Frankfurt, Ger, Jan 19, 30; m 50; c 2. ORGANOMETALLIC CHEMISTRY. *Educ:* Munich Tech Univ, BS, 55, PhD(chem), 57. *Prof Exp:* NSF fel phys org chem, Ga Inst Technol, 58-59; res chemist, Redstone Res Div, Rohm and Haas Co, 59-63; staff scientist, 63-68, res scientist, 68-70, mgr chem, 70-74, MGR ATLANTA RES CTR, US STEEL CORP, 74- *Mem:* AAAS; Am Chem Soc. *Res:* Organic and inorganic fluorine chemistry of nitrogen, phosphorous and sulphur. *Mailing Add:* US Steel Corp Atlanta Res Ctr 685 Indust Way Decatur GA 30033

WIESE, ALLEN F, b Eyota, Minn, Dec 16, 25; m 48; c 3. WEED SCIENCE. *Educ:* Univ Minn, BS, 49, MS, 51, PhD(agron), 53. *Prof Exp:* PROF AGRON, AGR EXP STA, TEX A&M UNIV, 53- *Concurrent Pos:* Res award, Weed Sci Soc Am, 80. *Mem:* AAAS; Am Soc Agron; fel Weed Sci Soc Am; South Weed Sci Soc. *Res:* Weed control methods in crop production. *Mailing Add:* Tex Agr Exp Sta Bushland TX 79012

WIESE, ALVIN CARL, b Milwaukee, Wis, Aug 13, 13; m 44; c 2. BIOCHEMISTRY. *Educ:* Univ Wis, BS, 35, MS, 37, PhD(biochem), 40. *Prof Exp:* Asst biochem, Univ Wis, 35-40; instr chem, Okla Agr & Mech Col, 40-42; spec res assoc, Univ Ill, 42-45, spec asst animal nutrit, 45-46; prof agr biochem & head dept, 46-72, prof biochem, 72-78, EMER PROF BIOCHEM, UNIV IDAHO, 78- *Mem:* AAAS; Am Chem Soc; Soc Exp Biol & Med; Poultry Sci Asn; Am Inst Nutrit. *Res:* Nutritional biochemistry; enzymology; effect of fluorides on enzymes; air pollution; trace minerals. *Mailing Add:* 721 S Lynn Moscow ID 83843

WIESE, HELEN JEAN COLEMAN, b San Antonio, Tex, Dec 10, 41; m 75. MEDICAL ANTHROPOLOGY. *Educ:* Univ Wis-Milwaukee, BA, 63; Stanford Univ, MA, 64; Univ NC, Chapel Hill, PhD(anthrop), 72. *Prof Exp:* Asst prof, 72-80, ASSOC PROF BEHAV SCI, COL MED, UNIV KY, 80- *Mem:* Soc Appl Anthrop; Soc Med Anthrop; Am Anthrop Asn; Asn Behav Sci Med Educ; Inst Soc Ethics Life Sci. *Res:* Cross-cultural variation in acceptable body image; effects of pharmaceutical counseling on patient compliance with chemotherapy for congestive heart failure; attitudes toward various contraceptive devices; rates of gonorrhea in two Kentucky counties. *Mailing Add:* Dept of Behav Sci Univ of Ky Col of Med Lexington KY 40506

WIESE, JOHN HERBERT, b Los Angeles, Calif, Jan 15, 17; m 42; c 2. GEOLOGY. *Educ:* Univ Calif, Los Angeles, AB, 40, MA, 41, PhD(struct geol), 47. *Prof Exp:* Geologist, US Geol Surv, 41-48; geologist, Richfield Oil Co, 48-59, supvr explor res, 59-66, sr geologist, Atlantic Richfield Co, 67-73; CONSULT GEOLOGIST, 73- *Concurrent Pos:* Vis indust prof, Southern Methodist Univ, 70-73. *Res:* Geology of Nevada; petroleum exploration; sedimentology; landslides; continental shelf resources; geology of central California coast. *Mailing Add:* 1595 Los Osos Valley Rd 16-C Los Osos CA 93402

WIESE, MAURICE VICTOR, b Columbus, Nebr, Sept 22, 40; m 63; c 3. PLANT PATHOLOGY, CROP LOSS ASSESSMENT. *Educ:* Univ Nebr, BS, 63, MS, 65; Univ Calif, PhD(plant path), 69. *Prof Exp:* Asst prof plant path, 69-74, assoc prof & wheat pathologist, Mich State Univ, 74-78; RES PROF & CROP LOSS COORDR, UNIV IDAHO, 78- *Mem:* Am Phytopath Soc; Am Soc Agron; Crop Sci Soc Am; Sigma Xi. *Res:* Pathogenesis, etiology and control of wheat diseases; assessment of losses in crops; comprehensive yield models; crop management. *Mailing Add:* Dept of Plant & Soil Sci Univ of Idaho Moscow ID 48823

WIESE, RICHARD ANTON, b Howells, Nebr, Apr 3, 28; m 54; c 7. SOIL FERTILITY. *Educ:* Univ Nebr, BS, 54, MS, 56; NC State Univ, PhD, 61. *Prof Exp:* From asst prof to assoc prof soil fertil, Univ Wis, 61-67; assoc prof agron, 67-74, PROF AGRON, UNIV NEBR, LINCOLN, 74- *Mem:* Am Soc Agron; Soil Sci Soc Am; Am Chem Soc; Soil Conserv Soc Am. *Res:* Plant nutrition as effected by soil release of nutrients. *Mailing Add:* 3440 Woodbine Ave Lincoln NE 68506

WIESE, ROBERT GEORGE, JR, b Boston, Mass, Sept 14, 33; m 58; c 4. GEOLOGY. *Educ:* Yale Univ, BS, 55; Harvard Univ, AM, 57, PhD(geol), 61. *Prof Exp:* Explor geologist, New Park Mining Co, 60-63; explor geologist, US Smelting Refining & Mining Co, 63-64; mem staff geol dept, 64-70, PROF GEOL & CHMN DEPT, MT UNION COL, 70- *Concurrent Pos:* Consult geologist. *Mem:* Am Inst Prof Geologists; Geol Soc Am; Am Inst Mining, Metall & Petrol Eng; Mineral Asn Can; Soc Econ Geol. *Res:* Petrology and geochemistry of White Pine copper deposit, Michigan; petrology of wallrock alteration; genesis of mineral deposits; coal geology, exploration, development; trace elements in coal; x-ray analysis of raw materials for ceramics. *Mailing Add:* 135 Overlook Dr Alliance OH 44601

WIESE, WARREN M(ELVIN), b Rochester, Minn, Apr 14, 29; m 48; c 4. MECHANICAL ENGINEERING. *Educ:* Univ Minn, BS, 50, MS, 52. *Prof Exp:* Teaching asst, Univ Minn, 50-52; res engr, Gen Motors Res Labs, 52-55, sr res engr, 56-65, sr liaison engr, 66-67, mgr air conditioning & automotive prod eng, Frigidaire Div, 67-72, asst chief engr, 72-75, CHIEF ENGR, DELCO AIR CONDITIONING DIV, GEN MOTORS CORP, 75- *Honors & Awards:* Springer Award, Soc Automotive Engrs, 59. *Mem:* Soc Automotive Engrs. *Res:* Engine combustion; fuel antiknock characteristics; deposit-induced ignition; engine rumble; vehicle exhaust emission; technical liaison; residential and automotive air conditioning systems. *Mailing Add:* Eng Dept Harrison Radiator Div Gen Motors Corp Dayton OH 45401

WIESE, WOLFGANG LOTHAR, b Tilsit, Ger, Apr 21, 31; US citizen; m 57; c 2. ATOMIC PHYSICS, PLASMA PHYSICS. *Educ:* Kiel Univ, BS, 54, PhD(physics), 57. *Prof Exp:* Res assoc physics, Univ Md, 58-59; physicist, 60-62, sect chief physics, 63-77, CHIEF ATOMIC & PLASMA RADIATION DIV, NAT BUR STANDARDS, 78- *Concurrent Pos:* Guggenheim fel, 66-67. *Mem:* Fel Optical Soc Am; Int Astron Union; fel Am Phys Soc. *Res:* Experimental plasma spectroscopy; stabilized arcs and pulsed plasma sources; atomic transition probabilities; spectral line broadening, atomic data for fusion. *Mailing Add:* Plasma Spectros Sect Nat Bur of Standards Washington DC 20234

WIESEL, TORSTEN NILS, b Upsala, Sweden, June 3, 24; div. PHYSIOLOGY. *Educ:* Karolinska Inst, Sweden, MD, 54. *Prof Exp:* Instr physiol, Royal Caroline Medico-Surg Inst & asst, Dept Child Psychiat, Hosp, 54-55; asst prof ophthal physiol, Johns Hopkins Univ, 58-59; assoc neurophysiol & neuropharmacol, 59-60, asst prof, 60-64, asst prof neurophysiol, Dept Psychiat, 64-67, prof physiol, 67-68, prof neurobiol, 68-74, ROBERT WINTHROP PROF NEUROBIOL, HARVARD MED SCH, 74-, CHMN DEPT, 73- *Concurrent Pos:* Fel ophthal, Med Sch, Johns Hopkins Univ, 55-58. *Honors & Awards:* Jules Stein Award, Trustees Prev of Blindness, 71; Rosenstiel Award, 72; Friedenwald Award, Asn Res Vision & Ophthal, 75; Karl Spencer Lashley Prize, Am Philos Soc, 77; Louisa Gross Horwitz Prize, Columbia Univ, 78; Dickson Prize, Univ Pittsburgh, 79; Ledlie Prize, Harvard Univ, 80; Nobel Prize in Med, 81. *Mem:* Nat Acad Sci; Am Physiol Soc; Am Acad Arts & Sci; Swed Physiol Soc; AAAS. *Res:* Neurophysiology, especially the visual system. *Mailing Add:* Dept of Neurobiol Harvard Med Sch Boston MA 02115

WIESENDANGER, HANS ULRICH DAVID, b Zurich, Switz, Jan 13, 28; nat US; m 54; c 4. PHYSICAL CHEMISTRY. *Educ:* Swiss Fed Inst Technol, dipl, 51, DrScTech, 54. *Prof Exp:* Tech adv inst phys therapy, Zurich Univ, 53-55; fel, Univ Calif, Los Angeles, 55-56; sr res chemist, Kaiser Aluminum & Chem Corp, 57-59; phys chemist, Stanford Res Inst, 59-66; mkt mgr sci instrument dept, Electronics Assocs, Inc, 66-70; dir mkt, Uthe Technol Int, 70-72; dir int mkt; Barnes-Hind Pharmaceut, Inc, 72-74; consult, 74-75; dir mkt, Plessy Environ Systs, Inc, 75-77; DIR INT MKT, CHEMETRICS CORP, 77- *Concurrent Pos:* Consult, 54-55, 71-77 & 81- *Mem:* Am Chem Soc; Am Vacuum Soc. *Res:* Surface chemistry; ultra high vacuum; radiochemistry; isotopes; tracer methods; catalysis; instrumentation; mass spectrometry; semiconductor processing equipment; process control; environmental monitoring; clinical laboratory instrumentation; clinical chemistry; technoeconomics; international marketing; long range planning; technology assessment and transfer; new ventures; acquisitions and business opportunities analysis. *Mailing Add:* 1151 Buckingham Dr Los Altos CA 94022

WIESENFELD, JOEL, b New York, NY, Apr 9, 18; m 45; c 2. CIVIL ENGINEERING, MECHANICS. *Educ:* City Col New York, BCE, 40; Mass Inst Technol, SM, 41; Polytech Inst Brooklyn, PhD(appl mech), 53. *Prof Exp:* Stress analyst, Curtiss-Wright Corp, NJ, 41-45; sr stress analyst, Repub Aviation Corp, NY, 45-46; from instr to assoc prof, 46-58, chmn, Dept Civil & Environ Eng, 70-80, PROF CIVIL ENG, RUTGERS UNIV, 58-, ASST DEAN FRESHMAN, 80- *Mem:* Am Soc Civil Engrs; Am Soc Eng Educ; Nat Soc Prof Engrs; Am Water Works Asn. *Res:* Structural design and analysis; computer techniques applied to structural problems; construction engineering; water distribution system operation. *Mailing Add:* Rutgers Univ PO Box 909 Piscataway NJ 08854

WIESENFELD, JOHN RICHARD, b New York, NY, July 26, 44. CHEMICAL KINETICS, PHOTOCHEMISTRY. *Educ:* City Col New York, BS, 65; Case Inst Technol, PhD(chem), 69; Cambridge Univ, MA, 70. *Prof Exp:* US Air Force fel phys chem, Cambridge Univ, 69-70, NSF fel, 70-71, Stokes res fel, Pembroke Col, 70-72; asst prof, 72-77, ASSOC PROF CHEM, CORNELL UNIV, 78- *Concurrent Pos:* US Hon Ramsay fel, Ramsay Mem Trust, UK, 71; Henry & Camille Dreyfus Teacher-Scholar, 77-; Alfred P Sloan Found Res Fel, 77-79. *Mem:* AAAS; Am Chem Soc. *Res:* Gas phase kinetics of electronically excited atoms and molecules in defined quantum states; energy storage and transfer in chemical lasers; environmental chemistry. *Mailing Add:* Dept Chem Cornell Univ Ithaca NY 14853

WIESER, HELMUT, b Austria, July 4, 35; Can citizen; m 67; c 2. SPECTROSCOPY, CHEMISTRY. *Educ:* Univ BC, BSc, 62; Univ Alta, PhD(chem), 66. *Prof Exp:* Session instr, 66-68, asst prof, 68-74, ASSOC PROF CHEM, UNIV CALGARY, 74- *Concurrent Pos:* Dozent fel, Alexander von Humboldt Found, Ger, 74, 75. *Mem:* AAAS; Chem Inst Can. *Res:* Molecular spectroscopy and structure; infrared and Raman spectroscopy. *Mailing Add:* Dept of Chem Univ of Calgary Calgary AB T2N 1N4 Can

WIESINGER, FREDERICK P(AUL), structural engineering, deceased

WIESMEYER, HERBERT, b Chicago, Ill, Jan 12, 32; m 54; c 2. MICROBIOLOGY. *Educ:* Univ Ill, BS, 54; Wash Univ, St Louis, PhD, 59. *Prof Exp:* NSF fel, Johns Hopkins Univ, 59-61; fel, McCollum-Pratt Inst, 61; NATO fel, 61-62; asst prof, 62-67, ASSOC PROF MOLECULAR BIOL, VANDERBILT UNIV, 67- *Mem:* Am Soc Microbiol; Genetics Soc Am. *Res:* Bacterial physiology. *Mailing Add:* Dept of Molecular Biol Vanderbilt Univ Nashville TN 37203

WIESNER, J(EROME) B, b Detroit, Mich, May 30, 15; m 40; c 4. ELECTRICAL ENGINEERING. *Educ:* Univ Mich, BS, 37, MS, 38, PhD(eng), 50. *Hon Degrees:* EngD, Polytech Inst Brooklyn, 61; DSc, Univ Mich & Lowell Tech Inst, 62, Univ Mass, 64, Brandeis Univ & Lehigh Univ, 65 & Northwestern Univ, 66; DEng, Rensselaer Polytech Inst, 72. *Prof Exp:* Assoc dir broadcasting, Univ Mich, 37-40; chief engr, Library of Cong, 40-42; mem staff, Radiation Lab, Mass Inst Technol, 42-45; mem staff & group leader, Los Alamos Sci Lab, Univ Calif, 45-46; from asst prof to prof elec eng, Mass Inst Technol, 46-61, asst dir res lab electronics, 47-50, assoc dir, 50-52, dir, 52-61; spec asst sci & technol to President, 61-64, dir, Off Sci & Technol, 62-64; dean sci, 64-66, provost, 66-71, PRES, MASS INST TECHNOL, 71- *Concurrent Pos:* Mem, President's Sci Adv Comt. *Mem:* Nat Acad Sci; Nat Acad Eng; AAAS; Am Philos Soc; Am Geophys Union. *Res:* Electronics; radar; acoustics; theory of communications. *Mailing Add:* Rm 3-208 Off of the Pres 77 Massachusetts Ave Cambridge MA 02139

WIESNER, KAREL, b Prague, Czech, Nov 25, 19; Can citizen; m 42; c 1. CHEMISTRY. *Educ:* Charles Univ, Prague, RNDr, 45. *Hon Degrees:* DSc, Univ NB, Fredericton, 70 & Univ Western Ont, 72. *Prof Exp:* Asst phys chem, Charles Univ, Prague, 45-46; fel, Swiss Fed Inst Technol, 46-47, Rockefeller fel, 47-48; from asst prof chem to prof org chem, Univ NB, 48-62; dir chem res, Ayerst Labs, Montreal, 62-64; RES PROF CHEM, UNIV NB, FREDERICTON, 64-, UNIV PROF, 77- *Honors & Awards:* Medal, Chem Inst Can, 63. *Mem:* Am Chem Soc; Chem Inst Can; fel Royal Soc Can; Brit Chem Soc; Swiss Chem Soc. *Res:* Synthesis and structure determination of natural products; study of fast reactions by polarography. *Mailing Add:* 814 Burden Fredericton NB E3B 4C4 Can

WIESNER, LEO, b Vienna, Austria, May 3, 13; nat US; m 58; c 1. PHYSICS, ELECTRONIC ENGINEERING. *Educ:* Univ Vienna, PhD, 37. *Prof Exp:* Res physicist, Harlem Hosp, NY, 39-43 & Int Electronics Indust, Inc, 43-45; electronics engr, Tuck Electronic Corp, 45-47 & Devenco Inc, 47-51; sr gyro engr, Reeves Instrument Corp, 51-62; mgr appl sci, Technol Group, Timex Corp, Waterbury, 62-78; ENG CONSULT, 78- *Mem:* Am Phys Soc; Inst Elec & Electronics Engrs. *Res:* Electro-optical displays; electronic watches; gyros, accelerometers and related inertial devices. *Mailing Add:* 115-01 Grosvenor Rd Kew Gardens NY 11418

WIESNER, LOREN ELWOOD, b Estelline, SDak, Nov 13, 38; m 59; c 3. SEED PHYSIOLOGY. *Educ:* SDak State Univ, BS, 60, MS, 63; Ore State Univ, PhD(agron), 71. *Prof Exp:* Asst agron, SDak State Univ, 63, asst county agt, 63-64; asst prof seed technol, Mont State Univ, 64-68; res asst agron, Ore State Univ, 68-70; assoc prof, 70-80, PROF SEED PHYSIOL, MONT STATE UNIV, 80- *Mem:* Am Soc Agron; Crop Sci Soc Am; Asn Off Seed Analysts; Asn Off Seed Cert Agencies; Sigma Xi. *Res:* Seed research related to production, technology, physiology and ecology. *Mailing Add:* Dept of Plant & Soil Sci Mont State Univ Bozeman MT 59717

WIESNER, RAKOMA, b New York City, NY, May 21, 20; m 58; c 1. BIOCHEMISTRY. *Educ:* Brooklyn Col, BA, 40, MA, 50; Columbia Univ, PhD(biochem), 62. *Prof Exp:* Technician clin lab, Brooklyn Jewish Hosp, 42-47; res asst zool, Columbia Univ, 47-50, res worker biochem, 50-62; res assoc enzymol, Inst Muscle Dis, 62-67; res assoc biochem, Mt Sinai Sch Med, 69-74; res assoc biochem, Columbia Univ, 74-76; RES SCIENTIST, DEPT ENVIRON MED, NY UNIV MED CTR, 76- *Mem:* Am Chem Soc. *Res:* Nucleic acid biochemistry; control mechanisms of enzymes. *Mailing Add:* 115-01 Grosvenor Rd Kew Gardens NY 11418

WIESNET, DONALD RICHARD, b Buffalo, NY, Feb 7, 27; m 52; c 4. GEOLOGY, HYDROLOGY. *Educ:* Univ Buffalo, BA, 50, MA, 51. *Prof Exp:* Asst, Univ Buffalo, 50-51; geologist, US Geol Surv, 52-54, chief manuscript rev sect, 54-55, geophys br, 56-57, asst to geol map ed, 57-59, asst chief br tech illustrations, 59-61, geohydrol map ed, 61-64, proj geologist, 65-67; oceanogr, Naval Oceanog Off, 67-68, res hydrologist, 68-71, sr res hydrologist, 71-80, CHIEF LAND SCI BR, NAT ENVIRON SATELLITE SERV, 80- *Concurrent Pos:* Mem comt hydrol, US Water Resources Coun, 68-71; rapporteur remote sensing of hydrol elements, Comn Hydrol, World Meteorol Orgn, 72-76; mem work group remote sensing in hydrol, US Nat Com, Int Hydrol Decade, 72-76; mem remote sensing comt, Int Field Year on Great Lakes, 72-75; int comt remote sensing & data transmission for hydrol, Int Asn Hydrol Res, 81-; prin investr, Heat Capacity Map Mission, NASA, 78-80. *Mem:* Fel Geol Soc Am; Am Soc Photogram; Int Glaciol Soc; Antarctican Soc; Am Geophys Union. *Res:* Satellite hydrology; remote sensing of hydrologic parameters such as snow, ice, soil moisture, floods, coastal hydrology; hydrologic maps. *Mailing Add:* Nat Oceanic & Atmospheric Admin Nat Environ Satellite Serv S/RE12 Washington DC 20233

WIEST, STEVEN CRAIG, b Harrisburg, Pa, Aug 4, 51. ORNAMENTAL HORTICULTURE, PLANT PHYSIOLOGY. *Educ:* Cornell Univ, BS, 73, MS, 75, PhD(agron), 79. *Prof Exp:* Res asst ornamental hort, Cornell Univ, 73-77, res asst agron, 77-78; asst prof hort, Rutgers Univ, New Brunswick, 78-80; ASST PROF, DEPT HORT, KANS STATE UNIV, 80- *Honors & Awards:* Kenneth Post Award, Am Soc Hort Sci, 78. *Mem:* Am Soc Plant Physiologists; Am Soc Hort Sci. *Res:* Biophysical and biochemical responses of plant cells to environmental stresses, especially those stresses induced directly by such meteorological conditions as low temperature and drought. *Mailing Add:* Dept Hort Kans State Univ Manhattan KS 66506

WIEST, WALTER GIBSON, b Price, Utah, Feb 16, 22; m 48; c 7. BIOCHEMISTRY. *Educ:* Brigham Young Univ, AB, 48; Univ Wis, MS, 51, PhD(biochem), 52. *Prof Exp:* Asst biochem, Univ Wis, 48-52; from instr to assoc prof, Univ Utah, 52-64; assoc prof, 64-68, PROF BIOCHEM IN OBSTET & GYNEC, SCH MED, WASH UNIV, 68- *Concurrent Pos:* USPHS spec fel, Univ Cologne, 59-60. *Mem:* Am Soc Biol Chem; Endocrine Soc; Soc Gynec Invest. *Res:* Biosynthesis, metabolism and mode of action of steroid hormones, especially progesterone; application of radioisotopic techniques to steroid biochemistry. *Mailing Add:* 4911 Barnes Hosp Plaza St Louis MO 63110

WIETING, TERENCE JAMES, b Chicago, Ill, Sept 4, 35; m 70; c 3. PHYSICS. *Educ:* Mass Inst Technol, BS, 57; Harvard Univ, BD, 62; Cambridge Univ, PhD(physics), 69. *Prof Exp:* Res staff mem physics, Naval Supersonic Lab, Mass Inst Technol, 58-60; res scientist, Mithras, Inc, Mass, 62-63; Nat Acad Sci-Nat Res Coun res assoc, 69-71; head, Optical Interactions Sect, Naval Res Lab, 71-80. *Concurrent Pos:* Invited prof, Ecole Polytechnique Federale, Lausanne, Switz, 77-78. *Mem:* Am Phys Soc; Sigma Xi; AAAS. *Res:* Optical properties of metals; physics of low-dimensional materials; Raman scattering; lattice dynamics. *Mailing Add:* Metal Physics Br Naval Res Lab Washington DC 20375

WIEWIOROWSKI, TADEUSZ KAROL, b Sopot, Poland, Nov 3, 35; US citizen; m 62; c 2. CHEMISTRY. *Educ:* Loyola Univ, La, BS, 59; Tulane Univ La, PhD(chem), 65. *Prof Exp:* ASST MGR RES & DEVELOP, FREEPORT MINERALS CO, 59- *Mem:* Am Chem Soc. *Res:* Inorganic and physical chemistry; process development; hydrometallurgy; management of chemical research and development; solvent extraction. *Mailing Add:* Res & Develop Lab Freeport Minerals Co Belle Chasse LA 70037

WIGEN, PHILIP E, b LaCrosse, Wash, May 11, 33; m 54; c 3. SOLID STATE PHYSICS, MAGNETISM. *Educ:* Pac Lutheran Col, BA, 55; Mich State Univ, PhD(physics), 60. *Prof Exp:* Assoc res scientist, Lockheed Res Labs, Calif, 60-63, res scientist, 63-65; assoc prof physics, 65-71, PROF PHYSICS, OHIO STATE UNIV, 71- *Concurrent Pos:* Consult, Res Labs, Battelle Mem Inst, 67-70, Drackett Co, 71-74, A F Avionics Lab, WPAB, 74-78 & Airtron/Litton, 81- *Mem:* Am Phys Soc; Am Asn Physics Teachers; Inst Elec & Electronics Eng; AAAS; Am Asn Univ Professors. *Res:* Magnetism in metals and insulators; paramagnetic resonance. *Mailing Add:* Dept Physics Ohio State Univ 174 W 18th Ave Columbus OH 43210

WIGFIELD, DONALD COMPSTON, b Godalming, Eng, June 13, 43; m 66. CHEMICCAL TOXICOLOGY. *Educ:* Univ Birmingham, BSc, 64; Univ Toronto, PhD(org chem), 67. *Prof Exp:* Fel, Univ BC, 67-68, teaching fel, 68-69; asst prof chem, 69-72, assoc prof, 72-78, PROF CHEM, CARLETON UNIV, 78-, DIR, OTTAWA-CARLETON INST RES & GRAD STUDIES CHEM, 81- *Concurrent Pos:* Vis assoc prof, Univ Victoria, 75-76. *Mem:* Am Chem Soc; fel Royal Soc Chem; fel Chem Inst Can. *Res:* Identification of modes of action and reaction mechanisms involved in the toxic action of metal ion and organic toxicants. *Mailing Add:* Dept of Chem Carleton Univ Ottawa ON K1S 5B6 Can

WIGGANS, DONALD SHERMAN, b Lincoln, Nebr, July 14, 25; m 51; c 4. BIOCHEMISTRY. *Educ:* Univ Nebr, BSc, 49; Univ Ill, PhD(chem), 52. *Prof Exp:* Instr biochem, Yale Univ, 52-54; from asst prof to assoc prof, 54-61, PROF BIOCHEM, UNIV TEX HEALTH SCI CTR, DALLAS, 61-, ASST DEAN CONTINUING EDUC, 78- *Concurrent Pos:* Vis prof, Southern

Methodist Univ, 64-66 & Univ Tex, Arlington, 67-74. *Mem:* Am Chem Soc; Am Soc Biol Chemists; Soc Exp Biol & Med; Am Inst Nutrit. *Res:* Intermediary metabolism of amino acids and peptides; mechanism of protein synthesis. *Mailing Add:* Dept Biochem Univ Tex Health Sci Ctr Dallas TX 75235

WIGGANS, SAMUEL CLAUDE, b Lincoln, Nebr, Sept 2, 22; m 57; c 2. PLANT PHYSIOLOGY, AGRONOMY. *Educ:* Univ Nebr, BS, 47; Univ Wis, MS, 48, PhD(plant physiol), 51. *Prof Exp:* Asst agron, Univ Wis, 47-49, asst bot, 49-51; asst prof agron & bot, Iowa State Univ, 51-58; assoc prof hort, Okla State Univ, 58-62; chmn, Dept Hort Sci, Univ Vt, 62-65, prof hort, 62-80, chmn, Dept Plant & Soil Sci, 65-80; agronomist, plant sciences, 80-81, HORTICULTURIST, COOP STATE RES SERV, USDA, WASHINGTON, DC, 81- *Concurrent Pos:* Mem, nat coun therapy & rehab through hort; mem, Coun Agr Sci & Technol. *Mem:* Am Soc Hort Sci; Am Soc Agron; Am Soc Plant Physiol. *Res:* Growth regulation; fertilizer placement and techniques; photoperiod and temperature. *Mailing Add:* Plant Sci Coop State Res Serv USDA 6440 S Bldg Washington DC 20250

WIGGER, H JOACHIM, b Hagen, Ger, May 29, 28; m 57; c 2. MEDICINE, PATHOLOGY. *Educ:* Johanneum Col, Lueneburg, Ger, BA, 49; Univ Hamburg, DMSc, 54. *Prof Exp:* Assoc dir labs, Children's Hosp, Washington, DC, 62-64; assoc, 64-67, asst prof, 67-69, ASSOC PROF PATH, COLUMBIA UNIV, 69- *Concurrent Pos:* Consult, USPHS Hosp, Staten Island, 66-; asst attend pathologist, Presby Hosp, New York, 67-69, assoc attend pathologist, 69- *Mem:* NY Acad Sci. *Res:* Pediatric and developmental pathology. *Mailing Add:* 622 W 168th St New York NY 10032

WIGGERS, KENNETH DALE, b Davenport, Iowa, Oct 17, 42; m 70. NUTRITION. *Educ:* Iowa State Univ, BS, 65, PhD(nutrit physiol), 71. *Prof Exp:* Fel path, 71-72, training fel path, Univ BC, 72-73; assoc nutrit, 73-75, ASST PROF NUTRIT, DEPT ANIMAL SCI, IOWA STATE UNIV, 75- *Mem:* Am Dairy Sci Asn; Am Heart Asn; Sigma Xi. *Res:* Experimental atherosclerosis and lipid metabolism in swine, rats and in young ruminants. *Mailing Add:* 313 Kildee Hall Iowa State Univ Ames IA 50011

WIGGERT, BARBARA NORENE, b Cleveland, Ohio, Jan 7, 38; m 58; c 4. BIOCHEMISTRY, VISUAL SCIENCE. *Educ:* Univ Wis-Madison, BA, 59; Harvard Univ, PhD(biochem), 63. *Prof Exp:* Fel biochem, Dept Physiol Chem, 63-65; NIH fel, 75-76, staff fel, 76-78, RES CHEMIST BIOCHEM, NAT EYE INST, NIH, 78- *Mem:* Am Chem Soc; Asn Res Vision & Ophthal; Sigma Xi; Am Soc Biol Chemists. *Res:* Uptake, binding and translocation of retinoids such as vitamin A and its analogs, into ocular tissues. *Mailing Add:* Nat Inst of Health Lab of Vision Res Bethesda MD 20205

WIGGERT, DJIMITRI, b Milwaukee, Wis, Feb 24, 34; m 58; c 4. ELECTRICAL ENGINEERING. *Educ:* Univ Wis, BS, 56, MS, 58, PhD(info theory), 66. *Prof Exp:* Staff mem programming & simulation, Lincoln Lab, Mass Inst Technol, 59-63; sr scientist, Wayland Lab, Raytheon Co, 65-67; asst prof elec eng, Univ Mass, 67-69; sr staff engr, Advan Systs Anal Off, Magnavox Co, Md, 69-72; proj dir, B-K Dynamics, Inc, 72-73, sr systs engr, Systs Consults, Inc, 73-75; mem tech staff, Mitre Corp, 75-80; ENGR, APPL PHYSICS LAB, JOHNS HOPKINS UNIV, 80- *Concurrent Pos:* Lectr, Goddard Space Flight Ctr, NASA, 70-71. *Mem:* Inst Elec & Electronics Engrs; Sigma Xi. *Res:* Statistical communications; convolutional codes and decoding; data distribution networks. *Mailing Add:* Appl Physics Lab Johns Hopkins Univ Johns Hopkins Rd Laurel MD 20810

WIGGILL, JOHN BENTLEY, b Durban, SAfrica, Mar 5, 30; div; c 2. CHEMICAL ENGINEERING, OIL & GAS EXPLORATION. *Educ:* Univ Cape Town, BSc, 52; Cambridge Univ, PhD(chem eng), 59. *Prof Exp:* Jr lectr chem, Univ Cape Town, 53, temp lectr chem eng & appl chem, 54-55; res chem engr, Socony Mobil Oil Co, 60-61; res engr, Exp Sta, 61-66, sr res engr, 66-68, asst div supt, Sabine River Works, Tex, 68-72, RES SUPVR, POLYMER INTERMEDIATES DEPT, E I DU PONT DE NEMOURS & CO, INC, 72-, MGR EXPLOR, 77- *Mem:* Am Chem Soc; Am Inst Chem Engrs; fel Royal Soc Arts; fel Royal Soc Chem; SAfrican Chem Inst. *Res:* Extrusion; polymer chemistry; rate processes; catalysis; kinetics; mass transfer and diffusional processes. *Mailing Add:* 625 Killburn Rd Wilmington DE 19803

WIGGIN, EDWIN ALBERT, b Exeter, NH, Aug 11, 21; m 47; c 2. CHEMISTRY. *Educ:* Univ NH, BS, 43. *Prof Exp:* Asst, SAM Labs, Columbia Univ, 43-45; res chemist, Carbide & Carbon Chem Co, 45-48; chief tech develop br, Isotopes Div, AEC, 48-54; EXEC V PRES, ATOMIC INDUST FORUM, 54- *Concurrent Pos:* Mem adv comt install info, AEC, 53-54, mem adv comt isotope & radiation develop, 58-60 & 70-72. *Mem:* AAAS; Am Chem Soc; Am Nuclear Soc; Inst Nuclear Mat Mgt. *Res:* Application of atomic energy and radioactive by-products. *Mailing Add:* 7101 Wisconsin Ave Atomic Indust Forms Washington DC 20014

WIGGIN, HENRY CARVEL, genetics, plant breeding, see previous edition

WIGGIN, NORMAN JACK BRIDGMAN, immunology, see previous edition

WIGGINS, ALVIN DENNIE, b Harrisburg, Ill, May 5, 22; m 50; c 6. MATHEMATICAL STATISTICS. *Educ:* Univ Calif, Berkeley, AB, 51, MA, 53, PhD(statist), 58. *Prof Exp:* Res asst statist & assoc biostatist, Sch Pub Health, Univ Calif, Berkeley, 54-57; instr math, Ctr Grad Studies, Univ Wash, 58-63; assoc res biostatistician & lectr biostatist, Sch Pub Health, Univ Calif, Berkeley, 63-69; asst prof biostatist, 69-73, ASSOC PROF BIOSTATIST, UNIV CALIF, DAVIS, 73- *Concurrent Pos:* Sr statistician, Hanford Labs Oper, Gen Elec Co, 57-63. *Mem:* Inst Math Statist; Biomet Soc; Am Statist Asn; fel Royal Statist Soc. *Res:* Mathematical models of biological phenomena; statistical theory of estimation; application of stochastic processes to problems of health, medicine and biology; design and analysis of experiments; stochastic differential equations in biology. *Mailing Add:* Div Statist Univ Calif Davis CA 95616

WIGGINS, EARL LOWELL, b Ringwood, Okla, July 11, 21; m 45; c 4. PHYSIOLOGY. *Educ:* Okla State Univ, BS, 47, MS, 48; Univ Wis, PhD(physiol of reprod), 51. *Prof Exp:* Asst, Univ Wis, 48-50; animal geneticist, Sheep Exp Sta, USDA, Idaho, 50-56; assoc prof, 56-73, PROF ANIMAL SCI, AUBURN UNIV, 73- *Mem:* AAAS; Am Soc Animal Sci; Am Genetic Asn; Soc Study Reproduction. *Res:* Puberty and related phenomena in sheep and swine; artificial insemination in swine; causes of reproductive failure in ewes; factors affecting the breeding season in ewes; reproduction, breeding and genetics in farm animals. *Mailing Add:* Dept of Animal & Dairy Sci Auburn Univ Auburn AL 36830

WIGGINS, EDWIN GEORGE, b Palo Alto, Calif, June 12, 43; m 65; c 2. MARINE ENGINEERING, MECHANICAL ENGINEERING. *Educ:* Purdue Univ, BS, 65, MS, 68, PhD(mech eng), 76. *Prof Exp:* Asst engr, USS Massey, US Navy, 65-66, ship supt, Charleston Naval Shipyard, 71-74, chief engr, USS Sampson, 74-76, maintenance plan officer, US Navy, 76-78; dept head marine eng, Moody Col, 78-81; DEPT HEAD ENG, US MERCHANT MARINE ACAD, 82- *Mem:* Am Soc Mech Engrs; Soc Naval Architects & Marine Engrs; Am Soc Eng Educ. *Res:* Measurement of characteristics of incompressible turbulent boundary layers. *Mailing Add:* Dept Eng US Merchant Marine Acad Kings Point NY 11024

WIGGINS, ERNEST JAMES, b Trenton, Ont, Nov 25, 17; m 45; c 2. PHYSICAL CHEMISTRY, CHEMICAL ENGINEERING. *Educ:* Queen's Univ, Ont, BSc, 38; McGill Univ, PhD(phys chem), 46. *Prof Exp:* Supt eng develop sect, Atomic Energy Proj, Nat Res Coun, 46-48; head munitions & eng sect, Suffield Exp Sta, Defence Res Bd, 48-52; sr chemist, Stanford Res Inst, 52-58; head chem div, Sask Res Coun, 58-61; asst dir, Chem Div, Ont Res Found, 61-62; dir res, Res Coun Alta, 62-77, CONSULT MEM, ALTA OIL SANDS TECHNOL & RES AUTHORITY, 77- *Mem:* Am Chem Soc; Am Inst Aeronaut & Astronaut; Arctic Inst NAm; Chem Inst Can; Brit Soc Chem Indust. *Res:* Chemical process development; environmental studies; energy resource development. *Mailing Add:* 8208 117th St Edmonton AB T6G 1R2 Can

WIGGINS, GLENN BLAKELY, b Toronto, Ont, Jan 29, 27; m 49; c 3. ENTOMOLOGY, FRESH WATER BIOLOGY. *Educ:* Univ Toronto, BA, 49, MA, 50, PhD, 58. *Prof Exp:* Asst biologist, Nfld Fisheries Res Sta, Fisheries Res Bd Can, 50-51; asst cur, Dept Entom, 52-61, from asst cur in chg to assoc cur in chg, 61-64, CUR DEPT ENTOM, ROYAL ONT MUS, 64-; PROF ZOOL, UNIV TORONTO, 68- *Concurrent Pos:* Vis prof, Univ Minn, 70, 72 & 74 & Univ Mont, 81. *Mem:* Entom Soc Can (vpres, 80-81, pres, 82); Can Soc Zool; Soc Syst Zool; NAm Benthol Soc; Entom Soc Am. *Res:* Systematic entomology; aquatic entomology, especially trichoptera; biology of temporary pools; domicilary invertebrates; evolution. *Mailing Add:* Royal Ont Mus 100 Queen's Park Toronto ON M5S 2C5 Can

WIGGINS, JAMES WENDELL, b Fayette, Ala, May 9, 42; m 64; c 2. SEISMIC IMAGING, IMAGE PROCESSING. *Educ:* Univ Ala, BS, 63; Johns Hopkins Univ, PhD(physics), 68. *Prof Exp:* Res assoc physics, Johns Hopkins Univ, 68-69, biophysics, 69-73, NIH spec fel, 73-74, asst prof biophysics, 74-80, assoc prof biophys, 80-81. *Mem:* Biophys Soc; Am Phys Soc; AAAS; Electron Micros Soc Am. *Res:* Methods of data collection and processing in seismic imaging; physical modeling of geological structure and stratigraphy for acoustic imaging study; image processing techniques applicable to geological, biological and other areas. *Mailing Add:* Sunset View Dr RD 4 Valencia PA 16059

WIGGINS, JAMES WILLIAM, b Paris, Ark, Mar 5, 40. INORGANIC CHEMISTRY. *Educ:* Univ Ark, Fayetteville, BS, 62; Univ Fla, PhD(chem), 66. *Prof Exp:* Res grant, Univ Calif, Riverside, 66-68; interim asst prof chem, Univ Fla, 68-69; asst prof, 69-73, PROF CHEM & INORG CHEM, UNIV ARK, LITTLE ROCK, 73-, ASSOC DEAN, COL SCI, 80- *Mem:* Am Chem Soc. *Res:* Boron-nitrogen-carbon chemistry, synthesis of compounds; mechanisms of reactions leading to unusual structures; water quality in Arkansas and the effect of changing the stream beds on the water quality. *Mailing Add:* Col Sci Univ of Ark Little Rock AR 72204

WIGGINS, JAY ROSS, b Baltimore, Md, Apr 12, 47; m 72; c 1. CARDIAC PHARMACOLOGY. *Educ:* Bucknell Univ, BS, 69; Columbia Univ, PhD(pharmacol), 75. *Prof Exp:* Res assoc, Rockefeller Univ, 73-75; asst prof pharmacol, Univ SFla, 76-80, assoc prof, 80-81; ASST DIR PHARMACOL, BERLEX LABS, INC, 82- *Mem:* AAAS; Am Soc Pharmacol & Exp Therapeut; Am Heart Asn. Biophys Soc; Int Soc Heart Res. *Res:* Electrophysiology and pharmacology of cardiac arrhythmias; mechanisms of excitation-contraction coupling in cardiac muscle. *Mailing Add:* Berlex Labs Inc 110 E Hanover Ave Cedar Knolls NJ 07927

WIGGINS, JOHN, b Bellevue, Nebr, Oct 25, 49; m 77. HEAVY ION PHYSICS. *Educ:* Univ Ga, BS, 75; Ind Univ, Bloomington, MS, 80, PhD(physics), 81. *Prof Exp:* Res asst, Cyclotron Facil, Ind Univ, 75-81, res assoc, 81; RES STAFF, LAB NUCLEAR SCI, MASS INST TECHNOL, 81- *Mem:* Sigma Xi; NY Acad Sci; Am Phys Soc; AAAS; Am Asn Physics Teachers. *Res:* Experimental intermediate energy nuclear physics; reaction mechanism of protons with nuclei, excitation and decay of giant resonances in nuclei and decay of nuclei at high excitation; nuclear structure and properties from proton and heavy ion induced reactions. *Mailing Add:* Rm 26-413 Lab Nuclear Sci Mass Inst Technol Cambridge MA 02139

WIGGINS, JOHN H(ENRY), JR, b Tulsa, Okla, May 12, 31; m 78; c 2. STRUCTURAL DYNAMICS, GEOPHYSICS. *Educ:* Stanford Univ, BS, 53; St Louis Univ, MS, 55; Univ Ill, PhD(civil eng), 61. *Prof Exp:* Physicist spec weapons ctr, US Air Force, 55-58; sr res engr, Jersey Prod Res Co, 61-64; tech prog dir sonic boom & earthquake effects, res div, John A Blume & Assocs, 64-66; tech dir environ res, Datacraft Inc, 66; PRES, J H WIGGINS CO, 66- *Honors & Awards:* Moisseiff Award, Am Soc Civil Engrs, 65. *Mem:* Am Inst Aeronaut & Astronaut; Soc Explor Geophysicists; Am Soc Mech Engrs; Am Inst Mining, Metall & Petrol Engrs; Am Geophys Union. *Res:* Nuclear weapons effects; earthquake engineering and seismology; oil well drilling and exploration geophysics; sonic boom effects; risk assessment. *Mailing Add:* J H Wiggins Co 1650 S Pacific Coast Hwy Redondo Beach CA 90277

WIGGINS, JOHN SHEARON, b Chicago, Ill, Feb 8, 15. SPACE PHYSICS. *Educ:* Earlham Col, AB, 36; Calif Inst Technol, MS, 38; Univ Southern Calif, PhD(physics), 56. *Prof Exp:* Lectr physics, Univ Southern Calif, 41-43; from instr to asst prof, Univ Redlands, 44-46; asst prof, Univ Okla, 46-50; lectr physics, Univ Southern Calif, 50-56, asst prof, 57-58; mem tech staff, Semiconductor Div, Hughes Aircraft Co, 58-63; mem tech staff, Space Sci Dept, 65-80, MEM TECH STAFF, SPACE SYSTS DIV, TRW SYSTS, 80- *Concurrent Pos:* UNESCO vis prof, Concepcion Univ, Chile, 64. *Mem:* Am Phys Soc; Am Asn Univ Professors; Sigma Xi. *Res:* Photoelectricity; electron microscopy; optical, beta-ray and gamma-ray spectroscopy; linear accelerator; semiconductor devices; space physics; space science instrumentation; payload design, test and integration; radiation damage and measurement; spacecraft charging. *Mailing Add:* Space Sci Dept R5/1280 TRW Systs Redondo Beach CA 90278

WIGGINS, PETER F, b New York, NY, July 18, 35; m 65; c 1. NUCLEAR ENGINEERING. *Educ:* State Univ NY Maritime Col, BMarE, 58; NY Univ, MME, 61; Univ Md, PhD(nuclear eng), 70. *Prof Exp:* Asst inst eng, State Univ NY Maritime Col, 58-61; asst prof eng sci, State Univ NY Agr & Technol Col, Farmingdale, 61-62; asst prof nuclear eng, 62-71, assoc prof naval systs eng, 71-76, chmn dept, 76-81, PROF NAVAL SYSTS ENG, US NAVAL ACAD, 76- *Concurrent Pos:* NSF sci fac fel, 69-70. *Mem:* Am Soc Eng Educ; Soc Naval Archit & Marine Engrs; Am Nuclear Soc; Am Soc Nuclear Engrs; Sigma Xi. *Res:* Neutron activation analysis; capture gamma ray studies using isotopic source, for example californium-252 for mineral exploration. *Mailing Add:* Dept of Naval Systs Eng US Naval Acad Annapolis MD 21402

WIGGINS, RALPHE, b Broadwater, Nebr, Apr 4, 40. GEOPHYSICS. *Educ:* Colo Sch Mines, GpE, 61; Mass Inst Technol, PhD(geophys), 65. *Prof Exp:* Proj dir geophys, Geoscience, Inc, 65-66; res assoc, Mass Inst Technol, 66-70; asst prof, Univ Toronto, 70-73; assoc prof, Univ BC, 73-75; sr res geophysicist, Western Geophys Co, 75-77; prin geophysicist, Del Mar Tech Assocs, 77-78; SR RES ASSOC, MOBIL RES & DEVELOP CORP, 78- *Mem:* Am Geophys Union; Soc Explor Geophys; Seismol Soc Am; Geol Soc Am; fel Royal Astron Soc. *Res:* Seismology; computer applications for interpretation and inversion of geophysical observations. *Mailing Add:* Mobil FRL PO Box 900 Dallas TX 75221

WIGGINS, RICHARD CALVIN, b Portsmouth, Va, June 26, 45; m 75. NEUROCHEMISTRY, DEVELOPMENTAL NEUROBIOLOGY. *Educ:* Duke Univ, BS, 67, PhD(anat), 73. *Prof Exp:* Res assoc neurol, Sch Med, Univ Miami, 72-73; res assoc neurochem, Med Sch, Univ NC, 73-75; asst prof, 76-81, ASSOC PROF NEUROBIOL & ANAT, MED SCH, UNIV TEX, 81- *Concurrent Pos:* NIH res career develop award, 79. *Mem:* Am Soc Neurochem; Int Soc Neurochem; Am Soc Neurosci; Am Asn Anatomists; Am Asn Phys Anthropologists. *Res:* Biological chemistry of myelin; effects of environmental perturbation on brain development. *Mailing Add:* Dept Neurobiol & Anat PO Box 20708 Houston TX 77025

WIGGINS, THOMAS ARTHUR, b Indiana, Pa, Feb 24, 21; m 53; c 2. OPTICS. *Educ:* Pa State Univ, BS, 42, PhD(physics), 53; George Washington Univ, MS, 49. *Prof Exp:* Instr physics, George Washington Univ, 48-50; from asst prof to assoc prof, 53-63, PROF PHYSICS, PA STATE UNIV, UNIVERSITY PARK, 63- *Mem:* Fel Am Phys Soc; fel Optical Soc Am. *Res:* High resolution and high precision molecular spectra of simple molecules, especially secondary wavelength standards; theory of rotation-vibration of molecules in the infrared; spontaneous and stimulated light scattering. *Mailing Add:* 104 Davey Lab Dept of Physics Pa State Univ University Park PA 16802

WIGGINS, VIRGIL DALE, b Tulsa, Okla, June 25, 31; m 52; c 3. PALYNOLOGY. *Educ:* Univ Okla, BS, 57, MS, 62. *Prof Exp:* Sr palynological technician, Sun Oil Co Prod Res, 58-59; explor palynologist, 59-69, sr explor palynologist, Alaskan Div, 69-81, STAFF EXPLOR PALYNOLOGIST, WESTERN REGION, CHEVRON USA, 81- *Concurrent Pos:* Alaskan mem, Int Palynological Comn Working Group P3, 74- *Mem:* Am Asn Stratig Palynologists. *Res:* Application of palynology to arctic petroleum exploration. *Mailing Add:* Chevron USA Inc PO Box 3862 San Francisco CA 94119

WIGGS, ALFRED JAMES, zoology, physiology, see previous edition

WIGH, RUSSELL, b Weehawken, NJ, Nov 17, 14; m 39; c 3. MEDICINE, RADIOLOGY. *Educ:* Rutgers Univ, BS, 35; Harvard Med Sch, MD, 39. *Prof Exp:* Asst demonstr radiol, Jefferson Med Col, 46-49, instr, 49-50, assoc, 50, asst prof, 50-52; asst prof, Col Physicians & Surgeons, Columbia Univ, 52-54, assoc prof, 54-56; prof & chmn dept, Med Col Ga, 56-63; dir dept radiol, Bartholomew County Hosp, 63-71; assoc prof radiol, Sch Med, Ind Univ, Indianapolis, 72-77; prof, 77-80, EMER PROF RADIOL, MED COL GA, 80- *Concurrent Pos:* Consult, Vet Admin Hosps, New York, 55-56 & Augusta, Ga, 56-63 & Battey State Hosp, Rome, 56-62; clin prof, Sch Med, Univ Louisville, 67-72. *Honors & Awards:* Cert of Merit, Am Roentgen Ray Soc, 51. *Mem:* Radiol Soc NAm; AMA; fel Am Col Radiol. *Res:* Photofluorographic detection of silent gastric neoplasms; clinical radiological investigations of various body systems. *Mailing Add:* Dept of Radiol Med Col of Ga Augusta GA 30901

WIGHAM, J(OHN) M(ALCOLM), civil engineering, hydrology, see previous edition

WIGHT, HEWITT GLENN, b Murray, Utah, Feb 8, 21; m 43; c 4. SYNTHETIC ORGANIC CHEMISTRY. *Educ:* Univ Utah, BS, 43; Univ Calif, PhD(chem), 55. *Prof Exp:* PROF CHEM, CALIF POLYTECH STATE UNIV, SAN LUIS OBISPO, 52- *Mem:* Am Chem Soc. *Res:* Chemical education; organic syntheses. *Mailing Add:* Dept of Chem Calif Polytech State Univ San Luis Obispo CA 93407

WIGHT, JERALD ROSS, b Brigham City, Utah, Oct 5, 31; m 54; c 7. RANGE SCIENCE. *Educ:* Utah State Univ, BS, 53, MS, 59; Univ Wyo, PhD(range sci), 66. *Prof Exp:* Lab technician olericult, Univ Calif, 58-63; RANGE SCIENTIST, AGR RES SERV, USDA, 65- *Mem:* Soil Conserv Soc Am; Am Soc Agron; Soc Range Mgt. *Res:* Plant, soil, climate and animal relationships in range ecosystems, with emphasis on improving productivity. *Mailing Add:* Agr Res Serv USDA 1175 S Orchard Boise ID 83705

WIGHTMAN, ARTHUR STRONG, b Rochester, NY, Mar 30, 22; m; c 2. MATHEMATICAL PHYSICS. *Educ:* Yale Univ, BA, 42; Princeton Univ, PhD(physics), 49. *Hon Degrees:* DSc, Swiss Fed Inst Technol, 69. *Prof Exp:* Instr physics, Yale Univ, 43-44; from instr to assoc prof, 49-60, prof math physics, 60-71, THOMAS D JONES PROF MATH PHYSICS, PRINCETON UNIV, 71- *Concurrent Pos:* Nat Res Coun fel, Inst Theoret Physics, Copenhagen, 51-52; NSF fel, Naples, 56-57; vis prof, Paris, 57; vis prof, Inst Advan Study Sci, Bures-sur-Yvette, 63-64 & 68-69; vis prof, Ecole Polytechnique Palaiseau, 77-78. *Mem:* Nat Acad Sci; AAAS; Am Math Soc; Am Phys Soc; Fedn Am Sci (treas, 54-56). *Res:* Elementary particle physics; quantum field theory; mathematical physics; functional analysis. *Mailing Add:* Dept of Physics Princeton Univ Box 708 Princeton NJ 08540

WIGHTMAN, FRANK, b Padiham, Eng, Jan 22, 28; Can citizen; m 56; c 5. PLANT PHYSIOLOGY. *Educ:* Univ Leeds, BSc, 48, PhD(plant physiol), 54. *Hon Degrees:* DSc, Univ Leeds, 81. *Prof Exp:* Sr sci officer plant physiol, Agr Res Coun Unit, Wye Col, Univ London, 52-58; Nat Res Coun Can fel, Nat Res Coun Lab, Univ Sask, Can, 58-59; assoc prof, 60-66, chmn dept, 68-71, PROF BIOL, CARLETON UNIV, 66- *Concurrent Pos:* Nuffield Found vis fel, Univ Col, Univ London, 65-66; vis prof, Univ Lausanne, 66 & Univ Calif, Santa Cruz, 74-75. *Mem:* Can Soc Plant Physiol (pres, 79-80); Am Soc Plant Physiol; Brit Soc Exp Biol; Scand Soc Plant Physiol. *Res:* Biosynthesis and physiological activity of indole and phenyl plant growth hormones; characterization of enzymes catalyzing amino acid metabolism; characterization of hormonal substances regulating flower induction and lateral root initiation. *Mailing Add:* Dept of Biol Carleton Univ Ottawa ON K1S 5B6 Can

WIGHTMAN, JAMES PINCKNEY, b Ashland, Va, May 14, 35; m 56; c 4. COLLOID & SURFACE CHEMISTRY. *Educ:* Randolph-Macon Col, BS, 55; Lehigh Univ, MS, 58, PhD(chem), 60. *Prof Exp:* Res assoc fuel sci, Pa State Univ, 60-62; PROF CHEM, VA POLYTECH INST & STATE UNIV, 62- *Concurrent Pos:* Vis res prof, Univ Bristol, 75-76. *Mem:* Am Chem Soc; Sigma Xi; Am Vacuum Soc; Int Asn Colloid & Interface Scientists; reactions of atoms with solids; thermodynamics of adhesion; electron spectroscopic chemical analysis of solids surfaces. *Res:* Surface chemistry focuses on the interaction of liquids and gases with solid surfaces and on the characterization of those solids, applications include adhesion, lubrication, coal liquefaction and desalination. *Mailing Add:* 1300 Westover Dr Blacksburg VA 24060

WIGHTMAN, ROBERT HARLAN, b Ottawa, Ont, Jan 24, 37; m 61; c 3. ORGANIC CHEMISTRY. *Educ:* Univ NB, BSc, 58, PhD(org chem), 62. *Prof Exp:* Nat Res Coun Can overseas fel org chem, Imp Col, Univ London, 62-63; res assoc, Stanford Univ, 63-65; asst prof, 65-69, ASSOC PROF ORG CHEM, CARLETON UNIV, 69- *Mem:* Am Chem Soc; Chem Inst Can. *Res:* New synthetic organic methods; syntheses of organic compounds of biological and theoretical interest. *Mailing Add:* 70 Kamloops Ottawa ON K1V 7C9 Can

WIGHTON, JOHN L(ATTA), b Vancouver, BC, June 15, 15. MECHANICAL ENGINEERING. *Educ:* Univ BC, BA, 35, BASc, 44; Univ Mich, MSE, 52, PhD(mech eng), 55. *Prof Exp:* Design engr, Hudson Bay Mining & Smelting Co, Man, 44-47; dist engr, B F Sturtevant Co, Ont, 47-49; design engr, Consol Mining & Smelting Co, BC, 49-51; proj engr, Standard Oil Co, Ind, 55-58; dir labs mech eng, Univ BC, 58-67; dir labs, Dept Mech Eng, Ahmadu Bello Univ, Nigeria, 67-69; DIR ENG LABS, FAC ENG, UNIV REGINA, 69- *Concurrent Pos:* Lab consult, Mech Eng Dept, Chulalongkorn Univ, Bangkok, Nat Polytech Sch, Ecuador, 74-75, Tehran Polytech, Tehran, Iran, 76-77 & Univ Americas, Puebla, Mexico, 81. *Mem:* Am Soc Eng Educ; Sigma Xi. *Res:* Heating and ventilating; fluid dynamics; particle technology; laboratory management and development. *Mailing Add:* Fac of Eng Univ of Regina Regina SK S4S 0A2 Can

WIGINGTON, RONALD L, b Topeka, Kans, May 11, 32; m 51; c 4. RESEARCH & DEVELOPMENT MANAGEMENT, INFORMATION SYSTEMS. *Educ:* Univ Kans, BS, 53, PhD(elec eng), 64; Univ Md, MS, 62; Harvard Bus Sch, AMP, 77. *Prof Exp:* Mem tech staff, Bell Tel Labs, Inc, 53-54; supvry electronic engr, Nat Security Agency, US Dept Defense, 54-65, sr engr, 65-68; DIR RES & DEVELOP, CHEM ABSTR SERV, AM CHEM SOC, 68- *Concurrent Pos:* Adj assoc prof comput info sci, Ohio State Univ, 70-78; mem Nat Acad Sci Comput Sci & Eng Bd, 69-72, comt on data for sci & technol, Int Coun Sci Unions Task Group on Comput Use, 68-77 & comn for coord Nat Bibliog Control, 75-; Dept Defense consult, 68-; trustee, Ohio Col Libr Ctr, 78-; pres, Nat Fedn Abstracting & Indexing Serv, 82. *Mem:* Inst Elec & Electronics Engrs; Am Chem Soc; Sigma Xi. *Res:* High speed instrumentation; transmission line theory; electronic devices/techniques for switching/storage of information; computer system organization; design/evaluation; displays and man-machine communications; simulation; computerized information systems; research and development management. *Mailing Add:* Res & Develop Chem Abstr Serv PO Box 3012 Columbus OH 43210

WIGINTON, CARROLL LAMAR, b Burnsville, Miss, June 5, 35; m 57; c 4. MATHEMATICS. *Educ:* Univ Tenn, BS, 59, MS, 61, PhD(math), 64. *Prof Exp:* Consult math, Oak Ridge Nat Lab, 61-65; asst prof, Space Inst, Univ Tenn, 64-65; asst prof, 65-69, ASSOC PROF MATH, UNIV HOUSTON, 69- *Concurrent Pos:* Consult, Math Res Inc, Houston, Tex, 65-77, gen mgr, 77- *Mem:* Am Math Soc; Math Asn Am. *Res:* Applied mathematics; engineering; functional analysis. *Mailing Add:* Dept of Math Univ of Houston Houston TX 77004

WIGLE, ERNEST DOUGLAS, b Windsor, Ont, Oct 30, 28; m 58; c 5. MEDICINE, CARDIOLOGY. *Educ:* Univ Toronto, MD, 53; FRCP(C), 58. *Prof Exp:* McLaughlin Found fel cardiol, Univ Toronto, 59-60; sr res assoc, Ont Heart Found, 63-66; from asst prof to assoc prof, 66-72, PROF MED, UNIV TORONTO, 72- *Concurrent Pos:* Dir cardiovasc unit, Toronto Gen Hosp, 64-72, dir div cardiol, 72-; fel coun clin cardiol, Am Heart Asn, 65- *Mem:* Fel Am Col Physicians; Asn Am Physicians; Am Soc Clin Invests; Am Fedn Clin Res; Can Soc Clin Invest. *Res:* Muscular subaortic stenosis, hemodynamics, pharmacology and electrocardiography; hemodynamics of acute valvular insufficiency; cardiomyopathy; ventricular aneurysm; heart catheterization; automated assessment of left ventricular function; ritral valve prolapse. *Mailing Add:* Eaton N 12 217 Toronto Gen Hosp Toronto ON M5G 1L7 Can

WIGLER, PAUL WILLIAM, b New York, NY, Aug 26, 28; m 52; c 4. BIOCHEMISTRY. *Educ:* Queens Col, NY, BS, 50; Brooklyn Col, MA, 52; Univ Calif, Berkeley, PhD(biochem), 58. *Prof Exp:* Jr res biochemist, Virus Lab, Univ Calif, Berkeley, 58; NIH fel chem Univ Wis, 58-60; asst prof, Sch Med, Univ Okla, 60-63, assoc prof, 63-66; assoc prof res, 66-68, res prof, 68-78, PROF MED BIOL, MEM RES CTR, UNIV TENN, KNOXVILLE, 78- *Concurrent Pos:* Biochemist, Okla Med Res Found, 60-63, assoc mem, 63-66; Pub Health Serv res career develop award, 66. *Mem:* Am Soc Biol Chemists; Am Chem Soc. *Res:* Mechanism of cell membrane transport of nucleosides. *Mailing Add:* Dept Med Biol Mem Res Ctr Univ of Tenn Ctr Health Sci Knoxville TN 37920

WIGLEY, NEIL MARCHAND, b Mt Vernon, Wash, Feb 16, 36; c 4. MATHEMATICAL ANALYSIS. *Educ:* Univ Calif, Berkeley, BA, 59, PhD(math), 63. *Prof Exp:* Staff mem math, Los Alamos Sci Lab, 63-65; asst prof, Univ Ariz, 65-67; assoc prof, Univ NC, 67-68; fel, Alex V Humboldt Found, Univ Bonn, 68-70; assoc prof, 70-74, PROF MATH, UNIV WINDSOR, 74- *Mem:* Am Math Soc. *Res:* Partial differential equations. *Mailing Add:* Dept of Math Univ of Windsor Windsor ON N9B 3P4 Can

WIGLEY, ROLAND L, b Blawenburg, NJ, Oct 4, 23; m 56; c 2. MARINE ECOLOGY. *Educ:* Univ Maine, BS, 49; Cornell Univ, PhD(ichthyol), 53. *Prof Exp:* Fishery biologist, Dept Conserv & Econ Develop, NJ, 52-53; supervisory fishery res biologist, Nat Marine Fisheries Serv, 53-80; CONSULT, 80- *Concurrent Pos:* Consult, Aquatic Sci Info Retrieval Ctr, Taft Lab, RI, 61-64 & John Wiley & Sons, NY, 66-; US deleg, Protein Resources Panel, US-Japan Coop Prog Natural Resources, 75-76; shellfisheries consult, Food & Agr Orgn, UN; mem adv panel 5, Int Comn, Northwest Atlantic Fisheries Comn; US rep shellfish & benthos comt, Int Coun Explor Sea, 73-75, US mem introd nonindigenous marine organisms panel, 74-; adv, New Eng Fishery Mgt Coun, 78. assoc ed, Nat Shellfisheries Asn Proc; assoc ed, Fishery Bull. *Mem:* Am Soc Ichthyologists & Herpetologists; Soc Syst Zool; Am Fisheries Soc; Am Soc Limnol & Oceanog. *Res:* Ecological aspects of offshore marine benthonic animal communities; taxonomy and geographic distribution of marine fishes and invertebrate organisms. *Mailing Add:* 35 Wilson Rd Woods Hole MA 02543

WIGNALL, GEORGE DENIS, b Bradford, Eng, July 16, 41; m 70; c 2. POLYMER PHYSICS, SMALL ANGLE SCATTERING. *Educ:* Univ Sheffield, BS, 62, PhD(physics), 66. *Prof Exp:* Fel, Harwell Atomic Energy Ctr, 66-68, Calif Inst Technol, 68-69; lab mgr, Imperial Chem Industs, Ltd, 69-79; RES SCIENTIST POLYMER PHYSICS, NAT CTR SMALL ANGLE SCATTERING, OAK RIDGE NAT LAB, 79- *Concurrent Pos:* Lectr, Univ Tenn, Knoxville, 81- *Mem:* Am Chem Soc; Am Phys Soc. *Res:* Structure of synthetic polymers and blends including molecular configuration and domain structure; small angle x-ray and neutron scattering. *Mailing Add:* Nat Ctr Small Angle Scattering Res Oak Ridge Nat Lab PO Box X Oak Ridge TN 37830

WIGNER, EUGENE PAUL, b Budapest, Hungary, Nov 17, 02; nat US; m 36, 41; c 2. MATHEMATICAL PHYSICS. *Educ:* Tech Hochsch, Berlin, DrIng, 25. *Hon Degrees:* Twenty-one from US & foreign cols & univs, 49-73. *Prof Exp:* Asst, Tech Hochsch, Berlin, 26-27, privatdocent, 28-30, N B Ausserord prof theoret physics, 30-33; asst, Univ Göttingen, 27-28; lectr math physics, Princeton Univ, 30, prof, 30-36; prof physics, Univ Wis, 37-38; Thomas D Jones prof math physics, Palmer Phys Lab, 38-71, EMER THOMAS D JONES PROF MATH PHYSICS, PRINCETON UNIV, 71- *Concurrent Pos:* Sci guest, Kaiser Wilhelm Inst Berlin, 31 & Metall Lab, Chicago, 42-45; dir res & develop, Clinton Labs, Tenn, 46-47; Lorentz lectr, Inst Lorentz, Leiden, 57; dir harbor proj civil defense, Nat Acad Sci, 63; dir course 29, Int Sch Physics Enrico Fermi, 63; dir, Civil Defense Res Proj, Oak Ridge, Tenn, 64-65; Kramers prof, State Univ Utrecht, 75. Consult, Off Sci Res & Develop, 41-42, Oak Ridge Nat Lab & Exxon Nuclear Co; mem vis comt, Nat Bur Stand, 47-51; gen adv comt, AEC, 52-57, 59-64; vis prof, La State Univ, 71- *Honors & Awards:* Nobel Prize in Physics, 63; Medal for Merit, 46; Franklin Medal, Franklin Inst, 50; Fermi Award, 58; Atoms for Peace Award, 60; Max Planck Medal, Ger Phys Soc, 61; George Washington Award, Am Hungarian Studies Found, 64; Semmelweiss Medal, Am Hungarian Med Asn, 65; Nat Medal Sci, 69; Albert Einstein Award, 72. *Mem:* Nat Acad Sci; Am Math Soc; fel Am Phys Soc (vpres, 55, pres, 66); Am Acad Arts & Sci; Am Philos Soc. *Res:* Application of group theory of quantum mechanics; rate of chemical reactions; theory of metallic cohesion; nuclear structure and reactions; philosophical implications of quantum mechanics. *Mailing Add:* Dept of Math Physics Jadwin Hall Princeton Univ PO Box 708 Princeton NJ 08540

WIGTON, ROBERT SPENCER, b Omaha, Nebr, Nov 1, 11; m 37; c 2. MEDICINE. *Educ:* Univ Nebr, BSc, 32, MA & MD, 35. *Prof Exp:* Instr, Sch Med, Univ Pa, 38-42; prof, 46-77, PROF EMER NEUROL & PSYCHIAT, COL MED, UNIV NEBR, OMAHA, 77- *Concurrent Pos:* Fel neurol, Hosp Univ Pa, 37-40; resident, Pa Hosp, 40-42; consult, Union Pac RR, 53-77. *Mem:* AAAS; AMA; Am Psychiat Asn. *Res:* Clinical neuropsychiatry; neurophysiology in relation to behavior. *Mailing Add:* Dept of Neurol & Psychiat Univ of Nebr Col of Med Omaha NE 68105

WIIG, ELISABETH HEMMERSAM, b Esbjerg, Denmark, May 22, 35; US citizen; m 58; c 2. SPEECH PATHOLOGY. *Educ:* State Sem Enmdrupborg, Denmark, BS, 56; Case-Western Reserve Univ, MA, 60, PhD(speech path), 67. *Prof Exp:* Instr phonetics, Univ Bergen, Norway, 60-64; asst prof speech path, Univ Mich, 68-70; PROF COMMUN DIS, BOSTON UNIV, 70- *Concurrent Pos:* NIH fel, Univ Mich, 67-68. *Mem:* Am Am Speech & Hearing Asn; Coun Except Children; Acad Aphasia. *Res:* Language disorders and learning disabilities; acquired aphasia in adults; congenital language disorders in children. *Mailing Add:* Dept Commun Dis 48 Cummington St Boston MA 02215

WIIST, WILLIAM HENRY, b Sherman, Tex, Mar 2, 47. HEALTH EDUCATION, EPIDEMIOLOGY. *Educ:* Southern Missionary Col, BA, 69; Walla Walla Col, MS, 73; Loma Linda Univ, MPH, 75, DHSc, 75. *Prof Exp:* Lectr health sci, San Diego State Univ, 75; ASST PROF HEALTH EDUC, UNIV UTAH, 75- *Concurrent Pos:* Fel, Grad Sch Pub Health, Univ Pittsburgh, 78- *Mem:* Soc Pub Health Educ; Am Pub Health Asn. *Res:* Planning and evaluation of health education programs in the primary prevention of cardiovascular disease. *Mailing Add:* Dept of Epidemiol Univ of Pittsburgh Pittsburgh PA 15261

WIITA, PAUL JOSEPH, b Bronx, NY, Feb 18, 53; m 78. ASTROPHYSICS, THEORETICAL PHYSICS. *Educ:* Cooper Union, NY, BS, 72; Princeton Univ, MA, 74, PhD(physics), 76. *Prof Exp:* Res asst physics, Princeton Univ, 75-76; res assoc, Enrico Fermi Inst, Univ Chicago, 76-79; ASST PROF ASTRON, UNIV PA, 79- *Concurrent Pos:* Instr, Adler Planetarium, Chicago, 77; Compton lectr, Enrico Fermi Inst, Univ Chicago, 77; NSF-NATO fel, Inst Astron, Univ Cambridge, 77-78; vis fel, Copernicus Astron Ctr, Warsaw, 78 & Tata Inst Fundamental Res, India, 81. *Mem:* Am Phys Soc; Am Astron Soc; Royal Astron Soc. *Res:* Problems in theoretical astrophysics, including radio galaxies, quasars, relativistic beams, black holes, rotating stars, star formation and planetary system formation. *Mailing Add:* Dept of Astron Univ of Pa Philadelphia PA 19104

WIITALA, STEPHEN ALLEN, b Vancouver, Wash, Oct 3, 46; m 68; c 1. ALGEBRA, COMPUTER SCIENCE. *Educ:* Western Wash Univ, BAEd, 68, MA, 71; Dartmouth Col, PhD(math), 75. *Prof Exp:* asst prof math, Nebr Wesleyan Univ, 75-80; ASST PROF MATH, NORWICH UNIV, 80- *Mem:* Am Math Soc; Math Asn Am. *Res:* Quadratic forms on vector spaces of characteristic two; representation theory of finite groups; mathematics and computer science education. *Mailing Add:* Dept Math Norwich Univ Northfield VT 05663

WIITANEN, WAYNE ALFRED, b Detroit, Mich, May 6, 35; m 73; c 1. BIONICS, COMPUTER SCIENCES. *Educ:* Harvard Univ, AB, 68, MA, 69, PhD(biol), 72. *Prof Exp:* Consult comput sci, 67-68; vpres, Mgt Eng Inc, 69-71; asst prof biol, Univ Ore, 71-77, asst prof comput sci, 73-77, assoc prof biol, 77-80, interim dir univ comput, 77-80; SR RES SCIENTIST, COMPUT SCI DEPT, GEN MOTORS RES LABS, 80- *Mem:* AAAS; Inst Elec & Electronics Engrs; Soc Comput Simulation. *Res:* Applications of computers and mathematics to biological problems with special emphasis on the mammalian nervous system; dynamical biological systems simulation. *Mailing Add:* Comput Sci Dept Gen Motors Res Labs Warren MI 48044

WIJANGCO, ANTONIO ROBLES, b Manila, Philippines, Apr 6, 44; m 67. HIGH ENERGY PHYSICS. *Educ:* Ateneo de Manila Univ, AB, 65; Columbia Univ, MS, 71, PhD(physics), 76. *Prof Exp:* Res assoc, Nevis Labs, Columbia Univ, 75-78; RES ASSOC PHYSICS, BROOKHAVEN NAT LAB, 78- *Concurrent Pos:* Vis scientist, Ecole Polytech, France & Europ Coun Nuclear Res, Geneva, Switz, 76- *Res:* Photon beams of energy, 100-400 Giga-electron volts as a probe of nuclear and sub-nuclear matter. *Mailing Add:* Brookhaven Nat Lab Upton NY 11973

WIJNEN, JOSEPH M H, b Wittem, Netherlands, Sept 22, 20; US citizen; m 67; c 2. PHYSICAL CHEMISTRY, PHOTOCHEMISTRY. *Educ:* Cath Univ Louvain, Lic Sci, 46, Dr Sci(chem), 48. *Prof Exp:* Lectr chem, Cath Univ Louvain, 48-49; Nat Res Coun Can fel photochem, 49-51; res assoc, NY Univ, 51-53; Nat Res Coun Can res officer, 53-55; res assoc chem, Celanese Corp Am, 55-58; sr fel photochem, Mellon Inst, 58-63; PROF CHEM, HUNTER COL, 63- *Concurrent Pos:* Consult, US Bur Mines, Pittsburgh, Pa, 61-63; NSF res grants, 67-69 & 70-72; vis prof, Univ Bonn, 69-70, Univ Amsterdam, 76-77. *Mem:* Am Chem Soc; Nat Combustion Inst; fel Am Inst Chemists. *Res:* Primary processes in photochemical reactions; free radical reactions; kinetics of free radical induced polymerization reactions. *Mailing Add:* Dept of Chem Hunter Col New York NY 10021

WIJSMAN, ROBERT ARTHUR, b Hague, Netherlands, Aug 20, 20; m 53; c 3. MATHEMATICAL STATISTICS. *Educ:* Delft Inst Technol, Netherlands, Ir, 45; Univ Calif, PhD(physics), 52. *Prof Exp:* Lectr med physics, Univ Calif, 52-53, instr math, 53-54, res statistician, 54-55, lectr statist & pub health, 55-56, actg asst prof statist, 56-57; from asst prof to assoc prof, 57-65, PROF STATIST, UNIV ILL, URBANA, 65- *Concurrent Pos:* Vis prof, Columbia Univ, 67-68. *Mem:* Inst Math Statist; Am Math Soc; Am Statist Asn. *Res:* Sequential and multivariate analysis. *Mailing Add:* 310 Altgeld Hall Univ Ill Urbana IL 61801

WIKJORD, ALFRED GEORGE, b Flin Flon, Man, July 15, 43; m 68. NUCLEAR CHEMISTRY. *Educ:* Univ Manitoba, BSc, 64, MSc, 65; McGill Univ, PhD(chem), 69. *Prof Exp:* NATO sci fel, Strasbourg Macromolecular Res Ctr, France, 69-70; res officer, Anal Sci Br, 70-80, HEAD NUCLEAR WASTE IMMOBILIZATION SECT, WHITESHELL NUCLEAR RES ESTAB, ATOMIC ENERGY CAN LTD, 80- *Mem:* Chem Inst Can; Am Vacuum Soc; NAm Thermal Anal Soc; Can Nuclear Soc; Mat Res Soc. *Res:* Chemistry of nuclear reactors; heavy water production; management of nuclear wastes. *Mailing Add:* Anal Sci Br Whiteshell Nuclear Res Estab Pinawa MB R0E 1L0 Can

WIKLER, ABRAHAM, psychiatry, deceased

WIKSWO, JOHN PETER, JR, b Lynchburg, Va, Oct 6, 49; m 70; c 2. BIOPHYSICS, MEDICAL PHYSICS. *Educ:* Univ Va, BA, 70; Stanford Univ, MS, 73, PhD(physics), 75. *Prof Exp:* Res fel cardiol, Med Sch, Stanford Univ, 75-77; ASST PROF PHYSICS, VANDERBILT UNIV, 77- *Concurrent Pos:* Res fel, Bay Area Heart Res Comt, 75-77. *Mem:* Am Phys Soc; Am Heart Asn; Biophys Soc; Inst Elec & Electronics Engrs; Sigma Xi. *Res:* Application of electric and magnetic measurements and electromagnetic theory to study the propagation of electrical activity in muscle and nerves; development of instrumentation and analysis techniques for neuromagnetism, magnetocardiography and electrocardiography. *Mailing Add:* Dept of Physics & Astron Box 1807 Sta B Nashville TN 37235

WIKSWO, MURIEL ANASTASIA, cell biology, see previous edition

WIKTOR, TADEUSZ JAN, b Stryj, Poland, Sept 9, 20; US citizen; m 48; c 3. VIROLOGY. *Educ:* Sch Vet Med, Alfort & Univ Paris, DrVetMed, 46; Inst Trop Med, Alfort, France, cert trop vet med, 46. *Prof Exp:* Asst path, Sch Vet Med, Alfort, France, 46-47; dir lab microbiol, Vet Lab, Kisenyi, Belgian Congo, 47-49, Vet Lab, Stanleyville, 49-55, Vet Lab, Astrida, 55-58 & Vet Lab, Elizabethville, 58-60; Food & Agr Orgn expert virol, Animal Husb Res Inst, WPakistan, 60-61; assoc mem virol rabies, 61-75, mem, 75-77, PROF, WISTAR INST ANAT & BIOL, 77- *Concurrent Pos:* Mem, expert comt rabies, WHO, 63; assoc prof, Sch Vet Med, Univ Pa, 67. *Res:* Animal pathology, viral and bacterial diseases, epidemiology, vaccine development and production; research on rabies virus. *Mailing Add:* 36th St at Spruce Philadelphia PA 19104

WIKUM, DOUGLAS ARNOLD, b Stoughton, Wis, Oct 3, 33; m 58; c 4. ECOLOGY, BIOLOGY. *Educ:* Univ Wis-Stevens Point, BS, 61, Univ SDak, MA, 65; Univ NDak, PhD(biol), 72. *Prof Exp:* Asst prof biol, Univ Wis-Stout, 66-74; ecologist, Stone & Webster Eng Corp, Boston, 74-76; assoc prof, 76-80, PROF BIOL, UNIV WIS-STOUT, 80- *Concurrent Pos:* Consult ecologist, NUS Corp, Pittsburgh, Pa, 73; res, US Forest Serv, 7-81. *Mem:* Am Inst Biol Sci; Ecol Soc Am; Sigma Xi. *Res:* Chemical and physical properties of soils; plant community structure; litter production; water quality; sewage disposal in bog ecosystems. *Mailing Add:* Dept of Biol Univ of Wis-Stout Menomonie WI 54751

WILANSKY, ALBERT, b St John's, Nfld, Sept 13, 21; nat US; m 69; c 5. MATHEMATICS. *Educ:* Dalhousie Univ, MA, 44; Brown Univ, PhD(math), 47. *Prof Exp:* Demonstr physics, Dalhousie Univ, 42-44; instr math, Brown Univ, 46-48; from asst prof to prof, 48-78, UNIV DISTINGUISHED PROF MATH, LEHIGH UNIV, 78- *Concurrent Pos:* Consult, Frankford Arsenal, 57-58; Fulbright vis prof, Reading Univ, 72-73. *Honors & Awards:* Ford Prize, Math Asn Am, 69. *Mem:* Am Math Soc; Math Asn Am. *Res:* Pure mathematics; analysis; summability; linear topological space; Banach algebra; functional analysis. *Mailing Add:* Dept of Math Lehigh Univ Bethlehem PA 18015

WILBAND, JOHN TRUAX, petrology, geochemistry, see previous edition

WILBANKS, JOHN RANDALL, b Foreman, Ark, June 10, 38; m 62; c 2. PETROLOGY, STRUCTURAL GEOLOGY. *Educ:* NMex Inst Mining & Technol, BS, 60; Tex Tech Univ, MS, 66, PhD(geol), 69. *Prof Exp:* Geologist, NMex State Hwy Dept, 61-63; teaching asst geol, Tex Tech Univ, 63-65, res assoc geol, Marie Byrd Land, 67-69, co-investr & NSF Antarctic grant, 69-70, vis asst prof geol, 70-71; chmn dept, 71-74, ASSOC PROF & CHMN DEPT GEOSCI, UNIV NEV, LAS VEGAS, 71- *Honors & Awards:* US Antarctic Serv Medal, Off Polar Progs, NSF, 70. *Mem:* Geol Soc Am; Nat Asn Geol Teachers. *Res:* Petrology and structure of metamorphic complexes; Marie Byrd Land, Antarctica; morphology of metamorphic zircons; tectonics of the southern great basin. *Mailing Add:* Dept of Geosci Univ of Nev Las Vegas NV 89154

WILBARGER, EDWARD STANLEY, JR, b Billings, Mont, Feb 21, 31; m 59; c 2. PHYSICS, FLUIDS. *Educ:* Va Mil Inst, BS, 52; US Naval Postgrad Sch, MS, 56, Univ Calif-Santa Barbara, PhD, 80. *Prof Exp:* Chief indust hyg sect, Off Surgeon Gen, US Army, 56-58; engr physicist, Proj Res Aviation Med, US Naval Med Res Inst, 58-59; engr physicist, Bioastronaut Res Unit, Ord Missile Command, US Army, Redstone Arsenal, 59, chief inspections, Health & Safety Br, Off Chief Engrs, 59-60; head bioinstrumentation group, Corp, 60-62, sr res physicist, Aerospace Opers Dept, AC Electronics Defense Res Labs, 62-71, sr res physict, 71-75, HEAD ANAL & DESIGN, AELOPHYS DEPT, DELCO ELECTRONICS DIV, GEN MOTORS CORP, 75- *Concurrent Pos:* Lectr fluid mech, Univ Calif, Santa Barbara, 79-81. *Mem:* Sigma Xi; Am Acad Mech. *Res:* Control engineering; measurement methods; physiological response to stress; design and fabrication of control systems; mobility systems analysis for off-road vehicles; analysis and design of auto safety systems; computational fluid dynamics; hypervelocity interior ballistics and fluid dynamics; hypervelacity impact. *Mailing Add:* 3830 Ctr Ave Santa Barbara CA 93110

WILBER, CHARLES GRADY, b Waukesha, Wis, June 18, 16; m 52; c 6. PHYSIOLOGY. *Educ:* Marquette Univ, BSc, 38; Johns Hopkins Univ, MA, 41, PhD(gen physiol), 42. *Prof Exp:* Lab asst zool, Marquette Univ, 38-39; asst, Johns Hopkins Univ, 40-42; instr, St Louis Univ, 42, assoc prof physiol & dir biol labs, 49-52; asst prof, Fordham Univ, 46-49; chief animal ecol br, Chem Corps Med Labs, US Army Chem Ctr, Md, 52-56, comp physiol br, Chem Res & Develop Labs, 56-60; prof physiol & dean, Grad Sch, Kent State Univ, 61-64; dir marine labs & prof, Univ Del, 64-67; PROF ZOOL, COLO STATE UNIV, 67-, DIR FORENSIC SCI LAB, 74- *Concurrent Pos:* Leader, Fordham Arctic Exped, 48; assoc, Univ Pa, 53-60; prof lectr, Loyola Col, 57-60; mem corp, Marine Biol Lab, Woods Hole; mem panel environ physiol, US Dept Army; mem life sci comt, Nat Acad Sci-Air Res & Develop Command; consult, USPHS; dep coroner, Larimer County, Colo; dir, Ecol Consults, Inc, 72-74; toxicologist, Thorne Ecol Inst, 72- *Mem:* Fel Am Acad Forensic Sci; Am Physiol Soc; fel NY Acad Sci. *Res:* Biochemistry of body fluids; chemistry of metabolism; comparative aspects of environmental physiology; climatic adaption; forensic biology; wound ballistics; environmental quality; environmental pathology; comparative toxicology; oceanography. *Mailing Add:* 900 Edwards Ft Collins CO 80524

WILBER, JOE CASLEY, JR, b Jonesboro, Ark, Feb 28, 29; m 51. CHEMISTRY, SCIENCE EDUCATION. *Educ:* Memphis State Col, BS, 50, MA, 53; Univ Ga, EdD, 61. *Prof Exp:* Teacher pub schs, Tenn, 50-51 & 53-56; teacher & chmn sci dept, pub sch, Ga, 56-59; from asst prof to assoc prof chem, Ga Southern Col, 60-70; teacher chem & chmn dept sci, Wingate Col, 70-73; assoc prof, 73-80, PROF CHEM, PAUL D CAMP COMMUNITY COL, 80- *Mem:* AAAS. *Res:* General chemistry; qualitative analysis, a non-sulfide scheme. *Mailing Add:* Dept of Chem Paul D Camp Community Col PO Box 737 Franklin VA 23851

WILBER, LAURA ANN, b Memphis, Tenn, May 26, 34. AUDIOLOGY, SPEECH PATHOLOGY. *Educ:* Univ Southern Miss, BS, 55; Gallaudet Col, MS, 58; Northwestern Univ, PhD(audiol), 64. *Prof Exp:* Teacher hard of hearing & deaf, McKinley Elem Sch, Bakersfield, Calif, 55-57; speech therapist & coordr spec educ, US Army Dependent Sch Syst, Heidelberg, Ger, 57-61; res asst audiol, Northwestern Univ, 61-64; asst res audiologist, Univ Calif, Los Angeles, 64-70; asst prof, Albert Einstein Col Med, 70-75, dir hearing & speech serv, 75-76, assoc prof rehab med, 71-77; PROF AUDIOL, COORDR HEARING CLINICS & HEAD AUDIOL & HEARING IMPAIRMENT, NORTHWESTERN UNIV, EVANSTON, ILL, 78- *Concurrent Pos:* Spec instr, Calif State Col, Los Angeles & Univ Southern Calif, 65-70; dir audiol clin, Hosp, Univ Calif, Los Angeles, 68-69; chmn, Clin Sch-Coun New York, 72-73; mem, Dir Hosp Speech & Hearing, Prog Asn & Soc Ear, Nose & Throat Advan in Children; US rep, Int Stand Orgn; mem, Am Nat Stand Inst; adj assoc prof, City Univ New York, 74-76; actg chmn commun dis, Northwestern Univ, 81. *Mem:* Am Speech & Hearing Asn; Acoust Soc Am; Am Auditory Soc; Sigma Xi. *Mailing Add:* Dept Commun Dis Northwestern Univ Evanston IL 60201

WILBORN, WALTER HARRISON, b Arbyrd, Mo, May 20, 35; m 57; c 3. HUMAN ANATOMY. *Educ:* Harding Col, BA, 57; St Louis Univ, MS, 62; Univ Tenn, PhD(anat), 67. *Prof Exp:* From asst prof to assoc prof anat, Med Ctr, Univ Ala, Birmingham, 67-73; assoc prof, 73-75, PROF ANAT, COL MED, UNIV S ALA, & DIR EM CTR, 76- *Concurrent Pos:* NIH res grant, 67-72. *Mem:* Am Asn Anat; Am Soc Cell Biol; Histochem Soc. *Res:* Ultrastructure and cytochemistry; cutaneous pathology; secretory mechanisms; reproductive biology. *Mailing Add:* Dept of Anat Univ SAla Col of Med Mobile AL 36688

WILBRAHAM, ANTONY CHARLES, b Chester, Eng, July 26, 36; m 65; c 1. BIOCHEMISTRY. *Educ:* Carlett Park Col, Eng, cert chem & physics, 59; Royal Soc Chem, grad chem, 62, res dipl chem, 65, FRSC, 72. *Prof Exp:* Anal technician chem, Shell Refining Co, Eng, 53-60; res assoc chem, Univ SFla, 66-67; vis asst prof, Eckerd Col, 67-68; asst prof, 68-72, assoc prof, 72-79, PROF CHEM, SOUTHERN ILL UNIV, EDWARDSVILLE, 79- *Concurrent Pos:* Res fel chem, Univ Manchester, 73-74. *Mem:* Fel Royal Soc Chem; Am Chem Soc. *Res:* Polar effects in model substrates of alpha chymotrypsin; carbon-13 labelling of active site amino acid residues in chymotrypsin. *Mailing Add:* Dept Chem Southern Ill Univ Edwardsville IL 62026

WILBUR, DANIEL SCOTT, b Bath, NY, Mar 18, 50; m 74; c 1. RADIOPHARMACEUTICAL CHEMISTRY. *Educ:* Portland State Univ, BS, 73; Univ Calif, Irvine, PhD(chem), 78. *Prof Exp:* MEM RES STAFF, LOS ALAMOS NAT LAB, 78- *Concurrent Pos:* Adj prof, Chem Dept, Univ NMex, 81-82. *Mem:* Am Chem Soc; Soc Nuclear Med. *Res:* Development of new radiopharmaceuticals, including design and synthesis of potential radiopharmaceuticals with concurrent studies involving new radiolabeling techniques. *Mailing Add:* Med Radioisotope Res MS-E514 Los Alamos Nat Lab Los Alamos NM 87545

WILBUR, DAVID WESLEY, b Hinsdale, Ill, Dec 15, 37; m 68; c 1. BIOPHYSICS, MEDICINE. *Educ:* Pac Union Col, BA, 61; Univ Calif, Berkeley, PhD(biophys), 65; Loma Linda Univ, MD, 71; Am Bd Internal Med, cert, 75. *Prof Exp:* Biophysicist, Lawrence Radiation Lab, Univ Calif, 65-67; asst prof physiol & biophys, Sch Med, Loma Linda Univ, 67-69, med intern, 71-72, med resident, 72-74, res assoc biomath, 69-74; Am Cancer Soc med oncol clin fel, Roswell Park Mem Inst, 74-76; MEM, MED ONCOL, DEPT INTERNAL MED, LOMA LINDA UNIV, 76- *Concurrent Pos:* Donner fel, 61-62. *Mem:* Am Col Physicians; AAAS; Am Soc Clin Oncol; Sigma Xi; AMA. *Res:* Cancer chemotherapy; computer simulation of cell population kinetics; role of immunology in cancer. *Mailing Add:* Dept of Internal Med Loma Linda Univ Loma Linda CA 92354

WILBUR, DONALD LEE, b Chicago, Ill, Apr 28, 66; c 2. NEUROENDOCRINOLOGY. *Educ:* Ind State Univ, BS, 68, MA, 70; Med Univ SC, PhD(anat), 74. *Prof Exp:* Asst prof anat, Sch Med, Tex Tech Univ, 74-76; ASSOC PROF ANAT, MED UNIV SC, 76- *Concurrent Pos:* Consult, Environ Protection Agency, 78- *Mem:* Am Asn Anatomists; Histochem Soc; Sigma Xi. *Res:* Electron microscopic, immunocytochemical studies of the pituitary gland and circumventricular organs, correlated with radioimmunoassayable levels of circulating hormones; mechanisms of hormone synthesis and release. *Mailing Add:* Med Univ SC 171 Ashley Ave Charleston SC 29425

WILBUR, DWIGHT LOCKE, b Harrow-on-the-Hill, Eng, Sept 18, 03; m 28; c 3. GASTROENTEROLOGY. *Educ:* Stanford Univ, AB, 23; Univ Pa, MD, 26; Univ Minn, MS, 33. *Hon Degrees:* DSc, Dartmouth Col, 73. *Prof Exp:* Resident physician, Univ Pa Hosp, 26-28; 1st asst, Sect Path Anat, May Clin, Rochester, Minn, 29-30, 1st asst, Div Med, 31-33, assoc, Sect Path Anat & from instr to asst prof med, 33-37; from asst clin prof to clin prof, 37-69, EMER PROF MED, SCH MED, STANFORD UNIV, 69- *Concurrent Pos:* Consult physician, Mayo Clin, 31-37; asst vis physician, Stanford Serv, San Francisco Hosp, 37-60; assoc ed, Gastroenterology, 43-51; ed, Calif Med, 46-67; chief med serv, French Hosp, 46-73, emer chief, 73-; expert consult, Letterman Gen Hosp, Dept Army, 46-76, emer consult, 76-; assoc clin prof med, Col Physicians & Surgeons, Sch Dent, Stanford Univ, 48-51; consult, US Naval Hosp, Oakland & SPac Hosp, 50-70; mem bd, Mayo Asn, 51-64; mem civilian health & med adv coun, Dept Defense, 53-59; trustee, Mayo Found, 64-71, emer pub trustee, 71-79; mem, Nat Adv Comn Health Manpower, 66-67; ed-in-chief, Post Grad Med, 69-73. *Honors & Awards:* Julius Friedenwald Medal, Am Gastroenterol Asn, 66; Alfred Stengel Mem Award, Am Col Physicians, 70. *Mem:* Sr mem Inst Med-Nat Acad Sci; master Am Col Physicians; Am Gastroenterol Asn (secy, 47-52, 2nd vpres, 52-53, 1st vpres, 53, pres, 54-55); AMA; fel & hon mem Int Col Dentists. *Mailing Add:* Suite 602 655 Sutter St San Francisco CA 94102

WILBUR, HENRY MILES, b Bridgeport, Conn, Jan 25, 44; m 67, 81; c 1. ZOOLOGY, ECOLOGY. *Educ:* Duke Univ, BS, 66; Univ Mich, Ann Arbor, PhD(zool), 71. *Prof Exp:* Univ Mich Soc Fels jr fel, Div Reptiles & Amphibians, Mus Zool, Univ Mich, Ann Arbor, 71-73; asst prof, 73-77, ASSOC PROF ZOOL, DUKE UNIV, 77- *Concurrent Pos:* Edwin S George scholar, Edwin S George Reserve, Mich, 68-69. *Honors & Awards:* Stove Award, Am Soc Ichthyol & Herpet, 70. *Mem:* AAAS; Ecol Soc Am; Soc Study Evolution; Brit Ecol Soc; Am Soc Ichthyol & Herpet. *Res:* Evolutionary ecology; evolution of species interactions and life histories. *Mailing Add:* Dept of Zool Duke Univ Durham NC 27706

WILBUR, JAMES MYERS, JR, b Philadelphia, Pa, Oct 31, 29; m 60; c 3. ORGANIC CHEMISTRY. *Educ:* Muhlenberg Col, BS, 51; Univ Pa, PhD, 59. *Prof Exp:* Res chemist, J T Baker Chem Co, NJ, 51-53; NIH fel cancer chemother, Univ Minn, 58-60; res chemist, E I du Pont de Nemours & Co, 60-62; fel, Univ Ariz, 62-63; assoc prof chem, 63-66, PROF CHEM, SOUTHWEST MO STATE UNIV, 66- *Mem:* Am Chem Soc. *Res:* Medicinal chemistry; cancer chemotherapy; organic mechanisms; polymers. *Mailing Add:* Dept of Chem Southwest Mo State Univ Springfield MO 65802

WILBUR, JOHN B(ENSON), b Oakland, Maine, July 25, 04. CIVIL ENGINEERING. *Educ:* Mass Inst Technol, BS, 26, MS, 28, ScD(civil eng), 33. *Prof Exp:* Bridge designer, Maine Cent RR, 28-39 & NY Cent RR, 29-30; from instr to prof civil eng, 30-60, acting head dept, 44-46, head dept, 46-60, consult prof eng, 60-70, sr lectr civil eng, 70-75, EMER PROF ENG, MASS INST TECHNOL, 70- *Concurrent Pos:* Chief engr, Smith-Putman Wind Turbine Proj, S Morgan Smith Co, Pa, 40-45; expert consult, US Dept Army, 46-55; consult, Fay Spofford & Thorndike, Boston, 48-58; dean eng, Am Univ Beirut, 64; in charge joint proj regional planning, Mass Inst Technol & Ottauquechee Regional Planning & Develop Comn. *Mem:* Fel Am Soc Civil Engrs; Am Soc Eng Educ; Soc Exp Stress Anal; fel Am Acad Arts & Sci. *Res:* Structural analysis; building frame stress analysis; suspension bridge analysis; mechanical solution of simultaneous equations; model analysis of structures; theory of statically indeterminate structure. *Mailing Add:* PO Box 14 Hancock NH 03449

WILBUR, KARL MILTON, b Binghamton, NY, May 7, 12; m 46; c 2. PHYSIOLOGY. *Educ:* Ohio State Univ, BA, 35, MA, 36; Univ Pa, PhD(zool), 40. *Prof Exp:* Asst zool, Ohio State Univ, 35-36; instr, Univ Pa, 39-40; Rockefeller fel, NY Univ, 40-41; instr zool, Ohio State Univ, 41-42, asst prof physiol, Med Sch, Dalhousie Univ, 42-44; assoc prof zool, 46-50, PROF ZOOL, DUKE UNIV, 50- *Concurrent Pos:* Physiologist, AEC, 52-53. *Mem:* Am Physiol Soc; Am Soc Naturalists; Soc Gen Physiol; Am Soc Zoologists. *Res:* Cellular physiology; calcification in marine organisms; cell division. *Mailing Add:* Dept of Zool Duke Univ Durham NC 27706

WILBUR, L(ESLIE) C(LIFFORD), b Johnston, RI, May 12, 24; m 50; c 4. MECHANICAL ENGINEERING. *Educ:* Univ RI, BS, 48; Stevens Inst Technol, MS, 49. *Prof Exp:* From instr to asst prof mech eng, Duke Univ, 49-57; assoc prof, 57-61, PROF MECH ENG, WORCESTER POLYTECH INST, 61-, DIR NUCLEAR REACTOR FACILITY, 59- *Mem:* Am Soc Mech Engrs; Am Soc Eng Educ; Am Nuclear Soc. *Res:* Nuclear reactor technology; thermodynamics. *Mailing Add:* PO Box 97 Berlin MA 01503

WILBUR, LYMAN D, b Los Angeles, Calif, April 27, 00; m 25. RIVER DIVERSION, CONSTRUCTION. *Educ:* Stanford Univ, BA, 21. *Hon Degrees:* LLD, Col Idaho, 62; DSc, Univ Idaho, 67. *Prof Exp:* Draftsman & asst eng field eng, City San Francisco, 21-24; designer, Merced Irrig Dist, 24-26; design eng, East Bay Munic Utility Dist, 26-29; asst to chief consult eng, Mid Asia Water Econ Serv, 29-31; dist engr eng, Morison-Knudsen Co, Inc, 32-39, div engr, 40-42, dist mgr, 42-47, chief eng, 47-52, vpres eng, 53-60, vpres foreign oper, 60-65, vpres, 65-70; CONSULT, 71- *Concurrent Pos:* Exec vpres, pres & chmn, Int Eng Co, Inc, Div Morrison-Knudsen Co, Inc, 56-70, constuct mgr, 39-41, resident partner, 65-66. *Mem:* Nat Acad Eng; Am Soc Civil Engrs; Nat Soc Prof Engrs; Soc Am Mil Engrs. *Mailing Add:* 4502 Hillcest Dr Boise 83705

WILBUR, PAUL JAMES, b Ogden, Utah, Nov 8, 37; m 60; c 2. MECHANICAL ENGINEERING. *Educ:* Univ Utah, BS, 60; Princeton Univ, PhD(aeronaut & mech sci), 68. *Prof Exp:* Assoc prof, 64-68, PROF MECH ENG, COLO STATE UNIV, 68- *Concurrent Pos:* Nuclear Power engr, US Atomic Energy Comn. *Mem:* Am Soc Mech Engrs; Am Inst Aeronaut & Astronaut. *Res:* Electric propulsion in space applications. *Mailing Add:* Dept of Mech Eng Colo State Univ Ft Collins CO 80521

WILBUR, RICHARD SLOAN, b Boston, Mass, Apr 8, 24; m 51; c 3. MEDICINE. *Educ:* Stanford Univ, BA, 43, MD, 46. *Prof Exp:* Intern, San Francisco County Hosp, 46-47; resident, Stanford Hosp, 49-51 & Univ Pa Hosp, 51-52; mem staff, Palo Alto Med Clin, 52-69; dep exec vpres, AMA, Chicago, 69-71; asst secy defense for health & environ, 71-73; dep exec vpres, AMA, 73-74; sr vpres, Baxter Labs, Inc, Deerfield, Ill, 74-76; EXEC VPRES, COUN MED SPECIALTY SOCS, 76- *Concurrent Pos:* Assoc prof med, Med Sch, Stanford Univ, 52-69 & Med Sch, Georgetown Univ, 71-; mem bd dirs, Medic Alert Found & Nat Adv Cancer Coun & secy, Cont Med Educ, 81-; mem bd visitors, Postgrad Med Sch, Drew Univ. *Honors & Awards:* Scroll of Merit, Nat Med Asn, 71. *Mem:* Inst Med-Nat Acad Sci; hon fel Int Col Dent; fel Am Col Physicians; Am Gastroenterol Asn; Am Soc Internal Med. *Mailing Add:* Coun of Med Specialty Socs PO Box 70 Lake Forest IL 60045

WILBUR, ROBERT DANIEL, b Glendale, Calif, May 7, 31; m 52; c 3. AGRICULTURAL RESEARCH MANAGEMENT, PLANT PROTECTION. *Educ:* Calif State Polytech Col, BS, 54; Iowa State Univ, PhD(animal nutrit, bact), 59. *Prof Exp:* Asst nutrit & bact, Iowa State Univ, 54-59, fel, 59; res nutritionist, 59-67, group leader nutrit & physiol, 67-76, mgr pesticides res, 76-80, mgr animal res, 80-81, DIR INT PLANT INDUST, AM CYANAMID CO, 81- *Concurrent Pos:* Consult, tech mgt. *Mem:* AAAS; Am Soc Animal Sci. *Res:* Nutrition and physiology of domesticated animals; crop physiology. *Mailing Add:* Agr Res Div Am Cyanamid Co Box 400 Princeton NJ 08540

WILBUR, ROBERT LYNCH, b Annapolis, Md, July 4, 25; m 55; c 6. PLANT TAXONOMY. *Educ:* Duke Univ, BS, 46, AM, 48; Univ Mich, PhD, 52. *Prof Exp:* Asst bot, Duke Univ, 46-47, Univ Hawaii, 47-48 & Univ Mich, 48-52; asst prof, Univ Ga, 52-53; asst prof & cur herbarium, NC State Col, 53-57; from asst prof to assoc prof bot, 57-70, chmn dept, 71-78, PROF BOT, DUKE UNIV, 70- CUR, HERBARIUM, 57- *Mem:* Am Soc Plant Taxon; Int Asn Plant Taxon. *Res:* Taxonomy and phytogeography of vascular plants; flora of the southeastern United States and Central America. *Mailing Add:* 265 Biol Sci Bldg Duke Univ Dept of Bot Durham NC 27706

WILBURN, NORMAN PATRICK, b Whittier, Calif, Mar 28, 31; m 56; c 4. CHEMICAL & ELECTRICAL ENGINEERING. *Educ:* Calif Inst Technol, BS, 53, MS, 54, PhD, 58. *Prof Exp:* Engr, Hanford Labs, Gen Elec Co, 58-65; res assoc, Pac Northwest Labs, Battelle Mem Inst, 65-70; res assoc, Hanford Eng Develop Labs, 70-75, mgr, 76-80, ADV ENGR, WESTINGHOUSE-HANFORD CO, 81- *Res:* Development of mathematical models of chemical and thermohydraulic processes; development of on-line digital computer systems; software engineering; large scale scientific software development. *Mailing Add:* 1922 Harris Richland WA 99352

WILCE, ROBERT THAYER, b Carbondale, Pa, Dec 9, 24; m 56. BOTANY. *Educ:* Univ Scranton, BS, 50; Univ Vt, MS, 52; Univ Mich, PhD(bot), 57. *Prof Exp:* Instr bot, Univ Mich, 57-58, fel, Horace Rackham Grad Sch, 58-59; from instr to prof, 59-76, PROF BOT, UNIV MASS, AMHERST, 76- *Mem:* Phycol Soc Am. *Res:* Systematic morphology, distribution and ecology of the attached algae of arctic and subarctic areas, especially the Canadian eastern arctic and northwest Greenland. *Mailing Add:* Dept of Bot Univ of Mass Amherst MA 01003

WILCHINSKY, ZIGMOND WALTER, b New York, NY, Aug 26, 15; m 40; c 1. POLYMER PHYSICS. *Educ:* Rutgers Univ, BS, 37, MS, 39; Mass Inst Technol, PhD(physics), 42. *Prof Exp:* Asst physics, Rutgers Univ, 37-39; mem staff radiation lab, Mass Inst Technol, 42-45; sect head, US Naval Res Lab, Washington, DC, 43-46; sr res assoc, Exxon Chem Co, 46-80. *Mem:* AAAS; Am Phys Soc; Am Chem Soc; Am Crystallog Asn; NY Acad Sci. *Res:* Structure of plastics; rubber technology; x-ray diffraction; physical chemistry of catalysts; adsorption; development of microwave generators; vacuum tube development. *Mailing Add:* 301 S Wood Ave Linden NJ 07036

WILCOCK, DONALD F(REDERICK), b Brooklyn, NY, Sept 24, 13; m 38; c 1. ENGINEERING. *Educ:* Harvard Univ, BS, 34; Univ Cincinnati, DEngSci, 40. *Prof Exp:* Res chemist, Sherwin-Williams Co, Ill, 39-42 & Res Lab, Gen Elec Co, NY, 42-45; eng group leader, Thomson Lab, 45-53; mgr mat & chem process eng serv dept, Gen Eng Lab, Gen Elec Co, 53-60, consult engr, Ord Dept, 60-65; dir bearings, lubricant & seal technol, Mech Technol Inc, 65-68, dir technol develop, 69-78; PRES, TRIBOLOCK INC, 78- *Concurrent Pos:* Ed, J Lubrication Technol. *Honors & Awards:* Centennial Medal, Am Soc Mech Engrs, 81. *Mem:* Fel Am Soc Mech Engrs; fel Am Soc Lubrication Engrs. *Res:* Air bearings; magnetic bearings; bearing design and testing; lubricant testing and development; cryogenics. *Mailing Add:* Tribolock Inc 1949 Hexam Rd Schenectady NY 12309

WILCOX, ARCHER CARL, chemistry, biochemistry, deceased

WILCOX, BENJAMIN A, b Anaconda, Mont, June 18, 34; m 55; c 3. MATERIALS SCIENCE, METALLURGY. *Educ:* Wash State Univ, BS, 56; Stanford Univ, MS, 58, PhD(mat sci), 62. *Prof Exp:* Phys metallurgist, Stanford Res Inst, 56-58; NSF fel, Cambridge Univ, 62-63; fel metals sci, Battelle Mem Inst, 63-71, div chief, High Temperature Mat & Processes Div, 71-73, mgr metals sci sect, Battelle Columbus Labs, 73-74; ceramics prog dir, 74-79, HEAD, METALL POLYMERS & CERAMICS SECT, NSF, 79- *Concurrent Pos:* Vis scientist, Imp Col Sci & Technol & Nat Phys Lab, Eng, 73. *Mem:* Am Soc Metals; Am Ceramic Soc; Am Inst Mining, Metall & Petrol Engrs. *Res:* Deformation and fracture of crystalline solids; high temperature creep, substructural strengthening; dispersion strengthened metals; laser-materials interactions; high temperature corrosion. *Mailing Add:* NSF Div of Mat Res 1800 G St NW Washington DC 20550

WILCOX, BENSON REID, b Charlotte, NC, May 26, 32; m 59; c 4. CARDIOVASCULAR SURGERY, THORACIC SURGERY. *Educ:* Univ NC, Chapel Hill, BA, 53, MD, 57. *Prof Exp:* From instr to assoc prof, 63-71, PROF SURG, UNIV NC, CHAPEL HILL, 71-, CHIEF DIV CARDIOVASC & THORACIC SURG, 69- *Concurrent Pos:* NIH fel, Univ NC, Chapel Hill, 63-64 & grant, 68-74; Markle scholar, 67-72; consult, NC Sanatorium Syst, 64- *Mem:* Am Asn Thoracic Surg; Am Col Surg; Am Surg Asn; Soc Thoracic Surg; Soc Univ Surg. *Res:* Application of biomathematical and engineering principles to the study of the circulation; pulmonary circulation in heart disease; surgical anatomy of congenital heart disease. *Mailing Add:* Div Cardiothoracic Surg 108 Burnett-Womack Bldg 229H Chapel Hill NC 27514

WILCOX, BRUCE ALEXANDER, b Hackensack, NJ, May 21, 48; m 76; c 3. BIOGEOGRAPHY, CONSERVATION BIOLOGY. *Educ:* Univ Calif, San Diego, AB, 73, PhD(biol), 79; Yale Univ, MS, 75. *Prof Exp:* RES ASSOC, DEPT BIOL SCI, STANFORD UNIV, 70- *Concurrent Pos:* Appointee, Int Union Conserv Nature & Natural Resources, Servival Serv Comn, 81-; prin investr, Indonesia/US Bilateral Res Sci Mgt Biosphere Reserves, 82-; consult,

US Man & the Biosphere Prog & UN Environ Prog, 82- *Mem:* AAAS. *Res:* Island biogeography; population ecology and genetics; application of population biology to biological conservation. *Mailing Add:* Dept Biol Sci Stanford Univ Stanford CA 94305

WILCOX, CALVIN HAYDEN, b Cicero, NY, Jan 29, 24; m 47; c 3. MATHEMATICS. *Educ:* Harvard Univ, AB, 51, AM, 52, PhD(math), 55. *Prof Exp:* Mathematician, Air Force Cambridge Res Ctr, 53-55; from instr to assoc prof math, Calif Inst Technol, 55-61; prof math & mem US Army Math Res Ctr, Univ Wis, 61-66; prof math, Univ Ariz, 66-69 & Univ Denver, 69-71; PROF MATH, UNIV UTAH, 71- *Concurrent Pos:* Vis prof, Inst Theoret Physics, Univ Geneva, 70-71, Univ Liege, 73, Univ Stuttgart, 74, 76-77, Kyoto Univ, 75. ed, Rocky Mountain J Math, 75-78; Alexander von Humboldt Found US sr scientist award, 76-77; Ecole Polytehique Federate, Lausanne, 79, Univ Bonn, 80. *Mem:* AAAS; Am Math Soc; Soc Indust & Appl Math. *Res:* Applied mathematics and mathematical physics, especially theories of wave propagation and scattering in classical and quantum physics; boundary value problems for partial differential equations. *Mailing Add:* Dept of Math Univ of Utah Salt Lake City UT 84112

WILCOX, CHARLES FREDERICK, JR, b Providence, RI, July 20, 30; m 57; c 3. PHYSICAL CHEMISTY, ORGANIC CHEMISTRY. *Educ:* Mass Inst Technol, BS, 52; Univ Calif, Los Angeles, PhD(org chem), 57. *Prof Exp:* NSF fel, Harvard Univ, 57; from instr to assoc prof, 57-74, PROF CHEM, CORNELL UNIV, 74- *Concurrent Pos:* Guggenheim fel, 66-67; vis prof, Calif Inst Technol, 67; asst ed, J Am Chem Soc, 65-66. *Mem:* Am Chem Soc; The Chem Soc. *Res:* Physical aspects of organic chemistry. *Mailing Add:* Dept of Chem Cornell Univ Ithaca NY 14853

WILCOX, CHARLES HAMILTON, b Rochester, NY, May 21, 29. THEORETICAL PHYSICS, ENGINEERING MANAGEMENT. *Educ:* Duke Univ, BS, 50; Univ Ill, MS, 52; Univ Southern Calif, 70. *Prof Exp:* Res physicist & lectr physics, Eng Exp Sta, Ga Inst Technol, 52-53; sr mem tech staff & assoc mgr theoret studies dept, Res Labs, 53-67, mgr tech planning, Aerospace Group, 67-70, dir corp independent res & develop, 70-74, DIR ENG & PROG DEVELOP, AEROSPACE GROUPS, HUGHES AIRCRAFT CO, 74- *Concurrent Pos:* Lectr, Univ Southern Calif, 55-59 & Univ Calif, Los Angeles, 61-63; consult, Stanford Res Inst, 73-76. *Mem:* AAAS; Am Phys Soc; Inst Elec & Electronics Eng; Sigma Xi; Inst Mgt Sci. *Res:* Scattering and diffraction of electromagnetic waves; radiowave propagation and geophysics; technology planning and development. *Mailing Add:* 10520 Draper Ave Los Angeles CA 90064

WILCOX, CHARLES JULIAN, b Harrisburg, Pa, Mar 28, 30; m 55; c 2. DAIRY SCIENCE. *Educ:* Univ Vt, BS, 50; Rutgers Univ, MS, 55, PhD(animal genetics), 59. *Prof Exp:* Res asst dairy sci, Rutgers Univ, 50 & 53-55; owner & mgr dairy farm, 55-56; res asst dairy sci, Rutgers Univ, 56-59; asst prof dairy sci & assoc geneticist, 59-71, PROF DAIRY SCI & GENETICIST, UNIV FLA, 71- *Mem:* Am Dairy Sci Asn; Am Soc Animal Sci; Am Inst Biol Sci; Latin Am Asn Animal Prod. *Res:* Quantitative genetics of productive traits of farm animals, including milk yield and composition, reproductive performance, birth weights, gestation lengths, heat tolerance, type conformation, disease resistance, maternal and fetal effects, life span and livability. *Mailing Add:* Dept Dairy Sci Univ Fla Gainesville FL 32611

WILCOX, CHRISTOPHER STUART, b UK, Sept 15, 42; m 64; c 2. NEPHROLOGY, CLINICAL PHARMACOLOGY. *Educ:* Oxford Univ, BA, 66, BMBCh & MA, 68; London Univ, PhD(med & physiol), 74. *Prof Exp:* House physician gen med, Middlesex Hosp, 69; house surgeon surg & urol, Cent Middlesex Hosp, 69-70; clin asst med hyper & nephrol, Middlesex Hosp, 70-75; ASST PROF MED CLIN PHARMACOL, BRIGHAM & WOMEN'S HOSP, 80- *Concurrent Pos:* House physician neurol, Middlesex Hosp, 70, lectr neurol studies, 70-71; house physician chest dis, Brompton Hosp, 70; asst prof med, Harvard Med Sch, 80- *Mem:* Physiol Soc; Brit Pharmacol Soc; Renal Asn; Am Fedn Clin Res; Am Soc Nephrol. *Res:* Regulation of body fluids and electrolytes and renal vascular resistance; hypertension; autonomic insufficiency; chronic kidney disease. *Mailing Add:* Brigham & Women's Hosp 75 Francis St Boston MA 02115

WILCOX, CLIFFORD LAVAR, b Archer, Idaho, Apr 15, 25; m 45; c 5. DAIRY HUSBANDRY. *Educ:* Utah State Univ, BS, 51; Univ Minn, MS, 57, PhD(dairy husb), 59. *Prof Exp:* Asst dairying, 56-59, instr dairy husb, 60, exten dairy specialist, 60-65, asst dir agr exp sta, 68-72, SUPT, AGR EXP STA, UNIV MINN, 65- *Mem:* Am Dairy Sci Asn. *Res:* Dairy cattle breeding. *Mailing Add:* Univ Minn Agr Exp Sta 1605-160 St W Rosemount MN 55068

WILCOX, DONALD BROOKS, b Walden, NY, Feb 23, 11; m 35; c 3. INDUSTRIAL ENGINEERING. *Educ:* Pa State Univ, BS, 33; Ga Inst Technol, MS, 39; Emory Univ, LLB, 52. *Prof Exp:* Instr mech eng, Ga Inst Technol, 36-40, instr indust eng, 46-52; assoc prof & acting head dept, Univ Ala, 41-42; prof, Univ Fla, 52-75; PRIVATE CONSULT & EXPERT WITNESS, 75- *Concurrent Pos:* Consult, Fla Indust Comn. *Mem:* Am Soc Eng Educ; Am Inst Indust Engrs; Am Soc Safety Engrs; Soc Advan Mgt; Am Soc Prof Engrs. *Res:* Accident prevention engineering; engineering contracts and specifications; engineering economy and law. *Mailing Add:* 1120 NE Fifth Terrace Gainesville FL 32601

WILCOX, ETHELWYN BERNICE, b Wyoming, Iowa, Mar 19, 06. NUTRITION. *Educ:* Iowa State Univ, BS, 31, MS, 37, PhD(nutrit), 42. *Prof Exp:* Teacher high sch, 32-36; asst & supvr animal nutrit lab, Iowa State Univ, 37-42; asst home economist, Exp Sta, Wash State Univ, 42-43; from asst prof to prof nutrit, 43-71, fac hon res lectr, 59, head dept food & nutrit, 65-71, EMER PROF NUTRIT, UTAH STATE UNIV, 71- *Honors & Awards:* Spec Fac Award, Utah State Univ, 64. *Mem:* Am Home Econ Asn; Am Dietetic Asn; Inst Food Technologists; Am Inst Nutrit. *Res:* Nutritional status of population groups; lipid metabolism; chemical components of venison flavor. *Mailing Add:* 788 Hillcrest Ave Logan UT 84321

WILCOX, FLOYD LEWIS, b Lodi, NY, Dec 17, 37; m 57; c 2. SCIENCE EDUCATION. *Educ:* Houghton Col, BS, 65; Univ Miami, Coral Gables, MS, 67; State Univ NY Binghamton, PhD(chem), 71. *Prof Exp:* From assoc prof to prof sci chem, Cent Wesleyan Col, 70-77; INSTR CHEM & PHYSICS, WINSTON-SALEM/FORSYTH COUNTY SCHS, 77- *Mem:* Am Chem Soc; Am Sci Affil; Nat Sci Teachers Asn. *Res:* Water pollution analysis aimed at monitoring local streams and lakes; new and novel teaching methods and aids; new methods for the removal of foreign substances from natural or industrial waters. *Mailing Add:* 1615 Miller St Winston-Salem NC 27103

WILCOX, FRANK H, b Norwich, Conn, June 15, 27; m 60; c 2. GENETICS. *Educ:* Univ Conn, BS, 51; Cornell Univ, MS, 53, PhD(animal genetics), 55. *Prof Exp:* Assoc prof poultry physiol, Univ Md, 55-67; PROF LIFE SCI, IND STATE UNIV, TERRE HAUTE, 67- *Concurrent Pos:* Poultry Sci travel award to World Poultry Cong, Australia, 62; USPHS res fel, 75-76; vis investr, Jackson Lab, 75-76. *Mem:* Genetics Soc Am; Am Soc Human Genetics; World Poultry Sci Asn. *Res:* Biochemical genetics, especially electrophoretic variants in vertebrates. *Mailing Add:* Dept of Life Sci Ind State Univ Terre Haute IN 47809

WILCOX, GARY LYNN, b Ventura, Calif, Jan 7, 47; m 70. BIOCHEMICAL GENETICS. *Educ:* Univ Calif, Santa Barbara, BA, 69, MA, 72, PhD(molecular biol), 72. *Prof Exp:* Res assoc biol, Univ Calif, Santa Barbara, 72-74; asst prof, 74-77, assoc prof bact, 77-80, PROF MICROBIOL BACT, UNIV CALIF, LOS ANGELES, 80- *Concurrent Pos:* Am Can Soc fac res award, 77. *Mem:* Am Soc Microbiol; Genetics Soc Am; Am Soc Biol Chemists. *Res:* Molecular basis of positive and negative regulation of L-arabinose utilization in E coli; protein nucleic acid interactions; genetic engineering. *Mailing Add:* Dept of Microbiol Univ of Calif Los Angeles CA 90024

WILCOX, GERALD EUGENE, b Wautoma, Wis, July 17, 25; m 49; c 3. SOIL FERTILITY. *Educ:* Univ Wis, BS, 49, MS, 51, PhD, 53. *Prof Exp:* Asst agronomist, Northern La Hill Farm Exp Sta, La State Univ, 53-57; assoc prof, 57-71, PROF HORT & AGRON, PURDUE UNIV, LAFAYETTE, 71- *Concurrent Pos:* Plant nutritionist, US Agency Int Develop, Brazil, 75-77. *Mem:* Soil Sci Soc Am; Am Soc Hort Sci; Int Soil Sci Soc. *Res:* Mineral nutrition and fertilization of vegetable crops, especially tomatoes and potatoes; soil fertility; culture and mechanization of tomato production; nutrient film technique for tomato, lettuce and cucumber production. *Mailing Add:* Dept of Hort Purdue Univ West Lafayette IN 47906

WILCOX, GLADE, b Macomb, Ill, Oct 18, 13; m 40; c 5. ELECTRONIC ENGINEERING. *Educ:* Univ Western Ill, BS, 37; Univ Ill, MS, 47, MEd, 51; Univ Ind, EdD(voc educ, indust mgt), 56. *Prof Exp:* Instr indust educ, Ind State Teachers Col, 47-50; assoc prof, Agr & Mech Col, Tex, 50-51; eng adminr, Thordarson-Meissner, Ill, 51-53; elec engr in charge qual control, Sarkes Tarzian Inc, Ind, 54-55; assoc prof elec eng, 55-65, PROF ELEC ENG, WESTERN MICH UNIV, 65- *Concurrent Pos:* Mem rev panels, NSF, 70 & 72; consult citizens band transceivers, Robyn Int, 71- *Mem:* Sr mem Inst Elec & Electronics Engrs; Am Soc Eng Educ. *Res:* The use of kits in technical education; direct conversion transceivers; apparatus for preventing simultaneous transmission and channel selection in a transmitter or transceiver; means for tuning a loaded coil antenna to a specific frequency within the antenna band width; single side band radio apparatus. *Mailing Add:* Dept of Elec Eng Western Mich Univ Kalamazoo MI 49008

WILCOX, HAROLD KENDALL, b Wichita, Kans, Aug 9, 42; m 66; c 2. METHODS DEVELOPMENT, HAZARDOUS WASTE TESTING. *Educ:* Sterling Col, BA, 64; Univ Southern Calif, PhD(chem), 71. *Prof Exp:* Prof chem, Calif Baptist Col, 70-73; chemist, San Bernadino County Air Pollution Control Dist, 73-75; prog mgr, Northrop Serv, Inc, 75-79; SECT HEAD, MIDWEST RES INST, 79- *Concurrent Pos:* Lectr, Riverside City Col, 74-77. *Mem:* Air Pollution Control Asn. *Res:* Test methods for stationary source emissions; development of analysis methods; testing of specialized air pollution sources. *Mailing Add:* Midwest Res Inst 425 Volker Blvd Kansas City MO 64110

WILCOX, HARRY HAMMOND, b Canton, Ohio, May 31, 18; m 41; c 3. ANATOMY. *Educ:* Univ Mich, BS, 39, MS, 40, PhD(zool), 48. *Prof Exp:* Assoc prof biol, Morningside Col, 47-48; assoc anat, Sch Med, Univ Pa, 48-52; from asst prof to prof anat, Univ Tenn, Memphis, 52-67, Goodman prof, 67-80. *Mem:* Am Soc Zool; Am Asn Anat. *Res:* Effects of aging on the nervous system; internal ear; central nervous system pathways. *Mailing Add:* 1031 Marcia Rd Memphis TN 38117

WILCOX, HENRY G, b Hornell, NY, Jan 26, 33; m 66; c 2. BIOCHEMISTRY, PHARMACOLOGY. *Educ:* Univ Fla, PhD(biochem), 64. *Prof Exp:* Asst prof, 68-74, assoc prof pharmacol, Vanderbilt Univ, 74-77; ASSOC PROF PHARMACOL, UNIV MO, 77- *Concurrent Pos:* NIH fel pharmacol, Vanderbilt Univ, 64-67. *Res:* Plasma lipoprotein metabolism, structure and function; methodology for lipoprotein isolation and analysis; hormonal control of lipid metabolism and transport. *Mailing Add:* Dept of Pharmacol Univ Mo Med Ctr Columbia MO 65212

WILCOX, HOWARD ALBERT, b Minneapolis, Minn, Nov 9, 20; m 43; c 3. PHYSICS, ENVIRONMENTAL MANAGEMENT. *Educ:* Univ Minn, BA, 43; Univ Chicago, MA & PhD(physics), 48. *Prof Exp:* Instr physics, Harvard Univ & Radcliffe Col, 43-44; jr scientist, Los Alamos Sci Lab, NMex, 44-46; asst, Inst Nuclear Studies, Univ Chicago, 46-48; from instr to asst prof & mem staff radiation lab, Univ Calif, 48-50; res physicist & head guided missile develop div, US Naval Ord Test Sta, 50-55, head weapons develop dept, 55-58, asst tech dir res & head res dept, 58-59; dep dir defense res & eng, Off Secy Defense, Washington, DC, 59-60; dir res & eng defense res labs, Gen Motors Corp, 60-66, tech dir adv power systs, Res Labs, 66-67; physicist, US Naval Weapons Ctr, China Lake, 71-74; mgr ocean food & energy farm proj, US Naval weapons ctr & undersea ctr, 72-77; STAFF SCIENTIST, ENVIRON SCI DEPT, NAVAL OCEAN SYST CTR, 77-; TECH & MGT

CONSULT, 67- *Concurrent Pos:* Vpres, Minicars, Inc, Goleta, 68-74. *Mem:* AAAS; fel Am Phys Soc. *Res:* Production of mesons in nuclear collisions; guided missile system engineering; oceanography; hypervelocity flight physics; lunar and terrestrial vehicles; advanced power systems; technical management; earth's energy balance. *Mailing Add:* 882 Golden Park Ave San Diego CA 92106

WILCOX, HOWARD JOSEPH, b Plattsburgh, NY, Oct 20, 39. MATHEMATICS. *Educ:* Hamilton Col, AB, 61; Univ Rochester, PhD(math), 66. *Prof Exp:* Asst prof math, Univ Conn, 65-67; asst prof, Amherst Col, 67-70; from asst prof to assoc prof, 72-78, chmn dept, 76-80, PROF MATH, WELLESLEY COL, 78- *Mem:* Am Math Soc; Math Asn Am. *Res:* Topological groups; general topology. *Mailing Add:* Dept Math Wellesley Col Wellesley MA 02181

WILCOX, HUGH EDWARD, b Manchester, Calif, Sept 2, 16; m 38; c 5. PLANT PHYSIOLOGY. *Educ:* Univ Calif, BS, 38, PhD, 50; Syracuse Univ, MS, 40. *Prof Exp:* Asst, State Univ NY Col Forestry, Syracuse, 38-40; technician, Dept Forestry, Univ Calif, 41-42; physicist, Radiation Lab, 42-45; physicist & ord engr, US Naval Ord Test Sta, 45-46; assoc prof forest prod & wood technologist, Ore State Col, 46-50; res assoc & proj leader, Res Found, State Univ NY, 50-54; assoc prof forestry, 54-59, PROF FORESTRY, STATE UNIV NY COL ENVIRON SCI & FORESTRY, 59- *Mem:* AAAS; Soc Am Foresters; Bot Soc Am; Am Soc Plant Physiol. *Res:* Growth periodicity; dormancy; physiology of cambial activity; wound healing and regeneration; growth and differentiation of roots; mycorrhiza. *Mailing Add:* Dept of Environ & Forest Biol Col of Environ Sci & Forestry Syracuse NY 13210

WILCOX, JAMES RAYMOND, b Minneapolis, Minn, Jan 20, 31; m 55; c 2. PLANT BREEDING, GENETICS. *Educ:* Univ Minn, BA, 53, MS, 59; Iowa State Univ, PhD(plant genetics), 61. *Prof Exp:* Res geneticist, Inst Forest Genetics, Forest Serv, USDA, 61-66, SUPVY RES GENETICIST, AGR RES SERV, USDA, PURDUE UNIV, WEST LAFAYETTE, 66- *Mem:* AAAS; fel Am Soc Agron; Am Genetic Asn; Crop Sci Soc Am. *Res:* Soybean breeding and genetics. *Mailing Add:* Room 2-307 Lilly Hall Purdue Univ Dept of Agron West Lafayette IN 47906

WILCOX, JAROSLAVA ZITKOVA, b Prague, Czech, June 8, 42; US citizen; m 72; c 2. PHYSICS. *Educ:* Czech Univ, Prague, Dipl Ing, 66; Univ Calif, Los Angeles, MS, 70, PhD(physics), 72. *Prof Exp:* Res assoc physics, Inst Physics, Czech Acad Sci, Prague, 66-68; asst prof physics, Tufts Univ, 72-74; MEM PROF STAFF APPL PHYSICS, RES GROUP, TRW SYSTS & ENERGY, 74- *Concurrent Pos:* Res assoc, Dept Physics, Univ Calif, Los Angeles, 72. *Mem:* Am Phys Soc. *Res:* General physics; solid state physics; physics of semiconductor devices; applied optics; material science. *Mailing Add:* TRW Defense & Space Systs Group One Space Park Redondo Beach CA 90278

WILCOX, JOHN MARSH, b Iowa City, Iowa, Jan 31, 25; m 55; c 2. SOLAR PHYSICS. *Educ:* Iowa State Col, BS, 48; Univ Calif, Berkeley, PhD(physics), 54. *Prof Exp:* Physicist, Lawrence Radiation Lab, Univ Calif, Berkeley, 51-64, res physicist, Space Sci Lab, 64-71; RES PHYSICIST & ADJ PROF, INST PLASMA RES, STANFORD UNIV, 71- *Concurrent Pos:* Vis physicist, Royal Inst Technol, Stockholm, Sweden, 61-62; assoc ed, J Geophys Res. *Mem:* AAAS; Am Phys Soc; Am Geophys Union; Am Astron Soc; Royal Astron Soc. *Res:* Solar and interplanetary magnetic fields; solar wind; photospheric magnetic fields; photospheric supergranulation and chromospheric network; solar wind interactions with geomagnetic field. *Mailing Add:* Stanford Univ Inst Plasma Res Via Crespi Stanford CA 94305

WILCOX, JOSEPH CLIFFORD, b McLean, Ill, June 18, 30; m 52; c 2. FOOD SCIENCE, FOOD MICROBIOLOGY. *Educ:* Univ Ill, BS, 52, MS, 54; Inst Mgt, Ill Benedictine Col, grad, 70. *Prof Exp:* Bacteriologist, 56-58, sect head sausage develop, Res & Develop Dept, Food Res Div, Armour & Co, 58-76; MGR FOOD PROD DEVELOP, GROCERY PRODS DIV, MILES LABS INC, 76- *Mem:* AAAS; Inst Food Technologists. *Res:* Bacteriological, chemical and radiological warfare decontamination; application of bacteriological principles in development and study of food products and associated problems; research in fresh, semidry and dry sausage items; utilization of nonmeat proteins; develop cholesterol-free food analog products. *Mailing Add:* Miles Labs Inc 900 Proprietors Rd Worthington OH 43085

WILCOX, KENT WESTBROOK, b NC, 1945. VIROLOGY. *Educ:* Duke Univ, BS, 67; Johns Hopkins Univ, MA, 69, PhD(microbiol), 74. *Prof Exp:* ASST PROF MICROBIOL, MED COL WIS, 79- *Mem:* Am Soc Microbiol; AAAS. *Res:* Regulation of viral gene expression in cells infected by herpes simplex virus. *Mailing Add:* Dept Microbiol Med Col Wis 8701 Watertown Plank Rd Milwaukee WI 53226

WILCOX, LEE ROY, b Chicago, Ill, June 8, 12; m 40; c 2. ALGEBRA, SCIENCE EDUCATION. *Educ:* Univ Chicago, SB, 32, SM, 33, PhD(math), 35. *Prof Exp:* Mem sch math, Inst Advan Study, 35-36, asst, 36-38; instr math, Univ Wis, 38-40; from asst prof to prof, 40-77, dir Ctr Educ Develop, 69-77, PROF EMER MATH, ILL INST TECHNOL, 77- *Mem:* Am Math Soc; Asn Am. *Res:* Theory of lattices; foundations of mathematics; abstract algebra; mathematics education. *Mailing Add:* 1404 Forest Ave Wilmette IL 60091

WILCOX, LOUIS VAN INWEGEN, JR, b Orange, NJ, Aug 24, 31; m 56; c 3. ECOLOGY. *Educ:* Colgate Univ, AB, 53; Cornell Univ, MS, 58, PhD(plant path), 61. *Prof Exp:* Asst plant physiol, Cornell Univ, 55-57; asst plant path, 57-61; asst prof biol, Lycoming Col, 61-65; assoc prof, Earlham Col, 65-71; dir, Fahkahatchee Environ Studies Ctr, 71-73; dir environ qual prog, Hampshire Col, 73-76; prof & chmn, Ctr Environ Sci, 76-78, dean, 78-80, PRES, UNITY COL, 80- *Concurrent Pos:* Consult, Coastal Enterprises, Inc, 80-81 & Maine Audubon Farm Study Proj, 79; mem, bd dirs, Ctr Human Ecol Studies, 79-81. *Mem:* Am Asn Geol; Sigma Xi. *Res:* Mangrove ecology. *Mailing Add:* Unity Col Unity ME 04988

WILCOX, LYLE C(HESTER), b Lansing, Mich, Aug 8, 32; m 52; c 3. SYSTEMS ENGINEERING, COMPUTER SCIENCE. *Educ:* Tri-State Col, BSEE, 54; Mich State Univ, MSEE, 58, PhD(elec eng), 63. *Prof Exp:* Fac mem elec eng, Tri-State Col, 52-54 & Mich State Univ, 55-63; dir opers, Vet Admin, Ark, 64-65; assoc prof elec eng, & Draper prof elec & mech eng, Clemson Univ, 65-66, head dept elec eng, 66-72, assoc dean prof studies, 70-73, prof elec & comput eng, 66-80, dean eng, Col Eng, 73-80; PRES, UNIV SOUTHERN COLO, 80- *Concurrent Pos:* NSF fac fel, 59-61; Ford Found fel, 62-63. *Mem:* AAAS; Inst Elec & Electronics Engrs; Am Soc Mech Engrs. *Res:* Application of systems theory to problems in control and biomedical and operations research; design and use of specialized instrumentation for data acquisition systems used in the study of multi-terminal components; general digital analog simulation from the hybrid point of view. *Mailing Add:* Univ Southern Colo Pueblo CO 81001

WILCOX, MARION ALLEN, b Dillon, SC, Oct 12, 17; m 42; c 3. ZOOLOGY. *Prof Exp:* Mus technician, Med Mus, Armed Forces Inst Path, 50-60; med plastic exhibit specialist, NIH, 60-69, HEAD MED MODELS & MOULAGE LAB, DIV RES SERVS, MED ARTS SECT, NIH, 69- *Res:* Applications of plastics to medical technology; museum technology. *Mailing Add:* Med Arts Sect Bldg 10 B2-L332 NIH Div of Res Serv Bethesda MD 20205

WILCOX, MARION WALTER, b Broken Arrow, Okla, Aug 17, 22; m 48; c 2. ENGINEERING MECHANICS. *Educ:* Univ Notre Dame, BSCE, 48, ScD(eng sci), 61; Ill Inst Technol, MSCE, 56. *Prof Exp:* Assoc res engr, Armour Res Found, Ill Inst Technol, 51-54; designer, Kaiser Aluminum Corp, 54-55; tech supvr dynamics, Bendix Prod Div, Bendix Aviation Corp, 55-58; sr engr, Gen Dynamics/Ft Worth, Tex, 58-61; assoc prof mech eng, Univ Ariz, 61-62; assoc prof, 62-66, PROF SOLID MECH & MECH ENG, SOUTHERN METHODIST UNIV, 66- *Concurrent Pos:* Consult, Ling-Temco-Vought Corp, 62-, Off Res Anal, Holloman AFB, NMex, 64-65, Socony Mobil Oil Co, Inc, 65-66 & Koelling Universal Joints, Inc, 65-72. *Mem:* Am Soc Eng Educ; Am Acad Mech; Am Inst Aeronaut & Astronaut; Soc Eng Sci. *Res:* Thermoelasticity and elastodynamics. *Mailing Add:* 3163 Whirlaway Rd Dallas TX 75229

WILCOX, MERRILL, b Milwaukee, Wis, Oct 10, 29; m 62; c 2. PLANT PHYSIOLOGY. *Educ:* Univ Md, BS, 52, MS, 54; NC State Univ, PhD(agron, plant physiol), 61. *Prof Exp:* Biol aide marine biol, Chesapeake Biol Lab, Univ Md, 56-57; from asst prof to assoc prof agron, 60-72, PROF AGRON, UNIV FLA, 72- *Concurrent Pos:* Grants, Am Cancer Soc, 63-66, NSF, 63-65 & Geigy Chem Corp, 70-78. *Mem:* AAAS; Am Soc Plant Physiol; Weed Sci Soc Am; Scand Soc Plant Physiol; Plant Growth Regulator Working Group; Am Chem Soc. *Res:* Structure-activity relationships and metabolism of herbicides and plant growth regulators; abscission by Glyoxime; tobacco growth regulation by Benzyldinitroanilines; hybridization in cocosoid palms. *Mailing Add:* Herbicide Lab Dept of Agron Univ of Fla Gainesville FL 32611

WILCOX, PAUL DENTON, b Salt Lake City, Utah, Mar 4, 35; m 61; c 1. CERAMIC ENGINEERING, METALLURGY. *Educ:* Univ Utah, BS, 58, PhD(ceramic eng), 62. *Prof Exp:* supvr active ceramic mat div, 62-80, SUPVR INITIA NATTING & PYROTECHNICS, SANDIA LABS, 80- *Concurrent Pos:* Adj prof, Univ NMex, 69-70. *Mem:* Am Ceramic Soc; Int Pyrotech Soc. *Res:* Piezoelectrics; ferroelectrics; glass; glass ceramics; thermoelectrics; acoustic surface waves; ceramic varistors; materials science technology; explosives and propellants; pyrotechnics. *Mailing Add:* 1501 Cedar Ridge Dr NE Albuquerque NM 87112

WILCOX, RAY EVERETT, b Janesville, Wis, Mar 31, 12; m 42; c 4. GEOLOGY. *Educ:* Univ Wis, PhB, 33, PhM, 37, PhD(geol), 41. *Prof Exp:* Geologist, State Geol Surv, Wis, 35-39 & Jones & Laughlin Steel Corp, 41-42; GEOLOGIST, US GEOL SURV, 46- *Mem:* AAAS; fel Geol Soc Am; fel Mineral Soc Am; Brit Mineral Soc; Geochem Soc. *Res:* Igneous petrology; volcanology; volcanic ash chronology; petrographic methods; optical crystallography. *Mailing Add:* US Geol Surv PO Box 25046 Denver CO 80225

WILCOX, ROBERTA ARLENE, b Hopkinton, RI, Nov 12, 32. MEDICAL STATISTICS. *Educ:* Univ RI, BS, 54; Johns Hopkins Univ, ScM, 58. *Prof Exp:* Biostatistician, State Dept Health, NY, 57-59; res statistician, Lederle Labs, Am Cyanamid Co, 59-66; sr biostatistician, Med Div, Ciba-Geigy Corp, 66-72; biostatistician, Pfizer Cent Res, Pfizer Inc, 72-77, sr res scientist clin res, 77-80. *Mem:* Am Statist Asn; Biomet Soc; Inst Math Statist; NY Acad Sci. *Res:* Experimental design and analysis applicable to medical and drug research. *Mailing Add:* 6908 Wilton Dr Ft Worth TX 76133

WILCOX, RONALD BRUCE, b Seattle, Wash, Sept 23, 34; m 58; c 2. BIOCHEMISTRY, ENDOCRINOLOGY. *Educ:* Pac Union Col, BS, 57; Univ Utah, PhD(biochem), 62. *Prof Exp:* Res fel med, Mass Gen Hosp & Harvard Med Sch, 62-65; from asst prof to assoc prof, 65-73, PROF BIOCHEM, SCH MED, LOMA LINDA UNIV, 73- *Mem:* AAAS; Sigma Xi; Endocrine Soc. *Res:* Biochemistry and metabolism of hormones; hormone related carcinogenesis. *Mailing Add:* Dept of Biochem Loma Linda Univ Sch of Med Loma Linda CA 92354

WILCOX, RONALD ERWIN, b Ft Wayne, Ind, Jan 6, 29; m 59; c 3. GEOLOGY. *Educ:* Iowa State Univ, BS, 50, MS, 52; Columbia Univ, PhD(petrol), 58. *Prof Exp:* Asst geol, Iowa State Univ, 50-52 & Columbia Univ, 52-54; res geologist, Humble Oil & Refining Co, 56-64; sr res geologist, Esso Prod Res Co, 64-72; CONSULT GEOLOGIST, 72- *Concurrent Pos:* Lectr, Univ Houston, 72-75, adj prof, 75; assoc prof, Inst Environ Studies, La State Univ, 77- *Honors & Awards:* President's Award, Am Asn Petrol Geologists, 75. *Mem:* Fel AAAS; fel Geol Soc Am; Am Asn Petrol Geologists; Am Geophys Union. *Res:* Structural geology; petrology; structure of continental margins; salt tectonics; orogenic belts; metamorphism. *Mailing Add:* PO Box 17140A Baton Rouge LA 77401

WILCOX, ROY CARL, b Alexandria, Va, Feb 4, 33; m 65; c 2. PHYSICAL METALLURGY. *Educ:* Va Polytech Inst, BS, 55, MS, 59; Univ Mo-Rolla, PhD(metall eng), 62. *Prof Exp:* Metallurgist, Naval Ord Lab, 55-56; instr metall, Va Polytech Inst, 57-59, 62, assoc prof, 62-68, assoc dir, Continuing Educ Ctr, 68-69; ASSOC PROF MAT, AUBURN UNIV, 69- *Mem:* Am Soc Metals; Am Inst Mining, Metall & Petrol Engrs. *Res:* Deformation of textures of cobalt; study of titanium-aluminum alloys; fracture studies of adhesive bonded joints. *Mailing Add:* 1219 Old Mill Rd Auburn AL 36830

WILCOX, THOMAS JEFFERSON, b San Francisco, Calif, Oct 2, 42; m 72; c 2. PHYSICS. *Educ:* Univ Calif, Berkeley, BA, 64; Univ Calif, Los Angeles, MS, 66, PhD(physics), 72. *Prof Exp:* Res physicist plasma/particle physics, Univ Calif, Los Angeles, 72-73; mem tech staff plasma physics, TRW Systs Group, 73-75; MEM TECH STAFF PHYSICS, R&D ASSOCS, 75- *Mem:* Am Phys Soc. *Res:* Plasma physics; radiation transport; optics; electromagnetism; mathematical physics. *Mailing Add:* R&D Assocs 4640 Admiralty Way Marina del Rey CA 90291

WILCOX, W(ILLIAM) R(OSS), b Manhattan, Kans, Jan 14, 35; m 68; c 4. CHEMICAL ENGINEERING, MATERIALS SCIENCE. *Educ:* Univ Southern Calif, BEng, 56; Univ Calif, Berkeley, PhD(chem eng), 60. *Prof Exp:* Instr chem eng, Univ Calif, Berkeley, 60; mem tech staff, Pac Semiconductors Inc, 60-62; mem tech staff, Aerospace Corp, 62-65, head crystal technol sect, 65-68; assoc prof mat sci & chem eng, Univ Southern Calif, 68-74, prof, 74-75; PROF CHEM ENG & CHMN DEPT, CLARKSON COL TECHNOL, 75- *Concurrent Pos:* Lectr, Eve Col, Univ Calif, Los Angeles, 62-65; res asst, Lawrence Radiation Lab, Univ Calif, Berkeley, 57-59; consult, NASA, various industs & univs; vis prof, Dept Physics, Univ Estadual de Compinas, Brazil, 75. *Mem:* Am Inst Chem Engrs; Am Soc Eng Educ; Am Asn Crystal Growth. *Res:* Growth of electronic crystals; crystallization of chemicals. *Mailing Add:* Clarkson Col Technol Potsdam NY 13676

WILCOX, WEBSTER WAYNE, b Berkeley, Calif, Oct 28, 38; m 60; c 2. FOREST PRODUCTS PATHOLOGY, WOOD BIODETERIORATION. *Educ:* Univ Calif, Berkeley, BS, 60; Univ Wis-Madison, MS, 62, PhD(plant path), 65. *Prof Exp:* Plant pathologist, US Forest Prod Lab, Wis, 60-64; from asst to assoc forest prod pathologist, 64-77, lectr, 64-75, FOREST PROD PATHOLOGIST & PROF FORESTRY, UNIV CALIF, BERKELEY, 77- *Concurrent Pos:* Fulbright-Hays sr fel, Ger, 73-74. *Honors & Awards:* Forest Prod Res Soc Award, 65. *Mem:* Forest Prod Res Soc; fel Int Acad Wood Sci; Soc Wood Sci & Technol; Am Inst Biol Sci; Int Asn Wood Anatomists. *Res:* Wood deterioration; microscopy of wood decay. *Mailing Add:* Forest Prod Lab Univ Calif 47th & Hoffman Blvd Richmond CA 94804

WILCOX, WESLEY C, b St Anthony, Idaho, July 19, 25; m 48; c 4. MICROBIOLOGY. *Educ:* Univ Utah, BA, 51, MS, 55; Univ Wash, PhD(microbiol), 58. *Prof Exp:* Donner fel med res, Western Reserve Univ, 58-59, USPHS fel prev med, 59-60; assoc microbiol, Univ Pa, 60-62, asst prof, 62-63; asst prof, Univ Vt, 63-65; PROF MICROBIOL, UNIV PA, 65-, CHMN DEPT, 76-, HEAD LAB MICROBIOL, 80- *Concurrent Pos:* Res career develop award, Univ Pa, 60-63. *Mem:* Am Asn Immunol; Am Soc Microbiol. *Res:* Virology; immunology; biochemistry. *Mailing Add:* Dept of Microbiol Univ of Pa Sch of Vet Med Philadelphia PA 19174

WILCOX, WESLEY CRAIN, b Bloomington, Ill, Apr 8, 26; m 48; c 5. AGRONOMY, BOTANY. *Educ:* Univ Ill, BS, 50, MS, 51. *Prof Exp:* Field supvr, Found Dept, 51-55, plant breeder, Res Dept, 55-66, mgr spec proj res, 66-71, MGR QUAL CONTROL & ASSOC RELATIONS, QUAL CONTROL DEPT, FUNK SEEDS INT, 71- *Mem:* AAAS; Am Soc Agron; Crop Sci Soc Am. *Res:* High quality seed of hybrid corn, sorghum, soybeans, sunflowers and farm seeds. *Mailing Add:* Funk Seeds Int Qual Control Dept 1300 W Washington St Bloomington IL 61701

WILCOX, WILLIAM JENKINS, JR, b Harrisburg, Pa, Jan 26, 23; m 46; c 3. ENGINEERING PHYSICS. *Educ:* Washington & Lee Univ, BA, 43; Univ Tenn, MS, 58. *Prof Exp:* Chemist, Tenn Eastman Corp, 43-48; chemist, 48-49, tech asst to lab dir, 49-55, head dept physics, 55-67, prog mgr, 67-69, PROD PLANTS TECH DIR, NUCLEAR DIV, UNION CARBIDE CORP, 69- *Mem:* AAAS; Am Chem Soc; Sigma Xi; fel Am Inst Chemists; NY Acad Sci. *Res:* Isotope separation processes, research and development; structure of porous materials; materials development. *Mailing Add:* Nuclear Div Union Carbide Corp Oak Ridge TN 37830

WILCOXSON, ROY DELL, b Columbia, Utah, Jan 12, 26; m 49; c 4. PLANT PATHOLOGY. *Educ:* Utah State Univ, BS, 53; Univ Minn, MS, 55, PhD(plant path), 57. *Prof Exp:* Asst prof, 57-66, PROF PLANT PATH, UNIV MINN, ST PAUL, 66- *Concurrent Pos:* Spec staff mem, Rockefeller Found; vis prof, Indian Agr Res Inst, New Delhi. *Mem:* Am Phytopath Soc; Indian Phytopath Soc. *Res:* Diseases of forage crops and cereal crops; cereal rust diseases. *Mailing Add:* Dept Plant Path Univ Minn St Paul MN 55101

WILCZEK, FRANK ANTHONY, b Queens, NY, May 15, 51; m 73; c 1. THEORETICAL PHYSICS. *Educ:* Univ Chicago, BS, 70; Princeton Univ, MA, 72, PhD(physics), 74. *Prof Exp:* Asst prof physics, Princeton Univ, 74-77; mem, Inst Advan Studies, 77-78; assoc prof, 78-80, PROF PHYSICS, PRINCETON UNIV, 80- *Concurrent Pos:* Adv comt, Brookhaven Nat Lab, 78-81. *Res:* High energy physics; quantum field theory. *Mailing Add:* Dept of Physics Princeton Univ Princteon NJ 08540

WILD, BRADFORD WILLISTON, b Fall River, Mass, Dec 5, 27. OPTOMETRY, OPTICS. *Educ:* Brown Univ, AB, 49; Columbia Univ, BS, 51, MS, 52; Ohio State Univ, PhD(physiol optics), 59. *Prof Exp:* From instr to asst prof optom & physiol optics, Ohio State Univ, 59-63, assoc prof optom & physiol optics, 63-69; dean, Col Optom, Pac Univ, 69-74; ASSOC DEAN, SCH OPTOM, MED CTR, UNIV ALA, BIRMINGHAM, 74- *Concurrent Pos:* Res psychologist, Gen Vision Sect, US Naval Med Res Lab, Conn. *Mem:* Optical Soc Am; Am Optom Asn; Am Acad Optom (pres, 78-80). *Res:* Physiological optics, especially retinal interaction, border phenomena and problems of visibility. *Mailing Add:* Sch of Optom Univ of Ala Med Ctr Birmingham AL 35294

WILD, GAYNOR (CLARKE), b Winner, SDak, Nov 10, 34; m 73; c 2. BIOCHEMISTRY. *Educ:* SDak Sch Mines & Technol, BS, 55; Tulane Univ, PhD(biochem), 62. *Prof Exp:* Fel biochem, Clayton Found Biochem Inst, Univ Tex, 62-63; res assoc, Rockefeller Univ, 63-65, asst prof, 65-67; ASST PROF BIOCHEM, SCH MED, UNIV NMEX, 67- *Mem:* AAAS. *Res:* Neurochemistry; receptor structure and function; enzymology; lipid biochemistry. *Mailing Add:* Dept of Biochem Univ of NMex Sch of Med Albuquerque NM 87131

WILD, GENE MURIEL, b Fremont, Nebr, Oct 15, 26; m 48; c 4. BIOCHEMISTRY. *Educ:* Iowa State Univ, BS, 48, MS, 50, PhD(biochem), 53. *Prof Exp:* Sr biochemist, 53-73, RES SCIENTIST, ELI LILLY & CO, 73- *Res:* Purification process research in antibiotics; chemical analysis and paper chromatography of antibiotics and related materials. *Mailing Add:* Antibiotics Develop Dept Eli Lilly & Co Indianapolis IN 46206

WILD, JACK WILLIAM, b Woonsocket, SDak, June 8, 23; m 45; c 2. PHYSICS. *Educ:* SDak State Col, BS, 48; Univ Kans, MS & PhD(physics), 52. *Prof Exp:* Asst, Univ Kans, 48-52; physicist, Nat Bur Stand, 52-53; proj leader, Diamond Ord Fuze Labs, 53-54; mgr br off, Frederick Res Corp, 54-56; sr engr, Cook Res Labs, 56-57, staff engr, 57-61; adv engr, Westinghouse Elec Corp, 61-63, dir space systs, 63-67, mgr space sci, 67; prin engr, Hq, NASA, 67-68, dir mission planning & opers, 68-70, dir advan prog studies, 70-76, chief, 76-80, DEP DIR, SPACE SHUTTLE UPPER STAGES DIV, HQ, NASA, 81- *Honors & Awards:* Exceptional Service Award, NASA, 76. *Mem:* Sigma Xi. *Res:* Effect of external treatments on electret charges; contact electrification of dusts; aircraft cockpit and space systems instrumentation; space systems integration. *Mailing Add:* 16630 Emory Lane Rockville MD 20853

WILD, JAMES ROBERT, b Sedalia, Mo, Nov 24, 45. MOLECULAR BIOLOGY. *Educ:* Univ Calif, Davis, BA, 67; Univ Calif, Riverside, PhD(biol), 71. *Prof Exp:* Res biochemist, Univ Calif, Riverside, 72; microbiologist, Naval Med Res Inst, Nat Naval Med Ctr, 72-75; asst prof genetics, 75-80, ASSOC PROF BIOCHEM & GENETICS, TEX A&M UNIV, 80- *Mem:* Am Soc Microbiol; Genetics Soc Am; Environ Mutagen Soc; Sigma Xi; Fedn Am Scientists. *Res:* Pyrimidine biosynthesis; nucleotide biosynthesis; regulation of gene expression. *Mailing Add:* Genetics Div Tex A&M Univ Plant Sci Dept College Station TX 77843

WILD, JOHN FREDERICK, b Erie, Pa, June 20, 42; m 66; c 2. NUCLEAR CHEMISTRY. *Educ:* Pa State Univ, BS, 64; Mass Inst Technol, PhD(nuclear chem), 68. *Prof Exp:* Res chemist, Knolls Atomic Power Lab, 68-69; RES CHEMIST, LAWRENCE LIVERMORE LAB, 69- *Mem:* Am Chem Soc. *Res:* Nuclear chemistry with emphasis on decay and chemical properties of isotopes of elements above Z 96. *Mailing Add:* Lawrence Livermore Lab Livermore CA 94550

WILD, JOHN FREDERICK, b Wallingford, Conn, Nov 30, 26; m 65; c 3. PHYSICS. *Educ:* Yale Univ, BS, 50, MS, 51, PhD(physics), 58. *Prof Exp:* From instr to asst prof physics, Trinity Col, Conn, 57-62; asst prof, 62-67, ASSOC PROF PHYSICS, WORCESTER POLYTECH INST, 67- *Mem:* Am Phys Soc; Am Asn Physics Teachers. *Res:* Wave functions for valence electron of neutral caesium for Fermi-Thomas central field; quantum mechanics; color vision; Foucault knife-edge test; tuned percussion instruments; solar heating. *Mailing Add:* Physics Dept Worcester Polytech Inst Worcester MA 01609

WILD, JOHN JULIAN, b Syndenham, Eng, Aug 11, 14; US citizen; m 68; c 3. CLINICAL MEDICINE, ULTRASOUND. *Educ:* Cambridge Univ, BA, 36, MA, 40, MB, BChir, 42, PhD(investigative med), 71. *Prof Exp:* Res assoc, Dept Surg, Univ Minn, 46-51, res assoc med diag ultrasound, Dept Elec Eng, 51-53; dir res, St Barnabas Hosp, Minneapolis, 53-60; dir medico-technol res unit, Minn Found, St Paul, 60-63; DIR MED DIAG ULTRASOUND, MEDICO-TECHNOL RES INST, MINNEAPOLIS, 65- *Concurrent Pos:* Res fel, Marion Ordway Found, St Paul, 46-47 & USPHS, 47-49; prin investr, Nat Adv Cancer Coun, 50-60, Nat Heart Inst, 57-60 & Gen Med Sci Div, 62-63. *Honors & Awards:* Pioneer Award, Am Inst Ultrasound Med, 78. *Mem:* Fel Am Inst Ultrasound Med; AMA. *Res:* Clinical research; physical detection of disease and deteriorative processes; originated ultrasonic pulse-echo tissue characterization, cancer detection and diagnosis of the breast and colon; originated pulse-echo measurement of biological tissues. *Mailing Add:* Medico-Technol Res Inst #1100 E 36th St Minneapolis MN 50407

WILD, ROBERT LEE, b Sedalia, Mo, Oct 9, 21; m 43; c 3. SOLID STATE PHYSICS. *Educ:* Cent Mo State Col, BS, 43; Univ Mo, MA, 48, PhD(physics), 50. *Prof Exp:* Asst instr physics, Univ Mo, 49; asst prof, Univ NDak, 50-53; from asst prof to assoc prof, 53-63, chmn dept, 63-68, PROF PHYSICS, UNIV CALIF, RIVERSIDE, 63- *Concurrent Pos:* NSF fel, Univ Ill, 59-60; vis prof, Tech Univ Denmark, 67-68 & Univ Münster, 75. *Mem:* Am Phys Soc; Am Asn Physics Teachers; Sigma Xi. *Res:* Small angle x-ray scattering by liquids and solids; optical and transport properties of solids. *Mailing Add:* Dept of Physics Univ of Calif Riverside CA 92502

WILD, WAYNE GRANT, b Waterville, Kans, Aug 9, 17; m 39; c 4. PHYSICS, MATHEMATICS. *Educ:* SDak State Univ, BS, 40; Univ Wis, MS, 48; Univ Ill, MA, 67. *Prof Exp:* Prof physics & head dept, Buena Vista Col, 48-67, chmn natural sci div, 53-67; assoc prof physics, 67-69, ASSOC PROF MATH, UNIV WIS-STEVENS POINT, 69- *Mem:* Sigma Xi; Am Math Asn. *Res:* Thermionic emission. *Mailing Add:* Dept of Math Univ of Wis Stevens Point WI 54481

WILDASIN, HARRY LEWIS, b York Co, Pa, Oct 10, 23; m 45, 70; c 2. BIOCHEMISTRY. *Educ:* Pa State Univ, PhD(dairy), 50. *Prof Exp:* Asst prof dairying, Univ Conn, 49-52; dir qual control, Whiting Milk Co, Boston, 52-57; DIR QUAL CONTROL & GOVT RELS, H P HOOD, INC, BOSTON, 57- *Mem:* AAAS; Am Dairy Sci Asn; NY Acad Sci; Nat Environ Health Asn; Am Pub Health Asn. *Res:* Frozen milk; lactose; milk proteins; surface active agents; antibiotics; salmonella; radioactive elements in milk. *Mailing Add:* 23 Oxbow Rd Lexington MA 02173

WILDBERGER, WILLIAM CAMPBELL, b Boston, Mass, Dec 8, 14; m 42; c 2. MEDICAL ADMINISTRATION, PSYCHIATRY. *Educ:* Boston Univ, BS, 37, MD, 40. *Prof Exp:* Mem pract group med, Perry Clin, 46-50; clin dir pediat & psychiat, Woodward State Hosp-Sch, 58-61, actg supt admin & psychiat, 61-63, supt psychiat admin, 63-69; CHIEF ADMITTING, VET ADMIN HOSP, DES MOINES, 69- *Concurrent Pos:* Mem, White House Conf on Ment Retardation, 62. *Mem:* Fel Am Asn Ment Deficiency; AMA; Am Hosp Asn; Am Psychiat Asn. *Res:* Child psychiatry, pediatrics and administration in mental retardation. *Mailing Add:* 2118 Second St PO Box 357 Perry IA 50220

WILDE, ANTHONY FLORY, b New York, NY, May 16, 30; m 72. PHYSICAL CHEMISTRY. *Educ:* Yale Univ, BS, 52; Ind Univ, PhD(phys chem), 59. *Prof Exp:* Res chemist, Monsanto Res Corp, 59-63; res chemist, US Army Natick Labs, 63-68, RES CHEMIST, ARMY MAT & MECH RES CTR, 68- *Mem:* Am Chem Soc; Soc Exp Stress Anal; NY Acad Sci. *Res:* Polymer rheology, especially dynamic mechanical and optical properties of organic polymers and elastomers; stress wave propagation, fracture and energy dissipation in materials; dielectric and piezoelectric properties of organic polymers; sorption and diffusion of liquids in polymers. *Mailing Add:* Org Mat Lab Army Mat & Mech Res Ctr Watertown MA 02172

WILDE, CARROLL ORVILLE, b Elmhurst, Ill, June 5, 32; m 52, 71; c 4. MATHEMATICS. *Educ:* Ill State Univ, BS, 58; Univ Ill, Urbana, PhD(math), 64. *Prof Exp:* Instr math, SDak Sch Mines & Technol, 58-59 & Col Wooster, 59-61; asst prof, Univ Minn, Minneapolis, 64-68; assoc prof, 68-75, PROF MATH, NAVAL POSTGRAD SCH, 75-, CHMN DEPT, 76- *Concurrent Pos:* Vis prof, US Mil Acad, West Point, 79-80. *Mem:* Am Math Soc; Math Asn Am; Sigma Xi; Soc Indust Appld Math. *Res:* Functional analysis; digital image processing; scientific computation. *Mailing Add:* Dept of Math Naval Postgrad Sch Monterey CA 93940

WILDE, CHARLES EDWARD, JR, b Boston, Mass, Nov 5, 18; m 44; c 3. BIOLOGY. *Educ:* Dartmouth Col, AB, 40; Princeton Univ, MA, 47, PhD(biol), 49. *Hon Degrees:* MA, Univ Pa, 72. *Prof Exp:* Instr zool, Dartmouth Col, 40-41 & Princeton Univ, 46-49; from asst prof to prof zool, Sch Dent Med, Univ Pa, 49-75, prof embryol, Dept Biol & Dept Path, 57-75; PROF ZOOL, UNIV RI, 75-, CHMN DEPT, 75- *Concurrent Pos:* Guggenheim Mem Found fel, 57-58; guest investr, Strangeways Res Lab, Cambridge Univ, 57-58; consult, Dept Animal Genetics, Univ Edinburgh, 57; trustee, Mt Desert Island Biol Lab, dir, 67-70, pres, 77- *Mem:* AAAS; Am Soc Zoologists; Soc Develop Biol; Soc Cell Biol; Int Inst Embryol. *Res:* Differentiation of organs in vitro; tissue culture; metabolite control of cell differentiation; embryology of the head; cytochimeras of muscle; temporal relations of energy flow; RNA and protein synthesis in morphogenesis and differentiation; molecular and genomic control of symmetry in embryogenesis; the ontogeny of euryhalinity. *Mailing Add:* Dept of Zool Univ of RI Kingston RI 02881

WILDE, D(OUGLASS) J(AMES), b Chicago, Ill, Aug 1, 29; m 56; c 1. OPTIMIZATION, COMPUTER GRAPHICS. *Educ:* Carnegie Inst Technol, BS, 48; Univ Wash, MS, 56; Univ Calif, PhD, 60. *Prof Exp:* Chem engr, Pittsburgh Coke & Chem Co, 48-50 & Union Oil Co, 54-56; asst, Univ Calif, 57-58, instr chem eng, 58-59, lectr, 59-60; Fulbright lectr, Ecole Nat Superieure Indust Chimiques, 60-61; asst prof, Univ Tex, 61-62; assoc prof, 63-67, prof chem eng, 67-72, assoc dean 78-80, PROF MECH ENG DESIGN, STANFORD UNIV, 72- *Concurrent Pos:* Vis assoc prof, Yale Univ, 63. *Honors & Awards:* Lanchester Prize, Opers Res Soc Am, 68; Maynard Prize, Am Inst Indust Engrs. *Mem:* Am Soc Mech Engrs. *Res:* Optimization theory; optimal design. *Mailing Add:* Dept Mech Eng Stanford Univ Stanford CA 94305

WILDE, GARNER LEE, b Spring Creek, Tex, Sept 29, 26; m 51; c 2. GEOLOGY. *Educ:* Tex Christian Univ, BA, 50, MA, 52. *Hon Degrees:* DSc, Tex Christian Univ, 76. *Prof Exp:* Jr geologist, Humble Oil & Refining Co, Exxon Co, USA, 52-53, from assoc paleontologist to paleontologist, 53-63, sr res geologist, 63-67, prof geologist, 67-71, prof geologist, Hq Staff, 71-76, sr explor geologist, 76-81; MGR, EXPLOR DIV, PERMIAN BASIN, HARPER OIL CO, 81- *Concurrent Pos:* Lectr, Case Western Reserve Univ, 63; vis lectr, Tex Tech Univ, 67, 78 & Univ Mo, 69; mem bd dirs, Cushman Found Foraminiferal Res, 70-75, pres, 74-75; vis lectr, Kans State Univ, 71 & Rensselaer Polytech Inst, 71; adj prof geol, Tex Christian Univ, 76- *Mem:* Fel Geol Soc Am; Soc Econ Paleontologists & Mineralogists; Am Asn Petrol Geologists. *Res:* Stratigraphic and paleontological studies on late Paleozoic Fusulinid Foraminifera, Calcareous algae and Mesozoic Calcareous Nannofossils. *Mailing Add:* PO Box 1600 Midland TX 79701

WILDE, GERALD ELDON, b Ballinger, Tex, Dec 7, 39. ENTOMOLOGY. *Educ:* Tex Tech Col, BS, 62; Cornell Univ, PhD(entom), 66. *Prof Exp:* Res asst entom, Cornell Univ, 62-66; ASSOC PROF ENTOM & RES ENTOMOLOGIST AGR RES STA, KANS STATE UNIV, 66- *Mem:* Entom Soc Am. *Res:* Economic entomology; field crops insects. *Mailing Add:* Dept of Entom Kans State Univ Manhattan KS 66506

WILDE, KENNETH ALFRED, b Cedar City, Utah, Mar 4, 29; m 61; c 2. PHYSICAL CHEMISTRY. *Educ:* Univ Utah, BS, 50, PhD(chem), 53. *Prof Exp:* Res chemist, Redstone Res Labs, Rohm and Haas Co, 53-70, res chemist, Res Div, 70-75; sr scientist, Radian Corp, 75-78; CONSULT, 78- *Mem:* Am Chem Soc. *Res:* Chemical kinetics in electric discharges; combustion wave theory; high temperature thermodynamics and kinetics; aerothermodynamics; mass transfer process simulation; solution thermodynamics and process simulation. *Mailing Add:* 3604 Laurel Lodge Lane Austin TX 78731

WILDE, PAT, b Chicago, Ill, Sept 25, 35. OCEANOGRAPHY. *Educ:* Yale Univ, BS, 57; Harvard Univ, AM, 61, PhD(geol), 65. *Prof Exp:* Geologist, Shell Oil Co, 57-59; res geologist, Scripps Inst Oceanog, 60-62; lectr ocean eng, Univ Calif, Berkeley, 64-68, asst prof, 68-75, res oceanogr, 66-75, res engr, 64-66; res scientist & oceanogr, Lawrence Berkeley Lab, 75-77, RES SCIENTIST, INST MARINE RESOURCES, UNIV CALIF, BERKELEY, 77- *Concurrent Pos:* Consult, Coastal Res Panel Earthquake Eng, Nat Acad Eng, 65-67; adv tech adv bd, Dept Eng, City & County of San Francisco, 70- *Mem:* AAAS; Geol Soc Am; Am Geophys Union; Marine Technol Soc; Geochem Soc. *Res:* Marine electrochemistry; sediment transport in marine environments. *Mailing Add:* Inst of Marine Resources Univ of Calif Berkeley CA 94720

WILDE, RICHARD EDWARD, JR, b Los Angeles, Calif, Jan 7, 31; m 60; c 3. VIBRATIONAL RELAXATION, HETEROGENEOUS PHOTOCATALYSIS. *Educ:* Univ Calif, Los Angeles, BS, 56; Univ Wash, PhD(chem), 61. *Prof Exp:* Res assoc, Johns Hopkins Univ, 61-63; asst prof chem, 63-67, assoc prof, 67-79, PROF CHEM, TEX TECH UNIV, 79- *Mem:* Am Chem Soc; Am Phys Soc; The Chem Soc. *Res:* Infrared and Raman spectroscopy of nonmetal hydrides; vibrational relaxation in liquids and solids; heterogeneous photocatalysis. *Mailing Add:* Dept of Chem Tex Tech Univ Lubbock TX 79409

WILDE, WALTER SAMUEL, b Toronto, Ont, Feb 12, 09; US citizen; m 36; c 3. MEDICAL PHYSIOLOGY. *Educ:* Miami Univ, AB, 31; Univ Minn, MA, 33, PhD(zool), 37. *Prof Exp:* Asst zool & physiol, Univ Minn, 31-33; instr zool, Miami Univ, 33-34; asst zool & physiol, Univ Minn, 34-37; teaching fel physiol, Univ Rochester, 37-38; instr zool, Univ Wyo, 38-39; from instr to asst prof physiol, Sch Med, La State Univ, 39-45; res assoc, Carnegie Inst, 45-47; sr physiologist, NIH, 47; from assoc prof to prof physiol, Tulane Univ, 47-56; prof, 56-75, EMER PROF PHYSIOL, UNIV MICH, ANN ARBOR, 75- *Concurrent Pos:* Guest lectr, Mt Desert Island Biol Lab, 56. *Mem:* Fel AAAS; fel Soc Exp Biol & Med; fel Am Physiol Soc. *Res:* Interstitial and capillary albumin; ion transport and kidney; renal stop flow method; blood-brain barrier and aqueous humor. *Mailing Add:* 151 Bayview Ave Naples FL 33940

WILDEMAN, THOMAS RAYMOND, b Madison, Wis, May 11, 40; m 65; c 2. ANALYTICAL CHEMISTRY, GEOCHEMISTRY. *Educ:* Col St Thomas, BS, 62; Univ Wis, PhD(phys chem), 67. *Prof Exp:* Lectr chem, Univ Wis, 66-67; asst prof, 67-73, assoc prof, 73-79, PROF CHEM, COLO SCH MINES, 79- *Concurrent Pos:* Consult, US Geol Surv, 70- *Mem:* AAAS; Am Chem Soc; Geochem Soc. *Res:* Properties of trace elements in inorganic solids; isotopic, radiochemical and atomic absorption analysis; geochemistry of trace elements in rocks and waters. *Mailing Add:* Dept of Chem Colo Sch of Mines Golden CO 80401

WILDENTHAL, BRYAN HOBSON, b San Marcos, Tex, Nov 4, 37; c 3. PHYSICS. *Educ:* Sul Ross State Col, BA, 58; Univ Kans, PhD(physics), 64. *Prof Exp:* Res assoc physics, Rice Univ, 64-66; US Atomic Energy Comn fel, Oak Ridge Nat Lab, 66-68; asst prof, Tex A&M Univ, 68-69; assoc prof, 69-72, PROF PHYSICS, MICH STATE UNIV, 72- *Concurrent Pos:* Sr US fel, Humboldt Found, Univ Munich, 73; vis scientist, Brookhaven Nat Lab, 74, Max Planck Inst Nuclear Physics, Heidelberg, 76, Gesellschaft für Schwereionforschung, Darmstadt, 77; vis prof, Univ Paris, 77; fel, John Simon Guggenheim Mem Found, 77; prog assoc, physics div, NSF, 78. *Mem:* Am Phys Soc; Sigma Xi. *Res:* Study of the low lying quantum states of atomic nuclei via direct reaction experiments and shell model theory. *Mailing Add:* Cyclotron Lab Mich State Univ East Lansing MI 48824

WILDENTHAL, KERN, b San Marcos, Tex, July 1, 41; m 64; c 2. PHYSIOLOGY, INTERNAL MEDICINE. *Educ:* Sul Ross Col, BA, 60; Univ Tex Southwestern Med Sch Dallas, MD, 64; Cambridge Univ, PhD(cell physiol), 70. *Prof Exp:* Intern, Bellevue Hosp-NY Univ, 64-65; resident, Parkland Hosp-Univ Tex Southwestern Med Sch Dallas, 65-66; vis scientist, Strangeways Res Lab, Cambridge Univ, 68-70; from asst prof to prof physiol & internal med, 70-75, dean, Grad Sch Biomed Sci, 76-80, PROF INTERNAL MED & PHYSIOL & DEAN, SOUTHWESTERN MED SCH, UNIV TEX HEALTH SCI CTR DALLAS, 80- *Concurrent Pos:* Guggenheim Found fel, Univ Cambridge, Eng, 75-76. *Mem:* Am Soc Clin Invest; Int Soc Heart Res; Royal Soc Med, Gt Brit; Am Physiol Soc; Am Col Cardiol. *Res:* Cardiac physiology and metabolism. *Mailing Add:* Off of Dean Univ of Tex Health Sci Ctr Dallas TX 75235

WILDER, CLEO DUKE, JR, b Macon, Ga, Sept 24, 25; m 50; c 2. VERTEBRATE ZOOLOGY. *Educ:* Univ NC, AB, 48; Univ Tenn, MS, 51; Univ Fla, PhD, 62. *Prof Exp:* Instr biol, Presby Col, SC, 51-53; asst, Univ Fla, 55-57 & 58-59; asst prof, Memphis State Univ, 59-62; asst zool, Va Polytech Inst, 62-69; ASSOC PROF BIOL, MURRAY STATE UNIV, 69- *Mem:* Am Soc Ichthyologists & Herpetologists; Am Soc Mammal; Soc Study Amphibians & Reptiles; Animal Behav Soc; Herpetologists' League. *Res:* Taxonomy, ecology, distribution, behavior and evolution of amphibians, reptiles and mammals; aggression in vertebrates; ecology of stream drainage systems in western Kentucky. *Mailing Add:* Dept of Biol Murray State Univ Murray KY 42071

WILDER, DAVID RANDOLPH, b Lorimor, Iowa, June 11, 29; m 51; c 4. CERAMIC ENGINEERING, METALLURGY. *Educ:* Iowa State Univ, BS, 51, MS, 52, PhD(ceramic eng), 58. *Prof Exp:* Jr ceramic engr, Ames Lab, Iowa State Univ, 52-55, ceramic engr, 55-57, res assoc, 57-58, engr, 58-61, sr engr, 61-66, div chief, Ceramic & Mech Eng Div, 66-73, instr ceramic eng, Iowa State Univ, 55-57, from asst prof to assoc prof, 57-61, chmn dept ceramic eng, 61-64, head dept, 64-75, sr engr, Ames Lab, Dept Energy, 73-81, PROF CERAMIC ENG, IOWA STATE UNIV, 61-, CHMN DEPT MAT SCI & ENG, 75- *Mem:* Am Soc Eng Educ; fel Am Ceramic Soc; Nat Inst Ceramic Engrs. *Res:* High temperature properties and processing of ceramic materials. *Mailing Add:* Dept of Mat Sci & Eng Iowa State Univ Ames IA 50011

WILDER, DONALD RICHARD, b Kodaikanal, SIndia, Apr 20, 32; US citizen; m 56; c 3. MATHEMATICS, OPTICS. *Educ:* Oberlin Col, BA, 53; Univ Rochester, MS, 64. *Prof Exp:* With apparatus & optical div, 53-54, 57-60, res physicist, 60-67, SR RES PHYSICIST, RES LABS, EASTMAN

KODAK CO, 67- *Mem:* AAAS; Optical Soc Am; Math Asn Am; Soc Photog Sci & Eng. *Res:* Geometrical optics; theory of Hamilton's characteristic functions as applied to lens design. *Mailing Add:* Eastman Kodak Co Res Labs 1669 Lake Ave Rochester NY 14650

WILDER, HARRY D(OUGLAS), b Westfield, Wis, Aug 22, 32; m 59; c 5. PULP & PAPER SCIENCE, CHEMICAL ENGINEERING. *Educ:* Univ Wis, BS, 55; Inst Paper Chem, MS, 57, PhD, 60. *Prof Exp:* Res aide chem eng, Inst Paper Chem, 59-65; asst dir res & develop, Albemarle Paper Co, Va, 66, dir, 67-68; dir pulp & paper res, Ethyl Corp, 68-76; sr sci assoc, 77-79, CHIEF RES, ASSOC SCOTT PAPER CO, 79- *Mem:* Am Inst Chem Engrs; Tech Asn Pulp & Paper Indust. *Res:* Pulping methods and rates; pulp bleaching; pulping and bleaching chemical generation; pulping research; fiber properties research. *Mailing Add:* Scott Paper Co Scott Plaza Philadelphia PA 19113

WILDER, JAMES ANDREW, JR, b Washingtin, DC, Dec 19, 50; m 73. MATERIALS SCIENCE, GLASS SCIENCE. *Educ:* Cath Univ Am, BSE, 73, MSE, 75, Phd(mat sci), 78. *Prof Exp:* MEM STAFF GLASS CERAMIC RES, SANDIA LABS, 78- *Mem:* Am Ceramic Soc. *Res:* Phase separation and crystallization in glass; glass-to-metal sealing. *Mailing Add:* Sandia Labs Div 5845 Albuquerque NM 87115

WILDER, JOSEPH R, b Baltimore, Md, Oct 5, 20; c 5. SURGERY. *Educ:* Dartmouth Col, BS, 42; Columbia Univ, MD, 45. *Prof Exp:* Chief & dir, Surg Serv, Wright Patterson Hosp, 52-54; fel cardiovasc res, Karolinska Inst, Sweden, 54-55; asst prof surg, New York Med Col, 55-58; dir gen surg, Hosp Joint Dis & Med Ctr, 59-80; PROF SURG, MT SINAI SCH MED, 67- *Concurrent Pos:* Med adv, NY State Legislature, 65-75; examiner, Am Bd Surg, 70-75; consult, US Off Economic Opportunity, 75-80. *Mem:* Am Bd Surg; Fel Am Col Surgeons; Am Med Asn. *Res:* Selective surgical intervention in management of penetrating wounds of the abdomen. *Mailing Add:* 1212 Fifth Ave New York NY 10029

WILDER, MARTIN STUART, b Brooklyn, NY, May 20, 37; m 64; c 1. MICROBIOLOGY. *Educ:* Brooklyn Col, BS, 60; Univ Kans, MA, 63, PhD(microbiol), 66. *Prof Exp:* Res aide microbiol, Sloan-Kettering Inst Cancer Res, 60-61; Nat Acad Sci-Nat Res Coun res assoc, Microbiol Div, US Dept Army, 66-68; asst prof microbiol, 68-74, ASSOC PROF MICROBIOL, UNIV MASS, AMHERST, 74- *Concurrent Pos:* Nat Acad Sci grant, 74. *Mem:* Am Soc Microbiol; Reticuloendothelial Soc; NY Acad Sci. *Res:* Pathogenesis and pathology of infectious diseases; interactions of platelets, bacteria and leukocytes. *Mailing Add:* Dept of Microbiol Univ of Mass Amherst MA 01003

WILDER, PELHAM, JR, b Americus, Ga, July 20, 20; m 45; c 3. ORGANIC CHEMISTRY. *Educ:* Emory Univ, AB, 42, MA, 43; Harvard Univ, MA, 47, PhD(org chem), 50. *Prof Exp:* From instr to prof chem, 49-68, PROF CHEM & PHARMACOL, DUKE UNIV, 68- *Concurrent Pos:* Consult, NSF, 60-68, E I du Pont de Nemours & Co, Inc, 66-69 & Res Triangle Inst, 68-; Gov Sci Adv Comt, 62-64; mem advan placement chem comt, Col Entrance Exam Bd, 68-74, chmn, 69-74, mem advan placement standing comt, 69-72; assoc, Comt Prof Training, Am Chem Soc. *Mem:* Am Chem Soc. *Res:* Stereochemical studies; kinetic, thermodynamic control and mechanism of organic reactions; quantitative structure-activity relationship studies in pharmacology. *Mailing Add:* Dept of Chem Duke Univ Durham NC 27706

WILDER, RAYMOND LOUIS, b Palmer, Mass, Nov 3, 96; m 21; c 4. MATHEMATICS. *Educ:* Brown Univ, PhB, 20, MS, 21; Univ Tex, PhD(math), 23. *Hon Degrees:* DSc, Bucknell Univ, 55 & Brown Univ, 58; LLD, Univ Mich, 80. *Prof Exp:* Asst math, Brown Univ, 20-21; instr, Univ Tex, 21-24; asst prof, Ohio State Univ, 24-26; from asst prof to prof, 26-47, res prof, 47-67, EMER PROF MATH, UNIV MICH, ANN ARBOR, 67-; RES ASSOC, UNIV CALIF, SANTA BARBARA, 69- *Concurrent Pos:* Researcher, Inst Advan Study, 33-34; Guggenheim fel, Univ Tex, 40-41; vis prof, Univ Southern Calif, 47; res assoc, Calif Inst Technol, 49-50; Taft Mem lectr, Univ Cincinnati, 58 & 78; vis res prof, Fla State Univ, 61-62; mem comt sci & pub policy, Nat Acad Sci, 65-67. *Honors & Awards:* Lester R Ford Award & Distinguished Serv Award, Math Asn Am, 73. *Mem:* Nat Acad Sci; AAAS (vpres math sect, 48); Am Math Soc (vpres, 50, pres, 55-56); Am Math Asn (pres, 65-66); Am Anthrop Asn. *Res:* Cultural anthropology; culturological evolution of mathematics. *Mailing Add:* Dept of Math Univ of Calif Santa Barbara CA 93106

WILDER, RUSSELL MORSE, medicine, psychiatry, see previous edition

WILDER, THOMAS C(UNNINGHAM), metallurgy, electrochemistry, see previous edition

WILDER, VIOLET MYRTLE, b Granville, Iowa, Apr 8, 08. BIOCHEMISTRY. *Educ:* Univ Nebr, BA, 28, MA, 34, PhD(biochem), 38. *Prof Exp:* Res chemist, Dr G A Young, Omaha, 38-40; instr biochem, Univ Ark, 40; dir, Lab Maternal & Child Health, Univ Nebr, 40-43 & 46-47; instr physiol chem, Woman's Med Col Pa, 43-46; from asst prof to assoc prof, 47-73, ASSOC PROF BIOCHEM, COL MED, UNIV NEBR MED CTR, OMAHA, 73- *Mem:* AAAS; Am Chem Soc; fel Am Asn Clin Chem. *Res:* Enzyme-hormone relationships; clinical chemistry. *Mailing Add:* 2045 S 18th St Lincoln NE 68502

WILDES, PETER DRURY, b Fall River, Mass, Feb 27, 45; m 68; c 2. PHOTOCHEMISTRY, SOLAR ENERGY. *Educ:* Rice Univ, BA, 66; Univ NC, Chapel Hill, PhD(org chem), 71. *Prof Exp:* Res assoc chem, Johns Hopkins Univ, 71-73; sr res assoc, Boston Univ, 73-78; sr res engr, 78-80, SR RES SCIENTIST, ARCO-SOLAR INC, 80- *Concurrent Pos:* Asst prof chem, Boston Univ, 77-78. *Mem:* Am Chem Soc; Inter-Am Photochem Soc. *Res:* Development of solar energy; luminescent materials. *Mailing Add:* ARCO-Solar Inc 20554 Plummer St Chatsworth CA 91311

WILDEY, ROBERT LEROY, b Los Angeles, Calif, Aug 22, 34; m 59; c 3. ASTRONOMY, ASTROPHYSICS. *Educ:* Calif Inst Technol, BS, 57, MS, 58, PhD(astron), 62. *Prof Exp:* Res engr, Jet Propulsion Lab, Calif Inst Technol, 59-60, res fel & lectr astron & geol, Mt Wilson & Palomar Observ & div geol sci, Calif Inst Technol, 62-65, astronr & astrophysicist, Ctr Astrogeol, Us Geol Serv, 65-72; assoc prof, 72-80, PROF ASTROPHYS & ASTRON, NORTHERN ARIZ UNIV, 80- *Concurrent Pos:* Consult, United Electrodynamics Corp, 62-63, Aeronutronics Div, Ford Motor Co, 63-64, World Book Encycl Sci Serv, 63-64 & US Geol Surv, 72-; vis prof, Univ Calif, Berkeley, 66; mem planetary astron panel, Space Sci Bd, Nat Acad Sci, 67- *Mem:* Am Astron Soc; Am Geophys Union; fel Geol Soc Am; Int Astron Union; fel Royal Astron Soc. *Res:* infrared studies substantiating Jupiter as a star; first mapping of the Moon in Heiligenschein magnitude; Apollo and Mariner-Mars experimenter; gravitation and cosmology; photoclinometry; automated digital photogrammetry and photoclinometry; radiative transfer theory; synthetic aperture radar signal processing. *Mailing Add:* Observ for Astron & Astrophys Northern Ariz Univ Flagstaff AZ 86001

WILDFEUER, MARVIN EMANUEL, b Bronx, NY, Apr 16, 36; m 67; c 2. FERMENTATION PRODUCTS, ANTIBIOTIC PURIFICATION DEVELOPMENT. *Educ:* Queen's Col, NY, BS, 57; Iowa State Univ, MS, 59; Univ Del, PhD(chem), 63. *Prof Exp:* NIH fel molecular biol, Univ Calif, San Diego, 63-65; res scientist, Sansum Clin & Res Found, 65-67; sr chemist, 68-80, RES SCIENTIST, ELI LILLY & CO, 80- *Mem:* Am Chem Soc. *Res:* Responsible for production scale antibiotic purification technology, especially macrolide, beta-lactam and polyether antibiotics; development of new isolation procedures from fermentation broth; antibiotic derivatization. *Mailing Add:* Dept TL969 Eli Lilly & Co Lafayette IN 47902

WILDI, BERNARD SYLVESTER, b Columbus, Ohio, May 23, 20. ORGANIC CHEMISTRY. *Educ:* Ohio State Univ, BSc, 43, PhD(org chem), 48. *Prof Exp:* Res chemist, Nat Defense Res Comt, Ohio State Univ, 43-44 & Manhattan Proj, Los Alamos Sci Lab, NMex, 44-47; Nat Res Coun fel, Harvard Univ, 48-49; mem fac, Fla State Univ, 49-50; mem staff, 50-53, group leader, 53-65, mgr life sci, 65-69, DISTINGUISHED SCI FEL, MONSANTO CO, 69- *Mem:* AAAS; Am Chem Soc. *Res:* Structure of natural products; chemical spectroscopy; organic synthesis. *Mailing Add:* 1234 Folger Kirkwood MO 63122

WILDIN, MAURICE W(ILBERT), b Hutchinson, Kans, June 24, 35; m 58; c 2. MECHANICAL ENGINEERING, HEAT TRANSFER. *Educ:* Univ Kans, BSME, 58; Purdue Univ, MS, 59, PhD(mech eng), 63. *Prof Exp:* From asst prof to assoc prof mech eng, 61-72, grad adv, 66-67, chmn dept, 69-73, PROF MECH ENG, UNIV NEW MEX, 72-, GRAD ADV, 82- *Mem:* Am Soc Heating Refrigeration & Air Conditioning Engrs; Am Soc Mech Engrs. *Res:* Radiative heat transfer from solid bodies, including directional and spectral effects; conduction heat transfer. *Mailing Add:* 720 Montclaire Dr NE Albuquerque NM 87110

WILDING, LAWRENCE PAUL, b Winner, SDak, Oct 1, 34; m 56; c 4. SOIL SCIENCE, AGRONOMY. *Educ:* SDak State Univ, BSc, 56, MSc, 59; Univ Ill, PhD(soils), 62. *Prof Exp:* Asst agron, SDak State Univ, 56-59; Campbell Soup Co fel plant sci, 59-62; from asst prof to prof agron, Ohio State Univ, 62-76; PROF AGRON, TEX A&M UNIV, 76- *Concurrent Pos:* Fel, Univ Guelph, 72. *Mem:* Fel Am Soc Agron; Soil Sci Soc Am; Int Soc Soil Sci; Clay Minerals Soc; Soil Conserv Soc Am. *Res:* Soil classification and genesis among different climatic, chronologic and topographic sequences; origin, depth distributions, properties and radiocarbon age of soil opal phytoliths; statistical variability in soil physical and chemical parameters; clay mineralogy; sediment mineralogy and soil erosion; microfabric and micropedology of soil habitats. *Mailing Add:* Dept Soil & Crop Sci Tex A&M Univ College Station TX 77843

WILDING, MORRIS DEAN, b Sugar, Idaho, June 15, 28; m 51; c 7. BIOCHEMISTRY, FOOD SCIENCE. *Educ:* Utah State Univ, BS, 52, MS, 56; Univ Wis, PhD(biochem), 59. *Prof Exp:* Res chemist veg oil & protein foods, Swift & Co, 59-63, dept head veg protein, 63-67, res mgr, 67-74, int proj res veg & food protein prod, 67-70, food consult, 75; RES MGR, KRAFT INC, 75- *Concurrent Pos:* Agency Int Develop grants, 67, 69 & 74. *Mem:* Am Cereal Chemists; Inst Food Technologists; Am Chem Soc; Food Protein Coun; Am Asn Oil Chemists. *Res:* Vegetable protein food products and processes; protein nutrition; food product development; international food development. *Mailing Add:* Kraft Inc 801 Waukegan Rd Glenview IL 60025

WILDMAN, GARY CECIL, b Middlefield, Ohio, Nov 25, 42; m 65; c 2. POLYMER CHEMISTRY. *Educ:* Thiel Col, AB, 64; Duke Univ, PhD(phys chem), 70. *Prof Exp:* Res chemist, Hercules Inc, 68-71; assoc prof polymer sci, 71-78, chmn dept, 71-75, PROF POLYMER SCI, UNIV SOUTHERN MISS, 78-, DEAN COL SCI & TECHNOL, 76- *Mem:* Am Chem Soc; Am Crystallog Asn; Sigma Xi; Fedn Socs Paint Technol; Soc Plastics Engrs. *Res:* Structure-property relationships of synthetic polymers; x-ray diffraction studies of single crystals and polymeric materials; surface coatings. *Mailing Add:* Univ of Southern Miss Box 5165 Southern Sta Hattiesburg MS 39406

WILDMAN, GEORGE THOMAS, b Grasmere, NH, Nov 14, 35. CHEMICAL ENGINEERING, ORGANIC CHEMISTRY. *Educ:* Univ NH, BS, 57; NY Univ, MS, 62; Mass Inst Technol, ScD(chem eng), 73. *Prof Exp:* Chem engr, Merck Sharp & Dohme Res Labs, 57-62, sr chem engr, 62-65, eng assoc chem eng, 65-68, res fel, 68-72, sect mgr, Chem Eng Res & Develop Dept, 72-77, tech serv mgr, 77-80, MFG MGR, MERCK & CO INC, 80- *Concurrent Pos:* Educ counr, Mass Inst Technol, 75- *Mem:* Am Inst Chem Engrs; Am Chem Soc. *Res:* Organic chemical process research and development; heterogeneous catalysis; oxidations; synthesis of heterocyclic compounds; antibiotic isolation; liquid ion exchange; coal liquefaction and gasification. *Mailing Add:* 2068 Old Raritan Rd Westfield NJ 07090

WILDMAN, PETER JAMES LACEY, b London, Eng, Sept 7, 36; m 63; c 1. SPACE PHYSICS, SENSORS. *Educ:* Univ Durham, Eng, BSc, 58, PhD(physics), 68. *Prof Exp:* Res physicist space physics, Air Force Geophys Lab, 68-79; MEM STAFF, BRIT AEROSPACE, ENGLAND, 79- *Mem:* Inst Physics (UK). *Res:* Instrumentation for electrical and optical measurements from space vehicles; investigation of processes in ionosphere and magnetosphere. *Mailing Add:* 32 Bannetts Tree Crescent Alveston Avon BS12 2LY England

WILDMAN, WILLIAM COOPER, organic chemistry, see previous edition

WILDMANN, MANFRED, b Karlesruhe, Ger, Apr 16, 30; US citizen; m 54; c 3. MECHANICAL ENGINEERING, COMPUTER SYSTEMS. *Educ:* City Col NY, BS, 54; Univ Calif, Los Angeles, MS, 57. *Prof Exp:* Res specialist inertial guidance, Autonetics Div, NAm Aviation, Inc, Calif, 54-62; mgr mech sect, Sunnyvale, 62-69, mgr Terabit Memory Systs Dept, 69-73, MGR RES DEPT, AMPEX CORP, REDWOOD CITY, 73- *Mem:* Am Soc Mech Engrs. *Res:* Lubrication, handling and control of flexible media; large computer memory systems; gas lubrication; foil bearing; inertial components. *Mailing Add:* Ampex Corp 401 Broadway Redwood City CA 94063

WILDMAN-SWENSON, RUTH BOWMAN, b Wilkes-Barre, Pa, July 16, 24; m 47, 80; c 2. AQUATIC BIOLOGY. *Educ:* Mt Holyoke Col, AB, 46; Univ Ill, Urbana, MS, 47; Iowa State Univ, PhD(cell biol, bot), 69. *Prof Exp:* Asst chemist, Ill Geol Survey, 47-49; res asst chem biochem, Univ Wis-Madison, 49-50; from asst prof to assoc prof bot, 69-77, PROF BOT, IOWA STATE UNIV, 77-, ASST DEAN COL SCI & HUMANITIES, 75- *Concurrent Pos:* Univ res grants, Iowa State Univ, 71-72 & 73-74; Iowa State Water Resources Res Inst grant, 72-78; dir, NSF Women in Sci Workshop, 77; mem bd trustees, Argonne Univ Asn, 77-80; mem, Iowa Comn, Am Coun Educ-Nat Indent Prog, 79. *Mem:* Am Soc Limnol Oceanog; Phycol Soc Am; Sigma Xi; Am Inst Biol Sci. *Res:* Role of blue-green algae in aquatic ecology; algal cytology and physiology; bioconcentration of chemical and energy-associated pollutants; effects of strip-mining on aquatic systems. *Mailing Add:* Dept Bot Iowa State Univ Ames IA 50011

WILDNAUER, RICHARD HARRY, b New Kensington, Pa, Feb 14, 40; m 66; c 1. DERMATOLOGY, PHARMACEUTICALS. *Educ:* St Vincent Col, BS, 62; WVa Univ, PhD(biochem), 66; Rider Col, MBA, 74. *Prof Exp:* Fel, Univ Kans, 66-67; sr scientist, Johnson & Johnson Res Labs, 67-73, sr group leader, 73-77; new prod dir, McNeil Pharmaceut, 77-79; DIR NEW PROD DEVELOP, JANSSEN PHARMACEUT, 79- *Mem:* NY Acad Sci; Soc Invest Dermat; Med Mycol Soc Am. *Res:* Enzyme kinetics and mechanisms; skin physiology and biochemistry; membrane transport properties; wound healing; physical polymer characterizations; medical mycology; pharmaceutical new product development. *Mailing Add:* New Prod Janssen Pharmaceut New Brunswick NJ 08903

WILDS, ALFRED LAWRENCE, b Kansas City, Mo, Mar 1, 15; m 37. ORGANIC CHEMISTRY. *Educ:* Univ Mich, BS, 36, MS, 37, PhD(org chem), 39. *Prof Exp:* Asst chem, Univ Mich, 37-39, DuPont fel, 39-40; from instr to assoc prof chem, 40-46, PROF CHEM, UNIV WIS-MADISON, 46- *Concurrent Pos:* Co-off investr, Nat Defense Res Comt, Univ Wis-Madison, 42-45; Guggenheim fel, 57. *Mem:* AAAS; Am Chem Soc; Royal Soc Chem; Swiss Chem Soc. *Res:* Modern organic synthesis; new methods, integrated syntheses, stereochemistry of catalytic hydrogenations, metal reductions; synthesis of natural products, steroids, hormone analogs; reactions of diazoketones; nuclear magnetic resonance studies. *Mailing Add:* Dept of Chem Univ of Wis Madison WI 53706

WILDS, PRESTON LEA, b Aiken, SC, Dec 18, 26; m 50, 63; c 4. OBSTETRICS & GYNECOLOGY. *Educ:* Yale Univ, BA, 49; Univ Pa, MD, 53; Am Bd Obstet & Gynec, dipl, 62. *Prof Exp:* Asst obstet & gynec, Sch Med, La State Univ, 54-57; pvt pract, SC, 57-59; clin instr, Med Col Ga, 59, from instr to prof, 59-78; PROF OBSTET & GYNEC, EASTERN VA MED SCH, 78- *Mem:* Fel Am Col Obstet & Gynec; AMA. *Res:* Programmed instruction; fetal physiology. *Mailing Add:* Dept of Obstet & Gynec Eastern Va Med Sch 600 Gresham Dr Norfolk VA 23507

WILDT, DAVID EDWIN, b Jacksonville, Ill, Mar 12, 50; m 70. REPRODUCTIVE PHYSIOLOGY. *Educ:* Ill State Univ, BS, 72; Mich State Univ, MS, 73, PhD(animal husb, physiol), 75. *Prof Exp:* Res asst reproductive physiol, Endocrine Res Univ, Mich State Univ, 72-75; fel reproductive physiol, Inst Comp Med, Baylor Col Med, 75-79; FEL COMP REPROD ENDOCRINOL, NIH, 79- *Mem:* Sigma Xi; Am Soc Animal Sci; Soc Study Reproduction; Am Soc Vet Physiol & Pharmacol; Int Primatological Soc. *Res:* Relationships of reproductive behavior; gonadotropin and steroid hormone concentrations and time of ovulation in canine, feline and nonhuman primate species; laparoscopy; development and use of frozen semen techniques for the preservation of captive wild mammal species. *Mailing Add:* Vet Res Br Div Res Serv Nat Inst Health Bethesda MD 20014

WILDUNG, RAYMOND EARL, b Van Nuys, Calif, Feb 24, 41; m 61; c 2. SOIL SCIENCE, ENVIRONMENTAL CHEMISTRY. *Educ:* Calif State Polytech Col, San Luis Obispo, BS, 62; Univ Wis-Madison, MS, 64, PhD(soil sci), 66. *Prof Exp:* NIH fel, Univ Wis-Madison, 66-67; sr res scientist, Soil-Sediment Sci, 67-71, prog leader, 71-75, MGR ENVIRON CHEM, BATTELLE PAC NORTHWEST LABS, 75- *Concurrent Pos:* Grants, USDA, 68-70, Environ Protection Agency, 68-71, US Dept Energy; 68-, Nat Inst Environ Health Sci, 71-; affil prof, Wash State Univ & Calif State Univ; comt accessory elements, chmn, oil shale panel, comt, soil as mineral resource, Nat Acad Sci; mem exec comt coord solid waste mgt, US Dept Energy Oil Shale Task Force. *Mem:* AAAS; Am Chem Soc; Am Soc Agron; Int Soc Soil Sci; Soil Sci Soc Am. *Res:* Soil-sediment science; fate and behavior of pollutants, including pesticides, petroleum and synfuel residuals, metals and metal complexes in soils, plants, sediments and waters. *Mailing Add:* Battelle Pac Northwest Labs PO Box 999 Richland WA 99352

WILE, HOWARD P, b New York, NY, Jan 4, 11; m 35; c 2. RESEARCH ADMINISTRATION. *Educ:* Dartmouth Col, AB, 32. *Prof Exp:* Mem staff admin, Mass Inst Technol, 44-46; adminr res, Polytech Inst Brooklyn, 46-65; exec dir comt govt rels, Nat Asn Col & Univ Bus Officers, 65-76; RETIRED. *Concurrent Pos:* Consult, Am Coun Educ; chmn grant admin adv comt, Dept Health, Educ & Welfare, 67-73; mem res & develop study group, Comn Govt Procurement, 71-72; consult, Com Fed Paperwork, 76-77 & NSF, 77-79; instr, Surv Course Grants Admin, HEW, 77-79 & Dept Energy, 78-79; prof adv, Nat Coun Univ Res Adminr, 78- *Res:* Governmental relations. *Mailing Add:* 2515 Q St NW Washington DC 20007

WILEMSKI, GERALD, b Dunkirk, NY, Oct 15, 46. PHYSICAL CHEMISTRY. *Educ:* Canisius Col, BS, 68; Yale Univ, PhD(chem), 72. *Prof Exp:* Res assoc, Dept Eng & Appl Sci, Yale Univ, 72-74; res assoc & vis asst prof chem, Dartmouth Col, 74-77; PRIN SCIENTIST, PHYS SCI INC, 77- *Mem:* Am Phys Soc; Electrochem Soc; AAAS; Sigma Xi. *Res:* Statistical mechanics; thermodynamics; electrochemical systems; polymer solutions. *Mailing Add:* Phys Sci Inc 30 Commerce Way Woburn MA 01801

WILEN, SAMUEL HENRY, b Brussels, Belgium, Mar 6, 31; nat US; m 60; c 2. ORGANIC CHEMISTRY. *Educ:* City Col New York, BS, 51; Univ Kans, PhD(chem), 56. *Prof Exp:* Asst instr chem, Univ Kans, 51-52, asst, 53-55; res assoc, Univ Notre Dame, 55-57; from instr to assoc prof, 57-71, PROF CHEM, CITY COL NEW YORK, 71- *Concurrent Pos:* Sci assoc, State Univ Groningen, 68-69; guest researcher, Free Univ Brussels, 75-76. *Mem:* AAAS; Am Chem Soc; Royal Soc Chem. *Res:* Chemistry of heterocyclic compounds; stereodiemistry; resolving agents and optical resolutions. *Mailing Add:* Dept of Chem City Col of New York New York NY 10031

WILENSKY, ROBERT, b Brooklyn, NY, Mar 26, 51. COMPUTER SCIENCE. *Educ:* Yale Univ, BA, 72, PhD(comput sci), 78. *Prof Exp:* ASST PROF COMPUT SCI, UNIV CALIF, BERKELEY, 78- *Mem:* Asn Comput Mach. *Res:* Atrificial intelligence; natural language process; computer situation of human thought processes. *Mailing Add:* Dept of Elec Eng & Comput Sci Univ of Calif Berkeley CA 94720

WILES, ALFRED BARKSDALE, b Flora, Miss, Oct 8, 18; m 49; c 1. PLANT PATHOLOGY. *Educ:* Miss State Col, BS, 40; Univ Ark, MS, 42; Univ Wis, PhD(plant path), 51. *Prof Exp:* Asst plant path, Univ Ark, 40-42 & Univ Wis, 48-50; assoc plant pathologist, Agr Exp Sta, 50-64, adj prof plant path, 64-77, EMER ADJ PROF & RES PLANT PATH, MISS STATE UNIV, 77-; RES PLANT PATHOLOGIST, USDA, 64- *Concurrent Pos:* Assoc plant pathologist, USDA, 50-64. *Mem:* AAAS; Am Phytopath Soc. *Res:* Diseases of cotton; disease resistance in cotton; seed treatment chemicals; pathology of seed. *Mailing Add:* Dept of Plant Path Miss State Univ 204 C Dorman Forestry Plant Sci Bldg Mississippi State MS 39762

WILES, DAVID M, b Springhill, NS, Dec 28, 32; m 57; c 2. POLYMER CHEMISTRY. *Educ:* McMaster Univ, BSc, 54, MSc, 55; McGill Univ, PhD(phys chem), 57. *Prof Exp:* Nat Res Coun Can & Can Ramsay Mem fels, Univ Leeds, 57-59; asst res officer, High Polymer Sect, 59-61, assoc res officer, 61-67, sr res officer, 67-74, HEAD TEXTILE CHEM SECT, NAT RES COUN CAN, 66-, DIR DIV CHEM, 75- *Honors & Awards:* Dunlop Lectr Award, Chem Inst Can, 81; Textile Sci Award, Textile Tech Fedn Can, 80. *Mem:* Am Chem Soc; Fiber Soc; Chem Inst Can; Can Inst Textile Sci; Royal Soc Chem. *Res:* Polymerization kinetics and mechanisms; synthesis of stereoregular polymers; polymer structure; photodegradation of fiber forming macromolecules; polymer stabilization; fiber morphology; modification of fibers; polymer surface studies; microbiological deterioration. *Mailing Add:* Div of Chem Nat Res Coun of Can Ottawa ON K1A 0R9 Can

WILES, DONALD ROY, b Truro, NS, Aug 30, 25; m 52; c 3. INORGANIC CHEMISTRY. *Educ:* Mt Allison Univ, BSc, 46, BEd, 47; McMaster Univ, MSc, 50; Mass Inst Technol, PhD(chem), 53. *Prof Exp:* Chemist, Eldorado Mining & Refining Ltd, Can, 47-48; res assoc radiochem, Chem Inst, Oslo, Norway, 53-55; res assoc metall chem, Univ BC, 55-59; from asst prof to assoc prof nuclear inorg chem, 59-69, PROF CHEM, CARLETON UNIV, 69-, CHMN CHEM DEPT, 79- *Concurrent Pos:* Vis scientist, Inst Hot Atom Chem, Nuclear Res Ctr, Karlsruhe, Ger, 69-70. *Mem:* Am Chem Soc; Chem Inst Can; Royal Soc Chem; Norweg Chem Soc. *Res:* Dissolution kinetics of metals and oxides; hot atom chemistry in organic solids; nuclear fission; radiochemistry; environmental radiochemistry of radium, thorium; Massbauer spectroscopy; analytical radiochemistry of radium and thorium. *Mailing Add:* Dept of Chem Carleton Univ Ottawa ON K1S 5B6 Can

WILES, MICHAEL, b Sheffield, Eng, May 8, 40; m 63; c 2. PARASITOLOGY, FRESHWATER ECOLOGY. *Educ:* Univ Leeds, BSc, 62, PhD(zool), 65. *Prof Exp:* Res scientist, Fisheries Res Bd, Can, 65-67; asst prof freshwater ecol, 67-72, assoc prof, 72-80, PROF FRESHWATER ECOL, ST MARY'S UNIV, NS, 80- *Mem:* Can Soc Zool; Brit Soc Parasitol. *Res:* Parasitic larvae of freshwater molluscs; parasites of freshwater fishes of Eastern Canada; culture of freshwater fishes in laboratory; marine ecology; parasites of Northwestern Atlantic marine fishes. *Mailing Add:* Dept of Biol St Mary's Univ Halifax NS B3H 3C3 Can

WILES, ROBERT ALLAN, b Quincy, Mass, Apr 6, 29; m 51; c 5. INDUSTRIAL ORGANIC CHEMISTRY. *Educ:* Univ NH, BS, 51, MS, 55; Mass Inst Technol, PhD(chem), 58. *Prof Exp:* Res chemist, Sun Oil Co, 57-59; res chemist, Solvay Process Div, 59-64, res supvr, 64-70, res supvr indust chem div, 66-68, mgr process res, 71-80, mgr specialty chem div, 60-80, SR RES ASSOC, ALLIED CHEM CO, ALLIED CORP, 81- *Mem:* Am Chem Soc. *Res:* fluorochemicals and process research and development. *Mailing Add:* 169 Euclid Ave Hamburg NY 14075

WILETS, LAWRENCE, b Oconomowoc, Wis, Jan 4, 27; c 3. THEORETICAL PHYSICS, NUCLEAR PHYSICS. *Educ:* Univ Wis, BS, 48; Princeton Univ, MA, 50, PhD(physics), 52. *Prof Exp:* Res assoc theoret physics, Proj Matterhorn, Princeton Univ, 51-53; res assoc, Lawrence

Livermore Lab, Univ Calif, 53; NSF fel, Inst Theoret Physics, Copenhagen, 53-55; mem staff, Los Alamos Sci Lab, 55-58; mem, Inst Advan Study, Princeton Univ, 57-58; assoc prof, 58-68, PROF THEORET PHYSICS, UNIV WASH, 68- *Concurrent Pos:* Consult, Los Alamos Sci Lab, 58-, Lawrence Livermore Lab, Univ Calif, 58- & Oak Ridge Nat Lab, 65-; NSF sr fel, Weizmann Inst Sci, 61-62; vis prof, Princeton Univ, 69 & Calif Inst Technol, 71; J S Guggenheim fel, Univ Lund & Weizmann Inst Sci, 76-77; Nordita prof, Univ Lund, 76. *Mem:* Fel Am Phys Soc; AAAS; Am Asn Univ Prof; Fedn Am Scientists. *Res:* Atomic quarks and quantum chromodynamics; meson physics; nuclear structure and manybody theory; nuclear reactions; heavy ions and fission. *Mailing Add:* Dept of Physics FM-15 Univ of Wash Seattle WA 98195

WILEY, ALBERT LEE, JR, b Forest City, NC, June 9, 36; m 60; c 4. RADIATION THERAPY. *Educ:* NC State Univ, BS, 58; Univ Rochester, MD, 63; Univ Wis, Madison, PhD(radiobiol), 72; Am Bd Radiol, cert, 68; Am Bd Nuclear Med, cert, 75; Am Bd Sci Nuclear Med, cert, 80. *Prof Exp:* Nuclear engr, Nuclear Prod Div, Lockheed Aircraft, Ga, 58; intern med & surg, Med Ctr, Univ Va, 63-64; Nat Cancer Inst fel radiation therapy, Med Ctr, Stanford Univ, 64-65, radiation therapy & nuclear med, Univ Wis Hosps, 65-68; med dir, US Naval Radiol Defense Lab, San Francisco, Calif, 68-69; asst prof radiation therapy, Univ Tex, M D Anderson Hosp, Houston, 72-73; assoc prof radiol & human oncol, Med Sch, Univ Wis, Madison, 76-79; ASSOC DIR & CLIN DIR RADIATION ONCOL & PROF HUMAN ONCOL, RADIOL & MED PHYSICS, MED SCH, UNIV WIS, MADISON, 79- *Concurrent Pos:* Vis prof, Cent Hosp & Radiation Clinics, Univ Helsinki, 79; consult, Nat Cancer Inst, 81 & Adv Comt Reactor Safeguards, Nuclear Regulatory Comn, 81-; tech adv, Dept Health & Human Serv, State Wis, 81-; bd dir, Int Clin Hyperthermia Soc, 81- *Mem:* Soc Nuclear Med; Am Col Radiol; Health Physics Soc; Inst Elec & Electronic Engrs; Am Soc Law & Med. *Res:* New radiation services and techniques in the treatment of cancer; the use of nuclear medicine and computerized tomography for improving the quality control in cancer treatment; use of nuclear reactors in medical research. *Mailing Add:* K4 B100 CSC Radiation Oncol Med Ctr Univ Wis Madison WI 53792

WILEY, BILL BEAUFORD, b St Joseph, Mo, Nov 12, 23; m 45; c 2. MICROBIOLOGY, IMMUNOLOGY. *Educ:* Univ Kans, BA, 49, MA, 50; Univ Rochester, PhD(microbiol), 56. *Prof Exp:* Asst dir Rochester Health Bur Labs, Med Ctr, Univ Rochester, 50-56; asst prof microbiol, Univ Sask, 56-62; from asst prof, to assoc prof, 62-78, PROF MICROBIOL, MED CTR, UNIV UTAH, 78- *Concurrent Pos:* Med Res Coun Can fel, Univ Sask, 57-62; Nat Inst Allergy & Infectious Dis fel, Univ Utah, 63- *Mem:* AAAS; Can Soc Microbiol; Am Soc Microbiol; NY Acad Sci; Sigma Xi. *Res:* Encapsulation and virulence of staphylococcus aureus staphylococcal scalded skin syndrome; sphingomyelinases of staphylococcal toxins. *Mailing Add:* Dept of Microbiol Univ Utah Med Ctr Salt Lake City UT 84132

WILEY, DON CRAIG, b Akron, Ohio, Oct 21, 44. BIOPHYSICS. *Educ:* Tufts Univ, SB, 66; Harvard Univ, PhD(biophys), 71. *Prof Exp:* Asst prof biochem & molecular biol, 71-75, assoc prof biochem, 75-80, PROF BIOCHEM & BIOPHYSICS, HARVARD UNIV, 80- *Concurrent Pos:* Jane Sloan Coffin Fund grant, Harvard Univ, 72-73; fel, Europ Molecular Biol, 76. *Mem:* AAAS. *Res:* X-ray diffraction; structure of macromolecules and assemblies of macromolecules; viral membrane glycoproteins. *Mailing Add:* Dept of Biochem Harvard Univ Cambridge MA 02135

WILEY, DOUGLAS WALKER, b Shanghai, China, Apr 8, 29; m 50; c 4. ORGANIC CHEMISTRY. *Educ:* Univ Richmond, BS, 49; Columbia Univ, MA, 52; Yale Univ, PhD(chem), 55. *Prof Exp:* RES CHEMIST, CENT RES DEPT, E I DU PONT DE NEMOURS & CO, INC, 55- *Mem:* Am Chem Soc. *Res:* Synthesis, structure and mechanism in area of fluorocarbons, cyanocarbons and exploratory process chemistry. *Mailing Add:* Cent Res Dept Exp Sta E I du Pont de Nemours & Co Inc Wilmington DE 19898

WILEY, E(DWARD) O(RLANDO), III, b Corpus Christi, Tex, Aug 15, 44; m 77; c 2. ICHTHYOLOGY, SYSTEMATIC BIOLOGY. *Educ:* Southwest Tex State Univ, BS, 66; Sam Houston State Univ, MS, 72; City Univ New York, PhD(biol), 76. *Prof Exp:* asst cur fishes, 76-80, ASSOC CUR FISHES, MUS NATURAL HIST, UNIV KANS, 76-, ASSOC PROF BIOL SCI, 78- *Honors & Awards:* Stoye Award Ichthyol, Am Soc Ichthyologists & Herpetologists, 76. *Mem:* Am Soc Ichthyologists & Herpetologists; Soc Syst Zool; fel Linnean Soc London. *Res:* Phylogenetic relationships in killifishes and various groups of fossil fishes; theory and practice of phylogenetic systematics, such as cladism; evolutionary theory and its relationship to systematics and biogeography. *Mailing Add:* Mus of Natural Hist Univ of Kans Lawrence KS 66045

WILEY, JACK CLEVELAND, b Evansville, Ind, Mar 17, 40; m 65; c 2. COMPUTER AIDED DESIGN. *Educ:* Purdue Univ, Lafayette, BS, 62, PhD(eng sci), 68; Univ Ill, Urbana, MS, 64. *Prof Exp:* Asst prof theoret & appl mech, Univ Ill, Urbana, 67-72; sr res engr, Tech Ctr, Deere & Co, 72-79, MGR ENG MATH, TECH CTR, DEERE & CO, 80- *Concurrent Pos:* Presidential exchange exec, US Dept Com, 79-80. *Mem:* Am Soc Mech Engrs; Soc Mfg Engrs; Am Acad Mech. *Res:* Mechanism and vehicle mechanics; computer graphics and geometric modeling; computer aided design and manufacturing. *Mailing Add:* Deere & Co Tech Ctr 3300 River Dr Moline IL 61265

WILEY, JAMES C, JR, b Higginsville, Mo, Mar 4, 38; m 62; c 2. RADIOCHEMICAL SYNTHESIS. *Educ:* Univ Mo, Kansas City, BS, 68. *Prof Exp:* Technician, 62-65, jr chemist, 65-68, asst chemist, 68-71, assoc chemist, 71-76, sr chemist, 76-81, PRIN CHEMIST, MIDWEST RES INST, 81- *Concurrent Pos:* Prin investr, Nat Cancer Inst, 76- *Mem:* Am Chem Soc; AAAS; Sigma Xi. *Res:* Synthesis of labeled and unlabeled carcinogenic polycyclic aromatic hydrocarbon metabolites. *Mailing Add:* 1105 S 14th Terr Blue Springs MO 64015

WILEY, JOHN DUNCAN, b Nashville, Tenn, Mar 23, 42. SOLID STATE PHYSICS. *Educ:* Ind Univ, BS, 64; Univ Wis, MS, 65, PhD(physics), 68. *Prof Exp:* Mem tech staff, Optical & Magnetic Mat Dept, Bell Tel Labs, 68-74; res assoc, Max Planck Inst Solid State Res, 74-75; ASSOC PROF ELEC & COMPUT ENG, UNIV WIS-MADISON, 76- *Mem:* Am Vacuum Soc; Am Phys Soc; Inst Elec & Electronics Engrs. *Res:* Transport properties of semiconductors; optical properties of semiconductors; growth and characterization of semiconductor crystals. *Mailing Add:* Dept of Elec & Comput Eng Univ of Wis Madison WI 53706

WILEY, JOHN ROBERT, b San Angelo, Tex, Oct 10, 46; m 68; c 1. NUCLEAR CHEMISTRY. *Educ:* Univ Houston, BS, 69; Purdue Univ, PhD(nuclear chem), 74. *Prof Exp:* RES CHEM SEPARATIONS, SAVANNAH RIVER PLANT, E I DU PONT DE NEMOURS & CO, INC, 74- *Mem:* Am Chem Soc; AAAS. *Res:* Management of nuclear plant wastes. *Mailing Add:* Savannah River Lab E I du Pont de Nemours & Co Inc Aiken SC 29801

WILEY, LORRAINE, b Sacramento, Calif. PLANT PHYSIOLOGY. *Educ:* Sacramento State Col, AB, 64; Univ Calif, Davis, MS, 66, PhD(plant physiol), 71. *Prof Exp:* Asst prof bot, Howard Univ, 71-72; asst prof, 72-76, assoc prof, 76-81, PROF BIOL, CALIF STATE UNIV, FRESNO, 81- *Concurrent Pos:* Res botanist, Univ Calif, Davis, 71. *Mem:* Am Soc Plant Physiol. *Res:* Plant protein metabolism; seed physiology; stress physiology. *Mailing Add:* Dept Biol Calif State Univ Fresno CA 93740

WILEY, LYNN M, b Tucson, Ariz, Feb 24, 47; m 69. DEVELOPMENTAL BIOLOGY. *Educ:* Univ Calif, Irvine, BS, 68, MS, 71; Univ Calif, San Francisco, PhD(anat), 75. *Prof Exp:* Lab technician electron micros, Univ Calif, Irvine, Calif Col Med, 69-71; cell biologist mammalian develop, San Francisco Med Ctr, Univ Calif, 75-78; mem fac, Univ Va, 78-80; MEM FAC, UNIV CALIF, DAVIS, 80- *Concurrent Pos:* Res Career Develop Award, NIH, 80-84. *Mem:* AAAS; Fedn Am Scientists; Soc Develop Biol; Am Asn Anatomists; Am Soc Cell Biol. *Res:* Cell surface in early mammalian development; origin of primary germ layers; regulation of cell determination. *Mailing Add:* Dept Human Anat Univ Calif Davis CA 95616

WILEY, MARTIN LEE, b Pittsburg, Kans, May 12, 35; m 63; c 3. ICHTHYOLOGY. *Educ:* Pittsburg State Univ, BS, 59, MS, 60; George Washington Univ, PhD(zool), 69. *Prof Exp:* Sci asst fisheries biol, Inter-Am Trop Tuna Comn, 61-62; mus technician ichthyol, Div Fishes, US Nat Mus, 66-67; fisheries res biologist, Bur Com Fisheries Ichthyol Lab, 67-68; managing ed, Chesapeake Sci, 68-77, ASST PROF ICHTHYOL, CHESAPEAKE BIOL LAB, 68- *Concurrent Pos:* Co-investr res contract, Naval Ord Lab, 73-74 & 75-76; ed proc, Estuarine Res Fedn, 75-78; managing ed, Estuaries, Estuarine Res Fedn, 78-80. *Mem:* Am Soc Ichthyologists & Herpetologists; Atlantic Estuarine Res Soc; Estuarine Res Fedn. *Res:* Structure and physiology of fish swimbladders; how fish adapt to changes in hydrostatic pressure and effects of underwater explosions; biology of fishes. *Mailing Add:* Chesapeake Biol Lab Box 38 Solomons MD 20688

WILEY, MICHAEL DAVID, b Long Beach, Calif, Nov 28, 39; m 61; c 2. ORGANIC CHEMISTRY. *Educ:* Univ Southern Calif, BS, 61; Univ Wash, PhD(org chem), 69. *Prof Exp:* Asst prof, 68-74, ASSOC PROF CHEM, CALIF LUTHERAN COL, 74- *Concurrent Pos:* SRC res assoc, Univ Liverpool, Eng, 81. *Mem:* AAAS; Am Chem Soc; Royal Soc Chem. *Res:* Reaction mechanisms; carbcations. *Mailing Add:* Dept Chem Calif Lutheran Col Thousand Oaks CA 91360

WILEY, PAUL FEARS, b Sullivan, Ill, June 21, 16; m 38, 75; c 4. ORGANIC CHEMISTRY. *Educ:* Univ Ill, BS, 38, MS, 39; Univ Minn, PhD(org chem), 44. *Prof Exp:* Jr chemist, Merck & Co, Inc, NJ, 39-41; sr res chemist, Allied Chem Corp, 44-46; res chemist, Eli Lilly & Co, 46-58, res assoc, 58-60; res assoc, Res Labs, 60-76, SR SCIENTIST, UPJOHN CO, 76- *Mem:* Am Chem Soc. *Res:* Chemistry of antibiotics and natural products. *Mailing Add:* Res Labs Upjohn Co Kalamazoo MI 49001

WILEY, RICHARD HAVEN, b Mattoon, Ill, May 10, 13; m 40; c 2. CHEMISTRY. *Educ:* Univ Ill, AB, 34, MS, 35; Univ Wis, PhD(chem), 37; Temple Univ, LLB, 43. *Prof Exp:* Res chemist, E I du Pont de Nemours & Co, Inc, 37-45; assoc prof chem, Univ NC, 45-49; prof & chmn dept, Univ Louisville, 49-65; prof chem, Hunter Col, 65-80, exec officer doctoral prog, 65-68. *Concurrent Pos:* NSF sr fel, Imp Col, Univ London, 57-58; vis prof, City Col New York, 63-64; consult; res proj dir with NSF, AEC, NIH, Off Naval Res, Off Ord Res, Bur Naval Ord & NASA; vis scholar, Stanford Univ, 78-79. *Honors & Awards:* Award, Am Chem Soc, 65. *Mem:* AAAS; Am Chem Soc. *Res:* Polymer chemistry; organic synthesis; mass spectrometry. *Mailing Add:* 8 Roosevelt Circle Palo Alto CA 94306

WILEY, RICHARD HAVEN, JR, b Wilmington, Del, June 14, 43; m 71; c 2. SOCIOBIOLOGY, ETHOLOGY. *Educ:* Harvard Univ, BA, 65; Rockefeller Univ, PhD(animal behav), 70. *Prof Exp:* Fel animal behav, Rockefeller Univ, 70-71; asst prof, 71-76, assoc prof, 76-81, PROF ZOOL, UNIV NC, CHAPEL HILL, 81- *Concurrent Pos:* Res grants, Nat Inst Mental Health, NSF, 69-83; mem bd dir, NC Botanical Garden & Orgn Tropical Studies, 78- *Mem:* AAAS; Animal Behav Soc; Ecol Soc Am; Soc Study Evolution; Am Soc Naturalists. *Res:* Comparative studies and ecology of vertebrate social organization; behavioral mechanisms of aggression and affiliation; acoustic communication. *Mailing Add:* Dept Zool Univ NC Chapel Hill NC 27514

WILEY, ROBERT A, b Ann Arbor, Mich, Sept 5, 34; m 55; c 3. MEDICINAL CHEMISTRY. *Educ:* Univ Mich, BS, 55; Univ Calif, San Francisco, PhD(pharmaceut chem), 62. *Prof Exp:* From asst prof to assoc prof, 62-71, PROF MED CHEM, UNIV KANS, 71- *Mem:* Am Chem Soc; Am Pharmaceut Asn; Soc Toxicol. *Res:* Relationship between biological activity and chemical properties among drugs; chemical aspects of drug metabolism. *Mailing Add:* Dept of Med Chem Univ of Kans Lawrence KS 66045

WILEY, ROBERT CRAIG, b Washington, DC, Nov 14, 24; m 51; c 3. FOOD SCIENCE, FOOD ENGINEERING. *Educ:* Univ Md, BS, 49, MS, 50; Ore State Univ, PhD(food tech), 53. *Prof Exp:* Asst, Ore State Univ, 51-52; food specialist, US Dept Navy, 53; from asst prof to assoc prof, 53-69, PROF HORT, UNIV MD, COLLEGE PARK, 69- *Concurrent Pos:* Fulbright-Hays sr lectr, Univ Belgrade, Yugoslavia, 79. *Honors & Awards:* Woodbury Res Award co-recipient, 61, 62; H W Wiley Medal, US Food & Drug Admin, 81. *Mem:* Am Soc Hort Sci; Inst Food Technol. *Res:* Measurement of structural and textural characteristics of foods; measurement of polysaccharides, fatty acids and enzymes in fruits and vegetables; aroma analyses by gas liquid chromatography; thermal processing of foods. *Mailing Add:* Dept Hort Food Sci Prog Univ of Md Col of Agr College Park MD 20742

WILEY, RONALD LEE, b Dayton, Ohio, Oct 4, 37; m 81; c 1. RESPIRATORY PHYSIOLOGY, PULMONARY PHYSIOLOGY. *Educ:* Miami Univ, Ohio, BS, 59; Univ Ky, PhD(physiol, biophys), 66. *Prof Exp:* Teacher, Talawanda High Sch, Ohio, 59-62; instr physiol & NIH fel, Marquette Univ, 66-67; asst prof, Wright State Univ Med Sch, Dayton, 74-76; asst prof, 67-71, assoc prof zool & physiol, 71-76, PROF ZOOL, MIAMI UNIV, 76-; prof, Med Sch, Wright State Univ, Dayton, 76-80. *Concurrent Pos:* Mem med staff, McCullough-Hyde Mem Hosp, Oxford, Ohio, 73- *Mem:* Am Physiol Soc; Am Thoracic Soc. *Res:* Control of respiration; perception of respiratory sensations. *Mailing Add:* Dept Zool Miami Univ Oxford OH 45056

WILEY, SAMUEL L, b Springfield, Ohio, Dec 24, 37; div. COMPUTER APPLICATIONS IN INSTRUCTION. *Educ:* Capital Univ, BS, 59; Ohio State Univ, PhD(physics), 68. *Prof Exp:* Instr physics, Capital Univ, 64-67; asstprof, 68-71, chmn, Dept Physics & info sci, 73-75 & 77-78, from assoc prof to prof physics, 71-78, dir, Comput Ctr, 78-79, DEAN, SCH SCI MATH & TECHNOL, 79- *Concurrent Pos:* Lectr, Otis Art Inst, 72-73. *Mem:* AAAS; Am Asn Physics Teachers; Asn Comput Mach. *Res:* Theoretical physics; phase transitions and cooperative phenomena; Ising and Heisenberg models of magnetic systems; computer applications in physics teaching. *Mailing Add:* Sch Sci Math & Technol Calif State Univ Dominguez Hills Carson CA 90747

WILEY, WILLIAM CHARLES, b Monmouth, Ill, Aug 7, 24; m 44; c 2. ENGINEERING, PHYSICS. *Educ:* Univ Ill, BS, 49. *Prof Exp:* Dir, Appl Physics Lab, Bendix Corp, 49-68, assoc dir, Planning Res Labs, 68-69, asst gen mgr, Sci Instruments & Equip Div, 69-71; VPRES & CHIEF TECH OFFICER, LEEDS & NORTHRUP CO, 71- *Concurrent Pos:* Dir, Univ City Sci Ctr. *Mem:* Fel Instrument Soc Am; AAAS; Inst Elec & Electronics Engrs; Ind Res Inst. *Res:* Advanced sensing techniques; electronics; instrumentation; mass spectrometry; electron multipliers. *Mailing Add:* Leeds & Northrup Co Dickerson Rd North Wales PA 19454

WILEY, WILLIAM LEE, organic chemistry, see previous edition

WILEY, WILLIAM RODNEY, b Oxford, Miss, Sept 5, 32; m 52; c 1. MICROBIOLOGY, BIOCHEMISTRY. *Educ:* Tougaloo Col, BS, 54; Univ Ill, MS, 60; Wash State Univ, PhD(bact), 65. *Prof Exp:* Coord Life Sci Prog, Pac Northwest Labs, 65-71 & Battelle Mem Inst, 71-74, mgr, biol dept, 74-79, DIR, RES, PAC NORTHWEST LABS, BATTELLE MEM INST, 79- *Concurrent Pos:* Adj prof, 68-75. *Mem:* AAAS; Fedn Am Scientists; Am Soc Microbiol; Am Soc Biol Chem. *Res:* Microbial metabolism, particularly the factors which control intracellular pool formation and membrane transport of amino acids and sugars in microorganisms and mammalian cells; develoment environmental engineering; biotechnology; geoscience; analytical chemistry. *Mailing Add:* Pac Northwest Lab Battelle Mem Inst PO Box 999 Richland WA 99352

WILFONG, ROBERT EDWARD, b Wayne Co, Ill, Jan 3, 20; m 38; c 5. CHEMISTRY. *Educ:* Univ Wis, BS, 41, MS, 42, PhD(phys chem), 44. *Prof Exp:* Res chemist, Va, 44-48, res supvr, 48-51, res mgr, 51-53, tech supt, 53-59, lab dir, 59-64, tech mgr, 64-71, TECH DIR, E I DU PONT DE NEMOURS & CO, INC, WILMINGTON, DEL, 71- *Honors & Awards:* Award of Merit, Nat Defense Res Comt. *Mem:* AAAS; Am Chem Soc; NY Acad Sci. *Res:* Photosynthesis; submarine detection; kinetics of rocket propellant decomposition; modified rocket propellants; infrared spectroscopy; new textile fibers, Orlon, Nylon and Dacron; aromatic polyamides. *Mailing Add:* Rte 2 Anvill Hills Kennett Square PA 19348

WILFRET, GARY JOE, b Sacramento, Calif, Oct 13, 43; m 68; c 2. PLANT BREEDING, GENETICS. *Educ:* Univ Hawaii, BS, 65, PhD(hort), 68. *Prof Exp:* Asst prof biol, Ga South Col, 68-69; asst geneticist, 69-74, assoc geneticist, 74-79, GENETICIST, AGR RES & EDUC CTR, UNIV FLA, BRADENTON, 79- *Mem:* Am Soc Hort Sci; Am Asn Trop Biol; Bot Soc Am; Tissue Cult Asn; Am Hort Soc. *Res:* Breeding of ornamental plants for disease resistance and adaptation to subtropical conditions; hybridizing Dendrobium species to determine sexual compatability, to examine meiotic behavior and to clarify genome relationships. *Mailing Add:* Agr Res & Educ Ctr Univ of Fla 5007 60th St E Bradenton FL 33508

WILGRAM, GEORGE FRIEDERICH, b Vienna, Austria, Apr 12, 24; nat US; m 56; c 3. PHYSIOLOGY, DERMATOLOGY. *Educ:* Univ Vienna, MD, 51; Univ Toronto, MA, 53, PhD, 57. *Prof Exp:* Lectr physiol, Univ Toronto, 57-58; asst prof exp path, Univ Chicago, 58-59; res assoc dermat, Harvard Med Sch, 59-60, asst prof, 61-67; PROF DERMAT, TUFTS UNIV, 67- *Mem:* Am Soc Exp Path; Soc Exp Biol & Med; Am Heart Asn. *Res:* Genetics of keratinization and pigmentation. *Mailing Add:* New Eng Med Ctr Hosp Boston MA 02116

WILGUS, DONOVAN RAY, b La Plata, Mo, Aug 11, 21; m 52; c 3. ORGANIC CHEMISTRY. *Educ:* Northeast Mo State Teachers Col, AB, 42; Univ Colo, PhD, 51. *Prof Exp:* From assoc res chemist to supv res chemist, 51-66, SR RES ASSOC, CHEVRON RES CO, 66- *Mem:* Am Chem Soc. *Res:* Diels-Alder reaction; lubricating oil additives; synthetic oils. *Mailing Add:* Apt #5 611 Liberty El Cerrito CA 94530

WILGUS, HERBERT SEDGWICK, b Brooklyn, NY, Dec 2, 05; m 26; c 6. POULTRY SCIENCE. *Educ:* Cornell Univ, BS, 26, PhD(poultry nutrit), 30. *Prof Exp:* From asst poultry nutrit to investr, Cornell Univ, 26-36; prof poultry husb & head dept, Colo Agr & Mech Col & chief poultry sect, Exp Sta, 36-50, assoc dir Exp Sta, 45-47; dir res & nutrit, Peter Hand Found, 50-58; res, Ray Ewing Co, 58-61, vpres tech sales serv & res, 61-62; mgr tech agr serv, Hoffmann-La Roche, Inc, 62-70; consult, 71-80; RETIRED. *Mem:* AAAS; Am Soc Animal Sci; fel Poultry Sci Asn; World Poultry Sci Asn. *Res:* Poultry nutrition; calcium; phosphorus; manganese; iodine; riboflavin; protein quality; egg quality; incubation; vitamins. *Mailing Add:* 377 Highland Ave San Rafael CA 94901

WILHEIT, THOMAS TURNER, b Dallas, Tex, Apr 10, 41; m 66; c 1. MICROWAVE PHYSICS, ATMOSPHERIC PHYSICS. *Educ:* Univ South, BA, 63; Wash Univ, St Louis, MA, 63; Mass Inst Technol, PhD(physics), 70. *Prof Exp:* PHYSICIST MICROWAVE, GODDARD SPACE FLIGHT CTR, 71- *Concurrent Pos:* Resident res assoc, Nat Acad Sci, 70-71. *Honors & Awards:* Medal Exceptional Sci Achievement, NASA, 74. *Mem:* Inst Elec & Electronics Engrs; Am Meterol Soc; AAAS. *Res:* Passive microwave remote sensing of the earth's surface and atmosphere. *Mailing Add:* Code 946 NASA Goddard Space Flight Ctr Greenbelt MD 20771

WILHELM, ALAN ROY, b Buffalo, NY, Oct 30, 36. MICROBIOLOGY, VIROLOGY. *Educ:* Stanford Univ, AB, 58; Univ Wis, Madison, MS, 65, PhD(bact), 67. *Prof Exp:* Microbiologist, US Army, 67-69; from asst prof to assoc prof, 69-77, PROF BIOL SCI, CALIF STATE UNIV, CHICO, 77- *Mem:* Sigma Xi; AAAS; Am Soc Microbiol. *Res:* Arboviruses; herpes viruses; viral infection of poikilothermic cells. *Mailing Add:* Dept of Biol Sci Calif State Univ First & Normal St Chico CA 95926

WILHELM, DALE LEROY, b Greenview, Ill, June 20, 26; m 51; c 4. INORGANIC CHEMISTRY. *Educ:* Univ Ill, BS, 51; Univ Tenn, MS, 52, PhD(chem), 54. *Prof Exp:* From asst prof to assoc prof chem, Univ WVa, 54-63; assoc prof, Cornell Col, 63-66; asst dean, Liberal Arts Col, 73-78, chmn chem dept, 74-78, PROF CHEM, OHIO NORTHERN UNIV, 66-, V PRES ACAD AFFAIRS, 78- *Mem:* AAAS; Am Chem Soc; The Chem Soc. *Res:* Heteropolyanions; electrophoresis in stabilized media. *Mailing Add:* Dept Chem Ohio Northern Univ Ada OH 45810

WILHELM, EUGENE J, JR, b St Louis, Mo, July 25, 33. BIOGEOGRAPHY, HUMAN ECOLOGY. *Educ:* St Louis Univ, BS, 59; La State Univ, Baton Rouge, MA, 61; Tex A&M Univ, PhD(geog), 71. *Prof Exp:* Instr geog, DePaul Univ, 62-63; asst prof, St Louis Univ, 63-65; asst prof, McGill Univ, 65-68; vis lectr, Univ Va, 68-69 & 71-72; assoc prof, 72-76, PROF GEOG, SLIPPERY ROCK STATE COL, 76- *Concurrent Pos:* Vis prof ecol, Univ Sierra Leone, sr Fulbright-Hays Awardee, 76-77. *Mem:* Asn Am Geog. *Res:* Cultural and natural history of Appalachia; ecological problems in national park areas; ethnobiology; human ecology; folk geography. *Mailing Add:* Dept of Geog Slippery Rock State Col Slippery Rock PA 16057

WILHELM, JAMES MAURICE, b Redfield, SDak, May 20, 40; m 69. MICROBIOLOGY, MOLECULAR BIOLOGY. *Educ:* SDak Sch Mines & Technol, BS, 62; Case Western Reserve Univ, PhD(biochem), 68. *Prof Exp:* Am Cancer Soc fel biophys, Univ Chicago, 68-70; asst prof microbiol, Sch Med, Univ Pa, 70-73; asst prof, 73-79, ASSOC PROF MICROBIOL, SCH MED, UNIV ROCHESTER, 79- *Mem:* Am Soc Cell Biol; Am Soc Microbiol. *Res:* Protein synthesis; control of viral replication; cell biology. *Mailing Add:* Dept of Microbiol Univ of Rochester Sch of Med Rochester NY 14642

WILHELM, RUDOLF ERNST, b Hanover, Ger, Dec 26, 26; US citizen; m 52; c 3. ALLERGY, IMMUNOLOGY. *Educ:* Univ Ill, Chicago, MD, 51; Am Bd Internal Med, dipl, 61. *Prof Exp:* Asst resident internal med, Detroit Receiving Hosp, Mich, 52-53; resident allergy, Roosevelt Hosp Inst, NY, 57; resident internal med, Henry Ford Hosp, Detroit, 58-59; instr med, Sch Med, La State Univ, New Orleans, 59-60; asst prof med, 60-64, asst prof dermat, 64-66, ASSOC PROF DERMAT, SCH MED, WAYNE STATE UNIV, 66-; CHIEF, ALLERGY SECT, OAKWOOD HOSP, 77- *Concurrent Pos:* Consult, USPHS Hosp, Detroit, 62-69; chief, Allergy Sect, Vet Admin Hosp, Allen Park, 60-77; secy, Dept Med, Oakwood Hosp, Dearborn, 65-67. *Mem:* Fel Am Col Physicians; fel Am Acad Allergy. *Res:* Delayed-type allergic skin reactions such as atopic eczema and contact dermatitis; methods and mechanics of allergy hyposensitization injections; anti-allergic drug treatment; methods of medical education in allergy and internal medicine. *Mailing Add:* Wilhelm Allergy Clin 751 S Military Rd Dearborn MI 48124

WILHELM, STEPHEN, b Imperial Co, Calif, Apr 19, 19; m 44; c 2. PLANT PATHOLOGY. *Educ:* Univ Calif, AB, 42, PhD(plant path), 48. *Prof Exp:* Instr plant path & jr plant pathologist, Exp Sta, 48-50, asst prof & asst plant pathologist, 50-56, assoc prof & assoc plant pathologist, 56-60, PROF PLANT PATH & PLANT PATHOLOGIST, UNIV CALIF, BERKELEY, 60- *Concurrent Pos:* Guggenheim fel, 58-59. *Mem:* AAAS; fel Am Phytopath Soc. *Res:* Verticilium wilt; diseases of small fruit; root infecting fungi; soil fumigation. *Mailing Add:* Dept of Plant Path Univ of Calif Berkeley CA 94720

WILHELM, WALTER EUGENE, b St Louis, Mo, May 16, 31; m 61; c 3. PARASITOLOGY, PROTOZOOLOGY. *Educ:* Harris Teachers Col, BA, 55; Univ Ill, MS, 59; Univ Southern Ill, PhD(zool), 65. *Prof Exp:* Lectr embryol, Univ Southern Ill, 62-63; asst prof, 64-68, ASSOC PROF BIOL, MEMPHIS STATE UNIV, 68- *Concurrent Pos:* NSF fel parasitol, Univ Ill, 67. *Mem:* Soc Protozool; Am Soc Parasitol. *Res:* Parasitic helminths and protozoa, particularly those which may be used as agents of biological control; ecology of free-living protozoa; biology of limax amoebae. *Mailing Add:* Dept of Biol Memphis State Univ Memphis TN 38152

WILHELM, WILLIAM JEAN, b St Louis, Mo, Oct 5, 35; m 57; c 5. STRUCTURAL & CIVIL ENGINEERING. *Educ:* Ala Polytech Inst, BME, 58; Auburn Univ, MS, 63; NC State Univ, PhD(struct eng), 68. *Prof Exp:* Struct engr, Palmer & Baker Engrs, Inc, 58-59 & 59-60; instr eng graphics, Auburn Univ, 60-61 & 62-64; teaching asst civil eng, NC State Univ, 66-67; from asst prof to prof civil eng, WVa Univ, 67-79, assoc chmn dept, 70-74, chmn dept, 74-79; DEAN, COL ENG, WICHITA STATE UNIV, 79- *Concurrent Pos:* NSF grants, 69-73; Am Iron & Steel Inst res grant, 68-73; Expanded Shale Clay & Slate Inst res grant, 71 & 72. *Mem:* Fel Am Concrete Inst; fel Am Soc Civil Engrs; Am Soc Eng Educ; Prestressed Concrete Inst; Nat Soc Prof Engrs. *Res:* Reinforced and prestressed concrete with particular emphasis on torsional and bond behavior for both normal weight and light-weight aggregate concrete. *Mailing Add:* Col Eng Wichita State Univ Wichita KS 67208

WILHELMY, JERRY BARNARD, b Sewickley, Pa, July 31, 42; m 64. NUCLEAR CHEMISTRY, NUCLEAR PHYSICS. *Educ:* Univ Ariz, BSChE, 64; Univ Calif, Berkeley, PhD(nuclear chem), 69. *Prof Exp:* Fel nuclear chem, Lawrence Berkeley Lab, 69-72; MEM STAFF NUCLEAR CHEM, LOS ALAMOS SCI LAB, 72- *Mem:* Am Chem Soc; Am Phys Soc. *Res:* Properties of nuclear fission; fission barriers; fission product spectroscopy, fission produced neutrons. *Mailing Add:* 120 Dos Brazos Los Alamos NM 87544

WILHITE, DOUGLAS LEE, b Owensboro, Ky, July 29, 44; m 67; c 3. PHYSICAL CHEMISTRY, QUANTUM CHEMISTRY. *Educ:* Univ Mo-Columbia, BS, 66; State Univ NY Stonybrook, PhD(phys chem), 71. *Prof Exp:* Fel quantum chem, Aerospace Res Labs, Wright-Patterson AFB, Ohio, 71-73; SR RES CHEMIST PHOTOG SCI, PHOTO PROD DEPT, RES & DEVELOP DIV, E I DU PONT DE NEMOURS & CO, 73- *Concurrent Pos:* Vis res chemist, Technol Inc, 71-72; Nat Res Coun assoc, 72-73. *Mem:* Am Phys Soc. *Res:* Fundamental processes involved in the photographic process as well as work toward designing more efficient photographic systems. *Mailing Add:* 1105 Piper Rd Wilmington DE 19803

WILHITE, ELMER LEE, b Owensbord, Ky, July 29, 44; m 66; c 3. PLUTONIUM CHEMISTRY, OFF-GAS. *Educ:* Univ Mo, BS, 66; Washington Univ, MA, 69. *Prof Exp:* Chemist, Savannah River Lab, 69-79, res chemist, 79-80, tech supvr, Environ Monitoring, 80-81, RES SUPVR, ANAL DEVELOP DIV, SAVANNAH RIVER LAB, E I DU PONT DE NEMOURS, 81- *Mem:* Am Chem Soc; Health Physics Soc. *Res:* Environmental assessment of transuranic element migration form buried solid waste; melting and off-gas processing of high-level defense nuclear waste. *Mailing Add:* 773-A B-152 Savannah River Lab E I Du Pont de Nemours & Co Inc Aiken SC 19801

WILHM, JERRY L, b Kansas City, Kans, Apr 27, 30; m 55; c 2. LIMNOLOGY, ECOLOGY. *Educ:* Kans State Teachers Col, BS, 52, MS, 56; Okla State Univ, PhD(zool), 65. *Prof Exp:* Teacher high sch, Kans, 56-62; US AEC fel, Oak Ridge, Tenn, 65-66; PROF ZOOL, SCH BIOL SCI, OKLA STATE UNIV, 66- *Concurrent Pos:* Biol consult, Am Inst Biol Sci Film Series, 61-62; Fulbright fel, NZ, 79. *Mem:* Am Soc Limnol & Oceanog; Ecol Soc Am. *Res:* Biological effects of oil refinery effluents. *Mailing Add:* Dept Zool Okla State Univ Stillwater OK 74078

WILHOFT, DANIEL C, b Newark, NJ, Nov 16, 30; m 51; c 2. ZOOLOGY. *Educ:* Rutgers Univ, AB, 56; Univ Calif, Berkeley, MA, 58, PhD(zool), 63. *Prof Exp:* From instr to assoc prof, 62-69, chmn dept zool & physiol, 69-75, PROF ZOOL, RUTGERS UNIV, NEWARK, 69- *Mem:* AAAS; Am Soc Zool; fel Zool Soc London. *Res:* Ecology of fresh-water turtles; reptilian endocrinology. *Mailing Add:* Dept of Zool & Physiol Rutgers Univ Newark NJ 07102

WILHOIT, EUGENE DENNIS, b Frankfort, Ky, Jan 28, 31; m 58; c 1. PHYSICAL CHEMISTRY. *Educ:* Univ Ky, BS, 53, PhD(phys chem), 56. *Prof Exp:* From res chemist to sr res chemist, Polychem Dept, 56-67, admin asst technol dept, 67, asst div supt, 67-69, div supt res, 69-75, GEN TECH SUPT, E I DU PONT DE NEMOURS & CO, INC, 75- *Mem:* AAAS; Am Chem Soc. *Res:* Electrochemistry and electrolytic conductance; reactions and synthesis of polymer intermediates; nonaqueous solutions; oxidation mechanisms. *Mailing Add:* 213 Tracy Lane Victoria TX 77901

WILHOIT, JAMES CAMMACK, JR, b Tulsa, Okla, Dec 22, 25; m; c 4. MECHANICAL ENGINEERING. *Educ:* Rice Inst Technol, BS, 48; Tex A&M Univ, MS, 51; Stanford Univ, PhD(eng mech), 54. *Prof Exp:* Instr mech eng, Tex A&M Univ, 49-51; sr aerophys eng, Convair, Tex, 53-54; from asst prof to assoc prof mech eng, 54-70, PROF MECH ENG, RICE UNIV, 70- *Mem:* Am Soc Mech Engrs. *Mailing Add:* Dept of Mech Eng Rice Univ Houston TX 77001

WILHOIT, RANDOLPH CARROLL, b San Antonio, Tex, Oct 16, 25; m 48; c 3. THERMODYNAMICS, PHYSICAL BIOCHEMISTRY. *Educ:* Trinity Univ, Tex, AB, 47; Univ Kans, MA, 49; Northwestern Univ, PhD, 52. *Prof Exp:* Fel phys chem, Univ Ind, 52-53; asst prof, Tex Tech Col, 53-57; assoc prof, NMex Highlands Univ, 57-60, prof, 60-64; ASSOC PROF CHEM & ASSOC DIR THERMODYN RES CTR, TEX A&M UNIV, 64- *Concurrent Pos:* Assoc ed, J Chem & Eng Data of Am Chem Soc, 71- *Mem:* AAAS; Am Chem Soc; Calorimetry Conf. *Res:* Thermochemistry; molecular structure; energetics of biochemical reactions. *Mailing Add:* Dept of Chem Tex A&M Univ College Station TX 77840

WILHOLD, GILBERT A, b East St Louis, Ill, Dec 9, 34; m 62; c 3. PHYSICS, MECHANICS. *Educ:* St Louis Univ, BS, 57. *Prof Exp:* Engr, McDonnell Aircraft Corp, Mo, 57-60 & Chrysler Corp, Ala, 60-62; engr, 62-63, tech asst anal & theoret acoust, 63, tech asst to lab dir, 63-66, dep br chief unsteady fluid mech, 66-69 & Unsteady Gas Dynamics Br, 69-77, AEROPHYS DIV ASST, MARSHALL SPACE FLIGHT CTR, NASA, 77- *Concurrent Pos:* Consult to private firms, fed, state & local govt & univ. *Mem:* Assoc fel Am Inst Aeronaut & Astronaut; sr mem Inst Environ Sci. *Res:* Acoustic noise generated by rocket exhausts and air flow over space vehicle surfaces during flight; random process theory and application; data reduction and analysis; aeroelasticity; fluid mechanics; structural dynamics and vibrations; sonic boom and its environmental effects; unsteady fluid flow in high performance pumps and aeroelastically induced loads. *Mailing Add:* 2604 Pitkin Lane Huntsville AL 35810

WILIMOVSKY, NORMAN JOSEPH, b Chicago, Ill, Sept 9, 25; m 47; c 4. ICHTHYOLOGY, FISHERIES. *Educ:* Univ Mich, BS, 48, MA, 49; Stanford Univ, PhD, 56. *Prof Exp:* Head fish & game off, Mil Govt, Bavaria, Ger, 46; assoc ichthyologist, Fisheries Surv Brazil, 50-51; prin investr, Arctic Invests, Stanford Univ, 51-54, res assoc, 55-56; chief marine fisheries invests, US Fish & Wildlife Serv, Alaska, 56-60; assoc prof, Fisheries & Zool, 60-64, dir, Inst Fisheries, 63-66, PROF FISHERIES, UNIV BC, 64- *Concurrent Pos:* Mem comt proj Chariot, AEC, 60-66; staff specialist, US Coun Marine Resources & Eng Develop, 67-68; mem, Environ Protection Bd, 70-76. *Mem:* Fel AAAS; Am Soc Ichthyol & Herpet; Am Fisheries Soc; Am Soc Limnol & Oceanog; fel Arctic Inst NAm. *Res:* Systematics of fishes; fisheries; ecology of ice; development and management of tropical multispecies fisheries; underwater instrumentation; history of biological exploration; science policy formulation. *Mailing Add:* Inst Resource Ecol Univ BC Vancouver BC V6T 1W5 Can

WILK, LEONARD STEPHEN, b Adams, Mass, Sept 29, 27; m 60; c 3. ELECTRICAL ENGINEERING, INSTRUMENTATION. *Educ:* Mass Inst Technol, SB & SM, 55. *Prof Exp:* Group leader missile guid, Instrumentation Lab, Mass Inst Technol, 55-60, asst dir space guid, 60-67, assoc dir instrumentation, Measurement Systs Lab, 67-74; STAFF ENGR, CHARLES STARK DRAPER LAB, INC, 74- *Mem:* Am Inst Aeronaut & Astronaut. *Res:* Inertial navigation and guidance; system analysis and testing; gravity gradiometry; magnetic suspension systems; control systems; experimental tests of gravitation theories. *Mailing Add:* 555 Tech Sq MS 88 Cambridge MA 02139

WILK, SHERWIN, b New York, NY, Aug 25, 38; m 63; c 2. BIOCHEMISTRY, PHARMACOLOGY. *Educ:* Syracuse Univ, BS, 60; Purdue Univ, MS, 62; Fordham Univ, PhD(biochem), 67. *Prof Exp:* Res asst biochem, Mt Sinai Hosp, 62-67; assoc prof, 69-80, PROF PHARMACOL, MT SINAI SCH MED, 80- *Concurrent Pos:* NIH fel, Sch Med, Cornell Univ, 67-69; NIH res career develop award, Mt Sinai Sch Med, 69- *Mem:* AAAS; Am Soc Pharmacol & Exp Therapeut; Am Soc Neurochem; Am Chem Soc. *Res:* Metabolism of gamma glutamyl compounds; peptidases and proteinases in the central nervous system; metabolism of catecholamines in central nervous system. *Mailing Add:* Dept of Pharmacol Mt Sinai Sch of Med New York NY 10029

WILK, STANISLAS FRANCOIS JEAN, b Thaumiers, France, May 17, 46; French & Can citizen; m 71; c 2. MATHEMATICAL PHYSICS, NUCLEAR PHYSICS. *Educ:* Univ Grenoble, BSc, 68, MSc, 70, Dr(physics), 73. *Prof Exp:* Fel, Dept Physics & Ctr Interdisciplinary Studies Chem Physics, Univ Western Ont, 73-75; fel, 75-76, res asst, 76-77, asst prof, 77-80, ASSOC PROF PHYSICS, DEPT PHYSICS & CYCLOTRON LAB, UNIV MAN, 80- *Concurrent Pos:* Nat Res Coun Can operating grants, 77-81 & 81-84. *Mem:* Am Phys Soc; Can Asn Physicists. *Res:* Concepts and mathematics for the formulation of a practical but rigorous many-body scattering theory. *Mailing Add:* Dept of Physics Univ of Man Winnipeg MB R3T 2N2 Can

WILK, WILLIAM DAVID, b Pittsburgh, Pa, Mar 6, 42; m 70; c 3. INORGANIC CHEMISTRY. *Educ:* Thiel Col, BA, 64; Northwestern Univ, PhD(chem), 68. *Prof Exp:* From asst prof to assoc prof, 68-78, PROF CHEM, CALIF STATE COL, DOMINGUEZ HILLS, 78- *Mem:* The Chem Soc; Nat Sci Teachers Asn. *Res:* Ligand substitution effects on cobalt III complexes. *Mailing Add:* 730 Muskingum Ave Pacific Palisades CA 90272

WILKE, CHARLES R, b Dayton, Ohio, Feb 4, 17; m 45. CHEMICAL ENGINEERING. *Educ:* Univ Dayton, BS, 40; State Col Wash, MS, 42; Univ Wis, PhD(chem eng), 44. *Prof Exp:* Assoc engr, Union Oil Co, Calif, 44-45; instr chem eng, State Col Wash, 45-46; from instr to assoc prof, 46-53, chmn dept, 53-63, PROF CHEM ENG, UNIV CALIF, BERKELEY, 53-, RES ASSOC, LAWRENCE BERKELEY LAB, 50- *Concurrent Pos:* Indust consult, 52-; commencement speaker, Univ Dayton, 61; mem adv bd, Petrol Res Fund, 64-67; mem Calif Bd Registr Prof Engrs, 64-72, pres, 67-68. *Honors & Awards:* Colburn Award, Am Inst Chem Engrs, 51, Walker Award, 65. *Mem:* Nat Acad Eng; AAAS; Am Inst Chem Engrs; Am Chem Soc; Am Soc Eng Educ. *Res:* Mass transfer operations; separation and purification of materials; electrostatic precipitation; biochemical engineering; kinetics and scale-up of microbial processes. *Mailing Add:* Dept Chem Eng 110 Gilman Hall Univ of Calif Berkeley CA 94720

WILKE, FREDERICK WALTER, b Pana, Ill, Sept 13, 33; m 56; c 4. MATHEMATICS. *Educ:* Drury Col, AB, 54; Wash Univ, MA, 59; Univ Mo, Columbia, MA, 60, PhD(math), 66. *Prof Exp:* Instr math, Southwest Mo State Col, 63-65; asst prof, 65-73, ASSOC PROF MATH, UNIV MO, ST LOUIS, 73- *Mem:* Am Math Soc; Math Asn Am. *Res:* Finite projective planes, especially translation planes. *Mailing Add:* Dept of Math Univ of Mo 8001 Natural Bridge Rd St Louis MO 63121

WILKE, ROBERT NIELSEN, b San Diego, Calif, July 7, 41; m 73; c 2. CHEMICAL INFORMATION, INFORMATION ANALYSIS. *Educ:* San Diego State Univ, BS, 64; Case Western Reserve Univ, PhD(org chem), 71. *Prof Exp:* Res assoc electrochem, Youngstown State Univ, 71-72, cancer res, Univ Chicago, 72-74; sr chemist, Velsicol Chem Corp, 74-80; RES INFO SCIENTIST, STANDARD OIL CO, 80- *Mem:* Am Soc Info Scientists; Am Chem Soc; Royal Soc Chem. *Res:* Retrieval and analysis of information related to petroleum industry. *Mailing Add:* Standard Oil Co PO Box 400 Naperville IL 60566

WILKEN, DAVID RICHARD, b Amarillo, Tex, Feb 20, 34; m 55; c 3. BIOCHEMISTRY. *Educ:* Blackburn Col, BA, 55; Univ Ill, MS, 58; Mich State Univ, PhD(biochem), 60. *Prof Exp:* From asst prof to assoc prof biochem, Okla State Univ, 62-66; asst prof, 66-72, ASSOC PROF PHYSIOL CHEM, UNIV WIS, MADISON, 72-; RES CHEMIST, LAB EXP PATH, VET ADMIN HOSP, 66- *Concurrent Pos:* Nat Found fel, Inst Enzyme Res, Univ Wis, 60-62. *Mem:* Am Soc Biol Chem; Am Chem Soc. *Res:* Diabetes; glycoprotein biosynthesis; pantothenic acid metabolism; enzymology. *Mailing Add:* Vet Admin Hosp 2500 Overlook Terr Madison WI 53705

WILKEN, DIETER H, b Los Angeles, Calif, Apr 12, 44. SYSTEMATIC BOTANY. *Educ:* Calif State Univ, Los Angeles, BA, 67; Univ Calif, Santa Barbara, PhD(biol), 71. *Prof Exp:* Res asst, Los Angeles State & County Arboretum, 66-67; asst prof biol, Occidental Col, 71-73; asst prof biol, 73-76, ASSOC PROF BOT, COLO STATE UNIV, 76- *Concurrent Pos:* Cur, Colo State Univ Herbarium, 73- *Mem:* Bot Soc Am; Am Soc Plant Taxon; Int Soc Plant Taxon. *Res:* Systematics of higher plants within field of cytology, biochemistry, anatomy and breeding behavior; ecology and evolutionary dynamics of populations. *Mailing Add:* Dept of Bot & Plant Path Colo State Univ Ft Collins CO 80523

WILKEN, DONALD RAYL, b New Orleans, La, Apr 25, 38; m 58; c 1. PURE MATHEMATICS. *Educ:* Tulane Univ, BS, 58, PhD(math), 65; Univ Calif, Los Angeles, MA, 62. *Prof Exp:* NSF fel, Brandeis Univ, 65-66; instr math, Mass Inst Technol, 66-68; from asst prof to assoc prof, 68-75, PROF MATH, STATE UNIV N Y ALBANY, 75- *Res:* Functional and complex analysis. *Mailing Add:* Dept of Math State Univ of N Y Albany NY 12203

WILKEN, LEON OTTO, JR, b Waterbury, Conn, Oct 21, 24; m 46. PHARMACEUTICS, BIOPHARMACEUTICS. *Educ:* Loyola Univ, La, BS, 51; Univ Tex, MS, 53, PhD(pharm), 63. *Prof Exp:* Spec instr pharm, Univ Tex, 53-63; assoc prof, 63-72, head, Pharmaceut Div, 73-77, PROF PHARM, AUBURN UNIV, 72- *Concurrent Pos:* Pharm consult, Vet Admin Hosp, Tuskegee, Ala, 74- *Mem:* Am Asn Cols Pharm; Am Pharmaceut Asn; Am Chem Soc. *Res:* Enteric coated and sustained release dosage forms; investigations of plants known in folk-medicine for actual therapeutic value; time-dose distribution of selected mycotoxins in the rat; bioavailability and stability related to dosage forms. *Mailing Add:* Dept of Pharm Auburn Univ Auburn AL 36830

WILKENFELD, JASON MICHAEL, b Brooklyn, NY, May 28, 39; m 62; c 2. SOLID STATE PHYSICS. *Educ:* Columbia Col, AB, 60; NY Univ, MS, 65, PhD(physics), 72. *Prof Exp:* Programmer analyst, Syst Develop Corp, 63; res asst physics, Radiation & Solid State Lab, NY Univ, 65-70; fel physics, New Eng Inst, 70-72; staff physicist, 73-77, group leader, 77-78, DEPT MGR, IRT CORP, 78- *Concurrent Pos:* Lectr physics, Hunter Col, City Univ New York, 66-69 & NY Univ, 69. *Mem:* Am Phys Soc. *Res:* Nuclear and space radiation effects in materials and systems; electrical properties of dielectrics; positron annihilation as a morphological probe. *Mailing Add:* IRT Corp PO Box 80817 San Diego CA 92138

WILKENING, GEORGE MARTIN, b New York, NY, Dec 31, 23; m 50; c 5. ENVIRONMENTAL HEALTH. *Educ:* Queen's Col, NY, BS, 49; Columbia Univ, MS, 50. *Prof Exp:* Indust hygienist, State Health Dept, Va, 50-51; indust hygienist, Esso Res & Eng Co, 52-56, sr indust hygienist, Esso Standard Oil Co, 56-61; asst chief indust hygienist, Humble Oil & Ref Co, 61-63; head indust hyg & safety admin, 63-64, HEAD ENVIRON HEALTH & SAFETY DEPT, BELL LABS, INC, 64-, DIR, ENVIRON HEALTH & SAFETY CTR, 80- *Concurrent Pos:* Lectr, Columbia Univ, 59-; mem, Safety Tech Adv Bd, Am Nat Stand Inst, 65-; chmn, Laser Hazards Stand Comt, 68-; mem, Environ Radiation Adv Comt, Environ Protection Agency, 67-72; tech electronic prod radiation stand comt mem, Dept Health, Educ & Welfare, 68-; mem, Nat Coun Radiation Protection & Measurements, 73-79; chmn, Tech Comt Lasers, Int Electrotech Comn, 73-; chmn, Sci Comt Microwaves, Nat Coun Radiation Protection & Measurements, 75; mem study group on non-ionizing radiations, Int Radiation Protection Asn, 75, Nat Acad Sci/Nat Res Coun comt on biosphere effects extremely low frequency radiation, 76 & panel on effects radiation from Pave Paws Radar, 78, exec comt, Safety & Health Standards Mgt Bd, Am Nat Standards Inst; adj assoc prof environ med, NY Univ; consult armed forces epidemiol bd, Dept Defense, Washington, DC, 77; mem, Electromagnetic Radiation Mgt Adv Coun, Nat Telecommunications & Info, 79- *Mem:* AAAS; Sigma Xi; Acoust Soc Am; Am Indust Hyg Asn; fel NY Acad Sci. *Res:* Dosimetry of exposure to electromagnetic radiations, including acoustical noise; industrial toxicology; biological effects of chemical, physical and biological agents in the environment; development of standards for permissible levels of exposure to environmental agents. *Mailing Add:* Environ Health & Safety Dept Bell Labs Murray Hill NJ 07974

WILKENING, LAUREL LYNN, b Richland, Wash, Nov 23, 44. METEORITICS, PLANETARY SCIENCES. *Educ:* Reed Col, BA, 66; Univ Calif, San Diego, PhD(chem), 70. *Prof Exp:* Am Asn Univ Women fel, Tata Inst Fundamental Res, India & Max Planck Inst Chem, 71; res assoc chem, Enrico Fermi Inst, Univ Chicago, 72-73; asst prof, 73-78, ASSOC PROF PLANETARY SCI, UNIV ARIZ, 78-, HEAD, PLANETARY SCI DEPT & DIR LUNAR & PLANETARY LAB, 81- *Honors & Awards:* Nininger Meteorite Award, Ariz State Univ, 70. *Mem:* AAAS; fel Meteoritical Soc; Am Geophys Union; Am Astron Soc; Asn Women Sci. *Res:* Chemistry and mineralogy of meteorites, asteroids and comets; cosmochemistry. *Mailing Add:* Lunar & Planetary Lab Univ of Ariz Tucson AZ 85721

WILKENING, MARVIN C, b Malone, Tex, July 1, 20; m 43; c 4. ANIMAL NUTRITION, BIOCHEMISTRY. *Educ:* Univ Tex, AB, 41; Agr & Mech Col, Tex, MS, 47. *Hon Degrees:* ScD, Athens Col, 56. *Prof Exp:* Res chemist, Dow Chem Co, Tex, 41-44; asst to dir res, Security Mills, Tenn, 47-50; dir res, Ala Flour Mills, 50-66; dir tech serv, Nebr, 67-75, NONRUMINANT NUTRITIONIST & CONSULT, CONAGRA, INC, 75- *Mem:* Fel AAAS; Am Chem Soc; Am Soc Animal Sci; Poultry Sci Asn. *Res:* Application of basic animal nutrition and management research. *Mailing Add:* ConAgra Inc PO Box 2207 Decatur AL 35601

WILKENING, MARVIN HUBERT, b Oak Ridge, Mo, Mar 13, 18; m 42; c 2. RADON & DAUGHTER PROD. *Educ:* Southeastern Mo Univ, BS, 39; Ill Inst Technol, MS, 43, PhD(nuclear physics), 49. *Prof Exp:* Teacher high sch, Mo, 39-41; physicist, Manhattan Proj, 42-45; instr physics, Ill Inst Technol, 46-48; assoc prof physics, 48-52, prof physics & geophys & head dept, 52-68, PROF PHYSICS & DEAN GRAD STUDIES, N MEX INST MINING & TECHNOL, 67- *Concurrent Pos:* Mem, Fermi group at first nuclear reactor, Chicago, 42 & 46; mem subcomn ions, Aerosols & Radioactivity, Int Comn Atmospheric Elec; mem, Nat Comn Radiation Protection; mem, NMex Radiation Tech Adv Comt. *Honors & Awards:* Cert Serv, Off Sci Res Develop, 46. *Mem:* Fel AAAS; fel Am Phys Soc; NY Acad Sci; Am Geophys Union; Am Meteorol Soc. *Res:* Radon and its daughter products; the natural radiation environment; atmospheric electricity-ions and aerosols; tracer studies of atmospheric systems; local climatology; radioactive wastes. *Mailing Add:* 1218 South Dr Socorro NM 87801

WILKENS, GEORGE A(LBERT), b North Bergen, NJ, June 29, 09; m 46; c 2. CHEMICAL ENGINEERING. *Educ:* Columbia Univ, AB, 29, BS, 30, CE, 31, PhD(chem eng), 33. *Prof Exp:* From res chemist to chief chemist, Arlington Plant, Polychem Dept, E I du Pont de Nemours & Co, Inc, Wilmington, 33-57, plastics consult, Chestnut Run Lab, 57-74; CONSULT ACRYLIC PLASTICS, 74- *Mem:* Am Chem Soc; Am Inst Chem Engrs; Am Soc Testing & Mat. *Res:* Agitation; organic synthesis; cellulose plastics; acrylic and dental resins; dyes; pigments; polymerization. *Mailing Add:* 213 Sypherd Dr Newark DE 19711

WILKENS, JERREL L, b Lorraine, Kans, Aug 5, 37; m 68; c 2. INVERTEBRATE NEUROPHYSIOLOGY, INVERTEBRATE MUSCLE PHYSIOLOGY. *Educ:* Univ Ottawa, Kans, BA, 59; Tulane Univ, MSc, 61; Univ Calif, Los Angeles, PhD(zool), 67. *Prof Exp:* NIMH fel, Brain Res Inst, Univ Calif, Los Angeles, 67-68; asst prof, 69-72, assoc prof, 72-81, PROF BIOL, UNIV CALGARY, 81- *Mem:* AAAS; Am Soc Zoologists; Can Soc Zool; Soc Neurosci. *Res:* Neuronal activity associated with hormone release; neurophysiology of crustacean motor systems; brachiopod neuromuscular physiology. *Mailing Add:* Dept Biol Univ Calgary Calgary AB T2N 1N4 Can

WILKENS, JOHN ALBERT, b New York, NY, Oct 28, 47; m 77. CHEMICAL ENGINEERING. *Educ:* Cornell Univ, BS, 69, MChE, 71; Mass Inst Technol, PhD(chem eng), 77. *Prof Exp:* Chem engr emission testing, US Environ Protection Agency, 70-72; RES ENGR, E I DU PONT DE NEMOURS & CO, INC, 77- *Mem:* Am Inst Chem Engrs; Am Chem Soc; Sigma Xi; Catalysis Soc. *Res:* Catalysis; reactor engineering; surface chemistry; filtration. *Mailing Add:* 138 Round Hill Rd Kennett Square PA 19348

WILKENS, LON ALLAN, b Ellsworth, Kans, Sept 7, 42; m 65; c 3. NEUROBIOLOGY. *Educ:* Univ Kans, Lawrence, BA, 65; Fla State Univ, PhD(physiol), 70. *Prof Exp:* Fel neurobiol, Univ Tex, Austin, 70-73; asst prof biol, Bryn Mawr Col, 73-75; asst prof biol, Univ Mo-St Louis, 75-80; MEM FAC, DEPT NEUROBIOL, RES SCH BIOL SCI, AUSTRALIAN NAT UNIV, 80- *Mem:* Am Soc Zoologists; Soc Neurosci; AAAS. *Res:* Neural basis of behavior, including circulatory, somatosensory and respiratory physiology in decapod crustaceans and in bivalve and cephalopod molluscs, specifically related to the function of central interneurons and mechanisms of integration. *Mailing Add:* Dept Neurobiol Res Sch Biol Sci Australian Nat Univ Canberra 2601 Australia

WILKENS, LUCILE SHANES, b Kansas City, Mo, May 19, 50; m 77. CHEMICAL ENGINEERING. *Educ:* Wash Univ, BS, 72; Mass Inst Technol, PhD(chem eng), 77. *Prof Exp:* RES ENGR, E I DU PONT DE NEMOURS & CO, INC, 77- *Mem:* Am Inst Chem Engrs; Am Chem Soc; Sigma Xi. *Res:* Colloid and surface chemistry; rheology; cryogenics. *Mailing Add:* 138 Round Hill Rd Kennett Square PA 19348

WILKERSON, CLARENCE WENDELL, JR, b Laredo, Tex, Aug 12, 44; m 65; c 1. TOPOLOGY. *Educ:* Rice Univ, BA, 66, PhD(math), 70. *Prof Exp:* Asst prof math, Univ Hawaii, Monoa, 70-72; res assoc, Swiss Fed Inst Technol, 72-73; res assoc, Carleton Univ, 73-74; instr, Univ Pa, 74-75, asst prof math, 75-77; PROF MATH, WAYNE STATE UNIV, 77- *Mem:* Am Math Soc. *Res:* Algebraic topology and homotopy theory of Lie groups, H-spaces and associated spaces. *Mailing Add:* Dept of Math Wayne State Univ Detroit MI 48202

WILKERSON, JOHN CHRISTOPHER, b Washington, DC, Mar 15, 26; m 58; c 2. PHYSICAL OCEANOGRAPHY. *Educ:* Univ Md, BS, 51. *Prof Exp:* Phys oceanogr, 60-62, from proj scientist to sr proj scientist, 62-67, proj mgr, 67-77, SR PROJ SCIENTIST, US NAVAL OCEANOG OFF, 77- *Concurrent Pos:* Proj mgr data mgt, US Naval Oceanog Off, 74-77. *Res:* Remote sensing; aircraft platforms; data management; satellites. *Mailing Add:* 4834 Butterworth Pl NW Washington DC 20016

WILKERSON, ROBERT C, b Orange, Tex, June 25, 18; m 42; c 1. PHYSICS, MATHEMATICS. *Educ:* Univ Okla, BS, 41. *Prof Exp:* Seismic comput, Geophys Party, Stanolind Oil & Gas Co, Okla, 41-43; spectroscopist, Sinclair Rubber Inc, Tex, 43-47; res & develop div, 47-49, group leader phys instruments, 49-55, anal res, 55, head anal sect, 55-65, ADMIN MGR, TECH CTR, CELANESE CHEM CO, NY, 65- *Mem:* Coblentz Soc. *Res:* Application of physical instruments in analytical support of organic chemistry research and development; development of application of computer systems for management information data and for technical information storage and retrieval systems. *Mailing Add:* 221 Rosebud Corpus Christi TX 78404

WILKERSON, ROBERT DOUGLAS, b Wilson, NC, Aug 5, 44; m 65; c 2. PHARMACOLOGY. *Educ:* Univ NC, Chapel Hill, BS, 67; Med Univ SC, MS, 69, PhD(pharmacol), 72. *Prof Exp:* Asst prof, Col Med, Univ South Ala, 73-76, assoc prof, 76-79; ASSOC PROF, MED COL OHIO, 79- *Mem:* AAAS; Am Soc Pharmacol & Exp Therapeut; Am Col Clin Pharmacol. *Res:* Cardiovascular pharmacology, especially antiarrhythmic drugs and pulmonary pharmacology, specifically shock lung. *Mailing Add:* Dept Pharamcol CS 10008 Med Col Ohio Toledo OH 43699

WILKERSON, THOMAS DELANEY, b Detroit, Mich, Feb 18, 32; div; c 3. PLASMA PHYSICS, SPACE PHYSICS. *Educ:* Univ Mich, BS, 53, MS, 54, PhD(physics), 62. *Prof Exp:* Consult, Proj Matterhorn, Princeton Univ, 59-60, mem proj res staff plasma, 60-61; from asst prof to assoc prof, 61-68, actg dir dept, 68-69, PROF PLASMA & SPACE PHYSICS, INST FLUID DYNAMICS & APPL MATH, UNIV MD, COLLEGE PARK, 68- *Concurrent Pos:* Consult, Radiation Div, US Naval Res Lab, 62-64; physics consult, Atlantic Res, 68-69; lectr, von Karman Inst, Brussels, 69; vpres, Versar, Inc, 69-70, consult, 70-; vis prof, Stanford Univ, 70; consult, Stanford Res Inst, 71; vis, Desert Res Inst, 71. *Mem:* Am Phys Soc; Am Astron Soc. *Res:* Laser-guided electrical discharges in gases, high-resolution absorption spectra of atmospheric gases; laser sounding of the atmosphere, infrared schlieren and interferometry; collision-induced spectroscopy in dense gases. *Mailing Add:* Inst for Phys Sci & Technol Univ of Md College Park MD 20740

WILKES, CHARLES EUGENE, b Worcester, Mass, Oct 9, 39; m 61; c 4. CHEMISTRY. *Educ:* Worcester Polytech Inst, BS, 61; Princeton Univ, PhD(phys chem), 64. *Prof Exp:* From res chemist to sr chemist, 64-69, sect leader, 69-73, sr res assoc, 73-74, sect mgr, Corp Res New Technol, 74-78, dir, Technol Assessment & Planning, 78-81, DIR CORP RES, RES CTR, B F GOODRICH CO, 81- *Mem:* Am Chem Soc. *Res:* Chemical physics; polymer characterization; x-ray diffraction; molecular spectroscopy; lab automation. *Mailing Add:* B F Goodrich Co Res Ctr Brecksville OH 44141

WILKES, GARTH L, b Syracuse, NY, May 22, 42; D; c 2. POLYMER SCIENCE. *Educ:* State Univ NY Col Environ Sci & Forestry, BS, 64; Univ Mass, Amherst, MS, 67, PhD(phys chem), 69. *Prof Exp:* From asst to assoc prof chem eng, Princeton Univ, 69-78; prof chem eng, 78-81, FWB PROF, VA POLYTECH INST & STATE UNIV, 81- *Concurrent Pos:* Res assoc, Textile Res Inst, 74- *Mem:* Am Inst Chem Eng; Am Chem Soc. *Res:* Property of synthetic and biopolymers. *Mailing Add:* Dept of Chem Eng Va Polytech Inst & State Univ Blacksburg VA 24061

WILKES, GLENN RICHARD, b Houtzdale, Pa, Mar 25, 37; m 61; c 2. INORGANIC CHEMISTRY. *Educ:* Pa State Univ, BS, 60; Univ Wis, PhD(inorg chem), 65. *Prof Exp:* Scholar, Univ Calif, Los Angeles, 65-66; RES SCIENTIST, EASTMAN KODAK CO, 66- *Mem:* Am Chem Soc; Am Crystallog Asn; The Chem Soc. *Res:* Crystal and molecular structure determination of organometallic compounds by single crystal x-ray diffraction studies; synthesis of metal carbonyls and their derivatives. *Mailing Add:* Indust Lab Eastman Kodak Co 1669 Lake Ave Rochester NY 14650

WILKES, HILBERT GARRISON, JR, b Los Angeles, Calif, Oct 2, 37; m 78. PLANT GENETICS. *Educ:* Pomona Col, BA, 59; Harvard Univ, PhD(biol), 66. *Prof Exp:* Asst prof biol, Tulane Univ, 66-70; asst prof, 70-73, ASSOC PROF BIOL, UNIV MASS, BOSTON, 73- *Concurrent Pos:* Mem, World Maize Germplasm Comn, Rockefeller Found & Food & Agr Orgn; exec comt, Assembly Life Sci, Nat Res Coun, 72-76; mem ed bd, J Econ Bot; Indo-Am fel, India, 78-79. *Mem:* Soc Study Econ Bot (secy, 73-75 & 75-77); Soc Study Evolution; Bot Soc Am; Soc Econ Bot; Indian Bot Soc. *Res:* Evolution under domestication in cultivated plants, especially maize and its wild relatives, teosinte and tripsacum. *Mailing Add:* Dept Biol Col II Univ Mass Boston MA 02125

WILKES, JAMES C, b Mar 13, 21; US citizen; m 45; c 6. BIOLOGY. *Educ:* Troy State Col, BS, 48; Univ Tenn, MS, 50; Univ Ala, PhD(bot), 54. *Prof Exp:* Prof biol, Tenn Wesleyan Col, 50-51; prof & head dept, Jacksonville State Univ, 52-56; ed adv med sci sch aviation med, Air Univ, 56-57; prof & head dept biol, Huntingdon Col, 57-60 & Miss State Col Women, 60-66; head dept, 68-77, PROF BIOL, TROY STATE UNIV, 66- *Res:* Bryophytes; radiation biology. *Mailing Add:* Dept of Biol Troy State Univ Troy AL 36081

WILKES, JAMES OSCROFT, b Southampton, Eng, Jan 24, 32; m 56. CHEMICAL ENGINEERING, DIGITAL COMPUTING. *Educ:* Cambridge Univ, BA, 54, MA, 60; Univ Mich, MS, 56, PhD(chem eng), 63. *Prof Exp:* Demonstr chem eng, Cambridge Univ, 57-60; from instr to assoc prof, 60-70, chmn dept, 71-77, PROF CHEM ENG, UNIV MICH, ANN ARBOR, 70- *Concurrent Pos:* Assoc, Trinity Col Music, London, Eng, 51. *Mem:* Soc Petrol Engrs; Am Inst Chem Engrs. *Res:* Applied numerical methods; fluid mechanics and heat transfer; metal casting; polymer processing; gas storage; two-phase flow. *Mailing Add:* Dept Chem Eng Univ Mich Ann Arbor MI 48109

WILKES, JOHN BARKER, b Berkeley, Calif, Jan 17, 16; m 38; c 2. PETROLEUM CHEMISTRY. *Educ:* Univ Calif, BS, 37; Stanford Univ, PhD(chem), 48. *Prof Exp:* Chemist, Poultry Prod of Cent Calif, 37-40; from res chemist to sr res chemist, 48-62, res assoc, 62-65, SR RES ASSOC, CHEVRON RES CO, 48- *Mem:* Am Chem Soc. *Res:* Kinetics; thermodynamics; catalysis; chemicals from petroleum; solubility theory. *Mailing Add:* 2935 Oxford Ave Richmond CA 94806

WILKES, JOHN STUART, b Panama, CZ, Mar 6, 47; m 71. ELECTROCHEMISTRY, ORGANIC CHEMISTRY. *Educ:* State Univ NY Buffalo, BA, 69; Northwestern Univ, Evanston, MS, 71, PhD(chem), 73. *Prof Exp:* Res chemist, Frank J Seiler Res Lab, US Air Force Acad, 73-75; asst prof chem, Univ Colo, Denver, 76-78; RES CHEMIST, FRANK J SEILER RES LAB, US AIR FORCE ACAD, 78- *Mem:* AAAS; Am Chem Soc. *Res:* Electrochemistry in molten salts; electroorganic synthesis, thermal decompostion of explosives and propellants. *Mailing Add:* Frank J Seiler Res Lab-NC US Air Force Acad Denver CO 80840

WILKES, JOSEPH WRAY, b Ft Worth, Tex, May 10, 22; m 47; c 3. COMPUTER SCIENCE, INDUSTRIAL ENGINEERING. *Educ:* Southern Methodist Univ, BS, 44; Washington Univ, St Louis, MS, 51, DSc(indust eng), 54. *Prof Exp:* Instr mech eng, Southern Methodist Univ, 48-49; lectr indust eng, Washington Univ, St Louis, 49-50, instr, 50-54; from asst prof to assoc prof, 54-64, asst to vpres & provost, Univ, 58-59, assoc dir, Comput Ctr, 60-62, actg dir, 62-65, dir, 65-72, head instr & res comput serv, 72-81, PROF INDUST ENG, UNIV ARK, FAYETTEVILLE, 64-, CHMN DEPT COMPUT SCI, 71- *Concurrent Pos:* Comput consult, Hwy Dept Ark, 61-65; ed consult, State Data Processing Comt, 62-63. *Mem:* Am Inst Indust Engrs; Asn Comput Mach; Am Soc Eng Educ. *Res:* Method and statistical analysis; production planning; operations research. *Mailing Add:* Eng 309 Univ of Ark Fayetteville AR 72701

WILKES, RICHARD JEFFREY, b Chicago, Ill, Oct 18, 45; m 70. EXPERIMENTAL HIGH ENERGY PHYSICS, COSMIC RAY PHYSICS. *Educ:* Univ Mich, BSE, 67; Univ Wis, MS, 69, PhD(physics), 74. *Prof Exp:* Res assoc & instr physics, 74-79, RES SCI & TECH DIR, COSMIC RAY LAB, UNIV WASH, 79- *Res:* High energy cosmic ray spectra and interactions, especially hadronic multiparticle production using nuclear emulsion and hybrid counter/bubble chamber emulsion techniques. *Mailing Add:* Dept of Physics FM-15 Univ of Wash Seattle WA 98195

WILKES, STANLEY NORTHRUP, b Corvallis, Ore, Jan 3, 27; m 58; c 3. PARASITOLOGY, MARINE ZOOLOGY. *Educ:* Ore State Univ, BS, 50, MS, 57, PhD(zool), 66. *Prof Exp:* Aquatic biologist, Res Div, Ore Fish Comn, 50-51 & 56-60; asst prof biol, E Carolina Col, 65-66; asst prof, 66-71, ASSOC PROF ZOOL, NORTHERN ARIZ UNIV, 71- *Mem:* Am Soc Parasitol; Am Micros Soc. *Res:* Taxonomy, life history studies and distribution of parasitic copepods of fishes, elasmobranchs and invertebrates; taxonomy of monogenetic Trematoda; taxonomy and ecology of marine invertebrates and fishes. *Mailing Add:* Dept of Biol Sci Box 5640 Northern Ariz Univ Flagstaff AZ 86001

WILKES, WILLIAM ROY, b Harvey, Ill, Feb 15, 39; m 59; c 3. ISOTOPE SEPARATION, FUSION TECHNOLOGY. *Educ:* DePauw Univ, AB, 59; Univ Ill, MS, 61, PhD(physics), 66. *Prof Exp:* Asst prof physics, Wake Forest Univ, 65-67; sr res physicist, 67-74, res specialist, 74-77, GROUP LEADER MOUND LAB, MONSANTO RES CORP, 79- *Mem:* AAAS; Am Phys Soc; Am Nuclear Soc. *Res:* Cryogenic isotope separation; Tritium technology; liquid helium; superconductivity. *Mailing Add:* Mound Lab Monsanto Res Corp Miamisburg OH 45342

WILKIE, BRUCE NICHOLSON, b Perth, Scotland, Jan 19, 41; Can citizen; m 66; c 1. IMMUNOLOGY, VETERINARY MEDICINE. *Educ:* Univ Guelph, DVM, 65; Cornell Univ, PhD(immunol), 71. *Prof Exp:* Res asst path, NY State Vet Col, Cornell Univ, 71; asst prof immunol, Univ Bern, 71-73; asst prof, 73-75, assoc prof, 75-80, PROF IMMUNOL, UNIV GUELPH, 80- *Mem:* Can Soc Immunol; Am Asn Immunologists. *Res:* Veterinary immunology and immunopathology. *Mailing Add:* Dept of Vet Microbiol & Immunol Univ of Guelph Guelph ON N1G 2W1 Can

WILKIE, CHARLES ARTHUR, b Detroit, Mich, Nov 21, 41; m 64; c 3. INORGANIC CHEMISTRY. *Educ:* Univ Detroit, BS, 63; Wayne State Univ, PhD(inorg chem), 67. *Prof Exp:* Asst prof, 67-74, ASSOC PROF CHEM, MARQUETTE UNIV, 74- *Mem:* Am Chem Soc; Royal Soc Chem; AAAS; Sigma Xi. *Res:* Organometallic chemistry; flame retardants; polymer chemistry; nuclear magnetic resonance spectroscopy. *Mailing Add:* Dept Chem Marquette Univ Milwaukee WI 53233

WILKIE, DONALD W, b Vancouver, BC, June 20, 31; m 56, 80; c 3. MARINE BIOLOGY. *Educ:* Univ BC, BA, 60, MSc, 66. *Prof Exp:* Asst res biologist, BC Fish & Game Dept, 60-61; asst cur, Vancouver Pub Aquarium, 61-63; cur, Philadelphia Aquarium, Inc, 63-65; AQUARIUM DIR, SCRIPPS INST OCEANOG, 65- *Mem:* Int Asn Aquatic Animal Med; Nat Marine Educ Asn; Am Asn Zool Parks & Aquariums; Am Cetacean Soc; Am Asn Zoologists. *Res:* Pigmentation and coloration of fishes; environmental physiology as it relates to maintenance of marine fishes and cetaceans; aquariology and methods of public education in aquaria and museums. *Mailing Add:* 4548 Cather Ave San Diego CA 92122

WILKIN, LOUIS ALDEN, b Bath, Maine, Mar 5, 39; m 60; c 3. ORGANIC CHEMISTRY. *Educ:* The Citadel, BS, 60; Clemson Univ, MS, 62, PhD(org chem), 65. *Prof Exp:* From chemist to sr chemist, 65-75, develop assoc, 75-76, GROUP LEADER, TENN EASTMAN CO, 76- *Mem:* Am Chem Soc. *Res:* Novel rearrangements of acetylenic alcohols and esters upon treatment with basic alumina. *Mailing Add:* 1122 Watauga St Kingsport TN 37660

WILKINS, BERT, JR, b Hattiesburg, Miss, Oct 8, 34; m 57; c 2. CHEMICAL ENGINEERING. *Educ:* Ga Inst Technol, BChE, 58, MS, 61, PhD(chem eng), 65. *Prof Exp:* Sr engr, Lockheed-Ga Co div, Lockheed Aircraft Corp, 63-64; sr engr, Humble Oil & Ref Co, 65-67; asst prof chem eng, Univ Mo-Columbia, 67-68; ASSOC PROF CHEM ENG, LA STATE UNIV, BATON ROUGE, 68-, COORDR ENERGY PROGS, 75- *Concurrent Pos:* NASA-Am Soc Eng Educ fac fel, NASA Manned Spacecraft Ctr, Tex, 68, 69; consult, 70-; mem environ adv panel, Gulf Universal Res Corp, 70-; NASA grant, La State Univ, Baton Rouge, 70-, NSF grant, 71- *Mem:* AAAS; Am Inst Chem Engrs. *Res:* Applied mathematics; transport phenomena; process design; bioengineering; ecological systems analysis. *Mailing Add:* 10341 Parkview Dr Baton Rouge LA 70815

WILKINS, BRIAN JOHN SAMUEL, b London, Eng, Feb 28, 37; Can citizen; m 61; c 3. PHYSICAL METALLURGY, THERMOMECHANICAL ANALYSIS. *Educ:* Univ London, BSc, 58, PhD(metall), 61. *Prof Exp:* Sci off fuel element develop, Dounreay Exp Reactor Estab, UK Atomic Energy Auth, 61-64; assoc res off mat develop, 64-80, sr res off mat & mech, 80, SECT HEAD MAT & ENG ANAL, WHITESHELL NUCLEAR RES ESTAB, ATOMIC ENERGY CAN LTD, 80- *Res:* Materials development; mathematical modelling (thermomechanical behavior, diffusion, deformation and fracture of solids) applied to reactor safety and nuclear waste management programs. *Mailing Add:* Whiteshell Nuclear Res Estab Pinawa MB R0E 1L0 Can

WILKINS, BRUCE TABOR, b Greenport, NY, June 21, 31; m 56; c 3. MARINE POLICY, RESOURCE EXTENSION ADMINISTRATION. *Educ:* Cornell Univ, BS, 52, PhD(resource planning), 67; Mont State Univ, MS, 56. *Prof Exp:* Res biologist, Mont Fish & Game Dept, 56-59; county agr agent, Broome County Exten Serv, NY, 59-63; exten specialist, 63-67, asst prof, 67-73, assoc prof, 73-80, PROF NATURAL ENERGY, CORNELL UNIV, 80- *Concurrent Pos:* Prog leader, NY Sea Grant Adv Serv, 72-, assoc dir, 75-; vis prof, Univ BC, 74; vis Sea Grant prof, Ore State Univ, 75 & Univ Hawaii, 81. *Mem:* Wildlife Soc; Am Fisheries Soc; Am Asn Univ Professors. *Res:* Relationships of human demands and natural resources, especially fish and wildlife resources; resource policy, particularly marine and recreational policy issues. *Mailing Add:* Dept of Natural Resources Fernow Hall Cornell Univ Ithaca NY 14853

WILKINS, CHARLES H(ENRY) T(ULLY), b Denver, Colo, Dec 10, 20; m 46; c 2. PHYSICAL METALLURGY. *Educ:* Va Mil Inst, BS, 42; Univ Pittsburgh, MS, 46, PhD(metall eng), 58. *Prof Exp:* Prod metallurgist, Carnegie-Ill Steel Corp, 42-46; metallurgist, Copperweld Steel Co, 46-48; fel, Mellon Inst, 48-56, sr fel, 56-61, advan fel, 56-60; head dept, 61-71, PROF METALL ENG, UNIV ALA, 61- *Concurrent Pos:* Consult, US Army Res Off-Durham & Atomic Energy Comn, Tenn. *Mem:* Am Soc Metals; Am Inst Mining, Metall & Petrol Engrs; Am Foundrymen's Soc; Am Soc Eng Educ. *Res:* Heat treatment of alloys; rubber-to-metal bonding; strip polishing processes; surface roughness; fatigue; vacuum deposition; high-temperature modular printed circuitry; alloy development; levitation melting; dispersion hardening; hot hardness. *Mailing Add:* Dept of Metall Eng Univ of Ala Col of Eng University AL 35486

WILKINS, CHARLES LEE, b Los Angeles, Calif, Aug 14, 38; m 66. ANALYTICAL CHEMISTRY. *Educ:* Chapman Col, BS, 61; Univ Ore, PhD(chem), 66. *Prof Exp:* From asst prof to assoc prof, Univ Nebr, Lincoln, 67-76, prof chem, 76-81; PROF CHEM, UNIV CALIF, RIVERSIDE, 81- *Concurrent Pos:* Vis assoc prof, Univ NC, Chapel Hill, 74-75. *Mem:* Am Chem Soc; Am Soc Test & Mat; Am Soc Mass Spectros; Soc Appl Spectros. *Res:* Pattern recognition application in chemistry; mass spectrometry; nuclear magnetic resonance spectroscopy and computer applications to chemical problems and laboratory automation. *Mailing Add:* Dept of Chem Univ Calif Riverside CA 92521

WILKINS, CLETUS WALTER, JR, b Asheville, NC, June 23, 45; m 69; c 2. ORGANIC CHEMISTRY, POLYMER CHEMISTRY. *Educ:* Morgan State Univ, BS, 69; Pa State Univ, MS, 74, PhD(chem), 76. *Prof Exp:* MEM TECH STAFF MAT RES, BELL LABS, 76- *Mem:* Am Chem Soc; AAAS. *Res:* Photochemistry in thin polymer films; solid state photochemistry; organometallic chemistry. *Mailing Add:* Bell Labs 600 Mountain Ave Murray Hill NJ 07974

WILKINS, CURTIS C, b La Crosse, Wis, Oct 28, 35; m 54; c 3. PHYSICAL CHEMISTRY. *Educ:* Wis State Univ, BS, 57; Mich State Univ, PhD(chem), 64. *Prof Exp:* Asst prof chem, WVa Wesleyan Col, 62-65; assoc prof, 65-70, PROF CHEM, WESTERN KY UNIV, 70- *Concurrent Pos:* NSF res participation fel, Univ Tenn, 65. *Mem:* Am Chem Soc. *Res:* Dilute solution properties of stereo-regular polymers; flame photometry studies of trace elements. *Mailing Add:* Dept of Chem Western Ky Univ Bowling Green KY 42101

WILKINS, DALE EDWARD, engineering, agriculture, see previous edition

WILKINS, EBTISAM A M SEOUDI, b Monofia, Egypt, Mar 10, 45; US citizen; m 74; c 1. BIOENGINEERING, CHEMICAL ENGINEERING. *Educ:* Cairo Univ, BSc, 65, MSc, 68; Univ Va, MSc, 73, PhD(chem eng), 76. *Prof Exp:* Res eng metall, Nat Res Ctr, Cairo, Egypt, 65-68; res specialist biomed eng, Div Biomed Eng, Univ Va, 69-73, res asst chem eng, Dept Chem Eng, 73-76; fel bioenergetics, Dept Kinesiology, Simon Fraser Univ, 76-80; MEM FAC, UNIV NMEX, 80- *Res:* Drug effects at cellular level, using cell culture, artificial lipid membrane techniques, especially carotenoids and skeletal muscle cells; effect of electric magnetic fields on bone fracture repair; modelling of blood flow in bones. *Mailing Add:* Univ NMex Albuquerque NM 87131

WILKINS, EUGENE MORRILL, b Hugo, Okla, Oct 5, 22; m 49; c 2. METEOROLOGY. *Educ:* Univ Chicago, MS, 49; Univ Okla, PhD(meteorol), 63. *Prof Exp:* Res scientist, US Weather Bur, 50-59; sr scientist, Ling-Temco-Vought, Inc, Tex, 59-71, SR SCIENTIST, ADVAN TECHNOL CTR, LTV AEROSPACE CORP, 71- *Concurrent Pos:* NSF res grants, 61-63, 65-67, 71-73; adj prof, Univ Okla, 65-; air pollution consult, Tex Pub Health Serv. *Mem:* Am Meteorol Soc; Am Geophys Union; Am Inst Aeronaut & Astronaut. *Res:* Atmospheric turbulence and diffusion; physics of the high atmosphere; severe storm research; satellite meteorology; weather modification. *Mailing Add:* Advan Technol Ctr Vought Corp PO Box 226144 Dallas TX 75266

WILKINS, GEORGE STANLEY, chemical engineering, see previous edition

WILKINS, HAROLD, b Cobden, Ill, Nov 3, 33. HORTICULTURE, PLANT PHYSIOLOGY. *Educ:* Univ Ill, BS, 56, MS, 57, PhD(hort, plant physiol), 65. *Prof Exp:* Res horticulturist, Gulf Coast Exp Sta, Univ Fla, 65-66; from asst prof to assoc prof hort, 66-74, PROF HORT SCI & LANDSCAPE ARCHIT, UNIV MINN, ST PAUL, 74- *Concurrent Pos:* Consult, Gas Chromatography Sch, Fisk Univ, 65. *Honors & Awards:* Lauri Award, 67 & 78; Port Award, 80. *Mem:* Am Soc Hort Sci. *Res:* Post harvest physiology; respiration and ethylene emanation in aging floral tissue; physiology of lilies in response to photoperiod and cold treatments; physiology of flowering. *Mailing Add:* Dept of Hort Col of Agr Univ of Minn St Paul MN 55101

WILKINS, J ERNEST, JR, b Chicago, Ill, Nov 27, 23; wid; c 2. MATHEMATICS. *Educ:* Univ Chicago, SB, 40, SM, 41, PhD(math), 42; NY Univ, BME, 57, MME, 60. *Prof Exp:* Instr math, Tuskegee Inst, 43-44; from assoc physicist to physicist, Manhattan Proj, Metall Lab, Univ Chicago, 44-46; mathematician, Am Optical Co, 46-50; sr mathematician, Nuclear Develop Corp Am, 50-55, mgr physics & math dept, 55-57, asst mgr res & develop, 58-59 & mgr, 59-60; asst chmn, Theoret Physics Dept, Gen Atomic Div, Gen Dynamics Corp, 60-65, asst dir lab, 65-70; distinguished prof appl math physics, Howard Univ, 70-77; assoc gen mgr, 77-80, DEP GEN MGR, EG&G IDAHO, INC, 80- *Mem:* AAAS; Am Math Soc; Optical Soc Am; Am Nuclear Soc; Soc Indust & Appl Math. *Res:* Differential and integral equations; Bessel functions; nuclear reactors; calculus of variation. *Mailing Add:* EG&G Idaho Inc PO Box 1625 Idaho Falls ID 83415

WILKINS, JUDD RICE, b Chicago, Ill, Dec 12, 20; m 50; c 2. MICROBIOLOGY, BIOENGINEERING. *Educ:* Univ Ill, BS, 46, MS, 47, PhD(bact), 50. *Prof Exp:* Asst prof, Med Sch, Univ SDak, 50-51; res investr, Upjohn Co, 51-57; sr res scientist, Booz-Allen Appl Res, 57-64; dept head bact, Eye Res Found, Bethesda, Md, 64-66; RES MICROBIOLOGIST, NASA LANGLEY RES CTR, 66- *Honors & Awards:* Spec Achievement & Outstanding Performance Awards, NASA, 76. *Mem:* Am Soc Microbiol; Am Water Works Asn. *Res:* Pollution monitoring; microbial detection methods; instrumentation development; life support systems; man in closed environments; electrochemistry; operations research; mathematical models. *Mailing Add:* 281 Little Town Quarter Williamsburg VA 23185

WILKINS, MICHAEL GRAY, b Northampton, Eng, Sept 9, 38; m 74; c 1. COMPUTER MODELLING, COMPUTER APPLICATIONS. *Educ:* Univ Manchester, BSc, 61; Univ Ill, Urbana, PhD(biophys), 70. *Prof Exp:* Consult comput sci, 63-65; asst prof biomed eng & physiol, Univ Va, 69-75; res scientist, Dept Kinesiol, Simon Fraser Univ, 77-78; CONSULT, 75-; res physicist, Univ Dayton Res Inst, 78-81; SR ANALYST, ROCKETDYNE/ROCKWELL, AIR FORCE WEAPONS LAB/ARAO, KIRKLAND AFB, NMEX, 81- *Concurrent Pos:* Nat Acad Sci travel grant, Moscow Biophys Cong, Kiev, 72; pres, Middle East Technol Inc, 75-77; assoc dir, Omnitechnol Ctr, Inc, 75-77; adj prof, Col Eng, Univ NMex, 79-81. *Mem:* Asn Comput Mach. *Res:* Applications computers and codes, to analysis and modelling of high energy laser systems and optical components; computer structural mechanics; management of computer facilities; structure and analysis of large biological systems; computer applications in life sciences. *Mailing Add:* Wilkins 643 Fairway Rd NW Albuquerque NM 87107

WILKINS, PETER OSBORNE, b Toronto, Ont, June 28, 21; US citizen; m 47. MICROBIOLOGY. *Educ:* Rochester Univ, BM, 49; Univ Hawaii, MS, 58; Univ Pa, PhD(microbiol), 62. *Prof Exp:* From instr to asst prof microbiol, NJ Col Med, 62-68; asst prof, 68-75, ASSOC PROF MICROBIOL, UNIV WESTERN ONT, 75- *Concurrent Pos:* NSF res fel, 62-64; NIH res grant, 64-; Med Res Coun Can res grant, 70- *Mem:* AAAS; Am Soc Microbiol. *Res:* Microbial physiology; membrane transport; psychrotrophic bacteria. *Mailing Add:* Dept of Bact & Immunol Univ of Western Ont London ON N6A 5B8 Can

WILKINS, RALPH G, b Southampton, Eng, Jan 7, 27; m 51; c 2. INORGANIC CHEMISTRY. *Educ:* Univ Southampton, BSc, 47, PhD(chem), 50; Univ London, DSc(chem), 61. *Prof Exp:* Res chemist, Imp Chem Indust, Eng, 49-52; res assoc inorg chem, Univ Southern Calif, 52-53; from lectr to sr lectr, Sheffield Univ, 53-62; guest prof, Max Planck Inst Phys Chem, 62-63; prof, State Univ NY Buffalo, 63-73; head dept, 73-76, PROF CHEM, N MEX STATE UNIV, 76- *Mem:* Am Chem Soc; The Chem Soc. *Res:* Mechanisms of transition metal complexes and metalloenzyme reactions. *Mailing Add:* Dept of Chem NMex State Univ Las Cruces NM 88003

WILKINS, RAYMOND LESLIE, b Boston, Mass, Jan 13, 25; m 50; c 2. RESEARCH MANAGEMENT. *Educ:* Univ Chicago, AB, 51, MS, 54, PhD(chem), 57. *Prof Exp:* Sr scientist, 56-68, head instrument technol lab, 68-73, mgr, Chem Process Res Dept, 74-78, mgr, Process Control Anal Dept, 79-81, MGR SPEC PROJ, ROHM AND HAAS CO, 82- *Concurrent Pos:* Mem, Pa Governor's Sci Adv Comt, 69-75, chmn health care delivery panel, 69-71. *Mem:* Electron Micros Soc Am; NY Acad Sci; fel Royal Micros Soc; Am Chem Soc. *Res:* Correlation of the microstructure of heterogeneous organic plastics, polymers and emulsions with their gross properties; mechanisms of polymer formation; sustainable strategies for applying advanced control systems to chemical processes. *Mailing Add:* Rohm & Haas Co PO Box 584 Bristol PA 19007

WILKINS, ROGER LAWRENCE, b Newport News, Va, Dec 14, 28; m 55; c 1. CHEMICAL PHYSICS. *Educ:* Hampton Inst, BS, 51; Howard Univ, MS, 52; Univ Southern Calif, PhD(chem physics), 67. *Prof Exp:* Aeronaut scientist, NASA, Ohio, 52-55; sr tech specialist, Rocketdyne Div, NAm Aviation, Inc, 55-60; sr staff scientist, Aerophys Dept, Aerodyn & Propulsion Res Lab, 60-80, SR STAFF SCIENTIST, CHEM KINETICS DEPT, AEROPHYSICS LAB, AEROSPACE CORP, 80- *Mem:* Combustion Inst. *Res:* Chemical lasers; application of quantum, statistical and classical mechanics to treatment of energy transfer processes in chemical reactions; application of computers to calculate properties of molecules from first principles. *Mailing Add:* Chem Kinetics Dept Aerophysics Lab 2400 El Segundo Blvd El Segundo CA 90245

WILKINS, RONALD WAYNE, b Roscoe, Tex, Aug 29, 43; m 66; c 1. PHYSICS, COMPUTER SCIENCE. *Educ:* Harvard Univ, AB, 65; Univ Ill, Urbana, MS, 67, PhD(physics), 73. *Prof Exp:* Fel physics, Univ Kans, 73-75; mem staff, Ind Univ, 75-77; MEM STAFF PLASMA PHYSICS, LOS ALAMOS SCI LAB, 77- *Mem:* Am Phys Soc; Sigma Xi. *Res:* Solid state physics, especially equation of state computer control and data acquisition. *Mailing Add:* Los Alamos Sci Lab MS 639 PO Box 1663 Los Alamos NM 87545

WILKINS, TRACY DALE, b Sparkman, Ark, July 25, 43; m 65. MICROBIOLOGY. *Educ:* Univ Ark, BS, 65; Univ Tex, PhD(microbiol), 69. *Prof Exp:* Fel germ-free res, Med Ctr, Univ Ky, 69-71; asst prof, 72-75, assoc prof, 75-80, PROF MICROBIOL, ANAEROBE LAB, VA POLYTECH INST & STATE UNIV, 80- *Res:* Anaerobic bacteriology; clinical methodology; antimicrobial susceptibility testing; intestinal microbiology; antibiotics; colon cancer. *Mailing Add:* Dept Anaerobic Microbiol Va Polytech Inst & State Univ Blacksburg MA 24601

WILKINSON, ARTHUR, b Saginaw, Mich, Aug, 14, 25; m 62. MATHEMATICS, COMPUTER SCIENCE. *Educ:* Temple Univ, BS, 50, EdM, 54; Lehigh Univ, EdD, 72. *Prof Exp:* Teacher high sch, NJ, 51-52 & Pa, 52-53, head dept, 53-65; assoc prof, 65-73, PROF MATH & COMPUT SCI, E STROUDSBURG STATE COL, 73- *Concurrent Pos:* Dir res, Stroudsburg Res Assocs, Inc, 74- *Mem:* Math Asn Am; Brit Comput Soc. *Res:* Applied mathematics; statistics; system analysis; computer sciences; military systems; logical design and scientific programming of electronic computer systems; military applications of electronic computer technology. *Mailing Add:* Dept of Math E Stroudsburg State Col East Stroudsburg PA 18301

WILKINSON, BRIAN JAMES, b Huddersfield, Eng, Aug 10, 46. MICROBIAL BIOCHEMISTRY, MEDICAL MICROBIOLOGY. *Educ:* Univ Col Wales, BSc, 67; Univ Sheffield, PhD(microbiol), 71. *Prof Exp:* Res assoc biochem & microbiol, Univ Ky, 70-73; res fel biochem, Cambridge Univ, 73-76; asst prof med & microbiol, Univ Minn, 76-78; asst prof, 79-81, ASSOC PROF MICROBIOL & CHEM, ILL STATE UNIV, 81- *Concurrent Pos:* Broodbank res fel, Cambridge Univ, 73-76. *Mem:* Am Soc Microbiol; Soc Gen Microbiol; Soc Exp Biol & Med; Sigma Xi; fel Am Acad Microbiol. *Res:* Bacterial cell surface, nature and role in pathogenicity; intrinsic resistance to penicillin; staphylococci. *Mailing Add:* Dept of Biol Sci Ill State Univ Normal IL 61761

WILKINSON, BRUCE H, b Lancaster, Pa, June 2, 42. SEDIMENTOLOGY. *Educ:* Univ Wyo, BS, 65, MS, 67; Univ Tex, PhD(geol), 74. *Prof Exp:* Geologist asst oil shale, US Geol Surv, 65; geologist petrol, Gulf Oil Co, 67-69; asst prof, 73-79, ASSOC PROF GEOL, UNIV MICH, ANN ARBOR, 79- *Mem:* Geol Soc Am; Sigma Xi. *Res:* Source and distribution of Holocene sediments of the Texas Gulf Coast and of Michigan; source and distribution of contemporary lacustrine carbonates; evolution; oceanic chemistry. *Mailing Add:* Dept of Geol & Mineral Univ of Mich Ann Arbor MI 48104

WILKINSON, BRUCE W(ENDELL), b Shelby, Ohio, Aug 9, 28; m 53; c 2. CHEMICAL & NUCLEAR ENGINEERING. *Educ:* Ohio State Univ, BChE, 51, PhD(chem eng), 58. *Prof Exp:* Chem engr, Dow Chem Co, 54-59, staff asst, 59-63, proj coordr, 63-65; from asst prof to assoc prof chem eng, 65-77, PROF CHEM ENG, MICH STATE UNIV, 77-, ASSOC DIR, DIV ENG RES, 81- *Mem:* Am Inst Chem Engrs; Am Nuclear Soc; Am Soc Eng Educ; Sigma Xi; Nat Soc Prof Engrs. *Res:* Radioisotope applications; nuclear fuel processing; nuclear power; energy; environmental effects of energy. *Mailing Add:* Dept of Chem Eng Mich State Univ East Lansing MI 48824

WILKINSON, CHARLES BROCK, b Richmond, Va, Jan 16, 22; m 45; c 1. MEDICINE, PSYCHIATRY. *Educ:* Va Union Univ, BS, 41; Howard Univ, MD, 44; Univ Colo, MS, 50. *Prof Exp:* From intern to resident internal med, Freedmen's Hosp, Washington, DC, 45-47; resident psychiat, Univ Colo, 47-50; from instr to asst prof neuropsychiat, Col Med, Howard Univ, 50-55; staff physician, Rollman Receiving Ctr, Cincinnati, Ohio, 58-59; dir adult outpatient serv, Greater Kansas City Ment Health Found, 59-60, dir training, 60-69, assoc dir found, 63-68; clin assoc prof, 59-65, chmn dept, 67-69, asst dean, 71-80, PROF PSYCHIAT, SCH MED, UNIV MO-KANSAS CITY, 65-, ASSOC DEAN, 81-; EXEC DIR, GREATER KANSAS CITY MENT HEALTH FOUND, 68- *Concurrent Pos:* Lectr, Sch Social Work, Howard Univ, 53-55; asst prof, Med Ctr, Univ Kans, 59-65; consult, Family & Children's Serv, Kans, 62-65; mem, Nat Adv Coun, NIMH, 66-70 & US Nat Comt Vital & Health Statist, 72-; consult to ed staff, Psychiat Annals, 70-; consult, Region IV, Fed Aviation Admin, 70-; mem bd trustees, Am Psychiat Asn, 71-74, treas, 76-80; mem bd govs, Group Advan Psychiat, 73-75; consult, Psychiat Educ Br, NIMH, 74-; mem, Panel Behav Sci, Nat Res Coun, Nat Acad Sci, 75-; coord, Task Panel, Orgn & Struct Ment Health Serv, President's Comn Ment Health, 77-78. *Mem:* Fel Am Psychiat Asn; AMA; Nat Med Asn; Am Group Psychother Asn; Pan-Am Med Asn. *Res:* Family dynamics and family therapy; psychiatry and the community; evaluation of psychiatric efforts in community mental health; racism and its effects; studies of black single parent female headed families; human ecology. *Mailing Add:* 600 E 22nd St Kansas City MO 64108

WILKINSON, CHRISTOPHER FOSTER, b Yorkshire, Eng, Feb 9, 38; m 76; c 1. ENTOMOLOGY, ORGANIC CHEMISTRY. *Educ:* Univ Reading, BSc, 61; Univ Calif, Riverside, PhD(entom), 65. *Prof Exp:* UK Civil Serv Comn sr res fel insecticide chem, Pest Infestation Lab, Agr Res Coun, Eng, 65-66; from asst prof to assoc prof, 66-78, PROF INSECT TOXICOL, CORNELL UNIV, 78-, DIR, INST COMPARATIVE & ENVIRON TOXICOL, 80- *Mem:* Soc Toxicol; Am Chem Soc; Soc Environ Toxicol & Chem. *Res:* Structure-activity relationships and mode of action of insecticide synergists; biochemistry; comparative biochemistry of microsomal drug metabolism; toxicology. *Mailing Add:* Dept of Entom Cornell Univ Ithaca NY 14853

WILKINSON, DANIEL R, b Glasgow, Ky, May 30, 38; m 61; c 2. PLANT PATHOLOGY, PLANT BREEDING. *Educ:* Western Ky Univ, BS, 61; Clemson Univ, MS, 63; Univ Ill, PhD(plant path), 67. *Prof Exp:* PLANT PATHOLOGIST, PIONEER HI-BREED INT, INC, 67- *Mem:* Am Phytopath Soc. *Res:* Breeding for disease and insect resistance; genetics. *Mailing Add:* Dept of Corn Breeding Pioneer Hi-Bred Int Inc Johnston IA 50131

WILKINSON, DAVID IAN, b Cookstown, Northern Ireland, Dec 17, 32; m 57; c 2. BIOCHEMISTRY. *Educ:* Queens Univ, Belfast, BS, 54, PhD(chem), 57. *Prof Exp:* USPHS res fel chem, Wayne State Univ, 57-58 & Univ Calif, Los Angeles, 58-59; res chemist, Brit Drug Houses, Eng, 59-61; NIH res grant & res fel chem, res assoc biochem, 63-73, ADJ PROF DERMAT, SCH MED, STANFORD UNIV, 73- *Concurrent Pos:* Fulbright fel, 57-59; NIH res grant dermat, Sch Med, Stanford Univ, 71-73. *Mem:* The Chem Soc; Am Chem Soc; Soc Invest Dermat. *Res:* Skin lipids; prostaglandins; metabolism of fatty acids in skin; polyunsaturated fatty acids. *Mailing Add:* Dept of Dermat Stanford Univ Sch of Med Stanford CA 96305

WILKINSON, DAVID TODD, b Hillsdale, Mich, May 13, 35; div; c 2. PHYSICS, COSMOLOGY. *Educ:* Univ Mich, BSE, 57, MSE, 59, PhD(physics), 62. *Prof Exp:* Lectr physics, Univ Mich, 62-63; from instr to assoc prof, 63-71, PROF PHYSICS, PRINCETON UNIV, 72- *Concurrent Pos:* Alfred P Sloan Found fel, 66-68; John Simon Guggenheim fel, 77-78. *Mem:* Fel Am Phys Soc; Am Astron Soc. *Res:* Atomic physics, properties of electrons and positrons; gravitation and relativity; primeval galaxies; cosmic microwave radiation. *Mailing Add:* Jadwin Hall Princeton Univ Princeton NJ 08544

WILKINSON, GRANT ROBERT, b Derby, Eng, Aug 27, 41; c 4. PHARMACOLOGY. *Educ:* Univ Manchester, BSc, 63; Univ London, PhD(pharmaceut chem), 66. *Prof Exp:* Asst prof pharm, Col Pharm, Univ Ky, 68-71; assoc prof, 71-77, PROF PHARMACOL, SCH MED, VANDERBILT UNIV, 77- *Concurrent Pos:* USPHS fel, Univ Calif, San Francisco, 66-68. *Mem:* AAAS; Am Soc Pharmacol & Exp Therapeut; NY Acad Sci; Am Pharmaceut Asn. *Res:* Clinical pharmacology; application of analytical methodology, drug metabolism and pharmacokinetics. *Mailing Add:* Dept of Pharmacol Vanderbilt Univ Sch of Med Nashville TN 37232

WILKINSON, JACK DALE, b Ottumwa, Iowa, Jan 27, 31; m 53; c 5. MATHEMATICS, EDUCATION. *Educ:* Univ Northern Iowa, BA, 52, MA, 58; Iowa State Univ, PhD(math, educ), 70. *Prof Exp:* PROF MATH, UNIV NORTHERN IOWA, 62- *Concurrent Pos:* Consult, 64-; mem comt affiliated groups, Nat Coun Teachers Math, 74-77. *Mem:* Am Educ Res Asn. *Res:* Activity learning; attitudes toward mathematical learning; learning styles in mathematics education; problem solving and applications of mathematics in the elementary and junior high schools. *Mailing Add:* Dept of Math Univ of Northern Iowa Cedar Falls IA 50613

WILKINSON, JAMES FREEMAN, agronomy, see previous edition

WILKINSON, JOHN EDWIN, b Tacoma, Wash, Nov 11, 42; m 66; c 2. ANALYTICAL CHEMISTRY, ENVIRONMENATL CHEMISTRY. *Educ:* Univ Puget Sound, BS, 64, MS, 78. *Prof Exp:* MGR ENVIRON RELATIONS & SR ANAL CHEMIST, DEPT SCI & TECHNOL, REICHHOLD CHEM INC, 66- *Concurrent Pos:* Chlorodioxin specialist, Am Wood Preservers Inst, 73-, chmn, Environ Progs Task Group, 78- *Mem:* Am Chem Soc; Am Wood Preservers Inst; AAAS. *Res:* Chlorodioxins present in chlorophenols; kemetic and analytical chemical study in the reduction of chlorodioxins in pentachlorophenol; phenol formaldehyde; urea formaldehyde; polyester resins. *Mailing Add:* 2340 Taylor Way Tacoma WA 98401

WILKINSON, JOHN PETER DARRELL, b Englewood, NJ, Nov 24, 38. ENGINEERING MECHANICS, TECHNICAL MANAGEMENT. *Educ:* Cambridge Univ, BA Hons, 60, MS, 64; Yale Univ, MEng, 61, DEng, 64. *Prof Exp:* Specialist dynamics, NAm Aviation, 64-67; consult struct, Space Div, 67-68; mech engr solid mech, Corp Res & Develop, 68-72, mgr solid mech, Corp Res & Develop, 72-79, mgr liaison oper, 79-80, MGR RES & DEVELOP APPLN OPER, GEN ELEC CO, 80- *Concurrent Pos:* Adj prof, Polytech Inst NY, 71-72. *Mem:* Am Soc Mech Engrs. *Res:* Structural vibrations; dynamics; mechanical behavior of materials; fracture mechanics; technology transfer; research and development policy. *Mailing Add:* Corp Res & Develop Gen Elec Co Schenectady NY 12301

WILKINSON, JOHN WESLEY, b Bexley, Ont, Nov 1, 28; m 53; c 2. MATHEMATICAL STATISTICS. *Educ:* Queen's Univ, Ont, BA, 50, MA, 52; Univ NC, PhD(math statist), 56. *Prof Exp:* Statistician, Can Industs, Ltd, 52-53; asst prof math, Queen's Univ, Ont, 56-58; res mathematician, Res Labs, Westinghouse Elec Corp, 58-64, fel mathematician, 64-65; prof statist, 65-70; chmn opers res & statist, 70-76, PROF MGT, RENSSELAER POLYTECH INST, 70- *Concurrent Pos:* Consult, Can Industs, Ltd, 56-58, Watervliet Arsenal, Bendix Corp, Kamyr, Inc, 72-, Shaker Res Corp, 72-, NY State Depts Transp, Health, Budget, 72- & NY State Legis Comn Expenditure Rev; assoc ed, Technometrics, 70-77, ed, 78-80. *Mem:* Inst Math Statist; Inst Mgt Sci; Am Inst Decision Sci; Am Soc Qual Control; fel Am Statist Asn. *Res:* Statistical design of experiments; statistical inference; mathematical modeling; statistical applications to problems of environment and energy. *Mailing Add:* Sch Mgt Rensselaer Polytech Inst Troy NY 12181

WILKINSON, JOSEPH RIDLEY, b Palatka, Fla, Sept 24, 17; m 41; c 2. ANALYTICAL CHEMISTRY. *Educ:* The Citadel, BS, 41; Univ Ga, MS, 49; Fla State Univ, PhD, 55. *Prof Exp:* Instr gen chem, 46-49, asst prof gen & anal chem, 49-55, assoc prof anal chem, 55-60, PROF ANAL CHEM, THE CITADEL, 60-, HEAD DEPT CHEM, 68- *Mem:* Am Chem Soc. *Res:* Nuclear inorganic chemistry; gamma ray spectroscopy; colorimetric methods of analysis. *Mailing Add:* Dept of Chem The Citadel Charleston SC 29409

WILKINSON, MICHAEL KENNERLY, b Palatka, Fla, Feb 9, 21; m 44; c 3. SOLID STATE PHYSICS. *Educ:* The Citadel, BS, 42; Mass Inst Technol, PhD(physics), 50. *Prof Exp:* Res assoc, Res Lab Electronics, Mass Inst Technol, 48-50; res physicist, 50-64, assoc dir, 64-72, DIR SOLID STATE DIV, OAK RIDGE NAT LAB, 72- *Concurrent Pos:* Neely vis prof, Ga Inst Technol, 61-62 & prof, 62- *Mem:* AAAS; fel Am Phys Soc; Am Crystallog Asn; Sigma Xi. *Res:* Neutron diffraction and spectrometry; magnetic properties of solids; dynamical properties of crystal lattices; x-ray diffraction; physical electronics. *Mailing Add:* Solid State Div Oak Ridge Nat Lab PO Box X Oak Ridge TN 37830

WILKINSON, PAUL KENNETH, b Oneonta, NY, Oct 19, 45; m 67; c 2. BIOPHARMACEUTICS, PHARMACODYNAMICS. *Educ:* Univ Conn, BS Pharm, 69; Univ Mich, Ann Arbor, MS & PhD(pharm), 75. *Prof Exp:* Dep chief pharmacist, USPHS, 69-71; asst, Sch Pharm, Univ Mich, Ann Arbor, 71-75; asst prof, Sch Pharm, Auburn Univ, 75-76; ASST PROF PHARMACEUT, SCH PHARM, UNIV CONN, 76- *Mem:* Am Pharmaceut Asn; Acad Pharmaceut Sci; Am Asn Cols Pharm; Sigma Xi. *Res:* Study of ethyl alcohol concentrations in various segments of the vascular system and evaluation of the kinetics of the oral absorption of ethanol in fasting subjects. *Mailing Add:* Sch of Pharm Box 4-92 Univ of Conn Storrs CT 06268

WILKINSON, PAUL R, b Calcutta, India, Apr 16, 19; m 47; c 5. ENTOMOLOGY. *Educ:* Cambridge Univ, BA, 41, MA, 45, PhD, 68. *Prof Exp:* Entomologist, Colonial Insecticide Res Unit, Uganda, 46-49; res officer, Commonwealth Sci & Indust Res Orgn, Australia, 50-62; RES SCIENTIST, CAN DEPT AGR, 62- *Mem:* Ecol Soc Am; Acarolog Soc Am; Entomol Soc Am; Entom Soc Can. *Res:* Acarology, ecology, physiology and control of ticks and biting flies. *Mailing Add:* Can Dept of Agr Res Sta Lethbridge AB T1S 4B1 Can

WILKINSON, RALPH RUSSELL, b Portland, Ore, Feb 20, 30; m 56. TECHNOLOGY AND RISK ASSESSMENT. *Educ:* Reed Col, BA, 53; Univ Ore, Eugene, PhD(phys chem), 62; Univ Mo-Kansas City, MBA, 74. *Prof Exp:* Sr res chemist, Sprague Elec Co, Tektronix Inc, MacDermid Inc & Chemagro Agr Div, Mobay Chem Corp, 61-72; res chemist, US Vet Hosp, 73-75; assoc chemist technol assessment, 75-80, SR SCIENTIST, MIDWEST RES INST, 80- *Mem:* Am Chem Soc; Sigma Xi; NY Acad Sci. *Res:* Technology and risk assessment; organotins; aryl phosphates; chemical economics; pesticides; PCBs; biodegradation; hazardous wastes. *Mailing Add:* Midwest Res Inst 425 Volker Blvd Kansas City MO 64110

WILKINSON, RAYMOND GEORGE, b Duluth, Minn, June 2, 22; m 48; c 3. ORGANIC CHEMISTRY. *Educ:* Harvard Univ, BS, 43; Univ Mich, MS, 48, PhD(org chem), 52. *Prof Exp:* From res chemist to sr res chemist, Lederle Div, Am Cyanamid Co, 51-62, group leader process improv, 62-66; asst to managing ed, Subject Index Div, Chem Abstracts Serv, Ohio State Univ, 66-68; SR RES CHEMIST, LEDERLE DIV, AM CYANAMID CO, 68- *Mem:* Am Chem Soc. *Res:* Synthesis of steroids, tetracyclines and their degradation products; antituberculosis agents; antimalarials; antitumor; immunomodulating agents. *Mailing Add:* Lederle Labs Am Cyanamid Co Middletown Rd Pearl River NY 10965

WILKINSON, RICHARD FRANCIS, JR, genetics, developmental biology, see previous edition

WILKINSON, ROBERT CLEVELAND, JR, b Grand Rapids, Mich, Oct 2, 23; m 48; c 3. ENTOMOLOGY, ECOLOGY. *Educ:* Mich State Univ, BS, 49, MS, 50; Univ Wis, PhD(entom), 61. *Prof Exp:* Entomologist, State Dept Agr, Mich, 51-53; supvr, Off State Entomologist, Wis, 53-57; res asst entom, Univ Wis, 57-60; from asst entomologist to assoc entomologist, 60-70, PROF ENTOM, UNIV FLA, 71- *Concurrent Pos:* Res grants, St Regis Paper Co, Prosper Energy Corp, US Navy, Buckeye Cellulose Corp, Ford Found, SE Coastal Plains Comn, Southern Forest Dis & Insect Res Coun, Ctr Trop Agr, US Forest Serv. *Mem:* AAAS; Entom Soc Am; Soc Am Foresters; Entom Soc Can. *Res:* Forest entomology; bionomics of pine sawflies and bark beetles. *Mailing Add:* Dept of Entom & Nemat 3103 McCarty Hall Univ of Fla Gainesville FL 32611

WILKINSON, ROBERT EUGENE, b Oilton, Okla, Oct 24, 26; m 51; c 2. PLANT PHYSIOLOGY, WEED SCIENCE. *Educ:* Univ Ill, BS, 50; Univ Okla, MS, 52; Univ Calif, Davis, PhD(plant physiol), 56. *Prof Exp:* Plant physiologist, Crops Res Div, Agr Res Serv, USDA, Ark, 57-62 & NMex, 62-65, assoc agronomist, 65-73, AGRONOMIST, EXP STA, USDA, GA, 73- *Concurrent Pos:* Sr Fulbright-Hayes Lectr appl ecol, Univ Turku, Finland, 74-75; consult, ESAWQ, Piricacicaba, Sao Paulo, Brazil, 78. *Mem:* AAAS; Weed Sci Soc Am; Am Soc Plant Physiol. *Res:* Absorption; translocation; herbicide response; environmental response of plants and effect of herbicides on metabolism. *Mailing Add:* Dept Agron Ga Exp Sta Experiment GA 30212

WILKINSON, ROBERT HAYDN, b Keighley, Eng, Feb 10, 26; m 56; c 4. INSTRUMENTATION. *Educ:* Univ London, BSc, 48; Syracuse Univ, MEE, 61; Mass Inst Technol, ScD(instrumentation), 65. *Prof Exp:* Apprentice engr, Keighley Lifts, Ltd, Eng, 41-47, jr engr, 47-48; sci officer, Radar Res Estab, 49-51; engr, Eng Elec Co, 51-53; engr, Short Bros & Harland, Northern Ireland, 53-54; sr engr, air arm div, Westinghouse Elec Corp, 54-59; prin engr, Link div, Gen Precision Inc, 58-61; PRIN ENGR, C S DRAPER LAB, MASS INST TECHNOL, 61- *Concurrent Pos:* Lectr, Northeastern Univ, 65-67. *Mem:* Inst Elec & Electronics Engrs; Brit Inst Elec Eng. *Res:* Thermal errors in instruments; methods of measurement of instrument parameters; analog function generator techniques; design of electromechanical sensors; design of servos and controls; measurement and modelling of instrument noise processes. *Mailing Add:* C S Draper Lab 555 Technology Sq Cambridge MA 02139

WILKINSON, RONALD CRAIG, b Augusta, Ga, Oct 1, 43; m 67. FOREST GENETICS, PHYSIOLOGY. *Educ:* Univ Wash, BS, 65; Yale Univ, MF, 66; Mich State Univ, PhD(forest genetics), 70. *Prof Exp:* RES PLANT GENETICIST, NORTHEASTERN FOREST EXP STA, US FOREST SERV, 70- *Mem:* AAAS; Soc Am Foresters; Phytochem Soc NAm. *Res:* Controlled and natural hybridization; comparative physiology of species, ecological races and hybrids; natural variation and adaptation; genetic and physiological resistance to insects and diseases; biochemical systematics. *Mailing Add:* US Forest Serv Box 640 Durham NH 03824

WILKINSON, STANLEY R, b West Amboy, NY, Mar 28, 31; m 57; c 3. AGRONOMY, SOIL SCIENCE. *Educ:* Cornell Univ, BS, 54; Purdue Univ, MS, 56, PhD(soil fertil, plant nutrit), 61. *Prof Exp:* Instr soil fertil & plant nutrit, Purdue Univ, 57-60; res soil scientist, Pasture Res Lab, 60-65, RES SOIL SCIENTIST, SOUTHERN PIEDMONT CONSERV RES CTR, AGR RES SERV, USDA, 65- *Mem:* Am Soc Agron; Soil Sci Soc Am; Int Soc Soil Sci. *Res:* Mineral nutrient requirements of corn, soybeans, forage grasses and legumes; biuret toxicity to corn; root growth response to fertilizer; competitive phenomena between forage species; grazing systems research; land application of wastes and environmental quality. *Mailing Add:* Southern Piedmont Conserv Res Ctr Box 555 Watkinsville GA 30677

WILKINSON, THOMAS PRESTON, b Gisburn, Eng, Mar 14, 41; m 66; c 2. PHYSICAL GEOGRAPHY. *Educ:* Univ Durham, BSc, 63; Univ Newcastle, PhD(geomorphol), 72. *Prof Exp:* From lectr to asst prof, 67-73, ASSOC PROF GEOG, CARLETON UNIV, 73- *Concurrent Pos:* Vis lectr, Univ Liverpool, 72-73. *Res:* Fluvial geomorphology; geography curricula; environmental management. *Mailing Add:* Dept Geog Carleton Univ Ottawa ON K1S 5B6 Can

WILKINSON, THOMAS ROSS, b Baltimore, Md, Aug 20, 37; m 65; c 3. MICROBIOLOGY. *Educ:* Univ Notre Dame, BS, 59; Univ Md, College Park, MS, 62; Wash State Univ, PhD(microbiol), 70. *Prof Exp:* Technician aerobiol, Naval Biol Lab, Univ Calif, Berkeley, 65-66; from asst prof to prof path & immunol, SDak State Univ, 70-81, head, Dept Microbiol, 75-81; ASSOC DEAN, COL AGR, ASSOC DIR, AGR EXP STA & PROF MICROBIOL, NDAK STATE UNIV, 81- *Mem:* Sigma Xi; Am Soc Microbiol; NY Acad Sci. *Res:* Rapid isolation technique for Listeria monocytogenes; survival of pathogens on metal surfaces; miniature cell systems for virus isolation and epidemiology of enclosed environments; epidemiology of Listeria and pathogenesis of Listeria L-forms; alcohol fuel production by a small farm scale plant. *Mailing Add:* Col Agr NDak State Univ Fargo ND 58105

WILKINSON, W(ILLIAM) C(LAYTON), b Tefte, Ind, Dec 17, 14; m 46; c 4. ELECTROMAGNETIC ENGINEERING. *Educ:* Purdue Univ, BSEE, 41. *Prof Exp:* Res engr, RCA Victor Co, RCA Corp, 41-42 & RCA Labs, 42-61, eng supvr, Missile & Surface Radar Div, 61-77, eng supvr astro electronics, 77-80; PRES, SPACE ANTENNA TECH INC, 80- *Mem:* Sr mem Inst Elec & Electronics Engrs. *Res:* Computer aided design of antennas and microwave systems for space communications satellites and systems. *Mailing Add:* 55 Littlebrook Rd N Princeton NJ 08540

WILKINSON, WILLIAM H(ADLEY), b Galt, Ont, Dec 1, 27; US citizen; m; c 5. MECHANICAL ENGINEERING. *Educ:* Rensselaer Polytech Inst, BME, 49, MME, 52. *Prof Exp:* Instr mech eng, Rensselaer Polytech Inst, 49-55, asst prof, 55-56; proj engr, 56-58, asst consult, 58-60, assoc staff engr, 60-64, fel, 64-70, PRIN MECH ENGR, COLUMBUS LABS, BATTELLE MEM INST, 70- *Concurrent Pos:* Engr, Am Locomotive Co, 53-54. *Mem:* Soc Automotive Engrs; Am Soc Mech Engrs. *Res:* Thermodynamic cycles and conversion systems; flow phenomena; comfort conditioning; advanced system synthesis and modeling; mechanisms; gearing; advanced vehicle propulsion systems. *Mailing Add:* Battelle Mem Inst Columbus Labs 505 King Ave Columbus OH 43201

WILKINSON, WILLIAM KENNETH, b Newcastle, Ind, Jan 17, 18; m 42; c 5. ORGANIC CHEMISTRY, POLYMER CHEMISTRY. *Educ:* DePauw Univ, AB, 40; Northwestern Univ, MS, 47, PhD(org chem), 48. *Prof Exp:* Training supvr, Trojan Powder Co, 41-43; res chemist, Firestone Tire & Rubber Co, 43-45; from res chemist to res assoc, 48-65, RES FEL, BENGER LAB, TEXTILE FIBERS DEPT, E I DU PONT DE NEMOURS & CO, 65- *Mem:* Am Chem Soc. *Res:* Rubber and textile fibers; explosives; acetylene chemistry. *Mailing Add:* 1010 Glenwood Blvd Waynesboro VA 22980

WILKINSON, WILLIAM LYLE, b Sikeston, Mo, Jan 18, 21; m 45, 69; c 6. OPERATIONS RESEARCH. *Educ:* US Naval Postgrad Sch, BS & MS, 55. *Prof Exp:* SR STAFF SCIENTIST, GEORGE WASHINGTON UNIV, 65- *Concurrent Pos:* Lectr, Univ Calif, Los Angeles, 65-66. *Mem:* Opers Res Soc Am. *Res:* Transportation networks in logistics research; computer-based management information systems; quantitative evaluation of weapon systems and tactics; man-computer systems; military sciences. *Mailing Add:* 1309 Alps Dr McLean VA 22102

WILKNISS, PETER EBERHARD, b Berlin, Ger, Sept 28, 34; US citizen; m 63; c 2. OCEANOGRAPHY, RADIOCHEMISTRY. *Educ:* Munich Tech Univ, MS, 59, PhD(radiochem), 61. *Prof Exp:* Prog mgr, Nat Ctr Atmospheric Res Prog, NSF, 75-76, prog mgr, Ocean Sediment Coring Prog, 76-80, team mgr, Ocean Drilling Proj team, 80, dir, Div Ocean Drilling Progs, 80-81, SR SCI ASSOC, OFF DIR, NSF, 81- *Concurrent Pos:* NSF, Nat Res Coun, Marine bd liaison mem, 78-81. *Mem:* AAAS; Sigma Xi; Am Geophys Union. *Res:* Radio and nuclear chemistry, solid propellants, oceanography, marine geochemistry, satellite images applied to meteorology, air/sea interactions; anthropogenic impact on the global environment, natural radioactivity in the troposphere; radiochemistry applied to oceanography. *Mailing Add:* Ocean Sediment Coring Prog NSF 1800 G St NW Washington DC 20550

WILKOFF, LEE JOSEPH, b Youngstown, Ohio, Oct 17, 24; m 53; c 1. MICROBIOLOGY, BIOCHEMISTRY. *Educ:* Roosevelt Univ, BS, 48; Univ Chicago, PhD(microbiol), 63. *Prof Exp:* Chemist, H Kramer & Co, 48-49; res asst biochem, Ben May Lab Cancer Res, Univ Chicago, 49-52 & Dept Med, 54-60; biochemist, Vet Admin Hosp, Hines, Ill, 52-54; dir microbiol lab, Woodard Res Corp, 63-64; sr microbiologist, 64-70, HEAD CELL BIOL DIV, SOUTHERN RES INST, 70- *Mem:* AAAS; Am Asn Cancer Res; Soc Exp Biol & Med; Am Soc Microbiol; Tissue Cult Asn. *Res:* Cell biology and chemotherapy of tumor cells; effect of anticancer drugs on the kinetic behavior of tumor cells; cellular sites of action of anticancer agents. *Mailing Add:* Cell Biol Div Southern Res Inst 2000 Ninth Ave S Birmingham AL 35205

WILKOV, ROBERT SPENCER, b New York, NY, Feb 2, 43; m 64; c 2. COMPUTER SCIENCE. *Educ:* Columbia Univ, BS, 64, MS, 66, PhD(elec eng), 68. *Prof Exp:* Res asst elec eng, Columbia Univ, 67-68; mem res staff comput sci, 68-72, MGR NETWORK ANAL, IBM RES CTR, 72- *Concurrent Pos:* Consult, Otis Elevator Co, 63-68; lectr, Univ Conn, 69-70; adj asst prof, City Col NY, 70- *Mem:* AAAS; Inst Elec & Electronics Engrs. *Res:* Applications of graph theory and queuing theory in the analysis and synthesis of voice and data communication systems. *Mailing Add:* IBM Corp 1000 Westchester Ave White Plains NY 10604

WILKOWSKE, HOWARD HUGO, b Zachow, Wis, Sept 10, 17; m 48; c 3. DAIRY BACTERIOLOGY. *Educ:* Tex Tech Col, BS, 40, MS, 42; Iowa State Col, PhD, 49. *Prof Exp:* Assoc prof dairy mfg & assoc dairy technologist, Agr Exp Sta, Inst Food & Agr Sci, Univ Fla, 50-57, asst dir, Agr Exp Sta, 57-68, asst dean res, 68-79, dir Internal Energy Mgt, 80-81; RETIRED. *Concurrent Pos:* Mem adv coun, Ctr Trop Agr, US AID dairy specialist, Costa Rica, 58, Ghana, 69 & Venezuela, 71. *Mem:* AAAS; Am Soc Microbiol; Am Dairy Sci Asn. *Res:* Antibiotics in dairy products; continuous and automatic manufacture of fermented dairy products; bacteriophage of dairy microorganisms; agricultural research administration. *Mailing Add:* Inst Food & Agr Sci Univ Fla Bldg 810 Rm 6 Gainesville FL 32611

WILKS, JOHN WILLIAM, b Kenosha, Wis, July 5, 44. REPRODUCTIVE ENDOCRINOLOGY. *Educ:* Univ Wis-Madison, BS, 66; Cornell Univ, PhD(physiol), 71. *Prof Exp:* SR RES SCIENTIST REPRODUCTIVE ENDOCRINOL, FERTIL RES, UPJOHN CO, 70- *Concurrent Pos:* Vis assoc prof, Dept Cell Biol, Baylor Col Med, 81. *Mem:* Am Fertil Soc; Endocrine Soc; AAAS; Soc Study Reproduction; NY Acad Sci. *Res:* Physiologic and pharmacologic control of ovarian function; mechanism of steroid hormone action; endocrinology of the menstrual cycle. *Mailing Add:* Fertil Res Upjohn Co Kalamazoo MI 49001

WILKS, LOUIS PHILLIP, b Dayton, Ohio, June 28, 13; m 38; c 3. CHEMISTRY. *Educ:* Univ Dayton, BS, 35. *Prof Exp:* Instr chem, Univ Dayton, 35; res chemist, Thomas & Hochwalt Lab, 35-38; res chemist, Velsicol Chem Corp, 38-40, dir labs, 40-46, tech dir, 46-56, vpres, 56-66, dir new prod develop, 56-63, dir long range tech planning, 63-70, dir corp long-range planning, 70-78; CONSULT, 78- *Mem:* AAAS; Am Chem Soc; Commercial Develop Asn; Planning Exec Inst. *Res:* Products from petrochemical by-products; agricultural chemicals; research management and corporate planning. *Mailing Add:* 9530 Lamon Place Skokie IL 60077

WILL, CLIFFORD MARTIN, b Hamilton, Ont, Can, Nov 13, 46; m 70; c 2. THEORETICAL ASTROPHYSICS. *Educ:* McMaster Univ, BSc, 68; Calif Inst Technol, PhD(physics), 71. *Prof Exp:* Instr physics, Calif Inst Technol, 71-72; fel, Enrico Fermi Inst, Univ Chicago, 72-74; ASST PROF PHYSICS, STANFORD UNIV, 74- *Concurrent Pos:* Res fel, Calif Inst Technol, 71-72; Sloan Found res fel, 75. *Mem:* Am Phys Soc; Am Aston Soc; Sigma Xi. *Res:* General relativity theory and its applications to astrophysics. *Mailing Add:* Dept of Physics Stanford Univ Stanford CA 94305

WILL, FRITZ, III, b Richmond, Va, Oct 24, 26; m 54; c 2. ANALYTICAL CHEMISTRY. *Educ:* Univ Va, BS, 49, MS, 51, PhD(chem), 53. *Prof Exp:* Asst chem, Univ Va, 47-51; res chemist, Res Labs, Aluminium Co Am, 53-65; res chemist, 65-69, mgr, Anal Chem Div, Philip Morris Res Ctr, 69-79, mgr beverage res & develop, 80-81, COORDR ANAL CHEM TOBACCO PROCESS, PHILIP MORRIS INC, 82- *Honors & Awards:* Medal, Am Inst Chemists, 49. *Mem:* Am Chem Soc; Soc Appl Spectros; Sigma Xi. *Res:* Analytical methods; spectrophotometry; ultraviolet and visual absorption spectroscopy; nuclear magnetic resonance spectroscopy. *Mailing Add:* Philip Morris Res Ctr PO Box 26583 Richmond VA 23261

WILL, FRITZ GUSTAV, b Breslau, Ger, Jan 12, 31; m 58; c 3. ELECTROCHEMISTRY. *Educ:* Munich Tech Univ, BS, 53, MS, 57, PhD(phys chem), 59. *Prof Exp:* Res scientist, Eng Res & Develop Labs, US Dept Army, Va, 59-60; electrochemist, 60-69, mgr electrochem mat & reactions unit, 69-72, MEM RES STAFF, RES & DEVELOP CTR, GEN ELEC CO, 72- *Concurrent Pos:* Div ed, J Electrochem Soc, 74- *Honors & Awards:* Battery Res Award, Electrochem Soc, 64. *Mem:* Electrochem Soc. *Res:* Electrochemical instrumentation; electrocatalysis; electrode kinetics; fuel cells; batteries; solid electrolyte; zinc-halogen; electrochemical sensors. *Mailing Add:* Gen Elec Res & Develop Ctr PO Box 8 Schenectady NY 12301

WILL, JAMES ARTHUR, b Wauwatosa, Wis, Nov 2, 30; m 53; c 3. PHYSIOLOGY. *Educ:* Univ Wis, BS, 52, MS, 53, PhD(vet sci), 67; Kans State Univ, DVM, 60. *Prof Exp:* Vet, Columbus Vet Hosp, Wis, 60-67; from asst prof to assoc prof, 67-74, chmn dept, 74-78, PROF VET SCI, UNIV WIS-MADISON, 74- MEM STAFF, CARDIOVASC RES LAB, 74- *Concurrent Pos:* NIH spec fel, New Med Sch, Univ Liverpool, 72-73; mem coun basic sci & circulation, Am Heart Asn; mem comt primary pulmonary hypertension, WHO; consult to domestic & foreign co. *Mem:* AAAS; Am Vet Med Asn; sr mem Am Fedn Clin Res; Asn Am Vet Med Col (pres); Am Physiol Soc. *Res:* Cardiopulmonary physiopathology, particularly relationship between function and disease under natural and altered environmental conditions or with impairment of function by a disease process. *Mailing Add:* Dept of Vet Sci 1655 Linden Dr Madison WI 53706

WILL, JOHN JUNIOR, b Cincinnati, Ohio, Aug 13, 24; m 46; c 3. HEMATOLOGY. *Educ:* Univ Cincinnati, MD, 47. *Prof Exp:* Intern med, Presby Hosp, New York, 47-48; resident internal med, Cincinnati Gen Hosp, 48-50; asst chief med serv, Travis AFB, 50-52; from instr to prof med, 52-76, PROF INTERNAL MED, COL MED, UNIV CINCINNATI, 76- *Concurrent Pos:* Fel, Nutrit & Hemat Lab, Cincinnati Gen Hosp, 52-55, co-dir, Hemat Lab, 57-, clinician, Outpatient Dept & chief clinician, Hemat Clin. *Mem:* Am Fedn Clin Res. *Res:* Nutrition; relationship of vitamin B-12 folic acid and ascorbic acid to the absorption and utilization of versene in iron deficiency anemia; nuclease inhibitors in human white blood cells in leukemia and other disease states; effect of antimetabolites on leukemia in rats and humans; cancer chemotherapy. *Mailing Add:* Dept of Med Univ of Cincinnati Cincinnati OH 45221

WILL, PAUL ARTHUR, b Weslaco, Tex, Feb 9, 46; m 70; c 2. FOOD SCIENCE & TECHNOLOGY. *Educ:* Tex A&M Univ, BS, 70; Okla State Univ, MS, 74, PhD(food sci), 78. *Prof Exp:* INSTR MEAT SCI, OKLA STATE UNIV, 78-; ASST PROF & DIR, SUL ROSS STATE UNIV, 78- *Mem:* Am Meat Sci Asn; Inst Food Technologists; Am Animal Sci Asn; Sigma Xi. *Res:* Efficiency of red meat production; palatibility of the produced product; method of fabrication and processing; physical and chemical properties of meat. *Mailing Add:* PO Box C 158 Alpine TX 79830

WILL, PETER CRAIG, b Red Oak, Iowa, Aug 11, 47; m 69; c 1. ELECTROLYTE TRANSPORT, ENDOCRINOLOGY. *Educ:* Northwest Mo State Univ, BS, 69; Univ Mo, PhD(biochem), 75. *Prof Exp:* Fel, Oak Ridge Nat Lab, 74-76; sr res assoc, 76-80, INSTR ANAT, CASE WESTERN RESERVE UNIV, 80- *Mem:* AAAS; Am Chem Soc; Tissue Cult Asn; Am Inst Chemists. *Res:* Mechanism of steroid regulation of electrolyte transport in the intestines; regulation of electrolyte transport during the development of the amphibious embryo and laval. *Mailing Add:* Dept Anat Case Western Reserve Univ Cleveland OH 44106

WILL, PETER MILNE, b Peterhead, Scotland, Nov 2, 35; m 59; c 3. COMPUTER SCIENCE, ELECTRICAL ENGINEERING. *Educ:* Aberdeen Univ, BScEng, 58, PhD(elec eng), 60. *Prof Exp:* Mem res staff automatic control, Res Labs Assoc Elec Industs, Ltd, Eng, 61-62; proj leader indust electronics & control, AMF Brit Res Labs, 62-64; sr res physicist, Morehead Patterson Res Ctr, Am Mach & Foundry Co, Conn, 64-65; mem res staff comput sci, T J Watson Res Ctr, IBM Corp, 65-80; DIR PROD SYSTS ENG, SCHLUMBERGER WELL SERV, 80- *Concurrent Pos:* Lectr, Univ Conn, Stamford Exten, 66-71. *Res:* Application of computers to non-traditional fields; image processing; bandwidth compression; robotry; robot vision; multispectral imagery. *Mailing Add:* Schlumberger Well Serv 5000 Gulf Freeway Houston TX 77001

WILL, THEODORE A, b Orange, NJ, Aug 9, 37. SOLID STATE PHYSICS. *Educ:* Johns Hopkins Univ, AB, 59; Univ Chicago, SM, 61; Case Western Reserve Univ, PhD(physics), 68. *Prof Exp:* Asst prof physics, Heidelberg Col, 62-64 & Grinnell Col, 68-72; vis prof, Mat Res Ctr, Nat Univ Mex, 72-74; MEM FAC, MAT RES CTR, NAT UNIV MEX, 74-,HEAD DEPT MAT SCI, 77- *Mem:* Am Phys Soc; Mex Phys Soc; Am Asn Physics Teachers. *Res:* Electron phonon interaction in PbTl and PbBi from superconductor tunneling measurements; electron tunneling. *Mailing Add:* Ciudad Univ AP 70-337 Mexico 20 DF Mexico

WILLARD, DANIEL, b Baltimore, Md, Aug 22, 26; m 58; c 2. PHYSICS. *Educ:* Yale Univ, BS, 49, MS, 50; Mass Inst Technol, PhD(physics), 54. *Prof Exp:* Res assoc physics, Brookhaven Nat Lab, 54-55; instr, Swarthmore Col, 55-58; assoc prof, Va Polytech Inst, 58-61; opers res analyst, Opers Res Off, Johns Hopkins Univ, 61 & Res Anal Corp, Va, 61-63; OPERS RES ANALYST, OFF UNDER SECY US ARMY, 63- *Concurrent Pos:* Consult, Langley Res Ctr, NASA, 59-61. *Mem:* Am Phys Soc; Royal Astron Soc. *Res:* Cosmic rays; heavy unstable particles; radio astronomy; mathematical models of combat; operations research; systems analysis. *Mailing Add:* Off Under Secy Army Dept of the Army Washington DC 20310

WILLARD, DANIEL EDWARD, b Cincinnati, Ohio, Oct 24, 34; m 78; c 3. ENVIRONMENTAL ECOLOGY. *Educ:* Stanford Univ, AB, 60, Univ Calif, Davis, PhD(zool), 66. *Prof Exp:* Lectr biol, Univ Tex, Austin, 66-67, asst prof bot & zool, 67-70; asst prof, Univ Wis-Madison, 70-72, assoc scientist, 72-77; ASSOC PROF, SCH PUB & ENVIRON AFFAIRS, IND UNIV, BLOOMINGTON, 77- *Concurrent Pos:* Lectr, San Diego Zool Soc, 60; vis asst prof, Inst Marine Sci, Univ Ore, 72-73; consult, Ore Pub Utility Comn, 75-76 & Wis Attorney Gen Off, 73- *Mem:* Ecol Soc Am; Human Ecol Soc; AAAS; Am Behav Soc; Am Inst Biol Sci. *Res:* Impacts of energy development on biological systems; dynamics of wetlands; human impact on wildlife; management of endangered species; ecological regulation. *Mailing Add:* Sch of Pub & Environ Affairs Ind Univ Bloomington IN 47405

WILLARD, EDWARD PAYSON, III, industrial engineering, operations research, see previous edition

WILLARD, H(ARRY) L(ENTZ), b Fairfield, Ill, Jan 16, 14; m 44; c 3. CHEMICAL ENGINEERING. *Educ:* Univ Ill, BS, 35. *Prof Exp:* Asst org synthesis, Mellon Inst, 35-36; asst tech div, Carbide & Carbon Chem Co, 36-39; asst tech dir, Tar & Chem Div, Koppers Co, 40-42; from fel to admin fel, Mellon Inst, 46-57; assoc tech dir, Union Carbide Develop Co, 57-60, asst mgr res admin, Union Carbide Corp, NY, 60-64, tech mgr, Chem & Plastics, 64-69; dir, Chappaqua Res Assocs, 69-71; asst to pres, NY Ocean Sci Lab, 71-79; CONSULT, 79- *Concurrent Pos:* Dir chem develop, Corn Prod Co, 46-57. *Mem:* AAAS; Am Chem Soc; Am Inst Chem Engrs. *Res:* Organic chemistry; chemical rocket propulsion; environmental contaminants; military research and development; land conservation. *Mailing Add:* 50 Egypt Close East Hampton NY 11937

WILLARD, HARVEY BRADFORD, b Worcester, Mass, Aug 9, 25; m 50; c 2. NUCLEAR PHYSICS. *Educ:* Mass Inst Technol, SB, 48, PhD(physics), 50. *Prof Exp:* Physicist, Oak Ridge Nat Lab, 50-57, co-dir, High Voltage Lab, 57-63, assoc dir physics div, 63-67; chmn dept physics, Case Western Reserve Univ, 67-71, dean sci & vprovost, Case Inst Technol, 70-76, prof physics, 67-81; HEAD NUCLEAR SCI, NSF, 81- *Mem:* AAAS; Fel Am Phys Soc. *Res:* Nuclear scattering; reaction and polarization phenomena; energy levels of nuclei; the few nucleon problem; Van de Graaff accelerators; medium energy studies of proton-proton scattering and meson production with polarized beams and targets. *Mailing Add:* Physics Div NSF 1800 S St NW Washington DC 20550

WILLARD, JAMES MATTHEW, b St Johnsbury, Vt, Nov 18, 39; m 61; c 3. BIOCHEMISTRY. *Educ:* St Michael's Col, Vt, AB, 61; Cornell Univ, PhD(biochem), 67. *Prof Exp:* Res assoc biochem, Case Western Reserve Univ, 66-69; asst prof biochem, Col Med, Univ Vt, 69-75; asst prof, 75-77,

ASSOC PROF BIOL, CLEVELAND STATE UNIV, 77-, ASST DEAN ARTS SCI, 81- *Res:* Preparation and effect of certain analogues of phosphoribosyl pyrophosphate on de novo purine synthesis; zeolites as dietary supplement; dietary use of fructose; predictive method of catalysis (intermedion theory). *Mailing Add:* Dept Biol Cleveland State Univ Cleveland OH 44115

WILLARD, JOHN ELA, b Oak Park, Ill, Oct 31, 08; m 37; c 4. PHYSICAL CHEMISTRY. *Educ:* Harvard Univ, SB, 30; Univ Wis, PhD(phys chem), 35. *Prof Exp:* Instr chem, Avon Sch, 30-32 & Haverford Col, 35-37; from instr to prof, 37-47, dean, Grad Sch, 58-63, Vilas res prof, 63-79, chmn, Dept Chem, 70-72, EMER PROF CHEM, UNIV WIS-MADISON, 79- *Concurrent Pos:* Assoc sect chief, Plutonium Chem Sect, Metall Lab, Univ Chicago, 42-44, dir pile chem div, 45-46; area supvr, Hanford Eng Works, E I du Pont de Nemours & Co, Inc, 44-45; consult, Oak Ridge Nat Lab, 46-49; mem, Phys Chem Panel, Off Naval Res, 48-50, Surv Comt, AEC, 49 & Isotope Distrib Adv Comt, AEC, 53-57; secy, Nuclear Chem Sect, Int Cong Pure & Appl Chem, 51; mem partic inst exec bd, Argonne Nat Lab, 50-53, chmn, 52-53, chem div vis comt, 58-64; mem adv bd, Gordon Res Confs, 55-60, chmn conf radiation chem, 68; assoc ed, Chem Reviews, 55-58 & Radiation Res, 65-68; mem bd vis chem div, Brookhaven Nat Lab, 56-59; mem panel on basic res & grad educ, President's Sci Adv Comt, 59-60 & on basic res & nat goals, Nat Acad Sci, 64-65. *Honors & Awards:* Award, Nuclear Appl in Chem, Am Chem Soc, 59. *Mem:* Am Chem Soc (chmn div phys & inorg chem, 57); Am Phys Soc; Radiation Res Soc; AAAS. *Res:* Radiation chemistry; photochemistry; chemical effects of nuclear transformations; nature and reactions of trapped intermediates. *Mailing Add:* Dept Chem Univ Wis Madison WI 53706

WILLARD, PAUL EDWIN, b Ogdensburg, NY, Sept 11, 19; m 43; c 2. ORGANIC CHEMISTRY. *Educ:* Univ Chicago, BS, 41. *Prof Exp:* Res chemist, Gen Labs, US Rubber Co, NJ, 41-44 & Celanese Corp Am, 44-47; res chemist, Ohio-Apex, Inc, 47-50, from asst res dir to res dir, Ohio-Apex Div, 50-57, tech mgr, 57-58, mgr applns, Tech Serv Lab, Org Chem Div, 58-62, asst dir govt liaison, NJ, 62-65, mgr ceramic fibers res & develop, 65-69, sr res chemist, 69-74, RES ASSOC, FMC CORP, 74- *Mem:* Am Chem Soc; Nat Asn Corrosion Engrs. *Res:* Hydrogen peroxide; thermosetting plastics, especially rheology; plastics testing and applications; composite materials; ceramic fibers; thermal analysis. *Mailing Add:* 20 Jericho Dr Trenton NJ 08690

WILLARD, PAUL W, b Marshalltown, Iowa, Mar 21, 33; m 52; c 4. TOXICOLOGY, PHARMACOLOGY. *Educ:* Iowa State Univ, BS, 55; Univ Iowa, PhD(physiol), 59; Ind Univ, MBA, 68; Am Bd Toxicol, dipl, 81. *Prof Exp:* Nat Heart Inst fel physiol, Lankenau Hosp, Philadelphia, Pa, 59-61; sr scientist, Div Pharmacol Res, Eli Lilly & Co, 61-69; clin res coordr, Med Prods Div, 3M Co, 69-75; dir regulatory affairs, Medtronic Inc, 75-77; supvr toxicol serv, 78-80, MGR PROD REGULATORY TOXICOL, 3M CO, 80- *Mem:* Am Physiol Soc; Am Soc Pharmacol & Exp Therapeut; Soc Toxicol; Am Col Toxicol; Am Indust Hyg Asn. *Res:* Cardiovascular pharmacology, physiology and toxicology; regulatory affairs; industrial toxicology; product toxicology. *Mailing Add:* Toxicol Serv 220-2E 3M Ctr St Paul MN 55101

WILLARD, ROBERT JACKSON, b Brockton, Mass, Mar 21, 29; m 54; c 2. GEOLOGY, RESEARCH ADMINISTRATION. *Educ:* Boston Univ, AB, 51, AM, 53, PhD(geol), 58. *Prof Exp:* Instr geol, Wellesley Col, 56-57; from instr to asst prof, Univ Ark, 57-63; geologist, 63-67, head, Fabric Anal Lab, 68-74, geologist & contract tech proj officericer, Advan Mining Div, 74-76, staff engr, Minerals Environ Tech, Headquarters, 77-78, geologist & contract tech proj off, Environ Assessment & Ground Control Div, 78-79, STAFF ENGR & PHYSICAL SCIENTIST, ADMIN DIV, TWIN CITIES MINING RES CTR, US BUR MINES, 80- *Concurrent Pos:* Nat Park Serv study grant, 60-61. *Mem:* Geol Soc Am; Am Soc Mining, Metall & Petrol Eng. *Res:* petrofabrics; electron fractography; improvements in longwall mining techniques and equipment; operational technical standards in deep ocean mining; relation of rock fabric to various deformation and fragmentation tests; analysis of Vermont & New York State industry; evaluation of coal deposits in the Narragansett Basin of Massachusetts and Rhode Island. *Mailing Add:* US Bur of Mines 5629 Minnehaha Ave S Minneapolis MN 55417

WILLARD, STEPHEN, b Syracuse, NY, Nov 1, 41; m 63; c 2. MATHEMATICS. *Educ:* Univ Rochester, AB, 62, MA, 64, PhD(math), 65. *Prof Exp:* Asst prof math, Lehigh Univ, 65-66 & Case Western Reserve Univ, 66-69; ASSOC PROF MATH, UNIV ALTA, 69- *Mem:* Am Math Soc; Math Asn Am. *Res:* Convergence structures; mapping properties of topological spaces; generalizations of compactness; absolute Borel and analytic sets in topological spaces; set theory. *Mailing Add:* Dept of Math Univ of Alta Edmonton AB T6G 2G1 Can

WILLARD, THOMAS MAXWELL, b Beaumont, Tex, Aug 30, 37; m 59; c 2. INORGANIC CHEMISTRY, ANALYTICAL CHEMISTRY. *Educ:* Lamar Univ, BS, 59; Tulane Univ, PhD(inorg chem), 64. *Prof Exp:* Fac mem, 64-65, PROF CHEM, FLA SOUTHERN COL, 81-, CHMN DEPT, 65- *Concurrent Pos:* Rotary Int group study exchange fel, Japan, 73. *Mem:* Am Chem Soc. *Res:* Interactions between very weak acids and very weak bases in non-polar media. *Mailing Add:* Dept Chem Fla Southern Col Lakeland FL 33802

WILLARD, WILLIAM KENNETH, b Hagerstown, Md, Nov 5, 29; m 61; c 2. ECOLOGY. *Educ:* Univ Ga, BSF, 57, MS, 60; Univ Tenn, PhD(zool), 65. *Prof Exp:* From asst prof to assoc prof zool, Clemson Univ, 65-75; PROF ZOOL & CHMN DEPT BIOL, TENN TECHNOL UNIV, 75- *Mem:* AAAS; Ecol Soc Am; Am Inst Biol Sci. *Res:* Effects of radiations on populations; fate of radioactive materials in the environment; population dynamics; ecosystem analysis; radiation ecology; bioenergetics of food chain relationships; ecological strategies in mammalian population dynamics. *Mailing Add:* Dept Biol Tenn Technol Univ Cookeville TN 38501

WILLARDSON, LYMAN S(ESSIONS), b Ephraim, Utah, May 10, 27; m 48; c 6. AGRICULTURAL ENGINEERING. *Educ:* Utah State Univ, BS, 50, MS, 55; Ohio State Univ, PhD(agr eng), 67. *Prof Exp:* Irrig engr, United Fruit Co, 52-54; irrig engr, Agr Exp Sta, Univ PR, 54-57; agr engr, Agr Res Serv, USDA, Ohio, 57-67, res leader drainage, Imp Valley Conserv Res Ctr, 67-74; PROF AGR & IRRIG ENG, UTAH STATE UNIV, LOGAN, 74- *Mem:* AAAS; Am Soc Civil Engrs; Am Soc Agr Engrs; Nat Soc Prof Engrs; Int Comn Irrig & Drainage. *Res:* Engineering research on problems associated with irrigation and drainage of agricultural lands; drainage and salinity of irrigated lands. *Mailing Add:* Dept of Agr & Irrig Eng Utah State Univ Logan UT 84322

WILLARDSON, ROBERT KENT, b Gunnison, Utah, July 11, 23; m 47; c 3. SOLID STATE PHYSICS. *Educ:* Brigham Young Univ, BS, 49; Iowa State Col, MS, 51. *Prof Exp:* Instr physics, Brigham Young Univ, 47-48 & Iowa State Col, 48-49; res physicist, Ames Lab, AEC, 49-51; prin physicist, Battelle Mem Inst, 51-56, asst chief, Phys Chem Div, 56-60; chief scientist, Res Ctr, Bell & Howell Co, 60-64, dir solid state res, 64-67, dir mat res, 67-69, gen mgr electronic mat div, 69-73, pres, Electronic Mat Corp, 73; asst to gen mgr, Electronic Mat Div, 73-77, mgr electronic mat, Div Sales, 77-81, MGR PLANNING, COMINCO AM INC, 81- *Mem:* Am Phys Soc; Electrochem Soc; Am Chem Soc; Inst Elec & Electronics Eng; Int Soc Hybrid Microelectronics. *Res:* Preparation, electrical and optical properties of high purity metals, alloys and semiconductors; analysis, control and effects of impurities and lattice defects in these materials; electronic transport phenomena in semiconductors. *Mailing Add:* Div Electronic Mat Cominco Am Inc E 15128 Euclid Ave Spokane WA 99216

WILLBANKS, EMILY WEST, b Ft Lauderdale, Fla, Nov 25, 30; m 59. COMPUTER SCIENCE, MATHEMATICS. *Educ:* Duke Univ, BS, 52; Univ NMex, MS, 57. *Prof Exp:* Eng aide math, Pratt-Whitney Aircraft Co, 52-54; STAFF MEM MATH & COMPUT, LOS ALAMOS NAT LAB, 54- *Mailing Add:* Los Alamos Nat Lab PO Box 1663 Los Alamos NM 87545

WILLCOTT, MARK ROBERT, III, b Muskogee, Okla, July 23, 33; m 55; c 4. ORGANIC CHEMISTRY. *Educ:* Rice Univ, BA, 55; Yale Univ, MS, 59, PhD(chem), 63. *Prof Exp:* Asst prof chem, Emory Univ, 62-64; from asst prof to assoc prof, 65-73, PROF CHEM, UNIV HOUSTON, 73- *Concurrent Pos:* NIH fel, Univ Wis, 64-65; Guggenheim fel, 72-73; consult, Upjohn Co, 65- & Aldrich Chem Co, 72-; adj prof med, Baylor Col Med, 78-; adj prof chem, Rice Univ, 81- *Mem:* Am Chem Soc; Royal Soc Chem. *Res:* Thermal rearrangements of organic compounds; nuclear magnetic resonance spectroscopy; magnetic resonance imaging; nuclear magnetic resonances in medicine. *Mailing Add:* Dept of Chem 3800 Cullen Blvd Houston TX 77004

WILLCOX, ALFRED BURTON, b Sioux Rapids, Iowa, Sept 18, 25; m 48; c 4. MATHEMATICS. *Educ:* Yale Univ, MA, 49, PhD(math), 53. *Prof Exp:* From instr to prof math, Amherst Col, 53-68, exec dir comt undergrad prog math, 63-64; EXEC DIR, MATH ASN AM, 68- *Concurrent Pos:* Vis asst prof, Univ Chicago, 57-58; vis lectr, Uppsala Univ, Sweden, 67-68. *Mem:* AAAS; Am Math Soc; Math Asn Am (vpres, 64-66); Nat Coun Teachers Math. *Res:* Banach algebras. *Mailing Add:* Math Asn Am 1529 Eighteenth St NW Washington DC 20036

WILLDEN, CHARLES RONALD, b Neola, Utah, Sept 30, 29; m 50; c 3. GEOLOGY. *Educ:* Univ Utah, BS, 51, MS, 52; Stanford Univ, PhD(geol), 60. *Prof Exp:* Geologist, US Geol Surv, Colo, 52-68; sr geologist, Vanguard Explor Co, 68-72; GEOLOGIST, SILVER RESOURCES CORP, 72- *Mem:* Geol Soc Am; Soc Econ Geol; Am Asn Petrol Geol. *Res:* Structural and economic geology. *Mailing Add:* 8750 Kings Hill Dr Salt Lake City UT 84121

WILLE, JOHN JACOB, JR, b New York, NY, June 24, 37; m 61; c 4. CELL BIOLOGY. *Educ:* Cornell Univ, BA, 60; Univ Ind, PhD(genetics), 65. *Prof Exp:* Resident res assoc cell biol, Biol Div, Argonne Nat Lab, 65-66, fel, 66-68; asst prof biol sci, Univ Cincinnati, 68-72; NIH spec fel, Univ Chicago, 72-73, res assoc, Dept Biophys, 73-75; asst prof zool & physiol, La State Univ, 75-80; SR RES ASSOC, DEPT CELL BIOL, MAYO CLIN, 80- *Res:* Developmental genetics of unicellular organisms; molecular biology of biological rhythms; cancer cell biology. *Mailing Add:* Dept Cell Biol Mayo Clin Rochester MN 55901

WILLEBOORDSE, FRISO, b Bandung, Indonesia, July 31, 35; m 58; c 4. ANALYTICAL CHEMISTRY. *Educ:* Univ Indonesia, BS, 54; Univ Amsterdam, Drs, 57, PhD(anal chem), 69. *Prof Exp:* Lectr inorg chem, Univ Natal, 60-61, sr lectr anal chem, 61-62; res chemist, WVa, Union Carbide Corp, Bound Brook, NJ, 62-69, res scientist, Bound Brook, 69-72, group leader anal res chem & plastics, 72-80; DIR, ANAL RES & COMPUT SERV, W R GRACE & CO, COLUMBIA, MD, 81- *Concurrent Pos:* Vis prof, Rutgers Univ, 73-74 & 79-80. *Mem:* Am Chem Soc; Royal Netherlands Chem Soc. *Res:* Polymer characterization, polarography; differential chemical kinetics. *Mailing Add:* 5468 Wingborne Ct Columbia MD 21045

WILLEFORD, BENNETT RUFUS, JR, b Greenville, SC, Oct 28, 21. PHYSICAL CHEMISTRY. *Educ:* Emory Univ, BA, 43; Univ Wis, MS, 49, PhD(phys chem), 50. *Prof Exp:* Jr chemist, Shell Develop Co, 43-46; asst, Univ Wis, 46-50; from asst prof to assoc prof, 50-61, PROF CHEM, BUCKNELL UNIV, 61- *Concurrent Pos:* Res fel, Univ Minn, 56-57; consult, US Fish & Wildlife Serv, 60-64; NSF sci fac fel, Univ Munich, 62-63; res assoc, Univ NC, Chapel Hill, 69-70; guest prof, Inorganic Chem Lab, Univ Oxford, Eng, 77-78 & Anorgenisch-Chem Inst, Tech Univ Munchen, 78. *Mem:* Am Chem Soc. *Res:* Structure of metal coordination compounds; organometallic chemistry. *Mailing Add:* Dept of Chem Bucknell Univ Lewisburg PA 17837

WILLEKE, KLAUS, b Essen, Ger, Mar 26, 41; m 68; c 1. AEROSOL SCIENCE & TECHNOLOGY. *Educ:* Univ NH, BS, 63; Stanford Univ, MS, 64, PhD(aeronaut & astronaut), 69; Von Karman Inst, dipl, 66. *Prof Exp:* Fel, Max Planck Inst Plasma Physics, Ger, 69-70; asst prof mech eng, Univ Minn,

70-76; assoc prof environ health & adj prof chem eng, 76-81, PROF ENVIRON HEALTH, UNIV CINCINNATI, 81- *Concurrent Pos:* Vis asst prof, Dept Chem Eng, Kyoto Univ, Japan, 73; mem, Occupational Safety & Health Study Sect, Nat Inst Occupational Safety & Health, 78-80. *Mem:* Am Indust Hyiene Asn; AAAS; Air Pollution Control Asn; Am Asn Aerosol Res. *Res:* Particle slicing and classification; aerosol generation and sampling; asbestos fibers; particle deposition in lung; therapeutic aerosols; respirator protection of workers; dust control. *Mailing Add:* ML 56 107 Kettering Lab Dept Environ Health Univ Cincinnati Cincinnati OH 45267

WILLEMOT, CLAUDE, b Ghent, Belg, Dec 26, 33; Can citizen; m 66; c 4. PLANT LIPID METABOLISM, STRESS PHYSIOLOGY. *Educ:* McGill Univ, MSc, 63, PhD(plant physiol), 64. *Prof Exp:* Nat Res Coun Can fel, Nat Inst Agr Res, Versailles, France, 64-65 & Univ Calif, Davis, 65-67; RES SCIENTIST PLANT PHYSIOL, RES STA, CAN DEPT AGR, 67- *Concurrent Pos:* Lectr, Fac Agr, Laval Univ, 68-; assoc ed, Can J Biochem, 75-79; mem staff, Dept Sci & Indust Res, New Zealand, 79-80. *Mem:* Can Soc Plant Physiol (secy-treas, 71-72, secy, 72-73); Am Soc Plant Physiol; Soc Cryobiol. *Res:* Mechanism of plant frost hardiness; plant lipid metabolism; winter hardiness of crop plants, mainly alfalfa and wheat. *Mailing Add:* Agr Can Res Sta 2560 Boul Hochelaga Ste-Foy PQ G1V 2J6 Can

WILLEMS, JAN C, b Bruges, Belg, Sept 18, 39; m 65; c 2. SYSTEMS ENGINEERING, CONTROL ENGINEERING. *Educ:* Univ Ghent, Electromech Engr, 63; Univ RI, MSc, 65; Mass Inst Technol, PhD(elec eng), 68. *Prof Exp:* Asst prof elec eng, Mass Inst Technol, 68-73; PROF, UNIV GRONINGEN, NETHERLANDS, 73- *Concurrent Pos:* Sr vis fel, dept appl math & theoret physics, UK Sci Res Coun, 70-71. *Mem:* Fel Inst Elec & Electronics Engrs; Soc Indust & Appl Math; Dutch Math Soc; Dutch Gen Systs Soc. *Res:* Control theory; stability theory; optimal control; mathematical system theory. *Mailing Add:* Univ Groningen Math Inst Postbus 800 9700 AV Groningen Netherlands

WILLEMS, NICHOLAS, b Aardenburg, Netherlands, Jan 6, 24; US citizen; m 48; c 5. CIVIL & STRUCTURAL ENGINEERING. *Educ:* Delft Univ Technol, MSc, 46; Univ Pretoria, MComm, 53; Univ Kans, PhD(eng mech), 63. *Prof Exp:* Asst engr, Hague Munic, 46-48; engr, Transvaal Prov Rd Dept, 48-51; construct engr, SAfrican Coal & Oil Corp, 51-52; resident engr, van Niekerk, Kleyn & Edwards, 52-54, jr partner & consult, 54-60; asst prof civil eng, 60-61, instr, 61-63, from assoc prof to prof, 63-75, chmn dept, 72-75, PROF CIVIL ENG, UNIV KANS, 75- *Concurrent Pos:* Consult, indust & state & fed govt, 60-67; Ford Found grant, 63. *Mem:* Am Soc Civil Engrs; Sigma Xi. *Res:* Structural analysis; plates; shells; dynamic loading; vibrations and matrix analysis. *Mailing Add:* 1305 Engel Rd Lawrence KS 66044

WILLEMSEN, HERMAN WILLIAM, b Huissen, Holland, Dec 23, 45; Can citizen. PHYSICS. *Educ:* Univ Waterloo, BSc, 70; Univ Toronto, MSc, 72, PhD(physics), 75. *Prof Exp:* Res assoc physics, Univ Toronto, 75-76; res assoc, Argonne Nat Lab, 76-79; SCIENTIST PHYSICS, BELL NORTHERN RES, 79- *Mem:* Can Asn Physicists; Am Phys Soc. *Res:* Superconductivity; phase transitions; defects in insulators; mass memory systems. *Mailing Add:* 1130 Allenmede Cresent Ottawa ON K2B 8H3 Can

WILLEMSEN, ROGER WAYNE, b Oskaloosa, Iowa, Jan 14, 44; m 66; c 2. PHYSIOLOGICAL ECOLOGY, BOTANY. *Educ:* Cent Col, Iowa, BA, 66; Kans State Col, Pittsburg, Kans, MS, 68; Univ Okla, PhD(bot), 71. *Frof Exp:* Grants, 72-73, asst prof bot, Rutgers Univ, New Brunswick, 71-78; MEM STAFF, LILLY RES LABS, 78- *Mem:* Ecol Soc Am; Am Inst Biol Sci; Torrey Bot Club; Bot Soc Am; Weed Sci Soc Am. *Res:* The physiology and ecology of weed seed germination; allelopathy; old-field succession; agricultural pest control. *Mailing Add:* Calif Res Sta 7521 W Calif Ave Fresno CA 93706

WILLENBROCK, FREDERICK KARL, b New York, NY, July 19, 20; m 44. ENGINEERING. *Educ:* Brown Univ, BS, 42; Harvard Univ, MA, 47, PhD(appl physics), 50. *Prof Exp:* Res fel & lectr, Harvard Univ, 50-55, from asst dir labs, Div Eng & Appl Physics to dir labs & assoc dean div, 54-67; prof & provost fac eng & appl sci, State Univ NY, Buffalo, 67-70; dir, Inst Appl Technol, Nat Bur Standards, 70-76; dean, Sch Eng & Appl Sci, 76-81, CECIL GREEN PROF ENG, SOUTHERN METHODIST UNIV, 76- *Mem:* Nat Acad Eng; Am Phys Soc; AAAS; Am Soc Eng Educ; Inst Elec & Electronics Eng. *Res:* Engineering education technology and public policy. *Mailing Add:* Sch Eng & Appl Sci Southern Methodist Univ Dallas TX 75275

WILLENKIN, ROBERT L, b Oceanside, NY, Feb 12, 31; m 64; c 4. ANESTHESIOLOGY, PHYSIOLOGY. *Educ:* Hofstra Univ, BA, 51; State Univ NY, MD, 55. *Prof Exp:* Fel anesthesiol, Yale Univ, 60-61; fel physiol, Univ Wash, 62-63; asst prof anesthesiol, Sch Med, Yale Univ, 63-68; assoc prof, Albany Med Col, 68-73; assoc clin prof, 73-79, CLIN PROF, DEPT ANESTHESIA, UNIV CALIF, SAN FRANCISCO, 79- *Mem:* AAAS; Am Soc Anesthesiol. *Res:* Cardiovascular physiology. *Mailing Add:* Dept of Anesthesiol Univ of Calif San Francisco CA 94143

WILLENS, RONALD HOWARD, b Chicago, Ill, Oct 31, 31; m 56; c 2. PHYSICAL METALLURGY, SOLID STATE PHYSICS. *Educ:* Calif Inst Technol, BS, 53, MS, 54, PhD(eng sci, physics), 61. *Prof Exp:* Res fel mat sci, Calif Inst Technol, 61-63, from asst prof to assoc prof, 63-67; vis mem, 64-65, MEM TECH STAFF, BELL LABS, 67- *Honors & Awards:* Mathewson Gold Medal, Am Inst Mining, Metall & Petrol Engrs, 64. *Mem:* Am Inst Mining, Metall & Petrol Engrs; Am Soc Metals; Brit Inst Metals; Am Phys Soc. *Res:* Metastable phases by rapid quenching from the melt; superconductivity; electro-magnetic transport properties of metals; phase transformations; defects in solids. *Mailing Add:* Bell Labs Murray Hill NJ 07974

WILLER, RODNEY LEE, b Albany, Ore, Nov 27, 48; m 74. STEREOCHEMISTRY, ENERGETIC MATERIALS. *Educ:* East Carolina Univ, BS, 70, MS, 74; Univ NC, PhD(org chem), 76. *Prof Exp:* Res assoc, Mich State Univ, 76-78; asst prof, Tex Tech Univ, 78-80; RES CHEMIST, ORG CHEM, NAVAL WEAPONS CTR, 80- *Mem:* Am Chem Soc; Sigma Xi; AAAS; NY Acad Sci. *Res:* Synthesis and characterization of high density energetic materials with potential application as propellant and explosive ingrediants. *Mailing Add:* Res Dept Code 3853 Naval Weapons Ctr China Lake CA 93555

WILLERMET, PIERRE ANDRE, b Mineola, NY, Aug 21, 41; m 63; c 2. LUBRICATION, TRIBOLOGY. *Educ:* Widener Univ, BS, 67; Univ Pa, PhD(phys chem), 72. *Prof Exp:* RES SCIENTIST, ENG & RES STAFF, FORD MOTOR CO, 72- *Mem:* Sigma Xi; Am Chem Soc; Am Soc Lubrication Engrs. *Res:* Tribology; chemistry of friction and wear in lubricated contacts; thermo oxidative degradation of hydrocarbons and lubricant additives; friction losses in automotive engines and drive trains; polymer and ceramic composites. *Mailing Add:* 11400 Melrose Ave Livonia MI 48150

WILLERTZ, LOTHAR ERNEST, b Detroit, Mich, Oct 10, 39; m 62; c 3. PHYSICAL METALLURGY. *Educ:* Mich State Univ, BS, 61; Carnegie Inst Technol, MS, 66, PhD(metall), 68. *Prof Exp:* Develop engr, Magnetic Mat Sect, Gen Elec Corp, 61-64; sr engr, 68-80, PRIN ENGR METALL, RES & DEVELOP CTR, WESTINGHOUSE ELEC CORP, 80- *Honors & Awards:* Templin Award, Am Soc Testing & Mat, 75. *Mem:* Am Soc Metals; Metall Soc; Am Soc Testing & Mat. *Res:* Mechanical properties of materials, particularly the areas of fatigue, corrosion fatigue and high frequency fatigue; damping, internal friction and their inter-relationships. *Mailing Add:* Res & Develop Ctr 1310 Beulah Rd Pittsburgh PA 15235

WILLETT, COLIN SIDNEY, b Danbury, Eng, Jan 11, 35; US citizen; c 2. PHYSICAL SCIENCE, LASERS. *Educ:* City Univ London, BS, 63; Univ London, PhD(physics), 67. *Prof Exp:* PHYSICIST LASERS, HARRY DIAMOND LABS, DEPT ARMY, ADELPHI, 67- *Res:* Atomic collision processes; gas discharge physics; laser systems research and analysis. *Mailing Add:* 9556 Frederick Rd Ellicott City MD 21043

WILLETT, DOUGLAS W, b Adams County, NDak, May 25, 37; m 59; c 5. MATHEMATICS. *Educ:* SDak Sch Mines & Technol, BS, 59; Calif Inst Technol, PhD(math), 63. *Prof Exp:* From asst prof to assoc prof math, Univ Alta, 62-66; assoc prof, 66-72, PROF MATH, UNIV UTAH, 72- *Concurrent Pos:* Vis prof, Univ Alta, 71-72. *Mem:* Soc Indust & Appl Math; Can Math Cong. *Res:* Ordinary differential equations and mathematical analysis. *Mailing Add:* Dept of Math Univ of Utah Salt Lake City UT 84112

WILLETT, HILDA POPE, b Decatur, Ga, July 15, 23; m 56; c 2. MICROBIOLOGY. *Educ:* Woman'sCol Ga, AB, 44; Duke Univ, MA, 46, PhD(microbiol), 49. *Prof Exp:* Instr microbiol, 48-50, assoc, 50-52, from asst prof to assoc prof, 52-64, PROF BACT, SCH MED, DUKE UNIV, 64-, DIR, GRAD STUDIES, 80- *Mem:* Am Soc Microbiol; Am Acad Microbiol. *Res:* Vitamin and amino acid metabolism of virulent and avirulent Mycobacterium tuberculosis; mode of action of isoniazid. *Mailing Add:* Dept of Microbiol Duke Univ Med Ctr Durham NC 27710

WILLETT, JAMES DELOS, b Stockton, Calif, Jan 16, 37; c 2. CHEMISTRY. *Educ:* Univ Calif, Berkeley, BA, 59; Mass Inst Technol, PhD(org chem), 65. *Prof Exp:* Jr chemist res, Merck, Sharp & Dohme Res Labs, 59-61; fel chem, Stanford Univ, 65-68; asst prof chem, 68-73; assoc prof chem, Univ Idaho, 73-78, prof chem & biochem, 78-80; grants assoc, 80-81, STAFF ASST DEP DIR, DIV RES RESOURCES, NIH, 81- *Concurrent Pos:* NIH fel, 65-68; NIH career develop award, Nat Inst Aging, 75-80. *Mem:* Am Chem Soc; Soc Nematologists; Am Aging Asn; AAAS. *Res:* Nematodes as models for the study of the effects of senescence on hormonal control systems. *Mailing Add:* Bldg 31 Rm 5B48B Div Res Resources NIH Bethesda MD 20205

WILLETT, JOSEPH ERWIN, b Albany, Mo, June 9, 29; m 55; c 3. PLASMA PHYSICS. *Educ:* Univ Mo, BA, 51, MA, 53, PhD(physics), 56. *Prof Exp:* From asst to instr physics, Univ Mo, 53-55, Stewart fel, 55; physicist & aeronaut res engr, US Naval Ord Lab, Md, 56-58; res scientist, McDonnell Aircraft Corp, 58-61, instr, McDonnell Eve Sch, 60-61; staff scientist, Gen Dynamics/Ft Worth, Tex, 61-65; assoc prof, 65-81, PROF PHYSICS, UNIV MO-COLUMBIA, 81- *Concurrent Pos:* Instr & adj prof, Tex Christian Univ, 62-64. *Honors & Awards:* Superior Accomplishment Award, US Naval Ord Lab, 58. *Mem:* Am Phys Soc. *Res:* Theoretical studies of the interaction of electromagnetic waves with plasmas; electrostatic and hydromagnetic waves; stimulated raman and brillouin scattering; instabilities in magnetized plasmas; plasma heating; controlled fusion. *Mailing Add:* Dept of Physics Univ of Mo Columbia MO 65211

WILLETT, LYNN BRUNSON, b Colorado Springs, Colo, Aug 2, 44; m 66; c 1. ANIMAL PHYSIOLOGY, DAIRY SCIENCE. *Educ:* Colo State Univ, BS, 66; Purdue Univ, Lafayette, MS, 68, PhD(animal physiol), 71. *Prof Exp:* Asst prof, 71-77, ASSOC PROF DAIRY SCI, OHIO AGR RES & DEVELOP CTR, OHIO STATE UNIV, 77- *Concurrent Pos:* Ed, Pharmacol & Toxicol Sect, J Animal Sci. *Mem:* Am Dairy Sci Asn; Am Soc Animal Sci. *Res:* Elimination; metabolism and toxicity of halogenated hydrocarbons, particularly polybrominated biphenyls and polychlorinated biphenyls by cattle; steroid hormone relationships in cattle. *Mailing Add:* Dept Dairy Sci Ohio Agr Res & Develop Ctr Ohio State Univ Wooster OH 44691

WILLETT, NORMAN P, b Paterson, NJ, Apr 13, 28; m 56; c 3. MICROBIOLOGY. *Educ:* Rutgers Univ, BS, 49; Syracuse Univ, MS, 52; Mich State Univ, PhD(microbiol), 55. *Prof Exp:* Asst dent med, Harvard Univ, 55-57; sr res microbiologist, Squibb Inst Med Res, 57-60; res microbiologist, Bzura, Inc, 60-62; sr res assoc, Lever Brothers, 62-63; chief microbiologist, Food & Drug Res Inc, 63; res assoc, Sch Vet Med, Univ Pa, 63-66; assoc prof, Sch Pharm, 66-73, PROF MICROBIOL, SCH DENT, TEMPLE UNIV, 73-, HEAD DEPT, 67- *Concurrent Pos:* Mem, Am Asn Dent Schs. *Mem:* AAAS; Am Soc Microbiol; Am Chem Soc; Soc Indust Microbiol; NY Acad Sci. *Res:* Biochemical basis of pathogenicity; physiology of streptococci; antibiotic biosynthesis; biochemistry and microbiology of saliva; organic acid and antibiotic fermentation; chemotherapy. *Mailing Add:* 604 Pine Tree Rd Jenkintown PA 19046

WILLETT, RICHARD MICHAEL, b Louisville, Ky, May 2, 45; m. MATHEMATICS. *Educ:* US Air Force Acad, BS, 67; NC State Univ, MA, 69, PhD(math), 71. *Prof Exp:* Teaching asst math, NC State Univ, 67-71, instr, 71-72; asst prof, 72-77, ASSOC PROF MATH, UNIV NC, GREENSBORO, 77- *Res:* Finite field theory; error-correcting codes. *Mailing Add:* Dept of Math Univ of NC Greensboro NC 27412

WILLETT, ROGER, b Northfield, Minn, July 13, 36; m 57; c 6. PHYSICAL CHEMISTRY, CHEMICAL PHYSICS. *Educ:* St Olaf Col, BA, 58; Iowa State Univ, PhD(chem, physics), 62. *Prof Exp:* From instr to assoc prof, 62-72, chmn dept, 74-80, PROF CHEM, WASH STATE UNIV, 72- *Mem:* Am Chem Soc; Am Crystallog Asn; Sigma Xi. *Res:* X-ray diffraction and crystallography; magnetic susceptibility and interactions; chemical bonding; molecular and electronic structure; electronic spectra and electron spin resonance studies of transition metal ions. *Mailing Add:* Dept of Chem Wash State Univ Pullman WA 99164

WILLETTE, GORDON LOUIS, b Dighton, Mass, Dec 19, 33. PETROLEUM CHEMISTRY. *Educ:* Brown Univ, ScB, 55; Univ Minn, PhD(org chem), 59. *Prof Exp:* Chemist, Res Labs, Rohm and Haas Co, 59-76; dir res & develop, Hatco Chem Corp, 76-80; NEW VENTURE MGR SYNTHETIC LUBRICANTS, UNIROYAL CHEM CO, 80- *Mem:* Am Chem Soc; Am Soc Lubrication Engrs; Soc Advan Educ. *Res:* Polymer synthesis; ATF and motor oil formulation, synthetic lubricants and plasticizers. *Mailing Add:* Spencer St Uniroyal Chem Naugatuck CT 06770

WILLETTE, ROBERT EDMOND, b Grand Rapids, Mich, Aug 15, 33; div; c 3. MEDICINAL CHEMISTRY, ORGANIC CHEMISTRY. *Educ:* Ferris State Col, BS, 55; Univ Minn, PhD(pharmaceut chem), 60. *Prof Exp:* Spec instr med chem, Ferris State Col, 59-61; NIH res fel, Australian Nat Univ, 61-63; res officer, Div Org Chem, Commonwealth Sci & Indust Res Orgn, 63-64; res assoc med chem, Univ Mich, 65-66; from asst prof to assoc prof, Sch Pharm, Univ Conn, 66-72; chemist, Div Res, 72-81, DIR, DUO RES, NAT INST DRUG ABUSE, 81- *Mem:* AAAS; Am Pharmaceut Asn; Am Chem Soc; The Chem Soc. *Res:* Isolation and structure determination of natural products; synthesis of heterocyclic compounds of medicinal interest, particularly analgetics and narcotic antagonists and alkylating and acylating agents related to cancer; drug development. *Mailing Add:* 139 Lafayette Ave Annapolis MD 21401

WILLEY, ANN MORRIS, human genetics, see previous edition

WILLEY, CLIFF RUFUS, b Hornell, NY, Nov 20, 35; m 57; c 5. SOIL PHYSICS. *Educ:* Cornell Univ, BS, 57, MS, 59; Univ Wis-Madison, PhD(soil physics), 62. *Prof Exp:* Soil scientist, Agr Res Serv, USDA, 62-73; chief solid waste serv, 73-74, CHIEF TECH SERV, MD ENVIRON SERV, DEPT NATURAL RESOURCES, 74- *Concurrent Pos:* Assoc prof agr eng, NC State Univ, 67-73. *Mem:* Sigma Xi. *Mailing Add:* Md Environ Serv 60 West St Annapolis MD 21401

WILLEY, JOAN DEWITT, b Summit, NJ, May 10, 48. MARINE CHEMISTRY, ANALYTICAL CHEMISTRY. *Educ:* Duke Univ, BSc, 69; Dalhousie Univ, PhD(chem oceanog), 75. *Prof Exp:* Fel geochem, Mem Univ Nfld, 74-75; vis scientist marine geol, Bedford Inst, 76-77; asst prof, 77-81, ASSOC PROF CHEM & MARINE SCI, UNIV NC, WILMINGTON, 81- *Concurrent Pos:* Consult, Am Inst Chemists. *Mem:* Am Chem Soc; AAAS; Systs Eng Evaluation & Res Soc. *Res:* Sediment and interstitial water chemistry in estuaries, including seasonal variations; marine chemistry of silica; reactions between sediments and seawater. *Mailing Add:* Univ of NC Dept of Chem PO Box 3725 Wilmington NC 28406

WILLEY, ROBERT BRUCE, b Long Branch, NJ, Sept 15, 30; m 56. ANIMAL BEHAVIOR, ENTOMOLOGY. *Educ:* NJ State Teachers Col, BA, 52; Harvard Univ, PhD(biol), 59. *Prof Exp:* Teacher high sch, NJ, 52-54; from asst prof to assoc prof biol, Ripon Col, 59-65; ASSOC PROF BIOL, UNIV ILL, CHICAGO, 65- *Concurrent Pos:* Res grants, Sigma Xi, 62 & 67, NSF, 64-66, 72-74 & 75-76; mem bd trustees, Rocky Mountain Biol Lab, 63-, vpres, 72-76, pres, 77-80. *Mem:* Am Soc Zool; Soc Study Evolution; Entom Soc Am; Pan-Am Acridological Soc; Animal Behav Soc. *Res:* Invertebrate behavior; interspecific behavior and evolution of sympatric insect populations; animal communication systems. *Mailing Add:* Dept of Biol Sci Box 4348 Univ Ill Chicago IL 60680

WILLEY, RUTH LIPPITT, b Wickford, RI, May 11, 28; m 56. PHYCOLOGY, HYDROBIOLOGY. *Educ:* Wellesley Col, BA, 50; Radcliffe Col, PhD(biol), 56. *Prof Exp:* Docent mus educ, Peabody Mus Natural Hist, Yale Univ, 50-52; instr zool, Wellesley Col, 56-57; res fel opthal, Mass Eye & Ear Infirmary, 57-58; comm histologist, Triarch Prod, 59-60; asst prof, 65-71, ASSOC PROF BIOL SCI, UNIV ILL, CHICAGO, 71- *Concurrent Pos:* Mem, Rocky Mountain Biol Lab, Colo, 58-, secy, 66-68, mem bd trustees, 75-78, environ officer, 79- *Mem:* Electron Microscope Soc Am; Am Soc Cell Biol; Am Micros Soc; Entom Soc Am; Phycol Soc Am. *Res:* Evolution and ecology of aquatic insects, especially the Odonata; ultrastructure and ecology of euglenoid algae. *Mailing Add:* Dept of Biol Sci Univ of Ill Box 4348 Chicago IL 60680

WILLHAM, RICHARD LEWIS, b Hutchinson, Kans, May 4, 32; m 54; c 2. ANIMAL BREEDING. *Educ:* Okla State Univ, BS, 54; Iowa State Univ, MS, 55, PhD(animal breeding), 60. *Prof Exp:* Asst prof animal breeding, Iowa State Univ, 59-63; assoc prof, Okla State Univ, 63-66; PROF ANIMAL BREEDING, IOWA STATE UNIV, 66-, CHARLES F CURTISS ASST PROF AGR, 80- *Concurrent Pos:* AEC grant, Iowa State Univ, 59-63. *Mem:* Biomet Soc; Am Soc Animal Sci. *Res:* Beef cattle breeding; evaluation of the results of selection and crossbreeding; beef improvement federation work with national sire evaluation program development in beef industry. *Mailing Add:* Dept of Animal Sci Iowa State Univ Ames IA 50010

WILLHITE, GLEN PAUL, b Waterloo, Iowa, July 18, 37; m 59; c 5. CHEMICAL & PETROLEUM ENGINEERING. *Educ:* Iowa State Univ, BS, 59; Northwestern Univ, PhD(chem eng), 62. *Prof Exp:* From res scientist to sr res scientist, Continental Oil Co, 62-70; assoc prof chem & petrol eng, 69-75, PROF CHEM & PETROL ENG, UNIV KANS, 75- *Concurrent Pos:* Co-dir, Tertiary Oil Recovery Proj, 74-; consult, Off Technol Assessment, 76-78. *Mem:* Am Inst Chem Engrs; Soc Petrol Engrs. *Res:* Transport processes in porous media; environmental heat transfer; numerical solutions of partial differential equations; enhanced oil recovery processes. *Mailing Add:* Dept of Chem & Petrol Eng Univ of Kans Lawrence KS 66045

WILLHOIT, DONALD GILLMOR, b Kansas City, Mo, Feb 5, 34; m 56; c 4. RADIATION HEALTH. *Educ:* William Jewell Col, AB, 56; Univ Wash, 58; Univ Pittsburgh, ScD(radiation health), 64. *Prof Exp:* Assoc scientist & health physicist, Westinghouse Testing Reactor, 58-60; radiation safety off, Univ Pittsburgh, 60-61, teaching fel, 61-64; asst prof radiol health, Sch Pub Health, 64-68, ASSOC PROF RADIATION BIOPHYS, UNIV NC, CHAPEL HILL, 68-, DIR HEALTH & SAFETY, 74- *Mem:* Health Physics Soc; Radiation Res Soc; Am Indust Hyg Asn. *Res:* Tumor and normal cell kinetics; radiation dose-rate and fractionation effects, late effects. *Mailing Add:* Health & Safety Off Univ of NC Chapel Hill NC 27514

WILLIAMS, AARON, JR, b Newark, NJ, Jan 29, 42. PHYSICAL GEOGRAPHY. *Educ:* Fla State Univ, BS, 65; Univ Mo, MA, 67; Univ Okla, PhD(geog), 71. *Prof Exp:* Meteorologist, US Weather Bur, 66; instr geog, 67-69, asst prof, 71-77, ASSOC PROF GEOG, UNIV S ALA, 77- *Mem:* Am Asn Geog; Am Meteorol Soc. *Res:* Climatology of coastal and tropical environments; radar climatology. *Mailing Add:* Dept of Geol & Geog Univ of SAla Mobile AL 36688

WILLIAMS, ALAN EVAN, b Mechanicsburg, Pa, Oct 4, 52. ISOTOPE GEOCHEMISTRY, GEOTHERMICS. *Educ:* Juniata Col, ScB, 74; Brown Univ, MSc, 76, PhD(geol), 80. *Prof Exp:* Res geochemist, 79-80, ASST RES GEOCHEMIST, INST GEOPHYSICS & PLANETARY PHYSICS, UNIV CALIF, RIVERSIDE, 80- *Concurrent Pos:* Vis lectr, Univ Redlands, 80; adj lectr, Univ Calif, Riverside, 81- *Mem:* Am Geophys Union; Geol Soc Am; Geothermal Resources Coun. *Res:* Stable isotopic constraints on systems of water-rock interaction: geothermal systems, ore bodies, shallow intrusives, and ophiolites. *Mailing Add:* Inst Geophysics & Planetary Physics Univ Calif Riverside CA 92521

WILLIAMS, ALBERT J, JR, b Media, Pa, Feb 28, 03; m 37; c 2. ELECTRICAL ENGINEERING. *Educ:* Swarthmore Col, AB, 24. *Prof Exp:* Engr transformers, Bell Tel Labs, 24-27; res engr measurement & control, Leeds & Northrup Co, 27-34, chief elec div res dept, 34-51, assoc dir res, 51-55, sci adv, 55-68; CONSULT, 68- *Concurrent Pos:* Consult, Leeds & Northrup Co, 68-76. *Honors & Awards:* John Price Wetherill Medal, Franklin Inst, 52; Morris E Leeds Award, Inst Elec & Electronics Engrs, 68; Rufus Oldenburger Medal, Am Soc Mech Engrs, 72. *Mem:* Fel Inst Elec & Electronics Engrs; fel Franklin Inst; fel Am Soc Mech Engrs; Am Phys Soc; Sigma Xi. *Res:* Measurements; recorders; control; measurements with extended range and precision; science of golf; aids to functioning of man's body, especially breathing, hearing, seeing, coma and perceiving; aiding man's perception of numbers. *Mailing Add:* Albert J Williams Jr Consult 901 Llanfair Rd Ambler PA 19002

WILLIAMS, ALBERT JAMES, III, b Philadelphia, Pa, Oct 17, 40; m 63; c 1. OCEANOGRAPHY, OCEAN ENGINEERING. *Educ:* Swarthmore Col, BA, 62; Johns Hopkins Univ, PhD(physics), 69. *Prof Exp:* Investr, 69-71, asst scientist, 71-75, ASSOC SCIENTIST, OCEAN ENG, WOODS HOLE OCEANOG INST, 75- *Mem:* AAAS; Am Geophys Union. *Res:* Ocean microstructure, mixing and thermohaline convection; stress and velocity structure in the benthic boundary layer; oceanographic, optical, acoustic, and electronic instrumentation. *Mailing Add:* Woods Hole Oceanog Inst Woods Hole MA 02543

WILLIAMS, ALBERT SIMPSON, b York Co, SC, Jan 23, 24; m 46. PLANT PATHOLOGY. *Educ:* Emory Univ, AB, 48; Univ Tenn, MS, 49; NC State Univ, PhD(plant path), 54. *Prof Exp:* Asst prof biol, Athens Col, 50; plant pathologist, State Plant Bd, Miss, 50-51; asst, NC State Univ, 51-54; assoc prof plant path, Va Polytech Inst, 54-68; exten prof plant path, 68-75, PROF & CHMN HORT DEPT, UNIV KY, 75- *Mem:* Am Phytopath Soc; Am Soc Nematol; Soc Europ Nematol; Am Soc Hort Sci. *Mailing Add:* Dept Hort Univ Ky Lexington KY 40546

WILLIAMS, ANNA MARIA, b Tampa, Fla, June 29, 27. MICROBIOLOGY. *Educ:* Univ Ala, BS, 48; Univ Wis, MS, 51, PhD(bact), 54. *Prof Exp:* Antibiotics lab supvr, Merck & Co, Inc, 48-50; res asst bact, Univ Wis, 50-54; Fulbright res grant, biophys res group, Univ Utrecht, 54-55; proj assoc, McArdle Mem Inst Cancer Res, Univ Wis-Madison, 55-57, res assoc med, Sch Med, 57-64, asst prof, 64-69, ASSOC PROF LIFE SCI, UNIV WIS-PARKSIDE, 69- *Mem:* AAAS; Am Chem Soc; Am Soc Microbiol; Am Inst Biol Sci. *Res:* Nucleic acid metabolism; leukemia; cancer chemotherapy; bacterial enzymes. *Mailing Add:* Dept of Life Sci Univ of Wis-Parkside Kenosha WI 53140

WILLIAMS, ARDIS MAE, b Boston, Mass, June 8, 19; m 49; c 1. PHYSICAL CHEMISTRY. *Educ:* Mt Holyoke Col, AB, 41; Vassar Col, AM, 46. *Prof Exp:* Chemist, Harvard Med Sch, 41-42; teacher, Low Heywood Sch, 42-44; lectr chem, Vassar Col, 44-46; lectr, Barnard Col, 46-48; res chemist, Merck & Co, 48-49; res chemist, Med Col Va, 50-54; teacher, Tatnall Sch, 63-67; ASSOC PROF CHEM, WEST CHESTER STATE COL, 67- *Mem:* AAAS; Am Chem Soc. *Res:* Surface area and adsorption by activated carbon; relationship of structure and adsorption of organic molecules. *Mailing Add:* Dept of Chem West Chester State Col West Chester PA 19380

WILLIAMS, ARTHUR LEE, b Sawyerville, Ala, July 16, 47; m 69; c 1. MOLECULAR BIOLOGY, MOLECULAR GENETICS. *Educ:* Ala State Univ, BS, 69; Atlanta Univ, MS, 71; Purdue Univ, PhD(molecular biol), 75. *Prof Exp:* Lab instr biol, Atlanta Univ, 69-70; teaching asst cell biol, Purdue Univ, 74-75; asst prof biol, Ala State Univ, 75-77, chairperson gen biol, 76-77; asst prof biol, Murray State Univ, 77-80; ASST PROF BIOL, UNIV KY, 80- *Concurrent Pos:* Prin investr, NIH res grant, 77-78. *Mem:* Am Soc Biog Res; Am Soc Microbiol; Nat Inst Sci; NY Acad Sci. *Res:* Biochemical and genetic investigation of the substrate induction of the ilvC gene expression of Escherichia coli. *Mailing Add:* Dept Microbiol Univ Ky Lexington KY 40506

WILLIAMS, ARTHUR OLNEY, JR, b Providence, RI, Apr 7, 13; m 38; c 1. PHYSICS. *Educ:* Mass Inst Technol, BS, 34; Brown Univ, ScM, 36, PhD(physics), 37. *Prof Exp:* From instr to asst prof physics, Univ Maine, 37-42; from asst prof to prof, 42-75, chmn dept, 56-60, 62-63, Hazard prof, 75-78, EMER PROF PHYSICS, BROWN UNIV, 78- *Concurrent Pos:* Mem, RI AEC, 55-68; vis res prof, Underwater Acoutics, Naval Postgrad Sch, Monterey, Calif, 81-82. *Mem:* Fel Am Phys Soc; fel Acoust Soc Am. *Res:* Physical acoustics. *Mailing Add:* Dept of Physics Brown Univ Providence RI 02912

WILLIAMS, ARTHUR ROBERT, b Feb 20, 41; US citizen; m 62; c 3. SOLID STATE PHYSICS. *Educ:* Dartmouth Col, AB, 62; Harvard Univ, PhD(solid state physics), 69. *Prof Exp:* Appl mathematician, Info Res Inc, Mass, 67-68; fel, 68-69, STAFF PHYSICIST, WATSON RES CTR, IBM CORP, 69- *Mem:* Am Phys Soc. *Res:* Effective one-electron theory of Fermi surface and optical data for solids. *Mailing Add:* IBM Watson Res Ctr Yorktown Heights NY 10598

WILLIAMS, AUSTIN BEATTY, b Plattsburg, Mo, Oct 17, 19; m 46; c 1. SYSTEMATIC ZOOLOGY. *Educ:* McPherson Col, AB, 43; Univ Kans, PhD(zool), 51. *Prof Exp:* Asst genetics, Univ Wis, 43-44; teacher pub schs, Kans, 44-46; shrimp investr, Inst Fisheries Res, Univ NC, 51-52, asst prof, 52-55; asst prof, Univ Ill, 55-56; assoc prof, Inst Fisheries Res, Univ NC, 56-63, prof, Inst Marine Sci, 63-71; SYST ZOOLOGIST, NAT SYSTS LAB, NAT MARINE FISHERIES SERV, 71- *Concurrent Pos:* Adj prof, Univ NC, Chapel Hill, 71- *Mem:* AAAS; Am Soc Zool; Ecol Soc Am; Soc Syst Zool; Estuarine Res Fedn (secy, 72-73, vpres, 80-01). *Res:* Taxonomy; ecology; life histories of decapod crustacea; special reference to western Atlantic region; estuarine ecology. *Mailing Add:* Nat Systs Lab US Nat Mus Nat Marine Fisheries Serv Washington DC 20560

WILLIAMS, BENJAMIN HAYDEN, b Davenport, Iowa, Dec 18, 21; m 46; c 5. ANATOMY, ORTHODONTICS. *Educ:* Ohio State Univ, DDS, 46, MSc, 49; Univ Ill, MS, 51; Am Bd Orthod, dipl. *Prof Exp:* Fel, Univ Ill, 50-51; from instr to assoc prof, 51-64, PROF ORTHOD & CHMN DEPT, COL DENT, OHIO STATE UNIV, 64- *Concurrent Pos:* Staff mem, Children's Hosp, Columbus, Ohio, 61-; mem bd med, State Crippled Children's Servs, Ohio, 66-; mem orthod sect, Am Asn Dent Schs. *Mem:* Int Asn Dent Res; Am Asn Orthod. *Res:* Cranio-facial growth and development; growth predictions; dental development and eruption; normal and abnormal growth. *Mailing Add:* Dept of Dent Ohio State Univ Col of Dent Columbus OH 43210

WILLIAMS, BENNIE B, b Scranton, Tex, Jan 16, 22; m 48; c 4. MATHEMATICS. *Educ:* Howard Payne Col, BA, 48; Univ Tex, MA, 53, PhD(math), 66. *Prof Exp:* From instr to asst prof math, Howard Payne Col, 48-61; asst prof, 66-71, ASSOC PROF MATH, UNIV TEX, ARLINGTON, 71- *Mem:* Am Math Soc; Math Asn Am. *Res:* Foundations of mathematics; ordinary differential equations. *Mailing Add:* Dept of Math Univ Tex Box 19408 Arlington TX 76019

WILLIAMS, BOBBY JOE, b Idabel, Okla, Nov 3, 30; m 57; c 4. PHYSICAL ANTHROPOLOGY, POPULATION GENETICS. *Educ:* Univ Okla, BA, 53, MA, 57; Univ Mich, PhD(anthrop, human genetics), 65. *Prof Exp:* Asst prof anthrop, Univ Wis, Milwaukee, 63-65; from asst prof to assoc prof, 65-77, PROF ANTHROP, UNIV CALIF, LOS ANGELES, 77- *Mem:* AAAS; Am Anthrop Asn; Am Asn Phys Anthrop. *Res:* Human population genetics; human evolution; population processes in simple societies. *Mailing Add:* Dept of Anthrop Univ of Calif Los Angeles CA 90024

WILLIAMS, BROWN F, b Evanston, Ill, Dec 22, 40. SOLID STATE PHYSICS. *Educ:* Univ Calif, Riverside, BA, 62, MA, 64, PhD(physics), 66. *Prof Exp:* Mem tech staff, 66-68, leader electron emission, 68-70, mgr electro-optics lab, 70-73, head quantum electronics res, 73-77, dir energy systs res lab, 77-79, STAFF VPRES, DISPLAY & ENERGY SYSTS, RCA LABS, 79- *Honors & Awards:* Outstanding Achievement Award, RCA Corp, 68, David Sarnoff Award, 70. *Mem:* Inst Elec & Electronic Engrs; Sigma Xi; AAAS; Am Phys Soc. *Res:* Electro-optic devices; optical information recording; solar energy; television picture tubes; electron optics. *Mailing Add:* Energy Systs Res Lab RCA Labs Princeton NJ 08540

WILLIAMS, (GEORGE) BRYMER, b Denver, Colo, Oct 17, 13; m 40; c 3. CHEMICAL ENGINEERING. *Educ:* Univ Mich, BS, 36, PhD(chem eng), 49. *Prof Exp:* Chem engr, M W Kellogg Co, NY, 40-47; from asst prof to assoc prof chem eng, 48-56, PROF CHEM & METALL ENG, UNIV MICH, ANN ARBOR, 56- *Mem:* Am Chem Soc; Am Soc Eng Educ; Am Inst Chem Engrs; Am Inst Mining, Metall & Petrol Engrs; Chem Inst Can. *Res:* Process design; natural resource utilization; petroleum processing. *Mailing Add:* Col Eng Univ Mich Ann Arbor MI 48109

WILLIAMS, BYRON BENNETT, JR, b Donaldsonville, Ga, Sept 2, 22; m 49; c 2. PHARMACOLOGY. *Educ:* Univ Fla, BS, 45, MS, 47, PhD, 51. *Prof Exp:* PROF PHARMACOL, AUBURN UNIV, 51-, HEAD PHARMACOL & TOXICOL DEPT, 80- *Mem:* Am Pharmaceut Asn. *Res:* Antihistamines; autonomics; psychopharmacology. *Mailing Add:* Dept of Pharm Auburn Univ Auburn AL 36830

WILLIAMS, BYRON LEE, JR, b Guantanamo Bay, Cuba, Aug 29, 20; m 42; c 3. ORGANIC CHEMISTRY. *Educ:* E Tex State Teachers Col, BS, 40, MS, 42; Univ Okla, PhD(org chem), 53. *Prof Exp:* Teacher pub sch, Tex, 40-42; chem engr, Chem Warfare Serv, US Dept Army, 42-44, chem engr, Chem Corps, 46-47; assoc prof chem, E Tex State Teachers Col, 47-41; asst, Res Found, Univ Okla, 51-53; assoc prof chem, E Tex State Teachers Col, 53-54; res chemist, 54-59, Monsanto Co, from asst dir res to assoc dir res, Plastics Div, 59-64, dir process tech & eng dept, Hydrocarbons Div, 64-65, dir res, Hydrocarbons & Polymers Div, 65-67, dir corp res dept, 67-76; gen mgr, Technol Div, Monsanto Textiles Co, 76-81; DIR, FEEDSTOCK TRANSITION, MONSANTO CO, 81- *Mem:* Am Chem Soc. *Res:* Isolation, chemical characterization and identification of flavonoid type chemical compounds from selected natural products using ion exchange, adsorption and paper chromatography; synthesis of pigments and demethylation studies; hydrolytic enzyme studies of natural glycosides. *Mailing Add:* 609 Mosley Rd Creve Coeur MO 63141

WILLIAMS, CALVIT HERNDON, JR, b Houston, Tex, Dec 28, 36; m 59; c 4. PHYSICAL CHEMISTRY, ANALYTICAL CHEMISTRY. *Educ:* Univ St Thomas, Tex, BA, 58; Brown Univ, PhD(chem), 64; Am Bd Indust Hyg, dipl. *Prof Exp:* Fel chem, Rice Univ, 64-66; tech staff mem, Sandia Labs, 66-70; asst prof chem, State Univ Campinas, Brazil, 71-76; lab dir, Aer-Aqua Labs, 76-77; SR SCIENTIST, RADIAN CORP, 77- *Mem:* Sigma Xi; Am Chem Soc; Am Indust Hyg Asn; Am Inst Chem; Am Soc Mass Spectrometry. *Res:* High energy crossed-molecular-beam reaction kinetics; thermodynamics of high temperature processes; mass spectrometry and gas chromatography applied to environmental and biomedical analysis; chemical aspects and comprehensive practice of industrial hygiene; occupational and environmental health. *Mailing Add:* Radian Corp 8500 Shoal Creek Blvd Austin TX 78766

WILLIAMS, CARL JAMES, JR, b Parkersburg, WVa, Feb 5, 30; div; c 3. PHOTOGRAPHIC CHEMISTRY. *Educ:* Marietta Col, BS, 51; Ohio State Univ, MS, 55; Univ Notre Dame, PhD(org chem), 58. *Prof Exp:* Chemist, 51-52, from res chemist to sr res chemist, 58-68, res assoc, 68-70, TECH ASSOC, EASTMAN KODAK CO, 70- *Mem:* Am Chem Soc. *Res:* Development of new and improved color photographic products, embodying all phases of photographic chemistry. *Mailing Add:* Eastman Kodak Co Kodak Off B-9 Rochester NY 14650

WILLIAMS, CARL L, b Murphysboro, Ill, Dec 11, 19; m 48; c 2. CHEMICAL ENGINEERING. *Educ:* Purdue Univ, BS, 49. *Prof Exp:* Engr, Merck & Co, 49-55; plant engr, Ayerst Labs, Div, Am Home Prod Corp, 55-57; engr, 57-58, asst to vpres eng, 58-59, proj engr, 59-61, proj mgr, 61-63, asst dir process eng, 63-67, asst vpres proj eng, 67-69, sr vpres eng & opers, 69-74, exec vpres, 74, pres, 74-78, CHMN, SCIENTIFIC DESIGN CO, 78- *Mem:* Am Chem Soc; Am Inst Chem Engrs; Soc Chem Indust. *Res:* Engineering management. *Mailing Add:* Scientific Design Co Two Park Ave New York NY 10016

WILLIAMS, CAROL ANN, b Stratford, NJ, Oct 3, 40. ASTRONOMY, CELESTIAL MECHANICS. *Educ:* Conn Col, BA, 62; Yale Univ, PhD(astron), 67. *Prof Exp:* Assoc res engr & consult, Jet Propulsion Lab, 64 & 65; part-time instr physics, Conn Col, 66-67; res staff astronr, Yale Univ, 67-68; asst prof, 68-73, ASSOC PROF ASTRON, UNIV S FLA, TAMPA, 73- *Mem:* Am Astron Soc; Sigma Xi. *Res:* Astrometry. *Mailing Add:* Dept of Astron Univ of SFla Tampa FL 33620

WILLIAMS, CARROLL BURNS, JR, b St Louis, Mo, Sept 24, 29; m 58; c 3. FOREST ENTOMOLOGY. *Educ:* Univ Mich, BS, 55, MS, 57, PhD(forestry), 63. *Prof Exp:* Entomologist, Pac Northwest Forest & Range Exp Sta, US Forest Serv, Ore, 57-58, res forester, 58-60, forestry sci lab, 61-65, res entomologist, Pac Southwest Forest & Range Exp Sta, Calif, 65-68, leader insect impact proj, Forest Insect & Dis Lab, Northeastern Exp Sta, Conn, 68-72, res entomologist, Pac Southwest Forest & Range Exp Sta, Calif, 72-75, PROJ LEADER, PIONEERING RES UNIT, INTEGRATED MGT SYSTS FOREST INSECT & DIS, PAC SOUTHWEST FOREST & RANGE EXP STA, CALIF, US FOREST SERV, 75- *Concurrent Pos:* Lectr, Sch Forestry, Yale Univ, 69-71; consult, NSF, 71-74. *Mem:* Soc Am Foresters; Ecol Soc Am; Entom Soc Am. *Res:* Evaluate and predict impact of forest insect and disease on forest resources; modelling pest management systems; computer simulation experiments of insect and disease control techniques and strategies; forest management decision models. *Mailing Add:* 1960 Addison St PO Box 245 Berkeley CA 94701

WILLIAMS, CARROLL MILTON, b Richmond, Va, Dec 2, 16; m 41; c 3. BIOLOGY. *Educ:* Univ Richmond, BS, 37; Harvard Univ, AM, 38, PhD(biol), 41, MD, 46. *Hon Degrees:* DSc, Univ Richmond, 60. *Prof Exp:* Fel, Soc Fels, 41-46, from asst prof to prof zool, 46-66, chmn dept, 59-62, chmn subdept cellular & develop biol, 72-73, BENJAMIN BUSSEY PROF BIOL, HARVARD UNIV, 66- *Concurrent Pos:* Lowell lectr, 48; Harvey lectr, 52; Dakin lectr, 64; Thomas lectr, 67; Nieuwland lectr, 67; Murlin lectr, 67; Delafield lectr, 70; David Rivett Mem lectr, 73; consult, NSF, 54-59; Guggenheim fel, 55-56; trustee, Radcliffe Col, 61-63. *Honors & Awards:* Res Prize, AAAS, 50; Boylston Medal, Harvard Med Sch, 61, George Ledlie Prize, Harvard Univ, 67; Howard Taylor Ricketts Award, Univ Chicago, 69. *Mem:* Nat Acad Sci (chmn, sect zool, 70-73, coun, 73-76); Inst Med Nat Acad Sci; fel AAAS; fel Am Acad Arts & Sci (mem coun, 52-55 & 74-78); fel Entom Soc Am. *Res:* Physiology of insects with special reference to endocrinology of growth and metamorphosis. *Mailing Add:* Biol Lab Harvard Univ Cambridge MA 02138

WILLIAMS, CHARLES EUGENE, b Muskogee, Okla, June 29, 30; c 3. TECHNICAL MANAGEMENT. *Educ:* Henderson State Teachers Col, BS, 52; Univ Va, PhD(physics), 61. *Prof Exp:* US Army, 52-65; physicist, Lawrence Livermore Lab, Calif, 61-63, test group dir, Nev Test Site, 63-69, dep mgr, 69-76; MGR, IDAHO OPERS OFF, US DEPT ENERGY, 76- *Concurrent Pos:* Actg asst secy energy & tech, US Dept Energy, 79. *Res:* Nuclear reactor safety; spent fuel storage and reprocessing; waste management; alternate energies; safety. *Mailing Add:* US Dept Energy Idaho Opers Off 550 Second St Idaho Falls ID 83401

WILLIAMS, CHARLES HADDON, JR, b Washington, DC, June 29, 32; m 62; c 2. BIOCHEMISTRY. *Educ:* Univ Md, BS, 56; Duke Univ, PhD(biochem), 61. *Prof Exp:* Am Cancer Soc fel, Dept Biochem, Sheffield Sci Sch, 61-63; from instr to assoc prof, 63-79, PROF BIOL CHEM, UNIV MICH, ANN ARBOR, 79-; res chemist, 63-74, coordr res, 77-79, SUPVRY RES CHEMIST, GEN MED RES, VET ADMIN MED CTR, ANN ARBOR, 74- *Mem:* AAAS; Am Chem Soc; Am Soc Biol Chemists. *Res:* Mechanism of action and structure of flavoproteins; roles of various amino acid residues in catalysis by flavoproteins and in their structures. *Mailing Add:* Gen Med Res Vet Admin Med Ctr 2215 Fuller Rd Ann Arbor MI 48105

WILLIAMS, CHARLES HERBERT, b Aurora, Mo, Jan 21, 35; m 56; c 3. BIOCHEMISTRY. *Educ:* Univ Mo-Columbia, BS, 57, MS, 67, PhD(agr chem), 68. *Prof Exp:* Asst prof biochem, Dept Anesthesiol, Univ Wis-Madison, 70-73 & Inst Enzyme Res, 70-72; RES ASSOC, DEPT HUMAN NUTRIT, UNIV MO-COLUMBIA, 73- *Concurrent Pos:* Trainee, Inst Enzyme Res, Univ Wis-Madison, 68-70; Fulbright lectr, Peru, 71; fel toxicol, Univ Mo-Columbia. *Res:* Malignant hyperpyrexia and surfactant system of the lung; biochemistry of malignant hyperthermia; role of glycoproteins in the lung. *Mailing Add:* 412 Manor Columbia MO 65201

WILLIAMS, CHARLES MELVILLE, b Regina, Sask, Mar 18, 25; m 53; c 3. PHYSIOLOGY, GENETICS. *Educ:* Univ BC, BSA, 49, MSA, 52, Ore State Col, PhD(genetics), 55. *Prof Exp:* Assoc prof animal physiol, 55-67, HEAD DEPT ANIMAL SCI, UNIV SASK, 67-, PROF ANIMAL SCI, 77- *Mem:* Am Soc Animal Sci; Can Soc Animal Prod; fel Agr Inst Can. *Res:* Effect of low environmental temperatures on farm animals. *Mailing Add:* Dept Animal Sci & Poultry Sci Univ Sask Saskatoon SK S7H 0W0 Can

WILLIAMS, CHARLES WESLEY, b Palestine, Ark, Feb 18, 31; m 59; c 2. ELECTRONIC ENGINEERING. *Educ:* Univ Tenn, BSEE, 59, MSEE, 63. *Prof Exp:* Design engr, Mead Res Labs, Ohio, 59-60; develop engr, Oak Ridge Nat Lab, 60-63; sr develop engr, 63-67, engr & mgr electronics res & develop, 67-80, DIR RES, ORTEC, LTD, 80- *Mem:* Inst Elec & Electronics Engrs; Nat Soc Prof Engrs. *Res:* Nuclear research instrumentation, especially sub-nanosecond time measurements and linear circuit design. *Mailing Add:* Ortec Ltd 100 Midland Rd Oak Ridge TN 37830

WILLIAMS, CHRISTINE, b Miami, Fla, Mar 20, 43; c 3. PEDIATRICS, PREVENTIVE MEDICINE. *Educ:* Univ Pittsburgh, BS, 63, MD, 67; Harvard Univ, MPH, 69. *Prof Exp:* Resident, Johns Hopkins Sch Hyg & Pub Health, 70-71, vis scientist, Karolinska Inst, Stockholm, 71-72; resident pediat, Hosp Med Col Pa, 72-73, pediatrician, Children & Youth Comprehensive Care Clin, 74-75; dir child health, Am Health Found, 75-80; DEP COMNR HEALTH, WESTCHESTER COUNTY DEPT HEALTH, 81- *Res:* Child health. *Mailing Add:* Westchester County Dept Health 150 Grand St White Plains NY 10601

WILLIAMS, CHRISTOPHER NOEL, b York, Eng, Dec 25, 35; Can citizen; m 60; c 4. GASTROENTEROLOGY. *Educ:* Royal Col Physicians & Surgeons London, MRCS & LRCP, 60; Royal Col Physicians & Surgeons Can, FRCP(C), 68; FACP, 76. *Prof Exp:* Fel med, Univ Pa, 69-71; lectr, 69-72, asst prof, 72-76, assoc prof, 76-82, PROF MED, DALHOUSIE UNIV, 82-, ASSOC PHYSICIAN MED, VICTORIA GEN HOSP, 76- *Concurrent Pos:* MacLaughlin fel, Univ Pa, 69-70, Med Res Coun fel, 70-71; asst physician med, Victoria Gen Hosp, 69-76; dir, Gastrointestinal Res Lab, Dalhousie Univ, 71-; consult gastroenterol, Camp Hill Hosp, Halifax, 73-; grants in aid, Med Res Coun Can, 71- & Nat Health & Welfare Can, 73-; consult, Halifax Infirmary, 78-; head prog dir gastroenterol, Dalhousie Univ, 81. *Mem:* Can Med Asn; Can Asn Gastroenterol; Can Soc Clin Res; Am Gastroenterol Asn; Am Asn Study Liver Dis. *Res:* Detailed kinetic studies of bile acid metabolism in health and disease, particularly liver and inflammatory bowel disease; application of 3-alpha, 7-alpha, 12-alpha hydroxysteroid dehydrogenases to bile analysis; dietary and biochemical factors and prevalence of gallstones in Caucasians and Canadian Indians. *Mailing Add:* 5849 University Ave Rm C-D 1 Clin Res Ctr Halifax NS B3H 4H7 Can

WILLIAMS, CHRISTOPHER P S, b Medford, Ore, Oct 12, 31; m 57; c 3. PEDIATRICS, MEDICINE. *Educ:* Univ Ore, BA, 53, MD, 58. *Prof Exp:* Asst prof pediat, Sch Med, Univ Wash, 62-68; ASSOC PROF PEDIAT, CRIPPLED CHILDREN'S DIV, MED SCH, UNIV ORE, 68- *Res:* Medical education. *Mailing Add:* Dept of Pediat Univ of Ore Med Sch Portland OR 97201

WILLIAMS, CLARKE, b New York, NY, May 4, 02; m 27, 33; c 3. NUCLEAR ENGINEERING, PHYSICS. *Educ:* Williams Col, AB, 22; Mass Inst Technol, BS, 24; Columbia Univ, PhD(physics), 35. *Hon Degrees:* ScD, Williams Col, 64. *Prof Exp:* Jr civil engr, Duke-Price Power Co, 24-25 & New York Cent RR, 25-26; asst, Columbia Univ, 26-30; tutor, City Col New York, 30-35, from instr to asst prof physics, 36-48; asst chmn nuclear reactor group, 46-51, assoc chmn, Reactor Sci & Eng Dept, 51-52, chmn, Nuclear Eng Dept, 52-62, dep dir, 62-67, EMER DEP DIR, BROOKHAVEN NAT LAB, 67-; RES ADMINR, MARINE RESOURCES COUN, NASSAU-SUFFOLK REGIONAL PLANNING BD, 67- *Concurrent Pos:* Mem sci staff, Off Sci Res & Develop, Columbia Univ, 41-44; group leader, Manhattan Proj, Carbide & Carbon Chem Co, 44-46; sr scientist, Los Alamos Sci Lab, NMex, 47-48; mem, State Adv Comt Atomic Energy, NY, 56-59, Gen Adv Comt, 66-70 & bd trustees, Williams Col, 67, emer mem, 72; mem atomic safety & licensing bd panel, US Atomic Energy Comn, 67-; mem comt radioactive waste mgt, Nat Acad Sci, 68- *Mem:* Fel AAAS; Am Phys Soc; fel Am Nuclear Soc (pres, 64-65); Fedn Am Sci; NY Acad Sci. *Res:* Physics teaching; nuclear engineering research; reactor technology; marine regional planning research. *Mailing Add:* 200 S Country Rd PO Box W Bellport NY 11713

WILLIAMS, CLAYTON DREWS, b St Louis, Mo, Oct 22, 35; m 59; c 4. THEORETICAL PHYSICS, SOLID STATE PHYSICS. *Educ:* Rice Inst, BA, 57; Wash Univ, PhD(physics), 61. *Prof Exp:* Asst prof, 61-64, ASSOC PROF PHYSICS, VA POLYTECH INST & STATE UNIV, 64- *Mem:* Am Phys Soc. *Res:* Many-body problem; solid-state theory. *Mailing Add:* Dept of Physics Va Polytech Inst & State Univ Blacksburg VA 24061

WILLIAMS, CLYDE MICHAEL, b Marlow, Okla, Oct 8, 28; m 53; c 4. PHYSIOLOGY. *Educ:* Rice Inst, BA, 48; Baylor Univ, MD, 52; Oxford Univ, DPhil(physiol), 54. *Prof Exp:* Tech dir radioisotope lab, Vet Admin Hosp, Pittsburgh, Pa, 58-60; res radiol, 60-63, from asst prof to assoc prof, 63-65, PROF RADIOL & CHMN DEPT, COL MED, UNIV FLA, 65- *Mem:* Am Physiol Soc; Soc Nuclear Med; Am Roentgen Ray Soc; Radiol Soc NAm. *Res:* Metabolism of aromatic amines; gas chromatography of aromatic acids; use of computer for medical diagnosis. *Mailing Add:* Dept of Radiol Univ of Fla Col of Med Gainesville FL 32610

WILLIAMS, COLIN JAMES, b London, Eng, May 12, 38. PHYSICAL CHEMISTRY, INORGANIC CHEMISTRY. *Educ:* Univ London, BSc, 60, PhD(phys chem, inorg chem), 60 & Imp Col, dipl, 63. *Prof Exp:* Res chemist, Cent Res Div, Mobil Oil Corp, NJ, 63-66; RES CHEMIST, CAHN INSTRUMENT CO, 67- *Mem:* Am Chem Soc; assoc mem Royal Soc Chem. *Res:* Physical and inorganic chemical properties of zeolites and their spectroscopic and catalytic properties; thermoanalysis; diffuse reflectance spectroscopy; physical adsorption. *Mailing Add:* 15042 A Parkway Loop Tustin CA 92680

WILLIAMS, CONRAD MALCOLM, b Warsaw, NC, March 1, 36; m 67; c 1. SOLID STATE PHYSICS. *Educ:* Morgan State Col, BS, 58; Howard Univ, MS, 65, PhD(physics), 72. *Prof Exp:* Res solid state physicist, Div Math Sci, US Naval Res Lab, 60-80; div sci personnel improv, 80-81, ASSOC DIR SOLID STTATE PHYSICS, DIV MAT RES, NAT SCI FOUND, 81- *Concurrent Pos:* adj prof physics, Howard Univ, 74-80, adj prof elec eng, 80- *Mem:* Sigma Xi; Am Phys Soc; Inst Elec & Electronics Engrs. *Res:* Solid state physics; physics of metals; ferromagnetism (thin films and bulk materials); low temperature; low temperature properties; irradiation effects metals; metal alloys; semiconductors; ion implantation in the ferromagnetic films. *Mailing Add:* Div Mat Res Nat Sci Found Washington DC 20550

WILLIAMS, CURTIS ALVIN, JR, b Moorestown, NJ, June 26, 27; m 60; c 3. BIOLOGY, NEUROBIOLOGY. *Educ:* Pa State Univ, BS, 50; Rutgers Univ, PhD(zool), 54. *Prof Exp:* Waksman fel & USPHS fel, Pasteur Inst, Paris, 52-54, USPHS fel, Carlsberg Lab, Copenhagen, 54-55; Carlsberg Lab, Copenhagen, 54-55; res assoc microbiol, Rockefeller Inst, 55-57; With Nat Inst Allergy & Infectious Dis, 57-60; from asst prof to assoc prof biochem genetics, Rockefeller Univ, 60-69; dean natural sci, 69-80, PROF BIOL, STATE UNIV NY COL PURCHASE, 69-, CHMN, DEPT BIOL, 80- *Concurrent Pos:* Adj prof, Rockefeller Univ, 70-78 & Sch Med, NY Univ, 76-; hon res fel neuroimmunol, Univ Col, London, 78; vis res fel cell biol, Albert Einstein Col Med, 79-80. *Mem:* Am Soc Microbiol; Soc Neurosci; Am Asn Immunologists. *Res:* Immunology; immunochemistry; microbiology; neurobiology; cellular biology. *Mailing Add:* Purchase NY 10577

WILLIAMS, CURTIS CHANDLER, III, b New York, NY, Sept 30, 26; m 55; c 2. CHEMICAL ENGINEERING. *Educ:* Yale Univ, BEng, 48; Mass Inst Technol, SM, 50, ScD(chem eng), 53. *Prof Exp:* Engr, Emeryville Res Ctr, Shell Develop Co, 53-59, supvr process eng, 59-64, sr technologist, Mfg Res Dept, Shell Oil Co, 64-65, head petrol processing dept, Emeryville Res Ctr, Shell Develop Co, 65-67, chief technologist, Wood River Refinery, Shell Oil Co, Ill, 67-71, mgr facilities, 71-74, MGR PROCESS ENG-REFINING, SHELL DEVELOP CO, 74- *Concurrent Pos:* Chmn tech data subcomt, API Refining Dept, 65-; mem bd dirs, Fractionation Res, Inc & Heat Transfer Res, Inc, 75- *Honors & Awards:* Cert of Appreciation, Am Petrol Inst, 77. *Mem:* AAAS; Am Chem Soc; Am Inst Chem Engrs. *Res:* Design of petroleum refining and petrochemical processes. *Mailing Add:* Shell Develop Co PO Box 3105 Houston TX 77001

WILLIAMS, DALE GORDON, b Chicago, Ill, Aug 9, 29; m 52. PHYSICAL CHEMISTRY. *Educ:* Beloit Col, BS, 51; Univ Minn, MS, 54; Univ Iowa, PhD, 57. *Prof Exp:* Engr, Linde Co Div, Union Carbide Corp, 56-58; res aide, Inst Paper Chem, 59-62, res assoc & assoc prof chem, 62-75; res scientist, 75-81, SR RES SCIENTIST, UNION CAMP CORP, 81- *Mem:* Am Chem Soc; Tech Asn Pulp & Paper Indust; Sigma Xi. *Res:* The application of physical chemistry to paper science and technology. *Mailing Add:* Union Camp Corp PO Box 412 Princeton NJ 08540

WILLIAMS, DANIEL CHARLES, b Compton, Calif, Dec 15, 44; m 64; c 2. CELL BIOLOGY, ELECTRON MICROSCOPY. *Educ:* Calif State Univ, Long Beach, BS, 67; Iowa State Univ, PhD(cell biol), 72. *Prof Exp:* Asst microbiologist, Purex Corp, 66-67; res engr microbiol, NAm Aviation, Inc, 67-72; instr cell & develop biol, Kans State Univ, 72-74; asst prof develop biol, Univ Notre Dame, 74-76; SR SCIENTIST, LILLY RES LABS, 76- *Concurrent Pos:* NIH fel, 67-71 & 72-74; consult, BioInfo Assocs, 72-74. *Mem:* Sigma Xi; Am Soc Cell Biol; Electron Micros Soc Am. *Res:* Structure-function relationships and control mechanisms associated with cellular and developmental processes. *Mailing Add:* Dept of Cell Biol Eli Lilly & Co Indianapolis IN 46206

WILLIAMS, DANIEL FRANK, b Redmond, Ore, Nov 20, 42; c 2. MAMMALOGY, NONGAME WILDLIFE MANAGEMENT. *Educ:* Cent Wash State Col, BA, 66; Univ NMex, MS, 68, PhD(zool), 71. *Prof Exp:* Asst prof, 71-75, assoc prof biol sci, 75-80, PROF ZOOL SCI, CALIF STATE COL, STANISLAUS, 80- *Concurrent Pos:* Res assoc, Carnegie Mus Natural Hist; assoc ed, Mammalian Species, 78- *Mem:* Am Soc Mammal; Ecol Soc Am; Soc Syst Zool; Wildlife Soc. *Res:* Systematics and evolution of mammals; ecology of mammals; evolution of chromosome morphology in mammals; conservation of mammals. *Mailing Add:* Dept Biol Sci Calif State Col Stanislaus Turlock CA 95380

WILLIAMS, DARRELL DEAN, physiology, see previous edition

WILLIAMS, DARRYL MARLOWE, b Denver, Colo, Apr 3, 38; m 66; c 3. HEMATOLOGY, ONCOLOGY. *Educ:* Baylor Univ, MS & MD, 64. *Prof Exp:* House officer med, Affil Hosps, Baylor Univ, 64-66; house officer med, Univ Utah, 66-68, fel hemat, 68-73, asst prof med, 73-77; assoc prof, 77-81,

PROF MED, LA STATE UNIV, SHREVEPORT, 81- *Concurrent Pos:* Chief hemat & oncol, La State Univ, Shreveport, 77-, asst dean res, 81- *Mem:* Am Col Physicians; Am Soc Hemat; Am Inst Nutrit; Am Soc Clin Nutrit; Am Fedn Clin Res. *Res:* Biological effects of copper; manifestations of copper deficiency; interactions of copper, iron, and hemoglobin synthesis. *Mailing Add:* PO Box 33932 Shreveport LA 71130

WILLIAMS, DAVID ALLEN, b Wakefield, Mass, Dec 22, 38; m 62; c 4. MEDICINAL CHEMISTRY. *Educ:* Mass Col Pharm, BS, 60, MS, 62; Univ Minn, Minneapolis, PhD(med chem), 68. *Prof Exp:* Sr scientist, Med Chem Div, Mallinckrodt Chem Works, 67-69; asst prof biochem, 69-77, ASSOC PROF MED CHEM, MASS COL PHARM, 77-, CHMN, DEPT CHEM & PHYSICS, 81- *Mem:* AAAS; Am Chem Soc; NY Acad Sci. *Res:* Stereochemistry of drug action; application of structure activity relationships to derivatives of biogenic amines; analgesics; high performance liquid chromatography analytical methods development. *Mailing Add:* Mass Col Pharm 179 Longwood Ave Boston MA 02115

WILLIAMS, DAVID BERNARD, b Leeds, Eng, July 25, 49; m 76; c 1. ENGINEERING, MATERIALS SCIENCE. *Educ:* Cambridge Univ, BA, 70, MA, 73, PhD(mat sci), 74. *Prof Exp:* Sci Res Coun fel mat sci, Cambridge Univ, 74-76; asst prof, 76-79, ASSOC PROF METALL & MAT ENG, LEHIGH UNIV, 79- *Mem:* Electron Micros Soc Am; Am Soc Metals; Am Inst Metals Engrs; Meteoritical Soc; fel Royal Micros Soc. *Res:* Application of transmission and scanning transmission electron microscopy to the study of phase transformations in metals and ceramics. *Mailing Add:* Dept of Metall & Mat Eng Lehigh Univ Bethlehem PA 18015

WILLIAMS, DAVID C, physics, see previous edition

WILLIAMS, DAVID CARY, b Santa Monica, Calif, June 22, 35; m 62. NUCLEAR CHEMISTRY, NUCLEAR PHYSICS. *Educ:* Harvard univ, AB, 57; Mass Inst Technol, PhD(nuclear chem), 62. *Prof Exp:* Fel nuclear chem, Princeton Univ, 62-64; mem staff, Los Alamos Sci Lab, 64-66; MEM TECH STAFF, SANDIA LABS, 66- *Mem:* Am Nuclear Soc; AAAS; Am Phys Soc; Am Chem Soc. *Res:* Nuclear reactions, nuclear decay schemes and nuclear reaction spectroscopy; fast reactor safety research; statistical models of nuclear reactions; atmospheric tracer studies. *Mailing Add:* Div 5425 Sandia Labs Albuquerque NM 87115

WILLIAMS, DAVID DOUGLAS F, b Bushey, Eng, May 13, 30; US citizen; m 52; c 6. HORTICULTURE. *Educ:* Univ Reading, BSc & dipl hort, 52; Univ Wis, Madison, PhD(bot & hort), 62. *Prof Exp:* Technician hort, Cent Exp Farm, Ottawa, Can, 52-53; res off fruit breeding, Exp Sta, Morden, Man, 53-56; proj asst hort, Univ Wis, Madison, 56-61; asst horticulturalist & supt hort, Maui Br Sta, Univ Hawaii, 62-67; plant breeder, Pineapple Res Inst Hawaii, 68-71, dir, 71-73; RES DIR & QUAL CONTROL MGR, MAUI LAND & PINEAPPLE CO, 73- *Concurrent Pos:* Lectr, Maunaolu Col Maui, 67. *Res:* Effect of cultural, handling and cannery practices on the yield and quality of pineapple products. *Mailing Add:* 517 Olinda Rd Makawao HI 96768

WILLIAMS, DAVID EMERTON, b Victor, Idaho, Apr 12, 15; m 42; c 4. SOIL CHEMISTRY. *Educ:* Univ Utah, BS, 39, MS, 41; Univ Minn, PhD(soil chem), 46. *Prof Exp:* Asst chem, Univ Utah, 39-41; asst soil chem, Univ Minn, 41-44; from asst soil chemist to assoc soil chemist, 46-63, SOIL CHEMIST, UNIV CALIF, BERKELEY, 63-, LECTR SOILS & PLANT NUTRIT & PLANT PHYSIOL, 77- *Mem:* Soil Sci Soc Am; Sigma Xi. *Res:* Soil as a treatment system for municipal organic wastes; study of soil organic matter; fixed potassium in soils and method by which plants extract same; manganese, boron and silicon interactions in plant nutrition. *Mailing Add:* Dept of Soils & Plant Nutrit Univ of Calif Berkeley CA 94720

WILLIAMS, DAVID FRANCIS, b New Orleans, Lam Sept 4, 38; m 64; c 2. MEDICAL ENTOMOLOGY. *Educ:* Univ Southwest La, BS, 64, MS, 67; Univ Fla, PhD(entom), 69. *Prof Exp:* Asst prof biol, Greensboro Col, 69-71; res entomologist, WFla Arthropod Res Lab, State Fla, 71-74; location & res leader, Fed Exp Sta, Sci & Educ Admin-Agr Res, USDA, St Croix, 74-77; location & res leader, 77-80, RES ENTOMOLOGIST, INSECTS AFFECTING MAN & ANIMALS LAB, USDA, GAINESVILLE, FLA, 80- *Concurrent Pos:* Adj asst prof entomol, Univ Fla, 79- *Mem:* Entom Soc Am; Am Mosquito Control Asn; Am Registry Prof Entomologists. *Res:* Bioloy, population dynamics and control of biting flies affecting man and animals; use of the sterile male techniques to control Stomoxys calcitrans on an island involving mass rearing, irradiating, releasing and monitoring results; evaluation of chemicals, bait formulations, equipment and methods of application in laboratory and field conditions and development of non-contaminating methods and integrated pest management programs for the control of the imported fire ant. *Mailing Add:* Sci & Educ Admin-Agr Res USDA PO Box 14565 Gainesville FL 32604

WILLIAMS, DAVID G(ERALD), b Hackensack, NJ, Feb 6, 35; m 76; c 1. SYSTEMS ANALYSIS, UNDERWATER ACOUSTICS. *Educ:* Univ Mich, BA, 62, MSE, 58, PhD(physics), 66. *Prof Exp:* Sr scientist underwater acoust, Gen Dynamics/Elec Boat, 65-69; systs analyst, Mystic Oceanog Co, 69-71; PHYSICIST SYSTS ANAL, NAVAL UNDERWATER SYSTS CTR, 71- *Concurrent Pos:* Instr physics, SE Br, Univ Conn, 67-69. *Mem:* Acoust Soc Am. *Res:* Military systems analysis; war gaming and tactical development; systems performance modelling. *Mailing Add:* Naval Underwater Systs Ctr New London CT 06320

WILLIAMS, DAVID JAMES, b Syracuse, NY, Feb 20, 43; m 65; c 3. PHYSICAL CHEMISTRY. *Educ:* Le Moyne Col, NY, BS, 64; Univ Rochester, PhD(phys chem), 68. *Prof Exp:* Scientist, 68-75, MGR PHYS CHEM, CORP RES LABS, XEROX CORP, 75- *Mem:* Am Chem Soc; Am Phys Soc. *Res:* Mechanistics of photogeneration and transport of electronic charge in organic and polymeric materials; pulsed nuclear magnetic resonance; electron spin resonance; electrical measurements; optical spectroscopy. *Mailing Add:* 73 W Church St Fairport NY 14450

WILLIAMS, DAVID JAMES, b Glendora, NJ, Mar 19, 47; m 70; c 3. HORTICULTURE, PLANT PHYSIOLOGY. *Educ:* Del Valley Col, BS, 69; Rutgers Univ, MS, 71, PhD(hort), 74. *Prof Exp:* Res asst hort, Rutgers Univ, 69-74, teaching asst, 70-74; asst prof, 74-80, ASSOC PROF HORT, UNIV ILL, 80- *Concurrent Pos:* Res grants, J M Rhoades Co, 77-78, NCent Region Pesticide Impact Assessment Prog, 78-79, 79-80 & 80-81, Abbott Labs, ICI & Stauffer Chem Co, Monsanto. *Mem:* Am Soc Hort Sci; Weed Sci Soc Am; Int Plant Propagator's Soc; Int Soc Arboricult. *Mailing Add:* 1107 Dorner Dr Univ of Ill Urbana IL 61801

WILLIAMS, DAVID JOHN, b Salem, Mass, Mar 2, 37; m 71. CHEMICAL ENGINEERING, POLYMER SCIENCE. *Educ:* Lehigh Univ, BS, 59; Case Western Reserve Univ, MS, 62, PhD(polymer sci), 64. *Prof Exp:* Prof chem eng, City Col, City Univ New York, 64-74; TECH ASST RES & DEVELOP DIV, AM HOECHST CORP, 74- *Concurrent Pos:* Consult, Mameco Int, Ohio, 62-; NSF res grant, City Col New York, 65-72, Am Chem Soc res grant, 70-72, univ res grant, 70-72; consult, Goodyear Tire & Rubber Co, 71-73. *Mem:* Am Chem Soc. *Res:* Emulsion polymerization and latex technology; polystyrene technology. *Mailing Add:* Am Hoechst Corp 289 N Main St Leominster MA 01453

WILLIAMS, DAVID JOHN, III, b Cordele, Ga, Sept 22, 27; m 48; c 3. THERIOGENOLOGY. *Educ:* Univ Ga, DVM, 53, BSA, 61; Auburn Univ, MS, 63; Royal Vet Col, Sweden, FRVC, 65; Am Col Theriogenologists, dipl, 71. *Prof Exp:* Pvt pract vet med, 53-60; instr vet med & surg, Sch Vet Med, Univ Ga, 61; from instr to assoc prof, Auburn Univ, 61-66; assoc prof, 66-73, PROF VET MED & SURG, COL VET MED, UNIV GA, 73- *Concurrent Pos:* Am Vet Med Asn fel, 64-65; Auburn Univ grant, 65-66; Animal Dis res grants, 67-70, 71-72. *Mem:* Am Vet Med Asn; Soc Theriogenologists; Am Col Theriogenologists. *Res:* bovine and equine reproduction; fat necrosis of bovine as influenced by ecological system. *Mailing Add:* Dept of Med & Surg Univ of Ga Col of Vet Med Athens GA 30602

WILLIAMS, DAVID LEE, b Oakland, Calif, Oct 11, 39; div; c 1. GEOPHYSICS, OCEANOGRAPHY. *Educ:* Univ Tex, BA, 62; Mass Inst Technol & Woods Hole Oceanog Inst, PhD(marine geophys), 74. *Prof Exp:* Fel, Woods Hole Oceanog Inst, 74; GEOPHYSICIST, US GEOL SURV, 74- *Mem:* Sigma Xi; Am Geophys Union. *Res:* Terrestial heat flow; thermal evolution of the Earth; young volcanic systems; geothermal energy. *Mailing Add:* Br of Regional Geophys Stop 964 Box 25046 Fed Ctr Denver CO 80225

WILLIAMS, DAVID LEE, b Kinston, Pa, Feb 22, 46. GENETIC ENGINEERING, ATHEROSCLEROSIS. *Educ:* Univ Calif, Berkeley, AB, 67; Univ Ill, Urbana, PhD(cell biol), 72. *Prof Exp:* Rockefeller Found fel reprod biol, Med Ctr, Univ Calif, San Francisco, 72-74; asst prof, 74-80, ASSOC PROF PHARMACOL SCI, STATE UNIV NY STONY BROOK, 80- *Mem:* Harvey Soc; NY Acad Sci. *Res:* Steroid hormone action; regulation of gene expression; molecular biology and regulation of apolipoprotein genes; molecular biology of atherosclerosis. *Mailing Add:* Dept Pharmacol Sci Health Sci Ctr State Univ NY Stony Brook NY 11794

WILLIAMS, DAVID LLEWELYN, b Hawarden, Wales, Apr 25, 37; m 62; c 2. METAL PHYSICS. *Educ:* Univ Col NWales, BSc, 57; Cambridge Univ, PhD(superconductivity), 60. *Prof Exp:* Nat Res Coun Can fel, 60-62, from instr to assoc prof, 62-71, assoc dean grad studies, 75-81, PROF PHYSICS, UNIV BC, 71- *Concurrent Pos:* Nat Res Coun sr fel, Copenhagen Univ & Bristol Univ, 69-70; Killam fel, SIN, Switzerland, 78-79. *Mem:* Am Phys Soc; Can Asn Physicists. *Res:* Nuclear magnetic resonance; positron annihilation in metal single crystals; muon spin rotation. *Mailing Add:* Dept Physics Univ BC Vancouver BC V6T 1W5 Can

WILLIAMS, DAVID LLOYD, b Springfield, Mass, Aug 15, 35; m 64. DENTAL RESEARCH. *Educ:* Trinity Col, BS, 57; Northwestern Univ, PhD(anal chem), 62. *Prof Exp:* Sr res chemist, Monsanto Res Corp, Monsanto Co, 61-67, New Enterprise Div, 67-69; sr res chemist, Am Hosp Supply Corp, 69-70; res assoc dent, Tufts Univ, 70; PROG MGR BIOMED, ABCOR INC, 70- *Concurrent Pos:* Consult, Joslin Diabetes Found, 74- *Mem:* Electrochem Soc; Am Chem Soc; Int Asn Dent Res; AAAS. *Res:* Dental caries (enzymes and fluoride delivery), and caries measurement instrumentation; delivery of progesterone for contraception and carcinogens for research purposes. *Mailing Add:* ABCOR Inc 850 S Main St Wilmington MA 01887

WILLIAMS, DAVID NOEL, b Lewisburg, Tenn, Oct 10, 34; m 56; c 2. MATHEMATICAL PHYSICS. *Educ:* Maryville Col, BA, 56; Univ Calif, Berkeley, PhD(theoret physics), 64. *Prof Exp:* Engr, Lockheed Missile Systs Div, Calif, 56-58; fel, Swiss Fed Inst Technol, 63-65, Nuclear Res Ctr, Saclay, France, 65-66 & Inst Adv Study, Princeton Univ, 66-67; asst prof theoret physics, 67-74, ASSOC PROF PHYSICS, UNIV MICH, ANN ARBOR, 74- *Mem:* Am Phys Soc. *Res:* Holomorphic, Lorentz covariant functions; analytic S matrix theory; analytic parametrization of higher spin scattering amplitudes; applications of functional analysis in the scattering theory and quantum field theory of elementary particles. *Mailing Add:* Dept of Physics Univ of Mich Ann Arbor MI 48109

WILLIAMS, DAVID TREVOR, b Slough, Eng, Oct 4, 40; m. ENVIRONMENTAL CHEMISTRY. *Educ:* Univ Bristol, BSc, 61; Queen's Univ, MSc, 63, PhD(chem), 66. *Prof Exp:* Res scientist food chem, Foods Directorate, 69-75, RES SCIENTIST ENVIRON CHEM, ENVIRON HEALTH DIRECTORATE, HEALTH & WELFARE, CAN, 75- *Mem:* Royal Soc Chem; Chem Inst Can. *Res:* Identification of organic contaminants in air and drinking water; effects of water treatment procedures on the organic contaminants of drinking water. *Mailing Add:* Environ Health Directorate Tunneys Pasture Ottawa ON K1G 3Z8 Can

WILLIAMS, DEAN E, b Iowa City, Iowa, Feb 18, 24; m 44; c 3. SPEECH PATHOLOGY, AUDIOLOGY. *Educ:* Univ Iowa, BA, 47, MA, 49, PhD(speech path), 52. *Prof Exp:* From asst prof to assoc prof speech path, Fla State Univ, 49-53; res assoc, Univ Iowa, 51-52; asst prof, Ind Univ, 53-58; PROF SPEECH PATH, UNIV IOWA, 58- *Concurrent Pos:* Mem adv panel speech path & audiol, US Voc Rehab Admin, 60-62; consult rev panel speech & hearing, Neurol & Sensory Dis Serv Proj, 64-67 & perinatal res, Nat Inst Neurol Dis & Blindness; mem bd dirs, Am Bd Exam Speech Path & Audiol. *Mem:* Fel Am Speech & Hearing Asn; Int Soc Gen Semantics. *Res:* Stuttering, especially onset and development of the problem and improved remedial procedures. *Mailing Add:* Johnson Speech & Hearing Ctr Woolf Ave Iowa City IA 52240

WILLIAMS, DENIS R, b London, Eng, Feb 4, 41; m 64; c 2. THEORETICAL CHEMISTRY, ACADEMIC ADMINISTRATION. *Educ:* Sheffield Sci Sch, BSc, 62, PhD(chem), 65. *Prof Exp:* Res assoc chem, Vanderbilt Univ, 65-67; from asst prof to assoc prof chem, 67-76, assoc dean grad sch & coordr res & serv, 72-76, PROF CHEM, UNIV COLO, DENVER, 76- *Concurrent Pos:* Univ Colo educ experimentation grant, 67-70; NSF res grant, 69-71 & 71-73; vis prof, Rijksunversiteit Utretcht, Holland, 76-77. *Honors & Awards:* Pub Understanding of Sci-Mus Exhibit, NSF, 74. *Res:* Substituent effects in aromatic hydrocarbons; high resolution ultraviolet spectroscopy of aromatic hydrocarbons; lattice energy of crystalline hydrocarbons; infra-red spectrum of liquid water; D-orbital participation in cyclic organic sulfides. *Mailing Add:* Dept of Chem 1100 14th St Denver CO 80202

WILLIAMS, DONALD BENJAMIN, b New York, NY, Aug 8, 33; m 56; c 2. BIOLOGY. *Educ:* Maryville Col, BA, 55; Emory Univ, MS, 57, PhD(biol), 59. *Prof Exp:* From asst prof to assoc prof biol, Maryville Col, 58-61; asst prof, 61-67, ASSOC PROF BIOL, VASSAR COL, 67- *Mem:* Soc Protozool; NY Acad Sci. *Res:* Ecology, physiology, ultrastructure and genetics of ciliated protozoa; effects of radiation and antimetabolites on various protozoan life stages. *Mailing Add:* Dept of Biol Vassar Col Poughkeepsie NY 12601

WILLIAMS, DONALD ELMER, b Kansas City, Mo, Mar 7, 30. X-RAY CRYSTALLOGRAPHY. *Educ:* William Jewell Col, AB, 50; Iowa State Univ, PhD(chem), 64. *Prof Exp:* Res asst chem, Iowa State Univ, 57-62, from asst chemist to assoc chemist, 62-67; assoc prof, 67-71, PROF CHEM, UNIV LOUISVILLE, 71- *Concurrent Pos:* Vis prof, State Univ Utrecht, The Netherlands, 80-81. *Mem:* AAAS; Am Chem Soc; Am Crystallog Asn; Am Phys Soc. *Res:* Intermolecular forces in crystals; protein folding; hydrogen bonding. *Mailing Add:* Dept of Chem Univ of Louisville Louisville KY 40292

WILLIAMS, DONALD ERROL, b Detroit, Mich, May 12, 28; m 53; c 3. PHYSICAL CHEMISTRY. *Educ:* Colgate Univ, BA, 51; Princeton Univ, PhD(phys chem), 57. *Prof Exp:* Asst chem, Princeton Univ, 51-54; sr chemist, Merck Sharp & Dohme Res Labs, 54-65; head phys & anal chem sect, Strasenburgh Labs Div, Wallace & Tiernan, Inc, 65-68; mgr chem develop, Xerox MDO, 68-70; asst dir qual control, Ayerst Labs Div, Am Home Prod Corp, 70-71, dir, 71-74; dir qual, Bristol Labs Div, Bristol-Myers Co, 74-77; CORP DIR CHEM QUAL ASSURANCE, TECHNICON INSTRUMENTS, 77- *Mem:* Am Chem Soc; Am Soc Qual Control. *Res:* Physical and analytical chemistry of pharmaceuticals; laboratory automation; physical biochemistry. *Mailing Add:* Technicon Instruments Corp Benedict Ave Tarrytown NY 10591

WILLIAMS, DONALD HOWARD, b Ellwood City, Pa, Mar 9, 38; m 60; c 2. INORGANIC CHEMISTRY. *Educ:* Muskingum Col, BS, 60; Ohio State Univ, PhD(inorg chem), 64. *Prof Exp:* Asst prof chem, Univ Ky, 64-69; dir summer sch, 72-78, PROF CHEM, HOPE COL 69-, DIR INST ENVIRON QUAL, 70-, CHMN CHEM DEPT, 79- *Concurrent Pos:* Grants, Res Corp, NY, 65-; water resources inst, US Dept Interior, 66-68; Petrol Res Found & W K Kellogg Found. *Mem:* Am Chem Soc; Inst Environ Sci. *Res:* Stereochemistry of transition metal complexes; environmental chemistry. *Mailing Add:* Dept of Chem Hope Col Holland MI 49423

WILLIAMS, DONALD J, b Fitchburg, Mass, Dec 25, 33; m 53; c 3. SPACE PHYSICS, NUCLEAR PHYSICS. *Educ:* Yale Univ, BS, 55, MS, 58, PhD(nuclear physics), 62. *Prof Exp:* Sr staff physicist, Appl Physics Lab, Johns Hopkins Univ, 61-65; sect head auroral & trapped radiation, Goddard Space Flight Ctr, NASA, 65-68, head particle physics sect, 68-69, head particle physics br, 69-70; DIR, SPACE ENVIRON LAB, ENVIRON RES LABS, NAT OCEANIC & ATMOSPHERIC ADMIN, 70- *Concurrent Pos:* Lectr, Univ Colo, Boulder; prin investr, Europ Space Agency Int Sun Earth Explorer Prog, Galileo Prog & Open Prog, NASA. *Honors & Awards:* Leigh Page Mem Prize, Yale Univ, 58; Nat Oceanic & Atmospheric Admin Res & Achievement Award, 74. *Mem:* Am Geophys Union; Am Phys Soc. *Res:* Nuclear scattering and excitations; earth's trapped particle population and magnetic field configuration; solar flares and cosmic rays; interplanetary physics; interaction of interplanetary medium with Earth's environment; space plasma instabilities. *Mailing Add:* Space Environ Lab NOAA Environ Res Labs R43 Boulder CO 80302

WILLIAMS, DONALD ROBERT, b Morristown, NJ, June 12, 48; m 70; c 3. ORGANIC CHEMISTRY, POLYMER CHEMISTRY. *Educ:* Brown Univ, ScBChem, 70; Mass Inst Technol, ScM, 72; Colo State Univ, PhD(chem), 78. *Prof Exp:* Res chemist dental polymers, Kendall Co, 72-74; RES CHEMIST PLASTICS, ROHM & HAAS CO, 78- *Res:* Asymmetric synthesis; polymer research (continuous flow, emulsion polymerizations, extrusion). *Mailing Add:* Rohm & Haas Labs PO Box 219 Bristol PA 19007

WILLIAMS, DOUGLAS FRANCIS, b Long Branch, NJ, Dec 14, 48; m 75. GEOLOGICAL OCEANOGRAPHY, MICROPALEONTOLOGY. *Educ:* Brown Univ, BA, 71; Univ RI, PhD(oceanog), 76. *Prof Exp:* Res assoc geochem, Dept Geol Sci, Brown Univ, 76-77; ASST PROF GEOL & MARINE SCI, UNIV SC, 77- *Mem:* AAAS; Am Geophys Union; Geol Soc Am; Sigma Xi. *Res:* Marine micropaleontology; stable isotope geochemistry of carbonates; paleoclimatology. *Mailing Add:* Dept of Geol Univ of SC Columbia SC 29208

WILLIAMS, DUANE ALWIN, b Marshfield, Wis, Apr 6, 35; m 57; c 2. CHEMICAL ENGINEERING. *Educ:* Univ Wis-Madison, BS, 56, MS, 57, PhD(chem eng), 61. *Prof Exp:* Tech serv engr lubricant additives, Enjay Labs, 57-58; fel, Univ Wis-Madison, 61-62; res chem engr pulp & paper, Kimberly-Clark Corp, 62-64; sr res engr & dir explor res, Rocket Res Corp, 64-71; sr res scientist pulp & paper, 71-76, SUPVR CONSUMER PROD RES & DEVELOP, KIMBERLY-CLARK CORP, 76- *Mem:* Am Inst Chem Engrs. *Res:* Solid waste management; reaction control systems and gas generation systems for aerospace and commercial applications; pulp mill unit operations; thermal radiation; solar energy utilization. *Mailing Add:* 632 Kessler Dr Neenah WI 54956

WILLIAMS, DUDLEY, b Covington, Ga, Apr 12, 12; m 37; c 2. MOLECULAR SPECTROSCOPY, PLANETARY ATMOSPHERES. *Educ:* Univ NC, AB, 33, MA, 34, PhD(physics), 36. *Prof Exp:* Instr physics, Univ Fla, 36-38, asst prof phys sci, 38-41; staff mem, Radiation Lab, Mass Inst Technol, 41-43; asst prof physics, Univ Okla, 43-44; staff mem, Los Alamos Sci Lab, Calif, 44-46; from assoc prof to prof physics, Ohio State Univ, 46-63, actg chmn dept, 52-53 & 58-59; prof & head dept, NC State Univ, 63-64; REGENT'S DISTINGUISHED PROF PHYSICS, KANS STATE UNIV, 64- *Concurrent Pos:* Guggenheim fel, Univ Amsterdam & Oxford Univ, 56; NSF sr fel, Univ Liege, 61-62. *Mem:* Fel Am Phys Soc; fel Optical Soc Am (vpres, 77, pres-elect, 78, pres, 79); Am Asn Physics Teachers. *Res:* Infrared spectroscopy; microwave transmission; mass spectroscopy; nuclear and atmospheric physics; planetary atmospheres; determination of nuclear magnet moments. *Mailing Add:* Dept of Physics Kans State Univ Manhattan KS 66506

WILLIAMS, E(DGAR) P, b Pierpont, Ohio, Aug 17, 18; div; c 4. MISSILE DESIGN, HYPERSONIC AERODYNAMICS. *Educ:* Oberlin Col, AB, 40; Calif Inst Technol, MS & AeroEng, 42. *Prof Exp:* Asst wind tunnel, Calif Inst Technol, 40-42; aerodyn engr, Douglas Aircraft Co, 42-48; head missiles aerodyn, Rand Corp, 49-55, head aerodyn, 56-63; chief aeromech br, McDonnell Douglas Astronaut Co, 63, chief engr aero-thermodyn dept, 64-66, staff asst to dir advan missile & reentry systs, 67-72, sr staff engr, 72-74; engr, CDI Corp, 77-78; DESIGN SPECIALIST, POMONA DIV, GEN DYNAMICS, 78- *Concurrent Pos:* Lectr, Univ Calif, Los Angeles, 56-58. *Mem:* Assoc fel Am Inst Aeronaut & Astronaut. *Res:* Aerodynamics, particularly hypersonic aerodynamics, glide and reentry vehicles. *Mailing Add:* 6721 Cory Dr Huntington Beach CA 92647

WILLIAMS, E(DWIN) T(HOMAS), b Brooklyn, NY, Mar 18, 18; m 44; c 3. CHEMICAL ENGINEERING. *Educ:* Univ Pa, BS, 39; Univ Toronto, MASc, 44; Pa State Univ, PhD(chem eng), 52. *Prof Exp:* Instr chem eng, Univ Toronto, 40-45, lectr, 45-47; instr, Carnegie Inst Technol, 47-48; instr, Pa State Univ, 48-52, assoc prof, 55-60; design engr, Shell Develop Co, 52-55; prof chem & chem eng & head dept, 60-62, vpres, 62-67, PROF CHEM & CHEM ENG, MICH TECHNOL UNIV, 67- *Mem:* Am Chem Soc; Am Soc Eng Educ; Am Inst Chem Engrs; Am Inst Chem. *Res:* Production of protein and energy from biomass. *Mailing Add:* Dept of Chem & Chem Eng Mich Technol Univ Houghton MI 49931

WILLIAMS, EBENEZER DAVID, JR, b Nanticoke, Pa, June 30, 27; m 54; c 1. TEXTILE CHEMISTRY. *Educ:* Swarthmore Col, AB, 47; Univ Pa, MA, 49, PhD(org chem), 52. *Prof Exp:* Asst instr chem, Univ Pa, 47-52; from res chemist to sr res chemist, 52-63, tech supvr, 63-66, res assoc, 66-74, DEVELOP FEL, TEXTILE RES LAB, TEXTILE FIBERS DEPT, E I DU PONT DE NEMOURS & CO, INC, 74- *Mem:* Am Chem Soc; Sigma Xi. *Res:* Polymer chemistry; synthetic textiles; mechanism of dyeing; dyeing technology of synthetic fibers. *Mailing Add:* Textile Res Lab E I du Pont de Nemours & Co Inc Wilmington DE 19898

WILLIAMS, EDDIE ROBERT, b Chicago, Ill, Jan 6, 45; m; c 2. MATHEMATICS. *Educ:* Ottawa Univ, BA, 66; Columbia Univ, PhD(math), 71. *Prof Exp:* Instr math, Intensive Summer Studies Prog, Columbia Univ, 70; ASST PROF MATH, NORTHERN ILL UNIV, 70- *Concurrent Pos:* Asst to vpres acad affairs, San Diego State Univ. *Mem:* NY Acad Sci; Am Math Soc. *Res:* Pure mathematics; several complex variable theory; mathematics education; mathematics for the disadvantaged student. *Mailing Add:* Dept of Math Northern Ill Univ De Kalb IL 60115

WILLIAMS, EDMOND BRADY, b Charlotte, NC, Aug 12, 43; m 67; c 2. BIOCHEMISTRY, ORGANIC CHEMISTRY. *Educ:* Duke Univ, BS, 65; Univ NC, Chapel Hill, PhD(org chem), 70. *Prof Exp:* NIH fel microbiol, Med Ctr, Univ Calif, San Francisco, 70-72; fel chem, Univ Ariz, 72-73; instr, Baylor Univ, 73-74; asst prof chem, Univ Wis-Oshkosh, 74-80; ASSOC PROF CHEM, COL ST CATHERINE, 80- *Mem:* Am Chem Soc; Sigma Xi; AAAS. *Res:* Synthesis of peptides; protein isolation and modification; enzyme kinetics. *Mailing Add:* Col St Catherine St Paul MN 55105

WILLIAMS, EDWARD JAMES, b Denver, Colo, June 25, 26; m 60; c 2. BIOPHARMACEUTICS, PHARMACOKINETICS. *Educ:* Regis Col, BS, 48; Univ Notre Dame, MS, 50; Purdue Univ, PhD(phys chem), 59. *Prof Exp:* Chief test design & eval serial chem munitions, US Army Chem Corps, 52-54; fel biochem, Med Sch, Marquette Univ, 59-60 & biophys chem, Purdue Univ, 60-63; assoc prof chem, St Norbert Col, 63-71; RES ASSOC PHARM & DIR DRUG DEVELOP LAB, PURDUE UNIV, 79- *Mem:* Sigma Xi. *Res:* Design of new drug dosage forms. *Mailing Add:* 1933 Vinton St Lafayette IN 47904

WILLIAMS, EDWIN BRUCE, b Ladoga, Ind, Nov 3, 18; m 40; c 1. PHYTOPATHOLOGY. *Educ:* Wabash Col, AB, 50; Purdue Univ, MS, 52, PhD(plant path), 54. *Prof Exp:* From asst prof to assoc prof, 54-69, PROF PLANT PATH, PURDUE UNIV, LAFAYETTE, 69-, PLANT PATHOLOGIST, 54- *Mem:* Am Phytopath Soc; Am Pomol Soc. *Res:* Genetics of Venturia inaequalis; breeding apples for disease resistance. *Mailing Add:* Dept of Bot & Plant Path Purdue Univ West Lafayette IN 47906

WILLIAMS, ELEANOR RUTH, b Ropesville, Tex, Apr 23, 24. NUTRITION, FOODS. *Educ:* Tex Woman's Univ, BS, 45; Iowa State Univ, MS, 47; Cornell Univ, PhD(nutrit), 63. *Prof Exp:* Res assoc nutrit, Tex Agr Exp Sta, 48-49; instr food & nutrit, Southern Methodist Univ, 49-51; from instr to asst prof, Cornell Univ, 51-59; assoc prof, Univ Nebr, 63-65; assoc prof nutrit, Teachers Col, Columbia Univ, 65-72; assoc prof, State Univ NY Col Buffalo, 72-74; assoc prof nutrit, 74-76, ASSOC PROF FOOD NUTRIT & INST ADMINR, UNIV MD, 76- *Mem:* AAAS; Soc Nutrit Educ. *Res:* B vitamins and reproduction in the rat; non-specific nitrogen intake; adequacy of cereal protein for man; nutrition education. *Mailing Add:* Dept of Food Nutrit & Inst Admin Univ of Md College Park MD 20740

WILLIAMS, ELIOT CHURCHILL, b Chicago, Ill, Nov 9, 13; m 45; c 4. INVERTEBRATE ZOOLOGY, ANIMAL ECOLOGY. *Educ:* Cent YMCA Col, BA, 35; Northwestern Univ, PhD(zool), 40. *Prof Exp:* Instr zool, Cent YMCA Col, 35-36; asst dir, Chicago Acad Sci, 40-47; asst prof biol, Roosevelt Univ, 47-48; assoc prof, 48-57, chmn, Div Sci, 76-79, PROF ZOOL, WABASH COL, 57- *Concurrent Pos:* Lectr, Roosevelt Univ, 46-47; Ford Found fel, Johns Hopkins Marine Sta, Stanford Univ, 54-55; consult, Fed Chem Co, 54-76. *Mem:* AAAS; Am Soc Zool; Ecol Soc Am; Am Inst Biol Sci; Sigma Xi. *Res:* Animal populations; cave animals; pigmentation in cave planarians; taxonomy and ecology of Symphyla; radioisotope cycling; energy relationships in ecosystems; meiofauna of coral reefs. *Mailing Add:* Dept of Biol Wabash Col Crawfordsville IN 47933

WILLIAMS, ELMER LEE, b Ironton, Ohio, Apr 14, 29; m 57; c 3. PHYSICAL CHEMISTRY. *Educ:* Ohio Univ, BS, 51, MS, 55; Ind Univ, PhD(phys chem), 59. *Prof Exp:* Asst chem, Ind Univ, 55-58; develop engr, Sylvania Elec Prods, Inc Div, Gen Tel & Electronics Corp, 58-60; phys chemist, Owens-Ill, Inc, 60-79; PROJ MGR, MIDLAND-ROSS CORP, 79- *Mem:* Am Chem Soc; Am Ceramic Soc; Electrochem Soc. *Res:* Diffusion of ions and atoms in glass and molten silicates; oxygen of mass 18 work and tracer work in the solid state; semiconductors; gas lasers; gas discharge displays; propose, plan and manage research and development engineering projects in energy and glass furnace areas. *Mailing Add:* Thermo Systs-Tech Ctr Midland-Ross Corp 900 N Westwood Toledo OH 43696

WILLIAMS, EMMETT LEWIS, JR, b Lynchburg, Va, June 6, 33; m 57; c 3. SOLID STATE PHYSICS. *Educ:* Va Polytech Inst, BS, 56, MS, 62; Clemson Univ, PhD(mat eng), 66. *Prof Exp:* Assoc aircraft engr, Lockheed-Ga Co, 56-57; mat engr, Atomic Energy Div, Babcock & Wilcox Co, 57-59; asst prof metall eng, Va Polytech Inst, 59-64; res asst ceramic eng, Clemson Univ, 64-65; res scientist, Union Carbide Nuclear Corp, 65-66; prof physics, Bob Jones Univ, 66-79, chmn dept, 73-79; mat engr, Continental Tel Labs, 79-81; ASSOC SCIENTIST, LOCKHEED-GA CO, 81- *Concurrent Pos:* Consult, Inland Motors, 61-64, Leaders Am Sci, 66, Continental Tel Labs, 70-72, Polysci Corp & Electrotech Corp. *Mem:* Creation Res Soc (vpres, 72-); Sigma Xi. *Res:* Solid state, surface physics; thermodynamics; formation of limestone stalactites in laboratory; thermodynamics of living organisms. *Mailing Add:* Metall & Failure Anal Group Lockheed-Ga Co Marietta GA 30063

WILLIAMS, ERNEST EDWARD, b Easton, Pa, Jan 7, 14. HERPETOLOGY, ECOLOGY. *Educ:* Lafayette Col, BS, 33; Columbia Univ, PhD(zool), 49. *Prof Exp:* Asst zool, Columbia Univ, 40-42 & 46-48; from instr to assoc prof, 49-70, cur reptiles & amphibians, Mus Comp Zool, 57-80, PROF BIOL, HARVARD UNIV, 70-, ALEXANDER AGASSIZ PROF ZOOL, 72- *Concurrent Pos:* Guggenheim fel, 52-53 & 81-82. *Mem:* AAAS; Am Soc Ichthyol & Herpet; Soc Syst Zool; Soc Study Evolution; fel Am Acad Arts & Sci. *Res:* Taxonomy, paleontology and morphology of reptiles; West Indian paleontology and zoogeography; evolution. *Mailing Add:* Mus of Comp Zool Harvard Univ Cambridge MA 02138

WILLIAMS, EUGENE G, b New Haven, Conn, June 9, 25; m 52; c 2. GEOLOGY, MINERALOGY. *Educ:* Lehigh Univ, BA, 50; Univ Ill, MS, 52; Pa State Univ, PhD, 57. *Prof Exp:* Instr geol, Kent State Univ, 52-53; instr, 54-55, res assoc, 56-57, from asst prof to assoc prof, 57-71, PROF GEOL, PA STATE UNIV, 71- *Mem:* Geol Soc Am; Am Asn Petrol Geol. *Res:* Stratigraphy and petrography of upper Paleozoic rocks of eastern United States. *Mailing Add:* Dept of Geosci Pa State Univ University Park PA 16802

WILLIAMS, EUGENE H(UGHES), b New Bern, NC, Jan 13, 12; m 40; c 2. CHEMICAL ENGINEERING. *Educ:* NC State Col, BS, 34; Inst Paper Chem, Lawrence, MS, 37. *Prof Exp:* Chem engr, Munising Paper Co, 37-49; supt printing, Milprint, Inc, 49-52; chem engr, Pulp & Paper, Detroit Sulphite Pulp & Paper Co, 52-54; tech dir, Detroit Div, Scott Paper Co, 54-65, tech specialist, 65-72; tech specialist, S D Warren Co, 72-77; RETIRED. *Mem:* Am Chem Soc; Am Inst Chem; Tech Asn Pulp & Paper Indust; Paper Indust Mgt Asn. *Res:* Pulp and paper chemistry; quality control and development. *Mailing Add:* 1920 Raymond St Dearborn MI 48124

WILLIAMS, EVAN THOMAS, b New York, NY, May 17, 36; m 59; c 2. ANALYTICAL CHEMISTRY. *Educ:* Williams Col, BA, 58; Mass Inst Technol, PhD(chem), 63. *Prof Exp:* Civil engr, Res Estab Res, Roskilde, Denmark, 63-65; prof to assoc prof, 65-75, PROF CHEM, BROOKLYN COL, 76-, CHMN DEPT, 81- *Concurrent Pos:* Consult, Geosci Instruments Corp, 66-72; mem exec bd, New York City Coun on the Environ, 73-76. *Mem:* AAAS; Am Chem Soc; Am Phys Soc; Geochem Soc; NY Acad Sci. *Res:* Trace element analysis; environmental applications; proton-induced x-ray emission; radiocarbon dating. *Mailing Add:* Dept Chem Brooklyn Col Brooklyn NY 11210

WILLIAMS, F(ORD) CAMPBELL, b Nanaimo, BC, Dec 28, 21; m 55; c 2. CHEMICAL ENGINEERING. *Educ:* Univ BC, BASc, 43, MASc, 46; Univ Iowa, PhD(chem eng), 48. *Prof Exp:* Instr chem eng, Univ Iowa, 47-48; asst prof, Univ Calif, 48-52; prof chem eng & tech consult, Nat Petrol Coun, Brazil, 52-55; head prof & head res, Petroleo Brasileiro SA, 55-65; consult chem engr, Consultores Industriais Associados, 65-70; VPRES, NATRON CONSULTORIA E PROJETOR SA, 70-, VPRES TECHNOL, 80- *Mem:* Am Inst Chem Engrs. *Res:* Phase equilibria; extraction; petroleum process and product development; engineering design; process research. *Mailing Add:* Natron-Consultoria e Projetos S A Teofilo Otoni 63-11 Rio de Janeiro Brazil

WILLIAMS, FERD ELTON, b Erie, Pa, June 9, 20; m 48; c 5. PHYSICS. *Educ:* Univ Pittsburgh, BS, 42; Princeton Univ, MA, 45, PhD(phys chem), 46. *Prof Exp:* Res chemist, Res Labs, Radio Corp Am, 42-46; asst prof chem, Univ NC, 46-48; res assoc, Res Lab, Gen Elec Co, 48-49, mgr, Light Prod Sect, 49-59, theoret physicist, Gen Physics Dept, 59-61; prof, 61-62, chmn dept, 61-77, H FLETCHER BROWN PROF PHYSICS, 62- *Concurrent Pos:* Prin investr, Army Res Off & Army Engrs res grants, 62-; mem adv comt solid state physics, Oak Ridge Nat Labs, 63-67; ed-in-chief, J Luminescence, 69-; indust & govt consult, Picatinny Arsenal; vis prof, Univs Liege, Paris & Nijmegen, 75-79, Univ Tokyo, 77, Univ Paris, 78 & Tech Univ Berlin, 80 & 81; chmn comt, Int Conf Luminescence, 69-; lectr NATO, Erice, Sicily, 74, 77, 79 & 81. *Honors & Awards:* Humboldt Prize, Fed Repub Ger, 81. *Mem:* Fel AAAS; fel Optical Soc Am; fel Am Phys Soc; Am Chem Soc; Am Asn Physics Teachers. *Res:* Solid state physics; semiconductivity; luminescence; chemical physics. *Mailing Add:* 1008 Dixon Dr Christine Manor Newark DE 19711

WILLIAMS, FLOYD JAMES, phytopathology, see previous edition

WILLIAMS, FLOYD JAMES, b Electra, Tex, Jan 9, 20; m 55; c 2. GEOLOGY. *Educ:* Univ Calif, BS, 43; Colo Sch Mines, MS, 51; Columbia Univ, PhD(geol), 58. *Prof Exp:* Mining engr, Bradley Mining Co, Idaho, 43; mining engr, Idaho-Md Mines Corp, Calif, 46-47; explosives engr, Hercules Powder Co, 47-48; chief reconnaissance sect, Salt Lake eExplor Br, Div Raw Mat, USAEC, 52-54; geologist, Standard Oil Co, Calif, 56-58; assoc prof geol, Univ Redlands, 58-66; supvr spectrog, Kaiser Steel Corp, Calif, 66-72; head dept geol, 72-76, assoc prof, 76-80, CHMN, DIV SCI, SAN BERNARDINO VALLEY COL, 80-, ASSOC PROF GEOL, 80- *Concurrent Pos:* NSF fel & res assoc geol & geophys, Univ Calif, Berkeley, 63-64; consult geol, City of San Bernardino, Calif, 74- *Mem:* Geol Soc Am; AAAS. *Res:* Criteria for active faults, earthquake prediction. *Mailing Add:* Dept of Geol San Bernardino Valley Col San Bernardino CA 92403

WILLIAMS, FORMAN A(RTHUR), b New Brunswick, NJ, Jan 12, 34; m 55; c 6. COMBUSTION, FLUID DYNAMICS. *Educ:* Princeton Univ, BSE, 55; Calif Inst Technol, PhD(eng sci), 58. *Prof Exp:* Asst prof mech eng, Harvard Univ, 58-64; mem tech staff, Inst Defense Anal, 63-64; assoc prof aerospace eng, Univ Calif, San Diego, 64-67, prof, 67-81; PROF MECH & AEROSPACE ENG, PRINCETON UNIV, 81- *Concurrent Pos:* NSF fel, Imp Col, Univ London, 62; Guggenheim fel, Univs Sydney & Madrid, 70-71; Alexander von Humboldt US sr scientist award, 81. *Honors & Awards:* Silver Combustion Medal, Combustion Inst, 78. *Mem:* Am Phys Soc; Am Inst Aeronaut & Astronaut; Soc Indust & Appl Math; Combustion Inst. *Res:* Aerothermochemistry; combustion theory; heat and mass transfer; fire research; mathematical methods. *Mailing Add:* Dept Mech & Aerospace Eng Princeton Univ Princeton NJ 08544

WILLIAMS, FRANCIS, b Whitley Bay, Eng, May 14, 27; m 57. FISHERIES, BIOLOGICAL OCEANOGRAPHY. *Educ:* Univ Durham, BSc, 51, MSc, 55; Univ Newcastle, Eng, DSc(marine fisheries), 64. *Prof Exp:* Prin sci officer, Pelagic Fish & Fisheries, E African Marine Fisheries Res Orgn, Zanzibar, 51-62; dir Guinean Trawling Surv, Orgn African Unity, Lagos, Nigeria, 62-66; mgr pelagic fisheries surv W Africa, dept fisheries, Food & Agr Orgn UN, Rome, Italy, 66-68; assoc res biologist, Scripps Inst Oceanog, Univ Calif, San Diego, 68-73; chmn div fisheries & appl estuarine ecol, 73-74, chmn div biol & living resources, 74-78, PROF MARINE SCI, ROSENSTIEL SCH MARINE & ATMOSPHERIC SCI, UNIV MIAMI, 73- *Mem:* Sci fel Zool Soc London; Marine Biol Asn UK; Challenger Soc; Am Fisheries Soc; fel Am Inst Fishery Res Biol. *Res:* Exploratory fishing surveys; fish taxonomy; correlation of fish and fisheries with environment. *Mailing Add:* Rosentiel Sch Marine & Atmos Sci Univ Miami Miami FL 33149

WILLIAMS, FRANK LYNN, b Peoria, Ill, Oct 6, 45. CHEMICAL ENGINEERING, CATALYSIS. *Educ:* Northwestern Univ, BS, 68; Stanford Univ, MS, 70, PhD(chem eng), 73. *Prof Exp:* Res engr catalysis, Gen Motors Res Labs, 72-77; asst prof, 77-80, ASSOC PROF CHEM ENG, UNIV NMEX, 80- *Concurrent Pos:* Consult, Sandia Nat Labs, 77- *Honors & Awards:* Kokes Award, NAm Catalysis Soc, 74. *Mem:* Am Inst Chem Engrs; Am Chem Soc; Am Vacuum Soc; NAm Catalysis Soc. *Res:* Methane recovery from coalbeds; heterogenous surface chemistry during catalytic reactions; in-situ energy production; methane recovery from coalbeds. *Mailing Add:* Dept Chem & Nuclear Eng Univ NMex Albuquerque NM 87131

WILLIAMS, FRED DEVOE, b New York, NY, Dec 16, 36; m 57; c 3. BACTERIOLOGY, BIOCHEMISTRY. *Educ:* Rutgers Univ, BA, 60, MS, 62, PhD(bact), 64. *Prof Exp:* Instr bact, Rutgers Univ, 63-64; from asst prof to assoc prof, 64-75, PROF BACT, IOWA STATE UNIV, 75-, CHMN, DEPT MICROBIOL, 81- *Mem:* AAAS; Am Soc Microbiol; Sigma Xi. *Res:* Biosynthesis of folic acid-like compounds by microorganisms and the metabolic regulation of these biosynthetic pathways; physiology and biochemistry of microbial behavior. *Mailing Add:* Dept Microbiol Iowa State Univ Ames IA 50011

WILLIAMS, FRED EUGENE, b Wichita Falls, Tex, Oct 23, 41; m 64; c 2. FOOD INTAKE CONTROL, DENTAL EDUCATION. *Educ:* Arlington State Col, BS, 66; Baylor Univ, PhD(physiol), 72. *Prof Exp:* Asst prof, 72-77, ASSOC PROF PHYSIOL, BAYLOR COL DENT, 77- *Mem:* Sigma Xi; AAAS; Am Physiol Soc; Am Asn Dental Schs. *Res:* Effects of liver denervation, hypothalamic lesions, hormones and other chemical agents on feeding behavior. *Mailing Add:* Dept of Physiol Baylor Col of Dent Dallas TX 75246

WILLIAMS, FREDERICK MCGEE, b Washington, DC, Jan 10, 34; m 55; c 4. BIOLOGY. *Educ:* Stanford Univ, AB, 55; Yale Univ, PhD(biol), 65. *Prof Exp:* Asst prof biol, Lehigh Univ, 63-64; from asst prof to assoc prof zool, Univ Minn, Minneapolis, 64-70; ASSOC PROF BIOL, PA STATE UNIV, UNIVERSITY PARK, 70- *Concurrent Pos:* NASA-Am Inst Biol Sci fel, 65-66; chmn grad prog ecol, Pa State Univ, 74-80. *Mem:* Am Soc Naturalists;

AAAS; Ecol Soc Am; Am Soc Zool; Am Inst Biol Sci. *Res:* Theoretical and experimental population dynamics; theory of ecosystem structure and stability; environmentally induced shape changes in algal cells; mathematical biology; mechanisms of competition and predation; fish population models sensitive to environmental alterations. *Mailing Add:* Dept Biol Pa State Univ University Park PA 16802

WILLIAMS, FREDERICK WALLACE, b Cumberland, Md, Sept 24, 39; m 64; c 2. ANALYTICAL CHEMISTRY. *Educ:* Univ Ala, BS, 61, MSc, 63, PhD(chem), 65. *Prof Exp:* Nat Acad Sci-Nat Res Coun fel, 65-66, res chemist, 66-73, SUPV RES CHEMIST, US NAVAL RES LAB, DC, 73- *Mem:* AAAS; Am Chem Soc; Combustion Inst. *Res:* Fundamental mechanisms of combustion. *Mailing Add:* 13408 Colwyn Rd Ft Washington MD 20022

WILLIAMS, FREDRICK DAVID, b Winnipeg, Man, Sept 1, 37; m 64; c 3. POLYMER CHEMISTRY, PHYSICAL CHEMISTRY. *Educ:* Univ Man, BSc, 59, MSc, 61, PhD(chem), 62. *Prof Exp:* Ital Govt res scholarship, Inst Indust Chem, Milan Polytech Inst, 62-63; res chemist, Allis-Chalmers Mfg Corp, 63-65; asst prof, 65-69, ASSOC PROF CHEM, MICH TECHNOL UNIV, 69- *Mem:* Am Chem Soc. *Res:* Polymer chemistry. *Mailing Add:* Dept Chem Mich Technol Univ Houghton MI 49931

WILLIAMS, GARETH, b Rhos, Wales, Apr 28, 37; US citizen; m 65; c 2. APPLIED MATHEMATICS. *Educ:* Univ Wales, BSc, 59, PhD(math), 62. *Prof Exp:* Asst prof math, Univ Fla, 62-65; from asst prof to assoc prof, Univ Denver, 65-73; assoc prof, 73-76, PROF MATH, STETSON UNIV, 76- *Mem:* Am Math Soc; Am Math Asn; Tensor Soc Gt Brit. *Res:* Relativity; differential geometry; mathematical models; computer science; linear algebra. *Mailing Add:* Dept of Math Stetson Univ Deland FL 32720

WILLIAMS, GARY LYNN, b Carlsbad, NMex, Feb 25, 50. REPRODUCTIVE ENDOCRINOLOGY, REPRODUCTIVE PHYSIOLOGY. *Educ:* NMex State Univ, BS, 72, MS, 74; Univ Ariz, PhD(animal physiol), 78. *Prof Exp:* ASST PROF PHYSIOL & ENDOCRINOL, DEPT ANIMAL SCI, NDAK STATE UNIV, 78- *Mem:* Am Soc Animal Sci; Soc Study Reproduction; Am Dairy Sci Asn; Sigma Xi. *Res:* Reproductive endocrinology of the postpartum bovine; neuroendocrine-ovarian relationships. *Mailing Add:* Dept Animal Sci NDak State Univ Fargo ND 58105

WILLIAMS, GARY MURRAY, b Regina, Sask, May 7, 40; US citizen; m 66; c 3. PATHOLOGY, TOXICOLOGY. *Educ:* Washington & Jefferson Col, BA, 63; Univ Pittsburgh, MD, 67. *Prof Exp:* Instr path, Med Sch, Harvard Univ, 67-69; staff assoc carcinogenesis, Nat Cancer Inst, 69-71; asst prof path, Fels Res Inst & Med Sch, Temple Univ, 71-75; res assoc prof, 75-80, RES PROF PATH, NEW YORK MED COL, 80-; ASSOC DIR & CHIEF DIV EXP PATH & TOXICOL, NAYLOR-DANA INST DIS PREV, AM HEALTH FOUND, 75- *Concurrent Pos:* Int Agency Res on Cancer res training fel, Wenner-Gren Inst, Stockholm, Sweden, 71-72; from intern to resident path, Mass Gen Hosp, 67-69. *Honors & Awards:* Sheard-Sanford Award, Am Soc Clin Path, 67. *Mem:* Am Asn Cancer Res; Am Asn Pathologists; Int Acad Path; Soc Exp Biol & Med; Soc Toxicol. *Res:* The genetic and carcinogenic effects of chemicals with emphasis on cell culture techniques. *Mailing Add:* Naylor-Dana Inst for Dis Prev 1 Dana Rd Am Health Found Valhalla NY 10595

WILLIAMS, GENE R, b Yuba City, Calif, Nov 10, 32; m 54, 69; c 2. PLANT PHYSIOLOGY, PLANT BIOCHEMISTRY. *Educ:* Univ Calif, BS, 57, MS, 59, PhD(plant physiol), 63. *Prof Exp:* Lectr bot, Univ Calif, 61-62; Am Cancer Soc fel biochem, Biol Div, Oak Ridge Nat Lab, 63-65; asst prof, 65-68, ASSOC PROF BOT, IND UNIV, BLOOMINGTON, 68- *Mem:* AAAS; Am Soc Plant Physiol. *Res:* Plant metabolism, protein and nucleic acid synthesis, amino acid activation and chloroplast development; effects of light on plant development. *Mailing Add:* Dept of Biol Ind Univ Bloomington IN 47401

WILLIAMS, GENEVA HYLAND, b Champaign, Ill, Dec 25, 34. DEVELOPMENTAL BIOLOGY, REPRODUCTIVE BIOLOGY. *Educ:* Univ Mo, AB, 55; Vanderbilt Univ & Peabody Col, MAT, 56; Wash Univ, PhD(embryol), 67. *Prof Exp:* Teacher high sch, Mo, 56-59; asst prof zool, Univ Toronto, 64-70; res assoc pharmacol, Pa State Univ, 70-74, instr obstet & gynec, 74-80; ASST PROF BIOL, VILLANOVA UNIV, 81- *Concurrent Pos:* Nat Res Coun Can oper res grant, 66-69. *Mem:* AAAS; NY Acad Sci; Tissue Cult Asn. *Res:* Regulation of enzyme activity in tissues of developing vertebrates; role of prolactin in uterine function; amniotic fluid phospholipids and fetal lung maturity. *Mailing Add:* Dept Biol Villanova Univ Villanova PA 19085

WILLIAMS, GEORGE, JR, b Benton, La, June 15, 31; m 57. BOTANY. *Educ:* Southern Univ, BS, 57; Univ NH, MS, 59, PhD(bot), 63. *Prof Exp:* Asst bot, Univ NH, 57-63; PROF BIOL, SOUTHERN UNIV, BATON ROUGE, 63- *Mem:* Am Soc Plant Physiol. *Res:* Plant growth as modified by light quality and chemical factors, particularly growth hormones. *Mailing Add:* Dept of Biol Southern Univ Baton Rouge LA 70813

WILLIAMS, GEORGE ABIAH, b Brooklyn, NY, Apr 1, 31; div; c 3. SOLID STATE PHYSICS. *Educ:* Colgate Univ, BA, 52; Univ Ill, PhD, 56. *Prof Exp:* Res assoc physics, Stanford Univ, 56-59; mem tech staff, Bell Tel Labs, NJ, 59-63; vis asst prof physics, Cornell Univ, 63-64; assoc prof, 64-70, PROF PHYSICS, UNIV UTAH, 70-, ASSOC CHMN, PHYSICS DEPT, 74- *Concurrent Pos:* NSF res grant, 72-74; Air Force Off Sci Res grant, 65-70; vis prof physics, Univ Minn, 79 & Univ Calif, Berkeley, 80. *Mem:* Am Phys Soc. *Res:* Wave propagation in solid state plasmas; plasma effects in solids; superconductivity; solid helium-3. *Mailing Add:* Dept of Physics Univ of Utah Salt Lake City UT 84112

WILLIAMS, GEORGE ARTHUR, b Wilcox, Ariz, Jan 14, 18; m 43; c 3. GEOLOGY, ENGINEERING. *Educ:* Tex Western Col, BS, 43; Univ Ariz, PhD(geol), 51. *Prof Exp:* Engr, Asarco Mining Co, Inc, Mex, 46; geologist, Peru Mining Co, 46-48, supt, Kearney Mine, 48; geologist, US Geol Surv, 51-57; assoc prof, 57-65, PROF GEOL ENG & HEAD DEPT GEOL, UNIV IDAHO, 65- *Concurrent Pos:* Gov appointed, Control Bd, Idaho Bur Mines & Geol; actg dir, Idaho Mining & Mineral Resources Res Inst, 81- *Mem:* Fel AAAS; fel Geol Soc Am; Soc Econ Paleont & Mineral; Soc Econ Geol; Am Asn Petrol Geol. *Res:* Economic geology; sedimentation; stratigraphy. *Mailing Add:* Dept of Geol Univ of Idaho Moscow ID 83843

WILLIAMS, GEORGE CHRISTOPHER, b Charlotte, NC, May 12, 26; m 50; c 4. ZOOLOGY. *Educ:* Univ Calif, Berkeley, AB, 49, MA, Los Angeles, 52, PhD, 55. *Prof Exp:* From instr to asst prof natural sci, Mich State Univ, 55-60; assoc prof, 60-66, PROF BIOL SCI, STATE UNIV N Y STONY BROOK, 66- *Mem:* AAAS; Soc Study Evolution; Am Soc Ichthyol & Herpet; Am Soc Limnol & Oceanog; Am Fisheries Soc. *Res:* Evolution; marine ecology; ichthyology; animal behavior; population genetics. *Mailing Add:* Dept of Ecol & Evolution State Univ of NY Stony Brook NY 11794

WILLIAMS, GEORGE HARRY, b Schenectady, NY, Nov 7, 42; m 67; c 1. COMPUTER SCIENCE. *Educ:* Union Col, BSEE & BA, 65; Yale Univ, MS, 66, PhD(eng, appl sci), 70. *Prof Exp:* ASSOC PROF ELEC ENG & COMPUT SCI, UNION COL, 70- *Concurrent Pos:* NSF res initiation grant, Union Col, 71-72; prin investr grant, NSF, 72-73. *Mem:* Inst Elec & Electronics Engrs; Asn Comput Mach. *Res:* Automata theory, logic design, computer-aided design and artificial intelligence. *Mailing Add:* Dept Elec Eng & Comput Sci Union Col Schenectady NY 12308

WILLIAMS, GEORGE JACKSON, III, b Corpus Christi, Tex, July 14, 38; m 61; c 2. PLANT ECOLOGY. *Educ:* Tex A&I Univ, BS, 61; George Peabody Col, MA, 66; Univ Tex, Austin, PhD(bot), 69. *Prof Exp:* Asst prof gen biol, Univ Denver, 69-72; asst prof, 72-75, ASSOC PROF GEN BIOL & BOT, WASH STATE UNIV, 75- *Concurrent Pos:* NSF grant grassland biome, Int Biol Prog, Pawnee Nat Grasslands, Colo State Univ, 71-72 & 74-75, grant physiol ecol C3 and C4 grasses, 74-76. *Mem:* AAAS; Bot Soc Am; Am Sco Plant Physiol; Ecol Soc Am. *Res:* Physiological and biochemical adaptations of plant populations; colonizing plant species and ecotypic differentiation. *Mailing Add:* Prog in Gen Biol & Dept of Bot Wash State Univ Pullman WA 99163

WILLIAMS, GEORGE KENNETH, b Detroit, Mich, July 8, 32; m 54; c 4. MATHEMATICS. *Educ:* Univ Ky, BAE, 55, MA, 58; Univ Va, PhD(math), 64. *Prof Exp:* Teacher high sch, Mich, 55-56; asst prof math, Madison Col, 58-60 & Univ Notre Dame, 64-68; assoc prof, 68-72, PROF MATH, SOUTHWESTERN AT MEMPHIS, 72- *Mem:* Am Math Soc; Math Asn Am. *Res:* Complex analysis; topology. *Mailing Add:* Dept of Math Southwestern at Memphis Memphis TN 38112

WILLIAMS, GEORGE NATHANIEL, b Kingsland, Ga, May 17, 47; m 70; c 1. INORGANIC CHEMISTRY, ORGANIC CHEMISTRY. *Educ:* Savannah State Col, BS, 69; Tuskegee Inst, MS, 72; Howard Univ, PhD(inorg chem), 78. *Prof Exp:* Lab technician chem, Union Camp Corp, 70; instr, 72-75, ASST PROF CHEM, SAVANNAH STATE COL, 78- *Mem:* Am Chem Soc; Am Inst Chemists. *Res:* Metal incorporation and the anation reactions of porphyrins. *Mailing Add:* Savannah State Col Box 20016 Savannah GA 31404

WILLIAMS, GEORGE RAINEY, b Atlanta, Ga, Oct 25, 26; m 50; c 4. MEDICINE. *Educ:* Northwestern Univ, BS, 47, BMed, 50, MD, 51. *Prof Exp:* Instr surg, Johns Hopkins Hosp, 57-58; from asst prof to assoc prof, 58-63, PROF SURG, UNIV OKLA, 63-, CHMN DEPT SURG, 74- *Concurrent Pos:* Markle scholar, 60. *Mem:* Soc Univ Surg; Am Surg Asn; Soc Vascular Surg; Am Asn Thoracic Surg; Am Col Surgeons. *Res:* Cardiovascular surgery. *Mailing Add:* Dept Surg Univ Okla Health Sci Ctr Oklahoma City OK 73190

WILLIAMS, GEORGE RONALD, b Liverpool, Eng, Jan 4, 28; m 52; c 3. BIOCHEMISTRY. *Educ:* Univ Liverpool, PhD(biochem), 51, DSc, 69. *Prof Exp:* Worshipful Co Goldsmith's traveling fel, Banting & Best Dept Med Res, Univ Toronto, 52-53; res assoc, Johnson Found Med Biophys, Univ Pa, 53-55; Med Res Coun res assoc path, Oxford Univ, 55-56; asst prof biochem, Banting & Best Dept Med Res, 56-61, assoc prof, 61-66, chmn dept, 70-77, PROF BIOCHEM, UNIV TORONTO, 66-, CHMN DIV LIFE SCI, 78- *Concurrent Pos:* Vis prof geochem, Lamont-Doherty Geol Observ, Columbia Univ, 77-78. *Mem:* Can Biochem Soc (pres, 71-72); Can Soc Cell Biol; fel Royal Soc Can; Geochem Soc; Brit Biochem Soc. *Res:* Geobiochemistry; catalysis in natural waters; environmental homeostasis; control systems in biochemical and geochemical reaction networks. *Mailing Add:* Div Life Sci Univ Toronto Scarborough Col West Hill ON M1C 1A4 Can

WILLIAMS, GEORGE W, b Nashville, Tenn, Oct 31, 46. BIOSTATISTICS. *Educ:* Bucknell Univ, BS, 68; George Washington Univ, MA, 70; Univ NC, PhD(biostatist), 72. *Prof Exp:* Assoc prof, 78-81, PROF BIOSTATIST, UNIV MICH, ANN ARBOR, 81-; CHMN, DEPT BIOSTATIST, CLEVELAND CLIN, OHIO, 80- *Mem:* Soc Clin Trials; Am Statist Asn; Am Pub Health Asn; Biomet Soc; Soc Epidemiol Res. *Res:* Clinical trials; statistical methods in epidemiology. *Mailing Add:* Dept Biostatist Cleveland Clin Found 9500 Enclid Ave Cleveland OH 44136

WILLIAMS, GERALD ALBERT, b Plankinton, SDak, Apr 1, 21; m 50; c 3. MEDICAL RESEARCH, ENDOCRINOLOGY. *Educ:* SDak State Col, BS, 45; George Washington Univ, MD, 49. *Prof Exp:* Instr med, Sch Med, Univ Va, 57-59; from asst prof to assoc prof, 59-69, PROF MED, UNIV ILL COL MED, 69- *Concurrent Pos:* Chief nuclear med serv & endocrinol sect, Vet Admin West Side Hosp, Chicago, 59-; attend physician, Univ Ill Hosp, 59-, chief endocrinol, 67- *Mem:* Am Fedn Clin Res; fel Am Col Physicians; Endocrine Soc; Soc Exp Biol & Med; Cent Soc Clin Res. *Res:* Parathyroid physiology; calcium metabolism; thyroid disorders. *Mailing Add:* Vet Admin West Side Hosp 820 S Damen Ave PO Box 8195 Chicago IL 60680

WILLIAMS, GLEN NORDYKE, b Port Arthur, Tex, Nov 15, 38; m 60; c 5. COMPUTER SCIENCE, CIVIL ENGINEERING. *Educ:* Tex A&M Univ, BS, 60, MEng, 61, PhD(civil eng), 65. *Prof Exp:* Systs engr, IBM Corp, 65; asst prof, 69-77, ASSOC PROF COMPUT SCI, TEX A&M UNIV, 77- *Mem:* Am Soc Civil Engrs; Asn Comput Mach. *Res:* Fluid networks; slope stability; numerical analysis; computer applications; information systems. *Mailing Add:* Dept of Comput Sci Tex A&M Univ College Station TX 77843

WILLIAMS, GLENN C(ARBER), b Princeton, Iowa, Oct 9, 14; m 39; c 2. CHEMICAL ENGINEERING. *Educ:* Univ Ill, BS, 37, MS, 38; Mass Inst Technol, ScD(chem eng), 42. *Prof Exp:* Res chem engr, Univ Ill, 37; from asst instr to instr, 38-42, from asst prof to assoc prof, 42-54, PROF CHEM ENG, MASS INST TECHNOL, 54- *Concurrent Pos:* Mem, Nat Adv Comt Aeronaut, 44 & 49; mem adv comt, Army Ord Res & Develop; res adv comt chem energy systs, NASA, 60-; mem comt, Motor Vehicle Emissions, Nat Acad Sci, 71-74. *Honors & Awards:* Egerton Medal, Combustion Inst. *Mem:* Am Chem Soc; Am Inst Chem Engrs; Am Inst Aeronaut & Astronaut; Combustion Inst (pres); Am Acad Arts & Sci. *Res:* Mass and heat transfer; high-output combustion. *Mailing Add:* Dept of Chem Eng Mass Inst of Technol Cambridge MA 02139

WILLIAMS, GRAHEME JOHN BRAMALD, b Auckland, NZ, Jan 8, 42; m 69; c 1. STRUCTURAL CHEMISTRY, CRYSTALLOGRAPHY. *Educ:* Univ Auckland, BSc, 66, MSc Hons, 67; Univ Alta, PhD(biochem), 72. *Prof Exp:* Fel chem, Univ Montreal, 72-73; res assoc chem, 73-78, assoc chemist, 78-80, CHEMIST, BROOKHAVEN NAT LAB, 81-; PROD MGR, ENRAF-NONIUS SERV CORP, 81- *Mem:* Am Crystallog Asn; Am Chem Soc; Am Mineral Soc. *Res:* Application of crystallography to structural problems in chemistry and biochemistry, enzymes, drugs and metabolites; crystallographic technique, improved computational methods and instrumentation. *Mailing Add:* ENRAF/NONIUS Serv Corp 390 Central Ave Bohemia NY 11716

WILLIAMS, HAROLD, b St John's, Nfld, Mar 14, 34; m 58; c 3. GEOLOGY. *Educ:* Mem Univ Nfld, BSc, 56, MSc, 58; Univ Toronto, PhD(geol), 61. *Prof Exp:* Res scientist, Geol Surv Can, Ont, 61-68; assoc prof, 68-71, PROF GEOL MEM UNIV NFLD, 71- *Honors & Awards:* R J W Douglas Medal, Can Soc Petrol Geologists, 81. *Mem:* Royal Soc Can; Geol Soc Am; fel Geol Asn Can. *Res:* Regional geology; ophiolite suites; continental margins; Appalachian geology. *Mailing Add:* Dept of Geol Mem Univ of Nfld St John's NF A1B 3X5 Can

WILLIAMS, HAROLD EDWARD, plant pathology, deceased

WILLIAMS, HAROLD HENDERSON, b Blanchard, Pa, Aug 29, 07; m 35; c 3. BIOCHEMISTRY. *Educ:* Pa State Univ, BS, 29; Cornell Univ, PhD(nutrit), 33. *Prof Exp:* Asst, Cornell Univ, 29-33; Sterling fel, Yale Univ, 33-35; res assoc, Children's Fund Mich, 35-39, from asst dir to assoc dir res lab, 39-45; prof, 45-73, head dept, 55-64, EMER PROF BIOCHEM, CORNELL UNIV, 73- *Concurrent Pos:* Mem nutrit res adv comt, USDA, 51-61; comt amino acids, Food & Nutrit Bd, Nat Acad Sci-Nat Res Coun, 52-72; nutrit study sect, NIH, 58-62, study sect comt nutrit & med res, Brazil, 62; spec organizing comt, conf fish & nutrit, Food & Agr Orgn, UN, Italy, 61, expert panel milk qual, 63-73; grad educ grants panel, US Bur Com Fisheries, 65-67 & exec comt, Off Biochem Nomenclature, 65-73; vis comt biol & phys sci, Western Reserve Univ, 65-67; overseas corresp, Nutrit Abstr & Rev, 57-71; Am Soc Biol Chem rep, div biol & agr, Nat Res Coun, 65-67. *Honors & Awards:* Borden Award, Am Inst Nutrit, 53. *Mem:* Am Soc Biol Chem; Am Chem Soc; Am Inst Nutrit. *Res:* Amino acid and protein metabolism; selenium metabolism in microorganisms. *Mailing Add:* 1060 Highland Rd Ithaca NY 14850

WILLIAMS, HARRY EDWIN, b Los Angeles, Calif, Mar 11, 30; m 55; c 4. MECHANICAL ENGINEERING. *Educ:* Univ Santa Clara, BME, 51; Calif Inst Technol, MS, 52, PhDPhD(mech eng), 56. *Prof Exp:* Fulbright scholar math, Univ Manchester, 56-57; res engr, Jet Propulsion Lab, Calif Inst Technol, 57-60; from asst prof to assoc prof eng, Harvey Mudd Col, 60-66; liaison scientist, Off Naval Res, London, 66-67; assoc prof eng, 67-71, PROF ENG, HARVEY MUDD COL, 71- *Concurrent Pos:* Consult, Jet Propulsion Lab, Calif Inst Technol, 60-66 & 68-71 & Naval Weapons Ctr, China Lake, 72- *Mem:* Am Soc Mech Engrs. *Res:* Analysis of linear and elastic shells and thin rings. *Mailing Add:* Dept of Eng Harvey Mudd Col Claremont CA 91711

WILLIAMS, HARRY LEVERNE, b Watford, Can, Nov 16, 16; m 46; c 2. POLYMER SCIENCE, POLYMER ENGINEERING. *Educ:* Univ Western Ont, BA, 39, MSc, 40; McGill Univ, PhD(phys chem), 43. *Prof Exp:* Res chemist, London Asn War Res, 40-41 & Res & Develop, Polysar Ltd, 46-55, supvr to asst mgr, 55-59 & 61-64, projs mgr, 59-61, prin scientist, 64-67; PROF APPL CHEM, DEPT CHEM ENG, UNIV TORONTO, 67- *Concurrent Pos:* Fel, Univ Western Ont, 43-46. *Honors & Awards:* Dunlop Award, Macromolecular Sci Div, Chem Inst Can, 77. *Mem:* Fel Royal Soc Chem; fel AAAS; sr mem Soc Plastics Engrs; fel Chem Inst Can; fel Plastics & Rubber Inst. *Res:* Structure, properties and uses of synthetic high polymers, specifically rheological, viscoelastic, optical, acoustical, electrical, and thermal; foams, blends and composites. *Mailing Add:* Dept Chem Eng & Appl Chem Univ Toronto Toronto ON M8S 1A4 Can

WILLIAMS, HARRY THOMAS, b Hampton, Va, July 22, 41; m 75; c 5. THEORETICAL PHYSICS. *Educ:* Univ Va, BS, 63, PhD(physics), 67. *Prof Exp:* Res assoc nuclear physics, Nat Bur Stand, 67-69; guest prof, Univ Erlangen-Nürenberg, 70; staff scientist, Kaman Sci div, Kaman Sci Corp, 71-73; asst prof, 74-80, ASSOC PROF PHYSICS, WASHINGTON & LEE UNIV, 80- *Mem:* Sigma Xi. *Res:* Effect of baryon resonance admixtures in nuclear wave function upon nuclear properties and reactions; response of circular loop antennae to electromagnetic fields. *Mailing Add:* Dept of Physics Washington & Lee Univ Lexington VA 24450

WILLIAMS, HENRY WARRINGTON, b Dallas, Tex, July 10, 34; m 58; c 4. ZOOLOGY, ANIMAL BEHAVIOR. *Educ:* Southern Methodist Univ, BS, 55; Utah State Univ, MS, 61, PhD(behavior), 66. *Prof Exp:* Assoc prof, 64-70, chmn div natural sci & math, 73-79, PROF BIOL, WESTMINSTER COL, MO, 70- *Concurrent Pos:* Vis prof ecol, Col Natural Resources, Utah State Univ, Logan, 78- *Mem:* AAAS; Animal Behav Soc; Am Ornith Union; Cooper Ornith Soc; Am Asn Univ Prof (pres, 67-68 & 74-75). *Res:* Investigations in the field of animal behavior with particular concern for sound communication in avian species. *Mailing Add:* Div of Natural Sci & Math Westminster Col Fulton MO 65251

WILLIAMS, HIBBARD E, b Utica, NY, Sept 28, 32; m; c 2. MEDICAL GENETICS. *Educ:* Cornell Univ, AB, 54, MD, 58. *Prof Exp:* Intern & asst resident med, Mass Gen Hosp, 58-60; clin assoc arthritis & metab dis & sr asst surgeon, NIH, 60-62; resident med, Mass Gen Hosp, 62-63, chief resident & teaching asst, Sch Med, Harvard Univ, 63-64, instr, 64-65; from asst prof to assoc prof, 65-72, prof med, Sch Med, Univ Calif, San Francisco, 72-78; prof med & chmn dept, Cornell Med Col, 78-80; PROF MED & DEAN, SCH MED, UNIV CALIF, DAVIS, 80- *Concurrent Pos:* Markle scholar, 68-73; chief med serv, San Francisco Gen Hosp; physician-in-chief, NY Hosp, 78- *Mem:* Am Soc Clin Invest (secy-treas); Asn Am Physicians; Am Fedn Clin Res. *Res:* Inborn errors of metabolism. *Mailing Add:* Sch Med Univ Calif Davis CA 95616

WILLIAMS, HUGH COWIE, b London, Ont, July 23, 43; m 67; c 1. MATHEMATICS, COMPUTER SCIENCE. *Educ:* Univ Waterloo, BSc, 66, Math, 67, PhD(math), 69. *Prof Exp:* Nat Res Coun Can fel, York Univ, 69-70; ASSOC PROF COMPUT SCI, UNIV MAN, 70- *Res:* Application of the computer to problems arising in the theory of numbers. *Mailing Add:* 1 Selwyn Ft Gry Winnipeg MB R3T 3N1 Can

WILLIAMS, HUGH HARRISON, b Boston, Mass, Dec 4, 44; m 70; c 1. EXPERIMENTAL HIGH ENERGY PHYSICS. *Educ:* Haverford Col, BS, 66; Stanford Univ, PhD(physics), 71. *Prof Exp:* Res assoc physics, Brookhaven Nat Lab, 71-73, assoc physicist, 73-74; asst prof, 74-78, ASSOC PROF PHYSICS, UNIV PA, 78- *Mem:* Am Phys Soc. *Res:* Experimental study of elementary particles, their nature and interactions, with particular emphasis on the study of weak interactions. *Mailing Add:* Dept of Physics Univ of Pa Philadelphia PA 19104

WILLIAMS, HULEN BROWN, b Lauratown, Ark, Oct 8, 20; m 42; c 2. PHYSICAL CHEMISTRY. *Educ:* Hendrix Col, AB, 41; La State Univ, MS, 43, PhD(chem), 48. *Prof Exp:* From instr to assoc prof, 43-57, admin asst to dean, 52-56, PROF CHEMISTRY, LA STATE UNIV, BATON ROUGE, 57- HEAD DEPT, 56-, DEAN COL CHEM & PHYSICS, 68- *Honors & Awards:* Coates Award, Am Chem Soc, 63. *Mem:* Am Chem Soc; Electron Micros Soc Am; Am Inst Chemists. *Res:* Light scattering of latices; proteins; protein metal complexes; organic reaction mechanisms. *Mailing Add:* 470 Castle Kirk Ave Baton Rouge LA 70808

WILLIAMS, J(AMES) RICHARD, b Millen, Ga, July 7, 41; m 64; c 4. NUCLEAR & MECHANICAL ENGINEERING. *Educ:* Ga Inst Technol, BS, 62, MS, 64 & 65, PhD(nuclear eng), 67. *Prof Exp:* From asst prof to assoc prof mech & nuclear eng, 67-75, PROF MECH ENG & ASSOC DEAN RES, COL ENG, GA INST TECHNOL, 75- *Concurrent Pos:* NASA res grants, 67-72. *Mem:* Am Nuclear Soc; Am Inst Aeronaut & Astronaut; Am Soc Mech Engrs; Int Solar Energy Soc; Nat Soc Prof Engrs. *Res:* Advanced energy conversion; nuclear magnetohydrodynamic power studies; advanced reactors; air pollution impact evaluation; solar energy. *Mailing Add:* Col of Eng Ga Inst of Technol Atlanta GA 30332

WILLIAMS, JACK A, b Wichita, Kans, June 29, 26; m 49; c 4. ORGANIC GEOCHEMISTRY. *Educ:* Univ Kans, AB, 50, PhD(org chem), 54. *Prof Exp:* Chemist, Standard Oil Co, Ind, 53-57; CHEMIST, RES CTR, AMOCO PROD CO, 57- *Res:* Organic geochemistry of petroleum and associated sedimentary substances. *Mailing Add:* 7317 E 59th St Tulsa OK 74145

WILLIAMS, JACK L R, b Edmonton, Alta, Oct 25, 23; nat US; m 50; c 5. ORGANIC CHEMISTRY. *Educ:* Univ Alta, BSc, 46; Univ Ill, PhD(org chem), 48. *Prof Exp:* Spec asst, Off Rubber Reserve, Univ Ill, 46-48; Du Pont fel, Univ Wis, 48-49; res chemist, 49-55, from res assoc to sr res assoc, 55-68, SR LAB HEAD, EASTMAN KODAK CO, 68- *Mem:* Am Chem Soc. *Res:* Organic synthesis; rubber chemistry; high pressure reactions; oxo synthesis; catalytic hydrogenation; high polymer chemistry; organic photochemistry; photochemistry of boron. *Mailing Add:* Div of Chem Eastman Kodak Co Res Labs Rochester NY 14650

WILLIAMS, JACK MARVIN, b Delta, Colo, Sept 26, 38; m 58; c 3. INORGANIC CHEMISTRY, STRUCTURAL CHEMISTRY. *Educ:* Lewis & Clark Col, BS, 60; Wash State Univ, MS, 64, PhD(phys-inorg chem), 66. *Prof Exp:* Resident res assoc neutron & x-ray diffraction anal, Argonne Nat Lab, 66-68, from asst chemist to assoc chemist, 68-72, chemist, 72-77, SR CHEMIST & GROUP LEADER, CHEM DIV, ARGONNE NAT LAB, 77- *Concurrent Pos:* Guest prof, Univ Copenhagen, Denmark, 80, Univ Mo, 80 & 81; chmn, Gordon Res Conf Inorg Chem, 80; treas, Inorg Div, Am Chem Soc, 82-85. *Mem:* Am Crystallog Asn; Am Chem Soc; Am Phys Soc; AAAS. *Res:* Inorganic chemistry and neutron and x-ray diffraction as applied to the elucidation of the nature of chemical bonding; synthesis and characterization of synthetic metals; chemical bonding. *Mailing Add:* Chem Div Argonne Nat Lab 9700 S Cass Ave Argonne IL 60439

WILLIAMS, JAMES C(LIFFORD), III, b Ocala, Fla, Oct 11, 28; m 51; c 2. AEROSPACE ENGINEERING. *Educ:* Va Polytech Inst, BS, 51, MS, 55; Univ Southern Calif, PhD(eng), 62. *Prof Exp:* Aeronaut res intern, Nat Adv Comt Aeronaut, 51; teaching fel fluid mech, Va Polytech Inst, 53-54; aeronaut engr, NAm Aviation Co, Inc, 54-57; res scientist, Univ Southern Calif, 57-62; PROF AEROSPACE ENG, NC STATE UNIV, 62-, ASSOC HEAD DEPT MECH & AEROSPACE ENG, 72- *Concurrent Pos:* Consult,Systs Corp Am,

Calif, 58-, Tech Prod Div, Waste King Corp, 60-61, Marquardt Corp, 61-64, Guid & Control Div, Litton Systs, Inc, 62-64, Corning Glass Co, NC, 64-65, Missile & Space Systs Div, Douglas Aircraft Co, Calif, 65-66 & Northrop Space Lab, Ala, 66- *Mem:* Assoc fel Am Inst Aeronaut & Astronaut. *Res:* Boundary layer theory including internal viscous flows; gas dynamics; magnetohydrodynamics; aerodynamics. *Mailing Add:* Dept of Mech & Aerospace Eng NC State Univ Raleigh NC 27607

WILLIAMS, JAMES CARL, b Covington, La, 35; m 63; c 4. ANIMAL PARASITOLOGY. *Educ:* Southeastern La Col, BS, 57; La State Univ, Baton Rouge, MS, 62; La State Univ, New Orleans, PhD(med parasitol), 69. *Prof Exp:* From instr to assoc prof, 57-78, PROF VET PARASITOL, LA STATE UNIV, BATON ROUGE, 78- *Mem:* Am Asn Vet Parasitologists; World Asn Advan Vet Pathol; Am Soc Parasitol. *Res:* Immunology of helminth infections; immunologic aspects of host-parasite relationships; epidemiology of parasitism in ruminants; chemotherapy and management control of parasitism in ruminants. *Mailing Add:* Dept of Vet Sci La State Univ Baton Rouge LA 70803

WILLIAMS, JAMES CASE, b Salina, Kans, Dec 7, 38; m 60; c 2. METALLURGY, MATERIALS SCIENCE. *Educ:* Univ Wash, BS, 62, MS, 64, PhD(metall eng), 68. *Prof Exp:* Res engr metall, Boeing Co, 62-68; mem tech staff, Rockwell Sci Ctr, 68-70, group leader, 70-73; prog mgr technol, Aerospace Group Staff, Rockwell Int, 73-75; from assoc prof to prof metall, Carnegie-Mellon Univ, 75-81, PRES, MELLON INST, 81- *Concurrent Pos:* Consult, Air Force Mat Lab, 75-, Garrett Air Res, 77-, Kelsey-Hayes Co, 76- & Westinghouse Co, 77-; adv, Air Force Off Sci Res, 76-; chmn, US deleg, Int Ti Conf, Moscow, 76; co-chmn, US deleg, Int Ti Cong, Kyoto, 80. *Honors & Awards:* Adams Award, Am Welding Soc, 79. *Mem:* Am Soc Metals; Am Inst Mining, Metall & Petrol Engrs; Am Welding Soc; Am Soc Eng Educ; Am Asn Defense Preparedness. *Res:* Physical metallurgy of Ti alloys; phase transformations; fracture and fatigue; electron microscopy; strengthening mechanisms; microstructure especially property relationships, powder metallurgy, welding. *Mailing Add:* Mellon Inst 4400 Fifth Ave Pittsburgh PA 15213

WILLIAMS, JAMES D, b Pratt, Kans, June 8, 32; m 56; c 4. ELECTRICAL ENGINEERING, SOLID STATE PHYSICS. *Educ:* Mass Inst Technol, BS & MS, 60; Purdue Univ, PhD(elec eng), 63. *Prof Exp:* Engr, Gen Radio Co, Mass, 57-59; asst elec eng, Mass Inst Technol, 59-60; instr, Purdue Univ, 60-63; staff mem, 63-66, proj leader adv develop, 66-67, proj leader hybrid microcircuits, 67-68, proj leader semiconductor devices, 68-69, div supvr semiconductor circuits, 69-75, DIV SUPVR, INTRUSION DETECTION SYSTS, SANDIA CORP, 75- *Concurrent Pos:* Instr, Franklin Inst, Boston, 59-60; assoc prof, Univ NMex, 67-68. *Mem:* Inst Elec & Electronics Engrs; Am Phys Soc; Am Soc Testing & Mat; Am Vacuum Soc. *Res:* Hybrid microcircuits; development of thin film processes and devices for application of components to hybrid microcircuits; development of semiconductor devices and integrated circuits for use in complex weapon systems; intrusion detection systems. *Mailing Add:* 9101 Aspen Ave NE Albuquerque NM 87112

WILLIAMS, JAMES EARL, JR, b Freesport, Pa, June 1, 38; m 58; c 3. PHYSICAL CHEMISTRY. *Educ:* Univ Pittsburgh, BS, 65, MS, 72. *Prof Exp:* Scientist chem, 65-73, sr scientist, 73-75, group leader chem, 73-79, SECT HEAD, ALUMINUM CO AM, 79- *Mem:* Am Chem Soc; Fedn Socs Coating Technol; Aluminum Asn; Steel Struct Painting Coun. *Res:* Development of new and improved product grades and manufacturing processes for aluminum pigment and flake powders, and development of new and improved aluminum-pigmented coating systems. *Mailing Add:* Alcoa Labs Alcoa Tech Ctr Alcoa Center PA 15069

WILLIAMS, JAMES GARNER, see Keeton-Williams, James G

WILLIAMS, JAMES GERARD, b New Kensington, Pa, April 12, 41. GEODYNAMICS, SOLAR SYSTEM DYNAMICS. *Educ:* Calif Inst Technol, BS, 63; Univ Calif, Los Angeles, PhD(planetary & space sci), 69. *Prof Exp:* mem tech staff, NAm Rockwell, 62-68; RES SCIENTIST, JET PROPULSION LAB, CALIF, 69- *Mem:* Int Astron Union; Am Geophys Union; Am Astron Soc. *Res:* Lunar laser range data; orbit of moon; rotations of earth and moon; dynamical evolution of asteroid orbits; asteroid families; main belt morphology; planet crossing asteroids. *Mailing Add:* Jet Propulsion Lab 264-720 4800 Oak Grove Dr Pasadena CA 91109

WILLIAMS, JAMES HENRY, JR, b Los Angeles, Calif, July 14, 18; m 39; c 2. AGRONOMY. *Educ:* Ore State Col, BS, 49; Iowa State Col, MS, 50, PhD(agron), 52. *Prof Exp:* Res assoc, Iowa State Col, 50-52; from asst prof to assoc prof agron, Univ Nebr, Lincoln, 52-72, PROF AGRON, UNIV NEBR, LINCOLN, EAST CAMPUS, 72- *Mem:* Am Soc Agron; Crop Sci Soc Am; Soc Econ Bot; AAAS. *Res:* Soybean breeding. *Mailing Add:* 319 Keim Hall Univ Nebr East Campus Lincoln NE 68583

WILLIAMS, JAMES HENRY, JR, b Newport News, Va, Apr 4, 41; m 75; c 1. MECHANICAL ENGINEERING. *Educ:* Mass Inst Technol, SB, 67, SM, 68; Univ Cambridge, PhD(mech eng), 70. *Prof Exp:* Apprentice machinist, Newport News Shipbuilding & Dry Dock Co, 60-61, apprentice designer, 61-65, mech designer, 65, sr design engr, 68-70; assoc prof, 70-80, PROF MECH ENG, MASS INST TECHNOL, 80- *Concurrent Pos:* NSF res initiation grant, Mass Inst Technol, 72-74, du Pont-Young fac grant, 72-73, Edgerton Professorship, 73-75. *Honors & Awards:* Charles F Bailey Awards, Bronze, 61, Silver, 62, Gold, 63; Teetor Award, Soc Automotive Engrs, 74. *Res:* Applied mechanics and materials, shell theory; earthquake isolation research, nondestructive evaluation and composite materials. *Mailing Add:* Dept of Mech Eng Rm 3-360 77 Massachusetts Ave Cambridge MA 02139

WILLIAMS, JAMES HUTCHISON, b Westerville, Ohio, Feb 20, 22; m 43; c 4. OBSTETRICS & GYNECOLOGY. *Educ:* Otterbein Col, AB, 44; Ohio State Univ, MD, 46, MMSc, 52; Am Bd Obstet & Gynec, dipl. *Prof Exp:* From instr to assoc prof, 55-70, assoc dir, Inst Perinatal Studies, 60-64 & Ctr Perinatal Studies, 65-70, PROF OBSTET & GYNEC, OHIO STATE UNIV, 70-, ASSOC DEAN COL MED, 61- *Mem:* Fel Am Col Surg; fel Am Col Obstet & Gynec. *Res:* Perinatal morbidity and mortality; selection of medical students; medical student evaluation in education. *Mailing Add:* Col of Med Ohio State Univ Columbus OH 43210

WILLIAMS, JAMES LOVON, JR, b Salem, Ind, May 16, 29; m 52; c 3. WEED SCIENCE, PLANT PHYSIOLOGY. *Educ:* Purdue Univ, Lafayette, BS, 57, MS, 59, PhD(plant path), 61. *Prof Exp:* From instr to assoc prof, 60-71, PROF WEED SCI, PURDUE UNIV, LAFAYETTE, 71- *Mem:* Weed Sci Soc Am; Am Soc Agron; Crop Sci Soc Am. *Res:* Weed control systems to minimize pollution potential from weeds and their control; effects of soil properties and climatic factors on control systems; fate of herbicides in soil and water. *Mailing Add:* Dept of Bot & Plant Path Purdue Univ Lilly Hall Life Sci West Lafayette IN 47907

WILLIAMS, JAMES MARVIN, b Denver, Colo, Apr 27, 34; m 61; c 2. NUCLEAR & CHEMICAL ENGINEERING. *Educ:* Univ NMex, BS, 57, MS, 64. *Prof Exp:* Staff mem, Los Alamos Sci Lab, 60-69; chief, Systs Studies Br, Off Safeguards & Mat Mgt, US AEC, 69-72; assoc group leader, Laser Div, Los Alamos Sci Lab, 72-74; asst dir develop & technol, Off Magnetic Fusion Energy, Dept of Energy, 74-78; div leader, systs, Anal & Assessment Div, 78-79, ASST DIR PLANNING & ANAL, LOS ALAMOS NAT LAB, 79- *Mem:* Am Nuclear Soc. *Res:* Development of fusion plasma heaters, magnets and materials; interdisciplinary policy research and analysis; technology assessment; energy systems modeling and economic analysis. *Mailing Add:* Los Alamos Nat Lab Mail Stop 195 PO Box 1663 Los Alamos NM 87545

WILLIAMS, JAMES STANLEY, b Coronado, Calif, Oct 12, 34; m 56; c 3. STATISTICS. *Educ:* Wash State Univ, BS, 55; Agr & Mech Col Tex, MS, 57; NC State Col, PhD(exp & math statist), 61. *Prof Exp:* Instr genetics, Agr & Mech Col, Tex, 56-57; statistician, Res Triangle Inst, NC, 60-62; PROF STATIST, COLO STATE UNIV, 62-, CHMN DEPT, 77- *Concurrent Pos:* Assoc ed, Biometrics, 72- *Mem:* Fel Am Statist Asn; Biomet Soc; Inst Math Statist. *Res:* Theory of statistical inference; multivariate analysis; indexing theory; population genetics. *Mailing Add:* Dept of Statist Colo State Univ Ft Collins CO 80521

WILLIAMS, JAMES THOMAS, b Martinsville, Va, Nov 10, 33; m 62; c 2. MEDICINE. *Educ:* Howard Univ, BS, 54, MD, 58; Am Bd Internal Med, dipl, 67, 74 & 80, cert endocrinol & metab, 72. *Prof Exp:* Intern, Philadelphia Gen Hosp, 58-59; resident internal med, DC Gen Hosp, 59-60 & Freedmen's Hosp, 60-62 & 64-65; fel endocrinol, 65-67, asst prof med, 67-74, ASSOC PROF MED, HOWARD UNIV, 74- *Mem:* Fel Am Col Physicians; Endocrine Soc; Am Diabetes Asn. *Res:* Clinical endocrinology and metabolic diseases. *Mailing Add:* Howard Univ Hosp 2041 Georgia Ave NW Washington DC 20060

WILLIAMS, JEAN PAUL, b New York, NY, Dec 29, 18; m 45. ANALYTICAL CHEMISTRY. *Educ:* Kent State Univ, BS, 40; Univ NC, PhD(chem), 50. *Prof Exp:* Chemist, Nat Bur Standards, 42-45; instr chem, Univ NC, 45-50; res chemist, Corning Glass Works, 50-57, mgr, Tech Serv Res Dept, 57-64, mgr, Instrumental Anal Res Dept, 64-73, mgr anal serv res, 73-81; RETIRED. *Mem:* AAAS; Am Chem Soc; Am Ceramic Soc; Soc Appl Spectros; Microbeam Anal Soc. *Res:* Inorganic chemical, instrumental and x-ray analysis; classical wet methods; polarography; flame spectrophotometry; glass property measurements; microscopy; mass spectrometry; electron microprobe analysis; atomic absorption and emission. *Mailing Add:* 1824 Cedar Ave Canon City CO 81212

WILLIAMS, JEFFREY F, b Bristol, Eng, Aug 28, 42; m 64. PARASITOLOGY, IMMUNOLOGY. *Educ:* Univ Bristol, BVSc, 64; Univ Pa, PhD(parasitol), 68. *Prof Exp:* Parasitologist, Pan-Am Health Orgn, Buenos Aires, Arg, 68-71; from asst prof to assoc prof microbiol, 71-77, dean res vet med, 77-79, PROF MICROBIOL & PUBHEALTH ASST, MICH STATE UNIV, 77- *Concurrent Pos:* dir, Sudan Proj on Collaborative Res on Tropical Dis, 79- *Mem:* Brit Soc Immunol; Am Soc Parasitol; Royal Soc Trop Med; Am Soc Trop Med. *Res:* Mechanisms of resistance to helminth infections in domestic animals and man. *Mailing Add:* Dept of Microbiol & Pub Health Mich State Univ East Lansing MI 48824

WILLIAMS, JEFFREY WALTER, b Argyle, Wis, Oct 4, 51; m 73. ENZYMOLOGY, BIOTECHNOLOGY. *Educ:* Univ Wis, Madison, BS, 73, PhD(pharm biochem), 77. *Prof Exp:* Fel biochem, Australian Nat Univ, 79; res fel, Univ Sussex, 79-80; ASST PROF MED CHEM, OHIO STATE UNIV, 80- *Concurrent Pos:* Prin investr, Ohio State Univ, 81- *Res:* Characterization and tight-binding inhibition of enzymes involved in antibiotic inactivation, cancer chemotherapy and drug metabolism; biochemical mechanisms of heavy metal detoxification by bacteria. *Mailing Add:* Col Pharm Ohio State Univ Columbus OH 43210

WILLIAMS, JEROME, b Toronto, Ont, July 15, 26; m 53; c 2. PHYSICAL OCEANOGRAPHY. *Educ:* Univ Md, BS, 50; Johns Hopkins Univ, MA, 52. *Prof Exp:* Res staff asst, Chesapeake Bay Inst, Johns Hopkins Univ, 52-56; physicist, Vitro Labs, 56-57; asst prof physics, 57-64, assoc prof oceanog, 64-72, res prof environ protection, 72-74, PROF OCEANOG, US NAVAL ACAD, 74- *Concurrent Pos:* Res assoc, Chesapeake Bay Inst, Johns Hopkins Univ, 57-71; tech ed, Naval Inst, 66-75. *Mem:* AAAS; Marine Technol Soc; Am Geophys Union; Instrument Soc Am; Estuarine Res Fedn (vpres, 71-73, secy, 73-75). *Res:* Underwater transparency; oceanographic instrumentation; environmental protection. *Mailing Add:* Dept of Oceanog US Naval Acad Annapolis MD 21402

WILLIAMS, JESSE BASCOM, b Lone Oak, Tex, Oct 24, 17; m 44; c 3. ANIMAL SCIENCE. *Educ:* Okla State Univ, BS, 47; Pa State Univ, MS, 48, PhD(dairy husb), 50. *Prof Exp:* Res asst dairy husb, Pa State Univ, 48-50; asst prof, NDak State Univ, asst dairy husbandman, Agr Exp Sta, 50-55; from asst prof to assoc prof, 55-61, PROF ANIMAL SCI, UNIV MINN, ST PAUL,

61- *Mem:* Fel AAAS; Am Soc Animal Sci; Am Dairy Sci Asn. *Res:* Infant ruminant nutrition; synthetic diets; mechanical feeding devices; heat treatment of dried skim milk powders; immunoglobulin absorption patterns. *Mailing Add:* Dept of Animal Sci Univ of Minn St Paul MN 55101

WILLIAMS, JIMMY CALVIN, b Palestine, Tex, Oct 26, 43; m 67; c 5. MICROBIOLOGY, BIOCHEMISTRY. *Educ:* Tex A&M Univ, BS, 69, MS, 71, PhD(biochem), 73. *Prof Exp:* Res assoc cancer, Lab Exp Oncol, Riley Cancer Wing, Ind Sch Med, 73-74; microbiologist, Naval Med Res Inst, Nat Naval Med Ctr, 74-78; BIOCHEMIST, NIH, NAT INST ALLERGY & INFECTIOUS DIS, ROCKY MOUNTAIN LAB, 78- *Concurrent Pos:* Vis instr, Lab Exp Oncol, Ind Sch Med, 74, vis asst prof, 75- *Mem:* Sigma Xi; Nat Am Soc Microbiol; NY Acad Sci; AAAS. *Res:* Molecular biology of rickettsiae entailing detailed analysis of structure-function immunology and the biochemical strategy of obligate intracellular activity of cytoplasmic, phagosomal and phagolysosomal pathogens; basic biology of rat hepatomas with emphasis on the biosynthesis of pyrimidine enzymes and a combined chemotherapy approach to the problems of rapid cellular proliferation. *Mailing Add:* Nat Inst Health Rocky Mountain Lab Hamilton MT 59840

WILLIAMS, JOEL LAWSON, b Sarecta, NC, Nov 10, 41; m 62; c 2. POLYMER CHEMISTRY. *Educ:* NC State Univ, BS, 65, MS, 67, PhD(polymer sci), 70. *Prof Exp:* Sr chemist polymer res, Camille Dreyfus Lab, Research Triangle Inst, 62-74; HEAD MAT SCI DEPT, BECTON DICKINSON RES CTR, RESEARCH TRIANGLE PARK, NC, 74- *Concurrent Pos:* Adj prof chem eng, NC State Univ, 72- *Mem:* Am Chem Soc. *Res:* Permeability and diffusion in membranes, polymer synthesis and characterization with special emphasis on the utilization of radiation chemistry as a tool for graft modification of polymeric substrates, ionic polymerization, high-energy irradiation applications, irradiation grafting and blood compatibility of polymers. *Mailing Add:* Becton Dickinson Res Ctr Box 12016 Research Triangle Park NC 27709

WILLIAMS, JOEL MANN, JR, b Suffolk, Va, Apr 6, 40; m 62; c 2. FUEL SCIENCE, PHYSICAL ORGANIC CHEMISTRY. *Educ:* Col William & Mary, BS, 62; Northwestern Univ, Evanston, PhD(org chem), 66. *Prof Exp:* NSF fel, Univ Minn, Minneapolis, 66-67, asst prof chem, 67-68; res chemist, Benger Lab, E I du Pont de Nemours & Co, Inc, Va, 68-72; MEM STAFF, LOS ALAMOS NAT LAB, 72- *Mem:* Sigma Xi. *Res:* Environmental chemistry associated with the disposal of energy related wastes; trace element release from coals, oil shales, uranium and their associated coal and coal wastes, especially trace elements of environmental concern; wastes; geothermal energy and uranium mill tailings. *Mailing Add:* CMB-8 MS 734 Los Alamos Nat Lab Univ of Calif Los Alamos NM 87545

WILLIAMS, JOEL QUITMAN, b Lake Charles, La, Mar 6, 22; m 47; c 2. PHYSICS. *Educ:* Centenary Col, BS, 43; Ga Inst Technol, MS, 48; Duke Univ, PhD(physics), 52. *Prof Exp:* From asst prof to assoc prof, 46-49, 51-70, PROF PHYSICS, GA INST TECHNOL, 70- *Mem:* Am Phys Soc; Am Asn Physics Teachers. *Res:* Microwave spectroscopy. *Mailing Add:* Sch of Physics Ga Inst of Technol Atlanta GA 30332

WILLIAMS, JOHN A(RTHUR), b San Bernardino, Calif, Aug 24, 29; m 59. HYDROMECHANICS, CIVIL ENGINEERING. *Educ:* Univ Calif, Berkeley, BS, 52, ME, 54, PhD(civil eng), 65. *Prof Exp:* From asst prof to assoc prof civil eng, 63-72, PROF CIVIL ENG, UNIV HAWAII, 72- *Concurrent Pos:* Asst engr, Hawaii Inst Geophys, 64-66, assoc researcher, 69; proj mgr, Water Resources Res Ctr, 68-76. *Mem:* Am Soc Civil Engrs; Am Geophys Union. *Res:* Hydromechanics; water waves; groundwater movement; geophysical fluid mechanics. *Mailing Add:* Dept Civil Eng Univ Hawaii 2540 Dole St Honolulu HI 96822

WILLIAMS, JOHN ALBERT, b Springfield, Ill, Mar 28, 37; m 59; c 2. ASTRONOMY. *Educ:* Univ Mich, AB, 49; Univ Calif, Berkeley, PhD(astron), 63. *Prof Exp:* NSF fel, Univ Calif, Berkeley & Princeton Univ, 63-64; from instr to asst prof astron, Univ Mich, Ann Arbor, 64-70; ASSOC PROF PHYSICS, ALBION COL, 70- *Mem:* AAAS; Am Astron Soc. *Res:* Photometry of astronomical objects; quantitative spectral classification; interstellar matter. *Mailing Add:* Dept of Physics Albion Col Albion MI 49224

WILLIAMS, JOHN ANDREW, b Des Moines, Iowa, Aug 3, 41; m 65; c 2. PHYSIOLOGY. *Educ:* Cent Wash State Col, BA, 63; Univ Wash, MD & PhD(physiol, biophys), 68. *Prof Exp:* Staff assoc, Clin Endocrinol Br, Nat Inst Arthritis & Metab Dis, 69-71; asst prof, 72-74, assoc prof, 74-79, PROF PHYSIOL, UNIV CALIF, SAN FRANCISCO, 79- *Concurrent Pos:* NIH fel, Dept Pharmacol, Univ Utah, 68-69; Helen Hay Whitney Found fel, Univ Cambridge, 71-72; USPHS grants, Univ Calif, San Francisco, 73-84, Nat Cystic Fibrosis Found grant, 74-77; assoc dir, Cell Biol Res Lab, Mt Zion Hosp & Med Ctr, San Francisco, 79- *Mem:* Endocrine Soc; Am Soc Cell Biol; Am Physiol Soc; Am Soc Clin Investr. *Res:* Cellular physiology; endocrinology. *Mailing Add:* Dept Physiol Univ Calif Sch Med San Francisco CA 94143

WILLIAMS, JOHN C(HAMBERLIN), electrical engineering, see previous edition

WILLIAMS, JOHN C, b Hazard, Ky, June 18, 25; m 57; c 1. ZOOLOGY. *Educ:* Mich State Univ, BS, 53; Univ Ky, MS, 57; Univ Louisville, PhD(biol), 63. *Prof Exp:* Instr biol, Mary Washington Col, Univ Va, 56-57; asst prof, Transylvania Col, 57-59; from asst prof to prof, Murray State Univ, 62-69; assoc prof, 69-72, PROF BIOL, EASTERN KY UNIV, 72- *Concurrent Pos:* Mussel Fishery Invests grant, Tenn, Ohio & Green Rivers, 66-69; Commercial Fisheries Invests of Ky River grant, 72-74. *Mem:* Am Fisheries Soc; Am Soc Ichthyol & Herpet. *Res:* Fisheries biology; mammalogy; herpetology; natural history of freshwater mussels. *Mailing Add:* Dept of Biol Sci Eastern Ky Univ Richmond KY 40475

WILLIAMS, JOHN CASWELL, plant genetics, statistics, see previous edition

WILLIAMS, JOHN COLLINS, JR, b Jackson, Tenn, Jan 19, 45; c 2. ORGANIC CHEMISTRY, PHYSICAL CHEMISTRY. *Educ:* Millsaps Col, BS, 67; Tulane Univ, PhD(chem), 72. *Prof Exp:* Instr chem, Sch Arts & Sci, Tulane Univ, 68-71; asst prof, 72-77, ASSOC PROF CHEM, RI COL, 77- *Mem:* Am Chem Soc; Sigma Xi. *Res:* Synthetic, physical and theoretical chemistry and cytotoxicity of organophosphorus heterocycles; P-31 nuclear magnetic resonance; polarography; photochemistry of aromatic phosphines; group theory and isomerization reactions; educational approaches to introductory spectroscopy. *Mailing Add:* RI Col Dept of Phys Sci 600 Mt Pleasant Ave Providence RI 02908

WILLIAMS, JOHN DELANE, b Ordway, Colo, Oct 26, 38; m 58, 80; c 2. STATISTICS, EDUCATIONAL PSYCHOLOGY. *Educ:* Univ Northern Colo, BA, 59, MA, 60, PhD(appl statist), 66. *Prof Exp:* Instr math, Western Wyo Community Col, 62-65; from asst prof to assoc prof, 66-71, PROF STATIST, UNIV NDAK, 71- *Concurrent Pos:* Sr consult, Comput Ctr, Univ NDak, 72-, statist consult, Proj Reclamation, 76- *Mem:* Am Statist Asn; Am Educ Res Asn; Am Psychol Asn. *Res:* Appl statist in multiple linear regression; statistical application in areas of species diversity, coal reclamation, and educational psychology. *Mailing Add:* Ctr Teaching & Learning Univ of NDak Grand Forks ND 58201

WILLIAMS, JOHN ERNEST, b Dublin, Ireland, Mar 27, 35; m 57; c 2. METALLURGY, MECHANICAL ENGINEERING. *Educ:* Col Advan Technol, Birmingham, Eng, ACT, 61; Univ Birmingham, PhD(metall), 64. *Prof Exp:* Res asst metall, Int Nickel Corp, Eng, 52-58; res fel metal cutting, Univ Birmingham, 61-64, sr res fel, 64-67; lectr, Brunel Univ, 67-70; ASSOC PROF MECH ENG, UNIV CONN, 70- *Concurrent Pos:* Consult, Cornell Univ, 69 & Gen Elec Corp, 71-72. *Mem:* Am Soc Mech Engrs; Brit Inst Metallurgists. *Res:* Materials and mechanical engineering with particular reference to manufacturing and design engineering. *Mailing Add:* Dept of Mech Eng Univ of Conn Storrs CT 06268

WILLIAMS, JOHN F, JR, b Louisville, Ky, Oct 25, 31; m 66. INTERNAL MEDICINE, CARDIOLOGY. *Educ:* Ind Univ, Indianapolis, MD, 56. *Prof Exp:* Intern med, Univ Minn Hosps, 56-57; resident internal med, Med Ctr, Ind Univ, Indianapolis, 57-59, from asst prof to assoc prof internal med, Sch Med, 65-70; PROF MED & DIR DIV CARDIOL, UNIV TEX MED BR GALVESTON, 70- *Concurrent Pos:* Am Heart Asn res fel cardiol, Med Ctr, Ind Univ, Indianapolis, 59-61; USPHS res fel, 61-63; fel, Cardiol Br, Nat Heart Inst, 63-65; chief cardiovasc res lab, Vet Admin Hosp, Indianapolis, 65-70. *Mem:* Am Soc Clin Invest; Am Physiol Soc; Am Fedn Clin Res; fel Am Col Cardiol; fel Am Col Physicians. *Res:* Cardiovascular physiology and pharmacology. *Mailing Add:* Div Cardiol Univ Tex Med Br Galveston TX 77550

WILLIAMS, JOHN FREDERICK, b York, SC, May 14, 23; m 45; c 2. CHEMISTRY. *Educ:* Univ SC, BS, 44; Clemson Univ, MS, 51; Univ Va, PhD(chem), 54. *Prof Exp:* Instr chem, Clemson Univ, 49-51; sr chemist anal chem, Res Dept, Liggett & Myers Tobacco Co, 54-60, res supvr anal chem, Res Dept, Liggett & Myers Inc, 60-80; STATE CHEMIST & DIR LAB, GA DEPT AGR, 80- *Mem:* Am Chem Soc; Coblentz Soc; Soc Appl Spectros; Asn Food & Drug Officials. *Res:* Development and application of chromatographic, spectrophotometric, automatic and classical methods of analysis in the study of natural products. *Mailing Add:* Lab Div Georgia Dept Agr Atlanta GA 30334

WILLIAMS, JOHN PAUL, b Laramie, Wyo, Aug 11, 46; m 67; c 2. INORGANIC CHEMISTRY. *Educ:* Univ Wyo, BS, 69, MS, 70; Ohio State Univ, PhD(inorg chem), 75. *Prof Exp:* Fel inorg chem, Univ Wis, 75-76; mem staff chem, Univ Cincinnati, 76-77; mem staff inorg chem, Ind Univ-Purdue Univ, Indianapolis, 77-79; ASST PROF CHEM, UNIV CINCINNATI, 79- *Mem:* Am Chem Soc. *Res:* Syntheic studies of organotransition metal isocyanide complexes. *Mailing Add:* Dept Chem Univ Cincinnati Cincinnati OH 45231

WILLIAMS, JOHN PETER, b London, Eng, Apr 17, 39; m 63; c 2. PLANT BIOCHEMISTRY, CYTOLOGY. *Educ:* Univ Leicester, BSc, 60; Univ London, PhD(plant physiol & cytol) & dipl, Imp Col, 63. *Prof Exp:* Asst prof, 63-68, assoc prof, 68-76, PROF BOT, UNIV TORONTO, 76- *Mem:* Am Soc Plant Physiol; Can Soc Plant Physiol. *Res:* Structure and function of chloroplasts; metabolism; lipid content and development; aspects of photosynthesis. *Mailing Add:* Dept of Bot Univ of Toronto Toronto ON M5S 1A1 Can

WILLIAMS, JOHN RODERICK, b Birmingham, Eng, July 5, 40; m 74; c 2. SYNTHETIC ORGANIC CHEMISTRY. *Educ:* Univ Western Australia, BSc, 62, PhD(org chem), 66. *Prof Exp:* Vis fel org photochem, NIH, 66-67; NIH fel & res assoc, Columbia Univ, 67-68; asst prof, 68-74, assoc prof, 74-81, PROF ORG CHEM, TEMPLE UNIV, 81- *Concurrent Pos:* Vis prof, State Univ Ghent, Belgium, 81. *Mem:* Am Chem Soc; assoc mem Royal Australian Chem Inst; fel The Chem Soc. *Res:* Photosensitivity and photobiology; synthesis of natural products; marine and steroid chemistry. *Mailing Add:* Dept of Chem Temple Univ Philadelphia PA 19122

WILLIAMS, JOHN T, b Bristol Twp, Ohio, Aug 2, 23; m 49; c 2. PHYSICAL CHEMISTRY. *Educ:* Hamline Univ, BS, 44; Univ Minn, MS, 49; Iowa State Col, PhD(chem), 54. *Prof Exp:* From asst prof to assoc prof, 54-63, PROF CHEM, COLO SCH MINES, 63- *Mem:* Am Chem Soc; AAAS. *Res:* Thermodynamics; phase equilibrium. *Mailing Add:* Dept of Chem & Geochem Colo Sch of Mines Golden CO 80401

WILLIAMS, JOHN WARREN, b Woburn, Mass, Feb 10, 98; m 25; c 1. PHYSICAL BIOCHEMISTRY. *Educ:* Worcester Polytech Inst, BS, 21; Univ Wis, MS, 22, PhD(chem), 25. *Hon Degrees:* DSc, Worcester Polytech Inst, 73. *Prof Exp:* Asst chem, 21-25, from instr to prof, 25-68, EMER PROF CHEM, UNIV WIS-MADISON, 68- *Concurrent Pos:* Nat Res Coun fel, Copenhagen Univ & Univ Leipzig, 27-28; Int Educ Bd fel, Univ Uppsala, 34-

35, Nobel guest prof, 68; vis prof, Calif Inst Technol, 46-47 & 53-54; Guggenheim fel, Copenhagen Univ, Oxford & Calif Inst Technol, 56-57; mem comt colloid sci, Nat Res Coun. *Honors & Awards:* Kendall Award, Am Chem Soc, 55. *Mem:* Nat Acad Sci; Am Chem Soc; Am Soc Biol Chem. *Res:* Physical chemistry of the proteins and high polymers. *Mailing Add:* Dept Chem Univ Wis Madison WI 53706

WILLIAMS, JOHN WATKINS, III, b Alexandria, La, Mar 11, 42; m 70. CYTOGENETICS. *Educ:* Univ Southwestern La, BS, 65; La State Univ, MS, 68, PhD(genetics zool), 71. *Prof Exp:* Res assoc genetics, La State Univ, 68-70; asst prof, 71-74, ASSOC PROF GENETICS & EMBRYOL, TUSKEGEE INST, 74- *Mem:* AAAS; Genetics Soc Am; Sigma Xi. *Res:* Nature of DNA sequences in lateral loop axes of T viridescens lampbrush chromosomes and the chromosomal incorporation of exogenous DNA in Drosophila polytene chromosomes; banding of amphibian chromosomes. *Mailing Add:* Dept of Biol Tuskegee Inst Tuskegee Institute AL 36088

WILLIAMS, JOHN WESLEY, b Mobile, Ala, Dec 31, 44; m 67; c 2. ORGANIC CHEMISTRY. *Educ:* Univ Ala, BS, 67; Univ Ill, MS, 70, PhD(org chem), 73. *Prof Exp:* Rockefeller Found fel, Dept Entom, Univ Ill, 73-75; sr chemist org chem, Abbott Labs, 75-79; SR RES CHEMIST, STAUFFER CHEM CO, 79- *Mem:* Am Chem Soc; AAAS. *Res:* Synthetic organic chemistry especially industrial and agricultural fungicides and bactericides. *Mailing Add:* Stauffer Chem Co 1200 S 47th St Richmond CA 94804

WILLIAMS, JOHN WHARTON, b Wichita, Kans, May 3, 45; m 68. GEOLOGY. *Educ:* Col William & Mary, BS, 67; Stanford Univ, MS, 68, PhD(geol), 70. *Prof Exp:* Geologist, Calif Div Mines & Geol, 71-76; asst prof, 76-80, ASSOC PROF GEOL, SAN JOSE STATE UNIV, 80- *Mem:* AAAS; Geol Soc Am; Asn Eng Geologists. *Res:* Detection, analysis and delineation of geologic hazards as to provide for the proper location and construction of engineering works. *Mailing Add:* Dept of Geol San Jose State Univ San Jose CA 95192

WILLIAMS, JOSEPH BURTON, b San Angelo, Tex, June 11, 46; m 76. ECOLOGY, BIOLOGY. *Educ:* David Lipscomb Col, BA, 69; Univ Ill, MA, 72, PhD(ecol), 76. *Prof Exp:* Vis instr biol, Univ Ill, 75-76; ASST PROF ECOL, PEPPERDINE UNIV, 77- *Mem:* Ecol Soc Am; Am Ornithologists Union; Cooper Ornith Soc; Sigma Xi. *Res:* Community organization in birds; ecological energetics; pollination ecology. *Mailing Add:* Dept of Natural Sci Pepperdine Univ Malibu CA 90265

WILLIAMS, JOSEPH FRANCIS, b Indianapolis, Ind, April 7, 38; m 67; c 2. IMMUNOPHARMACOLOGY, PHARMACOKINETICS. *Educ:* Ind Univ, AB, 62; Univ Utah, PhD(pharmacol), 71. *Prof Exp:* Fel pharmacol, Univ Minn, 70-72; asst prof, 72-78, ASSOC PROF PHARMACOL, UNIV SFLA, 78- *Mem:* Sigma Xi; Int Soc Study Xenobiotics. *Res:* Mechanisms involved in the regulation of the hepatic mixed function oxidase system; the interrelationship between the hepatic parenchyma and kupffer cell; effects of immunoactive substances on hepatic cellular metabolic activity. *Mailing Add:* Dept Pharmacol & Therapeut Col Med Univ SFla Tampa FL 33612

WILLIAMS, JOSEPH JOHN, b Toronto, Ont, Oct 7, 43; m 68; c 3. MATHEMATICS. *Educ:* Univ Toronto, BSc, 66, MSc, 67, PhD(math), 70. *Prof Exp:* Asst prof, 70-76, ASSOC PROF MATH, FAC SCI, UNIV MAN, 76-, ASSOC PROF APPL MATH, 78- *Res:* Theory of infinite matrices; differential equations; C algebras. *Mailing Add:* Dept of Appl Math Fac of Sci Univ of Man Winnipeg MB R3T 2N2 Can

WILLIAMS, JOSEPH LEE, b New Bern, NC, Nov 2, 36; m 62; c 4. FOOD CHEMISTRY, LIPID CHEMISTRY. *Educ:* Morehouse Col, BS, 60; Tuskegee Inst Technol, MS, 62; Univ Ill, Urbana, PhD(food sci), 70. *Prof Exp:* George Washington Carver fel, Carver Found, Tuskegee Inst Technol, 60-62; chemist, Monsanto Co, 63-66; USPHS fel, Burnsides Res Lab, Univ Ill, 68-70; dir multidisciplinary labs, Sch Vet Med, Tuskegee Inst Technol, 70-72; SR SCIENTIST, RES & DEVELOP DIV, KRAFTCO CORP, 72- *Concurrent Pos:* Consult & mgr audiovisual & multimedia learning resource ctr for sci & med stud & individualized study progs, Tuskegee Inst Technol, 70-72; Ninth Annual George Washington Carver lectr, 71. *Mem:* Fel AAAS; Am Chem Soc; Am Oil Chem Soc; fel Am Inst Chemists; Inst Food Technologists. *Res:* Food science and lipid chemistry as it relates to the feeding of the public; biochemical utilization by man and the nutritional impact upon man; flavor constituents in edible oils, shelf life of products; correlation of physical and sensory method for evaluation of flavor components in edible oils; application of chemometrics to edible oil quality. *Mailing Add:* Edible Oil Prod Lab R&D Div Kraft Inc 801 Waukegan Rd Glenview IL 60025

WILLIAMS, JOSEPHINE LOUISE, b Bowling Green, Ky, May 23, 26. PHYSICAL CHEMISTRY, SURFACE CHEMISTRY. *Educ:* Western Ky Univ, BS, 47; Northwestern Univ, MS, 50; Univ Cincinnati, BS, 58. *Prof Exp:* Res assoc heterocyclics, Dept Chem, Western Ky Univ, 47-48; sr chemist, Cimcool Div, 50-55, sr res chemist, Cent Res Div, 55-57, sr res supvr abrasives, Metal Working Fluids, 57-71, sr res supvr, Com Develop Dept, 71-75, sr res assoc, 75-77, mgr, Com Develop Dept, 77-79, DIR APPL SCI RES & DEVELOP, CINCINNATI MILACRON INC, 79- *Mem:* Am Chem Soc. *Res:* Chemistry of friction, lubrication and wear; mechanisms of wear of abrasives and bonded abrasives; metal working fluids and processes; corrosion, surfactants, emulsions, electrode processes; plastics processing and equipment research and development. *Mailing Add:* Dept 97B Cincinnati Milacron Inc Cincinnati OH 45209

WILLIAMS, JOY ELIZABETH P, b Blackshear, Ga, June 12, 29; m 59; c 2. BACTERIOLOGY, BIOCHEMISTRY. *Educ:* Univ Ga, BS, 50, MS, 58, PhD(bact), 61. *Prof Exp:* Teacher high sch, Ga, 52-57; USPHS fel biol div, Oak Ridge Nat Lab, 61-63; res assoc bact, 63-66, asst prof, 66-68, mgr biol automated info, Comput Ctr, 68-70, ASST PROF MICROS & ASSOC DIR HONS PROG, UNIV GA, 70- *Concurrent Pos:* Mem, Nat Collegiate Hons Coun. *Mem:* AAAS; Am Soc Microbiol; NY Acad Sci. *Res:* Bacterial metabolism of alginic and mannuronic acids; formic hydrogenlyase systems in bacteria; bacterial degradation of organic synthetic sulfur compounds; sulfur metabolism in bacteria. *Mailing Add:* Hons Prog Univ of Ga Athens GA 30601

WILLIAMS, JULIAN, geoenvironmental science, deceased

WILLIAMS, KEITH C(HARLES), b Shorncliffe, Eng, Sept 29, 36; m 63. CHEMICAL ENGINEERING. *Educ:* Univ Birmingham, BSc, 58, PhD(chem eng), 62; Univ Del, MBA, 71. *Prof Exp:* Res engr, 62-67, res supvr, 67-72, consult supvr, 72-76, SR RES SUPVR, E I DU PONT DE NEMOURS & CO, INC, 76- *Mem:* Am Inst Chem Engrs; Brit Inst Chem Engrs. *Res:* Process development; reactor engineering; low energy separations; coal gasification; polymer processing. *Mailing Add:* Eng Technol Lab Bldg 304 E I Du Pont de Nemours Exp Sta Wilmington DE 19898

WILLIAMS, KENNETH BOCK, b Petersburg, Tex, Jan 18, 30; m 52; c 2. PLANT TAXONOMY, ZOOLOGY. *Educ:* Abilene Christian Col, BS, 50; Univ Tex, MA, 59; Univ Ariz, PhD(bot), 67. *Prof Exp:* Asst prof, 67-73, ASSOC PROF BIOL, ABILENE CHRISTIAN COL, 73- *Res:* Biosystematic studies in the Gramineae. *Mailing Add:* Dept of Biol Abilene Christian Col Sta ACC Abilene TX 79601

WILLIAMS, KENNETH L, b Saybrook, Ill, Sept 4, 34; m 54; c 3. ZOOLOGY. *Educ:* Univ Ill, Urbana, BS, 60, MS, 61; La State Univ, Baton Rouge, PhD(zool), 70. *Prof Exp:* Instr comp anat & biol, Millikin Univ, 62-64; assoc prof, 66-79, PROF ZOOL & BIOL, NORTHWESTERN UNIV, 79- *Concurrent Pos:* Sigma Xi grant, La State Univ, 66; NSF fel, Northwestern State Univ, 68, Sigma Xi grant, 71; US Forest Serv grants, 79 & 80. *Mem:* Am Soc Ichthyol & herpet; Soc Study Amphibians & Reptiles; Soc Syst Zool. *Res:* Systematics and anatomy. *Mailing Add:* Dept of Biol Sci Northwestern State Univ Natchitoches LA 71457

WILLIAMS, KENNETH ROGER, b New York, NY, Aug 23, 22; m 49; c 1. TEXTILE PHYSICS. *Educ:* Columbia Univ, AB, 48, MA, 49. *Prof Exp:* Res physicist, 49-63, RES ASSOC, E I DU PONT DE NEMOURS & CO, INC, 63- *Mem:* Opers Res Soc Am; Am Phys Soc. *Res:* Mechanical properties of fibers; high polymer physics; economic analysis of new ventures; design of experiments. *Mailing Add:* Textile Res Lab E I du Pont de Nemours & Co Inc Wilmington DE 19898

WILLIAMS, KENNETH STUART, b Croydon, Eng, Aug 20, 40; m 62; c 3. MATHEMATICS. *Educ:* Univ Birmingham, BSc, 62; Univ Toronto, MA, 63, PhD(math), 65. *Hon Degrees:* DSc, Univ Birmingham, 79. *Prof Exp:* Lectr math, Univ Manchester, 65-66; from asst prof to assoc prof, 66-75, PROF MATH, CARLETON UNIV, 75-, CHMN DEPT, 80- *Mem:* Math Asn Am; Can Math Cong; Am Math Soc. *Res:* Theory of numbers. *Mailing Add:* Dept of Math Carleton Univ Ottawa ON K1S 5B6 Can

WILLIAMS, KIMBERLY EVE, see Thomas, Kimberly W

WILLIAMS, LANSING EARL, b Spencer, WVa, Aug 8, 21; m 46; c 2. PLANT PATHOLOGY. *Educ:* Morris Harvey Col, BSc, 50; Ohio State Univ, MSc, 52, PhD(bot, plant path), 54. *Prof Exp:* Lab asst, Morris Harvey Col, 49-50; lab asst, Ohio State Univ, 50-52, from instr to assoc prof, 54-65, PROF BOT & PLANT PATH, OHIO STATE UNIV & OHIO AGR RES & DEVELOP CTR, 65-, ASSOC CHMN DEPT, 68- *Mem:* AAAS; Am Phytopath Soc; Sigma Xi; Nat Res Soc. *Res:* Corn viruses and stalk rot; mycotoxins; relation of soil fungal flora to soil-borne plant pathogens. *Mailing Add:* Dept Plant Path Ohio Agr Res & Develop Ctr Wooster OH 44691

WILLIAMS, LARRY G, b Moscow, Idaho, Jan 8, 35; m 56; c 2. AGRICULTURAL ENGINEERING. *Educ:* Univ Idaho, BS, 56, MS, 59. *Prof Exp:* Asst prof, 56-71, assoc prof, 71-80, PROF AGR ENG, UNIV IDAHO, 80- *Mem:* Am Soc Agr Eng. *Res:* Agricultural mechanization and automation; materials handling and agricultural processing. *Mailing Add:* Dept of Agr Eng Univ of Idaho Moscow ID 83843

WILLIAMS, LARRY GALE, b Lincoln, Nebr, Sept 28, 39; m 62; c 2. GENETICS. *Educ:* Univ Nebr, Lincoln, BS, 61, MS, 63; Calif Inst Technol, PhD(biochem), 68. *Prof Exp:* NIH fel bot, Univ Mich, Ann Arbor, 67-71; ASST PROF BIOL, KANS STATE UNIV, 71- *Mem:* AAAS. *Res:* Plant cell and tissue culture. *Mailing Add:* Div of Biol Kans State Univ Manhattan KS 66502

WILLIAMS, LAWRENCE ERNEST, b Youngstown, Ohio, Nov 29, 37; m 66; c 2. NUCLEAR MEDICINE, BIOPHYSICS. *Educ:* Carnegie-Mellon Univ, BS, 59; Univ Minn, Minneapolis, MS, 62, PhD(physics), 65. *Prof Exp:* Sr sci officer, Rutherford High Energy Lab, Eng, 65-68; asst prof physics, Western Ill Univ, 68-70; asst prof radiol, Univ Minn, Minneapolis, 73-77, prof, 78-80; IMAGING PHYSICIST, CITY OF HOPE, DUARTE, CALIF, 80- *Concurrent Pos:* NIH spec fel nuclear med, Nuclear Med Clin, Univ Minn, Minneapolis, 71-73; NIH grant, 74. *Mem:* Soc Nuclear Med; Sigma Xi; Am Asn Physicists in Med. *Res:* Computers; nuclear giant resonance; phospholipid vesicles; transit time distributions of physiological systems; image enhancement; microwaves. *Mailing Add:* Diag Radiol City of Hope Duarte CA 91010

WILLIAMS, LEAH ANN, b Clarksburg, WVa, July 20, 32. DEVELOPMENTAL BIOLOGY. *Educ:* WVa Univ, AB, 54, MS, 58, PhD(biol), 70. *Prof Exp:* Instr anat & physiol, Exten, Pa State Univ, 58-59; instr gen zool, anat & physiol, W Liberty State Col, summer 59; from instr to asst prof, 59-73, ASSOC PROF BIOL, W VA UNIV, 73- *Concurrent Pos:* NSF sci fac develop grant, 77-78. *Mem:* Int Soc Differentiation; AAAS; Am Soc Zool; Soc Develop Biol; Sigma Xi. *Res:* Regeneration; control mechanisms in the regenerative processes in the eyes of newts; evolutionary studies of the lens proteins. *Mailing Add:* Dept of Biol WVa Univ Morgantown WV 26506

WILLIAMS, LEAMON DALE, b Flippin, Ark, Sept 28, 35; m 61; c 3. FOOD SCIENCE, BIOCHEMISTRY. *Educ:* Univ Ark, BS, 58, MS, 61; Mich State Univ, PhD(food sci), 63. *Prof Exp:* Res chemist, Foods Div, Anderson, Clayton & Co, Tex, 63-67; sect head, CPC Int Inc, 67-69; dir food res, 69-78, VPRES RES, CENT SOYA CO, INC, 78- *Honors & Awards:* MacGee Award, Am Oil Chem Soc, 63. *Mem:* Poultry Sci Asn; Inst Food Technologists; Am Oil Chem Soc; Am Chem Soc. *Res:* Organic chemistry of lipids; esterifiability of hydroxyls; interesterification and development of fat based derivatives; protein chemistry; food research; animal nutrition. *Mailing Add:* Cent Soya Co Inc 1300 Fort Wayne Bank Bldg Fort Wayne IN 46802

WILLIAMS, LELAND HENDRY, b Columbia, SC, Feb 24, 30; m 52; c 2. MATHEMATICS, COMPUTER SCIENCE. *Educ:* Univ SC, BS, 50; Univ GA, MS, 51; Duke Univ, PhD(math), 61. *Prof Exp:* Mathematician, Redstone Arsenal, 51-53; res assoc math & vis asst prof, Duke Univ, 60-62; math consult comput, Fla State Univ, 62-64, asst dir comput ctr, 64-66, asst prof math, Univ, 62-66; dir comput ctr & assoc prof math, Auburn Univ, 66-70; PRES & DIR, TRIANGLE UNIVS COMPUT CTR, 70- *Concurrent Pos:* assoc dir & lectr, NSF comput inst, Fla State Univ, 66; adj assoc prof, Duke Univ, Univ NC, Chapel Hill & NC State Univ, 70-; dep dir, Edinburgh Regional Comput Ctr & vis prof, Univ Edinburgh, Scotland, 76-77. *Mem:* Math Asn Am; Am Sci Affil; Am Math Soc; Asn Comput Mach. *Res:* Numerical analysis; nonnumeric mathematical computation; computation center management. *Mailing Add:* Triangle Univs Comput Ctr Box 12076 Research Triangle Park NC 27709

WILLIAMS, LEO, JR, b Perthshire, Miss, Feb 25, 26; m 50; c 2. ELECTRICAL ENGINEERING, ELECTRONICS. *Educ:* Univ Ill, Urbana-Champaign, BSEE, 50, MSEE, 53. *Prof Exp:* Prof elec eng & chmn dept, Prairie View A&M Col, Tex, 54-56; PROF ELEC ENG, NC A&T STATE UNIV, 56- *Concurrent Pos:* NSF fac sci fel, Univ Ill, 59-60; consultproposal eval, NSF, 61; consult, Western Elec Co, 66-67, IBM Corp, 69 & Gen Elec Co, 71-; Westinghouse Educ Found grant, NC A&T State Univ, 69-70, NASA grant, 70-73. *Honors & Awards:* James Fund Award, 52. *Mem:* Instrument Soc Am; Int Soc Hybrid Microelectronics; Am Soc Eng Educ; Simulation Coun. *Res:* Solid state electronics, microelectronics and metallic oxides. *Mailing Add:* Dept of Elec Eng NC A&T Univ Greensboro NC 27411

WILLIAMS, LESLEY LATTIN, b New Bedford, Mass, Aug 10, 39. PHYSICAL CHEMISTRY. *Educ:* Hollins Col, AB, 61, Univ Wis-Madison, PhD(chem), 68. *Prof Exp:* From asst prof to assoc prof, 68-78, PROF CHEM, CHICAGO STATE UNIV, 78- *Concurrent Pos:* Lectr, Univ Md, Munich Campus, 71-72. *Mem:* AAAS; Sigma Xi; Am Phys Soc. *Res:* Nuclear magnetic resonance relaxation mechanisms in inorganic fluorides, including solvent effects; solution thermodynamics; hexafluorides. *Mailing Add:* Dept of Phys Sci Chicago State Univ Chicago IL 60628

WILLIAMS, LEWIS DAVID, b Hopkinsville, Ky, Apr 2, 44; m 71. CHEMISTRY. *Educ:* Univ Chicago, BS, 66; Harvard Univ, PhD(org chem), 71. *Prof Exp:* Atholl McBean fel chem, Stanford Res Inst, 70-71; Presidential Intern, Western Regional Res Lab, Agr Res Serv, USDA, Albany, 72-73; asst lab dir, 73-80, LAB DIR, DIAG DATA INC, MOUNTAIN VIEW, 80- *Mem:* Am Chem Soc. *Res:* Physical organic chemistry; structure-reativity relationships; biochemistry. *Mailing Add:* Diagnostic Data Inc 518 Logue Ave Mountain View CA 94043

WILLIAMS, LLOYD BAYARD, b Corvallis, Ore, Sept 28, 13; m 41; c 2. MATHEMATICAL ANALYSIS. *Educ:* Reed Col, BA, 35; Univ Chicago, SM, 39. *Prof Exp:* Instr math, Ga Inst Technol, 40-42; from instr to asst prof, Hamilton Col, 42-47; from asst prof to assoc prof, Reed Col, 47-57; assoc prof, Wesleyan Univ, 57-58; prof, 58-80, EMER PROF MATH, REED COL, 80- *Mem:* Math Asn Am. *Res:* Preparation of undergraduate mathematics courses, primarily in analysis; convolution quotients in differential equations. *Mailing Add:* Dept of Math Reed Col Portland OR 97202

WILLIAMS, LORETTA ANN, b Denver, Colo, Aug 7, 53. GEOLOGY & GEOPHYSICS. *Educ:* State Univ NY Stony Brook, BS, 76; Princeton Univ, MA, 78, PhD(geol & geophys), 81. *Prof Exp:* RES AFFIL, APPL EARTH SCI DEPT, STANFORD UNIV, 81- *Mem:* Sigma Xi; Int Asn Sedimentologists. *Res:* Depositional environments and diagenesis of biogenic sediments; fine-gained sediments in wrench fault regimes. *Mailing Add:* Appl Earth Sci Dept Stanford Univ Stanford CA 94305

WILLIAMS, LORING RIDER, b Buckhannon, WVa, Jan 6, 07; m 41; c 2. INORGANIC CHEMISTRY. *Educ:* WVa Wesleyan Col, BS, 27; WVa Univ, MS, 32; Univ Ill, PhD(inorg chem), 39. *Prof Exp:* Teacher high sch, WVa, 27-31; instr chem, Alderson-Broaddus Col, 32-34; teacher high sch, WVa, 34-38; teacher chem univ high sch, Univ Ill, 38-39; from instr to prof chem, 39-72, chmn dept, 57-61, EMER PROF CHEM, UNIV NEV, RENO, 72- *Mem:* Am Chem Sco. *Res:* Distribution of selenium in plants and soils. *Mailing Add:* 4975 Malapi Way Sparks NV 89431

WILLIAMS, LOUIS GRESSETT, b Owensboro, Ky, Oct 28, 13; m 42; c 2. FRESH WATER ECOLOGY, ALGOLOGY. *Educ:* Marshall Univ, AB, 37; Duke Univ, MA, 40, PhD(biol), 48. *Prof Exp:* Asst, Marshall Col, 37-38; teacher high sch, Fla, 39-40 & NC, 40-41; asst, Duke Univ, 46-47; instr bot, Univ NC, 48; assoc prof biol, Furman Univ, 48-58; in charge, USPHS Plankton Prog, Nat Water Qual Network, Ohio, 58-65; in charge plankton prog, Nat Water Qual Lab, Minn, 65-67; prof biol, 67-79, EMER PROF BIOL, UNIV ALA, TUSCALOOSA, 79- *Concurrent Pos:* Carnegie grant, 49; Ford Found fel, Univ Calif, 51-52. *Honors & Awards:* Jefferson Award, 51. *Mem:* Fel AAAS; Bot Soc Am; Am Soc Limnol & Oceanog; Ecol Soc Am; Phycol Soc Am. *Res:* Water quality assessment by species diversity and toxicity bioassay on the Great Lakes and major rivers of the United States. *Mailing Add:* 1246 Northwood Lake Northport AL 35476

WILLIAMS, LUTHER STEWARD, b Sawyerville, Ala, Aug 19, 40; m 63. MOLECULAR BIOLOGY. *Educ:* Miles Col, BA, 61; Atlanta Univ, MS, 63; Purdue Univ, PhD(molecular biol), 68. *Prof Exp:* Lab instr biol, Spelman Col, 61-62; lab instr, Atlanta Univ, 62-63, instr, 63-64; teaching asst, Purdue Univ, 64-66; Am Cancer Soc fel, State Univ NY Stony Brook, 68-69; asst prof, Atlanta Univ, 69-70; asst prof, 70-73, assoc prof, 73-80, PROF BIOL SCI, PURDUE UNIV, WEST LAFAYETTE, 80-, ASST PROVOST, 76- *Concurrent Pos:* NSF teaching asst, 62-63; NIH career develop award, Purdue Univ, 71-75; assoc prof biol, Mass Inst Technol, 73-74; mem, Microbiol Training Comt, Nat Inst Gen Med Sci, 71-74; chmn, MARC Prog, Nat Inst Gen Med Sci, 75-76. *Mem:* AAAS; Am Soc Microbiol; NY Acad Sci; Am Chem Soc; Am Soc Biol Chemists. *Res:* Physiological role of aminoacyl-transfer RNA synthetases and transfer RNA's in bacterial metabolism. *Mailing Add:* Dept of Biol Sci Purdue Univ West Lafayette IN 47907

WILLIAMS, LYMAN O, b State College, Pa, Apr 1, 34; m 63; c 2. STRUCTURAL GEOLOGY. *Educ:* Univ Ga, BS, 56, Univ Iowa, MS, 59, PhD(geol), 62. *Prof Exp:* Explor geologist, Calif Co, 61-63; asst prof geol, Monmouth Col, 63-64; assoc prof, Eastern Tenn State Univ, 64-69; assoc prof, 69-73, PROF GEOL, MONMOUTH COL, 73-, DEPT CHMN, 77- *Mem:* Geol Soc Am. *Res:* Petrology and structure of crystalline rock terranes; remote sensing of environment. *Mailing Add:* Dept of Geol Monmouth Col Monmouth IL 61462

WILLIAMS, LYNN ALAN, b Chardon, Ohio, Dec 19, 47. ENOLOGY, BIOCHEMICAL ENGINEERING. *Educ:* Vanderbilt Univ, BE, 69; Univ Calif, Berkeley, PhD(chem eng), 77. *Prof Exp:* Researcher biotechnol, Dept Bacteriol, Karolinska Inst, Stockholm, Sweden, 76-78; ASST PROF ENOL, UNIV CALIF, DAVIS, 79- *Mem:* Sigma Xi; Am Inst Chem Engrs; Am Chem Soc; Am Soc Microbiol; Am Soc Enologists. *Res:* Application of chemical engineering to production of wine, brandy and other distilled beverages; biochemical engineering, especially as applied to bioconversions. *Mailing Add:* Dept of Viticult & Enol Univ of Calif Davis CA 95616

WILLIAMS, LYNN DOLORES, b Seattle, Wash, Mar 20, 44. MATHEMATICAL ANALYSIS. *Educ:* Lewis & Clark Col, BS, 66; Univ Ore, MS, 70, PhD(math), 72. *Prof Exp:* Vis asst prof math, Univ Ore, 72-73; asst prof, La State Univ, Baton Rouge, 73-77; asst prof, Converse Col, Spartanburg, SC, 77-78; RES ANALYST, BOEING AEROSPACE CO, 78- *Mem:* Am Math Soc; Sigma Xi; Math Asn Am; Asn Women in Math. *Res:* Functional analysis, especially Banach algebras of operators, Fredholm operator theory and approximate identities in Banach algebras. *Mailing Add:* 3417 42nd Ave SW Seattle WA 98116

WILLIAMS, LYNN ROY, b Detroit, Mich, Apr 23, 45; m 67; c 1. MATHEMATICS. *Educ:* King Col, BA, 67; Univ Ky, MA, 68, PhD(math), 71. *Prof Exp:* Asst prof math, La State Univ, Baton Rouge, 71-75; asst prof, 75-77, ASSOC PROF MATH, IND UNIV, SOUTH BEND, 77- *Mem:* Am Math Soc. *Res:* Functional analysis; Hp theory; harmonic analysis. *Mailing Add:* Dept of Math Ind Univ South Bend IN 46615

WILLIAMS, MARION JACK, b Hochheim, Tex, Oct 18, 28; m 46; c 2. THORACIC SURGERY, SURGERY. *Educ:* Univ Houston, BA, 49; Univ Tex, MD, Dallas, 53. *Prof Exp:* Resident, Univ Tex Southwestern Med Sch Dallas, 56-60; resident US Air Force, 60-, asst chief surg, Carswell AFB Hosp, Tex, 60-62, chief, Itazuke Air Base Hosp, Japan, 62-65, resident thoracic-cardiovasc surg, Wilford Hall Med Ctr, 65-67, chief thoracic surg, Med Ctr, Keesler AFB, 67-74, chmn dept surg & dir surg residency, 68-74; prof surg, 74-78, chief thoracic-cardiovasc surg, 75-78, CLIN PROF SURG, MED SCH, TULANE UNIV, 78- ACTG CHIEF SURG, 75- *Concurrent Pos:* Res fel surg, Univ Tex Southwestern Med Sch Dallas, 54; assoc clin prof surg, Med Sch, Tulane Univ, 67-; sr consult, Surgeon Gen, US Air Force, 68-; consult surg, Charity Hosp, New Orleans, Vet Admin Hosp, Alexandria, La, Huey P Long Charity Hosp & Lallie Kemp Charity Hosp. *Mem:* Soc Thoracic Surg; fel Am Col Surg; AMA. *Res:* Fluid and electrolyte balance; clinical surgery. *Mailing Add:* Suite 915 2633 Napoleon New Orleans LA 70115

WILLIAMS, MARION PORTER, b Salem, Ind, Jan 24, 46; m 68. FOOD SCIENCE. *Educ:* Purdue Univ, BS, 68, PhD(food sci), 73. *Prof Exp:* From sr food scientist to sr res scientist, 73-75, mgr int res & prod develop, 75-78, asst dir prod develop, Res Labs, Carnation Co, 78; dir new prod develop, Res Ctr, Anderson Clayton Foods, 78-81; DIR PROD DEVELOP, RES & DEVELOP, DART & KRAFT, INC, 81- *Mem:* Inst Food Technologists. *Res:* Development of new products and maintenance improvement of current product lines, other than dairy/cheese products. *Mailing Add:* Dart & Kraft Inc 801 Waukegan Rd Glenview IL 60025

WILLIAMS, MARSHALL HENRY, JR, b New Haven, Conn, July 15, 25; m 48; c 4. PHYSIOLOGY, INTERNAL MEDICINE. *Educ:* Yale Univ, BS, 45, MD, 47. *Prof Exp:* Intern, Presby Hosp, New York, 47-48, asst resident med, 48-49; asst resident, New Haven Hosp, Conn, 49-50, asst, 50; chief respiratory sect, Dept Cardiorespiratory Dis, Army Med Serv Grad Sch, Walter Reed Army Hosp, 52-55; dir cardiorespiratory lab, Grasslands Hosp, Valhalla, NY, 55-59; vis asst prof physiol, 55-59, assoc prof med & physiol, 59-66, PROF MED, ALBERT EINSTEIN COL MED, 66- *Concurrent Pos:* NIH trainee, New Haven Hosp, Conn, 50; dir chest serv, Bronx Munic Hosp Ctr, New York, 59- *Mem:* AAAS; Am Physiol Soc; Am Thoracic Soc; Am Soc Clin Invest; Am Heart Asn. *Res:* Respiratory and clinical cardiopulmonary physiology. *Mailing Add:* Albert Einstein Col of Med Yeshiva Univ New York NY 10461

WILLIAMS, MARSHALL VANCE, b Memphis, Tenn, Mar 22, 48; m 70; c 2. TUMOR BIOLOGY, VIROLOGY. *Educ:* Memphis State Univ, BS, 70, MS, 73; Univ Ga, PhD(microbiol), 76. *Prof Exp:* Cancer res scientist I, Roswell Park Mem Inst, 76-78; ASST PROF MICROBIOL, KIRKSVILLE COL OSTEOP MED, MO, 78- *Concurrent Pos:* Adj asst prof, Northeast Mo State Univ, 79-; consult, Bio-Diesel Fuels Iowa, Inc, 81- *Mem:* Am Soc

Microbiol; Soc Indust Microbiol. *Res:* Deoxyuridine metabolism in neoplastic cells and cells infected with herpes simplex virus; amino acid transport and drug resistance in bacteria. *Mailing Add:* Dept Microbiol & Immunol Kirksville Col Osteop Med Kirksville MO 63501

WILLIAMS, MARTHA E, b Chicago, Ill. INFORMATION SCIENCES. *Educ:* Barat Col, AB, 55; Loyola Univ, 57. *Prof Exp:* Assoc chemist, Chem Dept, Ill Inst Technol, 61, asst supvr, 61-68, mgr, Info Sci, 62-72, Comput Search Ctr, 68-72; DIR, INFO RETRIEVAL RES LAB, & PROF INFO SCI, COORD SCI LAB, UNIV ILL, 72-, AFFIL, COMPUT SCI DEPT, 79- *Concurrent Pos:* Mem, Comt Chem Info, 70-73, chmn & mem, Large Data Base Subcomt, 71-73, Ad Hoc Panel, Info Storage & Retrieval, 77, Numerical Data Adv Bd, 79-82 & Nat Res Coun/Nat Acad Sci; Ed, Annual Rev Info Sci & Tehcnol, 75-, & Online Rev, 77-; vpres, Eng Info, Inc, 78-80, chmn bd, 80-82; mem bd regents, Nat Libr Med, 78-82, chmn bd, 81-82. *Mem:* Fel AAAS; Am Chem Soc; Am Soc Info Sci; Asn Comput Mach; Asn Sci Info Dissemination Ctr, (vpres, 71-73, pres, 75-77, past pres, 77-79). *Res:* Online retrieval systems; computer readable databases; systems analysis and design; chemical information systems. *Mailing Add:* RR 1 Box 194 Monticello IL 61856

WILLIAMS, MARY ANN, b Albany, NY, May 18, 25. NUTRITION, BIOCHEMISTRY. *Educ:* Iowa State Col, BS, 46; Cornell Univ, MS, 50; Univ Calif, PhD, 54. *Prof Exp:* Asst pathologist, Univ Ky, 49-51; asst nutrit, Univ Calif, 51-54; res assoc, McCollum-Pratt Inst, Johns Hopkins Univ, 54-55; from instr to asst prof, 55-63, assoc prof, 63-75, PROF NUTRIT, UNIV CALIF, BERKELEY, 75- *Concurrent Pos:* Guggenheim fel, 63-64. *Mem:* AAAS; Am Chem Soc; Am Inst Nutrit; Soc Exp Biol & Med. *Res:* Essential fatty acid metabolism and functions. *Mailing Add:* Dept of Nutrit Sci 119 Morgan Hall Univ of Calif Berkeley CA 94720

WILLIAMS, MARY BEARDEN, b Lexington, Ky, Aug 29, 36. EVOLUTIONARY BIOLOGY, PHILOSOPHY OF SCIENCE. *Educ:* Reed Col, BA, 58; Univ Pa, MA, 61; Univ London, PhD(math biol) & DIC, 67. *Prof Exp:* Res assoc biomath, Univ Tex M D Anderson Hosp & Tumor Inst, 63-64; asst prof, NC State Univ, 67-73; vis asst prof hist & philos sci, Ind Univ, 73-74; asst prof philos, Ohio State Univ, 74-76; mem hon fac, Freshman Honors Prog, 76-78, ASSOC PROF LIFE & HEALTH SCI, UNIV DEL, 78- *Mem:* Am Soc Nat; Soc Study Evolution; Math Asn Am; Philos Sci Asn; Soc Syst Zool. *Res:* Axiomatization of evolutionary theory; logical status of evolutionary predictions; evolution of population self-regulation; philosophy of biology; bioethics. *Mailing Add:* Life & Health Sci Univ of Del Newark DE 19711

WILLIAMS, MARY CARR, b Port Arthur, Tex, Dec 25, 26; m 51; c 1. STEROID CHEMISTRY. *Educ:* Tex Woman's Univ, BA & BS, 49; St Mary's Univ, MS, 75. *Prof Exp:* Res chemist lipid metab, Dept Biochem & Biophys, Tex A&M Univ, 49-63; res scientist, 63-78, assoc found scientist, steroid metab, Dept Clin Sci & Reproductive Biol, 78-81, ASSOC FOUND SCIENTIST LIPID METAB, DEPT CARDIOPULMONARY DIS, 82- *Mem:* Am Chem Soc. *Res:* Metabolism of natural and synthetic steroid hormones; chromotography of steroids and lipids. *Mailing Add:* Southwest Found Res & Educ PO Box 28147 San Antonio TX 78284

WILLIAMS, MARY LOUISE MONICA FRITTS, b Detroit, Mich, Apr 16, 40; m 68; c 1. ANATOMY, EMBRYOLOGY. *Educ:* Univ Detroit, BS, 62, MS, 64; Wayne State Univ, PhD(embryol, anat), 71. *Prof Exp:* Instr microbiol & embryol, Mercy Col, Mich, 64-67, asst prof, 67-68; asst prof microbiol, Univ Detroit, 68-69; ASST PROF ANAT, MED SCH, WAYNE STATE UNIV, 71-, ASST PROF MORTUARY SCI, 76- *Mem:* AAAS; Genetics Soc Am; Am Soc Microbiol; Soc Develop Biol. *Res:* Primordial germ cells; gonadal development; tissue culture. *Mailing Add:* Dept of Anat Wayne State Univ Detroit MI 48202

WILLIAMS, MAX L(EA), JR, b Aspinwall, Pa, Feb 22, 22; m 67; c 3. AERONAUTICS. *Educ:* Carnegie Inst Technol, BS, 42; Calif Inst Technol, MS, 47, AeE, 48, PhD, 50. *Prof Exp:* Lectr aeronaut, Calif Inst Technol, 48-50, res fel, 50-51, from asst prof to prof, 51-65; prof eng & dean eng, Univ Utah, 65-73, distinguished prof eng, 73; PROF ENG & DEAN SCH ENG, UNIV PITTSBURGH, 73- *Concurrent Pos:* Ed in chief, Int J Fracture, 65-; mem exec comt, Int Cong Fracture, 65-; sci dir, NATO Advan Study Inst, Italy, 67; mem biomat adv comn, Nat Inst Dent Res, 67-70; mem chem rocket adv comt, NASA, 68-73; pres, Utah Eng & Develop Corp, 69-79; mem eng adv comn, NSF, 69-72; NSF sr fel, Imp Col, Univ London, 71-72; Sigma Xi nat lectr, 72; mem nat mat adv bd, Nat Res Coun & chmn, Coun on Mat Structures & Design, 75-77; assoc mem, Defense Sci Bd, 75-76; consult & lectr in field, Dir Terra Tek Inc, Salt Lake City, 73-77; adv, Regional Indust Develop Corp, Pittsburgh, 73-; chmn, Pa Adv Comn I-79 Bridge Failure, 77; dir, MPC Corp, Pittsburgh, 74-; chmn struct design task group, Automation Res Prog, Orbiting Syst Test Plan Comn, 78-79; dir, US Nat Comn World Energy Conf, 79- & Automation Syst Inc, 81- *Honors & Awards:* Adhesion Res Award, Am Soc Testing & Mat, 75. *Mem:* AAAS; Soc Exp Stress Anal; Am Chem Soc; Am Inst Aeronaut & Astronaut; Am Soc Eng Educ. *Res:* Continuum mechanics with application to fracture of solids and interaction with chemical structure of materials. *Mailing Add:* Benedum Eng Hall Univ of Pittsburgh Pittsburgh PA 15261

WILLIAMS, MAX W, b Cardston, Alta, Aug 24, 30; US citizen; m 54; c 4. PLANT PHYSIOLOGY, HORTICULTURE. *Educ:* Utah State Univ, BSc, 54, MSc, 57; Wash State Univ, PhD(hort), 61. *Prof Exp:* Res asst, Utah State Univ, 54-55; actg supt, Utah Tree Fruit Exp Sta, 55-58; res asst, Wash State Univ, 58-61; RES LEADER, TECH ADV & PLANT PHYSIOLOGIST, AGR RES SERV, USDA, 61- *Mem:* Am Soc Hort Sci; Int Soc Hort Sci. *Res:* Chemical thinning of apples; growth retardants; cytokinins; auxins. *Mailing Add:* Sci & Educ Admin-Agr Res USDA 1104 N Western Ave Wenatchee WA 98801

WILLIAMS, MERLIN CHARLES, b Howard, SDak, July 20, 31; m 59; c 4. METEOROLOGY, ENGINEERING. *Educ:* SDak State Univ, BS, 53; Univ Chicago, cert, 54; Univ Wyo, MS, 62; Stanford Univ, MSA, 81. *Prof Exp:* Instr civil eng, SDak State Univ, 57-58; instr & res asst weather eng, 58-59; engr, US Bur Reclamation, 59-61; asst civil eng, Univ Wyo, 61-62, proj dir weather modification res, 62-66; dir weather modification res, Fresno State Col Found, 66-71; dir, SDak State Weather Control Comn, 71-74; DIR, OFF WEATHER MODIFICATION PROGS, ENVIRON RES LABS, NAT OCEANIC & ATMOSPHERIC ADMIN, 74- *Concurrent Pos:* Consult adv bd weather modification, NSF, 75- *Mem:* Am Soc Civil Eng; Am Meteorol Soc; Am Geophys Union; Weather Modification Asn (pres, 69). *Res:* Water resources research to investigate increasing water supplies, including weather modification research, fluid mechanics and hydrology; basic hydrometeorological studies; mountain meteorology; snow physics; hurricane modification (abatement), boundary layer dynamics. *Mailing Add:* ERL-NOAA Off Weather Modification Progs Boulder CO 80302

WILLIAMS, MICHAEL, b London, Eng, Jan 3, 47. NEUROCHEMISTRY, PHARMACOLOGY. *Educ:* Univ London, BSc, 71, PhD(neurochem), 74. *Prof Exp:* Res assoc neurochem, Univ NC, Chapel Hill, 74-76; sr res neurochemist, 76-80, RES FEL PHARMACOL, MERCK INST, 80- *Mem:* Am Soc Pharmacol & Exp Therapeuts; Soc Neurosci; AAAS; Am Soc Neurochem. *Res:* Synaptic transmission; receptor function; cyclic nucleotides and protein phosphorylation. *Mailing Add:* Neuropsychopharmacol Sect Merck Inst West Point PA 19486

WILLIAMS, MICHAEL C(HARLES), b Milwaukee, Wis, June 11, 37; m 61; c 4. RHEOLOGY, VISCOELASTICITY. *Educ:* Univ Wis-Madison, BS, 59, MS, 60, PhD(rheology), 64. *Prof Exp:* Fel polymer solutions, Inst Theoret Sci, Univ Ore, 64-65; from asst prof to assoc prof chem eng, 65-72, PROF CHEM ENG, UNIV CALIF, BERKELEY, 72- *Concurrent Pos:* mem, career guid comt, 68-, San Francisco Bay area eng coun, 68-, chmn, 70-73; vis prof rheol, Univ Nat Del Sur, Bahia Blanca, Arg, 70; consult, pvt indust, govt & litagation; prin investr, numerous res grants & contracts, NSF, NIH, NASA, Off Naval Res & Petrol Res Fund. *Mem:* Am Inst Chem Engrs; Am Chem Soc; Soc Rheol; Am Soc Eng Educ; Soc Plastics Engrs. *Res:* Viscoelastic fluid phenomena; biomedical engineering; rheology of polymer melts and solutions; processing fluid mechanics of viscoelastic liquids and inclastic slurries; mechanical and dynamic properties of solid and liquid block copolymers; hemolytic and other damage to flowing blood; biomaterials. *Mailing Add:* Dept of Chem Eng Univ of Calif Berkeley CA 94720

WILLIAMS, MICHAEL D, nuclear engineering, see previous edition

WILLIAMS, MICHAEL EUGENE, b Ina, Ill, Aug 4, 40; m 68. VERTEBRATE PALEONTOLOGY. *Educ:* Mo Sch Mines & Metall, Rolla, BS, 63; Univ Kans, MS, 72; Univ Kans, PLD, 79. *Prof Exp:* CUR VERT PALEONT, CLEVELAND MUS NATURAL HIST, 76- *Mem:* Soc Vert Paleont; Paleont Soc; Int Paleont Union. *Res:* Paleozoic fishes with special emphasis on chondrichthyans; sedimentation and environments of deposition of various black shale units. *Mailing Add:* Cleveland Mus of Natural Hist Wade Oval Univ Circle Cleveland OH 44106

WILLIAMS, MICHAEL JOHN, textile chemistry, see previous edition

WILLIAMS, MICHAEL LEDELL, b Paragould, Ark, Sept 11, 43; m 63; c 2. ENTOMOLOGY, SYSTEMATICS. *Educ:* Ark State Univ, BS, 67; Va Polytech Inst & State Univ, MS, 69, PhD(entom), 72. *Prof Exp:* Asst entomologist, Md Dept Agr, 71-73; ASSOC PROF, DEPT ZOOL-ENTOM, AUBURN UNIV, 73- *Concurrent Pos:* Sigma Xi res award, 69. *Mem:* Entom Soc Am; Sigma Xi. *Res:* Insular speciation of scale insects of the Galapagos Islands; systematics and morphology of New World Coccidae (Homoptera: Coccoidea); natural host plant resistance to scale insects; scale insects of Alabama; insects of ornamental plants. *Mailing Add:* Dept of Zool-Entom Auburn Univ Auburn AL 36830

WILLIAMS, MILES COBURN, b Osage City, Kans, Jan 28, 29; m 53; c 2. PLANT PHYSIOLOGY. *Educ:* Kansas State Univ, BS & MS, 51; Univ Ill, PhD(agron), 56. *Prof Exp:* PLANT PHYSIOLOGIST, SCI & EDUC ADMIN-AGR RES SERV, USDA, 56- *Mem:* Weed Sci Soc Am; Soc Range Mgt; Am Soc Agron; Coun Agr Sci & Technol. *Res:* Biochemical and physiological research on poisonous range weeds, especially methods of chemical and biological control; Astragalus, Delphinium. *Mailing Add:* Sci & Educ Admin-Agr Res Serv USDA Dept Biol Utah State Univ Logan UT 84322

WILLIAMS, MILTON F(RIEL), b New Orleans, La, June 13, 16; m 42; c 1. CHEMICAL ENGINEERING. *Educ:* Tulane Univ, BS, 36, BE, 37, MS, 38. *Prof Exp:* Asst phys chemist, US Bur Mines, 40-42, assoc coal prep engr, 42-46; assoc chem engr, Oliver Iron Mining Div, US Steel Co, 46-53, supvr Res Lab, 53-60, mgr, Raw Mat Res Lab, Columbia-Geneva Steel Div, 60-65, chief res engr minerals beneficiation, res lab, 65-80. *Mem:* Am Inst Mining, Metall & Petrol Engrs. *Res:* Mineral beneficiation. *Mailing Add:* 225 N 26 Ave E Duluth MN 55812

WILLIAMS, MYRA NICOL, b Dallas, Tex, June 8, 41; m 68; c 2. MOLECULAR BIOPHYSICS. *Educ:* Southern Methodist Univ, BS, 64; Yale Univ, MS, 65, PhD(molecular biophys), 68. *Prof Exp:* Res fel biophys, 69-76, asst to pres, 76-78, dir sci planning, 78-80, SR DIR SCI & STRATEGIC PLANNING, MERCK SHARP & DOHME RES LABS, 80- *Mem:* Biophys Soc; Am Soc Biol Chemists. *Res:* Structure and function of proteins; biophysical and biochemical studies on dihydrofolate reductase, including nuclear magnetic resonance, fluorescence and ultraviolet difference spectroscopic studies, chemical modifications and enzyme kinetics. *Mailing Add:* Merck Sharp & Dohme Res Labs Rahway NJ 07065

WILLIAMS, NEAL THOMAS, b East Orange, NJ, Mar 16, 21; m 48; c 2. ENGINEERING PHYSICS. *Educ:* Cornell Univ, AB, 48. *Prof Exp:* Supvr magnetron eng, Westinghouse Elec Co, 42-44, develop engr, 48-51; res assoc, Radiation Lab, Columbia Univ, 44-48, assoc res physicist, 52; mem tech staff, Bell Tel Labs, Inc, 51-52; chief engr, L L Constantin & Co, 52-53; res engr, T A Edison, Inc, 53-60; chief engr, Seal-A-Metic, Inc, 60-65; div mgr, Platronics, Inc, 65-66; PRES, PLATRONICS-SEALS, INC, CLIFTON, 66- *Mem:* Am Phys Soc; sr mem Inst Elec & Electronics Eng; NY Acad Sci. *Res:* Microwave magnetrons and electronics; traveling wave tubes and backward oscillators; radar duplexers; gas discharges; metal-ceramic seals; low voltage x-rays. *Mailing Add:* PO Box 1002 5 Skyline Dr Hopatcong NJ 07843

WILLIAMS, NOREEN, b Brunswick, Maine, June 21, 55. BIOENERGETICS, ENZYME MECHANISMS. *Educ:* Univ Maine Orono, BS, 77; NY Univ, MS, 79, PhD(biol & biochem), 81. *Prof Exp:* FEL, SCH MED, JOHNS HOPKINS UNIV, 81- *Mem:* Biophys Soc; NY Acad Sci; AAAS. *Res:* Mechanism of action of the mitochondrial F1-ATPase employing photoaffinity analogs of adenine nucleotides and kinetic methods. *Mailing Add:* Dept Physiol Chem Sch Med Johns Hopkins Univ 725 N Wolfe St Baltimore MD 21205

WILLIAMS, NORMAN DALE, b Nebr, Nov 4, 24; m 47; c 2. PLANT GENETICS. *Educ:* Univ Nebr, BS, 51, MS, 54, PhD(agron), 56. *Prof Exp:* Assoc genetics, Argonne Nat Lab, 54-56, res assoc, 56; GENETICIST, SCI & EDUC-AGR RES SERV, USDA, 56- *Concurrent Pos:* Adj Prof, NDak State Univ, 61- *Mem:* AAAS; Am Soc Agron; Am Genetic Asn; Crop Sci Soc Am; Genetics Soc Am. *Res:* Genetic studies of host-parasite relationships, especially wheat and wheat stem rust; mutation induction. *Mailing Add:* USDA Walster Hall State Univ Sta Fargo ND 58102

WILLIAMS, NORMAN EUGENE, b Grove City, Pa, July 29, 28; m 53; c 2. ZOOLOGY. *Educ:* Youngstown State Univ, AB, 52; Brown Univ, ScM, 54; Univ Calif, Los Angeles, PhD(zool), 58. *Prof Exp:* Instr, 57-59, from asst prof to assoc prof, 59-67, PROF ZOOL, UNIV IOWA, 67- *Concurrent Pos:* NIH ser fel, Carlsberg Found, Denmark, 63-64 & Dept Biol Struct, Univ Wash, 66-67. *Mem:* Soc Protozool; Am Soc Cell Biol. *Res:* Cellular development; synthesis and assembly of organellar proteins; electron microscopy. *Mailing Add:* Dept of Zool Univ of Iowa Iowa City IA 52240

WILLIAMS, OLWEN, b Union, Conn, Jan 19, 17. VERTEBRATE ECOLOGY. *Educ:* Alfred Univ, BFA, 41; Univ Colo, MA, 51, PhD(zool), 52. *Prof Exp:* Instr sci, Putney Sch, Vt, 42-48; from instr to assoc prof biol, 51-67, PROF BIOL, UNIV COLO, BOULDER, 67- *Concurrent Pos:* Fulbright lectr, Pierce Univ Col, Athens, Greece, 65-66. *Mem:* AAAS; Am Ornith Union; Am Soc Mammal; Animal Behav Soc; Ecol Soc Am. *Res:* Avain and mammalian population and behavioral ecology; ecoenergetics of rodents and shrews; micotine biology. *Mailing Add:* Dept of EPO Biol Univ of Colo Boulder CO 80309

WILLIAMS, OREN FRANCIS, b Oakland City, Ind, Mar 5, 20; m 50; c 2. INORGANIC CHEMISTRY. *Educ:* Univ Toledo, BE, 43; Univ Ill, MS, 47, PhD(chem), 51. *Prof Exp:* Chemist, State Geol Surv, Ill, 44-47; res chemist, Food Mach & Chem Corp, 51-59; chemist, NIH, 59-61; asst prog dir chem, 61-64, PROG DIR INORG CHEM, NSF, DC, 64- *Mem:* Fel AAAS; Am Chem Soc. *Res:* Organic chemistry; agricultural chemicals; organic fluorine and coordination compounds; research administration. *Mailing Add:* Prog Dir Inorg Chem NSF 1800 G St NW Washington DC 20550

WILLIAMS, OWEN WINGATE, b Trouville, France, Aug 24, 24; US citizen; m 46; c 5. GEODESY, GEOPHYSICS. *Educ:* Kalamazoo Col, AB, 48. *Prof Exp:* Geod engr, Army Map Serv, Washington, DC, 48-55; phys scientist, Aeronaut Chart & Info Center, Dept Air Force, 55-57, phys scientist & chief, Terrestrial Sci Lab, Air Force Cambridge Res Labs, Hanscom AFB, 57-72; asst dep dir plans, Requirements & Technol, 72-76, dep dir systs & technol, 76-79, DEP DIR MGT & TECHNOL, DEFENSE MAPPING AGENCY, WASHINGTON, DC, 79- *Concurrent Pos:* Guest lectr, Acad Sci USSR, 66. *Honors & Awards:* Meritorious Civilian Serv Award, US Air Force, 73. *Mem:* Fel AAAS; Am Geophys Union; fel Am Cong Surv & Mapping; Earth Sci Technol Asn. *Res:* Theory, instrumentation and test of optical and laser celestial geodetic techniques; gravimetry; cartography; crustal physics. *Mailing Add:* 4703 Ponderosa Dr Annandale VA 22003

WILLIAMS, PATRICIA BELL, b Detroit, Mich. PHARMACOLOGY. *Educ:* Col Pharm, Univ Mich, BS, 68; Med Col Va, Va Commonwealth Univ, PhD(pharmacol), 72. *Prof Exp:* Lab asst pharmacol, Health Sci, Med Col Va, Va Commonwealth Univ, 68-70, teaching asst, 70-71; asst prof, 72-78, ASSOC PROF PHARMACOL, EASTERN VA MED SCH, 78- *Concurrent Pos:* Consult, United Drug Abuse Coun & Health Adv Coord Comt, Model Cities Comprehensive Health Sci Proj, 72; lectr, Sch Continuing Educ, Univ Va, 72; asst prof nursing & dent hyg, Old Dom Univ, 72-74; Tidewater Heart Asn res grant, 75; Am Heart Asn/Va Affil res grant, 76-77; Nat Inst Heart Lung & Blood Inst grant, 76- *Mem:* AAAS; Asn Am Med Cols; Asn Women in Sci; Am Fedn Clin Res. *Res:* Cardiovascular pharmacology and physiology of vascular smooth muscle with particular interest in the etiology and treatment of hypertension and peripheral vascular disease. *Mailing Add:* Dept of Pharmacol Eastern Va Med Sch PO Box 1980 Norfolk VA 23501

WILLIAMS, PATRICK KELLY, b San Angelo, Tex, July 31, 43; m 68. ECOLOGY. *Educ:* Univ Tex, Austin, BA, 66; Univ Minn, Minneapolis, MS, 69; Ind Univ, Bloomington, PhD(zool), 73. *Prof Exp:* Asst prof, 73-80, ASSOC PROF BIOL, UNIV DAYTON, 80- *Mem:* Ecol Soc Am; Am Soc Mammalogists; Am Soc Ichthyologists & Herpetologists. *Res:* Experimental population ecology on rodents with emphasis on natural regulation and management. *Mailing Add:* Dept of Biol Univ of Dayton Dayton OH 45469

WILLIAMS, PAUL HUGH, b Vancouver, BC, May 6, 38; m 63. PLANT PATHOLOGY, PLANT GENETICS. *Educ:* Univ BC, BSA, 59; Univ Wis, PhD(plant path), 62. *Prof Exp:* From asst prof to assoc prof, 62-71, PROF PLANT PATH, UNIV WIS-MADISON, 71- *Concurrent Pos:* J S Guggenheim fel, 77-78. *Honors & Awards:* Jakob Eriksson Medal, Swed Acad Sci, 81. *Mem:* Am Phytopath Soc; Am Genetics Asn; Am Soc Hort Sci. *Res:* Genetics and cytology of host-parasite relations and resistance breeding for disease resistance in vegetables; crucifer genetics. *Mailing Add:* Dept of Plant Path Univ of Wis Madison WI 53706

WILLIAMS, PETER J, b Croydon, Eng, Sept 27, 32; m 57; c 3. SOIL PHYSICS, GEOTECHNICAL SCIENCE. *Educ:* Cambridge Univ, BA, 54, MS, 58; Univ Stockholm, Fil Lic & Fil Dr, 69. *Prof Exp:* Res off soil mech sect, Div Bldg Res, Nat Res Coun Can, 57-69; assoc prof geog, 69-71, PROF GEOG, CARLETON UNIV, 71-, DIR GEOTECH SERV LAB, 79- *Concurrent Pos:* Royal Norweg Coun Sci & Indust Res fel, Norweg Geotech Inst, 63-65; lectr several univs in UK, Sweden, Norway, US & Can; consult & geotech adv, Northern Pipelines, Can Govt. *Mem:* Can Asn Geog; Norweg Geotech Soc; Can Geotech Soc; Can Soc Soil Sci. *Res:* Physics of freezing soils and application to engineering, especially Northern pipelines; geomorphology, especially frost action. *Mailing Add:* Geotech Sci Lab Carleton Univ Ottawa ON K1S 5B6 Can

WILLIAMS, PETER M, b New York, NY, July 17, 27; m 58; c 3. CHEMICAL OCEANOGRAPHY. *Educ:* Washington & Lee Univ, BS, 49; Univ Calif, Los Angeles, MS, 58, PhD(oceanog), 60. *Prof Exp:* Asst res chemist, Smith, Kline & French Labs, 49-51; lab technician, Citrus Exp Sta, Univ Calif, Riverside, 53-54; asst prof marine chem, Inst Oceanog, Univ BC, 60-63; asst res chemist, 63-69, assoc res chemist, 69-76, RES CHEMIST, INST MARINE RESOURCES, UNIV CALIF, SAN DIEGO, 76- *Mem:* Am Geophys Union; Am Chem Soc; Am Soc Limnol & Oceanog; AAAS; Goechem Soc. *Res:* Organic chemistry of sea water with respect to dissolved and patriculate organic matter derived from marine organisms. *Mailing Add:* Inst of Marine Resources A-018 Univ of Calif San Diego La Jolla CA 92093

WILLIAMS, PHARIS EDWARD, b Seligman, Mo, July 13, 41; m 61; c 4. THEORETICAL PHYSICS. *Educ:* Univ Colo, BS, 68; Naval Postgrad Sch, MS, 76. *Prof Exp:* Course supvr nuclear weapons training, Nuclear Weapons Training Group, Pacific, 72-74; instr thermodynamics, US Navel Acad, 76-78; NAVAL RES ASSOC, LOS ALAMOS NAT LAB, 78- *Mem:* Sigma Xi. *Res:* Dynamic theory containing current theories as special subsets with applications in the areas of electromagnetism, elementary particles, nuclear structure, and plasma physics. *Mailing Add:* Los Alamos Nat Lab MS 245 Los Alamos NM 87545

WILLIAMS, PHILIP CARSLAKE, b Mountain Ash, Wales, May 26, 33; Can citizen; m 70; c 4. ANALYTICAL CHEMISTRY. *Educ:* Univ Wales, BS, 54, PhD(agr biochem), 58. *Prof Exp:* Res officer, Agr Res Inst, Wagga Wagga, NSW, 58-64; fel cereal chem, Nat Res Coun Can, 64-65; RES SCIENTIST, GRAIN RES LAB, CAN GRAIN COMN, 65- *Concurrent Pos:* Consult, Int Ctr Agr Res, Syria, 75-, Int Develop Res Ctr, 74- *Mem:* Am Asn Cereal Chemists. *Res:* Near-infrared reflectance spectroscopic analysis of cereal grains, oilseals, pulses, and derived products; planning and design of large-scale analytical operations; applied statistical analysis. *Mailing Add:* Grain Res Lab 1404-303 Main St Winnipeg MB R3C 3G9 Can

WILLIAMS, PHLETUS P, b Junior, WVa, Aug 3, 33; m 60; c 3. MICROBIOLOGY, BIOCHEMISTRY. *Educ:* Davis & Elkins Col, BS, 55; Univ Md, MS, 59; NDak State Univ, PhD(animal nutrit), 68. *Prof Exp:* Microbiologist beef cattle res br, Animal Husb Res Div, Md, 59-60, dairy cattle res br, 60-61, beef cattle res br, 61-64, prof bact, 72-73, MICROBIOLOGIST, METAB & RADIATION RES LAB, N DAK STATE UNIV, SCI & EDUC ADMIN-AGR RES, USDA, 64- ADJ PROF BACT, 73- *Mem:* AAAS; Am Soc Animal Sci; Am Soc Microbiol; Brit Soc Gen Microbiol. *Res:* Development of rumen protozoal controlled bovines; chemical, physiological, cultural and metabolical study of rumen bacteria and protozoa; microbial metabolic fate studies with lipoidal and pesticidal compounds. *Mailing Add:* 2905 Edgewood Dr Fargo ND 58102

WILLIAMS, RALPH C, JR, b Washington, DC, Feb 17, 28; m 51; c 4. INTERNAL MEDICINE, IMMUNOLOGY. *Educ:* Cornell Univ, AB, 50, MD, 54. *Prof Exp:* Guest investr immunol, Rockefeller Inst, 61-63; from asst prof to prof med, Med Sch, Univ Minn, Minneapolis, 63-69; PROF MED & CHMN DEPT, SCH MED, UNIV NMEX, 69- *Concurrent Pos:* Consult, Bur Hearings & Appeals, Soc Security Admin, 65- *Mem:* Am Rheumatism Asn; Am Fedn Clin Res; Am Soc Clin Invest; Am Asn Immunol; Soc Exp Biol & Med. *Res:* Rheumatic diseases; immunopathology; immunoglobulin abnormalities and their relation to disease. *Mailing Add:* Dept of Med Seventh Floor Bernalillo County Med Ctr Albuquerque NM 87106

WILLIAMS, RALPH EDWARD, b Ontario, Ore, July 20, 43; m 63. PHYTOPATHOLOGY. *Educ:* Univ Idaho, BS, 65, MS, 69; Wash State Univ, PhD(plant path), 72. *Prof Exp:* Res asst plant path, Dept Plant Sci, Univ Idaho, 65-66, Wash State Univ, 66-68; res plant pathologist, Forest Serv, USDA, 67-70; weed control specialist, Latah County, Idaho, 70; PLANT PATHOLOGIST, FOREST PEST MGT, FOREST SERV, USDA, 70- *Res:* Develop growth impact methodology; conduct survey and analyse survey data for root disease centers in forests of northern Idaho and western Montana; develop models for root disease center occurrence; design and establish root disease management evaluations. *Mailing Add:* c/o Idaho City Stage Boise ID 83707

WILLIAMS, RAY CLAYTON, b Louisville, Ky, July 17, 44. PERIODONTOLOGY, MICROBIOLOGY. *Educ:* Samford Univ, AB, 66; Univ Ala, Birmingham, DMD, 70; Harvard Univ, cert periodont, 73. *Prof Exp:* Res fel periodont, Sch Dent Med, Harvard Univ, 70-73; res fel microbiol, Forsyth Dent Ctr, Boston, Mass, 70-74; instr, 74-78, ASST PROF PERIODONT, SCH DENT MED, HARVARD UNIV, 79-, ACTG CHMN

DEPT, 81- *Concurrent Pos:* Consult, WRoxbury Vet Admin Hosp, Mass, 77-80, attend physician, 80-; consult, Children's Hosp Med Ctr, 81- *Mem:* Am Acad Periodont; Int Asn Dent Res; Am Soc Microbiol. *Res:* Microbial etiology of periodontal disease; pharmacologic interception of peridontal diseases. *Mailing Add:* Dept Periodont 188 Longwood Ave Boston MA 02115

WILLIAMS, RAYMOND CRAWFORD, b Kansas City, Mo, Sept 22, 24; m 59; c 1. VETERINARY ANATOMY. *Educ:* Kans State Col, DVM, 46; Cornell Univ, MS, 55, PhD, 61. *Prof Exp:* Instr, 46-54, from asst prof to assoc prof, 54-64, PROF ANAT & HISTOL, SCH VET MED, TUSKEGEE INST, 64- *Mem:* AAAS; Am Vet Med Asn; Am Asn Vet Anat; World Asn Vet Anat; Southern Soc Anatomists. *Res:* Descriptive vertebrate anatomy; fetal size and age relationships; dentition development; anatomical museum methods. *Mailing Add:* Dept Anat Sch Vet Med Tuskegee Inst AL 36088

WILLIAMS, REED CHESTER, b Chicago, Ill, June 10, 41. ANALYTICAL CHEMISTRY. *Educ:* Lawrence Univ, BA, 63; Univ Wash, PhD(chem), 68. *Prof Exp:* RES CHEMIST, E I DU PONT DE NEMOURS & CO, INC, 68- *Mem:* Am Chem Soc; Sigma Xi. *Res:* Analytical chemistry; application of high speed liquid column chromatography to the separation and quantitation of complex mixtures. *Mailing Add:* Glasgow B100 E I du Pont de Nemours & Co Inc Wilmington DE 19898

WILLIAMS, RICHARD, b Chicago, Ill, Aug 5, 27; m 61; c 3. PHYSICAL CHEMISTRY. *Educ:* Miami Univ, AB, 50; Harvard Univ, PhD(phys chem), 54. *Prof Exp:* Instr chem, Harvard Univ, 55-58; MEM TECH STAFF, RCA LABS, 58- *Concurrent Pos:* Fulbright lectr, Sao Carlos Sch Eng, 69. *Honors & Awards:* Callinan Prize, Electrochem Soc. *Mem:* Fel Am Phys Soc; Brazilian Acad Sci. *Res:* Electrical properties of insulators; liquid crystals; luminescence of organic molecules; physical chemistry of surfaces. *Mailing Add:* RCA Labs Princeton NJ 08540

WILLIAMS, RICHARD ALVIN, b North Canton, Ohio, July 21, 36; m 72. ELECTRICAL ENGINEERING, COMPUTER SCIENCE. *Educ:* Ohio State Univ, BSEE, 59, MSc, 61, PhD(elec eng), 65. *Prof Exp:* Staff mem reliability eng, Sandia Corp, NMex, 59-60; assoc supvr electrosci lab, Ohio State Univ, 60-68, asst prof elec eng, 66-68; ASSOC PROF ELEC ENG, UNIV AKRON, 66-; ENG SPECIALIST, GOODYEAR AEROSPACE CORP, 79- *Res:* Communications; communication satellite systems; computers, simulation programming and application; environmental engineering; electric power systems; transportation; aerospace electronics. *Mailing Add:* Dept of Elec Eng Univ of Akron Akron OH 44325

WILLIAMS, RICHARD ANDERSON, b Akron, Ohio, July 21, 31; m 51; c 5. TEXTILE CHEMISTRY. *Educ:* Wabash Col, AB, 53; Univ Rochester, PhD(chem), 57. *Prof Exp:* Res chemist, Patent Div, 56-60, sr res chemist, Nylon Tech Div, 60-68, supvr res, Qiana Tech Div, 68-71, supvr res & develop, Orlon-Lycra Tech Div, 71-72, patent supvr, Patent Liaison Div, Textile Fibers Dept, 72-77, DEVELOP ASSOC, CARPET FIBERS TECH DIV, E I DU PONT DE NEMOURS & CO, 77- *Mem:* Am Asn Textile Chem & Color; Am Chem Soc. *Res:* Olefin-forming elimination reactions; polymer chemistry; synthetic fibers and applications. *Mailing Add:* RD 2 Box 36 Hockessin DE 19707

WILLIAMS, RICHARD BIRGE, b Monticello, NY, Feb 5, 29; m 51, 66; c 2. MARINE ECOLOGY. *Educ:* Univ Buffalo, BA, 51; Univ Wis, MS, 52; Harvard Univ, PhD(biol), 62. *Prof Exp:* Oceanogr, US Naval Hydrographic Off, 52-54; biologist, Biophys Div, Army Chem Ctr, 54-57; fishery biologist, Radiobiol Lab, US Bur Commercial Fisheries, 62-67; health physicist, Oak Ridge Nat Lab, 67-68; fishery biologist, Atlantic Estuarine Fisheries Ctr, Nat Marine Fisheries Serv, 68-72; PROG DIR BIOL OCEANOG, NSF, 72- *Concurrent Pos:* Adj asst prof, NC State Univ, 66-70, adj assoc prof, 70- *Mem:* AAAS; Am Soc Limnol & Oceanog; Ecol Soc Am. *Res:* Measurement of rate of production of estuarine plants; analysis of estuarine food webs. *Mailing Add:* Nat Sci Found 1800 G St NW Washington DC 20550

WILLIAMS, RICHARD JOHN, b Hazleton, Pa, May 24, 44; m 66. SCIENCE ADMINISTRATION, PLANETARY & EARTH SCIENCES. *Educ:* Lehigh Univ, BA, 66; Johns Hopkins Univ, MA, 68, PhD(geochem), 70. *Prof Exp:* Space scientist lunar studies, 70-73, sr space scientist lunar and planetary studies, 73-78, SUPVRY SPACE SCIENTIST, JOHNSON SPACE CTR, NASA, 79- *Honors & Awards:* Sigma Xi. *Mem:* Am Inst Aeronaut & Astronaut; Am Geophys Union. *Res:* Theoretical and experimental petrology; space industrialization; science and technology policy. *Mailing Add:* SN7 Johnson Space Ctr NASA Houston TX 77058

WILLIAMS, RICHARD KELSO, b Chattanooga, Tenn, Oct 20, 38; m 66. MATHEMATICS. *Educ:* Vanderbilt Univ, BA, 60, MA, 62, PhD(math), 65. *Prof Exp:* From asst prof to assoc prof, 65-77, chmn dept, 78-80, PROF MATH, SOUTHERN METHODIST UNIV, 77- *Mem:* Math Asn Am; Am Math Soc. *Res:* Complex function theory; topology. *Mailing Add:* Dept Math Southern Methodist Univ Dallas TX 75275

WILLIAMS, RICHARD M, physical oceanography, atmospheric physics, see previous edition

WILLIAMS, RICHARD SUGDEN, JR, b New York, NY, Dec 6, 38; m 60; c 2. SATELLITE GLACIOLOGY, GEOLOGIC REMOTE SENSING. *Educ:* Univ Mich, Ann Arbor, BS, 61, MS, 62; Pa State Univ, PhD(geol), 65. *Prof Exp:* Proj scientist geol, Air Force Cambridge Res Labs, 65-68, res geologist, 68-69, br chief, 69-71; GEOLOGIST, US GEOL SURV, 71- *Concurrent Pos:* Geologist, UNESCO, 71-; assoc ed, J Photogram Eng & Remote Sensing, 76-77. *Honors & Awards:* Alan Gordon Mem Award, Am Soc Photogram, 78. *Mem:* Fel Geol Soc Am; fel Iceland Sci Soc; Am Geophys Union; Am Soc Photogram; Int Glaciological Soc. *Res:* Remote sensing of dynamic geological phenomena and geologic hazards; chiefly photogeologic and thermal infrared studies of volcanoes, geothermal areas and glaciers with aircraft and satellite (LANDSAT, NOAA) sensors with particular emphasis on active geologic and geomorphic processes in Iceland; author of over 50 scientific publications. *Mailing Add:* US Geol Surv Reston VA 22092

WILLIAMS, RICHARD TAYLOR, b Tarboro, NC, May 27, 46. SOLID STATE PHYSICS. *Educ:* Wake Forest Univ, BS, 68; Princeton Univ, MA, 71, PhD(physics), 74. *Prof Exp:* PHYSICIST, NAVAL RES LAB, 69- *Mem:* Am Phys Soc; AAAS. *Res:* Effects of ionizing radiation in insulating solids, particularly time-resolved studies of exciton self-trapping and defect formation in halide crystals; vacuum-ultraviolet spectroscopy of solids. *Mailing Add:* Optical Mat Br Naval Res Lab Washington DC 20375

WILLIAMS, RICKEY JAY, b Muskogee, Okla, May 13, 42. PHYSICAL INORGANIC CHEMISTRY. *Educ:* Tex Christian Univ, BA, 64, MD, PhD(phys chem), 68. *Prof Exp:* Fel Los Alamos Sci Lab, 68-70 & Baylor Univ, 70-71; asst prof, 71-74, assoc prof, 74-80, PROF & HEAD DEPT CHEM, PHYSICS GEOL & GEOPHYSICS, MIDWESTERN STATE UNIV, 80- *Mem:* Am Crystallog Asn; Am Chem Soc. *Res:* Crystal structure studies of inorganic compounds. *Mailing Add:* Dept of Chem Midwestern State Univ Wichita Falls TX 76308

WILLIAMS, ROBERT ALLEN, b Cleveland, Ohio, Apr 25, 45. NUCLEAR CHEMISTRY. *Educ:* Oberlin Col, BA, 66; Carnegie-Mellon Univ, MS, 69, PhD(nuclear chem), 72. *Prof Exp:* Res assoc nuclear chem, 72-73, presidential intern, 73-74, STAFF MEM NUCLEAR CHEM, LOS ALAMOS SCI LAB, UNIV CALIF, 74- *Mem:* Am Chem Soc; Am Phys Soc; Sigma Xi. *Res:* Pionic nuclear reactions; neutron activation analysis; nuclear spectroscopy; computer applications. *Mailing Add:* 1063 48th St Los Alamos NM 87544

WILLIAMS, ROBERT BRUCE, b Washington, DC, Apr 30, 38; m 61; c 3. PHYSICAL OCEANOGRAPHY. *Educ:* San Diego State Col, BS, 64; Univ Calif, San Diego, MS, 68, PhD(eng sci), 73. *Prof Exp:* Lab technician, Univ Calif, San Diego, 60-66, assoc engr, 66-74; oceanogr, NATO, Italy, 74-77; SPECIALIST MARINE PHYSICS, UNIV CALIF, SAN DIEGO, 78- *Res:* Oceanographic underwater acoustics, turbulence and thermal microstructure; small computer systems at sea data collection and processing; ultra high frequency atmospheric propagation. *Mailing Add:* Marine Phys Lab Univ of Calif La Jolla CA 92093

WILLIAMS, ROBERT CALVIN, b Key West, Fla, May 1, 44; m 69. ANALYTICAL CHEMISTRY, PHYSICAL CHEMISTRY. *Educ:* Univ Kans, BS, 66; Univ Wis-Madison, PhD(phys chem), 72. *Prof Exp:* Instr chem, Univ Nebr-Lincoln, 72-74; sr chemist, Cent Res Labs, 3M Co, 74-79; res specialist, 79, SR RES & DEVELOP CHEMIST, BF GOODRICH CHEM GROUP, 79- *Concurrent Pos:* Res assoc, Univ Nebr-Lincoln, 72-74. *Mem:* Am Chem Soc; Am Phys Soc; Soc Appl Spectros; Coblentz Soc; AAAS. *Res:* Computer coupled instrumentation and instrumental methods of analysis; molecular spectroscopy, particularly infrared and mass spectroscopy; infrared normal coordinate analysis; analytical applications of fourier transform infrared spectroscopy; polymer chemistry. *Mailing Add:* Avon Lake Tech Ctr PO Box 122 Aron Lake OH 44012

WILLIAMS, ROBERT D(OWNES), b Cambridge, Mass, Nov 23, 11; m 41; c 2. METALLURGY. *Educ:* Harvard Univ, AB, 34; Mass Inst Technol, MS, 37. *Prof Exp:* Asst instr mech eng, Mass Inst Technol, 36-37; assoc, Univ Ill, 37-42; res engr welding, Res Div, Battelle Mem Inst, 42-44, asst supvr, 44-54, supvr res contract admin & security off, 54-57, supvr contract off, 57-65, mgr contracts dept, 65-71, asst bus mgr, 71-74, mgr, Internal Auditing Dept, 74-76; RETIRED. *Honors & Awards:* Award, Resistance Welder Mfrs Asn, 46. *Mem:* Sigma Xi; Am Inst Mining, Metall & Petrol Engrs. Engrs. *Mailing Add:* 8 Canterbury Village Columbus OH 43201

WILLIAMS, ROBERT DEE, b Wingate, Ind, June 4, 32; m 60; c 2. VETERINARY MEDICINE, MICROBIOLOGY. *Educ:* Wabash Col, AB, 54; Purdue Univ, DVM, 65, MS, 68, PhD(microbiol), 71. *Prof Exp:* Sanitarian, Ind State Bd Health, 56-60; veterinarian, Food & Drug Admin, 71-75; res veterinarian, Com Solvents Corp, 75-76; DIR ANIMAL SCI RES, INT MINERALS & CHEM CORP, 76- *Concurrent Pos:* Am Vet Med Asn fel, Purdue Univ, 65-66, NIH fel, 67-70. *Mem:* Am Vet Med Asn; Am Asn Indust Veterinarians; Am Soc Microbiol; Int Soc Ecotoxicol & Environ Safety. *Res:* New drugs for animals; toxicology. *Mailing Add:* Int Minerals & Chem Corp PO Box 207 Terre Haute IN 47808

WILLIAMS, ROBERT EARL, physical chemistry, see previous edition

WILLIAMS, ROBERT ELLIS, b Grenada, Miss, Apr 9, 30; m 67; c 3. BIOLOGY. *Educ:* Memphis State Univ, BA, 56; Ohio State Univ, MA, 57, PhD, 61. *Prof Exp:* Res assoc, Ohio State Res Found, 60; entomologist, Army Biol Labs, 61-63, chief insect biol res br, 63-65; asst head microbiol br, Off Naval Res, 65-66, prof officer biol countermeasures, 66-67, head virol dept, Naval Med Res Unit 3, Cairo, Egypt, 68-73; PATRON, ANTIOCH COL, 73- *Mem:* Am Soc Trop Med & Hyg; Entom Soc Am; Am Mosquito Control Asn. *Res:* Entomology; arbovirology; ecology. *Mailing Add:* Glaydin Sch Leesburg VA 22075

WILLIAMS, ROBERT ELVIN, b Bloomfield, Mo, Dec 28, 35; m 58; c 3. MATHEMATICS. *Educ:* Univ Mo, BS, 59, MA, 61, PhD(math), 65. *Prof Exp:* Asst prof math, Westminster Col, Mo, 63-65; ASST PROF MATH, KANS STATE UNIV, 65- *Mem:* Am Math Soc; Math Asn Am. *Res:* Near-rings; prime rings and quotient rings; divisibility in Cohn rings. *Mailing Add:* Dept of Math Kans State Univ Manhattan KS 66506

WILLIAMS, ROBERT FONES, b Bessemer, Ala, July 27, 28; m 52; c 1. TOPOLOGY. *Educ:* Univ Tex, BA, 48; Univ Va, PhD(math), 54. *Prof Exp:* Asst prof math, Fla State Univ, 54-55; vis lectr, Univ Wis, 55-56; asst prof, Purdue Univ, 56-59; NSF fel & mem Inst Adv Study, 59-61; asst prof, Univ Chicago, 61-63; assoc prof, 63-67, PROF MATH, NORTHWESTERN UNIV, EVANSTON, 67- *Concurrent Pos:* NSF grant, Univ Geneva, 68-69 & Inst Advan Sci Study, Bures-sur-Yvette, France, 70, 72-73. *Mem:* Am Math Soc. *Res:* Transformation groups; toplogical dynamics; global analysis; differentiable dynamical systems. *Mailing Add:* Dept of Math Northwestern Univ Evanston IL 60201

WILLIAMS, ROBERT GLENN, b Teaneck, NJ, Oct 14, 37; m 65; c 3. OCEANOGRAPHY. *Educ:* NY Univ, BA, 60, MS, 65, PhD(oceanog), 71. *Prof Exp:* Asst res scientist oceanog, NY Univ, 60-61 & 63-65; oceanogr, US Naval Underwater Systs Ctr, New London, Conn, 65-72; prog coordr oceanog, Rockville, Md, 72-74, dep chief scientist, Ship Oceanogr, 74, oceanogr, Ctr Environ Assessment Serv, 74-81, PHYS SCIENTIST, ENG DEVELOP OFF, NAT OCEANIC & ATMOSPHERIC ADMIN, 81- *Concurrent Pos:* Instr environ sci, Frederick Community Col, Md, 81. *Mem:* Am Geophys Union; Am Soc Limnol & Oceanog. *Res:* Air-sea interaction and dynamic studies of the tropical oceans, and continental shelves, with emphasis on exchange of heat and moisture with the atmosphere on time scales of several weeks; surface wind wave measurement system analysis; underwater acoustics; development of acoustic ocean current measurement systems. *Mailing Add:* 6501 Lafeyette Ave TE 2 Eng Develop Off Nat Oceanic & Atmospheric Admin Riverdale MD 20737

WILLIAMS, ROBERT HACKNEY, b Providence, RI, Jan 3, 15; m 42; c 2. ORGANIC CHEMISTRY. *Educ:* Univ NC, AB, 35, MA, 37; Temple Univ, PhD(chem), 53. *Prof Exp:* Res chemist, Mobil Res & Develop Lab, 38-42, sr res chemist, Cent Res Div Lab, 46-72, asst to admin mgr, Cent Res Div, Mobil Res & Develop Corp, 72-75; RETIRED. *Concurrent Pos:* VChmn, Punta Gorda-Charlotte Water & Sewer Bd, 78-81; mem water adv bd, Southwest Fla Regional Planning Coun, 78-81. *Mem:* Am Chem Soc; Am Inst Chem. *Res:* Petroleum additives; hydrocracking; lube oil manufacture and composition; radiation chemistry of hydrocarbons; application of nuclear radiation to petroleum processing; radiation and photochemical induced organic chemical reactions; oxidation of hydrocarbons. *Mailing Add:* 1615 Via Bianca Punta Gorda Isles Punta Gorda FL 33950

WILLIAMS, ROBERT HAWORTH, b Seattle, Wash, Mar 31, 14; m 39, 54; c 3. PLANT PHYSIOLOGY. *Educ:* Univ Wash, Seattle, BS, 35, MS, 40; Cornell Univ, PhD(plant physiol), 41. *Prof Exp:* Asst bot, Cornell Univ, 36-38, instr, 38-41; from asst prof, Univ Miami, Fla, 41-54, prof marine biol, 50-54, asst dir marine lab, 42-51; prof marine sci, Fla State Univ, 54-55; prof, 55-80, EMER PROF BIOL, UNIV MIAMI, 80- *Concurrent Pos:* Asst, US Frozen Pack Lab, Wash, 35. *Mem:* Am Soc Limnol & Oceanog; Phycol Soc Am. *Res:* Carbon dioxide absorption of roots; carbohydrates of the large brown algae; physiology of fern spore germination; ecology of marine algae of Florida. *Mailing Add:* Dept of Biol Univ of Miami Coral Gables FL 33124

WILLIAMS, ROBERT J(AMES), b Iron Mountain, Mich, Sept 12, 23; m 47; c 4. INDUSTRIAL ENGINEERING. *Educ:* Mich State Univ, BSME, 47, MSME, 53. *Prof Exp:* Instr mech eng, Univ Colo, 48-51; sr indust engr, Boeing Airplane Co, 51-54; from asst prof to assoc prof mech eng, Univ Colo, 52-61, chmn dept, 56-61; indust engr, Fry & Assocs, 61-63; assoc prof, 63-77, PROF ENG DESIGN & ECON EVAL, UNIV COLO, BOULDER, 77- *Concurrent Pos:* Consult, Vet Admin Hosp, Seattle, 53, Boeing Airplane Co, 58, Mountain States Tel & Tel Co, 59-, Babcock & Wilcox Co, Ohio, 60 & Govt of India, 61-63. *Mem:* Am Soc Mech Engrs; Am Soc Eng Educ; Am Inst Indust Engrs; Opers Res Soc Am. *Res:* Process engineering; engineering economics. *Mailing Add:* Dept of Eng Design & Econ Eval Univ of Colo Boulder CO 80302

WILLIAMS, ROBERT JACKSON, b Iowa City, Iowa, June 13, 31; m 74; c 3. PHYSIOLOGY, ECOLOGY. *Educ:* Univ Wis-Madison, BA, 53, MA, 61; Univ Md, College Park, PhD(zool), 67. *Prof Exp:* Cryobiologist, Am Found Biol Res, Wis, 60-62; biologist, Naval Med Res Inst, Md, 63-67; RES SCIENTIST CRYOBIOL, BLOOD RES LAB, AM NAT RED CROSS, 67- *Mem:* AAAS; Am Physiol Soc; Soc Cryobiol; Am Soc Plant Physiol; Biophys Soc. *Res:* Mechanisms of cell freezing injury; effects of low temperature on geographical distribution; instrumentation. *Mailing Add:* Blood Res Lab Am Int Red Cross 9312 Old Georgetown Rd Bethesda MD 20014

WILLIAMS, ROBERT K, b Ft Worth, Tex, Jan 6, 28; m 52; c 3. ENTOMOLOGY, CELL BIOLOGY. *Educ:* Agr & Mech Col Tex, BS, 48, MS, 56, PhD(entom), 59. *Prof Exp:* Asst county agent in training, Agr Exten Serv, Agr & Mech Col, Tex, 48, asst county agent, Agr Exten Serv & Wood County, 48, Agr exten Serv & Bowie County, 50 & Agr Exten Serv & Eastland County, 52-54, res asst entom, Col, 54-58; PROF BIOL, E TEX STATE UNIV, 58- *Concurrent Pos:* NSF Col Sci Improv Prog grant, Dept Physiol Chem, Univ Wis, 69-70. *Res:* Physiology; cell physiology; molecular biology. *Mailing Add:* Dept of Biol East Tex State Univ Commerce TX 75428

WILLIAMS, ROBERT K(ETTERING), b Chicago, Ill, Aug 4, 17; m 41; c 2. CHEMICAL ENGINEERING. *Educ:* Princeton Univ, BS, 40. *Prof Exp:* From res engr to sr res engr, Fuels & Lubricants Dept, Res Labs Div, Gen Motors Corp, 43-52, asst head, 52-55; head mech testing dept, 55-62, asst dir eng, 62-65, exec asst to pres, 65-66, V PRES CORP PLANNING & DEVELOP, LUBRIZOL CORP, 66- *Mem:* Soc Automotive Engrs. *Res:* Development and testing of fuels and lubricants. *Mailing Add:* Box 786 CCNC Pinehurst NC 28374

WILLIAMS, ROBERT L, b Buffalo, NY, July 22, 22; m 49; c 2. PSYCHIATRY, NEUROLOGY. *Educ:* Alfred Univ, BA, 44; Albany Med Col, Union Univ, NY, MD, 46. *Prof Exp:* Chief, Air Force Neurol Ctr, Lackland AFB Hosp, 52-55, chief neuropsychiat serv, 53-55, chief consult, Off Surgeon Gen, US Air Force, 55-58; from assoc prof to prof psychiat & neurol, Col Med, Univ Fla, 58-72, chmn dept psychiat, 64-72; prof psychiat & chmn dept, 72-76, actg chmn neurol dept, 76-77, PROF NEUROL, BAYLOR COL MED, 76- *Concurrent Pos:* Mem, Nat Adv Ment Health Coun & Nat Adv Neurol Dis & Blindness Coun, 55-58; Fla rep, Comn Ment Illness, Southern Regional Educ Bd, 64-72, chmn, 71-72; psychiat consult, Indust Security Prog, Dept Defense & consult psychiat & neurol, Surgeon Gen, US Air Force, 66- *Mem:* Fel AAAS; AMA; fel Am Psychiat Asn; fel Am Acad Neurol; Am Electroencephalog Soc. *Res:* Psychophysiology of sleep; medical education. *Mailing Add:* Baylor Col of Med Tex Med Ctr Houston TX 77030

WILLIAMS, ROBERT LEROY, b St Thomas, Ont, July 9, 28; m 51; c 3. PHYSICS. *Educ:* Univ Western Ont, BSc, 51; Univ BC, MA, 52, PhD(physics), 56. *Prof Exp:* Sci officer, Defense Res Bd Can, 55-59; group leader physics, RCA Victor Co, 59-63; chief physicist, Simtec Ltd, 63-65, gen mgr, 65-66; mem sci staff physics, 66-69, BR MGR DETECTOR DEVELOP, TEX INSTRUMENTS INC, 69- *Mem:* Am Phys Soc; sr mem Inst Elec & Electronics Eng. *Res:* Physics of infrared and nuclear particle detectors; development of detectors; diode, transistor and bulk structures. *Mailing Add:* 830 Northlake Dr Richardson TX 75080

WILLIAMS, ROBERT LLOYD, b Coshocton, Ohio, Mar 16, 33; m 59; c 4. INDUSTRIAL ENGINEERING, OPERATIONS RESEARCH. *Educ:* Ohio State Univ, BS & MS, 60, PhD(indust eng), 64. *Prof Exp:* Res assoc & instr indust eng, Ohio State Univ, 60-64; PROF INDUST & SYSTS ENG & CHMN DEPT, OHIO UNIV, 67- *Concurrent Pos:* Mem Z-94 comt indust eng terminology, Am Nat Standards Inst, 66-; Hwy & Econ Growth res grant, 66-69; res contract, effects Hwy Warning Signs, 78-82. *Mem:* Am Inst Indust Engrs; Opers Res Soc Am. *Res:* Transportation systems. *Mailing Add:* Dept of Indust & Systs Eng Ohio Univ Athens OH 45701

WILLIAMS, ROBERT MACK, b Idalou, Tex, Dec 30, 31; m 53; c 4. FOOD SCIENCE & TECHNOLOGY. *Educ:* Tex Tech Univ, BS, 54; Mich State Univ, MS, 58, PhD(food technol), 61. *Prof Exp:* Prod foreman dairy, Kroger Co, Marion, Ind, 61-63 & Indianapolis, 63-64, mgr qual control, 64-65 & Springdale, Ohio, 65-66, mgr spec proj admin staff, Cincinatti, 66-68, prod mgr dairy, St Louis, 68-69, mgr prod develop & tech serv, Mfg Div, 69-72, dir res & develop, 72-78, VPRES RES & DEVELOP, MGF DIV, KROGER CO, CINCINNATI, 78- *Mem:* Am Dairy Sci Asn; Am Dairy Cultured Prod Asn. *Res:* Utilization of acid whey, hydrolosate as a fermentation substitute for bakers yeast; decaffeination of coffee and tea, using carbon dioxide; continuous blending of nitrous oxide with soft-serve ice cream mix for over-run control and soft-serve ice cream dispensers. *Mailing Add:* 1212 State Ave Cincinnati OH 45204

WILLIAMS, ROBERT PIERCE, b Chicago, Ill, Oct 27, 20; m 44; c 2. MICROBIOLOGY. *Educ:* Dartmouth Col, AB, 42; Univ Chicago, SM, 46, PhD(bact, parasitol), 49; Am Bd Med Microbiol, cert. *Prof Exp:* Asst bact, Univ Chicago, 46-47, cur, 47-49; instr, Univ Southern Calif, 49-51; from asst prof to assoc prof, 51-63, actg chmn dept, 61-66, PROF MICROBIOL, BAYLOR COL MED, 63- *Concurrent Pos:* Lectr, Univ Houston, 64; vis mem grad fac, Col Vet Med, Tex A&M Univ, 65-; consult, Vet Admin Hosp & M D Anderson Hosp, 57- *Mem:* AAAS; Am Soc Microbiol (pres-elect, 82); Am Chem Soc; fel Am Acad Microbiol; Brit Soc Gen Microbiol. *Res:* Bacterial pigments, particularly prodigiosin and porphyrins; virulence versus avirulence of microorganisms; microbial nutrition; host-parasite relationships in bacterial infections; pathogenesis of gonorrhea. *Mailing Add:* Dept Microbiol Baylor Col Med Houston TX 77030

WILLIAMS, ROBERT WALTER, b Palo Alto, Calif, June 3, 20; m 46, 58, 69; c 3. EXPERIMENTAL HIGH-ENERGY PHYSICS. *Educ:* Stanford Univ, AB, 41; Princeton Univ, MA, 43; Mass Inst Technol, PhD(physics), 48. *Prof Exp:* Lab asst, Princeton Univ, 41-42; from jr physicist to assoc physicist, Manhattan Proj, Princeton Univ & Los Alamos Sci Lab, 42-46; res assoc, Mass Inst Technol, 46-48, from asst prof to assoc prof, 48-59; PROF PHYSICS, UNIV WASH, 59- *Concurrent Pos:* sci assoc, Europ Orgn Nuclear Res, 67-68, 74-75 & 81-82; trustee, Univ Res Asn, 78- *Mem:* Fel Am Phys Soc; fel Am Acad Arts & Sci. *Res:* Elementary particle physics using high-energy accelerators; cosmic rays; elementary particles. *Mailing Add:* Physics FM-15 Univ of Wash Seattle WA 98195

WILLIAMS, ROBIN, b Southampton, Eng, July 10, 41; US citizen; m 65; c 2. COMPUTER SCIENCE, DISTRIBUTED PROCESSING. *Educ:* Univ London, BSc, 62; NY Univ, MS, 68, PhD(comput sci), 71. *Prof Exp:* Staff mem optical character recognition, Mullard Res Labs, Philips Co, Eng, 62-64, staff mem comput memories, Philips Res Labs, 64-67; asst prof & instr comput sci, NY Univ, 67-72; mgr distrib comput, 72-80, MGR, DATABASE & DISTRIB SYSTS DEPT, IBM RES, 80- *Mem:* Asn Comput Mach; Inst Elec & Electronics Engrs. *Res:* Computer graphics; distributed processing; database management systems. *Mailing Add:* IBM Res K55-282 5600 Cottle Rd San Jose CA 95193

WILLIAMS, ROBIN O('DARE), b Greensboro, NC, Dec 26, 27; m 53; c 4. METALLURGY, THERMODYNAMICS. *Educ:* Univ Tenn, BS, 48, MS, 50; Carnegie-Mellon Univ, PhD(metall), 55. *Prof Exp:* Metallurgist, Oak Ridge Nat Lab, 48-51, consult, 51-54; res assoc, Res Lab, Gen Elec Co, 54-56; sr res supvr, Cincinnati Milling Mach Co, 56-59; METALLURGIST, OAK RIDGE NAT LAB, 59- *Mem:* Am Soc Metals. *Res:* Preferred orientation of deformed metals; precipitation hardening of alloys; stored energy of deformation; structure and thermodynamics of solid solutions; x-ray diffraction; order-disorder; software development and data reduction; spinodal decomposition. *Mailing Add:* 906 W Outer Dr Oak Ridge TN 37830

WILLIAMS, ROBLEY COOK, b Santa Rosa, Calif, Oct 13, 08; m 31; c 2. BIOPHYSICS, MOLECULAR BIOLOGY. *Educ:* Cornell Univ, AB, 31, PhD(physics), 35. *Prof Exp:* Asst physics, Cornell Univ, 29-35; from instr to asst prof astron, Observ, Univ Mich, 35-45, from assoc prof to prof physics, 45-50; assoc dir, Virus Lab & res biophysicist, 50-76, prof biophys, 50-59 & virol, 59-64, chmn dept molecular biol, 64-69, prof molecular biol, 64-76, EMER PROF, UNIV CALIF, BERKELEY, 76- *Concurrent Pos:* Vpres & consult, Evaporated Metal Films Corp, 35-56; res assoc, Off Sci Res & Develop, 41-42; coun mem, Int Union Pure & Appl Biophys, 61-69, pres, Comn Molecular Biophys, 61-69; Nat Acad Sci rep, UN Educ Sci & Cultural Orgn, 63-69; mem bd trustees, Deep Springs Col, 68-, chmn, 71- *Honors & Awards:* Longstreth Medal, Franklin Inst, 39, Scott Award, 54. *Mem:* Nat Acad Sci; Biophys Soc(pres, 58 & 59); Electron Micros Soc Am(pres, 51). *Res:* Electron microscopy of biological objects; development of techniques for electron microscopy of virus particles. *Mailing Add:* Dept of Molecular Biol Univ of Calif Berkeley CA 94720

WILLIAMS, ROBLEY COOK, JR, b Ann Arbor, Mich, Oct 15, 40; m 68; c 2. PHYSICAL BIOCHEMISTRY, CYTOSKELETON BIOCHEMISTRY. *Educ:* Cornell Univ, BA, 62; Rockefeller Univ, PhD(phys biochem), 68. *Prof Exp:* Nat Inst Arthritis & Metab Diseases fel, State Univ NY Buffalo, 67-68; from asst prof to assoc prof biol, Yale Univ, 69-76; ASSOC PROF MOLECULAR BIOL, VANDERBILT UNIV, 76- *Concurrent Pos:* Mem study sect biophys & biophys chem, NIH, 77-81, chmn, 79-81; fac assoc, US Antarctic Res Prog, McMurdo Sta, 79 & 81. *Mem:* Am Soc Cell Biol; Am Chem Soc; Biophys Soc; Am Soc Biol Chemists. *Res:* Protein-protein association and structure-function relationships in proteins. *Mailing Add:* Dept of Molecular Biol Vanderbilt Univ Nashville TN 37235

WILLIAMS, ROGER JOHN, b Ootacumund, India, Aug 14, 93; US citizen; m 16, 53; c 4. BIOCHEMISTRY, NUTRITION. *Educ:* Univ Redlands, BS, 14; Univ Chicago, MS, 18, PhD(biochem), 19. *Hon Degrees:* DSc, Univ Redlands, 34, Columbia Univ, 42, Ore State Univ, 56. *Prof Exp:* Res chemist, Fleischmann Co, Ill, 19-20; from asst prof to prof chem, Univ Ore, 20-32; prof, Ore State Univ, 32-39; prof chem, 39-71, dir, Clayton Found Biochem Inst, 40-63, EMER PROF CHEM, UNIV TEX, AUSTIN, 71-, RES SCIENTIST, CLAYTON FOUND BIOCHEM INST, 71- *Concurrent Pos:* Mem, Food & Nutrit Bd, 49-53; comt probs alcohol, Nat Res Coun, 49-53; med adv bd, Muscular Dystrophy Asn Am, Inc, 52-; res & med comt, Nat Multiple Sclerosis Soc, 60- *Honors & Awards:* Mead Johnson Award, Am Inst Nutrit, 41; Chandler Medal, Columbia Univ, 42. *Mem:* Nat Acad Sci; AAAS; Am Soc Biol Chem; Am Chem Soc(pres, 57); Soc Exp Biol & Med. *Res:* Pantothenic acid yeast nutrilites; folic acid; avidin; microbiological assay methods for B vitamins; B vitamins in normal and malignant tissues; nutrition of fungi; etiology of alcoholism; humanics; biochemical individuality. *Mailing Add:* Clayton Found Biochem Inst Univ of Tex Austin TX 78712

WILLIAMS, ROGER LEA, b Hamilton, Ohio, Jan 5, 41; c 2. CLINICAL PHARMACOLOGY, INTERNAL MEDICINE. *Educ:* Oberlin Col, BA, 63; Univ Chicago, MD, 67. *Prof Exp:* Intern med, Univ Chicago Hosps & Clins, 67-68, resident, 67-71; fel clin pharmacol, 74-77, ASST PROF MED & PHARM, UNIV CALIF, SAN FRANCISCO, 77- *Concurrent Pos:* Consult, Rev Panel New Drug Regulation, HEW, 76-77 & Task Force, Calif Citizen Action Group, 77-78. *Mem:* Am Fedn Clin; Am Soc Clin Pharmacol & Therapeut. *Res:* Clinical research drug risk and efficacy for new and established drug products; academic clinical drug investigation. *Mailing Add:* Drug Studies Unit 926-S Univ of Calif San Francisco CA 94143

WILLIAMS, ROGER NEAL, b Amityville, NY, Apr 3, 35; m 59; c 3. ENTOMOLOGY. *Educ:* Tex Tech Univ, BS, 57; La State Univ, MS, 64, PhD(entom), 66. *Prof Exp:* Res trainee entom, United Brands Co, Honduras, 58-62; res asst, La State Univ, 62-66; res entomologist, IRI Res Inst, Brazil, 66-68; asst prof, Ohio State Univ, Brazil, 68-73; ASSOC PROF ENTOM, OHIO AGR RES & DEVELOP CTR & OHIO STATE UNIV, 74- *Mem:* Entomol Soc Am; Int Orgn Biol Control; Soc Entom Brazil. *Res:* Biology and control of small fruit insect pests with chemicals and natural enemies; biological control of insect tropical pastures and ranges; natural enemies of fire ants and sap beetles. *Mailing Add:* Dept Entom Ohio Agr Res & Develop Ctr Wooster OH 44691

WILLIAMS, ROGER STUART, b San Diego, Calif, Feb 15, 41; m 74; c 2. CLINICAL NEUROLOGY, NEUROPATHOLOGY. *Educ:* Emory Univ, MD, 66. *Prof Exp:* Med intern, Grady Mem Hosp, Atlanta, Ga, 66-67, med resident, 67-68; med officer, US Navy, 68-70; neurol resident, Mass Gen Hosp, Boston, Mass, 70-73; instr, 73-78, ASST PROF NEUROL, HARVARD MED SCH, 78- *Concurrent Pos:* Res fel neurol, Mass Gen Hosp, 73-76; res fel neurosci, Joseph P Kennedy, Jr Mem Found, 74-76; assoc neurologist, McLean Hosp, Belmont, Mass, 75-; clin assoc neurol, Mass Gen Hosp, 75-; investr, Schizophrenia Res Found of the Scottish Rite, 78-80; asst neurol, Mass Gen Hosp, 78- *Mem:* Am Acad Neurol; Epilepsy Found Am; Soc Neurosci. *Res:* Experimental neuropathology of the developing nervous system. *Mailing Add:* Eunice Kennedy Shriver Ctr 200 Trapelo Rd Waltham MA 02154

WILLIAMS, ROGER TERRY, b Covina, Calif, June 15, 36; m 64; c 3. DYNAMIC METEOROLOGY. *Educ:* Univ Calif, Los Angeles, AB, 59, MS, 61, PhD(meterol), 63. *Prof Exp:* Ford Found fel, Univ Calif, Los Angeles, 63-64; res assoc meteorol, Mass Inst Technol, 64-66; asst prof, Univ Utah, 66-68; assoc prof, 68-74, PROF METEOROL, NAVAL POSTGRAD SCH, 74- *Concurrent Pos:* Mem, FGGE Adv Panel, Nat Res Coun, 74- *Mem:* AAAS; Am Geophys Union; Am Meteorol Soc. *Res:* Numerical weather prediction; dynamics of the atmosphere and other geophysical systems; application of numerical methods; dynamics of atmospheric waves and fronts. *Mailing Add:* Code 63 Wu Naval Postgrad Sch Monterey CA 93940

WILLIAMS, ROGER WRIGHT, b Great Falls, Mont, Jan 24, 18; m 43; c 2. MEDICAL ENTOMOLOGY, PARASITOLOGY. *Educ:* Univ Ill, BS, 39, MS, 41; Columbia Univ, PhD(med entom), 47; London Sch Hyg & Trop Med, cert appl parasitol & entom, 57. *Prof Exp:* Jr sci asst, Div Cereal Crops, Bur Entom & Plant Quarantine, USDA, 41; asst biol, Cornell Univ, 42; from res asst to res assoc parasitol, 44-48, from asst prof to assoc prof med entom, 48-66, actg head div trop med, 70, PROF PUB HEALTH, MED ENTOM, SCH PUB HEALTH, COLUMBIA UNIV, 66- *Concurrent Pos:* NSF sr fel, 56; fel trop med, La State Univ, 57; spec consult, USPHS, Alaska, 49, consult, Ga, 52; corp mem, Bermuda Biol Sta Res, 58-; consult, US Nat Park Serv, Virgin Island Govt & Jackson Hole Preserve, Inc, 59 & 61; consult, Rockefeller Found, WI, 63, mem field staff, Nigeria, 64-65; consult, WHO, Burma, 66. *Mem:* Fel AAAS; Entom Soc Am; Am Soc Parasitol; Am Mosquito Control Asn; Am Soc Trop Med & Hyg. *Res:* Biology, physiology control and taxonomy of arthropods of medical importance; biology and chemotherapy of helminths. *Mailing Add:* Div of Trop Med Sch of Pub Health Columbia Univ Col of Phys & Surg New York NY 10032

WILLIAMS, RONALD ALVIN, b Somerset, Pa, Aug 4, 42; m 64; c 2. BIOMEDICAL ENGINEERING, ELECTRICAL ENGINEERING. *Educ:* Pa State Univ, BS, 64, MS, 66, PhD(elec eng), 70. *Prof Exp:* Res bioengr, Columbus Labs, Battelle Mem Inst, 70-72, assoc chief bioeng sci & biochem div, 72-74; mgr prod explor, 76-78, VPRES & GEN MGR, FENWAL PROD SYSTS, 78- *Mem:* Inst Elec & Electronics Engrs; Asn Advan Med Instrumentation. *Res:* Blood cell separation; blood collection, processing and storage; medical instrumentation development. *Mailing Add:* Fenwal Labs Div of Baxter Labs Rte 120 & Wilson Rd Round Lake IL 60073

WILLIAMS, RONALD LEE, b Koleen, Ind, June 26, 36; m 57; c 4. PHARMACOLOGY, PHYSIOLOGY. *Educ:* Butler Univ, BS, 59, MS, 61; Tulane Univ, PhD(pharmacol), 64. *Prof Exp:* Asst prof, 66-70, ASSOC PROF PHARMACOL, LA STATE UNIV MED CTR, NEW ORLEANS, 71-, CONJOINT ASSOC PROF MED, 78- *Concurrent Pos:* La Heart Asn grants-in-aid, 65-66, 67-68 & 74-75; USPHS res contract, 68. *Mem:* AAAS; Am Pharmaceut Asn; Am Soc Pharmacol & Exp Therapeut; Soc Exp Biol & Med; NY Acad Sci. *Res:* Effect of autonomic drugs and neurotransmitters upon renal function and the relationships between hemodynamics and tubular changes. *Mailing Add:* Dept Pharmacol La State Univ Med Ctr New Orleans LA 70119

WILLIAMS, RONALD LLOYDE, b Northfield, Minn, May 7, 44; m 64; c 2. PHYSICAL CHEMISTRY, ENVIRONMENTAL CHEMISTRY. *Educ:* St Olaf Col, BA, 66; Iowa State Univ, PhD(phys chem), 70. *Prof Exp:* Fel, Univ Calif, Irvine, 70-72; RES CHEMIST, GEN MOTORS RES LAB, 72- *Mem:* Am Chem Soc; Soc Automotive Engrs. *Res:* Reaction kinetics; hot atom reactions; unregulated emissions from tires, brakes, refrigeration systems and diesel automobiles. *Mailing Add:* Environ Sci Dept Gen Motors Res Labs Warren MI 48090

WILLIAMS, RONALD WENDELL, b Atlanta, Ga, Nov 9, 39; m 63; c 2. SOLID STATE PHYSICS. *Educ:* Christian Bros Col, BSc, 62; Iowa State Univ, PhD(physics), 66. *Prof Exp:* Instr physics, Iowa State Univ, 66-67; staff scientist, Oak Ridge Nat Lab, 67-70; ASSOC PROF ELEC ENG, UNIV VT, 70- *Res:* Band structure and transport properties of metals. *Mailing Add:* Dept of Elec Eng Univ of Vt Burlington VT 05401

WILLIAMS, ROSS EDWARD, b Carlinville, Ill, June 28, 22; m 58; c 3. PHYSICS. *Educ:* Bowdoin Col, BS, 43; Columbia Univ, MA, 47, PhD(physics), 55. *Prof Exp:* Sr res engr, Sperry Prod Inc, 47-49; consult physicist, Paul Rosenberg Assocs, 53-60; sr res assoc, Oceanog Acoustics & Signal Processing, 60-65, asst dir, 65-66, ASSOC DIR, OCEANOG ACOUSTICS & SIGNAL PROCESSING, HUDSON LABS, COLUMBIA UNIV, 66-, PROF OCEAN ENG, 68-, LECTR ELEC ENG, 66- *Concurrent Pos:* Mem, Comt Undersea Warfare, Nat Res Coun-Nat Acad Sci; consult, Naval Res Lab & Nat Acad Sci; chmn bd dirs, Ocean & Atmospheric Sci, Inc, 68- *Mem:* Acoust Soc Am; Am Phys Soc; Am Soc Photogram; sr mem Inst Elec & Electronics Eng. *Res:* Oceanography; acoustic propagation; surveillance system design; signal processing techniques; aerial reconnaissance; automatic mapping; optical data processing; electronic design. *Mailing Add:* 23 Alta Pl Yonkers NY 10710

WILLIAMS, ROY EDWARD, b Cookeville, Tenn, Feb 12, 38; m 59. HYDROGEOLOGY. *Educ:* Ind Univ, Bloomington, BSc, 61, MA, 62; Univ Ill, Urbana, PhD(hydrogeol), 66. *Prof Exp:* Teaching asst phys geol, Ind Univ, Bloomington, 63-64; teaching asst eng geol, Univ Ill, Urbana, 64-66; asst prof, 66-70, PROF HYDROGEOL & HYDROGEOLOGIST, UNIV IDAHO, 70- *Concurrent Pos:* Res asst, Ill State Geol Surv, 64-66; grants, Idaho Water Resources Res Inst & Univ Idaho Res Comt, 66- & Idaho Short Term Appl Res Fund, 68- *Mem:* Am Geophys Union. *Res:* Studies of pollution of ground and surface water and the relation between ground water flow systems and certain engineering problems. *Mailing Add:* Col of Mines Univ of Idaho Moscow ID 83843

WILLIAMS, ROY LEE, b Portsmouth, Va, Feb 20, 37; m 57; c 1. ORGANIC CHEMISTRY. *Educ:* Col William & Mary, BS, 60; Univ Del, PhD(org chem), 65. *Prof Exp:* Res chemist, Am Cyanamid Co, NJ, 64-65; from asst prof to assoc prof, 65-73, PROF CHEM, OLD DOM UNIV, 73-; ASST PROF PHARMACOL, EASTERN VA MED SCH, 77- *Concurrent Pos:* Res grant, Army Med Res Inst, Walter Reed Hosp, Washington, DC, 66-68; consult, Chem & Physics Br, Langley Res Ctr, NASA, Va, 65- *Mem:* Am Chem Soc; fel The Chem Soc; Int Soc Heterocyclic Chem. *Res:* Heterocyclic, organic synthesis, including heterocyclic polymers; medicinals; synthetics. *Mailing Add:* Alfriend Lab Dept of Chem Old Dom Univ Norfolk VA 23508

WILLIAMS, RUSSELL RAYMOND, b Lost Creek, WVa, Apr 11, 26; m 53; c 3. PARASITOLOGY, INVERTEBRATE ZOOLOGY. *Educ:* Ohio State Univ, BSc, 55, MSc, 57, PhD(zool), 63. *Prof Exp:* Lab unit operator, B F Goodrich Chem Co, 45-50; from asst instr to instr zool, Ohio State Univ, 57-63; from asst prof to assoc prof, 63-67, PROF BIOL, WAYNESBURG COL, 67-, CHMN DEPT, 70-, PREMED ADV, 73- *Concurrent Pos:* Res Corp grant, 64-66; vis prof, Univ Northern Colo, 68-; partic, Res Corp Conf for New Sci Chairmen, 71. *Mem:* AAAS; Am Soc Parasitol; Wildlife Dis Asn; Am Micros Soc; Am Inst Biol Sci. *Res:* Life history and taxonomic studies on trematodes. *Mailing Add:* Dept of Biol Waynesburg Col Waynesburg PA 15370

WILLIAMS, SCOTT WARNER, b Staten Island, NY, Apr 22, 43. MATHEMATICS. *Educ:* Morgan State Col, BS, 64; Lehigh Univ, MS, 67, PhD(math), 69. *Prof Exp:* Instr, Pa State Univ, 68-69; res assoc, Pa State Univ, 69-71; asst prof, 71-77, ASSOC PROF MATH, STATE UNIV NY BUFFALO, 77- *Mem:* Am Math Soc. *Res:* General topology, completeness, paracompactness, linearly ordered spaces and Baire spaces; algebra, groups and categories. *Mailing Add:* Dept of Math State Univ NY Buffalo NY 14214

WILLIAMS, SIDNEY ARTHUR, b Ann Arbor, Mich, Dec 26, 33; m 57; c 1. MINERALOGY. *Educ:* Mich Technol Univ, BS, MS, 57; Univ Ariz, PhD(mineral), 62. *Prof Exp:* Instr mineral, Mich Technol Univ, 60-61, asst prof, 61-63; mineralogist, Silver King Mines, Inc, 63-65; dir res explor geol, Phelps Dodge Corp, 65-82; CONSULT, 82- *Concurrent Pos:* Mineralogist, Brit Mus Natural Hist, 71. *Mem:* Fel Mineral Soc Am; Mineral Asn Can; Brit Mineral Soc; Soc Econ Geol. *Res:* Descriptive mineralogy and crystallography; petrology of altered rocks related to ore deposits. *Mailing Add:* PO Box 872 Douglas AZ 85607

WILLIAMS, STANLEY A, b Lawrence, Kans, May 14, 32; m 58; c 2. THEORETICAL PHYSICS. *Educ:* Nebr Wesleyan Univ, BA, 54; Rensselaer Polytech Inst, PhD(physics), 62. *Prof Exp:* NSF fel, Univ Birmingham, 62-63; asst prof, 63-67, assoc prof, 67-76, PROF PHYSICS, IOWA STATE UNIV, 76-; MEM STAFF, AMES LAB, ENERGY RES & DEVELOP ADMIN, 76- *Concurrent Pos:* Assoc scientist, Ames Lab, 63-67, scientist, 67- *Mem:* Am Phys Soc; Am Asn Physics Teachers. *Res:* Mathematical physics, principally the application of group theoretic techniques to nuclear and elementary particle physics; structure of fission fragment nuclei. *Mailing Add:* Dept of Physics Iowa State Univ Ames IA 50010

WILLIAMS, STANLEY CLARK, b Long Beach, Calif, Aug 24, 39; m 65; c 3. ECOLOGY. *Educ:* San Diego State Col, AB, 61, MA, 63; Ariz State Univ, PhD(zool, 68. *Prof Exp:* Asst prof, 67-70, assoc prof, 70-74, PROF BIOL, SAN FRANCISCO STATE UNIV, 74- *Concurrent Pos:* Res assoc, Calif Acad Sci, 67-; NSF grants, Mexico, 68-72; lectr, Moss Landing Marine Sta, 72-73; mem Int Ctr Arachnological Documentation; ecol consult, Mill Valley, Calif. *Mem:* Am Archeol Soc; Ecol Soc Am. *Res:* Invertebrate ecology; scorpion systematics; urban ecology; medical entomology; biostatistics and data analysis. *Mailing Add:* Dept of Biol San Francisco State Univ San Francisco CA 94132

WILLIAMS, STEPHEN EARL, b Borger, Tex, Apr 27, 48; m 75. SOIL MICROBIOLOGY, SOIL BIOCHEMISTRY. *Educ:* NMex State Univ, BS, 70, MS, 72; NC State Univ, PhD(soil sci), 77. *Prof Exp:* Plant physiologist soils, Rocky Mountain Forest & Range Exp Sta, Forest Serv, USDA, Albuquerque, NMex, 72; res & teaching assoc, NC State Univ, 75-76; ASST PROF SOILS, UNIV WYO, 76- *Concurrent Pos:* Prin investr, US Dept Energy, Laramie Energy Technol Ctr, Wyo, 77- *Mem:* Am Soc Agron; Soil Sci Soc Am. *Res:* Symbiotic associations between plants and microorganisms such as mycorrhizae and symbiotic nitrogen fixation; revegetation of devastated lands; microbial degradations of organic constituents in waste waters produced from fossil fuel processing. *Mailing Add:* Univ of Wyo Div of Plant Sci PO Box 3354 Laramie WY 82071

WILLIAMS, STEPHEN EDWARD, b St Louis, Mo, Oct 9, 42; m 68. PLANT PHYSIOLOGY. *Educ:* Cent Col, Mo, BA, 64; Univ Tenn, Knoxville, MS, 66; Wash Univ, PhD(biol), 71. *Prof Exp:* Lectr plant physiol, Cornell Univ, 70-73; ASST PROF BIOL, LEBANON VALLEY COL, 73- *Mem:* AAAS; Am Soc Plant Physiol; Bot Soc Am. *Res:* Polar transport of auxin; electrophysiology, plant sensory physiology, excitable plant cells; carnivorous plants, especially Droseraceae, electron microscopy; canavanine synthesis and metabolism in legumes. *Mailing Add:* Dept of Biol Lebanon Valley Col Annville PA 17003

WILLIAMS, STEVEN FRANK, b Tacoma, Wash, May 8, 44; m 66. FISHERIES, ICHTHYOLOGY. *Educ:* Univ Wash, BS, 66; Univ Calif, Los Angeles, MA, 68; Ore State Univ, PhD(fisheries), 74. *Prof Exp:* Res biologist fisheries, US Peace Corps, Chile, 68-70; ASST PROF BIOL, ST CLOUD STATE UNIV, 74- *Concurrent Pos:* Res asst fisheries, Ore State Univ, 70- *Mem:* AAAS; Am Fisheries Soc. *Res:* Natural distribution and abundance of fishes and factors which affect them; fish culture, especially optimum culture conditions. *Mailing Add:* Dept of Biol St Cloud State Univ St Cloud MN 56301

WILLIAMS, TERENCE HEATON, b Oldham, Eng, Jan 5, 29; m 56; c 3. NEUROANATOMY, ELECTRON MICROSCOPY. *Educ:* Univ Manchester, MB, ChB, 53; Univ Wales, PhD(anat), 60. *Prof Exp:* House surgeon, Manchester Univ & Royal Infirmary, 53-54; jr registr surg, London Hosp, 55-56; asst lectr anat, Univ Col, Dublin, 57-58; lectr, Univ Wales, 58-61; lectr & sr lectr exp neurol, Univ Manchester, 61-68; vis lectr electron microscopy of nerv syst, Harvard Med Sch, 65-66; prof neuroanat, Sch Med, Tulane Univ, 68-73; PROF ANAT & HEAD DEPT, COL MED, UNIV IOWA, 73- *Concurrent Pos:* Brit Med Res Coun traveling fel, Harvard Med Sch, 64-65; Peck Sci Res award; NIH res awards, 69- *Honors & Awards:* DSc, Univ Manchester, 77. *Mem:* Soc Neurosci; Am Asn Anat; Anat Soc Gt Brit & Ireland. *Res:* Neuropeptidergic systems; plasticity of nervous system; small intensely fluorescent cells of sympathetic ganglia; electromicroscopy of the nervous system. *Mailing Add:* Dept Anat Univ Iowa Col Med Iowa City IA 52242

WILLIAMS, THEODORE BURTON, b Youngstown, Ohio, Sept 9, 49; m 71; c 2. ASTRONOMY. *Educ:* Purdue Univ, BS, 71; Calif Inst Technol, PhD(astron), 75. *Prof Exp:* Res assoc astron, Princeton Univ, 75-77, mem res staff, 77-79; ASST PROF, DEPT PHYSICS & ASTRON, RUTGERS UNIV, 79- *Mem:* Am Astron Soc; Int Astron Union. *Res:* Structure and dynamics of individual galaxies; development of astronomical detector systems. *Mailing Add:* Dept Physics & Astron Rutgers Univ Piscataway NJ 08854

WILLIAMS, THEODORE J(OSEPH), b Black Lick, Pa, Sept 2, 23; m 46; c 4. AUTOMATIC CONTROL, CHEMICAL ENGINEERING. *Educ:* Pa State Univ, BS, 49, MS, 50, PhD(chem eng), 55; Ohio State Univ, MSEE, 56. *Prof Exp:* Asst prof chem eng, US Air Force Inst Technol, 53-56; sr eng supvr, Monsanto Co, 56-65; PROF ENG & DIR LAB APPL INDUST CONTROL, PURDUE UNIV, 65- *Concurrent Pos:* Vpres, Simulation Coun, 60-62; vis prof automatic control, Wash Univ, 62-65; vpres, Am Automatic Control Coun, 63-65, pres, 65-67; surv lectr, Int Fedn Automatic Control, Basel, Switz, 63 & Warsaw, Poland, 69; mem bd gov, Am Fedn Info Processing Socs, 65-80, pres, 76-80; plenary lectr, Conf Chem Eng Frankfort, Ger, 70. *Honors & Awards:* Sir Harold Hartley Medal, Inst Measure & Control, London, 75; Silver Core Award, Int Fedn Info Processing, 77. *Mem:* Fel Instrument Soc (vpres, 65-67, pres, 69); Am Chem Soc; Am Soc Eng Educ; fel Am Inst Chem Engrs; Inst Elec & Electronics Eng. *Res:* Industrial process dynamics and automatic control; application of digital computers to industrial process control and management; theory of separation processes, particularly distillation. *Mailing Add:* Lab for Appl Indust Control 334 Potter Ctr Purdue Univ West Lafayette IN 47907

WILLIAMS, THEODORE L, b Denver, Colo, Oct 9, 39; c 2. ELECTRICAL ENGINEERING. *Educ:* Mass Inst Technol, BS, 60; Drexel Inst, MS, 64; Pa State Univ, PhD(control systs), 66. *Prof Exp:* Staff engr, Gen Atronics Corp, 60-64; instr elec eng, Drexel Inst, 64; teaching asst & instr, Pa State Univ, 64-67; asst prof, 67-72, ASSOC PROF ELEC ENG, UNIV ARIZ, 72- *Concurrent Pos:* Consult, Burr-Brown Res, 78. *Mem:* AAAS; Inst Elec & Electronics Engrs; Am Soc Eng Educ. *Res:* Design of computer control systems; instrumentation and computational aspects of control systems. *Mailing Add:* Dept of Elec Eng Univ of Ariz Tucson AZ 85721

WILLIAMS, THEODORE P, b Marianna, Pa, May 24, 33; m 56; c 5. BIOPHYSICS, PSYCHOBIOLOGY. *Educ:* Muskingum Col, BS, 55; Princeton Univ, MA, 57, PhD(phys chem), 59. *Prof Exp:* Res assoc chem, Brown Univ, 59-61, fel psychol, 61-63, asst prof biol & med sci, 63-66; assoc prof biol sci, 66-73, actg chmn dept, 70-71, PROF BIOL SCI, FLA STATE UNIV, 73-, CO-DIR PSYCHOBIOL PROG, 71- *Concurrent Pos:* NIH grant, 63-74 & 78-84; Nat Acad Sci exchange fel, USA-USSR, 73; NSF grant, 74-83; Energy Res & Develop Admin grant, 78-82. *Mem:* Asn Res Vision Ophthalmol. *Res:* Visual processes; sensory mechanisms; fast chemical reactions. *Mailing Add:* Rm 511 Inst Molecular Biophys Fla State Univ Tallahassee FL 32306

WILLIAMS, THEODORE ROOSEVELT, b Washington, DC, Oct 23, 30; m 54; c 4. ANALYTICAL CHEMISTRY. *Educ:* Howard Univ, BS, 52; Pa State Univ, MS, 54; Univ Conn, PhD, 60. *Prof Exp:* Asst instr chem, Univ Conn, 56-59; from instr to assoc prof, 59-66, PROF CHEM, COL WOOSTER, 66- *Concurrent Pos:* Res assoc, Harvard Univ, 67-68, Sloan vis prof chem, 69-70; vis prof, Univ Conn, 72-73 & Case Western Reserve Univ, 77-78; chmn anal div grad fel comt, Am Chem Soc, 73- *Honors & Awards:* Mfg Chemists Asn Award, 78; Martha Holden Jennings Found Award, 80. *Mem:* Am Chem Soc. *Res:* Electroanalytical chemistry. *Mailing Add:* Dept of Chem Col of Wooster Wooster OH 44691

WILLIAMS, THEODORE SHIELDS, b Kansas City, Kans, June 2, 11; m 36; c 2. VETERINARY MEDICINE. *Educ:* Kans State Univ, DVM, 35; Iowa State Univ, MS, 46. *Prof Exp:* Col vet, Prairie View State Col, 36; vet inspector, Meat Inspection Div, USDA, 36-45; head dept, 45-51, dean sch, 47-72, PROF PATH & PARASITOL, SCH VET MED, TUSKEGEE INST, 45- *Concurrent Pos:* Consult, Vet Admin Hosp, Tuskegee, Ala; vis prof path, NY State Vet Col, Cornell Univ, 73. *Mem:* Am Asn Vet Med Cols (pres, 69-70); Am Vet Med Asn. *Res:* Pathological lesions associated with tissue invading migratory parasites in animals. *Mailing Add:* Sch of Vet Med Tuskegee Inst Tuskegee Inst AL 36088

WILLIAMS, THOMAS ELLIS, b Plymouth, Pa, Feb 11, 29; m 52; c 2. GEOLOGY. *Educ:* Rochester Univ, BA, 51; Southern Methodist Univ, MS, 57; Yale Univ, PhD(geol), 62. *Prof Exp:* Instr, 59-62, from asst prof to assoc prof, 62-70, chmn dept, 74-78, PROF GEOL, SOUTHERN METHODIST UNIV, 70- *Mem:* Paleont Soc; Geol Soc Am. *Res:* Paleontology of fusuline foraminifers. *Mailing Add:* Dept of Geol Sci Southern Methodist Univ Dallas TX 75275

WILLIAMS, THOMAS FRANCON, b Denbighshire, Wales, Jan 30, 28; m 59; c 2. PHYSICAL CHEMISTRY. *Educ:* Univ London, BSc, 49, PhD(chem), 60. *Prof Exp:* From sci officer to prin sci officer, Chem Div, Atomic Energy Res Estab, Harwett, Eng, 49-61; from asst prof to prof, 61-74, DISTINGUISHED SERV PROF CHEM, UNIV TENN, KNOXVILLE, 74- *Concurrent Pos:* Assoc, Northwestern Univ, 57-59; NSF vis scientist, Kyoto Univ, 65-66; Guggenheim fel, Royal Inst Technol, Sweden, 72-73. *Mem:* Am Chem Soc; The Chem Soc. *Res:* Electron spin resonance studies of trapped radicals; free radical reactions at low temperature; electronic structure of radicals; radiation chemistry; radiation-induced ionic polymerization. *Mailing Add:* Dept Chem Univ Tenn Knoxville TN 37916

WILLIAMS, THOMAS FRANKLIN, b Belmont, NC, Nov 26, 21; m 51; c 2. INTERNAL MEDICINE. *Educ:* Univ NC, BS, 42; Columbia Univ, MA, 43; Harvard Univ, MD, 50. *Prof Exp:* Asst chem, Columbia Univ, 42-43; asst med, Johns Hopkins Univ, 51-53 & Boston Univ, 53-54; from instr to prof, Sch Med, Univ NC, 56-68; PROF MED, UNIV ROCHESTER, 68-; MED DIR, MONROE COMMUNITY HOSP, 68- *Concurrent Pos:* Res fel, Sch Med, Univ NC, 54-56, Markle scholar, 57-61; fel physiol, Vanderbilt Univ, 66-67. *Mem:* Inst of Med Nat Acad Sci; AAAS; Am Geriatrics Soc; Am Pub Health Asn; Am Col Physicians. *Res:* Diseases of metabolism, especially for chronic illness and aging; metabolic and renal physiology. *Mailing Add:* Monroe Community Hosp 435 E Henrietta Rd Rochester NY 14603

WILLIAMS, THOMAS HENRY, b Jamaica, WI, Apr 21, 34; m 67; c 2. STRUCTURAL CHEMISTRY. *Educ:* Univ WI, BSc, 56; Yale Univ, MS, 60, PhD(chem), 61. *Prof Exp:* Fel Univ Notre Dame, 61-62; res chemist, 63-74, RES FEL, HOFFMANN-LA ROCHE INC, NUTLEY, 75- *Mem:* Am Chem Soc. *Res:* Structural elucidation of natural products; applications of nuclear magnetic resonance spectroscopy in organic chemistry. *Mailing Add:* 340 Kingsland St Nutley NJ 07110

WILLIAMS, THOMAS R(AY), b Price, Utah, Feb 23, 26; m 68; c 2. ELECTRICAL ENGINEERING. *Educ:* Univ Okla, BSEE, 46; Princeton Univ, MSE, 49, PhD, 54. *Prof Exp:* Instr elec eng, 48-49, lectr, 52-54, asst prof, 54-60, asst chem dept, 70-75, ASSOC PROF ELEC ENG,

PRINCETON UNIV, 60- *Res:* Communication theory; detection of signals in noise; stochastic processes; noise mechanisms and properties of noise in electronic devices. *Mailing Add:* Dept of Elec Eng & Comput Sci Princeton Univ Princeton NJ 08540

WILLIAMS, THOMAS WALLEY, JR, b Ventnor, NJ, Nov 28, 09; m 35; c 2. HUMAN ANATOMY. *Educ:* Univ Pittsburgh, BS, 34, MS, 36, PhD(anat), 39. *Prof Exp:* Instr anat, Sch Med, Univ Pittsburgh, 39-44; asst prof anat & histol, Sch Med, Univ WVa, 44-48, assoc prof anat, 48-56, prof microanat & chmn dept, 56-65, prof, 66-72, EMER PROF ANAT, UNIV WVA, 72- *Mem:* Am Asn Anat; Microcirc Soc. *Res:* Microcirculation, angioarchitecture and human microanatomy. *Mailing Add:* Dept of Anat WVa Univ Med Ctr Morgantown WV 26506

WILLIAMS, TIMOTHY C, b New York, NY, May 7, 42. BEHAVIOR, ETHOLOGY. *Educ:* Swarthmore Col, BA, 64; Harvard Univ, AM, 66; Rockefeller Univ, PhD(animal behav), 68. *Prof Exp:* Asst prof biol, State Univ NY, Buffalo, 69-75; ASSOC PROF BIOL, SWARTHMORE COL, 76- *Concurrent Pos:* Scientist, Woods Hole Oceanog Inst, 68-74; invest, Marine Biol Labs, 75-78. *Res:* Radar studies of bird orientation and migration, especially over major oceans. *Mailing Add:* Dept Biol Swarthmore Col Swarthmore PA 19081

WILLIAMS, TODD ROBERTSON, b Washington, DC, Nov 3, 45; m 67; c 1. POLYMER CHEMISTRY. *Educ:* Cornell Univ, AB, 67; Univ Calif, Los Angeles, PhD(org chem), 71. *Prof Exp:* Fel, Syntex Res Co, 71-72; sr chemist med chem, 72-77, supvr biomat res, 77-79, RES SPECIALIST, 3M CO, 79- *Mem:* Am Chem Soc. *Res:* Optical polymers. *Mailing Add:* 3M Ctr Bldg 201-2W-17 3M Co St Paul MN 55144

WILLIAMS, TOM VARE, b Philadelphia, Pa, Dec 27, 38; m 63; c 3. PLANT BREEDING, PLANT PATHOLOGY. *Educ:* Univ Conn, BS, 60; Rutgers Univ, MS, 63, PhD(plant breeding), 66. *Prof Exp:* Agronomist, Soil Conserv Serv, USDA, 66-67; res horticulturist, Birds Eye Div, Gen Foods Corp, 67-70; res dir seed dept, Agr Chem Div, FMC Corp, 70-77; PROJ LEADER & VEGETABLE BREEDER, NORTHRUP KING CO, 77- *Mem:* Am Soc Agron; Am Soc Hort Sci; Am Genetic Asn. *Res:* Vegetable variety development. *Mailing Add:* Northrup King Co Box 1389 Homestead FL 33030

WILLIAMS, VERNON, b Augusta, Ga, Nov 10, 26; m 69; c 1. MATHEMATICS, EDUCATION. *Educ:* Paine Col, BA, 49; Univ Mich, Ann Arbor, MA, 54; Okla State Univ, EdD, 69. *Prof Exp:* Instr, Paine Col, 49-54 & Fla A&M Univ, 54-56; from asst prof to assoc prof, Southern Univ, Baton Rouge, 56-69, prof math, 69-80; PROF MATH, SETON HALL UNIV, 80- *Concurrent Pos:* Adv, Math Sect, La Educ Asn, 71- *Mem:* Am Math Asn. *Res:* Number theory; educational technology as devoted to higher education as well as secondary education. *Mailing Add:* Seton Hall Univ 309 Heywood Ave Orange NJ 07050

WILLIAMS, VICK FRANKLIN, b Pittsburg, Tex, Apr 30, 36; m 62; c 2. ANATOMY. *Educ:* Austin Col, BA, 58; Univ Tex, MD & PhD(anat), 64. *Prof Exp:* Intern path, Charity Hosp La, New Orleans, 64-65; from instr to asst prof anat, Univ Tex Southwestern Med Sch Dallas, 65-70; assoc prof anat, Dent Sch, Univ Tex, San Antonio & Univ Tex Med Sch, San Antonio, 70-73; assoc prof, 73-79, PROF ANAT, UNIV TEX HEALTH SCI CTR, SAN ANTONIO, 79- *Honors & Awards:* Borden Award, 64. *Mem:* AAAS; Am Asn Anat; Am Soc Cell Biol; Electron Micros Soc Am; Soc Neurosci. *Res:* Ultrastructure of the central nervous system of mammals. *Mailing Add:* Dept of Anat Univ of Tex Health Sci Ctr San Antonio TX 78284

WILLIAMS, WALLACE TERRY, b Vincent, Ala, July 7, 42; m 70; c 1. CLINICAL NUTRITIONIST. *Educ:* Southern Univ, BS, 64; NDak State Univ, MS, 66; Univ Maine, PhD(nutrit biochem), 69. *Prof Exp:* Asst prof nutrit sci, State Univ NY Buffalo, 69-71, assoc prof, 72-75, prof & chmn, 75-76; sci adminr, Div Assoc Health, NIH, 76-77; prof & chmn family & consumer resources, 77-81, INTERIM DEAN, COL LIB ARTS, WAYNE STATE UNIV, 81- *Concurrent Pos:* Consult, Div Assoc Health Professors, NIH, 69-81, Nat Cancer Inst, 80- & Health Resources Admin, 81-; actg chief clin nutrit, Wayne State Univ Med Ctr, 79-80. *Mem:* Am Dietetic Asn; AAAS; Soc Nutrit Educ. *Res:* Effects of diet on lipid metabolism; bio-nutritional status of children and adult populations; the effects of diet on elevation of blood lipids. *Mailing Add:* Wayne State Univ Detroit MI 48202

WILLIAMS, WALTER FORD, b Yazoo City, Miss, Oct 7, 27; m 50, 81; c 3. PHYSIOLOGY. *Educ:* Univ Mo, BS, 50, MS, 51, PhD(dairy physiol), 55. *Prof Exp:* Asst, Univ Mo, 53-55, res assoc, 55-57; from asst prof to assoc prof, 57-69, prof diary physiol, 69-76, PROF DAIRY SCI, UNIV MD, COLLEGE PARK, 76- *Concurrent Pos:* USPHS fel, Nat Cancer Inst, 55-57. *Mem:* AAAS; Am Dairy Sci Asn; Soc Study Reproduction; Am Soc Animal Sci. *Res:* Reproductive processes; endocrine regulation of metabolism in relation to reproduction, growth and lactation in domestic and wild mammals. *Mailing Add:* Dept of Dairy Sci Animal Sci Ctr Univ of Md College Park MD 20740

WILLIAMS, WALTER JACKSON, JR, b Elkhart, Ind, Jan 17, 25; m 44; c 3. ELECTRICAL ENGINEERING. *Educ:* Purdue Univ, Lafayette, BS, 48, MS, 50, PhD(elec eng), 54. *Prof Exp:* Instr, Purdue Univ, 48-54; from engr to prin engr, Fed Lab, Int Tel & Tel Corp, 54-60; chmn dept elec eng, Ind Inst Technol, 61-64, dean eng, 63-67, vpres & acad dean, 67-75, interim pres, 70-71; sr tech adv, 75-80, DIR ENG, AEROSPACE-OPTICAL DIV, ITT CORP, FT WAYNE, 80- *Concurrent Pos:* Consult, Int Tel & Tel Corp, Magnavox Co & Bowmar Instrument Corp. *Mem:* Inst Elec & Electronics Engrs; Nat Soc Prof Engrs; Am Soc Eng Educ. *Res:* Systems analysis with emphasis on feedback control. *Mailing Add:* 3100 E Pontiac Ft Wayne IN 46803

WILLIAMS, WAYNE WATSON, b Powersville, Mo, Dec 14, 22; m 44; c 7. ENGINEERING, GEOLOGY. *Educ:* Iowa State Univ, BS, 51, MS, 53. *Prof Exp:* Res asst soils, Eng Exp Sta, Iowa State Univ, 51-53; found engr, Univ Iowa, 53-65; assoc prof civil eng, 65-76, PROF CIVIL ENG, KANS STATE UNIV, 76- *Concurrent Pos:* NSF res asst, Tex A&M Univ, 67; vis prof, Univ Houston, 77-78. *Mem:* Am Soc Testing & Mat; Am Soc Eng Educ; Am Soc Prof Engrs; Int Asn Housing. *Res:* Foundations of structures; shearing resistance; swelling clays; deep foundation; building and construction failures. *Mailing Add:* Dept of Civil Eng Kans State Univ Manhattan KS 66502

WILLIAMS, WELLS ELDON, b Cadillac, Mich, July 8, 19; m 44. FISHERIES. *Educ:* Mich State Univ, BS, 53, MS, 54, PhD(fisheries, wildlife), 58. *Prof Exp:* Asst fisheries & wildlife, 54-56; from instr to asst prof, 56-70, ASSOC PROF NATURAL SCI, MICH STATE UNIV, 70- *Res:* Freshwater ecology; habitat improvement; food conversion and growth rates of fishes; pond culture; physiology of freshwater fishes. *Mailing Add:* Dept of Natural Sci Mich State Univ East Lansing MI 48824

WILLIAMS, WENDELL STERLING, b Lake Forest, Ill, Oct 27, 28; m 52; c 2. SOLID STATE PHYSICS, MATERIALS SCIENCE. *Educ:* Swarthmore Col, BA, 51; Cornell Univ, PhD(physics), 56. *Prof Exp:* Physicist, Leeds & Northrup Co, 51; asst, Cornell Univ, 52-55; physicist, Union Carbide Corp, 56-65, 66-67; sr res visitor, Dept Metall, Cambridge Univ, 65-66; assoc prof, 67-69, co-chmn, Bioeng Comt, 71, PROF PHYSICS & CERAMIC ENG & BIOENG, UNIV ILL, URBANA, 69-, PRIN INVESTR, MAT RES LAB, 67-, DIR, PROG ANCIENT TECHNOL & ARCHAEOL MAT, 80- *Concurrent Pos:* Nat Sci Foun lectr, Univ PR, 61; mem, Mat Sci Comt, Argonne Ctr Educ Affairs, Argonne Nat Lab, 71-; mem adv comt, Metals & Ceramics Div, Oak Ridge Nat Lab, 72-74; task coordr energy res, Div Materials Res, Nat Sci Found, 74-75; consult, Kennametal Inc, sect head metall & mat, Div Mat Res, NSF, 77-78. *Mem:* AAAS; fel Am Phys Soc; fel Am Ceramic Soc; Bioelectrical Repair & Growth Soc; Mat Res Soc. *Res:* Electrical, thermal and mechanical properties of refractory hard metals; high-strength fibers; defects in solids; low and high temperature thermal conductivity; electrical properties of bone; electrical modification of osteoporosis; implant materials; archaeological materials. *Mailing Add:* Materials Res Lab Univ Ill Urbana IL 61801

WILLIAMS, WILLIAM ARNOLD, b Johnson City, NY, Aug 2, 22; m 43; c 3. AGRONOMY. *Educ:* Cornell Univ, BS, 47, MS, 48, PhD(agron), 51. *Prof Exp:* Instr, 51-53, from asst prof to assoc prof, 54-64, PROF AGRON, UNIV CALIF, DAVIS, 65- *Concurrent Pos:* Fulbright scholar, Australia, 60; Rockefeller fel, Cent & SAm, 66; mem staff, Res Vessel Alpha Helix, Amazon Exped, 67. *Mem:* Am Soc Agron; Crop Sci Soc Am; Soil Sci Soc Am; Am Soc Plant Physiol; Ecol Soc Am. *Res:* Systems analysis of annual-type range growth and utilization. *Mailing Add:* Dept of Agron & Range Sci Univ of Calif Davis CA 95616

WILLIAMS, WILLIAM DONALD, b Macon, Ga, Apr 22, 28; m 52; c 4. PHYSICAL CHEMISTRY. *Educ:* Harding Col, BS, 50; Univ Ky, MS, 52, PhD(chem), 54. *Prof Exp:* Assoc prof chem, 54-63, PROF CHEM & CHMN DEPT PHYS SCI, HARDING COL, 63- *Mem:* AAAS; Am Chem Soc. *Res:* Chemistry and kinetics of flames. *Mailing Add:* Dept of Chem Harding Col Searcy AR 72143

WILLIAMS, WILLIAM JAMES, b Rio Grande, Ohio, May 9, 35; m 61; c 2. ELECTRICAL ENGINEERING, PHYSIOLOGY. *Educ:* Ohio State Univ, BEE, 58; Univ Iowa, MS, 61, PhD(elec eng), 63; Univ Mich, MS, 66. *Prof Exp:* Res engr, Battelle Mem Inst, 58-60; teaching asst elec eng, Univ Iowa, 60-63; sr res specialist commun theory, Emerson Elec Mfg Co, 63-64; lectr elec eng, 64-65, asst prof elec eng & bioeng, 65-69, assoc prof elec & comput eng & bioeng, 69-73, PROF ELEC & COMPUT ENG & BIOENG, UNIV MICH, ANN ARBOR, 73-, DIR BIOELEC SCI LAB, 68- *Concurrent Pos:* Rackham fel & award, 66-67; vis scientist, Sch Med, Johns Hopkins Univ, 74. *Mem:* Inst Elec & Electronics Engrs; Soc Neurosci. *Res:* Electrical and communication biophysics; neurocybernetics; application of signal processing and systems analysis techniques to biological problems, particularly the nervous system; computer applications. *Mailing Add:* Bioelec Sci Lab Dept Elec Comput Eng Univ Mich 5070F Ann Arbor MI 48109

WILLIAMS, WILLIAM JOSEPH, b Bridgeton, NJ, Dec 8, 26; m 50; c 3. MEDICINE, BIOCHEMISTRY. *Educ:* Univ Pa, MD, 49. *Prof Exp:* Intern, Hosp Univ Pa, 49-50; sr instr microbiol, Sch Med, Western Reserve Univ, 52; resident med, Hosp Univ Pa, 54-55; assoc med, Sch Med, Univ Pa, 55-56, from asst prof to prof, 56-69; PROF MED & CHMN DEPT, STATE UNIV NY UPSTATE MED CTR, 69- *Concurrent Pos:* Am Cancer Soc fel physiol chem, Sch Med, Univ Pa, 50-52, Am Philos Soc Daland fel res clin med, 55-57; Markle scholar, 57-62; USPHS res career develop award, 63-68; asst prof, Sch Med, Wash Univ, 59-60; mem hemat training comt, Nat Inst Arthritis & Metab Dis, 64-68, res career prog comt, 68-72 & thrombosis adv comt, 69-73, chmn, 71-73; mem adv coun, Nat Arthritis Metab & Digestive Dis, NIH, 75-79; vis prof, Med Dept, Monash Univ, Melbourne, Australia, 80; vis scientist, Walter & Eliza Hall Med Res, Melbourne, Australia, 80. *Mem:* Am Soc Hemat; Am Soc Clin Invest; Am Fedn Clin Res; Am Soc Biol Chem; Asn Am Physicians. *Res:* Internal medicine; hematology; blood coagulation; blood cell metabolism. *Mailing Add:* Dept of Med State Univ of NY Upstate Med Ctr Syracuse NY 13210

WILLIAMS, WILLIAM LANE, b Rock Hill, SC, Dec 23, 14. ANATOMY. *Educ:* Wofford Col, BS, 35; Duke Univ, MA, 39; Yale Univ, PhD(anat), 41. *Prof Exp:* Asst anat, Sch Med, Yale Univ, 39-40; instr, Sch Med & Dent, Univ Rochester, 41-42; instr, Sch Med, Yale Univ, 42-43; asst prof, Sch Med, La State Univ, 43-45; from asst prof to assoc prof, Univ Minn, Minneapolis, 45-58; prof anat & chmn dept, 58-80, EMER PROF ANAT, MED CTR, UNIV MISS, 80- *Concurrent Pos:* Donner Found fel anat, Sch Med, Yale Univ, 42-43; asst vchancellor, Med Ctr, Univ Miss, 75-80. *Mem:* Am Soc Exp Path; Am Physiol Soc; Soc Exp Biol & Med; Am Asn Anat; Am Inst Nutrit. *Res:* Endocrinology, experimental pathology; nutrition; cardiovascular disease; hepatic liposis. *Mailing Add:* Cndm J2 3975 I 55 N Jackson MS 39216

WILLIAMS, WILLIAM LAWRENCE, b St Cloud, Minn, June 14, 19; div; c 2. BIOCHEMISTRY. *Educ:* Univ Minn, BS, 42; Univ Wis, MS, 47, PhD(biochem), 49. *Prof Exp:* Asst prof biochem, NC State Univ, 49-50; res biochemist, Lederle Lab, 50-59; res assoc prof, 59-60, res prof, 60-76, MEM FAC BIOCHEM, UNIV GA, 76- *Concurrent Pos:* NIH career develop award, 62-, res grant, 64-67, training grant, 65-70; indust consult; dir, Reproduction Res Labs. *Mem:* Am Soc Biol Chem; Brit Soc Study Fertil; Soc Study Reproduction; Am Fertil Soc; Am Physiol Soc. *Res:* Animal reproduction. *Mailing Add:* Dept Biochem Boyd Grad Studies Ctr Univ Ga Athens GA 30601

WILLIAMS, WILLIAM LEE, b Chickasha, Okla, May 28, 37; m 59; c 2. ATOMIC PHYSICS. *Educ:* Rice Inst, BA, 59; Dartmouth Col, MA, 61; Yale Univ, PhD(physics), 65. *Prof Exp:* From instr to assoc prof, 65-77, PROF PHYSICS, UNIV MICH, ANN ARBOR, 77- *Mem:* Am Phys Soc. *Res:* High precision atomic physics of hydrogenic atoms; atomic lifetime measurements. *Mailing Add:* Dept of Physics Univ of Mich Ann Arbor MI 48109

WILLIAMS, WILLIAM MICHAEL, organic chemistry, see previous edition

WILLIAMS, WILLIAM NORMAN, b Detroit, Mich, June 18, 39. SPEECH PATHOLOGY. *Educ:* Fla State Univ, BA, 63, MS, 64; Univ Fla, PhD(speech path audiol), 69. *Prof Exp:* Res assoc speech physiol, Dept of Commun Dis, 65-66, asst prof, 71-77, ASSOC PROF SPEECH PHYSIOL, DEPT BASIC DENT SCI, COL DENT, UNIV FLA, 77- *Concurrent Pos:* Res clin consult, Audiol-speech path, Vet Admin Hosp, Gainesville, Fla, 71-; WHO fel, Sweden & WGer, 75. *Mem:* Am Speech & Hearing Asn; Am Cleft Palate Asn; Am Asn Phonetic Sci. *Res:* Radiographic assessment of oral motor function of normal subjects and individuals with oral facial-communicative disorders; basic research in assessing oral sensory-perceptual integrity. *Mailing Add:* Dept of Basic Dent Sci Univ of Fla Col of Dent Gainesville FL 32610

WILLIAMS, WILLIAM ORVILLE, b Carlsbad, NMex, Oct 19, 40; m 60. MATHEMATICS, MECHANICS. *Educ:* Rice Univ, BA, 62, MS, 63; Brown Univ, PhD(appl math), 67. *Prof Exp:* Assoc res engr, Houston Res Lab, Humble Oil & Ref Co, 64; asst prof, 66-70, assoc prof, 70-76, PROF MATH, CARNEGIE-MELLON UNIV, 76- *Mem:* Soc Natural Philos; Am Math Soc; Math Asn Am. *Res:* Foundations of continuum mechanics; thermodynamics. *Mailing Add:* Dept of Math Carnegie-Mellon Univ Pittsburgh PA 15213

WILLIAMS, WILLIAM THOMAS, b San Marcos, Tex, Dec 22, 24; m 51; c 1. BIOCHEMISTRY, CELL PHYSIOLOGY. *Educ:* Southwest Tex State Univ, BS, 47; Tex A&M Univ, MS, 51, PhD(biochem), 65. *Prof Exp:* Instr chem, Tex A&M, 47-48; res asst biochem, Tex Agr Exp Sta, 58-61, res chemist, Marine Lab, Tex A&M Univ, 61-62; res biologist, US Air Force Sch Aerospace Med, Brooks AFB, 63-64, res chemist, 64-72, ASSOC FOUND SCI, SOUTHWEST FOUND RES EDUC, 73- *Mem:* Fel Am Inst Chemists; Am Inst Biol Sci; fel AAAS; Am Chem Soc; Am Soc Microbiol. *Res:* Regulation of cell metabolism and growth; nitrogen nutrition and metabolism; analytical biochemistry. *Mailing Add:* Southwest Res Inst 6220 Culebra Rd San Antonio TX 78284

WILLIAMS, WILLIE ELBERT, b Jacksonville, Tex, June 6, 27; m 51; c 2. MATHEMATIC STATISTICS, COMPUTER SCIENCE. *Educ:* Huston-Tillotson Col, BS, 52; Tex Southern Univ, MS, 53; Mich State Univ, PhD(math educ), 72. *Prof Exp:* Teacher math, Lufkin Independent Schs, 53-59 & Case Western Reserve Univ, 64-73; dept chmn, Cleveland Bd Educ, 60-73; ASSOC PROF MATH, FLA INT UNIV, 73- *Mem:* Math Asn Am; Nat Coun Teachers Math. *Res:* Teacher effectiveness in mathematics and how children learn mathematics. *Mailing Add:* Fla Int Univ Tamiami Trail Miami FL 33199

WILLIAMS-ASHMAN, HOWARD GUY, b London, Eng, Sept 3, 25; nat US; m 59; c 4. BIOCHEMISTRY. *Educ:* Cambridge Univ, BA, 46; Univ London, PhD, 59. *Prof Exp:* Biochemist, Chester Beatty Res Inst, Eng, 49-50; from asst prof to prof biochem, Univ Chicago, 53-64; prof pharmacol & exp therapeut & prof reprod biol, Sch Med, Johns Hopkins Univ, 64-69; prof biochem & physiol, 69-73, MAURICE GOLDBLATT PROF BIOL SCI, PRITZKER SCH MED, UNIV CHICAGO, 73- *Concurrent Pos:* Am Cancer Soc scholar, 53-57; USPHS res career award, 62-64. *Honors & Awards:* Amory Prize, Am Acad Arts & Sci, 75. *Mem:* Am Soc Biol Chem; Am Soc Pharmacol & Exp Therapeut; fel Am Acad Arts & Sci; Brit Biochem Soc; Am Asn Cancer Res. *Res:* Mechanism of hormone action; reproductive physiology; chemical pathology. *Mailing Add:* Ben May Lab for Cancer Res Pritzker Sch Med Univ Chicago Chicago IL 60637

WILLIAMSON, ARTHUR ELRIDGE, JR, b Montgomery, Ala, July 6, 26; m 51; c 2. ELECTROOPTICS. *Educ:* Auburn Univ, BEP, 50, MS, 51. *Prof Exp:* Res engr, NAm Aviation, Inc, 51-52; instr physics, Univ Richmond, 52-53; res physicist, Southern Res Inst, 53-55; asst prof physics & res proj dir, Ga Inst Technol, 55-59; chief, Electrooptics Lab, Martin Marietta Corp, 59-73; HEAD, ELECTRO OPTICS SECT, SOUTHERN RES INST, 73- *Mem:* Am Phys Soc; Optical Soc Am. *Res:* Optics. *Mailing Add:* Southern Res Inst 2000 Ninth Ave S Birmingham AL 35205

WILLIAMSON, ASHLEY DEAS, b Columbus, Ga, June 16, 47; m 73; c 1. LASER SPECTROSCOPY. *Educ:* Emory Univ, BS, 68; Calif Inst Technol, PhD(chem), 76. *Prof Exp:* Sci & eng asst, US Army Chem Ctr, Edgewood Arsenal, Md, 69-71; res & teaching asst, Calif Inst Technol, 71-75; scientist, Oak Ridge Nat Lab, 75-79; sr chemist, 79-80, SECT HEAD, SOUTHERN RES INST, 81- *Mem:* Am Phys Soc; Am Chem Soc; Optical Soc Am. *Res:* Air pollution control and measurement; particulate sampling and measurement; chemical and physical transformation of condensible vapors in process emissions; laser spectroscopy; multiphoton excitation and ionization; mass spectrometry; gaseous ion chemistry; vacuum ultraviolet spectroscopy. *Mailing Add:* Southern Res Inst Box 3307-A 2000 Ninth Ave S Birmingham AL 35255

WILLIAMSON, CHARLES EDWARD, b Newport, Ind, May 29, 15; m 42; c 3. PLANT PATHOLOGY. *Educ:* Wabash Col, AB, 37; Cornell Univ, PhD(plant path), 49. *Prof Exp:* Asst prof plant path, NY State Col Agr & Life Sci, Cornell Univ, 48-72, assoc prof, 72-80. *Mem:* Am Phytopath Soc. *Res:* Diseases of ornamentals, including those caused by nematodes, soil fumigants and soil treatments. *Mailing Add:* 210 E Ringfactory Rd Belair MD 21014

WILLIAMSON, CHARLES ELVIN, b Portsmouth, Va, Dec 5, 26; m 52; c 6. BIO-ORGANIC CHEMISTRY, ONCOLOGY. *Educ:* Col William & Mary, BS, 50; Johns Hopkins Univ, PhD(bio-org chem), 70. *Prof Exp:* res chemist, Res Labs, Edgewood Arsenal, 52-79; PRES, JUNGLE-GEMS, INC, 79- *Concurrent Pos:* Res assoc, Siani Hosp Baltimroe, 55-; res assoc, Johns Hopkins Univ Sch Med, 72- *Res:* Microenvironmental forces at biologic binding sites; reactions at cell surfaces; hydrophobic and electrostatic catalyses; neoplastic changes and cancer chemotherapy; tissue culture and micropropagation of plants. *Mailing Add:* 210 E Ring Factory Rd Bel Air MD 21014

WILLIAMSON, CHARLES WESLEY, b Blue Earth, Minn, Sept 2, 24; m 44; c 5. PLASTICS CHEMISTRY. *Educ:* Kenyon Col, AB, 49; Rensselaer Polytech Inst, PhD(phys chem), 53. *Prof Exp:* Chemist, E I du Pont de Nemours & Co, Inc, 53-56, plastic technologist, 56-59; sr chemist, 59-63, res assoc polymer processing, 63-67, sr res assoc plastics fabrication, 68-74, SR RES ASSOC, PLASTICS TECHNOL DIV, EXXON CHEM CO, 74- *Mem:* Am Chem Soc; Soc Plastics Engrs. *Res:* Polymerization of polyolefins; viscoelastic properties of polymer melts; morphology of thermoplastics; polyolefin film fabrication process development; film fabrication and solution casting of high temperture plastics. *Mailing Add:* Exxon Chem Co Plastics Technol Div PO Box 4255 Baytown TX 77520

WILLIAMSON, CLARENCE KELLY, b McKeesport, Pa, Jan 19, 24; m 51; c 2. MICROBIOLOGY. *Educ:* Univ Pittsburgh, BS, 49, MS, 51, PhD, 55. *Prof Exp:* Instr bact, Sch Pharm, Univ Pittsburgh, 51-55; from asst prof to assoc prof, 55-63, chmn dept microbiol, 62-72, PROF MICROBIOL, MIAMI UNIV, 63-, DEAN, COL ARTS & SCI, 71- *Concurrent Pos:* Consult, Warren-Teed Prod Co, 54-64; consult ed, World Publ Co, 65-68; mem, Com Arts & Sci, Nat Asn State Univ & Land-Grant Col, 75- *Mem:* AAAS; Am Soc Microbiol; fel Am Acad Microbiol; Coun Cols of Arts & Sci (pres, 77-78). Brit Soc Gen Microbiol. *Res:* Microbic dissociation, Pseudomonas aeruginosa; classification and polysaccharides of viridans streptococci; post-streptococcal nephritis. *Mailing Add:* Col of Arts & Sci Miami Univ Oxford OH 45056

WILLIAMSON, CLAUDE F, b Henderson, Tex, Mar 29, 33; m 59. NUCLEAR PHYSICS. *Educ:* Univ Tex, BS, 55, MA, 56, PhD(physics), 59. *Prof Exp:* Physicist, Saclay Nuclear Res Ctr, France, 60-62; res asst prof nuclear physics, Nuclear Physics Lab, Univ Wash, 62-66; res physicist, Lab Nuclear Sci, 66-75, SR RES SCI, DEPT PHYSICS, MASS INST TECHNOL, 75- *Mem:* AAAS; Am Phys Soc. *Res:* Fast neutron physics; nuclear reaction gamma rays; nuclear structure by electron scattering. *Mailing Add:* Rm 26-431 Mass Inst Technol 77 Massachusetts Ave Cambridge MA 02139

WILLIAMSON, CRAIG EDWARD, b Boston, Mass, July 20, 53; m 74. AQUATIC ECOLOGY, POPULATION BIOLOGY. *Educ:* Dartmouth Col, AB, 75, PhD(biol), 81; Mt Holyoke Col, MA, 77. *Prof Exp:* ASST PROF BIOL, LEHIGH UNIV, 81- *Mem:* AAAS; Ecol Soc Am; Am Soc Limnol & Oceanog; Sigma Xi. *Res:* The role of selective predation in structuring freshwater zooplankton communities, particularly interactions between microzooplankton, invertebrate predators and larval fish; morphological and behavioral mechanisms regulating selective predation in zooplankton communities. *Mailing Add:* Dept Biol Williams Hall 31 Lehigh Univ Bethlehem PA 18015

WILLIAMSON, DALE EUGENE, b Dodge City, Kans, July 4, 48; m 75. INORGANIC CHEMISTRY. *Educ:* Bethany Nazarene Col, BS, 70; Univ Kans, PhD(inorg chem), 74. *Prof Exp:* Researcher catalysis, Univ Kans, 74-75; PROF CHEM, NORTHWEST NAZARENE COL, 75- *Mem:* Am Chem Soc. *Res:* Complexes of cobalt as oxygen carriers; catalysts for the oxidation of phosphines. *Mailing Add:* 308 N Midland Nampa ID 83651

WILLIAMSON, DAVID GADSBY, b Honolulu, Hawaii, June 12, 41; m 63; c 2. CHEMICAL KINETICS. *Educ:* Univ Colo, Boulder, BA, 63; Univ Calif, Los Angeles, PhD(phys chem), 66. *Prof Exp:* Chemist, Nat Bur Standards, Colo, 63; teaching & res asst chem, Univ Calif, Los Angeles, 63-66; fel, Nat Res Coun Can, 67-68; from asst prof to assoc prof, 68-76, PROF CHEM, CALIF POLYTECH STATE UNIV, SAN LUIS OBISPO, 76- *Concurrent Pos:* Res grant, Environ Protection Agency, 72. *Mem:* Am Chem Soc. *Res:* Ozone chemistry and the chemistry of free radicals of importance to atmospheric chemistry; development of energy sources alternate to petroleum products. *Mailing Add:* Dept of Chem Calif Polytech State Univ San Luis Obispo CA 93407

WILLIAMSON, DAVID LEE, b Humboldt, Nebr, July 17, 30; m 68; c 2. GENETICS. *Educ:* Nebr State Teachers Col, Peru, AB, 52; Univ Nebr, MS, 55, PhD(zool), 59. *Prof Exp:* Instr biol, Dana Col, 55-56; Fulbright scholar, Lab Genetics, Gif-sur-Yvette, France, 59-60; asst prof genetics, Univ Utah, 60-61; NIH fel, Yale Univ, 61-64; res fel, Med Col Pa, 64-66, asst prof, 66-71; assoc prof, 71-81, PROF ANAT SCI, STATE UNIV NY STONY BROOK, 81- *Mem:* AAAS; Am Soc Nat; Genetics Soc Am; Soc Study Evolution; Int Soc Mycoplasmologists. *Res:* Maternally inherited traits in Drosophila; biology of spiroplasmas. *Mailing Add:* Dept of Anat Sci State Univ NY Stony Brook NY 11794

WILLIAMSON, DENIS GEORGE, b Trail, BC, June 9, 41; m 62; c 3. BIOCHEMISTRY. *Educ:* Univ BC, BSc, 63, PhD(biochem), 68. *Prof Exp:* Med Res Coun fel, 68-71, lectr, 71-72, asst prof, 72-76, assoc prof, 76-81, PROF BIOCHEM, UNIV OTTAWA, 81- *Mem:* Can Biochem Soc. *Res:* Metabolism of steroid hormones; steroid conjugates; purification and characterization of steroid dehydrogenases. *Mailing Add:* Dept of Biochem Univ of Ottawa Ottawa ON K1N 9A9 Can

WILLIAMSON, DONALD ELWIN, b Lansing, Mich, Oct 24, 13; m 40; c 3. INSTRUMENTATION, BIOMEDICAL ENGINEERING. *Educ:* Carleton Col, AB, 35; Univ Mich, MS, 36. *Prof Exp:* Res physicist, Dept Eng Res, Univ Mich, 36, res engr, 44-45; mgr, Profilometer Div, Physicists Res Co, 36-44; res engr, Lincoln Park Industs, 45-47; chief engr & assoc dir res, Baird Assocs, Inc, Mass, 47-52; pres & treas, Williamson Develop Co, 53-60; sci adv to pres, Cordis Corp, 60-79; RETIRED. *Concurrent Pos:* Chmn, Gordon Res Conf Instrumentation, 56. *Mem:* Am Soc Mech Eng; Optical Soc Am. *Res:* Roughness measurement; optics; infrared instruments; physiological and cardiovascular instrumentation. *Mailing Add:* 13001 Old Cutler Rd Miami FL 33156

WILLIAMSON, DOUGLAS HARRIS, b Croydon, Eng, Mar 3, 24; m 52; c 2. GEOLOGY. *Educ:* Aberdeen Univ, BSc, 50, PhD, 52. *Prof Exp:* Lectr geol, Aberdeen Univ, 50-53; asst prof, Mt Allison Univ, 53-54, Sr James Dunn prof & head dept, 54-66; head dept, 66-74, assoc dean sci, 69-72, PROF GEOL, LAURENTIAN UNIV, 66-, DEAN SCI, 72- *Concurrent Pos:* Nat Res Coun Can major equip grant, 65, operating grants, 65 & 66; Geol Surv Can grant, Univ NB, 62, NB Res & Productivity Coun grant, 62-66; mem subcomt, Nat Adv Comt Res Geol Sci in Can, 56-57; mem, Comt Deans Arts & Sci, 69-; mem, Coun Ont Univs, 70-72; Univ res grants officer, 70- *Mem:* AAAS; Nat Asn Geol Teachers; Can Inst Mining & Metall; fel Brit Geol Soc. X-ray crystallography; petrogenesis and synthesis of metamorphic mineral assemblages; mineralogy of fluorspar; exploration of mineral resources of Ontario; geology of Pre-Carboniferous rocks of Southern New Brunswick. *Mailing Add:* Dean's Off Fac of Sci II Laurentian Univ Sudbury ON P3E 2C6 Can

WILLIAMSON, EDWARD P, b Lee Co, Fla, July 1, 33; m 58; c 3. ELECTRICAL ENGINEERING, COMMUNICATIONS. *Educ:* Univ Fla, BEE, 55, MSE, 60, PhD(elec eng), 65. *Prof Exp:* Engr, Bendix Radio Div, 55-56; asst prof elec eng, 65-70, ASSOC PROF ELEC ENG, TULANE UNIV, 70- *Concurrent Pos:* Res scientist, Kaman Nuclear Div, Colo, 67. *Mem:* Inst Elec & Electronics Engrs. *Res:* Radar system theory; statistical communication theory; communication system signal design and modulation techniques; optimization, estimation and decision theory as applied to communication and radar systems; remote sensing systems. *Mailing Add:* Dept of Elec Eng Tulane Univ New Orleans LA 70118

WILLIAMSON, FRANCIS SIDNEY LANIER, b Little Rock, Ark, Feb 6, 27; m 78; c 3. ZOOLOGY, PUBLIC HEALTH ADMINISTRATION. *Educ:* San Diego State Col, BS, 50; Univ Calif, MA, 55; Johns Hopkins Univ, ScD, 68. *Prof Exp:* Mus technician vert zool, Univ Calif, 53-55; med biologist, Arctic Health Res Ctr, USPHS, 55-64; dir, Chesapeake Bay Ctr Environ Studies, Smithsonian Inst, 68-75; NIH fel & res assoc, 64-68, assoc pathobiol, Sch Hyg & Pub Health, Johns Hopkins Univ, 65-77; comnr, Dept Health & Social Serv, Alaska, 75-78; prog mgr polar biol & med, 78-79, CHIEF SCIENTIST, POLAR SCI SECT, NAT SCI FOUND, 79- *Concurrent Pos:* Consult, Avian ecol, AEC, 59-61; instr, Anchorage Community Col, Univ Alaska, 61-64; consult ecol, Battelle Mem Inst, 67-74; adv, Chesapeake Bay Study, US Army Corps Engrs, 69-75; ed, Biosci, Am Inst Biol Sci, 70 & Condor, Cooper Ornith Soc, 71-74; consult, Md Dept Nat Resources, 72-73; adv environ qual comn, Gov Sci Adv Coun, Md, 72-73. *Honors & Awards:* Exceptional Serv Award, Smithsonian Inst, 75. *Mem:* Fel AAAS; Ecol Soc Am; Cooper Ornith Soc; Fel Am Ornith Union; Wilson Ornith Soc. *Res:* Taxonomy, behavior, distribution, parasites and viral diseases of birds; taxonomy, distribution, and life histories of helminths; medical helminthology; estuarine ecology; environmental planning. *Mailing Add:* Div of Polar Progs Nat Sci Found Washington DC 20550

WILLIAMSON, FRANK SHAVER, JR, inorganic chemistry, see previous edition

WILLIAMSON, FREDERICK DALE, b Poplar, Mont, Apr 15, 38; m 59; c 3. PAINT CHEMISTRY. *Educ:* NDak State Univ, BS, 60, MS, 62, PhD(polymers & coatings chem), 66. *Prof Exp:* Chemist, Glidden Co, 62; res chemist, Missiles & Space Systs Div, McDonnell Douglas Corp, 66-68; tech dir paints & coatings, Midland Div, Dexter Corp, 68-71; tech dir paints & coatings, O'Brien Corp, 71-76; mgr res & develop, Cargill, Inc, 76-78; OWNER & GEN MGR, ANDERSON PAINT CO, 78- *Mem:* Fedn Soc Paint Technol; Nat Paint & Coatings Asn. *Res:* Polymer synthesis; high temperature-resistant coatings; coatings rheology; high energy-curable coatings systems; water-borne resins and coating systems. *Mailing Add:* 156 Williams Rd Salinas CA 93905

WILLIAMSON, HAROLD EMANUEL, b Racine, Wis, Aug 8, 30; m 57; c 3. PHARMACOLOGY. *Educ:* Univ Wis, BS, 53, PhD(pharmacol, toxicol), 59. *Prof Exp:* Asst pharmacol, Univ Wis, 55-59, proj assoc, 59-60; from instr to assoc prof, 60-70, PROF PHARMACOL, COL MED, UNIV IOWA, 70- *Mem:* AAAS; Am Soc Pharmacol & Exp Therapeut; Am Fedn Clin Res; Soc Exp Biol & Med; Am Soc Nephrology. *Res:* Renal pharmacology and physiology, especially the effect of diuretics and hormones on electrolyte and water transport. *Mailing Add:* Dept of Pharmacol Univ of Iowa Col of Med Iowa City IA 52242

WILLIAMSON, HUGH A, b Kemp, Tex, Aug 11, 32; m 56; c 4. PHYSICS. *Educ:* North Tex State Univ, BA, 54; Univ Tex, PhD(physics, math), 62. *Prof Exp:* Res scientist, Molecular Physics Res Lab & Mil Physics Res Lab, Univ Tex, 60-63, res fel, 62-63; res scientist, Res Lab, United Aircraft Corp, 63-65, sr res scientist, 65-67; from asst prof to assoc prof, 67-74, PROF PHYSICS, CALIF STATE UNIV, FRESNO, 74- *Res:* Atomic and molecular structure; gaseous electronics; electron scattering processes off neutral atoms including elastic, inelastic and free-free scattering processes. *Mailing Add:* Dept of Physics Calif State Univ Fresno CA 93740

WILLIAMSON, HUGH A, b Williamsport, Pa, Apr 20, 27; m 60; c 2. ORGANIC CHEMISTRY, SCIENCE EDUCATION. *Educ:* Bucknell Univ, AB, 60, MA, 61; Cornell Univ, EdD(sci ed, chem), 66. *Prof Exp:* Teacher high sch, Pa, 50-55; PROF CHEM, LOCK HAVEN STATE COL, 55-, ASSOC DEAN ARTS & SCI, 73- *Mem:* Nat Asn Res Sci Teaching. *Res:* Synthesis of cyclooctatetraene compounds; reductions of epoxides. *Mailing Add:* Dept of Chem Lock Haven State Col Lock Haven PA 17745

WILLIAMSON, JAMES LAWRENCE, b Rebecca, Ga, Feb 28, 29; m 49; c 3. ANIMAL SCIENCE, ANIMAL NUTRITION. *Educ:* Univ Ga, BSA, 51; Univ Ill, MS, 52, PhD, 57. *Prof Exp:* Mgr, Beef Cattle & Sheep Res Div, 58-59, mgr, Livestock Res Dept, 59-60, dir res, 64-67, V PRES & DIR RES, CHOW DIV, RALSTON PURINA CO, 67- *Concurrent Pos:* Mem nutrit coun, Am Feed Mfrs Asn. *Mem:* Am Soc Animal Sci; Am Dairy Sci Asn; Poultry Sci Asn. *Res:* Animal nutrition and management. *Mailing Add:* Chow Div Ralston Purina Co Checkerboard Sq St Louis MO 63188

WILLIAMSON, JERRY ROBERT, b Danville, Ill, Feb 14, 38; m 65; c 1. ORGANIC CHEMISTRY, POLYMER CHEMISTRY. *Educ:* Univ Ill, Urbana, BA, 60; Univ Iowa, MS, 63, PhD(org polymer chem), 64. *Prof Exp:* Petrol Res Fund res fel polymer res, Univ Iowa, 61-62, teaching asst gen & org chem, 62-64; asst prof chem & actg chmn div sci, Jarvis Christian Col, 64-66; res fel, Tex Christian Univ, 66-67; asst prof, 67-70, ASSOC PROF CHEM, EASTERN MICH UNIV, 70- *Concurrent Pos:* Partic, State Tech Serv Prog, Mich, 67- *Mem:* AAAS; Am Chem Soc. *Res:* Organic polymer chemistry, thermally stable materials; polymer analysis via gel permeation chromatography. *Mailing Add:* Dept of Chem Eastern Mich Univ Ypsilanti MI 48197

WILLIAMSON, JOHN HYBERT, b Clarkton, NC, Apr 28, 38; m 63; c 2. GENETICS. *Educ:* NC State Col, BS, 60; Cornell Univ, MS, 63; Univ Ga, PhD(zool), 66. *Prof Exp:* Fel biol, Oak Ridge Nat Lab, 66-67; mem fac life sci, Univ Calif, Riverside, 67-69; asst prof, 69-72, assoc prof, 72-76, acad admin officer biol dept, 74-76, head dept, 76-78, PROF ZOOL, UNIV CALGARY, 76- *Mem:* Genetics Soc Can; Genetics Soc Am. *Res:* Chromosome mechanics; radiation biology; developmental genetics; enzymology. *Mailing Add:* Dept of Biol Univ of Calgary Calgary AB T2N 1N4 Can

WILLIAMSON, JOHN RICHARD, b Coventry, Eng, Sept 18, 33; m 61; c 3. BIOCHEMISTRY, BIOPHYSICS. *Educ:* Oxford Univ, BA, 56, MA, 59, PhD(biochem), 60. *Prof Exp:* Dept demonstr biochem, Oxford Univ, 60-61; independent investr, Baker Clin Res Lab, Harvard Univ, 61-63; assoc phys biochem, 63-65, from asst prof to prof phys biochem, Johnson Res Found, 65-76; PROF BIOCHEM, & BIOPHYSICS, SCH MED, UNIV PA, 75- *Concurrent Pos:* USPHS fel, 61-63; Am Heart Asn grant, 66-72; NIH res grants & contract, 71-; estab investr, Am Heart Asn, 67-72, mem coun basic sci. *Mem:* Am Soc Biol Chem; Am Diabetes Asn; Brit Biochem Soc; NY Acad Sci; Am Physiol Soc. *Res:* Mode of action of hormones and drugs; control of metabolic pathways; effect of hormones on cells and hormone interactions in animal cells; role of anion transport across mitochondrial membranes; myocardial ischemia. *Mailing Add:* Dept of Biochem & Biophys Univ of Pa Philadelphia PA 19174

WILLIAMSON, JOHN W, b Tulsa, Okla, Oct 26, 33; m 61; c 3. MECHANICAL ENGINEERING. *Educ:* Univ Okla, BSc, 55; Ohio State Univ, MSc, 59, PhD(mech eng), 65. *Prof Exp:* Test engr, NAm Aviation, Inc, 56-57; instr mech eng, Ohio State Univ, 57-60, 61-64, res asst, 60-61; from asst prof to assoc prof mech eng, 64-77, PROF MECH ENG & MAT SCI, VANDERBILT UNIV, 77- *Concurrent Pos:* Consult, Aerospace Struct Div, Avco Corp, 66- & E I du Pont de Nemours & Co, Inc, 69. *Mem:* Am Soc Eng Educ; Am Soc Mech Engrs. *Res:* Fluid mechanics, specifically aspects of turbulent fluid flow; energy utilization studies. *Mailing Add:* Dept of Mech Eng Vanderbilt Univ Nashville TN 37235

WILLIAMSON, KENNETH DALE, b Drumright, Okla, Sept 4, 20; m 46; c 3. PHYSICAL CHEMISTRY. *Educ:* Univ Okla, BS, 47, MS, 48; Univ Tex, PhD(chem), 54. *Prof Exp:* Chemist, Petrol Exp Sta, US Bur Mines, Okla, 48-50; spec instr chem, Univ Tex, 53; res chemist, 53-66, group leader res, 66-71, RES SCIENTIST, UNION CARBIDE CORP, 71- *Concurrent Pos:* Asst prof, Morris Harvey Col, 56-59 & WVa State Col, 62-64. *Mem:* AAAS; Am Chem Soc; Sigma Xi. *Res:* Physical properties of gas hydrates; physical properties of pure compounds and mixtures; thermodynamics; calorimetry; kinetics of pyrolysis of hydrocarbons; catalysis. *Mailing Add:* 1022 Sand Hill Dr St Albans WV 25177

WILLIAMSON, KENNETH DONALD, JR, b Williamsport, Pa, July 30, 35; m 58; c 3. SYSTEMS ANALYSIS, CRYOGENIC ENGINEERING. *Educ:* Pa State Univ, BS, 57, MS, 60, PhD(chem eng), 61. *Prof Exp:* Mem staff polymers, Union Carbide Corp, 61; mem staff cryog, 61-74, assoc group leader, 74-79, asst div leader technol assessment, 79-80, GROUP LEADER TECHNOL ASSESSMENT, LOS ALAMOS NAT LAB, 80- *Res:* Fast pulsed superconducting magnetic energy storage systems for the national fusion program, hydrogen energy systems and nuclear systems. *Mailing Add:* Los Alamos Nat Lab PO Box 1663 MS595 Los Alamos NM 87545

WILLIAMSON, KENNETH LEE, b Tarentum, Pa, Apr 13, 34; m 56; c 3. ORGANIC CHEMISTRY, STRUCTURAL CHEMISTRY. *Educ:* Harvard Univ, BA, 56; Univ Wis, PhD(org chem), 60. *Prof Exp:* NIH fel, Stanford Univ, 60-61; from asst prof to assoc prof, 61-69, dept chmn, 78-81, PROF CHEM, MT HOLYOKE COL, 69- *Concurrent Pos:* Mem grad faculty, Univ Mass, 62-; vis prof, Cornell Univ, 66; NSF sci faculty fel & fel Univ Liverpool, 68-69; vis assoc, Calif Inst Technol, 75; secy, Exp Nuclear Magnetic Resonance Spectroscopy Confs, 73-78, chmn exp nuclear magnetic resonance spectros conf, 79; fel, John Simon Guggenheim Found, 75-76; vis prof, Univ Utah, 76 & Oxford Univ, Eng, 76; mem, Comt Hazardous Substances in the Labs, Nat Res Coun, 81-82. *Mem:* Am Chem Soc; Sigma Xi; AAAS. *Res:* Conformational analysis by means of nuclear magnetic resonance spectroscopy; structural studies on insulin by nuclear magnetic resonance, Xenon nuclear magnetic resonance. *Mailing Add:* Dept of Chem Mt Holyoke Col South Hadley MA 01075

WILLIAMSON, LUTHER HOWARD, b Osyka, Miss, Oct 9, 36; m 57; c 3. PHYSICAL CHEMISTRY, OIL FIELD CHEMISTRY. *Educ:* La State Univ, BS, 59, MS, 62, PhD(phys chem), 65. *Prof Exp:* Res chemist corrosion, Mobil Res & Develop Corp, 65-70, sr res chemist corrosion, Water Chem, 70-78; STAFF ENGR CORROSION, MAT ENG, SUPERIOR OIL CO, 78- *Mem:* Am Chem Soc; Nat Asn Corrosion Engrs. *Res:* Surface chemistry; corrosion, corrosion inhibition, electrochemistry of corrosion; hydrogen embrittlement; sulfide stress corrosion cracking; water chemistry, oilfield chemistry, chemistry of scale formation; water pollution, air pollution; environmental science. *Mailing Add:* 108 Kirkwood Conroe TX 77301

WILLIAMSON, MERRITT A(LVIN), b Littleton, NH, Apr 1, 16; m 43; c 6. METALLURGY, AERONAUTICS. *Educ:* Yale Univ, BE, 38, MS, 40, PhD(metall), 46; Calif Inst Technol, MS, 45; Univ Chicago, MBA, 53. *Prof Exp:* Metallurgist, Scovill Mfg Co, Conn, 37-42 & Remington Arms Co Div, E I du Pont de Nemours & Co, 42-44; proj officer, US Naval Ord Test Sta, Calif, 45-46; dir tech res, Solar Aircraft Co, Calif, 46-48; assoc dir develop, Pullman-Standard Car Mfg Co, Ind, 48-52; dir res, Burroughs Adding Mach Co, 52-54, mgr res div, Burroughs Corp, 54-56; dean col eng, Pa State Univ, 56-66, prof eng, 59-66; prof mgt, Grad Sch Mgt, 69-77, ORRIN HENRY INGRAM DISTINGUISHED PROF ENG MGT & DIR STUDIES IN ENG MGT, VANDERBILT UNIV, 66- *Concurrent Pos:* Spec lectr, Univ Pa, 54-59 & Univ Mo-Rolla, 80; consult, 56-; secy-treas, Nat Conf Admin Res, 56-63, chmn, 64-65; chmn, Inst for Cert Eng Technicians, 61-63; ed, Eng Mgt Int, 79- *Honors & Awards:* James H McGraw Award, Am Soc Eng Educ, 74. *Mem:* Fel AAAS; Am Soc Eng Educ (vpres, 65-66, pres, 69-70); Nat Soc Prof Engrs; Am Soc Eng Mgt (vpres, 79-81, pres, 81-); Am Inst Mining, Metall & Petrol Engrs. *Res:* Metallurgy of brass alloys; etch markings in brass; metallic deformation and reflectivity; rockets and jet propulsion; guided missiles; corrosion; technical management. *Mailing Add:* 889 Gen Geol Patton Rd Nashville TN 37221

WILLIAMSON, PENELOPE ROSE, b New York, NY, Feb 6, 43; m 68; c 1. PSYCHOSOMATIC MEDICINE, HUMAN ECOLOGY. *Educ:* Antioch Col, BA, 65; Johns Hopkins Univ, ScD(ecol), 69. *Prof Exp:* Asst prof ment hyg, Sch Hyg & Pub Health, Johns Hopkins Univ, 69-78, asst prof med psychol, Dept Psychiat & Behav Sci, 73-77, asst prof, Sch Health Serv, 74-77; asst prof psychiat & med, Sch Med, Univ Rochester, 77-78; ASST PROF FAMILY MED & PSYCHOL, DEPT FAMILY MED, UNIV WASH SCH MED, 78- *Concurrent Pos:* Smithsonian Inst fel, Chesapeake Bay Ctr Environ Studies, Edgewater, Md, 69-70, Nat Audubon Soc grant, 70-72; asst prof, Eve Col, Johns Hopkins Univ, 73-77. *Mem:* Ecol Soc Am; Environ Design Res Asn. *Res:* Application of ecological methods and theory to the study of human behavior in urban areas; evaluation of behavioral science clinical teaching on health practitioner competencies and patient outcome. *Mailing Add:* Dept of Family Med RF-30 Univ of Wash Sch of Med Seattle WA 98195

WILLIAMSON, PETER GEORGE, b Hemel, UK, May 5, 52. EVOLUTIONARY BIOLOGY, BIOSTRATIGRAPHY. *Educ:* Univ Bristol, BSc, 74, PhD(geol), 79. *Prof Exp:* Res fel, NATO, 79-81; ASST PROF GEOL, HARVARD UNIV, 82- *Mem:* Soc Syst Zool; Geologists Asn; Malacological Soc London; Conchological Soc; Palaeont Asn. *Res:* Quantification of evolutionary mode and tempo in certain well-preserved mollusc sequences in East Africa and Germany; biostratigraphy of the East African hominid deposits; theoretical geometry of shell-coiling. *Mailing Add:* Mus Comp Zool Harvard Univ 26 Oxford St Cambridge MA 02138

WILLIAMSON, RALPH EDWARD, b Wilson, NC, Dec 28, 23; m 46; c 2. PLANT PHYSIOLOGY. *Educ:* NC State Univ, BS, 48; Univ Wis, MS, 50, PhD(bot), 58. *Prof Exp:* Botanist, Chem Corps, Dept Army, 48-49, plant physiologist, 50-51, 53-57 & Soil & Water Conserv Res Div, 57-74, PLANT PHYSIOLOGIST, TOBACCO RES LAB, USDA, OXFORD, NC, 74- *Mem:* Am Soc Plant Physiol; Am Soc Agron; Soil Sci Soc Am. *Res:* Determine major organic constituents of leaf tobacco that, if eliminated or reduced through breeding, cultural, processing, or curing techniques, would result in tobacco varieties less harmful to the consumer. *Mailing Add:* 716 Currituck Dr Raleigh NC 27609

WILLIAMSON, RALPH ELMORE, b Tulsa, Okla, July 8, 17; m 53; c 1. ASTRONOMY. *Educ:* Phillips Univ, AB, 38; Drake Univ, MA, 39; Univ Chicago, PhD(theoret astrophys), 43. *Prof Exp:* Instr astron, Yerkes Observ, Univ Chicago, 42-43, instr physics, US Air Force, 43-44; instr astron, US Navy, Cornell Univ, 44-46; lectr, David Dunlap Observ, Univ Toronto, 46-47, from asst prof to assoc prof, 47-53; MEM STAFF, LOS ALAMOS SCI LAB, 53- *Concurrent Pos:* Consult, Radio Astron Proj, Cornell Univ, 47-53. *Mem:* Am Astron Soc. *Res:* Theory of stellar atmospheres; stellar dynamics and interiors; radio astronomy; electronic computers; weapons physics and design. *Mailing Add:* Los Alamos Sci Lab Los Alamos NM 87545

WILLIAMSON, RICHARD EDMUND, b Chicago, Ill, May 23, 27; m 50. MATHEMATICS. *Educ:* Dartmouth Col, AB, 50; Univ Pa, AM, 51, PhD, 55. *Prof Exp:* Res asst, Univ Pa, 55-56; instr, 56-58, from asst prof to assoc prof, 58-66, PROF MATH, DARTMOUTH COL, 66- *Concurrent Pos:* Res fel, Harvard Univ, 60-61. *Mem:* Am Math Soc. *Res:* Analysis. *Mailing Add:* Dept of Math Dartmouth Col Hanover NH 03755

WILLIAMSON, ROBERT BRADY, b New Rochelle, NY, Nov 19, 33; m 59; c 3. CIVIL ENGINEERING. *Educ:* Harvard Univ, AB, 56, SB, 59, PhD(appl physics), 65. *Prof Exp:* Asst prof civil eng, Mass Inst Technol, 65-68; ASSOC PROF CIVIL ENG, UNIV CALIF, BERKELEY, 68- *Mem:* Am Soc Civil Engrs; Am Soc Testing & Mat; Soc Fire Protection Engrs; Am Ceramic Soc. *Res:* Morphology of solidified materials; fracture of materials; fire research and testing; theory of learning and programmed instruction. *Mailing Add:* Div of Struct Eng & Struct Mech Univ of Calif Berkeley CA 94720

WILLIAMSON, ROBERT EMMETT, b Ashland, Kans, June 9, 37; div; c 3. GEOMETRY, TOPOLOGY. *Educ:* Univ Ariz, BS, 59; Univ Calif, Berkeley, PhD(math), 63. *Prof Exp:* Mem, Inst Adv Study, 63-65; vis prof, Univ Warwick, 65-66; asst prof, Yale Univ, 66-69; ASSOC PROF MATH, CLAREMONT GRAD SCH, 69- *Concurrent Pos:* Nat Acad Sci-Air Force Off Sci Res fel, 63-64. *Mem:* Am Math Soc. *Res:* Algebraic model of surgery; singularities of smooth maps. *Mailing Add:* Dept Math Claremont Grad Sch Claremont CA 91711

WILLIAMSON, ROBERT MARSHALL, b Madison, Wis, Feb 2, 23; m 50. PHYSICS. *Educ:* Univ Fla, BS, 43, PhD(physics), 51. *Prof Exp:* Res assoc, Duke Univ, 51-53, from asst prof to assoc prof physics, 53-62; PROF PHYSICS, OAKLAND UNIV, 62- *Concurrent Pos:* Fulbright lectr, Univ Catania, 59-60. *Mem:* Am Phys Soc. *Res:* Nuclear spectroscopy. *Mailing Add:* Dept of Physics Oakland Univ Rochester MI 48063

WILLIAMSON, ROBERT SAMUEL, b Cincinnati, Ohio, June 18, 22. PHYSICS. *Educ:* Queens Col, BS, 45; NY Univ, MS, 48; Polytech Inst Brooklyn, PhD(physics), 57. *Prof Exp:* Tutor, 52-56, instr, 56-60, from asst prof to assoc prof, 60-68, from asst dean to assoc dean admin, 68-72, PROF PHYSICS, QUEENS COL, NY, 68- *Mem:* Am Phys Soc; Am Asn Physics Teachers; Am Crystallog Asn; Inst Elec & Electronics Eng. *Res:* X-ray crystallography; electronics. *Mailing Add:* Dept of Physics Queens Col Flushing NY 11367

WILLIAMSON, SAMUEL JOHNS, b West Reading, Pa, Nov 6, 39; m 66. LOW TEMPERATURE PHYSICS. *Educ:* Mass Inst Technol, SB, 61, ScD(physics), 65. *Prof Exp:* Res staff mem solid state physics, Nat Magnet Lab, Mass Inst Technol, 65-66; Nat Acad Sci-Nat Res Coun fel, Dept Physics of Solids, Fac Sci, Univ Paris, Orsay, France, 66-67; res staff mem, Sci Ctr Div, N Am Aviation, 67-70; lectr, Univ Calif, Santa Barbara, 70-71; assoc prof, 71-76, PROF PHYSICS, NY UNIV, 76- *Mem:* fel Am Phys Soc; Sigma Xi; AAAS; NY Acad Sci. *Res:* Polarimetry; magnetism; de Haas-Van Alphen effect and Fermi surface studies; superconductivity; ultra low temperature physics; biomagnetism; meuromagnetism; fundamentals of air pollution; light and color in nature and art. *Mailing Add:* Dept of Physics NY Univ 4 Washington Pl New York NY 10003

WILLIAMSON, STANLEY GILL, b Manhattan, Kans, Aug 28, 38; m 65. MATHEMATICS. *Educ:* Calif Inst Technol, BS, 60; Stanford Univ, MS, 62; Univ Calif, Santa Barbara,PhD(math), 65. *Prof Exp:* From asst prof to assoc prof, 65-75, PROF MATH, UNIV CALIF, SAN DIEGO, 75- *Mem:* Soc Indust Appl Math. *Res:* Combinatorial analysis; computation. *Mailing Add:* Dept of Math Univ of Calif San Diego La Jolla CA 92037

WILLIAMSON, STANLEY MORRIS, b Chattanooga, Ten, Mar 18, 36; m 66. CHEMISTRY. *Educ:* Univ NC, BS, 58; Univ Wash, PhD(chem), 61. *Prof Exp:* Asst prof chem, Univ Calif, Berkeley, 61-65, from asst prof to assoc prof, 65-74, PROF CHEM, UNIV CALIF, SANTA CRUZ, 74-, DEAN GRAD DIV, 72- *Mem:* AAAS; Am Chem Soc; Royal Soc Chem. *Res:* Fluorine chemistry of compounds of sulfur, nitrogen, oxygen and xenon including preparations and properties. *Mailing Add:* Div of Natural Sci Cowell Col Univ of Calif Santa Cruz CA 95064

WILLIAMSON, SUSAN, b Boston, Mass, Dec 29, 36. MATHEMATICS. *Educ:* Radcliffe Col, AB, 58; Brandeis Univ, AM, 61, PhD(math), 63. *Prof Exp:* Instr, Cardinal Cushing Col, 62-63; asst prof math, Boston Col, 63-64; scholar hist sci, Harvard Univ, 64-65; from asst prof to assoc prof, 65-71, dean col, Regis Col, 73-75, PROF MATH, REGIS COL, MASS, 71- *Mem:* Am Math Soc; Math Asn Am; Asn Women Math. *Res:* Associative algebras; commutative rings. *Mailing Add:* Dept Math Regis Col Weston MA 02193

WILLIAMSON, THOMAS GARNETT, b Quincey, Mass, Jan 27, 34; m 61; c 3. NUCLEAR ENGINEERING. *Educ:* Va Mil Inst, BS, 55; Rensselaer Polytech Inst, MS, 57; Univ Va, PhD(physics), 60. *Prof Exp:* Nuclear engr, Alco Prod, Inc, NY, 57-58; dir, Reactor Facil, 77-79, PROF NUCLEAR ENG, UNIV VA, 60-, CHMN NUCLEAR ENG & ENG PHYSICS DEPT, 77- *Concurrent Pos:* Consult, Gen Atomic Div, Gen Dynamics Corp, 66 & Combustion Eng, Conn, 71, 72; mem, Syst Nuclear Safety & Operating Comt, Va Elec & Power Co, 75-; mem reactor safety comt, Babcock & Wilcox Co, 76- *Mem:* Am Nuclear Soc. *Res:* Radioactive isotope usage; neutron activation analysis; radiation shielding. *Mailing Add:* Dept of Nuclear Eng Univ of Va Charlottesville VA 22901

WILLIAMSON, WALTON E, JR, b Corpus Christi, Tex, May 21, 44; m 65. FLIGHT MECHANICS, OPTIMIZATION. *Educ:* Stanford Univ, BS, 66; Univ Tex, Austin, MS, 67, PhD(aerospace eng), 70. *Prof Exp:* Asst prof optimal control, Univ Tex, Austin, 70-73; MEM TECH STAFF, SANDIA LABS, ALBUQUERQUE, 74- *Mem:* Am Inst Aeronaut & Astronaut. *Res:* Numerical methods for optimal control; shuttle reentry optimization. *Mailing Add:* Sandia Labs Div 5635 PO Box 5800 Albuquerque NM 87185

WILLIAMSON, WILLIAM, JR, b Newport, RI, Jan 20, 34; m 57; c 2. ATOMIC PHYSICS, ASTROPHYSICS. *Educ:* San Francisco State Col, BA, 55; Univ Calif, Berkeley, MA, 58; Univ Colo, PhD(physics), 63. *Prof Exp:* Physicist, US Naval Radiol Defense Lab, Calif, 56-58; Fulbright fel, Frascati Labs, Italy, 61-62; asst physics, Univ Colo, 62-63; fel, Inst Sci & Tech, Univ Mich, 63-64, instr, 64-65; asst prof physics & astron, 65-69, assoc prof, 69-75, PROF PHYSICS, UNIV TOLEDO, 75- *Concurrent Pos:* Vis prof, Univ Adelaide, 71-72. *Mem:* Am Astron Soc; Am Phys Soc; Am Asn Physics Teachers; Italian Phys Soc. *Mailing Add:* Ritter Astrophys Res Ctr Univ of Toledo Toledo OH 43606

WILLIAMSON, WILLIAM BURTON, Frederick, Okla, Apr 29, 46; m 67; c 3. HETEROGENEOUS CATALYSIS. *Educ:* Tex Tech Univ, BS, 69; Tex A&M Univ, PhD(phys chem), 76. *Prof Exp:* SR RES SCIENTIST, SCI RES, FORD MOTOR CO, 76- *Mem:* Am Chem Soc; Sigma Xi. *Res:* Basic and applied laboratory research on potential automotive emission catalysts (heterogeneous catalysis) for the reduction of nitric oxide and oxidation of carbon monoxide and hydrocarbons. *Mailing Add:* 264 Surrey Heights Westland MI 48185

WILLIAMSON, WILLIAM O(WEN), b Luton, Eng, Jan 30, 11; m 58; c 1. CERAMICS, PETROLOGY. *Educ:* Univ London, BSc, 30 & 31, PhD(geol), 33, DSc(geol, indust chem), 58. *Prof Exp:* Chief asst ceramics, North Staffordshire Col Technol, Eng, 34-42; res chemist, Univ Birmingham, 42-45; prof officer ceramics, Univ Witwatersrand, 45-47; prin res officer, Chem Res Labs, Commonwealth Sci & Indust Res Orgn, Australia, 47-59; assoc prof ceramic tech, 59-65, prof ceramic sci, 65-76, EMER PROF CERAMIC SCI, PA STATE UNIV, UNIVERSITY PARK, 76- *Mem:* Fel Am Ceramic Soc; Royal Inst Chem. *Res:* Solid state technology; rheology and surface chemistry; high temperature reactions; materials in ancient and modern cultures. *Mailing Add:* 222 Steidle Pa State Univ University Park PA 16802

WILLIARD, PAUL GREGORY, b Mt Carmel, Pa, Dec 18, 50; m 79. ORGANIC CHEMISTRY, STRUCTURAL CHEMISTRY. *Educ:* Bucknell Univ, BS & MS, 72; Columbia Univ, MPhil, 74, PhD(chem), 76. *Prof Exp:* NIH trainee chem, Mass Inst Technol, 76-78, fel, 78-79; ASST PROF CHEM, BROWN UNIV, 79- *Mem:* Am Chem Soc; British Chem Soc. *Res:* Total synthesis of natural products; synthetic methods; x-ray crystallography. *Mailing Add:* Box H Dept Chem Brown Univ Providence RI 02912

WILLIFORD, WILLIAM OLIN, b San Pedro, Calif, July 18, 33; m 71. MATHEMATICAL STATISTICS. *Educ:* Pepperdine Col, BA, 57; Fla State Univ, MS, 59; Va Polytech Inst & State Univ, PhD(statist), 67. *Prof Exp:* Instr math, Fla State Univ, 59-62; asst prof, Roanoke Col, 62-63; NIH fel, 64-67; asst prof statist, Univ Ga, 67-76, asst prof comput sci, 74-76; SR BIOSTATISTICIAN, COOP STUDIES PROG COORD CTR, VET ADMIN HOSP, MD, 77- *Mem:* Am Statist Asn; Inst Math Statist; Biomet Soc; Math Asn Am; Soc Clin Trials. *Res:* Bayesian inference; accident statistics; cooperative clinical trials. *Mailing Add:* Coop Studies Prod Coord Ctr Vet Admin Hosp Perry Point MD 21902

WILLIG, MICHAEL ROBERT, b Pittsburgh, Pa, June 7, 52. QUANTITATIVE BIOLOGY, POPULATION & EVOLUTIONARY BIOLOGY. *Educ:* Univ Pittsburgh, BS, 74, PhD(biol), 82. *Prof Exp:* Res fel ecol, Brazilian Nat Acad Sci, 76-78; vis prof terrestrial ecol, LaRoch Col, 79; ASST PROF ECOL & BIOMET, LOYOLA UNIV, 81- *Mem:* Ecol Soc Am; Am Soc Naturalists; Soc Study Evolution; Am Soc Mammalogists; AAAS. *Res:* Application of statistical techniques to answer questions of interest in population biology, ecology, behavior and evolution including population estimation, biogeography, conservation and mammalian systematics. *Mailing Add:* Dept Biol Sci Loyola Univ Box 28 New Orleans LA 70118

WILLIGER, ERVIN JOHN, b Szeged, Hungary, June 18, 27; US citizen; m 51; c 4. PLASTICS CHEMISTRY, RUBBER CHEMISTRY. *Educ:* Budapest Tech Univ, dipl chem eng, 50. *Prof Exp:* Res assoc polymers, Inst Plastics Res, Budapest Tech Univ, 50-56; res & develop chemist, Naugatuck Chem, US Rubber Co, 57-63; polymer chemist, Lucidol Div, Wallace & Tiernan, Inc, 63-65; sr res chemist, Res Ctr, Gen Tire & Rubber Co, 65-69; mgr tech serv & mkt, Union Process Co, Akron, 69-73; sr res chemist, res & develop ctr, B F Goodrich Co, 73-80; MGR SCI & TECHNOL, BEARFOOT CORP, WADSWORTH, OHIO, 80- *Mem:* Nat Soc Prof Eng; Am Chem Soc; Soc Plastics Eng. *Res:* Preparative polymer chemistry of thermoplastics and thermosets; structure behavior study of reinforced plastics; preparation and application of unsaturated polyesters and epoxy resins; study of peroxides and other free radical sources; toughening and fatigue of reinforced composites; technology of liquid elastomers; rubber compounding; adhesives and coatings. *Mailing Add:* 665 Fairwood Dr Tallmadge OH 44278

WILLIGES, GEORGE GOUDIE, b Sioux City, Iowa, May 18, 24; m 47; c 1. PLANT PATHOLOGY, PLANT TAXONOMY. *Educ:* Univ Corpus Christi, BA, 55; Tex A&I Univ, MA, 59; Tex A&M Univ, PhD(plant path), 69. *Prof Exp:* Teacher biol, Sinton Independent Sch Dist, 55-60; assoc prof, 61-77, chmn dept, 77-,80, PROF BIOL, TEX A&I UNIV, 77- CUR HERBARIUM, 71- *Concurrent Pos:* Mem bd dir, Tex Systs Natural Labs, 77. *Mem:* AAAS; Am Phytopath Soc. *Res:* Pathogenic variability, physiological and environmental effects on growth and reproduction of Sclerotium rolfsii; Fusarium diseases of cacti. *Mailing Add:* Dept of Biol Tex A&I Univ Kingsville TX 78363

WILLIGES, ROBERT CARL, b Richmond, Va, Mar 19, 42; m 65; c 1. HUMAN FACTORS ENGINEERING. *Educ:* Wittenberg Univ, AB, 64; Ohio State Univ, MA, 66, PhD(eng psychol), 68. *Prof Exp:* Asst human factors, Ohio State Univ, 64-68; from asst prof to assoc prof aviation & psychol, Univ Ill, 68-76; PROF INDUST ENG & PSYCHOL, VA POLYTECH INST & STATE UNIV, 76- *Concurrent Pos:* Asst dir human factors, Hwy Traffic Safety Ctr, Univ Ill, 68-70, assoc head human factors, Aviation Res Lab, 72-76; mem hwy res bd, Nat Acad Sci, 68-70; ed, Human Factors, 76-79. *Honors & Awards:* Jerome H Ely Award, Human Factors Soc, 74. *Mem:* Human Factors Soc (pres, 82-83); Am Psychol Asn; Inst Indust Engrs. *Res:* Research methodology; human performance research; computer-augmented training; human-computer interface; design of computer-generated displays. *Mailing Add:* Dept of Indust Eng & Oper Va Polytech Inst & State Univ Blacksburg VA 24061

WILLIMS, BILL GARY, b San Francisco, Calif, Nov 28, 44. RECOMBINANT DNA. *Educ:* Calif State Col, Heyward, BS, 68; Univ Wis-Madison, PhD(molecular biol), 77. *Prof Exp:* Fel, Dept Biochem, Roske Inst Molecular Biol, 77-78; scientist, Dept Recombinant Molecular Res, CETUS Corp, 78-82; SR SCIENTIST, DEPT MOLECULAR BIOL, ARCO PLANT CELL RES INST, 82- *Mem:* Am Soc Microbiol; NY Acad Sci. *Res:* Molecular genetical basis of plant response to environmental stress, the interactions between those responses and the mechanisms by which plants alter levels of metabolic flux. *Mailing Add:* 6560 Trinity Court Dublin CA 94566

WILLINGHAM, ALLAN KING, b Washington, DC, July 11, 41; m 67. BIOCHEMISTRY. *Educ:* George Washington Univ, BS, 63; St Louis Univ, PhD(biochem), 70. *Prof Exp:* Fel biochem, Res Inst Hosp Joint Dis, New York, 70-71; instr, 71-75, asst prof biochem, Col Med, Univ Nebr, Omaha, 75-76; asst prof, 76-78, ASSOC PROF BIOCHEM, KIRKSVILLE COL OSTEOP MED, 78- *Concurrent Pos:* USPHS res grant, Nat Heart, Lung & Blood Inst, 74-80; res grant, Am Osteop Asn, 81-82. *Mem:* AAAS; Sigma Xi. *Res:* Interconversion of phylloquinone and its 2, 3- epoxide and its relationship to the vitamin K-dependent carboxylation of glutamic acid residues to form active clotting proteins; post-translational synthesis and secretion of vitamin K-dependent clotting proteins. *Mailing Add:* Dept of Biochem Kirksville Col Osteop Med Kirksville MD 63501

WILLINGHAM, CHARLES ALLEN, b Longview, Tex, Apr 17, 34; m 55; c 2. MARINE ECOLOGY, MARINE BIOLOGY. *Educ:* NTex State Univ, BA, 58, MA, 59; Univ Miami, PhD(marine sci), 65. *Prof Exp:* Instr biol, ECent State Col, Okla, 59-60; res scientist microbiol petrol prod, Jersey Prod Res Co, Esso, 60; MARINE BIOLOGIST MARINE ECOL, WILLIAM F CLAPP LABS, BATTELLE MEM INST, 65- *Mem:* Am Soc Microbiol; AAAS; Ecol Soc Am; Am Fisheries Soc; Am Inst Biol Sci. *Res:* Fundamental and applied research on the microbiology of natural marine products, biofouling ecology, materials deterioration and estuarine ecology. *Mailing Add:* William F Clapp Labs Inc Battelle Mem Inst Drawer AH Duxbury MA 02332

WILLINGHAM, CHARLES B(AYNARD), JR, b Washington, DC, Jan 24, 39; m 60; c 3. MATERIALS SCIENCE, CERAMICS. *Educ:* Pa State Univ, BS, 60; Mass Inst Technol, ScD(ceramics), 66. *Prof Exp:* Asst prof mat sci, Rensselaer Polytech Inst, 66-68; PRIN RES SCIENTIST, RES DIV, RAYTHEON CO, 68- *Concurrent Pos:* Lectr, State Art Prog, Northeastern Univ, 73-82. *Mem:* Sigma Xi. *Res:* Advanced material fabrication techniques; thin film deposition, crystal growth, chemical vapor deposition; preparation and characterization of infrared optical materials. *Mailing Add:* Res Div Raytheon Co 131 Spring St Lexington MA 02173

WILLINGHAM, FRANCIS FRIES, JR, b Winston-Salem, NC, June 3, 42; m 70. TAXONOMIC BOTANY, ORNAMENTAL HORTICULTURE. *Educ:* Univ NC, Chapel Hill, AB, 65; Wake Forest Univ, MA, 67, PhD(biol), 73. *Prof Exp:* Instr biol, Pine Crest Prep Sch, 67-69 & Salem Col, 69-71; plant taxonomist, Dept Hort, Callaway Gardens, Ga, 73-74, dir greenhouse opers, 74-78; gen mgr, Res Farms, Houston Tex, 79-80; PRES, PHYTOTECH, INC, 81- *Concurrent Pos:* Instr philos sci, Gov's Sch NC, 69-72; Hort Res Inst grant, 77-78. *Mem:* Bot Soc Am; Am Fern Soc; Am Soc Plant Taxonomists; Am Soc Hort Sci; Sigma Xi. *Res:* Taxonomy of ornamental horticulture plant materials and tissue culture of ornamentals. *Mailing Add:* 7517 Alabonson Houston TX 77088

WILLIS, CARL BERTRAM, b Charlottetown, PEI, Nov 27, 37; m 62; c 2. PLANT PATHOLOGY. *Educ:* McGill Univ, BSc, 59; Univ Wis-Madison, PhD(plant path), 62. *Prof Exp:* RES SCIENTIST PLANT PATH, AGR CAN, 62- *Mem:* Can Phytopath Soc; Agr Inst Can; Soc Nematol. *Res:* Forage crops diseases; factors affecting root rots of forage legumes. *Mailing Add:* Agr Can Res Sta PO Box 1210 Charlottetown PE C1A 7M8 Can

WILLIS, CARL RAEBURN, JR, b Madison, Wis, Apr 5, 39; m 60; c 4. PHARMACY, PHARMACEUTICAL CHEMISTRY. *Educ:* Purdue Univ, BS, 61, MS, 64, PhD(indust pharm), 66. *Prof Exp:* Teaching asst bionucleonics & mfg pharm, Purdue Univ, 61-62, teaching assoc pharmaceut chem, 62-63; sr pharmaceut chemist, Warren-Teed Pharmaceut, Inc, Rohm and Haas Co, 66-69; supvr prod develop,Pharm Res & Develop Div, Ciba Pharmaceut Co, 69, mgr process & mat technol, 70-71; mgr prod develop, Pharmaceut Div, Ciba-Geigy Corp, 71-72; assoc dir, Drug Regulatory Affairs, Sterling Drug Inc, 72-76, dep dir, 76-78; dir, Drug Regulatory Affairs, Cooper Labs, Inc, 78-79; DIR, DRUG REGULATORY AFFAIRS, BERLEX LABS, INC, 79- *Mem:* AAAS; Am Pharmaceut Asn; Acad Pharmaceut Sci; Am Chem Soc; Sigma Xi. *Res:* Industrial pharmacy; pharmacokinetics; biopharmaceutics; pharmaceutical dosage form research and development; package materials research and development; drug regulatory affairs. *Mailing Add:* Berlex Labs Inc 110 E Hanover Ave Cedar Knolls NJ 07927

WILLIS, CHARLES RICHARD, b Westertown, NY, July 7, 28; m 54; c 2. PHYSICS. *Educ:* Syracuse Univ, BA, 51, PhD, 58. *Prof Exp:* From asst prof to assoc prof, 57-68, PROF PHYSICS, BOSTON UNIV, 68- *Mem:* Am Phys Soc. *Res:* Statistical mechanics; laser physics; classical many-body problems; quantum optics. *Mailing Add:* 30 Solon St Newton Highland MA 02161

WILLIS, CHRISTOPHER JOHN, b Sutton, Eng, June 6, 34; m 60; c 3. INORGANIC CHEMISTRY. *Educ:* Cambridge Univ, BA, 55, PhD(chem), 58, MA, 59. *Prof Exp:* Fel chem, Univ BC, 58-60, lectr, 60-61; lectr, 61-62, asst prof, 62-66, assoc prof, 66-82, PROF CHEM, UNIV WESTERN ONT, 82- *Concurrent Pos:* Nat Res Coun Can res grant. *Mem:* Chem Inst Can. *Res:* Synthesis and study of fluorinated alchols, alkoxides and related fluorinated ligands. *Mailing Add:* Dept of Chem Univ of Western Ont London ON N6A 5B7 Can

WILLIS, CLIFFORD LEON, b Chanute, Kans, Feb 20, 13; m 47; c 1. GEOLOGY. *Educ:* Univ Kans, BS, 39; Univ Wash, PhD(geol), 50. *Prof Exp:* Geophysicist, Carter Oil Co, 39-42, geologist, 46-47; instr geol, Univ Wash, 50-52, asst prof, 53-54; chief geologist, Harza Eng Co, Chicago, 54-68, vpres, 68-81; CONSULT GEOLOGIST, 81. *Concurrent Pos:* Consult geologist, US, Turkey, Greece & Iraq, 51- *Honors & Awards:* Haworth Distinguished Alumnus Award, Univ Kans, 63. *Mem:* Geol Soc Am: Am Asn Petrol Geol; Am Inst Mining, Metall & Petrol Eng; Brit Geol Asn; Int Soc Rock Mech. *Res:* Engineering geology; structural geology; geophysics. *Mailing Add:* 16 Briar Rd Golf IL 60029

WILLIS, CLIVE, b London, Eng, July 31, 39; Can citizen; m 62; c 2. PHYSICAL CHEMISTRY. *Educ:* Univ Liverpool, BSc Hons, 61, PhD(phys chem), 64. *Prof Exp:* Fel, Univ Calif, Los Angeles, 64-65; res assoc chem physics, Comn Atomic Energy, 65-66; res officer phys chem, Atomic Energy Can Ltd, 66-71; lectr chem, Univ West Indies, 71-73; RES OFFICER PHYS CHEM, NAT RES COUN CAN, 73- *Mem:* Chem Inst Can. *Res:* Laser chemistry; gas phase kinetics; photochemistry; radiation chemistry; discharge phenomena. *Mailing Add:* Div Chem Nat Res Coun Can Sussex Dr Ottawa ON K1A 0R6 Can

WILLIS, D(ONALD) ROGER, b Sutton Coldfield, Eng, Feb 12, 33; m 57; c 2. AERONAUTICAL SCIENCE. *Educ:* Oxford Univ, BA, 53, MA, 57; Princeton Univ, MSE, 57, PhD(aeronaut eng), 59. *Prof Exp:* Res assoc aeronaut sci, Royal Inst Technol, Sweden, 59-61 & Princeton Univ, 61-63; from asst prof to assoc prof, 63-70, PROF ENG SCI, UNIV CALIF, BERKELEY, 70- *Concurrent Pos:* Guggenheim fel, 66. *Mem:* Soc Indust & Appl Math. *Res:* Mathematical theory of rarefied gas dynamics; numerical fluid dynamics. *Mailing Add:* Dept of Mech Eng Univ of Calif Berkeley CA 94720

WILLIS, DAVID EDWIN, b Cleveland, Ohio, Mar 13, 26; m 48; c 4. GEOPHYSICS, GEOLOGY. *Educ:* Western Reserve Univ, BS, 50; Univ Mich, Ann Arbor, MS, 57, PhD, 68. *Prof Exp:* Computer seismic explor, Keystone Explor Co, 50-52, party chief, 52-54, asst supvr, 54-55; res assoc, Univ Mich, Ann Arbor, 55-60, assoc res geophysicist, 60-63, res geophysicist, 63-68, actg head geophys lab, 65-67, assoc prof geol & head geophys lab, 68-70; assoc prof geol, 70-73, chmn dept geol sci, 72-76, PROF GEOL, UNIV WIS-MILWAUKEE, 73- *Concurrent Pos:* Lectr, Univ Mich, Ann Arbor, 63-64; geophysicist, Union Oil Co, Int, 80-81. *Mem:* Soc Explor Geophys; Am Geophys Union; Seismol Soc Am; fel Geol Soc Am. *Res:* Seismic and acoustic wave propagation; earthquake seismology; ground vibration studies; geophysical exploration. *Mailing Add:* Dept of Geol Sci Univ of Wis Milwaukee WI 53201

WILLIS, DAVID LEE, b Pasadena, Calif, Mar 15, 27; m 50; c 3. BIOLOGY, RADIATION BIOLOGY. *Educ:* Biola Col, BTh, 49, BA, 51; Wheaton Col, Ill, BS, 52; Calif State Univ Long Beach, MA, 54; Ore State Univ, PhD(radiation biol), 63. *Prof Exp:* Teacher high sch, Calif, 52-57; instr biol, Fullerton Col, 57-61; from asst prof to assoc prof, 62-71, PROF BIOL, ORE STATE UNIV, 71-, CHMN DEPT, 69- *Concurrent Pos:* Consult, Comn Undergrad Educ Biol Sci, NSF, 66-70; vis investr, Oak Ridge Nat Lab, 68-69; consult, Portland Gen Elec Co, 70-72. *Mem:* Radiation Res Soc; Health Physics Soc; AAAS; fel Am Sci Affiliation (pres, 75). *Res:* Freshwater radioecology; radionuclide cycling in amphibians; radiation effects on reptiles and amphibians; general applications of radiotracer techniques to biology. *Mailing Add:* Dept Gen Sci Ore State Univ Corvallis OR 97331

WILLIS, DAWN BUTLER, microbiology, biochemistry, see previous edition

WILLIS, FRANK MARSDEN, b Philadelphia, Pa, Sept 5, 26; m 48; c 3. BIOMEDICAL ENGINEERING. *Educ:* Drexel Univ, BS, 51. *Prof Exp:* Asst develop engr, Res & Develop, Atlantic Refining Co, 51-55; area engr oil refining, Mobil Oil Co, 55-57; chief engr, Clark Cooper Co, Inc, 57-59; res engr explosives, Res & Develop, Eastern Lab, 59-62, supt eng & design, 62-65, sect head eng, 65-70, res supv, Polymer Res Develop Lab, 70-78, SR ENGR ASSOC BIOMED, RES & DEVELOP, ENG DEVELOP LAB, E I DU PONT DE NEMOURS & CO, INC, DEL, 78- *Concurrent Pos:* Consult, Lawrence Pump & Engine Co, 59-60; pub rel dir, Safety Div, Am Defense Preparedness Asn, 69-78. *Mem:* Am Soc Mech Engrs. *Res:* Clinical and theraputic biomedical process; equipment and device research; development and mechanical design. *Mailing Add:* E I Du Pont Co Eng Develop Lab 101 Beech St Wilmington DE 19898

WILLIS, FRENCH HOKE, physics, deceased

WILLIS, GROVER C, JR, b Kansas City, Mo, May 25, 21; m 41; c 3. PHYSICAL CHEMISTRY, ELECTROCHEMISTRY. *Educ:* Whittier Col, BA, 52; Univ Ore, MA, 55, PhD(chem), 57. *Prof Exp:* Petrol inspector, Gen Petrol Corp, Calif, 41-43; chemist, W C Hardesty Co, 46-51; assoc, Univ Ore, 53-55, res assoc, 55-57; from asst prof to assoc prof, 57-67, PROF PHYS & ANAL CHEM, CALIF STATE UNIV, CHICO, 67- *Mem:* Am Chem Soc. *Res:* Anodic oxide formation kinetics; mechanism; reaction rates, thermodynamics, adsorption phenomena and diffusion processes at dropping mercury electrodes; electrochemical instrumentation. *Mailing Add:* 612 Acacia Lane Chico CA 95926

WILLIS, GUYE HENRY, b Los Angeles, Calif, July 1, 37; m 60; c 2. SOIL CHEMISTRY. *Educ:* Okla State Univ, BS, 61; Auburn Univ, MS, 63, PhD(soil chem), 65. *Prof Exp:* RES SOIL SCIENTIST, SOIL & WATER POLLUTION RES DIV, AGR RES SERV, USDA, 65- *Mem:* Am Soc Agron; Soil Sci Soc Am; Am Chem Soc. *Res:* Fate of agricultural chemicals, including pesticides and fertilizers, in the environment; soil chemistry-plant nutrition relationships. *Mailing Add:* Soil & Water Pollution Res Div Univ Sta Baton Rouge LA 70893

WILLIS, HAROLD LESTER, b McPherson, Kans, Oct 20, 40. ENTOMOLOGY. *Educ:* Kans State Teachers Col, BA, 62; Univ Kans, PhD(entom), 66. *Prof Exp:* From asst prof to assoc prof, 66-77, PROF ZOOL, UNIV WIS-PLATTEVILLE, 77-, CHMN, DEPT BIOL, 78- *Mem:* AAAS. *Res:* Bionomics, taxonomy and zoogeography of Nearctic tiger beetles. *Mailing Add:* Dept of Biol Univ of Wis Platteville WI 53818

WILLIS, ISAAC, b Albany, Ga, July 13, 40; m 65; c 2. DERMATOLOGY. *Educ:* Morehouse Col, BS, 61; Howard Univ, MD, 65. *Prof Exp:* Assoc dermat, Sch Med, Univ Pa, 69-70; head internal med res team & dermatologist, Letterman Army Inst, US Army Med Corps, 70-72; res assoc & clin instr dermat, Sch Med, Univ Calif, 70-72; asst prof med dermat, Sch Med, Johns Hopkins Univ, 72-73; asst prof, Vet Admin Hosp, Atlanta, 73-75, assoc prof med dermat, Sch Med, Emory Univ & chief dermat, 75-81. *Concurrent Pos:* Asst attend physician, Philadelphia Gen Hosp, 69-70; Dermat Found res award, Univ Pa, 70; attend physician, Univ Calif Med Ctr, 70-72; attend physician, Johns Hopkins Hosp, Baltimore City Hosps & Good Samaritan Hosp, 72-73; consult & lectr dermat, Bur Med & Surg, US Dept Navy, 72-75; consult asst to Prof Dermat, Howard Univ Col Med, 72-; mem Formulary Task Force, Nat Prog Dermat, Am Fedn Clin Res. *Honors & Awards:* Dohme Chem Co Award, Dermat Sect, Nat Med Asn, 67. *Mem:* Am Med Asn; Nat Med Asn; Am Acad Dermat; Am Fedn Clin Res; Am Dermat Asn. *Res:* Phototherapy, photochemotherapy; acute and chronic effects of ultraviolet light, including carcinogenesis; effects of light on bacteria and fungi, and effects of heat and humidity on skin. *Mailing Add:* 1141 Regency Rd NW Atlanta GA 30327

WILLIS, JAMES BYRON, b Marietta, Ohio, Jan 24, 18; m 40; c 2. CERAMIC ENGINEERING. *Educ:* Ohio State Univ, BCerE, 39. *Prof Exp:* Ceramic res engr ceramic coatings, Pemco Corp, 40-45, serv mgr, 45-59, dir eng serv, 59-62, sales mgr, Pemco Div, Glidden Co, 62-65, dir develop labs, 65-68, DIR RES & DEVELOP, PEMCO PROD GROUP, SCM CORP, 68- *Mem:* Fel Am Ceramic Soc; Sigma Xi. *Res:* Ceramic coating materials and processes; ceramic colorants; casting floxes for heavy metals. *Mailing Add:* SCM Corp Pemco Prod Group 5601 Eastern Ave Baltimore MD 21224

WILLIS, JAMES STEWART, JR, b West Point, NY, Feb 9, 35; m 59; c 2. PHYSICS. *Educ:* US Mil Acad, BS, 58; Rensselaer Polytech Inst, MS, 64, PhD(physics), 66. *Prof Exp:* US Army, 58-, from instr to asst prof, 66-69, assoc prof, 70-80, PROF PHYSICS, US MIL ACAD, 80- *Mem:* AAAS; Am Asn Physics Teachers; Am Soc Eng Educ; Am Phys Soc. *Res:* Type II superconductivity; electron spin resonance studies on color centers and other defects in crystals. *Mailing Add:* Dept of Physics US Mil Acad West Point NY 10996

WILLIS, JEFFREY OWEN, b Long Branch, NJ, June 1, 48; m 69. HIGH PRESSURE PHYSICS, ELECTRONIC STRUCTURE OF METALS. *Educ:* Univ Ill, Urbana-Champaign, BS, 70, MS, 71, PhD(physics), 76. *Prof Exp:* Res assoc, Naval Res Lab, Nat Res Coun, 75-77; mem staff, Los Alamos Sci Lab, 78-79, MEM STAFF, GROUP CMB-5, LOS ALAMOS NAT LAB, 80- *Mem:* Am Phys Soc; Sigma Xi. *Res:* Magnetic and superconductive properties of differential and frequency metals under conditions of ultralow temperatures and high pressures as a probe of electronic structure. *Mailing Add:* Group CMB-5 MS G730 Los Alamos Nat Lab PO Box 1663 Los Alamos NM 87545

WILLIS, JOHN STEELE, b Long Beach, Calif, Jan 19, 35; m 58. PHYSIOLOGY, ZOOLOGY. *Educ:* Univ Calif, Berkeley, AB, 56; Harvard Univ, AM, 58, PhD(biol), 61. *Prof Exp:* Nat Heart Inst fel biochem, Oxford Univ, 61-62; from asst prof to assoc prof, 62-72, PROF PHYSIOL, UNIV ILL, URBANA, 72-, PROF NUTRIT SCI, 81- *Concurrent Pos:* Nat Inst Gen Med Sci res grants, 63-; mem physiol study sect, NIH, 69-73; consult, Basic Sci Rev Bd, Vet Admin, 75-78; assoc ed, Am J Physiol Cell, 76-81. *Mem:* Brit Soc Exp Biol; Soc Gen Physiol; Am Soc Zool; Am Physiol Soc. *Res:* Cold resistance of tissues of hibernating mammals; active cation transport; cell physiology of nutrition. *Mailing Add:* Dept of Physiol Univ of Ill Urbana IL 61801

WILLIS, JUDITH HORWITZ, b Detroit, Mich, Jan 2, 35; m 58. DEVELOPMENTAL BIOLOGY, INSECT PHYSIOLOGY. *Educ:* Cornell Univ, AB, 56; Radcliffe Col, AM, 57, PhD(biol), 61. *Prof Exp:* USPHS res fel, Harvard Univ, 60-61 & Oxford Univ, 61-62; from instr to assoc prof entom, 63-77, prof genetics & develop, 77, PROF ENTOM, UNIV ILL, URBANA, 77- *Concurrent Pos:* Mem, Aging Review Comt, NIH, 76-80. *Mem:* AAAS; Am Soc Cell Biol; Soc Develop Biol; Am Soc Zool; Tissue Culture Asn. *Res:* Endocrine action in insect metamorphosis. *Mailing Add:* Dept Genetics & Develop 515 Morrill Hall Univ of Ill Urbana IL 61801

WILLIS, LLOYD L, II, b Frederick, Okla, June 10, 43; m 67; c 2. BIOLOGY. *Educ:* Phillips Univ, BS, 65; Univ Va, Med, 67. *Prof Exp:* Teacher gen sci, Roanoke City Pub Sch Syst, 65-68; sci teacher, Pickens Co Pub Sch, 68-69; asst prof biol, Va Western Community Col, 69-70; res asst, Bot Dept, Univ NC, 70-73; asst prof, 74-77, ASSOC PROF BIOL, PIEDMONT VA COMMUNITY COL, 77- *Mem:* Am Inst Biol Sci; Ecol Soc Am; Nat Sci Teachers Asn; Soc Col Sci Teachers; Am Rhododendron Soc. *Res:* Science education biology; innovative teaching techniques; development of required out of class activities; development of independent study courses; development of support-services for part-time faculty in biology. *Mailing Add:* Piedmont Va Community Col Rt 6 Box 1-A Charlottesville VA 22901

WILLIS, PARK WEED, III, b Seattle, Wash, Nov 18, 25; m 48; c 6. CARDIOVASCULAR DISEASES, INTERNAL MEDICINE. *Educ:* Univ Pa, MD, 48. *Prof Exp:* Intern, Pa Hosp, 48-50; resident internal med, Univ Hosp & Med Sch, Univ Mich, Ann Arbor, 52-53, jr clin instr, Med Sch, 53-54, from instr to assoc prof, 54-65, asst prof postgrad med, 57-59, dir, Div Cardiol, 69-77, prof internal med, 65-79; PROF INTERNAL MED & DIR SECT CARDIOL, COL HUMAN MED, MICH STATE UNIV, 79- *Concurrent Pos:* Attend physician, Vet Admin Hosp, Ann Arbor, 54-59, consult, 59-79; consult health serv, Univ Mich, 56-79; fel Am Heart Asn Councils Clin Cardiol, Epidemiol & Atherosclerosis; consult cardiol, US Surg Gen; lectr & consult, Nat Naval Med Ctr, Bethesda, Md. *Honors & Awards:* Jacob Ehrenzeller Award, Pa Hosp, 82. *Mem:* Asn Univ Cardiologists (pres, 79-80); fel Am Col Cardiol; fel Am Col Physicians. *Res:* Clinical cardiology. *Mailing Add:* 1016 Martin Pl Ann Arbor MI 48104

WILLIS, PHYLLIDA MAVE, b Wallington, Eng, Mar ll, 18; nat US. PHYSICAL CHEMISTRY. *Educ:* Mt Holyoke Col, AB, 38; Smith Col, AM, 40; Columbia Univ, PhD(phys chem), 46. *Prof Exp:* Teacher sci, Knox Sch, NY, 40-42; asst chem, Columbia Univ, 42-44; from instr to asst prof, Wellesley Col, 46-54; assoc prof & head dept, Newcomb Col, Tulane Univ,

54-60; chmn, Dept Chem, Physics & Astron, 60-79, WHITAKER PROF CHEM, HOOD COL, 60- *Concurrent Pos:* Am Asn Univ Women fel, Oxford Univ, 51-52; NSF fac fel, Univ Minn, 58. *Mem:* AAAS; Am Chem Soc; Soc Appl Spectros; Am Asn Physics Teachers. *Res:* Molecular spectroscopy. *Mailing Add:* Dept of Chem Physics & Astron Hood Col Frederick MD 21701

WILLIS, ROLAND GEORGE, physical organic chemistry, see previous edition

WILLIS, RONALD PORTER, b Cowley, Wyo, Sept 20, 26; m 53; c 5. GEOLOGY. *Educ:* Univ Wyo, BS, 52, MA, 53; Univ Ill, PhD(geol), 58. *Prof Exp:* Geologist, Richfield Oil Corp, 53-55; asst, Univ Ill, 55-57; geologist, Richmond Explor Co, 58-61; chief geologist, Bahrain Petrol Co, 61-65; regional geologist, Amoseas, Tripoli, Libya, 65; geologist, Chevron Oil Co, Okla, 65-67; PROF GEOL, UNIV WIS-EAU CLAIRE, 67- *Concurrent Pos:* Fulbright lectr, Univ Benin, Nigeria, 76-77. *Mem:* Geol Soc Am; Am Asn Petrol Geol. *Res:* Stratigraphy; sedimentation; petroleum geology. *Mailing Add:* Dept of Geol Univ of Wis Eau Claire WI 54701

WILLIS, SUZANNE EILEEN, b New Brunswick, NJ, May 25, 51. ELEMENTARY PARTICLE PHYSICS. *Educ:* Mount Holyoke Col, BA, 72; Yale Univ, MPhil, 74, PhD(physics), 79. *Prof Exp:* RES ASSOC, FERMI NAT ACCELERATOR LAB, 79- *Mem:* Am Phys Soc; AAAS. *Res:* Elementary particle physics-photo production of charm and other high-mass final states; rare decay modes of the moon; neutrino oscillations and decay. *Mailing Add:* Dept Physics Fermi Nat Accelerator Lab PO Box 500 Batavia IL 60510

WILLIS, VICTOR MAX, b Weston, Mo, Aug 3, 27; m 52; c 2. ORGANIC CHEMISTRY. *Educ:* Univ Ill, BS, 50. *Prof Exp:* mgr develop sect, 49-80, DIR FORMULATION, CONSUMER DIV, SHERWIN WILLIAMS CO, 80- *Mem:* Am Chem Soc; AAAS; Fedn Socs Paint Technol. *Res:* Water dispersed coatings systems; pigment dispersion systems; surfactant systems; organic physical chemistry related to coatings pigments and polymers and properties. *Mailing Add:* 604 Forsythe Ave Calumet City IL 60409

WILLIS, WAYNE OWEN, b Paonia, Colo, Jan 21, 28; m 51; c 4. SOIL PHYSICS. *Educ:* Colo State Univ, BS, 52; Iowa State Univ, MS, 53, PhD(soil physics), 56. *Prof Exp:* Asst soils res, Iowa State Univ, 52-53; agent soils res, Iowa, 53-56, res soil scientist, Wash, 56-57 & Salinity Lab, Calif, 57-58, res soil scientist, Northern Great Plains Res Ctr, NDak, 58-68, supvry soil scientist and res leader, 68-76, supvry soil scientist & tech adv, 76-81, SUPVRY SOIL SCIENTIST & RES LEADER, SCI & EDUC ADMIN-AGR RES, USDA, 81- *Mem:* Fel Am Soc Agron; Am Geophys Union; Can Soc Soil Sci; Int Soil Sci Soc; fel Soil Conserv Soc Am. *Res:* Interrelationships of soil water, soil temperature, plant growth and frozen soils; water conservation; dryland agriculture; crop yield prediction. *Mailing Add:* Agr Res Serv USDA PO Box E Ft Collins CO 80522

WILLIS, WILLIAM DARRELL, JR, b Dallas, Tex, July 19, 34; m 60; c 1. NEUROPHYSIOLOGY, NEUROANATOMY. *Educ:* Tex A&M Univ, BS & BA, 56; Univ Tex, MD, 60; Australian Nat Univ, PhD(physiol), 63. *Prof Exp:* From asst prof to prof anat, Southwestern Med Sch, Univ Tex, Dallas, 63-70, chmn dept, 64-70; PROF ANAT & PHYSIOL & CHIEF COMP NEUROBIOL, MARINE BIOMED INST, UNIV TEX MED BR GALVESTON, 70-, DIR INST, 78- *Concurrent Pos:* NIH res fel, Australian Nat Univ, 60-62 & Univ Pisa, 62-63; Nat Inst Neurol Dis & Blindness res grant, 63-; mem neurol B study sect, NIH, 68-72, chmn, 70-72, mem neurol disorders prog, proj rev comt, 72-76; chief ed, J Neurophysiol, 78- *Mem:* AAAS; Am Asn Anat; Am Physiol Soc; Am Pain Soc (treas, 78-81, pres-elect, 81); Soc Neurosci. *Res:* Electrophysiology of the vertebrate spinal cord; somatic sensory pathways; pain mechanisms and descending control of pain transmission. *Mailing Add:* Off of Dir 200 University Blvd Galveston TX 77550

WILLIS, WILLIAM HILLMAN, b Trenton, Tenn, Oct 28, 08; m 34; c 2. SOILS, BACTERIOLOGY. *Educ:* Union Univ, Tenn, AB, 30; Iowa State Col, MS, 31, PhD(soil bact), 33. *Prof Exp:* Asst soil technologist, Soil Conserv Serv, USDA, 34-38, assoc soil scientist flood control surv, 38-42; from assoc agronomist to agronomist, 42-66, assoc prof, 42-48, prof agron, 48-79, head dept, 66-79, EMER PROF, LA STATE UNIV, BATON ROUGE, 79- *Concurrent Pos:* Chmn, Southern Regional Soil Res Comt, 73-75. *Mem:* Am Chem Soc; Soil Sci Soc Am; Am Soc Agron; Sigma Xi. *Res:* Soil microbiology; nitrogen fertilization and nutrition of rice; biological nitrogen fixation; microbial nitrate reduction. *Mailing Add:* Dept of Agron La State Univ Baton Rouge LA 70803

WILLIS, WILLIAM J, b Ft Smith, Ark, Sept 15, 32; m 58; c 3. PHYSICS. *Educ:* Yale Univ, BS, 54, PhD, 58. *Prof Exp:* Physicist, Brookhaven Nat Lab, 58-65; prof physics, Yale Univ, 65-73; PHYSICIST EUROP COUN NUCLEAR RES, GENEVA, SWITZ, 73- *Concurrent Pos:* Physicist, Europ Orgn Nuclear Res, 61-62. *Mem:* Am Phys Soc. *Res:* Elementary particle physics; weak interactions of strange particles, resonances and high energy collisions. *Mailing Add:* CERN EP-Div Geneva 1211 Switzerland

WILLIS, WILLIAM RUSSELL, b Moundsville, WVa, Feb 14, 26; m 46; c 4. PHYSICS. *Educ:* WVa Wesleyan Col, BS, 48; Okla State Univ, MS, 50, PhD(chem physics), 54. *Prof Exp:* Chemist, Oak Ridge Nat Lab, 52-55; assoc prof physics, W Liberty State Col, 55-56; prof, WVa Wesleyan Col, 56-65; asst prog dir, NSF, 65-66; sci fac fel, Univ Colo, 66-67; PROF PHYSICS & CHMN DEPT, NORTHERN ARIZ UNIV, 67- *Concurrent Pos:* Consult, Oak Ridge Nat Lab, 55-56, 58-65 & NSF, 67- *Mem:* AAAS; Am Asn Physics Teachers. *Res:* Diffusion in solids; molecular physics; ellipsometry. *Mailing Add:* PO Box 6010 Flagstaff AZ 86011

WILLIS, WILLIAM VAN, b Morganton, NC, Oct 15, 37. INORGANIC CHEMISTRY, ANALYTICAL CHEMISTRY. *Educ:* Ga Inst Technol, BS, 60; Univ Tenn, MS, 63, PhD(chem), 66. *Prof Exp:* Res assoc radiation & radiochem, Eng Exp Sta, Ga Inst Technol, 59-61; sci writer nuclear decontamination, Univ Tenn, 63-64; USAEC res fel, 66-67; ASSOC PROF CHEM, CALIF STATE UNIV, FULLERTON, 67- *Concurrent Pos:* Mem, State Regional Water Qual Control Bd. *Mem:* Am Chem Soc. *Res:* Neutron activation analysis; radiochemical tracer analysis; transition metal transport in biological systems. *Mailing Add:* Dept of Chem Calif State Univ Fullerton CA 92634

WILLIS, WILLIAM W, nuclear physics, solid state electronics, see previous edition

WILLIS-CARR, JUDITH IONE, immunobiology, human anatomy, see previous edition

WILLISTON, JOHN STODDARD, b Ft Madison, Iowa, July 23, 34; m 61. NEUROPHYSIOLOGY. *Educ:* Univ Wis-Madison, BS, 61; Calif State Univ, San Francisco, MA, 65; Univ Southern Calif, PhD(physiol, psychol), 68. *Prof Exp:* NIMH fel, Univ Calif, San Francisco, 68-70; asst prof, 70-75, ASSOC PROF PHYSIOL & BEHAV BIOL, SAN FRANCISCO STATE UNIV, 75- *Concurrent Pos:* Res physiologist, Univ Calif, San Francisco, 76-78. *Mem:* AAAS; Am Psychol Asn; Soc Neurosci; Am Soc Zool. *Res:* Neurological substrates of behavioral plasticity; neuroelectrical activity; neuroethology; psychotrophic drugs. *Mailing Add:* Dept of Biol San Francisco State Univ San Francisco CA 94132

WILLITS, CHARLES HAINES, b Camden, NJ, June 25, 23; m 45; c 2. ORGANIC CHEMISTRY. *Educ:* Wheaton Col, Ill, BS, 44; Ohio State Univ, MS, 48; Ore State Univ, PhD(org chem), 55. *Prof Exp:* Res engr, Battelle Mem Inst, 48-51; from asst prof to assoc prof, 55-70, actg chmn dept, 60-69, PROF CHEM, RUTGERS UNIV, CAMDEN, 70-, CHMN DEPT, 70- *Mem:* Am Chem Soc; Am Sci Affil. *Res:* Synthesis of purine derivatives; mechanism of Hofmann degradation of amides; Fries rearrangement of higher esters. *Mailing Add:* Dept Chem Col Arts & Sci Rutgers Univ 406 Penn St Camden NJ 08102

WILLKE, THOMAS ALOYS, b Rome City, Ind, Apr 22, 32; m 54; c 6. MATHEMATICAL STATISTICS. *Educ:* Xavier Univ, Ohio, AB, 54; Ohio State Univ, MS, 56, PhD(math), 60. *Prof Exp:* Res mathematician, Nat Bur Stand, 61-63; asst prof math, Univ Md, 63-66; assoc prof, 66-72, dir statist lab, 71-73, PROF MATH, OHIO STATE UNIV, 72-, VPROVOST, COL ARTS & SCI, 73- *Concurrent Pos:* Lectr, Univ Md, 61-63. *Mem:* Math Asn Am; Inst Math Statist; Am Statist Asn. *Res:* Design and analysis of experiments. *Mailing Add:* Col Arts & Sci Ohio State Univ Columbus OH 43210

WILLMAN, JOSEPH F(RANK), b Brownsville, Tex, Dec 3, 31; m 56; c 3. ELECTRICAL ENGINEERING, UNDERWATER ACOUSTICS. *Educ:* Univ Tex, BS, 57, MS, 58, PhD(elec eng), 62. *Prof Exp:* Aerophys engr, Gen Dynamics/Ft Worth, 58-61; res engr, Defense Res Lab, Univ Tex, 61-62; sr res engr, Southwest Res Inst, 62-69; spec res assoc, 69-80, ASST DIR, APPL RES LABS, UNIV TEX, AUSTIN, 80- *Mem:* Am Geophys Union; Inst Elec & Electronics Engrs; Acoust Soc Am. *Res:* Systems analysis; signal processing; underwater acoustics; sonar systems; radar systems; radio wave propagation; the ionosphere; electromagnetic compatibility. *Mailing Add:* Appl Res Labs Univ Tex PO Box 8029 Austin TX 78712

WILLMAN, VALLEE L, b Greenville, Ill, May 4, 25; m 52; c 9. SURGERY. *Educ:* Univ Ill, BS, 47; St Louis Univ, MD, 51; Am Bd Surg, dipl, 57; Bd Thoracic Surg, dipl, 61. *Prof Exp:* Sr instr, 57-58, from asst prof to assoc prof, 58-64, PROF SURG, SCH MED, ST LOUIS UNIV, 64-, CHMN DEPT, 69- *Concurrent Pos:* McBride fel cancer, Sch Med, St Louis Univ, 56-57; attend physician, Vet Admin Hosp, 57- & St Louis City Hosp, 60- *Mem:* Soc Univ Surg; Am Surg Asn; Am Physiol Soc; Int Cardiovasc Soc. *Res:* Cardiovascular surgery and extracorporeal circulation; author or coauthor of over 210 publications. *Mailing Add:* St Louis Univ Med Ctr 1325 S Grand Blvd St Louis MO 63104

WILLMAN, WARREN WALTON, b Chicago, Ill, May 24, 43. APPLIED MATHEMATICS. *Educ:* Univ Mich, BA, 65, BSE, 65; Harvard Univ, PhD(appl math), 69. *Prof Exp:* Mathematician, Shell Develop Co, Shell Oil Co, 69-70; OPERS RES ANALYST, US NAVAL RES LAB, 71- *Res:* Stochastic optimal control theory, estimation theory. *Mailing Add:* US Naval Res Lab Code 7931 Washington DC 20375

WILLMANN, ROBERT B, b Seguin, Tex, May 7, 31; m 62. PARTICLE PHYSICS. *Educ:* Tex A&M Univ, BS, 54; Univ Wis, PhD(physics), 60. *Prof Exp:* Res assoc physics, Univ Wis, 60-61; from asst prof to assoc prof, 61-71, PROF PHYSICS, PURDUE UNIV, LAFAYETTE, 71- *Mem:* Am Phys Soc. *Res:* Weak and strong interactions in particle physics. *Mailing Add:* Dept of Physics Purdue Univ West Lafayette IN 47907

WILLMARTH, WILLIAM W(ALTER), b Highland Park, Ill, Mar 25, 24; m 59; c 4. FLUID MECHANICS. *Educ:* Purdue Univ, BS, 49; Calif Inst Technol, MS, 50, PhD(aeronaut eng), 54. *Prof Exp:* From res fel to sr res fel aeronaut eng, Calif Inst Technol, 54-58; assoc prof, 58-61, PROF AERONAUT ENG, UNIV MICH, ANN ARBOR, 61- *Concurrent Pos:* Consult, Rand Corp, 54-66, Gen Motors Res Lab, 70-74, Bendix Aerospace Systs Div, 73-76 & Bendix Res Labs, 75-77; vis fel, Joint Inst Lab Astrophys, Boulder, 63-64. *Mem:* Am Inst Aeronaut & Astronaut; Am Phys Soc. *Res:* Condensation of gases; transonic flow; turbulent boundary layer; unsteady aerodynamics; aerodynamic sound; scientific instruments for fluid mechanical measurements. *Mailing Add:* Dept of Aerospace Eng Univ of Mich Ann Arbor MI 48109

WILLMERT, KENNETH DALE, b Kossuth Co, Iowa, Oct 25, 42; m 68. MECHANICAL ENGINEERING. *Educ:* Iowa State Univ, BS, 64; Case Inst Technol, MS, 66; Case Western Reserve Univ, PhD(mech eng), 70. *Prof Exp:* Asst prof, 70-76, ASSOC PROF MECH ENG, CLARKSON COL TECHNOL, 76- *Mem:* Am Soc Mech Engrs. *Res:* Mechanical design; optimization applied to mechanical and structural systems; kinematic analysis and synthesis; finite element techniques applied to vibration problems. *Mailing Add:* Dept of Mech Eng Clarkson Col Technol Potsdam NY 13676

WILLMES, HENRY, b Bocholt, Ger, Aug 30, 39; US citizen; m 66; c 3. NUCLEAR PHYSICS. *Educ:* Univ Calif, Los Angeles, BS, 61, MA, 62, PhD(physics), 66. *Prof Exp:* Res physicist, Aerospace Res Labs, Wright-Patterson AFB, 65-68; asst prof, 69-73, assoc prof, 73-80, PROF PHYSICS, UNIV IDAHO, 80-, CHMN DEPT, 75- *Mem:* Am Phys Soc. *Res:* Few nucleon systems; nuclear structure; applications of nuclear technology. *Mailing Add:* Dept of Physics Univ of Idaho Moscow ID 83843

WILLMS, CHARLES RONALD, b Rupert, Idaho, June 26, 33; m 55; c 4. BIOCHEMISTRY. *Educ:* Univ Tex, BA, 55; Southwest Tex State Col, MA, 56; Tex A&M Univ, PhD(biochem), 59. *Prof Exp:* Asst prof chem, Southwest Tex State Col, 59-62; res scientist assoc, Clayton Found Biochem Inst, Univ Tex, 62-64; assoc prof, 64-68, chmn dept, 68-75, PROF CHEM, SOUTHWEST TEX STATE UNIV, 68- *Mem:* AAAS; Am Chem Soc; NY Acad Sci; Sigma Xi. *Res:* Enzyme and protein chemistry; carbohydrate metabolism; characterization and isolation of proteolytic enzymes. *Mailing Add:* Dept of Chem Southwest Tex State Univ San Marcos TX 78666

WILLNER, DAVID, b Vienna, Austria, July 2, 30; m 54; c 2. ORGANIC CHEMISTRY. *Educ:* Hebrew Univ, Israel, MSc, 56, PhD(org chem), 59. *Prof Exp:* From res asst to res assoc org chem, Weizmann Inst, 59-64; scientist, New Eng Inst Med Res, Conn, 64-66; SR RES SCIENTIST, BRISTOL LABS, 66- *Concurrent Pos:* Asst org chem, Bar-Ilan Univ, Israel, 57-59, lectr org chem & reaction mechanism, 62-63; fel, Dept Chem, Univ Southern Calif, 59-61 & Calif Inst Technol, 61-62. *Mem:* Am Chem Soc. *Res:* Medicinal chemistry; structure elucidation and synthesis of natural products and physiological active compounds, antibiotics and lipids; reaction mechanisms; photochemistry. *Mailing Add:* Bristol Labs Syracuse NY 13201

WILLOUGHBY, DONALD S, b Napanee, Ont, Sept 20, 24; m 49; c 3. MEDICAL BACTERIOLOGY, IMMUNOLOGY. *Educ:* Queen's Univ, Ont, BA, 47, Hons, 48, MA, 49; Univ Minn, Minneapolis, PhD(bact), 60. *Prof Exp:* Asst bact, Fisheries Res Bd Can, 49-51; control chemist, Anglo-Can Drug Co, Ont, 52-54; scientist, Defence Res Bd Can, 54-56; supvr, Prov Pub Health Lab, Sask, 59-61; res scientist, Defence Res Bd Can, 61-71; SUPVR REGIONAL PUB HEALTH LABS, PROV ONT, 71-; DIR LAB SERV BR, ONT MINISTRY HEALTH, 74-; DIR LAB & SPECIMEN COLLECTION CTR LICENSING, TORONTO, 80- *Mem:* Am Soc Microbiol; Can Soc Microbiol; Can Pub Health Asn. *Res:* Medical microbiology. *Mailing Add:* Labs Br Ministry of Health Box 9000 Terminal A Toronto ON M2K 2R6 Can

WILLOUGHBY, RALPH ARTHUR, b Santa Rosa, Calif, Aug 15, 23; m 47; c 2. MATHEMATICS. *Educ:* Univ Calif, AB, 47, PhD(math), 51. *Prof Exp:* From asst prof to assoc prof math, Ga Inst Technol, 51-55; mem staff, Atomic Energy Div, Babcock & Wilcox Co, 55-57; MEM STAFF, MATH SCI DEPT, THOMAS J WATSON RES CTR, IBM CORP, 57- *Concurrent Pos:* Res partic, Math Panel, Oak Ridge Nat Lab, 54, consult, 54-55. *Mem:* Soc Indust & Appl Math. *Res:* Numerical analysis. *Mailing Add:* 14 Garey Dr Chappaqua NY 10514

WILLOUGHBY, RUSSELL A, b Tilston, Man, July 7, 33; m 54; c 3. VETERINARY MEDICINE. *Educ:* Univ Toronto, DVM, 57; Cornell Univ, PhD(vet path), 65. *Prof Exp:* Pvt pract vet med, Grenfell, Sask, 57-61; asst prof clin vet med, Ont Vet Col, Toronto, 61-62; res asst vet path, Cornell Univ, 62-65; assoc prof, 65-67, PROF CLIN VET MED, ONT VET COL, UNIV GUELPH, 67-, ASSOC DEAN RES, 79- *Mem:* Am Vet Med Asn; Am Asn Vet Clinicians; Can Vet Med Asn; Am Col Vet Internal Med (secy, 72-). *Res:* Environmental effects on animals, including heavy metal toxicity, the effects of intensification and the interaction between pollutants and infectious agents. *Mailing Add:* Dept of Clin Studies Ont Vet Col Univ of Guelph Guelph ON N1G 2W1 Can

WILLOUGHBY, SARAH MARGARET C(LAYPOOL), b Bowling Green, Ky, Oct 15, 17; div; c 3. CHEMICAL ENGINEERING, ORGANIC CHEMISTRY. *Educ:* Univ Western Ky, BS, 38; Purdue Univ, PhD(chem eng), 50. *Prof Exp:* Chemist, Devoe-Raynolds Co, Inc, 40-42; jr engr, Curtiss-Wright Corp, 42-44; res chemist, Monsanto Chem Co, 50-52; asst prof, 54-55, ASSOC PROF CHEM, UNIV TEX, ARLINGTON, 55-, ASSOC DIR, CTR MICROCRYSTAL POLYMER SCI, 75- *Mem:* Sigma Xi; fel Am Inst Chem; Am Chem Soc; Soc Women Engrs. *Res:* Protective coatings; organic polymer chemistry; education in chemical engineering; professional registration standards. *Mailing Add:* Dept of Chem Univ of Tex Arlington TX 76019

WILLOUGHBY, STEPHEN SCHUYLER, b Madison, Wis, Sept 27, 32; m 54; c 2. MATHEMATICS EDUCATION. *Educ:* Harvard Univ, AB, 53, AMT, 55; Columbia Univ, EdD(math educ), 61. *Prof Exp:* Teacher math & sci, Newton Pub Schs, Mass, 54-57; teacher math, Greenwich Pub Schs, Conn, 5759; instr educ & math, Univ Wis-Madison, 60-61, asst prof, 61-65; PROF EDUC & MATH, NY UNIV, 65-, CHMN DEPT MATH EDUC, 67- *Concurrent Pos:* Consult, NSF, 73-77. *Mem:* Math Asn Am; Nat Coun Teachers Math (pres, 82-84). *Res:* Learning and teaching mathematics. *Mailing Add:* 932 Shimkin Hall NY Univ New York NY 10003

WILLOWS, ARTHUR OWEN DENNIS, b Winnipeg, Man, Mar 26, 41; m 63; c 3. NEUROPHYSIOLOGY. *Educ:* Yale Univ, BS, 63; Univ Ore, PhD(biol), 67. *Prof Exp:* Asst prof, Univ Ore, 67-68, res assoc neurophysiol, 68-69; from asst prof to assoc prof, Univ Wash, 69-75, prof zool, 75-80, dir, Friday Harbor Labs, 73-80; MEM STAFF NEUROBIOL PROG, NSF, 80- *Mem:* Soc Gen Physiol; Soc Neurosci; Am Physiol Soc. *Res:* Neuroethology; neurophysiological basis of behavior. *Mailing Add:* Neurobiol Prog Nat Sci Found Washington DC 20550

WILLS, CHRISTOPHER J, b London, Eng, Mar 23, 38; m 65; c 1. GENETICS, BIOLOGY. *Educ:* Univ BC, BA, 60, MSc, 62; Univ Calif, Berkeley, PhD(genetics), 65. *Prof Exp:* NIH fel genetics, Univ Calif, Berkeley, 65-66; asst prof biol, Wesleyan Univ, 66-72; assoc prof, 72-78, PROF BIOL, UNIV CALIF, SAN DIEGO, 78- *Concurrent Pos:* NIH res grant, 67; Guggenheim fel, 77-78; var grants, NSF, NIH & Dept Energy. *Mem:* AAAS; Genetics Soc Am; Am Soc Naturalists. *Res:* Maintenance of genetic variability in natural populations; production, through selection in the laboratory, and characterization of isoenzymes in yeast; regulation of yeast isoenymes; biochemistry. *Mailing Add:* Dept of Biol Univ of Calif at San Diego La Jolla CA 92037

WILLS, DONALD L, b Peoria, Ill, May 12, 24; m 46; c 2. GEOLOGY. *Educ:* Univ Ill, BS, 49, MS, 51; Univ Iowa, PhD(geol), 71. *Prof Exp:* Assoc dir, Ill Dept Conserv, 77-79; DIR FINANCE & BUS, MONMOUTH COL, 79- *Concurrent Pos:* Environ consult, 71- *Mem:* Am Inst Prof Geol; Sigma Xi; Nat Asn Geol Teachers; Geol Soc Am. *Res:* Biostratigraphic studies of Mississippian Chesterian series. *Mailing Add:* Dept of Geol Monmouth Col Monmouth IL 61462

WILLS, GENE DAVID, b Birmingham, Ala, Apr 11, 34; m 66; c 2. PLANT PHYSIOLOGY, BIOCHEMISTRY. *Educ:* Auburn Univ, BS, 57, MS, 62; Okla State Univ, PhD(bot), 67. *Prof Exp:* Asst bot, Auburn Univ, 59-62 & Okla State Univ, 63-66; PLANT PHYSIOLOGIST WEED CONTROL, DELTA BR EXP STA, 67- *Mem:* Weed Sci Soc Am; Sigma Xi. *Res:* Chemical weed control including studies on ecology and anatomy of weeds and effects of environment on translocation and toxicity of radiolabeled and non-radiolabeled herbicides in weeds. *Mailing Add:* Delta Br Exp Sta PO Box 197 Stoneville MS 38776

WILLS, GEORGE B(AILEY), b Canton, Mo, Nov 24, 28; m 54; c 3. CHEMICAL ENGINEERING. *Educ:* Mass Inst Technol, BS, 54; Univ Wis, MS, 55, PhD(chem eng), 62. *Prof Exp:* Engr, Mallinckrodt Chem Works, 55-57 & Bjorksten Res Labs, 57-61; asst res engr, Phillips Petrol Co, 61-64; PROF CHEM ENG, VA POLYTECH INST & STATE UNIV, 64- *Concurrent Pos:* Consult, A O Smith Corp, 60 & Electrotech Corp, 66- *Mem:* AAAS; Am Inst Chem Engrs; Am Chem Soc. *Res:* Mass transfer; electrochemistry; catalysis. *Mailing Add:* Dept of Chem Eng Va Polytech Inst & State Univ Blacksburg VA 24061

WILLS, JAMES E, JR, b Tucumcari, NMex, Mar 20, 16. PHYSICS. *Educ:* Miss Col, BA, 36; Univ Va, MA, 38; Univ Tex, PhD(physics), 56. *Prof Exp:* Instr physics, Ga Sch Technol, 38-39; asst prof, Baylor Univ, 46-51; from assoc prof to prof, Stetson Univ, 56-64; chmn dept, 65-72, prof, 64-80, EMER PROF PHYSICS, UNIV NC, ASHEVILLE, 80- *Mem:* Am Phys Soc. *Res:* Fast neutron spectroscopy. *Mailing Add:* Dept of Physics Univ of NC Ashevelle NC 28803

WILLS, JOHN G, b Greeley, Colo, Feb 4, 31; m 54; c 5. THEORETICAL PHYSICS, NUCLEAR PHYSICS. *Educ:* San Diego State Col, AB, 53; Univ Wash, MS, 56, PhD(physics), 63. *Prof Exp:* Staff mem, Los Alamos Sci Lab, 56-60; res asst, 63-64, from asst prof to assoc prof, 64-76, PROF PHYSICS, IND UNIV, BLOOMINGTON, 76- *Res:* Nuclear theory. *Mailing Add:* Dept of Physics Ind Univ Bloomington IN 47405

WILLS, NANCY KAY, b Wytheville, Va, Aug 27, 49. PHYSIOLOGY, NEUROSCIENCE. *Educ:* Ohio State Univ, BS, 71; Univ Va, MA, 73, PhD(physiol psychol), 77. *Prof Exp:* Res asst neurophysiol, Dept Physiol & Brain Res Inst, Univ Calif, Los Angeles, 74-76; fel physiol, Med Br, Univ Tex, 76-77; fel physiol, Med Sch, 77-80, RES ASSOC FAC PHYSIOL, YALE UNIV, 80- *Concurrent Pos:* NIH fel, 78-80. *Mem:* Biophys Soc; Soc Gen Physiologists; NY Acad Sci. *Res:* Electrophysiology of ion transport across epithelia. *Mailing Add:* Dept of Physiol 333 Cedar St New Haven CT 06510

WILLS, ROGER R, b England. CERAMICS ENGINEERING. *Educ:* Manchester Univ, BSc, 65, PhD(metall), 68. *Prof Exp:* SECT MGR, CERAMICS & MAT PROCESSING SECT, BATTELLE MEM LAB, 68- *Mem:* Am Ceramic Soc; Nat Inst Ceramic Engrs. *Res:* Development of new ceramics; fracture mechanics; development of advanced processing techniques. *Mailing Add:* 505 King Ave Columbus OH 43201

WILLS, WIRT HENRY, b Petersburg, Va, Feb 12, 24; m 54; c 4. DISEASES OF ORNAMENTALS. *Educ:* Univ Richmond, BA, 50; Duke Univ, MA, 52, PhD(bot), 54. *Prof Exp:* From asst prof to assoc prof, 54-68, PROF PLANT PATH, VA POLYTECH INST & STATE UNIV, 69- *Mem:* Am Phytopath Soc. *Res:* Ecology of root diseases; biological control of fungal pathogens in soil-less media. *Mailing Add:* Dept of Plant Path & Physiol Va Polytech Inst & State Univ Blacksburg VA 24061

WILLSON, ALAN NEIL, JR, b Baltimore, Md, Oct 16, 39; m 62; c 3. ELECTRICAL ENGINEERING, APPLIED MATHEMATICS. *Educ:* Ga Inst Technol, BEE, 61; Syracuse Univ, MSEE, 65, PhD(elec eng), 67. *Prof Exp:* Instr, Syracuse Univ, 65-67; assoc engr, IBM Corp, 61-64; mem tech staff, Math & Statist Res Ctr, Bell Labs, 67-72; PROF ENG & APPL SCI, UNIV CALIF, LOS ANGELES, 72-, ASST DEAN GRAD STUDIES, SCH ENG & APPL STUDIES, 77- *Concurrent Pos:* Ed, Inst Elec & Electronics Engrs Transactions on Circuits & Systs, 77-79. *Mem:* Inst Elec & Electronics Engrs; Soc Indust & Appl Math; Am Soc Eng Educ. *Res:* Theory of nonlinear transistor networks; stability and instability theory for nonlinear distributed networks; studies of nonlinear effects in digital filters. *Mailing Add:* Sch of Eng & Appl Sci Univ of Calif 6730 Boelter Hall Los Angeles CA 90024

WILLSON, CARLTON GRANT, b Vallejo, Calif, Mar 30, 39; m 75. RADIATION CHEMISTRY, POLYMER SYNTHESIS. *Educ:* Univ Calif, Berkeley, BS, 62, PhD(chem), 73; San Diego State Univ, MS, 69. *Prof Exp:* Chemist, Aerojet Gen Corp, Sacramento, 62-64; instr chem & math, Fairfax High Sch, Los Angeles, 65-66; asst prof chem, Long Beach State Univ, 74-75, Univ Calif, San Diego, 76-78; MGR, RES LAB, IBM CORP, 78- *Mem:* Am

Chem Soc; Sigma Xi; Am Inst Mech Eng. *Res:* Synthetic and mechanistic studies associated with radiation sensitive organic materials, monomers and polymers and their application to resist materials. *Mailing Add:* IBM Res Lab K42/282 5600 Cottle Rd San Jose CA 95193

WILLSON, CLYDE D, b Omaha, Nebr, May 7, 35; m 54; c 4. ORGANIC CHEMISTRY, MOLECULAR BIOLOGY. *Educ:* Univ Calif, Berkeley, BA, 56, PhD(chem), 60. *Prof Exp:* NIH fel bact genetics & protein synthesis, Pasteur Inst, Paris, 60-62; asst prof biochem, Univ Calif, Berkeley, 62-68, res fel entom, Miller Inst, 68-69; INSTR LIFE SCI, LANEY COL, 69- *Concurrent Pos:* Vis prof biol, Brandeis Univ, 74-75. *Res:* Heterocyclic organic chemistry; bacterial enzyme regulation and genetic control; characterization of messenger RNA; biochemistry of communication substances in insects. *Mailing Add:* Dept of Life Sci Laney Col 900 Fallon St Oakland CA 94607

WILLSON, DAN LEROY, b Parson, Kans, Aug 25, 23. BIOLOGY. *Educ:* Kans State Teachers Col, BS, 48, MS, 49; Univ Okla, PhD(bot), 58. *Prof Exp:* Instr biol, Okla Mil Acad, 48-55; assoc prof, Cent State Univ, 58-61 & Cent Wash State Univ, 61-68; dean natural & appl sci & dean grad studies, 78, PROF BIOL & DEAN ARTS & SCI, WINONA STATE UNIV, 68- *Mem:* AAAS; Ecol Soc Am; Am Physcol Soc Am. *Res:* Cytology, morphology and taxonomy of algae, especially ecology of soil algae. *Mailing Add:* Winona State Univ Winona MN 55987

WILLSON, DONALD BRUCE, b Bloomington, Ind, Oct 25, 41; m 65; c 4. PHYSICAL INORGANIC CHEMISTRY, EXTRACTIVE METALLURGY. *Educ:* Geneva Col, BA, 63; Tufts Univ, PhD(chem), 69. *Prof Exp:* Lab instr chem & res asst, Tufts Univ, 64-69; res assoc Air Force Off Sci Res, Geneva Col, 69; chemist, Kawecki-Berylco Industs, Inc, Pa, 70-73, proj leader-group leader, 74; tech mgr, M&R Refractory Metals Inc, Winslow, 75-76, tech dir, 76-81; STAFF RES ENG, ANACONDA MINERALS CO, 81- *Mem:* Am Inst Mining, Metall & Petrol Engrs; Am Chem Soc. *Res:* Extractive metallurgy and physical, inorganic and analytical chemistry of the refractory, transition, rare earth and noble metals and their compounds. *Mailing Add:* 3732 N Tres Lomas Pl Tucson AZ 85715

WILLSON, JOHN ELLIS, b Scranton, Pa, May 4, 29; m 55; c 3. VETERINARY MEDICINE, TOXICOLOGY. *Educ:* Pa State Univ, BS, 50; NY State Vet Col, DVM, 54; Am Bd Toxicol, dipl, 81. *Prof Exp:* Intern, Angell Mem Animal Hosp, Boston, Mass, 57-58, mem staff, 58-61; head dept pharmacol, John L Smith Mem Cancer Res, Chas Pfizer & Co, Inc, NJ, 61-63; sr pathologist, 63-66, ASST DIR, JOHNSON & JOHNSON RES FOUND, NEW BRUNSWICK, 66- *Concurrent Pos:* Mem coun accreditation, Am Asn Accreditation of Lab Animal Care, 72-76; mem adv coun, Inst Lab Animal Resources, Div Biol Sci, Assembly of Life Sci, Nat Res Coun-Nat Acad Sci, 74-77. *Honors & Awards:* Philip B Hoffman Res Scientist Award, Johnson & Johnson, 72. *Mem:* Am Vet Med Asn; Soc Toxicol; Am Asn Indust Vet; Am Asn Lab Animal Sci. *Res:* Toxicology of foods, drugs and cosmetics; ethylene oxide sterilant residues; laboratory animal husbandry and medicine. *Mailing Add:* 42 Addison Dr Basking Ridge NJ 07920

WILLSON, JOHN TUCKER, b Bismarck, NDak, Aug 26, 24; m 47; c 3. ANATOMY. *Educ:* George Washington Univ, BS, 48, MS, 49; Univ Colo, PhD(anat), 53. *Prof Exp:* Asst, 51-53, from instr to assoc prof, 53-75, PROF ANAT, SCH MED, UNIV COLO, DENVER, 75- *Mem:* AAAS; Am Asn Anat; Am Soc Cell Biol; Microcirc Soc. *Res:* Microcirculation, intravascular erythrocyte agglutination, reproduction, fertility and sterility and fine structure. *Mailing Add:* Dept of Anat Univ of Colo Med Ctr Denver CO 80220

WILLSON, KARL STUART, b Cleveland, Ohio, June 11, 10; m 33; c 3. ELECTROCHEMISTRY, CORROSION. *Educ:* Western Reserve Univ, BA, 31, MA, 32, PhD(chem), 35. *Prof Exp:* Asst quant anal, Western Reserve Univ, 31-35; res chemist, Ansul Chem Co, 35-44; res chemist, Manhattan Proj, Harshaw Chem Co, 44-46, res chemist & supvr electroplating res, 46-52; mgr res & develop div, Gen Dry Batteries, Inc, 52-59; group leader phys chem, Lubrizol Corp, 59-62; assoc dir electroplating res & develop, Harshaw Chem Co, 62-69, sr res assoc, 70-75; CHEM CONSULT, 75- *Mem:* Am Chem Soc; Electrochem Soc; Am Electroplaters Soc; Am Inst Chem. *Res:* Dry battery technology; refrigerant and other gases; uranium compounds; electroplating and corrosion; fire extinguisher chemistry; chemistry of gases; lubricating materials; phosphate coatings. *Mailing Add:* c/o Dept of Chem Case Western Reserve Univ Cleveland OH 44106

WILLSON, LEE ANNE MORDY, b Honolulu, Hawaii, Mar 14, 47; m 69; c 2. ASTRONOMY. *Educ:* Harvard Univ, AB, 68; Univ Mich, MS, 70, PhD(astron), 73. *Prof Exp:* Instr, 73-75, asst prof, 75-79, PROF ASTROPHYS, DEPT PHYSICS, IOWA STATE UNIV, 79- *Concurrent Pos:* Annie J Cannon Award, Am Astron Soc, 80-81. *Mem:* Int Astron Union; Am Astron Soc. *Res:* Problems of stellar atmospheres, particularly theories of mass loss, extended atmospheres, and variable stars. *Mailing Add:* Dept Physics Iowa State Univ Ames IA 50011

WILLSON, MARY FRANCES, b Madison, Wis, July 28, 38; m 72. ECOLOGY, EVOLUTION. *Educ:* Grinnell Col, BA, 60; Univ Wash, PhD(zool), 64. *Prof Exp:* Asst prof to assoc prof zool, Univ Ill, Urbana-Champaign, 65-77, PROF ECOL, ETHOLOGY & EVOLUTION, UNIV ILL, URBANA, 77- *Concurrent Pos:* Res grants, Chapman Fund, Am Mus Natural Hist, 64 & 79 & Univ Ill Res Bd, 66-70, 77 & 81; vis prof, Univ Minn, 78 & 80. *Mem:* Ecol Soc Am; Am Ornith Union; Brit Ecol Soc; Cooper Ornith Soc; Am Soc Naturalists. *Res:* Evolutionary ecology. *Mailing Add:* Dept Ecol Ethology Univ Ill Urbana IL 61801

WILLSON, PHILIP JAMES, b Detroit, Mich, Apr 23, 26; m 48, 76; c 3. HIGH TEMPERATURE CHEMISTRY, CERAMICS. *Educ:* Wayne State Univ, BA, 51. *Prof Exp:* Technician electronics, US Navy, 45-46 & Gen Motors Corp, 48-50; chemist, 51-55, RES SUPVR CHEM, CHRYSLER RES, 56- *Mem:* Am Ceramic Soc; Soc Automotive Engrs. *Res:* High temperature structural ceramic materials for turbine engine applications; automotive catalysts for emission control; friction studies. *Mailing Add:* Chrysler Corp Res C I M S 418-19-18 PO Box 1118 Detroit MI 48231

WILLSON, RICHARD ATWOOD, b Minneapolis, Minn. GASTROENTEROLOGY. *Educ:* Univ Minn, BA, 58, BS, 59, MD, 62, MS, 69, Am Bd Internal Med, cert, 70. *Prof Exp:* Intern, Mary Fletcher Hosp, 62-63; resident internal med, Univ Vt, 63-64; resident, Mayo Clin, 66-68, NIH res fel gastroenterol, 68-71; res fel, Liver Unit, Dept Med, King's Col Hosp Med Sch, London, 72-73; asst prof, 73-77, ASSOC PROF MED, UNIV WASH, 77-; HEAD DIV GASTROENTEROL, HARBORVIEW MED CTR, SEATTLE, 73- *Mem:* Am Gastroenterol Asn; Am Asn Study Liver Dis; Am Fedn Clin Res. *Res:* Treatment of acute fulminant hepatic failure and the study of hepatic injury secondary to drugs and drug metabolism. *Mailing Add:* Dept of Med Univ of Wash Seattle WA 98195

WILLSON, WARRACK GRANT, b San Francisco, Calif, July 15, 43; m 63; c 2. FUEL ENGINEERING, PHYSICAL CHEMISTRY. *Educ:* Univ Northern Colo, BA, 65; Univ Wyo, PhD(chem, physics), 71. *Prof Exp:* Asst prof phys chem, Upper Iowa Col, 70-71; res scientist coal gasification, Univ Wyo, 71-73; res phys chemist reactor eng, E I du Pont de Nemours & Co, Inc, 73-76; sr res chemist coal liquefaction, Occidental Res Corp, Calif, 76-78; proj mgr liquefaction, 78-79, MGR GASIFICATION & LIQUEFACTION, DEPT ENERGY, GRAND FORKS ENERGY TECHNOL CTR, NDAK, 79- *Concurrent Pos:* Adj prof chem eng, Univ NDak, 80- *Mem:* Am Chem Soc; Sigma Xi. *Res:* Conversion of abundant domestic fossil resources and carbonaceous wastes into economically and environmentally acceptable alternate energy sources through direct combustion, gasification and liquefaction, with primary emphasis on coal liquefaction. *Mailing Add:* Grand Forks Energy Technol Ctr Univ Sta PO 8213 Grand Forks ND 58202

WILLWERTH, LAWRENCE JAMES, b Melrose, Mass, Oct 3, 32; m 56; c 3. PLASTICS CHEMISTRY. *Educ:* Lowell Technol Inst, BS, 72, MS, 75. *Prof Exp:* Jr chemist plastics, Nat Polychem Inc, Mass, 55-60; chemist, Avco Corp, Mass, 60-66; TECH MGR CHEM-PLASTICS, K J QUINN & CO INC, MALDEN, MASS, 66- *Concurrent Pos:* Instr polymer characterization, Eve Div, Lowell Technol Inst, 72- *Mem:* Am Chem Soc; Am Inst Chemists; Soc Plastics Engrs. *Res:* Research and development of polyurethane plastics; attainment of specific properties through rearrangement and addition of various species to the polymer backbone. *Mailing Add:* 19 Post Rd North Hampton NH 03862

WILMARTH, VERL RICHARD, economic geology, see previous edition

WILMER, HARRY A, b New Orleans, La, Mar 5, 17; m 45; c 5. PSYCHIATRY. *Educ:* Univ Minn, BS, 38, MS, 40, MD, 41, PhD(path), 44. *Prof Exp:* Chief psychiat, Palo Alto Clin, Calif, 49-51; prof psychiat, Sch Med, Univ Calif, 64-69; sr psychiatrist, Scott & White Clin, Temple, Tex, 69-72; PROF PSYCHIAT, UNIV TEX HEALTH SCI CTR, 72- *Concurrent Pos:* Consult, Mayo Clin, Mayo Found, 57-58 & Dept Corrections, State Calif, 61-65; ed, Hosp & Community Psychiat, 65-68; Guggenheim fel, Jung Inst, Zurich Switz, 69-70; dir, Int Film Festival-Symp Cult & Psychiat, Univ Tex Health Sci Ctr, 71-78; Nat Endowment Arts grant, 74, Nat Endowment Humanities grant, 78; Rockwell Fund, 80, 81 & 82; pres & dir, Inst Humanities, Salado, Tex, 80- *Mem:* Am Psychiat Asn; Int Asn Anal Psychologists; Am Acad Psychoanalysis; Am Col Psychiatrists; Inter-regional Soc Anal Psychologists. *Res:* Schizophrenia; therapeutic community; dreams. *Mailing Add:* Univ Tex Health Sci Ctr San Antonio TX 78284

WILMER, MICHAEL EMORY, b Washington, DC, Oct 11, 41. INFORMATION SCIENCE. *Educ:* Cath Univ Am, BSEE, 63, MSEE, 67, PhD(elec eng), 68. *Prof Exp:* PRIN SCIENTIST IMAGE PROCESSING, PALO ALTO RES CTR, XEROX CORP, 67- *Mem:* Sigma Xi; Inst Elec & Electronics Engrs. *Res:* Digital processing of images and speech for enhancement, compression and recognition. *Mailing Add:* Xerox Palo Alto Res Ctr 3333 Coyote Hill Rd Palo Alto CA 94304

WILMOT, GEORGE BARWICK, b Waterbury, Conn, Oct 27, 28; m 53; c 7. PHYSICAL CHEMISTRY. *Educ:* Rensselaer Polytech Inst, BS, 51; Mass Inst Technol, PhD(phys chem), 54. *Prof Exp:* Res chemist, Naval Ord Sta, 54-73, RES CHEMIST, NAVAL SURFACE WEAPONS CTR, 73- *Mem:* AAAS; Am Chem Soc; Am Phys Soc. *Res:* Infrared and Raman spectroscopy; propellant combustion; thermodynamics; lasers. *Mailing Add:* Propellant Sci Div Naval Surface Weapons Ctr Indian Head MD 20640

WILMOTH, JAMES HERDMAN, biology, deceased

WILMS, ERNEST VICTOR, b Winnipeg, Man, Apr 21, 36. ENGINEERING MECHANICS. *Educ:* Univ Man, BSc, 58; Univ Ill, MS, 60, PhD(theoret & appl mech), 63. *Prof Exp:* Res engr, Can Armament Res & Develop Estab, 58-59; from res asst to res assoc theoret & appl mech, Univ Ill, Urbana, 59-62; asst prof mech eng, Univ Sask, 62-64; res engr, Babcock & Wilcox Res Ctr, Ohio, 64-65; from asst prof to assoc prof eng mech, Univ Ala, 65-68; ASSOC PROF CIVIL ENG, UNIV MAN, 68- *Concurrent Pos:* Consult, Army Res Off, NC, 67-68. *Mem:* Am Inst Aeronaut & Astronaut. *Res:* Solid and fluid mechanics; dynamics and vibrations. *Mailing Add:* Dept of Civil Eng Univ of Manitoba Winnipeg MB R3T 2N2 Can

WILMS, HUGO JOHN, JR, b Gunskirchen, Austria, June 23, 22; US citizen; m 50; c 3. ELECTRICAL ENGINEERING, UNDERSEA WARFARE. *Educ:* Marquette Univ, BEE, 50; Univ Mo, MS, 52. *Prof Exp:* Proj leader underwater acoustics, US Navy Underwater Systs Ctr, 51-54, develop supvr sonar systs, 54-61, sr mem syst anal staff, 61-68, consult tech dir staff, 68-71, head plans & goals div, 71-74, sci adv to comdr, US 6th Fleet, 74-75, antisubmarine warfare adv to comdr, 75-76, head prog & mgt planning staff, 76-79; CONSULT, 80- *Concurrent Pos:* Tech consult; comdr, Oper Test & Eval Force, Norfolk, Va, 61; consult, Adv Sea Based Deterrance Summer

Study, US Navy, 64; chmn Captor tech rev comt, Undersea Warfare Res & Develop Planning Coun, 66. *Mem:* AAAS; Inst Elec & Electronics Engrs; NY Acad Sci. *Res:* Acoustic propagation in the sea; underwater acoustic sound sources, calibrations and measurements. *Mailing Add:* One Clarks Falls Rd North Stonington CT 06359

WILMSEN, CARL WILLIAM, b Galveston, Tex, Nov 20, 34; m 60; c 2. ELECTRICAL ENGINEERING. *Educ:* Tex A&M Univ, BS, 56; Univ Tex, Austin, BS, 60, MS, 62, PhD(elec eng), 67. *Prof Exp:* Test engr, Gen Dynamics Corp, 56-59; res engr, Tracor, Inc, 60-62; from asst prof to assoc prof elec eng, 66-77, PROF ELEC ENG, COLO STATE UNIV, 77- *Mem:* Am Phys Soc; Am Vacuum Soc. *Res:* Current transport through thin solid insulinsulators; metal-insulator-semiconductor devices; Auger and XPS analysis; oxide growth on semiconductor. *Mailing Add:* Dept of Elec Eng Colo State Univ Ft Collins CO 80523

WILNER, GEORGE DUBAR, b New York, NY, Dec 7, 40. HEMATOLOGY, PATHOLOGY. *Educ:* Northwestern Univ, BS, 62, MD, 65. *Prof Exp:* From instr to prof path, Col Physicians & Surgeons, Columbia Univ, 69-78; ASSOC PROF PATH & ASST PROF MED, SCH MED, WASH UNIV, 78- *Mem:* Am Heart Asn. *Res:* Hemostasis and thrombosis. *Mailing Add:* Washington Univ 660 S Euclid Ave St Louis MO 63110

WILNER, JOHN T, b New York, NY, Dec 13, 12; m 39; c 3. ELECTRICAL ENGINEERING. *Educ:* Newark Col Eng, BS, 34. *Prof Exp:* Engr, Gen Elec Co, 35-36; TV engr, Columbia Broadcasting Syst, NY, 37-43, head transmitter develop group, 45-48; vpres & dir broadcast eng, Hearst Corp, Md, 49-69; dir eng, NJ Pub Broadcasting Authority, 69-79; CONSULT, 79- *Concurrent Pos:* Group leader transmitter dept, Harvard Univ, Eng, 44-45. *Honors & Awards:* Award, Nat Asn Broadcasters, 59. *Mem:* Soc Motion Picture & TV Engrs; Inst Elec & Electronics Engrs; Soc Broadcast Engrs; Asn Fed Commun Engrs. *Res:* Radio and television broadcasting. *Mailing Add:* Continental Lane Washington Crossing NJ 08608

WILPIZESKI, CHESTER ROBERT, b Forty Fort, Pa, Aug 20, 30; m 56; c 3. AUDITORY PHYSIOLOGY, DEAFNESS. *Educ:* Univ Pa, AB, 57, PhD(psychol), 65. *Prof Exp:* Res assoc otolaryngol, Jefferson Med Col, 61-65; res psychologist, Wilmington, Del, 66-69; assoc prof, 69-76, PROF OTOLARYNGOL, THOMAS JEFFERSON UNIV, 76- *Concurrent Pos:* NIH res grants, Jefferson Med Col, 69-70 & 72-78. *Mem:* Am Neurotology Soc; AAAS; Acoust Soc Am. *Res:* Animal models and techniques for the study of experimental deafness; laser surgery of the ear; mystagmns; vestibular physiology. *Mailing Add:* Dept of Otolaryngol Thomas Jefferson Univ Philadelphia PA 19107

WILSDORF, DORIS KUHLMANN, b Bremen, Ger, Feb 15, 22; US citizen; M 50; c 2. MATERIALS SCIENCE. *Educ:* Univ Göttingen, Dipl, 46, Dr rer nat, 47; Univ Witwatersrand, DSc(phys metall), 55. *Prof Exp:* Res assoc, Dept Metall, Univ Göttingen, 48 & H H Wills Phys Lab, Bristol Univ, 49-50; lectr physics, Univ Witwatersrand, 50-56; from assoc prof to prof metall eng, Univ Pa, 57-63; prof eng physics, 63-66, UNIV PROF APPL SCI, UNIV VA, 66- *Mem:* Fel Am Phys Soc; Am Soc Eng Educ; Ger Metall Soc; Am Inst Mining & Metall Engrs. *Res:* Theory of crystal defects, crystal plasticity, radiation damage; theory of liquids. *Mailing Add:* 109 Dept of Physics Univ of Va Charlottesville VA 22901

WILSDORF, HEINZ G(ERHARD) F(RIEDRICH), b Pennekow, Ger, June 25, 17; nat US; m 50; c 1. MATERIALS SCIENCE, PHYSICS. *Educ:* Univ Berlin, Dipl, 44; Univ Göttingen, Dr rer nat, 47; Univ Witwatersrand, DSc, 54. *Prof Exp:* Res asst physics, Univ Göttingen, 47-49; prin res officer, Nat Phys Lab, SAfrica, 50-56; tech dir solid state sci labs, Franklin Inst, Pa, 56-65; prof mat sci, 63-66, chmn dept, 63-76, WILLS JOHNSON PROF MAT SCI, UNIV VA, 66- *Concurrent Pos:* Mem, space processing ad hoc adv subcomt, NASA, 75. *Mem:* AAAS; fel Am Phys Soc; Electron Micros Soc Am; fel Am Soc Metals; Am Inst Mining, Metall & Petrol Engrs. *Res:* Metallurgy; x-ray crystallography; electron diffraction; electron microscopy; metal physics, especially plastic deformation and fracture; thin films; biomaterials. *Mailing Add:* Dept of Mat Sci Thornton Hall Univ of Va Charlottesville VA 22901

WILSEY, NEAL DAVID, b Tunkhannock, Pa, July 27, 37; m 61; c 4. PHYSICS. *Educ:* Hartwick Col, BA, 61; Colo State Univ, MS, 64, PhD(physics), 67. *Prof Exp:* Res physicist solid state physics, 67-74, HEAD ELECTRONIC MAT SECT, RADIATION EFFECTS BR, US NAVAL RES LAB, 74- *Concurrent Pos:* Instr, Univ Md, 71-72; vis scientist, Inst Study Defects in Solids, State Univ NY Albany, 78-79. *Mem:* Am Phys Soc. *Res:* Radiation effects, defects in solids; magnetic materials. *Mailing Add:* US Naval Res Lab Code 6627 Washington DC 20375

WILSHIRE, HOWARD GORDON, b Shawnee, Okla, Aug 19, 26; div; c 3. PETROLOGY, SURFACE PROCESSES. *Educ:* Univ Okla, BA, 52; Univ Calif, Berkeley, PhD(geol), 56. *Prof Exp:* Lectr geol, Univ Sydney, 56-60; res fel, Australian Nat Univ, 61; GEOLOGIST, US GEOL SURV, 61- *Mem:* Geol Soc Am; AAAS; Am Geophys Union. *Res:* Structure and petrology of igneous and sedimentary rocks; petrology and processes of the upper mantle; effects of human uses of arid lands and rates of recovery. *Mailing Add:* US Geol Surv 345 Middlefield Rd Menlo Park CA 94025

WILSKA, ALVAR P, b Parikkala, Finland, Mar 14, 11; m 35; c 5. PHYSICS. *Educ:* Univ Helsinki, DrMed, 38. *Prof Exp:* Lectr physiol, Univ Helsinki, 40-44, prof, 44-58; vis prof cell res, La State Univ, 59-60; PROF PHYSICS, UNIV ARIZ, 60- *Concurrent Pos:* Fel, Rockefeller Inst Med Res, 40-41; head, Wihuri Res Inst, Finland, 44-47; consult, Philips Electronic Instruments, Inc, 60- *Mem:* Fel AAAS. *Res:* Experimental physiology; electrophysiology; microelectrodes; medical physics; optics; electron optics. *Mailing Add:* Dept of Physics Univ of Ariz Tucson AZ 85721

WILSON, ALAN CHANEY, biochemistry, see previous edition

WILSON, ALBERT E, b Glenwood Springs, Colo, Jan 17, 27; m 52; c 5. NUCLEAR ENGINEERING. *Educ:* Univ Colo, BS, 50; Univ NMex, MS, 59; Univ Okla, PhD(eng sci), 64. *Prof Exp:* Physicist, Nat Bur Standards, 51-55; staff mem, Los Alamos Sci Lab, 55-59; from instr to asst prof nuclear eng, Univ Okla, 59-66; prof nuclear eng & chmn dept, 66-76, PROF ENG & NUCLEAR SCI & DEAN SCH ENG, IDAHO STATE UNIV, 76- *Mem:* Am Nuclear Soc; Am Soc Eng Educ; Nat Soc Prof Engrs. *Res:* Nuclear engineering education, especially instrumentation, kinetics and control of nuclear reactor systems. *Mailing Add:* Sch of Eng Idaho State Univ Pocatello ID 83201

WILSON, ALEXANDER THOMAS, b Wellington, NZ, Feb 8, 30. PALEOCLIMATOLOGY, ISOTOPIC CHEMISTRY. *Educ:* Victoria Univ, NZ, BS, 49, MS, 50; Univ Calif, Berkeley, PhD(phys chem), 54; Univ Waikato, NZ, DSc, 81. *Prof Exp:* Trainee, Chem Div, NZ Dept Sci & Indust Res, 47-50; teaching asst thermodynamics, Univ Calif, Berkeley, 51-54; res chemist, Div Nuclear Sci, Dept Sci & Indust Res, 57-59; assoc prof appl chem, Univ Wellington, 60-69; dean sci, Univ Waikato, 69-79; DIR RES, DUVAL CORP, SUBSID PENNZOIL, 79- *Concurrent Pos:* Dir, Antartic Res Unit, Univ Waikato, 69-79; res assoc, Dept Geosci, Univ Ariz, 80- *Honors & Awards:* Easterfield Medal, NZ Inst Chem, 63. *Mem:* Soc Mining Entrs. *Res:* Hydrometallurgical research. *Mailing Add:* 4715 E Fort Lowell Tucson AZ 85712

WILSON, ALLAN CHARLES, b Ngaruawahia, NZ, Oct 18, 34; m 58; c 2. BIOCHEMISTRY, ZOOLOGY. *Educ:* Univ Otago, NZ, BSc, 55; Wash State Univ, MS, 57; Univ Calif, Berkeley, PhD(biochem), 61. *Prof Exp:* Fel biochem, Brandeis Univ, 61-64; from asst prof to assoc prof, 64-72, PROF BIOCHEM, UNIV CALIF, BERKELEY, 72- *Concurrent Pos:* NSF grants, 65-; NIH grants, 74-; mem, Alpha Helix Exped, New Guinea, 69; Guggenheim Mem Found award, Weizmann Inst Sci & Univ Nairobi, 72-73; assoc ed, Biochem Genetics, 75- & J Molecular Evolution, 78- *Mem:* Am Soc Biol Chem; Soc Syst Zool. *Res:* Immunochemistry of proteins; molecular and genetic basis of organismal evolution. *Mailing Add:* 401 Biochem Bldg Univ of Calif Berkeley CA 94720

WILSON, ALMA MCDONALD, b Colonia Pacheco, Chihuahua, Mex, Aug 29, 29; US citizen; m 52; c 7. PLANT PHYSIOLOGY. *Educ:* Brigham Young Univ, BA, 54; Univ Calif, Davis, PhD, 62. *Prof Exp:* Plant physiologist, Agr Res Serv, USDA, Wash State Univ, 62-72, PLANT PHYSIOLOGIST, AGR RES SERV, USDA, COLO STATE UNIV, 72- *Mem:* Am Soc Plant Physiologists; Soc Range Mgt; Am Soc Agron. *Res:* Physiology of seed germination; metabolic effects of temperature and moisture stress on higher plants; forage species in relation to seedling establishment on semiarid lands. *Mailing Add:* 304 Dartmouth Trail Ft Collins CO 80521

WILSON, ANDREW ROBERT, b Dublin, Ireland, Sept 13, 41; US citizen; m 68. PLASMA PHYSICS. *Educ:* Trinity Col, Univ Dublin, BA, 62, MA, 65; Oxford Univ, DPhil(physics), 68. *Prof Exp:* Fr Govt boursier nuclear physics, Inst Fourier, Grenoble, 62-63; fel solid state physics, Lincoln Lab, Mass Inst Technol, 68-70; systs engr, Elec Supply Bd, Dublin, Ireland, 70-71; PROG MGR PLASMA PHYSICS, SYSTS, SCI & SOFTWARE, 71- *Mem:* Am Phys Soc; Inst Elec & Electronics Engrs. *Res:* Hydromagnetic theory; system generated electromagnetic theory; radiation transport. *Mailing Add:* Systs Sci & Software PO Box 1620 La Jolla CA 92038

WILSON, ANDREW STEPHEN, b Doncaster, Eng, Mar 26, 47; m 75; c 1. ASTRONOMY. *Educ:* Univ Cambridge, BA, 69, MA & PhD(radio astron), 73. *Prof Exp:* Res fel radio astron, State Univ Leiden, 73-75; res fel astron, Univ Sussex, 75-78; asst prof, 78-81, ASSOC PROF ASTRON, UNIV MD, COLLEGE PARK, 81- *Mem:* Fel Royal Astron Soc; fel Am Astron Soc. *Res:* Crab nebula; radio sources; active galactic nuclei. *Mailing Add:* Dept of Astron Univ of Md College Park MD 20742

WILSON, ANGUS, b Mexico, Maine, Aug 13, 20. RUBBER CHEMISTRY. *Educ:* Georgetown Univ, BS, 41. *Prof Exp:* Control & anal chemist, E I du Pont de Nemours & Co, Inc, 41-43; prod supvr, Joseph E Seagrams & Sons, Inc, 47-48; control lab supvr, Govt Lab, Univ Akron, 49-52; rubber chemist, US Army Natick Res & Develop Command, 52-68, head rubber technol group, 68-74, head, Rubber & Plastics Group, 74-80; RETIRED. *Mem:* Am Chem Soc; Sigma Xi. *Res:* Development of methods of testing rubber and elastomeric materials; compounding of phosphazene elastomers; evaluation of experimental elastomers for possible end item applications. *Mailing Add:* 8 Bowdoin Rd Ipswich MA 01938

WILSON, ARCHIE FREDRIC, b Los Angeles, Calif, May 7, 31; m 66; c 2. PULMONARY DISEASES, PULMONARY PHYSIOLOGY. *Educ:* Univ Calif, Los Angeles, BA, 53; Univ Calif, San Francisco, MD, 57, PhD(physiol), 67. *Prof Exp:* Asst prof internal med, Univ Calif, Los Angeles, 67-70; from asst prof to assoc prof, 70-79, PROF INTERNAL MED & PHYSIOL, UNIV CALIF, IRVINE, 79-, CHMN DEPT, 78- *Mem:* Am Therapeut Soc; Am Fedn Clin Res; Am Col Physicians. *Res:* Asthma; airway physiology and pathophysiology; bronciodilator aerosols; physiology of transcendental meditation. *Mailing Add:* Dept Med Univ Calif Med Ctr Orange CA 92668

WILSON, ARCHIE SPENCER, b Tekoa, Wash, Jan 19, 21; m 44; c 3. CHEMISTRY. *Educ:* Iowa State Univ, BS, 46; Univ Chicago, MS, 50, PhD, 51. *Prof Exp:* Asst chem, Iowa State Univ, 43-46; res assoc, Gallium Proj, US Dept Navy, 48-49; asst, Univ Chicago, 49-50; instr chem, Univ Nebr, 50-51; sr scientist, Gen Elec Co, 51-65; sr res scientist, Pac Northwest Labs, Battelle Mem Inst, 64-71; assoc chmn dept, 71-78, PROF CHEM, UNIV MINN, MINNEAPOLIS, 71- *Concurrent Pos:* US sci adv, Int Conf Peaceful Uses Atomic Energy, Geneva, 58; mem, US-UK Ruthenium Conf, 58. *Mem:* Am Chem Soc; AAAS. *Res:* Crystal structure of compounds of uranium; ruthenium chemistry; solvent extraction of the actinide elements. *Mailing Add:* Univ Minn Dept Chem 207 Pleasant St SE Minneapolis MN 55455

WILSON, ARMIN GUSCHEL, b Sapulpa, Okla, Dec 13, 16; m 43; c 2. ORGANIC CHEMISTRY, MEDICINAL CHEMISTRY. *Educ:* Rice Inst, BA, 39, MA, 41; Harvard Univ, PhD(org chem), 45. 45. *Prof Exp:* Org chemist, Off Sci Res & Develop, Harvard Univ, 45-47 & Merck & Co, Inc, NJ, 47-52; dept head res div, Bristol-Myers Co, 52-68; chmn math & sci, Mercer County Community Col, 68-69; teacher & counr urban univ prog, Grad Sch Educ, 69-72, PROF ACAD FOUND, LIVINGSTON COL, RUTGERS UNIV, NEW BRUNSWICK, 72- *Concurrent Pos:* Instr, Union Jr Col; chmn, Gordon Conf Med Chem, 67. *Mem:* Am Chem Soc; fel NY Acad Sci. *Res:* Synthetic organic chemistry; structure-action relationships of drugs; reaction mechanisms; photochemistry; nature of science; relationship of science and poetry. *Mailing Add:* 249 Harrison Ave Highland Park NJ 08904

WILSON, BARBARA ANN, b West Lafayette, Ind, Sept 7, 48. SOLID STATE PHYSICS. *Educ:* Mt Holyoke Col, BA, 68; Univ Wis-Madison, PhD(physics), 78. *Prof Exp:* MEM TECH STAFF SOLID STATE PHYSICS, BELL LABS, 78- *Mem:* Sigma Xi; Am Physical Soc. *Res:* Energy transfer in solids; far infrared properties of semiconductor inversion layers; amorphous semiconductors. *Mailing Add:* Bell Labs Murray Hill NJ 07974

WILSON, BARRY WILLIAM, b Brooklyn, NY, Aug 20, 31; m 56. CELL BIOLOGY, NEUROBIOLOGY. *Educ:* Univ Chicago, BA, 50; Ill Inst Technol, BS & MS, 57; Univ Calif, Los Angeles, PhD(zool), 62. *Prof Exp:* Asst zool, Ill Inst Technol, 56-57; asst, Univ Calif, Los Angeles, 57-58, USPHS cardiovasc trainee, 58, fel, 59-61, jr res zoologist, 62; asst prof poultry husb & animal physiol & asst biologist, Exp Sta, 62-68, assoc prof avian sci & animal physiol & assoc biologist, 68-72, PROF AVIAN SCI, ANIMAL PHYSIOL & PHYS MED & REHAB, UNIV CALIF, DAVIS, 72- *Mem:* Am Soc Cell Biol; Soc Neurosci; Soc Develop Biol; Soc Toxicol; Tissue Cult Asn. *Res:* Cell growth and development; emphasis on muscle and nerve using cell culture and intact animals; regulation of acetylcholinesterase and other molecules of nerve, muscle; muscular dystrophy and pesticide action. *Mailing Add:* Dept Avian Sci Univ Calif Davis CA 95616

WILSON, BASIL W(RIGLEY), b Cape Town, SAfrica, June 16, 09; nat US; m 41; c 4. COASTAL ENGINEERING, PHYSICAL OCEANOGRAPHY. *Educ:* Cape Town Univ, BSc, 31, DSc(eng), 53; Univ Ill, MS, 39, CE, 40. *Prof Exp:* Jr engr, SAfrican Rwys & Harbors, 32-33, asst to res engr, Chief Civil Engrs Dept, 33-41, asst res engr, 41-52; from assoc prof to prof eng oceanog, Tex A&M Univ, 53-61; mem sr staff, Nat Eng Sci Co, Calif, 61-63, assoc dir, 64; dir eng oceanog, Sci Eng Assocs, 64-68; CONSULT OCEANOG ENGR, 68- *Concurrent Pos:* Mem, Permanent Int Asn Navig Congs & deleg, London, 57 & Baltimore, 61; coastal eng seminar, US-Japan Coop Sci Prog, Japan, 64; US lectr, NATO Adv Study Inst Berthing & Mooring Ships, Lisbon, Portugal, 65 & Wallingford, Eng, 73; A E Snape Mem Lectr, SAfrican Inst Civil Engrs, 75. *Honors & Awards:* Wellington Prize, Am Soc Civil Engrs, 52, Norman Medal, 69; Inst Award, SAfrican Inst Civil Engrs, 59; Overseas Premium Award, Brit Inst Civil Engrs, 68. *Mem:* fel AAAS; fel Am Soc Civil Engrs; fel Brit Inst Civil Engrs; fel SAfrican Inst Civil Engrs; Sigma Xi. *Res:* Track stresses; stability of railway vehicles on track; rail steel; economics of railway location; coastal engineering; ocean wave prediction; wave forces on structures; storm tide prediction; coastal seiches and oscillation in harbors; model engineering; ship mooring problems; tsunami waves. *Mailing Add:* 529 Winston Ave Pasadena CA 91107

WILSON, BENJAMIN JAMES, b Pennsboro, WVa, Jan 7, 23; m 78; c 4. MICROBIOLOGY. *Educ:* Univ WVa, AB, 43, MS, 47; George Washington Univ, PhD(microbiol), 55. *Prof Exp:* Med bacteriologist, Biol Warfare Labs, Ft Detrick, 49-51, chief microbiol br, 51-59; assoc prof biol, David Lipscomb Col, 59-65; from asst prof to assoc prof, 63-75, PROF BIOCHEM, SCH MED, VANDERBILT UNIV, 75- *Concurrent Pos:* Consult nutrit sect, Off Int Res, NIH, 65-67 & Food & Drug Admin, 72-; mem subcomt toxicants occurring naturally in foods, Nat Acad Sci, 68-74; contrib ed, Nutrit Reviews, 73-; mem adj fac, Col Vet Med, Univ Tenn, Knoxville, 79- *Mem:* Am Soc Microbiol; Am Chem Soc; Soc Toxicol; NY Acad Sci. *Res:* Mycotoxins; natural toxicants; microbial toxins. *Mailing Add:* Dept of Biochem Vanderbilt Univ Sch of Med Nashville TN 37232

WILSON, BILLY RAY, b SC, Apr 1, 22; m 47; c 1. ENTOMOLOGY. *Educ:* Clemson Col, BS, 42; Rutgers Univ, PhD(entom), 59. *Prof Exp:* Entomologist, Bur Entom & Plant Quarantine, USDA, 48-51 & Qm Res & Develop Labs, US Dept Army, 51-54; asst, 54-59, assoc res specialist, 59-66, chmn bur conserv & environ sci, 63-69, prof entom, 63-77, chmn, Dept Entom & Econ Zool, 71-77, RES PROF ENTOM & ECON ZOOL, RUTGERS UNIV, NEW BRUNSWICK, 77- *Mem:* Entom Soc Am; Am Inst Biol Sci. *Res:* Insect physiology; insect resistance to insecticides; biology; biochemistry; environmental science. *Mailing Add:* 709 N 2nd Ave Highland Park NJ 08904

WILSON, BOYD CHESTER, forest genetics, see previous edition

WILSON, BRAYTON F, b Cambridge, Mass, May 27, 34; m 60; c 2. BOTANY, FORESTRY. *Educ:* Harvard Univ, AB, 55, MF, 57; Australian Forestry Sch, dipl forestry, 59; Univ Calif, Berkeley, PhD(bot), 61. *Prof Exp:* Forest botanist, Harvard Univ, 61-67; asst prof, 67-72, ASSOC PROF FORESTRY, UNIV MASS, AMHERST, 72- *Mem:* AAAS; Bot Soc Am; Am Soc Plant Physiol. *Res:* Tree growth. *Mailing Add:* Dept of Forestry Univ of Mass Amherst MA 01003

WILSON, BURTON DAVID, b Los Angeles, Calif, Oct 20, 32; m 58; c 3. ORGANIC CHEMISTRY. *Educ:* Univ Calif, Los Angeles, BS, 54; Univ Ill, PhD, 58. *Prof Exp:* CHEMIST, EASTMAN KODAK CO, 57- *Mem:* Am Chem Soc. *Res:* Development and production problem solving on chemicals for photographic end uses. *Mailing Add:* Eastman Kodak Co 343 State St Rochester NY 14650

WILSON, BYRON J, b Jackson, Wyo, Feb 2, 31; m 58; c 7. INORGANIC CHEMISTRY. *Educ:* Idaho State Univ, BS, 56; Southern Ill Univ, MA, 58; Univ Wash, PhD(chem), 61. *Prof Exp:* Asst prof chem, Vanderbilt Univ, 61-65; from asst prof to assoc prof, 65-72, PROF CHEM, BRIGHAM YOUNG UNIV, 72- *Mem:* Am Chem Soc. *Res:* Inorganic free-radical research; paper deterioration research. *Mailing Add:* 545 E 3050 North Provo UT 84601

WILSON, CARL C, b Halfway, Ore, Mar 17, 15; m 42; c 2. FOREST MANAGEMENT. *Educ:* Univ Idaho, BS, 39; Univ Calif, Berkeley, MS, 41. *Prof Exp:* Fire control asst, Lassen Nat Forest, US Forest Serv, Calif, 46-49 & Plumas Nat Forest, 49, forester, Angeles Nat Forest, 49-55, res forester & proj leader forest fire res, Calif Forest Exp Sta, 56-57, chief forest fire res div, 57-62, asst dir forest fire & eng res & chief forest fire lab, Pac Southwest Forest & Range Exp Sta, 62-73, asst dir & nat fire specialist, Coop Fire Control, State & Pvt Forestry, US Forest Serv, 73-78; FOREST FIRE CONSULT, 78- *Concurrent Pos:* Consult fire mgt, Food & Agr Orgn-UN Environ Prog, UN, Rome, Italy, 75, Calif Dept Forestry, 78-80 & Ministry Natural Resources, Ont Can, 80. *Mem:* Soc Am Foresters; Am Soc Range Mgt; Am Forestry Asn. *Res:* Forest fire science; detection and control of forest fires for the protection of the human environment; author or coauthor of more than 40 technical papers in forestry and forest fire management. *Mailing Add:* 3 Maybeck Twin Dr Berkeley CA 94708

WILSON, CAROL MAGGART, b Burley, Idaho, Oct 26, 36; m 59; c 2. PHARMACOGENETICS, BIOCHEMICAL GENETICS. *Educ:* Northwestern Univ, BA, 58; Wayne State Univ, PhD(biochem), 63. *Prof Exp:* Fel microbiol, Emory Univ, 63-64, biochem, 64-66; asst prof chem, Wheaton Col, 67-68; clin chemist, RI Hosp, 69-70; res assoc molecular biol, Univ Tex, Dallas, 71-73; res assoc, 74-76, instr, 76-78, ASST PROF PHARMACOL & INTERNAL MED, UNIV TEX HEALTH SCI CTR, DALLAS SOUTHWESTERN MED SCH, 78- *Res:* Pharmacogenetics; control of eukaryotic gene expression; genetic and hormonal regulation of renin activity and structure. *Mailing Add:* Univ Tex Health Sci Ctr 5323 Harry Hines Blvd Dallas TX 75325

WILSON, CARROLL KLEPPER, b Denton, Tex, Aug 24, 17; m 41; c 2. MATHEMATICS. *Educ:* NTex State Col, BA, 37; Univ Tex, MA, 40. *Prof Exp:* Teacher pub schs, Tex, 37-41; instr radar, US Civil Serv, 41-43; actg chmn div math & natural sci, 56-60, head dept math, 60-74, assoc prof, 46-75, PROF MATH, EASTERN NMEX UNIV, 75- *Mem:* Math Asn Am. *Res:* Analysis. *Mailing Add:* Dept of Math Eastern NMex Univ Portales NM 88130

WILSON, CHARLES B, b Neosho, Mo, Aug 31, 29; m 56; c 3. MEDICINE. *Educ:* Tulane Univ, BS, 51, MD, 54. *Prof Exp:* Resident path, Tulane Univ, 55-56, instr neurosurg, 60-61; resident, Ochsner Clin, 56-60; instr, La State Univ, 61-63; from asst prof to prof, Univ Ky, 63-68; PROF NEUROSURG, UNIV CALIF, SAN FRANCISCO, 68- *Mem:* Am Asn Neurol Surg; Am Asn Neuropath; Soc Neurol Surg. *Res:* Brain tumor chemotherapy; tissue culture. *Mailing Add:* Dept of Neurosurg Univ of Calif Med Ctr San Francisco CA 94143

WILSON, CHARLES ELMER, b Passaic, NJ, Aug 2, 31; m 58; c 3. NOISE CONTROL, MACHINE DESIGN. *Educ:* NJ Inst Technol, BS, 53, MS, 58; NY UNiv, BS, 62; Polytech Inst NY, PhD(mech eng, 70. *Prof Exp:* Engr, Otis Elevator Co, 53-54; armament & electron officer, US Air Force, 54-56; engr, Bendix Corp, 56; PROF MECH ENG, MACH DESIGN, MECHANISMS, NOISE CONTROL, NJ INST TECHNOL, 56- *Concurrent Pos:* Prin investr, NSF, NASA & other foundations & industs, 64-81; consult mach design, var indust firms, 65-; consult noise control, Indust Firms & Govt Agencies, 72-; vis fel, Inst Sound & Vibration Res, Univ Southampton, Eng, 77. *Mem:* Acoust Soc Am; Am Inst Physics. *Res:* Community noise; industrial noise control; hearing protection; transportation noise prediction and control; adhesives and vibration. *Mailing Add:* 19 Highview Terrace Cedar Grove NJ 07009

WILSON, CHARLES L, plant pathology, see previous edition

WILSON, CHARLES MAYE, b Mt Olive, NC, Oct 16, 16. MYCOLOGY. *Educ:* Univ Va, BSc, 41, MA, 42; Harvard Univ, PhD(biol), 50. *Prof Exp:* Nat Res Coun fel, Univ Calif, 50-51; instr biol, Harvard Univ, 51-53; from asst prof to assoc prof bot, 53-62, chmn, Dept Biol, 62-70, PROF BOT, MCGILL UNIV, 62- *Concurrent Pos:* Vis prof, Univ Calif, 57. *Mem:* Bot Soc Am; Mycol Soc Am. *Res:* Cytology and life cycles of the lower fungi. *Mailing Add:* Dept Biol McGill Univ 1205 Dr Penfield Ave Montreal PQ H3A 1B1 Can

WILSON, CHARLES NORMAN, b Seattle, Wash, Mar 28, 47. MATERIALS SCIENCE, PHYSICAL CHEMISTRY. *Educ:* Univ Wash, BS, 69, MS, 70, PhD(ceramic eng), 74. *Prof Exp:* Ceramic engr glass technol, Penberthy Electromelt Co, Seattle, Wash, 68-69; SR SCIENTIST CERAMIC NUCLEAR MAT, RES & DEVELOP, WESTINGHOUSE HANFORD CO, 74- *Mem:* Am Ceramic Soc. *Res:* Fabrication and characterization of ceramic materials including oxide nuclear fuels, boron carbide, ceramic nuclear waste forms, and lithium ceramics for fusion reactor tritium breeding; solar cell materials characterization; biomaterials and bone physical chemistry. *Mailing Add:* Westinghouse Hanford Co PO Box 1970 Richland WA 99352

WILSON, CHARLES OREN, b Salt Lake City, Utah, May 9, 26; div; c 4. CLINICAL CHEMISTRY. *Educ:* Stanford Univ, BS, 49. *Prof Exp:* Prod chemist, Transandino Co, Calif, 49-51; res chemist, Nat Bur Stand, 51-52; sr res chemist, Olin Mathieson Chem Corp, NY, 52-54 & Calif, 54-59; sr res chemist, Nat Eng Sci Corp, 59-61 & Am Potash & Chem Corp, 61-68; chemist, Electro-Optical Systs, Inc, 68-69 & Int Chem & Nuclear Corp, 69-70; mgr qual control, Reagents Qual Control, 70-77, TECH SPECIALIST, REAGENTS PROCESS SUPPORT, ANAL SYSTS, ABBOTT DIAG DIV, 77- *Concurrent Pos:* Consult, 67- *Mem:* Am Chem Soc. *Res:* Organoboron and organophosphorus chemistry; exotic fuels and polymers; infrared spectroscopy; mass spectrometry; rare earth research; solvent cal extraction; quality control of clinical diagnostic reagents. *Mailing Add:* Abbott Diag Div Anal Systs Reagents Process Support 820 Mission St South Pasadena CA 91030

WILSON, CHARLES R, b Baltimore, Md, Jan 25, 29; m 59; c 3. GEOPHYSICS. *Educ:* Case Inst Technol, BS, 51; Univ NMex, MS, 56; Univ Alaska, PhD(geophys), 63. *Prof Exp:* PROF PHYSICS, GEOPHYS INST, UNIV ALASKA, 59- *Concurrent Pos:* Fulbright grant, Paris, 63-64; vis scientist, Nat Ctr Atmospheric Res, 68-69. *Mem:* Am Geophys Union. *Res:* Magnetic storms; geomagnetic micropulsations; auroral infrasonics. *Mailing Add:* Geophys Inst Univ of Alaska Fairbanks AK 99701

WILSON, CHARLES WOODSON, III, b Columbus, Ohio, Nov 20, 24; m 48; c 4. PHYSICS. *Educ:* Univ Mich, BSE, 47, MS, 48; Wash Univ, PhD(physics), 52. *Prof Exp:* Res assoc, Stanford Univ, 52; res physicist, Prod Dept, Res Div, Texaco Inc, 52-56; physicist, Res & Develop Dept, Chem Div, Union Carbide Corp, 56-62, res scientist, 62-64, group leader, 64-65; PROF PHYSICS & POLYMER SCI, HEAD PHYSICS DEPT & RES ASSOC, INST POLYMER SCI, UNIV AKRON, 65- *Mem:* AAAS; Am Phys Soc; Am Asn Physics Teachers. *Res:* Nuclear and electron spin resonance; high polymer physics; energy utilization and conservation. *Mailing Add:* Dept of Physics Univ of Akron Akron OH 44325

WILSON, CHRISTINE SHEARER, b Orleans, Mass. NUTRITION. *Educ:* Brown Univ, BA, 50; Univ Calif, Berkeley, PhD(nutrit, anthrop), 70. *Prof Exp:* Asst ed, Nutrit Rev, Sch Pub Health, Harvard Univ, 51-56; nutrit analyst, USDA, 57-58; asst res nutritionist, 70-71, res assoc nutrit anthrop, 71-74, asst res nutritionist, 74, ASST RES NUTRITIONIST, DEPT EPIDEMIOL & INT HEALTH, UNIV CALIF, SAN FRANCISCO, 75-, LECTR, 74-, LECTR, PROG MED ANTHROP, 77- *Concurrent Pos:* Consult, Soc Nutrit Educ, 71-72, 79 & 81; USPHS spec res fel, 72-73; lectr, Dept Anthrop, Univ Calif, Riverside, 73; vis prof, Dept Family Studies, Univ Guelph, 78; vis asst prof, Home Econ Dept, San Francisco State Univ, 79; mem, Behav Factors Panel, US Dept Agr Competitive Grants Prog, 79; contrib ed, Nutrit Rev, 79- *Mem:* Am Anthrop Asn; Am Inst Nutrit; Soc Med Anthrop; Soc Nutrit Educ. *Res:* Food in the culture; social influences on nutritional status; ethnographic field research on diet and nutritional health; dietary factors in breast cancer. *Mailing Add:* Dept of Int Health Univ of Calif San Francisco CA 94143

WILSON, CLAUDE E, b Starkey, NY, Jan 29, 39; m 60; c 1. ANALYTICAL CHEMISTRY. *Educ:* Harpur Col, BA, 60; Columbia Univ, MA, 61, PhD(chem), 66. *Prof Exp:* Instr chem, Drew Univ, 64-65; asst prof, Univ Pittsburgh, 65-71; ASST PROF CHEM, IND UNIV-PURDUE UNIV, INDIANAPOLIS, 71- *Mem:* AAAS; Am Chem Soc. *Res:* Electrochemical analysis of metals in natural water systems; use of mini and micro-computers in analytical research and teaching. *Mailing Add:* Dept of Chem Ind Univ-Purdue Univ Indianapolis IN 46205

WILSON, CLAUDE LEONARD, b Ottawa, Kans, Nov 30, 05; m 27; c 1. MECHANICAL ENGINEERING. *Educ:* Kans State Univ, BS, 25, ME, 29, MS, 33. *Prof Exp:* From asst prof to assoc prof mech eng, Prairie View Agr & Mech Univ, 25-33, supt bldgs & utilities, 33-41, dean eng, 41-66, dean, Col, 66-70, vpres, 70-74; ENG CONSULT, BOVAY ENGRS, INC, 75- *Mem:* Am Soc Mech Engrs; Am Soc Eng Educ; Am Soc Testing & Mat; Nat Soc Prof Engrs. *Res:* Thermodynamics and heat power; heating and air conditioning; structural analysis and design. *Mailing Add:* PO Box 2848 Prairie View TX 77445

WILSON, CLYDE LIVINGSTON, b Ohio, July 29, 22; m 51; c 2. SOIL PHYSICS. *Educ:* Ohio State Univ, BS, 47, BAE, 48, PhD(agron), 52. *Prof Exp:* Asst soils, Ohio State Univ, 48-52; from res agronomist to res specialist, 52-72, sr res specialist, 72-79, AGRON SYSTS MGR, MONSANTO CO, 79- *Mem:* Am Soc Agron; Am Soc Agr Engrs; Soil Sci Soc Am; Weed Sci Soc Am; Coun Agr Sci & Technol. *Res:* Saturated water flow in tiled lands; chemical coil conditioners; herbicide investigations. *Mailing Add:* 1530 Lynkirk Lane Kirkwood MO 63122

WILSON, COLON HAYES, JR, b Marshallberg, NC, Apr 10, 32; m 56; c 3. RHEUMATOLOGY, INTERNAL MEDICINE. *Educ:* Duke Univ, BA, 52, MD, 56. *Prof Exp:* From intern to asst resident med, Univ Va Hosp, 56-58; resident, Edward J Meyer Mem Hosp, Buffalo, NY, 61-63; res instr, State Univ NY Buffalo, 64-66; from asst prof to assoc prof rheumatology, 66-73, asst prof phys med, 66-74, PROF MED, MED SCH, EMORY UNIV, 74-, DIR, DIV RHEUMATOLOGY & IMMUNOL, 66- *Concurrent Pos:* Fel, Buffalo Gen Hosp, State Univ NY Buffalo, 63-66; Nat Inst Arthritis & Metab Dis prog grant, Edward J Meyer Mem Hosp, Buffalo; actg med dir, Arthritis Found, 77-79. *Mem:* Am Fedn Clin Res; Am Rheumatism Asn; Reticuloendothelial Soc; fel Am Col Physicians. *Res:* Significance of various patterns of antinuclear antibody fluorescence with respect to specific diagnosis and prognosis on various collagen vascular diseases; the efficacy of early synovectomy in rheumatoid arthritis in prevention of late deformity and preservation of function. *Mailing Add:* Dept Med Sch Med Emory Univ Atlanta GA 30303

WILSON, COYT TAYLOR, b Fulton, Miss, July 27, 13; m 36; c 2. PLANT PATHOLOGY. *Educ:* Ala Polytech Inst, BS, 38, MS, 41; Univ Minn, PhD(plant path), 46. *Prof Exp:* Instr bot, Ala Polytech Inst, 40-41; instr plant path, Univ Minn, 41-43; asst plant pathologist, Exp Sta, Auburn Univ, 44-47, prof plant path & plant pathologist, 47-51, asst dean, Col Agr & assoc dir, Agr Exp Sta, 51-64; from assoc dir to dir, Va Agr Exp Sta, 64-66; assoc dean, Res Div, Va Polytech Inst & State Univ, 66-71, exec assoc dean, 71-78, dir agr & life sci res, 66-78; RETIRED. *Concurrent Pos:* AID short term res consult, Ministry Agr, Iran, 60, Turkey, 66 & EPakistan. *Mem:* AAAS. *Mailing Add:* 2010 Linwood Lane NW Blacksburg VA 24060

WILSON, CURTIS MARSHALL, b Stillwater, Minn, Sept 11, 26; m 52; c 4. PLANT BIOCHEMISTRY. *Educ:* Univ Minn, BS, 48, MS, 51; Univ Wis, PhD(bot), 54. *Prof Exp:* Asst, Univ Minn, 48-51; from asst prof to assoc prof plant physiol, Rutgers Univ, 54-59; assoc prof, 66-72, PROF PLANT PHYSIOL, UNIV ILL, URBANA, 72-; RES CHEMIST, AGR RES SERV, USDA, 59- *Mem:* AAAS; Am Soc Plant Physiol; Am Asn Cereal Chemists. *Res:* Plant biochemistry; plant nucleases; seed development and storage proteins. *Mailing Add:* Dept Agron Univ Ill Urbana IL 61801

WILSON, CYNTHIA, b Gillingham, Eng, Aug 31, 26; Can citizen. CLIMATOLOGY. *Educ:* Univ London, BA, 47, teachers dipl, 48; McGill Univ, MSc, 58; Laval Univ, PhD, 72. *Prof Exp:* Teacher high sch, Eng, 48-54; res asst meteorol & climat, Meteorol Res Group, McGill Univ, 54-62; asst prof climat, Inst Geog, 64-67, assoc prof climat & researcher, Ctr Nordic Studies, Laval Univ, 67-75; CONSULT CLIMAT, 76-*Concurrent Pos:* Expert, Cold Regions Res & Eng Lab, US Army, 62-66; under contract to Meteorol Serv Can, 66-68. *Honors & Awards:* Darton Prize, Royal Meteorol Soc, 63. *Mem:* Am Meteorol Soc; Can Meteorol Soc; Arctic Inst NAm; Royal Meteorol Soc; Am Quaternary Asn. *Res:* Meteorology and climatology of cold regions; historical climatology. *Mailing Add:* PO Box 887 Sta B Ottawa ON K1P 5P9 Can

WILSON, DANA E, b Chicago, Ill, Oct 5, 37; m 60; c 3. MEDICINE, METABOLISM. *Educ:* Oberlin Col, AB, 57; Western Reserve Univ, MD, 62. *Prof Exp:* Intern & asst resident internal med, Boston City Hosp, Mass, 62-64, sr resident, 66-67; clin assoc allergy & infectious dis, NIH, 64-66; asst prof clin nutrit & human metab, Mass Inst Technol, 69-71; asst prof, 71-74, ASSOC PROF MED, COL MED, UNIV UTAH, 74- *Concurrent Pos:* Fel diabetes & metab, Thorndike Mem Lab, Harvard Med Sch, 67-69. *Mem:* AAAS; Am Fedn Clin Res; Am Diabetes Asn. *Res:* Diabetes and metabolism; lipoproteins and lipid transport. *Mailing Add:* Dept of Med Univ of Utah Col of Med Salt Lake City UT 84112

WILSON, DARCY BENOIT, b Rhinebeck, NY, May 14, 36; m 57; c 3. IMMUNOLOGY, IMMUNOBIOLOGY. *Educ:* Harvard Univ, AB, 58; Univ Pa, PhD(zool), 62. *Prof Exp:* Assoc, 63-65, from asst prof to assoc prof path & med genet, 66-74, PROF PATH & HUMAN GENET, SCH MED, UNIV PA, 74- *Concurrent Pos:* Res fel transplantation immunol, Wistar Inst, Univ Pa, 62-63, res fel med genet, Sch Med, 65-66; Helen Hay Whitney Found fel, 64-67; USPHS career develop award, 67-72. *Mem:* Am Asn Immunol. *Res:* Immunology of tissue transplantation, particularly immunologic behavior of lymphoid cells in vitro and in vivo. *Mailing Add:* Dept of Path Univ of Pa Sch of Med Philadelphia PA 19174

WILSON, DAVID BUCKINGHAM, b Cambridge, Mass, Jan 15, 40; m 63; c 3. BIOCHEMISTRY. *Educ:* Harvard Univ, BA, 61; Stanford Univ, PhD(biochem), 65. *Prof Exp:* Jane Coffin Childs fel biochem, Sch Med, Johns Hopkins Univ, 65-67; asst prof, 67-74, ASSOC PROF BIOCHEM, CORNELL UNIV, 74- *Mem:* Am Soc Biol Chemists; Am Soc Microbiol. *Res:* Regulation of gene expression in microorganisms; bacterial membrane biochemistry and genetic engineering; mechanisms of host cell lysis by bacteriophage lambda; cloning of thermophillic cellulase gene; regulation of galactose enzyme synthesis in Esherichia coli and yeast and the mechanisms of binding protein transport systems in Esherichia coli. *Mailing Add:* Dept of Biochem Wing Hall Cornell Univ Ithaca NY 14850

WILSON, DAVID E, b Meade, Kans, Aug 5, 29; m 56; c 2. MATHEMATICS. *Educ:* Kans State Col, Pittsburg, AB, 51, MS, 54; Univ Kans, PhD(math), 67. *Prof Exp:* Asst prof math, Univ Hawaii, 61-65; asst prof, 66-70, ASSOC PROF MATH, WABASH COL, 70- *Mem:* Am Math Soc; Math Asn Am. *Res:* Quasicon-formal mappings in n-space. *Mailing Add:* Dept of Math Wabash Col Crawfordsville IN 47933

WILSON, DAVID EVERETT, b Greenwich, Conn, May 27, 29; m 61; c 2. CELL PHYSIOLOGY, PROTOZOOLOGY. *Educ:* Univ Fla, BS, 61; Univ Calif, Los Angeles, PhD(zool), 66. *Prof Exp:* Technician, Fla State Plant Bd, 58-59; res asst protozool, Phelps Sanit Eng Lab, Univ Fla, 60-61 & Univ Calif, Los Angeles, 61-62; assoc prof biol, Cent Col, Iowa, 66-80. *Concurrent Pos:* NIH fel protozool, 66; NSF grant comput curric develop in biol sci, 70-72; chmn Conduit Biol Comt, 72-74. *Mem:* AAAS; Soc Protozool; Am Soc Zoologists. *Res:* Physiology and taxonomy of the Heliozoa; electrophysiology; physiology of meditation. *Mailing Add:* RR 4 Box 137-A Ottumwa IA 52501

WILSON, DAVID F, b Wray, Colo, Mar 28, 38; m 62. BIOCHEMISTRY. *Educ:* Colo State Univ, BS, 59; Ore State Univ, PhD(biochem), 64. *Prof Exp:* USPHS fel phys biochem, Johnson Res Found, 64-67, Pa Plan scholar, Sch Med, 67-69, res assoc, 67-68, asst prof, 68-72, assoc prof, 72-80, PROF BIOCHEM & BIOPHYS, MED SCH, UNIV PA, 80- *Honors & Awards:* Eli Lilly Award, Am Chem Soc, 71. *Mem:* Am Soc Biol Chemists; Biophys Soc. *Res:* Mitochondrial electron transport and energy conservation; cellular energy metabolism. *Mailing Add:* Dept of Biochem & Biophys Univ of Pa Med Sch Philadelphia PA 19104

WILSON, DAVID FRANKLIN, b Queens Village, NY, Feb 23, 41; m 65; c 3. NEUROPHYSIOLOGY. *Educ:* Hofstra Univ, BA, 63; Univ Del, MA, 66, PhD(biol sci), 68. *Prof Exp:* USPHS fel, Northwestern Univ, 68-69; from asst prof to assoc prof, 69-78, PROF ZOOL, MIAMI UNIV, 78- *Concurrent Pos:* USPHS grants, 70-72 & 73-75. *Mem:* Am Physiol Soc; Sigma Xi. *Res:* Examination of neuromuscular transmission using intracellular recording techniques. *Mailing Add:* Dept Zool Miami Univ Oxford OH 45056

WILSON, DAVID GEORGE, b Spokane, Wash, Dec 15, 19; m 42; c 3. RANGE CONSERVATION, RESEARCH ADMINISTRATION. *Educ:* Univ Idaho, BS, 47; Agr & Mech Col, Tex, MS, 50, PhD(range mgt), 61. *Prof Exp:* Dep fire warden, Clearwater Timber Protective Asn, 47; instr range mgt, Agr & Mech Col, Tex, 47-48, asst prof, 49-50; from instr to assoc prof range mgt & plants, Univ Ariz, 53-64; range consult, 64-65; res coordr, 65-76, ECOLOGIST/BOTANIST, US BUR LAND MGT, 76- *Mem:* Soc Range Mgt. *Res:* Natural resources. *Mailing Add:* US Bur Land Mgt Denver Fed Ctr Bldg 50 Denver CO 80225

WILSON, DAVID GEORGE, b St Catharines, Ont, Dec 3, 21; m 44; c 2. PLANT BIOCHEMISTRY. *Educ:* Univ Toronto, BA, 44; Queen's Univ, Ont, BA, 49, MA, 50; Univ Wis, PhD(biochem), 53. *Prof Exp:* Agr scientist, Conn Agr Exp Sta, 53-56; PROF BOT, UNIV WESTERN ONT, 56- *Mem:* AAAS; Am Soc Plant Physiol; Can Soc Plant Physiol. *Res:* Organic acids and amino acid metabolism in plants; biochemistry of cellulose and lignin degradation. *Mailing Add:* Dept of Plant Sci Univ of Western Ont London ON N6A 5B8 Can

WILSON, DAVID GORDON, b Sutton Coldfield, UK, Feb 11, 28; m 63; c 2. MECHANICAL ENGINEERING. *Educ:* Univ Birmingham, BSc, 48; Univ Nottingham, PhD(heat transfer), 53. *Prof Exp:* Sr res asst fluid mech & heat transfer, Univ Nottingham, 52-53; sr gas turbine engr, Brush Elec Eng Co, Ltd, UK, 53-55; Commonwealth Fund fel, Mass Inst Technol & Harvard Univ, 55-57; sr gas turbine designer, Ruston & Hornsby, Ltd, UK, 57-58; sr lectr thermodyn, fluid mech & mach design, Univ Ibadan, 58-60; tech dir, London Br, Northern Res & Eng Corp, 60-61, tech dir & vpres, Mass, 61-66; assoc prof thermodyn, dynamics & design, 66-71, PROF MECH ENG, MASS INST TECHNOL, 71- *Honors & Awards:* Hall Prize, Brit Inst Mech Engrs, 54, Weir Prize, 55. *Mem:* Am Soc Mech Engrs; Brit Inst Mech Engrs. *Res:* Heat transfer and fluid dynamics, especially with regard to turbomachinery; economic and design studies in solid-waste treatment, legislation and transportation and highway safety; solid-waste management; bicycling science; turbomachinery design. *Mailing Add:* Rm 3-447 Mass Inst of Technol Cambridge MA 02139

WILSON, DAVID J, b Ames, Iowa, June 25, 30; m 52; c 5. PHYSICAL CHEMISTRY. *Educ:* Stanford Univ, BS, 52; Calif Inst Technol, PhD(chem), 58. *Prof Exp:* From instr to prof chem, Univ Rochester, 57-69; PROF CHEM, VANDERBILT UNIV, 69-, PROF ENVIRON ENG, 77- *Concurrent Pos:* Alfred P Sloan fel, 64-66. *Mem:* Am Chem Soc; Am Phys Soc. *Res:* Energy transfer in gases; homogeneous gas reactions; pesticide and heavy metal residues; foam flotation; math modelling of unit operations in sanitary engineering. *Mailing Add:* Dept Chem Vanderbilt Univ Nashville TN 37235

WILSON, DAVID LOUIS, b Washington, DC, Jan 11, 43; m 67. NEUROSCIENCES, MOLECULAR BIOLOGY. *Educ:* Univ Md, College Park, BS, 64; Univ Chicago, PhD(biophys), 69. *Prof Exp:* Asst prof, 72-76, assoc prof, 76-81, PROF PHYSIOL & BIOPHYS, MED SCH, UNIV MIAMI, 81- *Concurrent Pos:* Helen Hay Whitney fel, Calif Inst Technol, 69-72; NIH grant, 72-74, 75-78, 78-81 & 80-85, NSF grant, 82-85. *Mem:* AAAS; Am Physiol Soc; Biophys Soc; Soc Neurosci; Am Soc Neurochem. *Res:* Protein synthesis in neurons; axonal transport; theoretical neuroscience; nerve regeneration. *Mailing Add:* Sch Med Univ Miami PO Box 016430 Miami FL 33101

WILSON, DAVID ORIN, b Portland, Ore, Apr 19, 37; m 56; c 3. SOIL MICROBIOLOGY, PLANT NUTRITION. *Educ:* Wash State Univ, BS, 59, MS, 63; Univ Calif, Davis, PhD(bact nutrit), 69. *Prof Exp:* Scientist, Soil Conserv Serv, USDA, Wash, 59-60 & Biol Lab, Hanford Labs, Gen Elec Co, 62-64; res assoc agron, Cornell Univ, 69-71; asst prof, 71-79, PROF, GA EXP STA, UNIV GA, 79- *Mem:* Am Soc Agron; Soil Sci Soc Am. *Res:* Microelement nutrition of plants and bacteria; symbiotic nitrogen fixation; rhizobial legume inoculants; soil microbial nitrogen transformations. *Mailing Add:* Dept of Agron Ga Exp Sta Univ of Ga Experiment GA 30212

WILSON, DONALD ALAN, b San Francisco, Calif, Sept 16, 30; m 57; c 3. BIOCHEMISTRY, MICROBIAL PHYSIOLOGY. *Educ:* San Jose State Col, BA, 59; Western Reserve Univ, PhD(microbiol), 65. *Prof Exp:* Fel microbiol, Pioneering Res Div, US Army Natick Labs, 65-66; assoc, 66-67, asst prof, 67-70, ASSOC PROF MICROBIOL, CHICAGO MED SCH, 70- *Res:* Microbial enzymology. *Mailing Add:* Dept of Microbiol Chicago Med Sch 3333 Greenbay Rd North Chicago IL 60064

WILSON, DONALD BENJAMIN, b Rowley, Alta, June 12, 25; m 48; c 4. FORAGE CROPS. *Educ:* Univ Alta, BSc, 50; Utah State Univ, MS, 54; Ore State Univ, PhD(farm crops), 60. *Prof Exp:* Res officer, 50-68, HEAD PLANT SCI SECT, AGR CAN RES STA, LETHBRIDGE, 68- *Concurrent Pos:* Coordr, Forage Crops, chmn, Expert Comt Forage Crops; actg dir, Res Sta, Lethbridge. *Mem:* Can Soc Agron; Agr Inst Can. *Res:* Forage crop production and animal grazing; management of irrigated pastures and administration of agricultural research. *Mailing Add:* Agr Can Res Sta Lethbridge AB T1S 4B1 Can

WILSON, DONALD BRUCE, b Monticello, Iowa, Nov 4, 33; m 56; c 4. CHEMICAL ENGINEERING. *Educ:* Univ NMex, BS, 56; Princeton Univ, MA, 63, PhD(chem eng), 65. *Prof Exp:* Engr, Phillips Petrol Co, 59-61; assoc prof, 64-75, PROF CHEM ENG, N MEX STATE UNIV, 75- *Res:* Macroscopic crystallization; design and optimization; thermodynamics of phase transformations. *Mailing Add:* Dept of Chem Eng NMex State Univ Las Cruces NM 88001

WILSON, DONALD LAURENCE, b Hamilton, Ont, Oct 2, 21; m 45; c 6. MEDICINE. *Educ:* Queen's Univ, Ont, MD, CM, 44; Univ Toronto, MA, 48; FRCP(C), 51. *Prof Exp:* From asst prof to assoc prof, 52-67, PROF MED, QUEEN'S UNIV, ONT, 67-, HEAD, DEPT MED, 76- *Concurrent Pos:* Attend physician, Kingston Gen Hosp, 52-; pres, Coun Col Physicians & Surgeons, Ont, 65-66; pres, Ont Med Asn, 73-74. *Mem:* Endocrine Soc; Am Diabetes Asn; NY Acad Sci; Can Soc Clin Invest; Can Med Asn (pres, 79-80). *Res:* Endocrinology and diseases of metabolism. *Mailing Add:* Dept of Med Queen's Univ Kingston ON K7L 3N6 Can

WILSON, DONALD RICHARD, b Plaistow, NH, Feb 8, 36; m 56; c 3. ORGANIC CHEMISTRY, POLYMER CHEMISTRY. *Educ:* Univ Wash, BS, 58; Univ Calif, Los Angeles, PhD(org chem), 62. *Prof Exp:* Mgr control lab, Am Marietta Co, Wash, 57-58; from res chemist to sr res chemist, E I du Pont de Nemours & Co, Inc, Del, 61-67; sr scientist, Xerox Corp, Webster, 67, res mgr org & polymer chem, 68, develop mgr org & polymer mat, 68-70, technol prog mgr advan xerography, 70-71, prin scientist xerographic mat, 71-72, mgr explor graphic sci, 72-75; RES DIR CHEM & CATALYSIS, CELANESE RES CO, 75- *Mem:* Am Chem Soc. *Res:* Organic and polymer synthesis-reaction mechanisms; stereochemistry; organometallics; textile fiber chemistry; high temperature fibers; xerography; xerographic imaging materials; triboelectricity. *Mailing Add:* Celanese Res Co PO Box 1000 Summit NJ 07901

WILSON, DORIS BURDA, b Cleveland, Ohio, July 1, 37; m 68. ANATOMY, EMBRYOLOGY. *Educ:* Ohio Wesleyan Univ, BA, 59; Radcliffe Col, MA, 60; Harvard Univ, PhD(biol), 63. *Prof Exp:* Teaching fel biol, Harvard Univ, 60-62; asst prof zool, San Diego State Col, 63-65; asst prof anat, Sch Med, Stanford Univ, 65-69; res anatomist & lectr, Sch Med, Univ Calif, San Diego, 69-73; assoc prof anat, Sch Med, Univ Calif, Davis, 73-75; assoc prof surg/anat, 75-77, PROF SURG/ANAT, SCH MED, UNIV CALIF, SAN DIEGO, 77- *Concurrent Pos:* Fulbright vis prof, Taiwan, 70-71. *Mem:* AAAS; Histochem Soc; Teratology Soc; Am Soc Zool; Am Asn Anat. *Res:* Developmental biology; neuroembryology; teratology. *Mailing Add:* Dept of Surg/Anat M-004 Univ of Calif San Diego La Jolla CA 92093

WILSON, DWIGHT ELLIOTT, JR, b Greensburg, Pa, June 7, 32; m 53; c 4. GENETICS. *Educ:* Yale Univ, BS, 53, PhD(biophys), 56. *Prof Exp:* From asst prof to assoc prof, 56-68, PROF BIOL, RENSSELAER POLYTECH INST, 68- *Concurrent Pos:* NIH fel, 66-67. *Mem:* Am Soc Human Genetics; Am Soc Microbiol. *Res:* Somatic cell genetics. *Mailing Add:* Dept of Biol Rensselaer Polytech Inst Troy NY 12181

WILSON, EDGAR BRIGHT, b Gallatin, Tenn, Dec 18, 08; m 35 & 55; c 6. CHEMICAL PHYSICS. *Educ:* Princeton Univ, BS, 30, AM, 31; Calif Inst Technol, PhD(phys chem), 33; Harvard Univ, MA, 36. *Hon Degrees:* Dr, Free Univ Brussels, 75, Dickinson Col & Univ Bologna, 76, Columbia Univ, 79 & Princeton Univ, 81. *Prof Exp:* Fel, Calif Inst Technol, 33-34; jr fel, 34-36, from asst prof to prof, 36-48, Richards prof chem, 48-79, EMER PROF CHEM, HARVARD UNIV, 79- *Concurrent Pos:* Res dir, Underwater Explosives Res Lab, Woods Hole, 42-44; res dir, Weapons Systs Eval Group, 52-53; hon trustee, Woods Hole Oceanog Inst. *Honors & Awards:* Prize, Am Chem Soc, 37; Debye Award, Am Chem Soc, 62, Norris Award, 66, G N Lewis Award, Calif Sect, Pauling Award, 72; Rumford Medal, Am Acad Arts & Sci, 73; Nat Medal of Sci, 75; Feltrinelli Award, Rome, 76; Ferst Award, Sigma Xi, 77; Pittsburgh Spectros Conf Award, 77; Plyler Award, Am Phys Soc, 78; Richards Medal, NE Sect Am Chem Soc, 78; Welch Found Award, 78. *Mem:* Nat Acad Sci; Am Chem Soc; fel Am Phys Soc; Am Acad Arts & Sci; Int Acad Quantum Molecular Sci. *Res:* Quantum mechanics in chemistry; molecular dynamics; microwave spectroscopy. *Mailing Add:* Harvard Chem Labs 12 Oxford St Cambridge MA 02138

WILSON, EDMOND WOODROW, JR, b Selma, Ala, Jan 18, 40; m 65; c 1. PHYSICAL CHEMISTRY. *Educ:* Auburn Univ, BS, 62; Univ Ala, Tuscaloosa, MS, 65, PhD(phys chem), 68. *Prof Exp:* Temporary instr gen chem, Univ Ala, Tuscaloosa, 66-68; res assoc biophys chem, Univ Va, 68-70; asst prof, 70-73, assoc prof, 73-79, PROF PHYS CHEM, HARDING UNIV, 79- *Concurrent Pos:* Vis assoc prof, Okla State Univ, 77. *Mem:* Am Chem Soc; Calorimetry Conf; Sigma Xi. *Res:* Calorimetry and spectroscopy of biological molecules containing transition metal ions. *Mailing Add:* Dept of Phys Sci Harding Univ Searcy AR 72134

WILSON, EDWARD BRUCE, b London, Ont, Aug 16, 16; m 42; c 4. MINING ENGINEERING, OPERATIONS RESEARCH. *Educ:* Univ Toronto, BASc, 40; Queen's Univ, Ont, MSc, 65. *Prof Exp:* Contract engr, Hollinger Consol Gold Mines Ltd, Timmins, Ont, 46-51, standards engr, 51-55, budget analyst, 55-57; chief indust eng, Denison Mines Ltd, Elliot Lake, 57-62; instr mining eng, Univ Toronto, 63-64; from lectr to asst prof, 64-68, assoc prof, 68-79, prof, 79-81, EMER PROF MINING ENG, QUEEN'S UNIV, ONT, 81- *Mem:* Can Inst Mining & Metall; Am Inst Mining, Metall & Petrol Engrs Soc Mining Engrs. *Res:* Reliability theory and replacement theory applications in heavy industry; computer graphics in mining; haulage system studies by Monte Carlo simulation using general purpose simulation system V. *Mailing Add:* Dept of Mining Eng Goodwin Hall Queen's Univ Kingston ON K7L 3N6 Can

WILSON, EDWARD CARL, b Daytona Beach, Fla, Jan 25, 29. INVERTEBRATE PALEONTOLOGY. *Educ:* Univ Calif, Berkeley, BA, 58, MA, 60, PhD(paleont), 67. *Prof Exp:* Cur paleont & chmn div invert, Natural Hist Mus San Diego, 64-67; CUR INVERT PALEONT, LOS ANGELES COUNTY MUS NATURAL HIST, 67- *Mem:* Paleont Soc; Brit Paleont Asn. *Res:* Late Paleozoic corals. *Mailing Add:* Los Angeles Count Mus Natural Hist 900 Exposition Blvd Los Angeles CA 90007

WILSON, EDWARD MATTHEW, b Content, Jamaica, Dec 19, 37; m 62; c 2. DAIRY SCIENCE. *Educ:* McGill Univ, BScAgr, 64, MSc, 66; Ohio State Univ, PhD(dairy sci), 69. *Prof Exp:* Res asst animal genetics, McGill Univ, 64-66; res assoc dairy sci, Ohio State Univ, 66-69; asst prof animal sci, Tuskegee Inst, 69-73; prin physiologist, Coop State Res Serv, USDA, 73-74; DEAN, COOP RES & HEAD, DEPT AGR & NATURAL RESOURCES, LINCOLN UNIV, 74-, DEAN, COL APPL SCI & TECHNOL, 78- *Concurrent Pos:* Mem, Task Force to Repub SAfrica, 74; mem, US Agr Educ Team, Peoples Repub China, 80. *Mem:* Am Dairy Sci Asn. *Res:* Genetic polymorphisms of bovine blood and milk proteins; immunological properties of seminal proteins and their implications in the reproductive process. *Mailing Add:* Dept of Agr & Natural Resources Lincoln Univ Jefferson City MO 65101

WILSON, EDWARD OSBORNE, b Birmingham, Ala, June 10, 29; m 55; c 1. BEHAVIORAL BIOLOGY, EVOLUTIONARY BIOLOGY. *Educ:* Univ Ala, BS, 49, MS, 50; Harvard Univ, PhD(biol), 55; Duke Univ & Grinnell Col, DSc Hons, 78. *Hon Degrees:* DSc, Duke Univ, Grinnell Col, Lawrence Univ, Univ WFla; LHD, Univ Ala. *Prof Exp:* Biologist, State Dept Conserv, Ala, 49; Soc Fels jr fel, 53-56, from asst prof to prof zool, 56-77, FRANK B

BAIRD, JR, PROF SCI, HARVARD UNIV, 77- *Concurrent Pos:* Mem expeds, WIndies & Mex, 53, New Caledonia, 54, Australia & New Guinea, 55, Ceylon, 55 & Surinam, 61; Charles and Martha Hitchcock Prof, Univ Calif, Berkeley, 72; John Simon Guggenheim fel, 77. *Honors & Awards:* Cleveland Prize, AAAS, 67; Mercer Award, Ecol Soc Am, 71; Founders' Mem Award, Entom Soc Am, 72; Nat Med of Sci, 76; Leidy Medal, 78; Carr Medal, 78. *Mem:* Nat Acad Sci; fel Am Acad Arts & Sci; fel Am Philos Soc; Soc Study Evolution (pres, 73); Am Genetic Asn. *Res:* Classification, ecology and behavior of ants; speciation; general sociobiology; chemical communication in animals; biogeography. *Mailing Add:* Mus Comp Zool Harvard Univ Cambridge MA 02138

WILSON, ELWOOD JUSTIN, JR, b New York, NY, Nov 28, 17; m 41; c 4. ORGANIC CHEMISTRY. *Educ:* Princeton Univ, AB, 38, MA, 40, PhD(chem), 41. *Prof Exp:* Corn Industs Res Found fel, NIH, 41-42; proj engr, Sperry Gyroscope Co, NY, 42-44; sr chemist, Exp, Inc, 46-47, secy, 47-49, vpres, 49-54; res dir, Detroit Controls Co, 54-59; pres, Adv Tech Labs Div, Am Radiator & Stand Sanit Corp, 59-64; PRES, E J WILSON ASSOCS, INC, 64-; PRES, EPOXON PRODS, INC, 71- *Concurrent Pos:* Vpres, Flight Res, Inc, 53-54; chmn & dir, Data Cartridge, Inc, 65-67. *Mem:* AAAS; Am Chem Soc. *Res:* Proteins; carbohydrates; fuels; combustion; synthetic organic chemistry; interior ballistics; rockets; petrochemicals; aerospace instruments; nuclear reactors; general and technical management; building materials. *Mailing Add:* 1125 Westridge Dr Portola Valley CA 94025

WILSON, ERIC LEROY, b Sharon, Pa, Mar 17, 35; m 59; c 2. MATHEMATICS. *Educ:* Westminster Col, Pa, BS, 57; Vanderbilt Univ, PhD(math), 66. *Prof Exp:* From instr to asst prof, 62-70, chmn dept, 73-76, assoc prof, 70-80, PROF MATH, WITTENBERG UNIV, 80- *Concurrent Pos:* Asst prof, Univ of the South, 67-68. *Mem:* Math Asn Am; Nat Speleol Soc. *Res:* Loop isotopy; graph theory. *Mailing Add:* Dept of Math Wittenberg Univ Springfield OH 45501

WILSON, EUGENE M, b Buckhannon, WVa, May 4, 28; m 51; c 2. PLANT PATHOLOGY. *Educ:* Univ WVa, BS, 51, MS, 54; Univ Calif, PhD(plant path), 58. *Prof Exp:* Asst plant path, Univ WVa, 51 & Univ Calif, 54-58; plant pathologist, Cent Res Lab, United Fruit Co, Mass, 58-60; technologist, Shell Chem Co, 60-72; plant pathologist pesticide regulation, 72-73, chief plant path sect, Off Pesticide Progs, 73-74, PROD MGR, US ENVIRON PROTECTION AGENCY, 74- *Mem:* Am Phytopath Soc. *Res:* Physiology of fungi; plant disease control; host parasite relationship; biological control of plant pests. *Mailing Add:* 5 De Forest Ave New City NY 10956

WILSON, EUGENE MADISON, b Cheyenne, Wyo, July 25, 43; m 65; c 3. CIVIL ENGINEERING. *Educ:* Univ Wyo, BS, 65, MS, 66; Ariz State Univ, PhD(civil eng, transp), 72. *Prof Exp:* Petrol engr, Texaco, Inc, 66-67; instr civil eng & staff asst transp, Ariz State Univ, 68-69; transp planner, Ariz Hwy Dept, 69-70; asst prof civil eng & res assoc transp, Univ Iowa, 70-74; assoc prof, 74-79, PROF CIVIL ENG, UNIV WYO, 79- *Concurrent Pos:* Mem, Transp Res Bd, Nat Acad Sci-Nat Res Coun. *Mem:* Am Soc Civil Engrs; Am Inst Planners; Inst Traffic Engrs. *Res:* Urban transportation planning; traffic assignment; public transportation planning; behavioral and sensitivity studies in transportation planning. *Mailing Add:* 1667 N 15th St Laramie WY 82070

WILSON, EVELYN H, b Philadelphia, Pa, Oct 8, 21; m 43; c 2. ORGANIC CHEMISTRY. *Educ:* Bryn Mawr Col, AB, 42; Radcliffe Col, AM, 44, PhD(org chem), 46. *Prof Exp:* Res chemist, Merck & Co, Inc, 46-53; sr scientist, Johnson & Johnson, 53-59; lectr chem, Westfield Sr High Sch, NJ, 49-65; sci supvr, New Brunswick Pub Schs, 65-67; assoc prof sci educ, 67-72, PROF SCI EDUC & ASSOC V PRES PROG DEVELOP & BUDGETING, RUTGERS UNIV, NEW BRUNSWICK, 72- *Res:* Educational planning and administration; philosophy of science; science education. *Mailing Add:* Off of Prog Develop & Budgeting Rutgers Univ Old Queens Campus New Brunswick NJ 08903

WILSON, EVERETT D, b Covington, Ind, July 13, 28; m 50; c 4. PHYSIOLOGY, ENDOCRINOLOGY. *Educ:* Ind State Teachers Col, BS, 50, MS, 51; Purdue Univ, PhD(physiol, endocrinol), 60. *Prof Exp:* Teacher pub sch, Ind, 48-50 & 55-56, supvr, 56-57; asst biol, Purdue Univ, 57-58, res asst, 58-60; asst prof zool, Southern Ill Univ, 60-61; assoc prof, 62-64, PROF, SAM HOUSTON STATE UNIV, 64- DEAN COL SCI, 65- *Concurrent Pos:* Lalor res fel, 61; NATO fel, Nat Med Res Inst, 62; chief, Grants Br Pop & Reproduction Ctr, Nat Inst Child Health, NIH, 71-72; adv, Oak Ridge Pop Res Inst, 72-74. *Mem:* Am Soc Zoologists; Endocrine Soc; Am Soc Animal Sci; Brit Soc Study Fertil. *Res:* Factors affecting mammalian reproduction. *Mailing Add:* Col of Sci Sam Houston State Univ Huntsville TX 77340

WILSON, F WESLEY, JR, b Washington, DC, Apr 22, 39. MATHEMATICS. *Educ:* Univ Md, College Park, BS, 61, PhD(math), 64. *Prof Exp:* Res assoc math, Div Appl Math, Brown Univ, 64-66; asst prof, Univ Mich, Ann Arbor, 66-67; asst prof, 67-69, assoc prof, 69-80, PROF MATH, UNIV COLO, BOULDER, 80- *Concurrent Pos:* Vis assoc prof, Univ Md, College Park, 70-71. *Mem:* Am Math Soc. *Res:* Applications of differential topology to problems of nonlinear ordinary differential equations; analytical problems in differential topology; numerical methods for solving differential equations, multidimensional interpolation and applications in meteorology and geophysical data analysis. *Mailing Add:* Dept of Math Univ of Colo Boulder CO 80309

WILSON, FLOYD DEE, experimental pathology, hematology, see previous edition

WILSON, FOREST RAY, II, b Wichita Falls, Tex, Aug 1, 41. HUMAN PHYSIOLOGY, COMPARATIVE ANIMAL PHYSIOLOGY. *Educ:* Tex Wesleyan Col, BA, 66; Tex Christian Univ, MS, 69; Univ Ill, PhD(physiol), 73. *Prof Exp:* asst prof, 73-80, ASSOC PROF PHYSIOL, BAYLOR UNIV, 80- *Concurrent Pos:* Prin investr, Monsanto Found Cancer Res grant, 77- *Mem:* AAAS; Am Zool Soc; Sigma Xi; Isozyme Soc. *Res:* Effects of hyperbaric hydrogen and antihormones on cancer; many physiological problems faced by man including prostaglandins, extra-renal sites of erythropoietin production, lethality of megadoses of vitamines; molecular mechanisms of temperature acclimation in poikilotherms. *Mailing Add:* Dept of Biol Baylor Univ Waco TX 76703

WILSON, FRANK B, b Detroit, Mich, Jan 8, 29; m 50; c 7. SPEECH, AUDIOLOGY. *Educ:* Bowling Green Univ, BS, 50; Northwestern Univ, PhD, 56. *Prof Exp:* Speech & hearing clinician, Cerebral Palsy Ctr, Ohio, 51-53, actg dir, 52-53; res asst, Lang Inst, Northwestern Univ, 55-57; asst prof speech, St Louis Univ, 57-59; coordr speech & hearing, Spec Dist for Educ & Training Handicapped Children, St Louis County, Mo, 59-65; dir div speech path, Dept Otolaryngol, Jewish Hosp St Louis, Mo, 66-72; dir res, Spec Sch Dist St Louis County, 73-77; PROF & DEAN REHAB MED, UNIV ALTA, 77- *Concurrent Pos:* Consult, US Off Res, 63-; assoc prof, Wash Univ, 68. *Mem:* Fel Am Speech & Hearing Asn; Am Cleft Palate Asn. *Res:* Articulatory behavior of the retarded child and the efficacy of speech therapy; hearing deviation among orthopedically handicapped children; basis of nonorganic articulation disorders in children; voice disorders in school-age children. *Mailing Add:* Dept of Rehab Med Univ of Alta Edmonton AB T6G 2E1 Can

WILSON, FRANK CHARLES, b Ironwood, Mich, June 29, 27; m 50; c 3. POLYMER CHEMISTRY, X-RAY CRYSTALLOGRAPHY. *Educ:* Ripon Col, AB, 52; Mass Inst Technol, BS, 52, PhD(phys chem), 57. *Prof Exp:* SR RES CHEMIST POLYMERS, PLASTIC PROD & RESINS DEPT, E I DU PONT DE NEMOURS & CO, INC, 57- *Mem:* Am Chem Soc; Am Crystallog Asn. *Res:* Structure and morphology of polymers and polymer blends by wide-angle and small-angle x-ray diffraction techniques. *Mailing Add:* Plastic Prod & Resins Dept Du Pont Exp Sta Bldg 323 Wilmington DE 19898

WILSON, FRANK CRANE, b Rome, Ga, Dec 29, 29; m 51; c 3. MEDICINE, ORTHOPEDIC SURGERY. *Educ:* Vanderbilt Univ, AB, 50; Med Col Ga, MD, 54; Am Bd Orthop Surg, dipl, 67. *Prof Exp:* Instr orthop surg, Columbia Univ, 63; from instr to assoc prof, 64-71, PROF ORTHOP SURG, SCH MED, UNIV NC, CHAPEL HILL, 71- *Concurrent Pos:* Markle scholar, 66-71; consult, Watts Hosp, Durham, NC, 65-; chief div orthop surg, NC Mem Hosp, 67- *Honors & Awards:* Nicholar Andry Award, 72. *Mem:* AAAS; Am Col Surg; Asn Am Med Col; Am Acad Orthop Surgeons; Am Orthop Asn. *Res:* Trauma; infections of bones and joints; rheumatoid arthritis. *Mailing Add:* Div Orthop Surg NC Mem Hosp Chapel Hill NC 27514

WILSON, FRANK DOUGLAS, b Salt Lake City, Utah, Dec 17, 28; m 50; c 8. PLANT GENETICS. *Educ:* Univ Utah, BS, 50, MS, 53; Wash State Univ, PhD(bot), 57. *Prof Exp:* Asst biol & genetics, Univ Utah, 51-53; asst bot, Wash State Univ, 53-56, asst agron, 56, jr animal scientist, 56-57; PLANT GENETICIST, WESTERN COTTON RES LAB, AGR RES SERV, USDA, 57- *Concurrent Pos:* Consult, Agron Exp Sta, Int Coop Admin, Cuba, 59- *Mem:* AAAS; Crop Sci Soc Am; Asn Taxon Study Trop African Flora. *Res:* Insect resistance in cotton; taxonomy of Hibiscus section Furcaria. *Mailing Add:* Western Cotton Res Lab 4135 E Broadway Phoenix AZ 85040

WILSON, FRANK JOSEPH, b Pittsburgh, Pa; c 2. ANATOMY, CELL BIOLOGY. *Educ:* St Vincent Col, BA, 64; Univ Pittsburgh, PhD(anat, cell biol), 69. *Prof Exp:* Muscular Dystrophy Asn fel, Univ Birmingham, 70-72; asst prof anat, 72-78, ASSOC PROF ANAT, RUTGERS MED SCH, COL MED & DENT NJ, 78- *Mem:* Am Asn Anatomists; AAAS; Am Soc Zoologists. *Res:* Immunochemistry and biochemistry of the contractile proteins. *Mailing Add:* Dept Anat Rutgers Med Sch Piscataway NJ 08854

WILSON, FREDDIE ELTON, b Lenexa, Kans, Dec 23, 37; m 61; c 1. ENDOCRINOLOGY. *Educ:* Univ Kans, BA, 58, MA, 60; Wash State Univ, PhD(zoophysiol), 65. *Prof Exp:* Instr biol, Lewis & Clark Col, 60-61; asst prof zool, 65-71, ASSOC PROF BIOL, KANS STATE UNIV, 71- *Concurrent Pos:* Physiologist, Agr Exp Sta, Kans State Univ, 65-79; consult, Oak Ridge Grad Sch Biomed Sci, Univ Tenn, 78. *Mem:* AAAS; Am Soc Zoologists; Coun Biol Ed; Int Soc Neuroendrocinol; fel AAAS. *Res:* Avian reproductive physiology; neuroendocrine control of annual reproductive cycles; photoperiodism. *Mailing Add:* Div of Biol Kans State Univ Manhattan KS 66506

WILSON, FREDERICK ALBERT, b Boston, Mass, May 5, 28. FIELD GEOLOGY, GEOPHYSICS. *Educ:* Brooklyn Col, BA, 66, MA, 70; George Washington Univ, PhD(geol), 81. *Prof Exp:* Lectr earth sci, Brooklyn Col, 68 & mineral field geol, York Col, City Univ New York, 70-71; geologist, US Geol Surv, 72-81; ASST PROF MINERAL PETROL & FIELD GEOL, HOWARD UNIV, 81- *Concurrent Pos:* Lectr, Howard Univ, 72, Washington Tech Inst, 76 & Howard Univ, 80-81. *Mem:* Am Geophys Union; Geol Soc Am; Asn Geoscientists Intern Develop. *Res:* Exploration geophysical methods of aeroradioactivity, aeromagnetics and gravity to interpret geology in deeply weathered complex terrains; Caribbean geology. *Mailing Add:* Dept Geol & Geog Howard Univ Washington DC 20059

WILSON, FREDERICK ALLEN, b Winchester, Mass, Aug 22, 37; m 62; c 2. GASTROENTEROLOGY. *Educ:* Colgate Univ, Hamilton, NY, 59; Albany Med Col, NY, MD, 63. *Prof Exp:* Intern med, Hartford Hosp, Conn, 63-64, residency, 64-66; fel gastroenterol, Albany Med Col, NY, 66-67; chief gastroenterol, US Army Hosp, Ft Jackson, SC, 67-69; fel gastroenterol, Southwestern Med Sch, Univ Tex, Dallas, 69-72; asst prof med, Vanderbilt Univ, Nashville, 72-76, assoc prof, 76-82; PROF MED, MILTON S HERSHEY MED CTR, PA STATE UNIV, HERSHEY, 82- *Mem:* Am Gastroenterol Asn; Am Fedn Clin Res; Am Asn Study Liver Dis; Am Soc Clin Invest. *Res:* Gastroenterology involving the cellular and subcellular aspects of bile acid intestinal transport. *Mailing Add:* Div Gastroenterol Milton S Hershey Med Ctr Pa State Univ Hershey PA 17033

WILSON, FREDERICK SUTPHEN, b Trenton, NJ, Feb 12, 27; m 50; c 3. FAMILY MEDICINE. *Educ:* Dickinson Col, ScB, 48; Thomas Jefferson Univ, MD, 53. *Prof Exp:* Dir clin invest, McNeil Labs, 69-71, dir med serv, 71-74; ASST PROF COMMUNITY MED, MED CTR, TEMPLE UNIV, 74- *Concurrent Pos:* Physician-in-chief & dir family pract ctr/family pract residency prog, Abington Mem Hosp, 74-; med dir, William H Rorea, Inc, 76- *Mailing Add:* 1338 Jercho Rd Abington PA 19001

WILSON, GARY AUGUST, b Chicago, Ill, Dec 13, 42; m 65; c 1. MOLECULAR GENETICS, MICROBIOLOGY. *Educ:* Ill State Univ, Normal, BS, 65; Univ Chicago, MS, 68, PhD(microbiol), 70. *Prof Exp:* Fel, Sch Med, Univ Rochester, 70-72, from instr to asst prof microbiol, 72-78, assoc prof, 78-80. *Concurrent Pos:* Am Cancer Soc res grant, 72-, fac res award, 79; vis asst prof, Inst Gulbenkian de Ciencia, Portugal, 74, vis prof, 76. *Mem:* Am Soc Microbiol; AAAS; Sigma Xi. *Res:* DNA mediated transformation in Bacillus subtilis; restriction endonucleases; gene cloning. *Mailing Add:* 54401 Susquehanna Rd Elkhart IN 46514

WILSON, GEOFFREY LEONARD, b London, Eng, Oct 26, 24; nat US; m 55; c 2. ACOUSTICS. *Educ:* Oxford Univ, BA, 45, MSc, & MA, 49; Loughborough Univ, PhD, 75. *Prof Exp:* Sci off, Royal Naval Sci Serv, Brit Admiralty, Clarendon Lab, Oxford Univ, 44-48, H M Underwater Detection Estab, 48-51 & Torpedo Exp Estab, 52-53; design engr, Can Westinghouse Co, Ont, 53-59; asst prof, 59-65, ASSOC PROF ENG RES, PA STATE UNIV, 65- *Concurrent Pos:* Vis res fel, Loughborough Univ Technol, Eng, 68-69; mem, Grad Fac Acoust, Pa State Univ, 75-; vis scientist, Inst Nat Sci Appliquees, Lyon, France, 82. *Mem:* Acoust Soc Am; fel Audio Eng Soc; sr mem Inst Elec & Electronics Engrs; fel Brit Inst Elec Engrs; fel Brit Inst Acoust. *Res:* Acoustics, especially underwater acoustics and transducer and array design. *Mailing Add:* Appl Res Lab Pa State Univ Box 30 State College PA 16801

WILSON, GEORGE PORTER, III, b Flint, Mich, Nov 10, 27; c 4. VETERINARY SURGERY, IMMUNOLOGY. *Educ:* Univ Ill, BS, 51; Univ Pa, VMD, 55; Ohio State Univ, MSc, 59. *Prof Exp:* Intern vet med, Angell Mem Animal Hosp, 55-56; from instr to assoc prof, 56-69, PROF VET CLIN SCI, COL VET MED, OHIO STATE UNIV, 69-; PROF MICROBIOL, COL BIOL SCI, 67- *Concurrent Pos:* Ohio State Univ Develop Fund grant, 67-; Mark Morris Found grant, 68; Am Cancer Soc instnl grant, 68-69; vis scientist, Nat Cancer Inst, Environ Epidemiol Br, 78 & Armed Forces Inst Path, 79. *Mem:* AAAS; Am Vet Med Asn; Am Col Vet Surg; NY Acad Sci. *Res:* Veterinary surgery, especially cancer research as related to immunology and epidemiology. *Mailing Add:* 1935 Coffey Rd Columbus OH 43210

WILSON, GEORGE RODGER, b Commercial Point, Ohio, July 10, 23; m 46; c 4. AGRICULTURE, ANIMAL SCIENCE. *Educ:* Ohio State Univ, BS, 48, MS, 56, PhD(animal sci), 63. *Prof Exp:* County agent, Butler County, Ohio, 48-54; from asst prof to assoc prof, 54-72, PROF ANIMAL SCI, OHIO STATE UNIV, 72- *Mem:* Am Soc Animal Sci. *Res:* Animal breeding, physiology and production. *Mailing Add:* Dept of Animal Sci Ohio State Univ Columbus OH 43210

WILSON, GEORGE SPENCER, b Bronxville, NY, May 23, 39; m 64. ANALYTICAL CHEMISTRY. *Educ:* Princeton Univ, BA, 61; Univ Ill, MS, 63, PhD, 65. *Prof Exp:* NIH fel, Univ Ill, 65-66, instr, 66-67; asst prof, 67-72, assoc prof, 72-80, PROF CHEM, UNIV ARIZ, 80- *Res:* Analytical applications of biochemical reactions; electrochemical synthesis of unusual or unstable products; oxidation-reduction and acid-base reactions in nonaqueous solvents; development of computer-controlled instrumentation. *Mailing Add:* Dept of Chem Univ of Ariz Tucson AZ 85721

WILSON, GERALD GENE, b Blue Hill, Nebr, Mar 18, 28; m 52; c 4. CHEMICAL ENGINEERING, GAS TECHNOLOGY. *Educ:* Univ Kans, BS, 49; Ill Inst Technol, MS & MGas Tech, 51. *Prof Exp:* Engr, North Shore Gas Co, 51-55; assoc chem engr, Inst Gas Technol, 55-56, supvr dist res, 56-60, sr dist engr, 60-63, coordr indust educ, 63-65, mgr indust educ, 65-69, asst dir educ, 69-77, DIR INDUST EDUC, ILL INST TECHNOL, 77- *Concurrent Pos:* Mem subcomt on distribution design & develop, Oper Sect, Am Gas Asn, 62- *Honors & Awards:* Award of Merit, Am Gas Asn, 66. *Mem:* Am Soc Eng Educ; Nat Asn Corrosion Engrs. *Res:* Internal pipeline coatings; sealants for cast iron bell joints; gas industry leak control technology; techniques for solution of network flow problems; pipeline flow behavior; engineering economics. *Mailing Add:* Inst Gas Technol 3424 S State St Chicago IL 60616

WILSON, GERALD LOOMIS, b Springfield, Mass, Apr 29, 39; m 58; c 3. ELECTRICAL ENGINEERING. *Educ:* Mass Inst Technol, SB, 61, SM, 63, ScD(mech eng & magnetohydrodynamics), 65. *Prof Exp:* From asst prof elec eng to assoc prof, 65-75, DIR ELEC POWER SYSTS ENG LAB, MASS INST TECHNOL, 75- *Concurrent Pos:* Ford Found fel, 65-66; consult, Dynatech Corp, 65-66 & Am Elec Power Serv Corp, Mass, 66-67. *Mem:* Inst Elec & Electronics Engrs. *Res:* Magnetohydrodynamic energy conversion; electrohydrodynamics; electromechanics; electric power engineering. *Mailing Add:* Elec Power Systs Eng Lab Mass Inst of Technol Cambridge MA 02139

WILSON, GLENN RHODES, b Altamont, Ill, Nov 10, 21. ORGANIC CHEMISTRY, BIOCHEMISTRY. *Educ:* Univ Ill, BS, 43; Univ Iowa, PhD(org chem), 51. *Prof Exp:* Res chemist, Res Labs, Ethyl Corp, Mich, 51-54 & Nat Cylinder Gas Co, Ill, 54-55; sr res engr, Sci Lab, Ford Motor Co, Mich, 54-59; scientist, Monsanto Res Corp, Mass, 59-65 & Dayton Lab, Ohio, 65-72; scientist, Monsanto Textile Co, 72-78; SCIENTIST, MONSANTO CHEM INTERMEDIATES CO, 78- *Mem:* AAAS; Am Chem Soc; NY Acad Sci. *Res:* Fatty alcohols; lubricants; organosilicon and polymer chemistry. *Mailing Add:* 12034 Charter House Lane St Louis MO 63141

WILSON, GOLDER NORTH, b Frederick, Okla, Oct 29, 44; m 67; c 2. BIOCHEMISTRY, GENETICS. *Educ:* Univ Ill, BS, 66; Univ Chicago, PhD(biochem), 70, MD, 72. *Prof Exp:* Intern pediat, New Eng Med Ctr, 72-73; res assoc hematol, NIH, 73-75; resident pediat, 75-76, fel, 76-77, ASST PROF PEDIAT, UNIV MICH, ANN ARBOR, 77- *Res:* Human DNA, its structure and transcription. *Mailing Add:* Holden K2015 Univ Hosp Univ of Mich Ann Arbor MI 48109

WILSON, GORDON, JR, b Bowling Green, Ky, Sept 13, 25; m 53; c 2. ORGANIC CHEMISTRY. *Educ:* Western Ky State Col, BS, 47; Univ Ky, MS, 49; Purdue Univ, PhD(org chem), 58. *Prof Exp:* Instr chem, Univ Minn, Duluth, 49-54; res chemist, Dow Chem Co, 57-61; assoc prof, 61-65, head, Dept Chem, 65-78, PROF CHEM, WESTERN KY UNIV, 65- *Mem:* AAAS; Am Chem Soc. *Res:* Organic fluorine compounds; polymer chemistry, especially polyelectrolytes. *Mailing Add:* Dept of Chem Western Ky Univ Bowling Green KY 42101

WILSON, GREGORY BRUCE, b Columbus, Ohio, Oct 15, 48. CELLULAR IMMUNOLOGY, INBORN ERRORS OF METABOLISM. *Educ:* Univ Calif Los Angeles, BA, 71, PhD(biol-cell biol & immunol), 74. *Prof Exp:* Res asst, Dept Biol, Univ Calif Los Angeles, 72, Dept Microbiol & Immunol, 72-73, Dept Biol, 73-74, res fel, 74; res fel, dept med, Univ Calif San Francisco, 74-75; assoc, 75-76, asst prof, 76-79, ASSOC PROF IMMUNOL, DEPT BASIC & CLIN IMMUNOL & MICROBIOL, MED UNIV SC, 79-, ASSOC PROF PEDIAT, 82- *Concurrent Pos:* Mem, Grad Educ Comt, Med Univ SC, 78-, Molecular, Cellular Biol & Pathobiol Fac, 79-, Univ Grad Fac, 76-; mem, Combined Fed Campaign, Nat Health Agencies, 80-, Subcomt Pub Info, 81; chmn, Med & Sci Adv Comt, Cystic Fibrosis Found, 79-80, vchmn, 80-82, comt mem, 82-, bd dirs, 79-, Five Year Plan Comt, 80, Patient Serv Comt, 80, 81 & Speaker Bur Comt, 80, 81; Basil O'Connor grant award, Nat Found March Dimes, 76-79; res fel, Nat Cystic Fibrosis Found, 74-76. *Mem:* AAAS; Sigma Xi; Soc Exp Biol & Med; Reticuloendothelial Soc; NY Acad Sci. *Res:* Role of soluble mediators of cellular immunity in lymphocyte maturation, regulation of the inflammatory response and the development of cell-mediated immune responsiveness; cystic fibrosis as a primary host defense abnormality or immune deficiency disease; structure and mechanism of action of transfer factor. *Mailing Add:* Dept Basic & Clin Immunol & Microbiol Med Univ SC 171 Ashley Ave Charleston SC 29425

WILSON, GUSTAVUS EDWIN, JR, b Philadelphia, Pa, Oct 6, 39; m 61; c 4. BIO-ORGANIC CHEMISTRY. *Educ:* Mass Inst Technol, SB, 61; Univ Ill, Urbana, PhD(chem), 64. *Prof Exp:* From instr to assoc prof chem, Polytech Inst NY, 64-75, prof, 75-80; MEM FAC, CHEM DEPT, CLARKSON COL, NY, 79- *Concurrent Pos:* Petrol Res Fund res grants, 64-68; adj assoc prof, Rockefeller Univ, 72-, adj prof, 76- vis assoc prof, Univ Pa, 74-75; res scholar, Am Cancer Soc, 74-75; vis prof, Washington Univ, 78-79. *Mem:* AAAS; Am Chem Soc; Royal Soc Chem; fel NY Acad Sci. *Res:* Mechanistic and synthetic studies in organic sulfur chemistry; application of organic chemistry to biological problems; magnetic resonance in chemistry and biochemistry. *Mailing Add:* Dept of Chem Polytech Inst of New York Brooklyn NY 11201

WILSON, HAROLD ALBERT, b Tilton, Ill, Oct 10, 05; m 37; c 2. MICROBIOLOGY. *Educ:* La State Univ, BS, 32, MS, 33; Iowa State Col, PhD(soil microbiol), 37. Prof agr, Panhandle Agr & Mech Col, 35-36; instr & asst, Iowa State Col, 37-38; prof agron, Southwestern La Inst, 38-44; soil conservationist, Soil Conserv Serv, USDA, 44-47; assoc prof bact, WVa Univ & assoc bacteriologist, Exp Sta, 47-57, prof & bacteriologist, 57-72, EMER PROF BACT, WVA UNIV, 72- *Mem:* Am Soc Agron; Am Soc Microbiol; Soil Sci Soc Am. *Res:* Microbiology of sanitary landfills and sewage decomposition in acid mine water. *Mailing Add:* 1297 Fairlawns Morgantown WV 26505

WILSON, HAROLD FREDERICK, b Columbiana, Ohio, Aug 15, 22; m 49; c 4. ORGANIC CHEMISTRY. *Educ:* Oberlin Col, AB, 47; Univ Rochester, PhD(chem), 50. *Prof Exp:* Res chemist, 50-57, lab head, 57-63, res supvr, 63-68, from asst dir res to dir res, 68-72, VPRES, ROHM AND HAAS CO, 72-, CHIEF SCIENTIFIC OFFICER, 81- *Concurrent Pos:* Mem bd dirs, Indust Res Inst, 79-82 & Coun Chem Res, 81. *Res:* Insecticides; herbicides; growth regulators. *Mailing Add:* 3 Joining Brook Spring House PA 19477

WILSON, HARRY DAVID BRUCE, b Winnipeg, Man, Nov 10, 16; m 41; c 3. ECONOMIC GEOLOGY. *Educ:* Univ Man, BSc, 36; Calif Inst Technol, MS, 39, PhD, 42. *Prof Exp:* Res & explor geologist, Int Nickel Co, Can, 41-47; asst prof geol, Univ Man, 47-49; geologist, Africa & Europe, 49-51; assoc prof, 51-57, head dept, 65-72, PROF GEOL, UNIV MAN, 57- *Concurrent Pos:* Mem, Nat Res Coun Can, 69-72; consult, Falconbridge Nickel Mines Ltd & Selco Mining Co Ltd; dir, Selco Mining Co Ltd & Man Mineral Resources Ltd. *Mem:* Soc Econ Geologists (pres, 76); Geol Soc Am; Geol Asn Can (pres, 65-66); Can Inst Mining & Metall; Royal Soc Can. *Res:* Geology and geochemistry of ore deposits; structure and origin of continental crust. *Mailing Add:* Dept of Earth Sci Fac Sci Univ of Man Winnipeg MB R3T 2N2 Can

WILSON, HARRY W(ALTON), JR, b Homestead, Pa, Nov 15, 24; m 47; c 2. CHEMICAL ENGINEERING. *Educ:* Univ Pittsburgh, BSChE, 48. *Prof Exp:* Develop engr, Goodyear Tire & Rubber Co, 48-50; process engr, Koppers Co, Inc, 50-56; sect head process develop, 56-64, mgr process eng, 64-68, MGR ENG, CALLERY CHEM CO DIV, MINE SAFETY APPLIANCES CO, 68- *Mem:* Am Inst Chem Engrs. *Res:* Chemical process development; new process design. *Mailing Add:* Box 557 Rd 2 Valencia PA 16059

WILSON, HENRY R, b Webbville, Ky, Mar 6, 36; m 59; c 2. REPRODUCTIVE PHYSIOLOGY, ENVIRONMENTAL PHYSIOLOGY. *Educ:* Univ Ky, BS, 57, MS, 59; Univ Md, PhD(poultry physiol), 62. *Prof Exp:* Asst prof poultry, 62-67, asst poultry physiologist, 62-67, assoc prof & assoc poultry physiologist, 67-74, PROF & POULTRY

PHYSIOLOGIST, UNIV FLA, 74- *Mem:* Soc Exp Biol & Med; Soc Study Reproduction; Wildlife Soc; Poultry Sci Asn; World Poultry Sci Asn. *Res:* Reproduction in male chickens; heat tolerance in chickens; delaying sexual maturity in chickens; management techniques, fertility and hatchability; game birds. *Mailing Add:* Dept of Poultry Sci Univ of Fla Gainesville FL 32611

WILSON, HERBERT ALEXANDER, JR, b Inverness, Miss, Jan 14, 14; m 41; c 2. MANAGEMENT CONSULTANT, AEROSPACE ENGINEERING. *Educ:* Ga Inst Technol, BS, 34. *Prof Exp:* Aeronaut res engr, Langley Mem Aeronaut Lab, Nat Adv Comt Aeronaut, Va, 37-43, head, full scale wind tunnel, 43-54, chief unitary plan wind tunnel div, 54-61, mgr, Proj Fire, Langley Res Ctr, NASA, 61-64, chief appl mat & physics div, 64-70, acting chief, Environ & Space Sci Div, 70-71, asst dir for space, 70-72; exec secy, res & develop incentives study, Nat Acad Eng, Washington, DC, 72-74, consult, 74-75; consult, Argonne Nat Lab, 77-78; consult, Booz-Allen & Hamliton, Inc, Bethesda, 78-79; RETIRED. *Concurrent Pos:* Mem subcomt helicopters, Nat Adv Comt Aeronaut, 47-48; consult, 79- *Honors & Awards:* Except Serv Award, NASA & Spec Serv Award, Langley Res Ctr, 66. *Mem:* Assoc fel Am Inst Aeronaut & Astronaut. *Res:* Space science studies of near earth space and upper atmosphere environmental factors; applications of aerospace knowledge to solution of public sector problems, facilities for research; technical management planning. *Mailing Add:* 3 Holly Dr Newport News VA 23601

WILSON, HOWARD LE ROY, b Salem, Ore, Dec 8, 32; m 60; c 3. MATHEMATICS. *Educ:* Willamette Univ, BA, 54; Univ Ill, MS, 60, PhD(educ), 66. *Prof Exp:* Teacher high sch, Ore, 55-56; from instr to asst prof math, Eastern Ore Col, 56-64; asst prof, 64-68, assoc prof math & sci educ, 68-80 PROF MATH & MATH EDUC, ORE STATE UNIV, 80- *Concurrent Pos:* Expert in math, Field Sta, Papua, New Guinea, UN Educ Sci & Cult Orgn, 71-73. *Res:* Mathematics education and teacher training. *Mailing Add:* Dept Sci Educ Ore State Univ Corvallis OR 97331

WILSON, HOWELL KENNETH, b Savannah, Ga, Aug 28, 37. MATHEMATICS. *Educ:* Ga Inst Technol, BS, 60; Univ Minn, PhD(math), 64. *Prof Exp:* From asst prof to assoc prof math, Ga Inst Technol, 64-69; assoc prof, 69-73, PROF MATH, SOUTHERN ILL UNIV, EDWARDSVILLE, 73- *Mem:* Am Math Soc; Soc Indust Appl Math. *Res:* Ordinary differential equations. *Mailing Add:* Dept of Math Southern Ill Univ Edwardsville IL 62026

WILSON, HUGH DANIEL, b Alliance, Ohio, Aug 15, 43; m 70; c 1. SYSTEMATIC BOTANY, ETHNOBOTANY. *Educ:* Kent State Univ, BA, 70, MA, 72; Ind Univ, Bloomington, PhD(bot), 76. *Prof Exp:* Asst prof bot, Univ Wyo, 76-77; ASST PROF BIOL, TEX A&M UNIV, 77- *Mem:* Am Soc Plant Taxonomists; Soc Econ Bot; Soc Study Evolution; Bot Soc Am; Am Inst Biol Sci. *Res:* Angiosperm biosystematics with emphasis on species complexes that include domesticated taxa. *Mailing Add:* Dept of Biol Tex A&M Univ College Station TX 77843

WILSON, HUGH HAYES, ceramics engineering, see previous edition

WILSON, HUGH REID, b Ft Monmouth, NJ, Apr 20, 43. VISUAL PSYCHOPHYSICS. *Educ:* Wesleyan Univ, Conn, BA, 65; Univ Chicago, MA, 68, PhD(chem physics), 69. *Prof Exp:* Fel, 69-72, from instr to asst prof, 72-80, ASSOC PROF BIOPHYS & THEORET BIOL, UNIV CHICAGO, 81- *Concurrent Pos:* NIH grant, 78-81 & 78-83; NSF grants, 82-85. *Mem:* Asn Res Vision & Opthal; AAAS; Optical Soc Am. *Res:* Processing of spatial and temporal information by the human visual system; stereopsis and binocular vision; mathematical models of human visual functions. *Mailing Add:* Dept Biophys & Theoret Biol Univ of Chicago Chicago IL 60637

WILSON, IRWIN B, b Yonkers, NY, May 8, 21; m 52; c 2. BIOCHEMISTRY. *Educ:* City Col New York, BS, 41; Columbia Univ, AM, 47, PhD(phys chem), 48. *Prof Exp:* Jr chemist, Picatinny Arsenal, NJ, 42; res assoc, Columbia Univ, 42-45; chemist, Union Carbide & Carbon Corp, 45; instr chem, City Col New York, 46-49; assoc, Col Physicians & Surgeons, Columbia Univ, 48-49, from asst prof to prof biochem, 49-66; PROF CHEM, UNIV COLO, BOULDER, 66- *Honors & Awards:* Asn Res Nerv & Ment Dis Award, 58. *Mem:* Am Chem Soc; Am Soc Biol Chem; Am Acad Neurol. *Res:* Enzymology; protein chemistry; nerve function; peptide hormones. *Mailing Add:* Dept of Chem Univ of Colo Boulder CO 80309

WILSON, J(AMES) W(OODROW), b Commerce, Tex, Apr 5, 16; m 43; c 3. CHEMICAL ENGINEERING, MATHEMATICS. *Educ:* Stephen F Austin State Col, BA, 35; Univ Tex, BS, 39; Agr & Mech Col, Tex, MS, 41. *Prof Exp:* Instr chem, Agr & Mech Col, Tex, 42; instr chem eng, Columbia Univ, 46-49; from asst prof to prof, 49-77, EMER PROF CHEM ENG, NAVAL POSTGRAD SCH, 77- *Mem:* Am Chem Soc; Am Inst Chem Engrs. *Res:* Explosives; rocket propellants; heat transfer; thermodynamics; fuels and lubricants. *Mailing Add:* 3435 Oak Cluster Lane San Antonio TX 78253

WILSON, JACK BELMONT, b Morgantown, WVa, Dec 1, 21; m 43; c 6. PLANT PATHOLOGY. *Educ:* WVa Univ, BS, 53, MS, 54, PhD(plant path), 57. *Prof Exp:* Instr plant path, Univ Md, 56-57, asst prof, 57-62; res plant pathologist, Potato Handling Res Ctr, USDA, Maine, 62-67; assoc prof plant path & exten plant pathologist & entomologist, WVa Univ, 67-69; asst br chief, Hort Crops Res Br, Mkt Qual Res Div, 69-73, asst area res dir, NE Region, Agr Res Serv, 73-74, AREA DIR, N ATLANTIC AREA, NE REGION, FED RES, SCI & EDUC AGENCY, USDA, 74- *Concurrent Pos:* Assoc prof, Univ Maine, 66-67. *Mem:* Am Phytopath Soc; Potato Asn Am; Europ Asn Potato Res. *Res:* Diseases of potatoes and ornamental plants; plant disease and insect diagnosis. *Mailing Add:* US Plant & Soil Nutrit Lab Cornell Univ ARS USDA Tower Rd Ithaca NY 14853

WILSON, JACK CHARLES, b Waterloo, Iowa, Dec 17, 28; m 48; c 4. ALGEBRA. *Educ:* Iowa State Teachers Col, BA, 51; Univ Iowa, MS, 54; Case Western Reserve Univ, PhD(math), 60. *Prof Exp:* Instr math, Cent Col, Iowa, 53-56; asst prof, Fenn Col, 56-59; assoc prof, Cent Col, Iowa, 59-65 & Earlham Col, 65-70; PROF MATH, UNIV NC, ASHEVILLE, 70- *Mem:* Am Math Soc; Math Asn Am. *Res:* Pure mathemtics; functions on algebras. *Mailing Add:* Dept of Math Univ of NC Asheville NC 28804

WILSON, JACK HAROLD, b Toronto, Ont, May 2, 43; m 65; c 2. BIOCHEMISTRY, MICROBIOLOGY. *Educ:* McGill Univ, BSc, 64; McMaster Univ, PhD(molecular biol), 68. *Prof Exp:* Res scientist, 68-73, res biochemist, Res Labs, Uniroyal Ltd, 73-74, res biochemist, Corp Planning & Plantations Div, Uniroyal Inc, 74-76, mgr planning stratetgies agr chem, 76-78, DIR MKT, UNIROYAL CHEM, 78- *Concurrent Pos:* Consult, Int Bank Reconstruct & Develop, 72. *Res:* Antimicrobial agents; plant pathology; mode of agricultural chemical action; plant protein; novel protein sources; plant disease losses. *Mailing Add:* Uniroyal Chem Elmira ON N3B 3A3 Can

WILSON, JACK LOWERY, b Looxahoma, Miss, June 24, 43; m 66; c 3. ANATOMY. *Educ:* Univ Southern Miss, BS, 64; Univ Miss, MS, 67, PhD(anat), 68. *Prof Exp:* From instr to asst prof, 68-74, ASSOC PROF ANAT, MED UNITS, UNIV TENN, MEMPHIS, 74- *Mem:* Am Asn Anat. *Res:* Relations of age and sex hormones to the dietary induction, high fat and low protein components of cardiac and hepatic lesions in mice, also study of the fine structure of these lesions; cerebrovascular spasm. *Mailing Add:* Dept of Anat Univ of Tenn Med Units Memphis TN 38163

WILSON, JACK MARTIN, b Camp Atterbury, Ind, June 29, 45; m 69; c 2. CHEMICAL PHYSICS, BIOPHYSICS. *Educ:* Thiel Col, AB, 67; Kent State Univ, MA, 70, PhD(physics), 72. *Prof Exp:* Res asst physics liquid crystals, Liquid Crystal Inst, Kent State Univ, 69, instr physics, Columbiana Co Br, 69-70, res asst physics liquid crystals, Liquid Crystal Inst, 70-72; asst prof, 72-78, ASSOC PROF PHYSICS, SAM HOUSTON STATE UNIV, 78-, CHMN DEPT, 80- *Concurrent Pos:* Consult in Forensic Sci, 75- *Honors & Awards:* Sigma Xi Res Award, 74. *Mem:* Am Inst Physics; Sigma Xi; AAAS. *Res:* Studying the structure of Sickle Cell hemoglobin; physics with application to police science; Mössbauer spectroscopy of liquid crystals. *Mailing Add:* Dept of Physics Sam Houston State Univ Hunstville TX 77340

WILSON, JAMES, JR, organic chemistry, see previous edition

WILSON, JAMES ALBERT, b Boston, Mass, Jan 28, 29. PHYSIOLOGY, BIOCHEMISTRY. *Educ:* Northeastern Univ, BS, 53; Univ Mich, MS, 55, PhD(zool), 59. *Prof Exp:* Res assoc zool, Univ Mich, 58-59; asst prof physiol, 59-72, ASSOC PROF PHYSIOL, OHIO UNIV, 72- *Mem:* AAAS; Am Inst Biol Sci; Am Soc Zoologists. *Res:* Pressure-temperature pH effects on the activity of adenosine-triphosphatases from rabbit tissues; contractility of glycerol-extracted muscle fibers and related enzyme activity; factors affecting muscle relaxation. *Mailing Add:* Dept of Zool & Microbiol Ohio Univ Athens OH 45701

WILSON, JAMES ALEXANDER, b Walters, Okla, Nov 19, 30; m 54; c 4. PLANT BREEDING. *Educ:* Okla State Univ, BS, 52, MS, 54; Tex A&M Univ, PhD(plant breeding), 58. *Prof Exp:* Instr agron, Tex A&M Univ, 54-57; asst prof, Ft Hays Exp Sta, Kans State Univ, 57-61; RES AGRONOMIST, DEKALB AGRESEARCH INC, 61- *Mem:* Am Asn Cereal Chem; Am Soc Agron. *Res:* Wheat breeding; genetics; cytology and management. *Mailing Add:* DeKalb AgResearch Inc 1831 Woodrow Ave Wichita KS 67203

WILSON, JAMES BLAKE, b Albion, Mich, Feb 9, 24; m 49; c 4. APPLIED MATHEMATICS. *Educ:* Univ Fla, BS, 48, PhD(appl math), 57; Cornell Univ, MS, 51. *Prof Exp:* Instr mech, Cornell Univ, 50; instr, Dept Ord, US Mil Acad, 51-54; asst math, Univ Fla, 54-56; asst prof, 57-63, assoc prof, 63-80, PROF MATH, NC STATE UNIV, 80-, ASST HEAD, 78- *Mem:* Am Math Soc; Math Asn Am. *Res:* Elasticity; mechanics; numerical analysis. *Mailing Add:* 1311 Greenwood Circle Cary NC 27511

WILSON, JAMES BRUCE, b Washington, DC, Sept 22, 29. COMPUTER SCIENCE, BIOMEDICAL ENGINEERING. *Educ:* George Washington Univ, BEE, 58. *Prof Exp:* From res asst to res assoc, George Washington Univ, 58-60; sr res scientist, Nat Biomed Res Found, 60-76; RES ASSOC, GEORGETOWN UNIV, 76- *Mem:* Pattern Recognition Soc (secy, 66-). *Res:* Systems and circuit design of biomedical scanner; computer programming for pattern recognition; switching circuit theory and logical design; Boolean algebra; information retrieval; research-planning methodology. *Mailing Add:* Nat Biomed Res Found Georgetown Univ Med Ctr Washington DC 20007

WILSON, JAMES DENNIS, b The Dalles, Ore, Feb 28, 40; m 62; c 2. ORGANIC CHEMISTRY. *Educ:* Harvard Univ, AB, 62; Univ Wash, PhD(chem), 66. *Prof Exp:* MGR RES & DEVELOP, DETERGENTS & PHOSPHATES DIV, MONSANTO CO, 66- *Mem:* AAAS. *Res:* Correlation of molecular structure with physical properties, especially solid-state electrical, magnetic and olfactory properties; synthesis of unsaturated nitrogen- and sulfur-compounds. *Mailing Add:* Res & Develop 800 N Lindbergh Blvd St Louis MO 63166

WILSON, JAMES FRANKLIN, b Christopher, Ill, Oct 27, 20; m 43; c 2. MICROBIOLOGY, GENETICS. *Educ:* Southern Ill Univ, BS, 44; Iowa State Col, MS, 46; Stanford Univ, PhD, 59. *Prof Exp:* Instr biol, Hartnell Col, 46-64; PROF BIOL, UNIV NC, GREENSBORO, 64- *Mem:* AAAS; Genetics Soc Am. *Res:* Application of microsurgical techniques to the study of heterocaryosis and cytoplasmic heredity in Neurospora crassa. *Mailing Add:* Dept of Biol Univ of NC Greensboro NC 27412

WILSON, JAMES GRAVES, b Clarksdale, Miss, Apr 2, 15; m 41; c 3. EMBRYOLOGY, TERATOLOGY. *Educ:* Miss Col, BA, 36; Univ Richmond, MA, 38; Yale Univ, PhD(anat), 42. *Hon Degrees:* DSc, Med Col Wis, 75. *Prof Exp:* Asst anat & primate biol, Sch Med, Yale Univ, 39-42; from instr to asst prof anat, Sch Med & Dent, Univ Rochester, 42-50; from assoc prof to prof, Col Med, Univ Cincinnati, 50-55; prof & head dept, Col Med, Univ Fla, 55-66; prof, 66-80, EMER PROF RES PEDIAT & ANAT, COL MED, UNIV CINCINNATI, 80-; DIV HEAD PATH EMBRYOL, INST DEVELOP RES, CHILDREN'S HOSP RES FOUND, 80- *Concurrent Pos:* Mem comt postdoctoral fels med sci, Nat Res Coun, 57-61; mem develop biol training comt, NIH, 59-62, human embryol & develop study sect, 62-66 & anat sci training comt, 66-; mem fac, Teratol Workshop, Univ Fla, 64, Univ Calif, 65, Univ Colo, 66 & int workshops, Copenhagen Univ, 66 & Kyoto Univ, 69; mem & chmn sci group testing drugs teratogenicity, WHO, 66; mem adv comt protocols safety eval, Food & Drug Admin, 67-; mem toxicol adv comt, Food & Drug Admin, 75-; mem sci adv bd, Nat Ctr Toxicol Res, 73-; mem Basil O'Conner Starter Grant Selection Comt, NFS. *Mem:* AAAS; Teratology Soc; Environ Mutagen Soc; Europ Teratology Soc; Am Asn Anat. *Res:* Experimental and human teratology, especially mechanisms of drug teratogenicity; use of non-human primates in teratological studies; embryology of malformations; experimental production of malformations with vitamin A deficiency; mechanisms of teratogenesis; x-rays; anemia. *Mailing Add:* Children's Hosp Res Found Elland Ave & Bethesda Cincinnati OH 45229

WILSON, JAMES LARRY, b Jackson, Tenn, Feb 9, 42; , 73. FISHERIES MANAGEMENT, AQUACULTURE. *Educ:* Union Univ, BS, 64; Univ Fla, MS, 67; Univ Tenn, PhD(zool), 70. *Prof Exp:* Asst prof, 70-75, ASSOC PROF FISHERIES, DEPT FORESTRY, WILDLIFE & FISHERIES, BIOL, UNIV TENN INST AGR, 75- *Concurrent Pos:* Lectr, Tech Aqua Biol Sta, Career Awareness Inst, 78-79. *Mem:* Am Fisheries Soc. *Res:* Management strategies for improvement of game fish yields in Tennessee waters; develop methods for economic rearing and marketing of aquatic animals with economic potential (aquaculture); maximizing production of commercially raised fishes. *Mailing Add:* Dept Forestry Wildlife & Fisheries PO Box 1071 Univ Tenn Inst Agr Knoxville TN 37901

WILSON, JAMES LEE, b Waxahachie, Tex, Dec 1, 20; m 44; c 3. GEOLOGY. *Educ:* Univ Tex, BA, 42, MA, 44; Yale Univ, PhD(geol), 49. *Prof Exp:* Jr geologist, Carter Oil Co, 43-44; assoc prof geol, Univ Tex, 49-52; res geologist, Shell Develop Co & Shell Int Res, 52-66; Wiess prof geol, Rice Univ, 66-78; PROF GEOL, UNIV MICH, 79- *Mem:* Fel Geol Soc Am; Paleont Soc; Soc Econ Paleont & Mineral (pres, 75-76); Am Asn Petrol Geol. *Res:* Cambrian paleontology; Paleozoic biostratigraphy; carbonate petrography and petrology; sedimentology of carbonate strata. *Mailing Add:* Dept Geol 1006 C C Little Bldg Ann Arbor MI 48109

WILSON, JAMES LESTER, b Nashville, Tenn, July 18, 25; m 48; c 2. ZOOLOGY. *Educ:* George Peabody Col, BS, 51, MA, 52; Vanderbilt Univ, PhD, 59. *Prof Exp:* Instr biol & phys sci, Ark State Col, 52-54; asst, Vanderbilt Univ, 55-56; from assoc prof to prof biol & chmn div sci & math, Belmont Col, 56-67; assoc prof, 67-70, PROF ZOOL, TENN STATE UNIV, NASHVILLE, 70- *Honors & Awards:* Sullivan Award, George Peabody Col, 51. *Mem:* Fel AAAS; Acarological Soc Am. *Res:* Taxonomy; life history and ecology of water mites; hydracarology. *Mailing Add:* Dept of Zool Tenn State Univ Nashville TN 37203

WILSON, JAMES R, b Berkeley, Calif, Oct 21, 22; m 49; c 5. THEORETICAL ASTROPHYSICS. *Educ:* Univ Calif, BS, 43, PhD(physics), 52. *Prof Exp:* Physicist, Sandia Corp, 52-53; PHYSICIST, LAWRENCE LIVERMORE LAB, UNIV CALIF, 53- *Mem:* Fel Am Phys Soc; AAAS. *Res:* Astrophysics; gravitational radiation; relativity; design of nuclear explosives. *Mailing Add:* 737 S M St Livermore CA 94550

WILSON, JAMES RUSSELL, b Pittsburgh, Pa, Jan 10, 33. BEHAVIORAL BIOLOGY. *Educ:* Univ Calif, Berkeley, AB, 59, PhD(psychol), 68. *Prof Exp:* Res psychologist, Univ Calif, Berkeley, 63-66; res assoc psychol, Univ Colo, Boulder, 66-68; instr psychol, Univ Calif, Santa Cruz 69; asst prof, 69-74, ASSOC PROF PSYCHOL, UNIV COLO, BOULDER, 74- *Concurrent Pos:* Assoc researcher, Univ Hawaii, 74- *Mem:* Genetics Soc Am; Behav Genetics Asn. *Res:* Genetic analysis of behavioral phenotypes, including reading disability, aggression, sexual behavior, alcohol use and cognitive abilities. *Mailing Add:* Inst for Behav Genetics Univ Colo Box 447 Boulder CO 80309

WILSON, JAMES STEWART, b Mich, June 3, 32; m 54; c 3. BOTANY. *Educ:* Kalamazoo Col, BA, 54; Univ Mich, MS, 57, PhD(bot), 61. *Prof Exp:* From asst prof to assoc prof, 59-70, PROF BIOL, EMPORIA STATE UNIV, 70- *Mem:* AAAS; Am Soc Plant Taxon; Bot Soc Am; Int Asn Plant Taxon. *Res:* Biosystematics of flowering plants with emphasis on population ecology. *Mailing Add:* Dept of Biol Emporia Kans State Col Emporia KS 66801

WILSON, JAMES WILLIAM, b Rice, Va, Oct 21, 19; m 50; c 4. MEDICINAL CHEMISTRY. *Educ:* Hampden-Sydney Col, BS, 41; Univ Va, MS, 44, PhD(org chem), 46. *Prof Exp:* Asst chem, Univ Va, 41-43; res chemist, 46-53, asst sect head org chem, 53-54, head med chem sect, 54-66, staff dir, 66-67, ASSOC DIR CHEM, SMITH KLINE & FRENCH LABS, 67- *Mem:* AAAS; Am Chem Soc; NY Acad Sci; Soc Chem Indust. *Res:* Medicinal chemistry; analgesics; cardiovascular drugs; psychopharmacological, diuretic and anti-inflammatory agents. *Mailing Add:* 15 Kinterra Rd Wayne PA 19087

WILSON, JAMES WILLIAM ALEXANDER, b Glasgow, Scotland, Dec 24, 44; m 70; c 3. ELECTRICAL ENGINEERING. *Educ:* Heriot-Watt Univ, BSc, 67; Univ Edinburgh, PhD(elec eng), 71. *Prof Exp:* Fel elec eng, Univ Toronto, 71-73; sr engr static power conversion, Reliance Elec Co, Cleveland, 73-76; elec engr, 76-78, unit mgr power circuits & drives, 78-81, BR MGR POWER CIRCUITS & SYSTS, GEN ELEC CO CORP RES & DEVELOP, 81- *Mem:* Inst Elec & Electronics Engrs; assoc mem Brit Inst Elec Engrs. *Res:* Development of advanced static power conversion techniques and applications. *Mailing Add:* Gen Elec Co PO Box 43 Schenectady NY 12301

WILSON, JEAN DONALD, b Wellington, Tex, Aug 26, 32. INTERNAL MEDICINE. *Educ:* Univ Tex, BA, 51, MD, 55; Am Bd Internal Med, dipl, 64. *Prof Exp:* From intern to asst resident internal med, Parkland Mem Hosp, Dallas, 55-58; clin assoc clin biochem, Nat Heart Inst, 58-60; from instr to assoc prof internal med, 60-68, PROF INTERNAL MED, UNIV TEX HEALTH SCI CTR DALLAS, 68- *Concurrent Pos:* Estab investr, Am Heart Asn, 60-65; ed, J Clin Invest, 72-77. *Honors & Awards:* Oppenheimer Award, Endocrine Soc, 72; Amory Prize, Am Acad Arts & Sci, 77. *Mem:* Am Soc Clin Invest; Am Fedn Clin Res; Am Soc Biol Chem; Endocrine Soc; Asn Am Physicians. *Res:* Mechanism of action of steroid hormones; sexual differentiation; androgen physiology. *Mailing Add:* Dept of Internal Med Univ of Tex Health Sci Ctr Dallas TX 75235

WILSON, JERRY D(ICK), b Coshocton, Ohio, May 6, 37; Div; c 2. SCIENCE WRITING, PHYSICS. *Educ:* Ohio Univ, BS, 62, PhD(physics), 70; Union Col, MS, 65. *Prof Exp:* Mat behav physicist dielectrics, Gen Elec Co, 63-66; asst prof physics, Ohio Univ, 70-75; assoc prof, 75-80, PROF PHYSICS, LANDER COL, 80- *Concurrent Pos:* Fel, Ohio Acad Sci, 72. *Mem:* Am Asn Physics Teachers; Nat Sci Teachers Asn; Am Med Technologists. *Res:* Science writing and science teaching, particularly for non-science students. *Mailing Add:* Dept of Sci & Math Lander Col Greenwood SC 29646

WILSON, JERRY LEE, b Heavener, Okla, Jan 30, 38; m 61; c 2. BIOCHEMISTRY. *Educ:* Okla State Univ, BS, 61; Univ Okla, PhD(chem), 67. *Prof Exp:* USPHS res fel, Univ Calif, Davis, 67-69; asst prof, 69-74, ASSOC PROF CHEM, CALIF STATE UNIV, SACRAMENTO, 74- *Mem:* Am Chem Soc. *Res:* Plant biochemistry; enzymology; protein chemistry. *Mailing Add:* Dept of Chem Calif State Univ Sacramento CA 95819

WILSON, JOAN BRUSH, clinical diagnostics manufacturing, see previous edition

WILSON, JOE BRANSFORD, b Dallas, Tex, June 29, 14; m 44; c 2. BACTERIOLOGY. *Educ:* Univ Tex, BA, 39; Univ Wis, MS, 41, PhD(bact), 47; Am Bd Microbiol, dipl. *Prof Exp:* Instr bact, Univ Tex, 39; asst, 39-42, from instr to assoc prof, 46-55, assoc dean grad sch, 65-69, chmn dept, 68-73, PROF BACT, UNIV WIS-MADISON, 55-, PROF MED MICROBIOL, 77- *Concurrent Pos:* Mem tech adv panel, Off Asst Secy Defense, 52-63. *Mem:* Fel AAAS; Am Soc Microbiol; Soc Exp Biol & Med; Am Asn Immunol; fel Am Acad Microbiol. *Res:* Metabolism and pathogenesis of Brucella, Cocci, Vibrio and Leptospira. *Mailing Add:* Dept of Bacteriol Univ of Wis Madison WI 53706

WILSON, JOE ROBERT, b Colfax, La, Apr 5, 23; m 44; c 3. CIVIL & CONSTRUCTION ENGINEERING. *Educ:* US Naval Acad, BS, 44; Rensselaer Polytech Inst, MCE, 48; Univ Tex, PhD(civil eng), 67. *Prof Exp:* Co commander, Naval Construct Battalion 105 & US Naval Civil Eng Corps, 48-50, proj engr, Pub Works Ctr, Va, 50-52, dir design div, Potomac River Naval Command Pub Works, 52-53, mgr construct div, Off in Charge Construct, Spain, 53-55, dir pub works, Naval Air Sta, Ala, 56-58, staff engr, Off Chief of Naval Opers, 58-60, dir pub works, Naval Sta, CZ, 60-62, dist civil engr, 15th Naval Dist, 62-64; PROF CIVIL ENG, LA TECH UNIV, 66-, HEAD DEPT, 75- *Mem:* Fel Am Soc Civil Engrs; Water Pollution Control Fedn; Am Soc Eng Educ. *Res:* Hydraulics; water pollution control systems; mixing and dispersion phenomena. *Mailing Add:* Dept of Civil Eng La Tech Univ Ruston LA 71270

WILSON, JOHN CHARLES, organic polymer chemistry, see previous edition

WILSON, JOHN CLELAND, b Galt, Ont, June 8, 35; m 64; c 4. SMALL COMPUTERS. *Educ:* Univ Toronto, BASc, 58; Univ Waterloo, MSc, 62, PhD(math), 66. *Prof Exp:* Analyst, KCS Data Control Ltd, Ont, 58-62; asst prof math, Univ Waterloo, 66-70, assoc dir comput ctr, 68-70; dir, Univ Toronto, 70-76, assoc prof comput sci, Comput Ctr, 70-76, dir student record serv, 76-79; COMPUT SCIENTIST, COMPUT SYSTS GROUP, UNIV WATERLOO, 80- *Concurrent Pos:* Nat Res Coun fels, Univ Waterloo, 67 & Univ Toronto, 72; Dept Univ Affairs fel, Univ Waterloo, 68. *Mem:* Asn Comput Mach; Can Info Processing Soc; Inst Elec & Electronics Engrs. *Res:* Microcomputer hardware and software; computer language implementation. *Mailing Add:* Comput Sci Group Univ Waterloo Waterloo ON N2L 3A1 Can

WILSON, JOHN D(OUGLAS), b Edinburgh, Scotland, Aug 21, 35; m 57; c 3. ELECTRICAL ENGINEERING. *Educ:* Univ Edinburgh, BSc, 56; Univ WI, PhD(elec eng), 67. *Prof Exp:* Electronic engr, Bristol Aircraft Ltd, Eng, 56-59; lectr elec eng, Univ WI, 62-67; assoc prof, 67-76, PROF ELEC ENG, ROYAL MIL COL CAN, 76-, HEAD DEPT, 78- *Concurrent Pos:* Can Defence Res Bd grant, 68- *Mem:* Inst Elec & Electronics Engrs; assoc Brit Inst Electronic & Radio Engrs. *Res:* Pattern recognition; digital data processing; microcomputers. *Mailing Add:* Dept of Elec Eng Royal Mil Col of Can Kingston ON K7L 2W3 Can

WILSON, JOHN DRENNAN, b Peoria, Ill, Mar 29, 38; m 67; c 1. PHYSIOLOGY, RADIOBIOLOGY. *Educ:* Carleton Col, BA, 60; Univ Ill, Urbana, MS, 63, PhD(physiol), 66. *Prof Exp:* Res assoc radiobiol, Univ Tex, Austin, 66-72; asst prof, 72-76, ASSOC PROF RADIOBIOL, MED COL VA, 76- *Mem:* AAAS; Radiation Res Soc. *Res:* Lethal and mutagenic effects of radiation on microorganisms; effects of accelerated particles on mammalian systems. *Mailing Add:* Dept of Radiol Med Col of Va Richmond VA 23298

WILSON, JOHN EDWARD, b Ft Wayne, Ind, Apr 27, 39; m 64; c 3. NEUROCHEMISTRY, ENZYMOLOGY. *Educ:* Univ Notre Dame, BS, 61; Univ Ill, MS, 62, PhD(biochem), 64. *Prof Exp:* From asst prof to assoc prof, 67-75, PROF BIOCHEM, MICH STATE UNIV, 75- *Concurrent Pos:* NSF fel, Univ Ill, Urbana, 64-65. *Mem:* Am Soc Biol Chem; Am Soc Neurochem; Int Soc Neurochem; Am Chem Soc. *Res:* Brain hexokinase; brain mitochondria; regulation of energy metabolism in brain. *Mailing Add:* Dept of Biochem Mich State Univ East Lansing MI 48824

WILSON, JOHN ERIC, b Champaign, Ill, Dec 13, 19; m 47; c 3. BIOCHEMISTRY. *Educ:* Univ Chicago, SB, 41; Univ Ill, MS, 44; Cornell Univ, PhD(biochem), 48. *Prof Exp:* Asst chem, Univ Ill, 41-44; asst biochem, Med Col, Cornell Univ, 44-48, res assoc, 48-50; from asst prof to assoc prof biochem, 50-65, dir, Neurobiol Prog, 72-73, PROF BIOCHEM, SCH MED, UNIV NC, CHAPEL HILL, 65- *Mem:* Fel AAAS; Am Chem Soc; Am Soc Biol Chem; Am Soc Neurochem; Soc Neurosci. *Res:* Effects of experience and behavior on brain metabolism; neurochemistry. *Mailing Add:* Dept Biochem Sch Med Univ NC Chapel Hill NC 27514

WILSON, JOHN F, b Niagara Falls, NY, Dec 23, 22; m 50; c 8. MEDICINE, PATHOLOGY. *Educ:* Univ Cincinnati, MD, 52. *Prof Exp:* Intern pediat, Univ Ark Hosp, 52-53; resident, Children's Hosp, Cincinnati, Ohio, 55-57; instr, Univ Cincinnati, 57-58; from instr to asst prof pediat, 58-68, instr path, 67-68, ASST PROF PATH, UNIV UTAH, 68-, ASSOC PROF PEDIAT, 73-; PATHOLOGIST & DIR LABS, PRIMARY CHILDREN'S HOSP, 69- *Concurrent Pos:* Smith Kline & French fel hemat, 57-59; from co-prin investr to prin investr gastrointestinal tract in iron deficiency anemia NIH grants, 61-66, prin investr, copper metab in acute leukemia, 63-64; mem comn child nutrit, Food & Nutrit Bd, Nat Res Coun, 64-66; resident path, Univ Utah, 66-69; assoc prog dir, Children's Cancer Study Group A, NIH, Univ Utah, 70-77, path of record, Non-Hodgkins Lymphoma Study, 77- *Mem:* AMA; Am Soc Hemat; Am Fedn Clin Res; Am Soc Clin Path; Col Am Path. *Res:* Iron and copper metabolism in iron deficiency; childhood malignancies. *Mailing Add:* Primary Children's Hosp 320 12th Ave Salt Lake City UT 84103

WILSON, JOHN HOWARD, b July 27, 44; US citizen; m 65; c 1. BIOCHEMISTRY, GENETICS. *Educ:* Wabash Col, AB, 66; Calif Inst Technol, PhD(biochem, genet), 72. *Prof Exp:* asst prof, 73-79, ASSOC PROF BIOCHEM, BAYLOR COL MED, 79- *Concurrent Pos:* Damon Runyon fel biochem, Med Ctr, Stanford Univ, 71-73. *Res:* Genetic recombination in somatic cells. *Mailing Add:* Dept Biochem Baylor Col Med Houston TX 77030

WILSON, JOHN HUMAN, b Wills Point, Tex, Feb 24, 00; m 24; c 2. EXPLORATION GEOPHYSICS. *Educ:* Colo Sch Mines, EM, 23. *Prof Exp:* Geologist, Midwest Ref Co, Colo, 23-26; geologist & geophysicist, Huasteca Petrol Co, Mex, 26-27; asst prof geophys, Colo Sch Mines, 28-29; consult geologist & geophysicist, 29-34; pres, Colo Geophys Corp, 34-37; vpres, Independent Explor Co, Piper Petrol Co, Woodson Oil Co & Wilson Explor Co, 38-61; PRES, PIPER PETROL CO & WILSON EXPLOR CO, 61- *Concurrent Pos:* Explor consult, 50- *Mem:* Soc Explor Geophys (secy-treas, 36); Am Asn Petrol Geol; assoc Am Inst Mining, Metall & Petrol Eng. *Res:* Design of geophysical equipment; incipient metamorphism of sediments; seismic velocities; exploration techniques. *Mailing Add:* 1212 W El Paso St Ft Worth TX 76102

WILSON, JOHN NEVILLE, b Portland, Maine, June 13, 18; m 44; c 3. PHYSICS, RESOURCE MANAGEMENT. *Educ:* Rice Inst, BA, 40; Harvard Univ, AM, 41. *Prof Exp:* Res chemist, E I du Pont de Nemours & Co, Va, 41, res physicist, 42-43, tech specialist, Manhattan Dist, Del, 43-44, sr supvr, Wash, 44-45, res physicist, Va, 45-50, tech specialist, Del, 50-51, SC, 51-53, res supvr, Appl Physics Div, Savannah River Plant, 53, res mgr, 54-70, supt Planning & Anal Dept, Savannah River Plant, 70-80; RETIRED. *Concurrent Pos:* Asst physicist, Nat Defense Res Comt, Radio & Sound Lab, Univ Calif, 41-42; assoc physicist, Clinton Labs, Tenn, 44. *Mem:* Soc Rheol. *Res:* Rayon spinning, yarn structure and physical testing; health physics; oceanography; radiation and chemical process instrumentation; electronics; non-destructive testing; computer models for finance and control of large industrial plant and laboratory. *Mailing Add:* 1208 Abbeville Ave NW Aiken SC 29801

WILSON, JOHN PHILLIPS, b Stamford, Conn, June 5, 16; m 40; c 1. MATHEMATICS. *Educ:* Univ Southern Miss, BA, 57; Johns Hopkins Univ, MEd, 60, MS, 70. *Prof Exp:* Res staff asst, Ballistic Anal Lab, Inst Coop Res, Johns Hopkins Univ, 57-62, res assoc, 62-67, res scientist, 67-69; sr res analyst, Thor Div, Falcon Res & Develop Co, Baltimore, 69-81; RETIRED. *Concurrent Pos:* Consult terminal ballistic testing, 81- *Mem:* Am Defense Preparedness Asn. *Res:* Military operations analysis: target vulnerability, weapon lethality, weapons systems evaluation, terminal ballistic evaluation of large caliaber weapons; geo and celestial navigation for surface vessels; merchant marine industry-shipboard operations. *Mailing Add:* 722 Shelley Rd Towson MD 21204

WILSON, JOHN RANDALL, b Miami, Fla, June 12, 34; m 59; c 3. PHYSICAL CHEMISTRY. *Educ:* Univ Fla, BS, 56; Univ Wis, MS, 59, PhD(chem), 65. *Prof Exp:* Asst prof chem, Franklin Col, 59-62, Miami Univ, 64-67 & Asheville-Biltmore Col, 67-68; assoc prof, 68-72, PROF CHEM, SHIPPENSBURG STATE COL, 72-, CHMN DEPT, 77- *Mem:* AAAS; Am Chem Soc. *Res:* Radiation chemistry; mechanisms of exchange reactions; photochemistry; scientific education in Latin America. *Mailing Add:* Dept of Chem Shippensburg State Col Shippensburg PA 17257

WILSON, JOHN SHERIDAN, b Morgantown, WVa, June 17, 44; m 65; c 4. COAL PROCESSES. *Educ:* WVa Univ, BS, 66, MS, 68, PhD(chem eng), 75. *Prof Exp:* Proj leader & engr, Bur Mines, US Dept Interior, 68-76; res supvr, Combustion Res & Develop Br, Res & Develop Admin, 76-77, asst dir, Energy Conversion & Utility Div, 77-79, DIR, COAL PROJ MGR DIV, MORGANTOWN ENERGY TECH CTR, US DEPT ENERGY, 79- *Concurrent Pos:* Proj mgr, Combustion Res & Develop Br, Res & Develop Admin, Dept Energy, 76. *Mem:* Am Chem Soc; Am Soc Mech Engrs; Sigma Xi. *Res:* Coal combustion and furnace analysis; design and operation of fluidized-bed coal combustion; coal gasification; environmental effluent control from coal conversion and utilization processes. *Mailing Add:* Morgantown Energy Technol Ctr US Dept Energy PO Box 880 Morgantown WV 26505

WILSON, JOHN SHIRLEY, inorganic chemistry, see previous edition

WILSON, JOHN T, b Gainesville, Tex, Apr 27, 38; m 62; c 3. PEDIATRICS, PHARMACOLOGY. *Educ:* Tulane Univ La, BS, 60, MS & MD, 63. *Prof Exp:* From intern to resident clin pediat, Palo Alto-Stanford Med Ctr, Palo Alto, Calif, 63-65; res assoc biochem pharmacol, Univ Iowa, 65-66; res assoc biochem pharmacol & endocrinol, Nat Inst Child Health & Human Develop, Bethesda, Md, 66-68; attend pediatrician & dir lab perinatal med pharmacol, Children's Hosp, San Francisco, 69-70; assoc prof, Med Sch, Vanderbilt Univ, 70-77; PROF PEDIAT & PHARMACOL & CHIEF, SECT CLIN PHARMACOL, SCH MED, LA STATE UNIV, 78- *Concurrent Pos:* Fel neonatal med & dir lab develop pharmacol, Children's Hosp, San Francisco, 68-69; NIH res career develop award, 69 & 72; lectr, Med Ctr, Univ Calif, San Francisco, 69-70; res assoc, J F Kennedy Ctr, 70- *Mem:* AAAS; Soc Pediat Res; Am Soc Pharmacol & Exp Therapeut; Am Soc Clin Pharmacol & Therapeut; Am Acad Pediat. *Res:* Pediatric clinical pharmacology, drug metabolism. *Mailing Add:* Dept of Pharmacol PO Box 33932 Shreveport LA 71130

WILSON, JOHN THOMAS, b Tucson, Ariz, Oct 30, 44; m 69. MOLECULAR BIOLOGY, BIOCHEMISTRY. *Educ:* Univ Ariz, BS, 69, PhD(genetics), 74. *Prof Exp:* Fel human genetics, Med Sch, Yale Univ, 74-76, res assoc, 76-78; ASSOC PROF CELL & MOLECULAR BIOL, MED COL GA, 78- *Concurrent Pos:* NIH fel, 75-77. *Mem:* Am Soc Microbiologists; AAAS; Am Chem Soc; Genetics Soc Am; Biophys Soc. *Res:* Structura and organization of human hemoglobin genes through molecular cloning. *Mailing Add:* Dept of Cell & Molecular Biol Med Col of Ga Augusta GA 30901

WILSON, JOHN THOMAS, JR, b Birmingham, Ala, June 2, 24; m 68. ENVIRONMENTAL MEDICINE, PREVENTIVE MEDICINE. *Educ:* Howard Univ, BS, 46; Columbia Univ, MD, 50; Univ Cincinnati, ScD(indust med), 56. *Prof Exp:* Physician, Div Indust Hyg, NY State Dept Labor, 55-56 & Sidney Hillman Health Ctr, New York, 56-57; chief bur occup health, Santa Clara County Health Dept, Calif, 57-61; life sci adv, Lockheed Aircraft Corp, 61-67, head biol sci res labs, Lockheed Missiles & Space Co, 67-69; asst prof community & prev med, Sch Med, Stanford Univ, 69-71; prof community health pract & chmn dept, Col Med, Howard Univ, 71-74; PROF ENVIRON HEALTH & CHMN DEPT, SCH PUB HEALTH & COMMUNITY MED, UNIV WASH, 74- *Concurrent Pos:* Nat Med Fel fel, 53-55; fel indust med, Univ Cincinnati, 53-56; lectr, Sch Pub Health, Univ Calif, Berkeley, 59-61. *Mem:* Fel Indust Med Asn; fel Am Col Physicians; Am Acad Occup Med; Am Indust Hyg Asn. *Res:* Occupational and environmental medicine; toxicology; industrial hygiene. *Mailing Add:* Sch Pub Health & Community Med Univ Wash Dept Environ Health Seattle WA 98195

WILSON, JOHN TUZO, b Ottawa, Ont, Oct 24, 08; m 38; c 2. GEOPHYSICS, TECTONICS. *Educ:* Univ Toronto, BA, 30; Univ Cambridge, MA, 32, ScD, 58; Princeton Univ, PhD(geol), 36. *Hon Degrees:* LLD, Carleton Univ, 58, Simon Fraser Univ, 78; DSc, Univ Western Ont, 58, Acadia Univ, Mem Univ Newf, 68, McGill Univ, 74, Univ Toronto, 77, Laurentian Univ, 78, Middlebury Col, 81; ScD, Franklin & Marshall Col, 69; DUniv, Univ Calgary, 74. *Prof Exp:* Asst geologist, Geol Surv Can, 36-39; prof geophys, Univ Toronto, 46-74; prin, Erindale Col, 67-74; DIR-GEN, ONT SCI CENTRE, 74- *Concurrent Pos:* Vis prof, Australian Nat Univ, 50 & 65; pres, Int Union Geol & Geophys, 57-60; mem, Nat Res Coun Can, 58-64; mem, Defence Res Bd Can, 60-66; distinguished lectr, Univ Toronto, 74-77. *Honors & Awards:* Miller Medal, Royal Soc Can, 56; Blaylock Medal, Can Inst Mining & Metal, 59; Bucher Medal, Am Geophys Union, 68; Penrose Medal, Geol Soc Am, 69; Companion Award, Order Can, 74; J J Carty Medal, Nat Acad Sci, 75; Wollaston Medal, Geol Soc London, 78; M Ewing Medal, Am Geophys Union, 80 & Soc Explor Geophysics, 81; A G Huntsman Award, Bedford Inst Oceanog, 81. *Mem:* Foreign assoc Nat Acad Sci; fel Geol Soc Am; fel Royal Soc Can (pres, 72-73); fel Royal Soc; foreign mem Am Philos Soc. *Res:* Physics of the earth; continental structure. *Mailing Add:* Ont Sci Centre 770 Don Mills Road Don Mills ON M3C 1R7 Can

WILSON, JOHN WILLIAM, b Arkansas City, Kans, Aug 6, 40; m 62; c 1. THEORETICAL HIGH ENERGY PHYSICS, HEALTH PHYSICS. *Educ:* Kans State Univ, BS, 62; Col William & Mary, MS, 69, PhD(physics), 75. *Prof Exp:* Aerospace technologist simulation, 63-70, space scientist space physics, 70-76, SR RES SCIENTIST ENERGY SYSTS, LANGLEY RES CTR, NASA, 76- *Concurrent Pos:* Adj asst prof physics, Old Dominion Univ, 75-80, adj assoc prof, 80- *Honors & Awards:* NASA spec achievement, 75. *Res:* High-energy heavy ion reaction theory; high-energy transport theory; health physics aspects of high-altitude aircraft and space operations and dosimetry; nuclear induced plasmas and radiolysis; nuclear pumped and electral pumped laser kinetics; solar pumped laser kinetics; author or coauthor of over 75 technical articles and reports. *Mailing Add:* NASA Langley Res Ctr Mail Stop 160 Hampton VA 23665

WILSON, JOHN WILLIAM, III, b New York, NY, May 10, 43; m 66. ZOOGEOGRAPHY, PALEONTOLOGY. *Educ:* Amherst Col, BA, 66; Univ Chicago, PhD(evolutionary biol), 72. *Prof Exp:* Asst prof, 72-78, ASSOC PROF BIOL, GEORGE MASON UNIV, 78- *Mem:* AAAS; Soc Study Evolution; Soc Vert Paleont; Am Soc Mammal; Ecol Soc Am. *Res:* Zoogeography of mammals; latitudinal gradients; paleoecology of mammals; changes in resource utilization of mammals during late Cretaceous and Cenozoic; Pleistocene extinctions. *Mailing Add:* Dept of Biol George Mason Univ Fairfax VA 22030

WILSON, JOSEPH EDWARD, b Hannibal, Mo, Jan 8, 20; m 45; c 4. PHYSICAL CHEMISTRY. *Educ:* Univ Chicago, BS, 39; Univ Rochester, PhD(phys chem), 42. *Prof Exp:* Res chemist, Goodyear Aircraft Corp, 42-46, Argonne Nat Lab, 46-47 & Firestone Tire & Rubber Co, 47-50; sr chemist, Bakelite Co Div, Union Carbide & Carbon Corp, 50-57 & J T Baker Chem Co, 57; develop supvr, Atlas Powder Co, 58-61; proj mgr, Kordite Co, 61-64; res dir, Pollock Paper Div, St Regis Paper Co, 64-67; assoc prof, 67-71, PROF PHYS CHEM, BISHOP COL, 71- *Concurrent Pos:* Plastics consult, 67- *Mem:* Am Chem Soc. *Res:* Photochemistry; polymerization; stability of polymers; radiation chemistry of plastics; synthesis of blood-compatible plastics for use in artificial organs. *Mailing Add:* Dept of Chem Bishop Col Dallas TX 75241

WILSON, JOSEPH WILLIAM, b Massena, NY, Apr 11, 34. ORGANIC CHEMISTRY. *Educ:* Mass Inst Technol, BS, 56; Ind Univ, PhD(chem), 61. *Prof Exp:* Res assoc, Univ Wis, 61-63; asst prof, 63-70, ASSOC PROF CHEM, UNIV KY, 70- *Mem:* Am Chem Soc. *Res:* organic photochemistry. *Mailing Add:* Dept of Chem Univ of KY Lexington KY 40506

WILSON, KARL A, b Buffalo, NY, Jan 19, 47; m 74. BIOCHEMISTRY. *Educ:* State Univ NY Buffalo, BA, 69, PhD(biochem), 73. *Prof Exp:* Res assoc biochem, Roswell Park Mem Inst, 73-74; res assoc biochem, Purdue Univ, West Lafayette, 74-76; asst prof & assoc fel, Ctr Biochem Res, 76-80, ASST PROF & ASSOC FEL, SEMANTIC CELL GENETICS & BIOCHEM, STATE UNIV NY BINGHAMTON, 80- *Concurrent Pos:* NSF grad fel, 69-72. *Mem:* AAAS; Sigma Xi; Am Soc Plant Physiol. *Res:* Mechanism and physiology of proteases and their protein inhibitors; molecular evolution of proteins and protein sequencing; physiology of seed germination. *Mailing Add:* Dept of Biol Sci State Univ NY Binghamton NY 13901

WILSON, KATHERINE WOODS, b Los Angeles, Calif, Feb 8, 23. AIR POLLUTION. *Educ:* Univ Calif, BS, 44, MS, 45; Univ Calif, Los Angeles, PhD(chem), 48. *Prof Exp:* Asst prof chem, WVa Univ, 48-53 & Pepperdine Col, 53-54; mem staff, Los Angeles County Air Pollution Control Dist, 54-55; lectr chem & assoc res chemist, Univ Calif, Los Angeles, 55-62; phys chemist, Stanford Res Inst, 62-71; staff officer, Univ Calif, Riverside, 71-72; supv air pollution chemist, Air Pollution Control Serv, San Diego County, 73-74; dir air qual studies, Copley Int Corp, 74-76; dir, Chem & Metal Dept, Pac Environ Serv, 76-80; CONSULT, 80- *Mem:* Am Chem Soc; Air Pollution Control Asn. *Res:* Air pollution; cotton chemistry; chemical analysis of agricultural products. *Mailing Add:* PO Box 33014 San Diego CA 92103

WILSON, KATHRYN JAY, b Virginia, Minn, June 21, 48; m 69. PLANT ANATOMY, PLANT MORPHOLOGY. *Educ:* Univ Wis-Madison, BA, 71; Ind Univ, Bloomington, MA, 76, PhD(plant sci), 76. *Prof Exp:* ASST PROF BIOL, IND UNIV-PURDUE UNIV, INDIANAPOLIS, 76- *Concurrent Pos:* Res grants, Ind Univ-Purdue Univ, 77-78, NSF, 81-84. *Mem:* AAAS; Am Inst Biol Sci; Am Bot Soc. *Res:* Development of non-articulated laticifer system of the Ascelpiadaceae, with special emphasis on cytodifferentiation of the laticifer as a unique cell type in whole plants and tissue culture. *Mailing Add:* Dept of Biol 1201 E 38th St Indianapolis IN 46223

WILSON, KENNETH ALLEN, b Rio de Janeiro, Brazil, Apr 15, 28; US citizen. PLANT MORPHOLOGY, SYSTEMATIC BOTANY. *Educ:* Miami Univ, BA, 51; Univ Hawaii, MS, 53; Univ Mich, PhD(bot), 58. *Prof Exp:* Botanist, Gray Herbarium & Arnold Arboretum, Harvard Univ, 57-60; from asst prof to assoc prof, 60-67, assoc dean, Sch Letters & Sci, 66-73, PROF BOT, CALIF STATE UNIV, NORTHRIDGE, 67- *Mem:* Bot Soc Am; Am Soc Plant Taxon; Am Fern Soc; Int Asn Plant Taxon. *Res:* Taxonomy; pteridophytes. *Mailing Add:* Dept Bot Calif State Univ Northridge CA 91330

WILSON, KENNETH CHARLES, b Vancouver, BC, Feb 9, 37; m 62; c 2. CIVIL ENGINEERING, FLUID MECHANICS. *Educ:* Univ BC, BASc, 59; Univ London, MSc & DIC, 61; Queen's Univ, Ont, PhD(civil eng), 65. *Prof Exp:* Hydraul engr, Ingledow, Kidd & Assocs, BC, 61-63 & Int Power & Eng, 65-66; consult hydraul engr, Dept External Affairs, Govt Can, 66-68; sr hydraul engr, T Ingledow & Assocs, Consult Engrs, 68-70; assoc prof, 71-80, PROF CIVIL ENG, QUEEN'S UNIV, ONT, 80- *Mem:* Eng Inst Can. *Res:* Sediment transport in rivers, canals and pipelines; blockage, plug flow and sliding beds in pipelines. *Mailing Add:* Dept of Civil Eng Queen's Univ Kingston ON K7L 3N6 Can

WILSON, KENNETH GEDDES, b Waltham, Mass, June 8, 36. PHYSICS. *Educ:* Harvard Univ, AB, 56; Calif Inst Technol, PhD(physics), 61. *Prof Exp:* Jr fel, Harvard Univ, 59-62; Ford Found fel, Europ Orgn Nuclear Res, Geneva, Switz, 62-63; from asst prof to assoc prof, 63-71, PROF PHYSICS, CORNELL UNIV, 71-, MEM STAFF, LAB ATOMIC & SOLID STATE PHYSICS, 77- *Concurrent Pos:* Mem staff, Stanford Linear Accelerator Ctr, 69-70. *Mem:* Nat Acad Sci; Am Phys Soc. *Res:* Elementary particle theory. *Mailing Add:* Cornell Univ Ithaca NY 14853

WILSON, KENNETH GLADE, b Payson, Utah, May 18, 40; m 59; c 3. BOTANY. *Educ:* Univ Utah, BS, 62, PhD(molecular biol), 68. *Prof Exp:* Reliability engr, Hercules Powder, 62-63; PROF BOT, MIAMI UNIV, 67- *Mem:* Am Genetic Asn; Am Soc Plant Physiologists; Sigma Xi; Tissue Culture Asn. *Res:* Function and inheritances of plastids in higher plants; plastid functions of amino acid biosynthesis. *Mailing Add:* Dept Bot Miami Univ Oxford OH 45056

WILSON, KENNETH SHERIDAN, b Waterloo, Iowa, May 1, 24; m 48, 62; c 1. MYCOLOGY, PLANT PATHOLOGY. *Educ:* Colo Col, BS, 49; Univ Wyo, MS, 50; Purdue Univ, PhD(mycol), 54. *Prof Exp:* Asst, Colo Col, 46-49 & Univ Wyo, 49-50; asst, 52-53, from instr to assoc prof, 54-71, PROF BIOL SCI, PURDUE UNIV, CALUMET CAMPUS, 71- *Mem:* AAAS; Mycol Soc Am; Bot Soc Am; Soc Indust Microbiol; Am Soc Microbiol. *Res:* Mycological taxonomy; plant taxonomy; plant morphology; microbiological ecology. *Mailing Add:* Dept of Biol Sci Purdue Univ Calumet Campus Hammond IN 46323

WILSON, KENT RAYMOND, b Philadelphia, Pa, Jan 14, 37. CHEMICAL PHYSICS. *Educ:* Harvard Col, AB, 58; Univ Strasbourg, dipl, 59; Univ Calif, Berkeley, PhD(chem), 64. *Prof Exp:* Res fel chem, Harvard Univ, 64-65; res chemist, Nat Bur Stand, 65; asst prof phys chem, 65-71, assoc prof, 71-77, PROF PHYS CHEM, UNIV CALIF, SAN DIEGO, 77- *Concurrent Pos:* Sloan res fel, 70-72; mem comt comput in chem, Div Chem & Chem Technol, Nat Res Coun, 70-72; mem comput & biomath sci study sect, NIH, 71-74; mem panel photochem oxidants, ozone & hydrocarbons, Nat Res Coun, 73-74. *Mem:* Am Phys Soc; Am Chem Soc. *Res:* Molecular dynamics of chemical reactions, particularly in solution; specialized computer systems for solution of scientific problems; computer animation; archaeological chemistry; air pollution. *Mailing Add:* Dept of Chem Univ of Calif San Diego La Jolla CA 92093

WILSON, L KENNETH, b Sacramento, Calif, Sept 22, 10; m 35; c 1. EXPLORATION GEOLOGY. *Educ:* Stanford Univ, AB, 32. *Prof Exp:* Geologist gold mining, Mother Lode Mining Dist, Calif, 32-35; geologist, Calumet & Hecla Copper Co, 35-38; mgr, Auburn Chicago Mine, Calif, 38-39; geologist, Cord Mining Interests, 39-43 & Am Smelting, 43-60; CONSULT GEOLOGIST, 60- *Concurrent Pos:* Gov app, Western Gov Mining Adv Coun, 67- *Mem:* Fel Geol Soc Am; Am Inst Prof Geologists; Am Inst Mining, Metall & Petrol Engrs; Am Asn Petrol Geologists. *Res:* Exploration geology, domestic mineral resources; assistance to legal counsel in mining law, litigation, utilization and acquisition of mineral property. *Mailing Add:* PO Box 7123 Menlo Park CA 94025

WILSON, LARRY EUGENE, b Wapakoneta, Ohio, Nov 17, 35; m 58; c 2. ANALYTICAL CHEMISTRY. *Educ:* Ohio State Univ, BSc, 57, PhD(anal chem), 62. *Prof Exp:* Anal chemist, Dow Chem Co, Mich, 63-64; asst prof chem, Mich State Univ, 64-65; anal chemist, Dow Chem Co, Mich, 65-66, supvr control lab, 66-67, coordr lab technician training, 67-69; asst prof, 69-72, ASSOC PROF CHEM, LANCASTER BR, OHIO UNIV, 72- *Mem:* Am Chem Soc. *Res:* Acid-base equilibria; methods of teaching. *Mailing Add:* Dept of Chem Lancaster Br Ohio Univ Lancaster OH 43130

WILSON, LARRY KITTRELL, b Russellville, Ky, Apr 15, 34; m 57; c 2. MICROWAVE THEORY & TECHNIQUES. *Educ:* Ga Inst Technol, BEE, 55, MSEE, 58; Vanderbilt Univ, PhD(elec eng), 64. *Prof Exp:* Sr engr, Sperry Microwave Electronics Co, 59-61; from asst prof to assoc prof elec eng, 64-73, chmn div elec & comput sci, 72-75, PROF ELEC ENG, VANDERBILT UNIV, 73- *Concurrent Pos:* Consult, Sperry Microwave Electronics Co, Fla, 61-64, Brown Eng Co, Ala, 65- & Sci-Atlanta, Inc, Ga, 66-; NSF fel exp solid state physics, Mass Inst Technol, 65; mem tech comn magnetic mat, Int Electrotech Comn, 74-; rep, Int Affil Coun, Adv Aircraft Elec Syst, 80-, vchmn, 82. *Mem:* AAAS; Inst Elec & Electronics Engrs; Am Phys Soc; Am Ceramic Soc; Am Soc Eng Educ; NY Acad Sci. *Res:* Microwave theory and techniques; magnetics and magnetic materials; microwave solid state devices; electrical magnetic properties of materials. *Mailing Add:* Box 1687 Sta B Vanderbilt Univ Nashville TN 37235

WILSON, LAUREN R, b Yates Center, Kans, May 4, 36; m 59; c 2. INORGANIC CHEMISTRY, ENVIRONMENTAL CHEMISTRY. *Educ:* Baker Univ, BS, 58; Univ Kans, PhD(inorg chem), 63. *Prof Exp:* Asst prof, 63-70, chmn dept, 70-77, PROF CHEM, OHIO WESLEYAN UNIV, 70-, DEAN ACAD AFFAIRS, 77- *Concurrent Pos:* Mem staff, Oak Ridge Nat Lab, 72-73; vis prof, Ohio State Univ, 68, 76-77. *Mem:* Am Chem Soc; Royal Soc Chem. *Res:* Synthesis of transition metal compounds; electrocatalysis of chemically modified electrodes; metal ions in natural and biological systems. *Mailing Add:* Dept of Chem Ohio Wesleyan Univ Delaware OH 43015

WILSON, LAURENCE EDWARD, b Aberdeen SDak, June 29, 30; m 57; c 3. INORGANIC CHEMISTRY. *Educ:* Western Wash Col Educ, BA, 52; Univ Wash, PhD(chem), 57. *Prof Exp:* Instr chem, Amherst Col, 56-59; from asst prof to assoc prof, San Jose State Col, 59-63; assoc prof, 63-80, PROF CHEM, KALAMAZOO COL, 80-, CHMN DEPT, 63- *Mem:* AAAS; Am Chem Soc. *Mailing Add:* Dept of Chem Kalamazoo Col Kalamazoo MI 49007

WILSON, LAWRENCE ALBERT, JR, b Mt Hope, WVa, Mar 19, 25; m 49; c 3. CHEMICAL & PETROLEUM ENGINEERING. *Educ:* Purdue Univ, BS, 49, PhD(chem eng), 52. *Prof Exp:* Engr, Staple Develop Plant, Am Viscose Corp, 52-53, develop supvr, 53-54; res engr, 54-56, group leader petrol res, 56-62, sr res engr, 62-66, sect supvr, 66-72, staff engr, 72-76, MGR PROD RES DEPT, GULF RES & DEVELOP CO, 76- *Concurrent Pos:* Lectr, Univ Pittsburgh, 64- *Mem:* Am Chem Soc; Am Inst Mining, Metall & Petrol Engrs. *Res:* Petroleum production. *Mailing Add:* Gulf Res & Develop Co PO Drawer 2038 Pittsburgh PA 15230

WILSON, LELAND LESLIE, b Williamsburg, Ky, June 13, 14; m 38; c 3. CHEMISTRY. *Educ:* Eastern Ky State Col, BS, 34; Univ Ky, MS, 41; Peabody Col, PhD(sci educ), 51. *Prof Exp:* Instr high sch, Ky, 35-36 & Fla, 36-42; radio theory, US Air Force Tech Sch, Univ Chicago, 42-43; asst prof sci, Eastern Ky State Col, 46-49, 51-52; prof physics, Ga Teachers Col, 52-55; assoc prof, 55-59, prof, 59-80, head dept, 68-75, EMER PROF CHEM, UNIV NORTHERN IOWA, 80- *Mem:* AAAS; Am Chem Soc; Nat Sci Teachers Asn. *Res:* Chemical instrumentation; metal chelate stability; molecular models and demonstrations for chemistry teaching. *Mailing Add:* Dept of Chem Univ of Northern Iowa Cedar Falls IA 50613

WILSON, LENNOX NORWOOD, b Quebec City, Que, Feb 15, 32; US citizen; m 58; c 3. FLUID DYNAMICS, ACOUSTICS. *Educ:* Univ Toronto, BASc, 53, MASc, 54, PhD(aerophys), 59. *Prof Exp:* Res asst, Inst Aerophys, Univ Toronto, 53-59; res engr, Armour Res Found, Ill, 59-62; head aerochem, Defense Res Labs, Gen Motors Corp, Calif, 62-66; mgr fluid dynamics & acoust, IIT Res Inst, Ill, 66-71; prof mech & aerospace eng, Univ Mo-Columbia, 71-73; actg head aerospace eng, 78-79, PROF AEROSPACE ENG, IOWA STATE UNIV, 73- *Mem:* Assoc fel Am Inst Aeronaut & Astronaut. *Res:* Turbulence; combustion; shock tubes; chemical kinetics; aerodynamic noise; noise control; engineering acoustics. *Mailing Add:* Dept of Aerospace Eng Iowa State Univ Ames IA 50010

WILSON, LEON WILLIAM, JR, environmental research, see previous edition

WILSON, LEONARD GILCHRIST, b Orillia, Ont, June 11, 28. HISTORY OF MEDICINE. *Educ:* Univ Toronto, BA, 49; Univ London, MSc, 55; Univ Wis, PhD(hist sci), 58. *Prof Exp:* Lectr biol, Mt Allison Univ, 50-53; vis instr hist sci, Univ Calif, 58-59; vis asst prof, Cornell Univ, 59-60; from asst prof to assoc prof hist med, Sch Med, Yale Univ, 60-67; PROF HISTORY OF MED & HEAD DEPT, UNIV MINN, MINNEAPOLIS, 67-, . *Mem:* AAAS; Am Asn Hist Med; Am Hist Asn; Hist Sci Soc; Soc Hist Technol. *Res:* History of biology; history of physiology in the seventeenth century; history of fever. *Mailing Add:* Dept History Med Univ Minn Minneapolis MN 55455

WILSON, LEONARD RICHARD, b Superior, Wis, July 23, 06; m 30; c 2. GEOLOGY, PALYNOLOGY. *Educ:* Univ Wis, PhB, 30, PhM, 32, PhD(bot), 36. *Prof Exp:* Asst, Wis Geol & Natural Hist Surv, 31-35; from instr to prof geol & bot, Coe Col, 35-46; prof geol & head dept geol & mineral, Univ Mass, 46-56; prof geol, NY Univ, 56-57; prof, 57-62, res prof, 62-67, George Lynn Gross res prof geol & geophysics, 68-78, EMER PROF GEOL & GEOPHYS, UNIV OKLA, 68-, CUR MICROPALEONT & PALEOBOT, STOVALL MUS, 71- *Concurrent Pos:* Melhaup scholar, Ohio State Univ, 39-40; consult, Carter Oil Co, 46-56; leader, Am Geog Soc Greenland Ice Cap Exped, 53; res assoc, Am Mus Natural Hist, 57-78; geologist, Okla Geol Surv, 57-78, emer geologist, 78-; adj prof, Univ Tulsa; consult, Jersey Prod Res Corp, 56-62, Humble Oil Co, 63-64 & Sinclair Oil Co, 63-69; consult geologist, 78- *Honors & Awards:* VI Gunnar Erdtman Int Medal, Palynology Soc India, 73. *Mem:* Fel Geol Soc Am; Am Bot Soc; Am Asn Petrol Geol; hon mem Nat Asn Geol Teachers; hon mem Am Asn Stratig Palynologists. *Res:* Stratigraphic and paleoecologic palynology. *Mailing Add:* Dept of Geol Univ of Okla Norman OK 73019

WILSON, LESLIE, b Boston, Mass, June 29, 41; div; c 1. PHARMACOLOGY, BIOCHEMISTRY. *Educ:* Mass Col Pharm, BS, 63; Tufts Univ, PhD(pharmacol), 67. *Prof Exp:* Asst prof pharmacol, Sch Med, Stanford Univ, 69-75; assoc prof biochem, 75-78, PROF BIOCHEM UNIV CALIF, SANTA BARBARA, 78- *Concurrent Pos:* USPHS fel, Univ Calif, Berkeley, 67-69; Nat Inst Neurol Dis & Stroke res grant, 70-; Am Cancer Soc grant, 70- *Mem:* AAAS; Am Soc Pharmacol & Exp Therapeut; Am Soc Cell Biol. *Res:* Mechanism and regulation of microtubule assembly and function; mechanism of action of antimitotic chemical agents. *Mailing Add:* Dept Biol Sci Univ Calif Santa Barbara CA 93106

WILSON, LESTER A, JR, b Charleston, SC, Apr 30, 17; m 45; c 4. MEDICINE. *Educ:* Col William & Mary, BS, 38; Med Col SC, MD, 42. *Prof Exp:* From asst prof to assoc prof, 51-65, PROF OBSTET & GYNEC, SCH MED, UNIV VA, 65- *Mailing Add:* Dept of Obstet & Gynec Univ Va Sch Med Charlottesville VA 22903

WILSON, LINDA S WHATLEY, b Washington, DC, Nov 10, 36; m 57, 70; c 1. CHEMISTRY, RESEARCH ADMINISTRATION. *Educ:* Tulane Univ, BA, 57; Univ Wis, PhD(inorg chem), 62. *Prof Exp:* Res assoc inorg chem, Univ Wis, 62; Nat Inst Dent Res trainee phys chem & res assoc molecular spectros, Univ Md, 62-64, res asst prof, Molecular Spectros, 64-67; vis res fel, Univ Southampton, 67; vis asst prof, Univ Mo-St Louis, 67-68; asst to vchancellor res, Wash Univ, 68-69, asst vchancellor res, 69-74, assoc vchancellor res, 74-75; ASSOC VCHANCELLOR RES, UNIV ILL, URBANA, 75-, ASSOC DEAN, GRAD COL, 78- *Concurrent Pos:* Mem, Gen Res Support Adv Comt, NIH, 71-75, chmn, 74-75; mem, Comt Govt Relations, Nat Asn Cols & Univ Bus Officers, 71-, chmn, 73-75; co-chmn, Panel Eval Div Res Resources, NIH, 75-76; mem, Procurement Policy Adv Comt, Energy Res & Develop Admin, 76-77, Bd-Coun Comt Chem & Pub Affairs, Am Chem Soc, 78-82, Nat Adv Coun Res Resources, NIH, 78-82 & Nat Comn Res, 78-80; mem dirs adv coun, NSF, 80-; mem comt gov & asn affairs, Coun Grad Schs, 81-84; mem comt govt univ rel in support of sci, Nat Acad Sci, 81-82. *Mem:* AAAS; Am Chem Soc. *Res:* Molecular spectroscopy; spectroscopic studies of molecular interactions; charge transfer complexes; coordination compounds and hydrogen bonded species; optical studies at high pressures. *Mailing Add:* 506 W Florida Ave Urbana IL 61801

WILSON, LON JAMES, b Mojave, Calif, Sept 4, 44. INORGANIC CHEMISTRY, BIOINORGANIC CHEMISTRY. *Educ:* Iowa State Univ, BS, 66; Univ Wash, PhD(inorg chem), 71. *Prof Exp:* Teaching asst chem, Univ Wash, 66-68; vis asst prof, Univ Ill, 71-73; asst prof, 73-78, ASSOC PROF CHEM, RICE UNIV, 78- *Concurrent Pos:* NIH fel, Univ Ill, 71-73; indust consult, Monsanto Chem Co, St Louis, 75- *Mem:* The Chem Soc; Am Chem Soc. *Res:* Magnetic and redox properties of transition metal compounds; Mössbauer spectroscopy; iron and copper containing metalloproteins and their synthetic analogs. *Mailing Add:* Dept of Chem Rice Univ Houston TX 77001

WILSON, LORENZO GEORGE, b Appleton, NY, July 25, 38; m 62; c 3. HORTICULTURE, VEGETABLE CROPS. *Educ:* Cornell Univ, BS, 61; Wash State Univ, MS, 64; Mich State Univ, PhD(hort), 69. *Prof Exp:* Res assoc postharvest physiol, United Fruit Co, 63-66; plant physiologist, United Brands Co, 69-75; PROF HORT & EXTEN HORT SPECIALIST VEG CROPS, HORT DEPT, NC STATE UNIV, 75- *Concurrent Pos:* Consult banana prod & postharvest produce handling, Cent & SAm. *Mem:* Am Soc Hort Sci; Sigma Xi; Potato Asn Am. *Res:* Investigations to determine optimum cultural practices for potato and sweet potato production in North Carolina, including the use of fertilizers, pesticides and harvesting, handling and storage techniques for enhanced quality maintenance; bananas. *Mailing Add:* Dept Hort Sci NC State Univ Raleigh NC 27607

WILSON, LORNE GRAHAM, b Saskatoon, Sask, Oct 23, 29; US citizen; m 57; c 2. SOIL PHYSICS, HYDROLOGY. *Educ:* Univ BC, BS, 51; Univ Calif, MS, 57, PhD(soil sci), 62. *Prof Exp:* Asst specialist irrig drainage, Univ Calif, 56-58; from asst hydrologist, to assoc hydrologist, 62-67, HYDROLOGIST, WATER RESOURCES RES CTR, UNIV ARIZ, 67- *Res:* Survey of drainage problems in San Joaquin Valley, California; simultaneous flow of air and water during infiltration in soils; subsurface flow characteristics during natural and artificial recharge in stratified sediments. *Mailing Add:* Water Resources Res Ctr Univ of Ariz Tucson AZ 85721

WILSON, LOUIS FREDERICK, b Milwaukee, Wis, Nov 22, 32; m 56; c 4. ENTOMOLOGY. *Educ:* Marquette Univ, BS, 55, MS, 57; Univ Minn, PhD(entom), 62. *Prof Exp:* Instr cytol & parasitol, Marquette Univ, 54-57; state entomologist, Minn, 58; CHIEF INSECT ECOLOGIST, NORTH CENT FOREST EXP STA, US FOREST SERV, 58-; asst prof forestry, 67-73, asst prof entom, 69-73, ASSOC PROF FORESTRY, MICH STATE UNIV, 73-, ASSOC PROF ENTOM, 73- *Mem:* Entom Soc Am; Entom Soc Can. *Res:* Insect ecology and behavior; population dynamics; insect impact. *Mailing Add:* 900 Longfellow Dr East Lansing MI 48823

WILSON, LOWELL D, b Pampa, Tex, May 11, 33; m 60; c 2. ENDOCRINOLOGY, BIOLOGICAL CHEMISTRY. *Educ:* Johns Educ: Univ Calif, Berkeley, AB, 55; Univ Chicago, MD, 60; Univ Southern Calif, PhD(biochem), 68. *Prof Exp:* From instr to asst prof med, Sch Med, Univ Southern Calif, 66-68; from asst prof to assoc prof med & biol chem, 68-77, PROF MED & BIOL CHEM, SCH MED, UNIV CALIF, DAVIS, 77- *Mem:* Endocrine Soc; Am Fedn Clin Res; Am Chem Soc; Am Soc Biol Chem. *Res:* Biochemistry; metabolic control processes; hormone action. *Mailing Add:* Dept of Internal Med Univ of Calif Sch of Med Davis CA 95616

WILSON, LOWELL L, b Egan, Ill, Jan 3, 36; m 55; c 3. ANIMAL SCIENCES. *Educ:* Wis State Univ, BS, 60; SDak State Univ, MS, 62, PhD(animal sci), 64. *Prof Exp:* Res asst animal genetics, SDak State Univ, 60-64; livestock specialist, Purdue Univ, 64-66; assoc prof animal prod, 66-71, PROF ANIMAL SCI, PA STATE UNIV, UNIVERSITY PARK, 71- *Honors & Awards:* Meat Animal Mgt Award, Am Soc Animal Sci, 73. *Mem:* AAAS; Am Genetic Asn; Am Soc Animal Sci; Am Meat Sci Asn. *Res:* Selection indices for beef cattle and estimations of genetic parameters from use of selected sires; ranch x sire and sex x sire interactions; beef cattle and sheep behavior; forage utilization with ruminants; recycling of waste materials through ruminants. *Mailing Add:* 238 Webster Dr State College PA 16802

WILSON, LYNN HAROLD, polymer chemistry, see previous edition

WILSON, LYNN O, b Wilmington, Del, July 9, 44. APPLIED MATHEMATICS. *Educ:* Oberlin Col, AB, 65; Univ Wis, PhD(appl math), 70. *Prof Exp:* MEM TECH STAFF MATH RES, BELL LABS, 70- *Mem:* Am Phys Soc; Soc Indust & Appl Math. *Res:* Mathematical physics; partial differential equations; crystal growth; acoustic waveguides, optical waveguides; electromagnetic theory. *Mailing Add:* Bell Labs 600 Mountain Ave Murray Hill NJ 07974

WILSON, MCCLURE, b Ogden, Utah, July 30, 24; m 50; c 2. RADIOLOGY. *Educ:* Univ Ark, BS, 47, MD, 48. *Prof Exp:* From asst prof to assoc prof radiol, Univ Tex Med Br, 55-63; radiologist, Scott & White Clin, Temple, Tex, 63-64; assoc prof radiol, 64-69, PROF RADIOL, UNIV TEX MED BR GALVESTON, 69- *Mem:* AMA; Radiol Soc NAm; Am Roentgen Ray Soc. *Mailing Add:* Dept of Radiol Univ of Tex Med Br Galveston TX 77550

WILSON, MARION EVANS, b Irwin, Pa, Nov 6, 16. MEDICAL MICROBIOLOGY, CLINICAL MICROBIOLOGY. *Educ:* Temple Univ, BSMT, 39; Smith Col, MA, 47; Boston Univ, PhD(med sci), 51. *Prof Exp:* Instr microbiol & immunol, State Univ NY Downstate Med Ctr, 51-54; asst dir microbiol & serol, St Luke's Hosp, New York, 54-65; dir microbiol & serol, Mt Sinai Hosp, Miami Beach, 65-66; chief microbiologist, 66-71, ASST DIR BUR LABS, NEW YORK CITY DEPT HEALTH, 71- *Concurrent Pos:* Consult microbiol, Social Security Admin, Bur Health Ins, US Dept Health, Educ & Welfare, 72; mem adv comt, Prof Exam Serv, Nat Clin Lab Technologist Exam, 74-75. *Mem:* Fel & dipl Am Acad Microbiol; Am Soc Microbiol; Am Pub Health Asn; fel NY Acad Sci. *Res:* Areas of public health interest, particularly gonorrhea detection; development and conduct of laboratory improvement methods, especially proficiency testing techniques. *Mailing Add:* New York City Dept Health Bur Labs 455 First Ave New York NY 10016

WILSON, MARJORIE PRICE, b Pittsburgh, Pa, Sept 25, 24; m 51; c 2. MEDICINE. *Educ:* Univ Pittsburgh, MD, 49. *Prof Exp:* Intern, Med Ctr, Univ Pittsburgh Hosp, 49-50, resident, Children's Hosp, 50-51; resident, Jackson Mem Hosp, Sch Med, Univ Miami, 54-56; chief, Contractual Res Sect, Res & Educ Serv, Vet Admin, 52-53, chief, Residency & Internship Div, Educ Serv, 56, chief prof training div, 56-60, asst dir, Educ Serv, 60; chief training br, Extramural Prog, Nat Inst Arthritis & Metab Dis, NIH, 60-63, asst to assoc dir training, Off of Dir, 63-64; assoc dir extramural prog, Nat Libr Med, 64-67; assoc dir prog develop, Off Prog Planning & Eval, Off of Dir, NIH, Bethesda, 67-69, asst dir prog planning & eval, 69-70; dir, Dept Inst Develop, Asn Am Med Col, 70-81; SR ASSOC DEAN, SCH MED, UNIV MD, BALTIMORE, 81- *Concurrent Pos:* Grants & contracts var agencies, 72-; mem adv bd, Fogarty Int Ctr, NIH, 72-73; mem bd vis, Sch Med, Univ Pittsburgh, 74-; mem bd trustees, Anal Serv, Inc, Arlington, 76- *Honors & Awards:* Superior Performance Award, HEW. *Mem:* Inst Med-Nat Acad Sci; Am Fedn Clin Res; AAAS; Inst Elec & Electronics Engrs; Asn Am Med Col. *Res:* Management of medical systems, including education, research and health care; leadership roles and decision making in academic medicine. *Mailing Add:* Sch Med Univ Md 655 W Baltimore St Baltimore MD 21201

WILSON, MARK ALLAN, b Berkeley, Calif, Nov 26, 56; m 76. INVERTEBRATE PALEONTOLOGY, BIOSTRATIGRAPHY. *Educ:* Col Wooster, Ohio, BA, 78; Univ Calif, Berkeley, PhD(paleont), 82. *Prof Exp:* Res geologist, Chevron Oil Field Res Co, 78; teaching asst paleont, Univ Calif, Berkeley, 79-81; instr, 81-82, ASST PROF GEOL, COL WOOSTER, OHIO, 82- *Concurrent Pos:* Ed, Paleo Biol J, 80-81. *Mem:* Paleont Soc; Geol Soc Am; Sigma Xi; AAAS. *Res:* Paleozoic invertebrate fossil communities in relation to sedimentary environments deduced through sedimentary petrology; evolution and systematics of late Paleozoic trilobites, application of paleoecology to biostratigraphy. *Mailing Add:* Dept Geol Col Wooster Wooster OH 44691

WILSON, MARK CURTIS, b Ware, Mass, Sept 19, 21. ENTOMOLOGY. *Educ:* Univ Mass, BS, 44; Ohio State Univ, MS, 46. *Prof Exp:* Field Aide, Div Truck Crops Invests, Bur Entom & Plant Quarantine, US Dept Agr, 45; asst zool, Ohio State Univ, 44-47; from asst prof to assoc prof, 47-69, PROF ENTOM, PURDUE UNIV, W LAFAYETTE, 69- *Concurrent Pos:* Consult, Adv Comt, Alfalfa Seed Coun, Food & Agr Orgn, Rumania, 71. *Mem:* Entom Soc Am. *Res:* Insect pest management; economic insect thresholds; host plant resistance. *Mailing Add:* Dept of Entom Purdue Univ West Lafayette IN 47907

WILSON, MARK VINCENT HARDMAN, b Toronto, Ont, Feb 11, 46; m 70; c 3. VERTEBRATE PALEONTOLOGY. *Educ:* Univ Toronto, BSc, 68, MSc, 70, PhD(geol), 74. *Prof Exp:* Asst prof biol, Queen's Univ, Kingston, Ont, 74-75; asst prof zool, 75-81, ASSOC PROF ZOOL & ADJ ASSOC PROF GEOL, UNIV ALTA, 81- *Concurrent Pos:* Res assoc, Dept Vert Palaeont, Royal Ont Mus, 74-; mem, Alta Paleontol Adv Comt, 78-81; assoc ed, Paleontographica Canadiana, 81- *Mem:* Soc Vert Paleont; Can Soc Zoologists; Am Soc Ichthyologists & Herpetologists; Soc Syst Zool; Soc Study Evolution. *Res:* Fossil fishes, especially Tertiary freshwater teleosts; zoological systematics; paleoecology of lacustrine sediments; Tertiary insects; anatomy and evolution of recent fishes. *Mailing Add:* Dept of Zool Univ of Alta Edmonton AB T6G 2E9 Can

WILSON, MARLENE MOORE, b Austin, Tex, July 4, 47; m 70; c 1. HUMAN ANATOMY, NEUROENDOCRINOLOGY. *Educ:* Univ St Thomas, BA, 69; Baylor Col Med, PhD(anat), 75. *Prof Exp:* Res asst neuropharmacol, Med Sch, Univ Tex, San Antonio, 69-70; res assoc neuroendocrinol, Health Sci Ctr, Univ Ore, 74-75, res fel endocrinol, 75-76; asst prof, 76-80, ASSOC PROF BIOL, UNIV PORTLAND, 80- *Concurrent Pos:* Teaching asst, Baylor Col Med, 70-72; instr anat, Health Sci Ctr, Univ Ore, 74-75; clin res asst prof med, Ore Health Sci Univ, 79-; consult, Providence Med Ctr, 79- *Mem:* Am Asn Anatomists; Endocrine Soc; Am Physiol Soc; Soc Neurosci; Geront Soc Am. *Res:* Regulation of pituitary secretion of ACTH by the nervous system; circadian rhythmicity and the role of the hippocampus in regulating the pituitary-adrenal axis. *Mailing Add:* Univ Portland 5000 N Willamette Blvd Portland OR 97203

WILSON, MARTIN, b Berlin, Ger, June 12, 13; US citizen; m 47; c 2. CHEMISTRY. *Educ:* Univ Geneva, DSc(constitution of starch), 39. *Prof Exp:* Res chemist, Palestine Potash Co, 43-48, Bonneville Ltd, Utah, 48-55, Kennecott Copper Corp, Utah, 55-56 & Nat Potash Co, NMex, 56; from res chemist to sr res chemist, US Borax Res Corp, 56-62, sr scientist, 62-79; CONSULT, 79- *Mem:* Am Chem Soc. *Res:* Potash refining; phase equilibrium; beneficiation of fluorspar ores and molybdenite ores. *Mailing Add:* 9 Orchard St Irvine CA 92714

WILSON, MARVIN CRACRAFT, b Wheeling, WVa, Aug 7, 43; m 66; c 2. PHARMACY, PHARMACOLOGY. *Educ:* WVa Univ, BS, 66; Univ Mich, Ann Arbor, PhD(pharmacol), 70. *Prof Exp:* Res assoc, Dept Psychiat, Univ Chicago, 70; asst prof, 70-73, assoc prof, 73-80, PROF PHARMACOL, SCH PHARM, UNIV MISS, 80- *Concurrent Pos:* Mem, Int Study Group Invest Drugs as Reinforcers. *Mem:* Sigma Xi; Am Asn Cols Pharm; Am Soc Pharmacol & Exp Therapeut; Soc Stimulus Properties of Drugs. *Res:* Neurochemical, neurophysiological and neuropharmacological factors which mediate psychomotor stimulant self-administration behavior; pharmacokinetics of stimulant self-administration; effects of central nervous system drugs on positively and negatively reinforced behavior and group behavior of non-human primates. *Mailing Add:* Dept Pharmacol Univ Miss Sch Pharm University MS 38677

WILSON, MASON P, JR, b Albany, NY, Jan 15, 33; m 55; c 2. FLUID MECHANICS, HEAT TRANSFER. *Educ:* State Univ NY Albany, BS, 57; Univ Conn, MS, 60, PhD(mech eng), 68. *Prof Exp:* Mathematician, Res & Develop Lab, Elec Boat Div, Gen Dynamics Corp, 57-58, engr, 58-62; sr anal engr advan propulsion group, Pratt & Whitney Aircraft, United Aircraft Corp, 62-64, admin supvr heat transfer, 64; res engr, Neptune Res Lab, Neptune Meter Co, 64-68; assoc prof fluid mech & heat transfer, 68-76, PROF MECH ENG & APPL MECH & DIR, UNIV RI, 76- *Concurrent Pos:* Consult, Neptune Res Lab, Neptune Meter Co, 68- *Mem:* Am Soc Mech Engrs. *Res:* Fluidics; thermodynamics; thermophysical properties; flow instrumentation. *Mailing Add:* Dept of Mech Eng & Appl Mech Univ of RI Kingston RI 02881

WILSON, MATHEW KENT, b Salt Lake City, Utah, Dec 22, 20; m 44; c 1. PHYSICAL CHEMISTRY. *Educ:* Univ Utah, BS, 43; Calif Inst Technol, PhD(phys chem), 48. *Prof Exp:* Asst, Off Sci Res & Develop, Calif Inst Technol, 43-46; instr chem, Harvard Univ, 48-51, asst prof, 51-56; prof & chmn dept, Tufts Univ, 56-66; head chem sect, 66-74, head, Off Energy-Related Gen Res, 74; dep asst dir planning & eval, Math & Phys Sci & Eng Directorate, 75-77, DIR OFF PLANNING & RESOURCES MGT, NAT SCI FOUND, 77- *Concurrent Pos:* Guggenheim fel & Fulbright scholar, King's Col, London, 54-55; mem, Adv Coun Col Chem, 63-66; ed, Spectrochimia Acta, 64- *Mem:* AAAS; Am Chem Soc; Optical Soc Am; fel Am Acad Arts & Sci. *Res:* Molecular spectroscopy. *Mailing Add:* Nat Sci Found 1800 G St NW Washington DC 20550

WILSON, MERLE R(OBERT), b Rochester, NY, July 16, 32; m 56; c 4. MECHANICAL ENGINEERING. *Educ:* Fenn Col, BME, 55. *Prof Exp:* Study engr, Pipe Mach Co, 53-54; asst engr, Bell Aircraft Co, 54; assoc mech engr, Cornell Aeronaut Lab, 55-63, res engr, 63-66; sr reliability engr, 66-70, SR DESIGN ENGR, MOOG INC, 70- *Res:* Design and evaluation of servo valves and servo activators relating to military, space and commercial applications; stress and fatigue analysis; finite element analysis and fracture mechanics; design and evaluation of test techniques for purposes of product development and design verification. *Mailing Add:* Moog Inc Proner Airport East Aurora NY 14052

WILSON, MICHAEL FRIEND, b Morgantown, WVa, Jan 13, 27; m 54; c 5. CARDIOLOGY, NUCLEAR MEDICINE. *Educ:* WVa Univ, AB, 49; Univ Pa, MD, 53. *Prof Exp:* From intern to resident med, Presby Hosp, Philadelphia, 53-55; resident physician internal med, Med Ctr, Temple Univ, 55-57; from asst prof to assoc prof physiol & biophys, Col Med, Univ Ky, 60-65; prof physiol & biophys & chmn dept, Med Ctr, WVa Univ, 65-76, clin prof med, 73-76; ASSOC CHIEF STAFF RES, VET ADMIN HOSP, OKLAHOMA CITY, 76-, PROF MED & ASSOC PROF NUCLEAR MED, 76-, DIR NUCLEAR CARDIOL, OKLA MEM HOSP & OKLAHOMA CITY VET ADMIN MED CTR, 79- *Concurrent Pos:* Fel physiol & cardiol, Med Ctr, Temple Univ, 57-58; res fel physiol & biophys, Sch Med, Univ Wash, 58-60; vis prof, Sch Med, Univ Nottingham, 72-73. *Mem:* Fel Am Col Cardiol; Am Physiol Soc; Biophys Soc; Pavlovian Soc NAm; Am Heart Asn. *Res:* Neurocirculatory control, cardiovascular dynamics and behavior correlates; renal blood flow and function; coronary artery disease. *Mailing Add:* Vet Med Ctr 151 921 NE 13th St Oklahoma City OK 73104

WILSON, MICHAEL JOHN, b Iowa City, Iowa, June 3, 42; m 69. ENDOCRINOLOGY, CELL BIOLOGY. *Educ:* St Ambrose Col, BA, 64; Univ Iowa, MS, 67, PhD(zool), 71. *Prof Exp:* NIH fel biochem, Harvard Univ, 71-73; res assoc, 73-75, ASST PROF LAB MED & PATH, UNIV MINN, MINNEAPOLIS, 75- *Mem:* Am Soc Zoologists; Am Physiol Soc; Int Soc Differentiation; Am Soc Cell Biol; Endocrine Soc. *Res:* Site and mode of action of hormones; in particular, the subcellular sites of hormone interaction in induction of specific effects and the cellular organelle response and role in mediating these effects. *Mailing Add:* Toxicol Res Lab Vet Admin Hosp Minneapolis MN 55417

WILSON, MIRIAM GEISENDORFER, b Yakima, Wash, Dec 3, 22; m 47; c 5. MEDICINE, PEDIATRICS. *Educ:* Univ Wash, BS, 44, MS, 45; Univ Calif, MD, 50; Am Bd Pediat, dipl. *Prof Exp:* From intern to resident pediat, Los Angeles County Hosp, 50-54; pvt pract, 54-56; sr physician, Bur Maternal & Child Health, Los Angeles County Health Dept, 57-58; asst prof pediat, Sch Med, Univ Calif, Los Angeles, 58-65, asst prof maternal & child health, Sch Pub Health, 60-65; assoc prof pediat, 65-69, PROF PEDIAT, SCH MED, UNIV SOUTHERN CALIF, 69-; CHIEF GENETICS DIV & DIR CYTOGENETICS LAB, PEDIAT PAVILION, LOS ANGELES COUNTY-UNIV SOUTHERN CALIF MED CTR, 65- *Mem:* Am Acad Pediat; Am Pediat Soc; Am Pub Health Asn; Am Soc Human Genetics. *Res:* Medical genetics and cytogenetics; medical problems of the newborn and premature infant; growth and development of the infant and child; maternal and child health. *Mailing Add:* Dept Pediat Univ Southern Calif Med Ctr Los Angeles CA 90033

WILSON, MONTE DALE, b Pomeroy, Wash, Nov 16, 38; m 62; c 2. GEOLOGY. *Educ:* Brigham Young Univ, BS, 62; Univ Idaho, MS, 68, PhD(geol), 70. *Prof Exp:* Geophysicist, Can Magnetic Reduction, Ltd, Alta, 62-63 & US Army Ballistics Res Labs, 63-65; teacher high schs, Idaho, 65-67; instr geol, Univ Idaho, 68-69; PROF GEOL, BOISE STATE UNIV, 69- *Concurrent Pos:* Mem, Idaho Bd Registration Prof Geologists, 75-80. *Mem:* Am Asn Petrol Geol; Am Quaternary Asn; Nat Asn Geol Teachers; Geol Soc Am. *Res:* Glacial and periglacial geomorphology; field geology and mapping in Northern Rocky Mountains. *Mailing Add:* Dept of Geol Boise State Univ Boise ID 83725

WILSON, NANCY KEELER, b Walton, NY, Apr 20, 37; m 59; c 3. NUCLEAR MAGNETIC RESONANCE SPECTROSCOPY. *Educ:* Univ Rochester, BS, 59; Carnegie-Mellon Univ, MS, 62, PhD(chem), 66. *Prof Exp:* Res assoc chem, Ohio State Univ, Columbus, 66-67; res assoc & lectr chem, Univ NC, Chapel Hill, 67-69; sr staff fel chem, Nat Inst Environ Health Sci, 70-74; RES CHEMIST, US ENVIRON PROTECTION AGENCY, 74- *Concurrent Pos:* Instr, Point Park Jr Col, 62-63; lectr math, Carnegie-Mellon Univ, 63-65; fac affil, Colo State Univ, 76-77. *Mem:* Am Chem Soc; Am Inst Chemists; NY Acad Sci; Sigma Xi. *Res:* Applications of nuclear magnetic resonance and other spectroscopic techniques to problems in physical organic chemistry; problems of environmental concern, toxicology and metabolism; author or coauthor of over 30 publications. *Mailing Add:* 1109 Archdale Dr Durham NC 27707

WILSON, NIGEL HENRY MOIR, b Kent, Eng, Aug 8, 44; m 70; c 1. TRANSPORTATION. *Educ:* Imp Col, Univ London, BSc, 65; Mass Inst Technol, SM, 67, PhD(civil eng), 69. *Prof Exp:* Res asst, 66-68, instr, 68-69, asst prof, 69-80, PROF CIVIL ENG, MASS INST TECHNOL, 80- *Concurrent Pos:* Fulbright travel award, 65-71; consult, Mass Bay Transit Authority Study, Boston Urban Observ, 71-72; mem, Transp Res Forum. *Mem:* Opers Res Soc Am; Regional Sci Asn. *Res:* Transportation systems analysis; urban transportation; airport systems. *Mailing Add:* Rm 1-177 77 Massachusetts Ave Cambridge MA 02139

WILSON, NIXON ALBERT, b Litchfield, Ill, May 20, 30; m 63; c 2. ACAROLOGY. *Educ:* Earlham Col, BA, 52; Univ Mich, MWM, 54; Purdue Univ, PhD(entom), 61. *Prof Exp:* Animal ecologist, Plague Res Labs, Hawaii State Dept Health, 61-62; acarologist, B P Bishop Mus, 62-69; from asst prof to assoc prof, 69-75, PROF BIOL, UNIV NORTHERN IOWA, 75- *Concurrent Pos:* USPHS res grants, B P Bishop Mus, 67-69; grant, Univ Northern Iowa, 69-79; res assoc, Fla State Collection of Arthropods, Fla Dept Agr & Consumer Servs, 70-; zool ed, Procelleraria, Iowa Acad Sci, 76- *Mem:* Am Soc Mammal; Am Soc Parasitol; Acarological Soc Am. *Res:* Ectoparasites of vertebrates, especially mites; ecology of bats. *Mailing Add:* Dept of Biol Univ of Northern Iowa Cedar Falls IA 50614

WILSON, ONSLOW HARUS, cell biology, see previous edition

WILSON, OSCAR BRYAN, JR, b Tex, Aug 15, 22; m 45; c 3. PHYSICS. *Educ:* Univ Tex, BS, 44; Univ Calif, Los Angeles, MA, 48, PhD, 51. *Prof Exp:* Mem tech staff, Hughes Aircraft Co, 51-52; physicist, Soundrive Engine Co, 52-57; assoc prof, 57-62, PROF PHYSICS, NAVAL POSTGRAD SCH, 62- *Mem:* AAAS; Am Phys Soc; Acoust Soc Am; Inst Elec & Electronics Engrs. *Res:* Physical acoustics; underwater acoustics. *Mailing Add:* Dept of Physics Naval Postgrad Sch Monterey CA 93940

WILSON, P DAVID, b Roswell, NMex, Oct 4, 33; m 65; c 1. STATISTICS, BIOMATHEMATICS. *Educ:* Univ Colo, Boulder, BA, 56; Univ Minn, Minneapolis, MS, 63; Johns Hopkins Univ, PhD(biostatist), 70. *Prof Exp:* Res assoc, Med Sch, Univ Md, Baltimore, 64-66; consult, Nat Coun Stream Improvement, 67; consult, Dept Surg, Ctr Study Trauma, Med Sch, Univ Md, Baltimore, 67-71; asst prof biomet, Med Col Va, 70-71; math statistician, Bur Drugs, Food & Drug Admin, Dept Health, Educ & Welfare, 71-72; asst prof, Dept Surg, Med Sch, Univ Md Ctr Study Trauma, 72-74, asst prof, Dept Epidemiol & Prev Med, 74-81, ASSOC PROF, MED SCH, UNIV MD,

BALTIMORE, 81- *Concurrent Pos:* Consult, Huntingdon Res Ctr, Baltimore, 73-76; lectr, Dept Biostatist, Sch Hyg & Pub Health, Johns Hopkins Univ, 73- *Mem:* Biomet Soc; Am Statist Asn. *Res:* Mathematics, statistics and computing in biomedical research. *Mailing Add:* 206 Upnor Rd Baltimore MD 21212

WILSON, PAUL ROBERT, b Chicago, Ill, Oct 25, 39. MATHEMATICS. *Educ:* Univ Cincinnati, BA, 61, MA, 62; Univ Ill, PhD(math), 67. *Prof Exp:* Asst prof math, Univ Nebr, Lincoln, 67-71; asst prof math, Alma Col, 71-80; ASSOC PROF MATH, ROCHESTER INST TECHNOL, 80- *Mem:* Am Math Soc. *Res:* Algebra, statistics. *Mailing Add:* Dept Math Rochester Inst Technol 1 Lomb Dr Rochester NY 14623

WILSON, PEGGY MAYFIELD DUNLAP, b Austin, Tex, Mar 24, 27; m 75. SURFACE CHEMISTRY. *Educ:* Univ Tex, BS, 48, PhD(chem), 52. *Prof Exp:* Spec instr chem, Univ Tex, 52-53; sr res technologist, 53-67, RES ASSOC, MOBIL RES & DEVELOP CORP, 67- *Concurrent Pos:* Dir, Stone Gap Indust Corp, 68-; State Republican Committeewoman, 71-; dir, JayBee Mfg Co, 80- *Mem:* Nat Asn Corrosion Engrs; Am Chem Soc; Soc Petrol Engrs. *Res:* Interfacial tension and contact angles; tertiary oil recovery; corrosion; wellstream processing. *Mailing Add:* Mobil Res & Develop Corp PO Box 900 Dallas TX 75221

WILSON, PERRY BAKER, b Norman, Okla, Feb 24, 27; div; c 3. HIGH ENERGY PHYSICS. *Educ:* Wash State Univ, BS, 50, MS, 52; Stanford Univ, PhD(physics), 58. *Prof Exp:* Staff physicist, Linfield Res Inst, Ore, 58-59; res assoc accelerator physicist, High Energy Physics Lab, Stanford Univ, 59-64, assoc dir opers, 64-68; vis scientist, Europ Orgn Nuclear Res, Geneva, Switzerland, 68-69, 77-78; sr res assoc, 69-74, ADJ PROF, STANFORD LINEAR ACCELERATOR CTR, STANFORD UNIV, 74- *Concurrent Pos:* Consult, Gen Atomic Div, Gen Dynamics Corp, Calif, 63-64, Phys Electronics Labs, 64 & US Naval Postgrad Sch, 64-65; mem staff, Varian Assocs, 74-77. *Mem:* AAAS; sr mem Am Phys Soc; Inst Elec & Electronics Eng. *Res:* Theory and design of linear electron accelerators and storage rings for high energy particle physics; theory and design of superconducting accelerators. *Mailing Add:* Stanford Linear Accelerator Ctr PO Box 4349 Stanford CA 94305

WILSON, PERRY WILLIAM, bacteriology, biochemistry, deceased

WILSON, PHILO CALHOUN, b Westfield, Mass, Jan 29, 24; m 47; c 3. STRATIGRAPHY, MARINE GEOLOGY. *Educ:* Williams Col, AB, 48; Cornell Univ, MS, 50; Wash State Univ, PhD(stratig), 54. *Prof Exp:* From geologist to staff geologist, Sohio Petrol Co, 54-60; area geologist, Champlin Oil Co, 60-63; assoc prof, 63-64, chmn dept, 67-73, prof earth sci, 64-78, DISTINGUISHED TEACHING PROF & CHMN DEPT, STATE UNIV NY COL ONEONTA, 78- *Concurrent Pos:* Mem selection panels rev of NSF Proposals, 65-66 & 70. *Mem:* Am Asn Petrol Geol. *Res:* Sedimentation; regional stratigraphic analysis; Pennsylvanian system of Wyoming. *Mailing Add:* 70 Dietz Oneonta NY 13820

WILSON, RAPHAEL, b Trenton, NJ, Apr 25, 25. MEDICAL BACTERIOLOGY. *Educ:* Univ Notre Dame, BS, 48; Univ Tex, MA, 51, PhD(bact), 54. *Prof Exp:* From instr to assoc prof biol, St Edward's Univ, 48-59, dean col, 51-58, dir testing & guid, 58-59; from asst prof to assoc prof biol, Univ Notre Dame, 59-71; prof pediat, Baylor Col Med, 71-76; prof biol, Univ Portland, 76-78, pres, 78-81; DIR SPEC PROGS, UNIV SAN FRANCISCO, 81- *Concurrent Pos:* Vis prof, Univ Ulm, Ger, 69-70 & Baylor Col Med, 70-71. *Mem:* Transplantation Soc; Radiation Res Soc; Am Soc Microbiol; Soc Exp Biol & Med; Soc Exp Hemat. *Res:* Germfree life; protection against radiation damage; role of the thymus; clinical gnotobiology and immunology; gastrointestinal microflora. *Mailing Add:* Univ San Francisco 2130 Fulton St San Francisco CA 94117

WILSON, RAY FLOYD, b Lee Co, Tex, Feb 20, 26; m 57; c 2. ANALYTICAL CHEMISTRY, PHYSICAL CHEMISTRY. *Educ:* Houston-Tillotson Col, BS, 50; Tex Southern Univ, MS, 61; Univ Tex, PhD(chem), 53. *Prof Exp:* Asst, Univ Tex, 51-53; assoc prof, 53-57, PROF CHEM, TEX SOUTHERN UNIV, 57- *Concurrent Pos:* Grants, Res Corp, 53-55, NSF, 54, 56 & Welch Found, 57, 59. *Mem:* Am Chem Soc. *Res:* Interaction of platinum elements with certain organic reagents. *Mailing Add:* Dept of Chem Tex Southern Univ Houston TX 77004

WILSON, RICHARD, b London, Eng, Apr 29, 26; m 52; c 6. PHYSICS. *Educ:* Oxford Univ, BA, 46, MA & DPhil(physics), 49; Harvard Univ, MA, 56. *Prof Exp:* Res lectr physics, Christ Church, Oxford Univ, 48-53, res off, Clarendon Lab, 53-55; from asst prof to assoc prof, 55-61, PROF PHYSICS, HARVARD UNIV, 61- *Concurrent Pos:* Res assoc, Univ Rochester, 50-51 & Stanford Univ, 51-52; Guggenheim fel, 61 & 69; Fulbright fel, 61 & 69; trustee, Univs Res Asn, 68-74; consult, Energy Res Develop Agency, 75-77, Nuclear Regulatory Comn, Nat Res Coun, 75- & Electric Power Res Inst, 75-76. *Mem:* Am Phys Soc; Am Acad Arts & Sci. *Res:* Elementary particle physics; environmental physics. *Mailing Add:* Lyman 231 Harvard Univ Cambridge MA 02138

WILSON, RICHARD BARR, b Lincoln, Nebr, Apr 21, 21; m 48; c 2. PATHOLOGY. *Educ:* Univ Nebr, AB, 43, MD, 45; Am Bd Path, dipl, 57. *Prof Exp:* Staff physician, Univ Nebr, Lincoln, 47-52; resident path, Univ Hosp, 53-57, assoc, Col Med, 57-62, from asst prof to assoc prof, 62-70, PROF PATH, COL MED & HEAD ELECTRON MICROS SECT, EPPLEY INST CANCER RES, UNIV NEBR, OMAHA, 70- *Concurrent Pos:* Attend pathologist, Vet Admin Hosp, Omaha, 60- *Mem:* Col Am Path; Am Soc Clin Path; Electron Micros Soc Am; Int Acad Path; Am Soc Nephrology. *Res:* Renal disease and biopsies; electron microscopy of human biopsies; morphological studies; animal carcinogenesis; ultrastructure of human neoplasms. *Mailing Add:* Eppley Inst for Cancer Res Univ of Nebr Med Ctr Omaha NE 68105

WILSON, RICHARD FAIRFIELD, b Pittsburgh, Pa, Nov 26, 30; m 52; c 6. GEOLOGY. *Educ:* Yale Univ, BS, 52; Stanford Univ, MS, 54, PhD(geol), 59. *Prof Exp:* Geologist, US Geol Surv, 55-62; asst prof geol, 62-66, ASSOC PROF GEOSCI, UNIV ARIZ, 66- *Mem:* AAAS; Paleont Soc; Geol Soc Am. *Res:* Stratigraphy; sedimentation; study of sedimentary rocks. *Mailing Add:* Dept of Geosci Univ of Ariz Tucson AZ 85721

WILSON, RICHARD FERRIN, b Dundurn, Sask, Jan 8, 20; nat US; m 43; c 4. ANIMAL SCIENCE. *Educ:* Iowa State Col, BS, 43; Univ Ill, MS, 47, PhD(animal sci), 49. *Prof Exp:* Asst animal sci, Univ Ill, 46-49; assoc prof animal husb, SDak State Col, 49-52, actg chmn dept, 51-52; assoc prof, 52-56, PROF ANIMAL SCI, OHIO STATE UNIV, 57-, IN CHARGE SWINE, 52- *Mem:* Am Soc Animal Sci. *Res:* Swine management, nutrition, physiology and breeding; swine production with emphasis on nutrition and physiology involving toxic feeds resulting from molds. *Mailing Add:* 2029 Fyffe Rd Columbus OH 43210

WILSON, RICHARD GARTH, b Montreal, Que, July 30, 45; m 67; c 2. CLIMATOLOGY. *Educ:* McGill Univ, BSc, 66, MSc, 68; McMaster Univ, PhD(climat), 71. *Prof Exp:* Lectr climat, Dept Geog, Queen's Univ, 67-68; lectr, Dept Geog, McGill Univ, 70-71, asst prof, 71-75; supvr climate inventory, Climate & Data Serv, BC Environ & Land Use Comt Secretariat, 75-78; mgr climate div, Resource Anal Br, 78-79, DIR, AIR STUDIES BR, BC MINISTRY ENVIRON, 79- *Mem:* Can Meteorol Soc. *Res:* Solar and terrestrial radiation, evaporation, snow melt, snow mapping, topoclimatology; climate network design; acidic precipitation. *Mailing Add:* BC Ministry Environ Parliament Bldg Victoria BC V8V 1X4 Can

WILSON, RICHARD HANSEL, b Madison, Wis, Aug 18, 39; m 64; c 2. PLANT PHYSIOLOGY, BIOCHEMISTRY. *Educ:* Carleton Col, BA, 61; NC State Univ, MS, 64; Ore State Univ, PhD(plant physiol), 67. *Prof Exp:* USPHS fel plant physiol, Univ Ill, Urbana, 67-68; asst prof, Univ Tex, Austin, 68-74; res specialist, Monsanto Chem Co, 74-78; FIELD SCIENTIST, FIELD DEVELOP, EASTERN REGION, VELSICOL CHEM CORP, 78- *Mem:* Weed Soc Am. *Res:* Herbicides. *Mailing Add:* Velsicol Chem Corp 5802 NW 57th Way Gainesville FL 32601

WILSON, RICHARD HEILBRON, b Decatur, Ohio, May 15, 19; m 42; c 2. AGRICULTURAL EDUCATION, AGRICULTURAL ECONOMICS. *Educ:* Ohio State Univ, BS, 43, MA, 51, PhD, 55. *Prof Exp:* Instr high sch, 47-50; res fel agr educ, 51-53, instr, 53-57, from asst prof to assoc prof, 57-69, PROF AGR EDUC, OHIO STATE UNIV, 69- *Res:* Educational evaluation and research; adult education; farm management; agronomy. *Mailing Add:* Dept of Agr Educ Ohio State Univ Columbus OH 43210

WILSON, RICHARD HOWARD, b Spearville, Kans, June 24, 42; m 62; c 1. ZOOLOGY, ANIMAL BEHAVIOR. *Educ:* Kans State Univ, BS, 64, MS, 65; Utah State Univ, PhD(zool), 71. *Prof Exp:* Instr, Prince Makonnen Sec Sch, 65-66; from instr to asst prof biol, 66-76, ASSOC PROF BIOL, UNIV WIS-STOUT, 76- *Mem:* AAAS; Animal Behav Soc; Am Ornith Union; Cooper Ornith Soc; Wilson Ornith Soc. *Res:* Animal communication; display postures and signaling mechanisms in birds. *Mailing Add:* Dept of Biol Univ of Wis-Stout Menomonie WI 54751

WILSON, RICHARD LEE, b Marshalltown, Iowa, Sept 18, 39; m 60; c 3. ENTOMOLOGY. *Educ:* Univ Northern Iowa, BA, 61; Tex A&M Univ, MS, 65; Iowa State Univ, PhD(entom), 71. *Prof Exp:* Teacher, Independent Sch Dist, Iowa, 65-68; res entomologist, Agr Res Serv, USDA, Phoenix, Ariz, 71-77; res entomologist, Okla State Univ, 77-80, RES ENTOMOLOGIST, AGR RES SERV, IOWA STATE UNIV, USDA, AMES, 80- *Mem:* Entom Soc Am; Sigma Xi. *Res:* Host plant resistance; development of resistant plant introductions to several insect pests. *Mailing Add:* Regional Plant Introduction Sta Iowa State Univ Ames IA 50011

WILSON, RICHARD MAC, electrochemistry, physical chemistry, see previous edition

WILSON, RICHARD MICHAEL, b Gary, Ind, Nov 23, 45; m 66. MATHEMATICS. *Educ:* Ind Univ, Bloomington, AB, 66; Ohio State Univ, MS, 68, PhD(math), 69. *Prof Exp:* From asst prof to assoc prof, 69-74, PROF MATH, OHIO STATE UNIV, 74- *Concurrent Pos:* Res fel, A P Sloan Found, 75-77. *Mem:* Math Asn Am; Am Math Soc; Soc Indust & Appl Math. *Res:* Combinatorial mathematics, with emphasis on combinatorial designs and related structures. *Mailing Add:* Dept of Math 231 W 18th Ave Columbus OH 43210

WILSON, ROBERT BURTON, b Salt Lake City, Utah, June 29, 36; m 62; c 2. EXPERIMENTAL PATHOLOGY. *Educ:* Utah State Univ, BS, 58; Wash State Univ, DVM, 61; Univ Toronto, PhD(physiol), 67. *Prof Exp:* Intern vet med, Angell Mem Animal Hosp, 62-63; asst prof animal sci, Brigham Young Univ, 63-64; res investr, Hosp for Sick Children, 64-67, asst scientist, 67-69; assoc prof nutrit & animal path, Mass Inst Technol, 69-73; prof vet path, Univ Mo, 73-76; PROF MICROBIOL & PATH & CHMN DEPT, WASH STATE UNIV, 76- *Concurrent Pos:* Lectr physiol, Univ Toronto, 67-69; Mary Mitchell res award, 63; mem, Coun on Arteriosclerosis, Am Heart Asn. *Mem:* Am Vet Med Asn; Am Inst Nutrit; Am Heart Asn. *Res:* Nutrition; diabetes; carcinogenesis; cardiovascular diseases; experimental pathology of nutrition and cardiovascular diseases. *Mailing Add:* Col Vet Med Wash State Univ Pullman WA 99163

WILSON, ROBERT D(OWNING), b Portchester, NY, July 9, 21; m 44; c 3. COMMUNICATIONS, ELECTRICAL ENGINEERING. *Educ:* Rensselaer Polytech Inst, BEE, 42; Cornell Univ, MS, 51. *Prof Exp:* Instr electronics, US Naval Acad, 46-47; res assoc elec eng, Cornell Univ, 47-51, asst prof, 51-56; mgr indust components div, Raytheon Co, 56-60, corp officer, 60-61; dir eng, US Sonics, 61-62; mgr systs support, Raytheon Co, 62-65, prog mgr, 65-66, mgr space systs develop, 66-69, prin engr, 69-74; ELEC PROD ENGR, ILL GAS & ELEC CO, 74- *Concurrent Pos:* Vpres, Zialite

Corp, 45-58, pres, 58-74; consult, Gen Elec Co, 51-56. *Mem:* Sr mem Inst Elec & Electronics Engrs; Am Inst Aeronaut & Astronaut. *Res:* Electronics; semiconductors; radio astronomy; vacuum tubes. *Mailing Add:* Ill Gas & Elec Co PO Box P Bettendorf IA 52722

WILSON, ROBERT E, b Norristown, Pa, Jan 16, 37; m 63. ASTROPHYSICS. *Educ:* Univ Pa, AB, 58, MS, 60, PhD(astron), 63. *Prof Exp:* Asst prof astron, Georgetown Univ, 63-66; Nat Res Coun sr res assoc, Inst Space Studies, 72-74; assoc prof astron, Univ SFla, 66-70, prof, 70-75; prof physics & astron, 75-79, PROF ASTRON, UNIV FLA, 79- *Concurrent Pos:* Consult, Goddard Space Flight Ctr, NASA, 65-70; res grants, NASA, 66-69 & 76-78 & NSF, 70-73, 77-79 & 80-81; Alexander von Humboldt Found sr scientist award, 79; Shapley vis lectr, Am Astron Soc, 81- *Mem:* Am Astron Soc; Int Astron Union; Royal Astron Soc. *Res:* Theory and observation of binary stars; stellar structure and evolution. *Mailing Add:* Dept of Astron Univ of Fla Gainesville FL 32611

WILSON, ROBERT E(LWOOD), b Decatur, Ill, July 2, 26; m 49. CHEMICAL ENGINEERING. *Educ:* Univ Ill, AB, 48, BS, 49, PhD(chem eng), 52; Univ Minn, MS, 50. *Prof Exp:* Proj leader eng res, Corn Prod Refining Co, 52-54; from assoc prof to prof chem eng, Univ Dayton, 54-61, head dept, 54-61; mgr eng & develop, Thomas J Lipton, Inc, 61-62, assoc dir develop, 62-64; assoc dir res & develop, Int Minerals & Chem Corp, Ill, 64-67; SR VPRES & MEM BD DIRS, HEIDRICK & STRUGGLES INC, CHICAGO, 67- *Concurrent Pos:* Consult, US Air Force, 55-56, US Navy, 59-60 & Eng Exp Sta, Univ Wis, 59-60. *Mem:* Am Chem Soc; Am Soc Eng Educ; Inst Nuclear Mgt; Am Inst Chem Engrs. *Res:* Fluid mechanics; high temperature; bioengineering and transport processes. *Mailing Add:* 11 Brunswick Lane Deerfield IL 60015

WILSON, ROBERT EUGENE, b Denton, Tex, Apr 16, 32; m 56; c 3. MICROBIOLOGY, ECOLOGY. *Educ:* North Tex State Univ, BS, 52, MS, 56; Univ Tex, PhD(microbiol), 63. *Prof Exp:* Instr biol, Col Arts & Indust, 56-59; from asst prof to assoc prof, 63-70, PROF BIOL, E TEX STATE UNIV, 70- *Mem:* Sigma Xi; Am Inst Biol Sci. *Res:* Cytotoxicity of staphylococcal toxins towards mammalian cells in vitro; changes in serum proteins following x-irradiation; effects of electromagnetic fields on plants and animals. *Mailing Add:* Dept Biol ETex State Univ ETex Sta Commerce TX 75428

WILSON, ROBERT FRANCIS, b Scranton, Pa, Aug 9, 34; m 72; c 7. THORACIC SURGERY, CARDIOVASCULAR SURGERY. *Educ:* Lehigh Univ, BA, 57; Temple Univ, MD, 58. *Prof Exp:* From instr to assoc prof, 63-71, PROF SURG, SCH MED, WAYNE STATE UNIV, 71-, DIR AFFIL PROG THORACIC SURG, 71-, ASST DEAN DETROIT GEN HOSP AFFAIRS, 72-; CHIEF SECT THORACIC & CARDIOVASC SURG, HARPER HOSP, 72- *Concurrent Pos:* Markle scholar acad med; pres med staff, Detroit Gen Receiving Hosp, 72-74. *Mem:* Soc Univ Surg; Am Asn Thoracic Surg; Am Asn Surg Trauma; Am Col Surg; Am Col Chest Physicians. *Res:* Shock; respiratory failure; fluid and electrolytes. *Mailing Add:* Sch of Med Dept of Surg Wayne State Univ Detroit MI 48202

WILSON, ROBERT G, b Galesburg, Ill, Aug 30, 30; m 53; c 3. CHEMISTRY, BIOCHEMISTRY. *Educ:* Knox Col, AB, 52; Purdue Univ, MS, 56; Okla State Univ, PhD(chem), 61. *Prof Exp:* Res chemist, Nat Cancer Inst, 63-67; from asst prof to assoc prof, 67-81, PROF BIOCHEM, COL MED NJ, 81- *Concurrent Pos:* NIH fel biochem, Brandeis Univ, 61-63. *Mem:* Sigma Xi; Am Asn Univ Professors; Am Soc Biol Chem; Am Asn Cancer Res. *Res:* Initiation of RNA synthesis; effect of mutagens and carcinogens upon transcription. *Mailing Add:* Dept Biochem Col Med NJ Newark NJ 07103

WILSON, ROBERT GRAY, b Wooster, Ohio, Apr 7, 34; m 57; c 2. ELECTRONICS, NUCLEAR PHYSICS. *Educ:* Ohio State Univ, BSc, 56, PhD(physics), 61. *Prof Exp:* Prin physicist, Battelle Mem Inst, 54-58; res asst, Res Found, Ohio State Univ, 58-60; sr physicist, NAm Aviation/Rocketdyne, 61-63; SR MEM TECH STAFF, RES LABS, HUGHES AIRCRAFT CO, 63- *Mem:* Am Phys Soc; Inst Elec & Electronics Eng. *Res:* Ion implantation; semiconductor devices and integrated circuits; electron and ion emission from surfaces; scanning acoustic microscopy; experimental low energy nuclear physics. *Mailing Add:* Dept Electron Device Physics Hughes Res Labs 3011 Malibu Canyon Rd Malibu CA 90265

WILSON, ROBERT HALLOWELL, b Baltimore, Md, July 30, 24; m 48; c 2. ENVIRONMENTAL HEALTH. *Educ:* Univ Rochester, BS, 45. *Prof Exp:* Jr scientist, Atomic Energy Proj, 46-51, instr indust hyg & toxicol & asst scientist, Atomic Energy Proj, 51-56, scientist, 56-62, chief engr, 62-76, ASST PROF RADIATION BIOL & BIOPHYS, SCH MED & DENT, UNIV ROCHESTER, 56-, CHIEF ENVIRON HEALTH & SAFETY, CHIEF SAFETY OFFICER, UNIV, 75- *Mem:* AAAS; Am Nuclear Soc; Health Physics Soc; Soc Study Amphibians & Reptiles; Am Indust Hyg Asn. *Res:* Generation, sampling and behavior of aerosols; control of radiation hazards; air safety considerations of nuclear weapons transport and storage; environmental impact of mercury. *Mailing Add:* Sch of Med & Dent Univ of Rochester Rochester NY 14642

WILSON, ROBERT JAMES, b Edmonton, Alta, Feb 5, 15; m 41; c 2. BACTERIOLOGY, IMMUNOLOGY. *Educ:* Univ BC, BA, 35, MA, 37; Univ Toronto, MD, 42, DPH, 46. *Prof Exp:* Assoc hyg & prev med, 47-48, from asst prof to assoc prof, 48-71, prof health admin & microbiol, 71-75, PROF MICROBIOL PARASITOL, FAC MED, UNIV TORONTO, 75- *Concurrent Pos:* Res assoc, Connaught Labs Ltd, 48-56, res mem, 56-57, from asst dir to assoc dir, 57-72, chmn & sci dir, 72-78, hon chmn & consult to pres, 78- *Honors & Awards:* Defries Award, Can Pub Health Asn, 80. *Res:* Staphylococcal food poisoning; staphylococcus toxoid; pertussis vaccine and multiple antigens; multiple antigens contained in poliomyelitis vaccine; clinical trials of live oral poliomyelitis virus vaccine; clinical studies of penicillin. *Mailing Add:* Connaught Labs Ltd 1755 Steeles Ave W Willowdale ON M2N 5T8 Can

WILSON, ROBERT JOHN, b St Louis, Mo, Apr 23, 35; m 57; c 5. RADIOLOGICAL PHYSICS, NUCLEAR MEDICINE. *Educ:* St Mary's Univ, Tex, BS & BA, 56; Wash Univ, PhD(physics), 63. *Prof Exp:* Res assoc physics, Wash Univ, 63-66; res physicist, US Naval Radiol Defense Lab, San Francisco, 66-69; asst prof radiol, 69-72, assoc prof nuclear med, 72-78, PROF RADIOLOGY, UNIV TENN, MEMPHIS, 78- *Mem:* Am Asn Physicists in Med; Am Phys Soc; Soc Nuclear Med; Am Col Radiol; Radiol Soc NAm. *Mailing Add:* Dept of Radiology Univ of Tenn Memphis TN 38163

WILSON, ROBERT LAKE, b Gallipolis, Ohio, July 2, 24; m 50; c 2. GEOLOGY. *Educ:* Wheaton Col, AB, 48; Univ Iowa, MS, 50; Univ Tenn, PhD, 67. *Prof Exp:* Asst geol, Univ Iowa, 49-50 & Univ Tenn, 50-52; area geologist, Tenn Div Geol, 52-55; from instr to assoc prof geol, 55-66, PROF GEOL & GEOG, UNIV TENN, CHATTANOOGA, 66- *Concurrent Pos:* NSF fac fel, 60-61. *Mem:* Soc Econ Paleontologists & Mineralogists; Nat Speleol Soc; Geol Soc Am; Nat Asn Geol Teachers; Am Asn Petrol Geol. *Res:* Paleozoic stratigraphy and sedimentation of Southern Appalachians; economic geology of the eastern United States. *Mailing Add:* Dept Geol Univ Tenn Chattanooga TN 37402

WILSON, ROBERT LEE, b Champaign, Ill, Mar 7, 17; m 40; c 4. MATHEMATICS. *Educ:* Univ Fla, AB, 38; Univ Wis, MA, 40, PhD(math), 47. *Prof Exp:* Asst math, Univ Wis, 39-41, 46-47; from instr to asst prof, Univ Tenn, 47-56; sr aerophys engr, Gen Dynamics/Convair, Tex, 56-58; prof math, 58-79, EMER PROF, OHIO WESLEYAN UNIV, 79- *Concurrent Pos:* Adj prof, Tex Christian Univ, 56-58; vis prof & dir comput ctr, Univ Ibadan, 66-68, Univ Western Australia & Washington Univ, 81. *Mem:* AAAS; Am Math Soc; Math Asn Am; Asn Comput Mach. *Res:* Galois theory; numerical analysis; computing; matrix theory. *Mailing Add:* Rte 1 Box 57-L Lexington VA 24450

WILSON, ROBERT LEE, b Washington, DC, Jan 16, 46; m 67; c 1. ALGEBRA. *Educ:* Am Univ, BA, 65; Yale Univ, PhD(math), 69. *Prof Exp:* Instr math, Courant Inst Math Sci, NY Univ, 69-71; from asst prof to assoc prof, 71-80, PROF MATH, RUTGERS UNIV, NEW BRUNSWICK, 80- *Mem:* Am Math Soc; Math Asn Am. *Res:* Lie algebras over fields of prime characteristic; Kac-Moody Lie algebras. *Mailing Add:* Dept of Math Rutgers Univ New Brunswick NJ 08903

WILSON, ROBERT LEE, JR, b Auburn, Ala, Jan 3, 42; m 62; c 2. MATHEMATICS. *Educ:* Ohio Wesleyan Univ, BA, 62; Univ Wis-Madison, MA, 63, PhD(math), 69. *Prof Exp:* Asst prof math, Univ Wis-Madison, 69-75; ASSOC PROF MATH, WASHINGTON & LEE UNIV, 75- *Mem:* Am Math Soc; Math Asn Am. *Res:* Combinatorics; graph theory; universal algebra; microcomputers; generalizations of group theory. *Mailing Add:* Dept of Math Washington & Lee Univ Lexington VA 24450

WILSON, ROBERT NORTON, b Walla Walla, Wash, Oct 7, 27; m 56; c 1. MATHEMATICAL PHYSICS, ATMOSPHERIC PHYSICS. *Educ:* Whitman Col, AB, 48; Stanford Univ, MS, 50, PhD(physics, math), 60. *Prof Exp:* Res scientist, Microwaves, Kane Eng Labs, Calif, 60-65 & Atmospheric Physics, Lockheed Res Lab, 65-71; res scientist, Radiative Transfer & Hydrodynamics, Mission Res Corp, 71-75; RES SCIENTIST, NEW MILLENNIUM ASSOCS, 75- *Mem:* Am Phys Soc; Am Inst Physics. *Res:* Electromagnetic theory and experimentation; multiple quantum effect physics; non-equilibrium statistical mechanics; hydrodynamics; magnetohydrodynamics; radiation physics; acoustic gravitation waves; interaction of electromagnetic radiation with relativistically moving plasma fronts; ground water flow; optical fluorescence detection systems. *Mailing Add:* 16 W Mountain Dr Santa Barbara CA 93103

WILSON, ROBERT PAUL, b Revere, Mo, Dec 28, 41; m 62; c 3. BIOCHEMISTRY. *Educ:* Univ Mo, Columbia, BSEd, 63, MS, 65, PhD(biochem), 68. *Prof Exp:* Instr agr chem, Univ Mo-Columbia, 68-69; from asst prof to assoc prof biochem, 69-77, PROF BIOCHEM, MISS STATE UNIV, 77-, HEAD BIOCHEM DEPT, 79- *Honors & Awards:* Res Award, Catfish Farmers Am, 81. *Mem:* AAAS; Am Inst Nutrit; Am Chem Soc. *Res:* Comparative toxicity and metabolism of ammonia; fish biochemistry and nutrition. *Mailing Add:* Dept of Biochem Miss State Univ Drawer BB Mississippi State MS 39762

WILSON, ROBERT RATHBUN, b Frontier, Wyo, Mar 4, 14; m 40; c 3. PHYSICS. *Educ:* Univ Calif, AB, 36, PhD(physics), 40. *Hon Degrees:* MA, Harvard Univ, 46; DSc, Notre Dame, Univ Bonn, WGer. *Prof Exp:* From instr to asst prof physics, Princeton Univ, 40-46, in tech chg isotron develop proj, 42-43; physicist, Los Alamos Sci Lab, 43-46, leader cyclotron group, 43-44, head exp res div, 44-46; assoc prof physics, Harvard Univ, 46-47; prof physics & dir lab nuclear studies, Cornell Univ, 47-67; prof, Dept Physics & Enrico Fermi Inst Nuclear Studies, Univ Chicago, 67-80, dir, Fermi Nat Accelerator Lab, 67-78; MICHAEL POPIN PROF, COLUMBIA UNIV, 80- *Concurrent Pos:* Mem, Comt Atomic Casualties, Nat Res Coun, 48-51; exchange prof, Univ Paris, 54-55; mem, Steering Comt, Proj Sherwood, US AEC, 58- *Honors & Awards:* Elliot Cresson Medal, Franklin Inst. *Mem:* Nat Acad Sci; Am Phys Soc; Am Acad Arts & Sci; Am Philos Soc. *Res:* Nuclear and particle physics. *Mailing Add:* 916 Stewart Ave Ithaca NY 14850

WILSON, ROBERT STEVEN, b Hartford, Conn, Dec 26, 42; m 66; c 3. PHYSICAL CHEMISTRY. *Educ:* Brown Univ, BS, 62, PhD(phys chem), 68. *Prof Exp:* Fel phys chem, Yale Univ, 68-69; asst prof, 69-73, ASSOC PROF PHYS CHEM, NORTHERN ILL UNIV, 73- *Concurrent Pos:* Res prof, Solid State Sci Div, Argonne Nat Lab, 71- *Mem:* Am Phys Soc; Am Chem Soc. *Res:* Statistical mechanics of irreversible processes; optical properties of impurity systems; critical transport properties of fluids. *Mailing Add:* Dept of Chem Northern Ill Univ De Kalb IL 60115

WILSON, ROBERT WARREN, b Oakland, Calif, July 26, 09; wid; c 2. VERTEBRATE PALEONTOLOGY. *Educ:* Calif Inst Technol, BS, 30, MS, 32, PhD(vert paleontol), 36. *Prof Exp:* Asst geol, Calif Inst Technol, 30-34, Sterling res fel, 36-37, fel, 37-39; from instr to asst prof geol, Univ Colo, 39-46, Nat Res Coun fel, 46-47; assoc prof zool & assoc cur vert paleont, Univ Kans, 47-61; prof paleont & dir mus geol, SDak Sch Mines & Technol, 61-75; vis prof, Tex Tech Univ, 75-77; Rose Morgan vis prof, 77, ASSOC MUS NATURAL HIST, UNIV KANS, 77-, EMER PROF, 80- *Concurrent Pos:* Guggenheim fel, London, 56-57; Fulbright sr res scholar, Univ Vienna, 67-68. *Honors & Awards:* Arnold Guyot Mem Award, Nat Geog Soc, 74. *Mem:* Fel Geol Soc Am; Paleont Soc; Soc Vert Paleont (secy-treas, 54, pres, 55); Am Soc Mammal. *Res:* Tertiary mammalian faunas. *Mailing Add:* Mus of Natural Hist Univ of Kans Lawrence KS 66045

WILSON, ROBERT WOODROW, b Houston, Tex, Jan 10, 36; m 58; c 3. RADIO ASTRONOMY. *Educ:* Rice Univ, BA, 57; Calif Inst Technol, PhD(physics), 62. *Prof Exp:* Res fel radio astron, Calif Inst Technol, 62-63; mem tech staff, 63-76, DEPT HEAD, BELL LABS, 76- *Honors & Awards:* Nobel Prize in Physics, 78; Herschel Medal, Royal Astron Soc, London; Henery Draper Medal, Nat Acad Sci. *Mem:* Nat Acad Sci; Am Acad Arts & Sci; Am Phys Soc; Int Sci Radio Union; Am Astron Soc. *Res:* Problems related to the galaxy; absolute flux and background temperature measurements; millimeter-wave measurements of interstellar molecules. *Mailing Add:* Bell Labs PO Box 400 Holmdel NJ 07733

WILSON, RONALD HARVEY, b Belle Fourche, SDak, Oct 2, 32; m 55; c 3. EXPERIMENTAL SOLID STATE PHYSICS, ENERGY CONVERSION. *Educ:* SDak State Univ, BS, 56, MS, 58; Rensselaer Polytech Inst, PhD(physics), 64. *Prof Exp:* Physicist, Flight Propulsion Lab, Gen Elec Co, 58-59, res trainee, Physics Res Lab, 59-61, physicist, Gen Eng Lab, 61-62; teaching asst physics, Rensselaer Polytech Inst, 62-63; PHYSICIST, GEN ELEC RES & DEVELOP CTR, 63- *Mem:* AAAS; Am Phys Soc; Electrochem Soc. *Res:* Physics and properties of thin films; physics of semiconductor devices; semiconductor processing; energy conversion processes; photoelectrochemistry; solar energy. *Mailing Add:* Gen Elec Res & Develop Ctr PO Box 8 Schenectady NY 12301

WILSON, RONALD WAYNE, b Iowa Falls, Iowa, Aug 4, 39. BOTANY, MYCOLOGY. *Educ:* Iowa State Univ, BS, 61; Mich State Univ, PhD(bot), 65. *Prof Exp:* USPHS fel, Med Ctr, Ind Univ, 65-67; from asst prof to assoc prof natural sci, 67-77, PROF NATURAL SCI, MICH STATE UNIV, 77- *Mem:* AAAS; Am Inst Biol Sci. *Res:* general-liberal studies in science; lysine metabolism. *Mailing Add:* Dept of Natural Sci Mich State Univ East Lansing MI 48823

WILSON, SHIRLEY LANE, b Barryton, Mich, Sept 7, 18. PLANT PHYSIOLOGY, PLANT PATHOLOGY. *Educ:* Mich State Col, BS, 50; Univ Ill, MS, 51, PhD(bot), 54. *Prof Exp:* Asst, Univ Ill, 51-53; asst plant physiologist, Conn Agr Exp Sta, 54-55; asst prof bot, Southern Ill Univ, 55-63; asst prof, 63-76, ASSOC PROF BOT, DRAKE UNIV, 76- *Mem:* Am Soc Plant Physiol; Bot Soc Am; Sigma Xi. *Res:* Photoperiodism; control of algal blooms; plant pigments; bioelectric currents in mimosa; flower opening rhythms. *Mailing Add:* Dept of Biol Drake Univ Des Moines IA 50311

WILSON, SLOAN JACOB, b Dallas, Tex, Jan 22, 10; m 48; c 4. INTERNAL MEDICINE. *Educ:* Wichita State Univ, AB, 31, MS, 32; Univ Kans, BS, 34, MD, 36; Am Bd Internal Med, dipl, 48. *Prof Exp:* From intern to asst resident, Ohio State Univ Hosp, 36-38, resident res med, 38-39, instr path, 39-40; from asst prof to assoc prof med, 46-59, prof, 59-70, EMER PROF INTERNAL MED, UNIV KANS MED CTR, KANSAS CITY, 70- *Mem:* AAAS; Soc Exp Biol & Med; fel AMA; fel Am Col Physicians; Am Soc Hemat. *Res:* Blood hematology. *Mailing Add:* Univ of Kans Med Ctr 39th St & Rainbow Blvd Kansas City KS 66103

WILSON, STANLEY D(EWOLF), b Sacramento, Calif, Aug 12, 12; m 43; c 3. CIVIL ENGINEERING. *Educ:* Harvard Univ, SM, 48. *Prof Exp:* Asst hwy engr, State Div Hwy, Calif, 33-42; asst prof soil mech & found eng, Harvard Univ, 48-53; consult, Shannon & Wilson, 54-78; RETIRED. *Concurrent Pos:* Vis lectr, Univ Ill, 58-; affiliate prof, Univ Wash, Seattle, 77-; consult engr, 78- *Honors & Awards:* Terzaghi Award, Am Soc Civil Engrs, 78. *Mem:* Nat Acad Eng; fel Am Soc Civil Engrs; Int Soc Soil Mech & Found Eng; Am Inst Consult Engrs. *Res:* Shear strength and compaction characteristics of fine grained soils; field measurements and instrumentation for large dams. *Mailing Add:* 9606 12th Ave NW Seattle WA 98117

WILSON, STANLEY PORTER, b Andalusia, Ala, Sept 4, 31; m 53; c 1. POPULATION GENETICS. *Educ:* Auburn Univ, BS, 54, MS, 58; Okla State Univ, PhD(genetics), 61. *Prof Exp:* Nat Acad Sci-Nat Res Coun fel, Purdue Univ, 61-63; coordr regional poultry breeding proj, US Dept Agr, 63-65, leader, Genetics Invest, Poultry Res Br, Animal Husb Res Div, Agr Res Ctr, Md, 65-67; dir, Pioneering Res Lab, Purdue Univ, 67-75; assoc dir & asst dean, Agr Exp Sta, Auburn Univ, 75-80; VPRES AGR, HOME ECON & VET MED, 80- *Mem:* AAAS; Genetics Soc Am; Poultry Sci Asn; Am Soc Animal Sci; Am Genetic Asn. *Res:* Selection studies with tribolium, mice, poultry and swine; effects of mating systems on selection and genetic parameters. *Mailing Add:* 410 Cross Creek Rd Auburn AL 36830

WILSON, STEPHEN ROSS, b Oklahoma City, Okla, Mar 13, 46; m 67; c 2. SYNTHETIC ORGANIC CHEMISTRY. *Educ:* Rice Univ, BA, 69, MA, 72, PhD(org chem), 72. *Prof Exp:* NIH fel org chem, Calif Inst Technol, 72-74; asst prof org chem, Ind Univ, Bloomington, 74-78, assoc prof, 78-80; ASSOC PROF ORG CHEM, NY UNIV, 80- *Concurrent Pos:* Sigma Xi res award, Rice Univ, 72. *Mem:* Royal Soc Chem; Am Chem Soc. *Res:* Development of new approaches to the synthesis of naturally occurring compounds of biological significance, and the structure elucidation and total synthesis of such substances. *Mailing Add:* Dept Chem NY Univ Washington Square New York NY 10003

WILSON, STEVEN PAUL, b New Castle, Pa, Oct 12, 50; m 72; c 1. NEUROCHEMISTRY. *Educ:* Univ Pittsburgh, BS, 72; Duke Univ, PhD(biochem), 76. *Prof Exp:* Guest worker, Nat Heart, Lung & Blood Inst, NIH, 76-78, staff fel, 78-79; vis scientist, Dept Med Biochem, Wellcome Res Labs, Burroughs Wellcome Co, Research Triangle Park, NC, 79-81; ASST MED RES PROF, DEPT PHARM, DUKE UNIV MED CTR, DURHAM, NC, 82- *Concurrent Pos:* Fel neurol, Sch Med & Dent, George Washington Univ, 76-78. *Mem:* Soc Neurosci. *Res:* Biochemical aspects of neurotransmitter secretion and synapse formation; regulation of catecholamine and opioid peptide biosynthesis, neurobiology of adrenal chromaffin cells. *Mailing Add:* Dept Pharmacol Box 3813 Duke Univ Med Ctr Durham NC 27710

WILSON, THEODORE A(LEXANDER), b Elgin, Ill, June 20, 35. AERONAUTICAL ENGINEERING, BIOMECHANICS. *Educ:* Cornell Univ, BEngPhysics, 58, PhD(aeronaut eng), 62. *Prof Exp:* Res scientist, Avco-Everett Res Lab, 62-63 & Jet Propulsion Lab, 63-64; from asst prof to assoc prof aeronaut & eng mech, 64-72, PROF AEROSPACE ENG & MECH, UNIV MINN, MINNEAPOLIS, 72- *Mem:* Am Physiol Soc. *Res:* Respiratory mechanics; acoustics; fluid mechanics. *Mailing Add:* Dept of Aerospace Eng & Mech Univ of Minn Minneapolis MN 55455

WILSON, THOMAS EDWARD, b Chicago, Ill, Feb 20, 42; m 66; c 2. ENVIRONMENTAL & CHEMICAL ENGINEERING. *Educ:* Northwestern Univ, BS, 64, MS, 67; Ill Inst Technol, PhD(environ eng), 69. *Prof Exp:* Asst prof environ eng, Rutgers Univ, New Brunswick, 67-70; CONSULT POLLUTION CONTROL & WATER TREATMENT, GREELEY & HANSEN, 70- *Mem:* Am Inst Chem Engrs; Int Asn Water Pollution Res; Water Pollution Control Fedn; Am Soc Civil Engrs; Am Water Works Asn. *Res:* Pollution control; advanced waste treatment; physical-chemical treatment processes; solids and sludge disposal; industrial waste treatment; treatment plant operations. *Mailing Add:* Greeley & Hansen 222 S Riverside Plaza Chicago IL 60606

WILSON, THOMAS G(EORGE), b Annapolis, Md, Jan 19, 26; m 49; c 3. ELECTRICAL ENGINEERING. *Educ:* Harvard Univ, AB, 47, SM, 49, ScD(elec eng), 53. *Prof Exp:* Physicist, US Naval Ord Lab, 48, elec engr, US Naval Res Lab, 49-53; mgr res & develop, Magnetics, Inc, 53-59; assoc prof, 59-63, chmn dept, 64-70, PROF ELEC ENG, DUKE UNIV, 63- *Mem:* Inst Elec & Electronics Engrs. *Res:* Magnetic devices, materials and amplifiers; nonlinear electromagnetics; energy conversion. *Mailing Add:* Dept of Elec Eng Duke Univ Durham NC 27706

WILSON, THOMAS GORDON, insect physiology, genetics, see previous edition

WILSON, THOMAS HASTINGS, b Philadelphia, Pa, Jan 31, 25; m 52; c 2. PHYSIOLOGY. *Educ:* Univ Pa, MD, 48; Sheffield Univ, 51-53, PhD(biochem), 53. *Prof Exp:* Instr physiol, Univ Pa, 49-50; instr biochem, Wash Univ, 56-57; assoc physiol, 57-59, from asst prof to assoc prof, 59-68, PROF PHYSIOL, HARVARD MED SCH, 68- *Mem:* Am Soc Biol Chem; Am Physiol Soc; Brit Biochem Soc. *Res:* Active transport of materials across cell membranes. *Mailing Add:* Dept of Physiol Harvard Med Sch Boston MA 02115

WILSON, THOMAS KENDRICK, b Highland Park, Mich, June 2, 31; m 52; c 5. PLANT MORPHOLOGY. *Educ:* Ohio Univ, BS, 53, MS, 55; Ind Univ, PhD(bot), 58. *Prof Exp:* Asst bot, Ohio Univ, 53-55 & Ind Univ, 55-58; from asst prof to assoc prof, Univ Cincinnati, 58-68; assoc prof, 68-74, PROF BOT, MIAMI UNIV, 74- *Mem:* AAAS; Bot Soc Am; Int Soc Plant Morphol; Int Asn Plant Taxon. *Res:* Comparative morphology of angiosperms; origin and phylogeny of vascular plants; evolution. *Mailing Add:* Dept of Bot Miami Univ Oxford OH 45056

WILSON, THOMAS LEE, b Wyoming, Ohio, Nov 4, 09; m 37; c 2. PHYSICAL CHEMISTRY. *Educ:* Col Wooster, BS, 30; Univ Wash, MS, 34; Univ Chicago, PhD(chem), 35. *Prof Exp:* Res chemist, Gen Labs, US Rubber Co, 35-42, dept head, 42-54, admin asst, Res & Develop Dept, 54-58, mgr res ctr, 58-65; from asst prof to assoc prof chem, Montclair State Col, 66-76, chmn dept, 71-73, dean, Sch Math & Sci, 73-76. *Mem:* AAAS; Am Chem Soc; fel Am Inst Chem. *Res:* Oceanography; reaction rates of gaseous decomposition; rubber and inorganic chemistry. *Mailing Add:* 7 Rockbrook Dr Camden ME 04843

WILSON, THOMAS PUTNAM, b New York, NY, Sept 4, 18; m 44, 80; c 1. HETEROGENOUS CATALYSIS. *Educ:* Amherst Col, BA, 39; Harvard Univ, PhD(chem physics), 43. *Prof Exp:* Res chemist, Manhattan Proj, M W Kellogg Co, NJ, 43-44; res chemist, Kellex Corp, 44-45; res chemist, Manhattan Proj & S A M Labs, Chems & Plastics Div, 45-46 & 46-62, asst dir res, 62-72, res assoc, 72-73, CORP RES FEL, RES & DEVELOP DEPT, ETHYLENE OXIDE/GLYCOL DIV, UNION CARBIDE CORP, 73- *Mem:* Am Chem Soc; Catalysis Soc. *Res:* kinetics and catalysis; catalytic reaction mechanisms; ethylene polymerization; catalyst development and characterization. *Mailing Add:* Res & Develop Dept Ethylene Oxide/Glycol Div Union Carbide Corp PO Box 8361 South Charleston WV 25303

WILSON, THORNTON ARNOLD, b Sikeston, Mo, Feb 8, 21; m 44; c 3. AERONAUTICS. *Educ:* Iowa State Col, BS, 43; Calif Inst Technol, MS, 48. *Prof Exp:* Mem staff, 43-57, asst chief tech staff & proj eng mgr, 57-58, vpres & mgr Minuteman br, Aerospace Div, 62-64, vpres opers & planning, 64-66, exec vpres & dir, 66-68, PRES, BOEING CO, 68-, CHIEF EXEC OFFICER & CHMN BD, 72- *Concurrent Pos:* Sloan fel, Mass Inst Technol, 52-53; mem bd gov, Iowa State Univ Found. *Mem:* Nat Acad Eng; fel Am Inst Aeronaut & Astronaut. *Mailing Add:* Boeing Co PO Box 3707 Seattle WA 98124

WILSON, TIMOTHY LUCIAN, metallurgy, see previous edition

WILSON, TIMOTHY M, b Columbus, Ohio, Aug 3, 38; m; c 2. SOLID STATE PHYSICS. *Educ:* Univ Fla, BS, 61, PhD(chem physics), 66. *Prof Exp:* Fel solid state physics, Univ Fla, 66-68, asst prof chem, 68-69; from asst prof to assoc prof physics, 69-78, asst dir exten, Col Arts & Sci, 77-79, PROF PHYSICS, OKLA STATE UNIV, 78-, ASSOC DIR EXTEN, COL ARTS & SCI, 79- *Concurrent Pos:* Res staff mem, Solid State Div, Oak Ridge Nat Lab, 74-75. *Mem:* Am Phys Soc; Sigma Xi; Nat Univ Continuing Educ Asn; Am Asn Physics Teachers. *Res:* Theoretical studies of the optical and magnetic properties of impurities and defects in crystalline solids. *Mailing Add:* Dept Physics Okla State Univ Stillwater OK 74078

WILSON, VERNON EARL, b Plymouth Co, Iowa, Feb 16, 15; m 47; c 2. MEDICAL ADMINISTRATION, FAMILY MEDICINE. *Educ:* Univ Ill, BS, 50, MS & MD, 52. *Prof Exp:* Asst pharmacol, Univ Ill, 50-52; intern, Univ Hosp, Chicago, 52-53; asst prof, Sch Med, Univ Kans, 53-59, asst dean sch med, 57-59, actg dean sch med & actg dir med ctr, 59; prof pharmacol, Univ Mo-Columbia, 59-70, dean sch med & dir med ctr, 59-67, exec dir health affairs, 67-68, vpres acad affairs, 68-70; adminr, Health Serv & Ment Health Admin, Dept Health Educ & Welfare, Md, 70-73; prof community health, Univ Mo-Columbia, 73-74; vchancellor med affairs, Vanderbilt Univ, 74-81; RETIRED. *Concurrent Pos:* Exec officer, Mo State Crippled Children's Serv, 60-68; mem exec coun, Am Asn Med Cols, 61-67; mem, Am Bd Family Pract, 62-74; consult, USPHS, 65-69; coun mem med educ, AMA, 67-75; coordr, Mo Regional Med Prog, 66-68; mem coun fed relationship, Am Asn Univ, 68-70; ed, Continuing Educ for Family Physician, 73-75; mem liaison comt, Grad Med Educ, 73-75. *Mem:* AMA; hon mem Acad Anesthesiol. *Res:* Renal pharmacology; medical education; public health administration. *Mailing Add:* Box 196 Rte #1 Ashland MD 65010

WILSON, VERNON ELDRIDGE, b Roanoke, Va, July 3, 18; m 53; c 2. GENETICS, PHYTOPATHOLOGY. *Educ:* Colo State Univ, BS, 47, MS, 49; Iowa State Univ, PhD(agron) & PhD(phytopath), 55. *Prof Exp:* Proj leader & phytopathologist, USDA, Univ Idaho, 52-62; proj leader & phytopathologist, USDA, Wash State Univ, 62-80. *Concurrent Pos:* Consult, WPakistan Agr Pulse Res, 71. *Mem:* Am Genetic Asn; Am Soc Agron; Am Phytopath Soc; Am Soc Hort Sci; Crop Sci Soc Am. *Res:* Developing high protein pulse crops through genetic approaches; program development for improved agricultural research. *Mailing Add:* SE 766 Ridgeview Ct Pullman WA 99163

WILSON, VICTOR JOSEPH, b Berlin, Ger, Dec 24, 28; m 53; c 2. NEUROPHYSIOLOGY. *Educ:* Tufts Col, BS, 48; Univ Ill, PhD(physiol), 53. *Prof Exp:* Res assoc, 56-58, from asst prof to prof neurophysiol, 58-69, PROF NEUROPHYSIOL, ROCKEFELLER UNIV, 69- *Mem:* Am Physiol Soc; Soc Neurosci. *Res:* Organization and synaptic transmission in the central nervous system, particularly the spinal cord and brain stem; vestibular system. *Mailing Add:* Rockefeller Univ 1230 York Ave New York NY 10021

WILSON, WALTER DAVIS, b Merced, Calif, Oct 20, 35; m 59; c 3. ATOMIC PHYSICS. *Educ:* Univ Calif, Berkeley, BS, 57, PhD(nuclear eng), 66. *Prof Exp:* Chem engr, Aerojet Gen Nucleonics, Calif, 58-59; mem tech staff high-altitude nuclear effects, Aerospace Corp, 65-69; PROF PHYSICS, CALIF POLYTECH STATE UNIV, SAN LUIS OBISPO, 69- *Concurrent Pos:* Tech consult, Sci Applns, Inc, Calif, 71-75. *Mem:* Am Inst Physics. *Res:* High altitude physics, particularly electromagnetic field propagation, chemistry and trapped radiation; plasma physics; nuclear reactor theory. *Mailing Add:* Dept of Physics Calif Polytech Univ San Luis Obispo CA 93407

WILSON, WALTER ERVIN, b Salem, Ore, Apr 1, 34. RADIOLOGICAL PHYSICS. *Educ:* Willamette Univ, BA, 56; Univ Wis, MS, 58, PhD(physics), 61. *Prof Exp:* RADIATION PHYSICIST, PAC NORTHWEST LABS, BATTELLE MEM INST, 64- *Concurrent Pos:* Fel, Basel Univ, 61-62 & Univ Wis, 62-64. *Mem:* Health Physics Soc; Radiation Res Soc; Am Asn Physicists in Med; Am Phys Soc. *Res:* Radiation effects and radiological sciences. *Mailing Add:* Pac Northwest Labs Battelle Mem Inst PO Box 999 Richland WA 99352

WILSON, WALTER LEROY, b Phoenixville, Pa, Sept 1, 18; m 44; c 2. PHYSIOLOGY. *Educ:* Pa State Teachers Col, West Chester, BS, 41; Univ Pa, PhD(zool), 49. *Prof Exp:* Biologist, Off Sci Res & Develop, Univ Pa, 43-44, asst instr zool, 46-47; biologist, Manhattan Proj, Columbia Univ, 44-46; instr physiol & biophys, Col Med, Univ Vt, 49-52, from asst prof to assoc prof, 52-65; PROF BIOL SCI, OAKLAND UNIV, 65- *Concurrent Pos:* Lectr, Middlebury Col, 52-53; mem corp, Marine Biol Lab, Woods Hole. *Mem:* Am Physiol Soc; Soc Gen Physiol; Am Soc Zoologists. *Res:* Effects of high temperature on living systems; protoplasmic viscosity changes during cell division; the release of anticoagulant substances from living cells and the inhibitory action of these anticoagulants on cell division; role of cellular cortex in stimulation and cell division. *Mailing Add:* Dept of Biol Oakland Univ Rochester MI 48063

WILSON, WALTER LUCIEN, JR, b Montgomery, Ala, Apr 26, 27; m 47; c 2. MATHEMATICS. *Educ:* Univ Ala, AB, 50, MA, 51; Univ Calif, Los Angeles, PhD(math), 59. *Prof Exp:* Res engr, NAm Aviation, Inc, Calif, 59-60; ASSOC PROF MATH, UNIV ALA, 60- *Mem:* Am Math Soc; Math Asn Am. *Res:* Calculus of variations; numerical analysis; linear programming. *Mailing Add:* Dept of Math Univ of Ala University AL 35486

WILSON, WALTER R, b South Bend, Ind, May 3, 19; m 44; c 3. ENGINEERING PHYSICS. *Educ:* Univ Mich, BS, 41. *Prof Exp:* Test engr, Res Lab, 41-42, develop engr, Transformer & Allied Prod Lab, 42-49, elec sect head, Switchgear & Control Lab, 49-54, mgr eng res, 54-56, mgr eng, High Voltage Switchgear Dept, 56-61, consult engr, 61-68, mgr elec & mech eng res, Power Delivery Div, 68-76, SR CONSULT & STANDARDS ENGR, GEN ELEC CO, 76- *Concurrent Pos:* US deleg, Int Electro-Tech Comn, Madrid, 59-72. *Honors & Awards:* Alfred Noble Prize, Am Soc Civil Engrs, 44. *Mem:* Nat Soc Prof Engrs; Am Mgt Asn; fel Inst Elec & Electronics Engrs. *Res:* High voltage electrical power equipment; dielectrics, magnetics, gaseous discharges and electric contact phenomena; electrical and mechanical instrumentation. *Mailing Add:* 6901 Elmwood Ave Philadelphia PA 19142

WILSON, WILBUR WILLIAM, b Ferriday, La, Jan 10, 48; m 69; c 2. PHYSICAL CHEMISTRY. *Educ:* Northeast La State Col, BS, 69; Univ NC, PhD(phys chem), 73. *Prof Exp:* Asst prof, 74-80, PROF CHEM, MISS STATE UNIV, 80- *Mem:* Am Chem Soc; Sigma Xi. *Res:* Laser light scattering by macromolecules. *Mailing Add:* Box 3348 Mississippi State MS 39762

WILSON, WILFRED J, b Ferndale, Calif, Mar 4, 30; m 68. EMBRYOLOGY. *Educ:* Sacramento State Col, AB, 52; Univ Calif, Davis, MA, 58, PhD(zool), 64. *Prof Exp:* Teaching asst zool, Univ Calif, Davis, 58-61, assoc, 61-63; from asst prof to assoc prof, 63-70, PROF ZOOL, SAN DIEGO STATE UNIV, 70- *Concurrent Pos:* Shell merit fel, Stanford Univ, 69; vis lectr, Burma, 71; Fulbright lectr, US Dept of State, Nat Taiwan Univ, 70-71. *Mem:* Am Soc Zool. *Res:* General and invertebrate biology; crustacean water balance; teaching methods in human biology; early animal development. *Mailing Add:* Dept of Zool San Diego State Univ San Diego CA 92182

WILSON, WILLIAM AUGUST, JR, b St Louis, Mo, July 3, 24; m 54; c 4. NEUROPSYCHOLOGY. *Educ:* Univ Calif, AB, 43, PhD(psychol), 56; Yale Univ, MD, 53. *Prof Exp:* Vis instr, psychol, Wesleyan Univ, 50-51; res assoc neurophysiol, Inst of Living, 53-56, dir dept exp psychol, 56-58; vis asst prof psychol, Univ Calif, 58; asst prof, Univ Colo, 59-60; assoc prof, Bryn Mawr Col, 60-64; assoc dean grad sch, 71-72, prof biobehav sci, 69-77, PROF PSYCHOL, UNIV CONN, 64-, ASSOC DEAN COL LIB ARTS & SCI, 78- *Concurrent Pos:* Mem exp psychol res review comt, NIMH, 69-73, chmn, 71-73. *Mem:* AAAS; Am Psychol Asn; Inst Math Statist; Animal Behav Soc; Soc Neurosci. *Res:* Neurological determinants of behavior, especially intersensory effects in perception and learning; function of regions of association cortex and the mechanisms of learning. *Mailing Add:* Dept of Psychol Univ of Conn Storrs CT 06268

WILSON, WILLIAM BUFORD, marine biology, see previous edition

WILSON, WILLIAM CURTIS, b Orlando, Fla, Dec 29, 27; m 52; c 1. PLANT PHYSIOLOGY. *Educ:* Cornell Univ, BS, 49; Univ Fla, MAgr, 58, PhD(fruit crops), 66. *Prof Exp:* Asst mgr agr res, Fla Agr Res Inst, 57-61; adj assoc horticulturist, Citrus Exp Sta, Agr Res & Educ Ctr, Univ Fla, 66-77; res scientist II, 77-80, RES SCIENTIST III, FLA DEPT CITRUS, 80- *Concurrent Pos:* Merck & Co grant, 69; Julian C Miller award, Asn Southern Agr Workers, Inc, 66; Ciba-Geigy grants, 70-72; adj assoc prof, Agr Res & Educ Ctr, Univ Fla, 74-81, adj horticulturist, 81- *Mem:* Am Soc Hort Sci; Int Soc Citricult; Plant Growth Regulator Soc Am (secy, 80-81). *Res:* Abscission chemicals to facilitate easier removal of citrus fruit to aid mechanical or hand harvesting; acidity reduction and cold hardy chemicals. *Mailing Add:* Fla Dept Citrus 700 Exp Sta Rd Lake Alfred FL 33850

WILSON, WILLIAM D, b Pittsburgh, Pa, Nov 8, 25; m 49; c 5. PARASITOLOGY. *Educ:* Dickinson Col, BS, 50; Univ Kans, MA, 53; Mich State Univ, PhD(microbiol, pub health), 57. *Prof Exp:* Instr, Mich State Univ, 56-57; prof biol, State Univ NY Col Oneonta, 57-81; RETIRED. *Mailing Add:* PO Box 97 Unadille NY 13849

WILSON, WILLIAM DENNIS, b New York, NY, July 20, 40; m 60, 73; c 2. SOLID STATE PHYSICS. *Educ:* Queens Col, NY, BS, 63, MA, 65; City Univ New York, PhD(physics), 67. *Prof Exp:* Res physicist, Queens Col, NY, 67 & 68-69; fel physics, City Univ New York, 67-68; RES PHYSICIST, LIVERMORE NAT LABS & SANDIA NAT LABS, 69-, DIV SUPVR, THEORET DIV, 74- *Concurrent Pos:* Consult, Lawrence Radiation Lab, Calif, 67-69. *Mem:* Am Phys Soc. *Res:* Interatomic potentials; defects in solids; hydrogen and helium in metals; diffusion. *Mailing Add:* Sandia Labs Theoret Div 8341 Livermore CA 94550

WILSON, WILLIAM ENOCH, JR, b El Dorado, Ark, Jan 15, 33; m 63; c 2. ATMOSPHERIC CHEMISTRY. *Educ:* Hendrix Col, BA, 53; Purdue Univ, PhD(phys chem), 57. *Prof Exp:* Instr chem, Wis State Univ-La Crosse, 55-56; Fulbright res fel, Inst Technol, Munich, Ger, 57-58; sr chemist, Appl Physics Lab, Johns Hopkins Univ, 58-67; assoc fel, Battelle Mem Inst, 67-71; chief atmospheric aerosol res sect, 71-75, chief aerosol res br, 75-77, SCI DIR REGIONAL FIELD STUDIES OFF, ENVIRON PROTECTION AGENCY, 77- *Concurrent Pos:* Adj assoc prof, Environ Sci & Eng Dept, Sch Pub Health, Univ NC, 73- *Mem:* AAAS; Am Chem Soc; Am Meteorol Soc; Sigma Xi; Air Pollution Control Asn. *Res:* Sources, formation, dynamics, transport, removal, and effects of atmospheric pollutants; atmospheric chemistry and physics; molecular spectroscopy; chemical kinetics and thermodynamics pertinent to combustion, propulsion, and air pollution. *Mailing Add:* Environ Protection Agency Regional Field Studies Off MD-84 Research Triangle Park NC 27711

WILSON, WILLIAM EWING, b New Orleans, La, Nov 8, 32; m 61; c 3. MOLECULAR PHARMACOLOGY. *Educ:* King Col, AB, 54; Univ Tenn, MS, 56, PhD(biochem), 59. *Prof Exp:* Res assoc biochem, Okla State Univ, 59-60, instr, 61-63; res biochemist, Radio Isotope Serv, Vet Admin Hosp, Little Rock, 63-64, chief, Biochem Sect, Southern Res Support Ctr, 64-68; asst prof biochem, Sch Med, Univ Ark, Little Rock, 63-68; res chemist, Anal & Synthetic Chem Br, 68-73, res chemist, Environ Toxicol Br, 73-76, RES CHEMIST, LAB BEHAVIORAL & NEUROL TOXICOL, NAT INST ENVIRON HEALTH SCI, 76- *Mem:* AAAS; Am Chem Soc; NY Acad Sci. *Res:* Interaction of chemicals with membranal enzymes; molecular pharmacology of drugs and environmental agents; analytical biochemistry; neurochemistry; solution interactions. *Mailing Add:* Lab of Behav & Neurol Toxicol Nat Inst of Environ Health Sci Research Triangle Park NC 27709

WILSON, WILLIAM JAMES FITZPATRICK, b Aberdeen, Scotland, Feb 13, 46; Can citizen; m 81. STELLAR EVOLUTION, MASS LOSS. *Educ:* Univ BC, BSc, 68; Univ Waterloo, MSc, 70; Univ Calgary, PhD(astrophysics), 77. *Prof Exp:* FEL & INSTR PHYSICS & ASTRON, UNIV CALGARY, 77- *Mem:* Can Astron Soc. *Res:* Computation of massive star evolution from the zero-age main sequence to helium exhaustion, with mass loss due to radiation pressure and convective and rotational turbulent pressure; origin of Wolf-Rayet stars. *Mailing Add:* Dept Physics Univ Calgary Calgary AB T2N 1N4 Can

WILSON, WILLIAM JEWELL, b St Joseph, Mo, Dec 14, 32; m 57; c 5. RADIOLOGY. *Educ:* William Jewell Col, AB, 54; Univ Mo-Columbia, MD, 58. *Prof Exp:* Intern, St Albans Hosp, Long Island & US Naval Hosp, 58-59; resident, Univ Mo-Columbia Hosp, 62-65, instr radiol, Univ, 64-65; asst prof cardiovasc radiol & dir dept, Univ Va, 66-67; asst prof diag radiol, 67-68; found prof radiol & chmn dept, Med Ctr, Univ Nebr, Omaha, 68-73; DIR RADIOL, LONG BEACH MEM HOSP, 73- *Concurrent Pos:* USPHS res fel, Univ Mo, 64-65; USPHS advan res fel cardiovasc radiol, Univ Minn, Minneapolis, 65-66; Markle scholar acad med, 67; chmn subcomt comput in diag radiol, Nat Ctr Radiol Health, 67-68; mem subcomt comput based diag radiol info, Am Bd Radiol, 71-73, chmn cardiovasc comt, Nat Bd Examr, 71-74. *Mem:* Radiol Soc NAm; Asn Univ Radiol; Am Col Radiol; AMA; fel Am Col Cardiol. *Res:* Cardiovascular radiology including physical properties of generating and analyzing radiant images; pharmacologic effects of contrast materials utilized in clinical angiography; aberrations in subsegmental arterial perfusion of organs; computer techniques in radiology. *Mailing Add:* Mem Hosp Med Ctr 2801 Atlantic Ave Long Beach CA 90801

WILSON, WILLIAM JOHN, b Spokane, Wash, Dec 16, 39; c 2. RADIO ASTRONOMY. *Educ:* Univ Wash, BSEE, 61; Mass Inst Technol, MSEE, 63, PhD(elec eng), 70. *Prof Exp:* MEM TECH STAFF MILLIMETER-WAVE RADIO ASTRON & ELEC ENG, AEROSPACE CORP, 70- *Concurrent Pos:* User's Comt, Nat Radio Astron Observ, 71-; asst prof elec eng, Univ Tex, Austin, 76-77. *Mem:* Am Astron Soc; Int Union Radio Sci; Int Astron Union. *Mailing Add:* Aerospace Corp PO Box 92957 Los Angeles CA 90009

WILSON, WILLIAM MARK DUNLOP, b Glasgow, Scotland, Jan 23, 49; Brit citizen; m 73. AGRICULTURE, ANIMAL SCIENCE. *Educ:* Univ Glasgow, BSc hons, 71; Univ Ill, Urbana, MS, 73, PhD(animal sci), 75. *Prof Exp:* Asst animal sci & ruminant nutrit, Univ Ill, Urbana, 71-75; AGR PROJS OFFICER, WORLD BANK, 75- *Mem:* Am Soc Animal Sci; Brit Soc Animal Prod. *Res:* Facets of animal science and agronomy which relate to agriculture in developing countries; appraisal and supervision of agricultural projects in developing countries in Latin America, South Asia, and the Middle East. *Mailing Add:* World Bank 1818 H St NW Washington DC 20433

WILSON, WILLIAM PRESTON, b Fayetteville, NC, Nov 6, 22; m 51; c 5. PSYCHIATRY. *Educ:* Duke Univ, BS, 43, MD, 47. *Prof Exp:* Intern, Gorgas Hosp, CZ, 47-48; staff psychiatrist, State Hosp, Raleigh, NC, 48-49; instr psychiat & asst resident, Sch Med, Duke Univ, 49-52, resident neurol, 52, assoc psychiat & chief resident, 52-54, asst prof psychiat, 55-58; assoc prof, dir psychiat res labs & consult, Hogg Found, Med Br, Univ Tex, 58-60; assoc prof psychiat, 58-61, PROF PSYCHIAT, MED CTR, DUKE UNIV, 61-, DIR NEUROPHYSIOL LABS, 58-; DIR PSYCHIAT RES LABS & STAFF PSYCHIATRIST, VET ADMIN HOSP, 58- *Concurrent Pos:* Fel med, Duke Univ, 52-54; NIH fel, Montreal Neurol Inst, McGill Univ, 54-55; mem, Am Bd Qual EEG, 69-, secy-treas, 71-74. *Mem:* AAAS; AMA; Am Psychiat Asn; Am Psychopath Asn; Asn Res Nerv & Ment Dis. *Res:* Clinical psychiatry and neurochemistry; clinical and experimental neurophysiology; electroencephalography. *Mailing Add:* Dept of Psychiat Box 3838 Duke Univ Med Ctr Durham NC 27710

WILSON, WILLIAM ROBERT DUNWOODY, b Belfast, Northern Ireland, Sept 11, 41; US citizen; m 67; c 2. TRIBOLOGY, PLASTICITY. *Educ:* Belfast Tech Col, HNC, 64; Queens Univ, Belfast, BS, 63, PhD(mech eng), 67. *Prof Exp:* Student apprentice, Harland & Wolff Ltd, Belfast, 59-63; sr res scientist, Colubus Div, Battelle Mem Inst, 67-71; prof, Univ Mass, Amherst, 71-81; PROF MECH & NUCLEAR ENG, NORTHWESTERN UNIV, 81- *Mem:* Am Soc Mech Engrs; Am Soc Lubrication Engrs; Soc Mfg Engrs. *Res:* Manufacturing processes and tribology in particular lubrication of metal forming processes, computer aided process and material selection. *Mailing Add:* Mech & Nuclear Eng Dept Northwestern Univ Evanston IL 60201

WILSON, WILLIAM SOLOMON, physical chemistry, deceased

WILSON, WILLIAM THOMAS, b Midvale, Utah, July 22, 32; m 58; c 5. INVERTEBRATE PATHOLOGY, ENTOMOLOGY. *Educ:* Colo Agr & Mech Col, BS, 55; Colo State Univ, MS, 57; Ohio State Univ, PhD(entom), 67. *Prof Exp:* Asst entom, Colo State Univ, 55-57, from instr to asst prof, 60-65; asst, Ohio State Univ, 65-67; asst res pathobiologist, Univ Calif, Irvine, 67-68; RES ENTOMOLOGIST, SCI & EDUC ADMIN-AGR RES, USDA & MEM GRAD FAC, UNIV WYO, 68- *Mem:* Bee Res Asn; Soc Invert Path; Entom Soc Am. *Res:* Chemotherapeutic treatment of insect diseases; invertebrate microbiology; impact of pesticides on bees; diseases and toxicology of the honey bee. *Mailing Add:* Bee Dis Invests USDA Univ Sta Box 3168 Laramie WY 82071

WILSON, WOODROW, JR, theoretical chemistry, see previous edition

WILT, FRED H, b South Bend, Ind, Dec 12, 34; m 57; c 1. ZOOLOGY. *Educ:* Ind Univ, AB, 56; Johns Hopkins Univ, PhD(biol), 59. *Prof Exp:* Fel, Carnegie Inst Technol, 59-60; assoc prof biol, Purdue Univ, 60-64; assoc prof, 64-71, PROF ZOOL, UNIV CALIF, BERKELEY, 71- *Concurrent Pos:* NIH spec fel, 63-64; fel, Guggenheim Found, 75. *Mem:* Soc Develop Biol; Am Soc Cell Biol; Am Soc Zoologists. *Mailing Add:* Dept of Zool Univ of Calif Berkeley CA 94720

WILT, JAMES WILLIAM, b Chicago, Ill, Aug 28, 30; m 53; c 5. ORGANIC CHEMISTRY. *Educ:* Univ Chicago, AB, 49, MSc, 53, PhD(chem), 54. *Prof Exp:* Instr chem, Univ Conn, 55; from instr to assoc prof, 55-66, chmn dept, 70-77, PROF CHEM, LOYOLA UNIV CHICAGO, 66- *Mem:* Am Chem Soc; Sigma Xi. *Res:* Rearrangements in organic chemistry; reaction mechanisms; diazoalkane chemistry; free radical chemistry; chemistry of bicyclic compounds. *Mailing Add:* Dept of Chem Loyola Univ 6525 N Sheridan Rd Chicago IL 60626

WILT, JOHN CHARLES, b Moose Jaw, Sask, Feb 20, 20; m; c 4. BACTERIOLOGY. *Educ:* Univ Man, MD, 45, MSc, 50; Am Bd Path, dipl, 50; FRCP(C). *Prof Exp:* Demonstr, 46-53, assoc prof bact, 54-56, prof & head dept, 57-69, PROF MED MICROBIOL & HEAD DEPT, FAC MED, UNIV MAN, 69-, ASSOC DEAN FAC MED & DIR DEPT CLIN MICROBIOL, HEALTH SCI CTR, 67-, DIR LAB & X-RAY UNITS, 77- *Concurrent Pos:* Asst pathologist, Winnipeg Gen Hosp, 46-53, dir dept bact, 67-; consult bacteriologist, Man Dept Health, Children's Hosp Winnipeg, Grace Hosp & Winnipeg Gen Hosp. *Mem:* Fel Am Col Physicians; Can Soc Microbiol; Can Pub Health Asn; Can Asn Med Microbiol (vpres, 57-58); Can Asn Path. *Res:* General microbiology, especially virology. *Mailing Add:* Dept of Med 770 Bannatyne Ave Winnipeg MB R3T 2N2 Can

WILT, PAXTON MARSHALL, b Louisville, Ky, July 8, 42; m 67. MOLECULAR SPECTROSCOPY. *Educ:* Centre Col Ky, BA, 64; Vanderbilt Univ, PhD(physics), 67. *Prof Exp:* From asst prof to assoc prof, 67-76, PROF CHEM PHYSICS, CENTRE COL KY, 76- *Concurrent Pos:* Consult, Res Corp Am, 67. *Res:* Molecular vibration-rotation spectres of small polyatomic molecules. *Mailing Add:* Dept of Chem Physics Centre Col of Ky Danville KY 40422

WILTBANK, WILLIAM JOSEPH, b Clifton, Ariz, Jan 1, 27; m 47; c 5. HORTICULTURE, PLANT PHYSIOLOGY. *Educ:* NMex State Univ, BSAgr, 50; Univ Fla, PhD(fruit crops), 67. *Prof Exp:* Instr voc agr, NMex State Dept Voc Educ, 50-53; instr hort, NMex State Univ, 53-54, ext horticulturist, 54-59; hort adv, US Agency Int Develop, Costa Rica, 59-64; res asst, 64-68, from asst prof to assoc prof, 68-79, actg chmn dept, 77-79, PROF FRUIT CROPS, UNIV FLA, 79- *Honors & Awards:* Gourley Award, Am Soc Hort Sci, 71. *Mem:* Am Soc Hort Sci; Am Inst Biol Sci; Int Soc Hort Sci; Int Soc Citricult. *Res:* Physiology of plant reproduction; plant tolerance to temperature and water stress; mineral nutrition of plants. *Mailing Add:* Dept of Fruit Crops Univ of Fla Gainesville FL 32611

WILTON, ARTHUR CHARLES, b Carragana, Sask, Jan 18, 24; US citizen; m 57; c 3. CYTOGENETICS, PLANT BREEDING. *Educ:* Univ BC, BSA, 49; Univ Sask, MSc, 54; Univ Man, PhD(plant breeding), 63. *Prof Exp:* Asst res officer agron, Can Dept Agr, BC, 49-55; asst exp officer clover breeding, Welsh Plant Breeding Sta, 55-56; agronomist, Univ Alaska, Palmer Ctr, 57-66; asst res officer cotton breeding, Univ Calif, Davis, 66-67; overseas agr adv, Md, 67-70, turf breeder & res agronomist, 70-72, res agronomist forage breeding, Pasture Res Sta, University Park, Pa, 72-74, team leader & botanist agrostologist, Food & Agr Orgn, Kenya, 74-75, RES GENETICIST, NORTHERN GREAT PLAINS RES LAB, SCI & EDUC ADMIN-AGR RES, USDA, MANDAN, NDAK, 76- *Concurrent Pos:* Adj prof soil physics, Dept Agron, Col Agr, Pa State Univ, 74-77. *Mem:* Genetics Soc Can; Soc Range Mgt; Am Soc Agron; Crop Sci Soc Am. *Res:* Breeding legumes for rangeland. *Mailing Add:* Northern Great Plains Res Lab Box 459 Mandan ND 58554

WILTON, DONALD ROBERT, b Lawton, Okla, Oct 25, 42; m 65; c 3. ELECTRICAL ENGINEERING. *Educ:* Univ Ill, Urbana, BS, 64, MS, 66, PhD(elec eng), 70. *Prof Exp:* Mem tech staff, Ground Systs Group, Hughes Aircraft Co, 65-67; PROF ELEC ENG, UNIV MISS, 70-, NAT SCI FOUND RES INITIATION GRANT, 72- *Mem:* Inst Elec & Electronics Engrs; Electromagnetics Soc. *Res:* Electromagnetic theory; numerical methods applied to electromagnetics; antennas. *Mailing Add:* Dept of Elec Eng Univ of Miss University MS 38677

WILTS, CHARLES H(AROLD), b Los Angeles Co, Calif, Jan 30, 20; m 47; c 3. ELECTRONICS. *Educ:* Calif Inst Technol, BS, 40, MS, 41, PhD(elec eng), 48. *Prof Exp:* Res staff mem, 42-45, asst prof appl mech, 47-52, assoc prof elec eng, 52-57, exec officer for elec eng, 72-75, PROF ELEC ENG, CALIF INST TECHNOL, 57- *Mem:* Inst Elec & Electronics Engrs. *Res:* Design and use of analog computers; feedback control systems; ferromagnetism in metals and alloys; anisotropy and ferromagnetic resonance in thin films. *Mailing Add:* Dept of Elec Eng Calif Inst of Technol Pasadena CA 91125

WILTS, JAMES REED, b Marshalltown, Iowa, June 7, 23; m 50. PHYSICS. *Educ:* Iowa State Col, BS, 44; Calif Inst Technol, MS, 49, PhD(physics), 52. *Prof Exp:* Fel, Calif Inst Technol, 52-53; physicist, Gen Elec Co, NY, 53-54; sr electronics engr, Gen Dynamics/Convair, Calif, 54-55; asst prof elec eng, Mich State Univ, 55-56; assoc prof, Colo State Univ, 56-57; staff physicist, Int Bus Mach Corp, NY, 57-62; PHYSICIST, NAVAL OCEAN SYSTS CTR, 63- *Mem:* Am Phys Soc. *Res:* Ionospheric and plasma physics; physics of fluids; statistical communication theory. *Mailing Add:* Naval Ocean Systs Ctr Code 9234 San Diego CA 92152

WILTSCHKO, DAVID VILANDER, b Portland, Ore, Feb 5, 49; m 81. TECTONICS, TECTONOPHYSICS. *Educ:* Univ Rochester, BA, 71; Brown Univ, MSc, 74, PhD(geol), 77. *Prof Exp:* Vis asst prof, 77-79, ASST PROF STRUCTURAL GEOL, UNIV MICH, 79- *Mem:* Geol Soc Am; Am Geophys Union. *Res:* Tectonics of mountain belts, focusing on the mechanism of the continent structures; strain magnitudes and stress directions in deformed rocks; theoretical model of thrust sheet motion; mechanisms of fault zones. *Mailing Add:* Dept Geol Sci 1006 C C White Bldg Univ Mich Ann Arbor MI 48109

WILTSE, JAMES CORNELIUS, b Tannersville, NY, Mar 16, 26; m 50; c 2. MILLIMETER WAVES, LASERS. *Educ:* Rensselaer Polytech Inst, BEE, 47, MEE, 52; Johns Hopkins Univ, PhD(eng), 59. *Prof Exp:* Engr, Gen Elec Co, 47-48; instr elec eng, Rensselaer Polytech Inst, 48-51; instr, Johns Hopkins Univ, 53-54, res assoc, 54-58; mgr microwaves & antennas, Electronic Commun, Inc, 59-63, dir advan develop, 63-64; prin scientist & mgr microwaves, radar, optics & lasers, Martin Marietta Corp, 64-73, dir res & technol, 73-78, dir electronics eng, 76; PRIN RES ENGR, ENG EXP STA, GA INST TECHNOL, 78- *Concurrent Pos:* Instr, Naval Reserve Off Sch, Fla, 66-69; mem vis comt, Dept Elec Eng, Univ Fla, 69-70, 73 & 78; mem external adv comt, Ga Inst Technol, 76-78. *Honors & Awards:* Auth of the Year Award, Martin Marietta Corp, 67, Engr of the Year Award, 70. *Mem:* Fel Inst Elec & Electronics Engrs. *Res:* Microwave and millimeter wave technology, antennas, electromagnetic theory, lasers, infrared and electro-optics with applications to radar, communications, guidance and electronic countermeasures; guided wave propagation; microwave and millimeter-wave technology and communications; lasers, infrared, and optics; quantum electronics; atmospheric propagation; radiometry; radar; antennas; signal processing. *Mailing Add:* Eng Exp Sta Ga Inst Technol Atlanta GA 30332

WILTSHIRE, CHARLES THOMAS, b Kansas City, Mo, Apr 5, 41; m 62; c 4. AQUATIC ECOLOGY. *Educ:* Culver-Stockton Col, BA, 63; Drake Univ, MA, 65; Univ Mo-Columbia, PhD(zool), 73. *Prof Exp:* From asst prof to assoc prof, 66-76, PROF BIOL & CHMN DIV NATURAL SCI, CULVER-STOCKTON COL, 76- *Mem:* AAAS; Am Soc Zoologists; Am Inst Biol Sci. *Res:* Taxonomy and natural history of conchostracans, such as Cyzicus; ecology of the middle Mississippi River. *Mailing Add:* Dept of Biol Culver-Stockton Col Canton MO 63435

WIMAN, FRED HAWKINS, b Roscoe, Tex, Jan 30, 48; m 78. EVOLUTIONARY ECOLOGY, AQUATIC ECOLOGY. *Educ:* Tex Tech Univ, BA, 70; Univ Wis-Madison, PhD(zool), 78. *Prof Exp:* Asst prof biol, Univ Houston, 78-79; lectr environ sci, Univ Mich, 80; lectr zool, Univ Wis, Madison, 81. *Mem:* Soc Study Evolution; Am Soc Naturalists; Soc Syst Zoologists. *Res:* Evolutionary ecology and biogeography of aquatic organisms; evolution of reproductive isolating mechanisms. *Mailing Add:* 2215 Packard Apt 4 Ann Arbor MI 48104

WIMBER, DONALD EDWARD, b Greeley, Colo, Jan 2, 30; m 57; c 2. BOTANY, CYTOLOGY. *Educ:* San Diego State Col, BA, 52; Claremont Col, MA, 54, PhD(bot), 56. *Prof Exp:* Res assoc, Dos Pueblos Orchid Co, 54-57; res collabr, Brookhaven Nat Lab, 57-60, asst biologist, 61-63; res collabr, Royal Cancer Hosp, 60-61; assoc prof, 63-68, PROF BIOL, UNIV ORE, 68- *Concurrent Pos:* NIH fel, 58-61, career develop award, 66-71. *Mem:* Bot Soc Am. *Res:* Chromosome structure; genetics and cytology of orchids; localization of gene function. *Mailing Add:* Dept of Biol Univ of Ore Eugene OR 97403

WIMBER, R(AY) TED, b Salina, Utah, Feb 27, 35; m 56; c 7. METALLURGY, MATERIALS SCIENCE. *Educ:* Univ Utah, BS, 56, PhD(metall), 59. *Prof Exp:* From instr to asst prof metall, Wash State Univ, 59-61; sr engr, Hercules Powder Co, Utah, 61-62; res engr, Varian Assocs, Calif, 62-64; res staff engr, Solar Div, Int Harvester Co, 64-67; from assoc prof to prof mech eng, Mont State Univ, 67-74; SCIENTIST, DEERE & CO TECH CTR, 74- *Honors & Awards:* NASA Award, 69. *Mem:* Am Soc Metals; Metall Soc; Soc Mfg Engrs. *Res:* Reaction kinetics; surface chemistry; high-temperature materials; coatings. *Mailing Add:* Deere & Co Tech Ctr 3300 River Dr Moline IL 61265

WIMBERLEY, STANLEY, b Detroit, Mich, Dec 22, 27. MARINE GEOLOGY, OCEANOGRAPHY. *Educ:* Johns Hopkins Univ, BA, 52; Univ Tex, MA, 54; Univ Southern Calif, PhD(geol), 64. *Prof Exp:* Res technician, Chesapeake Bay Inst, Johns Hopkins Univ, 51-52; sedimentologist, Gulf Res & Develop Co, 54-58; res assoc, Allan Hancock Found, Univ Southern Calif, 59-61; asst prof geol, Univ PR, 62-65 & Univ South Fla, 65-67; ASSOC PROF GEOL, CHAPMAN COL, 67- *Mem:* Geol Soc Am; Soc Econ Paleont & Mineral; Am Asn Petrol Geol. *Res:* Detrital sediments of barrier islands, beaches and continental shelf; sea floor topography. *Mailing Add:* Dept of Geol Chapman Col Orange CA 92666

WIMBUSH, (A H) MARK, HOWARD, b Nairobi, Kenya, June 26, 36; US citizen; m 66; c 2. PHYSICAL OCEANOGRAPHY. *Educ:* Oxford Univ, BA, 57, MA, 64; Univ Hawaii, MA, 63; Univ Calif, San Diego, PhD(phys oceanog), 69. *Prof Exp:* Res assoc phys oceanog, Inst Geophys & Planetary Physics, La Jolla, 69-70; NSF fel, Inst Oceanog Sci, Eng, 70-71; from asst prof to assoc prof phys oceanog, Nova Univ, 71-77; ASSOC PROF PHYS OCEANOG, GRAD SCH OCEANOG, UNIV RI, 77- *Res:* Oceanic turbulence, tides and waves; dynamics of shelf and slope regions and interaction of bottom boundary layer flow with underlying sediment. *Mailing Add:* Grad Sch Oceanog South Ferry Rd Narragansett RI 02882

WIMENITZ, FRANCIS NATHANIEL, b Philadelphia, Pa, Mar 9, 22; m 44; c 1. PHYSICS, ENGINEERING. *Educ:* Temple Univ, BA, 49, MA, 51. *Prof Exp:* Physicist acoust, Nat Bur Standards, 51-53; physicist mine fuze develop, Diamond Ord Fuze Lab, 53-58; res supvr nuclear weapons effects, Harry Diamond Labs, 58-64, chief, Nuclear Weapon Effects Br, 64-70, chief, Nuclear Weapons Effects Prog Off, 70-80; FAC MEM, GEORGE WASHINGTON UNIV, 80- *Mem:* AAAS. *Res:* Nuclear weapons effects; radiation transport; nuclear weapons electromagnetic pulse measurement; operations research; nuclear weapons effects simulation. *Mailing Add:* 1024 Chiswell Lane Silver Spring MD 20901

WIMER, BRUCE MEADE, b Tuckerton, NJ, Aug 31, 22; m 50; c 3. INTERNAL MEDICINE, HEMATOLOGY. *Educ:* Franklin & Marshall Col, BS, 43; Jefferson Med Col, MD, 46; Am Bd Internal Med, dipl; Am Bd Hemat, dipl, 72. *Prof Exp:* Intern, Hosp, Jefferson Med Col, 46-47, resident internal med & hemat, 48-51; asst internal med & hemat, Guthrie Clin, Sayre, Pa, 53-59; pvt pract, Summit, NJ, 59-61; assoc med dir, Squibb Inst Med Res, 61-62; CHIEF HEMAT & ONCOL, LOVELACE BATAAN MED CTR, 62- *Mem:* AMA; fel Am Col Physicians; Am Soc Hemat; Int Soc Hemat. *Res:* Cancer immunotherapy, especially adoptive leukocyte therapy; therapeutic applications of bone marrow curettage; oncology; hematologic therapeutics; hemolytic characteristics of the McLeod phenotype. *Mailing Add:* Lovelace Bataan Med Ctr 5200 Gibson Blvd SE Albuquerque NM 87108

WIMER, CYNTHIA CROSBY, b Boston, Mass, Oct 23, 33; m 57; c 3. BEHAVIOR GENETICS. *Educ:* Wellesley Col, BA, 55; McGill Univ, MA, 58; Rutgers Univ, PhD(psychol), 61. *Prof Exp:* res assoc psychol, Inst Develop Studies, NY Med Col, 61 & Jackson Lab, 63-69; ASSOC RES SCIENTIST, DIV NEUROSCI, CITY OF HOPE MED CTR, 69- *Mem:* Am Psychol Asn; Behav Genetics Asn; AAAS; Sigma Xi. *Res:* Behavior genetics; biometrics; neuroanatomical correlates of behavior. *Mailing Add:* Div of Neurosci City of Hope Med Ctr 1500 E Duarte Rd Duarte CA 91010

WIMER, DAVID CARLISLE, b Champaign, Ill, July 20, 26; m 55; c 1. ANALYTICAL CHEMISTRY, ORGANIC CHEMISTRY. *Educ:* Univ Ill, BS, 51. *Prof Exp:* From chemist to sr chemist, 51-65, group leader invest drugs res, 65-70, ANAL RES CHEMIST, ANAL RES DEPT, ABBOTT LABS, N CHICAGO, 70- *Res:* Acid-base interactions; non-aqueous solvent chemistry; functional group analysis, particularly organic nitrogen functions; thin layer chromatography; organic and inorganic qualitative analysis; ultraviolet absorption spectra of inorganic and organic compounds. *Mailing Add:* 2312 11th St Winthrop Harbor IL 60096

WIMER, LARRY THOMAS, b Stuttgart, Ark, Dec 20, 36; m 59; c 3. INSECT PHYSIOLOGY. *Educ:* Phillips Univ, BA, 57; Rice Inst, MA, 59; Univ Va, PhD(physiol), 63. *Prof Exp:* Instr biol, Northwestern Univ, 62-64; asst prof, 64-70, assoc prof, 70-77, PROF BIOL & CHMN DEPT, UNIV SC, 77- *Mem:* AAAS; Am Soc Zoologists. *Res:* Insect developmental physiology; hormonal regulation of developmental metabolic systems. *Mailing Add:* Dept Biol Univ SC Col Arts & Sci Columbia SC 29208

WIMER, RICHARD E, b Tulare, Calif, Apr 8, 32; m 57; c 3. BEHAVIORAL GENETICS, NEUROGENETICS. *Educ:* San Jose State Col, AB, 52; Ohio Univ, MSc, 53; McGill Univ, PhD(psychol), 59. *Prof Exp:* Instr psychol, Douglass Col, Rutgers Univ, 58-60; sr res assoc psychiat, NY Med Col, 60-61; assoc staff scientist, Jackson Lab, 61-65, staff scientist, 65-69; SR RES SCIENTIST & CHIEF BEHAV GENETICS SECT, DIV NEUROSCI, CITY OF HOPE MED CTR, 69- *Mem:* Am Psychol Asn; Genetics Soc Am; Am Genetic Asn; Soc Neurosci; Behav Genetics Asn. *Res:* Genetic variations in brain structure and correlated behavioral function. *Mailing Add:* City of Hope Med Ctr Div of Neurosci 1500 E Duarte Rd Duarte CA 91010

WIMMER, DONN BRADEN, b Pittsburg, Kans, Oct 14, 27; m 49; c 3. COMBUSTION CHEMISTRY, FUEL CHEMISTRY. *Educ:* Univ Kans, BS, 50, MS, 51. *Prof Exp:* Res chemist, 51-65, sr res chemist, 65-77, SECT SUPVR COMBUSTION, PHILLIPS PETROL CO, 77- *Concurrent Pos:* Mem, Eng & Sci Adv Comt, Coord Res Coun, Air Qual Comt, Am Petrol Inst, 76- *Honors & Awards:* Arch T Colewell Award, Soc Automotive Engrs, 74. *Mem:* Int Inst Combustion. *Res:* Reciprocating engine combustion and atmospheric photochemistry. *Mailing Add:* Phillips Res Ctr Phillips Petrol Co Bartlesville OK 74004

WIMMER, ECKARD, b Berlin, Ger, May 22, 36; m 65; c 2. MOLECULAR BIOLOGY, VIROLOGY. *Educ:* Univ Göttingen, diplom chemist, 59, PhD(org chem), 62. *Prof Exp:* Asst org chem, Univ Göttingen, 62-64; res fel biochem, Univ BC, 64-66; res assoc molecular biol, Univ Ill, 66-68; from asst prof to assoc prof microbiol, Sch Med, St Louis Univ, 68-74; ASSOC PROF MICROBIOL, SCH BASIC HEALTH SCI, STATE UNIV NY STONY BROOK, 74- *Concurrent Pos:* Vis prof, Mass Inst Technol, 69. *Mem:* Am Soc Microbiol. *Res:* Molecular biology of animal and bacterial viruses; biochemistry of nucleic acids; cell biology. *Mailing Add:* Sch of Basic Health Sci State Univ of NY Stony Brook NY 11790

WIMS, ANDREW MONTGOMERY, b Phila, Pa, Apr 29, 35; m 59; c 4. PHYSICAL CHEMISTRY, POLYMER CHEMISTRY. *Educ:* Howard Univ, BS, 57, MS, 59, PhD, 67. *Prof Exp:* Res chemist, Nat Bur Standards, 60-68; DEPT RES SCIENTIST, GEN MOTORS RES LAB, 69- *Mem:* Am Chem Soc; Am Inst Chem; Am Soc Test & Mat; Sigma Xi. *Res:* Characterization of polymeric materials; light scattering; electron microscopy; electron spectroscopy; x-ray diffraction. *Mailing Add:* Anal Chem Dept Gen Motors Res Labs 12 Mile & Mound Rds Warren MI 48090

WIMSATT, WILLIAM ABELL, b Washington, DC, July 28, 17; m 40; c 6. HISTOPHYSIOLOGY, REPRODUCTIVE BIOLOGY. *Educ:* Cornell Univ, AB, 39, PhD(hist, embryol), 43. *Prof Exp:* Asst histol & embryol, Cornell Univ, 40-43; asst anat, Med Sch, Harvard Univ, 43-44, instr, 44-45; from asst prof to assoc prof, 45-50, mem bd trustees, 60-65, PROF ZOOL, CORNELL UNIV, 51- *Concurrent Pos:* Res collabr, Brookhaven Nat Lab, 54-59; Guggenheim fel, 62-63. *Mem:* Fel AAAS; Am Asn Anat; Histochemical Soc; Sigma Xi. *Mailing Add:* Div of Biol Sci Sect of Genetics & Develop Cornell Univ Ithaca NY 14853

WINANS, RANDALL EDWARD, b Battle Creek, Mich, Jan 11, 49; m 75. ORGANIC CHEMISTRY. *Educ:* Mich Technol Univ, BS, 71; Cornell Univ, MS, 73, PhD(chem), 76. *Prof Exp:* Fel, 75-77, asst chemist, 77-80, CHEMIST/GROUP LEADER, ARGONNE NAT LAB, 80- *Concurrent Pos:* Consult, Gas Res Inst, 79-80. *Mem:* Am Chem Soc; AAAS. *Res:* Organic chemistry of coals and other fossil fuels; applications of mass spectrometry. *Mailing Add:* Chem Div Argonne Nat Lab Argonne IL 60439

WINANS, SARAH SCHILLING, b Hannibal, Mo, Apr 23, 41; m 65. NEUROANATOMY, NEUROPSYCHOLOGY. *Educ:* Cornell Univ, BA, 63, PhD(anat), 69. *Prof Exp:* Instr anat, State Univ NY Downstate Med Ctr, 68-70; asst prof, 70-75, ASSOC PROF ANAT, UNIV MICH, ANN ARBOR, 75- *Mem:* AAAS; Am Asn Anatomists; Soc Neurosci. *Res:* Structure and function of the olfactory and vomeronasal pathways in the central nervous systems. *Mailing Add:* Dept of Anat Univ of Mich Med Sci II Ann Arbor MI 48109

WINAWER, SIDNEY J, b New York, NY, July 9, 31. INTERNAL MEDICINE, GASTROENTEROLOGY. *Educ:* NY Univ, BA, 52; State Univ NY, MD, 56. *Prof Exp:* Asst med, Harvard Med Sch, 62-64, instr, 65-66; asst prof, 66-72, CLIN ASSOC PROF MED, MED COL, CORNELL UNIV, 72- *Concurrent Pos:* Fel med, Boston City Hosp, 62-64, assist physician, 65-66; NIH spec fel, 65-67; asst physician, New York Hosp, 66-; dir gastrointestinal lab, 72-; asst clinician, Sloan-Kettering Inst. *Mem:* Fel Am Col Physicians; Am Gastroenterol Asn; Am Soc Gastrointestinal Endoscopy; Am Fedn Clin Res; Am Col Gastroenterol. *Res:* Clinical investigation in gastrointestinal diseases, particularly morphology, physiology, cell proliferation and other aspects of gastritis; malabsorptive studies such as massive bowel resection; clinical and investigative aspects of gastrointestinal and liver cancer. *Mailing Add:* Mem Hosp 1275 York Ave New York NY 10021

WINBORN, WILLIAM BURT, b Victoria, Tex, Oct 6, 31; m 53; c 1. ANATOMY. *Educ:* Univ Tex, BS, 56; La State Univ, PhD(anat), 63. *Prof Exp:* From instr to asst prof anat, Med Units, Univ Tenn, Memphis, 63-68; asst prof, 68-69, ASSOC PROF ANAT, UNIV TEX HEALTH SCI CTR SAN ANTONIO, 69- *Mem:* AAAS; Electron Micros Soc Am; Am Soc Cell Biol; Am Asn Anatomists. *Res:* Electron microscopic studies of Islets of Langerhans and of the gastrointestinal tract; cytochemistry of the gastrointestinal tract. *Mailing Add:* 2915 Deer Ledge San Antonio TX 78230

WINBOW, GRAHAM ARTHUR, b Sedgley, Eng, Oct 31, 43; m 77; c 1. GEOPHYSICS, THEORETICAL PHYSICS. *Educ:* Cambridge Univ, BA, 65, PhD(physics), 68. *Prof Exp:* Sci Res Coun fel, Univ London, 68-69; NATO fel, Europ Orgn Nuclear Res, Geneva, Switz, 69-70; sr res assoc, Daresbury Lab, Warrington, Eng, 70-75; fel physics, Rutgers Univ, 75-78; sr res physicist geophys, 78-80, res specialist, 80-81, RES SUPVR, EXXON PROD RES CO, 81- *Mem:* Am Phys Soc; Soc Explor Geophys. *Res:* Propagation of sound in liquids and solids; applied mathematics. *Mailing Add:* Exxon Prod Res Co PO Box 2189 Houston TX 77001

WINBURY, MARTIN M, b New York, NY, Aug 4, 18; m 42; c 2. PHARMACOLOGY, PHYSIOLOGY. *Educ:* Long Island Univ, BS, 40; Univ Md, MS, 42; NY Univ, PhD(physiol), 51. *Prof Exp:* Economist, US Bur Mines, 42-44; mem staff biochem & pharmacol, Merck Inst Therapeut Res, 44-47; pharmacologist, Div Biol Res, G D Searle & Co, 47-55; sr pharmacologist, Schering Corp, 55-58, dir dept pharmacol, 58-61, assoc dir biol res, 61; dir, Dept Pharmacol, 61-82, DIR SCI DEVELOP, WARNER LAMBERT CO, 82- *Concurrent Pos:* Mem vis fac, Col Physicians & Surgeons, Columbia Univ; mem vis fac, Rutgers Univ. *Mem:* Soc Exp Biol & Med; Am Soc Pharmacol & Exp Therapeut; Am Chem Soc; Am Heart Asn; Am Col Cardiol. *Res:* Pharmacology and physiology of cardiovascular, coronary and autonomic agents; distribution myocardial flow; microcirculation. *Mailing Add:* Warner Lambert 2800 Plymouth Rd Ann Arbor MI 48105

WINCH, FRED EVERETT, JR, b Mass, June 16, 14; m 39; c 3. FORESTRY, SILVICULTURE. *Educ:* Univ Maine, BS, 36; Cornell Univ, MS, 37. *Prof Exp:* Forestry specialist, Soil Conserv Serv, USDA, 38-40, farm planning technician, 40-43; from asst prof to prof forestry, Cornell Univ, 43-76, actg head, Dept Natural Resources, 72-73, actg assoc dir agr exten, 73-74; CONSULT, FOREST MGT & ENVIRON MGT, 76- *Mem:* Fel Soc Am Foresters. *Res:* Plantation establishment and early growth; maple syrup and Christmas tree production; forest recreation, resource development and conservation; land use inventory analysis and planning; forest tax impacts. *Mailing Add:* Warner Rd Bradford NH 03221

WINCHELL, C PAUL, b Ionia, Mich, Oct 14, 21; m 46; c 3. MEDICINE. *Educ:* Univ Mich, MD, 45. *Prof Exp:* From instr to assoc prof, 51-71, PROF MED, SCH MED, UNIV MINN, MINNEAPOLIS, 71- *Concurrent Pos:* Consult cardiol, Vet Hosp, Minneapolis & Off Hearings & Appeals, Social Security Admin. *Mem:* Am Heart Asn; Am Fedn Clin Res; Am Col Physicians. *Res:* Cardiovascular diseases. *Mailing Add:* Univ Hosps Univ of Minn Minneapolis MN 55455

WINCHELL, HARRY SAUL, b Coaldale, Pa, Mar 1, 35; m 64; c 4. MEDICAL PHYSICS, NUCLEAR MEDICINE. *Educ:* Bucknell Univ, BA, 54; Hahnemann Med Col, MD, 58; Univ Calif, Berkeley, PhD(biophys), 61. *Hon Degrees:* DSc, Bucknell Univ, 72. *Prof Exp:* Intern, San Francisco Hosp, Univ Calif, 58-59; univ fel, Univ Calif, Berkeley, 59-61; resident, Mt Sinai Hosp, NY, 61-62; assoc res physician, Donner Lab, Univ Calif, Berkeley, 62-73, lectr med physics, Univ, 66-73; exec vpres & dir res & develop, Medi-Physics, Inc, 72-78, consult, 78-79. *Concurrent Pos:* NSF fel, Univ Calif, Berkeley, 59-60, NIH fel, 60-61; spec consult, Sealab II Exp, La Jolla, Calif, 65. *Honors & Awards:* George Von Hevesy Award, Europ Orgn Nuclear Med, 69. *Mem:* Fel Am Col Physicians; Am Fedn Clin Res; Soc Nuclear Med; Soc Exp Biol & Med. *Mailing Add:* #1 Via Oneg Lafayette CA 94549

WINCHELL, HORACE, b Madison, Wis, Jan 1, 15; m 37. MINERALOGY, GEOLOGY. *Educ:* Univ Wis, BA & MA, 36; Harvard Univ, MA, 37, PhD(mineral, crystallog), 41. *Prof Exp:* Asst geologist, City Bd Water Supply, Honolulu, 38-40; res crystallographer, Hamilton Watch Co, 41-45; from instr to asst prof, 45-51, ASSOC PROF MINERAL & CUR MINERAL, PEABODY MUS, YALE UNIV, 51- *Concurrent Pos:* Asst, Conn Geol Natural Hist Surv, 46-52. *Mem:* AAAS; fel Geol Soc Am; fel Mineral Soc Am; Geochem Soc; Soc Econ Geol. *Res:* Physical properties of sapphire; sapphire jewel bearing; diamond dies, design and crystallography; grading of diamond powder; mineralogy of Connecticut; petrology of Oahu, Hawaii; systematic mineralogy; optical mineralogy and crystallography. *Mailing Add:* 2161 Yale Sta New Haven CT 06520

WINCHELL, P(ETER) G(RUT), b Ossining, NY, July 27, 29; m 50; c 2. METALLURGY. *Educ:* Univ Chicago, AB, 48; Mass Inst Technol, BS, 53, PhD(metall), 58. *Prof Exp:* Instr phys metall, Mass Inst Technol, 53-55; from asst prof metall eng to assoc prof mat sci & metall eng, 58-67, PROF MAT SCI & METALL ENG, PURDUE UNIV, WEST LAFAYETTE, 67- *Concurrent Pos:* Vis prof, Cornell Univ, 67-68. *Mem:* Am Soc Metals; Am Inst Mining, Metall & Petrol Engrs. *Res:* Structure and properties of crystalline solids, particularly mechanical properties. *Mailing Add:* Sch of Mat Sci & Metall Eng Purdue Univ West Lafayette IN 47907

WINCHELL, ROBERT E, b Wichita, Kans, Sept 21, 31; m 58; c 3. MINERALOGY, CRYSTALLOGRAPHY. *Educ:* Stanford Univ, BS, 56; Mich Col Mining & Technol, MS, 59; Ohio State Univ, PhD(mineral), 63. *Prof Exp:* Jr eng geologist, Bridge Dept, Calif Div Hwys, 57-58; res scientist, AC Spark Plug Div, Gen Motors Corp, 63-66; assoc prof, 66-72, PROF GEOL & MINERAL, CALIF STATE UNIV, LONG BEACH, 72- *Mem:* Mineral Soc Am; Brit Mineral Soc. *Res:* Mineral synthesis and characterization; optical, x-ray and morphological crystallography; x-ray diffraction; electron microscopy; phase equilibrium studies; crystal chemistry, growth and structure analysis; solid state and materials science. *Mailing Add:* Dept of Geol Sci Calif State Univ Long Beach CA 90804

WINCHESTER, ALBERT MCCOMBS, b Waco, Tex, Apr 20, 08; m 34; c 1. BIOLOGY. *Educ:* Baylor Univ, AB, 29; Univ Tex, MA, 31, PhD(zool), 34. *Prof Exp:* Instr zool, Univ Tex, 32-34; prof, Lamar Col, 34-35; head dept biol, Ouachita Baptist Col, 35-36; head dept, Tenn State Teachers Col, 36-37; head dept biol & chmn div sci, Okla Baptist Univ, 37-43; prof zool, Baylor Univ, 43-46; head biol dept, Stetson Univ, 46-61; consult, Biol Sci Curric Study, Am Inst Biol Sci, Univ Colo, 61-62; PROF BIOL, UNIV NORTHERN COLO, 62- *Concurrent Pos:* Rockefeller fel; Carnegie grant, 48; AAAS vis lectr, 64-; mem, Colo Bd Exam Basic Sci, 66- *Mem:* AAAS; Genetics Soc Am; Am Soc Human Genetics; Am Eugenics Soc. *Res:* Genetics; effects of x-ray on Drosophila; induced sex ratio variation in Drosophila; radiation; human genetics. *Mailing Add:* Dept of Biol Univ of Northern Colo Greeley CO 80639

WINCHESTER, JOHN, b Chicago, Ill, Oct 8, 29; m 58; c 1. PHYSICAL CHEMISTRY. *Educ:* Univ Chicago, AB, 50, SM, 52; Mass Inst Technol, PhD(chem), 55. *Prof Exp:* Fulbright grant, Neth, 55-56; from asst prof to assoc prof geochem, Mass Inst Technol, 56-66; assoc prof meteorol & oceanog, Univ Mich, Ann Arbor, 67-69, prof oceanog & asst dir Great Lakes Res Div, 69-70; chmn dept, 70-77, PROF OCEANOG, FLA STATE UNIV, 70- *Concurrent Pos:* Vis lectr, Lamont Geol Observ, Columbia Univ, 59; res partic, Oak Ridge Inst Nuclear Studies & Oak Ridge Nat Lab, 58, 59 & 61; Fulbright vis prof, Taipei, 62-63; vis scientist, Inst Marine Sci, Univ Alaska, 64; vis prof, La Plata, 66. *Mem:* Am Chem Soc; Geochem Soc; Geol Soc Am; Am Phys Soc; Am Geophys Union. *Res:* Activation analysis; atmospheric and marine geochemistry. *Mailing Add:* Dept of Oceanog Fla State Univ Tallahassee FL 32306

WINCHESTER, RICHARD ALBERT, b Denver, Colo, Nov 20, 21; m 47; c 3. AUDIOLOGY, SPEECH PATHOLOGY. *Educ:* Univ Denver, BA, 47, MA, 48; Univ Southern Calif, PhD(audiol, speech path), 57. *Prof Exp:* Resident audiol & speech path, Orthop Hosp, Los Angeles, 48-50; asst prof, Univ Denver, 50-53; res audiologist, Walter Reed Army Med Ctr, 53-54; dir hearing & speech clin, Vet Admin Hosp, San Francisco, 54-55, res audiologist, Vet Admin Regional Off, Los Angeles, 55-58; asst prof audiol, Sch Med, Temple Univ, 59-63; DIR DIV COMMUN DISORDERS & RES AUDIOLOGIST, CHILDREN'S HOSP PHILADELPHIA, 63-; ASST PROF AUDIOL, SCH MED, UNIV PA, 64- *Concurrent Pos:* Dir audiol & speech path, Otologic Group Philadelphia, 59-66; consult, Pa Acad Ophthal & Otolaryngol, 60-; spec lectr, Univ Md, 63-64. *Mem:* AAAS; Am Speech & Hearing Asn; assoc fel Am Acad Ophthal & Otolaryngol; Am Cleft Palate Asn; Am Audiol Soc. *Res:* Speech in deafness; auditory perception in brain injury; nonorganic deafness; deafness in otosclerosis; congenital mixed deafness; hearing patterns in vestibular disorders; central auditory functions; sound spectrography and cleft palate speech; auditory behavior in infancy and early childhood. *Mailing Add:* 726 Clyde Circle Bryn Mawr PA 19010

WINCHURCH, RICHARD ALBERT, b Newark, NJ, June 18, 36; m 61; c 2. IMMUNOLOGY, MICROBIOLOGY. *Educ:* Seton Hall Univ, AB, 58, MS, 67; Rutgers Univ, PhD(microbiol), 70. *Prof Exp:* Sr scientist microbiol, Smith, Kline & French Labs, 70-71, assoc sr investr pharmacol, 71-73; staff fel immunol, Baltimore Cancer Res Ctr, Nat Cancer Inst, 73-76, sr staff fel, 76-77; ASST PROF SURG IMMUNOL, SCH MED, JOHNS HOPKINS UNIV, 77- *Concurrent Pos:* Dir, Microbiol Lab, Baltimore Regional Burn Ctr, Baltimore City Hosps, 78- *Mem:* Am Asn Immunologists; Reticuloendothelial Soc; NY Acad Sci; AAAS. *Res:* Cellular immunology; lymphocyte cyclic adenosine monophosphate metabolism; tumor immunology; autoimmune disease; infectious diseases. *Mailing Add:* Dept of Surg 4940 Eastern Ave Baltimore MD 21224

WINCKLER, JOHN RANDOLPH, b North Plainfield, NJ, Oct 27, 16; m 43; c 5. PHYSICS. *Educ:* Rutgers Univ, BS, 42; Princeton Univ, PhD(physics), 46. *Hon Degrees:* Doctor, Univ Paul Sabatier, France, 72. *Prof Exp:* Res physicist, Johns-Manville Corp, NJ, 37-42; instr physics, Palmer Lab, Princeton Univ, 46-49; from asst prof to assoc prof, 49-58, PROF PHYSICS, UNIV MINN, MINNEAPOLIS, 58- *Concurrent Pos:* Guggenheim fel, Meudon Observ, 65-66; mem math & phys sci div comt, NSF. *Honors & Awards:* Am Inst Aeronaut & Astronaut 62; Spade Sci Award, 62; Arctowski Medal, Nat Acad Sci, 78. *Mem:* Fel AAAS; fel Am Phys Soc; fel Am Geophys Union; Int Acad Astronaut. *Res:* High speed flow of gases and shock waves; geomagnetic effects and energy spectrum of primary cosmic rays; atmospheric total radiation; solar produced cosmic rays and energetic processes in solar flares; geomagnetic storm influences on energetic particles in the magnetosphere. *Mailing Add:* Sch of Physics & Astron Univ of Minn Minneapolis MN 55455

WINCKLHOFER, ROBERT CHARLES, b Newark, NJ, Dec 14, 26; m 49; c 2. POLYMER PHYSICS. *Educ:* Columbia Univ, BS, 53. *Prof Exp:* Engr, Cent Res Lab, 53-61, group leader, 61-64, res supvr, 64, Fibers Div, Tech Dept, 64-68, mgr res, 68-70, tech dir heavy denier nylon, 70-72, tech dir advan technol, 72-77, RES ASSOC, FIBERS & PLASTICS CO, TECH DEPT, ALLIED CHEM CORP, 77- *Mem:* AAAS. *Res:* Fiber polymer physics; crystallization kinetics; polymer characterization; differential thermal analysis of polymers. *Mailing Add:* Fibers & Plastics Co Tech Dept Allied Chem Corp PO Box 31 Petersburg VA 23803

WINDEKNECHT, THOMAS GEORGE, b Owosso, Mich, Feb 13, 35; m 58; c 3. COMPUTER SCIENCE, SYSTEMS ENGINEERING. *Educ:* Univ Mich, BSE, 58, MSE, 59; Case Western Reserve Univ, PhD(systs eng), 64. *Prof Exp:* Mem tech staff systs eng, Space Technol Labs, Inc, 59-62; from asst prof to assoc prof, Case Western Reserve Univ, 64-70; prof elec eng, Mich Technol Univ, 70-72; prof info & comput sci, Ga Inst Technol, 72-73; PROF MATH SCI, MEMPHIS STATE UNIV, 73- *Concurrent Pos:* NSF grant, Case Western Reserve Univ, 67-69 & Mich Technol Univ, 70-72. *Mem:* Asn Comput Mach; Inst Elec & Electronics Engrs. *Res:* Microcomputer programming and graphics; dynamic system theory; theory of computation. *Mailing Add:* Dept of Math Sci Memphis State Univ Memphis TN 38152

WINDELL, JOHN THOMAS, b Hammond, Ind, Apr 4, 30; m 59; c 3. AQUATIC BIOLOGY. *Educ:* Ind Cent Col, BS, 53; Ind Univ, MA, 58, PhD(limnol), 65. *Prof Exp:* Teacher, Griffith High Sch, 55-58; asst prof biol, Ind Cent Col, 58-62; assoc zool, Ind Univ, Bloomington, 62-65; asst prof, Ind Univ Northwest, 65-66; assoc prof, 66-70, PROF BIOL, UNIV COLO, BOULDER, 70- *Concurrent Pos:* Ind Univ fac fel, 66; partic, Int Symp Biol Basis Freshwater Fish Prod, Reading, Eng, 66. *Honors & Awards:* Lieber Mem Teaching Award, Ind Univ, 65. *Mem:* AAAS; Am Soc Limnol & Oceanog; Wetland Soc Am; Am Fisheries Soc. *Res:* Ecological physiology; biological basis of fish production; food consumption in fishes; conversion coefficients and the ecology of fishes; fish physiology, feeding, digestion, nutrition, population ecology, stream and wetland biology and habitat restoration. *Mailing Add:* Dept of EPO Biol Univ of Colo Boulder CO 80309

WINDELS, CAROL ELIZABETH, b Long Prarie, Minn, July 12, 48; m 70. PHYTOPATHOLOGY. *Educ:* St Cloud State Univ, BA, 70; Univ Minn, MS, 72, PhD(plant path), 80. *Prof Exp:* Jr scientist, 73-74, asst scientist, 74-77, assoc scientist, 77-80, SCIENTIST, DEPT PLANT PATH, UNIV MINN, 80- *Mem:* Am Phytopath Soc. *Res:* Ecology and taxonomy of fusarium species; root rot, stalk rot, and other diseases of corn; biological seed treatment of corn and vegetables to control seed and seedling diseases. *Mailing Add:* Dept Plant Path 209 Stakman Hall Univ Minn 1519 Gortner Ave St Paul MN 55108

WINDER, CHARLES GORDON, b Ottawa, Ont, June 13, 22; m 48; c 2. GEOLOGY. *Educ:* Univ Western Ont, BSc, 49; Cornell Univ, MS, 51, PhD(geol), 53. *Prof Exp:* Lectr, 53-56, from asst prof to assoc prof, 56-64, head dept, 65-71, PROF GEOL, UNIV WESTERN ONT, 64- *Mem:* Fel Geol Soc Am; Soc Econ Mineral & Paleont; Am Asn Petrol Geologists; fel Geol Asn Can. *Res:* Stratigraphy of southern Ontario; conodonts; carbonate petrology; Canadian geologists; creation-evolution controversy. *Mailing Add:* Dept of Geol Univ of Western Ont London ON N6A 5B7 Can

WINDER, DALE RICHARD, b Marion, Ind, Aug 27, 29; m 53. SOLID STATE PHYSICS. *Educ:* DePauw Univ, AB, 51; Univ Nebr, MA, 54; Case Inst Technol, PhD(physics), 57. *Prof Exp:* Lab & teaching asst physics, DePauw Univ, 50-51, Univ Nebr, 51-54 & Case Inst Technol, 54-57; physicist, Nat Carbon Res Labs, Union Carbide Corp, 57-60; asst prof, 60-64, ASSOC PROF PHYSICS, COLO STATE UNIV, 64- *Concurrent Pos:* Physicist, Boulder Lab, Nat Bur Standards, 62-69; Idaho Nuclear Corp-Asn Western Univs fac appointee, 67. *Mem:* Am Phys Soc; Am Asn Physics Teachers; Am Crystallog Asn. *Res:* Photoelectric effect; lattic dynamics; crystal growth; radiation damage; nuclear fuels and moderators; transport property measurements. *Mailing Add:* Dept of Physics Colo State Univ Ft Collins CO 80523

WINDER, ROBERT OWEN, b Boston, Mass, Oct 9, 34; div; c 2. COMPUTER SCIENCE. *Educ:* Univ Chicago, AB, 54; Univ Mich, BS, 56; Princeton Univ, MS, 58, PhD(math), 62. *Prof Exp:* Engr comput, RCA Corp, 57-58, mem tech staff, RCA Labs, 58-69, head group, 69-75, dir microprocessors, Solid State Div, 75-78; mgr microcomput, 78-80, DIR ADV DEVELOP, EXXON ENTERPRISES, INC, 81- *Honors & Awards:* David Sarnoff Award, RCA Corp, 76. *Mem:* Fel Inst Elec & Electronics Engrs. *Mailing Add:* 24 Deer Path Princeton NJ 08540

WINDER, WILLIAM CHARLES, b Salt Lake City, Utah, Nov 16, 14; m 39. FOOD SCIENCE, DAIRY INDUSTRY. *Educ:* Utah State Univ, BS, 46, MS, 48; Univ Wis, PhD(dairy indust), 49. *Prof Exp:* Plant supt, Winder Dairy, Utah, 34-45; from instr to assoc prof, 49-60, prof food sci, 60-81, EMER PROF FOOD SCI, UNIV WIS-MADISON, 81- *Mem:* Am Dairy Sci Asn; Sigma Xi. *Res:* Effects of ultrasound on food products; physical and chemical effects of freezing and drying food products; analysis of foods. *Mailing Add:* Dept of Food Sci Univ of Wis Madison WI 53706

WINDES, S(TEPHEN) L(OCKHART), b Winnetka, Ill, Dec 5, 11; m 36; c 3. COMMUNICATIONS, RADIO ENGINEERING. *Educ:* Bucknell Univ, BS, 33, MS, 34. *Prof Exp:* Radio operator, Radio-Marine Corp Am, Ohio, 30-34; electronic engr, C F Burgess Lab, Ill, 34-35; seismol observer, US Bur Mines, 35-42, physicist, 42-51; commun engr, US Dept Interior, 51-77; RETIRED. *Concurrent Pos:* Rep, Inter-Dept Radio Adv Comt, US Dept Interior, 42-77. *Res:* Seismic effects of quarry blasting; damage from air blasts; physical properties of rocks; frequency management. *Mailing Add:* 9302 Flower Ave Silver Spring MD 20901

WINDHAGER, ERICH E, b Vienna, Austria, Nov 4, 28; US citizen; m 56; c 2. PHYSIOLOGY, BIOPHYSICS. *Educ:* Univ Vienna, MD, 54. *Prof Exp:* Fel biophys, Harvard Med Sch, 56-58; instr physiol, Med Col, Cornell Univ, 58-61; vis scientist, Biochem Inst, Univ Copenhagen, 61-63; from asst prof to assoc prof physiol, 63-69, prof, 69-78, MAXWELL M UPSON PROF PHYSIOL & BIOPHYS, MED COL, CORNELL UNIV, 78-, CHMN DEPT PHYSIOL 73- *Concurrent Pos:* Career scientist, Res Coun New York, 63-71 & Irma Hirschl Found, 73-78; sect ed, Am J Physiol, 69-74. *Honors & Awards:* Homer W Smith Award. *Mem:* Am Physiol Soc; Biophys Soc; Int Soc Nephrology; Harvey Soc; Am Soc Nephrology. *Res:* Renal tubular transfer of electrolytes; electrophysiology of the nephron; micropuncture techniques and nephron function; kidney, water and electrolytes. *Mailing Add:* Dept Physiol Cornell Univ Med Col New York NY 10021

WINDHAM, MICHAEL PARKS, b Houston, Tex, Sept 23, 44; m 70; c 2. MATHEMATICS. *Educ:* Rice Univ, BA, 66, MA & PhD(math), 70. *Prof Exp:* Instr math, Univ Miami, 70-71; asst prof, 71-77, ASSOC PROF MATH, UTAH STATE UNIV, 77- *Mem:* Soc Indust & Appl Math; Math Asn Am. *Res:* Pattern recognition; stochastic differential equations. *Mailing Add:* Dept of Math Utah State Univ Logan UT 84321

WINDHAM, PAT MORRIS, b Roscoe, Tex, Sept 3, 20. PHYSICS. *Educ:* NTex State Col, BS, 47, MS, 51; Rice Inst, PhD(physics), 55. *Prof Exp:* Asst prof physics, Tex Tech Col, 55-56; asst prof physics, NTex State Univ, 56-59, assoc prof, 59-80. *Mem:* Am Phys Soc; Am Asn Physics Teachers. *Res:* Low energy nuclear physics; charge exchange studies; negative ions. *Mailing Add:* RFD 1 Denton TX 76203

WINDHAM, RONNIE LYNN, b Jasper, Tex, Mar 2, 43; m 72. ANALYTICAL CHEMISTRY. *Educ:* Pan Am Univ, BA, 65; Eastern NMex Univ, MS, 69; Tex A&M Univ, PhD(anal chem), 71. *Prof Exp:* proj chemist, Jefferson Chem Co, 71-81; SUPVR ANAL CHEM, TEXACO CHEM CO, AUSTIN LABS, 81- *Mem:* Am Chem Soc. *Res:* atomic absorption spectrophotometry; ion chromatography; trace analysis; isotachophoresis. *Mailing Add:* 11608 January Dr Austin TX 78753

WINDHAM, STEVE LEE, b Miss, Sept 19, 22; m 48; c 3. HORTICULTURE. *Educ:* Miss State Col, BS, 43, MS, 48; Mich State Col, PhD(hort), 53. *Prof Exp:* Asst, Miss State Col, 47-48; asst horticulturist 48-51, assoc horticulturist, 53-61, HORTICULTURIST, TRUCK CORPS BR, MISS AGR EXP STA, MISS STATE UNIV, 61-, ADJ ASSOC PROF HORT, 74- *Concurrent Pos:* Asst, Mich State Col, 51-53. *Res:* Vegetable crop response and utilization of nutrient elements. *Mailing Add:* Truck Crops Exp Sta Miss State Univ Crystal Springs MS 39059

WINDHEUSER, JOHN JOSEPH, b Bonn, Ger, Dec 2, 26; US citizen; m 51; c 4. PHYSICAL PHARMACY. *Educ:* Rutgers Univ, Newark, BSc, 51; Univ Wis-Madison, MS, 59, PhD(pharm), 61. *Prof Exp:* Res pharmacist, Ciba Pharmaceut Co, NJ, 51-57; asst prof pharm, Univ Wis-Madison, 61-63; dir pharm res & develop, Sandoz Pharmaceut, NJ, 63-66; assoc prof pharm, Univ Wis-Madison, 66-72; dir pharm res & develop, Alza Corp, 72-74; SR VPRES, INTERx RES CORP, 74- *Mem:* AAAS; Am Pharmaceut Asn; fel Acad Pharmaceut Sci. *Res:* Physical chemistry of solutions; drug interaction in solution; biopharmaceutics of cancer-chemotherapeutic agents; drug analysis. *Mailing Add:* INTERx Res Corp 2201 W 21st St Lawrence KS 66044

WINDHOLZ, THOMAS BELA, b Arad, Romania, Jan 10, 23; US citizen; m 48; c 2. ORGANIC CHEMISTRY. *Educ:* Univ Cluj, MS, 47. *Prof Exp:* Res chemist, Chinoin Pharmaceut Co, Budapest, 48-50; sr res chemist, Res Inst Pharmaceut Indust, 51-54, sect head, 55-56; res chemist, Res Labs, Celanese Corp Am, NJ, 57-59; sr res chemist, 60-63, sect head, 64-69, assoc dir, 70-72, dir, Int Regulatory Affairs, 72-75, dir, Proj Planning & Mgt, 75-80, SR DIR HUMAN HEALTH PROD DEVELOP, RES LABS, MERCK & CO, INC, 81- *Mem:* Am Chem Soc. *Res:* Synthetic organic chemistry; steroids and other natural products; medicinal chemistry, metabolism; international relations and management. *Mailing Add:* Merck & Co Res Labs Rahway NJ 07065

WINDHOLZ, WALTER M, b Gorham, Kans, Apr 25, 33; m 61; c 3. MATHEMATICS. *Educ:* Ft Hays Kans State Col, AB, 53; Kans State Univ, MS, 58. *Prof Exp:* Mathematician, Thiokol Chem Corp, Utah, 61-65; MATHEMATICIAN, KAMAN SCI CORP, 65- *Mem:* Math Asn Am. *Res:* Applied mathematics; structural dynamics. *Mailing Add:* 1338 Whitehouse Dr Colorado Springs CO 80904

WINDHORST, DOROTHY BAKER, b Pawhuska, Okla, Mar 25, 28; c 2. DERMATOLOGY, IMMUNOLOGY. *Educ:* Univ Chicago, MD, 54. *Prof Exp:* Asst prof dermat, Univ Minn, 62-68; from asst prof to assoc prof med, Univ Chicago, 68-73; med officer, Nat Cancer Inst, 72-76; dir clin res dermat, 76-80, DIR, BIOMED DATA SYSTS, HOFFMANN-LA ROCHE INC, 80- *Concurrent Pos:* Mem training grants comt, Nat Inst Arthritis, Metab & Digestive Dis, 72-73; mem subcomt arsenic, Comt Med & Biol Effects of Environ Pollutants, Nat Acad Sci, 74-76; clin prof dermat, Col Physicians & Surgeons, Columbia Univ. *Mem:* Am Asn Immunologists; Am Fedn Clin Res; Soc Invest Dermat; Am Dermat Asn. *Res:* Clinical research for drug efficacy and safety; human phagocyte function; genetic defects in defense mechanisms. *Mailing Add:* Dept of Biomed Data Systs Hoffmann-La Roche Inc Nutley NJ 07110

WINDING, CHARLES CALVERT, b Minneapolis, Minn, Aug 12, 08; m 36. CHEMICAL ENGINEERING. *Educ:* Univ Minn, BChE, 31, PhD(chem eng), 35. *Prof Exp:* From instr to prof chem eng, 35-75, asst dir, Sch Chem Eng, 47-57, dir, 57-70, EMER PROF CHEM ENG, CORNELL UNIV, 75- *Concurrent Pos:* Consult, Tide Water Oil Co, 38-45 & 48-54, Rome Cable Corp, 51-62 & B F Goodrich Co, 52-56; consult, Cowles Chem Co, 58-68, mem bd dirs, 59-68; mem staff, US Rubber Reserve. *Mem:* Am Chem Soc; Am Soc Eng Educ; distinguished mem Soc Plastics Engrs; fel Am Inst Chem Engrs; fel Am Inst Chemists. *Res:* Adsorption; heat transfer; fluid flow; polymerization; polymeric materials. *Mailing Add:* Olin Hall Sch of Chem Eng Cornell Univ Ithaca NY 14850

WINDISCH, RITA M, b Pittsburgh, Pa. CLINICAL CHEMISTRY. *Educ:* Duquesne Univ, BS, 60, PhD(chem), 64. *Prof Exp:* Chief clin chemist path, 65-80, DEP CHIEF CLIN CHEM & CRITICAL CARE PATH, MERCY HOSP, 80- *Concurrent Pos:* Clin prof, Sch Med Technol, Carlow Col, 65-; clin prof, Sch Med Technol, Duquesne Univ, 69-; med staff affil, Div Clin Chem & Critical Care, Dept Path, Mercy Hosp, 69- *Mem:* Am Asn Clin Chemists; Am Chem Soc. *Res:* Diabetes, clinical chemistry and toxicology. *Mailing Add:* Dept of Path Mercy Hosp Locust St Pittsburgh PA 15219

WINDLE, WILLIAM FREDERICK, b Huntington, Ind, Oct 10, 98; m 23; c 2. ANATOMY. *Educ:* Denison Univ, BS, 21; Northwestern Univ, MS, 23, PhD(anat), 26. *Hon Degrees:* ScD, Denison Univ, 47. *Prof Exp:* From asst to assoc prof anat, Med Sch, Northwestern Univ, 22-35, prof micros anat, 35-42, prof neurol & dir neurol inst, 42-46; prof anat & chmn dept, Sch Med, Univ Wash, Seattle, 46-47; prof anat & chmn dept, Sch Med, Univ Pa, 47-51, vis res prof, 51-52; sci dir, Baxter Lab, Inc, 51-53; chief, Lab Neuroanat Scis, NIH, 54-60, asst dir, Nat Inst Neurol Dis & Blindness, 60-61, chief lab perinatal physiol, NIH, San Juan, PR, 61-63; res prof rehab med & dir res, NY Univ Med Ctr, 63-71; RES PROF, DENISON UNIV, 71- *Concurrent Pos:* Guest investr, Cambridge Univ, 35-36; vis prof, Univ Tenn, 41; Commonwealth vis prof, Univ Louisville, 44; Harvey lectr, 45; lectr, Postgrad Assembly Gynec, Univ Southern Calif, 47; mem res adv bd, United Cerebral Palsy Asns, 55-64, human embryol & develop study sect, NIH, 55-58, sci rev comn, Div Health Res Facils & Resources, 64-67; ed, 58-75, emer ed, Exp Neurol, 75-; mem hon fac med, Univ Chile, 61; prof ad honoren, Univ PR, 62-65; vis prof, Univ Calif, Los Angeles, 70-; chmn sci adv comt, Nat Paraplegia Found, 70-73. *Honors & Awards:* Weinstein Award, United Cerebral Palsy Asns, 57; Albert Lasker Award Basic Med Res, 68; Award, Asn Res Nerv & Ment Dis, 71; William T Wakeman Basic Res Award, Nat Paraplegia Found, 72; Paralyzed Vet Asn Am Res Award, 72; Henry Gray Award, Am Asn Anatomists, 77. *Mem:* AAAS; Am Physiol Asn; Soc Exp Biol & Med; Am Asn Anat; Am Neurol Asn. *Res:* Embryology and histology of the nervous system; development of behavior; fetal physiology; cerebral anoxia; regeneration in the central nervous system. *Mailing Add:* 229 S Cherry St Granville OH 43023

WINDLER, DONALD RICHARD, b Centralia, Ill, Feb 4, 40; m 63; c 1. PLANT TAXONOMY. *Educ:* Southern Ill Univ, Carbondale, BS, 63, MA, 65; Univ NC, Chapel Hill, PhD(bot), 70. *Prof Exp:* From asst to assoc prof, 69-77, PROF BIOL, TOWSON STATE Univ, 77-, CUR HERBARIUM, 69- *Mem:* Int Asn Plant Taxonomists; Am Soc Plant Taxon; Torrey Bot Club; Sigma Xi. *Res:* Systematics of Leguminosae, Crotalaria, Mucuna and Neptunia; flora of Maryland and Delaware; Lichens of Maryland; plant distribution in the Eastern United States. *Mailing Add:* Herbarium Towson State Univ Baltimore MD 21204

WINDMUELLER, HERBERT GEORGE, b Westphalia, Ger, July 5, 31; nat US; m 58; c 2. BIOCHEMISTRY. *Educ:* Va Polytech Inst, BS, 52, MS, 56, PhD(biochem), 58. *Prof Exp:* Asst, Va Polytech Inst, 54-57; NIH fel biochem, Brandeis Univ, 58-61; BIOCHEMIST, NAT INST ARTHRITIS, DIABETES, DIGESTIVE & KIDNEY DIS, 61- *Mem:* Am Inst Nutrit; Am Soc Biol Chemists; Am Chem Soc; Am Heart Asn. *Res:* Development of methods to study small intestine by vascular perfusion; pefusion of isolatedl livers; biosynthesis of lipids, apolipoproteins and lipoproteins; glutamine/metabolism; metabolism of luminal and vascular substrates by small intestine. *Mailing Add:* Nat Inst of Arth Met & Dig Dis Bethesda MD 20014

WINDOM, HERBERT LYNN, b Macon, Ga, Apr 23, 41; m 63; c 2. OCEANOGRAPHY. *Educ:* Fla State Univ, BS, 63; Univ Calif, San Diego, MS, 65, PhD(earth sci), 68. *Prof Exp:* PROF OCEANOG, SKIDAWAY INST OCEANOG & GA INST TECHNOL, 68- *Mem:* Am Soc Limnol & Oceanog; Int Coun Explor of the Sea. *Res:* Marine environmental quality; chemical oceanography; marine biogeochemistry of trace elements; marine sediments; environmental effects of dredging. *Mailing Add:* Skidaway Inst Oceanog Box 13687 Savannah GA 31406

WINDSOR, DONALD ARTHUR, b Chicago, Ill, Mar 22, 34; m 63, 69; c 4. INFORMATION SCIENCE, SYSTEMS SCIENCE. *Educ:* Univ Ill, Urbana, BS, 59, MS, 60. *Prof Exp:* Res asst parasitol, Dept Zool, Univ Ill, Urbana, 62-64; unit leader, 66-67, doc sect chief, 67-74, info scientist III, 74-81, GROUP LEADER, RES & DEVELOP DEPT, NORWICH-EATON PHARMACEUT, 81-; RES DIR, SciAESTHETICS INST, 69- *Mem:* AAAS; NY Acad Sci; Am Soc Info Sci; Soc Gen Systs Res; Asn Comput Mach. *Res:* Applications of general systems principles to the investigation of real-world phenomena; computer simulation of biological systems; evolution models; reconstructability; reconstructability analysis of pharmacological effects; information transfer using bibliometric traits; complexity measurements of ecological situations. *Mailing Add:* SciAesthetics Inst PO Box 604 Norwich NY 13815

WINDSOR, DONALD MONTGOMERY, b Chicago, Ill, Aug 4, 44; m 71. ANIMAL BEHAVIOR. *Educ:* Purdue Univ, BS, 66; Cornell Univ, PhD(animal behav), 72. *Prof Exp:* Fel, Orgn Trop Studies, 72-73; fel, 73-75, ZOOLOGIST, SMITHSONIAN TROP RES INST, 75- *Res:* Ecological and genetical factors influencing reproductive success of the wasp, Polistes versicolor, in Panama. *Mailing Add:* Smithsonian Trop Res Inst PO Box 2072 Balboa CZ

WINDSOR, EMANUEL, b Gloucester, Mass, Sept 2, 13; m 47; c 3. BIOCHEMISTRY. *Educ:* Calif Inst Technol, BS, 38, MS, 48, PhD(biochem), 51. *Prof Exp:* Asst biochem, Sansum Clin, 38-41; sr sci aide, Phys & Chem Mat Test, US Eng Labs, 41-43; anal chemist, Gooch Labs, 43-44; res biochemist, Huntington Mem Hosp, 47-48; asst microbiol, Calif Inst Technol, 48-49; chief clin lab, Delos Comstock X-ray & Clin Labs, 50-51; res fel biol, Calif Inst Technol, 51-53; sr biochemist, Riker Labs, 53-70; clin biochemist, Los Angeles County-Olive View Med Ctr, 71-81. *Concurrent Pos:* Mem, Coun on Arteriosclerosis, Am Heart Asn, 80- *Mem:* AAAS; Am Heart Asn; Am Asn Clin Chemists. *Res:* Lipid metabolism; cardiovascular disease; enzyme induction; clinical laboratory methodology; liver microsomal enzymes. *Mailing Add:* 6421 Nagle Ave Van Nuys CA 91401

WINDSOR, JOHN GOLAY, JR, b Chester, Pa, Nov 20, 47. ENVIRONMENTAL CHEMISTRY, MARINE SCIENCE. *Educ:* PMC Col, Pa, BS, 69; Col William & Mary, MA, 72, PhD(marine sci), 77. *Prof Exp:* Res asst, Va Inst Marine Sci, 72-74; res assoc, Mass Inst Technol, 76-78; SR PROJ SCIENTIST, NORTHROP SERVS, INC, 78- *Mem:* Am Chem Soc; AAAS; Am Soc Mass Spectrometry; Geochem Soc; Sigma Xi. *Res:* Application of modern instrumental methods, for example gas chromatography and mass spectrometry to trace organic analysis of environmental mixtures such as air, soil, water and sediments. *Mailing Add:* Northrop Serv Inc PO Box 12313 Research Triangle Park NC 27709

WINDSOR, MAURICE WILLIAM, b Kent, Eng, Feb 28, 28; m 53; c 3. PHOTOCHEMISTRY, PHOTOSYNTHESIS. *Educ:* Univ Cambridge, BA, 52, PhD(phys chem), 55, MS, 57. *Prof Exp:* Res assoc, Calif Inst Technol, 55-58, Univ Sheffield, Eng, 56-67; mgr, Chem Sci Dept, TRW Systs, Redondo Beach, Calif, 58-71; prof & chmn dept, 71-74, PROF CHEM & CHEM PHYSICS, WASH STATE UNIV, 74- *Concurrent Pos:* Guest scientist, Nat Bur Standards, 58-59; prin investr, Sch Aerospace Med, Off Naval Res, Army Res Off, Air Force Off Sci Res, Nat Sci Found, 60-; consult, Appl Photophysics, London Eng, 74-77; sr vis fel, Royal Inst, LondonEng, 78-79; vis prof, Univ Paris, Orsay, 797. *Mem:* AAAS; Am Chem Soc; Royal Soc Chem; Royal Inst London; Inter-Am Photochem Soc. *Res:* Laser photochemistry and photobiophysics; design and development of instrumentation for ultrafast (nanosecond to picosecond) flash photolysis and kinetic spectroscopy; study of primary events, including electron transfer, in photosyntbesis and related model systems. *Mailing Add:* Dept Chem Wash State Univ Pullman WA 99164

WINDSOR, RICHARD ANTHONY, b Baltimore, Md, Aug 7, 43; m 78; c 3. PUBLIC HEALTH. *Educ:* Morgan State Univ, BS, 69; Univ Ill, MS, 70, PhD(educ res & evaluation), 72; Johns Hopkins Univ, MPH, 76. *Prof Exp:* Asst prof, Col Educ, Ohio State Univ, 72-75; asst prof pub health, Sch Hyg & Pub Health, Johns Hopkins Univ, 76-77; ASSOC PROF, SCH PUB HEALTH, RES SCI DIABETES RES & TREATMENT CTR & COMPREHENSIVE CANCER CTR, UNIV ALA, BIRMINGHAM, 77- *Mem:* Am Pub Health Asn; Soc Pub Health Educ. *Res:* Research and evaluation of patient and community education programs. *Mailing Add:* Sch Pub Helath Univ Ala Birmingham AL 35294

WINE, JEFFREY JUSTUS, b Pittsburgh, Pa, Feb 10, 40; m 66. NEUROSCIENCES. *Educ:* Univ Pittsburgh, BS, 66; Univ Calif, Los Angeles, PhD(psychol), 71. *Prof Exp:* NIH fel, Dept Biol Sci, 71-72, asst prof psychol, 72-78, ASSOC PROF PSYCHOL, STANFORD UNIV, 78- *Mem:* Am Psychol Asn; Soc Neurosci; Int Brain Res Orgn; Soc Exp Biol; AAAS. *Res:* Neurophysiological and neuroanatomical analysis of invertebrate behavior. *Mailing Add:* Dept of Psychol Stanford Univ Stanford CA 94305

WINE, PAUL HARRIS, b Detroit, Mich, Mar 18, 46; m 74. CHEMICAL PHYSICS. *Educ:* Univ Mich, BS, 68; Fla State Univ, PhD(phys chem), 74. *Prof Exp:* Robert A Welch fel chem, Univ Tex, Dallas, 74-76; res scientist, 77-81, SR RES SCIENTIST, ENG EXP STA, GA INST TECHNOL, 81- *Mem:* Am Chem Soc; Am Phys Soc; Inter-Am Photochem Soc. *Res:* Gas phase kinetics; photochemistry; reaction dynamics; lasers; spectroscopy. photochemistry of small molecules. *Mailing Add:* Molecular Sci Group Eng Exp Sta Ga Inst Technol Atlanta GA 30332

WINE, RUSSELL LOWELL, b Indian Springs, Tenn, Aug 17, 18; m 42; c 3. STATISTICS. *Educ:* Bridgewater Col, BA, 41; Univ Va, MA, 45; Va Polytech Inst, PhD(statist), 55. *Prof Exp:* Instr math, Univ Va, 43-45, Amherst Col, 45-46 & Univ Okla, 46-47; asst prof, Washington & Lee Univ, 47-52; assoc prof statist, Va Polytech Inst, 55-57; assoc prof, 57-60, PROF STATIST, HOLLINS COL, 60- *Mem:* Fel AAAS; Am Statist Asn; Biomet Soc. *Res:* Least squares; design of experiments; multiple tests; sample surveys. *Mailing Add:* Dept of Statist Hollins College Hollins College VA 24020

WINEFORDNER, JAMES D, b Geneseo, Ill, Dec 31, 31; m 57; c 3. ANALYTICAL CHEMISTRY. *Educ:* Univ Ill, BS, 54, MS, 55, PhD(anal chem), 58. *Prof Exp:* Fel, Univ Ill, 58-59; from asst prof to assoc prof, 59-67, PROF CHEM, UNIV FLA, 67- *Honors & Awards:* Meggers Award in Spectros, 69; Am Chem Soc Award Anal Chem, 73; Pittsburgh Spectrol Soc Award, 73; Am Chem Soc Anal Div Award Chem Instrumentation, 78; Anachem Award, 80; Theophilus Redwood Award, 81. *Mem:* Soc Appl Spectros; Am Chem Soc. *Res:* Atomic, ionic and molecular emission; absorption; fluorescence spectroscopy; gas chromatographic detectors; trace analysis. *Mailing Add:* Dept of Chem Univ of Fla Gainesville FL 32611

WINEGARD, WILLIAM CHARLES, b Hamilton, Ont, Sept 17, 24; m 47; c 3. METALLURGY. *Educ:* Univ Toronto, BASc, 49, MASc, 50, PhD(metall), 52. *Hon Degrees:* LLD, Univ Toronto, 71; DEng, Mem Univ, 76. *Prof Exp:* Spec lectr, 50-52, lectr, 52-54, from asst prof to prof metall, Univ Toronto, 54-67, asst dean sch grad studies, 64-67; pres & vchancellor, Univ Guelph, 67-75; vchmn, 76-77, CHMN, ONT COUN ON UNIV AFFAIRS, 78- *Concurrent Pos:* Vis prof, Cambridge Univ, 59-60; consult, Ont Fire Marshall, 50-65, A D Lettle Inc, 60-67; ed, Can Metall Quart, 64-67; gov, Int Develop Res Ctr, 74-80; mem, govt Ont Res Found, 78-; fel Guelph, 78. *Honors & Awards:* Alcan Award, Can Inst Mining & Metall, 67. *Mem:* Fel Am Soc Metals; Can Inst Mining & Metall; Can Coun Prof Engrs. *Res:* Solidification of pure metals and alloys; grain boundary migration. *Mailing Add:* RR 1 Georgetown ON L7G 4S4 Can

WINEGARTNER, EDGAR CARL, b Cleveland, Ohio, Jan 28, 27; m 49; c 2. COMBUSTIBILITY OF SOLIDS. *Educ:* Ohio State Univ, BMetE, 49. *Prof Exp:* Plant engr beryllium prod, Brush Beryllium Co, 49-51; res engr corrosion, Exxon Co, 51-62; res engr wood technol, 62-65, RES ASSOC COAL COMBUSTION, EXXON RES & ENG CO, 65- *Mem:* Am Soc Mech Engrs; Soc Mining Engrs; Am Soc Metals; Combustion Inst; Nat Asn Corrosion Engrs. *Res:* Investigation of combustion related properties of coal and solid by-products from synthetic fuels, including combustibility, fouling and slagging; size preparation of coal for synthetic fuels processes. *Mailing Add:* Exxon Res & Eng Co PO Box 4255 Baytown TX 77520

WINEGRAD, SAUL, b Philadelphia, Pa, Mar 15, 31; m 63; c 2. PHYSIOLOGY. *Educ:* Univ Pa, BA, 52, MD, 56. *Prof Exp:* Intern, Peter Bent Brigham Hosp, 56-57; sr asst surgeon, NIH, 57-59, fel, Nat Heart Inst, 59-60, surgeon, NIH, 60-61; hon res assoc, Univ Col, Univ London, 61-62; from asst prof to assoc prof physiol, 62-69, PROF PHYSIOL, SCH MED, UNIV PA, 69- *Concurrent Pos:* Assoc, Sch Med, George Washington Univ, 58-61; NSF sr fel, Univ Col, Univ London, 71-72. *Mem:* Am Physiol Soc; Soc Gen Physiol; Biophys Soc; Cardiac Muscle Soc. *Res:* Cardiovascular and muscle physiology. *Mailing Add:* Sch Med Univ Pa 37th & Hamilton Walk Philadelphia PA 19104

WINEHOLT, ROBERT LEESE, b York, Pa, Sept 20, 39; m 62; c 3. ORGANIC CHEMISTRY. *Educ:* Gettysburg Col, AB, 61; Univ Del, PhD(org chem), 66. *Prof Exp:* Fel, Duke Univ, 66; sr chemist, Hoffman LaRoche, Inc, 67-73, Mallinckrodt, Inc, 73-76; RES ASSOC, CROMPTON & KNOWLES, 77- *Mem:* Am Chem Soc. *Res:* Process development for organic chemicals to plant production. *Mailing Add:* 39 Dorchester Dr Wyomissing PA 19610

WINEK, CHARLES L, b Erie, Pa, Jan 13, 36; m 60; c 3. TOXICOLOGY, PHARMACOLOGY. *Educ:* Duquesne Univ, BS, 57, MS, 59; Ohio State Univ, PhD(pharmacol), 62. *Prof Exp:* Res assoc phytochem, Ohio State Univ, 59-62; res toxicologist, Procter & Gamble Col, 62-63; from asst prof pharmacol & toxicol to assoc prof toxicol, 63-69, PROF TOXICOL, DUQUESNE UNIV, 69-; CHIEF TOXICOLOGIST, ALLEGHENY COUNTY CORONER'S OFF, 66- *Concurrent Pos:* Consult, Dept Anesthesiol, St Francis Hosp, 67-; mem panel ther, Poison Control Ctrs, Dept Health; mem adv comt lab act, Pa Dept Health; mem adv bd, Drug Res Proj, Franklin Inst, Philadelphia; fac mem, Bur Narcotics & Dangerous Drugs, Police Educ Prog; adj prof, Sch Med, Univ Pittsburgh; ed at large toxicol, Marcel Dekker, Inc, New York; ed, Toxicol Newslett, Sch Pharm, Duquesne Univ; ed, Toxicol Ann, 74. *Mem:* Soc Toxicol; Am Acad Forensic Sci; Acad Pharmaceut Sci; Am Asn Poison Control Ctrs; Drug Info Asn. *Res:* Toxicity of antifungal agents; safety evaluations; rapid methods of toxicological analyses. *Mailing Add:* Dept of Pharmacol Duquesne Univ Pittsburgh PA 15219

WINELAND, WILLIAM CLEMARD, physics, research administration, deceased

WINEMAN, ALAN STUART, b Wyandotte, Mich, Nov 17, 37; m 64; c 2. APPLIED MECHANICS, APPLIED MATHEMATICS. *Educ:* Univ Mich, BSE, 59; Brown Univ, PhD(appl math), 64. *Prof Exp:* From asst prof to assoc prof, 64-75, PROF APPL MECH, UNIV MICH, 75- *Mem:* Am Acad Mech; Soc Rheol; Am Soc Mech Engrs; Soc Natural Philos. *Res:* Viscoelasticity; numerical methods; nonlinear elasticity; biomechanics. *Mailing Add:* Dept Mech Eng & Appl Mech Univ of Mich Ann Arbor MI 48109

WINEMAN, ROBERT JUDSON, b Chicago, Ill, 1919; m 44; c 5. BIO-ORGANIC CHEMISTRY, BIOMATERIALS. *Educ:* Williams Col, AB, 41; Univ Mich, MS, 42; Harvard Univ, PhD(chem), 49. *Prof Exp:* Chemist, E I du Pont de Nemours & Co, 42-43; res chemist, Monsanto Chem Co, 49-53, res group leader, 54-60, Monsanto Res Corp, Mass, 60-61, dir, Boston Lab, 61-69; dir biomed res labs, Am Hosp Supply Corp, 69-70; assoc chief, Artificial Kidney-Chronic Uremia Prog, Nat Inst Arthritis, Metab & Digestive Dis, 70-78, DIR, CHRONIC RENAL DIS PROG, NAT INST ARTHRITIS, DIABETES, DIGESTIVE & KIDNEY DIS, 79- *Concurrent Pos:* Instr, Northeastern Univ, 52-53. *Mem:* AAAS; Am Chem Soc; Am Soc Artificial Internal Organs. *Res:* Organic synthesis; steroids; amino acids; sulfur compounds; medical devices; artificial organs. *Mailing Add:* Nat Inst Health Rm 621 Westwood Bldg Bethesda MD 20205

WINER, ALFRED D, b Lynn, Mass, Dec 24, 26; m 55; c 2. BIOCHEMISTRY. *Educ:* Northeastern Univ, BS, 48; Purdue Univ, MS, 50; Duke Univ, PhD(biochem), 57. *Prof Exp:* Instr org chem, Univ Mass, 50-51; USPHS fel, Med Nobel Inst, Sweden, 58-60; ASSOC PROF BIOCHEM, MED CTR, UNIV KY, 65- *Concurrent Pos:* USPHS career develop award, 60-70. *Mem:* Am Chem Soc; Am Soc Biol Chemists. *Res:* Mechanism of action of dehydrogenase-coenzyme complexes; hormonal effects on enzymes in spermatogenesis. *Mailing Add:* Dept of Biochem Univ of Ky Med Ctr Lexington KY 40506

WINER, ARTHUR MELVYN, b New York, NY, May 5, 42. ATMOSPHERIC CHEMISTRY, AIR POLLUTION. *Educ:* Univ Calif, Los Angeles, BS, 64; Ohio State Univ, PhD(phys chem), 69. *Prof Exp:* Asst res chemist, 71-75, assoc res chemist, 76-80, RES CHEMIST, STATEWIDE AIR POLLUTION RES CTR, UNIV CALIF, RIVERSIDE, 80-, ASST DIR, 78- *Concurrent Pos:* Fel chem, Univ Calif, Berkeley, 70-71, prin investr, 79-, consult, 79- *Mem:* Optical Soc Am; AAAS; Am Chem Soc; Coblentz Soc; Sigma Xi. *Res:* Applications of longpath infrared and optical spectroscopy and chemical kinetics to atmospheric systems; environmental chamber studies of transformations and transport of trace pollutants. *Mailing Add:* Statewide Air Pollution Res Ctr Univ of Calif Riverside CA 92521

WINER, BETTE MARCIA TARMEY, b Boston, Mass, Feb 21, 40; m 63; c 2. PHYSICS, POWER SYSTEM ENGINEERING. *Educ:* Univ Maine, BS, 61; Univ Md, PhD(physics), 69. *Prof Exp:* Staff physics, Lincoln Labs, Mass Inst Technol, 59-63, staff, Nat Magnet Labs, 70-72; engr anal, Bedford Labs, Raytheon, 72-74; SR STAFF PHYSICS & ENG, ARTHUR D LITTLE INC, 74- *Concurrent Pos:* Vis prof, Univ Md, Catonsville, 69- & Univ Lowell, 70-72. *Mailing Add:* Arthur D Little Inc Acorn Park Cambridge MA 02140

WINER, HERBERT ISAAC, b New York, NY, Sept 19, 21; m 43, 70; c 4. FORESTRY. *Educ:* Yale Univ, BA, MF, 49, PhD, 56. *Prof Exp:* Instr forestry, Sch Forestry, Yale Univ, 52-56, asst prof lumbering, 56-64; sci consult, Pulp & Paper Inst Can, 63-64, forester, Forest Eng Res Inst Can, 64-65, sr forester, 65-71, dir, Logging Res Div, 71-75, res dir, 75-76, sr forest engr, Eastern Div, 76-78; MGR WOODLANDS OPER RES, MEAD CORP, 79- *Concurrent Pos:* Mem, Int Union Forest Res Orgns. *Mem:* Soc Am Foresters; Can Inst Forestry; Forest Hist Soc; Sigma Xi. *Res:* Application of operations research to forest management; forest history. *Mailing Add:* Woodlands Oper Res Mead Corp Courthouse Plaza NE Dayton OH 45406

WINER, JEFFERY ALLAN, b Minneapolis, Minn, Nov 16, 45. NEUROANATOMY, NEUROSCIENCES. *Educ:* Univ Ariz, BA, 67; Univ Tenn, PhD(physiol psychol), 74. *Prof Exp:* Fel neuroanat, Dept Psychol, Duke Univ, 74-76; res assoc, Dept Anat, Harvard Med Sch, 76-77; res assoc neuroanat, Health Ctr, Univ Conn, 77-80; MEM FAC, DEPT PHYSIOL & ANAT, UNIV CALIF, 80- *Concurrent Pos:* NIMH fel, USPHS, 74-77. *Res:* Neuroanatomy of the central auditory and visual systems, including Golgi, electron microscopic and axoplasmic transport methods applied to the morphology and development of the auditory thalamus, midbrain and cerebral cortex. *Mailing Add:* Dept Physiol & Anat Univ Calif Berkeley CA 94720

WINER, RICHARD, b Rochester, NY, Sept 16, 16; m 42; c 2. CHEMICAL ENGINEERING. *Educ:* Univ Ill, BS, 39. *Prof Exp:* Tech asst, Radford Ord Works, Hercules Powder Co, Va, 42-45, chem engr, Hercules Inc, Exp Sta, Del, 45-46, supvr propellant dept, Allegany Ballistics Lab, 46-53, dir develop, propellants & rockets, 53-59, asst plant mgr, 59-63, dir develop, Chem Propulsion Div, 63-66, dir eng & res, Indust Systs Dept, 66-77, dir, Res Ctr, 78-81; RETIRED. *Honors & Awards:* Distinguished Pub Serv Medal, US Dept Navy, 53. *Mem:* AAAS; Am Chem Soc. *Res:* Solid propellants; rockets; chemical research. *Mailing Add:* 211 Churchill Dr Wilmington DE 19803

WINER, WARD OTIS, b Grand Rapids, Mich, June 27, 36; m 57; c 4. MECHANICAL ENGINEERING, PHYSICS. *Educ:* Univ Mich, BSE, 58, MSE, 59, PhD(mech eng), 62; Cambridge Univ, PhD(physics), 64. *Prof Exp:* Demonstr, Univ Cambridge, 61-63; from asst to assoc prof mech eng, Univ Mich, 63-69; assoc prof, 69-71, PROF MECH ENG, GA INST TECHNOL, 71- *Concurrent Pos:* Consult, var indust. *Honors & Awards:* Melville Medal, Am Soc Mech Engrs, 75. *Mem:* Am Soc Lubrication Engrs; Am Soc Mech Engrs. *Res:* Tribology; high pressure lubricant rheology; fluid mechanics; heat transfer. *Mailing Add:* Sch of Mech Eng Ga Inst of Technol Atlanta GA 30332

WINESTOCK, CLAIRE HUMMEL, b US, July 7, 32; m 56; c 1. ORGANIC CHEMISTRY. *Educ:* Univ Utah, BS, 52; Univ Wis, PhD(org chem), 56. *Prof Exp:* Res assoc biochem, Columbia Univ, 56-59; res fel chem, Univ Utah, 59, res assoc biochem, Col Med, 60-61, res instr, 61-65; grants assoc, NIH, 65-66, health scientist adminr, Nat Inst Arthritis & Metab Dis, 66-69, EXEC SECY & REFERRAL OFFICER, VIROL STUDY SECT, DIV RES GRANTS, NIH, 69- *Mem:* AAAS; Am Chem Soc. *Res:* Organic synthesis; chemistry of natural products; science administration. *Mailing Add:* Div of Res Grants Nat Insts of Health Bethesda MD 20205

WINET, HOWARD, b Chicago, Ill, Sept 13, 37; m 68. ORTHOPEADICS, BIORHEOLOGY. *Educ:* Univ Ill, BS, 59; Univ Calif, Los Angeles, MA, 62, PhD(zool), 69. *Prof Exp:* Res fel eng sci, Calif Inst Technol, 69-73, res biophysicist eng sci, 73-77; assoc prof physiol, Southern Ill Univ, Carbondale, 77-80; ASSOC PROF RES ORTHOP, OBSTET & GYNEC, SCH MED, UNIV SOUTHERN CALIF, LOS ANGELES, 80- *Concurrent Pos:* Adv, Nat Sci Comt, Calif State Comn Teacher Preparation & Licensing, 72-77; vis res assoc eng sci, Calif Inst Technol, 78-; mem spec reproduction study sect, NIH, 78-; prin investr res grant, NIH, 78- *Mem:* Am Soc Andrology; Am Physiol Soc; Am Soc Biomech; Biophys Soc; Soc Exp Biol Med Eng. *Res:* Biophysical fluid mechanics of muco-ciliary systems, transit and propulsion of gametes; blood form in bone, vascular role in osteogenesis. *Mailing Add:* 2400 Flower St Orthop Hosp Univ Southern Calif Los Angeles CA 90007

WINETT, JOEL M, b Boston, Mass, Mar 1, 38; m 65; c 3. COMPUTER & MANAGEMENT SCIENCE. *Educ:* Mass Inst Technol, BSEE, 60, EE, 65; Columbia Univ, MSEE, 61. *Prof Exp:* Mem comput systs group, Lincoln Lab, Mass Inst Technol, 61-73, mem radar systs group, 73-74; mgr sci comput, Anal Sci Corp, 74-79; mgr sci appl support, Sanders Assoc, 79-81; PROD MGR, BGS SYSTS, 81- *Concurrent Pos:* Instr, Northeastern Univ, 67-69. *Mem:* Inst Elec & Electronics Engrs; Asn Comput Mach. *Res:* Effective use of computers for scientific problem solving; compatible batch and interactive operating systems emphasizing human engineered control language; user documentation and training aids; system measurement and operations procedures. *Mailing Add:* 10 Berkeley Rd Framingham MA 01701

WINFIELD, ARNOLD FRANCIS, b Chicago, Ill, Sept 29, 26; m 51; c 2. BIOCHEMISTRY. *Educ:* Howard Univ, BS, 49. *Prof Exp:* Chemist, Ord Corps, US Dept Army, 52-53; chemist, 53-69, biochemist, 69-71, MGR REGULATORY AFFAIRS ADMINR, CONSUMER DIV, ABBOTT LABS, 71- *Mem:* Am Chem Soc; Regulatory Affairs Profs Soc; Am Soc Qual Control. *Mailing Add:* Dept 490 Abbott Labs PO Box 68 Abbott Park North Chicago IL 60064

WINFIELD, JOHN BUCKNER, b Kentfield, Calif, Mar 19, 42; m 69; c 3. IMMUNOLOGY, RHEUMATOLOGY. *Educ:* Williams Col, BA, 64; Cornell Univ, MD, 68. *Prof Exp:* Intern internal med, New York Hosp, 68-69; staff assoc immunol, NIH, 69-71; resident, 71-73, instr, 74-75, assoc prof internal med, Univ Va, 76-78; assoc prof, 78-81, PROF INTERNAL MED, UNIV NC, CHAPEL HILL, 81-, CHIEF, DIV IMMUNOL & RHEUMATIOLOGY, 78- *Concurrent Pos:* Fel immunol, Rockefeller Univ, 73-75; fel, Arthritis Found, 73-76, sr investr, 76-79. *Mem:* Am Fedn Clin Res; fel Am Col Physicians; Am Rheumatology Asn; Am Asn Immunol; Am Soc Clin Invest. *Res:* Clinical immunology; auto immune diseases. *Mailing Add:* Div Immunol & Rheumatology Univ NC at Chapel Hill Chapel Hill NC 27514

WINFREE, ARTHUR T, b St Petersburg, Fla, May 5, 42; c 2. PHYSICAL CHEMISTRY, PHYSIOLOGY. *Educ:* Cornell Univ, BS, 65; Princeton Univ, PhD(biol), 70. *Prof Exp:* Asst prof math biol, Univ Chicago, 69-72; assoc prof biol, 72-78, PROF BIOL, PURDUE UNIV, 78- *Concurrent Pos:* Vis prof, Univ Sussex & Med Res Coun Lab Molecular Biol, Cambridge, Eng, 71; res career develop award, NIH, 73-78; vis prof biochem, Med Univ SC, 76-77; assoc ed, J Theoret Biol, 78-; dir res, Inst Natural Philos, 79-; vis prof natural sciences, Univ Calif, Berkeley, 80-81. *Res:* Chemical oscillations and waves; circadian clocks and temporal organization; pattern formation in chemical and developmental systems. *Mailing Add:* Dept of Biol Sci Purdue Univ West Lafayette IN 47907

WINFREY, J C, b Post, Tex, Feb 10, 27; m 47; c 1. ORGANIC CHEMISTRY, ANALYTICAL CHEMISTRY. *Educ:* ETex State Teachers Col, BS & MS, 49. *Prof Exp:* Teacher high sch, Tex, 49-51; chemist, Eagle-Picher Lead Co, 51 & Lone Star Gas Co, 51-56; res chemist, Dow Chem Co, 56-62; anal chemist, Res Dept, Signal Oil & Gas Co, 62-68; anal sect supvr res mgt, Signal Chem Co, 69-71; chief chemist, Geneva Industs, Inc, 71-73; gen mgr & corp secy, Anal Serv, Inc, 73-75; consult, 75-76; lab mgr, Val Verde Corp, 76-77; staff, 77-80, DIR HYDROCARBON SERV, SOUTHERN PETROL LABS, 80- *Concurrent Pos:* Mem, Adv Comt Proj, 44, Am Petrol Inst, 68-71; anal consult, Haines & Assocs, 71. *Mem:* Am Chem Soc; Am Soc Lubrication Engrs; Am Soc Testing Mat; Hort Eng & Sci Soc. *Res:* Instrumental analytical chemistry; organic synthesis of amines and epoxides; gas chromatography; thin layer chromatography; liquid chromatography; mass spectrometry; infrared spectrometry; computer applications in analytical chemistry; spectrochemical analysis of used lube oils. *Mailing Add:* 5215 Georgi Lane Houston TX 77092

WINFREY, RICHARD CAMERON, b Albany, Calif, June 18, 35; m 59; c 4. MECHANICAL ENGINEERING, COMPUTER AIDED DESIGN. *Educ:* Univ Calif, Berkeley, BSME, 63; Univ Calif, Los Angeles, MS, 65, PhD(eng), 69. *Prof Exp:* Mem tech staff, Hughes Aircraft Co, Calif, 63-69; asst prof mech eng, Naval Postgrad Sch, 69-71; mech engr, Naval Civil Eng Lab, 71-72; proj engr Burroughs Corps, 72-75; prin engr, 75-80, CONSULT ENGR, DIGITAL EQUIP CORP, 80- *Mem:* Am Soc Mech Engrs; Sci Res Soc Am; Inst Elec & Electronics Engrs. *Res:* Dynamics of elastic machinery. *Mailing Add:* Digital Equip Corp ML 1-3/E58 Maynard MA 01754

WING, BRUCE LARRY, b Coeur d'Alene, Idaho, Aug 7, 38. BIOLOGICAL OCEANOGRAPHY, MARINE INVERTEBRATE TAXONOMY. *Educ:* San Diego State Col, AB, 60; Univ RI, PhD(oceanog), 76. *Prof Exp:* Fishery biologist zooplankton, US Bur Com Fisheries, 62-75, CHIEF INVESTR OCEANOG, AUKE BAY LAB, NAT MARINE FISHERIES SERV, 75- *Honors & Awards:* C Y Conkel Award, Auke Bay Fisheries Lab, 77. *Mem:* Fel Am Inst Fishery Res Biologists; AAAS; Am Fisheries Soc; Am Soc Limnol & Oceanog; Sigma Xi. *Res:* Effect of environmental variation on plankton composition and fishery productivity; taxonomy of Alaskan marine invertebrates; ellobiopsids. *Mailing Add:* Nat Marine Fisheries Serv PO Box 155 Auke Bay AK 99821

WING, ELIZABETH S, b Cambridge, Mass, Mar 5, 32; m 57; c 2. ZOOLOGY. *Educ:* Mt Holyoke Col, BA, 55; Univ Fla, MS, 57, PhD(zool), 62. *Prof Exp:* Asst cur zoo-archaeol, 61-74, asst prof anthrop, Univ Fla, 70-75; assoc cur Fla State Mus, 74-78; ASSOC PROF ANTHROP, UNIV FLA, 75-; CUR, FLA STATE MUS, 78- *Concurrent Pos:* NSF grants, 61-64, 66-68, 69-73 & 75, co-investr, 61-64; Caribbean Res Prog grant, 64 & 65; Ctr Latin Am Studies res grant, 66. *Mem:* Am Soc Mammal; Soc Am Archaeol; AAAS. *Res:* Identification and analysis of faunal remains excavated from Indian sites in Southeastern United States and Latin America; prehistoric subsistence and animal domestication in the Andes. *Mailing Add:* Fla State Mus Univ of Fla Gainesville FL 32601

WING, GEORGE MILTON, b Rochester, NY, Jan 21, 23; m 72. APPLIED MATHEMATICS. *Educ:* Univ Rochester, BA, 44, MS, 47; Cornell Univ, PhD(math), 49. *Prof Exp:* Scientist, Los Alamos Sci Lab, Univ Calif, 45-46, mem staff, 51-58, 81-; instr math, Univ Rochester, 46-47; instr, Univ Calif, Los Angeles, 49-51, asst prof, 51-52; assoc prof, Univ NMex, 58-59; mem staff, Sandia Corp, 59-64; prof math, Univ Colo, 64-66 & Univ NMex, 66-73; vis prof, Tex Tech Univ, 75-76; prof & chmn, 77-78, PROF, SOUTHERN METHODIST UNIV, 78- *Concurrent Pos:* Consult, Los Alamos Sci Lab, 58-59 & 64-81, Sandia Corp, 58-59, E H Plesset Assocs, 58-59 & 65-69 & Rand Corp, 58-65; mem, Panel Phys Sci & Eng, Comt Undergrad Prog Math, 63-67. *Mem:* AAAS; Am Math Soc; Math Asn Am; Soc Indust & Appl Math. *Res:* Transport theory; integral equations. *Mailing Add:* 107 Tunyo Los Alamos NM 87544

WING, JAMES, b Highland Park, Mich, July 8, 29; m 57; c 2. NUCLEAR CHEMISTRY. *Educ:* Univ Tenn, BS, 51; Purdue Univ, MS, 53, PhD(chem), 56. *Prof Exp:* Asst chemist, Argonne Nat Lab, 55-65, assoc chemist, 65-69; res chemist, Anal Div, Nat Bur Standards, 69-75; nuclear chemist, 75-78, SR CHEM ENGR, US NUCLEAR REGULATORY COMN, 78- *Concurrent Pos:* Fulbright lectr, Chinese Univ Hong Kong, 64-65. *Mem:* Am Phys Soc; Am Chem Soc. *Res:* Nuclear mass systematics; nuclear activation analysis; cross sections and mechanisms of nuclear reactions; radioactivities of new isotopes; carrier-free radiochemical separation techniques; toxic vapor detection systems; computer automation of laboratory experiments; computer-aided information storage and retrieval; chemical safety for nuclear reactor operation. *Mailing Add:* US Nuclear Regulatory Comn Washington DC 20555

WING, JAMES MARVIN, b Anniston, Ala, Mar 17, 20; m 46, 76; c 1. ANIMAL NUTRITION. *Educ:* Berea Col, BS, 46; Colo State Univ, MS, 48; Iowa State Univ, PhD(dairy husb), 52. *Prof Exp:* From asst prof to assoc prof, 51-66, PROF DAIRY SCI, UNIV FLA, 66- *Mem:* Am Soc Animal Sci; Am Dairy Sci Asn. *Res:* Nutrition; digestibility of carotenoids; nucleic acids; medicated feeds; ensilability; digestibility and consumption of herbage; climatic adaptation of cattle; optimum levels of carbohydrates for cattle; evaluation of by-product feed stuffs; environmental quality and the animal industries; international development in Colombia, El Salvador, Paraguay, Viet Nam and Dominican Republic. *Mailing Add:* Dairy Res Unit Univ of Fla Rte 3 Box 73 Gainesville FL 32601

WING, JANET E (SWEEDYK) BENDT, b Detroit, Mich, Oct 12, 25; m 72; c 4. NUCLEAR REACTOR SAFETY ANALYSIS. *Educ:* Wayne State Univ, Detroit, BS, 47; Columbia Univ, MS, 50. *Prof Exp:* Engr, Gen Motors, 44-48; mathematician, Manhattan Proj, Columbia Univ, 50-51; mem res staff, 51-57, MEM RES STAFF, LOS ALAMOS NAT LAB, 68-, ASST GROUP LEADER, 80- *Concurrent Pos:* Proj leader, Los Alamos Nat Lab, 78-81. *Mem:* Women Sci & Eng; AAAS; Sigma Xi. *Res:* Mathematical modeling and computer solutions of physical systems; radiation-hydrodynamics and transport theory; applications to nuclear weapon design and testing; underground containment of nuclear explosions; pulsations of Cepheid stars. *Mailing Add:* Reactor Safety Anal Group Q-7 MS K556 Los Alamos Nat Lab Los Alamos NM 87545

WING, JOHN FAXON, b Lincoln, Nebr, Jan 27, 34; m 56; c 4. NAVAL ARCHITECTURE, MARINE ENGINEERING. *Educ:* Mass Inst Technol, BS, 55; Harvard Univ, MBA, 57. *Prof Exp:* Proj engr, Alcoa Steamship Co, 57-61; engr, Shipbldg Div, Bethlehem Steel Co, 61-64; sr engr, 64-65, proj engr, 65-66, prin engr, 66-67, res dir, 67-70, vpres, 70-72, sr vpres, 72-81, MANAGING OFFICER TRANSP CONSULT, BOOZ-ALLEN & HAMILTON, INC, 81- *Concurrent Pos:* Lectr, Univ Mich, 66. *Mem:* Soc Naval Archit & Marine Engrs. *Res:* Management consulting in transportation; research and analysis of maritime operations. *Mailing Add:* Booz-Allen & Hamilton Inc 4330 E-W Hwy Bethesda MD 20814

WING, MERLE WESLEY, b Ft Fairfield, Maine, Aug 14, 16; m 70. ENTOMOLOGY. *Educ:* Univ Maine, BS, 39; Univ Minn, PhD(entom), 67. *Prof Exp:* Asst prof zool, NC State Univ, 42-45 & 46-51; actg asst prof, Tulane Univ, 45-46; asst prof biol, Middle Tenn State Col, 58-60; assoc prof zool, State Univ NY Col Cortland, 60-63; lectr entom, Cornell Univ, 63-67; assoc prof biol, Slippery Rock State Col, 67-69; assoc prof, 69-72, PROF BIOL, GENEVA COL, 72- *Mem:* AAAS; Am Soc Zoologists; Am Inst Biol Sci; Biomet Soc; Am Statist Asn. *Res:* Systematics and evolution of social insects, especially Hymenoptera, Formicidae. *Mailing Add:* Dept of Biol Geneva College Beaver Falls PA 15010

WING, OMAR, b Detroit, Mich, Mar 2, 28; m 53; c 2. ELECTRICAL ENGINEERING, COMPUTER SCIENCE. *Educ:* Univ Tenn, BS, 50; Mass Inst Technol, MS, 52; Columbia Univ, DEng, 59. *Prof Exp:* Asst elec eng, Mass Inst Technol, 50-52; mem tech staff, Bell Tel Labs, NJ, 52-56; from instr to assoc prof, 56-76, PROF ELEC ENG, COLUMBIA UNIV, 76- *Concurrent Pos:* Fulbright vis lectr, Inst Electronics, Chiao Tung Univ, 61; Ford Found eng resident, Thomas J Watson Res Ctr, IBM Corp, 65-66; vis prof, Tech Univ Denmark, 73. *Mem:* Inst Elec & Electronics Engrs. *Res:* Network theory; computer design of networks; design automation; computer simulation of systems; distributed parameter networks; digital filters; computer analysis of large networks. *Mailing Add:* Dept of Elec Eng Columbia Univ New York NY 10027

WING, ROBERT EDWARD, b Bridgeport, Conn, Nov 29, 41; div; c 2. CHEMISTRY. *Educ:* Millikin Univ, BA, 63; Southern Ill Univ, Carbondale, PhD(biochem), 67. *Prof Exp:* Northern Regional Lab grant, Southern Ill Univ, Carbondale, 67-68; RES CHEMIST, BIOMAT CONVERSION LAB, NORTHERN REGIONAL RES CTR, USDA, 68- *Concurrent Pos:* Res assoc, Peoria Sch Med, Univ Ill Col Med, 71-; instr, Bradley Univ, 73- *Honors & Awards:* Indust Res-100 award, 78. *Mem:* Am Chem Soc; Sigma Xi; Am Electroplaters Soc. *Res:* Water pollution of heavy metal ions; reactive carbohydrate polymers; carbohydrate thin-layer chromatography and enzyme interactions; carbohydrate slow release pesticide formulations. *Mailing Add:* Biomat Conversion Lab USDA Northern Regional Res Ctr Peoria IL 61604

WING, ROBERT FARQUHAR, b New Haven, Conn, Oct 31, 39; m 63; c 3. ASTRONOMY. *Educ:* Yale Univ, BS, 61; Univ Calif, Berkeley, PhD(astron), 67. *Prof Exp:* From asst prof to assoc prof, 67-76, PROF ASTRON, OHIO STATE UNIV, 76- *Concurrent Pos:* Mem bd, Asn Univs for Res in Astron, Inc, 81- *Mem:* Int Astron Union; Am Astron Soc; fel Royal Astron Soc. *Res:* Spectroscopy and photometry of cool stars, especially Mira variables; infrared spectra; determination of chemical composition and effective temperature. *Mailing Add:* Dept Astron Ohio State Univ Columbus OH 43210

WING, WILLIAM HINSHAW, b Ann Arbor, Mich, Jan 11, 39; c 2. ATOMIC PHYSICS, MOLECULAR PHYSICS. *Educ:* Yale Univ, BA, 60; Rutgers Univ, New Brunswick, MS, 62; Univ Mich, Ann Arbor, PhD(physics), 68. *Prof Exp:* Res staff physicist, Yale Univ, 68-70, res assoc physics, 70-72, asst prof, 72-74; assoc prof physics, 74-78, PROF PHYSICS & OPTICAL SCI, UNIV ARIZ, 78- *Concurrent Pos:* Res Corp Cottrell grant, 71; Nat Bur Standards, US Dept Com Precision Measurement grants, 74 & 80; Am Chem Soc petrol res grant, 77; vis prof & Joint Inst Lab Astrophysics fel, Univ Colo, 79-80 & Mass Inst Technol, 80; assoc prof, Ecole Normale Superieure, 81; J S Guggenheim fel, 80-81; Alexander von Humboldt sr scientist award. *Mem:* Am Phys Soc; Inst Elec & Electronics Eng; fel Optical Soc Am. *Res:* Fundamental physical constants; simple atomic and molecular physics; lasers; particle beams; chemical physics; computer sciences. *Mailing Add:* Dept Physics & Optical Sci Ctr Univ Ariz Tucson AZ 85721

WINGARD, DEBORAH LEE, b San Diego, Calif, Aug 20, 52; m 76; c 1. EPIDEMIOLOGY. *Educ:* Univ Calif, Berkeley, BA, 74, MS, 76, PhD(epidemiol), 80. *Prof Exp:* Res specialist, Social Res Group, Sch Pub Health, Univ Calif, Berkeley, 76-77; epidemiologist, Human Pop Lab, Calif State Dept Health Serv, 77-78; ASST PROF, DIV EPIDEMIOL, DEPT COMMUNITY & FAMILY MED, UNIV CALIF, SAN DIEGO, 80- *Concurrent Pos:* Epidemiologist, Lipid Res Clin, Calif, 81- *Mem:* Soc Epidemiol Res; Am Pub Health Asn. *Res:* The interaction of biological and pyschosocial factors in the maintenance of health, through the study of sex differences in morbidity and mortality. *Mailing Add:* Dept Community & Family Med M-007 Univ Calif San Diego La Jolla CA 92093

WINGARD, LEMUEL BELL, JR, b Pittsburgh, Pa, July 10, 30; m 65. BIOCHEMISTRY, BIOENGINEERING. *Educ:* Cornell Univ, BChE, 53, PhD(biochem eng), 65. *Prof Exp:* Res engr, Jackson Lab, E I du Pont de Nemours & Co, 56-58 & Seaford Nylon Plant, 58-61; asst prof chem eng, Cornell Univ, 65-66; assoc prof, Univ Denver, 66-67; from asst prof to assoc prof chem eng, 67-75, adj prof chem eng, 76-77, from assoc prof to prof pharmacol, 72-81, PROF PHARMACOL & ANESTHESIOL, SCH MED, UNIV PITTSBURGH, 81- *Concurrent Pos:* NIH spec fel, Sch Pharm, State Univ NY Buffalo, 70-72; chmn confs enzyme eng, Eng Found, 71 & 73; sabbatical leave, vis assoc prof, Dept Pharmacol, Sch Med, Yale Univ, 79-80. *Mem:* Fel AAAS; Am Inst Chem Engr; NY Acad Sci; Am Chem Soc; Biomed Eng Soc. *Res:* Pharmacokinetics; immobilized enzymes; cells and drugs; mechanisms of anticancer drugs. *Mailing Add:* Dept Pharmacol Sch Med Univ Pittsburgh Pittsburgh PA 15261

WINGARD, PAUL SIDNEY, b Akron, Ohio, Jan 10, 30; m 53; c 5. PHYSICAL GEOLOGY. *Educ:* Miami Univ, AB, 52, MS, 55; Univ Ill, PhD(geol), 61. *Prof Exp:* Instr geol, Kans State Univ, 57-61, asst prof, 61-66; assoc prof geol & asst dean lib arts, 66-67, PROF GEOL & ASSOC DEAN COL ARTS & SCI, UNIV AKRON, 67- *Mem:* AAAS; Geol Soc Am. *Res:* Geochronology and geology of south central Maine; geology of central and southern Colorado; post-Pleistocene geology and life of northern Ohio. *Mailing Add:* 3904 Kent Rd Stow OH 44224

WINGARD, ROBERT EUGENE, JR, b Montgomery, Ala, Sept 18, 46. ORGANIC CHEMISTRY, POLYMER CHEMISTRY. *Educ:* Auburn Univ, BS, 68; Ohio State Univ, PhD(org chem), 71. *Prof Exp:* Res chemist, 74-75, sr res chemist, 76, SR RES SCIENTIST ORG CHEM, DYNAPOL, 77- *Concurrent Pos:* Fel org chem, Harvard Univ, 72-73, NIH fel, 72-74. *Mem:* Am Chem Soc; AAAS. *Res:* Synthetic and mechanistic organic chemistry; chemistry of functionalized polymers. *Mailing Add:* Dynapol 1454 Page Mill Rd Palo Alto CA 94304

WINGATE, CATHARINE L, b Boston, Mass, Sept 7, 22. RADIOLOGICAL PHYSICS, MEDICAL PHYSICS. *Educ:* Simmons Col, BS, 43; Harvard Univ, MA, 48; Columbia Univ, PhD(biophys), 61. *Prof Exp:* Res asst radiation physics, Mass Inst Technol, 43-45; sr technician, Woods Hole Oceanog Inst, 45-46; instr physics, Univ Conn, New London, 48-49; res asst med biophys, Sloan-Kettering Inst Cancer Res, 49-51; instr physics, Adelphi Col, 51-54; res scientist radiol physics, Col Physicians & Surgeons, Columbia Univ, 54-63; radiol physicist, Naval Radiol Defense Lab, 63-66; sr res scientist biophys, NY Univ, 66-67; assoc radiol physicist, Brookhaven Nat Lab, 67-70; asst prof radiol physics, Sch Med & asst dean, Sch Basic Health Sci, State Univ NY Stony Brook, 70-74, res asst prof radiol physics, Sch Med, 74-75, res assoc prof radiol, 75-78; MEM STAFF, HEALTH SCI ADMIN, NIH, 78- *Concurrent Pos:* Consult, Vet Admin Hosp, Northport, NY, 71-74 & Radiation Study Sect, NIH, 76-78; physicist, Nassau County Med Ctr, East Meadow, NY, 74-78; collabr, Brookhaven Nat Lab, 74-78; review ed, Med Phys, 79- *Mem:* AAAS; Radiation Res Soc; Biophys Soc; NY Acad Sci; Am Asn Physicists in Med. *Res:* Measurement of ionization parameters; measurement of microscopic dose distributions at a bone-soft tissue interface and around charged particle beams; thermo luminescence; neutron dosimetry; calcium uptake in stressed bone; clinical dosimetry; proton Bragg peak localization for therapy. *Mailing Add:* NIH Westwood Bldg 5333 Westbard Ave Bethesda MD 20205

WINGATE, CLARENCE ALEXANDER, JR, b Charlotte, NC, Nov 9, 30; m 55; c 4. AERODYNAMICS. *Educ:* NC State Univ, ME, MSME, 58. *Prof Exp:* Jr engr, Boeing Airplane Co, 52-54; instr thermodyn, NC State Univ, 56-58; assoc engr, 58-62, sr engr, 62-76, proj supvr satellite thermal design, 66-76, SUPVR THERMAL DESIGN, APPL PHYSICS LAB, JOHNS HOPKINS UNIV, 76- *Mem:* Am Inst Aeronaut & Astronaut. *Res:* Ramjet performance analysis; heat transfer; internal aerodynamics. *Mailing Add:* Appl Physics Lab Johns Hopkins Rd Laurel MD 20810

WINGATE, FREDERICK HUSTON, b Provo, Utah, Dec 21, 32; m 71. GEOLOGY, BOTANY. *Educ:* Univ Utah, BS, 56, MS, 61; Univ Okla, PhD(bot), 74. *Prof Exp:* Subsurface geologist oil explor, Chevron Oil Co, 61-66; WESTERN REGION PALYNOLOGIST BIOSTRATIG, CITIES SERV CO, 73- *Mem:* Am Asn Stratig Palynologists. *Res:* Palynology, involving organic- and siliceous-walled microfossil studies with application to solution of bistratigraphic and hydrocarbon generation problems. *Mailing Add:* 3052 S Ivan Way Denver CO 80227

WINGATE, MARTIN BERNARD, b London, Eng, m; c 2. OBSTETRICS & GYNECOLOGY. *Educ:* Univ London, MB, BS, 48, MD, 64; FRCS, 53; FRCS(E), 55; FRCS(C), 66. *Prof Exp:* House surgeon orthop, St Mary's Hosp, London, 48-50 & Obstet Unit, Whittington Hosp, 50-51; demonstr anat, St Mary's Hosp Med Sch, 51-52, prosecutor, 52, sr house officer surg, Hosp, 52-53; house surgeon, Cent Middlesex Hosp, 53-54; locum surg registr, Royal Northern Hosp, 54-55; locum surg registr obstet & gynec, Middlesex Hosp & Hosp for Women, 56-58; sr registr, Southampton Gen Hosp, 58-60; first asst, St George's Hosp, 58-62; sr registr obstet & gynec, Queen Charlotte & Chelsea Hosps, 62-63; asst examr obstet & gynec, Univ Bristol, sr lectr & consult, United Bristol Hosps & Univ Bristol & examr, Cent Midwives Bd, 63-66; assoc prof obstet & gynec, Univ Man, 67-71; prof, Temple Univ, 69-71; prof obstet & gynec & pediat, Thomas Jefferson Univ, 71-75; prof obstet & gynec & pediat, Albany Med Col, 75-77; PROF OBSTET & GYNEC & ASST DEAN, STATE UNIV NY, BUFFALO, 77-, ASST DEAN CONTINUING EDUC, 80- *Concurrent Pos:* Res fel obstet & pediat, Guy's Hosp Med Sch, 62-63. *Mem:* Can Med Asn; Sob Obstet & Gynaec Can; fel Am Col Obstet & Gynec. *Res:* Genetics of human aberrations and malignant lesions of the cervix; surgery of infertility and the transplantation of reproductive organs together with means of modification of the rejection phenomena. *Mailing Add:* Dept of Obstet & Gynec Childrens Hosp Buffalo NY 14222

WINGELETH, DALE CLIFFORD, b Cleveland, Ohio, June 8, 43; m 64; c 2. INORGANIC CHEMISTRY, CLINICAL CHEMISTRY. *Educ:* Cleveland State Univ, BES, 66; Univ Colo, Boulder, PhD(inorg chem), 70. *Prof Exp:* Clin biochemist, St Joseph Hosp, Denver, 70-72; clin chemist, St Lawrence Hosp, Mich, 72; forensic chemist, Poisonlab Inc, 72, vpres & tech dir, Poisonlab Div, Chemed Corp, 72-77; PRES, DALE C WINGELETH, PhD, INC, 77- *Mem:* Am Chem Soc; Royal Soc Chem; Am Asn Clin Chemists; Am Acad Forensic Sci; Forensic Sci Soc. *Res:* Inorganic hydrides; clinical toxicology. *Mailing Add:* 201 Cedarbrook Rd Boulder CO 80302

WINGENDER, RONALD JOHN, b Menominee, Mich, Sept 30, 36; div; c 2. ANALYTICAL CHEMISTRY. *Educ:* Univ Wis, BS, 59, PhD(anal chem), 69; Univ Iowa, MS, 61. *Prof Exp:* Chemist, Forest Prod Lab, 61-64; chemist, Ansul Co, Wis, 69, mgr anal res, 69-72; sect head chem, Indust Bio-Test Labs, 72-78; lab & res dir, Clin Bio-Tox Labs, 78-79; CHEMIST, ARGONNE NAT LAB, 79- *Mem:* Fel Am Inst Chemists; Am Chem Soc; Int Asn Great Lakes Res. *Res:* Proton nuclear magnetic resonance of cobalt II and nickel II aminopolycarboxylic acid and polyamine complexes; development of pesticide residue analytical procedures; development of analytical procedures for trace organic pollutants; identification of organic pollutants by gas chromatography and mass spectrometry; development of analytical procedures for drugs in biological fluids. *Mailing Add:* 822 Holmes Ave Deerfield IL 60015

WINGER, MILTON EUGENE, b Mayville, NDak, Aug 28, 31; m 54; c 2. MATHEMATICS, STATISTICS. *Educ:* Mayville State Col, BS, 53; Univ NDak, MS, 56; Iowa State Univ, PhD(statist), 72. *Prof Exp:* Inspector eng, US Army Corps Engrs, 57; asst prof math, Univ NDak, 60-68; instr statist, Iowa State Univ, 68-70; assoc prof, 71-78, PROF MATH, UNIV NDAK, 78-, ADV DEPT STATIST, 71- *Concurrent Pos:* Statist consult, Inst Appl Math & Statist, 74-; vis lectr, Inst Math Statist, 76-77. *Mem:* Math Asn Am; Am Statist Asn. *Mailing Add:* Dept of Math Univ of NDak Grand Forks ND 58201

WINGER, PARLEY VERNON, b Driggs, Idaho, Dec 11, 41; m 67. AQUATIC BIOLOGY, FISHERIES. *Educ:* Idaho State Univ, BS(med) & BS(zool), 66, MS, 68; Brigham Young Univ, PhD(aquatic biol), 72. *Prof Exp:* Res assoc aquatic biol, Brigham Young Univ, 72-73; asst prof, Tenn Technol Univ, 74-78; LEADER FIELD RES UNIT AQUATIC BIOL, COLUMBIA NAT FISHERY RES LAB, US FISH & WILDLIFE SERV, 78- *Concurrent Pos:* Prin investr fisheries, Ctr Health & Environ Studies, Brigham Young Univ, 72-74 & Tenn Valley Authority, 74-76; adj asst prof, Univ Ga, 78- *Mem:* Am Fisheries Soc; Am Soc Limnol & Oceanog; AAAS; Soc Int Limnol. *Res:* Effects of habitat alteration on aquatic ecosystems; mitigation techniques to enhance aquatic environments; effect of acid mine drainage and chemical contaminants on aquatic populations; population dynamics of benthic macroinvertebrates. *Mailing Add:* US Fish & Wildlife Serv Sch Forest Resources Univ Ga Athens GA 30602

WINGERT, LOUIS EUGENE, b Kimball, SDak, Feb 3, 24; m 52; c 3. CHEMICAL ENGINEERING. *Educ:* SDak Sch Mines & Technol, BS, 44. *Prof Exp:* Res engr, Deere & Co, Ill, 46-47; chem engr, Duro Tank Co, 47-48; bd plant engr, US Gypsum Co, Ohio, 48-51, qual supvr, 51-53, qual supt, Que, 53-57; sr chem engr, Minn Mining & Mfg Co, 57-68; RES CHEM ENGR, KIMBERLY-CLARK CORP, NEENAH, 68- *Mem:* Am Chem Soc. *Res:* Gypsum products; thermographic copy paper; lime; paper coatings. *Mailing Add:* 1525 Riverdale Dr Appleton WI 54911

WINGET, CARL HENRY, b Noranda, Que, Sept 28, 38; m 64; c 2. FOREST ECOLOGY, TREE PHYSIOLOGY. *Educ:* Univ NB, BScF, 60; Univ Wis, MSc, 62, PhD(forestry, bot), 64. *Prof Exp:* Prof forestry & geod, Laval Univ, 67-73; res scientist, 64-67 & 73-75, prog mgr, 75-78, DIR, LAURENTIAN FORESTRY RES CTR, CAN FORESTRY SERV, 78- *Mem:* Can Inst Forestry. *Res:* Forest resource management; silviculture of tolerant northern hardwoods. *Mailing Add:* Laurentian Forest Res Ctr Box 3800 Ste Foy PQ G1V 4C7 Can

WINGET, CHARLES M, b Garden City, Kans, Dec 26, 25; c 2. AEROSPACE SCIENCES. *Educ:* San Francisco State Col, BA, 51; Univ Calif, PhD, 57. *Prof Exp:* Chemist poultry husb, Univ Calif, 51-53, res asst, 53-56, jr res poultry physiologist, 56-57, res fel, 57-59; assoc prof avian physiol, Ont Agr Col, Univ Guelph, 59-63; res scientist, 63-67, PROJ SCIENTIST, BIOSATELLITE PROJ, NASA-AMES RES CTR, MOFFETT FIELD, 67- *Concurrent Pos:* Nat Inst Neurol Dis & Blindness fel, 57-59; lectr, Univ Calif, Davis, 64-; adj prof physiol, Sch Med, Wright State Univ, 75-81; prof pharmacol, Sch Pharm, Fla A&M Univ, 75- *Mem:* Poultry Sci Asn; Biophys Soc; Aerospace Med Asn; Int Soc Chronobiol; Am Physiol Soc. *Res:* Rhythms and social schedule; hypokinesis and drugs in humans; bird and monkey response to change in photoperiod; physiological changes associated with aeronautical environment; biotelemetry; biorhythm data acquisition and reduction. *Mailing Add:* Biomed Res Div 239-7 NASA Ames Res Ctr Moffett Field CA 94035

WINGET, GARY DOUGLAS, b Dayton, Ohio, Mar 27, 39; m 60; c 3. PLANT BIOCHEMISTRY, PLANT PHYSIOLOGY. *Educ:* Miami Univ, AB, 61, MA, 63; Mich State Univ, PhD(bot), 68. *Prof Exp:* Res chemist, Mound Lab, Monsanto Res Corp, 63-64; asst prof, 66-71, ASSOC PROF BIOL SCI, UNIV CINCINNATI, 71- *Concurrent Pos:* Vis assoc prof biochem, molecular & cell biol, Cornell Univ, 75. *Mem:* Am Soc Photobiol; Am Chem Soc; Am Soc Plant Physiologists. *Res:* Inhibitors of photosynthesis; mechanism of photophosphorylation; physiological action of phlorizin. *Mailing Add:* Dept of Biol Sci Univ of Cincinnati Cincinnati OH 45221

WINGET, JAMES L(YLE), physics, electrical engineering, deceased

WINGET, ROBERT NEWELL, b Monroe, Utah, July 11, 42; m 64; c 7. AQUATIC ECOLOGY, BIOLOGY. *Educ:* Univ Uath, BS, 67, MS, 68, PhD(biol sci), 70. *Prof Exp:* RES ASSOC AQUATIC ECOL, BRIGHAM YOUNG UNIV, 70- *Concurrent Pos:* Proj dir insect control, Div Parks & Recreation, State of Utah, 69-71; consult water qual mgt, US Forest Serv, Intermountain Region, 72-; consult, Cent Utah Proj, US Bur Reclamation, 73-, Vaughn Hansen Assocs, Utah, 77-78 & Sandia Proj, Eastern NMex Univ, 77-78; dir thermal study, Utah Power & Light Co, 74-76, consult aquacult, 77-; consult impact anal, Westinghouse Corp, 74-76; consult water qual, Eyring Res Inst, 75-, stream reclamation, Coastal States Energy Co, 79-, water qual, Getty Mineral Resources Co, 80- & Homestake Mining Co, 81- *Mem:* Am Fisheries Soc; Water Pollution Control Fedn; NAm Benthol Soc. *Res:* Environmental impact analyses, especially fisheries resources, water quality and water quality standards; aquaculture using thermal effluents; macroinvertebrate community dynamics. *Mailing Add:* Dept Zool Brigham Young Univ Provo UT 84602

WINGFIELD, EDWARD CHRISTIAN, b Charlottesville, Va, Nov 17, 23; m 47; c 3. PHYSICS, SCIENCE ADMINISTRATION. *Educ:* Univ Va, BA, 46, MA, 49; Univ NC, PhD(physics), 54. *Prof Exp:* Asst prof physics, Univ Richmond, 49-51; physicist, Savannah River Lab, E I du Pont de Nemours & Co, 54-62; chief, Instrumentation Develop & Serv, 62-65, asst mgr eng opers, 65-79, SR CONSULT, UNITED TECHNOLOGIES RES CTR, 79- *Res:* Instrumentation; reactor physics; simulation by computers; aerodynamic testing; management of research and development activities. *Mailing Add:* 38 Midwell Rd Wethersfield CT 06109

WINGO, CURTIS W, b Fair Grove, Mo, Aug 30, 15; m 52; c 2. ENTOMOLOGY. *Educ:* Southwestern Mo State Teachers Col, AB, 36; Univ Mo, MA, 39; Iowa State Col, PhD(entom), 51. *Prof Exp:* assoc prof entom, Univ Mo-Columbia, 51-59, prof, 59-80. *Mem:* Am Entomol Soc. *Res:* Biology and control of insect parasites of man and domestic animals. *Mailing Add:* RR 7 Columbia MO 65201

WINGO, WILLIAM JACOB, b Ladonia, Tex, July 17, 18; m 40; c 2. BIOCHEMISTRY. *Educ:* Univ Tex, BA, 38, MA, 40; Univ Mich, PhD(biochem), 46. *Prof Exp:* Tutor biochem, Med Br, Univ Tex, 38-39, instr, 39-41, 45-48, lectr biochem & nutrit, 48-54, asst prof biochem, Postgrad Sch Med, 50-54, res assoc, M D Anderson Hosp Cancer Res, 48-50, assoc biochemist, 50-54; ASSOC PROF BIOCHEM, MED COL & SCH DENT, UNIV ALA, BIRMINGHAM, 54- *Mem:* AAAS; Am Soc Biol Chemists; Am Chem Soc; Soc Exp Biol & Med; Soc Protozool. *Res:* Chemistry and metabolism of amino acids; growth and metabolism of ciliate Protozoa; histochemistry; apparatus development. *Mailing Add:* Dept of Biochem Univ of Ala Sch of Med Birmingham AL 35294

WINGROVE, ALAN SMITH, b Hanford, Calif, Mar 4, 39. ORGANIC CHEMISTRY. *Educ:* Univ Calif, Berkeley, BS, 60; Univ Calif, Los Angeles, PhD(chem), 64. *Prof Exp:* NSF fel, 64-65; asst prof chem, Univ Tex, Austin, 65-71; lectr & sci researcher & writer, 71-73; ASSOC PROF CHEM & CHMN DEPT, TOWSON STATE UNIV, 73- *Mem:* Sigma Xi; Am Chem Soc; Royal Chem Soc. *Res:* Chemistry of second row elements and participation in solvolysis and base-catalyzed cleavages; destabilized carbonium ions; carbenophiles; stereochemistry; synthetic methods. *Mailing Add:* Dept Chem Towson State Univ Baltimore MD 21204

WINHOLD, EDWARD JOHN, b Brantford, Ont, Jan 3, 28; nat US; m 51; c 3. PHYSICS. *Educ:* Univ Toronto, BA, 49; Mass Inst Technol, PhD(physics), 53. *Prof Exp:* Asst physics, Mass Inst Technol, 49-53, res staff mem, Lab Nuclear Sci, 53-54; from instr to asst prof physics, Univ Pa, 54-57; from asst prof to assoc prof, 57-69, PROF PHYSICS, RENSSELAER POLYTECH INST, 69- *Concurrent Pos:* Vis staff mem, Atomic Energy Res Estab, Harwell, Eng, 68-69 & lab nuclear sci, Mass Inst Technol, 82. *Mem:* Am Phys Soc. *Res:* Experimental nuclear and intermediate energy physics. *Mailing Add:* Dept of Physics Rensselaer Polytech Inst Troy NY 12181

WINICK, HERMAN, b New York, NY, June 27, 32; m 53; c 3. SYNCHROTRON RADIATION. *Educ:* Columbia Univ, AB, 53, PhD(physics), 57. *Prof Exp:* Asst physics, Columbia Univ, 53-54, asst, Nevis Cyclotron Lab, 54-57; res assoc & instr physics, Univ Rochester, 57-59; res fel, Cambridge Electron Accelerator, Harvard Univ, 59-65, sr res assoc & lectr, 65-73, asst dir, 73; DEP DIR, STANFORD SYNCHROTRON RADIATION LAB, STANFORD UNIV, 73- *Mem:* Am Phys Soc. *Res:* Meson scattering; bremstrahlung research; accelerator design and development; colliding beams; synchrotron radiation production and experimentation. *Mailing Add:* 853 Talman Dr Stanford CA 94305

WINICK, MYRON, b New York, NY, May 4, 29; m 64; c 2. PEDIATRICS, NUTRITION. *Educ:* Columbia Univ, AB, 51; Univ Ill, Urbana, MS, 52; State Univ NY Downstate Med Ctr, MD, 56. *Prof Exp:* From asst resident pediat to chief resident, Med Col, Cornell Univ, 57-60; Bank Am-Giannini Found fel, Stanford Univ, 62-63, attend pediatrician & instr pediat, Med Col, 63-64; asstprof, Med Col, Cornell Univ, 64-68, dir, Birth Defects Treatment Ctr, 64-71, from assoc prof to prof pediat & nutrit, 68-71; ROBERT R WILLIAMS PROF NUTRIT, PROF PEDIAT & DIR INST HUMAN NUTRIT, COL PHYSICIANS & SURGEONS, COLUMBIA UNIV, 72-, DIR, CTR NUTRIT, GENETICS & HUMAN DEVELOP, 75- *Concurrent Pos:* NIH spec fel, 63-64; vis prof, Univ Chile, 67; USPHS career develop award, 69-71; mem comt nutrit, brain develop & behav, Nat Acad Sci, 71-79; consult, Pan-Am Health Orgn, 66. *Honors & Awards:* E Mead Johnson Award Pediat Res, 70. *Mem:* Soc Pediat Res; Am Pediat Soc; Am Inst Nutrit; Am Soc Clin Nutrit; Am Acad Pediat. *Res:* Effects of early malnutrition on subsequent growth and development, particularly of the brain; study of brain growth and subsequent behavior. *Mailing Add:* Inst Human Nutrit Columbia Univ 701 W 168th St New York NY 10032

WINICOUR, JEFFREY, b Providence, RI, Apr 12, 38; m 64; c 1. THEORETICAL PHYSICS. *Educ:* Mass Inst Technol, BS, 59; Syracuse Univ, PhD(physics), 64. *Prof Exp:* Res asst, Syracuse Univ, 59-64; res physicist, Aerospace Res Labs, 64-72; ASSOC PROF PHYSICS, UNIV PITTSBURGH, 72- *Concurrent Pos:* Res assoc, Ctr Philos Sci, 77- *Mem:* Am Phys Soc. *Res:* General relativity; equations of motion; gravitational radiation. *Mailing Add:* Dept Physics Univ Pittsburgh Pittsburgh PA 15260

WINICOV, HERBERT, b Brooklyn, NY, Mar 14, 35; div; c 2. ORGANIC CHEMISTRY. *Educ:* Univ Pa, BA, 56; Univ Wis, PhD(chem), 61. *Prof Exp:* Sr chemist, 60-68, SR INVESTR, SMITH, KLINE & FRENCH LABS, 68- *Mem:* AAAS; Am Chem Soc. *Res:* Organic synthesis and process development of pharmaceuticals; applications of computer technology and statistical methods to the planning and optimization of chemical syntheses. *Mailing Add:* Smith Kline & French Labs 1500 Spring Garden St Philadelphia PA 19101

WINICOV, ILGA, b Riga, Lativia, May 16, 35; US citizen. NUCLEIC ACID BIOCHEMISTRY, MOLECULAR GENETICS. *Educ:* Univ Pa, Philadelphia, AB, 56, PhD(microbiol), 71; Univ Wis-Madison, MS, 58. *Prof Exp:* Assoc, Inst Cancer Res, Philadelphia, 72-74, res assoc, 74-76; res asst prof biochem, Fels Res Inst & Dept Biochem, Sch Med, Temple Univ, Philadelphia, 76-79; ADJ ASST PROF BIOCHEM, SCH MED, UNIV NEV, RENO, 79- *Mem:* Am Soc Microbiol; Am Soc Biol Chemists; Am Asn Cancer Res. *Res:* Eucaryotic gene expression at the level of RNA transcription and processing; characterization of processing products and enzymes in cultured mammalian cells; rRNA, tRNA and mRNA processing. *Mailing Add:* Dept Biochem Sch Med Univ Nev Reno NV 89557

WINICUR, DANIEL HENRY, b New York, NY, May 6, 39; m 60; c 2. CHEMICAL PHYSICS. *Educ:* City Col New York, BME, 61; Univ Conn, MSME, 63; Univ Calif, Los Angeles, PhD(chem dynamics), 68. *Prof Exp:* Res engr, Space Systs Div, Hughes Aircraft Co, 63-64; Shell Oil fel chem dynamics, A A Noyes Lab Chem Physics, Calif Inst Technol, 68-70; asst prof, 70-76, ASSOC PROF PHYS CHEM, UNIV NOTRE DAME, 76-, ASST DEAN, COL SCI, 79- *Mem:* AAAS; Am Chem Soc; Am Phys Soc. *Res:* Kinetics and spectroscopy of free-radical species in flames; molecular beam studies of chemical reactions; excited atomic and molecular states; energy transfer processes. *Mailing Add:* Dept of Chem Univ of Notre Dame Notre Dame IN 46556

WINICUR, SANDRA, b New York, NY, Oct 4, 39; m 60; c 2. CELL PHYSIOLOGY. *Educ:* Hunter Col, BA, 60; Univ Conn, MS, 63; Calif Inst Technol, PhD(biochem), 71. *Prof Exp:* Asst prof, 70-77, ASSOC PROF BIOL, IND UNIV, SOUTH BEND, 77- *Mem:* Am Soc Cell Biol; Am Inst Biol Sci. *Res:* Variations in salivary amylase activity; motility in Protozoa. *Mailing Add:* Dept Biol Ind Univ South Bend IN 46634

WINIKOFF, BEVERLY, b New York, NY, Aug 26, 45; m 73. PUBLIC HEALTH, NUTRITION. *Educ:* NY Univ, MD, 71; Harvard Univ, AB, 66, MPH, 73. *Prof Exp:* Intern, Gen Rose Mem Hosp, Denver, 71-72; res fel, Dept Nutrit, Sch Pub Health, Harvard Univ, 73-74; prog assoc & nutrit specialist, Rockefeller Found, 74-75, asst dir health sci, 75-78; MED ASSOC, INT PROGS, POP COUN, 78- *Mem:* Am Pub Health Asn. *Res:* Development and implementation of nutrition policies and programs; lactation; maternal child health. *Mailing Add:* The Pop Coun One Dag Hammarskjold Plaza New York NY 10017

WINJE, RUSSELL A, b Britton, SDak, Aug 24, 32; m 59; c 2. FUSION RESEARCH. *Educ:* Univ Minn, BSEE, 61. *Prof Exp:* Staff engr, Argonne Nat Lab, 61-68 & Fermi Nat Accelerator Lab, 68-76; STAFF ENGR, PLASMA PHYSICS LAB, PRINCETON UNIV, 76- *Mem:* Inst Elec & Electronics Engrs. *Mailing Add:* Plasma Physics Lab PO Box 451 Princeton NJ 08544

WINJUM, JACK KEITH, b Platte, SDak, Feb 5, 33; m 54; c 3. FOREST CULTURE. *Educ:* Ore State Univ, BS, 55; Univ Wash, MS, 61; Univ Mich, PhD(forest ecol), 65. *Prof Exp:* Forester, US Forest Serv, 55; forest technologist, Forestry Res Ctr, 58-63, regeneration ecologist, 63-73, mgr forest regenerator res, 73-77, mgr forest cult res, Technol Ctr, 77-80, MGR MT ST HELEN'S RES & DEVELOP, WESTERN FORESTRY RES CTR, WEYERHAEUSER CO, 80- *Concurrent Pos:* Affil assoc prof, Col Forest Resources, Univ Wash, Seattle, 80- *Mem:* Soc Am Foresters; Sigma Xi. *Res:* Cone and seed yield of Douglas fir; ecology of forest nurseries; stock handling and field out planting of seedlings in the regeneration period of Douglas fir management; forest regeneration ecology. *Mailing Add:* Western Forestry Res Ctr Weyerhaeuser Co PO Box 420 Centralia WA 98531

WINKEL, CLEVE R, b Logan, Utah, Mar 20, 32; m 55; c 6. BIOCHEMISTRY, ORGANIC CHEMISTRY. *Educ:* Utah State Univ, BS, 54, MS, 55; Brigham Young Univ, PhD, 70. *Prof Exp:* PROF CHEM, RICKS COL, 59-, CHMN DIV NATURAL SCI, 72- *Res:* Enzymology; enzyme mechanism; medical biochemistry. *Mailing Add:* Dept of Chem Ricks College Rexburg ID 83440

WINKEL, DAVID EDWARD, b Sibley, Iowa, Mar 10, 31; m 53; c 3. PHYSICAL CHEMISTRY, COMPUTER SCIENCE. *Educ:* Iowa State Univ, PhD(chem), 57. *Prof Exp:* From asst prof to assoc prof chem, 57-71, dir div comput serv, 72-77, head dept comput sci, 74-77, PROF CHEM & COMPUT SCI, UNIV WYO, 71- *Concurrent Pos:* Vis prof, Ind Univ, 62-63 & 71. *Res:* Nature of adsorption of gases on metals; computer architecture. *Mailing Add:* Dept Chem Univ Wyo Laramie WY 82070

WINKELHAKE, JEFFREY LEE, b Champaign, Ill, Oct 5, 45. IMMUNOCHEMISTRY, BIOCHEMISTRY. *Educ:* Univ Ill, Urbana-Champaign, BS, 67, MS, 69, PhD(immunochem), 74. *Prof Exp:* Res asst immunol, Walter Reed Army Inst Res, 69-72; res assoc fel cell biol, Jane Coffin Childs Mem Fund Med Res, Salk Inst Biol Studies, 74-76; asst prof,

76-80, ASSOC PROF MICROBIOL, MED COL WIS, 80- *Concurrent Pos:* Instr hemat & serol, US Army Med Training Ctr, San Antonio, 69-70; assoc scientist, Ctr Great Lakes Res, Univ Wis-Milwaukee, 78- *Mem:* Am Chem Soc; Am Asn Immunologists; Am Asn Cancer Res; Am Soc Biol Chemists; Biochem Soc London. *Res:* Immunoglobulin structure and effector functions; homeostasis of immune effector systems; evolutionary aspects; protein and carbohydrate chemistry; the physical biochemistry of antibody molecules; antibody metabolism; immune complexes. *Mailing Add:* Dept of Microbiol PO Box 26509 Milwaukee WI 53226

WINKELMANN, FREDERICK CHARLES, b Brooklyn, NY, Apr 11, 41; m 68; c 2. HIGH ENERGY PHYSICS. *Educ:* Mass Inst Technol, BS, 62, PhD(physics), 68. *Prof Exp:* Res assoc physics, Lab Nuclear Sci, Mass Inst Technol, 68-69; res assoc, Stanford Linear Accelerator Ctr, 69-72; RES ASSOC PHYSICS, LAWRENCE BERKELEY LAB, UNIV CALIF, 72- *Mem:* Am Phys Soc. *Res:* Elementary particle research using bubble chambers and spectrometers; phenomenology of strong interactions. *Mailing Add:* Lawrence Berkeley Lab Univ of Calif Berkeley CA 94720

WINKELMANN, JOHN ROLAND, b Champaign, Ill; m 62; c 2. VERTEBRATE ZOOLOGY, MAMMALOGY. *Educ:* Univ Ill, Urbana, BS, 54; Univ Mich, Ann Arbor, MA, 60, PhD(zool), 71. *Prof Exp:* Asst prof, 63-80, ASSOC PROF BIOL, GETTYSBURG COL, 80- *Concurrent Pos:* Fac fel grant for res in Mex, Gettysburg Col, 72-73. *Mem:* AAAS; Soc Study Evolution; Am Soc Mammal. *Res:* Biology of nectar-feeding bats. *Mailing Add:* Dept of Biol Gettysburg Col Gettysburg PA 17325

WINKELMANN, RICHARD KNISELY, b Akron, Ohio, July 12, 24; m; c 4. DERMATOLOGY. *Educ:* Univ Akron, BS, 47; Marquette Univ, MD, 48; Univ Minn, PhD(dermat), 56. *Prof Exp:* Res assoc chem, Wash Univ, 49, res assoc anat, 50; asst pub health officer, USPHS, Ala, 52-54; from instr to asst prof dermat, 56-65, assoc prof, 64-73, PROF DERMAT, MAYO GRAD SCH MED, UNIV MINN, 65-, PROF ANAT, 73-, CONSULT SECT DERMAT, MAYO FOUND, 56-, ROBERT H KIECKHEFER PROF DERMATOL, 75- *Concurrent Pos:* Instr & res assoc, Med Col, Univ Ala, 53-54; chmn dept dermat, Mayo Clin. *Res:* Anatomy. *Mailing Add:* Mayo Clin 200 SW First St Rochester MN 55901

WINKELSTEIN, WARREN, JR, b Syracuse, NY, July 1, 22; m 47; c 3. MEDICINE, EPIDEMIOLOGY. *Educ:* Univ NC, BA, 43; Syracuse Univ, MD, 47; Columbia Univ, MPH, 50. *Prof Exp:* Dist health officer, Erie County Health Dept, NY, 50-51; regional rep pub health div, Tech & Econ Mission, Mutual Security Agency, Cambodia, Laos & Viet Nam, 51-53; dir div commun dis control, Erie County Health Dept, NY, 53-56; from asst prof to prof prev med, Sch Med, State Univ NY Buffalo, 56-69, chief dept epidemiol, Chronic Dis Res Inst, 57-64; PROF EPIDEMIOL & DEAN SCH PUB HEALTH, UNIV CALIF, BERKELEY, 68- *Concurrent Pos:* Spec res fel, Nat Heart Inst, 56-67, career develop award, 62-68; dep health comnr, Erie County Health Dept, 59-62; mem heart dis control prog adv comt & air pollution training comt, USPHS, 62-65; mem subcomt, Nat Comt Health Statist, 65-; mem res comt, Am Heart Asn, 66-71. *Mem:* AAAS; fel Am Pub Health Asn; Am Col Prev Med; Am Col Prev Med. *Res:* Epidemiology of cardiovascular diseases; air pollution and cancer. *Mailing Add:* Dept of Epidemiol Univ of Calif Sch Pub Health Berkeley CA 94720

WINKER, JAMES A(NTHONY), b Randall, Minn, Dec 16, 28; m 53; c 5. AERONAUTICS, METEOROLOGY. *Educ:* Univ Minn, BAeroE & BBA, 52. *Prof Exp:* Jr engr, Mech Div, Gen Mills, Inc, 51-54; sr engr, 56-60, chief engr, 60-66, res mgr, 66-68, VPRES APPL TECHNOL DIV, RAVEN INDUSTS, INC, 68- *Mem:* Am Inst Aeronaut & Astronaut. *Res:* Scientific ballooning; atmospheric decelerators; aerial recovery systems; earth and space inflatables. *Mailing Add:* 2805 Poplar Dr Sioux Falls SD 57105

WINKERT, JOHN WYNIA, b Brooklyn, NY, Dec 27, 29; m 51; c 4. PHYSIOLOGY, CHEMISTRY. *Educ:* Polytech Inst Brooklyn, BS, 51; NY Univ, MS, 57, PhD(physiol), 60. *Prof Exp:* Instr physiol, NY Med Col, 60-64; asst prof pharmacol, State Univ NY Buffalo, 64-67; assoc prof physiol, Meharry Med Col, 67-72; asst prin supvr Morris Hepatoma Proj, Col Med, Howard Univ, 72-73, asst prof zool, 73-74; RES INVESTR BIOCHEM DIV, ARMED FORCES INST PATH, 74- *Concurrent Pos:* Helen Hay Whitney Found fel, NY Med Col, 61-64; NIH trainee nucleic acid & chromatin chem, Dept Obstet & Gynec, Vanderbilt Univ, 71-72; assoc prof biol sci, Bowie State Col, 74-75; sci res coordr, Washington Hosp Ctr, 75-78; guest lectr physiol, Uniformed Univ Health Sci, Washington, DC, 77- *Mem:* AAAS; Am Physiol Soc; NY Acad Sci; Am Inst Biol Sci; Am Soc Zoologists. *Res:* Effects of carcinogens on cancer cells; lactate on hematopoiesis; antimalarials on potassium fluxes; micro-electrophoresis of erythrocyte membrane proteins; mechanisms of cryoinjury and cryopreservation of enzymes; pH changes in frozen buffers by indicator dyes and NMR; purine nucelotide cycle enzymes of leukocytes; energy metabolism of migrating granulocytes; cryopreservation of granulocytes. *Mailing Add:* Biochem Div Air Force Inst of Path Washington DC 20306

WINKLER, BARRY STEVEN, b New York, NY, Apr 17, 45; m 66; c 1. PHYSIOLOGY. *Educ:* Harpur Col, BA, 65; State Univ NY Buffalo, MA, 68, PhD(physiol), 71. *Prof Exp:* Instr physiol, Sch Med, State Univ NY Buffalo, 70-71; asst prof, 71-78, ASSOC PROF BIOL SCI, OAKLAND UNIV, 78- *Res:* Physiology of the retina; analysis of ionic and metabolic contributions to photoreceptor potentials. *Mailing Add:* Inst Biol Sci Oakland Univ Rochester MI 48063

WINKLER, BRUCE CONRAD, b Milwaukee, Wis, Sept 25, 37; m 59; c 2. BIOCHEMISTRY. *Educ:* Valparaiso Univ, BA, 59; Iowa State Univ, MS, 62; Univ Okla, PhD(biochem), 67. *Prof Exp:* Instr chem, Cent State Univ, 62-64; fel biochem, Univ Alta, 67-69; asst prof biochem, Kansas City Col Osteop Med, 69-73, actg chmn dept, 73-78; ASST PROF CHEM, UNIV TAMPA, 78- *Res:* Muscle phosphorylase; clinical chemistry, especially proteins and enzymes. *Mailing Add:* Dept of Chem 401 W Kennedy Blvd Tampa FL 33606

WINKLER, DELOSS EMMET, b Atchison, Kans, Feb 4, 14; m 41; c 2. POLYMER CHEMISTRY. *Educ:* Univ Kans, AB, 36, MA, 39, PhD(chem), 41. *Prof Exp:* Teacher high sch, Kans, 36-37; asst instr chem, Univ Kans, 37-39; chemist, Shell Develop Co, 41-70; real estate salesman, 71-72; chemist, Spinco Div, 72, SR RES CHEMIST, BECKMAN INSTRUMENTS, INC, 72- *Concurrent Pos:* Consult, Polymer Chem & Technol, 79- *Mem:* Am Chem Soc. *Res:* Vapor phase catalysis; plastics; rubber; oxidation of hydrocarbons; chromatographic polymers for separation of amino acids and polymers for solid phase synthesis of peptides. *Mailing Add:* 133 Lombardy Lane Orinda CA 94563

WINKLER, ERHARD MARIO, b Vienna, Austria, Jan 8, 21; nat US; m 53; c 2. ENVIRONMENTAL GEOLOGY. *Educ:* Univ Vienna, PhD, 45. *Prof Exp:* Asst eng geol, Vienna Tech Univ, 40-45; sci asst geol, Vienna Tech Univ, 46-48; from instr to assoc prof, 48-73, PROF GEOL, UNIV NOTRE DAME, 73- *Honors & Awards:* E B Burwell Jr Award, Geol Soc Am, 75. *Mem:* Fel AAAS; fel Geol Soc Am. *Res:* Decay of stone monuments. *Mailing Add:* Dept of Earth Sci Univ of Notre Dame Notre Dame IN 46556

WINKLER, ERNST HANS, physics, deceased

WINKLER, EVA MARIA, b Ger, June 15, 15; m 40. PHYSICS. *Educ:* Univ Halle, Dr rer nat(physics), 41. *Prof Exp:* Res assoc atomic & molecular physics, Ger Army Res Ctr, Peenemünde, 41-43; res assoc atomic & molecular physics, Univ Halle, 43-44 & Ger Army Res Ctr, Kochel, 44-45; aeronaut res engr, US Naval Ord Lab, US Naval Surface Weapons Ctr, White Oak, 47-56, chief hypersonics group, 56-74, high-temperature aerodyn group, 60-74, chief hypersonics group & high-temperature aerodyn group, 74-75; consult, Winkler & Assocs, 75-81; RETIRED. *Res:* Physics of high temperature gases. *Mailing Add:* 12490 Lime Kiln Rd Fulton MD 20759

WINKLER, HERBERT H, b Highland Park, Mich, June 18, 39; m 61; c 1. MICROBIOLOGY, BIOCHEMISTRY. *Educ:* Kenyon Col, BA, 61; Harvard Univ, PhD(physiol), 66. *Prof Exp:* NSF fel physiol chem, Sch Med, Johns Hopkins Univ, 66-68; from asst prof to assoc prof microbiol, Sch Med, Univ Va, 68-77; PROF MICROBIOL, COL MED, UNIV S ALA, 77- *Concurrent Pos:* NIH res career develop award. *Mem:* Am Soc Microbiol; Am Soc Biol Chemists; Soc Exp Biol & Med; Tissue Cult Asn. *Res:* Transport of molecules across biological membranes; biology of rickettsiae. *Mailing Add:* Dept of Microbiol Univ of SAla Col of Med Mobile AL 36688

WINKLER, LEONARD P, b New York, NY. ELECTRICAL ENGINEERING, COMPUTER SCIENCES. *Educ:* Polytech Inst Brooklyn, BSEE, 65, MSEE, 67, PhD(elec eng), 71. *Prof Exp:* Res fel, Polytech Inst Brooklyn, 69-70; asst prof eng sci, Richmond Col, NY, 70-77; ASSOC PROF ENG SCI, COL STATEN ISLAND, CITY UNIV NEW YORK, 77- *Concurrent Pos:* NSF res grant, 72. *Mem:* Inst Elec & Electronics Engrs; Sigma Xi. *Res:* Traffic control; water pollution control; communications-computer systems; numerical optimization techniques; stochastic processes; microcomputers. *Mailing Add:* Col of Staten Island Staten Island NY 10301

WINKLER, LOUIS, b Elizabeth, NJ, Sept 7, 33; m 57. ASTRONOMY. *Educ:* Rutgers Univ, BS, 55; Adelphi Univ, MS, 59; Univ Pa, PhD(astron), 64. *Prof Exp:* Engr, Am Bosch Arma Corp, 56-59; proj engr, Philco Corp, 59-64; ASST PROF, PA STATE UNIV, 64- *Mem:* Am Astron Soc; fel Am Antiquarian Soc. *Res:* Double stars; astronomy and astrology of early America; United States of America seismic histories. *Mailing Add:* Dept of Astron Pa State Univ University Park PA 16802

WINKLER, MARVIN HOWARD, b Brooklyn, NY, Dec 17, 26; m 53; c 3. BIOPHYSICAL CHEMISTRY. *Educ:* NY Univ, BA, 49, MS, 51, PhD, 54. *Prof Exp:* Res assoc immunochem, Roswell Park Mem Inst, 54-58; asst & assoc investr, Protein Found, Inc, 58-66; asst prof biochem, Albert Einstein Col Med, 66-67; assoc prof immunochem, 76-77, ASSOC RES PROF, DEPT NEUROL, DEPT MED, MT SINAI SCH MED, 77- *Concurrent Pos:* Res assoc, Dept Biochem, Harvard Med Sch, 62-66; asst head dept microbiol, Montefiore Hosp, Bronx, NY, 66-67; consult, Brockton Vet Admin Hosp, Mass, 63-; Protein Found, Inc, 66- *Mem:* AAAS; Am Chem Soc; Soc Exp Biol & Med; Am Soc Biol Chemists; Am Asn Immunologists. *Res:* Protein small molecule interactions; immunochemistry; fluorescence. *Mailing Add:* Mt Sinai Sch of Med 100th St & Fifth Ave New York NY 10029

WINKLER, MAX ALBERT, b San Antonio, Tex, May 19, 31; m 53; c 4. PHYSICS, MATHEMATICS. *Educ:* St Mary's Univ, BS, 57; Univ Tex, Austin, MA, 62. *Prof Exp:* Physicist, Gen Elec Co, 57-59; MEM STAFF PHYSICS, LOS ALAMOS SCI LAB, 62- *Res:* Optical engineering; lens design; nondestructive testing. *Mailing Add:* Los Alamos Sci Lab Box 1663 Los Alamos NM 87545

WINKLER, NORMAN WALTER, b Englewood, NJ, May 28, 35; m 80; c 2. BIOCHEMISTRY, DERMATOLOGY. *Educ:* Univ Rochester, AB, 57; Univ Chicago, MD, 65, PhD(biochem), 70. *Prof Exp:* Res asst fibrinolysis, Sloan-Kettering Inst Cancer Res, 58-59; from intern to resident internal med, Univ Chicago Hosps & Clins, 68-70; USPHS fel dermat, Med Sch, Univ Ore, 70-72; chief dermat serv, Buffalo Vet Admin Hosp, 73-76; CHIEF, DERMAT SERV, SOUTH BUFFALO MERCY HOSP, 76- *Concurrent Pos:* Asst prof dermat, Sch Med, State Univ NY, Buffalo, 72-76. *Mem:* AAAS; Am Acad Dermat; Soc Invest Dermat. *Res:* Enzymology; membrane receptors in cutaneous disease; keratinocyte differentiation. *Mailing Add:* 4174 N Buffalo Rd Orchard Park NY 14127

WINKLER, PAUL, ichthyology, physiological ecology, see previous edition

WINKLER, PAUL FRANK, b Nashville, Tenn, Nov 10, 42; div; c 2. ASTROPHYSICS. *Educ:* Calif Inst Technol, BS, 64; Harvard Univ, AM, 65, PhD(physics), 70. *Prof Exp:* Asst prof, 69-77, ASSOC PROF PHYSICS, MIDDLEBURY COL, 77-, CHMN DEPT, 80- *Concurrent Pos:* Vis scientist, Mass Inst Technol, 73-74, res affil, 74-78, vis scientist, 78-80; Alfred P Sloan

Found res fel, 76-80. *Mem:* Am Phys Soc; Am Astron Soc; Int Astron Union. *Res:* Supernova remnants; galactic and extragalactic x-ray sources; atomic and molecular physics; solid waste separation technology. *Mailing Add:* Dept Physics Middlebury Col Middlebury VT 05753

WINKLER, PETER MANN, b Pasadena, Calif, Nov, 9, 46; m 73; c 2. COMPUTABILITY. *Educ:* Harvard Univ, BA, 68; Yale Univ, PhD(math), 75. *Prof Exp:* Mathematician, Dept Defense, 68-70; asst prof math, Stanford Univ, 75-77; ASST PROF MATH & COMPUT SCI, EMORY UNIV, 77- *Concurrent Pos:* Consult math, Navig Sci, Inc, 78- *Mem:* Am Math Soc; Math Asn Am; Asn Symbolic Logic. *Res:* Mathematical logic and computability; combinatorics; automated navigation. *Mailing Add:* Dept Math & Comput Sci Emory Univ Atlanta GA 30322

WINKLER, ROBERT RANDOLPH, b Washington, DC, June 16, 33; m 55; c 3. ORGANIC CHEMISTRY. *Educ:* Univ Md, BS, 55; Univ Mich, MS, 60, PhD(org chem), 62. *Prof Exp:* Phys sci aide plant indust sta, Agr Res Serv, USDA, Md, 55, chemist, 57-58; teaching asst & res fel, Univ Mich, 58-61; asst prof, 61-66, ASSOC PROF ORG CHEM, OHIO UNIV, 66- *Mem:* Sigma Xi; AAAS; Am Chem Soc. *Res:* Chemical education; mechanism and stereochemistry of carbonyl condensation reactions. *Mailing Add:* Dept of Chem Ohio Univ Athens OH 45701

WINKLER, SHELDON, b New York, NY, Jan 25, 32; m 61; c 2. DENTISTRY. *Educ:* NY Univ, BA, 53, DDS, 56. *Prof Exp:* From instr to asst prof denture prosthesis, Col Dent, NY Univ, 58-68; asst prof removable prosthodont, State Univ NY, Buffalo, 68-70, assoc prof removable prosthodont, 70-79; PROF REMOVABLE PROSTHODONT & CHMN DEPT, TEMPLE UNIV, PHILADELPHIA, 79- *Concurrent Pos:* Dir mat res, CMP Industs, Inc, 63-65, consult, 65-66; lectr, New York Community Col, 67-68; consult, Coe Labs, Inc, Ill, 67-; consult dent auxiliary training progs, Bd Coop Educ Serv, Cheektowaga, NY, 70-79; consult, Dental Lab Technol, Erie Community Col, Buffalo, NY, 78-; mem, Bd Consults, Quintessence Int, 80-; consult, Personal Prod Div, Lever Bros Co, NY, 81- *Mem:* Fel Am Col Dent; Am Prosthodont Soc; Am Dent Asn; Am Acad Plastics Res Dent. *Res:* Dental resins and alloys; preservation and embedment of specimens in methyl methacrylate; demineralization of bone; geriatric dentistry; laser radiation applications in dentistry. *Mailing Add:* Sch of Dent 3223 N Broad St Philadelphia PA 19140

WINKLER, VIRGIL DEAN, b Danvers, Ill, Feb 9, 17; m 43; c 2. GEOLOGY. *Educ:* Univ Ill, AB & BS, 38, MS, 39, PhD(geol), 41. *Prof Exp:* Instr geol, Univ Ill, 38-39; paleontologist, Creole Petrol Corp, 41-45, chief paleontologist, 45-55, paleont coordr, 55-56, eval geologist, 56-61, eval & opers geologist, 61-63, spec studies & eval geologist, 63-76; GEOL ADV, LAGOVEN S A, 76- *Concurrent Pos:* Prof, Cent Univ Venezuela, 58-59 & 66- *Mem:* AAAS; Paleont Soc; Soc Econ Paleont & Mineral; Geol Soc Am; Asn Geol, Mineral & Petrol, Venezuela (vpres, 54-55, secy-treas, 59-60). *Res:* Paleontology of Paleozoic rocks; world-wide occurrence of oil; Mesozoic and Cenozoic stratigraphy of Venezuela. *Mailing Add:* Aptdo 80537 Prados del Este Caracas 1080A Venezuela

WINKLEY, DONALD CHARLES, b Geneva, Ill, Apr 9, 38; m 62; c 1. INORGANIC CHEMISTRY. *Educ:* Northwestern Univ, BS, 61; Univ Tenn, PhD(chem), 65. *Prof Exp:* Res chemist inorg res & develop, 65-69, supvr metals applns, 69-71, MGR METALS APPLNS, INORG RES & DEVELOP, FMC CORP, 71- *Res:* Chemistry of peroxygen chemicals and applications of peroxygen chemicals in metal treating and ore processing; in situ leaching of uranium-chemistry, kinetics and computer simulation of leach process. *Mailing Add:* FMC Corp PO Box 8 Princeton NJ 08540

WINN, ALDEN L(EWIS), b Portsmouth, NH, Jan 26, 16; m 41; c 2. ELECTRONICS. *Educ:* Univ NH, BS, 37; Mass Inst Technol, MS, 48. *Prof Exp:* Engr & acct phys plant eval, New Eng Gas & Elec Syst, 37-40; asst elec eng, Mass Inst Technol, 45-47, instr, 47-48; from asst prof to assoc prof, 48-54, chmn dept, 52-67, PROF ELEC ENG, UNIV NH, 54- *Mem:* Am Soc Eng Educ; Inst Elec & Electronics Engrs. *Res:* Oceanographic instrumentation; semiconductor devices and circuits. *Mailing Add:* Dept of Elec Eng Univ of NH Durham NH 03824

WINN, C BYRON, b Canton, Mo, Nov 21, 33; m 58; c 3. AERONAUTICAL ENGINEERING, ELECTRICAL ENGINEERING. *Educ:* Univ Ill, Urbana, BS, 58; Stanford Univ, MS, 60, PhD(aeronaut eng), 67. *Prof Exp:* Engr, Lockheed Missiles & Space Co, 58-60; engr, Martin Marietta Co, 60-62; engr Lockheed Missiles & Space Co, 62-63; res asst, Stanford Univ, 63-67; assoc prof, 67-77, assoc dir Univ Comput Ctr, 70-77, PROF MECH ENG, COLO STATE UNIV, 77- *Concurrent Pos:* NASA res grant satellite geodesy, Colo State Univ, 67-71, remote sensing in hydrol, 70-72, Off Water Resources res grant optimal control of storm sewer syst, 70-72; consult, Space Res Corp, Que, 70-72, MEPPSCO, Inc, Mass, 71 & US Air Force, Wright-Patterson AFB, 71-72; vis assoc prof, Univ Newcastle, NSW, 72. *Honors & Awards:* Tech Paper Award, Am Inst Aeronaut & Astronaut, 67. *Mem:* Am Inst Aeronaut & Astronaut. *Res:* Optimal control theory and applications; satellite geodesy; simulation. *Mailing Add:* Dept of Mech Eng Colo State Univ Ft Collins CO 80523

WINN, EDWARD BARRIERE, b Baltimore, Md, Dec 27, 22; m 49; c 4. TECHNICAL MANAGEMENT, CHEMISTRY. *Educ:* Univ SC, BSEE, 46; Univ Va, MS, 47; Univ Minn, PhD(physics), 50. *Prof Exp:* Elec engr, Westinghouse Elec Corp, 46; asst, Univ Minn, 48-50; res physicist, Textile Fibers Dept, E I du Pont de Nemours & Co, 50-58, res supvr, 58-62, tech mgr, du Pont de Nemours Int, SA, 62-70; independent consult, 70-74 & SNIA Viscosa SpA, 74-77; consult, Diamond Shamrock France, 78-80; EUROP DIR, CHEM INDUST DIV, SRI INT, ZURICH, SWITZERLAND, 80- *Mem:* Am Phys Soc; Am Chem Soc; Sigma Xi. *Res:* Physics of high polymers; textile fibers; processing and applications technology of synthetic fibers; physics of electrical insulating materials; electrical insulation technology; industrial and technical marketing; new business ventures in textile, polymers and chemicals. *Mailing Add:* 25 ch de Trembley 1197 Prangins Switzerland

WINN, HENRY JOSEPH, b Lowell, Mass, Mar 2, 27; m 53; c 6. IMMUNOLOGY. *Educ:* Ohio State Univ, BA, 48, MS, 50, PhD(bact), 52. *Prof Exp:* Fel med & bact, Ohio State Univ, 52-54; fel chem, Calif Inst Technol, 54-55; res assoc, Jackson Mem Lab, 55-57, staff scientist, 57-65; assoc immunologist, Mass Gen Hosp, 65-73; asst prof bact, 65-70, assoc prof microbiol & molecular genetics, 69-77; SR ASSOC SURG, HARVARD MED SCH, 77- IMMUNOLOGIST, MASS GEN HOSP, 73- *Mem:* Am Asn Immunologists. *Res:* Immunology of homotransplantation; immunogenetics. *Mailing Add:* Dept of Surg Harvard Univ Cambridge MA 02138

WINN, HOWARD ELLIOTT, b Winthrop, Mass, May 1, 26; m 51; c 3. BIOLOGICAL OCEANOGRAPHY, BIOACOUSTICS. *Educ:* Bowdoin Col, AB, 48; Univ Mich, MS, 50, PhD(zool), 55. *Prof Exp:* Specialist, Am Mus Natural Hist, 54-55; from asst to prof zool, Univ Md, 55-65; PROF OCEANOG & ZOOL, UNIV RI, 65- *Concurrent Pos:* Guggenheim fel, 62-63. *Mem:* AAAS; Am Inst Biol Sci; Am Soc Ichthyol & Herpet; Animal Behav Soc; Am Soc Mammal. *Res:* Comparative animal behavior; biology of fishes; sounds in animals; behavior and sounds of whales. *Mailing Add:* Grad Sch of Oceanog Univ of RI Kingston RI 02881

WINN, HUGH, b St Louis, Mo, Apr 7, 18; m 39; c 2. CHEMICAL & MATERIALS ENGINEERING. *Educ:* Mich Col Mining & Technol, BS, 40; Case Inst Technol, MS, 44, PhD(chem eng), 48. *Prof Exp:* Res engr, Saran Develop Lab, Dow Chem Co, 41-42; asst prof chem eng & dir plastics lab, Case Inst Technol, 42-48; group leader, Firestone Tire & Rubber Co, 48-50 & Defense Res Div, 50-55; mgr nose cone design eng, Missile & Space Vehicle Dept, 55-58, mgr res opers & applns, Aerosci Lab, 58-59, mgr data processing & comput, 59-63, mgr corp eng, 63-71, mgr eng, Lamp Glass Dept, 71-78, PROJ MGR GLASS RESOURCE PLANS & PROG, LAMP GLASS PROD DEPT, GEN ELEC CO, 78- *Concurrent Pos:* Consult, Martin Co, Md, 42, Ohio Chem Co, 44-47 & Frankford Arsenal, 55-58. *Mem:* Am Chem Soc; Soc Plastics Engrs; Am Inst Chem Engrs. *Res:* Plastics formulation; evaluation and fabrication; rubber oxidation, compounding and evaluation; high explosive effects; space environment; engineering design and space vehicles; scientific computation and test data reduction; materials and processes. *Mailing Add:* 6524 Kingswood Dr Lyndhurst OH 44124

WINN, MARTIN, b Brooklyn, NY, Jan 25, 40; m 66; c 2. MEDICINAL CHEMISTRY. *Educ:* Cooper Union Univ, BChE, 61; Northwestern Univ, PhD(org chem), 65. *Prof Exp:* SR CHEMIST, ABBOTT LABS, 65- *Mem:* Am Chem Soc. *Res:* Pharmaceuticals; nonclassical aromatic systems; heterocycles; psychotropic drugs; antihypertensive drugs, diuretics. *Mailing Add:* Dept 466 Abbott Labs Research Div North Chicago IL 60064

WINN, WILLIAM PAUL, b Los Angeles, Calif, Apr 24, 39. ATMOSPHERIC PHYSICS. *Educ:* Univ Calif, Berkeley, BS, 61, PhD(physics), 66. *Prof Exp:* Fel physics, Nat Ctr Atmospheric Res, 66-70; from asst prof to assoc prof physics, 70-77, CHMN DEPT PHYSICS, N MEX INST MINING & TECHNOL, 77- *Mem:* Am Geophys Union; Am Asn Physics Teachers; AAAS; Int Solar Energy Soc. *Res:* Thunderstorms. *Mailing Add:* Dept Physics N Mex Inst Mining & Technol Socorro NM 87801

WINNER, ROBERT WILLIAM, b Columbus, Ohio, Apr 5, 27; m 51; c 2. AQUATIC ECOLOGY, TOXICOLOGY. *Educ:* Ohio State Univ, PhD(wildlife mgt), 57. *Prof Exp:* Instr zool, 57-59, asst prof biol, 59-65, assoc prof zool, 65-69, PROF ZOOL, MIAMI UNIV, 69- *Mem:* Am Soc Limnol & Oceanog; Soc Environ Toxicol & Chem; Int Soc Limnol. *Res:* Evaluation of the effects of toxic chemicals, especially heavy metals on freshwater populations, communities, and ecosystems; evaluating factors which control the structure of freshwater planktonic communities. *Mailing Add:* Dept Zool Miami Univ Oxford OH 45056

WINNETT, GEORGE, b New York, NY, Jan 4, 23; m 48; c 2. ENVIRONMENTAL SCIENCES, ANALYTICAL CHEMISTRY. *Educ:* Pa State Col, BS, 47; NY Univ, MA, 51. *Prof Exp:* Chemist, Queens Gen Hosp, NY, 48-49; Lutheran Hosp, New York, 49-50; lab asst & teacher high schs, 50-52; control chemist, Valspar Corp, Valentine Paint Co, 52-53, res chemist, 53-55; serv chemist, Reichold Chem, Inc, 55-57; asst prof, 57-62, assoc prof agr chem, 62-72, ASSOC RES PROF PESTICIDE RESIDUES, RUTGERS UNIV, 72- *Concurrent Pos:* Smithsonian Inst consult, Microanal Lab & Pesticide Monitoring Proj, Univ Tehran, Iran, 71; assoc prof, Univ Montpellier, France, 80-81. *Mem:* AAAS; Am Chem Soc; Sigma Xi (secy, 66-69, vpres, 70, pres, 71); Asn Offs Anal Chem. *Res:* Methodology for microanalysis of pesticide residues in soil and foodstuffs, using gas chromatograph, spectrometers, atomic absorption and miscellaneous allied equipment. *Mailing Add:* Dept of Entom & Econ Zool Rutgers Univ PO Box 231 New Brunswick NJ 08903

WINNICK, JACK, b Chicago, Ill, Sept 20, 37. CHEMICAL ENGINEERING. *Educ:* Univ Ill, BS, 58; Univ Okla, MS, 60, PhD(chem eng), 63. *Prof Exp:* From asst prof to assoc prof chem eng, Univ Mo-Columbia, 63-67, prof, 71-79; Cramer Wilson La Pierre prof eng, 79-80, PROF CHEM ENG, GA INST TECHNOL, 79- *Concurrent Pos:* NSF res grants, 64-; consult, NASA Manned Spacecraft Ctr, 66-; vis prof, Univ Calif, Berkeley, 69-70 & Univ Calif, Los Angeles, 76-77; Petrol Res Fund grant, 70-; NASA grants, 72-; Dept Energy grant, 77-80. *Mem:* Am Inst Chem Engrs; Am Chem Soc; AAAS; Sigma Xi. *Res:* High pressure behavior of liquids and liquid mixtures; fixed-bed adsorption systems for manned spacecraft; electrochemical engineering; fuel cells. *Mailing Add:* Dept Chem Eng Ga Inst Technol Atlanta GA 30332

WINNIE, DAYLE DAVID, b Brandon, Wis, July 20, 35; m 57; c 2. MECHANICAL ENGINEERING, ELECTRONICS. *Educ:* Univ Wis, BS, 58. *Prof Exp:* Aircraft maintenance officer, Charleston AFB, SC, 59-60; prod engr electromech design, Centralab Div, Globe Union Inc, Milwaukee, 60-64; develop engr automatic processing equip, Stoelting Bros Co, Kiel, 64-69; sr res engr, 69-81, STAFF ENGR ELECTROMECH, SOUTHWEST RES INST, 81- *Mem:* Sigma Xi; Am Soc Mech Engrs. *Res:* Electromechanical design; spaceflight mass measurement equipment; automatic machinery design and development; automatic direction finding systems; sub-sea hyperbaric and single atmosphere systems; geophysical anomaly detection systems; automated continuous dairy processing equipment. *Mailing Add:* Southwest Res Inst 8500 Culebra Rd San Antonio TX 78228

WINNIFORD, ROBERT STANLEY, b Portland, Ore, Oct 10, 21; m 44; c 4. PHYSICAL CHEMISTRY. *Educ:* Ore State Col, BS, 43; Calif Inst Technol, MS, 48; Univ Tenn, PhD, 51. *Prof Exp:* Instr chem, Univ Tenn, 47-49; res chemist, Calif Res Corp, Standard Oil Co Calif, 51-63; asst prof chem, 63-67, assoc prof, 67-77, chmn dept, 71-80, RPOF CHEM, WHITWORTH COL, WASH, 77- *Mem:* Am Chem Soc; Sigma Xi. *Res:* Colloid and surface chemistry; nonaqueous solutions; asphalt chemistry and rheology. *Mailing Add:* W 830 Hawthorne Rd Spokane WA 99218

WINNIK, MITCHELL ALAN, b Milwaukee, Wis, July 17, 43. ORGANIC CHEMISTRY, PHOTOCHEMISTRY. *Educ:* Yale Univ, BA, 65; Columbia Univ, PhD(org chem), 69. *Prof Exp:* USPHS fel, Calif Inst Technol, 69-70; asst prof, 70-75, assoc prof, 75-80, PROF ORG CHEM, UNIV TORONTO, 80- *Mem:* AAAS; Am Chem Soc; Chem Inst Can. *Res:* Organic photochemistry, polymer conformation and dynamics; luminescence techniques in polymer science; application of fluorescence, phosphorescence and organic photochemical reactions to the study of polymer conformation and dynamics. *Mailing Add:* Dept of Chem Univ of Toronto Toronto ON M5S 1A1 Can

WINNINGHAM, JOHN DAVID, b Mexia, Tex, Dec 28, 40; m 63; c 1. MAGNETOSPHERIC PHYSICS. *Educ:* Tex A&M Univ, BS, 63, MS, 65, PhD(physics), 70. *Prof Exp:* From res asst to res sci asst physics, Univ Tex, Dallas, 66-71, res assoc, 71-73, res scientist, 73-80; MGR, EXP SPACE PHYSICS, SOUTHWEST RES INST, SAN ANTONIO, TEX, 80- *Concurrent Pos:* Consult, Los Alamos Sci Lab, Univ Calif, 74- *Mem:* Am Geophys Union. *Res:* Investigation of the source and acceleration mechanisms of corpuscular fluxes that produce the aurora and concomitant physical processes by means of rocket and satellite instruments. *Mailing Add:* Southwest Res Inst Drawer 28510 San Antonio TX 78284

WINOGRAD, NICHOLAS, b New London, Conn, Dec 27, 45; c 77. ANALYTICAL CHEMISTRY. *Educ:* Rensselaer Polytech Inst, BS, 67; Case Western Reserve Univ, PhD(chem), 70. *Prof Exp:* Asst prof, Purdue Univ, West Lafayette, 70-75, assoc prof chem, 75-79; PROF, PA STATE UNIV, UNIVERSITY PARK, 79- *Concurrent Pos:* Res grants, Res Corp, 70-72, Am Chem Soc, 70-73, NSF, 71- & Air Force Off Sci Res, 72-; Sloan fel, 74-77; Guggenheim fel, 77-78. *Mem:* Am Chem Soc; Electrochem Soc. *Res:* Characterization of solid surfaces; x-ray photoelectron spectroscopy; secondary ion mass spectrometry; theory of ion impact phenomena on solids. *Mailing Add:* Dept of Chem Pa State Univ University Park PA 16802

WINOGRAD, SHMUEL, b Israel, Jan 4, 36; m 58; c 2. MATHEMATICS. *Educ:* NY Univ, PhD(math), 68. *Prof Exp:* MEM STAFF, DEPT MATH, T J WATSON RES CTR, IBM CORP, 61- *Concurrent Pos:* McKay lectr, Univ Calif, Berkeley, 67-68; IBM fel, 72; vis prof, Israel Inst Technol, 72- *Honors & Awards:* W Wallace McDowell Award, 74. *Mem:* Nat Acad Sci; Inst Elec & Electronics Engrs; Asn Comput Mach; Am Math Soc; Math Asn Am. *Res:* Computer mathematics; reliable computations; complexity of computations. *Mailing Add:* Math Sci Dept T J Watson Res Ctr PO Box 218 Yorktown Heights NY 10598

WINOGRAD, TERRY ALLEN, b Takoma Park, Md, Feb 24, 46; m 68. COMPUTER SCIENCE. *Educ:* Colo Col, BA, 66; Mass Inst Technol, PhD(appl math), 70. *Prof Exp:* Instr math, Mass Inst Technol, 70-71, asst prof elec eng, 71-73; asst prof, 73-79, ASSOC PROF COMPUT SCI & LING, STANFORD UNIV, 79- *Concurrent Pos:* Consult, Palo Alto Res Ctr, Xerox Corp, 73-; mem, Comput Sci & Eng Res Study Panel Artificial Intel, NSF, 75. *Mem:* Asn Comput Ling. *Res:* Artificial intelligence; computational linguistics; cognitive modelling. *Mailing Add:* Dept Comput Sci Stanford Univ Stanford CA 94305

WINOKUR, GEORGE, b Philadelphia, Pa, Feb 10, 25; m 51; c 3. PSYCHIATRY. *Educ:* Johns Hopkins Univ, BA, 44; Univ Md, MD, 47; Am Bd Psychiat & Neurol, dipl, 53. *Prof Exp:* From instr to prof psychiat, Sch Med, Wash Univ, 51-71; PROF PSYCHIAT & HEAD DEPT, COL MED, UNIV IOWA & DIR, IOWA PSYCHIAT HOSP, 71- *Concurrent Pos:* From asst psychiatrist to assoc psychiatrist, Barnes Hosp, 55-71; attend, Malcolm Bliss Psychiat Hosp. *Honors & Awards:* Anna Monika Prize Res Affective Disorder; Hofheimer Prize Psychiat Res, Am Psychiat Asn; Paul Hoch Award, Am Psychopath Asn. *Mem:* Soc Biol Psychiat; fel Am Psychiat Asn; Psychiat Res Soc; Asn Res Nerv & Ment Dis; Am Psychopath Asn. *Res:* Conditioning and habituation; sexual variables in psychiatric patients and controls; genetics and epidemiological studies of psychiatric diseases. *Mailing Add:* Iowa Psychiat Hosp 500 Newton Rd Iowa City IA 52240

WINOKUR, MORRIS, b Philadelphia, Pa, Nov 8, 10; m 36; c 3. BIOLOGY. *Educ:* City Col New York, BS, 31; NY Univ, MSc, 33, EdD, 38; Columbia Univ, PhD(bot), 46. *Prof Exp:* From tutor to instr biol, City Col New York, 33-47; from asst prof to assoc prof, 47-67, supvr div biol, 57-68, PROF BIOL & CHMN DEPT, BARUCH COL, 68-, DEAN SUMMER SESSION, 69-, ASSOC DEAN LIB ARTS, 70- *Concurrent Pos:* Fel, Cold Spring Harbor, 31 & Marine Biol Lab, Woods Hole, 32; vis scholar, Columbia Univ, 47-48. *Mem:* AAAS; Bot Soc Am; Am Soc Plant Physiol; Nat Sci Teachers Asn; Nat Asn Biol Teachers. *Res:* Science orientation; cytology of protozoa; comparative physiology of green alga Chlorella. *Mailing Add:* Dept of Biol Baruch Col New York NY 10010

WINOKUR, ROBERT MICHAEL, b Minneapolis, Minn, July 2, 42. ZOOLOGY. *Educ:* Macalester Col, BA, 65; Ariz State Univ, MA, 67; Univ Utah, PhD(biol), 72. *Prof Exp:* Teaching fel biol, Univ Utah, 67-72, asst res prof, 72-73; instr zool, Univ New Eng, Australia, 74-78; ASST PROF BIOL, UNIV NEV, LAS VEGAS, 78- *Honors & Awards:* Dwight D Davis Award, Am Soc Zoologists, 73. *Mem:* Am Soc Zoologists; Am Soc Ichthyologists & Herpetologists; Soc Study Amphibians & Reptiles; Soc Study Evolution. *Res:* Comparative morphology of lower vertebrates with emphasis on the microscopic anatomy and integumentary specialization of reptiles. *Mailing Add:* Dept of Biol Sci Univ of Nev Las Vegas NV 89154

WINRICH, LONNY B, b Eau Claire, Wis, July 10, 37; m 61; c 5. COMPUTER SCIENCE, APPLIED MATHEMATICS. *Educ:* Wis State Univ, Eau Claire, BS, 60; Univ Wyo, MS, 62; Iowa State Univ, PhD(appl math), 68. *Prof Exp:* Physicist, Boulder Labs, Nat Bur Standards, 60-62; mathematician, Aerospace Div, Honeywell, Inc, 62-64; instr math & comput sci, Iowa State Univ, 64-68; asst prof comput sci, Univ Mo-Rolla, 68-71; assoc prof, 71-77, PROF COMPUT SCI, UNIV WIS-LA CROSSE, 77-, CHMN DEPT, 71- *Concurrent Pos:* Lectr, Viterbo Col; consult, Dairyland Power Co & St Norbert Col. *Mem:* Asn Comput Mach; Asn Educ Data Systs. *Res:* Matrix computations; programming languages; medical computing. *Mailing Add:* Dept of Comput Sci Univ of Wis-La Crosse La Crosse WI 54601

WINSBERG, GWYNNE ROESELER, b Chicago, Ill, Nov 28, 30; m 50; c 2. EPIDEMIOLOGY. *Educ:* Univ Chicago, MS, 62, PhD(biopsychol), 67. *Prof Exp:* Instr biol, Univ Chicago, 65-67; asst prof anat, Med Sch, Northwestern Univ, Chicago, 67-71, asst prof community health & prev med, 71-76; ASSOC PROF COMMUNITY & FAMILY MED & ASSOC DEAN, STRITCH SCH MED, LOYOLA UNIV OF CHICAGO, 76- *Concurrent Pos:* Lectr, Ill Col Optom, 62-67; consult, Ill Dept Ment Health, 69-72; USPHS grant, Fac Inst Med Care Orgn, Univ Mich, 73 & 74; Nat Endowment Humanities grant, Univ Pa, 74; spec asst to regional health adminr, Region V, USPHS, 74-76; secy, bd trustees, North Communities Health Plan, Inc, Evanston, 76-; sr policy analyst, Off of the Secy, Dept Health Human Serv, Washington, DC, 79-81; vpres, Health Policy Div, Woodward Group, Chicago, 81- *Mem:* Am Pub Health Asn; Am Soc Trop Med & Hyg; Asn Teachers Prev Med; Nat Asn Community Health Centers. *Res:* Social and medical epidemiology; medical care organization; health policy and legislation; rural health care delivery. *Mailing Add:* 5533 N Glenwood Chicago IL 60640

WINSBERG, LESTER, b Montreal, Que, Jan 31, 21; nat US; m 49; c 4. NUCLEAR SCIENCE. *Educ:* Univ Chicago, BS, 42, PhD(chem), 47. *Prof Exp:* Jr scientist, Metall Lab, 43-45 & Los Alamos Sci Lab, 45-46; assoc physicist, Argonne Nat Lab, 47-50; sr scientist, Weizmann Inst, 50-52, 54-55 & Inst Nuclear Studies, Univ Chicago, 52-54; res scientist, Lawrence Radiation Lab, Univ Calif, 55-60; PROF PHYSICS, UNIV ILL, CHICAGO CIRCLE, 61- *Concurrent Pos:* Assoc chemist, Argonne Nat Lab, 60-64, consult, 64- *Mem:* Am Phys Soc. *Res:* Nuclear fission; neutron diffraction; natural radioactivity; meson interactions; high energy nuclear and heavy ion induced reactions; stopping of heavy ions; nuclear physics-high energy spallation reactions. *Mailing Add:* Univ of Ill Box 4348 Chicago IL 60680

WINSCHE, WARREN EDGAR, b Brooklyn, NY, Jan 26, 17; m 42; c 3. NUCLEAR ENGINEERING. *Educ:* Polytech Inst Brooklyn, BChE, 39; Univ Rochester, MChE, 40; Univ Ill, PhD(chem eng), 43. *Prof Exp:* Engr, Nat Res Coun, Univ Ill, 43-45 & Clinton Labs, Monsanto Chem Co, Tenn, 45-46; head div pile eng & asst chmn reactor dept, Brookhaven Nat Lab, 46-52; engr & res mgr atomic energy div, E I du Pont de Nemours & Co, 52-62; chmn nuclear eng dept, 62-68, chmn dept appl sci, 68-75, assoc dir, 75-79, DEP DIR, BROOKHAVEN NAT LAB, 79- *Mem:* Fel Am Nuclear Soc. *Res:* Chemistry and engineering of nuclear reactions; environmental problems in energy production; new energy technologies. *Mailing Add:* Brookhaven Nat Lab Upton NY 11973

WINSLOW, ALFRED EDWARDS, b Clinton, Mass, Oct 8, 19; m 44; c 2. ORGANIC CHEMISTRY. *Educ:* Worcester Polytech Inst, BS, 41; Mass Inst Technol, PhD(org chem), 47. *Prof Exp:* Jr chemist, Tenn Eastman Corp, 44-45; asst, Sugar Res Found, Mass Inst Technol, 45-47; res chemist, Union Carbide Chem Co, 47-64; RES & DEVELOP CHEMIST, BORDEN CHEM CO, 64- *Mem:* Am Chem Soc; Am Soc Qual Control. *Res:* Water soluble polymers; condensation polymerizations; reactions in aqueous media; paper resins; binders; applications orientated experimental designs; resin analyses; manufacturing procedures and quality control. *Mailing Add:* Borden Chem Co Adhes & Chem Div 6210 Camp Ground Rd Louisville KY 40216

WINSLOW, CHARLES ELLIS, JR, b Norfolk, Va, July 2, 28; m 50; c 2. CHEMICAL ENGINEERING. *Educ:* Va Polytech Inst, BS, 50; NC State Univ, MS, 52, PhD(chem eng), 56. *Prof Exp:* Chem engr, 56-58, group leader, 58-64, mgr process develop, 64-72; assoc dir res, 72-75, DIR DEVELOP, VA CHEM INC, 75- *Mem:* Am Inst Chem Engrs. *Res:* Inorganic and organic process development and equipment design; chemistry of sulfur dioxide bases on or derived from reducing agents. *Mailing Add:* Va Chem Inc Portsmouth VA 23703

WINSLOW, DOUGLAS NATHANIEL, b Lakewood, Ohio. CIVIL ENGINEERING. *Educ:* Purdue Univ, BSCE, 64, MSCE, 69, PhD(construct mat), 73. *Prof Exp:* ASSOC PROF CIVIL ENG, PURDUE UNIV, 73- *Mem:* Am Concrete Inst; Am Soc Testing & Mat; Am Ceramic Soc. *Res:* Microstructure, durability and test methods for various construction materials (cement, concrete, bricks and bituminous mixtures); mercury intrusion porosimetry. *Mailing Add:* Sch Civil Eng Purdue Univ Lafayette IN 47907

WINSLOW, FIELD HOWARD, b Proctor, Vt, June 10, 16; m 45; c 3. ORGANIC CHEMISTRY, POLYMER CHEMISTRY. *Educ:* Middlebury Col, BS, 38; RI State Col, MS, 40; Cornell Univ, PhD(org chem), 43. *Prof Exp:* Res chemist, Manhattan Proj, Columbia Univ, 43-45; MEM TECH STAFF, BELL LABS, INC, 45- *Concurrent Pos:* Adj prof, Stevens Inst Technol, 64-67; ed, Macromolecules, 67- *Mem:* Fel AAAS; Am Chem Soc; fel NY Acad Sci. *Res:* Photochemistry; organic semiconductors; polymer morphology and chemical reactivity; deterioration and stabilization of rubbers and plastics; fluorocarbons. *Mailing Add:* Bell Labs Inc Murray Hill NJ 07974

WINSLOW, GEORGE HARVEY, b Washington, DC, June 21, 16; m 44; c 2. PHYSICS. *Educ:* Carnegie Inst Technol, BS, 38, MS, 39, DSc, 46. *Prof Exp:* Instr physics, Carnegie Inst Technol, 38, res physicist, 43-46; assoc physicist, Argonne Nat Lab, 46-81; RETIRED. *Mem:* Am Phys Soc. *Res:* Magnetic moments by molecular beams; high speed deformation of metals; shaped charges; solid state; attempts to find requantization of space quantized atoms at collision; alpha decay theory high temperature physical chemistry. *Mailing Add:* 4124 W 100th St Oak Lawn IL 60453

WINSLOW, JOHN DURFEE, b Ft Monroe, Va, June 21, 23; m 52. GEOLOGY. *Educ:* Brown Univ, AB, 49; Univ Ill, PhD, 57. *Prof Exp:* Hydrologist, Water Resources Div, US Geol Surv, 50-74; planning officer, NCent Region, US Dept Interior, 74-75; phys scientist, Land Info & Anal, US Geol Surv, 75-80; CONSULT, GROUND WATER HYDROL, 80- *Concurrent Pos:* Eng geologist, State Geol Surv, Ind, 58-59; assoc prof, Univ Kans, 63-71; co-dir course on ground water, UNESCO, Buenos Aires, Arg, 65, course on appl geol, Medellin, Colombia, 66; int prof ground water, Pan-Am Health Orgn, Santiago, Chile, 66; mem adv panel hydrol, Arg Pampa, Nat Acad Sci, 70-71. *Honors & Awards:* Antarctic Serv Medal, Us Antarctic Res Prog, US Dept Interior, 69. *Mem:* Geol Soc Am; Am Geophys Union. *Res:* Hydrology; ground water and engineering geology. *Mailing Add:* US Geol Surv Nat Ctr MS-704 Reston VA 22091

WINSLOW, LEON E, b Centralia, Ill, Nov 17, 34; m 59; c 6. MATHEMATICAL ANALYSIS. *Educ:* Marquette Univ, BS, 56, MS, 60; Duke Univ, PhD(math), 65. *Prof Exp:* Asst physics, Marquette Univ, 56-57, Comput Ctr, 58-59; prin physicist, Battelle Mem Inst, 57-58; instr math, Rockhurst Col, 59-60; asst, Duke Univ, 60-64, res assoc spec projs numerical anal, 64-65; asst prof math, Rockhurst Col, 65-66; asst prof comput sci, Univ Notre Dame, 66-72; assoc prof comput sci, Wright State Univ, 72-81; PROF COMPUT SCI, UNIV DAYTON, 81- *Mem:* Math Asn Am; Am Math Soc; Asn Comput Mach. *Res:* Systems analysis. *Mailing Add:* Dept of Comput Sci Wright State Univ Dayton OH 45431

WINSLOW, RICHARD EDWARD, mathematics, see previous edition

WINSOR, FREDERICK JAMES, b Ilion, NY, Aug 22, 21; m 42; c 5. METALLURGY. *Educ:* Rensselaer Polytech Inst, BMetE, 42, MMetE, 44, PhD(metall), 46. *Prof Exp:* Asst, Rensselaer Polytech Inst, 42-46; res metallurgist, Armour Res Found, 46-48; supvr welding res, Standard Oil Co, Ind, 48-51; res engr, E I du Pont de Nemours & Co, 51-59; mgr welding lab, 59-69, DIR, WELDING DEVELOP LAB, FOSTER WHEELER CORP, 69- *Mem:* Am Soc Metals; Am Welding Soc. *Res:* Welding and metallurgical research and development; manufacturing and fabrication engineering. *Mailing Add:* Foster Wheeler Energy Corp 110 S Orange Ave Livingston NJ 07039

WINSOR, LAURISTON P(EARCE), b Johnston, RI, Dec 30, 14; m 42; c 3. ELECTRICAL ENGINEERING. *Educ:* Brown Univ, ScB, 36; Harvard Univ, MS, 37, ScD(elec eng), 46. *Prof Exp:* Asst elec eng, Grad Sch Eng, Harvard Univ, 38-40; instr, Case Inst Technol, 40-46; from asst prof to assoc prof, 46-53, PROF ELEC ENG, RENSSELAER POLYTECH INST, 53-, DIR SPEC PROJS, OFF CONTINUING STUDIES, 76- *Mem:* Am Soc Eng Educ; Inst Elec & Electronics Engrs. *Res:* Electromechanical energy conversion and control; arc reignition. *Mailing Add:* Dept of Elec & Systs Eng Rensselaer Polytech Inst Troy NY 12181

WINSOR, PAUL, IV, b Philadelphia, Pa, Mar 13, 54. DIELECTRIC PHENOMENA, ELECTROCHEMISTRY. *Educ:* Bowdoin Col, BA, 76; Brown Univ, PhD(chem), 81. *Prof Exp:* RES ASSOC, CHEM DEPT, BROWN UNIV, 81- *Mem:* Am Chem Soc; AAAS; Sigma Xi. *Res:* Experimental investigation of electrical response characteristics (dielectric behavior) of liquids, including electrolyte solutions and polymer solutions. *Mailing Add:* Box H Chem Dept Brown Univ Providence RI 02912

WINSTEAD, JACK ALAN, b Dixon, Ky, June 13, 32; m 56; c 3. TOXICOLOGY, BIOCHEMISTRY. *Educ:* Univ Ky, BS, 54; Okla State Univ, MS, 59; Univ Ill, PhD(chem), 64. Educ: Res officer chem, Mat Lab, US Air Force, Wright-Patterson AFB, Ohio, 54-57, asst prof, Air Force Acad, 59-62, res biochemist, Sch Aerospace Med, 64-68, res chemist, Frank J Seiler Res Lab, US Air Force Acad, 68-70, dir, Directorate Chem Sci, 70-72, dep dir, Toxic Hazards Div, Aerospace Med Res Lab, Wright-Patterson AFB, 72-75; prof assoc, Nat Acad Sci, 75-78; DIR TOXICOL REV, COSMETIC, TOILETRY & FRAGRANCE ASN, 78- *Prof Exp:* Res officer chem, Mat Lab, US Air Force Acad, 59-62, res chemist, Sch Aerospace Med, 64-68, Frank J Seiler Res Lab, 68-70, dir, Directorate Chem Sci, 70-72, dep dir, Toxic Hazards Div, Aerospace Med Res Lab, Wright-Patterson AFB, 72-75; prof assoc, Nat Acad Sci, 75-78; dir toxicol rev, Cosmetic, Toliletry & Fragrance Asn, 78-80; PRIN SCIENTIST, HEALTH EFFECTS & BIOASSAY DIV, TRACOR JITCO, 80- *Mem:* Soc Toxicol; Am Soc Biol Chemists; AAAS; Radiation Res Soc; Am Chem Soc. *Res:* Structure and function of proteins; radiation biochemistry; organic synthesis and toxicology. *Mailing Add:* Health Effects & Bioassay Div Tracor Jitco 1776 E Jefferson St Rockville MD 20852

WINSTEAD, JANET, b Wichita Falls, Tex, Mar 13, 32. MYCOLOGY. *Educ:* Midwestern Univ, BS, 53; Ohio Univ, MS, 55; Univ Tex, Austin, PhD(bot), 70. *Prof Exp:* Instr biol, Ky Wesleyan Col, 56-57; asst prof, Atlantic Christian Col, 57-65; ASSOC PROF BIOL, JAMES MADISON UNIV, VA, 69- *Mem:* Am Inst Biol Sci; Mycol Soc Am. *Res:* Monospore culture of myxomycetes. *Mailing Add:* Dept Biol James Madison Univ Harrisonburg VA 22807

WINSTEAD, JOE EVERETT, b Wichita Falls, Tex, Mar 17, 38; m 80; c 2. BOTANY, ECOLOGY. *Educ:* Midwestern Univ, BS, 60; Ohio Univ, MS, 62; Univ Tex, Austin, PhD(bot), 68. *Prof Exp:* Instr biol, Delta Col, 62; asst prof, 68-72, assoc prof, 72-78, PROF BIOL, WESTERN KY UNIV, 78- *Mem:* Ecol Soc Am; Bot Soc Am; Sigma Xi. *Res:* Ecotype differentiation of plant species; natural revegetation of stripmines; differentiation of wood cell types and wood anatomy; environmental physiology. *Mailing Add:* Dept of Biol Western Ky Univ Bowling Green KY 42101

WINSTEAD, MELDRUM BARNETT, b Lincolnton, NC, Oct 19, 26; m 59; c 3. ORGANIC CHEMISTRY. *Educ:* Davidson Col, BS, 46; Univ NC, MA, 49, PhD(chem), 52. *Prof Exp:* Instr chem, Davidson Col, 46-47; asst, Univ NC, 47-50; from asst prof to assoc prof, 52-69, PROF CHEM, BUCKNELL UNIV, 69- *Concurrent Pos:* Res grants, DuPont res fel, 51-52, Res Corp, 54-56, AAAS, 59-60 & Petrol Res Fund, 61-62; consult, Glyco Chem, Inc, 58 & Sadtler Res Labs, 59-70; vis chem assoc, Calif Inst Technol, 67-68; USPHS spec res fel, 67-68; res assoc, Lawrence Berkeley Lab, Univ Calif, Berkeley, 68-69; vis scientist, Medi-Physics, Inc, Calif, 72-78 & Israel Resources Corp, Ltd, Haifa, Israel, 81-82; Bucknell fac res fel, 70-71 & 78-79. *Honors & Awards:* USPHS Award, Nat Inst Gen Med Sci, 74 & 77. *Mem:* Sigma Xi; Am Chem Soc; Coblentz Soc. *Res:* Organic medicinals; preparation and scintigraphic study of pharmaceuticals containing short-lived radiocarbon-11. *Mailing Add:* Dept of Chem Bucknell Univ Lewisburg PA 17837

WINSTEAD, NASH NICKS, b Durham, Co, NC, June 12, 25; m 49; c 1. PLANT PATHOLOGY. *Educ:* NC State Col, BS, 48, MS, 51; Univ Wis, PhD(plant path), 53. *Prof Exp:* From asst prof to assoc prof, 53-60, vchancellor, 74-81, PROF PLANT PATH, NC STATE UNIV, 60-, PROVOST, 74-, ACTG CHANCELLOR, 81- *Concurrent Pos:* Dir, Inst Biol Sci & asst dir res, NC Agr Exp Sta, 65-67, asst provost, NC State Univ, 67-73, assoc provost, 73-74; Phillips Found internship acad admin, Ind Univ, 65-66; mem, Comt Planned Res Basic Bio-sci during manned earth-orbiting missions, Am Inst Biol Sci-NASA, 65-67; mem, Bd Dirs, Consortium Cooperating Raleigh Cols, 69-, pres, 71-73; res award, Sigma Xi, 61. *Mem:* AAAS; Am Phytopath Soc; Am Inst Biol Sci; Sigma Xi. *Res:* Vegetable diseases; breeding for resistance; physiology of parasitism. *Mailing Add:* Rm 109 Holladay Hall NC State Univ Raleigh NC 27650

WINSTEN, SEYMOUR, b Jersey City, NJ, June 14, 26; m 49; c 3. BIOCHEMISTRY. *Educ:* Rutgers Univ, AB, 48, PhD(microbiol, physiol), 56; NY Univ, MSc, 50; Am Bd Clin Chem, dipl. *Prof Exp:* Asst, Merck Inst Therapeut Res, 50-56; assoc microbiol, Univ Pa, 56-57; HEAD DEPT CHEM, ALBERT EINSTEIN MED CTR, 57-; DIR LABS, MOSS REHAB HOSP, 75- *Concurrent Pos:* Consult, Atlantic City Hosp, Mass Rehab Hosp, Surgeon Gen US & Walson Gen Hosp; assoc prof biochem, Sch Med, Temple Univ, 70-76; consult, Deborah Heart & Lung Ctr. *Honors & Awards:* John Gunther Reinhold Award, 68. *Mem:* Fel Am Asn Clin Chem. *Res:* Clinical chemistry; immunochemistry; chemical diagnosis of disease; mycology; endocrine chemistry and its relationship to various disease processes. *Mailing Add:* Div of Lab Albert Einstein Med Ctr Philadelphia PA 19141

WINSTON, ANTHONY, b Washington, DC, Dec 5, 25; m 52; c 4. POLYMER CHEMISTRY. *Educ:* George Washington Univ, BS, 50; Duke Univ, MA, 52, PhD, 55. *Prof Exp:* Res chemist, Armstrong Cork Co, 54-59; from asst prof to assoc prof, 59-75, PROF CHEM, WVA UNIV, 75- *Concurrent Pos:* Res assoc, Water Res Inst, WVa Univ, 75- *Mem:* AAAS; Am Chem Soc. *Res:* Polymer synthesis and reactions; metal complexing polymers; selective chelating ion exchange resins; stereochemistry; hemiacetal equilibria; wood plastic combinations. *Mailing Add:* Dept of Chem WVa Univ Morgantown WV 26506

WINSTON, ARTHUR WILLIAM, b Toronto, Ont, Feb 11, 30; US citizen; m 49; c 4. PHYSICS, MATHEMATICS. *Educ:* Univ Toronto, BASc, 51; Mass Inst Technol, PhD(physics), 54. *Prof Exp:* Eng physicist, Nat Res Coun Can, 49-51; res asst, Mass Inst Technol, 51-54; sr engr, Schlumberger Well Surv Corp, 54-57; sr engr, Nat Res Corp, 57-59; chief scientist, Allied Res Assocs, Inc, 59-61; pres, Space Sci, Inc, 61-65; pres, 65-75, chmn, Ikor, Inc, 75-79; PRES, WINCOM CORP, 79- *Concurrent Pos:* Lectr, Northeastern Univ, 57-65, adj prof, 65-; mem Int Dept Com First Trade Mission to Europe on Pollution Controls; judge Mass State Sci Fair. *Mem:* Am Inst Aeronaut & Astronaut; Inst Elec & Electronics Engrs; Am Geophys Union; Am Phys Soc; Am Inst Mining, Metall & Petrol Engrs. *Res:* Electromagnetic propagation and measurements; nuclear physics applied to geophysics; thin film technology; microprocessors; pollution control devices and systems. *Mailing Add:* Wincom Corp 23 Shepard St Lawrence MA 01842

WINSTON, DONALD, b Washington, DC, Apr 4, 31. GEOLOGY. *Educ:* Williams Col, BA, 53; Univ Tex, MA, 57, PhD(geol), 63. *Prof Exp:* From instr to asst prof, 61-70, ASSOC PROF GEOL, UNIV MONT, 70- *Mem:* AAAS; Soc Econ Paleont Mineral. *Res:* Sedimentary petrology, particularly carbonate petrology of Pennsylvanian rocks and modern carbonate areas; stratigraphy and sedimentation, particularly Precambrian rocks; Cambrian paleontology. *Mailing Add:* Dept of Geol Univ of Mont Missoula MT 59812

WINSTON, HARVEY, b Newark, NJ, Aug 11, 26; m 49; c 2. PHYSICAL CHEMISTRY. *Educ:* Columbia Univ, AB, 45, MA, 46, PhD(chem), 49. *Prof Exp:* Asst chem, Columbia Univ, 45-49; Jewett fel, Univ Calif, 49-50, instr chem, 50-51; asst prof, Univ Calif, Los Angeles, 51-52; mem tech staff, Hughes Aircraft Co, 52-58, mgr mat res lab, Semiconductor Div, 58-60; assoc dir quantum electronics lab, Quantatron, Inc, 61, vpres, Quantum Tech Labs, Inc, 61-63; mgr, 63-69, SR SCIENTIST, CHEM PHYSICS DEPT, HUGHES RES LABS, 69- *Mem:* Fel Am Phys Soc; sr mem Inst Elec & Electronics Engrs. *Res:* Solid state spectroscopy; lasers and laser systems; semiconductor physics and devices. *Mailing Add:* 3011 Malibu Canyon Rd Malibu CA 90265

WINSTON, JAMES J, b New York, NY, Mar 17, 15; m 40; c 2. FOOD CHEMISTRY. *Educ:* City Col New York, BS, 36. *Prof Exp:* Chemist, Jacobs Cereal Labs, Inc, 36-38, chief chemist, 39-49; dir food labs, Jacobs-Winston Labs, Inc, 50-70, PRES, WINSTON LABS INC, 70- *Concurrent Pos:* Dir res, Nat Macaroni Mfrs Asn, 50; lectr, City Col New York, 60. *Mem:* AAAS; Am Asn Cereal Chemists; fel Am Inst Chemists; Inst Food Technologists; NY Acad Sci. *Res:* Food chemistry, enrichment, sanitation, macaroni, egg noodles, lecithin and cereals; new product development; meat and fish technology. *Mailing Add:* PO Box 361 25 Mt Vernon St Ridgefield Park NJ 07660

WINSTON, JOHN S(TANTON), b Denver, Colo, Feb 16, 16; m 42; c 3. PHYSICAL METALLURGY. *Educ:* Cornell Col, AB, 37; Univ Chicago, MA, 39; Univ Mo, MSc, 50. *Prof Exp:* Instr metall, Ill Inst Technol, 41-42; instr math, Valparaiso Univ, 46; asst prof physics, Morningside Col, 46-48; instr metall, Mo Sch Mines, 49-51; physicist, US Bur Mines, 51-52; from asst prof to prof metall, Mackay Sch Mines, Univ Nev, Reno, 52-64, chmn depts mining & metall, 58-64; prof, Maden Faculties, Tech Univ Istanbul, 64-66; prof, 66-78, EMER PROF METALL, MACKAY SCH MINES, UNIV NEV, RENO, 78- *Concurrent Pos:* Res metallurgist, US Bur Mines, 55-61 & 66-78. *Mem:* Am Soc Metals. *Res:* High purity refractory metals; refractory metal alloys; effects of interstitial metal additions; powder metallurgy; x-ray metallography. *Mailing Add:* RR 1 Maquon IL 61458

WINSTON, JOSEPH, b Newark, NJ, Mar 8, 21; m 46; c 2. ELECTRICAL ENGINEERING. *Educ:* Newark Col Eng, BS, 43; Harvard Univ & Mass Inst Technol, dipl, 43; Stevens Inst Technol, MS, 49. *Prof Exp:* Motor design engr, Crocker-Wheeler Div, Joshua Hendy Corp, NJ, 46-49 & Star-Kimble Motor Div, Miehle Printing Press Co, 49-52; proj engr, Fairchild Camera & Instrument Corp, NY, 52-54; motor design group leader, Airborne Accessories Corp, NJ, 54; ASSOC PROF ELEC ENG, NJ INST TECHNOL, 55- *Concurrent Pos:* Motor design consult, Airborne Accessories Corp, 54-57, Walter Kidde Corp, 57-58, Bendix Aviation Corp, 58-59 & McLean Eng Labs, 64-; chief engr, Instrument Components of NJ, Inc, 59-62; consult, elec motors & electromagnetic devices, Nash Controls Div, Simmonds Precision, radar & antenna drive motor probs, Lockheed Electronics Corp & electromagnetic servovalve actuators, Marotta Sci Controls; motor design consult, SDD Magnetics, Albuquerque, 76- *Mem:* Sr mem Inst Elec & Electronics Engrs; Am Soc Eng Educ. *Res:* Electric machine design and accelerated testing of electric power connectors; basic transducers; electric power distribution; electric machinery. *Mailing Add:* NJ Inst of Technol 323 High St Newark NJ 02138

WINSTON, PAUL WOLF, b Chicago, Ill, Aug 9, 20; m 48; c 1. BIOLOGY. *Educ:* Univ Mass, BS, 48; Northwestern Univ, MS, 50, PhD, 52. *Prof Exp:* Instr, Brown Univ, 51-52; from instr to assoc prof, 52-68, PROF BIOL, UNIV COLO, BOULDER, 68- *Mem:* AAAS; Soc Environ Geochem & Health; Am Soc Zoologists; Soc Exp Biol; Am Physiol Soc. *Res:* Humidity relations and water balance of terrestrial arthropods, especially cuticular control of water exchange with air; physiology of molybdenum and toxicity of chronic exposure to trace metals in mammals. *Mailing Add:* Dept of EPO Biol Univ of Colo Boulder CO 80302

WINSTON, ROLAND, b Moscow, USSR, Feb 12, 36; US citizen; m 57; c 3. EXPERIMENTAL PHYSICS, PARTICLE PHYSICS. *Educ:* Shimer Col, BA, 53; Univ Chicago, BS, 56, MS, 57, PhD(physics), 63. *Prof Exp:* Asst prof physics, Univ Pa, 63-64; from asst prof to assoc prof, 64-75, PROF PHYSICS, UNIV CHICAGO, 75- *Concurrent Pos:* Sloan Found fel, 67-69; Guggenheim fel, 77-78. *Mem:* Fel Am Phys Soc. *Res:* Elementary particle physics; leptonic decays of hyperons; muon physics, especially hyperfine effects in muon capture by complex nuclei; solar energy concentrators; infra-red detectors; optics of visual receptors. *Mailing Add:* Dept of Physics Univ of Chicago Chicago IL 60637

WINSTON, VERN, b Gordon, Nebr, Apr 30, 48; m 70; c 2. VIROLOGY, CELL CULTURE. *Educ:* Univ Nebr-Lincoln, BS, 70, PhD(microbiol), 76. *Prof Exp:* Res assoc, Kans State Univ, 76-80; ASST PROF MICROBIOL, IDAHO STATE UNIV, 81- *Mem:* Am Soc Microbiol; Sigma Xi. *Res:* Viral diseases of fish; immunodiagnostic methods of indentifying infectious pancreatic necrosis virus; genetics of the bacterium sphaerotilus natans and its bacteriophages. *Mailing Add:* Dept Microbiol & Biochem Idaho State Univ Box 8094 Pocatello ID 83209

WINSTROM, LEON OSCAR, b Holland, Mich, Apr 8, 12; m 38; c 3. PHYSICAL CHEMISTRY, TEXTILE CHEMISTRY. *Educ:* Hope Col, AB, 34; Carnegie Inst Technol, MS, 37, DSc(phys chem), 38. *Prof Exp:* Instr, Carnegie Inst Technol, 37-38; res chemist, Nat Aniline Chem Div, Allied Chem Corp, 38-53, asst supvr, 53-57, sr scientist, 57-58, group leader, 58-64, res supvr, 64-68, sr res assoc, Spec Chem Div, 68-71; mgr res & develop, Flock Div, Malden Mills, Lawrence, 71-80. *Honors & Awards:* Schoellkopf Medal, 66. *Mem:* Am Chem Soc; ammination by reduction; recovery of organic oxidation products. *Res:* Vapor and liquid phase hydrogenation and oxidation; ammination by reduction; recovery of organic oxidation products. *Mailing Add:* 57 Maple St East Aurora NY 14052

WINTER, ALEXANDER J, b Vienna, Austria, June 21, 31; nat US; m 59; c 3. IMMUNOBIOLOGY. *Educ:* Univ Ill, DVM, 55; Univ Wis, PhD(med & vet path), 59. *Prof Exp:* From asst to assoc prof vet sci, Pa State Univ, 59-63; assoc prof, 63-66, PROF VET MICROBIOL, NY STATE VET COL, CORNELL UNIV, 66- *Concurrent Pos:* Mem, Bacteriol & Mycol Sect, NIH, 71-75. *Mem:* Conf Res Workers Animal Dis; Am Soc Microbiol; AAAS. *Res:* Microbial and immunologic factors affecting animal reproduction; bacterial virulence mechanisms. *Mailing Add:* NY State Col of Vet Med Cornell Univ Ithaca NY 14853

WINTER, CHARLES ERNEST, b Colorado Springs, Colo, Sept 9, 14; m 37; c 2. MICROBIOLOGY. *Educ:* Colo Col, BA, 36, MA, 38; Univ Md, MS, 45, PhD(bact), 47. *Prof Exp:* Instr biol, China Training Inst, Kiangsu, China, 39-42, prof biol sci, 47-50; prof, Southern Jr Col, 42-43; asst prof, Washington Missionary Col, 43-45; bacteriologist, US Fish & Wildlife Serv, 45-47; from asst prof to assoc prof, 50-61, PROF MICROBIOL, LOMA LINDA UNIV, 61- *Concurrent Pos:* Mem, Am Asn Dent Schs. *Mem:* AAAS; Am Soc Microbiol; Am Pub Health Asn; Asn Am Med Cols. *Res:* Medical microbiology; immunology. *Mailing Add:* Dept of Microbiol Loma Linda Univ Loma Linda CA 92354

WINTER, CHARLES GORDON, b Hanover, Pa, Dec 28, 36; m 58; c 3. BIOCHEMISTRY, MEMBRANES. *Educ:* Juniata Col, BS, 58; Univ Mich, MS, 63, PhD(biochem), 64. *Prof Exp:* Technician, Metab Res Unit, Univ Mich, Ann Arbor, 58-60; Childs Mem Fund Med Res fel phys chem, Sch Med, Johns Hopkins Univ, 64-66; asst prof, 66-73, ASSOC PROF BIOCHEM, SCH MED, UNIV ARK, LITTLE ROCK, 73- *Concurrent Pos:* Hon res assoc, Harvard Univ, 78-79. *Mem:* Am Soc Biol Chemists; AAAS; Am Chem Soc; Biophys Soc. *Res:* Structure and function of alkali-cation-dependent adenosinetriphosphatase. *Mailing Add:* Dept Biochem Univ Ark Med Sci Little Rock AR 72201

WINTER, CHESTER CALDWELL, b Cazenovia, NY, June 2, 22; m 45; c 3. MEDICINE. *Educ:* Univ Iowa, BA, 43, MD, 46; Am Bd Urol, dipl. *Prof Exp:* Asst prof surg, Sch Med, Univ Calif, Los Angeles, 58-61; PROF UROL, COL MED, OHIO STATE UNIV, 61- *Concurrent Pos:* Mem staff, Univ Hosp, 61- & Children's Hosp, 61- *Mem:* Am Urol Asn; Am Col Surg; Soc Univ Urol; Soc Univ Surg; Am Asn Genito-Urinary Surg. *Res:* Urological surgery; renal hypertension; diagnostic isotopes in urology. *Mailing Add:* Div of Urol 456 Clinic Dr Columbus OH 43210

WINTER, DAVID ARTHUR, b Windsor, Ont, June 16, 30; m 58; c 3. BIOMEDICAL ENGINEERING, ELECTRICAL ENGINEERING. *Educ:* Queen's Univ, Ont, BSc, 53, MSc, 61; Dalhousie Univ, PhD(physiol), 67. *Prof Exp:* From lectr to asst prof elec eng, Royal Mil Col, Ont, 58-63; from asst prof to assoc prof, NS Tech Col, 63-69; assoc prof surg, Univ Man, 69-74, adj prof elec eng, 70-74; assoc prof kinesiology, 74-76, PROF KINESIOLOGY, UNIV WATERLOO, 76- *Concurrent Pos:* Can Coun fel med, eng & sci, Dalhousie Univ, 66-68. *Mem:* Inst Elec & Electronics Eng; Can Med & Biol Eng Soc (pres, 70-74); Int Soc Electrophys Kinesiol; Int Soc Biomech; Can Soc Biomech. *Res:* Signal processing of biological signals; medical image processing; electromyography; biomechanics; locomotion studies; assessment pathological gait. *Mailing Add:* Dept of Kinesiology Univ of Waterloo Waterloo ON N2L 3G1 Can

WINTER, DAVID F(ERDINAND), b St Louis, Mo, Nov 9, 20; m 44; c 2. ELECTRICAL ENGINEERING. *Educ:* Wash Univ, BS, 42; Mass Inst Technol, MS, 48. *Prof Exp:* Mem staff, Radiation Lab, Mass Inst Technol, 42-45, res assoc elec eng, Wash Univ, 48-51, assoc prof, 51-54, prof, 55; sr engr, Spec Contract, US Naval Ord Plant, Ind, 50-52, proj head, 52-53; consult, Moloney Elec Co, 51-54, sect engr electronics, 54-57, vpres, chief engr & dir res, 55-66, vpres res & develop, 66-73, vpres eng, 73-74; V PRES RES & DEVELOP, ITT BLACKBURN, 74- *Concurrent Pos:* Affil prof, Wash Univ, 55- *Mem:* Fel Inst Elec & Electronics Engrs; Nat Soc Prof Engrs. *Res:* High voltage magnetic components for power industry; specialized high power radar and communications; electrical connectors for power industry. *Mailing Add:* ITT Blackburn 1525 Woodson Rd St Louis MO 63114

WINTER, DAVID JOHN, b Painesville, Ohio, May 2, 39; m 65; c 1. MATHEMATICS. *Educ:* Antioch Col, BA, 61; Yale Univ, MS, 63, PhD(math), 65. *Prof Exp:* Instr math, Yale Univ, 65-67; NSF fel, Univ Bonn, 67-68; from asst prof to assoc prof, 68-74, PROF MATH, UNIV MICH, ANN ARBOR, 74- *Concurrent Pos:* Vis assoc prof, Calif Inst Technol, 72-73. *Mem:* Am Math Soc. *Res:* Algebra. *Mailing Add:* Dept of Math 4200 Angell Hall Univ of Mich Ann Arbor MI 48104

WINTER, DAVID LEON, b New York, NY, Nov 10, 33; m 73; c 5. RESEARCH ADMINISTRATION. *Educ:* Columbia Col, AB, 55; Wash Univ, MD, 59. *Prof Exp:* Surg intern, Sch Med, Wash Univ, 59-60; Nat Inst Neurol Dis & Blindness fel, Baylor Univ, 60-62; med res officer, Nat Inst Neurol Dis & Blindness, 62-64; neurophysiologist, Walter Reed Army Inst Res, 64-66, chief dept neurophysiol, 66-71; dep dir life sci, Ames Res Ctr, Moffett Field, Calif, 71-74, dir life sci, NASA HQ, DC, 74-79; DIR MED RES, DANDOZ, INC, 79- *Honors & Awards:* Hans Berger Prize, Am Electroencephalog Soc, 64. *Mem:* AAAS; Am Physiol Soc; Soc Neurosci; Aerospace Med Asn; Am Soc Clin Pharmacol & Therapeut. *Res:* Somatosensory systems; visceral reflexes; autonomic nervous system; psychophysiology; aerospace physiology. *Mailing Add:* Med Res Sandoz Inc East Hanover NJ 07936

WINTER, DONALD CHARLES, b Brooklyn, NY, June 15, 48; m 69; c 2. OPTICS. *Educ:* Univ Rochester, BS, 69; Univ Mich, MS, 70, PhD(physics), 72. *Prof Exp:* Mem res staff optics, 72-74, sect ha head optics technol, 74-77, MGR OPTICS DEPT, TRW DEFENSE & SPACE SYSTS GROUP, 77- *Mem:* Optical Soc Am. *Res:* High energy laser optics; optical components; laser diagnostics; interferometry and optical testing; optical system design and optimization. *Mailing Add:* Bldg 01 Rm 1260 One Space Park Redondo Beach CA 90278

WINTER, DONALD F, b Buffalo, NY, Oct 6, 31; m 57; c 3. APPLIED MATHEMATICS. *Educ:* Amherst Col, BA, 54; Harvard Univ, MA, 59, PhD(appl physics), 62. *Prof Exp:* Mathematician, Air Force Cambridge Res Labs, 54-56; engr, Missile Systs Lab, Sylvania Elec Prod, Inc, 56-58, eng specialist, Appl Res Lab, 58-62, sr eng specialist, 62-63; mem staff, Geo-astrophys Lab, Boeing Sci Res Labs, 63-70; assoc prof, Ctr Quantitative Sci & Dept Oceanog, 70-74, PROF OCEANOG & APPL MATH, UNIV WASH, 74- *Concurrent Pos:* Vis lectr, Univ Manchester, 66-67. *Res:* Applied analysis; methods of mathematical physics with applications to solar system astronomy; hydrodynamical and biological processes in oceanography; growth and transport processes in biological systems. *Mailing Add:* Dept of Oceanog Univ of Wash Seattle WA 98195

WINTER, GEORGE, b Vienna, Austria, Apr 1, 07; m 31; c 1. STRUCTURAL ENGINEERING. *Educ:* Munich Tech Univ, Dipl Ing, 30; Cornell Univ, PhD(struct eng), 40. *Hon Degrees:* Dr Ing Eh, Munich Tech Univ, 69. *Prof Exp:* Designer struct eng, Rella & Neffe, Vienna, 30-32; foreign tech consult, USSR var orgn, 32-38; res investr, 38-40, from asst prof to prof struct eng, 40-75, dept chmn, 48-70, CLASS 1912 EMER PROF STRUCT ENG, CORNELL UNIV, 75- *Concurrent Pos:* Consult, Am Iron & Steel Inst, 50-;

vis prof, Calif Inst Technol, 50 & Univ Calif, Berkeley, 69; Guggenheim fel, 56-57; vis scientist, Cambridge Univ, 56; vis lectr, Univ Liege, 57; chmn, Struct Stability Res Coun, 74-78. *Honors & Awards:* Moisseif Award, Am Soc Civil Engrs, 48, Croes Medal, 61; Wason, Turner & Howard Medals, Am Concrete Inst, 65, 72 & 81; Tech Meeting Award, Am Iron & Steel Inst, 50. *Mem:* Nat Acad Eng; Am Acad Arts & Sci; hon mem Am Soc Civil Engrs; hon mem Am Concrete Inst. *Res:* Structural mechanics; structural stability; strength and performance of cold-formed thin-walled steel structures; strength and performance of reinforced concrete structures. *Mailing Add:* Sch of Civil & Environ Eng Cornell Univ Ithaca NY 14853

WINTER, HARRY CLARK, b New Britain, Conn, Feb 26, 41; m 77. BIOCHEMISTRY. *Educ:* Pa State Univ, BS, 62; Univ Wis, MS, 64, PhD(biochem), 67. *Prof Exp:* NSF fel cell physiol, Univ Calif, Berkeley, 67-68; asst prof biochem, Pa State Univ, 68-75; LECTR BIOL CHEM, UNIV MICH, ANN ARBOR, 75- *Mem:* Am Chem Soc; Am Soc Plant Physiologists; Am Peanut Res & Educ Soc. *Res:* Biological nitrogen fixation; photosynthesis; biosynthetic pathways of plants and bacteria; enzyme mechanisms. *Mailing Add:* Dept Biol Chem Box 034 Univ Mich Ann Arbor MI 48109

WINTER, HENRY FRANK, JR, b Wooster, Ohio, Dec 25, 36. PHYSIOLOGY. *Educ:* Case Inst Technol, BSc, 58; Baylor Univ, MSc, 62, PhD(physiol, biochem, anat), 65. *Prof Exp:* Asst prof, 65-72, assoc prof physiol, 73-80, PROF PHYSIOL & BIOMED SCI, SCH DENT MED, WASH UNIV, 80- *Mem:* AAAS; Am Physiol Soc; Int Asn Dent Res. *Res:* Oral biology, neurophysiology; instrumentation for medical research; growth and development. *Mailing Add:* Dept of Physiol Wash Univ Sch Dent Med St Louis MO 63110

WINTER, HERBERT, b Vienna, Austria, July 31, 24; US citizen; m 46; c 2. CONTROL & ELECTRICAL ENGINEERING. *Educ:* City Col New York, BEE, 49; Univ Mich, MSE, 50. *Prof Exp:* Instr elec eng, City Col New York, 49; engr, 50-54, syst engr, 54-57, group chief systs oper & preliminary design, 57-59, dynamic anal hypersonic glider, 59-60, supvr preliminary design electromech systs, 60-65, PRIN SCIENTIST, BELL AEROSPACE TEXTRON, 66- *Mem:* Inst Elec & Electronics Engrs; Am Inst Navig. *Res:* Application of optimal control and filtering to inertial navigation; optimization of oceanic air traffic; computer simulation of atmospheric propagation of laser beams. *Mailing Add:* High Energy Laser Technol PO Box 1 Zone B49 Buffalo NY 14240

WINTER, IRWIN CLINTON, b Clinton, Okla, July 17, 10; m 38; c 4. PHARMACOLOGY. *Educ:* Allegheny Col, BS, 31; Northwestern Univ, MS, 33, PhD, 34; Univ Tenn, MD, 41. *Prof Exp:* Asst physiol chem, Med Sch, Northwestern Univ, 31-34, fel, 34-35; physiologist, Res Dept, Parke, Davis & Co, Mich, 35-36; instr physiol & pharmacol, Col Med, Baylor Univ, 36-39; assoc prof pharmacol, Sch Med, Univ Okla, 39-42; dir clin res, 46-75, med dir, 59-75, vpres med affairs, 62-75, CONSULT, G D SEARLE & CO, 75- *Concurrent Pos:* Mem coun arteriosclerosis, Am Heart Asn; consult, PMA Found, 75- *Mem:* Soc Exp Biol & Med; Am Soc Pharmacol & Exp Therapeut; AMA; Am Rheumatism Asn; Am Fedn Clin Res. *Res:* Liver damage and fat metabolism; physiology and pharmacology of micturition; autonomic pharmacology. *Mailing Add:* G D Searle & Co 4711 Golf Rd PO Box 1045 Skokie IL 60076

WINTER, JEANETTE, b New York, NY, Dec 19, 17. MICROBIOLOGY. *Educ:* Brooklyn Col, BA, 37; NY Univ, PhD(microbiol), 60. *Prof Exp:* Instr, 64-68, asst prof, 68-71, ASSOC PROF MICROBIOL, MED SCH, NY UNIV, 71- *Mem:* AAAS; Am Soc Microbiol. *Res:* Mechanism of competence for DNA uptake in bacterial transformation; role of nucleases in DNA integration during bacterial transformation of streptococci. *Mailing Add:* Dept of Microbiol NYU Med Sch 550 First Ave New York NY 10016

WINTER, JEREMY STEPHEN DRUMMOND, b Duncan, BC, Dec 11, 37; m 61; c 2. PEDIATRICS, ENDOCRINE PHYSIOLOGY. *Educ:* Univ BC, MD, 61; Am Bd Pediat, dipl, 67; FRCP(C), 68. *Prof Exp:* Intern & resident, Montreal Gen, Montreal Children's & Royal Victoria Hosp, 61-64; instr pediat, Univ Pa, 64-67; from asst prof to assoc prof, 67-78, PROF PEDIAT, UNIV MAN, 78- ENDOCRINOLOGIST, HEALTH SCI CTR, WINNIPEG, 71- *Concurrent Pos:* NIH fel endocrinol, Children's Hosp Philadelphia, 64-67; Med Res Coun grant, Univ Man, 67-; consult, St Boniface Hosp, 67-; scientist, Queen Elizabeth II Res Found, 72. *Mem:* Endocrine Soc; Soc Pediat Res; Can Soc Clin Invest; Am Fedn Clin Res; Can Pediat Soc. *Res:* Physiology of the pituitary-gonadal axis during fetal life, childhood and puberty. *Mailing Add:* Health Sci Ctr 678 William Ave Winnipeg MB R3E 0W1 Can

WINTER, JERROLD CLYNE, SR, b Erie, Pa, March 25, 37; m 60; c 4. PHARMACOLOGY. *Educ:* Univ Rochester, BS, 59; State Univ NY, PhD(pharmacol), 66. *Prof Exp:* Asst prof, 67-71, assoc prof, 71-76, PROF PHARMACOL, STATE UNIV NY, BUFFALO, 76- *Res:* Behavioral pharmacology. *Mailing Add:* 127 Farber Hall State Univ NY Buffalo NY 14214

WINTER, JOHN JAMES, b New York, NY, Nov 11, 40; m 68; c 3. PHYSICS. *Educ:* City Col New York, BS, 64; Fairleigh Dickinson Univ, MS, 69. *Prof Exp:* MEM PHYS SCI STAFF, ELEC TECH & DEVICES LAB, ELECTRONICS RES & DEVELOP COMMAND, US ARMY, 64- *Res:* Cryogenics and superconductivity; magnet materials semiconductor; semiconductors; rave earth-co magnets; computers. *Mailing Add:* Elec Tech & Devices Lab US Army Ft Monmouth NJ 07703

WINTER, JOSEPH, b New York, NY, July 26, 29; m; c 2. PHYSICAL METALLURGY. *Educ:* NY Univ, BME, 53, MS, 55, EngScD, 58. *Prof Exp:* Assoc res scientist metall, Res Div, NY Univ, 52-60; ASSOC DIR METALL DEPT, METALS RES LABS, OLIN CORP, 60- *Concurrent Pos:* Adj instr, Cooper Union, 56-61; adj assoc prof, New Haven Col, 62-70. *Honors & Awards:* John M Olin Award. *Mem:* Am Soc Metals; Am Inst Mining, Metall & Petrol Engrs; Brit Inst Metals. *Res:* Solid state bonding; nonferrous physical metallurgy. *Mailing Add:* Metals Res Labs 91 Shelton Ave New Haven CT 06504

WINTER, JOSEPH WOLFGANG, b Vienna, Austria, Oct 27, 15; nat US; m 41; c 2. CLINICAL MICROBIOLOGY. *Educ:* Univ Calif, BA, 47; Stanford Univ, MA, 49, PhD(bact), 50. *Prof Exp:* Asst, Stanford Univ, 48-50; bacteriologist, Virus Lab, State Dept Pub Health, Calif, 50-51 & Vet Admin Hosp, Oakland, Calif, 51-53; fel, New York Pub Health Res Inst, 54-56; MICROBIOLOGIST, BETH ISRAEL MED CTR, 56- *Concurrent Pos:* Lectr, Hunter Col, 57-65; asst prof, Mt Sinai Sch Med, 68- *Mem:* Am Soc Microbiol; Am Pub Health Asn; NY Acad Sci. *Res:* Clinical microbiology; virology; enteric bacteriology. *Mailing Add:* Beth Israel Med Ctr 10 Nathan D Perlman Pl New York NY 10003

WINTER, KARL A, b Yarmouth, NS, Dec 18, 28; m 57; c 3. RUMINANT NUTRITION. *Educ:* McGill Univ, BSc, 53, MSc, 56; Ohio State Univ, PhD(ruminant nutrit), 62. *Prof Exp:* Grain salesman, Toronto Elevators Ltd, 55-57; res officer ruminant nutrit, Agr Can, 57-65; field res mgr, Tuco Prod Co, Upjohn Co, 65-68; RES SCIENTIST CATTLE NUTRIT, AGR CAN, 68- *Mem:* Can Soc Animal Sci (pres, 81-82); Agr Inst Can (vpres, 76-77 & 80-81); Am Soc Animal Sci. *Res:* Nutrition of ruminant animals, especially the young calf; utilization of non-protein nitrogen and agricultural wastes in cattle feeding and trace elements in ruminant nutrition. *Mailing Add:* Res Sta Agr Can PO Box 1210 Charlottetown PE C1A 7M8 Can

WINTER, MARGARET CASTLE, b Providence, RI, Oct 26, 35; m 64; c 3. ORGANIC CHEMISTRY, ENVIRONMENTAL CHEMISTRY. *Educ:* Oberlin Col, AB, 57; Johns Hopkins Univ, MA, 59, PhD(org chem), 63. *Prof Exp:* Fel steroid biochem, Clark Univ & Worcester Found Exp Biol, 62-64; res assoc environ chem, Ctr Biol Natural Systs, Washington Univ & Univ Mo-St Louis, 73-75; ENVIRON CHEMIST POLLUTION ANAL, ENVIRODYNE ENGRS, 77- *Concurrent Pos:* Adj asst prof, Univ Mo-St Louis, 78. *Mem:* Am Chem Soc. *Res:* Analysis of organic pollutants in industrial and biological samples; gas chromatography-mass spectrometry. *Mailing Add:* Envirodyne Engrs 12161 Lackland Rd St Louis MO 63141

WINTER, NICHOLAS WILHELM, b Birmingham, Ala, Mar 7, 43; m 65; c 2. THEORETICAL CHEMISTRY, THEORETICAL PHYSICS. *Educ:* Northern Ill Univ, BS, 65; Calif Inst Technol, PhD(chem & physics), 70. *Prof Exp:* Atmospheric physicist, Jet Propulsion Lab, 71-73 & Aerospace Corp, 73-76; ATOMIC & MOLECULAR PHYSICIST, LAWRENCE LIVERMORE LAB, 76- *Concurrent Pos:* Fel, Battelle Mem Inst, 69-71; consult, Lawrence Livermore Lab, 71-75; res assoc, Calif Inst Technol, 72-75. *Mem:* Am Phys Soc. *Res:* Molecular structure; potential energy surfaces; excited states; reaction dynamics as applied to atmospheric and laser physics. *Mailing Add:* Lawrence Livermore Lab PO Box 808 Livermore CA 94550

WINTER, OLAF HERMANN, b Erfurt, Ger, Dec 1, 33. CHEMICAL ENGINEERING, CHEMISTRY. *Educ:* Brunswick Tech Univ, BS, 57; Hannover Tech Univ, MS, 60, PhD(chem eng), 63; Univ Akron, MBA, 69. *Prof Exp:* Sr res engr, Res Div, Goodyear Tire & Rubber Co, 63-71; asst to vpres res, Hydrocarbon Res Inc, Trenton Lab, Dynalectron Corp, 72-73; prin engr, 73-80, SR PRIN ENGR, PROCESS TECHNOLOGY PLANNING, THE LUMMUS CO, COMBUSTION ENG, INC, 80- *Concurrent Pos:* Teacher, Berlitz Sch Lang, 65-71. *Mem:* Am Chem Soc; Am Inst Chem Engrs; Ger Chem Soc. *Res:* Novel processing methods and equipment; pollution control; gasification and liquefaction of coal; economic evaluations; process planning; facilities planning for petroleum, petrochemical and chemical complexes; feasibility studies; identification of future technological and economic trends. *Mailing Add:* 380 Mountain Rd Union City NJ 07087

WINTER, PETER MICHAEL, b Sverdlovsk, Russia, Aug 5, 34; US citizen; m 64; c 2. ANESTHESIOLOGY. *Educ:* Cornell Univ, AB, 58; Univ Rochester, MD, 62; Am Bd Anesthesiol, dipl, 72. *Prof Exp:* USPHS res fel, Harvard Univ, 65-66; res assoc physiol, State Univ NY Buffalo, 66-67, asst res prof anesthesiol, 67-69; assoc prof anesthesiol, Sch Med, Univ Wash, 69-74, prof, 74-79; chief anesthesiol serv, Vet Admin Hosp, Seattle, 78-79; PROF ANESTHESIOL & CHMN DEPT, CRITICAL CARE MED, SCH MED, UNIV PITTSBURGH, 79-, ANESTHESIOLOGIST-IN-CHIEF, UNIV HEALTH CTR HOSP, PITTSBURGH, 79- *Concurrent Pos:* Consult, Virginia Mason Res Ctr, Seattle, 69-; Nat Heart & Lung Inst grant, Sch Med, Univ Wash, 71-74, res career develop award, 72-77. *Mem:* Am Col Chest Physicians; AMA; Am Soc Anesthesiol; Asn Univ Anesthetists; NY Acad Sci. *Res:* Respiration therapy; critical care medicine; hyperbaric physiology; oxygen toxicity. *Mailing Add:* Dept Anesthesiol CCM Univ Pittsburgh Sch Med Pittsburgh PA 15261

WINTER, ROBERT JOHN, b Toledo, Ohio, Oct 13, 45; m 72; c 1. PEDIATRIC ENDOCRINOLOGY. *Educ:* Amherst Col, BA, 67; Northwestern Univ, MD, 71. *Prof Exp:* Intern pediat, Hartford Hosp, Conn, 71-72; resident pediat, Boston City Hosp, 72-73; fel pediat endocrinol, Johns Hopkins Univ, 73-75; asst prof, 75-81, ASSOC PROF PEDIAT ENDOCRINOL, CHILDREN'S MEM HOSP & NORTHWESTERN UNIV, CHICAGO, 81- *Mem:* Endocrine Soc; Am Diabetes Asn; Acad Pediat; Am Diabetes Asn; Soc Pediat Res. *Res:* Disorders of growth and of glucose homeostasis; primarily clinical research. *Mailing Add:* Children's Mem Hosp 2300 Children's Plaza Chicago IL 60614

WINTER, ROLAND ARTHUR EDWIN, b Reval, Estonia, Aug 29, 35; US citizen; m 59; c 3. ORGANIC CHEMISTRY, POLYMER CHEMISTRY. *Educ:* Stuttgart Tech Univ, Cand chem, 57; Harvard Univ, AM, 61, PhD(org chem), 65. *Prof Exp:* Res chemist, J R Geigy AG, Basel, Switz, 65-66, res assoc, Geigy Chem Corp, NY, 66-69, group leader, 69-70, Ciba-Geigy Corp, 70-72, sr staff scientist, 72-78, RES MGR, CIBA-GEIGY CORP, 79- *Mem:* Am Chem Soc. *Res:* Synthetic organic chemistry; heterocyclic chemistry; high temperature polymers and plastic additives. *Mailing Add:* 23 Banksville Rd Armonk NY 10504

WINTER, ROLF GERHARD, b Düsseldorf, Ger, June 30, 28; nat US; m 51; c 3. NUCLEAR PHYSICS, ELEMENTARY PARTICLE PHYSICS. *Educ:* Carnegie-Mellon Univ, BS, 48, MS, 51, DSc, 52. *Prof Exp:* Asst physics, Carnegie Inst Technol, 46-51; instr, Western Reserve Univ, 51-52, asst prof, 52-54; from asst prof to assoc prof, Pa State Univ, 54-64; chmn dept, 66-72, PROF PHYSICS, COL WILLIAM & MARY, 64-, DEAN GRAD STUDIES, ARTS & SCI, 81- *Concurrent Pos:* Vis physicist & lectr, Carnegie Inst Technol, 55-56, Oxford Univ, 61-62, Univ Wis, 63, Univ Sask, 76, Swiss Inst Nuclear Res & Univ Zurich, 79-80. *Mem:* Fel Am Phys Soc. *Res:* Beta decay; quantum theory; intermediate energy nuclear physics. *Mailing Add:* Dept of Physics Col of William & Mary Williamsburg VA 23185

WINTER, RUDOLPH ERNST KARL, b Vienna, Austria, Nov 27, 35; US citizen; m 64; c 3. ORGANIC CHEMISTRY. *Educ:* Columbia Univ, AB, 57; Johns Hopkins Univ, MA, 59, PhD(org chem), 64. *Prof Exp:* NIH fel chem, Karlsruhe Tech Univ, 62-63 & Harvard Univ, 63-64; asst prof org chem, Polytech Inst Brooklyn, 64-69; ASSOC PROF ORG CHEM, UNIV MO-ST LOUIS, 69- *Concurrent Pos:* Vis res prof, Swiss Fed Univ, Zurich, 75-76. *Mem:* Am Chem Soc; The Chem Soc. *Res:* Chemistry of naturally occurring substances, especially terpenes and sesquiterpenes; isolation, structure, reactions and synthesis of natural substances; chemical ecology; photochemical and thermal reactions. *Mailing Add:* Dept of Chem Univ of Mo St Louis MO 63121

WINTER, STEPHEN SAMUEL, b Vienna, Austria, Feb 27, 26; US citizen; m 51; c 3. SCIENCE EDUCATION. *Educ:* Albright Col, BS, 48; Columbia Univ, PhD(phys chem), 53. *Prof Exp:* Res chemist, Atlas Powder Co, 52-53; asst prof chem, Northeastern Univ, 53-58; asst prof chem & educ, Univ Minn, 58-61; assoc prof educ, State Univ NY Buffalo, 61-66, prof, 66-71, dir teacher educ, 68-71; chmn dept, 71-78, PROF EDUC, TUFTS UNIV, 71- *Concurrent Pos:* NSF fac fel, Harvard Univ, 57-58, consult, Proj Physics, 64-70; consult & hon assoc prof, Nat Univ Paraguay, 65; consult, Div Sci Teaching, UNESCO, 69-71. *Mem:* Nat Sci Teachers Asn; Nat Asn Res Sci Teaching. *Res:* Measurements of outcomes of science instruction; effectiveness of multi-modal teaching. *Mailing Add:* Dept Educ Tufts Univ Medford MA 02155

WINTER, STEVEN RAY, b Belvidere, Ill, Jan 16, 44; m 70. AGRONOMY, PLANT PHYSIOLOGY. *Educ:* Univ Ill, BS, 66, MS, 68; Purdue Univ, PhD(agron), 71. *Prof Exp:* Asst prof, 71-78, ASSOC PROF CROP PROD, TEX A&M UNIV, 78- *Mem:* Am Soc Agron; Am Soc Sugar Beet Technol. *Res:* Production and physiology of sugar beets on the Texas high plains. *Mailing Add:* 4036 Ricardo Dr Amarillo TX 79109

WINTER, THOMAS C, JR, b East Grand Rapids, Mich, June 19, 34; m 56; c 2. SPACE PHYSICS, OPTICS. *Educ:* US Mil Acad, BS, 56; Univ Calif, Los Angeles, MA, 61, PhD(planetary & space physics), 66; George Washington Univ, MBA, 81. *Prof Exp:* Officer, US Army Corps Engrs, 56-76; mem staff, Coun Environ Qual, Exec Off President, 70-72, mil staff asst to dir, defense res & eng, Off Secy Defense, 73-76; mem fac, Sch Eng & Appl Sci, George Washington Univ, 76-79; CONSULT, VERSAR INC, 79- *Concurrent Pos:* Exec secy, High Energy Laser Review Group, Dept Defense Adv Comt, 73-76. *Honors & Awards:* Skylab Achievement Award, NASA, 74, Solar Sci Exp Team Group Achievement Award, 74. *Mem:* Sigma Xi. *Res:* Hydrogen geocorona; extreme ultraviolet solar spectrum. *Mailing Add:* 5941 Thomas Dr Springfield VA 22150

WINTER, THOMAS GREELEY, b Los Angeles, Calif, Apr 21, 27; m 61; c 4. PHYSICS. *Educ:* Stanford Univ, BS, 49; Cath Univ, MS, 61, PhD(physics), 63. *Prof Exp:* Appl engr, Westinghouse Elec Corp, 49-52; self employed, 52-56; proj engr, US Dept Defense, 56-59; from asst prof to assoc prof physics, Okla State Univ, 63-72; Kistler prof, 72-77, head dept, 75-77, RES ASSOC EARTH SCI, UNIV TULSA, 77-; PRES, TULSA GEOPHYS CO, 77- *Mem:* Acoust Soc Am; Soc Explor Geophysicists. *Res:* Acoustical imaging and propagation in earth materials. *Mailing Add:* Dept of Earth Sci Univ of Tulsa Tulsa OK 74104

WINTER, WILLIAM KENNETH, b Manitowoc, Wis, Apr 26, 26; m 63; c 2. PHYSICS. *Educ:* Univ Wis, BA, 50; Kans State Col, MS, 52, PhD(physics), 56. *Prof Exp:* RES PHYSICIST, PHILLIPS PETROL CO, 56- *Mem:* AAAS; Soc Petrol Eng. *Res:* Develop mathematical models for petroleum reservoir simulation. *Mailing Add:* 2312 Hill Dr Bartlesville OK 74003

WINTER, WILLIAM PHILLIPS, b Uniontown, Pa, Aug 17, 38; m 60; c 2. BIOCHEMISTRY. *Educ:* Pa State Univ, University Park, BS, 60, MS, 62, PhD(biochem), 65. *Prof Exp:* Instr biochem, Pa State Univ, University Park, 63-65; res assoc, Univ Wash, 65-67, actg asst prof, 67-69; res assoc, Med Sch, Univ Mich, Ann Arbor, 69-73, asst res scientist, 73-75, assoc res scientist human genetics, 75-77; SR BIOCHEMIST, CTR SICKLE CELL DIS, ASSOC PROF, DEPT MED & GRAD DEPT GENETICS, MED SCH, HOWARD UNIV, 77- *Concurrent Pos:* NIH fel, Univ Wash, 65-66, Am Cancer Soc fel, 66-67; investr, Howard Hughes Med Res Inst, 67-69. *Mem:* NY Acad Sci; AAAS; Am Chem Soc; Am Soc Hemat. *Res:* Structure and function of human blood proteins; structural abnormalities in proteins in inherited and congenital disease. *Mailing Add:* Dept Genetics Box 75 Col Med Howard Univ Washington DC 20059

WINTERBERG, FRIEDWARDT, b Berlin, Ger, June 12, 29. THEORETICAL PHYSICS. *Educ:* Univ Frankfurt, MS, 53; Univ Göttingen, PhD(nuclear physics), 55. *Prof Exp:* Group leader theoret physics, Res Reactor, Hamburg, Ger, 55-59; asst prof plasma physics & relativity, Case Univ, 59-63; assoc prof physics, 63-68, RES PROF PHYSICS, DESERT RES INST, UNIV NEV SYST, RENO, 68- *Mem:* Am Phys Soc; hon mem Hermann Oberth Soc. *Res:* Neutron physics; plasma physics; magnetohydrodynamics; intense relativistic electron and ion beams; thermonuclear microexplosions and inertial confinement fusion; nuclear rocket propulsion; general relativity; atmospheric physics; energy research. *Mailing Add:* Desert Res Inst Univ of Nev Syst Reno NV 89507

WINTERBOTTOM, W L, b Pittsburgh, Pa, Sept 27, 30; m 51; c 4. METALLURGY. *Educ:* Drexel Inst Technol, BSc, 58; Carnegie Inst Technol, PhD(metall), 62. *Prof Exp:* Staff scientist, 62-80, PRIN RES SCIENTIST, SCI LAB, FORD MOTOR CO, 80- *Mem:* Am Inst Mining, Metall & Petrol Engrs; Am Inst Chemists. *Res:* Surface physics; evaporation of solids; vapor-solid interactions; condensation and nucleation; catalysis; gas monitoring devices; metal joining; fluxless vacuum brazing of aluminum. *Mailing Add:* 26360 Powers Rd Farmington MI 48024

WINTERCORN, ELEANOR STIEGLER, b Morristown, NJ, Jan 15, 35; m 58. AUDIOLOGY, SPEECH PATHOLOGY. *Educ:* Rockford Col, BA, 56; Univ Wis, MS, 58; Univ Md, PhD, 69. *Prof Exp:* Clin instr speech path & phonetics, Rockford Col, 56-57; speech & hearing therapist, El Paso Cerebral Palsy Treatment Ctr, 58-59; audiologist, 60-66, supvr clin audiol, 66-70, asst chief audiol & speech path serv, 71-80, CHIEF, AUDIOLOGY & SPEECH PATH SERV, VET ADMIN MED CTR, DC, 80- *Concurrent Pos:* Mem res comt hearing aid eval processes, Am Speech & Hearing Asn, 66-67; Vet Admin rep comt hearing, bioacoust & biomech, Nat Res Coun-Nat Acad Sci, 68-71; res assoc & Vet Admin rep comt hearing, Bioacoust Lab, Univ Md, 68-72; res asst prof, Univ Md, 73-; dir, Vet Admin Nat Hearing Aid Testing Prog, 75- *Res:* Hearing aids; speech intelligibility. *Mailing Add:* Vet Admin Hosp 50 Irving St NW Washington DC 20422

WINTERNHEIMER, P LOUIS, b Evansville, Ind, Feb 9, 31; m 51; c 2. BOTANY. *Educ:* Purdue Univ, West Lafayette, BS, 53; Univ Iowa, MS, 55; Ind Univ, Bloomington, PhD(bot), 71. *Prof Exp:* Assoc prof, 57-70, PROF BIOL, UNIV EVANSVILLE, 70- *Mem:* Am Bot Soc. *Res:* Biosystematic studies of Oenothera biennis and other species. *Mailing Add:* Univ of Evansville PO Box 329 Evansville IN 47702

WINTERNITZ, WILLIAM WELCH, b New Haven, Conn, June 21, 20; m 49; c 3. MEDICINE. *Educ:* Dartmouth Col, AB, 42; Johns Hopkins Univ, MD, 45. *Prof Exp:* From instr to asst prof med & physiol, Yale Univ, 52-59; assoc prof med, Col Med, Univ Ky, 59-64, prof, 64-77; PROF & CHMN, DEPT INTERNAL MED, COL COMMUNITY HEALTH SCI, UNIV ALA, 77- *Mem:* Endocrine Soc; AMA; Am Diabetes Asn. *Res:* Endocrine regulation of metabolism. *Mailing Add:* PO Box 6291 University AL 35486

WINTERS, ALVIN L, b Enumclaw, Wash, Aug 26, 39; m 60; c 2. VIROLOGY, BIOCHEMISTRY. *Educ:* Kans State Teachers Col, BA, 64; Kans State Univ, MA, 68, PhD(virol), 69. *Prof Exp:* Instr biol, Kans State Univ, 69; asst prof microbiol, Univ Pa, 71-74; ASST PROF MICROBIOL, UNIV S FLA, TAMPA, 74- *Concurrent Pos:* Fel, Univ Pa, 69-71. *Mem:* Am Soc Microbiol; AAAS; Sigma Xi. *Res:* Viral pathogenesis biochemistry of viral infection. *Mailing Add:* 3223 Wyoming Ave Tampa FL 33611

WINTERS, C(HARLES) E(RNEST), b Pratt, Kans, July 15, 16; m 41; c 4. CHEMICAL ENGINEERING. *Educ:* Kans State Col, BS, 37; Mass Inst Technol, SM, 39, ScD(chem eng), 42. *Prof Exp:* Chem engr, Mallinckrodt Chem Works, Mo, 40-43; prin engr, Manhattan Dist, US Atomic Energy Comn, 43-47; sect chief technol div, Oak Ridge Nat Lab, Carbide & Carbon Chem Co, 47-49, dept head, Eng Res & Develop Technol Div, 49-51, dir exp eng div, 51-53, asst res dir, 53-55, asst lab dir, Union Carbide Nuclear Co, 55-61; res dir, Parma Res Lab, Ohio, Union Carbide Corp, 62-66, gen mgr, Fuel Cell Dept, 63-69, asst to vpres, Washington, DC, 69-78; CONSULT, 78- *Mem:* Am Chem Soc; fel Am Nuclear Soc; Am Inst Chem Engrs; fel Am Inst Chemists. *Res:* Electrochemical and nuclear engineering; energy generation. *Mailing Add:* 8800 Fernwood Rd Bethesda MD 20817

WINTERS, EARL D, b Rio Grande, Ohio, Aug 28, 37; m 60; c 1. PHYSICAL CHEMISTRY. *Educ:* Ohio Wesleyan Univ, BA, 59; Mass Inst Technol, PhD(phys chem), 65. *Prof Exp:* MEM TECH STAFF, BELL LABS, INC, 65- *Mem:* Am Chem Soc; Electrochem Soc; Electroplaters Soc. *Res:* Electrodeposition, etching and corrosion of metals. *Mailing Add:* R D 4 117 W Sawmill Rd Quakertown PA 18951

WINTERS, EDWARD PHILLIP, pharmacy, see previous edition

WINTERS, HARVEY, b Paterson, NJ, Aug 23, 42; m 65; c 1. MICROBIOLOGY, BIOCHEMISTRY. *Educ:* Fairleigh Dickinson Univ, BS, 64, MS, 66; Columbia Univ, PhD(chem biol), 71. *Prof Exp:* From instr to asst prof, 69-75, assoc prof, 75-79, PROF BIOL, FAIRLEIGH DICKINSON UNIV, 79- *Honors & Awards:* Roon Award, Soc Paint Technol, 73. *Mem:* Am Soc Microbiol; Soc Indust Microbiol; Sigma Xi. *Res:* Microbiology of aqueous coatings; microbiofouling of marine surfaces; desalination. *Mailing Add:* Dept of Biol Fairleigh Dickinson Univ Teaneck NJ 07666

WINTERS, LAWRENCE JOSEPH, b Chicago, Ill, June 11, 30; m 61; c 3. ORGANIC CHEMISTRY. *Educ:* Wash Univ, AB, 53; Univ Kans, PhD(chem), 59. *Prof Exp:* Asst chem, Univ Kans, 56-58; fel, Fla State Univ, 59-61; from asst prof to prof, Drexel Univ, 61-72, actg chmn dept, 68-69, asst dean grad sch, 69-71; PROF CHEM & CHMN DEPT, VA COMMONWEALTH UNIV, 72- *Mem:* Am Chem Soc. *Res:* Bipyridine chemistry; organic reaction mechanisms; structure-activity relationships; aliphatic nitro-compounds. *Mailing Add:* Dept of Chem Va Commonwealth Univ Richmond VA 23284

WINTERS, MARY ANN, b Paterson, NJ, Nov 14, 37. BIOCHEMISTRY. *Educ:* Seton Hill Col, BA, 67; Univ Pittsburgh, PhD(biochem), 72. *Prof Exp:* Teacher elem & high schs, Pa & Ariz, 56-66; from instr to asst prof, 67-76, ASSOC PROF CHEM, SETON HILL COL, 76- *Mem:* Am Chem Soc. *Res:* Purification of nucleic acid synthesizing enzymes and the isolation and identification of nucleic acids. *Mailing Add:* Seton Hill Col Greensburg PA 15601

WINTERS, RAY WYATT, b Takoma Park, Md, Feb 17, 42; m 67. PHYSIOLOGICAL PSYCHOLOGY. *Educ:* Mich State Univ, BS, 64, MA, 66, PhD(psychol), 69. *Prof Exp:* Asst prof, 69-74, assoc prof, 74-80, PROF PSYCHOL, UNIV MIAMI, 80- *Concurrent Pos:* NIH & NSF instnl grants, 69-, NIH grant, 72-80. *Mem:* Optical Soc Am. *Res:* Human psychophysical research in conjunction with animal neurophysiology, especially sensory systems and vision. *Mailing Add:* Dept of Psychol Univ of Miami Coral Gables FL 33124

WINTERS, ROBERT WAYNE, b Evansville, Ind, May 23, 26; m 48, 76; c 1. PEDIATRICS, NUTRITION. *Educ:* Ind Univ, AB, 48; Yale Univ, MD, 52. *Prof Exp:* Intern pediat, Univ Calif, 52-53; from asst to chief resident, Univ NC, 54-56; res fel med, Univ NC, 56-58; asst prof physiol, Univ Pa, 58-61; from assoc prof to prof pediat, Col Physicians & Surgeons, Columbia Univ, 61-81; MED DIR, HOME NUTRIT SUPPORT INC, 81- *Concurrent Pos:* Res fel, Univ Calif, 52-53; res fel biochem, Univ Pa, 58. *Honors & Awards:* E Mead Johnson Prize, 66; Borden Award, 74. *Mem:* Soc Pediat Res; Am Soc Clin Invest; Am Pediat Soc; Am Acad Pediat; Am Physiol Soc. *Res:* Renal and acid base physiology; metabolism of water and electrolytes; intravenous nutrition. *Mailing Add:* Home Nutrit Support Serv 201 Bloomfield Ave Verona NJ 07044

WINTERS, RONALD HOWARD, b Los Angeles, Calif, Apr 13, 42; m 76. PHARMACOLOGY. *Educ:* Calif State Univ, Northridge, BA, 63; Ore State Univ, PhD(pharmacol), 69. *Prof Exp:* Biochemist, Riker Labs, Inc, 64-65; asst to dean undergrad studies, Sch Pharm, Ore State Univ, 72-74, from instr to assoc prof, pharmacol, 68-76, asst dean, 74-76; ASSOC DEAN, COL HEALTH RELATED PROF, WICHITA STATE UNIV, 77- *Concurrent Pos:* Res grants, Ore Heart Asn, 70-72 & Ore Educ Coord Coun, 70-72. *Mem:* AAAS; Sigma Xi; Western Pharmacol Soc; NY Acad Sci; Am Soc Allied Health Professions. *Res:* Cardiovascular pharmacology; anesthesia. *Mailing Add:* Col of Health Related Prof Wichita State Univ Wichita KS 67208

WINTERS, RONALD ROSS, b Marion, Va, June 4, 41; m 60; c 2. NUCLEAR PHYSICS, ASTROPHYSICS. *Educ:* King Col, AB, 63; Va Polytech Inst & State Univ, PhD(physics), 67. *Prof Exp:* Assoc prof physics, Denison Univ, 66-80. *Concurrent Pos:* Consult, Oak Ridge Nat Lab, 72-74; dir, Sci Semester Prog, Great Lakes Col Asn, 75- *Mem:* Sigma Xi; Asn Advan Physics Teaching. *Res:* Measurement of neutron capture cross sections; s-process nucleosynthesis; origin of the earth-moon system. *Mailing Add:* 820 W Broadway Granville OH 43023

WINTERS, STEPHEN SAMUEL, b New York, NY, June 29, 20; m 43; c 2. GEOLOGY. *Educ:* Rutgers Univ, BA, 42; Columbia Univ, MA, 48, PhD(geol), 55. *Prof Exp:* Instr geol, Rutgers Univ, 48-49; from asst prof to assoc prof, 49-66, PROF GEOL, FLA STATE UNIV, 66-, DEAN DIV BASIC STUDIES, 64-, DIR HONORS PROG, 67- *Mem:* Fel Geol Soc Am; Paleont Soc; Soc Econ Paleont & Mineral; Am Asn Petrol Geol; Sigma Xi. *Res:* Stratigraphy and invertebrate paleontology of late Paleozoic. *Mailing Add:* Dept Geol 105 Dodd Hall Fla State Univ Tallahassee FL 32306

WINTERS, WALLACE DUDLEY, b New York, NY, June 20, 29; m 53; c 4. NEUROPHARMACOLOGY, CLINICAL PHARMACOLOGY. *Educ:* George Washington Univ, AB, 50; Univ Mich, Ann Arbor, MA, 52; Univ Wis-Madison, PhD(pharmacol), 54; Med Col Wis, MD, 58; Am Bd Med Toxicol, dipl. *Prof Exp:* Asst pharmacol, Univ Mich, Ann Arbor, 51-52 & Univ Wis-Madison, 52-54; instr, Med Col Wis, 54-58; intern, Milwaukee Hosp, Wis, 58-59; Ment Health trainee neuropharmacol, Univ Calif, Los Angeles, 59-61, res pharmacologist, 61-63, assoc prof pharmacol, Sch Med, 63-68, prof pharmacol & psychiat, 68-71; PROF PHARMACOL, PSYCHIAT, & EMERGENCY MED, SCH MED, UNIV CALIF, DAVIS, 71- *Concurrent Pos:* Ment Health Prog rep pharmacol, Univ Calif, Los Angeles, 61-71, mem, Brain Res Inst & chmn ment health training prog, Educ Comt, 65-71, mem brain res adv comt, 70-71; mem, Preclin Psychopharmacol Res Rev Comt, 65-69. *Honors & Awards:* A E Bennet Award, Soc Biol Psychiat, 66. *Mem:* AAAS; Am Soc Pharmacol & Exp Therapeut; Am Asn Clin Toxicol; Am Asn Poison Control Centers. *Res:* Neuropharmacological action of central nervous system acting drugs; models of psychosis; scheme of anesthetic, excitant, hallucinogen and convulsant drug action; circadian rhythm and drug actions; melatonin and analgesia. *Mailing Add:* Dept Pharmacol Sch Med Univ Calif Davis CA 95616

WINTERS, WENDELL DELOS, b Herrin, Ill. VIROLOGY, IMMUNOLOGY. *Educ:* Univ Ill, Urbana, BS, 62, MS, 66, PhD(med microbiol), 68. *Prof Exp:* Res asst med microbiol, Univ Ill Col Med, 63-65, teaching asst, 65-68; vis scientist, Nat Inst Med Res, London, 68-71; asst prof surg & med microbiol, Sch Med, Univ Calif, Los Angeles, 71-76; ASSOC PROF MICROBIOL, SCH MED, UNIV TEX HEALTH SCI CTR SAN ANTONIO, 76- *Concurrent Pos:* Biochemist, Chicago Bd Health, 63-68; microbiologist, Presby St Lukes Hosp, Chicago, 65-68; Med Res Coun Eng grant, Nat Inst Med Res, London, 68-69; Damon Runyon Mem Fund Cancer Res fel, 70-71; consult, Vet Admin Hosp, Sepulveda, Calif, 71-76 & Audie Murphy Mem Vet Admin Hosp, 78- *Mem:* Am Asn Immunologists; Am Asn Cancer Res; Am Soc Microbiol; Tissue Cult Asn; Brit Soc Gen Microbiol. *Res:* Mechanisms of virus assembly; immune responses to human cancer and immunotherapy substances. *Mailing Add:* Dept of Microbiol Sch Med Univ Tex Health Sci Ctr San Antonio TX 78284

WINTERSCHEID, LOREN COVART, b Manhattan, Kans, Oct 5, 25; m 48; c 6. THORACIC SURGERY, CARDIOVASCULAR SURGERY. *Educ:* Willamette Univ, BA, 48; Univ Pa, PhD(microbiol), 62. *Prof Exp:* Asst surg, 57-58, from instr to assoc prof, 58-72, asst dean clin affairs, 72-80, PROF SURG, SCH MED & DIR, UNIV HOSP, UNIV WASH, 72-, ASSOC DEAN CLIN AFFAIRS, 80- *Concurrent Pos:* Resident surgeon, Affil Hosps, Univ Wash, 55-62; NIH fel, 57-60; mem bd trustees, Willamette Univ, 60-; attend surgeon, Univ & King County Hosps, Seattle, 63. *Mem:* AMA. *Res:* General surgery. *Mailing Add:* Dept Surg RF-25 Univ Hosp Seattle WA 98195

WINTHROP, JOEL ALBERT, b Elizabeth, NJ, Oct 30, 42. APPLIED MATHEMATICS, ELECTRICAL ENGINEERING. *Educ:* Univ Calif, BA, 64, MA, 70, PhD(math), 71, MEE, 78. *Prof Exp:* Asst prof math, Univ Mo, 71-76; mem tech staff, Bell Tel Labs, 77-80. *Mem:* Am Math Soc; Math Asn Am; Soc Indust & Appl Math; Inst Elec & Electronics Engrs; Sigma Xi. *Res:* Digital signal processing. *Mailing Add:* 17-3254 C 3 AT/T 295 N Maple Ave Basking Ridge NJ 07920

WINTHROP, STANLEY OSCAR, b Cowansville, Que, June 22, 27; m 56; c 3. ORGANIC CHEMISTRY. *Educ:* McGill Univ, BEng, 48; Ga Inst Technol, MS, 49; Univ Tex, PhD(org chem), 51. *Prof Exp:* Res chemist, Sterling-Winthrop Res Inst, 52-54; head med chem, Ayerst Res Labs, 54-64; dir res & develop, Lever Bros, Can, 64-69; sci adv, Off Sci & Technol, Can Dept Indust, Trade & Com, 69-71; dir gen, air pollution control directorate, 71-77, DIR GEN, ENVIRON IMPACT CONTROL DIRECTORATE, CAN DEPT ENVIRON, 77- *Mem:* Fel Can Inst Chem; Can Res Mgt Asn. *Res:* Pharmaceuticals; nitrogen heterocycles; fats and oils; detergents; research administration. *Mailing Add:* Air Pollution Control Directorate Can Dept of the Environ Ottawa ON K1A 0H3 Can

WINTNER, CLAUDE EDWARD, b Princeton, NJ, Apr 8, 38; m 67; c 2. ORGANIC CHEMISTRY. *Educ:* Princeton Univ, AB, 59; Harvard Univ, MA, 60, PhD(chem), 63. *Prof Exp:* From instr to asst prof, Yale Univ, 63-68; asst prof, Swarthmore Col, 68-69; assoc prof, 69-76, PROF CHEM, HAVERFORD COL, 76- *Concurrent Pos:* Acad guest, Swiss Fed Inst Technol, Zürich, 72-73 & 76-77. *Res:* Organic synthesis; chemistry of the azo and azoxy groups. *Mailing Add:* 25 Railroad Ave Haverford PA 19041

WINTON, CHARLES NEWTON, b Raleigh, NC, Sept 22, 43; m 66; c 2. MATHEMATICS, COMPUTER SCIENCE. *Educ:* NC State Univ, BS, 65; Univ NC, Chapel Hill, MA & PhD(math), 69. *Prof Exp:* Asst prof math, Univ SC, 69-74; ASSOC PROF MATH SCI, UNIV N FLA, 74- *Mem:* Am Math Soc; Math Asn Am; Asn Comput Mach. *Res:* Ring structure theory, including quotient objects and various torsion theories; data base management systems; screen management. *Mailing Add:* Dept of Math Sci Univ of NFla Jacksonville FL 32216

WINTON, HENRY J, b Guthrie, Okla, Mar 29, 29; m 55; c 3. ELECTRICAL ENGINEERING. *Educ:* Purdue Univ, Lafayette, BS, 50; Univ Ill, Urbana, MS, 55; Univ Santa Clara, PhD(elec eng), 70. *Prof Exp:* Engr, Sperry Gyroscope Co, NY, 57-60; assoc prof, 61-76, PROF ELEC ENG, ROSE-HULMAN INST TECHNOL, 76- *Mem:* Inst Elec & Electronics Engrs; Am Soc Eng Educ. *Res:* Modeling and computer simulation of biological control systems. *Mailing Add:* Dept of Elec Eng 5500 Wabash Ave Terre Haute IN 47803

WINTON, LAWSON LOWELL, forest physiology, tissue culture, see previous edition

WINTON, RAYMOND SHERIDAN, b Raleigh, NC, Jan 4, 40; m 73. MOLECULAR SPECTROSCOPY. *Educ:* NC State Univ, BS, 62; Duke Univ, PhD(physics), 72. *Prof Exp:* Physicist electro-optics, US Army Electronics Command, 65-67; ASST PROF MATH & PHYSICS, COL, 72- *Mem:* Sigma Xi; Am Phys Soc; Math Asn Am. *Res:* High precision measurements in microwave molecular spectroscopy and saturation effects in molecular absorption spectra. *Mailing Add:* Dept of Physics Miss Col Clinton MS 39056

WINTROBE, MAXWELL MYER, b Halifax, NS, Oct 27, 01; nat US; m 27; c 2. INTERNAL MEDICINE. *Educ:* Univ Man, BA, 21, MD, 26, BSc, 27; Tulane Univ, PhD(internal med), 29; Am Bd Internal Med, dipl, 37. *Hon Degrees:* DSc, Univ Man, 58, Univ Utah, 67 & Med Col Wis, 74; MD, Univ Athens, Greece, 81. *Prof Exp:* Intern, King George Hosp, Winnipeg, 25 & Winnipeg Gen Hosp, 25-26; Bell fel, Univ Man, 26-27; instr med, Sch Med, Tulane Univ, 27-30; instr, Sch Med, Johns Hopkins Univ, 30-35, assoc, 35-43; prof internal med, 43-70, head dept, 43-67, dir lab study hereditary & metab disorders, 45-72, dir, Cardiovasc Res & Training Inst, 69-74, DISTINGUISHED PROF INTERNAL MED, SCH MED, UNIV UTAH, 70- *Concurrent Pos:* Asst vis physician, Charity Hosp, New Orleans, La, 27-30; asst physician, Johns Hopkins Hosp, 30-39, assoc physician, 39-43, physician in charge clin nutrit, gastrointestinal & hemopoietic disorders, 41-43; physician in chief, Salt Lake Gen Hosp, Utah, 43-65 & Med Ctr, Univ Utah, 65-67; chief consult, Vet Admin Hosp, 46-81; mem consult, AEC, 48-; spec consult to Surgeon Gen, US Army, 49, mem adv comt metab, 60, nutrit anemias adv drug reactions, WHO, spec consult nutritional anemias, 59-; mem comt revision, US Pharmacopoeia, 50-60, mem panel hemat, 61-65; mem comt res life sci, Nat Acad Sci, 66-; mem coun arthritis & metab dis & coun allergy & infectious dis, NIH, 67-70; vis prof, Univ Colo, 55, Tufts Univ & New Eng Med Ctr, 56, Univ NC, 61, Vanderbilt Univ & Ohio State Univ, 64, Univ Okla, 65, Emory Univ & Univ Ala, 69, Univ Rochester, 70, Univ Wash, 71, Southwestern Med Col & George Washington Univ, 72, Univ Fla, 73, Wake Forest Univ, Univ Ottawa & Univ PR, 74; Univ Toronto, McGill Univ, Univ Calif, Los Angeles & Harvard Univ, 75 & Dalhousie Univ, 81; Fulbright lectr, India, 56; Lambie Dew oration, Univ Sydney, 58; Pfizer lectr, Australia & NZ, 58; York lectr, Univ BC, 60; Thayer lectr & vis prof, Johns Hopkins Univ & Hosp, 66; Rosenthal lectr, Mt Sinai Hosp, New York, 67; Lilly lectr, Royal Col Physicians, London, 68; Falk lectr & vis prof, St John's Mercy Hosp, St Louis, Mo, 70; lectr & vis prof, Queen's Med Ctr, Hawaii & lectr, Palm Springs Acad Med, Calif, 71; Gifford-Hill lectr & vis prof, Univ Tex Southwest Med Sch Dallas; Canfield lectr, Univ Mich & vis distinguished prof, Med Ctr, George Washington Univ, 72; Redlich lectr, Cedars-Mt Sinai Hosp, Los Angeles, 80; Musser-Burch lectr, Tulane Univ, 81. *Honors & Awards:* Francis G Blake Mem Award, Asn Am Physicians, 65; Phillips Mem Award, Am Col Physicians, 67; Mayo Soley Award, Western Soc Clin Res, 70; Robert H Williams Award, Asn Prof Med, 73; Kober Medal, Asn Am Physicians, 74. *Mem:* Nat Acad Sci; Asn Am Physicians (vpres, 63-64, pres, 64-65); master Am Col Physicians; Asn Prof Med (pres, 65-66); Am Soc Hemat (vpres, 69, pres, 71-72). *Res:* Hematology; clinical and experimental nutrition, especially nutritional deficiencies in swine; leukemia and related neoplastic diseases; editor of many scientific journals and author of more than 400 scientific articles. *Mailing Add:* Univ of Utah Med Ctr 50 N Medical Dr Salt Lake City UT 84132

WINTROUB, HERBERT JACK, b Omaha, Nebr, Aug 22, 21; m 48; c 3. PHYSICS, ELECTRONICS. *Educ:* Univ Southern Calif, BS, 50. *Prof Exp:* Mem tech staff, Hughes Aircraft Co, 50-57; sr engr, Litton Indust, 57-58; mem sr tech staff, Space Tech Lab, TRW, Inc, 58-63; HEAD COMMUN SCI DEPT, ELECTRONICS RES LABS, AEROSPACE CORP, 63- *Concurrent Pos:* Consult, Sch Med, Univ Southern Calif, 65-, adj asst prof, 69-; mem adv group on electron devices, Dept Defense. *Mem:* Inst Elec & Electronics Engrs. *Res:* Electronic systems research and development in radar, communications, command and control; millimeter-wave and laser propagation and systems investigations; applications of electronics, electro-optics and imaging to cardiac research. *Mailing Add:* A2/1205 Aerospace Corp PO Box 92957 Los Angeles CA 90009

WINTTER, JOHN ERNEST, b Birmingham, Ala, Oct 31, 24; m 44; c 2. MEDICINAL CHEMISTRY. *Educ:* Howard Col, BS, 49; Univ Fla, MS, 50, PhD(pharmaceut chem), 52. *Prof Exp:* Asst pharm, Univ Fla, 50-52; assoc prof, 52-58, PROF PHARM, SCH PHARM, SAMFORD UNIV, 58-, DEAN, 72- *Mem:* Acad Pharmaceut Sci; Am Pharmaceut Asn. *Res:* Amino acids in sponge; alginic acid derivatives; sapote gum suspending properties; esters of amino acids; phthalimidoacetic acid esters; antifungal esters of thiomalic acid. *Mailing Add:* Sch of Pharm Samford Univ 800 Lakeshore Dr Birmingham AL 35209

WINTZ, P(AUL) A, b Batesville, Ind, Mar 7, 35; m 56; c 1. ELECTRICAL ENGINEERING. *Educ:* Purdue Univ, BSEE, 59, MSEE, 61, PhD(elec eng), 64. *Prof Exp:* Engr, Duncan Elec Co, 58-61; from instr to assoc prof, Purdue Univ, West Lafayette, 61-71, prof elec eng, 71-76, asst head res, 72-76. *Concurrent Pos:* Pres, Wintek Corp, 76- *Mem:* Am Soc Eng Educ; Inst Elec & Electronics Engrs. *Res:* Statistical communication theory; data and image processing; information handling. *Mailing Add:* Wintek Corp 1801 South St Lafayette IN 47904

WINTZ, WILLIAM A, JR, b Carville, La, June 7, 15; m 42; c 8. CIVIL ENGINEERING. *Educ:* La State Univ, BS, 36, MS, 38; Mass Inst Technol, SM, 51. *Prof Exp:* From instr to prof civil eng, La State Univ, Baton Rouge, 41-80; RETIRED. *Mem:* Am Soc Civil Engrs; Am Soc Eng Educ; Water Pollution Control Fedn; Am Water Works Asn. *Res:* Sanitary engineering; advanced surveying. *Mailing Add:* 1991 Hollydale Ave Baton Rouge LA 70808

WINZENREAD, MARVIN RUSSELL, b Indianapolis, Ind, Nov 22, 37; m 60; c 2. MATHEMATICS, EDUCATION. *Educ:* Purdue Univ, BS, 60; Univ Notre Dame, MS, 64; Ind Univ, Bloomington, EdD(math educ), 69. *Prof Exp:* Teacher high sch, Ind, 60-63; from instr to asst prof math, Northwest Mo State Col, 64-67; lectr, Ind Univ Indianapolis, 69; asst prof, 69-73, ASSOC PROF MATH, CALIF STATE UNIV, HAYWARD, 73- *Res:* Mathematics in the inner city school. *Mailing Add:* Dept of Math Calif State Univ 25800 Hillary St Hayward CA 94542

WINZER, STEPHEN RANDOLPH, b Orlando, Fla, Nov 19, 44; m 67; c 2. PETROLOGY, GEOCHEMISTRY. *Educ:* Antioch Col, BA, 67; Univ Alta, PhD(petrol & geochem), 73. *Prof Exp:* Res assoc planetol, Goddard Space Flight Ctr, NASA, 73-75; res scientist geol, 75-80, sr scientist, 80-81, MGR, AGGREGATES RES, MARTIN MARIETTA LABS, 81- *Concurrent Pos:* Resident res assoc, Nat Acad Sci-Goddard Space Flight Ctr, NASA, 73-75. *Mem:* Geol Soc Am; Geochem Soc; Am Geophys Union; AAAS; Soc Explosives Engrs. *Res:* Petrology, trace element chemistry and isotopic systematics of shock metamorphosed lunar and terrestrial rocks; fundamental mechanisms of fragmentation of rock by explosive loading and applications to blasting operations. *Mailing Add:* Martin Marietta Labs 1450 S Rolling Rd Baltimore MD 21227

WIORKOWSKI, JOHN JAMES, b Chicago, Ill, Sept 30, 43; m 66; c 1. STATISTICS. *Educ:* Univ Chicago, BS, 65, MS, 66, PhD(statist), 72. *Prof Exp:* Asst prof statist, Grad Prog Health Care Admin, US Army-Baylor Univ, 68-71; res assoc, Univ Chicago, 71-73; asst prof, Pa State Univ, 73-75; ASSOC PROF STATIST, UNIV TEX, DALLAS, 75- *Concurrent Pos:* Assoc dir, Statist Consult & Coop Res Ctr, Pa State Univ, 73-74, dir, 74-75; consult, Fed Energy Admin, 75; asst vpres, acad affairs, 79-; prog head, Math Sci, 78-79; fel acad admin, Am Coun Educ, 81-82. *Mem:* Sigma Xi; Am Statist Asn; Biomet Soc; Inst Math Statist. *Res:* Interest in applied statistics, specifically biostatistics, linear models, time series analysis, genetic statistics. *Mailing Add:* Grad Prog in Math Sci Univ of Tex Dallas PO Box 688 Richardson TX 75080

WIPF, FRANCES LOUISE, b Iola, Wis, Aug 18, 06. CYTOLOGY. *Educ:* Wis State Teachers Col, Oshkosh, BE, 30; Univ Wis, PhM, 33, PhD(bot, agr bact), 39. *Prof Exp:* Asst biol, Wis State Teachers Col, Oshkosh, 30-32; asst vet sci, 39-43, asst genetics, 43-47, instr, 47-49, instr vet sci, 49-55, asst prof, 55-72, EMER ASST PROF VET SCI, UNIV WIS-MADISON, 72- *Mem:* AAAS; Genetics Soc Am; Conf Res Workers Animal Dis. *Res:* Root nodules; fur farm animals; cytogenetics; histopathology; microtechnique. *Mailing Add:* 602 N Segoe Rd Apt 807 Madison WI 53705

WIPKE, WILL TODD, b St Charles, Mo, Dec 16, 40; c 2. CHEMISTRY. *Educ:* Univ Mo-Columbia, BS, 62; Univ Calif, Berkeley, PhD(chem), 65. *Prof Exp:* Res fel chem, Harvard Univ, 67-69; asst prof, Princeton Univ, 69-75; assoc prof, 75-81, PROF CHEM, UNIV CALIF, SANTA CRUZ, 81- *Concurrent Pos:* NIH res fel, Harvard Univ, 68-69; NIH spec res resource grant, Princeton Univ, 70-75 & Merck prof develop grant, 70-75; consult, Merck, Sharp & Dohme, 70-80, Molecular Design Ltd, 77-; mem bd adv, Chem Abstr Serv, 70-73; dir, NATO Advan Study Inst Comput Rep & Manipulation Chem Info, 73; mem, Nat Res Coun Comt Nat Res Comput Chem, 74-77. *Mem:* Am Chem Soc; Royal Soc Chem; Asn Comput Mach; Am Asn Art Intel. *Res:* Organic synthesis; computer assisted design of organic syntheses; computer assisted prediction of metabolism. *Mailing Add:* Dept of Chem Univ of Calif Santa Cruz CA 95064

WIRSEN, CARL O, JR, b Arlington, Mass, Aug 11, 42; m; c 2. MARINE MICROBIOLOGY, OCEANOGRAPHY. *Educ:* Univ Mass, BS, 64; Boston Univ, MA, 66. *Prof Exp:* Res assoc microbiol, Harvard Univ, 66-68; RES SPECIALIST MICROBIOL, WOODS HOLE OCEANOG INST, 68- *Mem:* Am Soc Microbiol; Am Soc Limnol & Oceanog; Sigma Xi. *Res:* The role of microorganisms in the deep sea environment and how the environmental parameters of temperature and pressure influence their activities; microbiological studies of deep sea hydrothermal vents. *Mailing Add:* Dept of Biol Woods Hole Oceanog Inst Woods Hole MA 02543

WIRSZUP, IZAAK, b Wilno, Poland, Jan 5, 15; US citizen; m 49; c 1. MATHEMATICS. *Educ:* Univ Wilno, Mag Philos, 39; Univ Chicago, PhD(math), 55. *Prof Exp:* Lectr math, Tech Inst, Wilno, Poland, 39-41; dir bur studies & spec statist, Cent Soc Purchase; dir Soc Anonyme des Monoprix, France, 46-49; from instr to assoc prof math, 49-65, PROF MATH, UNIV CHICAGO, 65- *Concurrent Pos:* Dir Surv East Europ Math Lit, proj Univ Chicago, under NSF grant, 56-; consult sch math study group, Yale Univ & Stanford Univ, 60, 61 & 66; Ford Found consult, Univ Math Progs, Colombia, SAm, 65 & 66; mem, US Comn Math Instr, 69-73; adv math, Encyclopaedia Britannica, 71- *Honors & Awards:* Quantrell Award, Univ Chicago, 58. *Mem:* Am Math Soc; Math Asn Am. *Res:* Mathematical analysis; international mathematics education. *Mailing Add:* Dept of Math Univ of Chicago Chicago IL 60637

WIRTA, ROY W(ILLIAM), b Big Lake, Wash, Mar 27, 21; m 46; c 3. REHABILITATION BIOMEDICAL ENGINEERING, BIOMECHANICS. *Educ:* Univ Wash, BSME, 47. *Prof Exp:* Test engr, Gen Elec Co, 47-48, develop engr, Gen Eng Lab, 48-52, process engr, 52-56, mech engr, 56-57, sr engr, Hanford Atomic Prod Oper, 57-61, electromech systs engr, Ord Dept, 61-64; sr eng specialist, Biocybernetics Lab, Philco-Ford Corp, Pa, 64-67; sr res scientist, Rehab Eng Ctr, Moss Rehab Hosp, Philadelphia, 67-77; BIOMECH ENGR, BIOMECHANICS, 77- *Concurrent Pos:* Res biomed engr, Vet Admin Med Ctr, San Diego, Calif, 78- *Mem:* Am Soc Mech Engrs. *Res:* Electromechanical devices; mechanical arts; integrated man-machine systems; human locomotion; measurement of impaired human performance. *Mailing Add:* 5570 Rab St La Mesa CA 92041

WIRTH, H JACK, b Boston, Mass, May 6, 23; m 47; c 3. COMMUNICATIONS, ELECTRONICS. *Educ:* Univ NMex, BS, 50, BBA, 51; Univ Calif, Los Angeles, MS, 58. *Prof Exp:* Engr, Simulators & Comput Sect, Navy Electronics Lab Ctr, 50-55, group leader, Data Transmission Sect, 56-59, group leader, Shape & Tech Ctr, Hague, Neth, 60-61; sect head, Adv Data Transmission Sect, 61-66, HEAD, SATELLITE COMMUN DIV, NAVY ELECTRONICS LAB CTR, 66- *Mem:* Sr mem Inst Elec & Electronics Engrs. *Res:* Communications and data transmission systems; coding theory; radio propagation; computer-to-computer links; satellite communications; modulation theory; information theory. *Mailing Add:* US Naval Electronic Lab 271 Catalina Blvd San Diego CA 92152

WIRTH, JAMES BURNHAM, b Teaneck, NJ, Jan 15, 41. PHYSIOLOGICAL PSYCHOLOGY, PSYCHIATRY. *Educ:* Cornell Univ, AB, 63, MD, 67; Cambridge Univ, PhD(physiol), 75. *Prof Exp:* Intern med, Cornell Univ Hosps, 67-68; resident neurol, Cleveland Metrop Gen Hosp, 68-69; fel physiol pscyhol, Inst Neurol Sci, Univ Pa, 71-73; res physiol, Cambridge Univ, 73-75; resident psychiat, 75-77, ASST PROF PSYCHIAT, JOHNS HOPKINS HOSP, 77- *Concurrent Pos:* Mem panel neurol behav, Nat Inst Neurol & Cardiovasc Dis & Stroke, 78. *Mem:* Am Physiol Soc; Am Psychiat Asn; Soc Neurosci; Sigma Xi; Eastern Physiol Asn. *Res:* Ingestive behavior, especially thirst, hunger and sodium appetite. *Mailing Add:* Dept Psychiat & Behav Sci 720 Rutland Ave Baltimore MD 21205

WIRTH, JOSEPH GLENN, b Onawa, Iowa, Nov 19, 34; m 53; c 1. ORGANIC CHEMISTRY. *Educ:* Univ Wash, BS, 59; Univ Mich, Ann Arbor, MS & PhD(chem), 65. *Prof Exp:* Chemist, Boeing Co, 58-62; res chemist, 65-71, MGR RES & DEVELOP PROD DEVELOP, SILICONE PROD DEPT, RES & DEVELOP CTR, GEN ELEC CO, 71- *Res:* Organic synthesis, nitrogen heterocycles; polymer synthesis; fluorescence, organosilicon chemistry. *Mailing Add:* Silicone Prods Dept Gen Elec Co Waterford NY 12188

WIRTH, WILLIS WAGNER, b Dunbar, Nebr, Oct 17, 16; m 42; c 2. ENTOMOLOGY. *Educ:* Iowa State Col, BS, 40; La State Univ, MS, 47; Univ Calif, PhD(entom), 50. *Prof Exp:* Instr biol, La Polytech Inst, 40-41; ENTOMOLOGIST, SYST ENTOM LAB, USDA, WASHINGTON, DC, 49- *Concurrent Pos:* Sr asst sanitarian, USPHS, 42-47; Fulbright res scholar, Australia, 56-57; courtesy prof entom, Univ Fla, 65-; vis prof entom, Univ Md, College Park, 74- *Mem:* Fel Entom Soc Am; Soc Syst Zool. *Res:* Systematic entomology; taxonomy of Diptera. *Mailing Add:* 806 Copley Lane Silver Spring MD 20904

WIRTHLIN, MILTON ROBERT, JR, b Little Rock, Ark, July 13, 32; m 54; c 5. PERIODONTICS, EPIDEMIOLOGY. *Educ:* Univ Calif, DDS, 56, MS, 68; Am Bd Periodont, dipl, 74. *Prof Exp:* US Navy gen dent officer, 56-68, exec officer, First Dent Co, Fleet Marine Force, 68-69, head, periodont, Naval Dent Clin, 69-73, exec officer, Third Dent Co, Fleet Marine Force, 73-74, chief epidemiol, Naval Dent Res Inst, 74-76, cmndg officer, 76-81, CMNDG OFFICER, NAVAL REGIONAL DENT CTR, SAN FRANCISCO, 81- *Concurrent Pos:* Sec proj officer, Bur Med & Surg, US Navy, 64-65, Dir fel, Naval Dent Clin, Long Beach, 71-72, consult periodont, Naval Regional Med Ctr, 74-76; clin asst prof periodont, Univ Southern Calif, 70-73; Comt Nat Health Legis, Western Soc Periodont, 72-73; clin asst & prof periodont, Univ Ill, 77-81. *Mem:* Am Dent Asn; Int Asn Dent Res; fel Int Col Dentists; Am Dent Asn. *Res:* Periodontal new attachment therapy through biological treatment of diseased root surfaces; wound healing; dental epidemiology; dental care delivery systems; experimental atherosclerosis affect on the supporting tissues of the teeth. *Mailing Add:* Naval Regional Dent Ctr Treasure Island Bldg 2557-2 San Francisco CA 94130

WIRTSCHAFTER, JONATHAN DINE, b Cleveland, Ohio, Apr 9, 35; m 59; c 5. OPHTHALMOLOGY, NEUROLOGY. *Educ:* Reed Col, BA, 56; Harvard Med Sch, MD, 60; Linfield Col, MS, 63. *Prof Exp:* Intern, Philadelphia Gen Hosp, 60-61; resident neurol, Good Samaritan Hosp, Portland, Ore, 61-63; resident ophthal, Johns Hopkins Hosp, 63-66; fel neurol, New York Neurol Inst, Columbia-Presby Med Ctr, New York, 66-67; from asst prof to assoc prof ophthal & neurol, Col Med, Univ Ky, 67-72, dir div ophthal, 67-74, prof ophthal & neurol, 72-77, chmn dept ophthal, 74-77; PROF OPHTHAL, NEUROL & NEUROSURG, COL MED, UNIV MINN, 77- *Concurrent Pos:* Attend surgeon, Vet Admin Hosp, Lexington, Ky, 67-69, consult surgeon, 69-77; vis prof, Hadassah Hosp & Hebrew Univ Jerusalem, 73-74. *Honors & Awards:* Honor Award, Am Acad Ophth, 80. *Mem:* Am Acad Neurol; fel Am Acad Ophthal; fel Am Col Surg; Asn Res Vision & Ophthal. *Res:* Clinical neuro-ophthalmology; interactive teaching methods in ophthalmology; retinal venous pathophysiology; strabismus diagnosis and management; biology of the pterygium. *Mailing Add:* Dept of Ophthal Univ of Minn Minneapolis MN 55455

WIRTZ, GEORGE H, b Kohler, Wis, Apr 29, 31; m 52; c 2. IMMUNOCHEMISTRY, BIOCHEMISTRY. *Educ:* Univ Wis, BS, 53, MS, 56; George Washington Univ, PhD(biochem), 62. *Prof Exp:* Biochemist, Walter Reed Army Inst Res, 58-62; fel biol, Johns Hopkins Univ, 62-63; from asst prof to assoc prof, 63-72, PROF BIOCHEM, MED CTR, WVA UNIV, 72- *Concurrent Pos:* Vis prof, Mainz Univ, 68; Am Cancer Soc Scholar, Nat Inst Allergy & Infectious Dis, NIH, 78-79. *Mem:* Am Soc Biol Chemists; Am Asn Immunol. *Res:* Complementology. *Mailing Add:* Dept Biochem WVa Univ Med Ctr Morgantown WV 26506

WIRTZ, GERALD PAUL, b Wisconsin Rapids, Wis, Dec 22, 37; m 61; c 3. SOLID STATE ELECTROCHEMISTRY, CATALYSIS. *Educ:* St Norbert Col, BS, 59; Marquette Univ, BME, 61; Northwestern Univ, PhD(mat sci), 66. *Prof Exp:* Res scientist, Airco Speer Div, Air Reduction Co, Inc, 66-68; ASSOC PROF CERAMIC ENG, UNIV ILL, URBANA, 68-, SR STAFF MEM, MAT RES LAB, 68- *Concurrent Pos:* Fulbright-Hays lectr, Univ Aveiro, 80; vis lectr, Mideast Tech Univ, Ankara Turkey, 80. *Mem:* Am Ceramic Soc. *Res:* Phase quilibria and transformations in oxide systems; magnetic properties of small ferrimagnetic particles; materials for thick-film hybrid microcircuitry; metallic conductivity in oxides; defect structures of oxides; solid electrolytes; heterogeneous catalysis. *Mailing Add:* Dept of Ceramic Eng Univ of Ill Urbana IL 61801

WIRTZ, JOHN HAROLD, b Sheboygan, Wis, Nov 13, 23; m 50. NATURAL HISTORY, VERTEBRATE ZOOLOGY. *Educ:* Loyola Univ, Ill, BS, 52; Univ Wyo, MS, 54; Ore State Univ, PhD, 61. *Prof Exp:* Asst prof, 57-70, ASSOC PROF NATURAL HIST & GEN BIOL, PORTLAND STATE UNIV, 70- *Mem:* AAAS; Nat Audubon Soc. *Res:* Visual behavior, mobility and orientation in sciurid rodents. *Mailing Add:* Dept of Biol Portland State Univ Portland OR 97207

WIRTZ, RICHARD ANTHONY, b New Brunswick, NJ, Aug 16, 44; m 66; c 1. MECHANICAL ENGINEERING. *Educ:* Newark Col Eng, BSME, 66; Rutgers Univ, MS, 68, PhD(heat transfer), 71. *Prof Exp:* Asst prof, 70-76, ASSOC PROF & EXEC OFFICER MECH ENG, CLARKSON COL TECHNOL, 76- *Concurrent Pos:* Prin investr grants, 73-80. *Mem:* Assoc Am Soc Mech Engrs; Am Phys Soc. *Res:* Numerical and physical experiments on free convection heat transfer. *Mailing Add:* Dept of Mech Eng Clarkson Col of Technol Potsdam NY 13676

WIRTZ, WILLIAM OTIS, II, b Montclair, NJ, Aug 16, 37; m 72. MAMMALOGY. *Educ:* Rutgers Univ, BA, 59; Cornell Univ, PhD(ecol, evolutionary biol), 68. *Prof Exp:* Res cur, Smithsonian Inst, 62-66; asst prof zool, 68-77, ASSOC PROF BIOL, POMONA COL, 77- *Mem:* Am Soc Mammalogists; Ecol Soc Am; Wildlife Soc; Am Soc Zoologists; Am Inst Biol Sci. *Res:* Mammalian population ecology and behavior, especially limiting factors in population dynamics; avian population ecology; evolution and systematics of mammals. *Mailing Add:* Dept Biol Pomona Col Claremont CA 91711

WISBY, WARREN JENSEN, b Denmark, Nov 14, 22; US citizen; m 62; c 2. FISHERY BIOLOGY. *Educ:* Univ Wis, BA, 48, MA, 50, PhD(zool), 52. *Prof Exp:* Res assoc zool, Univ Wis, 52-59; assoc prof marine biol, Inst Marine Sci, Univ Miami, 59-65; dir, Nat Fisheries Ctr & Aquarium Dept of Interior, 65-72; adj prof, Inst Marine Sci, 65-72, assoc dean, Sch Marine & Atmospheric Sci, 72-80, INTERIM DEAN, UNIV MIAMI, 80- *Mem:* Am Fisheries Soc; Am Soc Zool; Animal Behav Soc; Sigma Xi. *Res:* Behavior and sensory physiology of marine organisms. *Mailing Add:* Sch of Marine & Atmospheric Sci Univ of Miami 7600 Rickenbacker Causeway Miami FL 33149

WISCHMEIER, WALTER HENRY, b Lincoln, Mo, Jan 18, 11; m 47; c 2. SOIL CONSERVATION. *Educ:* Univ Mo, BS, 53; Purdue Univ, MS, 57. *Prof Exp:* Researcher, Soil & Water Conserv Res Div, Agr Res Serv, USDA, 40-61, res invests leader soil erosion, Corn Belt Br, 61-72, tech adv water erosion, North Cent Region, 72-75; assoc prof agr eng, 65-75, prof, 75-76, EMER PROF AGR ENG, PURDUE UNIV, WEST LAFAYETTE, 76- *Concurrent Pos:* Consult, soil erosion prediction and control, 76- *Honors & Awards:* Superior Serv Awards, USDA, 59 & 73. *Mem:* Am Soc Agron; fel Soil Conserv Soc Am; Am Soc Agr Eng. *Res:* Soil and water conservation; quantitative relationship of soil erosion to rainfall characteristics, topographic features, management, productivity level and factor interactions; conservation farm planning; runoff and soil-loss prediction equations. *Mailing Add:* 2009 Indian Trail Dr West Lafayette IN 47906

WISCHMEYER, CARL R(IEHLE), b Terre Haute, Ind, Oct 2, 16; m 45; c 3. ELECTRICAL ENGINEERING. *Educ:* Rose Polytech Inst, BS, 37, EE, 42, ScD, 70; Yale Univ, MEng, 39. *Prof Exp:* Lab asst elec eng, Yale Univ, 37-39; instr, Rice Inst Technol, 39-45; mem tech staff, Bell Tel Labs, Inc, 45-47; from asst prof to prof elec eng, Rice Univ, 47-68, master, Baker Col, 56-68, dir continuing studies, 68; DIR EDUC, BELL TEL LABS, 68- *Concurrent Pos:* Consult to indust, 43-68; NSF grant, Eindhoven Technol Univ, 62; mem tech staff, Bell Tel Labs, 63-64; bd mgrs, Rose Polytech Inst, 63-67. *Mem:* Am Soc Eng Educ; fel Inst Elec & Electronics Engrs; Am Soc Train & Develop Engrs. *Res:* Radio; electronics; instruments and equipment. *Mailing Add:* Bell Tel Labs Holmdel NJ 07733

WISCHNITZER, SAUL, b New York, NY, Apr 10, 30. BIOLOGY, ANATOMY. *Educ:* Yeshiva Univ, BA, 51; Univ Notre Dame, MS, 54, PhD(biol), 56. *Prof Exp:* Resident res assoc biol, Argonne Nat Lab, 56-57; from instr to asst prof anat, NY Med Col, 57-64; assoc prof, 64-68, asst to dean, 64-66, asst dean, 66-76, PROF BIOL, YESHIVA UNIV, 68-, ASSOC DEAN, 77- *Concurrent Pos:* USPHS spec res fel, 60-61, career res develop award, 62-69; adj prof, Hunter Col, 71-74. *Mem:* AAAS; Electron Micros Soc Am; Am Asn Anat; Am Soc Cell Biol; Royal Micros Soc. *Res:* Electron microscopy; fine structure of cells; oocytes; nuclear physiology. *Mailing Add:* Dept Biol Yeshiva Univ New York NY 10033

WISCOMBE, WARREN JACKMAN, b St Louis, Mo, Feb 4, 43; m 67; c 2. ATMOSPHERIC PHYSICS. *Educ:* Mass Inst Technol, SB, 64; Calif Inst Technol, MS, 66, PhD(appl math), 70. *Prof Exp:* Res scientist, Systs Sci Software, 69-74; RES SCIENTIST, NAT CTR ATMOSPHERIC RES, 74- *Res:* Radiative transfer in planetary atmospheres, particularly bearing on climate problems. *Mailing Add:* 6 Benthaven Pl Boulder CO 80303

WISDOM, NORVELL EDWIN, JR, b Oklahoma City, Okla, Apr 20, 37. PHYSICAL CHEMISTRY. *Educ:* Univ Tex, BS, 58, PhD(phys chem), 62. *Prof Exp:* Staff mem, Corp Res Labs, Exxon Res & Eng Co, 62-69; sr res chemist, Proj Norton Electroplating Tech, 69-72, group leader, 72-75, MGR PROD DEVELOP, COATED ABRASIVE DIV, NORTON CO, 75- *Honors & Awards:* Silver Medal, Am Electroplaters Soc, 72. *Mem:* Am Chem Soc; Sigma Xi. *Res:* Electroplating; electrochemical kinetics; coated abrasive product design. *Mailing Add:* Coated Abrasive Res & Develop Dept Norton Co Troy NY 12181

WISE, BURTON LOUIS, b New York, Nov 24, 24; m 59. NEUROSURGERY. *Educ:* Columbia Univ, AB, 44; New York Med Col, MD, 47. *Prof Exp:* Clin instr neurol surg, 54, from instr to assoc prof, 55-68, vchmn dept, 65-68, assoc clin prof neurosurg, Sch Med, Univ Calif, San Francisco, 68-77; CHIEF DEPT NEUROSCI, MT ZION HOSP & MT ZION NEUROL INST, 75- *Concurrent Pos:* Attend neurol surgeon, Ft Miley Vet Admin Hosp, San Francisco, 54-68 & San Francisco Gen Hosp, 58-69; consult neurosurgeon, Laguna Honda Home & Langley Porter Neuropsychiat Inst, 57-68 & Letterman Army Hosp, 58-; chief neurosurg, Mt Zion Hosp & Mt Zion Neurol Inst, 70-74. *Mem:* Am Asn Neurol Surg; AMA; Am Col Surg; Am Fedn Clin Res. *Res:* Metabolic responses to central nervous system lesions; brain stem mechanisms in salt and water homeostasis; effects of hypertonic solutions on cerebrospinal fluid pressure; neuroendocrinology; pediatric neurosurgery and hydrocephalus. *Mailing Add:* Mt Zion Hosp & Neurol Inst 1600 Divisadero St San Francisco CA 94115

WISE, CHARLES DAVIDSON, b Huntington, WVa, June 13, 26; m 47; c 1. INVERTEBRATE ZOOLOGY, LIMNOLOGY. *Educ:* Univ WVa, AB & MS, 50; Univ NMex, PhD(invert zool), 62. *Prof Exp:* Asst zool, Marshall Univ, 50-51; teacher high sch, WVa, 51-53; instr biol, Amarillo Col, 55-57; res scientist, Inst Marine Sci, Univ Tex, 58-60; asst biol, Univ NMex, 60-61; from asst prof to assoc prof, 61-72, PROF BIOL, BALL STATE UNIV, 72- *Concurrent Pos:* Ind State rep, 66-68; Ind State senator, 68-72; mem, Int Comt Recent Ostracoda, 63-73. *Mem:* Am Micros Soc; Nat Audubon Soc; Sigma Xi. *Res:* Ecology; biological oceanography; marine and freshwater ostracods, especially taxonomy and ecology. *Mailing Add:* Dept of Biol Ball State Univ Muncie IN 47306

WISE, DAVID HAYNES, b Mineral Wells, Tex, Apr 28, 45; m 67; c 2. POPULATION ECOLOGY. *Educ:* Swarthmore Col, BA, 67; Univ Mich, MS, 69, PhD(zool), 74. *Prof Exp:* Instr biol, Albion Col, 69-70; lectr zool, Univ Mich, 70-71; asst prof biol, Univ NMex, 74-76; asst prof, 76-81, ASSOC PROF BIOL SCI, UNIV MD, BALTIMORE COUNTY, 81- *Mem:* Ecol Soc Am; Am Arachnol Soc; Soc Study Evolution; Entom Soc Am. *Res:* Population dynamics and regulation of population density; experimental field studies of competition and predation; life history evolution. *Mailing Add:* Dept of Biol Sci Univ Md Baltimore County Catonsville MD 21228

WISE, DONALD L, b Indianapolis, Ind, May 27, 29; m 52; c 4. CELL PHYSIOLOGY. *Educ:* Wabash Col, AB, 51; NY Univ, MS, 54, PhD, 58. *Prof Exp:* Instr natural sci, Univ Chicago, 57-58; from instr to assoc prof biol, 58-66, PROF BIOL, COL WOOSTER, 66-, CHMN DEPT, 72- *Concurrent Pos:* Staff biologist, Comn Undergrad Educ Biol, 67-68; vis prof, George Washington Univ, 67-68; vis prof, Case Western Reserve Univ, 76-77; consult/examr N Cent Asn Col & Schs, 75- *Mem:* AAAS; Soc Protozool; Am Soc Zool; Am Inst Biol Sci. *Res:* Protozoan and cellular metabolism and physiology. *Mailing Add:* Dept of Biol Col of Wooster Wooster OH 44691

WISE, DONALD U, b Reading, Pa, Apr 21, 31; m 65; c 2. GEOLOGY. *Educ:* Franklin & Marshall Col, BS, 53; Calif Inst Technol, MS, 55; Princeton Univ, PhD(geol), 57. *Prof Exp:* From asst prof to prof geol, Franklin & Marshall Col, 57-68; chief scientist & dep dir, NASA Apollo Lunar Explor Off, 68-69; prof geol, Univ Mass, Amherst, 69-80. *Concurrent Pos:* Consult, NASA, 64-, Pa Geol Surv, 65-66, Geotech & Power Cos Seismic Risk, 72-, Nuclear Regulation Comn, 76-80, various oil co, 73-; vis scientist, Max Planck Inst, Heidelberg, 75 & Univ Rome, 76. *Mem:* AAAS; Geol Soc Am; Am Geophys Union. *Res:* Structural geology; structure and basement features of the middle Rocky Mountains; flow mechanics of rocks; structures of the Appalachian Piedmont; regional fracture analysis; lunar and planetary geology. *Mailing Add:* 253 Shutesbury Rd Leverett MA 01054

WISE, DWAYNE ALLISON, b Lewisburg, Tenn, Feb 5, 45; m 66; c 1. CYTOGENETICS. *Educ:* David Lipscomb Col, BA, 67; Fla State Univ, MS, 70, PhD(genetics), 72. *Prof Exp:* Res fel cytogenetics, Health Sci Ctr, Univ Tex, 73-74; instr zool, Duke Univ, 74-75, res assoc cell biol, 75-80; MEM FAC, DEPT BIOL SCI, MISS STATE UNIV, 80- *Concurrent Pos:* NIH fel, 75-77. *Mem:* Sigma Xi. *Res:* Investigation of the control of chromosome structure during the cell cycle and of chromosome distribution at meiosis and mitosis. *Mailing Add:* Dept Biol Sci Miss State Univ Mississippi State MS 39762

WISE, EDMUND MERRIMAN, JR, b Jersey City, NJ, Aug 10, 30; m 52; c 2. MICROBIAL BIOCHEMISTRY. *Educ:* Oberlin Col, BA, 52; Harvard Univ, PhD(biochem), 63. *Prof Exp:* Jr biologist, Parke, Davis & Co, 54-55; NIH fel, Med Sch, Tufts Univ, 64-66, from instr to asst prof molecular biol & microbiol, 65-73; SR RES MICROBIOLOGIST, BURROUGHS-WELLCOME CO, 73- *Concurrent Pos:* NIH fel, Med Sch, Harvard Univ, 63-64. *Mem:* AAAS; Am Chem Soc; Am Soc Microbiol. *Res:* Control of enzyme activity; bacterial cell wall synthesis and degradation; design of enzyme inhibitors; microbial cofactor biosynthesis. *Mailing Add:* Microbiol Dept Wellcome Res Labs Research Triangle Park NC 27709

WISE, EDWARD NELSON, b Athens, Ohio, May 30, 15; m 36; c 2. CHEMISTRY, RESEARCH ADMINISTRATION. *Educ:* Ohio Univ, BS, 37, MS, 38; Univ Kans, PhD(chem), 53. *Prof Exp:* Teacher chem & physics, Gallia Acad High Sch, 38-42; qual control chemist, Baker & Adamson Div, Gen Chem Co, 42; supvr, Standards Lab, WVa Ord Works, 42-45; res engr graphic arts, Battelle Mem Inst, 45-47; mem staff anal instrumentation, Los Alamos Sci Lab, 47-50; tech asst, Hercules Powder Co, 51; from asst prof to assoc prof, 52-61, assocxcoordrfrom assoc coordr to coordr res, 64-72, PROF CHEM, UNIV ARIZ, 61- *Mem:* Am Chem Soc. *Res:* Electrophoretic deposition of natural and synthetic rubbers; halftone and color separation techniques in the graphic arts; electrostatic image formation and development; xerography; analytical instrumentation; automatic titrimetry and coulometric analysis. *Mailing Add:* Dept of Chem Univ of Ariz Tucson AZ 85721

WISE, ERNEST GEORGE, b Dunkirk, NY, Sept 6, 20; m 50; c 2. RADIATION BIOLOGY, MICROBIOLOGY. *Educ:* State Univ NY Col Fredonia, BEd, 42; Columbia Univ, MA, 47; Syracuse Univ, PhD(sci educ), 60. *Prof Exp:* Instr sci & math, State Univ NY Col New Paltz, 47-48, prof biol, State Univ NY Col Oswego, 48-77; RETIRED. *Concurrent Pos:* AEC-NSF acad year fel radiation biol, Cornell Univ, 64-65; AEC equip grant, 68. *Mem:* Health Phys Soc; Int Radiation Protection Asn. *Res:* Science education from elementary grades through the college level. *Mailing Add:* 34 S Shore Dr Boiling Spring Lakes Southport NC 28461

WISE, GARY E, b Yuma, Colo, July 30, 42; m 62; c 1. CELL BIOLOGY. *Educ:* Univ Denver, BA, 64; Univ Calif, Berkeley, PhD(zool), 68. *Prof Exp:* NIH fel cell biol, Univ Colo, Boulder, 69-71; asst prof biol struct, 72-75, ASSOC PROF BIOL STRUCT, SCH MED, UNIV MIAMI, 75- *Mem:* Am Soc Cell Biol; Am Asn Anatomists. *Res:* Origin and function of cytoplasmic membranes, especially the Golgi apparatus; localization and function of macromolecules involved in nucleocytoplasmic interactions; sickled erythrocyte membranes. *Mailing Add:* Dept of Anat Sch Med Univ of Miami Miami FL 33101

WISE, GENE, b Willard, Ohio, Apr 13, 22; m 64; c 2. ORGANIC CHEMISTRY, PHYSICAL CHEMISTRY. *Educ:* Capital Univ, BS, 47; Western Reserve Univ, PhD(chem), 50. *Prof Exp:* From asst prof to assoc prof, 50-60, PROF CHEM, VA MIL INST, 60-, HEAD CHEM DEPT, 77- *Concurrent Pos:* Consult, Gen Tire & Rubber Co, 57-63 & Environ Sci Serv Admin, 67-68; sect councilor, Am Chem Soc, 74- *Mem:* Am Chem Soc. *Res:* Computer applications in chemistry; chemical kinetics; properties of polymers. *Mailing Add:* Dept of Chem Va Mil Inst Lexington VA 24450

WISE, GEORGE HERMAN, b Saluda, SC, July 7, 08; m 37; c 4. ANIMAL NUTRITION, ANIMAL PHYSIOLOGY. *Educ:* Clemson Col, BS, 30; Univ Minn, MS, 32, PhD(dairy husb), 37. *Prof Exp:* Asst dairy husb, Univ Minn, 33-36; assoc, Clemson Col, 37-44; from assoc prof to prof, Kans State Col, 44-47; assoc prof, Iowa State Col, 47-49; prof animal indust, 49-51, head nutrit sect, 49-66, William Neal Reynolds Prof, 51-74, EMER PROF ANIMAL SCI, NC STATE UNIV, 75- *Concurrent Pos:* Mem comt animal nutrit, Nat Res Coun, 51-53; consult, State Exp Sta Div, Agr Res Serv, USDA, 55-62; study leave, Univ Calif, Davis, 66-67. *Honors & Awards:* Award, Am Feed Mfrs Asn, 48; Borden Award, 49; Award of Honor, Am Dairy Sci Asn, 66. *Mem:* Fel Am Soc Animal Sci; Am Dairy Sci Asn (vpres, 63-64, pres, 64-65); Am Inst Nutrit; Soc Nutrit Educ; Nutrit Today Soc. *Res:* Nutrition and physiology of animals. *Mailing Add:* 229 Woodburn Rd Raleigh NC 27605

WISE, HAROLD B, b Hamilton, Ont, Feb 14, 37. SOCIAL MEDICINE, INTERNAL MEDICINE. *Educ:* Univ Toronto, MD, 61. *Prof Exp:* Physician, Prince Albert Clin, Sask, Can, 62-63; resident, Kaiser Found Hosp, San Francisco, Calif, 63-64, Montefiore Hosp & Med Ctr, Bronx, NY, 64-65; actg dir ambulatory serv & home care, Morrisania City Hosp, 65-66; dir health ctr, Dr Martin Luther King, Jr Health Ctr, 66-71; dir anal & develop health teams, Montefiore Hosp & Med Ctr, 71-77; ASSOC PROF COMMUNITY HEALTH, ALBERT EINSTEIN COL MED, 70- *Concurrent Pos:* Milbank Mem Fund fel; Albert Einstein Col Med, 67-72; dir internship & residency prog social med, Montefiore Hosp & Med Ctr, 69-, dir inst health team develop, 72-; dir, Family Ctr Health. *Mem:* Nat Inst Med. *Res:* Research into the family and the healing processes. *Mailing Add:* Albert Einstein Col of Med Dept of Community Health Bronx NY 10461

WISE, HENRY, b Ciechanow, Poland, Jan 14, 19; nat US; m 43, 60; c 6. PHYSICAL CHEMISTRY. *Educ:* Univ Chicago, SB, 41, SM, 44, PhD(phys chem), 47. *Prof Exp:* Res assoc, Univ Chicago, 41-46; dir field lab, NY Univ, 46-47; scientist, Nat Adv Comt Aeronaut, Ohio, 47-49; phys chemist, Calif Inst Technol, 49-55; chmn chem dynamics dept, 55-71, SCI FEL, SRI INT, 71- *Concurrent Pos:* Lectr sch eng, Stanford Univ, 60-; vis prof, Israel Inst Technol, 65; vis prof, Univ Calif, Berkeley, 77-78; mem comt motor vehicle emission, Nat Acad Sci; lectr chem eng, Univ Calif, Berkeley, 80- *Mem:* Am Chem Soc; Am Phys Soc; Catalysis Soc; The Chem Soc. *Res:* Heterogeneous catalysis; chemical kinetics. *Mailing Add:* Mat Sci SRI Int Menlo Park CA 94025

WISE, HUGH EDWARD, JR, b Lafayette, Ind, Oct 12, 30. ORGANIC CHEMISTRY. *Educ:* Vanderbilt Univ, BA, 52; Univ Fla, PhD(chem), 61. *Prof Exp:* Proj leader, Tech Serv Lab, Union Carbide Corp, NY, 61-66, proj specialist, 66-68; res chemist, Nalco Chem Co, Ill, 68-70; res chemist, 70-71, field serv supvr, res & develop, Waste Treatment Div, Clow Corp, 71-77; ENVIRON SCIENTIST, EFFLUENT GUIDELINES DIV, ENVIRON PROTECTION AGENCY, 78- *Mem:* Am chem Soc; Water Pollution Control Fedn. *Res:* Environmental science and engineering; waste treatment technology; occurence and predictability of priority pollutants; chemistry of priority pollutants. *Mailing Add:* US Environ Protection Agency 401 M St SW Washington DC 20460

WISE, JOHN HICE, b Marysville, Pa, Nov 6, 20; m 43; c 3. PHYSICAL CHEMISTRY. *Educ:* Haverford Col, BS, 42; Brown Univ, PhD(chem), 47. *Prof Exp:* Asst chem, Brown Univ, 42-43, res chemist, Off Sci Res & Develop & Manhattan Proj, 43-46; from instr to asst prof chem, Stanford Univ, 47-53; assoc prof, 53-61, dept head, 70, PROF CHEM, WASHINGTON & LEE UNIV, 61- *Concurrent Pos:* Vis assoc prof, Brown Univ, 59-60; vis prof, Hollins Col, 63-64; teacher, Univ Va, 63 & 65 & Stanford Univ, 66; fac res partic, Argonne Nat Lab, 72-73. *Mem:* Am Chem Soc; Am Phys Soc. *Res:* Absorption and emission spectroscopy; infrared spectrometry; atomic and molecular structure. *Mailing Add:* Dept of Chem Washington & Lee Univ Lexington VA 24450

WISE, JOHN JAMES, b Cambridge, Mass, Feb 28, 32; m 67; c 2. PHYSICAL INORGANIC CHEMISTRY, CHEMICAL ENGINEERING. *Educ:* Tufts Univ, BS, 53; Mass Inst Technol, PhD(chem), 65. *Prof Exp:* Res engr, 53-55, sr res engr, 56-62, group leader appl res, 65-68, asst mgr appl res, 68-69, supvr appl develop, 69-76, mgr process res & develop, 76-77, V PRES PLANNING, MOBIL RES & DEVELOP CORP, 77- *Mem:* AAAS; Am Inst Chem Engrs; Am Chem Soc. *Res:* Catalysis related to petroleum and petrochemical processes. *Mailing Add:* Mobil Res & Develop Corp 150 E 42nd St New York NY 10017

WISE, JOHN P, b Boston, Mass, Feb 9, 24; m 60; c 3. FISHERIES BIOLOGY, MARINE BIOLOGY. *Educ:* Suffolk Univ, AB, 50; Univ NH, MS, 53. *Prof Exp:* Biologist, Woods Hole Lab, Bur Com Fisheries, 53-60; Food & Agr Orgn biologist, Govt Arg, Brazil, Tunisia & Uruguay, 60-64; biologist, Southwest Fisheries Ctr, Nat Marine Fisheries Serv, 65-73, sr analyst, 73-81; BIOSTATISTICIAN, INT COMN CONSERV ATLANTIC TUNAS, 81- *Concurrent Pos:* Consult, Food & Agr Orgn, 59 & 75; lectr George Washington Univ. & 75. *Mem:* AAAS; fel Am Inst Fishery Res Biol. *Res:* Stocks of marine animals, involving studies of ecology, growth rates, mortality rates, predation and parasitology, directed at eventual exploitation by man for maximum sustained yield. *Mailing Add:* Doce de Octubre 5 Madrid 9 Spain

WISE, JOHN THOMAS, b Orangeburg, SC, Nov 29, 26; m 55; c 3. CHEMISTRY, PAPER CHEMISTRY. *Educ:* The Citadel, BS, 46; Purdue Univ, MS, 49. *Prof Exp:* Chemist, Thiokol Chem Co, 49-50; chemist, 52-57, sr chemist, 57-65, group leader res & develop, 65-69, mgr tech serv sect, 69-70, mgr lab serv, 70-73, res coordr, 73-79, TECH SERV MGR, RES & DEVELOP, SONOCO PROD CO, 79- *Concurrent Pos:* Instr, Univ SC, 60; chmn tech comt, Composite Can & Tube Inst, 80- *Mem:* Am Chem Soc; Tech Asn Pulp & Paper Indust. *Res:* Physical and chemical testing; pulp and paper; paper products; utilization of waste products; organic synthesis; instrumentation. *Mailing Add:* Res Lab Sonoco Prod Co Hartsville SC 29950

WISE, LAWRENCE DAVID, b Canton, Ohio, Oct 13, 40; m 67; c 3. ORGANIC CHEMISTRY. *Educ:* Manchester Col, BA, 62; Ohio State Univ, MS, 64, PhD(org chem), 67. *Prof Exp:* Res scientist org chem, Goodyear Tire & Rubber Co, 67-69; res scientist org chem, Warner-Lambert Res Inst, 69-77; RES SCIENTIST ORG CHEM, WARNER-LAMBERT/PARKE DAVIS RES, 77- *Mem:* Am Chem Soc. *Res:* Synthetic organic chemistry, particularly heterocycles directed toward drug design. *Mailing Add:* Parke Davis Res 2800 Plymouth Rd Ann Arbor MI 48105

WISE, LEIGH SWITZEN, biochemistry, see previous edition

WISE, LOUIS NEAL, b Slagle, La, Jan 27, 21; m 44; c 2. AGRONOMY. *Educ:* Northwestern State Col, BS, 42; La State Univ, BS, 46, MS, 47; Purdue Univ, PhD(agron), 50. *Prof Exp:* Asst, Purdue Univ, 47-50; asst prof, 50-53, from assoc agronomist to agronomist, Exp Sta, 50-66, dir regional res lab, 52-66, dean sch agr, 61-66, vpres agr & forestry, 66-74, PROF AGRON, MISS STATE UNIV, 53-, V PRES AGR, FORESTRY & VET MED, 74- *Mem:* Am Soc Agron. *Res:* Pasture production and management; seed research. *Mailing Add:* Miss State Univ PO Box 5386 Mississippi State MS 39762

WISE, MATTHEW NORTON, b Tacoma, Wash, Apr 2, 40; m 65. HISTORY OF PHYSICS, HISTORY OF SCIENCE. *Educ:* Pac Lutheran Univ, BS, 62; Wash State Univ, PhD(physics), 68. *Prof Exp:* Asst prof physics, Auburn Univ, 67-69 & Ore State Univ, 69-71; NSF sci fac fel hist of sci, Princeton Univ, 71-72; lectr, 75-78, ASST PROF HIST, UNIV CALIF, LOS ANGELES, 78- *Mem:* Am Phys Soc; Am Asn Physics Teachers; Hist Sci Soc. *Res:* History of nineteenth and twentieth century physical sciences. *Mailing Add:* Dept of Hist 405 Hilgard Ave Univ of Calif Los Angeles CA 90024

WISE, MILTON BEE, b Newland, NC, July 17, 29; m 51; c 3. ANIMAL NUTRITION. *Educ:* Berea Col, BS, 51; NC State Col, MS, 53; Cornell Univ, PhD(animal nutrit), 57. *Prof Exp:* Lab supvr, Berea Col, 47-51; asst, NC State Col, 52-53, res assoc, 53-54; asst, Cornell Univ, 54-55, instr animal husb, 55-57; from asst prof to prof animal sci, NC State Univ, 57-70; PROF ANIMAL SCI & HEAD DEPT, VA POLYTECH INST & STATE UNIV, 70- *Mem:* Am Soc Animal Sci. *Res:* Mineral and nutrient metabolism; forage utilization; physiology of digestion. *Mailing Add:* Dept of Animal Sci VA Polytech Inst & State Univ Blacksburg VA 24061

WISE, RALEIGH WARREN, b Plainfield, NJ, Sept 30, 28; m 57. RESEARCH ADMINISTRATION, RUBBER CHEMISTRY. *Educ:* Univ Va, BS, 51. *Prof Exp:* Anal chemist, 51-53, anal res chemist, 54-56, res group leader, 56-65, res sect mgr, 65-71, group mgr, Instrument & Equip Div, 71-74, dir, 74-75, DIR TECHNOL, RUBBER CHEM DIV, MONSANTO INDUST CHEM CO, 75- *Mem:* Am Chem Soc; Instrument Soc Am; fel Am Inst Chemists. *Res:* Instrumentation; chemical and elastomer research. *Mailing Add:* Monsanto Indust Chem Co 260 Springside Dr Akron OH 44313

WISE, RICHARD MELVIN, b Greentown, Ohio, Sept 27, 24; m 68; c 3. ORGANIC CHEMISTRY. *Educ:* Mt Union Col, BS, 49; Ohio State Univ, PhD(org chem), 55. *Prof Exp:* Res chemist, 55-58, sr res chemist, 58-72, RES SCIENTIST, GEN TIRE & RUBBER CO, 72- *Mem:* Am Chem Soc. *Res:* Organic research; synthesis of monomers; preparation of polymerization catalysts and polymers; tire cord adhesives. *Mailing Add:* 2780 Wright Rd Uniontown OH 44685

WISE, ROBERT IRBY, b Barstow, Tex, May 19, 15; m 40; c 3. BACTERIOLOGY, INTERNAL MEDICINE. *Educ:* Univ Tex, BA, 37, MD, 50; Univ Ill, MS, 38, PhD(bact), 42; Am Bd Internal Med, dipl, 57. *Hon Degrees:* DSc, Thomas Jefferson Univ, 80. *Prof Exp:* Asst, Div Animal Genetics, Exp Sta, Univ Ill, 38-39, asst instr bact, 39-42; dir, Wichita City-County Pub Health Lab, Tex, 42-43; dir, Houston Pub Health Lab, 43; asst prof bact, Sch Med, Univ Tex, 43-46, dir bact & serol labs, Univ Hosp, 46-50; asst surgeon, USPHS Hosp, New Orleans, La, 50-51; fel med, Univ Minn, 51-53, asst prof, 53-54, asst prof med & bact, 54-55; from asst prof to assoc prof med, 55-59, Magee prof med & head dept, 59-75; asst chief med staff, 75-77, CHIEF OF STAFF, VET ADMIN MED & REGIONAL OFF CTR, TOGUS, 77-; EMER MAGEE PROF MED, JEFFERSON MED COL, 75- *Concurrent Pos:* Bacteriologist, Univ Hosp, Univ Minn, 57-59; assoc mem comn streptococcal dis, Armed Forces Epidemiol Bd, 58-66; physician-in-chief, Thomas Jefferson Univ Hosp, 59-75; mem bd trustees, Magee Mem Hosp, Philadelphia, 59-75 & Drexel Univ, 66-75; mem, Greater Philadelphia Comt Med-Pharmaceut Sci, 63-75, chmn, 70-74; mem adv comt, Inter-Soc Comt Heart Dis Resources, 67-70; mem bd-adv comt registry of tissue reaction, Univs Assoc for Res & Educ on Path, Inc, 70-75; mem exec comt, Int Cong Internal Med, 71. *Mem:* Am Fedn Clin Res; fel Am Col Physicians; Asn Am Physicians; Am Infectious Dis Soc; Am Pharmaceut Asn. *Res:* Infectious diseases; chemotherapy; antibiotics. *Mailing Add:* Vet Admin Hosp Togus ME 04330

WISE, SHERWOOD WILLING, JR, b Jackson, Miss, May 31, 41; m 65. GEOLOGY, PALEONTOLOGY. *Educ:* Washington & Lee Univ, BS, 63; Univ Ill, MS, 65, PhD(geol), 70. *Prof Exp:* NSF fel, Swiss Fed Inst Technol, 70-71; asst prof, 71-75, assoc prof, 75-80, PROF GEOL, FLA STATE UNIV, 80- *Concurrent Pos:* NSF res grant, 72-; res grant, Petrol Res Fund, 73-80. *Honors & Awards:* Outstanding Paper Award, Soc Econ Paleont & Mineral, 71. Mem Am Asn Petrol Geol; Soc Econ Paleont & Mineral; Am Micros Soc; Geol Soc Am; Swiss Geol Soc. *Res:* Skeletal ultrastructure; taxonomy and biostratigraphy of calcareous nannoplankton; early diagenesis of carbonate and siliceous sediment; circum-Antarctic marine geology. *Mailing Add:* Dept of Geol Fla State Univ Tallahassee FL 32306

WISE, WALTER R(OBERTSON), JR, mechanical engineering, see previous edition

WISE, WILLIAM CURTIS, b Louisville, Ky, Nov 24, 40; m 63; c 2. PHYSIOLOGY, BIOPHYSICS. *Educ:* Transylvania Univ, AB, 63; Univ Ky, PhD(physiol & biophys), 67. *Prof Exp:* Physiologist, McDonnell-Douglas Corp, 67-68; asst prof, 68-73, assoc prof, 73-80, PROF PHYSIOL, MED UNIV SC, 80- *Concurrent Pos:* Koebig Trust grant physiol, Med Univ SC, 72-73; Nat Cancer Inst res career develop award, 74- *Mem:* Sigma Xi; Am Physiol Soc; Soc Gen Physiologists; Biophys Soc; Shock Soc. *Res:* Entodoxic shock; septic shock; renal and acid-base physiology. *Mailing Add:* Dept of Physiol Med Univ of SC Charleston SC 29403

WISE, WILLIAM STEWART, b Carson City, Nev, Aug 18, 33; m 55; c 3. MINERALOGY, PETROLOGY. *Educ:* Stanford Univ, BS, 55, MS, 58; Johns Hopkins Univ, PhD(geol), 61. *Prof Exp:* Instr geol, Stanford Univ, 58 & Johns Hopkins Univ, 60-61; from asst prof to assoc prof, 61-73, assoc dean, Col Letters & Sci, 79-81, PROF GEOL, UNIV CALIF, SANTA BARBARA, 73-, DEAN, ACAD SKILLS, 81- *Concurrent Pos:* Consult, US Geol Surv, 65-67 & Argonne Nat Lab, 79- *Mem:* fel Geol Soc Am; fel Mineral Soc Am; Mineral Asn Can; Mineral Soc Gt Brit. *Res:* Paragenesis of minerals, principally zeolites and associated minerals, barium silicates; petrology of oceanic volcanoes. *Mailing Add:* Dept of Geol Sci Univ of Calif Santa Barbara CA 93106

WISEMAN, BILLY RAY, b Sudan, Tex, Mar 28, 37; m 63; c 2. ENTOMOLOGY, HORTICULTURE. *Educ:* Tex Tech Col, BS, 59; Kans State Univ, MS, 61, PhD(entom), 67. *Prof Exp:* Res asst host plant resistance, Kans State Univ, 59-61 & 64-66; res entomologist, Southern Grains Invests, Okla, 66-67; RES ENTOMOLOGIST, SOUTHERN GRAIN INSECTS LAB, AGR RES SERV, USDA, 67- *Concurrent Pos:* Mem grad fac, Univ Ga & Univ Fla; courtesy prof, grad courses in plant resistance to insects, Univ Fla. *Mem:* Entom Soc Am. *Res:* Entomological research in host plant resistance of small grains, corn, sorghum and vegetable crops and the insects attacking these crops, including feeding stimulants, deterrents, food utilization, behavior and biology. *Mailing Add:* Southern Grain Insects Res Lab Ga Coastal Plain Exp Sta Tifton GA 31794

WISEMAN, CARL D, b Chicago, Ill, Oct 25, 25; m 49; c 3. PHYSICAL METALLURGY. *Educ:* Southern Methodist Univ, BS, 50; Univ Calif, MS, 55, PhD(metall), 57. *Prof Exp:* Res engr, Calif, 51-57; metallurgist, Gen Elec Co, 57-59 & Tex Instruments, Inc, 59-64; assoc prof eng mech, 64-69, PROF ENG MECH, UNIV TEX, ARLINGTON, 69- *Mem:* Am Soc Metals; Am Inst Mining, Metall & Petrol Engrs. *Res:* Plastic deformation of metals; nuclear reactor metallurgy; metal failure analysis; metallurgy of semiconductors and thermoelectric materials; surfaces of solids to fields of research. *Mailing Add:* Dept of Mech Eng Univ of Tex Arlington TX 76010

WISEMAN, EDWARD H, b Portsmouth, Eng, Nov 14, 34; m 57; c 4. BIOCHEMICAL PHARMACOLOGY. *Educ:* Univ Birmingham, BSc, 56, PhD(org chem), 59. *Prof Exp:* Fel, Ohio State Univ, 60; res chemist, 61-64, supvr biochem pharmacol, 64-67, asst to res vpres, 67, mgr biochem pharmacol, 67-71, dir pharmacol, 71-76, EXEC DIR RES ADMIN, PFIZER INC, 76- *Mem:* Am Rheumatism Asn; Am Soc Pharmacol & Exp Therapeut. *Res:* Non-steroidal anti-inflammatory agents; biochemistry of metabolic diseases. *Mailing Add:* Pfizer Inc Groton CT 06341

WISEMAN, GEORGE EDWARD, b Brooklyn, NY, May 28, 18; m 45; c 3. INORGANIC CHEMISTRY, ORGANIC CHEMISTRY. *Educ:* St Peter's Col, BS, 40; Polytech Inst Brooklyn, PhD(chem), 56. *Prof Exp:* Assoc prof chem, St John's Univ, NY, 46-59; chmn dept chem, 59-66, assoc grad dean, Conolly, 66-71, PROF CHEM, LONG ISLAND UNIV, 59- *Mem:* Am Chem Soc; fel Am Inst Chemists. *Res:* Preparation, properties and structures of organoselenium compounds; heterocyclic compounds; metallic derivatives of aromatic hydrocarbons. *Mailing Add:* Dept of Chem Long Island Univ Brooklyn NY 11201

WISEMAN, GORDON G, b Livingston, Wis, Feb 24, 17; m 42; c 2. PHYSICS. *Educ:* SDak State Univ, BS, 38; Univ Kans, MS, 41, AM, 47, PhD(physics), 50. *Prof Exp:* Instr physics, Culver-Stockton Col, 41-43; from instr to assoc prof, 43-64, PROF PHYSICS, UNIV KANS, 64- *Mem:* Am Phys Soc; Am Asn Physics Teachers. *Res:* Dielectrics; absorption microspectrophotometry; ferroelectricity. *Mailing Add:* Dept of Physics & Astron Univ of Kans Lawrence KS 66044

WISEMAN, GORDON MARCY, b Winnipeg, Man, Feb 24, 34; m 56. BACTERIOLOGY. *Educ:* Univ Man, BSc, 56, MSc, 61; Univ Edinburgh, PhD(bact), 63, DSc, 74. *Prof Exp:* Demonstr, 57-59, asst prof, 65-72, assoc prof, 72-75, PROF BACT, FAC MED, UNIV MAN, 75- *Concurrent Pos:* Med Res Coun fel bact, Fac Med, Univ Man, 64 & scholar, 65- *Mem:* Am Soc Microbiol; Can Soc Microbiol. *Res:* Neisseria gonorrhoeae; adhesion to host cells in relation to pathogenicity and virulence. *Mailing Add:* Dept Med Microbiol Univ Manitoba Winnipeg MB R3E 0W3 Can

WISEMAN, H(ARRY) A(LEXANDER) B(ENJAMIN), b Montreal, Que, Dec 27, 24; m 44; c 1. ENGINEERING MECHANICS. *Educ:* Univ Sask, BSc, 47; Wash State Univ, MS, 49; Pa State Univ, PhD(eng mech), 54. *Prof Exp:* Instr, Wash State Univ, 47-49; asst & res assoc, Pa State Univ, 49-54; res officer, Nat Res Coun Can, 54-55; assoc prof eng, Univ Del, 55-58; prof civil & mech eng, 58-76, prof biomed eng, Sch Med, 70-76, PROF MECH ENG, UNIV MIAMI, 76- *Mem:* Am Soc Eng Educ; Am Soc Mech Engrs; Nat Soc Prof Engrs; Am Soc Metals; Am Soc Artificial Internal Organs. *Res:* Biaxial and triaxial stress and strain relations; prestressed concrete; solid state studies of ultra high pressures; electron microscope metallography; high velocity stress-strain phenomena; photo stress and elasticity; biomedical engineering. *Mailing Add:* Dept of Civil & Mech Eng Univ of Miami Coral Gables FL 33124

WISEMAN, JOHN R, b Patriot, Ohio, May 4, 36; m 56; c 3. ORGANIC CHEMISTRY. *Educ:* Univ Colo, BS, 57; Stanford Univ, PhD(chem), 65. *Prof Exp:* NSF fel chem, Univ Calif, Berkeley, 64-65, lectr, 65-66, fel, 66; asst prof, 66-70, assoc prof, 70-76, PROF CHEM, UNIV MICH, 76- *Concurrent Pos:* Grants, Petrol Res Fund, 68-73; Res Corp grant, 68-69; Am Cancer Soc grant, 72-77, Nat Cancer Inst, 78-80. *Mem:* AAAS; Am Chem Soc; Royal Soc Chem. *Res:* strain of bicyclic bridgehead alkenes; reaction of carbonium ions; synthesis of natural products. *Mailing Add:* Dept of Chem Univ Mich Ann Arbor MI 48109

WISEMAN, LAWRENCE LINDEN, b Galion, Ohio, Apr 27, 44; c 2. DEVELOPMENTAL BIOLOGY. *Educ:* Hiram Col, AB, 66; Princeton Univ, MA, 69, PhD(biol), 70. *Prof Exp:* Nat Cancer Inst fel, Princeton Univ, 70-71; asst prof, 71-77, ASSOC PROF BIOL, COL WILLIAM & MARY, 77- *Concurrent Pos:* Vis scientist, Human Leukemia Prog, Ont Cancer Inst, Toronto, 74-75. *Mem:* AAAS; Soc Develop Biol; Am Soc Zool; Am Soc Cell Biol; Int Soc Develop Biologists. *Res:* Cell adhesion, cell movement; vertebrate embryology. *Mailing Add:* Dept of Biol Col of William & Mary Williamsburg VA 23185

WISEMAN, PARK ALLEN, b Amsden, Ohio, Dec 29, 18; m 42; c 1. ORGANIC CHEMISTRY. *Educ:* DePauw Univ, AB, 40; Purdue Univ, MA, 42, PhD(org chem), 44. *Prof Exp:* Asst org & phys chem, Purdue Univ, 40-42, Monsanto Chem Co res fel org chem, 44-46; res chemist, Firestone Tire & Rubber Co, Ohio, 46-47; from asst prof to assoc prof, 47-56, hed dept, 65-69, prof, 56-81, EMER PROF CHEM, BALL STATE UNIV, 81- *Concurrent Pos:* NSF vis prof, Tech Inst Northwestern Univ, 69-70. *Mem:* AAAS; Am Chem Soc. *Res:* High pressure oxidation of hydrocarbons; catalytic vapor-phase oxidation of hydrocarbons; fluorine chemistry; organic synthesis and natural products. *Mailing Add:* Dept of Chem Ball State Univ Muncie IN 47306

WISEMAN, RALPH FRANKLIN, b Washington, DC, Sept 1, 21; m 51; c 2. MICROBIOLOGY. *Educ:* Univ Md, BS, 49; Univ Hawaii, MS, 53; Univ Wis, PhD(bact), 56. *Prof Exp:* Lab asst, Nat Cancer Inst, 39-42, med bacteriologist, Nat Inst Dent Res, 49-51; asst bact, Univ Hawaii, 51-53; asst, Univ Wis, 53-55, instr, 55-56; from instr to assoc prof, 56-66, PROF MICROBIOL, UNIV KY, 66- *Concurrent Pos:* Vis prof, Hacettepe Univ, Turkey, 68-69 & Rega Inst

Med Res, Cath Univ, Louvain, 69. *Mem:* Am Soc Microbiol; Asn Gnotobiotics; fel Am Acad Microbiol. *Res:* Intestinal microbiology; germ free-like characteristics in antibiotic-treated animals; animal-microbial ecosystems. *Mailing Add:* Morgan Sch of Biol Sci Univ of Ky Lexington KY 40506

WISEMAN, ROBERT S, b Robinson, Ill, Feb 27, 24; m 47; c 1. ILLUMINATING ENGINEERING, ELECTRICAL ENGINEERING. *Educ:* Univ Ill, BSEE, 48, MSEE, 50, PhD(elec eng), 54. *Prof Exp:* Instr & asst prof elec eng, Miss State Col, 48-51; chief, Res Sect, US Army Eng Res & Develop Lab, 51-58, chief, Warfare Vision Br, 58-65; dir, Combat Serv, US Army Electronics Res & Develop Command, 65-68, dep for labs, 68-71, dir, RED/Army Electronics Labs, 71-78, tech dir, 78-79; dep sci & technol, Darcom, 79-80; DIR ELECTRONICS LAB, MARTIN MARIETTA AEROSPACE-ORLANDO DIV, 81- *Concurrent Pos:* Mem, Nat Res Coun comt on vision, 54- *Honors & Awards:* ERDL Res & Develop Leadership Award, Army ERDL, 61; Army Meritorious Award, Dept Army, 65, Army Res & Develop Achievement Award, 65, Army Except Serv Medal, 68; DOD Distinguished Serv Medal, Dept Defense, 69. *Mem:* AAAS; fel Illum Eng Soc; Sigma Xi; Inst Elec & Electronics Engrs; Am Soc Eng Educ; Armed Forces Commun & Electronics Asn. *Res:* Night vision; combat surveillance and target acquisition; electronics/signals warfare; atmospheric sciences; electronic technology and devices; illuminating engineering; electro-optics. *Mailing Add:* US Army Mat Develop & Readiness Command 5001 Eisenhower Ave Alexandria VA 22333

WISEMAN, WILLIAM H(OWARD), b Chillicothe, Ohio, May 11, 29; m 50; c 2. CHEMICAL ENGINEERING. *Educ:* Ohio State Univ, BSChE, 53; Lawrence Col, MS, 55, PhD, 58. *Prof Exp:* Asst tech dir, WVa Pulp & Paper Co, 58-59; asst paper mill supt, 59-61; prod mgr bd div, Brunswick Pulp & Paper Co, Ga, 61-65, asst gen prod mgr, 65-69, opers mgr, 69-71; plant mgr, 71-77, V PRES & GEN MGR BLEACHED OPERS, CONTINENTAL CAN CO, 77- *Mem:* Tech Asn Pulp & Paper Indust. *Res:* Pulp and paper technology. *Mailing Add:* Continental Group PO Box 1425 Augusta GA 30903

WISEMAN, WILLIAM JOSEPH, JR, b Summit, NJ, June 16, 43; m 65; c 2. OCEANOGRAPHY. *Educ:* Johns Hopkins Univ, BES, 64, MS, 66, MA, 68, PhD(oceanog), 69. *Prof Exp:* Instr geol, Univ NH, 69-70, asst prof earth sci, 70-71; asst prof, 71-75, assoc prof, 75-80, PROF MARINE SCI, LA STATE UNIV, BATON ROUGE, 80-, CHMN MARINE SCI, COASTAL STUDIES INST, 77- *Mem:* Am Geophys Union; Inst Elec & Electronics Engrs. *Res:* Estuarine and nearshore circulation. *Mailing Add:* Coastal Studies Inst La State Univ Baton Rouge LA 70803

WISER, CYRUS WYMER, b Wartrace, Tenn, Jan 14, 23; m 45; c 3. AQUATIC ECOLOGY, PHYSIOLOGY. *Educ:* Harding Col, BS, 45; George Peabody Col, MA, 46; Vanderbilt Univ, PhD(biol), 56. *Prof Exp:* Instr biol, David Lipscomb Col, 46-49; assoc prof, Jacksonville State Teachers Col, 49-51, 53-54; vis asst prof, Vanderbilt Univ, 54-55; assoc prof, 56-61, PROF BIOL, MID TENN STATE UNIV, 61- *Mem:* Sigma Xi. *Res:* Physiology, aquatic ecology and limnology; population studies of ponds and lakes; accumulation of radioactive isotopes by aquatic organisms. *Mailing Add:* Dept Biol Mid Tenn State Univ Murfreesboro TN 37130

WISER, EDWARD H(EMPSTEAD), b Fatehgarh, India, Jan 21, 31; US citizen; m 57; c 2. AGRICULTURAL ENGINEERING. *Educ:* Iowa State Univ, BS, 53; NC State Univ, MS, 58, PhD(agr eng), 64. *Prof Exp:* From instr to assoc prof agr eng, 57-76, PROF BIOL & AGR ENG, NC STATE UNIV, 76- *Mem:* Am Geophys Union; Am Soc Agr Engrs; Am Soc Agron; Soil Conserv Soc Am. *Res:* Prediction of water yield from agricultural watersheds; computer simulation of precipitation and streamflow; statistical methods in hydrology. *Mailing Add:* Dept of Biol & Agr Eng NC State Univ Raleigh NC 27607

WISER, HORACE CLARE, b Lewiston, Utah, Jan 26, 33; m 53; c 4. MATHEMATICS. *Educ:* Univ Utah, BA, 53, PhD(math), 61; Univ Wash, BS, 54. *Prof Exp:* From asst prof to assoc prof, 61-74, PROF MATH, WASH STATE UNIV, 74- *Mem:* Am Math Soc; Math Asn Am. *Res:* Undergraduate mathematics curriculum; point set topology. *Mailing Add:* Dept of Math Wash State Univ Pullman WA 99163

WISER, JAMES ELDRED, b Wartrace, Tenn, Dec 31, 15; m 41; c 1. ANALYTICAL CHEMISTRY. *Educ:* Mid Tenn State Col, BS, 38; Peabody Col, MA, 40, PhD(sci educ), 47. *Prof Exp:* Teacher high sch, Fla, 38-39 & Ala State Teachers Col, 40-41; teacher physics, Vanderbilt Univ, 42; teacher chem & physics, David Lipscomb Col, 42-46; PROF CHEM & HEAD DEPT CHEM & PHYSICS, MID TENN STATE UNIV, 46- *Concurrent Pos:* Instr, Peabody Col, 44; NSF panelist, 64, 68 & 71. *Mem:* AAAS; emer mem Am Chem Soc; Am Inst Chem. *Res:* Food chemistry; educational psychology. *Mailing Add:* Dept of Chem & Physics Mid Tenn State Univ Murfreesboro TN 37130

WISER, NATHAN, b Zurich, Switz, 1935; m 61; c 4. THEORETICAL PHYSICS, MATERIAL SCIENCE. *Educ:* Wayne State Univ, BS, 57; Univ Chicago, MS, 59, PhD(physics), 64. *Prof Exp:* Res assoc physics, Univ Ill, 64-65; sr res scientist, IBM Watson Res Ctr, 65-67; assoc prof, 67-74, PROF PHYSICS, BAR-ILAN UNIV, ISRAEL, 74- *Concurrent Pos:* Fel, NSF, 62-64; Res grant, Nat Bur Standards, 67-70, US-Israel Binational Sci Found, 71-81 & Israel Acad Sci, 76-81; vis prof, Univ Cambridge, Eng, 80-81. *Mem:* Fel Am Phys Soc; European Phys Soc; Israel Phys Soc. *Res:* Theory of metals, including their electrical, thermal and structural properties; liquid metals; condensed matter physics; theory of phase transitions; dielectric theory. *Mailing Add:* Dept Physics Bar-Ilan Univ Ramat-Gan 52100 Israel

WISER, THOMAS HENRY, b Minneapolis, Minn, May 17, 46. CLINICAL PHARMACY. *Educ:* Univ Minn, BS, 71, PharmD, 73. *Prof Exp:* ASST PROF CLIN PHARM, SCH PHARM, UNIV MD, 74-, ASSOC DIR PRIMARY CARE PROG, SCH MED, 75-; PHARMACIST, 71- *Concurrent Pos:* Clin pharm practicioner, Univ Md Hosp, 73-, clin pharm consult, 73-, co-dir, Anticoagulant clin, 76-, co-dir, Therapeut Probs Clin, 77-; clin pharm consult, Loch Raven Vet Admin Hosp, 74-, Baltimore City Jail, 77-, Critical Care Nurses' Asn, 78- & Am Pharmaceut Asn Policy Comt Prof Affairs, 78-; mem, Md Comn Nursing, 75-76. *Honors & Awards:* Outstanding Contrib Award, Md Comn Nurses, 76. *Mem:* Am Pharmaceut Asn; Am Asn Col Pharm; Am Asn Hosp Pharmacists. *Res:* Ambulatory care; medical audits; clinical pharmacy services; drug utilization; adverse reactions; patient education. *Mailing Add:* Univ of Med Sch of Pharm 636 W Lombard St Baltimore MD 21201

WISER, WENDELL H(ASLAM), b Fairview, Idaho, Dec 16, 22; m 47; c 5. FUEL ENGINEERING, PHYSICAL CHEMISTRY. *Educ:* Univ Utah, BS, 49, PhD(fuel eng), 52. *Prof Exp:* Res assoc explosives res, Univ Utah, 52-53; asst prof chem eng, Brigham Young Univ, 55-58; pres, Church Col, NZ, 60-65; assoc prof, 65-69, chmn dept, 66-70, PROF FUELS ENG, UNIV UTAH, 69- *Concurrent Pos:* Consult, Power Plant Div, Boeing Airplane Co, 56-58; US ed, Fuel, 70-78. *Honors & Awards:* Henry H Storch Award, Am Chem Soc, 78. *Mem:* Am Inst Aeronaut & Astronaut; fel Brit Interplanetary Soc; Am Chem Soc. *Res:* Jet engine fuels; rocket propellants; production of liquid and gaseous fuels from coal. *Mailing Add:* Dept Mining & Fuels Eng Univ Utah Salt Lake City UT 84112

WISER, WINFRED LAVERN, b Wartrace, Tenn, June 14, 26; m 74; c 2. OBSTETRICS & GYNECOLOGY. *Educ:* Middle Tenn Univ, BS, 49; Univ Tenn, MD, 52. *Prof Exp:* Intern, John Gaston Hosp, 53; resident obstet & gynec, Sch Med, Univ Miss, 62; asst prof, Med Ctr, Univ Miss, 67-68; assoc prof, Ctr Health Sci, Univ Tenn, 68-73, prof, 73-76; PROF & CHMN OBSTET & GYNEC, SCH MED, UNIV MISS, 76- *Concurrent Pos:* Dir gynec, Ctr Health Sci, Univ Tenn, 68-76, dep chmn obstet & gynec, 71-76, actg chmn, 74-76; Consult staff, Vet Admin Hosp & Methodist Rehab Ctr, 76- *Mem:* AMA; Am Soc Fertility & Sterility; Am Col Surgeons; Am Col Obstetricians & Gynecologists. *Res:* Gynecology; congenital anomalies of the uterus; infertility. *Mailing Add:* Dept Obstet & Gynec Sch Med Univ Miss 2500 N State St Jackson MS 39216

WISHINSKY, HENRY, b New York, NY, Feb 2, 19; m 47; c 4. BIO-ORGANIC CHEMISTRY. *Educ:* NY Univ, BA, 41, MS, 44; Georgetown Univ, PhD(org biochem), 51. *Prof Exp:* Res chemist, Wallace & Tiernan, Inc, NJ, 41-46; dir res develop, Universal Synthetics, Inc, NY, 46-49; chem dir endocrinol lab, Med Sch & Hosp, Georgetown Univ, 49-51; dir div biochem, Sinai Hosp Baltimore, 52-64; dir, Res Lab, Ames Div, 64-68, vpres res & develop, 68-77, vpres, Res & Develop Resources, Prof Prods Group, 77-78, VPRES SCI & REGULATORY AFFAIRS, PROF PROD GROUP, MILES LABS, INC, 78- *Concurrent Pos:* Lectr, Sinai Sch Nursing, Baltimore, 52-64; consult biochem, Lutheran Hosp, Baltimore, 54-64, Franklin Square Hosp, Baltimore, 56-64, James L Kernan Hosp, Baltimore, 62-64 & Guerin & Kime Clin Lab, Md, 61-64. *Mem:* AAAS; Am Asn Clin Chem; Am Asn Poison Control Ctrs; Asn Clin Sci; Am Chem Soc. *Res:* Proteins, steroids, instrumentation and laboratory design. *Mailing Add:* Sci & Regulatory Affairs Div Miles Labs Inc Elkhart IN 46514

WISHNER, LAWRENCE ARNDT, b New York, NY, Sept 7, 32; m 55; c 2. BIOCHEMISTRY. *Educ:* Univ Md, BS, 54, MS, 61, PhD(food chem), 64. *Prof Exp:* Asst dairy dept, Univ Md, 57-61, from asst prof to assoc prof chem, 61-68, chmn dept, 67-71, asst dean, 71-77, PROF CHEM, MARY WASHINGTON COL, 68- *Mem:* Am Chem Soc; Am Oil Chem Soc; Am Inst Chem; NY Acad Sci; Sigma Xi. *Res:* Light-induced oxidation of milk; thermal oxidation of fats; autoxidation of tissue lipids in vivo; biological antioxidants. *Mailing Add:* Dept Chem Mary Washington Col Fredericksburg VA 22401

WISHNETSKY, THEODORE, b New York, NY, July 5, 25; m 48; c 2. FOOD TECHNOLOGY, CRYOGENICS. *Educ:* Cornell Univ, BS, 49, MS, 50; Univ Mass, PhD(food technol), 58. *Prof Exp:* Res assoc, NY Agr Exp Sta, Geneva, 50-54; chemist, Eastman Chem Prod, Inc, 58-62; sr scientist, Air Prod & Chem, Inc, Pa, 62-68; ASSOC PROF FOOD SCI, MICH STATE UNIV, 68- *Mem:* Inst Food Technol; Soc Cryobiol. *Res:* Fruit and vegetable processing; processing and marketing of frozen foods; mechanism of changes in frozen foods; application of cryogenic technology to processing problems; low-temperature preservation of foods; controlled atmospheres; packaging. *Mailing Add:* Dept Food Sci & Human Nutrit Mich State Univ East Lansing MI 48824

WISHNIA, ARNOLD, b New York, NY, July 1, 31; m 52; c 3. BIOPHYSICAL CHEMISTRY, MOLECULAR BIOLOGY. *Educ:* Cornell Univ, AB, 52; NY Univ, PhD(biochem), 57. *Prof Exp:* Res assoc chem, Yale Univ, 56-59; from asst prof to assoc prof biochem, Dartmouth Med Sch, 59-66; ASSOC PROF CHEM, STATE UNIV NY, STONY BROOK, 66- *Concurrent Pos:* USPHS sr fel, Dept Natural Philos, Univ Edinburgh, 67. *Mem:* Am Soc Biol Chemists; Am Chem Soc; Biophys Soc. *Res:* Ribosome chemistry on five dollars a day. *Mailing Add:* Dept of Chem State Univ of NY Stony Brook NY 11794

WISHNICK, MARCIA M, b New York, NY, Oct 10, 38; m 60; c 1. GENETICS, PEDIATRICS. *Educ:* Barnard Col, BA, 60; NY Univ, PhD(biochem), 70, MD, 74. *Prof Exp:* Chemist, Lederle Labs, Am Cyanamid Co, 60-66; assoc biochem, Pub Health Res Labs, City of New York, 70-71; res assoc pharmacol, Sch Med, 71, ASST PROF PEDIAT, NY UNIV MED CTR, 77- *Concurrent Pos:* Resident pediat, NY Univ-Bellevue Med Ctr, 74-77, asst attending pediat, 77- *Mem:* AAAS; Am Soc Human Genetics; Am Acad Pediat; Am Med Women's Asn. *Res:* Inborn errors in metabolism. *Mailing Add:* 920 Park Ave New York NY 10028

WISIAN-NELSON, PATTY JOAN, b Cuero, Tex, Aug 22, 49; m 76; c 1. CHEMISTRY. *Educ:* Tex Lutheran Col, BS, 71; Univ Tex Austin, PhD(inorg chem), 76. *Prof Exp:* Res assoc, Duke Univ, 76-78; res assoc, Univ Tex, Arlington, 78; res assoc, 79-80, RES SCIENTIST, TEX CHRISTIAN UNIV, 80-, ASST PROF, 81- *Concurrent Pos:* Prin investr, Army Res Off grant, Tex Christian Univ, 80- *Mem:* Am Chem Soc; Sigma Xi. *Res:* Synthesis, characterization and reactivity of compounds containing the silicon-nitrogen-phosphorus linkage, particularly those that are precursors to polymeric polyphasphazenes with alkyl and/or aryl subsituents. *Mailing Add:* Dept Chem Tex Christian Univ Fort Worth TX 76129

WISMAN, EVERETT LEE, b Woodstock, Va, Oct 1, 22; m 48; c 3. POULTRY SCIENCE. *Educ:* Va Polytech Inst & State Univ, BS, 46; Cornell Univ, MS, 49; Pa State Univ, PhD(biochem, poultry husb), 52. *Prof Exp:* County agr agent, 47-48, PROF POULTRY SCI, VA POLYTECH INST & STATE UNIV, 52- *Concurrent Pos:* Bd trustees, Sci Mus of Va, 77-80. *Honors & Awards:* Distinguished Serv Award, Asn Acad Sci, AAAS, 71. *Mem:* Am Poultry Sci Asn; Am Inst Nutrit; Asn Acad Sci (pres, 79); AAAS. *Res:* Role of antibiotics, arsenicals and other feed additives in chick growth stimulation; evaluation of animal by-products in poultry rations. *Mailing Add:* Dept of Poultry Sci Va Polytech Inst & State Univ Blacksburg VA 24061

WISMAR, BETH LOUISE, b Cleveland, Ohio, Feb 18, 29. ANATOMY, MEDICAL EDUCATION. *Educ:* Western Reserve Univ, BSc, 51, MSc, 57; Ohio State Univ, PhD(anat), 61. *Prof Exp:* Instr embryol & histol, Col Med, 61-63, asst prof anat, Col Med & Col Arts & Sci, 63-69, ASSOC PROF ANAT, COL MED & COL ARTS & SCI, OHIO STATE UNIV, 69- *Res:* Comparative and human histology, especially cardiovascular and urogenital systems; audio-visual methods and programming in science education. *Mailing Add:* Dept of Anat Ohio State Univ Columbus OH 43210

WISMER, MARCO, b Switz, Dec 26, 21; nat US; m 52; c 2. POLYMER CHEMISTRY. *Educ:* Swiss Fed Inst Technol, PhD, 48. *Prof Exp:* Res chemist, Amercoat Corp, 49-51; tech mgr plastics div, Ciba Prod Corp, 51-56; res assoc, Springdale Res Ctr, 56-62, scientist, 62-64, dir advan res dept, 64-74, VPRES RES & DEVELOP, RES CTR, PPG INDUST, INC, 74- *Honors & Awards:* IR-100, Indust Res, 66 & 74. *Mem:* Am Chem Soc; Am Soc Test & Mat; Fedn Soc Paint Technol. *Res:* Synthesis of epoxy resins; polyester resins; polyester polyols; chlorinated compounds; urethane technology; epoxidation thecnology; synthetic organic chemistry; polyolefin chemistry; unsaturated polyesters; radiation technology and electrodeposition. *Mailing Add:* 1215 Applewood Dr Gibsonia PA 15044

WISMER, ROBERT KINGSLEY, b Atlantic City, NJ, June 18, 45; m 70; c 1. X-RAY CRYSTALLOGRAPHY, CHEMICAL EDUCATION. *Educ:* Haverford Col, BS, 67; Iowa State Univ, PhD(phys chem), 72. *Prof Exp:* Instr chem, Iowa State Univ, 72; systs analyst comput sci, Ames Lab, Energy Res & Develop Admin, 73; asst prof chem, Luther Col, Iowa, 73-74; asst prof chem, Denison Univ, 74-76; asst prof, 76-80, ASSOC PROF CHEM, MILLERSVILLE STATE COL, 80- *Mem:* Am Chem Soc; AAAS; Am Crystallog Asn. *Res:* Solution of the phase problem through deconvolution of the Patterson function, especially development of techniques adaptable to small computers; general chemistry author. *Mailing Add:* Dept of Chem Millersville State Col Millersville PA 17551

WISNER, JACKSON WARD, JR, b Baltimore, Md, Aug 7, 25; m 63; c 3. ORGANIC CHEMISTRY. *Educ:* Univ Vt, BS, 50, MS, 52; Western Reserve Univ, PhD(org chem), 57. *Prof Exp:* Chemist, 57-59, sr chemist, 59-64, res chemist, 64-72, SR RES CHEMIST, TEXACO RES CTR, 72- *Mem:* Am Chem Soc; Sigma Xi. *Res:* Evaluation of additives for lubricants; formulation of lubricants useful in automotive vehicles. *Mailing Add:* Texaco Res Ctr PO Box 509 Beacon NY 12508

WISNER, ROBERT JOEL, b Hannibal, Mo, Jan 18, 25; m 47; c 4. ALGEBRA. *Educ:* Univ Ill, BS, 48, MS, 49; Univ Wash, PhD(math), 53. *Prof Exp:* Assoc math, Univ Wash, 51-53, res mathematician, Pub Opinion Lab, 52-53; instr math, Univ BC, 53-54; from asst prof to assoc prof, Haverford Col, 54-60; assoc prof, Mich State Univ, Oakland, 60-63; assoc prof, 63-70, head dept math, 70-77, PROF MATH SCI, NMEX STATE UNIV, 70- *Concurrent Pos:* Consult, Burroughs Corp, 57-58; NSF fel & mem, Inst Advan Study, 59-60; ed, Rev, Soc Indust & Appl Math, 59- *Mem:* Am Math Soc; Soc Indust & Appl Math; Math Asn Am; Am Statist Asn; Can Math Cong. *Res:* Rings; Abelian groups; number theory. *Mailing Add:* Dept of Math NMex State Univ Las Cruces NM 88003

WISNIESKI, BERNADINE JOANN, b Baltimore, Md, Feb 26, 45. PHYSICAL BIOCHEMISTRY. *Educ:* Univ Md, College Park, BS, 67; Univ Calif, Berkeley, PhD(genetics), 71. *Prof Exp:* Damon Runyon Mem Fund fel, 71-73, Celeste Durand Rogers Mem Found fel, 73-74, actg asst prof, 74-75, asst prof, 75-80, ASSOC PROF MICROBIOL, UNIV CALIF, LOS ANGELES, 80- *Concurrent Pos:* Mem, Cancer Res Ctr, Univ Calif, Los Angeles, 75-, assoc mem, Molecular Biol Inst, 75- *Mem:* AAAS; Sigma Xi. *Res:* Function and physical structure of animal cell membranes; membrane alterations; photoreactive probes, spin labels and protein insertion into membranes; membrane fusion induced by viral proteins; protein toxins. *Mailing Add:* Dept of Microbiol Univ of Calif Los Angeles CA 90024

WISNIEWSKI, HENRYK MIROSLAW, b Luszkowko, Poland, Feb 27, 31; US citizen; m 54; c 2. NEUROPATHOLOGY, PATHOLOGY. *Educ:* Med Acad, Danzig, physician dipl, 55; Med Acad, Warsaw, Dr Med, 60, docent, 65. *Prof Exp:* Resident res fel, Med Acad, Gdansk, Poland, 55-58; from asst to assoc prof neuropath, head of lab & assoc dir, Inst Neuropath, Polish Acad Sci, Warsaw, 58-66; from res assoc to asst prof path, Albert Einstein Col Med, Yeshiva Univ, 66-69, assoc prof neuropath, 69-74, prof neuropath, 74-76; PROF PATH, STATE UNIV NY DOWNSTATE MED CTR, 76-; DIR NY STATE INST BASIC RES, STATEN ISLAND, 76- *Concurrent Pos:* Health Res Coun New York career scientist award, 70-72; Nat Multiple Sclerosis Soc fel, 71-74; NIH fel, 72-77; vis neuropathologist, Univ Toronto, 61-62; vis scientist, lab of Neuropath, Nat Inst Neurol Dis & Blindness, 62-63; consult, Merck Labs, Rahway, NJ, 72-74; dir Demyelinating Dis Unit, Med Res Coun, Newcastle-upon-Tyne, Eng, 74-76. *Honors & Awards:* Weil Award, Am Asn Neuropathologists, 69, Moore Award, 72. *Mem:* Am Asn Neuropath; Polish Asn Neuropath; Polish Asn Path; Am Asn Geront. *Res:* Light and ultrastructural studies of the pathological brain; experimental neuropathology; synaptic and axonal pathology; developmental neurobiology; mental retardation; pre and senile dementia; multiple sclerosis and other human and experimental demyelinating diseases. *Mailing Add:* NY State Inst Basic Res 1050 Forest Hill Rd Staten Island NY 10314

WISOTZKY, JOEL, b Chicago, Ill, Feb 17, 23; m 49; c 3. DENTISTRY, DENTAL RESEARCH. *Educ:* Cent YMCA Col, BS, 45; Loyola Univ, DDS, 47; Univ Rochester, PhD(exp path), 56. *Prof Exp:* Pvt pract, 48-49; sr asst dent surgeon, Fed Correctional Inst, Tex, 49-51; fel, Univ Rochester, 51-56; res assoc exp path, Dent Med Div, Colgate-Palmolive Co, 56-59; hon assoc res specialist, Bur Biol Res, Rutgers Univ, 57-59; assoc prof res dent med, Sch Dent, Case Western Reserve Univ, 59-63, prof med & dir dent res, 63-72, prof oral biol, 63-80, dir grad training & res, 72-80. *Concurrent Pos:* USPHS res fel, 52-56, career develop award, 59-65. *Mem:* AAAS; Am Soc Exp Path; Int Asn Dent Res. *Res:* Cariology; aging changes in oral tissues; phosphorescence of oral structures; electro-physiology; theoretical oral biology. *Mailing Add:* 3407 Blanche Cleveland Heights OH 44118

WISSBRUN, KURT FALKE, b Brackwede, Ger, Mar 19, 30; nat US. POLYMER SCIENCE, RHEOLOGY. *Educ:* Univ Pa, BS, 52; Yale Univ, MS, 53, PhD(phys chem), 56. *Prof Exp:* Dreyfus fel, Univ Rochester, 55-57; res chemist, 57-60, group leader, 60-62, res assoc, 62-72, SR RES ASSOC, CELANESE RES CO, SUMMIT, 72- *Concurrent Pos:* Adj prof chem eng, Univ Del, 74- *Mem:* Am Chem Soc; Soc Rheol. *Mailing Add:* 806 Morris Turnpike Apt 3P7 Short Hills NJ 07078

WISSEMAN, CHARLES LOUIS, JR, b Seguin, Tex, Oct 2, 20; m 41; c 4. MEDICAL MICROBIOLOGY. *Educ:* Southern Methodist Univ, BA, 41; Kans State Col, MS, 43; Southwestern Univ, MD, 46; Am Bd Path, dipl; Am Bd Microbiol, dipl. *Prof Exp:* Chief chemotherapeut res sect, Dept Virus & Rickettsial Dis, Army Med Serv Grad Sch, Walter Reed Army Med Ctr, DC, 48-54, asst chief dept, 52-54; asst prof med, 57-74, PROF MICROBIOL & HEAD DEPT, SCH MED, UNIV MD, BALTIMORE CITY, 54- *Concurrent Pos:* Instr med, Sch Med, Georgetown Univ & actg dir bact & serol labs, Univ Hosp, 50-54; dep dir comn rickettsial dis, Armed Forces Epidemiol Bd, 57-59, dir, 59-72; consult, Surgeon Gen, US Army, NIH, WHO & Pan-Am Health Orgn. *Mem:* Am Soc Microbiol; Infectious Dis Soc Am; Am Soc Trop Med & Hyg; Am Soc Clin Invest; Am Asn Immunol. *Res:* Infectious diseases; viral and rickettsial diseases; pathogenesis and immunity. *Mailing Add:* Dept of Microbiol Univ of Md Sch of Med Baltimore MD 21201

WISSEMAN, WILLIAM ROWLAND, b Halletsville, Tex, Nov 2, 32; m 59; c 3. PHYSICS. *Educ:* NC State Univ, BNuclearEng, 54; Duke Univ, PhD(physics), 59. *Prof Exp:* Res assoc & instr physics, Duke Univ, 59-60; mem tech staff, 60-75, BR MGR, TEX INSTRUMENTS, INC, 75- *Mem:* Am Phys Soc; Inst Elec & Electronics Engrs. *Res:* Electromagnetic wave propagation in solids; properties of semiconductors; solid state microwave sources. *Mailing Add:* 5747 Melshire Dr Dallas TX 75230

WISSING, THOMAS EDWARD, b Milwaukee, Wis, Aug 15, 40; m 69. FRESH WATER ECOLOGY. *Educ:* Marquette Univ, BS, 62, MS, 64; Univ Wis-Madison, PhD(zool), 69. *Prof Exp:* Asst aquatic ecol, Marquette Univ, 62-63, asst gen biol, 63-64; asst gen zool, Univ Wis, 64-65, Fed Water Pollution Control Admin trainee aquatic ecol, 65-69; from asst prof to assoc prof zool, 69-78, PROF ZOOL, MIAMI UNIV, 78- *Mem:* Am Fisheries Soc; Sigma Xi; Am Inst Biol Sci. Int Asn Theoret & Appl Limnol. *Res:* Fisheries biology; bioenergetics. *Mailing Add:* Dept of Zool Miami Univ Oxford OH 45056

WISSLER, EUGENE H(ARLEY), b Cherokee, Iowa, Dec 18, 27; m 51; c 3. CHEMICAL ENGINEERING. *Educ:* Iowa State Univ, BS, 50; Univ Minn, PhD(chem eng), 55. *Prof Exp:* From asst prof to assoc prof chem eng, 57-67, chmn dept, 69-70, assoc dean col eng, 70-76, PROF CHEM ENG, UNIV TEX, AUSTIN, 67- *Concurrent Pos:* NSF fac fel, Univ Mich, 61-62; consult. *Mem:* Am Inst Chem Engrs; Undersea Med Soc. *Res:* Aerosol properties; heat transfer in the human. *Mailing Add:* Dept of Chem Eng Univ of Tex Austin TX 78712

WISSLER, ROBERT WILLIAM, b Richmond, Ind, Mar 1, 17; m 40; c 4. PATHOLOGY. *Educ:* Earlham Col, AB, 39; Univ Chicago, MS, 43, PhD(path), 46, MD, 48; Am Bd Path, dipl, 51. *Hon Degrees:* DSc, Earlham Col, 59; MD, Univ Heidelberg, 73. *Prof Exp:* Asst chem, Earlham Col, 38-39; asst path, 41-43, from instr to prof, 43-72, chmn dept, 57-72, Donald N Pritzker, 72-77, DISTINGUISHED SERV PROF PATH, SCH MED, UNIV CHICAGO, 77- *Concurrent Pos:* Intern, Chicago Marine Hosp, 49-50; mem path study sect, USPHS, 57-61, consult, Surgeon Gen Path Training Comt, 63-68; mem comt path, Nat Acad Sci-Nat Res Coun, 58-69, chmn, 62-69; consult, Armed Forces Inst Path, 61-72, chmn sci adv comt, 66-67; secy-treas, Am Asn Chmn Med Sch Dept Path, 63-64, pres, 67-68; chmn coun arteriosclerosis, Am Heart Asn, 65-66; vpres-dir, Univs Assoc Res & Educ

Path, Inc, 65, pres, 69-71; chmn ad hoc comt animal models, Artificial Heart-Myocardial Infarction Prog, Nat Heart Inst & mem Vet Admin Eval & Rev Comt, Res in Path & Lab Med, 66; vchmn bd trustees, Am Asn Accreditation on Lab Animal Care, 67, chmn, 72-74; trustee, Am Bd Path, 68-, secy, 74; mem path adv coun, Vet Admin, 70-74; mem adv comt, Life Sci Res Off, 71-; mem nat adv food comt, Food & Drug Admin, 72-74. *Honors & Awards:* Award of Merit, Am Heart Asn, 71; Leadership Citation, Am Can Soc, 70; H P Smith Award, Am Soc Clin Path, 76; Distinguished Achievement Award, Mod Med, 77. *Mem:* Soc Exp Biol & Med; Am Soc Exp Path (vpres, 60-61, pres, 61-62); AMA; Am Asn Path & Bact (vpres, 67, pres, 68-69); Am Asn Cancer Res. *Res:* Protein, lipid nutrition and metabolism; cardiovascular disease; experimental induction and regression of atherosclerosis; cellular immunological reactions including tumor immunity; immunohistochemistry of atherosclerosis; lipoprotein arterial wall cell interaction. *Mailing Add:* Dept of Path Box 414 Univ of Chicago Chicago IL 60637

WISSNER, ALLAN, b New York, NY, Nov 14, 45. ORGANIC CHEMISTRY. *Educ:* Long Island Univ, BS, 67; Univ Pa, PhD(org chem), 71. *Prof Exp:* NIH fel chem, Cornell Univ, 72-74; RES CHEMIST, LEDERLE LABS, AM CYANAMID CO, 74- *Mem:* Am Chem Soc. *Res:* Medicinal chemistry. *Mailing Add:* Metab Dis Ther Res Sect Lederle Labs Pearl River NY 10965

WISSOW, LENNARD JAY, b Philadelphia, Pa, May 23, 21; m 46; c 2. CHEMISTRY. *Educ:* Pa State Col, BS, 42; Duke Univ, AM, 43, PhD(org chem), 45. *Prof Exp:* Asst instr chem & asst org chem res, Duke Univ, 43-45; res org chemist, Publicker, Inc, 45; res & develop chemist, Nat Foam Syst, Inc, Pa, 46-47; sr res & develop chemist, Merck & Co, Inc, 47-51; head develop res, Otto B May, Inc, 51-58; treas, 59-60, CHIEF CHEMIST, J & H BERGE, INC, 58-, PRES, 60- *Mem:* Am Chem Soc; Am Inst Chem; AAAS; Sigma Xi; NY Acad Sci. *Res:* Synthetic organic chemistry; fine organic chemicals and processes; pharmaceuticals; vat dyestuffs and intermediates; research and sales administration. *Mailing Add:* 11 E Gloucester Box 302 Harvey Cedars NJ 08001

WIST, ABUND OTTOKAR, b Vienna, Austria, May 23, 26; US citizen; m 63; c 2. THEORETICAL PHYSICS, THERMODYNAMICS. *Educ:* Graz Tech Univ, BS, 48; Univ Vienna, PhD(thermodyn), 51. *Prof Exp:* Technician physics, Vienna Tech Univ, 51-52; res & develop engr, Radiowerke Wien, Austria, 52-54 & Siemens & Halske AG, WGer, 54-58; dir res & develop precision lab instruments, Fisher Sci, Inc, 64-69; res assoc, Grad Sch Pub Health, Univ Pittsburgh, 70-72 & Dept Radiol, Sch Med, 72-73; ASST PROF COMPUT SCI & BIOPHYS, VA COMMONWEALTH UNIV, 73- *Concurrent Pos:* Adj prof chem, Va Commonwealth Univ, 76- *Mem:* Sr mem Inst Elec & Electronics Engrs; Am Chem Soc. *Res:* Physical and analytical chemistry; solid state devices; new computer systems; reaction kinetics; catalysis; precision instrumentation in chemistry, physics and medicine. *Mailing Add:* 9304 Farmington Dr Richmond VA 23229

WISTAR, RICHARD, b NJ, Nov 2, 05; m 33; c 3. CHEMISTRY. *Educ:* Haverford Col, BS, 28; Harvard Univ, AM, 31, PhD, 39. *Prof Exp:* Instr chem, Haverford Col, 32-35 & Bennington Col, 35-38; from assoc prof to prof, 39-71, EMER PROF CHEM, MILLS COL, 71- *Mem:* AAAS; Am Chem Soc. *Res:* Physical organic chemistry; reaction kinetics and mechanisms in organic chemistry. *Mailing Add:* Duck Cove Inverness CA 94937

WISTENDAHL, WARREN ARTHUR, b Jersey City, NJ, Mar 12, 20; m 45; c 3. PLANT ECOLOGY. *Educ:* Rutgers Univ, BSc, 52, PhD(bot), 55. *Prof Exp:* Asst bot, Rutgers Univ, 52-55; asst prof biol, Carthage Col, 55-56, assoc prof & head dept, 56-57; from asst prof to assoc prof bot, 57-67, chmn dept, 64-69, PROF BOT, OHIO UNIV, 67-; DIR, DYSART WOODS LAB, 67- *Concurrent Pos:* Div ed, Ohio J Sci, 78- *Mem:* AAAS; Ecol Soc Am; Torrey Bot Club; Bot Soc Am; Am Bryol & Lichenological Soc. *Res:* Analyses of upland and flood plain plant communities; plant succession; ecology of bryophytes. *Mailing Add:* Dept of Bot Porter Hall Ohio Univ Athens OH 45701

WISTREICH, GEORGE A, b New York, NY, Aug 12, 32; m 57; c 2. MICROBIOLOGY, ELECTRON MICROSCOPY. *Educ:* Univ Calif, Los Angeles, AB, 57, MS, 61; Univ Southern Calif, PhD(bact), 68. *Prof Exp:* Res asst zool, Univ Calif, Los Angeles, 58-60, res virologist, 60-61; from instr to asst prof biol, 61-71, ASSOC PROF LIFE SCI, EAST LOS ANGELES COL, 71-, CHMN DEPT, 72-, DIR ALLIED HEALTH SCI PROGS, 68- *Concurrent Pos:* Aerospace consult, Garrett Corp, Calif, 66-67; lectr, Upward Bound Prog, East Los Angeles Col, 68- *Mem:* Am Soc Microbiol; Am Inst Biol Sci; NY Acad Sci; fel Am Inst Chem; fel Royal Soc Health. *Res:* Insect pathology; virology and tissue culture; cytology and cytochemistry; undergraduate education in biological sciences; electron microscopy. *Mailing Add:* Dept of Life Sci East Los Angeles Col Monterey Park CA 91754

WISTREICH, HUGO ERYK, b Jasto, Poland, Aug 8, 30; nat US; m 58; c 3. FOOD SCIENCE. *Educ:* Inst Agr Tech, France, Ingenieur, 53; Rutgers Univ, MS, 57, PhD(food tech), 59. *Prof Exp:* Dir res, Reliable Packing Co, 58-60, Preservaline Mfg Co, 60-63 & Dubuque Packing Co, 63-64; vpres technol, 64-75, PRES, B HELLER & CO, 75- *Mem:* AAAS; Am Chem Soc; Inst Food Technol; Am Meat Sci Asn; Am Soc Testing & Mat. *Res:* Meat curing; electrical anesthesia in animals; food analysis; nutrition; food-meat biochemistry. *Mailing Add:* 10127 S Seeley Ave Chicago IL 60643

WISWALL, RICHARD H, JR, b Peabody, Mass, Mar 7, 16; m 46; c 5. PHYSICAL CHEMISTRY. *Educ:* Harvard Univ, AB, 37; Princeton Univ, PhD(chem), 41. *Prof Exp:* Chemist, Am Cyanamid Co, NJ, 40-43 & Union Carbide & Carbon Chem Corp, 46-49; chemist, Brookhaven Nat Lab, 49-79; RETIRED. *Concurrent Pos:* Consult, 79- *Mem:* Am Chem Soc; fel Am Nuclear Soc. *Res:* Chemistry of nuclear energy production; fluorine chemistry; fused salts; metal hydrides; energy storage. *Mailing Add:* 331 Beaver Dam Rd Brookhaven NY 11719

WISWELL, JOHN GORDON, endocrinology, deceased

WIT, ANDREW LEWIS, b Oceanside, NY, Jan 18, 42; m 65; c 1. CARDIOVASCULAR PHYSIOLOGY, PHARMACOLOGY. *Educ:* Bates Col, BS, 63; Columbia Univ, PhD(pharmacol), 68. *Prof Exp:* Res physiologist, USPHS Hosp, Staten Island, NY, 68-70; assoc, 70-71, asst prof, 71-74, assoc prof, 74-81, PROF PHARMACOL, COL PHYSICIANS & SURGEONS, COLUMBIA UNIV, 81- *Concurrent Pos:* Res assoc, Rockefeller Univ, 70-71, vis asst prof, 71-74, adj assoc prof, 74-; NY Heart Asn sr investr, Columbia Univ, 71-75, Am Heart Asn grant in aid, 72-76; NIH grants, 70- *Mem:* Am Heart Asn; Am Fedn Clin Res; Soc Gen Physiol; Am Physiol Soc; Int Soc Res Cardiac Metab. *Res:* Cardiac electrophysiology, pharmacology and arrhythmias. *Mailing Add:* Col Physicians & Surgeons Columbia Univ Dept Pharmacol New York NY 10034

WIT, LAWRENCE CARL, b Chicago, Ill, May 12, 44; m 68; c 3. PHYSIOLOGICAL ECOLOGY. *Educ:* Wheaton Col, BS, 66; Western Ill Univ, MS, 68; Univ Mo, PhD(zool), 75. *Prof Exp:* ASST PROF ZOOL, AUBURN UNIV, 76- *Mem:* AAAS. *Res:* Physiological mechanisms regulating mammalian and reptilian hibernation. *Mailing Add:* Dept of Zool & Entom Auburn Univ Auburn AL 36830

WITCHER, WESLEY, b Chatham, Va, July 9, 23; m 55; c 2. PLANT PATHOLOGY. *Educ:* Va Polytech Inst, BS, 49, MS, 58; NC State Col, PhD(plant path), 60. *Prof Exp:* Instr voc agr, Pittsylvania County Sch Bd, 49-54; asst county agent, Exten Serv, Va Polytech Inst, 54-56; asst, NC State Col, 57-60; PROF FOREST PATH, CLEMSON UNIV, 60-, VEG PATHOLOGIST, 81- *Mem:* Am Phytopath Soc; Soc Nematol. *Res:* Fungus-nematode complex of tobacco; diseases of highbush blueberries; forest diseases; vegetable diseases. *Mailing Add:* Dept of Plant Path & Physiol Clemson Univ Clemson SC 29631

WITCOFSKI, RICHARD LOU, b Peiping, China, Mar 29, 35; US citizen; m 56; c 2. MEDICAL BIOPHYSICS, NUCLEAR MEDICINE. *Educ:* Lynchburg Col, BS, 56; Vanderbilt Univ, MS, 60; Wake Forest Univ, PhD(anat), 67. *Prof Exp:* Res asst, 57-61, from instr to prof, 61-73, PROF RADIOL, BOWMAN GRAY SCH MED, 73- *Mem:* Soc Nuclear Med; Health Physics Soc; Radiation Res Soc; Am Asn Physicists in Med; Am Inst Ultrasonics in Med. *Res:* Radiation biology. *Mailing Add:* Dept of Radiol Bowman Gray Sch of Med Winston-Salem NC 27103

WITELSON, SANDRA FREEDMAN, b Montreal, Que, Feb 24, 40. NEUROPSYCHOLOGY. *Educ:* McGill Univ, BSc, 60, MSc, 62, PhD(psychol), 66. *Prof Exp:* Lectr psychol, Yeshiva Univ, 66; NIMH res fel, Sch Med, NY Univ, 66-68; instr, NY Med Col, 68-69; asst prof, 69-74, assoc prof psychol, 74-77, PROF, DEPT PSYCHIAT, SCH MED, MCMASTER UNIV, 77- *Concurrent Pos:* Ont Ment Health Found res grant, McMaster Univ, 70-79, assoc mem, Dept Psychol, 76-; US NIH, Nat Inst Neurol & Commun Disorders & Stroke contract, 77-; Clarke Inst res fund prize, 78. *Honors & Awards:* Morton Prince Award, Am Psychopath Soc; John Dewan Award, Ont Ment Health Found, 77. *Mem:* AAAS; Can Psychol Asn; Am Psychol Asn; Acad Aphasia; Int Neuropsychol Soc. *Res:* Perception; cognition; language; brain function; developmental psychology; neuroanatomy; sex differences. *Mailing Add:* Dept Psychiat McMaster Univ Hamilton ON L8N 3Z5 Can

WITHAM, ABNER CALHOUN, b Atlanta, Ga, Apr 28, 21; m 48. CARDIOLOGY. *Educ:* Emory Univ, AB, 42; Johns Hopkins Univ, MD, 45. *Prof Exp:* Intern internal med, Emory Univ, 45-46, asst resident, 48-51; res asst, Cardiovasc Lab, Brit Post-Grad Med Sch, London, 51-52; asst prof physiol, 52-55, resident med, 54-58, assoc prof, 58-64, PROF MED, MED COL GA, 64- *Mem:* AMA; Am Fedn Clin Res; Am Clin & Climat Asn. *Res:* Physiology of venoms; pulmonary circulation; congenital heart disease; vector cardiography. *Mailing Add:* Div of Cardiol Med Col of Ga Augusta GA 30902

WITHAM, FRANCIS H, b Waltham, Mass, Apr 26, 36; m 61; c 3. PLANT PHYSIOLOGY. *Educ:* Univ Mass, BS, 58, MA, 60; Ind Univ, PhD(plant physiol), 64. *Prof Exp:* Lectr plant physiol, Ind Univ, 63-64; from asst prof to assoc prof biol, 66-79, PROF & HEAD, DEPT HORT, PA STATE UNIV, 80- *Mem:* Am Soc Plant Physiol. *Res:* Biosynthesis, chemistry and mechanism of action of cytokinins and their interaction with nuleic acids. *Mailing Add:* Dept Hort Pa State Univ University Park PA 16802

WITHBROE, GEORGE LUND, b Green Bay, Wis, Dec 14, 38; m 64; c 2. ASTROPHYSICS, SOLAR PHYSICS. *Educ:* Mass Inst Technol, BS, 61; Univ Mich, MS, 63, PhD(astron), 65. *Prof Exp:* Res fel astron, 65-69, res assoc astron, 69-76, LECTR, HARVARD UNIV, 70-; ASTROPHYSICIST, SMITHSONIAN ASTROPHYS OBSERV, 73- *Concurrent Pos:* Mem, Comt Solar & Space Physics, Space Sci Bd, 81-; mem, Sci Study Team Adv Solar Observ, NASA. *Mem:* Int Astron Union; Am Astron Soc; Am Geophys Union. *Res:* Interpretation of solar and stellar visible, radio and EUV radiation; determination of solar chemical abundances; temperature density structure of solar atmosphere and terrestrial atmosphere; development of plasma diagnostic techniques. *Mailing Add:* Ctr Astrophysics 60 Garden St Cambridge MA 02138

WITHEE, WALLACE WALTER, b Minneapolis, Minn, Mar 12, 13; m 38; c 3. AERONAUTICAL ENGINEERING. *Educ:* Univ Minn, BS, 34. *Prof Exp:* Engr, Boeing Co, 36-38; layout engr, Consol Vultee, 38-40, group leader, 40-42, asst proj engr, 42-49, design specialist, 49-50, sr design group engr, 50-53, chief flight test engr, Gen Dynamics/Convair, 53-54, sr design group engr, 54-55, chief exp flight test, 55-56, asst chief flight test, 56-57, asst chief engr, Gen Dynamics/Astronaut, 57-60, sr asst chief engr, 60-61, vpres res, develop & eng, 61-62, vpres eng, 62-65, dir test opers, Gen Dynamics/Convair Aerospace, 65-66, dept prog dir advan intercontinental ballistic missile, 66-67, prog dir manned orbital space systs, 67-68, dir mil space progs, 68, dir advan space systs, 68-71, prog dir, res & applications modules, 71, dir res & applications progs, 72-76, subcontract proj dir, 76-78, DIR ENERGY PROGS & CONSULT, GEN DYNAMICS/CONVAIR AEROSPACE, 78-

Mem: Assoc fel Am Inst Aeronaut & Astronaut; Soc Automotive Engrs; Inst Environ Sci; Am Astronaut Soc; Am Nuclear Soc. *Res:* Technical management in the aerospace industry from conception of missile to system development. *Mailing Add:* Gen Dynamics/Convair Aerospace PO Box 80847 San Diego CA 92138

WITHER, ROSS PLUMMER, b Portland, Ore, Dec 29, 22; m 44; c 3. ORGANIC CHEMISTRY, PULP & PAPER TECHNOLOGY. *Educ:* Univ Ore, BS, 47, MA, 49; Stanford Univ, PhD(chem), 56. *Prof Exp:* SR RES CHEMIST, CENT RES DIV, CROWN ZELLERBACH CORP, 55- *Mem:* Am Chem Soc; Tech Asn Pulp & Paper Indust; Sigma Xi. *Res:* Cellulose chemistry; pulp and paper research; paper coatings research; specialty papers development. *Mailing Add:* Cent Res Div Crown Zellerbach Corp Camas WA 98607

WITHERELL, DONALD RAY, organic chemistry, see previous edition

WITHERELL, EGILDA DEAMICIS, b Fall River, Mass, Nov 1, 22; m 56. RADIOLOGICAL PHYSICS, NUCLEAR MEDICINE. *Educ:* Mass Inst Technol, SB, 44; Am Bd Radiol, dip, 53; Am Bd Health Physics, dipl, 60. *Prof Exp:* Mem staff physics, Radiation Lab, Mass Inst Technol, 44-45, mem staff math, Dynamic Anal & Control Lab, 46-47; asst instr chem, Northeastern Univ, 45-56; radiol physicist, Cancer Res Inst, New Eng Deaconess Hosp, Boston, Mass, 47-66 & Peter Bent Brigham Hosp, 66-67; RADIOL PHYSICIST, NEWTON WELLESLEY HOSP, NEWTON LOWER FALLS, 67- *Mem:* Am Col Radiol; Soc Nuclear Med; Am Asn Physicists Med; Health Physics Soc. *Res:* Radiological physics. *Mailing Add:* Newton Wellesley Hosp Newton Lower Falls MA 02162

WITHERELL, MICHAEL STEWART, b Toledo, Ohio, Sept 22, 49. ELEMENTARY PARTICLE PHYSICS. *Educ:* Univ Mich, BS, 68; Univ Wis, MA, 70, PhD(physics), 73. *Prof Exp:* Instr, 73-75, ASST PROF PHYSICS, PRINCETON UNIV, 75- *Mem:* Sigma Xi; Am Phys Soc. *Res:* Counter and spark chamber experiments in elementary particle physics. *Mailing Add:* Dept of Physics Princeton Univ PO Box 708 Princeton NJ 08540

WITHERS, PHILIP CAREW, b Adelaide, SAustralia, Dec 23, 51; m 77; c 1. COMPARATIVE PHYSIOLOGY, PHYSIOLOGICAL ECOLOGY. *Educ:* Univ Adelaide, BSc Hons, 72; Univ Calif, Los Angeles, PhD(biol), 76. *Prof Exp:* Fel zool, Univ Cape Town, 76-78; vis fel zool, Duke Univ, 78-79; ASST PROF BIOL, PORTLAND STATE UNIV, 79- *Mem:* Am Soc Zoologists; Australian Mammal Soc. *Res:* Comparative physiology of terrestrial vertebrates; energetics, water relations and ionic balance of amphibians, reptiles, birds and mammals. *Mailing Add:* Biol Dept Portland State Univ PO Box 751 Portland OR 97207

WITHERSPOON, JAMES DONALD, animal physiology, see previous edition

WITHERSPOON, JOHN PINKNEY, JR, b Hamlet, NC, Feb 28, 31; m 52; c 5. RADIATION ECOLOGY, PLANT ECOLOGY. *Educ:* Emory Univ, BS, 52, MS, 53; Univ Tenn, PhD(bot), 62. *Prof Exp:* Res asst biol, Emory Univ, 55-57; health physicist, 62, ECOLOGIST, OAK RIDGE NAT LAB, 62- *Mem:* Ecol Soc Am; Health Physics Soc. *Res:* Radiological impact assessments of nuclear fuel cycle facilities. *Mailing Add:* Health & Safety Res Div Oak Ridge Nat Lab Oak Ridge TN 37830

WITHERSPOON, PAUL A(DAMS), JR, b Pittsburgh, Pa, Feb 9, 19; m 46; c 3. GEOLOGICAL & PETROLEUM ENGINEERING. *Educ:* Univ Pittsburgh, BS, 41; Univ Kans, MS, 51; Univ Ill, PhD(geol, phys chem), 57. *Prof Exp:* Petrol prod engr, Phillips Petrol Co, 41-42 & 45-47, chem process engr, 42-45, petrol reservoir engr, 47-49; asst instr petrol eng, Univ Kans, 49-51, head div petrol eng, State Geol Surv, Ill, 51-57; prof petrol eng, 57-65, PROF GEOL ENG, UNIV CALIF, BERKELEY, 65-, HEAD EARTH SCI DIV & ASSOC DIR, LAWRENCE BERKELEY LAB, 77- *Concurrent Pos:* Mem subpanel nuclear waste disposal, panel on rock mech probs, US Nat Comn Rock Mech, Nat Res Coun, 77-78. *Honors & Awards:* Robert E Horton Award, Am Geophys Union, 69; O E Meinzer Award, Geol Soc Am, 76. *Mem:* Am Geophys Union; Geol Soc Am; Am Asn Petrol Geol; Am Inst Mining, Metall & Petrol Engrs. *Res:* Flow of fluids in porous and fractured rocks; regional groundwater flow; well hydraulics; underground storage of fluids; radioactive waste isolation; geothermal systems. *Mailing Add:* 320 Hearst Mining Bldg Univ of Calif Berkeley CA 94720

WITHERSPOON, SAMUEL MCBRIDGE, b Marion, SC, Dec 26, 26; m 52; c 2. ANESTHESIOLOGY. *Educ:* Clemson Col, BS, 54; Med Col SC, MD, 52. *Prof Exp:* Intern, Jefferson Davis Hosp, Houston, Tex, 52-53; pvt pract, SC, 53-57; resident, Med Ctr Hosps, 57-59, instr, 59-60, assoc, 60-63, asst prof, 63-66, ASSOC PROF ANESTHESIOL, MED UNIV SC, 66- *Mem:* Am Soc Anesthesiol; AMA; Int Anesthesia Res Soc. *Res:* Effective compounds applicable in the patient with intractable pain. *Mailing Add:* 6 Pierates Cruze Mt Pleasant SC 29464

WITHNER, CARL LESLIE, JR, b Indianapolis, Ind, Mar 3, 18; m 41; c 3. PLANT MORPHOGENETICS. *Educ:* Univ Ill, BA, 41; Yale Univ, MS, 43, PhD(bot), 48. *Prof Exp:* Asst instr bot, Yale Univ, 41-43, asst, 46-47; from instr to prof biol, 48-78, dep chmn dept, 60-64, actg chmn dept, 64-65, EMER PROF BIOL, BROOKLYN COL, 78- *Concurrent Pos:* Resident investr orchids, Brooklyn Bot Garden, 49-76; Guggenheim fel, 61-62; orchid consult, NY Bot Garden, 76-79; instr hort, Bellingham Voc-Tech Sch, 79-80; adj prof biol, Western Wash Univ, 82. *Mem:* Bot Soc Am; Am Soc Plant Physiol; Am Orchid Soc. *Res:* Orchids; physiology of higher plants in relation to growth and development. *Mailing Add:* 2015 Alabama St Bellingham WA 98226

WITHROW, CLARENCE DEAN, b Hutchinson, WVa, Mar 6, 27; m 53; c 3. PHARMACOLOGY. *Educ:* Davis & Elkins Col, BS, 48; Univ Utah, MS, 55, PhD(pharmacol), 59. *Prof Exp:* Res instr, 59-63, from instr to asst prof, 63-70, ASSOC PROF PHARMACOL, COL MED, UNIV UTAH, 70- *Mem:* AAAS; Am Soc Pharmacol & Exp Therapeut. *Res:* Acid-base metabolism, particularly intracellular pH regulation; renal pharmacology; mineralocorticoids; polarography. *Mailing Add:* Dept of Pharmacol Univ of Utah Col of Med Salt Lake City UT 84132

WITHSTANDLEY, VICTOR DEWYCKOFF, III, b New York, NY, Sept 1, 21; m 58; c 3. MOLECULAR SPECTROSCOPY. *Educ:* Cornell Univ, BA, 50; Univ Calif, Berkeley, MA, 52; Pa State Univ, DEd(physics), 66, PhD(physics), 72. *Prof Exp:* Asst seismologist, Geotech Corp, Tex, 52-56; res asst underwater acoustics, Ord Res Lab, Pa State Univ, 59-62; instr math, Juniata Col, 66-67; res asst, Ctr Air Environ Studies, Pa State Univ, 69-73; prin scientist, Scitek, Inc, 74-75; instr phys sci, Pa State Univ, 75-77; STAFF SCIENTIST, BACHARACH INSTRUMENT CO, PITTSBURGH, 78- *Mem:* Am Phys Soc; Am Geophys Union. *Res:* Seismic wave and underwater sound studies; magnetic anisotropies of single crystals; computer analysis of time series; optical engineering; infrared spectroscopy of molecules; remote sensing for geophysical and environmental studies. *Mailing Add:* 127 W Whitehall Rd State College PA 16801

WITIAK, DONALD T, b Milwaukee, Wis, Nov 16, 35; m 55; c 2. ORGANIC CHEMISTRY, MEDICINAL CHEMISTRY. *Educ:* Univ Wis, BS, 58, PhD(med chem), 61. *Prof Exp:* From asst prof to assoc prof med chem, Univ Iowa, 61-67; assoc prof, 67-71, PROF MED CHEM, COL PHARM, OHIO STATE UNIV, 71-, CHMN DEPT, 73- *Mem:* Am Chem Soc; Am Pharmaceut Asn; fel Acad Pharmaceut Sci. *Res:* Synthesis of biologically active compounds; stereo-structure activity relationships; hypolipidemic drugs; CNS drugs; carcinogenesis and anticancer agents. *Mailing Add:* Dept of Med Chem Ohio State Univ Col of Pharm Columbus OH 43210

WITKIN, EVELYN MAISEL, b New York, NY, Mar 9, 21; m 43; c 2. MICROBIAL GENETICS. *Educ:* NY Univ, AB, 41; Columbia Univ, MA, 43, PhD(zool), 47. *Hon Degrees:* DSc, NY Med Col, 78. *Prof Exp:* Res assoc bact genetics, Carnegie Inst, 46-49, mem staff genetics, 49-55; assoc prof med, Col Med, State Univ NY Downstate Med Ctr, 55-69, prof, 69-71; PROF BIOL SCI, DOUGLASS COL, RUTGERS UNIV, 71- *Concurrent Pos:* Am Cancer Soc fel, 47-49; res assoc, Carnegie Inst, 55-71, fel, 56; Waksman lectr, 59. *Honors & Awards:* Prix Charles-Leopold Mayer, Inst France Acad Sci, 77. *Mem:* Nat Acad Sci; Am Soc Microbiol; Genetics Soc Am; Am Soc Nat; Radiation Res Soc. *Res:* Mechanism of spontaneous and induced mutation in bacteria; genetic effects of radiation; enzymatic repair of DNA damage. *Mailing Add:* Dept of Biol Sci Rutgers Univ New Brunswick NJ 08903

WITKIN, GEORGE JOSEPH, b New York, NY, Dec 22, 15; m 40; c 2. DENTISTRY. *Educ:* NY Univ, AB, 38, DDS, 42; Am Bd Periodont, dipl; Am Bd Oral Path, dipl. *Prof Exp:* Asst, 46-47, from instr to assoc prof, 47-66, dir teacher training prog, Col Dent, 61-65, chmn dept peridontics & oral med, 66-76, PROF PERIODONTICS NY UNIV, 66-, ASSOC DEAN, 67- *Concurrent Pos:* Res fel periodontia, NY Univ, 42; mem attend staff, Univ Hosp; spec consult, Munic Civil Serv Comn, New York & USPHS; consult, US Vet Admin. *Mem:* Sci Res Soc Am; Am Dent Asn; fel Am Col Dent; Am Acad Periodont; fel Am Acad Oral Med. *Res:* Periodontia; dental education. *Mailing Add:* Col of Dent NY Univ New York NY 10003

WITKIN, STEVEN S, b Brooklyn, NY, Oct 19, 43; m 66. IMMUNOLOGY, REPRODUCTIVE BIOLOGY. *Educ:* Hunter Col, BA, 65; Univ Conn, MS, 67; Univ Calif, Los Angeles, PhD(microbiol), 70. *Prof Exp:* Staff assoc, Inst Cancer Res, Columbia Univ, 72-74; assoc, Sloan-Kettering Inst Cancer Res, 74-81; RES ASSOC PROF, MED COL, CORNELL UNIV, 81- *Concurrent Pos:* Fel, Roche Inst Molecular Biol, Nutley, NJ, 70-72. *Mem:* AAAS; Am Soc Microbiol; Soc Study Reproduction; Am Asn Immunologists; Am Fertil Soc. *Res:* Reproductive immunology; cancer; spermatozoa. *Mailing Add:* Dept Obstet/Gynec Cornell Med Col 515 E 71st St New York NY 10021

WITKIND, IRVING JEROME, b New York, NY, Mar 28, 17; m 42. ECONOMIC GEOLOGY. *Educ:* Brooklyn Col, BA, 39; Columbia Univ, MA, 41; Univ Colo, PhD(geol), 56. *Prof Exp:* GEOLOGIST, US GEOL SURV, 46- *Mem:* Geol Soc Am; Am Asn Petrol Geol. *Res:* Pleistocene geology; localization of sodium sulfate; geologic mapping for environmental purposes in Price 1 degree x 2 degree AMS Sheet, Central Utah; localization of uranium minerals; laccolithic mountains of southeastern Utah and central Montana; stratigraphy and structural geology of southwestern Montana and southeastern Idaho. *Mailing Add:* US Geol Surv Fed Ctr Denver CO 80225

WITKOP, BERNHARD, b Freiburg, Ger, May 9, 17; nat US; m 45; c 3. ORGANIC CHEMISTRY. *Educ:* Univ Munich, PhD(org chem), 40, ScD, 46. *Prof Exp:* Privat docent, Univ Munich, 46-47; Mellon Found fel, Harvard Univ, 47-48, instr, 48-50, USPHS spec fel, 50-51; vis scientist, NIH, 51-53, chemist, 53-55, CHIEF SECT METABOLITES, NAT INST ARTHRITIS, METAB & DIGESTIVE DIS, 55-, CHIEF LAB CHEM, 57- *Concurrent Pos:* Mem, Nat Acad Sci-Nat Res Coun, 59-62; vis prof, Kyoto Univ, 61 & Univ Freiburg, 62; mem, Bd Int Sci Exchange, Nat Acad Sci, 75-77; adj prof, Med Sch, Univ Md, Baltimore, 78-; Alexander von Humboldt US sr scientist award, Univ Hamburg, 79. *Honors & Awards:* Superior Serv Award, US Dept Health, Educ & Welfare, 67; Paul Karrer Gold Medal, Univ Zurich, 71; Order of Sacred Treasure (Kun-Ni-To), Emperor of Japan, 75. *Mem:* Nat Acad Sci; hon mem Pharmacol Soc Japan; Am Acad Arts & Sci; Am Chem Soc; Leopoldine Ger Acad Res Natural Sci. *Res:* Alkaloids; arrow and mushroom poisons; oxidation mechanisms; peroxides; ozonides; intermediary and labile metabolites; nonenzymatic selective cleavage of proteins and enzymes; photochemistry of amino acids and nucleotides; venoms of amphibians; biochemical mechanisms; dynamics of modified homopolynucleotides; stimulation of interferon. *Mailing Add:* Nat Inst of Arthritis Metab & Dig Dis Bethesda MD 20014

WITKOP, CARL JACOB, JR, b East Grand Rapids, Mich, Dec 27, 20; m 66; c 7. HUMAN GENETICS, ORAL PATHOLOGY. *Educ:* Mich State Col, BS, 44; Univ Mich, DDS, 49, MS, 54; Am Bd Oral Path, dipl, 57. *Prof Exp:* Asst dent surgeon & intern, US Marine Hosp, USPHS, Seattle, Wash, 49-50, sr asst dent surgeon, US Coast Guard Yard, Baltimore, 50; oral pathologist, Nat Inst Dent Res, 50-57, chief human genetics sect, 57-63, chief human genetics br, 63-66; PROF HUMAN & ORAL GENETICS & CHMN DIV, SCH DENT & PROF DERMAT, MED SCH, UNIV MINN, MINNEAPOLIS, 66- *Concurrent Pos:* Fel, Univ Mich, 52-54; consult, Children's Hosp, Washington, DC, 56-, Nat Found Congenital Malformation, 63- & Easter Seal Soc, 63-66; lectr, Schs Med & Dent, Howard Univ, 56-, Georgetown Univ & Johns Hopkins Univ; dent dir, Int Comt Nutrit Nat Develop, Chile, 60 & Paraguay, 65; chief dent sect, Inst Nutrit Cent Am, Panama & Guatemala, 64. *Mem:* Fel AAAS; Am Soc Human Genetics (secy, 68-70); Am Soc Dermat; Am Dent Asn; fel Am Acad Oral Path (vpres, 60, 72, pres elect, 73, pres, 74). *Res:* Albinism and pigment defects; exfoliative cytology; population isolates; congenital malformations; oral epidemiology and nutrition. *Mailing Add:* 9 Manitoba Rd Hopkins MN 55343

WITKOSKI, FRANCIS CLEMENT, b Scranton, Pa, Dec 19, 22; m 46; c 5. ORGANIC CHEMISTRY. *Educ:* Univ Scranton, BSc, 43; Bucknell Univ, MSc, 50. *Prof Exp:* From instr to asst prof org chem, Univ Scranton, 47-55; dir res, State Dept Hwy, Pa, 55-58, assoc dir res & testing, 58-60; secy & tech dir, Am Testing Labs, Inc, 60-63; PRES, MAT ENG & SERV CO, 63- *Concurrent Pos:* Mem, Comt Rigid Pavement Design & Comt Prestressed Concrete, Hwy Res Bd, Nat Acad Sci-Nat Res Coun. *Mem:* AAAS; Am Chem Soc; Am Soc Testing & Mat. *Res:* Chemistry of lignin; incinerated anthracite mine waste in asphalt pavements; engineering properties of construction materials. *Mailing Add:* Mat Eng & Serv Co 21st & Chestnut Sts PO Box 621 Camp Hill PA 17011

WITKOVSKY, PAUL, b Chicago, Ill, May 24, 37; m 64. SENSORY PHYSIOLOGY. *Educ:* Univ Calif, Los Angeles, BA, 58, MA, 60, PhD(physiol), 62. *Prof Exp:* NIH fel neurophysiol, Sci Res Inst, Caracas, Venezuela, 62-63; instr ophthal, Columbia Univ, 64-65, from asst prof to assoc prof physiol, 65-73; PROF ANAT SCI, STATE UNIV NY STONEY STONY BROOK, 75- *Concurrent Pos:* Res grants, Nat Inst Neurol Dis & Blindness, 64- & Nat Coun Combat Blindness, 66-67. *Mem:* AAAS; Asn Res Vision & Ophthal; Biophys Soc; Soc Neurosci. *Res:* Central nervous system organization of tactile sensation; neurophysiological organization of the retina. *Mailing Add:* Dept of Anat Sci State Univ NY Stony Brook NY 11790

WITKOWSKI, JOHN FREDERICK, b Beatrice, Nebr, Apr 30, 42; m 74; c 1. ENTOMOLOGY. *Educ:* Univ Nebr, BSc, 65, MSc, 70; Iowa State Univ, PhD(entom), 75. *Prof Exp:* Res rep agr chem, Chemagro Corp, 70-72; res assoc entom, Iowa State Univ, 72-75; ENTOMOLOGIST, UNIV NEBR, 75- *Mem:* Entom Soc Am. *Res:* The biology and chemical control of insects damaging corn and soybeans. *Mailing Add:* Northeast Sta Concord NE 68728

WITKOWSKI, JOSEPH THEODORE, b Ft Worth, Tex, Oct 29, 42; m 65; c 1. ORGANIC CHEMISTRY, MEDICINAL CHEMISTRY. *Educ:* NTex State Univ, BS, 65, MS, 66; Univ Utah, PhD(chem), 70. *Prof Exp:* Res chemist, Nucleic Acid Res Inst, ICN Pharmaceut, Inc, 69-77; RES CHEMIST, SCHERING CORP, 77- *Mem:* Am Chem Soc; Int Soc Heterocyclic Chem. *Res:* Synthesis and properties of nucleosides and heterocycles; synthesis of antiviral agents. *Mailing Add:* Schering Corp 60 Orange St Bloomfield NJ 07003

WITKOWSKI, ROBERT EDWARD, b Glassport, Pa, Jan 9, 41; m 63; c 2. MICROANALYTICAL CHEMISTRY. *Educ:* Univ Pittsburgh, BS, 62, MS, 73. *Prof Exp:* Res asst phys measurements, Mellon Inst, Pittsburgh, 62-63, jr fel infrared spectros, 63-67; assoc engr mass spectros, 67-71, engr liquid metal technol, 71-75, sr engr liquid metal technol, 75-80, FEL SCIENTIST MAT CHEM, WESTINGHOUSE RES LABS, 80- *Concurrent Pos:* Res assoc, Sect Minerals, Carnegie Mus Natural Hist, Pittsburgh, 74- *Honors & Awards:* Jacquet-Lucas Award & Gold Medal, 78. *Mem:* Am Chem Soc; Nat Asn Corrosion Engrs; Int Metallog Soc. *Res:* Sodium corrosion and mass transport studies via advanced instrumental microanalytical techniques; material studies for advanced design homopolar machines utilizing liquid metal slip rings; solar grade silicon production; chemical characterization. *Mailing Add:* Westinghouse Res Labs 1310 Beulah Rd Pittsburgh PA 15235

WITKUS, ELEANOR RUTH, b New York, NY, July 11, 18. BIOLOGY. *Educ:* Hunter Col, BA, 40; Boston Univ, MA, 41; Fordham Univ, PhD(cytol), 44. *Prof Exp:* Instr zool, Marymount Col, NY, 43-44; from instr to assoc prof bot & bact, 44-74, chmn dept, 72-78, PROF BIOL SCI, FORDHAM UNIV, 71- *Mem:* Bot Soc Am; Torrey Bot Club (corresp secy, 53-56). *Res:* Botanical cytology. *Mailing Add:* Dept of Biol Sci Fordham Univ New York NY 10458

WITLOCK, DALE RAY, b Chicago Heights, IL, Jan 2, 51; m 73. ELECTRON MICROSCOPY, PATHOLOGY. *Educ:* Monmouth Col, BA, 73; Univ Ga, MS, 75, PhD(poultry sci), 78. *Prof Exp:* MICROBIOLOGIST, ANIMAL PARASITOL INST, USDA, 78- *Mem:* Am Soc Parasitologists; Electron Micros Soc Am; NY Acad Sci; Am Asn Vet Parasitol. *Res:* Physiological interactions of the host-parasite relationship; mechanisms of parasite induced pathology; ultrastructural changes resulting from parasite infections of intestinal coccidia. *Mailing Add:* Barc-East Animal Parasitol Inst Beltsville MD 20705

WITMAN, GEORGE BODO, III, b Upland, Calif, July 19, 45; m 69; c 2. CELL BIOLOGY. *Educ:* Univ Calif, Riverside, BA, 67; Yale Univ, PhD(cellular & develop biol), 72. *Prof Exp:* NIH fel cell biol, Whitman Lab, Univ Chicago, 72-73; fel molecular biol, Lab Molecular Biol & Biophys, Univ Wis-Madison, 73-74; STAFF SCIENTIST, WORCESTER FOUND EXP BIOL, SHREWSBURY, MASS, 81- *Mem:* AAAS; Am Soc Cell Biol; Int Fedn Cell Biol. *Res:* Structure, composition, function and development of cell organelles; male reproduction; sperm maturation and motility. *Mailing Add:* Worcester Found Exp Biol 222 Maple Ave Shrewsbury MA 01545

WITMAN, ROBERT CHARLES, b Pottsville, Pa, Feb 15, 27; m 52; c 3. ORGANIC CHEMISTRY. *Educ:* Pa State Col, BS, 49, MS, 50; Univ Del, PhD, 53. *Prof Exp:* Res chemist phys org chem, Shell Chem Corp, 53-61, sr technologist prod develop, 61-63; dir com develop, 63-65, dir mkt, 65-69, mgr corp develop, 69-70, VPRES & TECH DIR, CARSTAB COPR, SUBSID THIOKOL CORP, 70- *Mem:* Soc Plastics Engrs; Am Chem Soc; Ges Deut Chemiker. *Res:* Organometallics; organic sulfur compounds; heat stabilizers and lubricants for other polyvinyl chloride and plastics. *Mailing Add:* 501 Reily Rd Cincinnati OH 45215

WITMER, EMMETT A(TLEE), b Bellefonte, Pa, Dec 20, 24; m 48; c 2. AERODYNAMICS. *Educ:* Pa State Univ, BS, 44, MS, 48; Mass Inst Technol, ScD(aeronaut eng), 51. *Prof Exp:* Aeronaut engr, Nat Adv Comt Aeronaut, Ohio, 44; instr appl aerodyn, Pa State Univ, 46-48; aeronaut engr, Naval Supersonic Lab, 49 & Aeroelastic & Struct Res Lab, 50, sr engr, 51-52, proj leader, 52-60, exec officer, 60-62, assoc prof, 60-70, prof, Aeronaut & Astronaut Inst, 70-76, DIR, AEROELASTIC & STRUCT RES LAB, MASS INST TECHNOL, 62-, PROF AERONAUT & ASTRONAUT, 76- *Concurrent Pos:* Consult, Am Sci & Eng Co, 61-, White Sands Missile Range, US Dept Army, 61-, Picatinny Arsenal, 63-, Arthur D Little, Inc, 64-, York Astro Inc, 66 & Watertown Arsenal, 66- *Mem:* Am Inst Aeronaut & Astronaut. *Res:* Aeroelasticity; structural dynamics; transient airloads on wing-body configurations; effects of blast and radiation from explosions on aircraft, missile and ground structures; chemical and nuclear explosion characteristics; dynamic behavior of solids; discrete-element and finite difference methods of static and dynamic elastic-plastic-thermal analysis of structures. *Mailing Add:* Dept of Aeronaut & Astronaut Eng Mass Inst of Technol Cambridge MA 02139

WITMER, HEMAN JOHN, b Bayonne, NJ, Apr 5, 44; m 70; c 2. VIROLOGY, BIOCHEMISTRY. *Educ:* Delaware Valley Col, BS, 65; Ind Univ, Bloomington, PhD(microbiol), 69. *Prof Exp:* NIH fel, McArdle Lab, Univ Wis-Madison, 69 & Ind Univ, Bloomington, 69-71, vis asst prof microbiol, 71, asst prof, Med Ctr, 71-72; asst prof, 72-77, ASSOC PROF BIOL SCI, UNIV ILL, CHICAGO CIRCLE, 77- *Res:* Controls of gene expression of coliphage T4; biosynthesis of unusual bases in DNA. *Mailing Add:* Dept of Biol Sci Univ of Ill at Chicago Circle PO Box 4348 Chicago IL 60680

WITMER, WILLIAM BYRON, b Clarksville, Tex, June 29, 31; m 55; c 3. INORGANIC CHEMISTRY, PHYSICAL CHEMISTRY. *Educ:* Tex A&M Univ, BS, 52, MS, 58, PhD(chem), 60. *Prof Exp:* Res chemist, Chemstrand Res Ctr, Monsanto Co, NC, 59-64, sr res chemist, 64, supvr spec anal lab, Textiles Div, Ala, 64-65, supt tech lab, 65-68, supt qual control, Decatur Plant, 68-70, qual control mgr, Lingen Plant, Monsanto (Deutschland), GMBH, WGer, 70-73, SUPT, TECH DEPT, SAND MOUNTAIN PLANT, MONSANTO TEXTILES CO, 73- *Mem:* Am Soc Qual Control. *Res:* Amine-halogen complexes; polymer characterizition techniques; polymer properties related to synthetic fiber production. *Mailing Add:* Monsanto Textiles Co Sand Mountain Plant Star Route Guntersville AL 35976

WITORSCH, RAPHAEL JAY, b New York, NY, Dec 12, 41; m 64; c 2. PHYSIOLOGY. *Educ:* NY Univ, AB, 63; Yale Univ, MS, 65, PhD(physiol), 68. *Prof Exp:* USPHS trainee, Sch Med, Univ Va, 68-69, NIH fel, 69-70; Asst prof, 70-79, ASSOC PROF PHYSIOL, MED COL VA, VA COMMONWEALTH UNIV, 79- *Concurrent Pos:* Dir first yr med curriculum, Med Col Va, 75-77; co-investr, NIH Grant Breast Cancer, 75-78; prin investr, NIH grant prolactin binding in normal & neoplastic prostate, 78- *Mem:* Endocrine Soc; Am Physiol Soc; Soc Exp Biol & Med; Histochem Soc. *Res:* Endocrinology; immunohistochemistry; hormone receptors in normal and neoplastic tissues. *Mailing Add:* Dept Physiol Box 551 Med Col Va Richmond VA 23298

WITRIOL, NORMAN MARTIN, b Brooklyn, NY, June 9, 40; m 66. THEORETICAL PHYSICS, MOLECULAR PHYSICS. *Educ:* Polytech Inst Brooklyn, BS, 61; Brandeis Univ, MA, 64, PhD(physics), 68. *Prof Exp:* Res physicist, Phys Sci Lab, US Army Missile Command, 68-77; asst prof, 77-79, ASSOC PROF PHYSICS, LA TECH UNIV, 79- *Concurrent Pos:* Asst prof, Univ Ala, Huntsville, 70-77; consult, Columbus Labs, Battelle Mem Inst, 78-79. *Mem:* Am Phys Soc; Am Asn Physics Teachers; AAAS; Optical Soc Am. *Res:* Quantum optics; molecular, chemical, quantum, mathematical, many-body and theoretical physics. *Mailing Add:* La Tech Univ PO Box 3169 Tech Sta Ruston LA 71272

WITSCHARD, GILBERT, b Morehead City, NC, Mar 13, 33; m 60; c 3. ORGANIC CHEMISTRY. *Educ:* Queens Col, BS, 57; Univ Pittsburgh, PhD(org chem), 63. *Prof Exp:* Res chemist, 63-70, SR RES CHEMIST, HOOKER CHEM CORP, NIAGARA FALLS, 70- *Mem:* Am Chem Soc. *Res:* Organo-phosphorus chemistry; fire retardance; polymer synthesis; polymers stabilization; powder coatings; polyvinyl chloride. *Mailing Add:* 2078 Long Rd Grand Island NY 14072

WITSCHEL, JOHN, b New York, NY, Apr 27, 48. PHYSICAL CHEMISTRY. *Educ:* Queens Col, NY, BA, 69; Tufts Univ, PhD(phys chem), 74. *Prof Exp:* Cosmetic distrib, Aqualin Inc, 67-69; res asst phys chem, Tufts Univ & Univ Okla, 69-73; DIR SPECTROS LAB, ARIZ STATE UNIV, 74-; PROF CHEM, MESA COMMUNITY COL, 76- *Concurrent Pos:* Consult utilization of Ariz State Univ Spectros Lab to consult for Motorola, Talley Indust, UniDynamics & Sperry Flight Systs, 74- *Res:* Identification of natural and synthetic products with multi-nuclear magnetic resonance spectroscopy. *Mailing Add:* Dept Chem Ariz State Univ Tempe AZ 85281

WITSCHI, HANSPETER RUDOLF, b Berne, Switz, Mar 17, 33. TOXICOLOGY. *Educ:* Univ Berne, MD, 60. *Prof Exp:* Asst path, Inst Forensic Med, Univ Berne, 61-64; res fel, Toxicol Res Unit, Med Res Coun, Eng, 65-66; res fel exp path, Univ Pittsburgh, 67-69; from asst prof to assoc prof toxicol & pharmacol, Fac Med, Univ Montreal, 69-77; SR RES STAFF MEM, BIOL DIV, OAK RIDGE NAT LAB, 77- *Mem:* Am Soc Pharmacol

& Exp Therapeut; Soc Exp Biol & Med; Soc Toxicol. *Res:* Experimental toxicology; biochemical pathology; interaction of drugs and toxic agents with organ function at the cellular level. *Mailing Add:* Biol Div PO Box Y Oak Ridge TN 37830

WITSENHAUSEN, HANS S, b Frankfurt, Ger, May 6, 30; US citizen; m 61; c 3. APPLIED MATHEMATICS. *Educ:* Free Univ Brussels, ICME, 53, lic sc phys, 56; Mass Inst Technol, SM, 64, PhD(elec eng), 66. *Prof Exp:* Asst elec eng, Free Univ Brussels, 53-57; appln engr, European Ctr, Electronic Assoc, Inc, 57-60, sr engr, Res Div, 60-63; res asst control theory & Lincoln Lab assoc, Electronic Systs Lab, Mass Inst Technol, 63-65; MEM TECH STAFF, MATH RES CTR, BELL LABS, 66- *Concurrent Pos:* Vis prof, Mass Inst Technol, 73; Vinton Hayes sr fel, Harvard Univ, 75-76. *Mem:* Inst Elec & Electronics Eng; Am Math Soc. *Res:* System theory; optimization; geometry; inequalities; information. *Mailing Add:* Bell Labs Murray Hill NJ 07974

WITT, ADOLF NICOLAUS, b Bad Oldesloe, Ger, Oct 17, 40; m 67; c 2. ASTROPHYSICS. *Educ:* Univ Hamburg, Vordiplom, 63; Univ Chicago, PhD(astrophys), 67. *Prof Exp:* From asst prof to assoc prof, 67-74, assoc dir, Ritter Observ, 72-76, dir, Ritter Observ, 76-79, chmn dept phys & astron, 79-81, PROF ASTRON, UNIV TOLEDO, 74- *Concurrent Pos:* Vis fel, Lab Atmospheric & Space Physics, Univ Colo, Boulder, 75-76. *Mem:* AAAS; Am Astron Soc; Int Astron Union. *Res:* Interstellar matter; spectral classification; photometry; astronomical instrumentation. *Mailing Add:* Dept of Physics & Astron Univ of Toledo Toledo OH 43606

WITT, DONALD JAMES, b Chicago, Ill, May 13, 49; m 73; c 2. VIROLOGY, TISSUE CULTURE. *Educ:* Loyola Univ, BS, 71; Ohio State Univ, MS, 73, PhD(virol), 76. *Prof Exp:* Res assoc, Dept Entom, Ohio State Univ, 76-77; sr scientist, Crop Protection Div, Sandoz Inc, 77-78; NIH fel, Dept Cellular Virol & Molecular Biol, Med Sch, 78-80, virologist, 80, MGR BIOCHEM & MOLECULAR BIOL, RES INST, UNIV UTAH, 80- *Mem:* Am Soc Microbiol; Soc Invert Path; Sigma Xi. *Res:* Molecular biology of infectious disease agents, especially viruses; development of diagnostic technology for the identification of infectious disease agents; development of artifical vaccines; application of microorganisms to regulate pest insect populations. *Mailing Add:* Univ Utah Res Inst 520 Wakara Way Salt Lake City UT 84108

WITT, DONALD REINHOLD, b LeMars, Iowa, Apr 15, 23; m 50; c 4. CHEMISTRY. *Educ:* Westmar Col, BS, 48; Univ SDak, MA, 50. *Prof Exp:* Res chemist, 50-62, GROUP LEADER CHEM, PHILLIPS PETROL CO, 62- *Mem:* Am Chem Soc. *Res:* Polymerization of olefins and diolefins to solid polymers; catalyst development related to such reactions. *Mailing Add:* Res Ctr 84-G Phillips Petrol Co Bartlesville OK 74003

WITT, ENRIQUE ROBERTO, b Buenos Aires, Arg, May 10, 26; nat US; m 55; c 2. ORGANIC CHEMISTRY. *Educ:* Univ Buenos Aires, Lic, 51, DrChem, 53. *Prof Exp:* Technician, E R Squibb & Sons, Arg, 51-52; res chemist, Arg AEC, 53-55; RES ASSOC, CELANESE CHEM CO, 56- *Mem:* AAAS; Am Chem Soc; Soc Econ Bot. *Res:* Synthetic lubricants; phosphorus compounds; polyester technology; environmental maintenance; anaerobic biological treatment of industrial wastes. *Mailing Add:* 1037 Brock Corpus Christi TX 78412

WITT, HOWARD RUSSELL, b Morden, Man, July 12, 29; m 56; c 3. ELECTRICAL ENGINEERING. *Educ:* Univ Toronto, BASc, 53; Princeton Univ, MSE, 59; Cornell Univ, PhD(elec eng), 62. *Prof Exp:* Asst prof elec eng, Cornell Univ, 62-67; assoc prof eng, 67-71, asst dean sch eng, 69-75, PROF ENG, OAKLAND UNIV, 71-, ASSOC DEAN SCH ENG, 75- *Mem:* Inst Elec & Electronics Engrs; Am Soc Eng Educ; Sigma Xi. *Mailing Add:* Sch of Eng Oakland Univ Rochester MI 48063

WITT, JOHN, JR, b Muskegon, Mich, Oct 5, 35; m 64. ORGANIC CHEMISTRY. *Educ:* Mich State Univ, BS, 57; Univ Ill, PhD(org chem), 61. *Prof Exp:* Res chemist, Ethyl Corp, 60-62; asst head chem process develop, 62-69, mgr spec synthesis & process develop, 69-72, mgr, synthesis develop, 72-78, DIR CHEM DEVELOP, G D SEARLE & CO, 78- *Mem:* Am Chem Soc. *Res:* Organic synthesis; steroids; heterocyclics; amino acids. *Mailing Add:* G D Searle & Co PO Box 5110 Chicago IL 60680

WITT, PETER NIKOLAUS, b Berlin, Ger, Oct 20, 18; m 49; c 2. PHARMACOLOGY. *Educ:* Univ Tübingen, MD, 46. *Prof Exp:* Asst, Univ Tübingen, 45-49; sr asst, Univ Berne, 49-56, privat-docent, 56; from asst prof to assoc prof pharmacol, Col Med, State Univ NY Upstate Med Ctr, 56-66; dir div res, NC Dept Ment Health, 66-81; RETIRED. *Concurrent Pos:* Rockefeller fel, Harvard Med Sch, 52-53; Lederle med fac award, 57-59; adj prof, NC State Univ & Univ NC, Chapel Hill, 66-81. *Honors & Awards:* Buergi Award, 56. *Mem:* Am Soc Pharmacol & Exp Therapeut; Ger Pharmacol Soc; Swiss Pharmacol Soc. *Res:* Effect of drugs on web building behavior of spiders; invertebrate behavior; effect of cardioactive drugs on ion movements in heart muscle; objective testing of fine motor behavior in healthy and diseased human subjects under the influence of drugs. *Mailing Add:* Div of Res NC Dept Ment Health Box 7532 Raleigh NC 27611

WITT, ROBERT MICHAEL, b Waukesha, Wis, Oct 3, 42; m 71; c 2. MEDICAL PHYSICS, RADIOLOGICAL SCIENCES. *Educ:* Univ Wis-Milwaukee, BS, 64; Univ Wis-Madison, MS, 66, PhD(radiol sci), 75. *Prof Exp:* Proj assoc med physics, Dept Radiol, Univ Wis-Madison, 75-77; PHYSICIST NUCLEAR MED, VET ADMIN MED CTR, 77-; ASST PROF RADIOL, MED CTR, IND UNIV, INDIANAPOLIS, 77- *Mem:* Am Asn Physicists in Med; AAAS; Soc Nuclear Med; Health Physics Soc; Inst Elec & Electronics Engrs. *Res:* Determination of body composition by photon absorptionmetry; quantitative and qualitative medical imaging. *Mailing Add:* Nuclear Med Clin 115A Vet Admin Med Ctr 1481 W Tenth St Indianapolis IN 46202

WITT, SAMUEL N(EWTON), JR, b Seminole, Okla, Jan 29, 28; m 47; c 3. ELECTRONIC ENGINEERING. *Educ:* Tenn Polytech Inst, BS, 50; Ga Inst Technol, MS, 54, PhD(elec eng), 62. *Prof Exp:* Instr elec eng, Tenn Polytech Inst, 50-51; res asst, Ga Inst Technol, 51-53, res engr, 53-61, lectr electronics, 56-61; vpres & chief engr, RMS Eng, Inc, 61-70; DIR ENG, DIGITAL PRODS GROUP, 70- *Mem:* Sr mem Inst Elec & Electronics Engrs. *Res:* Electronic circuits and systems design. *Mailing Add:* Digital Prods Group PO Box 8508 Atlanta GA 30306

WITTBECKER, EMERSON LAVERNE, b Freeport, Ill, Feb 25, 17; m 40; c 2. POLYMER CHMISTRY, TEXTILE CHEMISTRY. *Educ:* Univ Ill, AB, 39; Pa State Univ, MS, 41, PhD(org chem), 42. *Prof Exp:* Jr res assoc, 46-52, res assoc, 52-55, res mgr pioneering res, 55-60, Orlon-Lycra res, 60-64, DIR, CAROTHERS LAB, NYLON RES DIV, TEXTILE FIBERS DEPT, E I DU PONT DE NEMOURS & CO, 64- *Mem:* Am Chem Soc. *Res:* Condensation polymers; fibers. *Mailing Add:* 208 Hitching Post Dr Wilmington DE 19803

WITTCOFF, HAROLD, b Marion, Ind, July 3, 18; m 46; c 2. ORGANIC CHEMISTRY. *Educ:* DePauw Univ, AB, 40; Northwestern Univ, PhD(org chem), 43; Harvard Univ, cert mgt, 64. *Prof Exp:* Head chem res dept, Gen Mills Chem, Inc, 43-56, dir chem res, 56-68, vpres chem res & develop, 68-69, vpres & dir corp res, 69-74, spec adv to the pres, 74-78; DIR RES & DEVELOP, KOOR CHEM LTD, BEER-SHEVA, ISRAEL, 78- *Concurrent Pos:* Adj prof chem, Univ Minn, 73- *Mem:* Am Chem Soc; Am Oil Chem Soc; Fedn Socs Paint Technol; Com Develop Asn; Inst Food Technol. *Res:* Phosphatides; polymers; protective coatings; resins and plastics; research adminstration. *Mailing Add:* Koor Chem Ltd PO Box 60 Beer-Sheva Israel

WITTE, DAVID L, b San Diego, Calif, 43; m 66; c 2. BIOCHEMISTRY, PATHOLOGY. *Educ:* St Olaf Col, BA, 65; Iowa State Univ, PhD(biochem), 71; Univ Iowa, MD, 82. *Prof Exp:* ASST PROF PATH & CLIN CHEM, UNIV IOWA, 73- *Concurrent Pos:* Fel clin chem, Univ Iowa, 71-73. *Mem:* Am Asn Clin Chem; Am Soc Clin Path. *Res:* Diagnostic methods in clinical pathology. *Mailing Add:* Dept of Path Univ of Iowa Iowa City IA 52242

WITTE, JOHN JACOB, b Passaic, NJ, Mar 10, 32; m 68; c 3. PREVENTIVE MEDICINE, PEDIATRICS. *Educ:* Hope Col, AB, 54; Johns Hopkins Univ, MD, 59; Harvard Univ, MPH(microbiol), 66. *Prof Exp:* Intern & resident pediat, Johns Hopkins Univ, 59-62; med epidemiologist infectious dis, 62-65, asst chief immunization br, 66-70, chief, 70-74, dir immunization div, 74-77, MED DIR, BUR HEALTH EDUC, DIS CONTROL, 77- *Concurrent Pos:* Consult, Adv Comt Immunizing Agents, Can, 69- & Adv Comt Epidemiol, Can, 69- *Honors & Awards:* Commendation Medal, USPHS, HEW, 72. *Mem:* Fel Am Acad Pediat; Infectious Dis Soc; Am Col Preventive Med; Am Pub Health Asn. *Res:* Epidemiology of communicable and chronic diseases; smoking related diseases; development and field testing of vaccines; complications of vaccine administration. *Mailing Add:* Ctr for Dis Control Atlanta GA 30333

WITTE, LARRY C(LAUDE), b Jonesboro, Tex, Apr 27, 39; m 62; c 1. MECHANICAL ENGINEERING, MATHEMATICS. *Educ:* Arlington State Col, BSME, 63; Okla State Univ, MSME, 65, PhD(mech eng), 67. *Prof Exp:* Assoc aerodyn engr, Ling-Temco-Vought, Inc, 63-65; res assoc, Argonne Nat Lab, 65-66, asst mech engr, 66-67; from asst prof to assoc prof mech eng, 67-73, chmn dept, 72-76, PROF MECH ENG, UNIV HOUSTON, 73- *Concurrent Pos:* Heat transfer consult. *Honors & Awards:* Herbert Allen Award, Am Soc Mech Engrs, 75. *Mem:* Am Soc Mech Engrs; Am Nuclear Soc; Am Inst Astronaut & Aeronaut. *Res:* Boiling heat transfer; high flux heat transfer processes; explosive vapor formation; natural convection in irregular enclosures; thermodynamic efficiency of heat exchanges. *Mailing Add:* Dept Mech Eng Univ Houston Houston TX 77004

WITTE, MICHAEL, b Poland, Mar 15, 11; nat US; m 40; c 4. ORGANIC CHEMISTRY, POLLUTION CHEMISTRY. *Educ:* Loyola Univ, Ill, BS, 37; Univ Ill, MS, 38, PhD(org chem), 41. *Prof Exp:* Asst chem, Univ Ill, 38-41; res chemist, Nat Aniline Div, Allied Chem Corp, 41-47; prod supvr, Gen Aniline & Film Corp, 46-54, prod mgr, NJ, 54-56; pres, Simpson Labs, Inc, 57-59; pres, Carnegies Fine Chem Div, Rexall Drug & Chem Corp, 59-60; PRES, M WITTE ASSOCS, 60- *Concurrent Pos:* Chem consult. *Mem:* AAAS; Am Chem Soc. *Res:* Pharmaceutical intermediates; dyestuffs manufacture; biochemistry; chemical management; solar energy. *Mailing Add:* 420 River Rd Apt C-11 Chatham NJ 07928

WITTEBORN, FRED CARL, b St Louis, Mo, Dec 27, 34; m 57; c 1. PHYSICS, ASTROPHYSICS. *Educ:* Calif Inst Technol, BS, 56; Stanford Univ, MS, 58, PhD(physics), 65. *Prof Exp:* Res assoc physics, Stanford Univ, 65-68; res scientist, 69-70, chief astrophysics br, 70-74, RES SCIENTIST, NASA AMES RES CTR, 75- *Concurrent Pos:* Vis scholar, Stanford Univ, 70-75. *Mem:* Am Phys Soc; Am Astron Soc. *Res:* Infrared astronomy; gravity; atomic physics; low temperature physics. *Mailing Add:* Astrophys Br NASA Ames Res Ctr N-245-6 Moffett Field CA 94035

WITTEBORT, JULES I, b Findlay, Ohio, Jan 26, 17; m 42; c 2. PHYSICS, MATERIALS SCIENCE. *Educ:* Findlay Col, AB, 39. *Prof Exp:* Textile & rubber engr, Wright-Patterson Air Force Base, 39-46, physicist, 46-53, supvry physicist, 53-66, phys sci adminr, US Air Force Mat Lab, 66-75; RETIRED. *Concurrent Pos:* Adv & contribr, Off Critical Tables, Nat Acad Sci-Nat Res Coun, 56-; mem ad hoc comts, Mat Adv Bd, Nat Res Coun, 57-58 & 64-65. *Mem:* Am Phys Soc; Sigma Xi. *Res:* Development of synthetic rubber and textile materials for aeronautical applications; thermal, optical magnetic and electronic properties of materials; direction of manufacturing technology program for thermionic and solid state devices and electronic materials; magnetic and semiconductor materials; history of the physics of materials. *Mailing Add:* 3762 Storms Rd Dayton OH 45429

WITTEKIND, RAYMOND RICHARD, b Jamaica, NY, May 9, 29; m 60. ORGANIC CHEMISTRY. *Educ:* Polytech Inst Brooklyn, BS, 51; Columbia Univ, AM, 55, PhD, 59; Seton Hall Univ, JD. *Prof Exp:* Res chemist, McNeil Labs, Inc, 58-61; scientist, Warner-Lambert Res Inst, 61-73, sr scientist, 73-74; patent lawyer, Hoffman-LaRoche Inc, Nutley, 74-78; PATENT LAWYER, AM HOECHST CORP, SOMERVILLE, 78- *Mem:* Am Chem Soc; Royal Soc Chem; Swiss Chem Soc. *Res:* Synthesis of fused ring heterocyclic compounds; stereochemistry and mechanism of organic reactions. *Mailing Add:* 30 Valley View Dr Morristown NJ 07960

WITTELS, BENJAMIN, b Minneapolis, Minn, Jan 22, 26; m 55; c 2. PATHOLOGY, BIOCHEMISTRY. *Educ:* Univ Minn, BA, 48, MD, 52; Am Bd Path, dipl, 57; Am Bd Clin Path, dipl, 70. *Prof Exp:* Assoc prof, 60-70, PROF PATH, MED CTR, DUKE UNIV, 70- *Mem:* Am Asn Path & Bact; Am Col Path. *Res:* Cardiac metabolism; hematology. *Mailing Add:* Dept of Path Duke Univ Med Ctr Durham NC 27710

WITTELS, MARK C, b Minneapolis, Minn, July 14, 21; m 51; c 3. MINERALOGY, SOLID STATE PHYSICS. *Educ:* Univ Minn, BS, 47; Mass Inst Technol, PhD(geol, ceramic eng), 51. *Prof Exp:* Staff scientist, Oak Ridge Nat Lab, 51-63; sr solid state physicist, US AEC, 63-74; CHIEF, SOLID STATE PHYSICS & MAT CHEM BR, DIV MAT SCI, US DEPT ENERGY, 74- *Concurrent Pos:* Vis prof, Wash Univ, 68-69. *Mem:* Mineral Soc Am; Am Crystallog Asn; Am Phys Soc. *Res:* Radiation effects in crystalline solids and in lunar materials; x-ray diffraction instrumentation; crystal growth techniques; defects in crystals; stored energy in reactor-irradiated graphite. *Mailing Add:* Mat Sci Div G-256 US Dept of Energy Washington DC 20545

WITTEMANN, JOSEPH KLAUS, b Heilbronn, Ger, Nov 13, 41; US citizen; m 65; c 3. DENTISTRY, PSYCHOLOGY. *Educ:* State Univ NY, BS, 64; Ohio State Univ, MA, 67, PhD(coun), 72. *Prof Exp:* Psychologist, Ohio Penitentiary, 67-68; asst prof psychol, Ohio Dominican Col, 69-72, chmn dept, 70-71; PROF GEN DENT, MED COL VA, 72-, DIR OFF EDUC EVAL, PLANNING & RES, 74- *Concurrent Pos:* Consult Curriculum Develop, Fac Develop, Human Servs Mgt, Res Int Prof Women Dent; mem ad hoc comt learning environ, Asn Am Med Schs, 73- *Mem:* Int Asn Dent Res; Am Educ Res Asn; Am Asn Dent Sch. *Res:* Clinical skills teaching; evaluation research program; pain control and analgesia; institutional research and management; management organization development. *Mailing Add:* Box 566 Med Col Va Sta Richmond VA 23298

WITTEN, ALAN JOEL, b Malden, Mass, Dec 11, 49; m 75; c 1. FLUIDS. *Educ:* Univ Rochester, BS, 71, MS, 72, PhD(mech eng), 75. *Prof Exp:* Mem staff, Themal-Hydraulics Group, 75-78, mgr, Coal Gasification Environ Proj, 78-80, LEADER, APPL PHYS SCI GROUP, OAK RIDGE NAT LAB, 80- *Mem:* Am Geophys Union. *Res:* Geophysical fluid dynamics; ekman layers; diffusion equation with random ejection; atmospheric transport in complex terrain. *Mailing Add:* Bldg 2001 Oak Ridge Nat Lab Oak Ridge TN 37830

WITTEN, GERALD LEE, b Daviess County, Mo, May 12, 29; m 51; c 3. SCIENCE EDUCATION. *Educ:* Kans State Teachers Col, 56, MS, 58, EdS(phys sci), 62. *Prof Exp:* Teacher high sch, Kans, 56-62; ASSOC PROF PHYS SCI, EMPORIA KANS STATE COL, 62- *Mem:* Nat Sci Teachers Asn; Am Asn Physics Teachers. *Res:* Development of take home laboratory exercises for high school physics and general education physical science classes. *Mailing Add:* Dept of Phys Sci Emporia Kans State Col Emporia KS 66801

WITTEN, LOUIS, b Baltimore, Md, Apr 13, 21; m 48; c 4. PHYSICS. *Educ:* John Hopkins Univ, BE, 41, PhD(physics), 51; NY Univ, BS, 44. *Prof Exp:* Res assoc, Proj Matterhorn, Princeton Univ, 51-53; instr fluid mech, Univ Md, 52-53; staff scientist, Lincoln Lab, Mass Inst Technol, 53-54; prin scientist, Res Inst Advan Study, Martin Marietta Corp, Md, 54-65, assoc dir, 65-68; head dept physics, 68-74, PROF PHYSICS, UNIV CINCINNATI, 68- *Concurrent Pos:* Adj prof, Drexel Univ, 56-68; Fulbright lectr, Weizmann Inst Sci, Israel, 64-65; trustee, Gravity Res Found, 66-, vpres, 72- *Mem:* AAAS; Am Phys Soc; Am Math Soc; Am Asn Physics Teachers; Am Astron Soc. *Res:* General theory of relativity; statistical mechanics; theory of particles and fields. *Mailing Add:* Dept of Physics Univ of Cincinnati Cincinnati OH 45221

WITTEN, MAURICE HADEN, b Jamesport, Mo, Dec 5, 31; m 69; c 3. PHYSICS. *Educ:* Emporia State Univ, BA, 56; Univ Nebr, Lincoln, MA, 60; Univ Iowa, PhD(sci educ, physics), 67. *Prof Exp:* Engr, Int Business Mach Corp, 56-57; from instr to assoc prof physics, 60-69, PROF PHYSICS, FT HAYS STATE UNIV, 69-, CHMN DEPT, 70- *Mem:* Am Asn Physics Teachers; Nat Sci Teachers Asn. *Res:* Nuclear emulsion techniques; physics education. *Mailing Add:* Dept Physics Ft Hays State Univ Hays KS 67601

WITTEN, THOMAS A, b Tulsa, Okla, July 19, 16; m 43; c 9. INTERNAL MEDICINE, GASTROENTEROLOGY. *Educ:* Univ Tex, AB, 38, MD, 42. *Prof Exp:* Intern, Med Col Va, 42-43; house officer, Johns Hopkins Hosp, Baltimore, 46-47; resident, Univ Utah, 47-49; clin instr, 51-53, asst clin prof, 53-57, from asst prof to assoc prof, 57-75, PROF MED, SCH MED, UNIV COLO MED CTR, DENVER, 75- *Concurrent Pos:* Instr, Vet Admin Hosp, Grand Junction, Colo, 51-53, asst dir res lab, Vet Admin Hosp, Ft Logan, 51-53, asst chief med & chief gastroenterol, Vet Admin Hosp, Denver, 52-, assoc chief staff res & educ, 61-68. *Mem:* Fel Am Col Physicians; Am Fedn Clin Res; Am Gastroenterol Asn; AMA. *Res:* Studies in the effect of alcohol on metabolic processes. *Mailing Add:* Vet Admin Hosp Rm A501a 1055 Clermont Denver CO 80220

WITTEN, THOMAS ADAMS, JR, b Raleigh, NC, Aug 24, 44. THEORETICAL PHYSICS. *Educ:* Reed Col, AB, 66; Univ Calif, San Diego, PhD(physics), 71. *Prof Exp:* Instr physics, Princeton Univ, 71-74; foreign collabr, Comn Atomic Energy, Saclay, France, 74-75; ASST PROF PHYSICS, UNIV MICH, ANN ARBOR, 75- *Mem:* Am Phys Soc. *Res:* Renormalization scaling symmetry in extended matter; excitations of systems with long-range order. *Mailing Add:* 1049 Randall Lab Univ of Mich Ann Arbor MI 48109

WITTEN, THOMAS RINER, experimental nuclear physics, see previous edition

WITTENBACH, VERNON ARIE, b Belding, Mich, Dec 13, 45; m 68; c 2. PLANT PHYSIOLOGY. *Educ:* Mich State Univ, BS, 68, MS, 70, PhD(hort), 74. *Prof Exp:* RES BIOLOGIST, CENT RES & DEVELOP DEPT, E I DU PONT DE NEMOURS & CO, 74- *Mem:* Am Soc Plant Physiologists; Am Soc Hort Sci. *Res:* Physiology of plant senescence. *Mailing Add:* E I du Pont de Nemours & Co Cent Res & Develop Dept Exp Sta Wilmington DE 19801

WITTENBERG, ALBERT M, b Newark, NJ; m 61; c 2. PHYSICAL ELECTRONICS. *Educ:* Union Col, NY, BS; Johns Hopkins Univ, PhD(physics). *Prof Exp:* MEM TECH STAFF PHYSICS, BELL LABS, 55- *Mem:* Am Phys Soc; Soc Info Display. *Res:* Atomic structure of diatomic molecules; gaseous electronics; radiative heat transfer; optical spectroscopy; photoconductivity; interconnection technology; research and development in electron beam and solid state display systems. *Mailing Add:* 19 Exeter Rd Short Hills NJ 07078

WITTENBERG, BEATRICE A, b Berlin, Ger, Nov 6, 28; US citizen; m 54; c 3. BIOCHEMISTRY, PHYSIOLOGY. *Educ:* Univ Toronto, BA, 49, MA, 50; Western Reserve Univ, PhD(pharmacol), 54. *Prof Exp:* Res assoc physiol, Western Reserve Univ, 54-55; cancer res, Delafield Hosp, NY Univ, 55-56; asst prof physiol, 64-75; ASSOC PROF PHYSIOL, ALBERT EINSTEIN COL MED, 75- *Mem:* Am Soc Physiologists; Am Soc Biol Chem. *Res:* Heme proteins; oxygen supply; isolated adult heart cells. *Mailing Add:* Dept of Physiol Albert Einstein Col of Med Bronx NY 10461

WITTENBERG, JONATHAN B, b New York, NY, Sept 19, 23; m 54; c 3. BIOCHEMISTRY, PHYSIOLOGY. *Educ:* Harvard Univ, BS, 45; Columbia Univ, MA, 46, PhD, 50. *Prof Exp:* From instr to asst prof biochem, Western Reserve Univ, 52-55; asst prof, 55, from asst prof to assoc prof physiol, 56-65, PROF PHYSIOL, ALBERT EINSTEIN COL MED, 65- *Concurrent Pos:* NIH res fel, 52. *Res:* Porphyrins; swimbladders; retia mirabilia; oxygen transport; myoglobin; hemeproteins; hemoglobin. *Mailing Add:* Dept of Physiol Albert Einstein Col of Med Bronx NY 10461

WITTENBERG, LAYTON JUNIOR, b Toledo, Ohio, May 6, 27; m 53; c 3. PHYSICAL INORGANIC CHEMISTRY. *Educ:* Ohio State Univ, BS, 49; Univ Wis, PhD(chem), 53. *Prof Exp:* SR RES SPECIALIST, MOUND LAB, US DEPT ENERGY, MONSANTO RES CORP, 53- *Mem:* Am Chem Soc; Am Nuclear Soc; Solar Energy Soc. *Res:* Chemistry applied to energy systems; solar pond technology; fusion reactor fuel systems; liquid actinide metals. *Mailing Add:* Mound Labs Monsanto Res Corp PO Box 32 Miamisburg OH 45342

WITTENBERGER, CHARLES LOUIS, b Ogallala, Nebr, June 22, 30; m 56; c 3. BACTERIOLOGY, BIOCHEMISTRY. *Educ:* Univ Creighton, BS, 52, MS, 54; Ind Univ, PHD(bact), 59. *Prof Exp:* Vis scientist, NIH, 59-61, res mcirobiologist, 61-68, CHIEF MICROBIOL SECT, NAT INST DENT RES, 68- *Mem:* Am Acad Microbiol; Am Soc Microbiol; Am Soc Biol Chemists. *Res:* Microbial metabolism; electron transport in Hydrogenomonas species; intermediary metabolism of carbohydrates; biochemical regulation of microbial metabolism. *Mailing Add:* Lab of Microbiol Nat Inst of Dent Res Bethesda MD 20014

WITTER, JOHN ALLEN, b Jamestown, NY, Sept 2, 43; m 71. FOREST ENTOMOLOGY, INSECT ECOLOGY. *Educ:* Va Polytech Inst, BS, 65, MS, 67; Univ Minn, St Paul, PhD(entom), 71. *Prof Exp:* Res technician entom, Southeastern Forest Exp Sta, US Forest Serv, 66-67; res asst, Univ Minn, St Paul, 67-71, res fel, 71-72, instr forest entom, 72; asst prof, 72-76, ASSOC PROF FOREST ENTOM, SCH NATURAL RESOURCES, UNIV MICH, ANN ARBOR, 76- *Mem:* Entom Soc Am; Entom Soc Can; Soc Am Foresters. *Res:* Population dynamics of forest insects, parasites and predators of forest insects; defoliators; insect impact; tent caterpillars; insect behavior; spruce budworm; risk rating systems. *Mailing Add:* Samuel T Dana Bldg Sch of Natural Resources Univ of Mich Ann Arbor MI 48109

WITTER, LLOYD DAVID, b Chicago, Ill, May 15, 23; m 50; c 3. FOOD MICROBIOLOGY, FOOD SCIENCE. *Educ:* Univ Wash, Seattle, BS, 45, MS, 50, PhD(microbiol), 53. *Prof Exp:* Asst microbiol, Univ Wash, Seattle, 52-53; res chemist, Continental Can Co, Ill, 53-56; from asst prof to assoc prof, 56-67, PROF FOOD MICROBIOL, UNIV ILL, URBANA, 67- *Concurrent Pos:* Vis prof appl biochem, Univ Nottingham, Eng, 72; vis prof food microbiol, Univ Montevideo, Uruguay, 77; viSouth prof, Polytech S Bank London, 80; vis scientist, Food Res Asn, Eng, 80. *Mem:* Fel Am Acad Microbiol; Am Soc Microbiol; Am Dairy Sci Asn; Inst Food Technol; NY Acad Sci. *Res:* Microbiology of food and dairy products; psychrophilic bacteria; bacterial growth on solid surfaces; heat resistance and injury of bacteria; institutional foods; osmoregution in microorganisms. *Mailing Add:* Dept of Food Sci Univ of Ill Urbana IL 61801

WITTER, RICHARD L, b Bangor, Maine, Sept 10, 36; m 62; c 1. POULTRY PATHOLOGY. *Educ:* Mich State Univ, BS, 58, DVM, 60; Cornell Univ, MS, 62, PhD, 64. *Prof Exp:* Res vet, Regional Poultry Res Lab, 64-75, DIR, REGIONAL POULTRY RES LAB, AGR RES SERV, USDA, 75- *Concurrent Pos:* Asst prof, Mich State Univ, 64-71, assoc prof, 71- *Honors & Awards:* Am Asn Avian Path Award, 66 & 80; Res Award, Poultry Sci Asn, 71; Res Award, Sigma Xi, 75; Res Award, CPC Int, Inc, 76; Res Award, Mfg Asn Am Feed, 78. *Mem:* Am Vet Med Asn; Am Asn Avian Path; Conf Res Workers Animal Dis; Poultry Sci Asn; Sigma Xi. *Res:* Epizootiology and control of poultry diseases, especially virology and pathology; viral-induced neoplasia, especially Marek's disease and lymphoid leukosis of chickens. *Mailing Add:* Regional Poultry Res Lab 3606 E Mt Hope Rd East Lansing MI 48823

WITTERHOLT, EDWARD JOHN, b Osceola Mills, Pa, Nov 12, 35; m 57; c 5. APPLIED MATHEMATICS. *Educ:* Manhattan Col, BS, 57; Brown Univ, ScM, 59, PhD(appl math), 64. *Prof Exp:* Res proj mathematician, Schlumberger Technol Corp, 63-77; MEM STAFF, SEISMOGRAPH SERV CORP, TULSA, 77- *Mem:* Am Phys Soc; Acoust Soc Am. *Res:* Analysis of pressure and temperature phenomena in petroleum reservoirs; multi-phase fluid flow; acoustic wave propagation. *Mailing Add:* Seismograph Serv Corp PO Box 1590 Tulsa OK 74102

WITTERHOLT, VINCENT GERARD, b New York, NY, Sept 24, 32; m 54; c 6. ORGANIC CHEMISTRY. *Educ:* Queens Col, NY, BS, 53; Purdue Univ, PhD(org chem), 58. *Prof Exp:* Res chemist, Org Chem Dept, 58-68, res supvr, 69-73, sr supvr sulfur colors area, Chambers Works, 73-74, chief supvr, Azo Lab, 74-75, div head, Chem, Dyes & Pigments Dept, Jackson Lab, 75-80, RES SUPVR, BIOCHEM DEPT, EXP STA, E I DU PONT DE NEMOURS & CO, INC, 81- *Mem:* Am Chem Soc. *Res:* Organofluorine chemistry; dye chemistry; new dyes product and process development; photochemistry; fluorescence; photo stabilization; colloid chemistry; pharmaceuticals; agrichemicals. *Mailing Add:* Biochem Dept Exp Sta E I du Pont de Nemours & Co Inc Wilmington DE 19898

WITTERS, ROBERT DALE, b Cheyenne, Wyo, May 2, 29. PHYSICAL CHEMISTRY. *Educ:* Univ Colo, BA, 51; Mont State Univ, PhD(phys chem), 64. *Prof Exp:* Chemist, E I du Pont de Nemours & Co, 51-53; asst prof chem, State Univ NY Col Plattsburgh, 59-62 & Mont State Univ, 62-63; res fel, Harvey Mudd Col, 64-65; from asst prof to assoc prof, 65-78, PROF CHEM, COLO SCH MINES, 78- *Concurrent Pos:* Brown innovative teaching grant, 75. *Mem:* Am Chem Soc; Am Crystallog Asn; Sigma Xi. *Res:* X-ray crystallography. *Mailing Add:* Dept of Chem Colo Sch of Mines Golden CO 80401

WITTERS, WELDON L, b Dayton, Ohio, Dec 13, 29; m 59; c 2. REPRODUCTIVE PHYSIOLOGY, BIOLOGY. *Educ:* Ball State Univ, BS, 52, MS, 55; Purdue Univ, MS, 64, PhD(animal physiol), 67. *Prof Exp:* Teacher, High Schs, Ind, 55-67; from asst prof to assoc prof, 67-77, PROF ZOOL, OHIO UNIV, 77- *Concurrent Pos:* NSF travel grant, France, 68; res grant, Ohio Univ, 68-69; NSF grant biol educ, 70-72; consult drug educ, Ohio. *Mem:* Nat Asn Biol Teachers; Nat Sci Teachers Asn; Soc Study Reproduction; Am Soc Animal Sci. *Res:* Metabolic pathways functional in sperm; effect of metabolic inhibitors on sperm; hallucinogenic alkaloids metabolic effect on tissue; laboratory concepts taught with visuals and video tapes. *Mailing Add:* 47 Avon Pl Athens OH 45701

WITTES, JANET TURK, b Pittsburgh, Pa, May 12, 43; m 64; c 2. STATISTICS, BIOSTATISTICS. *Educ:* Radcliffe Col, BA, 64; Harvard Univ, MA, 65, PhD(statist), 70. *Prof Exp:* Res assoc, Sch Pub Health, Univ Pittsburgh, 70-72 & Dept Statist, George Washington Univ, 72-73; adj asst prof pub health, Dept Epidemiol, Sch Pub Health, Columbia Univ, 73-74; asst prof math, 74-77, ASSOC PROF MATH, HUNTER COL, 77- *Mem:* Biomet Soc; Am Statist Asn. *Res:* Applied statistical methodology, especially biostatistical techniques. *Mailing Add:* Dept Math Sci Hunter Col 695 Park Ave New York NY 10021

WITTICK, JAMES JOHN, b New York, NY, Aug 17, 30; m 56; c 4. ANALYTICAL CHEMISTRY, QUALITY CONTROL. *Educ:* Col Holy Cross, BS, 52; Tufts Univ, MS, 55; Univ Pa, PhD(chem), 66. *Prof Exp:* Chemist, Merck Sharp & Dohme Res Labs, NJ, 55-57, group leader phys & anal res, 57-60, unit head pharmaceut anal, Pa, 60-62, sr res chemist, 65-68, res fel, 68-70, assoc dir qual control, 70-80, DIR QUAL CONTROL OPERS, MERCK CHEM DIV, MERCK & CO, INC, 80- *Mem:* Am Chem Soc; AAAS. *Res:* Purity and structure determination of organic compounds; pharmaceutical analysis; electro-analytical chemistry; x-ray diffraction; chromatography. *Mailing Add:* Qual Control Dept Merck Chem Mfg Div Rahway NJ 07065

WITTIE, LARRY DAWSON, b Bay City, Tex, Mar 9, 43; m 72; c 2. DISTRIBUTED COMPUTER SYSTEMS, INTELLIGENT SYSTEMS. *Educ:* Calif Inst Technol, BS, 66; Univ Wis-Madison, MS, 67, PhD(comput sci), 73. *Prof Exp:* Systs programmer, Calif Inst Technol, 63-66 & IBM Corp, Sunnyvale, 66; NASA trainee comput sci, Univ Wis-Madison, 66-69, res asst, 69-72; asst prof comput sci, Purdue Univ, 72-73; asst prof, 73-79, ASSOC PROF COMPUT SCI, STATE UNIV NY BUFFALO, 79- *Concurrent Pos:* Nat lectr, Asn Comput Machinery, 78-79 & 79-80; prin investr, NSF, 77-81, Air Force, 82- & NASA, 82-; sci adv, Army, 81; consult industry, 77- *Mem:* Asn Comput Mach; Sigma Xi; Inst Elec & Electronics Engrs; Soc Neurosci. *Res:* Distributed operating systems to control modular computers; parallel information processing in networks, with emphasis on computer architecture interconnection techniques for efficient communications among millions of microcomputers; simulation of large brain models; neural distributed memory mechanisms. *Mailing Add:* Dept of Comput Sci 4226 Ridge Lea Rd Amherst NY 14226

WITTIG, GERTRAUDE CHRISTA, b Glauchau, Ger, Oct 4, 28; US citizen. ZOOLOGY, INSECT PATHOLOGY. *Educ:* Univ Tübingen, Dr rer nat(zool, bot, biochem), 55. *Prof Exp:* Teacher, Musterschule Glauchau, Ger, 46-47 & Preuniv Sch Neckarsulm, 55; Ger Res Asn res assoc, Zool Inst, Univ Tübingen, 56-58; res assoc entom, Univ Calif, Berkeley, 58-59; microbiologist, Insect Path Pioneering Lab, Entom Res Div, Agr Res Serv, USDA, Md, 59-62; res microbiologist, Forestry Sci Lab, Pac Northwest Forest & Range Exp Sta, US Forest Serv, Ore, 62-68; assoc prof biol sci, 68-75, PROF BIOL SCI, SOUTHERN ILL UNIV, EDWARDSVILLE, 75- *Concurrent Pos:* Lalor Found fel, 58; Ger Acad Exchange Serv & Ministry of Educ Baden-Württemburg res grants, 58; Fulbright travel grant, 58-59; consult, Univ Ariz, 61; assoc prof, Ore State Univ, 62-68. *Mem:* AAAS; Am Soc Cell Biologists; Entom Soc Am; Electron Micros Soc Am; Am Soc Zoologists. *Res:* Biological ultrastructure; morphology and histology of insects; insect pathology, particularly histopathological and ultrastructural problems. *Mailing Add:* Biol Sci Southern Ill Univ Edwardsville IL 62026

WITTIG, HEINZ JOSEPH, b Munich, Ger, May 19, 21; US citizen; m 60; c 4. ALLERGY, IMMUNOLOGY. *Educ:* Univ Munich, MD, 51; Am Bd Pediat, dipl, 56, cert allergy, 61. *Prof Exp:* Instr & fel pediat allergy, Univ Rochester, 57-58; fel, NY Univ, 58-60; clin asst prof, Sch Med, Seton Hall Univ, 60-64; asst prof pediat, Sch Med, WVa Univ, 64-68; chief, Div Pediat Allergy, Col Med, Univ Fla, 68, prof pediat, 68-80; WITH OCHSNER CLIN, 80- *Mem:* Fel Am Acad Allergy; fel Am Acad Pediat; Am Thoracic Soc. *Res:* Clinical immunology; bronchial asthma, etiology of intrinsic form; lymphocyte stimulation with various antigens, including cancer; macrophage inhibition; bronchial challenge procedures. *Mailing Add:* Ochsner Clin 1514 Jefferson Hwy New Orleans LA 70121

WITTIG, KENNETH PAUL, b Pittsburgh, Pa, Aug 19, 46; m 69. INVERTEBRATE PHYSIOLOGY. *Educ:* St Vincent Col, BS, 68; Kent State Univ, PhD(animal physiol), 74. *Prof Exp:* Teacher biol & chem, St Thomas Aquinas High Sch, 68-69; asst prof, 74-80, ASSOC PROF BIOL, SIENA COL, 80, CHMN DEPT, 79- *Mem:* AAAS; Sigma Xi; Am Inst Biol Sci; Am Soc Zoologists. *Res:* Investigation of the neuroendocrine control of calcium metabolism in the crayfish; salt metabolism in amphibians. *Mailing Add:* Dept of Biol Siena Col Loudonville NY 12211

WITTING, HARALD LUDWIG, b Duisburg, Ger, Sept 23, 36; US citizen; m 60; c 3. PLASMA PHYSICS. *Educ:* Mass Inst Technol, BS & MS, 59, ScD(plasma), 64. *Prof Exp:* PHYSICIST, GEN ELEC RES & DEVELOP CTR, 64- *Mem:* AAAS; Am Phys Soc. *Res:* Gas discharges; electrodes; plasma light sources. *Mailing Add:* Gen Elec Res & Develop Ctr PO Box 8 Schenectady NY 12305

WITTING, JAMES M, b Chicago, Ill, Jan 14, 38; m 62; c 3. PHYSICAL OCEANOGRAPHY, HYDRODYNAMICS. *Educ:* John Carroll Univ, BS, 59, MS, 60; Mass Inst Technol, PhD(physics), 64. *Prof Exp:* Assoc physicist, IIT Res Inst, 64-66, res physicist, 66; asst prof hydrodyn, Dept Geophys Sci, Univ Chicago, 66-70; phys sci adminr, Off Naval Res, 70-73, oceanogr, Phys Oceanog Prog, 72-73, HEAD, PHYS OCEANOG BR, US NAVAL RES LAB, 73- *Mem:* Am Phys Soc; Am Geophys Union. *Res:* Waves in dispersive media; water waves; undular bores; numerical modeling of oceanic circulation. *Mailing Add:* 9400 Athens Rd Fairfax VA 22030

WITTING, LLOYD ALLEN, b Chicago, Ill, May 18, 30; m 56; c 3. NUTRITION, LIPID CHEMISTRY. *Educ:* Univ Ill, BS, 52, MS, 53, PhD, 56. *Prof Exp:* Asst food technol, Univ Ill, 52-55; assoc biochemist, Am Meat Inst Found, Chicago, 55-57; proj assoc physiol chem, Univ Wis, 57-59; med res assoc, Mendel Res Lab, Elgin State Hosp, Ill, 59-68, actg dir, 68-70, res scientist, 69-72; assoc prof food sci & technol, Tex Woman's Univ, 72-74; consult, NTex Educ & Training Coop, Inc, 75-76; sr chemist, 76-77, TECH DIR BIOCHEM RES & MFG, SUPELCO INC, 77- *Concurrent Pos:* Asst prof, Col Med, Univ Ill, 62-72. *Mem:* Am Inst Nutrit; Am Oil Chem Soc; Am Soc Biol Chemists. *Res:* High performance liquid chromatography; polyunsaturated fatty acids; glycolipids; clinical and animal nutrition; chemistry and biochemistry of lipids; tocopherol; gas chromatography. *Mailing Add:* Supelco Inc Supelco Park Bellefonte PA 16823

WITTKE, DAYTON D, b Matador, Tex, Oct 9, 32; m 56; c 5. NUCLEAR & MECHANICAL ENGINEERING. *Educ:* Brigham Young Univ, BES, 56; Univ Ill, MS, 61, PhD(nuclear eng), 66. *Prof Exp:* Mech engr, Atomic Prod Div, Gen Elec Co, Wash, 56; res asst nuclear eng, Univ Ill, Urbana, 63-65; from asst prof to assoc prof mech & nuclear eng, Univ Nebr, Lincoln, 65-74; mgr, Opers Tech Support Serv, 74-77, mgr generating sta eng, 77-80, MGR, ENG DIV, OMAHA PUB POWER DIST, 80- *Concurrent Pos:* Tech consult, Omaha Pub Power Dist, 67-74; consult, Wittke & Assocs, 70- *Mem:* Am Nuclear Soc; Am Soc Mech Engrs; Am Soc Eng Educ. *Res:* Heat transfer and fluid flow problems associated with nuclear engineering applications. *Mailing Add:* Omaha Pub Power Dist 1623 Harney St Omaha NE 68102

WITTKE, JAMES PLEISTER, b Westfield, NJ, Apr 2, 28; m 52; c 2. OPTICAL PHYSICS. *Educ:* Stevens Inst Technol, ME, 49; Princeton Univ, MA, 52, PhD(physics), 55. *Prof Exp:* Instr physics, Princeton Univ, 54-55; MEM TECH STAFF, RCA LABS, 55- *Mem:* Fel Am Phys Soc; Inst Elec & Electronics Eng; Optical Soc Am. *Res:* Microwave spectroscopy; masers; lasers; fiber optics; optical instrumentation. *Mailing Add:* RCA Corp RCA Labs David Sarnoff Res Ctr Princeton NJ 08540

WITTKE, PAUL H, b Toronto, Ont, Aug 17, 34; m 60; c 2. ELECTRICAL ENGINEERING. *Educ:* Univ Toronto, BASc, 56; Queen's Univ, Ont, MSc, 62, PhD(elec eng), 65. *Prof Exp:* Defense sci serv officer radar, Defence Res Telecommun Estab, Ont, 56-60; res assoc statist commun theory, 60-65, asst prof elec eng, 65-67, ASSOC PROF ELEC ENG, QUEEN'S UNIV, ONT, 67-, HEAD COMMUN GROUP, 68- & HEAD DEPT ELEC ENG, 77- *Concurrent Pos:* Acad vis, Imp Col, Univ London, 71-72; chmn, Comn C, Int Union Radio Sci Can, 76- *Mem:* Inst Elec & Electronics Engrs. *Res:* Radar and electronic countermeasures; statistical communication theory; frequency-modulation systems. *Mailing Add:* Dept Elec Eng Queen's Univ Kingston ON K7L 3N6 Can

WITTKOWER, ANDREW BENEDICT, b London, Eng, Nov 7, 34; m 57; c 2. ATOMIC PHYSICS. *Educ:* McGill Univ, BSc, 55; Cambridge Univ, MSc, 59; Univ London, PhD(atomic physics), 67. *Prof Exp:* Proj physicist, High Voltage Eng Corp, 59-64, res physicist, 64-67, assoc dir res, 67-71; sr vpres, Extrion Corp, 71-75, mkt & asst gen mgr, Extrion Div, Varian Assoc, 75-78; vpres & gen mgr, Nova Assoc, 78-80; VPRES & GEN MGR, ION IMPLEMENTATION DIV, EATON CORP, 80- *Mem:* Fel Am Phys Soc; Brit Inst Physics. *Res:* Atomic physics applied to the development of ion accelerators; author or coauthor of over 100 publications. *Mailing Add:* Eaton Corp 57 Dodge Beverly MA 01915

WITTKOWER, ERIC DAVID, b Berlin, Ger, Apr 4, 99; nat Can; m 31; c 2. PSYCHIATRY. *Educ:* Univ Berlin, MD, 24; FRCPS, cert psychiat, 55. *Prof Exp:* Lectr psychosom med, Univ Berlin, 31; mem res staff, Cent Path Lab, Maudsley Hosp, London, Eng, 33-35; Sir Halley-Stewart res fel & physician, Tavistock Clin, 35; res fel psychiat, Nat Asn Prev Tuberc, Gt Brit, 45; psychiatrist, Dermat Dept, St Bartholomew's Hosp, London, 48; from asst prof to prof psychiat, 51-72, dir transcult 56, EMER PROF PSYCHIAT, McGILL UNIV, 72- *Concurrent Pos:* Consult, Royal Victoria & Montreal Gen Hosps, 51-; mem expert adv panel ment health, WHO, 64-69; consult, Queen Elizabeth Hosp, 65; mem bd, Fr-Am Inst Ment Health, Paris, 73. *Mem:* Fel Am Asn Social Psychiat; fel Royal Col Psychiatrists; Am Psychiat Asn; Can Psychoanal Soc (pres, 66-); Int Col Psychosom Med (pres, 72). *Res:* Psychosomatic medicine; transcultural psychiatry. *Mailing Add:* Sect Transcult Psychiat Studies McGill Univ 1033 Pine Ave W Montreal PQ H3A 1A1 Can

WITTLE, JOHN KENNETH, b Lancaster, Pa, July 20, 39; c 1. INORGANIC CHEMISTRY, ANALYTICAL CHEMISTRY. *Educ:* Franklin & Marshall Col, AB, 62; Purdue Univ, Lafayette, PhD(inorg chem), 68. *Prof Exp:* Inorg chemist, 67-68, proj engr, 68-72, mgr polymer technol, 72-75, MGR DIELECTRIC MAT LAB, GEN ELEC CO, 75- *Mem:* AAAS; Am Chem Soc; The Chem Soc; Am Inst Mining, Metall & Petrol Eng. *Res:* Insulation systems for electrical systems; decomposition of electrical insulation under electrical stress; materials application. *Mailing Add:* 2601 Crum Creek Dr Berwyn PA 19312

WITTLE, LAWRENCE WAYNE, b Mt Joy, Pa, Nov 20, 41; m 64, 77; c 2. PHYSIOLOGY. *Educ:* Lebanon Valley Col, BS, 63; Univ Va, PhD(biol), 68. *Prof Exp:* NIH fel, Inst Marine Sci, Univ Miami, 68-70; asst prof, 70-77, ASSOC PROF BIOL, ALMA COL, 77-, CHMN BIOL, 77- *Mem:* AAAS; Am Soc Zool; Int Soc Toxinology. *Res:* Physiological and pharmacological properties of marine toxins; parathyroid physiology of uradele amphibians. *Mailing Add:* Dept of Biol Alma Col Alma MI 48801

WITTLIFF, JAMES LAMAR, b Taft, Tex, June 15, 38; m 62; c 2. BIOCHEMISTRY. *Educ:* Univ Tex, Austin, BA, 61, PhD(molecular biol), 67; La State Univ, MS, 63. *Prof Exp:* USPHS fel biochem regulation, Oak Ridge Nat Lab, Tenn, 67-69; asst prof biochem, Sch Med & Dent, 69-74, assoc prof biochem & head sect endocrine biochem, Cancer Ctr, Univ Rochester, 75-76; PROF BIOCHEM & CHMN DEPT, SCH MED & DENT, UNIV LOUISVILLE, 76- *Concurrent Pos:* Vis prof, Univ Düsseldorf, Ger, 74 & Univ Innsbruck, Austria, 76. *Mem:* AAAS; Am Chem Soc; Am Asn Cancer Res; Am Soc Biol Chemists; Endocrine Soc. *Res:* Hormonal control of protein and nucleic acid synthesis; role of specific hormone receptors in target cell response. *Mailing Add:* Dept of Biochem Health Sci Ctr PO Box 35260 Louisville KY 40232

WITTMAN, JAMES SMYTHE, III, b Ft Bragg, NC, Mar 1, 43; m 65; c 4. BIOCHEMISTRY, NUTRITION. *Educ:* La Col, BA, 64; Tulane Univ, PhD(biochem), 70; Fairleigh Dickinson Univ, MBA, 78. *Prof Exp:* Chemist, Southern Regional Res Lab, USDA, 64-65; org chemist, US Customs Lab, La, 65-66; asst biochemist, Hoffmann-La Roche Inc, 68-70, sr biochemist, 70-77, clin res scientist, 77-79; tech dir, Batter-Lite Foods Inc, 80-81; INSTR, ROCK VALLEY COL, 81- *Concurrent Pos:* Consult food indust, 81- *Mem:* Am Inst Nutrit; Sigma Xi; Am Sci Affiliation; NY Acad Sci; AAAS. *Res:* Reduced-calorie food formulations; fructose; biochemical nutrition; regulation of intermediary metabolism and protein synthesis; clinical studies, vitamin E and calorie sweeteners. *Mailing Add:* Rock Valley Col Rockford IL 61101

WITTMAN, WILLIAM F, b Pittsburgh, Pa, Oct 10, 37; m 64; c 6. ORGANIC CHEMISTRY. *Educ:* Carnegie Inst Technol, BS, 59; Univ Nebr, PhD(org chem), 65. *Prof Exp:* Sr res chemist, 64-72, patent liaison specialist & patent agent, 72-76, patent & info supvr, 77, PATENT & RES ADMIN MGR, 3M CO, 78- *Res:* Pharmaceutical, agrichemical and biopolymer patents. *Mailing Add:* 270-3A Riker Labs 3M Co 3M Ctr St Paul MN 55101

WITTMANN, HORST RICHARD, b Worms, Ger, Jan 31, 36; US citizen; m 64; c 3. SOLID STATE ELECTRONICS. *Educ:* Graz Univ, PhD(physics), 64. *Prof Exp:* Asst exp physics, Graz Univ, 63-64; space physicist, Bölkow, Ger, 64-66; res scientist quantum electronics, Phys Sci Lab, Missile Command, Redstone Arsenal, Ala, 66-70; chief, Elec Br, US Army Res Off, 70-75, ASST DIR, ELECTRONICS DIV, US ARMY RES OFF, 75- *Concurrent Pos:* Res asst, Duke Univ, 71-73; adj prof, NC State Univ, 75-; Secy Army fel, 77; Fulbright fel, Tech Univ, Vienna, Austria, 77-78. *Mem:* Am Phys Soc; Inst Elec & Electronics Engrs. *Res:* Semiconductor lasers; solid state electronics; 3-5 compounds. *Mailing Add:* Electronics Div US Army Res Off Box 12211 Research Triangle Park NC 27709

WITTMUSS, HOWARD D(ALE), b Papillion, Nebr, July 15, 22; m 50; c 3. AGRICULTURAL ENGINEERING. *Educ:* Univ Nebr, BS, 47, MS, 50, PhD(soil physics, agr eng), 56. *Prof Exp:* Construct engr, Diamond Eng Co, Nebr, 47-49; irrig engr, Irrig Res Div, Soil Conserv Serv, USDA, 49-50; asst soil physics, 52-56, asst prof agr eng, 56-58, ASSOC PROF AGR ENG, UNIV NEBR, LINCOLN, 58- *Mem:* Am Soc Agr Engrs; Soil Conserv Soc Am. *Res:* Irrigation efficiency; soil structure; tillplant system of corn production; land shaping; soil and water conservation. *Mailing Add:* 214 Dept of Agr Eng Univ of Nebr Lincoln NE 68583

WITTNEBERT, FRED R, b Bayonne, NJ, July 8, 11; m 36; c 1. MECHANICAL ENGINEERING. *Educ:* Stevens Inst Technol, ME, 33. *Prof Exp:* From jr engr to works mgr, Sperry Prod, Inc, 33-41; chief engr, War Prod Div, Eversharp, Inc, 41-44; pres, Wittnebert-Jones Corp, 44-53; dir phys lab, Parker Pen Co, 53-54, dir labs, 54-58, tech dir, 58-67, vpres tech develop, 67-76. *Concurrent Pos:* Dir, Panoramic Corp, 67-76 & Omniflight Helicopters, Inc, 72-78; mem res adv comt & spec consult, Agency Int Develop, US State Dept, 74-78. *Res:* Metal flaw detection; engine and generator design; instrument development; control and servo design; capillary and surface phenomenon; research and engineering administration. *Mailing Add:* 3516 Crystal Springs Rd Janesville WI 53545

WITTNER, MASAKO, b Tokyo, Japan; m 62. IMMUNOLOGY, BIOCHEMISTRY. *Educ:* Univ Ill Med Ctr, MSc, 66; Toho Univ, DMSc(immunol biochem), 76. *Prof Exp:* Res asst biochem, Univ Ill Med Ctr, 59-62; res technologist immunol microbiol, 62-73, instr, 73-76, RES ASSOC & ASST PROF, LA RABIDA INST, DEPT PEDIAT, UNIV CHICAGO, 76- *Concurrent Pos:* Prin investr grant, Nat Inst Allergy & Infectious Dis, 77-78. *Mem:* Am Asn Immunologists; Am Soc Microbiol; AAAS. *Res:* Streptococcal immunobiology; lymphocyte hybridomas; streptococcal vaccine. *Mailing Add:* La Rabida Inst E 65th at Lake Michigan Chicago IL 60649

WITTNER, MURRAY, b New York, NY, Apr 23, 27; m 55; c 2. PHYSIOLOGY, PARASITOLOGY. *Educ:* Univ Ill, ScB, 48, ScM, 49; Harvard Univ, PhD, 55; Yale Univ, MD, 61. *Prof Exp:* Instr path & parasitol & consult path, 56-57, PROF PATH & PARASITOL & DIR PARASITOL LABS, ALBERT EINSTEIN COL MED, 67- *Concurrent Pos:* Career scientist, Health Res Coun, New York, 67-; attend physician, Bronx Munic Hosp Ctr, Lincoln Hosp & Albert Einstein Col Med Hosp; dir, Trop Dis Clin, Lincoln Hosp & Bronx Munic Hosp Ctr. *Mem:* Soc Protozool; Am Soc Cell Biol; Am Asn Path & Bact; Am Soc Zool; Am Soc Parasitol. *Res:* Physiology and biochemistry of oxygen poisoning; physiology of parasites; experimental pathology. *Mailing Add:* Dept of Path Albert Einstein Col of Med Bronx NY 10461

WITTROCK, DARWIN DONALD, b Primghar, Iowa, Oct 20, 49. HELMINTHOLOGY, ELECTRON MICROSCOPY. *Educ:* Univ Northern Iowa, BA, 71; Iowa State Univ, MS, 73, PhD(parasitol), 76. *Prof Exp:* ASST PROF BIOL, UNIV WIS-EAU CLAIRE, 76- *Mem:* Am Soc Parasitologists; Am Micros Soc. *Res:* Ultrastructural studies on organ systems of digenetic trematodes and helminthological surveys from mammals. *Mailing Add:* Dept Biol Univ Wis Eau Claire WI 54701

WITTRY, DAVID BERYLE, b Mason City, Iowa, Feb 7, 29; m 55; c 5. SEMICONDUCTOR PHYSICS, ELECTRON OPTICS. *Educ:* Univ Wis, BS, 51; Calif Inst Technol, MS, 53, PhD(physics), 57. *Prof Exp:* Res fel, Calif Inst Technol, 57-58; from asst prof to assoc prof, 59-69, PROF MAT SCI & ELEC ENG, UNIV SOUTHERN CALIF, 69- *Concurrent Pos:* Consult, Appl Res Labs Inc, 58-, Hughes Aircraft, 58-59, Exp Sta, E I du Pont de Nemours & Co, 62-, NAm Aviation, 61-63, Gen Tel & Electronics Res Labs, 66-72 & Electronics Res Div, Rockwell Int, 76-; Guggenheim fel, Univ Cambridge, 67-68; vis prof, Univ Osaha prefecture, 74. *Mem:* Inst Elec & Electronics Engrs; Am Phys Soc; Electron Micros Soc Am; Microbeam Anal Soc; Sigma Xi. *Res:* Scanning electron microprobe instrumentation; quantitative electron probe microanalysis, electron microprobe applications to solid state electronics, electron spectroscopy in TEM, secondary ion mass spectrometry. *Mailing Add:* Dept of Mat Sci VHE 602 Univ of Southern Calif Los Angeles CA 90007

WITTRY, ESPERANCE, b Marshall, Minn, Jan 13, 20. BIOLOGY. *Educ:* Col St Catherine, BA, 46; Univ Notre Dame, MS, 54, PhD(biol), 60. *Prof Exp:* Assoc prof, 60-71, PROF BIOL, COL ST CATHERINE, 71- *Res:* Physiology; radiation biology; neurophysiology. *Mailing Add:* Dept of Biol Col of St Catherine St Paul MN 55105

WITTRY, JOHN P(ETER), b Aurora, Ill, Sept 6, 29; m 51; c 6. AERONAUTICAL & ASTRONAUTICAL ENGINEERING. *Educ:* St Louis Univ, BS, 51; US Air Force Inst Technol, MS, 56; Univ Mich, AAE, 62. *Prof Exp:* US Air Force, 51-, proj off aircraft nuclear propulsion, Res & Develop Command, Wright-Patterson AFB, Ohio, 56-58, adv propulsion technologist, Atomic Energy Comn, Hq, Germantown, Md, 58-60, instr astronaut, US Air Force Acad, 62-72, assoc prof astronaut & head dept astronaut & comput sci, 73-78, prof & head, Dept Astronautics & Comput Sci, 73-78, CHMN ENG DIV & VDEAN FAC, US AIR FORCE ACAD, 78- *Mem:* Am Soc Eng Educ. *Res:* Space nuclear power systems; astrodynamics; inertial guidance and control systems. *Mailing Add:* Vice Dean Fac US Air Force Academy CO 80840

WITTSELL, LAWRENCE EUGENE, b Neosho County, Kans, Mar 2, 29; m 51; c 6. SOIL SCIENCE. *Educ:* Brigham Young Univ, BS, 57; Kans State Univ, MS, 59, PhD(agron), 64. *Prof Exp:* Res asst soil mgt, Kans State Univ, 56-62; asst agronomist, Trop Res Div, United Fruit Co, 62-65; plant nutritionist, Agr Res Lab, 65-72, agronomist, Pesticide Develop Dept & Plant Physiol Dept, 72-76, TRIAZINE PROD COORDR, PESTICIDE DEVELOP DEPT, BIOL SCI RES CTR, SHELL DEVELOP CO, 76- *Mem:* Am Soc Agron; Soil Sci Soc Am; Int Soc Soil Sci; Coun Agr Sci & Technol; Weed Sci Soc Am. *Res:* Effects of artificial compaction of the soil on growth of plants in field and greenhouse; weed control and other cultural practices in bananas; general fertilizer and plant nutrition investigations; research and development of herbicides. *Mailing Add:* Shell Develop Co PO Box 4248 Modesto CA 95352

WITTSON, CECIL L, b Camden, SC, Jan 14, 07; m 34; c 1. PSYCHIATRY. *Educ:* Univ SC, BS, 28; Med Col of SC, MD, 31; Am Bd Neurol & Psychiat, dipl, 48. *Prof Exp:* Staff psychiatrist, Cent Islip State Hosp, NY, 32-50; prof neurol & psychiat, 50-71, chmn dept, 50-64, dean col, 64-71, pres, Med Ctr, 68-71, EMER PROF NEUROL & PSYCHIAT, COL MED & EMER CHANCELLOR, MED CTR, UNIV NEBR, OMAHA, 72-; MED PROG DIR, HENNINGSON, DURHAM & RICHARDSON, INC, 72- *Concurrent Pos:* Attend psychiatrist, Out-Patient Dept, NY Psychiat Inst, 35-36; res consult, 46-; dir, Nebr Psychiat Inst, 50-64; chief clin servs, Nebr Bd Control, 51-64, dir ment health, 54-67; mem, Surgeon Gen Adv Comt Indian Health, 65-; nat adv comt alcoholism, US Dept Health, Educ & Welfare, 66- *Mem:* AAAS; fel Am Psychiat Asn; Asn Mil Surg US; Am Psychopath Asn; Am Asn Ment Deficiency. *Res:* Psychiatric selection; medical education. *Mailing Add:* 168 1/2 Queen St Charleston SC 29401

WITTWER, JOHN WILLIAM, b Columbus, Ohio, Apr 35; m 59; c 3. PERIODONTOLOGY. *Educ:* Ohio State Univ, DDS, 59, MSc, 65. *Prof Exp:* Instr periodont, Ohio State Univ, 61-64; asst prof, Sch Dent, Loyola Univ Chicago, 66-69; assoc prof, 69-75, PROF PERIODONT, SCH DENT, UNIV LOUISVILLE, 75- *Mem:* Int Asn Dent Res; Am Acad Periodont. *Mailing Add:* Health Sci Ctr Sch Dent Univ Louisville Louisville KY 40292

WITTWER, LELAND S, b Belleville, Wis, Apr 26, 19. ANIMAL NUTRITION. *Educ:* Mich State Univ, BS, 52; Cornell Univ, MS, 54, PhD(dairy prod), 56. *Prof Exp:* Asst prof animal sci, Univ Mass, 56-58; PROF ANIMAL SCI, UNIV WIS-RIVER FALLS, 58- *Mem:* Sigma Xi; AAAS; Am Dairy Sci Asn; Am Soc Animal Sci. *Mailing Add:* Dept of Animal Sci Univ of Wis Col Agr River Falls WI 54022

WITTWER, ROBERT FREDERICK, b Boonville, NY, Sept 18, 40; m 68; c 3. SILVICULTURE. *Educ:* State Univ NY Col Environ Sci & Forestry, BS, 66, PhD(forestry), 74. *Prof Exp:* Forester, NY State Dept Environ Conserv, 66-69; NDEA fel, State Univ NY Col Environ Sci & Forestry, 69-73; asst prof, 74-80, ASSOC PROF FORESTRY, UNIV KY, 80- *Mem:* Am Soc Agron; Soil Sci Soc Am; Soc Am Foresters. *Res:* Forest soil productivity; forest fertilization; nutrient cycling; nutrition of forest trees. *Mailing Add:* Dept Forestry Univ Ky Lexington KY 40546

WITTWER, SYLVAN HAROLD, b Hurricane, Utah, Jan 17, 17; m 38; c 4. HORTICULTURE. *Educ:* Utah State Agr Col, BS, 39; Univ Mo, PhD(hort), 43. *Prof Exp:* Asst, Univ Mo, 40-43, instr hort, 43-46; from asst prof to assoc prof, 46-51, PROF HORT, MICH STATE UNIV, 51-, DIR AGR EXP STA, 65- *Concurrent Pos:* Consult, Rockefeller Found, Mex, 68-69, Ford Found, Ceylon, 69- & UN Develop Prog, 71-; mem agr bd, Nat Acad Sci, 71-73; chmn bd agr & renewable resources, Nat Acad Sci-Nat Res Coun, 73-77; climate res bd, Nat Acad Sci, Nat Res Coun, 78-; mem, US Cong Food Adv Bd, Off Technol Assessment, 77-, Liaison Comt, food & agr, Int Inst Appl Systs Anal, 77-, NASA Adv Coun, space & terrestrial appl, 78- & V I Lenin All-Union Acad of Agr Sci, USSR, 78-; Tanner Lectr Award, Inst Food Technol, 80. *Honors & Awards:* Campbell Award, AAAS, 57. *Mem:* AAAS; Soc Develop Biol; Am Soc Hort Sci; Am Soc Plant Physiol; Bot Soc Am. *Res:* Physiology of reproduction in horticulture; plant growth regulators for improving fruit set and control flowering; nutrition of horticultural crops; radioisotopes in mineral nutrition of plants. *Mailing Add:* Agr Exp Sta Mich State Univ East Lansing MI 48824

WITTY, RALPH, b Windsor Mills, Que, Nov 19, 20; m 52; c 2. BIOCHEMISTRY, NUTRITION. *Educ:* McGill Univ, BS, 48, PhD(biochem), 51. *Prof Exp:* Res chemist, 51-56, group leader biochem, 56-68, ASST DIR RES, RES & DEVELOP LABS, CAN PACKERS INC, 68- *Concurrent Pos:* Vis scientist, Cambridge, Eng, 67-68. *Mem:* AAAS; Can Inst Food Sci; Nutrit Soc Can; Nutrit Today Soc. *Res:* Animal and human nutrition fats; oils; digestion and absorption of nutrients and availability of nutrients. *Mailing Add:* Can Packers Inc Res Ctr 2211 St Clair Ave W Toronto ON M6N 1K4 Can

WITZ, DENNIS FREDRICK, b Milwaukee, Wis, Dec 10, 38; m 71; c 4. MICROBIOLOGY. *Educ:* Carroll Col, Wis, BS, 61; Univ Wis-Madison, MS, 64, PhD(bact), 67. *Prof Exp:* RES ASSOC MICROBIOL, UPJOHN CO, 67- *Mem:* Am Soc Microbiol. *Res:* Process of biological nitrogen fixation by microorganisms; biosynthesis of antibiotics and secondary metabolites; production of antibiotics by fermentation. *Mailing Add:* 1400-89-1 Upjohn Co Kalamazoo MI 49081

WITZ, GISELA, b Breslau, Ger, Mar 16, 39; US citizen. CANCER. *Educ:* NY Univ, BA, 62, MS, 65, PhD(phys org chem), 69. *Prof Exp:* Fel biochem, Sloan-Kettering Inst Cancer Res, 69-70; assoc res scientist cancer res, NY Univ, 70-73, res scientist environ med, Med Ctr, 73-77, asst prof environ med, 77-80; ASST PROF COMMUN MED, RUTGERS MED SCH, 80- *Mem:* NY Acad Sci; Am Asn Cancer Res; Am Chem Soc. *Res:* Chemical carcinogenesis; fluorescence spectrophotometric determination of conformational states of mammalian plasma membranes; effect of tumor promoters on cell membranes. *Mailing Add:* UMD Rutgers Med Sch Dept Cancer & Commun Med Piscataway NJ 08854

WITZ, RICHARD L, b New Lisbon, Wis, Jan 12, 16; m 41; c 2. AGRICULTURAL ENGINEERING. *Educ:* Univ Wis, BS, 39; Purdue Univ, MS, 42. *Prof Exp:* Asst, Purdue Univ, 39-42; exten specialist, Mich State Univ, 42-45; from asst prof & asst agr engr to assoc prof agr eng & assoc agr engr, 45-57, PROF AGR ENG & AGR ENGR, EXP STA, N DAK STATE UNIV, 57- *Honors & Awards:* George W Kable Award, Am Soc Agr Engrs. *Mem:* Fel & sr mem Am Soc Agr Engrs; Am Soc Eng Educ. *Res:* Rural electrification; building design; sewage disposal; farm water treatment. *Mailing Add:* Dept of Agr Eng NDak State Univ Fargo ND 58105

WITZEL, DONALD ANDREW, b Artesian, SDak, Sept 9, 26. VETERINARY PHYSIOLOGY. *Educ:* Univ Minn, BS, 53, DVM, 57; Iowa State Univ, MS, 65, PhD(vet physiol), 70. *Prof Exp:* Res vet physiol, Nat Animal Dis Lab, 61-72, VET MED OFFICER PHYSIOL & TOXICOL, VET TOXICOL & ENTOM RES LAB, AGR RES SERV, USDA, 72- *Concurrent Pos:* Consult, Baylor Col Med, 72-74. *Mem:* AAAS; Am Vet Med Asn; NY Acad Sci; Am Soc Vet Physiologists & Pharmacologists. *Res:* Electrophysiological studies of the visual system of domestic animals as related to toxicological problems. *Mailing Add:* Vet Toxicol & Entom Res Lab PO Drawer GE College Station TX 77840

WITZELL, O(TTO) W(ILLIAM), b Baltimore, Md, Nov 14, 16; m 42. MECHANICAL ENGINEERING. *Educ:* Johns Hopkins Univ, BE, 37; Purdue Univ, MSME, 49, PhD, 51. *Prof Exp:* Marine engr, US Maritime Comn, 40-46; from instr to prof mech eng, Purdue Univ, 46-64; prof & chmn dept, Univ Calif, Santa Barbara, 64-66; PROF MECH ENG, DREXEL UNIV, 76-, DEAN, GRAD SCH, 66- *Concurrent Pos:* Consult, US Steel Corp, 57- & Allison Div, Gen Motors Corp, 58-59; prog dir, off inst prog, NSF, 62-63. *Mem:* AAAS; Am Soc Mech Engrs; Am Soc Eng Educ. *Res:* Determination of physical and chemical thermodynamic properties. *Mailing Add:* Grad Sch Drexel Univ 32nd & Chestnut Sts Philadelphia PA 19104

WITZGALL, CHRISTOPH JOHANN, b Hindelang, Ger, Feb 25, 29; US citizen; m 64; c 3. OPERATIONS RESEARCH, NUMERICAL ANALYSIS. *Educ:* Univ Munich, PhD(math), 58. *Prof Exp:* Res assoc math, Princeton Univ, 59-60, Univ Mainz, 60-62 & Argonne Nat Lab, 62; mathematician, Nat Bur Standards, 62-66 & Boeing Co, 66-73; MATHEMATICIAN, CTR APPL MATH, NAT BUR STANDARDS, 73- *Concurrent Pos:* Vis prof, Univ Tex, Austin, 71 & Univ Würzburg, 72; assoc ed, Math Prog, 73- *Mem:* Asn Comput Mach; Soc Indust & Appl Math; AAAS. *Res:* Further development of operations research, numerical analysis and programming languages as needed for planning and systems applications. *Mailing Add:* Ctr Appl Math Nat Bur of Standards Washington DC 20234

WITZIG, WARREN FRANK, b Detroit, Mich, Mar 26, 21; m 42; c 4. NUCLEAR ENGINEERING, PHYSICS. *Educ:* Rensselaer Polytech Inst, BS, 42; Univ Pittsburgh, MS, 44, PhD(physics), 52. *Prof Exp:* Res engr, Westinghouse Elec Corp, 42-46, from engr & scientist to proj mgr, Bettis Labs, 46-60; sr vpres & dir, NUS Corp, 60-67; PROF NUCLEAR ENG & HEAD DEPT, PA STATE UNIV, UNIVERSITY PARK, 67- *Concurrent Pos:* Mem nuclear standards bd, US Am Standards Inst, 65; mem comt radioactive waste mgt, Nat Acad Sci; mem, Pa Gov Adv Comt Nuclear Energy & Asn Am Univs Rev Comt on EBR II Fast Breeder Reactor. *Mem:* Inst Elec & Electronics Engrs; fel Am Nuclear Soc; Am Phys Soc; AAAS. *Res:* Nuclear reactor engineering and physics; reactor safety; nuclear safeguards; heat transfer; nuclear fuel costs; reactor plant siting; reactor design and operation. *Mailing Add:* 1330 Park Hills Ave State College PA 16801

WITZLEBEN, CAMILLUS LEO, b Dickinson, NDak, Apr 20, 32; m 56; c 6. PATHOLOGY. *Educ:* Univ Notre Dame, BS, 53; St Louis Univ, MD, 57. *Prof Exp:* Resident path, St Louis Univ, 57-60; NSF fel, Hosp Sick Children, London, Eng, 60-61; fel, Harvard Univ, 61-62; dir labs, Children's Hosp Med Ctr Northern Calif, 64-66; dir labs, Cardinal Glennon Mem Hosp Children, St Louis, 66-73; PROF PATH & PEDIAT, UNIV PA, 73-; DIR PATH, CHILDREN'S HOSP PHILADELPHIA, 73- *Concurrent Pos:* Consult, San Francisco Gen Hosp, 64-66; asst prof, Univ Calif, 64-66; from asst prof to prof, St Louis Univ, 66-73; NIH res grant, 68- *Mem:* Am Asn Path & Bact. *Res:* Hepatobiliary system; pediatric disease; heavy metals. *Mailing Add:* 229 Cornell Ave Swarthmore PA 19081

WIXOM, ROBERT LLEWELLYN, b Philadelphia, Pa, July 6, 24; m 49, 75; c 3. BIOCHEMISTRY, NUTRITION. *Educ:* Earlham Col, AB, 47; Univ Ill, PhD(biochem), 52. *Prof Exp:* Asst biochem, Univ Ill, 48-52; from instr to assoc prof, Sch Med, Univ Ark, 52-64; assoc prof, 64-72, PROF BIOCHEM, SCH MED, UNIV MO-COLUMBIA, 72- *Concurrent Pos:* Fel, Univ Ill, 55; Lalor Found res fel, 58; NIH spec res fel, 70-71; NIH res serv fel, 78-79. *Mem:* AAAS; Am Soc Biol Chemists; Am Chem Soc; Soc Exp Biol & Chem; Am Inst Nutrit. *Res:* Requirements and metabolism of essential amino acids in man; nutritional aspects of glycine in the chick; biosynthesis of amino acids in microorganisms and plants; inborn errors of amino acid metabolism; intravenous alimentation of amino acid solutions; role of histidine in man. *Mailing Add:* Dept Biochem Sch Med Univ of Mo Columbia MO 65212

WIXSON, BOBBY GUINN, b Abilene, Tex, Mar 19, 31; m 52; c 2. AQUATIC BIOLOGY, SANITARY ENGINEERING. *Educ:* Sul Ross State Col, BS, 60, MA, 61; Tex A&M Univ, PhD(biol oceanog), 67. *Prof Exp:* Asst instr sci, Sul Ross State Col, 58-60, instr, 60-61, dir col planetarium & asst to dean of men, 59-61; asst oceanog, Tex A&M Univ, 61-63, asst aquatic biol, 63-65, asst water pollution res, 65-67; from asst prof to assoc prof environ health, 67-72, PROF ENVIRON HEALTH, UNIV MO-ROLLA, 72-, DIR INT CTR, 69- *Concurrent Pos:* Consult, United Nations Environ Prog, US Environ Protection Agency. *Mem:* Nat Water Pollution Control Fedn; Am Water Resources Asn; Soc Environ Geochem & Health (secy-treas, 78-81). *Res:* Aquatic pollution and industrial waste disposal problems. *Mailing Add:* Rm 319 Eng Res Bldg Univ Mo Rolla MO 65401

WIXSON, ELDWIN A, JR, b Winslow, Maine, Nov 30, 31; m 54, 76. MATHEMATICS. *Educ:* Univ Maine, BS, 53; Colby Col, MST, 62; Temple Univ, MSEd, 62; Univ Mich, PhD, 69. *Prof Exp:* Teacher, High Sch, Maine, 53-54 & 57-60; TV teacher, Maine Dept Educ, 60-61; teacher, High Sch, Maine, 62-63; assoc prof math, Keene State Col, 63-65; assoc prof, 66-70, PROF MATH, PLYMOUTH STATE COL, 70-, CHMN DEPT, 66- *Mem:* Math Asn Am; Nat Coun Teachers Math. *Res:* Mathematics education, especially at the undergraduate college level. *Mailing Add:* Dept of Math Plymouth State Col Plymouth NH 03264

WIZENBERG, MORRIS JOSEPH, b Toronto, Ont, Apr 9, 29; US citizen; m 55; c 4. RADIOTHERAPY. *Educ:* Univ Toronto, MD, 53. *Prof Exp:* Resident obstet & gynec, Sinai Hosp, Baltimore, Md, 54-58; resident therapeut radiol, Univ Hosp, 59-61, from instr to assoc prof, Sch Med, 61-68, prof radiol & head div therapeut radiol, Univ Md, Baltimore City, 68-74; PROF RADIOL & ASSOC DIR RADIATION THERAPY, UNIV OKLA COL MED, OKLAHOMA CITY, 74- *Concurrent Pos:* Nat Cancer Inst spec fel, Sch Med, Univ Md, Baltimore City, 61-63; consult numerous hosps. *Mem:* Am Cancer Soc; fel Am Col Radiol; Am Radium Soc; Am Soc Therapeut Radiol; Radiol Soc NAm. *Res:* Clinical radiation therapy, hyperthermia. *Mailing Add:* PO Box 25606 Oklahoma City OK 73125

WNUK, MICHAEL PETER, b Katowice, Poland, Sept 12, 36; US citizen; m 64; c 1. ENGINEERING MECHANICS. *Prof Exp:* Asst prof physics, Tech Univ Krakow, 59-64, assoc prof, 64-66; asst prof, 66-67, assoc prof, 67-76, PROF MECH ENG, SDAK STATE UNIV, 76- *Concurrent Pos:* Sr res fel, Calif Inst Technol, 67-68; distinguished vis scholar, Cambridge Univ, 68-70; vis scholar, Acad Mining & Metall, Krakow, 74; Nat Acad Sci sponsored vis prof & co-ed of proceedings, Fac Technol & Metall, Univ Belgrade, 80; vis prof, Northwestern Univ, 80-81. *Mem:* Sigma Xi; NY Acad Sci. *Res:* Solid mechanics with particular emphasis on mechanics of fracture; initiation and subsequent propagation of fracture in non-linear range of material behavior (durtile and time-dependent fracture). *Mailing Add:* Mech Eng Dept SDak State Univ Brookings SD 57007

WOBESER, GARY ARTHUR, b Regina, Sask, Feb 12, 42; m 65; c 2. FISH PATHOLOGY, WILDLIFE PATHOLOGY. *Educ:* Univ Toronto, BSA, 63; Univ Guelph, MSc, 66, DVM, 69; Univ Sask, PhD(vet path), 73. *Prof Exp:* assoc prof, 73-78, PROF VET PATH, WESTERN COL VET MED, UNIV SASK, SASKATOON, 78- *Concurrent Pos:* Coun mem, Wildlife Dis Asn, 75-78, chmn student awards comt, 76. *Mem:* Wildlife Dis Asn; Can Soc Environ Biologists; Can Asn Vet Pathologists; Am Fisheries Soc; Can Vet Med Asn. *Res:* Diseases of free-living fish and wild life, and of cultured salmonid fishes, with particular emphasis on infectious, degenerative and toxic problems. *Mailing Add:* Dept Vet Path Western Col Vet Med Univ Sask Saskatoon SK S7N 0W0 Can

WOBSCHALL, DAROLD C, b Wells, Minn, Feb 24, 32; m 57; c 3. BIOPHYSICS, ELECTRICAL ENGINEERING. *Educ:* St Olaf Col, BA, 53; State Univ NY Buffalo, MA, 60, PhD(biophys), 66. *Prof Exp:* Res assoc physics, Univ Buffalo, 58-60; assoc physicist, Cornell Aeronaut Lab, 60-62; cancer res scientist, Roswell Park Mem Inst, 66-67; asst prof, 67-71, ASSOC PROF ENG & BIOPHYS, STATE UNIV NY BUFFALO, 71- *Concurrent Pos:* NIH spec fel, 66-67. *Mem:* AAAS; Am Phys Soc; Biophys Soc; Inst Elec & Electronic Eng. *Res:* Electrical and mechanical properties of membranes; bioengineering; electronics instrumentation. *Mailing Add:* 25 Blossom Heath Williamsville NY 14221

WOBUS, REINHARD ARTHUR, b Norfolk, Va, Jan 11, 41; m 67; c 2. GEOLOGY. *Educ:* Wash Univ, AB, 62; Harvard Univ, MA, 63; Stanford Univ, PhD(geol), 66. *Prof Exp:* From asst prof to assoc prof, 66-78, PROF GEOL, WILLIAMS COL, 78-, GEOLOGIST CENT ENVIRON GEOL BR, US GEOL SURV, 67- *Concurrent Pos:* Vis prof geol, Colo Col, 76; instr geol field course, Colo State Univ, 77- *Mem:* Fel Geol Soc Am; Nat Asn Geol Teachers. *Res:* Igneous and metamorphic petrology; Precambrian geology of Southern Rocky Mountains. *Mailing Add:* Dept of Geol Williams Col Williamstown MA 01267

WOCHOK, ZACHARY STEPHEN, b Philadelphia, Pa, Dec 29, 42; m 70. PLANT PHYSIOLOGY. *Educ:* La Salle Col, BA, 64; Villanova Univ, MS, 67; Univ Conn, PhD(plant physiol), 70. *Prof Exp:* From asst prof to assoc prof biol, Univ Ala, 71-76; proj mgr tissue cult technol, Weyerhaeuser Co, 76-78; dir res, Plant Resources Inst & Native Plants, Inc, 78-80; BUS DEVELOP MGR, MONSANTO CO, 80- *Concurrent Pos:* NIH fel, Yale Univ, 70-71; consult, Gulf States Paper Corp, 75-76; mem bd dirs, Int Jojaba Trade Asn, 79. *Mem:* Am Soc Plant Physiol; Bot Soc Am; Int Asn Plant Tissue Cult; Scand Soc Plant Physiol. *Res:* Amelioration of strip mined spoils; study of plant growth and development through in vitro methodology; cell determination in meristematic growth zones and development of applied tissue culture technology. *Mailing Add:* Monsanto Co 800 N Lindbergh Blvd St Louis MO 63167

WODARCZYK, FRANCIS JOHN, b Chicago, Ill, Dec 11, 44. SPECTROSCOPY, SURFACE ANALYSIS. *Educ:* Ill Inst Technol, BS, 66; Harvard Univ, AM, 67, PhD(chem), 71. *Prof Exp:* Lectr chem, Harvard Univ, 69; res assoc, Univ Calif, Berkeley, 71-73; res chemist, Cambridge Res Labs, US Air Force, 73-77, prog mgr, Off Sci Res, 77-78; MEM TECH STAFF, ROCKWELL INT SCI CTR, 78- *Concurrent Pos:* Lectr, Univ Calif, Berkeley, 73. *Mem:* Am Chem Soc; AAAS; Sigma Xi. *Res:* Atomic and molecular spectroscopy; energy transfer and reaction kinetics; laser physics and chemistry; surface analysis; thin film coatings research. *Mailing Add:* Rockwell Int Sci Ctr PO Box 1085 Thousand Oaks CA 91360

WODINSKY, ISIDORE, b New York, NY, Mar 6, 19; m 42; c 2. ONCOLOGY. *Educ:* Brooklyn Col, BA, 39; George Washington Univ, MS, 51. *Prof Exp:* Biologist, Nat Cancer Inst, 46-55, sci adminr, 55-57; HEAD CANCER CHEMOTHER RES, LIFE SCI SECT, ARTHUR D LITTLE, INC, 59- *Mem:* Int Union Against Cancer; Am Asn Cancer Res; Int Soc Chemother; NY Acad Sci. *Res:* Chemotherapy of cancer; carcinogenesis; biology and kinetics of experimental neoplasms; cryobiology. *Mailing Add:* Arthur D Little Inc Life Sci Sect 30 Memorial Dr Cambridge MA 02142

WODZICKI, ANTONI, b Krakow, Poland, July 15, 34; NZ citizen; m 62; c 4. GEOLOGY. *Educ:* Univ Otago, NZ, BE, 56; Univ Minn, MS, 61; Stanford Univ, PhD(geol), 65. *Prof Exp:* Geologist econ geol, NZ Geol Surv, 54-75, geologist petrol, 58-59; vis asst prof mineral & geochem, Portland State Univ, 75-76; vis asst prof mineral & econ geol, Univ Ore, 76-77; asst prof, 77-80, ASSOC PROF ECON GEOL & MINERAL, WESTERN WASH UNIV, 80- *Concurrent Pos:* Actg chief petrologist, NZ Geol Surv, 69-70; mem mineral resources comt, NZ Nat Develop Conf, 69-70; hon lectr, Victoria Univ, Wellington, 74-75; proj geologist, Nat Uranium Resource Eval, 78- *Mem:* Royal Soc NZ; NZ Geol Soc; NZ Geochem Group (chmn, 71-73). *Res:* Field geology, economic geology, petrology, geochemistry and particularly the application of these disciplines to the finding, evaluation and understanding of the origin of ore deposits. *Mailing Add:* Dept of Geol Western Wash Univ Bellingham WA 98225

WODZINSKI, RUDY JOSEPH, b Chicago, Ill, June 12, 33; m 56; c 3. MICROBIAL BIOCHEMISTRY. *Educ:* Loyola Univ, Ill, BS, 55; Univ Wis, MS, 57, PhD(bact), 60. *Prof Exp:* Asst bact, Univ Wis, 55-60; sr res scientist, Squibb Inst Med Res, New Brunswick, NJ, 60-62; res microbiologist, Int Minerals & Chem Corp, Ill, 62-64, supvr microbial biochem, 64-68, mgr animal sci, 68-70; prof biol sci, 70-75, Gordon J Barnett prof environ sci, 75-77, PROF BIOL SCI, UNIV CENT FLA, 77- *Concurrent Pos:* Mem bd dirs, Anaerobic Energy Systs Inc & Govt Energy Res Task Force, State Fla, 80- *Mem:* Am Soc Microbiol; fel Am Acad Microbiol; Sigma Xi. *Res:* Enzymology; molecular biology; virology; microbial genetics and physiology; fermentation; available moisture requirements of microorganisms; water and waste microbiology. *Mailing Add:* Dept of Biol Sci Univ Cent Fla Orlando FL 32816

WOEHLER, KARLHEINZ EDGAR, b Berlin, Ger, June 5, 30; m 56; c 1. PHYSICS. *Educ:* Univ Bonn, BS, 53; Aachen Tech Univ, Dipl, 55; Univ Munich, PhD(physics), 62. *Prof Exp:* Physicist commun technol, Siemens & Halske, Ger, 55-59; res assoc plasma physics, Max-Planck Inst Physics, 59-62; asst prof physics, US Naval Postgrad Sch, 62-64; sr res assoc, Inst Plasma Physics, 64-65; assoc prof physics, 65-72, chmn dept physics & chem, 74-79, PROF PHYSICS, NAVAL POSTGRAD SCH, 72- *Concurrent Pos:* Consult physicist, Atomics Int Div, NAm Aviation, Inc, 63-64; Nat Acad Sci res grant, Res Labs, NASA, 66; consult, Naval Electronics Lab Ctr, Calif, 68, 69 & 72. *Mem:* Am Phys Soc; AAAS; Sigma Xi. *Res:* Plasma physics; general relativity and cosmology. *Mailing Add:* Dept of Physics & Chem Naval Postgrad Sch Monterey CA 93940

WOEHLER, MICHAEL EDWARD, b Appleton, Wis, Feb 16, 45. IMMUNOLOGY, MEDICAL MICROBIOLOGY. *Educ:* Northwestern Univ, BA, 67; Marquette Univ, PhD(microbiol), 71. *Prof Exp:* Fel biochem, Univ Ga, 71-74; mem tech staff immunol, GTE Labs, Inc, 74-80; WITH PHARMACIA, INC, 80- *Mem:* Am Soc Microbiol; AAAS; Sigma Xi; NY Acad Sci. *Res:* Immunology, specifically structure function relationships of immunoglobulins G and E antibodies. *Mailing Add:* Pharmacia Inc 800 Centennial Ave Piscataway NJ 08854

WOEHRLE, HELMUT REINHARD, b Newark, NJ, Jan 6, 40; m 61; c 2. METALLURGY. *Educ:* Gen Motors Inst, Flint, BME, 63; Rensselaer Polytech Inst, MMetE, 63, PhD(phys metall), 65. *Prof Exp:* Sr res metallurgist, 65-67, supvr metall labs, 67-69, mgr metall eng, 70-71, CHIEF METALLURGIST, NEW DEPARTURE-HYATT BEARINGS DIV, GEN MOTORS CORP, 71- *Mem:* Am Soc Metals; Soc Automotive Engrs; Am Soc Testing & Mat. *Res:* Rolling contact fatigue; ferrous alloy development; ferrous heat treatment; martensitic transformations; failure analysis. *Mailing Add:* Gen Motors Corp 2509 Hayes Ave Sandusky OH 44870

WOELFEL, JULIAN BRADFORD, b Baltimore, Md, Dec 17, 25; m 48; c 3. DENTISTRY. *Educ:* Ohio State Univ, DDS, 48. *Prof Exp:* PROF DENT, COL DENT, OHIO STATE UNIV, 48- *Concurrent Pos:* Consult & Am Dent Asn res assoc, Nat Bur Stands, 57-63; consult, Vet Admin Hosp, Dayton, Ohio, 66-69 & Fed Penitentiary, Chillicothe, 65-66; pres, Carl O Boucher Prosthodontic Conf, 67- *Honors & Awards:* Int Asn Dent Res Award, 67. *Mem:* Am Prosthodont Soc; Am Dent Asn; Int Asn Dent Res; fel Am Col Dent; Acad Denture Prosthetics. *Res:* Prosthodontic dentistry; denture base resins; clinical evaluation of complete dentures; electromyography; jaw and denture movement; mandibular motion in three dimensions; accuracy of impression materials; soft and hard tissue and facial dimension changes beneath complete dentures during six years; computer analysis of mandibular resorption. *Mailing Add:* 4345 Brookie Ct Columbus OH 43214

WOELKE, CHARLES EDWARD, b Seattle, Wash, Jan 8, 26; m 47; c 2. FISHERIES, MARINE ECOLOGY. *Educ:* Univ Wash, BS, 50, PhD(fisheries), 68. *Prof Exp:* Aquatic biologist, Ore Fisheries Comn, 50-51; fisheries biologist, 51-64, res scientist fisheries, 68-75; chief res & develop, Wash Dept Fisheries, 75-79; ASST TO DIR, INTERGOVT AFFAIRS, 79- *Concurrent Pos:* Affil prof, Univ Wash, 69- *Mem:* Fel Am Inst Fishery Res Biol; Nat Shellfisheries Asn. *Res:* Molluscan commercial shellfish; bioassays with bivalve embryos; development of in situ bioassays with bivalve larvae; development of water quality standards and criteria; biometrics and ecological systems analysis. *Mailing Add:* 2378 Crestline Blvd Olympia WA 98502

WOERNER, DALE EARL, b Oak Hill, Kans, Jan 15, 26; m 50; c 6. ANALYTICAL CHEMISTRY. *Educ:* Kans State Univ, BS, 49; Univ Ill, MS, 51, PhD(anal chem), 53. *Prof Exp:* Asst chem, Univ Ill, 49-53; assoc prof, Hanover Col, 53-55; from asst instr to asst prof, Kans State Univ, 55-58; from asst prof to assoc prof, 58-66, PROF CHEM, UNIV NORTHERN COLO, 66- *Mem:* Am Chem Soc. *Res:* Amperometric titrations; spectroscopy. *Mailing Add:* Dept of Chem Univ of Northern Colo Greeley CO 80639

WOERNER, ROBERT LEO, b Evanston, Ill, Apr 21, 48. LASER ISOTOPE SEPARATION, FUSION TARGET FABRICATION. *Educ:* Mass Inst Technol, SB & SM, 71, PhD(physics), 74. *Prof Exp:* Fel liquid helium, Dept Physics, Mass Inst Technol, 74-75; mem tech staff physics, Bell Tel Labs, Holmdel, NJ, 75-76; PHYSICIST, LAWRENCE LIVERMORE LAB, 76- *Mem:* Am Phys Soc. *Res:* Integrated experiments to demonstrate the atomic vapor laser isotope separation process. *Mailing Add:* Lawrence Livermore Nat Lab Univ Calif Livermore CA 94550

WOERTZ, BYRON B, b Crandall, Ind, Sept 20, 13; m 40; c 4. CHEMICAL ENGINEERING. *Educ:* Univ Louisville, BS, 33; Mass Inst Technol, ScD(chem eng), 39. *Prof Exp:* Lab technician, Jones Dabney Co, Ky, 33-35; res assoc solar energy proj, Mass Inst Technol, 39-41; ENG ASSOC, UNION OIL CO CALIF, 41- *Mem:* Am Chem Soc; Am Inst Chem Engrs. *Res:* Natural gasoline plant design; efficency studies; gas processing research; development of selective solvents for removal of carbon dioxide and hydrogen sulfide from high pressure natural gas such as methyl cyanoacetate; process and design work on Beavon sulfur plant tail gas cleanup process. *Mailing Add:* Res Ctr Union Oil Co of Calif PO Box 76 Brea CA 92621

WOESSNER, DONALD EDWARD, b Milledgeville, Ill, Oct 6, 30; m 58. PHYSICAL CHEMISTRY, NUCLEAR MAGNETIC RESONANCE. *Educ:* Carthage Col, AB, 52; Univ Ill, PhD(chem), 57. *Prof Exp:* Asst phys chem, Univ Ill, 55-57, fel chem, 57-58; sr res technologist, 58-62, RES ASSOC, FIELD RES LAB, MOBIL RES & DEVELOP CORP, 62- *Honors & Awards:* W T Doherty Award, Am Chem Soc, 75. *Mem:* AAAS; Am Phys Soc; NY Acad Sci; Am Chem Soc. *Res:* Relationships of nuclear spin relaxation times in nuclear magnetic resonance and use in determining structure and motion in physical systems. *Mailing Add:* Field Res Lab Mobil Res & Develop Corp Dallas TX 75221

WOESSNER, JACOB FREDERICK, JR, biochemistry, see previous edition

WOESSNER, RONALD ARTHUR, b Pittsburgh, Pa, Apr 27, 37; m 56; c 3. FORESTRY, GENETICS. *Educ:* WVa Univ, BS, 63; NC State Univ, MS, 66, PhD(forest genetics), 68. *Prof Exp:* Asst prof plant & forest sci, Tex A&M Univ, 68-74, assoc prof forestry, 74, assoc geneticist, Tex Forest Serv, 68-74; supv res & devel, Jari Florestal, Amazon Basin, Nat Bulk Carriers Inc, 74-81; MGR, FOREST PRODUCTIVITY, MEAD CORP, 81- *Mem:* Soc Am Foresters; AAAS; Sigma Xi; Commonwealth Forestry Asn; Int Soc Trop Foresters. *Res:* Genetic improvement of pine and hardwood species, temperate and tropical; quantitative genetics of forest trees; provenance and progeny testing; seed orchards, genotype-environment interactions; inter-population crossing; wood density, nurseries and regeneration; herbicides for site preparation and release. *Mailing Add:* Mead Corp PO Box 508 Escanaba MI 49829

WOESTE, FRANK EDWARD, b Alexandria, Ky, Feb 11, 48. AGRICULTURAL ENGINEERING. *Educ:* Univ Ky, BSAE, 70, MSAE, 72; Purdue Univ, PhD(agr eng), 75. *Prof Exp:* Vis asst prof wood eng res, Wood Res Lab, Purdue Univ, West Lafayette, 75-77; ASST PROF WOOD ENG RES, VA POLYTECH INST & STATE UNIV, 77- *Mem:* Sigma Xi; Forest Prod Res Soc; Am Soc Testing & Mat; Am Soc Agr Engrs. *Res:* Engineered wood structures; lumber research; farm structures research; light frame building fire research. *Mailing Add:* Dept of Agr Eng Va Polytech Inst & State Univ Blacksburg VA 24061

WOFFORD, IRVIN MIRLE, b White Co, Ga, Dec 11, 16; m 38. AGRONOMY. *Educ:* Univ Ga, BSA, 48; Univ Fla, MSA, 49; Mich State Col, PhD(farm crops), 53. *Prof Exp:* Instr agron, Univ Fla, 49-51, asst agronomist, Exp Sta, 53-56; asst, Mich State Col, 51-53; dir agron, Southern Nitrogen Co, Inc, 56-64; MGR AGR PUB RELS, KAISER AGR CHEM, 64- *Mem:* Am Soc Agron. *Res:* Crop management and production; fertilizer studies; variety testing; date of planting; rotations; plant population studies. *Mailing Add:* PO Box 246 Savannah GA 31402

WOFSY, LEON, b Stamford, Conn, Nov 23, 21; m 42; c 2. CHEMISTRY, IMMUNOLOGY. *Educ:* City Col New York, BS, 42; Yale Univ, MS, 60, PhD(chem), 61. *Prof Exp:* PROF IMMUNOL, UNIV CALIF, BERKELEY, 64- *Mem:* Am Chem Soc. *Res:* Study of antibody specificity; mechanisms of cellular differentiation. *Mailing Add:* Dept of Bacteriol & Immunol Univ of Calif Berkeley CA 94720

WOFSY, STEVEN CHARLES, b New York, NY, June 24, 46. ATMOSPHERIC CHEMISTRY, AQUATIC CHEMISTRY. *Educ:* Univ Chicago, BS, 66; Harvard Univ, PhD(chem), 71. *Prof Exp:* Res assoc, Smithsonian Astrophys Observ, 71-74; lectr, 74-77, assoc prof, Div Appl Sci, 77-82, SR RES FEL, HARVARD UNIV, 82- *Concurrent Pos:* Res assoc, Nat Acad Sci, Nat Res Coun, 71-73; Stratospheric Adv Comt, NASA, 75-77, comt mem Earth Sci, Space Sci Bd, 82- *Mem:* Am Geophys Union; AAAS; Am Soc Limnol & Oceanog. *Res:* Photochemistry and biogeochemistry of atmospheric gases; gases and nutrients in marine and fresh waters; human impact on the global environment. *Mailing Add:* Pierce Hall Harvard Univ Cambridge MA 02138

WOGAN, GERALD NORMAN, b Altoona, Pa, Jan 11, 30; m 57; c 2. TOXICOLOGY. *Educ:* Juniata Col, BS, 51; Univ Ill, MS, 53, PhD(physiol), 57. *Prof Exp:* Instr physiol, Univ Ill, 56-57; asst prof, Rutgers Univ, 57-61; res assoc food toxicol, 61-62, from asst prof to assoc prof, 62-68, PROF TOXICOL, MASS INST TECHNOL, 68- *Mem:* Nat Acad Sci; AAAS; Am Inst Nutrit; Soc Toxicol; Am Asn Cancer Res. *Res:* Chemical carcinogenesis; physiological and biochemical responses to toxic substances; mechanisms of action of carcinogens and mutagens; environmental carcinogenesis. *Mailing Add:* Dept Nutrit & Food Sci Mass Inst Technol Cambridge MA 02139

WOGEN, WARREN RONALD, b Forest City, Iowa, Feb 19, 43; m 69; c 2. MATHEMATICS. *Educ:* Luther Col, Iowa, BA, 65; Ind Univ, Bloomington, MS, 67, PhD(math), 69. *Prof Exp:*Assoc prof, 69-80, PROF MATH, UNIV NC, CHAPEL HILL, 80- *Mem:* Am Math Soc; Math Asn Am. *Res:* Operator theory and operator algebras. *Mailing Add:* Dept of Math Univ of NC Chapel Hill NC 27514

WOGMAN, NED ALLEN, b Spokane, Wash, Oct 25, 39; m 59; c 3. NUCLEAR CHEMISTRY, PHYSICAL CHEMISTRY. *Educ:* Wash State Univ, BS, 61; Purdue Univ, PhD(phys chem), 66. *Prof Exp:* Sr res scientist, 65-68, mgr radiol chem, 68-72, res assoc, Pac Northwest Lab, 72-79, MGR RADIAL CHEM, BATTELLE MEM INST, 79- *Concurrent Pos:* Lectr, Joint Ctr Grad Study, Wash State Univ/Univ of Wash/Ore State Univ, 72-; mem sci comt, Nat Coun Radiation Protection, 73- *Mem:* Am Chem Soc. *Res:* Rates and mechanisms of biological, meteorological, oceanographic and ecological processes by natural and artificial radionuclides, including development of sensitive multidimensional gamma-ray spectrometer systems for trace radionuclide measurements. *Mailing Add:* Battelle Northwest Labs PO Box 999 Richland WA 99352

WOGRIN, CONRAD A(NTHONY), b Denver, Colo, Apr 16, 24; m 51; c 3. ELECTRICAL ENGINEERING, COMPUTER SCIENCE. *Educ:* Yale Univ, BE, 49, MEng, 51, DEng, 55. *Prof Exp:* From instr to assoc prof elec eng, Yale Univ, 51-66; PROF COMPUT & INFO SCI, UNIV MASS, AMHERST, 67-, DIR UNIV COMPUT CTR, 67- *Concurrent Pos:* Consult, Mitre Corp, 61-65, Goddard Space Flight Ctr, 65- & United Aircraft Corp Syst Ctr, 66- *Mem:* AAAS; Inst Elec & Electronics Engrs; Asn Comput Mach. *Res:* Digital computers; computer systems and languages; information and control systems. *Mailing Add:* Univ Comput Ctr Univ Mass Amherst MA 01003

WOHL, BERNARD G, b Philadelphia, Pa, July 20, 16; m 41; c 2. ORGANIC CHEMISTRY, MEDICINAL CHEMISTRY. *Educ:* Pa State Col, BS, 40; Temple Univ, MA, 46, PhD, 49. *Prof Exp:* Chemist, Distillers-Seagram Corp, 40-42; med chemist, Wyeth Inc, 42-46; res chemist, Fels & Co, 46-48 & Pyrene Corp, 48-52; dir res, Lemmon Pharmacal Co, 52-59; tech dir, Philadelphia Ampoule Labs, Inc, 59-61; TECH DIR, WOHL LAB, 61- *Concurrent Pos:* Lectr, Pa State Univ, 46-48; secy-treas, Cunningham Distributors & Murd Co, 66- *Mem:* AAAS; Am Chem Soc. *Res:* Organic medicinal application of Mennich reaction to medicinal chemistry. *Mailing Add:* 1222 Vilsmeier Rd Lansdale PA 19446

WOHL, MARTIN H, b New York, NY, Feb 12, 35; m 57; c 2. CHEMICAL ENGINEERING. *Educ:* Cornell Univ, BChE, 57. *Prof Exp:* Res engr, Plastics Div, Monsanto Co, 57-63, res specialist, Plastic Prod & Resins Div, 63-68, tech group leader process develop, 68-70, tech supt film, Fabricated Prod Div, Monsanto Com Prod Co, 70-75, mgr, Res & Technol, Fabricated Prod Div, Monsanto Plastics & Resins Co, 75-78, PROJ DIR, NEW PROD DEVELOP DEPT, MONSANTO PLASTICS & RESINS CO, 78- *Mem:* Am Inst Chem Engrs; Soc Rheol. *Res:* Process development research in the field of high polymers; fluid flow and heat transfer to non-Newtonian fluids; research and engineering administration. *Mailing Add:* Monsanto Co 800 N Lindbergh Blvd St Louis MO 63166

WOHL, PHILIP R, b 1944; US citizen; m; c 1. MATHEMATICS. *Educ:* Queens Col, NY, BA, 66; Cornell Univ, PhD(appl math), 71. *Prof Exp:* asst prof, NY Univ, 71-72; res assoc math, Carleton Univ, 72-74; asst prof, 74-80, ASSOC PROF & GRAD PROG DIR, OLD DOMINION UNIV, 80- *Mem:* Soc Indust & Appl Math; Math Asn Am. *Res:* Classical analysis and methods of ordinary and partial differential equations; perturbation methods in fluid mechanics; low Reynolds number hydrodynamics; blood flow and other flows of suspensions in tubes; biofluid mechanics; mathematical modelling in biology. *Mailing Add:* Dept Math Sci Old Dominion Univ Norfolk VA 23508

WOHL, RONALD A, b Basel, Switz, Nov 25, 36. ORGANIC CHEMISTRY, MEDICINAL CHEMISTRY. *Educ:* Univ Basel, PhD(org chem), 65. *Prof Exp:* Lectr org chem, Univ Basel, 65-66; res assoc, Yale Univ, 66-67; asst prof, Rutgers Univ, 67-74; sr org chemist, 74-76, sect head org chem, 76-79, SECT HEAD ORG CHEM, BERLEX LABS, 79- *Mem:* Am Chem Soc; Swiss Chem Soc. *Res:* Stereochemistry; cardiovascular drugs. *Mailing Add:* Cooper Labs Inc 110 E Hanover Ave Cedar Knolls NJ 07927

WOHLEBER, DAVID ALAN, b Pittsburgh, Pa, Oct 1, 40; m 61; c 4. CHEMISTRY. *Educ:* Univ Pittsburgh, BS, 62; John Carroll Univ, MS, 67; Kent State Univ, PhD(chem), 70. *Prof Exp:* Chemist anal chem, Develop Lab, Standard Oil Co, Ohio, 61-63, chemist polymer chem, Res Lab, 63-66; sr res scientist phys chem, 70-74, sect head, 74-79, mgr Extractive Metall Div, 79-81, MGR PROCESS CHEM & PHYSICS DIV, ALCOA TECH CTR, ALUMINUM CO AM, 81- *Mem:* Am Chem Soc; Sigma Xi. *Res:* Chlorination technolgoy; inorganic and physical chemistry of alumina refining and aluminum smelting; physical adsorption; polymer synthesis and characterization. *Mailing Add:* Alcoa Center PA 15069

WOHLERS, HENRY CARL, b New York, NY, Feb 2, 16; m 49; c 2. AIR POLLUTION, ENVIRONMENTAL AFFAIRS. *Educ:* St Lawrence Univ, BS, 39; Stanford Univ, PhD(phys chem), 49. *Prof Exp:* Asst chemist, Boyce Thompson Inst Plant Res, 36-37 & 39-40; assoc chemist, Gen Chem Co, 40-44; supvr, Ford, Bacon & Davis, 44; sr chemist, Dorr Co, 44-46; sr anal chemist, Stanford Res Inst, 49-61; dir tech serv, Bay Area Air Pollution Control Dist, 61-65; from assoc prof to prof environ sci, Drexel Univ, 65-72; CONSULT ENVIRON AFFAIRS, 72- *Concurrent Pos:* Consult to var UN orgn. *Mem:* Air Pollution Control Asn; Am Chem Soc. *Res:* All phases of air pollution and global environmental problems. *Mailing Add:* 36381 Row River Rd Cottage Grove OR 97424

WOHLFORD, DUANE DENNIS, b Newcastle, Ind, May 20, 37; m 66; c 3. GEOLOGY, PETROLOGY. *Educ:* Univ Wis, BS, 59; Univ Colo, PhD(geol), 65. *Prof Exp:* Asst prof geol, 64-74, ASSOC PROF EARTH SCI, STATE UNIV NY COL ONEONTA, 74- *Mem:* AAAS; Geol Soc Am. *Res:* Petrology of the Precambrian rocks of the southern Adirondack Mountains of New York. *Mailing Add:* Dept of Earth Sci State Univ of NY Col Oneonta NY 13820

WOHLFORT, SAM WILLIS, b Toledo, Ohio, June 8, 26; m 49; c 3. ANALYTICAL CHEMISTRY, MATERIALS SCIENCE. *Educ:* Univ Toledo, BS, 48; Ohio State Univ, MS, 50. *Prof Exp:* Asst instrumental & spectrog anal, Ohio State Univ, 50-53; chemist, Sharp-Schurtz Co, 53-56; chemist, Libbey-Owens-Ford Glass Co, 56-58, group leader anal res, 58-65; supvr anal methods & mfg processes res & develop, Milchem Inc, Tex, 65-69; supvr phys measurements dept, 69-73, supvr, Mat Technol Dept, 73-77, SUPVR PROCESS TECHNOL, GOODYEAR ATOMIC CORP, 77- Int Metallographic Soc. *Mem:* Int Metall Soc. *Res:* Electron microscopy; x-ray diffraction and fluorescence; ultraviolet, infrared and visible spectrophotometry; differential thermal analysis; thin films; corrosion protection; vacuum deposition; x-ray stress analysis; incipient failure detection; non-destructive testing; metallography; radwaste disposal; effluent treatment, especially gas, liquid and solid; UF6 containment. *Mailing Add:* Piketon OH 45661

WOHLGELERNTER, DEVORA KASACHKOFF, b Washington, DC, Apr 1, 41; m 67; c 7. MATHEMATICS. *Educ:* Yeshiva Univ, BA, 61, MA, 63, PhD(math), 70. *Prof Exp:* Asst prof, 70-77, ASSOC PROF MATH, BARUCH COL, 77- *Mem:* Am Math Soc. *Res:* Polynomial approximation of functions of a complex variable. *Mailing Add:* Dept of Math Baruch Col New York NY 10010

WOHLHIETER, JOHN ANDREW, b Pittsburgh, Pa, Mar 18, 32; m 61; c 2. BIOPHYSICS. *Educ:* Univ Pittsburgh, BS, 54, MS, 57, PhD(biophys), 60. *Prof Exp:* Res assoc biophys, Univ Pittsburgh, 54-59; res biochemist, 62-69, ASST CHIEF, DEPT BACT IMMUNOL, WALTER REED ARMY INST RES, 69- *Concurrent Pos:* Mem genetics fac grad prog, NIH, 68-70, mem microbial chem study sect, 69-76, chmn comt eval extramural prog mechanisms resistance antimicrobial agents, Nat Inst Allergy & Infectious Dis, 75; mem contract review comt bacterial dis, US Army Med Res &

Develop Command, 79; instnl bio safety comt, Walter Reed Inst Res, 81; ad hoc mem, Nat Inst Allergy & Infectious Dis. *Mem:* AAAS; Biophys Soc; Am Chem Soc; Am Soc Microbiol. *Res:* Genetic and molecular structure of the chromosomes of bacteria and their plasmids and viruses, with special emphasis on the enterobacteria; molecular and genetic methods, including recombinant DNA technology, are employed to analyze various aspects of bacterial virulence and to develop suitable vaccine strains. *Mailing Add:* Dept of Bact Immunol Walter Reed Army Inst Res Washington DC 20012

WOHLMAN, ALAN, b New York, NY, May 17, 36; m 58; c 3. BIOCHEMICAL PHYSIOLOGY. *Educ:* NY Univ, BA, 59; Princeton Univ, MS, 65, PhD(biol sci), 66. *Prof Exp:* Res scientist, Bellevue Med Ctr NY Univ, 56-59 & Denver Labs, Stanford, Conn, 59-62; fac biol, State Univ NY, Stony Brook, 66-67; dir res pharmaceut, Denver Labs, Toronto, 67-70; div dir, Connaught Labs, Univ Toronto, 70-74; dir qual control & head, Armour Pharm Co, Kankakee, Ill, 74-77; DIR RES, FRITO-LAY INC, DALLAS, 77- *Concurrent Pos:* NIH fel, Princeton Univ, 63-66. *Mem:* AAAS; Sigma Xi; Food Res Inst. *Res:* Technical management, cell biology, biochemistry, physiology, optics, basic food and drug research, food and drug stability, nutrition and regulatory affairs. *Mailing Add:* Frito-Lay 900 N Loop 12 Irving TX 75061

WOHLPART, KENNETH JOSEPH, b New York, NY. FOOD TECHNOLOGY. *Educ:* St Bonaventure Univ, BS, 53; Purdue Univ, MS, 58. *Prof Exp:* Res asst anal chem, Union Carbide Corp, 55-56; asst food technologist food prod develop, Gen Foods Corp, 57-60; food pilot plant mgr, Beech Nut Foods, 60-63; SR FOOD TECHNOLOGIST, PACKAGING DIV CUSTOMER PRODS LAB, ALUMINUM CO AM, 63- *Mem:* Inst Food Technologists. *Res:* Product-package interaction; sensory evaluation; package-process development. *Mailing Add:* 4113 Impala Dr Pittsburgh PA 15239

WOHLRAB, HARTMUT, b Berlin, WGer, July 2, 41; m 67; c 2. BIOCHEMISTRY. *Educ:* Rensselaer Polytech Inst, BS, 62; Stanford Univ, PhD(biophys), 68. *Prof Exp:* NIH trainee, Johnson Res Found, Univ Pa, 68-70; asst biochem, Univ Munich, 70-72; staff scientist, 72-81, SR STAFF SCIENTIST, BOSTON BIOMED RES INST, 81- *Concurrent Pos:* Estab investr, Am Heart Asn, 73-78; res assoc, Dept Biol Chem, Harvard Med Sch, 73- *Mem:* Geront Soc; Biophys Soc; Fedn Europ Biochem Socs; Am Aging Asn; AAAS. *Res:* Mitochondrial biochemistry; mitochondria in developing and aging, or senescent, tissues; function and molecular structure of membrane transport proteins. *Mailing Add:* Boston Biomed Res Inst 20 Staniford St Boston MA 02114

WOHLSCHLAG, DONALD EUGENE, b Bucyrus, Ohio, Nov 6, 18; m 43; c 3. MARINE ECOLOGY. *Educ:* Ind Univ, PhD, 49. *Prof Exp:* Asst chem & zool, Heidelberg Col, 40-41; res assoc, Univ Wis, 49; from asst prof to prof biol, Stanford Univ, 49-65; dir, Inst, 65-70, PROF ZOOL, MARINE SCI INST, UNIV TEX, 65- *Concurrent Pos:* Arctic fisheries researcher, Off Naval Res & Arctic Inst NAm, 52-53 & 54-55, Antarctic fishery biol researcher, 58-65, Gulf coastal fishery biol research, 65-; consult, Inst Ecol, 74-; ed, Contrib Marine Sci, Univ Tex Marine Sci Inst, 75- *Mem:* AAAS; Am Fisheries Soc; Am Soc Limnol & Oceanog; Am Soc Zoologists; Ecol Soc Am. *Res:* Ecology of fishes; metabolism and growth; population dynamics. *Mailing Add:* Marine Sci Inst Univ of Tex Port Aransas TX 78373

WOHLTMANN, HULDA JUSTINE, b Charleston, SC, Apr 10, 23. PEDIATRICS. *Educ:* Col Charleston, BS, 44; Med Col SC, MD, 49; Am Bd Pediat, dipl, 55. *Prof Exp:* From instr to asst prof pediat, Sch Med, Wash Univ, 53-61, USPHS spec res fel biochem, Univ, 61-63; asst prof pediat, 65-70, PROF PEDIAT, MED UNIV SC, 70- *Mem:* AAAS; fel Am Acad Pediat; Am Diabetes Asn; NY Acad Sci; Endocrine Soc. *Res:* Pediatric metabolism and endocrinology. *Mailing Add:* Dept of Pediat Med Univ of SC Charleston SC 29425

WOISARD, EDWIN LEWIS, b Newark, NJ, Jan 21, 26; m 53, 69; c 7. PHYSICS, OPERATIONS RESEARCH. *Educ:* Drew Univ, BA, 50; Lehigh Univ, MS, 52, PhD(physics), 59. *Prof Exp:* Instr physics, Moravian Col, 56-59; assoc res physicist, Res Lab, Whirlpool Corp, 59-61; proj leader, Weapons Systs Eval Div, Inst Defense Anal, DC, 61-67; exec vpres, John D Kettelle Corp, 67-70; pvt consult, 70-71; asst, Navy Net Assessment & Midrange Objectives, Off Chief Naval Opers, US Navy, 71-79; PRIN SCIENTIST, RAMCOR, INC, 79- *Mem:* Res Soc Am; Sigma Xi; AAAS; Opers Res Soc Am. *Res:* Thermoelectricity; solid state physics; microwave absorption; systems and defense analysis; planning and management of research and development. *Mailing Add:* 5020 King David Blvd Annandale VA 20030

WOJCICKI, ANDREW, b Warsaw, Poland, May 5, 35; nat US; m 68. INORGANIC CHEMISTRY, ORGANOMETALLIC CHEMISTRY. *Educ:* Brown Univ, BS, 56; Northwestern Univ, PhD(chem), 60. *Prof Exp:* Asst chem, Northwestern Univ, 56-58, assoc, 59; NSF fel inorg chem, Univ Nottingham, 60-61; from asst prof to assoc prof, 61-69, PROF INORG CHEM, OHIO STATE UNIV, 69- *Concurrent Pos:* Vis assoc prof, Case Western Reserve Univ, 67; US sr scientist award, Humboldt Found, Ger, 75-76; Guggenheim Found fel, 76. *Mem:* AAAS; Am Chem Soc; Royal Soc Chem. *Res:* Synthesis and mechanism of reactions of inorganic and organometallic compounds. *Mailing Add:* Dept of Chem Ohio State Univ Columbus OH 43210

WOJCICKI, STANLEY G, b Warsaw, Poland, Mar 30, 37; US citizen; m 61. HIGH ENERGY PHYSICS. *Educ:* Harvard Univ, AB, 57; Univ Calif, Berkeley, PhD(physics), 62. *Prof Exp:* Physicist, Lawrence Radiation Lab, Univ Calif, 61-66; from asst prof to assoc prof, 66-74, PROF PHYSICS, STANFORD UNIV, 74- *Concurrent Pos:* NSF fel, 64-65; Alfred P Sloan Found fel, 68-72; Guggenheim fel, 73-74; Alexander von Humnoldt sr scientist award, 80. *Mem:* Fel Am Phys Soc. *Res:* Resonances in high energy physics; candle power violation; electron-positron annihilations; muon production in hedronic interactions. *Mailing Add:* Dept of Physics Stanford Univ Stanford CA 94305

WOJCIECHOWSKI, BOHDAN WIESLAW, b Wilno, Poland, Jan 29, 35; Can citizen; m 59; c 2. CHEMICAL ENGINEERING, CATALYSIS. *Educ:* Univ Toronto, BASc, 57, MASc, 58; Univ Ottawa, PhD(phys chem), 60. *Prof Exp:* Fel photolysis, Nat Res Coun, 60-61; fel kinetics, Univ Ottawa, 61-62; sr res chemist, Res & Develop, Socony Mobil Oil Co, Inc, 62-65; from asst prof to assoc prof chem eng, 65-72, PROF CHEM ENG, QUEEN'S UNIV, ONT, 72- *Concurrent Pos:* UN Develop Prog tech expert, Brazil, 72; consult to petrol indust. *Mem:* AAAS; The Chem Soc; fel Chem Inst Can; Am Inst Chem Engrs; Catalysis Soc. *Res:* Kinetics; catalysis; absorption; petroleum refining; process design; oceanography; recovery of oils from sand and shale; mathematical systems for highly coupled reactions; Fischer Tropsch synthesis. *Mailing Add:* Dept of Chem Eng Queen's Univ Kingston ON K7L 3N6 Can

WOJCIK, ANTHONY STEPHEN, b Chicago, Ill, Sept 18, 45; m 69; c 2. DESIGN AUTOMATION, COMPUTER ARCHITECTURE. *Educ:* Univ Ill, Urbana-Champaign, BS, 67, MS, 68, PhD(comput sci), 71. *Prof Exp:* Asst prof, 71-76, assoc prof, 76-81, PROF COMPUT SCI, ILL INST TECHNOL, 81-, CHMN DEPT, 78- *Concurrent Pos:* Mem tech staff, Bell Tel Labs, 74. *Mem:* Sigma Xi; Asn Comput Mach; Inst Elec & Electronics Engrs. *Res:* Theory and application of multi-valued switching theory; computer architecture; reliable design of digital systems; design automation and digital systems; logic design; multiple-valued logic. *Mailing Add:* Dept Comput Sci Ill Inst Technol 10 W 31st St Chicago IL 60616

WOJCIK, JOHN F, b Ashley, Pa, Nov 12, 38; m 60; c 4. PHYSICAL CHEMISTRY. *Educ:* King's Col, Pa, BS, 60; Cornell Univ, PhD(phys chem), 65. *Prof Exp:* Asst prof chem, St Francis Col, Pa, 65-66; asst prof, 66-77, ASSOC PROF CHEM, VILLANOVA UNIV, 77- *Concurrent Pos:* Petrol Res Fund res grant, 66-68. *Mem:* Am Chem Soc. *Res:* Kinetics of chelation reactions; stability constants of ethylenediaminetetra acetate type complexes. *Mailing Add:* Dept of Chem Villanova Univ Villanova PA 19085

WOJNAR, ROBERT JOHN, b Thompsonville, Conn, Jan 29, 35; m 58; c 3. IMMUNOBIOLOGY, BIOCHEMISTRY. *Educ:* Univ Conn, BA, 56, MS, 60, PhD(biochem), 64. *Prof Exp:* NIH fel, Yale Univ, 63-65; staff scientist, Worcester Found Exp Biol, 65-68; res investr, 68-69, SR INVESTR BIOCHEM IMMUNOL, SQUIBB INST MED RES, 69- *Mem:* AAAS; NY Acad Sci. *Res:* Cellular immunology; inflammation; nucleic acids; immunopharmacology; allergy and drug hypersensitivity; steroid biology. *Mailing Add:* Squibb Inst for Med Res Princeton NJ 08540

WOJTOWICZ, JOHN ALFRED, b Niagara Falls, NY, Oct 12, 26; div; c 3. INDUSTRIAL CHEMISTRY. *Educ:* Univ Buffalo, BA, 54; Niagara Univ, MS, 66. *Prof Exp:* Analyst chem anal, E I du Pont de Nemours & Co, Inc, 45-50, develop analyst chem anal & process develop, 50-54, develop chemist, 54-56; res chemist inorg synthesis & chem kinetics, 56-61, sr res chemist org synthesis & process develop, 61-71, res assoc inorg & org synthesis & process develop, 71-77, CONSULT SCIENTIST INORG & ORG SYNTHESIS & PROCESS DEVELOP, OLIN CORP, 77- *Concurrent Pos:* Consult scientist, inorg & org synthesis & process develop. *Mem:* Am Chem Soc; Sigma Xi. *Res:* Organic and inorganic synthesis; process development. *Mailing Add:* Olin Corp 275 S Winchester Ave New Haven CT 06511

WOJTOWICZ, PETER JOSEPH, b Elizabeth, NJ, Sept 22, 31; m 53; c 3. THEORETICAL PHYSICS. *Educ:* Rutgers Univ, BSc, 53; Yale Univ, MS, 54, PhD(phys chem), 56. *Prof Exp:* Mem tech staff & theoret chem physicist, 56-78, HEAD ELECTRON OPTICS & DEFLECTION RES, RCA LABS, 78- *Mem:* Fel Am Phys Soc. *Res:* Statistical mechanics; theory of liquid and solid states; theory of magnetism and properties of magnetic substances; liquid crystals; electron optics and magnetic deflection in display systems. *Mailing Add:* RCA Labs Princeton NJ 08540

WOLAK, JAN, b Lubasz, Poland, Mar 8, 20; US citizen; m 59; c 3. MECHANICAL ENGINEERING. *Educ:* Univ London, BSc, 50; Wash Univ, MS, 60; Univ Calif, Berkeley, PhD(mech eng), 65. *Prof Exp:* Col apprenticeship, AEI-Gen Elec Co, Eng, 50-52, steam turbine design engr, 52-56; lectr mech eng, Wash Univ, 56-60; assoc, Univ Calif, Berkeley, 60-63, asst res specialist, Inst Eng Res, 63-65; asst prof mech eng, 65-69, ASSOC PROF MECH ENG, UNIV WASH, 69- *Mem:* Am Soc Mech Engrs; Brit Inst Mech Engrs; Am Soc Eng Educ; Soc Mfg Engrs. *Res:* Mechanical behavior of materials; metal removal and forming processes; erosion by abrasive particles; evaluation of large plastic strains; friction and wear. *Mailing Add:* Dept of Mech Eng FU-10 Univ of Wash Seattle WA 98195

WOLAVER, LYNN E(LLSWORTH), b Springfield, Ill, Mar 10, 24; m 49; c 2. ENGINEERING, MATHEMATICS. *Educ:* Univ Ill, BS, 49, MS, 50; Univ Mich, PhD(info & control eng), 64. *Prof Exp:* Instr elec eng, Univ Ill, 49-50; electronic engr, Wright Air Develop Ctr, US Dept Air Force, 50-51, electronic scientist, 51-56, aero-res engr, Aerospace Res Labs, 56-63, dep dir, Appl Math Lab, 63-67, dir, 67-71, chmn dept syst eng & assoc dean res, 71-79, PROF, AIR FORCE INST TECHNOL, US DEPT AIR FORCE, 63-, DEAN RES, 79- *Concurrent Pos:* Lectr eve sch, Wright State Univ, 64-71; mem, Midwestern Simulation Coun, 53- *Mem:* AAAS; Inst Elec & Electronics Engrs; Soc Indust & Appl Math; fel Brit Interplanetary Soc; Am Soc Eng Educ. *Res:* Navigation; astrodynamics; simulation; nonlinear system analysis; modeling nonlinear systems driven by random noise; bioengineering. *Mailing Add:* Air Force Inst Technol Dayton OH 45433

WOLBACH, ROBERT ALBERT, b New York, NY, Sept 3, 30; m 74; c 7. PHYSIOLOGY. *Educ:* Cornell Univ, BA, 51, PhD(physiol), 54; NY Univ, MD, 61. *Prof Exp:* Instr physiol, Sch Med, NY Univ, 56-60; USPHS spec fel, Copenhagen Univ, 61; from asst prof to assoc prof physiol, Col Med, Univ Utah, 62-78, asst to dean, 72-75; asst med dir, 79-80, ASSOC DIR CLIN RES, ABBOTT LABS, 80- *Concurrent Pos:* Mem, Mt Desert Island Biol Lab; mem, Utah Task Force Health & Ment Health for Span Speaking, 70-73; mem, Utah Migrant Health Policy Bd, 73-75, actg chmn, 75. *Mem:* AAAS; Int Soc Nephrology; Am Soc Nephrology; Am Physiol Soc. *Res:* Comparative physiology of excretion of vertebrates; metabolism of phosphorus, calcium and hydrogen ions; pathophysiology of cold injury. *Mailing Add:* Abbott Park North Chicago IL 60064

WOLBARSHT, MYRON LEE, b Baltimore, Md, Sept 18, 24; m 63; c 3. BIOPHYSICS, BIOMEDICAL ENGINEERING. *Educ:* St Johns Col, AB, 50; Johns Hopkins Univ, PhD(biol, biophys), 58. *Prof Exp:* Chief physicist, Naval Med Res Inst, 58-68; PROF OPHTHALMOL & BIOMED ENG, EYE CTR, DUKE UNIV, 68- *Concurrent Pos:* Guest scientist, Naval Med Res Inst, 54-58; res assoc, Psychiat Inst, Med Sch, Univ Md, 54-60; res fel biol, Johns Hopkins Univ, 58-63; consult, York Hosp, Pa, 63-68; mem exec panel, Nat Res Coun Armed Forces Comt Vision, 63-; chmn eye hazards subcomt, Laser Safety Comt, Am Nat Standards Inst, 68; US rep, Tech Comt 76 Laser Safety, Int Electro Tech Comn, 76-; mem, US Nat Comt Photobiol, 78- *Mem:* Am Physiol Soc; Inst Elec & Electronics Engrs; Soc Gen Physiol; Optical Soc Am; Royal Soc Med. *Res:* Laser safety; biomedical engineering applications to ophthalmology; structure and function of sense organs, especially vision, chemoreception, mechanoreception; electrophysiology of central nervous system. *Mailing Add:* Dept of Ophthal Duke Univ Eye Ctr Durham NC 27710

WOLBER, WILLIAM GEORGE, b Detroit, Mich, Feb 19, 27; m 50; c 5. INSTRUMENT ENGINEERING. *Educ:* Univ Mich, BS(chem eng) & BS(eng math), 49 & MS, 50. *Prof Exp:* Engr-group leader, Uniroyal Tire Div, 50-54; proj engr-prog mgr, 54-62, dept mgr, 62-66, sr prin engr, 66-73, sr res planner, 73-76, SR RES CONSULT, BENDIX RES LABS, 76- *Concurrent Pos:* Chmn, Invention & Patent Comt, Bendix Res Labs, 74-78, corp gatekeeper-instr, Bendix Corp, 77-; chmn, Transducer Subcomt & reader, Soc Automotive Engrs. *Honors & Awards:* Corp Tech Achievement Award, Bendix Corp, 75. *Mem:* Inst Elec & Electronic Engrs; Instrument Soc Am; Soc Automotive Engrs; Am Nat Standards Inst. *Res:* Research and development in measuring instruments and sensors; their application to control systems such as automobile engine control; theory and practice of precision instrument calibration. *Mailing Add:* Bendix Res Labs 20800 Civic Ctr Dr Southfield MI 48037

WOLBERG, DONALD LESTER, b New York, NY, Dec 18, 45; c 4. VERTEBRATE PALEONTOLOGY. *Educ:* New York Univ, BA, 68; Univ Minn, PhD(geol), 78. *Prof Exp:* Curator & teaching asst geol, New York Univ, 67-69; ed, Encyclopedia Britannica, 69-71; teaching assoc, Univ Minn, 71-75; ed & geologist, Minn Geol Survey, 75-76; geologist, Nat Biocentric, Inc, 76-77; asst prof, Univ Wis-River Falls, 77-78; PALEONTOLOGIST, NMEX BUR MINES & MINERAL RESOURCES, 78- *Concurrent Pos:* Res assoc, Minn Messenia Exped Greece, 71-73; conract writer & ed, Encyclopedia Britannica, 71-73. *Mem:* Soc Vert Paleont; Soc Econ Paleontologists & Mineralogists; Paleont Soc; Asn Geoscientists Int Develop; Sigma Xi. *Res:* Late Mesozoic and early Tertiary stratigraphy; paleontolgy and paleoecology of North America. *Mailing Add:* NMex Bur Mines & Mineral Resources Socorro NM 87801

WOLBERG, GERALD, b New York, NY, Aug 18, 37; m 67; c 2. IMMUNOLOGY, MICROBIOLOGY. *Educ:* NY Univ, BA, 58; Univ Ky, MS, 63; Tulane Univ, PhD(immunol), 67. *Prof Exp:* Fel immunol, Pub Health Res Inst of City of New York, 67-68, NIH fel, 68-70; MEM STAFF, WELLCOME RES LABS, BURROUGHS WELLCOME CO, 70- *Mem:* Am Asn Immunol; Am Soc Microbiol. *Res:* Immunosuppression; immunoactivation. *Mailing Add:* Burroughs Wellcome Co 3030 Cornwallis Rd Research Triangle Park NC 27709

WOLBERG, WILLIAM HARVEY, b July 10, 31; US citizen; m 55; c 6. SURGERY, ONCOLOGY. *Educ:* Univ Wis-Madison, BS, 53, MD, 56. *Prof Exp:* Intern, Ohio State Univ, 56-57; resident surg, 57-61, chmn gen surg, 72-75, from instr to assoc prof, 61-71, PROF SURG, UNIV WIS-MADISON, 71- *Concurrent Pos:* Consult merit rev bd oncol, Vet Admin, 72. *Mem:* Am Asn Cancer Res; Am Col Surg; Asn Acad Surg; Western Surg Asn. *Res:* Nucleic acid synthesis in human tumors; immune response to human tumors. *Mailing Add:* Dept of Surg Univ Wis Ctr Health Sci Madison WI 53792

WOLCOTT, JOHN H, aerospace medicine, see previous edition

WOLCOTT, MARK WALTON, b Mansfield, Ohio, Apr 16, 15; m 41; c 2. SURGERY, THORACIC SURGERY. *Educ:* Lehigh Univ, BA, 37; Univ Pa, MD, 41. *Prof Exp:* Instr surg, Grad Sch Med, Univ Pa, 50-52; assoc, Med Col Pa, 52-53; asst clin prof, Med Col Ga, 54-57; chief of surg, Vet Admin Hosp, Coral Gables, Fla, 57-64; chief of res in surg, Vet Admin Cent Off, DC, 64-70; PROF SURG, SCH MED, UNIV UTAH, 70-; CHIEF OF STAFF, VET ADMIN HOSP, SALT LAKE CITY, 70- *Concurrent Pos:* Assoc prof, Sch Med, Univ Miami, 57-64; asst clin prof, Med Sch, George Washington Univ, 65-70. *Mem:* Am Thoracic Soc; AMA; Soc Thoracic Surg; Am Col Surg; Am Col Chest Physicians. *Res:* Coagulation defects associated with thoracic surgery; deep hypothermia and extra corporeal circulation; tissue transplantation; clostridial infection and hyperbaric medicine. *Mailing Add:* 500 Foothill Blvd Salt Lake City UT 84113

WOLCOTT, ROBERT B, b Janesville, Wis, July 27, 14; m 46; c 2. DENTISTRY. *Educ:* Beloit Col, BS, 36; Marquette Univ, DDS, 41; Georgetown Univ, MS, 51. *Prof Exp:* Head oper dent, US Naval Dent Sch, 44-48 & 52-54; guestworker, Dent Mat Lab, Nat Bur Stand, 49-51; dent asst, Naval Training Ctr, Calif, 56-58; dir training div, Dent Res Labs, Md, 58 & Ill, 59-62; PROF RESTORATIVE DENT, CHMN & DIR CLIN, SCH DENT, CTR HEALTH SCI, UNIV CALIF, LOS ANGELES, 62- *Concurrent Pos:* Consult, Vet Admin, 66- *Mem:* Fel Am Col Dent; Am Dent Asn; Am Acad Restorative Dent; Int Asn Dent Res. *Res:* Clinical and laboratory investigations in development and utilization of dental materials. *Mailing Add:* Sch of Dent Univ of Calif Ctr for Health Sci Los Angeles CA 90024

WOLCOTT, THOMAS GORDON, b San Diego, Calif, Dec 22, 44; m 68; c 2. PHYSIOLOGICAL ECOLOGY, BIOTELEMETRY. *Educ:* Univ Calif, Riverside, BA, 66; Univ Calif, Berkeley, PhD(zool), 71. *Prof Exp:* Vis asst prof biol, Univ Calif, Riverside, 71-72; asst prof zool, 72-78, ASSOC PROF MARINE, EARTH & ATMOSPHERIC SCI, NC STATE UNIV, 78- *Concurrent Pos:* NSF grant, 77-80. *Mem:* AAAS; Am Soc Zoologists; Estuarine Res Fedn; Sigma Xi; Crustacean Soc. *Res:* Adaptations of marine invertebrates to their physical microhabitats; role of food quality in limiting growth and population density of land crabs; role of physical environmental factors on limitation of species range. *Mailing Add:* NC State Univ PO Box 5068 Raleigh NC 27650

WOLD, AARON, b NY, May 8, 27; m 57; c 3. INORGANIC CHEMISTRY. *Educ:* Polytech Inst Brooklyn, BS, 46, MS, 48, PhD(chem), 52. *Prof Exp:* Res assoc chem, Univ Conn, 51-52; from instr to asst prof, Hofstra Col, 52-56; mem staff, Lincoln Lab, Mass Inst Technol, 56-63; assoc prof, 63-67, prof eng & chem, 67-80, VERNON K KRIEBLE PROF CHEM, BROWN UNIV, 80- *Concurrent Pos:* Ed, J Solid State Chem, 68-75, mem adv bd, 75-; assoc ed, Inorg Chem, 74-76 & Mat Res Bull, 77-; consult, Exxon Res & Develop Labs, 76-, Dow Chem Co, Midland, Mich, 80- & Gen Telephone Labs, Waltham, Mass, 80- *Mem:* Am Chem Soc. *Res:* Solid state chemistry of rare earths and transition elements. *Mailing Add:* Dept Chem & Div Eng Brown Univ Providence RI 02912

WOLD, DONALD C, b Fargo, NDak, Sept 24, 33; m 56; c 3. ACOUSTICS. *Educ:* Univ Wis-Madison, BA, 55, MA, 57; Ind Univ, Bloomington, PhD(physics), 68. *Prof Exp:* Lectr physics, Forman Christian Col, WPakistan, 58-63, head dept, 61-63; asst res physicist, Univ Calif, Los Angeles, 68-69; assoc prof physics, 69-74, head dept, 70-74, PROF PHYSICS & CHMN DEPT PHYSICS & ASTRON, UNIV ARK, LITTLE ROCK, 74- *Concurrent Pos:* Proj dir energy conserv plan, State Ark, 76-77; HEW res fel, 78. *Honors & Awards:* Donaghey Urban Mission Award, 79. *Mem:* Acoust Soc Am; Am Phys Soc; Am Asn Physics Teachers; Asn Comput Mach; Inst Elec & Electronics Engrs. *Res:* Acoustics and perception of speech to investigate the properties of physiologically significant acoustical features of the voice, such as perturbations in the fundamental frequency and variations in the formant frequencies. *Mailing Add:* Dept of Physics & Astron Univ Ark 33rd & Univ Ave Little Rock AR 72204

WOLD, FINN, b Stavanger, Norway, Feb 3, 28; nat US; m 53; c 2. BIOCHEMISTRY. *Educ:* Okla State Univ, MS, 53; Univ Calif, PhD(biochem), 56. *Prof Exp:* Res assoc biochem, Univ Calif, 56-57; from asst prof to assoc prof, Univ Ill, 57-66; prof biochem, Med Sch, Univ Minn, Minneapolis, 66-74; head dept, Univ Minn, St Paul, 74-79, prof biochem, 74-81; ROBERT A WELCH PROF CHEM, MED SCH, UNIV TEX, HOUSTON, 82- *Concurrent Pos:* Lalor res award, 58; Guggenheim fel immunochem, London, Eng, 60-61; USPHS res career develop award, 61-66; vis prof chem, Nat Taiwan Univ, 71; consult biochem & molecular biol fel rev comt, Nat Inst Gen Med Sci, 66-70, consult biochem training comt, 71-74; consult biochem & biophys res eval comt, Vet Admin, 69-71, consult res serv merit rev basic sci, 72-75; consult res personnel comt, Am Cancer Soc, 74-77; vis prof biochem, Rice Univ, 74. *Mem:* AAAS; Am Soc Biol Chemists; Am Chem Soc; Brit Biochem Soc. *Res:* Protein chemistry; physical, chemical and biological properties of proteins; relation of protein structure and function; mechanism of enzyme action. *Mailing Add:* Dept of Biochem Molecular Biol Med Sch Univ Tex PO Box 20708 Houston TX 77025

WOLD, RICHARD JOHN, b Oshkosh, Wis, Oct 23, 37; m 60; c 2. MARINE GEOPHYSICS. *Educ:* Univ Wis, BS, 60, PhD(geophys), 66. *Prof Exp:* Lectr geophys, Univ Wis, 66-67; asst prof geol & geophys, 67-70, chmn dept geol sci, 70-72, assoc dean res, Grad Sch, 72-73, dir, Gt Lakes Res Facility, 73-75; assoc prof geol sci, Univ Wis-Milwaukee, 70-77; geophysicist, US Geol Surv, 77-80 & Br Electromagnetism & Geomagnetism, 80-82; CHIEF GEOPHYSICIST, WESTERN GEOPHYS CORP, 82- *Concurrent Pos:* Mem, Nat Adv Coun, Univ-Nat Oceanog Lab Syst, 74-75; assoc br chief, Off Marine Geol, Atlantic-Gulf of Mex Br, US Geol Surv, 75-78. *Mem:* Am Geophys Union; Soc Explor Geophys. *Res:* Geophysical studies in Great Lakes; geophysical and geological studies of inland lakes; marine geophysical instrumentation. *Mailing Add:* Weston Geophys Corp 1600 Broadwat Suite 1560 Denver CO 80439

WOLDA, HINDRIK, Netherlands, May 24, 31; m 58; c 4. POPULATION DYNAMICS, COMMUNITY ECOLOGY. *Educ:* Univ Groningen, Netherlands, BSc, 55, MSc, 58, PhD(ecol), 63. *Prof Exp:* Sci officer ecol, Univ Groningen, 58-68, reader, 68-71; BIOLOGIST, SMITHSONIAN TROP RES INST, 71- *Mem:* Dutch Royal Acad Sci; Am Soc Naturalists; AAAS; Ecol Soc Am; Int Asn Ecol. *Res:* Temporal and special variations in abundance of tropical insect species; diapeux in tropical beetles; synetics of leafhoppers. *Mailing Add:* Smithsonian Trop Res Inst PO Box 2072 Balboa Panama

WOLDE-TINSAE, AMDE M, b Ethiopia, Apr 9, 47. CIVIL ENGINEERING. *Educ:* Johns Hopkins Univ, BES, 70; Univ Calif, Berkeley, MS, 71; State Univ NY, Buffalo, PhD(civil eng), 76. *Prof Exp:* Res asst civil eng, Univ Calif, Berkeley, 71-72; teaching asst, State Univ NY, Buffalo, 72-75; instr, Erie Community Col, Buffalo, 74-76; vis asst prof civil eng & eng mech, McMaster Univ, 76-77; asst prof, 77-81, ASSOC PROF CIVIL ENG, IOWA STATE UNIV, 81- *Concurrent Pos:* Res fel, Iowa State Univ Res Found, 78-79. *Mem:* Am Soc Civil Engrs; Nat Soc Prof Engrs; Int Asn Bridge & Struct Eng; Earthquake Eng Res Inst; Can Soc Civil Eng. *Res:* Non-linear analysis and stability of pre-buckled domes; hysteretic behavior of externally reinforced masonry walls; limit analysis of nuclear reactor containment vessels; piling stresses in integral abutment bridges; effects of lightning discharge on structures; diaphragm strength of composite masonry walls. *Mailing Add:* Dept of Civil Eng Iowa State Univ Ames IA 50011

WOLDMAN, MICHAEL L, US citizen. BIOENVIRONMENTAL ENGINEERING. *Educ:* Mo Sch Mines, BS, 62; Okla State Univ, MS, 67. *Prof Exp:* Mem staff, Dow Chem Co, 62-65; PROJ ENGR, ROY F WESTON, INC, 67- *Mem:* Fed Water Pollution Control Fedn; Am Acad Environ Eng; Am Soc Civil Engrs. *Res:* Industrial hazardous waste; industrial and municipal wastewater plant design; water plant design. *Mailing Add:* Roy F Weston Inc Weston Way West Chester PA 19380

WOLDSETH, ROLF, b Trondheim, Norway, Jan 18, 30; US citizen; m 55; c 4. ATOMIC PHYSICS, NUCLEAR PHYSICS. *Educ:* Tech Univ Norway, BSc, 55; Wash Univ, St Louis, PhD(physics), 65. *Prof Exp:* Res physicist, Joint Estab for Nuclear Energy Res, Norway, 55-56; asst prof physics, Rensselaer Polytech Inst, 63-67 & Wake Forest Univ, 67-70; DIR APPLN LAB, KEVEX CORP, FOSTER CITY, CALIF, 70- *Mem:* Am Phys Soc. *Res:* Positron annihilation; x-ray spectra; photo-nuclear reactions; fast neutron induced reactions. *Mailing Add:* 220 Stilt Ct Foster City CA 94404

WOLEN, ROBERT LAWRENCE, b New York, NY, May 20, 28. PHARMACOLOGY. *Educ:* West Chester State Col, BS, 50; Univ Del, MS, 51, PhD(biochem), 60. *Prof Exp:* Lectr atomic energy, Oak Ridge Inst Nuclear Studies, 60-61; lab dir biochem, Res Inst, St Joseph Hosp, 61-62; res scientist, Lilly Res Labs, 62-65, res assoc pharmacol, 65-75, RES ADV PHARMACOL, LILLY LAB CLIN RES, 75-; ASSOC PROF PHARMACOL, SCH MED, IND UNIV, INDIANAPOLIS, 73- *Mem:* Am Chem Soc; Sigma Xi; Am Soc Pharmacol & Exp Therapeut; Am Asn Clin Chemists; Am Soc Chem Pharmacol & Therapeut. *Res:* Phase I clinical pharmacology including drug metabolism, pharmacokinetics, drug interactions and therapeutic drug analysis. *Mailing Add:* Lilly Lab for Clin Res Wishard Mem Hosp Indianapolis IN 46202

WOLF, A(LFRED) A(BRAHAM), b Philadelphia, Pa, July 21, 25; m 57; c 2. ELECTRICAL ENGINEERING. *Educ:* Drexel Univ, BSc, 48; Univ Pa, MSc, 54, PhD(elec eng), 58; Univ Juarez, Mex, ScD(biomed), 77, MD, 78. *Prof Exp:* Head anal group, Anti-Submarine Div, US Naval Air Develop Ctr, 49-54; asst prof elec eng, Univ Pa, 54-59; chief scientist & tech asst to vpres, Gen Dynamics/Electronics, 59-61; dir res, Emerson Radio & Phonograph Corp, Md, 61-63; distinguished prof elec eng, chmn grad res & actg dir sch continuing ed, Drexel Univ, 63-65; div coordr & tech dir, Aerospace Systs Div, Radio Corp Am, Mass, 65-67; assoc tech dir res, Naval Ship Res & Develop Ctr, 67-78; PRES, PRIME RES CORP, MD, 78- *Concurrent Pos:* Lectr, Drexel Univ, 58-59, vis prof, 65-66; vis assoc prof, Univ Rochester, 60-61; vis prof, Univ Md, 67-68; vis prof, George Washington Univ, 68-69, adj prof, 72-; asst secy, Int Mil Electronics Conf, DC, 62, secy, 63. *Mem:* Sr mem Inst Elec & Electronics Engrs; Sigma Xi (vpres, 60-61). *Res:* Mathematical theory of nonlinear systems; stochastic processes; theory of physical and human systems; mathematical analysis; superconductivity; high temperature superconducting organic compounds with high critical fields; etiology and pathogenesis of cancer; mechanism of division of biological cells; mathematical biology. *Mailing Add:* RFD 3 Box 327 Ferry Point Rd Annapolis MD 21403

WOLF, ALBERT ALLEN, b Nashville, Tenn, Sept 2, 35; m 56; c 4. ELEMENTARY PARTICLE PHYSICS. *Educ:* Vanderbilt Univ, BA, 58, MA, 60; Ga Inst Technol, PhD(physics), 66. *Prof Exp:* Physicist, Aladdin Electronics Div, Aladdin Industs, Inc, 58; engr, Sperry Rand, Inc, 59-61; instr physics, Ga Inst Technol, 61-64; asst prof, 65-69, ASSOC PROF PHYSICS, DAVIDSON COL, 69- *Concurrent Pos:* Guest prof, Univ Ulm, WGer, 71-72. *Mem:* Am Phys Soc; Am Asn Physics Teachers. *Res:* Quantization of non-linear fields. *Mailing Add:* Rte 1 Box 130 Davidson NC 28036

WOLF, ALFRED PETER, b New York, NY, Feb 13, 23; m 46; c 1. ORGANIC CHEMISTRY, NUCLEAR CHEMISTRY. *Educ:* Columbia Univ, BA, 44, MA, 48, PhD(chem), 52. *Prof Exp:* MEM STAFF, CHEM DEPT, BROOKHAVEN NAT LAB, 51-, CHMN DEPT, 82- *Concurrent Pos:* Adj prof, Columbia Univ, 53-; ed, J Labelled Compounds, 65-; consult, Univ Mass, 65-66, Philip Morris, 66-, NIH, 66 & Int Atomic Energy Agency, 69-; adv, Ital Nat Res Coun, 69-; mem eval panel, Nat Bur Standards, 72-; ed, Radiochim Acta, 77- & assoc ed, J Nuclear Med, 78-81; consult, Nat Bur Standards, 72-76 & adv panel chem, Nat Res Coun, 77-80; vis comn, Atomic Res Ctr, Julich, Ger, 80- & Los Alamos Nat Lab, 81- *Honors & Awards:* Award, Am Chem Soc, 71; Aebersold Award, Soc Nuclear Med, 81. *Mem:* Am Chem Soc; Royal Soc Chem; Soc Ger Chem; Soc Nuclear Med. *Res:* Radiopharmaceutical research and nuclear medicine; organic reaction mechanisms; chemical effects of nuclear transformations; chemistry of carbon-11, nitrogen-13, oxygen-15, fluorine-18 and iodine-123; accelerators for nuclide production and radiopharmaceutical production. *Mailing Add:* PO Box 1043 Setauket NY 11733

WOLF, BARRY MORTON, mechanical engineering, see previous edition

WOLF, BENJAMIN, b Deerfield, NJ, Dec 2, 13; m 40; c 2. SOIL CHEMISTRY. *Educ:* Rutgers Univ, BS, 35, MS, 38, PhD(soil chem), 40. *Prof Exp:* Asst instr soil chem, Rutgers Univ, New Brunswick, 40-41; soil chemist, Seabrook Farms Co, 41-49; CONSULT, DR WOLF'S AGR LABS, 49- *Concurrent Pos:* Consult veg & floricult crops, Cent Am, SAm & Caribbean; assoc ed, Commun Soil Sci & Plant Anal, 70- *Mem:* Fel AAAS; Soil Sci Soc Am; Am Soc Hort Sci. *Res:* Soil and plant analysis; herbicides. *Mailing Add:* Dr Wolf's Agr Labs 6851 SW 45th St Ft Lauderdale FL 33314

WOLF, BENJAMIN, b Detroit, Mich, June 27, 26; m 52; c 2. MICROBIOLOGY. *Educ:* Wayne State Univ, BS, 49; Univ Mich, MS, 52; Univ Pa, PhD(microbiol), 59. *Prof Exp:* From asst instr to asst prof, 57-69, assoc prof, 69-80, PROF MICROBIOL, SCH VET MED, UNIV PA, 80- *Mem:* Am Soc Microbiol. *Res:* Medical microbiology; immunology. *Mailing Add:* 250 S 17th Philadelphia PA 19102

WOLF, BEVERLY, b Chicago, Ill, Jan 14, 35. MICROBIOLOGY. *Educ:* Univ Colo, BA, 55; Univ Calif, Los Angeles, PhD(biochem), 59. *Prof Exp:* Guest investr, Rockefeller Inst, 59-61; res assoc, Harvard Univ, 61-63; asst res biologist, Univ Calif, Berkeley, 65-72; vis asst prof, Mills Col, 72-73; SR SCIENTIST, CETUS CORP, 73- *Res:* Biochemical genetics of neurospora; genetical transformation of pneumococcus; origin and direction of deoxyribonucleic acid synthesis in Escherichia coli; temperature sensitive DNA synthesis mutants of Escherichia coli; microbial antibiotic production. *Mailing Add:* Cetus Corp 600 Bancroft Way Berkeley CA 94710

WOLF, CAROL EUWEMA, b New Castle, Pa, June 11, 36; m 58; c 2. COMPUTER THEORY. *Educ:* Swarthmore Col, BA, 58; Cornell Univ, MA, 62, PhD(math), 64. *Prof Exp:* Asst prof math, State Univ NY Brockport, 68-75; ASST PROF COMPUT SCI, IOWA STATE UNIV, 75- *Mem:* Asn Comput Mach; Math Asn Am; Asn Symbolic Logic; Asn Women Math. *Res:* Study of one and two dimensional context-free grammers. *Mailing Add:* 3611 Ross Rd Ames IA 50010

WOLF, CHARLES TROSTLE, b West Reading, Pa, Mar 20, 30; m 53; c 3. MATHEMATICS. *Educ:* Millersville State Col, BS, 53; Univ Del, MS, 59. *Prof Exp:* Teacher, Pequea Valley High Sch, 53-56; asst math, Univ Del, 56-58; asst prof, Shippensburg State Col, 58-61; ASSOC PROF MATH, MILLERSVILLE STATE COL, 61- *Mem:* Am Asn Univ Prof; Nat Coun Teachers Math. *Res:* Modern mathematics for elementary teachers. *Mailing Add:* Dept of Math Millersville State Col Millersville PA 17551

WOLF, DALE DUANE, b Alma, Nebr, June 16, 32; m 52; c 4. AGRONOMY. *Educ:* Univ Nebr, BSc, 54, MSc, 57; Univ Wis, PhD(agron), 62. *Prof Exp:* Asst prof agron, Univ Conn, 62-67; asst prof, 67-71, ASSOC PROF AGRON, VA POLYTECH INST & STATE UNIV, 71- *Mem:* Am Soc Agron; Crop Sci Soc Am. *Res:* Forage crops; plant physiology. *Mailing Add:* Dept of Agron Va Polytech Inst & Sta Univ Blacksburg VA 24061

WOLF, DALE E, b Kearney, Nebr, Sept 6, 24; m 45; c 4. AGRONOMY. *Educ:* Univ Nebr, BSc, 43; Rutgers Univ, PhD(farm crops, weed control), 49. *Prof Exp:* Asst farm crops, Rutgers Univ, 46-49, assoc prof & assoc res specialist, 49-50; agronomist, USDA, 47-50; asst mgr agr chem res, 50-54, mgr, 54-56, asst dist sales mgr, 56-59, dist sales mgr, 60-64, sales mgr biochem, Del, 64-67, mgr, Planning Div, 67-68, asst dir, Agr Div, 68-70, dir, Indust Specialities Div, 71-72, dir mkt agrichem, 72-75, asst gen mgr, Biochem Dept, 75-78, gen mgr, Biochem Dept, 78-79, VPRES BIOCHEMICALS, E I DU PONT DE NEMOURS & CO, INC, 79-, CHMN BD, ENDO LAB, INC, SUBSID E I DU PONT DE NEMOURS & CO, INC, 79- *Mem:* Am Soc Agron; Nat Agr Chemicals Asn. *Res:* Agricultural chemicals; weed control. *Mailing Add:* B-14348 E I du Pont de Nemours & Co Inc Wilmington DE 19898

WOLF, DANIEL STAR, b Indianapolis, Ind, Aug 25, 49; m 77. OCEAN ENGINEERING, FRACTURE MECHANICS. *Educ:* Purdue Univ, BS, 71, MS, 73, PhD(aeronaut eng), 76. *Prof Exp:* Teaching asst aeronaut eng, Purdue Univ, 71-76; asst prof ocean eng, Fla Atlantic Univ, 76-79; ASST PROJ ENGR, GOVT PROD DIV, PRATT & WHITNEY AIRCRAFT, UNITED TECHNOL CORP, 79- *Res:* Fatigue crack propagation; solid mechanics structures. *Mailing Add:* Pratt & Whitney Aircraft Mail Stop E-40 West Palm Beach FL 33431

WOLF, DIETER, b Sindelfingen, WGer, Nov 3, 46. THEORETICAL SOLID STATE PHYSICS, MAGNETIC RESONANCE. *Educ:* Univ Stuttgart, Diplom, 70, Dr rer nat(physics), 73. *Prof Exp:* Res assoc mat sci, Max Planck Inst Metal Res, Stuttgart, 72-74; res asst prof physics, Univ Utah, 74-77; ASST SCIENTIST, MAT SCI DIV, ARGONNE NAT LAB, 77- *Mem:* Am Phys Soc. *Res:* Diffusion in crystals; theory of magnetic resonance and relaxation; atomic, molecular and defect motions in metals, metal oxides and ionic crystals studied by nuclear magnetic resonance; Mössbauer effect and quasielastic neutron scattering. *Mailing Add:* Mat Sci Div Argonne Nat Lab Argonne IL 60439

WOLF, DON PAUL, b Lansing, Mich, Aug 8, 39; m 67; c 2. BIOCHEMISTRY, REPRODUCTIVE BIOLOGY. *Educ:* Mich State Univ, BS, 61, MS, 62; Univ Wash, PhD(biochem), 67. *Prof Exp:* Fel biochem, Univ Geneva, 67-68 & Univ Calif, Davis, 68-71; asst prof obstet & gynec & biophys, 71-77, ASSOC PROF OBSTET & GYNEC, BIOCHEM & BIOPHYS, UNIV PA, 77- *Mem:* AAAS; Am Fertil Soc; Soc Study Reproduction; Am Soc Cell Biol; Am Soc Biol Chemists. *Res:* Characterization of reproductive processes; the role of cortical granules in fertilization and early development; sperm excluding mechanism operative in animal ova; isolation and characterization of cervical and tracheal mucin. *Mailing Add:* 307 Med Labs Univ Pa Div Reprod Biol Philadelphia PA 19174

WOLF, DUANE CARL, b Springfield, Mo, Apr 7, 46; m 68. SOIL MICROBIOLOGY. *Educ:* Univ Mo-Columbia, BS, 68; Univ Calif, Riverside, PhD(soils), 73. *Prof Exp:* Asst prof soils, Univ Md, College Park, 73-78; ASSOC PROF SOILS, UNIV ARK, FAYETTEVILLE, 79- *Mem:* Am Soc Agron; Soil Sci Soc Am; Am Soc Microbiol; AAAS. *Res:* Microbiology of sludge amended soils; evaluation of forest and grass buffer strips in improving the water quality of manure-polluted runoff; effect of salt fallout from cooling towers on soil. *Mailing Add:* Dept of Agron Univ of Ark Fayetteville AR 72701

WOLF, EDWARD D, b Quinter, Kans, May 30, 35; m 55; c 3. SURFACE PHYSICS. *Educ:* McPherson Col, BS, 57; Iowa State Univ, PhD(phys chem), 61. *Prof Exp:* Res assoc, Princeton Univ, 61-62; sr chemist, Atomics Int Div, NAm Aviation, Inc, 63-64, res specialist, 65, mem tech staff, Sci Ctr Div, 64-65; mem tech staff, Hughes Res Labs, Malibu, 65-67, sr staff chemist, 67-72, sect head electron beam surface physics, 72-74, sr scientist, 74-78; PROF & DIR, NAT RES & RESOURCE FACIL SUBMICRON STRUCT, CORNELL UNIV, 78- *Concurrent Pos:* Res assoc, Univ Calif, Berkeley, 68. *Mem:* Am Phys Soc; Electron Micros Soc Am; fel Inst Elec & Electronics Eng. *Res:* Ionic mobilities of high temperature inorganic liquids; magnetohydrodynamic energy conversion; field emission and scanning electron microscopy; scanning electron beam diagnostics and microfabrication. *Mailing Add:* 8 Highgate Circle Ithaca NY 14850

WOLF, EDWARD G(EORGE), b Brooklyn, NY, Oct 25, 19; m 52; c 1. ELECTRICAL ENGINEERING. *Educ:* Brooklyn Col, BA, 41; NY Univ, BEE, 47; Polytech Inst Brooklyn, MEE, 54. *Prof Exp:* Jr engr, Am Dist Tel Co, 41-44; from instr to asst prof elec eng, Pratt Inst Technol, 46-49; engr & head eng sect, 49-67, IN CHARGE ELEC MEASUREMENTS LAB,

SPERRY GYROSCOPE CO, 67- *Mem:* Inst Elec & Electronics Engrs. *Res:* Electrical measurements as applied to component measurements and qualification test; reliability engineering. *Mailing Add:* Sperry Gyroscope Co Marcuse Ave & Lakeville Rd Great Neck NY 11020

WOLF, EDWARD LINCOLN, b Cocoa, Fla, Nov 22, 36; m 58; c 2. CONDENSED MATTER PHYSICS, SPECTROSCOPY. *Educ:* Swarthmore Col, AB, 58; Cornell Univ, PhD(exp physics), 64. *Prof Exp:* Fel physics, Dept Physics & Coord Sci Lab, Univ Ill, Urbana, 64-66, res assoc, 67; sr physicist, Res Labs, Eastman Kodak Co, Rochester, 68-75; assoc prof, 75-80, PROF PHYSICS, AMES LAB, IOWA STATE UNIV, 81- *Concurrent Pos:* Vis fel, Cavendish Lab, Univ Cambridge, 73-74. *Mem:* Am Phys Soc; AAAS. *Res:* Superconductivity; electron tunneling; physics of surfaces and interfaces; ultra high vacuum; superconducting proximity effect; photoemission spectroscopy and electron energy loss spectroscopy. *Mailing Add:* 3611 Ross Rd Ames IA 50010

WOLF, ELIZABETH ANNE, b Leeds, UK; US citizen; m 54; c 2. NUCLEAR PHYSICS. *Educ:* Oxford Univ, BA, 51, PhD(nuclear physics), 55. *Prof Exp:* Dept demonstr physics, Clarendon Lab, Oxford Univ, 52-55, res staff, Lab Archaeol, 55-56; res assoc physics, Biophys Lab, Harvard Med Sch, 56-57; lectr, Univ Conn, Waterbury, 75-79; ASST PROF PHYSICS, SOUTHERN CONN STATE COL, 79- *Concurrent Pos:* Newsletter ed, New Eng Sect, Am Phys Soc, 81- *Mem:* Am Phys Soc; Am Asn Physics Teachers; Health Physics Soc. *Res:* Experimental nuclear physics; deuteron-deuteron interactron; inelastic neutron scattering; measurement of very low level radiation. *Mailing Add:* Physics Dept Southern Conn State Col New Haven CT 06515

WOLF, EMIL, b Prague, Czech, July 30, 22. MATHEMATICAL PHYSICS, OPTICS. *Educ:* Bristol Univ, BSc, 45, PhD(physics), 48; Univ Edinburgh, DSc(physics), 55. *Prof Exp:* Res asst optics, Cambridge Univ, 48-51; res asst & lectr math physics, Univ Edinburgh, 51-54; res fel theoret physics, Univ Manchester, 54-59; assoc prof optics, 59-61, PROF PHYSICS, UNIV ROCHESTER, 61-, PROF OPTICS, 78- *Concurrent Pos:* Guggenheim fel & vis prof, Univ Calif, Berkeley, 66-67; vis prof, Univ Toronto, 74-75; ed, Progress in Optics. *Honors & Awards:* Frederic Ives Medal, Optical Soc Am, 77; Albert A Michelson Medal, Franklin Inst, 80. *Mem:* Fel Optical Soc Am (pres, 78); Fel Am Phys Soc; fel Brit Inst Physics. *Res:* Theoretical optics; electromagnetic theory. *Mailing Add:* Dept of Physics & Astron Univ of Rochester Rochester NY 14627

WOLF, ERIC W, b Frankfurt am Main, Ger, Feb 20, 22; US citizen; m 49; c 2. COMPUTER SCIENCE, SYSTEMS SCIENCE. *Educ:* City Col New York, BEE, 49; Ohio State Univ, MS, 51. *Prof Exp:* Electronic scientist, Wright Air Develop Ctr, 49-53; res engr, Lincoln Lab, Mass Inst Technol, 53-59; tech adv tech ctr, Supreme Hq Allied Powers Europe, The Hague, 59-60; dir comput prog, Data & Info Systs Div, Int Tel & Tel Corp, 61-62, tech dir, 62-64; tech dir, Naval Command Systs Support Activity, 64-70; sr scientist, 70-80, MGR WASH OPERS, COMMUN SYSTS DIV, BOLT BERANEK & NEWMAN INC, 80- *Honors & Awards:* Prof Commendation, US Air Force Res & Develop Command, 56. *Mem:* Comput Soc; Commun Soc; Asn Comput Mach; Inst Elec & Electronics Engrs. *Res:* Design and development of computer-based information systems; computer communications; computer networks; information management; man-machine interaction in natural language. *Mailing Add:* Bolt Beranek & Newman Inc 1300 N 17th St Arlington VA 22209

WOLF, FRANK JAMES, b Xenia, Ohio, Nov 7, 16; m 42; c 3. ORGANIC CHEMISTRY. *Educ:* Miami Univ, AB, 38; Univ Ill, PhD(org chem), 42. *Prof Exp:* Sr chemist, Merck & Co, Inc, 42-59, asst dir microbiol, Merck Sharp & Dohme Res Labs, 59-70, dir animal drug metab & radiochem, 70-77, SR SCIENTIST, MERCK SHARP & DOHME RES LABS, 78- *Concurrent Pos:* Asst, Nat Defense Res Comt, 41-42. *Mem:* Am Soc Pharmacol & Exp Therapeut; Am Chem Soc. *Res:* Phthalides; substituted sulfaquinoxalines; benzotriazines; antibiotics; vitamin B-12; catalysis; biochemical separations; animal and human drug metabolism; animal tissue residue; mass spectroscopy; biochemical toxicology; pharmacokinetics. *Mailing Add:* 126 E Lincoln Ave Rahway NJ 07065

WOLF, FRANK LOUIS, b St Louis, Mo, Apr 18, 24; m 47; c 4. MULTIVARIATE ANALYSIS. *Educ:* Wash Univ, BS, 44, MA, 48; Univ Minn, PhD(math), 55. *Prof Exp:* Tech supvr chem eng, Carbon & Carbide Chem Corp, Tenn, 44-46; instr math, St Cloud State Col, 49-51; from instr to assoc prof, 52-67, PROF MATH, CARLETON COL, 67- *Concurrent Pos:* NSF fel, 60-61. *Mem:* AAAS; Math Asn Am; Am Statist Asn. *Res:* Multivariate descriptive statistics; statistical education. *Mailing Add:* Dept of Math Carleton Col Northfield MN 55057

WOLF, FRANKLIN KREAMER, b Norman, Okla, Sept 30, 35; m 62; c 3. INDUSTRIAL ENGINEERING, OPERATIONS RESEARCH. *Educ:* Iowa State Univ, BS, 57, PhD(eng valuation, statist), 70; Univ Wis, MS, 62. *Prof Exp:* Officer, US Army Corps Engrs, 57-59; engr, Rheem Semiconductor, 59-60; res asst, Univ Wis, 60; engr, Martin Co, Denver, 61-64; asst prof indust eng, Iowa State Univ, 64-70; assoc prof, 70-77, PROF INDUST ENG & CHMN, WESTERN MICH UNIV, 77- *Mem:* Am Inst Indust Engrs; Am Soc Eng Educ; Inst Mgt Sci; Opers Res Soc Am; Sigma Xi. *Res:* Engineering economics and study of life estimation and methods of depreciation for capital recovery in regulated industries. *Mailing Add:* Dept of Indust Eng Western Mich Univ Kalamazoo MI 49008

WOLF, FREDERICK TAYLOR, b Auburn, Ala, July 11, 15; m 45; c 2. BOTANY. *Educ:* Harvard Univ, AB, 35; Univ Wis, MA, 36, PhD(bot), 38. *Prof Exp:* Nat Res Coun fel, Harvard Univ, 38-39; from instr to assoc prof bot, 39-56, PROF BOT, VANDERBILT UNIV, 56-; RETIRED. *Mem:* Mycol Soc Am; Bot Soc Am; Am Soc Plant Physiol; Brit Mycol Soc; Int Soc Human & Animal Mycol. *Res:* Mycology; physiology of fungi; plant physiology. *Mailing Add:* Dept of Gen Biol Vanderbilt Univ Nashville TN 37235

WOLF, GEORGE, b Vienna, Austria, June 16, 22; nat US; m 48; c 3. NUTRITION, BIOCHEMISTRY. *Educ:* Univ London, BSc, 44; Oxford Univ, DPhil, 47. *Prof Exp:* Res fel, Chester Beatty Res Inst, Royal Cancer Hosp, Eng, 47-48, Harvard Univ, 48-50 & Univ Wis, 50-51; from asst prof to assoc prof animal nutrit, Univ Ill, Urbana, 51-62; assoc prof, 62-74, PROF NUTRIT & FOOD SCI, MASS INST TECHNOL, 74- *Concurrent Pos:* Guggenheim fel, 58-59. *Honors & Awards:* Osborne-Mendel Award, Am Inst Nutrit, 77. *Mem:* Am Soc Biol Chemists; Am Inst Nutrit. *Res:* Metabolism and function of vitamin A. *Mailing Add:* Dept of Nutrit & Food Sci Mass Inst of Technol Cambridge MA 02139

WOLF, GEORGE ANTHONY, JR, b East Orange, NJ, Apr 20, 14; m 39; c 2. MEDICINE. *Educ:* NY Univ, BS, 36; Cornell Univ, MD, 41; Am Bd Internal Med, dipl, 48. *Hon Degrees:* DSc, Union Univ, 65. *Prof Exp:* Intern med, New York Hosp, 41-42; asst, Med Col, Cornell Univ, 42-43, instr, 43, fel med res, 44-46, asst prof clin med, 49-52; prof clin med & dean, Col Med, Univ Vt, 52-61; prof med, Sch Med & vpres med & dent affairs, Tufts Univ, 61-66; dean & provost, Univ Kansas Med Ctr, Kansas City, 66-70; prof, 70-79, EMER PROF MED, COL MED, UNIV VT, 79- *Concurrent Pos:* Asst resident med, New York Hosp, 42-43, resident physician, 43-44, physician to out-patients, 44, asst attend physician & dir out-patient dept, 49-52; dir, Tufts New Eng Med Ctr, 61-66; attend physician, Med Ctr Hosp, Vt, 70-81, emer attend physician, 80- *Mem:* Harvey Soc; fel Am Col Physicians; fel NY Acad Med; Asn Am Med Cols (past pres). *Res:* Internal medicine. *Mailing Add:* Box 237 Nashville Rd Jericho VT 05465

WOLF, GEORGE L, b Cadjavica, Yugoslavia, July 17, 27; US citizen; m 62; c 1. VETERINARY PATHOLOGY. *Educ:* Univ Munich, DVM, 59; Ohio State Univ, MSc, 61, PhD(path), 65. *Prof Exp:* From instr to asst prof path, Ohio State Univ, 59-65; pathologist, Eastman Kodak Co, NY, 65-68; asst prof lab animal med, Col Med, Univ Cincinnati, 68-72; pathologist, Hoechst Pharmaceut, Inc, 72-73; PATHOLOGIST, MERCK SHARP & DOHME, 73- *Concurrent Pos:* Consult, Vet Admin, 68- *Mem:* Electron Micros Soc Am; Am Vet Med Asn. *Res:* Spontaneous and experimental canine cryptococcosis; Rocky Mountain spotted fever in monkeys. *Mailing Add:* Merck Sharp & Dohme West Point PA 19450

WOLF, GEORGE WILLIAM, b Newark, NJ, Jan 15, 43. ASTRONOMY. *Educ:* Univ Pa, BA, 65, MS, 67, PhD(astron), 70. *Prof Exp:* Res assoc astron, Mt John Observ, Univ Canterbury, NZ, 68-69; ASSOC PROF ASTRON, SOUTHWEST MO STATE UNIV, 71- *Concurrent Pos:* NSF fel, 77-78. *Mem:* Am Astron Soc. *Res:* Observational astronomy in the areas of linear and circular polarimetry, spectroscopy and photoelectric photometry of stars. *Mailing Add:* Dept Physics & Astron Southwest Mo State Univ Springfield MO 65802

WOLF, GERALD LEE, b Sidney, Nebr, Apr 2, 38; m 64; c 2. RADIOLOGY. *Educ:* Univ Nebr, BS, 62, MS, 64, PhD(physiol & pharmacol), 65; Harvard Univ, MD, 68. *Prof Exp:* Asst prof physiol, Col Med, Univ Nebr, Omaha, 68-69, asst prof physiol & med, 69-71, asst prof pharmacol & radiol & dir radiol res, 71-80; PROF RADIOL, UNIV PA MED CTR, 80- *Concurrent Pos:* Life Ins Med res fel, 64-69; intern, Col Med, Univ Nebr, 68-69; res consult, Omaha Vet Admin Hosp, 69-, clin investr, 70-73. *Mem:* Am Col Radiol; fel Am Soc Clin Pharmacol & Therapeut; Asn Am Med Cols; AMA; Am Soc Pharmacol & Exp Therapeut. *Res:* Renal and endocrine participation in electrolyte homeostasis; physiology of the pump-perfused dog kidney. *Mailing Add:* Dept Radiol Univ Pa Med Ctr Philadelphia PA 19104

WOLF, HAROLD HERBERT, b Quincy, Mass, Dec 19, 34; m 57; c 2. PHARMACOLOGY. *Educ:* Mass Col Pharm, BS, 56; Univ Utah, PhD(pharmacol, exp psychiat), 61. *Prof Exp:* From asst prof to assoc prof, 61-69, Kimberly prof pharmacol & chmn dept, Col Pharm, Ohio State Univ, 69-76; DEAN & PROF BIOCHEM PHARMACOL & TOXICOL, COL PHARM, UNIV UTAH, 76- *Concurrent Pos:* NIMH & Nat Inst Drug Abuse res grants, 63-; Am Asn Cols Pharm vis lectr, 64-; mem pharm rev comt, NIH, 69-71; Fulbright-Hays sr scholar, Univ Sains Malaysia, 74; mem, Joint Comn on Prescription Drug Use, 77-80, Biomed Res Support Comt, NIH, 78-79, bd of dir, Am Found for Pharmaceut Educ, 78, comt of pres, Asn of Acad Health Ctr, 78; external exam, Univ Sains, Malaysia, 80; Am Pharmaceut Asn Task Force Educ, 81- *Mem:* AAAS; Am Asn Col Pharm (pres, 78); Am Pharmaceut Asn; fel AAAS; fel Acad Pharmaceut Sci. *Res:* Investigation of effects of drugs on central nervous system; psychotropics, central nervous system stimulants, anticonvulsants, narcotic analgetics, thermoregulation and animal behavior. *Mailing Add:* Univ of Utah Col of Pharm Salt Lake City UT 84112

WOLF, HAROLD WILLIAM, b Chicago, Ill, July 13, 21; m 44; c 4. ENVIRONMENTAL HEALTH. *Educ:* Univ Iowa, BS, 49, MS, 50, DrPH, 65. *Prof Exp:* From sanit engr to sr sanit engr, Fed Water Pollution Control Admin, USPHS, Calif, 50-68, asst chief res & develop, Water Supply & Sea Resources, Ohio, 68, dir div criteria & standards, Bur Water Hygiene, Md, 68-70; PROF CIVIL ENG, TEX A&M UNIV, 70-, DIR ENVIRON SCI ENG, 75- *Concurrent Pos:* Res fel, Calif Inst Technol, 60-62; lectr, Univ Calif, Los Angeles, 65-66; dir, Dallas Water Reclamation Res Ctr, 70-75; mem, Nat Drinking Water Adv Coun, 75. *Mem:* AAAS; Sigma Xi; Am Soc Civil Eng; Am Pub Health Asn; Am Soc Microbiol. *Res:* Water quality criteria; air-borne pathogens. *Mailing Add:* 202 Civil Eng Bldg Tex A&M Univ College Station TX 77843

WOLF, HELMUT, b Einöd, Saar Region, Jan 19, 24; US citizen. MECHANICAL ENGINEERING, HEAT TRANSFER. *Educ:* Case Inst Technol, BSME, 48; Purdue Univ, MSME, 50, PhD(mech eng), 58. *Prof Exp:* Instr mech eng, Purdue Univ, 48-50; develop engr, Eastman Kodak Co, 50-53; res assoc heat transfer, Jet Propulsion Ctr, Purdue Univ, 53-58; prin scientist, N Am Aviation, Inc, 58-61; prof mech eng, 61-71, RAYMOND F GIFFELS DISTINGUISHED PROF ENG, UNIV ARK, FAYETTEVILLE, 71- *Concurrent Pos:* Resident res assoc, Argonne Nat Lab, 64-66; res grant & consult, Cent Transformer Corp, 66-67; staff adv, Inst Reactor Develop,

Nuclear Res Ctr, Karlsruhe, WGer, 70-71. *Mem:* Am Soc Mech Engrs; Am Nuclear Soc; Am Soc Eng Educ. *Res:* Heat transfer of forced and free-convection shear flows and conduction transfer. *Mailing Add:* Dept of Mech Eng Univ of Ark Fayetteville AR 72701

WOLF, HENRY, b Munich, Ger, Aug 30, 19; mat US; m 44; c 4. APPLIED MATHEMATICS, CELESTIAL MECHANICS. *Educ:* Univ Toronto, BA, 46, MA, 47; Brown Univ, PhD, 50. *Prof Exp:* Instr math, Univ Toronto, 46-48; res assoc appl math, Brown Univ, 48-50; from asst prof to assoc prof math, Hofstra Col, 50-56; prin engr, Repub Aviation Corp, 56-57, group engr, 57-58, sr group engr, 58-59, develop engr, Appl Math Sect, 59-60, chief numerical methods, 60-63; sr scientist & secy treas, 63-74, VPRES, ANAL MECH ASSOCS, JERICHO, 74- *Mem:* Am Math Soc. *Res:* Plastic wave propagation; interior ballistics and aeroelasticity; numerical analysis. *Mailing Add:* Anal Mech Assocs 50 Jericho Turnpike Jericho NY 11753

WOLF, IRA KENNETH, b New York, NY, Nov 14, 42; m 64; c 1. MATHEMATICS. *Educ:* Tufts Univ, BA, 64; Yale Univ, MA, 66; Rutgers Univ, PhD(math), 71. *Prof Exp:* ASST PROF MATH, BROOKLYN COL, 71- *Mem:* Math Asn Am. *Res:* Category theory. *Mailing Add:* Brooklyn Col Math Bedford Ave H Brooklyn NY 11216

WOLF, IRVING W, b Nashville, Tenn, July 12, 27; m 54; c 3. CHEMICAL ENGINEERING. *Educ:* Vanderbilt Univ, BE, 47, MS, 49; Ill Inst Technol, PhD(chem eng), 51. *Prof Exp:* Instr chem eng, Ill Inst Technol, 50-51; res & develop engr, Gen Elec Co, 51-55, consult heat transfer, 55-58, proj engr, 58-61, mgr functional films sect, 61-63; head mat res, 63-65, mgr mat & devices res, 65-71, corp consult, 71-72, mgr magnetic mat, Magnetic Tape Div, 72-78, MGR PLASTICS & CHEM ENG, AMPEX CORP, 72- *Mem:* AAAS; Inst Elec & Electronics Engrs; Electrochem Soc. *Res:* Electrodeposition of magnetic thin films for information storage; vacuum deposition and sputtering of thin films for electronic application. *Mailing Add:* Magnetic Tape Div Ampex Corp Redwood City CA 94063

WOLF, JACK KEIL, b Newark, NJ, Mar 14, 35; m 55; c 3. ELECTRICAL ENGINEERING. *Educ:* Univ Pa, BS, 56; Princeton Univ, MSE, 57, MA, 58, PhD(elec eng), 60. *Prof Exp:* Instr, Syracuse Univ, 60-62; assoc prof elec eng, NY Univ, 63-65; from assoc prof to prof, Polytech Inst Brooklyn, 65-73; chmn dept elec & comput eng, 73-75, PROF ELEC ENG, UNIV MASS, AMHERST, 73- *Concurrent Pos:* Consult, govt & indust, 63-; NSF sr fel, Univ Hawaii, 71-72; Guggenheim fel, 79-80. *Mem:* Fel Inst Elec & Electronics Engrs (pres, info theory group, 74). *Res:* Statistical communications theory; algebraic coding theory. *Mailing Add:* Dept of Elec & Comput Eng Univ of Mass Amherst MA 01003

WOLF, JAMES S, b Cleveland, Ohio, July 26, 33; m 57. METALLURGY. *Educ:* Case Inst Technol, BS, 54, MS, 60; Univ Fla, PhD(metall), 65. *Prof Exp:* Res scientist, Lewis Lab, NASA, 57-69; assoc prof mat eng, 69-77, PROF MAT ENG, CLEMSON UNIV, 77- *Mem:* Am Soc Metals; Am Inst Mining, Metall & Petrol Engrs; Brit Inst Metals; Nat Asn Corrosion Engrs. *Res:* High temperature oxidation and deformation of metals and alloys; biomedical materials; secondary metals. *Mailing Add:* Dept of Mat Eng Clemson Univ Clemson SC 29631

WOLF, JAMES STUART, b Chicago, Ill, Mar 1, 35; m 58; c 2. MEDICINE, SURGERY. *Educ:* Grinnell Col, AB, 57; Univ Ill, BS, 59, MD, 61. *Prof Exp:* USPHS res fel transplantation, 64-66, from instr to prof surg, Med Col Va, 67-76; chief surg, McGuire Vet Admin Hosp, 68-76; PROF SURG & CHMN DIV OF TRANSPLANTATION, NORTHWESTERN UNIV MED SCH, 76- CHIEF SURG, McGUIRE VET ADMIN HOSP, 68- *Concurrent Pos:* Attend surgeon, McGuire Vet Admin Hosp, 67-68, Northwestern Mem Hosp, Lakeside Vet Admin Hosp, Evanston Hosp, 76- *Mem:* Transplantation Soc; Am Soc Nephrology; Asn Acad Surg; fel Am Col Surg; Soc Univ Surg. *Res:* Transplantation immunology; clinical and experimental organ transplantation. *Mailing Add:* Northwestern Univ Med Sch Dept Surg 303 E Chicago Ave Chicago IL 60611

WOLF, JOSEPH A(LLEN), JR, b Tacoma, Wash, Nov 26, 33; m 60; c 1. APPLIED MECHANICS. *Educ:* Stevens Inst Technol, ME, 55; Univ Calif, Los Angeles, MS, 57; Mass Inst Technol, ScD(mech eng), 67. *Prof Exp:* Mem tech staff, Hughes Aircraft Co, 55-62; asst prof mech & struct, Univ Calif, Los Angeles, 66-71; sr res engr, 71-80, STAFF RES ENGR, ENG MECH DEPT, GEN MOTORS RES LABS, 80- *Mem:* Am Soc Mech Engrs. *Res:* Dynamics; mechanical and structural vibrations; structural-acoustic interaction. *Mailing Add:* Eng Mech Dept Gen Motors Tech Ctr Warren MI 48090

WOLF, JOSEPH ALBERT, b Chicago, Ill, Oct 18, 36. MATHEMATICS. *Educ:* Univ Chicago, BS, 56, MS, 57, PhD(geom), 59. *Prof Exp:* NSF fel math & mem, Inst Advan Study, 60-62; from asst prof to assoc prof, 62-66, PROF MATH, UNIV CALIF, BERKELEY, 66- *Concurrent Pos:* Alfred P Sloan res fels, 66-68, Miller Res Prof, 72. *Mem:* Am Math Soc; Swiss Math Soc. *Res:* Riemannian geometry, Lie groups and harmonic analysis. *Mailing Add:* Dept of Math Univ of Calif Berkeley CA 94720

WOLF, JULIUS, b Boston, Mass, Aug 15, 18; m 45; c 3. MEDICINE. *Educ:* Boston Univ, SB, 40, MD, 43. *Prof Exp:* Chief med serv, 54-72, CHIEF OF STAFF, VET ADMIN HOSP, BRONX, 72-; PROF CLIN MED, MT SINAI SCH MED, 68-, ASSOC DEAN VET ADMIN PROGS, 72- *Concurrent Pos:* Assoc clin prof med, Col Physicians & Surgeons, Columbia Univ, 62-68; chmn, Vet Admin Lung Cancer Study Group, 62- *Res:* Lung cancer chemotherapy. *Mailing Add:* Vet Admin Hosp 130 W Kingsbridge Rd Bronx NY 10468

WOLF, KATHLEEN A, b Dallas, Tex, Sept 10, 46. ENVIRONMENTAL SCIENCES, CHEMICAL ENGINEERING. *Educ:* Univ Washington, BS, 68; San Diego State Univ, MS, 71; Univ Southern Calif, PhD(chem), 80. *Prof Exp:* PHYS SCIENTIST, RAND CORP, 73- *Concurrent Pos:* Res asst chem, Univ Southern Calif, 76-80. *Mem:* Am Chem Soc. *Res:* Molecular structure, spectroscopy, chemical events important in toxic waste, pollution and alternating energy technologists. *Mailing Add:* Rand Corp 1700 Main St Santa Monica CA 90406

WOLF, KENNETH EDWARD, b Chicago, Ill, Oct 22, 21; m 48; c 3. MICROBIOLOGY. *Educ:* Utah State Univ, BS, 51, MS, 52, PhD(fish path), 56. *Prof Exp:* Microbiologist, Eastern Fish Dis Lab, US Fish & Wildlife Serv, 54-72, dir, 72-77; SR RES SCIENTIST, NAT FISH HEALTH RES LAB, 77- *Concurrent Pos:* Ed, Fish Health News. *Honors & Awards:* S F Snieszko Distinguished Service Award, Am Fisheries Soc, 81. *Mem:* AAAS; Am Soc Microbiol; Tissue Cult Asn; Wildlife Dis Asn; Int Asn Aquatic Animal Med. *Res:* Diseases of fishes, especially of viral etiology; methods of cultivation of fish cells and tissues; life cycle studies on salmonid whirling disease, myxosoma cerebralis; immunization of salmonids against ichthyophthiriasis. *Mailing Add:* US Fish & Wildlife Serv RD 3 Box 41 Kearneysville WV 25430

WOLF, LARRY LOUIS, b Madison, Wis, Oct 21, 38; m 65. SOCIAL SYSTEMS. *Educ:* Univ Mich, BS, 61; Univ Calif, Berkeley, PhD(zool), 66. *Prof Exp:* Assoc zool, Univ Calif, Berkeley, 64-66; Elsie Binger Naumberg res fel ornith, Am Mus Natural Hist, 66-67; from asst prof zool to assoc prof biol, 67-76, PROF BIOL, SYRACUSE UNIV, 76- *Concurrent Pos:* Ecol adv panel, NSF, 77-79. *Mem:* Am Ornith Union; Cooper Ornith Soc; Brit Ornith Union; Am Soc Naturalists; Brit Ecol Soc. *Res:* Ecological determinants of social systems, principally in birds and insects; community organization coevolution. *Mailing Add:* Dept of Biol Syracuse Univ Syracuse NY 13210

WOLF, LESLIE RAYMOND, b East Chicago, Ind, Feb 18, 49; m 72. ORGANIC CHEMISTRY, POLYMER CHEMISTRY. *Educ:* Lewis Univ, BA, 71; Pa State Univ, PhD(chem), 74. *Prof Exp:* Chemist, Rohm & Haas Co, 73-78; sr res chemist, DeSota, Inc, 78-81; STAFF RES CHEMIST, AMOCO OIL CO, 81- *Concurrent Pos:* Lectr chem, Eve Div, LaSalle Col, 74-78. *Mem:* Am Chem Soc; Am Soc Lubrication Engrs. *Res:* Polymer coatings and monomer research. *Mailing Add:* Amoco Res Ctr PO Box 400 Naperville IL 60566

WOLF, LOUIS W, b Saginaw, Mich, May 3, 28; m 52; c 4. ENGINEERING MECHANICS, APPLIED MATHEMATICS. *Educ:* Univ Mich, BSE, 52, MSE, 55, PhD(eng mech), 63. *Prof Exp:* Engr, Carrier Corp, 52-54; res assoc eng mech, Univ Mich, 54-61, instr, 55-60; res engr, Systs Div, Bendix Corp, 61-62; from asst prof, 62-65, ASSOC PROF MECH ENG, UNIV MICH-DEARBORN, 65- *Mem:* Asn Comput Mach; Soc Indust & Appl Math. *Res:* Fluid mechanics; nonlinear elastic shells; computer technology. *Mailing Add:* Dept of Mech Eng Univ of Mich Dearborn MI 48128

WOLF, MARVIN ABRAHAM, b Syracuse, NY, Dec 26, 25; m 54; c 2. MICROMETEOROLOGY. *Educ:* NMex Inst Mining & Technol, BS, 51; Univ Wash, MS, 62. *Prof Exp:* Assoc res engr, Boeing Airplane Co, Wash, 58-60; res meteorologist, Meteorol Res Inc, Calif, 60-63; physicist, Pac Missile Range, Calif, 63-66; res assoc, Pac Northwest Labs, Battelle-Mem Inst, 66-77; res assoc air res ctr, 77-80, ASSOC PROF, DEPT ATMOSPHERIC SCI, ORE STATE UNIV, 80- *Mem:* Am Meteorol Soc; Am Geophys Union; Sigma Xi. *Res:* Micrometeorological and mesometeorological processes which control the suspension, transport, diffusion and deposition of airborne materials from agricultural and industrial sources. *Mailing Add:* 654 NW Stewart Pl Corvallis OR 97330

WOLF, MATTHEW BERNARD, b Los Angeles, Calif, May 5, 35; m 60; c 2. PHYSIOLOGY. *Educ:* Univ Calif, Los Angeles, BSc, 57, MSc, 62, PhD(physiol), 67. *Prof Exp:* Sr engr, Bendix Corp, 58-63; asst prof biomed eng, Univ Southern Calif, 67-72; assoc prof eng, Univ Ala, Birmingham, 72-76; ASSOC PROF PHYSIOL, UNIV SC, 76- *Concurrent Pos:* Consult, Rand Corp, 61-72; USPHS fel, 63-67. *Mem:* Am Physiol Soc; Biomed Eng Soc. *Res:* Cell biophysics; ion transport. *Mailing Add:* Dept of Physiol Sch of Med Univ of SC Columbia SC 29208

WOLF, MERRILL KENNETH, b Cleveland, Ohio, Aug 28, 31; m 58. NEUROBIOLOGY, TISSUE CULTURE. *Educ:* Yale Col, BA, 45; Western Reserve Univ, MD, 56. *Prof Exp:* Intern med, Peter Bent Brigham Hosp, 56-57; res assoc, Nat Inst Neurol Dis & Blindness, 57-59; res fel neurol, Med Sch, Harvard Univ, 59-64, instr anat, 64-69, asst prof neuropath, 69-71, assoc prof, 71-72; PROF ANAT, MED SCH, UNIV MASS, 72-, PROF NEUROL, 78- *Concurrent Pos:* Lectr, Med Sch, Harvard Univ, 72-79; vis prof, Sch Med, Stanford Univ, 77. *Mem:* Am Asn Anatomists; Soc Neurosci; Tissue Cult Asn. *Res:* Neurological mutant mice with central nervous system disorders (organotypic culture and light and electromagnetic cytology); practical genetics. *Mailing Add:* Dept Anat Sch Med Univ Mass Worcester MA 01605

WOLF, MONTE WILLIAM, b Whittier, Calif, Sept 1, 49. ORGANIC CHEMISTRY. *Educ:* Univ Calif, Santa Barbara, BS, 71; Univ Southern Calif, PhD(org chem), 76. *Prof Exp:* Res org chem, Univ Calif, San Diego, 76-77; asst prof chem, Bethel Col, Minn, 77-78; vis asst prof, Univ Calif, San Diego, 78; ASSOC PROF CHEM, OGLETHORPE UNIV, 78- *Mem:* Sigma Xi; Am Chem Soc. *Res:* Photophysical processes of excited state aromatic ketones. *Mailing Add:* Oglethorpe Univ 4484 Peachtree Rd NE Atlanta GA 30319

WOLF, NEIL STEVEN, b Brooklyn, NY, Nov 15, 37; m 59; c 2. PLASMA PHYSICS. *Educ:* Queens Col, NY, BS, 58; Stevens Inst Technol, MS, 60, PhD(physics), 66. *Prof Exp:* Res assoc physics, Space Physics Labs, G C Dewey Corp, 65-67; asst prof, 67-72, chmn dept physics & astron, 74-77, assoc prof & coordr, Dept Sci, 72-80, PROF PHYSICS, DICKINSON COL, 80- *Concurrent Pos:* Res Corp Frederick Cottrell res grant, 67-; NSF fel, Univ Calif, Irvine, 81, vis assoc prof, 81-82; vis assoc prof, Univ Calif, Irvine, 81-82. *Mem:* Am Inst Physics. *Res:* Plasma physics related to control of instabilities in linear discharges immersed in strong magnetic fields; study of low frequency ionization waves which affect instabilities and plasma confinement. *Mailing Add:* Dept of Physics Dickinson Col Carlisle PA 17013

WOLF, NORMAN SANFORD, b Kansas City, Mo, July 22, 27; m 67, 76; c 1. EXPERIMENTAL PATHOLOGY, RADIOBIOLOGY. *Educ:* Kans State Univ, BS & DVM, 53; Northwestern Univ, PhD(exp path), 60; Am Col Lab Animal Med, dipl, 55. *Prof Exp:* Dir dept animal care, Med Sch, Northwestern Univ, 53-58; vis scientist, Pasteur Lab, Inst Radium, Paris,

60-61; consult radiation biol, Path & Physiol Sect, Biol Div, Oak Ridge Nat Lab, 61-62; res asst prof exp biol, Baylor Col Med, 62-68; ASSOC PROF PATH & MEM RADIOL SCI GROUP, SCH MED, UNIV WASH, 68- *Concurrent Pos:* NSF fel, Pasteur Lab, Inst Radium, Paris, 60-61; consult, Animal Quarters, Vet Admin Res Hosp, Chicago, 54-60 & Vet Admin Hosp, Seattle, 73-79. *Mem:* Radiation Res Soc; Am Soc Exp Path; Int Soc Exp Hemat. *Res:* Hematopoietic regeneration and transplantation following ionizing radiation; immune competence; hemopoietic stem cell identification; control of hematopoiesis by hematopoietic organ stroma; recovery after irradiation by cells and tissues; senescence of hemopoietic stem cells. *Mailing Add:* Dept of Path Univ of Wash Sch of Med Seattle WA 98195

WOLF, PAUL LEON, b Detroit, Mich, Oct 4, 28; m 52; c 3. PATHOLOGY. *Educ:* Wayne State Univ, BA, 48; Univ Mich, MD, 52; Am Bd Path, cert path anat & clin path, 60; Hebrew Univ, PhD(hons), 79. *Prof Exp:* Intern, Detroit Receiving Hosp, 52-53; resident path, Wayne State Univ Hosps, 56-60, from asst prof to prof, 60-68; dir clin lab, Med Ctr, Stanford Univ, 68-74; PROF PATH, UNIV CALIF, SAN DIEGO, 74- *Concurrent Pos:* Assoc, Detroit Receiving Hosp; mem staff, Dearborn Vet Admin Hosp. *Mem:* AMA; Am Soc Clin Path; Am Asn Path & Bact; Col Am Path. *Res:* Anatomic pathology; histochemistry; immunopathology; cancer immunology. *Mailing Add:* Univ Hosp PO Box 3548 225 W Dickensen San Diego CA 92103

WOLF, PAUL R, b Mazomanie, Wis, June 13, 34; m 59; c 3. PHOTOGRAMMETRY. *Educ:* Univ Wis-Madison, BSCE, 60, MSCE, 66, PhD(civil eng), 67. *Prof Exp:* Hwy engr, Wis Hwy Comn, 60-63; instr civil eng, Univ Wis-Madison, 63-67; asst prof, Univ Calif, Berkeley, 67-70; assoc prof, 70-77, PROF CIVIL & ENVIRON ENG, UNIV WIS-MADISON, 77- *Concurrent Pos:* Mem, panel geod & cartog, Nat Acad Sci, 72-74. *Honors & Awards:* Bausch & Lomb Photogram Award, 66; Talbert Abrams Award III, Am Soc Photogram, 71; Fennel Award, Am Cong Surv & Mapping, 79. *Mem:* Am Cong Surv & Mapping; Am Soc Photogram; Am Soc Civil Engrs. *Res:* Geodesy; cartography; least squares adjustments. *Mailing Add:* Dept of Civil & Environ Eng Univ of Wis Madison WI 53706

WOLF, PHILIP FRANK, b New York, NY, Apr 12, 38; div; c 3. PHYSICAL ORGANIC CHEMISTRY. *Educ:* NY Univ, BS, 60; Columbia Univ, MA, 61, PhD(org chem), 64. *Prof Exp:* Fel org chem, Yale Univ, 64-65; res chemist, 65-70, from proj scientist to res scientist, 70-74, group leader org chem, 74-76, sr res scientist, 76-77, ASSOC DIR RES & DEVELOP, UNION CARBIDE CORP, 77- *Mem:* Am Chem Soc. *Res:* Studies on oxidation-oxygen transfer mechanisms, substitution reactions of ethylene oxide, free radical telomerization, heterogeneous gas phase kinetics and Diels-Alder reactions. *Mailing Add:* Union Carbide Corp Tarrytown NY 10591

WOLF, RICHARD ALAN, b Pittsburgh, Pa, Nov 10, 39; m 71. SPACE PHYSICS, ASTROPHYSICS. *Educ:* Cornell Univ, BEngPhys, 62; Calif Inst Technol, PhD(nuclear astrophys), 66. *Prof Exp:* Res fel physics, Calif Inst Technol, 66; mem tech staff, Bel Tel Labs, 66-67; from asst prof to assoc prof space sci, 67-74, PROF Physics, SPACE PHYSICS & ASTRON, RICE UNIV, 74- *Concurrent Pos:* Mem, Inst Advan Study, 69 & 74-75. *Mem:* Am Phys Soc; Am Geophys Union. *Res:* Physics of the solar wind; magnetosphere and ionosphere. *Mailing Add:* Dept Space Physics & Astron Rice Univ Houston TX 77001

WOLF, RICHARD CLARENCE, b Lancaster, Pa, Nov 28, 26; m 52; c 2. PHYSIOLOGY, ENDOCRINOLOGY. *Educ:* Franklin & Marshall Col, BS, 50; Rutgers Univ, PhD(zool), 54. *Prof Exp:* Waksman-Merck fel, Rutgers Univ, New Brunswick, 54-55; Milton fel, Sch Dent Med, Harvard Univ, 55-56, USPHS fel, 56-57; asst prof physiol, Primate Lab, 57-61, assoc prof, 61-66, co-dir, 68-70, MEM ENDOCRINOL-REPROD PHYSIOL PROG, UNIV WIS-MADISON, 63-, DIR, 70-, PROF PHYSIOL, 66- CHMN DEPT, 71- *Concurrent Pos:* Mem res career award comt, NIH, 70-72, mem contract res & adv comt, 73-76; mem sci adv bd, Yerkes Regional Primate Res Ctr, Emory Univ, 72-; consult, Ford Found, 72- *Mem:* Soc Study Reprod; Endocrine Soc; Am Physiol Soc; Brit Soc Endocrinol; Brit Soc Study Fertil. *Res:* Endocrinology of pregnancy. *Mailing Add:* Dept of Physiol Univ of Wis Serv Mem Insts 470 N Charter St Madison WI 53706

WOLF, RICHARD EDWARD, JR, b Philadelphia, Pa, Mar 22, 41. MOLECULAR BIOLOGY. *Educ:* Univ Cincinnati, BA, 63, MS, 68, PhD(microbiol), 70. *Prof Exp:* Res fel microbiol & molecular genetics, Med Sch, Harvard Univ, 70-73, instr, 73-75; asst prof, 75-80, ASSOC PROF BIOL SCI, UNIV MD BALTIMORE COUNTY, 80- *Res:* Molecular mechanisms of growth rate-dependent regulation of gene expression. *Mailing Add:* Dept Biol Sci Univ Md Baltimore County Cantonsville MD 21228

WOLF, RICHARD EUGENE, b Dixon, Ill, June 25, 36; m 60; c 3. ORGANIC CHEMISTRY, POLYMER CHEMISTRY. *Educ:* Northern Ill Univ, BSEd, 57; Univ San Francisco, MS, 65; Univ Calif, Berkeley, PhD(chem), 68. *Prof Exp:* Sect leader org synthesis, 68-70, mgr, Long Range Res Dept, 70-74, res scientist, 74-77, contract & explor res mgr, 77-79, DIR INT LICENSING, DESOTO, INC, 79- *Concurrent Pos:* Chmn patent comt, DeSoto, Inc, 71-76, chmn basic res comt, 74-76. *Mem:* Am Chem Soc; Fedn Socs Paint Technol; Nat Micrographics Asn; fel Am Inst Chem. *Res:* Photochemistry; photoconduction in organic molecules; photopolymerization; emulsion polymerization; coatings technology; water treatment. *Mailing Add:* DeSoto Inc 1700 S Mt Prospect Rd Des Plaines IL 60018

WOLF, ROBERT LAWRENCE, b New York, NY, Aug 7, 28; m 57; c 1. PHYSIOLOGY, BIOCHEMISTRY. *Educ:* Duke Univ, BS, 50, MD, 52; Am Bd Internal Med, dipl, 66. *Prof Exp:* Intern med & surg serv, Mt Sinai Hosp, 52-53, chief resident path, 53-54, asst resident med, 56-57, chief resident, 57-58, clin asst, Mt Sinai Hosp & Mt Sinai Sch Med, 58-65, res asst, 60-66, ASST CLIN PROF MED, MT SINAI SCH MED, 66- *Concurrent Pos:* Arthritis & Rheumatism Found res fel, 58-59; res fel med, Mt Sinai Hosp, 58-61; AEC byprod mat license for res, 59-; var pharmaceut corps res grants, 59-; USPHS res grants, 59-; Lupus Erhthematosus Found, Inc res grants, 61-; mem coun high blood pressure res & coun circulation, Am Heart Asn; asst attend physician, Mt Sinai Hosp, 65-; Syntex Res Found res grants, 65-; Ciba Co res grant, 66; guest lectr, Nat Univ Colombia, 66, Cath Univ Chile, 66 & Inst Med Res, Univ SAm, Buenos Aires, 66; G D Searle & Co res grant, 66-68; Health Res Coun of City New York res grant, 66-69; US partic, Int Atomic Energy Agency Symp Radioimmunoassay & Related Procedures in Clin Med & Res, Istanbul, Turkey, 73; consult ed, AMA Drug Eval, 73-74. *Mem:* Am Nuclear Soc; Am Physiol Soc; fel Am Col Physicians; Am Soc Internal Med; Am Col Chest Physicians. *Res:* Hypertension; circulatory physiology and cardiology. *Mailing Add:* Dept of Med Mt Sinai Sch of Med New York NY 10029

WOLF, ROBERT OLIVER, b Mansfield, Ohio, Mar 14, 25; m 70; c 2. ORAL BIOLOGY. *Educ:* NCent Col, BA, 50; Ohio State Univ, MA, 52, DDS, 58. *Prof Exp:* Res asst physiol genetics, Ohio State Univ, 52-54; res asst oral biol, Col Dent, 57-58; comn officer, USPHS, 58; intern clin dent, USPHS Hosp, New Orleans, La, 58-59; investr salivary physiol & biochem, Human Genetics Br, Nat Inst Dent Res, 59-70, Oral Med & Surg Br, 70-73, Lab Oral Med, 73-77 & Clin Invest Br, 77-81; PRIN INVESTR, SALIVARY PHYSIOL & BIOCHEM, LAB BIOL STRUCT, NAT INST DENT RES, 81- *Concurrent Pos:* Clin assoc prof, Sch Dent, Georgetown Univ, 80- *Mem:* Am Dent Asn; Am Soc Human Genetics; Int Asn Dent Res; Am Inst Biol Sci; Potomac Appalachian Trail Club (pres, 74-76). *Res:* Human and animal salivary physiology, biochemistry, enzymology and genetics, especially isoamylases; human salivary gland disease, diagnosis and treatment. *Mailing Add:* Rm 2B-13 Bldg 10 Nat Inst of Dent Res Bethesda MD 20205

WOLF, ROBERT PETER, b Long Branch, NJ, Oct 27, 39; m 60; c 2. SOLID STATE PHYSICS, ENVIRONMENTAL PHYSICS. *Educ:* Mass Inst Technol, BS, 60, PhD(physics), 63. *Prof Exp:* From asst prof to assoc prof, 63-74, PROF PHYSICS, HARVEY MUDD COL, 74- *Concurrent Pos:* NSF sci faculty fel, Oxford Univ, 69-70; vis scientist, Mass Inst Technol, 76. *Res:* Energy resources; phase transitions; solar energy development; philosophy of science. *Mailing Add:* Dept of Physics Harvey Mudd Col Claremont CA 91711

WOLF, ROBERT STANLEY, b New York, NY, May 14, 46; m 75. MATHEMATICAL LOGIC. *Educ:* Mass Inst Technol, BS, 66; Stanford Univ, MS, 67, PhD(math), 74. *Prof Exp:* Vis asst prof math, Univ Ore, 73-74; vis scholar, Stanford Univ, 74-75; lectr math, 75-80, ASSOC PROF MATH, CALIF POLYTECH STATE UNIV, SAN LUIS OBISPO, 80- *Mem:* Am Math Soc; Asn Symbolic Logic. *Res:* Continuing study of set theories with intuitionistic logic; theory of infinite games, specifically Almost-Borel games; point-set topology, mathematical biology, artificial intelligence and mathematics education. *Mailing Add:* Dept of Math Calif Polytech State Univ San Luis Obispo CA 93407

WOLF, ROBERT V(ALENTIN), b St Louis, Mo, June 5, 29. METALLURGICAL ENGINEERING. *Educ:* Univ Mo, BS, 51, MS, 52. *Prof Exp:* From instr to assoc prof, 51-67, PROF METALL ENG, SCH MINES, UNIV MO-ROLLA, 67-, ASST DEAN, SCH MINES & METALL, 81- *Concurrent Pos:* Partner, Askeland, Kisslinger & Wolf. *Mem:* Am Soc Metals; Am Foundrymen's Soc; Am Inst Mining & Metall Engrs; Am Soc Nondestructive Testing; Am Welding Soc. *Res:* Metals casting; nondestructive testing. *Mailing Add:* Dept of Metall Eng Univ of Mo Rolla MO 65401

WOLF, STANLEY MYRON, b Washington, DC, July 12, 39; m 63; c 1. METALLURGICAL ENGINEERING, MATERIALS SCIENCE. *Educ:* Va Polytech Inst & State Univ, BS, 60; Cornell Univ, MS, 63; Mass Inst Technol, PhD(metall), 72. *Prof Exp:* Metallurgist res & develop, Mat & Control Div, Tex Instruments, 62-63; researcher, US Army Mat Res Agency, 64-66, chief data processing br, Eighth US Army Hq, 66-67, metallurgist, US Army Mat & Mech Res Ctr, 71-74; metallurgist res, AEC, 74-75; metallurgist, ERDA, 75-77; METALLURGIST, US DEPT ENERGY, 77- *Mem:* Am Inst Metall Engrs; Am Soc Metals; Nat Asn Corrosion Engrs; Am Soc Testing Mat. *Res:* Mechanical and structural stability of metals, ceramics and polymers, including glasses, coatings and weld/braze joints; aqueous and gaseous corrosion; powder metallurgy; structure-property-processing correlations; research administration and program management. *Mailing Add:* Mat Sci Div US Dept of Energy Washington DC 20545

WOLF, STEPHEN NOLL, b Biloxi, Miss, Dec 4, 44; m 74. ACOUSTICS. *Educ:* Lebanon Valley Col, BS, 66; Univ Md, PhD(molecular spectros), 72. *Prof Exp:* RES PHYSICIST UNDERWATER ACOUSTICS, US NAVAL RES LAB, 71- *Mem:* Sigma Xi. *Res:* At-sea experimental studies of acoustic propagation of sound in shallow water. *Mailing Add:* Code 5120 US Naval Res Lab Overlook Ave Washington DC 20375

WOLF, STEWART GEORGE, JR, b Baltimore, Md, Jan 12, 14; m 42; c 3. INTERNAL MEDICINE, PHYSIOLOGY. *Educ:* Johns Hopkins Univ, AB, 34, MD, 38. *Hon Degrees:* MD, Gothenburg Univ, 68. *Prof Exp:* Intern med, NY Hosp, 38-39, from asst resident to resident, 39-42; from asst prof to assoc prof med, Med Col, Cornell Univ, 46-52; prof med & consult prof psychiat, Sch Med, Univ Okla, 52-67, regents prof med, psychiat, neurol & behav sci, 67-70, head dept med, 52-69, prof physiol, Sch Med, 68-70; prof med, Univ Tex Syst, 70-77; dir, Marine Biomed Inst, 70-77; prof internal med & physiol, Univ Tex Med Br Galveston, 70-77; PROF MED, TEMPLE UNIV, V PRES MED AFFAIRS & MEM STAFF, ST LUKES HOSP, BETHLEHEM, PA, 77- *Concurrent Pos:* Res fel, Bellevue Hosp, 39-42; Nat Res Coun fel, Cornell Univ, 41-42; assoc vis neuropsychiatrist, Bellevue Hosp, 48-52; asst attend physician in charge psychosom clin, Cornell Univ, 46-52; mem comt psychiat, Nat Res Coun, 48-52, mem comt vet med probs, 51-52; head psychosom sect, Okla Med Res Found, 52-, head neurosci sect, 67-70; mem spec study group, Off Res & Develop, Dept Defense, 52-55; mem pharmacol & exp therapeut study sect, 56-57; mem comt prof educ, 56-63, chmn, 57-63; mem gen med study sect, NIH, 57-61, chmn gastroenterol training grant comt, 58-61; mem adv comt, Space Med & Behav Sci, NASA, 60-61 & Nat Adv Heart Coun,

61-65; mem coun ment health, AMA, 60-64; consult, Europ Off, Off Int Res, NIH, 63-64; mem adv comt admis, Nat Formulary, 65-69; mem bd regents, Nat Libr Med, 65-69, chmn, 68-69; mem comt int progs, Am Heart Asn, 65-, chmn, 65-70; mem educ & supply panel, Nat Adv Comn Health Manpower, 66-67; mem, Nat Adv Environ Health Sci Coun, 78 & 81; mem bd visitors, Dept Biol, Boston Univ, 78. *Honors & Awards:* Award, Am Gastroenterol Asn, 42; Hofheimer Prize, Am Psychiat Asn, 53; Award of Merit, Am Heart Asn, 64, Citation Int Achievement, 77; Distinguished Serv Citation, Univ Okla, 68. *Mem:* Am Psychosom Soc (past pres); Am Gastroenterol Asn (pres, 69-70); fel Am Col Physicians; Pavlovian Soc (pres, 66-67); Am Col Clin Pharmacol & Chemother (pres, 66-67). *Res:* Gastrointestinal, cardiovascular, sensory and neural physiology. *Mailing Add:* St Lukes Hosp 801 Ostrum St Bethlehem PA 18015

WOLF, STUART ALAN, b Brooklyn, NY, Sept 15, 43; m 65; c 2. SOLID STATE PHYSICS. *Educ:* Columbia Col, AB, 64; Rutgers Univ, MS, 66, PhD(physics), 69. *Prof Exp:* Res assoc physics, Case Western Reserve Univ, 69-72; RES PHYSICIST PHYSICS, US NAVAL RES LAB, 72- *Concurrent Pos:* Assoc prof & lectr, George Washington Univ, 79-; panel mem, Interagency Advan Power Group-Superconductivity Panel, 80-; vis scholar, Univ Calif, Los Angeles, 81-82. *Mem:* Am Phys Soc; Am Vacuum Soc; Sigma Xi. *Res:* Cryogenics; superconductivity; transport properties; vacuum system design; thin films; magnetic shielding; Josephison devices. *Mailing Add:* Naval Res Lab Code 6634 Washington DC 20375

WOLF, THOMAS, b Sept 10, 32; US citizen; m 59; c 2. ANALYTICAL CHEMISTRY. *Educ:* Cambridge Univ, BA, 55, MA, 61; Univ RI, PhD(anal chem), 66. *Prof Exp:* Chemist, Coates Bros, Eng, 55-57; lab supvr, Wymat Corp, NJ, 57-58; chemist, Enthone Inc, Conn, 58-59 & Eltex Res Corp, RI, 59-62; sr res chemist, 66-75, RES ASSOC, COLGATE-PALMOLIVE CO, 75- *Concurrent Pos:* Course dir, Ctr Prof Advan, 79- *Mem:* Am Chem Soc; Am Soc Testing & Mat. *Res:* Analytical research, with particular reference to liquid chromatography, to thermal analysis and to laboratory automation. *Mailing Add:* Colgate-Palmolive Co 909 River Rd Piscataway NJ 08854

WOLF, THOMAS MICHAEL, b Highland Park, Mich, Dec 28, 42; c 2. GENETICS, ENVIRONMENTAL BIOLOGY. *Educ:* Western Mich Univ, BS, 65; Wayne State Univ, MS, 67, PhD(genetics), 72. *Prof Exp:* Instr, 71-72, asst prof, 72-80, ASSOC PROF BIOL, WASHBURN UNIV, TOPEKA, 80- *Mem:* Genetics Soc Am. *Res:* Human karyo-typing and human histocompatibility genetics. *Mailing Add:* 2413 SE Alexander Topeka KS 66605

WOLF, WALTER, b Frankfort, Ger, May 25, 31; US citizen; m 55; c 2. RADIOCHEMISTRY, RADIOPHARMACY. *Educ:* Univ of the Repub, Uruguay, BSc, 49, MS, 52; Univ Paris, PhD, 56. *Prof Exp:* Asst chem, Univ of the Repub, Uruguay, 51-52; asst chem, Nat Cent Sci Res, France, 55-56, attache, 56; assoc prof org chem & biochem, Concepcion Univ, 56-58; traveling fel, McGill Univ, 58; res assoc, Amherst Col, 58-59; res assoc org chem, 59-62, vis asst prof pharmaecut chem, 61-62, from asst prof to assoc prof, 62-70, chmn dept biomed chem, 70-74, PROF BIOMED CHEM, UNIV SOUTHERN CALIF, 70-, DIR, RADIOPHARM PROG, 68-; DIR RADIOPHARM SERV, LOS ANGELES COUNTY-UNIV SOUTHERN CALIF MED CTR, 70- *Concurrent Pos:* Consult radiopharm, Int Atomic Energy Agency & US Vet Admin. *Honors & Awards:* G Czezniak Prize Nuclear Med, Israel, 80. *Mem:* Am Chem Soc; Soc Nuclear Med; Fr Soc Biol Chem; Radiation Res Soc; Acad Pharmaceut Sci. *Res:* New radiopharmaceuticals, especially in clinical pharmacology; chemistry and biochemistry of organic iodo compounds; radioiodination; electron spin resonance of free radicals; radiopharmacokinetics; chelation of radiometals. *Mailing Add:* Radiopharm Prog Sch Pharm Univ Southern Calif Los Angeles CA 90033

WOLF, WALTER ALAN, b New York, NY, Mar 9, 42; m 62; c 2. BIOCHEMISTRY, ORGANIC CHEMISTRY. *Educ:* Wesleyan Univ, BA, 62; Brandeis Univ, MA, 64, PhD(org chem), 67. *Prof Exp:* Fel, Mass Inst Technol, 67-70; asst prof biochem, Colgate Univ, 70-77; asst prof, 77-80, ASSOC PROF CHEM, EISENHOWER UNIV, 80- *Concurrent Pos:* Vis prof, State Univ NY Agr & Tech Col Morrisville, 71-72, State Agr Exp Sta, Geneva; ed, Chem Ed Compacts, J Chem Educ. res corp grant, Colgate Univ, 71-72. *Mem:* AAAS; Am Chem Soc; Royal Soc Chem. *Res:* Pheromone biosynthesis; vitamin B12 models; enzymology. *Mailing Add:* Dept of Chem Eisenhower Col Seneca Falls NY 13346

WOLF, WALTER J, b Hague, NDak, May 2, 27; m 49; c 5. BIOCHEMISTRY. *Educ:* Col St Thomas, BS, 50; Univ Minn, PhD(biochem), 56. *Prof Exp:* Assoc chemist, 56-58, chemist, 58-61, prin chemist, 61-68, LEADER MEAL PROD RES, NORTHERN REGIONAL RES CTR, USDA, 68- *Concurrent Pos:* Assoc ed, Cereal Chem, 70-73 & Cereal Sci Today, 70-73. *Mem:* AAAS; Am Asn Cereal Chemists; Am Chem Soc; Am Oil Chemists Soc; Inst Food Technologists. *Res:* Isolation and characterization of soybean proteins; protein interactions, denaturation and structure; food uses of soybean proteins. *Mailing Add:* Northern Regional Res Ctr 1815 N University St Peoria IL 61604

WOLF, WARREN WALTER, b Oakdale, Pa, Dec 10, 41; m 74; c 2. GLASS SCIENCE, CERAMICS ENGINEERING. *Educ:* Pa State Univ, University Park, BS, 63; Ohio State Univ, PhD(ceramic eng), 68; Xavier Univ, MBA, 77. *Prof Exp:* Res engr, Ferro Corp, 63-65; sr scientist glass technol, 68-75, supvr glass res & develop, 75-78, MGR GLASS RES & DEVELOP, OWENS-CORNING FIBERGLAS CORP, 78- *Mem:* Brit Soc Glass Technol; Am Ceramic Soc; Nat Inst Ceramic Engrs; AAAS. *Res:* Glass fibers, especially high tensile strength glass fibers; alkali resistant glass for portland cement reinforcement; textile fibers; glass surface chemistry; high temperature glass properties; glass structural investigations. *Mailing Add:* 8056 Eliot Dr Reynoldsburg OH 43068

WOLF, WAYNE ROBERT, b Kenton, Ohio, May 18, 43; m 71. ANALYTICAL CHEMISTRY, NUTRITION. *Educ:* Kent State Univ, BS, 65, PhD(chem), 69. *Prof Exp:* Res chemist, Aerospace Res Lab, US Air Force, Wright-Patterson AFB, Ohio, 67-71; Nat Res Coun assoc, 71-72, res chemist, Human Nutrit Res Div, Agr Res Serv, 71-75, RES CHEMIST, NUTRIENT COMPOSITION LAB, NUTRIT CTR, USDA, 75- *Mem:* AAAS; Am Chem Soc; Am Inst Chem. *Res:* Instrumental analytical methodology for nutrient content of foods, trace element nutrition, biological availability of trace elements; atomic absorption spectrometry; optical emission spectrometry; gas-liquid chromatography. *Mailing Add:* Nutrient Compos Lab Nutrit Ctr USDA Beltsville MD 20705

WOLF, WERNER PAUL, b Vienna, Austria, Apr 22, 30; nat US; m 54; c 2. PHYSICS. *Educ:* Oxford Univ, BA, 51, MA & DPhil(physics), 54. *Hon Degrees:* MA, Yale Univ, 65. *Prof Exp:* Res assoc physics, Clarendon Lab, Oxford Univ, 54-56, Imp Chem Industs res fel, 57-59; res fel appl physics, Harvard Univ, 56-57; univ lectr physics, Oxford Univ, 59-63; assoc prof, 63-65, prof physics & appl sci, 65-76, Becton prof & chmn, Dept Eng & Appl Sci, 76-81, BECTON PROF & CHMN, COUN ENG, YALE UNIV, 81- *Concurrent Pos:* Consult, Hughes Aircraft Co & E I du Pont de Nemours & Co, Inc, 57, Gen Elec Co, 60 & 66-, Mullard Res Labs, 61, Int Bus Mach Corp, 62-66 & IBM Watson Res Ctr, Yorktown Heights, 62-66; res collabr, Brookhaven Nat Lab, 66-; mem, Orgn Prog Comt, Int Congress on Magnetism, 67, Int Prog Comt, 78-79 & planning comt, 79-80; prog comt chmn, 68, Conf Magnetism & Magnetic Mat, 68, gen conf chmn, 71, adv comt chmn, 71-72; vis prof, Munich Tech Univ, 69; sr vis fel, Oxford Univ, 80. *Mem:* Am Asn Crystal Growth; fel Am Phys Soc; Sigma Xi; sr mem Inst Elec & Electronics Eng. *Res:* Magnetism; experimental and theoretical study of magnetic materials, especially at low temperatures; magnetic cooling, relaxation, microwave resonance, optical properties, crystal fields and anisotropy; magnetic thermal properties, critical points and magnetic phase transitions; synthesis of new materials and growth of single crystals. *Mailing Add:* Becton Ctr Yale Univ PO Box 2157 New Haven CT 06520

WOLFARTH, EUGENE F, b Washington, DC, June 24, 32; m 57; c 3. PHYSICAL ORGANIC CHEMISTRY. *Educ:* Univ Md, BS, 54; Ohio State Univ, PhD(chem), 61. *Prof Exp:* Res chemist res & develop command, Wright Patterson Air Force Base, Ohio, 57; asst instr chem, Ohio State Univ, 58-60; res assoc, Res Labs, 61-76, MGR, KODAK LEGAL DEPT, LITIGATION GROUP, EASTMAN KODAK CO, 76- *Mem:* Am Chem Soc. *Res:* Kinetics and reaction mechanisms; organic synthesis; color photography, the mechanisms of development and designing new film systems. *Mailing Add:* 19 Rippingale Rd Pittsford NY 14534

WOLFE, ALAN DAVID, b New York, NY, Mar 25, 29; m 69. BIOCHEMISTRY, MICROBIOLOGY. *Educ:* Queens Col, NY, BS, 52; Mass Inst Technol, SM, 56, George Washington Univ, JD, 62; Univ Md, College Park, PhD(microbiol), 70. *Prof Exp:* Molecular biologist, 58-76, ASST CHIEF BIOCHEM, WALTER REED ARMY INST RES, 76- *Concurrent Pos:* Secy Army fel, US Dept Defense, 72-73. *Mem:* Am Soc Microbiol; AAAS. *Res:* Molecular biology and pharmacology of malaria; biochemistry of bacterial toxins; protein and nucleic acid synthesis; the mode of action of growth inhibitors. *Mailing Add:* Dept of Biol Chem Walter Reed Army Med Ctr Washington DC 20012

WOLFE, ALLAN FREDERICK, b Olyphant, Pa, Oct 22, 38; m 63; c 3. INVERTEBRATE PHYSIOLOGY, HISTOLOGY. *Educ:* Gettysburg Col, BA, 63; Drake Univ, MA, 65; Univ Vt, PhD(zool), 68. *Prof Exp:* ASSOC PROF BIOL, LEBANON VALLEY COL, 68- *Mem:* AAAS; Am Soc Zool; Am Inst Biol Sci. *Res:* Histology and physiology of Artemia salina; invertebrate reproductive systems. *Mailing Add:* Dept of Biol Lebanon Valley Col Anneville PA 17003

WOLFE, ALLAN MARVIN, b New York, NY, Nov 4, 37; m 64; c 3. MEDICINE, METABOLISM. *Educ:* Cornell Univ, MB, 58; NY Univ, MD, 62. *Prof Exp:* Asst instr med, State Univ NY Downstate Med Ctr, 64-66; diabetes & arthritis consult & chief educ & info control prog, Nat Ctr Chronic Dis Control, 66-68; clin asst prof med, State Univ NY Downstate Med Ctr, 68-72; med dir, Arthritis Found, NY Chap, 68-70; dir med res infrared eng, Barnes Eng Co, 69-71, dir med mkt, 70-71; dir med res devices & instrumentation, Survival Technol Inc, 71-75; V PRES RES & DEVELOP PHARMACEUT, MCGAW LABS DIV, AM HOSP SUPPLY CORP, 75- *Concurrent Pos:* Prin investr, Voc Rehab Serv, 68-69, Arthritis Ctr Prog, Pub Health Serv, 69-72, Mayor's Orgn Task Force Comprehensive Health Planning, 70-72 & Sudden Cardiac Death & Onset Myocardial Infarction, 71-73. *Mem:* AMA; Am Soc Parenteral & Enteral Nutrit. *Res:* Human metabolism; amino acid chemistry; medical devices; parenteral pharmacologic agents. *Mailing Add:* McGaw Labs Div 2525 McGaw Ave Irvine CA 92714

WOLFE, BERNARD MARTIN, b Killdeer, Sask, Dec 31, 34; m 70. MEDICINE, BIOCHEMISTRY. *Educ:* Univ Sask, BA, 56; Oxford Univ, BM, BCh, 63, MA, 67; McGill Univ, MSc, 67; FRCPS(C), 68. *Prof Exp:* House physician & surgeon med, Guy's Hosp, London, Eng, 63-64; from jr asst resident to sr asst resident, Royal Victoria Hosp, Montreal, Que, 64-68; Med Res Coun Can centennial fel, Cardiovasc Res Inst, Med Ctr, Univ Calif, San Francisco, 68-70; asst prof, 70-73, assoc prof, 73-80, PROF MED, UNIV WESTERN ONT, 80- *Concurrent Pos:* Consult & chief endocrinol & metab, Univ Hosp, London, Ont, 72-; mem coun on arteriosclerosis, Am Heart Asn; hon lectr biochem, Univ Western Ont, 72-80. *Mem:* Can Soc Clin Invest; Can Soc Endocrinol & Metab; Am Fedn Clin Res; Can Med Asn. *Res:* Clinical investigation of the effects of diets and drugs on lipid, carbohydrate and amino acid metabolism in man and experimental animals. *Mailing Add:* 17 Metamora Crescent London ON N6G 1R2 Can

WOLFE, BERTRAM, b US, June 26, 27; m 50; c 3. NUCLEAR PHYSICS, NUCLEAR ENGINEERING. *Educ:* Princeton Univ, BA, 50; Cornell Univ, PhD(nuclear physics), 54. *Prof Exp:* Physicist, Eastman Kodak Co, 54-55; physicist, Nuclear Energy Div, Gen Elec Co, 55-56, mgr develop reactor physics, 57-59, mgr conceptual design & anal, 59-64, mgr plant eng & develop, Advan Prod Oper, 64-69; assoc dir, Pac Northwest Labs, Battelle Mem Inst, 69-70; vpres & tech dir, Wadco Corp, 70; gen mgr, Breeder Reactor Dept, 70-73, gen mgr, Fuel Recovery & Irradiation Prod Dept, 74-78, VPRES & GEN MGR, NUCLEAR ENERGY PROGS DIV, GEN ELEC CO, 78- *Concurrent Pos:* Mem, Atomic Indust Forum. *Mem:* AAAS; Am Phys Soc; fel Am Nuclear Soc. *Res:* Nuclear power technology; advanced energy technology. *Mailing Add:* 15453 Via Vaquero Monte Sereno CA 95030

WOLFE, CALEB WROE, b Washington, DC, Oct 22, 08; m 57; c 6. GEOLOGY. *Educ:* River Falls State Teachers Col, BE, 30; Harvard Univ, MA, 35, PhD(mineral), 40. *Prof Exp:* Asst, Harvard Univ, 37-41; from asst to prof, 41-74, EMER PROF GEOL, BOSTON UNIV, 74-; PROF GEOL, SALEM STATE COL, 74- *Concurrent Pos:* Prod engr, Raytheon Co, 44; crystallog consult, Lincoln Labs, 61-64. *Honors & Awards:* Neil Miner Award, Nat Asn Geol Teachers, Distinguished Alumnus Award, Univ Wis-River Falls, 78. *Mem:* Fel Geol Soc Am; fel Am Mineral Soc. *Res:* Geometrical crystallography; genetic mineralogy; mountain building geophysics. *Mailing Add:* Dept of Geol Salem State Col Salem MA 01970

WOLFE, CARVEL STEWART, b Minneapolis, Minn, June 11, 27; m 54; c 3. MATHEMATICS. *Educ:* Univ Ariz, BS, 50, MS, 51. *Prof Exp:* Asst math, Univ Wash, 51-53; asst prof, Shepherd State Col, 53-54; asst, Univ Md, 54-56; asst prof, 56-63, ASSOC PROF MATH, US NAVAL ACAD, 63- *Mem:* AAAS; Am Math Soc; Math Asn Am. *Res:* Numerical analysis; linear programming; integer programming. *Mailing Add:* Dept of Math US Naval Acad Annapolis MD 21402

WOLFE, CHARLES MORGAN, b Morgantown, WVa, Dec 21, 35; m 59; c 2. ELECTRICAL ENGINEERING, SOLID STATE ELECTRONICS. *Educ:* Univ WVa, BSEE, 61, MSEE, 62; Univ Ill, PhD(elec eng), 65. *Prof Exp:* Mem staff, Lincoln Lab, Mass Inst Technol, 65-75; PROF ELEC ENG, WASH UNIV, 75-, DIR SEMICONDUCTOR RES LAB, 79- *Honors & Awards:* Electronics Award, Electrochem Soc, 78. *Mem:* AAAS; Am Asn Univ Prof; fel Inst Elec & Electronics Engrs; Am Phys Soc; Electrochem Soc. *Res:* Preparation and characterization of semiconductor materials for solid state devices. *Mailing Add:* Wash Univ Box 1127 St Louis MO 63130

WOLFE, DAVID FRANCIS ZEKE, b Lost Creek, WVa, Dec 10, 37; m 60; c 3. PHYSICAL CHEMISTRY. *Educ:* WVa Wesleyan Col, BS, 60; Univ WVa, MS, 62, PhD(phys chem), 67. *Prof Exp:* Asst chem, Univ WVa, 60-62, part-time instr, 62-65; from instr to assoc prof, 65-77, PROF CHEM, WVA WESLEYAN COL, 77- *Concurrent Pos:* Vis asst prof, Univ WVa, 67 & 68. *Mem:* Am Chem Soc. *Res:* Grignard reactions of 9-phenanthrenemethyl magnesium chloride; transfer of force constants from pure to mixed halides of boron. *Mailing Add:* Dept of Chem WVa Wesleyan Col Buckhannon WV 26201

WOLFE, DAVID M, b Philadelphia, Pa, Oct 27, 38; m 65; c 2. HIGH ENERGY PHYSICS. *Educ:* Univ Pa, BA, 59, MS, 61, PhD(physics), 66. *Prof Exp:* Res assoc physics, Enrico Fermi Inst, Univ Chicago, 66-69; vis asst prof physics, Univ Wash, 69-71; from asst prof to assoc prof, 71-79, PROF PHYSICS, UNIV NMEX, 79- *Mem:* Am Phys Soc; Fedn Am Scientists; Sigma Xi. *Res:* Experimental research in the nucleon-nucleon and antinucleon-nucleon interactions. *Mailing Add:* Dept Physics & Astron Univ of NMex Albuquerque NM 87131

WOLFE, DOROTHY WEXLER, b Springfield, Ill, Aug 20, 20; m 42; c 1. MATHEMATICS. *Educ:* Univ Ill, BS, 41; Wayne State Univ, MA, 53; Univ Pa, PhD(math), 66. *Prof Exp:* Asst math, Univ Pa, 54-55; instr, Swarthmore Col, 62-64; asst prof, 65-69, ASSOC PROF MATH, WIDENER UNIV, 69- *Mem:* Am Math Soc; Math Asn Am. *Res:* Combinatorics; metric spaces. *Mailing Add:* Dept of Math Widener Univ Chester PA 19013

WOLFE, DOUGLAS ARTHUR, b Dayton, Ohio, July 6, 39; m 59; c 3. MARINE CHEMISTRY, POLLUTION BIOLOGY. *Educ:* Ohio State Univ, BSc, 59, MSc, 61, PhD(physiol chem), 64; Stanford Univ, MSc, 81. *Prof Exp:* Chief biogeochem prog, Radiobiol Lab, US Bur Com Fisheries, 64-70; dir estuarine res, Atlantic Estuarine Fisheries Ctr, Nat Marine Fisheries Serv, 70-75; staff dir ecol, 75-77, dep dir, Outer Continental Shelf Environ Assessment Prog, 77-81, DIR OPER PROGS, OFF MARINE POLLUTION ASSESSMENT, NAT OCEANIC & ATMOSPHERIC ADMIN, 81- *Concurrent Pos:* Adj asst prof, NC State Univ, 66-70, adj assoc prof, 70-75; chief scientist I marine biol, Nuclear Ctr, PR, 69-70; consult, Panel on Zinc, Nat Acad Sci, 73-75; proj mgr, Nat Oceanic & Atmospheric Admin-Environ Protection Agency, Energy Proj on Fate & Effects of Petrol, 75-80; mem, Nat Oceanic & Atmospheric Admin-Ctr Nat Exploitation of Oceans, Int Comn for Study of the Ecol Effects of the Amoco Cadiz Oil Spill, 78- *Mem:* Estuarine Res Fedn; Am Chem Soc; Ecol Soc Am; Am Malacol Union; Am Soc Limnol & Oceanog. *Res:* Comparative biochemistry of carotenoids and lipids; ecology and biology of molluscs; petroleum, radioisotopes and trace metals in marine environment. *Mailing Add:* Off Marine Pollution Assessment Nat Oceanic & Atmospheric Admin 325 Broadway Boulder CO 80303

WOLFE, EDWARD W, b Brooklyn, NY, Jan 21, 36; m 56; c 5. GEOLOGY. *Educ:* Col Wooster, BA, 57; Ohio State Univ, PhD(geol), 61. *Prof Exp:* Instr geol, Col Wooster, 59-61; GEOLOGIST, US GEOL SURV, 61- *Mem:* AAAS; Geol Soc Am; Sigma Xi; Am Geophys Union. *Res:* Areal geology and volcanology. *Mailing Add:* US Geol Surv 2255 N Gemini Dr Flagstaff AZ 86001

WOLFE, GORDON A, b Chicago, Ill, Sept 8, 31; m 56; c 2. SOLID STATE PHYSICS. *Educ:* Ill Inst Technol, BS, 60; Univ Mo, MS, 63, PhD(physics), 67. *Prof Exp:* Instr physics, Univ Mo, 64-67; asst prof, 67-74, ASSOC PROF PHYSICS, SOUTHERN ORE STATE COL, 74- *Mem:* AAAS; Am Asn Physics Teachers. *Res:* Anharmonic effects in crystals. *Mailing Add:* Dept of Physics Southern Ore State Col Ashland OR 97520

WOLFE, HARRY BERNARD, b Vancouver, BC, Dec 29, 27; m 52; c 4. OPERATIONS RESEARCH. *Educ:* Univ BC, BA, 49, MA, 51; Columbia Univ, PhD(physics), 56. *Prof Exp:* Sr staff mem oper res, Mass, 56-63, mgr, San Francisco Opers Res Group, Calif, 63-69, SR STAFF MEM, HEALTH CARE SECT, ARTHUR D LITTLE, INC, MASS, 69- *Mem:* Inst Mgt Sci; Opers Res Soc Am; Can Opers Res Soc. *Res:* Health care; hospitals; management science, including inventory and scheduling theory and marketing analysis; nuclear physics. *Mailing Add:* Arthur D Little Inc 35 Acorn Park Cambridge MA 02140

WOLFE, HARVEY, b Baltimore, Md, Apr 14, 38; m 59; c 4. OPERATIONS RESEARCH, STATISTICS. *Educ:* Johns Hopkins Univ, BES, 60, MSE, 62, PhD(opers res), 64. *Prof Exp:* Opers res asst, Johns Hopkins Hosp, 60-64, opers res assoc, 64; from asst prof to assoc prof, 64-72, PROF INDUST ENG, UNIV PITTSBURGH, 72- *Concurrent Pos:* Res assoc, Grad Sch Pub Health, Univ Pittsburgh, 64-67, adj assoc prof, 67-77, prof, 77-, mem grad fac, 66-; consult, Blue Cross Western Pa, 65-, dir res, 67-69; consult, Dept Med & Surg Study Group, Vet Admin, 66-72, Nat Ctr Health Serv Res, Dept Health, Educ & Welfare, 67-, Social Security Admin, 73- & Blue Cross/Blue Shield Greater New York, 75- *Mem:* Opers Res Soc Am; Am Inst Indust Engrs; Am Pub Health Asn; Inst Mgt Sci. *Res:* Applications of operations research to the health services. *Mailing Add:* Dept of Indust Eng Univ of Pittsburgh Pittsburgh PA 15261

WOLFE, HERBERT GLENN, b Uniontown, Kans, Mar 14, 28; m 50; c 3. DEVELOPMENTAL GENETICS. *Educ:* Kans State Univ, BS, 49; Univ Kans, PhD(zool), 60. *Prof Exp:* Assoc staff scientist physiol genetics, Jackson Lab, Maine, 60-63; from asst prof to assoc prof, 63-70, PROF PHYSIOL GENETICS, UNIV KANS, 70- *Concurrent Pos:* Mem genetics standards subcomt, Inst Lab Animal Resources, 65-68; NIH spec res fel, Harwell, Eng, 69-70; vis scientist, Worcester Found for Exp Biol, Shrewsbury, Mass, 77. *Mem:* Soc Develop Biol; Genetics Soc Am; Sigma Xi; Soc Study Reproduction. *Res:* Physiological genetics, specifically genetic control of physiological and developmental processes related to reproduction; blood proteins and hematopoiesis; pigmentation in mice; gene regulation of y chromosome length. *Mailing Add:* Dept Physiol & Cell Biol Univ Kans Lawrence KS 66045

WOLFE, HUGH CAMPBELL, b Parkville, Mo, Dec 18, 05; m 29; c 4. PHYSICS. *Educ:* Park Col, AB, 26; Univ Mich, MS, 27, PhD(physics), 29. *Hon Degrees:* ScD, Park Col, 62. *Prof Exp:* Asst physics, Univ Mich, 26-27, instr, 27-29; Nat Res Coun fel, Calif Inst Technol, 29-31; Lorentz Found fel, State Univ Utrecht, 31-32; Heckscher res asst, Cornell Univ, 32; instr, Ohio State Univ, 32-33; from instr to assoc prof physics, City Col New York, 34-49; prof & head dept, Cooper Union, 49-60; dir publ, Am Inst Physics, 60-70, tech asst publ & info, 71-72; CONSULT, 73- *Concurrent Pos:* Mem comn on symbols, units & nomenclature, Int Union Pure & Appl Physics, 61-77, chmn comn on publ, 66-72; mem adv panel, Int Standards Orgn, 63-80; chmn comt symbols, units & terminology, Nat Acad Sci, 62-73; chmn, Gordon Conf Sci Info Probs in Res, 65; mem metric adv comt, Am Nat Standards Inst, 70-76; mem metric practice comt, Am Nat Metric Coun, 73- *Mem:* Fel Am Phys Soc; Fedn Am Scientists; Am Asn Physics Teachers. *Res:* Applications of quantum theory; development of information systems. *Mailing Add:* 30 Lawrence Pkwy Tenafly NJ 07670

WOLFE, JAMES ALVIS, botany, ecology, see previous edition

WOLFE, JAMES F, b York, Pa, Oct 5, 36; m 59; c 2. ORGANIC CHEMISTRY, PHYSICS, OPTICS. *Educ:* Lebanon Valley Col, BS, 58; Ind Univ, PhD(org chem), 63. *Prof Exp:* Teaching asst org chem, Ind Univ, 58-60; res assoc, Duke Univ, 63-64; from asst prof to assoc prof, 64-74, PROF CHEM, VA POLYTECH INST & STATE UNIV, 74-, DEPT HEAD, 81- *Mem:* Am Chem Soc. *Res:* Use of multiple anions in organic synthesis; mechanisms of heteroaromatic nucleophilic substitution; synthesis of new medicinal agents. *Mailing Add:* Dept Chem Va Polytech Inst & State Univ Blacksburg VA 24061

WOLFE, JAMES FREDERICK, b Bell, Calif, Dec 1, 48; m 71; c 1. POLYMERS. *Educ:* Occidental Col, Calif, AB, 70; Univ Iowa, PhD(org chem), 75. *Prof Exp:* Vis scientist polymers, Mat Lab, Polymer Br Wright-Patterson AFB, 76; SR POLYMER CHEMIST, POLYMER SYNTHESIS RES, SRI INT, 76- *Mem:* Am Chem Soc. *Res:* Defining molecular structural requirements and developing synthesis conditions and techniques to give aromatic, heterocyclic polymers capable of liquid crystalline order; poly (p phenylene benzo bisthiazole) as a lightweight, high strength, high modulus, thermally stable fiber and film. *Mailing Add:* Polymer Sci Dept SRI Int 333 Ravenswood Ave Menlo Park CA 94025

WOLFE, JAMES H, b Salt Lake City, Utah, Jan 7, 22; m 56. MATHEMATICS. *Educ:* Univ Utah, BA, 42; Harvard Univ, MA, 43, PhD(math), 48. *Prof Exp:* PROF MATH, UNIV UTAH, 48- *Mem:* Am Math Soc. *Res:* Topology and integration theory; matrices. *Mailing Add:* Dept of Math Univ of Utah Salt Lake City UT 84112

WOLFE, JAMES LEONARD, b Milton, Fla, May 5, 40; m 63. VERTEBRATE ZOOLOGY, ANIMAL BEHAVIOR. *Educ:* Univ Fla, BS, 62; Cornell Univ, PhD(vert zool), 66. *Prof Exp:* Asst prof biol, Univ Ala, University, 66-68; asst prof zool, 68-70, assoc prof, 70-77, prof zool & adj assoc prof wildlife & fish, 77-81, DIR, RES CTR, NAT SPACE TECHNOL LAB, MISS STATE UNIV, 81- *Mem:* Animal Behav Soc; Am Soc Mammal; Ecol Soc Am. *Res:* Ecology and behavior of mammals. *Mailing Add:* Nat Space Technol Lab Miss State Univ Station MS 39529

WOLFE, JAMES PHILLIP, b Randolph Field, Tex, July 16, 43; m 66; c 3. SOLID STATE PHYSICS. *Educ:* Univ Calif, Berkeley, BA, 65, PhD(physics), 71. *Prof Exp:* Asst res physicist, Univ Calif, Berkeley, 71-76; from asst prof to assoc prof, 76-81, PROF PHYSICS, UNIV ILL, URBANA-CHAMPAIGN, 81- *Concurrent Pos:* Prin investr, Mat Res Lab, Univ Ill, 76-, Cottrell res grant, Res Corp, 77-78, NSF grant, 78- & Air Force Off Sci Res grant, 79- *Mem:* Fel Am Phys Soc. *Res:* Physics of semiconductors; optical and microwave studies of photo-excited phases; thermal transport in crystals; phonon imaging; electron and nuclear magnetic resonance in solids. *Mailing Add:* Dept of Physics Univ of Ill Urbana IL 61801

WOLFE, JAMES RICHARD, JR, b Elizabeth, NJ, Aug 6, 32; m 57; c 3. REACTION MECHANISMS, POLYMER SYNTHESIS. *Educ:* Mass Inst Technol, BS, 54; Univ Calif, PhD(chem), 58. *Prof Exp:* RES CHEMIST, E I DU PONT DE NEMOURS & CO, INC, 57- *Mem:* Am Chem Soc. *Res:* Polymers; physical organic chemistry; rubber vulcanization; thermoplastic elastomers. *Mailing Add:* Exp Sta Bldg 353 E I du Pont de Nemours & Co Wilmington DE 19898

WOLFE, JAMES WALLACE, b Ludlowville, NY, Apr 11, 32; m 54; c 2. NEUROPHYSIOLOGY, PSYCHOLOGY. *Educ:* Univ Calif, Riverside, BA, 63; Univ Rochester, PhD(psychol), 66. *Prof Exp:* Res psychologist, Army Med Res Lab, Ft Knox, Ky, 66-68; RES NEUROPHYSIOLOGIST, US AIR FORCE SCH AEROSPACE MED, 68- *Concurrent Pos:* Lectr, Univ Louisville, 67-68 & St Mary's Univ, Tex, 69- *Mem:* Int Brain Res Orgn; Soc Res Otolaryngol; Aerospace Med Asn; Barany Soc. *Res:* Cerebellar integration of sensory information; effects of drugs on electrophysiological responses; neurophysiological control of oculomotor function. *Mailing Add:* c/o Chief Vestibular Function US Air Force Sch Aerospace Med Brooks AFB TX 78235

WOLFE, JOHN A(LLEN), b Riverton, Iowa, June 3, 20; m 48; c 2. GEOLOGICAL & MINING ENGINEERING. *Educ:* Colo Sch Mines, GeolE & EM, 47, MS, 54. *Prof Exp:* Res geologist, Ideal Cement Co, 48-51, chief geologist, 51-63, dir explor, 63-65; PRES, TAYSAN COPPER, INC, 72- & PAN-ASEAN TECH SERVS, INC, 74- *Concurrent Pos:* Consult porphyry copper & other metals & nonmetallics, Philippines & Southeast Asia; geol consult, 65- *Mem:* Geol Soc Am; Am Inst Mining, Metall & Petrol Engrs; Mining & Metall Soc Am; Soc Econ Geol; Geol Soc Philippines. *Res:* Origin and nature of porphyry copper deposits and development of mineral deposits in tectonic environments; geomorphology; quaternary explosive volcanism; Philippine geochronology and mineral resource economics. *Mailing Add:* MCC PO Box 1868 Makati Metro-Manila Philippines

WOLFE, LAUREN GENE, b Kenton, Ohio, Nov 7, 39; m 66. PATHOLOGY. *Educ:* Ohio State Univ, DVM, 63, MS, 65, PhD(vet path), 68; Am Col Vet Path, dipl, 68. *Prof Exp:* Asst prof path, Univ Ill Med Ctr, 68-71; assoc prof microbiol, Rush-Presby-St Luke's Med Ctr, 71-74, prof, 74-81; PROF & HEAD PATH & PARASITOL, AUBURN UNIV, 81- *Concurrent Pos:* Asst microbiologist, Presby-St Luke's Hosp, 68-71. *Mem:* AAAS; Am Soc Microbiol; Am Asn Pathologists; Am Asn Immunol; Am Asn Cancer Res. *Res:* Experimental and comparative pathology; oncology. *Mailing Add:* Dept Path Parasitol 166 Greene Hall Auburn Univ AL 36849

WOLFE, LEONHARD SCOTT, b Auckland, NZ, Mar 3, 25; Can citizen; m 60; c 2. BIOCHEMISTRY, NEUROCHEMISTRY. *Educ:* Univ NZ, BSc, 47; Cambridge Univ, PhD(insect physiol, biochem), 52, ScD, 76; Univ Western Ont, MD, 58; FRCP(C), 72. *Prof Exp:* Jr lectr zool, Univ Canterbury, 49-50; assoc entomologist, Agr Res Inst, Can Dept Agr, 52-54; from asst prof neurochem to assoc prof neurol & neurosurg, 60-70, PROF NEUROL & NEUROSURG, MONTREAL NEUROL INST, McGILL UNIV, 70-, DIR, DONNER LAB EXP NEUROCHEM, 65- *Concurrent Pos:* Nat Res Coun Can med res fel, 59-60; Sister Elizabeth Kenny Found scholar, 60-61; med res assoc, Med Res Coun Can, 63-, mem grants comt neurol sci, 70-74, mem priorities selection & rev comt, 72-; hon lectr biochem, McGill Univ, 60-70, prof biochem, 71-; consult dermat res unit, Royal Victoria Hosp, Montreal, 65-67. *Mem:* Int Brain Res Orgn; Am Soc Biol Chemists; Can Biochem Soc; Can Physiol Soc; Int Soc Neurochem. *Res:* Entomology; biology and control of biting flies; insect cholinesterases; metabolism of insecticides; biochemistry and function of complex glycolipids in neurones; membranes; role of lipid anions in excitable tissues; convulsive states; biosynthesis, release and action of prostaglandins; biochemistry of lipid storage diseases and degenerative neurological diseases. *Mailing Add:* Montreal Neurol Inst 3801 University St Montreal PQ H3A 2B4 Can

WOLFE, PAUL JAY, b Mansfield, Ohio, Oct 2, 38; m 60; c 2. EXPLORATION GEOPHYSICS, NUCLEAR PHYSICS. *Educ:* Case Inst Technol, BS, 60, MS, 63, PhD(nuclear physics), 66. *Prof Exp:* Design engr, Lamp Div, Gen Elec Co, 60-61; asst prof physics, 66-71, chmn dept, 72-75, ASSOC PROF PHYSICS, WRIGHT STATE UNIV, 71- *Concurrent Pos:* NSF geophysicist fel, US Bur Mines, Denver, 79-80. *Mem:* Soc Explor Geophysicists; Am Asn Physics Teachers. *Res:* Seismic exploration techniques related to hydrocarbons and coal; guided waves in coal; subsurface cavity detection with seismic and gravity methods. *Mailing Add:* Dept of Physics Wright State Univ Dayton OH 45435

WOLFE, PETER EDWARD, b Hammonton, NJ, Apr 27, 11. GEOLOGY. *Educ:* Rutgers Univ, BS, 33; Princeton Univ, MA, 40, PhD(geol), 41. *Prof Exp:* Asst conservationist, USDA, 35-37; asst instr geol, Princeton Univ, 37-41, res assoc, 44-45; geologist, Nfld Dept Nat Resources, 41-44; from asst prof to assoc prof geol, 45-60, PROF GEOL, RUTGERS UNIV, NEW BRUNSWICK, 60- *Concurrent Pos:* Vis prof, Osmania Univ, India, 58-59; Fulbright fel, 58. *Mem:* Fel Geol Soc Am; Sigma Xi. *Res:* Geomorphology; geohydrology; environmental geology; pleistocene and periglacial research, Atlantic Coastal Plain. *Mailing Add:* 6 Mercer St Princeton NJ 08540

WOLFE, PETER NORD, b Lakewood, Ohio, July 24, 29; m 51; c 3. PHYSICS. *Educ:* Ohio Wesleyan Univ, BA, 51; Ohio State Univ, MS, 52, PhD(physics), 55. *Prof Exp:* NSF fel, 54-55; from res physicist to mgr systs physics Dept, Res Labs, Westinghouse Elec Corp, 55-72, mgr transformer technol, 72-75, mgr laser fusion activities, 75-78; staff mem, 78-80, PROJ LEADER, LOS ALAMOS NAT LAB, 80- *Mem:* Am Phys Soc; Inst Elec & Electronics Engrs. *Res:* High power lasers; power technology; applied physics; microwave spectra. *Mailing Add:* Univ of Calif Los Alamos Sci Lab Los Alamos NM 87545

WOLFE, PHILIP, b San Francisco, Calif, Aug 11, 27. APPLIED MATHEMATICS. *Educ:* Univ Calif, AB, 48, PhD, 54. *Prof Exp:* Instr math, Princeton Univ, 54-57; mathematician, Rand Corp, 57-66; MEM RES STAFF, IBM RES, 66-; PROF ENG MATH, COLUMBIA UNIV, 68- *Concurrent Pos:* Chmn, Math Prog Soc, 78-80, vchmn, 80-82. *Mem:* Fel AAAS; Am Math Soc; Soc Indust & Appl Math; Math Prog Soc; fel Econ Soc. *Res:* Mathematics of optimization; linear and nonlinear programming. *Mailing Add:* IBM Res PO Box 218 Yorktown Heights NY 10598

WOLFE, RALPH STONER, b New Windsor, Md, July 18, 21; m 50; c 3. MICROBIOLOGY. *Educ:* Bridgewater Col, BS, 42; Univ Pa, MS, 49, PhD, 53. *Prof Exp:* Asst instr microbiol, Univ Pa, 47-49, instr, 51-52; asst limnol, Acad Natural Sci, Pa, 49-50; from instr to assoc prof, 53-60, PROF MICROBIOL, UNIV ILL, URBANA, 61- *Concurrent Pos:* NSF fel, 58; Guggenheim fel, 60 & 75. *Mem:* Nat Acad Sci; Am Soc Microbiol; Am Acad Arts & Sci; Am Soc Biol Chemists. *Res:* Metabolism and physiology of bacteria; methanogens. *Mailing Add:* Dept Microbiol 131 Burrill Hall Urbana IL 61801

WOLFE, RAYMOND, b Hamilton, Ont, Apr 8, 27; m 54; c 3. SOLID STATE PHYSICS. *Educ:* Univ Toronto, BA, 49, MA, 50; Bristol Univ, PhD(physics), 55. *Prof Exp:* Physicist, Eastman Kodak Co, NY, 50-52; physicist, Gen Elec Co, Eng, 54-57; MEM TECH STAFF, BELL TEL LABS, 57-, SUPVR, MAGNETIC PROPERTIES GROUP, 67- *Concurrent Pos:* Ed, Appl Solid State Sci. *Mem:* Fel Am Phys Soc. *Res:* Theoretical and experimental solid state physics; transport and optical properties of semiconductors and metals; thermoelectric materials and devices; magnetic materials; magnetic bubble devices. *Mailing Add:* Solid State Device Lab Bell Tel Labs Murray Hill NJ 07974

WOLFE, RAYMOND GROVER, JR, b Oakland, Calif, June 1, 20; m 46; c 3. BIOCHEMISTRY. *Educ:* Univ Calif, AB, 42, MA, 48, PhD(biochem), 55. *Prof Exp:* Biochemist, Donner Lab, Univ Calif, 48-55; Nat Found Infantile Paralysis fel chem, Univ Wis, 55-56; from asst prof to assoc prof, 56-67, Lalor res fel, summer 56, PROF CHEM, UNIV ORE, 67- *Concurrent Pos:* Guggenheim fel, Inst Biochem, Univ Vienna, 63-64; vis prof, Bristol Univ, 70-71, Cornell Univ, 78-79. *Mem:* AAAS; Am Chem Soc; Am Soc Biol Chem. *Res:* Enzyme catalytic mechanism; structure-function relationship of polymeric enzymes; enzyme kinetics and inhibition; protein structure studies, particularly in dehydrogenases. *Mailing Add:* Dept of Chem Univ of Ore Eugene OR 97403

WOLFE, ROBERT KENNETH, b Chattanooga, Tenn, Sept 5, 29; m 59; c 2. COMPUTER SCIENCE, ENGINEERING. *Educ:* Ga Inst Technol, BChE, 52, PhD(chem eng), 56. *Prof Exp:* Res asst chem eng, Ga Inst Technol, 51-52; chem engr, Mallinckrodt Chem Works, 55-60; systs eng mgr comput, Int Bus Mach, 60-68; opers res mgr planning, Owens Ill, 68-73; PROF INDUST ENG, UNIV TOLEDO, 73- *Concurrent Pos:* Tenn Eastman fel, Ga Inst Technol, 52-54; res contracts, Ohio Dept Transp & Fed Hwy Admin, 75-; chmn systs eng PhD prog, Univ Toledo, 76-78. *Mem:* Sigma Xi; sr mem Am Inst Indust Engrs; Am Inst Chem Engrs. *Res:* Development and use of design and decision making models using computers and informations systems. *Mailing Add:* 4930 Spring Mill Ct Toledo OH 43615

WOLFE, ROBERT NORTON, b Falls City, Nebr, Feb 22, 08; m 33; c 2. PHYSICS. *Educ:* Parsons Col, BS, 30; Univ Rochester, MS, 32, PhD(physics), 35. *Prof Exp:* Physicist, Eastman Kodak Co, 35-73; RETIRED. *Concurrent Pos:* Pres, Rochester Coun Sci Socs, 65-67. *Mem:* Fel Optical Soc Am; Soc Photog Sci & Eng; Am Phys Soc. *Res:* Radioactivity; photographic sensitometry; microsensitometry; optical and photographic image structure. *Mailing Add:* 340 Cobbs Hill Dr Rochester NY 14610

WOLFE, ROGER THOMAS, b Mt Vernon, Ill, July 31, 32; m 56; c 2. ORGANIC CHEMISTRY. *Educ:* Bradley Univ, BS, 54; Rensselaer Polytech Inst, PhD(chem), 59; Salmon P Chase Col, JD, 69. *Prof Exp:* Lab asst anal chem, Bradley Univ, 52-54; asst gen & org chem, Rensselaer Polytech Inst, 54-56; res chemist, Sterling-Winthrop Res Inst, NY, 56-60, from assoc patent agent to patent agent, 60-65, patent agent, Hilton-Davis Chem Co Div, Sterling Drug Co, 65-66, asst dir res & develop, 66-69, vpres res & develop, 70-75, patent attorney, Hilton-Davis Chem Co Div, 69-77, vpres res admin & legal affairs, 75-77, ASST TO CORP DIR, GOV REGULATORY AFFAIRS, STERLING DRUG INC, 77- *Mailing Add:* Sterling Drug Inc 90 Park Ave New York NY 10016

WOLFE, STEPHEN JAMES, b San Francisco, Calif, Jan 30, 43. MATHEMATICS. *Educ:* Williams Col, BA, 65; Univ Calif, Riverside, MA, 67, PhD(math), 70. *Prof Exp:* Asst prof math, 70-75, ASSOC PROF MATH, UNIV DEL, 75- *Concurrent Pos:* Assoc ed, Annals Probability, 80-81. *Mem:* Am Math Soc; Math Asn Am; Inst Math Statist. *Res:* Probability limit theorems; infinitely divisible distribution functions; characteristic functions; stochastic processess. *Mailing Add:* Dept Math Univ Del Newark DE 19711

WOLFE, STEPHEN LANDIS, b Sept 23, 32; m 53; c 2. CELL BIOLOGY, ELECTRON MICROSCOPY. *Educ:* Bloomsburg State Col, BS, 54; Ohio State Univ, MS, 59; Johns Hopkins Univ, PhD(biol), 62. *Prof Exp:* NIH fel zool, Univ Minn, 62-63; asst prof, 63-68, ASSOC PROF ZOOL, UNIV CALIF, DAVIS, 68- *Concurrent Pos:* Vis prof, Yale Univ, 73. *Mem:* AAAS; Am Soc Cell Biol. *Res:* Fine and molecular structure of chromosomes in interphase, dividing and reproductive cells. *Mailing Add:* Dept Zool Univ Calif Davis CA 95616

WOLFE, STEPHEN MITCHELL, b Winter Haven, Fla, Nov 13, 49. PLASMA PHYSICS, LASER PHYSICS. *Educ:* Mass Inst Technol, SB, 71, PhD(physics), 77. *Prof Exp:* physicist, Francis Bitter Nat Magnet Lab, 77-80, PHYSICIST, PLASMA FUSION CTR, MASS INST TECHNOL, 80- *Mem:* Am Optical Soc. *Res:* Fusion research; plasma diagnostics; optically pumped lasers; cyclotron resonance masers. *Mailing Add:* Plasm Fusion Ctr 167 Albany St Mass Inst Technol Cambridge MA 02139

WOLFE, WALTER MCILHANEY, b Baltimore, Md, Aug 15, 21; m 45; c 3. OBSTETRICS & GYNECOLOGY. *Educ:* Univ Md, MD, 46; Am Bd Obstet & Gynec, dipl, 57. *Prof Exp:* Asst prof, 65-68, actg chmn dept, 69-72, ASSOC PROF OBSTET & GYNEC, SCH MED, UNIV LOUISVILLE, 68- *Concurrent Pos:* Proj dir family planning, Dept Health Educ & Welfare Grant, Louisville Gen Hosp, 71- *Mem:* Am Col Obstet & Gynec. *Res:* Applications of current technological and educational techniques to community reproductive health. *Mailing Add:* Dept of Obstet & Gynec 323 E Chestnut St Louisville KY 40202

WOLFE, WILLIAM LOUIS, JR, b Yonkers, NY, Apr 5, 31; m 55; c 3. OPTICS, ELECTRICAL ENGINEERING. *Educ:* Bucknell Univ, BS, 53; Univ Mich, MS, 56, MSE, 66. *Prof Exp:* Asst proj engr, Sperry Gyroscope Co, 52-53; from res asst to res assoc infrared & optics, Univ Mich, 53-57, from assoc res engr to res engr, 57-66, lectr elec eng, 62-66; chief engr, Honeywell Radiation Ctr, 66-68, mgr electro-optics Dept, Honeywell, Inc, 68-69; PROF OPTICAL SCI, UNIV ARIZ, 69- *Concurrent Pos:* Lectr, Northeastern Univ, 68-69; mem panel of comt undersea warfare-assessment electro optics, Nat Acad Sci; mem adv comt, Army Res Off, study panel on Army Countermine Adv Comt & adv comt, Nat Bur Stand & Air Force Systs Command; consult, var orgn. *Mem:* Fel Optical Soc Am; sr mem Inst Elec & Electronics Engrs. *Res:* Optical materials for infrared use; radiometry; space navigation using star trackers; electro-optical system design; infrared simulation; infrared reconaissance and surveillance systems; optical scattering. *Mailing Add:* Optical Sci Ctr Univ of Ariz Tucson AZ 85721

WOLFE, WILLIAM RAY, JR, b Grafton, WVa, Nov 16, 24; m 52; c 2. PHYSICAL CHEMISTRY. *Educ:* WVa Wesleyan Col, BS, 49; Western Reserve Univ, MS, 50, PhD(phys chem), 53. *Prof Exp:* Asst phys chem, Western Reserve Univ, 50-52; res chemist cent res dept, 52-60, chemist, Explosives Dept, 60-64, chemist develop dept, 65-68, RES ASSOC, POLYMER PROD DEPT, EXP STA, E I DU PONT DE NEMOURS & CO, INC, 68- *Mem:* Am Chem Soc. *Res:* Fused salt and aqueous electrochemistry; energy conversion; high temperature chemistry; catalysis; plastics processing; microwave and dielectric film. *Mailing Add:* Polymer Prod Dept Exp Sta E I du Pont de Nemours & Co Inc Wilmington DE 19898

WOLFENBARGER, DAN A, b White Plains, NY, Sept 23, 34; m 59; c 3. ENTOMOLOGY. *Educ:* Univ Fla, BSA, 56; Iowa State Univ, MS, 57; Ohio State Univ, PhD(entom), 61. *Prof Exp:* Entomologist agr exp sta, Tex A&M Univ, 61-65; ENTOMOLOGIST COTTON INSECT RES, AGR RES SERV, USDA, 65- *Mem:* Entom Soc Am. *Res:* Activity of and resistance and mode of inheritance to insecticides against tobacco budworm; effect of insect and plant growth regulators on tobacco budworm and boll weevil; effect of grandlure on populations of boll weevils. *Mailing Add:* Agr Res Serv USDA PO Box 1033 Brownsville TX 78520

WOLFENDEN, RICHARD VANCE, b Oxford, Eng, May 17, 35; US citizen; m 65; c 2. BIOCHEMISTRY. *Educ:* Princeton Univ, AB, 56; Oxford Univ, BA & MA, 60; Rockefeller Inst, PhD(biochem), 64. *Prof Exp:* Asst prof biochem, Princeton Univ, 64-70; assoc prof, 70-73, PROF BIOCHEM, SCH MED, UNIV NC, CHAPEL HILL, 73- *Concurrent Pos:* Mem, NSF Adv Panel Molecular Biol, 74-77; vis fel, Exeter Col, Oxford, 69, 76; consult, Merck & Co, 73-76 & Burroughs Welcome Co, 80- *Mem:* AAAS; Am Chem Soc; Am Soc Biol Chemists. *Res:* Physical organic chemistry in relation to enzyme-catalyzed reactions; analogs of intermediates in substrate transformation. *Mailing Add:* Dept of Biochem Univ of NC Sch of Med Chapel Hill NC 27514

WOLFENSTEIN, LINCOLN, b Cleveland, Ohio, Feb 10, 23; m 43, 57; c 3. THEORETICAL HIGH ENERGY PHYSICS. *Educ:* Univ Chicago, BS, 43, MS, 44, PhD(physics), 49. *Prof Exp:* Physicist, Nat Adv Comt Aeronaut, 44-46; instr physics, 48-49, from asst prof to prof, 49-78, UNIV PROF PHYSICS, CARNEGIE-MELLON UNIV, 78- *Concurrent Pos:* NSF sr fel, Europ Orgn Nuclear Res, Geneva, Switz, 64-65; vis prof, Univ Mich, 70-71; Guggenheim fel, 74-75; mem physics adv comt, NSF, 74-77. *Mem:* Nat Acad Sci; Am Phys Soc. *Res:* Nuclear collisions; weak interactions. *Mailing Add:* Dept of Physics Carnegie-Mellon Univ Pittsburgh PA 15213

WOLFERSBERGER, MICHAEL GREGG, b Northampton, Pa, June 14, 44; m 65. MEMBRANE BIOLOGY, ENERGY TRANSDUCTION MECHANISMS. *Educ:* Lebanon Valley Col, BS, 66; Temple Univ, PhD(biochem), 71. *Prof Exp:* Res assoc biochem, Lab Exp Dermat, Albert Einstein Med Ctr, Philadelphia, 71-73, assoc mem div res, 73-75; asst prof, Div Natural Sci & Math, Rosemont Col, 74-77; RES ASSOC BIOL, TEMPLE UNIV, 77- *Concurrent Pos:* Lectr, Cabrini Col, 76-77 & LaSalle Co, 81-; consult, Rohm and Haas Co, 79-80. *Mem:* AAAS; Am Chem Soc. *Res:* Active transepithelial solute transport. *Mailing Add:* Dept Biol Temple Univ Philadelphia PA 19122

WOLFF, ALBERT ELI, b New York, NY, Jan 4, 12; div; c 2. BIOSTATISTICS, EPIDEMIOLOGY. *Educ:* Syracuse Univ, BS, 35, MS, 36; NY Univ, MA, 53; Univ Tex, PhD(econ, bus statist), 62. *Prof Exp:* Prof statist, Loyola Univ, La, 47-50; asst prof, Univ NMex, 57-59; assoc prof, Tulsa Univ, 60-61 & St Michael's Col, NMex, 62-63; assoc prof, 63-70, prof epidemiol & community med, 70-77, prof, 70-79, EMER PROF BIOSTATIST & PUB HEALTH, MED CTR, UNIV ALA, BIRMINGHAM, 79- *Mem:* Am Statist Asn; Am Pub Health Asn. *Res:* Economic, administrative and social aspects of medicine, dentistry and related life sciences. *Mailing Add:* Dept of Biostatist Univ Ala Birmingham AL 35294

WOLFF, ARTHUR HAROLD, b Trenton, NJ, Dec 23, 19; m 46; c 3. ENVIRONMENTAL HEALTH. *Educ:* Mich State Univ, DVM, 42. *Prof Exp:* Res investr, Commun Dis Ctr, USPHS, 46-50, res biologist, Sanit Eng Ctr, 50-58, chief training br, Div Radiol Health, 58-60; consult, UN Food & Agr Orgn, Italy, 60-61; chief radiation bio-effects prog, Nat Ctr Radiol Health, USPHS, 61-68; asst dir res, Consumer Protection & Environ Health, Dept Health, Educ & Welfare, 68-69, asst dir radiation prog, US Environ Protection Agency, 69-71; assoc dean res, 77-80, PROF ENVIRON HEALTH & CHMN DEPT, SCH PUB HEALTH, UNIV ILL MED CTR, 71- *Concurrent Pos:* Fel, Duke Univ & Oak Ridge Inst Nuclear Studies, 50-51; exec secy, Nat Adv Comt Radiation, 59-61; consult & mem expert panels, UN Food & Agr Orgn, 60-63 & WHO, 61-; sci adv, US Environ Protection Agency, 80- *Honors & Awards:* K F Meyer Award, 73. *Mem:* AAAS; Am Vet Med Asn; Am Pub Health Asn; Nat Soc Med Res; NY Acad Sci. *Res:* Radiation biology; comparative oncology; environmental toxicology. *Mailing Add:* 4285 Embassy Park Dr NW Washington DC 20016

WOLFF, DAVID A, b Cleveland, Ohio, Nov 2, 34; m 58, 76; c 4. CELL BIOLOGY, VIROLOGY. *Educ:* Col Wooster, AB, 56; Univ Cincinnati, MS, 60, PhD(microbiol, virol), 65. *Prof Exp:* From asst prof to prof virol & microbiol, Ohio State Univ, 64-78; MEM STAFF, NAT INST HEALTH, 78- *Concurrent Pos:* res grant, 66-69; Am-Swiss Found Sci exchange lectr, Switz, 70; res leave, Univ Uppsala, Sweden, 71. *Mem:* AAAS; Am Soc Microbiol; Sigma Xi. *Res:* Viral-induced cytopathic effects and relation of lysosomal enzymes; purification of virus; electron microscopy of virus infected cells; purification of lysosomes; virus interactions with synchronized cells. *Mailing Add:* 2212 Lomond Ct Vienna VA 22180

WOLFF, DONALD JOHN, b New York, NY, Feb 23, 42. BIOCHEMISTRY, PHARMACOLOGY. *Educ:* Fordham Univ, BS, 63; Univ Wis, PhD(biochem), 69. *Prof Exp:* asst prof, 72-80, ASSOC PROF PHARMACOL, RUTGERS MED SCH, COL MED & DENT NJ, 80- *Concurrent Pos:* NIH trainee pediat, J P Kennedy, Jr Labs, Med Sch, Univ Wis, 68-72. *Mem:* AAAS. *Res:* Calcium-binding proteins; regulation of cyclic nucleotide metabolism by clacium ion. *Mailing Add:* Four Copper Hill Rd Bridgewater Township NJ 08807

WOLFF, EDWARD A, b Chicago, Ill, Oct 31, 29; m 51; c 3. ELECTRICAL ENGINEERING. *Educ:* Univ Ill, BSEE, 51; Univ Md, MS, 53, PhD, 61. *Prof Exp:* Electronic scientist, US Naval Res Lab, 51-54; proj engr, Md Electronic Mfg Corp, Litton Indust, 56-59 & Electromagnetic Res Corp, 59-61; staff consult & mgr, Space Eng Lab, Aero Geo Astro Corp, Keltec Indust, Inc, Md, 61-65, chief engr, 65-67; vpres, Geotronics, Inc, 67-71; head, Syst Study Off, 71-73, ASSOC CHIEF COMMUN & NAVIG DIV, NASA GODDARD SPACE FLIGHT CTR, 73- *Concurrent Pos:* Mem, Md Gov Sci Resources Adv Bd, treas, Joint Bd Sci Educ. *Mem:* Nat Soc Prof Engrs; fel Inst Elec & Electronics Engrs (pres, antennas & propagation soc, 77); Am Inst Aeronaut & Astronaut; Am Mgt Asn. *Res:* Antennas; microwave components; electromagnetic waves. *Mailing Add:* 1021 Cresthaven Dr Silver Spring MD 20903

WOLFF, ERNEST N, b St Paul, Minn. GEOLOGY, MINING ENGINEERING. *Educ:* Univ Alaska, BS, 41; Univ Ore, MS, 59, PhD(geol), 65. *Prof Exp:* Field asst, Alaska Territorial Dept Mines, 39-40; observer geophys, Carnegie Inst Dept Terrestrial Magnetism, 41-46; observer in chg, Univ Alaska, 46-48, res assoc & asst prof mining eng, Sch Mines, 51-57; asst prof geol, Colo State Univ, 59-66; assoc prof geol & mining eng, Univ Alaska, 66-67; assoc prof geol, Colo State Univ, 67-69; PROF EXPLOR ENG & ASSOC DIR, MINERAL INDUST RES LAB, UNIV ALASKA, 69- *Mem:* Am Inst Mining, Metall & Petrol Engrs; Sigma Xi. *Res:* Economic geology of Alaska; regional Alaskan economics. *Mailing Add:* Mineral Indust Res Lab Univ Alaska College AK 99701

WOLFF, FREDERICK WILLIAM, b Berlin, Ger, Aug 21, 20. PHARMACOLOGY, MEDICINE. *Educ:* Univ Durham, MB, BS, 46, MD, 57; Georgian USSR Acad Sci, dipl, 81. *Prof Exp:* House physician, Royal Victoria Infirmary, Univ Durham, 46-47; house physician, med registr & resident med officer, Southend-on-Sea Gen Hosp, Eng, 47-50; med registr, Whittington Hosp, 53-54; clin pharmacologist, Wellcome Res Inst, 55-59; asst prof med, Sch Med & Endocrine Clin, Johns Hopkins Univ, 59-63; PRES, INST DRUG DEVELOP, WASHINGTON, DC, 80-; PROF MED, SCH MED, GEORGE WASHINGTON UNIV, 65- *Concurrent Pos:* Sr res asst, Post-Grad Med Sch, Univ London & Whittington Hosp, 55-59; consult, Food & Drug Admin, DC & Children's Med Ctr, DC, 71- *Mem:* Am Diabetes Asn; Am Soc Pharmacol & Exp Therapeut; Am Fedn Clin Res; Am Heart Asn; Royal Soc Med. *Res:* Therapeutics; clinical pharmacology; endocrinology; diabetes; hypertension. *Mailing Add:* 800 Notley Rd Silver Spring MD 20904

WOLFF, GEORGE LOUIS, b Hamburg, Ger, Aug 24, 28; US citizen; m 53; c 2. GENETICS, TOXICOLOGY. *Educ:* Ohio State Univ, BS, 50; Univ Chicago, PhD(zool), 54. *Prof Exp:* Biologist, Nat Cancer Inst, 56-58; res assoc, Inst Cancer Res, 58-63, supvr animal colony, 58-68, asst mem, 63-72, geneticist, 68-72; chief mammalian genetics br, 72-74, chief div mutagenic res, 74-79, SR SCI COORDR GENETICS, NAT CTR TOXICOL RES, US FOOD & DRUG ADMIN, 79- *Concurrent Pos:* USPHS fel, Nat Cancer Inst, 54-56; prof assoc, Nat Acad Sci, 56-57; consult, Am Asn Accreditation Lab Animal Care, 70-75; mem, HEW subcomt, Environ Mutagenesis, 73-; asst prof biochem, Med Sch, Univ Ark, 73-81, assoc prof interdisciplinary toxicol, 81- *Mem:* Soc Toxicol; Am Asn Cancer Res; Am Genetic Asn; Environ Mutagen Soc; Genetics Soc. *Res:* Genetic aspects of regulation of metabolism in neoplastic and normal mammalian tissues; genetic aspects of toxicology; mouse genetics; chemical mutagenesis in the mammal. *Mailing Add:* Off Res Nat Ctr for Toxicol Res Jefferson AR 72079

WOLFF, GEORGE THOMAS, b Irvington, NJ, Nov 27, 47; m 72; c 2. AIR POLLUTION METEOROLOGY & CHEMISTRY. *Educ:* NJ Inst Technol, BSChe, 69; NY Univ, MS, 70; Rutgers Univ, PhD(environ sci), 74. *Prof Exp:* Assoc engr, Interstate Sanitation Comn, 73-77; SR STAFF SCIENTIST, RES

LABS, GEN MOTORS CORP, 77- *Mem:* Am Meteorol Soc; Air Pollution Control Asn; AAAS; NY Acad Sci. *Res:* Pollutant transport; chemical composition of aerosols; sources of aerosols; effect of aerosol composition on visibility; fate of air pollutants and acid precipitation. *Mailing Add:* Environ Sci Dept Gen Motors Res Labs Warren MI 48090

WOLFF, GUNTHER ARTHUR, b Essen, Ger, Mar 31, 18; nat US; m 45; c 2. PHYSICAL CHEMISTRY, SOLID STATE CHEMISTRY. *Educ:* Univ Berlin, BS, 44, MS, 45; Tech Univ, Berlin, ScD(theoret inorg chem), 48. *Prof Exp:* Res assoc, Fritz-Haber Inst, Ger, 44-50, sci asst head & dep chief, 50-53; consult & sr res scientist, Signal Corps Res & Develop Labs, US Dept Army, NJ, 53-60; sr group leader mat res solid state res dept, Harshaw Chem Co, Ohio, 60-63; dir mat res, Erie Tech Prod, Inc, 63-64; prin scientist, Tyco Labs, Inc, 64-70; consult chemist, Lighting Res & Tech Serv Oper, Gen Elec Co, East Cleveland, 70-77; sr scientist, Epidyne, Inc, 77-78; sr engr, Nat Semiconductor Corp, 78-81; CONSULT INDUST, 81- *Concurrent Pos:* Mem comn crystal growth, Int Union Crystallog, 66-75, mem, Am Comt Crystal Growth, 67-72. *Mem:* Am Asn Crystal Growth; Am Chem Soc; Electrochem Soc; fel Mineral Soc Am; fel Am Inst Chemists. *Res:* Crystal growth and dissolution, including evaporation and etching; crystal imperfections; electroluminescence and luminescence; semiconductors and ceramics; chemical bonding; solid state chemistry and physics. *Mailing Add:* 3776 N Hampton Rd Cleveland Heights OH 44121

WOLFF, HANNS H, b Berlin, Ger, Dec 19, 03; US citizen; m 40; c 2. ELECTRICAL ENGINEERING, ELECTROPHYSICS. *Educ:* Tech Univ Berlin, Dipl Ing, 28, Dr Ing, 45. *Prof Exp:* Asst to dir res & develop, Telephonfabrik AG, Ger, 28-29; sci asst to patent & consult engr, Univ Berlin, 29-30; from chief engr patent dept to exec in res info, Radio AG, 30-44; docent, Tech Univ Berlin, 46; court expert elec & electromech eng, Supreme Court Berlin, 46-47; chief res engr, Lavoie Labs, Inc, NJ, 47-51; chief engr, Gen Fuse, Inc, 51-53; chief engr & vpres, Leetronics Inc, NY, 53-56; staff engr, W L Maxson Corp, 56-60; chief electronics engr, Repub Aviation Corp, 60-63, tech dir, Naval Training Device Ctr, Port Washington, NY & Orlando, Fla, 63-75; CONSULT TRAINING DEVICES & SYSTS & PRES, TRAINING SYSTS ASSOCS, INC, 75- *Concurrent Pos:* Patent & consult engr, 34-47; adj prof, Polytech Inst Brooklyn, 59-66. *Mem:* Fel Inst Elec & Electronics Engrs; Sigma Xi. *Res:* Electrical measurements; standards; alternating current bridges and potentiometers; television systems; skin effect; power transport on long lines at extremely high voltages; induction accelerators; antennas, communications, radar, electron countermeasures and training equipment, devices, systems and complexes. *Mailing Add:* 8624 Caracas Ave Orlando FL 32817

WOLFF, IVAN A, b Louisville, Ky, Feb 10, 17; m 41; c 4. ORGANIC CHEMISTRY, RESEARCH ADMINISTRATION. *Educ:* Univ Louisville, BA, 37; Univ Wis, MA, 38, PhD(org chem), 40. *Prof Exp:* Fel biochem, Univ Wis, 40-41; asst chemist northern regional res lab bur agr chem & eng, Sci & Educ Admin Agr Res, USDA, 41-42, from assoc chemist to chemist, 43-48, unit leader, 48-54, asst head cereal crops sect, 54-58, chief indust crops lab northern utilization res & develop div, Agr Res Serv, 58-69, dir, 69-80, EMER DIR & ACTG DIR, RES CTR, AGR RES SERV, USDA, 81- *Concurrent Pos:* Mem subcomt natural toxicants food protection comt, Nat Acad Sci-Nat Res Coun, 70-74. *Honors & Awards:* Super Serv Award, USDA, 57. *Mem:* Am Chem Soc; Am Oil Chem Soc; Soc Econ Bot (pres, 64-65); Inst Food Technol. *Res:* Biochemistry, nutrition, processing utilization of farm commodities, and the constituents, components and derivatives from them; authored or coauthored over two hundred professional publications. *Mailing Add:* 600 E Mermaid Eastern Regional Res Ctr Agr Res Serv USDA Philadelphia PA 19118

WOLFF, JAMES A, b New York, NY, June 19, 14; m 46; c 4. PEDIATRICS, HEMATOLOGY. *Educ:* Harvard Univ, AB, 35; NY Univ, MD, 40; Am Bd Pediat, dipl, 48, cert pediat hemat-oncol, 74. *Prof Exp:* Intern, Lenox Hill Hosp, New York, 40-42; asst resident, Boston Children's Hosp, 45-47, chief resident outpatient dept, 47; asst pediatrician, Babies Hosp, New York, 48-51, from asst attend pediatrician to assoc attend pediatrician, 51-68; from assoc prof to prof clin pediat, 61-72, PROF PEDIAT, COL PHYSICIANS & SURGEONS, COLUMBIA UNIV, 72-; ATTEND PEDIATRICIAN, BABIES HOSP, 68- *Concurrent Pos:* Fel pediat hemat, Harvard Med Sch, 48; prin investr children's cancer study group A, NIH, 58-; consult, Englewood Hosp, NJ, 62-, Valley Hosp, Ridgewood, 66-, St Luke's Hosp, New York & Community Hosp, Sullivan County, 69-; mem, Sub-board Pediat Hemat-Ontology, Am Bd Pediat, 72-79; mem, Nat Wilms' Tumor Study Comt, 69-79; attend pediatrician & dir, Ctr Cancer & Blood Dis, Overlook Hosp, Summit, NJ, 81- *Mem:* Harvey Soc; Am Pediat Soc; Soc Pediat Res; Am Soc Hemat; Int Soc Hemat. *Res:* Pediatric hematology and oncology. *Mailing Add:* Babies Hosp Dept Pediat 3975 Broadway New York NY 10032

WOLFF, JAN, b Dusseldorf, Ger, Apr 25, 25; US citizen; m 55; c 2. BIOCHEMISTRY, ENDOCRINOLOGY. *Educ:* Univ Calif, BA, 45, PhD(physiol, biochem), 49; Harvard Univ, MD, 53. *Prof Exp:* Teaching asst, Univ Calif, 46 & res asst, 46-49; res asst, Harvard Univ, 54-55; surgeon, 55-58, sr surgeon, 58-63, MED DIR, NAT INSTS HEALTH, 63-, ASSOC CHIEF, CLIN ENDOCRINOL BR, 65- *Concurrent Pos:* NSF sr fel, London & Paris, 58-59; vis prof, Univ Naples, 68. *Mem:* Am Thyroid Asn; Am Soc Biol Chemists; Endocrine Soc; Am Soc Clin Invest. *Res:* Biochemistry and chemistry of thyroid hormone synthesis; properties and function of biological membranes, particularly thyroid membranes, and the relation of adenylate cyclase to receptors and membrane organization; transport; secretory mechanisms; microtubules and control of tubulin polymerization. *Mailing Add:* Rm 8N312 NIH Clin Ctr Bethesda MD 20014

WOLFF, JOHN B(RUNO), b Ger, May 5, 25; nat US; m 50; c 1. BIOPHYSICS. *Educ:* Hunter Col, AB, 50; Johns Hopkins Univ, MA, 51, PhD(biol), 55. *Prof Exp:* NIH fel, 52-54; biochemist, Smithsonian Inst, 54-58; vis scientist & res assoc, Nat Inst Arthritis & Metab Dis, 58-60, chemist, Nat Inst Neurol Dis & Blindness, 60-62, health scientist adminstr, 62-65, HEALTH SCIENTIST ADMINR, DIV RES GRANTS, NIH, 65- *Mem:* AAAS; Am Soc Biol Chemists; Biophys Soc (treas, 71-78. *Res:* Microbial and plant biochemistry; enzymology. *Mailing Add:* Westwood Bldg Room 236B 5333 Westbard Ave Bethesda MD 20205

WOLFF, JOHN SHEARER, III, b Rochester, NY, Feb 9, 41; m 63; c 2. BIOCHEMISTRY, VIROLOGY. *Educ:* Wittenberg Univ, AB, 62; Univ Cincinnati, PhD(biochem), 66. *Prof Exp:* Asst prof biol, Fed City Col, 69-70; sr investr, 70-71, LAB HEAD MOLECULAR BIOL, JOHN L SMITH MEM FOR CANCER RES, PFIZER, INC, 71- *Concurrent Pos:* Nat Inst Allergy & Infectious Dis fel immunochem, Col Med, Univ Ill, 68-69. *Mem:* AAAS; Am Chem Soc; Am Soc Microbiol; Reticuloendothelial Soc. *Res:* Relationships between biochemical and biological activities of tumor viruses, especially RNA tumor viruses. *Mailing Add:* 588 Baker Ct River Vale NJ 07675

WOLFF, MANFRED ERNST, b Berlin, Ger, Feb 14, 30; nat US; div; c 3. MEDICINAL CHEMISTRY. *Educ:* Univ Calif, BS, 51, MS, 53, PhD(pharmaceut chem), 55. *Prof Exp:* Asst, Univ Calif, 52-55; res fel, Univ Va, 55-57; sr med chemist, Smith Kline & French Labs, 57-60; from asst prof to assoc prof pharmaceut chem, 60-65, PROF PHARMACEUT CHEM, UNIV CALIF, SAN FRANCISCO, 65-, CHMN DEPT, 70- *Concurrent Pos:* Vis prof, Imperial Col Sci, London, 67-68; ed, Burger's Med Chem, 79-81. *Mem:* Am Chem Soc; Am Pharmaceut Asn; fel Am Acad Pharmaceut Sci. *Res:* Synthesis of potential anabolic, anti-inflammatory or anti-aldosterone hormone analogs; synthesis of aldosterone, of cardiac glycosides and aglycones; steroid chemistry and biochemistry. *Mailing Add:* Dept of Pharmaceut Chem Univ of Calif San Francisco CA 94143

WOLFF, MANFRED PAUL, b New York, NY, Apr 26, 38; m 62; c 2. GEOLOGY, SEDIMENTOLOGY. *Educ:* Hofstra Univ, BS, 61; Univ Rochester, MS, 63; Cornell Univ, PhD(geol), 67. *Prof Exp:* Grad instr, Cornell Univ, 64-67, from asst prof to assoc prof geol, 67-75, actg chmn dept, 71-75; assoc prof, 75-81, PROF GEOL, HOFSTRA UNIV, 81- *Concurrent Pos:* Wilson P Foss fel, Cornell Univ, 63-65; Am Penrose Bequest grant, Geol Soc Am, 66; mem adv comt, Nassau-Suffolk Regional Planning Bd, 66-69; NSF grant, 69; Hofstra Univ res award, 75-81. *Mem:* Geol Soc Am; Soc Econ Paleont & Mineral; Nat Asn Geol Teachers; Int Asn Sedimentol. *Res:* Ancient and recent clastic and carbonate depositional environments; physical stratigraphy; coastal processes; sedimentation; sedimentology; plate tectonics; marine geology; sedimentology of beaches, barrier islands and beaches; nearshore shelf. *Mailing Add:* Dept Geol Hofstra Univ Hempstead NY 11550

WOLFF, MARIANNE, b Berlin, Ger; US citizen; m 52; c 2. PATHOLOGY, SURGICAL PATHOLOGY. *Educ:* Hunter Col, BA, 48; Columbia Univ, MD, 52. *Prof Exp:* Intern med, Presby Hosp, New York, 52-53; asst resident lab, Mt Sinai Hosp, New York, 53-54, asst resident path, St Luke's Hosp, 54-56; from instr to asst prof surg path, Col Physicians & Surgeons, Columbia Univ, 56-70; asst surg pathologist, 68-71, ASSOC SURG PATHOLOGIST, PRESBY HOSP, NEW YORK, 71-; assoc prof clin surg path, 70-82, ASSOC PROF SURG PATH, COL PHYSICIANS & SURGEONS, COLUMBIA UNIV, 70-, PROF CLIN SURG PATH, 82- *Concurrent Pos:* Resident, Presby Hosp, 56-57; from asst pathologist to assoc pathologist, Roosevelt Hosp, New York, 57-68; mem, Arthur Purdy Stout Soc Surg Pathologist, 68- *Mem:* Fel Am Soc Clin Path. *Mailing Add:* Col of Physicians & Surgeons Columbia Univ Lab of Surg Path New York NY 10032

WOLFF, MILO MITCHELL, b Glen Ridge, NJ, Aug 9, 23; m 54; c 5. PHYSICS, ELECTRICAL ENGINEERING. *Educ:* Upsala Col, BS, 48; Univ Pa, MS, 53, PhD(physics), 58. *Prof Exp:* Electronic engr, Philco Corp, Pa, 49-51; lectr electronics, Community Col, Temple Univ, 52-53; instr physics, Univ Pa, 58; Univ Ky-Agency Int Develop asst prof, Bandung Tech Inst, Indonesia, 58-61, assoc prof, 62; res physicist, Mass Inst Technol, 63-69; prof physics, Nanyang Univ, Singapore, 70-72; mem tech staff, Aerospace Corp, Los Angeles, 72-75; chief, Sci & Technol Sect, Econ Comn Africa-UN, Addis Ababa, 75-78; MEM STAFF, INT TECHNOL ASN, LONG BEACH, 78- *Concurrent Pos:* Asia Found vis prof physics, Vidyalankara Univ, Ceylon, 66-68; mem, US-Pakistan Sci Surv Team, US NSF, 74; mem methane gas panel, Nat Acad Sci, 74. *Honors & Awards:* Apollo Navig Team Award, 69. *Mem:* Inst Elec & Electronics Engrs; Am Phys Soc. *Res:* Electronics; computer science; planetary optics; methods of cultural adaptation to technology in traditional societies; nuclear physics; space physics; upper atmosphere; technical development in Southeast Asia; polarized light; atmospheric and biological energy; economic development. *Mailing Add:* 1600 Nelson Ave Manhattan Beach CA 90266

WOLFF, NIKOLAUS EMANUEL, b Munich, Ger, July 7, 21; nat US; m 54; c 3. CHEMISTRY, ELECTRONICS. *Educ:* Munich Tech Univ, Cand, 48; Princeton Univ, MA, 51, PhD(chem), 52. *Prof Exp:* Asst instr, Princeton Univ, 50-52, instr chem, 52-53; res chemist, Jackson Lab & Exp Sta, E I du Pont de Nemours & Co, 53-58; mem tech staff, Labs, David Sarnoff Res Ctr, RCA Corp, 59-63, head mat processing res, 63-66; assoc lab dir, Process Res & Develop Lab, 67-68; mgr mat progs, Xerox Corp, 68-69, mgr photoreceptor technol, 69-71, mgr mat info technol group, 71-76; TECHNOL CONSULT TO MGT, 76- *Mem:* Fel AAAS; Am Chem Soc; Tech Asn Pulp & Paper Indust; fel Am Inst Chemists; Soc Photog Sci & Eng. *Res:* Steroid, fluorine and polymer chemistry; organometallics; electronic properties of organic materials; chemistry of recording media; electrophotography; solid state technology and integrated circuits. *Mailing Add:* PO Box 1003 Hanover NH 03755

WOLFF, PETER ADALBERT, b Oakland, Calif, Nov 15, 23; m 48; c 2. PHYSICS. *Educ:* Univ Calif, AB, 45, PhD(physics), 51. *Prof Exp:* Physicist, Bell Tel Labs, Inc, NJ, 52-68, dir, Electronics Res Lab, 68-70; dir, Res Lab Electronics, 76-81, PROF PHYSICS, MASS INST TECHNOL, 70-, DIR, FRANCIS BITTER NAT MAGNET LAB, 81- *Concurrent Pos:* Prof, Univ Calif, San Diego, 63-64. *Mem:* Fel Am Phys Soc. *Res:* Spin susceptibility of electron gas; theory of local moments in metals; plasma effects in solids; interaction of light with electrons in solids; infrared nonlinear optics. *Mailing Add:* Dept of Physics Mass Inst of Technol Cambridge MA 02139

WOLFF, PETER HARTWIG, b Krefeld, Ger, July 8, 26; US citizen; m 62; c 4. MEDICINE, PSYCHOBIOLOGY. *Educ:* Univ Chicago, BS, 47, MD, 50. *Prof Exp:* Asst psychiat, Harvard Med Sch, 56-59, instr, 58-61, assoc, 61-64, asst prof, 64-71; res assoc, 56-61, ASSOC, CHILDREN'S HOSP MED CTR, 61-, DIR RES, 64-; PROF PSYCHIAT, HARVARD MED SCH, 71- *Concurrent Pos:* Fel neurophysiol, Univ Chicago, 51-52; Kirby Collier Mem lectr, Rochester, NY, 63; instr, Boston Psychoanal Inst, 67-; Sandor Rado lectr, Columbia Univ, 69. *Honors & Awards:* Helen Sargent Prize, Menninger Found, 66; Felix & Helene Deutsch Prize, Boston Psychoanal Inst, 66. *Mem:* Fel Am Psychiat Asn. *Res:* Developmental psychobiology; biological basis of behavior. *Mailing Add:* Children's Hosp Med Ctr 300 Longwood Ave Boston MA 02115

WOLFF, RICHARD JAMES, b St Paul, Minn, Oct 17, 40; m 62. ASTROPHYSICS, COMPUTING. *Educ:* Carleton Col, BA, 62; Univ Calif, Berkeley, PhD(physics), 67. *Prof Exp:* Asst prof, 67-70, asst astronr, 70-72, ASSOC ASTRONR, UNIV HAWAII, 72- *Mem:* Optical Soc Am; Asn Comput Mach. *Res:* Stellar spectroscopy; instrumentation for telescopes and for reduction of astronomical data; operating system software for astronomy research. *Mailing Add:* Inst for Astron Univ of Hawaii 2680 Woodlawn Dr Honolulu HI 96822

WOLFF, ROBERT L, b Marion, Tex, Dec 12, 39; m 60; c 1. AGRICULTURE. *Educ:* Tex A&I Univ, BS, 66; Tex A&M Univ, MS, 68; La State Univ, Baton Rouge, PhD(agr), 71. *Prof Exp:* Asst prof agr, Tex A&I Univ, 66-72; asst prof, 72-77, ASSOC PROF AGR, SOUTHERN ILL UNIV, CARBONDALE, 77- *Mem:* Am Soc Agr Eng. *Res:* Agricultural mechanization. *Mailing Add:* Dept of Agr Industs Southern Ill Univ Carbondale IL 62901

WOLFF, ROGER GLEN, b Eureka, SDak, Sept 7, 32; m 59; c 2. GEOLOGY, HYDROLOGY. *Educ:* SDak Sch Mines & Technol, BS, 58; Univ Ill, MS, 60, PhD(geol), 61. *Prof Exp:* Res geologist, Water Resources Div, 61-80, DEP ASST CHIEF HYDROLOGIST RES, US GEOL SURV, 80- *Mem:* Am Geophys Union; Clay Minerals Soc; Geol Soc Am; Sigma Xi. *Res:* Role of confining layers in fluid and solute movement; regional tectonic stress determinations. *Mailing Add:* US Geol Surv Water Resources Div Reston VA 22092

WOLFF, RONALD GILBERT, b Lewiston, Idaho, Jan 17, 42. VERTEBRATE PALEONTOLOGY. *Educ:* Whitman Col, AB, 64; Univ Ore, MA, 66; Univ Calif, Berkeley, PhD(paleont), 71. *Prof Exp:* Fel anat, Univ Chicago, 71-72, res assoc, 72-73; asst prof zool, 73-78, ASSOC PROF ZOOL, UNIV FLA, 78- *Concurrent Pos:* Prin investr grant, Col Arts & Sci, Univ Fla, 77-79 & Div Environ Biol, Nat Sci Found, 78-79; co-investr grant, Nat Geog Soc, 78-79. *Mem:* Soc Vert Paleont; Paleont Soc; Sigma Xi; Ecol Soc Am; Am Soc Mammalogists. *Res:* Population and community ecology of mammals; environment of human evolution; late Tertiary and Quaternary vertebrate communities. *Mailing Add:* Dept of Zool Univ of Fla Gainesville FL 32611

WOLFF, SHELDON, b Peabody, Mass, Sept 22, 28; m 54; c 3. CYTOGENETICS, RADIOBIOLOGY. *Educ:* Tufts Col, BS, 50; Harvard Univ, MA, 51, PhD(biol), 53. *Prof Exp:* Biologist, Oak Ridge Nat Lab, 53-66, mem sr res staff, 65-66; PROF CYTOGENETICS, UNIV CALIF, SAN FRANCISCO, 66- *Concurrent Pos:* Mem subcomt radiobiol, Nat Acad Sci-Nat Res Coun, 61-77, mem space sci bd & mem comt nuclear sci, 74-77; vis prof, Univ Tenn, 62; mem comt 15 environ biol & chmn panel radiation biol of comt 15, Space Sci Bd, Nat Acad Sci, 62, mem comt postdoctoral fels div biol & agr, 62-65; consult spec facil prog, NSF, 62-64; mem exec comt, Nat Acad Sci-Nat Res Coun Space Biol Summer Study, 68, mem exec comt priorities study for NASA, 70, mem subcomt genetics effects adv comt to Environ Protection Agency, Div Med Sci, 70-; mem safe drinking water comt, Nat Acad Sci, 76-; prog chmn, XIII Int Cong Genetics; mem comt federal res ionizing radiation & mem comt chem environ mutagens, Nat Res Coun-Nat Acad Sci, 80-81. *Honors & Awards:* E O Lawrence Award, US AEC, 73. *Mem:* Environ Mutagen Soc (pres, 80-81); Genetics Soc Am; Radiation Res Soc; Bot Soc Am; Am Soc Cell Biol. *Res:* Chromosome structure; radiation genetics and cytology; chromosome structure; genetics and cytology. *Mailing Add:* Lab Radiobiol Univ Calif San Francisco CA 94143

WOLFF, SHELDON MALCOLM, b Newark, NJ, Aug 19, 30; m 56; c 3. INFECTIOUS DISEASES, IMMUNOLOGY. *Educ:* Univ Ga, BS, 52; Vanderbilt Univ, MD, 57; Am Bd Internal Med, dipl. *Prof Exp:* Intern med, Sch Med, Vanderbilt Univ, 57-58, asst resident, 58-59; sr resident, Bronx Munic Hosp Ctr & Albert Einstein Col Med, 59-60; clin assoc, Nat Inst Allergy & Infectious Dis, 60-62, clin investr, 62-63, sr investr, 63-65, head physiol sect, Lab Clin Invest, 64-74, clin dir & chief lab clin invest, 68-77; ENDICOTT PROF MED & CHMN DEPT, SCH MED & ADJ PROF INT HEALTH, FLETCHER SCH LAW & DIPLOMACY, TUFTS UNIV, 77-; PHYSICIAN-IN-CHIEF, NEW ENG MED CTR HOSP, 77- *Concurrent Pos:* Res asst, Sch Med, Vanderbilt Univ, 56-59; lectr, Sch Med, Georgetown Univ, 62-69, clin prof, 69-77; consult infectious dis, Nat Naval Med Ctr, Md, 70- *Honors & Awards:* Super Serv Award, NIH, 71; Squibb Award, 76. *Mem:* AAAS; Asn Am Phys; Am Col Phys; Invest. *Res:* Mechanisms of host responses. *Mailing Add:* Dept of Med 171 Harrison Ave Boston MA 02111

WOLFF, SIDNEY CARNE, b Sioux City, Iowa, June 6, 41; m 62. ASTROPHYSICS. *Educ:* Carleton Col, BA, 62; Univ Calif, Berkeley, PhD(astron), 66. *Prof Exp:* Res astronr, Lick Observ, Univ Calif, Santa Cruz, 67; from asst astronr to assoc astronr, 67-75, ASTRON, INST ASTRON, UNIV HAWAII, 75-, ASSOC DIR, 76- *Mem:* Am Astron Soc; Int Astron Union. *Res:* Stellar spectroscopy; photoelectric photometry; magnetic stars. *Mailing Add:* Inst for Astron Univ of Hawaii 2680 Woodlawn Dr Honolulu HI 96822

WOLFF, STEVEN, b New York, NY, Apr 15, 43. ORGANIC CHEMISTRY. *Educ:* Williams Col, BA, 65; Yale Univ, PhD(org chem), 70. *Prof Exp:* Fel org chem, Squibb Inst Med Res, 70-71; res assoc, 71-73, asst prof, 73-78, ASSOC PROF ORG CHEM, ROCKEFELLER UNIV, 78- *Mem:* Am Chem Soc; Royal Soc Chem. *Res:* Mechanistic organic photochemistry. *Mailing Add:* Rockefeller Univ 1230 York Ave New York NY 10021

WOLFF, THEODORE ALBERT, b Philadelphia, Pa, Feb 24, 43; m 62. ENTOMOLOGY, MEDICAL PARASITOLOGY. *Educ:* NMex Highlands Univ, BS, 65; Univ NC, Chapel Hill, MSPH, 69; Univ Utah, PhD(biol), 76. *Prof Exp:* Vol biol, Peace Corps, Malaysia, 65-68; environ scientist entom, NMex Environ Improv Agency, 69-72; teaching fel biol, Univ Utah, 72-74; environ scientist, NMex Environ Improv Agency, 74-76, dir radiation protection prog, 76-81; TECH STAFF MEM, SANDIA NAT LABS, 81- *Mem:* Assoc Sigma Xi; Am Mosquito Control Asn; Am Pub Health Asn. *Res:* Systematic studies of mountain Aedes mosquitoes; subgenus Ochlerotatus of Arizona and New Mexico. *Mailing Add:* 8117 Loma del Norte NE Albuquerque NM 87109

WOLFF, WILLIAM FRANCIS, b Newark, NJ, June 17, 21; m 48; c 4. ORGANIC CHEMISTRY. *Educ:* Yale Univ, BS, 47. *Prof Exp:* Res chemist, Standard Oil Co, Ind, 47-53; res chemist, Pa Salt Mfg Co, 53-54; res chemist, 54-58, sr proj chemist, 58-61, SR RES SCIENTIST, STANDARD OIL CO, IND, 61- *Mem:* AAAS; Am Chem Soc. *Res:* Hydrocarbon polymers; organic sulfur and chlorine compounds; carbons and aromatic complexes; heterogeneous catalysis. *Mailing Add:* Amoco Res Ctr Naperville IL 60540

WOLFGRAM, FREDERICK JOHN, b Los Angeles, Calif, Mar 18, 25; m 52; c 3. NEUROCHEMISTRY. *Educ:* Univ Calif, AB, 49; Calif Inst Technol, PhD(physiol), 52. *Prof Exp:* Jr res neurologist, 54-55, from asst res neurologist to assoc res neurologist, 55-64, assoc prof neurol, 64-70, PROF NEUROL, UNIV CALIF, LOS ANGELES, 70- *Concurrent Pos:* Nat Found Infantile Paralysis res fel, Johns Hopkins Univ, 52-54. *Mem:* Am Acad Neurol; Am Neurol Asn; Am Soc Neurochem; Int Soc Neurochem. *Res:* Myelin chemistry; demyelinating diseases; amyotrophic lateral sclerosis. *Mailing Add:* Reed Neurol Res Ctr Univ of Calif Sch of Med Los Angeles CA 90024

WOLFHAGEN, JAMES LANGDON, b Portland, Ore, Dec 9, 20; m 48; c 3. ORGANIC CHEMISTRY. *Educ:* Linfield Col, AB, 46; Univ Calif, Berkeley, PhD(chem), 51. *Prof Exp:* Chemist, Northwest Testing Labs, Ore, 41-42; asst prof chem, Whitworth Col, Wash, 49-52; from asst prof to assoc prof, 52-64, head dept, 67-75, PROF CHEM, UNIV MAINE, ORONO, 64- *Concurrent Pos:* Vis scientist, Forest Sci Lab, Tex A&M Univ, 76-77. *Mem:* AAAS; Am Chem Soc; Sigma Xi. *Res:* Reaction of alkali metals with dimethylformamide; synthesis and stereochemistry of glycidic esters; epoxidation reactions; carbonium ions; wood and pulping chemistry. *Mailing Add:* Dept of Chem Univ of Maine Orono ME 04473

WOLFLE, DAEL (LEE), b Puyallup, Wash, Mar 5, 06; m 29; c 3. SCIENCE POLICY. *Educ:* Univ Wash, BS, 27, MS, 28; Ohio State Univ, PhD(psychol), 31. *Hon Degrees:* DSc, Drexel Inst Technol, 56, Ohio State Univ, 57 & Western Mich Univ, 60. *Prof Exp:* Instr psychol, Ohio State Univ, 29-32; prof, Univ Miss, 32-36; examr biol sci, Univ Chicago, 36-39, from asst prof to assoc prof psychol, 38-45; exec secy, Am Psychol Asn, 46-50; dir, Comn Human Resources & Advan Training, Assoc Res Couns, 50-54; exec officer, AAAS, 54-70; actg dean archit & urban planning, 72-73, prof pub affairs, 70-76, EMER PROF PUB AFFAIRS, GRAD SCH PUB AFFAIRS, UNIV WASH, 76- *Concurrent Pos:* Civilian training adminr electronics, US Army Sig Corps, 41-43; tech aide, Off Sci Res & Develop, 44-46; mem or vchmn, Bd Trustees, Russell Sage Found, 61-78; mem or chmn, Bd Trustees, James McKeen Cattell Fund, 62-; trustee, Pac Sci Ctr Found, 62-80; mem ed adv bd, Sci Yearbk, Encycl Brittanica, 67-77; mem res adv comt, Am Coun Educ, 68-73; trustee, Biosci Info Servs, 68-74; mem or chmn, Geophys Inst Adv Comt, Univ Alaska, 69-; mem manpower inst, Nat Indust Conf Bd, 70; chmn rev comt sci resources studies, NSF, 72-73; mem comt grad med educ, Asn Am Med Cols, 72-75; mem, US-USSR Joint Group Experts Sci Policy, 73-78; mem comn human resources, Nat Acad Sci-Nat Res Coun, 74-78; mem bd trustees, Biol Sci Curriculum Stidu, 80- *Honors & Awards:* Montgomery lectr, Univ Nebr, 59; Walter Van Dyke Bingham lectr, Columbia Univ, 60; Herbert S Langfeld lectr, Princeton Univ, 69. *Mem:* AAAS (exec officer, 54-70); Am Psychol Asn (exec secy 46-50); Am Coun Educ (secy, 66-67). *Res:* Education, utilization, mobility, supply and demand trends of scientific and specialized personnel. *Mailing Add:* Grad Sch Pub Affairs Univ Wash Seattle WA 98195

WOLFLE, THOMAS LEE, b Eugene, Ore, Apr 24, 36; m 62; c 2. VETERINARY MEDICINE, ANIMAL BEHAVIOR. *Educ:* Tex A&M Univ, BS, 59, DVM, 61; Univ Calif, Los Angeles, MA, 67, PhD(physiol psychol), 70; Am Col Lab Animal Med, dipl, 66. *Prof Exp:* Vet primate colony mgt, Sch Aerospace Med, Brooks AFB, Tex, 61-65, chief comp toxicol lab, Aeromed Res Lab, Holloman AFB, 65-66; chief flight environ br, Aerospace Med Res Labs, Wright-Patterson AFB, Ohio, 70-73, asst chief weapons effects br, Sch Aerospace Med, Brooks AFB, Tex, 73-75; SR VET OFFICER, NIH, 75- *Concurrent Pos:* Adj prof psychol, Wright State Univ, 71-73, consult, Lab Animal Med, 72-73. *Mem:* Am Vet Med Asn; Am Soc Vet Ethol; AAAS; Am Asn Lab Animal Sci; assoc fel Col Vet Toxicol. *Res:* Animal behavior, canine medicine; impact of early non-specific environmental influences upon research on selected animal-disease models; identification of animal models of human disease. *Mailing Add:* Bldg 102 Rm 102 NIH Animal Ctr Bethesda MD 20205

WOLFMAN, EARL FRANK, JR, b Buffalo, NY, Sept 14, 26; m 46; c 3. SURGERY. *Educ:* Harvard Univ, BS, 46; Univ Mich, MD, 50; Am Bd Surg, dipl, 58. *Prof Exp:* From instr to asst prof surg, Univ Mich, 57-63, assoc prof, Med Sch, 63-66, asst to dean, 60-61, asst dean, 61-64; chmn div & dept & assoc dean, 66-78, PROF SURG, SCH MED, UNIV CALIF, DAVIS, 66- *Concurrent Pos:* Consult, Vet Admin Hosps, Travis AFB & Martinez, Calif, 66-; chief div surg serv, Sacramento Med Ctr, 66-78. *Mem:* Fel Am Col Surgeons; AMA; Soc Surg Alimentary Tract; Asn Acad Surg; Sigma Xi. *Mailing Add:* Dept Surg Univ Calif Sch Med Prof Bldg 4301 X St Sacramento CA 95817

WOLFORD, JACK ARLINGTON, b Brookville, Pa, Dec 5, 17; m 44; c 2. PSYCHIATRY. *Educ:* Allegheny Col, AB, 40; Univ Pa, MD, 43; Am Bd Psychiat, dipl, 53. *Prof Exp:* Intern med, Allegheny Gen Hosp, Pittsburgh, Pa, 43; resident psychiat, Warren State Hosp, 44-46, sr psychiatrist, 48-51, clin dir, 51-56; dir, Hastings State Hosp, Nebr, 56-58; asst prof psychiat, Sch Med, 58-69, chief social psychiat, Western Psychiat Inst & Clin, 58-72, dir community ment health, Retardation Ctr, 67-74, psychiatrist-in-chief & actg chmn dept psychiat, Sch Med, 72-73, PROF PSYCHIAT, SCH MED, UNIV PITTSBURGH, 69-, DIR ADULT SERV, WESTERN PSYCHIAT INST & CLIN, 72-, DIR COMMUNITY MENT HEALTH/MENT RETARDATION CTRS, 76- *Concurrent Pos:* Resident psychiat, Psychiat Inst & Clin, Pittsburgh, 53; asst prof psychiat, Univ Nebr, 56-58; vis fac sem, Lab Community Psychiat, Harvard Univ; mem, Governor's Adv Comt to Dept Welfare & Comn Ment Health; mem commun adv comt, NIMH; mem med adv comt, Gov Adv Comt Ment Health & Ment Retardation, Dept Pub Welfare & Comn Ment Health, 74 & 75, Comprehensive Comt Ment Health Planning, 75 & Pa Asn Community Ment Health & Ment Retardation Ctrs, 75; pres, Group for Advan Psychiat, 77-79; secy, Pa Asn Community Ment Health & Ment Retardaton Providers, 80- *Mem:* Fel Am Psychiat Asn (vpres, 75); fel Am Col Psychiat; AMA. *Res:* Social and community psychiatry; urban mental health and illness. *Mailing Add:* Western Psychiat Inst & Clin 3811 O'Hara St Pittsburgh PA 15261

WOLFORD, JAMES C, b Fairmont, Nebr, July 20, 20; m 50; c 3. MECHANICS, MECHANICAL ENGINEERING. *Educ:* Univ Nebr, BS, 47, MS, 52; Purdue Univ, PhD(kinematics), 56. *Prof Exp:* Test engr, Gen Elec Co, 47-48, design engr, 48-50; design engr, Cecil W Armstrong & Assocs, 50-51; from instr to asst prof mech, 54-58, assoc prof kinematics & mach design, 58-63, PROF KINEMATICS & MACH DESIGN, UNIV NEBR, LINCOLN, 63- *Mem:* Am Soc Mech Engrs; Am Soc Eng Educ; Sigma Xi. *Res:* Design of machine elements; kinematics of mechanisms. *Mailing Add:* Dept of Mech Eng Univ of Nebr Lincoln NE 68588

WOLFORD, JOHN HENRY, b Osgood, Ind, June 11, 36. AVIAN PHYSIOLOGY, POULTRY SCIENCE. *Educ:* Purdue Univ, BS, 58; Mich State Univ, MS, 60, PhD(avian physiol), 63. *Prof Exp:* From asst prof to assoc prof poultry sci, Mich State Univ, 63-74; prof animal & vet sci & chmn dept, Univ Maine, Orono, 74-80; PROF POULTRY SCI & DEPT HEAD, VA POLYTECH INST & STATE UNIV, 80- *Mem:* Poultry Sci Asn; Sigma Xi; World Poultry Sci Asn. *Res:* Reproductive physiology of the turkey breeder hen; physiological alterations of fatty liver syndrome in laying chickens. *Mailing Add:* Dept Poultry Sci Va Polytech Inst & State Univ Blacksburg VA 24060

WOLFORD, RICHARD KENNETH, b Pa, Jan 3, 32. CHEMISTRY. *Educ:* WVa Wesleyan Col, BS, 53; Univ Ky, MS, 55, PhD(chem), 59. *Prof Exp:* Asst chem, Univ Ky, 53-58; chemist, Nat Bur Standards, 58-66; PHYS SCI ADMINSTR, NAT OCEAN SURV, NAT OCEANIC & ATMOSPHERIC ADMIN, 66- *Mem:* AAAS; Am Chem Soc. *Res:* Oceanography. *Mailing Add:* Triangle Towers 4853 Cordell Ave Bethesda MD 20814

WOLFORD, THOMAS LOUIS, inorganic chemistry, see previous edition

WOLFOWITZ, JACOB, mathematics, deceased

WOLFRAM, LESZEK JANUARY, b Krakow, Poland, Feb 24, 29; US citizen; m 53; c 2. FIBER SCIENCE, PROTEIN CHEMISTRY. *Educ:* Politechnika, Lodz, Poland, BSc, 53, MSc, 55; Univ Leeds, PhD(protein chem), 61. *Prof Exp:* Chemist, Gillette Res Lab, Reading, UK, 61-63, sr chemist, ground leader & prin scientist, Gillette Res Inst, Rockville, Md, 63-72; sci liaison officer, Int Wool Secretariat, Australia, 72-73; asst dir res, Personal Care Div, The Gillette Co, Boston, 74-77; dir res, 77-79, VPRES RES, CLAIROL RES LABS, 79- *Concurrent Pos:* Assoc ed, J Soc Cosmetic Chemists, 78-79, ed, 79- *Mem:* Am Chem Soc; NY Acad Sci; Fiber Soc; Soc Cosmetic Chemists; AAAS. *Res:* Physical chemistry of synthetic polymers and proteins; structure of fibers and biological tissues; evaluative techniques for hair and skin; organ biosurfaces and their properties. *Mailing Add:* Clairol Res Labs 2 Blachley Rd Stamford CT 06902

WOLFRAM, THOMAS, b St Louis, Mo, July 27, 36. SOLID STATE PHYSICS. *Educ:* Univ Calif, Riverside, AB, 59, PhD(physics), 63; Univ Calif, Los Angeles, MA, 60. *Prof Exp:* Mem tech staff, Atomics Int, 60-63; mem tech staff, NAm Rockwell Sci Ctr, 63-68, group leader solid state physics, 68-72, dir physics & chem, Rockwell Int Sci Ctr, 72-74; PROF PHYSICS, UNIV MO, COLUMBIA, 74-, CHMN DEPT, 80- *Concurrent Pos:* Adj prof physics, Univ Calif, Riverside, 68-69. *Honors & Awards:* Distinguished Prof Award, Argonne Univ Asn, 77. *Mem:* Fel Am Phys Soc. *Res:* Lattice dynamics; spin waves; superconductivity; electronic and optical properties; physics and chemistry of surfaces; catalysis. *Mailing Add:* Dept of Physics Univ of Mo Columbia MO 65201

WOLFROM, GLEN WALLACE, b Freeport, Ill, Apr 8, 47; m 69; c 2. ANIMAL NUTRITION, BIOSTATISTICS. *Educ:* Western Ill Univ, BS, 69; Southern Ill Univ, MS, 72; Univ Mo-Columbia, PhD(animal nutrit), 76. *Prof Exp:* Mgr nutrit & chem, Contech Lab-Pet Inc, 76-78; RESEARCHER NUTRIT, INT MINERALS & CHEM CORP, 78- *Mem:* AAAS; Nutrit Today Soc; Am Soc Animal Sci. *Res:* Amino acid nutrition of ruminants. *Mailing Add:* Animal Sci Res Int Minerals & Chem Corp Terre Haute IN 47808

WOLFSBERG, KURT, b Hamburg, Ger, Nov 1, 31; nat US; m 55; c 3. RADIOCHEMISTRY, NUCLEAR CHEMISTRY. *Educ:* St Louis Univ, BS, 53; Wash Univ, St Louis, MA, 55, PhD(chem), 59. *Prof Exp:* STAFF MEM RADIOCHEM GROUP, LOS ALAMOS NAT LAB, 59-, ASSOC GROUP LEADER ISOTOPE GEOCHEM GROUP, 80- *Concurrent Pos:* Consult aircraft nuclear propulsion comt nuclear measurements & standards, US Air Force, 56-57; mem subcomt radiochem, Nat Acad Sci, 72-76; guest & Fulbright grantee, Univ Mainz, WGer, 74-75; Fulbright award, tech proj officer, Nev Terminal Waste Storage Proj, 78-79. *Mem:* AAAS; Am Chem Soc; fel Am Inst Chemists; Mat Res Soc. *Res:* Emanation techniques; mass and charge distribution in fission; high temperature diffusion of fission products; lanthanide and actinide chemistry; properties of very heavy nuclides; nuclear waste management, sorptive properties of geologic media, migration of radionuclides; geochemistry. *Mailing Add:* 303 Venado Los Alamos NM 87544

WOLFSBERG, MAX, b Hamburg, Ger, May 28, 28; nat US; m 57; c 1. ISOTOPE EFFECTS. *Educ:* Wash Univ, St Louis, AB, 48, PhD(chem), 51. *Prof Exp:* Asst chem, Wash Univ, St Louis, 48-50; assoc chemist, Brookhaven Nat Lab, 51-54, from chemist to sr chemist, 54-69; Regents' lectr, 68, PROF CHEM, UNIV CALIF, IRVINE, 69- *Concurrent Pos:* NSF sr fel, 58-59; vis prof chem, Cornell Univ, 63 & Ind Univ, 65; prof, State Univ NY Stony Brook, 66-69; Alexander von Humboldt award, 77. *Mem:* Am Chem Soc. *Res:* Theoretical chemistry; isotope effects, chemical reactions, electronic structure of molecules. *Mailing Add:* Dept of Chem Univ of Calif Irvine CA 92664

WOLFSON, BERNARD T, b Chicago, Ill, Mar 16, 19; m 42; c 2. ENERGY CONVERSION & UTILIZATION. *Educ:* Ill Inst Technol, BS, 40; Ohio State Univ, MS, 50, PhD, 60; Univ Southern Calif, cert mgt & finance, 69. *Prof Exp:* Chem & metall engr, Process Control Dept, Carnegie-Ill Steel Corp, Ind, 40-41; chem engr, Eng & Oper Div, Kankakee Ord Works, Ill, 41-42; tech supvr prod & inspection, Atlas Imp Diesel Engine Co, 42; rotary wing aircraft develop engr, Mech Br, Rotary Wing Unit, Propeller Lab, Wright Patterson AFB, Ohio, 42-44; aeronaut flight test engr, Flight Test Div, Ames Res Ctr, Moffett Field, Calif, 45-46; asst chief rotary wing aerodyn develop eng, Aerodyn Br, Rotary Wing Unit, Aircraft Lab, Wright Patterson AFB, 46-51, sr propulsion res scientist, Fluid Dynamics Res Br, Aerospace Res Lab, 51-61; aerospace propulsion scientist, Propulsion Div, Eng Sci Directorate, Air Force Off Sci Res, 61-66, actg dir div, 66-67, AEROSPACE PROPULSION SCIENTIST, PROPULSION DIV, ENG SCI DIRECTORATE, AIR FORCE OFF SCI RES, 67- *Concurrent Pos:* Mem panels & steering comts, Liquid Rocket Combustion Instability & Solid Rocket Combustion, Interagency Chem Rocket Propellants Group, Dept Defense Advan Res Projs Agency-NASA, 62-; adv panel air-breathing propulsion & power plants, NASA, 65-; ad hoc comt SRAMJET, Supersonic Combustion & Appln, Air Force Systs Command, 65-; Joint Army-Navy-Air Force-NASA Panels Liquid & Solid Rockets & Air-Breathing Combustion; magnetohydrodyn panel & working groups, Interagency Advan Power Group; mem steering group, Joint Army Navy NASA Air Force Interagency Propulsion Comt, 79- *Mem:* Combustion Inst; Am Inst Aeronaut & Astronaut; Sigma Xi. *Res:* Fuel-air deflagrations and explosions; alternative fuels; high speed reacting flow characterization; non-interference instrumentation and diagnostics; plasma propulsion and electric power generation; air-breathing propulsion; gas dynamic, electric, explosive-driven and magnetohydrodynamic lasers; plasma dynamics; combustion instability. *Mailing Add:* Air Force Off of Sci Res/NA Bolling AFB Washington DC 20332

WOLFSON, C JACOB, physics, see previous edition

WOLFSON, EDWARD A, b New York, NY, Feb 4, 26; m 55; c 3. PREVENTIVE MEDICINE, MEDICAL EDUCATION. *Educ:* Cornell Univ, AB, 48, MNS, 49, MD, 53; Columbia Univ, MPH, 71. *Prof Exp:* Pvt pract internal med, 57-69; prof prev med & community health & vchmn dept, Col Med NJ, 69-77, assoc dean health care, 72-75, dir, off primary health care educ, 75-77; PROF MED, DEAN CLIN CAMPUS, UPSTATE MED CTR/ UNIV CTR BINGHAMTON, 77- & PROF HEALTH CARE MGT, STATE UNIV NY, BINGHAMTON, 77- *Concurrent Pos:* Consult, Spec Action for Drug Abuse Prev, White House, 71, NY State Bd Med, 79- *Mem:* Fel Am Col Physicians; fel Am Col Prev Med. *Res:* Drug abuse; delivery of health care. *Mailing Add:* Off of Dean State Univ of NY Binghamton NY 13901

WOLFSON, JAMES, b Chicago, Ill, Mar 16, 43; m 71. PHYSICS. *Educ:* Grinnell Col, BA, 64; Mass Inst Technol, PhD(physics), 68. *Prof Exp:* Mem staff physics lab nuclear sci, Mass Inst Technol, 68-70, asst prof physics, 70-76; mem staff, Fermi Nat Accelerator Lab, 76-80. *Mem:* AAAS; Am Phys Soc. *Res:* Experimental high energy physics. *Mailing Add:* 694 Sterling Court Naperville IL 60540

WOLFSON, JOSEPH LAURENCE, b Winnipeg, Man, July 22, 17; m 44; c 2. NUCLEAR PHYSICS. *Educ:* Univ Man, BSc, 42, MSc, 43; McGill Univ, PhD(physics), 48. *Prof Exp:* Asst res officer physics, Atomic Energy Can, Ltd, Chalk River, 48-55; physicist, Jewish Gen Hosp, Montreal, Que, 55-58; assoc res officer, Nat Res Coun Can, 58-64; prof physics, Univ Sask, 64-74; dean sci, 74-80, PROF PHYSICS, CARLETON UNIV, OTTAWA, 80- *Mem:* Am Phys Soc; Can Asn Physicists. *Res:* Nuclear spectroscopy. *Mailing Add:* Carleton Univ Ottawa ON K1S 5B6 Can

WOLFSON, KENNETH GRAHAM, b New York, NY, Nov 21, 24; m 47; c 2. MATHEMATICS. *Educ:* Brooklyn Col, BA, 47; Johns Hopkins Univ, MA, 48; Univ Ill, PhD(math), 52. *Prof Exp:* From instr to assoc prof, 52-58, chmn dept, 61-75, PROF MATH, RUTGERS UNIV, 60-, DEAN, GRAD SCH, 75- *Mem:* Am Math Soc; Math Asn Am. *Res:* Spectral theory of differential equations; rings of linear transformations; structure of rings. *Mailing Add:* Grad Sch Rutgers Univ New Brunswick NJ 08903

WOLFSON, RICHARD LEO THOMAS, b San Francisco, Calif, Apr 13, 47; m 70; c 1. SOLAR PHYSICS, SOLAR ENERGY. *Educ:* Swarthmore Col, BA, 69; Univ Mich, MS, 71; Dartmouth Col, PhD(physics), 76. *Prof Exp:* Asst prof, 76-82, ASSOC PROF PHYSICS, MIDDLEBURY COL, 82- *Concurrent Pos:* Vis scientist, High Altitude Observ, Nat Ctr Atmospheric Res, 80-81; prin investr, NSF, Dept Energy, . *Mem:* Am Phys Soc; Am Asn Physics Teachers. *Res:* Theoretical work on magnetohydrohynamics of space plasmas, especially in application to the solar orona and solar wind; experimental work on control strategies for solar energy systems. *Mailing Add:* Dept Physics Middlebury Col Middlebury VT 05753

WOLFSON, ROBERT JOSEPH, b Philadelphia, Pa, Sept 11, 29; m 53; c 2. OTOLARYNGOLOGY. *Educ:* Temple Univ, BA, 52, MS, 61; Hahnemann Med Col, MD, 57. *Prof Exp:* PROF OTOLARYNGOL & BRONCHO-ESOPHAGOLOGY, & HEAD DEPT, MED COL PA, 69- *Mem:* Am Acad Ophthal & Otolaryngol; Am Otol Soc; Am Laryngol, Rhinol & Otol Soc; Royal Soc Med; AMA. *Mailing Add:* Dept of Surg Med Col of Pa Philadelphia PA 19129

WOLFSON, SEYMOUR J, b Detroit, Mich, Feb 13, 37; m 58; c 4. COMPUTER SCIENCE. *Educ:* Wayne State Univ, BS, 59, PhD(physics), 65; Univ Chicago, MS, 60. *Prof Exp:* Res assoc physics, Wayne State Univ, 63-65; sr scientist, Comput Sci Corp, 65-68; asst prof comput sci, 68-73, ASSOC PROF COMPUT SCI, WAYNE STATE UNIV, 73- *Concurrent Pos:* Consult, Comput Sci Corp, 68-71, Lincorp Corp, 72- & Dept Housing & Urban Develop, 75-; secy, Comput Sci Bd, 74-76 & New York Carpet World, 80; chmn, Nat Comput Conf Bd, 81-82. *Mem:* Am Phys Soc; Asn Comput Mach; Am Arbit Asn; Inst Elec & Electronics Engrs. *Res:* Computer networks and applications; numerical methods. *Mailing Add:* Dept of Comput Sci Wayne State Univ Detroit MI 48202

WOLFSON, SIDNEY KENNETH, JR, b Philadelphia, Pa, June 14, 31; m 58; c 3. NEUROSURGERY, BIOMEDICAL ENGINEERING. *Educ:* Univ Pa, AB, 51; Univ Chicago, MD, 58. *Prof Exp:* Resident surg, Univ Pa Hosp, 59-63, asst prof surg res, Sch Med, Univ Pa, 63-68; dir surg res, Michael Reese Hosp & Med Ctr, 68-71; assoc prof neurosurg, 71-77, DIR SURG RES, UNIV PITTSBURGH, 71-, PROF NEUROSURG, 78-, DIR, PERIPHERAL VASCULAR DIAG LAB, MONTEFIORE HOSP, 77- *Concurrent Pos:* Career Develop Award, Nat Heart & Lung Inst, 63; assoc prof surg, Univ Chicago, 69-71; chmn spec study sect, Nat Inst Arthritis & Metab Dis, 74-75; consult, Artificial Heart Assessment Panel, NIH, 74, Med Devices Prog, Nat Heart & Lung Inst, 73-74. *Mem:* Am Soc Artificial Internal Organs; Am Asn Neurol Surgeons; Soc Acad Surgeons; Soc Neurosci; Asn Advan Med Instrumentation. *Res:* Hypothermia and circulatory arrest; implantable biofuel cell for powering implanted devices, indwelling arterial oxygen electrode; artificial pancreas; cerebral blood flow; computerized hospital patient chart. *Mailing Add:* Dept of Surg Montefiore Hosp 3459 5th Ave Pittsburgh PA 15213

WOLGA, GEORGE JACOB, b New York, NY, Apr 2, 31; m 59; c 3. PHYSICS. *Educ:* Cornell Univ, BEngPhys, 53; Mass Inst Technol, PhD(physics), 57. *Prof Exp:* Asst physics, Mass Inst Technol, 53-56, instr, 57-60, asst prof, 60-61; from asst prof to assoc prof, 61-68, PROF ELEC ENG & APPL PHYSICS, CORNELL UNIV, 68- *Concurrent Pos:* Consult,Gen Elec, Sylvania & US Naval Res Lab, vpres-dir res, Lansing Res Corp, 64-; head, Laser Physics Br, US Naval Res Lab, 68-70. *Mem:* Am Phys Soc; Inst Elec & Electronics Engrs; Optical Soc Am. *Res:* Excited state spectroscopy; molecular physics; quantum electronics; molecular energy transfer and relaxation; modern optical spectroscopic instruments; infrared tunable lasers and spectroscopy; picosecond optoelectronics. *Mailing Add:* Dept of Elec Eng Cornell Univ Ithaca NY 14853

WOLGAMOTT, GARY, b Alva, Okla, July 23, 40; m 62; c 2. MICROBIOLOGY, MOLECULAR BIOLOGY. *Educ:* Northwestern State Col, Okla, BS, 63; Okla State Univ, PhD(microbiol), 68. *Prof Exp:* From asst prof to assoc prof microbiol, 68-75, PROF MICROBIOL, SOUTHWESTERN OKLA STATE UNIV, 75-, CHMN DEPT, DIV ALLIED HEALTH SCI, 77- *Concurrent Pos:* NSF fel col med, Univ Iowa, 71; NASA-Am Soc Eng Educ fel, Johnson Space Ctr, Houston, Tex; mem, Med Technol Rev Comt, Nat Accrediting Agency Clin Lab Sci. *Mem:* AAAS; Am Soc Microbiol. *Res:* Study of the mode of action of specific chemotheopeutic agents on the activities of microorganisms, including their physiology and microstructure; action of microbial hemolysins on tissue culture cells ultrastructure; virulence analysis of space flown microautoflora from astronauts. *Mailing Add:* Div Appl Health Sci Southwestern Okla State Univ Weatherford OK 73096

WOLGEMUTH, CARL HESS, b Bareville, Pa, Apr 18, 34; m 54; c 2. MECHANICAL ENGINEERING. *Educ:* Pa State Univ, BS, 56; Ohio State Univ, MS, 58, PhD(mech eng), 63. *Prof Exp:* Instr mech eng, Ohio State Univ, 56-63; from asst prof to assoc prof, 63-77, PROF MECH ENG, PA STATE UNIV, 77- *Honors & Awards:* Ralph R Teetor Award, Soc Automotive Engrs, 65. *Mem:* Soc Automotive Engrs; Combustion Inst; Am Inst Aeronaut & Astronaut. *Res:* Application of thermodynamics and heat transfer to the study of power-producing systems. *Mailing Add:* Dept of Mech Eng Pa State Univ University Park PA 16802

WOLGEMUTH, DEBRA JOANNE, b Lancaster, Pa, July 28, 47; m 70; c 1. DEVELOPMENTAL BIOLOGY, CELL BIOLOGY. *Educ:* Gettysburg Col, BA, 69; Vanderbilt Univ, MA, 71; Columbia Univ, MPhil, 72, PhD(human genetics), 77. *Prof Exp:* Res assoc reproductive physiol, Vanderbilt Univ, 71-72; fel RNA synthesis, Sloan-Kettering Inst Cancer Res, 77-78, molecular cell biol, Rockefeller Univ, 78-80; ASST PROF HUMAN GENETICS & DEVELOP, COLUMBIA UNIV, 80- *Mem:* Am Soc Cell Biol; Soc Develop Biol; Int Soc Develop Biologists; AAAS; NY Acad Sci. *Res:* Cellular and molecular biology of mammalian gametogenesis, fertilization, and early embryogenesis; elucidating the structure of sperm chromatin and the role of oocyte products in the activation of development. *Mailing Add:* Dept Human Genetics & Develop Col Physicians & Surgeons Columbia Univ 630 W 168th St New York NY 10032

WOLGEMUTH, KENNETH MARK, b Mechanicsburg, Pa, Dec 23, 43; m 70. MARINE GEOCHEMISTRY. *Educ:* Wheaton Col, BS, 65; Columbia Univ, MS, 69, PhD(geochem), 72. *Prof Exp:* Asst prof geol, Dickinson Col, 71-76; vis prof geophys, Fed Univ, Bahia, Brazil, 76-78; SR SCIENTIST, TERRA TEK, INC, 78- *Concurrent Pos:* Vis asst prof geol, World Campus Afloat, Chapman Col, 75; asst prof oceanog, Fla State Univ, 78. *Mem:* Geol Soc Am; Am Geophys Union; AAAS. *Res:* Trace element geochemistry of surface waters; geothermal well stimulation; geochemistry of hydrothermal systems; elastic moduli of tar sand for oil recovery. *Mailing Add:* Terra Tek Inc 420 Wakara Way Salt Lake City UT 84108

WOLGEMUTH, RICHARD LEE, b Lebanon, Pa, June 29, 45; m 68; c 4. PHYSIOLOGY, PHARMACOLOGY. *Educ:* Ashland Col, BSc, 68; Ohio State Univ, MS, 75, PhD(physiol), 75. *Prof Exp:* Jr pharmacologist, Warren-Teed Pharmaceut, Rohm & Haas, 69-74; teaching asst physiol, Ohio State Univ, 73-75; scientist I renal pharmacol, Rohm & Haas Co, 75-77; SR RES SCIENTIST DRUG METAB, ADRIA LABS INC, 77- *Concurrent Pos:* Consult, Nat Inst Occup Safety & Health, 75-76 & Poly Sci Inc, 76- *Res:* Gastrointestinal physiology especially pancreatic function, proteolytic enzymes and digestion, enteric bacteria; renal stones especially calcium and phosphorus metabolism, mechanism and treatment of urolithiasis; anthracycline metabolism and toxicity. *Mailing Add:* Adria Labs Inc Res Park PO Box 16529 Columbus OH 43216

WOLICKI, ELIGIUS ANTHONY, b Buffalo, NY, May 10, 27; m 54; c 4. NUCLEAR PHYSICS. *Educ:* Canisius Col, BS, 46; Univ Notre Dame, PhD(physics), 50. *Prof Exp:* Asst physics, Univ Notre Dame, 46-47, asst, 47-48; res assoc nuclear physics, Univ Iowa, 50-52; nuclear physicist, Nuclear Sci Div, 52-66, consult & actg assoc, 66-77, assoc supt, Radiation Technol Div, 77-81, ASSOC SUPT, CONDENSED MATTER & RADIAON SCI DIV, US NAVAL RES LAB, 81- *Concurrent Pos:* AEC fel, 48-50. *Honors & Awards:* Centennial of Sci Award, Univ Notre Dame, 65; Meritorious Civilian Serv Award, US Naval Res Lab, 71. *Mem:* Fel Am Phys Soc; Sigma Xi; Fed Prof Asn. *Res:* Nuclear reactions, and applications; electrostatic accelerators; radiation detectors; applications of nuclear radiation, nuclear techniques and ion beam accelerators; radiation damage, and radiation effects; radiation hardness assurance; single event upsets in VL sol devices. *Mailing Add:* Radiation Tech Div Code 6601 Naval Res Lab Washington DC 20375

WOLIN, ALAN GEORGE, b New York, NY, Apr 2, 33; m 54; c 4. FOOD SCIENCE. *Educ:* Cornell Univ, BS, 54, MS, 56, PhD, 58. *Prof Exp:* Sr proj leader yeast tech div, Fleischmann Labs, Standard Brands, Inc, 58-60; head dairy tech lab, Vitex Labs Div, Nopco Chem Co, 60-62; prod improv mgr, 62-67, QUAL COORDR, M&M CANDIES DIV, MARS, INC, 67- *Concurrent Pos:* Ed, J Appl Microbiol, 72-; mem res comt, Nat Confectioners Asn, 75-, tech comt, Grocery Mfrs Asn, 73- & NJ Pub Health Adv Comn, 73-75. *Mem:* Am Dairy Sci Asn; Am Soc Microbiol; Inst Food Technol; Soc Consumer Affairs Prof; Am Chem Soc. *Res:* Use of radioisotopes in study of food flavors; dairy starter cultures; enzymes; fermentation; antimicrobial agents in milk; food fortification; phosphatase activity of chocolate milk; natural bacterial inhibitors in raw milk. *Mailing Add:* 44 Stonehenge Rd Morristown NJ 07960

WOLIN, HAROLD LEONARD, b Brooklyn, NY, June 22, 27; m 56; c 3. MICROBIOLOGY, CLINICAL CHEMISTRY. *Educ:* Univ Calif, AB, 50, MA, 52; Cornell Univ, PhD(bact), 56. *Prof Exp:* Res scientist, Pac Yeast Prod Co, 56-57; instr, Hahnemann Med Col, 57-59; asst prof microbiol col med & dent, Seton Hall Univ, 59-63; CLIN ASSOC PROF MICROBIOL, COL MED & DENT, NJ, 63-; ASSOC DIR CLIN LAB, BROOKDALE HOSP CTR, BROOKLYN, NY, 63- *Mem:* Am Soc Microbiol; Brit Soc Gen Microbiol; Am Asn Clin Chem; Nat Acad Clin Biochem. *Res:* Clinical microbiology and chemistry; microbial physiology. *Mailing Add:* Dept Clin Labs Brookdale Hosp Med Ctr Brookdale Plaza Brooklyn NY 11212

WOLIN, LEE ROY, b Cleveland, Ohio, Dec 8, 27; m 50; c 3. PSYCHOLOGY, NEUROPHYSIOLOGY. *Educ:* Los Angeles State Col, BS, 50; Cornell Univ, PhD(psychol), 55. *Prof Exp:* Mem fac psychol, Sarah Lawrence Col, 55-59; res assoc develop, Child Study Ctr, Clark Univ, 59-60; res assoc, Cleveland Psychiat Inst, 60-69, dir lab neuropsychol, 69-73; asst prof neurosurg, 70-76, ASST CLIN PROF PHYSIOL, CASE WESTERN RESERVE UNIV, 76-; DIR LAB NEUROPSYCHOL & EEG, OHIO MENT HEALTH & MENT RETARDATION RES CTR, 73-; ADMIN DIR, DRUG ABUSE TREATMENT UNIT, CLEVELAND PSYCHIAT INST, 75- *Concurrent Pos:* Lectr, Lakewood High Exten, Ohio State Univ, 63-66 & Bedford Exten, Cleveland State Univ, 66; lectr, Kent State Univ, 65. *Mem:* AAAS; Am Psychol Asn; NY Acad Sci. *Res:* Neurophysiology of vision; behavioral and neurophysiological manifestations of brain disfunction; perceptual, cognitive and emotional aspects of neuropsychiatric disorders perception. *Mailing Add:* Cleveland Psychiatric Inst Hosp 1708 Aiken Ave Cleveland OH 44106

WOLIN, MEYER JEROME, b Bronx, NY, Nov 10, 30; m 55. MICROBIAL ECOLOGY, MICROBIAL PHYSIOLOGY. *Educ:* Cornell Univ, BS, 51; Univ Chicago, PhD(microbiol), 54. *Prof Exp:* NIH fel microbiol, Univ Minn, 54-55; fel, Univ Ill, Urbana, 55-56, from asst prof to assoc prof dairy sci, 56-67, assoc prof microbiol, 65-67, prof dairy sci & microbiol, 67-74; CHIEF RES SCIENTIST DIV LAB & RES, NY STATE HEALTH DEPT, 74- *Concurrent Pos:* NSF sr fel, Univ Newcastle, 64-65; mem microbial chem study sect, NIH, 71-75. *Mem:* AAAS; Am Chem Soc; Am Soc Microbiol; NY Acad Sci; Am Soc Biol Chem. *Res:* Microbial biochemistry and ecology; fermentations in anaerobic ecosystems; intestinal tract microbiology; interspecies interactions; hydrogen metabolism; methane production. *Mailing Add:* Div Labs & Res Empire State Plaza Albany NY 12201

WOLIN, SAMUEL, b New York, NY, Feb 12, 09; m 42; c 2. ELECTRONICS, PHYSICS. *Educ:* City Col New York, BS, 30, MS, 31; Columbia Univ, AM, 41. *Prof Exp:* Instr, Pub Schs, NY, 30-42; instr radio eng, Army Air Force Officers Div, Yale Univ, 42-44; instr elec commun, Radar Sch, Mass Inst Technol, 44-45; radio engr, Victor Div, Radio Corp Am, 45-46; res engr, Bartol Res Found, Franklin Inst, 46-47; electronics engr, US Naval Base Sta, Naval Air Mat Ctr, 47; electronic scientist, US Naval Air Develop Ctr, 47-57; sr electronic engr, McDonnell Aircraft Corp, Mo, 56-60; sr elec engr, Adv Systs Res Dept, Lockheed Electronics Co, 60-61; sr design staff engr, Boeing Co, Pa, 61-63; sr res engr, Brown Engr Co, Ala, 63-66; res engr, Boeing Co, Ala, 66-69; electronic engr, US Army Missile Command, Redstone Arsenal, 69-80; CONSULT SCIENTIST, 80- *Mem:* AAAS; sr mem Inst Elec & Electronics Engrs; Soc Indust & Appl Math. *Res:* Electronic systems engineering for space vehicles; guided missiles; aircraft and vertical takeoff and landing; applied electromagnetic theory; antennas; radomes; radio propagation; optics; reliability; applied mathematics. *Mailing Add:* 2205 Wimberly Rd NW Huntsville AL 35805

WOLINSKI, LEON EDWARD, b Buffalo, NY, Apr 3, 26; m 54; c 3. ORGANIC POLYMER CHEMISTRY. *Educ:* Univ Buffalo, BA, 49, PhD(chem), 51. *Prof Exp:* Res chemist film dept, E I du Pont de Nemours & Co, 51-57, staff scientist org polymer chem, 57-59, res assoc, 59-70; CORP DIR RES, PRATT & LAMBERT CO, 70- *Concurrent Pos:* Lectr, Canisius Col, 55-59. *Mem:* Am Chem Soc; Am Inst Chemists. *Res:* Grignard reagents; organo silicon chemistry; surface chemistry; adhesives; condensation and addition polymers; coatings; films. *Mailing Add:* 35 Parkview Terr Cheektowaga NY 14225

WOLINSKY, EMANUEL, b New York, NY, Sept 23, 17; m 47; c 2. INFECTIOUS DISEASES. *Educ:* Cornell Univ, BA, 38, MD, 41. *Prof Exp:* Intern med, New York Hosp, 43-44, resident, 44-45; asst dir tuberc res, Trudeau Lab, Trudeau Found, 46-56; asst prof med, 56-62, asst prof microbiol, 59-62, assoc prof, 62-68, PROF MED, SCH MED, CASE WESTERN RESERVE UNIV, 68-, PROF PATH, 81- *Concurrent Pos:* Director microbiol, Cleveland Metrop Gen Hosp, 59-; former mem tuberc panel, US-Japan Coop Med Sci Prog; former mem strep & staph comn, Armed Forces Epidemiol Bd; assoc ed, Am Rev Respiratory Dis. *Mem:* Am Soc Microbiol; Am Thoracic Soc; Infectious Dis Soc Am. *Res:* Medical microbiology and pulmonary diseases; tuberculosis bacteriology and experimental chemotherapy; infectious diseases. *Mailing Add:* Metrop Gen Hosp Cleveland OH 44109

WOLINSKY, HARVEY, b Cleveland, Ohio, June 3, 39. MEDICINE, PATHOLOGY. *Educ:* Western Reserve Univ, AB, 60; Univ Chicago, MD & MS, 63, PhD(path), 67. *Prof Exp:* Intern, Univ Chicago Hosps, 63-64; asst resident internal med, Mt Sinai Hosp, Cleveland, Ohio, 64-65; resident chest serv, Bronx Municipal Hosp Ctr, NY, 67-68; assoc, Albert Einstein Col Med, 68-70, assoc path, 69-70, asst prof med & path, 70-73, assoc prof med, 73-77, prof med & path, 77-81; CLIN PROF MED, MT SINAI SCH MED, 81- *Concurrent Pos:* USPHS res fel, Univ Chicago Hosps, 65-67; USPHS res career develop award, Nat Heart & Lung Inst, 72-77; assoc attend physician, Bronx Municipal Hosp Ctr, NY, 68-71, attend physician, 72-81; mem coun arteriosclerosis, Am Heart Asn, 70- & mem coun high blood pressure res, 72-; attend physician, Mt Sinai Hosp & Med Ctr, 81- *Mem:* Am Thoracic Soc; Am Soc Exp Path; Fedn Am Socs Exp Biol; Am Soc Clin Invest; NY Acad Sci. *Res:* Comparative pathology; structure, function and biochemistry of blood vessels; effects of hormonal and mechanical factors on blood vessel structure. *Mailing Add:* Dept Med Mt Sinai Sch Med New York NY 10029

WOLINSKY, IRA, b New York, NY, Mar 30, 38; m 65; c 2. NUTRITION, BIOCHEMISTRY. *Educ:* City Col New York, BS, 60; Kans Univ, MS, 65, PhD(biochem), 68. *Prof Exp:* Lectr, Hebrew Univ Hadassah Med Sch, 68-74; vis scientist, Dalton Res Ctr, Univ Mo, 74; assoc prof nutrit, Pa State Univ, 74-79; ASSOC PROF NUTRIT, UNIV HOUSTON, 79- *Concurrent Pos:* Adj assoc prof, Prog Nutrit & Dietetics, Sch Allied Health Sci, Univ Tex, Houston, 80- *Mem:* Am Inst Nutrit; Soc Exp Biol & Med; Sigma Xi; NY Acad Sci. *Res:* Nutritional biochemistry of bone; calcium metabolism. *Mailing Add:* Dept Human Develop Univ Houston Houston TX 77004

WOLINSKY, JOSEPH, b Chicago, Ill, Dec 3, 30; m 51; c 5. ORGANIC CHEMISTRY. *Educ:* Univ Ill, BS, 52; Cornell Univ, PhD, 56. *Prof Exp:* Proj assoc, Univ Wis, 56-58; from asst prof to assoc prof chem, 58-67, PROF CHEM, PURDUE UNIV, 67- *Mem:* Am Chem Soc. *Res:* Chemistry of terpenes, alkaloids and related natural products. *Mailing Add:* Dept of Chem Purdue Univ West Lafayette IN 47906

WOLK, COLEMAN PETER, b New York, NY, Sept 28, 36; m 65; c 1. DEVELOPMENTAL MICROBIOLOGY. *Educ:* Mass Inst Technol, SB & SM, 58; Rockefeller Inst, PhD(biol), 64. *Prof Exp:* Nat Acad Sci-Nat Res Coun res fel biol, Calif Inst Technol, 64-65; from asst prof to assoc prof, 65-74, PROF BOT, MICH STATE UNIV, 74- *Honors & Awards:* Darbaker Prize, Bot Soc Am. *Mem:* Phycol Soc Am; Am Soc Microbiol; Soc Develop Biol; Am Soc Plant Physiol. *Res:* Physiological, biochemical and genetic bases of development and nitrogen fixation in cyanobacteria. *Mailing Add:* MSU-DOE Plant Res Lab Mich State Univ East Lansing MI 48824

WOLK, ELLIOT SAMUEL, b Springfield, Mass, Aug 5, 19; m 50; c 3. MATHEMATICS. *Educ:* Clark Univ, AB, 40; Brown Univ, ScM, 47, PhD(math), 54. *Prof Exp:* Instr math, 50-56, from asst prof to assoc prof, 56-63, chmn dept, 67-73, PROF MATH, UNIV CONN, 63- *Concurrent Pos:* Consult elec boat div, Gen Dynamics Corp, 55-58. *Mem:* Am Math Soc; Math Asn Am. *Res:* Partially ordered sets; general topology. *Mailing Add:* Dept of Math Univ of Conn Storrs CT 06268

WOLK, ROBERT GEORGE, b New York, NY, Mar 10, 31; m 56; c 5. ORNITHOLOGY. *Educ:* City Col New York, BS, 52; Cornell Univ, MS, 54, PhD(vert zool), 59. *Prof Exp:* Asst prof biol, St Lawrence Univ, 57-63; assoc prof vert morphol & behav, Adelphi Univ, 63-67; cur life sci, Nassau County Mus, 67-78; EXEC DIR, NATURE SCI CTR, 78- *Mem:* Am Asn Mus; Am Ornith Union; Am Soc Zool. *Res:* Behavioral adaptations and functional morphology of birds; evolution, systematics and distribution of gulls, terns and skimmers; avian crepuscular vision. *Mailing Add:* 156 Surtees Rd Winston-Salem NC 27104

WOLKE, RICHARD ELWOOD, b East Orange, NJ, June 2, 33; m 64; c 2. VETERINARY PATHOLOGY. *Educ:* Cornell Univ, BS, 55, DVM, 62; Univ Conn, MS, 66, PhD(vet path), 68. *Prof Exp:* Vet, Am Soc Prev Cruelty Animals, 62-63; pvt practice, 63-64; NIH path trainee, Univ Conn, 64-68, res assoc, 68-69, res assoc icthyopath, 69-70; asst prof, 70-75, assoc prof icthyopath, 75-81, PROF AQUACULTURE & PATH, UNIV RI, 81-; ADJ PROF COMP MED, TUFTS UNIV, 81- *Concurrent Pos:* Conn Res Comn grant, Univ Conn, 69-70; Nat Oceanic & Atmospheric Admin Sea grant, Univ RI, 70-80; vis prof, Unit Aquatic Pathbiol, Stirling Univ, Scotland, 78-79. *Mem:* Wildlife Dis Asn; Int Asn Aquatic Animal Med; World Maricult Soc; Sigma Xi; NY Acad Sci. *Res:* Ichthyopathology; comparative pathology; inflammation. *Mailing Add:* Dept of Animal Path Peckham Res Lab Univ of RI Kingston RI 02881

WOLKE, ROBERT LESLIE, b Brooklyn, NY, Apr 2, 28; m 64; c 1. NUCLEAR CHEMISTRY, RADIOCHEMISTRY. *Educ:* Polytech Inst Brooklyn, BS, 49; Cornell Univ, PhD, 53. *Prof Exp:* Res assoc nuclear chem, Enrico Fermi Inst, Univ Chicago, 53-56; nuclear chemist, Gen Atomic Div, Gen Dynamics Corp, 56-57; from asst prof to assoc prof chem, Univ Fla, 57-60; dir, Wherrett Lab Nuclear Chem, 61-77, assoc prof, 60-67, PROF CHEM, UNIV PITTSBURGH, 67-, DIR, UNIV OFF FAC DEVELOP, 77- *Concurrent Pos:* Res partic, Oak Ridge Nat Lab, 58 & 59; vis prof, Univ PR, 70; vis prof, US AID, Univ Oriente, Venezuela, 73. *Mem:* Sigma Xi; Am Chem Soc; Am Asn Higher Educ. *Res:* Nuclear reactions; recoil studies, interaction of energetic ions with matter; natural radioactivity; marine radioactivity. *Mailing Add:* Off Fac Develop Univ Pittsburgh Pittsburgh PA 15260

WOLKEN, GEORGE, JR, b Jersey City, NJ, Nov 11, 44; m 67; c 2. CHEMICAL PHYSICS, THEORETICAL CHEMISTRY. *Educ:* Tufts Univ, BS, 66; Harvard Univ, PhD(chem physics), 71. *Prof Exp:* Fel, Max Planck Inst Aerodyn, Univ Göttingen, 71-72; asst prof chem, Ill Inst Technol, 72-74; MEM STAFF, BATTELLE MEM INST, 74- *Mem:* Am Chem Soc; Am Phys Soc. *Res:* Theoretical chemical kinetics, both of gas phase reactions and heterogeneous reactions. *Mailing Add:* Battelle Mem Inst 505 King Ave Columbus OH 43201

WOLKEN, JEROME JAY, b Pittsburgh, Pa, Mar 28, 17; m 45, 56; c 4. BIOPHYSICS. *Educ:* Univ Pittsburgh, BS, 46, MS, 48, PhD(biophys), 49. *Prof Exp:* Res fel, Mellon Inst, 43-47; res fel, Rockefeller Inst, 51-52; dir biophys res lab, Eye & Ear Hosp, Mellon Col Sci, 53-64, head dept biol sci, 64-67, PROF BIOPHYS, CARNEGIE-MELLON UNIV, 64- *Concurrent Pos:* AEC fel, 49-51; Am Cancer Soc fel, 51-53; asst prof sch med, Univ Pittsburgh, 53-57, from assoc prof to prof, 57-66; Nat Coun Combat Blindness fel, 57; career prof, USPHS, 62-64; guest prof, Pa State Univ, 63; vis prof, Univ Paris, 67-68, Univ Col, Univ London, 71, Pasteur Inst, Paris, 72 & Princeton Univ, 78. *Mem:* Fel AAAS; fel Optical Soc Am; Am Chem Soc; fel Am Inst Chemists; Soc Gen Physiol. *Res:* Photosynthesis; spectroscopy, optics and vision. *Mailing Add:* 5817 Elmer St Pittsburgh PA 15232

WOLKO, HOWARD STEPHEN, b Buffalo, NY, Apr 30, 25; m 50; c 4. MECHANICAL ENGINEERING, SOLID MECHANICS. *Educ:* Univ Buffalo, BS, 49, MS, 53; George Washington Univ, ScD(mech), 67. *Prof Exp:* Design engr, Sci Instruments Div, Am Optical Co, 50-52; res assoc exp mech, Cornell Aeronaut Lab, Cornell Univ, 52-55; chief struct res, Bell Aircraft Corp, 55-59; head solid mech, Eng Sci Directorate, Air Force Off Sci Res, 59-63; chief struct mech, Off Advan Res & Technol, NASA, 65-67; prof mech eng, Tex A&M Univ, 67-72; prof & chmn dept, Memphis State Univ, 72-73; asst dir sci & technol dept, 73-80, SPEC ADV AERONAUTICS DEPT, NAT AIR & SPACE MUS, SMITHSONIAN INST, 80- *Concurrent Pos:* Lectr, Univ Buffalo, 53-59. *Mem:* Soc Eng Sci; Soc Exp Stress Anal. *Res:* Coupled thermomechanics; continuum mechanics; biomedical engineering; materials science. *Mailing Add:* Nat Air & Space Mus Smithsonian Inst Washington DC 20560

WOLKOFF, A STARK, b Uniontown, Pa, Sept 2, 21; m 56. OBSTETRICS & GYNECOLOGY, PHYSIOLOGY. *Educ:* Univ Scranton, BS, 43; Hahnemann Med Col, MD, 50. *Prof Exp:* Instr obstet & gynec, Univ Louisville, 55-56; asst prof, State Univ NY Downstate Med Ctr, 56-57; asst prof gynec & obstet, Sch Med, Univ NC, 59-64; PROF GYNEC & OBSTET & ASST PROF PHYSIOL, UNIV KANS MED CTR, KANSAS CITY, 64- *Concurrent Pos:* Spec res fel physiol, Sch Med, Yale Univ, 57-58; consult, Kansas City Vet Hosp & Munsen Hosp, Ft Leavenworth. *Mem:* Fel Am Col Surgeons; fel Am Col Obstet & Gynec; AMA; Soc Gynec Invest. *Res:* Fetal and placental physiology using pregnant ewe and intrauterine catheterization techniques. *Mailing Add:* Dept of Obstet & Gynec Univ of Kans Sch of Med Kansas City KS 66103

WOLKOFF, AARON WILFRED, b Toronto, Ont, Feb 12, 44; m 66; c 2. ANALYTICAL CHEMISTRY, ENVIRONMENTAL CHEMISTRY. *Educ:* Univ Toronto, BSc, 65, MSc, 67, PhD(org chem), 71. *Prof Exp:* Fel, Inst Environ Sci & Eng, Univ Toronto, 71-72; teaching master math & chem, Seneca Col Appl Arts & Technol, 72-73; res scientist environ anal, Can Centre for Inland Waters, Dept Environ, 73-77; MEM STAFF, WATERS SCI LTD, 77- *Mem:* Am Chem Soc; Chem Inst Can. *Res:* Development of new analytical methods for environmental analysis with emphasis on the applications of high pressure liquid chromatography. *Mailing Add:* Waters Sci Ltd 6480 Viscount Rd Unit 4 Mississauga ON L4V 1H3 Can

WOLKOFF, HAROLD, b Brooklyn, NY, June 10, 23; m 49; c 2. MECHANICAL ENGINEERING. *Educ:* Polytech Inst Brooklyn, BME, 49; City Col New York, MBA, 56. *Prof Exp:* PROF ENG, NEW YORK CITY TECH COL, 51- *Mem:* Am Soc Eng Educ; Soc Mfg Engrs; Am Indust Arts Asn. *Res:* Strength of materials; engineering drawing. *Mailing Add:* Dept Mech Eng Technol 300 Jay St Brooklyn NY 11201

WOLL, EDWARD, b May 29, 14. MECHANICAL ENGINEERING. *Educ:* Rensselaer Polytech Inst, ME, 46. *Prof Exp:* VPRES & GEN MGR, GROUP ADVAN ENG DIV, GEN ELEC CO, 70- *Mem:* Nat Acad Eng. *Mailing Add:* Gen Elec Co 1000 Western Ave Lynn MA 01910

WOLL, HARRY JEAN, b Farmington, Minn, Aug, 25, 20; m 47; c 2. ELECTRICAL & ELECTRONICS ENGINEERING. *Educ:* NDak State Univ, BS, 40; Univ Pa, PhD(elec eng), 53. *Prof Exp:* Asst, Ill Inst Technol, 40-41; res & develop engr, 41-43, res & develop supvr, 53-58, mgr appl res, 58-63, chief engr, Aerospace Systs Div, 63-69, div vpres gov eng, Govt & Com Systs, 69-75, div vpres & gen mgr, Automated Systs, 75-81, STAFF VPRES & CHIEF ENGR, ELECTRONIC PROD, SYSTS & SERV, RCA, 81- *Concurrent Pos:* Chmn, Trustees for Moore Sch Elec Eng, Univ Pa, 76-; chmn, Aerospace Indust Asn Tech Coun, 77 & chmn, Fel Comt, 79-80. *Mem:* AAAS; fel Inst Elec & Electronics Engrs; assoc fel Am Inst Aeronaut & Astronaut. *Res:* Linear circuit theory; solid state circuits; communications; electro-optics; aerospace systems; automatic test systems. *Mailing Add:* David Sarnoff Res Ctr Princeton NJ 08540

WOLL, JOHN WILLIAM, JR, b Philadelphia, Pa, May 19, 31; m 52; c 2. MATHEMATICS. *Educ:* Haverford Col, BS, 52; Princeton Univ, PhD, 56. *Prof Exp:* Instr math, Princeton Univ, 56-57; asst prof, Lehigh Univ, 57-58, Univ Calif, 58-61 & Univ Wash, 61-68; PROF MATH, WESTERN WASH STATE UNIV, 68- *Mem:* Am Math Soc. *Res:* Functional analysis and stochastic processes. *Mailing Add:* Dept of Math Western Wash State Univ Bellingham WA 98225

WOLLA, MAURICE L(EROY), b Minot, NDak, May 13, 33; m 53; c 5. ELECTRICAL & COMPUTER ENGINEERING. *Educ:* NDak State Univ, BS, 56; Mich State Univ, PhD(elec eng), 66. *Prof Exp:* Instr elec eng, NDak State Univ, 56-58 & Mich State Univ, 58-65; assoc prof, Colo State Univ, 65-66; assoc prof, 66-72, PROF ELEC ENG, CLEMSON UNIV, 72- *Concurrent Pos:* US Dept Interior res grants, 67-69. *Mem:* Simulation Coun; Inst Elec & Electronics Engrs; Am Soc Eng Educ. *Res:* Analysis and simulation of physical systems; computer sciences; software engineering; educational computing systems; real-time computing systems. *Mailing Add:* Dept of Elec & Comput Eng Clemson Univ Clemson SC 29631

WOLLAN, DAVID STRAND, b Boston, Mass, Mar 25, 37; m 79; c 2. SCIENCE POLICY, SOLID STATE PHYSICS. *Educ:* Amherst Col, AB, 59; Univ Ill, MS, 61, PhD(physics), 66. *Prof Exp:* Asst prof physics, Va Polytech Inst & State Univ, 66-74; PHYSICIST, US ARMS CONTROL & DISARMAMENT AGENCY, 74- *Mem:* Am Phys Soc; Inst Elec & Electronics Engrs. *Res:* Electron and nuclear magnetic resonance in solids; strategic arms. *Mailing Add:* US Arms Control & Disarmament Agency Washington DC 20451

WOLLAN, JOHN JEROME, b Chicago, Ill, July 7, 42; div; c 2. LOW TEMPERATURE PHYSICS. *Educ:* St Olaf Col, BA, 64; Iowa State Univ, PhD(physics), 70. *Prof Exp:* Vis asst prof physics, Univ Ky, 70-73; Nat Res Coun assoc physics, Air Force Mat Lab, 73-74; STAFF MEM PHYSICS, LOS ALAMOS SCI LAB, 74- *Mem:* Am Phys Soc. *Res:* Development and evaluation of superconducting wire for magnetic energy transfer and storage applications for fusion power systems, in particular, static and fast pulse energy losses in superconducting wire. *Mailing Add:* CTR-9 MS 464 Los Alamos Sci Lab Los Alamos NM 87545

WOLLENBERG, BRUCE FREDERICK, b Buffalo, NY, June 14, 42; m 65; c 4. POWER SYSTEMS OPERATIONS. *Educ:* Rensselaer Polytech Inst, BEE, 64, MEng, 66; Univ Pa, PhD(systs eng), 74. *Prof Exp:* Engr, Leeds & Northrop Co, 66-70, sr engr, 70-74; SR ENGR, POWER TECHNOLOGIES INC, 74- *Concurrent Pos:* Adj assoc prof, Rensselaer Polytech Inst, 79- *Mem:* Sigma Xi; Inst Elec & Electronics Engrs. *Res:* Methods for secure and optical operation of electric power systems; software implementation; software implenetation; field testing. *Mailing Add:* Power Technologies Inc PO Box 1058 Schenectady NY 12301

WOLLENSAK, JOHN CHARLES, b Rochester, NY, Dec 16, 32; m 57; c 5. ORGANIC CHEMISTRY. *Educ:* Col Holy Cross, BS, 54; Mass Inst Technol, PhD(org chem), 58; Mich State Univ, MBA, 80. *Prof Exp:* Res chemist, 58-66, SUPVR CHEM RES, ETHYL CORP, 66- *Mem:* Am Chem Soc. *Res:* Organic synthesis; organometallics; research administration. *Mailing Add:* Ethyl Corp PO Box 341 Gulf States Rd Baton Rouge LA 70821

WOLLER, WILLIAM HENRY, b San Antonio, Tex, Feb 28, 33; m 58; c 3. PHYSICAL PHARMACY, COSMETIC CHEMISTRY. *Educ:* Univ Tex, Austin, BS, 55. *Prof Exp:* Mfg pharmacist drug prod, 56-64, res & develop scientist drugs & cosmetics, 65-73, RES & DEVELOP MGR DRUGS & COSMETICS, TEX PHARMACAL CO, DIV WARNER LAMBERT, MORRIS PLAINS, NJ, 74- *Mem:* Am Pharm Asn. *Res:* Development of vehicles for organic peroxides for use in the treatment of dermatological disorders; screening alpha hydroxy acids for use in treatment of icthyosis. *Mailing Add:* 3314 Yorktown San Antonio TX 78230

WOLLIN, GOESTA, b Ystad, Sweden, Oct 4, 22; nat US; m 50; c 1. CLIMATOLOGY, CHEMISTRY. *Educ:* Hermods Col, Sweden, Phil; Columbia Univ, MS, 53. *Prof Exp:* Newspaper reporter, Ystads Allehanda, 39-41; free lance writer, Swedish Newspapers, 45-50; asst, 50-56, RES CONSULT, LAMONT GEOL OBSERV, COLUMBIA UNIV, 56- *Mem:* AAAS; NY Acad Sci; Glaciol Soc; Explorers Club. *Res:* Holocene and pleistocene climates and marine sedimentation; micropaleontological research of marine sediments; the relationship between climatic changes and variations in the earth's magnetic field; chemical research on origin of life. *Mailing Add:* Snedens Landing Palisades NY 10964

WOLLMAN, HARRY, b Brooklyn, NY, Sept 26, 32; m 57; c 3. ANESTHESIOLOGY. *Educ:* Harvard Univ, AB, 54, MD, 58; Am Bd Anesthesiol, dipl, 64. *Prof Exp:* Intern med & surg, Univ Chicago Clins, 58-59; resident, Hosp Univ Pa, 59-63, assoc in anesthesia, Univ, 63-65, from asst prof to prof, 65-70, ROBERT DUNNING DRIPPS PROF ANESTHESIA & CHMN DEPT, SCH MED, UNIV PA, 72-, PROF PHARMACOL, 71- *Concurrent Pos:* NIH res trainee, 59-63; Pharmaceut Mfrs Asn fel, 60-61; consult, Vet Admin Hosp, Philadelphia, 63-64, 79- & Valley Forge Army Hosp, 65-66; mem pharm & toxicol training grants comt, NIH, 66-68, mem anesthesia training grants comt, 71-73, mem surg A study sect, 74-78; mem anesthesia drug panel drug efficacy study, Comt Anesthesia, Nat Acad Sci-Nat Res Coun, 70-71, mem comt adverse reactions to anesthesia drugs, 71-72; assoc ed, Anesthesiol, 70-75; prin investr, Anesthesia Res Ctr, Univ Pa, 72-78, prog dir anesthesia res training grant, 72-, chmn comt studies involving human beings, 72-76; chmn, Clin Pract Exec Com, 76-80; John Harvard scholar. *Honors & Awards:* Detur Award. *Mem:* Am Soc Anesthesiologists; Soc Acad Anesthesia Chmn (pres, 77-78); Am Physiol Soc; Sigma Xi; Asn Univ Anesthetists. *Res:* Circulatory physiology; cerebral blood flow and metabolism; regional blood flow during anesthesia. *Mailing Add:* Dept of Anesthesiol Hosp Univ of Pa Philadelphia PA 19104

WOLLMAN, SEYMOUR HORACE, b New York, NY, May 17, 15; m 44; c 3. PHYSIOLOGY, CYTOLOGY. *Educ:* NY Univ, BS, 35, MS, 36; Duke Univ, PhD(physics), 41. *Prof Exp:* Physicist, Bur Ord, US Dept Navy, 42-46; mem staff, Sloan-Kettering Inst, 46 & 47; Nat Cancer Inst fel, Rockefeller Inst, 48; BIOPHYSICIST, NAT CANCER INST, 48- *Mem:* Am Physiol Soc; Am Thyroid Asn; Am Soc Cell Biol; Europ Thyroid Asn. *Res:* Thyroid gland and thyroid tumors. *Mailing Add:* Nat Cancer Inst Bethesda MD 20205

WOLLMER, RICHARD DIETRICH, b Los Angeles, Calif, July 27, 38. OPERATIONS RESEARCH, STATISTICS. *Educ:* Pomona Col, BA, 60; Columbia Univ, MA, 62; Univ Calif, Berkeley, PhD(eng sci), 65. *Prof Exp:* Oper res sci, Rand Corp, 65-70; PROF, CALIF STATE UNIV, LONG BEACH, 70- *Concurrent Pos:* Consult, US Air Force Adv Bd Int Trans, 68-70; mem, Naval Res Adv Comt, 74-78; lectr, Univ Calif, Los Angeles, 70 & 74; res mathematician, Univ Southern Calif, 73-75; vis assoc prof, Stanford Univ, 76-77; mathematician, Elec Power Res Inst, 77; consult, McDonnell Douglas Corp, 78-80 & Logicon, 79-81. *Mem:* Opers Res Soc Am; Inst Mgt Sci; Math Prog Soc. *Res:* Mathematics programming; network flows; dynamic programming; Markov processes. *Mailing Add:* Calif State Univ 1250 Bellflower Blvd Long Beach CA 90840

WOLLNER, THOMAS EDWARD, b Rochester, Minn, Dec 30, 36; m 58; c 2. ORGANIC CHEMISTRY, POLYMER CHEMISTRY. *Educ:* St John's Univ, Minn, BA, 58; Wash State Univ, PhD(chem), 64. *Prof Exp:* Res mgr polymer res, 64-74, lab mgr polymer res, 74-77, dir Chem Res Lab, 77-81, DIR, INDUST & CONSUMER SECTOR RES LAB, CENT RES LABS, 3M CO, 81- *Mem:* Am Chem Soc; Sigma Xi. *Res:* Adhesives, binders and coatings; optical and electrical properties of organics. *Mailing Add:* 3M Bldg 201-15-11 PO Box 33221 St Paul MN 55133

WOLLSCHLAEGER, GERTRAUD, b Muenchen, Ger, Feb 28, 24; US citizen; m 48; c 3. MEDICINE, RADIOLOGY. *Educ:* Univ Munich, physicum, 54, MD, 57; State Univ NY, MD, 65. *Prof Exp:* Instr radiol, Albert Einstein Col Med, 61-64; from asst prof to assoc prof, Sch Med, Univ Mo-Columbia, 64-71; asst chief sect neuroradiol, William Beaumont Hosp, Royal Oak, Mich, 71-72; PROF RADIOL & NEURORADIOL, SCH MED, WAYNE STATE UNIV, 73- *Concurrent Pos:* Res fel radiol, Albert Einstein Col Med, Yeshiva Univ, 61-62, NIH spec fel neuroradiol, 62-64; res grant, Univ Mo-Columbia, 64-71; co-dir, NIH spec fel training prog, 67-71, consult, Crippled Children's Serv, 69-71. *Mem:* AAAS; Asn Univ Neuroradiol; Radiol Soc NAm; Inst Elec & Electronics Eng; AMA. *Res:* Postmortem cerebral angiography; cerebral microangiography; microtumor-circulation. *Mailing Add:* Dept Radiol Wayne State Univ Detroit MI 48202

WOLLSCHLAEGER, PAUL BERNHARD, medicine, radiology, deceased

WOLLUM, ARTHUR GEORGE, II, b Chicago, Ill, July 26, 37; m 60; c 2. SOILS, MICROBIOLOGY. *Educ:* Univ Minn, BS, 59; Ore State Univ, MS, 62, PhD(soils), 65. *Prof Exp:* Forester, Gifford Pinchot Nat Forest, USDA, 59-60, res forester, Pac Northwest Forest & Range Exp Sta, 60-61; asst soils, Ore State Univ, 64-65, asst prof, 65-67; asst prof, NMex State Univ, 67-71; assoc prof, 71-76, PROF SOILS, NC STATE UNIV, 76- *Concurrent Pos:* Vis prof, Ohio State Univ, 78-79. *Mem:* Soc Am Foresters; Soil Sci Soc Am; Am Soc Microbiol; Sigma Xi; Am Soc Agron. *Res:* Microbiology of nodule-formation of nonleguminous plants; ecology of nitrogen fixing plants in forested ecosystems; nitrogen cycle in forested ecosystems; microbiology of environmental pollution; rhizobial ecology. *Mailing Add:* Dept of Soil Sci NC State Univ Raleigh NC 27650

WOLLWAGE, JOHN CARL, b Chicago, Ill, Oct 11, 14; m 39; c 3. PAPER CHEMISTRY. *Educ:* Northwestern Univ, BS, 34; Lawrence Col, MS, 36, PhD(paper chem), 38. *Prof Exp:* Mem staff, Res Dept, Hammermill Paper Co, Pa, 36; mem staff chem res, Beveridge-Marvellum Co, Mass, 37; res chemist, Kimberly-Clark Corp, 39-40, 42, tech supt, Mill, 41-42, war prod develop, 43-45, mill mgr, 45-49, asst tech dir, 49-52, dir res, 52-55, mgr foreign opers, 55-59, gen mgr creped wadding mfg processes, Consumer Prod Div, 59-62, vpres mfg, 62-68, vpres, C W Mfg, Res & Eng, 68-71, vpres corp res & eng, 71-73; vpres res, Inst Paper Chem, 73-78; DIR, MEMLINE, INC, SURING, 78- *Concurrent Pos:* Dir, Upson Co, Lockport, NY, 78- *Mem:* Tech Asn Pulp & Paper Indust (pres, 63-64); Am Chem Soc; Can Pulp & Paper Asn; AAAS; Sigma Xi. *Res:* Alum and its effect on hydrogen ion concentration of paper; flocculation of paper making fibers. *Mailing Add:* 1712 N Drew St Appleton WI 54911

WOLLWAGE, PAUL CARL, b Appleton, Wis, Mar 15, 41; m 65; c 2. PULPING AND BLEACHING CHEMISTRY. *Educ:* St Olaf Col, BA, 63; Inst Paper Chem, MS, 66, PhD(chem), 69. *Prof Exp:* Sr res chemist, St Regis Tech Ctr, 69-79; BLEACHING SCIENTIST, WEYERHAUSER TECH CTR, 79- *Mem:* Tech Asn Pulp & Paper Indust. *Res:* Pulping and bleaching processes; pulp characterization; wood chemicals. *Mailing Add:* Weyerhaeuser Co WTC 1B40 Tacoma WA 98477

WOLMA, FRED J, b Albuquerque, NMex, Dec 10, 16; m 43; c 2. MEDICINE, SURGERY. *Educ:* Univ Tex, BA, 40, MD, 43; Am Bd Surg, dipl, 53. *Prof Exp:* Intern, Med Col Va, 43-44, resident surg, 47-48; res physician, St Mary's Infirmary, Galveston, Tex, 46-47; resident surg, 48-51, from instr to assoc prof, 51-69, chief div gen surg, 67-70, PROF SURG, UNIV TEX MED BR GALVESTON, 69- *Concurrent Pos:* Consult, USPHS Hosp, St Mary's Hosp & Galveston, Tex. *Mem:* AMA; Am Col Surg; Soc Surg Alimentary Tract; Am Asn Cancer Res; Am Asn Surg of Trauma. *Res:* Clinical medicine; peripheral vascular surgery. *Mailing Add:* Dept of Surg Univ of Tex Med Br Galveston TX 77550

WOLMAN, ABEL, b Baltimore, Md, June 10, 92; m 19; c 1. SANITARY ENGINEERING. *Educ:* Johns Hopkins Univ, BA, 13, BSE, 15. *Hon Degrees:* DE, Johns Hopkins Univ, 37, LLD, 69; DSc, Drexel Inst Technol, 57; DHumane Lett, Md Inst Col Art, 69. *Prof Exp:* Mem staff stream pollution, USPHS, 13; mem staff sewage disposal, Md State Dept Health, 14, from asst engr to div engr, 15-22, chief engr, 22-39; prof sanit eng & water resources, 37-62, chmn, Dept Sanit Eng, 37-62, EMER PROF SANIT ENG & WATER RESOURCES, JOHNS HOPKINS UNIV, 62- *Concurrent Pos:* Lectr, Johns Hopkins Univ, 21-27 & 36-37, Harvard Univ, 25, Princeton Univ, 25 & 29, Univ Chicago, 29 & Univ Southern Calif, 28, 31 & 33; ed-in-chief, J Am Water Works Asn, 21-37; consult to numerous Am cities, state & fed agencies, & 50 foreign govts, 29-; state engr, Fed Emergency Admin Pub Works, Md, 33-34; chmn, Md State Planning Comn, 34-45, Nat Water Resources Bd US, 35-41, Johns Hopkins Univ Team, Brazil Eval, Int Coop Admin, 60, Mission to Taiwan, Repub of China, Community Water Supplies, WHO, 61, Bd Tech Adv, Int Boundary & Water Comn US & Mex, El Paso, Tex, 76 & Task Force on Population Migration, City of Baltimore, 77; mem, Adv Comt Reactor Safeguards & Safety & Indust Health Adv Bd & chmn, Stack Gas Working Group, Gen Waste Probs, US Atomic Energy Comn, 47-60; ed, Am J Pub Health, 55; mem, Ind Mission, Orgn Govt Arg, 56-57; mem, Awards Comt, Nat Acad Eng, 75 & Adv Comt, Regional Planning Coun, Gen Develop Plan, Md, 75-77; mem, Comt Pub Eng Policy, 75; mem, Ed Adv Bd, Encycl Environ Sci & Eng, 76; mem, US Deleg, 31st World Health Assembly, Geneva, Switz, 78; Harben Lectr, Royal Inst Pub Health & Hygiene, London, England, 79; chmn, Expert Panel, Worldwide Prog Water Decade, Agency Int Develop, US Dept State, 79, bd review, Diversion Med Sea to Dead Sea, State Israel, 81; consult, Findings on Aswan High Dam & Nile River Behavior, Cairo, US State Dept, 79. *Honors & Awards:* Sedgwick Mem Medal, Am Pub Health Asn, 48; Spec Award, Lasker Found Am Pub Health Asn, 60; William Proctor Prize, Sci Res Soc Am, 67; Lewis L Dollinger Pure Environ Award, Franklin Inst, Philadelphia, 68; Publ Award, Am Water Works Asn, 73 & 77; Milton Stover Eisenhower Medal, 73; US Nat Medal of Sci, 74; Tyler Ecol Award, 76; Ben Gurion Award, Israel, 76; Harben lectr, Royal Inst Pub Health & Hyg, London, Eng, 79; Int Friendship Medal Award, Inst Water Engrs & Scientists England, 80. *Mem:* Nat Acad Sci; Nat Acad Eng; Am Soc Civil Engrs; hon fel Franklin Inst; fel AAAS. *Res:* General sanitation; stream pollution; water supply. *Mailing Add:* 209 Ames Hall Johns Hopkins Univ Baltimore MD 21218

WOLMAN, ERIC, b New York, NY, Sept 25, 31; m 63; c 2. DATABASE MANAGEMENT, CONGESTION THEORY. *Educ:* Harvard Univ, AB, 53, MA, 54, PhD(appl math), 57. *Prof Exp:* Mem tech staff, 57-66, head traffic systs anal dept, 66-68, head traffic res dept, 68-72, head network eng dept, 72-77, head, Opers Res Tech & Database Res Dept, 77-80, HEAD ADVAN COMPUT SYSTS DEPT, BELL LABS, 81- *Concurrent Pos:* Vis lectr, Harvard Univ, 64; mem comt fire res, Nat Acad Sci-Nat Res Coun, 66-70; mem ad hoc eval panel for fire prog, Nat Bur Standards, 71-74, mem eval panel, Inst Appl Technol, 74-78, Nat Eng Lab, 78-80 & Working Group on Info Technol, NSF, 80. *Mem:* Fel AAAS; Am Math Soc; Asn Comput Mach; Soc Indust & Appl Math; Opers Res Soc Am. *Res:* Applied probability; queuing theory; teletraffic theory. *Mailing Add:* Bell Labs WB 1L-353 Holmdel NJ 07733

WOLMAN, MARKLEY GORDON, b Baltimore, Md, Aug 16, 24; m 51; c 4. GEOLOGY. *Educ:* Johns Hopkins Univ, BA, 49; Harvard Univ, MA, 51, PhD(geol), 53. *Prof Exp:* GEOLOGIST, US GEOL SURV, 51-; PROF GEOG & CHMN DEPT GEOG & ENVIRON ENG, JOHNS HOPKINS UNIV, 58- *Honors & Awards:* Asn Am Geog Award, 72. *Mem:* Geol Soc Am; Am Geophys Union; Asn Am Geog; AAAS. *Res:* River morphology; water resources. *Mailing Add:* Dept of Geog & Environ Eng Johns Hopkins Univ Baltimore MD 21218

WOLMAN, SANDRA R, b New York, NY, Nov 23, 33; m 63; c 2. PATHOLOGY, CYTOGENETICS. *Educ:* Radcliffe Col, AB, 55; NY Univ, MD, 59. *Prof Exp:* Intern path, Bellevue Hosp, New York, 59-60, resident, 60-63; asst assoc pathologist, Morristown Mem Hosp, 64-66; asst pathologist, Monmouth Med Ctr, 66-67; asst prof clin path, 67-72, asst prof path, 72-76, ASSOC PROF PATH, SCH MED, NY UNIV, 76-; ASSOC ATTEND PATHOLOGIST, BELLEVUE & UNIV HOSPS, 76- *Concurrent Pos:* Teaching fel path, Sch Med, NY Univ, 62-64, Nat Cancer Inst res fel oncol, 63, Children's Cancer Res Found fel, 64; asst pathologist, Bellevue Hosp, 63-64, asst vis pathologist, 67-76. consult pathologist, Morristown Mem Hosp, 66-; assoc pathologist, French & Polyclin Hosps, 70-71; mem, Path B Study Sect, NIH, 76-80. *Mem:* AAAS; Am Soc Clin Path; Am Soc Human Genetics; Am Asn Cancer Res; Tissue Cult Asn. *Res:* Clinical cytogenetics; tumor cytogenetics; leukemic cell differentiation. *Mailing Add:* Dept of Path NY Univ Sch of Med New York NY 10016

WOLMAN, WILLIAM WOLFGANG, b Ger, Aug 5, 22; nat US; m 67; c 3. MATHEMATICAL STATISTICS. *Educ:* City Col New York, BBA, 46; Columbia Univ, AM, 49; Univ Rochester, PhD(math), 60. *Prof Exp:* Statistician, State Div Housing, NY, 47-50; head statist div, Off Naval Inspector Ord, Eastman Kodak Co, 50-55; head statist methodology & reliability, Qual Control Div, Bur Ord, US Dept Navy, 55-56, statistician consult, Bur Yards & Docks, 56-60; chief statistician, Off Reliability & Systs Anal, NASA, 60-66; CHIEF TRAFFIC SYSTS DIV, OFF RES & DEVELOP, FED HWY ADMIN, US DEPT TRANSP, DC, 66- *Concurrent Pos:* Prof lectr, George Washington Univ, 56-; vis prof, Univ Md, 78. *Mem:* Am Statist Asn; Inst Math Statist; Int Asn Statist in Phys Sci. *Res:* Probability theory; modern statistical methodology for problems in physical sciences; reliability theory in space technology; transportation research. *Mailing Add:* Traffic Systs Div Off Res & Develop Fed Hwy Admin Washington DC 20591

WOLNY, FRIEDRICH FRANZ, b Troppau, Czechoslovakia, Aug 24, 31; US citizen; m 56; c 1. ORGANIC POLYMER CHEMISTRY. *Educ:* Munich Tech Univ, BS, 54, MS, 55. *Prof Exp:* Group leader resin res, Sued-West-Chemie, WGer, 56-58, asst res & develop dir, 59-64; chemist, 65-68, group leader, 69-72, MGR RESIN RES, SCHENECTADY CHEM, INC, NY, 73- *Mem:* Electrochem Soc WGer; Am Chem Soc; Soc Automotive Eng. *Res:* Organic polymer chemistry, poly condensation products, phenol formaldehyde resins, applied in friction materials. *Mailing Add:* 823 Dean St Schenectady NY 12309

WOLOCHOW, HYMAN, b Richdale, Can, Feb 10, 18; nat US; m 43; c 2. MICROBIOLOGY. *Educ:* Univ Alta, BSc, 38, MSc, 40; Univ Calif, PhD(microbiol), 50. *Prof Exp:* Asst dairy bact, Univ Alta, 38-41; teaching asst bact, Univ Calif, 47-48 & plant nutrit, 48-50, asst res bacteriologist, 50-59; assoc bacteriologist, Naval Biol Lab, Naval Supply Ctr, Univ Calif, 59-73, assoc res bacteriologist, 73-80; RETIRED. *Concurrent Pos:* Consult, US Dept Defense. *Res:* Dairy bacteriology; enzyme chemistry; medical microbiology; aerobiology. *Mailing Add:* Naval Biosci Lab Naval Supply Ctr Oakland CA 94625

WOLOCK, FRED WALTER, b Whitinsville, Mass, Mar 8, 26. MATHEMATICAL STATISTICS. *Educ:* Holy Cross Col, BS, 47; Cath Univ, MS, 49; Va Polytech Inst, PhD(math statist), 64. *Prof Exp:* Instr math, Lewis Col, 53-54; instr, Iona Col, 54-56; instr, St John's Univ, NY, 56-57; instr, Worcester Polytech Inst, 57-60; asst prof math & statist, Boston Col, 64-65; assoc prof, 65-77, PROF MATH & STATIST, SOUTHEASTERN MASS UNIV, 77- *Concurrent Pos:* Consult, Nat Ctr Air Pollution Control, USPHS, 65- & Berkshire Hathaway Co, 66- *Mem:* Inst Math Statist; Am Statist Asn; Math Asn Am. *Res:* Experimental design and applications of statistics to biological and medical sciences; industrial applications of statistics. *Mailing Add:* Dept of Math Southeastern Mass Univ North Dartmouth MA 02747

WOLOCK, IRVIN, b Baltimore, Md, June 21, 23; m 51; c 3. MATERIALS ENGINEERING, COMPOSITES. *Educ:* Johns Hopkins Univ, BS, 43, ME, 49, DrEng, 50. *Prof Exp:* Res asst, SAM Labs, Columbia Univ, 43-44; chemist, Nat Bur Standards, 50-57; supvr mat res engr, Naval Res Lab, DC, 57-73, liaison scientist, Off Naval Res, London, 73-74, SUPVR MAT RES ENGR, NAVAL RES LAB, DC, 74- *Concurrent Pos:* Ed, J Soc Plastics Engrs, 58-64. *Mem:* Am Soc Testing & Mat; Soc Advan Mat & Process Eng; AAAS. *Res:* Failure behavior of plastics and composites; transparent plastics; composites applications. *Mailing Add:* 401 Scott Dr Silver Spring MD 20904

WOLONTIS, V(IDAR) MICHAEL, b Helsinki, Finland, May 28, 26; nat US; m 48; c 2. MATHEMATICS. *Educ:* Univ Helsinki, MA, 47; Harvard Univ, PhD(math), 49. *Prof Exp:* Asst prof math, Univ Kans, 49-53; mem staff, Bell Labs, Inc, 53-80, exec dir opers res & qual assurance, 70-80; RETIRED. *Mem:* Am Math Soc; Inst Mgt Sci. *Res:* Functions of a complex variable; digital computers; data processing and communications. *Mailing Add:* MaKonikey PO Box 278 Vineyard Haven MA 02568

WOLOSHIN, HENRY JACOB, b Philadelphia, Pa, Aug 23, 13; m 48; c 3. RADIOLOGY. *Educ:* Temple Univ, BS, 34, MD, 38; Am Bd Radiol, dipl, 47. *Prof Exp:* Instr, 47-48, assoc, 48-55, from asst prof to assoc prof, 55-65, PROF RADIOL, SCH MED, TEMPLE UNIV, 65-, ASSOC, UNIV HOSP, 47- *Mem:* AMA; Am Col Radiol. *Mailing Add:* Dept Radiol Temple Univ Hosp Philadelphia PA 19140

WOLOVICH, WILLIAM ANTHONY, b Hartford, Conn, Oct 15, 37; m 59; c 2. ELECTRICAL ENGINEERING, CONTROL SYSTEMS. *Educ:* Univ Conn, BS, 59; Worcester Polytech Inst, MS, 61; Brown Univ, PhD(elec sci), 70. *Prof Exp:* Systs analyst, Res Lab, United Aircraft Corp, 59-61; control systs engr, Electronics Res Labs, NASA, 64-70; from asst prof to assoc prof eng, 70-77, PROF ENG, BROWN UNIV, 77- *Mem:* Inst Elec & Electronics Engrs. *Res:* Linear multivariable control systems; computational methods for the analysis and synthesis of large scale systems; stability and optimization of dynamical systems. *Mailing Add:* Div of Eng Brown Univ Providence RI 02912

WOLOWYK, MICHAEL WALTER, b Rain-Amlech, Ger, Oct 26, 42; Can citizen; m 66; c 2. PHARMACOLOGY, CELL BIOLOGY. *Educ:* Univ Alta, BSc, 65, PhD(pharmacol), 69. *Prof Exp:* Asst prof clin pharm, 71-75, assoc prof pharm, 75-81, PROF PHARM, UNIV ALTA, 81-, HON ASST PROF PHARMACOL, 71-, SCI RES ASSOC, HOSP, 73- *Concurrent Pos:* Med Res Coun fel, Wellcome Res Labs, Beckenham, Eng, 69-71, physiol lab, Cambridge, Eng, 77-78. *Mem:* Pharmacol Soc Can; Micros Soc Can. *Res:* Physiology, pharmacology and morphology of smooth muscle and red blood cells, with particular reference to active transport and exchange of cations. *Mailing Add:* Dept of Clin Pharm Univ of Alta Fac of Pharm Edmonton AB T6G 2N8 Can

WOLPE, JOSEPH, b Johannesburg, SAfrica, Apr 20, 15; US citizen; m 48; c 2. PSYCHIATRY, PSYCHOLOGY. *Educ:* Univ Witwatersrand, MB & BCh, 39, MD, 48. *Prof Exp:* Lectr psychiat, Univ Witwatersrand, 50-59; prof sch med, Univ Va, 60-65; PROF PSYCHIAT, SCH MED, TEMPLE UNIV & EASTERN PA PSYCHIAT INST, 65- *Concurrent Pos:* Fel, Ctr Advan Study Behav Sci, Stanford Univ, 56-57; ed, J Behav Ther & Exp Psychiat, 70- *Mem:* Fel Am Psychiat Asn; Am Psychol Asn; Am Psychopath Asn; Asn Advan Behav Ther. *Mailing Add:* Temple Univ Med Sch & Eastern Pa Psychiat Inst 3300 Henry Ave Philadelphia PA 19129

WOLPERT-DEFILIPPES, MARY KATHERINE, pharmacology, see previous edition

WOLPOFF, MILFORD HOWELL, b Chicago, Ill, Oct 28, 42; m 66. PHYSICAL ANTHROPOLOGY. *Educ:* Univ Ill, Urbana, AB, 64, PhD(anthrop), 69. *Prof Exp:* Asst prof anthrop, Case Western Reserve Univ, 68-70; assoc prof, 70-78, PROF ANTHROP, UNIV MICH, ANN ARBOR, 78- *Concurrent Pos:* NSF res grant, Transvaal Mus, Nat Mus Kenya, 72; Am Philos Soc equip grant, 72-73; NSF, Rackham Found & Nat Acad Sci grants. *Mem:* Fel Am Asn Phys Anthrop; fel Am Anthrop Asn. *Res:* Paleoanthropology; human origins and evolution; evolution theory; biomechanics; computer analysis; dental variation; worldwide fossil hominid study. *Mailing Add:* Dept of Anthrop Univ of Mich Ann Arbor MI 48104

WOLSEY, WAYNE C, b Battle Creek, Mich, Nov 12, 36; m 65; c 2. INORGANIC CHEMISTRY. *Educ:* Mich State Univ, BS, 58; Univ Kans, PhD(chem), 62. *Prof Exp:* Sr res chemist chem div, Pittsburgh Plate Glass Co, Ohio, 62-65; asst prof chem, 65-72, assoc prof, 72-80, PROF CHEM,

MACALESTER COL, 80- *Concurrent Pos:* Vis asst prof, Ariz State Univ, 71-72; vis sr res fel, Bristol Univ, 78-79. *Mem:* AAAS; Am Chem Soc. *Res:* Coordination compounds; chemistry of chlorine and nitrogen compounds; laboratory computing; chemistry experiments. *Mailing Add:* Dept of Chem Macalester Col St Paul MN 55105

WOLSKY, ALAN MARTIN, b Brooklyn, NY, May 17, 43; m 69. PHYSICS. *Educ:* Columbia Col, AB, 64; Univ Pa, MS, 65, PhD(physics), 69. *Prof Exp:* Nat Res Coun fel math physics, Courant Inst Math Sci, NY Univ, 70, vis mem, 71; asst prof physics, Temple Univ, 71-75; MEM STAFF, ARGONNE NAT LAB, 75- *Mem:* Am Phys Soc; Int Asn Economists. *Res:* Feasibility of reducing petroleum consumption by using biomass as an alternative source of hydrocarbons and by recycling, recovering or upgrading industrial waste materials; mathematical economics; theory of social choice and input-output analysis. *Mailing Add:* Argonne Nat Lab 9700 Cass Ave Argonne IL 60439

WOLSKY, MARIA DE ISSEKUTZ, b Kolozsvar, Romania, June 17, 16; nat US; m 40; c 2. CELL BIOLOGY, HISTORY & PHILOSOPHY OF SCIENCE. *Educ:* Med Univ, Budapest, MD, 43. *Prof Exp:* Asst pharmacol, Univ Budapest, 38-39; res assoc, Hungarian Biol Res Inst, 40-45; from instr to prof biol, Manhattanville Col, 56-78; adj prof, NY Univ, 78-79, prof biol, 79-81; RETIRED. *Concurrent Pos:* Res assoc, Fordham Univ, 58-62. *Res:* Cell physiology; theories of evolution; cell differentiation. *Mailing Add:* Bedford Rd Greenwich CT 06830

WOLSKY, SUMNER PAUL, b Boston, Mass, Aug 21, 26; m 50; c 2. PHYSICAL CHEMISTRY. *Educ:* Northeastern Univ, BS, 47; Boston Univ, MA, 49, PhD(chem), 52. *Prof Exp:* Mem res staff, Raytheon Co, 52-61; dir lab phys sci, P R Mallory & Co, Inc, 61-74, dir res & develop lab phys sci, 74-76, vpres res & develop, 76-81; PRES, ANSUM ENTERPRISES, INC, 81- *Mem:* AAAS; Am Chem Soc; Am Phys Soc; Int Elec & Electronics Eng; Electrochem Soc. *Res:* Batteries; semiconductors; surface physics; physical electronics; sputtering; thin films; vacuum microbalances; environment; occupational health. *Mailing Add:* 950 De Soto Rd Suite 3B Boca Raton FL 33432

WOLSSON, KENNETH, b Paterson, NJ, Oct 12, 33. MATHEMATICS. *Educ:* Brooklyn Col, BS, 54; Columbia Univ, AM, 55; NY Univ, PhD(math), 62. *Prof Exp:* Prin res mathematician, Repub Aviation Corp, 62-63, sr res mathematician, 63-64; asst prof, 64-77, ASSOC PROF MATH, FAIRLEIGH DICKINSON UNIV, TEANECK, 77- *Mem:* Am Math Soc; Math Asn Am. *Res:* Partial and ordinary differential equations. *Mailing Add:* Dept of Math 1000 River Rd Fairleigh Dickinson Univ Teaneck NJ 07666

WOLSTENCROFT, RAMON DAVID, astrophysics, see previous edition

WOLSTENHOLME, DAVID ROBERT, b Bury, Eng, Nov 5, 37; m 63. MOLECULAR BIOLOGY, CELL BIOLOGY. *Educ:* Univ Sheffield, BSc, 58, PhD(genetics), 61, DSc(genetics), 73. *Prof Exp:* Fel zool, Univ Wis, 61-62, res assoc, 62-63; vis lectr genetics, Univ Groningen, 63-64; res fel biol, Beermann Div, Max Planck Inst Biol, 64-67; res assoc, Whitman Lab, Univ Chicago, 67-68; assoc prof, Kans State Univ, 68-70; assoc prof, 70-72, PROF BIOL, UNIV UTAH, 72- *Concurrent Pos:* Nat Inst Gen Med Sci res career develop award, Univ Utah, 72-76; mem, Molecular Biol Study Sect, NIH, 73-77. *Mem:* Brit Genetical Soc; Am Soc Cell Biol; Genetics Soc Am. *Res:* Structure, replication, recombination and evolution of mitochondrial DNA. *Mailing Add:* Dept of Biol Univ of Utah Salt Lake City UT 84112

WOLSZON, JOHN DONALD, b Chicago, Ill, Jan 27, 29; m 53; c 6. ANALYTICAL CHEMISTRY. *Educ:* Univ Ill, BS, 51; Pa State Univ, PhD(anal chem), 55. *Prof Exp:* Instr chem, Marshall Univ, 55-58; asst prof, Univ Mo, 58-63; ASSOC PROF CHEM, PURDUE UNIV, 63- *Mem:* Am Chem Soc; Water Pollution Control Fedn; Am Water Works Asn. *Res:* Methods of chemical analysis; water and waste water chemistry. *Mailing Add:* Sch Civil Eng Purdue Univ Lafayette IN 47907

WOLTEN, GERARD MARTIN, b Berlin, Ger, Nov 7, 20; nat US; m 42; c 1. PHYSICAL CHEMISTRY, FORENSIC SCIENCE. *Educ:* NY Univ, BA, 42, MS, 44, PhD(phys chem), 48. *Prof Exp:* Dir res develop, Tempil Corp, 44-56; sr tech specialist, Atomics Int Div NAm Aviation, Inc, 56-61; staff scientist, 61-74, MGR FORENSIC SCI SECT, AEROSPACE CORP, 74- *Mem:* Am Chem Soc; Am Crystallog Asn; Am Phys Soc; Am Acad Forensic Sci. *Res:* Phase equilibria and transformations; crystallography; high temperature x-ray diffraction; machine computations; inorganic structures; gunshot residues; explosives. *Mailing Add:* Anal Sci Dept Aerospace Corp 2350 E El Segundo Blvd El Segundo CA 90245

WOLTER, J REIMER, b Halstenbek, Ger, May 9, 24; US citizen; m 52; c 4. OPHTHALMOLOGY, PATHOLOGY. *Educ:* Univ Hamburg, MD, 49. *Prof Exp:* Intern med, Med Sch, Univ Hamburg, 49-50, resident instr ophthal, 50-53; res assoc path, 53-56, from asst prof to assoc prof ophthal, 56-64, PROF OPHTHAL, MED SCH, UNIV MICH, ANN ARBOR, 64- *Concurrent Pos:* Chief ophthal serv, Vet Admin Hosp, Ann Arbor, 62-; ed, J Pediat Ophthal, 67-81. *Mem:* AMA; Am Ophthal Soc; Am Acad Ophthal & Otolaryngol; Asn Res Ophthal; Ger Ophthal Soc. *Res:* Clinical ophthalmology; opthalmic pathology. *Mailing Add:* Dept Ophthal Univ Mich Med Ctr Ann Arbor MI 48109

WOLTER, JANET, b Chicago, Ill, Apr 24, 26; m 73. MEDICAL ONCOLOGY. *Educ:* Cornell Col, AB, 46; Univ Ill, MD, 50. *Prof Exp:* Instr med, Univ Ill Col Med, 55-57, clin asst prof, 57-70, asst prof med, 70-71; asst prof med, 71-76, ASSOC PROF MED, RUSH MED COL, PRESBY-ST LUKE'S MED CTR, 76- *Concurrent Pos:* Staff physician respiratory, Univ Ill Hosp, 55-57; tumor clin physician oncol, Univ Ill Res & Educ Hosp, 63; res assoc oncol, Presby-St Luke's Hosp, 63-66, consult oncol, 66; consult oncol, WSuburban Hosp, 66; asst attend physician, Presby-St Luke's Med Ctr, 67-70, assoc attend physician, 70-72, sr attend physician, 72, consult oncol, 72-; consult oncol, Copley Hosp, 72- *Mem:* Am Soc Clin Oncol; Am Asn Cancer Res; Eastern Coop Oncol Group; Nat Surg Adj Breast Proj. *Res:* Cancer chemotherapy. *Mailing Add:* 1753 W Congress Pkwy Chicago IL 60612

WOLTER, KARL ERICH, b New York, NY, Nov 8, 30. PLANT PHYSIOLOGY. *Educ:* State Univ NY Col Forestry, Syracuse, BS, 58; Univ Wis, PhD(plant physiol), 64. *Prof Exp:* RES PLANT PHYSIOLOGIST, FOREST PROD LAB, FOREST SERV, USDA, 63- *Concurrent Pos:* Vis prof, Iowa State Univ, 71-72; Japanese Sci & Technol grant; vis scientist, Tsukuba, Japan, 81-82. *Mem:* Am Soc Plant Physiol; Scand Soc Plant Physiol; Japanese Soc Plant Physiol. *Res:* Growth, differentiation and nutrition of plants and secondary cambium, specifically tree species; host pathogen interactions, action, and identification of plant cell wall degrading enzymes. *Mailing Add:* Forest Prod Lab FS USDA PO Box 5130 Madison WI 53705

WOLTERINK, LESTER FLOYD, b Marion, NY, July 28, 15; m 38; c 2. BIOPHYSICS. *Educ:* Hope Col, AB, 36; Univ Minn, MA, 40, PhD(zool), 43. *Prof Exp:* Lab asst, Hope Col, 34-36; asst, Univ Minn, 36-41; instr physiol, 41-45, from asst prof to assoc prof, 45-52, PROF PHYSIOL, MICH STATE UNIV, 52-, ASST EXP STA, 45- *Concurrent Pos:* Assoc physiologist, Argonne Nat Lab, Ill, 48; proj scientist biosatellite proj, Ames Res Ctr, NASA, 65-66; mem subcomt nitrogen oxides, Nat Acad Sci-Nat Res Coun, 73-75. *Mem:* Am Soc Zool; Biophys Soc; Am Physiol Soc; Radiation Res Soc; Brit Biol Eng Soc. *Res:* Biological rhythms, oscillatory time series; physiological models. *Mailing Add:* Dept of Physiol Mich State Univ East Lansing MI 48824

WOLTERMANN, GERALD M, b Bellevue, Ky, Nov 19, 47. INORGANIC CHEMISTRY. *Educ:* Thomas More Col, AB, 69; Univ Ky, PhD(inorg chem), 73. *Prof Exp:* Res fel bioinorg chem, Univ Ill, 73-75; res chemist, Englehard Minerals & Chem Corp, 75-80. *Concurrent Pos:* Res fel, Univ Ky, 73. *Mem:* Am Chem Soc. *Res:* Catalysis; especially metal and zeolite catalysis; enzymatic systems especially model systems involving coordination complexes; electron spin resonance as applied to inorganic coordination crystals. *Mailing Add:* 7422 Avery Rd Dublin OH 43017

WOLTERS, ROBERT JOHN, b St Louis, Mo, Nov 7, 40; m 70; c 2. PHARMACEUTICAL CHEMISTRY, PHARMACOLOGY. *Educ:* St Louis Col Pharm, BS, 65; NDak State Univ, MS, 68, PhD(pharmaceut chem), 71. *Prof Exp:* REV CHEMIST, US FOOD & DRUG ADMIN, ROCKVILLE, 71- *Mem:* Am Chem Soc; Am Pharmaceut Asn; Sigma Xi. *Res:* Synthesis of potential pharmaceutically active compounds; mescaline analogs. *Mailing Add:* 18645 Hedgegrove Terr Olney MD 20832

WOLTERSDORF, OTTO WILLIAM, JR, b Philadelphia, Pa, June 19, 35; m 57; c 2. MEDICINAL CHEMISTRY. *Educ:* Gettysburg Col, AB, 56; Pa State Univ, MS, 59. *Prof Exp:* Res assoc org synthesis, 59-65, from res chemist to sr res chemist, 65-73, RES FEL, MERCK SHARP & DOHME RES LABS, 73- *Mem:* Am Chem Soc. *Res:* Organic synthesis; radioisotope synthesis. *Mailing Add:* 200 Dorset Way Chalfont PA 18914

WOLTHUIS, ROGER A, b Champaign, Ill, Mar 30, 37; m 65; c 2. CARDIOVASCULAR PHYSIOLOGY. *Educ:* Univ Mich, BA, 63; Mich State Univ, MS, 65, PhD(physiol), 68. *Prof Exp:* Prin res scientist, Technol Inc, Cardiovasc Res Lab, NASA Johnson Space Ctr, 68-74; chief cardiovasc res internal med, Sch Aerospace Med, Brooks AFB, 74-80; SR STAFF SCIENTIST, MEDTRONIC INC, 80- *Concurrent Pos:* Partic, Apollo & Skylab Med Experiments. *Mem:* Am Col Cardiol; Am Heart Asn; Aerospace Med Asn; Am Physiol Soc; Inst Elec & Electronics Engrs. *Res:* Studies on man's physiological adaptation to normal and zero gravity environments; studies on exercise stress testing for detection of coronary artery disease; studies on hypertension and its treatment. *Mailing Add:* Medtronic Inc 3055 Old Highway Eight Minneapolis MN 55440

WOLTJER, LODEWYK, b Holland, Apr 26, 30; m; c 1. ASTROPHYSICS. *Educ:* Univ Leiden, PhD(astron), 57. *Prof Exp:* Res assoc, Yerkes Observ, Univ Chicago, 57-58 & Fermi Inst Nuclear Studies, 60; mem, Inst Advan Study, 59; lectr, Univ Leiden, 59-60; mem, Inst Advan Study, 61; prof theoret astrophys & plasma physics, Univ Leiden, 61-64; Rutherford prof astron & chmn dept, 63-77, ADJ PROF ASTRON, 63-77, COLUMBIA UNIV, 77- *Concurrent Pos:* Vis prof, Mass Inst Technol, 62-63 & Univ Md, 63. *Mem:* Int Astron Union; Am Astron Soc. *Res:* Galactic dynamics; radio astronomy. *Mailing Add:* Dept of Astron 109 Mem Libr Columbia Univ New York NY 10027

WOLTZ, FRANK EARL, b Bethlehem, Pa, Nov 29, 16; m 47; c 2. PHYSICAL CHEMISTRY. *Educ:* Bethany Col, WVa, BS, 38; Univ WVa, MS, 40, PhD(chem), 43; Ohio Univ, MS, 70. *Prof Exp:* Mat engr, Westinghouse Elec Corp, Pa, 42-44; lab mgr, Goodyear Synthetic Rubber Corp, Ohio, 44-47, res chemist, Goodyear Tire & Rubber Co, 47-50, rubber compounder, 50-53, supvr opers anal, Goodyear Atomic Corp, Piketon, 53-67, SUPT ENG DEVELOP, GOODYEAR ATOMIC CORP, PIKETON, 67- *Concurrent Pos:* Consult radiation adv bd, Ohio Dept Health, 74- *Mem:* Am Nuclear Soc. *Res:* Electrical insulating varnishes; analytical test methods; rubber manufacture; inert electrode systems; rubber compounding for use in tire manufacturing; fluid flow; material and energy optimization of gaseous diffusion processes; computer control of chemical processes; nuclear criticality safety. *Mailing Add:* 400 E Third St Waverly OH 45690

WOLTZ, SHREVE SIMPSON, b Clifton, Va, Apr 9, 24; m 47; c 2. HORTICULTURE. *Educ:* Va Polytech Inst, BS, 43; Rutgers Univ, PhD(soils, plant physiol), 51. *Prof Exp:* Dir fertilizer res, Baugh & Sons Co, 51-53; asst horticulurist, 53-62, assoc plant physiologist, 62-68, plant physiologist, Agr Res & Educ Ctr, Bradenton, 53-62, PROF PLANT PHYSIOL, UNIV FLA, 68- *Mem:* Am Soc Hort Sci; Am Soc Plant Physiol; Am Phytopath Soc; Scand Soc Plant Physiol. *Res:* Plant nutrition; gladiolus and chrysanthemum culture; soil fertility; physiology of disease. *Mailing Add:* Dept of Plant Path Univ of Fla Gainesville FL 32611

WOLVEN-GARRETT, ANNE M, b New York, NY, Feb 2, 25; m 78. TOXICOLOGY. *Educ:* Hunter Col, BA, 45. *Prof Exp:* Group leader pharmacol, Schering Corp, NJ, 45-47; group leader, Leberco Labs, NJ, 47-52, from asst dir to assoc dir labs, 52-72; mgr toxicol, Alza Res Corp, 72-75; sr toxicologist, Shell Chem Co, 75-76; environ toxicologist, Syntex Corp, 76-78; CONSULT TOXICOL & REGULATORY AFFAIRS, A M WOLVEN, INC, 78- *Concurrent Pos:* Round Table discussant, Gordon Conf Toxicol & Safety Eval, 70, chairperson, 76; lectr, Ctr Prof Advan, 72; consult toxicol, Nat Inst Drug Abuse, 74-75 & Ministry Health, Mex, 75; mem hazardous mat adv comt, Environ Protection Agency, 75-77, mem sci adv bd, 75-79; lectr, Howard Univ, 77. *Mem:* AAAS; Soc Toxicol; Soc Cosmetic Chem; Am Soc Microbiol. *Res:* Eye and skin irritation and absorption phenomena; pesticide toxicology. *Mailing Add:* 6560 Sentry Hill Trail NE Atlanta GA 30328

WOLVERTON, BILLY CHARLES, b Scott Co, Miss, Oct 13, 32; m 55; c 1. CHEMISTRY. *Educ:* Miss Col, BS, 60; Occidental Univ, PhD(environ eng), 78. *Prof Exp:* Res asst, Med Ctr, Univ Miss, 60-63; res chemist, US Naval Weapons Lab, 63-65; br chief res chemist, Air Force Armament Lab, 65-71; ENVIRON SCIENTIST, NAT SPACE TECHNOL LAB, BAY ST LOUIS, MISS, 71- *Concurrent Pos:* Mem Panel Unconventional Approaches to Aquatic Weed Control & Utilization, Nat Acad Sci, 75- *Honors & Awards:* Super Sci Achievement Award, Dept Navy, 65; Sci Achievement Award, Dept Air Force, 69, Spec Sci Achievement Award, 71; Sci Technol Utilization Award, Am Inst Aeronaut & Astronaut, 70; Except Sci Serv Medal, NASA, 75. *Res:* Vascular, aquatic plants plants as biological filtration systems for removing domestic and industrial pollutants from wastewater and the utilization of harvested plant material as renewable sources of feed, fertilizer and methane. *Mailing Add:* PO Box 51 Picayune MS 39466

WOLYNES, PETER GUY, b Chicago, Ill, Apr 21, 53. STATISTICAL MECHANICS. *Educ:* Ind Univ, AB, 71; Harvard Univ, PhD(chem physics), 76. *Prof Exp:* Fel, Mass Inst Technol, 75-76; asst prof, Harvard Univ, 76-79, assoc prof, 79-80; ASSOC PROF CHEM, UNIV ILL, URBANA-CHAMPAIGN, 80- *Concurrent Pos:* Vis scientist, Max Planck Inst Biophys Chem, 77. *Mem:* Am Phys Soc; Am Chem Soc. *Res:* Theory of chemical dynamic phenomena in condensed phases, especially kinetics, tunneling and electronic structure in liquids; theory of the glassy state; biophysical applications. *Mailing Add:* Sch Chem Sci Univ Ill 505 S Mathews Ave Urbana IL 61801

WOLYNETZ, MARK STANLEY, b Kitchener, Ont, Nov 11, 45. STATISTICS. *Educ:* Univ Waterloo, BMath, 69, MMath, 70, PhD(statist), 74. *Prof Exp:* Statistician rd safety, Ministry Transp Can, 74-75; STATISTICIAN AGR RES, DEPT AGR, CAN, 75- *Res:* Application of statistical techniques in agriculture research; specifically in problems of categorical data, data screening, censored observations. *Mailing Add:* Res Br Agr Can Heritage House 54 Ottawa ON K1A 0C6 Can

WOMACK, FRANCES C, b Owensboro, Ky, Mar 23, 31; m 53; c 2. GENETICS, ENZYMOLOGY. *Educ:* Vanderbilt Univ, BA, 52, MA, 55, PhD(biol), 62. *Prof Exp:* Asst prof genetics, 62-63 & 64-65, res assoc, 63-64, res assoc enzymol, 65-72, ASST PROF ENZYMOL, SCH MED, VANDERBILT UNIV, 72- *Res:* Protein structure, function and their relation to genetic information; bacteriophage genetics. *Mailing Add:* Dept of Microbiol Vanderbilt Univ Sch of Med Nashville TN 37203

WOMACK, JAMES E, b Anson, Tex, Mar 30, 41; m 63; c 2. GENETICS. *Educ:* Abilene Christian Col, BS, 64; Ore State Univ, PhD(genetics), 68. *Prof Exp:* From asst prof to assoc prof biol, Abilene Christian Col, 68-73; vis scientist, Jackson Lab, 73-75, staff scientist, 75-77; ASSOC PROF VET PATH & GENETICIST, INST COMP MED, TEX A&M UNIV, 77- *Mem:* AAAS; Genetics Soc Am; Am Genetics Asn; Am Soc Human Genetics. *Res:* Comparative gene mapping; radiation induced isozyme mutants; mammalian developmental genetics; genetics of lysosomal enzymes. *Mailing Add:* Dept Vet Path Tex A&M Univ College Station TX 77843

WOMBLE, DAVID DALE, b Coffeyville, Kans, Oct 10, 49; m 72. MOLECULAR BIOLOGY, BIOCHEMISTRY. *Educ:* Ohio Univ, BS, 71; Univ Wis-Madison, PhD(biochem), 76. *Prof Exp:* Trainee biochem, Univ Wis-Madison, 71-75, res asst, 75-76, res assoc molecular biol, 76-77, trainee pathobiol, 77-79, asst scientist molecular biol, 79-81; SR RES ASSOC, MED SCH, NORTHWESTERN UNIV, 81- *Mem:* Am Soc Microbiol; AAAS; Sigma Xi. *Res:* Nuclei acid structure and organization; regulation of replication and genetic expression. *Mailing Add:* Dept Molecular Biol Northwestern Univ Med Sch 303 E Chicago Ave Chicago IL 60611

WOMBLE, EUGENE WILSON, b High Point, NC, June 27, 31; m 59; c 4. MATHEMATICS. *Educ:* Wofford Col, BS, 52; Univ NC, Chapel Hill, MA, 59; Univ Okla, PhD(math), 70. *Prof Exp:* Teacher, Kernersville High Sch, 56-58; instr math, Wake Forest Col, 59-61; asst prof, Pfeiffer Col, 61-66; spec instr, Univ Okla, 69-70; prof, 70-72, CHARLES A DANA PROF MATH, PRESBY COL, 72- *Mem:* Math Asn Am; Nat Coun Teachers Math. *Res:* Foundations of convexity; convexity structures. *Mailing Add:* Dept of Math Presby Col Clinton SC 29325

WOMER, WALTER DALE, organic chemistry, see previous edition

WOMMACK, JOEL BENJAMIN, JR, b Benton, Ky, Dec 5, 42; m 67; c 2. AGRICULTURAL CHEMISTRY. *Educ:* David Lipscomb Col, BS, 64; Vanderbilt Univ, PhD(org chem), 68. *Prof Exp:* Res chemist, 68-74, res supvr, 74-76, res mgr, 76-78, gen supvr, 78-79, asst mgr, 80-81, SITE MGR, BIOCHEM DEPT, E I DU PONT DE NEMOURS & CO, INC, 81- *Mem:* Am Chem Soc. *Mailing Add:* 4560 Simon Rd Wilmington DE 19803

WONDERLING, THOMAS FRANKLIN, b Utica, Ohio, Feb 4, 15; m 41; c 2. AGRICULTURE. *Educ:* Ohio State Univ, BS, 39. *Prof Exp:* Teacher bd educ, Ohio, 39-45; farm mgr, Tiffin State Hosp, State Dept Pub Welfare, Ohio, 45-46, farm mgr, Lima State Hosp, 46-48; supt outlying farms, Ohio Agr Exp Sta, 48-63; coordr res opers, Ohio Agr Res & Develop Ctr, 63-69, coordr res opers & phys plant, 69-74; coordr res opers & supvr, North Appalachian Water Exp Sta, 74-79; RETIRED. *Mailing Add:* Ohio Agr Res & Develop Ctr Wooster OH 44691

WONENBURGER, MARIA JOSEFA, b La Coruna, Spain, July 19, 27. MATHEMATICS. *Educ:* Univ Madrid, Lic math, 50, Dr(math), 60; Yale Univ, PhD(math), 57. *Prof Exp:* Nat Res Coun Can fel, Queen's Univ, Ont, 60-62; from asst prof to assoc prof math, Toronto Univ, 62-66; prof, State Univ NY, Buffalo, 66-67; PROF MATH, IND UNIV, BLOOMINGTON, 67- *Res:* Algebra. *Mailing Add:* Dept of Math Ind Univ Bloomington IN 47401

WONES, DAVID R, b San Francisco, Calif, July 13, 32; m 58; c 4. PETROLOGY, GEOCHEMISTRY. *Educ:* Mass Inst Technol, SB, 54, PhD(geol), 60. *Prof Exp:* Bush fel, Carnegie Inst, 57-59; geologist, US Geol Surv, 59-67; assoc prof geol, Mass Inst Technol, 66-71; chief br exp geochem & mineral, 72-76, geologist, US Geol Surv, 71-77; PROF GEOL, VA POLYTECH INST & STATE UNIV, 77-, CHMN, DEPT GEOL SCI, 80- *Concurrent Pos:* Fel, Am Geophys Union, 79. *Mem:* Mineral Soc Am (pres, 79); Geochem Soc; Am Geophys Union; Geol Soc Am; Brit Mineral Soc. *Res:* Mineral synthesis; phase equilibria of systems applicable to rocks and minerals; plutonic rocks of Northern Appalachians. *Mailing Add:* Dept of Geol Sci Va Polytech Inst & State Univ Blacksburg VA 24061

WONG, ALAN YAU KUEN, b Hong Kong, Feb 6, 37; Can citizen; m 67; c 3. PHYSICS, BIOPHYSICS. *Educ:* Dalhousie Univ, BSc, 62, MSc, 63, PhD(biophys), 67. *Prof Exp:* Res assoc comput sci, 66-68, lectr biophys, 68-71, asst prof, 71-77, ASSOC PROF BIOPHYS, DALHOUSIE UNIV, 77- *Concurrent Pos:* Can Heart Found fel biophys & bioeng res lab, Dalhousie Univ, 68-71, Med Res Coun Can res scholar, 71-76; fel circulation, Am Heart Asn. *Mem:* Med & Biol Eng Soc Can; Biophys Soc; Soc Math Biol. *Res:* Excitation-contraction coupling of cardiac muscle; coronary flow; sodium-calcium exchange in excitable tissue; ventricular dynamics. *Mailing Add:* Dept Physiol & Biophysics Dalhousie Univ Halifax NS B3H 3S5 Can

WONG, ALFRED YIU-FAI, b Macao, Portugal, Feb 4, 37; m 65. PLASMA PHYSICS. *Educ:* Univ Toronto, BASc, 58, MA, 59; Univ Ill, MSc, 61; Princeton Univ, PhD(plasma physics), 63. *Prof Exp:* Res assoc plasma physics lab, Princeton Univ, 62-64; from asst prof to assoc prof physics, 64-72, PROF PHYSICS, UNIV CALIF, LOS ANGELES, 72- *Concurrent Pos:* Sloan res fel, 66-68. *Mem:* fel Am Phys Soc. *Res:* Waves and radiation from plasmas; nonlinear phenomena; confinement system and space plasmas. *Mailing Add:* Dept of Physics Univ of Calif Los Angeles CA 90024

WONG, BING KUEN, b Shanghai, China, Oct 4, 38; m 66; c 2. MATHEMATICAL ANALYSIS. *Educ:* Kans State Col, Pittsburg, AB, 61; Univ Ill, MA, 63, PhD(math), 66. *Prof Exp:* Asst prof math, Univ Western Ill, 65-66; asst prof, Rochester Inst Technol, 66-68; PROF MATH & COMPUT SCI & CHMN DEPT, WILKES COL, 68- *Mem:* Am Math Soc; Math Asn Am. *Res:* Analysis. *Mailing Add:* Dept of Math & Comput Sci Wilkes Col Wilkes-Barre PA 18703

WONG, BRENDAN SO, b Hong Kong, Feb 25, 47; US citizen; m 72; c 1. BIOPHYSICS, PHYSIOLOGY. *Educ:* Univ San Francisco, BS, 71; Southern Ill Univ, MA, 74, PhD(biophys), 78. *Prof Exp:* FEL BIOPHYS, NAT INST NEUROL & COMMUN DIS & STROKE, 78- *Mem:* Biophys Soc; Am Physiol Soc; AAAS. *Res:* Single-channel patch-clamp studies on tissue-cultured cells; voltage clamp studies on the marine worm myxicola; electrophysiology of acanthocephalans; study of water dynamics in biological systems using pulsed nuclear magnetic resonance. *Mailing Add:* Lab of Biophys NIH Bldg 36 Rm 2A29 Bethesda MD 20205

WONG, CHAK-KUEN, b Macao, China; m 70. COMPUTER SCIENCE, APPLIED MATHEMATICS. *Educ:* Univ Hong Kong, BA, 65; Columbia Univ, MA, 66, PhD(math), 70. *Prof Exp:* RES STAFF MEM COMPUT SCI, T J WATSON RES CTR, IBM CORP, 69- *Concurrent Pos:* Vis assoc prof, Univ Ill, Urbana, 72-73; vis prof, Columbia Univ, 78-79. *Honors & Awards:* Outstanding Invention Award, IBM Corp, 71. *Mem:* Am Math Soc; Inst Elec & Electronics Eng; NY Acad Sci; Asn Comput Mach. *Res:* Mathematical analysis; discrete and combinatorial mathematics; application of mathematics to computers and computing; analysis of optimum and near-optimum algorithms in computing; system impact of future computer memory technology; traffic scheduling in satellite communications system; very large scale integration algorithms. *Mailing Add:* T J Watson Res Ctr IBM Corp Yorktown Heights NY 10598

WONG, CHEUK-YIN, b Kwangtung, China, Apr 28, 41; m 66; c 3. PHYSICS. *Educ:* Princeton Univ, AB, 61, MA, 63, PhD(physics), 66. *Prof Exp:* Physicist, Oak Ridge Nat Lab, 66-68; res fel physics, Niels Bohr Inst, Copenhagen, Denmark, 68-69; PHYSICIST, OAK RIDGE NAT LAB, 69- *Mem:* Am Phys Soc. *Res:* Theoretical studies of nuclear stability, nuclear fission and nuclear reactions; dynamics of nuclear fluid. *Mailing Add:* Oak Ridge Nat Lab Oak Ridge TN 37830

WONG, CHI SONG, b Cheng Tak, Hunan, China, May 26, 38; m 66; c 3. MATHEMATICAL STATISTICS, OPERATOR THEORY. *Educ:* Nat Taiwan Univ, BS, 62; Univ Ore, MS, 66; Univ Ill, Urbana, MS, 67, PhD(functional anal), 69. *Prof Exp:* Tutor, Chinese Univ, Hong Kong, 62-65; asst prof math, Southern Ill Univ, Carbondale, 69-71; asst prof, 71-73, assoc prof, 73-76, PROF MATH, UNIV WINDSOR, 76- *Concurrent Pos:* Can Nat Res Coun fels, 72-76. *Mem:* Can Math Cong. *Res:* Using algebra, functional analysis, geometry and topology to characterize certain classes of self maps which have fixed points; mathematical analysis. *Mailing Add:* Dept of Math Univ of Windsor Windsor ON N9B 3P4 Can

WONG, CHIU MING, b Canton, China, July 8, 35; m 60; c 2. ORGANIC CHEMISTRY. *Educ:* Nat Taiwan Univ, BSc, 59; Univ NB, PhD(chem), 64. *Prof Exp:* Asst, Univ NB, 64, res fels, 64-65; res fels, Harvard Univ, 65-66; from asst prof to assoc prof, 66-75, PROF ORG CHEM, UNIV MAN, 75- *Mem:* Am Chem Soc. *Res:* Synthesis and structure-reactivity studies of anthracycline antitumor antibiotics. *Mailing Add:* Dept of Chem Univ of Man Winnipeg MB R3T 2N2 Can

WONG, CHIU-PING, b Canton, China, Dec 24, 43; m 76; c 1. POLYMER RHEOLOGY, VISCOELASTICITY. *Educ:* Chinese Univ, Hong Kong, BSc, 66; Univ Wis-Madison, PhD(phys chem), 70. *Prof Exp:* Res chemist polymer sci, Mellon Inst, Carnegie-Mellon Univ, 70-78; RES SCIENTIST RUBBER ENG, GEN TIRE & RUBBER CO RES CTR, 79- *Mem:* Am Chem Soc; Am Phys Soc; Soc Rheol. *Res:* Polymer physics; rubber and tire engineering; rheology and polymer processing; linear and nonlinear viscoelasticity; high modulus and heat resistant polymers; highly oriented fiber and film fabrication. *Mailing Add:* Res Ctr 2990 Gilchrist Rd Akron OH 44305

WONG, CHUEN, US citizen. PHYSICS. *Educ:* Chung Chi Col, Hong Kong, dipl sci, 60; Case Western Reserve Univ, PhD(physics), 67. *Prof Exp:* Demonstr physics, Chung Chi Col, Hong Kong, 60-63; instr, 67-70, ASST PROF PHYSICS, UNIV LOWELL, 70- *Mem:* Am Phys Soc; Optical Soc Am. *Res:* Experimental solid state physics; elastic constants; semiconductors. *Mailing Add:* Dept of Physics Univ Lowell Lowell MA 01854

WONG, CHUN-MING, b Hong Kong, Brit Crown Colony, Nov 12, 40; m 71. ORGANIC POLYMER CHEMISTRY. *Educ:* Univ Calif, Berkeley, BS, 65; Wayne State Univ, MS, 66; NDak State Univ, PhD(chem), 73. *Prof Exp:* Chemist, Inmont Corp, 66-70; Res chemist, E I du Pont de Nemours & Co, Inc, 74-80. *Mem:* Am Chem Soc. *Res:* Water dispersible organic coatings aimed at reducing pollution and saving energy. *Mailing Add:* 9250 25th Ave NW Seattle WA 98117

WONG, DAVID TAIWAI, b Hong Kong, Nov 6, 35; US citizen; m 63; c 3. BIOCHEMISTRY. *Educ:* Seattle Pac Col, BS, 60; Ore State Univ, MS, 64; Univ Ore, PhD(biochem), 66. *Prof Exp:* Fel biophys chem, Univ Pa, 66-68; sr biochemist, 68-72, res biochemist, 73-77, RES ASSOC, LILLY RES LABS, ELI LILLY & CO, 78- *Mem:* Biophys Soc; Int Soc Neurochem; Am Soc Neurochem; Am Soc Pharmacol & Exp Therapeut; Sigma Xi. *Res:* Biochemistry of neurotransmission; synthetic chemicals which block the uptake of specific neurotransmitters investigated as potentially useful therapeutic agents for mental disorders; chemicals of microbial origin which carry metal cations across biomembranes; fluoxetine for treatment of mental depression. *Mailing Add:* 1640 Ridge Hill Lane Indianapolis IN 46217

WONG, DAVID YUE, b Swatow, China, Apr 16, 34; US citizen; m 60; c 2. PHYSICS. *Educ:* Hardin-Simmons Univ, BA, 54; Univ Md, College Park, PhD(physics), 58. *Prof Exp:* Theoretical physicist, Univ Calif, Berkeley, 58-60, from asst prof to assoc prof, 60-67, PROF PHYSICS, UNIV CALIF, SAN DIEGO, 67- *Concurrent Pos:* Alfred P Sloan fel, Univ Calif, San Diego, 63-66. *Mem:* Am Inst Physics; Am Phys Soc. *Res:* Theoretical high energy physics. *Mailing Add:* Dept of Physics Univ of Calif San Diego La Jolla CA 92093

WONG, DENNIS MUN, b San Francisco, Calif, Dec 14, 44; m 69. CELLULAR IMMUNOLOGY. *Educ:* Calif State Univ, San Francisco, BA, 69, MA, 74; Georgetown Univ, PhD(microbiol), 77. *Prof Exp:* Fel, Naval Med Res Inst, 77-79; STAFF FEL, BUR BIOLOGICS, DIV BLOOD & BLOOD PROD, NIH, 80- *Mem:* AAAS; Am Soc Microbiol; NY Acad Sci; Am Asn Clin Histocompatibility Testing; Sigma Xi. *Res:* Cellular immunology; human histocompatibility antigens; immunogenetic system; development of hybridoma antibodies against cell surface antigens. *Mailing Add:* Bur Biologics Div Blood & Blood Prod NIH Bethesda MD 20205

WONG, DEREK CHUNG-FAT, b Shanghai, China, Jan 22, 46; m 72; c 1. OPERATIONS RESEARCH, MATHEMATICAL PROGRAMMING. *Educ:* Hong Kong Baptist Col, BSc, 68; Fla State Univ, MS, 75, PhD(statist), 77. *Prof Exp:* ASST PROF MATH PROG, NORTHERN ILL UNIV, 77- *Mem:* Inst Mgt Sci; Am Statist Asn; Inst Math Statist. *Res:* Optimization theory. *Mailing Add:* Dept of Math Sci Northern Ill Univ DeKalb IL 60115

WONG, DONALD TAI ON, b Honolulu, Hawaii, Nov 1, 26; m 54; c 2. IMMUNOLOGY. *Educ:* St Louis Univ, BS, 49; Wash Univ, PhD(microbiol), 53. *Prof Exp:* Res chemist, Dept Bact Microbial Chem Sect, Walter Reed Army Inst Res, Army Med Ctr, Washington, DC, 52-61; res chemist, Blood Antigen Lab, Div Animal Husb, Agr Res Ctr, Md, 61-65; RES CHEMIST, DEPT IMMUNOCHEM, DIV COMMUN DIS & IMMUNOL, WALTER REED ARMY INST RES, ARMY MED CTR, 65- *Mem:* AAAS; Am Chem Soc. *Res:* Oxidative metabolism in microorganisms; alternate pathways and carbon-2-carbon-2 condensation mechanisms; immunoglobulin specifity and structure; mechanisms involved with immediate type hypersensitivity reactions. *Mailing Add:* Dept Immunochem Div Commun Dis & Army Med Ctr Washington DC 20012

WONG, DOROTHY PAN, b Nanking, China, July 8, 37; US citizen; m 68. PHYSICAL CHEMISTRY. *Educ:* Univ Okla, BS, 57; Univ Minn, MS, 59; Case Inst Technol, PhD(phys chem), 64. *Prof Exp:* Res chemist, Continental Oil Co, 57; assoc chemist, Airforce Midway Lab, Univ Chicago, 59-60; asst prof phys chem, Calif State Col Fullerton, 64-65; res assoc quantum chem, Princeton Univ, 65-66; asst prof, 66-67, assoc prof, 68-73, PROF PHYS CHEM, CALIF STATE UNIV, FULLERTON, 70- *Mem:* Am Chem Soc; Am Phys Soc. *Res:* Non-empirical quantum mechanical calculations for geometry of molecules; molecular properties and rotation barriers of nitrogen compounds and for other molecules of current chemical interest. *Mailing Add:* Dept of Chem Calif State Univ 800 N State College Blvd Fullerton CA 92634

WONG, E(UGENE), b Nanking, China, Dec 24, 34; nat US; m 56; c 3. ELECTRICAL ENGINEERING, COMPUTER SCIENCE. *Educ:* Princeton Univ, BSE, 55, AM, 58, PhD(elec eng), 59. *Prof Exp:* Nat Sci Found fel, Cambridge Univ, 59-60; mem res staff, Int Bus Mach Corp, 60-62; from asst prof to assoc prof elec eng, 62-69, PROF ELEC ENG & COMPUT SCI, UNIV CALIF, BERKELEY, 69- *Concurrent Pos:* Guggenheim fel, Cambridge Univ, 68-69; consult, Ampex Corp; Vinton Hayes sr fel, Harvard Univ, 76-77; consult, Honeywell, Inc, 78- Mem: Fel Inst Elec & Electronics Engrs; Asn Comput Mach. *Mem:* Fel Inst Elec & Electronics Engrs; Asn Comput Mach. *Res:* Stochastic processes; data base systems. *Mailing Add:* Dept of Elec Eng & Comput Sci Univ of Calif Berkeley CA 94720

WONG, EDWARD HOU, b Hankow, China, Oct 5, 46; m 74. INORGANIC CHEMISTRY. *Educ:* Univ Calif, Berkeley, BS, 68; Harvard Univ, PhD(inorg chem), 74. *Prof Exp:* Res assoc boron chem, Univ Calif, Los Angeles, 74-76; asst prof, Fordham Univ, 76-78; ASST PROF CHEM, UNIV NH, 78- *Mem:* Am Chem Soc. *Res:* Polyhedral borane and carborane chemistry; transition metal complexes in catalysis; cluster chemistry. *Mailing Add:* Dept Chem Parsons Hall Univ NH Durham NH 03824

WONG, FULTON, b Kwangtung, China, Nov 9, 48. NEUROSCIENCES, VISUAL SCIENCES. *Educ:* Univ Redlands, Calif, BS, 72; Rockefeller Univ, NY, PhD(biophysics), 77. *Prof Exp:* Res assoc vision, Dept Biol Sci, Purdue Univ, 77-78, vis asst biol, 78-79; ASST PROF, DEPT PHYSIOL & BIOPHYSICS, MED BR, UNIV TEX, 79- *Concurrent Pos:* Mem, Marine Biomed Inst, 79- *Mem:* AAAS; Genetics Soc Am; Biophys Soc; Sigma Xi; Asn Res Vision & Ophthal. *Res:* Molecular mechanisms of phototransduction. *Mailing Add:* Marine Biomed Inst Galveston TX 77550

WONG, GEORGE SHOUNG-KOON, b Hong Kong, July 21, 35; Can citizen. ACOUSTICAL MEASUREMENTS, ENGINEERING METROLOGY. *Prof Exp:* Asst res officer physics, 66-70, assoc res officer, 70-79, SR RES OFFICER PHYSICS, NAT RES COUN, CAN, 79- *Concurrent Pos:* Chmn, Int Electrotech Comn Subcomt, Can Standards Coun, 81- *Mem:* fel Inst Elec Engrs UK; Acoust Soc am; Inst Mech Engrs UK. *Res:* Precision acoustical measurements, in particular on the primary acoustical standards calibration; one order of magnitude improvement in accuracy can be achieved with the system under development. *Mailing Add:* Physics Div Nat Res Coun Can Ottawa ON K1A 0R6 Can

WONG, GEORGE TIN FUK, b Hong Kong, Nov 29, 49; m 74. CHEMICAL OCEANOGRAPHY, ENVIRONMENTAL CHEMISTRY. *Educ:* Calif State Univ, Los Angeles, BS, 71; Mass Inst Technol, MS, 73; PhD(chem oceanog), 76. *Prof Exp:* ASST PROF OCEANOG, OLD DOMINION UNIV, 76- *Concurrent Pos:* Prin investr, US Dept Energy, 77- *Mem:* Am Soc Limnol & Oceanog; AAAS; Am Geophysics Union. *Res:* Trace elements; radiogeochemistry; physical and analytical chemistry of seawater; marine environmental chemistry. *Mailing Add:* Inst of Oceanog Old Dominion Univ Norfolk VA 23508

WONG, HANS KUOMIN, b Canton, Kwangtung, China, Apr 30, 36; US citizen; m 67; c 2. PHYSICAL & INORGANIC CHEMISTRY. *Educ:* NDak State Univ, BS, 59; Univ Minn, PhD(phys chem), 65. *Prof Exp:* Sr chemist, Itek Corp, 65-70; sr chemist phys chem, Olivetti Corp Am, 71-81; SR CHEMIST PHYS CHEM, BACHARACH INST CO, 81- *Mem:* Am Chem Soc. *Res:* Electrophotography; photoconductivity; dye sensitization mechanism; photochemistry. *Mailing Add:* Bacharach Inst Co 301 Alpha Dr Pittsburgh PA 15238

WONG, HARRY YUEN CHEE, b Kapaa, Hawaii, Oct 23, 17; m 43; c 3. PHYSIOLOGY, ENDOCRINOLOGY. *Educ:* Okla State Univ, BS, 42; Univ Southern Calif, MS, 47, PhD(endocrinol, physiol), 50. *Prof Exp:* Asst physiol, Univ Southern Calif, 46-48, lab assoc anat, 48-49; assoc prof biol, Andrews Univ, 49-51; dir basic endocrine res, Freedmen's Hosp, 52-60; instr zool, 51-52, from asst prof to assoc prof physiol, Sch Med, 52-66, PROF PHYSIOL, SCH MED, HOWARD UNIV, 66-, DIR ENDOCRINOL & METAB, 53- *Concurrent Pos:* Consult, Off Surgeon Gen, US Air Force, 63-; vis prof hormone lab, II Med Clin, Univ Hamburg, 69; vis scientist, Armed Forces Inst Path, DC, 70; fel, coun arteriosclerosis, Am Heart Asn; mem, Int Cong Physiol Sci, Int Cong Pharmacol, Int Cong Hormonal Steroids & Int Cong Endocrinol; consult to chief dept med & clin sci, Brooks AFB; fel coun arteriosclerosis, Am Heart Asn. *Honors & Awards:* Citation, Food & Drug Admin, 62; Cert Outstanding Achievement, US Air Force, 69. *Mem:* Am Physiol Soc; Endocrine Soc; NY Acad Sci; AMA. *Res:* Lipid mobilizing factor; factor of stress and exercise and sex hormones in atherosclerosis; enzymes, catecholamines and hormones of heart and adrenal glands; lipid changes in chickens, man and gerbils; chemical determination of androgens; toxicology of benzodiazepines in lipid metabolism and atherosclerosis. *Mailing Add:* Dept of Physiol & Biophys Howard Univ Washington DC 20059

WONG, HORNE RICHARD, b Hong Kong, Jan 9, 23; Can citizen; m 58; c 3. SAWFLY SYSTEMATICS, ENTOMOLOGY. *Educ:* Univ Man, BSA, 47; Mich State Univ, MS, 50; Univ Ill, PhD(entom), 60. *Prof Exp:* Sr agr asst, Can Dept Agr, 47-48, officer-in-charge forest insect surv, 49-52, res officer, 53-60; res officer, 61-65, RES SCIENTIST, NORTHERN FOREST RES CTR, CAN DEPT ENVIRON, 66- *Concurrent Pos:* Mem, Can Comt Common Names Insects, 58-70. *Mem:* AAAS; Entom Soc Am; Sigma Xi; Soc Study Evolution; Entom Soc Can. *Res:* Systematics, biology and phylogeny of Symphta; life history and habits of forest insects. *Mailing Add:* Northern Forest Res Ctr Can Dept Environ 5320 122 St Edmonton AB T6H 3S5 Can

WONG, JAMES B(OK), b Canton, China, Dec 9, 22; nat US; m 46; c 3. CHEMICAL ENGINEERING, ECONOMICS. *Educ:* Univ Md, BS, 49, BChE, 50; Univ Ill, MS, 51, PhD, 54. *Prof Exp:* Asst chem eng, Univ Ill, 50-53; chem engr, Standard Oil Co, Ind, 53-55; engr, Shell Develop Co, Calif, 55-61; sr planning engr, Chem Group, Dart Indust Inc, 61-64, prin planning engr, 64-66, supvr planning & econ, 66-67, mgr long range planning & econ,

67, chief economist, 67-72, dir econ & opers anal, 72-78, dir, Int Technol, 78-81; PRES, JAMES B WONG ASSOC, INC, 81- *Mem:* Am Chem Soc; Am Inst Chem Engrs. *Res:* Filtration of aerosols; fluid mechanics; process design; economics and planning; technologies on polyethylene, polypropylene, polystryrene and other polymers; general operations analysis; international licensing; technology transfer; technology transfer and product distribution, Asian and Pacific basin regions. *Mailing Add:* 2460 Venus Dr Los Angeles CA 90046

WONG, JAMES CHIN-SZE, b Hong Kong, Dec 5, 40; Can citizen. MATHEMATICS. *Educ:* Univ Hong Kong, BA, 63; Univ BC, PhD(math), 69. *Prof Exp:* Nat Res Coun Can fel, McMaster Univ, 69-71; asst prof, 71-75, ASSOC PROF MATH, UNIV CALGARY, 75- *Mem:* Can Math Cong; London Math Soc; Am Math Soc. *Res:* Functional analysis. *Mailing Add:* Dept of Math Univ of Calgary Calgary Can

WONG, JAMES RICHARD, b Rockville Ctr, NY, June 15, 51; m 74. TISSUE CULTURE, HORMONE ACTION. *Educ:* Princeton Univ, AB, 73; Yale Univ, MPhil, 76, PhD(biol), 78. *Prof Exp:* Cystic Fibrosis Found fel & scholar, Dept Biochem & Biophysics, Univ Calif, San Francisco, 79-80; ASST PROF BIOL, DEPT BOT & PROG MOLECULAR, CELLULAR & DEVELOP BIOL, OHIO STATE UNIV, 80- *Mem:* AAAS; Int Asn Plant Tissue Cult; Am Soc Plant Physiologists; Plant Molecular Biol Asn; Sigma Xi. *Res:* Biochemical and genetic studies of plant hormone action using cell culture variants; plant physiology and development; crop improvement via tissue culture. *Mailing Add:* Bot Dept Ohio State Univ 1735 Neil Ave Columbus OH 43210

WONG, JAMES SAI-WING, mathematical analysis, see previous edition

WONG, JEFFREY TZE-FEI, b Hong Kong, Aug 5, 37; Can citizen; m 61; c 3. BIOCHEMISTRY. *Educ:* Univ Toronto, BA, 59, PhD(biochem), 62. *Prof Exp:* From asst prof to assoc prof, 65-76, PROF BIOCHEM, FAC MED, UNIV TORONTO, 76- *Concurrent Pos:* Med Res Coun Can grant, Univ Toronto, 65- *Mem:* Can Soc Biochem; Am Soc Biochem. *Res:* Enzyme kinetics and mechanism; biochemical evolution; blood substitutes. *Mailing Add:* Dept of Biochem Univ of Toronto Fac of Med Toronto ON M5S 1A8 Can

WONG, JOE, b Hong Kong, Aug 8, 42; m 69; c 3. PHYSICAL CHEMISTRY, SOLID STATE SCIENCE. *Educ:* Univ Tasmania, BSc, 65, BSc Hons, 66; Purdue Univ, Lafayette, PhD(phys chem), 70. *Prof Exp:* Anal chemist, Australian Titan Prod, Tasmania, 62-63; res asst, Electrolytic Zinc Co Australasia, 63-64 & Dept Chem, Univ Tasmania, 64-65; res chemist, Electrolytic Zinc Co Australasia, Tasmania, 66; res asst chem, Walker Lab, Rensselaer Polytech Inst, 66-67 & Purdue Univ, Lafayette, 67-70; PHYS CHEMIST, CORP RES & DEVELOP, GEN ELEC CO, 70- *Concurrent Pos:* Adj lectr chem, Royal Hobart Col, 66; adj prof chem, State Univ NY, Albany, 80- *Honors & Awards:* 1st Prize Optical Micros, Am Ceramic Soc, 75 & 77. *Mem:* Am Chem Soc; Royal Australian Chem Inst; Am Phys Soc; AAAS. *Res:* Molten salt chemistry; thermodynamic and spectroscopic studies; spectroscopy of simple inorganic glasses; thin films; deposition and structure; impurity diffusion in semiconductors; microstructure of non-ohmic Zn0 ceramics; metallic glasses; EXAFS spectroscopy; coal science; synchrotron radiation research. *Mailing Add:* Gen Elec Co Res & Develop Ctr Bldg K1 Rm 3A34 PO Box 8 Schenectady NY 12301

WONG, JOHNNY WAI-NANG, b Hong Kong, Nov 22, 47. COMPUTER SYSTEMS. *Educ:* Univ Calif, BS, 70, MS, 71, PhD(comput sci), 75. *Prof Exp:* ASST PROF COMPUT SCI, UNIV WATERLOO, 75- *Res:* Modeling and analysis of computer systems and computer networks; distributed processing. *Mailing Add:* Dept Comput Sci Univ Waterloo Waterloo ON N2L 3G1 Can

WONG, KAI-WAI, b Aug 7, 38; Brit citizen. PHYSICS. *Educ:* Duke Univ, BS, 59; Northwestern Univ, MS, 60, PhD(physics), 63. *Prof Exp:* Res assoc physics, Northwestern Univ, 63; res assoc, Univ Iowa, 63-64; from asst prof to assoc prof, 64-72, PROF PHYSICS, UNIV KANS, 72- *Concurrent Pos:* Vis assoc prof, Univ Southern Calif, 69-71; vis prof, Univ Calif, Los Angeles, 72-73 & 79-80; hon prof, Univ Hong Kong, 81-82. *Mem:* Am Phys Soc. *Res:* Theoretical physics; many-body problems; statistical mechanics; high-energy theory. *Mailing Add:* Dept of Physics Univ of Kans Lawrence KS 66045

WONG, KAM WU, b Hong Kong, Mar 8, 40; m 70. PHOTOGRAMMETRY, GEODETIC SURVEYING. *Educ:* Univ NB, BSc, 64; Cornell Univ, MSc, 66, PhD(photogram), 68. *Prof Exp:* From asst prof to assoc prof, 67-76, PROF CIVIL ENG, UNIV ILL, URBANA-CHAMPAIGN, 76- *Honors & Awards:* Talbert Abrams Award, Am Soc Photogram, 70; Walter L Huber Res Prize, Am Soc Civil Engrs, 71. *Mem:* Am Soc Photogram; Am Soc Civil Engrs; Can Inst Surv. *Res:* Analytical photogrammetry; television mapping and display systems; geodetic surveying. *Mailing Add:* Dept Civil Eng Univ Ill 208 N Romine St Urbana IL 61801

WONG, KEITH KAM-KIN, b Hong Kong, Feb 11, 29; US citizen; m 61; c 2. BIOCHEMISTRY, PHYSIOLOGY. *Educ:* Southwestern at Memphis, BA, 55; Univ Tenn, MSc, 57; NY Univ, PhD(biol), 69. *Prof Exp:* Res asst chemother, Sloan-Kettering Inst Cancer Res, 57-58; mem staff biochem & drug metab, Worcester Found Exp Biol, 60-63; res assoc biochem pharmacol, Schering Corp, 63-66; res assoc exp hemat, NY Univ, 66-69; sr res investr drug metab, Squibb Inst Med Res, 69-79; SECT LEADER BIOCHEM, WALLACE LABS, CARTER-WALLACE INC, 79- *Mem:* AAAS; Am Chem Soc; NY Acad Sci. *Res:* Drug metabolism; biochemical pharmacology; biogenesis of erythropoietin; metabolism of biogenic amines; amino acid activation and transfer; protein synthesis; transformation of nucleic acid. *Mailing Add:* Dept of Drug Metab Squibb Inst New Brunswick NJ 08903

WONG, KIN FAI, b Kwangtung, China, Nov 6, 44; m 71. CHEMICAL ENGINEERING. *Educ:* Ariz State Univ, BSE, 65; Univ Ill, Urbana, MS, 67, PhD(chem eng), 70. *Prof Exp:* Res engr process develop, Western Res Ctr, Stauffer Chem Co, 70-76, sr res engr, De Guigne Tech Ctr, 76-80. *Mem:* Am Inst Chem Engrs; Am Chem Soc. *Res:* Thermodynamics of solutions; solvent effects on chemical reactions; process research and development on pesticides; process economics; waste product recovery and pollution control. *Mailing Add:* 12716 Serpintine Way Silver Spring MD 20904

WONG, KING-LAP, b Canton, China. PLASMA & NUCLEAR PHYSICS. *Educ:* Chinese Univ, Hong Kong, BSc, 68; Univ Del, MS, 70; Univ Wis, PhD(physics), 75. *Prof Exp:* Res assoc, Columbia Univ, 75-76; res assoc, 76-78, res staff, 78-80, RES PHYSICIST, PLASMA PHYSICS LAB, PRINCETON UNIV, 80- *Mem:* Am Phys Soc. *Res:* Linear and nonlinear plasma wavephenomena; RF plasma current geneation; RF plasma heating; toroidal plasma confinement; fusion. *Mailing Add:* Plasma Physics Lab Princeton Univ Princeton NJ 08544

WONG, KIN-PING, b China, Aug 14, 41; m 68; c 2. BIOCHEMISTRY, PHYSICAL CHEMISTRY. *Educ:* Univ Calif, Berkeley, BS, 64; Purdue Univ, PhD(physchem & biochem), 68. *Prof Exp:* Res fel phys biochem, Med Ctr, Duke Univ, 68-70; from asst prof to assoc prof chem, Univ SFla, Tampa, 70-75; assoc prof, 75-79, PROF BIOCHEM, UNIV KANS MED CTR, 79-, DEAN GRAD STUDIES, 80- *Concurrent Pos:* Am Cancer Soc res grant, Univ SFla, Tampa, 70-71, NIH biomed res grant, 71-72, Cottrell res grant, 71-, Damon Runyon cancer res grant, 72-74; USPHS res career develop award, Nat Inst Gen Med Sci, 73; vis scientist, Max Planck Inst Molecular Genetics, 73; European Molecular Biol Orgn sr fel, Wallenberg Lab, Univ Uppsala, Sweden, 75; res grants, Nat Inst Gen Med Sci & Nat Heart, Lung & Blood Inst, 74-; vis prof, Univ Tokyo, Hongo, 79. *Mem:* Am Soc Biol Chemists; Biophys Soc; Mid-Am Cancer Ctr. AAAS; AAAS; Am Chem Soc. *Res:* Physical biochemistry of protein and nucleic acids; mechanism of protein folding; ribosome structure; physicochemical studies of ribosomal proteins and RNAs; the molecular mechanism on the assembly of ribosome; mechanism of RNA folding; protein ageing; chemical carcinogenesis. *Mailing Add:* Dept of Biochem Univ of Kans Med Ctr Kansas City KS 66103

WONG, KWAN Y, b Hong Kong, June 12, 37; US citizen; m 66; c 2. ELECTRICAL & SYSTEMS ENGINEERING. *Educ:* Univ New South Wales, BS, 60, ME, 63; Univ Calif, Berkeley, PhD(elec eng), 66. *Prof Exp:* Mem res staff systs, 66-77, MGR, IBM RES LAB, SAN JOSE, CALIF, 77- *Mem:* Inst Elec & Electronics Engrs; Sigma Xi. *Res:* Image processing; data compression; pattern recognition. *Mailing Add:* Dept K54/282 5600 Cottle Rd San Jose CA 95193

WONG, LAN KAN, organic chemistry, pharmacology, see previous edition

WONG, MAURICE KING FAN, b Shanghai, China, Apr 9, 32. MATHEMATICAL PHYSICS. *Educ:* Univ Hong Kong, BSc, 54; Berhmans Col, AB, 58, MA, 61; Univ Birmingham, PhD(math physics), 64. *Prof Exp:* Res assoc, Inst Advan Studies, Dublin, 64-65; res fel res inst nat sci, Woodstock Col, Md, 65-68; asst prof, 69-72, assoc prof, 72-80, PROF MATH, FAIRFIELD UNIV, 80- *Concurrent Pos:* Fel, St Louis Univ, 69. *Mem:* AAAS; Am Phys Soc. *Res:* Lie groups; superconductivity; Mössbauer effect; elementary particles; nuclear physics; quantum theory. *Mailing Add:* Dept of Math Fairfield Univ Fairfield CT 06430

WONG, MING MING, b Singapore, Jan 3, 28; US citizen. PARASITOLOGY. *Educ:* Wilmington Col, Ohio, BS, 52; Ohio State Univ, MS, 53; Tulane Univ La, PhD(med parasitol), 63. *Prof Exp:* Med technologist, Good Samaritan Hosp, Zanesville, Ohio, 54-55; teacher, Diocesan Girls' Sch, Hong Kong, 55-56; demonstr parasitol & bact fac med, Univ Hong Kong, 56-59; teaching asst med parasitol med sch, Tulane Univ La, 59-63, NIH res fel trop med, 63-64, res assoc, 64-65; res assoc fac med, Univ Malaya, 64-65, lectr parasitol, 65-67; asst res parasitologist, 67-73, ASSOC RES PARASITOLOGIST, PRIMATE RES CTR, UNIV CALIF, DAVIS, 73- *Concurrent Pos:* WHO res grant, Univ Malaya, 66-67; NIH grants primate res ctr, Univ Calif, Davis, 70-75. *Mem:* Am Soc Parasitol; Am Soc Trop Med & Hyg; Royal Soc Trop Med & Hyg; Am Heartworm Soc; Am Soc Clin Pathologists. *Res:* Filariasis; primate parasitology; immunology of parasitic diseases. *Mailing Add:* Primate Res Ctr Univ of Calif Davis CA 95616

WONG, MORTON MIN, b Canton, China, Oct 2, 24; US citizen; m 56; c 4. ELECTROCHEMISTRY, HYDROMETALLURGY. *Educ:* Univ Calif, BS, 51. *Prof Exp:* Trainee, Am Potash & Chem Corp, 51-53; researcher, 53-54, asst proj leader, 54-56, res proj leader, 56-60, res group leader, 60-62, res proj coordr, 62-71, RES SUPVR, US BUR MINES, 71- *Concurrent Pos:* Vis lectr, People's Repub China, 81. *Mem:* Am Inst Mining, Metall & Petrol Eng; Am Inst Chem. *Res:* Fused-salt electrolysis of rare earths; hydrometallurgical and electrolytical processing of copper-lead-zinc sulfide ores; metallurgical treatment of titanium ore; benefication and extraction of platinum-group metals from ores. *Mailing Add:* 2281 Riviera St Reno NV 89509

WONG, NOBLE POWELL, b Baltimore, Md, Apr 30, 31; m 61; c 4. FOOD CHEMISTRY, NUTRITION. *Educ:* Univ Md, BS, 53; Pa State Univ, MS, 58, PhD(dairy sci), 61. *Prof Exp:* Res chem, Food & Drug Admin, 61-66; RES CHEMIST, US DEPT AGR, 66- *Mem:* Am Chem Soc; Am Dairy Sci Asn; Inst Food Technol. *Res:* Nutrition and composition of dairy products; bioavailability of minerals. *Mailing Add:* Dairy Prod Lab Bldg 157 Agr Res Ctr Beltsville MD 20705

WONG, PATRICK TIN-CHOI, b Hong Kong, Mar 9, 42; m 67; c 2. GENETICS. *Educ:* Univ Calif, Berkeley, BA, 64; Ore State Univ, MS, 66, PhD(genetics), 69. *Prof Exp:* Asst genetics, Ore State Univ, 64-69; RES SCIENTIST, CITY OF HOPE MED CTR, 70- *Concurrent Pos:* Fel biol, Biomed Inst, City of Hope Med Ctr, 69-70. *Res:* Behavior genetics; insect neurophysiology. *Mailing Add:* Dept of Biol City of Hope Med Ctr Duarte CA 91010

WONG, PATRICK YUI-KWONG, b Kiangsi, China, Nov 25, 44. BIOCHEMISTRY, BIOCHEMICAL PHARMACOLOGY. *Educ:* Nat Taiwan Norm Univ, BSc, 67; Univ Vt, PhD(biochem), 75. *Prof Exp:* Fel, Med Col Wis, 74-75; instr pharmacol, Col Basic Med Sci, Univ Tenn, Memphis, 75-79; ASSOC PROF, DEPT PHARMACOL, NY MED COL, VALHALLA, 79- *Concurrent Pos:* Vis scientist, Karolinska Inst, Stockholm, Sweden, 82-83. *Mem:* Am Chem Soc; Am Soc Biol Chemists; Am Soc Pharm & Exp Therapeut. *Res:* Control and regulation of prostaglandin synthesis and metabolism in cardiovascular disorders and inflammation process in arthritis. *Mailing Add:* Dept Pharmacol NY Med Col Valhalla NY 10595

WONG, PATRICK YU-PEI, b Amoy, China, Oct 27, 39; US citizen; m 67; c 3. GASTROENTEROLOGY. *Educ:* Univ Sydney, MBBs, 65. *Prof Exp:* From intern to resident, Loma Linda Univ Hosp, 67-70; NIH res fel, Harvard Med Sch, 70-72, instr med, 73-74; asst prof, 74-76, ASSOC PROF MED, ALBANY MED COL, 76- *Mem:* Am Fedn Clin Res; Am Asn Study Liver Dis; Am Gastroenterol Asn. *Res:* Study of interrelationship between the Kallibrein-Kinin and the renin angiotensin systems in normals and hypertensives. *Mailing Add:* 3838 Calif St San Francisco CA 94118

WONG, PAUL WING-KON, US citizen. PEDIATRICS, GENETICS. *Educ:* Univ Hong Kong, MD, 58; Univ Man, MSc, 67; Am Bd Pediat, dipl, 64. *Prof Exp:* Instr pediat, Children's Mem Hosp, Northwestern Univ, Chicago, 63-64; from asst prof to prof pediat, Chicago Med Sch, 67-73; prof pediat & dir metab unit, Abraham Lincoln Sch Med, Univ Ill Med Ctr, 73-76; PROF PEDIAT & DIR GENETIC SECT, RUSH MED SCH & PRESBY-ST LUKE MED CTR, CHICAGO, 76- *Concurrent Pos:* USPHS res fel biochem & med genetics, Northwestern Univ, Chicago, 62-64; Children's Res Fund fel, Ment Retardation Res Unit, Royal Manchester Children's Hosp, Eng, 65-67; attend physician, Cook County Hosp, Chicago, Ill, 65-72, consult, 72-; dir infant's aid perinatal res labs & premature & newborn nurseries, Mt Sinai Hosp, 67-73; attend physician, Univ Ill Hosp & Presby-St Luke Med Ctr, 73- *Mem:* Am Pediat Soc; Am Fedn Clin Res; Soc Pediat Res; Am Soc Human Genetics. *Res:* Metabolic diseases; human genetics. *Mailing Add:* Dept of Pediat Presby-St Luke Med Ctr Chicago IL 60612

WONG, PETER ALEXANDER, b Honan, China, Apr 9, 41; US citizen; m 66; c 1. CHEMICAL INSTRUMENTATION. *Educ:* Pac Union Col, BS, 62; Rensselaer Polytech Inst, PhD(chem), 69. *Prof Exp:* US AEC grant, Purdue Univ, 67-69; asst prof, 69-72, ASSOC PROF, CHEM, ANDREWS UNIV, 72- *Mem:* Am Chem Soc; Sigma Xi; Fedn Am Scientists. *Res:* Chemistry of cell membranes. *Mailing Add:* Dept of Chem Andrews Univ Berrien Springs MI 49104

WONG, PETER P, b Shanghai, China, Dec 12, 41; m 64; c 2. NITROGEN FIXATION, CELL-CELL RECOGNITION. *Educ:* San Francisco State Col, BS, 66; Ore State Univ, BA, 67, PhD(plant physiol), 71. *Prof Exp:* Res assoc biochem, Univ Wis, 70-72; res assoc agr chem, Wash State Univ, 72-74, instr bot, 74-76; asst prof, 76-80, ASSOC PROF BIOL, KANS STATE UNIV, 80- *Mem:* Am Plant Physiologists; Am Soc Microbiol; AAAS. *Res:* Physiology and biochemistry of legume root nodule development; mechanism of recognition between rhizobia and legumes. *Mailing Add:* Div Biol Kans State Univ Manhattan KS 66506

WONG, PO KEE, b Canton City, China, May 5, 34; US citizen; m 65; c 2. RESEARCH ADMINISTRATION, SCIENCE EDUCATION. *Educ:* Cheng-Kung Univ, Taiwan, BSc, 56; Univ Utah, MSc, 61; Calif Inst Technol, Degree Eng, 66; Stanford Univ, PhD(aeronaut & astronaut), 70. *Prof Exp:* Teaching asst thermodynamics elasticity, Cheng-Kung Univ, 58-59; res & teaching asst appl math & mech eng, Univ Utah, 59-61; res & teaching asst appl math, Calif Inst Technol, 61-65; sr scientist appl mech, Lockheed Missles & Space Co, 66-68; res asst aeronaut & astronaut eng, Stanford Univ, 68-70; lectr & researcher, Univ Santa Clara, 70 & 71 & Ames Ctr, NASA, 70; engr I, Breeder Reactor Dept, Gen Elec, Suunyvale, 72-73; specialist engr, Nuclear Serv Co, Campbell, Calif, 73; engr, Stone & Webster Eng Co, Boston, Mass, 74; PRES, SYST RES CO, BROOKLINE, MASS, 76- *Concurrent Pos:* Teacher math & sci, Hong Kong YMCA English Col, 59; consult, pressure transducer, Consolidated Electrodynamics Co, 62-65; consult, Flanco Serv, Inc & Air Res Co, Phoenix, 72-73; teacher math & sci, Boston Pub Sch, Mass, 79- *Mem:* Am Soc Mech Engrs. *Res:* Trajectory solid angle, generalized stream functions, magneto-viscoelasto dynamics and visco-elasto dynamics; formulation and solution of multi-reservoir transient problem; physical economic model by means of the solution of a system of indeterminate structures which provide impacts in science; mathematics and engineering. *Mailing Add:* 238 Cypress St S3 Brookline MA 02146

WONG, PUI KEI, b Canton, China, Nov 7, 35; m 67. MATHEMATICS. *Educ:* Pac Union Col, BS, 56; Carnegie Inst Technol, MS, 58, PhD(math), 62. *Prof Exp:* Instr math, Carnegie Inst Technol, 60-62; asst prof, Lehigh Univ, 62-64; from asst prof to assoc prof, 64-72, PROF MATH, MICH STATE UNIV, 72- *Mem:* Am Math Soc. *Res:* Stability and oscillation theory of differential equation; function-theoretic differential equations; non-linear boundary value problems. *Mailing Add:* Dept of Math Wells Hall Mich State Univ East Lansing MI 48824

WONG, RODERICK SUE-CHEUNG, b Shanghai, China, Oct 2, 44. MATHEMATICAL ANALYSIS. *Educ:* San Diego State Col, AB, 65; Univ Alta, PhD(math), 69. *Prof Exp:* Asst prof, 69-73, assoc prof, 73-79, PROF MATH, UNIV MAN, 79- *Concurrent Pos:* Nat Res Coun Can grant, Univ Man, 69- *Mem:* Soc Indust & Appl Math. *Res:* Asymptotic expansions; special functions. *Mailing Add:* Dept of Math Univ of Man Winnipeg MB R3T 2N2 Can

WONG, ROMAN WOON-CHING, b Canton, China, June 17, 48; m 73. ALGEBRA, MATHEMATICS. *Educ:* Chinese Univ, Hong Kong, BS, 70; Sam Houston State Univ, MA, 72; Rutgers Univ, PhD(math), 77. *Prof Exp:* Asst prof, Syracuse Univ, 77-78; ASST PROF MATH, WASHINGTON & JEFFERSON COL, 78- *Concurrent Pos:* NATO travel grant math conf, Univ Antwerp, 78; res grant, Am Philos Soc, 78-79. *Mem:* Am Math Soc. *Res:* Category theory and homological algebra; group rings and free algebras. *Mailing Add:* Dept of Math Washington & Jefferson Col Washington PA 15301

WONG, ROSIE BICK-HAR, b Shanghai, China; US citizen; m; c 2. BIOCHEMISTRY, IMMUNOLOGY. *Educ:* Mt Mary Col, BSc, 65; Med Col Wis, PhD(biochem), 69. *Prof Exp:* Res assoc biochem, Rockefeller Univ, 69-71; res assoc virol & immunol, Rutgers State Univ, 71-77; SCIENTIST IMMUNOL, AGR DIV, AM CYANAMID CO, 77- *Res:* Protein structure and function relationship; radioimmunoassay, transplantation antigen system in mouse; hybridoma; parasitology of chickens. *Mailing Add:* Agr Div Am Cyanamid Co Princeton NJ 08540

WONG, RUTH (LAU), b Hong Kong, Nov 25, 25; m 52; c 4. PATHOLOGY. *Educ:* Lingnan Univ, MD, 48. *Prof Exp:* Resident path, Children's Hosp, Washington, DC, 51-52; resident, Duke Univ Hosp, 52-53; resident, Michael Reese Hosp, 53-54; res asst, La Rabida Sanitarium, 55-56; res asst, Univ Chicago, 56-57; from asst prof to assoc prof, 57-69, PROF PATH, UNIV ILL COL MED, 69- *Concurrent Pos:* Fel, Michael Reese Hosp, Chicago, Ill, 54-55. *Mem:* Int Acad Path. *Res:* Surgical pathology; serotonin content of mast and enterochromaffin cells; relationship of mast cells to tissue response; medical information science; data retrieval of pathology records. *Mailing Add:* Dept of Path Univ of Ill Col of Med Chicago IL 60612

WONG, S(OON) Y(UCK), b San Antonio, Tex, Mar 4, 20; m 49; c 3. CHEMICAL ENGINEERING. *Educ:* Univ Tex, BS & MS, 43, PhD(chem eng), 49. *Prof Exp:* Sr res engr, Skelly Oil Co, 43-46; res assoc, Jefferson Chem Co, 50-53, staff engr, 53-56; tech asst to dir, 56-61, supt process lab, Petrol Prod Res & Develop Div, 61-63, supvr process develop sect, Petrochem Res Div, 64-65, proj coordr, Petrochem Dept, 66-68, asst to mgr, Petrol Prods Res Div, 68-72, tech asst to mgr proj develop, Res & Develop Dept, 72-76, PROJ COORDR, MINING RES DIV, CONTINENTAL OIL CO, 76- *Res:* Minerals extraction and coal processing projects. *Mailing Add:* Res & Develop Dept PO Box 1267 Ponca City OK 74601

WONG, SAMUEL SHAW MING, b Peking, China, May 10, 37; m 67; c 2. PHYSICS. *Educ:* Int Christian Univ, Tokyo, BA, 59; Purdue Univ, MS, 61; Univ Rochester, PhD(theoret physics), 68. *Prof Exp:* From asst prof to assoc prof, 69-78, PROF PHYSICS, UNIV TORONTO, 78- *Mem:* Am Phys Soc; Can Asn Physics. *Res:* Nuclear structure theory. *Mailing Add:* Dept of Physics Univ of Toronto Toronto ON M5S 1A1 Can

WONG, SHAN SHEKYUK, b Mankassar, Indonesia, May 10, 45; US citizen; m 73; c 2. BIOCHEMISTRY, CHEMISTRY. *Educ:* Ore State Univ, BS, 70; Ohio State Univ, PhD(biochem), 74. *Prof Exp:* Fel chem, Temple Univ, 74-76; instr, Ohio State Univ, 78, res assoc, 76-78; ASST PROF BIOCHEM, UNIV LOWELL, 78- *Mem:* Biophys Soc; Am Chem Soc; NY Acad Sci. *Res:* Mechanisms of enzyme action; regulation of enzyme activities. *Mailing Add:* Dept Chem 1 University Ave Lowell MA 01854

WONG, SHEK-FU, b Canton, China, Dec 5, 43; m 73. ATOMIC PHYSICS, MOLECULAR PHYSICS. *Educ:* Chung Chi Col, Chinese Univ Hong Kong, BSc, 65; Univ Del, PhD(physics), 72. *Prof Exp:* Instr physics, Chung Chi Col, Chinese Univ Hong Kong, 65-67; fel, 72-74, res staff, 74-75, asst prof, 75-78, ASSOC PROF, ENG & APPL SCI, YALE UNIV, 78- *Mem:* Am Phys Soc. *Res:* Crossed-beam electron impact experiments, with particular interest in the resonant vibrational and rotational excitation in small molecules. *Mailing Add:* Mason Lab Dept Eng & Appl Sci Yale Univ New Haven CT 06520

WONG, SHI-YIN, b Hoiping, Canton, China, Apr 27, 41; US citizen; m 67; c 1. ORGANIC CHEMISTRY. *Educ:* Univ Calif, Los Angeles, BS, 64; Univ Southern Calif, PhD(chem), 68. *Prof Exp:* MEM TECH STAFF, HUGHES RES LAB, HUGHES AIRCRAFT CO, MALIBU, CALIF, 69- *Concurrent Pos:* Air Force Off Sci Res fel, Hughes Res Lab, 72-73. *Res:* Electrohydrodynamics of liquid crystal; molecular correlation of liquid crystal. *Mailing Add:* Hughes Aircraft Co 3011 Malibu Canyon Rd Malibu CA 90265

WONG, SIU GUM, b San Francisco, Calif, Feb 21, 47. OPTOMETRY, PUBLIC HEALTH. *Educ:* Univ Calif, Berkeley, BS, 68, OD, 70, MPH, 72. *Prof Exp:* Res assoc community med, Sch Med, St Louis Univ, 72-73; asst prof optom & pub health, Col Optom, Univ Houston, 73-78; CHIEF AREA OPTOM SERV BR, INDIAN HEALTH SERV, 78- *Concurrent Pos:* Consult, Health Power Assoc, Inc, New Orleans, 74. *Mem:* Fel Am Acad Optom; Am Optom Asn; Am Pub Health Asn. *Res:* Community optometry. *Mailing Add:* 500 Gold Ave Rm 4018 Indian Health Serv Albuquerque NM 87102

WONG, STEWART, b Toronto, Ont, Jan 2, 30; m 59; c 2. PHARMACOLOGY. *Educ:* Univ Toronto, BA, 58, MA, 60; Purdue Univ, PhD(pharmacog), 63. *Prof Exp:* Assoc prof pharmacol, Col Pharm, NDak State Univ, 63-65; instr, Col Med, Univ Iowa, 65-67; sect head, Appl Sci Div, Litton Indust Inc, 68; sect head, Union Carbide Corp, 68-69; group leader pharmacol, McNeil Labs, Inc, Johnson & Johnson, 69-78; SR PRIN SCIENTIST, DEPT PHARMACOL, BOEHRINGER INGELHEIM, LTD, 79- *Mem:* AAAS; Am Soc Pharmacol & Exp Therapeut; NY Acad Sci. *Res:* Immunopharmacology experimental diseases; arthritis; inflammation and healing of soft and skeletal tissue; diabetes mellitus; cardiovascular and metabolic diseases; autonomic nervous system; natural product biosynthesis and biological activity. *Mailing Add:* 175 Briar Ridge Rd PO Box 368 Ridgefield CT 06877

WONG, TANG-FONG FRANK, b Canton, China, Jan 21, 44; m 69; c 2. THEORETICAL HIGH ENERGY PHYSICS. *Educ:* Chinese Univ Hong Kong, BSc, 65; Brown Univ, PhD(physics), 70. *Prof Exp:* Res assoc physics, Brookhaven Nat Lab, 69-71; res fel physics, Rutgers Univ, New Brunswick, 71-73, vis asst prof, 73-74, asst prof, 74-80; MEM STAFF, BELL LABS, 80-

Mem: Am Phys Soc. *Res:* High energy behavior of renormalizable field theories; symmetry and symmetry breaking in field theories; strong interaction phenomenology. *Mailing Add:* Bldg 5 Bell Labs 600 Mountain Ave Murray Hill NJ 07974

WONG, VICTOR KENNETH, b San Francisco, Calif, Nov 1, 38; m 64; c 3. PHYSICS. *Educ:* Univ Calif, Berkeley, BS, 60, PhD(physics), 66. *Prof Exp:* Fel physics, Ohio State Univ, 66-67, res assoc, 67-68; lectr, 68-69, asst prof physics, Univ Mich, Ann Arbor, 69-76; assoc prof, 76-82, chmn physics discipline, 79-80, PROF PHYSICS, UNIV MICH-DEARBORN, 82-, CHMN, DEPT NATURAL SCI, 80- *Mem:* Am Phys Soc. *Res:* Many-body theory; equilibrium properties of interacting bosons at low temperatures; two-band superconductors; liquid helium; superfluidity; quantum fluids; critical phenomena; surface phenomena; and dielectric formulation of Bose liquids. *Mailing Add:* Dept of Natural Sci Univ of Mich Dearborn MI 48128

WONG, WAI-MAI TSANG, b Hong Kong, Apr 14, 41; Brit citizen; m 69; c 1. POLYMER SCIENCE. *Educ:* Nat Taiwan Normal Univ, BSc, 65; Univ Guelph, MSc, 69; Case Western Reserve Univ, PhD(macromolecular sci), 74. *Prof Exp:* Teaching asst physics, Nat Taiwan Normal Univ, 64-67; res assoc polymer sci, Case Western Reserve Univ, 74-76; RES SCIENTIST POLYMER SCI, COLUMBUS DIV, BATTELLE MEM INST, 76- *Mem:* Am Phys Soc. *Res:* Structure-property relationship of synthetic and bio-polymers. *Mailing Add:* Columbus Div 505 King Ave Columbus OH 43201

WONG, WANG MO, b Canton, Kwangtung, China; US citizen; m 49; c 2. CHEMICAL ENGINEERING. *Educ:* Sun Yat-Sen Univ, BS, 39; Univ Iowa, MS, 49, PhD(chem eng), 54. *Prof Exp:* Chief chem engr, US Rubber Co, Joliet Arsenal, Ill, 55-60; res engr, US Borax & Chem Corp, Calif, 60-61; sr engr, Armour Pharmaceut Co, Kankakee, 61-77; CHEM ENGR, ARTHUR G MC KEE & CO, 77- *Mem:* Am Chem Soc; Am Inst Chem Engrs. *Res:* Research and process development in bench scale and pilot plant of organic and inorganic chemical process; specialization in continuous process development. *Mailing Add:* 4233 Oakwood Lane Matteson IL 60443

WONG, WARREN JAMES, b Masterton, NZ, Oct 16, 34; m 62; c 3. ALGEBRA. *Educ:* Univ Otago, NZ, BSc, 55, MSc, 56; Harvard Univ, PhD(math), 59. *Prof Exp:* Lectr math, Univ Otago, NZ, 60-63, sr lectr, 64; assoc prof, 64-68, PROF MATH, UNIV NOTRE DAME, 68- *Concurrent Pos:* Vis fel, Univ Auckland, 69. *Mem:* Am Math Soc; Math Asn Am; Australian Math Soc. *Res:* Finite group theory; groups of Lietype. *Mailing Add:* Dept Math Univ Notre Dame Notre Dame IN 46556

WONG, YIU-HUEN, b Hong Kong, May 9, 46; m 72. PHYSICS, MATERIALS SCIENCE. *Educ:* Mass Inst Technol, BS, 67; Univ Wis-Madison, MS, 69, PhD(physics), 73. *Prof Exp:* Res fel, Rutgers Univ, 73-76; asst prof physics, Wayne State Univ, 76-80; MEM STAFF, BELL LABS, 80- *Concurrent Pos:* Co-prin investr grant, Army Res Off, 78-79. *Mem:* Am Phys Soc; Soc Photo-Optical Instrument Eng. *Res:* Laser spectroscopy of matter; surface and subsurface characterization of solids; transport properties of condensed matter. *Mailing Add:* Bell Labs MS7B-511 600 Mountain Ave Murray Hill NJ 07974

WONG, YUEN-FAT, b Kwangtung, China, Sept 22, 35; US citizen; m 62; c 3. MATHEMATICS. *Educ:* Cornell Univ, PhD(math), 64. *Prof Exp:* ASSOC PROF MATH, DEPAUL UNIV, 64- *Concurrent Pos:* NSF fel, DePaul Univ, 65-67. *Mem:* Am Math Soc. *Res:* Algebraic topology. *Mailing Add:* Dept of Math DePaul Univ 2323 N Seminary Ave Chicago IL 60614

WONG-RILEY, MARGARET TZE TUNG, b Shanghai, China, Oct 20, 41; US citizen; m 70; c 1. NEUROANATOMY, ANATOMY. *Educ:* Columbia Univ, BS, 65, MA, 66; Stanford Univ, PhD(anat), 70. *Prof Exp:* asst prof anat & neuroanat, Univ Calif, San Francisco, 73-80, assoc prof anat, 80-81; ASSOC PROF ANAT, MED COL WIS, 81- *Concurrent Pos:* Fight for Sight fel, Univ Wis, 70-71; NIH fel, Lab Neurophysiol, Nat Inst Neurol Dis & Stroke, 72-73; Alexander Ryan Endowment Fund fel, Univ Calif, San Francisco, 74-75. *Mem:* AAAS; Soc Neurosci; Asn Am Anat. *Res:* Structural and functional organization of the mammalian visual system; functionally related metabolic adjustments in neurons as revealed by cytochrome oxidase histo-and cytochemistry. *Mailing Add:* Dept of Anat Med Col Wis Milwaukee WI 53226

WONHAM, W MURRAY, b Montreal, Que, Nov 1, 34. APPLIED MATHEMATICS, SYSTEMS ENGINEERING. *Educ:* McGill Univ, BEng, 56; Cambridge Univ, PhD(eng), 61. *Prof Exp:* Asst prof elec eng, Purdue Univ, 61-62; res mathematician, Res Inst Advan Study, 62-64; assoc prof appl math & eng, Brown Univ, 64-70; assoc prof, 70-72, PROF ELEC ENG, UNIV TORONTO, 72- *Concurrent Pos:* Consult, Electronics Res Ctr, NASA, Mass, 65-70. *Mem:* Fel Inst Elec & Electronics Engrs; Soc Indust & Appl Math. *Res:* Systems theory. *Mailing Add:* Dept of Elec Eng Univ of Toronto Toronto ON M5S 1A4 Can

WONNACOTT, THOMAS HERBERT, b London, Ont, Nov 29, 35; m 80; c 4. MATHEMATICAL & APPLIED STATISTICS. *Educ:* Univ Western Ont, BA, 57; Princeton Univ, PhD(math statist), 63. *Prof Exp:* Asst prof, Wesleyan Univ, 61-66; assoc prof math, 66-80, ASSOC PROF STATIST, UNIV WESTERN ONT, 80- *Mem:* Am Statist Asn. *Res:* Applications of statistics to medical and social science; textbook writing especially econometrics and introductory statistics. *Mailing Add:* Dept Statist Univ of Western Ont London ON N6A 5B9 Can

WONSIEWICZ, BUD CAESAR, b Buffalo, NY, Aug 23, 41; m 63; c 3. METALLURGY. *Educ:* Mass Inst Technol, SB, 63, PhD(metall), 66. *Prof Exp:* Asst prof metall, Mass Inst Technol, 66-67; MEM TECH STAFF, BELL TEL LABS, 67- *Mem:* AAAS; Am Inst Mining, Metall & Petrol Engrs; Am Soc Metals; Inst Elec & Electronics Engrs; Asn Computing Machinery. *Res:* software engineering; software quality and productivity; software methodology; software project management. *Mailing Add:* Bell Tel Labs Handel NJ 07733

WOO, CHIA-WEI, theoretical physics, see previous edition

WOO, CHING CHANG, b Canton, China, Dec 12, 15; US citizen; m 49; c 4. PETROLOGY, MINERALOGY. *Educ:* Nat Univ Peking, BS, 37; Univ Chicago, MS, 48, PhD(petrol, mineral), 52. *Prof Exp:* Asst stratig, paleont & struct geol, Nat Univ Chungking, 38-40; asst geologist, Geol Surv Szechwan, China, 40-42, chief paleontologist, 42-44; asst geol, Univ Chicago, 49-51; geologist & field engr, Crane Co, Ill, 52-55; chief geologist, Heavy Minerals Co, Tenn, 55-58; div geologist, SE US, Vitro Minerals Corp, 58-59, res geologist, 59-63; geologist, Washington, DC, 63-71, GEOLOGIST, US GEOL SURV, OFF MARINE GEOL, WOODS HOLE OCEANOG INST, 71- *Mem:* Geol Soc Am; Mineral Soc Am; Mineral Asn Can. *Res:* Geotectonics; sedimentary petrology of dried lake sediments; petrogenesis of metamorphic and sedimentary rocks; petrographic analysis; mineral economics and mineral benefication of ores and ore deposits, especially placer type; lunar regoliths of Apollo programs; continental shelf sediments. *Mailing Add:* Off of Marine Geol US Geol Surv Woods Hole Oceanog Inst Woods Hole MA 02543

WOO, CHUNG-HO, b Sept 7, 43; Can citizen; m 68. THEORETICAL PHYSICS, MATERIALS SCIENCE. *Educ:* Univ Hong Kong, BSc, 67; Univ Calgary, MSc, 69; Univ Waterloo, PhD(physics), 73. *Prof Exp:* asst res officer, 77-80, SR ASSOC RES OFFICER MAT SCI, WHITESHELL NUCLEAR RES ESTAB, ATOMIC ENERGY CAN LTD, PINAWA, 80- *Concurrent Pos:* Adj prof, Dept Physics, Univ Man, 78- *Res:* Radiation damage; defects and mechanical properties; dislocations and point-defect dislocation interaction; color centers; electronic states in metals; computer simulation and numerical analysis; molecular quantum chemistry; diffusion mechanisms in metals. *Mailing Add:* Mat Sci Br Atomic Energy of Can Ltd Pinawa MB R0E 1L0 Can

WOO, DAH-CHENG, b Shanghai, China, Dec 18, 21; US citizen. HYDRAULICS, HYDROLOGY. *Educ:* Hangchow Christian Col, BS, 44; Univ Mich, Ann Arbor, MA, 48, PhD(hydraul eng), 56. *Prof Exp:* Res asst struct & hydraul res, Univ Mich, Ann Arbor, 48-50; design engr, Ayres, Lewis, Norris & May, Consult Engrs, 51-56, hydraul engr, 57-62; proj engr, Univ Mich, Ann Arbor, 56-57; HYDRAUL ENGR, US FED HWY ADMIN, 62- *Mem:* Am Geophys Union; Am Soc Civil Engrs; Int Asn Sci Hydrol; Int Asn Hydraul Res; Int Water Resources Asn. *Res:* Urban water resources; small watershed hydrology. *Mailing Add:* US Fed Hwy Admin Washington DC 20590

WOO, GAR LOK, b Canton, China, Jan 14, 35; US citizen; m 64; c 2. ORGANIC CHEMISTRY. *Educ:* Univ Calif, Berkeley, BS, 59; Mass Inst Technol, PhD(org chem), 62. *Prof Exp:* Res chemist, 62-69, sr res chemist, 69-75, SR RES ASSOC, CHEVRON RES CO, RICHMOND, 75- *Mem:* Am Chem Soc. *Res:* Physical organic chemistry, mechanism, stereochemistry and synthesis; exploratory petrochemicals and surfactants; sulfur and organo-sulfur chemistry. *Mailing Add:* 200 Blackfield Dr Tiburon CA 94920

WOO, GEORGE CHI SHING, b Shanghai, China, Feb 15, 41; Can citizen; m 67; c 3. OPTOMETRY. *Educ:* Col Optom Ont, OD, 64; Ind Univ, Bloomington, MS, 68, PhD(physiol optics), 70. *Prof Exp:* Optometrist, Can Red Cross, 64-66; clin instr optom, Ind Univ, 66-67, teaching assoc physiol optics, 67-68, res asst, 68-69, res assoc & assoc instr, 69-70; asst prof, 70-74, assoc prof, 74-80, PROF OPTOM, UNIV WATERLOO, 80- *Mem:* Am Acad Optom; Am Optom Asn; Can Asn Optom. *Res:* Low vision; photometry; contrast sensitivity junction and optics of the eye; refraction. *Mailing Add:* Sch of Optom Univ of Waterloo Waterloo ON N2L 3G1 Can

WOO, JAMES T K, b Shanghai, China, June 7, 38. ORGANIC CHEMISTRY. *Educ:* Wabash Col, BA, 61; Univ Md, PhD(chem), 67. *Prof Exp:* Asst, Univ Md, 61-63, res asst, 63-66, fel, 66-67; res chemist, Dow Chem Co, Mich, 67-71; mem staff, Horizon Res Corp, 71-72; SCIENTIST, GLIDDEN DURKEE CO, 72- *Mem:* Am Chem Soc; AAAS; Sigma Xi. *Res:* Polymer chemistry; graft copolymer. *Mailing Add:* Dwight P Joyce Res Ctr Glidden Durkee Co Strongsville OH 44136

WOO, KWANG BANG, b Kyoto, Japan, Jan 25, 34; m 63; c 2. BIOMEDICAL ENGINEERING, ELECTRICAL ENGINEERING. *Educ:* Yonsei Univ, Korea, BE, 57, ME, 59; Ore State Univ, MS, 62, PhD(elec eng), 65. *Prof Exp:* Instr elec eng, Yonsei Univ, Korea, 59-60; res mem, Sci Res Inst, Ministry Defense, Korea, 57-60; res assoc, Ore State Univ, 65; asst prof elec eng & biomed eng, Wash Univ & res assoc, Ctr Biol Natural Systs, 66-71; sr staff fel, Off of Dept Dir, Div Cancer Treatment, Nat Cancer Inst, 71-76; SCIENTIST, BIOL MARKERS LAB, FREDERICK CANCER RES CTR, 76- *Concurrent Pos:* Fel biophys, Inst Sci Technol, Univ Mich, 65-66. *Mem:* AAAS; Inst Elec & Electronics Eng; NY Acad Sci; Biophys Soc. *Res:* Control mechanisms in metabolic processes; cell cycle kinetics and cancer therapy; tumor-marker interactions; nonlinear systems analysis and computer techniques. *Mailing Add:* Frederick Cancer Res Ctr PO Box B1 Frederick MD 21701

WOO, NORMAN TZU TEH, b Shanghai, China, Sept 28, 39. MATHEMATICS. *Educ:* Wabash Col, BA, 62; Southern Methodist Univ, MS, 64; Wash State Univ, PhD(math), 68. *Prof Exp:* PROF MATH, CALIF STATE UNIV, FRESNO, 68- *Mem:* Am Math Soc. *Res:* Number theory of mathematics. *Mailing Add:* Dept of Math Calif State Univ Shaw & Cedar Ave Fresno CA 93710

WOO, P(ETER) W(ING) K(EE), b Canton, China, June 22, 34; m 66; c 3. ORGANIC CHEMISTRY. *Educ:* Stanford Univ, BS, 55; Univ Ill, PhD(chem), 58. *Prof Exp:* From assoc res chemist to sr res chemist, Parke, Davis & Co, 58-71, res scientist, 71-77, RES ASSOC, PHARMACEUT RES DIV, WARNER-LAMBERT/PARKE-DAVIS, 77- *Mem:* Am Chem Soc. *Res:* Synthesis, isolation, and structural elucidation of medicinal agents: antibiotics and relate microbial metabolites, enzyme inhibitors, anti-inflamatory agents; chemistry of nucleosides, beta-lactams, aminoglycosides, carbohydrates, and macrolides. *Mailing Add:* Pharmaceut Res Div 2800 Plymouth Rd Ann Arbor MI 48105

WOO, SHIEN-BIAU, b Shanghai, China, Aug 13, 37; m 63; c 2. ATOMIC PHYSICS, MOLECULAR PHYSICS. *Educ:* Georgetown Col, BS, 57; Washington Univ, MA, 61, PhD(physics), 64. *Prof Exp:* Instr math, Univ Mo, St Louis, 61-62; res assoc physics, Joint Inst Lab Astrophys, Univ Colo, 64-66; asst prof, 66-70, ASSOC PROF PHYSICS, UNIV DEL, 70-, TRUSTEE, 76- *Concurrent Pos:* Consult, Control Data Corp & Mid-Atlantic Consortium Energy Res, 81 & various law firms, 79-81; prin investr grant, NSF, 78-81 & Asn Res Opthamal, 81-83. *Mem:* Am Phys Soc; Am Asn Physics Teachers; AAAS. *Res:* Inference of ion-molecule reaction cross sections from rate constants; ion velocity distributions; photodetachment of molecular negative ions. *Mailing Add:* Dept of Physics Univ of Del Newark DE 19711

WOO, TSE-CHIEN, b Nanking, China, Mar 6, 24, US citizen; m 57; c 2. APPLIED MECHANICS, APPLIED MATHEMATICS. *Educ:* Ord Eng Col, China, BS, 46; Univ Wash, MS, 54; Brown Univ, PhD(appl math), 60. *Prof Exp:* Res asst interior ballistics, Ballistics Res Inst, China, 46-48; res assoc weapon eng, Navy Res Inst, 48-51; sr develop engr, Taiwan Fertilizer Co, 51-52; res asst mech eng, Univ Wash, 53-54; res asst appl math, Brown Univ, 54-60; sr researcher basic eng, Glass Res Ctr, PPG Indust, Inc, 60-62, eng assoc, 62-64, sr eng assoc, 64-67; assoc prof, 68-71, PROF MECH ENG, UNIV PITTSBURGH, 71-, PROF MATH, 77- *Concurrent Pos:* Lectr, Univ Pittsburgh, 60-67; consult, Glass Res Ctr, PPG Indust, Inc, 68-; bd dirs, Mid-West Mech Conf, 71-75, co-chmn, 13th Mid-West Mech Conf, 73. *Mem:* Soc Rheology; Math Asn Am; Am Soc Mech Engrs; Sigma Xi; Am Acad Mech. *Res:* Finite elasticity; theory of viscoelasticity and its applications to the thermal stress problems of glass; viscoelastic properties of glass at elevated temperatures. *Mailing Add:* Dept of Mech Eng Univ of Pittsburgh Pittsburgh PA 15261

WOOD, ALBERT D(OUGLAS), b Providence, RI, June 8, 30; m 75; c 5. GAS DYNAMICS, AEROPROPULSION. *Educ:* Brown Univ, ScB, 51, PhD(eng), 59; Harvard Univ, MS, 53. *Prof Exp:* Instr eng, Brown Univ, 56-58; staff scientist, Res & Develop Div, Avco Corp, 58-64, chief exp gas dynamics sect, 64-66, prin res scientist, Avco Everett Res Lab, Mass, 66-69; fluid dynamicist, Boston Br Off, 69-81, dir sci, 81, DIR MECH DIV, OFF NAVAL RES, ARLINGTON, VA, 81- *Mem:* Sigma Xi. *Res:* Theoretical and experimental aerophysics; high temperature gas dynamics; chemical kinetics; laser technology; aerospace propulsion. *Mailing Add:* Off Naval Res Code 432 Mech Div 800 N Quincy St Arlington VA 22217

WOOD, ALBERT E(LMER), b Cape May Court House, NJ, Sept 22, 10; m 37; c 3. VERTEBRATE PALEONTOLOGY. *Educ:* Princeton Univ, BS, 30; Columbia Univ, MA, 32, PhD(geol), 35. *Hon Degrees:* MA, Amherst Col, 54. *Prof Exp:* Asst biol, Long Island Univ, 30-33, tutor, 33-34; from asst geologist to geologist, US Army Engrs, 36-41 & geologist, 46; from asst prof to prof, 46-70, chmn dept, 62-66, EMER PROF BIOL, AMHERST COL, 70- *Concurrent Pos:* Partic, Paleont Expeds, Western US, 28, 31-32 & 35; dir, Amherst Col Exped, 48, 57, 60, 63, 65 & 68; assoc cur vert paleont, Pratt Mus, Amherst Col, 48-70; NSF sr fel, Naturhistorisches Mus, Basel, Switz, 66-67; vis prof, Dept Paleont, Univ Calif, Berkeley, 72. *Mem:* Fel AAAS; Am Soc Mammalogists; Paleont Soc; fel Geol Soc Am; Soc Study Evolution. *Res:* Rodent and lagomorph classification, paleontology and evolution. *Mailing Add:* 20 Hereford Ave Cape May Court House NJ 08210

WOOD, ALLEN D(OANE), b Englewood, NJ, Aug 16, 35; m 57; c 4. MECHANICAL ENGINEERING. *Educ:* Purdue Univ, BSME, 57, MSME, 61, PhD(mech eng), 63. *Prof Exp:* RES SCIENTIST, LOCKHEED RES LAB, 63- *Mem:* Am Inst Aeronaut & Astronaut. *Res:* Instrumentation for remote measurement of automobile exhaust emissions; environmental pollution studies; electrically-powered vehicles; infrared systems; spectroscopy; lasers; shock tubes; gas dynamics. *Mailing Add:* Lockheed Res Lab 3251 Hanover D52-22 B201 Palo Alto CA 94304

WOOD, ALLEN JOHN, b Milwaukee, Wis, Oct 1, 25; m 49; c 2. ELECTRICAL ENGINEERING. *Educ:* Marquette Univ, BEE, 49; Ill Inst Technol, MSEE, 51; Rensselaer Polytech Inst, PhD(elec eng), 59. *Prof Exp:* Engr, Allis Chalmers Mfg Co, Wis, 49-50; asst, Ill Inst Technol, 50-51; eng analyst, Gen Elec Co, 51-59; mem tech staff, Hughes Aircraft Co, 59-60; sr engr, Elec Utility Eng Oper, Gen Elec Co, 60-69; PRIN ENGR & MEM BD DIR, POWER TECHNOL, INC, 69- *Concurrent Pos:* Adj prof, Rensselaer Polytech Inst, 68- *Mem:* AAAS; Nat Soc Prof Engrs; Inst Elec & Electronics Engrs; Tensor Soc; Am Nuclear Soc. *Res:* Engineering analysis of complex technical or economic systems; business and system planning simulations and studies. *Mailing Add:* 901 Vrooman Ave Schenectady NY 12309

WOOD, ANNE MICHELLE, b Cleveland, Ohio, Aug 4, 51. PHYCOLOGY, PHYTOPLANKTON ECOLOGY. *Educ:* Univ Corpus Christi, BA, 73; Univ Ga, PhD(zool), 80. *Prof Exp:* Res asst, Cent Power & Light, 73; engr tech II, Tex Water Qual Bd, 73-74; teaching asst, Univ Ga, 74-78, instr, 78; res asst, 80-81, FEL, UNIV CHICAGO, 81- *Concurrent Pos:* Consult, Cent Power & Light, 73-75, LGL, Inc, 78; res asst, Univ Ga, 76-80. *Mem:* Am Soc Limnol & Oceanog; Phycol Soc Am; Ecol Soc Am; Estuarine Res Fedn; Sigma Xi. *Res:* Phytoplankton ecology and evolution, particularly the effect of environmental parameters on production, distribution and physiology; the relationship of metallo-organic interractions with trace metal bioavailability; environmental impact assessment in marine systems. *Mailing Add:* Barnes Lab Univ Chicago 5630 S Ingleside Chicago IL 60637

WOOD, BENJAMIN W, b Cardston, Alta, Nov 13, 38; US citizen; m 59; c 6. BOTANY, RANGE SCIENCE. *Educ:* Brigham Young Univ, BS, 63, MS, 67; Ore State Univ, PhD(range sci), 71. *Prof Exp:* Asst prof biol, Boise Col, 67-68; instr range mgt, Ore State Univ, 69-70, asst prof, 70-71; ASST PROF BOT & RANGE SCI, BRIGHAM YOUNG UNIV, 71- *Concurrent Pos:* Navajo-Kaiparowits Power Generating Sta fel, Ctr Health & Environ Studies, Brigham Young Univ, 71- *Mem:* Soc Range Mgt. *Res:* Desert ecology; wildlife habitat improvement. *Mailing Add:* Dept of Bot & Range Sci Brigham Young Univ Provo UT 84602

WOOD, BOBBY EUGENE, b Martinsville, Va, May 9, 39; m 65; c 2. PHYSICS, MATHEMATICS. *Educ:* Berea Col, BA, 61; Vanderbilt Univ, MA, 64. *Prof Exp:* Engr aerospace, Aro, Inc, 64-80; ENGR AEROSPACE, ARVIN/CALSPAN, 80- *Mem:* Optical Soc Am; Am Inst Aeronaut & Astronaut. *Res:* Optical properties of materials, especially radiative properties of condensed gases on cryogenically cooled optical components. *Mailing Add:* Arvin/Calspan PWT-ATD MS 640 Arnold Air Force Station TN 37389

WOOD, BRUCE, b Kintnersville, Pa, Apr 9, 38; m 63; c 2. MATHEMATICS, MECHANICAL ENGINEERING. *Educ:* Pa State Univ, BS, 60; Univ Wyo, MS, 64; Lehigh Univ, PhD(math), 67. *Prof Exp:* Asst air pollution control engr, Bethlehem Steel Corp, 60-62; asst math, Univ Wyo, 63-64 & Lehigh Univ, 64-67; asst prof, 67-71, ASSOC PROF MATH, UNIV ARIZ, 71- *Mem:* Am Math Soc. *Res:* Linear approximation theory; summability theory; theory of complex variables; linear positive operators. *Mailing Add:* Dept of Math Univ of Ariz Tucson AZ 85721

WOOD, BRUCE WADE, b Morganfield, Ky, Oct 22, 51; m 75; c 2. TREE NUT PHYSIOLOGY & HORTICULTURE. *Educ:* Univ Ky, BS, 73, MS, 75; Mich State Univ, PhD(forestry), 79. *Prof Exp:* HORTICULTURIST, SCI EDUC, AGR RES SERV, USDA, 79- *Mem:* Am Soc Hort Sci. *Res:* Maximizing nut production of nut trees by regulating growth, flowering, fruit development, root stocks, mineral nutrition and culture; interrelationship of trees with insect and disease organisms. *Mailing Add:* USDA Southeastern Fruit & Tree Nut Res Lab Byron GA 31008

WOOD, BYARD DEAN, b Cardston, Alta, Mar 30, 40; US citizen; m 65; c 3. MECHANICAL ENGINEERING, HEAT TRANSFER. *Educ:* Utah State Univ, BS, 63, MS, 66; Univ Minn, Minneapolis, PhD(mech eng), 70. *Prof Exp:* Assoc prof heat transfer & exp methods, 70-80, PROF ENG, DEPT ENG, ARIZ STATE UNIV, 80- *Concurrent Pos:* consult, Solar Energy Res & Educ Found, 77-, Solar Rating & Cert Corp, Nat Bur Standards & ERG, Inc. *Mem:* Am Soc Mech Engrs; Am Soc Heating, Refrig & Air-Conditioning Engrs; Am Soc Eng Educ; Combust Inst; Solar Energy Soc. *Res:* Solar energy research, especially heat transfer and experimental methods in thermal and photovoltaic solar heating and cooling systems; fire research, especially heat and mass transfer associated with large turbulent flames. *Mailing Add:* Col of Eng & Appl Sci Ariz State Univ Tempe AZ 85281

WOOD, CALVIN DALE, b Salt Lake City, Utah, July 13, 33; m 55; c 5. NUCLEAR PHYSICS, SHOCK HYDRODYNAMICS. *Educ:* Univ Calif, Berkeley, AB, 57, PhD(high energy physics), 61. *Prof Exp:* Res asst high energy physics, Lawrence Radiation Lab, Univ Calif, Berkeley, 58-62, physicist, 61-62; asst prof physics, Univ Utah, 62-64; PHYSICIST, LAWRENCE LIVERMORE LAB, 64- *Concurrent Pos:* Consult, Utah Hwy Patrol Accident Invest Staff, 62-64 & Hill AFB Accident Invest Staff, 64. *Mem:* Am Phys Soc; Ital Phys Soc. *Res:* Shock hydrodynamics; neutron cross sections; high speed digital computers; nuclear processes; chemical high explosives; material properties under high strain rates. *Mailing Add:* Lawrence Livermore Lab PO Box 808 L-35 Livermore CA 94550

WOOD, CARL EUGENE, b Alice, Tex, Aug 28, 40; m 73; c 3. MARINE ECOLOGY, INVERTEBRATE ZOOLOGY. *Educ:* Tex A&M Univ, BS, 62, MS, 65; PhD(fisheries), 69. *Prof Exp:* Fishery technician, Nat Marine Fisheries Serv, 63-64; res asst limnol, Tex A&M Univ, 65-67; limnologist, Tenn Valley Authority, 67-69; ASSOC PROF INVERT & MARINE BIOL, TEX A&I UNIV, 69- *Concurrent Pos:* Maricult consult, Flato Corp, 73-74. *Mem:* Am Soc Limnol & Oceanog; Fedn Estuarine Res. *Res:* Marine invertebrate ecology; shrimp of the suborder Natantia systematics; primary productivity of estuaries. *Mailing Add:* Box 158 Dept of Biol Tex A&I Univ Kingsville TX 78363

WOOD, CARLOS C, b Turloc, Calif, 1913. ENGINEERING. *Educ:* Col Pac, BA, 31; Calif Inst Technol, MSME, 32, MSAE, 34. *Prof Exp:* Mem staff, Douglas Aircraft, 37-60; mem staff, Sikorsky Aircraft, 60-70; DIR & V PRES, CLAUDE C WOOD CO, 70- *Concurrent Pos:* Consult, 70-; mem sci adv comn, US Air Force; mem aerospace eng bd, Nat Acad Eng. *Mem:* Nat Acad Eng; Am Inst Aeronaut & Astronaut. *Mailing Add:* Claude C Wood Co 686 Lockeford St Lodi CA 95240

WOOD, CAROL SAUNDERS, b Pennington Gap, Va, Feb 9, 45. MATHEMATICAL LOGIC. *Educ:* Randolph-Macon Womans Col, AB, 66; Yale Univ, PhD(math), 71. *Prof Exp:* Gast dozent math, Univ Erlangen-Nürnberg, WGer, 71-72; lectr, Yale Univ, 72-73; vis instr, 70-71, ASST PROF MATH, WESLEYAN UNIV, 73- *Mem:* Am Math Soc; Math Asn Am; Asn Symbolic Logic. *Res:* Application of model theory to algebra, in particular to fields and to differential fields. *Mailing Add:* Dept of Math Wesleyan Univ Middletown CT 06457

WOOD, CARROLL E, JR, b Roanoke, Va, Jan 13, 21. BOTANY. *Educ:* Roanoke Col, BS, 41; Univ Pa, MS, 43; Harvard Univ, AM, 47, PhD(biol), 49. *Prof Exp:* Instr biol, Harvard Univ, 49-51; from asst prof to assoc prof bot, Univ NC, 51-54; assoc cur, 54-70, CUR, ARNOLD ARBORETUM, HARVARD UNIV, 70-, PROF BIOL, 72-, MEM FAC ARTS & SCI, 63- *Concurrent Pos:* Lectr biol, Harvard Univ, 64-72. *Mem:* Am Soc Plant Taxon; Bot Soc Am; Int Asn Plant Taxon. *Res:* Flora of southeastern United States; biosystematics and taxonomy of flowering plants. *Mailing Add:* 22 Divinity Ave Cambridge MA 02138

WOOD, CHARLES, b London, Eng, Nov 6, 24; US citizen; m 50; c 3. EXPERIMENTAL SOLID STATE PHYSICS. *Educ:* Univ London, BSc, 51, MSc, 55, PhD(physics), 62. *Prof Exp:* Physicist, Gen Elec Res Labs, Eng, 51-53 & Electronic Tubes Ltd, 53-54; dep group leader, Caswell Res Lab, Plessey Co, 54-56; group supvr, Res Div, Philco Corp, Pa, 56-60; sect head solid state prod group, Kearfott Div, Gen Precision Instruments, NJ, 60-61; dir thermoelec, Intermetallic Prod, Inc, 61-63; mgr, Mat Res Dept, Xerox Corp Res Labs, NY, 63-67; head dept, 67-70, PROF PHYSICS, NORTHERN ILL UNIV, 67- *Mem:* Am Phys Soc; Sigma Xi. *Res:* Semiconductors; photoconductors; thin films; crystal growth; Hall-effect devices; thermoelectricity; electrophotography. *Mailing Add:* Dept of Physics Northern Ill Univ De Kalb IL 60115

WOOD, CHARLES D, US citizen. AUTOMOTIVE ENGINEERING. *Educ:* Rice Univ, BS, 56; Southern Methodist Univ, MS, 62. *Prof Exp:* Test engr, Ling-Temco-Vought Inc, 58-61, propulsion engr, 61-62; sr res engr, Dept Automotive Res, 62-67, sect mgr, 67-74, DIR DEPT ENGINE & VEHICLE RES, AUTOMOTIVE RES DIV, SOUTHWEST RES INST, 74- *Mem:* Soc Automotive Engrs. *Res:* Engine development; development of off-highway equipment; fuel-air explosive devices for earthmoving, rock ripping, hard-facing deposition, ship propulsion, undersea seismic shock generation, dredging and pumping, minefield clearance and marine icebreaking. *Mailing Add:* Dept of Engine & Vehicle Res Southwest Res Inst PO Drawer 28510 San Antonio TX 78284

WOOD, CHARLES DONALD, b Ravena, Ky, Feb 4, 25; m; c 4. PHARMACOLOGY. *Educ:* Univ Ky, BS, 49, MS, 50; Univ NC, PhD(physiol), 57. *Prof Exp:* Neurophysiologist, Nat Inst Neurol Dis & Blindness, 53-55; instr physiol & pharmacol, Med Sch, Univ Ark, 57-59, from asst prof to assoc prof pharmacol, Med Ctr, 59-67; prof physiol & pharmacol, 67-77, PROF PHARMACOL & THERAPEUT, MED SCH, LA STATE UNIV, SHREVEPORT, 77-, HEAD MED COMMUN, 71- *Concurrent Pos:* Consult, US Naval Aerospace Med Inst, 62- *Mem:* Aerospace Med Asn. *Res:* Temporal lobe epilepsy; influence of temporal lobe structures on behavior; neuropharmacology; pulmonary edema; oxygen toxicity; neurogenic hypertension; antimotion sickness drugs; aerospace pharmacology; drugs and athletic performance. *Mailing Add:* Dept of Physiol & Pharmacol La State Univ Med Sch Shreveport LA 71107

WOOD, CHRISTOPHER MICHAEL, b Manchester, Eng, Feb 21, 47; Brit & Can citizen; m 71; c 2. COMPARATIVE PHYSIOLOGY. *Educ:* Univ BC, BSc, 68, MSc, 71; Univ East Anglia, PhD(comp physiol), 74. *Prof Exp:* Fel, Univ Calgary, 74-76; asst prof, 76-79, ASSOC PROF BIOL, MCMASTER UNIV, 79- *Concurrent Pos:* Int collab res fel, Nat Sci & Eng Res Coun, 82. *Mem:* Soc Exp Biol; Am Soc Zool; Can Soc Zool; AAAS. *Res:* Circulation, respiration, gas exchange, acid base regulation, osmoregulation and homeostasis in teleost fish and decapod crustaceans; environmental acid and heavy metal toxicology of fishes. *Mailing Add:* Dept of Biol McMaster Univ Hamilton ON L8S 4K1 Can

WOOD, COLIN, b Farnborough, Eng, Dec 20, 23; nat US; m 56; c 2. PATHOLOGY. *Educ:* Univ Birmingham, MB, ChB, 46, MD, 57. *Prof Exp:* Sr resident, Case Western Reserve Univ, 53-54; sr registr, Bernhard Baron Inst Path, London Hosp, Eng, 54-58; from asst prof to assoc prof, 58-70, prof path, Sch Med, Univ Md, Baltimore City, 70-78; PROF DERMATOPATH, SCH MED, STANFORD UNIV, 78- *Mem:* Am Col Path; Am Acad Dermat; Int Acad Path; Am Soc Dermatopath; Soc Invest Dermat. *Res:* Dermatopathology. *Mailing Add:* Dept of Dermat Stanford Univ Med Ctr Stanford CA 94305

WOOD, CORINNE SHEAR, b Baltimore, Md, Apr 14, 25; m 46; c 4. PHYSICAL ANTHROPOLOGY, MEDICAL ANTHROPOLOGY. *Educ:* Univ Calif, Riverside, BA, 68, PhD(anthrop), 73. *Prof Exp:* Res asst med, Johns Hopkins Univ, 50-55, Sinai Hosp, Baltimore, 55-58 & Johns Hopkins Univ, 59-61; med technologist, Riverside Community Hosp, Calif, 62-71; teaching asst anthrop, Univ Calif, Riverside, 68-70; asst prof, 73-76, ASSOC PROF ANTHROP, CALIF STATE UNIV, FULLERTON, 76- *Concurrent Pos:* Res mem, Univ Calif Med Ctr, San Francisco, 73; lectr, Univ Calif, Riverside, 74-75, lab consult, 75. *Mem:* Fel Am Anthrop Asn; Am Asn Phys Anthropologists; Med Anthrop Soc. *Res:* Human physiological variables related to disease and disease vectors; health conditions of American Indian populations; women, nutrition and health; interrelationship of human culture and disease. *Mailing Add:* Dept of Anthrop Calif State Univ Fullerton CA 92634

WOOD, CRAIG ADAMS, b Rochester, NY, Jan 31, 41; m 64; c 2. MATHEMATICS. *Educ:* Col Wooster, BA, 62; Fla State Univ, MS, 63, PhD(math), 67. *Prof Exp:* Instr math, Fla State Univ, 67-68; from asst prof to assoc prof, Okla State Univ, 72-73, NASA res grant, 69-70; assoc prof math sci & head div, Univ Houston, Victoria Campus, 73-76, assoc prof comput sci & math & dir, Comput Ctr, 77-78, prof, 78-80; PROF COMPUT SCI & CHMN DEPT, STEPHEN F AUSTIN STATE UNIV, 80- *Concurrent Pos:* Am Coun Educ fel, Acad Admin, 76-77. *Mem:* Am Math Soc; Math Asn Am; Asn Comput Mach. *Res:* Commutative ring theory in algebra; algebraic equations in numerical analysis. *Mailing Add:* Comput Sci Dept Stephen F Austin State Univ Nacogdoches TX 75962

WOOD, D(ONALD) L(INCOLN), b Franklin, Pa, May 27, 25; m 46; c 4. METALLURGY. *Educ:* Carnegie Inst Technol, BS, 49, MS, 51; Rensselaer Polytech Inst, PhD(metall), 57. *Prof Exp:* Asst, Metals Res Lab, Carnegie Inst Technol, 49-51; metallurgist, Res Lab, 51-63, liaison scientist, 63-66, PROJ DEVELOP MGR, RES & DEVELOP CTR, GEN ELEC CO, 66- *Mem:* Am Soc Metals. *Res:* Relation of mechanical behavior of materials to their structure; studies of the brittleness of intermetallic materials; internal ioxidation; corrosion. *Mailing Add:* Gen Elec Corp Res & Develop PO Box 8 Bldg K-1 Rm 3A30 Schenectady NY 12301

WOOD, DARRELL FENWICK, b Kentville, NS, May 13, 42; m 70; c 1. FOOD SCIENCE. *Educ:* McGill Univ, BSc, 63, MSc, 65; Univ BC, PhD(food sci), 73. *Prof Exp:* Res officer food sci, Can Dept Agr, 65-67; res officer, Atomic Energy Can Ltd, 67-70; res scientist food sci, 73-76, asst coordr food systs, 76-78, RES SCIENTIST FOOD SCI, 78- AGR CAN, 78- *Mem:* Can Inst Food Sci Technol; Inst Food Technologists. *Res:* Meat research and nutrition. *Mailing Add:* 46 Sullivan Ave Ottawa ON K2G 1V2 Can

WOOD, DARWIN LEWIS, b East Orange, NJ, July 21, 21; m 45; c 6. PHYSICS, CHEMISTRY. *Educ:* Princeton Univ, AB, 42; Ohio State Univ, PhD(physics, physiol), 50. *Prof Exp:* Physicist, Rohm and Haas Co, 42-46; fel, Univ Mich, 50-52, asst prof physics, 53-56; MEM TECH STAFF, CHEM DEPT, BELL LABS, INC, 56- *Mem:* Fel Optical Soc Am. *Res:* Polymers; proteins; optics; spectroscopy; crystal spectra; ions in crystals. *Mailing Add:* Chem Dept Bell Labs Inc PO Box 261 Murray Hill NJ 07974

WOOD, DAVID, b Woodlawn, Ill, Oct 10, 28; m 58; c 3. ANALYTICAL CHEMISTRY. *Educ:* Univ Ill, BS, 50; Univ Wis, PhD(chem), 56. *Prof Exp:* Chemist, Velsicol Chem Corp, 50-52; asst chem, Univ Wis, 52-56; chemist, Spencer Kellogg & Sons, Inc, 56-59; assoc res chemist, 59-75, RES CHEMIST & GROUP LEADER, STERLING-WINTHROP RES INST, 75- *Mem:* Am Chem Soc. *Res:* Synthetic organic chemistry; synthesis of pharmaceuticals; gas chromatography. *Mailing Add:* Sterling-Winthrop Res Inst Rensselaer NY 12144

WOOD, DAVID ALVRA, b Flora Vista, NMex, Dec 21, 04; m 37; c 5. PATHOLOGY. *Educ:* Stanford Univ, AB, 26, MD, 30. *Prof Exp:* Asst pharmacol, Stanford Univ, 28-29, from instr to assoc prof path, 30-51; from assoc prof to prof, Sch Med, 51-72, dir, Cancer Res Inst, 51-72, EMER PROF PATH, SCH MED & EMER DIR, CANCER RES INST, UNIV CALIF, SAN FRANCISCO, 72-; CONSULT, 77- *Concurrent Pos:* Spec consult, Nat Cancer Inst, 56-63; mem sci adv bd, Armed Forces Inst Path, 57-62; co-chmn, mem adv comt & spec consult, Cancer Control Prog, Bur State Serv, USPHS, 59-63; mem clin studies panel cancer chemother, Nat Cancer Inst, NIH, 59-64; mem US nat comt, Int Union Against Cancer, 61-64; mem histopath nomenclature & classification tumors comt, WHO, Tokyo, 69-74; mem US nat comt X, Int Cancer Cong, 70; fel selection comt, Int Agency Res Cancer, Lyon, 70-73; chmn, Approach 3, Objective 5, Nat Cancer Plan, 71-74; mem cadre & chmn path subcomt, Nat Large Bowel Cancer Proj, Nat Cancer Inst, 73-76. *Honors & Awards:* Am Cancer Soc Award, 50 & Distinguished Serv Award, 72; Award, Col Am Pathologists, 58; Lucy Wortham James Award, James Ewing Soc, 70. *Mem:* Fedn Am Socs Exp Biol; Am Cancer Soc (pres, 56-57); Am Asn Cancer Res; Col Am Pathologists (pres, 52-55); Asn Am Cancer Insts (pres, 70-72). *Res:* Neoplastic diseases; dual pulmonary circulation; exfoliative cytology; evaluation of cancer education in medical and dental schools; oral contraceptives and tumors of the breast, epidemiological and morphological correlations. *Mailing Add:* 54 Commonwealth Ave San Francisco CA 94118

WOOD, DAVID BELDEN, b Glendale, Calif, Nov 15, 35; m 56; c 3. ASTRONOMY. *Educ:* Univ Calif, Berkeley, AB, 57, PhD(astron), 63. *Prof Exp:* Mem tech staff astron, Bellcomm, Inc, 67-69, supvr astrophys, 69-71; mem adv plans staff, Goddard Space Flight Ctr, NASA, 71-76, opers res analyst, Appln Systs Anal Off, 76-80; MEM TECH STAFF, THEATER C 3 SYSTS, MITRE CORP, 80- *Mem:* AAAS; Am Astron Soc; Royal Astron Soc. *Res:* Eclipsing binary stars; extragalactic research; photoelectric photometry; space astronomy; operations research; computer modeling. *Mailing Add:* Mitre Corp MS 415 PO Box 208 Bedford MA 01730

WOOD, DAVID ELDON, b Ada, Okla, Dec 1, 39; div; c 3. BIOMEDICAL REAGENTS & ASSAYS, PHYSICAL CHEMISTRY. *Educ:* Okla State Univ, BS, 60; Calif Inst Technol, PhD(phys chem), 64. *Prof Exp:* Res chemist, Orlando Div, Martin-Marietta Corp, 63-65; res fel chem, Calif Inst Technol, 65-66; asst prof, Carnegie-Mellon Univ, 66-71; asst prof, Univ Conn, Storrs, 71-74, assoc prof chem, 74-77, prof chem & mem staff, Inst Mat Sci, 77-80; FOUNDER, COVALENT TECHNOL CORP, 80- *Concurrent Pos:* Am Chem Soc Petrol Res Fund grant, 66-68. *Mem:* Am Chem Soc. *Res:* Development of reagents for immuno assays; electron paramagnetic resonance; studies of structure and reactions of free radicals. *Mailing Add:* Covalent Technol Corp 575 Massar Ave San Jose CA 95116

WOOD, DAVID LEE, b St Louis, Mo, Jan 8, 31; m 60; c 2. FOREST ENTOMOLOGY, INSECT ECOLOGY. *Educ:* State Univ NY Col Forestry, Syracuse Univ, BS, 52; Univ Calif, Berkeley, PhD(entom), 60. *Prof Exp:* Asst entomologist, Boyce Thompson Inst Plant Res, 59-60; from lectr entom & asst entomologist to assoc prof entom & assoc entomologist, 60-70, PROF ENTOM & ENTOMOLOGIST, UNIV CALIF, BERKELEY, 70- *Mem:* AAAS; Sigma Xi; Entom Soc Am; Soc Am Foresters; Entom Soc Can. *Res:* Forest insect ecology and pest management; insect-host relationships, especially host selection behavior, insect pheromones and host resistance with special emphasis on bark beetles. *Mailing Add:* Dept of Entom Sci Univ of Calif Berkeley CA 94720

WOOD, DAVID OLIVER, b Rome, Ga. BACTERIAL GENETICS. *Educ:* Berry Col, BA, 72; Med Col Ga, MS, 75, PhD(microbiol), 78. *Prof Exp:* Res fel microbiol, Med Col, Va Commonwealth Univ, 77-79; ASST PROF MICROBIOL, UNIV SOUTH ALA, 79- *Mem:* Am Soc Microbiol. *Res:* Molecular basis of bacterial pathogenicity; pseudomonas visulence factors. *Mailing Add:* Dept Microbiol & Immunol Med Col Univ SAla Mobile AL 36688

WOOD, DAVID ROY, b Mar 3, 35; US citizen; m 67. SPECTROSCOPY. *Educ:* Friends Univ, AB, 56; Univ Mich, MS, 58; Purdue Univ, PhD(physics), 67. *Prof Exp:* Instr physics, Friends Univ, 58-59; instr amth & physics, Scattergood Sch, 59-61; res assoc physics, Purdue Univ, 67; asst prof, 67-74, ASSOC PROF PHYSICS, WRIGHT STATE UNIV, 74- *Mem:* Optical Soc Am. *Res:* Experimental atomic spectroscopy; analysis of the energy level structure of the lead atom and ion; Fabry-Perut interferometry and Zeeman effect analysis; spectral line profiles in the vacuum ultraviolet; spectra of multiply-ionized atoms. *Mailing Add:* Dept of Physics Wright State Univ Dayton OH 45431

WOOD, DAVID S(HOTWELL), b Akron, Ohio, May 21, 20; m 45; c 1. MATERIALS SCIENCE. *Educ:* Calif Inst Technol, BS, 41, MS, 46, PhD(mech eng), 49. *Prof Exp:* Asst, Calif Inst Technol, 42-44; staff engr, Univ Calif, 44-46; asst mach design, 46-49, lectr, 49-50, from asst prof to assoc prof mech eng, 50-61, assoc dean students, 68-74, PROF MAT SCI, CALIF INST TECHNOL, 61- *Mem:* AAAS; Am Soc Mech Engrs; Am Soc Metals; Am Inst Mining, Metall & Petrol Engrs. *Res:* Plastic strain waves in metals; mechanical properties of metals subjected to dynamic loading; dislocations in crystals. *Mailing Add:* Calif Inst Technol Pasadena CA 91109

WOOD, DAVID WELLS, b Amesville, Ohio, May 22, 38; m 70. MATERIALS SCIENCE, PHYSICAL CHEMISTRY. *Educ:* Univ of the Pac, BS, 60, MS, 61; Univ Utah, PhD(ceramic eng), 65. *Prof Exp:* Petrol Res Fund grant calorimetry, Univ of the Pac, 60-61; Army res grant high pressure chem, 63-65; res chemist, E I du Pont de Nemours & Co, Inc, 65-68; proj leader composites, Burlington Industs, 68-70, sr res chemist, Corp Res & Develop, 70-77, mem tech staff, Indust Div, 77-78, mgr qual control, Indust Div, 78-79; MGR NEW PROD, HEXCEL CORP, DUBLIN, CALIF, 79- *Mem:* AAAS; Am Chem Soc; Am Ceramic Soc; NAm Thermal Anal Soc; Soc Advan Mat & Process Eng. *Res:* Solid state chemistry and physics relating to polymers in the form of plastics and fibers or in conjunction with each other in composites. *Mailing Add:* Hexcel Corp 11711 Dublin Blvd Dublin CA 94566

WOOD, DENNIS STEPHENSON, b Farnworth, Eng, May 28, 34; m 70. STRUCTURAL GEOLOGY, TECTONICS. *Educ:* Univ Liverpool, BSc, 60; Univ Leeds, PhD(geol), 70. *Prof Exp:* Lectr geol, Univ Leeds, 62-67; vis prof, 67-68, assoc prof, 70-74, PROF GEOL, UNIV ILL, 75- *Mem:* Geol Soc Am; Geol Soc London. *Res:* Study and deformation of rocks; nature of deformation at high strain zones associated with plate margins; early history of the earth. *Mailing Add:* Dept of Geol Univ Ill Urbana IL 61801

WOOD, DERICK, b Bolton, Eng, July 19, 40. COMPUTER SCIENCE. *Educ:* Univ Leeds, BS, 63, dipl electronic comput, 64, PhD(math), 68. *Prof Exp:* Comput asst, Univ Leeds, 64-68; asst res scientist, Courant Inst Math Sci, NY Univ, 68-70; from asst prof to assoc prof comput sci, McMaster Univ, 70-78, prof, 78-82; PROF COMPUT SCI, UNIV WATERLOO, 82- *Mem:* Asn Comput Mach; Am Math Soc; Can Info Processing Soc; Inst Elec & Electronic Engrs; Europ Asn Comput Sci. *Res:* Formal language theory; data structure theory; analysis of algorythems; computational geometry; very large scale integration theory. *Mailing Add:* Dept of Appl Math McMaster Univ Hamilton ON L8S 4K1 Can

WOOD, DON CLIFTON, b Farmington, Utah, Mar 25, 23; m 46; c 5. BIOCHEMISTRY, COMPUTER SCIENCE. *Educ:* Brigham Young Univ, BS, 47, MS, 48; Cornell Univ, PhD(biochem), 52. *Prof Exp:* Biochemist, Ft Detrick, Md, 47-49 & Vet Admin Hosp, Salt Lake City, 52-60; dir biochem, St Vincent & Providence Hosp, Portland, 60-64; head res dept, Providence Hosp, 64-73; VPRES, MEDLAB COMPUT SERV, INC, 73- *Concurrent Pos:* Asst res prof, Col Med, Univ Utah, 52-60, assoc clin prof path, 75; res assoc surg, Med Sch, Univ Ore, 67, assoc prof, 70-73; clin chemist-consult, Cottonwood Hosp, 75; dir comput, Compucare, Inc, 77-; assoc prof path, Univ SFla, 77. *Mem:* Asn Res Vision & Ophthal; Am Asn Clin Chemists; NY Acad Sci. *Res:* Chemistry lens protein; clinical chemistry; mechanism of action of dimethyl sulfoxide; cancer. *Mailing Add:* 4010 Priory Circle Tampa FL 33624

WOOD, DON JAMES, b Northeast, Pa, July 28, 36; m 59; c 2. FLUID MECHANICS. *Educ:* Carnegie Inst Technol, BS, 58, MS, 59, PhD, 61. *Prof Exp:* Asst prof eng mech, Clemson Univ, 61-62; asst prof civil eng, Duke Univ, 62-66; PROF CIVIL ENG, UNIV KY, 66- *Concurrent Pos:* Res engr, NASA, 63-66; consult, NASA, 63-66. *Honors & Awards:* Huber Res Prize, Am Soc Civil Engrs, 75; Western Elec Fund, Am Soc Eng Educ, 76. *Mem:* Am Soc Civil Engrs; Am Soc Mech Engrs; Soc Eng Sci; Am Inst Aeronaut & Astronaut; Am Soc Eng Educ. *Res:* Fluid transients; water hammer problems; water distribution systems; hydrotransport. *Mailing Add:* Dept of Civil Eng Univ of Ky Lexington KY 40506

WOOD, DONALD EUGENE, b St Paul, Minn, Dec 26, 30; m 54; c 3. NUCLEAR PHYSICS. *Educ:* Univ Nev, BS, 51; Northwestern Univ, MS, 53, PhD(physics), 56. *Prof Exp:* Asst physics, Northwestern Univ, 51-55; physicist, Hanford Labs, Gen Elec Co, 55-58, sr physicist, 58-63; res scientist, Kaman Sci Corp, 63-68, mgr nuclear prod, 68-74, sr scientist, Nuclear Serv Prog, 74-78; STAFF SCIENTIST, ROCKWELL HANFORD OPERS, 78- *Concurrent Pos:* Lectr, Hanford Grad Ctr, Univ Wash, 58-63. *Mem:* Am Nuclear Soc; Am Phys Soc. *Res:* Nuclear fuel cycle safety; risk assessment probabilistic analysis; reliability prediction; activation analysis. *Mailing Add:* Rockwell Hanford Opers PO Box 800 Richland WA 99352

WOOD, DONALD ROY, b Keats, Kans, Apr 17, 21; m 43; c 2. AGRONOMY. *Educ:* Kans State Col, BS, 43; Colo State Univ, MS, 49; Univ Wis, PhD, 56. *Prof Exp:* From asst prof agron & asst agronomist to assoc prof agron & assoc agronomist, 47-63, PROF AGRON & AGRONOMIST, COLO STATE UNIV, 63- *Concurrent Pos:* Asst, Univ Wis, 50-51; res assoc, Univ Calif, 60-61; res assoc, Inst Nutrit Cent Am, Panama, 74. *Mem:* Fel AAAS; Genetics Soc Am; Genetics Soc Can; Am Soc Agron; Am Phytopath Soc. *Res:* Dry field bean breeding; dry bean disease resistance; breeding for improved nutritional value. *Mailing Add:* Dept of Agron Colo State Univ Ft Collins CO 80523

WOOD, EARL HOWARD, b Mankato, Minn, Jan 1, 12; m 36; c 4. PHYSIOLOGY. *Educ:* Macalester Col, BA, 34; Univ Minn, BS, 36, MS, 39, PhD(physiol), 40; MD, 41. *Hon Degrees:* DSc, Macalester Col, 50. *Prof Exp:* Instr physiol, Univ Minn, 39-40; Nat Res Coun fel pharmacol, Univ Pa, 41-42; instr pharmacol, Harvard Med Sch, 42; assoc prof physiol, 42-60, PROF PHYSIOL & MED, MAYO GRAD SCH MED, UNIV MINN, 42-; CONSULT, MAYO CLIN, 42- *Concurrent Pos:* Am Physiol Soc travel award, Int Physiol Cong, Oxford Univ; career investr, Am Heart Asn, 61-; vis scientist, Univ Bern, 65-66 & Univ Col, Univ London, 72-73. *Honors & Awards:* Car Wiggers Award, Am Physiol Soc; Gold Heart Award, Am Heart Asn. *Mem:* AAAS; Am Physiol Soc (pres, 80-81); Soc Exp Biol & Med; Am Heart Asn; hon fel Am Col Cardiol. *Res:* Electrolyte metabolism of cardiac and voluntary muscle; glucose reabsorption in amphibian kidney; effect of cardiac glycoside on electrolyte metabolism; cardiopulmonary effects of gravitational and inertial forces, aerospace medicine; computer based quantitative imaging techniques; cardiovascular and respiratory physiology of man. *Mailing Add:* Mayo Med Sch Rochester MN 55901

WOOD, EDWARD C(HALMERS), b Tucson, Ariz, Apr 30, 23; m 43; c 4. ENGINEERING. *Educ:* Univ Ariz, BA, 46, BSEE, 48. *Prof Exp:* Nuclear engr & mgr, Gen Elec Co, Wash, 49-62; mgr geophysics, Stanford Res Inst, 62-67, dir appl progs, 67-69, exec dir, Irvine, 70-72, staff scientist, 72-76; MEM STAFF, GEN ELEC CO, CALIF, 76- *Mem:* Am Nuclear Soc; Inst Elec & Electronics Engrs. *Res:* Institutional and environmental studies; management. *Mailing Add:* Gen Elec Co 310 Deguigne Dr Sunnyvale CA 94086

WOOD, EDWARD MORGAN, b Ft Washikie, Wyo, May 7, 26; m 50; c 5. COMPARATIVE PATHOLOGY, PATHOLOGY OF FISH. *Educ:* Ore State Univ, BS, 49; Cornell Univ, PhD(fishery biol), 52; Univ Wash, MD, 60. *Prof Exp:* Comp pathologist, US Fish & Wildlife Serv, 52-56; dir, E M Wood Diagnostic Labs, 64-69, Lab Procedures Northwest, Upjohn Co, 69-79; DIR PATH, WESTERN HOSP, 64- *Concurrent Pos:* Prin investr, Nat Cancer Inst, 61-64; Consult, NASA, 65-69. *Mem:* Am Soc Clin Pathologists. *Res:* Effects of pesticides, pollution and effects of lunar materials on fish. *Mailing Add:* 7318 89th Ave NW Gig Harbor WA 98335

WOOD, ELWYN DEVERE, b Everett, Wash, Sept 15, 34; m 66; c 2. MARINE GEOCHEMISTRY. *Educ:* Western Wash State Col, BA(chem) & BA(educ), 64; Univ Wash, MS, 66; Univ Alaska, PhD(chem oceanog), 71. *Prof Exp:* Oceanogr, Univ Wash, 66-67 & PR Nuclear Ctr, 70-75; OCEANOGR, OUTER CONTINENTAL SHELF OFF, BUR LAND MGT, DEPT INTERIOR, 75- *Mem:* Am Geophys Union; Geochem Soc. *Res:* Trace element chemistry in the marine environment; determination and evaluation of natural and induced radioactivity in the environment; design and administration of environmental studies on the outer continental shelf; evaluation of near-shore currents for the disposal of wastes. *Mailing Add:* 133 Crapemyrtle Rd Covington LA 70433

WOOD, EUNICE MARJORIE, b Venice, Calif, Sept 5, 27. CELL BIOLOGY, ELECTRON MICROSCOPY. *Educ:* Rutgers Univ, New Brunswick, BS, 48; Mt Holyoke Col, MA, 50; Harvard Med Sch, PhD(anat), 68. *Prof Exp:* Instr zool, Wellesley Col, 50-52; lectr, Barnard Col, Columbia Univ, 53-55; res technician hemat, City of Hope Med Ctr, Calif, 57-59; res assoc, Inst Cancer & Blood Res, 59-62; instr biol, Mt Holyoke Col, 62-63; USPHS fel, Med Sch, Univ Southern Calif, 67-68; from asst prof to assoc prof, 68-77, PROF BIOL, CALIF STATE UNIV, LONG BEACH, 77- *Concurrent Pos:* Electron micros consult oncol unit, Med Sch, Univ Southern Calif, 68-72. *Mem:* Am Soc Cell Biologists; Am Asn Anat. *Res:* Electron microscopy and cytochemistry of invertebrate glands. *Mailing Add:* Dept of Biol Calif State Univ 6101 E Seventh St Long Beach CA 90840

WOOD, F(REDERICK) B(ERNARD), b Sacramento, Calif, Dec 17, 17; m 42; c 2. ELECTRICAL ENGINEERING. *Educ:* Univ Calif, BS, 41, MS, 48, PhD(elec eng), 53. *Prof Exp:* Asst elec eng, Univ Calif, 40-41, asst resonator coupling, 49-52; mem staff radar, Mass Inst Technol, 41-46; staff engr, Res & Develop Lab, 52-58, staff engr, Advan Systs Develop Div Lab, 59-61, proj engr, 61-64, staff engr, 65-70, adv engr, 70-72, adv engr, Systs Develop Div, 72-75, adv engr, Systs Commun Div, 75-76, ADV ENGR, GEN PROD DIV, IBM CORP, 76- *Mem:* AAAS; Inst Elec & Electronics Engrs; Soc Social Responsibilities in Sci; Soc Gen Systs Res; NY Acad Sci. *Res:* Development of computer-communication systems; simulation; computer programming; information theory; data communication; cybernetics; philosophy of science. *Mailing Add:* 2346 Lansford Ave San Jose CA 95125

WOOD, FERGUS JAMES, b London, Ont, May 13, 17; nat US; m 46; c 2. TIDAL DYNAMICS, COASTAL FLOODING. *Educ:* Univ Calif, AB, 38. *Prof Exp:* Asst astron, Univ Mich, 40-42; instr physics & astron, Pasadena City Col, 46-48 & John Muir Col, 48-49; asst prof physics, Univ Md, 49-50; assoc physicist, Appl Physics Lab, Johns Hopkins Univ, 50-55; sci ed, Encycl Americana, 55-60; aeronaut & space res scientist & sci asst to dir off space flight progs, NASA, 60-61; prog dir foreign sci info, NSF, 61-62; phys scientist, Off Dir, US Coast & Geod Surv, 62-70; phys scientist, Nat Oceanic & Atmospheric Admin, 70-73, res assoc, Off Dir, Nat Ocean Surv, Rockville, Md, 73-77; GEOPHYS CONSULT TIDAL DYNAMICS, 78- *Res:* Environmental geoscience; wind-profile studies over navy ships at sea; perigean and proxigean spring tide analysis and potential for coastal flooding; gravitational-geophysical correlations; science education, history and film documentation. *Mailing Add:* 3103 Casa Bonita Dr Bonita CA 92002

WOOD, FORREST GLENN, b South Bend, Ind, Sept 13, 18; m 46, 79. MARINE ZOOLOGY. *Educ:* Earlham Col, AB, 40; Yale Univ, MS, 50. *Prof Exp:* Resident biologist, Lerner Marine Lab, BWI, 50-51; cur, Marine Studios & Res Lab, Marineland, Fla, 51-63; head marine biosci facil, Naval Missile Ctr, Calif, 63-70; sr scientist & consult, Ocean Sci Dept, 70, head marine biosci prog off, Under Sea Sci Dept, Naval Undersea Ctr, 72-77, STAFF SCIENTIST, BIOSCI DEPT, NAVAL OCEAN SYSTS CTR, 77- *Mem:* Soc Vert Paleontol; Am Soc Mammalogy; Sigma Xi; Soc Marine Mammalogy. *Res:* Behavior of marine mammals, sharks. *Mailing Add:* 2828 Upshur St 112 San Diego CA 92106

WOOD, FRANCIS ALOYSIUS, b Perryville, Mo, Nov 17, 32; m 54; c 7. RESEARCH ADMINISTRATION. *Educ:* Univ Mo, BS, 55, MS, 56; Univ Minn, PhD(plant path), 61. *Prof Exp:* Lab technician, US Forest Serv, Columbia, 55; teaching asst, Dept Bot, Univ Mo, 55-56; exp mycologist, US Am Chem Corp, 57-58; teaching asst, Dept Plant Path & Bot, Univ Minn, 58-59, res asst, 59-61; asst prof forest path, Dept Plant Path, Pa State Univ, 61-66, asst dir, Ctr Air Environ Studies, 65-67, assoc prof & res assoc, 67-70, prof, 70-72; prof & dept head, Dept Plant Path, Univ Minn, 72-77; PROF & DEAN RES, INST FOOD & AGR SCI, UNIV FLA, 77- *Concurrent Pos:* Consult, various orgn, 62-; vis prof, Dept Plant Path, Univ Calif, Berkeley, 68-69. *Mem:* Am Phytopath Soc. *Res:* Effects of photochemical air pollutants on woody species and forest ecosystems; impact of power plants on agricultural and forest ecosystems. *Mailing Add:* 3811 SW 82nd St Gainesville FL 32601

WOOD, FRANCIS C, JR, b Philadelphia, Pa, Oct 20, 28; m 58; c 2. INTERNAL MEDICINE, ENDOCRINOLOGY. *Educ:* Princeton Univ, AB, 50; Harvard Med Sch, MD, 54; Am Bd Internal Med, dipl, 63 & 74. *Prof Exp:* Intern, King County Hosp, Seattle, Wash, 54-55; resident, Vet Admin Hosp, 55-56; resident, Univ Wash Hosp, 60-61; from instr to asst prof, Sch Med, 61-68, asst prog dir, Clin Res Ctr, 62-64, prog dir, 64-70, assoc dean, 70-76, ASSOC PROF MED, SCH MED, UNIV WASH, 68-; DIR PHYSICIAN EDUC, PROVIDENCE MED CTR, SEATTLE, 76- *Concurrent Pos:* Res fel, Harvard Med Sch & Peter Bent Brigham Hosp, 58-60; chief of staff, Seattle Vet Admin Hosp, 70-76. *Mem:* Endocrine Soc; Am Diabetes Asn; fel Am Col Physicians. *Mailing Add:* Univ Wash Dept Med RG-20 Sch of Med Seattle WA 98195

WOOD, FRANCIS CLARK, b Wellington, SAfrica, Oct 1, 01; US citizen; m 26; c 3. MEDICINE. *Educ:* Princeton Univ, AB, 22; Univ Pa, MD, 26. *Hon Degrees:* DSc, Trinity Col, Dublin, 62, Princeton Univ, 64 & Univ Pa, 71. *Prof Exp:* Intern, Hosp, 26-28, from asst instr to prof med, Sch Med, 28-70, chmn dept, Hosp, 47-65, Frank Wistar Thomas prof med, Sch Med, 55, pres med bd, 61, EMER PROF MED, SCH MED, UNIV PA, 70- *Concurrent Pos:* Mem bd trustees, Assoc Univs, Inc, Brookhaven, 53-61; vis prof, Peter Bent Brigham Hosp, Boston, 55, Univ Ore, 57 & 63, Duke Univ, 58, Univ Ark, 64 & Northwestern Univ, Ill, 65; Hugh J Morgan vis prof, Vanderbilt Univ, 62. *Mem:* Am Clin & Climat Asn (pres, 56); master Am Col Physicians; Am Heart Asn; Am Soc Clin Invest; Asn Am Physicians (pres, 66). *Res:* Internal medicine; cardiovascular disease. *Mailing Add:* 216 Maloney Clin Bldg Hosp of Univ of Pa Philadelphia PA 19104

WOOD, FRANCIS EUGENE, b Kirksville, Mo, Sept 19, 32; m 55; c 4. ENTOMOLOGY. *Educ:* Univ Mo-Columbia, BS, 58, MS, 62; Univ Md, PhD(entom), 70. *Prof Exp:* Exten entomologist, Univ Mo-Columbia, 60-64, asst prof, 71-76, EXTEN ENTOMOLOGIST, UNIV MD, 64-, ASSOC PROF ENTOM, 76- *Mem:* Entom Soc Am. *Res:* Taxonomy of Coleoptera; household insects; youth entomology. *Mailing Add:* Dept of Entom Univ of Md College Park MD 20740

WOOD, FRANCIS PATRICK, b Seattle, Wash, June 18, 17. ELECTRICAL ENGINEERING. *Educ:* Gonzaga Univ, AB, 40; Alma Col, Calif, STL, 48; Stanford Univ, MS, 51. *Prof Exp:* Instr elec eng, Gonzaga Univ, 42-44; instr elec eng, High Sch, Wash, 50; from asst prof to assoc prof, 52-65, PROF ELEC ENG, SEATTLE UNIV, 65-, HEAD DEPT, 59- *Mem:* Am Soc Eng Educ; Inst Elec & Electronics Engrs. *Res:* Power system analysis; stability; control systems. *Mailing Add:* Dept Elec Eng Seattle Univ Seattle WA 98122

WOOD, FRANK BRADSHAW, b Jackson, Tenn, Dec 21, 15; m 45; c 4. ASTRONOMY. *Educ:* Univ Fla, BS, 36; Princeton Univ, MA, 40, PhD(astron), 41. *Prof Exp:* Res assoc, Princeton Univ, 46; Nat Res Coun fel, Steward Observ, Univ Ariz & Lick Observ, Univ Calif, 46-47; asst prof astron & asst astronr, Univ Ariz, 47-50; from assoc prof to prof astron, Univ Pa, 50-54, Flower prof & chmn dept, 54-68; assoc chmn dept, 71-76, PROF ASTRON & DIR OPTICAL ASTRON OBSERV, UNIV FLA, 68- *Concurrent Pos:* Mem comts, Int Astron Union, 38 & 42, mem orgn comt & chmn comt int progs, 42, pres comt, 42, 68-71; Fulbright fel, Mt Stromlo Observ, Australian Nat Univ, 57-58; exec dir, Flower & Cook Observ, Univ Pa, 50-54, dir, 54-68; NATO sr fel sci, 73; Am Astron Soc vis lectr astron, 73-; Fulbright fel, Inst Astron & Space Physics, Buenos Aires, Argentina, 77. *Mem:* Can Astron Soc; Am Astron Soc; Royal Astron Soc; hon mem Royal Astron Soc NZ. *Res:* Photoelectric photometry eclipsing binary stars; analysis of spectrophotometric data in the far ultraviolet as taken from the Copernicus satellite; emphasis on close double stars. *Mailing Add:* Dept Astron SSRB Univ Fla Gainesville FL 32611

WOOD, FREDERICK STARR, b Redding, Conn, Nov 21, 21; m 47. CHEMICAL ENGINEERING. *Educ:* Univ Va, BChE, 43. *Prof Exp:* Sect leader, Res Dept, Am Oil Co, 44-64, sr opers analyst, 64-72, sr opers analyst, Standard Oil Co, Ind, 72-77, sr oper researcher, 77-80; CONSULT STATIST, 80- *Mem:* Soc Automotive Engrs; Am Inst Chem Engrs; Am Statist Asn. *Res:* Fuels and lubrication process and development; design and analysis of experiments with computers. *Mailing Add:* Opers Res Standard Oil Co of Ind Rm 0901 200 E Randolph Chicago IL 60601

WOOD, GALEN THEODORE, b Philadelphia, Pa, Feb 7, 29; m 55; c 3. NUCLEAR PHYSICS. *Educ:* Washington Univ, BS, 51, PhD(physics), 56. *Prof Exp:* Physicist, Argonne Cancer Res Hosp, Univ Chicago, 55-57; NSF res fel nuclear spectros, Inst Theoret Physics, Univ Copenhagen, 57-59; asst prof physics & res nuclear spectros, Univ Pa, 59-65, NSF res grant radioactive nuclei, 63-65; assoc physicist, Argonne Nat Lab, 65-69; ASSOC PROF PHYSICS, CLEVELAND STATE UNIV, 69- *Mem:* Am Phys Soc. *Res:* Nuclear spectroscopy of radiations from radioactive decay and nuclear reactions, decay scheme, gamma-gamma directional and polarization correlations, magnetic moments, lifetimes and nuclear magnetic hyperfine fields; electron accelerator developments; nuclear spectroscopy. *Mailing Add:* Dept of Physics Cleveland State Univ Cleveland OH 44115

WOOD, GARNETT ELMER, b Gloucester, Va, Feb 14, 29; m 53; c 2. BIOCHEMISTRY. *Educ:* Va State Col, BS, 51, MS, 56; Georgetown Univ, PhD(chem), 66. *Prof Exp:* Res microbiologist, Div Vet Med, Walter Reed Army Med Ctr, 56-64; RES CHEMIST, DIV CHEM & PHYSICS, FOOD & DRUG ADMIN, 65- *Concurrent Pos:* Lectr chem, Univ DC, 73- *Mem:* AAAS; NY Acad Sci; Sigma Xi; Am Chem Soc; Am Oil Chemists Soc. *Res:* Chemistry of toxic and deleterious compounds that may arise in certain foods as a result of handling, storage and/or processing. *Mailing Add:* 1717 Verbena St NW Washington DC 20012

WOOD, GARY WARREN, b Rochester, NY, Sept 9, 41. IMMUNOLOGY. *Educ:* Kalamazoo Col, BA, 63; Univ Mich, MS, 65; State Univ NY Buffalo, PhD(microbiol), 71. *Prof Exp:* Fel immunol, 71-73, instr path, 73-74, asst prof, 74-79, ASSOC PROF PATH, UNIV KANS MED CTR, 79-, DIR, DIAG IMMUNOL LAB, 73- *Mem:* Am Asn Immunologists; Sigma Xi; Reticuloendothelial Soc. *Res:* Immunobiology of the maternal/fetal interrelationship; in situ immune response to tumors. *Mailing Add:* Dept Path Univ Kans Med Ctr 39th & Rainbow Blvd Kansas City KS 66103

WOOD, GENE WAYNE, b Bedford, Va, Oct 23, 40; m 65; c 2. WILDLIFE ECOLOGY. *Educ:* Va Polytech Inst & State Univ, BS, 63; Pa State Univ, MS, 66, PhD(agron), 71. *Prof Exp:* Instr wildlife mgt, Pa State Univ, University Park, 67-71, asst prof wildlife ecol, 71-74; from asst prof forestry to assoc prof, 74-81, PROF FORESTRY, BELLE W BARUCH RES INST, CLEMSON UNIV, 81- *Mem:* Ecol Soc Am; Wildlife Soc; Soc Am Foresters. *Res:* Effects of silvicultural practices on animal population and habitat; nutrient distribution in forest ecosystems. *Mailing Add:* Belle W Baruch Res Inst Clemson Univ Box 596 Georgetown SC 29440

WOOD, GEORGE MARSHALL, b Fairfield, Conn, Jan 20, 33; m 52; c 3. ENGINEERING SCIENCE, PHYSICS. *Educ:* Univ Ga, BS, 59; Rensselaer Polytech Inst, MS, 68, PhD(eng sci), 74. *Prof Exp:* RES SCIENTIST INSTRUMENTATION, NASA/LANGLEY RES CTR, 59- *Concurrent Pos:* Adj assoc prof nuclear eng, Rensselaer Polytech Inst, 75- *Mem:* Am Soc Mass Spectrometry; Am Chem Soc. *Res:* Mass spectrometry; analytical instrumentation; boundary layer analysis; ionization processes and charged particle behavior; surface chemistry; ion physics; metal oxide catalysis; gas-gas interactons; data enhancement through deconvolution methods. *Mailing Add:* Instrument Res Div NASA/Langley Res Ctr Hampton VA 23665

WOOD, GERRY ODELL, b Oklahoma City, Okla, Nov 19, 43; m 65. INDUSTRIAL HYGIENE, CHEMISTRY. *Educ:* Univ Okla, BSCh, 65; Univ Tex, Austin, PhD(phys chem), 69; Am Bd Indust Hyg, cert, 76. *Prof Exp:* Res asst phys chem, Kerr-McGee Res Ctr, Okla, 65; fel, 69-71, STAFF MEM CHEM, LOS ALAMOS NAT LAB, 72- *Mem:* Am Indust Hyg Asn; Am Chem Soc. *Res:* Air sampling techniques; analytical methods development; chemical kinetics; photochemistry; vapor adsorption in sorbent beds; dynamics of gas phase reactions. *Mailing Add:* Indust Hyg Group Los Alamos Nat Lab MS 486 Los Alamos NM 87545

WOOD, GLEN MEREDITH, b Dallas, Tex, Apr 17, 20; m 50; c 7. AGRONOMY. *Educ:* RI State Col, BS, 47; Rutgers Univ, MS, 48, PhD(agr), 50. *Prof Exp:* Asst, Rutgers Univ, 47-50; actg chmn dept agron, 53-55, assoc prof & assoc agronomist, 50-78, PROF AGRON & AGRONOMIST, UNIV VT, 78- *Concurrent Pos:* Golf Course Supts Asn Am res grants, 67, 68 & 71-74; assoc prof & assoc agronomist, Wash State Univ, 69-70; tech adv, Vol Tech Asst, 76-; vis prof, Cornell Univ, 80. *Mem:* Am Soc Agron; Crop Sci Soc Am; Int Turfgrass Soc; Am Forage & Grassland Coun. *Res:* Cold hardiness in ladino clover; physiological and environmental studies with birdsfoot trefoil, perennial ryegrass and other forage crops; forage utilization by poultry; turfgrass management; shade and drouth studies with turfgrasses; application of infrared photography to turfgrass research; cold hardiness studies with forage and turfgrasses; marginal land pasture renovation studies using sheep and goats. *Mailing Add:* Dept Plant & Soil Sci Univ Vt Burlington VT 05405

WOOD, GORDON HARVEY, b Trail, BC, Jan 30, 40; m 64; c 2. SCIENTIFIC NUMERIC DATABASES, PHYSICS. *Educ:* Univ BC, BASc, 63, MASc, 65, PhD(physics), 69. *Prof Exp:* res officer, 69-79, RES COUN OFFICER, NAT RES COUN CAN, 80- *Mem:* Can Asn Physicists; Chem Inst Can. *Mailing Add:* Nat Res Coun Montreal Rd Ottawa ON K1A 0S1 Can

WOOD, GORDON WALTER, b NS, Can, Apr 6, 33; m 56; c 2. ORGANIC CHEMISTRY, MASS SPECTROMETRY. *Educ:* Mt Allison Univ, BSc, 55, MSc, 56; Syracuse Univ, PhD(org chem), 62. *Prof Exp:* Elem sch teacher, NS, 51-52; chemist, Paints Div, Can Industs Ltd, 56-58; fel with A C Cope, Mass Inst Technol, 62-63; from asst prof to assoc prof, 63-75, PROF CHEM, UNIV WINDSOR, 75- *Concurrent Pos:* Vis assoc res scientist, Space Sci Lab, Univ Calif, Berkeley, 69-70; sr researcher, Dept Med Biochem, Fac Med, Univ Dijon, 76-77; assoc dean, Fac Grad Studies & Res, Univ Windsor, 79- *Mem:* Am Chem Soc; Royal Soc Chem; Am Soc Mass Spectrometry; fel Chem Inst Can. *Res:* Applications of field ionization and field desorption mass spectrometry to problems in organic and biochemistry; applications of gas chromatography/mass spectrometry to analysis, particularly of organic pollutants in the Great Lakes. *Mailing Add:* Dept Chem Univ Windsor Windsor ON N9B 3P4 Can

WOOD, HARLAND G, b Delavan, Minn, Sept 2, 07; m 29; c 3. BIOCHEMISTRY, MICROBIOLOGY. *Educ:* Macalester Col, BA, 31; Iowa State Col, PhD, 35. *Hon Degrees:* ScD, Macalester Col, 46 & Northwestern Univ, 72. *Prof Exp:* From instr to asst prof bact, Iowa State Col, 36-43; assoc prof physiol chem, Univ Minn, 43-46; prof biochem & dir, 46-65, dean sci, 67-69, univ prof, 70-78, PROF BIOCHEM, CASE WESTERN RESERVE UNIV, 65-, EMER UNIV PROF, 79- *Concurrent Pos:* Nat Res Coun fel, Univ Wis-Madison, 35-36; Fulbright fel, Univ Dunedin, 55; Commonwealth fel, Max Planck Inst, Munich, Ger, 62; mem adv coun, Life Ins Med Res Fund, 57-62; mem, NIH Training Grant Comt, 65-69; mem adv bd, Am Cancer Soc, 65-69; mem, President's Adv Comt, 67-71; mem coun, Int Union of Biochem, 67-76, secy gen, 70-73; NIH sr res fel, Univ Ga, 69; mem phys study sect, NIH, 73-77; Fulbright sr scholar, Australia, 76; assoc ed, Biochemistry, 76-78. *Honors & Awards:* Eli Lilly Award in Bact, 42; Carl Neuberg Medal, 52; Bayerischen Akademie, Ger, 63; Modern Med Award for Distinguished Achievement, 68; Lynen Lectr & Medal, 72; Sr US Scientist Award, Humboldt Found, Munich, Ger, 79. *Mem:* Nat Acad Sci; Am Acad Arts & Sci; Am Soc Biol Chemists (pres, 59); Am Chem Soc; Soc Am Microbiol. *Res:* Tracer studies with labeled compounds; structure of enzymes; mechanism of enzyme action; role of biotin, B-12 and metals. *Mailing Add:* Dept Biochem Case Western Reserve Univ Cleveland OH 44106

WOOD, HAROLD SINCLAIR, b Washington, DC, Aug 4, 22. CHEMICAL ENGINEERING. *Educ:* Cornell Univ, BChE, 44. *Prof Exp:* Asst, Geol Lab, Univ Kans, 41; phys chemist, Univ Okla, 42; chem engr, Standard Oil Co, Ind, 44-50; head supvr eng lab, Res & Develop Dept, Mid-Continent Petrol Corp, 50-55; owner, Remwood Chem Co, Okla, 55-58; process engr, Refining &

Chem Div, Bechtel Corp, Calif, 58-61; head process design gas plant construct, 61-77, CHIEF ENGR, MALONEY-CRAWFORD TANK CORP, 77- *Mem:* Am Chem Soc; Am Inst Chem Engrs. *Res:* Commercial desalting unit employing fiberglass as contacting agent; petroleum, natural gas and their products. *Mailing Add:* 217 E 24th St Tulsa OK 74114

WOOD, HARRY ALAN, b Albany, NY, Apr 24, 41; div; c 2. PLANT VIROLOGY. *Educ:* Middlebury Col, AB, 63; Purdue Univ, MS, 65, PhD(plant virol), 68. *Prof Exp:* RES SCIENTIST, BOYCE THOMPSON INST PLANT RES, 68- *Mem:* Am Phytopath Soc; Am Soc Microbiol. *Res:* Physical and biological properties of insect and plant viruses with special interest in insect virus genetics. *Mailing Add:* Boyce Thompson Inst Plant Res Cornell Univ-Tower Rd Ithaca NY 14850

WOOD, HARRY BURGESS, JR, b Washington, DC, July 30, 19; m 46; c 1. ORGANIC CHEMISTRY. *Educ:* Washington & Lee Univ, AB, 42; Ohio State Univ, MS, 47, PhD(chem), 50. *Prof Exp:* Supvr prod control, Res & Develop, Merck & Co, Inc, 42-45; res assoc & spec asst carbohydrate chem & micro org anal, Ohio State Univ, 47-48, asst gen chem, 48-49 & org chem, 49-50; res chemist chem natural prod, Nat Heart Inst, 50-53 & carbohydrate chem, Nat Inst Arthritis & Metab Dis, 53-61, chief drug develop br, 61-78, CHIEF OFF EXTRAMURAL RES & RESOURCES, DCT, NAT CANCER INST, NIH, 78- *Mem:* AAAS; Am Chem Soc; Am Soc Hort Sci; Royal Soc Chem; Fr Soc Therapeut Chem. *Res:* Carbohydrate and medicinal chemistry; synthetic and structural chemistry of natural products; degradation and structure determinations; cancer chemotherapy. *Mailing Add:* 9125 Sevenlocks Rd Bethesda MD 20014

WOOD, HENDERSON KINGSBERRY, b Huntington, WVa, Feb 24, 13; m 38; c 1. GENETICS, PHYSIOLOGY. *Educ:* Ohio Wesleyan Univ, BA, 37; Fisk Univ, MA, 40; Ind Univ, PhD(zool), 53. *Prof Exp:* Instr biol, Ala State Teachers Col, 40-44; from instr to asst prof, Fisk Univ, 44-48; prof biol, Tenn State Univ, 48-80, head, Dept Biol Sci, 56-80. *Concurrent Pos:* Grad consult, Tenn State Univ, 52-62. *Mem:* Am Genetic Asn; Nat Inst Sci. *Res:* Protozoan genetics; physiology of Protozoa. *Mailing Add:* 3949 Drakes Branch Rd Nashville TN 37218

WOOD, HENRY NELSON, b Passaic, NJ, June 24, 25; m 51; c 3. BIOCHEMISTRY. *Educ:* Wagner Col, BS, 49; NC State Col, MS, 51; Purdue Univ, PhD(biochem), 55. *Prof Exp:* Res assoc, 55-62, asst prof, 62-67, ASSOC PROF PLANT BIOL, ROCKEFELLER UNIV, 67- *Mem:* Harvey Soc; Am Soc Biol Chemists. *Res:* Biochemistry and physiology of growth processes. *Mailing Add:* Rockefeller Univ 66th St & York Ave New York NY 10021

WOOD, HOUSTON GILLEYLEN, III, b Tupelo, Miss, Oct 4, 44; m 65; c 2. APPLIED MATHEMATICS, FLUID DYNAMICS. *Educ:* Miss State Univ, BA, 65, MS, 67; Univ Va, PhD(appl math), 78. *Prof Exp:* Engr isotope separation theory, Oak Ridge Gaseous Diffusion Plant, Union Carbide Corp, 67-73; res engr gas centrifuge theory res lab eng sci, Univ Va, 73-77; ENGR GAS CENTRIFUGE THEORY & FLUID DYNAMICS, OAK RIDGE GASEOUS DIFFUSION PLANT, NUCLEAR DIV, UNION CARBIDE CORP, 77- *Mem:* Soc Indust & Appl Math; Math Asn Am. *Res:* Rotating flows; singular integral equations and partial differential equations. *Mailing Add:* Nuclear Div PO Box P Oak Ridge TN 37830

WOOD, HOWARD JOHN, b Baltimore, Md, July 19, 38; m 61, 77; c 3. ASTRONOMY. *Educ:* Swarthmore Col, BA, 60; Ind Univ, MA, 62, PhD(astron), 65. *Prof Exp:* Res asst, Sproul Observ, 57-59, Goethe Link Observ, 58-62 & Lowell Observ, 62-63; from instr to assoc prof astron, Univ Va, 64-70; staff astronr, Europ Southern Observ, Santiago, Chile, 70-75; Fulbright vis prof, Univ Observ, Vienna, 75-77; vis asst prof dept astron, Ind Univ, Bloomington, 78-81; ASST TO DIR, CERRO TOLOLO, INTERAM OBSERV, LA SERENA, CHILE, 82- *Concurrent Pos:* Guest investr, McDonald Observ, 59-60, Lowell Observ, 62-65 & Kitt Peak Nat Observ, 63-69; NSF grants, 66-70, 79-82; guest prof, Univ Observ Vienna, 80-81. *Mem:* Am Astron Soc; fel Royal Astron Soc; Sigma Xi. *Res:* Photoelectric and spectrophotometric studies of the Balmer lines in the spectra of the magnetic and related stars; Zeeman spectroscopy of magnetic stars; photometric studies of asteroids; photography of Mars. *Mailing Add:* 17 River Hill Rd Louisville KY 40207

WOOD, IRWIN BOYDEN, b Concord, NH, Apr 27, 26; m; c 3. PARASITOLOGY. *Educ:* Univ NH, BS, 49, MS, 51; Kans State Univ, PhD(parasitol), 58. *Prof Exp:* Asst zoologist, Univ NH, 50; chemist, 52-54, parasitologist, 54-56, res parasitologist & group leader, Agr Div, 58-64, mgr animal res & develop, Cyanamid Int, 64-74, DIR ANIMAL PROD RES & DEVELOP, CYANAMID INT, AM CYANAMID CO, WAYNE, 74-, PRIN SCIENTIST, PARASITIC CHEMOTHERAPHY & IMMUNOL AGR RES DIV, PRINCETON, 77- *Mem:* Am Soc Parasitologists; World Asn Advan Vet Parasitologists. *Res:* Chemotherapy and physiology of helminths; host-parasite relations; bacterial chemotherapy; acaricides; animal health and feed product development. *Mailing Add:* Am Cyanamid Co 859 Budan Ave Wayne NJ 07470

WOOD, J(UDSON) A(RTHUR), b Utica, NY, Aug 28, 28; m 49; c 5. CHEMICAL ENGINEERING. *Educ:* Syracuse Univ, BChE, 49, MChE, 51. *Prof Exp:* Jr engr, Mathieson Chem Corp, 50-54, pilot plant supvr, Olin Corp, 54-60, sr engr, 60-63, proj mgr, 64-65, sect mgr process develop, Chem Group, 65-71, tech dir, 71-73, mgr res & develop, Chem Group, Charleston Technol Ctr, 74-82, MGR TECHNOL SERV, PROCESS TECHNOL, SE, CHEM GROUP, OLIN CORP, 82- *Mem:* Am Inst Chem Engrs. *Res:* Heavy inorganics; urethane chemicals; fertilizers; polyvinyl chloride. *Mailing Add:* Olin Corp PO Box 248 Charleston TN 37310

WOOD, JACK SHEEHAN, b St Albans, Vt, Oct 31, 31; m 58; c 2. ENVIRONMENTAL PHYSIOLOGY. *Educ:* Univ Maine, Orono, BS, 54; Mich State Univ, MA, 60, PhD(ecol, animal physiol), 63. *Prof Exp:* From asst prof to assoc prof, 63-75, PROF BIOMED SCI, WESTERN MICH UNIV, 75-, DIR PUB SERV, 81- *Concurrent Pos:* Water qual dir, Mich SCent Planning & Develop Region, 75- *Mem:* AAAS; Wildlife Soc; Am Inst Biol Sci; Soc Exp Biol & Med. *Res:* Physiological response to adverse environmental conditions, including general systematic stress responses, reproductive inhibition and related phenomena in vertebrates; water quality management. *Mailing Add:* Dept of Biomed Sci Western Mich Univ Kalamazoo MI 49001

WOOD, JACKIE DALE, b Picher, Okla, Feb 16, 37; m 56; c 2. PHYSIOLOGY, ZOOLOGY. *Educ:* Kans State Col Pittsburg, BS, 64, MS, 66; Univ Ill, PhD(physiol), 69. *Prof Exp:* Asst prof biol, Williams Col, 69-71; from asst prof physiol to assoc prof, Univ Kans Med Ctr, Kansas City, 71-78, prof, 78-79; PROF & CHMN, PHYSIOL DEPT, SCH MED, UNIV NEV, RENO, 79- *Mem:* AAAS; Am Gastroenterol Asn; Am Soc Zool; Soc Neurosci; Am Physiol Soc. *Res:* Gastrointestinal neurobiology. *Mailing Add:* Dept of Physiol Sch Med Univ Nev Reno NV 89557

WOOD, JAMES ALAN, b Richmond, Va, Sept 16, 39; m 65; c 1. MATHEMATICAL ANALYSIS. *Educ:* Georgetown Univ, BS, 61; Univ Va, MA, 63, PhD(math), 66. *Prof Exp:* From instr to asst prof math, Georgetown Univ, 65-69; asst prof, 69-72, ASSOC PROF MATH, VA COMMONWEALTH UNIV, 72- *Concurrent Pos:* NSF res grant, 68-70 & NSF-Nat Inst Educ grant, 80-82. *Mem:* Am Math Soc. *Res:* Operational calculus and dynamical systems; multiplier theory. *Mailing Add:* 10250 Gwynnbrook Rd Richmond VA 23235

WOOD, JAMES ALEXANDER, b Melfort, Sask, Sept 20, 16; m; c 2. PHARMACY. *Educ:* Univ Sask, BSP, 46; Univ Wash, Seattle, MS, 52, PhD, 58. *Prof Exp:* From instr to assoc prof, 46-63, PROF PHARM, UNIV SASK, 63- *Mem:* Can Pharmaceut Asn; Asn Fac Pharm Can. *Res:* Surface free energy values as parameters in the prediction of adhesive bond strengths developed by tablet film coatings; diffusion of medicaments in and from dermatologic preparations. *Mailing Add:* Col of Pharm Univ of Sask Saskatoon SK S7N 0W0 Can

WOOD, JAMES BRENT, III, b Oct 25, 42; US citizen; m 69; c 1. ORGANIC CHEMISTRY, GENERAL CHEMISTRY. *Educ:* Univ Denver, BS, 65; Univ Ariz, MS, 70, PhD(chem), 71. *Prof Exp:* Asst prof chem, Mobile Col, 71-73; ASSOC PROF CHEM & HEAD DEPT, PALM BEACH ATLANTIC COL, 73-, CHMN, DIV NATURAL SCI & MATH, 76- *Concurrent Pos:* Instr physics, Palm Beach Jr Col, 74- *Mem:* Am Chem Soc. *Res:* Chemical education. *Mailing Add:* Palm Beach Atlantic Col 1101 S Olive Ave West Palm Beach FL 33401

WOOD, JAMES C, JR, b Spartanburg, SC, Aug 21, 39; m 64; c 2. SOLID STATE PHYSICS. *Educ:* Clemson Univ, BS, 61, MS, 63; Univ Va, PhD(physics), 66. *Prof Exp:* Res physicist, Cent Res Div, Am Cyanamid Co, Conn, 66-71; sr res scientist, TRW Eastern Res Lab, 71-73; HEAD DEPT SCI TEACHING PHYSICS & PHYS SCI, TRI-COUNTY TECH COL, 73-, ACTG HEAD NUCLEAR ENG DEPT, 78- *Mem:* Am Phys Soc; Am Asn Physics Teachers; Sigma Xi. *Mailing Add:* Tri-County Tech Col Pendleton SC 29670

WOOD, JAMES DOUGLAS, b Aberdeen, Scotland, Jan 25, 30; m 56; c 3. NEUROCHEMISTRY. *Educ:* Aberdeen Univ, BSc, 51, PhD(biochem), 54. *Prof Exp:* Res officer, Can Dept Agr, 54-57; assoc scientist, Fisheries Res Bd, Can, 57-61; head biochem group, Defence Res Med Labs, Can, 61-63, head physiol chem sect, 63-68; PROF BIOCHEM & HEAD DEPT, UNIV SASK, 68- *Concurrent Pos:* Mem, Med Res Coun, Can, 76-82. *Mem:* Am Soc Neurochem; Int Soc Neurochem; Can Biochem Soc. *Res:* Gamma-aminobutyric acid metabolism; oxygen toxicity. *Mailing Add:* Dept Biochem Univ Sask Saskatoon SK S7N 0W0 Can

WOOD, JAMES EDWIN, III, medicine, see previous edition

WOOD, JAMES KENNETH, b Boulder, Colo, Jan 29, 42; m 66; c 2. SYNTHETIC ORGANIC CHEMISTRY. *Educ:* Colo State Univ, BS, 64; Kans State Col, MS, 65; Ohio State Univ, PhD(chem), 69. *Prof Exp:* Asst prof, 69-74, ASSOC PROF CHEM, UNIV NEBR AT OMAHA, 74- *Mem:* Am Chem Soc. *Res:* Synthesis of novel and biologically active compounds; development of new synthetic techniques and methods; development of new methods for the resolution of racemates. *Mailing Add:* Dept of Chem Univ of Nebr at Omaha Omaha NE 68182

WOOD, JAMES LEE, b Cordele, Ga, Sept 5, 40; m 60; c 4. INORGANIC CHEMISTRY, THERMOCHEMISTRY. *Educ:* Vanderbilt Univ, BA, 62, PhD(inorg chem), 66. *Prof Exp:* Res fel chem, Rice Univ, 65-66; asst prof, 66-69, ASSOC PROF CHEM, DAVID LIPSCOMB COL, 69- *Concurrent Pos:* Sr fel, Rice Univ, 71-73; Indust Res 100 Award, Indust Res Mag; actg dir, Hazardous Mat Training Inst, State Tenn, 78-, consult hazardous mat, Off Civil Defense. *Mem:* Am Chem Soc. *Res:* Thermodynamics and reaction calorimetry; fluorine chemistry; coordination compounds. *Mailing Add:* Dept of Chem David Lipscomb Col Nashville TN 37203

WOOD, JAMES MANLEY, JR, b Birmingham, Ala, July 5, 27; m 53; c 3. PHYSICAL CHEMISTRY. *Educ:* Howard Col, BA, 47; Univ Wis, PhD, 52. *Prof Exp:* Res chemist, La, 52-69, RES ASSOC, ETHYL CORP, 69- *Mem:* Am Chem Soc. *Res:* Molecular spectra; electrochemistry of fused salts; high energy batteries; decomposition of organometallic compounds, vapor plating; zeolite chemistry; high temperature chemistry. *Mailing Add:* Ethyl Corp PO Box 341 Baton Rouge LA 70821

WOOD, JAMES W, b Seattle, Wash, Jan 22, 25; m 53; c 2. BIOLOGY. *Educ:* Univ Wash, BS, 50, MS, 58. *Prof Exp:* Aquatic biologist, Fish Comn Ore, 50-55, fish pathologist, 55-60; fish pathologist, 60-70, supvr fish cult res, 70-77, FISH QUAL CONTROL SUPVR, WASH STATE DEPT FISHERIES, 77- *Concurrent Pos:* Consult, Int Pac Salmon Fisheries Comn, 64-65, Can Dept Fisheries, 66 & Repub of Chile Dept Fisheries, 70-71. *Mem:* Am Fisheries Soc; Am Inst Fishery Res Biol; Wildlife Dis Asn. *Res:* Infectious and nutritional diseases of salmonid fishes. *Mailing Add:* Wash State Dept of Fisheries Univ of Wash Seattle WA 98195

WOOD, JEANIE McMILLIN, see McMillin-Wood, Jeanie

WOOD, JOE GEORGE, b Victoria, Tex, Dec 8, 28; c 1. ANATOMY. *Educ:* Univ Houston, BS, 53, MS, 58; Univ Tex, Galveston, PhD(anat), 62. *Prof Exp:* Asst biol, Univ Houston, 56-58; instr anat, Dent Br, Univ Tex, 61 & Sch Med, Yale Univ, 62-63; asst prof, Sch Med, Univ Ark, 63-66; assoc prof, Univ Tex Med Sch, San Antonio, 66-70, asst dean acad develop, 67-69; dir prog neurostruct & function, 70-75, PROF NEUROBIOL & ANAT & CHMN DEPT, UNIV TEX MED SCH, HOUSTON, 70- *Concurrent Pos:* USPHS trainee, Univ Tex, Galveston & Sch Med, Yale Univ, 62-63; mem neuroanat vis scientist prog, USPHS, 65-66; consult to vchancellor health affairs, Univ Tex, 68-70. *Mem:* Am Asn Anat; Soc Exp Biol & Med; Electron Micros Soc Am; Soc Neurosci; Histochem Soc. *Res:* Histochemistry and cytochemistry of neurons; histochemical and electron microscopic localization of biogenic amines and their relation to nerve function in animals under stress and drug administration. *Mailing Add:* Dept Neurobiol & Anat Univ Tex Med Sch PO Box 20708 Houston TX 77030

WOOD, JOHN ARMSTEAD, JR, b Roanoke, Va, July 28, 32; c 2. GEOCHEMISTRY. *Educ:* Va Polytech Inst, BS, 54; Mass Inst Technol, PhD(geol), 58. *Prof Exp:* Geologist, Smithsonian Astrophys Observ, 59; Am Chem Soc-Petrol Res Fund fel, Cambridge Univ, 59-60; geologist, Smithsonian Astrophys Observ, 60-62; res assoc, Enrico Fermi Inst Nuclear Studies, Univ Chicago, 62-65; GEOLOGIST, SMITHSONIAN ASTROPHYS OBSERV, 65-, ASSOC DIR, HARVARD-SMITHSONIAN CTR ASTROPHYSICS, 81- *Concurrent Pos:* Res assoc, Harvard Col Observ, 60-; vchmn, Lunar Sample Anal Planning Team, 71-73; prof in pract geol, Dept Geol Sci, Harvard Univ, 76- *Honors & Awards:* NASA Medal for Exceptional Sci Achievement, 73; J Lawrence Smith Award, Nat Acad Sci, 76; Frederick C Leonard Award, Meteoritical Soc, 78. *Mem:* Fel AAAS; fel Am Geophys Union; Meteoritical Soc (pres, 70-72); Am Astron Soc; Int Astron Union. *Res:* Study of meteorites as samples of primordial planetary material; lunar petrology and geophysics; origin of the planets. *Mailing Add:* Smithsonian Astrophys Observ 60 Garden St Cambridge MA 02138

WOOD, JOHN D(UDLEY), b Brooklyn, NY, Dec 5, 30; m 56, 81; c 6. PHYSICAL METALLURGY, MATERIALS SELECTION. *Educ:* Case Inst Technol, BS, 53; Lehigh Univ, MS, 59, PhD(metall eng), 62. *Prof Exp:* Student engr, Long Lines Dept, Am Tel & Tel Co, 53-54; prod metallurgist, Kaiser Aluminum & Chem Corp, 56-58; instr phys metall, Lehigh Univ, 60-61; res metallurgist, Alcoa Res Labs, Aluminum Co Am, 61-62; asst prof metall eng, 62-65, assoc prof metall, 65-78, PROF METALL, LEHIGH UNIV, 78- *Concurrent Pos:* Consult, Aluminum Div, Howmet Corp, 65-; mat engr, Allied Chem Corp, 76-77; course dir & lectr, Ctr Prof Adv, 78- *Mem:* Am Inst Mining, Metall & Petrol Engrs; Am Soc Metals; Am Soc Testing & Mat; Brit Inst Metals. *Res:* Physical metallurgy of aluminum alloys; corrosion and stress corrosion; selection of materials; failure analysis; non-destructive evaluation. *Mailing Add:* Dept of Metall & Mat Eng Lehigh Univ Bethlehem PA 18015

WOOD, JOHN EDWARD, III, b Lynchburg, Va, May 20, 16; m 46. ORGANIC CHEMISTRY. *Educ:* Lynchburg Col, AB, 36; Mass Inst Technol, PhD(org chem), 39. *Prof Exp:* Res chemist, Standard Oil Develop Co, 39-41; plant technol supvr, Standard Oil Co La, 41-42, asst supvr synthetic alcohol plants, 42-45; gen foreman synthetic alcohol & olefin extraction plants, Esso Standard Oil Co, 45-49, head process eng, 50-52, asst head tech div, 52-53, head petrol prod div, 54, head chem prod div, 54-55, asst gen mgr, Chem Prod Dept, 55-56, gen mgr, 56-58; pres, Enjay Co, Inc, 58-60 & Enjay Chem Co Div, Humble Oil & Refining Co, 60-65; pres, Chem Div, 65-69, exec vpres chem & metallics, 65-72, vpres oil & gas, 72-81, CONSULT, VULCAN MAT COL, 81- *Mem:* Am Chem Soc; Am Inst Chem Engrs; Soc Chem Indust; Am Inst Chemists. *Res:* Friedel-Crafts reaction. *Mailing Add:* Vulcan Mat Co PO Box 7497 Birmingham AL 35223

WOOD, JOHN GRADY, b Atlanta, Ga, Aug 1, 42. NEUROBIOLOGY. *Educ:* Ga State Univ, BS, 67; Emory Univ, PhD(anat), 71. *Prof Exp:* Fel neurobiol, Inst Animal Physiol, Cambridge, Eng, 71-73 & City of Hope Med Ctr, Duarte, Calif, 73-74; asst prof anat, 74-76, assoc prof, 76-80, ADJ ASSOC PROF ANAT, CTR HEALTH SCI, UNIV TENN, 80- *Concurrent Pos:* Fel, Nat Multiple Sclerosis Soc, 71-72 & Multiple Sclerosis Soc Gt Brit & Northern Ireland, 72-73; independent res fel neurobiol, Friday Harbor Marine Labs, Friday Harbor, Wash, 74; Alfred P Sloan Found res fel, 76. *Mem:* Am Asn Anat; Soc Neurosci; Am Soc Cell Biol; Am Soc Neurochem; Am Soc Zoologists. *Res:* The fine structural immunocytochemical localization of carbohydrates and membrane antigens in the nervous system; the role of glycoproteins in myelin structure and function; properties of reaggregating sponge cells and nerve cells; the localization of proteins involved in neurotransmission. *Mailing Add:* Dept of Anat Ctr Health Sci Univ of Tenn Memphis TN 38163

WOOD, JOHN HENRY, b Calgary, Alta, Nov 18, 24; nat US; m 50; c 2. PHARMACEUTICS. *Educ:* Univ Man, BSc, 46, MSc, 47; Ohio State Univ, PhD(phys chem), 50. *Prof Exp:* Proj chemist, Colgate-Palmolive Co, 50-53; sr res assoc chem, Rensselaer Polytech Inst, 53-54; proj chemist, Colgate-Palmolive Co, 54-56, group leader, 56-57; head phys chem sect, Prod Div, Bristol-Myers Co, NJ, 57-61, head phys chem dept, 61-65, asst dir res & develop labs, 65-67, dir chem res, 67-69; PROF PHARM, MED COL VA, VA COMMONWEALTH UNIV, 69- *Concurrent Pos:* Mem comt rev, US Pharmacopoeia, 70-75. *Mem:* Am Chem Soc; Soc Rheol; fel Soc Cosmetic Chemists; Am Pharmaceut Asn; fel Acad Pharmaceut Sci. *Res:* Drug micellar phenomena; rheology; physical pharmacy; biopharmaceutics and pharmacokinetics; pharmacogenetics; saturation and competitive metabolism. *Mailing Add:* 1504 Cedarbluff Dr Richmond VA 23233

WOOD, JOHN HERBERT, b Michigan City, Ind, Oct 12, 29; m 59; c 3. SOLID STATE PHYSICS. *Educ:* Purdue Univ, BS, 51; Mass Inst Technol, PhD(solid state physics), 58. *Prof Exp:* Res assoc solid state physics, Mass Inst Technol, 58-62, asst prof, 62-66, dir coop comput lab, 64-65; consult, 65-66, STAFF MEM, LOS ALAMOS SCI LAB, 66- *Concurrent Pos:* Res assoc, Atomic Energy Res Estab, Harwell, Eng, 74-75. *Mem:* Am Phys Soc. *Res:* Calculation of atomic wave functions and energy levels; calculation of energy band structures; calculation of molecular structure via complete neglect of differential overlap and scattered wave methods. *Mailing Add:* Group CMB-5 MS 730 Los Alamos Sci Lab Los Alamos NM 87545

WOOD, JOHN KARL, b Logan, Utah, July 8, 19; m 47; c 4. PHYSICS. *Educ:* Utah State Agr Col, BS, 41; Pa State Col, MS, 42, PhD(physics), 46. *Prof Exp:* Asst petrol refining, Pa State Univ, 44-46; optical engr, Bausch & Lomb Optical Co, NY, 46-48; from asst prof to assoc prof physics, Univ Wyo, 48-56; PROF PHYSICS, UTAH STATE UNIV, 56- *Concurrent Pos:* NSF sci fac fel, Sweden, 66. *Mem:* Am Phys Soc; Am Soc Metals; Optical Soc Am. *Res:* Crystal orientation in metals studies by means of x-rays; Raman spectroscopy; pole figures of the effect of some cold rolling mill variables on low carbon steel; light; molecular and atomic physics; general mathematics; sound. *Mailing Add:* Dept Physics Utah State Univ Logan UT 84322

WOOD, JOHN LEWIS, b Homer, Ill, Aug 7, 12; m 41; c 2. BIOCHEMISTRY. *Educ:* Univ Ill, BS, 34; Univ Va, PhD(org chem), 37. *Hon Degrees:* DSc, Blackburn Univ, 55. *Prof Exp:* Asst biochem, Med Sch, George Washington Univ, 37-38; asst, Med Col, Cornell Univ, 38-39; assoc chemist, Eastern Regional Res Lab, Bur Agr Chem & Eng, USDA, 41-42; asst biochem, Med Col, Cornell Univ, 42-44, asst prof, 44-46; assoc prof, Col Med, Univ Tenn, Memphis, 46-50, prof biochem, Med Units, 50-71, head dept biochem, 52-55, chmn dept, 55-67, alumni distinguished serv prof biochem, Ctr Health Sci, 71-80, assoc dean, Grad Sch-Med Sci, 78-79; sr staff scientist, Life Sci Res Off, Fedn Am Soc Exp Biol, 80-81; CONSULT LIFE SCI, 81- *Concurrent Pos:* Finney-Howell fel, Harvard Univ, 39-41; Guggenheim fel, 54; USPHS spec res fel, 65; Nat Acad Sci-Polish Acad Sci exchange visitor, 70. *Mem:* AAAS; Am Chem Soc; Am Soc Biol Chemists; Soc Exp Biol & Med; Am Asn Cancer Res. *Res:* Biochemistry of amino acids; proteins; carcinogenesis; thiocyano derivatives; sulfur compounds. *Mailing Add:* 49 Sevier St Memphis TN 38111

WOOD, JOHN MARTIN, b Huddersfield, Eng, Mar 22, 38; m 62; c 2. BIOCHEMISTRY, INORGANIC CHEMISTRY. *Educ:* Univ Leeds, BSc, 61, PhD(biochem), 64. *Prof Exp:* Lectr org chem, Leeds Col Technol, Eng, 61-63; res assoc microbiol, Univ Ill, Urbana, 64-66, from asst prof to prof biochem, 66-74; PROF BIOCHEM & ECOL & DIR, FRESHWATER BIOL INST, UNIV MINN, 74- *Honors & Awards:* Gold Medal Chem, Synthetic Org Chem Mfrs Asn US, 72. *Mem:* Am Chem Soc; AAAS; Freshwater Soc. *Res:* The environmental chemistry of trace metals in water and the mechanism of action of metallo-enzymes. *Mailing Add:* Ecol Behav Biol 108 Zool Bldg Univ Minn 318 Church St SE Navarre MN 55391

WOOD, JOHN STANLEY, b Stoke-on-Trent, Eng, Oct 9, 36; m 62; c 2. CHEMISTRY. *Educ:* Univ Keele, BA, 58; Univ Manchester, PhD(chem), 62. *Prof Exp:* Res assoc chem, Mass Inst Technol, 62-64; lectr, Univ Southampton, 64-70; PROF CHEM, UNIV MASS, AMHERST, 70- *Mem:* Royal Soc Chem; Am Crystallog Asn. *Res:* Inorganic chemistry; x-ray crystallography; studies of stereochemistries and electron structures of inorganic compounds. *Mailing Add:* Dept of Chem Univ of Mass Amherst MA 01003

WOOD, JOSEPH M, b Richmond, Ind, May 2, 21; m 57; c 2. BOTANY, PALEOBOTANY. *Educ:* Ind Univ, BA, 53, PhD(plant morphol, paleobot), 60; Univ Mich, MSc, 56. *Prof Exp:* From instr to assoc prof bot & paleobot, 57-73, asst dir div biol sci, 71-75, PROF BIOL SCI, UNIV MO-COLUMBIA, 73- *Mem:* Paleont Soc; Paleont Asn; Int Asn Angiosperm Paleobot; Int Orgn Palaeobotanists; Am Asn Stratig Palynologists. *Res:* Paleozoic and Mesozoic plant macro/micro fossil morphology, anatomy, evolutionary, ecological, and stratigraphic studies. *Mailing Add:* Div of Biol Sci Tucker Hall Univ of Mo Columbia MO 65211

WOOD, JULIE HAN, b Bhamo, Burma, June 16, 38; m 70. TEXTILE ENGINEERING & CHEMISTRY. *Educ:* Univ Rangoon, BSc, 61; Clemson Univ, MS, 65, PhD(chem), 68. *Prof Exp:* Teacher, Ave Maria Convent High Sch, 54-55; asst lectr textile eng, Rangoon Inst Technol, 60-61; Burmese State scholar, Clemson Univ, 62-67; res chemist, Burlington Industs, Inc, 68-72 & Ciba-Geigy Corp, 72-77; RES CHEMIST, SEARS, ROEBUCK & CO, 78- *Mem:* Am Asn Textile Chem & Colorists. *Res:* Fiber chemistry; chemical finishing of textiles; dyeing; textile and color technology. *Mailing Add:* D817 Sears Roebuck & Co 1633 Broadway New York NY 10019

WOOD, KENNETH GEORGE, b Niagara Falls, Ont, Jan 11, 24; nat US; m 48; c 3. LIMNOLOGY. *Educ:* Univ Toronto, BA, 47, MA, 49; Ohio State Univ, PhD(hydrobiol), 53. *Prof Exp:* Asst prof biol, Buena Vista Col, 53-55 & RI Col, 55-56; prof, Thiel Col, 56-65; assoc prof, 65-71, PROF BIOL, STATE UNIV NY COL FREDONIA, 71- *Concurrent Pos:* Sabbatical leave, Calspan Corp, NY, 72-73; Fulbright scholar, Madurai-Kamaraj Univ, Madurai, India, 80-81. *Mem:* Ecol Soc Am; NAm Benthological Soc; Int Asn Great Lakes Res; Am Soc Limnol & Oceanog; Int Asn Theoret & Appl Limnol. *Res:* Ecology of aquatic animals; primary productivity; inorganic carbon dioxide. *Mailing Add:* Dept of Biol State Univ of NY Fredonia NY 14063

WOOD, KURT ARTHUR, b Springfield, Minn, July 2, 56; m 79. VIBRATIONAL SPECTROSCOPY, CONDENSED PHASES. *Educ:* Univ Calif, Davis, BS, 77, Berkeley, PhD(chem), 81. *Prof Exp:* ASST PROF CHEM, ST OLAF COL, 81- *Mem:* Am Phys Soc; Am Chem Soc; Am Sci Affil. *Res:* Applications of spectroscopy, particularly vibrational spectroscopy, to intra-and intermolecular interactions of molecules in condensed phases, to energy transfer and to the structure of matter. *Mailing Add:* Dept Chem St Olaf Col Northfield MN 55057

WOOD, LANGLEY HARRISS, b Lynchburg, Va, Aug 22, 24; m 51; c 5. ENVIRONMENTAL PHYSIOLOGY. *Educ:* Col William & Mary, BS, 49; Columbia Univ, AM, 50; Cornell Univ, PhD(biol), 65. *Prof Exp:* Instr sociol, Winthrop Col, 50-51; pvt bus, 52-56; researcher, Bur Commercial Fisheries, US Fish & Wildlife Serv, 56-57; res asst biol, Woods Hole Oceanog Inst, 57-58, Inst Fish Res, Univ NC, 59 & Lerner Lab, Am Mus Natural Hist, 59-60; assoc marine scientist & head dept, Va Inst Marine Sci, 61-67, sr marine scientist & head dept environ physiol, 67-69; prof zool & chmn dept, Univ NH, 69-72; DIR ENVIRON STUDIES PROG, SWEET BRIAR COL, 72- *Concurrent Pos:* From asst prof to assoc prof, Col William & Mary, 61-69; asst prof, Univ Va, 63-69. *Mem:* AAAS; Am Soc Limnol & Oceanog; Am Soc Zoologists; Animal Behav Soc; Estuarine Res Soc. *Res:* Physiological and behavioral effects upon marine organisms of changes in sensory and biochemical characteristics of environment. *Mailing Add:* Box Z Sweet Briar Col Sweet Briar VA 24595

WOOD, LAWRENCE ARNELL, b Peekskill, NY, Jan 15, 04; m 51; c 2. PHYSICS. *Educ:* Hamilton Col, AB, 25; Cornell Univ, PhD(physics), 32. *Prof Exp:* From asst to instr physics, Cornell Univ, 27-35; res physicist, 35-43, chief rubber sect, 43-62, CONSULT RUBBER, NAT BUR STANDARDS, 62- *Concurrent Pos:* Deleg, Int Rubber Technol Conf, London, 38, 48 & 62, Kuala Lumpur, Malaysia, 68 & Rio de Janeiro, Brazil, 74. *Honors & Awards:* Meritorious Serv Award, US Dept Com, 58. *Mem:* Fel Am Phys Soc; Am Chem Soc. *Res:* Semiconductors; Hall effect; blocking layer photocells; physics and technology of polymers, especially synthetic rubbers and natural rubber. *Mailing Add:* Polymers Div Nat Bur of Standards Washington DC 20234

WOOD, LEONARD ALTON, b Gratiot Co, Mich, Aug 22, 22; m 42, 77; c 3. GEOLOGY, GROUND WATER HYDROLOGY. *Educ:* Mich State Univ, BS, 46. *Prof Exp:* Geologist, Water Resources Div, US Geol Surv, Mich, 46-51, Tex, 52-63, Colo, 63-67, Washington, DC, 67-74 & Reston, Va, 74-80, coordr subsurface waste disposal studies, 71-78, staff hydrologist, Water Resources Div, 67-80; CONSULT HYDROGEOLOGIST, 80- *Mem:* Geol Soc Am; Am Asn Petrol Geologists; Am Geophys Union; Asn Eng Geologists; Am Inst Prof Geologists. *Res:* Occurrence of ground water; relation of ground water to surface water in Colorado; contamination of ground water; protection of ground water resources. *Mailing Add:* 431 Blair Rd NW Vienna VA 22180

WOOD, LEONARD E(UGENE), b Burr Oak, Kans, June 10, 23; m 47. CIVIL ENGINEERING. *Educ:* Kans State Univ, BS & MS, 49; Purdue Univ, PhD(civil eng), 56. *Prof Exp:* Instr appl mech, Kans State Univ, 49-53; from instr to asst prof eng mat, 55-59, assoc prof, 59-80, PROF ENG MAT, PURDUE UNIV, 80- *Concurrent Pos:* Consult, Tech Studies Adv Comt, Bldg Res Adv Bd, Nat Acad Sci-Nat Res Coun, 57-61, mem, Transp Res Bd. *Mem:* Am Soc Testing & Mat; Asn Asphalt Paving Technol; Am Soc Eng Educ. *Res:* Engineering materials; rock mechanics; corrosion studies; viscoelastic behavior of bituminous mixes. *Mailing Add:* Sch of Civil Eng Purdue Univ Lafayette IN 47907

WOOD, LEONARD E(UGENE), b Elwood, Ind, Nov 2, 27; m 58; c 4. ENVIRONMENTAL SCIENCES, GEOLOGY. *Educ:* Univ Ky, BS, 52, MS, 57; Mich State Univ, PhD(geol), 58. *Prof Exp:* Instr geol, Mich State Univ, 55-58; staff geologist, Mobil Oil Co, 58-61, US Geol Surv, 62-63 & Army Res Off, 63-65; prog mgr environ sci, Adv Res Projs Agency, Thailand, 65-72; CHIEF, ENVIRON CONTROL GROUP, OFF OF RES, FED HWY ADMIN, 72- *Concurrent Pos:* Instr exten, Univ Va, 64-65; adv ed, J Develop Areas, 68- *Res:* Management in environmental sciences; geology, soils, water resources, vegetation, fauna and meteorology in United States, Europe and Southeast Asia; geologic considerations in excavation; environmental research on high elevations; highways and the bio-environment; highway environmental interface, especially air, noise, water, ecology. *Mailing Add:* Fed Hwy Admin Environ Control Group HRS-42 Washington DC 20490

WOOD, LOUIS L, b Washington, DC, July 26, 31; m 58, 68; c 3. ORGANIC CHEMISTRY. *Educ:* Univ Del, BS, 53; Ohio State Univ, PhD(org chem), 59. *Prof Exp:* Res chemist, W R Grace & Co, Washington Res Ctr, Clarkville, 58-81; CHEM ADV, PURIFICATION ENG INC, COLUMBIA, MD, 81- *Mem:* Am Chem Soc; AAAS. *Res:* Polymers; organic chemical synthesis; textile applications; foam technology; immobilzation of cells; enzymes; monoclonal antibodies. *Mailing Add:* 11760 Gainsborough Rd Rockville MD 20854

WOOD, LOWELL THOMAS, b Ada, Okla, Sept 8, 42; m 66; c 2. PHYSICS, SCIENCE EDUCATION. *Educ:* Univ Kans, BS, 64; Univ Tex, Austin, PhD(physics), 68. *Prof Exp:* Asst prof physics, Univ Tex, Austin, 68-69; asst prof, 69-73, chmn dept, 75-80, ASSOC PROF PHYSICS, UNIV HOUSTON, 73- *Concurrent Pos:* NASA grant, Univ Houston, 70-78 & NSF grant, 72-77. *Mem:* Am Phys Soc; Optical Soc Am. *Res:* Thermomagnetic torques in gases; electromagnetic properties of materials; physics of optical fibers. *Mailing Add:* Dept Physics Univ Houston Houston TX 77004

WOOD, MARGARET GRAY, b Jamaica, NY, May 23, 18; m 50; c 3. MEDICINE, DERMATOLOGY. *Educ:* Univ Ala, BA, 41; Woman's Med Col Pa, MD, 48. *Prof Exp:* Assoc, 53-68, from asst prof to assoc prof, 68-77, PROF DERMAT, SCH MED, UNIV PA, 78- *Concurrent Pos:* Assoc, Grad Div Med Dermat, Univ Pa, 53-66, assoc prof, 66-71; asst prof, Woman's Col Pa, 58-66, vis asst prof, 66-; asst vis physician, Philadelphia Gen Hosp, 54-70, consult, 70-77; consult, Philadelphia Vet Hosp, 66-; consult, Dent Sch, Univ Pa, 66-, consult, Vet Sch Med, 70- *Mem:* Histochem Soc; Soc Invest Dermat; AMA; Am Med Women's Asn; Am Acad Dermat. *Res:* Histochemistry; dermatopathology. *Mailing Add:* Dept of Dermat Hosp of Univ of Pa Philadelphia PA 19104

WOOD, NANCY ELIZABETH, b Martins Ferry, Ohio. SPEECH PATHOLOGY. *Educ:* Ohio Univ, BS, 43, MS, 47; Northwestern Univ, PhD(speech path), 52. *Prof Exp:* Assoc prof lang path, Case Western Reserve Univ, 52-60; consult specialist, Off Educ, Dept Health, Educ & Welfare, 60-62, chief neurol & sensory dis res, USPHS, 62-64; prof commun dis, 65-74, PROF SURG, SCH MED, UNIV SOUTHERN CALIF, 65-, DIR COMMUN DIS, 71-, PROF & RES DIR, SCH JOUR, 75- *Concurrent Pos:* Asst dir, Cleveland Hearing & Speech Ctr, 52-56, coordr clin serv, 56-59, dir lang dis, 59-60. *Mem:* AAAS; Soc Res Child Develop; fel Am Speech & Hearing Asn; fel Am Psychol Asn. *Res:* Language development, disorders and pathology; differential diagnosis of young children; aphasia; mental retardation; hearing loss; test design; communication science research; memory, perception and auditory processing. *Mailing Add:* Univ of Southern Calif 734 W Adams Blvd Los Angeles CA 90007

WOOD, NORMAN KENYON, b Perth, Ont, Dec 1, 35; m 69; c 1. ORAL PATHOLOGY. *Educ:* Univ Toronto, DDS, 58; Cook County Hosp, Chicago, dipl oral surg, 65; Northwestern Univ, MS, 66, PhD(oral path), 68; Am Bd Oral Surg, dipl, 70; Am Bd Oral Path, dipl, 71. *Prof Exp:* Pvt pract, 58-62; res assoc biol mat, Dent Sch, Northwestern Univ, 67-68; asst prof oral path, 68-70, assoc prof oral diag, 70-76, PROF ORAL DIAG, DENT SCH, LOYOLA UNIV CHICAGO, 76-, CHMN DEPT, 70- *Concurrent Pos:* Consult, Hines Vet Admin Hosp, Ill, 71- *Mem:* Am Acad Oral Path. *Res:* Oral embryology, induction of cleft palates in fetal mice; implantology, tissue compatibility studies on implant materials. *Mailing Add:* Loyola Univ of Chicago Dent Sch 2160 First Ave Maywood IL 60153

WOOD, NORRIS PHILIP, b Binghamton, NY, July 8, 24; m 55; c 2. BACTERIOLOGY. *Educ:* Hartwick Col, BS, 49; Cornell Univ, MNS, 51; Univ Pa, PhD(microbiol), 55. *Prof Exp:* From asst prof to assoc prof microbiol, Agr & Mech Col Tex, 55-63; from asst prof to assoc prof bact, 63-72, PROF MICROBIOL, UNIV RI, 72-, CHMN DEPT, 70- *Concurrent Pos:* Res partic, Oak Ridge Nat Lab, 58 & 62; mem, State Adv Comt Regional Med Prog, 66-76. *Mem:* AAAS; Am Chem Soc; Am Soc Microbiol. *Res:* Bacterial physiology; intermediary metabolism; chemistry of microorganisms; microbial ecology. *Mailing Add:* Dept of Microbiol Univ of RI Kingston RI 02881

WOOD, OBERT REEVES, II, b Sacramento, Calif, Jan 18, 43. ELECTRICAL ENGINEERING, QUANTUM ELECTRONICS. *Educ:* Univ Calif, Berkeley, BS, 64, MS, 65, PhD(elec eng), 69. *Prof Exp:* MEM TECH STAFF LASER RES, BELL TEL LABS, 69- *Mem:* Am Phys Soc; Optical Soc Am; Inst Elec & Electronics Engrs; AAAS; Sigma xi. *Res:* Quantum electronics; nonlinear optics; plasma physics. *Mailing Add:* Rm 4C-434 Bell Tel Labs Holmdel NJ 07733

WOOD, ORIN LEW, b Hurricane, Utah, Apr 26, 36; m 57; c 4. QUARTZ RESONATOR TRANSDUCERS. *Educ:* Brigham Young Univ, BS, 58; Univ Calif, Los Angeles, MS, 62; Univ Utah, PhD(radiation biophys), 68. *Prof Exp:* Sr engr, Sperry Utah Co, 62-65; res scientist, Fluidonics Res Lab, ITE-Imperial Corp, 65-67, dir res biomed eng, Bio-Logics Inc, 67-69; assoc prof & collab environ pollution, Utah State Univ, 69-71; prog dir radiologic technol, Weber State Col, 70-75; VPRES, TECHNOLOGICS ASSOCS, 76-, CHIEF EXEC OFFICER, QUARTEX, INC, 79- *Concurrent Pos:* Consult, O Lew Wood Assocs, 69- *Mem:* AAAS. *Res:* Development of biomedical and air pollution instrumentation. *Mailing Add:* 811 E Woodshire Circle Murray UT 84107

WOOD, PAULINE J, b Springdale, Pa, Nov 7, 22. DEVELOPMENTAL BIOLOGY, HISTOLOGY. *Educ:* Adrian Col, BS, 51; Univ Mich, MS, 54, PhD(zool), 60. *Prof Exp:* Instr zool, Univ Mich, 58-59; res instr embryol, Dent Sch, Univ Wash, 59-61; asst prof zool, Knox Col, 61-62; from asst prof to assoc prof, 62-73, PROF ZOOL, UNIV DETROIT, 73- *Mem:* AAAS; Am Soc Zoologists; Am Inst Biol Sci; Reticuloendothelial Soc. *Res:* Phylogeny of mesenchymal and hemopoietic cells. *Mailing Add:* Dept of Biol Univ of Detroit Detroit MI 48221

WOOD, PETER DOUGLAS, b London, Eng, Aug 25, 29; m 53; c 1. BIOCHEMISTRY, CHEMISTRY. *Educ:* Univ London, BSc, 52, MSc, 56, PhD(chem), 62, DSc, 72. *Prof Exp:* Chemist, Weston Res Labs, Eng, 52-55; res chemist, Imp Chem Industs Australia & NZ, 56-59; res asst chem, Univ Sask, 59; res assoc, Inst Metab Res, Oakland, Calif, 62-68; ADJ PROF MED, MED CTR, STANFORD UNIV, 69- *Concurrent Pos:* Fel coun arteriosclerosis, Am Heart Asn, 68; dep dir, Stanford Heart-Dis Prev Prog, 71- *Mem:* Fel Royal Soc Chem; Am Inst Nutrit; Am Soc Clin Nutrit; Am Heart Asn; Am Oil Chem Soc. *Res:* Lipid chemistry, metabolism and methodology; exercise. *Mailing Add:* 730 Welch Rd Suite B Stanford Univ Stanford CA 94305

WOOD, PETER JOHN, b Barnard Castle, Durham, Eng, Aug 20, 43. CARBOHYDRATE CHEMISTRY, FOOD SCIENCE. *Educ:* Univ Birmingham, BS, 65, PhD(carbohydrate chem), 69. *Prof Exp:* RES SCIENTIST CARBOHYDRATES, FOOD RESEARCH INST, 69- *Mem:* Royal Inst Chem; Am Asn Cereal Chemists. *Res:* Connective tissue glycosaminoglycans; polysaccharides of potato cell wall; rapeseed carbohydrates; oat endosperm cell wall polysaccharides; analytical methodology; use of boronate esters for glc analysis and methanol analysis; dye-binding by polysaccharides. *Mailing Add:* Res Br Food Res Inst Agr Can Ottawa ON K1A 0C6 Can

WOOD, RANDALL DUDLEY, b Palmer, Ky, Aug 3, 36; m 59; c 1. BIOCHEMISTRY, ORGANIC CHEMISTRY. *Educ:* Univ Ky, BS, 59, MS, 61; Tex A&M Univ, PhD(biochem), 65. *Prof Exp:* Scientist, Oak Ridge Assoc Univs, 66-70; assoc prof, Stritch Sch Med, Loyola Univ Chicago & Hines Vet Admin Hosp, 70-71; assoc prof med & biochem, Sch Med, Univ Mo-Columbia, 71-76; PROF BIOCHEM, TEX A&M UNIV, COLLEGE STATION, 76- *Concurrent Pos:* AEC fel, 65-66. *Mem:* AAAS; Am Asn Cancer Res; Am Chem Soc; Am Oil Chem Soc; Am Soc Biol Chemists. *Res:*

Lipid biochemistry and metabolism of normal, tumor and embryonic tissues; biosynthesis, metabolism and occurrence of alkyl glyceryl ethers and plasmalogens; structural and metabolic relationships between molecular species of various classes; the metabolic fate of unnatural dietary fatty acids in processed foods. *Mailing Add:* Dept Biochem & Biophys Univ Tex A&M College Station TX 65201

WOOD, RAYMOND ARTHUR, b Middletown, NY, Nov 28, 24. ZOOLOGY, PARASITOLOGY. *Educ:* Mt St Mary's Col, Md, BS, 50; Univ Notre Dame, MS, 53, PhD, 55. *Prof Exp:* Instr & spec lectr anat & physiol, Ind Univ, 54-55; asst prof, Pan Am Col, 55-56; PROF ZOOL & CHMN DIV, ORANGE COUNTY COMMUNITY COL, 56- *Concurrent Pos:* NSF grants, Bermuda Biol Sta, 56, Comp Anat Inst, Harvard Univ, 63, Col Biol Inst, Williams Col, 66, Marine Lab, Duke Univ, 65, 67 & Marine Labs, Naples, Italy, 70; Sigma Xi grant, 57. *Mem:* Fel AAAS; Am Soc Parasitologists; Am Soc Zoologists; Soc Syst Zool; fel Royal Soc Trop Med & Hyg. *Res:* Systematics of monogenea. *Mailing Add:* Div of Biol & Health Sci Orange County Community Col Middletown NY 10940

WOOD, REGINALD KENNETH, b Unity, Sask, July 12, 37; m 58; c 3. CHEMICAL ENGINEERING. *Educ:* Univ Sask, BE, 58; Univ Alta, MSc, 60; Northwestern Univ, PhD(chem eng), 63. *Prof Exp:* Res engr, Can Chem Co Ltd, 59-60; res assoc foam separation, Northwestern Univ, 62-63; asst prof chem eng, Univ Ottawa, 63-66; from asst prof to assoc prof, 66-72, PROF CHEM ENG, UNIV ALTA, 72- *Concurrent Pos:* Guest worker, Control Eng Div, Warren Spring Lab, Stevenage, Eng, 72-73. *Mem:* Am Inst Chem Engrs; Can Soc Chem Engrs; Instrument Soc Am; Soc Comput Simulation; Am Soc Eng Educ. *Res:* Dynamics and control of chemical and mineral process systems. *Mailing Add:* Dept of Chem Eng Univ of Alta Edmonton AB T6G 2E1 Can

WOOD, REUBEN ESSELSTYN, physical chemistry, deceased

WOOD, RICHARD ELLET, b Farmington, Utah, Mar 3, 28; m 48; c 5. NUCLEAR PHYSICS, ENERGY SYSTEMS. *Educ:* Univ Utah, BS, 52, PhD(physics), 55. *Prof Exp:* Res assoc neutron cross sects, Brookhaven Nat Lab, 53-54; nuclear engr, Gen Elec Co, 55-56, supvr low power test opers, 56-59, supvr initial eng test opers, 59-60, supvr anal, Idaho Test Sta, Air Craft Nuclear Propulsion Dept, 60-61, physicist, Atomic Power Equip Dept, 61-62, mgr, Idaho Eng, Nuclear Mat & Propulsion Oper, Idaho Test Sta, 62-68; chief nuclear eng br, Idaho Opers Off, AEC, 68-74; dir, Reactor Support Div, US Energy Res & Develop Admin, 74-76, DIR, ENERGY & TECHNOL DIV, US DEPT ENERGY, 76- *Mem:* Am Nuclear Soc. *Res:* Nuclear engineering and neutron physics. *Mailing Add:* US Dept of Energy 550 Second St Idaho Falls ID 83401

WOOD, RICHARD FROST, b Lebanon, Tenn, June 6, 31; m; c 3. PHYSICS. *Educ:* Fordham Univ, BS, 53; Ohio State Univ, MS, 56, PhD(physics), 59. *Prof Exp:* Res specialist, Opers Res, NAm Aviation, Inc, 58-60; asst prof physics, Univ Fla, 60-62; RES SCIENTIST & HEAD THEORY SECT, SOLID STATE DIV, OAK RIDGE NAT LAB, 62- *Concurrent Pos:* Vis prof, Univ Uppsala, 60-61, NSF fel, 61-62. *Mem:* AAAS; fel Am Phys Soc. *Res:* Theoretical solid state physics; lattice defects; lattice dynamics; optical properties and electronic structure of solids. *Mailing Add:* Solid State Div Oak Ridge Nat Lab Oak Ridge TN 37830

WOOD, RICHARD LEE, b Ft Dodge, Iowa, Sept 8, 30; m 55; c 3. VETERINARY MICROBIOLOGY. *Educ:* Univ Mo-Columbia, DVM, 61; Iowa State Univ, MS, 66, PhD(vet microbiol), 70. *Prof Exp:* RES VET, NAT ANIMAL DIS CTR, AGR RES SERV, USDA, 61- *Mem:* Am Vet Med Asn; Am Soc Microbiol; Conf Res Workers Animal Dis. *Res:* Epizootiology and pathogenesis of swine erysipelas and streptococcal lymphadenitis of swine. *Mailing Add:* Nat Animal Dis Ctr PO Box 70 Ames IA 50010

WOOD, RICHARD LYMAN, b Allamore, Tex, Jan 2, 29; m 51; c 2. CYTOLOGY. *Educ:* Linfield Col, BA, 50; Univ Wash, PhD(zool), 57. *Prof Exp:* From instr to asst prof anat, Univ Wash, 59-64; assoc prof, Univ Minn, Minneapolis, 64-70; prof, Sch Med, Univ Miami, 70-74; PROF ANAT, SCH MED, UNIV SOUTHERN CALIF, 74- *Concurrent Pos:* NIH fel, Univ Wash, 57-59; NIH res grant, Dept Biol Struct, Univ Wash, 60-64 & Dept Anat, Univ Minn, 64-70; NSF res grant, Dept Anat, Univ Southern Calif, 78- *Mem:* Am Soc Zool; Am Soc Cell Biol; Am Asn Anat; Electron Micros Soc Am; Soc Develop Biol. *Res:* Fine structure; cellular anatomy by electron microscopy; animal cytology and histology. *Mailing Add:* Dept Anat Univ Southern Calif Sch Med Los Angeles CA 90033

WOOD, ROBERT CHARLES, b Lakewood, Ohio, May 7, 29. BACTERIOLOGY. *Educ:* Lehigh Univ, BA, 51, MS, 52; Univ Md, PhD, 55. *Prof Exp:* Sr res microbiologist, Wellcome Res Labs, Burroughs Wellcome & Co, 56-60; asst prof microbiol, Sch Med, George Washington Univ, 60-64; asst prof, 64-65, ASSOC PROF MICROBIOL, UNIV TEX MED BR GALVESTON, 65- *Concurrent Pos:* Res fel bact physiol, Univ Pa, 55-56. *Mem:* AAAS; Am Soc Microbiol. *Res:* Chemotherapy; mechanisms of action of drugs; folic acid metabolism; comparative aspects of bacterial physiology; membrane permeability; bacterial genetics. *Mailing Add:* Dept Microbiol Univ Tex Med Br Galveston TX 77550

WOOD, ROBERT E(MERSON), b Providence, RI, Oct 2, 16; m 43; c 5. CHEMICAL ENGINEERING. *Educ:* Univ RI, BS, 37; La State Univ, MS, 39, PhD(phys chem), 42. *Prof Exp:* Chem engr, Labs, Esso Standard Oil Co, 41-52, sect head, 52-54, asst dir, 54-57, assoc dir, 57-61; asst head, Technol Div, Baton Rouge Refinery, Humble Oil & Refining Co, 61-62; dir anal div, NJ, 62-64, assoc dir, Enjay Labs, 64, assoc mgr, Baytown Res & Develop Div, 65-66, res coordr chem staff, NJ, 66-67, MGR ENJAY POLYMER LABS, EXXON RES & ENG CO, NJ, 67- *Mem:* Am Chem Soc; Am Inst Chem Engrs. *Res:* Dipole moment measurements; thermoplastics; low temperature polymerization; emulsion polymerization; synthetic rubber; petroleum refining; research administration. *Mailing Add:* Technol Dept Box 599 Exxon Chem Co Linden NJ 07036

WOOD, ROBERT E, b Philadelphia, Pa, May 16, 38; m 62; c 2. INDUSTRIAL ENGINEERING. *Educ:* Ga Inst Technol, BS, 60, MS, 62, PhD(physics), 65. *Prof Exp:* From asst prof to assoc prof physics, Emory Univ, 64-75; sr opers res analyst, 75-76, MGR INDUST ENG, SOUTHERN RWY SYST, 76- *Concurrent Pos:* Consult, Ga Inst Technol, 65, fel chem, 66; consult, Allied Gen Nuclear Serv, 73-75 & Aston Co, 75-76. *Mem:* AAAS; Am Phys Soc; Sigma Xi. *Res:* Application of models to transportation industry. *Mailing Add:* Southern Rwy Syst 125 Spring St Rm 815 Atlanta GA 30303

WOOD, ROBERT HEMSLEY, b Brooklyn, NY, May 8, 32; div; c 2. PHYSICAL CHEMISTRY. *Educ:* Calif Inst Technol, BS, 53; Univ Calif, PhD(chem), 57. *Prof Exp:* From instr to assoc prof, 57-70, chmn dept, 69-71, PROF CHEM, UNIV DEL, 70- *Mem:* Am Chem Soc. *Res:* Solution thermodynamics; electrolytes, non-electrolytes, non-aqueous, and high temperature. *Mailing Add:* Dept of Chem Univ of Del Newark DE 19711

WOOD, ROBERT M(CLANE), b Ithaca, NY, Apr 4, 28; m 51; c 2. AERONAUTICAL ENGINEERING. *Educ:* Univ Colo, BS, 49; Cornell Univ, PhD(exp physics), 53. *Prof Exp:* Asst elem physics, Cornell Univ, 49-50, asst solid state physics, 51-53; res engr automatic control systs, Douglas Aircraft Co, Santa Monica, 53-54 & Missile & Space Systs Div, 56-63, dep chief engr advan space technol, 63-64, asst dir sci & future systs res & develop, 64-66, dep dir res & develop, 66-71, ASST DIR DETECTION, DESIGNATION & DISCRIMINATION, McDONNELL DOUGLAS ASTRONAUT CO, 71- *Concurrent Pos:* Consult, Flight Refueling, Inc, 55. *Mem:* Am Astronaut Soc; Am Inst Aeronaut & Astronaut; Am Phys Soc. *Res:* Heat transfer; missile and space system design, research management and radar discrimination. *Mailing Add:* McDonnell Douglas Astronaut Co 5301 Bolsa Ave Huntington Beach CA 92647

WOOD, ROBERT MANNING, b Bronxville, NY, May 13, 38; c 2. ATOMIC PHYSICS, MOLECULAR PHYSICS. *Educ:* Princeton Univ, AB, 60; Univ Wis, PhD(physics), 64. *Prof Exp:* Res assoc physics, Univ Wis, 64-66; asst prof, 66-80, ASSOC PROF PHYSICS, UNIV GA, 80- *Mem:* Am Phys Soc. *Res:* Ion-atom and ion-molecule collisions. *Mailing Add:* Dept Physics Univ Ga Athens GA 30602

WOOD, ROBERT WINFIELD, b Detroit, Mich, Dec 29, 31; m 59; c 3. RADIATION BIOPHYSICS. *Educ:* Univ Detroit, BS, 53; Vanderbilt Univ, MA, 55; Cornell Univ, PhD(biophys), 61. *Prof Exp:* Radiol physicist, AEC, 62-73; MGR PHYS & TECHNOL PROGS, OFF HEALTH & ENVIRON RES, US DEPT ENERGY, 73- *Concurrent Pos:* Nat Inst Gen Med Sci fel, 61-62. *Mem:* Am Soc Nuclear Med; Health Physics Soc; Radiation Res Soc; Am Asn Physicists in Med. *Res:* Electron spin resonance, aromatic hydrocarbon negative ions and irradiated biological compounds; radiological physics; dosimetry; biomedical instrumentation. *Mailing Add:* Off Health & Environ Res US Dept of Energy Washington DC 20545

WOOD, RODNEY DAVID, b Lansing, Mich, Aug 19, 32; m 61; c 4. CHEMICAL ENGINEERING. *Educ:* Yale Univ, BE, 54; Mich State Univ, MS, 59; Northwestern Univ, PhD(chem eng), 63. *Prof Exp:* Instr mech eng, Mich State Univ, 56-59; asst prof, Univ Nebr, 62-64; res engr, Tex Instruments Inc, 64-70; sr engr, Sherwin Williams Chem, 70-72, tech dir, 73-77; dir process eng, 77-80, MGR STERILE DRUGS, MEAD JOHNSON & CO, 80- *Honors & Awards:* Award, Am Inst Chem Engrs, 64. *Mem:* Am Chem Soc; Am Inst Chem Engrs; Sigma Xi. *Res:* Thermodynamics, food, and pharmaceutical processing. *Mailing Add:* 524 S Plaza Dr Evansville IN 47715

WOOD, ROGER CHARLES, b Minneapolis, Minn, Jan 17, 32; m 54; c 4. COMPUTER SCIENCE, APPLIED MATHEMATICS. *Educ:* Univ Minn, BS, 54, MS, 56; Univ Calif, Los Angeles, PhD(eng), 66. *Prof Exp:* Dynamics engr, Ryan Aeronaut Co, 54-57, sr dynamics engr, 57-58, sr opers res engr, 58-59; res engr, Univ Calif, Los Angeles, 64-65; opers res analyst, Syst Develop Corp, 59-60, sect head, 60-61, opers res scientist, 61-65; from asst prof to assoc prof elec eng, 65-72, chmn dept, 71-75, PROF ELEC ENG & COMPUT SCI, UNIV CALIF, SANTA BARBARA, 72- *Concurrent Pos:* Consult, GE Tempo, 66-68, Gen Motors Res Lab, 68-73, Human Factors Res Corp, 68-74, Gen Res Corp, 77-80 & US Navy, 76-; mem bd dir, Concordia Historical Inst Systs, 78- *Mem:* Inst Elec & Electronics Engrs; Opers Res Soc Am; Asn Comput Mach; Simulation Coun. *Res:* Analog, hybrid and digital computer applications; quantization theory; time sharing system scheduling; operations research; communications theory; simulation; computer architecture. *Mailing Add:* Dept of Elec Eng & Comput Sci Univ of Calif Santa Barbara CA 93106

WOOD, RONALD MCFARLANE, b New York, NY, Oct 11, 15; m 43; c 2. MEDICAL MICROBIOLOGY. *Educ:* McGill Univ, BSc, 39; Johns Hopkins Univ, PhD(biol), 49; Am Bd Med Microbiol, dipl, 62. *Prof Exp:* Microbiologist, Royal Victoria Hosp, 39-40; res microbiologist, Ayerst McKinna & Harrison, Ltd, 40-41; from instr to assoc prof ophthal, Sch Med, Johns Hopkins Univ, 49-63; CHIEF MICROBIAL DIS LAB, STATE DEPT PUB HEALTH, CALIF, 64- *Concurrent Pos:* Asst prof, Sch Hyg & Pub Health, Johns Hopkins Univ, 51-56; assoc prof, Sch Med, Univ Fla, 63-64. *Honors & Awards:* Barnett Cohen Award, 62. *Mem:* AAAS; fel Royal Soc Health; fel Am Pub Health Asn; Am Soc Microbiol; Nat Tuberc & Respiratory Dis Asn. *Res:* Immunology; public health; infectious diseases. *Mailing Add:* Microbial Dis Lab State Calif Dept Pub Health Berkeley CA 94704

WOOD, SCOTT EMERSON, b Ft Collins, Colo, Apr 9, 10; m 36; c 1. PHYSICAL CHEMISTRY. *Educ:* Univ Denver, BS, 30, MS, 31; Univ Calif, PhD(chem), 35. *Prof Exp:* Res assoc chem, Mass Inst Technol, 35-40; from instr to asst prof, Yale Univ, 40-48; from assoc prof to prof, 48-75, admin officer & vchmn dept, 60-62, actg assoc dean for res, 62-64, EMER PROF CHEM, ILL INST TECHNOL, 75- *Concurrent Pos:* Consult, Argonne Nat Lab, 60-; vis prof, Univ Col, Dublin, 66-67. *Mem:* AAAS; Am Chem Soc; Am Phys Soc. *Res:* Vapor pressures of nonaqueous solutions; density and coefficient of expansion of solutions; index of refraction; theory and thermodynamics of nonaqueous solutions; chromatography; paper electrochromatography; fused salts. *Mailing Add:* 6728 Mesa Grande Ave El Paso TX 79912

WOOD, SHERWIN FRANCIS, protozoology, medical entomology, deceased

WOOD, SPENCER HOFFMAN, b Portland, Ore, Nov 18, 38; m 61; c 3. GEOLOGY. *Educ:* Colo Sch Mines, GE, 64; Calif Inst Technol, MS, 70, PhD(geol), 75. *Prof Exp:* Seismol engr, Geophys Serv, Mobil Oil Corp, 64-65, geophysicist, Mobil Oil Libya, Ltd, 65-68; instr geol, Occidental Col, 74-76; geologist, US Geol Surv, Nat Ctr Earthquake Res, 76-77; asst prof, 78-80, ASSOC PROF GEOL, BOISE STATE UNIV, 80- *Concurrent Pos:* Vis asst prof geol, Univ Ore, 76. *Mem:* AAAS; Geol Soc Am; Am Geophys Union; Am Quaternary Asn; Sigma Xi. *Res:* Quaternary geology and geomorphology, neotectonics, geology of geothermal areas, tephrochronology and obsidian dating. *Mailing Add:* Dept Geol & Geophys Boise State Univ 1910 Univ Dr Boise ID 83725

WOOD, STEPHEN CRAIG, b Cleveland, Ohio, Sept 28, 42; m 67; c 3. PHYSIOLOGY. *Educ:* Kent State Univ, BS, 64, MA, 66; Univ Ore, PhD(physiol), 70. *Prof Exp:* Nat Res Coun res assoc physiol, Submarine Med Res Lab, Groton, Conn, 70-71; asst prof zoophysiol, Aarhus Univ, 71-72; asst prof physiol, Southern Ill Univ, Edwardsville, 72-74; asst prof, 74-79, ASSOC PROF PHYSIOL, SCH MED, UNIV NMEX, 79- *Concurrent Pos:* Sr vis res fel, Marine Biol Lab, Plymouth, Eng, 72; Danish Natural Sci Res Coun grant, Comoro Islands Coelacanth Exped, 72. *Mem:* Am Physiol Soc; Underseas Med Soc; Am Soc Zoologists. *Res:* Diving physiology; comparative physiology of respiration and blood gas transport; metabolism and function of red blood cells; environmental physiology. *Mailing Add:* Dept of Physiol Univ of NMex Sch of Med Albuquerque NM 87131

WOOD, STEPHEN LANE, b Logan, Utah, July 2, 24; m 47; c 3. ENTOMOLOGY. *Educ:* Utah State Univ, BS, 46, MS, 48; Univ Kans, PhD(entom), 53. *Prof Exp:* High sch instr, Utah, 48-50; asst instr biol, Univ Kans, 50-53; syst entomologist, Can Dept Agr, 53-56; from asst prof to assoc prof, 56-68, PROF ZOOL & ENTOM, BRIGHAM YOUNG UNIV, 68- *Concurrent Pos:* Ed, Great Basin Naturalist, 70- *Mem:* AAAS; Entom Soc Am; Coleopterists' Soc. *Res:* Systematics of Scolytidae. *Mailing Add:* Life Sci Mus Brigham Young Univ Provo UT 84602

WOOD, SUSAN, b Snainton, Eng, Jan 13, 48; US citizen. MATERIALS SCIENCE ENGINEERING. *Educ:* Victoria Univ, BSc Hon, 69; Univ Pittsburgh, MS, 73, PhD(mat eng), 76. *Prof Exp:* Sr engr, 76-80, MGR, RES & DEVELOP CTR, WESTINGHOUSE, 80- *Mem:* Am Nuclear Soc; Asn for Women in Sci; Am Inst Mining, Metal & Petrol Engrs. *Res:* Radiation damage analyses of pressure vessel steals, fusion reactor and breeder reactor materials; microstructural evaluation; mechanical property besting of radioactive and ion-implanted specimens. *Mailing Add:* Res & Develop Ctr Westinghouse 1310 Beulah Rd Pittsburgh PA 15235

WOOD, THOMAS HAMIL, b Atlanta, Ga, June 22, 23; m 51; c 3. BIOPHYSICS. *Educ:* Univ Fla, BS, 46; Univ Chicago, PhD(biophys), 53. *Prof Exp:* Res assoc, Univ Chicago, 53; from asst prof to assoc prof, 53-63, PROF PHYSICS, UNIV PA, 63- *Concurrent Pos:* NSF sr fel, Inst Radium, Paris, 61-62; vis prof, Univ Leicester, 67-68 & Ein Shams Univ, Cairo, Egypt, 80-81. *Mem:* Biophys Soc; Radiation Res Soc; Genetics Soc Am. *Res:* Effects of radiations on microorganisms; influence of temperature and protective agents; cellular freezing; bacterial conjugation; genetic recombination. *Mailing Add:* Dept of Physics Univ of Pa Philadelphia PA 19104

WOOD, THOMAS KENNETH, b Cleveland, Ohio, June 12, 42; m 65; c 2. BEHAVIORAL ECOLOGY, INSECT SYSTEMATICS. *Educ:* Wilmington Col, AB, 64; Cornell Univ, PhD(entom), 68. *Prof Exp:* Prof biol, Wilmington Col, 68-80; MEM FAC, DEPT ENTOM & APPL ECOL, UNIV DEL, 80- *Concurrent Pos:* NSF grant, 75-80. *Mem:* Entom Soc Am; Animal Behav Soc; Entom Soc Can; AAAS. *Res:* Parental care in insects, host-plant interaction; membracid-ant associations, membracid systematics. *Mailing Add:* Dept Entom & Appl Ecol Univ Del Newark DE 19711

WOOD, TIMOTHY E, b San Francisco, Calif, Aug 27, 48. ROOT SYMBIOSES, SOIL BIOGEOCHEMISTRY. *Educ:* Univ Calif, Santa Barbara, BA, 70; Yale Univ, MFS, 72, PhD(forest ecol), 80. *Prof Exp:* Res asst forest ecol, Yale Univ, 72-74; res assoc, Wood Hole Marine Biol Lab, 75-76; SR ECOLOGIST SOILS ECOL, NATIVE PLANTS, INC, 81- *Res:* Mineral nutrition of natural plant communities, including root systems, soil chemistry, and soil microbiology; symbiotic root associations involving mycorrhizal fungi, Frankia actomycenes, and Rhizobium bacteria. *Mailing Add:* Plant Resources Inst 360 Wakara Way Salt Lake City UT 84108

WOOD, TIMOTHY SMEDLEY, b Port Washington, NY, Dec 4, 42; m 64; c 2. INVERTEBRATE ZOOLOGY. *Educ:* Earlham Col, AB, 64; Univ Colo, PhD(zool), 71. *Prof Exp:* Asst prof, 71-76, ASSOC PROF BIOL SCI, WRIGHT STATE UNIV, 76-, DIR, ENVIRON STUDIES PROG, 75- *Mem:* AAAS; Am Soc Zoologists; Am Micros Soc; Int Asn. *Res:* Aquatic community ecology; structure and function of animal colonies, with emphasis on the Ectoprocta. *Mailing Add:* Dept of Biol Sci Wright State Univ Dayton OH 45435

WOOD, VAN EARL, b New York, NY, May 25, 33; m 58; c 2. PHYSICS. *Educ:* Union Col, BS, 55; Case Inst Technol, MS, 59, PhD(physics), 61. *Prof Exp:* Fel, 60-73, PRIN PHYSICIST, COLUMBUS LABS, BATTELLE MEM INST, 73- *Mem:* Am Phys Soc. *Res:* Theoretical solid-state physics and materials science; related applied mathematics. *Mailing Add:* 7332 S Section Line Rd Delaware OH 43015

WOOD, VINCENT TUNSTALL, b Phoenix, Ariz, Aug 6, 49. METEOROLOGY, COMPUTER SCIENCE. *Educ:* Univ St Thomas, BA, 73; Tex A&M Univ, MS, 77. *Prof Exp:* RES METEOROLOGIST, NAT SEVERE STORMS LAB, NAT OCEANIC & ATMOSPHERIC ADMIN, 76- *Mem:* Am Meteorol Soc. *Res:* Tornado formation; severe thunderstorms; Doppler weather radar. *Mailing Add:* Nat Severe Storms Lab NOAA 1313 Halley Circle Norman OK 73069

WOOD, WALLACE D(EAN), b Owego, NY, Dec 28, 10; m 37; c 2. ENGINEERING. *Educ:* Rochester Inst Technol, EE, 32; Cornell Univ, AB, 36. *Prof Exp:* Res engr, Taylor Instrument Co, 36-40, dir, 40-70, dir, Taylor Instrument Process Control Div, Standards Lab, Sybron Corp, 70-74. *Mem:* Instrument Soc Am; Nat Soc Prof Engrs; Am Soc Mech Engrs. *Res:* Automatic control analysis; design and maintenance of calibrating standards; test and process equipment. *Mailing Add:* 154 Clover Hills Dr Rochester NY 14618

WOOD, WARREN WILBUR, b Pontiac, Mich, Apr 9, 37; m 61; c 1. GEOCHEMISTRY, HYDROLOGY. *Educ:* Mich State Univ, BS, 59, MS, 62, PhD(geol), 69. *Prof Exp:* Geologist II, Mich Hwy Dept, 62-63; res hydrologist, US Geol Surv, 64-77, asst chief off radiohydrol, 77-78; assoc prof, Dept Geosci, Tex Tech Univ, 78-81; RES HYDROLOGIST, US GEOL SURV, 81- *Concurrent Pos:* Consult hydrologist, 78-81. *Mem:* Am Geophys Union; Geochem Soc; fel Geol Soc Am; Nat Water Well Asn. *Res:* Geochemistry of ground water; artifical recharge; solute transport; hydrology of radioactive waste isolation. *Mailing Add:* US Geol Surv Nat Ctr MS432 Reston VA 22092

WOOD, WILLIAM BAINSTER, b Surry Co, NC, Feb 7, 31; m 52; c 4. MEDICINE. *Educ:* Univ NC, BS, 53, MD, 56. *Prof Exp:* Intern, NC Mem Hosp, Chapel Hill, 56-57, resident internal med, 57-59; assoc physiol, George Washington Univ, 61-63; from instr to asst prof, 63-68, ASSOC PROF MED, SCH MED, UNIV NC, CHAPEL HILL, 68- *Concurrent Pos:* Fel chest dis, Sch Med, Univ NC, 59-60; attend physician, consult & dir pulmonary lab, NC Mem Hosp, Chapel Hill, 63-; attend physician, Gravely Sanatorium, 63-; sr scientist, Wrightsville Maine-Biomed Lab, 66-; hon sr lectr, Cardio Thoracic Inst, London, Eng, 73-74; dir med educ & res, Eastern NC Hosp, 74-, med dir, Wilson, NC, 75- *Mem:* Am Thoracic Soc; AMA; Am Fedn Clin Res; Am Soc Internal Med. *Res:* Pulmonary diseases; morphology of lung in disease; mechanics and control of respiration; effects of hyperbaric atmospheres on respiration; respiratory physiology in deep sea diving; immunological and hypersensitivity lung diseases. *Mailing Add:* Sch of Med Univ of NC Chapel Hill NC 27514

WOOD, WILLIAM BARRY, III, b Baltimore, Md, Feb 19, 38; m 61; c 2. BIOCHEMISTRY, GENETICS. *Educ:* Harvard Univ, AB, 59; Stanford Univ, PhD(biochem), 64. *Prof Exp:* Air Force Off Sci Res, Nat Acad Sci-Nat Res Coun fel molecular biol, Univ Geneva, 63-64; from asst prof to prof, Calif Inst Technol, 65-77; PROF & CHMN, DEPT MOLECULAR, CELLULAR & DEVELOP BIOL, UNIV COLO, 77- *Concurrent Pos:* Guggenheim fel, Dept Molecular, Cellular & Develop Biol, Univ Colo, Boulder, 75-76. *Honors & Awards:* US Steel Award, Nat Acad Sci, 69. *Mem:* Nat Acad Sci; AAAS; Am Acad Arts & Sci; Am Soc Biol Chemists; Soc Develop Biol. *Res:* Genetic control of macromolecular assembly; morphogenesis, structure and function of bacterial viruses; developmental genetics of invertebrates. *Mailing Add:* Univ Colo Campus Box 347 Boulder CO 80309

WOOD, WILLIAM BOOTH, b New York, NY, Sept 9, 22. PHYSIOLOGY. *Educ:* Ft Hays Kans State Col, MS, 51; Univ Kans, PhD(physiol, anat), 59. *Prof Exp:* Lab asst physiol, Univ Kans, 55-56, asst, 56-58, res assoc, 58, asst instr, 58-59; from instr to assoc prof, 59-73, PROF PHARMACOL, COL MED, UNIV TENN, MEMPHIS, 73- *Mem:* AAAS; assoc Am Physiol Soc; Am Soc Pharmacol & Exp Therapeut. *Res:* Respiratory physiology and pharmacology of cardiovascular system. *Mailing Add:* Dept of Pharmacol Univ of Tenn Ctr for Health Sci Memphis TN 38163

WOOD, WILLIAM EDWIN, b Plainfield, NJ, Mar 25, 47; m 71; c 3. MATERIALS SCIENCE. *Educ:* Univ Notre Dame, BS, 69; Univ Calif, Berkeley, MS, 70, DEngr, 73. *Prof Exp:* Asst prof, 73-77, assoc prof, 77-81, PROF MAT SCI, ORE GRAD CTR, 81- *Mem:* Am Soc Metals; Am Welding Soc. *Res:* Physical mechanical metallurgy; alloy developmental design; ferrous and non ferrous materials. *Mailing Add:* Ore Grad Ctr 19600 NW Walker Rd Beaverton OR 97123

WOOD, WILLIAM IRWIN, b Bloomington, Ind, Nov 8, 47; m 73. BIOCHEMISTRY, MOLECULAR BIOLOGY. *Educ:* Cornell Univ, BA, 70; Harvard Univ, MA, 71, PhD(biochem), 77. *Prof Exp:* Comn officer comput sci, USPHS, NIH, 71-73, staff fel biochem, 78-81; SCIENTIST, GENENTECH, INC, 82- *Mem:* AAAS. *Res:* Control of gene expression in eucaryotes, transcription and enzymology; computers in biomedical research. *Mailing Add:* Genentech Inc 460 Point San Bruno Blvd South San Francisco CA 94080

WOOD, WILLIAM WAYNE, b Terry, Mont, Nov 1, 24; m 46; c 5. STATISTICAL MECHANICS. *Educ:* Mont State Col, BS, 47; Calif Inst Technol, PhD(chem), 51. *Prof Exp:* Staff mem, Los Alamos Sci Lab, 50-58, group leader, 58-71, staff mem, 71-81; ASSOC PROF, DEPT PHYSICS, CARROLL COL, HELENA, MONT, 81- *Concurrent Pos:* Vis prof, Univ Colo, 69-70. *Mem:* AAAS; Sigma Xi; fel Am Phys Soc. *Res:* Theory of optical activity; detonation; Monte Carlo and molecular dynamics methods in statistical mechanics. *Mailing Add:* Physics Dept Carroll Col Helena MT 59601

WOOD, WILLIS A, b Johnson City, NY, Aug 6, 21; m 47; c 3. MICROBIOLOGY, BIOCHEMISTRY. *Educ:* Cornell Univ, BS, 47; Ind Univ, PhD, 50. *Prof Exp:* From asst prof to assoc prof dairy bact, Univ Ill, 50-58; prof agr chem, 58-61, chmn dept biochem, 68-74, PROF BIOCHEM, MICH STATE UNIV, 61- *Concurrent Pos:* Dir, Gilford Instrument Labs;

chmn res inst & spec profs adv comt, Nat Inst Dent Res; pres, Neogen Corp, 81- *Honors & Awards:* Lilly Award, Am Soc Microbiol, 55. *Mem:* Am Chem Soc; Am Soc Microbiol; Am Soc Biol Chemists. *Res:* Chemical activities of microorganisms; amino acid metabolism; enzymology; protein structure; instrumentation. *Mailing Add:* Rm 410 Dept of Biochem Mich State Univ East Lansing MI 48824

WOODALL, DAVID MONROE, b Perryville, Ark, Aug 2, 45; m 66. NUCLEAR ENGINEERING, ENGINEERING PHYSICS. *Educ:* Hendrix Col, BA, 67; Columbia Univ, MS, 68; Cornell Univ, PhD(appl physics), 75. *Prof Exp:* Nuclear engr, Westinghouse Nuclear Energy Systs, 68-70; asst prof mech eng, Univ Rochester, 74-77; asst prof nuclear eng, 77-78, assoc prof, 78-79, ASSOC PROF & CHMN CHEM & NUCLEAR ENG, UNIV NMEX, 80- *Mem:* Am Phys Soc; Am Nuclear Soc; Am Soc Mech Engrs. *Res:* Plasma physics, laser-plasma interaction experiments; x-ray imaging. *Mailing Add:* Dept of Chem & Nuclear Eng Univ of NMex Albuquerque NM 87131

WOODALL, HUNTER, JR, b Raleigh, NC, June 14, 30; m 56, 77; c 2. PHYSICS GENERAL. *Educ:* NC State Univ, BIE, 58, MS, 59. *Prof Exp:* Asst indust eng, NC State Univ, 58-59; opers analyst, Tech Opers Inc, 59-61, team leader weapons anal, 61-62, div chief test & exp, 62-65; staff mem, Mitre Corp, 65-68; chief combat support, Off Asst Vchief Staff, Army, 68-70, asst dep under secy army opers res, 70-80, RES DEVELOP & AQUISITION ANALYSIS OFFICER, DEPT ARMY, 80- *Mem:* Opers Res Soc Am. *Res:* Queuing theory; weapons analysis; war gaming; mathematical modeling; computer systems; test and experimentation; Monte Carlo analysis; experimental statistics; methodology of complex problem formulation and solution; military operations research; command, control, communications and intelligence systems. *Mailing Add:* 11920 Gainsborough Rd Potomac MD 20854

WOODALL, WILLIAM ROBERT, JR, b Augusta, Ga, May 29, 45; m 66; c 2. FUEL CHEMISTRY, ENVIRONMENTAL SCIENCE. *Educ:* Univ Ga, BS, 67, MS, 69, PhD(entom), 72. *Prof Exp:* Ecol consult, 72, environ specialist, 72-78, supvr, Environ Ctr, 78-80, MGR, POWER SUPPLY LABS, GA POWER CO, 80-; MGR POWER SUPPLY LBS, 80- *Mem:* Ecol Soc Am; Soc Power Indust Biologists (pres, 77-78). *Res:* Thermal effects; ecology of large rivers, their floodplains, oxbow lakes and swamps; invasion of exotic bivalves; entrainment and impingement of aquatic organisms; larval fish and invertebrate drift; nutrient cycling; coal chemistry. *Mailing Add:* Ga Power Co 17/333 PO Box 4545 Atlanta GA 30302

WOODARD, HELEN QUINCY, b Detroit, Mich, Aug 8, 00. BIOCHEMISTRY, RADIOBIOLOGY. *Educ:* Stetson Univ, BS, 20; Columbia Univ, AM, 21, PhD(chem), 25. *Prof Exp:* Res chemist, 25-56, assoc biochemist, 56-66, EMER ASSOC BIOCHEMIST, MEM CTR CANCER & ALLIED DIS, 66-; CONSULT, SLOAN-KETTERING INST, 68- *Concurrent Pos:* Asst mem, Sloan-Kettering Inst, 48-60, assoc mem, 60-68; asst prof, Med Col, Cornell Univ, 52-64, assoc prof, 64-68. *Mem:* AAAS; Am Chem Soc; Radiation Res Soc; Am Asn Cancer Res; Health Physics Soc. *Res:* Chemical effects of gamma and x-rays; serum and tissue phosphatases; clinical biochemistry in bone disease; effects of radiation on bone; metabolism of bone-seeking isotopes; biological effects of radiation. *Mailing Add:* Sloan-Kettering Inst 1275 York Ave New York NY 10021

WOODARD, HENRY HERMAN, JR, b Salisbury, Mass, Dec 18, 25; m 49; c 2. GEOLOGY. *Educ:* Dartmouth Col, AB, 47, AM, 49; Univ Chicago, PhD, 55. *Prof Exp:* Geologist, US Geol Surv, 47-49 & State Develop Comn, Maine, 50-51; assoc prof geol, 53-66, chmn div natural sci & math, 62-66, PROF GEOL & CHMN DEPT, BELOIT COL, 66- *Concurrent Pos:* Geologist, Geol Surv Nfld, 55 & US Geol Surv, 57. *Mem:* Geol Soc Am; Geochem Soc; Nat Asn Geol Teachers; Am Geophys Union. *Res:* Diffusion in naturally occurring silicates; geology of Newfoundland and Boulder batholith; structure and petrology of southwestern Maine; contact alteration associated with tertiary stocks in central Colorado; marine sanidines from Ordovician of Wisconsin; structural geology and petrology of the eastern contact zone vermilion batholith, Minnesota. *Mailing Add:* Dept of Geol Beloit Col Beloit WI 53511

WOODARD, JAMES CARROLL, b Birmingham, Ala, Nov 19, 33. NUTRITION, COMPARATIVE PATHOLOGY. *Educ:* Auburn Univ, DVM, 58; Mass Inst Technol, PhD(nutrit, path), 65. *Prof Exp:* Parasitologist, Fla Vet Diag Lab, Fla Livestock Bd, 58-59; instr vet path, Auburn Univ, 61-62; res assoc, Mass Inst Technol, 63-65; NIH fel, 65-66, asst prof, 66-70, head dir comp path, 74-80, assoc prof, 78, PROF PATH, COL MED & VET MED, UNIV FLA, 78- *Mem:* Am Vet Med Asn; Int Acad Path; Am Inst Nutrit; Am Soc Exp Path; NY from asst prof to assoc prof, 66-78, pathology, biochemical relationships of disease to microscopic pathology. *Mailing Add:* Div of Comp Path Univ of Fla Gainesville FL 32610

WOODARD, KENNETH EUGENE, JR, b Middletown, Ohio, Oct 7, 42; m 69; c 3. ELECTROCHEMICAL ENGINEERING. *Educ:* Univ Cincinnati, BS, 65. *Prof Exp:* Prod & develop engr chloralkali, Olin Mathieson Chem Corp, 65-69; prod supvr chloralkali & fluorocarbons, Vulcan Mat Co, 69-74; sect mgr chloralkali, 74-75, mgr electrochem develop chloralakali, Olin Corp Chem Group, 75-79, mgr electrochem technol, Olin Corp, 79-81. *Mem:* Electrochem Soc; Int Electrochem Soc. *Mailing Add:* Olin Corp Chem Group PO 248 Charleston TN 37310

WOODARD, RALPH EMERSON, b Nelsonville, Ohio, May 27, 21; m 43; c 3. RESEARCH ADMINISTRATION, REACTOR PHYSICS. *Educ:* Wittenberg Col, BA, 53; Oak Ridge Sch Reactor Technol, dipl, 57; Indust Col Armed Forces, dipl, 70; George Washington Univ, MSBA, 71. *Prof Exp:* Res physicist, Wright Air Develop Ctr, US Dept Air Force, 53-56, gen physicist, Oak Ridge Nat Lab, 56-57, nuclear physicist, Wright Air Develop Ctr, 57-61, gen engr res & tech plans, Aeronaut Systs Div, 61-63, supvry physicist & dep dir gen physics res lab, Aerospace Res Labs, 63-71, phys sci adminr, 71-75, phys sci adminr, Air Force Wright Aeronaut Labs, 75-79, phys sci adminr, Air Force Mat Lab, 80-82; RETIRED. *Concurrent Pos:* Instr, Wittenberg Col, 57-58. *Mem:* Am Phys Soc. *Res:* Laboratory management; plasma physics; solid state physics; mathematics; chemistry; fluid mechanics; metallurgy and ceramics; energy conversion; research management. *Mailing Add:* 305 Gordon Rd Springfield OH 45504

WOODARD, ROBERT LOUIS, b South Bristol, NY, June 16, 17; m 44; c 2. SCIENCE EDUCATION, ASTRONOMY. *Educ:* Syracuse Univ, BS, 39; State Univ NY Col Geneseo, MS, 56; Cornell Univ, PhD(sci educ), 63. *Prof Exp:* Boy's worker, Woods Run Settlement House, Pa, 39-41; supt parks, Greensboro, NC, 46-47; self-employed, 47-49; munic engr, Naples, NY, 49-51; elem & jr high sch teacher, NY, 53-57; assoc prof, 60-64, prof phys sci & astron, 64-76, DIR INSTNL RES, 67- *Mem:* Nat Asn Res Sci Teaching; Asn Instnl Res; Am Asn Higher Educ. *Mailing Add:* Off of Instnl Res Indiana Univ Indiana PA 15701

WOODBREY, JAMES C, b Sebago Lake, Maine, Oct 16, 34; m 56; c 3. POLYMER SCIENCE, MATERIALS SCIENCE. *Educ:* Univ Maine, BS, 56; Mich State Univ, PhD(phys chem, physics, org chem), 60. *Prof Exp:* Sr res chemist, Res Div, W R Grace & Co, Md, 60-61; sr res chemist, Plastics Div, Fund Res, Mass, 61-65, res specialist & res projs leader, Explor & Fund Mats Res, Cent Res Dept, Mo, 65-67, sr res specialist & res projs leader, Composites Res & Develop, New Enterprise Div, 67-69, sci fel & res projs mgr, Polymer & Composite Mats Res, 69-77, New Prod Develop Dept, 77-, SR SCI FEL & RES PROJS MGR, PLASTICS & RESINS CO, MONSANTO CO, 80- *Mem:* Am Chem Soc; AAAS. *Res:* Chemical, physical and mechanical properties, molecular and solid-state structures and preparations of macromolecular and composite materials; magnetic resonance and vibrational spectros; solution thermodynamics; surface physical chemistry. *Mailing Add:* Monsanto Co Res Ctr 800 N Lindbergh Blvd St Louis MO 63166

WOODBRIDGE, DAVID DAVIS, b Seattle, Wash, Jan 29, 22; m 50; c 3. PHYSICS, METEOROLOGY. *Educ:* Univ Wash, BS, 49; Ore State Univ, MS, 51, PhD(physics), 56. *Prof Exp:* Asst physics, Ore State Univ, 51-54; asst prof, Colo Sch Mines, 54-57; chief space environ br, Res Projs Lab, Ballistic Missile Agency, US Dept Army, 57-60, dir exp progs, Requirement & Plans Div, Rocket & Guided Missile Agency, 60-61; staff scientist, Chance Vought, Tex, 61-62; dir res & head physics dept, 62-69, prof sci educ & physics, Dir Univ Ctr Pollution Res & head Dept Sci Educ, Fla Inst Technol, 69-77; staff scientist, Watson & Assocs, Inc, 77-78; MGR ENVIRON ANALYSIS GROUP, HITTMAN ASSOCS INC, COLUMBIA, MD, 78- *Concurrent Pos:* Consult, High Altitude Observ, Univ Colo, 56-57; prof, Exten Div, Univ Ala, 57-61; vis lectr, Washington Univ, 60; pollution consult, Envirolab, Inc, Fla, 71- *Mem:* Am Meteorol Soc; Am Inst Aeronaut & Astronaut; Am Asn Physics Teachers; Am Geophys Union; Solar Energy Soc. *Res:* Pollution abatement; irradiation of waste water; physics of atmosphere and space; effects of solar storms on high-level circulation patterns; extra low frequency radiation; energy conversion. *Mailing Add:* 5333 High Tor Hill Columbia MD 21045

WOODBRIDGE, JOSEPH ELIOT, b Philadelphia, Pa, July 15, 21; m 49; c 6. CLINICAL CHEMISTRY, PHYSICAL CHEMISTRY. *Educ:* Princeton Univ, PhD(chem), 48. *Prof Exp:* Chemist, Manhattan Proj, 44; from res chemist to group leader, Atlantic Refining Co, 46-60; dir res, Hartman-Leddon Co, 60-66; res dir, Sadtler Res Labs, Inc, Pa, 66-68; dir clin res, Worthington Biochem Corp, NJ, 68-71; vpres diag prod, Princeton Biomedix Inc, 71-81; PRES, ALLADIN DIAGNOSTICS INC, 81- *Mem:* Am Chem Soc; Am Asn Clin Chemists; Sigma Xi; Am Soc Clin Pathol. *Res:* Synthetic detergents; petrochemicals; clinical reagents; mass spectrometry. *Mailing Add:* 84 Bayard Lane Princeton NJ 08540

WOODBURN, MARGY JEANETTE, b Pontiac, Ill, Sept 5, 28. FOOD SCIENCE, MICROBIOLOGY. *Educ:* Univ Ill, Urbana, BS, 50; Univ Wis, Madison, MS, 56, PhD(exp foods), 59. *Prof Exp:* Instr foods & nutrit, Univ Wis, Madison, 56-57; from assoc prof to prof, Purdue Univ, 59-69; PROF & HEAD DEPT FOODS & NUTRIT, SCH HOME ECON, ORE STATE UNIV, 69-, ASSOC DEAN RES, 80- *Concurrent Pos:* Nat Res Coun res assoc, Ft Detrick, Md, 68. *Honors & Awards:* Borden Award, 76. *Mem:* Am Dietetic Asn; Am Home Econ Asn; Am Pub Health Asn; Am Soc Microbiol; Inst Food Technol. *Res:* Food microbiology; staphylococcal enterotoxins; foodborne pathogenic bacteria. *Mailing Add:* Dept Foods & Nutrit Sch Home Econ Ore State Univ Corvallis OR 97331

WOODBURN, RUSSELL, b Central City, Ky, Feb 16, 07; m 33; c 2. CIVIL ENGINEERING. *Educ:* Univ Ky, BS, 29. *Prof Exp:* Field engr, Erie RR Co, 29-30 & Mo State Hwy Dept, 30-33; engr soil & water res & field opers, US Dept Agr, 33-56, dir sedimentation lab, Agr Res Serv, Miss, 56-61, chief southern br, Soil & Water Conserv Res Div Ga, 61-64; assoc coordr res & dir eng exp sta, 64-72, from assoc prof to prof civil eng, 64-72, EMER PROF CIVIL ENG, UNIV MISS, 72- *Concurrent Pos:* Alderman & commissioner, Elec Power, Water & Sewer Depts, Oxford, Miss, 73-81. *Mem:* Fel Am Soc Agr Engrs. *Res:* Soil and water conservation and research; engineering education and structures; research administration. *Mailing Add:* Box 283 University MS 38677

WOODBURN, WILTON A, b Pittsburgh, Pa, Nov 2, 26; m 56; c 3. MECHANICAL ENGINEERING. *Educ:* Carnegie Inst Technol, BS, 47, MS, 56. *Prof Exp:* Res engr, Eng Design Div, Alcoa Res Labs, 47-65 & Fabricating Metall Div, 65-72, eng assoc, 72-80, SR TECH SPECIALIST, FABRICATING TECHNOL DIV, ALCOA TECH CTR, ALUMINUM CO AM, 80- *Mem:* Am Soc Mech Engrs. *Res:* Fabricating processes, particularly hot and cold rolling; computerized control for preset, guage and flatness. *Mailing Add:* Fabricating Technol Div Alcoa Labs Alcoa Center PA 15069

WOODBURNE, MICHAEL O, b Ann Arbor, Mich, Mar 8, 37; m 60; c 2. VERTEBRATE PALEONTOLOGY, STRATIGRAPHY. *Educ:* Univ Mich, BS, 58, MS, 60; Univ Calif, Berkeley, PhD(paleont), 66. *Prof Exp:* Mus technician vert paleont, Univ Calif, Berkeley, 62-65, mus scientist, 65-66; res assoc, Princeton Univ, 66; from lectr to asst prof, 66-71, assoc prof, 71-77, PROF GEOL, UNIV CALIF, RIVERSIDE, 78- *Mem:* Soc Vert Paleont; Am Soc Mammal; Paleont Soc; Soc Study Evolution; Geol Soc Am. *Res:* Mammalian paleontology, including Australian marsupials; biostratigraphy and paleontology of the Mojave Desert. *Mailing Add:* Dept of Geol Sci Univ of Calif Riverside CA 92502

WOODBURNE, RUSSELL THOMAS, b London, Ont, Nov 2, 04; US citizen; m 34; c 3. ANATOMY. *Educ:* Univ Mich, AB, 32, MA, 33, PhD(anat), 35. *Prof Exp:* From instr to prof, 36-74, chmn dept, 58-73, EMER PROF ANAT, MED SCH, UNIV MICH, ANN ARBOR, 75- *Mem:* Am Asn Anat (secy-treas, 64-72, pres, 74-75); Can Asn Anat. *Res:* Structure of mammalian midbrain; pleura; blood vessels of pancreas, liver, urinary bladder, ureter and urethra. *Mailing Add:* Dept Anat 5810 Med Sci II Bldg Univ of Mich Med Sch Ann Arbor MI 48109

WOODBURY, DIXON MILES, b St George, Utah, Aug 6, 21; m 45; c 3. PHARMACOLOGY. *Educ:* Univ Utah, BS, 42, MS, 45; Univ Calif, PhD(zool), 48. *Prof Exp:* Asst zool, Univ Calif, 44-47; res instr physiol & pharmacol, 47-50, asst res prof, 50-53, assoc res prof pharmacol, 53-59, assoc prof, 59-61, PROF PHARMACOL, COL MED, UNIV UTAH, 61-, CHMN DEPT, 72- *Concurrent Pos:* USPHS grant, Col Med, Univ Utah, 47-50; NIH res career award, 62-; Nat Neurol Res Found scientist, Univ Utah, 58; mem pharmacol training comt, NIH, 61-65; mem adv panel on epilepsies, Surgeon Gen, USPHS, 66-69; mem prog proj comt A, Nat Inst Neurol Dis & Stroke, 67-71, comt anticonvulsants, 68- & vis scientist, Epilepsy Sect, 78; prof, State Univ Leiden, 68; mem neurobiol merit rev bd, Vet Admin, 72-74; mem prof adv bd & nat bd dirs, Epilepsy Found Am, 73-; distinguished res prof, Univ Utah, 73-74. *Mem:* Am Soc Pharmacol & Exp Therapeut; Endocrine Soc; Soc Neurosci; Am Soc Neurochem; Int Soc Neurochem. *Res:* Brain electrolyte metabolism; convulsive disorders; endocrinology; effects of hormones on the nervous system; neurochemistry; development of the nervous system; blood-brain barrier; metabolism of drugs. *Mailing Add:* Dept of Pharmacol Univ of Utah Col of Med Salt Lake City UT 84132

WOODBURY, ERIC JOHN, b Washington, DC, Feb 9, 25; m 46; c 3. PHYSICS. *Educ:* Calif Inst Technol, BS, 47, PhD(physics), 51. *Prof Exp:* Asst, Calif Inst Technol, 47-51; mem tech staff, 51-53, group head & sr staff engr, Electronics Dept, Guided Missile Lab, 53-60, sr staff physicist, Radar & Missile Electronics Lab, 61-62, sr scientist, 62-63, asst dept mgr, Laser Develop Dept, 63-66, mgr laser dept, 66-69, mgr laser develop dept, 69-72, mgr tactical laser systs lab, 72-76, CHIEF SCIENTIST, LASER SYSTS DIV, HUGHES AIRCRAFT CO, 76- *Concurrent Pos:* Mem indust adv comt, Tech Educ Res Ctr, 72-75. *Mem:* Am Phys Soc; fel Inst Elec & Electronics Engrs; Sigma Xi. *Res:* Noise in electronic systems; application of solid state to electronic devices; electronic systems for use in missiles and satellites; experimental nuclear physics; optical masers; laser systems and components. *Mailing Add:* 18621 Tarzana Dr Tarzana CA 91356

WOODBURY, GEORGE WALLIS, JR, b Oct 13, 37; US citizen; m 60; c 2. PHYSICAL CHEMISTRY. *Educ:* Univ Idaho, BS, 59; Univ Minn, PhD(phys chem), 64. *Prof Exp:* Res assoc chem, Univ Minn, 64-65 & Cornell Univ, 65-66; from asst prof to assoc prof, 66-74, PROF CHEM, UNIV MONT, 74- *Mem:* Am Chem Soc; Am Phys Soc. *Res:* Statistical mechanics of cooperative phenomena. *Mailing Add:* Dept of Chem Univ of Mont Missoula MT 59801

WOODBURY, HENRY HUGH, b Paterson, NJ, Sept 24, 28; m 55; c 7. PHYSICS. *Educ:* Calif Inst Technol, BS, 49, PhD(physics), 53. *Prof Exp:* PHYSICIST, RES & DEVELOP CTR, GEN ELEC CO, 53- *Mem:* Fel Am Phys Soc. *Res:* Solid state physics, particularly research and development on semiconducting materials. *Mailing Add:* Res & Develop Ctr Gen Elec Co Box 8 Schenectady NY 12301

WOODBURY, JOHN F L, b London, Eng, Dec 22, 18; Can citizen; m 43; c 3. MEDICINE. *Educ:* Dalhousie Univ, BSc, 39, MD, CM, 43; Royal Col Physicians Can, cert, 52; FRCP(C), 72. *Prof Exp:* Assoc prof, 46-49, PROF MED & DIR RHEUMATIC DIS UNIT, DALHOUSIE UNIV, 69- *Mem:* Fel Am Col Physicians; Am Rheumatism Asn; Can Rheumatism Asn; Can Med Asn. *Res:* Etiology and immunology of arthritis. *Mailing Add:* Suite 8-016 Victoria Gen Hosp Halifax NS B3H 2Y9 Can

WOODBURY, JOHN WALTER, b St George, Utah, Aug 7, 23; m 49; c 4. PHYSIOLOGY, BIOPHYSICS. *Educ:* Univ Utah, BS, 43, MS, 47, PhD(physiol), 50. *Prof Exp:* Lab asst physics, Univ Utah, 42-43; staff mem, Radiation Lab, Mass Inst Technol, 43-45; res asst physiol, Univ Utah, 45-47; from instr to asst prof physiol, Sch Med, Univ Wash, 50-57, from assoc prof to prof physiol & biophys, 57-73; PROF PHYSIOL, COL MED, UNIV UTAH, 73- *Mem:* AAAS; Am Physiol Soc; Biophys Soc; Inst Elec & Electronics Eng; Soc Neurosci. *Res:* Electrophysiology of excitable tissues; ion transport through membranes; characteristics of anion channels; anion permeability. *Mailing Add:* Dept of Physiol Sch Med Univ Res Park 410 Chipeta Way Salt Lake City UT 84108

WOODBURY, LOWELL ANGUS, b St George, Utah, Oct 11, 10; m 36; c 4. MEDICAL STATISTICS. *Educ:* Univ Utah, BS, 33, MS, 34; Univ Mich, PhD(zool), 40. *Prof Exp:* Res assoc anat, Sch Med, Univ Utah, 45-46, asst prof physiol, 46-52; chief biostatistician, Atomic Bomb Casualty Comn, 52-58; statistician, WHO, 59-70; assoc res prof, Div Radiobiol, Col Med, Univ Utah, 70-76; CONSULT MED STATIST & EPILEPSY, 70- *Mem:* Am Statist Asn; Biomet Soc; Am Physiol Soc. *Res:* Bone micromorphommetry; stereology; epidemiology of convulsive disorders; clinical drug trials; health information systems. *Mailing Add:* Box 116 Toquerville UT 84774

WOODBURY, MAX ATKIN, b St George, Utah, Apr 30, 17; m 47; c 4. BIOMATHEMATICS, COMPUTER SCIENCE. *Educ:* Univ Utah, BS, 39; Univ Mich, MS, 40, PhD(math), 48; Univ NC, Chapel Hill, MPH. *Prof Exp:* Instr math, Univ Mich, 47-49; Off Naval Res grant & mem, Inst Advan Study, 49-50; res assoc math & econ, Princeton Univ, 50-52; assoc prof statist, Univ Pa, 52-54; prin investr, Logistics Res Proj, George Washington Univ, 54-56; res prof math, Col Eng, NY Univ, 56-62, prof exp neurol, Med Ctr, 63-65; PROF BIOMATH, MED CTR, DUKE UNIV, 66-, PROF COMPUT SCI, 71- *Concurrent Pos:* Gov & indust consult, 51-; mem opers res adv coun, New York, 64-68; mem diag radiol adv group, Nat Cancer Inst, 74-77; sr fel, Ctr Study Aging & Human Develop, 75-; mem several nat comts weather modification & NIH & Food & Drug Admin study sects. *Mem:* Fel AAAS; fel Inst Math Statist; fel Am Statist Asn. *Res:* Computing; statistics; models in biology and medicine; quantitative models of information about biomedical systems require mathematics, probability and basic sciences for formulation, statistics of estimation of parametrics and testing, computing and numerical analysis for calculation. *Mailing Add:* Biomath Duke Univ Med Ctr PO Box 3200 Durham NC 27710

WOODBURY, RICHARD C, b Salt Lake City, Utah, Apr 19, 31; m 54; c 6. SOLID STATE ELECTRONICS. *Educ:* Univ Utah, BS, 56; Stanford Univ, MS, 58, PhD(elec eng), 65. *Prof Exp:* Engr, Oscilloscope Circuit Design, Hewlett-Packard Co, Calif, 56-59; asst prof elec eng, Brigham Young Univ, 59-62; res assoc, Stanford Electronics Labs, 62-65; from asst prof to assoc prof, 65-72, PROF ELEC ENG, BRIGHAM YOUNG UNIV, 72- *Concurrent Pos:* Nat Sci Found grants, 68-72; res consult, Eyring Res Inst, Provo, Utah, 75-78. *Mem:* Inst Elec & Electronics Engrs. *Res:* Magnetic devices; silicon monolithic integrated circuits; silicon and cadmium sulfide photovoltaic cells; radiation hardening of silicon electron voltaic and photovoltaic cells. *Mailing Add:* Dept of Elec Eng 458 CB Brigham Young Univ Provo UT 84602

WOODCOCK, ALFRED HERBERT, b Atlanta, Ga, Sept 7, 05; m 41; c 3. OCEANOGRAPHY. *Hon Degrees:* DSc, Long Island Univ, 61. *Prof Exp:* Technician, Woods Hole Oceanog Inst, 31-42, res assoc, 42-46, oceanogr, 46-63; res assoc geophys, Hawaii Inst Geophys, 63-72, RES AFFIL, DEPT OCEANOG, UNIV HAWAII, 72- *Mem:* AAAS; fel Am Meteorol Soc; assoc Am Geophys Union. *Res:* Marine meteorology; air-sea interaction; sea-salt nuclei in marine air and their role in cloud, rain and fog formation; Hawaii Alpine Lake, permafrost and mountain breathing studies. *Mailing Add:* Dept Oceanog Univ Hawaii Honolulu HI 96822

WOODCOCK, CHARLES MARTIN, b Newark, NJ, Aug 9, 20. FOOD SCIENCE. *Educ:* Univ Mass, BSc, 42; Ohio State Univ, MSc, 47. *Prof Exp:* Instr food freezing & preserv, Ohio State Univ, 46-47; proj leader, Packaging Res Sect, Cent Labs, 47-53, head, 53-58, lab mgr, Post Div, 58-72, SR RES SPECIALIST, TECH CTR, GEN FOODS CORP, 72- *Mem:* Sigma Xi; Inst Food Technologists; Packaging Inst; Soc Packaging & Handling Engrs. *Res:* Packaging of foodstuffs including papers, films, foils, glass and shipping containers; product and process improvement of cereals and beverage powders. *Mailing Add:* Tech Ctr Gen Foods Corp Cranbury NJ 08519

WOODCOCK, CHRISTOPHER LEONARD FRANK, b Essex, Eng, July 9, 42; m 64; c 3. CELL BIOLOGY, BIOCHEMISTRY. *Educ:* Univ Col, Univ London, BSc, 63, PhD(bot), 66. *Prof Exp:* Res fel biophys, Univ Chicago, 66-67; res fel bot, Harvard Univ, 67-69, lectr biol, 69-72; asst prof, 72-75, assoc prof, 75-78, PROF ZOOL, UNIV MASS, AMHERST, 78- *Mem:* Am Soc Cell Biol. *Res:* Cell ultrastructure and function; information processing in cells; chromatin structure and function. *Mailing Add:* Dept of Zool Univ of Mass Amherst MA 01003

WOODFIELD, F(RANK) W(ILLIAM), JR, b Astoria, Ore, Mar 1, 18; m 44; c 3. CHEMICAL ENGINEERING. *Educ:* Ore State Col, BS, 39; Columbia Univ, MS, 40. *Prof Exp:* Chem engr process eng & eng res, E I du Pont de Nemours & Co, Inc, 40-47; increasing responsibility group leader to mgr eng develop, Gen Elec Co, 47-55, mgr reactor mat develop, 55-62, specialist contract admin, 62-63, mgr programming, 64; dep staff mgr programming & tech develop, Pac Northwest Lab, Battelle Mem Inst, 65-66, mgr develop, Fast Flux Test Facility, 67-68, asst lab dir tech serv, 68-70, mgr facilities planning & eng, 70-73, prog mgr plenum fill exp, 74; mgr res & technol ctr, 75-81, MGR LOGISTICS, EXXON NUCLEAR CO INC, 81- *Mem:* Am Chem Soc; Am Nuclear Soc; Am Inst Chem Engrs. *Res:* Chemical engineering diffusional operations; technical and administrative management of research and development in a broad-spectrum laboratory. *Mailing Add:* Exxon Nuclear Co Inc 2101 Horn Rapids Rd Richland WA 99352

WOODFILL, MARVIN CARL, b Los Angeles, Calif, June 13, 38; m 80; c 5. ELECTRICAL ENGINEERING. *Educ:* Iowa State Univ, BS, 59, MS, 61, PhD(elec eng), 64. *Prof Exp:* Asst prof elec eng, Iowa State Univ, 59-64; from asst prof to assoc prof, 66-74, PROF ELEC ENG, ARIZ STATE UNIV, 74- *Concurrent Pos:* Engr consult, Sperry Flight Systs, Ariz, 66-67, semiconductor prod div, Motorola, Inc, 68-70, govt electronics div, 71, St Joseph's Hosp & Med Ctr, Phoenix, 70- & City of Prescott, 79- *Mem:* Inst Elec & Electronics Engrs. *Res:* Development of mini-micro computer systems for engineering and medical applications. *Mailing Add:* Col of Eng Sci Ariz State Univ Tempe AZ 85281

WOODFIN, BEULAH MARIE, b Chicago, Ill, June 22, 36. BIOCHEMISTRY. *Educ:* Vanderbilt Univ, BA, 58; Univ Ill, Urbana, MS, 60, PhD(biochem), 63. *Prof Exp:* Res assoc biochem, Univ Mich, 63-66, instr, 66-67; ASST PROF BIOCHEM, SCH MED, UNIV N MEX, 67- *Concurrent Pos:* USPHS fel, Univ Mich, 63-65. *Mem:* AAAS; Am Chem Soc; NY Acad Sci. *Res:* Correlation of activity and structure of enzymes; experimental mouse model of Reye's syndrome. *Mailing Add:* Dept of Biochem Univ of NMex Sch of Med Albuquerque NM 87131

WOODFORD, DAVID A(UBREY), b Cleethorpes, Eng, Sept 17, 37; m 61; c 3. PHYSICAL METALLURGY. *Educ:* Univ Birmingham, BSc, 60, PhD(metall), 63. *Hon Degrees:* DSc, Univ Birmingham, 81. *Prof Exp:* Res fel, Univ Birmingham, 63-64; res metallurgist, Mat & Processes Lab, 64-73, STAFF METALLURGIST, CORP RES & DEVELOP, GEN ELEC CO, 73- *Concurrent Pos:* Assoc ed, J Eng Mat & Tech, 74- & Fatigue Eng Mat & Struct, 78- *Honors & Awards:* A H Geisler Award, 72. *Mem:* Am Soc Metals; Am Soc Testing & Mat; Am Soc Mech Engrs. *Res:* High temperature mechanical properties; creep and radiation damage; strain aging superplasticity; temper embrittlement; thermal fatigue; cavitation erosion; environmental embrittlement; author or coauthor of 60 publications. *Mailing Add:* Corp Res & Develop Bldg K-1 Gen Elec Co Schenectady NY 12301

WOODFORD, JAMES B(EACH), JR, b Calif, Feb 27, 28; m 56; c 3. ELECTRICAL ENGINEERING. *Educ:* Carnegie Inst Technol, BSc, 48, MS, 39, DSc(elec eng), 50. *Prof Exp:* Assoc prof elec eng, Carnegie Inst Technol, 50-60; assoc group dir advan orbital systs, Calif, 60-71, PRIN DIR DATA SYSTS & TELECOMMUN, EASTERN TECH DIV, AEROSPACE CORP, WASHINGTON, DC, 71- *Mem:* Inst Elec & Electronics Engrs. *Res:* Electronics; communications; system engineering; satellite systems. *Mailing Add:* 11218 Wedge Dr 955 L'Enfant Plaza Southwest Washington DC 20024

WOODFORD, VERNON RICH, JR, biochemistry, deceased

WOODFORD, WARREN JAMES, b Roanoke, Va, Mar 18, 46. FORENSIC CHEMISTRY, TOXICOLOGY. *Educ:* East Carolina Univ, BS, 68; Emory Univ, MS, 70, PhD(chem), 73. *Prof Exp:* Fel med chem, Dept Medicinal Chem, Sch Pharm, Univ Kans, 73-74; res assoc chem, Dept Chem, Emory Univ, 74-75; DIR, WEB RES, ATLANTA, GA, 75- *Concurrent Pos:* Res award, Nat Cancer Inst, 73; vis scientist & guest seminar speaker, Metro Police Forensic Sci Lab, Scotland Yard, 75, 77 & 79; lectr chem, Chem Dept, Emory Univ, 76-77; instr clin chem, Sch Pharm, Mercer Univ, 77-78; bd dir, Metrop Atlanta Coun Alcohol & Drugs, 79-82. *Mem:* Am Chem Soc; AAAS. *Res:* Chemical testing for court purposes; chemical analyses of tangible evidence. *Mailing Add:* 585 Lakeshore Dr NE Atlanta GA 30307

WOODGATE, BRUCE EDWARD, b Eastbourne, Sussex, Eng, Feb 19, 39; m 65; c 2. ASTROPHYSICS. *Educ:* Univ London, BSc, 61, PhD(astron), 65. *Prof Exp:* From res asst to res assoc physics, Univ Col, Univ London, 65-71; sr res assoc, Columbia Univ, 71-74, assoc dir Astrophys Lab, 72-74; sci systs analyst, 74-75, ASTROPHYSICIST, GOODARD INST SPACE STUDIES, NASA, 75- *Concurrent Pos:* Mem working group, NASA Outlook for Space Study, 74. *Mem:* Am Astron Soc; Fel Royal Astron Soc. *Res:* X-ray astronomy; astronomy of galaxies and their interstellar medium; solar physics and solar-terrestrial relations; remote sensing of earth resources. *Mailing Add:* Code 683 Goddard Space Flight Ctr NASA Greenbelt MD 20771

WOODHAM, DONALD W, b Jacksonville, Ala, July 9, 29; m 54; c 1. ANALYTICAL CHEMISTRY. *Educ:* Jacksonville State Univ, BS, 54; Am Inst Chemists, cert, 73. *Prof Exp:* Chem aide, Phosphate Develop Works, Tenn Valley Authority, 54-55, control chemist, 55-57; res chemist, Pesticide Chem Br, Entom Res Div, 57-65, res chemist, Plant Pest Control Div, Miss, 65-67, supvry chemist, 67-70, chemist in-chg plant pest control prog, Animal & Plant Health Inspection Serv, 70-75, lab supvr, Pink Bollworm Rearing Facil, Animal & Plant Health Inspection Serv, Agr Res Serv, USDA, 75-77; NEW PEST DETECTION & SURV STAFF, USDA APHIS PPQ, 78- *Mem:* AAAS; Am Chem Soc; Entom Soc Am; Am Inst Chemists; Sigma Xi. *Res:* Analysis of phosphorous intermediates used in the synthesis of nerve gas; pesticide residues in crops; animal products and miscellaneous materials; analysis of environmental samples for pesticide and herbicide residues; development of new methods for the analysis of pesticides and pesticide residues; confirmation methods for identification purposes; methods utilized in the rearing, irradiation and shipment of pink bollworm moths. *Mailing Add:* USDA APHIS PPQ 659 Federal Bldg Hyattsville MD 20782

WOODHOUR, ALLEN F, b Newark, NJ, Feb 21, 30; m 55; c 1. VIROLOGY, BACTERIOLOGY. *Educ:* St Vincent Col, AB, 52; Cath Univ Am, MS, 54, PhD(bact), 56. *Prof Exp:* Bacteriologist, Walter Reed Army Inst Res, 56-57; res assoc virol, Charles Pfizer & Co, Inc, 57-60; res assoc, 60-64, asst dir, Dept Virus Dis, 64-66, dir viral vaccine res, 66-73, asst dir virus & cell biol res, 68-73, sr dir & asst area head virus cell biol res, 74-78, EXEC DIR BACT VACCINES & ADMIN AFFAIRS, VIRUS & CELL BIOL RES, MERCK INST THERAPEUT RES, 78- *Mem:* AAAS; Am Asn Immunol; Sigma Xi; Int Asn Biol Stand; Am Soc Microbiol. *Res:* Use of adjuvants in immunology; metabolizable vegetable oil water-in-oil adjuvant; respiratory viruses for vaccine development; development of bacterial vaccines; antivirals. *Mailing Add:* Merck Inst of Therapeut Res West Point PA 19486

WOODHOUSE, BERNARD LAWRENCE, b Norfolk, Va, Aug 14, 36; m 64; c 2. PHARMACOLOGY. *Educ:* Howard Univ, BS, 58, MS, 63, PhD(pharmacol), 73. *Prof Exp:* Instr zool, A&T Col NC, 63-64; from instr to asst prof, 64-73, assoc prof, 73-81, PROF BIOL, SAVANNAH STATE COL, 81- *Concurrent Pos:* Hoffmann-La Roche res grant & NIH res grant, 75- *Res:* Study of the mechanism of the antihypertensive effects of beta adrenergic blocking drugs on various species of animals. *Mailing Add:* Dept of Biol Savannah State Col Savannah GA 31404

WOODHOUSE, EDWARD JOHN, b Norwich, Eng, Apr 22, 39. CHEMISTRY, TOXICOLOGY. *Educ:* Univ Nottingham, BSc, 61, PhD(chem), 64. *Prof Exp:* Res assoc inorg chem, Ore State Univ, 64-67; sr chemist, 67-74, prin chemist, 74-80, HEAD BIOANALYTICAL CHEM SECT, MIDWEST RES INST, 80- *Mem:* AAAS; Am Chem Soc; NY Acad Sci; Int Asn Forensic Toxicol. *Res:* Radiochemistry; analytical chemistry; solvent extraction; analysis of drugs in body fluids and dosage form; marijuana chemistry and metabolism; analysis and metabolism distribution of xenobiotics in animal systems. *Mailing Add:* Midwest Res Inst 425 Volker Blvd Kansas City MO 64110

WOODHOUSE, JOHN CRAWFORD, b New Bedford, Mass, Apr 29, 98; m 27; c 2. CHEMISTRY. *Educ:* Dartmouth Col, BA, 21, MA, 23; Harvard Univ, AM, 24, PhD(chem), 27. *Hon Degrees:* MA, Dartmouth Col, 61. *Prof Exp:* Instr chem, Dartmouth Col, 21-23; from asst to instr, Harvard Univ, 23-25; consult, 26-28; chemist, Ammonia Dept, E I du Pont de Nemours & Co, 28-42, asst dir chem div, Grasselli Chem Dept, 42, dir, 43-44, dir tech div, 44-50, dir atomic energy div, 50-62; CONSULT ATOMIC ENERGY & CHEM, 62-; COUNR & SECY BD, COL MARINE STUDIES, UNIV DEL, 72- *Concurrent Pos:* Overseer, Thayer Sch Eng, Dartmouth Col, 56, trustee, Col, 60; consult mem steering comt, Panel Tech Adv, US Dept Defense, 58. *Mem:* Am Chem Soc; Am Nuclear Soc; Am Inst Chem Engrs; Brit Soc Chem Indust. *Res:* Corrosion; gaseous adsorption; high pressure; organic and inorganic polymers; biological chemotherapy; nuclear metallurgy and nuclear power; use of nuclear isotopes; marine studies. *Mailing Add:* Chocorua NH 03817

WOODHOUSE, WILLIAM WALTON, JR, b White Oak, NC, May 24, 10; m 34; c 2. SOILS. *Educ:* NC State Col, BS, 32, MS, 41; Cornell Univ, PhD(soils), 48. *Prof Exp:* From asst agronomist to assoc agronomist, 36-45, res assoc prof, 41-50, PROF AGRON, NC STATE UNIV, 51- *Concurrent Pos:* Mem erosion adv panel & chief eng, Shorline Mining Comn, NC Sedimentation Control Comn. *Mem:* Am Soc Agron; Soil Sci Soc Am. *Res:* Fertilization and management of pastures and forage plants; use of cover in the control of water on and in the soils; dune stabilization; land reclamation; marsh building. *Mailing Add:* Dept Soil Sci NC State Univ PO Box 5907 Raleigh NC 27650

WOODHULL, ANN MCNEAL, b Orange, NJ, Oct 20, 42. BIOPHYSICS, NEUROBIOLOGY. *Educ:* Swarthmore Col, BA, 64; Univ Wash, PhD(physiol, biophys), 72. *Prof Exp:* NIH fel physiol & biophys, Univ Wash, 72; asst prof, 72-78, ASSOC PROF BIOL, DIV NATURAL SCI, HAMPSHIRE COL, 78- *Concurrent Pos:* Lectr neurobiol, Harvard Univ, 75. *Mem:* Biophys Soc. *Res:* Chemical identity and molecular pharmacology of the neurotoxin of the salamander Notophthalmus viridescens. *Mailing Add:* Div of Natural Sci Hampshire Col Amherst MA 01002

WOODIN, SARAH ANN, b New York, NY, Dec 27, 45. MARINE ECOLOGY. *Educ:* Goucher Col, BA, 67; Univ Wash, PhD(marine ecol), 72. *Prof Exp:* Asst prof ecol, Univ Md, 72-75; asst prof ecol, Johns Hopkins Univ, 75-80; MEM FAC, DEPT BIOL, UNIV SC, 80- *Concurrent Pos:* Res grant, Div Biol Oceanog, NSF, 74-80; marine ed, Ecol & Ecological Monographs, 78-81. *Mem:* Ecol Soc Am; Am Soc Zool; AAAS; Am Soc Limnol & Oceanog. *Res:* Benthic ecology; life history strategies of organisms, particularly infauna; functional morphology of polychaetes; functional groups of infauna. *Mailing Add:* Dept Biol Univ SC Columbia SC 29208

WOODIN, TERRY STERN, b New York, NY, Dec 25, 33; m 54; c 5. BIOCHEMISTRY. *Educ:* Alfred Univ, BA, 54; Univ Calif, Davis, MA, 65, PhD(biochem), 67. *Prof Exp:* Res assoc biochem, Univ Calif, Davis, 67-68; adj asst prof, Univ Nev, Reno, 68-69, asst prof, 69-72; asst prof biochem, Humboldt State Univ, 72-77; ASSOC PROF, UNIV NEV, RENO, 77- *Mem:* AAAS; Am Chem Soc; Sigma Xi; Am Soc Plant Physiologists. *Res:* Sulfate metabolism in fungi; chorismate metabolism in plants; thermophilic fungi. *Mailing Add:* Univ Nev Reno NV 89557

WOODIN, WILLIAM GRAVES, b Dunkirk, NY, July 22, 14; m 40; c 2. ALLERGY. *Educ:* Cornell Univ, AB, 36, MD, 39. *Prof Exp:* Intern & asst resident med, Univ Hosps Cleveland, 39-41; asst, Med Col, Cornell Univ, 46, instr, 47-48; from instr to asst prof, 48-54, clin assoc prof, 54-63, CLIN PROF MED, STATE UNIV NY UPSTATE MED CTR, 63-, DIR ALLERGY CLIN, 48- *Concurrent Pos:* Fel, Roosevelt Hosp, New York, 47-48; consult hosps, 50- *Mem:* AMA; fel Am Acad Allergy; NY Acad Sci. *Mailing Add:* 109 S Warren St Syracuse NY 13202

WOODIN, WILLIAM HARTMAN, III, b New York, NY, Dec 16, 25; m 48, 77; c 4. ZOOLOGY. *Educ:* Univ Ariz, BA, 50; Univ Calif, MA, 56. *Prof Exp:* Dir, 54-71, EMER DIR, ARIZ-SONORA DESERT MUS, 72-; PRES, WOODIN LAB, 81- *Mem:* Fel AAAS. *Res:* Herpetology; taxonomy; desert ecology. *Mailing Add:* 3600 N Larrea Lane Tucson AZ 85715

WOODING, FRANK JAMES, b Pontiac, Ill, Feb 1, 41; m 64; c 3. AGRONOMY. *Educ:* Univ Ill, Urbana, BS, 63; Kans State Univ, MS, 66, PhD(agron), 70. *Prof Exp:* Res assoc plant physiol, Pa State Univ, 69-70; asst prof agron, 70-75, ASSOC PROF AGRON, AGR EXP STA, UNIV ALASKA, 75- *Mem:* Am Soc Agron; Crop Sci Soc Am; Soil Sci Soc Am. *Res:* Plant nutrition; plant growth under arctic and subarctic conditions; crop physiology; crop production. *Mailing Add:* Agr Exp Sta Univ of Alaska Fairbanks AK 99701

WOODING, WILLIAM MINOR, b Waterbury, Conn, Aug 24, 17; m 40; c 2. EXPERIMENTAL STATISTICS, CHEMISTRY. *Educ:* Polytech Inst Brooklyn, BChemE, 53. *Prof Exp:* Analyst inorg chem, Scovill Mfg Co, Conn, 36-40; technician, Am Cyanamid Co, 41-46, chemist, 46-51, res chemist, 51-56, coordr personnel admin serv, 56-57; asst chief chemist, Revlon, Inc, NY, 57-61, assoc res dir, 61-65; assoc res dir, 65-67, dir tech serv, Carter Prod Div, 67-75, CORP DIR, STATIST SERV, CARTER-WALLACE, INC, 75- *Mem:* AAAS; Am Chem Soc; fel Am Inst Chemists; fel Am Soc Qual Control; fel Soc Cosmetic Chem. *Res:* Experimental design and applied statistics, principally in medical and biological fields. *Mailing Add:* 24 Bertrand Dr Princeton NJ 08540

WOODLAND, BERTRAM GEORGE, b Mountain Ash, Wales, Apr 4, 22; m 52; c 2. STRUCTURAL GEOLOGY. *Educ:* Univ Wales, BSc, 42; Univ Chicago, PhD(geol), 62. *Prof Exp:* Exp officer, Ministry Home Security, Gt Brit Air Ministry, 43-46; res asst mineral surv, Ministry Town & Country Planning, 46-49; asst res officer, Ministry Housing & Local Govt, 49-54; from instr to asst prof geol, Univ Mass, 54-56; asst prof, Mt Holyoke Col, 56-58; assoc cur, Chicago Natural Hist Mus, 58-62; CUR, FIELD MUS NATURAL

HIST, 63- *Concurrent Pos:* Consult, Petrol Brasileiro Depex, Rio de Janeiro, Brazil, 55-56. *Mem:* Fel Geol Soc London; Geol Asn London. *Res:* Metamorphism; igneous rocks; cone-in-cone structure; tectonics and microstructures. *Mailing Add:* Dept of Geol Field Mus of Natural Hist Chicago IL 60605

WOODLAND, DOROTHY JANE, b Warren, Ohio, Sept 20, 08. PHYSICAL CHEMISTRY. *Educ:* Col Wooster, BS, 29; Ohio State Univ, MSc, 30, PhD(chem), 32. *Prof Exp:* Asst, Col Wooster, 28-29 & Ohio State Univ, 29-32; from instr to asst prof chem, Wellesley Col, 32-38; assoc prof & head dept, Western Col, 38-42, prof, 42-44; prof & head dept, 44-74, EMER PROF CHEM, JOHN BROWN UNIV, 74- *Mem:* Am Chem Soc. *Res:* Surface energy; relation between radius of curvature of droplets and surface energy. *Mailing Add:* Box 3048 John Brown Univ Siloam Springs AR 72761

WOODLAND, JOHN TURNER, b Melrose, Mass, June 26, 23. ZOOLOGY. *Educ:* Boston Univ, AB, 45, AM, 46; Harvard Univ, MA, 49, PhD(zool), 50. *Prof Exp:* From asst to instr biol, Boston Univ, 45-47; asst prof, Lebanon Valley Col, 50-52; assoc prof & chmn dept, Richmond Prof Inst, Col William & Mary, 52-55; asst prof, Northeastern Univ, 55-58; asst prof biol sci, Mass State Col, Salem, 58-63, assoc prof, 63-67, PROF BIOL, BOSTON STATE COL, 67- *Concurrent Pos:* NSF fac fel, 59-60. *Mem:* Am Soc Microbiol. *Res:* Insect embryology and histology; physiology of bacterial spores. *Mailing Add:* Dept of Biol Boston State Col Boston MA 02115

WOODLAND, WILLIAM CHARLES, b Highland Park, Mich, Nov 22, 19; m 44; c 3. PHYSICAL CHEMISTRY. *Educ:* Col Wooster, BA, 41; Carnegie Inst Technol, MS, 49, DSc(phys chem), 50. *Prof Exp:* Instr org microanal, NY Univ, 49-51; chemist, Jackson Lab, 51, Chambers Works, NJ, 51-64, color specialist, Washington Works, Parkersburg, WVa, 64-72, SR CHEMIST, WASHINGTON WORKS, E I DU PONT DE NEMOURS & CO, INC, PARKERSBURG, 72- *Res:* Thermoplastic resins; color technology; specialized analytical chemistry. *Mailing Add:* 9 Ashwood Dr Vienna WV 26101

WOODLEY, CHARLES LAMAR, b Atlanta, Ga, Sept 12, 41; m 64; c 1. BACTERIAL GENETICS. *Educ:* Ga State Univ, BS, 72, MS, 75; Univ Ga, PhD(microbiol), 80. *Prof Exp:* Lab technician, US Army Nutrit Labs, 64-66; lab technician, 66-72, MICROBIOLOGIST, CTR DIS CONTROL, 72- *Mem:* Am Soc Microbiol. *Res:* Genetic aspects of genus mycobacterium; organisms that cause tuberculosis. *Mailing Add:* 1430 Stoneleigh Hill Rd Lithonia GA 30058

WOODLEY, CHARLES LEON, b Montgomery, Ala, Jan 22, 44; m 66; c 1. BIOCHEMISTRY. *Educ:* Univ Ala, BS, 66, MS, 68; Univ Nebr, PhD(chem), 72. *Prof Exp:* Res assoc biochem, Univ Nebr, Lincoln, 71-74; ASST PROF BIOCHEM, UNIV MISS MED CTR, 74- *Mem:* Sigma Xi. *Res:* Control of protein synthesis initiation and translation in eukaryotic and viral systems. *Mailing Add:* Dept of Biochem Univ of Miss Med Ctr Jackson MS 39216

WOODLEY, ROBERT EARL, b Portland, Ore, Nov 22, 25; m 52; c 2. PHYSICAL CHEMISTRY. *Educ:* Ore State Univ, BS, 49; Univ Wash, MS, 51; Ore State Univ, PhD(chem), 65. *Prof Exp:* Engr, Gen Elec Co, 51-57; res fel chem, Ore State Univ, 57-60; sr engr, Gen Elec Co, 60-65; sr scientist, Battelle Mem Inst, 65-70; SR SCIENTIST, WESTINGHOUSE-HANFORD CO, 70- *Res:* Investigation of oxygen potential, composition relationships in mixed urania-plutonia and thoria-plutonia nuclear fuels; measurements of ceramic nuclear fuel chemical and physical properties. *Mailing Add:* Westinghouse-Hanford Co PO Box 1970 Richland WA 99352

WOODMAN, DANIEL RALPH, b Portland, Maine, Apr 20, 42; m 67. VIROLOGY, CLINICAL MICROBIOLOGY. *Educ:* Univ Maine, Orono, BS, 64; Univ Md, College Park, MS, 66, PhD(microbiol), 72. *Prof Exp:* Asst microbiol, Univ Md, College Park, 64-67; naval officer virol, Deseret Test Ctr, Salt Lake City, 67-69; instr, Univ Col, Univ Md, 70; exec officer, US Naval Unit, Ft Detrick, Md, 71-74, head virol div, 74-78, head microbiol br, Naval Med Res Inst, 78-80, HEAD MICROBIOL SECT, NAT NAVAL MED CTR, BETHESDA, 80- *Mem:* Am Soc Microbiol; Asn Mil Surgeons US; Am Soc Trop Med & Hyg; AAAS. *Res:* Animal virology with a special interest in viral immunology and chemotherapeutics; arbovirus replication and pathogenicity. *Mailing Add:* Microbiol Sect Lab Med Serv Nat Naval Med Ctr Bethesda MD 20014

WOODMAN, JAMES NELSON, silviculture, forest physiology, see previous edition

WOODMAN, PETER WILLIAM, b Glouster, Eng. ONCOLOGY, TOXICOLOGY. *Educ:* Univ Bath, BPharm, Hon, 70, PhD(molecular pharmacol & med chem), 74. *Prof Exp:* Systs analyst pharmaceut mfg, Eli Lilly, Eng, 69; teaching asst pharm & pharmacol, Univ Bath, 70-74; proj assoc oncol, McArdle Lab Cancer Res, 74-76; asst mem biochem & pharmacol, St Jude Childrens Hosp, 76-80; SR SCIENTIST BIOTECHNOL, DYNAMAC CORP, 80- *Concurrent Pos:* Mem ad hoc, Nat Large Bowel Cancer Proj, Nat Cancer Inst, 76-80, consult, Drug Synthesis & Chem Br, 80-; consult, Off Drinking Water, Environ Protection Agency, 80-81, Test Rules Develop Br, 81- *Mem:* NY Acad Sci; AAAS; Am Chem Soc; Soc Risk Anal. *Res:* Design and evaluation of medicinal, chemical, and environmental programs involving the metabolism, pharmacology, toxicology, pharmacokinetics, and oncogenicity of compounds. *Mailing Add:* Dynamac Corp Dynamac Bldg 11140 Rockville Pike Rockville MD 20852

WOODMANSEE, DONALD ERNEST, b Lexington, Ky, May 23, 41; m 64; c 2. CHEMICAL ENGINEERING, GEOCHEMISTRY. *Educ:* Univ Del, BChE, 63; Univ Ill, MS, 65, PhD(chem eng), 68. *Prof Exp:* CHEM ENGR FUELS RES, GEN ELEC CORP RES & DEVELOP CTR, 67-, MGR, GEOSCI BR, 80- *Honors & Awards:* Industrial Res 100, 77. *Mem:* Am Inst Chem Engrs. *Res:* Conversion of fossil fuels to clean energy forms; research on a one ton per hour, twenty atmosphere coal gasifier. *Mailing Add:* Gen Elec Corp Res & Develop Ctr PO Box 8 Schenectady NY 12345

WOODMANSEE, ROBERT ASBURY, b Cincinnati, Ohio, Mar 6, 26; m 49; c 3. MARINE ECOLOGY. *Educ:* Univ Miami, BS, 48, MS, 49; Western Reserve Univ, PhD(zool), 52. *Prof Exp:* Asst zool, Western Reserve Univ, 49-52, technician biochem, 52; oceanogr, US Naval Hydrog Off, 52-54; from asst prof to prof biol, Miss Southern Col, 54-64; assoc marine scientist, Va Inst Marine Sci, 64-65; from assoc prof to prof biol, Univ SAla, 65-72; HEAD ECOL SECT, GULF COAST RES LAB, 72- *Mem:* Am Soc Limnol & Oceanog; Ecol Soc Am. *Res:* Ecology of plankton; seasonal distribution and daily vertical migrations of zooplankton; distribution of planktonic diatoms in estuary; primary productivity. *Mailing Add:* Ecol Sect Gulf Coast Res Lab PO Box AG Ocean Springs MS 39564

WOODMANSEE, ROBERT GEORGE, b Albuquerque, NMex, Sept 11, 41; m 63; c 2. RANGE ECOLOGY, SYSTEMS ECOLOGY. *Educ:* Univ NMex, BS, 67, MS, 69; Colo State Univ, PhD(forest ecol & soils), 72. *Prof Exp:* Fel grassland ecol, 72-74, sr res ecologist, Natural Resource Ecol Lab, 74-78, asst dir grassland biome, 75-76, ASSOC PROF, DEPT RANGE SCI, COLO STATE UNIV, 78- *Concurrent Pos:* Consult interactions biochem cycles, Steering Comt, Swedish Univ Agr; prin investr, NSF. *Mem:* Ecol Soc Am; Am Soc Agron; Soc Range Mgt; AAAS; Am Inst Biol Sci. *Res:* Field experimentation and simulation modeling of nutrient cycling in grassland and agricultural ecosystems; long-term ecological. *Mailing Add:* Dept of Range Sci Colo State Univ Ft Collins CO 80523

WOODRIFF, ROGER L, b Bozeman, Mont. MATHEMATICS. *Educ:* Mont State Univ, BS, 64; Univ Wis-Milwaukee, MS, 65. *Prof Exp:* Asst math, Mont State Univ, 63-64; instructing asst, Univ Wis-Milwaukee, 64-65; vis instr, Mid East Tech Univ, Ankara, 65-67; asst prof, Humboldt State Col, 67-70; PROF MATH, MENLO COL, 70- *Concurrent Pos:* Comput & educ consult, Menlo Res Assoc, 81-; ed & rev, Math Texts, Harper & Rowe. *Mem:* Am Math Soc; Math Asn Am; Am Asn Univ Profs. *Res:* Algebraic topology. *Mailing Add:* Dept of Math Menlo Col Menlo Park CA 94025

WOODRING, JAY PORTER, b Philipsburg, Pa, Sept 29, 32; m 55; c 2. BIOCHEMISTRY. *Educ:* Pa State Univ, BS, 54; Univ Minn, MS, 58, PhD(entom & zool), 60. *Prof Exp:* From instr to assoc prof, 60-70, PROF ZOOL & PHYSIOL, LA STATE UNIV, BATON ROUGE, 71- *Concurrent Pos:* Humboldt scholar, 67-68. *Mem:* Am Soc Zool; Entomol Soc Am; AAAS. *Res:* Identify, characterize and study the functions of blood proteins in selected insect species; investigate the mechanisms regulating their titers and functions. *Mailing Add:* Dept Zool & Physiol La State Univ Baton Rouge LA 70803

WOODRING, WENDELL PHILLIPS, b Reading, Pa, June 13, 91; m 18, 65. GEOLOGY. *Educ:* Albright Col, AB, 10; Johns Hopkins Univ, PhD(geol), 16. *Hon Degrees:* DSc, Albright Col, 52. *Prof Exp:* Field asst, US Geol Surv, 13-16, geologist, 19-27; prof invert paleont, Calif Inst Technol, 27-30; geologist, US Geol Surv, 30-61; RES ASSOC, SMITHSONIAN INST, 61- *Concurrent Pos:* Geologist, Sinclair Cent Am Oil Corp, 17-18; geologist in chg, Haitian Geol Surv, 20-24; geol explor, Haiti, 20-21, 41-42 & Cuba, 42-43; paleontologist, Trop Oil Co, Colombia, 22. *Honors & Awards:* Penrose Medal, Geol Soc Am, 49; Thompson Medal, Nat Acad Sci, 67; Medal, Paleontol Soc, 77. *Mem:* Nat Acad Sci; AAAS; fel Geol Soc Am (pres, 53); Paleont Soc (pres, 48); Am Philos Soc. *Res:* Invertebrate paleontology; tertiary mollusks; stratigraphy; areal geology. *Mailing Add:* 6647 El Colegio Rd Goleta CA 93117

WOODROW, DONALD L, b Washington, Pa, Nov 25, 35; m 60; c 2. STRATIGRAPHY, SEDIMENTOLOGY. *Educ:* Pa State Univ, BS, 57; Univ Rochester, MS, 50, PhD(geol), 65. *Prof Exp:* From asst prof to assoc prof, 65-75, PROF GEOL, HOBART & WILLIAM SMITH COLS, 75- *Concurrent Pos:* NSF res grant, 68-78; Res Corp res grant, 69-75; vis res geologist, Univ Reading, 71-72 & 79-80; consult, var indust orgns, 74-; vis res fel, Univ Rochester, 80-82. *Mem:* Geol Soc Am; Am Asn Petrol Geologists; Soc Econ Paleontologists & Mineralogists; Int Asn Sedimentol. *Res:* Sedimentology of Paralic and lake sediments; Upper Devonian stratigraphy and sedimentology of the northern hemisphere; paleomagnetism of lake sediments; paleomagnetism. *Mailing Add:* Dept Geosci Hobart & William Smith Cols Geneva NY 14456

WOODRUFF, CALVIN WATTS, b Conn, July 16, 20; m 50; c 3. MEDICINE, PEDIATRICS. *Educ:* Yale Univ, BA, 41, MD, 44. *Prof Exp:* From instr to assoc prof pediat, Sch Med, Vanderbilt Univ, 50-60; PROF CHILD HEALTH, SCH MED, UNIV MO-COLUMBIA, 65- *Concurrent Pos:* Markle scholar med sci, Vanderbilt Univ, 52-58. *Mem:* Soc Pediat Res; Am Gastroenterol Asn; Am Inst Nutrit; Am Pediat Soc; Am Soc Clin Nutrit. *Res:* Nutritional anemias; metabolic aspects of growth; nutrition. *Mailing Add:* Dept Child Health Univ Mo Sch Med Columbia MO 65212

WOODRUFF, CHARLES MARSH, JR, b Columbia, Tenn, Aug 26, 44; m 73. PHYSICAL GEOLOGY. *Educ:* Vanderbilt Univ, BA, 66, MS, 68; Univ Tex, Austin, PhD(geol), 73. *Prof Exp:* Geologist, Tenn Div Geol, 69-70; RES SCIENTIST GEOL, BUR ECON GEOL, UNIV TEX, AUSTIN, 72- *Concurrent Pos:* Geol consult, Coastal Mgt Prog, Tex Gen Land Off, 74-76. *Mem:* Geol Soc Am; AAAS; Sigma Xi. *Res:* assessment of geothermal resources; basin analysis; regional tectonics and hydrodynamics. *Mailing Add:* Bur Econ Geol Univ Tex Univ Sta Box X Austin TX 78712

WOODRUFF, CLARENCE MERRILL, b Kansas City, Mo, Apr 8, 10; m 37; c 2. AGRONOMY. *Educ:* Univ Mo, BS, 32, MA, 39, PhD, 53. *Prof Exp:* Lab technician, Exp Sta, Univ Mo, 32-34; supt in chg soil conserv exp sta, USDA, 34-38; from instr to prof soils, 38-76, chmn dept, 67-70, EMER PROF AGRON, EXP STA, COL AGR, UNIV MO-COLUMBIA, 76- *Mem:* Am Soc Agron; Soil Sci Soc Am; assoc Am Geophys Union. *Mailing Add:* Dept of Agron Univ of Mo Columbia MO 65211

WOODRUFF, DAVID SCOTT, b Penrith, Eng, June 12, 43; Australian citizen; m 72. ECOLOGY, MEDICAL PARASITOLOGY. *Educ:* Univ Melbourne, BSc, 65, PhD(zool), 73. *Prof Exp:* Tutor biol, Trinity Col, Univ Melbourne, 66-69; Frank Knox fel biol, Harvard Univ, 69-71, Alexander Agassiz lectr biogeog, 72, res fel biol, Mus Comp Zool, 73-74; asst prof biol, Purdue Univ, 74-80; ASSOC PROF BIOL, UNIV CALIF, SAN DIEGO, 80- *Concurrent Pos:* Lectr ecol, Comn Exten Courses, Harvard Univ, 72-74; dir, Res Initiative & Support Prog Develop Ecol, Purdue Univ, 77- *Mem:* Soc Study Evolution; Am Soc Ichthyol & Herpetol; Soc Syst Zool; Ecol Soc Am; Soc Exp & Descriptive Malacol. *Res:* Genetic variation, population ecology and evolutionary biogeography of land snails; hybridization and evolutionary ecology of anuran amphibians; biological control of schistosomiasis. *Mailing Add:* Dept Biol Univ Calif San Diego La Jolla CA 92037

WOODRUFF, EDYTHE PARKER, b Bellwood, Ill, Jan 15, 28; m 50; c 2. TOPOLOGY. *Educ:* Univ Rochester, BA, 48, MS, 52; Rutgers Univ, New Brunswick, MS, 67; State Univ NY Binghamton, PhD(math), 71. *Prof Exp:* Asst prof, 71-80, ASSOC PROF MATH, TRENTON STATE COL, 80- *Concurrent Pos:* Mem, Inst Advan Study, 79-80 & 81. *Mem:* Am Math Soc; Math Asn Am; Asn Women Mathematicians. *Res:* Topology of Euclidean 3-space; monotone decompositions, P-lifting; crumpled cubes; shrinkable decompositions. *Mailing Add:* 11 Fairview Ave East Brunswick NJ 08816

WOODRUFF, GENE L(OWRY), b Conway, Ark, May 6, 34; m 61; c 2. NUCLEAR ENGINEERING. *Educ:* US Naval Acad, BS, 56; Mass Inst Technol, SM, 63, PhD(nuclear eng), 65. *Prof Exp:* Reactor supvr, Mass Inst Technol, 63-65; from asst prof to assoc prof, 65-76, from asst dir to dir, Nuclear Reactor Labs, 65-76, PROF NUCLEAR ENG, UNIV WASH, 76-, CHMN, DEPT NUCLEAR ENG, 81- *Concurrent Pos:* Consult, Pac Northwest Labs, Battelle Mem Inst, 67-70, Math Sci Northwest, 70- & Los Alamos Nat Lab, 77- *Mem:* Am Nuclear Soc. *Res:* Nuclear reactor physics, especially neutron spectra; fusion reactor engineering. *Mailing Add:* 303 Benson Hall BF-10 Univ of Wash Seattle WA 98195

WOODRUFF, HAROLD BOYD, b Bridgeton, NJ, July 22, 17; m 42; c 2. MICROBIOLOGY. *Educ:* Rutgers Univ, BS, 39, PhD(microbiol), 42. *Prof Exp:* Asst soil microbiol, Rutgers Univ, 38-42; res microbiologist, Merck Sharp & Dohme Res Labs, 42-46, head res sect, Microbiol Dept, 47-49, from asst dir to dir, 49-57, dir microbiol & natural prod res dept, 57-69, exec dir biol sci, Merck Inst Therapeut Res, 69-73, EXEC ADMINR, MERCK SHARP & DOHME RES LABS, MSD (JAPAN) CO, LTD, 73- *Concurrent Pos:* Lectr, US Off Educ; ed, Appl Microbiol, 53-62; mem bd dirs, Am Soc Microbiol Found, 72-74, pres, 74; mem bd trustees, Biol Abstracts, 72-77, treas, 74-77; mem sci adv comt, Charles F Kettering Res Lab, 72-75; mem exec bd, US Fedn Cult Collections, 73-76; mem bd trustees, Am Type Cult Collection, 81- *Honors & Awards:* Charles Thom Award, Soc Indust Microbiol, 73. *Mem:* Am Soc Microbiol (treas, 64-70); Soc Indust Microbiol (pres, 54-56); Am Chem Soc; Am Acad Microbiol; Brit Soc Gen Microbiol. *Res:* Antibiotics; physiology of microorganisms; production of chemicals by microorganisms; analytical procedures using microorganisms; isolation of natural products. *Mailing Add:* Merck Sharp & Dohme Res Labs PO Box 2000 Rahway NJ 07065

WOODRUFF, HUGH BOYD, b Plainfield, NJ, Mar 3, 49; m 73. ANALYTICAL & COMPUTER CHEMISTRY. *Educ:* Trinity Col, BS, 71; Univ NC, PhD(anal chem), 75. *Prof Exp:* Res assoc chem, Ariz State Univ, 75-77; sr res chemist anal chem, 77-82, RES FEL, DEPT COMPUT RESOURCES, MERCK SHARP & DOHME RES LABS, 82- *Mem:* Am Chem Soc; Coblentz Soc; Soc Appl Spectros. *Res:* Computer applications in chemistry; pattern recognition; intelligent computer systems for infrared spectral interpretation; image analysis. *Mailing Add:* Merck Sharp & Dohme Res Labs PO Box 2000 Rahway NJ 07065

WOODRUFF, JAMES DONALD, b Baltimore, Md, June 20, 12; m 39; c 3. OBSTETRICS & GYNECOLOGY. *Educ:* Dickinson Col, BS, 33; Johns Hopkins Univ, MD, 37. *Prof Exp:* From instr to assoc prof gynec, 42-60, from assoc prof to prof gynec & obstet, 60-75, assoc prof path, 63-75, RICHARD W TeLINDE PROF GYNEC & PATH, SCH MED, JOHNS HOPKINS UNIV, 75-, HEAD GYNEC PATH LAB, JOHNS HOPKINS HOSP, 51- *Concurrent Pos:* Chief gynecologist, Md Gen Hosp, 51-58 & Hosp for Women of Med, 58-62. *Mem:* Int Soc Study Vulvar Dis (pres, 73-75); Am Asn Obstet & Gynec (pres, 77); Am Gynec Soc; fel Am Col Obstet & Gynec. *Res:* Gynecologic pathology; study of functional activity of ovarian neoplasms and vulvar disease. *Mailing Add:* Johns Hopkins Hosp 601 N Broadway Baltimore MD 21205

WOODRUFF, JOHN H, JR, b Barre, Vt, Dec 14, 11; m 50; c 1. RADIOLOGY. *Educ:* Univ Vt, BS, 35, MD, 38. *Prof Exp:* Intern, US Marine Hosp, 38-39; resident radiol, Mary Fletcher Hosp, 39-40 & Royal Victoria Hosp, 40-41; asst prof, Univ Vt, 42-44; pvt pract, Calif, 46-50; clin instr, 50-52, asst prof, 52-54, assoc clin prof, 54-80, ADJ ASSOC PROF RADIOL, UNIV CALIF, LOS ANGELES, 80-; CHIEF RADIOL, US VET ADMIN HOSP, SEPULVEDA, 71- *Concurrent Pos:* Chief radiologist, Los Angeles, County Harbor Gen Hosp, 52-65; consult, Terminal Island Fed Prison, 57-65 & Long Beach Vet Admin Hosp, 59-68; radiologist, Univ Calif Med Ctr, 65-67; clin prof radiologic serv, Univ Calif, Irvine, 67-68, clin prof radiologic sci, 68-70; chief radiol, San Fernando Vet Admin Hosp, 68-71. *Mem:* Am Roentgen Ray Soc; Radiol Soc NAm; AMA; Am Col Radiol. *Res:* Radiologic aspects of diseases of kidneys, lungs, gastro-intestinal tract and of trauma to the abdomen and its contents. *Mailing Add:* 2618 Palos Verdes Dr W Palos Verdes Estates CA 90274

WOODRUFF, JOHN PAUL, b Shelby, Ohio, Feb 22, 42; m 67; c 1. COMPUTER SCIENCE, COMPUTATIONAL PHYSICS. *Educ:* Ohio State Univ, BS, 64. *Prof Exp:* PHYSICIST, LAWRENCE LIVERMORE NAT LAB, 64- *Mem:* AAAS; Asn Comput Mach; Inst Elec & Electronics Engrs. *Res:* Computational hydrodynamics and solid mechanics; computer programming methodology; software engineering; concurrent and applicative programming. *Mailing Add:* Lawrence Livermore Nat Lab PO Box 808 Livermore CA 94550

WOODRUFF, KENNETH LEE, b Phoenixville, Pa, Oct 10, 50; m 76. MINERAL ENGINEERING, METALLURGY. *Educ:* Pa State Univ, BS, 72. *Prof Exp:* Eng asst, Bethlehem Mines Corp, 70-71; staff consult & res engr, Nat Ctr Resource Recovery Inc, 72-75; proj mgr, Wehran Eng Corp, 75-76; PRES, RESOURCE RECOVERY SERV INC, 76- *Concurrent Pos:* Tech prog chmn, Ninth Nat Waste Processing Conf, Am Soc Mech Engrs, 78-80. *Mem:* Am Inst Mining, Metall & Petrol Engrs; Am Inst Chem Engrs; Am Inst Mech Engrs; Am Soc Testing & Mat; Am Asn Environ Prof. *Res:* Energy and materials recovery from municipal solid waste; unit operations and processes; hazardous waste reclamation and recovery systems; trommel for pre-processing of solid waste for resource recovery. *Mailing Add:* Resource Recovery Serv Inc 2500 Brunswick Pike Trenton NJ 08648

WOODRUFF, LAURENCE CLARK, b Kingman, Kans, Aug 5, 02; m 25; c 1. INSECT PHYSIOLOGY. *Educ:* Univ Kans, AB, 24, AM, 30; Cornell Univ, PhD(entom), 34. *Prof Exp:* Jr entomologist, Bur Entom, USDA, 24-28; instr entom, Univ Kans, 28-30; instr biol, Cornell Univ, 30-34; from asst prof to assoc prof entom, 34-42, resistrar, 42-46, dean men, 47-53, prof biol, 50-72, dean students, 53-67, EMER PROF BIOL, UNIV KANS, 72- *Concurrent Pos:* Ed, J Kans Entom Soc, 71- *Mem:* Fel Entom Soc Am; Nat Asn Biol Teachers. *Res:* Growth in insects; insect nutrition. *Mailing Add:* 2 Westwood Rd Lawrence KS 66044

WOODRUFF, MARVIN WAYNE, b New York, NY, Mar 9, 28; m 54; c 3. UROLOGY. *Educ:* Columbia Univ, BS, 51; NY Univ, MD, 55; Am Bd Urol, dipl, 64. *Prof Exp:* Intern surg, Bellevue Hosp, New York, 55-56, asst resident, 56-57; resident urol, Univ Mich Hosp, 57-58; clin instr, Univ Mich, 58-60; chief, Dept Urol, Roswell Park Mem Inst, 60-68; PROF SURG, ALBANY MED COL, 68-, DIR DIV UROL, ALBANY MED CTR HOSP, 68- *Concurrent Pos:* Dir clin studies sect, Kidney Dis Inst, NY State Dept Health, 68- *Honors & Awards:* Award, Am Urol Asn, 60. *Mem:* Am Urol Asn; fel Am Col Surg. *Res:* Estrogen-androgen antagonism of prostatic growth; renal handling of contrast media as determined by stop flow analysis; dialysis in infancy; renal excretion mechanism of nitrofurantoin. *Mailing Add:* Dept of Urol New Scotland Ave Albany NY 12208

WOODRUFF, RICHARD EARL, b Elk River, Idaho, July 3, 29; m 54; c 3. HORTICULTURE, PLANT PHYSIOLOGY. *Educ:* Wash State Univ, BS, 52, MS, 57; Mich State Univ, PhD, 59. *Prof Exp:* Asst hort, Tree Fruit Exp Sta, USDA, 54-55, Wash State Univ, 55-57 & Mich State Univ, 57-59; horticulturist, USDA, Tex, 59-60 & United Fruit Co, NJ, 60-63; head dept plant physiol, Tela RR Co, LaLima, Honduras, 63-70; plant physiologist, Inter-Harvest Inc, 70-72; DIR RES, TRANSFRESH CORP, 72- *Mem:* Am Soc Plant Physiol; Am Soc Hort Sci. *Res:* Post harvest physiology and handling of fruit. *Mailing Add:* TransFresh Corp PO Box 1788 Salinas CA 93901

WOODRUFF, RICHARD IRA, b Glen Ridge, NJ, Aug 19, 40; m 62; c 3. DEVELOPMENTAL BIOLOGY, REPRODUCTIVE BIOLOGY. *Educ:* Ursinus Col, BS, 62; West Chester State Col, MEd, 65; Univ Pa, PhD(biol), 72. *Prof Exp:* Teacher high sch, 62-66; from instr to assoc prof, 66-72, PROF BIOL, WEST CHESTER STATE COL, 72- *Concurrent Pos:* Res fel, Univ Pa, 72- *Mem:* AAAS; Am Soc Zoologists. *Res:* Developmental biology; electrophysiological events during egg formation. *Mailing Add:* Dept of Biol West Chester State Col West Chester PA 19380

WOODRUFF, RICHARD L, b Bakersfield, Calif, Oct 12, 25; m 50; c 3. PHYSICAL CHEMISTRY. *Educ:* Univ Calif, BS, 47. *Prof Exp:* Asst res chemist, Calif Res Corp, Stand Oil Co, Calif, 47-51; res technologist, Shell Oil Co, 51-55, res group leader, 55-64, chief res engr, 64-65, spec engr, 65-66, res dir, Shell Chem Co, NJ, 66-71, mgr prod develop-plastics, 71-72, res & develop coordr automotive lubricants, Shell Oil Co, 72-75, res & develop coordr indust lubricants, 72-78, sr staff econ specialist, Corp Planning, 78-80, PLANNING ADV, CORP PLANNING, SHELL OIL CO, 80- *Mem:* Soc Automotive Engrs. *Res:* Petroleum and petrochemical products and processes. *Mailing Add:* Shell Oil Co One Shell Plaza Box 2463 Houston TX 77002

WOODRUFF, ROBERT EUGENE, b Kennard, Ohio, July 20, 33; m 54; c 2. ENTOMOLOGY. *Educ:* Ohio State Univ, BSc, 56; Univ Fla, PhD(entom), 67. *Prof Exp:* Entomologist, Ky State Health Dept, 56-58; ENTOMOLOGIST, PLANT INDUST DIV, FLA DEPT AGR, 58- *Concurrent Pos:* Mem, Orgn Trop Studies, NSF, Costa Rica, 64; ed, Coleopterists Bulletin, 71-75; mem bd dirs, NAm Beetle Fauna Proj, 75-81; adj cur, Natural Sci, Fla State Mus, 76-; Nat Sci Found fossil amber insects, Dominican Republic, 77-78. *Mem:* Entom Soc Am; Soc Syst Zool; Asn Trop Biol; Coleopterists Soc (pres, 78). *Res:* Systematic entomology; taxonomy, ethology, ecology of beetles of the family Scarabaeidae, especially myrmecophilous and termitophilous species; fossil amber insects of the Dominican Republic. *Mailing Add:* 3517 NW 10th Ave Gainesville FL 32605

WOODRUFF, ROBERT WILSON, b Lagrange, Ohio, May 5, 25; m 50; c 2. POLYMER PHYSICS. *Educ:* Oberlin Col, AB, 47; Univ Rochester, PhD(optics), 54. *Prof Exp:* Res physicist, 54-66, sr res physicist, 66-81, RES ASSOC, E I DU PONT DE NEMOURS & CO INC, 81- *Mem:* Optical Soc Am; Soc Photog Sci & Eng. *Res:* Soft x-ray spectroscopy; vacuum evaporation techniques; optical-mechanical relationships in polymers; graphic arts reproduction systems; evaluation of photosensitive systems. *Mailing Add:* 11 Fairview Ave East Brunswick NJ 08816

WOODRUFF, RODGER KING, b Melrose Park, Ill, Nov 9, 40; m 63; c 3. METEOROLOGY, PHYSICAL OCEANOGRAPHY. *Educ:* Ore State Univ, BS, 63, MS, 67. *Prof Exp:* Commissioned officer, US Coast & Geod Surv, Environ Sci Serv Admin, 63-69; res scientist meteorol, 69-72, mgr atmospheric physics sect, 72-74, MGR APPL METEOROL SECT, PAC NORTHWEST LABS, BATTELLE MEM INST, 74- *Mem:* Am Meteorol Soc; Air Pollution Control Asn. *Res:* Atmospheric diffusion, transport, deposition, resuspension and turbulence; industrial siting and aircraft operations. *Mailing Add:* Appl Meteorol Sect Bombing Range Rd W Richland WA 99352

WOODRUFF, RONNY CLIFFORD, b Greenville, Tex, Mar 12, 43; m 65; c 1. GENETICS. *Educ:* ETex State Univ, BS, 66, MS, 67; Utah State Univ, PhD(zool), 71. *Prof Exp:* NIH reproduction & develop training grant, Univ Tex, Austin, 71-73, asst prof zool, 73-74; sr res asst genetics, Univ Cambridge, 74-76; res assoc zool, Univ Okla, 76-77; asst prof biol, 77-80, ASSOC PROF BIOL, BOWLING GREEN STATE UNIV, 80- *Mem:* Genetics Soc Am; Environ Mutagen Soc; Sigma Xi; Soc Study Evolution; Am Soc Naturalists. *Res:* Structure and function of the genetic material of higher organisms, particularly Drosophila melanogaster; mutagenesis. *Mailing Add:* Dept of Biol Sci Bowling Green State Univ Bowling Green OH 43402

WOODRUFF, SUSAN BEATTY, b Wakefield, RI, Aug 18, 40; m 63; c 2. THEORETICAL CHEMISTRY. *Educ:* Oberlin Col, AB, 62; Johns Hopkins Univ, MAT, 63; Univ Calif, Irvine, PhD(chem), 77. *Prof Exp:* MEM STAFF CHEM & FEL, LOS ALAMOS SCI LAB, 77- *Mem:* Am Chem Soc. *Res:* Chemical dynamics; chemical kinetics; classical trajectory methodology; quantum chemistry; potential energy surfaces; surface chemistry; computer capabilities. *Mailing Add:* Los Alamos Sci Lab Los Alamos NM 87545

WOODRUFF, TRUMAN OWEN, b Salt Lake City, Utah, May 26, 25; m 48. THEORETICAL SOLID STATE PHYSICS. *Educ:* Harvard Univ, AB, 47, BA, 50; Calif Inst Technol, PhD(physics), 55. *Prof Exp:* Res assoc physics, Univ Ill, 54-55; physicist, Res Lab, Gen Elec Co, 55-62; PROF PHYSICS, MICH STATE UNIV, 62- *Concurrent Pos:* Vis prof, Univ Ariz, 67; Fulbright fel, Univ Pisa, 68-69; consult, solid state physics. *Mem:* Fel Am Phys Soc. *Res:* Quantum mechanics; solid state physics, especially the quantum theory of solids; x-photon initiated reactions in solids; quantum mechanics and kinetics of the excitations of complex systems; applications of synchrotron radiation; reactions inside and on surface of solids. *Mailing Add:* Dept Physics Mich State Univ East Lansing MI 48824

WOODRUFF, WILLIAM LEE, b Seward, Nebr, Oct 21, 38; m 63; c 3. REACTOR PHYSICS. *Educ:* Nebr Wesleyan Univ, BA, 60; Univ Nebr, MS, 64; Tex A&M Univ, PhD(nuclear eng), 70. *Prof Exp:* Lab asst & technician physics, Nebr Wesleyan Univ, 60-63, vis lectr, 63-64; instr, Univ Omaha, 64-66; NUCLEAR ENGR, ARGONNE NAT LAB, 68- *Concurrent Pos:* Inst Atomic Energy, Brazil, 75- *Mem:* Am Nuclear Soc; Sigma Xi. *Res:* Methods and computer code development and physics analysis for design and safety of liquid metal and gas-cooled fast breeder reactors and for reduced enrichment research reactors. *Mailing Add:* Argonne Nat Lab 9700 S Cass Ave Argonne IL 60439

WOODS, ALAN CHURCHILL, JR, b Baltimore, Md, July 1, 18; m 44; c 4. SURGERY. *Educ:* Princeton Univ, AB, 40; Johns Hopkins Univ, MD, 43; Am Bd Surg, dipl, 51. *Prof Exp:* Intern & asst resident surgeon, Johns Hopkins Hosp, 44-45; resident surg, Henry Ford Hosp, 45-56; from asst resident surgeon to resident surgeon, Johns Hopkins Hosp, 48-49, surgeon & surgeon chg outpatient dept, 50; asst, 49, from instr to asst prof, 49-67, ASSOC PROF SURG, JOHNS HOPKINS UNIV, 67- *Concurrent Pos:* William Stewart Halsted fel surg, Johns Hopkins Univ, 49-50. *Mem:* fel Am Col Surgeons; Soc Head & Neck Surg. *Res:* Abdominal, head and neck surgery. *Mailing Add:* Dept of Surg Johns Hopkins Univ Baltimore MD 21205

WOODS, ALEXANDER HAMILTON, b Tuxedo, NY, July 26, 22; m 56; c 2. IMMUNOLOGY. *Educ:* Harvard Univ, BS, 44; Johns Hopkins Univ, MD, 52; Am Bd Internal Med, dipl, 60. *Prof Exp:* Instr med, Sch Med, Duke Univ, 55-56; asst prof med & microbiol, Med Ctr, Univ Okla, 58-64; prof immunol, 64-77, ASSOC PROF INTERNAL MED, COL MED, UNIV ARIZ, 64- *Concurrent Pos:* Res fel biochem, Duke Univ, 56-58; clin investr, Vet Admin Hosp, Oklahoma City, 59-61; dir res, Vet Admin Hosp, Tucson, 64-70; assoc chief staff, Vet Admin Hosp, Tuscon, 70-77. *Mem:* AAAS; Am Chem Soc; NY Acad Sci; Brit Biochem Soc. *Res:* Immunochemistry; hematology; cancer chemotherapy. *Mailing Add:* Dept of Internal Med Univ of Ariz Col of Med Tucson AZ 85721

WOODS, ALFRED DAVID BRAINE, b St John's, Nfld, July 16, 32; m 54; c 3. SOLID STATE PHYSICS, LOW TEMPERATURE PHYSICS. *Educ:* Dalhousie Univ, BSc, 53, MSc, 55; Univ Toronto, PhD(low temperature physics), 57. *Prof Exp:* Res fel low temperature physics, Univ Toronto, 57-58; res officer solid state physics, Atomic Energy Can Ltd, 58-78, head,Neutron & Solid State Physics Br, 71-78, 71-78; SR ADV TO THE EXEC VPRES, ATOMIC ENERGY CAN LTD, RES CO, 79- *Mem:* Am Phys Soc; Can Asn Physicists. *Res:* Dynamics of condensed matter using inelastic neutron scattering. *Mailing Add:* Atomic Energy of Can Ltd Res Co 275 Slater St Ottawa ON K1A 1E5 Can

WOODS, ALVIN EDWIN, b Murfreesboro, Tenn, Mar 17, 34; m 59; c 2. FOOD CHEMISTRY, BIOCHEMISTRY. *Educ:* Mid Tenn State Univ, BS, 56; NC State Univ, MS, 58, PhD(food flavor), 62. *Prof Exp:* From asst prof to assoc prof, 61-69, PROF CHEM, MID TENN STATE UNIV, 69- *Concurrent Pos:* Consult, Off Int Res, NIH, 65-67. *Mem:* Am Chem Soc; fel Am Inst Chemists. *Res:* Enzyme stereochemistry and kinetics; food flavors, metal ions in biological systems; organo phosphorous compounds; bromine in biological systems. *Mailing Add:* Dept of Chem Mid Tenn State Univ Murfreesboro TN 37132

WOODS, CALVIN E, civil engineering, see previous edition

WOODS, CHARLES WILLIAM, b Akron, Ohio, June 1, 28; m 61; c 2. ORGANIC CHEMISTRY. *Educ:* Ohio State Univ, BS, 51; Univ Md, PhD(org chem), 58. *Prof Exp:* Chemist, E I du Pont de Nemours & Co, Ky, 57-58; RES CHEMIST, ENTOM RES DIV, USDA, 59- *Mem:* AAAS; Am Chem Soc. *Res:* Synthesis of chemosterilants for insects; synthesis of radioactive organic compounds. *Mailing Add:* 34320 Underwood St Univ Park Hyattsville MD 20782

WOODS, CLIFTON, III, b Mecklenburg Co, NC, Aug 28, 44. PHYSICAL INORGANIC CHEMISTRY. *Educ:* NC Cent Univ, BS, 66; NC State Univ, MS, 69, PhD(chem), 71. *Prof Exp:* Asst prof chem, Univ Fla, 71-73, Bowling Green State Univ, 73-74; ASST PROF CHEM, UNIV TENN, 74- *Mem:* Am Chem Soc; Sigma Xi. *Res:* Interactions of metal complexes with biological molecules; electrochemical and Resonance Raman studies of organo-rhodium complexes. *Mailing Add:* Dept of Chem Univ of Tenn Knoxville TN 37916

WOODS, DALE, b Stone Co, Mo, Nov 1, 22. MATHEMATICS. *Educ:* Southwest Mo State Col, BS, 44; Okla State Univ, MS, 50, EdD, 61. *Prof Exp:* High sch teacher, Mo, 41-44 & Ill, 44-45; high sch prin, Nebr, 46-47; instr math, NDak State Univ, 47-51, Tex Western Col, 51-52 & Southern Miss Univ, 52-53; res mathematician, Halliburton Res Lab, 53-54; asst prof math, Memphis State Univ, 54-57 & Idaho State Univ, 57-59; assoc prof, 59-61, PROF MATH, NORTHEAST MO STATE UNIV, 61-, HEAD DIV MATH, 65- *Concurrent Pos:* Asst, Okla State Univ, 49-50, 57-58 & 60-61. *Mem:* Math Asn Am; Am Math Soc; Nat Coun Teachers Math. *Res:* Differential gemoetry and equations; theory of numbers. *Mailing Add:* Div of Math Northeast Mo State Univ Kirksville MO 63501

WOODS, DONALD LESLIE, b London, Eng, Mar 4, 44; Can citizen; m 68; c 2. PLANT BREEDING. *Educ:* Univ London, BPharm, 65, MPhil, 68; Univ Man, PhD(plant sci), 71. *Prof Exp:* Res assoc plant breeding, Dept Plant Sci, Univ Man, 71-76; res specialist plant chem, Dept Agron, Univ Minn, 76; RES SCIENTIST PLANT BREEDING, RES STA, AGR CAN, 77- *Mem:* Agr Inst Can. *Res:* Secondary plant metabolites; their biosynthesis, function, utilization, and environmental and genetic control. *Mailing Add:* Res Sta Agr Can 107 Science Crescent Saskatoon SK S7N 0X2 Can

WOODS, DONALD ROBERT, b Sarnia, Ont, Apr 17, 35; m 61; c 3. COLLOID & SURFACE CHEMISTRY. *Educ:* Queen's Univ, Ont, BSc, 57; Univ Wis, MS, 58, PhD(chem eng), 61. *Prof Exp:* Instr chem eng, Univ Wis, 59-60, Athlone fel, 61-63; asst prof chem eng, 64-68, assoc prof, 68-74, PROF CHEM ENG, McMASTER UNIV, 74- *Concurrent Pos:* C D Howe mem fel, van't Hoff Lab, State Univ Utrecht, 70-71. *Mem:* Am Inst Chem Engrs; Am Soc Eng Educ; Am Chem Soc; Am Asn Cost Engrs; Can Soc Chem Engrs. *Res:* Surface behavior; separation of immiscible liquid and liquid-solid systems for waste water treatment and chemical processing; properties of emulsions; stability and separation of emulsions; physical separations. *Mailing Add:* Dept of Chem Eng McMaster Univ Hamilton ON L8S 4L7 Can

WOODS, EDWARD JAMES, b Timmins, ON, Nov 9, 36; m 58; c 3. MATHEMATICS. *Educ:* Queen's Univ, BSc, 57; Princeton Univ, PhD(physics), 62. *Prof Exp:* Fel physics, Univ Alberta, 62-63; res assoc, Univ Md, 63-64, asst prof, 64-68; from asst prof to assoc prof, 68-76, PROF MATH, QUEEN'S UNIV, 76- *Concurrent Pos:* Vis prof, Heidelberg Univ, 76 & Kyoto Univ, 77. *Mem:* Can Math Soc. *Res:* Operator algebras, representations of the canonical commutation relations. *Mailing Add:* Dept of Math Queen's Univ Kingston ON K7L 3N6 Can

WOODS, FRANK ROBERT, b Mt Vernon, NY, June 20, 16; m 42; c 3. HYDRODYNAMICS, GAS DYNAMICS. *Educ:* NY Univ, BA, 41, MS, 47, PhD(physics), 55. *Prof Exp:* Instr physics, Univ NH, 48-53, from asst prof to assoc prof, 53-57; physicist, Boeing Airplane Co, 57-58; assoc prof physics, Mont State Col, 58-63; lectr aerospace eng & eng physics, Univ Va, 63-73, sr scientist, 63-69, prin scientist, Dept Aerospace Eng & Eng Physics, 69-73; master, Hill Sch, Pottstown, Pa, 73-81; ASSOC PROF PHYSICS, LOCK HAVEN STATE COL, 81-82. *Mem:* Am Phys Soc. *Res:* Hydrodynamics; scattering; theoretical hydrodynamics. *Mailing Add:* Lock Haven State Col Lock Haven PA 17745

WOODS, FRANK WILSON, b Covington, Va, Apr 1, 24; m 48; c 5. FOREST ECOLOGY, ENVIRONMENTAL SCIENCES. *Educ:* NC State Col, BS, 49; Univ Tenn, MS, 51, PhD, 57. *Prof Exp:* Instr, Univ Tenn, 52; res forester, Southern Forest Exp Sta, US Forest Serv, 53-58; asst prof silvicult, Duke Univ, 58-64, assoc prof forest ecol, 64-69; PROF FORESTRY, UNIV TENN, KNOXVILLE, 69- *Concurrent Pos:* Vis res partic, Oak Ridge Inst Nuclear Studies, 64; vis res assoc, Univ Calif, Los Angeles, 65; NSF-Soc Am Foresters vis lectr, 66; consult, Orgn Econ Develop, Portugal, 69- & Oak Ridge Nat Lab, 71- *Mem:* Soc Am Foresters; Int Asn Trop Biologists; fel AAAS; Int Asn Ecologists. *Res:* Silviculture of tropical plantations; effects of environment on tree growth; agroforestry; fuelwood production; biomass production by forests. *Mailing Add:* Univ Tenn Dept Forestry PO Box 1071 Knoxville TN 37901

WOODS, GEORGE THEODORE, b Tyro, Kans, Aug 21, 24; m 48; c 3. VETERINARY MEDICINE, PUBLIC HEALTH. *Educ:* Kans State Univ, DVM, 46; Univ Calif, MPH, 59; Purdue Univ, MS, 60. *Prof Exp:* Inspector animal dis eradication, Ill State Dept Agr, 46-47; supvr lab animal med, Med Sch, Northwestern Univ, 47-48; vet, 48-49; asst prof vet path & hyg, 49-59, assoc prof vet microbiol & pub health, 59-66, PROF VET MICROBIOL, PUB HEALTH & RES, COL VET MED, UNIV ILL, URBANA, 66- *Concurrent Pos:* Trainee, USPHS, 58-59; chmn adv comt, Nat Specific Pathogen Free Swine Cert Agency; collabr, USDA. *Mem:* Am Vet Med Asn; Am Pub Health Asn; Conf Pub Health Vets; Asn Teachers Vet Pub Health & Prev Med (pres); Am Asn Food Hyg Veterinarians. *Res:* Preventive veterinary medicine; epidemiology; viral respiratory diseases of cattle and swine; bovine myxovirus para-influenza 3. *Mailing Add:* Dept Vet Path & Hyg Col Vet Med Univ Ill Urbana IL 61801

WOODS, GERALDINE PITTMAN, b West Palm Beach, Fla; m 45; c 3. NEUROEMBRYOLOGY. *Educ:* Howard Univ, BS, 42; Radcliffe Col, MA, 43; Harvard Univ, PhD(neuroembryol), 45. *Hon Degrees:* DSc, Benedict Col, SC, 77, Talladega Col, 80. *Prof Exp:* Instr biol, Howard Univ, 45-46; SPEC CONSULT, NAT INST GEN MED SCI, NIH, 69- *Concurrent Pos:* Mem, Nat Adv Coun, Gen Med Sci Inst, NIH, 64-68; chmn, Defense Adv Comt Women in Serv, 68; mem bd trustees, Howard Univ, 68-, chmn, 75-; mem, Gen Res Support Prog Adv Comt, Div Res Resources, NIH, 70-73 & 77-78;

mem bd trustees, Calif Mus Found of Calif Mus Sci & Indust, 71-; mem air pollution manpower develop adv comt, Environ Protection Agency, 73-75; mem bd dirs, Robert Wood Johnson Health Policy Fels, Inst Med-Nat Acad Sci, 73-78, Nat Comn Cert Physicians Assts, 74-78; mem bd trustees, Atlanta Univ, 74- & mem Calif Post Sec Educ Comn, 74-78; mem bd trustees, Howard Univ, Washington, 68-75, chmn, 75-; mem bd dirs, Nat Ctr Higher Educ Mgt Systs, 77- *Mem:* Inst Med-Nat Acad Sci; AAAS; Fedn Am Scientists; Nat Inst Sci; Am Asn Univ Professors. *Res:* Encouraging the participation of minorities in the regular programs at the National Institutes of Health and developing two programs, Minority Biomedical Support Program and Minority Access to Research Careers, that would further assist colleges with minorities move into research and research training to project more participation in health and scientific careers. *Mailing Add:* 12065 Rose Marie Lane Los Angeles CA 90049

WOODS, J(OHN) M(ELVILLE), b Denver, Colo, May 14, 22; m 49; c 3. CHEMICAL ENGINEERING. *Educ:* Univ Kans, BS, 43; Univ Wis, PhD(chem eng), 53. *Prof Exp:* Instr chem eng, Univ Wis, 48-50; asst prof, Univ RI, 50-52; asst prof chem eng, Purdue Univ, 52-57, assoc prof, 57-77; CONSULT CHEM ENG, 77- *Mem:* Sigma Xi; Am Chem Soc; Am Inst Chem Engrs. *Res:* Applied reaction kinetics; process simulation and optimization. *Mailing Add:* 1626 Cranway Dr Houston TX 77055

WOODS, JAMES E, b Chicago, Ill, May 7, 26. ENDOCRINOLOGY, HISTOCHEMISTRY. *Educ:* Univ Ill, BS, 51; DePaul Univ, MS, 57; Loyola Univ, Chicago, PhD(anat), 64. *Prof Exp:* Res asst endocrinol, VioBin Corp, 51-52; res asst, Michael Reese Res Inst, Chicago, 53-54; res assoc histochem & endocrinol, Stritch Sch Med, Loyola Univ Chicago, 64-66; asst prof, 66-73, assoc prof, 73-80, PROF BIOL SCI, DEPAUL UNIV, 80- *Concurrent Pos:* Assoc ed, J Morphol. *Mem:* Sigma Xi; Endocrinol Soc; AAAS; Am Soc Zool; Soc Study Reproduction. *Res:* Reproductive endocrinology of adult and embryonic domestic fowl. *Mailing Add:* Dept of Biol Sci DePaul Univ Chicago IL 60614

WOODS, JAMES STERRETT, b Lewistown, Pa, Feb 26, 40; m 69. TOXICOLOGY, ENVIRONMENTAL EPIDEMIOLOGY. *Educ:* Princeton Univ, AB, 62; Univ Wash, PhD(pharmacol), 70; Univ NC, MPH, 78. *Prof Exp:* Res assoc pharmacol, Sch Med, Yale Univ, 70-72; head biochem toxicol sect, Lab Environ Toxicol, Nat Inst Environ Health Sci, NIH, 72-78; HEAD, EPIDEMIOL & ENVIRON HEALTH RES PROG, HEALTH & POP STUDY CTR, BATTELLE HUMAN AFFAIRS RES CTRS, 78-; AFFIL ASSOC PROF, DEPT ENVIRON HEALTH, UNIV WASH, 79- *Concurrent Pos:* Mem res panel, Coun Environ Qual, 73-76; rep toxicol info subcomt, HEW Coun Coord Toxicol & Related Progs, 74-78; mem panel, Nat Acad Sci, 77-81; chmn sci coun & mem bd dir, Pac Sci Ctr, 81- *Mem:* Am Asn Cancer; Am Soc Pharmacol & Exp Therapeute; Soc Toxicol; NY Acad Sci; Soc Exp Biol & Med. *Res:* Biochemical toxicology; environmental epidemiology; risk assessment in humans using biostatistical and experimental animal models. *Mailing Add:* Battelle Human Affairs Res Ctrs 4000 NE 41st St Seattle WA 98105

WOODS, JAMES WATSON, b Lewisburg, Tenn, Feb 20, 18; m 44; c 3. MEDICINE. *Educ:* Univ Tenn, BA, 39; Vanderbilt Univ, MD, 43; Am Bd Internal Med, dipl. *Prof Exp:* Instr, Sch Med, Univ Pa, 47-48; from asst prof to assoc prof, 53-64, PROF MED, SCH MED, UNIV NC, CHAPEL HILL, 64- *Concurrent Pos:* NIH spec fel, Dept Med, Vanderbilt Univ, 67-68; mem med adv bd, Coun High Blood Pressure Res, Am Heart Asn; consult, Social Security Admin Bur Hearings & Appeals, Dept Health, Educ & Welfare. *Mem:* AAAS; Am Fedn Clin Res; Am Clin & Climat Asn; fel Am Col Physicians; Southern Soc Clin Res. *Res:* Cardiology; pathogenesis of hypertension. *Mailing Add:* Dept of Med Univ of NC Sch of Med Chapel Hill NC 27514

WOODS, JIMMIE DALE, b Albuquerque, NMex, Oct 8, 33; m 56; c 3. MATHEMATICS, STATISTICS. *Educ:* US Coast Guard Acad, BS, 55; Trinity Col, Conn, MS, 63; Univ Conn, PhD(math statist), 68. *Prof Exp:* US Coast Guard, 51-, from instr to assoc prof math, US Coast Guard Acad, 60-68, asst head dept, 64-68, PROF MATH & HEAD DEPT, US COAST GUARD ACAD, 68- *Mem:* Am Statist Asn; Am Math Soc; Math Asn Am. *Res:* Application of matrix techniques to statistical distribution theory; mathematical modeling in management science. *Mailing Add:* RD 2 Box 136 Wheeler Rd Stonington CT 06378

WOODS, JOE DARST, b Knoxville, Iowa, Jan 2, 23; m 45; c 2. INORGANIC CHEMISTRY. *Educ:* Cent Col, Iowa, BS, 44; Iowa State Univ, MS, 50, PhD(chem), 54. *Prof Exp:* From instr to assoc prof, 52-64, chmn dept, 69-78, PROF CHEM, DRAKE UNIV, 64- *Concurrent Pos:* Fulbright-Hays lectr, St Louis Univ, Philippines, 67-68. *Mem:* AAAS; Am Chem Soc; Am Inst Chemists. *Res:* Mechanism of decomposition of chlorates; radioactive tracers; oxidation of metals; dissolution of metals in acids. *Mailing Add:* 4107 Ardmore Rd Des Moines IA 50310

WOODS, JOSEPH JAMES, b Camden, NJ, June 21, 43; m 68; c 2. PHYSIOLOGY. *Educ:* St Jospeh's Col, Pa, BS, 65; Rutgers Univ, PhD(physiol), 71. *Prof Exp:* From asst prof to assoc prof, 70-78, PROF BIOL, QUINNIPIAC COL, 78-, CHMN DEPT, 81- *Concurrent Pos:* NIH co-investr, 71-81. *Res:* Application of the principles of muscle biophysics to muscular exercise; muscle activity and oxygen consumption during varying rates of positive and negative work; muscle fatigue mechanisms using electromyogram indices. *Mailing Add:* Dept of Biol Quinnipiac Col PO Box 304 Hamden CT 06518

WOODS, KEITH NEWELL, b Wilmington, Del, Jan 28, 41; m 68; c 1. MATERIALS SCIENCE, CERAMICS. *Educ:* Stanford Univ, BS, 62; Univ Mich, MSE, 63; Northwestern Univ, PhD(math sci), 68. *Prof Exp:* Adv res engr, Appl Res Lab, Sylvania Elec Prods, Inc, 68-69; staff ceramist, Res & Develop Ctr, Gen Elec Co, 69-72, tech leader, Nuclear Fuels Dept, 72-77; MEM STAFF, EXXON NUCLEAR CO, INC, 77- *Mem:* Am Ceramic Soc; Am Inst Mining, Metall & Petrol Engrs; Am Soc Metals. *Res:* Physical properties of crystalline ceramics and glasses; electronic materials. *Mailing Add:* 2524 Albermarle Ct Richland WA 99352

WOODS, LAUREN ALBERT, b Aurora Co, SDak, Spet 10, 19; m 44; c 3. PHARMACOLOGY. *Educ:* Dakota Wesleyan Univ, BA, 39; Iowa State Col, PhD(org chem), 43; Univ Mich, MD, 49. *Prof Exp:* Asst, Nat Defense Res Comt, Iowa State Col, 43-44; from instr to prof pharmacol, Univ Mich, 46-60, actg chmn dept, 56; prof & head dept, Col Med, Univ Iowa, 60-70; vpres health sci, 70-76, assoc provost, Acad Med Col Va, 77-78, actg vpres health sci, 78-81, PROF PHARMACOL, VA COMMONWEALTH UNIV, 70-, VPRES HEALTH SCI, 81- *Mem:* AAAS; Am Chem Soc; Am Soc Pharmacol & Exp Therapeut; NY Acad Sci. *Res:* Metabolism of drugs; chemical structure; biological activity relationships; compounds affecting the central nervous system; mechanisms of development of tolerance and physical dependence to narcotics; radioactive tracer studies; histochemical distribution of drugs. *Mailing Add:* Box 549 Med Col Va Sta Va Commonwealth Univ Richmond VA 23298

WOODS, MARIBELLE, b Albany, Ga, Aug 16, 19. PHARMACOLOGY. *Educ:* Univ Chattanooga, BS, 42; Yale Univ, MS, 48. *Prof Exp:* Bioassayer, Chattanooga Med Co, 42-48, pharmacologist, 48-66; PHARMACOLOGIST, CHATTEM DRUG & CHEM CO, 66- *Concurrent Pos:* Pharmacologist, Brayten Pharmaceut Co, 48-73. *Mem:* Am Asn Lab Animal Sci; NY Acad Sci. *Res:* Laxative action of senna; premenstrual tension; uterine physiology; antacids. *Mailing Add:* 311 Guild Dr Chattanooga TN 37421

WOODS, MARY, b Webster Groves, Mo, Dec 22, 23. INORGANIC CHEMISTRY. *Educ:* Rosary Col, AB, 45; Univ Ill, MA, 47; Univ Wis, PhD(chem), 61. *Prof Exp:* Teacher, Trinity High Sch, Ill, 49-53; from instr to assoc prof chem, 53-73, PROF CHEM, ROSARY COL, 73- *Concurrent Pos:* Consult, Argonne Nat Lab, 75- *Mem:* Am Chem Soc. *Res:* Complex ion equilibria and kinetics; kinetics of redox reactions of actinide ions in solution. *Mailing Add:* Dept of Chem Rosary Col River Forest IL 60305

WOODS, PHILIP SARGENT, b Concord, NH, Nov 25, 21; div; c 2. CELL BIOLOGY, MOLECULAR BIOLOGY. *Educ:* Mich State Univ, BS, 47; Univ Wis, PhD(cytol), 52. *Prof Exp:* Head cellular res sect, Dept Radiobiol, US Army Med Res Lab, Ky, 52-53; USPHS fel, Columbia Univ, 53-55; assoc cytochemist biol dept, Brookhaven Nat Lab, 55-61; assoc prof biol sci, Univ Del, 61-67; PROF BIOL, QUEEN'S COL, NY, 67- *Mem:* Am Soc Cell Biol; Sigma Xi; Electron Micros Soc Am. *Res:* Biosynthesis of macromolecules; nucleic acid and protein metabolism within cells; autoradiography with tritium-labeled precursors; fine structure of cells and chromosomes; electron microscopy. *Mailing Add:* Dept of Biol Queen's Col Flushing NY 11367

WOODS, RALPH ARTHUR, b Norwich, Eng, Mar 26, 41; m 66; c 2. METALLURGY, WELDING ENGINEERING. *Educ:* Birmingham Univ, BSc, 63, PhD(metall), 66. *Prof Exp:* Mat engr, Sikorsky Helicopters Div, United Technologies Corp, 66-67; WELDING ENGR, KAISER ALUMINUM & CHEM CORP, 67- *Honors & Awards:* C H Jennings Mem Award, Am Welding Soc, 72. *Mem:* Am Soc Metals. *Res:* Aluminum welding research; aluminum alloy metallurgy. *Mailing Add:* Kaiser Aluminum & Chem Corp 6177 Sunol Blvd Pleasanton CA 94566

WOODS, RICHARD DAVID, b Lansing, Mich, Sept 4, 35; m 57; c 3. CIVIL ENGINEERING. *Educ:* Univ Notre Dame, BSCE, 57, MSCE, 62; Univ Mich, Ann Arbor, PhD(civil eng), 67. *Prof Exp:* Proj engr, Air Force Weapons Lab, NMex, 62-63; instr civil eng, Mich Technol Univ, 63-64; from asst prof to assoc prof, 67-77, PROF CIVIL ENG, UNIV MICH, ANN ARBOR, 77- *Concurrent Pos:* Consult, several indust firms & units of munic govt, 67-; Fed Ger Res Coun vis prof, Inst Soil & Rock Mech, Univ Karlsruhe, 71-72; found eng consult, Consumers Power Co, Mich, 72- *Honors & Awards:* Collingwood Prize, Am Soc Civil Engrs, 68. *Mem:* Am Soc Civil Engrs; Am Soc Eng Educ; Am Soc Testing & Mat. *Res:* Vibrations of soils; foundations and structures; seismology; earthquake engineering. *Mailing Add:* 2330 G G Brown Lab Univ of Mich Ann Arbor MI 48104

WOODS, ROBERT CLAUDE, b Atlanta, Ga, Mar 24, 40; m 63; c 2. PHYSICAL CHEMISTRY. *Educ:* Ga Inst Technol, BS, 61; Harvard Univ, AM, 62, PhD(phys chem), 65. *Prof Exp:* Instr chem, US Naval Acad, 65-67; from asst prof to assoc prof, 67-77, PROF CHEM, UNIV WIS-MADISON, 77- *Mem:* Am Chem Soc; Am Phys Soc. *Res:* Microwave spectroscopy of molecules with internal rotors and of transient species present in electrical discharges and related theoretical problems. *Mailing Add:* Dept of Chem Univ of Wis Madison WI 53706

WOODS, ROBERT JAMES, b London, Eng, Feb 8, 28; m 58; c 4. RADIATION CHEMISTRY, SCIENCE COMMUNICATIONS. *Educ:* Univ London, BSc, 49, PhD(org chem), 51; Imp Col London, dipl, 51. *Prof Exp:* Nat Res Coun Can fel, Prairie Regional Lab, Sask, 51-53; Univ NZ res fel, Victoria, NA, 53-54; res assoc, Univ Sask, 55-62; sr res fel, Royal Mil Col Sci, Eng, 62-63; from asst prof to assoc prof, 63-76, PROF CHEM, UNIV SASK, 76- *Concurrent Pos:* Vis prof, Saclay Nuclear Res Ctr, France, 72-73. *Mem:* Chem Inst Can; fel Royal Soc Chem; Can Nuclear Soc. *Res:* Radiation chemistry of organic compounds, both pure and in aqueous solution. *Mailing Add:* Dept of Chem & Chem Eng Univ of Sask Saskatoon SK S7N 0W0 Can

WOODS, ROGER DAVID, b Los Angeles, Calif, Mar 28, 24; m 52; c 3. THEORETICAL PHYSICS, COMPUTER SCIENCE. *Educ:* Univ Redlands, AB, 45; Univ Calif, Los Angeles, MA, 49, PhD, 54. *Prof Exp:* Res physicist, Univ Calif, Los Angeles, 54; asst prof physics, Univ Miami, 54-61; assoc prof, Univ Redlands, 61-65; assoc prof, 65-72, PROF PHYSICS, SAN BERNARDINO VALLEY COL, 72- *Mem:* AAAS; Am Phys Soc. *Res:* Nucleon-nuclei scattering; molecular structure; electron structure of atoms; energy bands in solids; generalized theory of gravitation; visible, ultraviolet and infrared spectroscopy; scientific computer application. *Mailing Add:* Dept of Physics San Bernardino Valley Col San Bernardino CA 92403

WOODS, ROY ALEXANDER, b Columbia, Mo, Oct 31, 13; m 34; c 1. PHYSICS, ELECTRONICS. *Educ:* Lincoln Univ, Mo, AB, 34; Boston Univ, AM, 46 & 48, EdD, 60. *Prof Exp:* Teacher high schs, Mo, 34-41; instr electronics & radar technician, US Navy, 42-45; prof physics & chmn div natural sci, Va State Col, 48-68; prof, 68-80, EMER PROF PHYSICS, NORFOLK STATE COL, 80- *Concurrent Pos:* Electronic engr, Lab Electronics Res & Develop, Mass, 52-53, 59-60. *Mem:* Am Asn Physics Teachers. *Res:* Instrumentation for naval radar. *Mailing Add:* Dept of Physics Norfolk State Col Norfolk VA 23504

WOODS, SHERWYN MARTIN, b Des Moines, Iowa, June 25, 32; m 71. PSYCHIATRY, PSYCHOANALYSIS. *Educ:* Univ Wis, BS, 54, MD, 57, PhD(psychoanal), 77; Am Bd Psychiat & Neurol, dipl, 65, cert psychoanal, 77. *Prof Exp:* Intern, Philadelphia Gen Hosp, 57-58; resident, Univ Hosps, Univ Wis Med Sch, 58-61, instr psychiat, Med Sch, 61; from asst prof to assoc prof, 63-74, PROF PSYCHIAT, SCH MED, UNIV SOUTHERN CALIF, 74-, DIR GRAD EDUC, 63-, DIR STUDENT PSYCHIAT SERV, 66- *Concurrent Pos:* NIMH career teacher award, 64-66; clin assoc, Southern Calif Psychoanal Inst, 64-68, mem, 68-, instr, 69-, supv & training analyst, 78-; examr, Am Bd Psychiat & Neurol, 67-; consult, Calif Dept Ment Hyg, 70-; pres, Am Asn Dir Psychiat Residency Training, 74-76. *Mem:* Fel Am Psychiat Asn; Group Advan Psychiat; Asn Advan Psychother; fel Am Col Psychiat. *Res:* Medical education; human sexuality; psychotherapy. *Mailing Add:* Dept of Psychiat Div Grad Educ Univ Southern Calif Sch of Med Los Angeles CA 90033

WOODS, STUART B, b Pathlow, Sask, Apr 26, 24; m 49; c 2. SOLID STATE PHYSICS. *Educ:* Univ Sask, BA, 44, MA, 48; Univ BC, PhD, 52. *Prof Exp:* Res officer physics, Nat Res Coun Can, 52-59; assoc prof, 59-65, PROF PHYSICS, UNIV ALTA, 65-, ASSOC DEAN FAC GRAD STUDIES & RES, 74- *Concurrent Pos:* Vis prof, Univ Bristol, 66-67 & Univ St Andrews, Scotland, 73-74. *Mem:* Am Phys Soc; Can Asn Physicists. *Res:* Low temperature and solid state physics, chiefly experimental transport properties in solids. *Mailing Add:* Dept of Physics Univ of Alta Edmonton AB T6G 2S1 Can

WOODS, THOMAS STEPHEN, b Florence, Ala, Dec 13, 44; m 66; c 2. ORGANIC CHEMISTRY. *Educ:* Auburn Univ, BS, 67; Univ Ill, PhD(org chem), 71. *Prof Exp:* Res chemist, Div Med Chem, Walter Reed Army Inst Res, 72-74; res chemist, Biochem Dept, 74-79, res supvr, 79-80, LAB ADMINR, E I DU PONT DE NEMOURS & CO, INC, 80- *Mem:* Am Chem Soc. *Res:* Synthesis of novel organic compounds of biological utility; heterocyclic chemistry; organosulfur and selenium chemistry; theories of tautomerism and resonance; organic photochemistry. *Mailing Add:* 1919 Floral Dr N Graylyn Crest Wilmington DE 19810

WOODS, W(ALLACE) KELLY, b Claremore, Okla, Dec 10, 12; m 37; c 4. NUCLEAR ENGINEERING. *Educ:* Stanford Univ, AB, 34; Mass Inst Technol, MS, 36, DSc(chem eng), 40. *Prof Exp:* Instr chem eng, Mass Inst Technol, 36-40; chem engr, Tech Div, Eng Dept, E I du Pont de Nemours & Co, 40-43, tech specialist, Explosives Dept, 43-46; tech & managerial assignments with plutonium prod reactors, Hanford Labs, Gen Elec Co, 46-55, mgr nuclear mat, Vallecitos Atomic Lab, 55-61 & prog, Hanford Labs, 61-63, consult engr, 63-65; consult engr, Douglas United Nuclear, Inc, Wash, 65-71; coordr, Ore Nuclear & Thermal Energy Coun, Ore State Govt, 71-75, energy site coordr, 75-78; PROF NUCLEAR ENG, ORE STATE UNIV, 78- *Mem:* Am Chem Soc; fel Am Nuclear Soc (treas, 59-61); Am Inst Chem Engrs. *Res:* Heat transfer to boiling liquids; fluid flow; irradiation effects in solids. *Mailing Add:* 714 Tillman Ave SE Salem OR 97302

WOODS, WALTER RALPH, b Grant, Va, Dec 2, 31; m 53; c 2. ANIMAL NUTRITION. *Educ:* Murray State Univ, BS, 54; Univ Ky, MS, 55; Okla State Univ, PhD, 57. *Prof Exp:* Instr, Okla State Univ, 56-57; from asst prof to assoc prof animal husb, Iowa State Univ, 57-62; from assoc prof to prof, Univ Nebr-Lincoln, 62-71; HEAD DEPT ANIMAL SCI, PURDUE UNIV, WEST LAFAYETTE, 71- *Mem:* Am Soc Animal Sci; Poultry Sci Asn; Am Inst Nutrit; Am Dairy Sci Asn; Sigma Xi. *Res:* Protein and nonprotein nitrogen utilization in beef cattle and sheep; energy utilization as influenced by diet composition and processing. *Mailing Add:* Dept of Animal Sci Purdue Univ West Lafayette IN 47907

WOODS, WENDELL DAVID, b Liberal, Kans, Dec 5, 32; m 64; c 2. BIOCHEMISTRY, PHYSIOLOGY. *Educ:* Univ Mo, BS, 58, MS, 59, PhD(biochem), 65. *Prof Exp:* Res asst, 63-66, from instr to asst prof, 66-73, ASSOC PROF OPHTHAL, SCH MED, EMORY UNIV, 73- *Concurrent Pos:* NIH grant vision, Emory Univ, 72- *Mem:* AAAS; Asn Res Ophthal; Am Chem Soc. *Res:* Biochemical mechanisms relating cyclic-nucleotide monophosphates and prostaglandins to fluid dynamics in the eye. *Mailing Add:* Lab for Ophthal Res Emory Univ Atlanta GA 30322

WOODS, WILLIAM BOONE, JR, b Louisville, Ky, Oct 5, 42. BIOCHEMICAL ENGINEERING, MICROBIOLOGY. *Educ:* Univ Mich, BS, 64, MSE, 74, PhD(chem eng), 76. *Prof Exp:* Sr microbiologist, 76-80, LAB MGR, TENNECO CHEM INC, 80- *Mem:* Am Inst Chem Engrs; Am Chem Soc; Am Soc Testing & Mat; Soc Indust Microbiol. *Res:* Development of industrial microbicides for use as preservatives in water based systems and for the prevention of bacterial, fungal or algal defacement of coating films and polymeric materials. *Mailing Add:* Tenneco Chem Inc Turner Pl PO Box 365 Piscataway NJ 08854

WOODS, WILLIAM GEORGE, b Superior, Wis, Dec 21, 31; m 52; c 3. PHYSICAL ORGANIC CHEMISTRY. *Educ:* Univ Calif, Los Angeles, BS, 53; Calif Inst Technol, PhD, 57. *Prof Exp:* Asst, Calif Inst Technol, 53-55; res chemist, Res Lab, Gen Elec Co, 56-58; sr res chemist, 58-74, mgr agr res & develop, 74-76, SR SCIENTIST, US BORAX RES CORP, 76- *Concurrent Pos:* Res officer, Commonwealth Sci & Indust Res Orgn, Melbourne, Australia, 62-63. *Mem:* Nat Asn Corrosion Eng; Am Chem Soc; Sigma Xi. *Res:* Carbonium ion and pyrolysis mechanism; semi-inorganic polymer systems; semi-empirical molecular orbital calculations; nuclear magnetic resonance spectroscopy; organometallic and organic synthesis; herbicide synthesis and metabolism; direct agricultural research programs; fire retardants and polymer additives; corrosion electro-chemistry. *Mailing Add:* US Borax Res Corp 412 Crescent Way Anaheim CA 92801

WOODSIDE, DONALD G, b Pittsburgh, Pa, Apr 28, 27; Can citizen; m 53; c 3. ORTHODONTICS. *Educ:* Dalhousie Univ, BSc, 48, DDS, 52; Univ Toronto, MSc, 56; FRCD(C), 67. *Prof Exp:* Assoc, 55-58, asst prof & actg head dept, 58-59, assoc prof, 59-61, actg head dept, 61-62, assoc dean, 70-73, PROF ORTHOD & HEAD DEPT, FAC DENT, UNIV TORONTO, 62- *Concurrent Pos:* Consult, Ont Hosp Crippled Children & Burlington Orthod Res Ctr, 62. *Mem:* Am Asn Orthod; Europ Orthod Soc; Edward H Angle Soc; Charles Tweed Found. *Res:* Human growth and development; study of human mandibular growth distance, velocity curves and growth direction to establish predicability factors; primate studies in relationship between bone induction and muscle activity and tonicity. *Mailing Add:* Dept of Orthod Univ of Toronto Fac of Dent Toronto ON M5C 1C6 Can

WOODSIDE, JOHN MOFFATT, b Toronto, Ont, Jan 23, 41; m 67; c 2. MARINE GEOPHYSICS, GEOLOGY. *Educ:* Queen's Univ, BSc, 64; Mass Inst Technol, MSc, 68; Cambridge Univ, PhD(geophys), 76. *Prof Exp:* Tech officer geophys, Geol Surv Can, 64; res asst marine geophys, Woods Hole Oceanog Lab, 66-68; sci officer, Bedford Inst Oceanog, 68-71; res asst, Dept Geod & Geophys, Cambridge Univ, 71-76; RES SCIENTIST MARINE GEOPHYS, ATLANTIC GEOSCI CTR, GEOL SURV CAN, 76- *Concurrent Pos:* IBM fel, Dept Geod & Geophys, Cambridge Univ, 75-76; mem bd dirs, Int Gravity Bur, 78-; sr geophysicist, Proj for Regional Offshore Prospecting in East Asia & Pacific, UN, 79-80. *Mem:* Fel Geol Asn Can; fel Royal Astron Soc; Am Geophys Union; Soc Explor Geophysicists; Am Geol Inst. *Res:* Dynamic aspects of evolution of ocean basins with particular emphasis on nature of passive continental margins, mid-ocean ridges, and subduction zones; areas of primary interest are Mediterranean Sea, Labrador Sea, Mid-Atlantic Ridge, Arctic and southwestern Pacific. *Mailing Add:* 46 Lyngby Ave Dartmouth NS B3A 3T8 Can

WOODSIDE, KENNETH HALL, b Northampton, Mass, June 18, 38; m 60; c 2. PHYSIOLOGY, BIOCHEMISTRY. *Educ:* Oberlin Col, AB, 59; Univ Rochester, PhD(biochem), 69. *Prof Exp:* Res assoc physiol, Col Med, Pa State Univ, 68-70, asst prof physiol & head multidiscipline labs, 70-76; asst prof med, Sch Med, Univ Miami, 76-79; res biochemist, Mt Sinai Med Ctr, Miami, 79-81; ASSOC PROF BIOCHEM & CHMN DEPT, SOUTHEASTERN COL OSTEOP MED, NORTH MIAMI BEACH, 81- *Mem:* Am Physiol Soc; AAAS; Am Toracic Soc; Sigma Xi. *Res:* Hormonal and non-hormonal regulation of protein biosynthesis and degradation; pulmonary macrophage function. *Mailing Add:* Southeastern Col Osteopathic Med 1750 NE 168 St North Miami Beach FL 33162

WOODSIDE, PHILIP RODMAN, b Mt Holly, NJ, June 8, 25; m 50; c 4. GEOLOGY, PETROLEUM ENGINEERING. *Educ:* Syracuse Univ, AB, 50; Rutgers Univ, MSc, 52. *Prof Exp:* Eval geologist, Creole Petrol Corp, Venezuela, 53-57; subsurface geologist, Am Overseas Petrol, Ltd, Libya, 57-58; explor mgr, Sharmex, Mex, 58-59; sr valuation engr oil & gas sect, Internal Revenue Serv, Washington, DC, 59-67; supvr final anal, Gen Bus Serv, Md, 69-71; sr petrol adv, UN, Ecuador, 71-75 & Pakistan, 75; asst dir, Energy & Minerals Div, US Gen Acct Off, 76-79; sr res geologist, US Geol Surv, 79-81; SR STAFF GEOLOGIST CHINA STUDIES, UNIV TEX, TYLER, 82- *Mem:* Soc Petrol Engrs; Am Asn Petrol Geologists. *Mailing Add:* Univ Tex Tyler TX 75701

WOODSIDE, WILLIAM, b Ft William, Ont, July 5, 31; m 53; c 3. PHYSICS, MATHEMATICS. *Educ:* Queen's Univ, Belfast, BSc, 51, MSc, 59, DSc, 62. *Prof Exp:* Asst Royal Naval Sci Serv, Baldock, Eng, 51 & Toronto, 53; master physics, Ridley Col, Can, 52-55; res officer, Nat Res Coun, Can, 54-58; res physicist, Gulf Res & Develop Co, 58-60; master math, Ridley Col, 60-66; asst prof, 66-70, ASSOC PROF MATH, QUEEN'S UNIV, ONT, 70-, CHMN ENG MATH, 80- *Mem:* Can Math Soc; Math Asn Am. *Res:* Optimization theory; operations research; mathematics; education; heat transfer in porous media. *Mailing Add:* Dept Math Queen's Univ Kingston ON K7L 3N6 Can

WOODSON, HERBERT H(ORACE), b Stamford, Tex, Apr 5, 25; m 51; c 3. ELECTRICAL ENGINEERING. *Educ:* Mass Inst Technol, SB & SM, 52, ScD, 56. *Prof Exp:* Elec engr, US Naval Ord Lab, Md, 52-54; asst elec eng, Mass Inst Technol, 54-55, from instr to prof, 55-71; Alcoa Found prof, 72-75, chmn dept, 71-81, PROF ELEC ENG, UNIV TEX, AUSTIN, 71-, DIR CTR ENERGY STUDIES, 77-; PROF ENG, TEXAS ATOMIC ENERGY RES FOUND, 80- *Concurrent Pos:* Mem bd dir, Stauffer Chem Co, 72- *Mem:* Nat Acad Eng; Am Soc Eng Educ; fel Inst Elec & Electronics Engrs. *Res:* Electrical energy conversion and control; power system engineering. *Mailing Add:* Eng Sci Bldg Univ of Tex Austin TX 78712

WOODSON, JOHN HODGES, b Hartford, Conn, May 25, 33; m 60; c 3. PHYSICAL CHEMISTRY, THEORETICAL CHEMISTRY. *Educ:* Wesleyan Univ, BA, 55; Northwestern Univ, PhD(phys chem), 59. *Prof Exp:* Asst prof chem, Wesleyan Univ, 59-61; from asst prof to assoc prof, 61-70, PROF CHEM, SAN DIEGO STATE UNIV, 70- *Mem:* Am Chem Soc; Sigma Xi. *Res:* Valence theory; kinetics of oscillating reactions; ion-selective electrodes. *Mailing Add:* Dept of Chem San Diego State Univ San Diego CA 92182

WOODSON, PAUL BERNARD, b St Louis, Mo, Jan 20, 49; div. NEUROBIOLOGY. *Educ:* Univ Calif, San Diego, BA, 70, PhD(neurosci), 75. *Prof Exp:* Scholar neurobiol, Dept Psychiat, Univ Calif, San Diego, 75-77; ASST PROF BIOL, UNIV SAN DIEGO, ALCALA PARK, 77- *Mem:* AAAS; Soc Neurosci; Am Soc Zoologists. *Res:* Mechanisms and modulations of synaptic transmission; correlations of synaptic and behavioral plasticities; pharmacology of synaptic transmission; synaptic tolerance phenomena; membrane fluidity as a physiological regulation point in synaptic transmission. *Mailing Add:* Dept of Biol Univ of San Diego Alcala Park San Diego CA 92110

WOODSTOCK, LOWELL WILLARD, b Harvey, Ill, July 6, 31; m 61; c 2. PLANT PHYSIOLOGY, BIOCHEMISTRY. *Educ:* Univ Ill, BS, 54; Univ Wis, PhD(bot), 59. *Prof Exp:* Nat Cancer Inst fel, Royal Bot Garden, Scotland, 59-61 & Univ Wis, 61-62; res assoc, Argonne Nat Lab, 62-63; res plant physiologist, USDA, 63-67, leader seed qual invests, 67-73, res plant physiologist, Agr Res Serv, 73-76; assoc tech dir, Agr & Water Res Ctr, Riyadh, Saudi Arabia, 76-78; RES PLANT PHYSIOLOGIST, SCI & EDUC ADMIN, USDA, 78- *Concurrent Pos:* Am Seed Res Found grant, 69-72; intergovt employee exchange act trainee, Ore State Univ, 73-74. *Mem:* AAAS; Bot Soc Am; Am Soc Plant Physiol; Asn Off Seed Anal; Japanese Soc Plant Physiologist. *Res:* Molecular basis of seed germination, vigor, dormancy and storage; freeze-drying seeds for better storage at high temperatures; biochemical and physiological basis of seed response o environmental stress. *Mailing Add:* BARC-West 006 USDA Sci & Educ Admin-Agr Res Beltsville MD 20705

WOODWARD, ARTHUR EUGENE, b Los Angeles, Calif, Oct 16, 25; m 52; c 1. PHYSICAL CHEMISTRY, POLYMER PHYSICS. *Educ:* Occidental Col, BA, 49, MA, 50; Polytech Inst Brooklyn, PhD(phys chem), 53. *Prof Exp:* Asst Occidental Col, 50; US Govt grantee chem, Cath Univ Louvain, 53-54; res fel, Harvard Univ, 54-55; asst prof, Pa State Univ, 55-59, from asst prof to assoc prof physics, 59-64; assoc prof chem, 64-66, PROF CHEM, CITY COL NEW YORK, 67- *Concurrent Pos:* Guggenheim fel, Queen Mary Col, London, 62-63. *Mem:* Am Chem Soc; Am Phys Soc; NY Acad Sci. *Res:* Physical and chemical properties of polymer crystals; low temperature dynamic mechanical properties; nuclear magnetic resonance of high polymers; polymer crystals. *Mailing Add:* Dept of Chem City Col of New York New York NY 10031

WOODWARD, CLARE K, b Houston, Tex, Dec 10, 41; m 67. BIOCHEMISTRY. *Educ:* Smith Col, BA, 63; Rice Univ, PhD(biol), 67. *Prof Exp:* Fel genetics, Univ Minn, St Paul, 67-68; fel phys chem, Univ Minn, Minneapolis, 68-70, asst prof lab med, Med Sch, 70-72; asst prof biochem, 72-77, ASSOC PROF BIOCHEM & BIOL SCI, UNIV MINN, ST PAUL, 78- *Mem:* Biophys Soc; Am Soc Biol Chemists. *Res:* Protein chemistry. *Mailing Add:* Dept of Biochem Univ of Minn St Paul MN 55101

WOODWARD, DAVID LEE, b Sioux City, Iowa, Feb 14, 40; m 59; c 2. PHARMACOLOGY. *Educ:* Utah State Univ, BS, 64; Univ Utah, PhD(pharmacol), 68. *Prof Exp:* Asst prof, Fac Dent, Univ Man, 69-70; res assoc, 70, ASSOC DIR, HOECHST-ROUSSEL PHARMACEUT INC, 70- *Concurrent Pos:* NIH trainee pharmacol, Univ Man, 68-69. *Mem:* AAAS; NY Acad Sci. *Res:* Cardiovascular-renal pharmacology. *Mailing Add:* Dept of Pharmacol Bldg L Hoechst-Roussel Pharmaceut Inc Somerville NJ 08876

WOODWARD, DAVID WILLCOX, b Oxford, NY, July 24, 13; m 38; c 1. ORGANIC CHEMISTRY. *Educ:* Amherst Col, AB, 34; Harvard Univ, PhD(org chem), 37. *Prof Exp:* Res chemist, Chem Dept, E I du Pont de Nemours & Co, Inc, 37-51, res supvr, Photo Prod Dept, 51-54, res mgr, 45-68, lab dir, Photo Prod Dept, 68-76; RETIRED. *Mem:* Am Chem Soc; Soc Photog Sci & Eng. *Res:* Photography; furane and polymer chemistry; cyanides; nitriles; photochemistry; photopolymerization; dyes. *Mailing Add:* 103 Taylor Lane Kennett Square PA 19348

WOODWARD, DONALD JAY, b Detroit, Mich, Aug 1, 40; m 63; c 3. PHYSIOLOGY. *Educ:* Univ Mich, BS, 62, PhD(physiol), 66. *Prof Exp:* From instr to assoc prof physiol, Dept Physiol & Ctr Brain Res, Sch Med & Dent, Univ Rochester, 66-75; PROF CELL BIOL & PHYSIOL, UNIV TEX HEALTH SCI CTR, DALLAS, 75- *Mem:* Am Physiol Soc; Neurosci Soc. *Res:* Developmental neurobiology; cerebellar neurophysiology and neuropharmacology. *Mailing Add:* Dept of Cell Biol 5323 Harry Hines Blvd Dallas TX 75235

WOODWARD, DOW OWEN, b Logan, Utah, Dec 1, 31; m 56; c 4. MOLECULAR BIOLOGY. *Educ:* Utah State Univ, BS, 56; Yale Univ, MS, 57, PhD(bot), 59. *Prof Exp:* Mem res staff radiobiol, Aerospace Med Ctr, US Air Force, 59-62; assoc prof, 62-74, PROF BIOL, STANFORD UNIV, 74- *Mem:* Genetics Soc Am; Am Soc Biol Chemists. *Res:* Biochemical genetics in microorganisms; membrane structure and function; cytoplasmic inheritance; biological rhythms; enzymology. *Mailing Add:* Dept of Biol Stanford Univ Stanford CA 94305

WOODWARD, EDWARD ROY, b Chicago, Ill, Sept 6, 16; m 39; c 2. SURGERY. *Educ:* Grinnell Col, BA, 38; Univ Chicago, MD, 42; Am Bd Surg, dipl, 51. *Prof Exp:* Asst resident, Univ Clins, Univ Chicago, 47-49, instr & resident, Grad Sch Med, 49-50 & 51-52, instr, 52-53; from asst prof to assoc prof, Med Ctr, Univ Calif, Los Angeles, 53-57; PROF SURG & HEAD DEPT, COL MED, UNIV FLA, 57- *Concurrent Pos:* Douglas Smith fel surg, Univ Chicago, 46-47; Markle scholar, 52-57. *Mem:* Am Physiol Soc; Soc Univ Surg; Am Surg Asn; Am Gastroenterol Asn; fel Am Col Surgeons. *Res:* Physiology of gastrointestinal tract. *Mailing Add:* Dept of Surg Univ of Fla Gainesville FL 32610

WOODWARD, ERVIN CHAPMAN, JR, b Long Beach, Calif, Apr 8, 23; m 49; c 2. RADIATION PHYSICS. *Educ:* Univ Calif, PhD(physics), 52. *Prof Exp:* PHYSICIST, LAWRENCE LIVERMORE LAB, UNIV CALIF, 52- *Mem:* Am Phys Soc. *Res:* Spectroscopy; hyperfine structure; nuclear spin and isotope shift; high speed optics. *Mailing Add:* Lawrence Livermore Lab Univ of Calif PO Box 808 Livermore CA 94550

WOODWARD, EUGENE C(LAYTON), JR, mechanical engineering, deceased

WOODWARD, FRED ERSKINE, b Boston, Mass, Aug 20, 21; m 44; c 4. SURFACE CHEMISTRY, ORGANIC POLYMER CHEMISTRY. *Educ:* Dartmouth Col, AB, 43; Univ Ill, MA, 44, PhD(org chem), 46. *Prof Exp:* Chemist, Gen Aniline & Film Corp, Pa, 46-48, sr chemist, Dyestuff & Chem Div, 48-54, mgr indust sect, Antara Tech Dept, 54-58, asst prog mgr appln res, 58-62; dir res & develop, Nopco Chem Co, NJ, 62-69; PRES, SURFACE CHEMISTS FLA, INC, 69- *Mem:* Am Chem Soc; Am Oil Chem Soc; Soc Lubrication Eng; Am Inst Mining & Metall Engrs; Am Asn Textile Chemists & Colorists. *Res:* Surface active agents; lubrication; defoaming; detergency; synthesis and applications research; surface chemistry of antimicrobial agents; mechanisms of clay dewatering; iodophors. *Mailing Add:* Surface Chemists Fla Inc Palm Beach Int Airport Bldg 541 West Palm Beach FL 33406

WOODWARD, HARRY W, b Norwich, Norfolk, Eng, Feb 1, 23; Can citizen; m 51; c 3. PETROLEUM GEOLOGY. *Educ:* Queen's Univ, Ont, BSc, 49; Univ Wis, PhD(geol), 53. *Prof Exp:* Sr staff geologist, Gulf Oil Can Ltd, 53-66; adminr oil & gas sect, 66-68, DIR NON-RENEWABLE RESOURCES BR, DEPT INDIAN & NORTHERN AFFAIRS, GOVT CAN, 68- *Res:* Resource management; surface structure and subsurface geology of Western Canada; resource development of Northern Canada. *Mailing Add:* Dept Indian & Northern Affairs Govt Can Ottawa ON K1A 0H4 Can

WOODWARD, J GUY, b Carleton, Mich, Nov 19, 14; m 45; c 3. PHYSICS. *Educ:* NCent Col, BA, 36; Mich State Col, MS, 38; Ohio State Univ, PhD(physics), 42. *Prof Exp:* Asst physics, Mich State Col, 36-39; asst physics, Ohio State Univ, 39-42; res physicist, Mfg Co, RCA Corp, 42, res engr, RCA Labs, 42-72, RES FEL, RCA LABS, 72- *Honors & Awards:* Emile Berliner Award, Audio Eng Soc, 68. *Mem:* Fel AAAS; Acoust Soc Am; Audio Eng Soc (pres, 71-72); fel Inst Elec & Electronics Engrs. *Res:* Physical optics; room and music acoustics; radio interference from motor vehicles; underwater sound; electroacoustic transducers; high fidelity phonograph systems; viscometry; video magnetic tape recording. *Mailing Add:* RCA Labs Princeton NJ 08540

WOODWARD, JAMES KENNETH, b Anderson, Mo, Feb 5, 38; m 60; c 2. PHARMACOLOGY. *Educ:* Southwest Mo State Col, BS & AB, 60; Univ Pa, PhD(pharmacol), 67. *Prof Exp:* Pharmacologist, Stine Lab, E I du Pont de Nemours & Co, Inc, Del, 63-67, res pharmacologist, 67-71; head cardiovasc-autonomic dis res, 71-72, head cardiovasc-respiratory dis res, 72-74, head pharmacol dept, Merrell-Nat Labs, 74-78, head preclin pharmacol dept, Merrell Res Ctr, 78-81, HEAD, PRECLIN PHARMACOL DEPT, MERRELL DOW RES CTR, MERRELL DOW PHARMACEUT INC, 81- *Concurrent Pos:* Lectr, Sch Med, Univ Pa, 67-71. *Mem:* NY Acad Sci. *Res:* Cardiovascular-autonomic pharmacology, especially etiology, pathology and treatment of hypertension; role of central nervous system and autonomic nervous system in control of cardiovascular function. *Mailing Add:* Preclin Pharmacol Dept 2110 E Galbraith Rd Cincinnati OH 45215

WOODWARD, JOE WILLIAM, b Teral, Okla, Oct 31, 37; m 58; c 3. CHEMICAL ENGINEERING. *Educ:* Tex A&M Col, BS, 60; Calif Inst Technol, MS, 61, PhD(chem eng), 65. *Prof Exp:* Sr res engr, US Army assigned to Jet Propulsion Lab, NASA, 65-66; CONSULT, E I DU PONT DE NEMOURS & CO, INC, 66- *Concurrent Pos:* Fel, Calif Inst Technol, 65-66. *Mem:* Am Inst Chem Engrs; Nat Soc Prof Engrs. *Res:* Polymer processing; rheology; mathematical models; computer process control. *Mailing Add:* 2726 Elizabeth Port Neches TX 77651

WOODWARD, JOHN MORRILL, b Concord, NH, Oct 16, 18; m 42; c 3. BACTERIOLOGY. *Educ:* Univ NH, BS, 41; Mass State Col, MS, 43; Univ Kans, PhD(bact, biochem), 49. *Prof Exp:* Asst bact, Univ Kans, 46-47; asst prof, Univ Maine, 49-51; assoc prof, 51-57, PROF MICROBIOL, UNIV TENN, KNOXVILLE, 57- *Concurrent Pos:* Consult, St Mary's Hosp, 51-54, Baptist Hosp, 55-59, Children's Hosp, 57- & Biol Div, Oak Ridge Nat Lab, 59-63. *Mem:* AAAS; Am Soc Microbiol; Am Acad Microbiol. *Res:* Role of restriction endonucleases in drug resistance of Neisseria gonorrhoeae; pathogenesis of Moraxella bovis in bovine keratoconjunctivitis; radiation injury and bacterial invasion of animal tissues; serological grouping of the serratia; new techniques in antibiotic sensitivity testing; pseudomonas infection in laboratory animals; bacterial endotoxins and host response to infection. *Mailing Add:* Dept of Microbiol Univ of Tenn Knoxville TN 37916

WOODWARD, KENT THOMAS, b Cleveland, Ohio, Dec 11, 23; m 49; c 3. RADIOTHERAPY. *Educ:* Clemson Univ, BS, 47; Univ SC, MD, 47; Univ Rochester, PhD(radiation biol), 66. *Prof Exp:* Intern, Boston City Hosp, Boston, Mass, 47-48; intern res med, Georgetown Univ Hosp, DC, 48-49; intern chest disease, Fitzsimons Army Hosp, Denver, Colo, 49, 50-51; intern med, Walter Reed Army Hosp, DC, 51-52; staff mem biomed res, Los Alamos Sci Lab, 52-56; chief biophys dept, Walter Reed Army Inst Res, 56-60, dir div nuclear med, 62-68; prog dir radiation, Nat Cancer Inst, 68-69; fel radiation ther, Univ Tex, M D Anderson Hosp & Tumor Inst Houston, 69-72; assoc prof, Med Univ SC, 72-73; assoc prof radiol, Univ Pa, 73-77; ASSOC PROF RADIATION THER, DUKE UNIV MED CTR, 78- *Mem:* AAAS; Am Med Asn; Radiation Res Soc; Health Physics Soc; fel Am Col Physicians. *Res:* Biological effects ionizing radiation on normal tissues and tumors. *Mailing Add:* Dept of Radiol Div of Radiation Ther Duke Univ Med Ctr Durham NC 27710

WOODWARD, LEE ALBERT, b Omaha, Nebr, Apr 22, 31; m 52; c 4. STRUCTURAL GEOLOGY. *Educ:* Univ Mont, BA, 58, MS, 59; Univ Wash, PhD(geol), 62. *Prof Exp:* Geologist, US Bur Reclamation, 58 & Pan Am Petrol Corp, 62-63; instr geol, Olympic Col, 63-65; from asst prof to assoc prof, 65-73, chmn dept, 70-76, PROF GEOL, UNIV NMEX, 73- *Concurrent Pos:* NSF fel, 58-61; Monsanto fel, 61-62; assoc ed, Geol Soc Am Bull, 77-82; NATO fel, 73. *Mem:* Geol Soc Am; Am Asn Petrol Geologists; Soc Mining Engrs. *Res:* Regional tectonics of western United States; mineral exploration. *Mailing Add:* Dept of Geol Univ of NMex Albuquerque NM 87106

WOODWARD, LEROY ALBERT, b Hartford, Conn, Nov 22, 16; m 42; c 2. PHYSICS. *Educ:* Ga Inst Technol, BS, 43; Univ Mich, MS, 47. *Prof Exp:* Mem sci staff, US Navy Underwater Sound Lab, Columbia Univ, 44; contract physicist, David Taylor Model Basin, US Dept Navy, DC, 45; from instr to asst prof physics, Ga Inst Technol, 47-51, assoc prof physics & res physicist,

Eng Exp Sta, 51-55; res physicist, Scripto, Inc, 55-58, dir res, 58-60; res asst prof physics, Eng Exp Sta, 60-63, asst prof, 63-65, ASSOC PROF PHYSICS, GA INST TECHNOL, 65- *Mem:* Royal Astron Soc Can; Am Asn Physics Teachers. *Res:* Optics and optical microscopy. *Mailing Add:* 834 Oakdale Rd NE Atlanta GA 30307

WOODWARD, PAUL RALPH, b Rockeville Center, NY, Aug 25, 46; m 72. ASTROPHYSICS, COMPUTATIONAL GAS DYNAMICS. *Educ:* Cornell Univ, BA, 67; Univ Calif, Berkeley, MA, 68, PhD(physics), 73. *Prof Exp:* Physicist physics, Lawrence Livermore Lab, 68-71; res assoc astron, Nat Radio Astron Observ, 74-75; res assoc, Leiden Observ, Neth, 75-78; PHYSICIST ASTROPHYS & COMPUT PHYSICS, LAWRENCE LIVERMORE LAB, 78- *Mem:* Int Astron Union. *Res:* Astrophysical gas dynamics relating to galactic structure and star formation; development of numerical methods for compressible gas dynamics. *Mailing Add:* Lawrence Livermore Lab PO Box 808 Livermore CA 94550

WOODWARD, RALPH STANLEY, b Williston, SC, Oct 1, 14; m 38; c 2. HORTICULTURE. *Educ:* Clemson Col, BS, 36; La State Univ, MS, 47. *Prof Exp:* Inspector, USDA, 36; tech asst, Univ Ark, 36-39; asst prof hort, La Polytech Inst, 39-42; prod supt, Fed Rubber Reserve Comn, 43-44; asst exten horticulturist, Univ, 45-47, asst hort & supt, NLa Exp Sta, 47-55, assoc, 55-58, prof hort & supt, 58-80, EMER PROF HORT & EMER SUPT, NORTH LA EXP STA, LA STATE UNIV, 80- *Mem:* Am Soc Hort Sci. *Res:* General agriculture; tree ripened peaches. *Mailing Add:* PO Box 557 Calhoun LA 71225

WOODWARD, RICHARD L(EWIS), sanitary engineering, deceased

WOODWARD, STEPHEN COTTER, b Atlanta, Ga, July 19, 35; m 57; c 2. PATHOLOGY. *Educ:* Emory Univ, MD, 59. *Prof Exp:* Pathologist, Georgetown Univ Hosp, 64-68; asst prof, 64-68, ASSOC PROF PATH, SCH MED, GEORGETOWN UNIV, 68-; PATHOLOGIST, HUNTER LAB, SIBLEY HOSP, 68- *Concurrent Pos:* Consult, Children's Hosp, 64-, Vet Admin Hosp, 65- & comt skeletal syst, Div Med Sci, Nat Res Coun, 68-; attend pathologist, DC Gen Hosp, 67- *Mem:* Col Am Path; Am Soc Clin Path; Am Soc Exp Path; AMA. *Res:* Fibroplasia; collagen elaboration; effects of endocrine and vulnerary agents upon wound repair; quality control methods for clinical laboratories. *Mailing Add:* Dept of Path Georgetown Univ Washington DC 20007

WOODWARD, THEODORE ENGLAR, b Westminster, Md, Mar 22, 14; m 38; c 4. MICROBIOLOGY, MEDICINE. *Educ:* Franklin & Marshall Col, BS, 34; Univ Md, MD, 38; Am Bd Internal Med, dipl. *Hon Degrees:* DSc, Western Med Col, 50 & Franklin & Marshall Col, 54. *Prof Exp:* Asst prof med, Sch Med & Univ Hosp, 46-48, assoc prof med & dir sect infectious dis, Sch Med, 48-54, prof med & head dept, Sch Med, 54-81, DISTINGUISHED PHYSICIAN, VET ADMIN HOSP, UNIV MD, 81- *Concurrent Pos:* Instr, Sch Med, Johns Hopkins Univ, 46-48, lectr, 48-54; attend physician, Vet Admin Hosp, 46-48, consult, 48-; consult, State Health Dept, Md, 50; mem comt int ctrs med res & training, USPHS, 61-62; mem US adv comt, US-Japan Coop Med Sci Prog, 65- *Mem:* Am Soc Clin Invest; AMA; Am Clin & Climat Asn; Am Asn Physicians; master Am Col Physicians. *Res:* Infectious and rickettsial diseases; enteric diseases including typhoid fever; internal medicine. *Mailing Add:* Dept Med Rm N3W40 Univ Md Hosp Baltimore MD 21201

WOODWARD, VAL WADDOUPS, b Preston, Idaho, July 26, 27; m 47, 67; c 3. GENETICS. *Educ:* Utah State Univ, BS, 50; Kans State Univ, MS, 50; Cornell Univ, PhD(genetics), 53. *Prof Exp:* NIH fel & guest assoc biologist, Brookhaven Nat Lab, 53-55; assoc prof genetics, Kans State Univ, 55-58; prof biol & chmn dept, Univ Wichita, 58-61; assoc prof, Rice Univ, 61-67; PROF GENETICS, UNIV MINN, ST PAUL, 67- *Concurrent Pos:* Fel, Birmingham Univ, 62-63. *Mem:* AAAS; Am Soc Cell Biol; Genetics Soc Am. *Res:* Gene-enzyme transport; cell wall; neurospora; self-assembly of membrane and other organelle proteins. *Mailing Add:* 250 Biosci Univ of Minn St Paul MN 55101

WOODWARD, WILLIAM MOONEY, b Hartford, Conn, Sept 19, 16; m 42; c 2. NUCLEAR PHYSICS. *Educ:* Columbia Univ, AB, 38; Princeton Univ, PhD(physics), 42. *Prof Exp:* Physicist, Manhattan Proj, Los Alamos Sci Lab, 43-46; asst prof physics, Mass Inst Technol, 46-48; assoc prof physics, Cornell Univ, 48-58, prof, 58-80, mem staff, Lab Atomic Solid State Physics, 78-80. *Mem:* Am Phys Soc. *Res:* Electron scattering; high energy physics. *Mailing Add:* 927 Cayuga Heights Rd Ithaca NY 14850

WOODWELL, GEORGE MASTERS, b Cambridge, Mass, Oct 23, 28; m 55; c 4. ECOLOGY, BOTANY. *Educ:* Dartmouth Col, AB, 50; Duke Univ, AM, 56, PhD(bot), 58. *Hon Degrees:* DSc, Williams Col, 77. *Prof Exp:* From asst bot to assoc prof, Univ Maine, 57-61; sr ecologist, Brookhaven Nat Lab, 61-75; DIR ECOSYSTS CTR, MARINE BIOL LAB, 75- *Concurrent Pos:* Assoc, Conserv Found, 58-61, mem bd trustees, 75-77; lectr, Sch Forestry, Yale Univ, 67-; founding mem bd trustees, Environ Defense Fund, 67-68 & 73-; mem, Inst Ecol, 70-71, vchmn, Natural Resources Defense Coun, 70-, World Wildlife Fund, 70-, chmn bd, 80-; chmn, Suffolk County Coun Environ Qual, 72. *Honors & Awards:* NY Bot Garden Sci Award, 75. *Mem:* Fel AAAS; Ecol Soc Am (vpres, 67, pres, 77-78); Am Inst Biol Sci; Brit Ecol Soc; Am Acad Arts & Sci. *Res:* Structure, function and development of terrestrial and marine ecosystems; environmental cycling of nutrients, radioactive isotopes and organic compounds, especially pesticides; ecological effects of ionizing radiation; biotic contributions to the global carbon cycle. *Mailing Add:* Ecosysts Ctr Marine Biol Lab Woods Hole MA 02543

WOODWICK, KEITH HARRIS, b Tappen, NDak, Jan 4, 27; m 51; c 3. INVERTEBRATE ZOOLOGY. *Educ:* Jamestown Col, BS, 49; Univ Wash, MS, 51; Univ Southern Calif, PhD(zool), 55. *Prof Exp:* Asst zool, Univ Wash, 49-51; instr, Univ Southern Calif, 54, asst, 54-55; from instr to assoc prof zool, 55-66, chmn dept, 65-69, PROF ZOOL, CALIF STATE UNIV, FRESNO, 66-, COORDR MARINE SCI, 68- *Mem:* Am Inst Biol Sci; Soc Syst Zool. *Res:* Systematics and larval development of polychaetes; Enteropneusta. *Mailing Add:* Dept of Biol Calif State Univ Fresno CA 93740

WOODWORTH, CURTIS WILMER, b Reading, Pa, Aug 30, 42; m 64; c 2. ORGANIC CHEMISTRY. *Educ:* Albright Col, BS, 64; Princeton Univ, PhD(chem), 69. *Prof Exp:* Res chemist, Am Cyanamid Co, Bound Brook, 68-73, group leader, 73-75, dept head, Lederle Labs, 75-79, SECT DIR, MED RES DIV, AM CYANAMID CO, PEARL RIVER, 79- *Mem:* Am Chem Soc. *Res:* Structure-reactivity relationships; process research and development on pharmaceuticals and fine chemicals; fermentation; proces development; biotechnology. *Mailing Add:* Am Cyanamid Co Med Res Div Lederle Labs Pearl River NY 10965

WOODWORTH, JOHN GEORGE, b Lockport, NY, Apr 16, 48. NUCLEAR PHYSICS. *Educ:* Trent Univ, BSc, 72, MSc, 74; Univ Toronto, PhD(physics), 78. *Prof Exp:* PHYSICIST NUCLEAR PHYSICS, LAWRENCE LIVERMORE LAB, 78- *Mem:* Am Phys Soc. *Res:* Nuclear modelling experimentalist. *Mailing Add:* Lawrence Livermore Lab L-405 PO Box 808 Livermore CA 94550

WOODWORTH, ROBERT CUMMINGS, b Cambridge, Mass, Nov 11, 30; m 52; c 3. BIOCHEMISTRY. *Educ:* Univ Vt, BS, 53; Pa State Univ, PhD(chem), 57. *Prof Exp:* Res chemist, Nat Inst Allergy & Infectious Dis, 56-60; from instr to assoc prof, 61-75, PROF BIOCHEM, COL MED, UNIV VT, 75- *Concurrent Pos:* USPHS fel, Clin Chem Lab, Malmo Gen Hosp, Sweden, 60-61; USPHS spec fel & vis prof, Inorg Chem Lab, Oxford Univ, 68-69; Fogarty Int sr fel, Oxford Univ, 76-77. *Mem:* Am Chem Soc; Am Soc Biol Chemists; Sigma Xi. *Res:* Protein structure-function; nature of iron-binding proteins; mechanisms of metal binding and release; role of bound anions, physiological function and structure. *Mailing Add:* Dept Biochem Univ Vt Given Med Bldg Burlington VT 05405

WOODWORTH, ROBERT HUGO, b Boston, Mass, Feb 24, 02; m 27; c 3. BIOLOGY. *Educ:* Mass Col, BS, 24; Harvard Univ, AM, 27, PhD(biol), 28. *Prof Exp:* Instr biol, Williams Col, 24 & 26; tutor biol, Harvard Univ, 27-35, from instr to asst prof bot, 27-35, cur bot garden, 29-35; chmn div sci, 36-46, mgr col farm, 42-45, interim pres, 76, PROF SCI, BENNINGTON COL, 35- *Concurrent Pos:* Vis prof, Hiram Col, 55-56, Univ Fla, 62-67, Williams Col, 63-64 & Southwestern at Memphis, 71-72. *Mem:* AAAS. *Res:* Chromosome number in birches and related species; biomicrocinematography. *Mailing Add:* Div of Sci Bennington Col Bennington VT 05201

WOODWORTH, WAYNE LEON, b Liberal, Kans, Jan 31, 40; m 62; c 3. MATHEMATICS. *Educ:* Kans State Univ, BS, 62, MS, 63; Iowa State Univ, PhD(math), 68. *Prof Exp:* From instr to assoc prof, 65-76, PROF MATH, DRAKE UNIV, 76-, CHMN DEPT, 72- *Mem:* Math Asn Am; Am Math Soc. *Res:* Measure and integration theory; operations research; functional analysis. *Mailing Add:* Dept of Math Drake Univ Des Moines IA 50311

WOODY, A-YOUNG MOON, b Pyungyang, Korea, Mar 7, 34; US citizen; m 65; c 2. CHEMISTRY, BIOCHEMISTRY. *Educ:* Univ Calif, Berkeley, BS, 59; Cornell Univ, PhD(biochem), 64. *Prof Exp:* Res assoc chem, Cornell Univ, 64-65; res assoc microbiol, Univ Ill, Urbana, 65-66; res assoc biochem, 67-69; res assoc develop biol, Dept Zool, Ariz State Univ, 72-74; RES ASSOC BIOCHEM, DEPT BIOCHEM, COLO STATE UNIV, FT COLLINS, 76- *Mem:* Am Chem Soc; Sigma Xi. *Res:* Structure and function of proteins and enzymes. *Mailing Add:* 2607 Shadow Court Ft Collins CO 80521

WOODY, CHARLES DILLON, b Brooklyn, NY, Feb 6, 37; m 59; c 2. NEUROPHYSIOLOGY. *Educ:* Princeton Univ, AB, 57; Harvard Med Sch, MD, 62. *Prof Exp:* Intern med, Strong Mem Hosp, Univ Rochester, 62-63; resident, Boston City Hosp, Mass, 63-64; res assoc, Lab Neurophysiol, NIH, 64-67, res officer, Lab Neural Control, 68-71; assoc prof anat, physiol & psychiat, 71-76, PROF ANAT & PSYCHIAT, MENT RETARDATION CTR, NEUROPSYCHIAT INST, UNIV CALIF, LOS ANGELES, 77- *Concurrent Pos:* Harvard Moseley fel & Nat Acad Sci exchange fel neurophysiol, Inst Physiol, Czech Acad Sci, 67-68; res fel neurol, Harvard Med Sch, 63-64. *Honors & Awards:* Nightingale Prize, Brit Biol Eng Soc & Int Fedn Med Electronics & Biol Eng, 69. *Mem:* AAAS; Am Physiol Soc; Soc Neurosci; Biomed Eng Soc. *Res:* Neurophysiology of learning and memory; neurophysiology of learned motor performance; electrophysiologic data analysis by linear filter techniques employing digital computers. *Mailing Add:* Ment Retardation Res Ctr Univ Calif Med Sch Los Angeles CA 90024

WOODY, CHARLES OWEN, JR, b Somerville, Tenn, Oct 28, 30; m 60; c 4. REPRODUCTIVE PHYSIOLOGY. *Educ:* Miss State Univ, BS, 57, MS, 59; NC State Univ, PhD(animal sci), 63. *Prof Exp:* Trainee endocrinol, Univ Wis-Madison, 63, proj assoc reproductive physiol, 64-68; assoc prof, 68-81, PROF ANIMAL INDUSTS, UNIV CONN, 81- *Mem:* Am Soc Animal Sci; Brit Soc Study Fertility; Soc Study Reproduction. *Res:* Corpus luteum physiology; testis growth and function. *Mailing Add:* Dept of Animal Industries Univ of Conn Storrs CT 06268

WOODY, CRAIG L, b Baltimore, Md, Mar 26, 51; m 73. PHYSICS. *Educ:* Johns Hopkins Univ, BA, 73, MA, 74, PhD(physics), 79. *Prof Exp:* Res asst physics, Johns Hopkins Univ, 74-78; res assoc physics, Stanford Linear Accelerator Ctr, 78-80; MEM STAFF, EUROP CTR NUCLEAR RES, 80- *Mem:* Am Phys Soc. *Res:* Elementary particle physics. *Mailing Add:* Europ Ctr Nuclear Res Ch 1211 Geneva 23 94305 Switzerland

WOODY, NORMAN COOPER, b Winnfield, La, June 15, 14; m 40. PEDIATRICS. *Educ:* Centenary Col, BS, 36; La State Univ, MD, 41; Am Bd Pediat, dipl, 48; Am Bd Neonatal Perinatal Med, dipl, 75. *Prof Exp:* Intern, Charity Hosp, New Orleans, La, 41-42; resident pediat, Tulane Serv, 45-47; instr, Sch Med, Tulane Univ, 47-48; pvt pract, Tex, 48-59; from asst prof to assoc prof, 59-64, prof, 64-80, EMER PROF PEDIAT, SCH MED, TULANE UNIV, 80- *Concurrent Pos:* Lederle med fac award, 62-65; asst vis physician, Charity Hosp, New Orleans, 59-67. *Mem:* Am Pediat Soc. *Res:* Human parasitology; neonatology; inborn metabolic errors. *Mailing Add:* Tulane Univ Sch of Med New Orleans LA 70112

WOODY, ROBERT WAYNE, b Newton, Iowa, Dec 5, 35; m 65; c 2. PHYSICAL CHEMISTRY, BIOCHEMISTRY. *Educ:* Iowa State Col, BS, 58; Univ Calif, Berkeley, PhD(chem), 62. *Prof Exp:* Res assoc phys chem, Cornell Univ, 62-64, Nat Inst Gen Med Sci fel, 63-64; asst prof, Univ Ill, Urbana, 64-70; from assoc prof to prof, Ariz State Univ, 70-75; PROF BIOCHEM, COLO STATE UNIV, 75- *Mem:* Am Phys Soc; AAAS; Am Chem Soc; Am Soc Biol Chemists; Biophys Soc. *Res:* Optical properties of molecules; structure of proteins; protein-nucleic acid interactions; interaction of small molecules with proteins. *Mailing Add:* Dept of Biochem Colo State Univ Ft Collins CO 80523

WOODYARD, JACK RAMON, b Los Angeles, Calif, Oct 18, 44; m 65; c 5. SOFTWARE SYSTEMS, ANALYTICAL CHEMISTRY. *Educ:* Colo State Univ, BS, 66; Univ Nev, Reno, MS, 68, PhD(physics), 74. *Prof Exp:* Physicist, Reno Metall Res Ctr, US Bur Mines, 71-78; OWNER, NOMAR-COMPUTER SOFTWARE CO, 78- *Concurrent Pos:* Adj asst prof, Univ Nev, Reno, 75- *Mem:* Optical Soc Am; Soc Appl Spectroscopy. *Res:* Computer applications and measurement theory for instrumental chemical analysis with particular emplasis on human engineering for the man-machine interface. *Mailing Add:* NOMAR PO Box 3030 Sparks NV 89431

WOODYARD, JAMES DOUGLAS, b San Antonio, Tex, Oct 8, 38. ORGANIC CHEMISTRY. *Educ:* Tex Christian Univ, BA, 61, MA, 63, PhD(chem), 67. *Prof Exp:* NSF fel Univ Ill, Chicago, 66-67; from asst prof to assoc prof, 67-78, PROF CHEM, WEST TEX STATE UNIV, 78- *Mem:* Am Chem Soc; Royal Soc Chem. *Res:* Reaction of carbenes and stereochemistry of carbene reactions; triplet state of organic molecules. *Mailing Add:* Dept Chem WTex State Univ Canyon TX 79016

WOODYARD, JAMES ROBERT, b Pittsburgh, Pa, July 18, 36; m 60; c 4. PHYSICS. *Educ:* Duquesne Univ, BEd, 60; Univ Del, MS, 62, PhD(physics), 66. *Prof Exp:* AEC fel, Oak Ridge Nat Lab, 65-67; asst prof physics, Univ Ky, 67-69; mem tech staff, Gen Tel & Electronics Labs, 69-71; asst prof physics, Univ Hartford, 71-72; asst prof, Trenton State Col, 72-75; ASSOC PROF, DIV SCI & TECHNOL, COL LIFELONG LEARNING, WAYNE STATE UNIV, 75- *Mem:* AAAS; Am Phys Soc; Am Vacuum Soc; Sigma Xi; Am Asn Physics Teachers. *Res:* Particle surface interactions; ultra high vacuum technique; instructional methods. *Mailing Add:* Col Lifelong Learning Wayne State Univ Detroit MI 48202

WOOFTER, HARVEY DARRELL, b Glenville, WVa, Jan 31, 23; m 44. WEED SCIENCE. *Educ:* WVa Univ, BS, 43; Ohio State Univ, MS, 49, PhD(agron), 53. *Prof Exp:* County agr agt, WVa, 43-44 & 46-48; asst agron, Ohio State Univ, 48-49; res agronomist, Chem Corps Biol Warfare Labs, US Dept Army, Md, 49-54; field res rep, Pittsburgh Coke & Chem Co, 54-56; field res rep, Chemagro Corp, 56-62, asst supvr field res, 62-64; mgr field res, Diamond Alkali Co, 64-66; mgr prod develop, Ciba Agrochem Co, Fla, 66-68; mgr, Fla Res Sta, Velsicol Chem Corp, 68-72, mgr agrochem sta, 72-76, MGR RES & DEVELOP, MAAG AGROCHEM, HOFFMAN-LA ROCHE, INC, 76- *Mem:* Am Soc Agron; Entom Soc Am; Weed Sci Soc Am; Aquatic Plant Mgt Soc; Plant Growth Regulator Soc Am. *Res:* Weed control; development of new herbicides, insecticides, fungicides, nematocides, bactericides, defoliants, desiccants and plant growth regulators. *Mailing Add:* Hoffman-La Roche Sci Inc PO Box X Vero Beach FL 32960

WOOL, IRA GOODWIN, b Newark, NJ, Aug 22, 25; m 50; c 2. BIOCHEMISTRY. *Educ:* Syracuse Univ, AB, 49; Univ Chicago, MD, 53, PhD(physiol), 54. *Prof Exp:* Intern med, Beth Israel Hosp, Boston, Mass, 54-55, asst resident, 55-56; from asst prof to assoc prof physiol, 57-65, assoc prof biochem, 64-65, PROF BIOCHEM, UNIV CHICAGO, 65-, A J CARLSON PROF BIOL SCI, 73- *Concurrent Pos:* Fel physiol, Harvard Univ, 56; Commonwealth Fund fel, Univ Chicago, 56-57; vis scientist, Dept Biochem, Cambridge Univ, 60-61; vis prof, Wayne State Univ, 64, 66 & Fla State Univ, 66; Lederle sci lectr, Lederle Labs, 66; vis fac mem, Mayo Grad Sch Med, 66; vis prof, Rutgers Univ, 67; ed, Vitamins & Hormones & J Biol Chem; vis res scientist, Max-Planck Inst Molecular Genetics, Berlin, Ger, 73-74; mem, Molecular Biol Study Sect, NIH, 74-78. *Honors & Awards:* Ginsburg Award, Univ Chicago, 52; Bernstein lectr, Beth Israel Hosp, Harvard Med Sch, 64; Alexander von Humboldt spec fel, Fed Repub Ger, 73-74. *Mem:* AAAS; Am Physiol Soc; Brit Biochem Soc; Am Soc Biol Chemists; Am Soc Cell Biol. *Res:* Regulation of protein synthesis; structure and function of eukaryotic ribosomes. *Mailing Add:* Dept of Biochem 920 E 58th St Chicago IL 60637

WOOLARD, HENRY W(ALDO), b Clarksburg, WVa, June 2, 17; m 41; c 2. FLUID DYNAMICS, AERODYNAMICS. *Educ:* Univ Mich, BS, 41; Univ Buffalo, MS, 54. *Prof Exp:* Aeronaut engr, Nat Adv Comt Aeronaut, 41-46; from asst prof to assoc prof aeronaut eng, Univ WVa, 46-48, actg head dept, 46-48; res aerodynamicist, Cornell Aeronaut Lab, Inc, 48-57; sr staff engr, Appl Physics Lab, Johns Hopkins Univ, 57-63; sr res specialist, Lockheed-Calif Co, 63-67; mem tech staff, TRW Systs Group, Calif, 67-70; pres, Beta Technol Co, Calif, 70-71; AEROSPACE ENGR, FLIGHT DYNAMICS LAB, WRIGHT-PATTERSON AFB, 71- *Concurrent Pos:* Lectr aerodynamics, Univ Buffalo, 55-57. *Mem:* Assoc fel Am Inst Aeronaut & Astronaut; Sigma Xi. *Res:* Numerous technical papers and reports, principally theoretical, on fluid dynamics and aerodynamics published in various journals. *Mailing Add:* 975 Thorndale Dr Dayton OH 45429

WOOLCOTT, WILLIAM STARNOLD, b Coffeyville, Kans, Apr 14, 22; m 46; c 2. VERTEBRATE ZOOLOGY. *Educ:* Austin Peay State Col, BS, 47; Peabody Col, MA, 48; Cornell Univ, PhD(vert zool), 55. *Prof Exp:* Asst prof biol, Carson-Newman Col, 49-53; assoc prof, 55-67, PROF BIOL, UNIV RICHMOND, 67- *Mem:* Am Soc Zool; Am Soc Ichthyol & Herpet. *Res:* Morphological and ecological aspects of fishes. *Mailing Add:* Dept Biol Univ Richmond Richmond VA 23173

WOOLDRIDGE, DAVID DILLEY, b Seattle, Wash, Mar 12, 27; m 48, 70; c 5. FOREST SOILS, FOREST HYDROLOGY. *Educ:* Univ Wash, BS, 50, PhD(forestry), 61. *Prof Exp:* Forester, Rayonier Inc, 50-52, res forester, 53-56; res forester, Forest Hydrol Lab, US Forest Serv, Wash, 56-68; ASSOC PROF FOREST HYDROL, COL FOREST RESOURCES, UNIV WASH, 68- *Concurrent Pos:* Asst prof, Univ Wash, 65-68; consult, King County Flood Control Div, 66-; consult local eng firms & US Corps Eng; res grants, Off Water Resources & Res & US Forest Serv, Wash State Dept Ecol, Environ Protection Agency & Wash State Dept Natural Resources. *Mem:* Sigma Xi; Am Chem Soc; Soc Am Foresters; Soil Sci Soc Am; Am Geophys Union. *Res:* Hydrologic data summary; turbidity-suspended sediment relations in forest streams; disposal of stabilized municipal-industrial sewage sludge; impacts of clear-cutting on soil nutrient balance; effects of slash burial on surface water quality; variability in soil properties under pristine western hemlock. *Mailing Add:* Col of Forest Resources Univ of Wash Seattle WA 98195

WOOLDRIDGE, DAVID PAUL, b Terre Haute, Ind, Dec 25, 31; m 56. ENTOMOLOGY. *Educ:* Ind Univ, BS, 56, PhD(zool), 62. *Prof Exp:* Asst prof biol, Wilkes Col, 62-63; asst prof zool, Southern Ill Univ, 63-67; assoc ed, Biol Abstr, 67-68; from asst prof to assoc prof, 68-78, PROF BIOL, PA STATE UNIV, 78- *Mem:* Entom Soc Am; Coleopterist's Soc. *Res:* Taxonomy and biochemistry of aquatic Coleoptera; systematics of world limnichidae. *Mailing Add:* 810 E Prospect Ave North Wales PA 19454

WOOLDRIDGE, DEAN E, b Chickasha, Okla, May 13. PHYSICS, ENGINEERING. *Educ:* Univ Okla, BA, MS; Calif Inst Technol, PhD(physics), 36. *Prof Exp:* Mem tech staff, Bell Tel Lab, 36-46; dir electronic res & develop, Hughes Aircraft Co, 46-53; pres, Thompson Ramo Wooldridge Inc, 53-62; RES ASSOC ENG, CALIF INST TECHNOL, 62- *Concurrent Pos:* Chmn, Nat Inst Health Study Comt, 64-65; mem bd trustees, Calif Inst Technol, 75-78. *Honors & Awards:* Raymond E Hackett Award, 55; Westinghouse Award, AAAS, 63. *Mem:* Nat Acad Sci; Nat Acad Eng; Am Phys Soc; Inst Elec & Electronics Engrs; Am Inst Aeronaut & Astronaut. *Mailing Add:* 4545 Via Esperanza Santa Barbara CA 93105

WOOLDRIDGE, GENE LYSLE, b Randalia, Iowa, Apr 16, 24; m 45; c 5. ATMOSPHERIC SCIENCES, PHYSICS. *Educ:* Upper Iowa Col, BS, 44; Mankato State Col, MS, 61; Colo State Univ, PhD(atmospheric sci), 70. *Prof Exp:* Instr physics, Rochester State Jr Col, Minn, 61-62; instr, Mankato State Col, 62-64, asst prof atmospheric sci, 65-67; assoc prof, 70-77, PROF ATMOSPHERIC SCI, UTAH STATE UNIV, 77- *Mem:* Am Meteorol Soc. *Res:* Mesoscale circulations and transport processes; mesoscale-macroscale and mesoscale-microscale energy interactions and mechanisms. *Mailing Add:* Dept of Soil Sci & Biometeorol Utah State Univ UMC 48 Logan UT 84322

WOOLDRIDGE, KENT ERNEST, b Waukegan, Ill, Apr 23, 42; m 68; c 2. MATHEMATICS. *Educ:* Univ Chicago, BS, 64; Univ Ill, Urbana, PhD(math), 75. *Prof Exp:* Asst prof math, 74-81, ASSOC PROF MATH, CALIF STATE COL, 81- *Mem:* Am Math Soc; Math Asn Am. *Res:* Number theory. *Mailing Add:* Dept of Math Calif State Col Turlock CA 95380

WOOLES, WALLACE RALPH, b Lawrence, Mass, Mar 8, 31; m 51; c 5. PHYSIOLOGY, PHARMACOLOGY. *Educ:* Boston Col, BS, 58, MS, 61; Univ Tenn, PhD(physiol), 63. *Prof Exp:* From instr to assoc prof pharmacol, Med Col Va, 63-70; PROF PHARMACOL & ASSOC VCHANCELLOR HEALTH AFFAIRS, E CAROLINA UNIV, 70- *Mem:* AAAS; Soc Toxicol; Int Soc Res Reticuloendothelial Systs; Am Soc Pharmacol & Exp Therapeut. *Res:* Radiation injury and lipid metabolism; alcohol and lipid metabolism; reticuloendothelial system and drug metabolism. *Mailing Add:* Sch of Med ECarolina Univ Greenville NC 27834

WOOLF, C R, b Cape Town, SAfrica, Jan 26, 25; Can citizen; m 52; c 3. PULMONARY DISEASES, INTERNAL MEDICINE. *Educ:* Univ Cape Town, BSc, 44, MB, ChB, 47, MD, 51; FRCP(C), 57; FRCP, 78. *Prof Exp:* Jr asst path, Univ Cape Town, 49, jr asst med, 50-51; house physician, Brompton Hosp, London, Eng & London Chest Hosp, 52-53; resident chest serv, Bellevue Hosp, New York, 53-54; res assoc, Ont Heart Found, 55-63; from asst prof to assoc prof, 63-73, PROF MED, UNIV TORONTO, 73-, DIR TRI-HOSP RESPIRATORY SERV, 63- *Concurrent Pos:* Francis Esther res fel cardio-respiratory, Univ Toronto, 54-55; AMA, Med Res Coun Can, Ont Heart Found, Ont Tuberc Asn & Can Tuberc Asn grants; sr physician, Toronto Gen Hosp, 58-; div postgrad training prog, Dept Med, Univ Toronto, Ont, Can. *Mem:* Am Thoracic Soc; Am Col Chest Physicians; Can Thoracic Soc. *Res:* Respiratory physiology; cardiac dyspnea; role of oxygen in the regulation of respiration; respiratory rehabilitation; effects of smoking; surgical treatment of emphysema. *Mailing Add:* Respiratory Div Off 101 College St Toronto ON M5G 1L7 Can

WOOLF, CHARLES MARTIN, b Salt Lake City, Utah, Aug 23, 25; m 50; c 4. GENETICS. *Educ:* Univ Utah, BS, 48, MS, 49; Univ Calif, PhD(genetics), 54. *Prof Exp:* Asst geneticist, Lab Human Genetics, Univ Utah, 50-51, dir, 57-61, res instr genetics, Univ, 53-55, asst prof, 55-59, assoc prof, 59-61; dean col lib arts, 73-75, assoc prof genetics, 61-64, PROF ZOOL, ARIZ STATE UNIV, 64-, VPRES GRAD STUDIES & RES & DEAN GRAD COL, 76- *Mem:* Am Soc Human Genetics (treas, 61-63); Genetics Soc Am. *Res:* Genetics of congenital malformation; consanguinity and genetic effects; drosophila behavior and developmental genetics. *Mailing Add:* Dept of Zool Ariz State Univ Tempe AZ 85281

WOOLF, HARRY, b New York, NY, Aug 12, 23; m 61; c 4. SCIENCE POLICY. *Educ:* Univ Chicago, BS, 48, MA, 49; Cornell Univ, PhD(hist sci), 55. *Hon Degrees:* DSc, Whitman Col, 79, Am Univ, 82. *Prof Exp:* Instr physics, Boston Univ, 53-55; from asst prof to prof hist, Univ Wash, 55-61; prof hist sci, Johns Hopkins Univ, 61-76, chmn, 6-72, provost, 72-76; DIR, INST ADVAN STUDY, 76- *Concurrent Pos:* Instr hist, Brandeis Univ, 54-55; trustee, Assoc Univ Inc, Brookhaven Nat Lab & Nat Radio Astron Observ, 72-; chmn of bd, Univ Res Asn, Inc, 79-; mem, Sci Adv Bd, Berlin, 81-, Corp Vis Comt, dept physics, Mass Inst Technol, 79-, Adv Coun, dept philosophy, Princeton Univ, 80-84 & Adv Bd, Stanford Humanities Ctr, 81-84. *Mem:* Sigma Xi; fel Am Philosphical Soc; AAAS; Royal Astron Soc; Hist Sci Soc. *Res:* History of science, with emphasis on physics and astronomy; issues involving the intersection of work, research and education with modern technology. *Mailing Add:* Inst Advan Study Olden Lane Princeton NJ 08540

WOOLF, J(ACK) R(OYCE), b Trinidad, Tex, June 10, 24; m 48; c 3. MECHANICAL ENGINEERING. *Educ:* Agr & Mech Col, Tex, BS & MS, 48; Purdue Univ, PhD, 51. *Prof Exp:* Asst instr, Agr & Mech Col, Tex, 47-48, prof mech eng & res engr, Eng Exp Sta, 56-57, asst to dean eng, 57; instr, Purdue Univ, 48-51; res engr, Consol Aircraft Co, 51-56; dean, 57-58, actg pres, 58-59, pres, 59-68, UNIV PROF MECH ENG, UNIV TEX, ARLINGTON, 68- *Concurrent Pos:* Lectr, Southern Methodist Univ, 53-56. *Mem:* Am Soc Mech Engrs; Am Soc Eng Educ. *Res:* Heat transfer; thermodynamics and transfer properties of fluids; aerothermodynamics. *Mailing Add:* 3115 Woodford Dr Arlington TX 76013

WOOLF, MICHAEL A, b Detroit, Mich, Feb 3, 38; m 60; c 2. LOW TEMPERATURE PHYSICS. *Educ:* Harvard Col, AB, 59; Univ Calif, Berkeley, PhD(physics), 64. *Prof Exp:* Mem tech staff physics, Bell Tel Labs, 64-66; asst prof, Univ Calif, Los Angeles, 66-71; CONSULT, 71- *Concurrent Pos:* Alfred P Sloan fel, 67-69; assoc prof physics, Hampshire Col, 75-80. *Res:* Tunneling in superconductors; light scattering in liquid helium. *Mailing Add:* 167 South St Northampton MA 01060

WOOLF, NEVILLE JOHN, b London, Eng, Sept 15, 32; US citizen; m 72; c 2. ASTROPHYSICS. *Educ:* Manchester Univ, BSc, 56, PhD(astrophys), 59. *Prof Exp:* Res assoc astron, Lick Observ, Univ Calif, 59-61; res assoc, Princeton Univ, 61-65; assoc prof, Univ Tex, 65-67; prof, Univ Minn, 67-74; PROF ASTRON, STEWARD OBSERV, UNIV ARIZ, 74- *Concurrent Pos:* Dir, Minn Observ, Univ Minn, 67-74; Nat Acad Sci/Nat Res Coun sr fel, NASA Goddard Inst Space Studies, 65-67; actg dir, Flandrau Planetarium, Univ Ariz, 77; actg dir, Multiple Mirror Telescope Observ, 78- *Mem:* Am Astron Soc; Int Astron Union. *Res:* Astrophysics, observational, theoretical and instrumental. *Mailing Add:* Steward Observ Univ of Ariz Tucson AZ 85721

WOOLF, WILLIAM BLAUVELT, b New Rochelle, NY, Sept 18, 32. MATHEMATICS. *Educ:* Pomona Col, BA, 53; Claremont Col, MA, 55; Univ Mich, PhD(math), 60. *Prof Exp:* Instr math, Mt San Antonio Jr Col, 54 & Univ Mich, 54-59; from instr to assoc prof, Univ Wash, 59-68; staff assoc, Am Asn Univ Profs, 68-69, assoc secy & dir admin, 69-79; MANAGING ED, MATH REVIEWS, 79- *Concurrent Pos:* Fulbright res scholar, Univ Helsinki, 63-64. *Mem:* Am Math Soc; AAAS; Math Asn Am. *Res:* Functions of a complex variable; mathematics education. *Mailing Add:* Math Reviews 611 Church St PO Box 8604 Ann Arbor MI 48107

WOOLFENDEN, GLEN EVERETT, b Elizabeth, NJ, Jan 23, 30; m 54; c 3. ORNITHOLOGY. *Educ:* Cornell Univ, BS, 53; Univ Kans, MA, 56; Univ Fla, PhD(zool), 60. *Prof Exp:* Instr biol, Univ Fla, 59-60; from instr to assoc prof zool, 60-70, PROF BIOL, UNIV SOUTH FLA, TAMPA, 70- *Concurrent Pos:* Res Soc Am res grant, 61; consult, Encephalitis Res Ctr, Tampa, 61-64; res assoc, Am Mus Natural Hist, 70- *Mem:* Am Ornith Union; Wilson Ornith Soc; Cooper Ornith Soc; Brit Ornith Union. *Res:* Behavioral ecology; communal breeding. *Mailing Add:* Dept of Biol Univ of South Fla Tampa FL 33620

WOOLFOLK, CLIFFORD ALLEN, b Riverside, Calif, June 5, 35; m 57; c 2. MICROBIOLOGY. *Educ:* Univ Calif, Riverside, BA, 57; Univ Wash, Seattle, MSc, 59, PhD(microbiol), 63. *Prof Exp:* Res asst microbiol, Univ Wash, 57-59 & 62-63; USPHS fel enzymol lab biochem, Nat Heart Inst, 63-65; asst prof, 65-68, ASSOC PROF MICROBIOL, UNIV CALIF, IRVINE, 68- *Mem:* AAAS; Am Soc Microbiol; Brit Soc Gen Microbiol; Am Chem Soc; Am Soc Biol Chemists. *Res:* Microbial physiology; hydrogenase and hydrogenase mediated reduction of inorganic compounds; cumulative feedback inhibition of glutamine synthetase from Escherichia coli; bacterial purine oxidizing enzymes. *Mailing Add:* Dept of Microbiol & Biochem Univ of Calif Irvine CA 92717

WOOLFOLK, ROBERT WILLIAM, b Riverside, Calif, Feb 9, 37; m 68; c 4. PHYSICAL CHEMISTRY. *Educ:* Univ Calif, Riverside, BA, 58; Univ Calif, Berkeley, PhD(phys chem), 64. *Prof Exp:* Staff scientist, Chem Syst Div, United Technol Corp, 63-65; PHYS CHEMIST & DIR BUS DEVELOP, SRI INT, 65- *Mem:* Am Chem Soc; Am Phys Soc; Am Inst Aeronaut & Astronaut. *Res:* Shock wave phenomenon; gas phase reaction kinetics; photochemistry; fluorine chemistry; explosive sensitivity; nonideal explosions; combustion and marketing research and development. *Mailing Add:* SRI Int 1611 N Kent St Arlington VA 22209

WOOLFORD, ROBERT GRAHAM, b London, Ont, Apr 14, 33; m 55; c 2. ORGANIC CHEMISTRY. *Educ:* Univ Western Ont, BSc, 55, MSc, 56; Univ Ill, PhD(org chem), 59. *Prof Exp:* From asst prof to assoc prof chem, 59-68, assoc dean sci, 67-75, PROF CHEM, UNIV WATERLOO, 68-, ASSOC CHMN DEPT, 77- *Concurrent Pos:* Res fel chem, Univ Ill, 56-58. *Mem:* Fel Chem Inst Can. *Res:* Electroorganic chemistry of halogenated carboxylic acids; synthesis of polymers. *Mailing Add:* Dept of Chem Univ of Waterloo Waterloo ON N2L 3G1 Can

WOOLHISER, DAVID A(RTHUR), b La Crosse, Wis, Jan 21, 32; m 57; c 3. CIVIL ENGINEERING. *Educ:* Univ Wis, BS(agr) & BS(civil eng), 55, PhD(civil eng), 62; Univ Ariz, MS, 59. *Prof Exp:* Asst agr engr, Univ Ariz, 55-58; hydraul engr, Agr Res Serv, USDA, 58-63; asst prof civil eng, Cornell Univ, 63-67; RES HYDRAUL ENGR, AGR RES SERV, USDA, 67- *Concurrent Pos:* Mem assoc faculty, Dept Civil Eng, Colo State Univ, 70-, mem staff, Eng Res Ctr, Foothills Campus. *Mem:* AAAS; Am Soc Civil Engrs; Am Soc Agr Engrs; Am Geophys Union. *Res:* Simulation of hydrologic systems, including numerical solutions of unsteady, spatially varied flow; hydrologic effects of surface mining. *Mailing Add:* Eng Res Ctr Colo State Univ Foothills Campus Ft Collins CO 80523

WOOLLAM, JOHN ARTHUR, b Kalamazoo, Mich, Aug 10, 39; m 65; c 2. PHYSICS, ELECTRICAL ENGINEERING. *Educ:* Kenyon Col, AB, 61; Mich State Univ, MS, 63, PhD(physics), 67; Case Western Reserve Univ, MS, 78. *Prof Exp:* Res physicist mat, Lewis Res Ctr, NASA, 67-74, head, Cryophysics Sect, 74-78, res physicist photovoltaics, 78-80; MEM FAC, DEPT ELEC ENG, UNIV NEBR, 80- *Concurrent Pos:* Asst, Mich State Univ, 61-62, res asst, 62-67; vis scientist, Mat Sci Ctr, Mass Inst Technol, 72 & Francis Bitter Nat Magnet Lab, 77-; adj scientist, Oberlin Col, 78-; consult, Wright Patterson AFB, 78-; mem, Interagency Adv Power Group. *Honors & Awards:* Achievement Awards, NASA/Lewis Res Ctr, 72 & 77. *Mem:* Am Phys Soc; Am Carbon Soc; Inst Elec & Electronics Engrs. *Res:* Physics of solids: electronic properties; superconductivity, magnetism; physical chemistry of trapped free radicals: magnetic resonance of atomic species; photovoltaics: energy conversion in Ga As; semiconductors. *Mailing Add:* Dept Elec Eng W194 Nebraska Hall Univ Nebr Lincoln NE 68588

WOOLLETT, ALBERT HAINES, b Oxford, Miss, Jan 23, 30; m 64; c 3. PHYSICS. *Educ:* Univ Miss, BA, 49, MS, 50; Univ Okla, PhD(physics), 56. *Prof Exp:* Asst prof physics, Fisk Univ, 56-57; instr, Reed Col, 57-59; assoc prof, High Point Col, 59-61; asst prof, Va Polytech Inst & State Univ, 61-63; asst prof, 63-72, ASSOC PROF PHYSICS, MEMPHIS STATE UNIV, 72- *Mem:* Am Asn Physics Teachers; Optical Soc Am; assoc mem Am Astron Soc. *Res:* Infrared and Raman spectroscopy; physical optics. *Mailing Add:* Dept of Physics Memphis State Univ Memphis TN 38152

WOOLLETT, RALPH STORER, b Newport, RI, Dec 30, 17. ACOUSTICS. *Educ:* Mass Inst Technol, SB, 39; Univ Conn, MS, 60, PhD, 67. *Prof Exp:* PHYSICIST, NAVAL UNDERWATER SYSTS CTR, 47- *Mem:* Acoust Soc Am; Inst Elec & Electronics Eng. *Res:* Magnetostriction; piezoelectricity; electromechanical transducers. *Mailing Add:* Naval Underwater Systs Ctr New London CT 06320

WOOLLEY, DONALD GRANT, b Magrath, Alta, Dec 12, 25; m 47; c 5. AGRONOMY, PHYSIOLOGY. *Educ:* Utah State Univ, BSc, 51, MSc, 56; Iowa State Univ, PhD(crop physiol), 59. *Prof Exp:* Asst prof agron, Iowa State Univ, 59-60; res officer, Can Dept Agr, 60-63; assoc prof, 63-67, PROF AGRON, IOWA STATE UNIV, 67-, HEAD, FARM MGT DEPT & CLASSIFICATION OFFICER, COL AGR, 76- *Concurrent Pos:* Consult, World Bank, SE Asia, 74-75. *Mem:* Am Soc Agron; Am Soc Crop Sci. *Res:* Crop physiology and climatology. *Mailing Add:* 1816 Bel Air Dr Ames IA 50010

WOOLLEY, DOROTHY ELIZABETH SCHUMANN, b Wapakoneta, Ohio, Feb 2, 29; m 50; c 3. PHYSIOLOGY, PHARMACOLOGY. *Educ:* Bowling Green State Univ, BS, 50; Ohio State Univ, MS, 56; Univ Calif, Berkeley, PhD(physiol), 61. *Prof Exp:* NSF fel, Univ Calif, Berkeley, 61-62, asst res physiologist, 62-65, lectr physiol, 63-64; from asst prof to assoc prof physiol & environ toxicol, 65-74, PROF ANIMAL PHYSIOL, UNIV CALIF, DAVIS, 74- *Concurrent Pos:* Lectr, Sch Med, Univ Calif, San Francisco, 60-65. *Mem:* AAAS; Am Physiol Soc; Endocrine Soc; Am Soc Pharmacol & Exp Therapeut. *Res:* Effects of hormones, drugs and neurotoxins on brain electrical activity, neurochemistry and behavior in rats and monkeys. *Mailing Add:* Dept of Animal Physiol Univ of Calif Davis CA 95616

WOOLLEY, EARL MADSEN, b Richfield, Utah, Apr 10, 42; m 66; c 8. PHYSICAL CHEMISTRY, ANALYTICAL CHEMISTRY. *Educ:* Brigham Young Univ, BS, 66, PhD(phys chem), 69. *Prof Exp:* Nat Res Coun Can fel, Univ Lethbridge, 69-70; assoc prof, 70-77, PROF ANAL & PHYS CHEM, BRIGHAM YOUNG UNIV, 77- *Mem:* Am Chem Soc. *Res:* Acid-base equilibria in aqueous-organic mixtures; hydrogen bonding in solutions; calorimetric and thermal methods of analysis. *Mailing Add:* Dept of Chem Brigham Young Univ Provo UT 84602

WOOLLEY, GEORGE WALTER, b Osborne, Kans, Nov 9, 04; m 36; c 3. GENETICS. *Educ:* Iowa State Col, BS, 30; Univ Wis, MS, 31, PhD(genet), 35. *Prof Exp:* Asst genet, Univ Wis, 31-35; res assoc, Jackson Mem Lab, 36-49, mem bd dirs, 37-49, vpres, 43-47, asst dir & sci adminr, 47-49; chief div steroid biol, Sloan-Kettering Inst, 49-58, chief div human tumor exp chemother, 58-61, chief div & head sect tumor biol, 61 66; head biol sci sect, 66-67, HEALTH SCIENTIST ADMINR & GENET PROG ADMINR, NAT INST GEN MED SCI, 66- *Concurrent Pos:* Fel, Univ Wis, 35-36; mem, Int Genet Cong, NY, 36 & Edinburgh, 39, Int Cancer Cong, Atlantic City, 39 & St Louis, 47, sect biol, Nat Res Coun, 54-57, bd trustees, Dalton Schs, Inc, NY, 56- & Mt Desert Island Biol Labs; vis assoc, Sloan-Kettering Inst Cancer Res, 48-49, assoc scientist, 66-; vis res assoc, Jackson Mem Lab, 49-53; prof, Sloan-Kettering Div, Med Col, Cornell Univ, 51-66; consult, Nat Cancer Inst, 56-60. *Mem:* Fel AAAS; Genet Soc Am; Am Asn Cancer Res; Am Soc Human Genet; fel NY Acad Sci. *Res:* Basic and human genetics; cancer; endocrinology. *Mailing Add:* Apt 336 Kenwood Pl 5301 Westbard Circle Washington DC 20816

WOOLLEY, JOSEPH TARBET, b Denver, Colo, Jan 25, 23; m 52; c 3. PLANT PHYSIOLOGY. *Educ:* Utah State Agr Col, BS, 48, MS, 52; Univ Calif, PhD(plant physiol), 56. *Prof Exp:* Asst prof, 56-65, ASSOC PROF PLANT PHYSIOL, UNIV ILL, URBANA, 65-; PLANT PHYSIOLOGIST, AGR RES SERV, USDA, 56- *Mem:* Am Soc Plant Physiol; Am Soc Agron; Soc Exp Biol. *Res:* Physics of water in plants and soils; reflection of light by leaves; soil-plant-atmosphere interactions. *Mailing Add:* Dept of Agron Univ of Ill Urbana IL 61801

WOOLLEY, LEGRAND H, b Salt Lake City, Utah, Apr 22, 31; m 53; c 4. ORAL PATHOLOGY, DENTISTRY. *Educ:* Univ Mo-Kansas City, DDS, 58; Univ Ore, MS, 66; Am Bd Oral Path, dipl, 73. *Prof Exp:* Asst prof path, Dent Sch, 66-70, sr clin instr dent & oral med, 67-71, assoc prof dent, Med Sch, 70-71, assoc prof path, Dent Sch, 70-75, chmn dept path, 76-80, PROF PATH, SCH DENT, ORE HEALTH SCI UNIV, 78-, DIR ORAL PATH GRAD PROG, 81- *Concurrent Pos:* Am Cancer Soc fel, 66-68; consult, Fairview Hosp, Salem, Ore, 66-68. *Mem:* Fel Am Acad Oral Path; Am Dent Asn. *Res:* Effects of therapeutic radiation on dental structures. *Mailing Add:* Oregon Health Sci Univ 611 SW Campus Dr Portland OR 97201

WOOLLEY, RONALD LEE, b Twin Falls, Idaho, July 23, 43; m 77; c 1. MECHANICAL ENGINEERING, COMPUTER SCIENCE. *Educ:* Brigham Young Univ, BES, 66, MS, 68; Stanford Univ, PhD(mech eng), 74. *Prof Exp:* Res assoc mech eng, Stanford Univ, 69-73; fel fluid dynamics, Ames Res Ctr, 74; TECH ASST PRES MECH ENG, BILLINGS ENERGY CORP, 75- *Concurrent Pos:* Mem fac, Brigham Young Univ, 74-78. *Mem:* Am Soc Mech Engrs; Am Soc Automotive Engrs; Sigma Xi. *Res:* Hydrogen use as a fuel in automotive applications. *Mailing Add:* Billings Energy Corp 2000 E Billings Ave Provo UT 84601

WOOLLEY, TYLER ANDERSON, b Los Angeles, Calif, Apr 3, 18; m 80; c 3. ZOOLOGY. *Educ:* Univ Utah, BS, 39, MS, 41; Ohio State Univ, PhD(entom), 48. *Prof Exp:* Sr asst comp anat, Univ Utah, 38-39; asst zool, Ohio State Univ, 46-47, asst instr, 47-48; from asst prof to assoc prof, 48-58, PROF ZOOL, COLO STATE UNIV, 58- *Res:* Acarology; Oribatei; taxonomy; biology; invertebrate zoology. *Mailing Add:* Dept of Zool & Entom Colo State Univ Ft Collins CO 80521

WOOLRIDGE, EDWARD DANIEL, b Jackson, Miss, June 7, 32; m 63; c 2. DENTISTRY, FORENSIC DENTISTRY. *Educ:* Lynchburg Col, BS, 53; Med Col Va, DDS, 57; George Washington Univ, MEd, 81; Am Bd Forensic Odontol, dipl, 71. *Prof Exp:* Private pract dent, Farmville, Va, 59-62; liaison officer, US Coast Guard Base, NY, 65-66, sr dent officer, 69-74; sr dent officer, US Coast Guard Acad, 74-77; CHIEF DENT OFFICER, US COAST GUARD HQ, 77- *Concurrent Pos:* Consult, Off Chief Med Examrs, Rockland, NY, 71-, vis asst prof, Med Univ SC, 75-; clin instr, Sch Dent Med, Tufts Univ, 76-; clin field instr, Baltimore Col Dent Surg, Univ Md, 78- *Honors & Awards:* Commendation Medal, USPHS, 73. *Mem:* Fel Am Col Dent; fel Am Acad Forensic Sci; Soc Med Jurisprudence. *Mailing Add:* Commandant G-KOM US Coast Guard Washington DC 20590

WOOLRIDGE, ROBERT LEONARD, medical bacteriology, immunology, see previous edition

WOOLSEY, CLINTON NATHAN, b Brooklyn, NY, Nov 30, 04; m 42; c 3. NEUROPHYSIOLOGY. *Educ:* Union Col, NY, AB, 28; Johns Hopkins Univ, MD, 33. *Hon Degrees:* ScD, Union Col, 68. *Prof Exp:* Asst physiol, Sch Med, Johns Hopkins Univ, 33-34, instr, 34-39, from assoc to assoc prof physiol, 41-48; Charles Sumner Slichter res prof neurophysiol, 48-75, dir lab neurophysiol, 60-73, biomed unit coordr, Waisman Ctr, 73-78; EMER PROF NEUROPHYSIOL, UNIV WIS-MADISON, 75- *Concurrent Pos:* Rockefeller Found fel, Johnson Found, Univ Pa, 38-39; fel neuromuscular physiol, Johns Hopkins Univ, 39-41; hon lectr, Albany Med Col, 66; hon mem fac med, Univ Chile. Spec consult, Ment Health Study Sect, NIH, 52-53 & neurol study sect, 53-56 & 57-58; mem nat adv coun, Nat Inst Neurol Dis & Blindness, 58-62, spec consult neurol prog proj comt, 63-67, mem bd sci counr, 65-69; mem div med sci, Nat Res Coun, 52-58 & Inter-Coun Adv Comt Career Res Professorships, 60-61; mem med exchange mission pharmacol & physiol of nerv syst, USSR, 58; US organizer, Int Brain Res Orgn-UNESCO vis sem, Chile, 66, workshop, Shanghai, China, 80 & workshop, Algiers, Algeria, 81; mem, Nat Acad Sci-Colciencias Panel Grad Educ & Res Biol, Colombian Univs, 72. *Honors & Awards:* Medalist, Univ Brussels, 68; James Arthur lectr, Am Mus Nat Hist, New York, 52; Hines lectr, Emory Univ, 61; Bishop lectr, Wash Univ, 61; Von Monakow lectr, Univ Zurich, 68; J Hughlings Jackson Mem lectr, Montreal Neurol Inst, 71; Donald D Matson lectr, Harvard Med Sch, 75. *Mem:* Nat Acad Sci; Am Physiol Soc; hon mem Am Neurol Asn; assoc Am Asn Neurol Surg; Soc Neurosci. *Res:* Cerebral localization; sensory and motor. *Mailing Add:* Dept of Neurophysiol 627 Waisman Ctr Univ of Wis Madison WI 53706

WOOLSEY, GERALD BRUCE, b Brooks, Ga, Aug 16, 37; m 60; c 3. PHYSICAL CHEMISTRY. *Educ:* Univ SC, BS, 60, PhD(phys chem), 67. *Prof Exp:* Chemist, Tenn Corp, Cities Serv Co, 60-63; res chemist, 67-69, develop supvr, 69-71, res supvr, 71-74, mfg supvr, 74-76, bus specialist, 76-78, STAFF RES CHEMIST, SAVANNAH RIVER LAB, E I DU PONT DE NEMOURS & CO, INC, 79- *Mem:* Am Chem Soc. *Res:* Thermodynamics of solutions; hydration in solutions of concentrated electrolytes; amide solutions; polyester films; nuclear waste disposal; nuclear propulsion. *Mailing Add:* Savannah River Lab E I du Pont de Nemours & Co Inc Aiken SC 29801

WOOLSEY, MARION ELMER, b Croft, Kans, July 27, 19; m 40; c 3. MICROBIOLOGY. *Educ:* Univ Tex, Austin, BA, 64, MA, 66, PhD(microbiol), 68. *Prof Exp:* Res assoc immunol, Univ Tex, Austin, 68, asst prof microbiol, 68-70; asst prof, 70-76, ASSOC PROF MICROBIOL, UNIV TULSA, 76- *Concurrent Pos:* NIH fel, Univ Tex, Austin, 68. *Mem:* Am Soc Microbiol. *Res:* Basic and applied research in medical microbiology, immunology and immunochemistry. *Mailing Add:* Dept of Life Sci Univ of Tulsa Tulsa OK 74104

WOOLSEY, NEIL FRANKLIN, b Tieton, Wash, Apr 30, 35; m 56; c 5. ORGANIC CHEMISTRY. *Educ:* Univ Portland, BS, 57; Univ Wis, PhD(org chem), 62. *Prof Exp:* NSF fel, Imp Col, London, 61-63; res assoc org chem, Iowa State Univ, 63-65; asst prof chem, 65-70, assoc prof, 70-77, PROF CHEM, UNIV NDAK, 77- *Mem:* Am Chem Soc. *Res:* Diazoketone and carbene reactions; organic photochemistry; structure, reactions and analytical chemistry of coal and coal derived materials. *Mailing Add:* Dept of Chem Univ of NDak Grand Forks ND 58202

WOOLSEY, ROBERT M, b Chicago, Ill, May 30, 31; m 67; c 1. MEDICINE, NEUROLOGY. *Educ:* St Louis Univ, BS, 53, MD, 57. *Prof Exp:* Intern med, St Louis Univ Hosp, 57-58; resident neurol, Univ Mich Hosp, 58-61; from instr to assoc prof, 62-75, PROF NEUROL, ST LOUIS UNIV, 75- *Concurrent Pos:* Fel neuropath, Col Physicians & Surgeons, Columbia Univ, 61-62. *Mem:* AMA; Asn Res Nerv & Ment Dis; Am Acad Neurol; Am Electroencephalog Soc; Am Paraplegia Soc. *Res:* Electroencephalography. *Mailing Add:* Dept of Neurol 1402 S Grand Blvd St Louis MO 63104

WOOLSEY, THOMAS ALLEN, b Baltimore, Md, Apr 17, 43; m 69; c 2. NEUROANATOMY. *Educ:* Univ Wis-Madison, BS, 65; Johns Hopkins Univ, MD, 69. *Prof Exp:* Intern surg, Barnes Hosp St Louis, Mo, 69-70; asst prof, 71-77, ASSOC PROF ANAT & NEUROBIOL, MED SCH, WASHINGTON UNIV, 77-, COORDR NEURAL SCI PROG, 80- *Concurrent Pos:* NIH fel anat, Med Sch, Wash Univ, 70-71, Nat Inst Neurol Dis & Stroke grant, 72-, consult NIH, NSF; reviewer Brain Res, J Comp Neurol Sci. *Mem:* Am Asn Anat; Soc Neurosci. *Res:* Structure and function of somatosensory areas of the cerebral cortex; computer applications to morphology. *Mailing Add:* Dept of Anat & Neurobiol Wash Univ Med Sch St Louis MO 63110

WOOLSON, EDWIN ALBERT, b Takoma Park, Md, Oct 2, 41; m 61; c 4. PESTICIDE CHEMISTRY. *Educ:* Univ Md, BS, 63, MS, 66, PhD(soil chem), 69. *Prof Exp:* Analyst soil testing, Univ Md, 62; phys sci aide, USDA, 62-63, chemist, 63-65, anal chemist, 65-67, RES CHEMIST, USDA, 67- *Honors & Awards:* USDA Superior Serv Award, 74. *Mem:* Am Chem Soc; Am Soc Agron; Soil Sci Soc Am; Weed Sci Soc Am; Coun Agr Sci Technol. *Res:* Behavior and fate of arsenic, herbicides and insecticides in soil and water; method development for pesticides in soils, plants and water; toxicity of pesticides to plants; impurities in pesticides; bioaccumulation. *Mailing Add:* Bldg 050 Agr Res Ctr-West USDA Beltsville MD 20705

WOOLSTON, DANIEL D, b Churchville, NY, Oct 18, 26; m 50; c 2. ELECTRONICS. *Educ:* Iowa State Col, BS, 51. *Prof Exp:* Physicist & electronic scientist, US Naval Ord Lab, 51-63; vpres, 63-75, PRES, UNDERWATER SYSTS, INC, 75- *Mem:* Inst Elec & Electronics Engrs. *Res:* Underwater telemetry; hydroacoustic mine research and development; underwater explosive perameter data gathering and analysis for underwater mine research programs; sediment velocimeter research, design and development of the instrumentation; underwater sound propagation studies. *Mailing Add:* 11810 Pittson Rd Wheaton MD 20906

WOONTON, GARNET ALEXANDER, physics, magnetic resonance, deceased

WOOSLEY, RAYMOND LEON, b Roundhill, Ky, Oct 2, 42; m 63; c 2. CLINICAL PHARMACOLOGY. *Educ:* Western Ky State Univ, BS, 64; Univ Louisville, PhD(pharmacol), 67; Univ Miami, MD, 73. *Prof Exp:* Sr pharmacologist, Meyer Labs, Inc, 68-69, dir res pharmaceut, 69-71; from intern to resident med, Vanderbilt Univ Hosp, 73-74, fel clin pharmacol, 74-75, asst prof, 75-76, ASSOC PROF MED, VANDERBILT UNIV, 76- *Concurrent Pos:* NIH fel pharmacol, Med Sch, Univ Louisville, 67-68, lectr, 69-71; instr med & clin pharmacol, Vanderbilt Univ, 75. *Mem:* Soc Exp Biol & Med; Am Soc Pharmacol & Exp Therapeut; fel Am Col Clin Pharmacol. *Res:* Drug induced lupus erythematosus; and clinical pharmacology of new antiarrhythmic drugs. *Mailing Add:* Dept of Clin Pharmacol Vanderbilt Univ Nashville TN 37232

WOOSLEY, ROYCE STANLEY, b Caneyville, Ky, June 17, 34; m 59; c 2. ORGANIC CHEMISTRY. *Educ:* Western Ky Univ, BS, 56; Univ Conn, MS, 59; Ohio Univ, PhD(org chem), 67. *Prof Exp:* Sect leader tech serv, Olin Mathieson Chem Corp, 58-62; from asst prof to assoc prof, 66-74, PROF CHEM, WESTERN CAROLINA UNIV, 74-, CHMN DEPT, 69- *Mem:* Am Chem Soc; Sigma Xi. *Res:* Chemical waste management and alternative sources of energy. *Mailing Add:* Dept Chem Western Carolina Univ Cullowhee NC 28723

WOOSLEY, STANFORD EARL, b Texarkana, Tex, Dec 8, 44; div. ASTROPHYSICS. *Educ:* Rice Univ, BA, 66, MS, 69, PhD(astrophys), 71. *Prof Exp:* Res assoc, Rice Univ, 71-73; res fel, Calif Inst Technol, 73-75; asst prof, 75-78, ASSOC PROF ASTRON, LICK OBSERV, UNIV CALIF, SANTA CRUZ, 78- *Concurrent Pos:* Consult, Lawrence Livermore Lab, 74-; NSF grants, 77-83. *Mem:* Am Phys Soc; Am Astron Soc. *Res:* Theoretical nuclear astrophysics, origin of the elements in explosive events such as supernovae; theoretical nuclear physics; gamma-ray astronomy; models for gamma-ray bursts. *Mailing Add:* Lick Observ Univ Calif Santa Cruz CA 95064

WOOSTER, HAROLD ABBOTT, b Hartford, Conn, Jan 3, 19; m 41, 68; c 4. INFORMATION SCIENCE. *Educ:* Syracuse Univ, AB, 39; Univ Wis, MS, 41, PhD(physiol chem), 43. *Prof Exp:* Asst, Toxicity Lab, Univ Chicago, 43-46; res assoc, Pepper Lab, Univ Pa, 46-47; sr fel, Mellon Inst, 47-56; dir res commun, Air Force Off Sci Res, 56-59, chief info sci div, 59-62, dir info sci, 62-70; chief res & develop br, 70-74, SPEC ASST PROG DEVELOP, LISTER HILL NAT CTR BIOMED COMMUN, NAT LIBR MED, 74- *Concurrent Pos:* Exec secy panel info sci & tech, Comt Sci & Tech Info, Off Dir Defense Res & Eng, 65-66; adj instr, Grad Sch Libr Sci, Drexel Inst Technol, 67. *Mem:* AAAS; Am Soc Info Sci. *Res:* Biomedical communications; computer-aided instruction; medical television; information storage and retrieval. *Mailing Add:* Lister Hill Nat Ctr Biomed Commun Nat Libr of Med 8600 Rockville Pike Bethesda MD 20209

WOOSTER, WARREN SCRIVER, b Westfield, Mass, Feb 20, 21; m 48; c 3. OCEANOGRAPHY. *Educ:* Brown Univ, BSc, 43; Calif Inst Technol, MS, 47; Univ Calif, PhD, 53. *Prof Exp:* Asst res oceanogr, Scripps Inst, Univ Calif, 51-58, assoc res oceanogr, 58-61; dir off oceanog, UNESCO, 61-63; prof oceanog, Scripps Inst Oceanog, Univ Calif, 63-73, chmn grad dept, 67-69; prof oceanog & dean, Rosenstiel Sch Marine & Atmospheric Sci, Univ Miami, 73-76; PROF MARINE STUDIES & FISHERIES, INST MARINE STUDIES, UNIV WASH, 76-, DIR, 81- *Concurrent Pos:* Dir invests, Coun Hydrobiol Invests, Peru, 57-58; vpres, Int Coun Explor Sea, 74-76 & 81- *Mem:* fel Am Geophys Union; fel Am Meteorol Soc. *Res:* Descriptive oceanography of the Pacific Ocean; physical, chemical and fishery oceanography; ocean affairs. *Mailing Add:* Inst of Marine Studies Univ of Wash Seattle WA 98105

WOOTEN, FRANK THOMAS, b Fayetteville, NC, Sept 24, 35; m 62; c 3. BIOMEDICAL ENGINEERING. *Educ:* Duke Univ, BS, 57, PhD(elec eng), 64. *Prof Exp:* Sr engr, Electronic Res Lab, Corning Glass Works, 64-67; res engr, 67-71, mgr biomed eng, 71-75, exec asst to pres, 75-80, VPRES, RES TRIANGLE INST, 80- *Mem:* Asn Advan Med Instrumentation; Inst Elec & Electronics Eng. *Res:* Medical instrumentation; analysis of pulmonary sound; technology transfer. *Mailing Add:* Res Triangle Inst PO Box 12194 Research Triangle Park NC 27709

WOOTEN, FREDERICK (OLIVER), b Linwood, Pa, May 16, 28; m 52; c 2. SOLID STATE PHYSICS. *Educ:* Mass Inst Technol, BS, 50; Univ Del, PhD(chem), 55. *Prof Exp:* Staff physicist, All Am Eng Co, 54-57; res chemist, Lawrence Livermore Lab, 57-72; vchmn dept appl sci, 72-73, PROF APPL SCI, UNIV CALIF, DAVIS, 72-, CHMN DEPT, 73- *Concurrent Pos:* Vis prof, Drexel Univ, 64; lectr, Univ Calif, Davis, 65-72; vis prof, Chalmers Univ Technol, Sweden, 67-68; consult, Lawrence Livermore Nat Lab, 72-; vis prof, Heriot-Watt Univ, Heriot-Watt Edinburgh, Scotland, 79. *Mem:* AAAS; Am Phys Soc. *Mailing Add:* Dept of Appl Sci Univ of Calif Davis CA 95616

WOOTEN, JEAN W, b Douglasville, Ga, Jan 11, 29; m 52; c 1. BOTANY. *Educ:* NGa Col, BS, 46; Fla State Univ, MS, 64, PhD(bot), 68. *Prof Exp:* Asst prof bot, Iowa State Univ, 68-74; asst prof, 74-77, ASSOC PROF BIOL, UNIV SOUTHERN MISS, 78- *Mem:* Am Soc Plant Taxonomists; Soc Study Evolution; Int Asn Plant Taxon; Bot Soc Am. *Res:* Evolution and systematics in aquatic vascular plants. *Mailing Add:* Dept of Biol Univ of Southern Miss Hattiesburg MS 39401

WOOTEN, WILLIS CARL, JR, b Homerville, Ga, Mar 9, 22; m 49; c 3. POLYMER CHEMISTRY. *Educ:* Univ NC, PhD(chem), 50. *Prof Exp:* Sr res chemist, 51-60, admin asst, 60-65, div head, res lab, 65-75, DIR, POLYMER RES DIV, TENN EASTMAN CO, 76- *Mem:* Am Chem Soc. *Res:* Synthetic fibers and plastics; organic chemistry. *Mailing Add:* Res Lab Tenn Eastman Co Kingsport TN 37662

WOOTTEN, HENRY ALWYN, b Salisbury, Md, May 3, 48. ASTRONOMY, ASTROPHYSICS. *Educ:* Univ Md, BS, 70; Univ Tex, MS, 76, PhD(astron), 78. *Prof Exp:* res fel astron, Calif Inst Technol, 78-81; RES ASSOC ASTRON, RENESSELAER POLYTECH INST, 82- *Mem:* Am Astron Soc. *Mailing Add:* Owens Valley Radio Observ Calif Inst of Technol Pasadena CA 91125

WOOTTEN, MICHAEL JOHN, b Somersham, Eng, Mar 2, 44; m 66; c 2. PHYSICAL CHEMISTRY, WATER CHEMISTRY. *Educ:* Univ Leicester, BS, 66, PhD(phys chem), 69. *Prof Exp:* Res fel chem, Carnegie-Mellon Univ, 69-71; sr res fel phys chem, Univ Southampton, Eng, 71-73; sr engr, Westinghouse Europe, Belg, 73-75, sr engr, 75-77, mgr, Westinghouse Res & Develop Ctr, Pittsburgh, 77-80, MGR, WESTINGHOUSE NUCLEAR TECHNOL DIV, PITTSBURGH, 80- *Mem:* Nat Asn Corrosion Engrs; Royal Inst Chem, Eng; Electrochem Soc Eng. *Res:* The physical chemistry of aqueous solutions at high temperatures and pressures with particular reference to power generation. *Mailing Add:* Westinghouse Nuclear Technol Div PO Box 855 Pittsburgh PA 15230

WOOTTON, DONALD MERCHANT, b Paonia, Colo, Apr 13, 16; m 41; c 1. PARASITOLOGY, ZOOLOGY. *Educ:* Santa Barbara State Col, BA, 41; Univ Wash, MS, 43; Stanford Univ, PhD(biol), 49. *Prof Exp:* Actg instr zool & bot, Santa Barbara State Col, 41-42, instr zool, 49-52; asst prof, Univ Calif, Santa Barbara, 52-56; prof, 57-80, dept chmn, 76-80, EMER PROF BIOL, CALIF STATE UNIV, CHICO, 80- *Mem:* Am Soc Parasitol. *Res:* Helminths; branchipods; limnology. *Mailing Add:* Dept of Biol Sci Calif State Univ Chico CA 95926

WOOTTON, JOHN FRANCIS, b Penn Yan, NY, May 31, 29; m 59; c 4. BIOCHEMISTRY. *Educ:* Cornell Univ, BS, 51, MS, 53, PhD(biochem), 60. *Prof Exp:* Clin chemist, Clifton Springs Sanitarium & Clin, NY, 56; Nat Found fel chem, Univ Col London, 60-62; from asst prof to assoc prof physiol chem, 62-70, prof physiol chem, 70-79, PROF BIOCHEM, NY STATE COL VET MED, 79-, ASSOC DEAN, GRAD SCH, CORNELL UNIV, 80- *Concurrent Pos:* Hon res asst, Univ London, 62; vis scientist, Lab Molecular Biol, Med Res Coun, Cambridge, Eng, 69-70; temp sr res assoc, Stanford Univ Med Sch, 77-78. *Mem:* Am Chem Soc; Am Soc Biol Chemists; AAAS; Sigma Xi. *Res:* Enzymology; proteolytic enzymes; relationship of enzyme structure to function. *Mailing Add:* Grad Sch 100 Sage Grad Ctr Cornell Univ Ithaca NY 14853

WOOTTON, PETER, b Peterborough, Eng, Apr 30, 24; m 47; c 3. MEDICAL PHYSICS, RADIOLOGY. *Educ:* Univ Birmingham, BSc, 44. *Prof Exp:* Physicist, Res & Develop Labs, Farrow's Br, Reckitt & Coleman Ltd, 44-48; radiation physicist, Royal Infirmary, Glasgow, Scotland, 48-51; instr radiol physics, Univ Tex M D Anderson Hosp, 51-53; radiation physicist, Tumor Inst, Swedish Hosp, Seattle, Wash, 53-64; from asst prof to assoc prof radiol, 64-72, PROF RADIOL, UNIV WASH, 72- *Concurrent Pos:* Instr, Med Sch, Univ Ore, 54-60, Univ Seattle, 56 & Penrose Cancer Hosp, Colorado Springs, Colo, 56-57; clin asst prof & radiation physicist, Univ Wash, 59-64; mem tech adv bd radiation control, Dept Health, Wash, 62-, US Nat Comt Med Physics, 64-, comt radiation ther studies, Hyperbaric Oxygen Steering Comt, Nat Cancer Inst, 65- & sci comt, 25, Nat Coun Radiation Protection & Measurements, 67- *Mem:* Am Asn Physicists in Med (pres, 78); Soc Nuclear Med; fel Am Col Radiol; Am Soc Therapeut Radiol; fel Brit Inst Physics. *Res:* Applications of radiation physics in medicine, especially dosimetry of all types of ionizing radiations and the effects of physical parameters such as high pressure oxygen and pulsed radiation in radiobiology; fast neutron therapy. *Mailing Add:* NN158 Univ Hosp RC-08 Univ of Wash Seattle WA 98195

WOPSCHALL, ROBERT HAROLD, b Glendale, Calif, May 1, 40; m 62; c 2. PHYSICAL CHEMISTRY. *Educ:* Harvey Mudd Col, BS, 62; Univ Wis, PhD(phys chem), 67. *Prof Exp:* RES CHEMIST, E I DU PONT DE NEMOURS & CO, INC, 66- *Mem:* Am Chem Soc. *Res:* Stationary electrode polarography; adsorption of electroactive species on electrodes and coupled chemical reactions; photopolymerization; electroless deposition; photoresists; printed circuits manufacturing; photographic science. *Mailing Add:* Photo Prod Dept E I du Pont de Nemours & Co Inc Wilmington DE 19898

WORDEN, DAVID GILBERT, b Minneapolis, Minn, Mar 9, 24; m 47; c 2. SOLID STATE PHYSICS, PLASMA PHYSICS. *Educ:* Earlham Col, AB, 50; Iowa State Univ, PhD(physics), 56. *Prof Exp:* Physicist, Gen Elec Res Lab, 56-61; mgr surface physics sect, Electro-Optical Systs, Inc, 61-65, electron device res sect, 65-66, electron & image device dept, 66-67; chmn, Dept Physics, NDak State Univ, 67-68, prof physics & acad vpres, 68-79; MGR, UNIV RELATIONS, GEN ELEC CORP RES & DEVELOP, 79- *Concurrent Pos:* Assoc part-time prof, Calif State Col, Los Angeles, 65-67. *Mem:* Am Soc Eng Educ. *Res:* Properties of thin films; physical and chemical adsorption; electron emission; ion production on surfaces; low energy gaseous electrical discharges in magnetic fields; university industry relationships; manpower; science and engineering policy. *Mailing Add:* 1178 Van Curler Ave Schenectady NY 12308

WORDEN, EARL FREEMONT, JR, b Portsmouth, NH, Nov 30, 31; m 60; c 1. PHYSICAL CHEMISTRY. *Educ:* Univ NH, BS, 53, MS, 55; Univ Calif, PhD(chem), 59. *Prof Exp:* CHEMIST, LAWRENCE LIVERMORE LAB, UNIV CALIF, 58- *Mem:* Am Chem Soc; Sigma Xi; Optical Soc Am; Soc Appl Spectros. *Res:* Atomic and molecular optical spectroscopy; laser isotope separation; laser spectroscopy of atoms. *Mailing Add:* Lawrence Livermore Lab Univ of Calif Livermore CA 94550

WORDEN, FREDERIC GARFIELD, b Syracuse, NY, Mar 22, 18; m 44; c 5. PSYCHIATRY. *Educ:* Dartmouth Col, AB, 39; Univ Chicago, MD, 42. *Prof Exp:* Intern med, Johns Hopkins Hosp, 42-43, from house officer to resident psychiat, 46-50; instr, Med Sch, Johns Hopkins Univ, 50-52; clin dir, Sheppard & Enoch Hosp, Towson, Md, 52-53; from asst prof to prof psychiat, Med Sch, Univ Calif, Los Angeles, 53-71, from assoc res psychiatrist to res psychiatrist, 56-61; prog dir, Neurosci Res Prog, Mass Inst Technol, 69-71, exec dir, 71-74, prof psychiat, 69-82, dir, Neurosci Res Prog, 74-81. *Concurrent Pos:* Career investr, NIMH, 56-61, mem behav sci & exp psychol study sects, 57-61, ment health career award comt, 61-66 & res scientist & mem develop rev comt, 71-74; mem comt brain sci, Nat Res Coun, 71-74; mem bd dirs fund for res in psychiat, Neurosci Res Prog, Mass Inst Technol, 73-76; mem, bd sci counrs, NIMH, 75- *Mem:* Am Psychiat Asn; Am Psychoanal Asn; AMA; NY Acad Sci; fel Am Acad Arts & Sci. *Res:* Relationships between brain function and behavior, especially auditory electrophysiology of attention, habituation and learning. *Mailing Add:* 45 Hilltop Rd Weston MA 02193

WORDEN, PAUL WELLMAN, JR, b San Angelo, Tex, Mar 1, 45. PHYSICS. *Educ:* Rice Univ, BA, 67; Stanford Univ, MS, 69, PhD(physics), 76. *Prof Exp:* Res asst, 68-76, scholar, 76-78, res assoc physics, 78-80, SR RES ASSOC, STANFORD UNIV, 80- *Mem:* AAAS; Am Phys Soc; Sigma Xi. *Res:* Experimental gravitation; equivalence principle; cryogenic applications to basic research. *Mailing Add:* W W Hansen Lab of Physics Stanford Univ Stanford CA 94305

WORDEN, RALPH EDWIN, b Berwyn, Nebr, Dec 23, 17; m 43; c 9. PHYSICAL MEDICINE. *Educ:* Univ Nebr, BS, 41, MD, 44; Univ Minn, MS, 49. *Prof Exp:* Instr phys med & rehab, Col Med, Univ Minn, 49-51; from asst prof to prof, Col Med, Ohio State Univ, 51-58; prof phys med, 58-67, PROF REHAB, DEPT MED, SCH MED, UNIV CALIF, LOS ANGELES, 67-, PROF, DEPT PSYCHIAT, 74- *Concurrent Pos:* Consult, St John's Hosp Chem Dependency Ctr, dir, substance abuse prog, Univ Calif Los Angeles Fac, staff and families; chmn, Ext Course, Studies in Alcoholism. *Mem:* AMA. *Res:* Physiological effects of physical agents; functional anatomy; alcoholism; rehabilitation. *Mailing Add:* Rehab Ctr Univ of Calif Sch of Med Los Angeles CA 90024

WORDEN, SIMON PETER, b Mt Clemens, Mich, Oct 21, 49. SOLAR PHYSICS. *Educ:* Univ Mich, BS, 71; Univ Ariz, PhD(astron), 75. *Prof Exp:* Res asst astron, Kitt Peak Nat Observ, 71-75; astrophysicist, Sacramento Peak Observ, Air Force Geophys Lab, 75-80; MEM FAC, DEPT ASTRON, UNIV CALIF, LOS ANGELES, 80- *Mem:* Am Astron Soc; Royal Astron Soc. *Res:* The study of large-scale convective motions on the sun and observation and interpretation of stellar phenomena related to solar surface activity; development of techniques for high resolution imaging through the Earth's atmosphere. *Mailing Add:* Dept Astron Univ Calif 405 Hilgard Ave Los Angeles CA 90024

WORDINGER, ROBERT JAMES, b Philadelphia, Pa, Feb 5, 45; m 74; c 2. ANATOMY, ELECTRON MICROSCOPY. *Educ:* Pa State Univ, BS, 67; Clemson Univ, MS, 69, PhD(animal physiol), 72. *Prof Exp:* Fel physiol, Sch Vet Med, Univ Pa, 72-73; asst prof biol, St Bonaventure Univ, 73-76; asst prof path, Sch Med Sci, Univ Ark, 76-77; asst prof, 78-80, ASSOC PROF ANAT, TEX COL OSTEOP MED, NORTH TEX STATE UNIV, 80- *Concurrent Pos:* Head histol, Nat Ctr Toxicol Res, 76-77; vchmn, Dept Anat, Tex Col Osteop Med, NTex State Univ, 79-82. *Mem:* Am Asn Anatomists; Soc Study Reproduction; Histochem Soc; AAAS; Electron Micros Soc Am. *Res:* Estrogenic changes in the mammalian reproductive system using histochemistry and electron microscopy; factors influencing in vitro embryo development and differentiation within mammals. *Mailing Add:* Dept Anat NTex State Univ Tex Col Osteop Med Ft Worth TX 76107

WOREK, WILLIAM MARTIN, b Joliet, Ill, May 7, 54. HEAT & MASS TRANSFER, ENERGY SYSTEMS. *Educ:* Ill Inst Technol, BS, 76, MS, 77, PhD(mech eng), 80. *Prof Exp:* Instr, 77-80, VIS ASST PROF MECH ENG, ILL INST TECHNOL, 80- *Mem:* Am Soc Mech Engrs; Am Soc Heating, Refrigeration & Air Conditioning Engrs; Sigma Xi. *Res:* Fundamental heat and mass transfer problems which are related to specific problems encountered in energy systems; design and simulation of hybrid heat transfer components and energy systems. *Mailing Add:* Dept Mech Eng Ill Inst Technol 10 W 32nd St Chicago IL 60616

WORF, DOUGLAS LOWELL, b Bowbells, NDak, Oct 20, 17; m 48; c 3. ENVIRONMENTAL SCIENCES, BIOMEDICAL ENGINEERING. *Educ:* Univ Toledo, BS, 38; Georgetown Univ, PhD(biochem), 53. *Prof Exp:* Fel org mat, Mellon Inst, 41-44; res analyst toxicol, Off Naval Res, 46-52; biochemist, AEC, 52-58; dir, Life Support Systs, NASA, 58-62; res dir environ pollution, Alaska Water Lab, USPHS, 65-67; sci adminr, Environ Protection Agency, NC State Univ, Raleigh, 71-77, vis prof & consult, 76-79; PROJ DIR INNOVATIVE SOLAR COLLECTOR, DEPT ENERGY GRANT, 80- *Concurrent Pos:* Mem, Interagency Comt US Partic Int Biol Yr, 67-68, Off Sci & Technol, President's Sci & Adv Comt, Environ Qual Comt Res Panel; US deleg, Spec Comt for Int Geophys Year. *Mem:* Am Chem Soc; Soc Environ Geochem & Health. *Res:* Administration of environmental pollution research including indoor air pollution, toxicology of chemicals and metals, health aspects of pesticides, auto emissions, administration of research grants and contracts; alternative energy sources, biomass, recycling solid wastes. *Mailing Add:* 109 Perth Ct Cary NC 27511

WORF, GAYLE L, b Garden City, Kans, Nov 17, 29; m 52; c 2. PLANT PATHOLOGY. *Educ:* Kans State Univ, BS, 51, MS, 53; Univ Wis, PhD(plant path), 61. *Prof Exp:* County agt, Kans State Univ, 55-58; plant pathologist, Iowa State Univ, 61-63; PLANT PATHOLOGIST, UNIV WIS-MADISON, 63- *Mem:* Am Phytopath Soc. *Res:* Interpreting current research in plant pathology and analyzing its application to field situations; diagnostic procedures; economical appraisal of disease outbreaks; effective control programs. *Mailing Add:* 285 Russell Labs Univ Wis Madison WI 53706

WORGUL, BASIL VLADIMIR, b New York, NY, June 30, 47; m 69; c 2. CELL BIOLOGY, RADIATION BIOLOGY. *Educ:* Univ Miami, BS, 69; Univ Vt, PhD(zool), 74. *Prof Exp:* Staff assoc, 74-75, NIH fel & res assoc cell biol, 75-78, ASST PROF, DEPT OPHTHAL, COL PHYSICIANS & SURGEONS, COLUMBIA UNIV, 78- *Concurrent Pos:* Adj prof, Dept Biol Sci, Fordham Univ. *Mem:* Soc Gen Physiol; Sigma Xi; AAAS; Asn Res Vision & Ophthal; Am Soc Cell Biol. *Res:* The cytopathomechanism of radiation cataractogenesis; control of growth and differentiation in ocular epithelia. *Mailing Add:* Col of Physicians & Surgeons Columbia Univ 630 W 168th St New York NY 10032

WORK, CLYDE E(VERETTE), b Bridgeport, Nebr, Jan 31, 24; m 48; c 5. MECHANICS. *Educ:* Univ Ill, BS, 45, MS, 48, PhD, 52. *Prof Exp:* Asst mech, Univ Ill, 46-47, instr, 47-51, res assoc, 51-52, asst prof, 52-53; assoc prof, Rensselaer Polytech Inst, 53-57; head dept, 57-69, prof eng mech, 57-68, ASSOC DEAN ENG, MICH TECHNOL UNIV, 69- *Concurrent Pos:* UNESCO expert eng mat, Maulana Azad Col Technol, Bhopal, India, 68-69; vis prof mech eng, Univ Ilorin, Nigeria, 78-79. *Honors & Awards:* Dudley Medal, Am Soc Testing & Mat, 54; Western Elec Award, Am Soc Eng Educ, 68. *Mem:* Am Soc Testing & Mat; fel Soc Exp Stress Anal (pres, 72-73); Am Soc Eng Educ; Am Acad Mechanics. *Res:* Mechanical behavior of engineering materials; fatigue of metals; effects of fluctuation in stress amplitude; temperature time effects; torsional loading. *Mailing Add:* Col of Eng Mich Technol Univ Houghton MI 49931

WORK, HENRY HARCUS, b Buffalo, NY, Nov 11, 11; m 45; c 4. PEDIATRICS, PSYCHIATRY. *Educ:* Hamilton Col, AB, 33; Harvard Univ, MD, 37; Am Bd Pediat, dipl, 47; Am Bd Psychiat & Neurol, dipl, 50, cert child psychiat, 60. *Prof Exp:* Psychiat serv adv, US Children's Bur, 47-49; assoc prof pediat & psychiat, Univ Louisville, 49-55; from assoc prof to prof psychiat, Univ Calif, Los Angeles, 55-72; DEP MED DIR, AM PSYCHIAT ASN, 72- *Mem:* Am Psychiat Asn; fel Am Orthopsychiat Asn; Am Pub Health Asn; Am Acad Pediat; Am Col Psychiat. *Res:* Identification of child with mother and other relatives. *Mailing Add:* Am Psychiat Asn 1700 18th St NW Washington DC 20009

WORK, JAMES LEROY, b Lancaster, Pa, Feb 6, 35; m 55; c 2. POLYMER CHEMISTRY, PHYSICAL CHEMISTRY. *Educ:* Franklin & Marshall Col, BA, 62; Univ Del, PhD(phys chem), 70. *Prof Exp:* res scientist, 52-77, RES ASSOC, ARMSTRONG CORK CO, LANCASTER, 77- *Mem:* Am Chem Soc. *Res:* Structure-property relationships in polymers and polymeric composites. *Mailing Add:* 845 Paramount Ave Lampeter PA 17537

WORK, RICHARD NICHOLAS, b Ithaca, NY, Aug 7, 21; m 48; c 3. POLYMER PHYSICS. *Educ:* Cornell Univ, BA, 42, MS, 44, PhD(appl physics), 49. *Prof Exp:* Asst physics, Cornell Univ, 44-46, 48-49; physicist, Nat Bur Standards, 49-51; res assoc, Plastics Lab, Princeton Univ, 51-56; from asst prof to assoc prof physics, Pa State Univ, 56-65; from asst dean to assoc dean, Col Lib Arts, 65-73, PROF PHYSICS, ARIZ STATE UNIV, 65-, CHMN DEPT, 77- *Concurrent Pos:* Consult, Thiokol Chem Corp, 54-55, White Sands Missile Range, 55-60, Sandia Corp, 65-69 & Acushnet Co, 74- *Mem:* Fel AAAS; fel Am Phys Soc; Am Asn Physics Teachers. *Res:* Relaxation phenomena and transitions in polymers; theory of dielectrics; electrical breakdown; instrumentation. *Mailing Add:* 413 E Geneva Dr Tempe AZ 85282

WORK, ROBERT WYLLIE, b Chicago, Ill, July 10, 07; m 34. POLYMER CHEMISTRY. *Educ:* Univ Ill, BS, 29; Cornell Univ, PhD, 32. *Prof Exp:* Chemist, Swift & Co, Ill, 29; asst chem, Cornell Univ, 29-32; res engr, Gen Elec Co, 33-41; chief chemist, Celanese Corp Am, 41-43, dir phys res, Res Lab, 43-52, asst mgr res, 52-54, asst mgr opers, Textile Div, 54-55, asst tech dir, 55-56; mgr tech res, Chemstrand Res Ctr, Inc, 57-64; dir textile res & prof textiles, 64-73, EMER PROF TEXTILES, NC STATE UNIV, 73- *Mem:* Am Micros Soc; Am Chem Soc; hon mem Fiber Soc; fel Brit Textile Inst; fel Am Inst Chem. *Res:* Man-made and spider fibers. *Mailing Add:* 12 David Clark Labs NC State Univ PO Box 5666 Raleigh NC 27650

WORK, STEWART D, b Chicago, Ill, Oct 17, 37; m 59; c 4. ORGANIC CHEMISTRY. *Educ:* Oberlin Col, AB, 59; Duke Univ, PhD(org chem), 63. *Prof Exp:* Fel, Duke Univ, 63 & Purdue Univ, 63-64; from asst prof to assoc prof, 64-73, PROF CHEM, EASTERN MICH UNIV, 73- *Mem:* Am Chem Soc. *Res:* Base-catalyzed condensation reactions; organo-silicon chemistry. *Mailing Add:* Dept of Chem Eastern Mich Univ Ypsilanti MI 48197

WORK, TELFORD HINDLEY, b Selma, Calif, July 11, 21; m; c 3. BIOLOGY, EPIDEMIOLOGY. *Educ:* Stanford Univ, AB, 42, MD, 46; Univ London, dipl, 49; Johns Hopkins Univ, MPH, 52. *Prof Exp:* Res assoc filariasis, Fiji Islands Colonial Med Serv, 49-51; staff mem virus labs, Rockefeller Found, NY, 52; mem, US Naval Med Res Unit 3, Egypt, 53-54; staff mem virus res ctr, Rockefeller Found, Poona, India, 54-55, dir, 55-58; staff mem virus labs, Rockefeller Found, NY, 58-60; chief virus & rickettsia sect, Commun Dis Ctr, USPHS, 61-67; prof infectious & trop dis, 66-69, prof immunol & microbiol, 69-71; vchmn sch pub health, 66-69, head div infectious & trop dis, 69-73, PROF INFECTIOUS & TROP DIS, MED MICROBIOL & IMMUNOL, MED CTR, UNIV CALIF, LOS ANGELES, 71- *Concurrent Pos:* Mem expert comt virus dis, WHO, 60-; dir, WHO Regional Arbovirus Lab, 61-66; assoc mem comn viral infections, Armed Forces Epidemiol Bd, 61-69; Pan-Am Health Orgn consult, Arg, 62, Venezuela, 64, Jamaica, 66; regents lectr, Univ Calif, Los Angeles, 63; consult, US Army Engrs Medico-Ecol Study, Atlantic-Pac Interoceanic Canal Studies, 67-, Fogarty sr int fel, Australia, 78-79; prof epidemiol & virol, Pahlavi Univ, Shiroz, Iran, 78; vis prof microbiol, Univ Western Australia, New Zealand, 78; Arbouiduses, Dept Environ, Papua, New Guinea, 78; epidemologist, Dept Health, Western Australia, 79; consult epidemial, Clark County Health Dist, 80. *Honors & Awards:* Richard Moreland Taylor Award, 81. *Mem:* AAAS; Cooper Ornith Soc; Am Ornith Union; Am Soc Trop Med & Hyg; Am Pub Health Asn. *Res:* Medical ecology, epidemiology and medicine of virus infections, especially arthropod-borne viruses; tropical medicine. *Mailing Add:* Ctr for the Health Sci Univ of Calif Med Ctr Los Angeles CA 90024

WORK, WILLIAM JAMES, b Carmel, Calif, Feb 23, 48; m 76. POLYMER CHEMISTRY, ORGANIC CHEMISTRY. *Educ:* Univ Santa Clara, BS, 70; Univ Ill, PhD(org chem), 76. *Prof Exp:* CHEMIST POLYMER CHEM, ROHM & HAAS CO, 76- *Mem:* Am Chem Soc; AAAS. *Res:* Morphology of polymer blends and composites; synthesis of grafted polymers. *Mailing Add:* Rohm & Haas Co PO Box 219 Bristol PA 19007

WORKER, GEORGE F, JR, b Ordway, Colo, June 1, 23; m 49; c 4. AGRONOMY, BOTANY. *Educ:* Colo State Univ, BS, 49; Univ Nebr, MS, 53. *Prof Exp:* Asst county agent, Nebr, 49-51, asst in agron, 53; SPECIALIST IN AGRON & SUPT, IMP VALLEY FIELD STA, UNIV CALIF, DAVIS, 53- *Concurrent Pos:* Consult. *Mem:* Am Soc Agron. *Res:* Grain sorghum production, plant function, breeding and adaption to desert climate; adaption of other field crops such as barley, sugar beets and flax to southwestern desert areas. *Mailing Add:* Imp Valley Field Sta 1004 E Holton Rd El Centro CA 92243

WORKMAN, GARY LEE, b Birmingham, Ala, Apr 21, 40; m 67; c 1. PHYSICAL CHEMISTRY. *Educ:* Col William & Mary, BS, 64; Univ Rochester, PhD(phys chem), 69. *Prof Exp:* Res fel chem, Ohio State Univ, 69-70; Nat Acad Sci res assoc, Marshall Space Flight Ctr, NASA, 70-72; dir, PBR Electronics, Inc, 72-76; prof sci technol, Athens State Col, 76-80; DIR TECH STUDIES & SR RES ASSOC, UNIV ALA, HUNTSVILLE, 80- *Mem:* Am Phys Soc; Am Chem Soc; Instrument Soc Am; Optical Soc Am. *Res:* Systems interfacing; electrooptics applications; solar photochemistry; reaction kinetics; spectroscopy; materials processing; robotics and industrial automation. *Mailing Add:* Univ Ala Huntsville AL 35807

WORKMAN, JOHN PAUL, b Salem, Ore, Feb 18, 43; m 64; c 2. RANGE MANAGEMENT, AGRICULTURAL ECONOMICS. *Educ:* Univ Wyo, BS, 65; Utah State Univ, MS, 67, PhD(range econ), 70. *Prof Exp:* Asst prof range econ, 70-75, assoc prof, 75-80, PROF RANGE ECON, UTAH STATE UNIV, 81- *Concurrent Pos:* Mem, Rangeland Mgt Comt, Nat Acad Sci. *Mem:* AAAS; Soc Range Mgt; Am Agr Econ Asn. *Res:* Economics of range utilization, range improvement and range livestock production. *Mailing Add:* Dept of Range Sci Utah State Univ Logan UT 84322

WORKMAN, MARCUS ORRIN, b Canton, Ohio, Sept 20, 40. INORGANIC CHEMISTRY. *Educ:* Manchester Col, BA, 62; Ohio State Univ, PhD(inorg chem), 66. *Prof Exp:* Teaching assoc chem, Ohio State Univ, 65-66; res assoc, Northwestern Univ, 66-67; asst prof chem, Univ Va, 67-74; ASSOC PROF CHEM, THOMAS NELSON COMMUNITY COL, 75- *Concurrent Pos:* Adv Res Projs Agency fel, 66-67. *Mem:* Am Chem Soc. *Res:* Coordination complexes of transition metals with polydentate ligands; complexes with oxide and sulfoxide donor atoms; complexes of lanthanides and actinides. *Mailing Add:* PO Box 9407 Hampton VA 23670

WORKMAN, MILTON, b Chicago Heights, Ill, Oct 1, 20; m 49; c 6. PLANT PHYSIOLOGY. *Educ:* Colo Agr & Mech Col, BS, 50; Univ Calif, PhD(plant physiol), 54. *Prof Exp:* Asst veg crops, Univ Calif, 50-54; from instr to assoc prof hort, Purdue Univ, 54-66; PROF HORT, COLO STATE UNIV, 66- *Res:* Pre and post harvest physiology. *Mailing Add:* Dept Hort Colo State Univ Ft Collins CO 80521

WORKMAN, RALPH BURNS, b Omaha, Nebr, June 25, 24; m 51; c 4. ECONOMIC ENTOMOLOGY, VEGETABLE CROPS. *Educ:* Colo State Univ, BS, 51, MS, 52; Ore State Univ, PhD(entom), 58. *Prof Exp:* Res asst entom, Colo State Univ, 52-55; asst entomologist, 58-67, ASSOC ENTOMOLOGIST, AGR RES CTR, UNIV FLA, 67- *Mem:* Entom Soc Am. *Res:* Economic entomology; biology and control of cruciferous and potato insects. *Mailing Add:* Agr Res Ctr Univ of Fla Hastings FL 32045

WORKMAN, WESLEY RAY, b Mich, Feb 1, 26; m 48; c 4. ORGANIC CHEMISTRY. *Educ:* Mich State Univ, BS, 49, MS, 50; Univ Minn, PhD(org chem), 54. *Prof Exp:* Sr chemist, 54-68, mgr photog sci & photo chem, 68-72, dir imaging, Res Div, 72-74, dir, Systs Res Lab, 74-78, DIR UNIV RELATIONS, CENT RES LABS, 3M CO, 78- *Mem:* Am Chem Soc; Soc Photog Scientists & Engrs. *Res:* Photochemistry. *Mailing Add:* 2672 Sumac Ridge St Paul MN 55110

WORKMAN, WILLIAM EDWARD, b Richmond, Va, May 13, 41; m 59; c 2. ENVIRONMENTAL GEOLOGY. *Educ:* Univ Va, BS, 62, MS, 64; Univ Tex, Austin, PhD(geol), 68. *Prof Exp:* Asst prof geol, Albion Col, 68-73; geoscientist, Palmer & Baker Engrs, Inc, 73-75; SUPVRY ENVIRON GEOLOGIST, US CORPS ENGRS, MOBILE, 75- *Concurrent Pos:* Sigma Xi-Sci Res Soc Am grants in aid of res, 63 & 66; geologist C, Va Div Mineral Resources, Charlottesville, 63-; consult, Palmer & Baker Engrs, Inc, 75-; environ consult to var pvt firms, 75- *Mem:* Sigma Xi. *Res:* Regional metamorphism in Llano Uplift, Texas; coastal erosion; engineering geology relative to coastal processes. *Mailing Add:* 204 Nichols Fairhope AL 36532

WORKMAN, WILLIAM GLENN, b Sheridan, Wyo, Mar 19, 47; m 72; c 2. NATURAL RESOURCE ECONOMICS. *Educ:* Univ Wyo, BS, 69; Utah State Univ, MA, 72, PhD(resource econ), 78. *Prof Exp:* Res asst econ, Utah State Univ, 69-72; asst prof 73-79, ASSOC PROF ECON, UNIV ALASKA, 79- *Concurrent Pos:* Assoc economist, Frank Orth & Assocs, Seattle, 80- *Mem:* Am Econ Asn; Asn Environ & Resource Econ. *Res:* Economic analysis of allocation of public funds in the provision of outdoor recreation opportunities; economic analysis of land use and public land use policy. *Mailing Add:* Dept of Econ Univ of Alaska Fairbanks AK 99701

WORL, RONALD GRANT, b Dunlap, Iowa, Jan 16, 38; m 60; c 3. ECONOMIC GEOLOGY. *Educ:* Utah State Univ, BS, 60; Univ Wyo, MA, 63, PhD(geol), 68. *Prof Exp:* Teaching asst, Univ Wyo, 62-64; asst prof petrol & mineral deposits, Colo State Univ, 66-67; geologist, Cent Mineral Resources, 67-73, GEOLOGIST, US GEOL SURV, 73- *Mem:* Soc Econ Geologists. *Res:* Distribution of minerals and elements in mineral deposits that formed at or near surface; structural petrology of migmatites; fluorine deposits, geologic and geochemical perspectives and commodity aspects; geology and economic aspects of massive sulfide, sedimentary copper and hydrothermal gold deposits of the Arabian Shield. *Mailing Add:* Box 25 Pinedale WY 82941

WORLEY, DAVID EUGENE, b Cadiz, Ohio, Aug 6, 29; m 68; c 2. PARASITOLOGY. *Educ:* Col Wooster, AB, 51; Kans State Univ, MS, 55, PhD(parasitol), 58. *Prof Exp:* Assoc res parasitologist, Parke, Davis & Co, 58-62; from asst prof to assoc prof, 62-72, PROF VET RES LAB, MONT STATE UNIV, 72- *Mem:* Am Soc Parasitol; Am Micros Soc; Wildlife Dis Asn. *Res:* Zoology; helminthology, including chemotherapy of parasitic infections and helminth life cycles. *Mailing Add:* Vet Res Lab Mont State Univ Bozeman MT 59715

WORLEY, FRANK L, JR, b Kansas City, Mo, Oct 9, 29; m 52; c 1. CHEMICAL ENGINEERING. *Educ:* Univ Houston, BS, 52, MS, 59, PhD(chem eng), 65. *Prof Exp:* Chem engr, Nyotex Chem, Inc, 52-55 & Stauffer Chem Co, 55-57; instr chem eng, Univ Houston, 57-59; Fulbright lectr, Univ Guayaquil & Cent Univ Ecuador, 59-61; from instr to assoc prof, 61-72, PROF CHEM ENG, UNIV HOUSTON, 72- *Concurrent Pos:* Vis scientist, Div Meteorol, Environ Protection Agency, 71. *Mem:* Am Inst Chem Engrs. *Res:* Fluid mechanics; turbulence properties of flow systems; modelling of atmospheric dispersion and reactions; air pollution control; computer aided design and analysis. *Mailing Add:* Dept of Chem Eng 3800 Cullen Blvd Houston TX 77004

WORLEY, JIMMY WELDON, b Bowie, Tex, May 2, 44; m 66; c 3. TRACE ORGANIC ANALYSIS, INDUSTRIAL HYGIENE. *Educ:* Midwestern State Univ, BS, 66; Univ Ill, Urbana-Champaign, PhD(org chem), 71. *Prof Exp:* Res assoc, Wesleyan Univ, 71; sr res chemist, 71-75, res specialist, 75-78, res group leader, 78-80, SR RES GROUP LEADER, MONSANTO CO, ST LOUIS, 80- *Mem:* Am Chem Soc. *Res:* Trace organic analysis to suppoprt agricultural chemicals; emphasis on new chromatographic and spectroscopic methods for characterizing and/or monitoring trace components in air, water, and solid waste samples. *Mailing Add:* Monsanto Co 800 N Lindbergh Blvd St Louis MO 63167

WORLEY, JOHN DAVID, b Texarkana, Tex, Dec 10, 38; m 63; c 4. BIOPHYSICAL CHEMISTRY. *Educ:* Hendrix Col, BA, 60; Univ Okla, PhD(phys chem), 64. *Prof Exp:* NIH fel biophys chem, Northwestern Univ, 64-66; asst prof chem, Univ Cincinnati, 66-70; asst prof, 70-77, ASSOC PROF CHEM, ST NORBERT COL, 78- *Mem:* Am Chem Soc. *Res:* Protein structure and denaturation in solution; solutions of nonelectrolytes; hydrogen bonding. *Mailing Add:* Dept of Chem St Norbert Col West De Pere WI 54115

WORLEY, JOSEPH FRANCIS, plant pathology, deceased

WORLEY, RAY EDWARD, b Robbinsville, NC, May 4, 32; m 55; c 3. HORTICULTURE, AGRONOMY. *Educ:* NC State Col, BS, 54, MS, 58; Va Polytech Inst, PhD(agron), 61. *Prof Exp:* Asst field crops, NC State Col, 56-58; instr agron, Va Polytech Inst, 58-61; asst horticulturist, 61-72, assoc horticulturist, 72-80, PROF HORT, GA COASTAL PLAIN EXP STA, 80- *Honors & Awards:* L M Ware Award, 81. *Mem:* Am Soc Hort Sci. *Res:* Pecan tree nutrition, management and physiology; vegetable and forage nutrition and physiology. *Mailing Add:* Hort Dept Ga Coastal Plain Exp Sta Tifton GA 31794

WORLEY, RICHARD DIXON, b Little Rock, Ark, Dec 24, 26; m 51; c 2. PHYSICS. *Educ:* Hendrix Col, BS, 49; Univ Ark, MA, 51; Univ Chicago, MS, 60; Univ Calif, Berkeley, PhD(physics), 63. *Prof Exp:* Nuclear physicist, Wright-Patterson AFB, Ohio, 51-54; nuclear engr, Douglas Air Craft Co, Calif, 57-59; sr physicist, Lawrence Radiation Lab, Univ Calif, 63-70; PHYSICIST, MASON & HANGER, PANTEX PLANT, SILAS MASON CO, 70- *Concurrent Pos:* teacher, Memphis State Univ. *Mem:* Am Phys Soc. *Res:* Characteristic x-ray production by ion bombardment of both polycrystalline and single-crystal targets; atomic beams and the hyperfine interaction; high explosive research and development. *Mailing Add:* Gen Dilevery Biggers AR 72413

WORLEY, ROBERT DUNKLE, b Trenton, NJ, Jan 24, 25; m 50; c 3. PHYSICS. *Educ:* Williams Col, AB, 49; Columbia Univ, AM, 51, PhD, 55. *Prof Exp:* From asst to lectr, Columbia Univ, 50-54; MEM STAFF, BELL LABS, INC, 54-, SUPVR, 60- *Mem:* Am Phys Soc; Acoust Soc Am. *Res:* Heat capacities of superconductors; sound transmission in the ocean; operations research; sonar systems. *Mailing Add:* 17 Knollwood Trail E Brookside NJ 07926

WORLEY, SMITH, JR, b Columbia, SC, June 14, 24; m 47; c 3. AGRONOMY. *Educ:* Clemson Col, BS, 49; Univ Ariz, MS, 53; La State Univ, PhD, 58. *Prof Exp:* Asst plant breeder, Univ Ariz, 49-55; res assoc agron, NC State Col, 55-56 & La State Univ, 56-58; RES AGRONOMIST, SOUTHERN REGION, AGR RES SERV, USDA, 58- *Honors & Awards:* Service Award, Am Soc Testing & Mat, 74. *Mem:* Am Soc Qual Control; Am Soc Testing & Mat. *Res:* Genetics of cotton quality; fiber technology; statistics; instrumentation for evaluation of components of fiber quality; textile quality control. *Mailing Add:* US Cotton Fiber Res Lab Univ Tenn Agr Campus Knoxville TN 37916

WORLEY, WILL J, b Gibson City, Ill, Aug 2, 19; m 54; c 3. THEORETICAL MECHANICS, APPLIED MECHANICS. *Educ:* Univ Ill, BS, 43, MS, 45, PhD, 52. *Prof Exp:* From instr to assoc prof, 43-60, PROF THEORET & APPL MECH, UNIV ILL, URBANA, 60-, PROJ DIR, NASA PROJ, 63- *Concurrent Pos:* Consult, Magnavox Co, Ind, 56-58, Ill, 58-65, Chris-Kaye Mfg Co, Ill, 57, A O Smith Corp, Wis, 59 & attorneys, Ill, 59-; proj dir, Wright Air Develop Ctr Nonlinear Mech Proj, 59-61; consult, IBM Corp, NY, 60-61 & 63-64, Calif, 61; pres, Worley Systs Inc, 77-; vis fel, Inst Sound & Vibration Res, Univ Southampton, Eng, 79. *Mem:* Acoust Soc Am; Am Soc Mech Eng. *Res:* Acoustical noise reduction; mechanical vibrations and nonlinear mechanics; static and dynamic behavior of plates and shells; optimum structural design; mechanical properties of materials; failure investigation of components and systems; systems approach to prevention and analysis of system failure. *Mailing Add:* 2106 Zuppke A3 Urbana IL 61801

WORLOCK, JOHN M, b Kearney, Nebr, Feb 15, 31; div; c 2. SOLID STATE PHYSICS. *Educ:* Swarthmore Col, BA, 53; Cornell Univ, PhD(physics), 62. *Prof Exp:* NSF fel, 62-63; actg asst prof physics, Univ Calif, Berkeley, 63-64; MEM TECH STAFF, BELL LABS, INC, 64- *Mem:* AAAS; Fedn Am Scientists; fel Am Phys Soc. *Res:* Lattice dynamics; transport and optical properties of non-metallic crystals; light scattering; phase transitions. *Mailing Add:* Bell Labs Inc Holmdel NJ 07733

WORMAN, JAMES JOHN, b Allentown, Pa, Feb 17, 40; m 61; c 4. ORGANIC CHEMISTRY. *Educ:* Moravian Col, BS, 61; NMex Highlands Univ, MS, 64; Univ Wyo, PhD, 68. *Prof Exp:* Instr chem, Moravian Col, 62-63; res asst, Univ Wyo, 65-67; asst prof, 67-72, assoc prof, 72-76, PROF CHEM, S DAK STATE UNIV, 77- *Mem:* Am Chem Soc; Royal Soc Chem. *Res:* Theoretical and experimental organic photochemistry, including syntheses and reaction of large ring nitrogen heterocycles. *Mailing Add:* Dept of Chem SDak State Univ Brookings SD 57006

WORMSER, ERIC M, b Ger, Apr 30, 21; nat US; m 47; c 2. ENGINEERING PHYSICS. *Educ:* Mass Inst Technol, BS, 42. *Prof Exp:* Test engr, Universal Camera Co, 42-45; physicist, Hillyer Instrument Co, 47-49 & Servo Corp Am, 49-52; chief engr, Barnes Eng Co, 52-58, vpres, 58-68, exec vpres, 68-76; PRES, WORMSER SCI CORP, 76- *Mem:* Optical Soc Am; Inst Elec & Electronics Engrs; Instrument Soc Am; NY Acad Sci; fel Optical Soc Am; fel Can Aeronaut & Space Inst. *Res:* Infrared instruments, systems and detector development. *Mailing Add:* Wormser Sci Corp 88 Foxwood Rd Stamford CT 06903

WORMSER, HENRY C, b Strasbourg, France, Sept 10, 36; US citizen; m 63; c 2. PHARMACEUTICAL CHEMISTRY. *Educ:* Temple Univ, BSc, 59, MSc, 61; Univ Wis, PhD(pharmaceut chem), 65. *Prof Exp:* From asst prof to assoc prof, 65-76, PROF PHARMACEUT CHEM, WAYNE STATE UNIV, 76- *Mem:* Am Chem Soc; Am Pharmaceut Asn. *Res:* Synthesis of model compounds to be used in study of drug-enzyme or drug-receptor site interactions in an effort to determine specific mechanisms of drug activity. *Mailing Add:* 5420 Hammersmith Dr West Bloomfield MI 48033

WORMUTH, JOHN HAZEN, b Cobleskill, NY, Dec 9, 44; m 67; c 2. BIOLOGICAL OCEANOGRAPHY. *Educ:* Hope Col, BA, 66; Scripps Inst Oceanog, PhD(oceanog), 71. *Prof Exp:* Biol oceanogr, Intersea Res Corp, 71-72; asst prof, 72-77, ASSOC PROF, TEX A&M UNIV, 77- *Mem:* Am Soc Limnol & Oceanog; Marine Biol Asn UK; AAAS; Am Geophys Union. *Res:* Ecology and sampling problems associated with cephalopods; neuston communities; zooplankton ecology, particularly pteropods. *Mailing Add:* Dept of Oceanog Tex A&M Univ College Station TX 77843

WORNARDT, WALTER WILLIAM, JR, paleontology, see previous edition

WORNICK, ROBERT C(HARLES), b Bellows Falls, Vt, June 13, 24; m 53; c 2. CHEMICAL ENGINEERING, FOOD TECHNOLOGY. *Educ:* Columbia Univ, BChE, 50. *Prof Exp:* Anal lab asst, Chas Pfizer & Co, Inc, 42 & 46-48, anal chemist, 49-50, head food & beverage sect, Tech Serv Dept, 51-53, head chem labs, Agr Res Dept, 53-59, prof engr, Agr Develop Dept, 60-65, dir develop res labs, Agr Div, 66-70, dir agr licensing, Pfizer Inc, 70-77, SCI DIR, PFIZER INT INC, 77- *Concurrent Pos:* Abstractor, Chem Abstr. *Mem:* Am Inst Chem Engrs; Nat Soc Prof Engrs; Am Chem Soc; Am Asn Feed Micros; Animal Nutrit Res Coun. *Res:* Vitamin enrichment, processing and preservation of foods; leavening agents, acidulants and antioxidants; micro-ingredient supplementation of animal feeds; feed processing and formulation; equipment evaluation; food and feed quality control; product development. *Mailing Add:* 13855 SW 78th Ct Miami FL 33158

WOROCH, EUGENE LEO, b Kenosha, Wis, Mar 18, 22; m 49; c 4. MEDICINAL CHEMISTRY. *Educ:* Univ Wis, BS, 44, MS, 45, PhD(org chem), 48; Univ Chicago, MBA, 71. *Prof Exp:* Proj dir natural prod, Wis Alumni Res Found, 48-49; group leader & consult, Bjorksten Labs, 49; res assoc natural prod, Mayo Clin, 49-51; group leader, Glidden Co, 51-58; head dept org chem res, 58-75, dir div antibiotic res, 75-77, DIR DIV SCI SERVS, ABBOTT LABS, 77- *Mem:* Am Chem Soc; AAAS; Am Soc Microbiol. *Res:* Natural products; steroids; antibiotics; peptides and structural chemistry. *Mailing Add:* Abbott Labs 1400 Sheridan Rd North Chicago IL 60064

WORONICK, CHARLES LOUIS, b Meriden, Conn, Dec 4, 30. BIOCHEMISTRY, CLINICAL CHEMISTRY. *Educ:* Univ Conn, BS, 53; Univ Calif, Berkeley, MS, 55; Univ Wis, PhD(biochem), 59. *Prof Exp:* Asst prof chem, Brown Univ, 62-66; assoc non-clin investr path, Pa Hosp, 66-68; BIOCHEMIST, MED RES LABS & DEPT MED, HARTFORD HOSP, 68- *Concurrent Pos:* NSF fel, 59-61; fel enzyme chem, Nobel Med Inst, Stockholm, 59-62; Nat Cancer Inst fel, 61-62; assoc path, Med Sch, Univ Pa, 66-68; consult staff biochem, Hartford Hosp, 68-; consult staff clin chem, John Dempsey Hosp, Conn, 75-; asst prof labs med, Sch Med, Univ Conn, Farmington, 73-; mem comn toxicol, Clin Chem Div, Subcomt Cholinesterases, Int Union Pure & Appl Chem, 76-81. *Mem:* Am Asn Clin Chem; Am Chem Soc; NY Acad Sci; fel Nat Acad Clin Biochem; AAAS. *Res:* Enzyme kinetics; equilibria and mechanisms; immunochemistry; leukocyte function. *Mailing Add:* Med Res Lab Hartford Hosp Hartford CT 06115

WORRALL, JOHN GATLAND, b Cleethorpes, Eng, May 22, 38; Can citizen. DENDROLOGY. *Educ:* Univ Durham, BSc, 59; Yale Univ, MF, 64, PhD(forestry), 69. *Prof Exp:* ASSOC PROF FORESTRY, UNIV BC, 68- *Res:* Environmental control of cambial activity; breakage of dormancy seeds and plants. *Mailing Add:* Fac of Forestry Univ of BC Vancouver BC V6T 1W5 Can

WORRALL, PAUL MICHAEL, b Dursley, Eng, Jan 17, 35; m 65; c 2. MEDICAL RESEARCH. *Educ:* Univ Birmingham, Eng, BS, 56, MB ChB, 59; Royal Col Surgeons & Physicians, MRCS LRCP, 60. *Prof Exp:* Dep med dir, Lederle Labs, Eng, 64-65; var, Bristol Labs, NY, 65-69; proj officer med, Army Investigational Drug Rev Bd, US Army, 69-71; dir med res, Bristol-Myers Int Div, 71-73; dir med res, 73-75, med dir, 75-78, VPRES & MED DIR MEAD JOHNSON CO, 78- *Mem:* Am Rheumatism Asn; AAAS; Brit Med Asn. *Res:* Management of drug development area (human use) in a major pharmaceutical company. *Mailing Add:* Mead Johnson Co Evansville IN 47721

WORRALL, RICHARD D, b Waterloo, Eng, May 31, 38; m 60; c 2. CIVIL & TRANSPORTATION ENGINEERING. *Educ:* Durham Univ, BSc, 60; Northwestern Univ, MS, 61, PhD(civil eng), 66. *Prof Exp:* Asst traffic engr, City Planning Dept, Newcastle, Eng, 61-62; sr res fel city & transp planning, Lower Swansea Valley Proj, Univ Wales, 62-63; res assoc transp planning & traffic flow theory, Northwestern Univ, Evanston, 63-69; MGR, PEAT MARWICK MITCHELL & CO, 69- *Concurrent Pos:* Mem, Hwy Res Bd, Nat Acad Sci-Nat Res Coun, 63-, mem comts land use eval, freeway opers & origin-destination, 66- *Mem:* Am Soc Civil Engrs. *Res:* Transportation and city planning; traffic flow theory; transportation systems control. *Mailing Add:* 2023 Peppermint Ct Reston VA 22090

WORRALL, WINFIELD SCOTT, b Cheltenham, Pa, Jan 12, 21; m 49; c 2. ORGANIC CHEMISTRY. *Educ:* Haverford Col, BS, 42; Harvard Univ, MA, 47, PhD(chem), 49. *Prof Exp:* Res chemist, Monsanto Chem Co, 50-54; from instr to assoc prof chem, Trinity Col, Conn, 54-64; assoc prof chem, 64-68, assoc prof gen sci studies, 68-77, PROF GEN SCI STUDIES, STATE UNIV NY COL PLATTSBURGH, 78- *Res:* Steroids; heterocyclics. *Mailing Add:* Dept of Gen Studies State Univ of NY Col Plattsburgh NY 12901

WORRELL, FRANCIS TOUSSAINT, b Hartford, Conn, Apr 19, 15; m 48; c 2. PHYSICS. *Educ:* Univ Mich, BSE, 36; Univ Pittsburgh, MS, 40, PhD(physics), 41. *Prof Exp:* Mem staff, Physicists Res Co, Mich, 36-37; asst, Univ Pittsburgh, 37-41; instr, Univ Tenn, 41-42; staff mem, Radiation Lab, Mass Inst Technol, 42-46; res assoc, Inst Metals, Univ Chicago, 46-47; asst prof physics, Rensselaer Polytech Inst, 47-55; assoc prof, DePauw Univ, 55-58; Fulbright lectr, Al-Hikma Univ Baghdad, 58-59; assoc prof, Beloit Col, 59-60; staff mem, Lincoln Lab, Mass Inst Technol, 60-63; prof physics, Univ Lowell, 63-80. *Concurrent Pos:* Vis lectr, Univ Bristol, 72-73 & Mass Maritime Acad, 81. *Mem:* AAAS; Am Asn Physics Teachers. *Res:* Design of experiments; structure of materials; thermionic emission; atmospheric optics. *Mailing Add:* 11 Old Salt Lane Yarmouth Port MA 02675

WORRELL, G(EORGE) RICHARD, b Tampa, Fla, Jan 4, 27; m 50, 79; c 3. CHEMICAL ENGINEERING. *Educ:* Mass Inst Technol, BS, 48, MS, 49; Univ Pa, PhD(chem eng), 63. *Prof Exp:* From jr to prin chem engr, Res & Develop Dept, Atlantic Refining Co, 49-65; head systs eng & eng res, ARCO Chem Div, 65-71, mgr simulation & anal, 71-75, coordr energy conserv & environ affairs, 75-78, prin engr, 78-81, REACTION TECHNOL SPECIALIST, ARCO CHEM CO, DIV ATLANTIC RICHFIELD CO, 81- *Mem:* Am Inst Chem Engrs. *Res:* Reaction kinetics; mass transfer; automatic control systems; computer simulation. *Mailing Add:* Aro Chem Co 3801 W Chester Pike Newtown Square PA 19073

WORRELL, JAY H, b Manchester, NH, July 14, 38; m 59; c 3. PHYSICAL INORGANIC CHEMISTRY, CHEMICAL ENGINEERING. *Educ:* Univ NH, BS, 61, MS, 63; Ohio State Univ, PhD(inorg chem), 66. *Prof Exp:* Res assoc chem, State Univ NY Stony Brook, 66-67; asst prof, 67-72, assoc prof, 72-78, PROF CHEM, UNIV SOUTH FLA, TAMPA, 78- *Concurrent Pos:* Res Corp NY res grant, 68- *Mem:* Am Chem Soc; Am Inst Chem Engrs. *Res:* Preparation, properties and theory of coordination compounds; stereochemistry and inorganic reaction kinetics for ligand substitution and oxidation reduction processes; applied industrial chemistry; chemical engineering. *Mailing Add:* Dept of Chem Univ of SFla Tampa FL 33620

WORRELL, JOHN MAYS, JR, b El Paso, Tex, Oct 3, 33; m 66; c 1. MATHEMATICS, MEDICINE. *Educ:* Univ Tex, BA, 54, MD, 57, PhD(math), 61. *Prof Exp:* Intern med, Denver Gen Hosp, Colo, 57-58; instr math, Univ Tex, 58-59; NSF fel, 61-62; mem tech staff math res, Sandia Corp, NMex, 62-72; PROF MATH, OHIO UNIV, 72-, DIR INST FOR MED & MATH, 75- *Concurrent Pos:* Consult clin med & biomed sci. *Mem:* Am Math Soc; Am Med Asn. *Res:* Problems having topological character; clinical medicine; biological processes. *Mailing Add:* Inst for Med & Math Ohio Univ Athens OH 45701

WORRELL, LEE FRANK, b Orleans, Ind, Feb 27, 13; m 34; c 1. PHARMACEUTICAL CHEMISTRY. *Educ:* Purdue Univ, BS, 35, PhD(pharmaceut chem), 40. *Prof Exp:* Assoc prof pharm, Drake Univ, 38-42; from instr to assoc prof, Univ Mich, 42-60; dean col pharm, 62-66, PROF PHARMACEUT CHEM, UNIV TEX, AUSTIN, 60- *Mem:* AAAS; Am Chem Soc; Am Pharmaceut Asn. *Res:* Analytical pharmaceutical chemistry. *Mailing Add:* Univ of Tex Col of Pharm Austin TX 78712

WORRELL, WAYNE L, b Rock Island, Ill, Oct 25, 37; m 68; c 2. MATERIALS CHEMISTRY, SOLID-STATE ELECTRCHEMISTRY. *Educ:* Mass Inst Technol, BS, 59, PhD(metall), 63. *Hon Degrees:* MA, Univ Pa, 71. *Prof Exp:* Fel metall, Univ Calif, Berkeley, 63-64, lectr, 64-65; from asst prof to assoc prof, 65-74, PROF MAT SCI, UNIV PA, 74- *Concurrent Pos:* Chmn comt high temp sci & technol, Nat Acad Sci-Nat Res Coun, 74-77; consult to indust & govt orgns; vis prof, Dept Chem, Univ Calif, Berkeley, 75-76; ed, Prog Solid State Chem, 77-; mem chem eng, Div Rev Comt, Argonne Nat Lab, 79- *Mem:* Am Inst Mining, Metall & Petrol Eng; Electrochem Soc; Am Soc Metals; Am Ceramic Soc. *Res:* Thermodynamics and kinetics of high-temperature reactions; thermodynamics of metallic alloys; corrosion at elevated temperatures; high-temperature materials chemistry; solid state electrochemistry. *Mailing Add:* Dept Mat Sci & Eng K1 Univ Pa Philadelphia PA 19104

WORREST, ROBERT CHARLES, b Hartford, Conn, July 6, 35; m 57; c 1. RADIATION BIOLOGY, MARINE ECOLOGY. *Educ:* Williams Col, BA, 57; Wesleyan Univ, MA, 64; Ore State Univ, PhD(radiation biol), 75. *Prof Exp:* Teacher, Canterbury Sch, Conn, 57-59, Belmont Hill Sch, Mass, 59-71; instr biol, 71-72, trainee environ health, 72-75, res assoc marine ecol, 75-77, asst prof, 77-81, ASSOC PROF RADIATION BIOL, ORE STATE UNIV, 81-; PROJ LEADER PHOTOBIOL PROG, US ENVIRON PROTECTION AGENCY, 80- *Concurrent Pos:* Prin investr, Assessment of Impact of Increased Solar Ultraviolet Radiation upon Marine Primary Producers, US Environ Protection Agency, 79-80; ad hoc panel biol & ecol effect, Nat Acad Sci, 80; invited participant, Biol Effects of Increases Solar Ultraviolet Radiation, Nat Acad Sci/Nat Res Coun, 81. *Mem:* Radiation Res Soc; AAAS; Am Soc Photobiol; Ecol Soc Am; Am Soc Limnol & Oceanog. *Res:* Assessment of the impact environmental stress factors (solar ultraviolet radiation, ionizing radiation, oil pollution, PCB's) upon freshwater and marine ecosystems and their constituent organisms; oversight of research projects determining the impact of solar ultraviolet radiation upon agricultural corps, terrestrial ecosystems and marine fisheries. *Mailing Add:* Environ Res Lab US EPA 200 SW 35th St Corvallis OR 97333

WORSHAM, ARCH DOUGLAS, b Culloden, Ga, Feb 22, 33; m 56, 82; c 5. WEED SCIENCE, PLANT PHYSIOLOGY. *Educ:* Univ Ga, BSA, 55, MS, 57; NC State Univ, PhD(crop sci), 61. *Prof Exp:* From exten asst prof to exten assoc prof, 60-67, assoc prof, 67-69, PROF CROP SCI, NC STATE UNIV, 69- *Concurrent Pos:* Res grants, 66-; consult, 67- *Honors & Awards:* Outstanding Publ Award, Weed Sci Soc Am, 75. *Mem:* Weed Sci Soc Am; Am Soc Agron; Am Soc Plant Physiologists; Sigma Xi. *Res:* Pesticides; crop science; weed science; basic and applied weed science research in agronomic crops and non-tillage crop production and specific weeds. *Mailing Add:* Dept of Crop Sci NC State Univ Raleigh NC 27650

WORSHAM, JAMES ESSEX, JR, b Newport News, Va, Apr 29, 25. PHYSICAL CHEMISTRY, BIOMEDICAL ENGINEERING. *Educ:* Univ Richmond, BS, 47; Vanderbilt Univ, MS, 49; Duke Univ, PhD(chem), 53. *Prof Exp:* Instr high sch, Va, 48-50; assoc prof chem, Hampden-Sydney Col, 53-54; from asst prof to assoc prof, 54-67, PROF CHEM, UNIV RICHMOND, 67-, DIR ACAD COMPUT, 74- *Concurrent Pos:* Res assoc, Mass Inst Technol, 59-60; consult, Dept Med, Med Col, Va, 63-, adj res prof med, 63-; Max Planck Inst fur Systs Physiol, Dortmund, WGer, 80. *Mem:* Am Chem Soc. *Res:* Molecular structure; neutron diffraction; solutions; biomedical instrumentation; control of circulation. *Mailing Add:* Dept of Chem Univ of Richmond Richmond VA 23173

WORSHAM, LESA MARIE SPACEK, b Sellersville, Pa, Dec 4, 50; m 73. PROTEIN CHARACTERIZATION. *Educ:* Ursinus Col, BS, 72; Univ NC Chapel Hill, PhD(chem), 77. *Prof Exp:* Consult atmosheric chem, Res Triangle Inst, 77-78; RES ASSOC BIOCHEM, QUILLEN-DISHNER COL MED EAST TENN STATE UNIV, 79- *Mem:* Am Chem Soc; Sigma Xi. *Res:* Isolation fatty acid synthetase from Euglena gracilis to determine its molecular weight and study its properties and to break down this complex to study its submits. *Mailing Add:* 525 Ranier Dr Kingsport TN 37663

WORSHAM, WALTER CASTINE, b Turbeville, SC, Aug 17, 38; m 59; c 2. TEXTILE CHEMISTRY. *Educ:* Col Charleston, BS, 61; Univ NC, PhD(phys chem), 66. *Prof Exp:* Chemist, Fiber Industs, Inc, 66-67; chemist, Emery Industs, Inc, Mauldin, 67-75, tech mgr, 75-79; VPRES & GEN MGR, ETHOX CHEM, INC, 79- *Mem:* Am Chem Soc; Am Asn Textile Chemists & Colorists. *Res:* Kinetics of photochemical reactions; chemistry of textile processing. *Mailing Add:* PO Box 5094 Sta B Ethox Chem Inc Greenville SC 29607

WORSLEY, THOMAS R, b Brooklyn, NY, June 1, 42. MARINE GEOLOGY, BIOSTRATIGRAPHY. *Educ:* City Col New York, BS, 65; Univ Tenn, MS, 67; Univ Ill, PhD(geol), 70. *Prof Exp:* Res prof oceanog, Univ Wash, 70-77, PROF GEOL, OHIO UNIV, 76- *Concurrent Pos:* NSF grant, 73-75, 75-77 & 77- *Mem:* Soc Econ Paleont & Mineralogy. *Res:* Computer application in marine micropaleontology; erosion-sedimentation of the globe. *Mailing Add:* Dept of Geol Ohio Univ Athens OH 45701

WORSTELL, HAIRSTON G(EORGE), b West Plains, Mo, Jan 5, 20; m 44; c 1. MECHANICAL ENGINEERING. *Educ:* Univ Okla, BSME, 50. *Prof Exp:* Design engr, Boeing Aircraft Co, Kans, 50-51; staff engr, Sandia Corp, NMex, 51-53; proj engr, Phillips Petrol Co, Okla, 53-59; staff engr, 59-66, asst group leader mech eng, 66-67, assoc group leader, 67-72, alt group leader, 72-77, CONSULT, LOS ALAMOS SCI LAB, 77- *Mem:* Am Vacuum Soc. *Res:* Mechanical design and supervision of fellow engineers in development of large ultra high vacuum linear accelerator systems employing unusual fabrication and metallurgical techniques. *Mailing Add:* 207 McDougal Belen NM 87002

WORT, ARTHUR JOHN, b Fordingbridge, Eng, Mar 26, 24; m 57; c 2. MICROBIOLOGY, MEDICINE. *Educ:* Univ Durham, MB, BS, 56; FRCP(C), 70, FRCPath, 77. *Prof Exp:* Demonstrator path, Univ Durham, 57-60; sr registrar microbiol, Royal Victoria Infirmary, 60-65; consult pathologist, N Tees Hosp, 65-68; asst prof, Univ Toronto, 68-70; ASST PROF, DALHOUSIE UNIV, 70-; HEAD, MICROBIOL DIV, IWK HOSP, 70- *Concurrent Pos:* Consult microbiol, Grace Hosp, 72- *Mem:* Am Soc Microbiol; Path Soc Gt Brit & Ireland; Can Pub Health Asn; Can Soc Microbiol; NY Acad Sci. *Res:* Epidemiology and immunology of pertussis; streptococci. *Mailing Add:* IWK Hosp PO Box 3070 Halifax NS B3S 3G9 Can

WORTH, DONALD CALHOUN, b Brooklyn, NY, Oct 20, 23; m 46; c 4. SOLAR ENERGY APPLICATIONS, SCIENCE EDUCATION. *Educ:* Carnegie Inst Technol, BS, 44; Yale Univ, MS, 48, PhD(physics), 49. *Prof Exp:* Instr physics, Berea Col, 50-52, assoc prof, 52-53; from asst prof to assoc prof, 54-60, dean, Col Liberal Arts, 70-74 & 76-80, PROF PHYSICS, INT CHRISTIAN UNIV, TOKYO, 60- *Concurrent Pos:* Vis asst prof, Ala Polytech Inst, 51; vis assoc prof, Univ Chicago, 53-54; NSF fel, Univ Va, 58-59; vis prof, Univ Wis, 63-64 & State Univ NY Stony Brook, 68-69; vis researcher, Lawrence Berkeley Nat Lab, Univ Calif, 81-82. *Mem:* Int Solar Energy Soc; Am Phys Soc; Am Asn Physics Teachers; e. *Res:* Low energy nuclear polarization studies, especially in nucleon-nucleon scattering; physics education; solar energy utilization. *Mailing Add:* Dept Physics Int Christian Univ 10-2 Osawa 3-Chome Mitaka-Shi Tokyo 181 Japan

WORTH, JAMES JUDSON BLACKLEY, b Charleston, WVa, Dec 11, 27; m 52; c 3. GEOPHYSICS, METEOROLOGY. *Educ:* Pa State Univ, BS, 52; Univ Mich, MS, 57. *Prof Exp:* Liaison off pres off, Pa State Univ, 51-52; indust engr, Armstrong Cork Co, 52-56; res assoc meteorol group, Eng Res Inst, Univ Mich, 56-57; engr, Commun Dept, Bendix Systs Div, Bendix Corp, 57-58, mgr eng group, 58-59, head meteorol & geophys dept, 59-62, asst gen mgr & dir proj mgt, 62-64, dir geophys lab, 64-68, assoc dir eng & environ sci, 68-70, dir indust develop, 70-71, VPRES, RESEARCH TRIANGLE INST, 71- *Concurrent Pos:* Am del, Int Geophys Conf, Helsinki, Finland, 60; mem atmospheric sci new tech comt, Nat Acad Sci, 61-62; adj asst prof, Dept Geol, Univ NC, 64-65, mem vis coun, 64-69, mem water resources res inst, 65-70; ad hoc sci adv comt geophys, US Army, 67-68. *Mem:* Am Meteorol Soc; Am Geophys Union; Royal Meteorol Soc; Explorers Club. *Res:* Engineering meteorology; micrometeorology; physical oceanography; atmospheric chemistry; environmental sciences. *Mailing Add:* Res Triangle Inst PO Box 12194 Research Triangle Park NC 27709

WORTH, ROBERT MCALPINE, b Kiangsi Prov, China, Aug 27, 24; US citizen; m 51; c 2. EPIDEMIOLOGY. *Educ:* Univ Calif, Berkeley, BA, 50, PhD(epidemiol), 62; Univ Calif, San Francisco, MD, 54; Harvard Univ, MPH, 58. *Prof Exp:* Intern med, Southern Pac Hosp, San Francisco, 54-55; resident family pract, San Mateo Community Hosp, 55-56; physician leprosy, Hawaii Dept Health, 56-57, asst chief chronic dis, 57, health officer, 58-60; PROF EPIDEMIOL, SCH PUB HEALTH, UNIV HAWAII, MANOA, 63- *Concurrent Pos:* Hooper Found res fel, Univ Hong Kong, 61-63; vis prof, Sch Med, Univ Calif, 69-70, Sch Pub Health, 76-77. *Mem:* Am Pub Health Asn. *Res:* Leprosy epidemiology and control; disease survey methodology; automation medical record systems for epidemiologic and quality control purposes; public health in modern China. *Mailing Add:* Univ of Hawaii Sch of Pub Health 1960 East-West Rd Honolulu HI 96822

WORTH, ROY EUGENE, b Broxton, Ga, Mar 24, 38; m 65; c 1. FUNCTIONAL ANALYSIS. *Educ:* Univ Ga, BS, 60, MA, 62, PhD(math), 68. *Prof Exp:* Asst prof math, WGa Col, 63-68; asst prof, 68-71, ASSOC PROF MATH, GA STATE UNIV, 71- *Mem:* Am Math Soc; Math Asn Am. *Res:* Banach semilinear spaces and semialgebras; applications of optimal control theory in economics, health care, etc. *Mailing Add:* Dept of Math Ga State Univ Atlanta GA 30303

WORTHAM, ALBERT WILLIAM, b Athens, Tex, Jan 18, 27; m 65; c 4. MATHEMATICS, STATISTICS. *Educ:* E Tex State Univ, BA, 47; Okla State Univ, MS, 49, PhD(math), 54. *Prof Exp:* Sr engr, Chance Vought Aircraft, 52-54, supvr systs eng, 54-57; mgr opers res, Tex Instruments, 57-58, mgr qual assurance, 58-59, mgr indust eng, 59-60, mgr planning & mgt systs, 60-61, mgr diode dept, 61-62; prof statist & indust eng, 62-63, chmn dept indust eng, 63-72, prof indust eng, Tex A&M Univ, 72-76; CORP STAFF, EDS WORLD CORP, 78- *Concurrent Pos:* Prof, Southern Methodist Univ, 58-61; consult, Fed Energy Admin, 74-75. *Mem:* Am Statist Asn; fel Am Soc Qual Control (exec secy, 61-62); Math Asn Am; Opers Res Soc Am; Am Inst Indust Engrs. *Res:* Planning; quality and inventory control; network theory. *Mailing Add:* PO Box 10 Wheelock TX 77882

WORTHEN, HOWARD GEORGE, b Provo, Utah, Dec 21, 25; m 50; c 5. PEDIATRICS, BIOCHEMISTRY. *Educ:* Brigham Young Univ, AB, 47; Northwestern Univ, MD, 51; Univ Minn, PhD, 61. *Prof Exp:* From instr to asst prof pediat, Univ Minn, 56-62; assoc prof, Med Col, Cornell Univ, 62-65; PROF PEDIAT, UNIV TEX HEALTH SCI CTR DALLAS, 65- *Mem:* Am Soc Exp Path; Electron Micros Soc Am; Harvey Soc; Soc Pediat Res; Am Soc Cell Biologists. *Res:* Renal disease; histochemistry; electron microscopy. *Mailing Add:* Dept of Pediat Univ of Tex Health Sci Ctr Dallas TX 75235

WORTHEN, LEONARD ROBERT, b Woburn, Mass, Dec 28, 25; m 55; c 3. MICROBIOLOGY. *Educ:* Mass Col Pharm, BS, 50; Temple Univ, MS, 52; Univ Mass, PhD(bact), 57. *Prof Exp:* Instr pharmacol, Sch Nursing, Holyoke Hosp, 55-57; asst prof pharm, 57-63, assoc prof pharmacog, 63-70, PROF PHARMACOG, UNIV RI, 70-, DIR ENVIRON HEALTH SCI PROG, 72- *Mem:* Am Pharmaceut Asn; Am Soc Pharmacog. *Res:* Fungal metabolites, particularly antibiotics and other metabolites of medicinal importance; natural products from marine sources. *Mailing Add:* Col of Pharm Univ of RI Kingston RI 02881

WORTHING, JURGEN, b Brooklyn, NY, Aug 11, 24; m 49; c 2. ELECTRICAL ENGINEERING. *Educ:* Polytech Inst Brooklyn, BEE, 48. *Prof Exp:* Staff engr, Servomechanisms, Inc, 48-55; staff engr, Repub Aviation Corp, 55; dir eng & sr vpres, Trio Labs, Inc, NY, 55-68; pres, Worthing Enterprises, 68-75; tech dir, NY State Legis Comn on Energy Systs, 75-78; TECH COUN, NY STATE ENERGY COMN, 78- *Mem:* Inst Elec & Electronics Engrs. *Res:* Cable television; medical instrumentation; energy legislation, its effects on production, distribution and use of energy, and socio-economic effects. *Mailing Add:* 75 Weaving Lane Wantagh NY 11793

WORTHINGTON, CHARLES ROY, b Penola, Australia, May 17, 25; m 59; c 3. BIOPHYSICS. *Educ:* Univ Adelaide, PhD(physics), 55. *Prof Exp:* Res assoc crystallog, Polytech Inst Brooklyn, 55-57; staff mem biophys, Biophys Res Unit, Med Res Coun, King's Col, Univ London, 58-61; from asst prof to assoc prof physics, Univ Mich, Ann Arbor, 61-69; prof chem & physics, 69-72, PROF PHYSICS & BIOL, MELLON INST SCI, CARNEGIE-MELLON UNIV, 72- *Concurrent Pos:* Consult, Nat Bur Standards, DC, 57-58. *Mem:* Biophys Soc; Am Crystallog Asn. *Res:* Membrane structure; molecular organization of biological systems and theories of biological mechanisms; x-ray biophysics and microscopy. *Mailing Add:* Mellon Inst of Sci Carnegie-Mellon Univ Pittsburgh PA 15213

WORTHINGTON, JAMES BRIAN, b Sandwich, Ill, Nov 29, 43; m 65; c 1. ANALYTICAL CHEMISTRY. *Educ:* Augustana Col, BA, 65; Purdue Univ, Lafayette, PhD(anal chem), 70. *Prof Exp:* Res chemist, 70-72, group leader environ anal, 72-75, mgr environ anal & comput serv, 75-76, mgr sci servs, 76-77, DIR ENVIRON AFFAIRS, DIAMOND SHAMROCK CORP, 77- *Honors & Awards:* Am Inst Chemists Award. *Mem:* Am Chem Soc. *Res:* Kinetic methods of analysis; design of chemical instrumentation; real time computer automation; environmental related analyses. *Mailing Add:* Diamond Shamrock Corp 717 N Harwood St Dallas TX 75243

WORTHINGTON, JOHN THOMAS, III, b Catonsville, Md, Feb 1, 24; m 49; c 2. HORTICULTURE. *Educ:* Univ Md, BS, 49, MS, 53. *Prof Exp:* Biol aide, Bur Plant Indust, USDA, 49-51, from jr horticulturist to horticulturist, 51-67, sr res horticulturist, 67-74, prin horticulturist, Mkt Res Div, Agr Mkt Serv, 74-79; RETIRED. *Mem:* Am Soc Hort Sci. *Res:* Fruits and vegetables, especially storage, market diseases and field studies on nursery stock, particularly strawberry plants; quality evaluation of fresh fruits and vegetables by light transmission methods. *Mailing Add:* 4600 Drexel Rd College Park MD 20740

WORTHINGTON, JOHN WILBUR, b Lexington, Ky, June 13, 18; m 43; c 2. ELECTRICAL ENGINEERING. *Educ:* Univ Ky, BSEE, 49. *Prof Exp:* Tech adv, Tech Training Command, Scott AFB, US Dept Air Force, Ill, 49-51, engr, Wright-Patterson AFB, 51-52, elec engr, Griffis AFB, 52-58, supv elec engr, Ground Elec Eng Installation Agency, 58-60, dep div chief, 60, proj elec engr, Rome Air Develop Ctr, 60-62; elec engr, opers res off, 62-74, ELEC ENGR, DEFENSE COMMUN ENG CTR, DEFENSE COMMUN AGENCY, 74- *Mem:* Sr mem Inst Elec & Electronics Engrs. *Res:* Operations research; war gaming; simulation; systems engineering; systems survivability/endurability. *Mailing Add:* 8416 Doyle Dr Alexandria VA 22308

WORTHINGTON, LAWRENCE VALENTINE, b London, Eng, Mar 6, 20; US citizen; m 52; c 2. OCEANOGRAPHY. *Prof Exp:* Hydrographic technician, 46-50, res assoc phys oceanog, 50-58, phys oceanogr, 58-63, sr scientist, 63-74, CHMN, DEPT PHYS OCEANOG, WOODS HOLE OCEANOG INST, 74- *Mem:* Am Geophys Union; AAAS. *Res:* General circulation of ocean and deep water problems. *Mailing Add:* Woods Hole Oceanog Inst 540 Woods Hole Rd Woods Hole MA 02543

WORTHINGTON, RALPH ERIC, b Coventry, Eng, July 28, 26; m 59; c 3. CHEMISTRY, FERTILIZER TECHNOLOGY. *Educ:* Univ Birmingham, Eng, BSc hons, 47, PhD(chem), 52. *Prof Exp:* Sci officer U metal prod, UK Atomic Energy Authority, 47-49, sr sci officer isotope separation, 52-55; chem res mgr clays, English Clays, Lovering & Pochin Ltd, Eng, 55-58; process develop mgr fertilizers, Assoc Chem Co, Eng, 58-63; tech dir fertilizers, Goulding Chem Ltd, Ireland, 63-76; V PRES TECH URANIUM EXTRACTION, URANIUM RECOVERY CORP, 77- *Concurrent Pos:* Res scholar, Birmingham Univ, Royal Aircraft Estab, 49-52; mem bd, Inst Indust Res & Standards, Ireland, 69-72. *Honors & Awards:* Award Technol Innovation, Govt Ireland, 72. *Mem:* Soc Chem Indust, UK; Am Chem Soc; Fertilizer Soc; Inst Chem Ireland. *Res:* Technology of recovery of secondary elements particularly related to phosphoric acid manufacture; general fertilizer technology. *Mailing Add:* UNC Recovery Corp PO 765 Mulberry FL 33860

WORTHINGTON, RICHARD DANE, b Houston, Tex, Sept 20, 41; m 64. MORPHOLOGY, HERPETOLOGY. *Educ:* Univ Tex, Austin, BA, 63; Univ Md, MS, 66, PhD(zool), 68. *Prof Exp:* USPHS trainee, Univ Chicago, 68-69; asst prof biol, 69-74, ASSOC PROF BIOL SCI, UNIV TEX, EL PASO, 74- *Mem:* Soc Syst Zool; Soc Study Evolution; Ecol Soc Am; Am Soc Ichthyologists & Herpetologists; Soc Study Amphibians & Reptiles. *Res:* Evolutionary biology of caudate amphibians; mountain floral of the southwest United States; evolutionary morphology; lizard ecology; ecology. *Mailing Add:* Dept of Biol Sci Univ of Tex El Paso TX 79968

WORTHINGTON, ROBERT EARL, b Kingston, Ga, Jan 2, 29; m 60; c 3. LIPID CHEMISTRY, FOOD SCIENCE. *Educ:* Berry Col, BSA, 52; NC State Col, MS, 55; Iowa State Univ, PhD(biochem), 62. *Prof Exp:* Res instr agr & biol chem, NC State Col, 55-56; assoc biochem & biophys, Iowa State Univ, 56-61, asst prof animal sci, 61-64; asst prof, 64-76, ASSOC PROF FOOD SCI, GA STA, UNIV GA, 76- *Mem:* AAAS; Am Chem Soc; Am Oil Chem Soc. *Res:* Lipid chemistry of foods. *Mailing Add:* Dept Food Sci Ga Sta Univ of Ga Experiment GA 30212

WORTHINGTON, THOMAS KIMBER, b New York, NY, Aug 4, 47. LOW TEMPERATURE PHYSICS. *Educ:* Franklin & Marshall Col, BA, 69; Wesleyan Univ, PhD(physics), 75. *Prof Exp:* FEL PHYSICS, RUTGERS UNIV, 75- *Mem:* Am Inst Physics. *Res:* Specific heat and thermal conductivity of granular aluminum films; magnetics. *Mailing Add:* IBM Thomas J Watson Lab PO Box 218 Yorktown Heights NY 10598

WORTHINGTON, WARD CURTIS, JR, b Savannah, Ga, Aug 8, 25; m 47; c 2. MEDICAL CENTER ADMINISTRATION, ANATOMY. *Educ:* The Citadel, BS, 52; Med Col SC, MD, 52. *Prof Exp:* Intern surg, Boston City Hosp, Mass, 52-53; instr anat, Sch Med, Johns Hopkins Univ, 53-56; asst prof, Col Med, Univ Ill, 56-57; from asst prof to assoc prof, 57-66, asst dean, 66-69, chmn dept, 69-77, assoc dean, 70-77, actg vpres acad affairs, 75-77, PROF ANAT, MED UNIV SC, 66-, VPRES ACAD AFFAIRS, 77- *Concurrent Pos:* NIH spec fel, Dept Human Anat, Oxford Univ, 64-65. *Mem:* AAAS; Am Asn Anat; Endocrine Soc; Am Physiol Soc; Asn Anat Chmn (secy-treas & pres, 71-76). *Res:* Anatomy and physiology of pituitary circulation; histology; neuroendocrinology. *Mailing Add:* Med Univ SC 171 Ashley Ave Charleston SC 29425

WORTHMAN, ROBERT PAUL, b Chicago, Ill, Aug 3, 19; m 46; c 2. VETERINARY ANATOMY. *Educ:* Kans State Univ, DVM, 43; Iowa State Univ, MS, 53. *Prof Exp:* Asst prof vet anat, Wash State Univ, 46-49 & Iowa State Univ, 49-53; from asst prof to assoc prof, PROF VET ANAT, WASH STATE UNIV, 65- *Mem:* Am Vet Med Asn; Am Asn Anat; Am Asn Vet Anatomists (pres, 75); World Asn Vet Anatomists (vpres, 75). *Res:* Veterinary surgical and functional anatomy; techniques of teaching museum specimen preparation. *Mailing Add:* Div of Anat Dept of VCAPP Wash State Univ Pullman WA 99163

WORTHY, LIONEL DORSEY, JR, b Ft Payne, Ala, Jan 19, 47; m 82. ACUTE TOXICITY. *Educ:* WVa Univ, BS, 74; Va Polytech & State Univ, MS, 77. *Prof Exp:* Teaching asst fish ecol, Va Polytech & State Univ, 74-75; res asst, Va Coop Fishery Res Unit, 75-77; sea grant asst ed food sci, Va Polytech & State Univ, 77-78; sr tech adv, Fisheries Ministry, Govt St Lucia, US Peace Corps, 78-80; DIR FIELD SERV, OLVER INC, 81- *Concurrent Pos:* Adv naturalist, St Lucia Naturalist Soc, 78-80; lectr marine sci, Univ West Indies, St Lucia, 79-80. *Mem:* Am Fisheries Soc. *Res:* Aquatic population dynamics and habitat manipulation, specializing in beuthic invertebrates; effects of toxic substances on aquatic organisms; monitoring industrial effluents for acute and chronic toxicity. *Mailing Add:* PO Box 319 Blacksburg VA 24060

WORTIS, MICHAEL, b New York, NY, Sept 28, 36; m 64; c 2. THEORETICAL PHYSICS, SOLID STATE PHYSICS. *Educ:* Harvard Univ, BA, 58, MA, 59, PhD(physics), 63. *Prof Exp:* Miller fel physics, Univ Calif, Berkeley, 62-64; NSF fel, Fac Sci, Univ Paris, 64-65; vis prof, Pakistan Atomic Energy Comn, WPakistan, 65; res asst prof, 66, from asst prof to assoc prof, 66-73, PROF PHYSICS, UNIV ILL, URBANA, 73- *Concurrent Pos:* A P Sloan Found fel, Univ Ill, Urbana, 67-69; Ford Found consult, Univ Islamabad, WPakistan, 71. *Honors & Awards:* Fulbright-Hays lectr, Pakistan, 78. *Mem:* Am Phys Soc. *Res:* Statistical physics; magnetic phenomena; phase transitions; phase transitions and related phenomena in strongly coupled and complex systems; surface and interface phenomena. *Mailing Add:* Dept of Physics Univ of Ill Urbana IL 61801

WORTMAN, BERNARD, b Brooklyn, NY, Apr 23, 24; m 52; c 3. BIOCHEMISTRY. *Educ:* Syracuse Univ, AB, 48; Univ Tex, MA, 51; Ohio State Univ, PhD(physiol), 55. *Prof Exp:* From res asst to res asst prof ophthal, Sch Med, Wash Univ, 55-65; res assoc prof, Albany Med Col, 65-66; res chemist, Food & Drug Admin, Washington, DC, 66-69; SCIENTIST ADMINR, NAT EYE INST, 69- *Concurrent Pos:* NIH spec fel, 60-61; estab investr, Am Heart Asn, 61-65; vis scientist, Am Physiol Soc, 63; consult to lab serv, Vet Admin Hosp, Albany, 65-66; res assoc prof, Med Sch, George Washington Univ, 67-70. *Mem:* Am Physiol Soc; Soc Gen Physiol; Am Soc Cell Biol; Am Chem Soc. *Res:* Cell physiology; general metabolism of cornea; biosynthesis of sulfated mucopolysaccharides in cornea; biochemistry of connective tissue; macromolecular biochemistry. *Mailing Add:* H H S Nat Inst Aging NIH Bldg 31 Rm 5C21 Bethesda MD 20205

WORTMAN, JIMMIE J(ACK), b NC, Feb 23, 36; m 54; c 1. SOLID STATE PHYSICS, ELECTRONICS. *Educ:* NC State Univ, BS, 60; Duke Univ, MS, 62, PhD(elec eng), 65. *Prof Exp:* Mem tech staff, Bell Tel Labs, 60-62; res engr, Res Triangle Inst, 62-68, mgr, Eng Physics Dept, 68-72, dir, Eng Div, 72-75, dir, Energy & Environ Res Div, 75-80. *Concurrent Pos:* Asst prof, exten div, NC State Univ, 62-63; lectr, Duke Univ, 64-70; adj prof, NC State Univ, 74. *Mem:* Am Phys Soc; Inst Elec & Electronics Engrs. *Res:* Semiconductor and thin film phenomena; devices; microelectronics; transducers; solar cells. *Mailing Add:* Rte 6 Box 192 Chapel Hill NC 27514

WORTMAN, LEO STERLING, JR, plant breeding, deceased

WORTMAN, ROGER MATTHEW, b Chicago, Ill, Dec 11, 32; m. PHYSICS. *Educ:* Univ Chicago, PhD(phys chem), 57. *Prof Exp:* Res physicist, Carnegie Inst Technol, 57-61; res scientist, Douglas Aircraft Co, Inc, 61-63; criminalist, Oakland Police Dept, Calif, 63-67; CHEMIST, SCI LIAISON & ADV GROUP, US ARMY, 67- *Res:* Field emission microscopy and radiation damage of surfaces; aerospace devices; scientific criminal investigation; military technology; research administration. *Mailing Add:* 3100 Twin Ct Bowie MD 20715

WORTS, GEORGE FRANK, JR, b Toledo, Ohio, Apr 24, 16; m 50; c 1. GEOLOGY, HYDROGEOLOGY. *Educ:* Stanford Univ, BS, 39. *Prof Exp:* Geologist, Ground Water Br, 40-50, geologist in charge, Long Beach, 52-56, dist geologist, Sacramento, 56-58, br area chief, Pac Coast Area, 58-62, dist chief, Nev, 62-74, PART-TIME, US GEOL SURV, 74- *Concurrent Pos:* Water-res eval, Azores, Guyana, Philippines, Isreal, Egypt & Korea. *Mem:* Fel Geol Soc Am; Am Geophys Union; Asn Eng Geol. *Res:* National and international hydrology, especially of arid regions; ground-water resources, particularly quantitative analysis, water quality, coastal hydrology and water management; direction of complex hydrologic studies and applied research. *Mailing Add:* 163 Tahoe Dr Carson City NV 89701

WORZALA, F(RANK) JOHN, b Milwaukee, Wis, Nov 13, 33; m 54; c 9. NUCLEAR METALLURGY. *Educ:* Univ Wis, BS, 56, MS, 58; Carnegie Inst Technol, MS, 62, PhD(metall eng), 65. *Prof Exp:* Engr, Hanford Labs, Gen Elec Co, Wash, 56-57; engr, Bettis Atomic Power Lab, Westinghouse Elec Corp, 58-65, res scientist, 66-67; NSF fel & res scientist, Grenoble Nuclear Res Ctr, France, 65-66; assoc prof nuclear mat, 67-77, PROF ENG METALL & MINING ENG, UNIV WIS-MADISON, 77- *Mem:* Am Nuclear Soc; Am Inst Mining, Metall & Petrol Engrs; Am Soc Metals. *Res:* Nuclear materials; irradiation damage in metals; fracture mechanics; applied superconductivity and superconducting materials. *Mailing Add:* Dept of Metall & Minerals Eng Univ of Wis Madison WI 53706

WORZEL, JOHN LAMAR, b West Brighton, NY, Feb 21, 19; m 41; c 4. GEOPHYSICS. *Educ:* Lehigh Univ, BS, 40; Columbia Univ, MA, 48, PhD, 49. *Prof Exp:* Res assoc, Woods Hole Oceanog Inst, 40-46; geodesist, Columbia Univ, 47-49, res assoc geol, 48-49, instr, 49-51, asst prof, 51-52, assoc prof geophys, 52-57, prof, 57-72, asst dir, Lamont Geol Observ, 57-64, actg dir, 64-65, assoc dir, 65-72; prof geophys & dep dir earth & planetary sci div, Marine Biomed Inst, Univ Tex Med Br, Galveston, 72-74; actg dir, Geophys Lab, Marine Sci Inst, Univ Tex, Austin, 74-75, prog geol sci, 72-79, prof marine studies, 75-79, dir, Geophhys Lab, Marine Sci Inst, 75-79; RETIRED. *Concurrent Pos:* Geophys consult, Off Naval Res, 50; mem, US Navy Deep Water Propagation Comt, 50-60; Guggenheim Found fel, 63; chmn spec study group, Int Union Geod & Geophys; prof geosci, Univ Tex, Dallas, 72-79; adj prof geol sci, Rice Univ, 74-77; pres, Palisades Geophys Inst, 74-; mem, US Nat Comt Int Geol Correlation Prog, 78-79. *Honors & Awards:* Meritorious Pub Serv Citation, US Navy, 64. *Mem:* AAAS; Seismol Soc Am; Soc Explor Geophysicists (vpres, 78-79); Am Physical Soc; Geol Soc Am. *Res:* Gravity at sea; seismic refraction and reflection at sea; underwater photography; tectonophysics; marine geophysics; marine instrumentation. *Mailing Add:* Geophys Lab Marine Sci Inst Univ of Tex 700 The Strand Galveston TX 77550

WOSILAIT, WALTER DANIEL, b Racine, Wis, Feb 4, 24; m 48; c 1. PHARMACOLOGY, BIOCHEMISTRY. *Educ:* Wabash Col, BA, 49; Johns Hopkins Univ, PhD(biol), 53. *Prof Exp:* Jr instr pharmacol, Western Reserve Univ, 53-56; asst prof, State Univ NY Downstate Med Ctr, 56-63, assoc prof, 63-65; assoc prof, 65-66, PROF PHARMACOL, SCH MED, UNIV MO-COLUMBIA, 66- *Concurrent Pos:* USPHS res grant, State Univ NY Downstate Med Ctr, 56-65; USPHS res grant, Sch Med, Univ Mo-Columbia, 65- *Mem:* Am Soc Biol Chemists; Am Soc Pharmacol & Exp Therapeut; Am Soc Clin Pharmacol & Therapeut; Soc Exp Biol & Med; Harvey Soc. *Res:* Anticoagulant interactions; pharmacokinetics. *Mailing Add:* Dept of Pharmacol Univ Mo Sch of Med Columbia MO 65212

WOSINSKI, JOHN FRANCIS, b North Tonawanda, NY, Dec 30, 30; m 56; c 2. MATERIAL SCIENCE, MINERALOGY. *Educ:* Denison Univ, BS, 53; Brown Univ, MS, 58. *Prof Exp:* Geologist mapping, US Geol Surv, 56-57; mineralogist glass, 58-60, supvr petrog, 61-64, supvr refractories, 65-67, MGR REFRACTORIES, CORNING GLASS WORKS, 67- *Concurrent Pos:* Prin investr Apollo 14-15 mission samples, NASA, 71-72; chmn refractories div, Am Ceramic Soc, 78-79. *Mem:* Geol Soc Am; Sigma Xi; Am Ceramic Soc; Am Soc Testing & Mat; Soc Glass Technol. *Res:* Develop, test, evaluate and recommend refractory materials used in corporate glass melting endeavors; glass-refractory manufacturing problems and archaeological excavations. *Mailing Add:* Corning Glass Works Main Plant 52-4 Corning NY 14830

WOSKE, HARRY MAX, b Reading, Pa, Feb 26, 24; m 72; c 7. INTERNAL MEDICINE, CARDIOLOGY. *Educ:* Columbia Univ, AB, 45; Long Island Col Med, MD, 48. *Prof Exp:* Instr med, Sch Med, Univ Pa, 55-57, assoc, 57-64, from adj asst prof to adj assoc prof, 64-69, assoc prof med & assoc dean, 69-73; assoc dean, 74, prof med & chief med serv, 73-76, ACTG DEAN, NJ-RUTGERS MED SCH, 75-; CHIEF CARDIOL, HUNTERDON MED CTR, NJ, 77- *Concurrent Pos:* NIH fel cardiol, Sch Med, Univ Pa, 55-57. *Mem:* Fel Am Col Physicians; fel Am Col Cardiol; fel NY Acad Sci; clin prof med, Rutgers Med Sch, 77- *Res:* Exercise projects. *Mailing Add:* Hunterdon Med Ctr Flemington NJ 08822

WOSKOBOINIKOW, PAUL PETER, b Montour Falls, NY, Apr 23, 50; m 76. LASERS, PLASMA PHYSICS. *Educ:* Rensselaer Polytech Inst, BS, 72, MS, 74, PhD(electrophysics), 76. *Prof Exp:* Res asst lasers, Rensselaer Polytech Inst, 72-75, asst electromagnetics, 75-76; staff scientist lasers & plasma diagnostics, Francis Bitter Nat Magnet Lab, 76-80, PROJ LEADER SUBMILLIMETER-WAVE PLASMA DIAGNOSTIC DEVELOP, PLASMA FUSION CTR, MASS INST TECHNOL, 80- *Mem:* Am Phys Soc; AAAS; Inst Elec & Electronics Engrs. *Res:* High power far-infrared laser development and research; plasma diagnostic of controlled fusion type plasmas; application of high-power submillimeter wave lasers to Thomson scattering plasma diagnostics. *Mailing Add:* Bldg NW14-4107 Mass Inst of Technol Cambridge MA 02139

WOSTMANN, BERNARD STEPHAN, b Amsterdam, Neth, Nov 6, 18; US citizen; m 46; c 5. BIOCHEMISTRY, NUTRITION. *Educ:* Univ Amsterdam, BS, 40, MS, 45, DSc, 48. *Prof Exp:* Instr org chem, Univ Amsterdam, 43, instr biochem, 45-48, lectr, 48-50, sci off, 48-55; from asst prof to assoc prof, 55-65, PROF BIOCHEM, UNIV NOTRE DAME, 65- *Concurrent Pos:* Asst dir, Neth Inst Nutrit, 48-55; Rockefeller res fel, 50-51. *Mem:* AAAS; Am Inst Nutrit; Soc Exp Biol & Med; Asn Gnotobiotics (pres, 66-68); NY Acad Sci. *Res:* Biochemical background of host-contaminant relationship; role of intestinal flora in nutrition. *Mailing Add:* Dept of Microbiol Lobund Lab Univ of Notre Dame Notre Dame IN 46556

WOTHERSPOON, NEIL, b New York, NY, Oct 24, 30; m 54; c 1. PHYSICAL CHEMISTRY, INSTRUMENTATION. *Educ:* Polytech Inst Brooklyn, BS, 52, PhD, 57. *Prof Exp:* Res scientist, Radiation & Solid State Lab, NY Univ, 57-68; asst prof biophys & bioeng, Mt Sinai Sch Med, 68-76; SR SCIENTIST, TECHNICON INSTRUMENTS CORP, 76- *Mem:* Am Chem Soc; Asn Comput Mach. *Res:* Instrumentation for physics, chemistry and biomedical sciences, including optical electronic and computer techniques for automated analysis; analog and digital data acquisition, interfacing and processing. *Mailing Add:* 14 Washington Place Apt 8-I New York NY 10003

WOTIZ, HERBERT HENRY, b Vienna, Austria, Oct 8, 22; nat US; m 47; c 3. ORGANIC CHEMISTRY, BIOCHEMISTRY. *Educ:* Providence Col, ScB, 44; Yale Univ, PhD(org chem), 51. *Prof Exp:* Instr, 51-53, asst prof, 53-55, assoc res prof, 55-61, assoc prof, 61-63, res assoc, R D Evans Mem Hosp, 55-68, PROF BIOCHEM, SCH MED, BOSTON UNIV, 63- *Concurrent Pos:* Res fel, R D Evans Mem Hosp, 50-55; USPHS sr res fel, 60-64 & res career develop fel, 65-69. *Mem:* Am Chem Soc; Am Soc Biol Chemists; Endocrine Soc; Am Asn Cancer Res. *Res:* Steroid metabolism and analysis; mechanism of hormone action, action of impeding estrogens. *Mailing Add:* Dept of Biochem Boston Univ Sch of Med Boston MA 02118

WOTIZ, JOHN HENRY, b Moravska Ostrava, Czech, Apr 12, 19; nat US; m 45; c 3. ORGANIC CHEMISTRY. *Educ:* Furman Univ, BS, 41; Univ Richmond, MS, 43; Ohio State Univ, PhD(org chem), 48. *Prof Exp:* Asst chem, Univ Richmond, 41-43 & Ohio State Univ, 43-44 & 46-47; from instr to assoc prof, Univ Pittsburgh, 48-57; prof chem & chmn dept, Marshall Univ, 62-67; chmn dept, 67-69, PROF CHEM, SOUTHERN ILL UNIV, 67- *Concurrent Pos:* With Fed Security Agency, 44; Nat Acad Sci exchange prof, numerous countries, 69-74; mem int activ comt, Am Chem Soc, 75- *Mem:* Hist of Sci Soc; Am Chem Soc (chmn, Hist Chem Div, 79-). *Res:* Propargylic rearrangement; radical ions from vicinal diamines; institutional research in eastern socialist southeast Asian and Pacific Ocean countries; history of chemistry. *Mailing Add:* Dept of Chem Southern Ill Univ Carbondale IL 62901

WOTSCHKE, DETLEF, b Treuenbrietzen, Ger, Apr 14, 44; m 69. COMPUTER SCIENCE, SYSTEMS SCIENCE. *Educ:* Univ Braunschweig, Vordiplom, 67, Diplom, 69; Univ Calif, Los Angeles, PhD(syst sci), 74. *Prof Exp:* Mgr safety eng, Tebera Tech Res & Consult, Braunschweig, 65-70; teaching & res assoc syst sci, Univ Calif, Los Angeles, 71-74; ASST PROF COMPUT SCI, PA STATE UNIV, 74- *Concurrent Pos:* Ger Acad Exchange Serv fel, 70; chmn arrangements, Eighth Ann Symp Theory Comput, Asn Comput Mach, 75-76; vis assoc prof comput sci, Univ Kaiserslautern, W Ger, 77-78. *Mem:* Asn Comput Mach; Ger Soc Comput Sci. *Res:* Formal languages; automata theory; theory of grammars and parsing; stochastic systems. *Mailing Add:* Dept of Comput Sci Pa State Univ University Park PA 16802

WOTT, JOHN ARTHUR, b Fremont, Ohio, Apr 10, 39; m 59; c 3. HORTICULTURE. *Educ:* Ohio State Univ, BS, 61; Cornell Univ, MS, 66, PhD(hort), 68. *Prof Exp:* Instr, Coop Exten Serv, Ohio State Univ, 61-64; res asst hort, Cornell Univ, 64-68; from asst prof to assoc prof hort, Purdue Univ, West Lafayette, 68-78, prof 78-81; PROF URBAN HORT, UNIV WASH, SEATTLE, 81- *Concurrent Pos:* County exten agent 4-H, Wood County, Bowling Green, Ohio, 61-64. *Mem:* Am Soc Hort Sci; Am Hort Soc; Int Plant Propagators Soc. *Res:* Nutrition of cuttings during propagation; application of nutrient mist; horticultural problems of homeowners, such as foliage plants, annuals and perennials; herbicides in annual flowers; morphological and physiological response of woody plants to flooding. *Mailing Add:* Ctr Urban Hort AR-10 Univ Wash Seattle WA 98195

WOTZAK, GREGORY PAUL, b New York, NY, Dec 12, 44; m 68; c 1. CHEMICAL ENGINEERING. *Educ:* Rensselaer Polytech Inst, BChE, 65; Princeton Univ, MS, 67, PhD(chem eng), 68. *Prof Exp:* From asst prof to assoc prof chem eng, Rensselaer Polytech Inst, 68-77, prof, 77-80; MEM FAC CHEM ENG, CLEVELAND STATE UNIV, 80- *Mem:* Am Inst Chem Engrs. *Res:* Chemical reaction engineering; stochastic simulation; transport phenomena; chemical physics. *Mailing Add:* Stillwell Hall Rm 409 Cleveland State Univ Cleveland OH 44115

WOUK, ARTHUR, b New York, NY, Mar 25, 24; m 44; c 2. MATHEMATICS. *Educ:* City Col New York, BS, 43; Johns Hopkins Univ, MA, 47, PhD(math), 51. *Prof Exp:* Instr math, Johns Hopkins Univ, 47-50 & Queens Col, NY, 50-52; mathematician, Proj Cyclone, Reeves Instrument Corp, 52-54; supvr math anal sect, Missile Systs Lab, Sylvania Elec Prod, Inc, 54-56, sr eng specialist, Appl Res Lab, Sylvania Electronic Systs Div, Gen Tel & Electronics Corp, 56-62; vis prof, Math Res Ctr, Univ Wis, 62-63; from assoc prof to prof appl math, Northwestern Univ, Evanston, 63-72; chmn dept, 72-77, PROF COMPUT SCI, UNIV ALTA, 72- *Concurrent Pos:* Ed, Commun, Asn Comput Mach, 58-64; consult, Appl Res Lab, Sylvania Electronic Systs Div, Gen Tel & Electronics Corp & Argonne Nat Lab, 63-69; ed, SIAM Rev, Soc Indust & Appl Math, 63- *Mem:* Am Math Soc; Soc Indust & Appl Math; Opers Res Soc Am; Asn Comput Mach. *Res:* Optimal control theory; numerical and functional analysis. *Mailing Add:* Dept of Comput Sci Univ of Alta Edmonton AB T5R 0E2 Can

WOUK, VICTOR, b New York, NY, Apr 27, 19; m 41; c 2. HIGH POWER ELECTRONICS, ELECTRIC HYBRID VEHICLES. *Educ:* Columbia Univ, BA, 39; Calif Inst Technol, MS, 40, PhD(elec eng), 42. *Prof Exp:* Res engr, Res Labs, Westinghouse Elec Corp, 42-45; circuit engr, NAm Philips Co, NY, 45-47; pres & chief engr, Beta Elec Corp, 47-57; vpres eng & res, Sorenson & Co, Inc, 57-60; pres, Electronic Energy Conversion Corp, 60-63; gen mgr electronic energy conversion dept, Gulton Industs, Inc, NY, 63-68, dir electronics res, 68-70; pres, Petro-elec Motors, Ltd, 70-76; PRES, VICTOR WOUK ASSOC, 76- *Concurrent Pos:* US rep tech comt elec rd vehicles, Int Electrotech Comn, 69; consult, Dept Energy, 76- *Mem:* Fel AAAS; Soc Automotive Engrs; Inst Elec & Electronics Engrs; Fedn Am Sci; NY Acad Sci. *Res:* Static electricity generation by gasoline; television amplifier and sweep circuits; high voltage power supplies; regulated alternating and direct current power supplies; electronic controls for electric vehicles; electric and hybrid vehicles. *Mailing Add:* 267 Fifth Ave New York NY 10016

WOURMS, JOHN BARTON, b New York, NY, Apr 30, 37; m 72. CELL BIOLOGY, DEVELOPMENTAL BIOLOGY. *Educ:* Fordham Univ, BS, 58, MS, 60; Stanford Univ, PhD(biol), 66. *Prof Exp:* Am Cancer Soc fel, Harvard Univ, 66-68; Nat Res Coun Can grant & asst prof cell develop biol, Dept Biol, McGill Univ, 68-71, res assoc, Dept Path, 71-72; assoc res scientist, NY Ocean Sci Lab, 72-80; MEM FAC, DEPT ZOOL, CLEMSON UNIV, 80- *Concurrent Pos:* Vis lectr, Biol Labs, Harvard Univ, 71-72. *Mem:* Am Soc Cell Biol; Am Soc Ichthyologists & Herpetologists; Soc Develop Biol; Int Soc Develop Biologists; Marine Biol Asn UK. *Res:* Cell differentiation; cell ultrastructure; reproduction and development of fishes and marine invertebrates; oogenesis; ultrastructure and chemistry of extra-cellular matrices; biology of annual fishes; evolutionary biology; elasmobranch biology; marine biomedical resources. *Mailing Add:* Dept Zool Clemson Univ Clemson SC 29631

WOVCHA, MERLE G, b Virginia, Minn, Dec 19, 38. BIOCHEMISTRY. *Educ:* Univ Minn, BA, 62, BS, 64, MS, 67, PhD(biochem), 71. *Prof Exp:* NIH fel, Dept Biol Chem, Univ Mich, 71-74; res scientist, 74-77, sr res scientist, 77-81, SR SCIENTIST, FERMENTATION RES & DEVELOP, UPJOHN CO, 81- *Mem:* Am Soc Microbiol. *Res:* Microbial sterol bioconversions; streptomycete metabolism and replication; bacteriophage biochemistry. *Mailing Add:* Fermentation Res & Develop UpJohn Co Kalamazoo MI 49001

WOYCHIK, JOHN HENRY, b Scranton, Pa, Mar 30, 30; m 53; c 2. BIOCHEMISTRY, PHYSIOLOGY. *Educ:* Univ Scranton, BS, 53; Univ Tenn, MS, 55, PhD(biochem), 57. *Prof Exp:* Chemist, Northern Regional Lab, 57-63, prin chemist, Eastern Mkt & Res Div, 63-74, CHIEF, DAIRY LAB, EASTERN REGIONAL RES CTR, USDA, 74- *Mem:* Am Chem Soc; Am Dairy Sci Asn; Am Soc Biol Chemists; Inst Food Technologists. *Res:* Isolation and characterization of milk and cereal proteins; glycoproteins; basic research on milk components and dairy product development. *Mailing Add:* Eastern Regional Res Ctr USDA 600 E Mermaid Lane Philadelphia PA 19118

WOYSKI, MARGARET SKILLMAN, b West Chester, Pa, July 26, 21; m 48; c 4. GEOLOGY. *Educ:* Wellesley Col, BA, 43; Univ Minn, MS, 45, PhD(geol), 46. *Prof Exp:* Instr geol, Univ Minn, 46; geologist, Mo Geol Surv, 46-48; instr geol, Univ Wis, 48-52; lectr, Calif State Col, Long Beach, 63-67; from asst prof to assoc prof, 67-74, prof geol, 74-77, chmn EARTH SCI, 78- Earth Sci, 73-76, PROF GEOL, CALIF STATE UNIV, FULLERTON, 74- *Concurrent Pos:* Lectr geol, Calif State Univ, Fullerton, 66-67. *Mem:* Mineral Soc Am; Nat Asn Geol Teachers; Geol Soc Am. *Res:* Intrusive rocks of central Minnesota; Precambrian sediments of Missouri; laboratory manuals for historical and physical geology; geologic guidebooks of Southern California; source locations of artifacts; petrology of peninsular range batholith. *Mailing Add:* Dept of Earth Sci Calif State Univ 800 N State College Blvd Fullerton CA 92634

WOZENCRAFT, JOHN MCREYNOLDS, b Dallas, Tex, Sept 30, 25; m 63; c 2. ELECTRICAL ENGINEERING, COMMUNICATIONS. *Educ:* US Mil Acad, BS, 46; Mass Inst Technol, SM & EE, 51, ScD, 57. *Prof Exp:* Asst elec eng, Mass Inst Technol, 55-57, from asst prof to prof, 57-72, head commun div, Lincoln Lab, 69-72; dean res, 72-76, PROF ELEC ENG, NAVAL POSTGRAD SCH, 76- *Mem:* Fel Inst Elec & Electronics Engrs. *Res:* Application of information theory to practical communication problems; algorithmic languages for digital computation. *Mailing Add:* Naval Postgrad Sch Monterey CA 93940

WOZNIAK, WAYNE THEODORE, b Chicago, Ill, Oct 13, 45; m 71; c 2. CHEMISTRY, SPECTROSCOPY. *Educ:* Ill Benedictine Col, BS, 67; Fla State Univ, PhD(phys inorg chem), 71. *Prof Exp:* Res assoc phys chem, Princeton Univ, 71-73; res assoc chem physics, Univ Ill, 73-75; res assoc biophys, 75-78, head, Physics Lab, 78-79, dir, 79-80, ASST SECY, COUN DENT MAT, INSTRUMENTS & EQUIP, AM DENT ASN, 80- *Concurrent Pos:* Instr, Univ Ill, 74. *Mem:* Am Chem Soc; Int Asn Dent Res; Intersoc Color Coun; Soc Appl Spectros. *Res:* Spectroscopy of dental materials and calcified tissue; resonance Raman spectroscopy; applications of vibrational spectroscopy to biological systems. *Mailing Add:* Am Dent Asn 211 E Chicago Ave Chicago IL 60611

WRAIGHT, COLIN ALLEN, b London, Eng, Nov 27, 45. BIOPHYSICS. *Educ:* Univ Bristol, BSc, 67, PhD(biochem), 71. *Prof Exp:* Fel biophys, State Univ Leiden, 71-72; assoc, Cornell Univ, 72-74; asst prof biol, Univ Calif, Santa Barbara, 74-75; asst prof, 75-81, ASSOC PROF BIOPHYS & BOT, UNIV ILL, URBANA-CHAMPAIGN, 81- *Mem:* Biophys Soc; AAAS; Am Soc Photobiol. *Res:* Membrane functions and mechanisms of electron and ion transport in biological energy conservation. *Mailing Add:* Depts of Biophys & Bot 289 Morrill Hall Univ of Ill Urbana IL 61801

WRANGELL, LEWIS J, b Milwaukee, Wis, July 30, 14; m 40; c 1. ANALYTICAL CHEMISTRY. *Educ:* Marquette Univ, BS, 36, MS, 39. *Prof Exp:* Chemist, Res Labs, Allis-Chalmers Mfg Co, Wis, 42-45, chemist-in-chg anal lab, 45-59, res chemist, 59-69; chief chem eng & sci, Geo J Meyer Mfg, 69-70; indust consult, 70-72; sr anal chemist, Reduction Systs Div, Allis-Chalmers Corp, 72-78; RETIRED. *Concurrent Pos:* Consult anal chem, 79- *Mem:* Fel Am Inst Chemists; Am Chem Soc. *Res:* Analytical chemistry of metallic materials; reactions of metals with gases at elevated temperatures; analysis of unusual and new compounds; analysis of direct reduced iron; electrodeposition of catalytic nickel powder. *Mailing Add:* 2325 N 86th St Wauwatosa WI 53226

WRASIDLO, WOLFGANG JOHANN, b Beuthen, Ger, Oct 31, 38; US citizen; m; c 2. POLYMER CHEMISTRY. *Educ:* San Diego State Univ, BA, 63; Univ Nurnberg, MS, 67. *Prof Exp:* Sr res chemist, Whittaker Corp, 63-65; res chemist, US Naval Ord Lab, 67-69; staff mem polymers, Sci Res Labs, Boeing Co, 69-71; STAFF CHEMIST, UOP, 71- *Honors & Awards:* Civilian Serv Award, US Naval Ord Lab, 70. *Mem:* Am Chem Soc. *Res:* Solid state polymers; synthesis and characterization of high temperature polymers; mechanical, thermal and morphological behavior of polymers; reverse osmosis membranes. *Mailing Add:* 1219 Coast Blvd #5 La Jolla CA 92037

WRATHALL, DONALD PRIOR, b Pittsburgh, Pa, Mar 9, 36; m 62; c 4. PHYSICAL CHEMISTRY. *Educ:* Brigham Young Univ, BA, 64, PhD(phys chem), 68. *Prof Exp:* NIH fel, Yale Univ, 67-68; SR RES CHEMIST, EASTMAN KODAK CO, 68- *Res:* Thermodynamics of reactions at solid-liquid interfaces and with macromolecules in solution. *Mailing Add:* Res Labs Eastman Kodak Co 1669 Lake Ave Rochester NY 14650

WRATHALL, JAY W, b Salt Lake City, Utah, May 12, 33; m 69; c 2. INORGANIC CHEMISTRY. *Educ:* Brigham Young Univ, BS, 57, MS, 59; Ohio State Univ, PhD(inorg chem), 62. *Prof Exp:* Asst prof chem, Univ Calif, Berkeley, 62-64 & Univ Hawaii, 64-69; assoc prof, Church Col Hawaii, 69-73, prof & div chmn, 74-, PROF PHYS SCI, 77- CHMN, BRIGHAM YOUNG UNIV, HAWAII CAMPUS, 74- *Mem:* Am Chem Soc. *Res:* Coordination chemistry; reactions of coordinated ligands; biological activity of transition metal complexes. *Mailing Add:* Brigham Young Univ Hawaii Campus Dept of Phys Sci Laie HI 96762

WRATHALL, JEAN REW, b Brooklyn, NY, Dec 3, 42; m 60; c 2. GENETICS, CELL BIOLOGY. *Educ:* Univ Utah, BS, 64, PhD(genetics, molecular biol), 69. *Prof Exp:* Asst prof biol, State Univ NY Col Geneseo, 69-70; from instr to asst prof genetics, Med Col, Cornell Univ, 70-74; res assoc, 74-75, ASST PROF ANAT, MED COL, GEORGETOWN UNIV, 75- *Concurrent Pos:* Damon Runyon Mem Fund fel, Cornell Univ, 71- *Mem:* AAAS; Soc Develop Biol; Soc Cell Biologists; Tissue Cult Asn. *Res:* Control of differentiated function in eukaryotic cells in culture; abnormal functions in malignant cells in culture; 5-bromodeoxyuridine suppression of melanin synthesis and tumorigenicity of melanoma cells. *Mailing Add:* Dept of Anat Georgetown Univ Med Col Washington DC 20007

WRAY, GRANVILLE WAYNE, b Elk City, Okla, Dec 16, 41; m 65. CELL BIOLOGY, BIOCHEMISTRY. *Educ:* Phillips Univ, BS, 63; Okla State Univ, MS, 65; Univ Tex, PhD(cell biol), 70. *Prof Exp:* Res asst biochem, Okla State Univ, 63-65; res asst, Univ Tex M D Anderson Hosp & Tumor Inst, 65-66; ASST PROF CELL BIOL, BAYLOR COL MED, 72- *Concurrent Pos:* Damon Runyon Cancer res fel, McArdle Lab Cancer Res, Univ Wis-Madison, 71-72. *Honors & Awards:* Mike Hogg Award, 68. *Mem:* AAAS; Am Chem Soc; Am Soc Cell Biologists. *Res:* Isolation, morphology and biochemistry of the mammalian metaphase chromosome. *Mailing Add:* Dept of Cell Biol Baylor Col of Med Houston TX 77030

WRAY, JAMES DAVID, b Norton, Kans, Oct 3, 36; c 1. ASTRONOMY. *Educ:* Univ MNex, BS, 59; Univ Cincinnati, MS, 62; Northwestern Univ, PhD(astron), 66. *Prof Exp:* Res assoc meteoritics, Univ NMex, 62-64, dir, Inst Meteoritics, 66-67; asst prof astron, Northwestern Univ, 67-72; RES SCIENTIST ASTRON, UNIV TEX, AUSTIN, 72- *Concurrent Pos:* Consult, Boller & Chivens Div, Perkin-Elmer Corp, 73- *Mem:* Int Astron Union; Am Astron Soc. *Res:* Space astronomy, ultraviolet stellar spectroscopy; extra-galactic research, surface distribution of color in galaxies; digital image processing; numerical data base management and applications. *Mailing Add:* Dept of Astron Univ of Tex Austin TX 78712

WRAY, JOE D, b Conway, Ark, Sept 30, 26; m 51; c 5. MATERNAL & CHILD HEALTH, NUTRITION. *Educ:* Stanford Univ, BA, 47, MD, 52; Univ NC, MPH, 67; Am Bd Pediat, dipl. *Prof Exp:* Intern, Charity Hosp La, New Orleans, 51-52; intern & resident pediat, Grace-New Haven Community Hosp, Conn, 54-56; chief resident, Hacettepe Children's Hosp, Ankara, Turkey, 56-58, assoc pediatrician, 58-61; vis prof pediat, Fac Med, Univ Valle, Cali, Colombia, 61-66; vis prof community med & pediat, Ramathibodi Hosp Med Sch, Mahidol Univ, Bangkok, Thailand, 67-74; fel, Ctr Advan Study Behav Sci, 74-75; vis prof maternal & child health & int health, Harvard Sch Pub Health, 75-78, sr lectr, 78-81, head, Dept Pop Sci, 78-80, dir, Off Int Health Prog, 79-81; PROF CLIN PEDIAT, COL PHYSICIANS & SURGEONS & PROF CLIN PUB HEALTH, SCH PUB HEALTH, COLUMBIA UNIV, 81-, DEP DIR, CTR POP & FAMILY HEALTH, 81- *Concurrent Pos:* Mem field staff health & pop, Rockefeller Found, NY, 60-76. *Mem:* Fel Am Acad Pediat; Am Pub Health Asn. *Res:* Infant and preschool child nutrition; growth and development; nutrition and infection; delivery of health services to children in developing countries; family planning. *Mailing Add:* Ctr Pop & Family Health Columbia Univ 60 Haven Ave New York NY 10032

WRAY, JOHN LEE, b Charleston, WVa, July 10, 25; m 52; c 1. GEOLOGY. *Educ:* Univ WVa, BS, 50, MS, 51; Univ Wis, PhD(geol), 56. *Prof Exp:* Teaching asst geol, Univ WVa, 48-51; geologist, WVa State Hwy Dept, 51-53; res asst chem, Univ Wis, 53-56; RES ASSOC, RES CTR, MARATHON OIL CO, 56- *Concurrent Pos:* Adj prof geol, Colo Sch Mines, 70- *Mem:* Geol Soc Am; Paleont Soc; Am Asn Petrol Geologists; Soc Econ Paleont & Mineral. *Res:* Paleontology; fossil algae; carbonate sedimentology; biostratigraphy. *Mailing Add:* Marathon Oil Co Res Ctr PO Box 269 Littleton CO 80160

WRAY, STEPHEN DONALD, b Eng. ORDINARY DIFFERENTIAL EQUATIONS. *Educ:* Univ Adelaide, BSc, 67; Flinders Univ, BSc, 68, MSc, 69, PhD(math), 74. *Prof Exp:* Asst prof math, Carleton Univ, 77-78 & Mt Allison Univ, 78-81; ASST PROF MATH, ROYAL ROADS COL, VICTORIA, BC, 81- *Mem:* Can Appl Math Soc. *Res:* Ordinary differential equations associated with formally symmetric ordinary differential expressions of Sturm-Liouville type. *Mailing Add:* Dept Math Royal Roads Col Victoria BC V0S 1B0 Can

WRAY, VIRGINIA LEE POLLAN, b Grove, Okla, Mar 20, 40; m 65. BIOCHEMISTRY. *Educ:* Okla State Univ, BS, 62, MS, 66; Univ Tex Grad Sch Biomed Sci Houston, PhD(biochem), 70. *Prof Exp:* Res asst biochem virol, Col Med, Baylor Univ, 66; RES ASST PROF CELL BIOL, BAYLOR COL MED, 73- *Concurrent Pos:* Fel, McArdle Lab Cancer Res, Univ Wis-Madison, 70-72. *Mem:* Am Soc Cell Biologists; Am Chem Soc. *Res:* Membrane biochemistry; composition and function of nuclear and plasma membranes. *Mailing Add:* Dept of Cell Biol Baylor Col of Med Houston TX 77030

WREDE, DON EDWARD, b Cincinnati, Ohio, Feb 13, 30; m 50; c 5. MEDICAL PHYSICS, BIOPHYSICS. *Educ:* Univ Cincinnati, BS, 57, MS, 60, PhD(biophys), 63; Am Bd Radiol, cert, 74. *Prof Exp:* Tech engr, Gen Elec Co, Ohio, 48-54; lectr physics, Univ Cincinnati, 58-62; assoc prof & chmn dept, Heidelberg Col, 62-66; Fulbright lectr, Cheng Kung Univ, Taiwan, 66-68; asst prof radiation med, A B Chandler Med Ctr, Univ Ky, Lexington, 69-72, assoc prof & chief clin physicist, 72-78, radiol physicist, 69-78. *Concurrent Pos:* NIH res fel, Radioisotope Lab, Gen Hosp, Univ Cincinnati, 68-69; med physics liaison, Australia & Taiwan, 74-78; vis lectr, Bowling Green State Univ, 63-64; vis scientist, NSF, 69-72. *Mem:* Am Soc Therapeut Radiol; Am Asn Physicists in Med; Radiol Soc NAm; Am Col Radiol; Bioelectromagnetic Soc. *Res:* Medical radiation dosimetry, particularly the study of irregular shaped fields from teletherapy devices; chemical protection from radiation; mathematical models of biological systems, particularly the endocrine. *Mailing Add:* King Faisal Spec Hosp & Res Ctr PO Box 3354 Riyad Saudi Arabia

WREDE, ROBERT C, JR, b Cincinnati, Ohio, Oct 19, 26; m 48; c 3. MATHEMATICS. *Educ:* Miami Univ, Ohio, BS, 49, MA, 50; Ind Univ, PhD(math), 56. *Prof Exp:* Instr math, Miami Univ, Ohio, 50-51; from instr to assoc prof, 55-63, PROF MATH, CALIF STATE UNIV, SAN JOSE, 63- *Concurrent Pos:* Consult phys & res lab, Int Bus Mach Corp, Calif, 56-58; Hunter's Point Radiation Lab, 60. *Mem:* Am Math Soc; Math Asn Am; Tensor Soc. *Res:* Relativity theory; differential geometry; vector and tensor analysis. *Mailing Add:* Dept of Math McQuarry Hall Calif State Univ San Jose CA 95114

WREFORD, STANLEY S, b Detroit, Mich, Mar 18, 49; m 67; c 1. CATALYTIC CHEMISTRY, CARBOXYLATION CHEMISTRY. *Educ:* Univ Mich, BS, 70; Mass Inst Technol, PhD(inorg chem), 74. *Prof Exp:* Asst prof inorg chem, Harvard Univ, 74-78, Univ Toronto, 78-80; GROUP LEADER INORG CHEM, E I DU PONT DE NEMOURS & CO, INC, 80- *Mem:* Am Chem Soc. *Res:* Homogeneous catalysis of carboxylation reactions. *Mailing Add:* Cent Res & Develop Dept E I Du Pont de Nemours & Co Inc Wilmington DE 19898

WREN, HENRY K, b Loganton, Pa, July 26, 26; m 61. ORGANIC CHEMISTRY. *Educ:* Fremont Col, BS, 56; Milan Polytech Inst, PhD(chem), 60; Am Inst Chemists, PC-A. *Prof Exp:* Head, Resin Dept, Perfection Paint & Chem Co, 60-61; chemist, Am Art Clay Co, 61-62; head sect, Sherwin-Williams Res Ctr, 62-64; dir res, Baltimore Paint & Chem Corp, 64-66; mat engr, RCA Magnetic Prod, 67; chemist, Naval Avionics Facil, Ind, 67-69 & Wren Res & Develop Corp, Mich, 69-70; mem staff, Sargent Paint, 70-75; chief chemist IVC Industrial Coatings, 76-77; chief chemist trade sales, Perfection Paint & Color Co, 76-77; group supvr chem coatings, Standard T-Chem Co, 75-77, instr paint technol, 77-78, group supvr resins, 78-80; MEM STAFF, ALLERTON CHEM DIV, VOPLEX CORP, ROCHESTER, NY, 80- *Concurrent Pos:* Teacher, Purdue Univ, Indianapolis, 68-69 & Ind Cent Col, 68-69. *Mem:* AAAS; fel Am Inst Chemists; Am Chem Soc; Info Coun Fabric Flammability. *Res:* Polymers; organic synthesis. *Mailing Add:* Allerton Chem Div Voplex Corp 763 Linden Ave Rochester NY 14625

WRENN, MCDONALD EDWARD, b New York, NY, Apr 16, 36; m 67; c 2. ENVIRONMENTAL HEALTH, RADIOLOGICAL HEALTH. *Educ:* Princeton Univ, AB, 58; NY Univ, MS, 62, PhD(nuclear eng, environ health), 67. *Prof Exp:* Res scientist, 62-67, from instr to asst prof, 67-72, biomed scientist radiobiol, Div Biomed & Environ Res, US Energy Res & Develop Admin, 73-75; ASSOC PROF ENVIRON MED, MED CTR, NY UNIV, 72- *Concurrent Pos:* Mem, Nat Coun Radiation Protection & Measurements, 71-; mem & former chmn N-13 comt, Am Nat Standards Inst, 72- *Mem:* Radiation Res Soc; Health Physics Soc; fel Am Pub Health Asn; Am Inst Biol Sci; Am Indust Hygiene Asn. *Res:* Biological effects of environmental agents on man and animals, particularly radiations and radioactive materials; environmental cycling and transport of trace and radioactive elements; mammalian metabolism of actinides and development of environmental radiation detection instruments. *Mailing Add:* Dept of Environ Med 550 First Ave New York NY 10016

WRENSCH, DANA LOUISE, b Greenwood, Miss, Oct 3, 46; m 74; c 2. ACAROLOGY, GENETICS. *Educ:* Ohio State Univ, BSc, 68, MS, 70, PhD(genetics), 72. *Prof Exp:* NIH trainee, 72-75, ADJ ASST PROF ENTOM, OHIO STATE UNIV, 78-; ASST PROF BOT & BACTERIOL, OHIO WESLEYAN UNIV, 81- *Concurrent Pos:* Consult, IBP, 72 & 73, Ministry Educ & Cult, Brazil, 78; lectr genetics, Ohio State Univ, 82. *Mem:* AAAS; Acarol Soc Am; Am Genetic Asn; Entom Soc Am. *Res:* Population biology and genetics of spider mites. *Mailing Add:* Arcarol Lab 484 W 12th Ave Ohio State Univ Columbus OH 43210

WRIDE, W(ILLIAM) JAMES, b Garfield, Wash, Dec 3, 21; m 48; c 3. CHEMICAL ENGINEERING. *Educ:* State Col Wash, BS, 43, MS, 46; Iowa State Col, PhD(chem eng), 48. *Prof Exp:* Asst chem & chem eng, State Col Wash, 41-42; co-owner, mgr & consult engr, Ames Eng & Testing Serv, 48-51; chem & process engr, 52-66, mgr chem eng fundamentals br, Res & Develop Dept, 66-72, mgr eng res br, 72-74, process technol consult, 74-77, MGR, ENG & TECHNOL, ENERGY MINERALS DIV, PHILLIPS PETROLEUM CO, 78- *Mem:* Am Inst Chem Engrs. *Res:* Mercaptan formation in petroleum distillates; polyolefin resin process development; petrochemical process optimization; kinetics and mass transfer; process design and economic evaluation; research and development of alternate energy sources. *Mailing Add:* 1353 S Keeler Bartlesville OK 74003

WRIEDE, PETER ARTUR, b Grossenhain, Ger, Jan 27, 44; US citizen; m 67; c 3. ORGANIC CHEMISTRY. *Educ:* Columbia Univ, AB, 65, MA, 66, PhD(chem), 69. *Prof Exp:* chemist, 69-74, res supvr, 74-77, TECH SERV SUPVR, E I DU PONT DE NEMOURS & CO, INC, 77- *Mem:* Am Chem Soc. *Res:* Photochemistry; photochemical pathways for reaction in solution and in the solid state. *Mailing Add:* E I du Pont de Nemours & Co Chestnut Run Wilmington DE 19898

WRIEDT, HENRY ANDERSON, b Melbourne, Australia, Feb 6, 28; nat US; m 53 & 60; c 3. PHYSICAL CHEMISTRY, METALS. *Educ:* Univ Melbourne, BMetE, 49; Mass Inst Technol, ScD(metall), 54. *Prof Exp:* Asst metall, Mass Inst Technol, 49-53; technologist, Appl Res Lab, 53-55, scientist, Edgar C Bain Lab Fund Res, 55-66, sr scientist, 66-72, sr scientist, Res Lab, 72-76, ASSOC RES CONSULT, RES LAB, US STEEL CORP, 76- *Mem:* Am Inst Mining, Metall & Petrol Eng. *Res:* Physical chemistry of metals; phase equlibria and gas-metal reactions in ferrous systems; thermodynamics of metallic systems. *Mailing Add:* US Steel Corp Res Lab Monroeville PA 15146

WRIGHT, ALAN CARL, b Bangor, Maine, Aug 16, 39; m 64; c 2. CHEMISTRY. *Educ:* Univ Maine, Orono, BS, 61; Univ Fla, PhD(chem), 66. *Prof Exp:* Res chemist, Cent Res Div, Am Cyanamid Co, 66-69; asst prof chem, 70-76, chmn dept earth & phys sci, 75-78, ASSOC PROF CHEM, EASTERN CONN STATE COL, 76- *Mem:* Am Chem Soc; Sigma Xi; AAAS. *Res:* Development of new laboratory experiments for organic chemistry involving compounds of biological interest; synthesis of organic fluorine compounds. *Mailing Add:* Dept of Phys Sci Eastern Conn State Col Willimantic CT 06226

WRIGHT, ALDEN HALBERT, b Missoula, Mont, Apr 23, 42; m 67; c 2. HOMOTOPY METHODS. *Educ:* Dartmouth Col, BA, 64; Univ Wis-Madison, PhD(math), 69. *Prof Exp:* Vis asst prof math, Univ Utah, 69-70; asst prof, 70-74, assoc prof, 74-81, PROF MATH, WESTERN MICH UNIV, 81- *Mem:* Math Prog Soc; Inst Mgt Sci; Am Math Soc. *Res:* Piecewise linear and differentiable homotopy mehtods for fixed point computation and solution of systems of nonlinear equations; finding all solutions to a system of polynomial equations; linear programming. *Mailing Add:* Dept of Math Western Mich Univ Kalamazoo MI 49008

WRIGHT, ANDREW, b Edinburgh, Scotland, Jan 28, 35; m 57; c 2. MOLECULAR BIOLOGY. *Educ:* Univ Edinburgh, BSc, 57, PhD(biochem), 60. *Prof Exp:* Fel biochem, Univ Minn, 60-62; fel biol, Mass Inst Technol, 63-67; PROF MOLECULAR BIOL, MED SCH, TUFTS UNIV, 67- *Mem:* Fedn Am Socs Exp Biol. *Res:* Structure and function of bacterial cell membranes and mechanisms of DNA replication. *Mailing Add:* Dept of Molecular Biol Tufts Univ Med Sch Boston MA 02111

WRIGHT, ANN ELIZABETH, b Mooringsport, La, Feb 20, 22; m 40; c 1. RADIOLOGICAL PHYSICS, BIOPHYSICS. *Educ:* Univ Houston, BA, 65; Univ Tex M D Anderson Hosp & Tumor Inst Houston, MS, 67, PhD(radiol physics), 70. *Prof Exp:* Instr radiol, Baylor Col Med, 68-70, asst prof radiol physics, 70-75; ASSOC PROF RADIOL, UNIV TEX MED BR GALVESTON, 75- *Concurrent Pos:* Consult physicist radiother, Vet Admin Hosp, Houston. *Mem:* Am Inst Physics; Am Asn Physicist in Med (treas, 73-75). *Res:* Radiological physics measurements using solid state devices; interaction of radiation with molecules and penetration in inhomogeneous mediums. *Mailing Add:* Dept of Radiol Univ of Tex Med Br Galveston TX 77550

WRIGHT, ANTHONY AUNE, b Los Angeles, Calif, Jan 4, 43; m 65. ANIMAL BEHAVIOR, PSYCHOPHYSICS. *Educ:* Stanford Univ, BA, 65; Columbia Univ, MA, 70, PhD(psychol), 71. *Prof Exp:* Instr psychol, Columbia Univ, 69-71; asst prof, Univ Tex, Austin, 71-72, asst prof, 72-76, ASSOC PROF NEURAL SCI, SENSORY SCI CTR, UNIV TEX HEALTH SCI CTR, HOUSTON, 76- *Mem:* Psychonomic Soc; Asn Res Vision & Ophthal; Sigma Xi. *Res:* Animal sensory processes; discrimination learning; theoretical psychophysics; color vision. *Mailing Add:* Sensory Sci Ctr UT Health Sci Ctr Tex Med Ctr 6420 Lamar Fleming Ave Houston TX 77030

WRIGHT, ARCHIBALD NELSON, b Toronto, Ont, May 22, 32; m 55; c 3. PHYSICAL CHEMISTRY. *Educ:* McGill Univ, BSc, 53, PhD, 57. *Prof Exp:* Grace Chem fel with Prof F S Dainton, Univ Leeds, 57-59; res fel with Prof C A Winkler, McGill Univ, 59-63; phys chemist, 63-68, mgr photochem br, Chem Lab, 68-72, mgr reactions & processes br, 72-73, mgr planning & resources, Mat Sci & Eng, Res & Develop Ctr, Gen Elec Co, 73-78; VPRES & DIR RES & DEVELOP, CARLEW CHEM LTD, MONTREAL, 78- *Mem:* Am Chem Soc; Am Phys Soc; Royal Soc Chem; NY Acad Sci; Chem Inst Can. *Res:* Gas phase kinetics, especially reactions of hydrogen and nitrogen atoms and excited nitrogen molecules; anionic polymerization; reactions at clean metal surfaces; photolysis; photopolymerization; polymer chemistry. *Mailing Add:* Carlew Chem Ltd 177 St Andre St St Remi de Napierville PQ J8G 1Z7 Can

WRIGHT, ARTHUR GILBERT, b Carthage, Ill, Jan 22, 09; m. ZOOLOGY. *Educ:* Carthage Col, AB, 32; Univ Ill, MS, 47. *Prof Exp:* Zoologist, Ill State Mus, 33-37; Rockefeller fel & mus asst, Biol Sect, Buffalo Mus Sci, 37-38; cur, Ill State Mus, 39-53 & exhibits, State Mus Fla, 53-60; supv exhibits specialist, Nat Park Serv, 61-63; asst chief, Off Exhibits, 63-69, sr museologist, 69-72, spec asst to dir, 72-73, writer ed, Off Exhibits Cent, 74-75, coordr mus studies, 77-78, CONSULT, NAT MUS NATURAL HIST, SMITHSONIAN INST, 75-; ASSOC PROF LECTR, DEPT ANTHROP, GEORGE WASHINGTON UNIV, 72- *Concurrent Pos:* Ed bd Sci Activities, 76- *Mem:* AAAS; Am Asn Mus; Philos Sci Asn. *Res:* Museum exhibit planning. *Mailing Add:* 12201 Galway Dr Silver Spring MD 20904

WRIGHT, BARBARA EVELYN, b Pasadena, Calif, Apr 6, 26; m 51; c 3. BIOCHEMISTRY, DIFFERENTIATION. *Educ:* Stanford Univ, PhD(microbiol), 51. *Prof Exp:* Biologist, Nat Heart Inst, 53-61; res assoc, Huntington Labs, Mass Gen Hosp, 61-67; res dir, Boston Biomed Res Inst, 67-82, RES PROF, DEPT MICROBIOL, UNIV MONT, 82- *Concurrent Pos:* Nat Res Coun fel, Carlsberg Lab, Copenhagen, Denmark, 50-51, Childs Mem Fund fel, 51-52; tutor, Harvard Univ & assoc prof, Harvard Med Sch; ed ann rev microbiol, Exp Mycol & J Bact; Found for Microbiol lectr, 70-71; Consult, Miles Lab, 80- *Mem:* Am Soc Biol Chem; Am Soc Microbiol. *Res:* Biochemical basis of differentiation in the slime mold; kinetic modelling of metabolic networks in steady state and while undergoing transitions, as in aging and development. *Mailing Add:* Microbiol Dept Univ Mont Missoula MT 59801

WRIGHT, BILL C, b Waterford, Miss, June 15, 30; m 59; c 3. SOIL SCIENCE. *Educ:* Miss State Univ, BS, 52, MS, 56; Cornell Univ, PhD(soil sci), 59. *Prof Exp:* From asst prof to assoc prof soil sci, Miss State Univ, 59-64; assoc soil scientist to assoc dir, Indian Agr Prog Rockefeller Found, 64-70, agr proj leader, Turkey, 70-77, PROG OFFICER AFRICA & MIDDLE EAST, INT AGR DEVELOP SERV, NEW YORK, 77- *Concurrent Pos:* Mem, Bd Sci & Technol for Int Develop, Nat Acad Sci, 80- *Mem:* Int Soc Soil Sci; Am Soc Agron; Soil Sci Soc Am; Indian Soc Agron; Indian Soil Sci Soc. *Res:* Soil-phosphorus reactions products; phosphate components of fertilizers; evaluation techniques for fertilizers in field and laboratory; fertilizer use and cultural management of cereal crops in India; wheat production in areas of low rainfall; organization and management of agricultural research and production in developing countries. *Mailing Add:* Int Agr Develop Serv 1133 Ave of Americas New York NY 10036

WRIGHT, BRADFORD LAWRENCE, b Colfax, Wash, May 10, 40; m 61; c 2. PHYSICS. *Educ:* Reed Col, BA, 61; Mass Inst Technol, PhD(physics), 67. *Prof Exp:* Asst prof physics, Mass Inst Technol, 67-70 & Middlebury Col, 70-74; MEM STAFF, LOS ALAMOS SCI LAB, 74- *Mem:* Am Phys Soc; Am Asn Physics Teachers. *Res:* Plasma physics; gaseous electronic. *Mailing Add:* MS 648 Los Alamos Sci Lab Los Alamos NM 87545

WRIGHT, BYRON TERRY, b Waco Tex, Oct 19, 17; wid; c 3. NUCLEAR PHYSICS. *Educ:* Rice Univ, BA, 38; Univ Calif, Berkeley, PhD(physics), 41. *Prof Exp:* Physicist, Navy Radio & Sound Lab, Calif, 41-42 & Manhattan Dist, Calif, Tenn & NMex, 42-46; from asst prof to assoc prof, 46-56, PROF PHYSICS, UNIV CALIF, LOS ANGELES, 56- *Concurrent Pos:* Fulbright res scholar, 56-57; Guggenheim fel, 63-64; Ford Found fel, Europ Orgn Nuclear Res, 63-64. *Mem:* Am Phys Soc. *Res:* Accelerators; nuclear structure. *Mailing Add:* Dept of Physics Univ of Calif Los Angeles CA 90024

WRIGHT, CHARLES CATHBERT, b Hanford, Calif, Dec 18, 19; m 41; c 3. CHEMISTRY. *Educ:* Univ Calif, Los Angeles, BA, 41. *Prof Exp:* Chemist, A R Maas Chem Co, 46-47, res chemist, 47-48; independent consult, 48-49; gen mgr, Oilwell Res, Inc, 49-50, pres, 50-72, chmn bd, 72-74; tech advr, Eng Dept, 74-77, SR ENG CONSULT, ARABIAN AM OIL CO, 77- *Concurrent Pos:* Lectr, Univ Southern Calif, 57-; pres, Am Coun Independent Labs, 64-66; dir water technol, Rhodes Corp, 66-68. *Honors & Awards:* Max Hecht Award, 77. *Mem:* Am Chem Soc; Am Water Works Asn; Am Inst Chemists; Am Soc Testing & Mat; Soc Petrol Eng. *Res:* Treatment of drilling fluids and the chemistry of oilwell production; oilfield corrosion control; water for subsurface injection. *Mailing Add:* PO Box 1151 San Ysidro CA 92073

WRIGHT, CHARLES DEAN, b Yankton, SDak, June 25, 30; m 52; c 4. POLYMER CHEMISTRY. *Educ:* Augustana Col, SDak, BA, 52; Univ Minn, PhD(org chem), 56. *Prof Exp:* Instr org chem, Univ Minn, 55-56; res chemist, 56-64, mgr res & new prod groups, 64-77, SR RES SPECIALIST, ADHESIVES, COATINGS & SEALERS DIV, 3M Co 77- *Mem:* Am Chem Soc. *Res:* Stereospecific polymers; oxidizers for rocket fuels; general polymer chemistry; adhesive compounding and testing; adhesion; new business development; relationships of science and Christianity; epoxy chemistry; cyanoacrylate chemistry. *Mailing Add:* 14 Oakridge Dr White Bear Lake MN 55110

WRIGHT, CHARLES GERALD, b Boynton, Pa, June 12, 30; m 53; c 1. ENTOMOLOGY. *Educ:* Univ Md, BS, 51, MS, 53; NC State Univ, PhD(entom), 58. *Prof Exp:* Entomologist, Wilson Pest Control, 58-63; from asst prof to assoc prof, 63-75, PROF ENTOM, NC STATE UNIV, 75- *Concurrent Pos:* Vchmn NC struct pest control comt. *Mem:* Entom Soc Am. *Res:* Urban and industrial entomology; cockroaches; rodent control. *Mailing Add:* Box 5215 NC State Univ Raleigh NC 27650

WRIGHT, CHARLES HUBERT, b Appleton City, Mo, Oct 30, 22; m 52; c 5. ANALYTICAL CHEMISTRY. *Educ:* Univ Mo, PhD(chem), 52. *Prof Exp:* Instr anal chem, Univ Mo, 52-54; chemist, US Radium Corp, 54-58; anal group leader, Spencer Chem Co, 58-66; supvr anal sect, Gulf Res & Develop Co, 66-71; sr res chemist, 71-80, RES ASSOC, PITTSBURG & MIDWAY COAL MINING CO, 80- *Mem:* AAAS; Am Chem Soc. *Res:* Analytical chemistry of fertilizers, herbicides, polymers and fuels. *Mailing Add:* Pittsburg & Midway Coal Mining Co 9009 W 67th St Merriam KS 66202

WRIGHT, CHARLES JOSEPH, b Montour Falls, NY, May 27, 38. ORGANIC MASS SPECTROMETRY. *Educ:* Univ Rochester, BS, 60; Mass Inst Technol, MS, 62. *Prof Exp:* Res chemist, 64-70, SR RES CHEMIST, RES LABS, EASTMAN KODAK CO, 70- *Mem:* Am Chem Soc; Am Soc Mass Spectrometry. *Res:* Synthetic organic chemistry; mass spectrometry of organic compounds; chemical modification of gelatin. *Mailing Add:* 1210 Majestic Way Webster NY 14580

WRIGHT, CHARLES R B, b Lincoln, Nebr, Jan 11, 37; div; c 2. ALGEBRA. *Educ:* Univ Nebr, BA, 56, MA, 57; Univ Wis, PhD(math), 59. *Prof Exp:* Res fel math, Calif Inst Technol, 59-60, instr, 60-61; from asst prof to assoc prof, 61-72, assoc dean, Col Liberal Arts, 73-77, PROF MATH, UNIV ORE, 72- *Concurrent Pos:* Vis prof math, Mich State Univ, 77. *Mem:* Am Math Soc; Math Asn Am. *Res:* Finite groups. *Mailing Add:* Dept of Math Univ of Ore Eugene OR 97403

WRIGHT, CHRISTINE SCHUBERT, molecular biology, structural chemistry, see previous edition

WRIGHT, CLARENCE PAUL, b Cliffside, NC, Apr 15, 39. GENETICS. *Educ:* Lenoir-Rhyne Col, BS, 62; Univ Utah, MS, 65, PhD(genetics), 68. *Prof Exp:* ASSOC PROF BIOL, WESTERN CAROLINA UNIV, 68- *Mem:* Genetics Soc Am. *Res:* Developmental genetics. *Mailing Add:* Dept of Biol Western Carolina Univ Cullowhee NC 28723

WRIGHT, DAVID ANTHONY, b Baltimore, Md, Aug 19, 41; m 62; c 3. DEVELOPMENTAL BIOLOGY, GENETICS. *Educ:* Univ Md, College Park, BS, 63; Univ Ill, Urbana, MS, 65; Wash Univ, PhD(biol), 68. *Prof Exp:* NIH fel med genetics, Univ Tex M D Anderson Hosp & Tumor Inst Houston, 68-70; asst prof biol, Univ Tex Grad Sch Biomed Sci Houston, 70-75; assoc biologist & asst prof biol, Univ Tex Cancer Ctr, M D Anderson Hosp & Tumor Inst, 75-80. *Mem:* AAAS; Am Soc Zoologists; Soc Develop Biol. *Res:* Patterns and control of gene expression during embryogenesis, especially of enzyme phenotypes in nuclear-cytoplasmic hybrids in amphibians. *Mailing Add:* 3906 Cheryl Lynne Houston TX 77045

WRIGHT, DAVID FRANKLIN, b Quincy, Mass, Feb 19, 29; m 52; c 1. PHYSICAL CHEMISTRY. *Educ:* Tufts Univ, BS, 51; Ohio State Univ, PhD(chem), 57. *Prof Exp:* PROF BASIC SCI & CHMN DEPT, MASS MARITIME ACAD, 69- *Mem:* Am Chem Soc. *Res:* Low temperature thermodynamics; clathrates of hydroquinone. *Mailing Add:* Dept of Basic Sci Mass Maritime Acad Buzzards Bay MA 02532

WRIGHT, DAVID GRANT, b Am Fork, Utah, Aug 21, 46; m 70; c 2. TOPOLOGY. *Educ:* Brigham Young Univ, BA, 70; Univ Wis-Madison, MA, 72, PhD(math), 73. *Prof Exp:* Lectr math, Univ Wis-Madison, 74; fel math, Mich State Univ, 74-76; ASST PROF, UTAH STATE UNIV, 76- *Mem:* Am Math Soc. *Res:* Geometric topology including piecewise linear topology and topological embeddings in manifolds. *Mailing Add:* Dept of Math Utah State Univ Logan UT 84322

WRIGHT, DAVID LEE, b Mattoon, Ill, Dec 1, 49; m 69; c 1. MATHEMATICS. *Educ:* David Lipscomb Col, BA, 71; Columbia Univ, MS, 73, PhD(math), 75. *Prof Exp:* Asst prof math, 75-81, ASSOC PROF MATH, WASH UNIV, 81- *Mem:* Sigma Xi; Am Math Soc. *Res:* Behavior of polynomial algebras, their automorphisms, their stable structure. *Mailing Add:* Dept of Math Wash Univ St Louis MO 63130

WRIGHT, DAVID PATRICK, b Pocahontas, Ark, Apr 11, 43; m 75. NUCLEAR PHYSICS. *Educ:* St Edward's Univ, BS, 65; Univ Tex, Austin, PhD(nuclear physics), 74. *Prof Exp:* Instr math, Univ Tex, Austin, 75-76; vis asst prof physics, Univ Southwestern La, 76-77; ASST PROF PHYSICS & MATH, ST EDWARD'S UNIV, 77- *Mem:* Am Phys Soc. *Res:* Nuclear structure; medical physics; energy studies. *Mailing Add:* Dept of Phys & Biol Sci PO Box 597 Austin TX 78704

WRIGHT, DENNIS CHARLES, b Flint, Mich, Oct 14, 39. NEUROSCIENCES. *Educ:* Univ Mich, Ann Arbor, BA, 60; Univ Calif, Berkeley, PhD(psychol), 69. *Prof Exp:* Asst prof, 68-73, ASSOC PROF PSYCHOL, UNIV MO-COLUMBIA, 73-, ASSOC CHAIR PSYCHOL, 81- *Mem:* Behav Teratology Soc; Psychonomic Soc. *Res:* Psychopharmacology; behavioral toxicology/teratology; biochemistry and electrophysiology of learning and memory. *Mailing Add:* Dept of Psychol Univ of Mo Columbia MO 65211

WRIGHT, DEXTER V(AIL), b Milford, Conn, Sept 12, 23; m 44; c 2. MECHANICAL ENGINEERING. *Educ:* Univ Conn, BSEE, 44; Univ Pittsburgh, MSEE, 47. *Prof Exp:* Res engr, 44-61, fel engr, 61-66, engr in charge mech vibrations, 66-67, MGR DYNAMICS, WESTINGHOUSE RES & DEVELOP CTR, 67- *Concurrent Pos:* Mem, Am Nat Standards S2 Comt. *Mem:* Am Soc Mech Engrs; Acoust Soc Am. *Res:* Vibration of machines and structures; noise control and acoustics; vibration and acoustic instrumentation; structural vibration due to fluid flow. *Mailing Add:* 104 Kings Dale Rd Pittsburgh PA 15221

WRIGHT, DONALD N, b Provo, Utah, Dec 6, 35; m 57; c 4. BACTERIOLOGY, BIOCHEMISTRY. *Educ:* Univ Utah, BS, 58; Iowa State Univ, PhD(bact), 64. *Prof Exp:* Chief bacteriologist & head serol div, Philadelphia Naval Hosp, Pa, 60-62; res bacteriologist, Naval Biol Lab, Calif, 64-69; assoc prof, 69-74, PROF MICROBIOL, BRIGHAM YOUNG UNIV, 74- *Mem:* AAAS; Am Soc Microbiol; Brit Soc Gen Microbiol; Am Oil Chem Soc. *Res:* Physiology of microorganisms, particularly growth, inhibition, taxonomy and aerosol behavior of the Mycoplasma; biochemical responses and growth rate control of microorganisms as a function of their environment. *Mailing Add:* Dept of Microbiol Brigham Young Univ Provo UT 84602

WRIGHT, DOUGLAS TYNDALL, civil engineering, see previous edition

WRIGHT, EDWARD KENNETH, b Bluefields, Nicaragua, Nov 9, 30; US citizen; m 58; c 2. OPERATIONS ANALYSIS, INDUSTRIAL MANAGEMENT. *Educ:* Mass Inst Technol, BS, 52; Carnegie Inst Technol, MS, 61. *Prof Exp:* Dept asst, Missile Div, NAm Aviation, Inc, 55-57; mech engr, Bettis Atomic Power Lab, Westinghouse Elec Corp, 57-59; consult, Westinghouse Elec Corp, 59-61; mech engr, Anal Serv, Inc, 61-64; engr, Sperry Rand Systs Group, Sperry Gyroscope Co, 64-65; mech engr, Anal Serv, Inc, 65-69; asst dir systs anal, 69-70, assoc dir syst definition, 70-71, staff engr strategic anal, 71-73, dir minuteman/site defense integration, Develop Planning Div, 73-75, prog mgr planning, Environ Energy Conserv Div, 76-81, PROF ENGR & STRATEGIC PETROL RES DIR, AEROSPACE CORP, 81- *Concurrent Pos:* Fel Ctr for Advan Eng Study, Mass Inst Technol, 75-76. *Mem:* AAAS; Inst Mgt Sci; Opers Res Soc Am; Am Nuclear Soc. *Res:* Nuclear reactors for submarines; operations analysis, operations research, cost-effectiveness analysis and weapon systems evaluation for present and proposed strategic aerospace systems and strategic planning. *Mailing Add:* Aerospace Corp 20030 Century Blvd Germantown MD 20767

WRIGHT, ELISABETH MURIEL JANE, b Ottawa, Ont, July 28, 26; m 58; c 3. MATHEMATICS. *Educ:* Univ Toronto, BA, 49, MA, 50, cert, 51; Wash Univ, PhD(educ), 57. *Prof Exp:* Specialist schs, Ont, 51-55; asst prof educ, Wash Univ, 57-61, asst prof math, 59-61; from asst prof to assoc prof, 63-72, PROF MATH, CALIF STATE UNIV, NORTHRIDGE, 72- *Concurrent Pos:* Consult, Santa Barbara Schs, 61-62 & Minn Nat Lab, State Dept Educ, 62-67. *Mem:* AAAS; Math Asn Am; Am Educ Res Asn. *Res:* Psychological problems in mathematics education; curriculum development. *Mailing Add:* Dept Math Calif State Univ Northridge CA 91324

WRIGHT, EVERETT JAMES, b Meriden, Conn, Sept 20, 29; m 51; c 1. ORGANIC CHEMISTRY. *Educ:* Hobart Col, BS, 51; Univ Del, MS, 54, PhD(chem), 57. *Prof Exp:* Chemist, Olin Industs, 51-52; RES CHEMIST, E I DU PONT DE NEMOURS & CO, 57- *Mem:* Am Chem Soc. *Res:* Organic nitrogen heterocycles; aliphatic nitrogen compounds; polymerization; textile chemicals; application techniques; fibers and fabrics; personnel and industrial relations. *Mailing Add:* 2615 Bardell Dr Wilmington DE 19808

WRIGHT, FARRIN SCOTT, b Fallston, NC, Dec 3, 36; m 57; c 3. AGRICULTURAL ENGINEERING, PLANT SCIENCE. *Educ:* Clemson Univ, BS, 59, MS, 61; NC State Univ, PhD(agr eng), 66. *Prof Exp:* Res asst agr eng, Clemson Univ, 57-59; res instr, NC State Univ, 60-66; AGR ENGR, USDA, 66- *Concurrent Pos:* Fel prog, Nat Cotton Coun, 59-60; mem, Suffolk City Sch Bd, 77- *Mem:* Am Soc Agr Engrs; Sigma Xi; Am Peanut Res & Educ Soc. *Res:* Agricultural research, development of concepts and improvement of peanut production equipment and peanut harvesting machinery. *Mailing Add:* USDA PO Box 7098 Suffolk VA 23437

WRIGHT, FARROLL TIM, b Hume, Mo, June 24, 41; m 65; c 4. STATISTICS, MATHEMATICS. *Educ:* Univ Mo, AB, 63, AM, 64, PhD(statist), 68. *Prof Exp:* Asst prof math, Univ Mo-Rolla, 67-68; asst prof statist, Univ Iowa, 68-71, assoc prof, 71-75; assoc prof math, 75-78, PROF MATH, UNIV MO-ROLLA, 78- *Mem:* Am Statist Asn; Inst Math Statist. *Res:* Order restricted inference; behavior of sums of independent variables; reliability and life testing. *Mailing Add:* Rolla MO

WRIGHT, FRANCIS HOWELL, b New York, NY, Jan 30, 08; m 69; c 2. PEDIATRICS. *Educ:* Haverford Col, BS, 29; Johns Hopkins Univ, MD, 33; Am Bd Pediat, dipl, 41. *Hon Degrees:* DMSc, Haverford Col, 80. *Prof Exp:* Asst pediat, Johns Hopkins Univ, 34-35; asst, Columbia Univ, 35-36, instr, 36-38; from asst prof to prof, Sch Med, Univ Chicago, 40-73, chmn dept, 46-62; exec secy, Am Bd Pediat, 69-77; RETIRED. *Concurrent Pos:* Fel bact & path, Rockefeller Inst, 38-40; mem, Am Bd Pediat, 62-67, from vpres to pres, 64-67. *Honors & Awards:* Jacoby Award, 80. *Mem:* AAAS; Am Pediat Soc; Soc Pediat Res (vpres, 52); Am Acad Pediat. *Res:* Virology; infant care; psychologic adjustment of infants and children. *Mailing Add:* 5739 Kimbark Ave Chicago IL 60637

WRIGHT, FRANCIS STUART, b Pittsfield, Mass, Feb 24, 29; m 58; c 4. PEDIATRIC NEUROLOGY. *Educ:* Univ Mass, BS, 51; Univ Rochester, MD, 55; Am Bd Pediat, dipl, 64; Am Bd Psychiat & Neurol, dipl & cert neurol, 66, cert child neurol, 72. *Prof Exp:* From asst prof to assoc prof, 68-76, PROF PEDIAT & NEUROL, MED CTR, UNIV MINN, MINNEAPOLIS, 76- *Concurrent Pos:* Fel pediat, Med Ctr, Univ Minn, Minneapolis, 56-58, Nat Inst Neurol Dis & Blindness spec fel pediat neurol, 60-63; consult, Minneapolis Pub Sch Syst, 65-; assoc, Grad Fac, Univ Minn, 67- *Res:* Developmental electrophysiology. *Mailing Add:* Dept of Neurol Univ of Minn Med Ctr Minneapolis MN 55455

WRIGHT, FRED BOYER, b Roanoke, Va, Dec 14, 25; m 48; c 2. MATHEMATICS. *Educ:* Univ NC, BA, 47, MA, 48; Univ Chicago, PhD(math), 53. *Prof Exp:* Instr math, Univ NC, 48-49; sr mathematician adv bd simulation, Univ Chicago, 53-54, consult systs res; from instr to prof math, Tulane Univ, 54-68; chmn dept, 68-76, PROF MATH, UNIV NC, CHAPEL HILL, 68- *Concurrent Pos:* Vis prof, Cambridge Univ, 58-59 & Northwestern Univ, 63; Sloan Found fel, 58-62; chmn comt regional develop, Nat Acad Sci-Nat Res Coun, 69-71, pregrad fel panel, 71-72; mem math adv panel, NSF, 71-; pregrad fel panel (chmn, 73-74), 71-74; actg chmn opers res curric, Univ NC, Chapel Hill, 72. *Mem:* Am Math Soc; Math Asn Am; London Math Soc. *Res:* Algebra; functional analysis; history of math. *Mailing Add:* Buttons Lane Chapel Hill NC 27514

WRIGHT, FRED(ERICK) D(UNSTAN), b Genoa, Italy, Mar 31, 16; US citizen; m 44; c 5. MINING ENGINEERING. *Educ:* Harvard Univ, BS, 38; Columbia Univ, MS, 42. *Prof Exp:* Shift boss, New Consol Goldfields, SAfrica, 38-39; supt, Johns-Manville Corp, NY, 39-41; mining engr, US Bur Mines, 46-53; tech dir, San Martin Mining Co, Inc, Mex, 53-54; prof mining eng, Univ Ill, Urbana, 54-67; prof, 67-81, EMER PROF MINING ENG, UNIV KY, 81- *Concurrent Pos:* Mining consult, 54- *Mem:* Am Inst Mining, Metall & Petrol Engrs; Am Soc Eng Educ. *Res:* Rock mechanics; strata control; design of underground structures; drilling, blasting, loading and transportation in mines; operations research. *Mailing Add:* 1059 Mackey Pike Univ of Ky Nicholasville KY 40356

WRIGHT, FRED MARION, b Aurora, Ill, Sept 29, 23; m 47. MATHEMATICS. *Educ:* Denison Univ, BA, 44; Northwestern Univ, MS, 49, PhD(math), 53. *Prof Exp:* Instr math, Denison Univ, 47; asst, Northwestern Univ, 47-51; from instr to assoc prof, 53-64, PROF MATH, IOWA STATE UNIV, 64- *Concurrent Pos:* Vis asst prof, Univ Mich, 57-58. *Mem:* Am Math Soc. *Res:* Continued fractions and function theory. *Mailing Add:* Dept of Math Iowa State Univ Ames IA 50010

WRIGHT, FREDERICK FENNING, b Princeton, NJ, Mar 16, 34. MARINE GEOLOGY, OCEANOGRAPHY. *Educ:* Columbia Univ, BS, 59, AM, 61; Univ Southern Calif, PhD(geol), 67. *Prof Exp:* Teaching asst geol, Columbia Univ, 59-61; res asst, Univ Southern Calif, 61-65; eng geologist, Div Water Resources, State of Calif, 65-66; asst prof marine sci, Inst Marine Sci, Univ Alaska, Fairbanks, 66-72, asst prof oceanog & exten oceanogr, Marine Adv Prog, Anchorage, 72-74; oceanog consult, 74-75; dir, Alaska Coastal Mgt Prog, Off Gov, State of Alaska, 75; ALASKA OCS RES MGT OFFICER, OUTER CONTINENTAL SHELF ENVIRON ASSESSMENT PROG, OFF GOV, STATE OF ALASKA & NAT OCEANIC & ATMOSPHERIC AGENCY, 75- *Concurrent Pos:* Asst dir, NSF Inst Oceanog, Marine Lab, Tex A&M Univ, 63; Geol Soc Am Penrose res grant, 64-66. *Mem:* Geol Soc Am; Am Geophys Union; Am Asn Petrol Geologists; Am Soc Limnol & Oceanog; Arctic Inst NAm. *Res:* Inshore oceanography and sedimentation in subarctic; fisheries oceanography; coastal resource management and planning. *Mailing Add:* Box 537 Douglas AK 99824

WRIGHT, FREDERICK HAMILTON, b Washington, DC, Dec 2, 12; m 70. PHYSICS. *Educ:* Haverford Col, BA, 34; Calif Inst Technol, PhD(physics), 48. *Prof Exp:* Aerodynamicist, Douglas Aircraft Co, Inc, 40-46; res engr, Jet Propulsion Lab, Calif Inst Technol, 46-59; div mgr & prog mgr, Space Gen Corp, 59-69; mem staff, Aerojet Electrosysts Co, Azusa, 69-78, CONSULT, 78- *Mem:* Am Inst Aeronaut & Astronaut; Am Phys Soc; Inst Elec & Electronic Engrs. *Res:* Sensor systems; fluids; geophysics. *Mailing Add:* 515 Palmetto Dr Pasadena CA 91105

WRIGHT, GEORGE CARLIN, b Shawsville, Md, Mar 3, 26; m 55; c 3. SYNTHETIC ORGANIC CHEMISTRY. *Educ:* Johns Hopkins Univ, BE, 47; Univ Del, MS, 55, PhD(chem), 58. *Prof Exp:* Chemist, Glenn L Martin Co, Md, 47-50; res chemist, Gen Aniline & Film Corp, Pa, 50; chemist, Army Chem Ctr, 51-52; res chemist, Gen Aniline & Film Corp, Pa, 52-53; SR RES CHEMIST, NORWICH PHARMACAL CO, 58- *Mem:* Am Chem Soc. *Res:* Polymerization and development chemistry; degradation of carbamates; organic synthesis; hydantoins; nitrofurans; hydrazidines; quinolines. *Mailing Add:* Norwich Pharmacal Co Norwich NY 13815

WRIGHT, GEORGE EDWARD, b Milwaukee, Wis, Oct 21, 41; m 65; c 3. MEDICINAL CHEMISTRY. *Educ:* Univ Ill, Chicago, BS, 63, PhD(chem), 67. *Prof Exp:* Sr res asst chem, Univ Durham, 66-68; asst prof med chem, Sch Pharm, Univ Md, Baltimore, 68-74; assoc prof, 74-78, actg assoc dean, 78-80, PROF PHARMACOL, MED SCH, UNIV MASS, 78-, DEAN GRAD STUDIES, 80- *Concurrent Pos:* Affil assoc prof chem, Clark Univ, 76-78, affil prof, 78-; vis prof, Inst Exp Physics, Univ Warsaw, 80-81. *Mem:* Am Chem Soc; The Chem Soc; Int Soc Heterocyclic Chem. *Res:* Synthesis and structure of heterocyclic compounds; nuclear magnetic resonance spectroscopy; DNA polymerase inhibitors. *Mailing Add:* 298 Highland St Worcester MA 01602

WRIGHT, GEORGE GREEN, b Ann Arbor, Mich, Aug 17, 16; m 57; c 3. IMMUNOLOGY, MICROBIOLOGY. *Educ:* Olivet Col, BA, 36; Univ Chicago, PhD(bact), 41. *Prof Exp:* Instr immunol, Univ Chicago, 41-42; vis investr, NIH, 46-48; med microbiologist, Ft Detrick, Md, 48-71; asst dir, 71-77, DIR BIOL LABS, MASS STATE DEPT PUB HEALTH, 77- *Concurrent Pos:* Logan fel Univ Chicago, 41-42; Nat Res Coun fel, Calif Inst Technol, 42-43, fel immunol, 43-46; US Secy Army res fel, Oxford Univ, 57-58; vis lectr applied microbiol, Harvard Sch Pub Health, 72-; lectr med, Sch Med, Tufts Univ, 72- *Mem:* Soc Exp Biol & Med; Am Soc Microbiol; Am Asn Immunol. *Res:* Elaboration, isolation and characterization of microbial antigens and toxins; production of biologics; general immunology and serology; immunity in anthrax; serum proteins. *Mailing Add:* Biologic Labs 375 South St Boston MA 02130

WRIGHT, GEORGE JOSEPH, b Allendale, Ill, June 4, 31; m 53; c 2. DRUG METABOLISM, BIOCHEMISTRY. *Educ:* Univ Ill, Urbana, BS, 52, PhD(animal nutrit & biochem), 60. *Prof Exp:* Med researcher human biochem, L B Mendel Res Lab, Elgin State Hosp, Ill, 60-62; biochemist toxicol & indust hyg, Biochem Res Lab, Dow Chem Co, Midland, Mich, 62-67; head, Drug Metab Dept, Merrell-Nat Labs, Richardson-Merrell, Inc, 67-79; DIR, DRUG METAB, A H ROBINS CO, 79- *Concurrent Pos:* Lectr chem, Eve Col, Univ Cincinnati, 70-72; consult clin and preclin pharmacol, Walter Reed Army Inst Res & Nat Cancer Inst. *Mem:* AAAS; Soc Toxicol; Am Soc Pharmacol & Exp Therapeut. *Res:* Drug disposition; bioavailability; biopharmaceutics; pharmacokinetics; enzymology; toxicology. *Mailing Add:* A H Robins Co 1211 Sherwood Ave Richmond VA 23220

WRIGHT, GEORGE LEONARD, JR, b Ludington, Mich, Feb 8, 37; m 64; c 2. IMMUNOCHEMISTRY, TUMOR IMMUNOLOGY. *Educ:* Albion Col, BA, 59; Mich State Univ, MS, 62, PhD(microbiol, path, biochem), 66. *Prof Exp:* Fel immunol & immunochem, Sch Med, George Washington Univ, 66-67, asst prof microbiol & immunochem, 67-73; assoc prof, 73-76, PROF DEPT MICROBIOL & IMMUNOL EASTERN VA MED SCH, 76-, DEP CHMN, DEPT MICRO/IMMUNOL, 76-, DIR IMMUNOL PROG, 75- *Concurrent Pos:* Sigma Xi award sci res, 66; spec consult, Vet Admin Hosp, Wilmington, Del, 66-73; deleg & rapporteur, Tuberc Panel, US-Japan Coop Med Sci Prog, Tokyo, 68 & 70; Hartford Found grant, 68-73; NIH grant, 72-74; Nat Cancer Inst contract, 75-78; Am Cancer Soc grant, 77-79; spec consult, Beckman Instruments; consult, Washington, DC Vet Admin & Children's Hosps; mem subcomt, US-Japan Med Sci Prog Stand Mycobact Antigens. *Honors & Awards:* NIH Career Develop Award, 75-80. *Mem:* AAAS; Am Asn Cancer Res; Am Soc Microbiol; Am Asn Immunologists. *Res:* Separation, isolation and immunobiological characterization of specific mycobacterial antigens; identification and isolation of human prostate tumor-associated antigens; monoclonial antibodies to urogenital cancer cells. *Mailing Add:* Dept of Microbiol & Immunol Lewis Hall 700 Olney Rd Norfolk VA 23507

WRIGHT, HAROLD E(UGENE), b Hillsdale, Mich, Dec 28, 20; m 49; c 2. MECHANICS. *Educ:* Univ Dayton, BME, 49; Univ Cincinnati, MS, 60; Mich State Univ, PhD, 66. *Prof Exp:* From instr to assoc prof mech eng, Univ Dayton, 49-62; assoc prof, 62-77, PROF MECH ENG, US AIR FORCE INST TECHNOL, 77- *Concurrent Pos:* Mech engr, Nat Cash Register Co, 51-52; combustion engr, City of Dayton, 52-53; maintenance dir, Miami Valley Hosp, 53-57. *Mem:* Am Soc Mech Engrs; Am Soc Eng Educ; Nat Soc Prof Engrs. *Res:* Gas dynamics; applied mechanics; heat transfer; shock tubes utilization, both gas and liquid drivers. *Mailing Add:* 7625 Rolling Oak Dr Centerville OH 45459

WRIGHT, HARRY TUCKER, JR, b Louisville, Ky, July 21, 29. PEDIATRICS, EPIDEMIOLOGY. *Educ:* Wake Forest Col, BS, 51, MD, 55; Univ Calif, Berkeley, MPH, 75. *Prof Exp:* From instr to assoc prof, 63-73, PROF PEDIAT, UNIV SOUTHERN CALIF, 73-, HEAD, DIV INFECTIOUS DIS & VIROLOGY, CHILDREN'S HOSP, LOS ANGELES, 75- *Concurrent Pos:* Teaching fel pediat, Case Western Reserve Univ, 58-59; NIH res training grant, 61-64. *Mem:* Am Acad Pediat; Am Fedn Clin Res; Soc Pediat Res; Am Pediat Soc; Am Soc Microbiol. *Res:* Clinical and laboratory studies of cytomegalovirus and other herpes viruses; central nervous system syndromes of viral etiology and newborn infections; virology; hospital acquired infections. *Mailing Add:* Childrens Hosp of Los Angeles PO Box 54700 Terminal Annex Los Angeles CA 90054

WRIGHT, HARVEL AMOS, b Mayflower, Ark, July 6, 33; m 54; c 2. MATHEMATICS. *Educ:* Ark State Teachers Col, BS, 54; Univ Ark, MA, 56; Univ Tenn, PhD, 67. *Prof Exp:* Teacher high sch, Ark, 55-56; instr math & physics, Ark State Teachers Col, 56-58; instr math, Univ Tenn, 58-62; physicist, 62-74, HEAD, BIOL & RADIATION PHYSICS SECT, OAK RIDGE NAT LAB, 74- *Concurrent Pos:* Vis scientist, Europ Ctr Nuclear Res, Switz, 71-72. *Mem:* Health Physics Soc; Radiation Res Soc. *Res:* Interaction of radiation with matter; dosimetry of ionizing radiation; plasma physics; theory of real variable. *Mailing Add:* Health & Safety Res Div Bldg 4500S Oak Ridge Nat Lab Oak Ridge TN 37830

WRIGHT, HASTINGS KEMPER, b Boston, Mass, Aug 22, 28; m 54; c 4. MEDICINE, PHYSIOLOGY. *Educ:* Harvard Univ, AB, 50, MD, 54. *Prof Exp:* Asst prof surg, Western Reserve Univ, 62-66; assoc prof, 66-72, PROF SURG, SCH MED, YALE UNIV, 72- *Concurrent Pos:* Crile fel surg, Western Reserve Univ, 61-62. *Mem:* AAAS; Soc Univ Surg; Am Fedn Clin Res; Am Gastroenterol Asn; Am Surg Asn. *Res:* Gastrointestinal fluid and electrolyte absorption. *Mailing Add:* Dept of Surg Yale-New Haven Hosp 333 Cedar St New Haven CT 06510

WRIGHT, HENRY ALBERT, b Modesto, Calif, June 1, 35; m 61; c 4. FIRE ECOLOGY, RANGE MANAGEMENT. *Educ:* Univ Calif, Davis, BS, 57; Utah State Univ, MS, 62, PhD(range mgt), 64. *Prof Exp:* Exten specialist range mgt, Univ Calif, Davis, 57-58; range aid, Intermountain Forest & Range Exp Sta, Boise, Idaho, 60-64, res assoc, 64-67; from asst prof to assoc prof, 67-74, prof, 74-78, HORN PROF RANGE MGT, TEX TECH UNIV, 78-, CHAIRPERSON RANGE & WILDLIFE MGT, 81- *Concurrent Pos:* Mem grad coun, Tex Tech Univ, 71-74; educ comt, Southwest Interagency Fire Coun, 71-, mem tenure & priviledge comt, 79-81. *Mem:* Soc Range Mgt. *Res:* Fire ecology particularly developing prescription techniques for burning rangeland communities and studying the effect of fire on their total ecosystem. *Mailing Add:* Dept of Range & Wildlife Mgt Tex Tech Univ Lubbock TX 79409

WRIGHT, HERBERT EDGAR, JR, b Malden, Mass, Sept 13, 17; m 43; c 5. PALEOECOLOGY. *Educ:* Harvard Univ, AB, 39, AM, 41, PhD(geol), 43. *Hon Degrees:* DSc, Trinity Col, Dublin, 66. *Prof Exp:* Instr geol, Brown Univ, 46-47; from asst prof to prof, 47-74, REGENTS' PROF GEOL, ECOL & BOT, UNIV MINN, MINNEAPOLIS, 74-, DIR LIMNOL RES CTR, 63- *Concurrent Pos:* Geologist, US Geol Surv, DC, 46-47; mem Boston Col-Fordham archaeol exped, 47; geologist, Minn Geol Surv, 48-63; Wenner-Gren fel, 51; geologist, US Geol Surv, DC, 52-53; mem archaeol exped, Oriental Inst, 51, 54-55, 60, 63, 64 & 70; Guggenheim Fel, 54-55. *Mem:* Geol Soc Am; Ecol Soc Am; Am Soc Limnol & Oceanog; Am Quaternary Asn (pres, 71-72); Glaciol Soc. *Res:* Geomorphology; Pleistocene geology and paleoecology; vegetation history; paleolimnology. *Mailing Add:* Dept of Geol Univ of Minn Minneapolis MN 55455

WRIGHT, HERBERT FESSENDEN, b Worcester, Mass, July 19, 17; m 41; c 1. MEDICINAL CHEMISTRY, BIOCHEMISTRY. *Educ:* Oberlin Col, AB, 40; Cornell Univ, MS, 42, PhD(org chem), 44; Am Inst Chem, cert. *Prof Exp:* Asst chem, Cornell Univ, 42-43, Off Sci Res & Develop antimalarial proj, 43-44; res chemist, Lever Bros Co, Mass, 44-45; res assoc, Mass Inst Technol, 45-46; instr chem, Tufts Col, 46-48; res chemist, Arthur D Little, Inc, 48-49; instr chem, Yale Univ, 49-52; sr res chemist, Olin Industs, 52-54; CONSULT CHEM, 54-; chmn dept, 67-79, dir environ studies, 70-79, PROF BIOL & PHYS SCI, UNIV NEW HAVEN, 66- *Concurrent Pos:* Pres & res dir, W Elsworth Co, Inc, 59-64; asst prof biol & phys sci, Univ New Haven, 64-65, assoc prof, 6S-66; dir, Univ Res Insts Conn, 67-77. *Mem:* AAAS; Am Chem Soc; NY Acad Sci; fel Am Inst Chem; Am Inst Biol Sci. *Res:* Synthetic drugs and vitamin A, organic ortho silicate esters; polymers; fungicides; antimetabolites; organic electrode reactions; organic synthetic methods; molecular biology; forensic science; biochemical genetics; nutrition. *Mailing Add:* Dept of Sci & Biol Univ New Haven 300 Orange Ave West Haven CT 06516

WRIGHT, HERBERT N, b Berwyn, Ill, May 23, 28; m 52; c 3. PSYCHOACOUSTICS, AUDIOLOGY. *Educ:* Grinnell Col, BA, 50; Ind Univ, MA, 53; Northwestern Univ, PhD(audiol), 58. *Prof Exp:* Res assoc otolaryngol, Northwestern, 56-58; res assoc blind mobility, Auditory Res Ctr, 60-61; from res instr to res assoc prof otolaryngol, 61-63, ASSOC PROF OTOLARYNGOL, STATE UNIV NY UPSTATE MED CTR, 63- *Concurrent Pos:* Res fel psychoacoustics, Cent Inst Deaf, St Louis, Mo, 58-60 & Syracuse Univ, 61-63. *Mem:* AAAS; Am Speech & Hearing Asn; Acoust Soc Am; Psychonomic Soc; Int Soc Audiol. *Res:* Psychoacoustics of individual differences, especially with reference to disorders of the auditory system; temporal factors of audition. *Mailing Add:* Dept of Otolaryngol & Commun Sci State Univ of NY Upstate Med Ctr Syracuse NY 13210

WRIGHT, IAN GLAISBY, b Fredericton, NB, Sept 15, 35; m 58; c 3. SYNTHETIC ORGANIC CHEMISTRY. *Educ:* Univ BC, BA, 57; Univ NB, Fredericton, MSc, 59; Univ Wis-Madison, PhD(org chem), 65. *Prof Exp:* Fel with A I Scott, Univ BC, 63-65; sr org chemist, 65-73, SR ORG CHEMIST PROCESS RES & DEVELOP DIV, LILLY RES LABS, ELI LILLY & CO, 73- *Mem:* AAAS; Am Chem Soc; Royal Soc Chem. *Res:* Chemistry and biological activity of cephalosporin antibiotics; chemistry of natural products from plant and microbiological sources. *Mailing Add:* Eli Lilly & Co Lilly Res Labs Indianapolis IN 46206

WRIGHT, JAMES ARTHUR, b Toronto, Ont, Dec 29, 41; m 70. GEOPHYSICS. *Educ:* Univ Toronto, BASc, 64, MSc, 65, PhD(physics), 68. *Prof Exp:* Nat Res Coun Can fel, Brunswick Tech Univ, 68-69; asst prof, 69-74, ASSOC PROF PHYSICS, MEM UNIV NFLD, 74- *Concurrent Pos:* Mem geomagnetism subcont, Assoc Comt Geod & Geophys, Nat Res Coun Can, 71-73. *Mem:* Can Soc Explor Geophysicists; Geol Soc Can; Am Geophys Union; Soc Explor Geophysicists. *Res:* Geomagnetism and the earth's interior; exploration geophysics; marine heat flow. *Mailing Add:* Dept Physics Mem Univ Nfld St Johns NF A1B 3X7 Can

WRIGHT, JAMES EDWARD, b Little Rock, Ark, Sept 6, 46; m 66; c 2. EXERCISE PHYSIOLOGY. *Educ:* Fairleigh Dickinson Univ, BS, 69; Miss State Univ, PhD(zool), 73. *Prof Exp:* Asst prof biol sci, Simon's Rock Early Col, 73-75; NIH fel & asst res physiologist exercise & environ physiol, Inst Environment Stress, Univ Calif, Santa Barbara, 75-77; staff, Exercise Physiol Div, US Army Res Inst Environ Med, 77-82; TECH EDITOR & SPECIAL ASST PUBL, WEIDER HEALTH & FITNESS CORP, WOODLAND HILLS, CALIF, 82- *Concurrent Pos:* Athletic training & nutritional consult, Sports Science Consult, Natick, Mass, 78; assoc ed, Nat Strength Conditioning Asn J, 81-; mem, Int Coun Phys Fitness Res, 80- *Mem:* AAAS; Am Col Sports Med. *Res:* Longitudinal and cross sectional investigation of functional physical and physiological changes produced by weight/strength training and body building; anabolic steroid and other ergogenic aid effects on muscle size, strength, endurance and performance; comparative responses of males and females to strength training and bodybuilding; occupational fitness requirements. *Mailing Add:* Weider Health & Fitness Corp 21100 Erwin Woodland Hills CA 91367

WRIGHT, JAMES ELBERT, b Kerrville, Tex, Oct 7, 40; m 62; c 2. MEDICAL ENTOMOLOGY, BACTERIOLOGY. *Educ:* Tex A&M Univ, BS, 63; Ohio State Univ, PhD(med entom, bact), 66; Am Registry Cert Entom, cert. *Prof Exp:* Res asst mosquitoes entom, Ohio State Univ, 63-66, res assoc, 66; RES ENTOMOLOGIST, RES LEADER BOLL WEEVIL RES LAB, SCI & EDUC ADMIN-AGR RES, USDA, 66- *Mem:* Fel AAAS; Entom Soc Am; Am Chem Soc; Soc Invert Path; Am Mosquito Control Asn. *Res:* Insect juvenile and molting hormones interrelationships; insect biochemistry; mosquito biology; diapause mechanisms; livestock arthropods; biting flies; stable fly and horn fly biology; studies on temperature and photoperiod; biology of livestock ticks; insect growth regulators; boll weevil and cotton insects; sterility; nutrition. *Mailing Add:* Boll Weevil Res Lab USDA Sci & Educ Admin-Agr Res PO Box 5367 Mississippi State MS 39762

WRIGHT, JAMES EVERETT, JR, b Deepstep, Ga, Apr 28, 23; m 48; c 3. GENETICS. *Educ:* Univ Ga, BS, 46; Cornell Univ, PhD(genetics), 50. *Prof Exp:* From instr to assoc prof, 49-60, PROF GENETICS, PA STATE UNIV, 60- *Mem:* AAAS; Genetics Soc Am; Am Fisheries Soc; Am Genetic Asn. *Res:* Genetics and breeding of fishes. *Mailing Add:* 202 Buckhout Lab Pa State Univ University Park PA 16802

WRIGHT, JAMES FOLEY, b Tulsa, Okla, Feb 9, 43; m 64; c 2. NUCLEAR SCIENCE, HYDRODYNAMICS. *Educ:* Cent State Univ, Okla, BS, 69; Iowa State Univ, PhD(nuclear chem), 74. *Prof Exp:* Fel physics, Ames Lab, Iowa, 74; scientist, Battelle Northwest Labs, 74-75; mem sci staff planning, Los Alamos Sci Lab, 75-80; MEM STAFF, TECH SYSTS, 80- *Concurrent Pos:* Dir, Nat Particle-Beam Study Group, 78-79. *Mem:* Am Phys Soc. *Res:* Directed energy weapons, nuclear weapons, plasma physics, systems analysis. *Mailing Add:* Tech Systs Suite 10 - 212 E Marcy Santa Fe NM 87501

WRIGHT, JAMES FRANCIS, b Philadelphia, Pa, Jan 18, 24; m 55; c 3. COMPARATIVE PATHOLOGY, TOXICOLOGY. *Educ:* Univ Pa, VMD, 51; Univ Calif, Davis, PhD(comp path), 69. *Prof Exp:* Vet in-chg animal quarantine, Plum Island Animal Dis Lab, USDA, NY, 54-57; vet, Nat Zool Park, Smithsonian Inst, 57-62; res scientist, USPHS, US Air Force Radiobiol Lab, Univ Tex, Austin, 62-64, Yerkes Regional Primate Res Ctr, Emory Univ, 64-65 & Radiobiol Lab, Univ Calif, Davis, 65-69; chief toxicol studies sect, Twinbrook Res Lab, 69-73, CHIEF PATH STUDIES SECT, HEALTH EFFECTS RES LAB, ENVIRON PROTECTION AGENCY, 73- *Concurrent Pos:* Adj assoc prof path, Sch Vet Med, NC State Univ, 79- *Mem:* Am Vet Med Asn; Am Asn Zoo Vets; Am Asn Lab Animal Sci; Wildlife Dis Asn; Radiation Res Soc. *Res:* Laboratory animal medicine; pathology and toxicology; diseases of wild animals; comparative radiation pathology. *Mailing Add:* 8508 E Lake Ct Raleigh NC 27612

WRIGHT, JAMES HAROLD, b Memphis, Tex, Nov 19, 26; m 50; c 3. CHEMICAL & NUCLEAR ENGINEERING. *Educ:* Tex Tech Col, BS, 48; Univ Pittsburgh, MS, 54, PhD(chem eng), 57. *Prof Exp:* Chief chemist, Moutray Oil Co, 44-45; plant chief engr, Gulf Oil Corp, 49-52; res chemist, Mellon Inst Indust Res, 52-56; fel scientist, Atomic Power Div, Westinghouse Elec Corp, 56-57, mgr adv reactor develop, 57-66, tech dir, Adv Reactor Div, 66-68, dir, Environ Systs Dept, 68-77, gen mgr, 77-80; PRES, ENERGY IMPACT ASSOCS, INC, 80- *Concurrent Pos:* Lectr, Univ Pittsburgh, 57-61; mem adv coun, comt govt sponsored res & develop, US House Rep, 62-63; mem, Tech Exchange Mission Atomic Power, USSR, 63; consult, Nat Water Comn, 70-; mem prog rev comt, Argonne Nat Lab, 71- *Mem:* Am Nuclear Soc; Am Chem Soc; Am Inst Chem Engrs; Am Soc Eng Educ. *Res:* Petroleum technology, especially processing natural gas; pioneering development in economic nuclear power; advanced reactor design and development; environmental impact of energy use. *Mailing Add:* Energy Impact Assocs Inc Box 1899 Pittsburgh PA 15230

WRIGHT, JAMES LOUIS, b Pleasant Grove, Utah, Aug 28, 34; m 58; c 7. AGRONOMY, AGRICULTURAL METEOROLOGY. *Educ:* Utah State Univ, BS, 59, MS, 61; Cornell Univ, PhD(soil physics), 65. *Prof Exp:* SOIL SCIENTIST, AGR RES SERV, USDA, 65-; ASSOC PROF RES CLIMATOL & AFFIL PROF SOILS, UNIV IDAHO, 70- *Mem:* Am Soc Agron; Soil Sci Soc Am; Sigma Xi. *Res:* Microclimate investigations to determine rate of evaporation of water from agricultural crops using energy balance and micrometeorological approaches. *Mailing Add:* Snake River Conserv Res Ctr Rte 1 Box 186 Kimberly ID 83341

WRIGHT, JAMES P, b St Petersburg, Fla, Apr 10, 34; m 56; c 3. ASTROPHYSICS. *Educ:* Univ Fla, BS, 56; Univ Chicago, PhD(chem), 61. *Prof Exp:* NSF-Nat Res Coun assoc, Inst Space Studies, 61-63; vis asst prof math, Math Res Ctr, Univ Wis, 63-64; astrophysicist, Smithsonian Astrophys Observ, 64-70; PROG DIR, NAT SCI FOUND, 70- *Concurrent Pos:* Lectr astron, Harvard Univ, 64-70. *Mem:* Am Phys Soc; Am Astron Soc; Int Astron Union. *Res:* Properties of high temperature gases in electromagnetic fields; theoretical cosmological world models; observable effects of use of general relativity theory; high energy astrophysics. *Mailing Add:* Nat Sci Found Rm 618 1800 G St Washington DC 20550

WRIGHT, JAMES R, b Riversdale, NS, July 19, 16; m 42; c 2. SOIL CHEMISTRY. *Educ:* McGill Univ, BSc, 40; Mich State Univ, MS, 48, PhD(soil chem), 53. *Hon Degrees:* DSc, Acadia Univ, 80. *Prof Exp:* Asst chemist, NS Dept Agr, 40-41, asst prov chemist, 45-50; head soil genesis sect, Soil Res Inst, Can Dept Agr, 51-61, dir, Kentville Res Sta, 61-78; CONSULT SOILS & AGR, 79- *Concurrent Pos:* Lectr, NS Agr Col, 45-50; prof, Acadia Univ, 65-75; asst dir gen, Res Br, Agr Can, 67-68; second vpres, Acadia Univ Inst. *Mem:* Am Soc Agron; Soil Sci Soc Am; fel Chem Inst Can; Can Soc Soil Sci (pres, 61-62); fel Agr Inst Can. *Res:* Chemical nature of soil organic matter; soil genesis, fertility and plant nutrition. *Mailing Add:* PO Box 668 Chester NS B0J 1J0 Can

WRIGHT, JAMES ROSCOE, b White Hall, Md, July 7, 22; m 50; c 2. ORGANIC CHEMISTRY. *Educ:* Md State Col Salisbury, BSEd, 46; Wash Col, BS, 48; Univ Del, MS, 49, PhD(chem), 51. *Prof Exp:* Res chemist, Southwest Res Inst, 51-52 & Chevron Res Corp, Stand Oil Co Calif, 52-60; from chemist to sr chemist, 60-66, phys sci adminstr, 66-72, dir, Ctr for Bldg Technol, 72-74, dep dir, Inst Appl Technol, 74-76, actg dir, 76-78, DEP DIR, NAT ENG LAB, NAT BUR STANDARDS, 78- *Concurrent Pos:* Asst prof, Trinity Univ, Tex, 51-52; Com Sci & Tech fel, US Patent Off, 64-65; pres, Int Union Testing & Res Labs Mat & Struct, 71-72, mem bur, 74-78 & del, 75-85; mem, USA/Egypt Working Group, Technol, Res & Develop, 76- *Honors & Awards:* Gold Medal Award, Dept Com, 75. *Mem:* Am Chem Soc; Am Soc Testing & Mat; Int Union Testing & Res Labs Mat & Struct (pres-elect, 81-82, pres, 82-85). *Res:* Organosilicon compounds; radiation effects on organic lubricants; emulsification of petroleum products; photochemical stability of organic building materials; application of performance concept in building research, codes and standards. *Mailing Add:* Nat Bur of Standards Bldg 225 Rm B-117 Washington DC 20234

WRIGHT, JAMES SHERMAN, b Seattle, Wash, Aug 27, 40; m 63; c 1. THEORETICAL CHEMISTRY. *Educ:* Stanford Univ, BS, 62; Univ Calif, Berkeley, PhD(chem), 68. *Prof Exp:* Nat Ctr Sci Res, France grant, Fac Sci, Orsay, France, 69-70; asst prof, 70-77, ASSOC PROF CHEM, CARLETON UNIV, 77- *Res:* Chemistry. *Mailing Add:* 1358 Normandy Circle Ottawa ON L1H 7N8 Can

WRIGHT, JANE COOKE, b New York, NY, Nov 30, 19; m 47; c 2. MEDICINE. *Educ:* Smith Col, AB, 42; NY Med Col, MD, 45. *Hon Degrees:* DrMedSci, Women's Med Col Pa, 65; DSc, Denison Univ, 71. *Prof Exp:* Sch physician, New York City Dept Health, 49; clinician, Cancer Res Found, Harlem Hosp, 49-52, dir, 52-55; from instr to asst prof res surg, Postgrad Med Sch, NY Univ, 55-61, adj assoc prof, 61-67, dir cancer chemother serv res, 55-67; assoc dean, 67-75, PROF SURG, NY MED COL, 67- *Concurrent Pos:* Clin asst vis physician, Harlem Hosp, 49, asst vis physician, 49-55; asst vis physician, 4th Surg Div, Bellevue Hosp, 55-59, assoc vis physician, 60-; asst attend physician, Univ Hosp, 56- & Manhattan Vet Admin Hosp, 63-; mem courtesy staff, Midtown Hosp, 62-; consult, Health Ins Plan, 62-, Boulevard Hosp, 63-, St Luke's Hosp, Newburgh, NY, 64- & St Vincent's Hosp, New York, 66-; mem, President's Comn Heart Dis, Cancer & Stroke, 64, Nat Adv Cancer Coun, 66-70 & Nat Coun Negro Women, 56 & 63; attend surg, Flower-Fifth Ave Hosps, 67-79, Metrop Hosp & Bird S Coler Mem Hosp, 67-; consult oncol, Wyckoff Heights Hosp, 69-; attend physician, Gen Surg Sect, Chemother, Grassland Hosp, 71-; attend surg, Lincoln Hosp, 79- *Honors & Awards:* Mademoiselle Award, 52; Spence Chapin Award, 58; Spirit Achievement Award, 65. *Mem:* AMA; Am Soc Clin Oncol (secy-treas, 64-); Am Asn Cancer Res; Nat Med Asn; NY Acad Sci. *Res:* Cancer chemotherapy. *Mailing Add:* NY Med Col 1249 Fifth Ave New York NY 10029

WRIGHT, JOE CARROL, b Benton, Ark, Feb 6, 33; m 53; c 4. ORGANIC CHEMISTRY. *Educ:* Ouachita Baptist Univ, BS, 54; Univ Ark, MS, 62, PhD(org mech), 66. *Prof Exp:* Asst prof chem, Mobile Col, 64-66; assoc prof, 66-72, PROF CHEM, HENDERSON STATE UNIV, 72-, DEAN SCH SCI, 69- *Mem:* Am Chem Soc; Royal Soc Chem. *Res:* Isotope effect studies in organic reaction mechanism determinations. *Mailing Add:* Off of the Dean Sch Sci Henderson State Univ Arkadelphia AR 71923

WRIGHT, JOHN CLIFFORD, b Livingston, Mont, Jan 29, 19; m 44; c 2. LIMNOLOGY. *Educ:* Mont State Univ, BS, 41; Ohio State Univ, PhD, 50. *Prof Exp:* From instr to assoc prof, 49-61, assoc coordr, Ctr Environ Studies, 71-73, PROF BOT, MONT STATE UNIV, 61- *Concurrent Pos:* NSF sr fel, 59-60; exec secy, XV Int Cong Limnol, 61-62; dir, Ctr Environ Studies, Mont State Univ, 66-71. *Mem:* AAAS; Ecol Soc Am; Am Soc Limnol & Oceanog; Int Asn Theoret & Appl Limnol. *Res:* Oceanography; ecology. *Mailing Add:* Dept of Biol Mont State Univ Bozeman MT 59715

WRIGHT, JOHN CURTIS, b Lubbock, Tex, Sept 17, 43; m 68; c 2. ANALYTICAL & PHYSICAL CHEMISTRY. *Educ:* Union Col, BS, 65; Johns Hopkins Univ, PhD(physics), 70. *Prof Exp:* Student fel, Purdue Univ, 70-72; asst prof, 72-78, ASSOC PROF CHEM, UNIV WIS, 78- *Honors & Awards:* William F Meggars Award, Optical Soc Am, 80. *Mem:* Sigma Xi; Am Chem Soc; Am Phys Soc. *Res:* Lasers in analytical chemistry; fluorescence methods; solid state chemistry; coherent Raman methods; energy transfer and relaxation processes. *Mailing Add:* Dept of Chem Univ of Wis Madison WI 53706

WRIGHT, JOHN CUSHING, animal behavior, see previous edition

WRIGHT, JOHN FOWLER, b London, Ont, July 28, 21; US citizen; m 49; c 2. PHYSICAL CHEMISTRY. *Educ:* Univ Western Ont, BSc, 45, MSc, 46. *Prof Exp:* RES ASSOC, RES LABS, EASTMAN KODAK CO, 46- *Mem:* Am Chem Soc. *Res:* Polymer synthesis; surface treatments of polymers; colloid chemistry; surface active agents. *Mailing Add:* 51 New Wickham Dr Penfield NY 14526

WRIGHT, JOHN JAY, b Torrington, Conn, July 10, 43; m 65; c 2. ATOMIC PHYSICS. *Educ:* Worcester Polytech Inst, BS, 65; Univ NH, PhD(physics), 70. *Prof Exp:* Fel lasers, Joint Inst Lab Astrophys, Colo, 69-70; asst prof, 70-77, PROF PHYSICS, UNIV NH, 77- *Mem:* Am Inst Physics; Am Phys Soc; Am Asn Physics Teachers. *Res:* Optical pumping; liquid crystals. *Mailing Add:* Dept of Physics Univ of NH Durham NH 03824

WRIGHT, JOHN MARLIN, b Long Beach, Calif, Feb 2, 37; m 58; c 2. CHEMICAL INSTRUMENTATION, MAGNETIC RESONANCE. *Educ:* Calif Inst Technol, BS, 60; Harvard Univ, PhD(chem), 67. *Prof Exp:* Res fel chem, Harvard Univ, 67-70; assoc specialist, 70-73, specialist & lectr chem, 73-79, SR DEVELOP ENGR CHEM, UNIV CALIF, SAN DIEGO, 79- *Mem:* Am Chem Soc; AAAS. *Res:* Application of nuclear magnetic resonance and mass spectrometry to chemical problems; development of new instrumental techniques. *Mailing Add:* Dept of Chem B-014 Univ Calif San Diego La Jolla CA 92093

WRIGHT, JOHN RICKEN, b Batesville, Ark, Jan 3, 39; m 64; c 1. BIOINORGANIC CHEMISTRY. *Educ:* Ark State Univ, BS, 60; Univ Miss, MS, 67, PhD(chem), 71. *Prof Exp:* Res assoc, Dept Bot, Wash Univ, 67-68; NIH fel, Fla State Univ, 72-73; ASSOC PROF CHEM, DEPT PHYS SCI, SOUTHEASTERN OKLA STATE UNIV, 73- *Mem:* Sigma Xi. *Res:* The metabolism and transport of biological forms of copper; pigmented, copper-containing antibody labels. *Mailing Add:* Dept of Phys Sci Southeastern Okla State Univ Durant OK 74701

WRIGHT, JOHNIE ALGIE, b Atlas, Ala, Feb 5, 24; m 49; c 2. HORTICULTURE. *Educ:* Tenn Polytech Inst, BS, 47; Iowa State Col, MS, 49; La State Univ, PhD, 60. *Prof Exp:* Asst prof hort, Tenn Polytech Inst, 49-53; assoc prof, 53-60, PROF HORT, LA TECH UNIV, 60-, ASSOC DEAN, COL LIFE SCI, 72-, PROF AGRON, 77-, HEAD DEPT AGRON & HORT, 77- *Concurrent Pos:* Asst, La State Univ, 60. *Mem:* Am Soc Hort Sci. *Res:* Nutrient culture of roses; methods of watering greenhouse roses; container nursery stock studies. *Mailing Add:* Dept of Hort La Tech Univ PO Box 5136 Ruston LA 71270

WRIGHT, JON ALAN, b Tacoma, Wash, Jan 18, 38; m 62; c 3. THEORETICAL PHYSICS, PARTICLE PHYSICS. *Educ:* Calif Inst Technol, BS, 59; Univ Calif, Berkeley, PhD(physics), 65. *Prof Exp:* Physicist, Aerospace Corp, 65; res assoc physics, Univ Calif, San Diego, 65-67; assoc prof, 67-73, PROF PHYSICS, UNIV ILL, URBANA, 73- *Mem:* Am Inst Physics. *Res:* Theoretical elementary particle physics; non-linear physics. *Mailing Add:* Dept Physics Univ Ill Urbana IL 61801

WRIGHT, JONATHAN WILLIAM, b Spokane, Wash, June 29, 16; m 40; c 1. FOREST GENETICS. *Educ:* Univ Idaho, BS, 38; Harvard Univ, MF, 39, AM, 41, PhD(genetics), 42. *Prof Exp:* Instr forestry, Purdue Univ, 42-45; geneticist, Northeastern Forest Exp Sta, US Forest Serv, Morris Arboretum, 46-57; prof forestry, Mich State Univ, 57-81; RETIRED. *Concurrent Pos:* Assoc ed, Silvae Genetica, 56- *Honors & Awards:* Barrington Moore Award, 81. *Mem:* Soc Am Foresters. *Res:* Interspecific hybridization and geographic variation in Pinus and Picea; genetic statistics. *Mailing Add:* 2034 Yuma Trail Okemos MI 48864

WRIGHT, JOSEPH D, b Trochu, Alta, Nov 11, 41; m 69; c 4. CHEMICAL ENGINEERING. *Educ:* Univ Alta, BSc, 63; Cambridge Univ, PhD(chem eng), 67. *Prof Exp:* Res engr, Shawinigan Chem Div, Gulf Oil Can, 67-69; asst prof 69-74, assoc prof, 74-78, PROF CHEM ENG, MCMASTER UNIV, 78-; MGR, MAT PROCESSING LAB, XEROX RES CENTRE CAN, 77- *Concurrent Pos:* Trustee CACHE Corp, chmn, CACHE Task Force on Real-time Comput; exec dir, Sheridan Res Park Asn, 79- *Mem:* Instrument Soc Am; Chem Inst Can; Am Inst Chem Engrs; Am Chem Soc; Can Soc Chem Eng. *Res:* Chemical plant simulation and control extending to direct digital control and optimization of chemical plants and simulations; computer process control. *Mailing Add:* Xerox Res Ctr Can 2660 Speakman Dr Mississauga Hamilton ON L5K 2L1 Can

WRIGHT, JOSEPH WILLIAM, JR, b Indianapolis, Ind, Oct 30, 16; m 42, 65; c 2. MEDICINE. *Educ:* Univ Mich, AB, 38, MD, 42. *Prof Exp:* Intern, Univ Mich Hosp, 42-43; resident, Ind Univ Hosp, 46-48; ASSOC PROF OTOLARYNGOL, SCH MED, IND UNIV, INDIANAPOLIS, 58- *Concurrent Pos:* Fel surg, Northwestern Univ, 55-56; consult, Off Surgeon Gen, US Army, 49-; chmn otolaryngol serv, Community Hosp, 57-62. mem bd trustees; mem, Ind State Hearing Comn; pres, Wright Inst Otol; consult, Crossroad Rehab Ctr, Indianapolis, Ind, & Indianapolis Speech & Hearing Ctr; consult mem, St Vincent's Hosp; pres, Am Coun Otolaryngol, 79-80; mem, Otosclerosis Study Group, 75- *Mem:* AMA; Am Acad Ophthal & Otolaryngol; Am Laryngol, Rhinol & Otol Soc; Pan-Am Med Asn; Int Col Surg. *Res:* Bioceramics as applied to otology; endolymphatic ducts in tomography. *Mailing Add:* 5506 E 16th St Indianapolis IN 46218

WRIGHT, KENNETH A, b Timmins, Ont, Apr 7, 36; m 59; c 3. ZOOLOGY, PARASITOLOGY. *Educ:* Univ Toronto, BA, 58, MA, 60; Rice Univ, PhD(parasitol, cytol), 62. *Prof Exp:* Res zoologist, Univ Calif, Riverside, 62-63, asst res nematologist, Univ Calif, Davis, 63-64; res scientist parasitol & cytol, Ont Res Found, 64-66; from asst prof to assoc prof, Sch Hyg, 66-75, assoc prof microbiol & parasitol, fac med, 75-79, ASSOC PROF, ZOOL DEPT, UNIV TORONTO, 79- *Concurrent Pos:* Assoc ed, Can Soc Zoologists, 74- *Mem:* Am Soc Parasitol; Soc Nematol; Can Soc Zoologists; Can Soc Microscopists. *Res:* Cytology of parasites, especially of nematodes; nematology. *Mailing Add:* Dept Zool Univ Toronto Toronto ON M5S 1A3 Can

WRIGHT, KENNETH JAMES, b Pittsburgh, Pa, Aug 26, 39; m 66; c 2. PHYSICAL INORGANIC CHEMISTRY, ENVIRONMENTAL SCIENCES. *Educ:* Portland State Univ, BS, 62; Univ Idaho, PhD(inorg chem), 72. *Prof Exp:* Anal & res chemist, Harvey Aluminum Corp, Ore, 63-66; chmn div phys sci, 72-77, INSTR CHEM & ENVIRON SCI, NORTH IDAHO COL, 71- *Concurrent Pos:* NSF trainee chem, Univ Idaho, 67, Nat Defense Educ Act fel, 68-70, consult, 78- *Mem:* Am Chem Soc; Sigma Xi. *Res:* Environmental effects of air and water pollutants; energy resources and conservation; science education methodologies; analytical chemistry of environmental pollutants. *Mailing Add:* Div Phys Sci N Idaho Col Coeur d'Alene ID 83814

WRIGHT, KENNETH OSBORNE, b Ft George, BC, Nov 1, 11; m 37 & 70; c 1. ASTROPHYSICS. *Educ:* Univ Toronto, BA, 33, MA, 34; Univ Mich, PhD(astron), 40. *Hon Degrees:* DSc, Nicolas Copernicus Univ, Torun, Poland, 73. *Prof Exp:* Asst astron, Univ Toronto, 33-34; asst, 36-40, astronomer, 40-60, asst dir, 60-66, dir, 66-76, GUEST WORKER, DOM ASTROPHYS OBSERV, 76- *Concurrent Pos:* Lectr, Univ BC, 43-44; spec lectr, Univ Toronto, 60-61; res asst, Mt Wilson & Palomar Observ, 62; chmn assoc comt astron, Nat Res Coun Can, 71-74. *Honors & Awards:* Gold Medal, Royal Astron Soc Can, 33. *Mem:* Int Astron Union; Am Astron Soc; Royal Astron Soc Can (pres, 64-66); fel Royal Soc Can; Can Astron Soc. *Res:* Stellar radial velocities; observations of stellar line intensities; curves of growth; stellar atmospheres, peculiar A-type stars; observation and analysis of atmospheres of giant eclipsing systems. *Mailing Add:* Dom Astrophys Observ 5071 W Saanich Rd Victoria BC V8X 4M6 Can

WRIGHT, LAUREN ALBERT, b New York, NY, July 9, 18. GEOLOGY. *Educ:* Univ Southern Calif, AB, 40, MS, 43; Calif Inst Technol, PhD(geol), 51. *Prof Exp:* From jr geologist to asst geologist, US Geol Surv, 42-46; assoc geologist, State Div Mines, Calif, 47-51, sr mining geologist, 51-54, supv mining geologist, 54-61; PROF GEOL, PA STATE UNIV, 61- *Mem:* Fel Geol Soc Am; Am Soc Econ Geologists; Am Inst Mining, Metall & Petrol Eng. *Res:* Geologic occurence, origin and economics of industrial minerals; stratigraphic-tectonic evolution of southwesterrn Great Basin; structural geology; extensional tectonics. *Mailing Add:* Dept of Geosci Pa State Univ University Park PA 16802

WRIGHT, LEMUEL DARY, b Nashua, NH, Mar 1, 13; m 41; c 5. BIOCHEMISTRY. *Educ:* Univ NH, BS, 35, MS, 36; Ore State Col, PhD(biochem), 40. *Prof Exp:* Asst biochem, Pa State Univ, 36-37; asst nutrit chemist, Ore State Col, 37-40; fel, Univ Tex, 40-41; instr biochem, Sch Med, Univ WVa, 41-42; res biochemist, Med Res Div, Merck Sharp & Dohme Div, 42-47, dir nutrit res, 47-50, dir microbiol chem, 50-56; PROF NUTRIT, CORNELL UNIV, 56- *Mem:* Am Chem Soc; Am Soc Biol Chemists; Soc Exp Biol & Med; Am Inst Nutrit. *Res:* Vitamin B complex; microbiological methods of assay; bacterial growth factors; biogenesis and metabolism of pyrimidines. *Mailing Add:* Div Nutrit Sci Cornell Univ Ithaca NY 14850

WRIGHT, LEON WENDELL, b Los Angeles, Calif, July 16, 23; m 50; c 4. ORGANIC CHEMISTRY. *Educ:* Univ Calif, Los Angeles, BS, 46, MS, 47; Univ Del, PhD(chem), 51. *Prof Exp:* Instr chem, Mont State Col, 47-49 & Univ Del, 49-51; res chemist, Houdry Process Corp, 51-56; from res chemist to sr res chemist, Atlas Chem Indust, Inc, 56-67, prin chemist, Chem Res Dept, 67-70, supvr, Org & Process Res Group, 70-77, PRIN CHEMIST, ICI US, INC, 77- *Mem:* Am Chem Soc; Sigma Xi. *Res:* Catalytic hydrogenation and hydrogenolysis; hetero and homogeneous activation of hydrogen; isomerization of polyhydric alcohols. *Mailing Add:* Chem Res Dept ICI Americas Inc Concord Pike & New Murphy Rd Wilmington DE 19897

WRIGHT, LOUIS EDGAR, b Buras, La, Oct 18, 40; m 69; c 2. THEORETICAL PHYSICS, NUCLEAR PHYSICS. *Educ:* La State Univ, BS, 61; Duke Univ, PhD(physics), 66. *Prof Exp:* Res assoc physics, Duke Univ, 66; prog mgr theoret physics, US Army Res Off-Durham, 66-69; asst prof physics, Duke Univ, 69-70; asst prof, 70-73, assoc prof, 73-80, PROF PHYSICS, OHIO UNIV, 80- *Concurrent Pos:* Vis physicist, Inst Theoret Physics, Univ Frankfurt, 68-69; Alexander von Humboldt fel, Inst Nuclear

Physics, Mainz Univ, 81-82. *Mem:* Am Phys Soc. *Res:* Theoretical nuclear physics; electron scattering, pion production, virtual photon spectra, bremsstrahlung and pair production. *Mailing Add:* Dept Physics Ohio Univ Athens OH 45701

WRIGHT, MADISON JOHNSTON, b Washington, DC, Apr 9, 24; m 54; c 4. AGRONOMY. *Educ:* Univ NC, BA, 47; Univ Wis, MS, 50, PhD(agron, bot), 52. *Prof Exp:* Asst prof agron, Univ Wis, 52-59; assoc prof, 59-68, chmn dept, 70-75, PROF AGRON, CORNELL UNIV, 68- *Mem:* Am Soc Agron; Crop Sci Soc Am; AAAS; Am Inst Biol Sci. *Res:* Crop management. *Mailing Add:* Dept of Agron Cornell Univ Ithaca NY 14853

WRIGHT, MARGARET HAGEN, b San Francisco, Calif; m 65; c 1. NONLINEAR PROGRAMMING, NUMERICAL ANALYSIS. *Educ:* Stanford Univ, BS, 64, MS, 65, PhD(comput sci), 76. *Prof Exp:* Develop engr, Sylvania Electron Syst, 65-71; SR RES ASSOC, STANFORD UNIV, 76- *Concurrent Pos:* Mem, Bd Dir, Special Interest Group Numerical Anal, Asn Comput Mach, 79-82; assoc ed, J Sci Statist Comput, Soc Indust & Appl Math, 81- *Mem:* Asn Comput Mach; Soc Indust & Appl Math; Math Prog Soc. *Res:* Methods for nonlinear programming, particularly unconstrained, linearly constrained and nonlinearly constrained optimization; mathematical software; numerical linear algebra; software library development. *Mailing Add:* Dept Opers Res Stanford Univ Stanford CA 94305

WRIGHT, MARGARET RUTH, b Rochester, NY, Mar 24, 13. ZOOLOGY. *Educ:* Univ Rochester, AB, 34, MS, 38; Yale Univ, PhD(zool), 46. *Prof Exp:* Asst, Univ Rochester, 36-38; histol technician, Med Sch, Yale Univ, 38-41, asst, Osborn Zool Lab, 42-43; instr biol, Middlebury Col, 43-46; from instr to prof, 46-78, EMER PROF ZOOL, VASSAR COL, 78- *Concurrent Pos:* Mem exped, Alaska, 36; grant, Nat Inst Neurol Dis & Blindness, 54-64; Vassar Col fels, 54-55, 63-64 & 68-69; cur, Natural Hist Mus, Vassar Col; vis scientist, Marine Biol Asn UK, Plymouth, Devon, 68-69, 76 & 81. *Mem:* AAAS; Am Soc Zool; Sigma Xi; NY Acad Sci. *Res:* Limnology and biogeography; experimental morphology; trophic action in sensory systems; ecology of cladocera. *Mailing Add:* Dept Biol Vassar Col Poughkeepsie NY 12601

WRIGHT, MARY LOU, b Milford, Mass, Dec 4, 34. DEVELOPMENTAL BIOLOGY, ENDOCRINOLOGY. *Educ:* Col Our Lady Elms, BS, 57; Univ Detroit, MS, 66; Univ Mass, PhD(develop biol), 72. *Prof Exp:* TEACHING & RES BIOL, COL OUR LADY ELMS, 58- *Concurrent Pos:* Sigma Xi Res Grant, 73; Res Corp grant, 76-78; consult, NSF, 81- *Mem:* Soc Develop Biol; Am Soc Zoologists; Tissue Cult Asn; AAAS. *Res:* Investigation of the influence of thyroxine and prolactin on cell population kinetics in Amphibian tadpole limb epidermis; study of biological rhythms of cell proliferation in amphibian eqidermis. *Mailing Add:* Col of Our Lady of Elms Chicopee MA 01013

WRIGHT, MAURICE ARTHUR, b Coventry, Eng, Aug 2, 35; m 60; c 3. METALLURGY. *Educ:* Univ Col Swansea, Wales, BSc, 59, PhD(metall), 62. *Prof Exp:* Staff scientist, metall, Tyco Labs Inc, Mass, 62-65; sr metallurgist, Norton Res Corp, 65-68; PROF METALL ENG, SPACE INST, UNIV TENN, 68- *Mem:* Am Soc Metals. *Res:* Mechanical properties of metals, ceramics and composite materials; study of fracture mechanisms and investigation of application of linear elastic fracture mechanics to composite materials. *Mailing Add:* Univ Tenn Space Inst Tullahoma TN 37388

WRIGHT, MAURICE MORGAN, b Assiniboia, Sask, July 29, 16; m 45; c 3. ELECTROCHEMISTRY. *Educ:* Univ BC, BA & BASc, 38; Princeton Univ, MA, 48, PhD(chem), 52. *Prof Exp:* Res chemist, Cominco, Ltd, 38-45 & 49-81; RETIRED. *Concurrent Pos:* Indust fel, Nat Res Coun Can, 49-52. *Mem:* Electrochem Soc; Am Chem Soc; Chem Inst Can. *Res:* Electrowinning and refining of metals; electrolytic hydrogen; ammonia synthesis; physical methods of analysis; deuterium separation, analysis and exchange reactions; reactive metals; anodic films; corrosion; protective coatings; lead-acid battery chemistry. *Mailing Add:* 1454 Willowdown Rd Oakville ON L6L 1X3 Can

WRIGHT, MELVYN CHARLES HARMAN, b Leicester, Eng, Sept 1, 44; Brit citizen. RADIO ASTRONOMY. *Educ:* Cambridge Univ, BA, 66, MA, 69, PhD(astron), 70. *Prof Exp:* Res assoc astron, Nat Radio Astron Observ, 70-72 & Calif Inst Technol, 72-77; RES ASTRONR, RADIO ASTRON LAB, 72- *Mem:* Fel Royal Astron Soc; Am Astron Soc. *Res:* Galactic and extragalactic radio astronomy; design and implementation of radio interferometers. *Mailing Add:* Radio Astron Lab Univ of Calif Berkeley CA 94720

WRIGHT, NORMAN SAMUEL, b BC, Dec 8, 20; m 49. PLANT PATHOLOGY. *Educ:* Univ BC, BSA, 44, MSA, 46; Univ Calif, PhD(plant path), 51. *Prof Exp:* Plant pathologist, Sci Serv, Plant Path Lab, 46-60, head plant path sect, 60-81, SR PLANT PATHOLOGIST, VANCOUVER RES STA, CAN DEPT AGR, 81- *Mem:* Potato Asn Am; Can Phytopath Soc; Agr Inst Can. *Res:* Potato viruses. *Mailing Add:* Agr Can Res Sta 6660 NW Marine Dr Vancouver BC V6T 1X2 Can

WRIGHT, OSCAR LEWIS, b Murphysboro, Ill, Apr 21, 17; m 39; c 3. ORGANIC CHEMISTRY, PHYSICAL CHEMISTRY. *Educ:* Southern Ill Univ, BEd, 38; Univ Mo, BS, 47, PhD(org & phys chem), 49. *Prof Exp:* Teacher pub sch, Ill, 39-40; anal chemist, Wis Steel Co, 40-41 & E I du Pont de Nemours & Co, 41-43; assoc prof, Southwest Mo State Col, 49-50; head dept chem, Col of Emporia, 50-52; org chemist, Continental Oil Co, 52-55, Pittsburgh Coke & Chem Co, 55-58 & MSA Res Corp Div, Mine Safety Appliance Co, 58-61; prof chem & chmn div sci & math, Rockhurst Col, 61-67; PROF CHEM & CHMN DEPT, NORTHEAST LA UNIV, 67- *Res:* Organic reactions of ion-exchange agents; steric factors in aromatic electrophilic substitution; organometallics; gas-solid reaction systems; effect of solvents in aromatic electrophilic substitution reactions. *Mailing Add:* Dept of Chem Northeast Sta Monroe LA 71209

WRIGHT, PAUL ALBERT, b Nashua, NH, June 15, 20; m 43; c 3. REPRODUCTIVE ENDOCRINOLOGY. *Educ:* Bates Col, SB, 41; Harvard Univ, AM, 42, PhD(endocrinol), 44. *Prof Exp:* Asst biol, Harvard Univ, 42-43, instr, 44-45; instr zool & physiol, Univ Wash, 45-46; instr biol sci, Boston Univ, 46-47; from instr to assoc prof zool, Univ Mich, 47-58; assoc prof, 58-62, endocrinologist, Agr Exp Sta, 58-68, chmn dept, Univ, 63-69, PROF ZOOL, UNIV NH, 62- *Mem:* AAAS; Am Soc Zoologists (treas, 65-68); Soc Exp Biol & Med; Soc Study Reproduction. *Res:* Ovulation in the frog; physiology of melanophores of Amphibia; blood sugar studies in lower vertebrates; control of corpus luteum life by the uterus. *Mailing Add:* Dept of Zool Univ of NH Durham NH 03824

WRIGHT, PAUL MCCOY, b Alfalfa Co, Okla, Sept 11, 04; m 30; c 3. PHYSICAL CHEMISTRY. *Educ:* Wheaton Col, Ill, BS, 26; Ohio State Univ, MS, 28, PhD(phys chem), 30. *Prof Exp:* Asst chem, Wheaton Col, Ill, 25-26; asst gen chem, Ohio State Univ, 26-28, asst phys chem, 28-29; from asst prof to prof chem, 29-70, actg chmn dept chem & geol, 39-40, chmn dept geol, 40-59, chmn dept chem, 40-69, dir field camp, SDak, 46-52 & 60, EMER PROF CHEM, WHEATON COL, ILL, 70- *Mem:* AAAS; Am Chem Soc; fel Am Inst Chemists. *Res:* Dimensions of vapor particles; eutectics of explosive mixtures; equilibria of glycerol esters; radiochemistry; color centers in rose quartz by electron paramagnetic resonance. *Mailing Add:* GoYe Village Apt 416 Tahlequah OK 74464

WRIGHT, PETER MURRELL, b Toronto, Ont, Sept 26, 32; m 55; c 4. CIVIL ENGINEERING. *Educ:* Univ Sask, BS, 54, MSc, 61; Univ Colo, Boulder, PhD(struct), 68. *Prof Exp:* Engr, Dorman-Long Ltd, Eng, 54-57; asst prof struct, Univ Sask, 57-66; PROF STRUCT, UNIV TORONTO, 68-, ASSOC DEAN ENG, 81- *Mem:* Eng Inst Can; Can Soc Civil Engrs (pres, 81-82). *Res:* Automatic design of steel building frames including member selection. *Mailing Add:* Dept Civil Eng Univ Toronto Toronto ON M5S 1A4 Can

WRIGHT, PHILIP LINCOLN, b Nashua, NH, July 9, 14; m 39; c 3. ZOOLOGY. *Educ:* Univ NH, BS, 35, MS, 37; Univ Wis, PhD(zool), 40. *Prof Exp:* From instr to assoc prof, 39-51, chmn dept, 56-69 & 70-71, PROF ZOOL, UNIV MONT, 51- *Concurrent Pos:* Ed, Gen Notes & Rev, J Mammal, 66-67; sabbatical leave, Africa, 70; vis Maytag prof zool, Ariz State Univ, 80. *Mem:* Am Soc Mammalogists; Am Soc Zoologists; Wildlife Soc; Soc Study Reproduction; fel AAAS. *Res:* Reproductive cycles of birds and mammals; especially Mustelidae. *Mailing Add:* Dept Zool Univ Mont Missoula MT 59812

WRIGHT, RAMIL CARTER, b Hastings, Nebr, May 16, 39; m 63. MICROPALEONTOLOGY, BIOSTRATIGRAPHY. *Educ:* Rice Univ, BA, 60; Univ Ill, MS, 62, PhD(geol), 64. *Prof Exp:* Asst dir, Waterways Exp Sta, Corps Engrs, 64-66; NSF fel, Museo Argentino de Ciencias Naturales, Argentina, 66-67; vis prof, Hamline Univ, St Paul, Minn, 68; from asst prof to assoc prof, Beloit Col, Wis, 68-76; ASSOC PROF GEOL, FLA STATE UNIV, 76-, ASSOC CHAIRPERSON, DEPT GEOL, 80- *Concurrent Pos:* Int Working Group, Int Geol Correlation Proj, 75-78. *Mem:* Geol Soc Am; Paleont Soc; AAAS; Sigma Xi. *Res:* Foraminiferal ecology and biostratigraphy; Miocene paleoenvironments. *Mailing Add:* Dept of Geol Fla State Univ Tallahassee FL 32306

WRIGHT, RICHARD DONALD, cell biology, see previous edition

WRIGHT, RICHARD N(EWPORT), b Syracuse, NY, May 17, 32; m 59; c 4. CIVIL ENGINEERING. *Educ:* Syracuse Univ, BS, 53, MS, 55; Univ Ill, PhD(civil eng), 62. *Prof Exp:* Jr engr, Pa RR Co, 53-54; from instr to assoc prof, 57-70, prof civil eng, Univ Ill, Urbana, 70-72 & 73-74; chief struct sect, 71-72, dep dir-tech, 72-73, DIR, CTR FOR BLDG TECHNOL, NAT BUR STAND, 74- *Concurrent Pos:* Secy, Column Res Coun, 62-66; adj prof civil eng, Univ Ill, Urbana, 74-79; mem bd, Int Coun Bldg Res, 80- *Mem:* Am Soc Eng Educ; fel Am Soc Civil Engrs; Int Union Testing & Res Labs Mat & Struct; Earthquake Eng Res Inst; Sigma Xi. *Res:* Analysis, behavior and design of structures; technologies for the formulation and expression of standards; performance criteria and measurement technology for buildings. *Mailing Add:* Ctr for Bldg Technol Nat Bur of Stand Washington DC 20234

WRIGHT, RICHARD T, b Haddonfield, NJ, June 28, 33; m 61; c 3. AQUATIC ECOLOGY. *Educ:* Rutgers Univ, AB, 59; Harvard Univ, PhD(biol), 63. *Prof Exp:* NSF fel, Inst Limnol, Univ Uppsala, 63-65; PROF BIOL, GORDON COL, 65- *Concurrent Pos:* NSF res grants, 66-71, 73-79 & 80-83; NSF sci fac fel, Ore State Univ, 69-70. *Mem:* Ecol Soc Am; Am Soc Limnol & Oceanog; Am Sci Affil; Am Soc Microbiologists. *Res:* Dissolved organic matter of natural waters and the microorganisms using, transforming and producing it. *Mailing Add:* Dept of Biol Gordon Col Wenham MA 01984

WRIGHT, ROBERT ANDERSON, b El Paso, Tex, July 22, 33; m 55; c 4. BOTANY. *Educ:* NMex State Univ, BS, 55, MS, 60; Univ Ariz, PhD(bot), 65. *Prof Exp:* PROF BIOL, W TEX STATE UNIV, 64- *Mem:* AAAS; Biomet Soc; Ecol Soc Am; Soc Study Evolution; Brit Ecol Soc. *Res:* Vegetation changes; statistical ecology; net primary productivity. *Mailing Add:* Dept of Biol WTex State Univ Canyon TX 79016

WRIGHT, ROBERT HAMILTON, b Vancouver, BC, Dec 26, 06; m 31; c 3. PHYSICAL CHEMISTRY. *Educ:* Univ BC, BA, 28; McGill Univ, MSc, 30, PhD(chem), 31. *Hon Degrees:* DSc, Univ NB, 73. *Prof Exp:* From asst prof to assoc prof chem, Univ NB, 31-41, prof phys chem, 41-46; head div chem, BC Res Coun, 46-62, head olfactory response invest, 62-71; CONSULT, FOOD & AGR ORGN, Fel Chem Inst Can; Can Entom Soc. *Res:* Fundamental and applied odor studies; physical basis of odors; insect attractants and repellents. *Mailing Add:* 6822 Blenheim St Vancouver BC V6N 1R7 Can

WRIGHT, ROBERT JAMES, b Bridgewater, Va, Dec 16, 18; m 46; c 4. GEOLOGY. *Educ:* Denison Univ, BA, 40; Columbia Univ, MA, 42, PhD(geol), 47. *Prof Exp:* Field geologist, US Geol Surv, Washington, DC, 42-44; lectr geol, Columbia Univ, 46-47; asst prof, St Lawrence Univ, 47-49; staff geologist, US AEC, NY, 49-50, chief geol br, Colo, 51-54; supvr explor, Climax Uranium Co, 54-58; mgr western explor, Am Metal Climax, Inc, 59-65, vpres, AMAX Explor, Inc, 65-68, mgr overseas mining activities group, AMAX, Inc, 68-73; consult geologist, Roan Consolidated Mines Ltd, Zambia, 73-75; chief geologist, Uranium Resources & Enrichment Div, US Dept Energy, 75-79; SR TECH ADV, DIV WASTE MGT, US NUCLEAR REGULATORY COMN, 79- *Mem:* Fel Geol Soc Am; Soc Econ Geol; Am Inst Mining, Metall & Petrol Eng. *Res:* Economic geology. *Mailing Add:* MS 609-SS US Nuclear Regulatory Comn Washington DC 20555

WRIGHT, ROBERT L, b Buckhannon, WVa, Sept 7, 30; m 52; c 1. ORGANIC CHEMISTRY, RUBBER CHEMISTRY. *Educ:* WVa Wesleyan Col, BS, 52. *Prof Exp:* Anal trainee, 52, res chemist, 55-64, sr res chemist, 64-75, res specialist, 75-80, SR RES SPECIALIST, MONSANTO CO, 80- *Mem:* Am Chem Soc. *Res:* Process development; exploratory synthesis in the field of rubber chemicals; product development of adhesive systems. *Mailing Add:* 95 Blue Hill Lane Fairlawn OH 44313

WRIGHT, ROBERT PAUL, paleoecology, invertebrate paleontology, see previous edition

WRIGHT, ROBERT RAYMOND, b Buffalo, NY, May 20, 31; m 60; c 3. SCIENCE POLICY. *Educ:* Syracuse Univ, BS, 57; Wayne State Univ, MA, 61, EdD, 64. *Prof Exp:* Asst dir instnl res, Wayne State Univ, 60-66; dir instnl res, State Univ NY Cent Staff, 66-72; consult univ sci & data eval, NSF, 72-73; dir instnl res, State Univ NY Cent Staff, 73-74; STAFF ASSOC & HEAD SCI INDICATORS UNIT, NSF, 74- *Concurrent Pos:* Chmn, Data Standards Comt, Asn Instnl Res, 67-69, mem, Comt Access to Fed Data, 72-73; mem, Comt Fed Reporting, Nat Asn Col & Univ Bus Officers, 67-69. *Mem:* AAAS; Asn Instnl Res; Soc Social Studies Sci. *Res:* Economics of research and development; sociology of science. *Mailing Add:* 10713 Shadowglen Trail Fairfax Station VA 22039

WRIGHT, ROBERT W, b Auburn, NY, Aug 2, 32; m 55. PHYSICAL ORGANIC CHEMISTRY, POLYMER CHEMISTRY. *Educ:* NY State Col Forestry, BS, 59, PhD(chem), 64. *Prof Exp:* Chemist, Owens-Ill, Inc, Ohio, 64-65, res chemist, 65-66, sect leader polymer chem, 66-69; group dir synthetic mat, 69-76, MGR ANAL SCI, CORP RES CTR, INT PAPER CO, 77- *Mem:* Am Chem Soc; Tech Asn Pulp & Paper Indust; Soc Plastics Engrs; Coun Agr & Chemurgic Res. *Res:* Plastics processing; polymer coatings and adhesives; polymer characterization; analytical chemistry. *Mailing Add:* Corp Res & Develop Div Int Paper Co Tuxedo Park NY 10987

WRIGHT, ROGER M, b Long Beach, Calif, Feb 19, 35; m 58; c 2. CHEMICAL ENGINEERING. *Educ:* Univ Calif, Berkeley, BS, 56, PhD(chem eng), 61. *Prof Exp:* Res engr, Lawrence Radiation Lab, Calif, 57-61; SR ENG SPECIALIST, AiRES MFG CO, 60- *Mem:* Am Inst Chem Engrs; Am Inst Aeronaut & Astronaut. *Res:* Heat transfer, including research in forced-convection boiling, compact heat exchangers and spacecraft thermal radiators; spacecraft environmental control systems; mass-transfer systems. *Mailing Add:* 6235 Monita St Long Beach CA 90803

WRIGHT, RUSSELL EMERY, b Muscatine, Iowa, June 19, 39; m 63; c 3. MEDICAL ENTOMOLOGY. *Educ:* Iowa State Univ, BSc, 63, MS, 66; Univ Wis-Ann Arbor, PhD(entom), 69. *Prof Exp:* From asst prof to assoc prof entom, Univ Guelph, 69-76; ASSOC PROF, OKLA STATE UNIV, 76- *Mem:* Entom Soc Am; Entom Soc Can; Am Mosquito Cent Asn. *Res:* Behavior, biology and control of insect pests of livestock; arthropod borne viruses. *Mailing Add:* Dept of Entom Okla State Univ Stillwater OK 74074

WRIGHT, SEWALL, b Melrose, Mass, Dec 21, 89; m 21; c 3. GENETICS, EVOLUTION. *Educ:* Lombard Col, BS, 11; Univ Ill, MS, 12; Harvard Univ, ScD(zool), 15. *Hon Degrees:* ScD, Univ Rochester, 42, Yale Univ, 49, Harvard Univ, 51, Knox Col, 57, Western Reserve Univ, 58, Univ Chicago, 59, Univ Ill, 61, Univ Wis, 65; LLD, Mich State Col, 55. *Prof Exp:* Sr animal husbandman, Animal Husb Div, Bur Animal Indust, USDA, 15-25; from assoc prof to prof, 26-37, Ernest D Burton distinguished serv prof, 38-54, EMER PROF ZOOL, UNIV CHICAGO, 55- *Concurrent Pos:* Mem exec comt, Div Biol & Agr, Nat Res Coun, 31-33; Hitchcock prof, Univ Calif, 43; Fulbright prof, Univ Edinburgh, 49-50; mem comt biol effects of radiation, Nat Acad Sci, 55-; Leon J Cole prof genetics, Univ Wis-Madison, 55-60, emer prof, 60-; pres, Int Cong Genetics, Montreal, 58. *Honors & Awards:* Weldon Mem Medal, Oxford Univ, 47; Elliot Medal, Nat Acad Sci, 47, Kimber Award, 56; Lewis Prize, Am Philos Soc, 50; Nat Medal Sci, 66; Darwin Medal & Award, Royal Soc Chem, 80. *Mem:* Nat Acad Sci; Genetic Soc Am (pres, 34); Am Soc Zool (pres, 44); Am Soc Naturalists (treas, 29-32, pres, 52); Soc Study Evolution (pres, 53). *Res:* Genetics of guinea pig and populations; theory of evolution; mathematical theory of population genetics. *Mailing Add:* 3905 Council Crest Madison WI 53711

WRIGHT, STEPHEN E, b Searcy, Ark, Mar 20, 42; m 65; c 2. ONCOLOGY, VIROLOGY. *Educ:* Hendrix Col, BA, 63; Univ Ark, MD, 76. *Prof Exp:* Instr med hematol/oncol, Sch Med, Univ Wash, 73-74, asst prof, 74-75; chief, oncol, Vet Admin Med Ctr, Salt Lake City, Utah, 75-82; ASST PROF MED MOLECULAR BIOL, COL MED, UNIV UTAH, 75-; RES ASSOC CANCER RES, VET ADMIN MED CTR, SALT LAKE CITY, UTAH, 82- *Concurrent Pos:* Prin investr, Southwest Oncol Group, 75-, Vet Admin Grant, 76-79 & 79-82. *Res:* Mechanisms of oncogenic transformation; tumor vaccine production; tumor antibody production. *Mailing Add:* Viral Oncol 111 Vet Admin Med Ctr Salt Lake City UT 84148

WRIGHT, STEPHEN GAILORD, b San Diego, Calif, Aug 13, 43; m 70. CIVIL ENGINEERING. *Educ:* Univ Calif, Berkeley, BS, 66, MS, 67, PhD(civil eng), 69. *Prof Exp:* Asst prof, 69-77, ASSOC PROF CIVIL ENG, UNIV TEX, AUSTIN, 77- *Mem:* Am Soc Civil Engrs. *Res:* Soil mechanics and foundations; slope stability; foundations for offshore structures. *Mailing Add:* Dept of Civil Eng Univ of Tex Austin TX 78712

WRIGHT, STEVEN MARTIN, b Oak Park, Ill, Aug 25, 53; m 75; c 2. FLUORINE CHEMISTRY. *Educ:* Elmhurst Col, BA, 75; Marquette Univ, PhD(inorg chem), 80. *Prof Exp:* ASST PROF CHEM, LAKELAND COL, 80- *Concurrent Pos:* Vis asst prof, Univ Wis-Milwaukee, 81-82; instr, Marquette Univ, 80-82. *Mem:* Am Chem Soc; AAAS; Sigma Xi; NY Acad Sci. *Res:* New synthetic methods to form new and existing graphite interalation compounds; interalaction of fluorides and graphite. *Mailing Add:* 2217 N 37th St Sheboygan WI 53081

WRIGHT, STUART JOSEPH, b Arvida, Que, Jan 17, 52; US citizen. TROPICAL ECOLOGY. *Educ:* Princeton Univ, BA, 74; Univ Calif, Los Angeles, PhD(biol), 80. *Prof Exp:* Fel trop biol, 80-81, RES ASSOC, SMITHSONIAN TROP RES INST, 81- *Concurrent Pos:* Vis asst prof ecol, Univ Mont, 81-82. *Mem:* Ecol Soc Am; Asn Trop Biol; Am Ornithologists Union. *Res:* Theoretical and empirical investigations of the relative abundances of species with emphasis on tropical communities of birds, lizards and trees. *Mailing Add:* Dept Zool Univ Mont Missoula MT 59812

WRIGHT, STUART R(EDMOND), b Calgary, Alta, Aug 13, 23; m 49; c 3. CHEMICAL ENGINEERING, CHEMISTRY. *Educ:* Univ Alta, BSc, 46, MSc, 47; Northwestern Univ, PhD, 50. *Prof Exp:* Engr, Aluminum Co Can, Ltd, 50-54; engr, 54-66, sr res engr, 66-69, res assoc chem, 69-74, RES ASSOC DIV ENG, E I DU PONT DE NEMOURS & CO, INC, 74- *Mem:* Am Inst Chem Engrs. *Res:* Industrial chemicals; dye intermediates. *Mailing Add:* 15 Marlton Rd Woodstown NJ 08098

WRIGHT, SYDNEY COURTENAY, b Vancouver, BC, Oct 16, 23; m 48; c 3. PHYSICS. *Educ:* Univ BC, BA, 43; Univ Calif, PhD(physics), 49. *Prof Exp:* NSF fel, 49-50, res assoc, 50-55, from asst prof to assoc prof, 55-68, PROF PHYSICS, ENRICO FERMI INST, UNIV CHICAGO, 69- *Concurrent Pos:* Consult, Brookhaven Nat Lab, 53 & Argonne Nat Lab, 57-60. *Mem:* Am Phys Soc. *Res:* Experimental particle physics; particle accelerator design. *Mailing Add:* Dept of Physics Univ Chicago 5801 S Ellis Ave Chicago IL 60637

WRIGHT, TERRY L, b Houston, Tex, July 9, 52. SYNTHETIC HETEROCYCLIC CHEMISTRY. *Educ:* Tex Christian Univ, BS, 74; Univ Chicago, MS, 75, PhD(org chem), 79. *Prof Exp:* Sr res chemist, 79-81, PROJ LEADER, WESTERN DIV, DOW CHEM USA, 81- *Mem:* Am Chem Soc. *Res:* Development of new areas of heterocyclic chemistry particularly the synthesis of new heterocyclic ring systems and for the design, synthesis and development of new pharmaceuticals. *Mailing Add:* Western Div Dow Chem USA Loveridge Rd Pittsburg CA 94565

WRIGHT, THEODORE ROBERT FAIRBANK, b Kodaikanal, India, Apr 10, 28; US citizen; m 51. DEVELOPMENTAL GENETICS. *Educ:* Princeton Univ, AB, 49; Wesleyan Univ, MA, 54, Yale Univ, PhD(zool), 59. *Prof Exp:* Asst prof biol, Johns Hopkins Univ, 59-65; assoc prof, 65-75, PROF BIOL, UNIV VA, 75- *Concurrent Pos:* Mem genetics study sect, NIH, 72-74; fel, Max Planck Inst Biol, 75-76. *Mem:* Fel AAAS; Genetics Soc Am; Soc Develop Biol; Am Soc Zoologists. *Res:* Developmental genetics of embryonic mutants in Drosophila; genetic and molecular analysis of the functional organizaion of the genome of Drosophila. *Mailing Add:* Dept of Biol Univ of Va Charlottesville VA 22901

WRIGHT, THOMAS L, b Chicago, Ill, July 26, 35; m 58; c 2. GEOLOGY, PETROLOGY. *Educ:* Pomona Col, AB, 57; Johns Hopkins Univ, PhD(geol), 61. *Prof Exp:* Geologist, Washington, DC, 61-64, staff geologist, Hawaiian Volcano Observ, Hawaii Nat Park, 64-69, geologist, Geol Div, Washington, DC, 69-74, WITH US GEOL SURV, RESTON, VA, 74- *Mem:* Mineral Soc Am; Geochem Soc; Am Geophys Union. *Res:* Igneous petrology; petrology and mineralogy of Hawaiian basalt; study of crystallization of basalt in the lava lakes of Kilauea volcano; chemical and stratigraphic study of the basalts of the Columbia River plateau. *Mailing Add:* US Geol Surv 959 Nat Ctr Reston VA 22092

WRIGHT, THOMAS OSCAR, b Jasper, Ala, July 9, 40; m 65. STRATIGRAPHY, STRUCTURE. *Educ:* Auburn Univ, BS, 65; George Washington Univ, MS, 71, PhD(geochem), 74. *Prof Exp:* Oceanogr, Nat Oceanog Data Ctr, 65-69; lectr geol, Bryn Mawr Col, 73-75; asst prof geol, Allegheny Col, 75-78; prog assoc geol, 78-80, PROG DIR STRUCTURE & TECTRONICS, NSF, 80- *Concurrent Pos:* Lectr, George Washington Univ, 73-75 & Carbon Lehigh Intermediate Sch Unit, 76-78; proj geologist explor, Cyprus Explor Ltd, 70- *Mem:* Geol Soc Am. *Res:* Geology and geochemistry of sedimentary rocks and modern analogs; teaching of geology; Ordovician clastic rocks of central Appalachians; sedimentology and structure of pre-cambrian and paleozoic rocks; northern Victoria Land; Antarctica. *Mailing Add:* Geol Prog Rm 602 Nat Sci Found Washington DC 20055

WRIGHT, THOMAS PAYNE, b Ft Worth, Tex, Dec 23, 43; m 66; c 3. PHYSICS, PLASMA PHYSICS. *Educ:* St Bonaventure Univ, BS, 66; NMex State Univ, MS, 68, PhD(physics), 69. *Prof Exp:* Staff mem physics, 69-80, SUPVR THEORET DIV, SANDIA NAT LABS, 80- *Mem:* Am Phys Soc. *Res:* Plasma waves and instabilities; electromagnetic theory; theory of kinetic equations; laser-plasma interaction; statistical mechanics; relativistic electron beams; magnetohydrodynamics; intense charged particle beam sources and transport. *Mailing Add:* Sandia Nat Labs PO Box 5800 Albuquerque NM 87185

WRIGHT, THOMAS PERRIN, JR, b Great Falls, SC, June 23, 39; m 61; c 2. TOPOLOGY. *Educ:* Davidson Col, AB, 60; Univ Wis, MA, 63, PhD(math), 67. *Prof Exp:* ASSOC PROF MATH, FLA STATE UNIV, 67- *Concurrent Pos:* NSF grant, Fla State Univ, 67-72. *Mem:* Am Math Soc. *Res:* Topology of manifolds. *Mailing Add:* 1808 Skyland Dr Tallahassee FL 32303

WRIGHT, THOMAS WILSON, b Fergus Falls, Minn, Oct 23, 33; m 55; c 3. MECHANICS. *Educ:* Cornell Univ, BCE, 56, MCE, 57, PhD(mech), 64. *Prof Exp:* Sr engr struct, AAI Corp, Md, 59-61; asst prof mech, Johns Hopkins Univ, 64-67; MECH ENGR, US ARMY BALLISTIC RES LABS, ABERDEEN PROVING GROUND, 67- *Mem:* Soc Natural Philos. *Res:* Nonlinear wave propagation and the mechanics of deformable media. *Mailing Add:* US Army Ballistic Res Labs Aberdeen Proving Ground MD 21005

WRIGHT, VERNON LEE, b Muscatine, Iowa, Feb 20, 41; m 66; c 3. BIOMETRICS, POPULATION DYNAMICS. *Educ:* Iowa State Univ, BS, 64; Purdue Univ, MS, 66; Wash State Univ, PhD(zool), 71. *Prof Exp:* Fel biometrics, Cornell Univ, 70-72; wildlife biometrician, Iowa Conserv Comn, 72-76; conserv res analyst, Ill Dept Conserv, 76-78; ASST PROF EXP STATIST, LA STATE UNIV, BATON ROUGE, 78- *Mem:* Wildlife Soc; Biometric Soc; Ecol Soc Am; Sigma Xi; AAAS. *Res:* Sampling from and modeling of naturally occurring populations; statistical aspects of wildlife management and administration; measuring peoples' attitudes toward conservation issues. *Mailing Add:* Dept Exp Statist La State Univ Baton Rouge LA 70803

WRIGHT, WALTER EUGENE, b Terre Haute, Ind, July 16, 24; m 51; c 5. BIOPHARMACEUTICS. *Educ:* Purdue Univ, BS, 48, MS, 50, PhD(pharmaceut chem), 53. *Prof Exp:* Sr biochemist, 53-65, res scientist, 65-69, RES ASSOC, ELI LILLY & CO, 69- *Mem:* Am Chem Soc; NY Acad Sci; Am Soc Microbiol. *Res:* Intestinal and drug absorption; active transport; study of the absorption, metabolism and excretion of new medicinal agents in experimental animals. *Mailing Add:* 7553 N Audubon Rd Indianapolis IN 46250

WRIGHT, WAYNE GORDON, b Yankton, SDak, June 13, 35; m 57; c 3. WEED SCIENCE, ENTOMOLOGY. *Educ:* SDak State Univ, BS, 57, MS, 61. *Prof Exp:* Asst mgr state seed lab, SDak State Univ, 57-62, mgr found seed stock div, 63-64, in charge of weed res, 64-66; regional tech specialist agr herbicides, Dow Chem Co, 67-71, field group leader, Dow Chem USA, 71-74, prod tech specialist, 74-78, REGIONAL MGR, AGR T S & D, DOW CHEM USA, 78- *Mem:* Weed Sci Soc Am. *Res:* Seed technology; crop production; weed control in crops and non-crop areas; brush control; harvest aid defoliation; insect and disease control in crops and ornamentals. *Mailing Add:* Dow Chem USA Continental Towers Bldg 11 1701 W Golf Rd suite 500 Rolling Meadows IL 60008

WRIGHT, WAYNE MITCHELL, b Sanford, Maine, July 12, 34; m 59; c 4. ACOUSTICS. *Educ:* Bowdoin Col, AB, 56; Harvard Univ, MS, 57, PhD(appl physics), 61. *Prof Exp:* Res fel, Harvard Univ, 61-62; from asst prof to assoc prof, 62-75, PROF PHYSICS & CHMN DEPT, KALAMAZOO COL, 75- *Mem:* Fel Acoust Soc Am; Am Asn Physics Teachers. *Res:* Physical acoustics; experimental studies of finite-amplitude sound phenomena in air. *Mailing Add:* Dept Physics Kalamazoo Col Kalamazoo MI 49007

WRIGHT, WELLESLEY HORTON, dentistry, periodontology, deceased

WRIGHT, WILBUR HERBERT, b Kansas City, Mo, Feb 28, 20; m 43; c 2. PHYSICS. *Educ:* Oberlin Col, AB, 42; Rutgers Univ, PhD(physics), 52. *Prof Exp:* From asst to instr physics, Rutgers Univ, 47-52; asst prof, Univ NH, 52-56; assoc prof, 56-60, PROF PHYSICS, COLO COL, 60- *Concurrent Pos:* NSF fac fel, Stanford Univ, 59-60. *Mem:* Am Phys Soc; Am Asn Physics Teachers. *Res:* Superconductivity; applied mathematics; measurement of small magnetic susceptibilities; non-equilibrium thermodynamics. *Mailing Add:* Dept of Physics Colo Col Colorado Springs CO 80903

WRIGHT, WILLIAM BLYTHE, JR, b Washington, DC, Sept 29, 18; m 48; c 2. PHARMACEUTICAL CHEMISTRY. *Educ:* Univ Va, BS, 39; Univ Mich, PhD(chem), 42. *Prof Exp:* Resin res chemist, Rohm and Haas Co, Pa, 42-47; pharmaceut res chemist, Bound Brook Labs, 47-55, PHARMACEUT RES CHEMIST, LEDERLE LABS, AM CYANAMID CO, 55- *Mem:* Am Chem Soc. *Res:* Coatings; plywood adhesives; ion exchange resins; pharmaceuticals. *Mailing Add:* 18 Clinton Pl Woodcliff Lake NJ 07675

WRIGHT, WILLIAM F(RED), b Salt Lake City, Utah, Nov 12, 18; m 55; c 2. MECHANICAL ENGINEERING. *Educ:* Vanderbilt Univ, BE, 40, MA, 41; Harvard Univ, MS, 47. *Prof Exp:* Instr appl math, 46-47, from instr to assoc prof, 47-70, PROF MECH ENG, VANDERBILT UNIV, 70- *Concurrent Pos:* Instr, US Naval Acad, 59-60. *Mem:* Am Soc Eng Educ; Am Soc Mech Engrs. *Res:* Mechanical design; heat transfer; thermodynamics. *Mailing Add:* Dept of Mech Eng Vanderbilt Univ Box 1597 Substa B Nashville TN 37235

WRIGHT, WILLIAM H(OWELL), b Caroll Co, Ga, July 8, 25; m 54; c 3. CHEMICAL ENGINEERING. *Educ:* Ga Inst Technol, BChE, 51, MS, 60. *Prof Exp:* Shift supvr, Merck & Co, Ltd, Va, 51-53; chem engr, Nitrogen Div, Allied Chem Corp, 54-58, eng supvr, 58-60, mgr opers eng, 60-63, tech supt, Fibers Div, 63-66, mgr process eng, 66-70, supvr, 70-77; MEM FAC, VA INTERMONT COL, 77- *Mem:* Am Inst Chem Engrs. *Res:* Thermal conductivity of metals and alloys at low temperature; chemical engineering design and operation of ammonia and related plants; chemical and fiber engineering design and operation of synthetic fiber plants. *Mailing Add:* Dept of Biol Va Intermont Col Bristol VA 24201

WRIGHT, WILLIAM HERBERT, III, b Newton, Mass, Feb 13, 43. STRUCTURAL GEOLOGY. *Educ:* Middlebury Col, BA, 65; Ind Univ, Bloomington, MA, 67; Univ Ill, Urbana, PhD(geol), 70. *Prof Exp:* Explor geologist, Chevron Oil Co, Colo, 66; from asst prof to assoc prof, 69-78, PROF GEOL, SONOMA STATE UNIV, 78- *Mem:* AAAS; Geol Soc Am; Am Geophys Union. *Res:* Folding, metamorphic structures; geology of geothermal energy resources; structural evolution of mountain belts; structure and geologic history of Calaveras Formation and Sierra Foothills Melange, Sierra Nevada, California. *Mailing Add:* Dept Geol Sonoma State Univ Rohnert Park CA 94928

WRIGHT, WILLIAM LELAND, b Darbyville, Ohio, Aug 14, 30; m 52; c 3. WEED SCIENCE. *Educ:* Ohio Univ, BS, 53, MS, 57; Purdue Univ, PhD(plant physiol), 64. *Prof Exp:* Plant physiologist, Dow Chem Co, Tex, 57-58; from plant physiologist to sr plant physiologist, 58-65, head plant sci res, 65-72, prod plans adv, Elanco Prod Co, 72-73, regulatory serv adv, 73-74, mgr agr regulatory serv, 74-76, dir, Agr Regulatory Serv, 76-80, DIR, GOVERNMENT AFFAIRS, ELI LILLY & CO, 80- *Mem:* Sigma Xi; Am Hort Soc; Am Soc Plant Physiologists; Weed Sci Soc Am. *Res:* Chemical weed control; plant growth regulation, insecticides and aquatic weed control; fate of herbicides in environment; product planning; regulatory affairs; government affairs. *Mailing Add:* 1901 L St NW Suite 705 Washington DC 22036

WRIGHT, WILLIAM RAY, b Iola, Wis, Agu 16, 41; m 63. SOIL MORPHOLOGY. *Educ:* Wis State Univ-River Falls, BS, 66; Univ Md, College Park, MS, 69, PhD(soils), 72. *Prof Exp:* Asst prof, 72-77, ASSOC PROF SOIL SCI, UNIV RI, 77- *Mem:* Am Soc Agron; Soil Sci Soc Am; Soil Conserv Soc Am. *Res:* Soil genesis, classification and land use. *Mailing Add:* Dept of Plant & Soil Sci Univ of RI Kingston RI 02881

WRIGHT, WILLIAM REDWOOD, b Philadelphia, Pa, Sept 17, 27; m 56; c 3. PHYSICAL OCEANOGRAPHY. *Educ:* Princeton Univ, BA, 50; Univ RI, MS, 65, PhD(oceanog), 70. *Prof Exp:* Teacher, RI Pvt Sch, 50-52; pub info officer, Woods Hole Oceanog Inst, 60-62, res asst phys oceanog, 62-70, asst scientist, 70-75; supvry oceanogr, Northeast Fisheries Ctr, Nat Marine Fisheries Serv, 76-81; PRES, BERMUDA BIOL STA RES, INC, 77-; OCEANOGRAPHER & ASSOC SCIENTIST, WOODS HOLE INST OCEANOG, 79- *Concurrent Pos:* Reporter, Auburn Citizen-Advertiser, NY, 52-54 & Providence J, RI, 54-60. *Mem:* AAAS; Am Geophys Union; Am Soc Limnol & Oceanog. *Res:* Deep circulation of the world oceans; coastal circulation. *Mailing Add:* Box 54 Woods Hole MA 02543

WRIGHT, WILLIAM ROBERT, b Cleveland, Ohio, Nov 24, 28. THEORETICAL PHYSICS. *Educ:* Harvard Univ, AB, 51, MA, 52, PhD(physics), 57. *Prof Exp:* Asst prof physics, Univ Kans, 57-61; assoc prof, 61-62, head dept, 62-66, PROF PHYSICS, UNIV CINCINNATI, 62- *Concurrent Pos:* Vis mem dept physics, Oxford Univ, 67-68. *Mem:* AAAS; Am Phys Soc; Am Asn Physics Teachers. *Res:* Solid state effects in nuclear orientation; Green's function techniques in magnetism; variational methods in statistical mechanics. *Mailing Add:* Dept of Physics Univ of Cincinnati Cincinnati OH 45221

WRIGHT, WILLIAM V(AUGHN), b Winston-Salem, NC, Sept 15, 31; m 55; c 3. COMPUTER SCIENCE, APPLIED MATHEMATICS. *Educ:* Duke Univ, BSEE, 53; Harvard Univ, SM, 54; Univ NC, PhD(comput sci), 72. *Prof Exp:* Assoc systs planner, Int Bus Mach Corp, 58-61, staff systs planner, 61-62, proj engr, 62-63, develop engr, 63-65, adv engr, 65-67, SR ENGR, IBM CORP, RESEARCH TRIANGLE PARK, 67- *Concurrent Pos:* Adj assoc prof comput sci, Univ NC, Chapel Hill, 72- *Mem:* Inst Elec & Electronics Engrs; Asn Comput Mach; Sigma Xi. *Res:* Computing systems architecture, design, and evaluation; computer applications in chemistry, crystallography, and biology; interactive computer graphics. *Mailing Add:* 107 E Poplar Ave Chapel Hill NC 27514

WRIGHT, WILLIAM VALE, b Long Beach, Calif, Dec 4, 29; m 71; c 4. ENGINEERING, AERONAUTICS. *Educ:* Calif Inst Technol, BS, 51, PhD(mech eng, physics), 55. *Prof Exp:* Res asst, Calif Inst Technol, 50-52; mem tech staff, Hughes Aircraft Co, 53-54; mgr semiconductor mats, TRW Semiconductors, Inc, 54-57, mgr solid state div, Electro Optical Systs, Inc, 57-60, vpres, 60-65; dir sci & eng, Environ Sci Serv Admin, 66-68; pres, Flight Test Res, Inc, 68-72; prog develop mgr autonetics, Rockwell Int Corp, 72-75; vpres, COR, Inc, 75-78; dir eng & develop, Ball Corp, 78-80; tech dir, Food Mach Group, FMC Corp, 80-81; PRES, COMPOWER SYSTS INC, 81- *Concurrent Pos:* Lectr, Univ Calif, Los Angeles, 55-60; lectr eng, Univ NC, Charlotte, 74-75. *Mem:* AAAS; Inst Elec & Electronics Engrs; Am Geophys Union; assoc fel Am Inst Aeronaut & Astronaut. *Res:* Research and engineering management; aeronautics; solid state materials and devices; computer sciences. *Mailing Add:* 2412 Cloister Dr Charlotte NC 28211

WRIGHT, WILLIAM WYNN, b Baltimore, Md, Aug 13, 23; m 45; c 5. CHEMISTRY. *Educ:* Loyola Col, Md, BS, 44; Georgetown Univ, MS, 46, PhD(biochem), 48. *Prof Exp:* Chemist, Nat Bur Stand, Washington, DC, 45; chief antibiotic chem br, 45-55, dir antibiotic control labs, 55-57, dir antibiotic res, 57-64, dep dir div antibiotics & insulin cert, 64-69, dep dir pharmaceut res & testing, 69-71, dir div drug biol, 71-75, dep assoc dir pharmaceut res & testing, Bur Drugs, 75-79, SR SCIENTIST, US PHARMACOPEIA, US FOOD & DRUG ADMIN, ROCKVILLE, MD, 79- *Concurrent Pos:* Mem, WHO Expert Panels on Antibiotics, 60-75 & Biol Stand, 75- *Honors & Awards:* Superior Serv Award, US Dept Health, Educ & Welfare, 64; Award of Merit, US Food & Drug Admin, 71. *Mem:* Fel AAAS; Am Chem Soc; fel Asn Off Anal Chemists (pres, 76-77); NY Acad Sci; fel Acad Pharmaceut Sci. *Res:* Antibiotic testing by chemical, physical, microbial and biological methods; absorption, excretion, distribution and tissue residues of antibiotics; bacterial susceptibility; pharmaceutical analysis. *Mailing Add:* 1301 Dilston Pl Silver Spring MD 20903

WRIGHT, WOODRING ERIK, b San Francisco, Calif, June 21, 49; m 71. CELL BIOLOGY, SEMATIC CELL GENETICS. *Educ:* Harvard Univ, BA, 70; Stanford Univ, PhD(med microbiol), 74, MD, 75. *Prof Exp:* Fel, Pasteur Inst, Paris, 75-78; ASST PROF CELL BIOL, UNIV TEX HEALTH SCI CTR, DALLAS, 78- *Concurrent Pos:* Prin investr, Am Heart Asn, 78-79 & 80-82, res grants, NIH, 78-, & Muscular Dystrophy Asn, 80-; Nat Inst Aging, Res Career Develop Award, 78; Lyndon Baines Johnson Award, Am Heart Asn, 78. *Mem:* Geront Soc; Tissue Cult Asn; Am Soc Cell Biol; AAAS. *Res:* Isolating purified populations of heterokaryins (fusion products) between essentially any types of cells, and using the phenotype of these heterokaryins to probe the mechanisms regulating cell differentiation and aging. *Mailing Add:* Dept Cell Biol & Internal Med Univ Tex Health Sci Ctr 5323 Harry Hines Blvd Dallas TX 75235

WRIGHTON, MARK STEPHEN, b Jacksonville, Fla, June 11, 49; m 68. PHOTOCHEMISTRY, INORGANIC CHEMISTRY. *Educ:* Fla State Univ, BS, 69; Calif Inst Technol, PhD(chem), 72. *Prof Exp:* From asst prof to assoc prof, 72-77, prof chem, 77-81, FREDERICK G KEYES PROF CHEM, MASS INST TECHNOL, 81- *Concurrent Pos:* Alfred P Sloan fel, 74-76 &

Dreyfus grant, 75-80; mem, Chem Res Eval Panel for Air Force Off Sci Res, 76-80; Standard Oil Co Calif vis energy prof, Calif Inst Technol, 77; distinguished vis lectr, Univ Tex, Austin, 77-; div ed, J Electrochem Soc, 80-; mem, Mat Res Coun, Defense Adv Res Proj Agency, 81- *Honors & Awards:* Herbert Newby McCoy Award, Calif Inst Technol, 72; Am Chem Soc Award, 80. *Mem:* AAAS; Am Chem Soc; Electrochem Soc. *Res:* Excited state processes in transition metal containing molecules; photoelectrochemistry; surface chemistry; catalysis; energy conversion. *Mailing Add:* Dept of Chem 6-335 Mass Inst of Technol Cambridge MA 02139

WRIST, PETER ELLIS, b Mirfield, Eng, Oct 9, 27; m 55; c 3. PHYSICS, MATHEMATICS. *Educ:* Univ Cambridge, BA, 48, MA, 52; Univ London, MSc, 52. *Prof Exp:* Res physicist, Brit Paper & Board Indust Res Asn, 49-52 & Que NShore Paper Co, Can, 52-56; res physicist, 56-60, assoc dir res, Cent Res Labs, 60-62, dir res, 62-65, mgr res & eng, 65-68, VPRES, MEAD CORP, 68- *Concurrent Pos:* Chmn bd gov, Nat Coun Paper Indust Air & Stream Improv, Inc. *Honors & Awards:* Smith Medal, 54; Weldon Medal, 56. *Mem:* Tech Asn Pulp & Paper Indust; NY Acad Sci; Brit Inst Physics. *Res:* Fluid mechanical behavior of fibre suspensions; high speed paper manufacture; filtration and associated problems. *Mailing Add:* Mead Corp Courthouse Plaza NE Dayton OH 45463

WRISTERS, HARRY (JAN), organometallic chemistry, see previous edition

WRISTON, JOHN CLARENCE, JR, b Boston, Mass, Aug 12, 25; m 45; c 4. BIOCHEMISTRY. *Educ:* Univ Vt, BS, 48; Columbia Univ, PhD(biochem), 53. *Prof Exp:* Nat Found Infantile Paralysis fel & instr biochem, Sch Med, Univ Colo, 53-55; from asst prof to assoc prof, 55-69, PROF CHEM, UNIV DEL, 69- *Mem:* Am Soc Biol Chemists. *Res:* Protein chemistry; structure and mechanism of action of L-asparaginase. *Mailing Add:* Dept of Chem Univ of Del Newark DE 19711

WROBEL, JOSEPH JUDE, b Chicago, Ill, Mar 18, 47; m 70; c 2. CHEMICAL PHYSICS. *Educ:* Loyola Univ, Chicago, BS, 68; Univ Fla, PhD(chem physics), 76. *Prof Exp:* RES PHYSICIST, EASTMAN KODAK CO RES LABS, 75- *Res:* Image storage and display systems. *Mailing Add:* Eastman Kodak Co Kodak Park Rochester NY 14650

WROBEL, JOSEPH STEPHEN, b Syracuse, NY, Aug 15, 39. SOLID STATE PHYSICS. *Educ:* Syracuse Univ, BS, 61, MS, 64, PhD(physics), 67. *Prof Exp:* Res asst physics, Syracuse Univ, 61-66; MEM TECH STAFF, TEX INSTRUMENTS INC, 66- *Mem:* Asn Comput Mach; Am Phys Soc. *Res:* Semiconductor materials; computer automation; photoconductivity; infrared physics. *Mailing Add:* Tex Instruments Inc PO Box 225621 MS 452 Dallas TX 75265

WROBEL, RAYMOND JOSEPH, b Chicago, Ill, Feb 7, 26; m 64; c 4. FOOD SCIENCE & TECHNOLOGY. *Educ:* DePaul Univ, BSc, 49. *Prof Exp:* Chemist pharmaceut, 49-53, chemist edible fats & oils, 53-66, CHEMIST-SECT HEAD CURED & PROCESSED MEATS, ARMOUR & CO, 66- *Mem:* Inst Food Technologists; Am Oil Chem Soc. *Res:* Cured and processed meats; edible fats and oils. *Mailing Add:* 6513 N 87th St Scottsdale AZ 85253

WROBEL, THEODORE FRANK, solid state physics, see previous edition

WROBEL, WILLIAM EUGENE, b Syracuse, NY. ENVIRONMENTAL ASSESSMENT, WATER QUALITY. *Educ:* Syracuse Univ, BA, 68; New York Univ, MS, 73. *Prof Exp:* Biologist, NY State Atomic & Space Develop Authority, 69-72; sr ecologist, Dames & Moore, 72-79; SR PROJ MGR, VTN ORE, INC, SUBID OF VTN CORP, 79- *Mem:* Am Soc Civil Eng; Am Mining Cong; Am Soc Limnol & Oceanog. *Res:* Performance and management of interdisciplinary environmental studies for mining and energy facilities, pipelines, refineries, dredging activities, shoreline and land developments, and pollution control facilities. *Mailing Add:* 4475 NW Metolius Ct Portland OR 97229

WROBLEWSKI, JOSEPH S, b Chicago, Ill, June 8, 48. BIOLOGICAL OCEANOGRAPHY. *Educ:* Univ Ill, BSc, 70; Fla State Univ, MSc, 72, PhD(oceanog), 76. *Prof Exp:* ASST PROF BIOL OCEANOG, DALHOUSIE UNIV, 76- *Concurrent Pos:* Prin investr, Natural Sci & Eng Res Coun Can, 76- & NSF, 81- *Mem:* Am Soc Limnol & Oceanog; Sigma Xi. *Res:* Numerical modeling of marine ecosystems; theory of plankton patchiness; ocean circulation-marine biomass interactions; numerical analysis; applied statistics; computer-generated movie productions. *Mailing Add:* Dept of Oceanog Dalhousie Univ Halifax NS B3H 4S1 Can

WROGEMANN, KLAUS, b Berlin, Ger, Dec 8, 40; m 67; c 3. BIOCHEMISTRY, GENETICS MEDICINE. *Educ:* Univ Marburg, MD, 66; Univ Man, PhD(biochem), 69. *Prof Exp:* Intern surg & med, Med Hosp, Hanover, Ger, 70; asst prof, 70-74, assoc prof, 74-79, PROF BIOCHEM, FAC MED, UNIV MAN, 79- *Concurrent Pos:* Muscular Dystrophy Asn Can res grant, Fac Med, Univ Man, 71-74, 74-77, 77-80 & 80-82; Can Heart Found res grants, 74-75, 75-76, 76-79 & 81-84; Med Res Coun res grant, 81-83. *Mem:* Can Biochem Soc; Am Chem Soc; Int Study Group Heart Res; AAAS. *Res:* Metabolism of normal and dystrophic heart and skeletal muscle; molecular basis of genetic diseases. *Mailing Add:* Dept of Biochem Univ of Man Winnipeg MB R3E 0W3 Can

WROLSTAD, RONALD EARL, b Oregon City, Ore, Feb 5, 39; m 77; c 2. FOOD SCIENCE, AGRICULTURAL CHEMISTRY. *Educ:* Ore State Univ, BS, 60; Univ Calif, Davis, PhD(agr chem), 64. *Prof Exp:* Grad scientist, Unilever Res Lab, Eng, 64-65; res assoc, 65-66, asst prof, 66-71 assoc prof, 71-80, PROF FOOD SCI, ORE STATE UNIV, 80- *Concurrent Pos:* Sabbatical leave, Plant Dis Div, Dept Sci & Indust Res, Auckland, NZ, 72-73; vis prof, Cornell Univ, 79-80. *Mem:* Inst Food Technol; Am Chem Soc. *Res:* Composition of foods as indices of authenticity and quality; sugars; anthocyanin pigments; flavonoids; acids; color degradation; adulteration. *Mailing Add:* Dept of Food Sci Ore State Univ Corvallis OR 97331

WRONA, WLODZIMIERZ STEFAN, b Deszno, Poland, Oct 16, 12; m 44; c 3. DIFFERENIAL GEOMETRY, APPLICATIONS OF MATHEMATICS. *Educ:* Jagiellonian Univ, MPh, 34, PhD(math), 45; Acad Mining & Metall, Cracow, docent, 49. *Prof Exp:* Asst lectr math, Acad Mining & Metall, Cracow, 32-45, from asst prof to assoc prof, 45-60; assoc prof, Warsaw Tech Univ, 60-65; prof, Univ Ghana, Legon, 65-66, Warsaw Tech Univ, 66-69 & Ahmadu Bello Univ, Nigeria, 69-70; prof, 78-80, EMER PROF MATH, CALIF STATE UNIV, HAYWARD, 80- *Concurrent Pos:* Brit Coun scholar, Univ Leeds, 47-48. *Honors & Awards:* S Zaremba Award, Polish Math Soc, 50. *Mem:* Am Math Soc; Polish Math Soc; Math Asn Am; NY Acad Sci; London Math Soc. *Res:* Published more than 50 papers in the field of metric differentiable manifolds (concerning mainly properties of curvature) and in the field of analysis. *Mailing Add:* Dept of Math Calif State Univ 25800 Carlos Bee St Hayward CA 94542

WRONSKI, CHRISTOPHER ROMAN, solid state physics, deceased

WROTENBERY, PAUL TAYLOR, b Pollok, Tex, Apr 24, 34; m 54; c 2. INFORMATION SYSTEMS. *Educ:* Univ Tex, BS, 58, MA, 62, PhD(physics, chem), 64. *Prof Exp:* Res scientist, Defense Res Labs, Tex, 58; sr scientist & proj dir, Tracor Inc, 58-64; sci consult & mgr, Int Bus Mach Corp, Dallas & Washington, DC, 64-68; dir comput serv dept, Tracor Inc, 68, sr vpres & dir, Tracor Comput Corp, 68-70; pres & chmn bd, United Systs Int, 70-74; pres, Equimatics Co, 74-76; dir, Informatics Inc, 74-76, group vpres & dir, 76-79; SR STAFF TO GOV & DIR BUDGET & PLANNING, STATE OF TEX, 79- *Res:* Surfaces and solid-liquid interfaces; semiconductor electrolyte interface properties; signal processing; management information systems; systems analysis; strategic planning, management development. *Mailing Add:* 3411 Monte Vista Austin TX 78731

WRUCKE, CHESTER THEODORE, JR, b Portland, Ore, Oct 24, 27; m 54; c 3. GEOLOGY. *Educ:* Stanford Univ, BS, 51, MS, 52, PhD, 66. *Prof Exp:* GEOLOGIST, US GEOL SURV, 52- *Mem:* Geol Soc Am. *Res:* Petrology of igneous and metamorphic rocks; structural geology. *Mailing Add:* US Geol Surv 345 Middlefield Rd Menlo Park CA 94025

WU, ADAM YU, b Nanking, Aug 2, 46. PHYSICS, CHEMICAL PHYSICS. *Educ:* Tunghai Univ, BS, 68; Univ Chicago, MS, 71, PhD(physics), 76. *Prof Exp:* RES ASSOC CHEM, NAT RES COUN CAN, 75- *Res:* High pressure neutron scattering experiments; high pressure ultrasonic experiments. *Mailing Add:* 49-653 Richmond Rd Ottawa ON K2A 3Y3 Can

WU, ALFRED CHI-TAI, b Chekiang, China, Jan 24, 33; m 67; c 2. THEORETICAL PHYSICS. *Educ:* Wheaton Col, BS, 55; Univ Md, PhD(physics), 60. *Prof Exp:* Mem, Inst Advan Study, 60-62; from asst prof to assoc prof, 62-80, PROF PHYSICS, UNIV MICH, ANN ARBOR, 80- *Concurrent Pos:* John Simon Guggenheim Mem Found fel, 68-69. *Mem:* Am Phys Soc. *Res:* Quantum field theory; particle physics. *Mailing Add:* Dept of Physics Univ of Mich Ann Arbor MI 48109

WU, ANGELA YUEN, computer science, see previous edition

WU, ANNA FANG, b Chengtu, China, Mar 25, 40; US citizen; m 66; c 1. MEDICINE, BIOCHEMISTRY. *Educ:* Cornell Univ, BA, 62; Mass Inst Technol, MS, 65, PhD(chem), 67; Univ Chicago, MD, 74; Am Bd Internal Med, cert, 77. *Prof Exp:* Res assoc biochem, Muscle Inst, 67-68; res assoc, Col Physicians & Surgeons, Columbia Univ, 68-71; resident, 75-77, instr, 77-79, assoc, 79-80, ASST PROF MED, MED SCH, NORTHWESTERN UNIV, 80- *Concurrent Pos:* Med dir employee health, Northwestern Mem Hosp, 79- *Mem:* Sigma Xi; Am Col Physicians; Am Occup Med Asn. *Res:* Synthetic peptides; synthetic nucleotides; fractionation of erythrocytes. *Mailing Add:* Dept Med Med Sch Northwestern Univ Chicago IL 60611

WU, CHANGSHENG, b Liaoning, Manchuria, China, Oct 3, 23; nat US; m 55; c 2. EXPLORATION GEOPHYSICS. *Educ:* Nat Southwestern Assoc Univs, China, 44; Univ Tex, BS, 47; Rice Univ, MA, 63, PhD(geophys), 66. *Prof Exp:* Seismologist, United Geophys Co, 47-51; party chief, Tex Seismog Co, 52-53; rev geophysicist, Precision Explor Co, 53-55 & Ralph E Fair, Inc, 55-56; seismic prospecting agent, Tech Assistance Admin, UN, 57-60; asst geophys, Rice Univ, 62-64; res geophysicist, Western Geophys Co, 66-69, sr res geophysicist, 69-74, SR STAFF SCIENTIST, WESTERN GEOPHYS CO, LITTON INDUSTS, INC, 74- *Mem:* Soc Explor Geophysicists. *Res:* Elastic wave propagation. *Mailing Add:* 2275 Woodland Springs Dr Houston TX 77077

WU, CHAU HSIUNG, b Taipei, Taiwan, Feb 10, 41; US citizen; m 66; c 2. PHARMACOLOGY, ELECTROPHYSIOLOGY. *Educ:* Nat Taiwan Univ, BS, 63; Univ Miami, MS, 68, PhD(pharmacol), 71. *Prof Exp:* Res assoc pharmacol, Med Ctr, Duke Univ, 74-75, asst adj prof, 75-76, asst med res prof, 76-77; ASST PROF PHARMACOL, MED SCH, NORTHWESTERN UNIV, 77- *Concurrent Pos:* Fel, Med Ctr, Duke Univ, 70-72, Muscular Dystrophy Asn fel, 72-74; NIH res career develop award, 81-86. *Mem:* Am Chem Soc; Biophys Soc; Soc Gen Physiologists; Soc Neurosci; Am Soc Pharmacol & Exp Therapeut. *Res:* Molecular mechanisms of drug actions on membrane excitation in nerves and muscles. *Mailing Add:* Dept of Pharmacol 303 E Chicago Ave Chicago IL 60611

WU, CHENG-WEN, b Taipei, Taiwan, June 19, 38; m 63; c 3. BIOPHYSICS, BIOCHEMISTRY. *Educ:* Nat Taiwan Univ, MD, 64; Case Western Reserve Univ, PhD(biochem), 69. *Prof Exp:* Assoc phys biochem, Cornell Univ, 69-71; from asst prof to assoc prof biophys, Albert Einstein Col Med , 72-78, prof biochem, 78-80; PROF PHARMACOL SCI, STATE UNIV NY STONY BROOK, 80- *Concurrent Pos:* NIH spec fel biophys, Yale Univ, 71-72; Am Cancer Soc res grant, Albert Einstein Col Med, 72-75, NIH res grant, 72-79 & res career develop award, 72-77; Irma T Hirschl Sci grant, 77-82. *Mem:* AAAS; Am Chem Soc; Am Soc Biol Chem; Biophys Soc; NY Acad Sci. *Res:* Regulation and mechanism of gene expression; carcinogenesis; optical studies of nucleic acid and protein interaction; fast reactions in biological systems; absorption and emission spectroscopy. *Mailing Add:* Dept Pharm Sci Heatlh Ctr State Univ NY Stony Brook NY 11794

WU, CHIEN-SHIUNG, b Shanghai, China, May 29, 12; nat US; m 42; c 1. PHYSICS. *Educ:* Nat Cent Univ, China, BS, 34; Univ Calif, PhD, 40. *Hon Degrees:* DSc, Princeton Univ, 58, Smith Col, 59, Goucher Col, 60, Rutgers Univ, 61, Yale Univ, 67, Russell Sage Col, 71, Harvard Univ, Bard Col & Adelphi Univ, 74, Dickinson Col, 75; LLD, Chinese Univ Hong Kong, 69. *Prof Exp:* PROF PHYSICS, COLUMBIA UNIV, 57- *Honors & Awards:* Res Award, Res Corp, 59; Award, Am Asn Univ Women, 60; Comstock Award, Nat Acad Sci, 64; Achievement Award, Chi-Tsin Cult Found, 65; Scientist of Year, Indust Res Magazine, 74; Tom Bonner Prize, Am Phys Soc, 75; Nat Sci Medal, 75; Wolf Prize in Physics, 78. *Mem:* Nat Acad Sci; hon fel Royal Soc Edinburgh; Am Phys Soc (pres, 75); Chinese Acad Sci. *Res:* Nuclear physics; non-conservation of parity in beta decay. *Mailing Add:* Dept of Physics Columbia Univ New York NY 10027

WU, CHIH, b Changsha, China, Apr 13, 36; m 66; c 4. STATISTICAL THERMODYNAMICS. *Educ:* Cheng Kung Univ, Taiwan, BS, 57, MS, 61; Univ Ill, PhD(mech eng), 66. *Prof Exp:* Instr eng, Cheng Kung Univ, 59-61; instr, Univ Ill, 61-66; from asst to assoc prof, 66-78, PROF ENG, US NAVAL ACAD, 78- *Concurrent Pos:* Prof phys, Loyola Col, Md, 66-69; prof, Johns Hopkins Univ, 68- *Mem:* Am Soc Mech Engrs; Am Soc Eng Educ; Chinese Soc Mech Engrs. *Res:* Transport properties; ionized gas; magnetohydrodynamics; multi-phase fluid; energy conversion; computer-assisted education. *Mailing Add:* 1705 Tarleton Way Crofton MD 21114

WU, CHII-HUEI, b Taichung, Taiwan, May 14, 41; US citizen; m 65; c 1. MEDICAL MICROBIOLOGY. *Educ:* Chung-Hsing Univ, BS, 63; Okla State Univ, MS, 68, PhD(microbiol), 70. *Prof Exp:* NIH & USPHS fel, Dept Biol, Yale Univ, 70-72; sr med microbiologist, Clin Path Lab, Faxton Hosp, Utica, NY, 72-76; chief microbiologist, Dept Path, Stamford Hosp, Stamford, Conn, 76-80; chief microbiologist, Columbia Med Lab, Bridgeport, Conn, 80-81; CHIEF MICROBIOLOGIST, DEPT LAB MED, METHODIST HOSP, INC, GARY, IND, 81- *Concurrent Pos:* Clin instr path, Dept Path, NY Med Col, Valhalla, NY, 77-80. *Mem:* Sigma Xi; Am Soc Microbiol. *Res:* Regulatory control mechanisms governing the synthesis of bacterial enzymes and medical microbiology and immunology. *Mailing Add:* Methodist Hosp 600 Grant St Gary IN 46404

WU, CHING KUEI, b Hopei, China, Feb 26, 19; m 38; c 4. BIOLOGY, GENETICS. *Educ:* Cath Univ, Peiping, BS, 41, MS, 43; Northern Ill Univ, cert advan study, 63; Brown Univ, PhD(biol), 65. *Prof Exp:* Teacher high sch, China, 43-45; asst prof biol, Prov Med Col Honan, China, 4S-47; dean study high sch, Normal Univ China, 47-55; instr biol, Univ Taiwan, 55-61; res asst, Wash Univ, St Louis, 61-63; res assoc, Brown Univ, 63-65; from asst prof to assoc prof, 65-79, PROF BIOL, ADRIAN COL, 79- *Mem:* AAAS; Genetics Soc Am; Am Genetic Asn. *Res:* Radiation genetics and chemical mutagens, especially behavior of chromosomes in Drosophila melanogaster and detection of mutagens in the environments. *Mailing Add:* Dept of Biol Adrian Col Adrian MI 49221

WU, CHING-HSONG, b Taipei, Taiwan, Apr 22, 39; m 67; c 2. CHEMICAL KINETICS. *Educ:* Nat Taiwan Univ, BS, 62; NMex Highland Univ, MS, 65; Univ Calif, Berkeley, PhD(chem), 69. *Prof Exp:* SR RES CHEMIST, SCI RES LAB, FORD MOTOR CO, DEARBORN, 69- *Mem:* Am Chem Soc. *Res:* Gas phase kinetics; free radical reactions; mechanism of smog formation; energy transfer; carbon dioxide laser induced chemical reactions; three-way catalyst research, characterization, and modeling. *Mailing Add:* 30691 Turtle Creek Dr Farmington Hills MI 48018

WU, CHING-YONG, US citizen. INDUSTRIAL ORGANIC CHEMISTRY. *Educ:* Nat Taiwan Univ, BS, 55; Univ Pittsburgh, PhD(chem), 61. *Prof Exp:* Nat Res Coun Can fel chem, 63-65; fel, Mellon Inst Sci, 65-67; res chemist, 67-71, SR RES CHEMIST, GULF RES & DEVELOP CO, 71- *Mem:* Am Chem Soc; Catalysis Soc. *Res:* Physical organic chemistry and petrochemical research; homogeneous and heterogeneous catalysis, polymer synthesis and new polymerization. *Mailing Add:* Gulf Res & Develop Co PO Drawer 2038 Pittsburgh PA 15230

WU, CHISUNG, b Chishan, Taiwan, Jan 1, 32; m 57, 72; c 2. ORGANIC CHEMISTRY. *Educ:* Nat Taiwan Univ, BSc, 55; Case Inst Technol, PhD(org chem), 60. *Prof Exp:* Res chemist, Harris-Intertype Corp, 59-61; res chemist, Chem & Plastics Opers Div, Union Carbide Corp, 61-65, proj scientist, 65-75, proj leader, 76-79, DEVELOP SCIENTIST, UNION CARBIDE CAN LTD, 79- *Concurrent Pos:* Adj asst prof, Rider Col, 72-73. *Mem:* Can Soc Chem Eng; Catalysis Soc; Sigma Xi; Chem Inst Can. *Res:* Organic synthesis; organophosphorus chemistry; polymer synthesis; organometallic chemistry; catalysis. *Mailing Add:* Union Carbide Can Ltd 10555 Metropolitan Blvd Montreal East PQ H1B 1A1 Can

WU, CHUNG, b Foochow, China, Dec 13, 19; nat US; m 50; c 4. BIOCHEMISTRY. *Educ:* Fukien Christian Univ, China, BS, 41; Univ Mich, MS, 48, PhD(biol chem), 52. *Prof Exp:* Res asst, Mayo Clin, 52-56; from instr to asst prof, 56-65, ASSOC PROF BIOL CHEM, MED SCH, UNIV MICH, ANN ARBOR, 65- *Mem:* Am Soc Biol Chem; Am Chem Soc; Am Asn Cancer Res. *Res:* Mechanisms of enzyme action; enzymology of cancer; metabolic controls; drug allergy. *Mailing Add:* 5685 Kresge Bldg Univ Mich Med Sch Ann Arbor MI 48109

WU, CHUNG PAO, b Kwantung, China, May 15, 42; US citizen; m 71; c 3. SOLID STATE ELECTRONICS. *Educ:* Yale Univ, BS, 65, MS, 66, PhD(physics), 68. *Prof Exp:* Res physicist, Electron Accelerator Lab, Yale Univ, 68-70; asst prof physics, Nanyang Univ, 70-72; MEM TECH STAFF INTEGRATED CIRCUIT TECHNOL, SARNOFF RES CTR, RCA CORP, 73- *Mem:* Am Phys Soc; Inst Elec & Electronics Engrs. *Res:* Development of methods which accurately control the generation and implantation of ions in solids; study and characterization of ion implantation and laser annealing techniques for semiconductor device fabrication. *Mailing Add:* Dept of Physics RCA Corp Princeton NJ 08540

WU, DAISY YEN, b Shanghai, China, June 12, 02; US citizen; m 24; c 5. NUTRITION, BIOCHEMISTRY. *Educ:* Ginling Col, China, BA, 21; Columbia Univ, MA, 23; Chinese-French Acad, China, dipl, 44; UN Lang Training Course, dipl, 63. *Prof Exp:* Asst biochem, Peking Union Med Col, 23-24; res assoc, Med Col Ala, 49-53; tech assoc nutrit, Food Conserv Div, UNICEF, 60-64; assoc pub health nutrit, Inst Human Nutrit, Columbia Univ, 64-71; RES ASSOC NUTRIT, ST LUKE'S HOSP CTR, 71- *Mem:* Am Inst Nutrit; fel Am Pub Health Asn; fel Royal Soc Health; Sigma Xi; NY Acad Sci. *Res:* Proteins and amino acids; metabolic studies in man; vegetarian diets and dietaries; development, design and administration of an information retrieval system. *Mailing Add:* 449 E 14th St New York NY 10009

WU, DAO-TSING, b Macau, China, Nov 6, 33. CHEMICAL ENGINEERING. *Educ:* Univ Calif, Berkeley, BS, 54; Princeton Univ, MSE, 56; Mass Inst Technol, DSc(chem eng), 62. *Prof Exp:* Res engr, 61-66, staff engr, 66-69, res supvr, 69-76, res assoc, 76-79, RES FEL, E I DU PONT DE NEMOURS & CO, INC, 79- *Mem:* Am Chem Soc. *Res:* Reactor design; process development; paint research; computer modeling and simulation. *Mailing Add:* E I du Pont de Nemours & Co Inc 3500 Grays Ferry Ave Philadelphia PA 19146

WU, ELLEN LEM, b Shanghai, China, Dec 6, 30; m 54; c 2. PHYSICAL CHEMISTRY. *Educ:* Carleton Col, BA, 54; Univ Minn, PhD(phys chem), 62. *Prof Exp:* Sr res chemist, Appl Res Div, 62-71, res assoc, 71-79, SR RES ASSOC, PROCESS RES & TECH SERV DIV, MOBIL RES & DEVELOP CORP, 79- *Mem:* Am Chem Soc; Am Crystallogrs Asn. *Res:* Catalysis research; physicochemical methods employed to elucidate nature of catalysts used in hydrocarbon conversion processes. *Mailing Add:* Res Dept Mobil Res & Develop Corp Paulsboro NJ 08066

WU, EN SHINN, b Kwangtung, China, Apr 20, 43. CHEMICAL PHYSICS. *Educ:* Nat Taiwan Univ, BS, 65; Cornell Univ, PhD(appl physics), 72. *Prof Exp:* Res assoc chem, Syracuse Univ, 72-74; asst prof, 74-79, ASSOC PROF PHYSICS, UNIV MD, BALTIMORE COUNTY, 79- *Mem:* Am Phys Soc; Biophys Soc; Sigma Xi. *Res:* General properties of simple fluids and fluid mixtures, in particular, their thermodynamic behaviors near the critical points; the experimental techniques employed are primarily light-scattering and small angle X-ray scattering. *Mailing Add:* Dept of Physics Univ Md Baltimore County Baltimore MD 21228

WU, FA YUEH, b China, Jan 5, 32; m 63; c 3. THEORETICAL PHYSICS. *Educ:* Chinese Naval Col, BS, 54; Nat Tsing Hua Univ, MS, 59; Wash Univ, PhD(physics), 63. *Prof Exp:* Res assoc physics, Wash Univ, 63; asst prof, Va Polytech Inst, 63-67; from asst prof to assoc prof, 67-75, PROF PHYSICS, NORTHEASTERN UNIV, 75- *Concurrent Pos:* Sr Fulbright res fel, Australian Nat Univ, 73; vis prof, Lorentz Inst & Delft Univ, 80. *Mem:* fel Am Phys Soc. *Res:* Many body theory; theory of quantum liquids; statistical mechanics; solid state theory. *Mailing Add:* Dept Physics Northeastern Univ Boston MA 02115

WU, FELICIA YING-HSIUEH, b Taipei, Taiwan, Feb 27, 39; US citizen; m 63; c 3. BIOPHYSICS, BIOCHEMISTRY. *Educ:* Nat Taiwan Univ, BS, 61; Univ Minn, MS, 63; Case Western Reserve Univ, PhD(org chem), 69. *Prof Exp:* Med technician biochem, US Naval Med Res Unit 2, Taipei, Taiwan, 63-65; res assoc biochem, Sect Biochem & Molecular Biol, Cornell Univ, 69-71; res assoc pharmacol, Yale Univ, 71; res fel, 72, assoc, 72-73, instr, 73-78, ASST PROF BIOPHYS, ALBERT EINSTEIN COL MED, YESHIVA UNIV, 78- *Mem:* Am Soc Biol Chem; Biophys Soc; Am Chem Soc; The Chem Soc. *Res:* Regulation and mechanism of gene transcription; carcinogenesis; optical studies of nucleic acid and protein interaction; fast reactions in biological systems; absorption and emission spectroscopy. *Mailing Add:* Dept of Biochem (U205) Albert Einstein Col of Med Bronx NY 10461

WU, FELIX F, b China, Dec 1, 43; US citizen. POWER SYSTEMS. *Educ:* Nat Taiwan Univ, BS, 65; Univ Pittsburgh, MS, 68; Univ Calif, Berkeley, PhD(elec eng & comput sci), 72. *Prof Exp:* Asst prof elec eng, Univ Pittsburgh, 72-74, asst prof elec eng & comput sci, Univ Calif, Berkeley, 74-78; engr, Pac Gas & Elec Co, 76-77; ASSOC PROF ELEC ENG & COMPUT SCI, UNIV CALIF, BERKELEY, 78- *Concurrent Pos:* Consult, Pac Gas & Elec Co, 77-, Solar Energy Res Inst, 80-81, Elec Power Res Inst, 81-82; vis prof, Shanghai Jiao Tung Univ, 80, Swiss Fed Inst Technol, 82. *Mem:* Inst Elec & Electronics Engrs; AAAS. *Res:* Analysis methods for electric power systems planning and operations. *Mailing Add:* Dept Elec Eng & Comput Sci Univ Calif Berkeley CA 94720

WU, FRANCIS TAMING, b Shanghai, China, May 27, 36; m 66. GEOPHYSICS. *Educ:* Nat Taiwan Univ, BS, 59; Calif Inst Technol, PhD(geophys), 66. *Prof Exp:* Asst prof geophys, Boston Col, 68-69; from asst prof to assoc prof, 70-76, PROF GEOPHYS, STATE UNIV NY, BINGHAMTON, 76- *Mem:* AAAS; Am Geophys Union; Seismol Soc Am. *Res:* Faulting as a dynamic phenomenon, its seismic radiation, rate of growth and driving mechanism; near source strong ground motion; fault gauge and mechanics of faulting. *Mailing Add:* Dept of Geol State Univ of NY Binghamton NY 13901

WU, HAI, b Tunghai, Kiangsu, China, Aug 22, 36; US citizen; m 66; c 3. MECHANICAL ENGINEERING, APPLIED MECHANICS. *Educ:* Nat Cheng Kung Univ, Taiwan, BS, 54; Univ Iowa, MS, 63; Case Inst Technol, PhD(fluid mech), 69. *Prof Exp:* Mech engr HVAC design, Syska & Hennessy, Engrs, 65; sr res engr fluid mech heat transfer, Mech Res Dept, Sci Res Lab, 69-75, prin res assoc engr engine anal, 76-80, PRIN STAFF ENGR, COMPUT MODELING & SIMULATION, SYST RES LAB, ENG & RES STAFF, FORD MOTOR CO, 80- *Concurrent Pos:* Vis lectr, Detroit Inst Technol, 74. *Mem:* Sigma Xi; Am Soc Mech Engrs. *Res:* Energy management, engine research, automotive safety, lubrication, squeeze films, computer modeling and system optimization. *Mailing Add:* E-2194 Sci Res Labs PO 2053 Ford Motor Co Dearborn MI 48121

WU, HENRY CHI-PING, b Fenghua, Chekiang, China, May 21, 35; m 65; c 3. BIOCHEMISTRY. *Educ:* Nat Taiwan Univ, MD, 60; Harvard Univ, PhD(biochem), 66. *Prof Exp:* Jane Coffin Childs Fund fel, Mass Inst Technol, 66-67, Med Found fel, 67-69; asst prof to prof microbiol, Univ Conn Health Ctr, 69-80; PROF MICROBIOL, UNIFORMED SERV UNIV HEALTH SCI CTR, 80- *Mem:* AAAS; Am Soc Microbiol; Am Soc Biol Chemists. *Res:* Biogenesis of membrane proteins in bacteria; biochemical and genetic studies of cell surface. *Mailing Add:* Uniformed Serv Univ Health Sci Ctr 4301 Jones Bridge Rd Bethesda MD 20814

WU, HSIN-I, b Tokyo, Japan, May 25, 37; m 64; c 2. MATHEMATICAL PHYSICS, BIOSYSTEMS MODELING. *Educ:* Tunghai Univ, Taiwan, BS, 60; Univ Mo, MS, 64, PhD(physics), 67. *Prof Exp:* From asst prof to assoc prof physics, Southeast Mo State Univ, 67-76; res assoc, 76-77, res scientist, 77-78, SR RES SCIENTIST BIOSYSTEMS, TEX A&M UNIV, 78- *Concurrent Pos:* Asst prof bioeng, Tex A&M Univ, 80-81, assoc prof, 81- *Mem:* Am Asn Physics Teachers; Am Crystallog Asn; NY Acad Sci; Am Asn Indust Engrs; Sigma Xi. *Res:* Small angle x-ray scattering theory; calculating the chord distribution function; theory of x-ray study of membranes; stomatal mechanics; forest succession problems; applied catastrophic theory in biological and ecological sciences. *Mailing Add:* Biosysts Res Div Dept Indust Eng Tex A&M Univ College Station TX 77843

WU, HUNG-HSI, b Hong Kong, May 25, 40; US citizen; m 76. MATHEMATICS. *Educ:* Columbia Col, AB, 61; Mass Inst Technol, PhD(math), 63. *Prof Exp:* Res assoc math, Mass Inst Technol, 63-64; mem, Inst Advan Study, 64-65; from asst prof to assoc prof, 65-73, PROF MATH, UNIV CALIF, BERKELEY, 73- *Concurrent Pos:* Alfred P Sloan fel, 71-73. *Mem:* Am Math Soc. *Res:* Differential geometry; complex manifolds. *Mailing Add:* Dept of Math Univ of Calif Berkeley CA 94720

WU, I-PAI, b Chingkaing Kaingsu, China, June 23, 33; m 63; c 2. HYDROLOGY, HYDRAULICS. *Educ:* Nat Taiwan Univ, BS, 55; Purdue Univ, MS, 60, PhD(civil eng), 63. *Prof Exp:* Hydraul engr, Ind Flood Control & Water Resources Comn, 61-62 & 63-64; asst prof civil eng, Chico State Col, 64-66; from asst prof to assoc prof agr eng, 66-76, assoc agr engr, 71-80, PROF AGR ENG, UNIV HAWAII, 76- *Concurrent Pos:* Fulbright prof, Dept Agr Eng, Univ Khartoum, Sudan, 79-80. *Mem:* Am Soc Agr Engrs; Am Soc Civil Engrs; Am Water Resources Asn. *Res:* Small watershed hydrology; hydraulics of surface irrigation; sprinkler irrigation; drip irrigation system design. *Mailing Add:* Dept Agr Eng Univ Hawaii 3050 Maileway Honolulu HI 96822

WU, JAIN-MING, aerospace engineering, see previous edition

WU, JAMES CHEN-YUAN, b Nanking, China, Oct 5, 31; nat US; m 57; c 2. MECHANICAL ENGINEERING. *Educ:* Gonzaga Univ, BS, 54; Univ Ill, MS, 55, PhD(mech eng, appl math), 57. *Prof Exp:* Mech engr, Wah Chang Corp, NY, 54; mem res staff, Mass Inst Technol, 57; asst prof, Gonzaga Univ, 57-59; chief res br, Douglas Aircraft Co, 59-65; PROF AEROSPACE ENG, GA INST TECHNOL, 65- *Concurrent Pos:* European Atomic Energy Comn sr vis fel, Ispra Res Ctr, Italy, 62-63; consult, Lockheed-Georgia Co, 76- *Mem:* Am Soc Eng Educ; Am Inst Aeronaut & Astronaut; Am Astronaut Soc. *Res:* Gas dynamics; thermodynamics; boundary layer theory; viscous flows; numerical analysis. *Mailing Add:* Sch of Aerospace Eng Ga Inst of Technol Atlanta GA 30332

WU, JANG-MEI GLORIA, analytical mathematics, see previous edition

WU, JIA-HSI, b Formosa, July 6, 26; m 56; c 1. PLANT PHYSIOLOGY, VIROLOGY. *Educ:* Univ Taiwan, BA, 50; Cornell Univ, MS, 52; Wash Univ, PhD(bot), 58. *Prof Exp:* Instr plant physiol, Univ Taiwan, 52-55; fel, Univ Wis, 58-59; asst botanist, Univ Calif, Los Angeles, 59-63; asst prof plant physiol, Tex Tech Col, 63-65; asst biologist, Univ Calif, San Diego, 65-66; asst prof cell physiol, 66-72, assoc prof cell physiol, 72-80, PROF BIOL SCI, CALIF STATE POLYTECH UNIV, POMONA, 80- *Concurrent Pos:* NSF grants, 64-68 & 70-72. *Res:* Cell physiology. *Mailing Add:* Dept of Biol Sci 3801 W Temple Ave Pomona CA 91768

WU, JIANN-LONG, b Chang-hua, Taiwan. RADIOCHEMISTRY, RADIOPHARMACEUTICAL. *Educ:* Fu-Jen Cath Univ, Taiwan, BS, 68; Northeast La Univ, MS, 72; Va Polytech Inst & State Univ, PhD(chem), 77. *Prof Exp:* Instr anal chem, Chem Dept, Northeast La Univ, 72; fel, Nuclear Med Dept, Med Ctr, Univ Mich, 77-79; RES SCIENTIST, MEDI-PHYSICS INC, SUBSID HOFFMANN-LA ROCHE, 79- *Mem:* Soc Nuclear Med; Am Chem Soc. *Res:* Design, synthesis and development of radiolabeled compounds for organ imaging and biological function studies. *Mailing Add:* Medi-Physics Inc 5801 Christie Ave Emeryville CA 94608

WU, JIN, b Nanking, China, Apr 9, 34; m 61; c 3. FLUID MECHANICS, HYDRAULIC ENGINEERING. *Educ:* Cheng-Kung Univ, Taiwan, BSc, 56; Univ Iowa, MSc, 61, PhD(mech, hydraul), 64. *Prof Exp:* Res scientist, Hydronautics, Inc, 63-66, sr res scientist, 66-69, head fluid motions div, 66-72, prin res scientist, 69-74, head geophys fluid dynamics div, 72-74; assoc prof, 74-75, prof, 75-80, H FLETCHER BROWN PROF MARINE STUDIES & CIVIL ENG, UNIV DEL, 80- *Concurrent Pos:* Consult, Hydronautics, Inc, 74- & US Naval Res Lab, 80-; adv, Taiwan Hydraulics Lab, Nat Cheng-Kung Univ, Taiwan, 75-; distinguished adj prof, Shandong Col Oceanog, China, 81- *Mem:* Am Geophys Union; Am Soc Civil Engrs. *Res:* Geophysical and environmental fluid dynamics; air-sea interaction; coastal and ocean engineering. *Mailing Add:* Col of Marine Studies Univ of Del Newark DE 19711

WU, JOHN NAICHI, b Soochow, China, Sept 10, 32; US citizen; m 61; c 2. MATERIALS SCIENCE ENGINEERING. *Educ:* Nat Taiwan Univ, BSME, 55; Univ Fla, MSEM, 61, PhD(eng sci), 65. *Prof Exp:* Sr res specialist appl mech, Babcock & Wilcox Co Res Ctr, 62-66, group supvr, 67-77; MGR, MAT & PROCESSES LAB, GEN ELEC CO, 77- *Mem:* Am Acad Mech; Am Soc Mech Engrs; Am Soc Acoust; Am Soc Metals. *Res:* Theoretical and experimental mechanics; mechanics of sandwich structures; finite element analysis; nonlinear mechanics and dynamics; earthquake engineering in terms of structural design; nuclear steam generating systems. *Mailing Add:* 139 Putnam Dr Erie PA 16511

WU, JOSEPH M, b China, Aug 1, 47; US citizen; m 75; c 1. GENE REGULATION, DEVELOPMENTAL CONTROL. *Educ:* McGill Univ, BS, 70; Fla State Univ, MS, 72, PhD(biol sci), 75. *Prof Exp:* Fel, Temple Univ, 76-77, res instr, 77-78; ASST PROF BIOCHEM, NY MED COL, 78- *Concurrent Pos:* Prin investr, NIH grants, 79- *Res:* Mechanism of eukaryotic protein synthesis regulation; molecular mechanism of interferon action. *Mailing Add:* Rm 127 Dept Biochem Basic Sci Bldg NY Med Col Valhalla NY 10595

WU, JOSEPH WOO-TIEN, b Taiwan, Repub China; US citizen; c 2. ORGANIC CHEMISTRY, ENZYMOLOGY. *Educ:* Tainan Cheng-Kung Univ, BS, 65; Worcester Polytech Inst, MS, 69; Univ Pa, PhD(chem), 72. *Prof Exp:* Fel enzymol dept biochem & human genetics, Univ Pa, 72-74; sr chemist bio-org chem, New Eng Nuclear Co, 74-76; SR SCIENTIST IMMUNOCHEM, INSTRUMENTATION LAB INC, 76- *Mem:* Am Chem Soc. *Res:* Modification of protein enzyme surface; organic and enzymatic reaction mechanism and analysis of biochemical compounds by antibody, enzyme and fluorometer. *Mailing Add:* 15032 Joshua Tree Rd Gaithersburg MD 20760

WU, JUNG-TSUNG, b Taiwan, China, Feb 17, 36; US citizen; m 65; c 2. REPRODUCTIVE BIOLOGY, EMBRYOLOGY. *Educ:* Nat Taiwan Univ, BS, 58; Univ Wis-Madison, MS, 66, PhD(endocrinol & reprod biol), 69. *Prof Exp:* Teaching asst zool, Nat Taiwan Univ, 60-62; fel reprod biol, Med Ctr, Univ Kans, 69-71; res assoc, 71-72, STAFF SCIENTIST REPROD BIOL, WORCESTER FOUND EXP BIOL, 72- *Mem:* Soc Study Reprod; AAAS. *Res:* Implantation; embryo development and transport; hybridization; pathenogenesis; fertilization. *Mailing Add:* Worcester Found Exp Biol Shrewsbury MA 01545

WU, KENNETH KUN-YU, b Kaohsiung, Taiwan, July 6, 41; US citizen; m 69; c 2. MEDICAL SCIENCE, BIOLOGY. *Educ:* Yale Univ, MS, 69; Nat Taiwan Univ, MD, 66. *Prof Exp:* From instr to asst prof, Univ Iowa, 73-76; assoc prof & chief coagulation & thrombosis unit, 76-81, PROF MED, RUSH MED COL, RUSH PRESBY ST LUKE'S MED CTR, 81- *Concurrent Pos:* Adv consult, NIH, 76-, mem prog proj rev comt, 76- *Mem:* Am Asn Immunol; Am Soc Hemat; Am Fedn Clin Res; Int Soc Thrombosis & Hemostasis. *Res:* Thrombosis and hemostasis; platelet physiology; pathophysiology and biochemistry. *Mailing Add:* Rush Presby St Luke's Med Ctr 1753 W Congress Pkwy Chicago IL 60612

WU, KUANG MING, b Taiwan, Nov 30, 49; m 74. STRUCTURAL MECHANICS, CONTINUUM MECHANICS. *Educ:* Nat Taiwan Univ, BS, 71; Princeton Univ, MS, 74, PhD(civil eng), 77. *Prof Exp:* ASSOC SR RES ENGR, GEN MOTORS RES LABS, 77- *Res:* Structural dynamics; elasticity; composite materials. *Mailing Add:* Dept 15 Gen Motors Res Labs Warren MI 48090

WU, LILIAN SHIAO-YEN, b Peiking, China, July 6, 47. APPLIED MATHEMATICS. *Educ:* Univ Md, BS, 68; Cornell Univ, MS, 72, PhD(appl math), 74. *Prof Exp:* RES STAFF APPL MATH, THOMAS J WATSON RES CTR, IBM CORP, 73- *Concurrent Pos:* Vis scientist, Marine Biol Lab, 75- *Mem:* Soc Indust & Appl Math. *Res:* Data analysis and statistics; game theory. *Mailing Add:* IBM Thomas J Watson Res Ctr Box 218 Yorktown Heights NY 10598

WU, MING TSUNG, b Taiwan, Rep China, Oct 9, 41; m 68; c 1. CHEMISTRY, FOOD SCIENCE. *Educ:* Nat Taiwan Univ, BS, 64, MS, 67; Utah State Univ, PhD(plant nutrit & biochem), 71. *Prof Exp:* Res assoc food sci, Utah State Univ, 71-72; res assoc food sci, Univ Ga, 72-73; RES ASST PROF FOOD SCI, UTAH STATE UNIV, 73- *Mem:* Am Soc Plant Physiol; Am Soc Microbiol; Inst Food Technol; Sigma Xi; Soc Econ Bot. *Res:* Food storage; postharvest physiology; mycotoxins; plant growth regulators; biochemistry and toxicology of potato toxicants. *Mailing Add:* Dept Nutrit & Food Sci Utah State Univ Logan UT 84322

WU, MING-CHI, b Nantou, Taiwan, Nov 13, 40; US citizen; m 68; c 2. BIOCHEMISTRY. *Educ:* Nat Taiwan Univ, BS, 63; Univ Wis-Madison, MS, 68, PhD(biochem), 70. *Prof Exp:* Res fel physiol chem, Sch Med, Johns Hopkins Univ, 69-71; res assoc biochem, Sch Med, Univ Pittsburgh, 71-73; res assoc hemat, Howard Hughes Med Inst, 74-80, asst prof med, Sch Med, Univ Miami, 75-80, assoc prof, 81-82; ASSOC PROF BIOCHEM, TEX COL OSTEOPATH MED, 82- *Mem:* Am Chem Soc; Am Fedn Clin Res; Sigma Xi; Am Soc Biol Chemists; Int Soc Exp Ment Hematol. *Res:* Control of granulopoiesis; proteases from cultured cancer cells. *Mailing Add:* Tex Col Osteopath Fort Worth TX 76102

WU, MIN-YEN, b Taiwan, China, Oct 1, 40; m 68; c 1. ELECTRICAL ENGINEERING, COMPUTER SCIENCE. *Educ:* Nat Taiwan Univ, BS, 62; Univ Ottawa, MSc, 65; Univ Calif, Berkeley, PhD(elec eng), 68. *Prof Exp:* Actg asst prof elec eng, Univ Calif, Berkeley, 68-69; asst prof, 69-74, ASSOC PROF ELEC ENG, UNIV COLO, BOULDER, 74- *Concurrent Pos:* Independent prof, IBM Corp, Boulder, 72-74, consult, 74-75. *Mem:* AAAS; Inst Elec & Electronics Engrs. *Res:* Control and system theory; social and economical systems; mathematical ecology. *Mailing Add:* Dept of Elec Eng Univ of Colo Boulder CO 80309

WU, MU TSU, b Changhwa, Taiwan, Oct 25, 29; US citizen; m 57; c 4. ORGANIC CHEMISTRY, MEDICINAL CHEMISTRY. *Educ:* Nat Taiwan Univ, BS, 51; Univ Md, PhD(pharmaceut chem), 61; Tohoku Univ, Japan, DSc(chem), 61. *Prof Exp:* Res chemist, Ord Res Inst, 51-58; res assoc pharmaceut chem, Univ Md, 58-62, assoc res prof, 64-65; res assoc chem,

Univ NH, 62-64; sr res chemist, 65-72, res fel, 72-78, SR RES FEL, MERCK & CO, INC, 78- *Mem:* AAAS; Am Chem Soc; Am Inst Chemists. *Res:* Synthetic organic and medicinal chemistry. *Mailing Add:* 35 Lance Dr Clark NJ 07066

WU, PEI-RIN, b Taoyuan, Taiwan, Feb 16, 35; US citizen; m 58; c 3. ELECTRICAL ENGINEERING, ELECTROMAGNETISM. *Educ:* Taipei Inst Technol, dipl, 55; Univ Tenn, MS, 60; Univ Mich, PhD(elec eng), 67. *Prof Exp:* Engr elec, Sintong Chem Works Inc, 56-59; asst prof elec eng, SDak Sch Mines & Technol, 60-64; res asst, Radiation Lab, Univ Mich, 66-67; MEM STAFF ELECTROMAGNETICS, LINCOLN LAB, MASS INST TECHNOL, 67- *Mem:* Inst Elec & Electronics Engrs. *Res:* Antennas; electromagnetics; scattering; radar data analysis; radar decoy designs; reentry physics and signatures; satellite signatures; identification; signature discrimination techniques. *Mailing Add:* Hiddenwood Path Lincoln MA 01773

WU, RAY J, b Peking, China, Aug 14, 28; nat US; m 56; c 2. BIOCHEMISTRY. *Educ:* Univ Ala, BS, 50; Univ Pa, PhD, 55. *Prof Exp:* Asst instr biochem, Univ Pa, 51-55, Damon Runyon fel cancer res, 55-57; from asst to assoc, Pub Health Res Inst New York, 57-61, assoc mem, 61-66; assoc prof, 66-72, assoc chmn sect, 75-77, chmn sect, 77-79, PROF BIOCHEM, MOLECULAR & CELL BIOL, CORNELL UNIV, 72- *Concurrent Pos:* NSF sr fel, MRC Lab, Cambridge, England, 71; vis assoc prof, Mass Inst Technol, 72. *Mem:* Am Chem Soc; Sigma Xi; Am Soc Biol Chem. *Res:* DNA sequence analysis; cancer research; recombinant DNA research; gene synthesis; enzymology. *Mailing Add:* Dept of Biochem Wing Hall Cornell Univ Ithaca NY 14850

WU, RICHARD LI-CHUAN, b Tainan, Taiwan, Aug 21, 40; m 68; c 1. PHYSICAL CHEMISTRY. *Educ:* Nat Cheng Kung Univ, Taiwan, BS, 63; Univ Kans, PhD(chem), 71. *Prof Exp:* Res chemist, Aerospace Res Labs, Wright-Patterson Air Force Base, 71-75; ADJ RES PROF ENG, CHEM & BREHM LAB, WRIGHT STATE UNIV, 75- *Concurrent Pos:* US Dept Energy res grant, 80-82. *Mem:* Am Chem Soc; Am Soc Mass Spectrometry; Sigma Xi; NY Acad Sci. *Res:* Mass Spectrometry; high temperature chemistry; chemical kinetics; vaporization processes; ion-molecule reactions; thermodynamics. *Mailing Add:* 384 Merrick Dr Xenia OH 45385

WU, ROY SHIH-SHYONG, b Shanghai, China, Nov 15, 44; US citizen. CELL BIOLOGY, BIOCHEMISTRY. *Educ:* Univ Calif, Berkeley, AB, 67; Albert Einstein Col Med, Bronx, NY, PhD(biochem), 72. *Prof Exp:* NIH fel develop biol, Dept Zool, Univ Calif, Berkeley, 72-74; fel cell biol, Children's Hosp, Oakland, Calif, 74-75; scientist cell biol, Biotech Res Lab Inc, Rockville, Md, 75-80; MEM STAFF, NIH, 80- *Mem:* AAAS; Am Soc Cell Biol; Am Chem Soc; Am Soc Biol Chemists; Soc Develop Biol. *Res:* Turnover rates of specific ribonucleic acids in mammary gland explants and epithelial cells; screening of new materials for anti-oncogenic virus related properties. *Mailing Add:* NCI Bldg 37 5D 17 Nat Inst Health Bethesda MD 20005

WU, SAU LAN YU, b Hong Kong, China; US citizen. HIGH ENERGY PHYSICS. *Educ:* Harvard Univ, PhD(physics), 70. *Prof Exp:* Res assoc, Mass Inst Technol, 70-72, res physicist, 73-77; asst prof, 77-80, Rohmes fel, 80, ASSOC PROF PHYSICS, PHYSICS DEPT, UNIV WIS-MADISON, 80- *Concurrent Pos:* Vis scientist, Brookhaven Nat Lab, 72-75, Cern, 75-77 & Deutsches Elektroneu-Synchrotron, 70-72 & 77- *Res:* Electron-positron colliding beam physics at high energies. *Mailing Add:* Dept Physics Univ Wis Madison WI 53706

WU, SHERMAN H, b Hupeh, China, Aug 21, 38; US citizen. ELECTRICAL & SYSTEMS ENGINEERING. *Educ:* Northwestern Univ, BSEE, 61, MS, 63, PhD(elec eng), 65. *Prof Exp:* Asst engr, Ill Bell Tel Co, 61-62; lectr systs eng, Univ Ill, Chicago, 64; staff engr, TRW Systs Group, Calif, 65; from asst prof to assoc prof elec eng, 65-76, PROF ELEC ENG, MARQUETTE UNIV, 76- *Concurrent Pos:* NSF grant, 66-68. *Mem:* Inst Elec & Electronics Engrs. *Res:* Nonlinear pulse-modulation in aerospace and physiological systems. *Mailing Add:* Dept of Elec Eng Col of Eng 1131 W Wisconsin Ave Milwaukee WI 53233

WU, SHI TSAN, b Nanchang, China, July 31, 34; m 64; c 2. AEROSPACE ENGINEERING. *Educ:* Nat Taiwan Univ, BS, 56; Ill Inst Technol, MS, 59; Univ Colo, PhD(aerospace eng sci), 67. *Prof Exp:* Res asst eng sci, Harvard Univ, 59-62; res fel aeronaut, NY Univ, 62-63; asst aerospace eng sci, Univ Colo, 63-64; res asst solar physics, High Altitude Observ, Nat Ctr Atmospheric Res, 64-67; from asst prof to assoc prof, 67-72, PROF AEROSPACE ENG SCI, UNIV ALA, HUNTSVILLE, 72- *Concurrent Pos:* Consult, Wyle Labs, 68-; sr Fulbright-Hays Scholar, 75-76; Australia-Am Educ Found prof space physics, La Trobe Univ, Australia, 75-76; solar physics coordr, Study of Interplanetary Phenomena & Spec Comt on Solar Terrestrial Physics. *Honors & Awards:* Outstanding Serv Award, Sigma Xi, 77. *Mem:* AAAS; Am Phys Soc; Am Geophys Union; assoc fel Am Inst Aeronaut & Astronaut. *Res:* Plasmadynamics; magnetohydrodynamics and its astrogeophysical applications; boundary layer type flows; kinetic theory; radiative gas dynamics and other fluid mechanics problems. *Mailing Add:* Univ of Ala PO Box 1247 Huntsville AL 35807

WU, SHIEN-MING, b Chekiang, China, Oct 28, 24; m 59; c 2. MECHANICAL ENGINEERING. *Educ:* Univ Wis, PhD(mech eng), 62. *Prof Exp:* Asst prof mech eng, 62-65, assoc prof, 65-68, prof mech eng & statist, 68-80, RES PROF, UNIV WIS-MADISON, 81- *Honors & Awards:* C R Richards Award, Am Soc Mech Engrs, 81. *Mem:* Am Soc Mech Engrs; Am Statist Asn. *Res:* Drilling and metal cutting; engineering statistics; stochastic processes; system analysis. *Mailing Add:* Dept of Mech Eng Univ of Wis Madison WI 53706

WU, SING-CHOU, b China, June 2, 36; m 64; c 2. STATISTICS, ECONOMETRICS. *Educ:* Nat Taiwan Univ, BA, 59; Utah State Univ, MS, 66; Colo State Univ, PhD(statist), 70. *Prof Exp:* Economist, Bank of China, 61-63; programmer, Comput Ctr, Utah State Univ, 65-66; asst statist, Colo State Univ, 66-69; from asst prof to assoc prof, 69-75, PROF STATIST, CALIF STATE POLYTECH UNIV, SAN LUIS OBISPO, 75- *Mem:* Am Statist Asn; Chinese Statist Soc; Japan Statist Soc. *Res:* Design of experiment; statistical computation. *Mailing Add:* Dept of Comput Sci & Statist Calif Polytech State Univ San Luis Obispo CA 93401

WU, SING-YUNG, b Cheng-tu, China, July 5, 39. ENDOCRINOLOGY, NUCLEAR MEDICNE. *Educ:* Univ Wash, PhD(exp path), 69; Johns Hopkins Univ, MD, 72. *Prof Exp:* Intern med, Univ Chicago, 71-72; resident, Univ Calif, Irvine, 72-73; instr, Univ Wash, 73-75; fel, Univ Calif, Los Angeles, 75-77; ASST PROF MED, UNIV CALIF, IRVINE, 77- *Concurrent Pos:* Staff physician, Vet Admin Med Ctr, Long Beach, 77- *Mem:* Am Thyroid Asn; Soc Nuclear Med; Soc Clin Res. *Res:* Biochemical study of endocrine physiology, the thyroid in particular; clinical application of radioisotopes: radioimmunoassay and radio-immune-detection of pathological foci including cancer. *Mailing Add:* 5901 E 7th St Long Beach CA 90822

WU, SOUHENG, b Taiwan, China, Jan 16, 36; m 65; c 1. PHYSICAL CHEMISTRY. *Educ:* Nat Cheng Kung Univ, BS, 58; Univ Kans, PhD(chem), 65. *Prof Exp:* Researcher, Taiwan Sugar Corp, 58-61; res chemist, 65-69, staff chemist, 69-71, RES ASSOC, E I DU PONT DE NEMOURS & CO, INC, 71- *Mem:* Am Phys Soc; Am Chem Soc; Soc Rheology. *Res:* Polymer physics; interfacial sciences; adhesion. *Mailing Add:* Exp Sta E I du Pont de Nemours & Co Inc Wilmington DE 19898

WU, SZU HSIAO ARTHUR, b Ho-Fei, China, Sept 15, 19; nat US; m 56; c 1. PHYSIOLOGY. *Educ:* Nat Cent Univ, China, BSc, 41; Ore State Col, MSc, 49, PhD(animal breeding), 52. *Prof Exp:* Instr, Oberlin Mem Sch, 44-45; asst, 47-52, instr physiol of reproduction, 52-57, asst prof animal sci, 57-66, assoc prof, 67-78, PROF ANIMAL SCI, ORE STATE UNIV, 78- *Mem:* Am Soc Animal Sci; Soc Study Reproduction; Electron Micros Soc Am. *Res:* Physiology of reproduction; physiology and ultrastructure of germ cells. *Mailing Add:* Dept of Animal Sci Ore State Univ Corvallis OR 97331

WU, TAI TE, b Shanghai, China, Aug 2, 35; m 66. BIOCHEMISTRY, MOLECULAR BIOLOGY. *Educ:* Univ Hong Kong, MB & BS, 56; Univ Ill, Urbana, BS, 58; Harvard Univ, SM, 59, PhD(eng), 61. *Prof Exp:* Res fel struct mech, Harvard Univ, 61-63; asst prof eng, Brown Univ, 63-65; res assoc biol chem, Harvard Med Sch, 65-66; from asst prof to assoc prof biomath, Med Col, Cornell Univ, 67-70; from assoc prof to prof physics & eng sci, 70-74, PROF BIOCHEM, MOLECULAR & CELL BIOL, ENG SCI & APPL MATH, NORTHWESTERN UNIV, 74- *Concurrent Pos:* Gordon McKay fel, Harvard Univ, 58; res scientist, Hydronaut, Md, 62; res fel biol chem, Harvard Med Sch, 64; chmn comt biophys, & mem comt biomed eng, Northwestern Univ, 72-80. *Honors & Awards:* Res Career Develop Award, NIH, 74; C T Loo scholar, China Inst, 59; Progress Award, Chinese Engrs & Scientists Asn Southern Calif, 71. *Mem:* Am Soc Biol Chem; Am Soc Microbiol; Biophys Soc. *Res:* Three-dimensional structures of macromolecules, especially those of antibodies; bacterial evolution; fractionation of erythrocytes. *Mailing Add:* Dept of Biochem & Molecular Biol Northwestern Univ Evanston IL 60201

WU, TAI TSUN, b Shanghai, China, Dec 1, 33; m 67. PHYSICS. *Educ:* Univ Minn, BS, 53; Harvard Univ, SM, 54, PhD(appl physics), 56. *Prof Exp:* Jr fel, Soc Fels, 56-59, from asst prof to assoc prof, 59-66, GORDON McKAY PROF APPL PHYSICS, HARVARD UNIV, 66- *Concurrent Pos:* Mem, Inst Advan Study, 58-59, 60-61 & 62-63; vis prof & NSF sr fel, Rockefeller Univ, 66-67; Guggenheim Mem Found fel, Deutsches Elektronen-Synchotron, Hamburg, Ger, 70-71; Kramers prof, Inst Theoret Physics, Univ Utrecht, Neth, 77-78. *Mem:* Am Phys Soc; Inst Elec & Electronics Eng. *Res:* Electromagnetic theory; statistical mechanics; elementary particles. *Mailing Add:* Rm 308 Gordon McKay Lab of Appl Sci Harvard Univ Cambridge MA 02138

WU, TAI WING, b Hong Kong; US citizen. BIOCHEMISTRY, BIOCHEMICAL ENGINEERING. *Educ:* Chinese Univ Hong Kong, BSc, 66; Univ Toronto, MSc, 68, PhD(biochem), 71. *Prof Exp:* Med Res Coun Can fel develop biol, 71-73; SR RES ASSOC CLIN BIOCHEM & BIOCHEM ENG, EASTMAN KODAK CO RES LABS, 73- *Concurrent Pos:* Referee publ, Can J Biochem, Nat Res Coun Can, 73-; referee papers, Biochem, J Biol Chem, 73-, Clin Chem, 81- *Mem:* Biophys Soc; Can Biol Socs; AAAS; Am Asn Clin Chem. *Res:* Mechanistic investigation of diverse biochemical phenomena of fundamental and practical interest; design and testing of totally novel techniques for clinical analyses; molecular characterization of unusual biomaterials; protein chemistry and enzymology. *Mailing Add:* Eastman Kodak Res Labs Bldg 59 1669 Lake Ave Rochester NY 14650

WU, TE-KAO, b Feng-Shan, Taiwan, Oct 12, 48; m 76; c 1. ELECTRICAL ENGINEERING. *Educ:* Nat Taiwan Univ, BEE, 70; Univ Miss, MS, 73, PhD(elec eng), 76. *Prof Exp:* Res assoc elec eng, Univ Miss, 76-78; scientist assoc res antenna eng, Lockheed Missiles & Space Co Inc, 78-80; SR STAFF ENGR, SPERRY MICROWAVE ELECTRONICS, 80- *Concurrent Pos:* Res asst, Univ Miss, 71-76; res fels, Army Res Orgn, 76-78 & Rome Air Develop Ctr, 76-78. *Mem:* Sigma Xi; Inst Elec & Electronics Engrs. *Res:* Electromagnetics; scattering; antennas; microwave biological effects; electromagnetic compatibiligy; electromagnetic pulses; microwave circuits and devices. *Mailing Add:* Sperry Microwave Electronics PO Box 4648 Clearwater FL 33518

WU, THEODORE YAO-TSU, b Changchow, China, Mar 20, 24; US citizen; m 50; c 2. FLUID MECHANICS, ENGINEERING SCIENCE. *Educ:* Chiao Tung Univ, BS, 46; Iowa State Col, MS, 48; Calif Inst Technol, PhD(aeronaut), 52. *Prof Exp:* Res fel appl mech, 52-55, from asst prof to assoc prof, 52-61, PROF ENG SCI, CALIF INST TECHNOL, 61- *Concurrent*

Pos: Mem, US deleg, Int Towing Tank Conf, 57-72; Guggenheim fel & vis prof, Univ Hamburg, 64-65. *Mem:* Fel Am Phys Soc; assoc fel Am Inst Aeronaut & Astronaut; Ger Soc Appl Math & Mech; Ger Soc Shipbldg. *Res:* Fluid mechanics of compressible, viscous, heat-conducting fluids, water waves, jets, cavity, wake, boundary layer and stratified flows; biophysical and geophysical fluid mechanics. *Mailing Add:* Dept of Eng Calif Inst of Technol Pasadena CA 91125

WU, TIEN HSING, b Shanghai, China, Mar 2, 23; nat US; m 52; c 2. CIVIL ENGINEERING. *Educ:* St John's Col, BS, 47; Univ Ill, MS, 48, PhD(civil eng), 51. *Prof Exp:* Civil engr, Deleuw, Cather & Co, Ill, 51-52; State Hwy Div, Ill, 52-53; from asst prof to prof civil eng, Mich State Univ, 53-65; PROF CIVIL ENG, OHIO STATE UNIV, 65- *Concurrent Pos:* Consult geotech eng. *Mem:* Am Soc Civil Engrs. *Res:* Soil mechanics; geotechnical engineering. *Mailing Add:* Dept of Civil Eng 2070 Neil Ave Columbus OH 43210

WU, TING KAI, b Nanking, China, Aug 5, 37; m 66; c 2. CHEMISTRY. *Educ:* Mt St Mary's Col, Md, BS, 60; Columbia Univ, MA, 61, PhD(phys chem), 65. *Prof Exp:* Res assoc, Columbia Univ, 65; res chemist, 65-72, sr res chemist, 72-78, SR RES SUPVR, E I DU PONT DE NEMOURS & CO, INC, 78- *Concurrent Pos:* Vis assoc prof, Nat Sci Coun China, Nat Taiwan Univ, 70-71. *Mem:* AAAS; Am Chem Soc; NY Acad Sci; Am Inst Physics; Soc Plastics Engrs. *Res:* Structure and properties of molecules and macromolecules; spectroscopic analyses of molecular structure; polymer characterization. *Mailing Add:* Polymer Prod Dept Exp Sta E I du Pont de Nemours & Co Inc Wilmington DE 19898

WU, TSE CHENG, b Hong Kong, Aug 21, 23; nat US; m 63; c 3. ORGANIC CHEMISTRY, POLYMER CHEMISTRY. *Educ:* Yenching Univ, China, BS, 46; Univ Ill, MS, 48; Iowa State Univ, PhD(org chem), 52. *Prof Exp:* From res asst to res assoc, Iowa State Univ, 48-53; res chemist, Textile Fibers Dept, E I du Pont de Nemours & Co, Inc, 53-60; res chemist, Silicone Prod Dept, Gen Elec Co, 60-71; sr res chemist, Abcor, Inc, 71-77; RES ASSOC, CORP RES CTR, ALLIED CORP, 77- *Mem:* Am Chem Soc; Sigma Xi. *Res:* Monomer and polymer syntheses; acrylic, vinyl, polyester, polycarbonate, polyamide, silicone, and bioabsorbable polymers; rubber, fiber, plastic, membrane, and coating; biomaterials and biomedical implantation devices; organometallic, organosilicon, and fluorine chemistry. *Mailing Add:* 14-E Dorado Dr Morristown NJ 07960

WU, TSU MING, b Taipei, Taiwan, Dec 18, 36; m; c 2. PHYSICS. *Educ:* Univ Taiwan, BS, 59; Univ Pa, PhD(physics), 66. *Prof Exp:* Fel physics, Case Western Reserve Univ, 66-68; asst prof, 68-71, assoc prof, 71-80, PROF PHYSICS, STATE UNIV NY BINGHAMTON, 80- *Mem:* Am Phys Soc. *Res:* Many-body problems in solid state physics, especially superconductivity and magnetism. *Mailing Add:* Dept of Physics State Univ of NY Binghamton NY 13901

WU, WEN-LI, polymer physics, see previous edition

WU, WILLIAM CHI-LIANG, b Shanghai, China, Dec 24, 32; US citizen; m 57; c 3. CHEMICAL ENGINEERING, POLYMER SCIENCE. *Educ:* Mass Inst Technol, SB, 54, SM, 55, ChE, 58. *Prof Exp:* Res asst, Fuels Res Lab, Mass Inst Technol, 55-57; res engr, US Indust Chem Co Div, Nat Distillers & Chem Corp, 57-59, proj leader, 59-61, res supvr, 61; develop engr, Mobil Chem Co Div, Mobil Oil Corp, 62-63, sr develop engr, 63, group leader polymer process develop, 63-67, sect leader, 67-68; res mgr polymer develop, Chemplex Co, 68-77; MGR RES & DEVELOP, MOBIL CHEM CO, 77- *Mem:* Am Inst Chem Engrs; Am Chem Soc; Soc Plastics Engrs. *Res:* Polymerization of ethylene; stereospecific polymerization of propylene and butene-1; polyesterification of terephthalic acid; chemical modifications of polyolefins; polymer additives; polymer blends. *Mailing Add:* Mobil Chem Co Macedon NY 14502

WU, WILLIAM GAY, b Portland, Ore, Feb 5, 31; m 57; c 3. MEDICAL MICROBIOLOGY, IMMUNOLOGY. *Educ:* Ore State Univ, BS, 49, MS, 61; Univ Utah, PhD(immunol, cell biol), 62. *Prof Exp:* Lab asst soil microbiol, Ore State Univ, 57-58, res asst vet microbiol, 58-59; res asst immunol, Univ Utah, 59-62; from asst prof to assoc prof, 62-70, chmn dept microbiol, 67-72, chmn dept biol, 76-81, PROF MICROBIOL, SAN FRANCISCO STATE UNIV, 70- *Concurrent Pos:* Res Corp grants, 64-65; NSF grants, 65-67; vis prof, Tulane Univ, 70-71. *Mem:* AAAS; Am Soc Microbiol; Am Asn Immunol. *Res:* Natural resistance mechanisms; cellular immunity; acute disease mechanisms. *Mailing Add:* Dept Biol San Francisco State Univ 1600 Holloway Ave San Francisco CA 94132

WU, WU-NAN, b Kaohsiung, Taiwan, Mar 16, 38; US citizen; m 71; c 1. PHARMACY. *Educ:* Kaohsiung Med Col, BS, 61; Ohio State Univ, PhD(pharm), 72. *Prof Exp:* Technician drug anal, Taiwan Prov Hyg Labs, 62-63; asst pharm, Taipei Med Col, 63-65; specialist, Bristol Res Inst Taiwan, 65-67; res scientist, 78-79, SR SCIENTIST DRUG METAB, MCNEIL PHARMACEUT INC, 79- *Concurrent Pos:* Res assoc, Col Pharm, Ohio State Univ, 67-72, researcher, 74-77; res fel, Col Pharm, Univ Fla, 73-74. *Mem:* Am Chem Soc; Am Pharmacog Soc. *Res:* Isolation and structural elucidation of biologically active natural products; drug metabolism. *Mailing Add:* McNeil Pharmaceut Inc 500 Office Center Dr Ft Washington PA 19034

WU, YAO HUA, b Soochow, China, July 16, 20; nat US; m 50; c 2. ORGANIC CHEMISTRY. *Educ:* Chiao Tung Univ, BS, 43; Univ Nebr, MS, 48, PhD(org chem), 51. *Prof Exp:* Pharmaceut chemist, Int Chem Works, Shanghai, 43-47; res chemist, Smith-Dorsey Co, 51-53; res chemist, 53-60, sr res fel, 60-70, dir chem res, 70-76, dir clin publ, 77-80, DIR RES PLANNING, MEAD JOHNSON & CO, 80- *Mem:* Am Chem Soc. *Res:* Synthetic pharmaceuticals. *Mailing Add:* Mead Johnson Res Ctr Evansville IN 47721

WU, YING VICTOR, b Peking, China, Nov 1, 31; nat US; m 60; c 1. PHYSICAL CHEMISTRY. *Educ:* Univ Ala, BS, 53; Mass Inst Technol, PhD(phys chem), 58. *Prof Exp:* Asst phys chem, Mass Inst Technol, 53-57; res assoc chem, Cornell Univ, 58-61; res chemist, 61-64, prin chemist, 64-76, SUPVR RES CHEMIST, NORTHERN REGIONAL LAB, USDA, 76- *Concurrent Pos:* Fel, Mass Inst Technol, 57-58. *Mem:* AAAS; Am Chem Soc; Am Asn Cereal Chemists; Am Soc Biol Chemists; Inst Food Technologists. *Res:* Physical chemistry of protein protein structure, cereal protein concentrates and isolates; optical rotatory disperson; hydrogen ion equilibria. *Mailing Add:* Northern Regional Lab 1815 N University St Peoria IL 61604

WU, YING-CHU LIN (SUSAN), b Peking, China, June 23, 32; m 59; c 3. THERMAL PHYSICS, FLUIDS. *Educ:* Nat Taiwan Univ, BS, 55; Ohio State Univ, MS, 59; Calif Inst Technol, PhD(aeronaut), 63. *Prof Exp:* Engr, Taiwan Hwy Bur, 55-56; sr engr, Electro-Optical Syst, Pasadena, Calif, 63-65; from asst prof to assoc prof, 65-73, PROF AEROSPACE, SPACE INST, UNIV TENN, 73- *Concurrent Pos:* Lab mgr, Res & Develop Lab, 77-81, adminr, Energy Conversion Res & Develop Ctr, 81- *Mem:* Assoc fel Am Inst Aeronaut & Astronaut; Am Soc Mech Engrs; Sigma Xi. *Res:* Magnetohydrodynamic power generation; physical phenomena occurring in magnetohydrodynamic generators. *Mailing Add:* Univ Tenn Space Inst Energy Conversion Div Tullahoma TN 37388

WU, YUNG-CHI, b Canton, China, Oct 3, 23; US citizen; m 45; c 2. THERMODYNAMICS. *Educ:* Sun Yat-Sen Univ, BS, 47; Univ Houston, MS, 52; Univ Chicago, PhD(chem), 57. *Prof Exp:* Chemist, Res & Develop Lab, Portland Cement Asn, 57-62, Watson Res Ctr, Int Bus Mach Corp, 63-66 & Oak Ridge Nat Lab, 66-67; CHEMIST, NAT BUR STANDARDS, 67- *Mem:* AAAS; Am Chem Soc; NY Acad Sci. *Res:* Electrolyte solutions; thermodynamics; bio-technology of heat transfer. *Mailing Add:* Nat Bur of Standards Washington DC 20234

WU, YUNG-KUANG, b Chung-li, Taiwan, Dec 15, 33; m 63; c 1. ELECTRICAL ENGINEERING. *Educ:* Nat Taiwan Univ, BS, 56; Kans State Univ, MS, 60; Univ Mich, PhD(elec eng), 65. *Prof Exp:* Asst res engr, Radiation Lab, Univ Mich, 64-65; asst prof elec eng, Southeastern Mass Univ, 65-68, assoc prof, 68-72; mem staff, Lincoln Lab, Mass Inst Technol, 72-74; mem staff, Charles Stark Draper Lab, 74-75; RES ENGR, NAT HWY TRAFFIC SAFETY ADMIN, DEPT OF TRANSP, 75- *Mem:* Sr mem Inst Elec & Electronics Engrs. *Res:* Electromagnetic compatibility; radar brake; electronic engine control systems; application of electromagnetic theory such as reentry blackout problems; magnetohydrodynamic boundary-layer control. *Mailing Add:* NHTSA/NRD-12 400 7th St SW Washington DC 20590

WUBBELS, GENE GERALD, b Lanesboro, Minn, Sept 21, 42; m 67; c 2. CHEMISTRY. *Educ:* Hamline Univ, BS, 64; Northwestern Univ, PhD(chem), 68. *Prof Exp:* Chmn dept chem, 68-80, ASSOC PROF ORG & BIOL CHEM, GRINNELL COL, 68- *Concurrent Pos:* Petrol Res Fund grant, 71-73; res assoc, State Univ NY Buffalo, 74-75; vis prof, Northwestern Univ, 75; res grant, Am Chem Soc-Petrol Res Fund, 74-77 & 78-80. *Mem:* Am Chem Soc. *Res:* Catalytic mechanisms for photosubstitution, photoreduction and photoaddition reactions of aromatic compounds. *Mailing Add:* Dept of Chem Grinnell Col Grinnell IA 50112

WUCHTER, RICHARD B, b Wadsworth, Ohio, July 21, 37; m 72. ORGANIC CHEMISTRY. *Educ:* Western Reserve Univ, AB, 59; Cornell Univ, PhD(org chem), 63. *Prof Exp:* Asst org chem, Cornell Univ, 60-62; group leader process res, 63-70, GROUP LEADER POLLUTION CONTROL CHEM SYNTHESIS, FLUID PROCESS LAB, ROHM AND HAAS CO, 70- *Mem:* Am Chem Soc. *Res:* Monomer synthesis and process development; plastics; modifiers for plastics; fibers; pollution control and ion exchange syntheses. *Mailing Add:* Fluid Process Lab Rohm and Haas Co Morristown & McKean Rd Spring House PA 19477

WUDL, FRED, b Cochabamba, Bolivia, Jan 8, 41; US citizen; m 67. ORGANIC CHEMISTRY, MATERIALS SCIENCE. *Educ:* Univ Calif, Los Angeles, BS, 64, PhD(chem), 67. *Prof Exp:* Fel org chem, Harvard Univ, 67-68; asst prof, State Univ NY, Buffalo, 68-73; MEM TECH STAFF, BELL LABS, 73- *Mem:* Am Chem Soc; Sigma Xi. *Res:* Organic conductors; organic synthesis; heterocycles; organometallic compounds and complexes. *Mailing Add:* Bell Labs 600 Mountain Ave Murray Hill NJ 07974

WUEBBLES, DONALD J, b Breese, Ill, Jan 28, 48; m 70; c 2. ATMOSPHERIC CHEMISTRY & PHYSICS. *Educ:* Univ Ill, BS, 70, MS, 72. *Prof Exp:* Res scientist, Nat Oceanic & Atmospheric Admin, 72-73, Univ Colo, Boulder, 73; RES SCIENTIST, LAWRENCE LIVERMORE NAT LAB, 73- *Concurrent Pos:* Prin investr, Environ Protection Agency, 79-; sci adv, Meetings on fluorocarbon, Orgn Econ Coop & Develop, 81; consult, Calif Air Resources Bd, 81-; lectr, Univ Calif, Irvine, 81. *Mem:* Am Geophys Union; Am Meteorol Soc. *Res:* Computational modelling of the physical, chemical, and radiative processes in the atmosphere; atmospheric ozone and athropogenic effects on it. *Mailing Add:* Lawrence Livermore Nat Lab L-262 Livermore CA 94550

WUENSCH, BERNHARDT J(OHN), b Paterson, NJ, Sept 17, 33; m 60; c 2. CRYSTALLOGRAPHY, CERAMICS. *Educ:* Mass Inst Technol, SB, 55, SM, 57, PhD(crystallog), 63. *Prof Exp:* Res fel crystallog, Inst Mineral Petrog, Univ Berne, 63-64; from asst prof to assoc prof, 64-74, PROF CERAMICS, MASS INST TECHNOL, 74- *Concurrent Pos:* Ford fel eng, 64-66; vis prof crystallog, Univ Saarland, Saarbrucken, Germany, 73; adv ed, Physics & Chem Minerals, 76-; assoc ed, J Mineral Asn Can, 78- & 80; ed, Zeit Kristallogr, 81-; vis scientist, Max Planck Inst fur Festkorperforschung, Ger, 81. *Mem:* Mineral Asn Can; Am Crystallog Asn; fel Am Ceramic Soc; fel Mineral Soc Am. *Res:* X-ray diffraction; crystal structure determination; relation between crystal structure and crystal properties; diffusion and point defects. *Mailing Add:* Dept of Mat Sci & Eng Mass Inst Technol Cambridge MA 02139

WUENSCHEL, PAUL CLARENCE, b Erie, Pa, May 13, 21; m 50; c 6. GEOPHYSICS. *Educ:* Colo Sch Mines, GeolEngr, 44; Columbia Univ, PhD(geol), 55. *Prof Exp:* Res assoc, Columbia Univ, 46-52; dir geol & geophys res, Res, Inc, 52-55; res assoc, 55-74, GEOPHYSICIST & SR SCIENTIST, GULF RES & DEVELOP CO, 74- *Mem:* Soc Explor Geophys; Seismol Soc Am; Acoust Soc Am; Am Geophys Union; Europ Asn Explor Geophys. *Res:* Seismology; potential, electrical and seismic methods of geophysical exploration. *Mailing Add:* 128 Marian Ave Glenshaw PA 15116

WUEPPER, KIRK DEAN, b Bay City, Mich, Mar 18, 38; m 67; c 3. DERMATOLOGY. *Educ:* Univ Mich, MD, 63; Am Bd Dermat, dipl, 70. *Prof Exp:* USPHS fel, Scripps Clin & Res Found, 68-70, assoc dermat & path, 70-72; assoc prof dermat, Med Sch, Univ Ore, 72-76, PROF DERMAT, OREGON HEALTH SCI UNIV, 76- *Concurrent Pos:* Res career develop award, 71-76. *Honors & Awards:* Charles W Burr Award for Res, 64. *Mem:* Am Asn Immunol; Am Soc Clin Invest; Soc Invest Dermat (secy-treas, 79-); Am Fedn Clin Res; Am Acad Dermat. *Mailing Add:* Dept Dermat Oregon Health Sci Univ Portland OR 97201

WUERKER, RALPH FREDERICK, b Los Angeles, Calif, Jan 18, 29; div; c 3. PHYSICS. *Educ:* Occidental Col, BA, 51; Stanford Univ, PhD(physics), 60. *Prof Exp:* Engr, AiRes, Inc, 56-58; mem tech staff, Res Lab, Ramo-Wooldridge, Inc, 58-59; mem sr staff, Res Lab, Space Technol Labs, Inc, 60-61; mem sr staff, Quantatron Corp, 61-62; MEM PROF STAFF, TRW SYSTS GROUP, TRW INC, REDONDO BEACH, 63- *Concurrent Pos:* Consult, Lawrence Livermore Labs, 73- *Honors & Awards:* Res Soc Award, TRW Systs, 66. *Mem:* Am Asn Physics Teachers; Am Phys Soc; Optical Soc Am. *Res:* Holography and coherent optics; plasma particle resonances; superconductivity; electrooptics; lasers; physical optics; plasma physics; electron and general experimental physics. *Mailing Add:* 15123 Cordary Ave Lawndale CA 90260

WUEST, PAUL J, b Philadelphia, Pa, Feb 26, 37; m 61; c 4. PLANT PATHOLOGY, MYCOLOGY. *Educ:* Pa State Univ, BS, 58, PhD(plant path), 63. *Prof Exp:* Asst, 58-63, asst prof, 64-68, assoc prof, 68-74, PROF PLANT PATH, PA STATE UNIV, 74- *Concurrent Pos:* Fel, Univ Guelph, 70-71; agr consult, 70- *Mem:* Am Phytopath Soc; Can Phytopath Soc; Soc Nematol; Mycol Soc Am; Am Mushroom Inst. *Res:* Diseases of the commercial mushroom; soil treatment and disease occurrence; fungicide tolerance; epidemiology; pest management; worker exposure to pesticides. *Mailing Add:* Dept of Plant Path Pa State Univ University Park PA 16802

WU-HUNTER, SHIRLEY SHAO-NING, biochemistry, see previous edition

WUJEK, DANIEL EVERETT, b Bay City, Mich, Oct 26, 39; m 66. BOTANY. *Educ:* Cent Mich Univ, BS, 61, MA, 62; Univ Kans, PhD(bot), 66. *Prof Exp:* From asst prof to assoc prof bot, Wis State Univ, La Crosse, 66-68; assoc prof, 68-73, PROF BOT, CENT MICH UNIV, 73-, RES PROF, 78-, PROF BOT, 80- *Concurrent Pos:* Wis State Univ fac grant, 66-68; NSF grant, 71-72 & 76-77; Cent Mich Univ fac res grant, 71-79. *Honors & Awards:* Dimond Award, Bot Soc Am, 75. *Mem:* AAAS; Bot Soc Am; Am Micros Soc; Phycol Soc Am; Int Phycol Soc. *Res:* Algal life history studies and electron microscopy, including ecology and relations to water quality. *Mailing Add:* Dept of Biol Cent Mich Univ Mt Pleasant MI 48859

WUKELIC, GEORGE EDWARD, b Steubenville, Ohio, Sept 17, 29; m 55; c 3. REMOTE SENSING, SPACE PHYSICS. *Educ:* WVa Univ, AB, 52. *Prof Exp:* Prin physicist, Columbus Div, 52-60, sr physicist, 60-72, assoc sect mgr, Space Systs & Appln Sect, 72-77, STAFF SCIENTIST, WATER & LAND RESOURCES DEPT, PAC NORTHWEST DIV, BATTELLE MEM INST, 77- *Mem:* Am Soc Photogram; Am Geophys Union. *Res:* Space; geophysics; remote sensing applications; satellite earth resource surveys. *Mailing Add:* Pac Northwest Div Battelle Blvd Richland WA 99352

WULBERT, DANIEL ELIOT, b Chicago, Ill, Dec 17, 41; m 63. MATHEMATICS. *Educ:* Knox Col, Ill, BA, 63; Univ Tex, MA, 64, PhD(math), 66. *Prof Exp:* Vis asst prof math, Univ Lund, 66-67; asst prof, Univ Wash, 67-74; assoc prof, 74-80, PROF MATH, UNIV CALIF, SAN DIEGO, 80- *Concurrent Pos:* Fel, Univ Lund, 66-67; NSF res grant, 68-; vis prof, Northwestern Univ, 77-80. *Mem:* Am Math Soc. *Res:* Approximation theory; functional analysis. *Mailing Add:* Dept of Math Univ of Calif at San Diego La Jolla CA 92093

WULF, OLIVER REYNOLDS, b Norwich, Conn, Apr 22, 97; m 22. METEOROLOGY, PHYSICS. *Educ:* Worcester Polytech Inst, BS, 20; Am Univ, MS, 22; Calif Inst Technol, PhD, 26. *Prof Exp:* Jr chemist, USDA, 20-22; asst, Calif Inst Technol, 23-26, Nat Res Coun fel chem, 26-27; Nat Res Coun fel, Univ Calif, 27-28; from assoc chemist to sr physicist, Bur Chem & Soils, USDA, 28-39; meteorologist, US Weather Bur, 39-63, res meteorologist, 63-65; res meteorologist, Inst Atmospheric Sci, Environ Sci Serv Admin, US Dept Com, 65-67; res assoc, 45-67, emer res assoc, 67-74, EMER SR RES ASSOC PHYS CHEM, CALIF INST TECHNOL, 74- *Concurrent Pos:* Guggenheim fel, Univs Berlin & Göttingen, 32-33; res assoc, Univ Chicago, 41-45. *Mem:* Nat Acad Sci; AAAS; fel Am Phys Soc; Am Meteorol Soc; Am Chem Soc. *Res:* Chemical kinetics; photochemistry; molecular structure; band spectra; atmospheric and solar physics; geomagnetism; meteorology of the upper atmosphere; general circulation. *Mailing Add:* Noyes Lab of Chem Physics Calif Inst of Technol Pasadena CA 91125

WULF, RONALD JAMES, b Davenport, Iowa, July 24, 28; m 59; c 3. TOXICOLOGY, PHARMACOLOGY. *Educ:* Univ Iowa, BS, 50, MS, 57; Purdue Univ, PhD(biochem), 64. *Prof Exp:* Res chemist, John Deere & Co, 50-52; asst pharmacol, Univ Iowa, 54-57; res pharmacologist, Lederle Labs, Am Cyanamid Co, NY, 57-61; teaching asst biochem, Purdue Univ, 61-64; assoc prof pharmacol, Univ Conn, 64-70; DIR BIOL RES, CARTER WALLACE INC, 70- *Mem:* AAAS; Am Chem Soc; Soc Toxicol. *Res:* Drug safety evaluations; chemically induced fibrinolysis; inhalation toxicology. *Mailing Add:* Carter Wallace Inc Cranbury NJ 08512

WULF, WILLIAM ALLAN, b Chicago, Ill, Dec 8, 39; m 61; c 2. COMPUTER SCIENCE. *Educ:* Univ Ill, BSc, 61, MSc, 63; Univ Va, DSc(comput sci), 68. *Prof Exp:* Instr comput sci, Univ Va, 63-68; from asst prof to assoc prof, 68-75, actg dept head, 78-79, PROF COMPUT SCI, CARNEGIE-MELLON UNIV, 75- *Concurrent Pos:* Chmn working group on syst implementation lang, Int Fedn Info Processing, 72-78; assoc ed, Transactions Prog Languages & Systs, 79- *Mem:* Asn Comput Mach; Inst Elec & Electronics Engrs; Int Fedn Info Processing. *Res:* Computer languages and their translators, operating systems, methodology and computer architecture. *Mailing Add:* Dept of Comput Sci Carnegie-Mellon Univ Pittsburgh PA 15213

WULFERS, THOMAS FREDERICK, b Cape Girardeau, Mo, Oct 4, 39; m 63. ORGANIC CHEMISTRY. *Educ:* St Louis Univ, BS, 61; Washington Univ, MA, 63; Univ Chicago, PhD(chem), 65. *Prof Exp:* Res chemist, Shell Oil Co, Mo, 65-72; sr res chemist, 72-80, MGR INDUST PROD RES, ATLANTIC RICHFIELD CO, ILL, 80- *Mem:* Am Chem Soc. *Res:* Petroleum products research. *Mailing Add:* Atlantic Richfield Co 400 E Sibley Blvd Harvey IL 60426

WULFF, BARRY LEE, b Mt Kisco, NY, Feb 17, 40; m 66; c 2. ECOLOGY, BOTANY. *Educ:* State Univ NY Cortland, BS, 65; Col William & Mary, MA, 68; Ore State Univ, PhD(bot), 70. *Prof Exp:* Asst prof, 70-76, ASSOC PROF BIOL, EASTERN CONN STATE COL, 76- *Mem:* AAAS; Am Bryolochical & Lichenological Soc; Mycol Soc Am. *Res:* Lichens; fungi; marine algae; structure and function of benthic aquatic plant communities. *Mailing Add:* Dept Biol Eastern Conn State Col Willimantic CT 06226

WULFF, CLAUS ADOLF, b Hamburg, Ger, July 20, 38; US citizen; m 60; c 2. PHYSICAL CHEMISTRY. *Educ:* Cornell Univ, AB, 59; Mass Inst Technol, PhD(phys chem), 62. *Prof Exp:* Fel, Inst Sci & Technol, Univ Mich, 62-63; asst prof chem, Carnegie Inst Technol, 63-65; from asst prof to assoc prof, 65-73, PROF CHEM, UNIV VT, 73- *Concurrent Pos:* Am-Scand Found fel, Univ Lund, 71-72. *Mem:* Am Chem Soc; Royal Soc Chem; Calorimetry Conf. *Res:* Low-temperature and solution calorimetry. *Mailing Add:* Dept of Chem Univ of Vt Burlington VT 05405

WULFF, JOHN LELAND, b Oakland, Calif, Mar 19, 32; m 68; c 4. MATHEMATICS. *Educ:* Sacramento State Col, AB, 54; Univ Calif, Davis, MA, 57, PhD(math), 66. *Prof Exp:* From instr to assoc prof, 55-68, chmn dept, 68-71, PROF MATH, CALIF STATE UNIV, SACRAMENTO, 69- *Res:* Measure theory and integration. *Mailing Add:* Dept of Math Calif State Univ Sacramento CA 95819

WULFF, VERNER JOHN, b Essen, Ger, Aug 16, 16; m 42; c 3. NEUROPHYSIOLOGY. *Educ:* Wayne Univ, AB, 38; Northwestern Univ, MA, 40; Univ Iowa, PhD(zool), 42. *Prof Exp:* Asst zool & comp vert anat, Wayne Univ, 36-38; asst zool, embryol & endocrinol, Northwestern Univ, 38-40; asst, Univ Iowa, 40-42, instr & assoc mammalian physiol, 46-47; asst prof mammalian neurophysiol, Univ Ill, 47-51; prof zool & chmn dept, Syracuse Univ, 51-60; ASSOC DIR RES, MASONIC MED RES LAB, 61- *Mem:* AAAS; Am Soc Zool; Soc Exp Biol & Med. *Res:* Electrophysiology of retinae; relation between photochemical events and retinal action potential. *Mailing Add:* Masonic Med Res Lab Bleeker St Utica NY 13501

WULFF, WOLFGANG, b Darmstadt, Ger, June 16, 33; m 64; c 2. MECHANICAL & AEROSPACE ENGINEERING. *Educ:* Winterthur Tech Univ, Switz, BSME, 58; Ill Inst Technol, MSME, 62, PhD(mech & aerospace eng), 68. *Prof Exp:* Proj engr, Escher-Wyss Ltd, Zurich, 58-60 & Eppi Precision Prod, Ill, 60-63; res engr, IIT Res Inst, 63-68; from asst prof to assoc prof mech eng, Ga Inst Technol, 68-74; SR SCIENTIST, BROOKHAVEN NAT LAB, 74- *Mem:* Am Soc Mech Engrs; Combustion Inst; Am Soc Eng Educ; Am Nuclear Soc. *Res:* Fabric flammability; thermal control of space vehicles; atmospheric vortices; thermohydraulics of reactor systems; nuclear power reactor safety. *Mailing Add:* Brookhaven Nat Lab Upton NY 11973

WULFMAN, CARL E, b Detroit, Mich, Nov 29, 30; m 52; c 4. THEORETICAL PHYSICS, THEORETICAL CHEMISTRY. *Educ:* Univ Mich, BS, 53; Univ London, PhD(org chem), 57. *Prof Exp:* Instr chem, Univ Tex, 56-57; assoc prof, Defiance Col, 57-61; chmn dept, 61-74, PROF PHYSICS, UNIV OF THE PAC, 61- *Concurrent Pos:* Vis mem, Ctr Theoret Studies, Coral Gables, Fla, 67; NSF sci fac fel, Oxford Univ, 67-68; vis prof, Japan Soc Promotion Sci, 74-75. *Mem:* AAAS; Am Chem Soc; Am Phys Soc; Am Asn Physics Teachers. *Res:* Transformation properties of dynamical equations; continuous groups; applications to chemical kinetics, atomic and molecular quantum mechanics. *Mailing Add:* Dept of Physics Univ of the Pac Stockton CA 95211

WULFMAN, DAVID SWINTON, b Detroit, Mich, Sept 1, 34; m 61; c 3. SYNTHETIC ORGANIC CHEMISTRY, PHYSICAL ORGANIC CHEMISTRY. *Educ:* Univ Mich, Ann Arbor, BS, 56; Dartmouth Col, AM, 58; Stanford Univ, PhD(chem), 62; Alliance Francaise, Paris, France, IVe, French, 74. *Prof Exp:* Res asst chem, Univ Mich, 54-56; sr develop engr, Hercules Inc, Utah, 61-63; from asst prof to assoc prof, 63-77, PROF CHEM, UNIV MO-ROLLA, 77- *Concurrent Pos:* Consult, Dept Chem, Stanford Univ, 69; lectr, Washington Univ, 70 & Chem Soc France, 75; res assoc, Ctr Nat Res Sci, Ecole Normale Superieure, Paris, 74-75. *Mem:* Am Chem Soc; Royal Soc Chem; Chem Inst Can. *Res:* Synthesis and study of theoretically important molecules; homogeneous catalysis; kinetics of photochemical processes; biological action of diazo compounds. *Mailing Add:* Dept of Chem Univ of Mo Rolla MO 65401

WULLSTEIN, LEROY HUGH, b Nampa, Idaho, Nov 23, 31; m 56; c 1. BOTANY, MICROBIOLOGY. *Educ:* Univ Utah, BS, 57; Ore State Univ, MS, 61, PhD(microbiol), 64. *Prof Exp:* Asst prof soil sci, Univ BC, 64-66; from asst prof to assoc prof, 66-75, PROF BOT, UNIV UTAH, 75-, ASSOC PROF BIOL, 80- *Concurrent Pos:* Sr Fulbright res fel nitrogen fixation, Ireland, 72-73; consult, Brookhaven Labs, 74- *Mem:* Am Soc Microbiol; Am Chem Soc; Soil Sci Soc Am. *Res:* Nitrogen transformations; oak ecology. *Mailing Add:* Dept of Biol Univ of Utah Salt Lake City UT 84112

WULPI, DONALD JAMES, b Oak Park, Ill, May 2, 24; m 49; c 4. METALLURGICAL ENGINEERING, MECHANICS. *Educ:* Lehigh Univ, BS, 49. *Prof Exp:* Res metallurgist, Eng Mat Res & Testing Lab, Int Harvester Co, 49-56, chief mat spec engr, Gen Off, 56-61, res engr, 61-66, mat engr eng res, 66-69, mat engr, Truck Group Eng, 69-71, head, Metall Lab, 71-80; METALL CONSULT, 80- *Honors & Awards:* Silver Cert, Am Soc Metals, 75. *Mem:* Fel Am Soc Metals; Am Soc Testing & Mat. *Res:* Studying mechanisms of failure; writing and teaching about analysis of failures and ways to prevent failures; selection of materials; mechanical testing. *Mailing Add:* 3919 Hedwig Dr PO Box 1109 Ft Wayne IN 46815

WUN, CHUN KWUN, b Canton, China, Feb 15, 40; US citizen; m 64; c 2. BACTERIOLOGY,ENVIRONMENTAL POLLUTION CONTROL.*Educ:* Chung Chi Col, Chinese Univ Hong Kong, BS, 64; Springfield Col, MS, 69; Univ Mass, Amherst, MS, 71, PhD(lipid chem), 74. *Prof Exp:* Asst educ officer sci, Educ Dept Hong Kong, 65-66; from asst instr to instr biol, Springfield Col, 68-70; res asst lipid chem, Univ Mass, Amherst, 70-73; asst prof biol, Springfield Col, 73-74, assoc res prof, 81-82; FEL, DEPT ENVIRON SCI, UNIV MASS, AMHERST, 75- *Concurrent Pos:* Adj asst prof biol, Springfield Col, 75- *Mem:* Am Soc Microbiol; Sigma Xi; Soc Appl Bacteriol. *Res:* Lipid metabolism, particularly triglyceride synthesis and its control in mycobacterium smegmatis; water pollution; the use of fecal sterols as an indicator of fecal pollution of water; column method for rapid extraction and gas-liquid chromatography quantitation of algal chlorophylls; new media for the isolation/identification of E coli and other enteric organisms; rapid procedure for the isolation and drug susceptibility determination of mycobacteria; recycling of agricultural and domestic wastes. *Mailing Add:* Dept of Environ Sci Univ of Mass Amherst MA 01002

WUNDER, BRUCE ARNOLD, b Monterey Park, Calif, Feb 10, 42; m 63; c 2. PHYSIOLOGICAL ECOLOGY, VERTEBRATE ZOOLOGY. *Educ:* Whittier Col, BA, 63; Univ Calif, Los Angeles, PhD(vert zool), 68. *Prof Exp:* NIH fel, Inst Arctic Biol, Univ Alaska, 68-69; asst prof, 69-76, ASSOC PROF ZOOL, COLO STATE UNIV, 76- *Concurrent Pos:* Small mammal ecologist, Biol Res Assocs, Inc & consult, Thorne Ecol Inst, 72-; assoc prof zool, Univ Mich Biol Sta, 76 & 78; prof zool, Univ Mont Biol Sta, 81; Alexander von Humboldt fel, Frankfurt, Germany, 79-80. *Mem:* AAAS; Am Soc Zoologists; Am Soc Mammalogists; Am Inst Biol Sci; Ecol Soc Am. *Res:* Temperature regulation and energetics; water balance and mechanisms of evaporative water loss, particularly in vertebrates; feeding strategies and distribution patterns in vertebrates. *Mailing Add:* Dept of Zool & Entom Colo State Univ Ft Collins CO 80523

WUNDER, CHARLES C(OOPER), b Pittsburgh, Pa, Oct 2, 28; m 62; c 3. PHYSIOLOGY, BIOPHYSICS. *Educ:* Washington & Jefferson Col, AB, 49; Univ Pittsburgh, MS, 52, PhD(biophys), 54. *Prof Exp:* Asst biophys, Univ Pittsburgh, 49-51; assoc physiol, 54-56, asst prof, 56-63, assoc prof physiol & biophys, 63-71, PROF PHYSIOL & BIOPHYS, UNIV IOWA, 71- *Concurrent Pos:* NIH res career develop award, 61-66; vis scientist & NIH spec fel, Mayo Clin, 66-67. *Mem:* Soc Exp Biol & Med; Am Soc Zoologists; Soc Develop Biol; Biophys Soc; Am Physiol Soc. *Res:* Environmental biophysics of growth and function; gravitational biology. *Mailing Add:* Physiol Res Lab Oakdale Campus Univ Iowa Oakdale IA 52319

WUNDER, WILLIAM W, b Lake Park, Iowa, June 4, 30; m 60; c 3. POPULATION GENETICS, BIOMETRICS. *Educ:* Iowa State Univ, BS, 58; Mich State Univ, MS, 64, PhD(dairy cattle breeding), 67. *Prof Exp:* Asst prof exten dairy sci, Univ Ky, 67-68; asst prof, 68-74, assoc prof, 74-79, PROF ANIMAL SCI, IOWA STATE UNIV, 79- *Mem:* Am Dairy Sci Asn. *Res:* Effects of environment on milk production and statistical methods of adjusting for or removing these effects in selecting dairy cattle for higher milk production. *Mailing Add:* Dept of Animal Sci 123 Kildee Hall Iowa State Univ Ames IA 50010

WUNDERLICH, BERNHARD, b Brandenburg, Ger, May 28, 31; nat US; m 53; c 2. POLYMER CHEMISTRY. *Educ:* Univ Frankfurt, BSc, 54; Northwestern Univ, PhD, 57. *Prof Exp:* Instr chem, Northwestern Univ, 57-58; from instr to asst prof, Cornell Univ, 58-63; assoc prof, 63-65, PROF CHEM, RENSSELAER POLYTECH INST, 65- *Concurrent Pos:* Consult, E I du Pont de Nemours & Co, Inc. *Honors & Awards:* Mettler Award for Thermal Anal, 71. *Mem:* Am Chem Soc; NAm Thermal Anal Soc; Int Confedn Thermal Anal; fel Am Phys Soc; NY Acad Sci. *Res:* Physical chemistry of the solid state of high polymers; transitions of high polymers at elevated temperatures and high pressures. *Mailing Add:* Chem Dept Rensselaer Polytech Inst Troy NY 12181

WUNDERLICH, FRANCIS J, b Philadelphia, Pa, Mar 9, 38; m 62; c 5. PHYSICAL CHEMISTRY. *Educ:* Villanova Univ, BS, 59; Georgetown Univ, PhD(chem), 64. *Prof Exp:* Res asst chem, Villanova Univ, 57-58, instr, 59; instr, Georgetown Univ, 59-61, res assoc, 61-63; fel molecular physics, 63-65; from asst prof to assoc prof physics & chem, Col Virgin Islands, 65-69; ASST PROF PHYSICS, VILLANOVA UNIV, 69- *Concurrent Pos:* Dir, NSF Grant, Undergrad Sci Equip Prog, Col Virgin Islands, 65-67, dir, Etelman Astron Observ, 66-67. *Honors & Awards:* Award, Am Inst Chemists, 59. *Mem:* Am Chem Soc; The Chem Soc. *Res:* Theoretical molecular physics; gas phase free radicals; laser-induced gas phase reactions. *Mailing Add:* Dept of Physics Villanova Univ Villanova PA 19085

WUNDERLICH, MARVIN C, b Decatur, Ill, May 8, 37; m 60; c 2. MATHEMATICS. *Educ:* Concordia Teachers Col, Ill, BS, 59; Univ Colo, PhD(math), 64. *Prof Exp:* Asst prof math, State Univ NY, Buffalo, 64-67; assoc prof, 67-72, PROF MATH, NORTHERN ILL UNIV, 72- *Concurrent Pos:* NSF res grant, 66-; vis, Univ Nottingham, 72-73. *Mem:* Am Math Soc; Asn Comput Mach. *Res:* Number theory; computing mathematics. *Mailing Add:* Dept of Math Northern Ill Univ De Kalb IL 60115

WUNDERLY, STEPHEN WALKER, b Cleveland, Ohio, May 24, 45; m 69. SYNTHETIC ORGANIC CHEMISTRY, PHYSICAL CHEMISTRY. *Educ:* Col Wooster, BA, 63; Univ Cincinnati, MS, 71, PhD(chem), 75. *Prof Exp:* Res assoc chem, Univ BC, 74-75, Univ Calif, San Francisco, 75-76 & Univ Southern Calif, 76-77; SR CHEMIST, BECKMAN INSTRUMENTS INC, 77- *Mem:* Am Chem Soc. *Res:* Photochemistry; alkaloid synthesis and biosynthesis; synthesis of polycyclic aromatics; emulsion chemistry and emulsifer properties; chemistry with solid phase supported reagents. *Mailing Add:* Beckman Instruments Inc Campus At Jamboree Irvine CA 92713

WUNDERMAN, IRWIN, b New York, NY, Apr 24, 31; m 51; c 3. ELECTROOPTICS, ELECTRONIC INSTRUMENTATION. *Educ:* City Col New York, BSEE, 52; Univ Southern Calif, MSEE, 56; Stanford Univ, EEE, 61, PhD(elec eng), 64. *Prof Exp:* Jr engr draftsman, Lockheed-Calif Co, 52, jr engr, 52-53, res engr, 53-56; lab sect leader, Hewlett Packard Co, 56-61, co-founder, Hewlett Packard Assocs, 61-65, lab mgr, Hewlett Packard Corp Labs, 65-67; pres & gen mgr, Cintra Inc, Cintra Physics Int, 67-71; RESEARCHER, SCIENTIST & AUTHOR, 71- *Honors & Awards:* Outstanding Invited Paper, Solid State Circuits Conf, Inst Elec & Electronics Engrs, 65; Nat Commendation Letter, 68. *Mem:* AAAS; sr mem Inst Elec & Electronics Engrs; Optical Soc Am; Am Inst Physics; Sigma Xi. *Res:* Electrooptics instrumentation; radiometry; photometry; optoelectronic solid state devices and circuits; computer architecture and systems; modeling of nonlinear physical systems; physics of optics and quanta; wave/particle dilemma; photons, granular mechanics and the classical origin of quanta theory in mathematical physics. *Mailing Add:* 655 Eunice Ave Mountain View CA 94040

WUNSCH, CARL ISAAC, b New York, NY, May 5, 41; m 70; c 2. PHYSICAL OCEANOGRAPHY. *Educ:* Mass Inst Technol, SB, 62, PhD(geophys), 66. *Prof Exp:* Lectr oceanog, 66-67, from asst prof to assoc prof, 67-75, prof, 75-76, head, Dept Earth & Planetary Sci, 77-81, CECIL & IDA GREEN PROF PHYS OCEANOG, MASS INST TECHNOL, 76- *Concurrent Pos:* Vis sr investr, Cambridge Univ, 69, 74-75 & 81-82; vis prof, Univ Wash, 80 & Harvard Univ, 80; ed, Monographs in Mech & Appli Math, Cambridge Univ Press, 81-; Fulbright award, 81-82; Guggenheim Found fel, 81-82. *Honors & Awards:* James B Macelwane Award, Am Geophys Union, 71; Founders Prize, Tex Instruments Found, 75. *Mem:* Nat Acad Sci; Am Geophys Union; Royal Astron Soc; Am Acad Arts & Sci. *Res:* internal waves; sea level, mixing processes, general circulation; tides; ocean acoustics. *Mailing Add:* Dept of Earth & Planetary Sci Mass Inst of Technol Cambridge MA 02139

WUNZ, PAUL RICHARD, JR, b Erie, Pa, Oct 18, 23; m 48; c 3. ORGANIC CHEMISTRY. *Educ:* Pa State Col, BS, 44, MS, 47; Univ Del, PhD(chem), 50. *Prof Exp:* Instr chem, Univ Del, 50; asst prof chem & head dept, Augsburg Col, 50-51; res chemist, Nopco Chem Co, 51-53; res chemist & group leader, Callery Chem Co, 53-57; from asst prof to assoc prof chem, Geneva Col, 57-65; chmn dept, 65-73, PROF CHEM, INDIANA UNIV PA, 65- *Mem:* Am Chem Soc; Sigma Xi. *Res:* Synthetic organic chemistry; organometallic compounds; pharmaceuticals, steroids; heterocyclic compounds. *Mailing Add:* Dept of Chem Indiana Univ of Pa Indiana PA 15705

WUONOLA, MARK ARVID, b Astoria, Ore, Oct 9, 47. ORGANIC CHEMISTRY, MEDICINAL CHEMISTRY. *Educ:* Mass Inst Technol, SB, 69; Harvard Univ, AM, 70, PhD(org chem), 73. *Prof Exp:* Res fel, Harvard Univ, 73-76; res chemist org chem, Cent Res & Develop Dept, 76-82, RES CHEMIST, BIOCHEM DEPT, E I DU PONT DE NEMOURS & CO, INC, 82- *Mem:* Am Chem Soc. *Res:* Chemistry of natural products; synthetic organic chemistry; heterocyclic chemistry. *Mailing Add:* Exp Sta Bldg 353 E I DuPont de Nemours & Co Inc Wilmington DE 19898

WUORI, ALBERT FREDERICK, b Houghton, Mich, July 25, 28; m 51; c 4. ENGINEERING. *Educ:* Mich Technol Univ, BSCE, 55, MS, 57 & 68. *Prof Exp:* Civil engr res, Snow Ice & Permafrost Res Estab, 55-61; supvry engr, 61-73, CHIEF, EXP ENG DIV, US ARMY COLD REGIONS RES & ENG LAB, 73- *Mem:* Am Soc Civil Engrs; Int Soc Terrain-Vehicle Systs. *Res:* Cold region engineering; snow and ice mechanics; soils mechanics; research management. *Mailing Add:* US Army Cold Regions Res & Eng Lab Hanover NH 03755

WUORINEN, JOHN H, JR, b New York, NY, Aug 9, 31; m 56; c 4. ELECTRICAL ENGINEERING. *Educ:* Columbia Univ, AB, 53, MS, 56, PhD(elec eng), 63. *Prof Exp:* Res asst elec eng, Electronics Res Lab, Columbia Univ, 54-56, instr, Univ, 56-62; mem tech staff, 62-64, supvr digital device integration, 64-68, head, Electronic Subsyst Design Dept, 68-74, head, Memory & Call Progress Syst Dept, 74-80, HEAD, SPECIAL SYSTS DEPT, BELL LABS, 81- *Concurrent Pos:* Chmn solid state circuits conf, Inst Elec & Electronics Engrs, 76-77. *Mem:* Inst Elec & Electronics Engrs. *Res:* Digital integrated circuits; solid state electronics; digital memory systems; telephone switching. *Mailing Add:* Bell Labs Whippany Rd Whippany NJ 07981

WURDACK, JOHN J, b Pittsburgh, Pa, Apr 28, 21; m 59; c 2. BOTANY. *Educ:* Univ Pittsburgh, BS, 42; Univ Ill, BS, 49; Columbia Univ, PhD, 52. *Prof Exp:* Asst bot, Univ Pittsburgh, 42; tech asst bot, NY Bot Garden, 49-52; from asst cur to assoc cur, 52-60, assoc cur, Div Phanerogams, 60-63, CUR BOT, NAT MUS NATURAL HIST, SMITHSONIAN INST, 63- *Concurrent Pos:* Mem exped, Venezuela, 50-59 & 72 & Peru, 62. *Mem:* Am Soc Plant Taxonomists; Torrey Bot Club; Int Asn Plant Taxon. *Res:* Taxonomy of Melastomataceae and flowering plants of northern South America. *Mailing Add:* Dept Bot Nat Mus of Natural Hist Smithsonian Inst Washington DC 20560

WURMSER, LEON, b Zurich, Switzerland, Jan 31, 31; US citizen; m 58; c 3. PSYCHOANALYSIS, DRUG ABUSE. *Educ:* Univ Basel, MD, 58. *Prof Exp:* Staff psychiatrist, Sheppard Pratt Hosp, Baltimore, 62-65; dir out patient, Smai, 66-69; dir, Drug Abuse Ctr, Johns Hopkins Hosp, 69-71; assoc prof, 71-77, DIR ALCOHOL & DRUG ABUSE & PROF PSYCHIAT, UNIV MD,

77- *Concurrent Pos:* Asst prof psychiat, Johns Hopkins Univ, 68-71, asst prof psychol, 79- *Mem:* Am Psychiat Asn; Am Psychoanal Asn; Swiss Med Soc; Swiss Psychiat Soc; AAAS. *Res:* Psychodynamics of compulsive substance abuse; shame, shame conflicts, and defense against shame; the defense against superego. *Mailing Add:* 721 W Redwood St Baltimore MD 21201

WURSIG, BERND GERHARD, b WGer, Nov 9, 48; m 69; c 1. BEHAVIORAL BIOLOGY, MARINE MAMMALOGY. *Educ:* Ohio State Univ, BSc, 71; State Univ NY, PhD(behav biol), 78. *Prof Exp:* fel, NIH & Univ Calif, Santa Cruz, 78-81. *Concurrent Pos:* Researcher, Nat Geog Soc, 74-77, biomed res fel, 77. *Mem:* Am Behav Soc; Explorer's Club; Am Soc Mamalogists; Natural History Soc. *Res:* Behavior and ecology of cetaceans and pinnipeds; movement and migration patterns of porpoises; tagging techniques for small cetaceans; comparison of wild and captive porpoise behavior; sociobiology and ecology of mammals. *Mailing Add:* Moss Landing Marine Labs Moss Landing CA 95039

WURST, GLEN GILBERT, b Mt Holly, NJ, Apr 17, 45. GENETICS. *Educ:* Juniata Col, BS, 67; Univ Pittsburgh, PhD(biol), 75. *Prof Exp:* Teaching asst biol, Univ Pittsburgh, 67-71, teaching fel, 71-75; ASST PROF BIOL, ALLEGHENY COL, 75- *Concurrent Pos:* Vis assoc res scientist, Johns Hopkins Univ, 80 & 81. *Res:* Developmental genetics of Drosophila Melanogaster. *Mailing Add:* Dept of Biol Allegheny Col Meadville PA 16335

WURST, JOHN CHARLES, b Defiance, Ohio, Jan 11, 36; m 58; c 3. CERAMIC ENGINEERING. *Educ:* Univ Dayton, BME, 57, MEngSc, 68; Univ Ill, Urbana, PhD(ceramic eng), 71. *Prof Exp:* Sr res ceramist, 57-75, ASSOC DIR, RES INST, UNIV DAYTON, 75- & ASSOC PROF, GRAD FACULTY, 73- *Concurrent Pos:* Consult mem comt coatings, Mat Adv Bd, Nat Acad Eng, 67-71. *Mem:* Fel Am Ceramic Soc; Sigma Xi; Nat Coun Univ Adminr; Nat Inst Ceramic Engrs; Ceramic Educ Coun. *Res:* High temperature protective coatings; corrosion; infrared transmitting materials; ceramics; sintering. *Mailing Add:* Univ of Dayton Res Inst Dayton OH 45469

WURSTER, CHARLES F, JR, b Philadelphia, Pa, Aug 1, 30. ENVIRONMENTAL SCIENCES, ENVIRONMENTAL TOXICOLOGY. *Educ:* Haverford Col, SB, 52; Univ Del, MS, 54; Stanford Univ, PhD(org chem), 57. *Prof Exp:* Asst, Univ Del, 52-54 & Stanford Univ, 54-57; Fulbright fel, Innsbruck Univ, 57-58; res chemist, Monsanto Res Corp, 59-62; res assoc, Dartmouth Col, 62-65; asst prof biol sci, 65-71, ASSOC PROF ENVIRON SCI, MARINE SCI RES CTR, STATE UNIV NY STONY BROOK, 71- *Mem:* AAAS. *Res:* Ecological and physiological effects of stable chemical pollutants; effects of chlorinated hydrocarbons on marine plankton communities. *Mailing Add:* Marine Sci Res Ctr State Univ of NY Stony Brook NY 11794

WURSTER, DALE E, b Sparta, Wis, Apr 10, 18; m 44; c 2. PHARMACY. *Educ:* Univ Wis, BS, 42, PhD, 47. *Prof Exp:* From instr to prof pharm, Univ Wis, 47-71; prof pharm & pharmaceut chem & dean col pharm, NDak State Univ, 71-72; PROF PHARM & DEAN COL PHARM, UNIV IOWA, 72- *Concurrent Pos:* Am Asn Cols Pharm-NSF vis scientist, 63-66; consult, USPHS, 66-72; mem revision comt, US Pharmacopoeia, 61-72. *Honors & Awards:* Indust Pharm Technol Award, Am Pharmaceut Asn Acad Pharmaceut Sci, 80. *Mem:* Acad Pharmaceut Sci; Am Pharmaceut Asn; hon mem Rumanian Soc Med Sci. *Res:* Physical factors influencing dissolution kinetics; diffusion kinetics in biological membranes, drug release mechanisms from pharmaceutical systems, percutaneous absorption, air-suspension microencapsulation coating and granulating technique. *Mailing Add:* Col of Pharm Univ of Iowa Iowa City IA 52240

WURSTER, DALE ERIC, b Madison, Wis, Jan 19, 51; m 75; c 1. SURFACE CHEMISTRY, DISSOLUTION KINETICS. *Educ:* Univ Wis, BS, 74; Purdue Univ, PhD(phys pharm), 79. *Prof Exp:* ASST PROF PHARM, SCH PHARM, UNIV NC, 79- *Mem:* Acad Pharmaceut Sci; Am Pharmaceut Asn; Am Chem Soc; Sigma Xi; Am Asn Col Pharm. *Res:* Surface phenomena, especially adsorption-desorption thermodynamics and dissolution mechanisms: applied to the performance of pharmaceutical dosage forms and dosage form excipients. *Mailing Add:* Beard Hall 200H Sch Pharm Univ NC Chapel Hill NC 27514

WURSTER, RICHARD T, horticulture, see previous edition

WURSTER, WALTER HERMAN, b Ger, Aug 17, 25; nat US. PHYSICS. *Educ:* Univ Buffalo, BA, 50, PhD, 57. *Prof Exp:* Res physicist, Cornell Aeronaut Lab, Inc, 55-61, prin physicist, 61-72, staff scientist, 72-74; MEM STAFF, CALSPAN CORP, 74- *Mem:* Am Phys Soc; Optical Soc Am. *Res:* Beta ray spectroscopy; absorption and emission spectroscopy of high temperature gases in infrared and ultraviolet; shock tube techniques and instrumentation; rocket plume radiation and chemistry. *Mailing Add:* Calspan Corp PO Box 400 Buffalo NY 14225

WURSTER-HILL, DORIS HADLEY, b Washington, DC, Sept 9, 32. CYTOGENETICS. *Educ:* George Washington Univ, BS, 54; Stanford Univ, MA, 56, PhD(biol), 58. *Prof Exp:* Res assoc endocrinol, 62-65, from res assoc & instr to res assoc & asst prof cytogenetics, 67-77, assoc prof cytogenetics, 77-80, RES ASSOC PROF PATH, DARTMOUTH MED SCH, 80- *Concurrent Pos:* USPHS trainee cytogenetics, Dartmouth Med Sch, 65-67; consult, Vet Admin Hosp, White River Jct, Vt, 69- *Mem:* AAAS; Am Soc Human Genetics. *Res:* Clinical and comparative mammalian cytogenetics. *Mailing Add:* Dept of Path Dartmouth Med Sch Hanover NH 03755

WURTELE, MORTON GAITHER, b Harrodsburg, Ky, July 25, 19; m 42; c 2. DYNAMIC METEOROLOGY. *Educ:* Harvard Univ, BS, 40; Univ Calif, Los Angeles, MA, 44, PhD, 53. *Prof Exp:* Asst prof meteorol, Mass Inst Technol, 53-58; assoc prof, 58-64, vchmn dept, 69-72, chmn dept, 72-76, PROF METEOROL, UNIV CALIF, LOS ANGELES, 64- *Concurrent Pos:* Fulbright grants, Univ Sorbonne, 49 & Hebrew Univ, Israel, 65; NATO sr fel, 62; consult, Atmospheric Sci Lab, White Sands Missile Range, 65-, Jet Propulsion Lab, 78- *Mem:* Am Meteorol Soc; Am Geophysics Union. *Res:* Small- and medium-scale atmospheric motions; sound propagation; atmospheric-ocean interaction. *Mailing Add:* Dept of Atmospheric Sci Univ of Calif Los Angeles CA 90024

WURTELE, ZIVIA SYRKIN, b New York, NY, Apr 1, 21; m 42; c 2. STATISTICS, ECONOMETRICS. *Educ:* Hunter Col, BA, 40; Univ Calif, Los Angeles, MA, 44; Columbia Univ, PhD(math statist), 54. *Prof Exp:* From asst res statistician to assoc res statistician, Univ Calif, Los Angeles, 59-65; consult econ & math models, Syst Develop Corp, 65-74; consult statist, Sci Appln, Inc, 74-76; SR RES SCIENTIST, PAN HEURISTIES, 76- *Concurrent Pos:* Res fel econ, Harvard Univ, 56-58. *Mem:* Inst Math Statist; NY Acad Sci. *Res:* Mathematical models of social science processes. *Mailing Add:* 432 E Rustic Rd Santa Monica CA 90402

WURTH, MICHAEL JOHN, b Highland Park, Ill, Mar 31, 37; m 65; c 1. ORGANIC CHEMISTRY, PHOTOGRAPHY. *Educ:* Lake Forest Col, BA, 64; Northwestern Univ, Evanston, PhD(org chem), 69. *Prof Exp:* ASSOC PROF CHEM, OKLAHOMA CITY UNIV, 68- *Mem:* Am Chem Soc. *Res:* Synthesis of new bicyclic heterocyclic compounds; photographic chemistry, especially emulsions and developing agents. *Mailing Add:* Dept of Chem Oklahoma City Univ Oklahoma City OK 73106

WURTH, THOMAS JOSEPH, b St Louis, Mo, June 13, 28; m 58; c 3. CHEMICAL ENGINEERING, RESEARCH & BUSINESS PLANNING. *Educ:* Washington Univ, St Louis, BS, 52; Univ Mo-Kansas City, MBA, 67. *Prof Exp:* Develop engr, Mathieson Chem Corp, NY, 52-53, proj engr, Olin Mathieson Chem Corp, Ill, 53-55, pilot plant supvr, 55-59; process engr, R W Booker & Assoc, Mo, 59-61; process engr, Austin Co, Ill, 61-63; res engr, Gulf Res & Develop Co, 63-66, sr proj engr, 66-69, planning specialist, Chem Dept, Develop Div, 69-71, dir planning, Develop Div, 71-75, mgr planning & bus anal, Spec Chem, 75-80, COORDR TECHNOL DEVELOP, SPEC CHEM, GULF OIL CHEM CO, 80- *Mem:* Am Asn Cost Engrs. *Res:* Management of chemical research and development projects, screening evaluation and coordinator of research and development projects; planning new business projects; process development of chemical processes; economic evaluation of chemical processes and research and development projects; process design of chemical plants. *Mailing Add:* 5054 Bayou Vista Dr Houston TX 77091

WURTMAN, JUDITH JOY, b Brooklyn, NY, Aug 4, 37; m 59; c 2. NUTRITION. *Educ:* Wellesley Col, BA, 59; Harvard Univ, MAT, 60; George Washington Univ, PhD(cell biol), 71. *Prof Exp:* Asst prof biol & nutrit, Newton Col, 72-74; RES SCIENTIST, MASS INST TECHNOL, 74-, FEL, DEPT NUTRIT, 74- *Concurrent Pos:* Consult nutrit educ, Newton Pub Schs, 72-74; NIH fel, 74-76; instr, Radcliffe Seminars-Harvard Exten Courses, 76-; counselor, Obesity Clin, 81-; commentator, Boston TV Sta, 81- *Mem:* Soc Nutrit Educ; Am Dietetic Asn; Nutrit Today; Inst Food Technol; Sigma Xi. *Res:* Regulation of food intake in laboratory animal and human, especially in obesity and other eating disorders. *Mailing Add:* Dept of Nutrit Mass Inst of Technol Cambridge MA 02139

WURTMAN, RICHARD JAY, b Philadelphia, Pa, Mar 9, 36; m 59; c 2. ENDOCRINOLOGY, NEUROBIOLOGY. *Educ:* Univ Pa, AB, 56; Harvard Med Sch, MD, 60. *Prof Exp:* Intern & asst resident med, Mass Gen Hosp, 60-62; res assoc, Lab Clin Sci, NIMH, 62-64, med res officer, 65-67; assoc prof, 67-70, prof endocrinol & metab, 70-80, PROF NEUROENDOCRINE REGULATIONS, MASS INST TECHNOL, 80- *Concurrent Pos:* Josiah Macy, Jr Found fel, Mass Gen Hosp, 60-62; res fel endocrinol, Mass Gen Hosp, 64-65; clin assoc med, Mass Gen Hosp, 65-; vis lectr, Am Chem Soc, 66; lectr, Harvard Med Sch, 69-; mem, Preclin Psychopharmacol Study Sect, NIMH, 71-75; Am Inst Biol Sci Adv panel, Biosci Prog, NASA; res adv bd, Parkinson's Dis, Am Parkinson's Dis Asn, Tourette Syndrome Asn; assoc, Neurosci Res Prog; chmn, Life Sci Adv Comt, NASA, 79-; Sterling vis prof, Boston Univ, 81. *Honors & Awards:* Am Therapeut Soc Prize, 66; Soc Biol Psychiat Prize, 66; John Jacob Abel Award, Am Soc Pharmacol Exp Therapeut, 68; Alvarenga Prize & Lect, Col Physicians Philadelphia, 70; Ernst Oppenheimer Prize, Endocrine Soc, 73; Foster Elting Bennett lectr, Am Neurol Asn, 74; Louis B Flexner lectr, 75; Pfizer lectr, State Univ NY Buffalo, 80; Zale lectr, Univ Tex, 80; MaCallum lectr, Univ Toronto, 81. *Mem:* Am Physiol Soc; Am Soc Pharmacol & Exp Therapeut; Am Soc Neurochem; Am Soc Biol Chem; Am Soc Clin Invest. *Res:* Neuroendocrinology; neuropharmacology; biological rhythms; pineal gland; catecholamines; amino acid metabolism; effects of nutrition on brain; biological effects of light; acetylcholine. *Mailing Add:* Dept of Nutrit & Food Sci Mass Inst of Technol E 25-604B Cambridge MA 02139

WURTZ, ROBERT HENRY, b St Louis, Mo, Mar 28, 36; div; c 2. NEUROPHYSIOLOGY, NEUROPSYCHOLOGY. *Educ:* Oberlin Col, AB, 58; Univ Mich, Ann Arbor, PhD(physiol psychol), 62. *Prof Exp:* Res assoc neurophysiol, Wash Univ, 62-65; res fel, Lab Neurophysiol, NIH, 65-66, res scientist, Lab Neurobiol, NIMH, 66-78, CHIEF, LAB SENSORIMOTOR RES, NAT EYE INST, 78- *Mem:* Am Physiol Soc; Int Brain Res Orgn; Soc Neurosci. *Res:* Neurophysiological basis of behavior, specifically the physiology of vision and movement. *Mailing Add:* Lab of Sensorimotor Res Bldg 36 Nat Eye Inst Bethesda MD 20205

WURZBURG, OTTO BERNARD, b Grand Rapids, Mich, Aug 1, 15; m 40; c 6. CARBOHYDRATE CHEMISTRY. *Educ:* Univ Mich, BS, 38, MS, 39. *Prof Exp:* Chemist & supvr cent control, Nat Starch Prod, Nat Starch & Chem Corp, 39-44, res chemist & supvr starch res, 45-55, assoc res dir, 56-68, vpres res, Starch Div, 68-73, sr vpres, 73-80; CONSULT, 80- *Concurrent Pos:* Mem bd dirs, Customaize Inc, 74- *Mem:* Am Chem Soc; Inst Food Technologists; Am Asn Cereal Chemists. *Res:* Starch; carbohydrates; industrial applications. *Mailing Add:* RR 1 Box 45 Felmly Rd Whitehouse Station NJ 08889

WUSKELL, JOSEPH P, b New York, NY, Nov 14, 38. CHEMISTRY. *Educ:* Univ Conn, BA, 60; Univ Minn, PhD(chem), 67. *Prof Exp:* Chemist, Merck Sharp & Dohme Res Labs, 60-62; sr chemist, Ott Chem Co, Corn Prod Co, 67-68; GROUP LEADER, QUAKER OATS CO, 68- *Mem:* Am Chem Soc; The Chem Soc. *Res:* Organic synthesis and reaction mechanisms. *Mailing Add:* John Stuart Res Labs 617 W Main St Barrington IL 60010

WUSSOW, GEORGE C, b Milwaukee, Wis, Mar 10, 23; m 49; c 3. ORAL SURGERY, ORAL PATHOLOGY. *Educ:* Marquette Univ, DDS, 49. *Prof Exp:* From instr to assoc prof, 53-67, PROF ORAL SURG, MARQUETTE UNIV, 67-, CHMN DEPT, 61-, LECTR, SCH DENT HYG, 70- *Concurrent Pos:* Attend oral surg, Vet Admin Ctr, Wood, Wis & mem consult staff, Milwaukee County Gen Hosp, 57-; consult, Great Lakes Naval Hosp, 70-; mem adv bd, Milwaukee Area Tech Col, 70- *Mem:* Am Soc Oral Surg; Am Acad Oral Path; fel Am Col Dent; Int Asn Oral Surg; fel Royal Soc Health. *Res:* Clinical evaluation of proteolytic enzymes in the management of impacted mandibular third molars. *Mailing Add:* Dept of Oral Surg Marquette Univ Sch of Dent Milwaukee WI 53233

WUST, CARL JOHN, b Providence, RI, July 2, 28; m 51; c 5. IMMUNOLOGY. *Educ:* Providence Col, BS, 50; Brown Univ, MSc, 53; Ind Univ, PhD(microbiol), 57. *Prof Exp:* Electron microscopist, Ind Univ, 53-55; NIH fel, Yale Univ, 57-59; biochemist, Biol Div, Oak Ridge Nat Lab, 59-70; assoc prof, 70-74, PROF MICROBIOL, UNIV TENN, KNOXVILLE, 74- *Mem:* AAAS; Am Soc Microbiol; Am Asn Immunologists; Sigma Xi; Soc Exp Biol & Med. *Res:* Antibody biosynthesis; leukemia antigens; immunity to viral infections. *Mailing Add:* Dept of Microbiol Univ of Tenn Knoxville TN 37996

WUTHIER, ROY EDWARD, b Rushville, Nebr, Nov 11, 32; m 56; c 2. BIOCHEMISTRY. *Educ:* Univ Wyo, BS, 54; Univ Wis, MS, 58, PhD, 60. *Prof Exp:* Asst biochem, Univ Wis, 55-60; res fel, Forsyth Dent Ctr, Harvard Med Sch, 60-63, asst mem staff & assoc biol chem, 63-69; assoc prof biochem, Depts Orthop Surg & Biochem, Col Med, Univ Vt, 69-75; PROF CHEM, COL ARTS & SCI & COORDR BIOCHEM, COL MED, UNIV SC, 75- *Mem:* AAAS; Am Soc Biol Chem; Am Chem Soc; Am Soc Bone & Mineral Res; Int Asn Dent Res. *Res:* Mechanism of calcification; lipid and membrane involvement in calcification; role of matrix resicles in calcification. *Mailing Add:* Dept Chem Phys Sci Ctr Univ SC Columbia SC 29208

WUTS, PETER G M, b Schiedamm, Holland, July 24, 50; US citizen; m 78; c 1. SYNTHETIC ORGANIC CHEMISTRY. *Educ:* Univ Washington, BS, 73; Northwestern Univ, PhD(chem), 78. *Prof Exp:* Fel chem, Calif Inst Technol, 78-80; ASST PROF CHEM, UNIV MICH, 80- *Concurrent Pos:* NIH fel, 80. *Mem:* Am Chem Soc. *Res:* Development of methodology and the total synthesis of natural products. *Mailing Add:* Dept Chem Univ Mich Ann Arbor MI 48109

WUU, TING-CHI, b Salt County, China, Sept 27, 34; US citizen; m 62; c 3. BIOCHEMISTRY. *Educ:* Nat Taiwan Univ, BSc, 58, MSc, 60; McGill Univ, PhD(biochem), 67. *Prof Exp:* Prof asst biochem res, McGill Univ, 67-69; asst prof, 69-74, ASSOC PROF BIOCHEM, MED COL OHIO, 75- *Mem:* AAAS. *Res:* Structure and function of peptides and proteins; brain, peptides and proteins; isolation and characterization of hormone-binding proteins of neurohypophysis; biological, chemical and physical properties of neurophysins and neurosecretory granules; biosynthesis of brain peptides and proteins. *Mailing Add:* Dept of Biochem Caller Serv No 10008 Toledo OH 43699

WYANT, GORDON MICHAEL, b Frankfurt, Ger, Mar 28, 14; m; c 5. ANESTHESIOLOGY. *Educ:* Univ Bologna, MD, 38; Royal Col Physicians & Surgeons Eng, dipl, 45; Am Bd Anesthesiol, dipl, 53; Royal Col Physicians & Surgeons Can, dipl anesthesiol, 52, FRCP(C), 63. *Prof Exp:* Asst prof anesthesia, Col Med, Univ Ill, 50-53; asst prof surg & head div anesthesia, Stritch Sch Med, Loyola Univ, Ill, 53-54; prof, 54-71, EMER PROF ANESTHESIA, UNIV SASK, 71- *Mem:* Am Soc Anesthesiol; fel Am Geriat Soc; Am Geog Soc; fel Am Col Anesthesiol; Can Anesthesiol Soc. *Res:* Related clinical and basic sciences of anesthesia; principle management. *Mailing Add:* Dept Anesthesia Univ Sask Col Med Saskatoon SK S7N 0X0 Can

WYANT, JAMES CLAIR, b Morenci, Mich, July 31, 43; m 71. OPTICS. *Educ:* Case Inst Technol, BS, 65; Univ Rochester, MS, 67, PhD(optics), 68. *Prof Exp:* Optical engr & head, Optical Eng Sect, Itek Corp, 68-74; assoc prof, 74-80, PROF OPTICS, OPTICAL SCI CTR, UNIV ARIZ, 80- *Concurrent Pos:* Assoc ed, J Optical Soc Am & Optical Eng; mem, Int Comn Optics, US Nat Comt. Am Inst Physics; Optical Soc Am; Soc Photo-Optical Instrumentation Engrs. *Res:* Interferometry; holography; optical testing; optical processing; optical properties of the atmosphere; active optics; application of microcomputer to optics. *Mailing Add:* Optical Sci Ctr Univ Ariz Tucson AZ 85721

WYATT, BENJAMIN WOODROW, b Farrar, Ga, Dec 24, 16; m 48; c 4. CHEMISTRY. *Educ:* Southwestern Univ, Tex, BS, 37; Univ Tex, MA, 40, PhD(org chem), 43. *Prof Exp:* Tutor chem, Univ Tex, 38-43; assoc mem & asst to patent agent, 43-50, patent agent, 50-61, from asst dir to assoc dir, 61-74, dir, Patent Div, 74-78, VPRES PATENTS, STERLING-WINTHROP RES INST, 78- *Mem:* Am Chem Soc. *Res:* Organic chemistry. *Mailing Add:* Sterling-Winthrop Res Inst Rensselaer NY 12144

WYATT, CAROLYN JANE, b Safford, Ariz, Mar 24, 38. FOOD SCIENCE. *Educ:* Univ Ariz, BS, 59; Ore State Univ, MS, 60, PhD(food sci), 66. *Prof Exp:* Res assoc, Flavor Chem Sect, Food Sci Dept, Ore State Univ, 60-66, asst prof food sci, 69-70; dept adminr, Dairy & Consumer Serv Div, Ore Dept Agr, 74-75; instr foods & nutrit, Chemeketa Community Col, 75-76; consumer officer, Ore Dept Agr, 71-76, asst adminr, Dairy Div, Consumer Affairs, 76-77; ASSOC PROF FOOD SCI, ORE STATE UNIV, 77- *Concurrent Pos:* mem, Western Regional Task Force Food Qual, 75, Ore Hort Adv Bd, 76-77, Sect Agr, Nat Consumer Adv Coun, 76, Sea Grant Adv Coun 76-77, and comt, Irradiation Mean-Natick Lab, 77; consult, Off Technol Assessment, US Congress, 77-78. *Mem:* Inst Food Technologists. *Res:* Effects of processing on food nutrients. *Mailing Add:* Food Sci & Technol Ore State Univ Corvallis OR 97331

WYATT, COLEN CHARLES, b Geneva, NY, Dec 10, 27; m 48; c 5. HORTICULTURE. *Educ:* Cornell Univ, BS, 53. *Prof Exp:* Sr res horticulturist, H J Heinz Co, 54-64; univ horticulturist & asst dir maintenance, Bowling Green State Univ, 65-66; plant breeder, Libby McNeill & Libby, Ohio, 67-72; PLANT BREEDER, PETO SEED CO, 72- *Mem:* Am Hort Soc; Am Forestry Asn. *Res:* Breeding tomatoes for disease resistance and mechanical harvest; breeding vegetable crops. *Mailing Add:* PO Box 1255 Rte 4 Woodland CA 95695

WYATT, ELLIS JUNIOR, b Norton, Kans, Oct 30, 30; m 53; c 3. PARASITOLOGY, INVERTEBRATE ZOOLOGY. *Educ:* Lewis & Clark Col, BS, 57; Ore State Univ, MS, 61, PhD(zool), 71. *Prof Exp:* Aquatic biologist, Ore State Fish Comn, 57, 58-60 & 61; asst prof biol, Cent Ore Col, 61-65 & 67-68; aquatic biologist, Ore State Fish Comn, 68-71; from asst prof to assoc prof, 71-77, chmn dept, 72-82, PROF BIOL, HAMLINE UNIV, 77- *Concurrent Pos:* Lab teaching asst, Ore State Univ, 57. *Mem:* AAAS; Am Soc Parasitologists; Am Soc Zoologists; Am Fisheries Soc. *Res:* Parasitic protozoa of fresh water fishes; bacteriology, helminthology, mycology, therapeutics and toxicology of fresh water fishes; ecology of fish parasitism. *Mailing Add:* Dept of Biol Hamline Univ St Paul MN 55104

WYATT, GERARD ROBERT, b Palo Alto, Calif, Sept 3, 25; m 51; c 3. INSECT PHYSIOLOGY, BIOCHEMISTRY. *Educ:* Univ BC, BA, 45; Cambridge Univ, PhD(natural sci), 50. *Prof Exp:* Sci officer, Insect Path Res Inst, Can Dept Agr, Ont, 50-54; asst prof biochem, Yale Univ, 54-60, from assoc prof to prof biol, 60-73; head dept, 73-75, PROF BIOL, QUEEN'S UNIV, ONT, 73- *Concurrent Pos:* Guggenheim Mem fel, 54. *Mem:* Am Soc Biol Chemists; fel Royal Soc Can. *Res:* Composition of nucleic acids; biochemistry and physiology of insects; composition of insect hemolymph; carbohydrate metabolism and its regulation; physiology of development; actions of insect hormones; insect vitellogenins; insect molecular biology. *Mailing Add:* Dept of Biol Queen's Univ Kingston ON K7L 3N6 Can

WYATT, JAMES L(UTHER), b Williamsburg, Ky, May 13, 24; m 46; c 2. METALLURGICAL ENGINEERING, CHEMICAL ENGINEERING. *Educ:* Univ Ky, BS, 47, MS, 48; Mass Inst Technol, ScD(metall), 53. *Prof Exp:* Instr metall, Univ Ky, 47-48; proj engr, Titanium Div, Nat Lead Co, 48-50; head dept metall eng, Horizons, Inc, 53-57; consult & assoc, Booz-Allen & Hamilton, 57-61; vpres prog develop, Armour Res Found, 61-63; vpres new prod develop, Joy Mfg Co, Pa, 63-67; vpres corp develop, Nat Gypsum Co, NY, 67-69; Max Factor & Co, Calif, 69-71; pres, Wyatt & Co, 71-72; PRES/OWNER, AMBASSADOR INDUSTS, INC, 72- *Concurrent Pos:* US rep, World Metall Cong Steelmaking, 51. *Mem:* Am Inst Mining, Metall & Petrol Engrs; Am Soc Metals; Marine Technol Soc. *Res:* Extractive and physical metallurgy of titanium, zinc, zirconium, uranium; development of heavy industrial machinery; mining and construction. *Mailing Add:* 32700 Coatsite Dr #203 Rancho Palos Verdes CA 90274

WYATT, JEFFREY RENNER, b Hampton, Va, Jan 1, 46; m 69. CHEMISTRY. *Educ:* Univ Calif, Riverside, AB, 63; Northwestern Univ, Evanston, PhD(chem), 71. *Prof Exp:* Teaching assoc chem, Univ Kans, 71-72; Nat Res Coun res fel, 72-73, RES CHEMIST, NAVAL RES LAB, 73- *Mem:* Am Chem Soc; Am Soc Mass Spectrometry. *Res:* Mass spectrometry; chemical dynamics; trace analysis; ion-molecule reactions. *Mailing Add:* Naval Res Lab Code 6110 Washington DC 20375

WYATT, JOHN POYNER, b Winnipeg, Man, Feb 25, 16; m 45; c 4. PATHOLOGY. *Educ:* Univ Man, MD, 38. *Prof Exp:* Coroner's pathologist, City of Toronto, Can, 46-49; prof path, Sch Med, St Louis Univ, 49-67; prof path & head dept, Med Col, Univ Man, 67-73; prof path, Col Med, Univ Ky, 73-80. *Concurrent Pos:* Fel path, Banting Inst, Univ Toronto, 39-41; Littauer fel, Harvard Med Sch, 45-46; lectr, Univ Toronto, 46-49; consult, Silicosis Bd, Ont Prov Govt, 46-49; chief pathologist, St Louis County, Mo, 49-67. *Mem:* Am Asn Path & Bact; Col Am Path; Path Soc Great Brit & Ireland; Int Acad Path. *Res:* Iron metabolism, particularly ferrodynamics of iron storage; chronic lung disease, particularly pneumoconioses and emphysema; virology, especially salivary gland virus. *Mailing Add:* 1825 Fielden Dr Lexington KY 40502

WYATT, PHILIP JOSEPH, b Los Angeles, Calif, Apr 16, 32; m 57; c 3. BIOPHYSICS, LIGHT SCATTERING. *Educ:* Univ Chicago, BA, 52, BS, 54; Univ Ill, MS, 56; Fla State Univ, PhD, 59. *Prof Exp:* Staff mem, Los Alamos Sci Lab, 59; prin scientist, Aeronutronic Div, Ford Motor Co, 59-62; dir adv planning, Plasmadyne Corp, 62-63; mem tech staff, DRC Inc, 63-66; sr sci specialist, EG&G, Inc, 66-68; PRES & CHMN, SCI SPECTRUM, INC, 68- *Concurrent Pos:* Vis lectr physics, Univ Calif, Santa Barbara, 81- *Mem:* Fel Am Phys Soc; fel Optical Soc Am; Am Soc Microbiol; Sigma Xi. *Res:* Light scattering studies of microparticles; development of new assays and identification techniques using resonance light scattering; antibiotic susceptibility testing; development of light scattering instrumentation; bioassays for antimicrobials in serum, antineoplastic drugs, drug residues in food, and toxicants in water. *Mailing Add:* PO Box 3003 Santa Barbara CA 93105

WYATT, RAYMOND L, b Salisbury, NC, Nov 23, 26; m 52; c 1. PLANT MORPHOLOGY, PLANT TAXONOMY. *Educ:* Wake Forest Col, BS, 48; Univ NC, MA, 54, PhD, 56. *Prof Exp:* Instr biol, Mars Hill Col, 48-52 & Univ NC, 55-56; from asst prof to assoc prof, 56-75, lectr, NSF Insts Sci Teachers, 59-60, PROF BIOL, WAKE FOREST UNIV, 75- *Mem:* AAAS. *Res:* Embryology of Asarum; floral morphology and phylogeny of Aristolochiaceae and Annonaceae; survival of American chestnut in North Carolina. *Mailing Add:* Dept of Biol Wake Forest Univ Reynolds Sta Winston-Salem NC 21703

WYATT, RICHARD JED, b Los Angeles, Calif, June 5, 39; c 2. PSYCHOPHARMACOLOGY. *Educ:* Johns Hopkins Univ, BA, 61, MD, 64; Am Bd Psychiat & Neurol, dipl. *Prof Exp:* Intern pediat, Western Reserve Univ Hosp, 64-65; resident psychiat, Mass Ment Health Ctr, Boston, 65-67; clin assoc, Sect Psychophysiol Sleep, Adult Psychiat Br, 67-68, clin assoc, Lab Clin Psychobiol, 68-69, res psychiatrist, Lab Clin Psychopharmacol, 69-71, chief, Lab Clin Psychopharmacol, 72-77, DIR, DIV SPEC MENTAL HEALTH RES, NAT INST MENT HEALTH, 77- *Concurrent Pos:* Teaching asst, Harvard Univ, 65-67; assoc prof psychiat, Med Ctr, Stanford Univ, 73-74; clin prof, Med Ctr, Duke Univ, 75- *Honors & Awards:* Harry Solomon Res Award, Mass Ment Health Ctr, Boston, 68; A E Bennett Award Clin Psychiat Res, Soc Biol Psychiat, 71; Psychopharmacol Award, Am Psychol Asn, 72; Stanley R Dean Award, Am Col Psychiat, 82. *Mem:* Am Psychiat Asn; Soc Psychophysiol Study Sleep; Psychiat Res Soc; Soc Biol Psychiat; Am Col Neuropsychopharmacol. *Res:* Etiology and treatment of major psychiatric disorders; neural plasticity; sleep and memory. *Mailing Add:* Rm 536 WAW Bldg Adult Psychiat Br St Elizabeth's Hosp NIMH Washington DC 20032

WYATT, ROBERT EDWARD, b Charleston, SC, July 15, 50. POPULATION BIOLOGY, PLANT SYSTEMATICS. *Educ:* Univ NC, AB, 72; Duke Univ, PhD(bot), 77. *Prof Exp:* asst prof biol, Tex A&M Univ, 77-79; ASST PROF BIOL, UNIV GA, 79- *Mem:* Am Soc Plant Taxonomists; Bot Soc Am; Soc Study Evolution; Ecol Soc Am; Am Soc Naturalists. *Res:* Reproductive biology of plants, especially Asclepias; population dynamics, breeding systems, pollination and fruit-set; plant biosystematics and evolutionary ecology. *Mailing Add:* Dept Bot Univ Ga Athens GA 30602

WYATT, ROBERT EUGENE, b Chicago, Ill, Nov 11, 38; m 64; c 1. THEORETICAL CHEMISTRY. *Educ:* Ill Inst Technol, 61; Johns Hopkins Univ, MA, 63, PhD(chem), 65. *Prof Exp:* NSF fel chem, Keele Univ, 65-66 & Harvard Univ, 66-67; from asst prof to assoc prof, 67-76, PROF CHEM, UNIV TEX, AUSTIN, 76- *Honors & Awards:* Prize Medal, Int Acad Quantum Molecular Sci, 80. *Mem:* AAAS; Am Chem Soc; Am Phys Soc; NY Acad Sci. *Res:* scattering theory; theoretical chemical dynamics; molecular multiphoton processes. *Mailing Add:* Dept of Chem Univ of Tex Austin TX 78712

WYATT, ROGER DALE, b Albemarle, NC, Apr 16, 48; m 68; c 2. MICROBIOLOGY, POULTRY SCIENCE. *Educ:* NC State Univ, BS, 70, MS, 72, PhD(micorbiol), 74. *Prof Exp:* Asst prof, 74-77, ASSOC PROF, DEPT POULTRY SCI, UNIV GA, 77- *Mem:* Poultry Sci Asn; Am Soc Microbiol. *Res:* Biological effects of dietary mycotoxins on poultry and evaluation of antifungal compounds for use in grain and poultry feeds. *Mailing Add:* Dept of Poultry Sci Univ of Ga Athens GA 30602

WYATT, STANLEY PORTER, JR, b Medford, Mass, Apr 20, 21; m 48; c 3. ASTRONOMY. *Educ:* Dartmouth Col, AB, 42; Harvard Univ, AM, 48, PhD(astron), 50. *Prof Exp:* Instr astron, Univ Mich, 50-53; from asst prof to assoc prof, 53-61, PROF ASTRON, UNIV ILL, URBANA, 61- *Mem:* Int Astron Union; Am Astron Soc. *Res:* Galactic astronomy; interplanetary matter. *Mailing Add:* Dept of Astron Univ of Ill Urbana IL 61801

WYCH, ROBERT DALE, b Kingsley, Iowa, Mar 3, 48; c 2. CROP PHYSIOLOGY, AGRONOMY. *Educ:* Iowa State Univ, BS, 70; Univ Calif, Davis, MS, 74, PhD(plant physiol), 77. *Prof Exp:* ASST PROF SMALL GRAIN PHYSIOL, DEPT AGRON & PLANT GENETICS, UNIV MINN, 77- *Mem:* Am Soc Plant Physiol; Am Soc Agron; Crop Sci Soc Am. *Res:* Influence of genotype and environment on nitrate uptake and nitrogen and carbohydrate storage, metabolism and mobilization in wheat, oats and barley. *Mailing Add:* Dept Agron & Plant Genetics Univ Minn St Paul MN 55108

WYCKOFF, DELAPHINE GRACE ROSA, b Beloit, Wis, Sept 11, 06; m 42. MICROBIOLOGY, BACTERIOLOGY. *Educ:* Univ Wis, PhB, 27, PhM, 28, PhD(bact), 38. *Prof Exp:* From instr to asst prof bact, NDak Agr Col, 28-37; from instr to assoc prof bact & bot, 38-57, prof bact, 57-72, EMER PROF BACT, WELLESLEY COL, 72- *Concurrent Pos:* Consult, Traveling Sci Teachers Prog, Oak Ridge Inst Nuclear Studies & Biol Sci Curric Study, Am Inst Biol Sci. *Mem:* Fel AAAS; Am Soc Microbiol; Am Acad Microbiol. *Res:* Physiological variation; induced mutations in actinomycetes; bactericidal agents; antibiotics from actinomycetes; biochemical activities of yeasts; marine halophilic bacteria; soil microbiology. *Mailing Add:* 78 Cedar St Newington CT 06111

WYCKOFF, HAROLD ORVILLE, b Traverse City, Mich, Apr 26, 10; m 40; c 2. PHYSICS. *Educ:* Univ Wash, BS, 34, PhD(physics), 40. *Prof Exp:* Jr physicist, Nat Bur Stand, 41-42, from asst physicist to assoc physicist, 42-43; expert consult, Ninth US Army Air Force, Europe, 43-45; physicist & asst chief, X-ray Sect, Nat Bur Stand, 45-49, chief, 49-53, chief radiation physics lab, 53-66; dep sci dir, Armed Forces Radiobiol Res Inst, 66-71; consult, Bur Radiol Health, 71-74; CONSULT RADIATION PHYSICS, 74- *Concurrent Pos:* Secy & mem, Int Comn Radiation Units & Measurements, 53-69, chmn, 69-; mem comt, Int Comn Radiol Protection, 53-69; mem adv comt, Health Physics Div, Oak Ridge Nat Lab, 62-69; mem bd, Nat Coun Radiation Protection & Measurements, 64-70; consult, Fed Aviation Agency, 71-74; mem US Delegation, Sci Comt Effects of Atomic Radiation, UN, 76- *Honors & Awards:* Bronze Star, 46; Silver Medal, Dept Com, 52, Gold Medal, 60; Gold Medal, Radiol Soc NAm, 63; Gold Medal, XIII Int Cong Radiol, 73; Gold Medal, Am Col Radiol, 76. *Mem:* Health Physics Soc; fel Am Phys Soc; Radiation Res Soc; assoc fel Am Col Radiol; Radiol Soc NAm (treas, 70-76). *Res:* Radiation physics; radiation protection and measurement. *Mailing Add:* 4108 Montpelier Rd Rockville MD 20853

WYCKOFF, HAROLD WINFIELD, b Niagara Falls, NY, Dec 3, 26; m 55; c 3. MOLECULAR BIOPHYSICS. *Educ:* Antioch Col, BS, 49; Mass Inst Technol, PhD(biophys), 55. *Prof Exp:* Res assoc biol, Mass Inst Technol, 55; NIH fel, Cambridge Univ, 56; res physicist, Am Viscose Corp, Pa, 57-63; ASSOC PROF MOLECULAR BIOPHYS, YALE UNIV, 63- *Mem:* Am Crystallog Asn; Biophys Soc. *Res:* Structure and function of biological macromolecules, especially enzymes, as determined by x-ray diffraction analysis. *Mailing Add:* Dept of Molecular Biophys Box 1937 Yale Station New Haven CT 06520

WYCKOFF, JAMES M, b Niagara Falls, NY, July 3, 24; m 47, 68; c 5. NUCLEAR PHYSICS. *Educ:* Antioch Col, BS, 48; Univ Rochester, MS, 52. *Prof Exp:* Electronics technician, Airborne Instruments Lab, 46-47; asst physics, Antioch Col, 47-48; res asst, Univ Rochester, 48-51; physicist, Nat Bur Stand, 51-67; health physicist, Stanford Linear Accelerator Ctr, 67-68; physicist, 68-71, coordr, Radiation Safety Prog, 71-76, LIAISON OFFICER, STATE & LOCAL GOVT AFFAIRS, NAT BUR STAND, 76- *Concurrent Pos:* Mem comt 22, Nat Coun Radiation Protection & Measurement, 66-72, mem off telecommun policy side effects subcomt, 72-75; mem, Interagency Comt Fed Guid Occup Exposures to Ionizing Radiation, 74-75; rep, Nat Conf State Legislatures' Model Interstate Tech Info Clearinghouse, 76-; adv comt mem, Booker T Washington Found Technol Com Ctr, 76-; rep & exec bd mem, Federal Lab Consortium Technol Transfer, 77-; exec secy comt mem, Federal Labs Off Sci & Technol Policy, 76-77. *Mem:* Am Phys Soc; Sigma Xi; Fedn Am Scientists. *Res:* Detection of high energy x-rays; measurement of attenuation coefficients; induced radioactivity and development of on-line computer system; application of measurements to safe and effective use of x-rays; radioactivity, ultraviolet light, lasers, electromagnetic and ultrasonic radiation sources; development of measurement systems adequate to the protection of those near such radiation sources; review of mechanisms of technology transfer. *Mailing Add:* Nat Bur of Stand Admin Bldg Rm A402 Washington DC 20234

WYCKOFF, RALPH WALTER GRAYSTONE, b Geneva, NY, Aug 9, 97; m; c 3. PHYSICAL CHEMISTRY, BIOPHYSICS. *Educ:* Hobart Col, BS, 16; Cornell Univ PhD(chem), 19. *Hon Degrees:* MD, Masaryk Univ, Brno, 47; ScD, Univ Strasbourg, 52, Hobart Col, 75. *Prof Exp:* Instr anal chem, Cornell Univ, 17-19; phys chemist, Carnegie Inst Geophys Lab, 19-27; assoc mem subdiv biophys, Rockefeller Inst, 27-38; with Lederle Labs, 38-40, assoc res dir, 40-42; tech dir, Reichel Labs, 42-43; lectr, Univ Mich, 43-45; sr scientist, NIH, 45, scientist dir, 46-52, sci attache, Am Embassy, Eng, 52-54, biophysicist, 54-59; PROF PHYSICS & BACT, UNIV ARIZ, 59-; CONSULT, DUVAL CORP, 61- *Concurrent Pos:* Res assoc, Calif Inst Technol, 21-22; dir res, Nat Ctr Sci Res, France, 58-62 & 69. *Honors & Awards:* Medal, Pasteur Inst. *Mem:* Nat Acad Sci; Fel AAAS; fel Am Chem Soc; fel Am Phys Soc; fel Am Acad Arts & Sci. *Res:* Structure of crystals; effect of radiation on cells; development of air-driven ultracentrifugation of proteins and viruses; electron microscopy; purification of viruses and macromolecules; ultra-soft x-rays; ultrastructure of fossils; application of x-ray and electron optical techniques to ore minerals. *Mailing Add:* Duval Corp 4715 E Fort Lowell Rd Tucson AZ 85712

WYCKOFF, ROBERT CUSHMAN, b Peoria, Ill, Feb 7, 13; m 42. PHYSICS, SPACE SCIENCE. *Educ:* Univ Ill, BS, 35, MS, 36. *Prof Exp:* Prof physics & head dept, Buena Vista Col, 38-47; instr, Univ Okla, 47-51; head sci & technol unit, Off Naval Intel, Europe, 51-57, sr ord analyst, 57-58; chief sci & technol br, Army Correlation Ctr, US Signal Intel Agency, Va, 58-60; head oper anal group, Res Anal Sect, Space Sci Div, Jet Propulsion Lab, Calif Inst Technol, 61-72; sr scientist, Electro-Optical Systs, Vista Lab, 72-78; CONSULT. *Concurrent Pos:* Chief ballistician, Des Moines Ord Plant, 42-43. *Mem:* Am Phys Soc. *Res:* Physical optics; high vacuum techniques; trace elements in biological tissue; planetary space mission planning/analysis; military and naval scientific and technical intelligence, collection/analysis. *Mailing Add:* PO Box 370 Garberville CA 95440

WYCKOFF, SUSAN, b Santa Cruz, Calif, Mar 18, 41; m 67. ASTRONOMY. *Educ:* Mt Holyoke Col, AB, 62; Case Inst Technol, PhD(astron), 67. *Prof Exp:* Fel, Inst Sci & Technol, Univ Mich, 67-68; asst prof physics, Albion Col, 68-70; res assoc astron, Univ Kans, 70-72; Smithsonian res fel, Wise Observ, Tel Aviv Univ, 72-75; prin res fel, Royal Greenwich Observ, 75-78; vis prof, Dept Astron, Ohio State Univ, 78-79; assoc prof, 79-82, PROF PHYSICS, AZ STATE UNIV, 82- *Concurrent Pos:* Hon lectr, Women Astron, Smith Col, 78; Millan found scholar, Denison Univ, 82; mem, comt comet spectroscopy, Int Astron Union; discipline specialist spectroscopy & spectrophotometry, Int Halley Watch, NASA, 82-, consult, Comput Sci Corp & Sci Appln. *Mem:* Am Astron Soc; Int Astron Union; Royal Astron Soc. *Res:* Spectroscopy of long-period variable stars, cool stars comets and supernovae; normal and active galaxies; quasars and cosmology. *Mailing Add:* Dept Physics Ariz State Univ Tempe AZ 85281

WYCOFF, SAMUEL JOHN, b Berry, Ala, Feb 25, 29. PUBLIC HEALTH, DENTISTRY. *Educ:* Univ Ala, Tuscaloosa, BS, 50; Univ Ala, Birmingham, DMD, 54; Univ Mich, Ann Arbor, MPH, 59; Am Bd Dent Pub Health, dipl, 65. *Prof Exp:* Staff dent officer, Div Dent Health, USPHS, Washington, DC, 59-63, regional prog dir, Boston, Mass, 63-65; assoc prof prev dent & community health & chmn dept, Sch Dent Loyola Univ Chicago, 67-69; PROF GEN DENT & CHMN DEPT, SCH DENT, UNIV SAN FRANCISCO, 69- *Concurrent Pos:* Fels, Univ Calif, San Francisco, 69-; consult, Coun Dent Educ, Am Dent Asn, 68- & Calif State Health Manpower Coun, 70-; mem comt acad affairs, Am Asn Dent Schs, 71-; mem tech adv comt, Calif State Dept Pub Health, 72-; mem, Pierre Fouchard Acad. *Honors & Awards:* H Trendley Dean Citation, 65. *Mem:* Am Dent Asn; fel Am Pub Health Asn; Am Asn Hosp Dent; fel Am Col Dent; Int Dent Fedn. *Res:* Epidemiology of oral disease; studies on health care delivery system and health manpower needs. *Mailing Add:* Univ of Calif Sch of Dent 532 Parnassus Ave San Francisco CA 94122

WYDEVEN, THEODORE, b Wausau, Wis, Jan 18, 36; m 63; c 2. PHYSICAL CHEMISTRY. *Educ:* Marquette Univ, BS, 58; Univ Wash, PhD(phys chem), 64. *Prof Exp:* RES SCIENTIST ENVIRON CONTROL SYSTS, NASA AMES RES CTR, 64- *Mem:* Am Chem Soc. *Res:* Research and development of advanced environmental control systems for purifying water, recycling oxygen and controlling atmospheric trace contaminants; development of plasma polymerized thin film technology. *Mailing Add:* 1130 Revere Dr Sunnyvale CA 94087

WYDOSKI, RICHARD STANLEY, b Nanticoke, Pa, Feb 3, 36; m 59; c 4. FISHERIES, ZOOLOGY. *Educ:* Bloomsburg State Col, BS, 60; Pa State Univ, MS, 62, PhD(zool), 65. *Prof Exp:* Teaching asst zool, Pa State Univ, 61-65; fisheries biologist, Bur Com Fisheries, US Fish & Wildlife Serv, 65-66; asst prof fisheries & asst leader coop fishery unit, Ore State Univ, 66-69; assoc prof fisheries & asst leader coop fishery unit, Univ Wash, 69-73; assoc prof wildlife sci & leader, Coop Fishery Unit, Utah State Univ, 73-80; MEM STAFF, NAT FISH CTR, LEETOWN, 80- *Mem:* Am Fisheries Soc; Am Inst Fishery Res Biol. *Res:* Aquatic ecology; reponses of fish populations to alterations of the aquatic environment; fish behavior and habit requirements; socio-economic studies as related to fish management. *Mailing Add:* Nat Fish Ctr-Leetown Box 41 Rte 3 Kearneysville WV 25430

WYETH, NEWELL CONVERS, b Wilmington, Del, Oct 13, 46; m 72; c 1. PHYSICS. *Educ:* Princeton Univ, AB, 67; Univ Calif, Berkeley, PhD(physics), 74. *Prof Exp:* Physicist appl physics, Eng Physics Lab, E I du Pont de Nemours & Co, 68-69; assoc scientist solid state physics, Inst Energy Conversion, Univ Del, 74-79; STAFF SCIENTIST, SCI APPLN, INC, 79- *Mem:* Am Phys Soc. *Res:* Photovoltaic solar cells; compound semiconductors; semiconductor interfaces; semiconductor device physics. *Mailing Add:* Electro-Optics Technol Div Sci Appln Inc 1710 Goodridge Dr McLean VA 22102

WYGANT, J(AMES) F(REDERIC), b Hornell, NY, Aug 4, 19; m 44; c 7. CERAMIC ENGINEERING, PETROLEUM TECHNOLOGY. *Educ:* Alfred Univ, BS, 41, MS, 48; Mass Inst Technol, ScD(ceramics), 50. *Prof Exp:* Chemist, Mo Portland Cement Co, 41-43; proj engr, Eng Res Dept, Standard Oil Co, Ind, 50-55, sect head res & develop dept, Am Oil Co, 55-62, asst dir res dept, 62-68, dir eng & explor res, Res & Develop Dept, 68-71, dir prod & explor res, 71-73; dir corp res, Standard Oil Co, Ind, 73-75, mgr corp serv, 75-79; CONSULT, 79- *Honors & Awards:* Purdy Award, Am Ceramic Soc, 52; Pace Award, Inst Ceramic Engrs, 59. *Mem:* Fel Am Ceramic Soc; Inst Ceramic Engrs; Am Inst Chem Engrs. *Res:* Non petroleum energy resources and processing; process industry refractories and insulations; industrial research evaluation and management; fireproofing; organic materials of construction; cements and concretes; corrosion protection; carbon; petroleum processing; advanced energy resources; alternative fossil fuels. *Mailing Add:* 1306 Francisco Dr Tallahasse FL 32304

WYGANT, JAMES CALVIN, b Guys Mills, Pa, Oct 3, 23; m 48; c 3. ORGANIC CHEMISTRY. *Educ:* Allegheny Col, BS, 48; Univ Mich, MS, 49, PhD(chem), 52. *Prof Exp:* RES CHEMIST, MONSANTO CO, 52- *Mem:* Am Chem Soc. *Res:* Product and process research and development; organic synthesis. *Mailing Add:* Monsanto Co 800 N Lindbergh Blvd St Louis MO 63166

WYKES, ARTHUR ALBERT, b Boston, Mass, May 21, 23; m 56; c 2. BIOCHEMICAL PHARMACOLOGY, TOXICOLOGY. *Educ:* Univ Ill, BS, 45; Univ Wis, MS, 49; Purdue Univ, PhD(pharmaceut chem, pharmacol, biochem), 57. *Prof Exp:* Res asst biochem, Res Div, Armour & Co, 45-46; res asst biochem, Univ Wis, 47-49; teaching asst pharmaceut chem, Purdue Univ, 49-51; res biochemist, Armour & Co, 51-52; sr res biochemist, Res Div, Int Minerals & Chem Corp, 52-53; sr res biochemist, Res Dept, Baxter Labs, Inc, 53-55; res asst pharmaceut chem, Purdue Univ, 55-57; res biochemist, Chem Pharmacol Sect, Abbott Labs, 57-61; chief & supvry res pharmacologist, biochem pharmacol sect, US Air Force Sch Aerospace Med, 61-67; sr pharmacologist, Chem & Life Sci Labs, Res Triangle Inst, 67-68; PHARMACOLOGIST & SR DRUG & TOXICOL LIT SPECIALIST, NAT LIBR MED, 68- *Concurrent Pos:* Assoc clin prof, Div Pharmacol & Physiol, Med Ctr, Duke Univ, 67-69; vis assoc prof pharmacol, Milton S Hershey Med Ctr, 71-76. *Mem:* Fel AAAS; Am Chem Soc; Int Soc Biochem Pharmacol; Soc Toxicol; Drug Info Asn. *Res:* Drug effects on biological, enzyme and metabolic systems at cellular and subcellular levels, especially as influenced by environmental agents, husbandry factors, other drugs and toxic chemicals; drug interactions; neurobiochemistry; pharmacology; enzymology; central nervous system drugs; drugs of abuse; biogenic amines; psychopharmacologic drugs and agents; drug, toxic agent and animal models; biomedical literature and computerized data. *Mailing Add:* 18900 Diary Rd Gaithersburg MD 20760

WYKLE, ROBERT LEE, b Belmont, NC, Mar 17, 40; m 71. BIOCHEMISTRY. *Educ:* Western Carolina Univ, BS, 63; Univ Tenn, Memphis, PhD(biochem), 70. *Prof Exp:* Teacher, Waynesville High Sch, 63-65; teaching asst biochem, Med Sch, Univ Tenn, 65-67; fel, Oak Ridge Assoc Univs, 68-70, assoc scientist, 70-71, scientist, 76-80; ASSOC PROF, DEPT BIOCHEM, BOWMAN GRAY SCH MED, 80- *Mem:* Am Soc Biol Chemists. *Res:* Biochemistry and function of lipids in normal and neoplastic cells with special interest in ether-linked lipids. *Mailing Add:* Dept Biochem Bowman Gray Sch Med Winston-Salem NC 27051

WYKOFF, MATTHEW HENRY, b Kewanee, Ill, Apr 11, 23; m 52; c 5. EXPERIMENTAL SURGERY, PHYSIOLOGY. *Educ:* Iowa State Univ, DVM, 46; Univ Mo, MS, 60. *Prof Exp:* Pvt pract, 46-50 & 52-57; asst prof vet anat, Univ Mo, 57-61; assoc prof physiol, Comp Animal Res Lab, Univ Tenn-AEC, 61-72; PRIN SCIENTIST VET SURG, ETHICON RES FOUND, 72- *Res:* Effects of ionizing irradiation on central nervous and cardiovascular systems; placental transfer; prenatal effects of ionizing irradiation; wound healing. *Mailing Add:* Ethicon Res Found Bridgewater NJ 08807

WYKOFF, W(ALTER) ROBERT, b Fresno, Calif, Aug 13, 20; m 42; c 4. NUCLEAR ENGINEERING. *Educ:* Univ Calif, BS, 42. *Prof Exp:* Exp test engr, Pratt & Whitney Aircraft, Conn, 46-47; res engr, Battelle Mem Inst, 47-49; res engr, Los Alamos Sci Lab, 49-57, group leader reactor eng, 57-67, assoc div leader reactor develop, 67-69; mgr sodium technol, Hanford Eng Develop Lab, 69-73, ADV ENGR, FFTF PLANT, WESTINGHOUSE-HANFORD CO, 73- *Concurrent Pos:* Mem liquid metals components working group, Atomic Energy Comn, 59-68. *Mem:* Am Nuclear Soc. *Res:* Fast reactor plant design and management overview of plant startup and acceptance testing; sodium technology aspects of plant performance; heat transfer; fluid flow. *Mailing Add:* 703 Lynnwood Loop Richland WA 99352

WYLD, HENRY WILLIAM, JR, b Portland, Ore, Oct 16, 28; m 55; c 3. PHYSICS. *Educ:* Reed Col, BA, 49; Univ Chicago, MS, 52, PhD(physics), 54. *Prof Exp:* Instr physics, Princeton Univ, 54-57; from asst prof to assoc prof, 57-63, PROF PHYSICS, UNIV ILL, URBANA, 63- *Concurrent Pos:* Consult, Space Tech Labs, Inc, Calif, 57-63; NSF sr fel, Oxford Univ, 63-64; Guggenheim fel, Europ Coun Nuclear Res, 71. *Mem:* Am Phys Soc. *Res:* Theoretical high energy and plasma physics. *Mailing Add:* Dept of Physics Univ of Ill Urbana IL 61801

WYLDE, RONALD JAMES, b St Louis, Mo, Feb 7, 21; m 47; c 3. INSTRUMENTATION. *Educ:* Washington Univ, St Louis, BA, 42; Univ Md, MS, 52. *Prof Exp:* Physicist, Underwater Acoust Div, Naval Ord Lab, US Dept Navy, 42-48, head physics br, Naval Gun Factory, 48-54, supt elec lab, Naval Eng Exp Sta, 54-57, head, Instrumentation Div, 57-63 & Elec Div, US Navy Marine Eng Lab, 63-68, head elec dept, Naval Ship Res & Develop Ctr, 68-71; CONSULT, 71- *Mem:* sr mem Inst Elec & Electronics Engrs. *Res:* Electronic circuitry of measuring systems; electromechanical transducers; amplitude-modulating transducers; electronic devices for physical measurement. *Mailing Add:* 322 Severn Rd Rte 1 Annapolis MD 21401

WYLER, JOHN STEPHEN, b Huntington, NY, Dec 26, 46; m 73; c 2. MECHANICAL ENGINEERING, FLUID MECHANICS. *Educ:* State Univ NY, Buffalo, BS, 68; Stanford Univ, MS, 69. *Prof Exp:* Develop engr instruments, Westinghouse Elec Corp, STD, 70-77; develop engr aerospace instruments, Aerospace Instruments & Elec Systs Div, 77-81, MGR ENG ACCESSORIES ENG, AIRCRAFT INSTRUMENTS DEPT, GEN ELEC CO, 81- *Mem:* Am Soc Mech Engrs. *Res:* Fluid flow and related instrumentaion; pressure, temperature and flow measurements; two-phase flow measurements; optics; ultrasonics. *Mailing Add:* Gen Elec Co 50 Fordham Rd Wilmington MA 01887

WYLER, OSWALD, b Scuol, Grisons, Switz, Apr 2, 22; m 60; c 3. MATHEMATICS. *Educ:* Swiss Fed Inst Technol, dipl, 47, Dr sc math, 50. *Prof Exp:* Asst inst geophys, Swiss Fed Inst Technol, 46-50; lectr math, Northwestern Univ, 51-53; from asst prof to assoc prof, Univ NMex, 53-65; PROF MATH, CARNEGIE-MELLON UNIV, 65- *Mem:* Am Math Soc; Math Asn Am; Swiss Math Soc. *Res:* Categorical algebra; categorical topology; theory of convergence spaces; continuous lattices. *Mailing Add:* Dept of Math Carnegie-Mellon Univ Pittsburgh PA 15213

WYLIE, AUBREY EVANS, b Carthage, Ark, Nov 21, 17; m 49; c 1. FORESTRY. *Educ:* Colo State Univ, BS, 46, MF, 47; State Univ NY Col Environ Sci & Forestry, PhD(wood sci), 50. *Prof Exp:* Instr assoc prof wood prod, Col Environ Sci & Forestry, State Univ NY, 50-56; prof, Mich State Univ, 56-68; vpres, Freeman Corp, 68-70; forest scientist, Sci & Educ Admin, USDA, 70-80; ADV UNDEVELOP PROG, FOOD& AGR ORGN, BURMA, 81- *Mem:* Soc Am Foresters; Forest Prod Res Soc. *Res:* Institutional and national planning of forestry research; review of institutional research programs; research budgeting, coordination of federal and state research. *Mailing Add:* USDA Rm 6418 S Bldg Washington DC 20250

WYLIE, CLARENCE RAYMOND, JR, b Cincinnati, Ohio, Sept 9, 11; m 35, 58; c 2. GEOMETRY. *Educ:* Wayne State Univ, BA & BS, 31; Cornell Univ, MS, 32, PhD(math), 34. *Prof Exp:* Instr & asst prof math, Ohio State Univ, 34-46; prof & head dept & actg dean col eng, US Air Force Inst Technol, 46-48; prof, Univ Utah, 48-69, head dept, 48-67; prof, 69-71, chmn dept, 70-76, Kenan prof math, 71-78, WILLIAM R KENAN, JR PROF EMER, FURMAN UNIV, 78- *Concurrent Pos:* Consult, Gen Elec Co, NY, 37 & Briggs Mfg Co, Mich, 41; mech engr, Wright Field Propellor Lab, Ohio, 43-46 & Aero Prod Div, Gen Motors Corp, 45-47; lectr, Educ Prog, Union Carbide Corp, 65-70. *Mem:* Fel AAAS; Am Math Soc; Math Asn Am; Am Soc Eng Educ. *Res:* Projective geometry, especially line geometry; applied mathematics, especially mechanical vibrations. *Mailing Add:* Rte 7 Merritt View Terrace Greenville SC 20609

WYLIE, DONALD P, atmospheric science, engineering, see previous edition

WYLIE, DOUGLAS WILSON, b Saskatoon, Sask, Nov 12, 26; nat US; m 51; c 4. PHYSICS. *Educ:* Univ NB, BSc, 47; Dalhousie Univ, MSc, 49; Univ Conn, PhD(solid state physics), 62. *Prof Exp:* Asst, Brown Univ, 49-50; instr, Univ NB, 50-51; from instr to prof, Univ Maine, 51-68; chmn dept, 68-73, PROF PHYSICS, WESTERN ILL UNIV, 68- *Mem:* AAAS; Am Phys Soc; Am Asn Physics Teachers; Can Asn Physicists. *Res:* Solid state physics; radiation damage; electron spin resonance. *Mailing Add:* Dept of Physics Western Ill Univ Macomb IL 61455

WYLIE, EDWIN J, b Cincinnati, Ohio, Oct 13, 18; m 45; c 3. SURGERY. *Educ:* Pomona Col, AB, 39; Harvard Med Sch, MD, 43. *Prof Exp:* From asst prof to assoc prof, 58-67, PROF SURG, SCH MED, UNIV CALIF, SAN FRANCISCO, 67-, VCHMN DEPT, 59-, CHIEF VASCULAR SURG, 55- *Concurrent Pos:* Consult, Vet Admin Hosp, Ft Miley, Calif, 51- *Mem:* Soc Vascular Surg; Soc Univ Surg; Am Surg Asn; Am Col Surg; Int Cardiovasc Soc. *Res:* Vascular surgery. *Mailing Add:* Dept of Surg San Francisco Med Ctr Univ of Calif Sch of Med San Francisco CA 94122

WYLIE, EVAN BENJAMIN, b Sask, Can, Jan 14, 31; US US citizen; m 55; c 3. HYDRAULICS, CIVIL ENGINEERING. *Educ:* Univ Denver, BS, 53; Univ Colo, MS, 55; Univ Mich, PhD(hydraul), 64. *Prof Exp:* Asst engr, City Engr Off, Englewood, Colo, 54-55; jr res off hydraul sect, Div Mech Eng, Nat Res Coun Can, 55-56; struct design engr, Ford Motor Co of Can, Ltd, 56-59; asst prof civil eng, Univ Denver, 59-62; from asst prof to assoc prof, 65-70, PROF CIVIL ENG, UNIV MICH, ANN ARBOR, 70- *Mem:* Am Soc Civil Engrs; Am Soc Mech Engrs; Am Soc Eng Educ; Int Asn Hydraul Res; Earthquake Eng Res Inst. *Res:* Basic and applied research in fluid transients in closed and open conduits, and fluid flow in porous media. *Mailing Add:* Dept of Civil Eng Rm 319 West Eng Univ of Mich Ann Arbor MI 48109

WYLIE, HAROLD GLENN, b Wingham, Ont, Oct 15, 27; m 53; c 2. ENTOMOLOGY. *Educ:* Univ Toronto, BA, 49; Univ Oxford, PhD(entom), 53. *Prof Exp:* Res scientist, Belleville, Ont, 49-50 & 51-72, RES SCIENTIST ENTOM, CAN DEPT AGR, WINNIPEG, 72- *Concurrent Pos:* Res scientist, Commonwealth Inst Biol Control, Zurich, 50-51. *Mem:* Entom Soc Can. *Res:* Parasitic hymenoptera and diptera; manipulation of insect parasites for pest control; host selection behavior of insect parasites. *Mailing Add:* 643 Silverstone Ave Winnipeg MB R3T 2V8 Can

WYLIE, KYRAL FRANCIS, b Akron, Ohio, Feb 24, 31; m 56. ENGINEERING, PHYSICS. *Educ:* Kent State Univ, BS, 58, MA, 60; Ohio State Univ, PhD(eng), 70. *Prof Exp:* Res physicist, Mound Lab, Ohio, 60-65, sr res physicist, 65-66; res fel, Ohio State Univ, 70; from asst prof to assoc prof mech eng, Univ Miss, 70-78; STAFF MEM, LOS ALAMOS NAT LAB, 78- *Concurrent Pos:* Consult physicist, Nuclear Med Lab, Grandview Hosp, Dayton, Ohio, 60-66. *Honors & Awards:* Cert appreciation, Am Nuclear Soc, 69. *Mem:* Am Soc Mech Engrs; Am Phys Soc; Health Physics Soc; Am Meteorol Soc. *Mailing Add:* Los Alamos Nat Lab Los Alamos NM 87544

WYLIE, RICHARD MICHAEL, b Louisville, Ky, June 17, 34; m 69. BIOLOGY, NEUROPHYSIOLOGY. *Educ:* Harvard Univ, BA, 56, MA, 58, PhD(biol), 62. *Prof Exp:* Fel neurophysiol, Univ Utah, 62-65, res assoc, 65-66; res assoc, Rockefeller Univ, 66-69; RES PHYSIOLOGIST, DEPT MED NEUROSCI, WALTER REED ARMY INST RES, 69- *Mem:* Soc Neurosci; assoc mem Am Physiol Soc. *Res:* Biophysics of sensory mechanisms; mechanisms of sensory discrimination in central nervous systems; integration in sensory and motor systems. *Mailing Add:* Dept Med Neurosci Walter Reed Army Inst Res Washington DC 20012

WYLIE, WILLIAM DICKEY, b Carthage, Ark, Nov 18, 14; m 40; c 4. ENTOMOLOGY. *Educ:* Univ Ark, BSA, 37; Cornell Univ, PhD(econ entom), 41. *Prof Exp:* Asst entom, Cornell Univ, 37-42; entomologist, US Sugar Corp, 42-45 & Everglades Exp Sta, Univ Fla, 46-47; asst prof, Univ & asst entomologist, Exp Sta, 47-49, assoc prof & assoc entomologist, 49-57, PROF ENTOM, UNIV & ENTOMOLOGIST, EXP STA, UNIV ARK, FAYETTEVILLE, 57- *Mem:* Entom Soc Am. *Res:* Biology and control of insects of fruit and vegetable crops. *Mailing Add:* Dept Entom Univ Ark Fayetteville AR 72701

WYLLIE, GILBERT ALEXANDER, b Saltcoats, Scotland, Jan 11, 28; US citizen; m 57; c 3. BIOLOGY, ECOLOGY. *Educ:* Col Idaho, BS, 58; Sacramento State Col, MA, 60; Purdue Univ, PhD(ecol), 63. *Prof Exp:* Assoc prof biol, WTex State Univ, 63-65; asst prof, 65-66, ASSOC PROF BIOL, BOISE STATE UNIV, 66- *Mem:* Ecol Soc Am. *Res:* Effects of environment on morphology, distribution, behavior of invertebrates and lower vertebrates. *Mailing Add:* Dept of Biol Boise State Univ Boise ID 83725

WYLLIE, PETER JOHN, b London, Eng, Feb 8, 30; m 56; c 3. GEOLOGY, GEOCHEMISTRY. *Educ:* Univ St Andrews, BSc, 52 & 55, PhD, 58. *Hon Degrees:* DSc, Univ St Andrews, 74. *Prof Exp:* Geologist, Brit NGreenland Exped, 52-54; asst lectr geol, Univ St Andrews, 55-56; asst geochem, Pa State Univ, 56-58, asst prof, 58-59; res fel, Leeds Univ, 59-60, lectr exp petrol, 60-61; assoc prof petrol, Pa State Univ, 61-65; master of col & assoc dean phys sci div, 72-73, PROF PETROL & GEOCHEM, UNIV CHICAGO, 65-, HOMER J LIVINGSTON PROF, 78-, CHMN GEOPHYS SCI, 80- *Concurrent Pos:* Mem, Int Comn Exp Petrol at High Pressures & Temperatures, 71-, chmn, 76-; adv panel earth sci, NSF, 75-78; mem, US Nat Comt Geol, 78-82; ed-in-chief, Minerals & Rocks, Springerverlag; ed, Smith-Wyllie series, Intermed Geol; ed, J Geol. *Honors & Awards:* Polar Medal for Geol Surv & Explor in Greenland; Award, Mineral Soc Am, 65. *Mem:* Geol Soc Am; Int Mineral Asn (2nd vpres, 78-82); Mineral Soc Am (vpres, 76-77, pres, 77-78); Asn Earth Sci Ed; Asn Geoscientists Int Develop. *Res:* Igneous and metamorphic petrology; experimental petrology; high pressure studies on hydrothermal systems; application of phase equilibrium studies to batholiths, andesites, kimberlites, and carbonatites. *Mailing Add:* Hinds Geophys Lab 5734 S Ellis Ave Chicago IL 60637

WYLLIE, THOMAS DEAN, b Hinsdale, Ill, Dec 4, 28; m 50; c 3. PLANT PATHOLOGY. *Educ:* San Diego State Col, AB, 52; Univ Minn, MS, 57, PhD(plant path), 60. *Prof Exp:* PROF PLANT PATH, UNIV MO-COLUMBIA, 60- *Mem:* Am Phytopath Soc. *Res:* Physiology of host-parasite interactions; mycotoxin and mycotoxicoses research; ecological relationships of non-specific soil borne pathogenic fungi on the soybean. *Mailing Add:* Dept of Plant Path 108 Waters Hall Univ of Mo Columbia MO 65201

WYLLY, ALEXANDER, b New York, NY, Sept 2, 20; m 43; c 2. OPERATIONS RESEARCH, COMPUTER SCIENCE. *Educ:* Ga Inst Technol, BS, 41; Mass Inst Technol, SM, 46; Calif Inst Technol, PhD(aerodyn eng), 51. *Prof Exp:* Aerodynamicist, Rand Corp, 46-51, chief missile preliminary designs, 51-54; vpres comput sci, Planning Res Corp, 54-69, vpres pac opers, 69-73; CONSULT, 73- *Concurrent Pos:* Trustee, Oceanic Found. *Mem:* Am Soc Info Sci. *Res:* Systems analysis; computer systems software design and applications. *Mailing Add:* 4069 Kulamanu St Honolulu HI 96816

WYLY, LEMUEL DAVID, JR, b Seneca, SC, Aug 9, 16; m 38; c 2. NUCLEAR PHYSICS. *Educ:* The Citadel, BS, 38; Univ NC, MA, 39; Yale Univ, PhD(physics), 49. *Prof Exp:* Instr physics, Ga Sch Technol, 39-41, asst prof, 46; asst instr, Yale Univ, 46-48; from assoc prof to prof, 49-58, REGENTS' PROF PHYSICS, GA INST TECHNOL, 58- *Concurrent Pos:* Consult, Oak Ridge Nat Lab, 52- *Mem:* Fel Am Phys Soc. *Res:* Nuclear energy levels; proportional and scintillation and solid state detectors; decay schemes of radioactive isotopes and from neutron capture. *Mailing Add:* Sch of Physics Ga Inst of Technol Atlanta GA 30332

WYMA, RICHARD J, b Grand Rapids, Mich, June 25, 36; m 64; c 3. PHYSICAL CHEMISTRY, INORGANIC CHEMISTRY. *Educ:* Hope Col, AB, 58; Univ Mich, MS, 60, PhD(phys chem), 64. *Prof Exp:* Asst prof chem, Geneva Col, 64-69; ASSOC PROF CHEM, IND-PURDUE UNIV, INDIANAPOLIS, 70- *Concurrent Pos:* consult, City of Indianapolis & Inst Adv Res, Ind-Purdue Univ, 76-80. *Mem:* Am Chem Soc; Soc Appl Spectros. *Res:* Application of molecular spectroscopy to structure determination and to bounding theories of inorganic systems; chemistry of sulfides, phosphines, boranes and transition metal complexes; analysis of air, solid wastes and commercial products. *Mailing Add:* 1125 E 38th St PO Box 647 Dept Chem Ind-Purdue Univ Indianapolis IN 46223

WYMAN, BOSTWICK FRAMPTON, b Aiken, SC, Aug 22, 41. MATHEMATICS. *Educ:* Mass Inst Technol, SB, 62; Univ Calif, Berkeley, MA, 64, PhD(math), 66. *Prof Exp:* Instr math, Princeton Univ, 66-68; asst prof, Stanford Univ, 68-72; ASSOC PROF MATH, OHIO STATE UNIV, 72- *Concurrent Pos:* Vis asst prof, Univ Oslo, 70-71; vis assoc prof, Univ Notre Dame, 78-79. *Mem:* Am Math Soc; Math Asn Am. *Res:* algebraic system theory; linear control system design; algebraic number theory. *Mailing Add:* Dept of Math Ohio State Univ Columbus OH 43210

WYMAN, DONALD, b Templeton, Calif, Sept 18, 03; m 27; c 4. HORTICULTURE. *Educ:* Pa State Col, BSA, 26; Cornell Univ, MSA, 31, PhD(hort), 35. *Prof Exp:* Instr, Pa State Univ, 27-29; investr, Cornell Univ, 29-31, instr, 31-35; horticulturist, 36-70, EMER HORTICULTURIST, ARNOLD ARBORETUM, HARVARD UNIV, 70- *Honors & Awards:* Coleman Award, Am Asn Nurserymen, 49 & 51; NY Hort Soc Distinguished Serv Award, 60; Garden Club Fedn Am Medal of Honor, 65; Veitch Medal, Royal Hort Soc, 69; George Robert White Medal of Honor, Mass Hort Soc, 70; Arthur Hoyt Scott Gold Medal, Swarthmore Col, 71; L H Bailey Medal, Am Hort Soc, 71. *Mem:* Am Soc Hort Sci (vpres, 52-53); Am Hort Soc (pres, 61-62); Am Asn Bot Gardens & Arboretums; fel Nat Recreation & Park Asn. *Res:* Ornamental horticulture; plant propagation; winter hardiness; selection of best varieties of woody plants for landscape use. *Mailing Add:* 59 Jericho Rd Weston MA 02193

WYMAN, GEORGE MARTIN, b Budapest, Hungary, Oct 13, 21; nat US; m 51; c 1. ORGANIC CHEMISTRY. *Educ:* Cornell Univ, AB, 41, MS, 43, PhD(org chem), 44. *Prof Exp:* Res chemist, Gen Chem Co, 44-45, Gen Aniline & Film Corp, 45-49 & Nat Bur Standards, 49-54; chief spectros sect, Qm Res & Develop Ctr, US Dept Army, 54-57, sci adv, European Res Off, 57-60, dir chem div, US Army Res Off, 60-77, CHIEF CHEM BR, EUROP RES OFF, 77- *Concurrent Pos:* Adj prof chem, Univ NC, Chapel Hill, 73-77. *Mem:* Am Chem Chem Soc; Int Am Photochem Soc; Europ Photochem Asn. *Res:* Spectrophotometry; cis-trans isomerization of conjugated compounds; organic photochemistry; excited state chemistry of dyes. *Mailing Add:* US Army Res & Standards Group Box 65 APO New York NY 09510

WYMAN, HAROLD ROBERTSON, b Yarmouth, NS, Nov 12, 05; wid; c 3. CHEMISTRY. *Educ:* Dalhousie Univ, BSc, 27; McGill Univ, MSc, 30. *Prof Exp:* Demonstr chem, McGill Univ, 27-28; asst chemist, Halifax Refinery, Imp Oil, Ltd, 30-38; consult chemist, 38-64; pres, Wyman & West Ltd, 64-73; lab mgr, Caleb Brett Can Ltd, 73-78; ASSOC, MACLAREN PLANSEARCH LTD, 79- *Mem:* AAAS; Am Chem Soc; fel Chem Inst Can; Marine Chem Asn. *Res:* Surface energy relationships; chemical analytical methods, especially identification of oil sources, detection and identification of drugs. *Mailing Add:* 5269 Kaye St Halifax NS B3K 1Y2 Can

WYMAN, JEFFRIES, b West Newton, Mass, June 21, 01; m 54; c 2. MOLECULAR BIOLOGY. *Educ:* Harvard Univ, AB, 23; Univ London, PhD, 27. *Prof Exp:* From instr to assoc prof zool, Harvard Univ, 28-51; sci adv, US Embassy, Paris, 51-54; dir, UNESCO Sci Off MidE, 55-58; GUEST PROF, BIOCHEM INST, UNIV ROME & ISTITUTO REGINA ELENA, 60- *Concurrent Pos:* Past secy gen, European Molecular Biol Orgn. *Mem:* Nat Acad Sci; Am Acad Arts & Sci. *Mailing Add:* Inst di Chimicam Biol Citta Universitaria 00185 Rome Italy

WYMAN, JOHN E, b Amsterdam, NY, Feb 20, 31; m 52; c 4. CHEMISTRY. *Educ:* Univ Mich, BS, 52, Purdue Univ, MS, 55, PhD, 56. *Prof Exp:* Res chemist, Linde Co, Union Carbide Corp, 56-58, res chemist, Union Carbide Chem Co, 58-59; res chemist, Spec Proj Dept, Monsanto Chem Co, 59-60, res group leader, Monsanto Res Corp, 60-65; MEM SCI STAFF, ITEK CORP, 65- *Res:* Photochemistry; complex transition element organometallic chemistry; metal carbonyls; propellant, explosive and inorganic chemistry; graphic arts, film and paper coatings. *Mailing Add:* 164 N Beacon Boston MA 02116

WYMAN, MARVIN E(UGENE), b North Branch, Minn, Apr 9, 21; m 55; c 2. NUCLEAR ENGINEERING, NUCLEAR PHYSICS. *Educ:* St Olaf Col, BA, 42; Univ Ill, MS, 43, PhD(physics), 50. *Prof Exp:* Asst physics, Univ Ill, 42-44 & 46-49; from asst prof to assoc prof, St Olaf Col, 49-53; mem staff, Los Alamos Sci Lab, 53-58; prof nuclear eng & physics, Univ Ill, Urbana, 58-75, chmn nuclear eng prog, 65-75, asst to dean long range planning, 75-77; ASSOC VPRES RES & SPONSORED PROGS, OLD DOMINION UNIV, 78- *Concurrent Pos:* Mem subcomt res reactors, Nat Acad Sci-Nat Res Coun, 61-70, chmn, 65-70, mem comt nuclear sci, 65-70; UN consult, Mex Nuclear Energy Comn, 63; mem fel bd, Atomic Energy Comn, 65-68, chmn, 67-68. *Mem:* Fel Am Phys Soc; Am Soc Eng Educ; fel Am Nuclear Soc; Am Inst Physics; Am Asn Physics Teachers. *Res:* Experimental reactor physics; fission physics; research administration. *Mailing Add:* Res & Sponsored Progs Old Dominion Univ Norfolk VA 23508

WYMAN, MAX, b Can, Apr 14, 16; m 40; c 1. MATHEMATICS. *Educ:* Univ Alta, BSc, 37; Calif Inst Technol, PhD(math), 40. *Prof Exp:* Munitions gauge inspector, Nat Res Coun Can, 40-41; lectr math, Univ Sask, 41-42; munitions gauge inspector, Nat Res Coun Can, 42-43; lectr math, 43-45, from asst prof to prof, 45-56, head dept math, 61-64, dean sci, 63-64, acad vpres, 64-69, pres, 69-74, UNIV PROF MATH, UNIV ALTA, 74- *Concurrent Pos:* Chmn, Alta Human Rights Comn, 74-79. *Mem:* Math Asn Am; fel Royal Soc Can; NY Acad Sci. *Res:* Relativity theory and asymptotics. *Mailing Add:* 844 Educ Bldg S Univ of Alta Edmonton AB T6G 2G5 Can

WYMAN, MILTON, b Cleveland, Ohio, Oct 11, 30; m 56; c 2. VETERINARY MEDICINE, OPHTHALMOLOGY. *Educ:* Ohio State Univ, DVM, 63, MS, 64; Am Col Vet Ophthal, dipl. *Prof Exp:* Res assoc ophthal, Cols Med & Vet Med, 62-64, instr vet ophthal, Col Vet Med, 64-66, from asst prof to prof vet ophthal & med, 66-75, CHIEF COMP VET OPHTHAL & MED, COL VET MED, OHIO STATE UNIV, 75- CHIEF SMALL ANIMAL SERV, 72-, ASSOC PROF OPHTHAL, COL MED, 72- *Mem:* Am Soc Vet Ophthal; dipl, Am Col Vet Ophthalmologists (past pres); Am Vet Med Asn; Am Asn Vet Clin. *Res:* Congenital ocular defects in dogs and their relationship to man; glaucoma in the basset hound; ocular fundus anomaly in collies; medical application of soft contact lenses in animals and man. *Mailing Add:* 2615 Carriage Rd Powell OH 43065

WYMAN, RICHARD VAUGHN, b Painesville, Ohio, Feb 22, 27; m 47; c 1. GEOLOGICAL ENGINEERING, ECONOMIC GEOLOGY. *Educ:* Case Western Reserve Univ, BS, 48; Univ Mich, MS, 49; Univ Ariz, PhD(geol eng), 74. *Prof Exp:* Geologist econ geol, NJ Zinc Co, 49; geologist, Cerro de Pasco Corp, 50-52; geologist, NJ Zinc Co, 52-53; geologist uranium, Western Gold & Uranium Inc, 53-54, chief geologist, 54-55, gen mgr, 55-57, vpres, 57-59; tunnel supt tunnel construct, Reynolds Elec & Eng Co, 61-63; construct supt, Sunshine Mining Co, 63-65; engr, Reynolds Elec & Eng Co, 65-67, asst mgr, 67-69; lectr, 69-74, assoc prof, 74-80, chmn dept, 76-80, PROF ENG, UNIV NEV, 80- *Concurrent Pos:* Pres explor geol, Intermountain Explor Co, 59-; consult, C K Geoenergy Corp, 77-; Univ Nev, Las Vegas Senate Res Grant Geothermal, 77-; mem peer rev comt, Nevada Nuclear Waste Isolation Proj, Dept Environ, 78- *Mem:* Am Inst Mining, Metall & Petrol Engrs; Am Soc Civil Engrs; Soc Econ Geol; Geol Soc Am; Asn Eng Geol. *Res:* Geothermal energy utilization; ore genesis; tunnel construction and design. *Mailing Add:* 610 Bryant Ct Boulder City NV 89005

WYMAN, ROBERT J, b Syracuse, NY, June 8, 40. DEVELOPMENTAL NEUROBIOLOGY, DEVELOPMENTAL GENETICS. *Educ:* Harvard Univ, AB, 60; Univ Calif, Berkeley, MA, 63, PhD(biophys), 65. *Prof Exp:* Math analyst, Tech Res Group, Inc, 59; NSF res fel appl sci, Calif Inst Technol, 66; asst prof, 66-70, assoc prof, 71-80, PROF BIOL, YALE UNIV, 80- *Concurrent Pos:* Vis scienitst, Nobel Inst, Stockholm, 70-71, Med Res Coun, Cambridge, Eng, 74 & Univ Basel, Switz, 77; mem staff physiol study sect, NIH, 76-80. *Mem:* Soc Neurosci; Int Brain Res Orgn; Sigma Xi; Brit Soc Exp Biol. *Res:* Genetics of Drosophila nervous system; neural generation of motor output in insects and vertebrates; computer analysis of neural data; developmental genetics. *Mailing Add:* Dept of Biol Yale Univ New Haven CT 06511

WYMAN, STANLEY M, b Cambridge, Mass, Aug 3, 13; m; c 4. MEDICINE, RADIOLOGY. *Educ:* Harvard Univ, AB, 35, MD, 39. *Prof Exp:* Radiologist, Mass Gen Hosp, 47-68; asst clin prof radiol, Harvard Med Sch, 54-75; vis radiologist, 68-77, radiologist, 77-81, SR RADIOLOGIST, MASS GEN HOSP, 81-; CLIN PROF RADIOL, HARVARD MED SCH, 77-; SR RADIOLOGIST, MASS GEN HOSP, 81- *Concurrent Pos:* Consult, US Navy, 57-73. *Honors & Awards:* Silver Medal, Roentgen Ray Soc, 52; Gold Medal, Am Col Radiol, 72; Gold Medal, Radiol Soc NAm, 74. *Mem:* Radiol Soc NAm (pres, 68); Roentgen Ray Soc; AMA; Am Col Radiol (pres, 71). *Res:* Cardiovascular radiology. *Mailing Add:* 575 Mt Auburn St Cambridge MA 02139

WYMER, JOSEPH PETER, b Marion, Va, July 31, 23; m 55; c 3. INDUSTRIAL ENGINEERING. *Educ:* Va Polytech Inst & State Univ, BSIE, 47; Univ Southern Calif, MSIE, 69. *Prof Exp:* Methods & standards engr, Brunswick, Balke-Collender, Va, 47-49; RCA Victor, Va, 49-51; mfg engr, Convair Div, Gen Dynamics Corp, Tex, 51-55; chief indust engr, O'Sullivan Rubber Corp, Va, 55-59; chief indust engr, Gen Instruments Corp, Va, 59; indust engr, Boeing Airplane Co, Wash, 59-61; PROF INDUST ENG & CHMN DEPT, CALIF STATE POLYTECH UNIV, POMONA, 61- *Concurrent Pos:* Indust eng consult, Lawry Foods, Inc, McDonnell Douglas Corp, Electronic Specialties, Taylor Corp & others, Southern Calif, 61- *Mem:* Am Inst Indust Engrs; Nat Soc Prof Engrs; Am Soc Eng Educ; Am Foundrymen's Soc. *Mailing Add:* Dept Indust Eng Calif State Polytech Univ Pomona CA 91768

WYMER, RAYMOND GEORGE, b Colton, Ohio, Oct 1, 27; m 48; c 4. RESEARCH ADMINISTRATION. *Educ:* Memphis State Col, BS, 50; Vanderbilt Univ, MA & PhD, 53. *Prof Exp:* Mem staff, Oak Ridge Nat Lab, 53-56; assoc prof, Ga Inst Technol, 56-58; chief nuclear chem, Indust Reactor Labs, 58-59; res chemist, 59-62, sect chief, 62-73, ASSOC DIR CHEM TECHNOL DIV, OAK RIDGE NAT LAB, 73- *Concurrent Pos:* Ed, Radiochimica Acta. *Mem:* Am Inst Chem Engrs; Sigma Xi; fel Am Nuclear Soc; Am Chem Soc. *Res:* Colloid, radiation, transuranium element and complex ion chemistry; kinetics; nuclear fuel cycle. *Mailing Add:* Chem Technol Div Oak Ridge Nat Lab Oak Ridge TN 37830

WYMORE, ALBERT WAYNE, b New Sharon, Iowa, Feb 1, 27; m 49; c 4. SYSTEM THEORY, SYSTEMS ENGINEERING. *Educ:* Iowa State Univ, BS, 49, MS, 50; Univ Wis, PhD(math), 55. *Prof Exp:* Consult, Pure Oil Co, 55-57; dir, Comput Ctr, 57-67, head dept systs eng, 59-74, PROF SYSTS ENG, UNIV ARIZ, 59- *Concurrent Pos:* Consult, RCA, 58 & 73, IBM, San Jose, 60-61, Lockheed, Ga, 69, Centro Agronomotrop de Invest y Ensenanza, Costa Rica, 75-76 & Gen Elec Tempo Ctr Advan Studies, 77-78. *Mem:* AAAS; Am Inst Indust Engrs; Am Math Soc. *Res:* Mathematical system theory; system design methodology; information systems; software engineering; agricultural systems; communication systems. *Mailing Add:* Dept of Systs & Indust Eng Univ of Ariz Tucson AZ 85721

WYMORE, CHARLES ELMER, b Iowa, Jan 2, 32; m 52; c 3. INORGANIC CHEMISTRY. *Educ:* Cent Col, Iowa, BA, 53; Univ Ill, PhD(chem), 57. *Prof Exp:* Res chemist, 56-63, proj leader, 63-68, group leader, 68-71, res mgr, 71-74, LAB, DIR, DOW CHEM CO, 74- *Mem:* Am Chem Soc; AAAS. *Res:* Coordination and organometallic chemistry; homogeneous catalysis; organic chemistry; heterogeneous catalysis. *Mailing Add:* Chem Process Lab Dow Chem Co 1776 Bldg Midland MI 48640

WYNBLATT, PAUL P, b Alexandria, Egypt, June 30, 35; m 59; c 2. MATERIALS SCIENCE, SURFACE SCIENCE. *Educ:* Univ Manchester, BScTech, 56; Israel Inst Technol, MS, 58; Univ Calif, Berkeley, PhD(metall), 66. *Prof Exp:* Res metallurgist, Israel Atomic Energy Comn Labs, 58-62; staff scientist res staff, Ford Motor Co, 66-81; PROF METALL ENG & MAT SCI, ENG & PUB POLICY, CARNEGIE-MELLON UNIV, 81- *Mem:* Am Soc Metals; Am Vacuum Soc; Am Inst Mining, Metall & Petrol Engrs-Metall Soc. *Res:* Dislocation dynamics and metal plasticity; volume and surface diffusion in metals; point defects in crystals; materials aspects of catalysis. *Mailing Add:* Dept Metall Eng & Mat Sci Carnegie-Mellon Univ Pittsburgh PA 15213

WYNDER, ERNST LUDWIG, b Ger, Apr 30, 22; nat US. PREVENTIVE MEDICINE, EPIDEMIOLOGY. *Educ:* NY Univ, BA, 43; Wash Univ, BS & MD, 50. *Prof Exp:* Intern, Georgetown Univ Hosp, 50; asst prof prev med, Grad Sch Med Sci, Med Col, Cornell Univ, 54-56, assoc prof, 56-69; PRES & MED DIR, AM HEALTH FOUND, 69- *Concurrent Pos:* Asst, Sloan-Kettering Inst Cancer Res, 52-54, assoc, 54-60, assoc mem, 60-69, assoc scientist, 69-71; jr asst resident, Mem Hosp for Cancer & Allied Dis, 51-52, sr asst resident, 52-54, clin asst physician, 54-64, asst attend physician, 64-69, consult epidemiologist, 69-; clin vis asst, James Ewing Hosp, 54-64, asst vis physician, 64-68; mem, Task Force Lung Cancer, Tobacco Working Group, 67-; mem, Nat Cancer Plan, 71; ed, Prev Med J, 72. *Mem:* AMA; Am Asn Cancer Res; Am Pub Health Asn; NY Acad Sci. *Res:* Environmental factors affecting major chronic disease development, preventive medical aspects. *Mailing Add:* Am Health Found 320 E 43rd St New York NY 10017

WYNDRUM, RALPH WILLIAM, JR, b Brooklyn, NY, Apr 20, 37; m 60; c 4. ELECTRICAL ENGINEERING, TELECOMMUNICATIONS. *Educ:* Columbia Univ, BS, 59, MS, 60, MS(bus admin), 78; NY Univ, EngScD(elec eng), 63. *Prof Exp:* Mem tech staff, 63-65, supvr explor circuit appln, 65-69, dept head loop transmission systs, 69-79, HEAD ADV TRANSMISSION SYSTS DEPT, BELL LABS, INC, 69- *Concurrent Pos:* Asst prof, NY Univ, 63-64; mem, Nat Basic Sci Comt, 66-70; adj prof, Newark Col Eng, 67-70; prof elec eng & comput sci, Stevens Inst Technol, 81-82. *Mem:* Fel Inst Elec & Electronics Engrs. *Res:* Network synthesis; integrated circuit design; telephone transmission design. *Mailing Add:* Bell Labs 1B 306 Whippany NJ 07981

WYNER, AARON D, b New York, NY, Mar 17, 39; m 63; c 4. ELECTRICAL ENGINEERING, MATHEMATICS. *Educ:* Queens Col, NY, BS, 60; Columbia Univ, BS, 60, MS, 61, PhD(elec eng), 63. *Prof Exp:* Asst prof elec eng, Columbia Univ, 63; mem tech staff, Math Res Ctr, 63-74, HEAD, COMMUN ANAL RES DEPT, BELL LABS, 74- *Concurrent Pos:* Consult, T J Watson Res Ctr & IBM Corp, 63; adj prof, Columbia Univ, 64-; Guggenheim fel, 66-67; vis scientist, Weizmann Inst Sci & Israel Inst Technol, 69-70; vis prof, Polytech Inst Brooklyn, 71. *Mem:* AAAS; Inst Elec & Electronics Engrs. *Res:* Communication theory; information theory; probability. *Mailing Add:* Bell Labs Murray Hill NJ 07974

WYNGAARD, JOHN C, b Madison, Wis, Dec 4, 38; m 65; c 2. FLUID DYNAMICS. *Educ:* Univ Wis-Madison, BSc, 61, MSc, 62; Pa State Univ, PhD(mech eng), 67. *Prof Exp:* Res physicist, Air Force Cambridge Res Labs, 67-75; physicist, Wave Propagation Lab, Nat Oceanic & Atmospheric Admin, Boulder, 75-79; PHYSICIST, MESOSCALE RES SECT, NAT CTR ATMOSPHERIC RES, 79-, HEAD, 81- *Concurrent Pos:* Vis assoc prof atmospheric sci, Univ Wash, 73; fel, Coop Inst Res Environ Sci, Boulder, 75-79. *Mem:* Am Meteorol Soc; Am Phys Soc; Sigma Xi. *Res:* The structure and dynamics of turbulent flows, particularly in the lower atmosphere. *Mailing Add:* Nat Ctr Atmospheric Res PO Box 3000 Boulder CO 80307

WYNGAARDEN, JAMES BARNES, b East Grand Rapids, Mich, Oct 19, 24; m 46; c 5. BIOCHEMISTRY, METABOLISM. *Educ:* Univ Mich, MD, 48. *Prof Exp:* Asst pharmacol, Med Sch, Univ Mich, 46-48; mem med house staff, Mass Gen Hosp, 48-52; vis investr, Pub Health Res Inst New York, 53; investr, Nat Heart Inst, 53-54 & Nat Inst Arthritis & Metab Dis, 54-56; assoc prof med & biochem, Sch Med, Duke Univ, 56-61, prof med & assoc prof biochem, 61-65; prof med & chmn dept, Univ Pa, 65-67; FREDERIC M HANES PROF MED & CHMN DEPT, DUKE UNIV, 67- *Concurrent Pos:* Dalton scholar med res, Mass Gen Hosp, 51; consult, Vet Admin Hosp, Durham, NC; consult, Off Sci & Technol, Exec Off of the President, 66-72; mem adv comt biol & med, AEC, 67-69; mem adv bd, Howard Hughes Med Inst, 69-; mem bd sci counrs, Nat Inst Arthritis, Metab & Digestive Dis, 71-74; mem, Nat Res Coun, 71- & President's Sci Adv Comt, 72-73; mem exec comn, Assembly of Life Sci, 72-77. *Mem:* Inst of Med of Nat Acad Sci; Am Soc Clin Invest; Nat Acad Sci; Am Acad Arts & Sci; Assoc Am Physicians (pres, 78-79). *Res:* Control of purine synthesis; purine metabolism in normal and gouty man; metabolism of iodine and steroids; oxalate synthesis; inborn errors of metabolism. *Mailing Add:* Dept of Med Duke Univ Med Ctr Durham NC 27710

WYNKOOP, RAYMOND, chemical engineering, chemistry, deceased

WYNN, CHARLES MARTIN, SR, b New York, NY, May 8, 39; m 66; c 3. ORGANIC CHEMISTRY, ACADEMIC ADMINISTRATION. *Educ:* City Col New York, BChE, 60; Univ Mich, MS, 63, PhD(chem), 65. *Prof Exp:* Instr gen chem, Univ Mich, 65-67; US Peace Corps lectr chem, Malayan Teachers' Col, 67-69; from asst prof to assoc prof phys sci, 69-74, asst to provost, 74-75, PROF PHYS SCI, OAKLAND COMMUNITY COL, 74-, CHMN DEPT, 69- *Mem:* Am Chem Soc; Am Asn Higher Educ; Am Educ Sci Asn. *Res:* Structural directivity in diene synthesis. *Mailing Add:* Dept of Phys Sci Oakland Community Col Farmington MI 48018

WYNN, CLAYTON S(COTT), b Plymouth, Ohio, Nov 12, 07; m 39; c 3. CHEMICAL ENGINEERING. *Educ:* Colo Col, AB, 30; Cornell Univ, PhD(chem eng), 35. *Prof Exp:* Asst chem, Cornell Univ, 30-35; chem engr, Air Reduction Sales Co, 35-45, admin engr, 45-50, sr chem engr, 50-60, mgr process eng, 60-72, CONSULT, AIRCO, INC, 72- *Mem:* Am Chem Soc; Am

Inst Chem Engrs. *Res:* Process design of plants; economic evaluation of projects; technical planning; catalytic oxidation; dehydration of alcohols and glycols; calcium carbide; vinyl acetate and polymers; acetylenic chemicals; anesthetic agents; waste water treatment with ozone. *Mailing Add:* 274 Woodbine Circle New Providence NJ 07974

WYNN, JAMES ELKANAH, b Pennington Gap, Va, Feb 7, 42; m 64; c 1. MEDICINAL CHEMISTRY, ANALYTICAL CHEMISTRY. *Educ:* Va Commonwealth Univ, BS, 64, PhD(med chem), 69. *Prof Exp:* Res fel med & anal chem, Med Col Va, 69; from asst prof to assoc prof med chem, 69-77, PROF PHARM, COL PHARM, UNIV SC, 77- *Concurrent Pos:* Comn prod scholar grant, Col Pharm, Univ SC, 70-71, lectr, Proj Upward Bound, 70- *Mem:* Am Chem Soc; Am Pharmaceut Asn; Am Asn Cols Pharm; Sigma Xi. *Res:* Organic chemistry; cancer chemotherapeutic agents of the alkylating type; synthesis, testing and correlation of activity with physical parameters; mechanism of dimenthyl sulfoxide interaction with isolated enzyme systems; synthesis of agents for urolithiasis treatment. *Mailing Add:* Col of Pharm Univ of SC Columbia SC 29208

WYNN, RALPH MATTHEW, b New York, NY, Nov 1, 30. OBSTETRICS & GYNECOLOGY. *Educ:* Harvard Univ, AB, 51; NY Univ, MD, 54; Am Bd Obstet & Gynec, dipl. *Prof Exp:* From instr to assoc prof obstet & gynec, State Univ NY Downstate Med Ctr, 61-68; prof obstet & gynec & head dept, Univ Ill Med Ctr, 68-78; PROF OBSTET & GYNEC & HEAD DEPT, UNIV ARK FOR MED SCI, 78- *Concurrent Pos:* USPHS res fel, 62-63; mem study sect, NIH; mem, Nat Med Comn Planned Parenthood-World Pop. *Honors & Awards:* Purdue Frederick Res Award, Am Col Obstet & Gynec, 67. *Mem:* Fel Am Asn Obstet & Gynec; fel Am Gynec Soc; Am Asn Anat; Asn Profs Gynec & Obstet; Soc Gynec Invest. *Res:* Electron microscopy; comparative anatomy of placenta; ultrastructure of placenta; fetal membranes; endometrium. *Mailing Add:* Dept of Obstet & Gynec Univ of Ark for Med Sci Little Rock AR 72201

WYNN, WILLARD KENDALL, JR, b Raleigh, NC, Mar 28, 32; m 63. PLANT PATHOLOGY. *Educ:* NC State Univ, BS, 55; Univ Fla, PhD(plant path), 63. *Prof Exp:* Assoc plant pathologist, Boyce Thompson Inst Plant Res, 63-68; ASSOC PROF PLANT PATH, UNIV GA, 68- *Mem:* Am Phytopath Soc; Am Plant Physiol. *Res:* Physiology of uredospore germination and rust infection. *Mailing Add:* Dept of Plant Path Univ of Ga Athens GA 30601

WYNNE, ELMER STATEN, b El Paso, Tex, Oct 23, 17; m 38, 78; c 2. MEDICAL MICROBIOLOGY. *Educ:* Univ Tex, BA, 38, MA, 44, PhD(bact), 48; Am Bd Microbiol, cert microbiol & bact. *Prof Exp:* Asst bact, Univ Tex, 38-39, tutor, 39-42, instr, 46, res assoc, 46-48, res bacteriologist, M D Anderson Hosp & Tumor Inst, 50-58, assoc prof microbiol, Dent Br, Univ, 58-59; asst prof, Univ Okla, 48-50; bacteriologist, US Air Force Sch Aerospace Med, 59-60, res prof bact & chief microbiol, 60-67, sr microbiologist, 68-69; assoc prof, Med Lab Technol, St Phillips Col, 70-76, prog dir, 70-75, prof, 76-82; RETIRED. *Mem:* AAAS; Am Soc Microbiol; fel Am Acad Microbiol. *Res:* Enteric bacteriology; bacterial antagonism; physiology of Clostridium spore germination; microbiological aspects of cancer research; aerospace microbiology; hand disinfection; live hybrid vaccine for bacillary dysentery. *Mailing Add:* 10514 Auldine San Antonio TX 78220

WYNNE, JOHNNY CALVIN, b Williamston, NC, May 17, 43; m 61; c 2. PLANT BREEDING, PLANT GENETICS. *Educ:* NC State Univ, BS, 65, MS, 68, PhD(crop sci), 74. *Prof Exp:* Instr, 68-74, asst prof, 74-78, ASSOC PROF CROP SCI, NC STATE UNIV, 78- *Honors & Awards:* Bailey Award, Am Peanut Res & Educ Asn. *Mem:* Am Soc Agron; Am Peanut Res & Educ Asn; Am Genetic Asn. *Res:* Improvement of cultivated peanuts through breeding for higher productivity, disease resistance, insect resistance, nitrogen fixation efficacy, and better quality; evolution and genetics of subspecific groups in peanuts. *Mailing Add:* Dept of Crop Sci NC State Univ Raleigh NC 27650

WYNNE, KENNETH JOSEPH, b Rumford, RI, Jan 17, 40; m 67; c 2. POLYMER SCIENCE, INORGANIC CHEMISTRY. *Educ:* Providence Col, BS, 61; Univ Mass, Amherst, MS & PhD(chem), 65. *Prof Exp:* Fel inorg chem, Univ Calif, Berkeley, 65-67; asst prof, Univ Ga, 67-73, SCI OFFICER, OFF NAVAL RES, 73- *Mem:* AAAS; Sigma Xi; Am Chem Soc. *Res:* Polymer chemistry; inorganic polymers; electroactive polymers; synthetic inorganic and organometallic chemistry; coordination chemistry. *Mailing Add:* Off of Naval Res Chem Prog 800 N Quincy St Arlington VA 22217

WYNNE, LYMAN CARROLL, b Lake Benton, Minn, Sept 17, 23; m 47; c 5. PSYCHIATRY, PSYCHOLOGY. *Educ:* Harvard Med Sch, MD, 47; Harvard Univ, PhD(soc psychol), 58. *Prof Exp:* Intern med, Peter Bent Brigham Hosp, Boston, 47-48; USPHS res fel, Harvard Univ, 48-49; Moseley traveling fel, London, Eng, 49-50; Rantoul fel psychol, Harvard Univ, 50; resident, Mass Gen Hosp, 51; psychiatrist, Lab Socio-Environ Studies, NIMH, Md, 52-54, Adult Psychiat, 54-71, chief family studies sect, 57-67, chief adult psychiat br, 61-71; chmn dept, 71-77, PROF PSYCHIAT SCH MED & DENT, UNIV ROCHESTER, 71- *Concurrent Pos:* Mem fac, Wash Sch Psychiat, 56-71; mem fac, Wash Psychoanal Inst, 60-71, teaching analyst, 66-71; consult & collab investr, WHO, 65-; mem-at-large, Div Behav Sci, Nat Res Coun, 69-72; psychiatrist-in-chief, Strong Mem Hosp, 71-77; mem rev comt career develop awards, NIMH, 72-76; vis lectr, Am Univ Beirut, 63-64. *Honors & Awards:* Commendation medal, USPHS, 65, Meritorious Serv Medal, 66; Fromm-Reichmann Award, Am Acad Psychoanal, 66; Hofheimer Prize, Am Psychiat Asn, 66; Salmon lectr, 73; Stanley R Dean Res Award, Am Col Psychiatrists, 76; McAlpin Res Achievement Award, 77. *Mem:* Am Psychiat Asn; Am Psychosom Soc; Am Orthopsychiat Asn; Psychiat Res Soc; Soc Life Hist Res Psychopath. *Res:* Family research and therapy; schizophrenia; cross-cultural studies; child development. *Mailing Add:* Dept of Psychiat Univ Rochester Sch Med & Dent Rochester NY 14642

WYNNE-EDWARDS, HUGH ROBERT, b Montreal, Que, Jan 19, 34; m 56, 72; c 4. GEOLOGY. *Educ:* Aberdeen Univ, BSc, 55; Queen's Univ, Ont, MA, 57, PhD(geol), 59. *Hon Degrees:* DSc, Mem Univ, 75. *Prof Exp:* Tech officer geol, Geol Surv Can, 58-59; lectr, Queen's Univ, Ont, 59-61, from asst prof to assoc prof, 61-68, prof geol & head dept geol sci, 68-72; prof geol & head, Dept Geol Sci, Univ BC, 72-77; asst secy, Ministry State for Sci & Technol, Govt Can, Ottawa, 77-79; sci dir, 79-80, VPRES & CHIEF SCI OFFICER, ALCAN INT LTD, MONTREAL, 80- *Concurrent Pos:* Vis fel, Aberdeen Univ, 65-66 & Univ Witwatersrand, 72; pres, Can Geosci Coun, 74; UN consult, India, 76; mem sci adv comt, Can Broadcasting Comn, 78-; mem, Conseil de la Politique Sci, Quebec, 81- *Mem:* Fel Geol Soc Am; fel Geol Asn Can; AAAS; Asn Sci & Technol Community Can (pres, 77); Royal Soc Can. *Res:* Resources and physical environment; science policies. *Mailing Add:* Alcan Int Ltd Box 6090 Pl Ville Marie Montreal PQ H3C 3H2 Can

WYNNEMER, D(ONALD) J(AMES), b Waseca, Minn, Dec 8, 28; m 51; c 4. CHEMICAL ENGINEERING. *Educ:* Univ Minn, BChE, 53, PhD(chem eng), 57. *Prof Exp:* Res chem engr, Humble Oil & Ref Co, 57-65, res assoc, Esso Res & Eng Co, Tex, 65-69, TECHNOL ADV, GAS DEPT, EXXON CORP, 69- *Mem:* Am Inst Chem Engrs; Am Chem Soc. *Res:* Technology and economics of natural gas processing and conversion; synthetic gas manufacture and liquified natural gas. *Mailing Add:* Gas Dept Exxon Corp New York NY 10020

WYNNYCKYJ, JOHN ROSTYSLAV, b Ukraine, Nov 4, 32; Can citizen; c 3. EXTRACTIVE METALLURGY, HIGH TEMPERATURE PROCESSES. *Educ:* McGill Univ, BEng, 56; Univ Toronto, MASc, 65, PhD(metall), 68. *Prof Exp:* Res engr, Int Nickel Co Can, 56-59; develop supvr, DuPont Can Ltd, 59-64; Nat Res Coun Can fel, Max Planck Inst Phys Chem, 68-69; ASSOC PROF CHEM ENG & EXTRACTIVE METALL, UNIV WATERLOO, 69- *Concurrent Pos:* Consult, several companies in metal extraction field. *Mem:* Can Inst Mining & Metall; Chem Inst Can; Can Soc Chem Engrs; Am Inst Mining, Metall & Petrol Engrs. *Res:* Chemistry and mechanisms of high temperature heterogeneous reactions significant in metals extraction; coal combustion and ash fouling; sintering, selective reduction; iron ore pelletizing; silicothermic production of magnesium metal. *Mailing Add:* Dept of Chem Eng Univ of Waterloo Waterloo ON N2L 3G1 Can

WYNSTON, LESLIE K, b San Diego, Calif, Jan 5, 34; m 63. BIOCHEMISTRY. *Educ:* San Diego State Col, BS, 55; Univ Calif, Los Angeles, MS, 58, PhD(physiol chem), 60. *Prof Exp:* Instr biochem, Med Sch, Northwestern Univ, 60-61; lectr, Med Sch, Univ Calif, San Francisco, 61-63; USPHS fel, Max Planck Inst Protein & Leather Res, 63-65; from asst prof to assoc prof chem, 65-75, PROF CHEM, CALIF STATE UNIV, LONG BEACH, 75- *Concurrent Pos:* Supvr, Metab Res Lab, Chicago Wesley Mem Hosp, 60-61; consult, NAm Aviation, Inc, 65-67; vis prof, Univ Zurich, 71-72; exchange prof, Nat Chung Hsing Univ Taiwan, 75-76. *Mem:* AAAS; Am Chem Soc; Soc Wine Educr; NY Acad Sci. *Res:* Protein purification and characterization; chemical isolation procedures; chromatographic and electrophoretic methods. *Mailing Add:* Dept of Chem Calif State Univ Long Beach CA 90840

WYNVEEN, ROBERT ALLEN, b Baldwin, Wis, July 24, 39; m 64; c 4. HEALTH PHYSICS, MEDICAL PHYSICS. *Educ:* Univ Wis-River Falls, BS, 61; Rutgers Univ, MS, 63, PhD(radiation biophysics), 72. *Prof Exp:* Health physicist, Argonne Nat Lab, 63-65; radiol health physicist, Rutgers Med Sch, Rutgers Univ, 65-76; HEALTH PHYSICS MGR, ARGONNE NAT LAB, 76- *Concurrent Pos:* Radiol health physics consult, Colgate-Palmolive Res Ctr, 68-76, Warner-Lambert Res Ctr, 72-76, Ortho Diag & Pharmaceut, Inc, 74-76 & Fusion Energy Corp, 75-76. *Mem:* Am Asn Physicists Med; Nat Health Physics Soc. *Res:* Immediate and transient effects of radiation, especially ionizing, microwave and laser, on biological systems' functions with emphasis on cellular energy production and active transport across membranes. *Mailing Add:* Health Physics Sect OHS Div Argonne Nat Lab 9700 S Cass Ave Argonne IL 60439

WYON, JOHN BENJAMIN, b London, Eng, May 3, 18; m 46; c 2. EPIDEMIOLOGY, DEMOGRAPHY. *Educ:* Cambridge Univ, BA, 40, MB, BCh, 42; Harvard Univ, MPH, 53. *Prof Exp:* Med officer, Friends Ambulance Unit, Ethiopia, 43-45; med missionary to India from Church Missionary Soc, London, 47-52; res assoc epidemiol, 53-58, instr, 58-60, res fel, 60-61, res assoc pop studies, 61-62, asst prof, 62-66, lectr pop studies & sr res assoc, Ctr Pop Studies, 66-71, SR LECTR POP STUDIES, SCH PUB HEALTH, HARVARD UNIV, 71- *Concurrent Pos:* Field dir, India-Harvard-Ludhiana Pop Study & asst prof, Christian Med Col, Ludhiana, India, 53-60. *Mem:* Am Pub Health Asn; fel Royal Soc Med; Int Union Sci Study Pop. *Res:* Population control; internal medicine; field research on births, deaths and migrations in urban United States and in rural developing countries; development of local education units to demonstrate implications of population changes. *Mailing Add:* Dept of Pop Sci 665 Huntington Ave Boston MA 02115

WYRICK, PRISCILLA BLAKENEY, b Greensboro, NC, Apr 28, 40. BACTERIOLOGY. *Educ:* Univ NC, Chapel Hill, BS, 62, MS, 67, PhD(bact), 71. *Prof Exp:* Technician clin microbiol, NC Mem Hosp, 62-64, asst supvr, 64-65, supvr in chg mycol & mycobact, 65-66; asst prof, 73-79, ASSOC PROF BACT, SCH MED, UNIV NC, CHAPEL HILL, 79- *Concurrent Pos:* Med Res Coun fel, Nat Inst Med Res, London, Eng, 71-73; consult, Dept Hosp Labs, NC Mem Hosp, 73- *Mem:* Am Soc Microbiol; Brit Soc Gen Microbiol; Am Acad Microbiol. *Res:* Bacterial L-forms; bacterial ultrastructure; pathogenesis of Chlamydia; medical microbiology. *Mailing Add:* Dept of Bact Univ of NC Sch of Med Chapel Hill NC 27514

WYRICK, RONALD EARL, b Kansas City, Mo, Nov 4, 44; m 66; c 2. BIOCHEMISTRY, ALLERGY. *Educ:* Calif State Col, Stanislaus, BA, 68; Univ Calif, Davis, PhD(biochem), 74. *Prof Exp:* Indust res allergist, 74-81, dir res, 77-81, VPRES SCI AFFAIRS, HOLLISTER-STIER LABS, SUBSID CUTTER LABS, WASH, 81- *Res:* Elucidation of allergy mechanisms to provide research directions for potential new treatments for the allergic condition. *Mailing Add:* Hollister-Stier Labs Box 3145 Terminal Annex Spokane WA 99220

WYRTKI, KLAUS, b Tarnowitz, Ger, Feb 7, 25; m 53; c 2. PHYSICAL OCEANOGRAPHY. *Educ:* Kiel Univ, PhD(phys oceanog), 50. *Prof Exp:* Scientist, Ger Hydrographic Inst, Hamburg, 50-51; res fel oceanog, Kiel Univ, 51-54; scientist, Inst Marine Res, Djakarta, 54-57; scientist, Int Hydrographic Bur, Monaco, 58; res officer, Commonwealth Sci & Indust Res Orgn, Australia, 58-61; res oceanogr, Scripps Inst, Univ Calif, 61-64; PROF OCEANOG, UNIV HAWAII, 64- *Concurrent Pos:* Ed, Atlas Phys Oceanog for Int Indian Ocean Exped, 65-; chmn, NPac Exp, 74- *Honors & Awards:* Rossenstiel Award, Univ Miami, 81. *Mem:* AAAS; Am Geophys Union; Am Meteorol Soc. *Res:* General circulation of the oceans; water masses; equatorial circulation; air-sea energy exchange; ocean-atmosphere interaction. *Mailing Add:* Dept of Oceanog Univ of Hawaii Honolulu HI 96822

WYSE, BENJAMIN DELANEY, b Columbia, SC, July 20, 27; m 52; c 2. ORGANIC CHEMISTRY. *Educ:* Erskine Col, AB, 48; Vanderbilt Univ, MA, 51; Univ SC, PhD(chem), 57. *Prof Exp:* Instr math, Erskine Col, 49-51; chemist, Celanese Corp, SC, 51-53; chemist, Tech Sect, 56-61, SR RES CHEMIST, TECH SECT, E I DU PONT DE NEMOURS & CO, INC, 61- *Mem:* Am Chem Soc. *Res:* Acrylic polymerization processes and reaction mechanisms; isocyanate chemistry; solution and melt spinning processes of elastomers and polyamides. *Mailing Add:* Tech Sect E I du Pont de Nemours & Co Inc Chattanooga TN 37401

WYSE, FRANK OLIVER, b Milwaukee, Wis, Apr 22, 30; m 67; c 3. MATHEMATICS. *Educ:* Harvard Univ, AB, 52; Princeton Univ, AM, 55; Ore State Univ, PhD(math), 64. *Prof Exp:* Instr math, Lehigh Univ, 55-58; from instr to asst prof, Ore State Univ, 58-70; prof & chmn dept, Talladega Col, 70-73; ASSOC PROF MATH, CLARK COL, 73- *Concurrent Pos:* Asst prof, Cleveland State Univ, 66-70. *Mem:* Am Math Soc. *Res:* Algebra; topology. *Mailing Add:* 1611 E Nancy Creek Dr Northeast Atlanta GA 30319

WYSE, GORDON ARTHUR, b San Jose, Calif, July 12, 40; m 63; c 3. ZOOLOGY, NEUROPHYSIOLOGY. *Educ:* Swarthmore Col, BA, 61; Univ Mich, MA, 63, PhD(zool), 67. *Prof Exp:* From instr to asst prof, 66-72, ASSOC PROF ZOOL, UNIV MASS, AMHERST, 72- *Concurrent Pos:* Nat Inst Neurol Dis & Stroke res grant, 69-; vis scholar, Stanford Univ, 72-73. *Mem:* AAAS; Brit Soc Exp Biol; Soc Gen Physiol; Am Soc Zoologists; Am Soc Mammal. *Res:* Comparative neurophysiology; neural integration of central and sensory information to control rhythmic and other behavior patterns; mechanoreception, propioception and chemoreception. *Mailing Add:* Dept of Zool Univ of Mass Amherst MA 01003

WYSE, JOHN PATRICK HENRY, b Kamloops, BC, July 28, 48; m 72; c 4. MEDICAL SCIENCE, ANATOMY. *Educ:* Univ BC, BSc, 71, MD, 75; Univ Calgary, PhD(med sci anat), 78. *Prof Exp:* asst prof, 78-81, ASSOC PROF ANAT, FAC MED, UNIV CALGARY, 81- *Concurrent Pos:* MRC grant, Med Res Coun Can, 78-80; Nat Retinitis Pigmentosa Found Can grant, 78-82; Alberta Mental Health grant & Alberta Heritage Found med res grant, 81; fel, Med Res Coun, 75-78. *Mem:* Asn Res Vision & Opthal; Soc Neurosci; Can Asn Anatomists. *Res:* Histological, functional and genetic investigation of inherited ophthalmic defects in the BW rat; dopamine neurochemisty of retina, hypothalamus and nigrostriatal system of BW rat; morphometric investigations of mechanisms regulating rod outer segment renewal in vertebrate retinae. *Mailing Add:* 3330 Hosp Dr NW Health Sci Ctr Dept Anat Calgary AB T2N 4N1 Can

WYSE, ROGER EARL, b Wauseon, Ohio, Apr 22, 43. PLANT PHYSIOLOGY, BIOCHEMISTRY. *Educ:* Ohio State Univ, BSAgr, 65; Mich State Univ, MS, 67, PhD(crop sci), 69. *Prof Exp:* Fel, Mich State Univ, 69-70; PLANT PHYSIOLOGIST, AGR RES SERV, USDA, 70- *Mem:* AAAS; Am Soc Plant Physiol; Am Soc Agron; Am Soc Crop Sci. *Res:* Physiological limitations to yeild in crop plants; oligosaccharide metabolism and mechanism of sucrose storage in beet roots; biochemical methods of testing for superior breeding lines. *Mailing Add:* USDA Agr Res Serv Crops Res Lab Utah State Univ Logan UT 84321

WYSHAK, GRACE, b Boston, Mass. BIOSTATISTICS. *Educ:* Smith Col, BA, 49; Harvard Univ, MSHyg, 56; Yale Univ, PhD(biomet), 64. *Prof Exp:* Res assoc epidemiol, Harvard Univ, 56-60; instr math, Albertus Magnus Col, 64-65; ASSOC PROF BIOMET, YALE UNIV, 65- *Concurrent Pos:* NIH res career develop award, 68-72; consult, NIH, 70-, Vet Admin Coop Studies Ctr, 72- & Radcliffe Inst Prog Health Care, 75. *Mem:* Sigma Xi; Am Statist Asn; Biomet Soc; Am Epidemiol Asn; Int Epidemiol Asn. *Res:* Inheritance of twinning; biometric and epidemiologic methods; statistical methods in virology; statistical applications in psychiatry. *Mailing Add:* 32 Commonwealth Ave Chestnut Hill MA 02167

WYSKIDA, RICHARD MARTIN, b Perrysburg, NY, Sept 2, 35; m 62; c 2. INDUSTRIAL ENGINEERING, OPERATIONS RESEARCH. *Educ:* Tri-State Col, BS, 60; Univ Ala, Tuscaloosa, MS, 64; Okla State Univ, PhD(indust eng), 68. *Prof Exp:* Elec engr, Philco Corp, 60-62; aerospace technol, Marshall Space Flight Ctr, NASA, 62-68; from asst prof to assoc prof, 68-78, PROF INDUST ENG, UNIV ALA, HUNTSVILLE, 78- *Concurrent Pos:* Consult, Gen Res Corp, Revere, Missile Command, Battelle Mem Inst & Mantech; part-time assoc prof, Ala A&M Univ, 71-76. *Mem:* Am Inst Indust Engrs; Opers Res Soc Am; Am Soc Eng Educ; Inst Mgt Sci. *Res:* Temperature sensitive cushioning systems; routing models; cost estimation models. *Mailing Add:* Dept of Indust & Syst Eng Univ of Ala Huntsville AL 35807

WYSOCKI, ALLEN JOHN, b Chicago, Ill, Dec 22, 36; m 63; c 2. INDUSTRIAL ORGANIC CHEMISTRY. *Educ:* Loyola Univ Chicago, BS, 58; Northwestern Univ, Evanston, PhD(org chem), 63. *Prof Exp:* Res chemist, IIT-Res Inst, 62-64; div res mgr, Soap & Household Prod Div, Armour-Dial, Inc, Phoenix, 64-77; TECH MGR, CHEM PROD DIV, DE SOTO, INC, 77- *Mem:* Am Chem Soc. *Res:* Development of detergents and other household products. *Mailing Add:* 715 E Cherry Lane Arlington Heights IL 60004

WYSOCKI, CHARLES JOSEPH, b Utica, NY, May 4, 47; m 68; c 2. REPRODUCTION, CHEMORECEPTION. *Educ:* Col Oswego, State Univ NY, BA, 73; Fla State Univ, Tallahasse, MS, 76, PhD(psychobiol), 78. *Prof Exp:* Fel vomeronasal organ & reproduction, 78-79, ASST MEM GENES & REPRODUCTION, MONELL CHEM SENSES CTR, UNIV PA, 80- *Concurrent Pos:* Lectr, Dept Biol, Univ Pa, 78-; asst prof, Dept Psychol, Rutgers Univ, 79-80. *Mem:* Asn Chemoreception Sci; Behav Genetics Asn; NY Acad Sci; Sigma Xi; Soc Neurosci. *Res:* Role of genetics in individual differences in odor perception; regulation of reproductive physiology and behavior by odors. *Mailing Add:* Monell Chem Senses Ctr Univ Pa 3500 Market St Philadelphia PA 19104

WYSOCKI, JOSEPH J(OHN), b Cohoes, NY, Aug 6, 28; m 57; c 3. ELECTRICAL ENGINEERING. *Educ:* Mass Inst Technol, BS & MS, 54. *Prof Exp:* Trainee, Naval Ord Lab, 51-54; res engr, RCA Labs, 54-67; SR SCIENTIST, SOLID STATE RES, XEROX CORP, 67- *Concurrent Pos:* Instr, Trenton Jr Col, 60-62. *Mem:* Inst Elec & Electronics Engrs. *Res:* Semiconductor and solar cell devices; transistors; diodes; radiation damage to solar cells; lithium-doped, radiation-resistant solar cells; liquid crystals; display devices; thin-film transistors; fabrication; testing and evaluation of solid-state devices of various types. *Mailing Add:* 544 Crest Circle Webster NY 14580

WYSOLMERSKI, THERESA, b West Rutland, Vt, Oct 25, 32. ZOOLOGY, ECOLOGY. *Educ:* Col St Rose, BS, 59; Univ Notre Dame, MS, 61; Rutgers Univ, New Brunswick, PhD(zool, ecol), 73. *Prof Exp:* Teacher, St John's Cath Acad, 56-59; instr chem, 59-60, asst prof biol, 61-66, ASSOC PROF BIOL, COL ST ROSE, 66- *Concurrent Pos:* Col rep, Hudson Valley Mohawk League Consortium, 69-70. *Mem:* Ecol Soc Am; Am Inst Biol Sci; Sigma Xi. *Res:* Distribution of animal populations and their energy impact on forest floors. *Mailing Add:* Col of St Rose Div Natural Sci 432 Western Ave Albany NY 12203

WYSONG, DAVID SERGE, b Glasgow, Ky, Apr 20, 34; m 58; c 5. PLANT PATHOLOGY. *Educ:* Colo State Univ, BS, 58, MS, 61; Univ Ill, PhD(plant path), 64. *Prof Exp:* ASSOC PROF PLANT PATH & EXTEN PLANT PATHOLOGIST, UNIV NEBR-LINCOLN, 64- *Mem:* Am Phytopath Soc. *Res:* Practical application of plant pathology. *Mailing Add:* 820 E Sanborn Dr Lincoln NE 68505

WYSS, MAX, b Zurich, Switz, Sept 10, 39; m 70; c 2. SEISMOLOGY. *Educ:* Swiss Fed Inst Technol, dipl, 64; Calif Inst Technol, MS, 68, PhD(geophysics), 70. *Prof Exp:* Res scientist geophysics, Univ Calif, San Diego, 70; res scientist seismology, Lamont-Doherty Geol Observ, Columbia Univ, 70-72, res assoc, 72-73; asst prof, 73-75, ASSOC PROF GEOL, UNIV COLO BOULDER, 75- *Concurrent Pos:* Ed, Pure & Appl Geophysics, 74; vis prof geophysics, Univ Karlsruhe, Ger, 75, Fed Inst Technol, Zuerick, 79. *Mem:* Am Geophys Union; Seismol Soc Am; Geol Soc Am. *Res:* Earthquake source mechanism; earthquake predictions; seismic risk. *Mailing Add:* Boulder CO

WYSS, ORVILLE, b Medford, Wis, Sept 10, 12; m 41; c 3. MICROBIOLOGY. *Educ:* Univ Wis, BS, 37, MS, 38, PhD(bact), 41. *Prof Exp:* Asst bact, Univ Wis, 37-41; res bacteriologist, Wallace & Teirnan Prod, 41-45; assoc prof bact, 45-48, chmn dept microbiol, 59-69, 75-76, PROF MICROBIOL, UNIV TEX, AUSTIN, 48- *Concurrent Pos:* Fulbright grant, Univ Sydney, 71; Tribhuvan Univ, Nepal, 78. *Mem:* AAAS; Am Chem Soc; Am Soc Microbiol (pres, 65); Am Soc Biol Chemists; Am Acad Microbiol. *Res:* Bacterial physiology and genetics; microbial survival. *Mailing Add:* Dept of Microbiol Univ of Tex Austin TX 78712

WYSS, WALTER, b Matzendorf, Switz, Mar 26, 38; m 61; c 4. MATHEMATICS, PHYSICS. *Educ:* Swiss Fed Inst Technol, dipl phys, 61, Dr Sc Nat(math physics), 65. *Prof Exp:* Instr physics, Swiss Fed Inst Technol, 61-66; instr, Princeton Univ, 66-68; from asst prof to assoc prof math & physics, 68-77, PROF PHYS, UNIV COLO, BOULDER, 77- *Concurrent Pos:* Swiss Nat Found stipend, Princeton Univ, 66-68; res fel, Univ Colo, Boulder, 69-70, NSF res grant, 70-72. *Mem:* Am Math Soc; Int Asn Math Phys; Sigma Xi. *Res:* Axiomatic theory of quantized fields; general relativity; functional analysis; infinite parameter lie groups; stochastic processes and combinatorics. *Mailing Add:* 2810 Iliff Boulder CO 80303

WYSSBROD, HERMAN ROBERT, b Louisville, Ky, Oct 17, 41; m 63. PHYSIOLOGY, BIOPHYSICS. *Educ:* Univ Louisville, BEE, 63, PhD(physiol), 68. *Prof Exp:* Asst prof physiol, 72-73, ASSOC PROF PHYSIOL & BIOPHYS, MT SINAI SCH MED, 74- *Concurrent Pos:* NIH res career develop award, Mt Sinai Sch Med, 72-77; asst prof biophys chem, Mt Sinai Grad Sch Biol Sci, City Univ New York, 68-73; vis asst prof, Rockefeller Univ, 71-73, vis assoc prof, 74-78; investr, NY Heart Asn, 77-81. *Mem:* AAAS; Am Physiol Soc; Am Chem Soc; Soc Exp Biol & Med; NY Acad Sci. *Res:* Conformation-function relationships of biologically active peptides; transmembrane transport. *Mailing Add:* Dept of Physiol & Biophys Mt Sinai Sch of Med New York NY 10029

WYSTRACH, VERNON PAUL, b St Paul, Minn, May 8, 19; m 49; c 4. ORGANIC CHEMISTRY. *Educ:* Univ Minn, BCh, 41; Univ Rochester, PhD(org chem), 44. *Prof Exp:* Res chemist, Am Cyanamid Co, 44-52, group leader, Res Div, 52-54, group leader, Basic Res Dept, 54-59, mgr chem synthesis sect, Contract Res Dept, 59-66, mgr appl res sect, 66-67, mgr prod res sect, Chem Dept, Cent Res Div, 67-72, prof mgr, Prod Develop Dept, Chem Res Div, 72-74, employment supvr, 74-81; RETIRED. *Concurrent Pos:* Am Cyanamid Co grant, Univ Cambridge, 61-62; adj assoc prof chem, Sacred Heart Univ, 81- *Res:* Cyanamide derivatives and nitrogen heterocycles; organic phosphorus compounds; rocket propellants and explosives; chemistry of adhesion; fire retardants. *Mailing Add:* 20 Westfield Rd Wilton CT 06897

WYSZECKI, GUNTER, b Tilsit, Ger, Nov 8, 25; Can citizen; m 54; c 2. PHYSICS, MATHEMATICS. *Educ:* Tech Univ Berlin, Dipl Ing, 51, Dr Ing(math), 53. *Prof Exp:* Fulbright scholar, Nat Bur Standards, DC, 53-54; physicist, Fed Inst Mat Test, Ger, 54-55; prin res officer, 55-80, ASST DIR, PHYSICS DIV & HEAD, OPTICS SECT, NAT RES COUN CAN, 80- *Concurrent Pos:* Chmn colorimetry comt, Int Comn Illum, 63-75; adj prof, Sch Optom, Fac Sci, Univ Waterloo, 69- *Honors & Awards:* Gold Medal, Asn Int de la Couleur, 79; Godlove Award, Inter-Soc Color Coun, 79; Bruning Award, Fedn Soc Coatings Technol, 79. *Mem:* Fel Optical Soc Am; fel Illum Eng Soc. *Res:* Colorimetry; photometry; color vision. *Mailing Add:* Div Physics Nat Res Coun Ottawa ON K1A 0R6 Can

WYTTENBACH, CHARLES RICHARD, b South Bend, Ind, Jan 28, 33; m 59; c 3. DEVELOPMENTAL BIOLOGY. *Educ:* Ind Univ, AB, 54, MA, 56; Johns Hopkins Univ, PhD(biol), 59. *Prof Exp:* From instr to asst prof anat, Univ Chicago, 59-66; asst prof zool, 66-70, assoc prof physiol & cell biol, 70-75, PROF PHYSIOL & CELL BIOL, UNIV KANS, 75-, CHMN DEPT, 76- *Concurrent Pos:* Managing ed, Univ Kans Sci Bull, 68-74; mem corp, Marine Biol Lab, Woods Hole, Mass. *Mem:* Soc Develop Biol; Am Soc Zoologists. *Res:* Developmental biology, particularly insecticide-induced teratogenesis in chicks; growth and morphogenesis in colonial hydroids. *Mailing Add:* Dept Physiol & Cell Biol Univ Kans Lawrence KS 66045

WYZGA, RONALD EDWARD, b New Bedford, Mass, Aug 10, 42; m 69; c 2. PUBLIC HEALTH. *Educ:* Harvard Col, AB, 64; Fla State Univ, MS, 66; Harvard Univ, ScD, 71. *Prof Exp:* Tech staff, Orgn Econ Coop & Develop, 71-75; prog mgr, 76, PROJ MGR, ELEC POWER RES INST, 75-, TECH MGR, 77- *Concurrent Pos:* Lectr, Am Col, Paris, 73-75. *Mem:* Am Statist Asn; Biomet Soc; Soc Risk Assessment. *Res:* Environmental risk assessment; health effects of air pollution; environmental cost-benefit analyses. *Mailing Add:* 4690 Smith Grade Santa Cruz CA 95060

WYZGOSKI, MICHAEL GARY, b Pontiac, Mich, Dec 25, 43; m 67; c 3. POLYMER SCIENCE, MATERIALS ENGINEERING. *Educ:* Oakland Univ, BS, 64; Univ Mich, MS, 70, PhD(mat eng), 73. *Prof Exp:* Plastics engr, Dow Chem Co, 66-68; RES ENGR, GEN MOTORS RES LAB, 73- *Mem:* Am Phys Soc; Am Chem Soc. *Res:* Durability of plastic and elastomeric materials, including oxidative and physical aging, stress cracking and ozone cracking. *Mailing Add:* Polymers Dept 12 Mile & Mound Rds Warren MI 48090

X

XINTARAS, CHARLES, b New Bedford, Mass, Sept 5, 28; m 57; c 2. INDUSTRIAL HEALTH. *Educ:* Harvard Univ, AB, 52; Univ Cincinnati, ScD(indust health), 64. *Prof Exp:* Res chemist, Filtrol Corp, 52-55; eng inspector, Los Angeles County, 55-59; pub health adv, USPHS, 59-62, pharmacologist brain res, 62-74, asst chief, Behav Motivation Factors Br, 71-76, chief, Support Serv Br, Nat Inst Occup Safety & Health, 76-80; SCIENTIST OCCUP MED, WHO, GENEVA, 81- *Concurrent Pos:* Consult behav toxicol, WHO; mem, Permanent Comn & Int Asn Occup Health, Soc Neurosci. *Res:* Behavioral toxicology; behavioral and neurophysiological indicators for the monitoring and early detection of potential industrial health and safety problems. *Mailing Add:* Occup Health/WHO 1211 Geneva 27 Switzerland

Y

YABLON, ISADORE GERALD, b Montreal, Que, May 30, 33; m 62; c 2. ORTHOPEDIC SURGERY. *Educ:* McGill Univ, BSc, 54; Univ Toronto, MD, 58. *Prof Exp:* Instr orthop, McGill Univ, 67-71; from asst prof to assoc prof, 71-78, PROF ORTHOP SURG, BOSTON UNIV SCH MED, 78- *Concurrent Pos:* Vis surgeon orthop, Univ Hosp, 71- & Boston City Hosp, 71- *Mem:* Am Acad Orthop Surg; Orthop Res Soc; Can Orthop Soc; Can Orthop Res Soc; fel Royal Col Physicians & Surgeons Can. *Res:* Developing technique of joint homografting for clinical application; methods to prevent graft rejection. *Mailing Add:* Univ Hosp 75 E Newton St Boston MA 02118

YABLON, MARVIN, b New York, NY, Oct 30, 35; m 68; c 2. APPLIED STATISTICS, PATTERN RECOGNITION. *Educ:* New York Univ, BEE, 57, MEE, 60, MS, 64, PhD(operatons res), 77. *Prof Exp:* Res engr, Grumman Corp, 62-69; operations res analyst, Roosevelt Hosp, 73-76; statistician, Med Ctr, New York Univ, 76-78; asst prof, 78-82, ASSOC PROF MATH, JOHN JAY COL, 82- *Concurrent Pos:* Consult, Med Ctr, New York Univ, 78- *Mem:* Sigma Xi; Am Statistical Asn; Inst Elec & Electronics Engrs; Operations Res Soc Am; Soc Indust & Appl Math. *Res:* Pattern recognition; applied statistics; stochastic processes; applications of operations research. *Mailing Add:* 35-17 172 St Flushing NY 11358

YABLONOVITCH, ELI, b Puch, Austria, Dec 15, 46; Can citizen. OPTICS, PHYSICAL CHEMISTRY. *Educ:* McGill Univ, BSc, 67; Harvard Univ, AM, 69, PhD(appl physics), 72. *Prof Exp:* Mem tech staff, Bell Labs, 72-74; asst prof appl physics, Harvard Univ, 74-76, assoc, 76-79; RES ASSOC, EXXON RES CTR, 79- *Honors & Awards:* Adolph Lomb Medal, Optical Soc Am, 78. *Mem:* Am Phys Soc; Am Chem Soc; Optical Soc Am; Inst Elec & Electronics Engrs. *Res:* Nonlinear optics; laser-plasma interaction; laser induced chemistry. *Mailing Add:* Exxon Res Ctr PO Box 45 Linden NJ 07036

YABLONSKI, MICHAEL EUGENE, b Minneapolis, Minn, July 11, 40; m 62; c 4. MEDICINE, PHYSIOLOGY. *Educ:* Univ Minn, BS, 65, MD, 67, PhD(physiol), 73. *Prof Exp:* Intern surg, Albert Einstein Col Med, 68; resident physician, Naval Air Develop Ctr, 71-73; resident ophthal, Univ Minn Hosps, 73-76; RES OPHTHAL MT SINAI SCH MED, 77- *Concurrent Pos:* Glaucoma fel, Wash Univ, St Louis, 76-77. *Res:* Transport physiology; transcapillary exchange; physiology of the eye and vision. *Mailing Add:* 1635 Hanover St Teaneck NJ 07666

YABLONSKY, HARVEY ALLEN, b New York, NY, Nov 24, 33; m 64; c 2. PHYSICAL CHEMISTRY. *Educ:* Brooklyn Col, BS, 54, MA, 58; Stevens Inst Technol, MS, 57, PhD(phys chem), 64; Am Inst Chem, cert. *Prof Exp:* Res chemist, NY State Dept Health, 55; lectr chem, Brooklyn Col, 55-56; teaching asst, Stevens Inst Technol, 56-59; lectr, Hunter Col, 60-63; asst prof, US Merchant Marine Acad, 63-64; head dept phys chem, Bristol Myers Prod Div, 64-69; PROF CHEM, DEPT PHYS SCI, KINGSBOROUGH COL, 69- *Concurrent Pos:* Res biochemist, Messinger Res Found, 56-58; lectr, Hunter Col, 63-64 & Rutgers Univ, 67-69; independent consult. *Mem:* Am Chem Soc; fel Am Inst Chem. *Res:* Kinetics of redox systems; structure of solutions; sorption at surfaces; complex ion chemistry; fiber and powder rheology; piezoelectricity of biological materials; nonuniform surface photometry; pharmacokinetics. *Mailing Add:* Dept of Phys Sci Kingsborough Col Brooklyn NY 11235

YABROFF, RONALD M, b Berkeley, Calif, Apr 24, 37; m 63; c 3. CHEMICAL ENGINEERING. *Educ:* Univ Colo, BS, 59; Cornell Univ, PhD(chem eng), 64. *Prof Exp:* Res engr, 64-70, patent specialist, 70-71, spec assignment mkt, 71-72, develop engr, Elastomers Dept, Deepwater, NJ, 72-77, develop engr, Elastomers Dept, Ky, 78-80, STAFF ENGR, POLYMER PROD DEPT, E I DU PONT DE NEMOURS & CO, INC, 80- *Mem:* Am Inst Chem Engrs. *Res:* Expression of fluids from fluid-solid combinations; formation of microporous polymeric structures; isocynate manufacture; polychloroprene manufacture; kinetics. *Mailing Add:* Polymer Prod Dept E I Du Pont de Nemours & Co Inc Louisville KY 40211

YACHNIN, STANLEY, b New York, NY, June 28, 30; m 60; c 2. INTERNAL MEDICINE, HEMATOLOGY. *Educ:* NY Univ, MD, 54; Am Bd Internal Med, dipl, 62. *Prof Exp:* House officer, Peter Bent Brigham Hosp, Boston, Mass, 54-55, jr asst resident med, 55-56, sr resident, 60-61; from asst prof to assoc prof, 61-69, head, Sect Hemat-Oncol, 66-81, PROF MED, SCH MED, UNIV CHICAGO, 69- *Concurrent Pos:* USPHS res fel, Peter Bent Brigham Hosp & Harvard Med Sch, 58-60; Markle scholar acad med, 63-68. *Mem:* AAAS; Am Soc Clin Invest; Am Fedn Clin Res; Am Soc Hemat; Asn Am Physicians. *Res:* Hemolytic anemias; complement; lymphocyte transformation; mitogenic proteins; paroxysmal nocturnal hemoglobinuria; alpha feto protein; cholesterol metabolism and cell growth. *Mailing Add:* Dept Med Univ Chicago Sch Med Chicago IL 60637

YACKEL, JAMES W, b Sanborn, Minn, Mar 6, 36; m 60; c 3. MATHEMATICS. *Educ:* Univ Minn, BA, 58, MA, 60, PhD(math), 64. *Prof Exp:* John Wesley Young res instr math, Dartmouth Col, 64-66; from asst prof to assoc prof, 66-76, PROF & ASSOC DEAN SCI, PURDUE UNIV, 76- *Mem:* Am Math Soc; AAAS; Inst Math Statist; Math Asn Am. *Res:* Stochastics processes and graph theory; probability theory; combinatorial theory. *Mailing Add:* Sci Admin Purdue Univ West Lafayette IN 47907

YACOE, J CRAIG, b Chicago, Ill, Aug 26, 20; m 43; c 4. CHEMICAL ENGINEERING. *Educ:* Univ Ill, BS, 41. *Prof Exp:* Supvr prod, Chambers Works, E I du Pont de Nemours & Co Inc, 41-48, chief supvr develop, 48-55, supt plant tech sect, 55-60, eng mgr res & develop, Jackson Lab, 60-66, asst mgr, Freon Prod Sales, 66-68, mgr food systs venture, 68-70, mgr diversification studies res & develop, 70-72, mgr, Int Dept, 72-77, mgr plan develop, 77-80. *Mem:* Am Chem Soc; Am Inst Chem Engrs. *Res:* Fluorinated hydrocarbons; organic chemicals; heavy chemicals and tetraethyl lead; fluidized solids; filtration; reaction design; food freezing. *Mailing Add:* Harvey Lane Chadds Ford PA 19317

YACOUB, KAMAL, b Nazareth, Palestine, Nov 11, 32; US citizen; m 64. ELECTRICAL ENGINEERING. *Educ:* Univ Pa, MSEE, 58, PhD(elec eng), 61. *Prof Exp:* Assoc elec eng, Moore Sch Elec Eng, Univ Pa, 61-63, asst prof, 63-66; from asst prof to assoc prof, 66-73, chmn dept, 72-76, PROF ELEC ENG, UNIV MIAMI, 73- *Honors & Awards:* Res Award, Am Soc Eng Educ. *Mem:* Inst Elec & Electronics Engrs; Am Soc Eng Educ. *Res:* Acoustic transmission fluctuations in Florida straits; tidal modulation of environmental and acoustic parameters; spectral analysis and modelling of relationships; relationship between partial and multiple coherence functions; estimation through order statistics; time series analysis. *Mailing Add:* Dept of Elec Eng PO Box 8294 Coral Gables FL 33124

YACOWITZ, HAROLD, b New York, NY, Feb 17, 22; m 41; c 3. NUTRITION. *Educ:* Cornell Univ, BS, 47, MNS, 48, PhD(animal nutrit), 50. *Prof Exp:* Assoc res biochemist, Parke, Davis & Co, 50-51; from asst prof to assoc prof poultry nutrit, Ohio State Univ, 51-55, assoc prof, Agr Exp Sta, 51-55; head nutrit res dept, Squibb Inst Med Res, 55-59; dir appl res, Nopco Chem Co, 59-61; RES ASSOC, FAIRLEIGH DICKINSON UNIV, 61- *Concurrent Pos:* Nutrit consult, 61-; owner, H Yacowitz & Co, nutrit assay & consult lab. *Mem:* Am Chem Soc; NY Acad Sci; Poultry Sci Asn; Am Soc Animal Sci; Am Inst Nutrit. *Res:* Vitamin B-12 microbiological assays; vitamin interrelationships; antibiotic absorption and effects of dietary antibiotics on chicks and hens; vitamin requirements; antifungal agents; calcium and fat metabolism in man and animals; atherosclerosis; nutritional value of human and animal foods; marine sources of animal protein. *Mailing Add:* 221 Second Ave Piscataway NJ 08854

YADAV, KAMALESHWARI PRASAD, b Burhiatikar, India, Jan 5, 37; m 57; c 2. ANALYTICAL BIOCHEMISTRY. *Educ:* Univ Bihar, BSc, 59; Univ Mo, MS, 61, PhD(biochem), 66. *Prof Exp:* Instr animal husb, Ranchi Agr Col, Bihar, 59-61; res asst agr chem, Univ Mo, 62-66; res biochemist, Falstaff Brewing Corp, 66-70, sr biochemist, 70-74; PRES, CHEMCO INDUSTS, INC, 74- *Mem:* Am Soc Brewing Chemists. *Res:* Brewing and fermentation. *Mailing Add:* 5122 Birch Hollow St Louis MO 63129

YADAV, RAGHUNATH P, b Kanpur, India, Jan 2, 35; m 64; c 2. ENTOMOLOGY. *Educ:* Agra Univ, BS, 56, MS, 58; La State Univ, PhD(entom), 64. *Prof Exp:* From asst prof to assoc prof entom, 64-74, ASSOC PROF BIOL, SOUTHERN UNIV, BATON ROUGE, 74- *Mem:* Entom Soc Am. *Res:* Artificial diet media for rearing of sugarcane borer; laboratory techniques for the detection of sugarcane borer resistance to insecticides; response of sweet corn hybrids to corn earworm damage in southern central Louisiana; possible antibiosis in sweet corn hybrids to corn earworm. *Mailing Add:* Dept of Biol Sci Southern Univ Baton Rouge LA 70813

YADAVALLI, SRIRAMAMURTI VENKATA, b Secunderabad, India, May 12, 24; US citizen; m 52. PHYSICS, ELECTRICAL ENGINEERING. *Educ:* Andhra Univ, India, BS, 42, MS, 45; Univ Calif, MS, 49, PhD(elec eng), 53. *Prof Exp:* Officer in charge, Physics & Chem Labs, Eng Res Dept, Hyderabad, India, 46-48; asst elec eng, Univ Calif, 49-52, lectr, 52, res engr, 59; physicist, Stanford Res Inst, 59-67, staff scientist, 67-68, staff scientist eng sci, 68-77; DIR RES, SHASTRA INC, 77- *Concurrent Pos:* Lectr, Exten, Univ Calif, 57-58; consult, Raytheon Co, 59-62, Litton Indust, 62-64, McGraw Hill Book Co, 62-70 & Rand Corp, 71- *Mem:* AAAS; Inst Elec & Electronic Eng; Am Inst Aeronaut & Astronaut; Am Phys Soc; NY Acad Sci. *Res:* Stochastic processes; electron and plasma physics; statistical and mathematical physics; electrohydrodynamics; optics; biomathematics. *Mailing Add:* Shastra Inc PO Box 1231 Palo Alto CA 94302

YADEN, SENKALONG, b Nagaland, India, Apr 21, 35. ZOOLOGY. *Educ:* Wilson Col, Bombay, India, BSc, 56; Univ Bombay, MSc, 58; Univ Minn, PhD(zool), 65. *Prof Exp:* Assoc prof, 67-80, PROF BIOL, JARVIS CHRISTIAN COL, 80- *Mem:* AAAS; NY Acad Sci; Am Inst Biol Sci. *Res:* Ecology of freshwater organisms. *Mailing Add:* Dept of Biol Jarvis Christian Col US Hwy 80 Hawkins TX 75765

YAEGER, JAMES AMOS, b Chicago, Ill, Aug 10, 28; m 52; c 4. HISTOLOGY. *Educ:* Ind Univ, DDS, 52, MS, 55; Univ Ill, PhD(anat), 59. *Prof Exp:* Instr anat & clin dent, 55-57; from asst prof to prof histol & head dept, Col Dent, Univ Ill, Chicago, 59-68; head dept, 68-78, PROF ORAL BIOL, SCH DENT MED, UNIV CONN, 68- *Concurrent Pos:* Resident assoc, Argonne Nat Lab, 63-64. *Mem:* Am Soc Cell Biol; Am Asn Anat; Int Asn Dent Res. *Res:* Physiology of mastication. *Mailing Add:* Dept of Oral Biol Univ of Conn Health Ctr Farmington CT 06032

YAEGER, ROBERT GEORGE, b Rochester, NY, Oct 25, 17; m 53; c 3. PARASITOLOGY. *Educ:* Univ Rochester, AB, 50; Univ Tex, MA, 52; Tulane Univ, PhD(parasitol, biochem), 55. *Prof Exp:* Instr bact & parasitol, Med Sch, Univ Tex, 52-54; from instr to assoc prof, 55-70, PROF PARASITOL & MED, SCH MED, TULANE UNIV, 70- *Concurrent Pos:* Vis prof, Sch Med, St George Univ, 79- *Mem:* Am Soc Parasitol; Am Soc Trop Med & Hyg; Soc Exp Biol & Med; Am Inst Nutrit; Soc Protozool. *Res:* Nutritional and immunological relationships of host and parasite; culture methods; Chagas' disease; other parasitic protozoa which infect man. *Mailing Add:* Dept of Trop Med Tulane Med Ctr New Orleans LA 70112

YAFET, YAKO, b Istanbul, Turkey, Jan 2, 23; nat US; m 49; c 3. SOLID STATE PHYSICS. *Educ:* Tech Univ Istanbul, ME, 45; Univ Calif, PhD(physics), 52. *Prof Exp:* Res assoc physics, Univ Ill, 52-54; physicist, Westinghouse Elec Corp Res Labs, 54-60; MEM TECH STAFF, BELL TEL LABS, INC, 60- *Mem:* Fel Am Phys Soc. *Res:* Electronic properties of semiconductors and metals; theoretical solid state physics. *Mailing Add:* Bell Tel Labs Inc PO Box 261 Rm 1d-334 Murray Hill NJ 07974

YAFFE, LEO, b US, July 6, 16; Can citizen; m 45; c 2. RADIOCHEMISTRY. *Educ:* Univ Man, BSc, 40, MSc, 41; McGill Univ, PhD, 43. *Hon Degrees:* DLett, Trent Univ. *Prof Exp:* Proj leader nuclear chem & tracer res, Atomic Energy Can, Ltd, 43-52; spec lectr radiochem, 52-54, assoc prof, 54-58, chmn dept chem, 65-72, vprin admin & prof fac, 74-81, MACDONALD PROF CHEM, MCGILL UNIV, 58- *Concurrent Pos:* Dir res, Int Atomic Energy Agency, Vienna, Austria, 63-65; res collabr, Brookhaven Nat Lab. *Mem:* Fel AAAS; fel Chem Inst Can; fel Royal Soc Can. *Res:* Nuclear chemistry; fission studies; chemistry applied to archaeology. *Mailing Add:* Dept of Chem McGill Univ Montreal PQ H3A 2K6 Can

YAFFE, ROBERTA, b Chelsea, Mass, Jan 2, 44. ORGANIC CHEMISTRY. *Educ:* Bryn Mawr Col, AB, 65; Mass Inst Technol, PhD(chem), 70. *Prof Exp:* Teaching asst org chem, Mass Inst Technol, 65-66; sr chemist, 69-75, res chemist, 75-81, PETROLEUM PROD RES, BEACON RES LABS, TEXACO, INC, 81- *Mem:* Am Chem Soc; Sigma Xi. *Res:* Non-crankcase automotive lubricants; aircraft lubricants; tractor transmission-differential-hydraulic lubricants. *Mailing Add:* Texaco Beacon Res Labs PO Box 509 Beacon NY 12508

YAFFE, RUTH POWERS, b Duluth, Minn, June 4, 27; m 76; c 2. RADIOCHEMISTRY. *Educ:* Macalester Col, BA, 48, PhD(phys chem), 51. *Prof Exp:* AEC fel radiochem, Ames Lab, 51-52; chemist, Oak Ridge Nat Lab, 52-53; instr chem, Univ Tenn, 55-56; from asst prof to assoc prof, 57-66, PROF CHEM, SAN JOSE STATE UNIV, 66-, COORDR NUCLEAR SCI FACIL, 72- *Concurrent Pos:* Consult radiation safety training, 80- *Mem:* Am Nuclear Soc; Am Chem Soc; Health Physics Soc. *Res:* Chemistry of ruthenium; environmental soil and water analysis for radionuclides; fast radiochemistry, nuclear spectroscopy. *Mailing Add:* Dept of Chem San Jose State Univ San Jose CA 95192

YAFFE, SUMNER J, b Boston, Mass, May 9, 23; c 4. PEDIATRICS, PHARMACOLOGY. *Educ:* Harvard Univ, AB, 45, MA, 50; Univ Vt, MD, 54; Am Bd Pediat, dipl, 60. *Prof Exp:* From intern to sr asst resident, Children's Hosp, Boston, 54-56; exchange resident, St Mary's Hosp, London, Eng, 56-57; from instr to asst prof pediat, Stanford Univ, 59-63; assoc prof, State Univ NY Buffalo, 63-66, prof pediat, 66-75, assoc chmn dept, 69-75; PROF PEDIAT & PHARMACOL, UNIV PA, 75-; HEAD DIV CLIN PHARMACOL, CHILDREN'S HOSP PHILADELPHIA, 75- *Concurrent Pos:* Res fel metab, Children's Hosp, Boston, 57-59; teaching fel pediat, Harvard Med Sch, 56; Fulbright scholar, St Mary's Hosp, London, Eng, 56-57; Am Heart Asn adv res fel, 60; Lederle med fac award, 62; attend pediatrician, Palo Alto-Stanford Hosp, 59, dir newborn nursery serv, 60, prof dir clin res ctr premature infants, 62; dir pediat renal clin, Stanford Med Ctr, 60; attend pediatrician, Children's Hosp, Buffalo, 63-75; prog dir, Clin Res Ctr for Children, 63; prog consult, Nat Inst Child Health & Human Develop, 63, mem training grant comt, 63, mem reprod biol comt, 65; on leave, Dept Pharmacol, Karolinska Inst, Stockholm, Sweden, 69-70; Jose Albert mem lectr, 81; fel, Japan Soc Prom Sci. *Mem:* Soc Pediat Res; Am Acad Pediat; Am Soc Clin Pharmacol & Therapeut; Am Pediat Soc; Am Soc Pharmacol & Exp Therapeut. *Res:* Pediatric clinical pharmacology; neonatal, perinatal, fetal and pediatric pharmacology; developmental pharmacology; drug metabolism; drug disposition in sick infants and children; bilirubin metabolism and binding albumin; drug effects upon the mother, fetus and infant. *Mailing Add:* Nat Inst Child Health & Human Develop Landow Bldg Rm 7C 03 7910 Woodmont Ave Bethesda MD 20205

YAGER, BILLY JOE, b Cameron, Tex, Dec 16, 32; m 53; c 4. PHYSICAL ORGANIC CHEMISTRY. *Educ:* Southwest Tex State Col, BS, 53; Tex A&M Univ, MS, 60, PhD(chem), 62. *Prof Exp:* Instr chem, Tex A&M Univ, 61-62; from asst prof to assoc prof, 62-71, PROF CHEM, SOUTHWEST TEX STATE UNIV, 71-, CHMN DEPT, 75- *Mem:* Am Chem Soc. *Res:* Solvent effects upon saponification rate constants; effect of solvent composition upon activity of reactants. *Mailing Add:* Dept of Chem Southwest Tex State Univ San Marcos TX 78666

YAGER, JAMES DONALD, JR, b Milwaukee, Wis, Dec 29, 43; m 68; c 1. CELL BIOLOGY, CHEMICAL CARCINOGENESIS. *Educ:* Marquette Univ, BS, 65; Univ Conn, PhD(develop biol), 71. *Prof Exp:* asst prof biol sci, Dartmouth Col, 74-77, ASST PROF PATH, DARTMOUTH MED SCH, 77- *Concurrent Pos:* Nat Cancer Inst fel oncol, McArdle Lab Cancer Res, Med Ctr, Univ Wis-Madison, 71-74; Nat Cancer Inst grant, 75-; Milheim Found res grant, 75. *Mem:* AAAS; Am Asn Cancer Res; Am Soc Cell Biologists; Sigma Xi. *Res:* Oncology. *Mailing Add:* Dept of Path Dartmouth Med Sch Hanover NH 03755

YAGER, PHILIP MARVIN, b Los Angeles, Calif, Aug 5, 38; m 73; c 2. EXPERIMENTAL HIGH ENERGY PHYSICS. *Educ:* Univ Calif, Berkeley, BA, 61; Univ Calif, San Diego, MS, 64, PhD(physics), 71. *Prof Exp:* From lectr to assoc prof, 68-75, PROF PHYSICS, UNIV CALIF, DAVIS, 81- *Mem:* AAAS; Am Phys Soc. *Res:* Hadronic interactions at high energy. *Mailing Add:* Dept of Physics Univ of Calif Davis CA 95616

YAGER, ROBERT EUGENE, b Carroll, Iowa, Apr 13, 30; m 55; c 2. SCIENCE EDUCATION, PLANT PHYSIOLOGY. *Educ:* State Col Iowa, BS, 50; Univ Iowa, MS, 53, PhD, 57. *Prof Exp:* Res asst plant physiol, 55-56, from instr to assoc prof sci educ, 56-67, PROF SEC EDUC, UNIV IOWA, 67- *Concurrent Pos:* Dir sec sci training prog, NSF, 59-, dir, In-Serv Inst, 61-, dir, Summer Inst, 63-, dir acad yr prog for sci supv, summer inst in-serv teachers, coop col sch sci prog & undergrad pre-serv teacher educ prog; ed, Jour Nat Asn Res Sci Teaching, 64- *Mem:* Nat Asn Res Sci Teaching; Nat Sci Teachers Asn; Nat Asn Biol Teachers. *Res:* Chemical control of abscission processes; effect of student interaction upon learning process; teacher affects upon learning outcomes; development of science curricula. *Mailing Add:* Dept of Sci Educ Univ of Iowa Iowa City IA 52240

YAGGEE, FRANK L, b Dearborn, Mich, Sept 4, 23; m 58. PHYSICAL METALLURGY, CHEMICAL ENGINEERING. *Educ:* Univ Mich, BS, 48, MS, 49. *Prof Exp:* Assoc metallurgist, Argonne Nat Lab, 49-53, staff metallurgist res & develop, 54-81. *Concurrent Pos:* Consult, Reactor Anal & Safety Div, Argonne Nat Lab, 73-81. *Mem:* Sigma Xi; Am Nuclear Soc; fel Am Soc Metals; fel Am Inst Chemists; Res Soc Am. *Res:* Mechanical and physical metallurgy of reactor fuels and cladding; reactor fuel development and fabrication; fuel element failure analysis; special mechanical test equipment; remote mechanical testing. *Mailing Add:* Argonne Nat Lab 9700 S Cass Ave Argonne IL 60439

YAGGY, PAUL FRANCIS, b Detroit, Mich, Aug 4, 23; m 45; c 4. AERONAUTICAL & ELECTRICAL ENGINEERING. *Educ:* San Jose State Col, BSEE, 63. *Prof Exp:* Aeronaut engr, 46-50 & 51-58, aeronaut engr large scale aerodyn br, 58-61, asst br chief, 61-65, tech dir, US Army Aeronaut Res Lab, 65-68, dir lab, 68-72, DIR LAB, US ARMY AIR MOBILITY RES & DEVELOP LAB, AMES RES CTR, NASA, 72- *Concurrent Pos:* Mem subcomt aircraft aerodyn, NASA, 67-70; mem fluid dynamics panel, Adv Group Aerospace Res & Develop, NATO, 67- *Mem:* Am Helicopter Soc; Soc Automotive Engrs; assoc fel Am Inst Aeronaut & Astronaut. *Res:* Research and development in aeronautical sciences with particular emphasis in aerodynamics and flight vehicles for air mobile systems development. *Mailing Add:* 1381 E Sheffield Ave Campbell CA 95008

YAGHJIAN, ARTHUR DAVID, b Jan 1, 43; US citizen; m 73. ELECTROMAGNETIC THEORY. *Educ:* Brown Univ, ScB, 64, ScM, 66, PhD(elec eng), 69. *Prof Exp:* Asst prof physics & elec eng, Hampton Inst, 69-70; Nat Res Coun res assoc, 71-73, ELECTRONICS ENGR, ELECTROMAGNETIC FIELDS DIV, NAT BUR STANDARDS, 73- *Mem:* Inst Elec & Electronics Engrs; Sigma Xi. *Res:* Develops theory, computer programs and error analyses for near-field antenna measurements and coupling; Solves electromagnetic scattering and radiation problems. *Mailing Add:* Electromagnetic Fields Div Nat Bur of Standards Boulder CO 80303

YAGI, FUMIO, b Seattle, Wash, July 14, 17; m 54. MATHEMATICS. *Educ:* Univ Wash, BS, 38, MS, 41; Mass Inst Technol, PhD(math), 43. *Prof Exp:* Fel, Inst Advan Study, 43; instr, Univ Wash, 46-49, asst prof, 49-53; mathematician, Ballistic Res Labs, Aberdeen Proving Ground, 53-56; sr res engr, Jet Propulsion Lab, Calif Inst Technol, 56-58, res specialist, 58-63; appl mathematician, Grumman Aircraft Eng Corp, Bethpage, NY, 63-66, mem systs anal staff, 66-67, group supvr systs anal, 67-77; RETIRED. *Concurrent Pos:* Lectr, Univ Md, 56, Univ Calif, Los Angeles, 57-61 & Adelphi Univ, 63-64 & 66; adj prof, C W Post Col, Long Island Univ, 66-77. *Mem:* Am Math Soc; Sigma Xi. *Res:* Analysis; space trajectory and guidance studies; systems performance and error analysis. *Mailing Add:* 2914 Sahalee Dr E Redmond WA 98052

YAGI, HARUHIKO, b Sendai, Japan, June 27, 39; m 69; c 2. ORGANIC CHEMISTRY, DRUG METABOLISM. *Educ:* Tohoku Univ, Japan, MS, 65, PhD(systhesis of isoquinoline alkaloid), 68. *Prof Exp:* Asst org synthesis, Pharmaceut Inst, Tohoku Univ, Japan, 68-69; res asst electrochem, Univ Conn, 69-70; res assoc chem kinetics, Johns Hopkins Univ, 70-71; VIS SCIENTIST DRUG METABOLISM & CARCINOGENESIS, LAB CHEM, NAT INST ARTHRITIS, DIGESTIVE & KIDNEY DIS, NIH, 71- *Concurrent Pos:* Fel, Univ Conn, 69-70 & Johns Hopkins Univ, 70-71. *Mem:* Pharmaceut Soc Japan; Am Chem Soc. *Res:* Carcinogenesis. *Mailing Add:* Lab Chem Rm 230 Bldg 4 NIAMD NIH Bethesda MD 20014

YAGLE, RAYMOND A(RTHUR), b Aspinwall, Pa, Dec 29, 23; m 54; c 3. NAVAL ARCHITECTURE, OCEAN ENGINEERING. *Educ:* Univ Mich, BSE, 44, MSE, 47. *Prof Exp:* Jr engr, Cornell Aeronaut Lab, Inc, 46; res engr, Frederic Flader, Inc, 47; res asst to res engr, 50-54, asst prof eng mech, 55-60, assoc prof naval archit & marine eng, 60-64, prof, 64-76, PROF MARINE ENG, ENG RES INST, UNIV MICH, ANN ARBOR, 76- *Concurrent Pos:* Consult, Rand Corp; chmn ship res comt, Nat Acad Sci-Nat Res Coun. *Mem:* Marine Technol Soc; Am Soc Naval Engrs; Soc Naval Archit & Marine Engrs; Am Soc Eng Educ. *Res:* Fuel sprays, atomization and combustion; fluid mechanics generally, resistance studies and naval architecture applications in particular; ship structures; computer applications. *Mailing Add:* Dept of Marine Eng Univ of Mich Ann Arbor MI 48109

YAGNIK, CHANDRAKANT M, solid state physics, material science, see previous edition

YAGUCHI, MAKOTO, b Yokohama, Japan, Oct 19, 30; m 60; c 1. PROTEIN CHEMISTRY, AGRICULTURAL CHEMISTRY. *Educ:* Tokyo Univ Agr, BAgr, 53; Univ Calif, Davis, MS, 57, PhD(agr chem), 63. *Prof Exp:* Res assoc protein chem, Purdue Univ, 63-64; res food technologist, Univ Calif, Davis, 64-65; asst res officer, 65-69, assoc res officer, 70-77, SR RES OFFICER, DIV BIOL SCI, NAT RES COUN CAN, 77- *Concurrent Pos:* Vis scientist, Max-Planck-Inst fur Malekulare Genetik, Berlin, 74-75; vis prof, Japan Soc Promotion Sci, 78. *Mem:* AAAS; Can Soc Microbiologists; Inst Food Technol; NY Acad Sci; Can Biochem Soc. *Res:* Amino acid sequence of ribosomal proteins and histones; proteins and enzymes from thermophilic and halophilic bacteria; structure and function of cellulases and amylases. *Mailing Add:* Div of Biol Sci Nat Res Coun Ottawa ON K1A 0R6 Can

YAHIKU, PAUL Y, b Honolulu, Hawaii, July 25, 38; m 65; c 1. STATISTICS. *Educ:* Pac Union Col, BA, 61; Univ Calif, Los Angeles, PhD(biostatist), 67. *Prof Exp:* Asst prof, 66-74, ASSOC PROF BIOSTATIST, LOMA LINDA UNIV, 74- *Mem:* Am Statist Asn; Biomet Soc. *Res:* Statistical methodology. *Mailing Add:* Dept of Biostatist Loma Linda Univ Loma Linda CA 92354

YAHIL, AMOS, b Tel Aviv, Israel, Nov 28, 43; m 72; c 2. ASTROPHYSICS, ASTRONOMY. *Educ:* Hebrew Univ, Jerusalem, BSc, 66; Calif Inst Technol, PhD(physics), 70. *Prof Exp:* Lectr, Tel Aviv Univ, 70-71; mem, Inst Advan Study, 71-73; lectr, Tel Aviv Univ, 73-75, sr lectr, 75-77; asst prof, 77-79, ASSOC PROF ASTROPHYS, STATE UNIV NY, STONY BROOK, 79-, COORDR ASTRON, 80- *Concurrent Pos:* Chercheur Invite, Univ Montreal, 75 & 76-77; vis assoc prof, Calif Inst Technol, 77 & 78; vis prof, Nordita, Copenhagen, 81; vis fel, Inst Astron, Cambridge, 81. *Mem:* Am Astron Soc; Int Astron Union. *Res:* Physical cosmology; dynamics and evolution of clusters of galaxies; galactic structure; x-ray sources; molecular clouds; supernovae. *Mailing Add:* Astron Prog ESS Bldg State Univ of NY Stony Brook NY 11794

YAHNER, JOSEPH EDWARD, b Chicago, Ill, June 16, 31; m 58; c 3. SOIL CLASSIFICATION. *Educ:* Purdue Univ, BS, 54; Ore State Univ, MS, 61, PhD(soils), 63. *Prof Exp:* Agronomist, Purdue Univ-Brazil Proj, US AID Contract, Vicosa, Brazil, 63-67, EXTEN AGRONOMIST, PURDUE UNIV, WEST LAFAYETTE, 67-, ASSOC PROF AGRON, 70- *Mem:* Am Soc Agron; Soil Conserv Soc Am. *Res:* Use of soil maps and soil information in land use planning; on-site waste disposal for homes or small commercial establishments; soil map use for land appraisal. *Mailing Add:* Dept of Agron Purdue Univ West Lafayette IN 47907

YAHNER, RICHARD HOWARD, b McKees Rocks, Pa, June 21, 49; m 72; c 2. WILDLIFE SCIENCES. *Educ:* Pa State Univ, BS, 71; Univ Tenn, MS, 73; Ohio Univ, PhD(zool), 77. *Prof Exp:* Fel, Smithsonian Inst, 77-78; asst prof, Univ Minn, 78-81; ASST PROF, PA STATE UNIV, 81- *Mem:* Am Soc Mammalogists; Wildlife Soc. *Res:* Effects of habitat alteration, manipulation, and fragmentation on behavioral ecology and community ecology of vertebrates; habitat management. *Mailing Add:* Forest Resources Sch & Lab Pa State Univ University Park PA 16802

YAHR, MELVIN DAVID, b New York, NY, Nov 18, 17; m 48; c 4. NEUROLOGY. *Educ:* NY Univ, AB, 39, MD, 43; Am Bd Psychiat & Neurol, dipl, 49. *Prof Exp:* Res asst, Col Physicians & Surgeons, Columbia Univ, 48-50, instr, 50-51, assoc, 51-53, from asst prof to assoc prof clin neurol, 53-70, from asst dean to assoc dean, 59-73, Merritt prof clin neurol, 70-73; HENRY P & GEORGETTE GOLDSCHMIDT PROF NEUROL & CHMN DEPT, MT SINAI SCH MED, 73- *Concurrent Pos:* Nat Res Coun res assoc & asst neurologist, Neurol Inst, Presby Hosp, 48-50, asst attend neurologist, 50-53, assoc attend, 53-61, attend, 61-; asst adj neurol serv, Lenox Hill Hosp, 48-49, adj, 49-54, assoc, 54-60; asst neurologist, Montefiore Hosp, 49-51; mem neurol study sect, NIH, 50-; consult, USPHS, 52-55 & Neuro-Psychiat Inst, NJ, 52-59; med dir, Parkinson's Dis Found, 58-73; mem comt drug ther in neurol, Nat Inst Neurol Dis & Blindness, 59- *Mem:* Am Epilepsy Soc; Am Neurol Asn (secy-treas); Asn Am Med Cols; Asn Res Nerv & Ment Dis; fel Am Acad Neurol. *Res:* Cause and treatment of epilepsy; cerebro-vascular diseases; Parkinsonism and multiple sclerosis. *Mailing Add:* Dept of Neurol Mt Sinai Sch of Med New York NY 10029

YAKAITIS, RONALD WILLIAM, b Baltimore, Md, Oct 13, 41; m 68; c 2. ANESTHESIOLOGY. *Educ:* Loyola Col, BS, 63; Univ Md, MD, 67. *Prof Exp:* Staff instr anesthesia, US Naval Hosp, Oakland, Calif, 71-73; asst prof, Med Univ SC, 73-75; asst prof anesthesia, Univ Ariz Med Ctr, 75-77; STAFF ANESTHESIOLOGIST, KINO COMMUNITY HOSP, TUCSON, 77- *Concurrent Pos:* Consult anesthesia, Univ Calif, San Francisco, 72-73, Vet Admin Hosp, Charleston, SC, 73-75 & Vet Admin Hosp, Tucson, Ariz, 75-; clin assoc, Univ Ariz Med Ctr, 77-; consult, Tucson Hosps Med Educ Prog, 78- *Mem:* Am Soc Anesthesiologists; Int Anesthesia Res Soc; Am Col Physicians; AMA. *Res:* Pulmonary ultramicroscopic and biochemical changes due to oxygen toxicity; cardiovascular drug pharmacokinetics during acid-base imbalance; new techniques for intraoperative anesthetic management. *Mailing Add:* Dept Anesthesiol Kino Community Hosp 2800 E Ajo Way Tucson AZ 85714

YAKAITIS-SURBIS, ALBINA ANN, b Harvey, Ill, Feb 16, 23; m 67. ANATOMY. *Educ:* Univ Chicago, BS, 45, MS, 49; Univ Minn, PhD(anat), 55. *Prof Exp:* Instr biol, Univ Akron, 46-47; instr, Univ Minn, 47-49, asst anat, 49-54; res assoc path, Med Sch, Univ Mich, 59-61; ASST PROF ANAT, SCH MED, UNIV MIAMI, 61- *Concurrent Pos:* George fel, Detroit Inst Cancer Res, 56-58; res assoc, Vet Admin Hosp, Miami, 64- *Mem:* Am Soc Hemat; Am Asn Anat. *Res:* Oncology; electron microscopy; pathology. *Mailing Add:* Dept Anat & Cell Biol Univ Miami Sch Med Miami FL 33101

YAKATAN, GERALD JOSEPH, b Philadelphia, Pa, May 20, 42; m 64; c 2. PHARMACY. *Educ:* Temple Univ, BS, 63, MS, 65; Univ Fla, PhD(pharmaceut sci), 71. *Prof Exp:* Asst prof pharm, Univ Tex, Austin, 72-76, assoc prof, 76-80, asst dir, Drug Dynamics Inst, 75-80; DIR PHARMACOKINETICS/DRUG METAB, WARNER-LAMBERT CO, 80- *Concurrent Pos:* Adj prof pharm, Univ Mich, 81- *Mem:* Am Pharmaceut Asn; Acad Pharmaceut Sci; fel Am Col Clin Pharmacol. *Res:* Pharmacokinetics; biopharmaceutics; analysis of drugs in biological fluids; drug metabolism. *Mailing Add:* Warner-Lambert Co 2800 Plymouth Rd Ann Arbor MI 48105

YAKEL, HARRY L, b Brooklyn, NY, July 24, 29. X-RAY CRYSTALLOGRAPHY. *Educ:* Polytech Inst Brooklyn, BS, 49; Calif Inst Technol, PhD(chem), 52. *Prof Exp:* Fel chem, Calif Inst Technol, 52-53; GROUP LEADER METALS & CERAMICS, OAK RIDGE NAT LAB, 53- *Mem:* AAAS; Am Chem Soc; Am Crystallog Asn; Mineral Soc Am; Sigma Xi. *Res:* Structural studies of solids using x-ray diffraction methods. *Mailing Add:* Oak Ridge Nat Lab PO Box X Oak Ridge TN 37830

YAKOWITZ, HARVEY, b Baltimore, Md, Feb 1, 39; m 60; c 2. METALLURGICAL ENGINEERING. *Educ:* Univ Md, College Park, BS, 59, MS, 62, PhD(mat sci), 70. *Prof Exp:* METALLURGIST, NAT BUR STANDARDS, 59- *Concurrent Pos:* Panel mem interagency bd, US Civil Serv Comn, 66-; US Dept Com vis res worker, Dept Eng, Cambridge Univ, 70-71. *Mem:* Electron Probe Anal Soc Am; Am Soc Metals. *Res:* Electron probe microanalysis; scanning electron microscopy; optical microscopy; divergent beam x-ray microdiffraction. *Mailing Add:* Nat Bur of Standards Washington DC 20234

YAKOWITZ, SIDNEY J, b San Francisco, Calif, Mar 8, 37; m 63; c 2. STATISTICS, COMPUTER SCIENCE. *Educ:* Stanford Univ, BS, 60; Ariz State Univ, MS, 65, MA, 66, PhD(elec eng), 67. *Prof Exp:* Fac assoc elec eng, Ariz State Univ, 65-66; asst prof systs eng, 66-68, assoc prof math, 68-71, ASSOC PROF SYSTS ENG, UNIV ARIZ, 68-, ASSOC PROF INDUST ENG, 71- *Concurrent Pos:* Nat Res Coun fel, Naval Postgrad Sch, 70-71. *Mem:* Inst Math Statist. *Res:* Sequential design of statistical experiments; statistical decision theory; applications to adaptive control theory; pattern recognition. *Mailing Add:* Dept of Systs Eng Univ of Ariz Tucson AZ 85721

YAKSH, TONY LEE, b San Angelo, Tex, June 14, 44; m 74; c 1. NEUROPHARMACOLOGY, NEUROPHYSIOLOGY. *Educ:* Ga Inst Technol, BS, 66; Univ Ga, MS, 68; Purdue Univ, PhD(neurobiol), 71. *Prof Exp:* Res asst, Purdue Univ, 67-71; mem res staff, Biomed Lab, US Army, Edgewood Arsenal, Md, 71-73; asst scientist, Sch Pharm, Univ Wis-Madison, 73-76; vis scientist, Dept Physiol, Univ Col, Univ London, 76-77; ASSOC CONSULT PHARMACOL & NEUROSURG, MAYO CLIN, 77- *Mem:* Am Physiol Soc; Int Asn Study Pain; Soc Neurosci; Sigma Xi. *Res:* Pharmacology of opiate action; physiology and pharmacology of pain transmission role of neuropeptides in behavior. *Mailing Add:* Mayo Clin 200 First St SW Rochester MN 55901

YAKUBIK, JOHN, b Fords, NJ, Sept 23, 28; m 52; c 2. PHARMACEUTICAL CHEMISTRY. *Educ:* Rutgers Univ, BS, 49; Purdue Univ, MS, 50, PhD(pharmaceut chem), 52. *Prof Exp:* Res assoc, Squibb Inst Med Res, 52-55; from scientist to sr scientist, Schering Corp, 55-61, mgr pharmaceut develop dept, 61-65, dir sci liaison, Schering Labs, 65-71, dir new prod planning, 71-74, dir corp prod develop, Schering Corp, Bloomfield, 74-79, dir bus develop, 79-80, dir int regulatory affairs, 80-81, DIR NEW PROD DEVELOP, PHARMACEUT PROD DIV, SCHERING PLOUGH INT, KENILWORTH, 82- *Mem:* AAAS; Soc Cosmetic Chem; Am Pharmaceut Asn; NY Acad Sci. *Res:* Pharmaceutical product development; pharmaceutical and medicinal chemistry; pharmacology. *Mailing Add:* Schering Plough Corp Galloping Hill Rd Kenilworth NJ 07033

YAKURA, JAMES K, b Los Angeles, Calif, Nov 1, 33; m 61; c 3. AERONAUTICAL ENGINEERING. *Educ:* Univ Calif, Los Angeles, BS, 55, MS, 57; Stanford Univ, PhD(aeronaut), 62. *Prof Exp:* Mem tech staff, Hughes Aircraft Co, 55-58, sr staff engr, 62-65; mem sr staff, Nat Eng Sci Co,

65-66; staff engr, 66-69, asst dir, 69-71, assoc systs planning dir, 71-72, dir, Vehicle Systs Off, 72-74, dir, Shuttle Interface Off, 75-77, ASSOC DIR, PAYLOAD INTEGRATION OFF, AEROSPACE CORP, EL SEGUNDO, 77- *Mem:* Am Inst Aeronaut & Astronaut. *Res:* Hypersonic aerodynamics. *Mailing Add:* 7732 Gonzaga Place Westminster CA 92683

YALE, CHARLES E, b Aurora, Ill, Mar 21, 25; m 48; c 4. MEDICINE, SURGERY. *Educ:* Univ Ill, Urbana, BS, 49; Case Western Reserve Univ, MD, 55; Univ Cincinnati, DSc(surg), 61. *Prof Exp:* Resident surg, Univ Cincinnati, 56-62, instr, 62-64; from asst prof to assoc prof, 64-72, PROF SURG, MED SCH, UNIV WIS-MADISON, 72-, VCHMN DEPT, 73- *Concurrent Pos:* NIH grant, Univ Wis-Madison, 66-71; clin investr surg, Cincinnati Vet Admin Hosp, 62-64; attend surgeon, Univ Wis Hosps, 64-, dir gnotobiotic lab, Univ Wis-Madison, 65-81. *Mem:* Soc Surg Alimentary Tract; Asn Gnotobiotics (pres, 70-71); Asn Acad Surg; Am Col Surg; AMA. *Res:* Gastrointestinal surgery; intestinal obstruction and strangulation; wound healing; surgical infections and septic shock; gnotobiotics; surgery for morbid obesity. *Mailing Add:* Dept of Surg Univ of Wis Med Sch Madison WI 53706

YALE, HARRY LOUIS, b Chicago, Ill, Dec 18, 13; m 43; c 3. ORGANIC CHEMISTRY. *Educ:* Univ Ill, BSc, 37; Iowa State Col, PhD(org chem), 40. *Prof Exp:* Res chemist, Nat Defense Res Comt, 40-41 & Shell Develop Co, 41-45; res chemist, Squibb Inst Med Res, 46-67, sr res fel, 67-79; CONSULT, 79- *Honors & Awards:* Lasker Award. *Mem:* Am Chem Soc; NY Acad Sci; Swiss Chem Soc. *Res:* Organometallic compounds; quinoline derivatives; furan; high temperature oxidation and chlorination of olefins; chelate compounds; explosives; antituberculous drugs; diuretics; ataractic agents; natural products. *Mailing Add:* Waksman Inst Microbiol Piscataway NJ 08854

YALE, IRL KEITH, b Billings, Mont, Mar 13, 39. MATHEMATICS. *Educ:* Univ Mont, BA, 60; Univ Calif, Berkeley, PhD(math), 66. *Prof Exp:* Instr math, Univ Mont, 64-65; asst prof, Morehouse Col, 66-67; asst prof, 67-73, assoc prof, 73-80, PROF MATH, UNIV MONT, 80- *Mem:* Am Math Soc; Math Asn Am. *Res:* Functional and harmonic analysis. *Mailing Add:* Dept of Math Univ of Mont Missoula MT 59812

YALE, PAUL B, b Geneva, NY, Apr 28, 32; m 53; c 5. MATHEMATICS. *Educ:* Univ Calif, Berkeley, BA, 53; Harvard Univ, MA & PhD(math), 59. *Prof Exp:* Asst prof math, Oberlin Col, 59-61; from asst prof to assoc prof, 61-74, PROF MATH, POMONA COL, 74- *Concurrent Pos:* NSF sci fac fel, 67-68. *Mem:* Am Math Soc; Math Asn Am; Asn Comput Mach. *Res:* Geometry; symmetry; group theory; computer graphics; numerical analysis. *Mailing Add:* Dept of Math Pomona Col Claremont CA 91711

YALE, SEYMOUR HERSHEL, b Chicago, Ill, Nov 27, 20; m 43; c 2. RADIOLOGY. *Educ:* Univ Ill, BS, 44, DDS, 45. *Prof Exp:* Asst clin dent, Col Dent, 48-49, from instr to asst prof, 49-54, assoc prof radiol & head dept, 56-57, prof, 57, mem fac grad col, 60, admin asst to dean col dent, 61-63, from asst dean to actg dean, 63-65, DEAN COL DENT, UNIV ILL MED CTR, 65- *Concurrent Pos:* Res consult, Hines Vet Admin Hosp, Ill, 59; consult, West Side Vet Admin Hosp, Chicago, 61-, dent proj sect, Nat Inst Radiol Health, 61-, div radiol health, Bur State Serv, 63- & Vet Admin Res Hosp, Chicago, 63-; mem sect comt dent film specifications, US Am Stand Inst, 59-, subcomt 16, Nat Comt Radiation Protection, 63-, gen res support adv comt, Dept Health, Educ & Welfare, 65-, Mayor's Comt Heart, Cancer & Stroke, Chicago & comt dent care ment ill, Ill State Dept Ment Health. *Mem:* AAAS; Am Dent Asn; Am Acad Dent Radiol; fel Am Col Dent; Int Asn Dent Res. *Res:* Morphology; radiographic anatomy; radiation biology and control. *Mailing Add:* PO Box 6998 Chicago IL 60680

YALKOVSKY, RALPH, b Chicago, Ill, Oct 11, 17. OCEANOGRAPHY. *Educ:* Univ Chicago, BS, 46, MS, 55, PhD(geol), 56. *Prof Exp:* Geologist, US Corps Engrs, Wash, 49-50; jr engr, State Div Hwys, Calif, 50-52; jr engr geophys comput, Western Geophys Co, 52-54; assoc geol engr, Crane Co, Ill, 55-56; asst prof geol, Mont State Univ, 56-61 & State Univ NY Col New Paltz, 61-62; from asst prof to assoc prof, 62-65, PROF GEOL, BUFFALO STATE UNIV COL, 65- *Concurrent Pos:* Res grant, Mont State Univ, 59-60 & 60-61; vis investr, Archives of Indies, Naval Mus Madrid, 59-60 & 68, Spanish Inst Oceanog, Spain, 59-60 & Royal Spanish Acad Hist, 68; vis scientist, US Coast Geodetic Surv ship Discoverer, 69; sci corresp, Nat Public Radio, WBFO, 75-78, UN press corresp, Geneva, 75, New York, 73, 76, 77, 79, 80 & 81; rep, KPBX, Radio, Spokane, 79-81; mem, Malaspina Expedition; vis investr, Mus Naval, Madrid, 81-82. *Mem:* Fel AAAS; Nat Asn Geol Teachers; Am Geophys Union; fel NY Acad Sci; Nat Sci Teachers Asn. *Res:* Marine geology and geochemistry of marine sediments; water resources; history of science; international law of the sea; public policy. *Mailing Add:* Dept of Geosci Physics Buffalo State Univ Col Buffalo NY 14222

YALKOWSKY, SAMUEL HYMAN, b New York, NY, Dec 5, 42; m 62; c 2. PHARMACEUTICAL CHEMISTRY. *Educ:* Columbia Univ, BS, 65; Univ Mich, Ann Arbor, MS, 68, PhD(pharm chem), 69. *Prof Exp:* SR RES SCIENTIST PHARMACY RES, UPJOHN CO, 69- *Mem:* Am Pharmaceut Asn; Am Chem Soc. *Res:* Physical chemistry of surfaces and micelles; solubility and related phenomena. *Mailing Add:* 8124 Brookwood Dr Portage MI 49002

YALL, IRVING, b Chicago, Ill, Jan 31, 23. MICROBIAL PHYSIOLOGY. *Educ:* Brooklyn Col, BA, 48; Univ Mo, MA, 51; Purdue Univ, PhD(bact), 55. *Prof Exp:* Asst bact, Univ Mo, 49-51; res fel, Purdue Univ, 54-56, resident res assoc biochem, Argonne Nat Lab, 56-57; from asst prof microbiol to assoc prof, 57-68, PROF MICROBIOL & MED TECHNOL, UNIV ARIZ, 68- *Mem:* Fel AAAS; Am Soc Microbiol; Am Chem Soc. *Res:* Phosphorus metabolism in wastewaters; intermediary metabolism of microorganisms; control of nucleic acids. *Mailing Add:* Dept of Microbiol Univ of Ariz Tucson AZ 85721

YALMAN, RICHARD GEORGE, b Indianapolis, Ind, Apr 16, 23; m 44; c 2. INORGANIC CHEMISTRY. *Educ:* Harvard Univ, BS, 43, MA, 47, PhD(chem), 49. *Prof Exp:* Jr chemist, Monsanto Chem Co, 44; res chemist & sr group leader, Mound Lab, 49-50; from asst prof to assoc prof chem, 50-61, chmn dept, 58 & 61-66, PROF CHEM, ANTIOCH COL, 61-, CHMN DEPT, 72- *Concurrent Pos:* Consult, Signal Corps, Air Force Off Sci Res Projs, Antioch, 50-58, Monsanto Co, 55 & Kettering Res Lab, 67-71; pres, Mad River Chem Co, 67-; consult, Yellow Springs Instrument Co, 71-72; vis scientist, Electronics Br, Avionics Lab, Wright-Patterson AFB, 79- *Mem:* AAAS; Am Chem Soc; Royal Soc Chem; Indian Chem Soc; Soc Chem Indust. *Res:* Kinetics; metal complexes; high temperature synthesis; metalloporphines; hydrothermal properties of oil shale. *Mailing Add:* Dept Chem Antioch Col Yellow Springs OH 45387

YALOVSKY, MORTY A, b Montreal, Que, May 14, 44; m 70; c 2. STATISTICS. *Educ:* McGill Univ, BSc, 65, MSc, 68, PhD(statist), 76. *Prof Exp:* Lectr math, 70-74, asst prof, 74-78, ASSOC PROF MGT SCI, MCGILL UNIV, 79- *Mem:* Am Statist Asn; Statist Soc Can. *Res:* Goodness-of-fit testing; regression models and time series analysis; applications of quantitative techniques to administrative sciences; biostatistics. *Mailing Add:* Fac of Mgt McGill Univ Montreal PQ H3A 1G5 Can

YALOW, ABRAHAM AARON, b Syracuse, NY, Sept 18, 19; m 43; c 2. PHYSICS, MEDICAL BIOPHYSICS. *Educ:* Syracuse Univ, AB, 39; Univ Ill, MS, 42, PhD(physics), 45. *Prof Exp:* Asst physics, Syracuse Univ, 39-41 & Univ Ill, 41-42; asst physicist, Nat Defense Res Comt, 43; asst physics, Univ Ill, 44-45; asst engr, Fed Telecommun Labs, NY, 45-46; asst prof physics, NY State Maritime Col, 47-48; from instr to assoc prof, 48-66, PROF PHYSICS, COOPER UNION, 66- *Concurrent Pos:* Consult physicist, Montefiore Hosp, 46- *Mem:* AAAS; Am Phys Soc; Am Asn Physics Teachers; assoc fel Am Col Radiol; Fedn Am Scientists. *Res:* Neutron resonance absorption and scattering; microwave transmission; medical applications of radioactive isotopes; Mössbauer effect. *Mailing Add:* Dept of Physics Cooper Union Sch of Eng & Sci New York NY 10003

YALOW, ROSALYN SUSSMAN, b New York, NY, July 19, 21; m 43; c 2. MEDICAL PHYSICS. *Educ:* Hunter Col, AB, 41; Univ Ill, MS, 42, PhD(physics), 45; Am Bd Radiol, dipl, 51. *Hon Degrees:* Various from US Univs, 74-81. *Prof Exp:* Instr physics, Univ Ill, 44-45; lectr & temp asst prof, Hunter Col, 46-50; physicist & asst chief, Radioisotope Serv, Vet Admin Hosp, Bronx, 50-70; res prof, Dept Med, Mt Sinai Sch Med, 68-74, distinguished serv prof, 74-79; DISTINGUISHED PROF AT LARGE, ALBERT EINSTEIN COL MED, YESHIVA UNIV, 79-; CHMN, DEPT CLIN SCI, MONTEFIORE HOSP & MED CTR, 80- *Concurrent Pos:* Consult, Radioisotope Unit, Vet Admin Hosp, Bronx, 47-50 & Lenox Hill Hosp, 52-62; secy, US Nat Comt Med Physics, 63-67; actg chief, Radioisotope Serv, Vet Admin Hosp, Bronx, 68-70, chief, Radioimmunoassay Res Lab, 69, Nuclear Med Serv, 70-80; mem, Med Adv Bd, Nat Pituitary Agency, 68-71; Int Atomic Energy Agency expert, Inst Atomic Energy, Sao Paulo, 70; mem, Endocrinol Study Sect, NIH, 69-72, Bd Sci Coun, Nat Inst Arhritis, Metab & Digestive Dis, 72-75 & 78-81, Task Force Immunol Dis, Nat Inst Allergy & Infectious Dis, 72-73; consult, New York City Dept Health, 72-; co-ed, Hormone & Metab Res, 73-; mem, Comt Eval of Nat Pituitary Agency, Nat Res Coun, 73-74; Albert Lasker Basic Med Res Award, 76; WHO consult, Radiation Med Ctr, Bombay, 78. *Honors & Awards:* Nobel Prize, 77; Middleton Award, 60; Lilly Award, Am Diabetes Asn, 61; Fed Woman's Award, 61; Van Slyke Award, Am Asn Clin Chem, 68; Gairdner Found Int Award, 71; Am Col Physicians Award, 71; Koch Award, Endocrine Soc, 72; sustaining mem lect award, Asn Mil Surgeons, 75; A Cressy Morrison Award, Natural Sci, NY Acad Sci, 75; Vet Admin Except Serv Award, 75; AMA Sci Achievement Award, 75; Am Asn Clin Chem Award, 75; Albion O Bernstein, MD Award, Med Soc, State NY, 74; Banting Medal, Am Diabetes Asn, 78. *Mem:* Nat Acad Sci; Am Acad Arts & Sci; Endocrine Soc (pres elect, 77-78, pres, 78-79); Am Asn Physicists in Med; fel NY Acad Sci. *Res:* Medical use of radioisotopes, radioimmunoassay and radiation chemistry. *Mailing Add:* Vet Admin Hosp 130 W Kingsbridge Rd Bronx NY 10468

YAM, LUNG TSIONG, b Canton, China, Apr 10, 36; US citizen; m 64; c 2. INTERNAL MEDICINE. *Educ:* Nat Taiwan Univ, MD, 60. *Prof Exp:* From instr to asst prof med, Sch Med, Tufts Univ, 67-72; assoc hemat, Scripps Clin & Res Found, 72-74; assoc prof, 74-80, PROF MED, UNIV LOUISVILLE, 80-; CHIEF HEMAT-ONCOL, VET ADMIN HOSP, 74- *Concurrent Pos:* Res assoc, New Eng Med Ctr Hosp, 68-72, head cytol & histochem, 70-72. *Mem:* Am Soc Hemat; Am Soc Histochem & Cytochem. *Res:* Use of morphologic approach to study problems related to hematology-oncology; use of cytochemistry, immunochemistry and electrophoresis for isoenzymes to identify the origin of normal and neoplastic cells. *Mailing Add:* Vet Admin Hosp 800 Zorn Ave Louisville KY 40206

YAMADA, ESTHER V, b London, Ont, July 19, 23; m 53; c 1. BIOCHEMISTRY. *Educ:* Univ Western Ont, BSc, 45, PhD(biochem), 51; McGill Univ, MSc, 47. *Prof Exp:* Nat Cancer Inst fel, Univ Western Ont, 52-55; res assoc, Karolinska Inst, Sweden, 55-57; res fel, NIH, 57-59; lectr, 59-60, asst prof, 60-66, assoc prof, 66-75, PROF BIOCHEM, FAC MED, UNIV MAN, 66- *Mem:* AAAS; Can Biochem Soc; Am Soc Biol Chemists; NY Acad Sci. *Res:* Transcription and translation; skeletal muscle metabolism; bioenergetics; membrane; bound enzymes; heart metabolism. *Mailing Add:* Dept Biochem Fac Med Univ Man Winnipeg MB R3E 0W3 Can

YAMADA, MASAAKI, b Japan, Aug 9, 42; m 71; c 2. PLASMA PHYSICS. *Educ:* Univ Tokyo, Japan, BS, 66, MS, 68; Univ Ill, PhD(physics), 73. *Prof Exp:* Res asst physics, Univ Ill, 69-73; res assoc, 73-75, res staff, 75-78, RES PHYSICIST, PLASMA PHYSICS, PLASMA PHYSICS LAB, PRINCETON UNIV, 78- *Mem:* Am Phys Soc; Phys Soc Japan. *Res:* Experimental studies of plasma physics, including spheronia K physics, general microinstabilities and transport properties of plasmas. *Mailing Add:* Plasma Physics Lab PO Box 451 Princeton Univ Forrestal Campus Princeton NJ 08540

YAMADA, RYUJI, b Hiroshima City, Japan, Jan 3, 32; m m 60; c 2. EXPERIMENTAL HIGH ENERGY PHYSICS, ACCELERATOR PHYSICS. *Educ:* Hiroshima Univ, Japan, BS, 54; Univ Tokyo, Japan, MS, 56, PhD(physics), 62. *Prof Exp:* Res assoc high energy physics, Inst Nuclear Study, Univ Tokyo, Japan, 56-68; res assoc, Brookhaven Nat Lab, 63-65; res assoc accelerator physics, Cornell Univ, 65-66; accelerator consult, 67, PHYSICIST HIGH ENERGY PHYSICS, FERMI NAT ACCELERATOR LAB, 68- *Mem:* Am Phys Soc; Phys Soc Japan. *Res:* Development of super conducting magnets for Energy Doubler Project and Colliding Detector; high energy experiments using existing 400 GeV Proton Synchrotron; construction of accelerators, including 16 inch cyclotron 1 GeV INS electron synchrotron, 10GeV Cornell Electron Synchrotron, and NAL 500 Gev Proton Synchrotron. *Mailing Add:* 1228 Modaff St Naperville IL 60540

YAMADA, SYLVIA BEHRENS, b Hamburg, Ger, May 7, 46; m 75. POPULATION ECOLOGY. *Educ:* Univ BC, BSc, 68, MSc, 71; Univ Ore, PhD(marine ecol), 74. *Prof Exp:* Biologist fisheries, Pac Biol Sta Fisheries & Marine Serv, Dept Environ Can, 74-79; asst prof, Wellesley Col, Mass, 80-81; ADJ PROF, SCH OCEANOG, ORE STATE UNIV, 81- *Concurrent Pos:* course coordr, Marine Ecol, Marine Biol Lab, Woods Hole, Mass, 80. *Mem:* Ecol Soc Am. *Res:* Incorporation and retension of trace elements in salmon tissue; ecology of intertidal mollusks, (Littorina sitkana, Littorina scutulata and Littorina planaxis, Littorina littorea, Littorina Saxatilits, Batillaria Attramentaria). *Mailing Add:* Sch Oceanog Ore State Univ Corvallis OR 97331

YAMADA, TETSUJI, Japanese citizen. METEOROLOGY, CIVIL ENGINEERING. *Educ:* Osaka Univ, BE, 65, ME, 67; Colo State Univ, PhD(civil eng), 71. *Prof Exp:* Fel civil eng, Colo State Univ, 71-72; mem res staff meteorol, Princeton Univ, 72-76; meteorologist, Argonne Nat Lab, 76-81; MEM STAFF, LOS ALAMOS NAT LAB, 81- *Mem:* Am Meteorol Soc; Meteorol Soc Japan; Royal Meteorol Soc. *Res:* Turbulence theory; numerical and physical modellings of mountain flows, sea breeze, urban heat island and air pollution; parameterization and numerical modelling of the planetary boundary layer. *Mailing Add:* Los Alamos Nat Lab MS D466 PO Box 1663 Los Alamos NM 87545

YAMADA, YOSHIKAZU, b Honokaa, Hawaii, May 20, 15; m 50; c 4. ORGANIC CHEMISTRY. *Educ:* Univ Hawaii, BS, 37; Univ Mich, MS, 38; Purdue Univ, PhD(chem), 50. *Prof Exp:* Res chemist, Davidson Corp, Ill, 50-53; from sr proj engr to res engr, Mergenthaler Linotype Co, NY, 53-59; sr res chemist, Bell & Howell Co, Ill, 59-60, prin res chemist, Res Labs, Calif, 60-72; PRES, YAMADA-GRAPHICS CORP, IRVINE, 72- *Mem:* AAAS; Am Chem Soc; Sigma Xi. *Res:* Photosensitive systems; graphic media. *Mailing Add:* 6151 Sierra Bravo Rd Irvine CA 92715

YAMAGISHI, FREDERICK GEORGE, b Reno, Nev, Sept 14, 43; m 68; c 2. ORGANIC CHEMISTRY. *Educ:* Univ Calif, Los Angeles, BS, 65, PhD(org chem), 72; Calif State Col, MS, 67. *Prof Exp:* Fel, Dept Physics, Univ Pa, 72-73, res assoc org chem, 73-74; MEM TECH STAFF ORG CHEM, HUGHES RES LAB, HUGHES AIRCRAFT CO, 74- *Mem:* Am Chem Soc. *Res:* Organic conductors; one-dimensional materials; conducting polymers. *Mailing Add:* Exp Study Dept 3011 Malibu Canyon Rd Malibu CA 90265

YAMAGUCHHI, TADANORI, b Miyazaki, Japan, Jan 17, 49. METAL OXIDE SEMICONDUCTOR. *Educ:* Miyakonojyo Tech Col, BSEE, 69. *Prof Exp:* Res engr, Semiconnductor Div, Sony Corp, Japan, 69-77; PROF SR ENGR, TEKTRONIX, INC, 78- *Res:* Device and technology development for advanced metaloxide semiconductor-large scale integration-very large scale integrations, including state-of-the-art device structure, also new device structure in n-channel metal oxide semiconductor, complementary metal oxide semiconductor, and high-voltage metal oxide semiconductor integrated circuits; investigation of metal oxide semiconductor device physics and modeling. *Mailing Add:* 5612 Southeast Drake Rd Hillsboro OR 97123

YAMAGUCHI, MASATOSHI, b San Leandro, Calif, Mar 12, 18; m 42; c 3. PLANT PHYSIOLOGY, BIOCHEMISTRY. *Educ:* Univ Calif, BS, 40, PhD(agr chem), 50. *Prof Exp:* Prin lab technician, 41 & 46-50, instr, 50-52, asst olericulturist, 50-58, assoc olericulturist, 58-64, lectr, 64-73, prof veg crops, 73-81, olericulturist, 64-81, EMER PROF, UNIV CALIF, DAVIS, 81- *Concurrent Pos:* Fulbright res scholar, 59-60; vis prof, Univ Man, 67-68; consult veg crops, Sao Paulo & Panama, Brazil, 75-76. *Mem:* Am Chem Soc; Am Soc Hort; Int Soc Hort Sci. *Res:* Chemical constituents and quality of vegetables; physiological disorders of vegetable crops; biochemistry and physiology of vegetable fruit development and ripening. *Mailing Add:* Dept of Veg Crops Univ of Calif Davis CA 95616

YAMAKAWA, KAZUO ALAN, b San Jose, Calif, June 18, 18; m 55. SOLID STATE PHYSICS. *Educ:* Stanford Univ, AB, 40; Princeton Univ, MA, 47, PhD(physics), 49. *Prof Exp:* Br chief, Ballistic Res Labs, Aburdeen, Md, 49-55; group head semiconductor develop, Hughes Res Labs, Malibu, Calif, 59-61; dept mgr laser mat, Electro Optical Syst, Pasadena, Calif, 61-63; group scientist semi conductor mat, Autometics, Amaheim, Calif, 63-68; SR MEM TECH STAFF PHOTOVOLTAICS, JET PROPULSION LABS, 70- *Mem:* Fel Am Phys Soc; Sigma Xi. *Mailing Add:* 1459 Bonita Terrace Monterey Park CA 91754

YAMAMOTO, DIANE MASA, b Madison, Wis, Nov 3, 46. MEDICINAL CHEMISTRY, ORGANIC CHEMISTRY. *Educ:* Univ Wis-Madison, BS, 68; Univ Calif, Berkeley, PhD(org chem), 73. *Prof Exp:* Res asst, Univ Calif, Berkeley, 69-73; res assoc, Univ Ariz, 73-75; sr chemist, Wyeth Labs Div, Am Home Prods Corp, 75-77; SCIENTIST, ORTHO PHARMACEUT CORP, JOHNSON & JOHNSON, 78- *Mem:* Am Chem Soc; Sigma Xi. *Res:* Chemistry of biologically active compounds, including design, synthesis, structure-activity relationships and pertinent mechanistic studies. *Mailing Add:* Ortho Pharmaceut Corp Chem Res Div Raritan NJ 08869

YAMAMOTO, HARRY Y, b Honolulu, Hawaii, Nov 26, 33; m 57; c 2. BIOCHEMISTRY, FOOD TECHNOLOGY. *Educ:* Univ Hawaii, BS, 55; Univ Ill, MS, 58; Univ Calif, Davis, PhD(biochem), 62. *Prof Exp:* Asst prof, 61-64, assoc prof, 65-70, PROF FOOD SCI, UNIV HAWAII, MANOA, 70- *Concurrent Pos:* USPHS spec fel, Charles F Kettering Res Lab, 68-69; vis scientist, Inst Animal Physiol, Babraham, Cambridge, Eng, 76. *Honors & Awards:* Samuel Cate Prescott Award, Inst Food Technologists, 69. *Mem:* Am Chem Soc; Am Soc Plant Physiol; Inst Food Technologists. *Res:* Carotenoid function; photosynthesis; food biotechnology. *Mailing Add:* Dept of Food Sci Univ of Hawaii Honolulu HI 96822

YAMAMOTO, HISASHI, organic chemistry, see previous edition

YAMAMOTO, JOE, b Los Angeles, Calif, Apr 18, 24; m 47; c 2. PSYCHIATRY. *Educ:* Univ Minn, BS, 46, MB, 48, MD, 49. *Prof Exp:* Asst prof psychiat, Sch Med, Univ Okla, 55-58, asst prof, 58-61; from asst prof to assoc prof psychiat, Sch Med, 58-66, mem fac, Psychoanal Inst, 66-69, prof psychiat, Sch Med, Univ Southern Calif, 69-77; PROF PSYCHIAT, UNIV CALIF, LOS ANGELES, 77-, DIR, ADULT AMBULATORY SERV, 77- *Concurrent Pos:* Clin dir, Adult Outpatient Psychiat Clin, Los Angeles County-Univ Southern Calif Med Ctr, 58-77. *Mem:* AAAS; fel Am Acad Psychoanal (pres, 78); fel Am Psychiat Asn; fel Am Col Psychiatrists; fel Am Asn Soc Psychiat. *Res:* Clinical and preventive psychiatry; social class factors, Asian/Pacific factors. *Mailing Add:* Dept Psychiat 760 Westwood Plaza Los Angeles CA 90024

YAMAMOTO, KEITH ROBERT, b Des Moines, Iowa, Feb 4, 46. MOLECULAR BIOLOGY. *Educ:* Iowa State Univ, BSc, 68; Princeton Univ, PhD(biochem sci), 73. *Prof Exp:* Res asst biochem, Dept of Biochem & Biophys, Iowa State Univ, 67-68; NIH trainee biochem sci, Princeton Univ, 68-73; fel biochem, Lab Gordon M Tomkins, 73-75, asst prof, 76-79, ASSOC PROF BIOCHEM, UNIV CALIF, SAN FRANCISCO, 79- *Concurrent Pos:* Fel, Helen Hay Whitney Found, 73-76; fel consult, Found Res Hereditary Dis, 74. *Honors & Awards:* Sterling lectr, 82. *Mem:* Am Soc Microbiol; Am Soc Biol Chemists; Am Soc Develop Biol. *Res:* Mechanisms of gene regulation in eukaryotic cells. *Mailing Add:* Dept Biochem & Biophys Univ Calif San Francisco CA 94143

YAMAMOTO, NOBUTO, b Tagawa City, Japan, Apr 25, 25; m 54; c 3. MICROBIOLOGY, BIOPHYSICS. *Educ:* Kurume Inst Technol, BS, 47; Kyushi Univ, MS, 53; Nagoya Univ, PhD(bact), 58. *Prof Exp:* Asst prof, Sch Med, Gifu Univ, 58-62; vis scientist molecular biol, NIH, 62-63; from asst prof to assoc prof microbiol, Fels Res Inst & Sch Med, Temple Univ, 63-71, prof, 71-80; MEM FAC, DEPT MICROBIOL, HAHNEMANN MED COL, 80- *Concurrent Pos:* Vis researcher virol, Inst Cancer Res, Philadelphia, 59-61; vis scientist, Dept Bact, Ind Univ, 61-62. *Mem:* Am Soc Microbiol; Am Asn Cancer Res. *Res:* Virology; genetics; cancer research; molecular biology. *Mailing Add:* Dept Microbiol Hahnemann Med Col 230 N Broad St Philadelphia PA 19102

YAMAMOTO, RICHARD, b Wapato, Wash, May 27, 27; m 50; c 7. VETERINARY MICROBIOLOGY, MYCOPLASMOLOGY. *Educ:* Univ Wash, BS, 52; Univ Calif, MA, 55, PhD(microbiol), 57. *Prof Exp:* Asst specialist vet pub health, Univ Calif, 57-58, asst res microbiologist, 59; asst prof vet serol & asst vet serologist, Ore State Univ, 59-61; asst microbiologist, 62-64, lectr, 64-67, assoc prof, 67-70, assoc microbiologist, 64-70, PROF & MICROBIOLOGIST, UNIV CALIF, DAVIS, 70- *Concurrent Pos:* Assoc ed, Poultry Sci, 67-72 & 80- & Avian Dis J, 75- *Honors & Awards:* Tom Newman Int Award, 67; Nat Turkey Fedn Res Award, 70. *Mem:* Am Soc Microbiol; Poultry Sci Asn; Am Asn Avian Path; Animal Health Asn; World Poultry Sci Asn. *Res:* Host parasite interactions (infection, immunity, epidemiology) with reference to avian and canine species; mycoplasmas and viruses; development of rapid diagnostic tools for avian diseases. *Mailing Add:* Dept of Epidemiol & Prev Med Univ of Calif Davis CA 95616

YAMAMOTO, RICHARD KUMEO, b Honolulu, Hawaii, June 29, 35; m 61; c 3. PHYSICS. *Educ:* Mass Inst Technol, SB, 57, PhD(physics), 63. *Prof Exp:* Res staff physics, 63-64, from instr to assoc prof, 64-75, PROF PHYSICS, MASS INST TECHNOL, 75- *Mem:* Fel Am Phys Soc. *Res:* High energy nuclear physics; bubble chamber and spectrometer techniques and automated scanning and measuring of bubble chamber film. *Mailing Add:* Dept of Physics Mass Inst of Technol Cambridge MA 02139

YAMAMOTO, RICHARD SUSUMU, b Honolulu, Hawaii, May 15, 20; m 46; c 1. BIOCHEMISTRY. *Educ:* Univ Hawaii, AB, 46; George Washington Univ, AM, 49; Johns Hopkins Univ, ScD, 54. *Prof Exp:* Res assoc biochem, Johns Hopkins Univ, 54-55; biochemist, Lab Nutrit & Endocrinol, Nat Inst Arthritis & Metab Dis, 55-62; biochemist biol, 62-70, biochemist etiology, Exp Path Br, 70-76, BIOCHEMIST, CARCINOGEN METABOLISM & TOXICOL BR, NAT CANCER INST, 76- *Mem:* AAAS; Am Inst Nutrit; Soc Exp Biol & Med; Am Asn Cancer Res; Am Asn Clin Chemists. *Res:* Vitamin B12; nutritional obesity; lipid metabolism; chemical carcinogenesis; nutrition and endocrines in carcinogenesis. *Mailing Add:* Rm 3-C-22 Bldg 37 Nat Cancer Inst Bethesda MD 20014

YAMAMOTO, ROBERT TAKAICHI, b Hawaii, May 26, 27. ENTOMOLOGY. *Educ:* Univ Hawaii, BA, 53; Univ Ill, MS, 55, PhD, 57. *Prof Exp:* Res assoc entom, Univ Ill, 57-60; mem staff, Entom Res Div, USDA, 60-65; ASSOC PROF ENTOM, NC STATE UNIV, 65- *Mem:* Entom Soc Am. *Res:* Insect physiology and behavior. *Mailing Add:* Dept of Entom NC State Univ PO Box 5126 Raleigh NC 27607

YAMAMOTO, SACHIO, b Petaluma, Calif, Dec 12, 32; m 58; c 3. MARINE CHEMISTRY, PHYSICAL CHEMISTRY. *Educ:* Univ Calif, Berkeley, BS, 55; Iowa State Univ, PhD(phys chem), 59. *Prof Exp:* Res chemist, Calif Res Corp, 59-63; res chemist, US Naval Radiol Defense Lab, 63-69, res chemist, Naval Undersea Ctr, 69-71, SUPVRY RES CHEMIST, NAVAL OCEAN SYSTS CTR, 71- *Mem:* Am Chem Soc; AAAS. *Res:* Environmental sciences; trace metal analysis; gas solubility; x-ray fluorescence analysis. *Mailing Add:* 3725 Notre Dame Ave San Diego CA 92122

YAMAMOTO, TATSUZO, b Hardieville, Alta, Feb 8, 28. MICROBIOLOGY. *Educ:* Univ Alta, BSc, 52, MSc, 55; Yale Univ, PhD(virol), 61. *Prof Exp:* Fel microbiol, Univ Toronto, 61-62; from asst prof to assoc prof virol, 62-74, PROF MICROBIOL, UNIV ALTA, 74- *Concurrent Pos:* Consult, Govt Can, 72-; Sabbatical Res Assoc Award, Can Int Develop Res Ctr, 79-80. *Mem:* Am Soc Microbiol; Am Fisheries Soc; Int Ozone Inst; Int Wildlife Asn; Electron Micros Soc Am. *Res:* Replication and structure of animal viruses; ozone inactivation of microorganisms; microbial diseases of fish; virus diseases of cattle. *Mailing Add:* Dept of Microbiol Univ of Alta Edmonton AB T6G 2E9 Can

YAMAMOTO, TERUO, b Honolulu, Hawaii, Nov 27, 24; c 1. GEOLOGY. *Educ:* Univ Mo-Kansas City, BA, 53; Ind Univ, BS, 56, MA, 57. *Prof Exp:* Geologist watershed mgt, Southern Forest Exp Sta, 57-59 & Pac Southwest Forest & Range Exp Sta, 59-66, GEOLOGIST WATERSHED MGT & MINED-LAND RECLAMATION, ROCKY MOUNTAIN FOREST & RANGE EXP STA, FOREST SERV, USDA, 66- *Mem:* Am Geophys Union; Soil Sci Soc Am; Agron Soc Am; AAAS. *Res:* Mined-land reclamation and watershed management. *Mailing Add:* Rocky Mt Forest & Range Exp Sta Sch of Mines Campus Rapid City SD 57701

YAMAMOTO, WILLIAM SHIGERU, b Cleveland, Ohio, Sept 22, 24; m 65; c 3. PHYSIOLOGY, COMPUTER SCIENCE. *Educ:* Park Col, AB, 45; Univ Pa, MD, 49. *Hon Degrees:* MS, Univ Pa, 71. *Prof Exp:* Instr physiol, Sch Med, Univ Pa, 52-53, assoc, 55-57, instr biostatist & asst prof physiol, 57-66, prof physiol, 66-70; prof physiol & biomath, Sch Med, Univ Calif, 70-71; PROF CLIN ENG & CHMN DEPT, SCH MED, GEORGE WASHINGTON UNIV, 71- *Concurrent Pos:* Mem study sect, NIH, 63-65, mem Nat Adv Coun Res Resources, 71-75; consult, Health Care Tech Div, Nat Ctr Health Serv Res & Develop, 68-80 & Am Col Preventive Med, 80- *Mem:* AAAS; Am Physiol Soc; Asn Comput Mach; Biomed Eng Soc. *Res:* Computer applications in health services; physiology of respiratory regulation by carbon dioxide homeostasis. *Mailing Add:* Dept Clin Eng George Washington Univ Med Ctr Washington DC 20037

YAMAMOTO, Y LUCAS, b Hokkaido, Japan, Jan 19, 28; Can citizen; m 58; c 3. NEUROSURGERY, NUCLEAR MEDICINE. *Educ:* Hokkaido Univ, BSc, 48, MD, 52; Yokohama Nat Univ, PhD(radiobiol), 61. *Prof Exp:* Intern med, Int Cath Hosp, Tokyo, Japan, 53; resident neurosurg, Med Ctr, Georgetown Univ, 54-58; res assoc nuclear med & radiobiol, Med Dept, Brookhaven Nat Lab, 58-61; res assoc neurosurg res, 61-68, from asst prof to assoc prof, 68-80, PROF NEUROL & NEUROSURG, MONTREAL NEUROL INST, MCGILL UNIV, 80- *Concurrent Pos:* Mem, Am Bd Nuclear Med, 73- *Mem:* Soc Nuclear Med; Radiation Res Soc; Am Col Nuclear Physicians; Can Neurosurg Soc. *Res:* Neurological science; cerebral circulation. *Mailing Add:* Montreal Neurol Inst 3801 University St Montreal PQ H3A 2B4 Can

YAMAMOTO, YASUSHI STEPHEN, b Topaz, Utah, Aug 6, 43. ORGANIC CHEMISTRY, PHOTOGRAPHIC CHEMISTRY. *Educ:* Univ Wis, BS, 65; Pa State Univ, PhD(org chem), 71. *Prof Exp:* sr res chemist, Eastman Kodak Co Res Labs, 71-78; ASSOC PROF CHEM, ROCHESTER INST TECH, 78- *Concurrent Pos:* Coordr experiential learning, Rochester Inst Technol, 78-81. *Mem:* Am Chem Soc. *Res:* Investigating synthesis of color couplers for photographic applications; mechanisms and rates of coupling. *Mailing Add:* 1009 Roosevelt East Rochester NY 14445

YAMAMURA, HENRY ICHIRO, b Seattle, Wash, June 25, 40; m 64; c 1. NEUROCHEMISTRY, NEUROPHARMACOLOGY. *Educ:* Univ Wash, BS, 64, MS, 68, PhD(pharmacol), 69. *Prof Exp:* Pharm intern, Seattle, Wash, 60-64, staff pharmacist, 64-66; spec lectr pharmacol, Seattle Pac Col, 66-67; asst prof, 75-77, ASSOC PROF, DEPT PHARMACOL, COL MED, UNIV ARIZ, 77- *Concurrent Pos:* NIMH spec fel pharmacol, Sch Med, Johns Hopkins Univ, 72-75; NIMH Res Scientist Develop Awardee, 75- *Mem:* AAAS; Soc Neurosci; Am Soc Neurochem; Am Soc Pharmacol & Exp Therapeut. *Res:* Release and uptake of brain neurohumoral transmitters; demonstration of brain neurotransmitter receptors and their alterations in neuropsychiatric disorders. *Mailing Add:* Dept Pharmacol Col of Med Univ of Ariz Tucson AZ 85724

YAMANAKA, WILLIAM KIYOSHI, b Kauai, Hawaii, Mar 19, 31; m 58; c 3. NUTRITION, COMMUNITY HEALTH. *Educ:* Univ Hawaii, BS, 55; Univ Calif, PhD(nutrit), 69. *Prof Exp:* Res assoc nutrit, Children's Hosp of East Bay, Oakland, Calif, 59-64; res asst, Univ Calif, Berkeley, 64-69; assoc prof nutrit, Univ Mo-Columbia, 69-75; MEM FAC, UNIV WASH, 75- *Concurrent Pos:* Nutrit adv, Delta Area Head Start, Mo, 69-74; adv, Sickle Cell Anemia Adv Bd, Mo, 74; Nutrit proj & policies in develop countries. *Mem:* Am Dietetic Asn; Soc Nutrit Educ; Am Soc Clin Path. *Res:* Role of lipids in cardiovascular disease; effect of protein malnutrition of growing mammalian organisms; applied nutrition programs in developing countries; nutrition for cancer patients. *Mailing Add:* DL-10 Univ of Wash Seattle WA 98195

YAMANE, GEORGE M, b Honolulu, Hawaii, Aug 9, 24; m 51; c 3. ORAL MEDICINE, ORAL PATHOLOGY. *Educ:* Haverford Col, AB, 46; Univ Minn, Minneapolis, DDS, 50, PhD(oral path), 63. *Prof Exp:* Asst chem & zool, Univ Hawaii, 43-44; asst oral path & diag, Univ Minn, Minneapolis, 51-53; asst prof oral path, Univ Ill, Chicago, 57-59; asst prof oral path, Univ Wash, 59-63, dir tissue lab, 60-63; prof oral diag, med & roentgenol & chmn div, Univ Minn, Minneapolis, 63-70; asst dean res & postdoc prog, 77-80, PROF ORAL MED & RADIOL & CHMN DEPT, COL DENT NJ, UNIV MED & DENT NJ, 70- *Concurrent Pos:* Consult, Children Orthop Hosp & Med Ctr, Seattle, 60-63, Vet Admin Hosps, American Lake, Wash, 62-63 & Minneapolis, 64-70 & div dent health, Wyo State Bd Health, 66-70. *Mem:* Fel AAAS; fel Am Acad Oral Path; fel Int Col Dent; Int Asn Dent Res; fel Am Col Dent. *Res:* Bone tissue formation; radiobiology; magnesium metabolism; psychosomatic etiology of oral lesions. *Mailing Add:* Dept Oral Med & Radiol Univ Med & Dent NJ Newark NJ 07103

YAMANOUCHI, TAIJI, b Tokyo, Japan, Aug 16, 31; m 61; c 2. PHYSICS. *Educ:* Tokyo Univ Ed, BS, 53, MS, 55; Univ Rochester, PhD(physics), 60. *Prof Exp:* Res assoc physics, Univ Rochester, 60-65, sr res assoc, 65-69; PHYSICIST, FERMI NAT ACCELERATOR LAB, 69- *Mem:* Am Phys Soc. *Res:* Experimental particle physics. *Mailing Add:* Fermi Nat Accelerator Lab PO Box 500 Batavia IL 60510

YAMASHIRO, STANLEY MOTOHIRO, b Honolulu, Hawaii, Nov 26, 41; m 64; c 2. BIOMEDICAL ENGINEERING. *Educ:* Univ Southern Calif, BS, 64, MS, 66, PhD(elec eng), 70. *Prof Exp:* Mem tech staff elec eng, Hughes Aircraft Co, 64-70; res assoc, 70-71, asst prof, 71-74, ASSOC PROF BIOMED ENG, UNIV SOUTHERN CALIF, 74- *Res:* Cardiopulmonary physiology; application of control theory and computer technology to biological systems. *Mailing Add:* Dept of Biomed Eng Univ of Southern Calif Los Angeles CA 90007

YAMASHIROYA, HERBERT MITSUGI, b Honolulu, Hawaii, Sept 14, 30; m 47; c 4. MICROBIOLOGY, VIROLOGY. *Educ:* Univ Hawaii, BA, 53; Univ Ill, Chicago, MS, 62, PhD(microbiol), 65; Registry of Medical Technologists, cert. *Prof Exp:* Med technician supvr clin lab, Atomic Bomb Casualty Comn, Nat Acad Sci-Nat Res Coun, Hiroshima, Japan, 56-58; assoc scientist, IIT Res Inst, 64-65, res scientist, 65-68, sr scientist, 68-71; asst prof path, 71-76; asst dir hosp lab, 71-76; ASSOC PROF PATH, UNIV ILL COL MED, 76-, HEAD VIROL LAB, UNIV ILL HOSP, 71- *Concurrent Pos:* Mem adv bd, Clin Lab & Blood Bank, State Ill, 79-; lectr microbiol, Cook County Grad Sch Med, 77- *Mem:* AAAS; Am Soc Microbiol; Am Soc Clin Path. *Res:* Tissue culture and its application to viruses and rickettsiae; tissue culture nutritional studies; immunologic techniques and the immune mechanism; diagnostic procedures in microbiology. *Mailing Add:* Dept of Path Univ of Ill at the Med Ctr Chicago IL 60680

YAMAUCHI, HIROSHI, b Honolulu, Hawaii, Mar 26, 23; m 60; c 2. THEORETICAL PHYSICS. *Educ:* Univ Hawaii, BS, 47; Harvard Univ, MA, 48, PhD(physics), 50. *Prof Exp:* From instr to asst prof physics, Colby Col, 50-54; theoret physicist, Nuclear Develop Assoc, Inc, NY, 54-55; from asst prof to assoc prof math, Univ Hawaii, 55-65; assoc prof math & physics, 66-69, PROF MATH & PHYSICS, CHAMINADE COL HONOLULU, 69- *Mem:* Am Phys Soc. *Res:* Foundations of quantum mechanics; quantum field theory; mathematical physics; theoretical nuclear physics. *Mailing Add:* Dept Math Chaminade Col 3140 Waialae Ave Honolulu HI 96816

YAMAUCHI, MASANOBU, b Maui, Hawaii, Mar 3, 31; m 58; c 2. INORGANIC CHEMISTRY. *Educ:* Univ Hawaii, BA, 53; Univ Mich, MS, 58, PhD(chem), 61. *Prof Exp:* Asst prof chem, Univ NMex, 60-65; from asst prof to assoc prof, 65-74, PROF CHEM, EASTERN MICH UNIV, 74- *Mem:* Am Chem Soc. *Res:* Chemistry of boron hydrides and related compounds. *Mailing Add:* Dept of Chem Eastern Mich Univ Ypsilanti MI 48197

YAMAUCHI, TOSHIO, b Newell, Calif, Feb 13, 45. MEDICAL GENETICS, PEDIATRICS. *Educ:* Northwestern Univ, BA, 66, PhD(biol sci), 72. *Prof Exp:* Fel med genetics, Univ Tex Syst Cancer Ctr, M D Anderson Hosp & Tumor Inst, 72-74, res assoc med genetics, 74-77, MEM STAFF, UNIV TEX MED SCH, 79- *Mem:* AMA; Am Acad Pediat. *Res:* Study of enzymes which are involved in the metabolism and activation of chemical carcinogens and the development of systems to study these enzymes in the human population. *Mailing Add:* Dept Pediat Univ Tex Med Sch Houston TX 77025

YAMAZAKI, HIROSHI, b Hokkaido, Japan, Sept 5, 31; m 61; c 3. BIOCHEMISTRY. *Educ:* Hokkaido Univ, BS, 54, MS, 56; Univ Wis, PhD(biochem), 60. *Prof Exp:* Proj assoc biochem, Univ Wis, 61-63, res assoc, 63-65; res officer biol, Atomic Energy Can Ltd, 65-67; asst prof, 67-70, assoc prof, 70-77, PROF BIOL, CARLETON UNIV, 77- *Res:* Control mechanisms of RNA and protein biosynthesis in bacteria. *Mailing Add:* Dept of Biol Carleton Univ Ottawa ON K1S 5B6 Can

YAMAZAKI, RUSSELL KAZUO, b Topaz, Utah, Nov 23, 42; m 66. BIOCHEMICAL PHARMACOLOGY. *Educ:* Col Wooster, BA, 64; Mich State Univ, PhD(biochem), 69. *Prof Exp:* Res assoc biochem, Case Western Reserve Univ, 69-71; vis asst prof pharmacol, Univ Va, 71-73, asst prof, 73-78; ASSOC PROF PHARMACOL, WAYNE STATE UNIV, 78- *Mem:* Am Soc Biol Chemists; Am Chem Soc; Am Soc Plant Physiologists; AAAS. *Res:* Actions of hormones on the metabolism of mitochondria, peroxisomes and lysosomes. *Mailing Add:* Dept Pharmacol Sch Med Wayne State Univ Detroit MI 48201

YAMAZAKI, WILLIAM TOSHI, b San Francisco, Calif, May 10, 17; m 42; c 3. CEREAL CHEMISTRY. *Educ:* Univ Calif, BS, 39, MS, 41; Ohio State Univ, PhD(agr chem), 50. *Prof Exp:* CHEMIST IN CHG SOFT WHEAT QUAL LAB, AGR RES SERV, USDA, OHIO AGR RES & DEVELOP CTR, 63- *Concurrent Pos:* Adj prof agron, Ohio State Univ & Ohio Agr Res & Develop Ctr, 57- *Mem:* AAAS; Am Asn Cereal Chem; Am Chem Soc. *Res:* Chemical and physical basis for processing quality in soft wheat and soft wheat flour. *Mailing Add:* USDA Agr Res Serv Ohio Agr Res & Develop Ctr Wooster OH 44691

YAMBERT, PAUL ABT, b Toledo, Ohio, May 15, 28; m 50; c 5. CONSERVATION. *Educ:* Univ Mich, BS, 50, MS, 51, MA, 55, PhD(conserv), 60. *Prof Exp:* Field scout exec, Boy Scouts of Am, 51-52; teacher, Ann Arbor High Sch, Mich, 53-57; prof natural resources, Wis State Univ, Stevens Point, 57-69; dean outdoor labs, 69-74, PROF FORESTRY DEPT, SOUTHERN ILL UNIV, CARBONDALE, 74- *Concurrent Pos:* Vis prof, Univ Mich, 63. *Res:* Environmental attitude and knowledge; interpretation for the handicapped; outdoor recreation. *Mailing Add:* Forestry Dept Southern Ill Univ Carbondale IL 62901

YAMDAGNI, RAGHAVENDRA, b Aligarh, India, June 30, 41. PHYSICAL CHEMISTRY, MASS SPECTROMETRY. *Educ:* Allahabad Univ, BSc, 57, MSc, 59, PhD, 65. *Prof Exp:* Res assoc, Cornell Univ, 65-68; res assoc mass spectrom, Univ Alta, 68-75; prof assoc, 75-78, SR INSTR, DEPT CHEM, UNIV CALGARY, 78- *Mem:* Am Soc Mass Spectrom. *Res:* Ion molecule reactions; thermodynamic and reaction kinetics studies. *Mailing Add:* Dept of Chem Univ of Calgary Calgary AB T2N 1N4 Can

YAMIN, MICHAEL, b New York, NY, Aug 24, 28. PHYSICAL CHEMISTRY, COMPUTER SCIENCES. *Educ:* Polytech Inst Brooklyn, BS, 49; Yale Univ, PhD(chem), 52. *Prof Exp:* Fel chem, Yale Univ, 52-53; fel glass sci, Mellon Inst, 53-56; MEM STAFF, BELL LABS, INC, 57- *Res:* Semiconductors and semiconductor devices; insulating thin films; computer aids to design. *Mailing Add:* Bell Labs Inc Murray Hill NJ 07974

YAMIN, SAMUEL PETER, b New York, NY, July 26, 38; m 65; c 2. PARTICLE PHYSICS. *Educ:* Mass Inst Technol, SB, 60; Univ Pa, MS, 61, PhD(physics), 66. *Prof Exp:* Res assoc physics, Brookhaven Nat Lab, 66-69; asst prof physics, Rutgers Univ, New Brunswick, 69-75; assoc physicist, 75-78, PHYSICIST, BROOKHAVEN NAT LAB, 78- *Mem:* Am Phys Soc. *Res:* Experimental elementary particle physics; particle beam optics; superconducting magnet design; musical acoustics. *Mailing Add:* Bldg 911B Brookhaven Nat Lab Upton NY 11973

YAMINS, JACOB LOUIS, b Fall River, Mass, Jan 8, 14; m 48; c 1. FOOD SCIENCE. *Prof Exp:* Res assoc, Res Lab Org Chem, Mass Inst Technol, 39-42; sr chemist, Nat Fireworks, Inc, Mass, 43-46; sr chemist, Biochem Div, Interchem Corp, NJ, 47-48; res chemist & proj leader, Res Labs Div, Nat Dairy Prod Corp, 48-49, asst to vpres & dir res, 50-54, asst to pres, 54-58; dept head fundamental studies, Res & Develop Div, Am Sugar Co, NY, 58-65, dir sci develop, 65-67; VIS PROF FOOD SCI, RUTGERS UNIV, NEW BRUNSWICK, 67-; CONSULT, 69- *Concurrent Pos:* Adv chem dept, Adelphi Col, 50-; abstractor, Chem Abstrs. *Mem:* Fel AAAS; Am Chem Soc; Sigma Xi; Soc Chem Indust; fel NY Acad Sci. *Res:* Protein hydrolysis and isolation of amino acids; vitamin syntheses; preparation of primary explosives; tall oil; sterol isolation and syntheses; tocopherols; flavors; syntheses of long chain surface active agents and bactericides; antioxidants; baked products; carbohydrates; food product development; nutrition; single cell proteins; packaging. *Mailing Add:* PO Box 150 Freeport NY 11520

YAN, GEORGE, b Oct 10, 42; Can citizen; m 69; c 3. ELECTRICAL ENGINEERING, TECHNICAL MANAGMENT. *Educ:* Univ BC, BASc, 65, PhD(elec eng), 70. *Prof Exp:* Engr electronics, Atomic Energy Can Ltd, 70-73, sect leader electronics res, 73-77, head electronic syst br, 77-81; CORP ENG MGR, PHILLIPS CABLES LTD, 81- *Concurrent Pos:* Mem paper rev comt, Inst Elec & Electronics Engrs Transactions on Nuclear Sci, 77-82; tech prog comt mem, Nuclear Sci Symp, Inst Elec & Electronics Engrs, 77-81 & Symp Nuclear Power Systs, 80; mem, Smart Instrumentation Panel, Advan Electrotechnol Appls Nuclear Power Plants, Inst Elec & Electronics Engrs/Nat Res Coun Working Conf, 80; Can rep int working group, Nuclear Power Plant Control & Instrumentation, Atomic Energy Agency, Vienna; chmn, Specialists Meeting on Distrib Systs Nuclear Power Plants, Int Atomic Energy Agency, Chalk River, Ont, 80; chmn, Int Atomic Energy Agency, Specialists' Meeting on Distrib Systs Nuclear Power Plants, Chalk River, Ont, 80; invited lectr, Man-Machine Interfacing in Nuclear Power & Indust Process Control, Mass Inst Technol, 81. *Res:* Semiconductor devices and materials; computer aided design and drafting; distributed computer architectures; data acquisition systems; control and safety systems for nuclear power plants. *Mailing Add:* Phillips Cables Ltd King St W Brockville ON K6V 5W4 Can

YAN, JOHNSON FAA, b Amoy, China, May 21, 34; m 70. PHYSICAL CHEMISTRY. *Educ:* Nat Taiwan Univ, BS, 59; Kent State Univ, MS, 65, PhD(chem), 67. *Prof Exp:* Chief lab, Hwa Ming Pulp & Paper Manufactory, Chu-nan, Taiwan, 59-62; res assoc & fel, Cornell Univ, 67-69; develop assoc pulp & paper, Bowaters Carolina Corp, 69-77; SCI SPECIALIST, WEYERHAEUSER CORP, 77- *Mem:* AAAS; Am Chem Soc. *Res:* Physical chemistry, surface and colloid; polymers; biopolymers; pulp and paper. *Mailing Add:* Weyerhaeuser Technol Ctr Tacoma WA 98477

YAN, MAN FEI, b Kwang Tung, China, Dec 26, 48; m 77; c 2. CERAMIC SCIENCE, PHYSICAL METALLURGY. *Educ:* Mass Inst Technol, BS, 70, ScD(mat sci & eng), 76; Univ Calif, Berkeley, MS, 71. *Prof Exp:* MEM TECH STAFF, BELL LABS, 76- *Honors & Awards:* Ross Coffin Purdy Award, Am Ceramic Soc, 80. *Mem:* Am Ceramics Soc; Am Soc Metals. *Res:* Sintering of solids; ceramic microstructures; grain boundaries; grain boundary migration; glass fibre processing; electronic ceramics; magnetic ferrites; varistors; ceramic capacitor. *Mailing Add:* Bell Labs Rm 6E212 600 Mountain Ave Murray Hill NJ 07974

YAN, MAXWELL MENUHIN, b Russia, May 20, 19; Can citizen; m 44; c 5. ORGANIC CHEMISTRY, WOOD SCIENCE. *Educ:* Univ Man, BSc, 40, MSc, 42; McGill Col, PhD(wood chem), 47. *Prof Exp:* Inspector asphalts, Can Nat Testing, 42; chemist oil refining, Imp Oil Regina, 42-45; MGR PANELBD RES, WOOD COMPOS BD, ABITIBI PAPER CO LTD, 47- *Concurrent Pos:* Mem comt fibrebd, Can Gov Specif Bd, 69-; mem, Nat Adv Comt Forest Prod Res, Can Forestry Serv, Ottawa, 71-78; chmn, Panelbd Res Prog Adv Comt, Fed Forest Prod Lab, Ottawa, 71-78; mem, US Joint Coatings, Forest Prod Indust Steering Comt, 73-; adj prof forest prod, Fac Forestry, Univ Toronto, 75- *Honors & Awards:* Pioneer Wood Award, Forest Prod Res Soc, 76. *Mem:* Forest Prod Res Soc; Can Pulp & Paper Asn; Soc Wood Sci & Technol; AAAS; Am Soc Testing & Mat. *Res:* Wood composition board; wood fiber utilization; hearboard; particle board; wood and lignin chemistry. *Mailing Add:* 61 Stonedene Blvd Willowdale ON M2R 3C8 Can

YAN, TSOUNG-YUAN, b Tainan, Taiwan, Sept 17, 33; m 61; c 1. CHEMICAL ENGINEERING. *Educ:* Nat Taiwan Univ, BS, 59; Purdue Univ, MS, 62, PhD(chem eng), 63. *Prof Exp:* Teacher, Tainan Sch, 52-55; res engr, Mobil Oil Corp, 62-65, sr res engr, 65-70, res assoc, 70-78, SR RES ASSOC, MOBIL RES & DEVELOP CORP, 78- *Mem:* Am Chem Soc; Sigma Xi. *Res:* Catalysis, petroleum refining; coal upgrading and utilization; uranium in-situ leaching and refining processes; biomass conversion; lube oil processing; environmental control; process evaluation. *Mailing Add:* Mobil Res & Develop Corp PO Box 1025 Princeton NJ 08540

YAN, TUNG-MOW, b Keelung, Taiwan, Nov 27, 36; m 64; c 2. HIGH ENERGY PHYSICS. *Educ:* Nat Taiwan Univ, BS, 60; Nat Tsinghua Univ, Taiwan, MS, 62; Harvard Univ, PhD(physics), 68. *Prof Exp:* Res assoc physics, Stanford Linear Accelerator Ctr, 68-70, vis scientist, 73-74; asst prof, 70-75, assoc prof, 76-81, PROF PHYSICS, CORNELL UNIV, 81- *Concurrent Pos:* Alfred P Sloan Found fel, 74-78. *Mem:* Am Phys Soc. *Res:* Structure of elementary particles and properties of quantum field theories. *Mailing Add:* Lab Nuclear Studies Cornell Univ Ithaca NY 14853

YANAGIMACHI, RYUZO, b Sapporo, Japan, Aug 27, 28; m 60. REPRODUCTIVE BIOLOGY. *Educ:* Hokkaido Univ, BSc, 53, DSc(biol), 60. *Prof Exp:* Res scientist, Worcester Found Exp Biol, 60-64; lectr biol, Hokkaido Univ, 64-66; from asst prof to assoc prof, 66-73, PROF ANAT, SCH MED, UNIV HAWAII, 73- *Mem:* Soc Study Reproduction; Am Asn Anat; Am Soc Cell Biol; Brit Soc Study Fertil. *Res:* Biology of reproduction, particularly biology and physiology of gametes and early development of mammals. *Mailing Add:* Dept Anat & Reproductive Biol Univ Hawaii Sch of Med Honolulu HI 96822

YANAGISAWA, SAMUEL T, b Berkeley, Calif, Feb 18, 22; m 52; c 3. ELECTRICAL ENGINEERING. *Educ:* Univ Calif, Berkeley, BSEE Hons, 42. *Prof Exp:* Qual control engr, Machlett Labs, Inc, 43-45, develop engr, 46-48, sr develop engr, 48-55, sect head spec prod eng, 55-57, chief engr display & storage tubes, 57-60, prod line mgr, 60-63; vpres eng & mfg, Warnecke Electron Tubes, Ill, 63-67; mgr, Imaging Sensors Div, Varo Inc, 67-68, gen mgr, Electron Devices Div, 68-72, vpres, Varo, Inc, 71-72, exec vpres & dir, 72-74, pres & chief exec off, 74-76, chmn bd & chief exec officer, 76-78, CHMN BD, PRES & CHIEF EXEC OFFICER, VARO, INC, 78-, PRES & DIR, ELECTRON DEVICES DIV, 72- *Mem:* Inst Elec & Electronics Engrs; Am Vacuum Soc; Am Mgt Asn; Sigma Xi. *Res:* Management; design, development and production engineering of high power transmitting and microwave tubes; circuitry; vacuum switches; storage and display tubes; supervoltage electron accelerators; image converters and intensifiers; crossed field tubes. *Mailing Add:* Varo Inc 2203 Walnut St Garland TX 75040

YANAI, HIDEYASU STEVE, b Tokyo, Japan, Feb 26, 28; nat US; m 56; c 2. ANALYTICAL CHEMISTRY, PHYSICAL CHEMISTRY. *Educ:* Tokyo Agr Col, BS, 47; Calif State Polytech Col, BS, 53; Univ Minn, PhD(phys chem), 58. *Prof Exp:* Sr scientist, 58-69, anal lab head, Res Div, 69-73, anal res proj leader, Res Div, 73-79, proj leader, Plastics Res Dept, 79-81, RES SECT MGR PLASTICS, ROHM AND HAAS CO, 81- *Mem:* Am Chem Soc. *Res:* Plastics, polymer chemistry or polymers. *Mailing Add:* 302 Kenwood Dr Moorestown NJ 08057

YANARI, SAM SATOMI, b Gilcrest, Colo, May 27, 23; m 51; c 3. IMMUNOLOGY, BIOCHEMISTRY. *Educ:* Univ Chicago, BS, 48, PhD, 52. *Prof Exp:* Res assoc, Univ Chicago, 52-53; res assoc, Armour & Co, 53-56; res assoc, Minn Mining & Mfg Co, 56-64; head, Biochem Dept, Armour Pharmaceut Co, Ill, 65-69; res dir & vpres, Wilson Labs, 69-72; DIR, RES LAB, DIV ALLERGY & CLIN IMMUNOL, HENRY FORD HOSP, DETROIT, 72- *Mem:* Am Chem Soc; Am Fedn Clin Res; Am Asn Clin Chem; Am Acad Allergy. *Res:* Mechanism of enzyme action; protein chemistry and structure; proteolytic enzymes; absorption and fluorescence spectroscopy; hormones; immunology. *Mailing Add:* Div of Allergy & Clin Immunol 2799 W Grand Blvd Detroit MI 48202

YANCEY, PAUL HERBERT, b Whittier, Calif, July 4, 51; m 78. ENVIRONMENTAL PHYSIOLOGY, COMPARATIVE BIOCHEMISTRY. *Educ:* Calif Inst Technol, BS, 73; Scripps Inst Oceanog, Univ Calif, PhD(marine biol), 78. *Prof Exp:* NATO fel physiol, Univ St Andrews, Scotland, 78-80; ASST PROF BIOL, WHITMAN COL, 81- *Mem:* AAAS; Soc Develop Biol; Am Inst Biol Sci. *Res:* Biochemical and physiological adaptations in muscle proteins of fishes to temperature and salinity; correlating changes in protein types and functions with changes in physiological functions under varying environmental conditions. *Mailing Add:* Biol Dept Whitman Col Walla Walla WA 99362

YANCEY, ROBERT JOHN, JR, b Austin, Tex, Sept 17, 48; m 69; c 1. VETERINARY MICROBIOLOGY, MICROBIAL PATHOGENESIS. *Educ:* Univ Tex, Austin, BA, 71, PhD(microbiol), 77. *Prof Exp:* Instr med & gen microbiol, Univ Tex, Austin, 76-77, res assoc, Dept Microbiol, 77-78; fel, Dept Microbiol & Immunol, Univ Tex Health Sci Ctr Dallas, 78-79, Sch Med, Univ Mo, 79-80; RES SCIENTIST VET THERAPEUT, UPJOHN CO, 80- *Concurrent Pos:* Coordr microbiol teaching labs, Univ Tex, Austin, 76-77; conf group leader med microbiol, Univ Tex Health Sci Ctr Dallas & bacteriol lab instr, 78-79; bacteriol lab lectr, Sch Med, Univ Mo, 79-80. *Mem:* Sigma Xi; Am Soc Microbiol; AAAS; NY Acad Sci. *Res:* Molecular mechanisms of bacterial pathogenesis including the role of ion and siderophores; mechanisms of exotoxin production; role of bacterial rootility; disease pathogenesis of slaphylococcal mosites. *Mailing Add:* 9690-190-40 Upjohn Co Kalamazoo MI 49001

YANCEY, THOMAS ERWIN, b Lowville, NY, July 24, 41; m 71; c 3. PALEONTOLOGY, SEDIMENTARY PETROLOGY. *Educ:* Univ Calif, Berkeley, BA, 66, MA, 69, PhD(paleont), 71. *Prof Exp:* Lectr, Univ Malaya, 71-75; prof geol, Idaho State Univ, 75-80; MEM STAFF, DEPT GEOL, TEX A&M UNIV, 80- *Concurrent Pos:* Consult. *Mem:* Geol Soc Am; Soc Econ Paleontologists & Mineralogists; Am Asn Petrol Geologists; Paleont Soc; Paleont Asn. *Res:* Paleoecology and systematics of Upper Paleozoic invertebrates, primarily molluscs and brachipods; studies of molluscs of all ages. *Mailing Add:* Dept of Geol Tex A&M Univ College Station TX 77843

YANCHICK, VICTOR A, b Joliet, Ill, Dec 3, 40; m 63; c 3. PHARMACY. *Educ:* Univ Iowa, BS, 62, MS, 66; Purdue Univ, PhD(pharm), 68. *Prof Exp:* Instr pharm, Purdue Univ, 66-68; asst prof, 68-72, assoc prof, 72-79, actg asst dean, 72-74, asst dean acad affairs, Col Phar, 74-81, assoc dean, 81, PROF PHARM, UNIV TEX, AUSTIN, 79- *Honors & Awards:* Parenteral Drug Asn Res Awards, 66 & 68. *Mem:* Am Pharmaceut Asn; Am Soc Hosp Pharmacists; Acad Pharmaceut Sci; Am Asn Cols Pharm. *Res:* Parenteral drugs, primarily inactivation by other agents; drug interactions and incompatibilities; drug-nutrient interactions; geriatric pharmacotherapeutics. *Mailing Add:* Col of Pharm Univ of Tex Austin TX 78712

YANCIK, JOSEPH J, b Mt Olive, Ill, Dec 1, 30; m 55; c 2. MINING ENGINEERING. *Educ:* Univ Ill, Urbana-Champaign, BS, 54; Mo Sch Mines, MS, 56; Univ Mo-Rolla, PhD(mining eng), 60. *Prof Exp:* Mining engr, St Joseph Lead Co, 55-58, res assoc mining, Mo Sch Mines, 58-60; mgr res & develop explosives, Monsanto Co, 60-70; asst dir mining, 72-77, CHIEF DIV MINING RES, US BUR MINES, US DEPT INTERIOR, WASHINGTON, DC, 70- *Concurrent Pos:* Mem, Emergency Minerals Admin, US Dept Interior, 71-; vpres res & tech servs, Nat Coal Asn, 77-; chmn bd, Bituminous Coal Res, Inc, 77-79, vchmn bd & pres, 79-81. *Mem:* Am Inst Mining, Metall & Petrol Engrs. *Res:* Mining research in areas of operations research in areas of operations, health and safety; explosives in areas of utilization, thermochemical and hydrodynamic properties; coal utilization. *Mailing Add:* 1703 James Payne Circle McLean VA 22101

YANDERS, ARMON FREDERICK, b Lincoln, Nebr, Apr 12, 28; m 48; c 2. GENETICS. *Educ:* Nebr State Col, AB, 48; Univ Nebr, PhD(zool), 53. *Prof Exp:* Res assoc genetics, Oak Ridge Nat Lab & Northwestern Univ, 53-54; biophysicist, US Naval Radiol Defense Lab, 55-58; assoc geneticist, Argonne Nat Lab, 58-59; assoc prof zool, Mich State Univ, 59-65, prof & asst dean col natural sci, 65-69; DEAN COL ARTS & SCI, UNIV MO-COLUMBIA, 69- *Concurrent Pos:* Vis scientist, Commonwealth Sci & Indust Res Orgn, Canberra, Australia, 66; mem bd dir & consult, Assoc Midwestern Univs, 66-68. *Mem:* AAAS; Am Soc Zoologists; Genetics Soc Am; Soc Study Evolution; Am Soc Naturalists. *Res:* Drosophila cytogenetics. *Mailing Add:* Col of Arts & Sci Univ of Mo Columbia MO 65201

YANEY, PERRY PAPPAS, b Columbus, Ohio, July 28, 31; m 61; c 3. ELECTRO-OPTICS. *Educ:* Univ Cincinnati, EE, 54, MS, 57, PhD(physics), 63. *Prof Exp:* Design engr, Baldwin Piano Co, Ohio, 54-55; res physicist, St Eloi Corp, 55-59; physicist, Electronics & Ord Div, Avco Corp, 59-62; Univ Cincinnati res fel, Wright-Patterson AFB, 62-63; assoc res physicist, Res Inst, 63-65, from asst prof to assoc prof physics, 65-77, PROF PHYSICS, UNIV DAYTON, 77- *Concurrent Pos:* Consult, Optical Spectros & Reheis Chem Co, 74; consult & vis scientist, Univ Southern Calif, 75. *Mem:* Am Inst Aeronaut & Astronaut; Am Phys Soc; Optical Soc Am; Inst Elec & Electronics Engrs; Am Asn Physics Teachers. *Res:* Laser probe measurements in combustion and flowing gases; optical and electrical properties of ions in crystals; Raman spectroscopy; lasers and their applications; electroluminescence in solids; electrooptical instrumentation techniques; Raman scattering in solids and gases. *Mailing Add:* Dept Physics Univ Dayton Dayton OH 45469

YANG, AN TZU, b Shanghai, China, Oct 5, 23; US citizen; m 52; c 2. DYNAMICS. *Educ:* Northwestern Col Eng, China, BS, 46; Ohio State Univ, MS, 50; Columbia Univ, DEngSc, 63. *Prof Exp:* Res engr, Columbia Univ, 55-56; vis prof, Inst Math, Univ Rio Grande do Sul, Brazil, 59-60; sr engr, Res & Develop Div, Am Mach & Foundry Co, 60-64; from asst prof to assoc prof eng, 64-71, NSF res grant, 66-69, PROF ENG, UNIV CALIF, DAVIS, 71- *Concurrent Pos:* NSF res grant, Stanford Univ, 70-71. *Mem:* Am Soc Mech Engrs. *Res:* Kinematic analysis and synthesis of mechanisms; dynamics of mechanical systems. *Mailing Add:* Dept of Mech Eng Univ of Calif Davis CA 95616

YANG, C(HENG) Y(I), b Tientsin, China, Dec 17, 30; m 61. STRUCTURAL DYNAMICS. *Educ:* Nat Taiwan Univ, BS, 53; Purdue Univ, MS, 58; Mass Inst Technol, DSc(civil eng), 62. *Prof Exp:* Asst civil eng, Nat Taiwan Univ, 54-56, Purdue Univ, 56-58 & Mass Inst Technol, 58-61, res engr, 61-62; asst prof, Univ Ill, 62-66; ASSOC PROF, UNIV DEL, 66- *Mem:* Assoc mem Am Soc Civil Engrs; Am Astronaut Soc; Am Soc Eng Educ; Soc Exp Stress Anal. *Res:* Wave propagation in solids investigated by method of characteristics; behavior of structural systems under deterministic and probabilistic loads; structural safety studies. *Mailing Add:* Dept of Civil Eng Univ of Del Newark DE 19711

YANG, CHANG-TSING, b Shanghai, China, Feb 15, 17; US citizen. CHEMICAL ENGINEERING, PHARMACEUTICAL CHEMISTRY. *Educ:* Nat Univ Chekiang, BS, 37; Univ Minn, Minneapolis, PhD(chem eng), 50. *Prof Exp:* Group leader, Res & Develop, Julius Hyman & Co, 51-54; res assoc air pollution, Univ Ill, 55-56; sr engr, Dow Chem Co, 56-60; pilot plant mgr, 60-63, sr engr, 63-76, PRIN ENGR, AM CYANAMID CO, 76- *Mem:* Am Chem Soc. *Res:* Vapor-liquid equilibrium; countercurrent multi-stage processes; polyester and polyolefin processes; process design and pollution control. *Mailing Add:* Am Cyanamid Co Wayne NJ 07470

YANG, CHAO-CHIH, b Changsha, China, Dec 17, 28; m 57; c 1. COMPUTER SCIENCE. *Educ:* Chinese Naval Col Technol, BS, 53; Nat Chiao Tung Univ, MS, 62; Northwestern Univ, MS, 64, PhD(elec eng), 66. *Prof Exp:* Asst prof elec eng & info sci, Wash State Univ, 66-67; prof comput sci, Nat Chiao Tung Univ, 67-71; scientist, Int Bus Mach, San Jose Res Lab, 71-72; assoc prof info sci, 72-79, PROF COMPUT & INFO SCI, UNIV ALA, BIRMINGHAM, 79- *Mem:* Inst Elec & Electronics Engrs; Asn Comput Mach; Sigma Xi. *Res:* Design, implementation and analysis of computer algorithms related to theory of computation, operating systems principles. *Mailing Add:* Dept Comput & Info Sci Univ Ala Univ Sta Birmingham AL 35294

YANG, CHAO-HUI, b Taichung, Taiwan, Aug 20, 28; m 63; c 2. MATHEMATICS. *Educ:* Nat Taiwan Univ, BS, 51; Univ Mich, MA, 55; Univ Cincinnati, PhD(math), 58. *Prof Exp:* Res fel, Inst Math Sci, NY Univ, 58-59, assoc res scientist, 59-61; lectr math, Rutgers Univ, 61-64; PROF MATH, STATE UNIV NY COL ONEONTA. *Mem:* Am Math Soc; Math Asn Am. *Res:* Maximal binary matrices; integral equations; integrability of trigonometric series; combinatorial and functional analyses. *Mailing Add:* Dept of Math State Univ of NY Col Oneonta NY 13820

YANG, CHARLES CHIN-TZE, b Shanghai, China, Aug 20, 22; US citizen; m 57; c 3. MECHANICS, METALLURGY. *Educ:* Henry Lester Inst Technol, BSc, 42; Univ Mich, Ann Arbor, MSE, 47; Univ Calif, Berkeley, PhD(mech eng, metall), 51. *Prof Exp:* Asst prof mech eng, Mass Inst Technol, 51-54; sr res engr, Ford Res Ctr, Ford Motor Co, 54-57; assoc prof, Univ Mich, Ann Arbor, 57-60; adv engr, Int Bus Mach Corp, 60-63; sr staff scientist, San Diego Div, Gen Dynamics Corp, 63-68, staff scientist, Pomona Div, 68-77; SR ENGR, GEN ELEC CO, CALIF, 77- *Concurrent Pos:* Sr staff specialist, Tech Resources Inc, 71- *Mem:* Am Soc Metals; Am Soc Mech Engrs. *Res:* Powder metallurgy, boron fibrous-aluminum powder composites; nitrocellulose tape metal processing and dinitrocellulose; structural design analysis and evaluation of engineered components, machineries, large steam turbine-generators, gas turbines, and nuclear reactors; statistics; dynamics; heat transfer. *Mailing Add:* Gen Elec Co 310 Deguigne Dr MC S24 Sunnyvale CA 94086

YANG, CHEN NING, b Hofei, Anhwei, China, Sept 22, 22; m 50; c 3. PHYSICS. *Educ:* Southwest Assoc Univ, China, BSc, 42; Univ Chicago, PhD(physics), 48. *Hon Degrees:* DSc, Princeton Univ, 58, Polytechnic Inst Brooklyn, 65, Univ Wroclaw, 75, Gustavus Adolphus Col, Minn, 75, Univ Md, 79 & Univ Durham, England, 79. *Prof Exp:* Instr physics, Univ Chicago, 48-49; mem, Inst Advan Study, 49-66; EINSTEIN PROF PHYSICS & DIR INST THEORET PHYSICS, STATE UNIV NY STONY BROOK, 66- *Honors & Awards:* Nobel Prize in Physics, 57; Einstein Award, 57; Rumford Prize, 80. *Mem:* Nat Acad Sci; Am Philos Soc; Am Phys Soc; Brazelian Acad Sci; Venezuelan Acad Sci. *Res:* Theoretical physics. *Mailing Add:* Inst for Theoret Physics State Univ of NY Stony Brook NY 11794

YANG, CHIA HSIUNG, b Peikang, Taiwan, Sept 24, 40; US citizen; m 69; c 3. NUCLEAR PHYSICS. *Educ:* Tunghai Univ, Taiwan, BSc, 62; Tsing Hua Univ, Taiwan, MSc, 65; Washington Univ, MA, 67, PhD(physics), 71. *Prof Exp:* From asst prof to assoc prof, 71-80, PROF PHYSICS, SOUTHERN UNIV, 80- *Concurrent Pos:* NASA res grant, 72-79. *Mem:* Sigma Xi; Am Phys Soc. *Res:* Microscopic study of isotropic superfluidity of neutron star matter by Yang and Clark method which combines Bardeen-Cooper-Schrieffer and correlated basis function theories. *Mailing Add:* 1062 Stoneleigh Dr Baton Rouge LA 70808

YANG, CHIH TED, b Chung King, China, Jan 23, 40; m 68. MORPHOLOGY, HYDROLOGY. *Educ:* Cheng Kung Univ, Taiwan, BS, 62; Colo State Univ, MS, 65, PhD, 68. *Prof Exp:* Assoc prof scientist, Ill State Water Surv, 68-74; hydraul engr, US Army Corp Engrs, 74-80; HYDRAUL ENGR, WATER & POWER RESOURCES SERV, ENG & RES CTR, US BUR RECLAMATION, 80- *Honors & Awards:* Robert E Horton Award, Am Geophys Union, 72; Walter L Hurber Res Prize, Am Soc Civil Engrs, 73. *Mem:* Am Geophys Union; Am Soc Civil Engrs. *Res:* Hydraulics, hydrology, morphology, sedimentation, hydraulic structure design. *Mailing Add:* US Bur Reclamation Code 3200 PO Box 25007 Denver CO 80202

YANG, CHING HUAN, b Hunan, China, Sept 7, 20; m 52; c 3. MECHANICS. *Educ:* Nat Cent Univ, China, BS, 43; Lehigh Univ, PhD(appl mech), 51. *Prof Exp:* Res assoc plasticity, Fritz Eng Lab, Lehigh Univ, 47-51; engr, Anaconda Copper Mining Co, 52-55; sr engr, Convair Div, Gen Dynamics Corp, 56-57, staff scientist, Sci Res Lab, 57-62; mem tech staff, Defense Res Corp, Calif, 62-68; PROF ENG, STATE UNIV NY, STONY BROOK, 68- *Mem:* Combustion Inst. *Res:* Applied mechanics; combustion theories; explosion phenomena; nonequilibrium thermodynamics; gaseous kinetics. *Mailing Add:* Dept of Mech State Univ of NY Stony Brook NY 11790

YANG, CHUI-HSU (TRACY), b Hunan, China, Nov 19, 38; US citizen; m 64; c 2. RADIATION BIOPHYSICS. *Educ:* Tunghai Univ, BS, 59; North Tex State Univ, MS, 64; Univ Ill, PhD(biophys), 67. *Prof Exp:* Appointee biol, Argonne Nat Lab, 67-69; BIOPHYSICIST, LAWRENCE BERKELEY LAB, UNIV CALIF, 69- *Mem:* Am Inst Biol Sci; Biophys Soc; Radiation Res Soc; Sigma Xi; AAAS. *Res:* Effects of radiation on membrane, development and longevity; mechanisms and kinetics of recovery; space biology; responses of cultured mammalian cells to heavy ions and other environmental factors; mechanisms of cell transformation in vitro by radiation and virus. *Mailing Add:* Bldg 74B Rm 106 Univ Calif Lawrence Berkeley Lab Berkeley CA 94720

YANG, CHUN CHUAN, b Taichung, Taiwan, Jan 25, 36; m 66; c 2. MECHANICAL ENGINEERING, FLUID DYNAMICS. *Educ:* Cheng-Kung Univ, BS, Taiwan, 59; Univ RI, MS, 65; Yale Univ, PhD(eng), 69. *Prof Exp:* Jr engr, Taiwan Mach Mfg Corp, 61-63; res asst heat transfer, Univ RI, 63-65; mem res staff geophys fluid dynamics, Yale Univ, 69-72; res scientist, Xonics, Inc, 72-74; RES ENGR, HEAT TRANSFER RES, INC, 74- *Mem:* Am Soc Mech Engrs; Sigma Xi. *Res:* Heat transfer and fluid mechanics in two-phase flow. *Mailing Add:* Heat Transfer Res Inc 1000 S Fremont Ave Alhambra CA 91802

YANG, CHUNG CHING, b Peiking, China, Sept 13, 38; US citizen; m 62; c 2. SOLID STATE PHYSICS, QUANTUM ELECTRONICS. *Educ:* Univ Calif, Los Angeles, BS, 66; Harvard Univ, MS, 67, PhD(solid state physics), 72. *Prof Exp:* Mem sci staff, 72-78, res mgr, 78-80, TECH RES MGR, XEROX CORP, 80- *Mem:* Am Phys Soc. *Res:* Quantum optics; phase transition; transport across materials interfaces. *Mailing Add:* Xerox Corp 1341 W Mockingbird Lane Dallas TX 75247

YANG, CHUNG SHU, b Peking, China, Aug 8, 41; m 66; c 2. BIOCHEMISTRY. *Educ:* Nat Taiwan Univ, BS, 62; Cornell Univ, PhD(biochem), 67. *Prof Exp:* Fel biochem, Scripps Clin & Res Found, 67-69; res assoc, Yale Univ, 69-71; asst prof, 71-75, assoc prof, 75-79, PROF BIOCHEM, COL MED NJ, 79- *Honors & Awards:* Fac Res Award, Am Cancer Soc. *Mem:* Am Soc Biochemists; Am Chem Soc; Am Soc Pharmacol; Am Inst Nutrit; Am Asn Cancer Res. *Res:* Mechanisms of biological oxygenation and carcinogen activation, etiology and modification of carcinogenesis. *Mailing Add:* Dept of Biochem Col of Med & Dent of NJ Newark NJ 07103

YANG, CHUNG-CHUN, b Kiang-su, China, Nov 21, 42; m 67; c 3. PURE MATHEMATICS, APPLIED MATHEMATICS. *Educ:* Nat Taiwan Univ, BS, 64; Univ Wis-Madison, MS, 66, PhD(math), 69. *Prof Exp:* Res assoc math, Mich State Univ, 69-70; RES MATHEMATICIAN, NAVAL RES LAB, 70- *Honors & Awards:* Res Publ Award, Naval Res Lab, 73. *Mem:* Am Math Soc; Japanese Math Soc. *Res:* Factorization theory in the function theory of one complex variable; applications of theory of meromorphic functions to some physical and engineering problems; pattern recognition and image processing in computer science area. *Mailing Add:* Naval Res Lab Washington DC 20375

YANG, CHUNG-TAO, b Pingyang, China, May 4, 23; m 57; c 3. MATHEMATICS. *Educ:* Chekiang Univ, BS, 46; Tulane Univ, PhD, 52. *Prof Exp:* Asst math, Chekiang Univ, 46-48; asst, Nat Acad Sci, China, 48-49; instr, Nat Taiwan Univ, 49-50; res assoc, Univ Ill, 52-54; mem staff, Inst Advan Study, 54-56; from asst prof to assoc prof, 56-61, PROF MATH, UNIV PA, 61-, CHMN DEPT, 80- *Mem:* Am Math Soc; Math Asn Am. *Res:* General and algebraic topology; topological and differential transformation groups. *Mailing Add:* Dept of Math Univ of Pa Philadelphia PA 19174

YANG, DA-PING, b Peiping, China, Oct 5, 33; US citizen; m 67; c 2. GENETICS, CELL BIOLOGY. *Educ:* Nat Taiwan Univ, BSc, 56; Ottawa Univ, Can, MSc, 64, PhD(genetics), 69. *Prof Exp:* Agronomist, Rice Res Inst, Taiwan; instr, Ottawa Univ, Can, 64-68; fel biol, Nat Res Coun, Can, 68-70; SR RES SCIENTIST & SUPVR, CYTOL LAB, WYETH LABS, INC, 71- *Mem:* AAAS; Tissue Cult Asn; Environ Mutagen Soc; NY Acad Sci. *Res:* Mammmalian cell culture and cytogenetics; genetic toxicology; mutagenesis; carcinogenesis; somatic cell genetics. *Mailing Add:* Div Res & Develop Wyeth Labs Inc PO Box 8299 Philadelphia PA 19101

YANG, DARCHUN BILLY, b Taipei, Taiwan, July 17, 45; m 71; c 2. HETEROGENEOUS CATALYSIS, HOMOGENEOUS CATALYSIS. *Educ:* Tamkang Univ, Taiwan, BS, 69; Furman Univ, MS, 73; Univ Ga, PhD(inorg chem), 77. *Prof Exp:* Anal technician, Alpha Lab, Can, 74-75; fel, Univ Ga, 78-80; SR CHEMIST, EXXON RES & ENG CO, 80- *Concurrent Pos:* Chem teacher, Mil Acad Taiwan & Shulin High Sch, 69-71. *Mem:* Am Chem Soc; Catalysis Soc. *Res:* Homogeneous and heterogeneous catalysis; new and improved catalysts, their catalytic performance, physical charaterization of catalyst and carrier diagnosis of catalyst decilivation and their use in processing operations. *Mailing Add:* Exxon Res & Eng Co PO Box 4255 Baytown TX 77520

YANG, DAVID CHIH-HSIN, b Hsinchiang, China, Jan 8, 47; m 71. BIOCHEMISTRY. *Educ:* Nat Taiwan Univ, BSc, 68; Yale Univ, PhD(biochem), 73. *Prof Exp:* Res assoc, The Rockefeller Univ, 73-75; asst prof, 75-81, ASSOC PROF BIOCHEM, GEORGETOWN UNIV, 81- *Mem:* Am Chem Soc; AAAS; Am Asn Univ Professors; Am Soc Biol Chemists; NY Acad Sci. *Res:* Structure of amino acyl-tRNA synthetases; conformational analysis of protein and nucleic acid; fluorescence spectroscopy; chemical modification of nucleic acid; animal lectins. *Mailing Add:* Dept of Chem Georgetown Univ Washington DC 20057

YANG, DOMINIC TSUNG-CHE, b Tainan, Taiwan, Oct 9, 33; US citizen; m 62; c 2. ORGANIC CHEMISTRY. *Educ:* St Benedict's Col, Kans, BS, 59; Univ Ga, PhD(org chem), 69. *Prof Exp:* Chemist, Nalco Chem Co, Ill, 59-64; instr toxicol & NIH res grant, VanderVanderbilt Univ, 68-70; asst prof org chem, 70-74, assoc prof, 74-79, PROF ORG CHEM, UNIV ARK, LITTLE ROCK, 79- *Mem:* Am Chem Soc; The Chem Soc. *Res:* Isolation and structure elucidation of fungal metabolites; organic synthesis. *Mailing Add:* Dept of Chem Univ of Ark Little Rock AR 72204

YANG, DOROTHY CHUAN-YING, b Shanghai, China, May 27, 18; US citizen; div; c 2. PEDIATRICS, NEUROLOGY. *Educ:* St Johns Univ, China, MD, 45; New York Med Col, MMSc, 50; Am Bd Pediat, dipl, 52. *Prof Exp:* Intern, St Luke's Hosp, Shanghai, China, 44-45; med resident, Govt Hosp, Free China, 45-46; resident pediat, Children's Ctr, New York, 47-48; asst resident, New Eng Hosp Women & Children, Boston, Mass, 48-49; asst resident, Syracuse Med Ctr, 49-50; instr pediat, New York Med Col, 52-54, assoc, 54-55, asst clin prof, 55-56, asst prof, 56-60; res neurol, Children's Hosp Philadelphia, 61-62; assoc prof pediat, New York Med Col, 64-69, asst prof neurol, 66-69; CLIN ASSOC PROF PEDIAT, STATE UNIV NY DOWNSTATE MED CTR, 69-; ASSOC DIR STANLEY S LAMM INST DEVELOP DIS, LONG ISLAND COL HOSP, 69- *Concurrent Pos:* Teaching & res fel, New York Med Col, 50-52; NIH spec fel pediat neurol, 60-63; asst pediatrician, Flower & Fifth Ave Hosp, New York, 54-60; pediatrician, Collab Study Neurol Dis & Blindness, NIH, 57-60, neurologist, 64-69; asst vis pediatrician, Metrop Hosp, New York, 58-60; spec training electroencephalog, Grad Hosp, Univ Pa, 62-63; assoc attend pediatrician, Flower & Fifth Ave & Metrop Hosps, 64-69, asst attend neurologist, 66-69; assoc vis pediatrician, Kings County Hosp Ctr, 71-; consult pediat neurol, St John's Episcopal Hosp, Brooklyn, NY, 72- *Mem:* Fel Am Acad Pediat; Child Neurol Soc; Am Acad Neurol; Am Med Electroencephalog Asn. *Mailing Add:* 110 Amity St Brooklyn NY 11201

YANG, EDWARD S, b Nanking, China, Oct 16, 36; US citizen; m 61; c 2. ELECTRONICS. *Educ:* Cheng Kung Univ, Taiwan, BS, 57; Okla State Univ, MS, 61; Yale Univ, PhD(eng & appl sci), 66. *Prof Exp:* Jr engr, Int Bus Mach Corp, 61-62, assoc engr, 62-63; asst electronics, Yale Univ, 63-65; from asst prof to assoc prof elec eng, 65-75, PROF ELEC ENG, COLUMBIA UNIV, 75- *Concurrent Pos:* Dir, NSF res grant & prin investr, 67-81, NASA res grant, 67-69; contracts, Dept Energy, 77-82 & Dept Defense, 77- *Mem:* Fel Inst Elec & Electronics Engrs. *Res:* Schottky Barriers, p-n junction, LED solar cell injection laser, device fabrication and physics. *Mailing Add:* Dept of Elec Eng Columbia Univ New York NY 10027

YANG, GENE CHING-HUA, b Kaohsuing, Taiwan, Feb 26, 38; US citizen; m 70; c 1. MICROBIOLOGY, INFECTIOUS DISEASE. *Educ:* Tunghai Univ, BS, 60; Northwestern Univ, MS, 66; Mich State Univ, PhD(microbiol), 70. *Prof Exp:* Asst prof, Med Ctr, Univ Tenn, 71-76; ASSOC PROF MICROBIOL & DIR MED TECHNOL PROG, SAGINAW VALLEY STATE COL, 76- *Concurrent Pos:* Mem bd, Dr Sun Yet Sen Inst, 77-; consult, St Luke's Hosp, Saginaw, 77- *Mem:* AAAS; Am Soc Med Technol; Am Soc Microbiol; Sigma Xi. *Res:* Pathogenic mechanism of enteric infection. *Mailing Add:* Dept of Microbiol Saginaw Valley State Col University Center MI 48710

YANG, GRACE L, b Queichow, China; m 64; c 2. STATISTICS. *Educ:* Univ Calif, Berkeley, MA, 63, PhD(statist), 66. *Prof Exp:* From asst prof to assoc prof, 73-78, PROF STATIST, UNIV MD, COLLEGE PARK, 78- *Mem:* Am Statist Asn; Inst Math Statist. *Res:* Mathematical statistics; biostatistics. *Mailing Add:* 6106 Neilwood Dr Rockville MD 20852

YANG, H(SUN) T(IAO), b Hangchow, China, May 19, 24; m 65; c 3. AEROSPACE ENGINEERING. *Educ:* Univ Wash, MS, 50; Calif Inst Technol, PhD(aeronaut, math), 55. *Prof Exp:* Res fel, Calif Inst Technol, 55-56; res assoc, Inst Fluid Dynamics, Univ Md, 56-58; res scientist, Eng Ctr, 58-63, ASSOC PROF AERONAUT ENG, UNIV SOUTHERN CALIF, 63- *Concurrent Pos:* Fulbright-Hays lectr, 64-65; consult various indust concerns. *Mem:* Am Phys Soc; Am Inst Aeronaut & Astronaut. *Res:* Fluid dynamics; aerodynamics. *Mailing Add:* Dept of Aerospace Eng Univ of Southern Calif Los Angeles CA 90007

YANG, HO SEUNG, b Korea, Dec 13, 47; m 74; c 2. FOOD SCIENCE & TECHNOLOGY, BIOCHEMICAL ENGINEERING. *Educ:* Seoul Nat Univ, BS, 69; Univ Minn, MS, 71; Mass Inst Technol, PhD(food sci), 76. *Prof Exp:* Res assoc, Mass Inst Technol, 76; res scientist, Watson Res Ctr, IBM, 76-78; SR RES CHEMIST, A E STALEY MFG CO, 78- *Mem:* Inst Food Technologists; Am Chem Soc; Soc Indust Microbiol. *Res:* Enzyme technology; carbohydrate and protein processing; fermentation; applied biochemistry; food process development. *Mailing Add:* A E Staley Mfg Co 2200 Eldorado St Decatur IL 62525

YANG, HOYA Y, b Amoy, China, June 3, 12; nat US; m 46; c 2. FOOD TECHNOLOGY. *Educ:* Nanking Univ, BS, 36; Ore State Col, MS, 40, PhD(food technol), 44. *Prof Exp:* From asst prof to prof, 43-77, EMER PROF FOOD SCI, ORE STATE UNIV, 77- *Concurrent Pos:* Consult, Food Industries. *Mem:* Am Chem Soc; Am Soc Enol; Inst Food Technologists; Am Soc Microbiol; Sigma Xi. *Res:* Food fermentation; food additives; food enzymes; food and food product analysis. *Mailing Add:* 1020 NW 30th Corvallis OR 97330

YANG, IN CHE, b Taiwan, Feb 7, 34; US citizen; m 66; c 3. NUCLEAR CHEMISTRY, INORGANIC CHEMISTRY. *Educ:* Nat Taiwan Univ, BSc, 56; Carleton Univ, MSc, 66; Univ Wash, PhD(nuclear & inorg chem), 71. *Prof Exp:* Radiochemist radiation ecol, Univ Wash, 72, res assoc isotope geol, 72-75, res asst prof, 75-78; radiochemist isotope hydrol, 78-80, RADIOCHEM SECT CHIEF, DENVER CENT LAB, WATER RESOURCE DIV, US GEOL SURV, 80- *Res:* Applications of radioactive and stable isotopes to geology and hydrology; geochronology using carbon-14; tritium and potassium-argon dating; stable isotope ratios in hydrology using oxygen-18/oxygen-16, carbon-13/carbon-12 and deuterium/hydrogen ratios. *Mailing Add:* US Geol Surv Denver Fed Ctr MS 407 Lakewood CO 80225

YANG, JEN TSI, b Shanghai, China, Mar 18, 22; m 49; c 2. BIOPHYSICAL CHEMISTRY. *Educ:* Nat Cent Univ, China, BS, 44; Iowa State Univ, PhD(biophys chem), 52. *Prof Exp:* Asst anal chem, Nat Cent Univ, China, 46-47; res assoc protein chem, Iowa State Univ, 52-54; res fel polypeptide & protein chem, Harvard Univ, 54-56; res chemist, Am Viscose Corp, 56-59; assoc prof biochem, Dartmouth Med Sch, 59-60; assoc prof, 60-64, PROF BIOCHEM, UNIV CALIF, SAN FRANCISCO, 64- *Concurrent Pos:* Guggenheim fel, 59-60. *Mem:* Am Chem Soc; Am Soc Biol Chemists; Biophys Soc. *Res:* Physical chemistry of biopolymers. *Mailing Add:* Cardiovasc Res Inst Rm 831 HSW Univ of Calif San Francisco CA 94143

YANG, JEONG SHENG, b Taiwan, July 11, 34; m 60; c 3. TOPOLOGY. *Educ:* Taiwan Normal Univ, BS, 58; Univ Ala, Tuscaloosa, MA, 63; Univ Miami, PhD(math), 67. *Prof Exp:* Asst math, Taiwan Normal Univ, 57-62; asst prof, La State Univ, New Orleans, 66-68; vis asst prof, Univ Miami, 68-69; asst prof, 69-73, ASSOC PROF MATH, UNIV SC, 73- *Mem:* Am Math Soc; Math Asn Am. *Res:* Function spaces; topological groups; transformation groups. *Mailing Add:* Dept Math & Statist Univ of SC Columbia SC 29208

YANG, JIH HSIN, b Formosa, 1937; m 71; c 1. CHEMICAL ENGINEERING, FOOD SCIENCE. *Educ:* Univ Ill, Urbana, BS, 63, MS, 66, PhD(food sci), 68. *Prof Exp:* Res proj engr foods, Procter & Gamble Co, 68-70; sr prod technologist, Kroger Co, 70-77; res & develop mgr, Food Producers Inc, 77-80; WITH THE DENMARK CO, 80- *Mem:* Am Inst Chem Engrs; Inst Food Technol. *Res:* Research and development of new foods and processes. *Mailing Add:* Denmark Co 5360 W 23rd St Minneapolis MN 55416

YANG, JOHN YUN-WEN, b Changsha, China, May 19, 30; US citizen; m 58; c 3. ENVIRONMENTAL CHEMISTRY. *Educ:* St Benedict's Col, Kans, BS, 52; Univ Kans, PhD(chem), 57. *Prof Exp:* Res assoc recoil carbon-14, Brookhaven Nat Lab, 57-59; sr chemist, US Naval Radiol Defense Lab, Calif, 59-60; res specialist, Atomics Int Div, NAm Aviation, Inc, 60-62, mem tech staff, Sci Ctr, 62-67; sr res scientist, Western NY Nuclear Res Ctr, 67-72; prin chemist, Environ Systs Dept, Calspan Corp, 72-76; SR CHEMIST, LINDE DIV, UNION CARBIDE CORP, 76- *Concurrent Pos:* Adj assoc prof, State Univ NY Buffalo, 70-76. *Mem:* Am Chem Soc; Am Nuclear Soc; NY Acad Sci. *Res:* Environmental air and water chemistry; physiocochemical methods of wastewater treatment; air pollution technology; radiation and isotope applications; water treatment and corrosion protection; radiation photochemistry; electrochemical processes. *Mailing Add:* Union Carbide Corp PO Box 44 Tonawanda NY 14150

YANG, JULIE CHI-SUN, b Beijing, China, June 10, 28. INORGANIC CHEMISTRY. *Educ:* Tsing Hua Univ, China, BS, 49; Ind Univ, MA, 52; Univ Ill, PhD, 55. *Prof Exp:* Asst chem, Ind Univ, 50-52; res chemist, Res Ctr, Johns-Manville Corp, 55-59, sr res chemist, 59-67, res assoc, 67-72; sr group leader, 72-74, RES MGR, CONSTRUCT PROD DIV, W R GRACE & CO, 75- *Concurrent Pos:* Mem, Hwy Res Bd, Nat Acad Sci-Nat Res Coun. *Mem:* Am Chem Soc; Am Ceramic Soc; Am Concrete Inst. *Res:* Inorganic silicate and cement chemistry; synthesis; properties; structures; material research; analytical instrumentation. *Mailing Add:* W R Grace & Co 62 Whittemore Ave Cambridge MA 02140

YANG, KEI-HSIUNG, b Taiwan, Dec 10, 40; US citizen; m 71; c 2. QUANTUM OPTICS, MEDICAL PHYSICS. *Educ:* Nat Taiwan Univ, BS, 64; Univ Notre Dame, MS, 67; Univ Calif, Berkeley, PhD(physics), 74. *Prof Exp:* Teaching asst, Univ Notre Dame, 65-67; teaching asst, Univ Calif, Berkeley, 67-69; mem tech staff res, Bell Tel Labs, Murray Hill, NJ, 69; res asst, Lawrence Berkeley Lab, 69-73; mem staff, Res & Develop Ctr, Gen Elec Corp, 73-79; MEM RES STAFF, T J WATSON RES CTR, IBM CORP, YORKTOWN HEIGHTS, NY, 79- *Mem:* Am Phys Soc. *Res:* Continuous tunable coherent vacuum ultraviolet source; medical x-ray devices; liquid crystal displays. *Mailing Add:* T J Watson Res Ctr IBM Corp PO Box 218 Yorktown Heights NY 10598

YANG, KWANG-TZU, b China, Nov 12, 28; nat US; m 53; c 5. MECHANICAL ENGINEERING. *Educ:* Ill Inst Technol, BS, 51, MS, 52, PhD(heat transfer), 55. *Prof Exp:* From asst prof to assoc prof, 56-62, chmn dept, 68-69, PROF MECH ENG, UNIV NOTRE DAME, 62-, CHMN DEPT AEROSPACE & MECH ENG, 69- *Concurrent Pos:* Consult, Dodge Mfg Corp, 56-; NSF res grants, 56-; Off Naval Res grant, 61-64. *Mem:* AAAS; Am Soc Mech Engrs; Am Soc Eng Educ. *Res:* Boundary-layer theory; nonlinear methods; forced and free convection; hydrodynamic stability; thermal radiation. *Mailing Add:* Dept of Aerospace & Mech Eng Univ of Notre Dame Notre Dame IN 46556

YANG, LAU SHAN, b China, June 2, 45; m 70; c 2. ORGANIC CHEMISTRY. *Educ:* Nat Taiwan Univ, BS, 67; Univ Chicago, PhD(chem), 74. *Prof Exp:* Fel, Rice Univ, 73-74 & Ohio State Univ, 74-76; SR RES CHEMIST, AM CAN CO, 76- *Mem:* Am Chem Soc. *Res:* Physical and synthetic organic chemistry. *Mailing Add:* Am Can Co 469 Harrison St Princeton NJ 08540

YANG, MAN-CHIU, b Hankow, China, Aug 16, 46; m 71; c 1. BIOCHEMISTRY. *Educ:* Chinese Univ Hong Kong, BSc, 70; Univ Nebr, PhD(chem), 74. *Prof Exp:* RES ASSOC, STATE UNIV NY BUFFALO, 74- *Mem:* Biophys Soc; Am Chem Soc. *Res:* Study of the intermediates and enzymic systems in oxidative phosphorylation and photophosphorylation. *Mailing Add:* 32 Rainbow Ave Chelmsford MA 01824

YANG, MARK CHAO-KUEN, b Tsuchuan, China, Dec 14, 42; m 68; c 1. STATISTICS. *Educ:* Nat Taiwan Univ, BS, 64; Univ Wis, MS, 67, PhD(statist), 70. *Prof Exp:* Asst prof, 70-75, ASSOC PROF STATIST, UNIV FLA, 75- *Concurrent Pos:* Consult, Redstone Arsenal, US Army Command, Ala, 72-73 & Offshore Power Co, Fla, 73-74. *Mem:* Am Statist Asn; Inst Math Statist; AAAS. *Res:* Applied probability; stochastic processes; time series analysis. *Mailing Add:* Dept of Statist Nuclear Sci Bldg Univ of Fla Gainesville FL 32601

YANG, NIEN-CHU, b Shanghai, China, May 1, 28; nat US; m 54; c 3. CHEMISTRY. *Educ:* St John's Univ, China, BS, 48; Univ Chicago, PhD, 52. *Prof Exp:* Res assoc, Mass Inst Technol, 52-55; res fel, Harvard Univ, 55-56; from asst prof to assoc prof, 56-63, PROF CHEM, UNIV CHICAGO, 63- *Concurrent Pos:* Alfred P Sloan fel, 60-64; Nat Cancer Inst fel, 73-74; Guggenheim fel, 74-75. *Honors & Awards:* Gregory & Freda Jalpern Award, NY Acad Sci, 81. *Mem:* AAAS; Am Chem Soc; Royal Soc Chem. *Res:* Photochemistry; chemistry of nucleic acids; organic synthesis. *Mailing Add:* Dept of Chem Univ of Chicago Chicago IL 60637

YANG, OVID Y H, b Korea; US citizen. PATHOLOGY, IMMUNOLOGY. *Educ:* Yonsei Univ, Korea, MD, 50; Univ Ottawa, PhD, 62. *Prof Exp:* Dir clin lab, Park Place Hosp, Port Arthur, Tex, 69-76; DIR CLIN LAB, TITUS COUNTY MEM HOSP, MT PLEASANT, TEX, 76- *Mem:* Am Soc Exp Path; Int Acad Path; Am Soc Clin Path; Col Am Path; AMA. *Res:* Chemical carcinogenesis; cancer immunology. *Mailing Add:* 106 Dessie Mt Pleasant TX 75455

YANG, RALPH TZU-BOW, b Chungking, China, Sept 18, 42; US citizen; m 72; c 1. CHEMICAL ENGINEERING, PHYSICAL CHEMISTRY. *Educ:* Nat Taiwan Univ, BS, 64; Yale Univ, MS, 68, PhD(chem eng), 71. *Prof Exp:* Res assoc, NY Univ, 71-72 & Argonne Nat Lab, 72-73; scientist, Alcoa Lab, Aluminum Co Am, 73-74; group leader, Brookhaven Nat Lab, 74-78; assoc prof, 78-81, PROF CHEM ENG, STATE UNIV NY, BUFFALO, 82- *Mem:* Am Inst Chem Engrs; Am Chem Soc. *Res:* Heterogeneous kinetics; surface chemistry; diffusion; coal conversion; air pollution control; advanced energy systems. *Mailing Add:* Dept of Chem Eng State Univ of NY Buffalo Amherst NY 14260

YANG, SEN-LIAN, b Taipei, Taiwan, Jan 10, 38; Chinese citizen; m 66; c 2. OBSTETRICS & GYNECOLOGY. *Educ:* Nat Taiwan Univ, MD, 63. *Prof Exp:* Resident obstet & gynec, Nat Taiwan Univ Hosp, 64-68; res fel immunol, US Naval Res Unit 2, 68-70; Ford Found fel reproductive biol & immunobiol, Dept Obstet & Gynec, Univ Pa, 70-71; resident obstet & gynec, Chicago Lying-in Hosp, Univ Chicago, 72-73; from instr to asst prof, 73-80, ASSOC PROF OBSTET & GYNEC, UNIV CHICAGO, 80- *Concurrent Pos:* Vis staff obstet & gynec, Nat Taiwan Univ Hosp, 68-70; fel reproductive biol & immunobiol, Chicago Lying-in Hosp, Univ Chicago, 73-74. *Mem:* Int Fedn Gynec & Obstet; Am Fertil Soc; Soc Study Reproduction; Am Col Obstetricians & Gynecologists; Asn Obstet & Gynec Repub China. *Res:* Immunobiology of reproductive medicine. *Mailing Add:* Dept Obstet & Gynec Univ Chicago 5841 S Maryland Ave Chicago IL 60637

YANG, SHANG, b Tainan, Formosa, Nov 10, 32; m 65; c 2. PLANT PHYSIOLOGY. *Educ:* Nat Taiwan Univ, BS, 56, MS, 58; Utah State Univ, PhD(plant biochem), 62. *Prof Exp:* Fel, Univ Calif, Davis, 62-63; res assoc biochem, NY Univ Med Ctr, 63-64 & Univ Calif, San Diego, 64-66; from asst biochemist to assoc biochemist, 66-74, PROF BIOCHEM & BIOCHEMIST, UNIV CALIF, DAVIS, 74- *Concurrent Pos:* NSF res grant, 67-; vis prof, Univ Konstanz, 74; NIH res grant, 75- *Honors & Awards:* Campbell Award, Am Inst Biol Sci, 69. *Mem:* AAAS; Am Soc Biol Chemists; Am Soc Plant Physiol; Am Soc Hort Sci. *Res:* Biosynthesis and hormonal action of ethylene; postharvest biochemistry of fruits and vegetables; biochemical effects of sulfur dioxide on vegetation. *Mailing Add:* Dept of Veg Crops Univ of Calif Davis CA 95616

YANG, SHAW-MING, b Tainan, Taiwan, May 10, 33; m 66; c 1. MICROBIOLOGY. *Educ:* Nat Taiwan Univ, BSA, 57, MSA, 59; Univ Wis-Madison, PhD(plant path), 65. *Prof Exp:* Res asst plant path, Nat Taiwan Univ, 55-57 & Univ Wis-Madison, 62-65; fel food microbiol, Nat Res Coun Can, 65-67; res scientist plant path, Can Dept Agr, 67-68; RES PLANT PATHOLOGIST, USDA, 68- *Mem:* Am Phytopath Soc; Mycol Soc Am. *Res:* Bacterial and fungal diseases of sugarcane; disease control; nitrogen fixation. *Mailing Add:* USDA SEA AR Conserv Prod Res Lab PO Drawer 10 Bushland TX 79012

YANG, SHEN KWEI, b Chung-King, China, May 4, 41; US citizen; m 68; c 1. PHYSICAL CHEMISTRY, BIOCHEMISTRY. *Educ:* Nat Taiwan Univ, BS, 64; Wesleyan Univ, MA, 69; Yale Univ, MPh, 70, PhD(biophys chem), 72. *Prof Exp:* Fel biochem, Yale Univ, 72-73; res fel chem, Calif Inst Technol, 73-75; sr staff fel, Nat Cancer Inst, NIH, 75-77; assoc prof, 77-81, PROF PHARMACOL, SCH MED, UNIFORMED SERV UNIV HEALTH SCI, 81- *Concurrent Pos:* USPHS traineeship, Yale Univ, 72. *Honors & Awards:* Sci Achievement Award, Chinese Med & Health Asn, 78. *Mem:* Am Soc Pharmacol & Exp Therapeut; Am Asn Cancer Res; Am Soc Biol Chemists; Int Soc Study Xenobiotics. *Res:* Environmental toxicology, drug metabolism and chemical carcinogenesis. *Mailing Add:* Dept of Pharmacol Uniformed Serv Univ Health Sci Bethesda MD 20814

YANG, SHIANG-PING, b Hankow, China, Mar 5, 19; nat US; m 60. NUTRITION. *Educ:* Nat Cent Univ, China, BS, 42; Iowa State Univ, MS, 49, PhD(nutrit), 56. *Prof Exp:* Animal husbandman, Nan-An Dairy Farms, China, 42-45; tech trainee, USDA, 45-46; sr animal husbandman, Chinese Nat Relief & Rehab Admin, 46-47; res assoc nutrit, Iowa State Univ, 49-56; chemist, Mead Johnson Res Ctr, 56-57; asst prof food & nutrit, Purdue Univ, 57-62; assoc prof, Va Polytech Inst, 62; prof, La State Univ, Baton Rouge, 63-69; chmn dept, 69-76, PROF FOOD & NUTRIT, TEX TECH UNIV, 69- *Concurrent Pos:* Fulbright lectr & vis prof, Nat Taiwan Univ, 59-60. *Mem:* Am Soc Animal Sci; Am Chem Soc; Am Inst Nutrit; Inst Food Technologists. *Res:* Diets and carcinogenesis; protein metabolism; nutritional improvement of dietary proteins; factors influencing the qualities of food. *Mailing Add:* Dept of Food & Nutrit Tex Tech Univ Lubbock TX 79409

YANG, SHI-TIEN, b Hsinchu, Taiwan, July 9, 46; US citizen; m 71; c 2. NUCLEAR REACTOR PHYSICS, NUCLEAR REACTOR SAFETY. *Educ:* Tunghai Univ, BS, 68; Mass Inst Technol, PhD(nuclear eng), 75. *Prof Exp:* Fel, Univ Calif, Los Angeles, 75-76; sr engr, Nuclear Serv Corp, 76-78; sr scientist, Sci Appl, Inc, 78-79; NUCLEAR ENGR, ARGONNE NAT LAB, 79- *Mem:* Am Nuclear Soc. *Res:* Core neutronics; kinetics analysis; general shielding analysis. *Mailing Add:* 9700 S Cass Ave Argonne IL 60439

YANG, SHUNG-JUN, b Tintsin, China, Jan 13, 34; US citizen; m 64; c 3. CELL BIOLOGY, RADIATION BIOLOGY. *Educ:* Taiwan Univ, BS, 55; Univ Toronto, MS, 58; NC State Col, PhD(genetics), 62. *Prof Exp:* Fel cytogenetics, Baylor Col Med, 62-63, instr, 63-64; res assoc radiation biol, Sch Med, Stanford Univ, 64-68; res assoc cell biol, Albert Einstein Col Med, 73-74; RADIATION BIOLOGIST, METHODIST HOSP, BROOKLYN, NY, 74- *Concurrent Pos:* Clin asst prof radiation biol, State Univ NY Downstate Med Ctr, 75- *Mem:* NY Acad Sci; Tissue Cult Asn. *Res:* Proliferation kinetics of mammalian cells in culture; cellular effects of anti-tumor agents. *Mailing Add:* Dept of Radiother Methodist Hosp 506 Sixth St Brooklyn NY 11215

YANG, SWE-WONG, b Taiwan, July 6, 47; m 76. PHYSICAL METALLURGY. *Educ:* Cheng-King Univ, Taiwan, BS, 69; Tenn Tech Univ, MS, 70; Univ Tenn, PhD(metall eng), 77. *Prof Exp:* STAFF MEM, CORP RES & DEVELOP CTR, GEN ELEC CO, 77- *Mem:* Am Soc Metals; Sigma Xi. *Res:* Oxidation of metals; mechanical properties of superalloys and stainless steels; phase transformations. *Mailing Add:* Corp Res & Develop Ctr Gen Elec Co Schenectady NY 12345

YANG, TAH TEH, b Shanghai, China, Aug 15, 27; m 63; c 2. FLUID MECHANICS. *Educ:* Shanghai Inst Technol, BS, 48; Okla State Univ, MS, 57; Cornell Univ, PhD(mech eng), 61. *Prof Exp:* Engr, Kaohsiung Harbor Bur, Taiwan, 49-55; proj engr, Wright Aeronaut Div, Curtiss Wright Corp, 60-62; from asst prof to assoc prof fluids, 62-69, PROF FLUIDS, CLEMSON UNIV, 69- *Concurrent Pos:* Prin investr, NSF grant, 63-64; US Army res grant, 63-66, res contract, 70-73; NASA grant, 69-72; consult, Singer Co, 76- & Avco Corp, 77-; res grants, US Air Force, 75-76, Singer Co, 77-79 & US Navy, 80-82. *Mem:* Am Soc Mech Engrs; Am Inst Aeronaut & Astronaut. *Res:* Thermal engineering. *Mailing Add:* Dept Eng 315 Riggs Hall Clemson Univ Clemson SC 29631

YANG, TSU-JU (THOMAS), b Fengshang, Taiwan, Repub China, Aug 14, 32; m 61; c 3. PATHOBIOLOGY, IMMUNOBIOLOGY. *Educ:* Nat Taiwan Univ, BVM, 55; Ministry Exam, Taipei, Taiwan, DVM, 59; McGill Univ, PhD(immunol), 71. *Prof Exp:* Assoc mem immunol, Academia Sinica Inst Zool, 61-64; res assoc cytogenetics, Dept Animal Biol, Univ Pa, 64-66; res fel immunol, Dept Microbiol, Univ Minn, 66-67; demonstr immunol, McGill Univ, 68-71; from asst prof to assoc prof immunol, Univ Tenn Mem Res Ctr, 71-75; assoc prof, 75-78, PROF PATHOBIOL, UNIV CONN, STORRS, 78- *Mem:* Am Asn Cancer Res; Am Soc Cell Biol; Am Asn Immunologists; Am Soc Microbiol; AAAS. *Res:* Tumor-host interaction in canine transmissible sarcoma; canine immunology; immunoregulatory role of lynphoid cells in hematopoiesis cancer and infections; mode of action of membrane reactive agents: antibodies and lectins. *Mailing Add:* Dept of Pathobiol Univ of Conn Storrs CT 06268

YANG, TSUTE, b Yangchow, China, Nov 16, 16; nat US; m 42; c 2. ELECTRICAL ENGINEERING, COMPUTER SCIENCE. *Educ:* Chiao Tung Univ, China, BS, 38; Harvard Univ, MS, 46; Univ Pa, PhD, 60. *Prof Exp:* Assoc prof elec eng, Univ Toledo, 46-53; sr engr, Remington Rand Univac, Pa, 53-57; asst prof elec eng, Univ Pa, 57-60; res engr, Radio Corp Am, NJ, 60-62; prof elec eng, Villanova Univ, 62-80; VIS PROF, DEPT ELEC & COMPUT ENG, UNIV CLEMSON, 80- *Concurrent Pos:* Consult, Tracor Corp, Pa, Naval Air Develop Ctr, Pa, NASA, Va & Burroughs Corp, Pa. *Mem:* Am Asn Univ Prof; Inst Elec & Electronics Engrs; Am Soc Eng Educ. *Res:* Network theory; computer architecture and design; communication systems. *Mailing Add:* Dept Elec & Comput Eng Univ Clemson Clemson SC 29631

YANG, WEI-HSUIN, b Apr 1, 36; m 64; c 2. MECHANICS, APPLIED MATHEMATICS. *Educ:* Cheng Kung Univ, Taiwan, BS, 58; Univ Wash, MS, 62; Stanford Univ, PhD(mech), 65. *Prof Exp:* Res engr, Boeing Co, 62; res fel, Calif Inst Technol, 64-65; from asst prof to assoc prof eng mech, 65-77, PROF APPL MECH, UNIV MICH, ANN ARBOR, 77- *Concurrent Pos:* Ed consult, Math Rev, 66-67; consult, Gen Motors Corp, 67- *Res:* Solid mechanics including elasticity, plasticity and viscoelasticity; large deformation and numerical analysis. *Mailing Add:* Dept of Eng Mech Univ of Mich Ann Arbor MI 48109

YANG, WEN JEI, b Formosa, China, Oct 14, 31; m 60; c 3. HEAT TRANSFER, BIOENGINEERING. *Educ:* Nat Taiwan Univ, BS, 54; Univ Mich, MS, 56, PhD(mech eng), 60. *Prof Exp:* Res engr, Sci Lab, Ford Motor Co, 57-58; res engr, Inst Indust Sci, Tokyo Univ, 60-61; lectr mech eng, 61-62, from asst prof to assoc prof, 62-70, PROF MECH ENG, UNIV MICH, ANN ARBOR, 70- *Concurrent Pos:* Consult, Tamano Works, Mitsui Shipbldg Co, Japan, 60-61, Tecumseh Prod Res Lab, 66-67, Atomic Power Div, Westinghouse Elec Corp, 67-68, Borg-Warner Mach, 68-71 & Environ Protection Agency, 70-72; ed-in-chief, Int J Biomed Eng, 71-73; consult, Ex-Cell-O, 76-80, Energy Develop Assocs, 79-80, Panasonic, 79-, Bendix Corp, 79-80 & KMMCO, 81- *Mem:* Japan Soc Flow Visualization; Am Soc Mech Engrs (secy, 78-); Sigma Xi. *Res:* Heat exchangers; heat transfer enhancement; interfacial stability; thermograph and digital image processing; thermal physiology; cardiovascular fluid mechanics; hyperthermia. *Mailing Add:* 3925 Waldenwood Dr Ann Arbor MI 48105

YANG, WEN-CHING, b Taipei, China, Nov 11, 39; m 68. CHEMICAL ENGINEERING. *Educ:* Nat Taiwan Univ, BS, 62; Univ Calif, Berkeley, MS, 65; Carnegie-Mellon Univ, PhD(chem eng), 68. *Prof Exp:* Sr engr, 68-76, FEL ENGR, WESTINGHOUSE ELEC CORP, PITTSBURGH, 76- *Mem:* Am Inst Chem Engrs; Am Chem Soc. *Res:* Mass transfer; thermodynamics; chemical vapor deposition and high temperature technology; fluidized bed technology; fluidized bed coal gasification and combustion; pneumatic transport. *Mailing Add:* 236 Mount Vernon Ave Export PA 15632

YANG, WEN-KUANG, b Taiwan, China, Oct 19, 36; m 63; c 2. BIOCHEMISTRY, MEDICINE. *Educ:* Nat Taiwan Univ, MD, 62; Tulane Univ, PhD(biochem), 66; Educ Coun Foreign Med Grad, cert, 62. *Prof Exp:* Vis investr enzym, 66-68, staff biochemist, 68-73, GROUP LEADER, BIOL DIV, OAK RIDGE NAT LAB, 73- *Concurrent Pos:* Res fel nutrit & metab, Sch Med, Tulane Univ, 63-66; Damon Runyon Mem res fel cancer, 66-68; lectr biomed sci, Oak Ridge Biomed Grad Sch, Univ Tenn, 69-; ad hoc mem, Review Comt & Study Sect, NIH, 77- *Mem:* Am Soc Biol Chem; Am Asn Cancer Res; Geront Soc; Formosan Med Asn. *Res:* Genetic expression in cancer tissues; host cell-RNA oncogenic virus interaction; enzymology of DNA synthesis in mammalian normal and tumor cells; isoaccepting transfer RNA of mammalian tissues; lectins for cell membrane research; molecular mechanisms of aging. *Mailing Add:* 15 Asbury Lane Oak Ridge TN 37830

YANG, WON-TACK, marine biology, see previous edition

YANICK, NICHOLAS SAMUEL, b Oakburn, Man, Dec 4, 07; nat US; m 53. PHYSICAL CHEMISTRY. *Educ:* Univ Man, BSc, 30, MSc, 32; NY Univ, PhD(chem), 35. *Prof Exp:* Chemist, Olin-Mathieson Corp, Va, 35-36; res chemist, US Gypsum Co, Ill, 36-38; chief chemist, Wahl-Henius Inst, Ill, 38-45; scientist, Metall Labs, Univ Chicago, 45; chief chemist, Chapman & Smith Co, 45-48; res chemist, John F Jelke Co, 49-51; sr scientist, Res & Develop Div, Kraft, Inc, 51-70; TECH CONSULT, 70- *Mem:* Am Chem Soc; Inst Food Technologists. *Res:* Colloid-chemical aspects of food products; solubilities; physico-chemical properties of organic compounds; winterization of vegetable oils, separation of fatty acids and fats; evaluation of edible proteins; vanilla; evaluation and formulation of retail and institutional, nutritive and dietetic food products; food ingredients application; food technology; development of industrial food products. *Mailing Add:* 1643 David Dr Escondido CA 92026

YANIV, SHLOMO STEFAN, b Poznan, Poland, Sept 11, 31; US citizen; m 59; c 2. HEALTH PHYSICS, RADIOLOGICAL PHYSICS. *Educ:* Israel Inst Technol, BS, 54, Ingenieur, 55; Univ Pittsburgh, MS, 65, DSc(radiation health), 69. *Prof Exp:* Radiation protection engr, Israel AEC, 58-62; univ health physicist, Grad Sch Pub Health, Univ Pittsburgh, 63-67, asst prof health physics & asst prof radiol, Sch Med, 69-72; sr health physicist, Prod Stand Br, Directorate Regulatory Stand, US AEC, DC, 72-75; TECH ASST TO DIR, DIV SAFEGUARDS FUEL CYCLE & ENVIRON RES, US NUCLEAR REGULATORY COMN, WASHINGTON, DC, 75- *Concurrent Pos:* Am Cancer Soc grant, Univ Pittsburgh, 71-72; radiol physicist, Montefiore Hosp, 67-72. *Mem:* Health Physics Soc; Am Asn Physicists in Med; Soc Nuclear Med. *Res:* Dose reduction in diagnostic radiology; environmental aspects of radionuclides use; application of short life radionuclides in nuclear medicine; radiation dosimetry; effects of population exposure to ionizing radiation. *Mailing Add:* 11216 Broad Green Dr Potomac MD 20854

YANIV, SIMONE LILIANE, b France, May 17, 38; US citizen; c 2. PSYCHOACOUSTICS, BIOACOUSTICS. *Educ:* Univ Pittsburgh, BS, 66, MS, 68, PhD(noise control psychoacoust), 72. *Prof Exp:* Noise pollution consult, Allegheny County Health Dept, 72-73; bioacoust scientist effects noise on people, US Environ Protection Agency, Noise Abatement & Control Off, 73-74; GROUP LEADER BLDG ACOUSTICS, NAT BUR STANDARDS, 74- *Mem:* Nat Acad Sci; Acoust Soc Am; Nat Res Coun. *Res:* Noise measurements; sound absorption, propagation and isolation. *Mailing Add:* Bldg 233 Rm A107 Nat Bur Standards Washington DC 20234

YANIV, ZOHARA, plant physiology, phytopathology, see previous edition

YANKAUER, ALFRED, b New York, NY, Oct 12, 13; m 48; c 3. PUBLIC HEALTH. *Educ:* Dartmouth Col, BA, 34; Harvard Univ, MD, 38; Columbia Univ, MPH, 47. *Prof Exp:* Dist health officer, New York City Dept Health, 48-50; asst prof prev med & pub health, Med Col, Cornell Univ, 48-50 & Sch Med, Univ Rochester, 50-52; dir bur maternal & child health, NY State Dept Health, 52-61; regional adv maternal & child health, Pan-Am Health Orgn, WHO, 61-66; sr lectr maternal & child health, 66-70, SR LECTR HEALTH SERV ADMIN, SCH PUB HEALTH, HARVARD UNIV, 70-; PROF COMMUNITY MED & PEDIAT, MED SCH, UNIV MASS, WORCESTER, 73- *Concurrent Pos:* Dir maternal & child health serv, Health Bur, Rochester, NY, 50-52; lectr, Albany Med Col, 52-61; WHO vis prof, Madras Med Col, India, 57-59; ed, Am J Pub Health, 75- *Honors & Awards:* Job Lewis Smith Award, Am Acad Pediat, 79. *Mem:* Fel Am Pub Health Asn; fel Am Acad Pediat. *Res:* Maternal and child health; school health; social medicine; health care. *Mailing Add:* Dept of Community & Family Med Univ of Mass Med Sch Worcester MA 01604

YANKEE, ERNEST WARREN, b Hayward, Calif, Nov 18, 43; m 65; c 2. ORGANIC CHEMISTRY, MEDICINAL CHEMISTRY. *Educ:* La Sierra Col, BA, 65; Univ Calif, Los Angeles, PhD(org chem), 70. *Prof Exp:* RES ASSOC ORG CHEM, UPJOHN CO, 70- *Mem:* Am Chem Soc. *Res:* Synthesis and structure-activity relationships of prostaglandins. *Mailing Add:* Upjohn Co Kalamazoo MI 49001

YANKEE, RONALD AUGUST, b Franklin, Mass, May 24, 34. MEDICINE. *Educ:* Tufts Univ, BS, 56; Yale Univ, MD, 60. *Prof Exp:* Intern med, Univ Va, 60-61; resident, Univ Mich, 62-63; sr investr, Nat Cancer Inst, 63-75; assoc prof, Sidney Farber Cancer Inst, Harvard Med Sch, 73-79; PROF, BROWN UNIV, 79-; DIR, RHODE ISLAND BLOOD CTR, 79- *Mem:* Transplantation Soc; Am Soc Hemat. *Res:* Bone marrow transplantation; histocompatibility; platelet transfusion therapy; cancer chemotherapy. *Mailing Add:* Rhode Island Blood Ctr 551 N Main St Providence RI 02940

YANKEELOV, JOHN ALLEN, JR, biochemistry, organic chemistry, deceased

YANKELL, SAMUEL L, b Bridgeton, NJ, July 4, 35; m 58; c 3. BIOCHEMISTRY, TOXICOLOGY. *Educ:* Ursinus Col, BS, 56; Rutgers Univ, MS, 57, PhD, 60; Univ Pa, Sch Dent Med, RDH, 81. *Prof Exp:* Instr, Georgian Court Col, 60; sr res biochemist, Colgate-Palmolive Co, 60-63; head dept biochem & pharmacol, Smith, Miller & Patch, 63-65; sr pharmacologist, Menley & James Res Labs, 66-67; sect head biol labs, Smith Kline & French Inter-Am Corp, 67-69; head dept biol sci, Menley & James Labs, 69-74; res asst prof, 74-81, RES ASSOC PROF, SCH DENT MED, UNIV PA, 81- *Mem:* Am Chem Soc; NY Acad Sci; Int Asn Dent Res; Am Soc Pharmacol & Exp Therapeut. *Res:* Nutrition; dermatology; dental research. *Mailing Add:* Univ of Pa Sch of Dent Med 4001 Spruce St Philadelphia PA 19104

YANKO, WILLIAM HARRY, b Monessen, Pa, Jan 6, 19; m 42; c 2. RADIOCHEMISTRY, ORGANIC CHEMISTRY. *Educ:* Geneva Col, BS, 40; Pa State Univ, PhD(org chem), 44. *Prof Exp:* Org res chemist, Cent Res Lab, Monsanto Chem Co, 43-46; org res chemist, Clinton Labs, Tenn, 46-47; radiochem res group leader, Cent Res Lab, Monsanto Chem Co, 47-60, group leader, 61-78, SR CHEMIST, MONSANTO RES CORP, 78- *Mem:* Am Chem Soc; NY Acad Sci; AAAS. *Res:* Synthetic antimalarials; anticancer drugs; radioisotopic synthesis. *Mailing Add:* Mound Facil Monsanto Res Corp Miamisburg OH 45342

YANKWICH, PETER EWALD, b Los Angeles, Calif, Oct 20, 23; m 45; c 3. PHYSICAL CHEMISTRY. *Educ:* Univ Calif, BS, 43, PhD(chem), 45. *Prof Exp:* Res chemist, Radiation Lab, Univ Calif, 44-46, instr chem, 47-48; from asst prof to assoc prof, 48-57, PROF CHEM, UNIV ILL, URBANA, 57-, VPRES, ACAD AFFAIRS, 77- *Concurrent Pos:* NSF fel, Calif Inst Technol & Brookhaven Nat Lab, 60-61. *Mem:* Fel AAAS; Sigma Xi; Am Chem Soc; fel Am Phys Soc. *Res:* Chemical kinetics; isotope effects. *Mailing Add:* Dept Chem Univ Ill Urbana IL 61801

YANNAS, IOANNIS VASSILIOS, b Athens, Greece, Apr 14, 35; m 68. PHYSICAL CHEMISTRY, POLYMER PHYSICS. *Educ:* Harvard Col, AB, 57; Mass Inst Technol, MS, 59; Princeton Univ, MA, 65, PhD(phys chem), 66. *Prof Exp:* Res phys chemist, W R Grace & Co, 59-63; asst prof mech eng, 66-68, DuPont asst prof, 68-69, assoc prof, 69-76, ASSOC PROF MECH, MASS INST TECHNOL, 76- *Concurrent Pos:* Polymer consult. *Mem:* AAAS; Am Chem Soc; Biomed Eng Soc; NY Acad Sci. *Res:* Physical chemistry of natural and synthetic polymers. *Mailing Add:* Dept of Mech Eng Rm 3-334 Mass Inst of Technol Cambridge MA 02139

YANNITELL, DANIEL W, b Johnson City, NY, Sept 26, 41; m 70; c 1. MECHANICS, APPLIED MATHEMATICS. *Educ:* Webb Inst Technol, BS, 62; Cornell Univ, PhD(mech), 67. *Prof Exp:* Res assoc & instr mech, Cornell Univ, 67; asst prof eng mech, 67-72, assoc prof eng sci, 72-77, ASSOC PROF MECH ENG, LA STATE UNIV, BATON ROUGE, 77- *Mem:* Am Acad Mech. *Res:* Fluid mechanics; analytical and computational fluid dynamics. *Mailing Add:* Dept of Mech Eng CEBA La State Univ Baton Rouge LA 70803

YANNONI, COSTANTINO SHELDON, b Boston, Mass, May 20, 35; m 66; c 5. MAGNETIC RESONANCE. *Educ:* Harvard Col, AB, 57; Columbia Univ, MA, 60, PhD(chem), 67. *Prof Exp:* Res chemist, Union Carbide Res Inst, 66-67; res chemist, Watson Res Ctr, 67-71, RES CHEMIST, RES LAB, IBM CORP, 71- *Concurrent Pos:* Chmn, Exp Nuclear Magnetic Relaxation Comt, 81-82. *Mem:* Am Chem Soc. *Res:* Structure and dynamics of reactive intermediates using high resolution solid state nuclear magnetic relaxation. *Mailing Add:* K34/281 IBM Res Lab 5600 Cottle Rd San Jose CA 95193

YANNONI, NICHOLAS, b Boston, Mass, Aug 3, 27; m 55; c 4. PHYSICAL CHEMISTRY. *Educ:* Boston Univ, BA, 54, PhD(chem), 61; Boston Col, MBA, 80. *Prof Exp:* Res fel chem, Mellon Inst, 54-55; staff scientist, Device Develop Corp, 60-61; physicist, 61-64, chief energetics br, 64-73, chief, opto-electronic physics br, Air Force Cambridge Res Labs, 74-79, CHIEF SIGNAL PROCESSING & TIMING DEVICES, ROME AIR DEVELOP CTR, 80- *Honors & Awards:* Am Inst Chemists Medal, 54. *Mem:* Sigma Xi; Am Crystallog Asn; Am Chem Soc; Am Phys Soc. *Res:* Crystal structure analysis; optics; atomic frequency/time standards; quartz oscillators. *Mailing Add:* Rome Air Develop Ctr L G Hanscom AFB Bedford MA 01731

YANO, FLEUR BELLE, US citizen. THEORETICAL PHYSICS. *Educ:* Columbia Univ, BS, 54; Univ Southern Calif, MA, 58; Univ Rochester, PhD(physics), 66. *Prof Exp:* From asst prof to assoc prof, 64-73, assoc dean instruction, Sch Letters & Sci, 78-79, PROF PHYSICS, CALIF STATE UNIV, LOS ANGELES, 73- *Concurrent Pos:* Res Corp grant, Calif State Univ, Los Angeles & State Univ Groningen, 72-73. *Mem:* Am Phys Soc; Fedn Am Sci. *Res:* Theoretical nuclear physics; radiative muon capture by complex nuclei; exchange currents in nuclear physics. *Mailing Add:* Dept of Physics Calif State Univ Los Angeles CA 90032

YANOFSKY, CHARLES, b New York, NY, Apr 17, 25; m 49; c 3. MOLECULAR BIOLOGY. *Educ:* City Col New York, BS, 48; Yale Univ, MS, 50, PhD(microbiol), 51. *Hon Degrees:* DSc, Univ Chicago, 80; DSc, Yale Univ, 81. *Prof Exp:* Res asst microbiol, Yale Univ, 51-54; asst prof, Sch Med, Western Reserve Univ, 54-58; assoc prof biol, 58-61, PROF BIOL, STANFORD UNIV, 61- *Concurrent Pos:* Lederle med fac award, 55-57; Am Heart Asn career investr, 69- *Honors & Awards:* Eli Lilly Award, 59; US Steel Found Award, 64; Howard Taylor Ricketts Award, 66; Lasker Med Res Award, 71; Nat Acad Sci Award Microbiol, 72; Louisa Gross Horwitz Prize, 76. *Mem:* Nat Acad Sci; AAAS; Am Acad Arts & Sci; Am Soc Microbiol; Genetics Soc Am. *Mailing Add:* Dept of Biol Sci Stanford Univ Stanford CA 94305

YANOW, GILBERT, b Los Angeles, Calif, Oct 15, 35; m 63; c 3. PHYSICS, SOLAR ENERGY. *Educ:* Univ Calif, Los Angeles, BA, 59; Univ Queensland, MS, 65; Australian Nat Univ, PhD(physics), 71. *Prof Exp:* Res specialist space sci, Douglas Aircraft Co, 56-63; lab instr physics, Univ Queensland, 64-65; sr lab instr, Australian Nat Univ, 65-71; sr engr, Martin Marietta, 71-72; res specialist, McDonnell Douglas Aircraft Co, 72-74; STAFF MEM PHYSICS, JET PROPULSION LAB, CALIF INST TECHNOL, 74- *Mem:* Int Solar Energy Soc; Am Radio Relay League; Sigma Xi. *Res:* Solar energy utilization; high speed gas dynamics; teaching methods. *Mailing Add:* Jet Propulsion Lab 4800 Oak Grove Dr Pasadena CA 91103

YANOWITCH, MICHAEL, b Minsk, Russia, Feb 1, 23; nat US; m 52; c 2. APPLIED MATHEMATICS. *Educ:* Cooper Union, BSE, 43; NY Univ, MS, 50, PhD(math), 53. *Prof Exp:* Elec engr, Philco Corp, 43-46; instr elec eng, Polytech Inst Brooklyn, 48-49; asst, Inst Math Sci, NY Univ, 50-52, assoc res scientist, 57-58; sr mathematician, Reeves Instrument Corp, 52-57; assoc prof math, 58-62, PROF MATH, ADELPHI UNIV, 62- *Concurrent Pos:* Consult, Surv Bur Corp, 59-60 & Grumman Aircraft Eng Corp, 61-63; vis scientist, Nat Ctr Atmospheric Res, 65-66. *Mem:* AAAS; Am Math Soc; Soc Indust & Appl Math; Math Asn Am. *Res:* Asymptotics; wave motion; atmospheric waves. *Mailing Add:* Dept of Math Adelphi Univ Garden City NY 11530

YANTIS, PHILLIP ALEXANDER, b Portland, Ore, Mar 30, 28; m 54; c 3. AUDIOLOGY. *Educ:* Univ Wash, BA, 50; Univ Mich, MA, 52, PhD(audiol), 55. *Prof Exp:* Res assoc physiol acoust, Univ Mich, 55-58, instr audiol, 57-60; from asst prof to assoc prof, Case Western Reserve Univ, 60-65; prog dir speech path & audiol, 68-74, PROF AUDIOL, UNIV WASH, 65- *Concurrent Pos:* Dir, Dept Audiol, Cleveland Hearing & Speech Ctr, 60-65; mem rev panel, Neurol & Sensory Dis Proj, USPHS, 67-69; field reader, Bur Educ Handicapped, HEW, 72-73, mem rev panel, Speech & Hearing Training, Rehab Serv Admin, 77-78; chmn Coun Prof Standards Speech-Lang Path & Adiol, 82-84. *Mem:* Acad Rehab Audiol; Acoust Soc Am; fel Am Speech-Lang-Hearing Asn (vpres, 69-71, pres, 75); Am Auditory Soc; Int Soc Audiol. *Res:* Detection of aural harmonics; bone conduction audiometry; speech audiometry; middle ear immittance. *Mailing Add:* Dept Speech & Hearing Sci JH-40 Univ Wash Seattle WA 98195

YANTIS, RICHARD P, b Westerville, Ohio, July 1, 32; m 59; c 2. MATHEMATICS, OPERATIONS RESEARCH. *Educ:* US Naval Acad, BS, 54; Univ NC, MA, 62; Ohio State Univ, PhD(indust eng), 66. *Prof Exp:* US Air Force, 54-74, intel officer, 54-56, instr navig, 56-60, from instr to assoc prof math, US Air Force Acad, 62-70, assoc prof opers res, US Air Force Inst Technol, 71-74; teacher, Columbus Acad, 75-76; ASSOC PROF MATH, OTTERBEIN COL, 76- *Concurrent Pos:* Proj leader underground coal mining proj, Battelle Mem Inst, 74-75, consult, 75- *Mem:* Inst Mgt Sci; Sigma Xi; Am Inst Indust Eng; Inst Mgt Sci. *Res:* Linear programming; integer linear programming. *Mailing Add:* 265 Storington Rd Westerville OH 43081

YANUSHKA, ARTHUR, b NY, Dec 2, 48. MATHEMATICS. *Educ:* Fordham Univ, BA, 70; Univ Ill, MS & PhD(math), 74. *Prof Exp:* Asst prof math, Univ Mich, 74-76 & Kans State Univ, 76-77; asst prof, 77-80, ASSOC PROF MATH, CHRISTIAN BROS COL, 80- *Concurrent Pos:* Prin investr, Math Sci Sect, NSF, 78, 79. *Mem:* Math Asn Am. *Res:* Finite geometry and combinatorics. *Mailing Add:* Dept of Math Christian Bros Col Memphis TN 38104

YAO, JAMES TSU-PING, b Shanghai, China, July 7, 32; m 58; c 3. STRUCTURAL ENGINEERING. *Educ:* Univ Ill, Urbana, BSCE, 57, MSCE, 58, PhD(struct), 61. *Prof Exp:* Res asst civil eng, Univ Ill, Urbana, 57-61; asst prof, Univ NMex, 61-64; preceptor mech, Columbia Univ, 64-65; from assoc prof to prof civil eng, Univ NMex, 65-71; PROF CIVIL ENG, PURDUE UNIV, WEST LAFAYETTE, 71- *Mem:* Am Soc Civil Engrs; Am Soc Mech Engrs; Am Soc Eng Educ; Int Asn Bridge & Struct Eng; Am Acad Mech. *Res:* Metals fatigue; application of probability theory in structural engineering. *Mailing Add:* Sch Civil Eng Purdue Univ West Lafayette IN 47907

YAO, JERRY SHI KUANG, b Peiping, China, Oct 12, 25; m 46; c 2. PHOTOGRAPHIC CHEMISTRY. *Educ:* Peking Univ, BS, 46; Mont State Col, PhD, 60. *Prof Exp:* Fel biochem, Mont State Col, 60-61; asst prof org & gen chem, Wis State Col, Stevens Point, 61-62; assoc prof, Dubuque, 62-63; res chemist, 63-66, tech specialist, Photo & Reprod Div, 66-76, GROUP LEADER RES & DEVELOP, GAF CORP, 76- *Mem:* Soc Photog Sci & Eng; Am Chem Soc. *Res:* Heterocyclic chemistry in relation to photography; silver halide emulsions. *Mailing Add:* GAF Corp Res & Develop Ctr 1361 Alps Rd Wayne NJ 07470

YAO, JOE, b Antung, China, Feb 11, 30; m 68. WOOD SCIENCE, WOOD CHEMISTRY. *Educ:* Chung Hsing Univ, Taiwan, BS, 54; Mont State Univ, MS, 58; NC State Univ, PhD(wood sci, wood technol), 65. *Prof Exp:* Asst prof, 63-70, ASSOC PROF WOOD SCI & TECHNOL, MISS STATE UNIV, 70-; ASSOC WOOD TECHNOLOGIST, MISS FOREST PROD UTILIZATION LAB, 70- *Concurrent Pos:* Asst forester, Miss Agr Exp Sta, 63-67; asst wood technologist, Miss Forest Prod Utilization Lab, 67-70; vis prof, Nat Chung Hsing Univ, Taiwan, 73-74. *Mem:* AAAS; Soc Wood Sci & Technol; Forest Prod Res Soc; Am Inst Chemists; NY Acad Sci. *Res:* Wood particleboard properties; wood capillary structure; water diffusion in wood; shrinkage and related properties; low grade hardwood utilization; utilization of recycled wood fiber material. *Mailing Add:* Dept of Wood Sci & Technol Miss State Univ Mississippi State MS 39762

YAO, KUAN MU, b Chekiang, China, Sept 25, 23; US citizen. SANITARY ENGINEERING. *Educ:* Pei-Yang Univ, BS, 47; Univ NC, MS, 55, PhD(sanit eng), 68. *Prof Exp:* Sr engr, Prov Govt Taiwan, 48-58; teaching fel water resources, Univ NSW, Australia, 59; sr lectr civil eng, Canterbury Univ, NZ, 60-65; res assoc sanit eng, Univ NC, 68; sr specialist, Camp, Dresser & McKee, Boston, 68-71; Sanit engr, 72-78, WATER QUAL MGT ADV, WHO, 79- *Concurrent Pos:* Consult water supply eng, Mil Construct Comn, Taiwan, 57-58; prof sanit eng, Univ Eng & Technol, Lahore, Pakistan, 72-75. *Mem:* Water Pollution Control Fedn. *Res:* Fundamental and practical studies of water filtration, tube settling and sewer hydraulics; mathematical modeling and computer application in engineering. *Mailing Add:* PO Box 2550 WHO Kuala Lumpur Malaysia

YAO, KUNG, b Hong Kong, Nov 24, 38; US citizen; m 69. COMMUNICATIONS, SYSTEMS ENGINEERING. *Educ:* Princeton Univ, BSE, 61, MA, 63, PhD(elec eng), 65. *Prof Exp:* Res asst commun eng, Princeton Univ, 63-65; Nat Acad Sci-Nat Res Coun res fel syst eng, Univ Calif, Berkeley, 65-66; asst prof commun eng, 66-72, assoc prof, 72-78, PROF COMMUN ENG, UNIV CALIF, LOS ANGELES, 78- *Concurrent Pos:* Prin investr, NSF initiation grant, 68-71 & Off Naval Res, 72- *Mem:* AAAS; Inst Elec & Electronics Engrs; Am Math Soc. *Res:* Research, teaching and consulting in communications theory and signal processing. *Mailing Add:* Dept Eng Boelter Hall 4531 Univ Calif Los Angeles CA 90024

YAO, MENT-CHAO, b Taiwan, Mar 21, 49; m. GENETICS. *Educ:* Nat Taiwan Univ, BS, 71; Univ Rochester, MS, 75, PhD(biol), 75. *Prof Exp:* Assoc cell biol, Yale Univ, 75-78; ASST PROF BIOL, WASHINGTON UNIV, 78- *Mem:* Am Soc Cell Biol; AAAS. *Res:* Changes in dosage and structure of genes during animal development, and their relationships to differentiation. *Mailing Add:* Dept Biol Washington Univ Lindell Blvd St Louis MO 63130

YAO, NENG-PING, b Shanghai, China, Oct 13, 38; m 67; c 1. CHEMICAL ENGINEERING, ELECTROCHEMISTRY. *Educ:* Univ Calif, Los Angeles, BS, 63, MS, 65, PhD(chem eng), 69; Univ Chicago, MBA, 79. *Prof Exp:* Res engr, Univ Calif, Los Angeles, 63-69; mem tech staff chem technol, Atomics Int Div, N Am Rockwell Corp, 69-71; sect head electrochem technol, Heliotek Div, Textron Inc, 71-72; mem staff, Chem Eng Div, 72-76, assoc dir energy storage prog, 76-77, DIR, OFF ELECTROCHEM PROJS, ARGONNE NAT LAB, 77- *Mem:* AAAS; Electrochem Soc; Am Chem Soc; Sigma Xi. *Res:* Electrochemical energy conversion systems; batteries and fuel cells; air and water pollution control systems. *Mailing Add:* Argonne Nat Lab 9700 S Cass Ave D-205 Argonne IL 60439

YAO, SHANG JEONG, b Canton, China, June 6, 34; US citizen. CHEMICAL PHYSICS, BIOMEDICAL SCIENCES. *Educ:* Taipei Inst Technol, Taiwan, Dipl chem eng, 55; Univ Ore, MA, 61; Univ Minn, Minneapolis, PhD, 66. *Prof Exp:* Asst prof phys sci, Wilbur Wright Col, Chicago City Col, 68-69; assoc surg res, Michael Reese Hosp & Med Ctr, Chicago, 69-71; asst prof, 71-79, RES ASSOC PROF NEUROL SURG, SCH MED, UNIV PITTSBURGH, 79- *Concurrent Pos:* Robert A Welch Found fel theoret chem, Tex A&M Univ, 66-67; fel, Northwestern Univ, Evanston, 67-68; instr, Univ Chicago, 70-71; sr res scientist, Montefiore Hosp, Pittsburgh, Pa, 71-; prin investr, John A Hartford Found grant, 77-80 & NIH, 79-81 & 81- *Mem:* Am Phys Soc; Am Soc Artificial Internal Organs; Soc Neurosci. *Res:* Irreversible thermodynamics; bioenergetics; quantum theory of enzyme specificity and theory of catalyst facilitated tunneling; implantable energy sources; neuroscience; electrochemical urea removal for hemodialysis; electrochemical sensors. *Mailing Add:* Dept of Neurol Surg Univ of Pittsburgh Pittsburgh PA 15261

YAO, SHI CHUNE, b Taiwan, Dec 31, 46. HEAT TRANSFER, NUCLEAR ENGINEERING. *Educ:* Nat Tsing Univ, Taiwan, BS, 68; Univ Calif, Berkeley, MS, 71, PhD(nuclear eng), 74. *Prof Exp:* Engr, Argonne Nat Lab, 74-77; asst prof, 77-80, ASSOC PROF MECH ENG, CARNEGIE-MELLON UNIV, 80- *Concurrent Pos:* Consult, Nuclear Ctr & Steam Turbine Div, Westinghouse Elec Co, 78- *Mem:* Am Soc Mech Engrs; Am Nuclear Soc; Am Inst Chem Engrs. *Res:* Two phase flow and heat transfer; droplet flow; particle flow; nuclear and coal applications; nuclear reactor thermal hydraulics; rod bundles; spray combustion. *Mailing Add:* Dept of Mech Eng Carnegie Mellon Univ Pittsburgh PA 15213

YAO, YORK-PENG EDWARD, b Canton, China, Sept 11, 37; m 65; c 4. THEORETICAL HIGH ENERGY PHYSICS. *Educ:* Univ Calif, Berkeley, BS, 60; Harvard Univ, MA, 63, PhD(physics), 64. *Prof Exp:* Assoc mem natural sci, Inst Advan Study, 64-66; asst prof physics, 66-72, assoc prof, 72-78, PROF PHYSICS, UNIV MICH, ANN ARBOR, 78- *Mem:* Am Phys Soc. *Res:* Quantum field theory; elementary particle physics. *Mailing Add:* Dept of Physics Univ of Mich Ann Arbor MI 48109

YAP, FUNG YEN, b Jamaica, WI, Oct 12, 33. ATMOSPHERIC SCIENCE, MARINE SCIENCE. *Educ:* Brandeis Univ, BA, 58; Johns Hopkins Univ, PhD(physics), 67. *Prof Exp:* Asst prof physics, Wilson Col, 66-74, chmn dept, 72-74; sr digital programmer, Comput Sci Technicolor Assocs, 74-76; mem tech staff, 76-77, sr mem, 77-78, tech mgr, 78-80, SR SCIENTIST, COMPUT SCI CORP, 80- *Concurrent Pos:* Proj dir, NSF Award for Purchase of Instnl Sci Equip for Physics Dept, Wilson Col, 68-70. *Mem:* Sigma Xi; Am Phys Soc; Am Asn Physics Teachers. *Res:* Satellite navigation and remote sensing; Atmospheric modelling; ozone modelling; solar ultraviolet flux determination by satellites; determination of temperature and humidity for storm prediction from satellite sounding measurements; determination of nuclear decay schemes; environmental pollution; artificial satellite image navigation; satellite remote sensing of ocean color. *Mailing Add:* Comput Sci Corp 8728 Colesville Rd Silver Spring MD 20910

YAP, PETER S K, biopharmaceutics, pharmacy, see previous edition

YAP, WILLIAM TAN, b Amoy, China, Aug 10, 34; US citizen; m 69; c 2. PHYSICAL CHEMISTRY. *Educ:* Mass Inst Technol, BS, 56, MS, 58, PhD(phys chem), 64. *Prof Exp:* Res chemist, Res Ctr, Hercules, Inc, 64-69; vis assoc biophys chem, NIH, 69-71; RES CHEMIST, NAT BUR STAND, 72- *Res:* Biophysical chemistry; solution properties of proteins and other macromolecules; electroanalytical chemistry. *Mailing Add:* 6204 Mori St McLean VA 22101

YAPEL, ANTHONY FRANCIS, JR, b Soudan, Minn, Aug 14, 37; m 60; c 3. DRUG DELIVERY SYSTEMS, BIOMATERIALS. *Educ:* St John's Univ, Minn, BA, 59; Univ Minn, Minneapolis, PhD(phys chem), 67. *Prof Exp:* Sr res chemist, 66-71, res specialist, 71-75, sr res specialist, 75-78, mgr biokinetics res, 78-81, MGR BIOMAT RES, MINN MINING & MFG CO, 81- *Concurrent Pos:* Mem bd dir, Univ Minn Inst Technol Alumni Asn, 75-77, vpres, 77-78, pres, 78-79; mem bd dir, St John's Univ Alumni Asn, 78-81, vpres, 80-81. *Mem:* Am Chem Soc; AAAS. *Res:* Fast reaction, temperature-jump relaxation and enzyme kinetics; physical chemistry of membranes; reverse osmosis phenomena; structure-activity correlations on biological systems; column chromatography; drug delivery systems; wound management studies; biomaterials. *Mailing Add:* Biosci Res Lab Minn Mining & Mfg Co St Paul MN 55144

YAPHE, WILFRED, b Lachine, Que, July 9, 21; m 46; c 3. BACTERIOLOGY. *Educ:* McGill Univ, BSc, 49, PhD(agr bact), 52. *Prof Exp:* Assoc res officer, Atlantic Regional Lab, Nat Res Coun Can, 52-66; assoc prof microbiol & immunol, 66-72, PROF MICROBIOL & IMMUNOL, McGILL UNIV, 72- *Mem:* Am Soc Microbiol; Can Soc Microbiol. *Res:* Marine microbiology; marine algae; bacterial decomposition of agar, carrageenin and other algal polysaccharides. *Mailing Add:* Dept Microbiol & Immunol McGill Univ 3775 University St Montreal PQ H3A 2B4 Can

YAQUB, ADIL MOHAMED, b Jordan, Jan 19, 28; nat US; m 51; c 2. ALGEBRA. *Educ:* Univ Calif, AB, 50, MA, 51, PhD(math), 55. *Prof Exp:* Asst, Univ Calif, 50-55; from instr to asst prof math, Purdue Univ, 55-60; assoc prof, 60-67, PROF MATH, UNIV CALIF, SANTA BARBARA, 67- *Mem:* Am Math Soc; Math Asn Am. *Res:* Algebraic structures; ring theory; number theory. *Mailing Add:* Dept of Math Univ of Calif Santa Barbara CA 93106

YAQUB, JILL COURTANEY DONALDSON SPENCER, b Almondsbury, Eng, Dec 17, 31; m 59. GEOMETRY. *Educ:* Oxford Univ, BA, 53, MA, 57, PhD(math), 60. *Prof Exp:* Asst lectr math, Royal Holloway Col, Univ London, 56-59; instr, Wash Univ, 60-61; asst prof, Tufts Univ, 61-63; from asst to assoc prof, 63-75, PROF MATH, OHIO STATE UNIV, 75- *Concurrent Pos:* Fel, Alexander von Humboldt Found, 70-71. *Mem:* Am Math Soc. *Res:* Non-Desarguesian planes, inversive planes and their automorphism groups. *Mailing Add:* Dept of Math Ohio State Univ Columbus OH 43210

YARAMANOGLU, MELIH, b Istanbul, Turkey, July 20, 47; m 73. MATHEMATICAL WATERSHED MODELING. *Educ:* Middle East Tech Univ, BS, 71, MS, 73; Univ Md, PhD(agr eng), 78. *Prof Exp:* Res assoc, 78-80, ASST PROF HYDROL, DEPT AGR ENG, UNIV MD, 80- *Mem:* Am Soc Agr Eng; Soc Comput Simulation. *Res:* Mathematical modeling of watersheds; hydrology; water quality. *Mailing Add:* Dept Agr Eng Univ Md College Park MD 20742

YARBOROUGH, LYMAN, b Cushing, Okla, Feb 13, 37; m 61; c 1. CHEMICAL ENGINEERING. *Educ:* Okla State Univ, BS, 59, MS, 61, PhD(chem eng), 64. *Prof Exp:* Staff res engr, 64-76, res supvr, Tulsa, 76-78, plant eng supvr, 78-81, MGR PROCESS ENG, AMOCO PROD CO, CHICAGO, 81- *Mem:* AAAS; Am Inst Chem Engrs; Am Chem Soc; Soc Petrol Engrs. *Res:* Thermodynamics and phase behavior of fluids; hydrocarbons and mixtures of hydrocarbons; natural gas processing plant design. *Mailing Add:* Amoco Prod Co PO Box 5340-A Mail Code 4507 Chicago IL 60680

YARBOROUGH, WILLIAM WALTER, JR, b Tylertown, Miss, Jan 6, 45; m 68. PLASMA PHYSICS. *Educ:* Univ Chattanooga, AB, 67; Vanderbilt Univ, PhD(physics), 74. *Prof Exp:* asst prof, 74-80, ASSOC PROF PHYSICS, PRESBY COL, 80-, CHMN, DEPT PHYSICS, 79- *Mem:* Am Asn Physics Teachers; Am Inst Physics. *Res:* Low energy theta pinch devices, particularly losses from such devices. *Mailing Add:* Dept Physics Presby Col Clinton SC 29325

YARBRO, CLAUDE LEE, JR, b Jackson, Tenn, Sept 26, 22; m 51; c 3. ECOLOGY. *Educ:* Lambuth Col, BA, 43; Univ NC, PhD(biochem), 54. *Prof Exp:* Actg prof math & physics, Lambuth Col, 46-47; instr physics, Union Col, Tenn, 48; instr biochem, Vanderbilt Univ, 49-51; asst, Univ NC, 51-54, res assoc, 54-57, instr, 54-60; biologist, Biol Br, Res & Develop Div, US AEC, 60-67, biol scientist, Res Contracts Br, Lab & Univ Div, 67-72, biol scientist, Res & Develop Admin, 72-76, LIFE SCIENTIST, OAK RIDGE OPERS, US DEPT ENERGY, 76- *Mem:* Ecol Soc Am; AAAS; fel Am Inst Chemists; Sigma Xi; NY Acad Sci. *Res:* Phospholipid chemistry and metabolism; mechanism of renal calculus; formation and physical chemistry of calcium phosphate; ecological succession on sandstone bluffs. *Mailing Add:* 147 Alger Rd Oak Ridge TN 37830

YARBROUGH, ARTHUR C, JR, b Mitchell, Ga, June 12, 28. ORGANIC CHEMISTRY, SCIENCE EDUCATION. *Educ:* Ga Southern Col, BS, 49; George Peabody Col, MA, 52. *Prof Exp:* Pub sch instr, Ga, 49-51 & 52-53; asst prof chem, Emory at Osford, 53-55; instr, George Peabody Col, 56-57; ASSOC PROF CHEM, TOWSON STATE COL, 57- *Concurrent Pos:* Consult var high & jr high schs, Md, 57-, Univ Md, 63 & Baltimore County Fire Dept, 67- *Mem:* Am Chem Soc. *Res:* Reactions of transition elements. *Mailing Add:* Dept of Chem Towson State Col Baltimore MD 21204

YARBROUGH, CHARLES GERALD, b Lumberton, NC, Oct 13, 39; m 60; c 2. ZOOLOGY. *Educ:* Wake Forest Univ, BS, 61, MA, 63; Univ Fla, PhD(zool), 70. *Prof Exp:* From instr to asst prof biol, Campbell Col, 64-75, assoc prof, 75-80; MEM FAC, DIV SCI & MATH, WINGATE COL, 80- *Concurrent Pos:* Chapman res grant, Am Mus Natural Hist, 64; AEC proj ecol researcher, Battelle Mem Inst, 68; vis grad prof, Univ Va, 75. *Mem:* Am Ornith Union; Cooper Ornith Soc. *Res:* Influence of physical factors, nutrients and heavy metals on biotic communities; metabolism and temperature regulation in vertebrates; ecological implications of energetics in animals. *Mailing Add:* Div Sci & Math Wingate Col Wingate NC 28174

YARBROUGH, DAVID WYLIE, b Long Beach, Calif, May, 7, 37. CHEMICAL ENGINEERING. *Educ:* Ga Inst Technol, BChE, 60, MS, 61, PhD(chem eng), 66. *Prof Exp:* From asst prof to assoc prof, 68-76, assoc dean, Grad Studies & Res, 76-79, PROF CHEM ENG, TENN TECHNOL UNIV, 76- *Concurrent Pos:* Mem res staff, Oak Ridge Nat Lab, 79-80. *Mem:* Am Inst Chem Engrs; Am Soc Eng Educ; Sigma Xi; Am Soc Testing & Mats. *Res:* Thermodynamics; physical properties; applied mathematics; energy conservation. *Mailing Add:* Col of Eng PO Box 5013 Tenn Technol Univ Cookeville TN 38501

YARBROUGH, GEORGE GIBBS, b Houston, Tex, Jan 20, 43; m 64; c 2. NEUROPHARMACOLOGY. *Educ:* Univ Houston, BS, 68; Vanderbilt Univ, PhD(pharmacol), 72. *Prof Exp:* Fel physiol, Univ Man, 72-73; from lectr to asst prof, Univ Sask, 73-75; res fel, 75-80, SR RES FEL NEUROPSYCHOPHARMACOL, MERCK INST THERAPEUT RES, 80- *Concurrent Pos:* Med Res Coun Can scholar, Univ Sask, 74-75. *Mem:* Am Soc Pharmacol & Exp Therapeut; Soc Neurosci. *Res:* Physiology and pharmacology of synaptic transmission in the mammalian central nervous system. *Mailing Add:* Merck Sharp & Dohme Res Labs West Point PA 19486

YARBROUGH, HENRY FLOYD, JR, b Richmond, Va, Jan 21, 24; m 46; c 2. BACTERIOLOGY. *Educ:* Univ Ill, BS, 50, MS, 51, PhD(bact), 53. *Prof Exp:* RES ASSOC, MOBIL RES & DEVELOP CORP, 53- *Mem:* Am Soc Microbiol; Sigma Xi. *Res:* Petroleum microbiology. *Mailing Add:* Mobil Res & Develop Corp Res Lab PO Box 900 Dallas TX 75221

YARBROUGH, KAREN MARGUERITE, b Memphis, Tenn, Mar 4, 38. GENETICS, MICROBIOLOGY. *Educ:* Miss State Univ, BS, 61, MS, 63; NC State Univ, PhD(genetics), 67. *Prof Exp:* Asst prof biol, 67-70, assoc prof, 70-81, PROF MICROBIOL & ACTG VPRES, ACADEMIC AFFAIRS, UNIV SOUTHERN MISS, 81-, DIR, INST GENETICS, 72- *Concurrent Pos:* Assoc prof biol, Univ Southern Miss, 70-71, asst dean & res coordr, Col Sci & Technol, 76-81. *Mem:* Genetics Soc Am; Am Genetic Asn; Sigma Xi; NY Acad Sci; Am Soc Human Genetics. *Res:* Population genetics; human genetics; dermatoglyphics. *Mailing Add:* PO Box 421 Univ Southern Miss Hattiesburg MS 39401

YARBROUGH, LYNN DOUGLAS, b Ft Worth, Tex, July 17, 30; m 61; c 3. COMPUTER SCIENCE. *Educ:* Rice Inst, BA, 53; Univ Ill, MS, 55. *Prof Exp:* Comput prog analyst, MacDonnell Aircraft Corp, 55; from sr engr to prin scientist, Space & Info Systs Div, NAm Aviation Inc, 55-65; asst dir, Comput Ctr, Harvard Univ, 65-67; sr scientist, Arcon Corp, 67-75; PRIN SOFTWARE ENGR, DIGITAL EQUIPMENT CORP, 75- *Mem:* Asn Comput Mach. *Res:* Design and development of computer operating systems, computer languages and computer graphic systems. *Mailing Add:* Digital Equip Corp 110 Spit Brook Rd Nashua NH 03061

YARBROUGH, LYNWOOD R, b Cherokee, Ala, July 26, 40; m 75. BIOCHEMISTRY, BIOPHYSICS. *Educ:* Univ Northwestern Ala, BS, 65; Purdue Univ, PhD(biochem, molecular biol), 71. *Prof Exp:* Res assoc molecular biol, Albert Einstein Col Med, 71-73, res assoc biophys, 73-75; asst prof, 75-80, ASSOC PROF BIOCHEM, MED CTR, UNIV KANS, 80- *Concurrent Pos:* Damon Runyon Found res fel, 72-74. *Mem:* Biophys Soc; Am Chem Soc; Sigma Xi; NY Acad Sci; Am Soc Biol Chemists. *Res:* Structure of tubulin genes and regulation of tubulin gene expression; assembly of subunit proteins. *Mailing Add:* Dept of Biochem Univ of Kans Med Ctr Kansas City KS 66103

YARD, ALLAN STANLEY, b Rocktown, NJ, Nov 18, 27; m 57; c 2. PHARMACOLOGY. *Educ:* Rutgers Univ, BS, 52; Med Col Va, PhD(pharmacol, biochem), 56. *Prof Exp:* Asst prof pharmacol, Rutgers Univ, 55-56; asst prof, Med Col Va, 56-60; sr scientist, Ortho Res Found, 60-63, Ortho res fel, 63-67; group chief, 67-73, dir acad & govt liaison, 73-75, ASST DIR, DRUG REGULATORY AFFAIRS, HOFFMANN-LA ROCHE INC, 75- *Concurrent Pos:* Mem coadj fac, Rutgers Univ, 63- *Mem:* AAAS; Am Soc Pharmacol & Exp Therapeut; Soc Study Reproduction; Am Chem Soc; NY Acad Sci. *Res:* Drug metabolism; effect of drugs on liver metabolism; synthesis of hydrazino compounds; biochemistry and pharmacology of the oviduct, uterus and fertility control agents. *Mailing Add:* Res Labs Hoffmann-La Roche Inc Nutley NJ 07110

YARDLEY, DARRELL GENE, b Gorman, Tex, Apr 15, 48; m 72; c 1. POPULATION GENETICS. *Educ:* Univ Tex, Austin, BA, 71, MA, 72; Univ Ga, PhD(zool), 75. *Prof Exp:* Instr human anat & physiol, Univ Ga, 75; ASST PROF ZOOL, CLEMSON UNIV, 75- *Mem:* Genetics Soc Am; Soc Study Evolution. *Res:* Laboratory, field and theoretical approaches to genetic mechanisms of evolution. *Mailing Add:* Dept of Zool Clemson Univ Clemson SC 29631

YARDLEY, DONALD H, b Estevan, Sask, Sept 9, 17; m 42. MINING ENGINEERING. *Educ:* Queen's Univ, Ont, BSc, 41 & 46, MSc, 47; Univ Minn, PhD(geol), 51. *Prof Exp:* Asst to chief engr, Hardrock Gold Mines, 41-42; field engr, Andowan Mines, 45-46; party chief, Can Geol Surv, 47-48; asst mining, Univ Minn, St Paul, 47-49, from instr to assoc prof, 49-77; PROF CIVIL & MINING ENG, UNIV MINN, MINNEAPOLIS, 77- *Res:* Geochemical exploration; heavy metals; geological engineering; economic geology. *Mailing Add:* Dept of Civil Eng Univ of Minn Minneapolis MN 55455

YARDLEY, JAMES THOMAS, III, b Taft, Calif, May 15, 42; m 66, 76; c 2. PHYSICAL CHEMISTRY. *Educ:* Rice Univ, BA, 64; Univ Calif, Berkeley, PhD(chem), 67. *Prof Exp:* Asst prof, 67-70, assoc prof chem, Univ Ill, Urbana, 74-77; sr chem physicist, 77-80, SR RES ASSOC, ALLIED CORP, 80- *Concurrent Pos:* Dreyfus Found teacher-scholar award, 70-75; Alfred P Sloan fel, 72-73. *Mem:* Am Phys Soc; Am Chem Soc. *Res:* Molecular spectroscopy; vibrational energy transfer; molecular lasers; molecular dynamics. *Mailing Add:* Corp Res Ctr Allied Corp PO Box 1021R Morristown NJ 07960

YARDLEY, JOHN FINLEY, b St Louis, Mo, Feb 1, 25; m 46; c 5. AERONAUTICAL ENGINEERING. *Educ:* Iowa State Col, BS, 44; Wash Univ, MS, 50. *Prof Exp:* Stress analyst aircraft design, McDonnell Aircraft Corp, 46-48, strength group engr, 48-51, proj stress engr, 51-54, chief strength engr, 54-58, proj engr Mercury capsule design, 58-60, base mgr spacecraft flight testing, Cape Canaveral, 60-64, Gemini Prog tech dir, 64-66, tech dir, 66-68, vpres & dep gen mgr, Eastern Div, McDonnell-Douglas Astronaut Co, 68-76; ASSOC ADMINR MANNED SPACE FLIGHT, NASA, 76- *Honors & Awards:* John J Montgomery Award, 63; NASA Pub Serv Awards, 63 & 66. *Mem:* Am Inst Aeronaut & Astronaut; Nat Acad Engrs. *Res:* Applied mechanics; integration of advanced systems into space vehicles. *Mailing Add:* NASA 600 Independence Ave Washington DC 20546

YARDLEY, JOHN HOWARD, b Columbia, SC, June 7, 26; m 52; c 3. PATHOLOGY. *Educ:* Birmingham-Southern Col, AB, 49; Johns Hopkins Univ, MD, 53; Am Bd Path, dipl, 59. *Prof Exp:* Intern internal med, Vanderbilt Univ Hosp, 53-54; from instr to assoc prof, 54-72, PROF PATH, SCH MED, JOHNS HOPKINS UNIV, 72-, ASSOC DEAN ACAD AFFAIRS, 77- *Concurrent Pos:* From asst resident to resident, Johns Hopkins Hosp, 54-58. *Mem:* Am Asn Path & Bact; Int Acad Path; Am Soc Exp Path; Am Gastroenterol Asn. *Res:* Gastrointestinal diseases; electron microscopy. *Mailing Add:* Dept of Path Johns Hopkins Hosp Baltimore MD 21205

YARGER, DOUGLAS NEAL, b Omaha, Nebr, July 13, 37; m 60; c 4. ATMOSPHERIC PHYSICS, METEOROLOGY. *Educ:* Iowa State Univ, BS, 59; Univ Ariz, MS, 62, PhD(meteorol), 67. *Prof Exp:* Asst prof, 67-71, assoc prof meteorol & climatol, 71-80, PROF METEOROL & AGRON, IOWA STATE UNIV, 80- *Mem:* Am Meteorol Soc; Optical Soc Am. *Res:* Radiative transfer in the atmosphere; physical meteorology. *Mailing Add:* 313 Curtiss Hall Iowa State Univ Ames IA 50010

YARGER, FREDERICK LYNN, b Lindsey, Ohio, Mar 8, 25; m 48; c 2. PHYSICS. *Educ:* Capital Univ, BSc, 50; Ohio State Univ, MSc, 53, PhD(physics), 60. *Prof Exp:* Res asst physics, Los Alamos Sci Lab, 52, mem staff, 53-55 & 56; sr engr, Columbus Div, NAm Aviation, Inc, Ohio, 56-58; res asst physics, Ohio State Univ, 58-60; supvry physicist, Nat Bur Standards, Colo, 60-64; sci specialist, Edgerton, Germeshausen & Grier, Inc, Nev, 64-65; sr res physicist, Falcon Res & Develop Co, Colo, 65-66; assoc prof, 66-76, PROF PHYSICS, NMEX HIGHLANDS UNIV, 76- *Concurrent Pos:* Vis staff mem, Los Alamos Sci Lab, 74-; vis prof, Nat Univ Mex, 68, 72, 77 & 81. *Mem:* Am Phys Soc; Optical Soc Am; Sigma Xi; Mex Phys Soc. *Res:* High pressure equations of state; molecular spectroscopy. *Mailing Add:* Dept of Physics & Math NMex Highlands Univ Las Vegas NM 87701

YARGER, HAROLD LEE, b Ypsilanti, Mich, Mar 15, 40; m 65; c 3. EXPLORATION GEOPHYSICS. *Educ:* Antioch Col, BS, 62; State Univ NY Stony Brook, MA, 65, PhD(physics), 68. *Prof Exp:* Instr physics, State Univ NY Stony Brook, 67-68; res assoc, Northwestern Univ, 68-69; res assoc, Univ, 69-70, res assoc geophys, 70-77, ASSOC GEOPHYS SCIENTIST, KANS GEOL SURV, UNIV KANS, 77-, ADJ ASSOC PROF PHYSICS & GEOL, 78- *Concurrent Pos:* NASA res contracts, 72-74 & 73-75; US Geol Surv res contract, 74-76 & 78-79; Ark Geol Comn res contract, 79-81. *Mem:* Geol Soc Am; Am Geophys Union; Am Phys Soc; Soc Explor Geophys. *Res:* Gravity and magnetics; remote sensing; airplane and satellite imagery for exploration and management of earth resources; high energy physics; bubble chamber work. *Mailing Add:* Kans Geol Surv Univ of Kans Lawrence KS 66044

YARIAN, DEAN ROBERT, b Warsaw, Ind, Oct 12, 33; m 54; c 7. ORGANIC CHEMISTRY. *Educ:* DePauw Univ, BA, 55; Univ Wash, PhD(chem), 60. *Prof Exp:* Asst lectr, Univ Wash, 58-59; sr chemist, Cent Res Lab, 60-65, sr chemist, Paper Prod Div, 65-70, chemist specialist, 70-78, MGR CARBONLESS PAPER DEVELOP, PAPER PROD LAB, 3M CO, ST PAUL, 78- *Mem:* Am Chem Soc. *Res:* Organic synthesis; imaging chemistry; colloids; paper chemistry; statistics. *Mailing Add:* 3M Ctr 234-1E-14 St Paul MN 55101

YARINGTON, CHARLES THOMAS, JR, b Sayre, Pa, Apr 26, 34; m 63; c 3. OTORHINOLARYNGOLOGY. *Educ:* Princeton Univ, AB, 56; Hahnemann Med Col, MD, 60; Am Bd Otolaryngol, dipl, 65. *Prof Exp:* Rotating intern, Rochester Gen Hosp, 60-61; res gen surg, Dartmouth Med Sch Affil Hosps, 61-62; asst otolaryngol, Sch Med, Univ Rochester, 62-63, instr, 63-65; chief, Eye, Ear, Nose & Throat Serv, US Army Hosp, Ft Carson, Colo, 65-67; asst prof, Sch Med WVa Univ, 67-68; from assoc prof to prof otorhinolaryngol & chmn dept, Col Med, Univ Nebr, Omaha, 68-74; CLIN PROF OTOLARYNGOL, UNIV WASH, 74-; HEAD & NECK SURGEON & CHIEF, DEPT OTOLARYNGOL, MASON CLIN, 74- *Concurrent Pos:* Res otolaryngol, Sch Med, Univ Rochester, 62-65; consult, Colo State Hosp, 65-67 & Vet Admin Hosp, WVa, 67-68; chief, Vet Admin Hosp, Omaha & Univ Nebr Hosp, Omaha, 68-74; chief ear, nose & throat, Mason Clin & Virginia Mason Hosp, 74-; consult, Surgeon Gen, US Air Force, 76- *Honors & Awards:* Prof Doctor Ignacio Barraquer Mem Award, 68; Honor Award, Am Acad Ophthal & Otolaryngol, 74. *Mem:* Fel Am Acad Facial Plastic & Reconstruct Surg; fel Am Col Surgeons; Soc Head & Neck Surgeons. *Res:* Clinical studies in the pathology and therapy of congenital and neoplastic defects in the head and neck; histopathology of salivary gland disease. *Mailing Add:* Mason Clin 1100 Ninth Ave Seattle WA 98101

YARINSKY, ALLEN, b Brooklyn, NY, May 6, 29; m 52; c 3. PARASITOLOGY, CHEMOTHERAPY. *Educ:* City Col New York, BS, 51; Columbia Univ, MS, 53; Univ NC, MS, 57, PhD, 61. *Prof Exp:* Med bacteriologist, Ft Detrick, Md, 54-56; res scientist, New York Dept Health, 61-65; res biologist, 66-69, head, Parasitol dept, 69-79, DIR QUAL ASSURANCE DEPT, STERLING-WINTHROP RES INST, 79- *Mem:* Am Soc Parasitol; Am Soc Trop Med & Hyg; Royal Soc Trop Med & Hyg. *Res:* Research on Clostridium botulinum type E toxin; immunological relationships of experimental Trichinella spirals infections; laboratory diagnosis of Protozoan and helminth infections; chemotherapy of parasitic infections; quality assurance. *Mailing Add:* Sterling-Winthrop Res Inst Rensselaer NY 12144

YARIS, ROBERT, b New York, NY, Oct 16, 35; m 64. PHYSICAL CHEMISTRY. *Educ:* Univ Calif, Los Angeles, BS, 58; Univ Wash, PhD(phys chem), 62. *Prof Exp:* Res assoc phys chem, Univ Minn, 62-64; from asst prof to assoc prof chem, 64-70, PROF CHEM, WASH UNIV, 70- *Concurrent Pos:* Alfred P Sloan fel, 66- *Mem:* Am Phys Soc. *Res:* Theoretical and quantum chemistry; time-dependent perturbation theory; many body theory. *Mailing Add:* Dept of Chem Wash Univ St Louis MO 63130

YARIV, A(MNON), b Tel Aviv, Israel, Apr 13, 30; nat US; m 54; c 2. SEMICONDUCTOR LASERS, INTEGRATED OPTICS. *Educ:* Univ Calif, Berkeley, BS, 54, MS, 56, PhD(elec eng), 59. *Prof Exp:* Asst, Univ Calif, Berkeley, 55-58; res assoc, 58-59; mem tech staff, Bell Tel Labs, 59-66; PROF ELEC ENG, CALIF INST TECHNOL, 66- *Concurrent Pos:* Indust consult. *Honors & Awards:* Quantum Electronics Award, Inst Elec & Electronics Engrs, 80. *Mem:* Fel Nat Acad Eng; fel Inst Elec & Electronics Engrs; fel Am Optical Soc; Am Phys Soc. *Res:* Lasers; nonlinear optics; optical modulation. *Mailing Add:* 2257 Homet Rd San Marino CA 91108

YARKONY, DAVID R, b Bronx, NY, Jan 28, 49. CHEMICAL PHYSICS. *Educ:* State Univ NY, Stony Brook, BA, 71; Univ Calif, Berkeley, PhD(chem), 75. *Prof Exp:* Res asst, Mass Inst Technol, 75-77; ASST PROF CHEM, JOHNS HOPKINS UNIV, 77- *Concurrent Pos:* Consult, Inst Comput Appln Sci & Eng, 78-79. *Res:* Electronic structure theory; energy transport in solids. *Mailing Add:* Dept of Chem Johns Hopkins Univ Baltimore MD 21218

YARLAGADDA, RADHA KRISHNA RAO, b Velpucherla, India, Apr 1, 38; m 66; c 3. ELECTRICAL ENGINEERING. *Educ:* Univ Mysore, BE, 59; SDak State Univ, MS, 61; Mich State Univ, PhD(elec eng), 64. *Prof Exp:* From asst prof to assoc prof, 66-78, PROF ELEC ENG, OKLA STATE UNIV, 78- *Concurrent Pos:* NSF res grant, 67-69; Air Force res grant, 81- *Honors & Awards:* Premium Award, Brit Inst Elec Engrs, 66. *Mem:* Inst Elec & Electronics Engrs. *Res:* Digital signal processing; communication theory. *Mailing Add:* Sch of Elec Eng Okla State Univ Stillwater OK 74074

YARMOLINSKY, MICHAEL BEZALEL, b New York, NY, Jan 18, 29; m 62; c 1. MOLECULAR BIOLOGY. *Educ:* Harvard Univ, AB, 50; Johns Hopkins Univ, PhD(biol), 54. *Prof Exp:* Instr pharmacol, Col Med, NY Univ, 54-55; res assoc, McCollum-Pratt Inst, Johns Hopkins Univ, 58-61, asst prof, 61-63; res chemist, NIH, 64-70; dir res, CNRS Rech Biol Molec, Paris, 70-76; DIR MOLECULAR GENETICS SECT, CANCER BIOL PROG, FREDERICK CANCER RES FAC, MD, 76- *Concurrent Pos:* NSF fel, Pasteur Inst, Paris, 63-64. *Mem:* Am Soc Biol Chemists. *Res:* Protein biosynthesis and its regulation; interactions between temperate bacteriophage and its host; replication control and partition of plasmids in bacteria. *Mailing Add:* Frederick Cancer Res Fac PO Box B Frederick MD 21701

YARMUSH, DAVID LEON, b New York, NY, June 10, 28. APPLIED MATHEMATICS. *Educ:* Harvard Univ, BA, 49; Princeton Univ, PhD(math), 59. *Prof Exp:* Mathematician chem & radiation labs, Army Chem Ctr, Md, 52-54; asst math, Princeton Univ, 54-56; mathematician, Tech Res Group, Inc, 56-67; res scientist, Courant Inst, NY Univ, 65-76; RES ASSOC, DEPT BIOL, COLUMBIA UNIV, 76- *Mem:* Am Math Soc. *Res:* Dynamic theory of games; radiation transport theory; structural vibrations and sound radiation; computer programming of deduction procedures; computer study of conformation of proteins. *Mailing Add:* Fairchild Ctr Columbia Univ New York NY 10027

YARNALL, JOHN LEE, b Elizabeth, NJ, Jan 27, 32; m 53; c 3. INVERTEBRATE ZOOLOGY, BIOLOGY. *Educ:* Univ Mont, BS, 53, MA, 62; Stanford Univ, PhD(biol), 72. *Prof Exp:* Asst prof, 69-72, assoc prof, 72-78, PROF BIOL, HUMBOLDT STATE UNIV, 78- *Mem:* AAAS; Am Soc Zoologists. *Res:* Invertebrate functional morphology and behavior, especially locomotion and feeding. *Mailing Add:* Dept of Biol Humboldt State Univ Arcata CA 95521

YARNELL, CHARLES FREDERICK, b Napoleon, Ohio, Sept 22, 39; div; c 4. PHYSICAL CHEMISTRY. *Educ:* Defiance Col, BS, 61; Mass Inst Technol, PhD(phys chem), 65. *Prof Exp:* STAFF MEM LEAD-ACID BATTERIES, BELL LABS, 65- *Mem:* Electrochem Soc. *Res:* Materials research on the positive and negative plate of the lead-acid battery; environmental assessment of oil placers of Alaska; production from Natural Petroleum Reserve Alaska. *Mailing Add:* Bell Labs 600 Mountain Ave Murray Hill NJ 07974

YARNELL, JOHN LEONARD, b Topeka, Kans, Mar 1, 22; m; c 4. SOLID STATE PHYSICS, NUCLEAR ENGINEERING. *Educ:* Univ Kans, AB, 47, AM, 49; Univ Minn, PhD(physics), 52. *Prof Exp:* Asst instr physics & math, Univ Kans, 47-49; asst, Univ Minn, 49-51; staff mem, Physics Div, Los Alamos Sci Lab, 52-65, group leader, Physics Div, 65-81; CONSULT, 81- *Mem:* Fel Am Phys Soc; Am Nuclear Soc. *Res:* Lattice dynamics; neutron diffraction; reactors; cryogenics; solid state physics. *Mailing Add:* 205 El Conejo Los Alamos NM 87544

YARNELL, RICHARD ASA, b Boston, Mass, May 11, 29; m; c 4. ANTHROPOLOGY, ETHNOBOTANY. *Educ:* Duke Univ, BS, 50; Univ NMex, MA, 58; Univ Mich, PhD(anthrop), 63. *Prof Exp:* From instr to assoc prof anthrop, Emory Univ, 62-71; assoc prof anthrop, 71-75, assoc chmn dept, 73-75, PROF ANTHROP, UNIV NC, CHAPEL HILL, 75- *Mem:* AAAS; Am Anthrop Asn; Soc Am Archaeol; Soc Econ Bot; Am Soc Ethnohist. *Res:* Analysis of archaeological plant remains; evolution of plant domestication; aboriginal plant utilization; cultural ecology; economic botany. *Mailing Add:* Dept of Anthrop Univ of NC Chapel Hill NC 27514

YARNS, DALE A, b Jackson, Minn, July 9, 30; m 54; c 2. ANIMAL PHYSIOLOGY. *Educ:* Univ Minn, BS, 56; SDak State Col, MS, 58; Univ Md, PhD(animal sci), 64. *Prof Exp:* Res asst dairy husb, SDak State Univ, 56-58; lab technician animal sci, Univ Calif, Davis, 58-61; animal husbandryman, Beef Cattle Br, USDA, 61-64; assoc res physiol, Animal Med Ctr, 64-66; asst prof, 66-72, ASSOC PROF PHYSIOL & CHMN DEPT BIOL, WAGNER COL, 72- *Res:* Comparative cardiac and ruminant physiology. *Mailing Add:* Dept of Biol Wagner Col Staten Island NY 10301

YAROSEWICK, STANLEY J, b Epping, NH, Sept 10, 39; m 64; c 2. ATOMIC PHYSICS, SPECTROSCOPY. *Educ:* Univ NH, BS, 61; Clarkson Col Technol, MS, 63, PhD(physics), 66. *Prof Exp:* Asst prof physics, Clarkson Col Technol, 66-69; assoc prof, 69-74, PROF PHYSICS, WEST CHESTER STATE COL, 74- *Mem:* Am Asn Physics Teachers. *Res:* Atomic emission spectra. *Mailing Add:* Dept Physics West Chester State Col West Chester PA 19380

YARRINGTON, ROBERT M, b Peoria, Ohio, Sept 26, 28; m 66; c 2. CHEMICAL ENGINEERING. *Educ:* Ohio State Univ, BSc, 51, MSc, 56, PhD(chem eng), 58. *Prof Exp:* Group leader res & develop, Am Cyanamid Co, 58-74; SECT HEAD RES & DEVELOP, ENGELHARD MINERAL & CHEM, 74- *Mem:* Am Inst Chem Engrs; Sigma Xi. *Res:* Research and development of catalytic processes related to the petroleum and energy fields. *Mailing Add:* 70 Wood Ave S Englehard Ind Div Iselin NJ 08830

YARUS, MICHAEL J, b Pikeville, Ky, Mar 2, 40; m 62; c 2. MOLECULAR BIOLOGY, BIOCHEMISTRY. *Educ:* Johns Hopkins Univ, BA, 60; Calif Inst Technol, PhD(biophys), 66. *Prof Exp:* USPHS & NIH fels biochem, Stanford Univ, 65-67; asst prof, 67-74, ASSOC PROF MOLECULAR, CELLULAR & DEVELOP BIOL, UNIV COLO, BOULDER, 74- *Concurrent Pos:* USPHS & NIH grant, 68- *Mem:* AAAS. *Res:* Minute viruses; transfer RNA; mammalian embryogeny. *Mailing Add:* Dept of MCD Biol Univ of Colo Boulder CO 80309

YARWOOD, CECIL EDMUND, plant pathology, deceased

YARZE, JOSEPH C(ARL), b Pottsville, Pa, Jan 22, 23; m 55; c 2. CHEMICAL ENGINEERING, CHEMISTRY. *Educ:* Pa State Univ, BS, 44, MS, 46; Cornell Univ, MChE, 47. *Prof Exp:* Res chem engr, Pilot Plant Develop, M W Kellogg Co, 47-51; supvr chem eng develop, Am Mach & Foundry Co, 51-53; mgr pilot plant develop, 53-75, SR PROCESS MGR, PULLMAN KELLOGG, PULLMAN, INC, 75- *Mem:* Sigma Xi (secy, 65, pres, 78); Am Inst Chem Engrs. *Res:* Plastics; fertilizers; petroleum; petrochemicals; heavy chemicals; reforming and other organic and inorganic processes; flue gas desulfurization. *Mailing Add:* 766 Evergreen Pkwy Union NJ 07083

YASAR, TUGRUL, b Ankara, Turkey, Sept 23, 41; div; c 3. ELECTRICAL ENGINEERING, THIN FILM TECHNOLOGY. *Educ:* Robert Col, Istanbul, BS, 63; Princeton Univ, MA, 67, PhD(elec eng in solid state sci), 68. *Prof Exp:* Res engr photoelectronics, Bendix Res Labs, 67-73; chief eng, Gen Instruments, 73-76; dir eng, 76-79, OPERS MGR, NAT MICRONETICS, INC, 79- *Concurrent Pos:* Mem affil fac, Col Eng, Wayne State Univ, 68-69; mem adv coun, Ulster Community Col, 79- *Mem:* Inst Elec & Electronics Engrs; Int Soc Hybrid Microelectronics; Am Vacuum Soc; Sigma Xi. *Res:* Photoemission from semiconductors; photoelectronic devices; imaging devices; amorphous semiconductors; ultrasonics; thin film technology; magnetic devices; semiconductor manufacturing technology. *Mailing Add:* Nat Micronetics Inc Semi-Films Rte 28 Box 188 West Hurley NY 12491

YASBIN, RONALD ELIOTT, b Brooklyn, NY, Apr 27, 47; m 72; c 2. INDUSTRIAL MICROBIOLOGY, PATHOGENIC MECHANISMS. *Educ:* Pa State Univ, BS, 68; Cornell Univ, MS, 70; Univ Rochester, PhD(microbiol), 74. *Prof Exp:* Asst prof microbiol & molecular genetics, Pa State Univ, 76-81; ASST PROF MICROBIOL, SCH MED, UNIV ROCHESTER, 81- *Concurrent Pos:* Vis scientist, Brookhaven Nat Lab, 79-82. *Mem:* Am Soc Microbiol; Environ Mutagen Soc; Genetics Soc; Sigma Xi. *Res:* The role of DNA repair systems in the production of mutations and carcinogenesis events; use of recombinant DNA technology to explore pathogenesis and secondary metabolites. *Mailing Add:* Box 672 Dept Microbiol Sch Med Univ Rochester Rochester NY 14642

YASHON, DAVID, b Chicago, Ill, May 13, 35; c 3. NEUROSURGERY. *Educ:* Univ Ill, BSM, 58, MD, 60; FRCS(C), 69. *Prof Exp:* Instr neurosurg, Univ Chicago, 65-66; asst prof, Case Western Reserve Univ, 66-69; assoc prof, 69-74, PROF NEUROSURG, OHIO STATE UNIV, 74- *Mem:* Cong Neurol Surg; Am Asn Neurol Surg; Soc Univ Surg; Am Acad Neurol; Asn Acad Surg. *Res:* Cerebral physiology and metabolism during circulatory deficiency; spinal cord injury and metabolic effects. *Mailing Add:* Dept Neurosurg Ohio State Univ Columbus OH 43210

YASKO, RICHARD N, b Conemaugh, Pa, Aug 29, 35; m 64. NUCLEAR PHYSICS. *Educ:* Pa State Univ, BS, 57, MS, 61, PhD(physics), 63. *Prof Exp:* Fel nuclear physics, Argonne Nat Lab, 63-64; asst prof physics, Villanova Univ, 64-67; adv physicist, IBM Corp, Endicott, 68-77; PROD ASSURANCE MGR, AVCO SYST DIV, AVCO CORP, 78- *Mem:* Am Phys Soc; Inst Elec & Electronics Eng; Am Vacuum Soc. *Res:* Surface physics; semiconductor device physics; ion implantation, spreading resistance diffusion profiling and capacitance; voltage testing of MO5 devices. *Mailing Add:* PO Box 53 Ipswich MA 01938

YASMINEH, WALID GABRIEL, b Amman, Jordan, Jan 21, 31; US citizen; m 60; c 3. BIOCHEMISTRY. *Educ:* Am Univ Cairo, BSc, 53; Univ Minn, Minneapolis, MSc, 63, PhD(biochem), 66. *Prof Exp:* From jr scientist to assoc scientist pediat, 59-65, asst prof lab med, 67-72, ASSOC PROF LAB MED, SCH MED, UNIV MINN, MINNEAPOLIS, 72- *Concurrent Pos:* Grad Sch grant, Sch Med, Univ Minn, Minneapolis, 68- *Mem:* Am Chem Soc. *Res:* Mammalian constitutive heterochromatin and repetitive DNA, nature, origin, function and relation to disease. *Mailing Add:* 2057 Woodbridge St Paul MN 55113

YASPAN, ARTHUR, b Youngstown, Ohio, Feb 2, 18; m 44; c 1. MATHEMATICS, OPERATIONS RESEARCH. *Educ:* Univ Chicago, MS, 38; Case Inst Technol, PhD(opers res), 61. *Prof Exp:* Res asst physics, Sonar Anal Sect, Div War Res, Columbia Univ, 44-47; instr math, Western Reserve Univ, 52-54; res asst opers res, Case Inst Technol, 56-58; asst prof math, Polytech Inst Brooklyn, 63-67, assoc prof, 67-72; assoc prof math, York Col, City Univ New York, 74-76. *Res:* Applied probability, with special reference to gambling theory. *Mailing Add:* 83-19 141st St Kew Gardens NY 11415

YASSO, WARREN E, b New York, NY, Oct 19, 30; m 57; c 2. GEOLOGY, GEOMORPHOLOGY. *Educ:* Brooklyn Col, BS, 57; Columbia Univ, MA, 61, PhD(geomorphol), 64. *Prof Exp:* Instr earth sci, Adelphi Univ, 61-64; asst prof geol, Va Polytech Inst, 64-66; ASSOC PROF SCI EDUC, TEACHERS COL, COLUMBIA UNIV, 66- *Concurrent Pos:* Prog dir educ, Nat Sea Grant Prog, Nat Oceanic & Atmospheric Admin, 78-79. *Mem:* AAAS; Geol Soc Am; Int Asn Sedimentol; Nat Asn Geol Teachers; Nat Sci Teachers Asn. *Res:* Coastal and continental shelf geological processes; curriculum research in earth sciences. *Mailing Add:* 528 Franklin Turnpike Ridgewood NJ 07450

YASUDA, HIROTSUGU, b Kyoto, Japan, Mar 24, 30; m 68; c 3. POLYMER CHEMISTRY, PHYSICAL CHEMISTRY. *Educ:* Kyoto Univ, BS, 53; State Univ NY Col Environ Sci & Forestry, MS, 59, PhD(polymer & phys chem), 61. *Prof Exp:* Fel, State Univ NY Col Environ Sci & Forestry, Syracuse, 61; chemist, Camille Dreyfus Lab, Res Triangle Inst, 61-63; res assoc, Ophthalmic Plastic Lab, Mass Eye & Ear Infirmary, 63-64 & Cedars-Sinai Med Ctr, 64-65; guest scientist, Royal Inst Technol, Sweden, 65-66; head membrane & med polymer sect, Camille Dreyfus Lab, Res Triangle Inst, 66-75, mgr polymer dept, 75-77; PROF CHEM ENG, UNIV MO-ROLLA, 78-, SR INVESTR MAT RES CTR, 78- *Mem:* Am Chem Soc; AAAS. *Res:* Preparation and characterization of polymers; transport phenomena through polymer membrane; biomedical application of polymers, membrane technology, plasma polymerization and surface modifications. *Mailing Add:* Dept of Chem Eng Univ of Mo Rolla MO 65401

YASUDA, STANLEY K, b Pahoa, Hawaii, Jan 7, 31; m 55; c 3. ANALYTICAL CHEMISTRY. *Educ:* Park Col, BA, 53; Kans State Univ, MS, 55, PhD(anal chem), 57. *Prof Exp:* MEM STAFF, LOS ALAMOS NAT LAB, 57- *Concurrent Pos:* Sr analyst, Chemagro Corp, 64. *Mem:* Fel Am Inst Chemists; Am Chem Soc. *Res:* Microanalytical methods for analysis of explosive and non-explosive materials, utilizing wet and instrumental techniques. *Mailing Add:* 75 San Juan Los Alamos NM 87544

YASUI, GEORGE, b Olympia, Wash, May 7, 22; m 50; c 4. CHEMICAL ENGINEERING. *Educ:* Univ Denver, BS, 44; Univ Mich, MS, 48; Univ Wash, PhD(chem eng), 57. *Prof Exp:* Chem engr, Varnish Lab, Sherwin-Williams Co, 44-45 & Chem Eng Div, Argonne Nat Lab, 48-54; res scientist, Lockheed Missiles & Space Co, 56-60, staff scientist, 60-62, mgr res & develop staff, 62-63, asst mgr nuclear eng, 63-64, sr staff engr, 64-71; proj engr, Environ Qual Eng, Inc, 71-72; STAFF ENGR, LOCKHEED MISSILES & SPACE CO, 72- *Mem:* Am Inst Chem Engrs. *Res:* Development of nosetips and heat shields for reentry vehicles; analyses and testing of materials exposed to nuclear weapons effects. *Mailing Add:* 3491 Janice Way Palo Alto CA 94303

YASUKAWA, KEN, b New York, NY, Sept 7, 49; m 72; c 1. ECOLOGY, ANIMAL BEHAVIOR. *Educ:* State Univ NY, Stony Brook, BS, 71; Ind Univ, MS, 75, PhD(zool), 77. *Prof Exp:* Fel animal behav, Field Res Ctr, Rockefeller Univ, 77-80; ASST PROF BIOL, DEPT BIOL, BELOIT COL, 80- *Mem:* Soc Am Naturalists; Animal Behav Soc; Ecol Soc Am; Am Ornithologists Union; Sigma Xi. *Res:* Avian behavioral ecology; evolution of mating systems; function and causation of aggression; territoriality; population regulation; dominance hierarchies; communication behavior; function and development of avian vocal behavior. *Mailing Add:* Dept Biol Beloit Col Beloit WI 53511

YASUMURA, SEIICHI, b New York, NY, Sept 28, 32; m 63; c 2. ENDOCRINOLOGY. *Educ:* Occidental Col, AB, 58; Univ Cincinnati, PhD(anat), 62. *Prof Exp:* Instr, 64-66, asst prof, 66-77, ASSOC PROF PHYSIOL, STATE UNIV NY DOWNSTATE MED CTR, 77- *Concurrent Pos:* Fel, State Univ Groningen, 62-63; NSF fel, State Univ NY Downstate Med Ctr, 63-64; res collabr, Brookhaven Nat Lab, 75-; consult, Nat Inst Environ Health Sci, 80-82. *Mem:* Endocrine Soc; Am Physiol Soc. *Mailing Add:* Dept of Physiol State Univ NY Downstate Med Ctr New York NY 11203

YASUNOBU, KERRY T, b Seattle, Wash, Nov 21, 25; m 52; c 1. BIOCHEMISTRY. *Educ:* Univ Wash, PhD(biochem), 54. *Prof Exp:* Res scientist, Univ Tex, 54-55; res assoc, Med Sch, Univ Ore, 55-58; asst prof chem, 58-62, assoc prof biochem, 62-64, PROF BIOCHEM, UNIV HAWAII, MANOA, 64- *Concurrent Pos:* NSF sr fel, 63-64; NIH sr fel, 71-72. *Mem:* Am Chem Soc; Am Soc Biol Chemists. *Res:* Enzymology, especially oxidative, heme-enzymes and proteolytic enzymes. *Mailing Add:* Dept Biochem-Biophys Univ of Hawaii at Manoa Honolulu HI 96822

YATES, ALBERT CARL, b Memphis, Tenn, Sept 29, 41; m 62; c 2. THEORETICAL PHYSICAL CHEMISTRY. *Educ:* Memphis State Univ, BS, 65; Ind Univ, Bloomington, PhD(chem physics), 68. *Prof Exp:* Res assoc chem, Univ Southern Calif, 68-69; from asst prof to assoc prof, Ind Univ, Bloomington, 69-74; assoc prof chem & assoc univ dean for grad educ & res, 74-76, PROF CHEM & UNIV DEAN FOR GRAD EDUC & RES, UNIV CINCINNATI, 76- *Mem:* Am Phys Soc; Am Chem Soc. *Res:* Collisions of charged particles with atomic and molecular systems; heavy-particle collisions; photo-absorption processes. *Mailing Add:* Dept of Chem Univ of Cincinnati Cincinnati OH 45221

YATES, ALFRED RANDOLPH, b Guelph, Ont, July 3, 28; m 52; c 4. FOOD MICROBIOLOGY. *Educ:* Univ Toronto, BSA, 50, MSA, 54; Univ Nottingham, PhD(microbiol), 65. *Prof Exp:* Control chemist, Cow & Gate, Ltd, 55-57; res officer food microbiol, Microbiol Div, Can Dept Agr, 57-59; teacher high schs, Ont, 59-61; res officer food microbiol, Plant Res Inst, 61-62, RES SCIENTIST, FOOD RES INST, CAN DEPT AGR, 62- *Concurrent Pos:* Food microbiol expert, Food & Agr Orgn UN, Food Technol Ctr, Malaysia, 72-73. *Mem:* Am Soc Microbiol; Can Inst Food Sci & Technol. *Res:* Dairy microbiology; physiology and ecology of bacteria and moulds. *Mailing Add:* Food Res Inst Res Br Can Dept Agr Cent Exp Farm Ottawa ON K1A 0C6 Can

YATES, ALLAN JAMES, b Calgary, Alta, May 23, 43; m 68; c 1. NEUROPATHOLOGY, NEUROCHEMISTRY. *Educ:* Univ Alta, MD, 67; Univ Toronto, PhD(neurochem), 72; FRCP(C). *Prof Exp:* Asst prof, 75-79, ASSOC PROF NEUROPATH, OHIO STATE UNIV, 79- *Mem:* Am Asn Neuropath; Am Soc Neurochem; Am Soc Path; Int Soc Neurochem; Int Soc Neuropath. *Res:* Physiological and biochemical aspects of glycolipids and their roles in diseases of the nervous system, with special reference to nerve degeneration, regeneration and gliomas. *Mailing Add:* 105 Upham Hall Ohio State Univ Columbus OH 43210

YATES, ANN MARIE, b Ogdensburg, NY, Sept 29, 40. ANALYTICAL CHEMISTRY. *Educ:* St Lawrence Univ, BS, 62; Ariz State Univ, PhD(chem), 66. *Prof Exp:* Asst prof anal chem, Ariz State Univ, 66-67; NIH res assoc inorg chem, Univ Pittsburgh, 67-68; dir labs, Chemalytics Inc, 68-74; mem chem fac, Maricopa County Community Col Dist, 76-77; MEM CHEM FAC, ARIZ STATE UNIV, 77- *Mem:* AAAS; Am Chem Soc; Sigma Xi. *Res:* Microanalytical techniques; x-ray fluorescence. *Mailing Add:* 1627 E Wesleyan Dr Tempe AZ 85282

YATES, CHARLIE LEE, b Harrellsville, NC, Apr 8, 36; m 58; c 3. FLUID MECHANICS, AEROCHEMISTRY. *Educ:* Va Polytech Inst & State Univ, BS, 58; Calif Inst Technol, MS, 59; Johns Hopkins Univ, PhD, 78. *Prof Exp:* Assoc engr, Westinghouse Elec Corp, 59-60; assoc engr, Appl Physics Lab, Johns Hopkins Univ, 60-64, sr engr, 64-79; ASSOC PROF, MECH ENG DEPT, VA POLYTECH INST & STATE UNIV, 79- *Mem:* Am Inst Aeronaut & Astronaut. *Res:* Surface gravity wave physics; wave-wave interactions. *Mailing Add:* Mech Eng Dept Va Polytech Inst & State Univ Blacksburg VA 24061

YATES, CLAIRE HILLIARD, b Cornwall, Ont, Mar 27, 20; m 42; c 3. ANALYTICAL CHEMISTRY, PHARMACEUTICAL CHEMISTRY. *Educ:* Sir George Williams Col, BSc, 46; McGill Univ, PhD(biochem), 51. *Prof Exp:* Prod chemist, Charles E Frosst & Co, Montreal, 41-47, res chemist, 48-69, ANAL UNIT HEAD, PHARMACEUT RES DEPT, MERCK FROSST CAN, 69-, RES FEL, 80- *Concurrent Pos:* Lectr, Sir George Williams Col, 48-61. *Mem:* Chem Inst Can. *Res:* Steroids; synthesis of radioactive organic substances; analyses of drug formulations; stability of drugs in dosage forms. *Mailing Add:* 994 Second Ave Verdun PQ H4G 2W8 Can

YATES, DAVID J C, b Newcastle-under-Lyme, Staffordshire, Eng, Feb 13, 27. SURFACE CHEMISTRY, CATALYSIS. *Educ:* Univ Birmingham, BSC, 49; Univ Cambridge, PhD(chem), 55, ScD, 68. *Prof Exp:* Res physicist, Kodak Labs, Middlesex, UK, 49-50; sci off, British Ceramic Res Asn, Staffordshire, UK, 50-51; res student & fel, Dept Colloid Sci, St Catherine's Col, Univ Cambridge, 51-58; res assoc metall & lectr, Sch Mines, Columbia Univ, 58-60; sr res fel, Nat Phys Lab, Teddington, Middlesex, UK, 60-61; RES ASSOC, CORP RES LAB, EXXON RES & ENG, LINDEN, NJ, 61- *Mem:* Fel Royal Inst Chem; fel Inst Physics UK. *Res:* Solid-gas interface; physical absorption by length charge techniques and infrared spectroscopy; Chemasorption on oxides and supported metals by infrared radiation electronic and scanning radar, and nuclear magnetic resonance. *Mailing Add:* Exxon Res & Eng PO Box 45 Linden NJ 07036

YATES, EDWARD CARSON, JR, b Raleigh, NC, Nov 3, 26; m 52; c 1. AEROSPACE ENGINEERING, ENGINEERING MECHANICS. *Educ:* NC State Univ, BS, 48, MS, 49; Univ Va, MS, 53; Va Polytech Inst & State Univ, PhD(eng mech), 59. *Prof Exp:* AEROSPACE ENGR, LANGLEY RES CTR, NASA, 49-; ASSOC PROF, GEORGE WASHINGTON UNIV, 68- *Concurrent Pos:* Lectr physics, Va Polytech Inst & State Univ, 59-67; adj assoc prof, NC State Univ, 64-75; assoc ed, J Aircraft, 72-78. *Honors & Awards:* Citation, Fed Aviation Admin, 64; Performance Award, NASA, 64 & Achievement Award, 67 & 69. *Mem:* Assoc fel Am Inst Aeronaut & Astronaut. *Res:* Subsonic, transonic and supersonic aerodynamics; unsteady aerodynamics; aeroelasticity; structural dynamics. *Mailing Add:* NASA Langley Res Ctr Hampton VA 23665

YATES, FRANCIS EUGENE, b Pasadena, Calif, Feb 26, 27; m 49; c 5. PHYSIOLOGY. *Educ:* Stanford Univ, BA, 47, MD, 51. *Prof Exp:* Intern, Philadelphia Gen Hosp, 50-51; instr physiol, Harvard Med Sch, 55-57, assoc, 57-59, asst prof, 59-60; from assoc prof to prof, Stanford Univ, 60-69, actg exec head dept physiol, 64-69; PROF BIOMED ENG, DEPT BIOMED ENG, UNIV SOUTHERN CALIF, 69-, DIR BIOMED ENG CTR, 77-; PROF CHEM ENG, MED & PHYSIOL, RALPH & MARJORIE CRUMP PROF MED ENG & DIR, CRUMP INST MED ENG, UNIV CALIF, LOS ANGELES, 80- *Concurrent Pos:* Res fel physiol, Harvard Univ, 53-55; Markle scholar med sci, Harvard Med Sch, 59; mem, physiol training comt, Nat Inst Gen Med Sci, 64-70, mem med scientist training prog comt, 71-73; vis prof, Stanford Univ, 69-; sect ed endocrinol & metab, Am J Physiol, 69-74; managing ed, Annals Biomed Eng, 71-74; consult prin scientist, Alza Corp; mem sci info prog adv comt, Nat Inst Neurol & Communicative Dis & Stroke, 76-; managing ed, Am J Physiol, Regulatory Integrative & Comp Physiol, 76-; mem, Space Biol Panel, NASA, 79-80; mem, Panel Basic Biomed Sci, Human Resources Comn, Nat Res Coun, 79-; mem adv bd biol, Harvey Mudd Col, 79- *Honors & Awards:* Upjohn Award, Endocrine Soc, 62. *Mem:* AAAS; Biomed Eng Soc (pres, 74-75); Am Physiol Soc; Endocrine Soc; NY Acad Sci. *Res:* Metabolism and inactivation of adrenal cortical hormones; analysis of endocrine feedback systems. *Mailing Add:* Crump Inst Med Eng Boelter Hall 6417 Univ Calif Los Angeles CA 90024

YATES, GEORGE KENNETH, b Chicago, Ill, Sept 24, 25; div; c 4. SPACE PHYSICS. *Educ:* Harvard Univ, AB, 50; Univ Chicago, MS, 55, PhD(physics), 64; Suffolk Univ, JD, 80. *Prof Exp:* RES PHYSICIST, AIR FORCE GEOPHYSICS LAB, 64- *Mem:* Am Phys Soc; Am Geophys Union. *Res:* Physics of the near space environment, especially particle radiation. *Mailing Add:* AFGL-PHG L G Hanscom AFB Bedford MA 01731

YATES, HAROLD W(ILLIAM), b Hagerstown, Md, Oct 17, 23; m 47; c 3. CHEMICAL ENGINEERING. *Educ:* Johns Hopkins Univ, BE, 44, MA, 50. *Prof Exp:* Jr instr physics, Johns Hopkins Univ, 44-47, asst optics, 47-50; physicist, Optics Div, US Naval Res Lab, 50-57; chief engr, Field Eng Dept, Barnes Eng Co, 57-67; DIR, OFF RES, NAT ENVIRON SATELLITE SERV, NAT OCEANIC & ATMOS ADMIN, 67- *Mem:* Optical Soc Am. *Res:* Optical properties of atmosphere; infrared transmission; refraction; scintillation military applications of infrared; target and background measurements; detection systems; tracking; optical instrument design for field research; photography; radiometry; spectroscopy. *Mailing Add:* Nat Environ Satellite Serv Nat Oceanic & Atmos Admin Washington DC 20233

YATES, HARRIS OLIVER, b Paducah, Ky, Apr 14, 34; m 54; c 3. BIOLOGY. *Educ:* David Lipscomb Col, BA, 56; George Peabody Col, MA, 57; Vanderbilt Univ, PhD(biol), 65. *Prof Exp:* Instr, 57-59, from asst prof to assoc prof, 63-68, PROF BIOL & CHMN DEPT, DAVID LIPSCOMB COL, 68- *Res:* Experimental plant taxonomy. *Mailing Add:* Dept of Biol David Lipscomb Col Nashville TN 37203

YATES, HARRY ORBELL, III, b Camden, NJ, May 15, 31; m 58; c 3. FOREST ENTOMOLOGY. *Educ:* Univ Maine, BS, 54; Duke Univ, MF, 58; Ohio State Univ, PhD(entom), 64. *Prof Exp:* Entomologist, US Forest Serv, Ga, 58-60, Ohio, 60-63, ENTOMOLOGIST, US FOREST SERV, GA, 63- *Mem:* Entom Soc Am. *Res:* Terminal feeding moths of the genus Rhyacionia; influence of pine oleoresin on insect attack; seed and cone insects. *Mailing Add:* Forestry Sci Lab Carlton St Athens GA 30602

YATES, JAMES T, b Forney, Tex, June 8, 40; m 61; c 2. GERIATRICS, DIAGNOSTIC AUDIOLOGY. *Educ:* Tex Tech Univ, BA(psychol) & BA(audiol), 65, MA, 66; Univ Denver, PhD(audiol), 70. *Prof Exp:* Teaching asst commun, Tex Tech Univ, 65-66; lab instr anat, Univ Denver, 66-69; dir audiol, Tex Tech Univ, 70-78; PROF & CHMN AUDIOL, SCH MED, UNIV HAWAII, 78- *Concurrent Pos:* Consult, various govt orgn & co, 70-78; prin investr grants & contracts, 70-; consult audiologist, Lubbock State Sch Ment Retardation, 72-75, WTex Rehab Ctr, 75-78. *Mem:* Fel Am Speech & Hearing Asn; Acoust Soc Am; Acad Rehab Audiol; Oceanog Soc. *Res:* Geriatric audiology; central auditory processing: development, deteriation and diagnosis of disorders of processing in children and adults. *Mailing Add:* 518 Pepeekeo Pl Honolulu HI 96825

YATES, JEROME DOUGLAS, b Center Point, Ark, Jan 5, 35; m 69; c 3. POULTRY NUTRITION. *Educ:* Univ Ark, BSA, 58, MS, 59; Mich State Univ, PhD(poultry nutrit), 64. *Prof Exp:* Nutrit technician, Mich State Univ, 59-63; res assoc nutrit & food sci, 64-68, RES SCIENTIST, CAMPBELL SOUP CO, 69- *Mem:* Poultry Sci Asn; World Poultry Sci Asn. *Res:* Poultry nutrition emphasizing the influence of nutrients and other dietary components on quality of poultry meat; mineral and amino acid nutrition. *Mailing Add:* Campbell Inst for Agr Res Fayetteville AR 72701

YATES, JOHN THOMAS, JR, b Winchester, Va, Aug 3, 35; m 58; c 2. PHYSICAL CHEMISTRY, SURFACE CHEMISTRY. *Educ:* Juniata Col, BS, 56; Mass Inst Technol, PhD, 60. *Prof Exp:* Res assoc chem, Mass Inst Technol, 60; instr & asst prof, Antioch Col, 60-63; Nat Res Coun-Nat Bur Standards res assoc, 63-65; staff mem, Phys Chem Div, Nat Bur Standards, 65-74, chief, Surface Processes & Catalysis Sect, 74-78; R K MELLON PROF CHEM, UNIV PITTSBURGH, 81-, DIR, PITTSBURGH SURFACE SCI CTR, 81- *Concurrent Pos:* Consult, Westgate Labs, Ohio, 63 & UOP, Inc, 81; vis examr, Swarthmore Col, 66; sr vis fel, Univ EAnglia, 70-71 & 72; trustee, Am Vacuum Soc, 74; mem bd dirs, Catalysis Soc, 76-81; Sherman Fairchild scholar, Calif Inst Technol, 77-78; chmn, Div Colloid & Surface Chem, Am Chem Soc, 80. *Honors & Awards:* Silver Medal, Dept of Com, 73; Samuel Wesley Stratton Award, Nat Bur Standards, 78. *Mem:* Am Chem Soc; Am Phys Soc; Am Vacuum Soc. *Res:* Spectra of adsorbed molecules; metal carbonyls; heterogeneous catalysis; kinetics of adsorption and desorption; electron impact studies of adsorbed species; electronic properties of the chemisorbed layer. *Mailing Add:* Surface Sci Div Nat Bur of Standards Washington DC 20234

YATES, KEITH, b Preston, Eng, Oct, 22, 28; Can citizen; m 53; c 3. PHYSICAL ORGANIC CHEMISTRY. *Educ:* Univ BC, BA, 56, MSc, 57, PhD(org chem), 59; Oxford Univ, DPhil(phys chem), 61. *Prof Exp:* From asst prof to assoc prof chem, 61-67, asst dean, Sch Grad Studies, 67-70, PROF CHEM, UNIV TORONTO, 68-, CHMN DEPT, 74- *Res:* Physical and theoretical organic chemistry; acidity functions and reaction mechanisms. *Mailing Add:* Dept of Chem Univ of Toronto Toronto ON M5S 1A1 Can

YATES, LELAND MARSHALL, b Stevensville, Mont, Feb 11, 15; m; c 4. PHYSICAL CHEMISTRY. *Educ:* Mont State Univ, BA, 38, MA, 40; Wash State Univ, PhD(chem), 55. *Prof Exp:* Instr chem & physics, Custer County Jr Col, 40-42 & 45-47; instr chem, Univ Mont, 47-49; asst, Wash State Univ, 49-51; from instr to assoc prof, 51-71, prof chem, 71-78, EMER PROF CHEM, UNIV MONT, 78- *Mem:* Am Chem Soc. *Res:* Equilibrium constants and thermodynamics of complex ions; analysis for small concentration of ions. *Mailing Add:* 610 Hastings Ave Univ of Mont Missoula MT 58901

YATES, PETER, b Wanstead, Eng, Aug 26, 24; m 50; c 3. ORGANIC CHEMISTRY. *Educ:* Univ London, BSc, 46; Dalhousie Univ, MSc, 48; Yale Univ, PhD(chem), 51. *Prof Exp:* Instr chem, Yale Univ, 51-52; from instr to asst prof, Harvard Univ, 52-60; PROF CHEM, UNIV TORONTO, 60- *Concurrent Pos:* Sloan Found fel, 57-60; vis prof, Yale Univ, 66; vis prof, Princeton Univ, 77; consult, Ciba-Geigy Pharmaceut Div. *Honors & Awards:* Centennial Medal, Govt Can, 67; Merck Sharp & Dohme lectr, Chem Inst Can, 63. *Mem:* Am Chem Soc; Royal Soc Chem; Chem Inst Can; Royal Soc Can. *Res:* Structural, synthetic and mechanistic organic chemistry, including natural and photochemical products, aliphatic diazo and heterocyclic compounds. *Mailing Add:* Dept of Chem Univ of Toronto Toronto ON M5S 1A1 Can

YATES, RICHARD ALAN, b Oakland, Calif, July 14, 30; m 58; c 1. BIOCHEMISTRY, MICROBIOLOGY. *Educ:* Univ Calif, Berkeley, BA, 52, PhD(biochem), 56. *Prof Exp:* RES BIOCHEMIST, CENT RES & DEVELOP DEPT, E I DU PONT DE NEMOURS & CO, INC, 56- *Mem:* Am Soc Microbiol; Inst Food Technologists; AAAS; NY Acad Sci. *Res:* Biochemical control mechanisms; microbial genetic alterations; production of feedstock chemicals from renewable sources; single cell protein production and adaptation for human foods. *Mailing Add:* Cent Res & Develop Dept Exp Sta Wilmington DE 19898

YATES, RICHARD LEE, b Red Oak, Iowa, June 15, 31; m 61; c 2. MATHEMATICS. *Educ:* Fla Southern Col, BS, 52; Univ Fla, MS, 54, PhD(math), 57. *Prof Exp:* Asst math, Univ Fla, 52-56; asst prof, Univ Houston, 57-60; from asst prof to assoc prof, Kans State Univ, 60-67; assoc prof & chmn math sect, 67-70, prof & acad dean, 70-75, exec asst to chancellor, 75-80, PROF, PURDUE UNIV, 80- *Mem:* Math Asn Am. *Res:* Classical number theory; modern algebra; lattice theory. *Mailing Add:* Purdue Univ Calumet Campus Hammond IN 46323

YATES, ROBERT DOYLE, b Birmingham, Ala, Feb 28, 31; m 55; c 2. CYTOLOGY. *Educ:* Univ Ala, BS, 54, MS, 56, PhD(anat), 60. *Prof Exp:* Instr gross anat & neuroanat, Univ Tex Med Br, Galveston, 61-64, from asst prof to prof microanat, 64-70; PROF ANAT & CHMN DEPT, SCH MED, TULANE UNIV, LA, 72- *Concurrent Pos:* Fel, Med Ctr, Univ Ala, 61-62; NIH career res develop award, 64. *Mem:* AAAS; Am Soc Cell Biol; Am Asn Anat; Am Soc Neuropath; Fedn Am Soc Exp Biol. *Res:* Electron microscopic studies of reversible alterations in the organelles and inclusions of cells subjected to experimentally induced stresses. *Mailing Add:* Dept Anat Sch Med Tulane Univ New Orleans LA 70112

YATES, ROBERT EDMUNDS, b Bisbee, Ariz, Aug 15, 26; m 47; c 4. PHYSICAL CHEMISTRY. *Educ:* Univ Ariz, BS, 48, MS 49; Mich State Univ, PhD(phys chem), 52. *Prof Exp:* Asst chem, Mich State Univ, 49-51; res engr, Dow Chem Co, 52-58; res chemist, Aerojet-Gen Corp, 58-61 & Rocket Power, Inc, 61-65; res chemist, Aerojet-Gen Corp, Calif, 66-67, chem specialist, 67-71; PHYSICIST, McCLELLAN AFB, SACRAMENTO, 71- *Mem:* Am Chem Soc. *Res:* Boron, fluorine and high temperature chemistry; thermodynamics and spectroscopy. *Mailing Add:* 7313 Pine Grove Way Folsom CA 95630

YATES, SHELLY GENE, b Altus, Okla, Feb 29, 32; m 54; c 4. CHEMISTRY, NATURAL PRODUCTS. *Educ:* Southwestern State Col, Okla, BS, 56; Okla State Univ, MS, 58. *Prof Exp:* ORG CHEMIST, NORTHERN REGIONAL RES CTR, AGR RES SERV, USDA, 58- *Mem:* Am Chem Soc. *Res:* Natural products; isolation, characterization and analysis. *Mailing Add:* 5619 N Plaza Dr Peoria IL 61614

YATES, STEVEN WINFIELD, b Memphis, Mo, Apr 19, 46; m 75. NUCLEAR CHEMISTRY, RADIOCHEMISTRY. *Educ:* Univ Mo-Columbia, BS, 68; Purdue Univ, Lafayette, PhD(chem), 73. *Prof Exp:* Res asst chem, Purdue Univ, Lafayette, 71-73; fel, Argonne Nat Lab, 73-75; asst prof chem, 75-79, ASSOC PROF CHEM, UNIV KY, 79- *Mem:* Am Chem Soc; Am Phys Soc. *Res:* Level structures of transitional and deformed nuclei; heavy-ion reactions; inelastic scattering and transfer reactions; nuclear isomerism and high-spin phenomena; neutron induced reactions; neutron scattering; nuclear spectroscopy. *Mailing Add:* Dept of Chem Univ of Ky Lexington KY 40506

YATES, VANCE JOSEPH, b Smithville, Ohio, Oct 25, 17; m 42; c 4. VETERINARY VIROLOGY. *Educ:* Ohio State Univ, BSc, 40, DVM, 49; Univ Wis, PhD, 60. *Prof Exp:* Instr high sch, Ohio, 40-41; asst prof animal path, 49-50, assoc prof & assoc res prof, 51-55, head dept, 51-79, PROF ANIMAL PATH & RES PROF, UNIV RI, 55- *Concurrent Pos:* Mem temp staff, Rockefeller Found, 63-64; vis prof dept exp biol, Baylor Col Med, 71-72. *Mem:* Am Vet Med Asn; Am Asn Avian Path. *Res:* Avian virology and pathology; oncogenicity of avian adenoviruses. *Mailing Add:* Dept Animal Path Univ RI Kingston RI 02881

YATES, WESLEY ROSS, physical chemistry, see previous edition

YATES, WILLARD F, JR, b Findlay, Ohio, June 20, 30; m 65; c 2. PLANT TAXONOMY, CYTOGENETICS. *Educ:* Eastern Ill Univ, BS, 58; Ind Univ, MA, 60, PhD(bot), 67. *Prof Exp:* Instr biol, Cumberland Col, 60-62; asst prof, Ball State Univ, 65-67; assoc prof, 67-78, PROF BOT, BUTLER UNIV, 78- *Mem:* AAAS; Bot Soc Am; Am Soc Plant Taxon; Torrey Bot Club; Am Inst Biol Sci. *Res:* Plant cytotaxonomy; phytochemistry; plant tissue culture. *Mailing Add:* Dept of Bot Butler Univ Indianapolis IN 46208

YATSU, EIJU, b Uchihara, Japan, July 10, 20; m 46; c 3. MINERALOGY, GEOLOGY. *Educ:* Tokyo Bunrika Univ, BSc, 45; Univ Tokyo, DSc, 57. *Prof Exp:* Asst prof earth sci, Chuo Univ, Tokyo, 54-57, prof eng geol, 58-66; vis prof geomorphology, Univ Ottawa, 66-67; assoc prof, 67-69, PROF GEOMORPHOLOGY, UNIV GUELPH, 69- *Concurrent Pos:* Vis assoc prof, La State Univ, 65-66. *Mem:* Am Geophys Union; Clay Minerals Soc; Geochem Soc. *Res:* Weathering of rocks and minerals; clay minerals; mechanical behaviors of unconsolidated rocks. *Mailing Add:* Dept of Geog Univ of Guelph Guelph ON N1G 2W1 Can

YATSU, FRANK MICHIO, b Los Angeles, Calif, Nov 28, 32; m 55; c 1. NEUROLOGY. *Educ:* Brown Univ, AB, 55; Case Western Reserve Univ, MD, 59. *Prof Exp:* From asst prof to assoc prof neurol, Univ Calif Med Ctr, San Francisco, 67-75, vchmn dept, 73-75; PROF NEUROL & CHMN DEPT, UNIV ORE HEALTH SCI CTR, 75- *Concurrent Pos:* Chief neurol serv, San Francisco Gen Hosp, 69-75; mem cardiovasc A res study comt, Am Heart Asn, 74-77; mem neurol disorders prog, Proj A Rev Comt, Nat Inst Neurol & Commun Disorders & Stroke, NIH, 75-79; mem adv coun, Epilepsy Ctr of Ore, 75- *Mem:* Am Acad Neurol; Am Neurol Asn; Am Soc Neurochem; Int Soc Neurochem. *Res:* Brain ischemia and atherosclerosis. *Mailing Add:* Dept of Neurol Univ of Ore Health Sci Ctr Portland OR 97201

YATSU, LAWRENCE Y, b Pasadena, Calif, Aug 2, 25; m 54; c 2. PLANT PHYSIOLOGY. *Educ:* Mich State Univ, BS, 49; Univ Calif, MS, 50; Cornell Univ, PhD, 60. *Prof Exp:* Chemist, Strong, Cobb & Co, 54-55; res assoc, Cornell Univ, 55-60; plant physiologist, Field Lab Tung Invest, USDA, 60-61, RES CHEMIST, SOUTHERN REGIONAL RES CTR, USDA, 61- *Concurrent Pos:* Adj assoc prof biol, Tulane Univ, 73- *Mem:* AAAS; Am Chem Soc; Bot Soc Am; Am Soc Plant Physiol; Am Inst Biol Scientists. *Res:* Cell biology; biochemistry. *Mailing Add:* 7611 Dalewood Rd New Orleans LA 70126

YATVIN, MILTON B, b New Brunswick, NJ, Nov 12, 30; m 52; c 3. PHYSIOLOGY, RADIOBIOLOGY. *Educ:* Rutgers Univ, BS, 52, MS, 54, PhD(endocrinol, reproductive physiol), 62. *Prof Exp:* Instr dairy sci, Rutgers Univ, 55-56; lectr reproductive physiol, Univ PR, 57-59; from instr to assoc prof, 63-71, PROF RADIOBIOL, MED SCH, UNIV WIS-MADISON, 71-, PROF HUMAN ONCOL, 77- *Concurrent Pos:* NIH fel endocrinol, Rutgers Univ, 62-63. *Mem:* Biophys Soc; Radiation Res Soc; Soc Exp Biol & Med; Am Physiol Soc. *Res:* Cell damage and repair after exposure to ionizing radiation; nucleic acid-membrane relationships in cells. *Mailing Add:* Depts of Radiol & Path Med Sch Univ of Wis Madison WI 53706

YAU, CHIOU CHING, b Taiwan, Dec 31, 34; US citizen; m 66; c 2. FIBER & POLYMER SCIENCE. *Educ:* Nat Cheng Kung Univ, Taiwan, BS, 58; Ga Inst Technol, MS, 66; NC State Univ, PhD(fiber & polymer sci), 72. *Prof Exp:* Chem engr, Chinese Petrol Corp, 60-65; res chemist, Am Enka Corp, Akzona, Inc, 66-69; mem tech staff, Emery Indust Inc, 72-77; res scientist, Kimberly-Clark Corp, 77-79; sr res chemist, Kendall Co, 79-81; PROG CHEMIST, GILLETTE CO, 81- *Mem:* Am Chem Soc; Soc Plastics Engrs; Am Asn

Textile Chemists & Colorists. *Res:* Polymer synthesis; polymer characterization by thermal analysis; structure and property relationships of polymers; fiber chemistry; flame retardants for fibers and plastics; nonwovens, polymer emulsions, coatings, ink chemistry, writing instruments. *Mailing Add:* Gillette Co Gillette Park Boston MA 02106

YAU, KING-WAI, b China, Oct 27, 48; m 75; c 2. NEUROPHYSIOLOGY, VISION. *Educ:* Princeton Univ, AB, 71; Harvard Univ, PhD(neurobiol), 76. *Prof Exp:* Res fel neurobiol, Sch Med, Stanford Univ, 76-79, physiol, Univ Cambridge, Eng, 79-80; ASST PROF PHYSIOL & BIOPHYSICS, UNIV TEX MED BR, 80- *Concurrent Pos:* Vis fel, Trinity Col, Univ Cambridge, 80-81; Rank Prize Funds, Eng, 80. *Mem:* Biophys Soc; Soc Neurosci; Asn Res Vision & Ophthal. *Res:* Retinal physiology. *Mailing Add:* Dept Physiol & Biophysics Univ Tex Med Br Galveston TX 77550

YAU, LEOPOLDO D, b Surigao, Philippines, Aug 15, 40; US citizen; m 71; c 1. SEMICONDUCTOR TECHNOLOGY, LITHOGRAPHY. *Educ:* Univ San Carlos, BS, 62; Univ Minn, MS, 65; Univ Ill, PhD(elec eng), 69. *Prof Exp:* Asst prof elec eng, Univ Phillipines, 70-71, Univ Ill, 71-73; staff, Bell Telephone Labs, 73-78; SR STAFF, INTEL, 78- *Mem:* Inst Elec & Electronics Engrs. *Res:* Deep level impurities in silicon; short-channel device model of mos-transistors; applications of electron-beam lithography; measurements of process-induced distortion in silicon; dynamic random access memory technology. *Mailing Add:* 8300 SW Woody End Durham OR 97223

YAU, SHING-TUNG, b Kwuntung, China, Apr 4, 49. MATHEMATICS. *Educ:* Univ Calif, Berkeley, PhD(math), 71. *Prof Exp:* Fel, Inst Advan Study, Princeton Univ, 71-72; asst prof math, State Univ NY, Stony Brook, 72-73; vis asst prof, Stanford Univ, 73-74, assoc prof, 74-77, prof math, 77-80; PROF, INST ADVAN STUDY, PRINCETON, 80- *Honors & Awards:* Veblen Prize, Am Mat Soc, 81; Certy Prize, Nat Acad Sci, 81. *Mem:* Am Math Soc. *Res:* Differential geometry. *Mailing Add:* Dept of Math Inst Advan Study Princeton NJ 08540

YAU, STEPHEN SIK-SANG, b Wusei, Kiangsu, China, Aug 6, 35; m 64; c 2. COMPUTER SCIENCE, ELECTRICAL ENGINEERING. *Educ:* Nat Taiwan Univ, BS, 58; Univ Ill, Urbana, MS, 59, PhD(elec eng), 61. *Prof Exp:* From asst prof to prof elec eng, 61-70, chmn dept comput sci, 72-77, PROF ELEC ENG & COMPUT SCI, NORTHWESTERN UNIV, EVANSTON, 70-, CHMN DEPT, 77- *Concurrent Pos:* Consult, Battelle Columbus Lab, 76-77 & Syst Develop Corp, 77. *Honors & Awards:* Levy Medal, Franklin Inst, 63; Golden Plate Award, Am Acad Achievement, 64. *Mem:* AAAS; Am Soc Eng Educ; Inst Elec & Electronics Engrs; Asn Comput Mach; Soc Indust & Appl Math. *Res:* Reliability and maintainability of computing systems; software engineering; computer architecture; fault tolerant computing; pattern recognition. *Mailing Add:* Dept of Elec Eng & Comput Sci Northwestern Univ Evanston IL 60201

YAU, WALLACE WEN-CHUAN, b Shianghai, China, Feb 20, 37; US citizen; m 61; c 2. ANALYTICAL CHEMISTRY, POLYMER PHYSICS. *Educ:* Nat Taiwan Univ, BS, 59; Univ Mass, PhD(phys chem), 66. *Prof Exp:* RES CHEMIST ANAL CHEM, CENT RES & DEVELOP DEPT, E I DU PONT DE NEMOURS & CO, INC, 65- *Mem:* Am Chem Soc. *Res:* Studies of polymer structures and properties using chromatographic, optical and mechanical characterization techniques. *Mailing Add:* Cent Res & Develop Dept E I du Pont de Nemours & Co Wilmington DE 19898

YAU, WEN-FOO, b Shanghai, China, June 11, 35; US citizen; m 62. ENGINEERING MECHANICS, APPLIED MATHEMATICS. *Educ:* Nat Taiwan Univ, BS, 58; Univ Mass, MS, 61; Princeton Univ, PhD, 65. *Prof Exp:* Instr civil eng, Univ Mass, 61-63; res assoc eng mech, Univ Ky, 65-66, asst prof, 66-69; res engr, Eastern Lab, 69-72, staff engr, 72-78, res staff engr, 78-81, RES ASSOC, SAVANNAH RIVER LAB, E I DU PONT DE NEMOURS & CO, INC, 81- *Mem:* Am Soc Mech Engrs. *Res:* Operation and safety considerations of the Savannah River Plant for production of nuclear materials. *Mailing Add:* Savannah River Lab E I du Pont de Nemours & Co Inc Aiken SC 29801

YAVERBAUM, SIDNEY, b New York, NY, Jan 28, 23; m 67; c 2. MEDICAL MICROBIOLOGY, IMMUNOCHEMISTRY. *Educ:* Univ Pa, PhD(med microbiol), 52. *Prof Exp:* Asst, Univ Pa, 51-52, res assoc, 52-53; fel microbiol, Boyce Thompson Inst Plant Res, 54-55; res med bacteriologist, Bio-Detection Br, Phys Defense Div, US Dept Army, Ft Detrick, 55-70; sr res biologist, Corning Glass Works, 70-76; mem staff, Wampole Div, Carter Wallace Inc, 76-80; MEM STAFF, TECHNICON, 80- *Mem:* AAAS; Am Soc Microbiol; Am Chem Soc; Sigma Xi; NY Acad Sci. *Res:* Cytology of yeasts, fungi and bacteria; genetics and nutrition of bacteria; assay of fungicides; physiology of aerobic sporeforming bacteria; biochemical composition of microorganisms; radioactive antibodies; solid-phase radioimmunoassay; immobilized enzyme research; automated instrumentation for microbiology. *Mailing Add:* Technicon 25F Tarrytown NY 10591

YAVORSKY, JOHN MICHAEL, b Renovo, Pa, June 11, 19. WOOD TECHNOLOGY. *Educ:* State Univ NY, BS, 42, MS, 47, PhD(wood eng), 55. *Prof Exp:* Res assoc & assoc prof wood utilization, State Univ NY Col Forestry, Syracuse, 48-56; chief wood utilization sect, Forestry Div, Food & Agr Orgn, UN, Rome, Italy, 57-63, proj mgr forestry proj, Lima, Peru, 63-67, sr proj officer, UN Spec Fund, NY, 67; PROF FORESTRY, STATE UNIV NY COL ENVIRON SCI & FORESTRY, SYRACUSE, 67-, DEAN SCH CONTINUING EDUC, 73- *Mem:* Forest Prod Res Soc; Soc Am Foresters; Soc Wood Sci & Technol. *Res:* Planning and supervision of continuing education activities in forestry and forest products technology; world forestry aspects of forest industries development. *Mailing Add:* State Univ of NY Col of Environ Sci & Forestry Syracuse NY 13210

YAVORSKY, PAUL M(ICHAEL), b Donora, Pa, Jan 6, 25; m 50; c 3. CHEMICAL ENGINEERING, PHYSICAL CHEMISTRY. *Educ:* Univ Pittsburgh, BS, 47, MS, 49, PhD, 56. *Prof Exp:* Asst eng & nuclear physics, Univ Pittsburgh, 47-49; chemist, Res Div, Consol Coal Co, Pa, 56-60, group leader, 60-71; res supvr explor eng, US Bur Mines, 71-73; asst dir coal liquefaction, US Off Coal Res, 73-74; DIV MGR, US ENERGY RES & DEVELOP ADMIN, US DEPT ENERGY, 74- *Honors & Awards:* Bituminous Coal Res Awards, 57 & 64. *Mem:* Am Chem Soc; Am Inst Chem Engrs. *Res:* Coal energy conversion; engineering development of liquefaction and gasification. *Mailing Add:* Pittsburgh Energy Tech Ctr 4800 Forbes Ave Pittsburgh PA 15213

YAWS, CARL LLOYD, b Yoakum, Tex, Oct 1, 38; m 58; c 4. CHEMICAL ENGINEERING, CHEMISTRY. *Educ:* Tex A&I Col, BS, 60; Univ Houston, MS, 63, PhD(chem eng), 65. *Prof Exp:* Res chem engr, Baytown Labs, Esso Res & Eng Co, Tex, 63-65; process develop engr, Res & Develop Dept, Ethyl Corp, La, 65-68; sr engr & mem tech staff, Chem Mat Div, Tex Instruments, Inc, 68-77; ASSOC PROF CHEM ENG, LAMAR UNIV, 77- *Mem:* Am Inst Chem Engrs; Am Chem Soc. *Res:* Chemicals; petrochemicals; petroleum refining; pollution control; solvent extractions; distillation; chlorination; fluorination; hydrogenation; desulfurization; catalytic reactions; chemical vapor deposition; fluorocarbons; chlorocarbons; specialty hydrocarbons; lubricants; gasolines; ultra purity silicon; carbides; nitrides. *Mailing Add:* Dept of Chem Eng PO Box 10053 Lamar Univ Beaumont TX 77710

YAYANOS, A ARISTIDES, b Buffalo, NY, Jan 31, 40; m 66; c 1. BIOPHYSICS, DEEP-SEA BIOLOGY. *Educ:* Univ Buffalo, BA, 61; Pa State Univ, MS, 65, PhD(biophysics), 67. *Prof Exp:* Fel, 67-68, asst res physiologist, 68-78, ASSOC RES BIOPHYSICIST, SCRIPPS INST OCEANOG, UNIV CALIF, SAN DIEGO, 78- *Concurrent Pos:* NIH res career develop award, 70-75. *Mem:* Am Chem Soc; Math Asn Am; Am Soc Microbiol; Biophys Soc; AAAS. *Res:* Physiology of deep-sea invertebrates; deep-sea microbiology; physics and biology at high pressures; radiation biology. *Mailing Add:* A-002 3115 MBIR Scripps Inst Oceanog La Jolla CA 92037

YAZICIGIL, HASAN, b Konya, Turkey, Nov 24, 52; m 77; c 1. GROUND-WATER MODELLING, SURFACE-WATER FORCASTING. *Educ:* Middle East Tech Univ, BS, 74; Iowa State Univ, MS, 77; Purdue Univ, PhD(systs eng), 80. *Prof Exp:* Soil surv proj engr, Gen Directorate Hwy Dept, Turkey, 74-75; proj asst, Iowa State Univ, 75-77; instr, Purdue Univ Sch Civil Eng, 77-80; res assoc, 80-81, ASST PROF HYDROGEOL ENG GEOL, SOUTHERN ILL UNIV, CARBONDALE COAL RES CTR, 81- *Concurrent Pos:* Consult engr, Willow Creek Consults, 81-, Sargent Limestone Quarry, 76-77; res assoc, Coal Res Ctr, Southern Ill Univ, 80- *Mem:* Am Geophys Union; Oper Res Soc Am; Nat Water Well Asn; Int Asn Hydrogeologists; Chambers Turkish Geol Engrs. *Res:* Ground water and surface water modelling; environmental modelling; optimal operations of surface and underground reservoir systems using forecasts. *Mailing Add:* RR6 Breckenridge Cts 5A Carbondale IL 62901

YCAS, MARTYNAS, b Voronezh, Russia, Dec 10, 17; nat US; m 45; c 3. BIOLOGY, COMPUTER APPLICATIONS. *Educ:* Univ Wis, BA, 47; Calif Inst Technol, PhD(embryol), 50. *Prof Exp:* Instr, Univ Wash, 50-51; biologist pioneering res labs, Corps, US Dept Army, 51-56; asst prof microbiol, Sch Med, 56-65, PROF MICROBIOL, SCH MED, STATE UNIV NY UPSTATE MED CTR, 65- *Concurrent Pos:* Vis prof, Univ Vilnius, Lithuanian Soviet Socialist Repub, 79. *Res:* Biochemical evolution; theoretical biology; computer applications to protein structure. *Mailing Add:* 109 Croyden Rd Syracuse NY 13224

YEADON, DAVID ALLOU, b New Orleans, La, Nov 10, 20; m 49; c 2. CHEMISTRY. *Educ:* Loyola Univ, La, BS, 40; Univ Detroit, MS, 42. *Prof Exp:* Asst & lab instr, Univ Detroit, 40-42; chemist, Gelatin Prod Corp, Mich, 42-43; chemist, Esso Standard Oil Co, La, res chemist, Esso Labs, 43-50; res chemist, Southern Regional Res Lab, Naval Store Div, USDA, 50; res chemist, Alpine Corp, Miss, 50-53; res chemist, Oilseed Crops Lab, 53-65, RES CHEMIST, COTTON FINISHES LAB, SOUTHERN REGIONAL RES LAB, USDA, 65- *Honors & Awards:* Superior Serv Awards, USDA, 67 & 73. *Mem:* Am Chem Soc; Sigma Xi; Am Asn Textile Chemists & Colorists. *Res:* Synthetic rubber; hydrocarbons; polymers, resins and coatings; chemistry, synthesis and applications of fats and oils; modifications to improve utilization of cotton; fire retardant cotton textiles. *Mailing Add:* 1460 Pressburg St New Orleans LA 70122

YEAGER, CHARLES LEVANT, b Rose City, Mich, Sept 12, 07; m 34. NEUROLOGY, PSYCHIATRY. *Educ:* Emanuel Missionary Col, Andrew, BS, 29; Col Med Evangelists, MD, 34; Univ Minn, MS, 40, PhD(neurol, psychiat), 44. *Prof Exp:* Dir clin psychiat & electroencephalog lab, Vet Admin Hosp, Waco, Tex, 46-47; lectr, 47-48, asst prof, 48-53, from asst clin prof to clin prof, 53-66, PROF PSYCHIAT IN RESIDENCE, SCH MED, UNIV CALIF, SAN FRANCISCO, 66-, PSYCHIATRIST & DIR ELECTROENCEPHALOG LAB, 47- *Concurrent Pos:* Consult, Vet Admin Hosp, 47-, Surgeon Gen, US Air Force, 49-57, Mt Zion Hosp, 51- & Marin Gen Hosp, 56-; dir electroencephalog labs, Calif State Hosps, 53- *Mem:* Am Electroencephalog Lab; Soc Exp Biol & Med; Sci Res Soc Am; Am Psychiat Asn; AMA. *Res:* Electroencephalography; neurophysiology; behavior. *Mailing Add:* Dept of Psychiat Univ of Calif Sch of Med San Francisco CA 94122

YEAGER, ERNEST BILL, b Orange, NJ, Sept 26, 24. ELECTROCHEMISTRY. *Educ:* Montclair State Col, BA, 45; Western Reserve Univ, MS, 46, PhD(phys chem), 48. *Prof Exp:* Asst physics & phys chem, 45-47, from instr to assoc prof chem, 48-58, actg chmn dept, 64-65, chmn dept, 69-72, chmn fac senate, 72-73, PROF CHEM, CASE WESTERN RESERVE UNIV, 58-, DIR CASE LABS ELECTROCHEM STUDIES, 76- *Concurrent Pos:* Consult, Union Carbide Corp, 55- & Gen Motors Corp, 70; vis prof & NATO fel, Univ Southampton, 68; mem comt undersea warfare,

Nat Acad Sci-Nat Res Coun, 63-73; rep mem phys sci div, Nat Res Coun, 69-73; mem comn electrochem, Int Union Pure & Appl Chem, 69-75; mem underwater sound adv group, Off Naval Res, 72-74. *Honors & Awards:* Acoust Soc Am Award, 56; Cert of Commendation, US Navy, 73. *Mem:* Fel AAAS; fel Acoust Soc Am (vpres, 67-68); Am Chem Soc; Int Soc Electrochem (vpres, 67-68, pres, 70-71); Electrochem Soc (vpres, 62-64, pres, 64-65). *Res:* Ultrasonics; electrode kinetics; electrolytes; relaxation spectroscopy. *Mailing Add:* Dept of Chem Case Western Reserve Univ Cleveland OH 44106

YEAGER, HOWARD LANE, b Pittsburgh, Pa, Dec 24, 43. MEMBRANE SCIENCE, ION EXCHANGE. *Educ:* Univ Pittsburgh, BS, 65; Univ Wis-Madison, MS, 67; Univ Alta, PhD(chem), 69. *Prof Exp:* Lectr anal chem, Univ Wis, 69-70; asst prof, 70-76, ASSOC PROF CHEM, UNIV CALGARY, 76- *Concurrent Pos:* Vis scientist, Nat Res Coun Can, 78-79. *Mem:* Am Chem Soc; Electrochem Soc; Chem Inst Can. *Res:* Transport in ion exchange membranes, ion exchange thermodynamics and synthetic membrane technology. *Mailing Add:* Dept Chem Univ Calgary Calgary AB T2N 1N4 Can

YEAGER, JOHN CALVIN, b Mt Pleasant, Mich, Nov 6, 47; m 74; c 2. PHYSIOLOGY. *Educ:* Miami Univ, BA, 69; Ohio State Univ, PhD(physiol), 74. *Prof Exp:* Fel, Mich State Univ, 74-76; ASST PROF PHYSIOL, EAST CAROLINA UNIV SCH MED, 76- *Concurrent Pos:* Cardiovasc Peer Rev, Nat Inst Occup Safety & Health, Physiol & Ergonomics Br, 77-78; mem, Am Heart Asn. *Mem:* Sigma Xi; Am Physiol Soc; Soc Exp Biol & Med. *Res:* Effects of alterations in blood gases and plasma electrolytes on coronary vascular autoregulation, hypertension, ischemic heart disease and various cardiomyopathies. *Mailing Add:* Dept Physiol East Carolina Sch Med Greenville NC 27834

YEAGER, JOHN FREDERICK, b Orange, NJ, Jan 3, 27; m 57; c 4. CHEMISTRY. *Educ:* NJ State Teachers Col, Montclair, BA, 49; Western Reserve Univ, MS, 51, PhD(phys chem), 53. *Prof Exp:* Res chemist, Nat Carbon Co, 53-60, res group leader, Consumer Prod Div, 60-65, res tech mgr primary batteries, 65-67, tech mgr Leclanche cells, 67-72, dir battery develop lab, Battery Prod Div, 72-75, DIR TECHNOL, BATTERY PROD DIV, UNION CARBIDE CORP, 76- *Mem:* Int Soc Electrochem; Electrochem Soc. *Res:* Electrochemistry; plating; batteries; fuel cells. *Mailing Add:* Union Carbide Corp Btry Prod Div PO Box 6056 Cleveland OH 44101

YEAGER, PAUL RAY, b Sherman, Tex, Feb 7, 31; m 56; c 2. PHYSICS, INSTRUMENT ENGINEERING. *Educ:* Austin Col, BA, 52; George Washington Univ, MS, 70. *Prof Exp:* Engr instrumentation, Nat Adv Comt Aeronaut, 52-55, sr proj engr, 55-59; leader vacuum measurements group, 59-63, head vacuum measurements sect, 63-69, head environ measurements sect, 69-74, HEAD GEN RES INSTRUMENTATION BR, NASA, 74- *Mem:* Am Vacuum Soc. *Res:* Mass spectrometry; vacuum instrumentation; thermal measurements. *Mailing Add:* MS 234 Langley Res Ctr NASA Hampton VA 23665

YEAGER, SANDRA ANN, b Philadelphia, Pa, Jan 4, 39. ORGANIC CHEMISTRY, BIOCHEMISTRY. *Educ:* Thiel Col, AB, 60; Univ NH, MS, 63, PhD(org chem), 68. *Prof Exp:* Asst prof chem, Hudson Valley Community Col, NY, 62-64; res asst, Children's Cancer Res Found, Boston, Mass, 68-69; asst prof chem, Pa State Univ, Mont Alto, 69-73; asst prof org & biochem, Wilson Col, 73-74; ASSOC PROF ORG & BIOCHEM, MILLERSVILLE STATE COL, 74- *Concurrent Pos:* Res assoc, Southwest Res Inst, San Antonio, Tex, 81. *Mem:* Am Chem Soc; World Future Soc; Nutrit Today Soc; Sigma Xi. *Res:* Analysis of biochemically important substances using varied chromatographic techniques; synthesis of possible cancer chemotherapeutics. *Mailing Add:* Millersville State Col Millersville PA 17551

YEAGER, VERNON LEROY, b Williston, NDak, Nov 20, 26; m 47; c 4. ANATOMY. *Educ:* Minot State Col, BS, 49; Univ NDak, PhD(anat), 55. *Prof Exp:* Teacher sci, Garrison High Sch, 49-51; prof anat, Univ NDak, 55-67; assoc prof, St Louis Univ, 67-68; Rockefeller Found vis prof, Mahidol Univ, Thailand, 68-71; PROF ANAT, ST LOUIS UNIV, 71- *Concurrent Pos:* NSF fel, Northwestern Univ, Chicago, 60; NIH grant, Univ NDak, 60-67. *Honors & Awards:* Hektoen Gold Medal, AMA, 78. *Mem:* Am Asn Anat; Sigma Xi. *Res:* Pathology of connective tissues. *Mailing Add:* Dept of Anat St Louis Univ Sch of Med St Louis MO 63104

YEAGLE, PHILIP L, US citizen. BIOLOGICAL MEMBRANES. *Educ:* St Olaf Col, BA, 71; Duke Univ, PhD(chem), 79. *Prof Exp:* Fel, Univ Va, 74-78; ASST PROF BIOCHEM, STATE UNIV NY, BUFFALO, 78- *Mem:* Am Chem Soc; Basic Sci Coun Am Heart Asn; Biophys Soc. *Res:* Structure of cell membranes and relations of structure to function, including phospholipid-protein interactions and cholesterol protein interactions in membranes using biochemical and licophysical techniques. *Mailing Add:* Dept Biochem State Univ NY Buffalo Sch Med Buffalo NY 14214

YEAKEY, ERNEST LEON, b Sikeston, Mo, Aug 5, 34; m 61; c 2. ORGANIC CHEMISTRY. *Educ:* Southeast Mo State Col, BS, 56; State Univ, Iowa, PhD(org chem), 60. *Prof Exp:* Res chemist, 60-67, supvr explor res, Jefferson Chem Co, 67-76, mgr res, 76-80, MGR NEW PROD DEVELOP, TEXACO CHEM CO, 80- *Mem:* Am Chem Soc. *Res:* Hydrogenation of nitriles to amines; reductive amination of alcohols to amines; synthetic routes to alpha olefins; catalytic synthesis of ethyleneamines; synthesis of heterocyclic amines. *Mailing Add:* Jefferson Chem Co PO Box 4128 N Austin Sta Austin TX 78751

YEANDLE, STEPHEN SAFFORD, b Bayonne, NJ, Sept 28, 29; m 66. BIOPHYSICS. *Educ:* Cornell Univ, BA, 51; Johns Hopkins Univ, PhD, 57. *Prof Exp:* NIH fel, Yale Univ, 58-59; asst prof physics, George Washington Univ, 59-65; BIOPHYSICIST, NAVAL MED RES INST, 65- *Mem:* Biophys Soc. *Res:* Biophysics of visual excitation; neurophysiology; biological applications of thermodynamics. *Mailing Add:* Naval Med Res Inst Bethesda MD 20814

YEARGAN, JERRY REESE, b Kirby, Ark, Jan 31, 40; m 59; c 2. ELECTRICAL ENGINEERING. *Educ:* Univ Ark, BSEE, 61, MSEE, 65; Univ Tex, Austin, PhD(elec eng), 67. *Prof Exp:* From asst engr to assoc engr, Tex Instruments, Inc, 61-63; res engr, Univ Tex, 66-67; from asst prof to assoc prof elec eng, 67-77, PROF ELEC ENG, UNIV ARK, FAYETTEVILLE, 77-, HEAD DEPT ELEC ENG, 80- *Mem:* Inst Elec & Electronics Engrs; Am Phys Soc; Am Soc Eng Educ. *Res:* Metal-oxide-semiconductor devices, particularly charge-coupled and optoelectronic metal-oxide-semiconductor devices. *Mailing Add:* SE 232 Dept of Elec Eng Univ of Ark Fayetteville AR 72701

YEARGAN, KENNETH VERNON, b Clanton, Ala, Feb 12, 47; m 72. ENTOMOLOGY, ECOLOGY. *Educ:* Auburn Univ, BS, 69; Univ Calif, Davis, PhD(entom), 74. *Prof Exp:* Asst prof, 74-79, ASSOC PROF ENTOM, UNIV KY, 79- *Mem:* Entom Soc Am; Entom Soc Can; Am Arachnological Soc; Int Orgn Biol Control; Ecol Soc Am. *Res:* Biological control of insect pests of soybeans and forage crops; theory and practice of population sampling; integrated pest management. *Mailing Add:* Dept Entom Univ Ky Lexington KY 40546

YEARGERS, EDWARD KLINGENSMITH, b Houma, La, Apr 27, 38; m 75; c 2. BIOPHYSICS. *Educ:* Ga Inst Technol, BS, 60; Emory Univ, MS, 62; Mich State Univ, PhD(biophys), 66. *Prof Exp:* US AEC res fel radiation physics, Oak Ridge Nat Lab, 66-67; NIH res fel theoret chem, Czech Acad Sci, 67; asst prof biol, 68-70, ASSOC PROF BIOL, GA INST TECHNOL, 70- *Res:* Molecular biophysics; protein structure; molecular aspects of aging. *Mailing Add:* Sch Biol Ga Inst Technol Atlanta GA 30332

YEARIAN, MASON RUSSELL, b Lafayette, Ind, July 5, 32; m 56, 65; c 3. NUCLEAR PHYSICS, HIGH ENERGY PHYSICS. *Educ:* Purdue Univ, BS, 54; Stanford Univ, MS, 56, PhD(physics), 61. *Prof Exp:* Res assoc physics, Univ Pa, 59-61; from asst prof to assoc prof, 61-71, PROF PHYSICS, STANFORD UNIV, 71-, DIR HIGH ENERGY PHYSICS LAB, 73- *Res:* Electron scattering from nuclei and nucleons; nucleon form factors; charge distribution in nuclei; high energy particle physics. *Mailing Add:* 921 Cottrell Way Stanford CA 94305

YEARIAN, WILLIAM C, b Lake Village, Ark, May 20, 37; m 60; c 1. ENTOMOLOGY. *Educ:* Univ Ark, Fayetteville, BS, 60, MS, 61; Univ Fla, PhD(entom), 66. *Prof Exp:* From asst prof to assoc prof, 65-74, PROF ENTOM, UNIV ARK, FAYETTEVILLE, 74- *Mem:* Soc Invert Path; Entom Soc Am. *Res:* Forest entomology; applied insect pathology. *Mailing Add:* Dept of Entom Univ of Ark Fayetteville AR 72701

YEARICK, ELISABETH STELLE, b Spokane, Wash, July 1, 13. NUTRITION, BIOCHEMISTRY. *Educ:* Univ Wis, BS, 34, MS, 35; Univ Iowa, PhD(nutrit), 60; Am Bd Nutrit, cert human nutrit. *Prof Exp:* Asst dir dietetics, Duke Hosp, 48-53, asst prof, Duke Univ, 53; assoc prof nutrit, Univ Iowa, 53-57; assoc prof, WVa Univ, 60-66; prof, 66-79, EMER PROF NUTRIT & FOODS, ORE STATE UNIV, 79- *Mem:* Am Inst Nutrit; Am Chem Soc; Am Dietetic Asn; Am Home Econ Asn. *Mailing Add:* 145 NW 16th #406 Corvallis OR 97330

YEAROUT, PAUL HARMON, JR, b Coeur d'Alene, Idaho, Sept 15, 24; m 49. MATHEMATICS. *Educ:* Reed Col, BA, 49; Univ Wash, MS, 58, PhD, 61. *Prof Exp:* Instr math, Reed Col, 51-52; instr exten ctr, Portland State Col, 52-55; asst prof, Knox Col, 59-62; assoc prof 62-67, PROF MATH, BRIGHAM YOUNG UNIV, 67- *Concurrent Pos:* Consult sch med, Univ Wash, 59-64. *Mem:* Math Asn Am. *Res:* Abstract algebra; theory and structure of groups and rings. *Mailing Add:* 328 TMCB Dept of Math Brigham Young Univ Provo UT 84602

YEARY, ROGER A, b Cleveland, Ohio, Apr 26, 32; m 53; c 4. TOXICOLOGY, PHARMACOLOGY. *Educ:* Ohio State Univ, DVM, 56; Am Col Lab Animal Med, dipl; Am Bd Vet Toxicol, dipl. *Prof Exp:* Staff sr toxicologist, Charles Pfizer & Co, Inc, Conn, 60-61; chief toxicol sect, Lakeside Labs Div, Colgate-Palmolive Co, Wis, 61-65; exten vet toxicologist, Coop Exten Serv, 65-67, assoc prof vet physiol & pharmacol, 67-72, PROF VET PHYSIOL & PHARMACOL, COL VET MED, OHIO STATE UNIV, 72- *Concurrent Pos:* Toxicol consult, Lakeside Labs Div, Colgate-Palmolive Co, 65-67 & Minn Mining & Mfg Co, 67-77; NIH res grants, toxicol study sect, 73-77; consult, Chemlawn Corp, 77-81 & O M Scott & Sons, 78-; dir Employee & Environ Health Chemlawn Corp, 81- *Mem:* AAAS; Am Soc Pharmacol & Exp Therapeut; Am Vet Med Asn; Soc Toxicol. *Res:* Drug toxicology; perinatal pharmacology. *Mailing Add:* Dept Vet Physiol & Pharmacol Ohio State Univ 1900 Coffey Rd Columbus OH 43210

YEATMAN, CHRISTOPHER WILLIAM, b Port Pirie, Australia, Aug 6, 27; m 54; c 4. FOREST GENETICS. *Educ:* Univ Adelaide, BSc, 51; Australian Sch Forestry, Canberra, dipl, 51; Yale Univ, MF, 57, PhD(forest genetics), 66. *Prof Exp:* Forester, Dept Woods & Forests, SAustralia, 51; forest officer, Forestry Comn Gt Brit, 51-53; asst, Petawawa Forest Exp Sta, 53-54, res forest officer, 54-66, RES SCIENTIST, PETAWAWA FOREST EXP STA, 66- *Concurrent Pos:* Mem & secy, Comt Forest Tree Breeding Can, 55-66, exec secy, 66-68. *Mem:* Biomet Soc; Can Inst Forestry; Genetics Soc Can. *Res:* Silviculture; plantation establishment; tree breeding and forest genetics; genecology. *Mailing Add:* Petawawa Forest Exp Sta Can Forestry Serv Chalk River ON K0J 1J0 Can

YEATMAN, HARRY CLAY, b Ashwood, Tenn, June 22, 16; m 49; c 2. ZOOLOGY. *Educ:* Univ NC, AB, 39, MA, 42, PhD(zool), 53. *Prof Exp:* Asst zool, Univ NC, 39-42, instr, 47-50; from asst prof to assoc prof biol, 50-59, chmn dept, 71-76, prof, 59-80, KENAN PROF BIOL, UNIV OF THE SOUTH, 80- *Concurrent Pos:* Consult, US Nat Mus, 48-, Woods Hole Oceanog Inst, 60- & SEATO, US Army, Thailand, 66-; consult, Univ Tehran, Iran, 72- & WHO, 76- *Mem:* AAAS; Soc Syst Zool; Am Soc Limnol & Oceanog; Am Soc Ichthyologists & Herpetologists; Am Ornith Union. *Res:* Limnology; taxonomy and ecology of freshwater and marine copepods. *Mailing Add:* Dept of Biol Univ of the South Sewanee TN 37375

YEATMAN, JOHN NEWTON, b Washington, DC, Apr 30, 20; m 54; c 2. FOOD SCIENCE. *Educ:* Univ Md, BS, 44; Univ Calif, Los Angeles, MS, 48. *Prof Exp:* Plant physiologist, USDA, 44-47; plant physiologist, Chem Corps, US Dept Army, Ft Detrick, 48-53; res food technol & leader, Qual Eval Invest, Agr Res Serv, USDA, 54-68, dir color res lab, Mkt Qual Res Div, 68-71; res food technol, Bur Foods, Div Food Technol, Food & Drug Admin, 71-75; CONSULT FOOD STANDS-QUAL EVAL, 75- *Mem:* Inst Food Technol; Inter-Soc Color Coun; Sigma Xi. *Res:* Research and development of methods for standards improvement by objectively measuring by physical and chemical means identity and quality factors in processed fruits and vegetables and their products; food standards and quality evaluation; instruments and inspection lighting. *Mailing Add:* 11106 Cherry Hill Rd Adelphi MD 20783

YEATS, FREDERICK TINSLEY, b Gadsden, Ala, Apr 4, 42; m 69; c 2. BOTANY. *Educ:* Miss Col, BS, 64; Univ Miss, MS, 67; Univ SC, PhD(biol), 71. *Prof Exp:* ASSOC PROF BIOL, HIGH POINT COL, 69- *Mem:* Sigma Xi; Am Inst Biol Sci. *Res:* Developmental morphology in fern gametophytes; embryology in the genus Smilax. *Mailing Add:* Dept of Biol High Point Col High Point NC 27262

YEATS, ROBERT SHEPPARD, b Miami, Fla, Mar 30, 31; m 52; c 5. GEOLOGY. *Educ:* Univ Fla, AB, 52; Univ Wash, MS & PhD(geol), 58. *Prof Exp:* Exploitation engr, Shell Oil Co, 58-62, sr prod geologist, 62-64, sr geologist, 64-67; from assoc prof to prof geol, Ohio Univ, 67-77; PROF & CHMN DEPT GEOL, ORE STATE UNIV, 77- *Concurrent Pos:* Consult, F Beach Leighton & Assocs, Calif & Energy Resources Br, US Geol Surv, 75; co-chief scientist, Deep Sea Drilling Proj, 73-78. *Mem:* AAAS; fel Geol Soc Am; Am Geophys Union; Seismological Soc Am; Am Asn Petrol Geol. *Res:* Structural evolution of Pacific continental margin of Americas; application of plate tectonics to petroleum accumulation; neotectonics: active folds and faults, particularly in contractile continental areas. *Mailing Add:* Dept of Geol Ore State Univ Corvallis OR 97331

YEATS, RONALD BRADSHAW, b Newcastle-upon-Tyne, Eng, Mar 17, 41; Can citizen; m 62; c 2. ORGANIC CHEMISTRY. *Educ:* Univ Durham, BSc, 62, PhD(org chem), 65. *Prof Exp:* Mayo fel, Univ Western Ont, 65-67, lectr org chem, 67-68; asst researcher, Univ Hosp Ctr, Univ Sherbrooke, 70-71; asst prof, 68-74, assoc prof, 78-80, PROF ORG CHEM, BISHOPS UNIV, LENNUXVILLE, QUE, CAN, 80-, CHMN DEPT, 81- *Mem:* The Chem Soc; Chem Inst Can. *Res:* Terpene synthesis; synthetic aspects of organic photochemistry; mechanism of solvolysis reactions; microbiological oxidation reactions. *Mailing Add:* Dept of Chem Bishop's Univ Lennoxville PQ S1M 1Z7 Can

YEATTS, FRANK RICHARD, b Altoona, Pa, Mar 5, 36; m 60; c 2. THEORETICAL PHYSICS. *Educ:* Pa State Univ, BS, 58; Univ Ariz, MS, 63, PhD(physics), 64. *Prof Exp:* Asst prof physics, 64-67, ASSOC PROF PHYSICS, COLO SCH MINES, 67- *Mem:* Am Geophys Union; Am Phys Soc; Am Asn Physics Teachers. *Res:* Theoretical geophysics. *Mailing Add:* Dept Physics Colo Sch Mines Golden CO 80401

YEATTS, LEROY BROUGH, JR, b Newport, Pa, Mar 28, 22; m 49; c 3. PHYSICAL INORGANIC CHEMISTRY. *Educ:* Lebanon Valley Col, BS, 43; Cornell Univ, MS, 45, PhD, 48. *Prof Exp:* Asst prof chem, Lafayette Col, 48-52; CHEMIST, OAK RIDGE NAT LAB, 52- *Mem:* Am Chem Soc. *Res:* High temperature aqueous electrolyte solutions; particle size determinations; polynuclear aromatic hydrocarbons in the environment; tobacco smoke chemistry. *Mailing Add:* 418 N Kingston Ave Rockwood TN 37854

YECK, ROBERT GILBERT, b La Valle, Wis, Dec 6, 20; m 44; c 2. AGRICULTURAL ENGINEERING. *Educ:* Univ Wis, BS, 48; Univ Mo, MS, 53, PhD(agr eng), 60. *Prof Exp:* Proj leader environ & animals, Agr Eng Div, USDA, 48-51, lab leader bioclimatic studies, 51-58, invests leader animal environ, 58-60, br chief livestock eng & rural housing, 70-72, staff scientist, waste mgt & microbiol, 72-75, STAFF SCIENTIST FARMSTEAD ENG & RURAL HOUSING, NAT PROG STAFF, SCI & EDUC ADMIN-AGR RES, USDA, 75- *Concurrent Pos:* Mem Agr bd, Nat Acad Sci, 71-74; consult, Food & Agr Orgn, UN, Italy, 64-67 & Agr Eng Grad Prog, Agrarian Univ, Peru, UN develop proj, 67-70; chmn, Int Symp Livestock Wastes, 71 & USDA Task Force Recycled Animal Wastes, 74; mem, President's Solar Domestic Pol Rev Group, 78. *Mem:* Fel Am Soc Agr Engrs; Sigma Xi. *Res:* Farmstead engineering; rural housing; waste management; solar energy; anaerobic fermentation processes; livestock shelters; environmental stress; bioclimatic studies. *Mailing Add:* Nat Prog Serv Sci & Educ Admin-Agr Res Beltsville Agr Res Ctr W Beltsville MD 20705

YEDINAK, PETER DEMERTON, b Bath, NY, Aug 20, 39; m 63; c 3. THEORETICAL PHYSICS, SOLID STATE PHYSICS. *Educ:* Union Col, BS, 62; Clark Univ, MA, 67, PhD(chem physics), 68. *Prof Exp:* Asst prof, 67-72, ASSOC PROF PHYSICS, WESTERN MD COL, 72- *Mem:* AAAS; Am Inst Physics; Am Asn Physics Teachers; Am Phys Soc. *Res:* Theoretical lattice dynamics; determination of transition rates for acoustical energy absorption by molecules in a solid containing isotopic defects. *Mailing Add:* Dept of Physics Western Md Col Westminster MD 21157

YEDLOUTSCHNIG, RONALD JOHN, b Centralia, Wash, Jan 14, 30; m 56; c 2. VETERINARY MEDICINE. *Educ:* Wash State Univ, DVM, 54. *Prof Exp:* Pvt pract, 57-60; field vet, Animal Health Div, USDA, 60-65, foreign animal dis epidemiologist, 65-66, trainee exotic dis, 66-67, PRIN VET, PLUM ISLAND ANIMAL DIS LAB, USDA, 67- *Res:* Exotic animal diseases. *Mailing Add:* Plum Island Animal Dis Lab PO Box 848 Greenport NY 11944

YEE, ALFRED A, b Aug 5, 25; US citizen. ENGINEERING. *Educ:* Rose-Hulman Inst Technol, BSCE, 48; Yale Univ, ME, 49. *Hon Degrees:* DE, Rose-Hulman Inst Technol, 76. *Prof Exp:* PRES, ALFRED A YEE & ASSOCS, INC, 53- *Concurrent Pos:* Dir, Pre-Stressed Concrete Inst, 69-72. *Mem:* Nat Acad Eng; fel Am Concrete Inst; fel Am Soc Civil Engrs. *Res:* Offshore and oceangoing vessels; reinforcing steel bar splices and concrete framing systems for high rise buildings; precast prestressed concrete construction. *Mailing Add:* Suite 810 1441 Kapiolani Blvd Honolulu HI 96814

YEE, JOHN ALAN, b Salt Lake City, Utah, Feb 11, 47; m 68; c 3. BONE BIOLOGY, CELL BIOLOGY. *Prof Exp:* Asst prof, 74-80, ASSOC PROF ANAT, TEX TECH UNIV HEALTH SCI CTR, 80- *Mem:* Am Asn Anatomists; Am Soc Bone & Mineral Res; AAAS. *Res:* Elucidating the factors which regulate bone cell functions and how cell function changes with age. *Mailing Add:* Dept Anat Tex Tech Univ Health Sci Ctr Lubbock TX 79430

YEE, KANE SHEE-GONG, b Kwangtung, China, Mar 26, 34; US citizen; m 62; c 2. APPLIED MATHEMATICS. *Educ:* Univ Calif, Berkeley, BS, 57, MS, 58, PhD(appl math), 63. *Prof Exp:* Assoc prof math, Univ Fla, 66-68; assoc prof, 68-73, PROF MATH, KANS STATE UNIV, 73- *Concurrent Pos:* Consult, Lawrence Livermore Lab, Univ Calif, 66-, grant, 70- *Mem:* Soc Indust & Appl Math. *Res:* Mathematical physics; numerical solution to partial differential equations. *Mailing Add:* Dept of Math Kans State Univ Manhattan KS 66502

YEE, SINCLAIR SHEE-SING, b China, Jan 20, 37; US citizen; m 61; c 2. BIOENGINEERING, MICROELECTRONICS. *Educ:* Univ Calif, Berkeley, BS, 59, MS, 61, PhD(elec eng), 65. *Prof Exp:* Res engr, Lawrence Livermore Lab, 64-66; from asst prof to prof elec eng, 66-77, DIR MICROTECHNOL LAB, UNIV WASH, 74- *Concurrent Pos:* Consult, Lawrence Livermore Lab, 66-75, Beckman Instruments, 77- & Tektronics Inc, 77-78; NIH spec res fels, Case Western Reserve Univ, 72-73 & Bioeng Ctr, Univ Wash, 73-74. *Mem:* Am Phys Soc; fel Inst Elec & Electronics Engrs. *Res:* Semiconductor physics and devices; bioinstrumentation; microelectronic devices. *Mailing Add:* Dept of Elec Eng Univ of Wash Seattle WA 98195

YEE, TIN BOO, b Canton, China, Feb 25, 15; US citizen. CHEMISTRY, CERAMICS. *Educ:* Ark State Col, BS, 38; Univ Ark, MS, 40; Univ Ill, AM, 50, PhD(chem), 54. *Prof Exp:* Chemist, Chem Warfare Serv, Huntsville Arsenal, Ala, 42-45; asst chemist, State Geol Surv, Ill, 45-55; RES CHEMIST, REDSTONE ARSENAL, 55- *Concurrent Pos:* Instr, Exten, Univ Ala, 60; vis res scientist, Union Indust Res Inst, Taiwan, 70-71. *Mem:* Am Chem Soc; Am Ceramic Soc. *Res:* Crystal growth studies by the thin film method in ceramic materials; solid rocket propellants; mutations in flowers and plants by radiations; material research in microelectronics. *Mailing Add:* 719 Erskine St NW Huntsville AL 35805

YEE, TUCKER TEW, b Toyshun, Canton, China, Mar 9, 36; US citizen; m 68; c 1. ORGANIC CHEMISTRY, PHYSICAL ORGANIC CHEMISTRY. *Educ:* Knox Col, Ill, BA, 60; Univ Mass, PhD(org chem), 64. *Prof Exp:* Res assoc, Princeton Univ, 64-65; res chemist, Eastern Lab, E I du Pont de Nemours & Co, Inc, 65-67; sr res chemist, Arco Chem Co Div, Atlantic Richfield Co, Pa, 67-72; RES CHEMIST, NAVAL WEAPONS CTR, CHINA LAKE, CALIF, 72- *Mem:* Sigma Xi; Am Chem Soc. *Res:* Chemistry of nitrogen containing heterocycles; radiochemical tracer technique; general organic syntheses; organic polymer syntheses and polymer applications. *Mailing Add:* 908 Sylvia Ave Ridgecrest CA 93555

YEE, WILLIAM C, b Boston, Mass, Sept 23, 28; m 54; c 3. CHEMICAL & ENVIRONMENTAL ENGINEERING. *Educ:* Tufts Univ, BS, 48; Univ Tenn, MS, 59. *Prof Exp:* Chemist, Allied Chem & Dye Corp, 48-52; chemist, 52-59, chem engr, 59-72, GROUP LEADER, OAK RIDGE NAT LAB, 72- *Concurrent Pos:* Session chmn, Gordon Conf on Water, 66. *Mem:* Sigma Xi; Am Inst Chem Engrs. *Res:* Environmental impact statement preparation; aquaculture; waste heat utilization; nutrition economics; nuclear desalination; agro-industrial complexes; waste and water treatment; ion exchange; radiation effects on metals; corrosion of nuclear materials; synthetic detergent technology. *Mailing Add:* 113 Westover Dr Oak Ridge TN 37830

YEEND, WARREN ERNEST, b Colfax, Wash, May 14, 36; m 64; c 1. GEOLOGY. *Educ:* Wash State Univ, BS, 58; Univ Colo, MS, 61; Univ Wis, PhD(geol), 65. *Prof Exp:* GEOLOGIST, US GEOL SURV, 65- *Honors & Awards:* Spec Achievement Award, US Geol Surv, 75. *Mem:* Geol Soc Am. *Res:* Surficial geology in an area of oil shade interest in western Colorado; geomorphology; gold bearing gravels of the Sierra Nevada; economic geology; engineering geology along the Trans-Alaska pipeline; mapping and copper resource evaluation in southern Arizona. *Mailing Add:* US Geol Surv 345 Middlefield Rd Menlo Park CA 94025

YEGULALP, TUNCEL MUSTAFA, b Konya, Turkey, Nov 5, 37; m 63; c 2. MINING ENGINEERING, OPERATIONS RESEARCH. *Educ:* Tech Univ Istanbul, MS, 61; Columbia Univ, DES(mining), 68. *Prof Exp:* Mining engr, Mineral Res & Explor Inst, Turkey, 61-63; res engr, Mobil Res & Develop Corp, 67-69; prog mgr, Mineral Res & Explor Inst, Turkey, 71-72; asst prof, 72-75, ASSOC PROF MINING, COLUMBIA UNIV, 75- *Mem:* Am Inst Mining, Metall & Petrol Engrs; Inst Mgt Sci; Opers Res Soc Am. *Res:* Mineral economics; hydraulic transport of coal in underground mines; earthquake forecasting. *Mailing Add:* Henry Krumb Sch of Mines Columbia Univ New York NY 10027

YEH, BILLY KUO-JIUN, b Foochow, China, Aug 28, 37; m 65; c 3. INTERNAL MEDICINE, CARDIOVASCULAR DISEASES. *Educ:* Nat Taiwan Univ, MD, 61; Univ Okla, MS, 63; Columbia Univ, PhD(pharmacol), 67; Am Bd Internal Med, dipl. *Prof Exp:* Intern med, Nat Taiwan Univ Hosp, 60-61; resident path, Med Ctr, Univ Okla, 63; teaching asst, Col Physicians & Surgeons, Columbia Univ, 64-67; asst resident, Emory Univ Affil Hosps, 68-69; staff cardiologist & chief sect clin pharmacol, Div Cardiol, Mt Sinai Med Ctr, Miami Beach, 69-71; assoc dir, Div Clin Investr, Miami Heart Inst, Miami Beach, 73-76; asst prof med, 70-73, asst prof pharmacol, 72-73, clin asst prof, 73-76, CLIN ASSOC PROF MED, SCH MED, UNIV MIAMI, 76-

Concurrent Pos: Fel, Univ Okla, 62-63; fel pharmacol, Col Physicians & Surgeons, Columbia Univ, 63-64; fel med, Sch Med, Emory Univ & Grady Mem Hosp, 67-68. *Mem:* Fel Am Col Physicians; fel Am Col Cardiol; Am Soc Pharmacol & Exp Therapeut; Am Physiol Soc; Am Fedn Clin Res. *Mailing Add:* 7110 SW 148th Terr Miami FL 33158

YEH, CHAI, b Hangchow, China, Sept 21, 11; nat US; m 36; c 2. ELECTRONICS. *Educ:* Chekiang Univ, BS, 31; Harvard Univ, MS, 34, ScD(commun), 36. *Prof Exp:* Asst, Harvard Univ, 35-36; assoc prof elec eng, Peiyong Univ, China, 36-37; prof, Tsinghua Univ, 37-48; vis prof, Univ Kans, 48-56; res engr, Inst Sci & Technol, 56-61, assoc prof elec eng, 61-64, PROF ELEC ENG, UNIV MICH, ANN ARBOR, 64- *Mem:* Sr mem Inst Elec & Electronics Engrs. *Res:* Microwave electronics and engineering; linear and nonlinear circuit analysis. *Mailing Add:* Dept of Elec & Comput Eng Univ of Mich Ann Arbor MI 48109

YEH, FRANCIS CHO-HAO, b Hankow, China, Dec 20, 45; m 69; c 1. QUANTITATIVE GENETICS, POPULATION GENETICS. *Educ:* Univ Calgary, BSc, 70, PhD(genetics), 74. *Prof Exp:* Geneticist quantitative genetics, 74-80, TECH ADV GENETICS, BC MINISTRY FORESTS, VICTORIA, 80- *Concurrent Pos:* Adj assoc prof, Dept Forest Sci, Univ Alberta, 80- *Mem:* NAm Quantitative Forest Genetics Group; Int Union Forestry Res Orgn; Can Tree Improvement Asn; Genetics Soc Can; Genetics Soc Am. *Res:* Genetic structure of forest tress and breeding theories. *Mailing Add:* 1083 Brookview Dr Victoria BC V8X 3W9 Can

YEH, GEORGE CHIAYOU, b Kagi, Taiwan, Oct 3, 26; US citizen; m 57; c 4. PHYSICAL CHEMISTRY, CHEMICAL PHYSICS. *Educ:* Taiwan Univ, BSc, 50; Univ Tokyo, DEng, 53; Univ Toronto, MSc, 55, PhD(chem engr), 57. *Prof Exp:* Lectr, Japanese Engrs Union, Tokyo, 51-53; assoc prof chem eng, Auburn Univ, 57-61; assoc prof, 61-63, dir res & patent affairs, 73-79, PROF CHEM ENG, VILLANOVA UNIV, 63- *Concurrent Pos:* Prin investr res grants, Petrol Res Fund, 63-65 & NASA, 65-69. *Honors & Awards:* Meritorious Serv Award, Am Inst Chemists, 72; Achievement Award, United Inventors & Scientists Am, 74. *Mem:* Fel Am Inst Chemists; AAAS; Am Inst Chem Engrs; Am Chem Soc; Japanese Soc Chem Eng. *Res:* Reactions at interfaces; interfacial phenomena; catalysis; quantum mechanics; solid state chemistry; electrochemical analysis; liquids separation; gas separation; energy conversion; vapor engine. *Mailing Add:* Dept of Chem Eng Villanova Univ Villanova PA 19085

YEH, GORDON C(HIEN)-K(UAN), b Chekiang, China, Aug 17, 23; US citizen; m 56; c 3. MECHANICS. *Educ:* Nat Cent Univ, China, BS, 45; Stanford Univ, MS, 48; Harvard Univ, SM, 49, ScD(appl mech), 51. *Prof Exp:* Mem tech staff aeronaut eng, Chinese Air Force, 45-47; mem res staff, Nat Adv Comt Aeronaut Proj, Harvard Univ, 50-51, asst eng math, 51; proj engr, Anal Eng Dept, Reed Res, Inc, 51-53, staff scientist, Reed Res, Inc & Reed Res Found, 54-59; mem tech staff, Ramo-Wooldridge Corp, 59-60 & Space Technol Labs, Inc, 60-63; mem tech staff, TRW Space Technol Labs, 63-65 & TRW Systs, 65-70; ENG SPECIALIST, BECHTEL POWER CORP, 70- *Concurrent Pos:* Consult, Reed Res Found, 60-62 & Space Sci Lab, TRW Systs, 70-71; mem instrnl staff, Univ Calif, Los Angeles, 66-; lectr, Dept Mech Eng, Loyola Univ Los Angeles, 71-73; prof appl mech & appl math, South Bay Univ, Los Angeles, 79- *Mem:* Am Soc Mech Engrs; Sigma Xi; Am Soc Eng Educ; Am Acad Mech. *Res:* Elasticity; plasticity; fluid mechanics; vibrations; structural dynamics; earthquake engineering; potential theory; electrocardiography; liquid sloshing; wave propagation; applied mathematics; structural mechanics in reactor technology; tornado and extreme wind; piping stress analysis. *Mailing Add:* 12400 E Imperial Hwy Bechtel Power Corp Norwalk CA 90650

YEH, GOUR-TSYH, b Lunhoutsun, Taiwan, Dec 5, 40; US citizen; m 71; c 1. HYDROSCIENCES, ATMOSPHERIC SCIENCES. *Educ:* Nat Taiwan Univ, BS, 64; Syracuse Univ, MS, 67; Cornell Univ, PhD(hydrol), 69. *Prof Exp:* Res assoc atmospheric diffusion, Cornell Univ, 69-71; vis res scientist air-sea interaction, NASA, Houston, 71-72; sr environ engr thermal hydraul, Ebasio Serv Inc, 72-73; sr hydraul-environ engr fluid mech, Stone & Webster Eng Corp, 73-77; RES SCIENTIST HYDROL, OAK RIDGE NAT LAB, 77- *Concurrent Pos:* Adj prof, Northeastern Univ, 74-75. *Mem:* AAAS; Am Soc Civil Engrs; Am Geophys Union; Am Meteolog Soc; Nat Soc Prof Engrs. *Mailing Add:* PO Box X Oak Ridge Nat Lab Oak Ridge TN 37830

YEH, GREGORY SOH-YU, b Shanghai, China, Apr 11, 33; US citizen; m 59; c 2. POLYMER PHYSICS, ELECTRON MICROSCOPY. *Educ:* Holy Cross Col, BS, 57; Cornell Univ, MS, 60; Case Inst Technol, PhD(polymer physics), 66. *Prof Exp:* Res physicist, Goodyear Res Ctr, 60-61; sr res physicist, Gen Res Ctr, 61-64; res fel, Case Inst Technol, 66-67; asst prof chem & metall eng, 67-69, assoc prof, 69-72, PROF MAT & METALL & CHEM ENG, UNIV MICH, ANN ARBOR, 72- *Concurrent Pos:* Fulbright fel, 73; Humboldt fel, 74. *Mem:* Am Phys Soc; Electron Micros Soc Am; Am Chem Soc. *Res:* Polymer structure and properties; morphology and crystal structure; mechanical properties of polymers; electron diffraction. *Mailing Add:* EE 2217 Chem Eng Univ of Mich Ann Arbor MI 48104

YEH, HERMAN JIA-CHAIN, b Taipei, Taiwan, Nov 15, 39. PHYSICAL CHEMISTRY. *Educ:* Cheng-Kung Univ, Taiwan, BS, 63; Univ Mass, Amherst, PhD(chem), 68. *Prof Exp:* Fel chem, Univ Mass, 68-69; vis fel, Lab Chem, 70-71, staff fel, 72-74, sr staff fel, 74-76, RES CHEMIST, NAT INST ARTHRITIS, METABOLISM & DIGESTIVE DIS, 76- *Mem:* AAAS; Am Chem Soc. *Res:* Nuclear magnetic resonance spectroscopy. *Mailing Add:* 6000 Marquette Terrace Bethesda MD 20817

YEH, HSIANG-YUEH, b Tainan Hsien, Taiwan, Apr 1, 40; m 69; c 1. MECHANICS. *Educ:* Cheng King Univ, Taiwan, BSE, 62; Univ NMex, MSCE, 67, PhD(civil eng), 69. *Prof Exp:* Jr engr, Taiwan Pub Works Bur, 63-65; asst prof civil eng, 69-77, NASA grants, 71-73, ASSOC PROF CIVIL ENG, PRAIRIE VIEW AGR & MECH COL, 77- *Mem:* Am Soc Civil Engrs; Nat Soc Prof Engrs; Am Soc Eng Educ. *Res:* Reliability analysis, random vibration and fatigue damage of structural systems. *Mailing Add:* PO Box 2244 Prairie View TX 77445

YEH, HSI-HAN, b Shanghai, China, Nov 10, 35; m 66; c 2. ELECTRICAL ENGINEERING, CONTROL SYSTEMS. *Educ:* Nat Taiwan Univ, BSc, 56; Chiao Tung Univ, MSc, 61; Univ NB, MSc, 63; Ohio State Univ, PhD(elec eng), 67. *Prof Exp:* Asst engr, Taiwan Power Co, 58-60; res assoc elec eng, Ohio State Univ, 66-67; asst prof, 67-73, ASSOC PROF ELEC ENG, UNIV KY, 73- *Concurrent Pos:* NSF res initiation grant, 68-69; fac res, NASA, 73-74 & Air Force Off Sci Res, 81; vis prof, Nat Chiao Tung Univ, 75-76. *Mem:* Inst Elec & Electronics Engrs; Sigma Xi. *Res:* Distributed-parameter systems; computer-controlled systems; learning and adaptive control systems; optimal control theory. *Mailing Add:* 3821 Hapgood Lane Lexington KY 40503

YEH, HSIN-YANG, b Hsin-Chu, Formosa, Jan 1, 30; US citizen; m 67; c 2. MATHEMATICAL PHYSICS, PARTICLE PHYSICS. *Educ:* Nat Taiwan Univ, BS, 52; Kyushu Univ, MS, 57; Univ NC, Chapel Hill, PhD(theoret physics), 60. *Prof Exp:* Res physicist nuclear data group, Nat Acad Sci-Nat Res Coun, Washington, DC, 60-61; sr scientist, Edgerton, Germeshausen & Grier, Inc, 61-63; prof physics, Moorhead State Univ, 66-80. *Mem:* Am Phys Soc; NY Acad Sci; Int Soc Gen Relativity & Gravitation. *Res:* Quantum field theory; nuclear physics; group theory. *Mailing Add:* 12722 Castleford Shadow Pk Cerritos CA 90701

YEH, HSUAN, b Shanghai, China, Dec 1, 16. MECHANICAL ENGINEERING, AERONAUTICAL ENGINEERING. *Educ:* Chiao-Tung Univ, BS, 36; Mass Inst Technol, SM, 44, ScD(mech eng), 50. *Prof Exp:* Instr mech eng, Mass Inst Technol, 48-50; res assoc, Johns Hopkins Univ, 50-52, from asst prof to assoc prof, 52-56; PROF MECH ENG, UNIV PA, 56-, DIR TOWNE SCH CIVIL & MECH ENG, 60- *Concurrent Pos:* Mem, Franklin Inst. *Mem:* Am Inst Aeronaut & Astronaut; Am Soc Eng Educ; Am Phys Soc; fel Am Soc Mech Engrs. *Res:* Turbomachinery; fluid and analytical mechanics; aerodynamics; magnetohydrodynamics. *Mailing Add:* Towne Sch of Civil & Mech Eng Univ of Pa Philadelphia PA 19104

YEH, HSU-CHI, b Taipei, Taiwan, Sept 30, 40; US citizen; m 66; c 2. AEROSOL SCIENCE, MECHANICAL ENGINEERING. *Educ:* Nat Taiwan Univ, BS, 63; Univ Minn, MS, 67, PhD(mech eng), 72. *Prof Exp:* Teaching asst mech eng, Univ Minn, 64-65, res asst mech eng & aerosol physics, 65-72; res assoc, 72-73, RES SCIENTIST AEROSOL PHYSICS, INHALATION TOXICOL RES INST, LOVELACE BIOMED & ENVIRON RES INST, 73- *Mem:* Health Physics Soc; AAAS; Am Indust Hyg Asn; Sigma Xi; Air Pollution Control Asn. *Res:* Aerosol science and technology; inhalation toxicity associated with inhaled aerosols and the particle deposition in mammalian lungs including mammalian airway morphometry. *Mailing Add:* Lovelace Inhalation Toxicol Res Inst PO Box 5890 Albuquerque NM 87185

YEH, HUN CHIANG, b Nanking, China, June 27, 35; m 65; c 2. METALLURGY, CERAMICS. *Educ:* Nat Taiwan Univ, BS, 58; Brown Univ, MS, 63; Ill Inst Technol, PhD, 66. *Prof Exp:* Sr metallurgist, Res & Develop Lab, Corning Glass Works, 66-69; asst prof metall eng, 69-75, actg chmn dept, 76-77, assoc prof metall eng, 75-80, PROF MAT SCI, CHMN ENG DEPT, CLEVELAND STATE UNIV, 80- *Mem:* Metall Soc; Am Ceramic Soc. *Res:* X-ray studies of metals and ceramics; mechanical behaviors of materials; grinding of metals; processing of refractory oxides and silicon nitrides. *Mailing Add:* Dept of Metall Eng Cleveland State Univ Cleveland OH 44115

YEH, JAMES JUI-TIN, b Tainan, Formosa, Apr 26, 27; US citizen. MATHEMATICS. *Educ:* Taiwan Univ, BS, 50; Univ Minn, MA, 54, PhD(math), 57. *Prof Exp:* Instr math inst technol, Univ Minn, 57-58 & Mass Inst Technol, 58-60; asst prof, Univ Rochester, 60-64; vis mem, Courant Inst Math Sci, NY Univ, 64-65; assoc prof, 65-68, PROF MATH, UNIV CALIF, IRVINE, 68- *Mem:* Am Math Soc. *Res:* Integration in function spaces; functional analysis; stochastic processes. *Mailing Add:* Dept of Math Univ of Calif Irvine CA 92717

YEH, K(UNG) C(HIE), b Hangchow, China, Aug 4, 30; m; c 4. ELECTRICAL ENGINEERING. *Educ:* Univ Ill, BS, 53; Stanford Univ, MS, 54, PhD(elec eng), 58. *Prof Exp:* Asst, Electronics Lab, Stanford Univ, 54-58; res assoc elec eng, 58-59, from asst prof to assoc prof, 59-67, assoc, Ctr Advan Study, 73-74, PROF ELEC ENG, UNIV ILL, URBANA, 67- *Concurrent Pos:* Mem, US Comn G, Int Sci Radio Union. *Honors & Awards:* Cert of Achievement Award, Inst Elec & Electronics Engrs, 68. *Mem:* Fel Inst Elec & Electronics Engrs; Am Geophys Union; Am Phys Soc; Am Meteorol Soc. *Res:* Propagation, ionosphere and plasma; radio propagation; ionospheric dynamics. *Mailing Add:* Rm 60B Dept of Elec Eng Univ of Ill Urbana IL 61801

YEH, KUO-CHEN, organic chemistry, see previous edition

YEH, KWAN-NAN, b Taichung, Taiwan, Feb 27, 38; m 65; c 2. TEXTILE CHEMISTRY. *Educ:* Nat Taiwan Univ, BS, 61; Tulane Univ, La, MS, 65; Univ Ga, PhD(chem), 70. *Prof Exp:* Cotton Found res assoc fel, Nat Bur Standards, 70-72, res chemist, 72-73; asst prof, 73-79, ASSOC PROF TEXTILES & CONSUMER ECON, UNIV MD, COLLEGE PARK, 79- *Mem:* Am Chem Soc; Am Asn Textile Chemists & Colorists; Textile Inst Fiber Soc. *Res:* Thermodynamics; thermochemistry; textile and polymer flammability; textile chemistry; dyeing and finishing. *Mailing Add:* Dept of Textiles & Consumer Econ Univ of Md College Park MD 20742

YEH, KWO-YIH, b Tao-yuan, Taiwan, Jan 20, 42; m 71. CELL CULTURE. *Educ:* Taiwan Normal Univ, BS, 65; Washington Univ, St Louis, PhD(biol), 75. *Prof Exp:* Instr biol, Chung-Li High Sch, Taiwan, 65-66; teaching asst develop biol, Taiwan Normal Univ, 67-71; res asst, Washington Univ, St Louis, 71-75, res assoc, 75-77, res asst prof, 77-78; SR RES SCIENTIST CELL BIOL, SOUTHERN RES INST, 78- *Mem:* AAAS; Am Soc Cell Biol; Am Soc Zoologists; Soc Develop Biol. *Res:* Developmental biology in vertebrates; structural and enzymic development of intestine; developmental endocrinology; cell proliferation and differentiation. *Mailing Add:* Southern Res Inst PO Box 3307-A Birmingham AL 35255

YEH, LAI-SU LEE, b Hunan, China, June 24, 42, US citizen; m 72; c 2. ENZYMOLOGY. *Educ:* Taiwan Normal Univ, BS, 65; Sacramento State Univ, MS, 69; Univ Calif, Davis, PhD(agr chem), 79. *Prof Exp:* Res assoc enzym, Dept Biochem, Univ Utah, 75-77, res specialist clin biochem, Dept Pediat, 77-78; RES SCIENTIST BIOCHEM, NAT BIOMED RES FOUND, 80- *Mem:* Am Chem Soc. *Mailing Add:* 11317 Stryver Ct Gaithersburg MD 20878

YEH, NOEL KUEI-ENG, b Malacca, Malaysia, Dec 15, 37; m 65; c 2. PARTICLE PHYSICS, MEDICAL PHYSICS. *Educ:* Williams Col, BA, 61; Yale Univ, MS, 62, PhD(physics), 66. *Prof Exp:* Res assoc physics, Nevis Labs, Columbia Univ, 66-68, instr univ, 68-69; from asst prof to assoc prof, 69-80, PROF PHYSICS, STATE UNIV NY BINGHAMTON, 80-, CHMN DEPT PHYSICS, APPL PHYSICS & ASTROPHYS, 81- *Concurrent Pos:* Vis res physicist, Max-Planck-Inst Physics & Astrophys, Munich, W Ger, 76-77. *Mem:* NY Acad Sci; Am Phys Soc. *Res:* Properties of mesons and hyperons; resonances; medical applications of particle beams; weak and strong interactions of elementary particles. *Mailing Add:* Dept of Physics State Univ of NY Binghamton NY 13901

YEH, PAI-T(AO), b Canton, China, Feb 5, 20; nat US; m 51; c 2. CIVIL ENGINEERING. *Educ:* Chekiang Univ, BS, 43; Purdue Univ, MSCE, 49, PhD, 53. *Prof Exp:* Asst engr, Chekiang Waterway Off, 43-44; engr, Kwak Wha Eng Develop Co, 44-48; res engr, 53-58, asst prof hwy eng, 59-65, ASSOC PROF HWY ENG, PURDUE UNIV, WEST LAFAYETTE, 65- *Mem:* AAAS; Am Soc Photogram; Sigma Xi; Am Soc Prof Engrs; Am Mil Eng. *Res:* Aerial photograph interpretation of engineering soils; hydrological problems. *Mailing Add:* Dept of Civil Eng Purdue Univ West Lafayette IN 47907

YEH, PAUL PAO, b Sun-Yang, China, Mar 25, 27; US citizen; m 53; c 4. ELECTRICAL & ELECTRONIC ENGINEERING. *Educ:* Univ Toronto, BASc, 51; Univ Pa, MS, 60, PhD(elec eng), 66. *Prof Exp:* Design engr, James R Kearny Corp Can Ltd, 51 & Can Gen Elec Co, 51-56; asst prof elec technol, Broome Technol Community Col-State Univ NY, Binghamton, 56-57; sr design engr, H K Porter Co, Inc, Pa, 57; transformer engr, I-T-E Circuit Breaker Co, 57-58 & Kuhlman Elec Co, Mich, 58-59; sr design engr, Fed Pac Elec Co, NJ, 59-61; chief engr, Eisler Transformer Co, 61; assoc prof elec eng, Newark Col Eng, 61-67; supvr performance anal, Autonetics Div, N Am Rockwell Corp, 67-70; advan systs engr, S3-A Avionics, Lockheed-Calif Co, 70-72; supvr module commun systs, Site Defense Prog, McDonnell Douglas Corp, Huntington Beach, 72-73; mem tech staff, Aerospace Corp, 73-78, SR STAFF ENGR ADVAN DEVELOP PROJ, LOCKHEED-CALIF CO, 78- *Concurrent Pos:* Consult, Eisler Transformer Co, NJ, 61-62, Standard Transformer Co, Ohio, 62, H K Porter Co, Inc, Va, 62-65, Consol Edison Co NY, Inc & Niagara Transformer Co, NY, 63-64 & Pub Serv Elec & Gas Co, NJ, 66; lectr, Calif State Univ, Long Beach, 67-73. *Honors & Awards:* Achievement Award, Lockheed-Calif Co. *Mem:* AAAS; sr mem Inst Elec & Electronics Engrs; Am Inst Aeronaut & Astronaut; Am Asn Univ Prof; Nat Mgt Asn. *Res:* Weapon deliver computer mechanization; air-to-air missile launch control problems; magnetic anomaly detection in antisubmarine warfare systems; communication and systems readiness verification as applied to antiballistic missile programs; Cruise missile launch and control. *Mailing Add:* Dept 7773 Bldg 90-1 Plant A-1 Lockheed Calif Co Box 551 Burbank CA 91520

YEH, PU-SEN, b Hualien, Taiwan, July 7, 35; m 64; c 3. AEROTHERMODYNAMICS, HEAT TRANSFER. *Educ:* Nat Taiwan Univ, BSME, 58; Univ Ill, MS, 62; Rutgers Univ, PhD(mech eng), 67. *Prof Exp:* ASSOC PROF ENG, JACKSONVILLE STATE UNIV, 67-, HEAD DEPT COMPUT SCI & ENG, 78- *Mem:* Am Soc Eng Educ; Am Soc Mech Engrs. *Res:* Ignition and combustion of liquid fuel droplets; heat transfer problem of underground residential transformer. *Mailing Add:* Dept Eng & Comput Sci Jacksonville State Univ Jacksonville AL 36265

YEH, RAYMOND T, b Hunan, China, Nov 5, 37; m 66; c 1. COMPUTER SCIENCE. *Educ:* Univ Ill, BS, 61, MA, 63, PhD(math), 66. *Prof Exp:* Asst prof comput sci, Pa State Univ, 66-69; assoc prof, 69-74, PROF COMPUT SCI & ELEC ENG, UNIV TEX, AUSTIN, 74-, CHMN DEPT COMPUT SCI, 75- *Concurrent Pos:* Ed transactions software eng, Inst Elec & Electronics Eng. *Mem:* Am Math Soc; Asn Comput Mach; Inst Elec & Electronics Eng. *Res:* Software engineering; data base management. *Mailing Add:* Dept of Comput Sci Univ of Tex Austin TX 78712

YEH, SAMUEL D J, b Kunming, China, Apr 23, 26; US citizen; m 59; c 2. BIOCHEMISTRY. *Educ:* Nat Defense Med Ctr, Shanghai, MD, 48; Johns Hopkins Univ, ScD(biochem), 60. *Prof Exp:* Instr med, Nat Defense Med Ctr, 48-53; asst resident, Lutheran Hosp, Md, 53-54; fel med, 54-57, from instr to asst prof biochem, Sch Hyg & Pub Health, Johns Hopkins Univ, 60-63; instr, Med Col, Cornell Univ, 63-69; asst attend physician, Mem Hosp, New York City, 69-70 & 72-75; asst prof med, Med Col, Cornell Univ, 69-76; ASSOC ATTEND PHYSICIAN, MEM HOSP, NEW YORK CITY, 75- *Concurrent Pos:* Assoc, Sloan-Kettering Inst, 63-71 & 71-; assoc prof clin med, Med Col Cornell Univ, 76- *Mem:* AAAS; Am Chem Soc; Am Inst Nutrit; Soc Nuclear Med; Am Col Nuclear Physicians. *Res:* Interrelationship between nutrients; intestinal absorption and marginal deficiencies; role of protein synthesis on metabolic functions; tumor localizing radionuclides. *Mailing Add:* 303 E 71st St Apt 4A New York NY 10021

YEH, SHU-YUAN, b Kwangtung, China, June 26, 26; US citizen; m 57; c 2. PHARMACEUTICAL CHEMISTRY, PHARMACOLOGY. *Educ:* Nat Defense Med Ctr, Taiwan, BS, 51; Univ Iowa, MS, 57, PhD(pharmaceut chem), 59. *Prof Exp:* Pharmacist, Army, Navy & Air Force Hosp, Taiwan, 51-52; clin, Off of President, Taiwan, 53-55; res asst pharm, Univ Iowa, 55-59, res assoc med, 59-63, from res instr to res asst prof drug metab, Col Med, 63-70; asst prof, Univ Ky, 71; PHARMACOLOGIST, ADDICTION RES CTR, NAT INST DRUG ABUSE, 72- *Mem:* AAAS; Am Pharmaceut Asn; Acad Pharmaceut Sci; Am Soc Pharmacol & Exp Med; NY Acad Sci. *Res:* Development of methods for detection, isolation and identification of drug and its metabolites in the biological fluids. *Mailing Add:* Addiction Res Ctr Nat Inst Drug Abuse PO Box 12390 Lexington KY 40583

YEH, WILLIAM WEN-GONG, b Szechwan, China, Dec 5, 38; m 67; c 2. WATER RESOURCES, HYDROLOGY. *Educ:* Cheng-Kung Univ, BS, 61; NMex State Univ, MS, 64; Stanford Univ, PhD(civil eng), 67. *Prof Exp:* Actg asst prof civil eng, Stanford Univ, 67; asst res engr eng syst, 67-69, asst prof, 69-73, assoc prof, 73-77, PROF ENG SYST, UNIV CALIF, LOS ANGELES, 77- *Concurrent Pos:* Asst res engr, Dry-Lands Res Inst, Univ Calif, Riverside, 72-73; lectureship, Consejo Nacional de Ciencia Y Tecnologia, Mexico, 73, Nat Polytech Inst, Mexico 81; expert water resources, Div Hydrol, Unesco, 74; Eng Found Fel Award, Eng Found, 81. *Mem:* Am Soc Civil Engrs; Am Geophys Union; Am Water Resources Asn. *Res:* Hydrology; water resources; operations research; optimal control; optimization of large-scale water resource systems. *Mailing Add:* 7619F Boelter Hall Univ Calif Los Angeles CA 90024

YEH, YIN, b Chungking, China, Nov 1, 38; US citizen; m 61; c 2. QUANTUM ELECTRONICS, CHEMICAL PHYSICS. *Educ:* Mass Inst Technol, BS, 60; Columbia Univ, PhD(physics), 65. *Prof Exp:* Res assoc physics, Columbia Radiation Lab, Columbia Univ, 65-66; Lawrence Radiation Lab fel, Lawrence Livermore Lab, 66-67, sr physicist, 67-72; assoc prof, 72-78, PROF APPL SCI, UNIV CALIF, DAVIS, 78- *Concurrent Pos:* Lectr, St Mary's Col, Calif, 67-68; lectr, Univ Calif, Davis, 71-72; consult, Lawrence Livermore Lab, 72- *Mem:* AAAS; Sigma Xi; Biophys Soc; Am Phys Soc. *Res:* Application of laser spectroscopy to study dynamic phenomena in chemical physics, biophysics and solid state physics. *Mailing Add:* Dept of Appl Sci Univ of Calif Davis CA 95616

YEHLE, CLIFFORD OMER, genetics, biochemistry, see previous edition

YEIGH, JOHN H, JR, b Bryn Mawr, Pa, Oct 19, 55; m 78. ENERGY CONSERVATION. *Educ:* Bucknell Univ, BS, 77; Drexel Univ, MBA, 81. *Prof Exp:* SR STAFF ENGR, MOBIL RES & DEVELOP CORP, SUBSID MOBIL CORP, 77- *Mem:* Am Inst Chem Engrs; Am Mgt Asn. *Res:* Petroleum refining including: process optimization, catalyst development, energy conservation, and economics. *Mailing Add:* 2 Lanark Rd Turnersville NJ 08012

YELENOSKY, GEORGE, b Vintondale, Pa, July 20, 29; m 63; c 3. PLANT PHYSIOLOGY. *Educ:* Pa State Univ, BS, 55, MS, 58; Duke Univ, DF, 63. *Prof Exp:* Res forester, Northeastern Forest Exp Sta, US Forest Serv, 55-56 & 58-61; Int Shade Tree Conf res fel, 63-64; PLANT PHYSIOLOGIST, CITRUS INVESTS, USDA, 64- *Mem:* Am Soc Plant Physiol; Am Soc Hort Sci. *Res:* Forestry; soil aeration and tree growth; cold hardiness of citrus trees; cryobiology membership. *Mailing Add:* USDA Agr Res Serv 2120 Camden Rd Orlando FL 32803

YELLEN, JAY, b New York, NY, Dec 17, 48; m 71; c 1. ALGEBRA. *Educ:* Polytech Inst Brooklyn, BS, 69, MS, 71; Colo State Univ, PhD(math), 75. *Prof Exp:* Teaching asst math, Polytech Inst Brooklyn, 69-71; teaching asst, Colo State Univ, 71-75; asst prof, Allegheny Col, 75-76; ASST PROF MATH, STATE UNIV NY COL, FREDONIA, 76- *Mem:* Am Math Soc. *Res:* Group representation theory, particularly groups of central type; algebraic coding theory. *Mailing Add:* Dept of Math Fredonia NY 16335

YELLIN, ABSALOM MOSES, b Tel-Aviv, Israel, July 25, 36; US citizen; m 66; c 2. PSYCHOPHYSIOLOGY, CHILD PSYCHIATRY. *Educ:* Univ Del, BA, 65, MA, 68, PhD(psychol), 70. *Prof Exp:* Scholar, Neuropsychiat Inst, Univ Calif, Los Angeles Sch Med, 69-71; asst res psychologist, Neuropsychiat Inst, Univ Calif, Los Angeles, 71-72; asst prof, Dept Psychiat, Univ Calif, Davis, 72-74; asst prof, 74-80, ASSOC PROF, DEPT PSYCHIAT, UNIV MINN, 80-, DIR, CLIN STUDIES UNIT, 74- *Mem:* Am Psychol Asn; AAAS; NY Acad Sci; Soc Psychophysiol Res. *Res:* Attention and information processing; hyperkinesis and other disorders involving attentional deficits, biorhythms, mental retardation, electroencephalograph and evoked potentials; child psychology and psychiatry; psychopharmacology. *Mailing Add:* Div Child & Adolescent Psychiat Univ Minn Box 95 Mayo Bldg Minneapolis MN 55455

YELLIN, EDWARD L, b Brooklyn, NY, July 2, 27; m 48; c 3. BIOENGINEERING, CARDIAC PHYSIOLOGY. *Educ:* Colo State Univ, BS, 59; Univ Ill, MS, 61, PhD(mech eng), 64. *Prof Exp:* Res assoc surg, 65-66, assoc surg & physiol, 66-68, asst prof, 68-72, assoc prof surg & physiol, 72-79, PROF SURG & ASSOC PROF PHYSIOL & BIOPHYS, ALBERT EINSTEIN COL MED, 79- *Concurrent Pos:* NIH sr fel cardiovasc tech, Univ Wash, 64-65. *Mem:* Am Physiol Soc; Biomed Eng Soc; Am Soc Mech Eng; Cardiovasc Syst Dynamics Soc; Am Soc Artificial Internal Organs. *Res:* Cardiac dynamics, particularly left ventricular filling and mitral valve dynamics; cardiac dynamics; application of fluid mechanics, particularly turbulence to cardiovascular physiology; natural and artificial heart valves. *Mailing Add:* 38 Lakeside Dr New Rochelle NY 10801

YELLIN, HERBERT, b New York, NY, May 27, 35; m 63; c 5. HEALTH SCIENCES, EXPERIMENTAL NEUROLOGY. *Educ:* City Col New York, BA, 56; Univ Calif, Los Angeles, PhD(anat & neurophysiol), 66. *Prof Exp:* Cytologist, Div Labs, Cedars of Lebanon Hosp, Los Angeles, 57-58; cytologist radiation path, Armed Forces Inst Path, US Army, 58-60; staff fel exp neurol, Nat Inst Neurol Dis & Blindness, NIH, 66-68; res physiologist trophic nerve functions, Nat Inst Neurol Dis & Stroke, NIH, 68-73; res physiologist neuronal develop & regeneration, Nat Inst Neurol & Communicative Dis & Stroke, NIH, 73-76; grants assoc sci admin, div res grants, 76-77, prog dir, Nat Eye Inst, 77-78, HEALTH SCIENTIST ADMIN, NAT INST NEUROL & COMMUN DIS & STROKE, HIH, 78- *Concurrent Pos:* Lectr anat, Sch Med & Dent, Georgetown Univ, 67-75; councilman assembly scientists, Nat Inst Neurolog & Communicative Dis & Stroke, NIH, 73-75. *Mem:* Am Asn Anatomists; Am Physiol Soc; Soc Neurosci; NY Acad Sci. *Res:* Sensorimotor characteristics of posture and locomotion; interrelationships of neurons and skeletal muscle. *Mailing Add:* Grants Assocs Prog Div of Res Grants NIH Bethesda MD 20014

YELLIN, JOSEPH, b Tel Aviv, Israel, April 21, 38; US citizen; m 68; c 2. PHYSICS, ARCHAEOLOGY. *Educ:* Univ Del, BS & BA, 60; Univ Calif, Berkeley, PhD(physics), 65. *Prof Exp:* Teaching asst physics, Univ Calif, Berkeley, 60-62, res asst, 62-65, res physicist, Lawrence Berkeley Lab, 65-73; ASSOC PROF PHYSICS & ARCHAEOL, HEBREW UNIV, JERUSALEM, ISRAEL, 73- *Concurrent Pos:* Vis sr lectr, Hebrew Univ, 70-71; vis assoc prof, Univ Calif, Los Angeles, 78-79; sr res assoc, Nat Res Coun, Jet Propulsion Lab, Pasadena, Calif, 80-82. *Mem:* Am Phys Soc; NY Acad Sci. *Res:* Experimental atomic physics including optical pumping, atomic beams beam-foil-level-crossing spectroscopy; gamma-ray spectroscopy with application to element analysis; provenance of ancient ceramics through chemical fingerprinting employing gamma-ray spectroscopy. *Mailing Add:* Dept Physics Hebrew Univ Jerusalem Israel

YELLIN, STEVEN JOSEPH, b San Francisco, Calif, Dec 27, 41. EXPERIMENTAL HIGH ENERGY PHYSICS. *Educ:* Calif Inst Technol, BS, 63, PhD(physics), 71. *Prof Exp:* Physicist, Deutsches Elektronen-Synchrotron, 71-73; asst rpof & asst res physicist, 73-80, ASSOC RPOF RESIDENCE & ASSOC RES PHYSICIST, UNIV CALIF, SANTA BARBARA, 80- *Res:* Electromagnetic interactions in elementary particle physics. *Mailing Add:* Dept of Physics Univ of Calif Santa Barbara CA 93106

YELLIN, TOBIAS O, b Tel Aviv, Israel, Aug 22, 34; US citizen; m 66; c 3. BIOCHEMISTRY, PHARMACOLOGY. *Educ:* Philadelphia Col Pharm, BS, 59, MS, 62; Univ Del, PhD(chem), 66. *Prof Exp:* Sr scientist, Abbott Labs, Ill, 66-71; sr pharmacologist, Smith Kline & French Labs, Pa, 71-73; head gastroenterol sect, Rorer Res Labs, Pa, 73-75; mgr gastroentestinal pharmacol, ICI Americas Inc, Wilmington, Del, 75-81; RES DIR BIOPROD OPER, BECKMAN INSTRUMENTS, INC, PALO ALTO, CALIF, 81- *Concurrent Pos:* Vis instr pharmacol, Med Col Pa, 73-81. *Mem:* AAAS; Am Chem Soc; Am Soc Pharmacol & Exp Therapeut. *Res:* Gastrointestinal pharmacology and biochemistry; histamine and histamine antagonists; biology and chemistry of peptides. *Mailing Add:* 4 Waterford Way Wallingford PA 19086

YELLIN, WILBUR, b Passaic, NJ, Nov 1, 32; m 77; c 3. PHYSICAL MEASUREMENTS, SPECTROSCOPY. *Educ:* Rutgers Univ, BSc, 54; Cornell Univ, PhD, 62. *Prof Exp:* Chemist, Nat Starch Corp, 54; asst chem, Cornell Univ, 54-58, res asst, 58-59; sr res chemist, Ozalid Div, Gen Aniline & Film Corp, 59-62; res chemist, 62-70, SECT HEAD PHYSICAL SCI, PROCTER & GAMBLE CO, 70- *Mem:* AAAS; Soc Appl Spectros; Coblentz Soc; Am Chem Soc. *Res:* Application of spectroscopic and physical measurement techniques to chemical problems and structure determinations; structure and physical properties of stratum corneum; metal ion complexes, photochemistry; Raman, infrared, uvlvis and mass spectrometry. *Mailing Add:* Winton Hill Tech Ctr Procter & Gamble Co Cincinnati OH 45224

YELLOTT, JOHN I(NGLE), b Bel Air, Md, Oct 25, 08; m 34, 51; c 2. MECHANICAL ENGINEERING, SOLAR ENERGY. *Educ:* Johns Hopkins Univ, BS, 31, MME, 33. *Prof Exp:* Instr mech eng, Univ Rochester, 33-34; from instr to asst prof, Stevens Inst Technol, 34-40; prof & head dept, Ill Inst Technol, 40-43; dir, Inst Gas Technol, Chicago, 43-45; dir res locomotive develop comt, Bituminous Coal Res, Inc, 45-55; asst dir, Stanford Res Inst, 56-58; PRES, YELLOTT ENG ASSOCS, INC, 58-, DIR, YELLOTT SOLAR ENERGY LAB, 61- *Concurrent Pos:* Headmaster, Phoenix Country Day Sch, 66-72, dir develop, 72-73; consult, Manhattan Proj, 43-46; exec dir, Asn Appl Solar Energy, 56-58; mem, Nat Res Coun, 67-70; prof archit, Ariz State Univ, 73-79, emer prof, 79- *Honors & Awards:* Gold Medal, Soc Mech Engrs, 40. *Mem:* Fel AAAS; Am Soc Mech Engrs; Am Soc Heating, Refrig & Air-Conditioning Engrs. *Res:* Supersaturated steam; high pressure reducing valves; process for pulverizing and gasifying coal; coal-fired gas turbine for locomotives; solar energy utilization and control. *Mailing Add:* 901 W El Caminito Dr Phoenix AZ 85021

YELON, ARTHUR MICHAEL, b New York, NY, Apr 15, 34; m 58; c 2. SOLID STATE PHYSICS. *Educ:* Cornell Univ, BA, 55; Case Inst Technol, MS, 59, PhD(physics), 61. *Prof Exp:* Asst physics, Case Inst Technol, 55-57, instr, 57-61; assoc mem res staff, Res Ctr, Int Bus Mach Corp, 61-62, mem res staff, 62-63; mem res staff, Lab Electrostatics & Metal Phys, Grenoble, France, 63-66; assoc prof appl sci, Yale Univ, 66-72; assoc prof eng physics, 72-74, PROF ENG PHYSICS, POLYTECH SCH MONTREAL, 74- *Mem:* Am Phys Soc; Am Vacuum Soc; Am Asn Physics Teachers; Inst Elec & Electronics Eng; Can Asn Physicists. *Res:* ferromagnetism; surface physics; electron tunneling; electronic properties and degradation of polymers; amorphous silicon; photovoltaics. *Mailing Add:* Dept Eng Physics Post Box 6079 Sta A Montreal PQ H3C 3A7 Can

YELON, WILLIAM B, b Brooklyn, NY, Aug 23, 44; m 66; c 2. EXPERIMENTAL SOLID STATE PHYSICS. *Educ:* Haverford Col, BA, 65; Carnegie Mellon Univ, MS, 67, PhD(physics), 70. *Prof Exp:* Fel physics, Brookhaven Nat Lab, 70-72; res physicist, Inst Laue-Langevin, 72-75; SR RES SCIENTISLEADER NEUTRON SCATTERING, UNIV RES REACTOR, 75- & ASSOC PROF PHYSICS, UNIV MO-COLUMBIA, 75- *Concurrent Pos:* Mem, Neutron Diffraction Comn, Int Union Crystalography, 77-; ed, Neutron Diffraction Newsletter, 77- *Mem:* Am Phys Soc; Am Crystallog Asn. *Res:* Neutron scattering; studies of phase transitions; dynamics and statics of nearly one and two dimensional systems; gamma ray diffraction; crystallography. *Mailing Add:* Univ Mo Res Reactor Res Park Columbia MO 65211

YELTON, DAVID BAETZ, b Cincinnati, Ohio, Jan 16, 45. MICROBIOLOGY. *Educ:* Mass Inst Technol, BS, 66; Univ Mass, Amherst, MS, 69, PhD(microbiol), 71. *Prof Exp:* Instr cell biol, Med Sch, Univ Md, 72-73; asst prof, 73-80, ASSOC PROF MICROBIOL, WEST VA UNIV MED CTR, 80- *Mem:* Am Soc Microbiol; AAAS. *Res:* Tumor virology; cell biology. *Mailing Add:* Dept of Microbiol Med Ctr W Va Univ Morgantown WV 26506

YEMMA, JOHN JOSEPH, b Youngstown, Ohio, July 14, 33; m 78; c 7. CYTOCHEMISTRY, CELL BIOLOGY. *Educ:* Youngstown State Univ, BS, 61; George Peabody Col, MA, 65; Pa State Univ, PhD(cytochem), 71. *Prof Exp:* Instr biol, Pa State Univ, 65-71; assoc prof, 71-80, PROF CELL BIOL, YOUNGSTOWN STATE UNIV, 80- *Concurrent Pos:* Youngstown State Univ res grant, 72-76; NIH trainee, 75. *Mem:* AAAS; Am Bot Soc; Am Inst Biol Sci; Sigma Xi. *Res:* Developmental biochemistry of biomembranes during stages of the cell cycle. *Mailing Add:* Dept of Cell Biol Youngstown State Univ Youngstown OH 44555

YEN, BELINDA R S, b Szechuen, China, Sept 2, 42; US citizen. IMMUNOLOGY. *Educ:* Southern Ill Univ, Carbondale, BS, 62; Univ Ark, Fayetteville, MS, 66, PhD(immunol), 71. *Prof Exp:* Am Heart Asn fel, 71-72, Arthritis Found res fel, 72-73; res assoc clin immunol, Sch Med, Case Western Reserve Univ, 73-74; res fel, 74-77, PROJ SCIENTIST, CLEVELAND CLIN FOUND, 77- *Mem:* AAAS; NY Acad Sci; Am Soc Microbiol. *Res:* Clinical immunology; regulation of immune response; tumor immunology. *Mailing Add:* Cleveland Clin 9500 Euclid Ave Cleveland OH 44106

YEN, BEN CHIE, b Canton, China, Apr 14, 35. HYDROLOGY, HYDRAULICS. *Educ:* Nat Taiwan Univ, BS, 56; Univ Iowa, MS, 59, PhD(mech & hydraul), 65. *Prof Exp:* Civil engr, Chinese Army Engr Br, 57-58; jr engr, Water Resources Planning & Develop Comn, Taiwan, 58; res assoc fluid mech, Inst Hydraul Res, Univ Iowa, 60-64 & Princeton Univ, 64-66; from asst prof to assoc prof hydraul, 66-76, PROF CIVIL ENG, UNIV ILL, URBANA-CHAMPAIGN, 76- *Concurrent Pos:* Vis prof, Univ Karlsruhe, Ger, 74-75; vis res fel, Hydraul Res Sta, UK, 75; dir, Second Int Conf on Urban Storm Drainage, 81. *Mem:* Am Soc Civil Engrs; Am Geophys Union; Int Asn Hydraul Res. *Res:* Open-channel hydraulics; sediment transport and deposition; surface water hydrology; probabilistics hydrology; risk and reliability analysis; flood drainage. *Mailing Add:* Dept of Civil Eng Univ Ill 208 N Romine St Urbana IL 61801

YEN, BEN-TSENG, b Canton, China, Jan 19, 32; m 65; c 2. CIVIL ENGINEERING. *Educ:* Nat Taiwan Univ, BS, 55; Lehigh Univ, MS, 59, PhD(struct eng), 63. *Prof Exp:* Res asst civil eng, Fritz Lab, 57-60, res assoc, 60-64, from asst prof to assoc prof, 64-77, PROF CIVIL ENG, LEHIGH UNIV, 77- *Concurrent Pos:* Consult industs, 61- *Mem:* Am Soc Civil Engrs; Struct Stability Res Coun (secy, 66-69). *Res:* Mechanical properties of materials; behavior and strength of civil engineering structures; fatigue and fracture of materials and structures. *Mailing Add:* Dept of Civil Eng Fritz Lab 13 Lehigh Univ Bethlehem PA 18015

YEN, BING CHENG, b Shantung Province, China, June 13, 34; m 64; c 3. CIVIL ENGINEERING, SOIL MECHANICS. *Educ:* Nat Taiwan Univ, BS, 56; Univ Utah, PhD(civil eng), 63. *Prof Exp:* Found engr, Utah State Hwy Dept, 62-63; asst prof civil eng, Univ Utah, 63-64; from asst prof to assoc prof, 64-78, PROF CIVIL ENG, CALIF STATE UNIV, LONG BEACH, 78- *Concurrent Pos:* Consult, Dept Engrs, Los Angeles County, 65-70 & Woodward-Clyde Consults, 72-78; Geotech consult. *Mem:* Am Soc Civil Engrs. *Res:* Soil mechanics and foundation engineering; i slope stability; earthquake effects on soil engineering; marine geomechanics; rock mechanics. *Mailing Add:* Dept of Civil Eng Calif State Univ Long Beach CA 90840

YEN, CHEN-WAN LIU, b Tainan, Taiwan, Jan 26, 32; US citizen; m 58; c 2. AEROSPACE SCIENCE. *Educ:* Nat Taiwan Univ, BS, 54; Mass Inst Technol, PhD(physics), 64. *Prof Exp:* Tech staff space sci, KMS Technol, 68-72; MEM TECH STAFF SPACE SCI, JET PROPULSION LAB, CALIF INST TECHNOL, 72- *Mailing Add:* 867 Marymount Lane Claremont CA 91711

YEN, CHIN-LIEN, fluid mechanics, hydrodynamics, see previous edition

YEN, DAVID HSIEN-YAO, b Tsingtao, Shantung, Apr 18, 34; m 64; c 3. APPLIED MATHEMATICS, ENGINEERING MECHANICS. *Educ:* Nat Taiwan Univ, BS, 56; Mich State Univ, MS, 61; NY Univ, PhD(math), 66. *Prof Exp:* Asst prof civil eng & mech, Bradley Univ, 61-62; from asst prof to assoc prof, 65-72, PROF MECH & MATH, MICH STATE UNIV, 72- *Concurrent Pos:* Vis scientist, Inst Comp Appln Sci & Eng, NASA Langley Res Ctr, 74. *Mem:* Am Math Soc; Am Soc Mech Engrs; Soc Indust Appl Math; Am Phys Soc. *Res:* Analytical and numerical studies of linear and nonlinear wave phenomena in various continuous media; methods of applied mathematics. *Mailing Add:* Dept of Math Mich State Univ East Lansing MI 48824

YEN, ELIZABETH HSI, mathematical statistics, see previous edition

YEN, HOWARD HONG-YUANG, b Taipei, Taiwan, May 18, 37; m 64; c 2. MECHANICAL ENGINEERING. *Educ:* Nat Taiwan Univ, BS, 60; Ga Inst Technol, MS, 64, PhD(mech eng), 69. *Prof Exp:* Res engr, Heat Technol Lab, Huntsville, Ala, 63-66 & Northrop Corp, 66; sr res engr, Skidaway Inst Oceanog, Ga, 68-70; sr staff engr, Space Support Div, Sperry Rand Corp, 70-77; CHIEF ANAL, SOLAR SYSTS DIV, WYLE LABS, 77- *Mem:* Am Soc Mech Engrs. *Res:* Heat transfer; thermodynamics; fluid mechanics. *Mailing Add:* Wyle Labs Solar Systs Div 7800 Governors Dr W Huntsville AL 35807

YEN, I-KUEN, b Singapore, May 29, 30; US citizen; m 58; c 2. CHEMICAL ENGINEERING. *Educ:* Nat Taiwan Univ, BS, 54; Mass Inst Technol, SM, 56, ScD(chem eng), 60. *Prof Exp:* Chem engr, Crucible Steel Co, 59-61; res scientist pollution control, Am Standard Corp, 61-64; group leader eng, C F Braun & Co, 64-68; dir contract res, 68-78, DIR HEALTH, SAFETY & ENVIRON, OCCIDENTAL RES CORP, 78- *Concurrent Pos:* Adj prof, Newark Col Eng, 61-62 & Stevens Inst Technol, 63-64. *Mem:* Am Inst Chem Engrs; Am Chem Soc. *Res:* Inorganic chemicals processing; health and safety; pollution control; process development; contract research; research management. *Mailing Add:* 2100 SE Main St Irvine CA 92714

YEN, JAMES T(SING-SEN), b Shanghai, China, Dec 24, 29; US citizen; m 57; c 1. FLUID MECHANICS. *Educ:* Cheng Kung Univ, Taiwan, BS, 53; Univ Minn, MS, 56, PhD(fluid mech), 61. *Prof Exp:* From asst prof to assoc prof aeronaut eng, NC State Col, 61-64; assoc prof space sci, Cath Univ, 64-66; SR RES SCIENTIST, RES DEPT, GRUMMAN AIRCRAFT ENG CORP, 66- *Concurrent Pos:* Dir res proj plasma dynamics, US Air Force, 62-66; vis consult, Aerospace Corp, 64. *Res:* Kinetic theory of highly nonequilibrium plasma; plasma-microwave interaction; magneto-plasma-dynamics; plasma flow and heat transfer; geophysical plasma dynamics. *Mailing Add:* Res Dept 111 Stewart Ave Bethpage NY 11714

YEN, LEWIS C, physical chemistry, chemical engineering, see previous edition

YEN, NAI-CHYUAN, b Shaohsing, China, Apr 12, 36; US citizen; m 67; c 3. ACOUSTICS, ELECTRICAL ENGINEERING. *Educ:* Cheng Kung Univ, BS, 57; Univ RI, MS, 62; Harvard Univ, PhD(appl physics), 71. *Prof Exp:* Elec engr electronics, Bendix Corp, 62-66; res physicist acoust, Naval Underwater Systs Ctr, 72-79; ocean engr, US Coast Guard Res & Develop Ctr, 79-82; RES PHYSICIST, NAVAL RES LAB, 82- *Mem:* Acoust Soc Am; Inst Elec & Electronics Engrs; AAAS; Soc Photo-optical Instrumentation Engrs; NY Acad Sci. *Res:* Radiation, transmission and reception of underwater acoustic waves; noise generation mechanisms and control; non-linear phenomena and oscillations; signal processing; electronic and electro-optics instrumentation. *Mailing Add:* Naval Res Lab 4555 Overlook Ave SW Washington DC 20375

YEN, PETER KAI JEN, b China, Feb 10, 22. DENTISTRY, BIOPHYSICS. *Educ:* West China Union Univ, DDS, 47; Harvard Univ, DMD, 54. *Prof Exp:* Intern children's dent, Forsyth Dent Infirmary, 49-50; asst oral path, 54-57, instr dent med, 57-61, clin assoc, 61-67, asst prof orthod, 67-70, ASSOC PROF ORTHOD, SCH DENT MED, HARVARD UNIV, 70- *Concurrent Pos:* Fel orthod, Forsyth Dent Infirmary, 50-52 & 55-57; assoc orthop, Med Ctr, Boston Children's Hosp, 65-74, sr assoc, 74- *Mem:* Fel AAAS; Am Dent Asn; Am Asn Orthod; NY Acad Sci; Int Asn Dent Res. *Res:* Cranio-facial growth and development; bone dynamics. *Mailing Add:* Harvard Sch of Dent Med 188 Longwood Ave Boston MA 02115

YEN, S C YEN, b Peking, China, Feb 22, 27; m 58; c 3. REPRODUCTIVE ENDOCRINOLOGY. *Educ:* Chee-Loo Univ, China, BS, 49; Univ Hong Kong, MD, 54, DSc, 80; Am Bd Obstet & Gynec, dipl, 66; Am Bd Reproductive Endocrinol, cert, 73. *Prof Exp:* Intern med, Queen Mary Hosp, Hong Kong, 54-55; resident obstet & gynec, Johns Hopkins Hosp, 56-60; instr, Johns Hopkins Univ, 58-60; chief dept, Guam Mem Hosp, 60-62; asst prof, Sch Med, Case Western Reserve Univ, 62-67, assoc prof reprod biol, 67-70; assoc dir obstet, Univ Hosps of Cleveland, 68-70; PROF OBSTET & GYNEC, UNIV CALIF, SAN DIEGO, 70-, CHMN DEPT, 72- *Concurrent Pos:* Teaching & res fels, Harvard Med Sch, 62. *Mem:* Endocrine Soc; Am Diabetes Asn; Am Soc Gynec Invest (pres, 81); fel Am Col Obstet & Gynec; Asn Am Physicians. *Res:* Obstetrics and gynecology. *Mailing Add:* Dept of Reproductive Med Univ of Calif Sch of Med La Jolla CA 92093

YEN, TEH FU, b Kunming, China, Jan 9, 27; US citizen; m 59. ENVIRONMENTAL SCIENCE, BIOCHEMICAL ENGINEERING. *Educ:* Cent China Univ, BS, 47; WVa Univ, MS, 53; Va Polytech, PhD(org chem), 56. *Prof Exp:* Asst, Cent China Univ, 47-48, Yunnan Univ, 48-49 & WVa Univ, 50-53; sr res chemist, Res Div, Goodyear Tire & Rubber Co, 55-59; fel petrol chem, Mellon Inst, 59-65, sr fel, Carnegie-Mellon Univ, 65-68; assoc prof, Calif State Univ, Los Angeles, 68-69; assoc prof, 69-80, PROF BIOCHEM, DEPT MED, UNIV SOUTHERN CALIF, 80-, PROF, DEPT ENG, 70- *Mem:* Sr mem Am Chem Soc; Am Inst Physics; Am Inst Chem Engrs; Am Soc Artificial Internal Organs; fel Royal Soc Chem. *Res:* Structure of large molecules by physical methods; biogeoorganic chemistry; geomicrobiology, fossil fuels science and technology, asphaltenes; biochemical energy conversion, energy and environment; biomaterials; heavy metals in environments; new energy sources. *Mailing Add:* Dept Chem Eng University Park Los Angeles CA 90007

YEN, TERENCE TSIN TSU, b Shanghai, China, May 2, 37; m 64; c 3. BIOCHEMISTRY, GENETICS. *Educ:* Nat Taiwan Univ, BS, 58; Univ NC, PhD(biochem, genetics), 66. *Prof Exp:* RES SCIENTIST, RES LABS, ELI LILLY & CO, 65- *Mem:* AAAS; Sigma Xi; Am Soc Biol Chem; Am Chem Soc. *Res:* Biochemical defects and treatment of metabolic diseases in higher organisms, obesity, diabetes and hypertension. *Mailing Add:* Lilly Res Labs 307 E McCarty St Indianapolis IN 46285

YEN, WILLIAM MAO-SHUNG, b Nanking, China, Apr 5, 35; m 78; c 1. SOLID STATE PHYSICS. *Educ:* Univ Redlands, BS, 56; Washington Univ, PhD(physics), 62. *Prof Exp:* Res assoc physics, Washington Univ, 62 & Stanford Univ, 62-65; from asst prof to assoc prof physics, 65-72, PROF PHYSICS, UNIV WIS-MADISON, 72- *Concurrent Pos:* Consult cent res dept, Varian Assocs, Calif, 63-65; vis prof inst solid state physics, Univ Tokyo, 71-72; sr vis fel, Stanford Univ, 74-75; physicist, Lawrence Livermore Lab, 74-75, consult, 75-; vis prof, Univ Paris, 76; consult, Argonne Nat Lab, 77-; vis scientist, Harvard Univ, 79; J S Guggenheim fel, 79-80; vis fel, Australian Nat Univ, 80; vis prof, Univ Fed Pernambuco, Brazil, 80 & Univ Calif, Santa Barbera, 81. *Mem:* Fel AAAS; fel Am Phys Soc; fel Optical Soc Am. *Res:* Solid state spectroscopy; spectroscopy in magnetic materials; quantum electronics; laser spectroscopy; ultraviolet spectra of solids. *Mailing Add:* Dept of Physics Sterling Hall Univ of Wis Madison WI 53706

YEN, YIN-CHAO, b China, 27; US citizen; m 60; c 3. ENGINEERING PHYSICS, EARTH SCIENCES. *Educ:* Nat Taiwan Univ, BS, 51; Kans State Col, MS, 56; Northwestern Univ, PhD(chem eng), 60. *Prof Exp:* Chem engr, 60-62, res chem engr, 62-67, res phys scientist, 67-68, SUPVRY RES PHYS SCIENTIST, US ARMY COLD REGIONS RES & ENG LAB, 68- *Concurrent Pos:* From adj asst prof to adj assoc prof, Univ NH, 65-71 & vis prof, 71-74. *Honors & Awards:* Civilian Qual Increase Award, US Army Cold Regions Res & Eng Lab, 64, 65 & 71, Civilian Spec Act Award, 65, Meritorious Performance Award, 65, Outstanding Performance Award, 71. *Mem:* AAAS; Sigma Xi; Am Inst Chem Engrs. *Res:* Thermophysical properties of snow and ice; effect of density inversion and thermal instability phenomena associated with the ice-water systems and heat transfer characteristics in snow and ice involving phase change. *Mailing Add:* Phys Sci Br Res Div US Army Cold Regions Res & Eng Lab Hanover NH 03755

YEN, YOU-HSIN EUGENE, b Keelung, Taiwan, Oct 14, 50; m 3; c 1. FIELDS & WAVES, COMMUNICATION THEORY. *Educ:* Nat Chiao-Tung Univ, BSEE, 72; Marquette Univ, Wis, MSEE, 77; Univ Wis-Madison, PhD(microwave commun), 81. *Prof Exp:* Manufacture supvr, Tex Instruments Taiwan Br, 74; qual assurance engr, Continental Tel Taiwan Br, 74-75; MEM TECH STAFF, BELL LABS, 81- *Mem:* Sigma Xi; Inst Elec & Electronics Engrs. *Res:* Electromagnetic compatibility in communication engineering: electromagnetic interference testing, radio frequency design and statistical communication engineering. *Mailing Add:* 111B White St Eatontown NJ 07724

YENCHA, ANDREW JOSEPH, b Pa, July 3, 38; m 67. PHYSICAL CHEMISTRY, CHEMICAL PHYSICS. *Educ:* Univ Calif, Berkeley, BS, 63, Univ Calif, Los Angeles, PhD(chem), 68. *Prof Exp:* Res asst chem, Dow Chem Co, Calif, 60-62; res asst, Univ Calif, Berkeley, 62-63, teaching asst, Los Angeles, 64-65, res asst, 65-68; fel, Yale Univ, 68-70; asst prof, 70-76, ASSOC PROF, STATE UNIV NY ALBANY, 76- *Mem:* Am Soc Mass Spectroscopy; Am Inst Physics; Am Chem Soc; Int Am Photochem Soc. *Res:* Molecular beam, molecular spectroscopy and penning ionization electron spectroscopy. *Mailing Add:* Dept Chem & Physics State Univ of NY Albany NY 12222

YENDOL, WILLIAM G, b Pomona, Calif, Feb 22, 31; m 59; c 2. ENTOMOLOGY. *Educ:* Calif State Polytech Univ, BS, 53; Purdue Univ, MS, 57, PhD(entom), 64. *Prof Exp:* Tech rep agr chem, L H Butcher Chem Co, 58-59; entomologist, Lake States Forest Exp Sta, 63-65; assoc prof, 65-71, PROF ENTOM RES, PESTICIDE LAB, PA STATE UNIV, UNIVERSITY PARK, 71- *Concurrent Pos:* Consult, US/USSR, 78 & AID, 80. *Mem:* Entom Soc Am; Soc Invert Path; Int Orgn Biol Control; Am Inst Biol Sci; Sigma Xi. *Res:* Insect pathology; biological control; insect pest management; biochemistry. *Mailing Add:* Pesticide Lab Dept Entom Pa State Univ University Park PA 16802

YENISCAVICH, WILLIAM, b Girardville, Pa, June 30, 34; m 54; c 2. METALLURGICAL ENGINEERING. *Educ:* Drexel Inst Technol, BS, 57; Carnegie-Mellon Univ, MS, 62, PhD(metall eng), 63. *Prof Exp:* Engr, Bettis Atomic Power Lab, Westinghouse Elec Corp, 57-62 & 63-66; group leader welding eng, Mat Systs Div, Union Carbide Corp, 66-67, mgr eng sci, 67-69, mgr process eng, 69-71; mgr welding eng, 71-76, mgr mat control, 76-80, MGR WELDING ENG, BETTIS ATOMIC POWER LAB, WESTINGHOUSE ELEC CORP, 80- *Concurrent Pos:* Vis asst prof mat sci & metall eng, Purdue Univ, 67-68; chmn basic res subcomt, high alloys comt, Welding Res Coun, 68-71; mem bd dirs, Metal Properties Coun, 69-72. *Mem:* Am Welding Soc; Am Soc Metals; Am Inst Mining, Metall & Petrol Engrs. *Res:* Irradiation damage in reactor fuels, control rods and structural materials; causes of cracking during welding and effects of small cracks on service performance; solidification of metals. *Mailing Add:* Bettis Atomic Power Lab PO Box 79 West Mifflin PA 15122

YENNIE, DONALD ROBERT, b Paterson, NJ, Mar 4, 24; m 50; c 2. THEORETICAL HIGH ENERGY PHYSICS. *Educ:* Stevens Inst Technol, ME, 45; Columbia Univ, PhD(physics), 51. *Prof Exp:* Instr physics, Stevens Inst Technol, 46-47; mem, Inst Advan Study, 51-52; from instr to asst prof, Stanford, 52-57; from assoc prof to prof, Univ Minn, Minneapolis, 57-64; PROF PHYSICS, CORNELL UNIV, 64-, MEM STAFF, LAB NUCLEAR STUDIES, 77- *Concurrent Pos:* NSF sr fel, 60-61; mem prog adv comt, Stanford Linear Accelerator Ctr, 65-68, vis scientist, 70-71; vis prof, Univ Paris VI, 78-79; Guggenheim fel, 78-79. *Mem:* Am Phys Soc; AAAS. *Res:* Quantum field theory; theory of high energy electromagnetic interactions; theory of Lamb shift and hyperfine splitting; renormalization theory; infrared divergence in quantum electrodynamics. *Mailing Add:* Newman Lab Cornell Univ Ithaca NY 14853

YENSEN, ARTHUR ERIC, b Nampa, Idaho, Oct 13, 44; m 66. ECOLOGY. *Educ:* Col Idaho, BS, 66; Ore State Univ, MA, 71; Univ Ariz, PhD(zool), 73. *Prof Exp:* asst prof biol, Millsaps Col, 73-78; ASST PROF BIOL, BOISE STATE UNIV, 78- *Mem:* Ecol Soc Am; Soc Study Evolution; Am Soc Mammalogists; Cooper Ornith Soc; Br Ecol Soc. *Res:* Community structure including species diversity, competition, niche utilization, especially mammals; biosystematics and evolution of Throscidae. *Mailing Add:* Dept of Biol Boise State Univ Boise ID 83725

YENTSCH, CHARLES SAMUEL, b Louisville, Ky, Sept 13, 27. MARINE BIOLOGY. *Educ:* Univ Louisville, BS, 50; Fla State Univ, MS, 53. *Prof Exp:* Asst marine biol, Fla State Univ, 52-53; asst biol oceanog, Univ Wash, 53-55; res assoc marine ecol, Woods Hole Oceanog Inst, 55-67; assoc prof oceanog, Nova Univ, 67-69, assoc prof marine biol, 69-71; prof marine sci & dir marine sta, Univ Mass, Amherst, 71-77; EXEC DIR, BIGELOW LAB OCEAN SCI, BOOTHBAY HARBOR, 77- *Mem:* Am Soc Limnol & Oceanog; Phycol Soc Am. *Res:* Marine phytoplankton ecology. *Mailing Add:* Off Exec Dir Bigelow Lab Ocean Sci Boothbay Harbor ME 04575

YEO, YUNG KEE, b Kyungbuk, Korea, Apr 24, 38; US citizen; m 64; c 2. SEMI-CONDUCTOR PHYSICS, LOW-TEMPERATURE PHYSICS. *Educ:* Seoul Nat Univ, BS, 61; Univ Southern Calif, PhD(physics), 72. *Prof Exp:* Res asst, Univ Southern Calif, 69-72, res assoc, 72; physicist, Develco Inc, 73-74; res assoc, Univ Ore, 74-77; resident scientist, Avionics Lab, Wright-Patterson AFB, 77-78; sr physicist, Systs Res Lab, 78-80; RES SCIENTIST, UNIVERSAL ENERGY SYSTS, 80- *Concurrent Pos:* Adj lectr, Air Force Inst Technol, 81. *Mem:* Am Phys Soc; Korean Scientists &

Engrs Asn Am; Asn Korean Physicist Am. *Res:* Ion-implantation techniques used for fabrication of electronic devices or opto-electronic applications; electrical properties of various ion-implanted compound semiconductors such as gallium arsenic and indium phosphorus. *Mailing Add:* 3646 Olde Willow Dr Dayton OH 45431

YEOMAN, LYNN CHALMERS, b Evanston, Ill, May 17, 43; m 66; c 3. BIOCHEMISTRY, IMMUNOLOGY. *Educ:* DePauw Univ, BA, 65; Univ Ill, Champaign, PhD(biochem), 70. *Prof Exp:* From instr to asst prof, 72-76, ASSOC PROF PHARMACOL, BAYLOR COL MED, 76- *Concurrent Pos:* NIH training grant & univ fel, Baylor Col Med, 70-72; prin investr, Cancer Prog Proj grant, 73- *Mem:* Am Asn Cancer Res; Am Soc Biol Chemists; Am Chem Soc; Sigma Xi; Tissue Cult Asn. *Res:* Structural and physical chemistry of the proteins of the nucleus and the nucleolus; non-histone chromosomal proteins and gene regulation; tumor markers. *Mailing Add:* Dept of Pharmacol Baylor Col of Med Houston TX 77030

YEOMANS, DONALD KEITH, b Rochester, NY, May 3, 42; m 70; c 1. ASTRONOMY. *Educ:* Middlebury Col, BS, 64; Univ Md, MS, 67, PhD(astron), 70. *Prof Exp:* Sr math analyst astron, Bendix Field Eng Corp, 70-72; tech supvr, Comput Sci Corp, 72-75; SR ENGR ASTRON, JET PROPULSION LAB, CALIF INST TECHNOL, 76- *Concurrent Pos:* Fel, Univ Md, 70; mem, NASA's Comets & Asteroids Sci Working Group, 74-82; discipline specialist astrometry, Int Halley Watch. *Mem:* Int Astron Union; Am Astron Soc; Hist Sci Soc. *Res:* Comet and asteroid orbit determination; interplanetary mission analysis; celestial mechanics; history of science. *Mailing Add:* 833 Chehalem Rd La Canada CA 91011

YEOWELL, DAVID ARTHUR, b London, Eng, Jan 3, 37; m 64. DRUGS. *Educ:* Bristol Univ, BSc, 58, PhD, 61. *Prof Exp:* Swiss Nat Fund fel org chem, Univ Zurich, 61-62; Imp Chem Indust res fel biogenetics, Univ Liverpool, 62-64; sr org chemist, Wellcome Res Labs, 64-68, sr develop chemist, Chem Develop Labs, 68-71, head develop res, 71-73, mgr chem develop labs, 73-81, DIR DEVELOP LABS, BURROUGHS WELLCOME CO, 81- *Mem:* Am Chem Soc; The Chem Soc. *Res:* Application of organic, physical and analytical chemical knowledge to devising economic and practical chemical and dosage form production scale processes for pharmaceuticals. *Mailing Add:* Burroughs Wellcome Co 3030 Cornwallis Rd Research Triangle Park NC 27709

YERANSIAN, JAMES A, b Chicago, Ill, Apr 8, 28; m 50; c 5. ANALYTICAL CHEMISTRY. *Educ:* Cornell Univ, BA, 48; Adelphi Univ, MS, 55. *Prof Exp:* Chemist, Nat Dairy Res Labs, Inc, 48-55; assoc chem, 55-58, proj leader food res, 58-60, sr chemist, 60-64, group leader coffee res, 64-65, sr group leader, 65-66, sr group leader, Flavor & Prod Develop, 66-68, SUPVR CORP ANAL LAB, FLAVOR & PROD DEVELOP, GEN FOODS CORP RES, 68- *Mem:* AAAS; Am Chem Soc. *Res:* Food analysis; coffee technology; analytical instrumentation and automation. *Mailing Add:* 25 Robin St Pearl River NY 10965

YERAZUNIS, STEPHEN, b Pittsfield, Mass, Aug 21, 22; m 54; c 2. CHEMICAL ENGINEERING. *Educ:* Rensselaer Polytech Inst, BChE, 47, MChE, 48, DChE, 52. *Prof Exp:* Engr, Manhattan Proj, Oak Ridge, Tenn, 43-46 & Gen Elec Co, Mass, 47; from instr to assoc prof chem eng, 48-63, assoc dean, Sch Eng, 66-79, PROF CHEM ENG, RENSSELAER POLYTECH INST, 63- *Concurrent Pos:* Consult, Knolls Atomic Power Lab, NY, 56-72, NY State Dept Ment Hyg, 68-72 & Jet Propulsion Lab, 77-78. *Mem:* Fel Am Inst Chem Engrs; Am Soc Eng Educ. *Res:* Mass and heat transfer; vapor-liquid equilibrium; activation of radio-nuclides and their transport; appraisal of electrical energy alternatives; guidance of an autonomous planetary rover. *Mailing Add:* Sch of Eng Rensselaer Polytech Inst Troy NY 12181

YERBY, ALONZO SMYTHE, b Augusta, Ga, Oct 14, 21; m 43; c 3. PUBLIC HEALTH, HEALTH ADMINISTRATION. *Educ:* Univ Chicago, BS, 41; Meharry Med Col, MD, 46; Harvard Univ, MPH, 48; Am Bd Prev Med, dipl, 53. *Hon Degrees:* DSc, Meharry Med Col, 77. *Prof Exp:* Asst to dir food res inst, Univ Chicago, 42-43; intern, Coney Island Hosp, Brooklyn, NY, 46-47; health officer-in-training, New York City Dept Health, 47-48; field med officer, UN Int Refugee Orgn, US Zone, Ger, 48-49, dep chief med affairs, Off US High Comnr Ger, 49-50; assoc med dir, Health Ins Plan Greater New York, 50-54, consult, 54; regional med consult, Off Voc Rehab, 54-57; dep comnr med affairs, NY State Dept Soc Welfare, 57-60; exec dir med servs, New York City Dept Health & med welfare adminr, Dept Welfare, 60-65 & coordr welfare servs, Dept Hosps, 64-65, comnr, Dept Hosps, 65-66; head dept, 66-75, PROF HEALTH SERV ADMIN, SCH PUB HEALTH, HARVARD UNIV, 66- *Concurrent Pos:* Staff physician, Sidney Hillman Health Ctr, New York, 51-53; adj asst prof admin med, Sch Pub Health, Columbia Univ, 60-66; lectr, Yale Univ, 65-66; mem, Surg Gen Adv Comt Urban Health Affairs, USPHS & task force on orgn community health servs, Nat Comn Health Servs, 63-66; mem summer study sci & urban develop, Dept Housing & Urban Develop & President's Off Sci & Tech, 66; adv comt on rels with state health agencies, Dept Health, Educ & Welfare, 66; mem, President's Nat Adv Comn Health Manpower, 66-67; mem nat pub health training coun, NIH, 69-71, consult, 71-, mem bd adv, John E Fogarty Int Ctr, 72-76, vis prof, 75; WHO consult health manpower training, Govt Sierra Leone, WAfrica, 70; found mem, Inst Med of Nat Acad Sci, mem Coun, 70-73; adv, Ministry Health Kuwait, 76; mem, Nat Prof Standards Rev Coun, OASH, HEW, 77-; dep asst, Sect Health for Intergovt Affairs & asst surg gen, US Dept Health & Human Serv/USPHS, 80-81. *Mem:* Fel Am Pub Health Asn; fel Am Col Prev Med; Am Pub Welfare Asn; NY Acad Med. *Res:* Health service administration; public health practice. *Mailing Add:* Dept Health Serv Admin Harvard Univ Sch Pub Health Boston MA 02115

YERG, DONALD G, b Lewistown, Pa, Mar 4, 25; m 48; c 3. METEOROLOGY. *Educ:* Pa State Univ, BS, 46, MS, 47, PhD(meteorol), 53. *Prof Exp:* Asst agr eng, Univ Calif, 47-48; instr math, Univ Alaska, 48-50; consult, Tech Info Div, Library of Cong, 51-52; asst ionosphere res, Pa State Univ, 52-53; lectr physics, Univ PR, 53-55; assoc prof, 55-60, PROF PHYSICS & DEAN GRAD SCH, MICH TECHNOL UNIV, 60- *Mem:* AAAS; Am Meteorol Soc; Int Soc Biometeorology; Am Geophys Union. *Res:* Meteorology of ionospheric regions; micrometeorology; biometeorology. *Mailing Add:* Grad Sch Mich Technol Univ Houghton MI 49931

YERG, RAYMOND A, b Jersey City, NJ, Apr 4, 17; m 46; c 3. AEROSPACE MEDICINE, OCCUPATIONAL MEDICINE. *Educ:* Seton Hall Col, BS, 38; Georgetown Univ, MD, 42; Harvard Univ, MPH, 55. *Prof Exp:* Comdr, 1st Missile Div, Vandenberg AFB, US Air Force, Calif, 59-61, dep bioastronaut Air Force Eastern Test Range, 61-65, comdr, Aerospace Med Res Lab, Wright-Patterson AFB, Ohio, 65-68, chief sci & tech div, Hq US Air Force, The Pentagon, 68-72; corp med dir, Am Can Co, 72-; corp med dir, Perlcin-Elmer Corp, 78-80; CORP MED DIR, AM STANDARD INC, 80- *Honors & Awards:* AMA Spec Aerospace Med Citation, 62; Air Force Asn Meritorious Award Support Mgt, 64. *Mem:* Fel Aerospace Med Asn; fel Am Col Prev Med; NY Acad Sci; fel Am Acad Occup Med; fel Am Occup Med Asn. *Mailing Add:* 160 Eden Rd Stamford CT 06907

YERGANIAN, GEORGE, b New York, NY, June 14, 23; m 50; c 2. BIOLOGY. *Educ:* Mich State Univ, BS, 47; Harvard Univ, PhD(biol), 50. *Prof Exp:* Instr bot, Univ Minn, 50-51; AEC fel, Brookhaven Nat Lab, 51-52 & Boston Univ, 52-53; USPHS res fel, Boston Univ & Children's Cancer Res Found, 53-54; res assoc, Children's Cancer Res Found, Children's Hosp Med Ctr, 54-78; res assoc path, Harvard Univ, 54-78; chief, Lab Cytogenetics & Esp Carcinogenesis, Sidney Farber Cancer Inst, 56-78; PROF, INST ENVIRON BIOMED SCI, NORTHEASTERN UNIV, 78- *Honors & Awards:* Prof Dikran H Kabakjian Sci Award, Armenian Students Asn, 77. *Mem:* Genetics Soc Am; Tissue Culture Asn; Am Soc Human Genetics; Am Asn Cancer Res; Am Soc Cell Biologists. *Res:* Mammalian cytogenetics with emphasis on dwarf species of hamsters. *Mailing Add:* Northeastern Univ 360 Huntington Ave Boston MA 02115

YERGER, RALPH WILLIAM, b Reading, Pa, July 31, 22; m 54; c 4. SYSTEMATIC ICHTHYOLOGY. *Educ:* Pa State Univ, BS, 43, MS, 47; Cornell Univ, PhD(zool), 50. *Prof Exp:* Teacher high sch, Pa, 43; instr biol, Pa State Univ, 47-48; instr nature study, Reading Mus, 48; from asst prof to assoc prof zool, 50-61, actg head dept, 53-55, assoc chmn undergrad studies, 75-77, assoc dean, Col Arts & Sci, 77-78, actg dean, Col Arts & Sci, 78-79, PROF BIOL, FLA STATE UNIV, 61- *Mem:* Am Soc Ichthyologists & Herpetologists; Am Inst Biol Scientist; Am Fisheries Soc. *Res:* Taxonomy, ecology and distribution of fresh and salt water fishes of the southeastern United States, Central America and the Caribbean. *Mailing Add:* Col of Arts & Sci Fla State Univ Tallahassee FL 32306

YERGEY, ALFRED L, III, b Philadelphia, Pa, Sept 17, 41; m 63; c 3. ION OPTICS, CHEMICAL KINETICS. *Educ:* Muhlenberg Col, BS, 63; Pa State Univ, PhD(chem), 67. *Prof Exp:* Res fel chem, Rice Univ, 67-69; chemist, Esso Res & Eng Co, NJ, 69-71; sr scientist, Sci Res Instruments Corp, 71-77; RES CHEMIST, NAT INST CHILD HEALTH & HUMAN DEVELOP, NIH, 77- *Mem:* AAAS; Am Chem Soc; Air Pollution Control Asn. *Res:* Ion/electron optics; chemical ionization kinetics; applications of mass spectrometry; heterogeneous reaction kinetics; non-isothermal method; stable isotope applications to clinical situations; quadrupole mass spectrometry. *Mailing Add:* NIH Bldg 6 Rm 136 Bethesda MD 20205

YERGIN, PAUL FLOHR, b New York, NY, Apr 21, 23; m 47; c 2. NUCLEAR PHYSICS. *Educ:* Union Univ, NY, BS, 44; Columbia Univ, MA, 49, PhD, 53. *Prof Exp:* Asst electronics res, Gen Elec Co, NY, 42; asst gen physics lab, Union Univ, NY, 42-43; physicist radiation lab, Columbia Univ, 44-45, mem sci staff, 45-52; instr physics, Univ Pa, 52-55, asst prof, 55-56; from asst prof to assoc prof, 56-74, PROF PHYSICS, RENSSELAER POLYTECH INST, 74- *Concurrent Pos:* Res affiliate, Lab Nuclear Sci 80-82. *Mem:* Am Phys Soc; Am Asn Physics Teachers; Sigma Xi; Am Asn Univ Profs. *Res:* Photonuclear reactions; neutron cross sections; photopron reactions. *Mailing Add:* Dept of Physics Rensselaer Polytech Inst Troy NY 12181

YERICK, ROGER EUGENE, b Kingsville, Tex, July 6, 32. ANALYTICAL CHEMISTRY. *Educ:* Tex Col Arts & Indust, BS, 53. *Prof Exp:* Res asst anal chem, Iowa State Univ, 53-57; asst prof chem, Tex Col Arts & Indust, 57-58; from asst prof to assoc prof, 58-65, PROF CHEM, LAMAR UNIV, 65-, DEAN COL SCI, 74- *Concurrent Pos:* Educ consult, Spec Training Div, Oak Ridge Assoc Univs, 62- *Mem:* AAAS; Am Chem Soc. *Res:* Analytical chemistry of chelates; analytical radiochemistry; analytical applications of liquid scintillation counting techniques. *Mailing Add:* Dept of Chem Lamar Univ Beaumont TX 77705

YERKES, WILLIAM D(ILWORTH), JR, b Wilkes Barre, Pa, May 29, 22; m 47; c 3. ENVIRONMENTAL SCIENCES. *Educ:* State Col Wash, BS, 48, PhD(plant path), 52. *Prof Exp:* Asst, State Col Wash, 48-52; asst plant pathologist, Mex Agr Prog, Rockefeller Found, 52-56, assoc plant pathologist, 56-60; microbiologist, Pioneering Res Lab, Kimberly-Clark Corp, 60-72; chmn, Dept Environ Sci, 72-79, MEM STAFF, SCH HEALTH SCI, GRAND VALLEY STATE COL, 80- *Mem:* Am Soc Civil Engrs; Water Pollution Control Fedn; Nat Environ Health Asn. *Res:* Ecology of water pollution; effects of pollutants on aquatic biota; solid and hazardous waste management; food sanitation. *Mailing Add:* Dept of Environ Sci CAS Grand Valley State Col Allendale MI 49401

YERMANOS, DEMETRIOS M, b Thessaloniki, Greece, June 29, 21; US citizen; m 55; c 3. GENETICS, PLANT BREEDING. *Educ:* Univ Thessaloniki, MS, 47; Iowa State Univ, MS, 52; Univ Calif, Davis, PhD(genetics), 60. *Prof Exp:* Agronomist, UN Relief & Rehab Admin, Greece, 45-47 & Econ Coop Admin, 53-55; asst specialist, Univ Calif, Davis, 56-60; from asst prof to assoc prof agron, 61-72, vchmn dept plant sci, 72-74, PROF AGRON, UNIV CALIF, RIVERSIDE, 72- *Concurrent Pos:* Res grants, NSF & USPHS, 63-65, Dept Health, Educ & Welfare, 71-74. *Mem:* Am Soc Agron. *Res:* Genetics and plant breeding of oil crops. *Mailing Add:* Dept of Plant Sci Univ of Calif Riverside CA 92502

YESAIR, DAVID WAYNE, b Newbury, Mass, Sept 9, 32; m 54; c 3. BIOCHEMISTRY. *Educ:* Univ Mass, BS, 54; Cornell Univ, PhD(biochem), 58. *Prof Exp:* Asst biochem, Cornell Univ, 55-57, res assoc, 58; res biochemist, Lederle Labs Div, Am Cyanamid Co, 59-61; NSF fel, Reading, Eng, 61-62; consult biochemist, 62-74, DIR BIOMOLECULAR SCI, ARTHUR D LITTLE, INC, 77- *Concurrent Pos:* Nat Cancer Inst spec res award, Inst Org Chem, Gif-sur-Yvette, France, 71-72; lectr, Mass Inst Technol, 72- *Mem:* Am Chem Soc; NY Acad Sci; Am Asn Cancer Res; Am Soc Pharmacol & Exp Therapeut; fel Am Inst Chemists. *Res:* Lipid biochemistry; cancer, obesity and diabetes; metabolism and mode of action of drugs affecting lipid metabolism; isolation, characterization and metabolic action of biologically active agents; development of drug delivery systems. *Mailing Add:* Biomolecular Sci Arthur D Little Inc Acorn Park Cambridge MA 02140

YESINOWSKI, JAMES PAUL, b LaSalle, Ill, Mar 22, 50. PHYSICAL CHEMISTRY, INORGANIC CHEMISTRY. *Educ:* Univ Ill, Urbana, BS, 71; Univ Cambridge, PhD(chem), 74. *Prof Exp:* Res assoc phys chem, Mass Inst Technol, 74-76; STAFF SCIENTIST, MIAMI VALLEY LABS, PROCTER & GAMBLE CO, 76- *Concurrent Pos:* Am Cancer Soc fel, 76. *Res:* High resolution NMR of solids; NMR studies of calcium phosphate chemistry related to biological mineralization; nuclear magnetic resonance spectroscopy of inorganic complexes, surfactant, phospholipid and liquid crystalline systems. *Mailing Add:* Miami Valley Labs PO Box 39175 Cincinnati OH 45247

YESKE, RONALD A, b Wisconsin Rapids, Wis, Oct 28, 46; m 68; c 1. MATERIALS SCIENCE ENGINEERING. *Educ:* Marquette Univ, BME, 68; Northwestern Univ, PhD(mat sci), 73. *Prof Exp:* Asst prof metall eng, Univ Ill, Urbana, 74-78; mgr corrosion res, Res & Develop Ctr, Westinghouse, 78-82; SR RES ASSOC & ASSOC PROF CORROSION, INST PAPER CHEM, 82- *Mem:* Nat Asn Corrosion Engrs; Am Soc Metals. *Res:* Mechanisms of corrosion, corrosion-assisted cracking and fatigue crack propagation; materials performance in power plant materials; materials for the pulp and paper industry. *Mailing Add:* Inst Paper Chem PO Box 1039 Appleton WI 54912

YESNER, RAYMOND, b Columbus, Ga, Apr 18, 14; m 47; c 3. PATHOLOGY. *Educ:* Harvard Univ, AB, 35; Tufts Col, MD, 41; Yale Univ, MA, 72. *Prof Exp:* Intern & res, Beth Israel Hosp, Boston, Mass, 41-44; pathologist & chief lab serv, Vet Admin Hosp, Newington, 47-53; from asst clin prof to assoc clin prof, Med Sch, Yale Univ, 49-64, assoc prof, 64-72, assoc dean, chief pathologist, Vet Admin Hosp, West Haven, 74-77; PROF PATH, MED SCH, YALE UNIV, 72-; DIR ANATOMIC PATH, VET ADMIN HOSP, WEST HAVEN, 77- *Concurrent Pos:* Consult pathologist, Coop Study of Prostate, Vet Admin, chmn path panel, Lung Cancer Chemother Study Group, 58-, mem path res eval comt, sr physician, 71-74; pathologist & chief lab serv, Vet Admin Hosp, West Haven, 53-74, chief staff, 69-74; chmn, WHO Lung Cancer Comt, Geneva, 77. *Mem:* AMA; Am Asn Path & Bact; Col Am Path; Int Acad Path. *Res:* Changes in blood viscosity; liver, lung and gastrointestinal disease; carcinoma of prostate and bladder. *Mailing Add:* Vet Admin Hosp W Spring St West Haven CT 06516

YESSIK, MICHAEL JOHN, b Webster, Mass, Nov 22, 41; m 70. SOLID STATE PHYSICS. *Educ:* Williams Col, BA, 62; Syracuse Univ, PhD(solid state sci), 66; Univ Cambridge, MA, 67. *Prof Exp:* NATO fel, Cavendish Lab, Univ Cambridge, 66-67, NSF fel, 67-68; sr res scientist physics, Sci Res Staff, Ford Motor Co, 68-75; mgr process develop, 75-77, mgr new prod develop, 77-80, DIR RES & DEVELOP, PHOTON SOURCES, INC, 80- *Mem:* Am Soc Metals; Sigma Xi; AAAS; Am Phys Soc; Inst Elec & Electronics Engrs. *Res:* Electronic and magnetic properties of metals and alloys; physical properties of high temperature ceramics; high-power gas laser development; materials processing using high-power lasers. *Mailing Add:* Photon Sources Inc 4651 Platt Rd Ann Arbor MI 48104

YETT, FOWLER REDFORD, b Johnson City, Tex, Oct 18, 19; m 45; c 3. APPLIED MATHEMATICS. *Educ:* Univ Tex, BS, 43, MA, 52; Iowa State Univ, PhD(appl math), 55. *Prof Exp:* Res chemist & chem engr, Manhattan Proj, 43-45; owner camera supply co, 46-49; teaching fel, Univ Tex, 49-52; instr math, Iowa State Univ, 52-55; asst prof, Long Beach State Col, 55-56 & Univ Tex, 56-65; chmn dept math, 65-68, PROF MATH, UNIV SOUTH ALA, 65- *Mem:* Am Math Soc; Math Asn Am. *Res:* Nonlinear differential equations. *Mailing Add:* Dept Math Univ South Ala Mobile AL 36688

YEUNG, EDWARD SZESHING, b Hong Kong, Feb 17, 48; m 71; c 1. ANALYTICAL CHEMISTRY, PHYSICAL CHEMISTRY. *Educ:* Cornell Univ, AB, 68; Univ Calif, Berkeley, PhD(chem), 72. *Prof Exp:* From instr to asst prof, 72-77, assoc prof, 77-81, PROF CHEM, IOWA STATE UNIV, 81- *Concurrent Pos:* Sloan Found fel, 74. *Mem:* Am Chem Soc; NAm Photochem Soc. *Res:* Pollution monitoring; high resolution spectroscopy; photochemistry. *Mailing Add:* Dept of Chem Iowa State Univ Ames IA 50011

YEUNG, KATHERINE LU, b Shanghai, China, July 28, 43; US citizen; m 68; c 2. CANCER, PHARMACOLOGY. *Educ:* Univ Houston, BS, 65, MS, 68. *Prof Exp:* Res asst, 68-75, res assoc, 75-80, ASST PHRAMACOLOGIST, CANCER CHEMOTHERAPY, UNIV TEX SYST CANCER CTR, 80- *Mem:* Sigma Xi; NY Acad Sci; Am Soc Pharm & Exp Therapeut; Am Asn Cancer Res. *Res:* Cancer chemotherapy; metabolism and distribution of antitumor agents in patients and experimental animals. *Mailing Add:* Univ Tex Syst Cancer Ctr M D Anderson Hosp & Tumor Inst Houston TX 77030

YEUNG, PATRICK PUI-HANG, b Kweiyang, China, Sept 26, 42; US citizen; m 70; c 1. ORGANIC CHEMISTRY, TEXTILE CHEMISTRY. *Educ:* Auburn Univ, BSc, 67; Ga Inst Technol, PhD(org chem), 75. *Prof Exp:* Res chemist dyes, Toms River Chem Corp, Ciba-Geigy Corp, 75-80; MEM STAFF, AM COLOR & CHEM CORP, 80- *Mem:* Am Chem Soc; Am Asn Textile Chemists & Colorists; AAAS. *Res:* Dyes and chemicals. *Mailing Add:* Am Color & Chem Corp Mt Vernon St Lock Haven PA 17745

YEUNG, REGINALD SZE-CHIT, b Hong Kong, Apr 30, 32; US citizen; m 66; c 1. CHEMICAL ENGINEERING, CHEMISTRY. *Educ:* Univ London, BSc, 54; Mass Inst Technol, SM, 59, ScD(chem eng), 61. *Prof Exp:* Engr, Cabot Corp, 61-63; ENGR, SHELL OIL CO, HOUSTON, 64- *Mem:* Am Chem Soc; Am Inst Chem Engrs. *Res:* Process development and design; reactor design; flame reactor design. *Mailing Add:* 10607 Creektree Dr Houston TX 77070

YEUNG, SHIU FONG, applied mathematics, see previous edition

YEVICH, JOSEPH PAUL, b McKees Rocks, Pa, Sept 20, 40; m 64; c 2. ORGANIC CHEMISTRY, MEDICINAL CHEMISTRY. *Educ:* Carnegie-Mellon Univ, BS, 62, MS, 67, PhD(org chem), 69. *Prof Exp:* Chemist, Gulf Res & Develop Corp, 62-65; sr scientist, 69-74, sr investr, 74-76, SR RES ASSOC, MEAD JOHNSON & CO, 76- *Mem:* AAAS; Am Chem Soc; Sigma Xi. *Res:* Design and synthesis of potential medicinal agents. *Mailing Add:* 8366 Birch Dr N Newburgh IN 47630

YEVICH, PAUL PETER, b Berwick, Pa, June 16, 24. HISTOPATHOLOGY. *Educ:* Pa State Univ, BA, 49. *Prof Exp:* Histologist chem warfare lab med directorate, Army Chem Ctr, US Dept Defense, 50-54, histopathologist, 54-60; res histopathologist physiol sect, Div Occup Health, US Dept Health, Educ & Welfare, 61-66; res biologist, Invert Sect, 67-71, RES TEAM LEADER, INVERT SECT, ENVIRON RES LAB, ENVIRON PROTECTION AGENCY, 71- *Mem:* Soc Invert Path. *Res:* Comparative histology and pathology; toxic effects of various compounds on cells and tissues of various species of animals; invertebrate histology and effects of toxic compounds on invertebrates; histopathologic effects of oil pollutants metals, organics and sewage sludge on marine life. *Mailing Add:* Environ Res Labs South Ferry Rd Narragansett RI 02882

YEVICK, GEORGE JOHANNUS, b Berwick, Pa, Apr 24, 22; m 45. PHYSICS. *Educ:* Mass Inst Technol, BSc, 42, DSc(physics), 47. *Hon Degrees:* MEng, Stevens Inst Technol, 58. *Prof Exp:* Staff mem, Radiation Lab, Mass Inst Technol, 44-46; from asst prof to assoc prof, 48-57, PROF PHYSICS, STEVENS INST TECHNOL, 57-, PROF ENG PHYSICS, 77- *Mem:* Am Phys Soc; Soc Photo-Optical Instrument Engr; NY Acad Sci. *Res:* Theory of elementary particles; dynamical theory of many interacting particles; causal theory of quantum mechanics; control of thermonuclear fusion. *Mailing Add:* Dept of Physics Stevens Inst of Technol Hoboken NJ 07030

YEZ, MARTIN S(IMON), b Chicago, Ill, Apr 25, 20; m 46; c 1. MECHANICAL ENGINEERING, AERONAUTICAL ENGINEERING. *Educ:* Ill Inst Technol, BSME, 46; DePaul Univ, MA, 51. *Prof Exp:* Eng draftsman, Pullman Standard Car Mfg Co, 46; chief power engr, Commonwealth Edison Co, 47-49; prof eng, Wright Br, Chicago City Jr Col, 50-51; eng designer, Northrop Aircraft Co, 51-54; PROF ENG, EL CAMINO COL, 54- *Mem:* Am Cong Surv & Mapping. *Res:* Drafting room practices; surveying; geology; plant propagation. *Mailing Add:* 4029 Via Larga Vista Palos Verdes Estates CA 90274

YFF, PETER, b Chicago, Ill, Mar 8, 24; m 51; c 4. MATHEMATICS. *Educ:* Roosevelt Univ, BS, 47; Univ Chicago, MS, 48; Univ Ill, PhD(math), 57. *Prof Exp:* Lectr math, Roosevelt Univ, 48-50; asst prof, Am Univ Beirut, 51-55, chmn dept, 52-55; asst, Univ Ill, 55-57; asst prof, Fresno State Col, 57-58; assoc prof, 58-64, PROF MATH, AM UNIV BEIRUT, 64- *Mem:* Am Math Soc; Math Asn Am; Edinburgh Math Soc. *Res:* Theory of groups; projective and Euclidean geometries. *Mailing Add:* Dept of Math Am Univ of Beirut Beirut Lebanon

YGUERABIDE, JUAN, b Laredo, Tex, Oct 9, 35; m 56; c 4. BIOCHEMISTRY, BIOPHYSICS. *Educ:* St Mary's Univ, Tex, BS, 57; Univ Notre Dame, PhD(phys chem), 62. *Prof Exp:* Res assoc, Radiation Lab, Univ Notre Dame, 61-63; mem res staff, Sandia Corp, NMex, 63-68; res assoc biochem, Stanford Univ, 68-69; lectr & res assoc biochem & biophys, Yale Univ, 69-72; ASSOC PROF BIOL, UNIV CALIF, SAN DIEGO, 72- *Concurrent Pos:* Fel, Radiation Lab, Univ Notre Dame, 62-63; consult prof chem, Univ NMex, 66-68; sci consult, Sandia Corp, NMex, 68-69. *Mem:* AAAS; Biophys Soc. *Res:* Structure, conformation and function of proteins and biological membranes; nanosecond fluorescence spectroscopy; mathematical physics. *Mailing Add:* Dept of Biol Univ of Calif at San Diego La Jolla CA 92093

YI, CHO KWANG, b Tomisaki City, Japan, Sept 10, 42; m 78; c 1. PLANNT BIOCHEMISTRY, PLANT PATHOLOGY. *Educ:* Kyungpook Nat Univ, Korea, BS, 65; Okla State Univ, MS, 72, PhD(plant physiol), 76. *Prof Exp:* Res assoc, 76-78, ASSOC PROF & PROJ DIR, SCI, EDUC & ADMIN, COOP STATE RES SERV, LANGSTON UNIV, OKLA, 79- *Mem:* Am Soc Plant Physiologists; Am Phytopath Soc; Sigma Xi; Photochem Soc NAm. *Res:* Biochemical study on the host-pathogen interaction during developmennt of bacterial blight disease in cotton plant, especially recognition mechanism by susceptible and-or resistant cultivars of cotton plant for Xanthomonas malvacearum, resulting in hypersensitive response. *Mailing Add:* Sci Educ Admin Coop State Res Serv PO Box 730 Langston OK 73050

YI, KONG SUNG, b Seoul, Korea, Apr 26, 45; m 72; c 2. CHEMICAL ENGINEERING, POLYMERIZATION ENGINEERING. *Educ:* Hanyang Univ, Korea, BS, 72; Univ Md, MS, 74, PhD(chem eng), 76. *Prof Exp:* Process engr, Signetics Co, Korea, 71-72; res asst chem eng, Univ Md, 73-76; ADVAN RES & DEVELOP ENGR, B F GOODRICH CO, 76- *Concurrent Pos:* NSF res grants, 72. *Mem:* Am Inst Chem Engrs. *Res:* Polymer reaction kinetics and engineering; mass transport in and through polymer media; chemical process development and design. *Mailing Add:* Chem Div B F Goodrich Co Independence OH 44131

YIAMOUYIANNIS, JOHN ANDREW, b Hartford, Conn, Sept 25, 42; m 62; c 6. BIOCHEMISTRY, STATISTICS. *Educ:* Univ Chicago, SB, 63; Univ RI, PhD(biochem), 67. *Prof Exp:* Fel develop biol, Western Reserve Univ Sch Med, 67-68; assoc ed, Chem Abst Serv, 68-72; SCI DIR, NAT HEALTH FEDN, 74-, EXEC DIR, NAT HEALTH ACTION COMN, 80- *Concurrent Pos:* Co-ed, Fluoride, 72-81; pres, Safe Water Found, 79- *Mem:* Am Chem Soc; Int Soc Fluoride Res. *Res:* Ganglioside biosynthesis; biochemical differentiation; subcellular particles; RNA synthesis in isolated nuclei; biological effects of inorganic fluoride; epidemiological ramifications of toxic substances. *Mailing Add:* Nat Health Fedn 6439 Taggart Pl Delaware OH 43105

YIANNIOS, CHRIST NICHOLAS, b Molai, Greece, Oct 10, 24; m 62; c 2. SYNTHETIC ORGANIC CHEMISTRY. *Educ:* Nat Univ Athens, BS, 51; Univ Ga, MS, 55. *Prof Exp:* Res chemist, Allied Chem Corp, 56-57, Cedars Lebanon Hosp, Los Angeles, Calif, 58-59 & Western Lacquer Corp, 59-60; res chemist, Olin Mathieson Chem Corp, 61-65, sr res chemist, 65-69; consult self-employed, 69-72, SR RES CHEMIST, CARBOLABS, INC, 73- *Mem:* Am Chem Soc; Sigma Xi. *Res:* Organic chemistry of sulfur; synthesis of biologically active compounds; synthesis of new chemicals for agricultural and pharmaceutical purposes. *Mailing Add:* 830 Blackstone Village Meriden CT

YIANNOS, PETER N, b Olympia, Greece, Nov 27, 32; US citizen; m 62; c 3. PHYSICAL CHEMISTRY, ENGINEERING. *Educ:* Univ Mo-Rolla, BS, 56; Lawrence Univ, MS, 58, PhD(phys chem), 60. *Prof Exp:* From res group leader to sr res group leader, Scott Paper Co, 60-65, sect head, 65-66, mgr pioneering res, 66-67; assoc prof eng, Widener Col, 67-69; mgr paper res, 69-73, dir paper res, 73-76, vpres prod develop, 76-79, vpres consumer res & develop, 79-81, VPRES INT RES & DEVELOP, SCOTT PAPER CO, 81- *Concurrent Pos:* Instr, Tech Develop Prog, Scott Paper Training Course, 64-69; lectr eng, Eve Div, PMC Cols, 66-67; tech consult, Scott Paper Co, 67-69; adj prof, Widener Col, 72-74. *Honors & Awards:* Albert Award, Tech Asn Pulp & Paper Indust. *Mem:* Am Chem Soc; Am Inst Chem Eng; Tech Asn Pulp & Paper Indust. *Res:* Molecular forces and surface phenomena; fibers and fiber bonding; wood technology and pulping; mechanical properties of fibers and sheet assemblies; technical management; materials science. *Mailing Add:* Scott Paper Co Res Div Philadelphia PA 19113

YIELDING, K LEMONE, b Auburn, Ala, Mar 25, 31; m 73; c 5. MOLECULAR BIOLOGY, MEDICINE. *Educ:* Ala Polytech Inst, BS, 49; Univ Ala, MS, 52, MD, 54. *Prof Exp:* Intern, Med Ctr, Univ Ala, 54-55; clin assoc, NIH, 55-57; resident, USPHS Hosp, 57-58; sr investr, Nat Inst Arthritis & Metab Dis, 58-64; prof biochem, assoc prof med & chief lab molecular biol, Med Ctr, Univ Ala, Birmingham, 64-79; CHMN & PROF ANAT MED, UNIV SOUTH ALA, MOBILE, 79- *Concurrent Pos:* Asst prof med, Georgetown Univ, 58-64; consult, USPHS, 64- *Mem:* AAAS; Am Soc Pharmacol & Exp Therapeut; Soc Exp Biol & Med; Am Soc Biol Chem; Am Asn Anatomists. *Res:* Molecular basis for biological regulation, including both genetic mechanisms and control of enzyme activity; elucidation of disease mechanisms and drug action in molecular terms. *Mailing Add:* Dept Anat Univ South Ala Mobile AL 36688

YIH, CHIA-SHUN, b Kweiyang, China, July 25, 18; nat US; m 49; c 3. MECHANICS. *Educ:* Nat Cent Univ, China, BS, 42; Univ Iowa, MS, 47, PhD(fluid mech), 48. *Prof Exp:* Asst, Nat Bur Hydraul Res, China, 42-43; jr bridge engr, Nat Bur Bridge Design, 43-45; instr, Nat Kweichow Univ, 45; asst, Inst Hydraul Res, Univ Iowa, 46-48, asst prof fluid mech & res engr, 52-54, assoc prof, 54-56; instr math, Univ Wis, 48-49; lectr, Univ BC, 49-50; assoc prof civil eng, Colo State Univ, 50-52; from assoc prof to prof eng mech, 56-68, STEPHAN P TIMOSHENKO UNIV PROF ENG MECH, UNIV MICH, ANN ARBOR, 68- *Concurrent Pos:* Res assoc, Nat Ctr Sci Res, Univ Nancy, France, 51-52; NSF sr fel, Cambridge Univ, 59-60; consult, Huyck Felt Co, 60-64; Guggenheim fel, 64; vis prof, Univ Paris, 70-71; von Humboldt award, 77; mem academia sinica, US Nat Acad Eng. *Honors & Awards:* Theodore Von Karman Medal, Am Soc Chem Engrs, 81. *Mem:* Fel Am Phys Soc; Int Asn Hydraul Res. *Res:* Fluid mechanics, especially flows of nonhomogeneous fluids, flows with general rotation, geophysical fluid mechanics and hydrodynamic stability. *Mailing Add:* Dept Mech Eng & Appl Mech Univ of Mich Ann Arbor MI 48109

YIH, ROY YANGMING, b Changsha, China, Oct 5, 31; nat US; m 60; c 3. AGRICULTURAL CHEMISTRY. *Educ:* Nat Taiwan Univ, BS, 56; Univ SC, MS, 59; Rutgers Univ, PhD(plant physiol, biochem), 63. *Prof Exp:* Sr scientist, 62-71, lab head, 72-73, proj leader, 73-81, RES SECT MGR, ROHM AND HAAS CO, SPRINGHOUSE, 81- *Mem:* Am Chem Soc; Weed Sci Soc Am. *Res:* Synthesis, evaluation and development of compounds as herbicides and plant growth regulators worldwide. *Mailing Add:* 94 Windover Lane Doylestown PA 18901

YII, ROLAND, b Chengtu, China, Aug 11, 19; m 54; c 3. ELECTRICAL ENGINEERING. *Educ:* Nanking Univ, BS, 45; Brown Univ, MS, 53; Univ Pa, PhD(elec eng), 65. *Prof Exp:* Mgr printing dept, Sprague Elec Co, 52-54; prog & dept mgr, Burroughs Corp, 55-65; prof elec eng, Villanova Univ, 65-68; prof, 68-77, RES SCIENTIST, UNIV FLA, 77- *Res:* Solid state electronic and magnetic circuits; computer logic and variable radix computer. *Mailing Add:* Dept of Elec Eng Univ of Fla Gainesville FL 32601

YILDIZ, ALAETTIN, b Surmene, Turkey, Jan 5, 22; US citizen. AERO-ASTRONAUTICS, CARDIOLOGY. *Educ:* Tech Univ West Berlin, MS, 56, PhD(fluid mech & heat transfer), 65. *Prof Exp:* Res eng aerodynamics, Res Lab, Siemens, Berlin, 60-62; asst prof & res assoc mech eng, Tech Univ West Berlin, 62-65; res scientist aeronaut & astronaut, Edcliff Instruments contractor NASA, 67-69; med scientist cardiol, City Hope Nat Med Ctr, Calif, 67-69, res, Univ Hosp, Vakifgureba, Turkey, 76-80 & scientist comn team, Fac Med, King Faisal Univ, 80-81; SCIENTIST MED SCI, ROYAL AL HADA HOSP, SAUDI ARABIA, 81- *Concurrent Pos:* fel aeronaut sci, Calif Inst Technol, Pasadena, 69; sci advisor, Prog Data Co, Calif & Univ Calif, Los Angeles, 71-76. *Mem:* Am Inst Aeronaut & Astronaut; Ger Engrs Asn; Turkish Engrs Asn; Am Soc Mech Engrs. *Res:* Resistance coefficient of intimal surface on normal and pathological human aortas with special emphasis on development of atherosclerosis and stenosis of vessels; potential role of hydro-dynamics of the structures of blood vessels; ballistics of spinning projectiles; establishing the dimensionless Yildiz-number related to aero-astronautics. *Mailing Add:* 2311 Nottingham Ave Los Angeles CA 90027

YIM, GEORGE KWOCK, WAH, b Honolulu, Hawaii, Jan 7, 30; m 52; c 5. PHARMACOLOGY. *Educ:* Univ Iowa, BS, 52, MS, 54, PhD(pharmacol), 56. *Prof Exp:* Instr pharmacol, Univ Iowa, 55-56; from asst prof to assoc prof, 56-70, PROF PHARMACOL, PURDUE UNIV, WEST LAFAYETTE, 70- *Concurrent Pos:* USPHS career develop award, 61-66; NIH spec fel, 66-67. *Mem:* AAAS; Am Pharmaceut Asn; Am Soc Pharmacol & Exp Therapeut; Soc Exp Biol & Med; Soc Neurosci. *Res:* Pharmacological control of appetite; inflammation; cardiovascular and central actions of neuro active agents; biochemical mechanisms of cancer cachexia and anorexia. *Mailing Add:* Dept of Pharmacol Purdue Univ Sch of Pharm Lafayette IN 47907

YIM, W(OONGSOON) MICHAEL, b Korea, Feb 13, 27; US citizen; m 56; c 4. MATERIALS SCIENCE. *Educ:* Mont Col Mineral Sci & Technol, BS, 51; Univ Wash, Seattle, MS, 53; Mass Inst Technol, ScD(phys metall, crystal physics), 61. *Prof Exp:* Instr, US Dept Defense, 53-56; res asst metall, Mass Inst Technol, 56-61; res metallurgist, Linde Tonawanda Labs, Union Carbide Corp, 61-62; MEM TECH STAFF, RCA LABS, DAVID SARNOFF RES CTR, 62- *Mem:* Am Phys Soc; Am Inst Mining, Metall & Petrol Engrs; fel Am Inst Chemists; Electrochem Soc. *Res:* Crystal growth of electronic materials; chemical and physical vapor deposition; sputtering; electrical properties; optical properties; photoconductivity; luminescence; thermoelectricity; crystal physics; phosphors; semiconductors; cermets. *Mailing Add:* RCA Labs David Sarnoff Res Ctr Princeton NJ 08540

YIN, BARBARA HSIN-HSIN, mathematical statistics, see previous edition

YIN, CHIH-MING, b Szechwan, China, July 2, 43; m 68; c 3. INSECT PHYSIOLOGY, INVERTEBRATE ENDOCRINOLOGY. *Educ:* Taiwan Nat Univ, BSc, 66; Univ Sask, PhD(biol), 72. *Prof Exp:* Fel entomol, Univ Mo-Columbia, 72-74, res assoc, 74-78; assoc, Cornell Univ, 78; ASST PROF ENTOM, UNIV MASS, AMHERST, 78- *Mem:* Entom Soc Am; Sigma Xi; AAAS. *Res:* Hormonal control of growth, development and diapause in insects. *Mailing Add:* Dept of Entom Univ of Mass Amherst MA 01003

YIN, FAY HOH, b Peking, China, Mar 10, 32; US citizen; m 59; c 2. VIROLOGY. *Educ:* Univ Wis-Madison, BA, 54, MS, 55, PhD(biochem), 60. *Prof Exp:* Res asst biochem, Univ Wis-Madison, 60; res assoc virol, Dept Path, Univ Pa, 63-65; RES CHEMIST, CENT RES DEPT, E I DU PONT DE NEMOURS & CO, INC, 66- *Mem:* Am Soc Microbiol. *Res:* Biochemical studies of arbovirus and picornavirus replication. *Mailing Add:* Cent Res Dept E I du Pont de Nemours & Co Inc Wilmington DE 19898

YIN, LO I, b Wuchang, China, Apr 19, 30; US citizen; m 58; c 2. PHYSICS. *Educ:* Cent China Univ, BA, 49; Carleton Col, BA, 51; Univ Rochester, MA, 52, BS, 56; Univ Mich, MS, 59, PhD(physics), 63. *Prof Exp:* Res physicist, Bendix Res Lab, Bendix Corp, 64-67; AEROSPACE TECHNOLOGIST, NASA GODDARD SPACE FLIGHT CTR, 67- *Concurrent Pos:* Vis prof chem, Univ Md, 72-76, adj prof, 77- *Honors & Awards:* IR-100 Award, 79; NASA Inventor of the Year, 80. *Mem:* Am Phys Soc; AAAS; Am Nuclear Soc; NY Acad Sci. *Res:* Atomic and nuclear physics; x-ray spectroscopy; x-ray and gamma-ray spectroscopy; x-ray and gamma-ray imaging; lixiscope, low intensity x-ray imaging scope. *Mailing Add:* Lab for Astron & Solar Physics Code 684 Greenbelt MD 20771

YIN, TOM CHI TIEN, b Kunming, China, Jan 7, 45; US citizen; m 72. NEUROPHYSIOLOGY, BIOENGINEERING. *Educ:* Princeton Univ, BSE, 66; Univ Mich, PhD(elec eng), 73. *Prof Exp:* Fel neurophysiol, State Univ NY, Buffalo, 74; fel physiol, Johns Hopkins Univ, 74-77; ASST PROF NEUROPHYSIOL, UNIV WIS-MADISON, 77- *Mem:* Soc Neurosci; Sigma Xi; Inst Elec & Electronics Engrs. *Res:* Neurophysiology of sensory and motor systems. *Mailing Add:* 283 Med Sci Bldg Univ of Wis Madison WI 53706

YING, ANDREW SUI-CHUN, b China, Jan 21, 26; m 57; c 3. MECHANICAL ENGINEERING. *Educ:* Carnegie Inst Technol, PhD(mech eng), 53. *Prof Exp:* Asst prof math, Carnegie Inst Technol, 52-55; designer, Pittsburgh Des Moines Steel Co, 55-58; FEL ENGR, WESTINGHOUSE ELEC CORP, 58- *Mem:* Am Soc Mech Engrs. *Res:* Stress analysis; hydrodynamic lubrication; superconducting turbine generators. *Mailing Add:* Res & Develop Ctr 401-2X38 Westinghouse Elec Corp Pittsburgh PA 15235

YING, KUANG LIN, b Kiangsu, China, June 12, 27; Can citizen; m 55; c 3. GENETICS, CYTOGENETICS. *Educ:* Nat Taiwan Univ, BSc, 52; Univ Sask, PhD(cytol, genetics), 61. *Prof Exp:* Sr specialist plant breeding & genetics, Sino-Am Joint Comn Rural Reconstruct, 61-64; Med Res Coun Can res assoc, Univ Sask, 64-67, from asst prof human cytogenetics to assoc prof, dept pediat, 73-78; dir cytogenetics & prenatal detection lab, Valley Children's Hosp & Guidance Clin, Fresno, Calif, 78-81; HEAD SECT CYTOGENETICS, DIV MED GENETICS, CHILDREN'S HOSP, LOS ANGELES, CALIF, 81-; ASSOC CLIN PROF, DEPT PEDIAT, SCH MED, UNIV SOUTHERN CALIF, LOS ANGELES, 81- *Concurrent Pos:* Assoc prof, Grad Sch, Nat Taiwan Univ, 62-63. *Mem:* Genetics Soc Can; Am Soc Human Genetics; Tissue Cult Asn. *Res:* Human cytogenetics; mammalian cytogenetics; prenatal detection of genetic disorders. *Mailing Add:* Div Med Genetics Children's Hosp 4650 Sunset Blvd Los Angeles CA 90027

YING, SEE CHEN, b Shanghai, China, Apr 4, 41; m 68. SOLID STATE PHYSICS. *Educ:* Univ Hong Kong, BSc, 63 & 64; Brown Univ, PhD(physics), 68. *Prof Exp:* Res assoc physics, Brown Univ, 68-69; asst res scientist, Univ Calif, San Diego, 69-71; asst prof, 71-75, assoc prof, 75-80, PROF PHYSICS, BROWN UNIV, 80- *Concurrent Pos:* Res fel, A P Sloan Found, 72; Alexander von Humboldt Found US sr scientist award, 76. *Res:* Theoretical solid state physics; electronic properties of surfaces and interfaces; phase transitions on surcases and low dimensional systems. *Mailing Add:* Dept of Physics Brown Univ Providence RI 02912

YING, WILLIAM H, b Shanghai, China, July 1, 35; m 64. CIVIL ENGINEERING. *Educ:* Cheng Kung Univ, Taiwan, BS, 57; Univ Mo-Rolla, MS, 61; Okla State Univ, PhD(civil eng), 65. *Prof Exp:* Engr, Chau & Lee Archit & Civil Engrs, Hong Kong, 57-58 & Pan-Ocean, Ltd, Okinawa, 58-60; asst prof mech math, 64-67, assoc prof civil eng, 67-72, PROF CIVIL ENG, CALIF STATE UNIV, LONG BEACH, 72- *Mem:* Am Soc Civil Engrs; Am Soc Eng Educ; Am Inst Aeronaut & Astronaut. *Res:* Solid mechanics, including plates and shells, elasticity and dynamics of structures. *Mailing Add:* Dept of Civil Eng 6101 E Seventh St Long Beach CA 90840

YINGST, HARVEY AUSTIN, physical inorganic chemistry, see previous edition

YINGST, JOSEPHINE YUDKIN, b Washington, DC, Jan 30, 48; m 70; c 1. MARINE ECOLOGY, BENTHIC ECOLOGY. *Educ:* Univ Calif, Berkeley, BA, 69; Univ Southern Calif, PhD(marine biol), 75. *Prof Exp:* Res asst biol, Univ Southern Calif, 69-70, teaching asst, 70-74; res assoc geol, Yale Univ, 75-80; RES SCIENTIST, WAYNE STATE UNIV, 80- *Mem:* AAAS; Am Soc Limnol & Oceanog; Am Geophys Union. *Res:* Animal-sediment relations including the biology of deposit-feeding organisms, the structure of food-webs on muddy seafloors, and decomposition processes; microbial activity in marine sediments. *Mailing Add:* Dept Biol Sci Wayne State Univ Detroit MI 48202

YINGST, RALPH EARL, b Lebanon, Pa, Aug 5, 29; m 64. INORGANIC CHEMISTRY. *Educ:* Univ Chicago, AB, 50; Lebanon Valley Col, BS, 55; Univ Pittsburgh, PhD(chem), 64. *Prof Exp:* Instr chem, Johnstown Col, 61-63; asst prof, 64-70, ASSOC PROF CHEM, YOUNGSTOWN STATE UNIV, 70- *Mem:* AAAS; Am Chem Soc. *Res:* Coordination compounds of metals with pyridine and substituted pyridines, especially those containing olefinic linkages, such as 2-vinylpyridine and 2-allylpyridine; optically active metal complexes, especially cobalt. *Mailing Add:* Dept of Chem Youngstown State Univ Youngstown OH 44555

YIP, CECIL CHEUNG-CHING, b Hong Kong, June 11, 37; m 60; c 2. BIOCHEMISTRY, ENDOCRINOLOGY. *Educ:* McMaster Univ, BSc, 59; Rockefeller Univ, PhD(biochem, endocrinol), 63. *Prof Exp:* Res assoc endocrinol, Rockefeller Univ, 63-64; from asst prof to assoc prof, 64-74, PROF ENDOCRINOL, BANTING & BEST DEPT MED RES, C H BEST INST, UNIV TORONTO, 74- *Concurrent Pos:* Med Res Coun Can med res scholar, 67-71. *Mem:* AAAS; Am Soc Biol Chem; Can Biochem Soc; Am Chem Soc. *Res:* Biosynthesis of proinsulin and insulin; hormone-receptor interaction. *Mailing Add:* C H Best Inst Univ of Toronto Toronto ON M5G 1L6 Can

YIP, GEORGE, b Oakland, Calif, Nov 14, 26; m 53; c 1. BIOCHEMISTRY, FOOD TECHNOLOGY. *Educ:* Univ Calif, Berkeley, BS, 51; Georgetown Univ, MS, 59. *Prof Exp:* Chemist, Nat Canners Asn, Calif, 51-52; chemist, Div Food Chem, 55-56, res chemist pesticides, 56-63, sect chief herbicides & plant growth regulators, 63-71, chief, Biochem Technol Br, 71-72, CHIEF, INDUST CHEM CONTAMINANT BR, DIV CHEM TECHNOL, FOOD & DRUG ADMIN, 72- *Mem:* Am Chem Soc; Asn Off Anal Chem. *Res:* Methods of analysis for industrial chemical contaminants in foods; identification of unknown contaminants including degradation products. *Mailing Add:* 5211 Kipling St Springfield VA 22151

YIP, JOSEPH W, b Hong Kong, Sept 17, 48; m 77; c 1. DEVELOPMENTAL NEUROBIOLOGY. *Educ:* Wash State Univ, BS, 71; Univ Calif, San Francisco, PhD(physiol), 77. *Prof Exp:* Fel neurobiol, Washington Univ, St Louis, 77-80; ASST PROF PHYSIOL, SCH MED, UNIV PITTSBURGH, 81- *Mem:* Soc Neurosci. *Res:* Specificity of synapse formation. *Mailing Add:* Dept Physiol Sch Med Univ Pittsburgh Pittsburgh PA 15261

YIP, KWOK LEUNG, b Canton, China, Sept 23, 44; m 72; c 2. PHYSICS, LASER TECHNOLOGY. *Educ:* Chung Chi Col, Chinese Univ Hong Kong, BSc, 65; Providence Col, MS, 70; Lehigh Univ, PhD(physics), 73. *Prof Exp:* Teacher physics, King's Col, Hong Kong, 66-68; res assoc physics, Univ Ill, Urbana, 73-75; assoc scientist physics, Webster Res Ctr, 75-76, TECH SPECIALIST PHYSICS, WILSON CTR TECHNOL, XEROX CORP, 76- *Mem:* Am Phys Soc. *Res:* Electro-optical, laser and fiber optic technology; laser beam scanning and recording systems; device modeling, characterization and simulation; systems analysis and systems engineering. *Mailing Add:* Wilson Ctr of Technol Xerox Corp Webster NY 14580

YIP, LILY CHUNG, b Canton, China, Aug 10, 37; US citizen; m 62; c 4. BIOCHEMISTRY, MICROBIOLOGY. *Educ:* Taiwan Normal Univ, BSc, 58; Univ Cincinnati, PhD, 65. *Prof Exp:* Instr biochem, Sch Med, Ind Univ, 67-69; res assoc, 70-73, ASSOC, SLOAN-KETTERING INST, 73- *Concurrent Pos:* Fel, Ind Univ, 65-67; asst prof, Cornell Med Sch, 73- *Mem:* Am Chem Soc; AAAS; Sigma Xi. *Res:* Enzymes involved in purine metabolic pathway; control mechanism of the metabolic process. *Mailing Add:* Sloan-Kettering Inst 410 E 68th St New York NY 10021

YIP, PATRICK CHEUNG-YUM, applied mathematics, nuclear physics, see previous edition

YIP, RODERICK WING, b Vancouver, BC, Oct 12, 37; m 63; c 4. PHYSICAL CHEMISTRY, ORGANIC CHEMISTRY. *Educ:* Univ BC, BSc, 60; Univ Western Ont, BSc, 61, PhD(chem), 65. *Prof Exp:* Jr res fel chem, Univ Sheffield, 65-66; asst res officer, Div Pure Chem, 66-71, assoc res officer, 71-80, SR RES OFFICER, DIV CHEM, NAT RES COUN CAN, 80- *Res:* Photophysics; photochemistry and photobiology. *Mailing Add:* Div Chem Nat Res Coun of Can Ottawa ON K1A 0R6 Can

YIP, SIDNEY, b Peking, China, Jan 28, 36; US citizen; m 58. NUCLEAR ENGINEERING. *Educ:* Univ Mich, BS, 58, MS, 59, PhD(nuclear eng), 62. *Prof Exp:* Res fel, Inst Sci Technol, Univ Mich, 62-63; res assoc eng physics, Cornell Univ, 63-65; from asst prof to assoc prof nuclear eng, 65-73, PROF NUCLEAR ENG, MASS INST TECHNOL, 73- *Concurrent Pos:* Alexander von Humboldt Found US sr scientist award, Ger. *Mem:* Fel Am Phys Soc; Am Nuclear Soc. *Res:* Computer molecular dynamics simulation; neutron physics and applications; non-equilibrium statistical mechanics and kinetic theory; radiation effects and uses. *Mailing Add:* Dept of Nuclear Eng 24-211 Mass Inst of Technol Cambridge MA 02139

YIRAK, JACK J(UNIOR), b Omaha, Nebr, Oct 10, 18; m 45; c 2. CHEMICAL ENGINEERING. *Educ:* Iowa State Col, BS, 40; Lawrence Col, MS, 42, PhD, 44. *Prof Exp:* Chem engr, Union Bag & Paper Corp, 44-48, group leader, 48-51, proj engr, Semi-Chem Pulp Mill, 51-54, asst pulp mill supt, 54-55; pulp mill proj engr, 55-60, construct proj engr, 60-64, asst construct engr, Bleached Div, Union Camp Corp, 64-66, construct proj mgr, 66-81, ASST TO PROJ DIR, UNION CAMP CORP, 81- *Mem:* Tech Asn Pulp & Paper Indust. *Res:* Pulp, paper and related products; tall oil. *Mailing Add:* 76 Westview Ave Greenville SC 29609

YNTEMA, CHESTER LOOMIS, anatomy, deceased

YNTEMA, JAN LAMBERTUS, b Neth, Oct 5, 20; m 48; c 4. PHYSICS. *Educ:* Free Univ, Amsterdam, NatPhilDrs, 48, DrPhysics, 52. *Prof Exp:* Res assoc physics, Princeton Univ, 49-52; asst prof, Univ Pittsburgh, 52-55; assoc physicist, 55-68, SR PHYSICIST, ARGONNE NAT LAB, 68- *Mem:* Am Phys Soc. *Res:* Radioactivity; gases at high temperatures; nuclear physics. *Mailing Add:* Argonne Nat Lab Argonne IL 60439

YNTEMA, MARY KATHERINE, b Urbana, Ill, Jan 20, 28. MATHEMATICS. *Educ:* Swarthmore Col, BA, 50; Univ Ill, AM, 61, PhD(math), 65. *Prof Exp:* Teacher, Am Col Girls, Istanbul, 50-54 & Columbus Sch Girls, Ohio, 54-57; programmer, Lincoln Lab, Mass Inst Technol, 57-58; teacher high sch, Mont, 59-60; asst prof math, Univ Ill, Chicago, 65-67; asst prof comput sci, Pa State Univ, 67-71; from asst prof to assoc prof, 71-81, coordr math systs prog, 75-77, 80-81, chmn fac senate, 77-78, PROF MATH, SANGAMON STATE UNIV, 81- *Mem:* Am Math Soc; Asn Comput Mach; Math Asn Am. *Res:* Automata; context-free languages. *Mailing Add:* Dept of Math Systs Sangamon State Univ Springfield IL 62708

YOAKUM, ANNA MARGARET, b Loudon, Tenn, Jan 13, 33. ANALYTICAL CHEMISTRY, PHYSICAL METALLURGY. *Educ:* Maryville Col, AB, 54; Univ Fla, MS, 56, PhD(anal chem), 60. *Prof Exp:* Supvr control lab, Greenback Indust, Inc, 56-59; sr res chemist, Chemstrand Res Ctr, Inc, 60-64; mem res staff, Oak Ridge Nat Lab, 64-69; EXEC V PRES & LAB DIR, STEWART LABS, INC, 67- *Mem:* Am Chem Soc; Soc Appl Spectros; NY Acad Sci; Am Soc Test & Mat; fel Am Inst Chem. *Res:* Analytical chemistry and trace analysis; research and method development in emission, flame, atomic absorption, x-ray fluorescence and infrared spectroscopy. *Mailing Add:* Stewart Labs Inc 5815 Middlebrook Pike Knoxville TN 37921

YOCH, DUANE CHARLES, b Parkston, SDak, Nov 4, 40; m 64; c 2. MICROBIOLOGY, BIOCHEMISTRY. *Educ:* SDak State Univ, BS, 63, MS, 65; Pa State Univ, PhD(microbiol), 68. *Prof Exp:* Asst res microbiologist, Agr Exp Sta, Dept Cell Physiol, Univ Calif, Berkeley, 68-69, assoc specialist, 70-78; asst prof, 78-80, ASSOC PROF, DEPT BIOL, UNIV SC, COLUMBIA, 80- *Mem:* Am Soc Microbiol. *Res:* Bioenergetics; investigations of electron transport coupled to nitrogenase in bacteria; nitrogen fixation; iron-sulfur proteins. *Mailing Add:* Dept of Biol Univ of SC Columbia SC 29208

YOCHELSON, ELLIS LEON, b Washington, DC, Nov 14, 28; m 50; c 3. INVERTEBRATE PALEONTOLOGY. *Educ:* Univ Kans, BS, 49, MS, 50; Columbia Univ, PhD, 55. *Prof Exp:* Asst, Univ Kans & Columbia Univ, 50-52; PALEONTOLOGIST, US GEOL SURV, 52- *Concurrent Pos:* Mem, Nat Res Coun, 57-71; treas, Int Paleont Asn, 71-75; organizer, NAm Paleontol Conv, 69, ed proceedings, 70-71; secy-gen, Ninth Int Cong Carboniferous Stratig & Geol, 79; Gilbert fel, US Geol Surv; vis prof, Univ Del, 81. *Mem:* AAAS; Paleont Soc (pres, 76); Soc Syst Zool (secy, 62-65). *Res:* Systematics and evolution of Paleozoic gastropods; phylogeny of Mollusca, especially early Paleozoic major taxa. *Mailing Add:* Rm E-317 US Nat Mus Washington DC 20560

YOCHELSON, LEON, b Buffalo, NY, July 23, 17; m 42; c 3. PSYCHIATRY. *Educ:* Univ Buffalo, AB, 38, MD, 42. *Prof Exp:* Clin prof psychiat, 59-69, chmn dept psychiat, 59-70, PROF PSYCHIAT & BEHAV SCI, SCH MED, GEORGE WASHINGTON UNIV, 59-; CHMN, PSYCHIAT INST AM, 69- *Concurrent Pos:* Guest lectr, Catholic Univ, 48-58; mem fac, Wash Sch Psychiat, 50-58; consult, Vet Admin, 52- & NIMH, 54-; supv & training analyst, Wash Psychoanal Inst, 59-; chmn prof assocs, Psychiat Inst Washington, DC, chmn inst, chmn found, 66-; chmn comt psychiat hosps, Am Fedn Hosps, 74-; consult, Off Voc Rehab, Dept Health, Educ & Welfare; vpres, Fedn Am Hosps, 76- *Mem:* Fel Am Psychiat Asn; Am Psychoanal Asn. *Res:* Psychoanalysis. *Mailing Add:* Psychiat Inst of Wash 2020 K St NW Washington DC 20006

YOCHIM, JEROME M, b Chicago, Ill, Feb 23, 33; m 57; c 2. ENDOCRINOLOGY, PHYSIOLOGY. *Educ:* Univ Ill, BS, 55, MS, 57; Purdue Univ, PhD(biol sci), 60. *Prof Exp:* NIH fel anat, Col Med, Univ Ill, 60-62; from asst prof to assoc prof physiol, 62-70, PROF PHYSIOL, UNIV KANS, 71- *Concurrent Pos:* NIH career develop award, 71-76. *Mem:* AAAS; Am Asn Anatomists; Am Physiol Soc; Soc Study Reprod; Endocrine Soc. *Res:* Physiology of reproduction. *Mailing Add:* Dept Physiol & Cell Biol Univ Kans Lawrence KS 66045

YOCKEY, HUBERT PALMER, b Alexandria, Minn, Apr 15, 16; m 46; c 3. THEORETICAL BIOLOGY, MOLECULAR BIOLOGY. *Educ:* Univ Calif, Berkeley, AB, 38, PhD(physics), 42. *Prof Exp:* Jr physicist, Nat Defense Res Comt, Calif, 41-42; physicist radiation lab, Univ Calif, 42-44; sr physicist, Tenn Eastman Corp, 44-46; group leader irradiation physics, NAm Aviation, Inc, 46-52; chief nuclear physics, Convair Div, Gen Dynamics Corp, Tex, 52-53; asst dir health & physics div, Oak Ridge Nat Lab, Tenn, 53-59; mgr res & develop div, Aerojet-Gen Nucleonics Corp, 59-62 & Hughes Res Labs, 63-64; chief, Reactor Br, 64-80, CHIEF, ARMY PALSE RADIATION DIV, ABERDEEN PROVING GROUND, 80- *Concurrent Pos:* Consult, Oak Ridge Nat Lab, 60. *Mem:* Am Phys Soc; Am Nuclear Soc; Radiation Res Soc; Health Phys Soc. *Res:* Application of information theory to origin of life, genetic code, calculated information content of cytochrome c aging and radiation effects; established fast pulsed reactor facility; radiation effects in ferroelectrics; solid state physics; pulsed reactors. *Mailing Add:* Army Pulse Radiation Facil STEAP MT-R Bldg 860 Aberdeen Proving Ground MD 21005

YOCOM, CHARLES FREDERICK, b Logan, Iowa, Oct 21, 14; m 39; c 3. WILDLIFE MANAGEMENT. *Educ:* Iowa State Univ, BS, 39; Wash State Univ, MS, 42, PhD, 49. *Prof Exp:* Lab technician, Iowa Coop Wildlife Res Unit, 39-40; game biologist, State Dept Game, Wash, 42-47; from instr to asst prof game mgt, Wash State Univ, 47-53; assoc prof wildlife mgt & head game mgt, 53-56, chmn div natural resources, 56-60, coordr, 60-61, prof, 58-78, EMER PROF WILDLIFE MGT, HUMBOLDT STATE UNIV, 78- *Concurrent Pos:* Sabbatical leave, NZ, Australia & other foreign countries, 68. *Mem:* Wildlife Soc; Cooper Ornith Soc; assoc Am Ornith Union. *Res:* Wildlife conservation; ornithology; mammalogy; aquatic biology; ecology; scientific illustrations; Canadian geese in Washington and illustrations of plants of the desert southwest. *Mailing Add:* 9909 Pleasant Valley Rd Sun City AZ 85351

YOCOM, PERRY NIEL, b Auburn, Maine, Sept 27, 30; m 62; c 3. INORGANIC CHEMISTRY. *Educ:* Pa State Univ, BS, 54; Univ Ill, PhD, 58. *Prof Exp:* Mem tech staff, 57-70, RES GROUP HEAD, DAVID SARNOFF RES CTR, RCA CORP, 70- *Concurrent Pos:* Lectr, Advan Study Inst, NATO, 72. *Honors & Awards:* David Sarnoff Award, Sci, 70. *Mem:* AAAS; Am Chem Soc; Electrochem Soc; Sigma Xi; Mineral Soc Am. *Res:* Chemistry of fused salts; crystal growth; defects in solids; rare earth phase chemistry; luminescence. *Mailing Add:* David Sarnoff Res Ctr RCA Corp Princeton NJ 08540

YOCUM, CHARLES FREDRICK, b Storm Lake, Iowa, Oct 31, 41; m 82; c 1. BIOCHEMISTRY. *Educ:* Iowa State Univ, BS, 63; Ind Univ, PhD(biochem), 71. *Prof Exp:* Biochemist protein chem, ITT Res Inst, 63-68; NIH Fel biochem, Cornell Univ, 71-73; asst prof, 73-77, ASSOC PROF BIOL, UNIV MICH, 78- *Mem:* Am Chem Soc; Am Soc Plant Physiologists; AAAS; Biophys Soc. *Res:* Mechanisms of photosynthetic electron transport and energy transduction in chloroplasts and blue-green algae. *Mailing Add:* Dept Cellular & Molecular Biol Div Biol Sci Univ Mich Ann Arbor MI 48104

YOCUM, CONRAD SCHATTE, b Swarthmore, Pa, Mar 29, 19; m 46; c 3. PLANT PHYSIOLOGY. *Educ:* Col William & Mary, BS, 40; Univ Md, MS, 47; Stanford Univ, PhD, 52. *Prof Exp:* Asst marine biol, Va Fisheries Lab, 46-47; asst plant physiol, Hopkins Marine Sta, 47-48; instr plant physiol, Harvard Univ, 52-55; asst prof, Cornell Univ, 55-61; assoc prof, 61-64, PROF PLANT PHYSIOL, UNIV MICH, ANN ARBOR, 64- *Mem:* Am Soc Plant Physiol. *Res:* Photosynthesis; respiration; tropisms; nitrogen fixation. *Mailing Add:* Dept of Bot Univ of Mich Ann Arbor MI 48109

YOCUM, RONALD HARRIS, b Darby, Pa, June 2, 39. CHEMISTRY. *Educ:* Gettysburg Col, BA, 61; Univ Pa, PhD(org chem), 65. *Prof Exp:* Dir res, Latin Am, 73-77, Designed Prod Dept, 77-78, dir prod res, 78-80, DIR RES, MICH DIV, DOW CHEM USA, 80- *Mem:* Am Chem Soc. *Mailing Add:* Res & Develop Mich Div 566 Bldg Dow Chem USA Midland MI 48640

YODAIKEN, RALPH EMILE, b Johannesburg, SAfrica, Aug 25, 26; US citizen. PATHOLOGY, OCCUPATIONAL HEALTH. *Educ:* Univ Witwatersrand, MB & BCh, 56; Johns Hopkins Univ, MPH, 76. *Prof Exp:* Lectr path, Univ Witwatersrand, 58-63; assoc pathologist, Buffalo Gen Hosp, NY, 63-67; assoc prof path, Sch Med, Univ Cincinnati, 68-71; prof path & assoc prof med, Sch Med, Emory Univ, 71-77; asst researcher, Johns Hopkins Univ, 76-76; SR MED OFFICER & CHMN SR ADV STAFF, NAT INST OCCUP SAFETY & HEALTH, 77- *Concurrent Pos:* Chief ultra structure res, Vet Admin Hosp, 71-76. *Mem:* Fel Am Col Preventive Med; Soc Occup & Environ Health; fel Am Col Path; fel Royal Micros Soc. *Res:* Vascular pathology with special reference to diabetes. *Mailing Add:* 7100 Oak Forest Lane Bethesda MD 20014

YODER, CHARLES FINNEY, b Cincinnati, Ohio, July 18, 43; m 70; c 2. CELESTIAL MECHANICS, PLANETOLOGY. *Educ:* Univ Calif, Santa Barbara, BA, 68, PhD(physics), 73. *Prof Exp:* Fel, Dept Earth & Space Sci, Univ Calif, Los Angeles, 73-76; MEM TECH STAFF, JET PROPULSION LAB, 76- *Mem:* Am Geophys Union; Am Astron Soc. *Res:* Effect of tidal friction and gravitational resonances on planetary satellites; rotational dynamics; core mantle coupling mechanisms. *Mailing Add:* Jet Propulsion Lab 4800 Oak Grove Dr Pasadena CA 91103

YODER, CLAUDE H, b West Reading, Pa, Mar 16, 40; m 66; c 2. INORGANIC CHEMISTRY. *Educ:* Franklin & Marshall Col, BA, 62; Cornell Univ, PhD(chem), 66. *Prof Exp:* Asst prof, 66-74, assoc prof, 74-80, PROF CHEM, FRANKLIN & MARSHALL COL, 80-, CHMN DEPT, 74- *Concurrent Pos:* Dreyfus Found teacher scholar, 71. *Mem:* AAAS; Am Chem Soc. *Res:* Bonding in organometallic compounds. *Mailing Add:* Dept of Chem Franklin & Marshall Col Lancaster PA 17604

YODER, DAVID LEE, b Bellefontaine, Ohio, June 23, 36; m 61; c 2. PLANT PATHOLOGY, SOIL MICROBIOLOGY. *Educ:* Goshen Col, BA, 60; Mich State Univ, MS, 68, PhD(plant path), 71. *Prof Exp:* Plant pathologist, Hunt-Wesson Foods, Inc, 71-78; PLANT BREEDER, GILROY FOODS, INC, 78- *Res:* Soil-borne plant diseases; disease of tomatoes; soil fungistasis; onion genetics and diseases of onion and garlic. *Mailing Add:* Gilroy Foods Inc Gilroy CA 95020

YODER, DONALD MAURICE, b Elkhart Co, Ind, Jan 3, 20; m 45; c 3. AGRICULTURAL CHEMISTRY. *Educ:* Wabash Col, BA, 42; Cornell Univ, PhD(plant path), 50. *Prof Exp:* Sr fel biol res div, Union Carbide Chem Co, 50-54, head div, 54-61, mem staff tech develop, Agr Chem Div, 61-67, sr analyst mkt res & technol deleg UAR, Union Carbide Tech Serv Co, 67-68; mgr prod develop agr chem, 68-74, MGR REGIST & TOXICOL, BASF-WYANDOTTE CORP, 74- *Concurrent Pos:* Fel, Boyce Thompson Inst Plant Res, 50. *Mem:* Am Chem Soc; Am Phytopath Soc; Am Inst Biol Sci. *Res:* Evaluation of organic chemicals for agricultural uses; agricultural chemicals and food; pesticide regulations. *Mailing Add:* Agr Chem Dept BASF-Wyandotte Corp PO Box 181 Parsippany NJ 07054

YODER, ELDON J, b Goshen, Ind, Dec 11, 18; m 43; c 4. CIVIL ENGINEERING. *Educ:* Purdue Univ, BSCE, 45, MSCE, 46. *Prof Exp:* Asst prof civil eng, Ohio State Univ, 48-49; from asst prof to assoc prof hwy eng, 49-61, PROF HWY ENG, PURDUE UNIV, 61- *Concurrent Pos:* Consult, US Army Corps Engrs, 52-, Pa Turnpike Comn, 54-59, US Bur Pub Rds, 58-59 & Govt Southern Rhodesia, 59; chmn dept soils, geol & found, Hwy Res Bd, Nat Acad Sci-Nat Res Coun. *Mem:* Am Soc Civil Engrs; Am Soc Eng Educ. *Res:* Highway engineering, primarily pavement design, soils, foundations and materials. *Mailing Add:* Civil Eng Bldg Purdue Univ West Lafayette IN 47907

YODER, ELMON EUGENE, b Wolford, NDak, Oct 10, 21; m 47; c 4. AGRICULTURAL ENGINEERING, CIVIL ENGINEERING. *Educ:* Ore State Univ, BS, 47 & 54, MS, 61. *Prof Exp:* Civil engr design, Consumers Power Inc, 48-54; agr engr, Khon Trup Agr Univ, Thailand, 54-56; civil engr, Ore State Univ, 57-61; AGR ENGR RES, USDA, LEXINGTON, 62- *Concurrent Pos:* Agr engr, Univ Ky, 65-66 & 76-78. *Mem:* Am Soc Agr Engrs; Tobacco Workers; Sigma Xi. *Res:* Tobacco mechanization and processing; improvement of tobacco combustion in health-related research. *Mailing Add:* Tobacco Div USDA Univ Ky Lexington KY 40504

YODER, HARRY WHITAKER, JR, b Chicago, Ill, Aug 2, 28; m 50; c 3. VETERINARY MEDICINE. *Educ:* Univ Ill, BS, 50; Iowa State Col, DVM, 54. *Prof Exp:* Asst prof vet res, Vet Res Inst, Iowa State Univ, 57-65; RES VET, SOUTHEAST POULTRY RES LAB, USDA, 65- *Mem:* Am Vet Med Asn; Am Asn Avian Path. *Res:* Poultry respiratory diseases, especially pleuropneumonia-like organism infections. *Mailing Add:* USDA SE Poultry Res Lab 934 College Station Rd Athens GA 30601

YODER, HATTEN SCHUYLER, JR, b Cleveland, Ohio, Mar 20, 21; m 59; c 2. PETROLOGY. *Educ:* Univ Chicago, SB, 41, cert(meteorol), 42 & 46; Mass Inst Technol, PhD(petrol), 48. *Hon Degrees:* ScD, Univ Paris, 81. *Prof Exp:* Petrologist, 48-71, DIR, CARNEGIE INST WASHINGTON GEOPHYS LAB, 71- *Concurrent Pos:* Vis prof, Calif Inst Technol, 58, Univ Tex, 64, Univ Colo, 66 & Univ Cape Town, 67. *Honors & Awards:* Columbia Univ Bicentennial Medal, 54; Mineral Soc Am Award, 54; Day Medal, Geol Soc Am, 62; Arthur L Day Prize & lectureship, Nat Acad Sci, 72; A G Werner Medal, Ger Mineral Soc, 72; Wollaston Medal, Geol Soc London, 79- *Mem:* Nat Acad Sci; Mineral Soc Am (pres, 72); Geol Soc Am; Am Geophys Union (pres, Volcanology, Geochem & Petrol Sect, 61-64); Geochem Soc. *Res:* Experimental petrology; phase equilibria in mineral systems; piezochemistry; properties of minerals at high pressure and high temperature; hydrothermal mineral synthesis. *Mailing Add:* Carnegie Inst Wash Geophys Lab 2801 Upton St NW Washington DC 20008

YODER, JAMES AMOS, b Chicago, Ill, April 18, 49; m 75; c 2. OCEANOGRAPHY. *Educ:* DePauw Univ, BA, 70; Univ RI, MS, 74, PhD(oceanog), 79. *Prof Exp:* Res assoc, 78-79, ASST RES PROF, SKIDAWAY INST OCEANOG, 79- *Mem:* Am Soc Limnol & Oceanog. *Res:* Photoplankton physiology; biological oceanography of continental shelves. *Mailing Add:* Skidaway Inst Oceanog PO Box 13687 Savannah GA 31406

YODER, JOHN MENLY, b Ft Wayne, Ind, Oct 4, 31; m 60; c 2. ENDOCRINOLOGY, IMMUNOCHEMISTRY. *Educ:* Purdue Univ, BS, 53, PhD(animal physiol), 61. *Prof Exp:* Res biochemist, Ames Co Div, 61-72, SR RES SCIENTIST, AMES CO DIV, MILES LABS, INC, 72- *Mem:* Am Chem Soc; NY Acad Sci. *Res:* Plant and animal physiology; silage fermentation; protein purification; characterization of proteins and polysaccharides by immunochemistry; gonadotropins; hepatitis antigen; antibody production; factor VIII. *Mailing Add:* Ames Res Lab 819 McNaughton St Elkhart IN 46514

YODER, LEVON LEE, b Middlebury, Ind, June 22, 36; m 60; c 1. ELEMENTARY PARTICLE PHYSICS. *Educ:* Goshen Col, BA, 58; Univ Mich, MA, 61, PhD, 63. *Prof Exp:* Asst prof physics & chmn dept, Millikin Univ, 63-65; assoc prof, 65-71, chmn dept, 65-76, PROF PHYSICS, ADRIAN COL, 71-, CHMN DEPT, 79- *Mem:* AAAS; Am Asn Physics Teachers. *Res:* High energy and cosmic ray physics. *Mailing Add:* 2499 Sword Hwy Adrian MI 49221

YODER, NEIL RICHARD, b Wichita, Kans, Mar 27, 37; m 68. PARTICLE PHYSICS. *Educ:* Kans State Teachers Col, BA, 59; Pa State Univ, PhD(physics), 69. *Prof Exp:* Instr physics, Mich State Univ, 65-67; SR RES ASSOC, UNIV MD, COLLEGE PARK, 67- *Mem:* Am Phys Soc. *Res:* Phenomenological analysis of moderate energy nucleon-nucleon data; application of computers to on-line analysis of nuclear physics experimental data. *Mailing Add:* Dept of Physics & Astron Univ of Md College Park MD 20742

YODER, OLEN CURTIS, b Fairview, Mich, Jan 26, 42; m 67. PLANT PATHOLOGY. *Educ:* Goshen Col, BA, 64; Mich State Univ, MS, 68, PhD(plant path), 71. *Prof Exp:* Asst prof, 71-77, ASSOC PROF PLANT PATH, CORNELL UNIV, 77- *Concurrent Pos:* USDA res grant, 72-75; Rockefeller Found res grant, 74 & 77-; USDA res grant, 78- *Mem:* AAAS; Am Phytopath Soc; Am Soc Plant Physiol; Int Soc Plant Path; Sigma Xi. *Res:* Physiology and genetics of plant disease; host-specific fungal toxins; control of post-harvest diseases. *Mailing Add:* Dept of Plant Path Cornell Univ Ithaca NY 14853

YODER, PAUL RUFUS, JR, b Huntingdon, Pa, Feb 6, 27; m 48; c 4. OPTICS. *Educ:* Juniata Col, BS, 47; Pa State Univ, MS, 50. *Prof Exp:* Assoc prof physics & math, Bridgewater Col, 50-51; physicist, US Army Frankford Arsenal, 51-61; proj engr, 61-67, ENG DEPT MGR, PERKIN-ELMER CORP, 67- *Concurrent Pos:* Lectr geometric optics, Univ Conn Exten, 77- *Mem:* Fel Optical Soc Am; Soc Photo-Optical Instrumentation Engrs. *Res:* Design, development, fabrication and test of specialized optical instrumentation. *Mailing Add:* 9 Bhasking Ridge Rd Wilton CT 06897

YODER, ROBERT E, b Richmond, Va, Jan 1, 30; m 52; c 3. HEALTH PHYSICS, INDUSTRIAL HYGIENE. *Educ:* Appalachian State Teachers Col, BS, 51; Harvard Univ, ScD(radiol health), 63. *Prof Exp:* Jr health physicist, Oak Ridge Nat Lab, 54-57; from instr to asst prof health physics, Sch Pub Health, Harvard Univ, 57-66; group leader & hazards control dept head, Lawrence Livermore Lab, Univ Calif, 65-72; asst dir nuclear facil, div oper safety, US AEC, 72-75; DIR HEALTH SAFETY & ENVIRON, ROCKWELL INT, ROCKY FLATS PLANT, COLO, 75- *Concurrent Pos:* Consult radiation safety, Mass, 58-64. *Mem:* AAAS; Health Physics Soc; Sigma Xi; NY Acad Sci. *Res:* Aerosol technology; basic properties of aerosols; physics and chemistry of small particles and their influence on health; radiation safety and environment protection program administration in nuclear research and production institutions. *Mailing Add:* PO Box 464 Golden CO 80401

YODER, WAYNE ALVA, b Grantsville, Md, July 6, 43; m 67; c 2. INVERTEBRATE ZOOLOGY, ENTOMOLOGY. *Educ:* Goshen Col, BA, 65; Mich State Univ, MS, 71, PhD(zool), 72. *Prof Exp:* Asst prof, 72-75, ASSOC PROF BIOL, FROSTBURG STATE COL, 75- *Mem:* Am Inst Biol Sci; Am Soc Zoologists; Entom Soc Am; Sigma Xi. *Res:* Systematic and ecological studies of the mites associated with silphid beetles. *Mailing Add:* Dept of Biol Frostburg State Col Frostburg MD 21532

YODH, GAURANG BHASKAR, b Ahmedabad, India, Nov 24, 28; nat US; m 54; c 3. PHYSICS. *Educ:* Univ Bombay, BSc, 48; Univ Chicago, MS, 51, PhD(physics), 55. *Prof Exp:* Instr physics, Stanford Univ, 54-56; res fel, Tata Inst Fundamental Res, India, 57-58; res physicist, Carnegie Inst Technol, 58-59, asst prof physics, 59-61; PROF PHYSICS, UNIV MD, COLLEGE PARK, 65- *Concurrent Pos:* Consult, US Naval Res Lab, DC, 65-69 & Argonne Nat Lab, 66-70; vis prof, Univ Ariz, 66-67; vis scientist, Goddard Space Flight Ctr, NASA, 76-77; prog officer elementary particle physics, NSF, 78-80. *Mem:* Fel Am Phys Soc. *Res:* Experimental and phenomenological study of high energy interactions of elementary particles and cosmic rays. *Mailing Add:* 1800 G St Washington DC 20550

YOERGER, ROGER R, b LeMars, Iowa, Feb 17, 29; m 71; c 4. AGRICULTURAL ENGINEERING. *Educ:* Iowa State Univ, BS, 49, MS, 51, PhD(agr eng), 57. *Prof Exp:* Instr & asst prof agr eng, Iowa State Univ, 49-56; assoc prof, Pa State Univ, 56-58; prof, 58-78, HEAD DEPT AGR ENG, UNIV ILL, URBANA, 78- *Honors & Awards:* Paper Award, Am Soc Agr Engrs, 67, 68, 70, 75 & 76. *Mem:* Fel Am Soc Agr Engrs; Am Soc Eng Educ; AAAS; Sigma Xi. *Res:* Off-road vehicles; noise reduction; vibration and operator comfort; field crop production equipment. *Mailing Add:* Dept Agr Eng Univ Ill 1208 W Peabody Dr Urbana IL 61801

YOESTING, CLARENCE C, b Apr 5, 12; US citizen; m 40; c 2. PHYSICS, SCIENCE EDUCATION. *Educ:* Cent State Col, Okla, BS, 36; Univ Okla, MEd, 47, EdD(sci educ), 65. *Prof Exp:* Teacher sci, Lacy Schs, Okla, 36-38, Loyal Schs, 38-40, Newkirk, Okla, 41-42 & Ponca Mil Acad, 45-47; prin & teacher, Tonkawa, Okla, 47-51; counr & teacher, Northeast High Sch, Oklahoma City, 51-61; PROF PHYSICS, CENT STATE UNIV OKLA, 61- *Mem:* Nat Sci Teachers Asn; Am Inst Physics; Am Asn Physics Teachers. *Mailing Add:* 1716 S Rankin Edmond OK 73034

YOFFA, ELLEN JUNE, b Boston, Mass, Aug 18, 51. VERY LARGE SCALE INTEGRATION DESIGN. *Educ:* Mass Inst Technol, BS, 73, PhD(physics), 78. *Prof Exp:* Fel, 78-80, RES STAFF MEM, THOMAS J WATSON RES CTR, IBM, 80- *Mem:* Am Phys Soc; Sigma Xi. *Res:* Creating tools for very large scale integration design automation, and construction of interactive systems for large scale circuit design, wiring, and data interchange standards. *Mailing Add:* IBM T J Watson Res Ctr PO Box 218 Yorktown Heights NY 10598

YOGORE, MARIANO G, JR, b Iloilo City, Philippines, Dec 29, 21; m 45; c 7. PARASITOLOGY, PUBLIC HEALTH. *Educ:* Univ Philippines, MD, 45; Johns Hopkins Univ, MPH, 48, DrPH, 57; Philippine Bd Prev Med & Pub Health, dipl, 56. *Prof Exp:* From instr to prof parasitol, Univ Philippines, 45-67; res assoc & asst prof, 67-69, RES ASSOC & PROF PARASITOL, UNIV CHICAGO, 69- *Concurrent Pos:* USPHS res fel, Dept Microbiol, Univ Chicago, 59-61; mem, Nat Res Coun Philippines, 57- *Mem:* Am Soc Trop Med & Hyg. *Res:* Immunity to parasitic diseases with special interest in schistosomiasis. *Mailing Add:* Comm Immunol Univ Chicago Box 414 950 E 59th St Chicago IL 60637

YOH, JOHN K, b Shanghai, China, Oct 9, 44; US citizen. PHYSICS. *Educ:* Cornell Univ, BA, 64; Calif Inst Technol, MS, 66, PhD(physics), 70. *Prof Exp:* Res asst high energy physics, Calif Inst Technol, 67-70; res assoc, Rutgers Univ, 70; NATO fel, Cern Europ Orgn Nuclear Res, 70-71, vis scientist, 71-73; res assoc, Columbia Univ, 73-77, asst prof, 77-80; SCIENTIST RES & ADMIN, FERMI NAT ACCELARATOR LAB, 80- *Res:* Colliding anti-proton project; experimental dileptons and high point physics. *Mailing Add:* MS 223 Fermi Nat Accelarator Lab PO Box 500 Batavia IL 60510

YOHE, CLEON RUSSELL, b New York, NY, July 8, 41; m 66; c 1. ALGEBRA. *Educ:* Univ Pa, AB, 62; Univ Chicago, MS, 63, PhD(math), 66. *Prof Exp:* Asst prof, 66-71, ASSOC PROF MATH, WASH UNIV, 71- *Mem:* AAAS; Am Math Soc. *Res:* Structure theory of rings, specifically structure of rings of endomorphisms of modules over commutative noetherian rings. *Mailing Add:* Dept of Math Wash Univ St Louis MO 63130

YOHE, JAMES MICHAEL, b Delaware, Ohio, June 8, 36; m 61; c 3. MATHEMATICS, COMPUTER SCIENCE. *Educ:* DePauw Univ, BA, 57; Univ Wis-Madison, MS, 62, PhD(math), 67. *Prof Exp:* Asst prof math, Math Res Ctr, Univ Wis-Madison, 67-68; asst prof, Pa State Univ, 68-69; proj assoc, Math Res Ctr, Univ Wis-Madison, 69-71, asst dir, 71-75, assoc dir, 75-78; DIR ACAD COMPUT, UNIV WIS-EAU CLAIRE, 79- *Concurrent Pos:* Lectr, Univ Wis, 71-72, asst prof comput sci, 73-74. *Mem:* Am Math Soc; Math Asn Am; Asn Comput Mach. *Res:* Computer systems programming; computer arithmetic; interval arithmetic; graph theory. *Mailing Add:* Acad Comput Servs Univ of Wis Eau Claire WI 54701

YOHN, CHARLES PHILIP, b Harrisburg, Pa, Aug 5, 28; m 53; c 2. MECHANICAL ENGINEERING. *Educ:* Cornell Univ, BME, 50. *Prof Exp:* Indust engr, 50-55, develop engr foil slitting, 55-63, supvr impact extrusion die design & develop, 63-66, mgr forge die mfg & develop, 66-75, eng assoc powder metall develop, 75-78, ENG ASSOC RES & DEVELOP PLANNING, ALUMINUM CO AM, 78- *Mem:* Sigma Xi; Soc Mfg Engrs. *Res:* Evaluation of research and development activities; long range forecasting and planning for research and development. *Mailing Add:* Alco Labs Aluminum Co of Am Alcoa Center PA 15069

YOHN, DAVID STEWART, b Shelby, Ohio, June 7, 29; m 50; c 5. MICROBIOLOGY. *Educ:* Otterbein Col, BS, 51; Ohio State Univ, MS, 53, PhD, 57; Univ Pittsburgh, MPH, 60. *Prof Exp:* Res assoc, Univ Pittsburgh, 56-60, asst res prof microbiol, Grad Sch Pub Health, 60-62; res prof, State Univ NY Buffalo, 62-71; assoc cancer res scientist, Roswell Park Mem Inst, 62-69; PROF VIROL, OHIO STATE UNIV, 69-, DIR, COMPREHENSIVE CANCER CTR, 73- *Concurrent Pos:* Consult, Nat Cancer Inst, 70-; mem med & sci adv bd & bd trustees, Leukemia Soc Am, 71-; secy gen, Int Asn Comp Res Leukemia & Related Dis, 74- *Mem:* AAAS; Am Soc Microbiol; Am Asn Cancer Res. *Res:* Mammalian and oncogenic viruses; virus host-cell relationships; tumor immunology. *Mailing Add:* Ohio State Univ Comprehensive Cancer Ctr Suite 357 1580 Cannon Dr Columbus OH 43210

YOHO, CLAYTON W, b Glen Dale, WVa, Dec 4, 24; m 49; c 3. ORGANIC CHEMISTRY. *Educ:* W Liberty State Col, BSc, 49; Univ Pittsburgh, MSc, 51, PhD(org chem), 57. *Prof Exp:* Jr fel org res, Mellon Inst Indust Res, 51-54; process develop chemist, Merck & Co, Inc, 57-60; res supvr org res, 65-71, STAFF RES SUPVR, JOHNSON WAX, 71-, SR CHEMIST, 60-, TECH INVESTR, 76-, SCI ASSOC, 82- *Mem:* AAAS; Am Chem Soc. *Res:* Process development work involving vitamins B-1, B-12, and gibrel; organic synthesis work in the areas of adhesives, insect repellents, insect attractants and insecticides; product development of oral hygiene products. *Mailing Add:* S C Johnson & Son Inc 1525 Howe St Racine WI 53403

YOHO, ROBERT OSCAR, b Solsberry, Ind, Sept 29, 13; m 34; c 3. PUBLIC HEALTH EDUCATION. *Educ:* Ind Univ, AB, 34, MA, 38, HSD, 57. *Prof Exp:* High sch teacher, Ind, 35-41; health educ consult, 41-45, dir div pub health educ, 45-68, dir bur pub health educ, rec & statist, 46-68, asst state health comnr, 68-78, DEP STATE HEALTH COMNR, IND STATE BD HEALTH, 78- *Concurrent Pos:* Instr, Med Sch, Ind Univ, Indianapolis & Butler Univ. *Mem:* Am Pub Health Asn; Am Asn Health, Phys Educ & Recreation. *Res:* Interrelation of services provided by rehabilitation agencies of Indiana. *Mailing Add:* 2318 N Fisher Ave Indianapolis IN 46224

YOHO, TIMOTHY PRICE, b Nov 8, 41. DEVELOPMENTAL BIOLOGY, ENTOMOLOGY. *Educ:* West Liberty State Col, BS, 67; WVa Univ, PhD(develop biol & entomol), 72. *Prof Exp:* Fel res, WVa Univ, 72-74; asst prof, 74-77, ASSOC PROF BIOL, LOCK HAVEN COL, 77- *Concurrent Pos:* Liaison dir, Pa Comt Correspon Creation Evolution Controversy, 80- *Mem:* Sigma Xi; Entomol Soc Am; Am Inst Biol Sci. *Res:* Electron microscopy; biochemistry; electrophysiology to study the photodynamic effect of light on dye-fed insects; death in visible light-exposed insects caused by food, drug and cosmetic dyes; danger to consumer and new insecticide development. *Mailing Add:* Dept Biol Lock Haven Col Lock Haven PA 17745

YOKE, JOHN THOMAS, b New York, NY, Feb 27, 28; m 56; c 3. INORGANIC CHEMISTRY. *Educ:* Yale Univ, BS, 48; Univ Mich, MS, 50, PhD(chem), 54. *Prof Exp:* Res chemist, Procter & Gamble Co, 56-58; instr chem, Univ NC, 58-59; asst prof, Univ Ariz, 59-64; assoc prof, 64-70, PROF CHEM, ORE STATE UNIV, 70- *Mem:* Am Chem Soc. *Res:* Inorganic synthesis; coordination chemistry; group V compounds; chemical binding; oxidation of ligands; catalysis. *Mailing Add:* Dept of Chem Ore State Univ Corvallis OR 97331

YOKEL, FELIX Y, b Vienna, Austria, July 13, 22; US citizen; m 46; c 3. GEOTECHNICAL ENGINEERING, STRUCTURAL ENGINEERING. *Educ:* Univ Conn, BS, 59, MS, 61, PhD(civil eng), 63. *Prof Exp:* Tech dir, Hazbani River Diversion Proj, 50-56; design engr, Griswold Eng, 56-60; chief found engr, John Clarkeson, Consult Engr, 60-63; sr partner, Clarkeson, Clough & Yokel, Consult Engrs, 63-68; res engr, 68-78, CHIEF GEOTECH

ENG, NAT BUR STANDARDS, 78- *Concurrent Pos:* Chmn masonry comt, Am Nat Standards Inst; chmn comt found & excavation standards, Am Soc Civil Engrs. *Honors & Awards:* Silver Medal, Dept Com, 76. *Mem:* Am Soc Civil Engrs. *Mailing Add:* Nat Bur Standards Washington DC 20234

YOKELSON, BERNARD JULIUS, b Brooklyn, NY, Sept 14, 24; m 46; c 2. ELECTRICAL ENGINEERING. *Educ:* Columbia Univ, BS, 48; Polytech Inst Brooklyn, MEE, 54. *Prof Exp:* Mem tech staff transmission & switching, 48-54, supvr switching syst & circuit develop, 54-59, head network & syst develop, 59-66, dir, Oper Systs Lab, 66-74 & Electronic Power Systs Lab, 74-76, dir, Local Switching Systs Lab, 76-80, DIR, TOLL DIGITAL SWITCHING LAB, BELL LABS, 80- *Mem:* Fel Inst Elec & Electronics Engrs; Sigma Xi. *Res:* Telephone communications; electronic switching systems; automation of telephone operator services; digital computers. *Mailing Add:* Bell Labs Rm 4E-301 Naperville IL 60566

YOKELSON, M(ARSHALL) V(ICTOR), b Brooklyn, NY, Nov 18, 18; m 53; c 2. METALLURGICAL ENGINEERING. *Educ:* City Col New York, BChE, 38; Polytech Inst Brooklyn, MMetE, 51. *Prof Exp:* Metallurgist, Chance Vought Corp, 47-48; res metallurgist, 48-56, res supvr, 56-57, chief metallurgist, 57-67, CHIEF METALL ENGR, GEN CABLE CORP, 67- *Mem:* Am Soc Metals; Am Inst Mining, Metall & Petrol Engrs; Brit Inst Metals; Metall Soc. *Res:* Work-hardening and annealing characteristics of copper; fabricating methods; laboratory evaluation and service behavior of metallic components of power and communications cables. *Mailing Add:* Gen Cable Co 160 Fieldcrest Ave Edison NJ 08818

YOKLEY, PAUL, JR, b Mitchellville, Tenn, Aug 3, 23; m 52; c 2. ZOOLOGY. *Educ:* George Peabody Col, BS, 49, MA, 50; Ohio State Univ, PhD(zool), 68. *Prof Exp:* Instr biol, 50-53, asst prof zool, 53-68, PROF ZOOL, UNIV NORTH ALA, 68- *Concurrent Pos:* Sci consult, Colbert Co Schs, 67-68; Tenn Game & Fish Comn res grant, 69-72; fisheries scientist, Am Fisheries Soc; Am Fisheries res scientist fel; consult, Tenn Valley Authority, 71- *Honors & Awards:* Res Award, Asn Southeastern Biologists, 70; State Conserv Educr Year, Ala Wildlife Fedn, 72. *Mem:* Soc Syst Zool; Am Malacol Union. *Res:* Life history and ecology of freshwater mussels; ecology of the freshwater mussels in the Tennessee River. *Mailing Add:* Dept of Biol Univ of NAla Box 5153 Florence AL 35630

YOKOSAWA, AKIHIKO, b Kofu, Japan, Nov 19, 27; US citizen; m 57; c 3. HIGH ENERGY PHYSICS. *Educ:* Tohoku Univ, Japan, BS, 51; Univ Cincinnati, MS, 53; Ohio State Univ, PhD(nuclear physics), 57. *Prof Exp:* Assoc prof physics, Ill State Univ, 57-59; physicist, 59-70, SR PHYSICIST, ARGONNE NAT LAB, 70- *Mem:* Fel Am Phys Soc. *Res:* Elementary particle physics. *Mailing Add:* Argonne Nat Lab 9700 S Cass Ave Argonne IL 60439

YOKOYAMA, MELVIN T, b Honolulu, Hawaii, Jan 22, 43. NUTRITION, MICROBIOLOGY. *Educ:* Univ Hawaii, BS, 66; Univ Ill, MS, 69, PhD(nutrit sci), 71. *Prof Exp:* Res asst dairy nutrit, Univ Ill, 66-69 & Nutrit Sci Prog, 66-71; res assoc nutrit biochem, Wash State Univ, 71-75; asst prof, 75-80, ASSOC PROF ANIMAL NUTRIT, MICH STATE UNIV, 80- *Mem:* Am Soc Animal Sci; Am Soc Microbiol; AAAS; Am Inst Nutrit. *Res:* Nutrition-microbiology. *Mailing Add:* Dept of Animal Husb Mich State Univ East Lansing MI 48823

YOKOYAMA, MITSUO, b Fukuoka, Japan, Mar 6, 27; m 55. IMMUNOLOGY, IMMUNOHEMATOLOGY. *Educ:* Juntendo Med Sch, Tokyo, MD, 50; Tokyo Med & Dent Univ, DMSc, 58. *Prof Exp:* Intern, Japanese Red Cross Cent Hosp, 51; staff, United Nat Blood Bank, 406 Med Gen Lab, Tokyo, 51-53; res asst, Tokyo Med & Dent Univ, 54-56, chief consult, 56-58, lectr, 59; res assoc, NIH, Japan, 58-59; vis scientist, NIH, US, 59-62; assoc res physician & vis res asst prof, Sch Med, Univ Calif, 62-63; assoc prof genetics, Univ Hawaii, 64-65, clin assoc prof med & genetics, 66-72; vpres sci affairs & dir labs, Kallestad Labs, 73-74; ASSOC PROF PATH & MICROBIOL, COL OF MED & COL BASIC MED SCI, UNIV ILL & HEAD CLIN IMMUNOL, UNIV HOSP LAB, 74- *Concurrent Pos:* Dir res, Kuakini Med Res Inst, 65-72; consult hemat, Tripler Army Med Ctr, Honolulu, Hawaii, 72. *Mem:* Am Asn Immunologists. *Res:* Blood group; human genetics; clinical immunology. *Mailing Add:* Clin Immunol Univ Hosp Lab Univ of Ill Med Ctr Chicago IL 60680

YOLDAS, BULENT ERTURK, b Turkey, Feb 19, 38; US citizen. CERAMICS, GLASS TECHNOLOGY. *Educ:* Ohio State Univ, BCerE, 63, MS, 64, PhD(glass & refractory), 66. *Prof Exp:* Sr engr mat sci, Owens-Ill Tech Ctr, 66-74; FEL SCIENTIST MAT SCI, WESTINGHOUSE RES LABS, 74- *Mem:* Am Ceramic Soc; Sigma Xi. *Res:* Coating technology for electronic and consumer products; formation of glass and ceramic materials by chemical polymerization; high surface area; catalytic materials; porous ceramic, metal-organic compounds; optics. *Mailing Add:* Westinghouse Elec Corp Res & Develop Ctr Pittsburgh PA 15235

YOLE, RAYMOND WILLIAM, b Middlesbrough, Eng, Feb 21, 27; Can citizen; m 57; c 4. STRATIGRAPHY, SEDIMENTOLOGY. *Educ:* Univ New Brunswick, BSc, 47; Johns Hopkins Univ, MA, 58; Univ BC, PhD(geol), 65. *Prof Exp:* Geologist, Calif Standard Co, Alta, 47-51, asst to vpres explor, 51-53, dist stratigr, 53-56; asst prof, 63-67, chmn dept, 67-70, ASSOC PROF GEOL, CARLETON UNIV, 67- *Concurrent Pos:* Vis res geologist, Univ Reading, 70-71; assoc ed, Can Soc Petrol Geol, 74-; vis prof, Fed Univ Pernambuco, Recife, Brazil, 76. *Mem:* Can Soc Petrol Geol; Petrol Soc; Can Inst Mining & Metall; fel Geol Asn Can; Am Asn Petrol Geol. *Res:* Petroleum geology; stratigraphy and tectonichistory Canadian cordillera; Paleozoic stratigraphy and sedimentology. *Mailing Add:* Dept of Geol Carleton Univ Ottawa ON K1S 5B6 Can

YOLKEN, HOWARD THOMAS, b Birmingham, Ala, Jan 29, 38; m 67; c 1. METALLURGY, MATERIALS SCIENCE. *Educ:* Univ Md, BS, 60, PhD(mat sci), 70. *Prof Exp:* Res metallurgist, 60-67, asst to dir, Inst Mat Res, 67-70, dep chief, Off Standard Ref Mat, 71-75, chief, Off Measurements Nuclear Technol, 76-80, CHIEF OFF HEALTH MEARUREMENTS, NAT BUR STANDARDS, 80- *Concurrent Pos:* Liaison mem comt mat specif, testing methods & standards, Nat Res Coun Mat Adv Bd, 74-75; mem tech adv comt nuclear safeguards, Int Atomic Energy Asn, 78 & 79. *Mem:* Am Phys Soc; AAAS. *Res:* Materials measurement and standards. *Mailing Add:* Nat Bur of Standards Washington DC 20234

YOLLES, SEYMOUR, b Brooklyn, NY, Oct 12, 14; m 40; c 2. CHEMISTRY. *Educ:* Brooklyn Col, BS, 35; Univ Miami, MS, 48; Univ NC, PhD(inorg chem), 51. *Prof Exp:* Anal chemist, US Testing Co, NJ, 37-38; tutor chem, Brooklyn Col, 38; res chemist, Colgate-Palmolive-Peet Co, NJ, 38-42, Ridbo Labs, 42-43 & Alrose Chem Co, RI, 43-45; consult chemist, 45-47; from instr to asst prof chem, Univ Miami, 47-52; staff chemist, Fabric & Finishes Dept, E I du Pont de Nemours & Co, Inc, 52-67; PROF CHEM, UNIV DEL, 67- *Concurrent Pos:* AEC asst, Univ NC, 50-51; adj prof, Univ Del, 56-67; consult, E I du Pont de Nemours & Co, Inc, 68- *Mem:* Am Chem Soc. *Res:* Organic and inorganic chemistry; reactions in liquid sulphur dioxide; quinoxalines; zirconium and hafnium; boron-phosphorus and silicon-phosphorus polymers; inorganic polymers; long time sustained release compositions for morphine antagonists. *Mailing Add:* Dept of Chem Univ of Del Newark DE 19711

YOLLES, STANLEY FAUSST, b New York, NY, Apr 19, 19; m 42; c 2. MEDICINE, PSYCHIATRY. *Educ:* Brooklyn Col, AB, 39; Harvard Univ, AM, 40; NY Univ, MD, 50; Johns Hopkins Univ, MPH, 57. *Prof Exp:* Parasitologist, Sector Malaria Lab, US Dept Army, 41-42, assoc dir, 42-44; intern, USPHS Hosp, Staten Island, NY, 50-51, resident psychiat, Lexington, Ky, 51-54; staff psychiatrist, Ment Health Study Ctr, NIMH, 54-55, from assoc dir to dir, 55-60, from assoc dir to dep dir extramural progs, 60-63, from dep dir to dir, NIMH, 63-70, assoc adminr for ment health, US Dept Health, Educ & Welfare, 68-70; chmn dept, 71-81, PROF PSYCHIAT & BEHAV SCI, STATE UNIV NY STONY BROOK, 71-, PSYCHIATRIST IN CHIEF, UNIV HOSP, 80- *Concurrent Pos:* Clin prof psychiat, George Washington Univ, 67-71; spec consult, NY City Bd Educ; mem, Prof Adv Bd, Int Comt Against Ment Illness, 68-, Nat Adv Panel, Am Jewish Comt, 69-72, Expert Adv Panel Ment Health, WHO, 69-81, Med Adv Comt, Am Joint Distribution Comt, 70-; trustee, NY Sch Psychiat; sr consult, Southside Hosp, Bay Shore, South Oaks Hosp, Amityville & Nassau County Med Ctr, NY. *Mem:* AAAS; fel Am Psychiat Asn; fel Am Pub Health Asn; fel Am Col Psychiat; fel NY Acad Sci. *Res:* Community mental health; mental health asministration; epidemiology of mental health. *Mailing Add:* 2 Soundview Ct Stony Brook NY 11790

YOLLES, TAMARATH KNIGIN, b New York, NY, Feb 27, 19; m 42; c 2. PUBLIC HEALTH. *Educ:* Bellevue Med Ctr, New York Univ, MD, 51. *Prof Exp:* Assoc dir, Malaria Lab, Sector, Trinadad, 43-45; dep dir, USPHS Outpatients Clinic, Washington, DC, 53, health maintenance officer, Off Surgeon Gen, 61-64, dir, Off Personnal Technol, HHS, 64-70, asst surgeon gen, 70-71; PROF COMMUN MED, SCH MED, HEALTH SCI CTR, STATE UNIV NY STONY BROOK, 71-, ASSOC DEAN CONTINUING MED EDUC, 74- *Concurrent Pos:* Consult, Health Serv & Mental Health Advan Lab, Dept HHS, 71-73; mem, Emergency Med Serv Comt, Nat Acad Sci, 75-; vchmn, Regional Emergency Med Serv Coun, 80- *Mem:* Am Col Emergency Physicians; AMA. *Res:* Malaria vectors in Guana and French Guana; sehistosomiasis. *Mailing Add:* Sch Med Health Sci Ctr State Univ NY Stony Brook NY 11794

YOLLICK, BERNARD LAWRENCE, b Toronto, Ont, Mar 24, 22; nat US; m 47; c 2. ANATOMY, SURGERY. *Educ:* Univ Toronto, MD, 45; Am Bd Surg, dipl, 57; Am Bd Otolaryngol, dipl, 67. *Prof Exp:* Instr anat, Col Med, Univ Sask, 47-49; clin asst prof, Col Med, Baylor Univ, 54-67; asst prof, Univ Tex Dent Sch, 54-61; lectr surg, Univ Tex Postgrad Sch Med, 57-67; ASST PROF OTOLARYNGOL, UNIV TEX HEALTH SCI CTR DALLAS, 67- *Concurrent Pos:* Fel surg, Am Cancer Soc, 53-54; consult, Houston Pulmonary Cytol Proj, 59 & Vet Admin Hosp, Dallas. *Mem:* Soc Human Genetics; Am Asn Anat; AMA; fel Am Col Surg; Am Soc Head & Neck Surg. *Res:* Induction of bone tumors in animals using heavy metals; experimental surgery in animals. *Mailing Add:* 4229 Bobbitt Dr Dallas TX 75229

YON, E(UGENE) T, b Mt Hope, WVa, Dec 29, 36; m 60; c 2. ELECTRICAL ENGINEERING, SOLID STATE ELECTRONICS. *Educ:* Univ Cincinnati, EE, 60; Case Western Reserve Univ, MS, 62, PhD, 65. *Prof Exp:* Sr staff engr, Electronics Div, Avco Corp, 65-67; asst prof elec eng, Case Western Reserve Univ, 67-70, assoc dir solid state electronics labs, 67-77, assoc prof, 70-77; V PRES, BOOZ, ALLEN & HAMILTON, INC, 78- *Concurrent Pos:* Consult, Avco Corp, 64-65 & 67-68, Babcock & Wilcox Corp, 67-, Am Radiation Res, Inc, 67-, Keithley Instruments, Inc, 68- & Solon Assocs, Inc, 68- *Mem:* Inst Elec & Electronics Engrs. *Res:* Semiconductor devices; biomedical engineering; technology, assessment and forecasting. *Mailing Add:* 8800 E Pleasant Valley Rd Cleveland OH 44131

YONAN, EDWARD E, b Beirut, Lebanon, Apr 15, 43; US citizen; m 72; c 2. ORGANIC SYNTHESIS. *Educ:* Univ Wis, BS, 70. *Prof Exp:* Chemist, Hodag Chem Corp, 72-73 & Velsicol Chem Corp, 73-76; SR CHEMIST, PPG INDUSTS, INC, 76- *Mem:* Am Chem Soc; Fire Retardant Chem Asn. *Res:* Organic synthesis and process development of agricultural chemicals such as herbicides, pesticides, phosgene, and related chemistry, carbonates, chloroformates, isocyanutes, and fire retardant additives. *Mailing Add:* PPG Indust Inc PO Box 66251 AMF-O'Hare Chicago IL 60666

YONAS, GEROLD, b Cleveland, Ohio, Dec 8, 39; m 61; c 2. PULSED POWER, INERTIAL FUSION. *Educ:* Cornell Univ, BS, 62; Calif Inst Technol, PhD(eng sci), 66. *Prof Exp:* Physicist & mgr electron beam res dept, Physics Int Co, 67-72; div supvr, 72-73, dept mgr fusion res, 73-78, DIR

PULSED ENERGY PROGS, SANDIA LABS, 78- *Concurrent Pos:* Mem adv bd, Am for Energy Independence; assoc ed, J Fusion Energy. *Mem:* Am Phys Soc; Am Nuclear Soc; Sigma Xi. *Res:* Fusion; intense electron and ion beams; pulsed high voltage technology; inertial confinement fusion; laser technology; plasma physics; high pressure physics. *Mailing Add:* Sandia Nat Labs Orgn 4200 Albuquerque NM 87115

YONCE, LLOYD ROBERT, b Roscoe, Mont, Sept 27, 24; m 48; c 2. PHYSIOLOGY. *Educ:* Mont State Col, BS, 49; Oregon State Univ, MS, 52; Univ Mich, PhD(physiol), 55. *Prof Exp:* Instr physiol, Ore State Univ, 51-52; instr, Med Sch, Univ Mich, 55-56; asst prof, 57-61, ASSOC PROF PHYSIOL, SCH MED, UNIV NC, CHAPEL HILL, 61- *Concurrent Pos:* Fel, Med Col Ga, 56-57; USPHS spec fel physiol, Univ Gothenburg. *Mem:* Am Phys Soc; Am Microcirculation Soc. *Res:* Cardiovascular physiology; neurophysiology; physiology of diving animals. *Mailing Add:* Dept of Physiol Univ of NC Sch of Med Chapel Hill NC 27514

YONDA, ALFRED WILLIAM, b Cambridge, Mass, Aug 10, 19; m 49, 75; c 4. MATHEMATICS. *Educ:* Univ Ala, BS, 52, MA, 54. *Prof Exp:* Mathematician, Rocket Res, Redstone Arsenal, Ala, 53 & US Army Ballistic Res Labs, Aberdeen Proving Ground, Md, 54-56; instr math, Temple Univ, 56-57; assoc scientist, Res & Adv Develop Div, Avco Corp, 57-59; sr proj mem tech staff, Radio Corp Am, 59-66; mgr comput anal & prog dept, Raytheon Corp, Bedford, 66-70, prin engr, Missile Systs Div, 70-73; MGR mgr systs anal & prog dept, Eastern Div, Waltham, Mass, 73-76, SOFTWARE ENG, ATLANTIC OPER, GTE SYLVANIA, WALTHAM, MASS, 76- *Concurrent Pos:* Hon fel, Advan Level Telecom Training Ctr, Fac, New Delhi, India. *Mem:* AAAS; Inst Elec & Electronics Engrs; Math Asn Am; Asn Comput Mach; NY Acad Sci. *Res:* Computer systems analysis; simulation; communications systems analysis; numerical analysis; telecommunications systems. *Mailing Add:* 12 Sunset Dr Medway MA 02053

YONEMOTO, ROBERT HIROSHI, b Oakland, Calif, Sept 7, 21; m 55; c 5. CANCER. *Educ:* Osaka Univ, MD, 47; Am Bd Gen Surg, cert, 58. *Prof Exp:* Asst surg, 58-62, assoc surg, 62-65, ASSOC DIR DEPT GEN & ONCOL SURG, CITY OF HOPE NAT MED CTR, 65-, DIR LAB SURG ONCOL, 75- *Concurrent Pos:* Fel, Thorndike Mem Lab, Harvard Med Sch, 54-55; NIH vis scientist, 73-74; assoc clin prof surg, Univ Calif, Irvine, 66-72 & Univ Calif, Los Angeles, 79- *Mem:* Fel Am Col Surgeons; James Ewing Soc; Am Asn Cancer Res; Am Soc Clin Oncol; Am Fedn Clin Res. *Res:* Immunotherapy of cancer; breast cancer; clinical surgical oncology; organ transplantation. *Mailing Add:* Dept of Gen & Oncol Surg City of Hope Nat Med Ctr Duarte CA 91010

YONETANI, TAKASHI, b Kagawa-ken, Japan, Aug 6, 30; US citizen; m 58; c 1. BIOCHEMISTRY, BIOPHYSICS. *Educ:* Osaka Univ, BA, 53, PhD(biochem), 61. *Prof Exp:* Res fel biochem, Johnson Found, Univ Pa, 58-61; Swedish Med Res Coun res fel, Nobel Med Inst, Stockholm, 62-64; from asst prof to assoc prof phys biochem, 64-68, PROF PHYS BIOCHEM, JOHNSON RES FOUND, UNIV PA, 68- *Concurrent Pos:* USPHS career develop award, 67-72. *Mem:* AAAS; Am Soc Biol Chemists; Am Chem Soc; Biophys Soc. *Res:* Purification, crystallization and characterization of cytochrome oxidase, alcohol dehydrogenase and cytochrome c peroxidase; determination of structure and function of these enzymes by spectrophotometry, electron spin resonance and x-ray diffraction techniques; heart disease; artificial hemoglobin; metalloporphyrin synthesis. *Mailing Add:* Johnson Res Found Univ Pa 37th & Hamilton Walk Philadelphia PA 19104

YONETZ, GERALD C(HARLES), b Manahgha, Minn, June 16, 20; m 43; c 4. CHEMICAL ENGINEERING. *Educ:* Mont State Col, BS, 42. *Prof Exp:* Chem engr, US Rubber Co, NC, 42-44; chem engr, Chem Corps, US Dept Army, 45-55, chief develop br, 55-70; vpres, Metronics Corp, 71-80; RETIRED. *Mailing Add:* 602 Schley Ave Frederick MD 21701

YONG, MAN SEN, b Sumatra, Indonesia, Mar 29, 41; Can citizen; m 65; c 2. PHARMACOLOGY. *Educ:* Nat Taiwan Univ, BSc, 62; Univ Alta, MSc, 64, PhD(pharmacol), 68. *Prof Exp:* ASST PROF PHARMACOL, McGILL UNIV, 71- *Concurrent Pos:* Med Res Coun Can fel, McGill Univ, 68-71, Can Heart Found res scholar, 71- *Mem:* Pharmacol Soc Can. *Res:* Peripheral and central adrenergic receptor mechanism; identification and characterization of adrenergic receptors of the uterus, vascular tissues and the central nervous system. *Mailing Add:* Dept of Pharmacol & Therapeut McGill Univ Montreal PQ H3A 2T5 Can

YONG, R(AYMOND), b Singapore, Apr 10, 29; Can citizen; m 61; c 2. CIVIL ENGINEERING. *Educ:* Washington & Jefferson Col, BA, 50; Mass Inst Technol, ScB, 52; Purdue Univ, MSc, 54; McGill Univ, MEng, 58, PhD(soil mech), 60. *Prof Exp:* From asst prof to assoc prof civil eng, 59-65, prof civil eng & appl mech, 65-73, WILLIAM SCOTT PROF CIVIL ENG & APPL MECH & DIR, GEOTECHNICAL RES CTR, MCGILL UNIV, 73- *Mem:* Am Soc Civil Engrs; assoc mem Brit Inst Civil Engrs. *Res:* Soil mechanics; soil physics; nonlinear mechanics; plasticity. *Mailing Add:* McGill Univ Geotech Res Ctr 817 Sherbrooke St W Montreal PQ H3A 2K6 Can

YONGE, KEITH A, b London, Eng, June 22, 10; m 47; c 4. PSYCHIATRY. *Educ:* McGill Univ, MD, CM, 48; Univ London, dipl psychol med, 52. *Prof Exp:* Mem staff psychiat, Med Res Coun, Eng, 51-52; dir, Ment Health Clin, Can, 52-54; from asst prof to assoc prof psychiat, Univ Sask, 55-57, clin dir, Univ Hosp, 55-57; prof & head dept, 55-75, EMER PROF PSYCHIAT, UNIV ALTA, 75- *Concurrent Pos:* Can Coun leave fel, 71-72. *Mem:* Psychiat Asn; Can Med Asn; Can Psychiat Asn; Can Ment Health Asn. *Res:* Basic and clinical psychiatry; phenomenology of depression; cognitive effects of cannabis; nature of human aggression. *Mailing Add:* 4345 Kingscote Rd RR 3 Cobble Hill BC V0R 1L0 Can

YONGUE, WILLIAM HENRY, b Charlotte, NC, Aug 21, 26; m 48; c 1. PROTOZOOLOGY, AQUATIC ECOLOGY. *Educ:* Johnson C Smith Univ, BS, 49; Univ Mich, MS, 62; Va Polytech Inst & State Univ, PhD(zool), 72. *Prof Exp:* Head dept sci, West Charlotte High Sch, 59-70; from instr to asst prof, 70-73, ASSOC PROF ZOOL, VA POLYTECH INST & STATE UNIV, 73- *Concurrent Pos:* Res assoc & proj scientist, Univ Mich Biol Sta, 69-75. *Mem:* Soc Protozoologists; Am Inst Biol Sci; Sigma Xi; fel AAAS; Nat Asn Biol Teachers. *Res:* The ecology of freshwater protozoans using polyurethane foam substrates for sampling and as microhabitats; lentic plankton dynamics; effects of heat and toxicants on protists; intracellular parasitism effects in blood of water snakes. *Mailing Add:* Dept Biol Va Polytech Inst & State Univ Blacksburg VA 24061

YONKE, THOMAS RICHARD, b Kankakee, Ill, Nov 30, 39; m 63; c 3. ENTOMOLOGY, SYSTEMATICS. *Educ:* Loras Col, BS, 62; Univ Wis, Madison, MS, 64, PhD(entom), 67. *Prof Exp:* Instr entom, Univ Wis, Madison, 66-67; asst prof, 67-71, assoc prof, 71-77, PROF ENTOM, UNIV MO-COLUMBIA, 77-, DIR, ENTOM RES MUS, 78-, CHMN DEPT, 80- *Concurrent Pos:* Pres grad fac senate, Univ Mo-Columbia, 80-81. *Mem:* Entom Soc Am; Soc Syst Zool; Entom Soc Can. *Res:* Biology and taxonomy of Hemiptera; taxonomy of immature Heteroptera; biology of Cicadellidae; taxonomy of Coreidae. *Mailing Add:* Dept of Entom Univ of Mo Columbia MO 65201

YONUSCHOT, GENE R, b Brooklyn, NY, Oct 29, 36; m 66; c 3. NUTRITION. *Educ:* Calif Polytech Inst, BS, 63; Univ Mo-Columbia, PhD(biochem), 69. *Prof Exp:* Instr biochem, Univ NC, 69-71; asst prof biochem, George Mason Univ, 71-76; chmn, Biochem Dept, WVa Sch Osteop Med, 76-78; ASSOC DEAN BASIC SCI, NEW ENGLAND COL OSTEOP MED, 78- *Res:* Acidic chromosomal proteins and t-RNA in relation to the control of cell division and differentiation; medical school curriculum; lanthanide series elements in biology. *Mailing Add:* New Eng Col of Osteop Med Biddeford ME 04005

YOO, BONG YUL, b Pusan, Korea, June 30, 35; Can citizen. PLANT PHYSIOLOGY, CELL BIOLOGY. *Educ:* Seoul Nat Univ, BSc, 58; Okla State Univ, MSc, 61; Univ Calif, Berkeley, PhD(bot), 65. *Prof Exp:* Nat Res Coun Can fel, 65-66; from asst prof to assoc prof, 66-77, PROF BIOL, UNIV NB, FREDERICTON, 77- *Mem:* Am Soc Cell Biol; Am Soc Plant Physiol; Bot Soc Am; Can Soc Cell Biol. *Res:* Biogenesis of plant cell organelles. *Mailing Add:* Dept of Biol Univ of NB Fredericton NB E3B 5A3 Can

YOO, MAN HYONG, b Seoul, Korea, June 27, 35; m 60; c 3. MATERIALS SCIENCE, METALLURGY. *Educ:* Mich State Univ, BS, 60, MS, 62, PhD(phys metall), 66. *Prof Exp:* Spec res grad asst, Mich State Univ, 61-65, res assoc, 65-67, res assoc mech metall, 66-67; RES STAFF SCIENTIST, METALS & CERAMICS DIV, OAK RIDGE NAT LAB, 67- *Mem:* Metall Soc Am; Am Soc Metals; Inst Mining, Metall & Petrol Engrs. *Res:* Deformation twinning; Dislocation theory and plastic deformation; mechanical properties; lattice defect theory; diffusion; radiation damage. *Mailing Add:* 966 W Outer Dr Oak Ridge TN 37830

YOO, TAI-JUNE, b Seoul, Korea, Mar 7, 35; US citizen; m 63; c 3. IMMUNOLOGY, INTERNAL MEDICINE. *Educ:* Seoul Nat Univ, MD, 59; Univ Calif, Berkeley, PhD(med physics), 63. *Prof Exp:* Teaching asst biophys, Div Med Physics, Univ Calif, Berkeley, 60-61, res asst, Lawrence Radiation Lab, 61-63; asst in med, Sch Med, Wash Univ, 63-66; sr cancer res scientist, Roswell Park Mem Inst, 66-68; res prof biol, Niagara Univ, 68-69; asst prof, 72-75, ASSOC PROF MED, COL MED, UNIV IOWA, 75- *Concurrent Pos:* NIH fel immunol, Wash Univ, 65-66; from intern to asst resident, Barnes Hosp, St Louis, Mo, 63-65; assoc resident, Sch Med, NY Univ, 68-69; clin investr, Vet Admin Hosp, Iowa City, Iowa, 72- *Mem:* AAAS; Biophys Soc; Am Asn Immunol; NY Acad Sci; Am Fedn Clin Res. *Res:* Molecular and cellular biology of immune phenomena; structure and function of antibody active site; interaction of ligand and protein; regulation in immune response; mechanism of action of immunopotentiator; immunologic and allergic disorders. *Mailing Add:* Div of Allergy & Immunol Univ of Iowa Col of Med Iowa City IA 52240

YOOD, BERTRAM, b Bayonne, NJ, Jan 6, 17; m 44; c 3. MATHEMATICAL ANALYSIS. *Educ:* Yale Univ, BS, 38, PhD(math), 47; Calif Inst Technol, MS, 39. *Prof Exp:* From instr to asst prof math, Cornell Univ, 47-53; from asst prof to prof, Univ Ore, 53-72; PROF MATH, PA STATE UNIV, 72- *Concurrent Pos:* Vis assoc prof, Univ Calif, 56-57; vis res assoc, Yale Univ, 58-59; mem, Inst Adv Study, 61-62; vis prof, Univ Edinburgh, 69-70, Weizmann Inst, Israel, 78-79. *Mem:* Am Math Soc. *Res:* Banach algebra; Banach spaces; analysis. *Mailing Add:* Dept of Math Pa State Univ University Park PA 16802

YOON, CHAI HYUN, b Korea, Aug 14, 20; nat US; m 53; c 2. GENETICS. *Educ:* Alma Col, AB, 50; Ohio State Univ, PhD(genetics), 53. *Prof Exp:* Res assoc genetics, Ohio State Univ, 53-55, instr, 55-56; asst prof biol, Lycoming Col, 56-58; from asst prof to assoc prof genetics, 59-66, PROF GENETICS, BOSTON COL, 66- *Mem:* AAAS; Genetics Soc Am; Am Genetic Asn. *Res:* Neuromuscular mutations in mice. *Mailing Add:* Great Rock Rd Sherborn MA 01770

YOON, DO YEUNG, b Inchon, Korea, Jan 22, 47; m 71; c 3. POLYMER CHEMISTRY. *Educ:* Seoul Nat Univ, BS, 69; Univ Mass, MS, 71, PhD(polymer sci), 73. *Prof Exp:* Res assoc chem, Stanford Univ, 73-75; RES SCIENTIST POLYMER MAT, RES LAB, IBM CORP, 75- *Mem:* Am Chem Soc; Am Phys Soc. *Res:* Conformational statistics and conformation-dependent properties of polymers; morphology and properties of polymers. *Mailing Add:* 511 Weybridge Dr San Jose CA 95123

YOON, HYO SUB, b Kyungbook, Korea, Apr 17, 35; US citizen; m 72. BIOENGINEERING, BIOMEDICAL ENGINEERING. *Educ:* Seoul Nat Univ, BS, 59; Univ Cincinnati, MS, 65; Pa State Univ, PhD(solid state sci), 71. *Prof Exp:* Res metallurgist, Sci Res Inst, Ministry Nat Defense, Korea, 59-62; res fel metall eng, Univ Cincinnati, 62-66; res asst solid state sci, Pa State Univ, 66-71; NIH trainee biophysics, 71-74, res assoc, 74-77, INSTR BIOMED ENG, RENSSELAER POLYTECH INST, 77- *Mem:* Am Soc Metals; Am Ceramic Soc; Inst Elec & Electronics Engrs; Am Crystallog Asn; Am Phys Soc. *Res:* Biomedical ultrasonics; biomechanics; calcified tissues; biomaterials; dental materials; nondestructive testing; elasticity; crystallography; animal ultrasound. *Mailing Add:* Ctr for Biomed Eng Rensselaer Polytech Inst Troy NY 12181

YOON, JI-WON, b Kangjin, Korea, Mar 28, 39; US citizen; m 68; c 2. DIABETES MELLITUS, VIRUS-INDUCED DISEASES. *Educ:* Chosun Univ, Korea, BS, 59, MS, 61; Univ Conn, Storrs, MS, 71, PhD(path), 73. *Prof Exp:* Asst prof cell biol, Chosun Univ, 65-67, assoc prof microbiol, Med Sch, 67-69; teaching asst, Univ Conn, Storrs, 69-73; res fel pathobiol, Sloan-Kettering Cancer Inst, 73-74; staff fel, 74-76, sr staff fel, 76-78, SR INVESTR VIROL, NIH, MD, 78- *Concurrent Pos:* Adj fac, Med Sch, Howard Univ, 79-82. *Mem:* Am Soc Microbiol; Genetics Soc Am; Tissue Culture Asn Am; NY Acad Sci; AAAS. *Res:* Role of viruses and autoantibodies in the pathogenesis of insulin dependent diabetes mellitus; cultivation and characterization of human, non-human primate and murine pancreatic beta cell cultures in microculture system; virus and cell interaction in the disease process in human and animal. *Mailing Add:* Rm 232 Bldg 30 NIH Bethesda MD 20205

YOON, JONG SIK, b Suwon, Korea, Jan 25, 37; US citizen; m 62; c 3. GENETICS, EVOLUTION. *Educ:* Yonsei Univ, Korea, BS, 61; Univ Tex, Austin, MA, 64, PhD(genetics), 65. *Prof Exp:* Res scientist assoc IV, Univ Tex, Austin, 62-65; res assoc oncol, M D Anderson Hosp, Univ Tex, 66-68; asst prof genetics & cytol, Yonsei Univ, Korea, 68-71; res scientist IV & V genetics, 71-74, instr cell biol, 74-75, res scientist genetics, Univ Tex, Austin, 75-78; ASSOC PROF, BIOL SCI, BOWLING GREEN STATE UNIV, 78- *Honors & Awards:* Young Scientist Award, Int Union Against Cancer, 70. *Mem:* Genetics Soc Am; Soc Study Evolution; AAAS; Sigma Xi; Am Genetic Asn. *Res:* Cytogenetics; mutation; oncogenetics; radiation genetics; genome organization, speciation and evolution of Drosophila and other species; genic balance between euchromatin and heterochromatin of chromosomes; sister chromatid exchange of mammalian and human chromosomes. *Mailing Add:* Dept of Biol Sci Bowling Green State Univ Bowling Green OH 43403

YOON, SUN, b Seoul, Korea, Jan 27, 49. FOOD SCIENCE, BIOCHEMISTRY. *Educ:* Yonsei Univ, Korea, BS, 71; Univ Ill, Urbana, MS, 74, PhD(food & nutrit), 78. *Prof Exp:* Res asst foods & nutrit, Univ Ill, Urbana, 71-78; asst prof foods & nutrit, Univ Fla, Lake Alfred, 78-80. *Mem:* Am Home Econ Asn; Am Dietetic Asn; Sigma Xi; Inst Food Technologists; Korean Scientists & Engrs Am. *Res:* Purification and characterization of food enzymes and their application to food processing; lipid oxidation; citrus processing. *Mailing Add:* 53 Foxoboro Lane E Amherst NY 14226

YORDY, JOHN DAVID, b St John's, Mich, Sept 17, 42; m 66; c 3. ORGANIC CHEMISTRY. *Educ:* Goshen Col, BA, 67; Mich State Univ, PhD(org chem), 74. *Prof Exp:* Teacher chem & math, Wesley High Sch, Oturkpo, Nigeria, 67-70; res scientist, Lubrizol Corp, 74-77; ASST PROF CHEM, GOSHEN COL, 77-, CHAIR, DIV NATURAL SCI, 81- *Mem:* Am Chem Soc. *Res:* Lubrication chemistry; synthesis and transformations of cyclopropanol derivatives; natural products isolation, identification and syntheses. *Mailing Add:* Dept Chem Goshen Col Goshen IN 46526

YORE, EUGENE ELLIOTT, b Columbus, Ohio, Mar 6, 39; c 2. CONTROL SYSTEMS, MECHANICAL ENGINEERING. *Educ:* Ohio State Univ, BSME, 62; Univ Calif, Berkeley, MS, 63, PhD(mech eng), 66. *Prof Exp:* Sr prin res scientist, Honeywell Inc, 66-70, sect chief, 70-73, mgr, 73-76, dir res, 76-78; dep sci & technol, asst secy of Army, 78-81; CORP DIR, ENG & MFG PROD, HONEYWELL INC, 81- *Concurrent Pos:* NASA trainee, Univ Calif, Berkeley, 64-66. *Mem:* Inst Elec & Electronics Engrs; Am Soc Mech Engrs; Am Inst Aeronaut & Astronaut; Am Defense Preparedness Asn. *Res:* Identification of dynamic systems and component parameter identification. *Mailing Add:* Honeywell Inc Honeywell Plaza Minneapolis MN 55408

YORIO, THOMAS, b New York, NY, Aug 27, 48; m 70; c 2. MEMBRANE PHYSIOLOGY, RENAL PHARMACOLOGY. *Educ:* Herbert H Lehman Col, BA, 71; City Univ NY, PhD(pharmacol), 75. *Prof Exp:* Res asst, Dept Opthal, Mt Sinai Sch Med, NY, 74-75, fel, 75-77; ASST PROF, DEPT PHARMACOL, TEX COL OSTEOP MED, 77- *Concurrent Pos:* Prin investr, Nat Kidney Found, 77-78, Am Heart Asn, 78-81, Nat Inst Arthritis, Metab & Digestive Dis, NIH, 79-82, minority hypertension res develop grant, Nat Heart, Lung & Blood Inst, 80-85. *Mem:* Sigma Xi; NY Acad Sci; Asn Res Vision & Opthal. *Res:* Hormonal regulation of epithelial transport of ions and water; role of lipid metabolism and prostaglandins in the response to aldosterone and antidiuretic hormone. *Mailing Add:* Dept Pharmacol Camp Bowie Montgomery Tex Col Osteop Med Ft Worth TX 76107

YORK, CARL MONROE, JR, b Macon, Ga, July 2, 25; m 52; c 3. PHYSICS. *Educ:* Univ Calif, Berkeley, AB, 46, MA, 50, PhD(physics), 51. *Prof Exp:* Fulbright fel physics, Univ Manchester, 51-52; res fel, Calif Inst Technol, 52-54; asst prof, Univ Chicago, 54-59; Ford Found & Guggenheim Found fel, Europ Orgn Nuclear Res, Geneva, 59-60; from assoc prof to prof, Univ Calif, Los Angeles, 60-69, asst chancellor res, 65-69, assoc dean grad div, 63-65; tech asst basic sci, Off Sci & Technol, Exec Off of the President, 69-72; vchancellor acad affairs, Univ Denver, 72-74; consult, 74-77; group leader conserv educ, Lawrence Berkeley Lab, 77-81; CONSULT, 81- *Concurrent Pos:* Consult, Argonne Nat Lab, 57-61, TRW Systs, Calif, 61-, Film Assocs, Calif, 62-, Lawrence Radiation Lab, 66, NSF, 72-76, Fedn Rocky Mountain States, 74-75, Colo Energy Res Inst, 75-76, Calif Energy Resource, Conserv & Develop Comn, 75-76, Pac Gas & Elec Co, 77- & Lawrence Livermore Nat Lab, 81- *Mem:* AAAS; Am Phys Soc. *Res:* Cosmic rays; elementary particles; positive sigma hyperon; high energy accelerator design; pion-nucleon scattering and production; muon decay and interactions; photo-production of pions; regional and state energy policies and plans; federal budgets for basic science and national science policy; validation of energy data bases and models. *Mailing Add:* 679 Carlston Ave Oakland CA 94610

YORK, CHARLES JAMES, b Calif, Sept 28, 19; m 44; c 4. VIROLOGY, BACTERIOLOGY. *Educ:* Univ Calif, AB, 43; Ohio State Univ, DVM, 48; Cornell Univ, PhD(virol, bact), 50. *Prof Exp:* Asst bact, Univ Calif, 41-43, bacteriologist, Vet Sci Dept, 43-44; sr bacteriologist, Med Res Dept, Ohio State Univ, 44-46, bacteriologist, Vet Col, 46; res assoc, Vet Virus Inst, Cornell Univ, 48-52; dir virus res lab, Pitman-Moore Co, Ind, 52-63; prof vet sci & head dept vet res lab, Mont State Univ, 63-65; dir inst comp biol, Zool Soc San Diego, 65-70; ASSOC PROF COMP PATH, MED SCH, UNIV CALIF, SAN DIEGO, 67- *Concurrent Pos:* Mem WHO. *Mem:* Soc Exp Biol & Med; Am Vet Med Asn; Tissue Cult Asn; US Animal Health Asn; Am Pub Health Asn. *Res:* Virus diseases of man and animals; comparative medicine for animal research models. *Mailing Add:* 5451 Yerba Anita Dr San Diego CA 92115

YORK, DEREK H, b Yorkshire, Eng, Aug 12, 36; m 61; c 1. GEOPHYSICS. *Educ:* Oxford Univ, BA, 57, DPhil(physics), 60. *Prof Exp:* Lectr, 60-62, from asst prof to assoc prof, 62-74, PROF PHYSICS, UNIV TORONTO, 74- *Concurrent Pos:* Chmn subcomt isotope geophys & mem comt geod & geophys, Nat Res Coun Can, 67. *Mem:* Am Geophys Union; Can Asn Physicists. *Res:* Isotopic geophysics; temporal evolution of continents; reversals of earth's magnetic field. *Mailing Add:* Dept of Physics Univ of Toronto Toronto ON M5S 2R8 Can

YORK, DONALD GILBERT, b Shelbyville, Ill, Oct 28, 44; m 66; c 3. ASTROPHYSICS. *Educ:* Mass Inst Technol, BA, 66; Univ Chicago, PhD(astrophysics), 70. *Prof Exp:* From res asst to res assoc, 70-72, RES STAFF ASTROPHYSICS, PRINCETON UNIV, 72- *Mem:* Int Astron Union; Am Astron Soc. *Res:* Determination physical properties of interstellar gas and dust, using ultraviolet and visual spectroscopic techniques in our own galaxy as well as distant galactic systems. *Mailing Add:* Princeton Univ Observ Princeton NJ 08540

YORK, DONALD HAROLD, b Moose Jaw, Sask, Jan 30, 44; m 65; c 3. NEUROPHYSIOLOGY, NEUROSCIENCE. *Educ:* Univ BC, BSc, 65, MSc, 66; Monash Univ, Australia, PhD(neurophysiol), 69. *Prof Exp:* Asst prof physiol, Queen's Univ, Ont, 68-75; ASSOC PROF PHYSIOL, SCH MED, UNIV MO-COLUMBIA, 75- *Concurrent Pos:* Med Res Coun Can grant, Queen's Univ, Ont, 69-72; scholar, Med Res Coun Can, 70. *Mem:* AAAS; Can Physiol Soc; Am Physiol Soc; Soc Neurosci; Pharmacol Soc Can. *Res:* Motor control; basal ganglia and movement; synaptic transmission in central nervous system. *Mailing Add:* Dept of Physiol Univ of Mo Sch of Med Columbia MO 65201

YORK, GEORGE KENNETH, II, b Tucson, Ariz, July 1, 25; m 47; c 5. MICROBIOLOGY. *Educ:* Stanford Univ, AB, 50; Univ Calif, PhD(microbiol), 60. *Prof Exp:* Asst bacteriologist, Nat Canners Asn, 51-53; actg asst prof, 58-60, asst prof food sci & technol, 60-66, EXTEN MICROBIOLOGIST, UNIV CALIF, DAVIS, 66- *Mem:* NY Acad Sci; Am Soc Microbiol; Inst Food Technol. *Res:* Food microbiology; intermediary metabolism of microbes; thermomicrobiology; modes of inhibition of microbes by chemicals; treatment and disposal of waste. *Mailing Add:* Dept of Food Sci & Technol Univ of Calif Davis CA 95616

YORK, GEORGE WILLIAM, b St Louis, Mo, Sept 26, 45; m 68; c 2. LASERS. *Educ:* St Louis Univ, BS, 67; Univ Mo, Rolla, MS, 69, PhD(physics), 71. *Prof Exp:* Res assoc physics, Joint Inst Lab Astrophys, 72-74; MEM STAFF PHYSICS, LOS ALAMOS SCI LAB, 74- *Mem:* Am Phys Soc; Laser Inst Am. *Res:* Development of high power gas lasers utilizing preionized electrical discharges in metal vapor system. *Mailing Add:* Los Alamos Sci Lab Lab L-10 MS-532 Los Alamos NM 87545

YORK, HERBERT FRANK, b Rochester, NY, Nov 24, 21; m 47; c 3. PHYSICS, SCIENCE POLICY. *Educ:* Univ Rochester, AB, 42, MS, 43; Univ Calif, PhD, 49. *Hon Degrees:* DSc, Case Western Reserve Univ, 60; LLD, Univ San Diego, 64; DrHumL, Claremont Grad Sch, 74. *Prof Exp:* Asst physics, Univ Rochester, 42-43; physicist, Radiation Lab, Univ Calif, 43-54, assoc dir, 54-58, dir, Livermore Lab, 54-58, asst prof physics, Univ, 51-54; dir advan res projs div, Inst Defense Anal & chief scientist, Advan Res Projs Agency, US Dept Defense, 58, dir defense res & eng, Off Secy Defense, 58-61; chancellor, 61-64 & 70-72, grad dean, 69-70 & 72-73, PROF PHYSICS, UNIV CALIF, SAN DIEGO, 65- *Concurrent Pos:* Mem sci adv bd, US Air Force, 53-57, ballistic missile adv comt, Secy Defense, 55-58 & sci adv panel, US Army, 56-58; mem, President's Sci Adv Comt, 57-58 & 64-67, vchmn, 65-67; mem gen adv comt, US Arms Control & Disarmament Agency, 61-69; mem bd trustees, Aerospace Corp, 62- & Inst Defense Anal, 65 & 67-; Guggenheim fel, 72-73; mem continuing comt, Conf Sci & World Affairs, 73-76; sr consult, Off Secy Defense, 77-; mem, Defense Sci Bd, 78-, US Ambassador, Comp Test Ban Talks, Geneva, 79-81. *Mem:* Am Phys Soc; Am Acad Arts & Sci; Am Inst Aeronaut & Astronaut; Inst Elec & Electronics Eng; Int Acad Astronaut. *Res:* Science and public affairs; disarmament problems. *Mailing Add:* 6110 Camino de la Costa La Jolla CA 92037

YORK, J(ESSE) LOUIS, b Plains, Tex, May 1, 18; m 45, 75; c 2. AIR POLLUTION CONTROL, ENVIRONMENTAL PERMITS. *Educ:* Univ NMex, BSE, 38; Univ Mich, MS, 40, PhD(chem eng), 50. *Prof Exp:* From instr to prof chem & metall eng, Univ Mich, 42-70, proj dir, Res Inst, 42-70; environ scientist, 70-80, CHIEF ENVIRON SCIENTIST, STEARNS-ROGER CORP, 80- *Concurrent Pos:* Mem bd, Colo Sch Mines Found, 73- *Mem:* Am Chem Soc; Am Soc Mech Engrs; Air Pollution Control Asn; Am Inst Chem Engrs; Nat Soc Prof Engrs. *Res:* Suspensions of fine particles; sprays; nozzles; combustion; air and water pollution control; entrainment; desalination; filtration; environmental studies and analyses. *Mailing Add:* Environ Sci Div PO Box 5888 Denver CO 80217

YORK, JAMES WESLEY, JR, b Raleigh, NC, July 3, 39; m 61; c 2. THEORETICAL PHYSICS, GRAVITATION. *Educ:* NC State Univ, BS, 62, PhD(physics), 66. *Prof Exp:* Asst prof physics, NC State Univ, Raleigh, 65-68; res assoc physics, Princeton Univ, 68-69, lectr, 69-70, asst prof, 70-73; assoc prof, 73-77, PROF PHYSICS, UNIV NC, CHAPEL HILL, 77- *Concurrent Pos:* Vis asst prof, Univ Maryland, 72; vis prof, Univ Paris, 76; vis scientist, Harvard-Smithsonian Ctr Astrophys, 77; vis prof, Univ Tex, 79; mem, Int Soc Gen Relativity & Gravitation, 80-83. *Honors & Awards:* Third Prize, Gravity Res Found, Mass, 75. *Mem:* Am Phys Soc; Am Asn Physics Teachers; AAAS. *Res:* Gravitation and relativity; mathematical, astrophysical and quantum theoretic aspects. *Mailing Add:* Dept of Physics & Astron Univ of NC Chapel Hill NC 27514

YORK, JOHN LYNDAL, b Morton, Tex, Aug 14, 36; m 58; c 2. BIOCHEMISTRY, PHYSICAL ORGANIC CHEMISTRY. *Educ:* Harding Col, BS, 58; Johns Hopkins Univ, PhD(biochem), 62. *Prof Exp:* NIH trainee, 62-64; biochemist, Stanford Res Inst, 64-65; asst prof biochem, Med Units, Univ Tenn, Memphis, 65-68; assoc prof, 68-77, PROF BIOCHEM, SCH MED, UNIV ARK, LITTLE ROCK, 77- *Concurrent Pos:* Vis prof, Karolinska Inst, Stockholm, 74-75; fel, Swedish Med Res Coun, 75. *Mem:* Am Soc Biol Chem; Am Chem Soc; Sigma Xi; AAAS. *Res:* Nature of the active site and mechanisms of action of non-heme iron proteins; Mossbauer effect; mechanisms of oxidation and oxygenation; structure and function of fibrinogen. *Mailing Add:* Dept Biochem Univ Ark Med Col Little Rock AR 72201

YORK, JOHN OWEN, b Parkin, Ark, July 11, 23; m 49; c 2. PLANT BREEDING, PLANT GENETICS. *Educ:* Miss State Univ, BS, 48, MS, 50; Tex A&M Univ, PhD(plant breeding), 62. *Prof Exp:* From instr to assoc prof, 52-68, PROF AGRON, UNIV ARK, FAYETTEVILLE, 68- *Mem:* Am Soc Agron; Am Genetic Asn. *Res:* Hybrid corn and grain sorghum breeding and production. *Mailing Add:* Dept Agron Univ Ark Fayetteville AR 72701

YORK, OWEN, JR, b Evansville, Ind, Oct 18, 27; m 48; c 2. ORGANIC CHEMISTRY. *Educ:* Evansville Col, BA, 48; Univ Ill, MA, 50, PhD(org chem), 52. *Prof Exp:* Asst, Univ Ill, 48-52; res chemist, Hercules Powder Co, 52-56; head dept chem, Ill Wesleyan Univ, 56-60; res supvr, W R Grace & Co, 60-61; assoc prof, 61-64, chmn dept, 64-73, reader & table leader, 64-72, chief reader, Advan Placement Chem, 72-76, PROF CHEM, KENYON COL, 64-, ASSOC DIR, READING-ADVAN PLACEMENT PROG EDUC TESTING SERV, 79- *Concurrent Pos:* NSF fel, Stanford Univ, 68-69. *Mem:* AAAS; Am Chem Soc; Royal Soc Chem. *Res:* Grignard reaction; oxidation; electrophilic substitution; isomerization of aromatic acids; synthetic photochemistry; catalysis. *Mailing Add:* Dept of Chem Kenyon Col Gambier OH 43022

YORK, SHELDON STAFFORD, b New Haven, Conn, Oct 29, 43; m 68; c 2. BIOPHYSICAL CHEMISTRY. *Educ:* Bates Col, BS, 65; Stanford Univ, PhD(biochem), 71. *Prof Exp:* Am Cancer Soc res fel chem, Calif Inst Technol, 70-72; ASST PROF CHEM, UNIV DENVER, 72- *Mem:* Am Chem Soc. *Res:* Protein - DNA recognition processes, specifically the conformational changes within the lac repressor protein which affect its ability to bind to the lac operator. *Mailing Add:* Dept of Chem Univ of Denver Denver CO 80208

YORKE, JAMES ALAN, b Peking, China, Aug 3, 41; US citizen; m 63; c 6. APPLIED MATHEMATICS, BIOMATHEMATICS. *Educ:* Columbia Univ, AB, 63; Univ Md, College Park, PhD(math), 66. *Prof Exp:* From res assoc to res assoc prof, 66-72, RES PROF MATH, INST PHYS SCI & TECHNOL, UNIV MD, COLLEGE PARK, 72- *Concurrent Pos:* Guggenheim fel, 80-81. *Mem:* AAAS; Am Math Soc; Math Asn Am; Soc Indust & Appl Math. *Res:* Qualitative ordinary differential equations; applications in epidemiology. *Mailing Add:* Inst Phys Sci & Technol Univ of Md College Park MD 20740

YORQUE, RALF RICHARD, b Toronto, Ont, Mar 15, 42; Can citizen; m 70; c 2. BIOLOGY, RESOURCE MANAGEMENT. *Educ:* Univ Toronto, BSc, 63; Univ McMurdo Sound, PhD(zool), 68. *Prof Exp:* Fel zool, Univ Calif, Berkeley, 68-69; from asst prof to assoc prof, 69-81, PROF ECOL, UNIV BC, 81- *Mem:* Ecol Soc Am; Brit Ecol Soc; Am Resource Ecol Soc (secy-treas, 75-77). *Res:* Dynamics of managed ecosystems; resource planning. *Mailing Add:* Inst Resource Ecol Univ BC Vancouver BC V6T 1W5 Can

YORTON, JOAN BANNISTER, organic chemistry, see previous edition

YOS, DAVID ALBERT, b Trenton, NJ, Apr 24, 23; m 46; c 2. BOTANY, HISTORY OF BIOLOGY. *Educ:* NY Univ, AB, 48; Univ Mo, MA, 52, MLS, 81; Univ Iowa, PhD(bot, plant anat), 60. *Prof Exp:* Instr biol, Burlington Col, 52-59; asst prof bot, Univ Wis-Green Bay, 60-62; teacher, High Sch, NJ, 63; from asst prof to assoc prof biol, Eastern N Mex Univ, 63-73, prof biol, 73-81, adj prof biol & sci librn, 81-82; SCI LIBRN, ILL STATE UNIV, NORMAL, 82- *Mem:* Sigma Xi; Spec Libraries Asn; Am Soc Info Sci. *Res:* Fluorescence microscopy of plant tissues; development of periderm; microtechnique; history of microscopy and photomicrography. *Mailing Add:* Sci Librn Ill State Univ Normal IL 61761

YOS, JERROLD MOORE, b Clinton, Iowa, Jan 1, 30; m 60; c 3. RE-ENTRY PHYSICS. *Educ:* Univ Nebr, AB, 52, MS, 54, PhD(physics), 56. *Prof Exp:* SR SCIENTIST, SYSTS DIV, AVCO CORP, 57- *Mem:* Am Phys Soc. *Res:* Electromagnetics; atomic physics; kinetic theory of gases; electrical discharges. *Mailing Add:* Avco Systs Div 201 Lowell St Wilmington MA 01887

YOSHIDA, AKIRA, b Okayama, Japan, May 10, 24; m 54. BIOCHEMISTRY, GENETICS. *Educ:* Univ Tokyo, MS, 47, DSc, 54. *Prof Exp:* From instr to asst prof chem, Univ Tokyo, 51-54, assoc prof chem & biochem, 54-60; res assoc biochem, Univ Pa, 61-63; res chemist, NIH, 63-65; res prof med genetics, Univ Wash, 64-72; DIR DEPT BIOCHEM GENETICS, CITY OF HOPE MED CTR, 72- *Concurrent Pos:* Rockefeller Found Int scholar, 55-56. *Mem:* AAAS; Am Soc Biol Chem; Int Soc Hemat; Soc Human Genetics. *Res:* Study on the changes of protein structure and properties of the enzymes due to mutation; regulatory mechanism of gene action. *Mailing Add:* Dept of Biochem Genetics City of Hope Med Ctr Duarte CA 91010

YOSHIDA, TAKESHI, b Fukuoka, Japan, July 24, 38; m 64; c 2. IMMUNOPATHOLOGY. *Educ:* Univ Tokyo, MD, 63, Dr Med Sci, 70. *Prof Exp:* Res mem immunol, Dept Tuberc, NIH, Tokyo, 64-71; asst prof, Dept Path, State Univ NY Buffalo, 71-74; asst prof, 74-75, assoc prof, 75-82, PROF PATH, UNIV CONN HEALTH CTR, 82- *Concurrent Pos:* Res assoc, Dept Path, NY Univ Med Ctr, 67-68; vis assoc, Lab Immunol, Nat Inst Allergy & Infectious Dis, Bethesda, 68-69, vis scientist, 71; Buswell fel, State Univ NY Buffalo , Buffalo, 71-74, asst dir, Ctr Immunol, 73-74; Nat Inst Allergy & Infectious Dis res career develop award, 75-80. *Mem:* Am Asn Immunologists; Am Asn Pathologists; Am Asn Univ Pathologists; Reticuloendotherial Soc; NY Acad Sci. *Res:* Mechanisms of cell-mediated immunity, biological and physicochemical characterizations of effector molecules produced in vitro by stimulated lymphocytes, and in vivo activities of lymphokines. *Mailing Add:* Dept of Path Univ of Conn Health Ctr Farmington CT 06032

YOSHIKAMI, DOJU, b Heart Mountain, Wyo. NEUROBIOLOGY, NEUROSCIENCE. *Educ:* Reed Col, BA, 65; Cornell Univ, PhD(biochem & molecular biol), 70. *Prof Exp:* NIH fel appl physics, Cornell Univ, 70-71; NSF fel neurobiol, Harvard Univ Sch Med, 71-73, instr, 73-76, prin res assoc, 76-78; asst prof, 78-81, ASSOC PROF BIOL, UNIV UTAH, 81- *Res:* Cellular and molecular neurobiology; structure and function of synapses. *Mailing Add:* Dept Biol Univ Utah Sch Med Salt Lake City UT 84112

YOSHIKAWA, HERBERT HIROSHI, b South Dos Palos, Calif, May 13, 29; m 60. NUCLEAR ENGINEERING, SOLID STATE PHYSICS. *Educ:* Univ Chicago, PhB, 48, MS, 51; Univ Pa, PhD(physics), 58. *Prof Exp:* Sr engr physics, Hanford Labs, Gen Elec Co, 58-65; mgr graphite res & develop radiation effects, Pac Northwest Lab, Battelle-Northwest Lab, 65-70; mgr mat eng, 70-78, MGR TECHNOL, HANFORD ENG DEVELOP LAB, WESTINGHOUSE HANFORD CO, 78- *Mem:* Am Nuclear Soc; Am Phys Soc; AAAS; Sigma Xi. *Res:* Technology of fast breeder, light water and fusion reactors; materials development, irradiation testing and reactor environment characterization. *Mailing Add:* Hanford Eng Develop Lab PO Box 1970 Richland WA 99352

YOSHIMOTO, CARL MASARU, b Honolulu, Hawaii, Apr 27, 22; m 57; c 2. ENTOMOLOGY. *Educ:* Iowa Wesleyan Col, BA, 50; Kans State Univ, MS, 52; Cornell Univ, PhD(entom), 55. *Prof Exp:* Entomologist, Entom Res Div, USDA, 55-57 & BP Bishop Mus, 58-69; SR RES SCIENTIST, DEPT ENVIRON, CAN FORESTRY SERV, 69- *Concurrent Pos:* Affil fac, Grad Sch, Univ Hawaii, 64-69; NSF grant, Brit Mus, London, Eng, 67-68. *Mem:* Entom Soc Am; Entom Soc Can; Sigma Xi. *Res:* Taxonomy of Hymenoptera; insect behavior and dispersal; zoogeography; biological control. *Mailing Add:* Biosysts Res Inst Cent Exp Farm Ottawa ON K1A 0C6 Can

YOSHIMURA, SEI, b Hilo, Hawaii, May 24, 22. CHEMOTHERAPY, VIROLOGY. *Educ:* Univ Hawaii, BS, 46. *Prof Exp:* Bacteriologist, Honolulu Health Dept, 47-49; lab technician, Hektoen Inst, Ill, 50-52; bacteriologist, Vet Admin Hosp, Minneapolis, Minn, 52-54 & Mt Sinai Hosp, Chicago, Ill, 54-55; virologist, Nepera Chem Co, Warner-Chillcott Co, 55-56; sect head microbiol, Grove Labs Div, Bristol-Myers Co, 56-65; SR RES ASST MICROBIOL, MERRELL NAT-LABS, RICHARDSON-MERRELL INC, 65- *Res:* Viral chemotherapy; medical microbiology; general toxicology; analgesics. *Mailing Add:* Infectious Dis Res Dept Merrell-Nat Labs 2110 E Galbraith Rd Cincinnati OH 45215

YOSHINAGA, KOJI, b Yokohama, Japan, Mar 20, 32; m 61. ENDOCRINOLOGY. *Educ:* Univ Tokyo, BSc, 55, MSc, 57, PhD(agr), 60. *Prof Exp:* Trainee physiol reproduction, Worcester Found Exp Biol, 61-64; vis scientist, Agr Res Coun Unit Reproduction Physiol & Biochem, Cambridge, 64-66; staff scientist, Worcester Found Exp Biol, 66-69; res assoc anat, Harvard Med Sch, 69, asst prof, 69-72, assoc prof, 72-79; HEALTH SCIENTIST ADMINR, REPRODUCTION SCI BR, POP RES, NAT INST CHILD HEALTH & HUMAN DEVELOP, NIH, 78- *Concurrent Pos:* Pop Coun fel, Worcester Found Exp Biol, 62-63; Pop Coun fel, Agr Res Coun Unit Reproduction Physiol & Biochem, Cambridge, 64-65, Lalor Found fel, 65-66. *Mem:* Am Asn Anat; Endocrine Soc; Soc Study Reproduction; Am Physiol Soc; Soc Study Fertil. *Res:* Endocrinology and physiology of reproduction in female animals, especially the mechanisms involved in ovo-implantation, ovarian function and relationship between the egg development and hormone action. *Mailing Add:* Reproduction Sci Br Landow Bldg 733 Bethesda MD 20205

YOSHINO, KOUICHI, b Matsuyama, Japan, Jan 1, 31. CHEMICAL PHYSICS, MOLECULAR SPECTROSCOPY. *Educ:* Tokyo Univ Educ, BS, 53, MS, 55, PhD(physics), 72. *Prof Exp:* Physicist, Indust Res Inst Kanagawa, Japan, 54-58 & Govt Indust Res Inst, Tokyo, 58-65; res physicist, Air Force Cambridge Res Lab, 65-76; RES ASSOC, HARVARD-SMITHSONIAN CTR ASTROPHYS, 76- *Concurrent Pos:* Res physicist, Wentworth Inst, 61-63. *Mem:* Phys Soc Japan; Spectros Soc Japan; Optical Soc Am. *Res:* Determination of properties of ground and excited electronic states of molecules or atoms by high resolution vacuum ultraviolet spectroscopy such as nitrogen, oxygen, carbon monoxide and rare gases. *Mailing Add:* Harvard-Smithsonian Ctr Astrophys 60 Garden St Cambridge MA 02138

YOSHINO, TIMOTHY PHILLIP, b Turlock, Calif, Apr 5, 48. PARASITOLOGY, IMMUNOBIOLOGY. *Educ:* Univ Calif, Santa Barbara, BA, 70, MA, 71, PhD(biol), 75. *Prof Exp:* Res assoc parasitol, Univ Calif, Santa Barbara, 71-73; res assoc invert immunol, Lehigh Univ, 75-77; ASST PROF ZOOL, UNIV OKLA, 78- *Concurrent Pos:* USPHS res fel, Nat Inst Allergy & Infectious Dis, 75. *Mem:* Am Soc Parasitologists; Soc Invert Path;

Am Soc Zoologists; AAAS; Int Soc Develop & Comp Immunol. *Res:* Humoral and cellular mechanisms of internal defense in bivalve and gastropod molluscs; immunobiology of schistosome-mollusc interactions. *Mailing Add:* Dept of Zool 730 Van Vleet Oval Univ Okla Norman OK 73019

YOSIM, SAMUEL JACK, b St Petersburg, Fla, Apr 21, 20; m 49; c 2. PHYSICAL CHEMISTRY. *Educ:* Univ Fla, BS, 48; Univ Chicago, MS, 49, PhD(phys chem), 52. *Prof Exp:* Assoc chemist, Argonne Nat Lab, 51-52; res chemist, 52-56, mgr pollution technol unit, 56-75, MGR ENVIRON CHEM UNIT, CHEM GROUP, ENERGY SYSTS GROUP, ROCKWELL INT, 75- *Res:* Molten salts, high temperature chemistry; nuclear chemistry; fuel chemistry. *Mailing Add:* 23812 Killion Woodland Hills CA 91364

YOSS, KENNETH M, b Hudson, Iowa, Jan 13, 26; m 55; c 3. ASTRONOMY. *Educ:* Univ Mich, BS, 48, MS, 50, PhD(astron), 53. *Prof Exp:* Asst prof astron & physics, Wilson Col, 52-53; from asst prof to assoc prof, La State Univ, 53-59; assoc prof astron, Mt Holyoke Col, 59-64; PROF ASTRON, UNIV ILL, URBANA, 64- *Mem:* Am Astron Soc; Int Astron Union. *Res:* Spectrophotometry of objective prism and slit spectra; spectral and luminosity classification. *Mailing Add:* Univ of Ill Observ Urbana IL 61801

YOSS, ROBERT EUGENE, b Spooner, Wis, Nov 28, 24; m 47; c 3. NEUROANATOMY, NEUROLOGY. *Educ:* Univ Tenn, MD, 48; Univ Mich, MS & PhD(neuroanat), 52. *Prof Exp:* From instr to asst prof anat, Med Sch, Univ Mich, 49-54; from asst prof to assoc prof, 57-70, PROF NEUROL, MAYO GRAD SCH MED, UNIV MINN, 70-, CONSULT, MAYO CLIN, 57- *Concurrent Pos:* Fel neruol, Mayo Grad Sch Med, Univ Minn, 55-57. *Mem:* Am Asn Anat. *Res:* Anatomy of spinal cord; narcolepsy. *Mailing Add:* Mayo Grad Sch of Med Univ of Minn Rochester MN 55901

YOST, FRANCIS LORRAINE, b Punxsutawney, Pa, Dec 18, 08; m 54. THEORETICAL PHYSICS. *Educ:* Univ Ky, BS, 29, MS, 31; Univ Wis, PhD(physics), 36. *Prof Exp:* Asst physics, Univ Wis, 31-36 & Purdue Univ, 36-37; physicist, US Rubber Co, Mich, 37-42; sr tech aide, Div 17, Nat Defense Res Comt, 43-44; Off Sci Res & Develop, Eng & France, 44-45, Washington, 45-46; chief math anal subdiv, US Naval Ord Lab, 46-47 & weapons anal div, 50-54; assoc prof physics, Ill Inst Technol, 47-51; prof physics, Univ Ky, 54-74, head dept, 54-65; RETIRED. *Concurrent Pos:* Vis prof, Univ Indonesia, 56-58. *Mem:* Am Phys Soc; Am Asn Physics Teachers. *Res:* Nuclear physics; physical properties of rubber; naval ordnance; guided missile lethalities. *Mailing Add:* 1320 E Cooper Dr Lexington KY 40502

YOST, FREDERICK GORDON, b Norwalk, Conn, Aug 29, 40; m 63; c 2. METALLURGY. *Educ:* Polytech Inst Brooklyn, BSMetE, 66; Iowa State Univ, PhD(metall), 72. *Prof Exp:* Engr metall, Pratt & Whitney Aircraft, 66-67; STAFF MEM METALL, SANDIA LABS, 72- *Mem:* Am Soc Metals; Am Inst Mining, Metall & Petrol Engrs. *Res:* Kinetics of solid state phase transformations in metals and alloys, especially those used in microelectronics. *Mailing Add:* Div 5832 Box 5800 Sandia Labs Albuquerque NM 87185

YOST, GAROLD STEVEN, b Denver, Colo, Sept 8, 49; m 78. DRUG METABOLISM, MEDICINAL CHEMISTRY. *Educ:* Bethel Col, BS, 71; Univ Hawaii, MS, 74; Colo State Univ, PhD(chem), 77. *Prof Exp:* Fel pharmaceut chem, Univ Calif, San Francisco, 77-78; instr chem, Towson State Univ, 78-81; ASST PROF, COL PHARM, WASH STATE UNIV, 81- *Concurrent Pos:* Vis lectr, Dept Pharmacol, Johns Hopkins Univ, 79-81. *Mem.* Am Chem Soc; Int Soc Study Xenobiotics; Sigma Xi. *Res:* Marine and terrestrial natural products including poisonous feedstocks; suicidal inhibitors of cytochrome P-450 and other enzymes; stereoselective drug metabolism involving cytochrome P-450 and glucuronyltransferase. *Mailing Add:* Dept Pharm Wash State Univ Pullman WA 99164

YOST, HENRY THOMAS, JR, b Baltimore, Md, Jan 22, 25; m 48; c 1. RADIATION GENETICS. *Educ:* Johns Hopkins Univ, AB, 47, PhD, 51. *Hon Degrees:* MA, Amherst Col, 65. *Prof Exp:* From instr to assoc prof, 51-65, prof biol, 65-76, RUFUS TYLER LINCOLN PROF BIOL, AMHERST COL, 76- *Concurrent Pos:* Pres WMass Health Planning Coun, 76-; pres Valley Health Plan, 75- NIH fel, Chester Beatty Res Inst, London, Eng, 62-63 & 69-70. *Mem:* Fel AAAS; Soc Develop Biol; NY Acad Sci; Bot Soc Am; Genetics Soc Am. *Res:* Investigation of the structure of the chromosome and other particulates; radiation biology. *Mailing Add:* 75 N East St Amherst MA 01002

YOST, JOHN FRANKLIN, b Brodbecks, Pa, Mar 21, 19; m 43; c 2. ORGANIC CHEMISTRY. *Educ:* Western Md Col, BS, 43; Johns Hopkins Univ, AM, 48, PhD(org chem), 50. *Hon Degrees:* DS, Western Md Col, 64. *Prof Exp:* Jr instr, Johns Hopkins Univ, 46-50; res chemist, Synthetic Rubber & Plastics Lab, US Rubber Co, 43-44 & 46; agr chemist & group leader, Agr Chem Labs, 50-57, mgr tech dept, Phosphate & Nitrate Div, 57, dir plant indust develop, Agr Div, 58-62, dir prod develop & govt registrn, 62-66, DIR AGR RES & DEVELOP, INT DEPT, AM CYANAMID CO, 66- *Mem:* Am Chem Soc. *Res:* Synthetic organic chemistry; agricultural product analysis, formulation and registration; pesticides, fertilizers, feed additives and veterinary products; research administration. *Mailing Add:* 21 Toth Lane Rocky Hill NJ 08553

YOST, JOHN R(OBARTS), JR, b Phoenixville, Pa, July 10, 23; m 47; c 2. CHEMICAL ENGINEERING. *Educ:* Ursinus Col, BS, 44; Univ Pa, MS, 49. *Prof Exp:* Process develop engr, Res Labs, Sharples Corp, 49-51; process develop engr, Merck & Co, 51-54; sect head, Process Eng, E R Squibb & Sons Div, Olin Mathieson Chem Corp, 54-61, head chem pilot plant, 61-67; vpres mfg, Ott Chem Co, 67-70, exec vpres, 70-73; PRES, MUSKEGON CHEM CO, 74- *Mem:* Am Chem Soc; Am Inst Chem Engrs. *Res:* Pharmaceutical compounds; unit processes leading to synthetic organic compounds; distillation and solvent extraction. *Mailing Add:* 1725 Warner St Whitehall MI 49461

YOST, ROBERT STANLEY, b Pottsville, Pa, Jan 24, 21; m 43; c 2. ORGANIC CHEMISTRY. *Educ:* Pa State Univ, BS, 42; Duke Univ, PhD(org chem), 48. *Prof Exp:* Chemist, Hercules Powder Co, 42-43; lab instr chem, Duke Univ, 43-44, chemist, 44-46 & 47-59, head process res group, Redstone Res Labs, 59-68, CHEMIST, RES LABS, ROHM AND HAAS CO, 68- *Mem:* Am Chem Soc. *Res:* Organic synthesis including synthetic resins and explosives; process research. *Mailing Add:* Res Labs Rohm & Haas Co Spring House PA 19477

YOST, WILLIAM A, b Dallas, Tex, Sept 21, 44; m 69; c 2. PSYCHOACOUSTICS, PSYCHOPHYSICS. *Educ:* Colo Col, BA, 66; Ind Univ, Bloomington, PhD(psychol), 70. *Prof Exp:* NSF fel, Univ Calif, San Diego, 70-71; asst prof speech psychol, Univ Fla, 71-74, assoc prof psychol, 74-77; assoc prof, 77-78, PROF PSYCHOL, LOYOLA UNIV, 79- *Concurrent Pos:* Mem & chmn, Comt Acoust Standards, 72-75. *Mem:* Acoust Soc Am; Am Psychol Asn; Sigma Xi; Int Audiol Soc; AAAS. *Res:* Binaural hearing; pitch perception; speech perception; auditory sensitivity and discrimination in young children; noise pollution. *Mailing Add:* Parmly Hearing Inst 6525 N Sheridan Rd Chicago IL 60626

YOST, WILLIAM JACQUE, b Fairview, WVa, Dec 23, 13; m 81; c 2. PHYSICS. *Educ:* Furman Univ, AB, 35, BS, 36; Syracuse Univ, MA, 38; Brown Univ, PhD(physics), 40. *Prof Exp:* Instr math, Furman Univ, 35-36 & physics, Syracuse Univ, 40-41; res physicist, Field Res Dept, Magnolia Petrol Co, 41-44, group leader, 44-46, res assoc, 46-52, tech adv to res dir, 52-54, dir res, Marathon Oil Co, 54-73; MGT CONSULT, 73- *Mem:* AAAS; Am Phys Soc; Soc Explor Geophys. *Res:* Theoretical quantum mechanics; infrared and ultraviolet spectroscopy; electromagnetic phenomena in conducting media; x-ray and electron diffraction; electromagnetic and elastic wave propagation theory. *Mailing Add:* PO Box 2870 Estes Park CO 80517

YOST, WILLIAM LASSITER, b Washington, DC, Mar 14, 23; m 51; c 4. ORGANIC CHEMISTRY. *Educ:* Univ Va, BS, 44, MS, 47, PhD(chem), 49. *Prof Exp:* AEC fel biol Sci, Calif Inst Technol, 49-50, NIH fel, 50-51; res chemist, US Naval Ord Test Sta, 51-52; sr chemist, Ciba Pharmaceut Co, 52-65, head appl math, 65-67, dir chem develop & appl math, 67-69; pres, Union Data Corp, 69-78; VPRES, ACTION BIOMED COMPUT, 78- *Mem:* AAAS; Am Chem Soc; Asn Comput Mach; NY Acad Sci. *Res:* Application of mathematics and computer techniques to the solution of problems arising in medical and pharmaceutical research. *Mailing Add:* 208 Schooley's Mountain Rd Long Valley NJ 07853

YOTIS, WILLIAM WILLIAM, b Almyros, Greece, Jan 17, 30; US citizen; m 57; c 3. MICROBIOLOGY. *Educ:* Wayne State Univ, BS, 54, MS, 56; Northwestern Univ, PhD(microbiol), 60. *Prof Exp:* Asst microbiol, Wayne State Univ, 54-56; clin bacteriologist, Univ Hosp, Univ Mich, 56-57; from instr to assoc prof, 60-72, interim chmn, 64-65, PROF MICROBIOL, MED SCH, LOYOLA UNIV CHICAGO, 73- *Concurrent Pos:* Res grants, NIH, 60-, Eli Lilly Res Labs, 65-66, Syntex Res Labs, 66- & Upjohn Co, 66-; consult, Am Type Cult Collection, 66-; mem ed bd Applied & Environ Microbiol; vis scientist, Argonne Nat Lab, 77- *Mem:* AAAS; Am Med Asn; Am Soc Microbiol; Am Asn Dent Res; NY Acad Sci. *Res:* Investigations on mechanisms of microbial pathogenicity; nonspecific host defense mechanisms; bactericidal activity of body fluids; staphylococcal host-parasite relationship; hormonal influence on infection; bacterial physiology; isotachophoresis and scanning isoelectric focusing of medically important proteins; cariostasis by fluoride. *Mailing Add:* Loyola Univ Med Sch 2160 S First Ave Maywood IL 60153

YOUD, THOMAS LESLIE, b Spanish Fork, Utah, Apr 2, 38; m 62; c 4. SOIL MECHANICS, EARTHQUAKE ENGINEERING. *Educ:* Brigham Young Univ, BES, 64; Iowa State Univ, PhD(civil eng), 67. *Prof Exp:* RES & CIVIL ENGR, US GEOL SURV, MENLO PARK, 67- *Mem:* Am Soc Civil Engrs; Int Soc Soil Mech & Found Engrs; Earthquake Eng Res Inst; Seismol Soc Am; Am Soc Testing & Mats. *Mailing Add:* US Geol Surv MS 98 345 Middlefield Rd Menlo Park CA 94025

YOUDELIS, W(ILLIAM) V(INCENT), b Edmonton, Alta, Aug 1, 31; m 56; c 2. PHYSICAL METALLURGY. *Educ:* Univ Alta, BSc, 52; McGill Univ, MEng, 56, PhD(metall eng), 58. *Prof Exp:* Mine engr, Steep Rock Iron Mines, Ont, 52-54; from asst prof to assoc prof phys metall, Univ Alta, 58-65; assoc prof, 65-68, PROF PHYS METALL, UNIV WINDSOR, 68-, HEAD DEPT ENG MAT, 72-; PRES, YOUDELIS ASSOCS INC, 77- *Mem:* AAAS; Am Soc Metals; Am Inst Mining, Metall & Petrol Engrs; Can Inst Mining & Metall; Metals Soc. *Res:* Solidification; kinetics of phase transformations; dental alloys; electronic materials. *Mailing Add:* Dept of Eng Mat Univ of Windsor Windsor ON N9B 3P4 Can

YOUKER, JAMES EDWARD, b Cooperstown, NY, Nov 13, 28; div; c 2. RADIOLOGY. *Educ:* Colgate Univ, AB, 50; Univ Buffalo, MD, 54; Am Bd Radiol, dipl, 60. *Prof Exp:* Asst prof radiol, Med Col Va, 61-63; from asst prof to assoc prof, Univ Calif, San Francisco, 64-68; PROF RADIOL & CHMN DEPT, MILWAUKEE COUNTY GEN HOSP, WIS, 68- *Concurrent Pos:* NIH res fel, Allmanna Sjukhuset, Malmo, Sweden, 62 & 63; attend radiologist, Proj HOPE, Indonesia, 58; USPHS grant dir, Training Radiologist & Technician Teams in Mammography, & co-dir, Training Prog Cardiovasc Radiol, 65-68. *Mem:* Radiol Soc NAm; Am Col Radiol; Asn Univ Radiol; Int Soc Lymphology. *Res:* Pulmonary function changes with lymphographic contrast media; pathology of congenital heart disease; chylous ascites and the spectrum of the disease. *Mailing Add:* Dept of Radiol Milwaukee County Gen Hosp Milwaukee WI 53202

YOUKER, JOHN, b Auburn, NY, Sept 7, 43; m 67; c 4. PHYSICAL CHEMISTRY, ANALYTICAL CHEMISTTRY. *Educ:* Rensselaer Polytech Inst, BS, 65, PhD(phys chem), 69. *Prof Exp:* Chemist, Coated Abrasive & Tape Div, Norton Co, 68-69; asst prof, 69-74, assoc prof, 74-81, PROF CHEM, HUDSON VALLEY COMMUNITY COL, 81- *Concurrent Pos:* Dep dir, Rensselaer County Off Disaster Preparedness, 81- *Mem:* Am Chem Soc; Sigma Xi. *Res:* Spectroscopy; analytical chemistry; environmental science. *Mailing Add:* Dept of Chem Hudson Valley Community Col Troy NY 12180

YOULE, RICHARD JAMES, b Concord, Calif, Sept 20, 52; m 81. PROTEIN TOXINS, CELL MEMBRANES. *Educ:* Albion Col, AB, 74; Univ SC, PhD(biol), 77. *Prof Exp:* Staff fel, NIMH, 78-80, SR STAFF FEL, SECT BIOPHYS CHEM, LAB NEUROCHEM, NIMH, NIH, 81- *Res:* The mechanism of protein toxins (ricin and diptheria), inhibition of protein synthesis and how they can be linked to cell surface binding species, such as monoclonal antibodies, to create cell-type-specific toxins; physiological role of ricin and lectins. *Mailing Add:* Sect Biophys Chem Lab Neurochem Bldg 36 Rm 3D30 NIH Bethesda MD 20205

YOUM, YOUNGIL, b Seoul, Korea, Jan 2, 42; m 68; c 3. KINEMATICS OF MECHANISMS, BIOMECHANICS. *Educ:* Utah State Univ, Logan, BS, 68; Univ Wis-Madison, MS, 70 & 73, PhD(eng mech), 76. *Prof Exp:* Res asst biomech, Univ Wis-Madison, 68-73; assoc res scientist bioeng, Univ Iowa, Iowa City, 74-78; asst prof, 78-80, ASSOC PROF MECH ENG, CATHOLOIC UNIV AM, WASHINGTON, DC, 80- *Concurrent Pos:* Consult, Nat Bur Standards, 79-81 & Walter Reed Army Med Ctr, 79- *Mem:* Am Soc Mech Engrs; Am Soc Biomech; Sigma Xi; Korean Soc Engrs & Scientists. *Res:* Three dimemsional (spatial) analysis of the mechanisms, kinematics, kinetics, vibrations and biomechanics of the human upper extremity (the hand, the elbow, the wrist joint); design of prosthetic limbs and total replacement of human articular joint; robotic research. *Mailing Add:* 3411 Fullerton St Beltsville MD 20705

YOUMANS, GARY RICHARD, b Hastings, Mich, Jan 17, 50. MICROBIOLOGY. *Educ:* Ind Univ, AB, 72; Northern Mich Univ, MA, 75; Univ Northern Colo, DA, 80. *Prof Exp:* Microbiologist, Fitzsimons Army Med Ctr, 79-80; ASST PROF, DEPT BIOL, WVA INST TECHNOL, 80- *Mem:* Am Soc Microbiol; AAAS; Sigma Xi. *Res:* Microbial ecology; denitrification rates in terrestrial ecosystems. *Mailing Add:* Dept Biol WVa Inst Technol Montgomery WV 25136

YOUMANS, HUBERT LAFAY, b Lexsy, Ga, Aug 2, 25; m 51; c 1. ANALYTICAL CHEMISTRY. *Educ:* Emory Univ, AB, 49, MS, 50; La State Univ, PhD(anal chem), 61. *Prof Exp:* Chemist, Savannah River Plant, E I du Pont de Nemours & Co, SC, 52-57; develop chemist, Sucrochem Div, Colonial Sugars Co, Lab, 57-58; asst prof chem, Ft Hays Kans State Col, 61-64; res chemist, Atlas Chem Indust, Inc, Del, 64-67; assoc prof chem, 67-78, PROF CHEM, WESTERN CAROLINA UNIV, 78- *Mem:* Am Chem Soc. *Res:* Absorptiometry; analytical separations; communications for chemistry students. *Mailing Add:* Chem Dept Western Carolina Univ Cullowhee NC 28733

YOUMANS, JULIAN RAY, b Baxley, Ga, Jan 2, 28; m 54; c 3. NEUROSURGERY. *Educ:* Emory Univ, BS, 49, MD, 52; Univ Mich, MS, 55, PhD(neuroanat), 57; Am Bd Neurol Surg, dipl, 60. *Prof Exp:* From asst prof to assoc prof neurosurg, Sch Med, Univ Miss, 59-63; from assoc prof to prof, Med Col SC, 63-67, chief div, 63-67; PROF NEUROSURG & CHIEF DEPT, SCH MED, UNIV CALIF, DAVIS, 67- *Mem:* AMA; Am Acad Neurol; Am Asn Surg of Trauma; Am Col Surg; Am Asn Automotive Med. *Res:* Physiology of cerebral blood flow. *Mailing Add:* Dept of Neurol Surg Univ of Calif Sch of Med Davis CA 95616

YOUMANS, WILLIAM BARTON, b Cincinnati, Ohio, Feb 3, 10; m 32; c 3. PHYSIOLOGY. *Educ:* Western Ky State Col, BS, 32, MA, 33; Univ Wis, PhD(animal med), 38; Univ Ore, MD, 44. *Prof Exp:* Instr biol, Western Ky State Col, 32-35; from asst to instr physiol, Univ Wis, 35-38; from instr to prof, Med Sch, Univ Ore, 38-52, head dept, 45-52; chmn dept, 52-71, prof, 52-76, EMER PROF PHYSIOL, SCH MED, UNIV WIS-MADISON, 76- *Concurrent Pos:* USPHS spec fel, 61-62; intern, Henry Ford Hosp, 44-45; mem physiol study sect, USPHS, 52-56, mem physiol training comt, 58-62. *Mem:* Am Physiol Soc; Am Soc Pharmacol & Exp Therapeut. *Res:* Innervation of intestine; gastrointestinal motility; visceral reflexes; cardiac innervation, neurohormones; angiotensin. *Mailing Add:* 162 Benson Rd Port Angeles WA 98362

YOUNATHAN, EZZAT SAAD, b Deirut, Egypt, Aug 25, 22; nat US; m 58; c 2. BIOCHEMISTRY. *Educ:* Univ Cairo, BSc, 44; Fla State Univ, MA, 53, PhD, 55. *Prof Exp:* Chemist, Govt Labs, Egypt, 44-50; Seagrams' Int Training Prog fel, 50-51; res asst, Fla State Univ, 51-55, asst prof, 58-59; res assoc, Col Med, Univ Ill, 55-57; asst prof biochem, Sch Med, Univ Ark, Little Rock, 59-63, assoc prof & actg head dept, 63-66; NIH spec fel & vis prof, Inst Enzyme Res, Univ Wis, 66-67; PROF BIOCHEM, LA STATE UNIV, BATON ROUGE, 68- *Concurrent Pos:* Vis prof, Dept Biochem, Univ Calif, Berkeley, 78. *Mem:* Am Soc Biol Chem; Am Chem Soc; Soc Exp Biol & Med; NY Acad Sci. *Res:* Mechanism of enzyme action; protein chemistry; control of carbohydrate metabolism; experimental diabetes. *Mailing Add:* Dept of Biochem La State Univ Baton Rouge LA 70803

YOUNATHAN, MARGARET TIMS, b Clinton, Mass, Apr 25, 26; m 58; c 2. FOOD SCIENCE, NUTRITION. *Educ:* Southern Miss Univ, BA, 46, BS, 50; Univ Tenn, MS, 51; Fla State Univ, PhD(food sci, nutrit), 58. *Prof Exp:* Instr food & nutrit, Ore State Univ, 51-55; Qm Food & Container Inst res fel, Fla State Univ, 58-59; instr pediat, Sch Med, Univ Ark, Little Rock, 62-65, asst prof, 65-68; assoc prof, 71-79, PROF FOOD & NUTRIT, LA STATE UNIV, BATON ROUGE, 79- *Concurrent Pos:* Consult, Ark State Health Dept, 62-68. *Mem:* Inst Food Technol; Am Home Econ Asn; Am Dietetic Asn. *Res:* Heme pigments; antioxidants; lipid oxidation; infant and child nutrition. *Mailing Add:* Dept of Food & Nutrit La State Univ Baton Rouge LA 70803

YOUNES, MUAZAZ A, b Zahleh, Lebanon, Sept 15, 51; Jordan citizen. ENDOCRINOLOGY, CLINICAL CHEMISTRY. *Educ:* Beirut Univ, BSc, 74; Am Univ Beirut, MSc, 76; Welch Nat Sch Med, PhD(endocrinol), 79. *Prof Exp:* Teaching asst biochem, Am Univ Beirut, 74-76, endocrinol, Welch Nat Sch Med, 76-79; fel, 79-81, INSTR ENDOCRINOL, BAYLOR COL MED, 81- *Mem:* Am Asn Clin Chem; Am Chem Soc; Am Fertility Soc; Am Soc Andrology. *Res:* Exploring the mechanism of action of steroid hormones in human term placenta, ovary and uterus; receptor analysis in areas of the female reproductive tract; reproductive endocrinology; high risk maternal medicine. *Mailing Add:* Dept Obstet & Gynec Baylor Col Med Houston TX 77030

YOUNG, AINSLIE THOMAS, JR, b Norman, Okla, Mar 3, 43; m 68. POLYMER CHEMISTRY, PHOTOCHEMISTRY. *Educ:* Memphis State Univ, BS, 66, MS, 68; Univ Ky, PhD(phys chem), 71. *Prof Exp:* Fel, Univ Calif, Berkeley, 71-73; fel, La State Univ, Baton Rouge, 73-74; res chemist polymer chem, Ctr Res Lab, Mead Corp, 74-80. *Mem:* Am Chem Soc; Sigma Xi; AAAS. *Res:* Physical chemical and chemical kinetic studies of photo-polymerization reactions. *Mailing Add:* 360 Cheryl Ave Los Alamos NM 87544

YOUNG, ALLEN MARCUS, b Ossining, NY, Feb 23, 42. ECOLOGY. *Educ:* State Univ NY New Platz, BA, 64; Univ Chicago, PhD(zool), 68. *Prof Exp:* Orgn Trop Studies, Inc fel for study in Costa Rica, Univ Chicago, 68-70; asst prof biol, Lawrence Univ, Appleton, Wis, 70-75; CUR & HEAD DEPT INVERTEBRATE ZOOL, MILWAUKEE PUB MUS, 75- *Concurrent Pos:* NSF fel for study in Costa Rica, Lawrence Univ, 71-74; NSF res grant, 75-; res assoc, Nat Mus Costa Rica, 75-; Am Cocoa Res Inst grant, 78- *Mem:* AAAS; Ecol Soc Am; Lepidop Soc; Asn Trop Biol. *Res:* Population biology and behavior of neotropical Lepidoptera and Cicadidae; ecology of laboratory populations of Tribolium; insect pollination of cocoa. *Mailing Add:* Dept Invertebrate Zool Milwaukee Pub Mus 800 W Wells St Milwaukee WI 53233

YOUNG, ALVIN BAU YUEN, b Honolulu, Hawaii, Oct 22, 42; m 69. SOLID STATE ELECTRONICS. *Educ:* Calif Inst Technol, BS, 64; Stanford Univ, MS, 65, PhD(elec eng), 69. *Prof Exp:* MEM RES STAFF, OPTOELECTRONICS DIV, FAIRCHILD CAMERA & INSTRUMENT CORP, 69- *Mem:* Electrochem Soc. *Res:* Light-emitting diodes, device physics and processing; epitaxial growth of III-V compounds. *Mailing Add:* Optoelectronics Div MS 50-502 3105 Alfred St Santa Clara CA 95050

YOUNG, ANDREW TIPTON, b Canton, Ohio, Apr 4, 35; m 54, 63, 68; c 2. ASTRONOMICAL PHOTOMETRY, PLANETARY ASTRONOMY. *Educ:* Oberlin Col, BA, 55; Harvard Univ, MA, 57, PhD(astron), 62. *Prof Exp:* Res fel, Observ, Harvard Univ, 60-65, lectr astron, Univ, 62-65; asst prof, Univ Tex, 65-67; mem tech staff, Aerospace Corp, 67-68 & Jet Propulsion Lab, 68-73; res scientist, Tex A&M Univ, 73-75, vis asst prof physics, 75-78, res scientist, 78-80; ADJ ASSOC PROF ASTRON, SAN DIEGO STATE UNIV, 81- *Concurrent Pos:* Co-investr TV experiments, Mariner Mars, 69 & 71; consult, NASA; assoc ed, Inter-Continental Aerospacecraft-Range Unlimited Systs, 77- *Mem:* Fel AAAS; Am Astron Soc; fel Royal Astron Soc; fel Optical Soc Am; Int Astron Union. *Res:* Observational astronomy; astronomical photometry and instrumentation; photomultipliers; scintillation; planetary physics. *Mailing Add:* Dept Astron San Diego State Univ San Diego CA 92182

YOUNG, ARCHIE RICHARD, II, b Camden, NJ, June 8, 28; m 51; c 7. INORGANIC CHEMISTRY. *Educ:* Lincoln Univ, Pa, AB, 49; Univ Pa, MS, 50, PhD(phys chem), 55. *Prof Exp:* Instr chem, Ft Valley State Col, 50-51 & Va Union Univ, 51-52; assoc prof, Tenn State Univ, 54-56; from res chemist to sr res chemist, Reaction Motors Div, Thiokol Chem Corp, NJ, 56-63, supvr inorg synthesis, 63-67; sr chemist, 67-68, sr res chemist, 68-80, STAFF CHEMIST, EXXON RES & ENG CO, LINDEN, 80- *Mem:* AAAS; NY Acad Sci. *Res:* Aluminum hydride and inorganic fluorine chemistry; fluorocarbons; fuel cells; solid state synthesis; ferrites. *Mailing Add:* Exxon Res & Eng Co US Hwy 1 & Park Ave Linden NJ 07036

YOUNG, ARTHUR, b New York, NY, Jan 4, 40; m 60; c 1. ASTRONOMY. *Educ:* Allegheny Col, BS, 60; Ind Univ, MA, 65, PhD(astron), 67. *Prof Exp:* From asst prof to assoc prof, 67-74, PROF ASTRON, SAN DIEGO STATE UNIV, 74- *Concurrent Pos:* Acad consult, Spitz Labs, 63-; vis staff scientist, High Altitude Observ, 81-82. *Mem:* Int Astron Union; Am Astron Soc. *Res:* Spectroscopy. *Mailing Add:* Dept of Astron San Diego State Univ San Diego CA 92115

YOUNG, ARTHUR WESLEY, b Shenandoah, Iowa, May 14, 04; m 29; c 3. AGRONOMY, SOILS. *Educ:* Iowa State Col, BS, 29, MS, 30, PhD(soil microbiol), 32. *Prof Exp:* Instr agr bact, Univ Tenn, 32-34; prof agron, Panhandle Agr & Mech Col, 34-35; from assoc prof to emer prof agron, Tex Tech Univ, 35-69, from actg head dept to head dept, 37-69; CONSULT, 69- *Concurrent Pos:* Consult, Bunge y Born, Argentina, 68-71; independent agr consult, 69-; chmn, State Seed & Plant Bd, Tex; res consult, Dept of Agr, Lubbock Christian Col, 75- *Honors & Awards:* Agr Chem Award, W Tex Agr Chem Inst, 69; Gerold W Thomas Outstanding Agriculturalist Award, Tex Tech Univ, 70. *Mem:* AAAS; Sigma Xi; Am Soc Agron; Soil Sci Soc Am; hon mem Int Crop Improve Asn (vpres, 58-59, pres, 60-61). *Res:* Soil bacteriology, chemistry and fertility; direction of microbial studies on influence of organic matter and fertilizer to selected soils. *Mailing Add:* 3305 45th St Lubbock TX 79413

YOUNG, AUSTIN HARRY, b Brighton, Mass, Oct 25, 28; m 58; c 2. PHYSICAL CHEMISTRY. *Educ:* Tufts Univ, BS, 50; Univ Wis, PhD(chem), 59. *Prof Exp:* Develop chemist, Fabrics & Finishes Dept, EI du Pont de Nemours & Co, 50-51, supvr, Explosives Dept, 51-52; res asst, Army Chem Ctr, Edgewood, Md, 53-54; from res chemist to sr res chemist, 58-69, res assoc, 69-78, SR SCIENTIST, A E STALEY MFG CO, 78- *Mem:* AAAS; Am Chem Soc; Am Asn Cereal Chem. *Res:* Starch, colloid, polymer and radiation chemistry; kinetics; polymer synthesis and characterization; coatings; chromatography; thermal analysis; rheology; radiotracer techniques; graphic arts; health physics. *Mailing Add:* Res & Develop Div AE Staley Mfg Co Decatur IL 62525

YOUNG, BERNARD THEODORE, b Tarentum, Pa, Apr 13, 30; m 55; c 5. PHYSICS. *Educ:* Slippery Rock State Col, BS, 52; Tex A&M Univ, MS, 61, PhD(physics), 64. *Prof Exp:* Res & develop engr, Tex Div, Dow Chem Co, 56-59; res asst physics, Tex A&M Univ, 60-63; from assoc prof to prof, Sam Houston State Col, 63-68, dir, 65-68; assoc dean, 68-70, PROF PHYSICS & DEAN GRAD SCH, ANGELO STATE UNIV, 70- *Concurrent Pos:* Mem elem transparency proj, Tex Educ Agency, 66-67. *Mem:* Am Phys Soc. *Res:* Molecular spectroscopy; atomic structure. *Mailing Add:* Off of Grad Dean Angelo State Univ San Angelo TX 76901

YOUNG, BING-LIN, b Honan, China, Feb 3, 37; m 64; c 1. HIGH ENERGY PHYSICS. *Educ:* Nat Taiwan Univ, BS, 59; Univ Minn, PhD(physics), 66. *Prof Exp:* Res assoc physics, Ind Univ, 66-68 & Brookhaven Nat Lab, 68-70; asst prof, 70-74, assoc prof, 74-79, PROF PHYSICS, IOWA STATE UNIV, 79- *Concurrent Pos:* Assoc physicist, Ames Lab, US AEC, 70-74, physicist, 74-79, sr physicist, 79- *Mem:* Am Phys Soc. *Res:* Theoretical physics of the elementary particles. *Mailing Add:* Dept of Physics Iowa State Univ Ames IA 50011

YOUNG, BOBBY GENE, b Cape Girardeau, Mo, Aug 3, 29; m 52; c 2. MICROBIOLOGY, GENETICS. *Educ:* Southeast Mo State Col, BS, 51; Johns Hopkins Univ, PhD(biol), 65. *Prof Exp:* Biologist, Nat Cancer Inst, 54-56, chemist, 56-62; teaching asst, Johns Hopkins Univ, 62-64; staff fel, Nat Cancer Inst, 65-66, res microbiologist, Div Biologics Standards, NIH, 66-69; assoc prof, 69-74, actg chmn dept, 70-71, 70-71, chmn dept, 71-75; PROF MICROBIOL, UNIV MD, COLLEGE PARK, 74- *Mem:* AAAS; Am Soc Microbiol. *Res:* Microbial genetics; cancer research, virology and interferon aspects of malignancy. *Mailing Add:* Dept of Microbiol Univ of Md College Park MD 20742

YOUNG, BRUCE ARTHUR, b Sydney, Australia, Jan 16, 39; m 65; c 2. AGRICULTURE, ANIMAL PHYSIOLOGY. *Educ:* Univ New Eng, Australia, BRurSc, 62, MRurSc, 65, PhD(physiol), 69. *Prof Exp:* From asst prof to assoc prof, 68-78, PROF ANIMAL PHYSIOL, UNIV ALTA, 78- *Mem:* Am Soc Animal Sci; Can Soc Animal Sci; Int Soc Biometeorol; Agr Inst Can. *Res:* Environmental physiology of animals; adaptation to physical environment; livestock production and energy metabolism in cold climates. *Mailing Add:* Dept of Animal Sci Univ of Alta Edmonton AB T6G 2E3 Can

YOUNG, C(HARLES), JR, b Washington, Pa, June 3, 23; m 47; c 2. ELECTRONICS, MECHANICAL ENGINEERING. *Educ:* Ill Inst Technol, BSME, 45; Mo Sch Mines, MSME, 50. *Prof Exp:* Instr mech eng, Univ RI, 46-47; from instr to asst prof, Mo Sch Mines, 47-51; design engr, 51-57, supvry electronics engr, 57-66, SR PROJ MGR SWIMMER SYSTS, US NAVAL ORD LAB, US NAVAL SURFACE WEAPONS CTR, 66- *Concurrent Pos:* Subj specialist electronics, Nat Home Study Coun, 62- *Mem:* Am Soc Mech Engrs; Am Ord Asn; Marine Technol Soc; Am Defense Preparedness Asn. *Res:* Application of electronic, mechanical and radioactive materials and principles to the design, development and production of combat swimmers' and divers' weapons. *Mailing Add:* Naval Surface Weapons Ctr Code U102 White Oak Silver Spring MD 20910

YOUNG, C(LARENCE) B(ERNARD) F(EHRLER), b Birmingham, Ala, May 13, 08; m 34; c 3. CHEMISTRY, ELECTROMETALLURGY. *Educ:* Howard Col, BS, 30; Columbia Univ, MS, 32, PhD, 34. *Prof Exp:* Asst chem, Howard Col, 27-30; lectr, Columbia Univ, 30-32; asst cur, Chandler Chem Mus, 32-34; tech dir, US Res Corp, NY, 34-37; dir, Nat Southern Prod Corp, 43-52, vpres, 44, exec vpres, 44-52; pres, Aply N Austin Co, 52-55 & Cracker Asphalt Corp, 55-69; PRES, YOUNG REFINING CORP, 71-, CHEM ENGR, 76- *Concurrent Pos:* Pres, Warrior Asphalt Corp, 49-55, Ala Southern Warehouses, 49-, Cytho Corp, 49-, M'Lady, Inc, 52-, Auromet Corp, NY, 53-56 & Abaca Chem Corp, 54-56; vpres, Findan Corp, 55-57. *Mem:* AAAS; Electrochem Soc; fel Inst Chemists. *Res:* Surface acting agents; chemistry for electroplating; metal finishing; production of fatty acids; resin and fatty acids from the Southern pine tree; refineries for production of petroleum light oils, asphalts and its products. *Mailing Add:* PO Box 775 Douglasville GA 30134

YOUNG, C(ECIL) G(EORGE), JR, b Baltimore, Md, Sept 26, 20; m 43; c 2. ELECTRONICS. *Educ:* US Mil Acad, BSc, 43; Univ Pa, MSEE, 48. *Prof Exp:* Supvr atomic weapons assembly team, Sandia Base, US Army, NMex, 48-49, proj head atomic weapons telemetry, Appl Physics Lab, Johns Hopkins Univ, 49-51, proj engr test instrumentation, Los Alamos Sci Lab, 51-52, tech asst to dir, Ballistic Res Labs, 52-53, chief atomic energy & supporting res, Off Chief Ord, Washington, DC, 53-55, rep nuclear power & propulsion, Reactor Div, Atomic Energy Comn, 55-56; dept head res div, McDonnell Aircraft Co, 56-60, mgr, Western Region Off, McDonnell Douglas Corp, 60-68, prog dir electromagnetic war- fare, 68-70, ASST TO V PRES ENG, SPACE SHUTTLE PROG, DOUGLAS AIRCRAFT CO, 70- *Res:* Guided missiles; reentry vehicles; spacecraft; nuclear weapons and effects; nuclear propulsion; radioisotopes. *Mailing Add:* 2105 Paseo Del Mar Palos Verdes Estates CA 90274

YOUNG, CHARITY LOUISE, b Chicago, Ill, Oct 4, 46. CELL BIOLOGY, BIOCHEMISTRY. *Educ:* Conn Col Women, BA, 68; Georgetown Univ, PhD(biol), 76. *Prof Exp:* From instr to asst prof biol, St Joseph's Col, Philadelphia, 75-77; res scientist, Nat Biomed Res Found, 77-80. *Res:* Protein evolution. *Mailing Add:* 2341 Lincolwood Dr Evanston IL 60201

YOUNG, CHARLES ALBERT, b Dodge Center, Minn, Oct 11, 11; m 50; c 2. INDUSTRIAL ORGANIC CHEMISTRY. *Educ:* Purdue Univ, BS, 33; Univ Notre Dame, MS, 34, PhD(org chem), 36. *Prof Exp:* Asst chem, Univ Notre Dame, 33-36; staff chemist, Jackson Lab, E I du Pont de Nemours & Co, Inc, 36-60, staff chemist, Exp Sta, 60-76. *Mem:* Am Chem Soc. *Res:* Synthetic rubber; organic water repellants; adhesives; dye synthesis and application; industrial and automotive finishes. *Mailing Add:* 111 Beech Lane Forest Brook Glen Wilmington DE 19804

YOUNG, CHARLES E(DWARD), b Perry County, Ind, Aug 5, 21; m 45; c 4. ELECTRONICS. *Educ:* Utah State Col, BS, 49; Purdue Univ, MS, 50. *Prof Exp:* Assoc res physicist, Cornell Aeronaut Lab, Inc, 49-56, res physicist, 56-58, sect head avionics, 58-63, br head navig, 63-71, asst prog mgr avionics, Dayton Opers, 71-76; asst prog mgr, Colspan Corp, 76-80; RETIRED. *Concurrent Pos:* Mem spec comt autopilot criteria, Radio Tech Comt for Aeronaut, 58-61. *Mem:* Sr mem Inst Elec & Electronics Engrs; Am Inst Aeronaut & Astronaut. *Res:* Air traffic and real time computer control systems; data links; submarine and antisubmarine warfare; low level and terrain avoidance systems for aircraft; radar systems; all-weather flying; navigation systems. *Mailing Add:* 1512 Chris Lane Westminster MD 21157

YOUNG, CHARLES EDWARD, b Petrolia, Ont, June 1, 41. CHEMICAL PHYSICS. *Educ:* Univ Toronto, BSc, 63; Univ Calif, Berkeley, PhD(chem), 66. *Prof Exp:* Res assoc chem, Mass Inst Technol, 66-68; mem tech staff, Bell Labs, 68-70; CHEMIST, ARGONNE NAT LAB, 70- *Mem:* Am Chem Soc; Am Phys Soc. *Res:* Reaction and excitation cross sections for supra thermal collisions of atoms and simple molecules studied by accelerated beam techniques, chemiluminescence and laser induced fluorescence; laser techniques as a diagnostic in sputtering studies of solid surfaces. *Mailing Add:* Chem Div Argonne Nat Lab Argonne IL 60439

YOUNG, CHARLES GILBERT, b Pa, Feb 25, 30; m 59; c 3. ENERGY INDUSTRY HARDWARE, TECHNOLOGY FUTURES. *Educ:* Elizabethtown Col, BA, 52; Univ Conn, MS, 56, PhD(physics), 61. *Prof Exp:* Physicist, Brookhaven Nat Lab, 56 & Navy Electronics Lab, Calif, 57; instr physics, Conn Col, 57-59; from res asst to instr, Univ Conn, 59-62; consult, Am Optical Co, 61-62, sr physicist, 62-65, mgr systs res dept, 65-70, gen mgr laser prod dept, 70-73, dir prod develop, 73-77; dir eng, Kollmorgen Corp, 77-79; asst tech mgr, 79-80, DIR TECHNOL DEVELOP COMBUSTION ENG, NEW ENG RES APPLN CTR, UNIV CONN, 80- *Concurrent Pos:* Adj instr, Sch Bus, Univ Conn, 80. *Mem:* Sr mem Inst Elec & Electronics Eng; Optical Soc Am; Am Phys Soc. Division management in design and construction of submarine periscopes and military sights, stabilized systems and electro-optic devices; Am Soc Mech Engrs; Am Nuclear Soc. *Res:* Metallic and non-metallic materials, coatings and composites, joining, automation, instrumentation, monitoring and control, nuclear, fossil and unconventional power generation, oil and gas, extraction hardware; multi-decade technology futures; numerous publications. *Mailing Add:* 17 Southwood Rd Storrs CT 06268

YOUNG, CHARLES STUART HAMISH, b Plymouth, UK, Feb 2, 44; m 70; c 1. ANIMAL VIRUS GENETICS, RECOMBINATION MECHANISMS. *Educ:* Oxford Univ, BA, 66, PhD(genetics), 69. *Prof Exp:* Lectr genetics, Biol Dept, Princeton Univ, 70-71; sci officer, Virol Inst Med Res Coun, 71-74; ASST PROF VIROL & GENETICS, DEPT MICROBIOL, COLUMBIA UNIV, 74- *Mem:* Am Soc Microbiol; Am Soc Virol. *Res:* Mechanisms of genetic recombination in eukaryotic cells using DNA containing aniaml viruses as model sytems. *Mailing Add:* Dept Microbiol Columbia Univ Health Sci Ctr New York NY 10032

YOUNG, CHARLES WESLEY, b Enid, Okla, Dec 2, 29; m 52; c 3. DAIRY HUSBANDRY. *Educ:* Okla State Univ, BS, 56; NC State Univ, MS, 58, PhD(animal indust), 61. *Prof Exp:* From asst prof to assoc prof, 60-69, PROF DAIRY HUSB, UNIV MINN, ST PAUL, 69- *Mem:* Am Dairy Sci Asn. *Res:* Systems of breeding in dairy cattle; relationship between size and production in dairy cattle; economics of selection for milk yield in dairy cattle. *Mailing Add:* Dept of Animal Sci Univ of Minn St Paul MN 55108

YOUNG, CHARLES WILLIAM, b Denver, Colo, Nov 19, 30; m 63; c 3. INTERNAL MEDICINE, CANCER. *Educ:* Columbia Univ, AB, 52; Harvard Univ, MD, 56. *Prof Exp:* Intern med, Second Med Div, Bellevue Hosp, New York, 56-57, resident, Second Med Div, Bellevue Hosp & Mem Hosp, 57-59; asst prof med, Med Col Cornell Univ, 66-76; from res assoc to assoc, 62-71, ASSOC MEM, SLOAN-KETTERING INST CANCER RES, 71-; ASSOC PROF MED, MED COL CORNELL UNIV, 76- *Concurrent Pos:* Attend physician, Mem Hosp, 78- *Mem:* AAAS; Am Asn Cancer Res; Am Soc Clin Oncol; Am Fedn Clin Res; NY Acad Sci. *Res:* Oncology; biochemical pharmacology; embryology. *Mailing Add:* Mem Sloan-Kettering Cancer Ctr 1245 York Ave New York NY 10021

YOUNG, CHESTER EDWIN, b Butler, Pa, Apr 24, 48; m 71; c 2. RESOURCE ECONOMICS, ECONMETRICS. *Educ:* Westminster Col, BA, 70; NC State Univ, ME, 72, PhD(econ), 74. *Prof Exp:* Instr econ, Meredith Col, 73; res asst econ, NC State Univ, 73-74; agr econ, 74-81, PROJ LEADER, ECON RES SERV, USDA, 81- *Concurrent Pos:* Adj asst prof, Dept Agr & Econ, Pa State Univ, 74- *Mem:* Am Agr Econ Asn. *Res:* Economics of land application of wastewaters investments in soil conservation practices; evaluation of agricultural nonpoint source pollution control. *Mailing Add:* Dept Agr Econ Weaver Bldg Pa State Univ University Park PA 16802

YOUNG, CLIFTON A, b 1943; US citizen. INORGANIC CHEMISTRY. *Educ:* Haverford Col, BA, 65; Dartmouth Col, MA, 67; Tufts Univ, PhD(chem), 77. *Prof Exp:* Mem res staff, P R Mallory Co Inc, 77-78; mem tech staff, GTE Labs Inc, Gen Tel & Electronics Corp, 78-80; asst prof, Tufts Univ, 80-81; ASST PROF, UNIV DALLAS, 81- *Mem:* Am Chem Soc; Electrochem Soc; AAAS. *Res:* Battery research; chemistry of metal-ammonia and other metal solutions; non-aqueous solvents; battery chemistry. *Mailing Add:* Chem Dept Univ Dallas Irving TX 75061

YOUNG, CLYDE THOMAS, b Durham, NC, Aug 22, 30; m 55; c 5. FOOD SCIENCE. *Educ:* NC State Univ, BS, 52, MS, 55; Okla State Univ, PhD(food sci), 70. *Prof Exp:* Instr chem & math, NC State Univ, 54-56; asst head claims dept, Anderson-Clayton & Co, Ga, 58-59; res chemist, Ga Inst Technol, 59-60; asst res chemist, Ga Sta, Univ Ga, 60-76; assoc prof, 76-80, PROF, NC STATE UNIV, 80- *Mem:* Am Peanut Res & Educ Asn; Am Chem Soc; Inst Food Technologists. *Res:* Major investigations in changes and variations in biochemical constituents of peanuts--factors affecting aroma, flavor, color, maturation and protein during development, harvesting, curing, storage and roasting. *Mailing Add:* Dept Food Sci NC State Univ Raleigh NC 27650

YOUNG, DALE W, b Perry, Utah, Apr 23, 18; m 42. PLANT PHYSIOLOGY. *Educ:* Utah State Univ, BS, 42, MS, 50; Iowa State Univ, PhD(plant physiol), 53. *Prof Exp:* Agronomist, USDA, 48-51; plant physiologist, Rohm and Haas Co, 53-60; supvr pesticide eval, Hooker Chem Corp, 60-66; mem field res staff, Chemagro, 66-67, mgr biol res, Kansas City, Mo, 68-72; mgr com develop, Gulf Oil Chem Co, Merriam, 73-80; MGR COM DEVELOP, OTSUKA CHEM CO, 80- *Mem:* Weed Sci Soc Am; Entom Soc Am. *Res:* Chemicals to increase food production. *Mailing Add:* 9639 Delmar Overland Park KS 66207

YOUNG, DANA, b Washington, DC, Oct 6, 04; m 30; c 2. MECHANICAL ENGINEERING. *Educ:* Yale Univ, BS, 26, MS, 30; Univ Mich, PhD(eng mech), 40. *Prof Exp:* Field engr, Marland Oil Co, 26-27; asst dist engr, Shell Petrol Corp, 27-28; instr eng mech, Yale Univ, 28-30; struct engr, United Engrs & Constructors, Inc, 30-34; prof civil eng & appl mech, Univ Conn, 34-42; prof eng mech, Univ Tex, 42-50; prof mech eng, Univ Minn, 50-53; chmn dept civil eng, Yale Univ, 53-55, Sterling prof civil eng, 53-62, dean sch eng, 55-59; sr vpres, 62-71, CONSULT, SOUTHWEST RES INST, 71- *Concurrent Pos:* Consult, Space Technol Labs, Inc, 54-62; mem comt ship struct design, Nat Res Coun, 55-63, adv comt to Nat Bur Standards, 56-61, div eng & indust res, 59-64 & spec comt appl res, US Air Force Sci Adv Bd, 61; comnr, Nat Comn Prod Safety, 68-70. *Mem:* Am Soc Civil Engrs; hon mem Am Soc Mech Engrs; Soc Exp Stress Anal; Am Inst Aeronaut & Astronaut. *Res:* Vibrations; theory of elasticity; structural mechanics; dynamics of rotating machines; pressure vessels and piping. *Mailing Add:* Southwest Res Inst 8500 Culebra Rd San Antonio TX 78228

YOUNG, DANIEL DAVID, b Toledo, Ohio, July 18, 44; m 67; c 1. LASER PHYSICS. *Educ:* Univ Toledo, BS, 67; Air Force Inst Technol, MS, 69, PhD(laser physics), 76. *Prof Exp:* Res scientist lasers, Air Force Avionics Lab, 69-71, physicist holography, 71-73 & 75-76, physicist target signatures, 76-77; PROG MGR COMMON LASER, AERONAUT SYSTS DIV, WRIGHT-PATTERSON AFB, 77- *Honors & Awards:* Air Force Systs Command Tech Achievement Award, 77. *Res:* Theory of holographic lens; nonlinear optics; dye lasers; solid state lasers. *Mailing Add:* ASD/AERA Wright-Patterson AFB Dayton OH 45433

YOUNG, DAVID A, b Carmel, Calif, Sept 26, 42. PHYSICAL CHEMISTRY. *Educ:* Pomona Col, BA, 64; Univ Chicago, PhD(chem), 67. *Prof Exp:* PHYSICIST, LAWRENCE LIVERMORE LAB, 67- *Mem:* Am Phys Soc. *Res:* Statistical mechanics of gases, liquids and solids. *Mailing Add:* Lawrence Livermore Lab PO Box 808 Livermore CA 94550

YOUNG, DAVID A(NTHONY), b Pittsburgh, Pa, Jan 6, 21; m 45; c 5. CHEMICAL ENGINEERING. *Educ:* Pa State Univ, BS, 42. *Prof Exp:* Chem engr, Sun Oil Co, 42-47 & Warwick Wax Co, 47-48; group leader, Chem Eng Process Develop Dept, Spencer Chem Co, 48-59; chief engr, Eng Sci Div, Am Metal Prod Co, 59-62; sect head solution polymerization, Gen Tire & Rubber Co, Ohio, 62-70; sr process engr, J F Pritchard & Co, Kansas City, 70-76; STAFF ENGR, KANSAS CITY DIV, BENDIX CORP, 76- *Concurrent Pos:* Instr, Kans State Teachers Col, 59. *Honors & Awards:* Spec commendation, US Secy Navy. *Mem:* Am Inst Chem Engrs. *Res:* Design, construction and start-up of new chemical plants; hydrogen sulfide and sulphur dioxide recovery from stack gases; evaporation and burning of pulp mill waste liquors; equipment design and procurement for new polymer facilities; pilot plant production of new polymers including polyethylenes, nylon, specialized poly BD's, propyleneoxide rubber and polyurides; treatment to detoxify chemical wastewater streams. *Mailing Add:* Bendix Inc 2100 Bannister Rd Kansas City MO 64131

YOUNG, DAVID ALLAN, b Wilkinsburg, Pa, May 26, 15; m 34; c 1. INSECT TAXONOMY. *Educ:* Louisville Univ, AB, 39; Cornell Univ, MS, 42; Univ Kans, PhD(entom), 51. *Prof Exp:* Instr, Louisville Univ, 46-48; asst, Univ Kans, 48-49; entomologist, Insect Identification & Parasite Introd Sect, Entom Res Br, Agr Res Serv, USDA, 50-57; assoc prof, 57-61, prof, 61-80, EMER PROF ENTOM, NC STATE UNIV, 80- *Mem:* Entom Soc Am. *Res:* Insect taxonomy; taxonomy of the Auchenorrhynchous Homoptera; reclassification of Cicadellinae (Homoptera: Auchenorrhyncha). *Mailing Add:* Dept of Entom NC State Univ Raleigh NC 27650

YOUNG, DAVID ALLEN, b Pomona, Calif, July 31, 46; c 2. BOTANY, BIOCHEMICAL SYSTEMATICS. *Educ:* Calif State Univ, Fullerton, BA, 71, MA, 72; Claremont Grad Sch & Univ Ctr, PhD(bot), 75. *Prof Exp:* Lab instr & instr bot, Calif State Univ, Fullerton, 70-72; res asst, Rancho Santa Ana Bot Garden, Claremont, Calif, 72-75; asst prof, Union Col, 75-76; asst prof, 76-80, PROF BOT, UNIV ILL, URBANA, 80- *Mem:* Bot Soc Am; Am Asn Plant Taxonomists; Int Asn Plant Taxonomists; Soc Study Evolution; Am Soc Naturalists. *Res:* Biochemical systematics of the angiosperms; angiosperm phylogeny; cladistics. *Mailing Add:* Dept of Bot Univ of Ill Urbana IL 61801

YOUNG, DAVID BRUCE, b Pittsburgh, Pa, Mar 13, 45; m 65; c 3. PHYSIOLOGY. *Educ:* Univ Colo, BA, 67; Ind Univ, PhD(physiol), 72. *Prof Exp:* From instr to asst prof, 72-77, ASSOC PROF PHYSIOL, SCH MED, UNIV MISS, 77- *Concurrent Pos:* NIH trainee, Sch Med, Univ Miss, 72-74. *Res:* Fluid and electrolyte balance control mechanisms; hypertension. *Mailing Add:* Dept of Physiol Univ of Miss Med Ctr Jackson MS 39216

YOUNG, DAVID CALDWELL, b Memphis, Tenn, June 18, 24; m 55; c 3. ORGANIC CHEMISTRY. *Educ:* Davidson Col, BS, 46; Univ Fla, MS, 48, PhD(chem), 50. *Prof Exp:* Chemist, Edgar C Britton Res Lab, 50-53, group leader, 53-62, patents coord, 62-65, asst to dir, 65-70, asst to dir chem biol res, 70-74, asst to dir pharmaceut res & develop, 74-76, sr res specialist, Hydrocarbons & Energy Res, 77-80, SR ENVIRON SPECIALIST, ENVIRON SERV DEPT, DOW CHEM CO, 81- *Mem:* AAAS; Am Chem Soc. *Res:* Leuckart reaction; phthalaldehydic acid; organic research and process development; chemical patents; environmental regulations. *Mailing Add:* 1223 Holyrood St Midland MI 48640

YOUNG, DAVID GRIER, b Dayton, Ohio, May 9, 40; m 69; c 2. ENTOMOLOGY. *Educ:* Univ Fla, BS, 62, MS, 70, PhD(entom), 77. *Prof Exp:* Med entomologist, Med Field Serv Sch, 63-66 & Atlantic-Pac Interoceanic Canal Surv, 66-68; assoc entomol, 75-77, ASST RES SCIENTIST ENTOM & NEMATOL, UNIV FLA, 77- *Honors & Awards:* Austin Award, Fla State Mus, 78. *Mem:* AAAS; Entom Soc Am. *Res:* Systematics of biting diptera, particularly their habits and role in transmission of disease pathogens. *Mailing Add:* Dept of Entom & Nematol Univ of Fla Gainesville FL 32611

YOUNG, DAVID MARSHALL, b Minot, ND, Aug 26, 42; m 63; c 4. PATHOLOGY. *Educ:* Colo State Univ, DVM, 66; Ohio State Univ, MS, 67, PhD(comp path), 70. *Prof Exp:* Comp pathologist, Lab Toxicol, Nat Cancer Inst, 73-77; PROF VET SCI & HEAD DEPT, MONT STATE UNIV, 77- *Concurrent Pos:* Sr staff fel, NIH, 70-73; consult pathologist, Statutory Adv Comt, Food & Drug Admin, Dept Health, Educ & Welfare, 71; mem fac, Found Advan Educ in the Sci, NIH, 72- *Honors & Awards:* C L Davis Jour Award, C L Davis Found Advan Vet Path, 73. *Mem:* AAAS; Int Acad Path; Am Asn Path; Am Vet Med Asn; Soc Pharmacol & Environ Path; Am Asn Cancer Res. *Res:* Comparative pathology; endocrine pathology; cancer; mineral metabolism; orthopedic pathology; animal models of human disease; toxicology. *Mailing Add:* Dept of Vet Sci Mont State Univ Bozeman MT 59717

YOUNG, DAVID MATHESON, b London, Eng, Apr 19, 28; m 53; c 6. ENVIRONMENTAL CHEMISTRY. *Educ:* Univ London, BSc, 48, PhD(chem), 49. *Prof Exp:* Asst lectr phys chem, St Andrews Univ, 49-51; res assoc, Amherst Col, 51-52; res fel, Nat Res Coun Can, 52-53; Royal Mil Col, Can, 53-54 & 55-56; Humboldt Scholar, Phys Chem Inst, Munich, 54-55; res chemist, 56-58, supvr res & develop lab, 58-65, asst res mgr, 65-72, mgr chem res & develop, 72-75, MGR ENVIRON AFFAIRS, DOW CHEM CAN, INC, 75- *Mem:* Chem Inst Can. *Res:* Physical adsorption of gases; boron chemistry; gas chromatography; heterogeneous catalysis; photochemistry. *Mailing Add:* 1315 Hillcrest-Nisbet Sarnia ON N7S 4T4 Can

YOUNG, DAVID MONAGHAN, JR, b Boston, Mass, Oct 20, 23; m 49; c 3. MATHEMATICS. *Educ:* Webb Inst Naval Archit, BS, 44; Harvard Univ, MA, 47, PhD(math), 50. *Prof Exp:* Instr & res assoc math, Harvard Univ, 50-51; mathematician, Aberdeen Proving Ground, 51-52; assoc prof math, Univ Md, 52-55; mgr math anal dept, Ramo-Wooldridge Corp, 55-58; prof math & dir comput ctr, 58-70, PROF MATH & COMPUT SCI & DIR CTR NUMERICAL ANAL, UNIV TEX, AUSTIN, 70- *Mem:* Am Math Soc; Soc Indust & Appl Math; Math Asn Am; Asn Comput Mach. *Res:* Numerical analysis, especially the numerical solution of partial differential equations by finite difference methods; high-speed computing. *Mailing Add:* Ctr Numerical Anal Univ of Tex Austin TX 78712

YOUNG, DAVID ROSS, oceanography, see previous edition

YOUNG, DAVID THAD, b Port of Spain, Trinidad, Apr 18, 43; US citizen; m 66; c 4. SPACE PHYSICS. *Educ:* Univ Southwestern La, BS, 64; Rice Univ, MS, 67, PhD(space physics), 70. *Hon Degrees:* Venia Docendi, Univ Bern, 80. *Prof Exp:* Grad fel, Dept Space Physics & Astron, Rice Univ, 64-70, res assoc, 70-71; vis scientist, Div Plasma Physics, Royal Inst Technol, Stockholm, 72; sr res assoc, Physikalisches Inst, Univ Bern, 72-81; MEM STAFF, SPACE PLASMA PHYSICS GROUP, LOS ALAMOS NAT LAB, 81- *Mem:* Am Geophys Union; Europ Geophys Soc. *Res:* Magnetospheric plasma physics, particularly the development of ion mass spectrometers for space flight and the analysis and application of this data. *Mailing Add:* Mail Stop 438 Box 1663 Los Alamos Nat Lab Los Alamos NM 87545

YOUNG, DAVIS ALAN, b Abington, Pa, Mar 5, 41; m 65; c 3. PETROLOGY, MINERALOGY. *Educ:* Princeton Univ, BSE, 62; Pa State Univ, MS, 65; Brown Univ, PhD(geol), 69. *Prof Exp:* Asst prof geol, NY Univ, 68-73; assoc prof geol, Univ NC, Wilmington, 73-78; ASSOC PROF GEOL, CALVIN COL, 78- *Concurrent Pos:* NSF instnl grant, NY Univ, 69-70. *Mem:* Mineral Soc Am; Geol Soc Am; Sigma Xi. *Res:* Precambrian igneous and metamorphic geology of New Jersey and southeastern Pennsylvania; petrology of syenites; history of geology in relation to Christianity. *Mailing Add:* Dept Physics Calvin Col Grand Rapids MI 49506

YOUNG, DELANO VICTOR, b Honolulu, Hawaii, Nov 17, 45; m 70; c 1. BIOCHEMISTRY OF TUMOR CELLS, CELL GROWTH CONTROL. *Educ:* Stanford Univ, BS, 67; Columbia Univ, PhD(biochem), 73. *Prof Exp:* Fel cell biol, Salk Inst Biol Studies, 73-75; ASST PROF CHEM, BOSTON UNIV, 75- *Mem:* AAAS; Sigma Xi; Am Soc Microbiol. *Res:* Peptide growth factors/hormones by transformed eukaryotic cells and the mechanisms by which these and other factors regulate growth in normal and transformed cells. *Mailing Add:* Dept of Chem 675 Commonwealth Ave Boston MA 02215

YOUNG, DENNIS LEE, b St Louis, Mo, Jan 22, 44; m 78. MATHEMATICAL STATISTICS. *Educ:* St Louis Univ, BS, 65; Purdue Univ, MS, 67, PhD(statist), 70. *Prof Exp:* Asst prof statist, NMex State Univ, 70-75; ASSOC PROF STATIST, ARIZ STATE UNIV, 75- *Mem:* AAAS; Inst Math Statist; Am Statist Asn. *Res:* Multivariate statistical analysis. *Mailing Add:* Dept Math Ariz State Univ Tempe AZ 85281

YOUNG, DONALD ALCOE, b Fredericton, NB, Oct 21, 29; m 55; c 3. GENETICS, PLANT BREEDING. *Educ:* McGill Univ, BSc, 52; Univ Wis, MS, 54, PhD(genetics), 57. *Prof Exp:* Res officer, 57-66, sect head potato breeding, 66-73, PROG MGR, CAN DEPT AGR, 73- *Concurrent Pos:* Mem, Work Planning Comt Potato Breeding, 59-; chmn, Work Planning Comt Potato Texture, 64- *Mem:* Potato Asn Am; Can Soc Hort Sci; Genetics Soc Can. *Res:* Potato breeding; sample selection as related to potato quality; disease resistance. *Mailing Add:* Can Dept of Agr Res Sta PO Box 20280 Fredericton NB E3B 5A3 Can

YOUNG, DONALD C, b Paducah, Ky, Feb 25, 33; m 51; c 4. INORGANIC CHEMISTRY, AGRICULTURAL CHEMISTRY. *Educ:* Univ Calif, Riverside, BA, 61, PhD(inorg chem), 66. *Prof Exp:* From res asst petrochem to sr res chemist, 53-69, sr res assoc, 69-74, sr res assoc fertilizer chem, 74-78, STAFF CONSULT, SCI & TECHNOL DIV, UNION OIL CO, 78- *Concurrent Pos:* Res scholar, Univ Calif, Riverside, 66-68. *Mem:* Am Chem Soc. *Res:* Chemistry and technology of polyphosphoric acid; transition-metal complexes in homogeneous catalysis; carborane chemistry; transition metal complexes of dicarbollide ion; fertilizer and soil chemistry. *Mailing Add:* Union Oil Co Union Oil Ctr Los Angeles CA 90017

YOUNG, DONALD CHARLES, b Fremont, Ohio, June 29, 44; m 68, 80; c 3. ANALYTICAL CHEMISTRY. *Educ:* Harvard Univ, AB, 66; Univ NC, Chapel Hill, PhD(anal chem), 71. *Prof Exp:* Res assoc chem, Purdue Univ, 71-72; asst prof chem, Oakland Univ, 72-78; PROJ CHEMIST, GULF OIL CO, 78- *Mem:* Am Chem Soc; Sigma Xi; Soc Appl Spectros. *Res:* Nuclear magnetic resonance methods of analysis; thermo analytical methods. *Mailing Add:* Gulf Sci & Technol Co PO Drawer 2038 Pittsburgh PA 15230

YOUNG, DONALD EDWARD, b Lake Zurich, Ill, June 13, 22; m 47; c 3. HIGH ENERGY PHYSICS. *Educ:* Ripon Col, BA, 46; Univ Minn, MS, 51, PhD(nucleon scattering), 59. *Prof Exp:* Asst physics, Univ Minn, 49-53; physicist, Labs, Gen Mills Co, 53-60; head, Physics Div, Midwestern Univs Res Asn, 60-67; prof physics, Univ Wis, 67; PHYSICIST, FERMI NAT ACCELERATOR LAB, 67- *Mem:* Am Phys Soc; Sigma Xi. *Res:* Proton linear accelerator design; high energy particle accelerators design and operation; magnetic field measurements; nuclear physics and radioactivity; proton-proton scattering; dosimetry; radiation damage; antiproton production and collection. *Mailing Add:* Fermi Nat Accelerator Lab PO Box 500 Batavia IL 60510

YOUNG, DONALD F(REDERICK), b Joplin, Mo, Apr 27, 28; m 50; c 5. ENGINEERING MECHANICS, BIOMEDICAL ENGINEERING. *Educ:* Iowa State Univ, BS, 51, MS, 52, PhD(eng mech), 56. *Prof Exp:* Res assoc, 52-53, from instr to assoc prof eng mech, 52-61, PROF ENG SCI & MECH, IOWA STATE UNIV, 61- *Mem:* Am Soc Eng Educ; Am Soc Mech Engrs. *Res:* Fluid mechanics; biomechanics. *Mailing Add:* Dept of Eng Mech Iowa State Univ Ames IA 50011

YOUNG, DONALD REEDER, b Logan, Utah, July 21, 21; m 46; c 4. PHYSICS. *Educ:* Utah State Agr Col, BA, 42; Mass Inst Technol, PhD(physics), 49. *Prof Exp:* Mem staff, Radiation Lab, Mass Inst Technol, 42-45, asst, Insulation Lab, 45-49; tech engr, 49-52, proj engr, 52-61, sr engr & mgr device & mat characterization, 61-71, RES STAFF MEM, IBM CORP, 71- *Concurrent Pos:* Alexander von Humboldt US sr scientist award, 80-81; mgr interface physics, IBM Corp, 77- *Mem:* Fel Am Phys Soc; sr mem Inst Elec & Electronics Engrs. *Res:* Electrical breakdown; ferroelectric materials; superconductors; semiconductors. *Mailing Add:* IBM Res Ctr Yorktown Heights NY 10598

YOUNG, DONALD RUDOLPH, b Chicago, Ill, Oct 29, 23; m 55; c 2. PHYSIOLOGY, METABOLISM. *Educ:* Loyola Univ, Ill, BS, 49; Univ Calif, Berkeley, MA, 51, PhD(physiol), 54. *Prof Exp:* Res physiologist poultry nitrit, Univ Calif, Berkeley, 54-55, asst prof physiol, 55; nutritionist, Qm Food & Container Inst, 55-57, head performance lab, 58-61, actg chief nutrit br, 61-62; res scientist, Biotechnol Div, 62-72; chief environ physiol, 72-76, RES SCIENTIST, BIOMED RES DIV, AMES RES CTR, NASA, 76- *Concurrent Pos:* Mem panel environ physiol, Dept Army, 57-62 & biomed exp working group, NASA, 63-65; lectr, Stanford Univ, 63- *Mem:* AAAS; Am Physiol Soc; Soc Exp Biol & Med; Aerospace Med Asn; NY Acad Sci. *Res:* Inert gases; nutritional requirements during stress conditions; methematical models of fat metabolism; carbohydrate turnover rate; bong biomechanics. *Mailing Add:* Biomed Res Div Ames Res Ctr NASA Moffett Field CA 94035

YOUNG, DONALD STIRLING, b Belfast, Northern Ireland, Dec 17, 33. CLINICAL PATHOLOGY. *Educ:* Aberdeen Univ, MB & ChB, 57; Univ London, PhD(chem path), 62. *Prof Exp:* Lectr mat med, Aberdeen Univ, 58-59; resident chem path, Royal Postgrad Med Sch London, 62-64; vis scientist, NIH, 65-67, chief clin chem, 67-77; HEAD CLIN CHEM, MAYO CLINIC, 77- *Concurrent Pos:* Chmn bd ed, Clin Chem, Am Asn Clin Chemists, 73-78, pres, 80. *Honors & Awards:* J H Roe Award, Am Asn Clin Chemists, 73, Ames Award, 77; Bernard Gerular Award, Am Asn Clin Chemists, 77; NIH Dir Award, 77; Gernard B Lambert Award, Gerart B Lambert Awards Orgn, 75; W Roman lectr, Australian Asn Clin Biochem, 79; Gerald T Evans Award, Acad Clin Lab Physicians & Scientists, 81. *Mem:* Sigma Xi; Brit Asn Clin Biochem; Am Asn Clin Chemists (pres, 80); Acad Clin Lab Physicians & Scientists; Int Fedn Clin Chemists (vpres, 82-). *Res:* Clinical chemistry; development and application of high resolution analytical techniques in the clinical laboratory; optimized use of the clinical laboratory. *Mailing Add:* Mayo Clin Rochester MN 55905

YOUNG, EARLE F(RANCIS), JR, b Pittsburgh, Pa, Aug 27; m 50; c 3. ENVIRONMENTAL CONTROL, PROCESS METALLURGY. *Educ:* Carnegie Inst Technol, BS, 49. *Prof Exp:* Res engr chem eng, Babcock & Wilcox Co, 49-51; res engr, Olin Mathieson Chem Corp, 51-54, proj group leader, 54-56; process engr, Jones & Laughlin Steel Corp, 56-57, sr develop engr, 57-58, res supvr, 58-61, supvr ore res, 61-65, asst dir chem & raw mat serv, Tech Serv Div, 65-69, dir environ control, 69-72, gen mgr, 73-76; dir environ affairs, 76-78, asst vpres environ affairs, 78-80, VPRES ENERGY & ENVIRON, AM IRON & STEEL INST, 80- *Concurrent Pos:* Instr, Carnegie Inst Technol, 57-58. *Mem:* Am Chem Soc; Am Inst Chem Engrs; Soc Mining Engrs; Am Iron & Steel Inst. *Res:* Upgrading of iron ores; fluid dynamics of steelmaking; air and stream pollution. *Mailing Add:* Am Iron & Steel Inst 1000 16th St NW Washington DC 20036

YOUNG, EDMOND GROVE, b Govans, Md, Oct 29, 17; m 46; c 3. FLUORINE CHEMISTRY. *Educ:* Univ Md, BS, 38, PhD(org chem), 43. *Prof Exp:* Asst chem, Univ Md, 38-43; chemist, Sharples Chem, Inc, Mich, 43-44; res chemist, E I du Pont de Nemours & Co, Inc, 44-48; tech sales, Kinetics Chem, Inc, 48-49, sales mgr aerosol propellants, 49-50; sales develop, Kinetic Chem Div, 50-52, mgr kinetic chem div, 52-57, mgr develop conf, 57-68, mgr develop conf & govt liaison, Develop Dept, 68-73, MGR BUS DEVELOP, CENT RES & DEVELOP DEPT, E I DU PONT DE NEMOURS & CO, INC, 73- *Concurrent Pos:* Mem, Franklin Inst. *Mem:* AAAS; Am Chem Soc; Com Develop Asn; Soc Chem Indust. *Res:* Reaction of metallo-organics; chemistry of fluorinated compounds; commercial chemical development and marketing. *Mailing Add:* Cent Res & Develop Dept Tenth & Market Sts Wilmington DE 19898

YOUNG, EDWARD JOSEPH, b Roselle, NJ, Feb 18, 23; m 55; c 2. GEOCHEMISTRY, MINERALOGY. *Educ:* Rutgers Univ, BS, 48; Mass Inst Technol, MS, 50, PhD(geol), 54. *Prof Exp:* GEOLOGIST, US GEOL SURV, 52- *Mem:* Am Geol Soc; Mineral Soc Am; soc Ecol Geol; Mineral Asn Can. *Res:* Petrology; geochemistry of apatite. *Mailing Add:* US Geol Surv Fed Ctr Denver CO 80225

YOUNG, EDWIN C(HARLES), b Derby, Conn, July 8, 19; m 45; c 1. MECHANICAL ENGINEERING. *Educ:* Yale Univ, BE, 42; Univ Tex, MS, 52, PhD, 54. *Prof Exp:* Res engr, United Aircraft Corp, Conn, 46-47; asst prof mech eng & res engr, Defense Res Lab, Univ Tex, 48-53; from chief develop engr to mgr eng res, Filament Struct Div, Black, Sivalls & Bryson, Inc, Okla, 53-65; consult, 65-67; prog mgr, Advan Composites & Mfg Res, Lockheed Ga Co, 67-75; RETIRED, 75- *Mem:* Am Soc Mech Engrs. *Res:* Thermodynamics; compressible flow; advanced composite design and fabrication. *Mailing Add:* 469 Terrell Mill Dr Marietta GA 30067

YOUNG, EDWIN H(AROLD), b Detroit, Mich, Nov 4, 18; m 44; c 2. CHEMICAL ENGINEERING. *Educ:* Univ Detroit, BChE, 42; Univ Mich, MSE, 49 & 51. *Prof Exp:* Jr chem engr, Wright Air Develop Ctr, 42-43; instr chem eng, Univ Detroit, 46-47; from instr to assoc prof chem & metall eng, 47-59, PROF CHEM & METALL ENG, UNIV MICH, ANN ARBOR, 59-; CONSULT ENGR, 47- *Honors & Awards:* Award, Nat Soc Prof Engrs, 77. *Mem:* Am Chem Soc; fel Am Soc Mech Engrs; fel Am Inst Chem Engrs; fel Am Inst Chemists. *Res:* Heat transfer; process design; design of process equipment. *Mailing Add:* Dept of Chem Eng Univ of Mich Ann Arbor MI 48104

YOUNG, ELEANOR ANNE, b Houston, Tex, Oct 8, 25. NUTRITION. *Educ:* Incarnate World Col, BA, 47; St Louis Univ, MEd, 55; Univ Wis, PhD(nutrit), 68. *Prof Exp:* Asst prof foods & Nutrit, Incarnate World Col, 53-63 & 68-72; sr res assoc, Univ Tex Health Sci Ctr, Dept Med, 68-72, asst prof med, 72-77; ASSOC PROF FOODS & NUTRIT, INCARNATE WORD COL, 72-; ASSOC PROF MED, UNIV TEX HEALTH SCI CTR, DEPT MED, SAN ANTONIO, 77- *Concurrent Pos:* Consult, Audie Murphy Vet Admin Hosp, San Antonio, 73- *Mem:* Am Inst Nutrit; Am Bd Human Nutrit; Am Soc Clin Nutrit; Am Dietetic Asn; Am Pub Health Asn. *Res:* Metabolic response and feeding-fasting intervals in man; metabolism of intravenously infused maltose; lactose intolerance; nutritional adaptations after partial small bowel resections. *Mailing Add:* Univ Tex Health Sci Ctr 7703 Floyd Curl San Antonio TX 78284

YOUNG, ELIZABETH BELL, b Franklinton, NC, July 2, 29; m. SPEECH PATHOLOGY, AUDIOLOGY. *Educ:* NC Col Durham, AB, 48, MA, 50; Ohio State Univ, PhD(speech sci, speech & hearing ther), 59. *Prof Exp:* Chmn dept English, Barber-Scotia Col, 48-53; chmn dept speech, Talladega Col, 53-55; asst prof, Va State Col, 56-57; prof speech correction & dir speech clin, Fla A&M Univ, 59; chmn dept English & speech, Fayetteville State Col, 59-63; asst prof speech path, Col Dent, Howard Univ, 63-64; chmn dept English & lang, Md State Col, 65-66; prof speech path, undergrad & grad prog & supvr speech & audiol training clin prog, 66-69, PROF SPEECH PATH, GRAD SCH & SUPVR SPEECH CLIN, CATH UNIV AM, 69- *Mem:* Fel Am Speech & Hearing Asn. *Res:* Pathology of speech and hearing mechanism and speech science; observations in the field of speech and hearing pathology and science. *Mailing Add:* 8104 W Beach Dr NW Washington DC 20012

YOUNG, ELTON THEODORE, b Brush, Colo, May 1, 40; m 62; c 2. MOLECULAR BIOLOGY. *Educ:* Univ Colo, BA, 62; Calif Inst Technol, PhD(biophys), 67. *Prof Exp:* Fel molecular biol, Univ Geneva, 67-69; asst prof, 69-75, ASSOC PROF BIOCHEM & GENETICS, UNIV WASH, 75- *Res:* Regulation of transcription and translation in bacteriophage. *Mailing Add:* Dept of Biochem Univ of Wash SJ-70 Seattle WA 98195

YOUNG, EUTIQUIO CHUA, b Del Gallego, Philippines, July 17, 32; m 61; c 3. MATHEMATICAL ANALYSIS. *Educ:* Far Eastern Univ, Manila, BS, 54; Univ Md, MA, 60, PhD(math), 62. *Prof Exp:* Asst prof math, Univ Conn, 61-62; head dept math, Far Eastern Univ, Manila, 62-64; assoc prof, De la Salle Col, Manila, 64-65; from asst prof math to assoc prof, 65-74, PROF MATH, FLA STATE UNIV, 74- *Mem:* Math Asn Am; Am Math Soc. *Res:* Cauchy problems, uniqueness of solutions of boundary value problems and comparison theorems for partial differential equations. *Mailing Add:* Dept Math & Comput Sci Fla State Univ Tallahassee FL 32306

YOUNG, EVIE FOUNTAIN, JR, b Baton Rouge, La, Sept 9, 28; m 57; c 3. PLANT BREEDING, AGRONOMY. *Educ:* La State Univ, BS, 51, MS, 53; Okla State Univ, PhD(plant breeding, genetics), 64. *Prof Exp:* Agronomist, Ibec Res Inst, 53-55 & NAR Farm, 55-56; asst agronomist, La State Univ, 56-59; agronomist, 59-63, RES AGRONOMIST, SCI & EDUC ADMIN-AGR RES, USDA, 63- *Concurrent Pos:* Instr, Okla State Univ, 59-63. *Res:* Genetics. *Mailing Add:* 4207 E Broadway Phoenix AZ 85040

YOUNG, FRANCIS ALLAN, b Utica, NY, Dec 29, 18; m 45; c 2. PSYCHOPHYSIOLOGY. *Educ:* Tampa Univ, BS, 41; Case Western Reserve Univ, MA, 45; Ohio State Univ, PhD(psychol), 49. *Prof Exp:* From instr to assoc prof, 48-61, PROF PSYCHOL, WASH STATE UNIV, 61-, DIR PRIMATE RES CTR, 57- *Concurrent Pos:* Nat Acad Sci-Nat Res Coun sr fel physiol psychol, 56-57; vis res prof, Med Sch, Univ Ore, 63-64; actg asst dir, Regional Primate Res Ctr, Univ Wash, 66-68; vis res prof, Med Sch, Univ Uppsala, 71. *Honors & Awards:* Apollo Award, Am Optometic Asn, 80. *Mem:* AAAS; Am Psychol Asn; Am Acad Optom; Asn Res Vision & Ophthal; Animal Behav Soc. *Res:* Vision and audition including comparative studies within primates; classical and instrumental conditioning; sexual behavior and genetics of behavior in primates. *Mailing Add:* Primate Res Ctr Wash State Univ Pullman WA 99164

YOUNG, FRANK, b Canton, China, Aug 8, 35; m 60; c 3. DIGITAL ELECTRONICS, ANALOG SERVOMECHANISMS. *Educ:* Hofstra Univ, BS, 62; Polytech Inst NY, MS, 70. *Prof Exp:* Elec engr, Sperry Rand, 57-65, Naval Appl Sci Lab, 65-70, Naval Electron Lab, 70-75; consult, 75-78; sr engr, TRW, Inc, 78; proj develop mgr, Comptek Res, 78-80; CHIEF ELECTRON ENGR, HUMPHREY INC, 80- *Concurrent Pos:* Instr comput, Coleman Col, 80-; consult digital appln. *Res:* Designed and developed high temperature (175 degrees C) North Seeker and magnetometer electronic instruments; designed digital Loran C naviagation receiver using 16 bit processor; designed error detection and correction systems; design magnetic tape certification unit. *Mailing Add:* 7296 Golfcrest Dr San Diego CA 92119

YOUNG, FRANK COLEMAN, b Roanoke, Va, June 10, 35; m 59; c 3. EXPERIMENTAL PLASMA PHYSICS, NUCLEAR DIAGNOSTICS. *Educ:* Johns Hopkins Univ, BA, 57; Univ Md, PhD(nuclear physics), 62. *Prof Exp:* NSF res fel, US Naval Res Lab, 62-63; from asst prof to assoc prof physics, Univ Md, 63-72; RES PHYSICIST, US NAVAL RES LAB, 72- *Mem:* Am Phys Soc; Inst Elec & Electronics Engr; Nuclear & Plasma Sci Soc. *Res:* Experimental nuclear physics; application of nuclear techniques to studies of hot dense plasmas. *Mailing Add:* Naval Res Lab 4555 Overlook Ave SW Washington DC 20375

YOUNG, FRANK E, b Mineola, NY, Sept 1, 31; m 56; c 5. PATHOLOGY, MICROBIOLOGY. *Educ:* State Univ NY, MD, 56; Western Reserve Univ, PhD(microbiol), 62. *Prof Exp:* From intern to resident path, Univ Hosps, Cleveland, Ohio, 56-60; from instr to asst prof, Western Reserve Univ, 62-65; from assoc mem to mem, Depts Microbiol & Exp Path, Scripps Clin & Res Found, 65-70; prof microbiol, path, radiation biol & biophys & chmn dept microbiol, 70-79, DEAN, SCH MED & DEN, UNIV ROCHESTER, 79-, VPRES HEALTH AFFAIRS, 81- *Concurrent Pos:* Am Cancer Soc res grant, 62-; NIH res grants, 65-, training grant, 70-; NSF res grant, 70-72; fac res assoc, Am Cancer Soc, 62-70; assoc prof, Univ Calif, San Diego, 67-70; dir clin microbiol labs, Strong Mem Hosp, 70-79, microbiologist-in-chief, 76-79; dir, Health Dept Labs, Monroe County, 70-79, mem bd, Am Asn Med Cols. *Mem:* Inst Med-Nat Acad Sci; Am Soc Microbiol; Am Soc Biol Chem; Am Soc Exp Path; Am Asn Path & Bact. *Res:* Mechanism of deoxyribonucleic and mediated transformation of bacterial and animal cells; regulation of bacterial cell surface; pathobiology of Neisseria gonorrhoeae. *Mailing Add:* Dept Microbiol Univ of Rochester Rochester NY 14642

YOUNG, FRANK GLYNN, b New York, NY, Dec 29, 16; m 41. CHEMISTRY, CATALYSIS. *Educ:* Dartmouth Col, AB, 37; Columbia Univ, PhD(org chem), 41. *Prof Exp:* Asst chem, Columbia Univ, 37-41; res chemist, 41-55, group leader radiation & isotope chem, 55-60, chem physics, Parma Res Labs, 60-63, SR RES SCIENTIST, UNION CARBIDE CORP, 63- *Mem:* Am Chem Soc; Am Soc Testing & Mat; fel Am Inst Chemists. *Res:* Mechanisms of catalytic processes; isotopic tracer studies; heterogeneous catalysis and surfaces. *Mailing Add:* Tech Ctr Union Carbide Corp Chem Div PO Box 8361 South Charleston WV 25303

YOUNG, FRANK HOOD, b Baltimore, Md, Dec 31, 39; m 61; c 4. MATHEMATICS. *Educ:* Haverford Col, BA, 61; Univ Pa, MA, 63, PhD(math), 68. *Prof Exp:* Instr math, Temple Univ, 65-68; asst prof, 68-74, chmn dept, 76-81, ASSOC PROF MATH, KNOX COL, ILL, 74- *Concurrent Pos:* Vis asst prof, Dept Comput Sci, Univ Ill, 73; Fulbright vis sr lectr, Dept Comput Sci, Univ Lagos, Nigeria, 75-76; vis assoc prof, Dept Comput Sci, Univ Iowa, 81-82. *Mem:* Am Math Soc; Asn Comput Mach; Soc Indust & Appl Math; Math Asn Am. *Res:* Analysis of algorithms; computer science education; linear algebra. *Mailing Add:* Dept of Math & Comput Sci Knox Col Galesburg IL 61401

YOUNG, FRANK NELSON, JR, b Oneonta, Ala, Nov 2, 15; m 43; c 2. BIOLOGY. *Educ:* Univ Fla, BS, 38, MS, 40, PhD(biol), 42. *Prof Exp:* Asst prof biol, Univ Fla, 46-49; from asst prof to assoc prof, 49-62, PROF ZOOL, IND UNIV, BLOOMINGTON, 62- *Concurrent Pos:* Guggenheim fel, 60-61; fel, La State Univ, 63. *Mem:* Am Soc Zool; Soc Study Evolution. *Res:* Taxonomy and ecology of aquatic Coleoptera; medical entomology; speciation and extinction of animals; land snails of genus Liguus. *Mailing Add:* Dept of Biol Ind Univ Bloomington IN 47405

YOUNG, FRANKLIN, b Beijing, China, Feb 1, 28; nat US. NUTRITION, BIOCHEMISTRY. *Educ:* Mercer Univ, AB, 51; Univ Fla, BSA, 52, MAgr, 54, PhD(nutrit), 60. *Prof Exp:* Asst vet sci, Univ Fla, 54-60, fel biochem, 60-61; res assoc, Bowman Gray Sch Med, 61-65, res instr prev med & assoc biochem, 65-66; ASSOC PROF FOOD & NUTRIT SCI, UNIV HAWAII, 66- *Mem:* Am Inst Nutrit. *Res:* Atherosclerosis, lipid metabolism, hypertension and human nutrition. *Mailing Add:* Dept of Food & Nutrit Sci Univ of Hawaii 2500 Dole St Honolulu HI 96822

YOUNG, FRANKLIN ALDEN, JR, b Harrisburg, Pa, Mar 14, 38; m 59; c 3. MATERIALS SCIENCE. *Educ:* Univ Fla, BIE, 60, MSE, 63; Univ Va, DSc(mat sci), 68. *Prof Exp:* Instr metall, Clemson Univ, 63-65, asst prof mat eng, 68-70; assoc prof, 70-75, PROF DENT MAT & CHMN DEPT, COL DENT MED, MED UNIV SC, 75- *Mem:* Am Soc Metals; Int Asn Dent Res; Sigma Xi. *Res:* Mechanical properties of alloys; materials of medicine and dentistry. *Mailing Add:* Col Dent Med 80 Barre St Charleston SC 29401

YOUNG, FRED M(ICHAEL), b Dallas, Tex, Aug 29, 40; m 63; c 2. HEAT TRANSFER, FLUID MECHANICS. *Educ:* Southern Methodist Univ, BSME, 63, MSME, 65, PhD(mech eng), 67. *Prof Exp:* Propulsion engr, Gen Dynamics/Ft Worth, 63-64; from asst prof to assoc prof mech eng, Lamar Univ, 67-74, dir grad eng studies, 72-74; head eng & appl sci, Portland State Univ, 74-79; DEAN ENG, LAMAR UNIV, 79- *Concurrent Pos:* Consult, Mobil Oil, Bethlehem Steel & Beaumont Yard. *Mem:* Am Soc Mech Engrs; Am Soc Eng Educ. *Res:* Two phase heat transfer; unsteady fluid flow; transient boiling. *Mailing Add:* Col Eng Box 10057 Lamar Univ Beaumont TX 77710

YOUNG, FREDERICK, physics, see previous edition

YOUNG, FREDERICK GRIFFIN, b Niagara Falls, Ont, Nov 7, 40; m 63; c 2. PETROLEUM GEOLOGY. *Educ:* Queen's Univ, Ont, BSc, 63; McGill Univ, MSc, 64, PhD(geol), 70. *Prof Exp:* Geologist, Hudson's Bay Oil & Gas Co, 64-66; res scientist stratig, Inst Sedimentary & Petrol Geol, Geol Surv Can, 69-78; sr staff geologist, 78-80, CHIEF GEOLOGIST, HOME OIL CO, LTD, 80- *Mem:* Am Asn Petrol Geologists; Soc Econ Paleont & Mineral; Can Soc Petrol Geologists; Int Asn Sedimentologists; Sigma Xi. *Res:* Physical stratigraphy; lithofacies analyses; geology of Upper Precambrian and Cambrian; clastic sedimentation; trace fossils; Mesozoic and Cenozoic geology of Mackenzie Delta area; petroleum geology. *Mailing Add:* Home Oil Co Ltd 324 Eighth Ave SW Calgary AB T2P 2Z5 Can

YOUNG, FREDERICK J(OHN), b Buffalo, NY, May 19, 31; m 54; c 3. ELECTRICAL ENGINEERING. *Educ:* Carnegie Inst Technol, BS, 53, MS, 54, PhD(elec eng), 56. *Prof Exp:* From instr to prof elec eng, Carnegie-Mellon Univ, 55-71; res engr, Labs, Westinghouse Elec Corp, 57-63, consult engr, 63-71, adv engr, 71-73; PROF ELEC ENG, PA STATE UNIV, 74- *Concurrent Pos:* Consult, Westinghouse Air Brake Co, 56, Union Switch & Signal Div, 57 & 60, Cornell Aeronaut Lab, Inc & Concrete Accessories Corp, 59, Oak Ridge Nat Labs, 74-, Westinghouse Res, 74-, Allied Chem Corp, 76-, TRW, Inc, 77-, ERDA, 77- & Mech Res, Inc, 77-; ed, Proceedings of Inst Elec & Electronics Engrs, 68; reviewer, Cent Br Math, E Ger Acad Sci, 70-; secy bd, Erebus Ltd, Eng, 75-; pres, Frontier Timber Co, 75- *Mem:* Inst Elec & Electronics Engrs. *Res:* Acoustical horns; electromagnetic field theory in ferrous media; magnetodydrodynamics; plasmadynamics; magneto-oceanography; magneto-mechanical devices. *Mailing Add:* 800 Minard Run Rd Frontier Timber Co Bradford PA 16701

YOUNG, FREDERICK WALTER, JR, b Hebron, Va, Sept 13, 24; m 50; c 2. PHYSICAL CHEMISTRY. *Educ:* Hampden-Sydney Col, BS, 44; Univ Va, PhD(chem), 50. *Prof Exp:* Instr, Hampden-Sydney Col, 44-46; res assoc, 50-51, chemist, Solid State Div, 56-69, ASSOC DIR SOLID STATE DIV, OAK RIDGE NAT LAB, 69- *Concurrent Pos:* Res assoc, Univ Va, 51-56. *Mem:* Fel AAAS; Am Crystallog Asn; fel Am Phys Soc; Am Asn Crystal Growth; Mat Res Soc. *Res:* Chemical properties of metal surfaces; observations of dislocations in metals; radiation damage in metals. *Mailing Add:* Gallaher Ferry Rd Rte 5 Lenoir City TN 37771

YOUNG, GAIL SELLERS, JR, b Chicago, Ill, Oct 3, 15; m 34, 68; c 1. MATHEMATICS. *Educ:* Univ Tex, BA, 39, PhD(math), 42. *Prof Exp:* Tutor pure math, Univ Tex, 38-39, instr, 39-42; from instr to asst prof math, Purdue Univ, 42-47; from asst prof to prof, Univ Mich, 47-59; prof, Tulane Univ, La, 59-70, head dept, 61-69; prof math, Univ Rochester, 70-80, chmn dept, 70-76 & 78-79; PROF & CHMN, DEPT MATH & STATIST, CASE WESTERN RESERVE UNIV, 80- *Concurrent Pos:* Mem, Nat Res Coun, 65-68 & 70-73, Conf Bd Math Sci, 66-70; chmn, US Comn Math Educ & Steering Coun, 75 & The Rochester Plan, 75-77. *Mem:* Fel AAAS; Am Math Soc; Math Asn Am (1st vpres, 66-68, pres, 70-71). *Res:* Topology; analysis; differential equations. *Mailing Add:* Dept Math & Statist Case Western Reserve Univ Cleveland OH 44106

YOUNG, GALE, b Baroda, Mich, Mar 5, 12; m 49; c 2. NUCLEAR PHYSICS. *Educ:* Milwaukee Sch Eng, BS, 33; Univ Chicago, BS & MS, 36. *Prof Exp:* Asst math biophys res, Univ Chicago, 36-40; head dept math & physics, Olivet Col, 40-42; physicist, Manhattan Dist Proj, Univ Chicago, 42-46; physicist, Clinton Labs, Tenn, 46-48; tech dir, Nuclear Develop Assocs, 48-55, vpres, Nuclear Develop Corp Am, 55-61; div vpres, United Nuclear Corp, 61-62; asst dir, 62-71, CONSULT, OAK RIDGE NAT LAB, 71- *Concurrent Pos:* Mem sci adv bd, US Dept Air Force, 54-58. *Mem:* Soc Indust & Appl Math; Math Asn Am. *Res:* Nuclear reactors; applied mathematics. *Mailing Add:* Oak Ridge Nat Lab Oak Ridge TN 37830

YOUNG, GEORGE ALLEN, civil engineering, deceased

YOUNG, GEORGE ANTHONY, b New York, NY, Nov 8, 19; m 49; c 4. METEOROLOGY, EXPLOSION PHENOMENA. *Educ:* NY Univ, BS, 48, MS, 49, PhD(meteorol), 65. *Prof Exp:* Res asst meteorol, NY Univ, 49-50; RES ASSOC, NAVAL SURFACE WEAPONS CTR, 50- *Mem:* Am Meteorol Soc. *Res:* Micrometeorology; hydrodynamics; turbulence; underwater explosions; environmental effects; effects of conventional and nuclear explosions in air and water, including military damage and environmental import. *Mailing Add:* 3611 Janet Rd Silver Spring MD 20906

YOUNG, GEORGE JAMISON, b Hornell, NY, Aug 31, 25; m 46; c 3. PHYSICAL CHEMISTRY. *Educ:* Rensselaer Polytech Inst, BS, 50; Lehigh Univ, MS, 52, PhD(phys chem), 54. *Prof Exp:* Instr phys chem, Lehigh Univ, 54-55; fel, Mellon Inst, 55-56; from asst prof to assoc prof, Pa State Univ, 56-58; prof chem, Alfred Univ, 58-61; pres, Surface Processes Corp, 61-69; DIR CORP ENG, PITNEY-BOWES, INC, 69- *Mem:* Royal Soc Chem. *Res:* Engineering science; operations analysis; research administration. *Mailing Add:* Pitney-Bowes Inc 69 Walnut St Stamford CT 06904

YOUNG, GEORGE ROBERT, b Monmouth, Ill, Mar 9, 25; m 46; c 4. BIOLOGICAL CHEMISTRY. *Educ:* Univ Ind, BS, 49, PhD(biol chem), 56; Northwestern Univ, MS, 52. *Prof Exp:* Fel biol chem, Univ Ind, 55-56; instr, Dent Br, Univ Tex, 56-57, asst prof, 57-62; assoc prof biochem & nutrit, Sch Dent, 62-68, coord grad studies, 67-72, PROF BIOCHEM & NUTRIT, SCH DENT, UNIV MO-KANSAS CITY, 68-, CHMN DEPT, 62-, PROF MED, SCH MED, 73- *Mem:* Am Chem Soc; Int Asn Dent Res. *Res:* Collagen and collagenase; invasiveness of cells; solubility of tooth enamel; nutrition and periodontal metabolism. *Mailing Add:* Dept Biochem & Nutrit Sch Dent Univ Mo 650 E 25th St Kansas City MO 64108

YOUNG, GERALD A, b Plainwell, Mich, Jan 9, 36; m 76; c 3. NEUROPSYCHOPHARMACOLOGY. *Educ:* Colo Col, BA, 58; Western Mich Univ, MA, 68; McMaster Univ, PhD(psychol), 73. *Prof Exp:* Res psychol, Kalamazoo State Hosp, 72-73; asst prof, Western Mich Univ, 73-74; res assoc, 74-81, SR RES ASSOC, UNIV MD, BALTIMORE, 81-

Concurrent Pos: Adj asst prof pharmacol, Univ Md, Baltimore, 78-79, adj assoc prof, 79- *Mem:* Am Soc Pharmacol & Exp Therapeut; Eastern Psychol Asn; Soc Neurosci. *Res:* Neuropsychopharmacology of psychoactive drugs; electroencephalogram spectral analysis; self-administration of drugs of abuse by experimental animals; behavioral pharmacology. *Mailing Add:* Dept Pharmacol & Toxicol Sch Pharm Univ Md 636 W Lombard St Baltimore MD 21201

YOUNG, GILBERT FLOWERS, JR, b Mayesville, SC, Sept 23, 22. NEUROLOGY, PEDIATRICS. *Educ:* Col Charleston, BA, 42; Univ NC, MA, 46, Med Col SC, MD, 47; Am Bd Pediat, dipl, 58; Am Bd Psychiat & Neurol, dipl, 66, cert neurol with spec competence child neurol, 69. *Prof Exp:* Intern, Med Col Va Hosp, 47-48; instr pharmacol, Univ NC, 48-49; resident pediat, Roper Hosp, Charleston, SC, 51-53; pvt pract, 53-56; resident child develop, Children's Hosp, Columbus, Ohio, 56-57; from asst prof to assoc prof pediat, 57-71, from asst prof to assoc prof neurol, 60-71, PROF NEUROL & PEDIAT, MED UNIV SC, 71- *Concurrent Pos:* Resident, Mass Gen Hosp, 60-63; consult, Med Univ SC Hosp & Roper Hosp, Charleston. *Mem:* AMA; Am Acad Pediat; Am Acad Neurol. *Res:* Child neurology and development; congenital encephalopathies. *Mailing Add:* Med Univ Hosp 80 Barre St Charleston SC 29403

YOUNG, GLENN REID, b Kingsport, Tenn, Aug 22, 51; m 80. NUCLEAR PHYSICS. *Educ:* Univ Tenn, BA, 73; Mass Inst Technol, PhD(physics), 77. *Prof Exp:* Fel Mass Inst Technol, 77-78; fel nuclear physics, 78-80, RES STAFF, OAK RIDGE NAT LAB, 80- *Mem:* Sigma Xi; Am Physical Soc. *Res:* Heavy ion macrophysics and reactions; isomeric and high spin nuclear spectroscopy; experimental tests of baryon number nonconservation. *Mailing Add:* Physics Div Bldg 6003 PO Box X Oak Ridge Nat Lab Oak Ridge TN 37830

YOUNG, GRANT MCADAM, b Glasgow, Scotland, Aug 23, 37; m 60; c 3. STRATIGRAPHY, SEDIMENTOLOGY. *Educ:* Glasgow Univ, BSc, 60, PhD(geol), 67. *Prof Exp:* Res demonstr geol, Univ Wales, 62-63; from lectr to assoc prof, 63-78, PROF GEOL, UNIV WESTERN ONT, 78- *Concurrent Pos:* Nat Res Coun Can & Geol Surv Can grants, Univ Western Ont, 65- *Mem:* Soc Econ Paleont & Mineral; Geol Soc Am; Geol Asn Can. *Res:* Stratigraphy and sedimentation of Precambrian supracrustal rocks; glaciogenic rocks in global correlation; Huronian rocks of Ontario; Upper Precambrian rocks of Arctic Canada and Canadian Cordillera. *Mailing Add:* Dept of Geol Univ of Western Ont London ON N6A 5B8 Can

YOUNG, H(ENRY) BEN, JR, b Rockdale, Tex, Oct 13, 13; m 41; c 2. MECHANICAL ENGINEERING. *Educ:* Rice Univ, BSME, 37; Harvard Univ, AMP, 58. *Prof Exp:* From mech engr to chief engr & dir overseas projs, Mission Mfg Co, Tex, 37-56; dir eng & res, W-K-M valve div, ACF Industs, Inc, 56-59, vpres eng & res, 59-63, vpres mgr & res, 63-65, vpres & gen mgr, W-K-M Valve Div, 65-72; dir capital expenditures, Marathon Mfg Co, Houston, 72-73; mgr & eng consult, Houston, 73-75; chmn bd dir & pres, CEO Chronister Valve Co, Houston, 75-77; mgt & eng consult, Houston, 77-78; VPRES ADMIN, LANZAGORTA INT INC, 78- *Mem:* Am Soc Mech Engrs; Nat Soc Prof Engrs. *Mailing Add:* 10122 Del Monte Houston TX 77042

YOUNG, HARLAND HARRY, b Portland, Ore, July 29, 08; m 32; c 2. ORGANIC CHEMISTRY. *Educ:* Reed Col, BA, 29; Mass Inst Technol, PhD(org chem), 32. *Prof Exp:* From anal chemist to res chemist, Swift & Co, 24-36, in charge new prod develop div, 36-39, asst to chief chemist, 39-41, asst chief chemist, 41-46, from asst dir res to dir res, 46-70; pres, Res Adv Serv, Inc, 71-82; RETIRED. *Mem:* Am Chem Soc; Am Leather Chem Asn; Am Inst Chem Engrs. *Res:* Adhesives; foods; fats; industrial oils; colloids; emulsions; detergents; proteins; in-plant pollution control; byproduct utilization. *Mailing Add:* 4724 Wolf Rd Western Springs IL 60588

YOUNG, HAROLD EDLE, b Arlington, Mass, Sept 4, 17; m 43; c 4. FORESTRY. *Educ:* Univ Maine, BS, 37; Duke Univ, MF, 46, PhD(tree physiol), 48. *Prof Exp:* Field asst, US Forest Serv, 37-40; from instr to assoc prof, 48-61, PROF FORESTRY, UNIV MAINE, 61- *Concurrent Pos:* Fulbright res scholar, Norway, 63-64; vis appointment, Dept Forestry, Australian Nat Univ, 68-69; consult, Off Opers Anal, US Air Force, 51-59. *Honors & Awards:* Hitchcock Award, Forest Prod Res Soc Am, 74; Burckhart-Medaille, Fac Forestery, Univ Gottingen, 80. *Mem:* Fel AAAS; Soc Am Foresters; Ecol Soc Am; Am Soc Plant Physiol; corresp mem Soc Forestry Finland. *Res:* Tree physiology and growth phenomena; soils; biomass studies within complete forest concept. *Mailing Add:* Complete Tree Inst Univ of Maine Orono ME 04473

YOUNG, HAROLD HENRY, b Malone, NY, Sept 11, 27; m 51; c 5. ANALYTICAL CHEMISTRY. *Educ:* St Michael's Col, Vt, BS, 51. *Prof Exp:* Chem tech, Works Lab, Gen Elec Co, 51-52; shift supvr, Ind Ord Works, E I du Pont de Nemours & Co, Inc, Ind, 52-54, lab supvr, Savannah River Plant, SC, 54-57; tech reviewer, Div Civilian Appln, Oak Ridge, Tenn, 57-58, non-destructive testing specialist, Div Isotopes Develop, Washington, DC, 58-59, isotopes training specialist, 59-62, nuclear educ & training specialist, 62-73, educ & training specialist, Div Biomed & Environ Res, 73-75, sr training coordr, Div Univ & Manpower Develop Progs, US AEC, 75-77, chief, Instnl Prog Br, Educ Progs Div, 77-82, CHIEF, LAB PROG BR, UNIV & IND PROG DIV, OFF ENERGY RES, US DEPT ENERGY WASHINGTON, DC, 82- *Mem:* Am Nuclear Soc; AAAS. *Res:* Quality control of nitrocellulose, plutonium and special nuclear materials; radioisotope and radiation applications. *Mailing Add:* Off Energy Res Dept Energy Washington DC 20545

YOUNG, HARRISON HURST, JR, b Drumright, Okla, Sept 24, 19; m 42; c 2. PHYSICAL CHEMISTRY. *Educ:* Princeton Univ, AB, 40; Columbia Univ, PhD(chem), 50; Fordham Univ, JD, 74. *Prof Exp:* Asst, Nat Defense Res Comt, 41-45; instr chem, Williams Col, Mass, 47-50; res group leader, Westvaco Div, Food Mach & Chem Corp, 50-52, res sect mgr, 52-56, asst to dir res, Westvaco Mineral Prod Div, 56-58, mgr detergent applns res, Inorg Res & Develop Dept, 59-62, tech recruitment mgr, Chem Div, 62-70, MEM STAFF CHEM GROUP, PATENT & LICENSING DEPT, FMC CORP, 70-, PATENT ATTORNEY, 75- *Mem:* Am Pat Law Asn; Am Chem Soc. *Res:* Reaction kinetics; industrial inorganic chemicals; detergent applications; agricultrual pesticides. *Mailing Add:* FMC Corp 2000 Market St Philadelphia PA 19103

YOUNG, HARRY CURTIS, JR, b East Lansing, Mich, Sept 6, 18; m 43; c 4. PLANT PATHOLOGY. *Educ:* Ohio State Univ, BSc, 40; Univ Minn, MSc, 43, PhD, 49. *Prof Exp:* Asst, Div Plant Path, Exp Sta, Univ Minn, 40-43 & 46-47; asst prof plant path, NY State Agr Exp Sta, Geneva, 47-50; assoc prof, 50-56, PROF PLANT PATH, OKLA STATE UNIV, 56- *Concurrent Pos:* Fel, Guggenheim Mem Found, 61; sr postdoctoral fel, Fulbright-Hays Prog, 69. *Mem:* Am Phytopath Soc; Am Soc Agron; Crop Sci Soc Am. *Res:* Pathology of cereal crops; breeding for disease resistance in cereal crops. *Mailing Add:* Dept of Bot & Plant Path Okla State Univ Stillwater OK 74074

YOUNG, HENRY H(ANS), b Des Moines, Iowa, June 28, 20; m 45. CHEMICAL ENGINEERING. *Educ:* Iowa State Univ, BS, 42. *Prof Exp:* Asst engr, Midwest Res Inst, 46-48, assoc engr, 48-55, sr engr, 55-65; res coordr, Res Found Kans, 65-67; INDUST SPECIALIST, UNIV MO-KANSAS CITY, 67- *Concurrent Pos:* Chief chem sect, Joint US-Brazil Mil Comn, Rio de Janeiro. *Mem:* Am Inst chem Engrs; Nat Soc Prof Engrs. *Res:* Combustion; heat transfer; filtration; extraction; evaporation; fire protection engineering; information transfer; research proposal evaluation. *Mailing Add:* Univ Mo Exten Ctr 4049 Pennsylvania Rm 200 Kansas City MO 64111

YOUNG, HEWITT H, b Willoughby, Ohio, May 16, 23; m 45; c 6. INDUSTRIAL & HUMAN FACTORS ENGINEERING. *Educ:* Case Inst Technol, BSME, 44, MSIE, 50; Ariz State Univ, PhD, 66. *Prof Exp:* Engr, Lamp Develop Lab, Gen Elec Co, Ohio, 46-48; instr graphics, Case Inst Technol, 48-50; indust engr jet engines, Tapco Div, Thompson Prod, Inc, Ohio, 50-53; prof indust eng, Purdue Univ, 53-67; chmn indust eng fac, 67-76, PROF ENG, ARIZ STATE UNIV, 67- *Concurrent Pos:* Chmn, Col-Indust Comt Mat Handling Educ, 66-68 & Nat Coun Indust Eng Acad Dept Heads, 71-72. *Mem:* Am Soc Eng Educ; fel Am Inst Indust Engrs (vpres, 72-75, 77-79). *Res:* Plant facilities; material handling; industrial mechanization; automatic control; optimization of manufacturing costs; computer-aided design; large-scale systems analysis; performance analysis; human engineering. *Mailing Add:* Dept of Indust Eng Ariz State Univ Tempe AZ 85281

YOUNG, HO LEE, b Canton, China, July 15, 20; nat US; m 49. PHYSIOLOGY. *Educ:* Lingnan Univ, BS, 43; Univ Calif, PhD, 54. *Prof Exp:* Asst gen biol & comp anat, Nat Med Col Shanghai, China, 44-49; student res physiologist, Univ Calif, 52-54, jr res physiologist, 54-56; res assoc radiol, Stanford Univ, 56-57; asst res physiologist, Med Ctr, Univ Calif, San Francisco, 57-63; res scientist, NASA Ames Res Ctr, 63-72; chief chem sect, 72-74, chief air sect, 74-76, chief lab br, 74, chief water sect, 76-79, REGION 9 QUAL ASSURANCE OFFICER, US ENVIRON PROTECTION AGENCY, 79- *Concurrent Pos:* San Francisco Heart Asn sr res fels, 60-62. *Mem:* Am Soc Microbiol; Am Chem Soc; Sigma Xi. *Res:* Cell physiology; cell particulates; cellular and fat metabolism; enzyme systems; protein synthesis; radiation effect on cells; electrolyte transport in skeletal muscle and isolated cells; effect of toxic materials and stresses on biochemical and physiological process of living systems. *Mailing Add:* 5978 Greenridge Rd Castro Valley CA 94546

YOUNG, HOBART PEYTON, b Evanston, Ill, Mar 9, 45. APPLIED MATHEMATICS, ECONOMICS. *Educ:* Harvard Univ, BA, 66; Univ Mich, PhD(math), 70. *Prof Exp:* Economist, Nat Water Comn, 71; assoc prof math, Grad Sch, City Univ New York, 71-75; res scholar & dep chmn, Int Inst Appl Systs Anal, 76-82; PROF PUB POLICY, UNIV MD, 82- *Concurrent Pos:* Vis prof, Univ Bonn, Univ Paris & Yale Univ; consult, numerous govt agencies; dir grants, US Army Res Off, 73-74 & NSF, 75-82. *Honors & Awards:* Lester R Ford Award, Math Asn Am, 76. *Mem:* Economet Soc; Am Polit Sci Asn; Opers Res Soc Am. *Res:* public economics; mathemattical models of voting and representation; environmental policy. *Mailing Add:* Int Inst Appl Systs Anal 2361 Laxenburg Austria

YOUNG, HONG YIP, b Wailuku, Hawaii, Nov 27, 10; m 37; c 3. AGRICULTURAL CHEMISTRY. *Educ:* Univ Hawaii, BS, 32, MS, 33. *Prof Exp:* Sci aide, Pineapple Res Inst, 33-40, from jr chemist to chemist, 40-67; from assoc agronomist to agronomist, 67-75, EMER AGRONOMIST, AGR EXP STA, COL TROP AGR, UNIV HAWAII, 75- *Concurrent Pos:* Vis scientist, Int Rice Res Inst, 65-66; consult, Indian Agr Res Inst, 68. *Mem:* AAAS; Am Chem Soc. *Res:* Plant, soil, hormone and pesticide residue analysis; mineral nutrition of plants. *Mailing Add:* 676 Hakaka St Honolulu HI 96816

YOUNG, HOWARD FREDERICK, b Fond du Lac, Wis, Nov 13, 18; m 42; c 3. ZOOLOGY. *Educ:* Univ Wis, BA, 46, MA, 47, PhD, 50. *Prof Exp:* Instr, Univ Ark, 50, asst prof, 50-53; assoc prof biol, Western Ill State Col, 53-55; from asst prof to assoc prof, 55-63, PROF BIOL, UNIV WIS, LA CROSSE, 63- *Concurrent Pos:* NSF grant, 59-60. *Mem:* Sigma Xi; Northeastern Bird Banding Asn; Wilson Ornith Soc; Am Ornith Union. *Res:* Ornithology; ecology; behavior; population. *Mailing Add:* Dept Biol Univ Wis La Crosse WI 54601

YOUNG, HOWARD SETH, b Birmingham, Ala, July 7, 24; m 45; c 7. PHYSICAL CHEMISTRY. *Educ:* Birmingham Southern Col, BS, 42; Brown Univ, PhD(chem), 48. *Prof Exp:* Chemist, 44-46 & 48-51, sr res chemist, 51-62, from res assoc to sr res assoc, 63-70, head eng res div, 70-75, HEAD PHYS & ANAL CHEM RES DIV, TENN EASTMAN CO, 75- *Mem:* Sigma Xi; Am Chem Soc. *Res:* Inorganic chemistry; catalysis. *Mailing Add:* 1909 E Sevier Ave Kingsport TN 37664

YOUNG, HUGH DAVID, b Ames, Iowa, Nov 3, 30; m 60; c 2. THEORETICAL PHYSICS. *Educ:* Carnegie Inst Technol, BS, 52, MS, 53, PhD(physics), 59, Carnegie-Mellon Univ, BFA, 72. *Prof Exp:* From instr to assoc prof physics, 56-76, head dept natural sci, 62-74, PROF PHYSICS, CARNEGIE-MELLON UNIV, 76- *Mem:* Am Phys Soc; Am Asn Physics Teachers. *Res:* Meson theory; new teaching materials for introductory college physics courses; administrative work in science education. *Mailing Add:* Dept of Physics Carnegie-Mellon Univ Pittsburgh PA 15213

YOUNG, IAN THEODORE, b Chicago, Ill, Dec 15, 43; m 77; c 3. ELECTRICAL ENGINEERING, ANALYTICAL CYTOLOGY. *Educ:* Mass Inst Technol, SB & SM, 66, PhD(elec eng), 69. *Prof Exp:* From instr to assoc prof elec eng, Mass Inst Technol, 67-79; group leader, Lawrence Livermore Lab, 78-81; PROF APPL PHYSICS, TECH UNIV DELFT, NETH, 81- *Concurrent Pos:* Vincent Hayes fel, Mass Inst Technol, 69-71, consult, Lincoln Labs, 72-78 & Coulter Biomed Res Corp, 75-78; fel, Neth Orgn Res, 75-77; guest prof, Tech Univ Neth, 75-76, Tech Univ Sweden, 76 & Tech Univ Lausanne, Switz, 80; mem cytol automation comn, Nat Cancer Inst, NIH, 77-81. *Mem:* Inst Elec & Electronics Engrs; Med & Biol Soc; Soc Anal Cytol. *Res:* Quantitative microscopy; image processing; pattern recognition; signal processing. *Mailing Add:* Dept Appl Physics Loreutzweg 1 Tech Univ Delft Delft 2600 GA Netherlands

YOUNG, IN MIN, b Seoul, Korea, July 13, 26; US citizen; m 53; c 3. AUDIOLOGY, PSYCHOACOUSTICS. *Educ:* Yonsei Univ, MD, 48; Jefferson Med Col, MSc, 66. *Prof Exp:* Instr otolaryngol, Sch Med, Yonsei Univ, 54-59; resident, Newark Eye & Ear Infirmary, NJ, 59-60; res audiologist, 60-65, from asst prof to assoc prof, 65-72, PROF AUDIOL, JEFFERSON MED COL, 72- *Concurrent Pos:* Dir, Hearing & Speech Ctr, Thomas Jefferson Univ Hosp, Philadelphia, 72-, audiologist, Affil Staff, 73-; consult otolaryngol, US Naval Hosp, Philadelphia; United Fund grant, 73-76. *Mem:* Acoust Soc Am; Am Speech & Hearing Asn; Am Neurotol Soc; Am Audiol Soc. *Res:* Auditory threshold and suprathreshold adaptation; Bekesy audiometry and marking. *Mailing Add:* Jefferson Med Col Thomas Jefferson Univ Philadelphia PA 19107

YOUNG, IRVING, b New York, NY, Aug 15, 22; m 48; c 3. MEDICINE, PATHOLOGY. *Educ:* Johns Hopkins Univ, AB, 43, MD, 46. *Prof Exp:* Asst pathologist, Kings County Hosp, Brooklyn, NY, 49-51; assoc dir labs, Div Path, 52-71, CHMN DIV LABS, ALBERT EINSTEIN MED CTR, 71-; CLIN PROF PATH, SCH MED, TEMPLE UNIV, 75- *Mem:* AMA. *Res:* Immunomorphologic correlation; histochemistry of chromosomes; surgical pathology. *Mailing Add:* Div of Labs Albert Einstein Med Ctr Philadelphia PA 19141

YOUNG, IRVING GUSTAV, b Brooklyn, NY, Dec 10, 19; m 41; c 2. ANALYTICAL CHEMISTRY, PHYSICAL CHEMISTRY. *Educ:* City Col New York, BS, 39; Polytech Inst Brooklyn, MS, 50; Temple Univ, PhD, 67. *Prof Exp:* Res asst, Bellevue Hosp, Columbia Univ, 39-42; asst chemist, Picatinny Arsenal, 42-44; battery technologist, US Elec Mfg Corp, 44-51; sr res chemist, Int Resistance Co, 51-56, sr res scientist, 59-64; chief chemist, Transition Metals & Chem Co, 56-57; asst res scientist, Leeds & Northrup Co, 57-59; res fel, Temple Univ, 64-65; chemist, Advan Technol Staff, Indust Div, Honeywell, Inc, 65-74, develop supvr, Honeywell Power Sources Ctr, 74-76; MGR, ENERGY PROGS, AM NAT STANDARDS INST, 76- *Mem:* Am Chem Soc; Instrument Soc Am; Air Pollution Control Asn; Water Pollution Control Fedn; Am Soc Test & Mat. *Res:* Electrochemistry; process analyzers; air and water pollution; standards coordination. *Mailing Add:* 22 Four Leaf Rd Levittown PA 19056

YOUNG, J LOWELL, b Perry, Utah, Dec 13, 25; m 50; c 4. SOIL BIOCHEMISTRY & BIOLOGY, SOIL CLAY MINERALOGY. *Educ:* Brigham Young Univ, BS, 53; Ohio State Univ, PhD(soils), 56. *Prof Exp:* Asst agron, Agr Exp Sta, Ohio State Univ, 53-56, fel agr biochem, Univ, 56-57; chemist, Agr Res Serv, USDA, 57-60; asst prof, 57-63, assoc prof, 63-78, PROF SOIL SCI, ORE STATE UNIV, 78-; RES CHEMIST, AGR RES SERV, USDA, 60- *Concurrent Pos:* Assoc ed, Soil Sci Soc Am J, 75-78. *Mem:* AAAS; Am Soc Agron; Soil Sci Soc Am; Clay Minerals Soc; Int Asn Study Clays. *Res:* Enzymes in cotyledons of germinating seeds; amino acids of soils, humic substances, root exudates; D-amino acids uptake and metabolism by higher plants; nitrogen and soil particulates as nonpoint-source pollutants eroded from agricultural lands; soil properrties affecting beneficial root-fungus symbroses (endomycorrhiza). *Mailing Add:* Dept of Soil Sci Ore State Univ Corvallis OR 97331

YOUNG, JACK PHILLIP, b Huntington, Ind, Oct 28, 29; m 55; c 5. ANALYTICAL CHEMISTRY. *Educ:* Ball State Teachers Col, BS, 50; Univ Ind, PhD(chem), 55. *Prof Exp:* CHEMIST, UNION CARBIDE NUCLEAR CO, 55- *Mem:* AAAS; Am Chem Soc; Sigma Xi. *Res:* Actinide chemistry; spectroscopy of solutions, molten salts, solid state compounds; laser spectroscopy; photoionization studies. *Mailing Add:* 100 Westlook Circle Oak Ridge TN 37830

YOUNG, JAMES ARTHUR, JR, b Tacoma, Wash, Feb 12, 21; m 43; c 2. PHYSICS, ELECTRICAL ENGINEERING. *Educ:* Calif Inst Technol, BS, 43; Univ Wash, PhD(physics), 53. *Prof Exp:* Res engr rocket instrumentation, Jet Propulsion Lab, Calif Inst Technol, 46-47; teaching fel physics, Univ Wash, 47-53; co-dir, Radio Res Lab, Bell Tel Labs, Holmdel, 53-76; sr design engr, Data Gen Corp, 76-80. *Mem:* Inst Elec & Electronics Engrs; Am Phys Soc. *Res:* Communications research; encoding, modulation transmission and switching of information signals, particularly for high radio frequency and optical media. *Mailing Add:* 13921 Silen Ave NE Bainbridge Island WA 98110

YOUNG, JAMES CHRISTOPHER F, b Charlottetown, PEI, Apr 1, 40; m 66; c 3. ANALYTICAL CHEMISTRY, MYCOTOXINS. *Educ:* Mt Allison Univ, BSc, 60; McMaster Univ, MSc, 62; Mass Inst Technol, PhD(org chem), 71. *Prof Exp:* Teacher sci, Kitchener-Waterloo Col & Voc Sch, 62-64; lectr chem, Sir Wilfred Laurier Univ, 64-66; RES SCIENTIST, CHEM & BIOL RES INST, AGR CAN, 72- *Concurrent Pos:* Rockefeller Found fel, NY Col Forestry, Syracuse Univ, 71-72. *Mem:* AAAS; Chem Inst Can; Am Chem Soc. *Res:* Natural product chemistry; organic chemistry analytical methodology; mycotoxins; ergot alkaloids; chemicals used in animal communication; insect pheromones. *Mailing Add:* Agr Can Chem & Biol Res Inst Ottawa ON K1A 0C6 Can

YOUNG, JAMES EDWARD, b Wheeling, WVa, Jan 18, 26; m 48; c 1. PARTICLE PHYSICS, NUCLEAR PHYSICS. *Educ:* Howard Univ, BS, 46, MS, 49; Mass Inst Technol, MS, 51, PhD(physics), 53. *Prof Exp:* Instr physics, Hampton Inst, 46-49; fel acoustics, Mass Inst Technol, 53-55; staff mem physics, Los Alamos Sci Lab, 57-70; PROF PHYSICS, INST THEORET PHYSICS, MASS INST TECHNOL, 70- *Concurrent Pos:* Shell B P fel, Univ Southampton, 56; consult, Gen Atomics, Calif, 57-58; Nat Acad Sci-Nat Res Coun & Ford fel, Bohr Inst, Copenhagen, 61-62; vis assoc prof, Univ Minn, 64; res asst, Oxford Univ, 65-66; visitor, Inst Theoret Physics, Mass Inst Technol, 68-69. *Mem:* Am Phys Soc. *Res:* Pion physics at intermediate energies; three-body relativistic models; multipheripheral equations for hadrons at high energies. *Mailing Add:* Ctr for Theoret Physics Mass Inst of Technol Cambridge MA 02139

YOUNG, JAMES FORREST, b Meadville, Pa, June 22, 43; m 71. LASER PHYSICS, ENGINEERING. *Educ:* Mass Inst Technol, BS, 65, MS, 66; Stanford Univ, PhD(elec eng), 70. *Prof Exp:* Res assoc, E L Ginzton Lab, 70-75, ADJ PROF ELEC ENG, STANFORD UNIV, 75- *Concurrent Pos:* Consult, Coherent, Inc, 70-75, Spectra-Physics Inc, 76- & Bell Tel Labs, 77- *Mem:* Am Inst Physics; fel Optical Soc Am; Inst Elec & Electronics Engrs. *Res:* Quantum electronics; nonlinear optics; experimental techniques and instruction. *Mailing Add:* Edward L Ginzton Lab Stanford Univ Stanford CA 94305

YOUNG, JAMES FREDERICK, mechanical engineering, deceased

YOUNG, JAMES GEORGE, b Milwaukee, Wis, July 18, 26; m 54; c 3. INDUSTRIAL PHARMACY. *Educ:* Univ Wis, BS, 48, MS, 49; Univ NC, PhD(pharm), 52. *Prof Exp:* Asst prof pharmaceut chem, Med Col Va, 51-54 & Univ Tenn, 56-58; sr chemist, Riker Labs, Inc, 58-60, dir prod develop, 60-72; DIR DEVELOP, G D SEARLE & CO, 72- *Mem:* AAAS; Am Chem Soc; Am Pharmaceut Asn; NY Acad Sci. *Res:* Pharmaceutical aerosol formulation; drug stabilization; general pharmaceutical development. *Mailing Add:* GD Searle & Co PO Box 5110 Chicago IL 60680

YOUNG, JAMES H, b LaFayette, Ky, Mar 19, 41; m 63; c 2. AGRICULTURAL ENGINEERING. *Educ:* Univ Ky, BSAE, 62, MSAE, 64; Okla State Univ, PhD(eng), 66. *Prof Exp:* From asst prof to assoc prof, 66-76, PROF BIOL & AGR ENG, NC STATE UNIV, 76- *Mem:* Am Soc Agr Engrs; Am Soc Eng Educ; Am Peanut Res Educ Soc. *Res:* Heat and mass transfer in biological materials including tobacco, wheat and peanuts; growth simulation of peanuts as affected by environment; automatic monitoring of weather parameters affecting crop production. *Mailing Add:* Dept of Biol & Agr Eng NC State Univ Raleigh NC 27607

YOUNG, JAMES HOWARD, b Norfolk, Va, May 9, 24; m 50; c 1. MATHEMATICS. *Educ:* Univ Va, BA, 48; Duke Univ, MA, 51. *Prof Exp:* Instr physics, Norfolk Div, Col William & Mary, 47-51; instr math, Johns Hopkins Univ, 55-69, res scientist, Inst Coop Res, 51-69; sr res analyst, Falcon Res & Develop, 69-81; SR RES ANALYST, KETRON, INC, 81- *Mem:* Am Math Soc. *Res:* Weapons systems analysis; military operations research. *Mailing Add:* 106 Regester Ave Baltimore MD 21212

YOUNG, JAMES R(ALPH), b Rushville, Ill, June 22, 30; m 52; c 1. ELECTRICAL ENGINEERING, MATHEMATICS. *Educ:* Univ Ill, BS, 56, MS, 57, PhD(elec eng), 60. *Prof Exp:* Instr elec eng, Univ Ill, 56-60; assoc prof, NMex State Univ, 60-65; SR RES ENGR, SRI INT, 65- *Concurrent Pos:* Elec engr, Barber Colman Co, Ill, 56-59. *Mem:* Inst Elec & Electronics Engrs. *Res:* Network theory; applications of topology to network synthesis; applications of dynamic programming techniques; analysis of linear systems. *Mailing Add:* 3433 Cowper Palo Alto CA 94306

YOUNG, JAMES ROGER, b Fordland, Mo, June 14, 23; m 45; c 3. PHYSICS. *Educ:* Park Col, AB, 46; Univ Mo, BA, 49, PhD(physics), 52. *Prof Exp:* Res physicist, Res Lab, 51-63, mgr advan develop vacuum prod, 63-64, mgr eng, 64-66, MGR PLASMA LIGHT SOURCES, RES & DEVELOP CTR, GEN ELEC CO, SCHENECTADY, 74- *Mem:* Am Vacuum Soc (treas, 73-); Am Phys Soc; Am Inst Physics. *Res:* Vacuum physics; physical electronics. *Mailing Add:* 422 Nott Rd Rexford NY 12148

YOUNG, JANIS DILLAHA, b Little Rock, Ark, July 12, 27; m 56; c 2. BIOCHEMISTRY, IMMUNOCHEMISTRY. *Educ:* Hendrix Col, BA, 49; Univ Okla, MS, 51; Univ Calif, Berkeley, PhD(biochem), 60. *Prof Exp:* Biochemist, Armour Labs, Chicago, Ill, 51-54; instr chem, Colby Col, 54-55; NIH trainee virol, Univ Calif, Berkeley, 59-61; assoc res scientist, Lab Med Entom, Kaiser Found Res Inst, 61-70; assoc res biochemist, Space Sci Lab & Adj Assoc Prof Immunol, Dept Bact & Immunol, Univ Calif, Berkeley, 71-79; assoc biochemist, Lowell Labs, McLean Hosp, Belmont, Ma, 79-82 RES ASSOC, DIV INFECTIOUS DIS CHILDREN'S HOSP MED CTR, 82-; RES ASSOC, DEPT BIOL CHEM, HARVARD MED SCH, 79- *Mem:* Am Chem Soc; Am Asn Immunol; Am Soc Biol Chemists. *Res:* Immunochemistry of proteins; post-translational reactions of proteins, particularly basic myelin protein, using peptide synthesis. *Mailing Add:* Div Infectious Dis Children's Hosp Med Ctr Boston MA 02115

YOUNG, JAY ALFRED, b Huntington, Ind, Sept 8, 20; m 42, 62; c 18. PUBLIC HEALTH. *Educ:* Univ Ind, BS, 39; Oberlin Col, AM, 40; Univ Notre Dame, PhD, 50. *Prof Exp:* Chief chemist, Asbestos Mfg Co, Ind, 40-42; ord engr, US War Dept, DC, 42-44; from instr to prof chem, King's Col, Pa, 49-69; vis prof, Carleton Univ, 69-70; Hudson Prof Chem, Auburn Univ,

70-75; vis prof chem, Fla State Univ, 75-77; mgr tech publ, Chem Mfrs Asn, DC, 77-80; CONSULT, 80- *Concurrent Pos:* Ed, Int J Chem Health & Safety, 80-; expert witness & tech consult in labeling hazardous chem & prod liability, 79- *Honors & Awards:* Centennial of Sci Award, Univ Notre Dame, 65; Excellence in Teaching Award, Mfg Chem Asn, 71. *Mem:* AAAS; Am Chem Soc. *Res:* Safe use, handling, precautionary labeling and disposal of chemicals; application of chemical reactions to manufacturing processes and to consumer uses and concomitant prevention of injury and property damage and loss. *Mailing Add:* 12916 Allerton Lane Silver Spring MD 20904

YOUNG, JAY MAITLAND, b Louisville, Ky, Nov 26, 44. IMMUNOASSAYS, ENZYMOLOGY. *Educ:* Vanderbilt Univ, BA, 66; Yale Univ, MS, 67, MPh, 68, PhD(chem), 71. *Prof Exp:* Asst prof chem, Bryn Mawr Col, 70-76; RES BIOCHEMIST & PROJ MGR, ABBOTT LABS, 77- *Concurrent Pos:* NIH fel, Oxford Univ, 71-72; vis scientist, Inst Cancer Res, Philadelphia, Pa, 75-76. *Mem:* AAAS; Am Chem Soc. *Res:* Radio-immuno assays; enzyme-immuno assays; antibody production and characterization. *Mailing Add:* Abbott Diag Div Abbott Park North Chicago IL 60064

YOUNG, JERRY H, b Fitzhugh, Okla, Aug 4, 31; m 52; c 1. ENTOMOLOGY. *Educ:* Okla State Univ, BS, 55, MS, 56; Univ Calif, Berkeley, PhD(parasitol), 59. *Prof Exp:* PROF ENTOM, OKLA STATE UNIV, 59- *Mem:* Entom Soc Am; Entom Soc Can. *Res:* Cotton insect control; mite morphology; Hymenoptera taxonomy; integrated and biological control of cotton insects. *Mailing Add:* Dept Entom Okla State Univ Stillwater OK 74074

YOUNG, JERRY WESLEY, b Mulberry, Tenn, Aug 19, 34; m 59; c 2. ANIMAL NUTRITION. *Educ:* Berry Col, BS, 57; NC State Univ, MS, 59, PhD(animal nutrit), 63. *Prof Exp:* Res asst animal nutrit, NC State Univ, 57-63; USPHS fel biochem, Inst Enzyme Res, Univ Wis, 63-65; asst prof animal nutrit, 65-70, assoc prof animal sci & biochem, 70-74, PROF ANIMAL SCI & BIOCHEM, IOWA STATE UNIV, 74- *Mem:* Am Chem Soc; Am Dairy Sci Asn; Am Inst Nutrit; Am Soc Animal Sci. *Res:* Volatile fatty acid metabolism in ruminants; mechanism and control of gluconeogenesis and interrelationships with lipid metabolism; lactation ketosis in the bovine. *Mailing Add:* Dept Animal Sci Iowa State Univ Ames IA 50010

YOUNG, JOHN A, b Washington, DC, July 4, 39; c 2. METEOROLOGY. *Educ:* Miami Univ, BA, 61; Mass Inst Technol, PhD(meteorol), 66. *Prof Exp:* NSF fel, Univ Oslo, 66; from asst prof to assoc prof, 66-75, NSF res grant, 71-81, PROF METEOROL, UNIV WIS-MADISON, 75- *Concurrent Pos:* Vis assoc prof, Mass Inst Technol, 73-74; mem, Global Atmospheric Res Prog, Nat Acad Sci, 73-78 & 80-83. *Mem:* AAAS; Am Meteorol Soc. *Res:* Dynamic meteorology, observations and monsoon dynamics; numerical modeling; planetary boundary layers; tropical field experiments. *Mailing Add:* Dept of Meteorol Univ of Wis Madison WI 53706

YOUNG, JOHN ALBION, JR, b Newport, RI, Aug 29, 09; m 37. PETROLEUM GEOLOGY. *Educ:* Brown Univ, PhB, 32, ScM, 34; Harvard Univ, PhD(geol), 46. *Prof Exp:* Asst geol, Brown Univ, 32-37; asst paleont, Harvard Univ, 37-39; instr geol, Mich State Col, 39-44; geologist, Sun Oil Co, 44-46; asst prof geol, Syracuse Univ, 46-47; geologist, Sun Oil Co, 47-50, staff geologist, 50-70; vpres, secy, dir & dir oil & gas div, Tax Shelter Adv Serv, Inc, Pa, 70-73; vpres, World Resources, 73-81; sr vpres explor & prod, 74-81, SR EXPLOR CONSULT, OMNI-EXPLOR INC, RADNOR, 81- *Mem:* Fel Geol Soc Am; Am Asn Petrol Geologists. *Res:* Petroleum geology; stratigraphy; subsurface geology. *Mailing Add:* PO Box 436 Hunters Lane Devon PA 19333

YOUNG, JOHN CANNON, b Salt Lake City, Utah, June 27, 28; m 56; c 4. GEOLOGY. *Educ:* Univ Utah, BS, 50, MS, 53; Princeton Univ, PhD(geol), 60. *Prof Exp:* Explor geologist, Standard Oil Co Calif, 50-54 & 59-61; chmn dept, 61-77, PROF GEOL, HUMBOLDT STATE UNIV, 61-; consult, 79-81; SR PROF GEOLOGIST, SUN EXPLOR CO, 81- *Mem:* AAAS; Am Asn Petrol Geologists; Nat Asn Geol Teachers; Geol Soc Am. *Res:* Regional stratigraphy and structural geology in the western United States; geomorphology; tectonics in Klamath Mountains. *Mailing Add:* 4795 McKinley Dr Boulder CO 80303

YOUNG, JOHN CHANCELLOR, b Sacramento, Calif, May 21, 38; m 63; c 2. NUCLEAR PHYSICS, ENVIRONMENTAL SCIENCES. *Educ:* Univ Calif, Berkeley, AB, 60; Univ Calif, Davis, MA, 67, PhD(physics), 69. *Prof Exp:* Asst prof physics, Univ Calif, Los Angeles, 68-70; assoc prof, Calif State Univ, Chico, 70-75; lab dir res & admin, 73-78, RES PHYSICIST & CONSULT RES & DEVELOP, TRACE ANAL LAB, 78- *Concurrent Pos:* Fac fel, Assoc Western Univ, 71 & Crocker Nuclear Lab, 72; Univ Calif, Davis, res grant, Res Corp, 71-72. *Mem:* Am Phys Soc; Soc Appl Spectros; AAAS. *Res:* Applications of energy dispersive x-ray fluorescence to trace elemental analysis; experimental nuclear physics. *Mailing Add:* Trace Anal Lab 3423 Investment Blvd 14 Hayward CA 94545

YOUNG, JOHN COLEMAN, b Leesville, La, July 13, 42; m 64; c 1. STATISTICS. *Educ:* Northwestern State Univ, BA, 64, MS, 65; Southern Methodist Univ, PhD(statist), 71. *Prof Exp:* Asst instr math, Northwestern State Univ, 64-65; asst prof, McNeese State Univ, 67-69; instr statist, Southern Methodist Univ, 69-71; from asst prof to assoc prof, 71-77, PROF MATH, McNEESE STATE UNIV, 77- *Mem:* Am Statist Asn. *Res:* Multivariate analysis; discrimination, analysis of variance and goodness of Fit test for multivariate populations. *Mailing Add:* 233 Greenway Lake Charles LA 70601

YOUNG, JOHN DAVIS, b Harrisonburg, Va, July 9, 21; m 46; c 3. ORGANIC CHEMISTRY. *Educ:* Univ NC, BS, 43; Univ Ill, PhD(org chem), 47. *Prof Exp:* Asst org chem, Univ Ill, 43-46, chemist, Off Rubber Reserve, 46-47; chemist, E I du Pont de Nemours & Co, Inc, 47-80. *Mem:* Soc Plastics Engrs; Soc Automotive Engrs. *Res:* Synthesis of substituted styrene monomers for polymerization studies; design development with plastic materials in automotive industry. *Mailing Add:* 975 Barcelona Dr Santa Barbara CA 93105

YOUNG, JOHN FALKNER, b Tyler, Tex, Apr 3, 40. PHARMACODYNAMICS, TOXICOLOGY. *Educ:* NTex State Univ, BA, 63; Univ Houston, BS, 66; Univ Fla, MS, 69, PhD(pharmaceut res), 73. *Prof Exp:* RES BIOLOGIST TERATOLOGY, NAT CTR TOXICOL RES, 73- *Honors & Awards:* Commendable Serv Award, Nat Ctr Toxicol Res, Food & Drug Admin, 74. *Mem:* Am Pharmaceut Asn; Soc Appl Spectros. *Res:* Application of the principles of pharmacokinetics to teratogenic research; development of the analytical procedures used to quantitate the chemicals from biological fluids and tissues; simulation of data on hybrid computer. *Mailing Add:* Teratology Div Nat Ctr for Toxicol Res Jefferson AR 72079

YOUNG, JOHN H, b Shamokin, Pa, Aug 16, 40. PHYSICS. *Educ:* Gettysburg Col, BA, 62; Univ NH, MS, 64; Clark Univ, PhD, 69. *Prof Exp:* Asst physics, Clark Univ, 64-66; asst prof, 70-77, ASSOC PROF PHYSICS, UNIV ALA, BIRMINGHAM, 77- *Mem:* Am Phys Soc. *Res:* Description of the gravitational field of a rotating mass in the general theory by exact means; two body problem in general relativity; three body nucleon problem. *Mailing Add:* Dept of Physics Univ of Ala Birmingham AL 35294

YOUNG, JOHN PAUL, b Baltimore, Md, Dec 20, 23; m 53; c 2. OPERATIONS RESEARCH. *Educ:* Univ Md, BS, 50; Johns Hopkins Univ, DEng(opers res), 62. *Prof Exp:* Indust engr, Westinghouse Elec Corp, 50-54; sr analyst opers res, 54-59, instr, 59-62, lectr, 62-64, asst dir, Opers Res Div, Hosp, 62-68, from asst prof to assoc prof, Pub Health Admin & Opers Res, 64-69, assoc provost, 68-72, actg vpres & provost, 70-71, prof, Pub Health Admin & Opers Res, 69-80, PROF HEALTH SERV, SCH HYG & PUB HEALTH, JOHNS HOPKINS UNIV, 80- *Concurrent Pos:* USPHS grant; consult, USPHS, 62-, mem health serv res study sect, 66-69, mem health care systs study sect, 69-72; consult, Vet Admin, 62-72, Hosp Coun of Md, 65-72, Am Hosp Asn, 66- & CSF, Ltd, 75-80; bd trustees, Chesapeake Res Consortium, 72-76; bd gov, Johns Hopkins Hosp, 72- *Mem:* Fel AAAS; Opers Res Soc Am; Am Pub Health Asn; Inst Mgt Sci; fel Royal Soc Health. *Res:* Operations research in health services. *Mailing Add:* Stebbins Bldg Johns Hopkins Univ Baltimore MD 21205

YOUNG, JOHN W(ATTS), b San Francisco, Calif, Sept 24, 30; m; c 2. ASTRONAUTICS, AERONAUTICAL ENGINEERING. *Educ:* Ga Inst Technol, BSAE, 52. *Hon Degrees:* LLD, Western State Univ Col Law, 69; DrApplSci, Fla Technol Univ, 70. *Prof Exp:* Pilot on first manned Gemini flight, 65, backup pilot for Gemini 6, occupied command pilot seat for Gemini 10 mission, 66, backup command module pilot for Apollo 7, command module pilot for Apollo 10, 69, backup spacecraft commander for Apollo, 13, spacecraft commander of Apollo 16, 72, backup spacecraft commander for Apollo 17, 72, ASTRONAUT, NASA, 62- *Honors & Awards:* Two NASA Distinguished Serv Medals, two Except Serv Medals, Manned Spacecraft Ctr Cert of Commendation, 70; Ivan C Kinchloe Award, Soc Exp Test Pilots, 72. *Mem:* Fel Am Astronaut Soc; assoc fel Soc Exp Test Pilots; Am Inst Aeronaut & Astronaut. *Mailing Add:* NASA Manned Spacecraft Ctr Houston TX 77058

YOUNG, JOHN W(ESLEY), JR, b Baltimore, Md, June 16, 24; m 50; c 1. COMPUTER SCIENCE. *Educ:* Albright Col, AB, 45; Harvard Univ, MS, 55. *Prof Exp:* Supvry analyst data processing, US Dept Defense, Washington, DC, 49-56; SR CONSULT ANALYST, SYSTS ENG, SCRIPPS RANCH, NCR CORP, 57- *Concurrent Pos:* Guest lectr, Univ Calif, Los Angeles, 66- *Mem:* Asn Comput Mach; Inst Elec & Electronics Engrs; Asn Comput Ling. *Res:* Design, application and programming of digital computers, especially problem formulation languages, simulation, artificial intelligence and operating systems; data base systems; query languages. *Mailing Add:* NCR Corp Scripps Ranch Dept 5500 16550 W Bernardo Dr San Diego CA 92127

YOUNG, JOHN WILLIAM, b Toronto, Ont, Nov 16, 12; nat US; m 39; c 1. MATHEMATICS, COMPUTER SCIENCE. *Educ:* Univ Fla, AB, 34, BS, 37, MA, 40, PhD(math), 52. *Prof Exp:* Prin & sch teacher, Fla, 34-42; instr math, Univ Fla, 46-52; appl sci rep, Int Bus Mach Corp, Ga, 54-55; mathematician & comput prog consult, Res Comput Ctr, NY, 55-57 & Missile Test Ctr, Radio Corp Am, 57-58; head anal & info processing, Res Div, Radiation, Inc, 59-60, head eng comput serv, 61-68, mem sr staff, 68-71; mem sr specialist staff, Data Systs Div, Martin Marietta Corp, Fla, 72-75; vis assoc prof comput sci, Fla Technol Univ, 75-76; MEM TECH STAFF, EDUC COMPUT CORP, ORLANDO, 76- *Concurrent Pos:* Consult, Sci Systs Serv, Melbourne, 76. *Mem:* Nat Coun Teachers Math; Math Asn Am; Asn Comput Mach. *Res:* Applications of electronic digital computers; computer performance measurement and evaluation; simulation of computer systems. *Mailing Add:* PO Box 1661 Melbourne FL 32901

YOUNG, JOSEPH HARDIE, b Salt Lake City, Utah, Aug 11, 18; m 66; c 1. BIOLOGY. *Educ:* Stanford Univ, PhD(biol), 54. *Prof Exp:* From instr to asst prof zool, Tulane Univ, 54-59; from asst prof to assoc prof biol, 59-65, chmn dept, 66-80, PROF BIOL, SAN JOSE STATE UNIV, 65- *Mem:* AAAS; Entom Soc Am; Am Soc Zool; Sigma Xi. *Res:* Insect embryology; arthropod morphology; marine biology. *Mailing Add:* Dept of Biol Sci San Jose State Univ San Jose CA 95112

YOUNG, JOSEPH MARVIN, b Marshall, Tex, Oct 16, 19; m 42; c 4. PATHOLOGY, ANATOMY. *Educ:* Harvard Univ, BS, 43; Johns Hopkins Univ, MD, 45. *Prof Exp:* Intern surg, Johns Hopkins Hosp, 45-46; resident surg, 46-51, resident path, 51-54, CHIEF LAB SERV, VET ADMIN HOSP, 54-; PROF PATH, UNIV TENN MED UNITS, MEMPHIS, 62- *Honors & Awards:* Spec Commendation Award, Chief Med Dir, Vet Admin Cent Off, 67. *Mem:* AAAS; Col Am Path; Am Asn Path & Bact; Am Soc Exp Path. *Res:* Joint reactions and spread of cancer. *Mailing Add:* Vet Admin Hosp Lab Serv 1030 Jefferson Ave Memphis TN 38104

YOUNG, KEITH PRESTON, b Buffalo, Wyo, Aug 18, 18; m 49; c 3. PALEONTOLOGY, STRATIGRAPHY. *Educ:* Univ Wyo, BA, 40, MA, 42; Univ Wis, PhD(stratig), 48. *Prof Exp:* From asst prof to assoc prof, 48-58, PROF GEOL, UNIV TEX, AUSTIN, 58- *Mem:* Paleont Soc; Geol Soc Am;

Soc Econ Paleont & Mineral; Am Asn Petrol Geol; Am Inst Prof Geologists. *Res:* Cretaceous stratigraphy and paleontology of southwestern North America; Cephalopods and rudists. *Mailing Add:* Dept of Geol Sci Univ of Tex Austin TX 78712

YOUNG, KENNETH CHRISTIE, b Rochester, NY, Nov 9, 41. CLOUD PHYSICS. *Educ:* Ariz State Univ, BS, 65; Univ Chicago, MS, 67, PhD(geophys), 73. *Prof Exp:* Fel, Nat Ctr Atmospheric Res, 73-74; asst prof, 74-80, ASSOC PROF ATMOSPHERIC SCI, UNIV ARIZ, 80- *Mem:* Am Meteorol Soc; Inst Atmospheric Sci. *Res:* Precipitation processes in clouds; ice phase nucleation; hail suppression; orographic precipitation and its enhancement; numerical simulations of microphysical processes in clouds. *Mailing Add:* Inst of Atmospheric Physics Univ of Ariz Tucson AZ 85721

YOUNG, KENNETH KONG, b Vancouver, BC, Mar 19, 37; m 67. HIGH ENERGY PHYSICS. *Educ:* Univ Wash, BSc, 59; Univ Pa, PhD(physics), 65. *Prof Exp:* Res assoc physics, Univ Mich, 65-67; from asst prof to assoc prof, 67-77, PROF PHYSICS, UNIV WASH, 77- *Mem:* Am Phys Soc. *Res:* Experimental weak interactions; time reverse invariance; particle physics. *Mailing Add:* Dept of Physics Univ of Wash Seattle WA 98195

YOUNG, LAURENCE RETMAN, b New York, NY, Dec 19, 35; m 60; c 3. BIOENGINEERING, INSTRUMENTATION. *Educ:* Amherst Col, AB, 55; Mass Inst Technol, BS, 57, MS, 59, ScD(instrumentation), 62; Univ Paris, cert, 58. *Prof Exp:* Engr, Instrumentation Lab, Mass Inst Technol, 56 & 58-60 & Sperry Gyroscope Co, 57; res asst sch med, Univ PR, 60-61; res asst biol servomech, Electronic Systs Lab, 61-62, from asst prof to assoc prof aeronaut & astronaut, 62-70, PROF AERONAUT & ASTRONAUT, MASS INST TECHNOL, 70- *Concurrent Pos:* Consult to various indust & govt orgns, 62-; mem exec comt, Conf Eng Med & Biol, 67; mem, Eng Biol & Med Training Comt, NIH, 70-73; vis prof, Swiss Fed Inst Technol, 72-73 & Univ Zurich, 72-73; mem staff, Conserv Nat Arts Metiers, France, 72-73; mem eng & clin care subcomt, Nat Acad Eng; mem cardiovasc panel, Nat Acad Sci; mem comt space biol & med, Space Sci Bd, Nat Res Coun, Nat Acad Sci, 74-; chmn vestibular panel, Nat Acad Sci, 77; Dryden lectr, Am Inst Aeronaut & Astronaut, 82. *Mem:* Fel Inst Elec & Electronics Engrs; Biomed Eng Soc; Nat Acad Eng. *Res:* Application of control theory to man-vehicle problems, especially orientation; flight simulators; space laboratory experimentation on vestibular function. *Mailing Add:* Rm 37-207 Man-Vehicle Lab Mass Inst of Technol Cambridge MA 02139

YOUNG, LAWRENCE DALE, b Lafayette, Ind, Sept 13, 50; m 72; c 3. ANIMAL SCIENCE, ANIMAL BREEDING. *Educ:* Purdue Univ, BS, 72; Okla State Univ, MS, 73, PhD(animal breeding), 75. *Prof Exp:* Res asst, Okla State Univ, 72-75; RES GENETICIST, US MEAT ANIMAL RES CTR, USDA, 76- *Concurrent Pos:* NDEA fel, Okla State Univ, 74-75. *Mem:* Am Soc Animal Sci. *Res:* Animal genetics; physiological genetics. *Mailing Add:* US Meat Animal Res Ctr PO Box 166 Clay Center NE 68933

YOUNG, LAWRENCE DALE, b Hartford, Ky, Apr 18, 51; m 71; c 2. NEMATOLOGY, PLANT BREEDING. *Educ:* Univ Ky, BS, 73; NC State Univ, MS, 75, PhD(plant path), 78. *Prof Exp:* Plant breeder, Pfizer Genetics, 78-79; PLANT PATHOLOGIST, AGR RES SERV, USDA, 79- *Concurrent Pos:* Adj asst prof, Univ Tenn, 80- *Mem:* Am Phytopath Soc; Crop Sci Am; Soc Nematologist. *Res:* Practical control measures for nematodes that reduce yield of soybeans by developing resistant cultivars and nongenetical methods such as crop rotation and use of nematicides. *Mailing Add:* Agr Res Serv USDA Nematol Res 605 Airways Blvd Jackson TN 38301

YOUNG, LAWRENCE EUGENE, b Waterville, Ohio, Mar 18, 13; m 40; c 4. MEDICINE. *Educ:* Ohio Wesleyan Univ, BA, 35; Univ Rochester, MD, 39; Am Bd Internal Med, dipl. *Hon Degrees:* DSc, Ohio Wesleyan Univ, 67 & Med Col Ohio, Toledo, 77. *Prof Exp:* From intern to asst resident med, Strong Mem Hosp, 39-41, asst bact, Sch Hyg & Pub Health, Johns Hopkins Univ & Hosp, 41-42; chief resident, Strong Mem Hosp, 42-43; instr med, 43-44, 46-47, from asst prof to assoc prof, 48-57, Charles A Dewey prof & chmn dept, 57-74, dir prog internal med, Univ Rochester Assoc Hosps, 74-78, alumni distinguished serv prof med, 74-78, EMER PROF MED, SCH MED & DENT, UNIV ROCHESTER, 78- *Concurrent Pos:* Buswell fel, 46-47; physician-in-chief, Strong Mem Hosp, 57-74; mem comt blood, Nat Res Coun, 51-53; hemat study sect mem, USPHS, 53-57; distinguished vis prof med, Univ S Fla, 78- *Mem:* Am Soc Clin Invest; Asn Am Physicians (vpres, 72-73, pres, 73-74); Am Fedn Clin Res; Asn Profs Med (pres, 66-67); fel Int Soc Hemat. *Res:* Hematology; patient care. *Mailing Add:* Dept of Internal Med Box 19 12901 N 30th St Tampa FL 33612

YOUNG, LEO, b Vienna, Austria, Aug 18, 26; US citizen; m 53; c 3. ELECTRONICS. *Educ:* Cambridge Univ, BA(math), 45, BA(physics), 47, MA, 50; Johns Hopkins Univ, MS, 56, DrEng, 59. *Prof Exp:* Lectr physics, Bradford Technol Col, 47-48; engr, A C Cossor, Ltd, 48-51; head, Microwave & Antenna Lab, Decca Radar, Ltd, 51-53; adv engr, Westinghouse Elec Corp, 53-60; head microwave tech prog, Stanford Res Inst, 60-73; STAFF CONSULT, NAVAL RES LAB, 73- *Concurrent Pos:* Consult, Westinghouse Elec Corp, Stanford Linear Accelerator Ctr, Varian & TRW Systs, 60-; lectr, Stanford Univ, 63; mem, US comn A, Int Union Radio Sci, 65-, mem, US nat comn, 78-; vis prof, Univ Leeds, 66, Israel Inst Technol, 70-71 & Univ Bologna, 71. *Honors & Awards:* Microwave Prize, Inst Elec & Electronics Engrs, 63. *Mem:* AAAS; fel Inst Elec & Electronics Engrs (exec vpres, 79). *Res:* Microwaves; optics; radar; filters; antennas. *Mailing Add:* Naval Res Lab Code 5203 Washington DC 20375

YOUNG, LEONA GRAFF, b New York, NY, Dec 22, 36; m 58; c 3. PHYSIOLOGY. *Educ:* Bryn Mawr Col, BA, 58; Univ SC, MS, 60; Emory Univ, PhD(physiol), 67. *Prof Exp:* Instr physiol, 67-68, USPHS fel biochem, 69-71, instr physiol, 71-72, asst prof, 72-76, ASSOC PROF PHYSIOL, SCH MED, EMORY UNIV, 76- *Concurrent Pos:* USPHS res grant, 72- *Mem:* Biophys Soc; Am Physiol Soc; AAAS; Am Soc Cell Biol. *Res:* Mammalian spermatozoan motility; fertility; immunological infertility; contraception; contractile proteins. *Mailing Add:* Dept of Physiol Emory Univ Sch of Med Atlanta GA 30322

YOUNG, LEONARD M, b Dallas, Tex, Oct 20, 35. GEOLOGY. *Educ:* Rice Univ, BA, 57; Univ Okla, MS, 60; Univ Tex, Austin, PhD(geol), 68. *Prof Exp:* Asst prof, 67-74, ASSOC PROF GEOL, NORTHEAST LA UNIV, 74- *Mem:* Soc Econ Paleontologists & Mineralogists; Nat Asn Geol Teachers. *Res:* Carbonate and terrigenous sedimentary petrology; sedimentary processes; textural parameters; sedimentary structures; fluid inclusion paleotemperatures. *Mailing Add:* Dept of Geol Northeast La Univ Monroe LA 71209

YOUNG, LEWIS BREWSTER, b Los Angeles, Calif, Feb 25, 43; m 66. ORGANIC CHEMISTRY. *Educ:* Univ Calif, Riverside, BA, 64; Iowa State Univ, PhD(org chem), 68. *Prof Exp:* NIH fel, Univ Colo, Boulder, 68-70; sr res chemist, 70-78, ASSOC, MOBIL CHEM CO, 78- *Mem:* Am Chem Soc. *Res:* Oxidation mechanisms; homogeneous catalysis; heterogeneous catalysis; ion-molecule reactions; catalysis by zeolites. *Mailing Add:* Mobil Chem Co PO Box 240 Edison NJ 08818

YOUNG, LINDA, b Oakland, Calif, Dec 20, 54. LASER SPECTROSCOPY. *Educ:* Mass Inst Technol, SB, 76; Univ Calif, Berkeley, PhD(chem), 81. *Prof Exp:* Res asst, Univ Calif, Berkeley, 76-81; RES ASSOC CHEM, JAMES FRANCK INST, UNIV CHICAGO, 81- *Mem:* Am Phys Soc. *Res:* Molecular dynamics using inducer fluorescence as a probe; vibrational energy transfer in the ground electronic state of impurities isolated in inert gas matrices and intramolecular dynamics of aromatic molecules in supersonic free jets. *Mailing Add:* James Franck Inst Univ Chicago Chicago IL 60637

YOUNG, LIONEL WESLEY, b New Orleans, La, Mar 14, 32; m 57; c 3. PEDIATRICS, RADIOLOGY. *Educ:* St Benedict's Col, Kans, BS, 53; Howard Univ, MD, 57. *Prof Exp:* From sr instr to asst prof radiol, 65-69, asst prof pediat, 66-69, assoc prof radiol & pediat, Med Ctr, Univ Rochester, 69-75; PROF RADIOL & PEDIAT, HEALTH CTR, UNIV PITTSBURGH, 75- *Concurrent Pos:* Nat Cancer Inst traineeship grant radiation ther, Med Sch, Univ Rochester, 59-60; Children's Bur, Dept Health, Educ & Welfare fel pediat radiol, Sch Med, Univ Cincinnati, 63-65; abstractor radiol, Am J Roentgenol & Radium Ther & Nuclear Med, 65-; clin consult, NY State Dept Health, 67-75; mem radiol training comt, Nat Inst Gen Med Sci, NIH, 71-73; pediat radiol consult, Comt Prof Self-Eval & Continuing Educ, Am Col Radiol, 72- *Honors & Awards:* Spec Paper Award, Soc Pediat Radiol, 69; Gold Cert, Nat Med Asn, 70. *Mem:* Radiol Soc NAm; Am Roentgen Ray Soc; Soc Pediat Radiol; Am Col Radiol; Asn Univ Radiol. *Res:* Magnification radiography and tomagraphy in pediatric radiology; radiology of renal hypoplasias and dysplasias; duodenal, pancreatic and renal injury from blunt trauma; skeletal dysplasias and metabolic bone disease in childhood. *Mailing Add:* Dept of Radiol Children's Hosp of Pittsburgh Pittsburgh PA 15213

YOUNG, LLOYD MARTIN, b Merricourt, NDak, Nov 9, 42; m 66; c 2. ACCELERATOR PHYSICS. *Educ:* Univ NDak, BS, 65, MS, 66; Univ Ill, PhD(physics), 72. *Prof Exp:* Res Assoc, Univ Ill, 72-74, asst prof physics, 74-79, sr res physicist, 77-79; PROJ LEADER, LOS ALAMOS NAT LAB, 79- *Mem:* Am Phys Soc. *Res:* Development of an electron accelerator having a 100% duty factor using a superconducting linac through which the beam is recirculated several times. *Mailing Add:* AT-1 (MSH817) Los Alamos Nat Lab Los Alamos NM 87545

YOUNG, LLOYD STEVEN, b Ossining, NY, Apr 11, 49. FOOD SCIENCE. *Educ:* Cornell Univ, BS, 71, PhD(food sci), 76. *Prof Exp:* Res food scientist, 75-76, sr res food scientist, 76-77, sr prod appl scientist, 77-80, MGR PROD APPLNS, ARCHER-DANIELS-MIDLAND CO, 80- *Mem:* Inst Food Technologists; Am Asn Cereal Chemists; Am Dairy Sci Asn; Am Soc Bariatric Physicians. *Res:* Development and application of food ingredients from corn, wheat and soybeans. *Mailing Add:* Archer-Daniels-Midland Co 4666 Fanies Pkwy Decatur IL 62526

YOUNG, LOUIS LEE, b El Paso, Tex, Nov 22, 41. FOOD SCIENCE. *Educ:* Tex A&M Univ, BS, 64, MS, 67, PhD(poultry prod technol), 70. *Prof Exp:* Res asst poultry nutrit, Tex Agr Exp Sta, 64-67; res fel poultry prod technol, Tex A&M Univ, 67-68; res assoc, Tex Agr Exp Sta, 68-71; RES FOOD TECHNOLOGIST, POULTRY PROD TECHNOL, RUSSELL RES CTR, AGR RES SERV, US DEPT AGR, 71- *Mem:* AAAS; Poultry Sci Asn; Inst Food Technol; Sigma Xi. *Res:* Food chemistry and microbiology; poultry processing; recovery and utilization of protein from food processing waste. *Mailing Add:* Russell Res Ctr Agr Res Serv US Dept of Agr PO Box 5677 Athens GA 30604

YOUNG, LYLE E(UGENE), b Branford, NDak, Oct 16, 19; m 42; c 4. ENGINEERING MECHANICS. *Educ:* Univ Minn, BA, 41, MS, 49. *Prof Exp:* Asst supvr track, Pa, RR, 41-42; instr graphics & surv, Univ Minn, 45-53; asst dean, Col Eng, 66-70, assoc dean, Col Eng & Technol, 70-79, PROF ENG MECH, UNIV NEBR-LINCOLN, 53-, ASSOC DEAN, COL ENG & TECHNOL, 81- *Mem:* Am Soc Eng Educ; Nat Soc Prof Engrs. *Res:* Mechanics of materials; concrete. *Mailing Add:* Col of Eng & Technol Univ of Nebr Lincoln NE 68588

YOUNG, M(ILTON) G(ABRIEL), b Coopersburg, Pa, Nov 29, 11; m 37; c 3. ELECTRONICS ENGINEERING, MATERIALS SCIENCE. *Educ:* Lehigh Univ, BS, 32; Harvard Univ, MS, 33. *Prof Exp:* Elec engr, Saucon Hosiery Mills, 33-34; asst chemist, Devoe & Raynolds Corp, 34-35; res engr, Hamilton Watch Co, 35-36; sr mfg engr, Western Elec Co, 36-40; instr elec eng, 40-42, from asst prof to prof & chmn dept, 42-73, actg dean sch eng, 51-52, dir, Nema-Univ Res Lab, 58-77, exec officer elec eng, 73-74, EMER PROF ELEC ENG, UNIV DEL, 74- *Concurrent Pos:* Consult, Triumph Explosives Co, 40-44, Bio-Chem Res Found, Franklin Inst, 42-45 & Gen Develop Corp, 50-; guest prof, Birla Eng Col, India, 57-58. *Mem:* Sr mem Inst Elec & Electronics Engrs. *Res:* Industrial electronics; ultrasonics. *Mailing Add:* 32 Sunset Rd Newark DE 19711

YOUNG, MAHLON GILBERT, b Texarkana, Tex, Nov 25, 19; m 40; c 4. CHEMISTRY. *Prof Exp:* Prod chemist, Fansteel Metall Corp, 40-42; control chemist pharmaceut, Abbott Labs, 45-52, opers supvr, Radio Pharmaceut Div, 52-59; group leader low-level radio anal, Nuclear Sci & Eng Corp, 59-60; appln engr, Fisher Sci Co, 60-66, sr appln chemist, Pa, 66-68, instrument specialist, 68-81; CONSULT. *Mem:* Am Chem Soc; fel Am Inst Chemists. *Res:* Synthesis of tagged organics; szilard-chalmers separations; instrumental analysis; nucleonics. *Mailing Add:* 3704 Southampton Ct Raleigh NC 27604

YOUNG, MARGARET CLAIRE, b Austin, Tex, Sept 23, 43; m 64; c 2. ANATOMY, PHYSIOLOGY. *Educ:* Univ Tex, BA, 64; Univ Tex Med Br Galveston, PhD(physiol), 69. *Prof Exp:* Res technician II physiol, 64-65, res assoc physiol, 69-70, instr anat, 70-71, ASST PROF ANAT, UNIV TEX MED BR, GALVESTON, 71- *Concurrent Pos:* Jeanne B Kempner fel, Univ Tex Med Sch, San Antonio, 69-70. *Mem:* AAAS; Am Asn Anat. *Res:* Autoradiographic evidence of leucocytic participation in nervous system injury; autoradiographic study of pathways of nerve fibers in and out of spinal cord. *Mailing Add:* Dept Anat Univ Tex Med Br Galveston TX 77550

YOUNG, MARTIN DUNAWAY, b Moreland, Ga, July 4, 09; m 38; c 2. PARASITOLOGY, MALARIOLOGY. *Educ:* Emory Univ, BS, 31, MS, 32; Johns Hopkins Univ, ScD(parasitol), 37; Am Bd Med Microbiol, dipl. *Hon Degrees:* DSc, Emory Univ, 63 & Mich State Univ, 75. *Prof Exp:* Jr zoologist, NIH, 37-40, dir malaria res lab, 41-50, in charge imported malaria studies, 43-46, dir, Malaria Sur Liberia, 48, sanitarian, 44-48, sr scientist, 48-50, scientist dir, 50-64, head sect epidemiol, Lab Trop Dis, Nat Inst Allergy & Infectious Dis, 50-61, asst chief lab parasite chemother, 61-62, assoc dir extramural prog, 62-64; dir, Gorgas Mem Lab, 64-74, dir res, Gorgas Mem Inst, 72-74; RES PROF PARASITOL, COL VET MED & DEPT IMMUNOL & MED MICROBIOL, COL MED, UNIV FLA, 74- *Concurrent Pos:* Vis prof, ETenn State Teachers Col, 39; lectr, Meharry Med Sch SC, 60 & Med Sch, Univ Panama, 64-69; vis prof, Ala Med Ctr, 65-; clin prof, Sch Med, La State Univ, 67-; consult, Int Coop Admin, India, 57, WHO, Rumania, 61, CZ Dept, 64-74 & US AID, Africa, 80; mem expert adv panel malaria, WHO, 50-; mem malaria adv panel, Pan Am Health Orgn, 57-68; mem Columbia Bd Health, SC, 60-61; mem malaria & parasitic dis comns, Armed Forces Epidemiol Bd, Dept Defense, 65-73; hon res assoc, Smithsonian Inst, 66-; res assoc, Gorgas Mem Lab, 74-77; mem bd dirs, Gorgas Mem Inst, 77-; prin investr, Effects Insect Pathogens on the Ability of Mosquitoes to Transmit Malaria, grant, USAID. *Honors & Awards:* Rockefeller Pub Serv Award, 53; Darling Medal & Prize, WHO, 63; Order of Manuel Amador Guerrero, Govt Panama, 74; Cert Merit, Gorgas Mem Inst Trop & Prev Med, Inc, 74; Gorgas Medal, Asn Mil Surgeons of US, 74; LePrince Award, Am Soc Trop Med & Hyg, 76. *Mem:* AAAS; Am Soc Parasitol (pres, 65); Am Soc Trop Med & Hyg (pres, 52); Royal Soc Trop Med & Hyg; Nat Malaria Soc. *Res:* Malaria parasitology, epidemiology and treatment; parasitic protozoa, helminths; parasitic diseases, especially biology, epidemiology and treatment. *Mailing Add:* 8421 NW Fourth Pl Gainesville FL 32601

YOUNG, MARVIN KENDALL, JR, b Tulia, Tex, Mar 28, 24; m 48; c 3. BIOCHEMISTRY. *Educ:* McMurry Col, BS, 46; Univ Tex, MA, 50, PhD(chem), 62; cert, Nat Registry Clin Chem & Am Bd Clin Chem. *Prof Exp:* Teacher high sch, Tex, 47-48; res scientist, Clayton Found Biochem Inst, Tex, 50-51; biochemist, Surg Res Unit, Brooke Army Med Ctr, Ft Sam Houston, Tex, 51-56, chief physiol sect, 56-57; clin chemist, Woman's Hosp, Detroit, Mich, 62-65, chmn dept biochem, Hutzel Hosp, 65-66; chmn biochem, Clin Path Labs, 66-73; dir, Health & Environ Technol, Inc, 73-74; dir, Bio-Sci Labs, Chicago Br, 74-76; AIR QUAL ASSURANCE COORDR, REGION V, US ENVIRON PROTECTION AGENCY, 77- *Concurrent Pos:* Affil instr, Sch Med, Wayne State Univ, 63-66; consult, Holy Cross, Seton & St David Hosps, Austin, 66-, spec lectr, Col Pharm, Univ Tex, Austin. *Mem:* Am Chem Soc; fel Am Asn Clin Chemists; fel Am Inst Chemists. *Res:* Body fluid distribution; intermediary metabolism of carbohydrates; enzymology; methodology in clinical chemistry, including spectrophotometric, radioisotopic, gas chromatographic and atomic absorption spectrometric methods. *Mailing Add:* 1247 Hailshaw Wheaton IL 60187

YOUNG, MARVIN P(LEASANT), b NC, Oct 22, 21; m 45; c 2. ELECTRICAL ENGINEERING. *Educ:* NC State Univ, BEE, 43. *Prof Exp:* Elec engr, Naval Gun Factory, DC, 43-44; radio engr, Naval Res Lab, 46-50, electronic scientist, 50-64, elec engr, 64-78; RETIRED. *Mem:* Sr mem Inst Elec & Electronics Engrs. *Res:* Nuclear instrumentation and reactor control systems; atomic weapons tests; digital computers and conversion devices; plasma physics research. *Mailing Add:* 7805 Lee Ave Alexandria VA 22308

YOUNG, MATT, b Brooklyn, NY, Jan 30, 41; m 64; c 2. OPTICS. *Educ:* Univ Rochester, BS, 62, PhD(optics), 67. *Prof Exp:* Res assoc optics, Univ Rochester, 67; asst prof physics, Univ Waterloo, 67-70; asst prof electrophys, Rensselaer Polytech Inst, 70-74; assoc prof natural sci, Verrazzano Col, 74-75; PHYSICIST, ELECTROMAGNETIC TECHNOL DIV, NAT BUR STANDARDS, 76- *Concurrent Pos:* Optics res corresp, Physics Teacher J, 73-76; tech ed, Optical Spectra, 74; consult, Holobeam, Inc, 74, Res & Develop Ctr, Gen Elec Co, 74-75 & NY State Energy Comn, 75; assoc ed, J Optical Soc Am, 74-79. *Honors & Awards:* Newton Award, 62. *Mem:* Sigma Xi; Optical Soc Am; AAAS; Am Asn Physics Teachers; Fedn Am Scientists. *Res:* Lasers; solar energy; physical optics; holography; coherent optics; optical communications; measurement technology; laser produced plasmas. *Mailing Add:* 3145 Fremont Boulder CO 80302

YOUNG, MAURICE DURWARD, b North Vancouver, BC, Sept 20, 12; m 54; c 2. PEDIATRICS, CARDIOLOGY. *Educ:* Cambridge Univ, BA, 33, MRSC & LRCP, 36, MA & MB, BCh, 38, MRCP, 44; FRCP(C), 48; FRCP(L), 76. *Prof Exp:* House physician & officer, London Hosp, 37-41; resident med officer, Warleywoods Hosp, 41-44; sr intern, Children's Mem Hosp, Montreal, Que, 46-47; from asst prof to prof, 53-78, assoc dean, 74-78, dean, Fac Med, 74-78, EMER PROF PEDIAT, UNIV BC, 78- *Concurrent Pos:* Fel pediat, Johns Hopkins Univ, 48-49; asst physician, Cardiac Clin, Johns Hopkins Hosp, 48-49; mem hon staff, Vancouver Gen Hosp; Queen's hon surgeon, 58-60; sr active staff mem, Children's Hosp, Vancouver. *Mem:* Can Pediat Soc; Can Med Asn; Can Cardiovasc Soc. *Res:* Pediatric cardiology. *Mailing Add:* 3181 Thompson Pl West Vancouver BC V7V 3E3 Can

YOUNG, MAURICE ISAAC, b Boston, Mass, Feb 10, 27; m 54; c 3. MECHANICAL & AEROSPACE ENGINEERING. *Educ:* Univ Chicago, PhB & SB, 49; Boston Univ, AM, 50; Univ Pa, PhD(eng mech), 60. *Prof Exp:* Sr dynamics engr, Helicopter Div, Bell Aerospace Corp, 51-54; chief dynamics res & develop, Vertol Aircraft Corp, 54-56; prin engr, Piasecki Aircraft Corp, 56-58; sect mgr appl mech, Govt & Indust Div, Philco Corp, 58-61; mgr advan technol, Vertol Div, Boeing Co, 61-68; PROF MECH & AEROSPACE ENG, UNIV DEL, 68- *Concurrent Pos:* Lectr, Southern Methodist Univ, 53; consult, Vertol Div, Boeing Co, 68-70; du Pont fac fel, Univ Del, 69, Univ Del Res Found grant, 70-71, US Army Res Off NC res grant, 71-; consult, Mech Res, Inc, 69-71, Textile Fibers Dept, E I Du Pont De Nemours & Co, Inc, 72-73, TM Develop, Inc, Pa, 76- & Bigham, Englar, Jones & Houston, New York, 78-81. *Mem:* Am Inst Aeronaut & Astronaut; Am Helicopter Soc. *Res:* Dynamics; vibrations; control dynamics; flight mechanics; aeroelasticity; rotary wing and vertical/short takeoff and landing mechanics; alternate energy dynamics; wind and ocean current and thermal. *Mailing Add:* Dept of Mech & Aerospace Eng Univ of Del Newark DE 19711

YOUNG, MICHAEL WARREN, genetics, see previous edition

YOUNG, MORRIS NATHAN, b Lawrence, Mass, July 20, 09; m 48; c 2. OPHTHALMOLOGY, SURGERY. *Educ:* Mass Inst Technol, BS, 30; Harvard Univ, MA, 31; Columbia Univ, MD, 35; Am Bd Ophthal, dipl. *Prof Exp:* Intern, Queen's Gen Hosp, NY, 35-37; resident ophthal, Harlem Eye & Ear Hosp, 38-40; asst flight surgeon, Maxwell Field, Ala, 41-42, sr eye, ear, nose & throat officer, Walter Reed Gen Hosp, Washington, DC, 42, chief eye, ear, nose & throat serv, 69th Sta Hosp, 42-44, chief eye, ear, nose & throat sect, 235th Gen Hosp, 44-45, med officer & mem staff, 301st Logistical Support Brigade, 66, dep comdr, 343rd Gen Hosp, 66-67, dep comdr & chief prof serv, 307th Gen Hosp, 67-69, staff med officer, 818th Hosp Ctr, 69; dir ophthal & attend, 69-80, EMER DIR OPHTHAL, BEEKMAN DOWNTOWN HOSP, NEW YORK CITY, 80- *Concurrent Pos:* Ophthalmologist & auth, 45-; attend & prof, Fr & Polyclin Med Sch & Health Ctr, 63-77; med adv, Dir Selective Serv, NY Dist, 65-; consult ophthalmologist, Beth Israel Med Ctr, New York 72- & St Vincent's Hosp & Med Ctr, 77- *Honors & Awards:* Grand Hospitaler, Knights of Malta, Order of St John of Jerusalem, 72; Order of Lafayette. *Mem:* AMA; Pan-Am Med Asn; Contact Lens Asn Ophthal; Am Acad Ophthal; Acad Comp Med. *Res:* Medicine; mnemonics and art of memory; science exhibits; illusion practices. *Mailing Add:* 170 Broadway New York NY 10038

YOUNG, MYRON H(WAI-HSI), b Shanghai, China, July 3, 29; US citizen; m 59; c 5. NUCLEAR ENGINEERING, MATHEMATICAL MODELING. *Educ:* La State Univ, BS, 53, MS, 57; NC State Col, PhD(nuclear eng), 63. *Prof Exp:* From instr to asst prof eng mech, La State Univ, 56-62; supvry nuclear engr, Air Force Flight Dynamics Lab, Wright-Patterson AFB, 63; from asst prof to assoc prof mech eng, 63-76, prof mech eng, 77-79, PROF MARINE SCI & NUCLEAR ENG, LA STATE UNIV, BATON ROUGE, 80- *Concurrent Pos:* Consult, Eng Physics Lab, Wright Air Develop Ctr, Wright-Patterson AFB, 59-60 & Air Force Flight Dynamics Lab, 64-65; consult, Systs Res Lab, Inc, 66- *Mem:* Am Nuclear Soc; Am Soc Eng Educ; Sigma Xi; Int Asn Math Modeling. *Res:* Estuarine hydrodynamic modeling; cumulative impact study on wet land environment; data management systems. *Mailing Add:* Nuclear Sci Ctr La State Univ Baton Rouge LA 70803

YOUNG, NANCY LIZOTTE, b Rumford, Maine. BIOCHEMISTRY. *Educ:* Antioch Col, BS, 59; Purdue Univ, PhD(develop biol), 74. *Prof Exp:* Fel biochem, Purdue Univ, 74-77; ASST PROF, DEPT MED, MED COL, CORNELL UNIV, 77- *Res:* Regulation of 3-hydroxy-3-methylglutaryl coenzyme A reductase and cholesterol synthesis in diabetes. *Mailing Add:* Dept of Med Cornell Univ Med Col New York NY 10021

YOUNG, NELSON FORSAITH, b Everett, Wash, Oct 17, 14; m 42; c 4. BIOCHEMISTRY. *Educ:* Univ Wash, BS, 36; NY Univ, PhD(biochem), 45. *Prof Exp:* Res chemist, Mem Hosp, 40-43; asst, Sloan-Kettering Inst, 45-48; from asst prof to assoc prof clin biochem, 48-56, PROF CLIN PATH, MED COL VA, 56-, LECTR BIOCHEM, 70- *Mem:* Am Soc Clin Path; Am Chem Soc. *Res:* Renal function; protein metabolism; radiation effects. *Mailing Add:* 8505 Rivermont Dr Richmond VA 23229

YOUNG, NORTON BRUCE, b Renton, Wash, Aug 11, 26; m 50; c 3. SPEECH PATHOLOGY, AUDIOLOGY. *Educ:* Univ Wash, BS, 50, MA, 53; Purdue Univ, PhD(speech path, audiol), 57. *Prof Exp:* Sr clinician speech path & audiol, Seattle Speech & Hearing Ctr, 54-55; asst prof, Univ, 55-60, instr audiol, Med Sch, 60-64, from instr to assoc prof audiol & pediat, 64-73, assoc prof speech path & audiol, Crippled Children's Div, 70-73, PROF PEDIAT, MED SCH & PROF SPEECH PATH & AUDIOL, CRIPPLED CHILDREN'S DIV, UNIV ORE, 73- *Mem:* Am Speech & Hearing Asn. *Res:* Pedo-audiology; psychoacoustics; organic disorders of speech; clinical audiology. *Mailing Add:* Dept of Speech Univ of Ore Med Sch Portland OR 97201

YOUNG, PAUL ANDREW, b St Louis, Mo, Oct 3, 26; m 49; c 10. ANATOMY. *Educ:* St Louis Univ, BS, 47, MS, 53; Univ Buffalo, PhD(anat), 57. *Prof Exp:* From asst to instr anat, Univ Buffalo, 53-57; from asst prof to assoc prof, 57-72, actg chmn dept, 69-73, PROF ANAT, SCH MED, ST LOUIS UNIV, 72-, CHMN DEPT, 73-, ASSOC PROF NEUROANAT IN NEUROL & PSYCHIAT, 67- *Mem:* AAAS; Am Asn Anat; Soc Neurosci. *Res:* Neuroanatomy, especially mammalian forebrain centers, basal ganglia, thalamus, cerebral cortex; degenerative and axoplasmic flow techniques; electron microscopy of nervous tissue. *Mailing Add:* Dept Anat St Louis Univ St Louis MO 63104

YOUNG, PAUL MCCLURE, b Seaman, Ohio, Feb 13, 16; m 42; c 2. MATHEMATICS. *Educ:* Miami Univ, AB, 37; Ohio State Univ, MA, 39, PhD(math), 41. *Prof Exp:* From instr to asst prof math, Miami Univ, 41-47; from assoc prof to prof, Kans State Univ, 47-62, assoc dean sch arts & sci, 56-62; vpres acad affairs, Univ Ark, 62-66; exec dir, Mid-Am State Univs Asn, 66-78; PROF MATH & VPRES UNIV DEVELOP, KANS STATE UNIV, 70- *Mem:* AAAS; Am Math Soc; Math Asn Am. *Res:* Analysis; approximation of functions by integral means; characterization of integral means. *Mailing Add:* Kans State Univ Manhattan KS 66506

YOUNG, PAUL RUEL, b St Marys, Ohio, Mar 16, 36; c 2. COMPUTER SCIENCES, MATHEMATICAL LOGIC. *Educ:* Antioch Col, BS, 59; Mass Inst Technol, PhD(math), 63. *Prof Exp:* Asst prof math, Reed Col, 63-66; prof comput & info sci & math & chmn dept comput info sci, Univ NMex, 78-79; from asst prof to PROF MATH & COMPUT SCI, PURDUE UNIV, LAFAYETTE, 66- *Concurrent Pos:* NSF fel, Stanford Univ, 65-66; vis prof, Univ Calif, Berkeley, 72-73; chmn adv bd comput sci, NSF, 79-80. *Mem:* Asn Comput Mach; Inst Elec & Electronics Engrs; Asn Symbolic Logic. *Res:* Theory of computational complexity and theory of algorithms. *Mailing Add:* Comput Sci Dept Purdue Univ Lafayette IN 47907

YOUNG, PETER CHUN MAN, b Hong Kong, Dec 19, 36; Can citizen; m 67; c 2. BIOCHEMISTRY. *Educ:* McGill Univ, BS, 61, MS, 63, PhD(biochem), 67. *Prof Exp:* Res assoc endocrinol, St Michael's Hosp, 67-71; asst prof endocrinol, 71-77, ASSOC PROF OBSTET & GYNEC, SCH MED, IND UNIV, INDIANAPOLIS, 77- *Mem:* AAAS. *Res:* Biochemistry of steroid hormones; reproductive endocrinology. *Mailing Add:* Dept Obstet & Gynec Ind Univ Med Ctr Indianapolis IN 46202

YOUNG, PHILIP ROSS, b Emory, Va, Oct 24, 40. ANALYTICAL CHEMISTRY. *Educ:* Emory & Henry Col, BS, 62; Va Polytech Inst & State Univ, MS, 71, PhD(chem), 76. *Prof Exp:* CHEMIST POLYMER RES, NASA LANGLEY RES CTR, 62- *Mem:* Am Chem Soc. *Res:* Using liquid and gel permeation chromatography techniques to characterize and evaluate new monomers and high performance polymers for aerospace applications. *Mailing Add:* NASA Langley Res Ctr Mail Stop 226 Hampton VA 23665

YOUNG, PHILLIP GAFFNEY, b Beeville, Tex, July 21, 37; m 60; c 3. NUCLEAR PHYSICS. *Educ:* Univ Tex, Austin, BS, 61, MA, 62; Australian Nat Univ, PhD(nuclear physics), 65. *Prof Exp:* Res fel nuclear physics, Australian Nat Univ, 65-66; res fel, 66-68, mem staff nuclear cross sect eval, 68-75, GROUP LEADER NUCLEAR CROSS SECT EVAL, LOS ALAMOS NAT LAB, 75- *Mem:* Am Phys Soc; Am Nuclear Soc. *Res:* Low energy nuclear physics; neutron-particle and charged-particle cross sections and polarization. *Mailing Add:* Group T-2 Los Alamos Nat Lab Los Alamos NM 87544

YOUNG, POH-SHIEN, b Chekiang, China, Jan 18, 26; m 59; c 5. PARTICLE PHYSICS. *Educ:* Nat Chi-Nan Univ, China, BS, 49; Okla State Univ, MS, 57; Univ Calif, Berkeley, PhD(physics), 65. *Prof Exp:* Asst physics, Okla State Univ, 55-57; nuclear physicist, Admiral Corp, Ill, 57 & Nuclear Chicago Corp, 57-59; instr physics, Univ Ill, Chicago, 59-60 & Oakland City Col, Calif, 60-62; asst, Univ Calif, Berkeley, 62-65, physicist, Lawrence Radiation Lab, 65-66; asst prof, 66-70, assoc prof, 70-80, PROF PHYSICS, MISS STATE UNIV, 80- *Mem:* Am Phys Soc. *Res:* Cosmic ray and reactor physics. *Mailing Add:* Dept of Physics Miss State Univ Mississippi State MS 39762

YOUNG, RALPH ALDEN, b Arickaree, Colo, July 14, 20; m 42; c 2. SOIL FERTILITY. *Educ:* Colo State Univ, BS, 42; Kans State Univ, MS, 47; Cornell Univ, PhD(agron), 53. *Prof Exp:* Instr soils, Kans State Univ, 47-48; asst prof soils, NDak State Univ, Univ & asst soil scientist, Exp Sta, 48-50 & 53-55, from assoc prof & assoc soil scientist to prof soils & soil scientist, 55-62; vis prof, Univ Calif, Davis, 62-63; chmn dept agr biochem & soil sci, 63-65, chmn div plant, soil & water sci, 65-75, PROF SOIL SCI, UNIV & SOIL SCIENTIST, NEV AGR EXP STA, UNIV NEV, RENO, 63-, ASSOC DIR, NEV AGR EXP STA, 75- *Mem:* Fel AAAS; Soil Sci Soc Am; Am Soc Agron; Soils Conserv Soc Am. *Res:* Fertilizer-water interactions; soil as a waste treatment system. *Mailing Add:* Nev Agr Exp Sta Univ of Nev Reno NV 89557

YOUNG, RALPH HOWARD, b Berkeley, Calif, Mar 22, 42; m 68; c 1. CHEMICAL PHYSICS, SOLID STATE PHYSICS. *Educ:* Calif Inst Technol, BS, 64; Stanford Univ, PhD(chem physics), 68. *Prof Exp:* Lectr chem, Stanford Univ, 68; asst prof, Jackson State Col, 68-70; lectr, Univ Calif, Riverside, 70; SR RES CHEMIST, CHEM PHYSICS LAB, EASTMAN KODAK CO, 71- *Mem:* Sigma Xi. *Res:* Photoconduction in organic solids; quantum chemistry; quantum axiomatics. *Mailing Add:* Chem Physics Lab Eastman Kodak Co Res Labs Rochester NY 14650

YOUNG, RAYMOND A, b Buffalo, NY, Mar 14, 45; m 62; c 2. WOOD CHEMISTRY. *Educ:* State Univ NY, BS, 66, MS, 68; Univ Wash, PhD(wood chem), 73. *Prof Exp:* Process supvr paper prod, Kimberly-Clark Corp, 68-69; Textile Res Inst fel, Princeton Univ, 73-74, staff scientist textiles, 74-75; ASST PROF FORESTRY, UNIV WIS-MADISON, 75- *Mem:* Tech Asn Pulp & Paper Indust; Fiber Soc. *Res:* Chemical modification of cellulose and high yield pulp fibers; bonding of cellulose fibers in blended flexible fiber composites such as nonwovens and synthetic papers. *Mailing Add:* Dept of Forestry Univ of Wis Madison WI 53706

YOUNG, RAYMOND H(YKES), b Bellefonte, Pa, June 23, 21. ELECTRICAL ENGINEERING. *Educ:* Bucknell Univ, BS, 43; Northwestern Univ, MS, 51, PhD(elec eng), 57. *Prof Exp:* Test engr, Gen Elec Co, 43-46; instr, 47-50, from asst prof to assoc prof, 53-70, PROF ELEC ENG, BUCKNELL UNIV, 70- *Mem:* Inst Elec & Electronics Engrs. *Res:* Switching theory; relation of electrical engineering to medical and biological sciences. *Mailing Add:* Dept of Elec Eng Bucknell Univ Lewisburg PA 17837

YOUNG, RAYMOND HINCHCLIFFE, JR, b Pennsauken, NJ, Nov 22, 28; m 53; c 4. CLAY MINERALOGY. *Educ:* Pa Mil Col, BS, 53; Univ Maine, MS, 55, PhD(org chem), 61. *Prof Exp:* Asst chemG U chem, Univ Maine, 53-54, res asst org chem, 54-55, instr chem, 55-60; res chemist, Bircham Bend Plant, Monsanto Co, 60-70; RES CHEMIST, FREEPORT KAOLIN CO, 70- *Honors & Awards:* A K Doolittle Award, Am Chem Soc, 72. *Mem:* AAAS; Am Chem Soc. *Res:* Surface modified kaolins; flame retardants; light scattering of pigments; computer science. *Mailing Add:* Freeport Kaolin Co PO Box 337 Gordon GA 31031

YOUNG, REGINALD H F, b Honolulu, Hawaii, May 17, 37; m 59; c 2. SANITARY & CIVIL ENGINEERING. *Educ:* Univ Hawaii, BS, 59, MS, 65; Wash Univ, DSc(environ & sanit eng), 67. *Prof Exp:* Jr engr, Paul Low Eng, 59; jr engr, Sunn, Low, Tom & Hara, Inc, 59, asst proj engr, 62-63; res asst pub health, 63, asst prof environ health & sanit eng, 66-69, assoc prof civil eng, 69-74, asst dir, Water Resources Res Ctr, 73-78, PROF CIVIL ENG, UNIV HAWAII, 74-, ASSOC DEAN, COL ENG, 79- *Mem:* Am Acad Environ Engrs; Am Soc Civil Engrs; Water Pollution Control Fedn; Am Water Works Asn; Sigma Xi. *Res:* Water quality management and pollution control; water and sewage treatment; industrial waste treatment; solid wastes management and control. *Mailing Add:* 2540 Dole St Co Eng Univ Hawaii at Manoa Honolulu HI 96822

YOUNG, REUBEN B, b Wilmington, NC, Apr 2, 30; m 53; c 3. MEDICINE, PEDIATRICS. *Educ:* Med Col Va, BS, 53, MD, 57. *Prof Exp:* Instr pediat, Univ Pa, 61-63; from asst prof to assoc prof, 63-71, dir med staff hosp & exec assoc dean, Sch Med, 77-79, PROF PEDIAT, MED COL VA, 71-, PROF GENETICS, 75-, ASSOC DEAN CONTINUING MED EDUC, 79- *Mem:* Am Acad Pediat; Endocrine Soc; Am Diabetes Asn. *Res:* Pediatric endocrinology and diabetology; catecholamine metabolism in children; hypoglycemia in children. *Mailing Add:* Off of the Dean Med Col of Va Box 65 Richmond VA 23298

YOUNG, RICHARD A, b Providence, RI, Aug 5, 40; m 64. GEOLOGY. *Educ:* Cornell Univ, BA, 62; Wash Univ, PhD(geol), 66. *Prof Exp:* Asst prof earth sci, 66-72, assoc prof, 72-79, PROF GEOL SCI, STATE UNIV NY COL GENESEO, 79-, CHMN DEPT, 77- *Concurrent Pos:* Prin investr geol mapping proj using Apollo Mission photog, NASA Contract, 72-75; vis faculty mem, Univ Canterbury, 72; hydrologist, US Geol Surv, 76-; Environ Protection Agency grant, 79-82. *Mem:* AAAS; Geol Soc Am. *Res:* Cenozoic geology, including sedimentation, geomorphology, glacial geology and vulcanism; lunar geology. *Mailing Add:* Dept of Geol Sci State Univ NY Col Geneseo NY 14454

YOUNG, RICHARD ACCIPITER, b Pittsburgh, Pa, Mar 24, 42; m 68; c 2. SOLID STATE PHYSICS. *Educ:* Lehigh Univ, BS, 64; Univ Chicago, PhD(physics), 68. *Prof Exp:* Res assoc, 68-69, asst prof, 69-74, Alfred P Sloan fel, 71-73, ASSOC PROF PHYSICS, UNIV ARIZ, 74- *Concurrent Pos:* Vis asst prof, Univ Calif, Berkeley, 72- *Mem:* Am Phys Soc. *Res:* Electronic transport properties of metals. *Mailing Add:* Dept of Physics Univ of Ariz Tucson AZ 85721

YOUNG, RICHARD D, b New York, NY, Mar 16, 24; m 50; c 2. PHYSICS, ELECTRICAL ENGINEERING. *Educ:* Princeton Univ, AB, 45; Calif Inst Technol, MS, 47, PhD(physics), 52. *Prof Exp:* Teaching asst, Calif Inst Technol, 48-50; mem tech staff, Hughes Aircraft Co, 50-54; mem sr staff, Ramo-Wooldridge Corp, TRW Space Technol Labs & Bunker-Ramo Corp, 54-64 & Informatics, Inc, 64-67; asst prog dir, Tracor, Inc, 67-68; dir systs eng, Digilinc Systs Corp, 68-69; mem sr staff, Synergetic Sci, Inc, 69-70; SR SCI SPECIALIST, DATA SYSTS DIV, LITTON INDUSTS, INC, VAN NUYS, 70- *Res:* Advanced systems engineering and systems analysis of military command and control systems, electronic countermeasures and radar; theoretical nuclear physics. *Mailing Add:* 4521 Larkwood Ave Woodland Hills CA 91364

YOUNG, RICHARD EDWARD, b Los Angeles, Calif, Aug 20, 38; m 63; c 2. BIOLOGICAL OCEANOGRAPHY. *Educ:* Pomona Col, BA, 60; Univ Southern Calif, MS, 64; Univ Miami, PhD(oceanog), 68. *Prof Exp:* Res asst oceanog, Inst Marine Sci, Univ Miami, 65-68, res scientist, 68; asst prof zool, Ohio Wesleyan Univ, 68-69; asst prof oceanog, 69-74, ASSOC PROF OCEANOG, UNIV HAWAII, MANOA, 74- *Mem:* AAAS; Marine Biol Asn UK. *Res:* Cephalopod, deep-sea and invertebrate biology. *Mailing Add:* Dept of Oceanog Univ of Hawaii at Manoa Honolulu HI 98622

YOUNG, RICHARD EVANS, dynamic meteorology, geophysics, see previous edition

YOUNG, RICHARD L, b Rushville, Ill, Nov 22, 32; m 53; c 3. ORGANIC CHEMISTRY. *Educ:* Univ Ill, BSc, 54; Brown Univ, PhD(org chem), 59. *Prof Exp:* Res chemist, Res Inst Med & Chem, 58-61; res assoc biochem, Col Agr, Univ Wis, 61-63; asst prof agr biochem, Univ Hawaii, 64-66; SECT LEADER ORG CHEM, NEW ENG NUCLEAR CORP, 66- *Mem:* Am Chem Soc. *Res:* Peptide synthesis; tritium and carbon-14 radiochemicals. *Mailing Add:* New Eng Nuclear Corp 549 Albany St Boston MA 02118

YOUNG, RICHARD LAWRENCE, b Proctor, Vt, Mar 12, 25; m 57; c 3. ANALYTICAL BIOCHEMISTRY, NEUROCHEMISTRY. *Educ:* Cath Univ Am, AB, 49; St Louis Univ, PhD(biochem), 56. *Prof Exp:* Trainee res & develop, SK&F Lab, 49-51, sr res scientist biochem, 56-59; Nat Inst Neurol Dis & Blindness spec trainee neurochem, Inst Living, 59-60, spec fel, Sch Med, Washington Univ, 60-62; res assoc, Inst Living, 62-66; sr biochemist pharmacol & biochem, 66-73, asst chief clin biochem, 73-74, RES FEL BIOCHEM, HOFFMANN-LA ROCHE INC, 74- *Mem:* AAAS; Am Chem Soc; Am Soc Neurochem. *Res:* Development and use of micromethods for investigating the disposition, metabolism and target effects of therapeutic agents in vivo; quantitative histochemistry, radioisotopes, radioimmunoassay; bioavailability and pharmacokinetics. *Mailing Add:* Dept of Biochem & Drug Metab Hoffmann-La Roche Inc Nutley NJ 07110

YOUNG, RICHARD WAIN, b Albany, NY, Dec 15, 29; m 55; c 4. ANATOMY. *Educ:* Antioch Col, BA, 56; Columbia Univ, PhD(anat), 59. *Hon Degrees:* Dr Sci, Univ Chicago, 80. *Prof Exp:* From asst prof to assoc prof, 60-68, PROF ANAT, SCH MED, UNIV CALIF, LOS ANGELES, 68- *Concurrent Pos:* NSF fel anat, Univ Bari & Caroline Inst, Sweden, 59-60; Markle scholar med sci, 62-67; guest investr anat, Dept Biol, Saclay Nuclear Res Ctr, France, 66-67; mem, Jules Stein Eye Inst, Univ Calif, Los Angeles. *Honors & Awards:* Fight for Sight Res Citation, 69; Friedenwald Award, Asn Res in Vision & Opthalmol, 76. *Mem:* Am Asn Anat; Am Soc Cell Biol; Asn Res Vision & Opthal. *Res:* Cell biology; radioisotope studies of ocular tissues. *Mailing Add:* Dept of Anat Univ of Calif Sch of Med Los Angeles CA 90024

YOUNG, ROBERT, JR, b Sept 14, 30; US citizen; m 55; c 3. VETERINARY MEDICINE. *Educ:* Univ Calif, BS, 53, MS, 56, DVM, 61. *Prof Exp:* Vet, Shell Develop Co, 61-67, dept head vet med, 67-69, dept head drug develop, 69-78; RESEARCHER, KEARLEY & YOUNG RES, 78- *Mem:* Am Vet Med Asn; Am Soc Animal Sci; Indust Vet Med Asn. *Res:* Drug development and secondary screening; growth regulators; anthelmintics and ectoparasiticides. *Mailing Add:* Kearley & Young Res PO Box 2089 Turlock CA 95380

YOUNG, ROBERT A, b New York, NY, June 8, 29; m 57, 69; c 1. PHYSICS, PHYSICAL CHEMISTRY. *Educ:* Univ Wash, BS, 51, PhD(physics), 59. *Prof Exp:* Res asst, Univ Wash, 53-59; engr, Boeing Airplane Co, 59-60; physicist, Stanford Res Inst, 60-62, sr physicist, 62-67, chmn atmospheric chem physics dept, 67-68; prof physics, York Univ, 68-75; dir res, Xonics, Inc, 75-79; FOUND, CHMN & PRES, QUANTATEC INT, INC, 79- *Concurrent Pos:* Consult, Dept Physics, Univ Wash, 59-60; vis fel, Joint Inst Lab Astrophys, Univ Colo, 66-67; chmn & pres, Intra-Space Int, 72-75; vis fel, Lab for Astrophys & Space Physics, Univ Colo, 74-75. *Mem:* AAAS; Am Phys Soc; Am Geophys Union. *Res:* Energy transfer; atomic and molecular processes and spectra; rocket experimentation; baloon, aircraft stratospheric measurements. *Mailing Add:* Quantatec Int Inc 9773 Variel Ave Chatsworth CA 91311

YOUNG, ROBERT ALAN, b St Cloud, Minn, Jan 24, 21; m 48, 77; c 3. SOLID STATE PHYSICS, CRYSTALLOGRAPHY. *Educ:* Polytech Inst Brooklyn, PhD(physics), 59. *Hon Degrees:* Dr, Univ Toulouse, France, 79. *Prof Exp:* Res asst prof & res physicist, Ga Inst Technol, 51-53; instr physics, Polytech Inst Brooklyn, 53-57; res assoc prof physics & head diffraction lab, 57-63, PROF PHYSICS & HEAD CRYSTAL PHYSICS BR, GA INST TECHNOL, 64- *Concurrent Pos:* Co-ed, J Appl Crystallog, 67-69, ed, 70-78; mem, US Nat Comt Crystallog, 69-74 & 76-78, chmn, 79-81. *Mem:* Int Asn Dent Res; fel Brit Inst Physics; French Soc Mineral & Crystallog; fel Am Phys Soc; Am Crystallog Asn (treas, 68-71, vpres, 72, pres, 73). *Res:* Crystal physics; x-ray, neutron and electron diffraction theory and applications; structural locations and roles of minor impurities; atomic scare mechanisms; aparites; tooth enamel; extension of methods for greater detail. *Mailing Add:* Sch of Physics Ga Inst of Technol Atlanta GA 30332

YOUNG, ROBERT ALAN, b Bombay, India, Jan 13, 35; US citizen; m 65; c 2. AGRICULTURAL ENGINEERING, SOIL SCIENCE. *Educ:* Purdue Univ, BS, 56; Univ Minn, MS, 60; SDak State Univ, PhD(agr eng), 72. *Prof Exp:* Res asst, 58-60, ASST PROF AGR ENG, UNIV MINN, 74-, AGR ENGR, NORTH CENT SOIL CONSERV RES CTR, AGR RES SERV, USDA, 68- *Mem:* Am Soc Agr Engrs; Soil Conserv Soc Am. *Res:* Effect of land-use practices on water quality; animal waste management research; basic mechanics of erosion and erosion modeling. *Mailing Add:* NCent Soil Conserv Rest Ctr Agr Res Serv USDA Morris MN 56267

YOUNG, ROBERT HAYWARD, b Andover, NB, Mar 18, 40; m 65; c 2. PHOTOCHEMISTRY, ORGANIC POLYMER CHEMISTRY. *Educ:* Mt Allison Univ, BSc, 62, MSc, 63; Mich State Univ, PhD(org chem), 67. *Prof Exp:* Asst prof org chem, Georgetown Univ, 67-73; GROUP LEADER, UNION CARBIDE CORP, 73- *Mem:* Am Chem Soc; Chem Inst Can. *Res:* Organic chemistry and photochemistry of singlet oxygen; polymer chemistry, adhesive bonding fundamentals; phenolic resin chemistry. *Mailing Add:* Union Carbide Corp One River Rd Bound Brook NJ 08805

YOUNG, ROBERT JOHN, b Calgary, Alta, Feb 10, 23; m 50; c 2. ANIMAL NUTRITION. *Educ:* Univ BC, BSA, 50; Cornell Univ, PhD(animal nutrit), 53. *Prof Exp:* Asst poultry nutrit, Cornell Univ, 50-53; res assoc, Banting & Best Dept Med Res, Univ Toronto, 53-56; res biochemist, Int Minerals & Chem Corp, Ill, 56-58 & Procter & Gamble Co, Ohio, 58-60; assoc prof animal nutrit & poultry husb, 60-65, head dept poultry sci, 65-76, PROF ANIMAL NUTRIT, NY STATE COL AGR & LIFE SCI, CORNELL UNIV, 65-, CHMN DEPT ANIMAL SCI, 76- *Mem:* PoulPoultry Sci Asn; Am Inst Nutrit. *Res:* Mineral metabolism; energy value of fats and fatty acids; nutrition and metabolism of protein and amino acids. *Mailing Add:* Dept Animal Sci Morrison Hall Cornell Univ Ithaca NY 14853

YOUNG, ROBERT L(YLE), b Neoga, Ill, Apr 3, 25; m 46, 69; c 3. MECHANICAL ENGINEERING, AEROSPACE ENGINEERING. *Educ:* Northwestern Univ, BS, 46, MS, 48, PhD(eng), 53. *Prof Exp:* Instr mech eng, Northwestern Univ, 48-53, asst prof, 53-57; from assoc prof to prof, 57-64, dir, Arnold Eng Develop Ctr Grad Prog, 57-64, assoc dean, Space Inst, 64-79, PROF MECH & AEROSPACE ENG, SPACE INST, UNIV TENN, 64- *Concurrent Pos:* Consult, US Air Force, 57- *Mem:* Am Soc Mech Engrs; Am Inst Aeronaut & Astronaut; Am Soc Eng Educ; Nat Soc Prof Engrs. *Res:* Heat transfer and fluid mechanics with current emphasis on solidification in near zero g environments. *Mailing Add:* Dept Aerospace Eng Univ Tenn Space Inst Tullahoma TN 37388

YOUNG, ROBERT LEE, b Houston, Tex, Apr 10, 34; m 56; c 5. ELECTRICAL ENGINEERING. *Educ:* La State Univ, Baton Rouge, BS, 56, MS, 58; Tex A&M Univ, PhD(elec eng), 66. *Prof Exp:* Instr elec eng, La State Univ, 58-59; from asst prof to assoc prof, Southwestern La Univ, 59-68; prof & chmn dept, Northern Ariz Univ, 68-71, asst dean col eng, 70-71; prof eng, Nicholls State Univ, 71-77; PROF ELEC ENG & ASST TO DEAN COL ENG, UNIV SOUTHWESTERN LA, 77- *Mem:* Inst Elec & Electronics Engrs; Am Soc Eng Educ. *Res:* Multivariable control systems; electronic systems. *Mailing Add:* Dept Elec Eng Col Eng Univ Southwestern La PO Box 43690 Lafayette LA 70504

YOUNG, ROBERT M, b Brooklyn, NY, Sept 10, 39. BIOCHEMISTRY, BIOLOGY. *Educ:* Brooklyn Col, BS, 60, MA, 65; Univ Pittsburgh, PhD(biochem), 71. *Prof Exp:* Sr res asst clin enzymol, Beth Israel Med Ctr, 60-65; asst prof, 70-75, assoc prof biol, 75-78, chmn dept, 75-79, PROF BIOL, RI COL, 78- *Concurrent Pos:* Lectr, Brooklyn Col, 62-65; res asst, Creedmoor State Hosp, 63-64. *Mem:* Sigma Xi; AAAS; Am Inst Biol Sci; Am Soc Microbiol; Am Soc Zoologists. *Res:* Ribosomal structure and function; protein and RNA synthesis; biosynthesis of folates and pteridines; use of enzymes for the diagnosis of cancer; lens proteins in anopthalmic mice. *Mailing Add:* Dept of Biol RI Col Providence RI 02908

YOUNG, ROBERT RICE, b Washington, Pa, Aug 26, 34; m 59; c 3. NEUROLOGY, NEUROPHYSIOLOGY. *Educ:* Yale Univ, SB, 56; Harvard Med Sch, MD, 61. *Prof Exp:* Intern, Peter Bent Brigham Hosp, Boston, 61-62; resident neurol, Mass Gen Hosp, 62-65; NIH spec fel neurophysiol, Oxford Univ, 65-67; DIR, CLIN NEUROPHYSIOL LAB, HARVARD MED SCH & MASS GEN HOSP, BOSTON, 68- *Concurrent Pos:* vis scientist clin neurophys, Swedish Med Res Coun, Uppsala Univ, 79; Josiah Macy, Jr Found fac scholar award, 79. *Mem:* Am Acad Neurol; Am Electroencephalog Soc; Am Neurol Asn; Am Asn Electromyog & Electrodiag; Soc Neurosci. *Res:* Discharge properties of spinal motoneurones, their synchronization to produce tremor, the role played by muscle spindle primary afferent discharge in that synchronization and those peripheral beta-adrenergic mechanisms which alter muscle mechanics to affect the behavior of muscle spindles. *Mailing Add:* Mass Gen Hosp Boston MA 02114

YOUNG, ROBERT SPENCER, b Charlottesville, Va, Apr 14, 22; m 45; c 4. GEOLOGY. *Educ:* Univ Va, BA, 50, MA, 51; Cornell Univ, PhD(geol), 54. *Prof Exp:* Field geologist, Va State Geol Surv, 52-53, stratigrapher-struct geologist, 53-56; regional geologist & br mgr, Roland F Beers, Inc, 56-59; from asst prof to assoc prof geol, Univ Va, 59-68, asst dean col, 60-64; pres, NAm Explor Inc, 64-79; PRES, EXPLOR SERV INC, 80- *Concurrent Pos:* Lectr, Harpur Col, State Univ NY, 54; partner, Beers & Young, 60-63; pres. *Mem:* Am Inst Prof Geologists; Am Asn Petrol Geologists; Soc Explor Geophysicists; Am Inst Mining, Metall & Petrol Engrs; Soc Econ Geologists. *Res:* Evaluation of energy resources of Gulf Coastal states; economic and structural studies of the Paleozoics in the Appalachians of the eastern United States; geological, geophysical and geochemical explorations for sulfide deposits in the United States. *Mailing Add:* Explor Serv Inc Rte 2 Box 68 Ruckersville VA 22968

YOUNG, ROBERT WESLEY, b New York, NY, Mar 31, 22; m 48; c 1. GLASS CHEMISTRY. *Educ:* State Univ NY Col Ceramics, BSc, 48; NMex Highlands Univ, MS, 51. *Prof Exp:* Methods engr, Taylor Instruments Co, 48-50; asst chem, NMex Highlands Univ, 50-51; res asst, Eng Exp Sta, Ohio State Univ, 51-53; sr glass technologist, Res Div, 53-60, sect head glass develop lab, 60-62, CHIEF RES ENGR, RES DIV, AM OPTICAL CO, 62- *Concurrent Pos:* Lectr, Annhurst Col, 69- *Mem:* Nat Inst Ceramic Engrs; Am Ceramic Soc; Am Soc Testing & Mat. *Res:* Glass laser; fiber optics; high purity melting; infra-red transmitting glasses. *Mailing Add:* PO Box 104 Childs Hill Rd Woodstock CT 06281

YOUNG, ROBERT WILLIAM, b Mansfield, Ohio, May 11, 08; m 47; c 3. PHYSICS, ACOUSTICS. *Educ:* Ohio Univ, BS, 30; Univ Wash, PhD(physics), 34. *Prof Exp:* Physicist, C G Conn, Ltd, 34-42; physicist, Div War Res, Univ Calif, 42-46, res assoc, Marine Phys Lab, 46; physicist, US Navy Electronics Lab, 46-67, consult acoust, Naval Undersea Ctr, 67-74, Physicist, Naval Ocean Systs Ctr, 74-77; CONSULT ARCHITECTURAL ACOUSTICS & NORSE COMMUN, 77- *Mem:* AAAS; fel Acoust Soc Am (vpres, 53-54, pres, 60-61). *Res:* Acoustics of wind musical instruments; piano strings and tuning; underwater ambient and ship noise and sound propagation; acoustical standards; techniques for analyzing sound; architectural acoustics; community noise measurement and description. *Mailing Add:* 1696 Los Altos Rd San Diego CA 92109

YOUNG, ROGER GRIERSON, b Moose Jaw, Sask, Dec 18, 20; nat US; m 54; c 3. COMPARATIVE BIOCHEMISTRY. *Educ:* Univ Alta, BSc, 43, MSc, 48; Univ Ore, PhD(chem), 52. *Prof Exp:* Rockefeller asst, Cornell Univ, 51-52, Geer res fel, 52-53; assoc biochemist, Ethicon, Inc, 53-55; asst prof, 55-60, ASSOC PROF ENTOM, CORNELL UNIV, 60- *Concurrent Pos:* Vis prof, Col Agr, Univ Philippines, 68-69. *Mem:* AAAS; Entom Soc Am; Am Chem Soc. *Mailing Add:* Dept of Entom Cornell Univ Ithaca NY 14853

YOUNG, ROLAND S, b Portage la Prairie, Man, Oct 23, 06; m 52. CHEMICAL ENGINEERING, INORGANIC CHEMISTRY. *Educ:* Univ Alta, BSc, 28, MSc, 30; Cornell Univ, PhD(inorg chem), 34. *Prof Exp:* Res chemist, Int Nickel Co Can, 34-40, chem engr, 53-57; chief res chemist, Anglo Am Corp SAfrica, 40-48; dir res, Diamond Res Labs, Johannesburg, 49-52; consult chem engr, 58-60; chem engr, Dept Mines & Petrol Resources, BC, 61-71; chem engr, UN, 71-72; CONSULT CHEM ENGR, 72- *Mem:* Am Chem Soc; Inst Chem Engrs; SAfrican Inst Mining & Metall; Am Inst Mining, Metall & Petrol Engrs; Royal Inst Chem. *Res:* Cobalt; metallurgy; analytical chemistry. *Mailing Add:* 1178 Beach Dr Victoria BC V8S 2M9 Can

YOUNG, RONALD JEROME, b Hong Kong, Aug 10, 32; m 62; c 2. REPRODUCTIVE BIOCHEMISTRY, REPRODUCTIVE TOXICOLOGY. *Educ:* Univ Sydney, BSc, 54; Univ NSW, PhD, 58. *Prof Exp:* Fel, Univ Wis, 58-62; lectr biochem, Monash Univ, 63-67; fel, Univ Calif, 67-70; assoc prof biol sci, Drexel Univ, 70-73; assoc prof reproductive biol, Med Ctr, Cornell Univ, 73-80. *Mem:* Am Soc Biol Chemists. *Res:* Biochemistry of fertilization; reproductive biology. *Mailing Add:* Cornell Univ Med Ctr 1300 York Ave New York NY 10021

YOUNG, ROSS DARELL, b Osceola, Iowa, July 22, 27; m 72; c 2. MECHANICAL ENGINEERING, BIOENGINEERING. *Educ:* Iowa State Col, BS, 53, MS, 55. *Prof Exp:* Automotive engr, Standard Oil Co Ind, 55-58; asst prof mech eng, 58-65, assoc prof bioeng, 68-72, assoc prof phys med & rehab, Sch Med, 70-78, ASSOC PROF MECH & AEROSPACE ENG, COL ENG, UNIV MO-COLUMBIA, 65- *Res:* Mechanical design; engineering history; blood handling, prosthetic and orthopedic devices; heart assisting devices; medical equipment; product liability consulting. *Mailing Add:* Dept of Mech Eng Col of Eng Univ of Mo Columbia MO 65201

YOUNG, ROY ALTON, b McAlister, NMex, Mar 1, 21; m 50; c 2. PLANT PATHOLOGY. *Educ:* NMex State Univ, BS, 41; Iowa State Univ, MS, 42, PhD(plant path), 48. *Hon Degrees:* LLD, NMex State Univ, 78. *Prof Exp:* From asst prof to prof bot & plant path, Ore State Univ, 48-76, head dept, 58-66, dean res, 66-70, actg pres, Univ, 69-70, vpres res & grad studies, 70-76; chancellor, Univ Nebr, Lincoln, 76-80; MANAGING DIR, BOYCE THOMPSON INST PLANT RES, CORNELL UNIV, 80- *Concurrent Pos:* Mem exec comt, Study Probs Pest Control: A Technol Assessment, Nat Acad Sci-Nat Acad Eng, 72-75; mem US nat comt man & biosphere, UNESCO, 73-; mem comt to rev int biol prog, Nat Acad Sci-Nat Res Coun, 74-76; mem bd dirs, Pac Power & Light Co, 74-, Boyce Thompson Inst Plant Res, 75, First Nat Bank Lincoln, 76-80 & First Bank Ithaca, 81-; mem, Nat Sea Grant Adv Comt, 78-80; mem NSF adv comt appl sci & res appln policy, 77-79; mem adv comt appl sci & eng, NSF, 80-81. *Mem:* Fel AAAS; fel Am Phytopath Soc. *Res:* Diseases of ornamentals and potatoes; soil-borne diseases; chemical control of plant diseases; administration. *Mailing Add:* Boyce Thompson Inst Cornell Univ Ithaca NY 14853

YOUNG, ROY E, b Lincoln, Nebr, Apr 9, 18; m 50; c 2. PLANT PHYSIOLOGY. *Educ:* Univ Calif, Los Angeles, PhD(biochem), 60. *Prof Exp:* Assoc biochemist, Univ Calif, Los Angeles, 60-66; asst prof biochem, 66-71, assoc prof plant physiol, 71-76, PROF PLANT PHYSIOL, UNIV CALIF, RIVERSIDE, 76- *Concurrent Pos:* Consult, Scripps Inst Oceanog, Univ Calif, San Diego, 65-66; sr fel, Dept Sci & Indust Res, Auckland, NZ, 66-67. *Mem:* AAAS; Am Chem Soc; Am Soc Plant Physiologists; Am Inst Biol Sci; Am Soc Hort Sci. *Res:* Biochemistry of fruit ripening; phosphate metabolism in ripening fruit; changes in mitochondria associated with ripening; extraction and characterization of isoenzymes of ripening fruit; ethylene production. *Mailing Add:* Dept of Plant Sci Univ of Calif Riverside CA 92502

YOUNG, ROY EDWARD, agricultural & biological engineering, see previous edition

YOUNG, RUSSELL DAWSON, b Huntington, NY, Aug 17, 23; m 54; c 4. OPTICS, SURFACE SCIENCE. *Educ:* Rensselaer Polytech Inst, BS, 53; Pa State Univ, MS, 56, PhD(physics), 59. *Prof Exp:* Res assoc, Pa State Univ, 59-61; mem staff, 61-73, CHIEF MECH PROCESSES DIV, NAT BUR STANDARDS, 73- *Honors & Awards:* Edward Uhler Condon Award, Nat Bur Standards, 74. *Mem:* Am Phys Soc; Optical Soc Am. *Res:* Physical characterization of surfaces; micrometrology. *Mailing Add:* Optics & Micrometrology Sect Nat Bur Standards Washington DC 20234

YOUNG, SANFORD TYLER, b Chicago, Ill, Apr 14, 36; m 61; c 2. ORGANIC CHEMISTRY, ANALYTICAL CHEMISTRY. *Educ:* Univ Ill, BS, 58; Univ Rochester, PhD(org chem), 63. *Prof Exp:* Res chemist, 62-68, sr res chemist, 68-74, res assoc, 74-81, SR RES ASSOC, AGR CHEM DIV, FMC CORP, 82- *Mem:* AAAS; Am Chem Soc. *Res:* Synthesis of biologically active materials and organic analytical chemistry. *Mailing Add:* Agr Chem Div FMC Corp Princeton NJ 08450

YOUNG, SETH YARBROUGH, III, b Victoria, Miss, June 8, 41; m 61; c 3. ENTOMOLOGY, VIROLOGY. *Educ:* Miss State Univ, BS, 63; Auburn Univ, PhD(entom), 67. *Prof Exp:* Res entomologist, Stored Prod Res Lab, Mkt Qual Res Div, USDA, Ga, 66-67; from asst prof to assoc prof, 67-76, PROF ENTOM, UNIV ARK, FAYETTEVILLE, 76- *Mem:* Entom Soc Am; Soc Invert Path. *Res:* Insect virology. *Mailing Add:* Dept of Entom Univ of Ark Fayetteville AR 72701

YOUNG, SHARON CLAIRENE, b Elk City, Okla, Aug 3, 42. ZOOLOGY, ANATOMY. *Educ:* Bethany Nazarene Col, BS, 64; Okla State Univ, MS, 65, PhD(entom), 69. *Prof Exp:* From asst prof to assoc prof, 68-73, PROF BIOL, BETHANY NAZARENE COL, 73- *Mem:* Nat Asn Biol Teachers; AAAS; Sigma Xi. *Res:* Thrips resistance in peanuts; behavior of maongatian gerbil; very low density tipoproteins. *Mailing Add:* Dept of Biol Bethany Nazarene Col Bethany OK 73008

YOUNG, SIMON NESBITT, b Godalming, Eng, Feb 2, 45; div; c 1. NEUROSCIENCES. *Educ:* Oxford Univ, BA, 67; London Univ, MS, 68, PhD(biochem), 71. *Prof Exp:* Res asst biochem, Inst Neurol, London Univ, 68-71; fel, 71-75, asst prof, 75-79, ASSOC PROF NEUROCHEM, DEPT PSYCHIAT, MCGILL UNIV, 79- *Concurrent Pos:* Fel, Que Med Res Coun, 72-73; J B Collip fel, McGill Univ, 73-75. *Mem:* Can Biochem Soc; Can Col Neuropsychophamacol. *Res:* Investigation of brain biogenic amine synthesis and function in experimental animals and in man. *Mailing Add:* Dept of Psychiat McGill Univ 1033 Pine Ave W Montreal PQ H3A 2T5 Can

YOUNG, STEPHEN DEAN, invertebrate physiology, marine biology, see previous edition

YOUNG, STEPHEN JAMES, b Long Beach, Calif, Feb 28, 42; m 65. ATMOSPHERIC PHYSICS. *Educ:* Univ Alaska, College, BS, 64, PhD(physics), 68. *Prof Exp:* Sr res asst physics, Geophys Inst, Univ Alaska, 67-68; res scientist, US Army Cold Regions Res & Eng Lab, 68-70; MEM TECH STAFF, AEROSPACE CORP, 71- *Mem:* Optical Soc Am. *Res:* Molecular physics and spectroscopy; radiative transfer. *Mailing Add:* Chem & Physics Lab Aerospace Corp Box 95085 Los Angeles CA 90045

YOUNG, STEVEN WILFORD, sedimentary petrology, see previous edition

YOUNG, STUART, b Haslington, Eng, Dec 30, 25; nat US; m 53. VETERINARY PATHOLOGY. *Educ:* Royal Vet Col, Univ London, MRCVS, 48; Royal Dick Sch Vet Studies, Univ Edinburgh, DVSM, 51; Mich State Univ, MS, 54; Univ Calif, Davis, PhD(path), 63. *Prof Exp:* Asst vet invest officer, Vet Invest Lab, North of Scotland Col Agr, 49-55; from asst pathologist to assoc pathologist, Vet Res Lab, Mont State Col, 55-61; assoc prof path, Univ Minn, 63-64; assoc prof path, 64-72, dir, NIH Grad Training Prog, 65-72, dir, NIH Vision Res Training Prog, 79-82, PROF PATH, COL VET MED & BIOMED SCI, COLO STATE UNIV, 72- *Concurrent Pos:* NIH spec res fel, Cambridge Univ, 59 & Univ Bern, Switz, 70-71. *Mem:* Teratol Soc; Asn Res Vision Ophthal; Am Asn Neuropath; Am Vet Med Asn; Conf Res Workers Animal Dis. *Res:* Metabolic and developmental disorders of central nervous system and eye; pathology of chronic, progressive pneumonopathies; pathogenesis of nutritional myopathies. *Mailing Add:* Dept of Path Colo State Univ Col Vet Med & Biomed Sci Ft Collins CO 80521

YOUNG, SUE ELLEN, b Port Arthur, Tex, Nov 28, 39; m 72. OPHTHALMOLOGY. *Educ:* Univ Tex, BA, 61; Univ Tex, Galveston, MD, 69. *Prof Exp:* From intern to resident ophthal, Univ Tex, Houston, 69-73; fel neuro ophthal, Johns Hopkins Hosp, 73-74; chief, Ophthal Serv, 75-81, ASST PROF OPHTHAL, UNIV TEX CANCER SYST, 74- *Concurrent Pos:* Fel, Columbia Presby Hosp, 74; asst prof, Univ Tex Med Br, Houston, 74-81. *Mem:* Am Acad Ophthal; Am Asn Ophthal; AMA. *Res:* Breast carcinoma metastatic to the choroid its value as a prognosic indicator and its management. *Mailing Add:* 900 Live Oak Ridge Austin TX 78746

YOUNG, SYDNEY SZE YIH, b Fukien, China, Nov 8, 24; m 54; c 1. QUANTITATIVE GENETICS, POPULATION GENETICS. *Educ:* Nantung Univ, BAgrSc, 47; Sydney Tech Col, FSTC, 51; Univ NSW, MSc, 56, DSc(genetics), 66; Univ Sydney, PhD(genetics), 59. *Prof Exp:* From res scientist to prin res scientist, Div Animal Genetics, Commonwealth Sci & Indust Res Orgn, 59-67; PROF GENETICS, OHIO STATE UNIV, 67- *Concurrent Pos:* Commonwealth Sci & Indust Res Orgn overseas fel, 63-64. *Mem:* Biomet Soc; Genetics Soc Am; AAAS. *Res:* Theoretical and experimental quantitative and population genetics; animal breeding; biostatistics. *Mailing Add:* Dept of Genetics Ohio State Univ Columbus OH 43210

YOUNG, THOMAS EDWARD, b Chaves Co, NMex, June 15, 28; m 60; c 2. NUCLEAR PHYSICS. *Educ:* Rice Univ, PhD(physics), 58. *Prof Exp:* Asst prof physics, Pac Col, Calif, 58-60 & Trinity Univ, Tex, 60-61; PHYSICIST, AEROJET NUCLEAR CO, 61- *Mem:* Am Asn Physics Teachers. *Res:* Neutron reactions and low energy charged particle reactions; radiation shielding. *Mailing Add:* 1184 Atlantic Idaho Falls ID 83401

YOUNG, THOMAS EDWIN, b Manheim, Pa, Sept 7, 24; m 45; c 1. ORGANIC CHEMISTRY. *Educ:* Lehigh Univ, BS, 49, MS, 50; Univ Ill, PhD(chem), 52. *Prof Exp:* Asst chem, Lehigh Univ, 49-50; res chemist, E I du Pont de Nemours & Co, 52-55; asst prof chem, Antioch Col, 55-58; from asst prof to assoc prof, 58-66, PROF CHEM, LEHIGH UNIV, 66- *Mem:* Am Chem Soc. *Res:* Heterocyclic chemistry; indoles; structure and reactivity of heteroaromatic compounds; organosulfur chemistry. *Mailing Add:* 1952 Pinehurst Rd Bethlehem PA 18018

YOUNG, TZAY Y, b Shanghai, China, Jan 11, 33; m 65. ELECTRICAL ENGINEERING. *Educ:* Nat Taiwan Univ, BS, 55; Univ Vermont, MS, 59; Johns Hopkins Univ, DrEng, 62. *Prof Exp:* Res assoc, Carlyle Barton Lab, Johns Hopkins Univ, 62-63; mem tech staff, Bell Tel Lab, 63-64; asst prof elec eng, Carnegie-Mellon Univ, 64-68, assoc prof, 68-74; PROF ELEC ENG, UNIV MIAMI, 74- *Mem:* Inst Elec & Electronics Engrs. *Res:* Communication theory; signal and information theory; pattern recognition; computer process of biological data. *Mailing Add:* Dept of Elec Eng Univ of Miami Coral Gables FL 33124

YOUNG, VERNON ROBERT, b Rhyl, Wales, Nov 15, 37; m 66; c 5. NUTRITION, BIOCHEMISTRY. *Educ:* Univ Reading, BSc, 59; Cambridge Univ, dipl agr, 60; Univ Calif, Davis, PhD(nutrit), 65. *Prof Exp:* Lectr nutrit biochem, 65-66, asst prof physiol chem, 66-72, assoc prof nutrit biochem, 72-76, PROF NUTRIT BIOCHEM, MASS INST TECHNOL, 76- *Concurrent Pos:* Prog mgt human nutrit, Competitive Res Grants Prog, USDA, 80-81. *Honors & Awards:* Mead Johnson Award, Am Inst Nutrit, 73; Borden Award, Am Inst Nutrit, 82. *Mem:* Am Inst Nutrit; Nutrit Soc; Am Soc Clin Nutrit; Geront Soc Am; Am Chem Soc. *Res:* Protein and clinical nutrition; muscle protein metabolism; nutrition and aging; study of trace minerals; nutrient bioavailability-use of stable isotopes. *Mailing Add:* Dept of Nutrit & Food Sci Mass Inst of Technol Cambridge MA 02139

YOUNG, VIOLA MAE (HORVATH), b Allegan, Mich, Oct 9, 15; m; c 2. MICROBIOLOGY. *Educ:* Mich State Col, BS, 36; Univ Ill, MS, 43; Loyola Univ, Ill, PhD, 53. *Prof Exp:* Technician, Ill Res & Educ Hosp, Chicago, 37-43; instr bact, Univ Chicago Med Sch, 43-45; bacteriologist & parasitologist, Mt Sinai Hosp & Res Found, Chicago, 45-47; res assoc, Sch Trop Med, PR, 47-48; parasitologist, Hektoen Inst, Cook County Hosp, Ill, 48-54; supvry bacteriologist, Dept Bact, Walter Reed Army Inst Res, 54-61; chief microbiol serv, Clin Path Dept, Clin Ctr, NIH, 61-68; head, Res Microbiol Sect, Baltimore Cancer Res Ctr, Clin Br, Nat Cancer Inst, 68-80; RETIRED. *Concurrent Pos:* Asst supv bacteriologist, State Hosp Serv, Ill, 43-44; dir lab, Presby Hosp, San Juan, PR, 47-48; lectr, Loyola Univ, Ill, 49-54; mem fac, Rackham Grad Sch, Univ Mich, 69-; mem, Am Bd Microbiol. *Mem:* Am Soc Microbiol; Am Soc Trop Med & Hyg; Soc Exp Biol & Med; Am Acad Microbiol; Sigma Xi. *Res:* All infectious agents causing diarrhea; ecology of intestinal tract; Pseudomonas aeruginosa; host-parasite relationships; normal antibodies and immunological response; infection prevention in cancer patients; interrelationships among microorganisms; opportunistic infections. *Mailing Add:* 5203 Bangor Dr Kensington MD 20895

YOUNG, WARREN C(LARENCE), b Mauston, Wis, Sept 7, 23; m 45; c 3. ENGINEERING MECHANICS. *Educ:* Univ Wis, BS, 44, MS, 48, PhD(eng mech), 56. *Prof Exp:* Instr, 47-56, assoc prof, 59-63, PROF ENG MECH, UNIV WIS-MADISON, 63- *Mem:* Soc Exp Stress Anal; Am Soc Eng Educ. *Res:* Experimental stress analysis; photoelasticity. *Mailing Add:* 537 Engineering Res Univ of Wis Madison WI 53706

YOUNG, WARREN HOYLE, JR, b Wilmington, NC, Oct 15, 39; m 62; c 3. AERODYNAMICS, FLUID MECHANICS. *Educ:* Duke Univ, BS, 61; NC State Univ, MS, 63, PhD(aerospace eng), 70. *Prof Exp:* Engr magnetohydrodynamics, Martin-Marietta Corp, 63-65; AEROSPACE ENGR AERODYNAMICS, STRUCTS LAB, US ARMY AERONAUT RES & TECHNOL LAB, NASA LANGLEY RES CTR, 70- *Mem:* Am Helicopter Soc. *Res:* Unsteady and viscous flow on helicopter rotors including aeroelastic and structural response. *Mailing Add:* NASA Langley Res Ctr MS 340 Hampton VA 23665

YOUNG, WARREN MELVIN, b Massillon, Ohio, Dec 30, 37; m 60; c 2. ASTRONOMY. *Educ:* Case Inst Technol, BS, 60; Ohio State Univ, MS, 61, PhD(astron), 71. *Prof Exp:* Assoc prof astron & planetarium dir, 62-80, PROF & CHMN DEPT PHYSICS & ASTRON, YOUNGSTOWN STATE UNIV, 80- *Mem:* Am Astron Soc; Int Soc Planetarium Educ. *Res:* Spectrum binary stars; photometry. *Mailing Add:* Dept of Physics & Astron Youngstown State Univ Youngstown OH 44555

YOUNG, WESLEY O, b Nampa, Idaho, Oct 7, 25; m 50; c 2. DENTISTRY. *Educ:* Northwest Nazarene Col, AB, 46; Univ Ore, DMD, 47; Univ Mich, Ann Arbor, MPH, 51; Am Bd Dent Pub Health, dipl, 57. *Prof Exp:* Pvt pract, Idaho, 47-50; dir dent health sect, Idaho Dept Health, 51-53; sr dent surgeon, Div Dent Resources, USPHS, 53-55; chief dent health sect, Idaho Dept Health, 55-63, head cleft palate rehab prog, 56-63, dir child health div, 60-63; prof community dent & chmn dept, Col Dent, Univ Ky, 63-71; PROF COMMUNITY DENT, SCH DENT, UNIV ALA, BIRMINGHAM, 72- *Concurrent Pos:* Consult, West Interstate Comn for Higher Educ, 56-58 & Idaho State Univ, 57-59; staff mem, Comn Surv Dent in US, Am Coun Educ, Ill, 60; lectr, dept dent hyg, Idaho State Univ, 62-63; exam mem, Am Bd Dent Pub Health, 66-70, pres, 70-71; mem, Nat Traineeship Adv Comt, USPHS, DC, 62, Nat Adv Coun Health, Bur Health Manpower, 67- & health serv res study sect, NIH, 64. *Honors & Awards:* Sippy Mem Award, Am Pub Health Asn, 60. *Mem:* Am Dent Asn; Am Soc Dent for Children (secy-treas, 59-60, vpres, 61, pres, 63-64); fel Am Col Dent; fel Am Pub Health Asn; Int Asn Dent Res. *Res:* Preventive dentistry; health service research; dental public health. *Mailing Add:* Dept of Community Dent Univ of Ala Sch of Dent Birmingham AL 35233

YOUNG, WILLIAM ALLEN, b St Marys, Ohio, May 21, 30. PETROLEUM GEOCHEMISTRY. *Educ:* Miami Univ, Ohio, BA, 52; Ohio State Univ, MSc, 54, PhD(chem), 57. *Prof Exp:* Res chemist, Carter Oil Co, 57-58, Jersey Prod Res Co, 58-64, Esso Prod Res Co, 64-66, sr res specialist, 66-72, res assoc, 72-75, sr res assoc, 75-78, res adv, 78-81, SR RES ADV, EXXON PROD RES CO, 81- *Mem:* AAAS; Am Asn Petrol Geol; Am Chem Soc. *Res:* Petroleum and organic geochemistry; clay-organic-water interactions; hydrogeology. *Mailing Add:* Exxon Prod Res Co PO Box 2189 Houston TX 77001

YOUNG, WILLIAM ANTHONY, b Cleveland, Ohio, Feb 10, 23; m 54; c 2. PHYSICAL CHEMISTRY, ENGINEERING MANAGEMENT. *Educ:* Univ Wash, Seattle, BS, 49, MS, 53. *Prof Exp:* Res chemist, Am Marietta Co, 53-54; chemist, Thermodyn Sect, Nat Bur Standards, 54-55; test engr, Douglas Aircraft Co, 55-56; res engr, Atomics Int Div, NAm Rockwell Corp, 56-57, sr res chemist, 57-68, mem tech staff, 68-71; mgr anal develop & testing lab, Nuclear Energy Div, 72-74, mgr anal technol develop, 74-81, MGR LAB AUTOMATION, WILMINGTON MFG DEPT, GEN ELEC CO, 81- *Mem:* Am Chem Soc; Am Phys Soc; Am Nuclear Soc; Sigma Xi; fel Am Inst Chem. *Res:* Metal hydrides; solid state chemistry; high temperature heterogeneous reactions; diffusion in solids; reaction kinetics; thermophysical properties; molecular structure; analytical chemistry; computer applications; environmental sciences; chemical safety. *Mailing Add:* M/C K51 Gen Elec Co PO Box 780 Wilmington NC 28402

YOUNG, WILLIAM BEN, b Camden, Mich, Oct 29, 34; m 59; c 2. PHYSICAL METALLURGY. *Educ:* Cent Mich Univ, BS, 56; Mich State Univ, BS, 61. *Prof Exp:* Teacher math & sci, Port Austin High Sch, 56-59; staff metallurgist, Linde Div, Union Carbide Corp, 61-67; CHIEF ENGR, MAT SCI DEPT, PERFECT CIRCLE DIV, DANA CORP, 67- *Mem:* Fel Am Soc Metals; Am Ceramic Soc; Soc Automotive Engrs. *Res:* Metallurgical development of wear resistant coatings applied by metallizing processes; plasma, flame spray and detonation gun processes. *Mailing Add:* Perfect Circle Div 1400 Dana Pkwy PO Box 1166 Richmond IN 47374

YOUNG, WILLIAM DONALD, JR, b Glen Ridge, NJ, Nov 2, 38. BACTERIOLOGY, SYSTEMATICS. *Educ:* Fairleigh Dickinson Univ, BS, 60, MS, 74. *Prof Exp:* Res asst parasitol, NY Med Col, 61-62; sci asst clin chem, Walter Reed Army Inst Res, 62-64; scientist bact, Warner Lambert Res Inst, Morris Plains, 64-77; CONSULT BACT, 77- *Mem:* Am Soc Microbiol. *Res:* Development of rapid biochemical tests for use in diagnostic bacteriology; use of computer technology in the identification of bacterial cultures. *Mailing Add:* 68 Gates Ave Montclair NJ 07042

YOUNG, WILLIAM GLENN, JR, b Washington, DC, Feb 26, 25; m 52; c 4. THORACIC SURGERY. *Educ:* Duke Univ, MD, 48; Am Bd Surg, dipl, 58; Am Bd Thoracic Surg, dipl, 58. *Prof Exp:* Resident surg, Dake Hosp, 56-57; from asst prof to assoc prof, 57-63, PROF SURG, MED CTR, DUKE UNIV, 63- *Concurrent Pos:* Mem sr surg staff, Duke Hosp, 57-; attend surgeon, Vet Admin Hosp, Durham, NC, 57-; consult, Watts Hosp, Durham, 58- & Womack Army Hosp, Ft Bragg, 59- *Mem:* Soc Vascular Surg; Soc Univ Surg; AMA; Am Asn Thoracic Surg; fel Am Col Surg. *Res:* Cardiovascular surgery, application of moderate and profound hypothermia in cardiovascular surgery. *Mailing Add:* Dept of Surg Duke Univ Med Ctr Durham NC 27710

YOUNG, WILLIAM GOULD, chemistry, deceased

YOUNG, WILLIAM IRVING, b Vineland, NJ, Dec 15, 39; m 67; c 2. MEDICAL GENETICS. *Educ:* Pa State Univ, BS, 61; Univ Minn, MS, 66, PhD(human genetics), 74. *Prof Exp:* Geneticist, Minn Dept Health, 65-68; NIMH trainee behav genetics, Univ Minn, 68-73; ASST PROF CLIN GENETICS & BEHAV SCI, DEPT PSYCHIAT & BEHAV SCI, EASTERN VA MED SCH, 74- *Mem:* Am Soc Human Genetics; Behav Genetics Asn. *Res:* Behavioral genetics; genetic factors in Parkinson's disease; hyperkinetic syndrome; alcoholism. *Mailing Add:* Dept Psychiat & Behav Sci Eastern Va Med Sch Norfolk VA 23501

YOUNG, WILLIAM JOHNSON, II, b Lynn, Mass, Dec 10, 25; m 50; c 2. GENETICS, ANATOMY. *Educ:* Amherst Col, BA, 50, MA, 52; Johns Hopkins Univ, PhD(biol), 56. *Prof Exp:* Res assoc biol, Johns Hopkins Univ, 56-57, from asst prof to assoc prof anat, Sch Med, 57-66, assoc prof biophys, 66-68; PROF ANAT & CHMN DEPT, COL MED, UNIV VT, 68- *Mem:* Genetics Soc Am; Am Soc Human Genetics; Am Genetic Asn; Am Asn Anat. *Res:* Drosophila biochemical genetics; cytogenetics. *Mailing Add:* Dept of Anat Univ of Vt Col of Med Burlington VT 05401

YOUNG, WILLIAM PAUL, b Spokane, Wash, Oct 11, 13; m 42; c 3. SURGERY. *Educ:* Univ Wis, BS, 37, MS, 39, MD, 41. *Prof Exp:* Intern, Res Hosp, Kansas City, Mo, 41-42; res surg, Univ Wis Hosps, 46-49, instr surg, Univ, 50; chief surg serv, Southeast Fla State Tuberc Hosp, Lantana, 51; chief surg serv, Vet Admin Hosp, Madison, Wis, 52; from asst prof to assoc prof, 53-56, PROF SURG, CARDIOVASC SURG SECT, MED SCH, UNIV WIS-MADISON, 56- *Concurrent Pos:* USPHS trainee, Univ Wis Hosps, 49-50; consult, Vet Admin. *Mem:* AMA; Am Heart Asn; Am Col Surg; Am Asn Thoracic Surg. *Res:* Cardiovascular surgery; pulmonary hypertension associated with congenital heart disease; homografts; myocardial revascularization and studies of anticoagulation techniques. *Mailing Add:* Dept of Surg Sch of Med 1239 Wellesley Rd Madison WI 53705

YOUNG, WILLIAM RAE, b Lawton, Mich, Oct 30, 15; m 37; c 3. ELECTRICAL ENGINEERING. *Educ:* Univ Mich, Ann Arbor, BSEE, 37. *Prof Exp:* Mem tech staff, Bell Tel Labs, 37-50, supvr classified mil systs, 50-52, supvr switching syst studies, 52-54, supvr data systs planning, 54-56, head dept, 56-61, head, Dept Switching Systs Studies, 61-70, head, Dept Mobile Systs Eng, 70-80; RETIRED. *Mem:* Fel Inst Elec & Electronics Engrs. *Res:* Mobile radio, propagation studies and system planning for vehicular and portable communications. *Mailing Add:* 1 Kingfisher Dr Middletown NJ 07748

YOUNG, WILLIAM ROBERT, b East Rochester, NY, Oct 20, 26; m 49; c 3. ECONOMIC ENTOMOLOGY. *Educ:* Univ Rochester, BA, 51; Cornell Univ, PhD(entom), 55. *Prof Exp:* From asst entomologist to entomologist, 55-75, AGR PROJ LEADER & FOUND REP TO THAILAND, ROCKEFELLER FOUND, 75- *Mem:* Entom Soc Am. *Res:* Economic entomology; pests of cereal crops; biology; ecology; population studies; host plant resistance to insects. *Mailing Add:* Rockefeller Found GPO Box 2453 Bangkok Thailand

YOUNGBERG, CHESTER THEODORE, b Seattle, Wash, Mar 26, 17; m 41; c 4. FOREST SOILS. *Educ:* Wheaton Col, BS, 41; Univ Mich, MF, 47; Univ Wis, PhD(soils), 51. *Prof Exp:* Asst soils, Univ Wis, 47-51, forest soils specialist, Weyerhaeuser Timber Co, 51-52; assoc prof soils, Ore State Univ, 52-57; forestry specialist, Monsanto Chem Co, 57-58; prof forest soils, Ore State Univ, 58-82; CONSULT FOREST SOILS, 82- *Concurrent Pos:* Exchange prof, NC State Univ, 69-70. *Mem:* Soc Am Foresters; fel Am Soc Agron; Soil Sci Soc Am; Sigma Xi. *Res:* Soil-vegetation relationships; forest humus; symbiotic nitrogen fixation in non-leguminous plants; tree nutrition; slope-stability. *Mailing Add:* 841 NW Merrie Dr Corvallis OR 97330

YOUNGBLOOD, BETTYE SUE, b Powhatan, Ala, Dec 6, 26. ORGANIC CHEMISTRY. *Educ:* Auburn Univ, BS, 46; Univ Ala, MS, 49, PhD(chem), 57. *Prof Exp:* High sch teacher, Ala, 46-50; instr chem, Univ Miss, 50-52; high sch teacher, Ala, 56-57; asst ed chem nomenclature, Chem Abstr Serv, 57-59, assoc ed, 59-62; asst prof, 62-65, PROF CHEM, JACKSONVILLE STATE UNIV, 65- *Mem:* AAAS; Am Chem Soc; fel Am Inst Chemists. *Res:* Reaction mechanisms of aliphatic sulfonyl chlorides and derivatives; organic nomenclature of steroids and alkaloids. *Mailing Add:* Dept Chem Jacksonville State Univ Jacksonville AL 36265

YOUNGBLOOD, DAVE HARPER, b Waco, Tex, Oct 30, 39. PHYSICS. *Educ:* Baylor Univ, BS, 61; Rice Univ, MA, 63, PhD(physics), 65. *Prof Exp:* Fel, Argonne Nat Lab, 65-67; assoc prof, 67-77, PROF PHYSICS, CYCLOTRON INST, TEX A&M UNIV, 77-, DIR, CYCLOTRON INST, 78- *Mem:* Fel Am Phys Soc. *Res:* Nuclear spectroscopy and reaction theory; nuclear physics; grant resonances. *Mailing Add:* Cyclotron Inst Tex A&M Univ College Station TX 77843

YOUNGBLOOD, MICHAEL PHILLIP, b Ridgeland, SC, Apr 3, 51; m 72; c 2. KINETICS, ELECTROCHEMISTRY. *Educ:* Univ Ga, BS, 73; Purdue Univ, PhD(chem), 79. *Prof Exp:* Engr, Western Elec Co, 73-74; RES CHEMIST, EASTMAN KODAK RES LABS, 79- *Mem:* Sigma Xi. *Res:* Kinetics and mechamisms of reactions of transition metal complexes and of reactions of radio-active organic compounds. *Mailing Add:* Res Labs Eastman Kodak Co Rochester NY 14650

YOUNGBLOOD, WILLIAM ALFRED, b Waco, Tex, June 24, 25; m 49; c 2. ELECTRONICS, COMMUNICATIONS ENGINEERING. *Educ:* Univ Tex, BA & BSEE, 48, MSEE, 50; Mass Inst Technol, ScD(info theory), 58. *Prof Exp:* Asst res geophysicist, Humble Oil & Refining Co, 49-51; instr elec eng, Mass Inst Technol, 52-58, asst prof, 58-59; assoc prof, Univ Tex, 59-62; sr engr, Tracor, Inc, 62-65; dep proj mgr AN/BQQ-2 Sonar Proj, 65-71, chief engr, Navships Temp/Rewson Proj, 71-76, DEP PROJ MGR & TECH DIR REWSON, NAVAL SHIP SYSTS COMMAND, 76- *Concurrent Pos:* Consult, Sperry Gyroscope Co, 57-58, 59-60, Polaroid Corp, 58 & Tex Instruments, Inc, 59-60. *Honors & Awards:* Navy Superior Civilian Serv Award. *Mem:* Inst Elec & Electronics Engrs; Am Soc Naval Engrs. *Res:* Communication theory, underwater acoustics. *Mailing Add:* Dept Navy Naval Elec Systs Command Washington DC 20360

YOUNGDAHL, CARL KERR, b Chicago, Ill, Aug 14, 34; m 63; c 3. APPLIED MECHANICS, REACTOR ENGINEERING. *Educ:* Univ Chicago, AB, 53; Ill Inst Technol, BS, 56, MS, 57; Brown Univ, PhD(appl math), 60. *Prof Exp:* Mathematician, 60-74, SR MATHEMATICIAN, ARGONNE NAT LAB, 74- *Concurrent Pos:* Vis lectr, Ill Inst Technol, 63-64. *Mem:* Sigma Xi; Am Soc Mech Engrs; Am Acad Mech. *Res:* Pressure transients in reactor piping systems; dynamic plastic deformation of reactor components; thermoelasticity; fusion reactor structural analysis. *Mailing Add:* Components Tech Div Argonne Nat Lab Argonne IL 60439

YOUNGDAHL, PAUL F, b Brockway, Pa, Oct 8, 21; m 43; c 3. MECHANICAL ENGINEERING. *Educ:* Univ Mich, BSE, 42, MSE, 49, PhD(mech eng), 61. *Prof Exp:* Asst sr engr, E I du Pont de Nemours & Co, 42-43 & 46-48; teaching fel & instr, Univ Mich, 48-53; dir res, Mech Handling Systs, Mich, 53-62; from assoc prof to prof mech eng, Univ Mich, Ann Arbor, 62-74; CONSULT MECH ENGR, 74- *Concurrent Pos:* Staff consult, Mech Handling Systs, 62-; design consult, Liquid Drive Corp, 62-; patent & prod liability law suit consult & expert witness; sr lectr mech eng, San Jose State Univ, 77- *Mem:* AAAS; Am Soc Mech Engrs; Am Soc Eng Educ; Nat Soc Prof Engrs. *Res:* System design criteria, specifically directed at automation of mass manufacturing chemical process equipment. *Mailing Add:* 501 Forest Ave No 1002 Palo Alto CA 94301

YOUNGDALE, GILBERT ARTHUR, b Detroit, Mich, Jan 15, 29; m 56; c 5. ORGANIC CHEMISTRY. *Educ:* Univ Detroit, BS, 54, MS, 56; Wayne State Univ, PhD(org chem), 59. *Prof Exp:* RES ASSOC MED CHEM, UPJOHN CO, 59- *Mem:* Am Hypoglycemic agents. *Mailing Add:* 1702 Greenbriar Dr Kalamazoo MI 49008

YOUNGER, DANIEL H, b Flushing, NY, Sept 30, 36; m 65; c 3. MATHEMATICS. *Educ:* Columbia Univ, AB, 57, BS, 58, MS, 59, PhD(elec eng), 63. *Prof Exp:* Sloan fel, Princeton Univ, 63-64; res engr, Res & Develop Ctr, Gen Elec Co, NY, 64-67; assoc prof math, 68-75, chmn dept combinatorics & optimization, 78-79, PROF MATH, UNIV WATERLOO, 75- *Concurrent Pos:* Managing ed, J Combinatorial Theory, 68-75; vis scholar, Mass Inst Technol, 81-82. *Res:* Graph theory, especially minimax theory of directed graphs; algorithms; use of computer in combinatorial mathematics. *Mailing Add:* Dept of Combinatorics Univ of Waterloo Waterloo ON N2L 3G1 Can

YOUNGER, STEPHEN MICHAEL, b Baltimore, Md, Nov 2, 51; m 74; c 2. ATOMIC PHYSICS, THEORETICAL PHYSICS. *Educ:* Cath Univ Am, BA, 73; Univ Md, MS, 76, PhD(physics), 78. *Prof Exp:* PHYSICIST PHYSICS, NAT BUR STANDARDS, 74- *Concurrent Pos:* Res assoc, Nat Res Coun/Nat Bur Standards, 78-79. *Res:* Theory of atomic structure; atomic transition probabilities; electron-atom scattering; relativistic atomic structure calculations. *Mailing Add:* Atomic & Plasma Radiation Div Nat Bur of Standards Washington DC 20234

YOUNGGREN, NEWELL A, b River Falls, Wis, Mar 15, 15; m 41; c 2. BIOLOGY. *Educ:* River Falls State Col, BE, 37; Univ Wis, MPh, 40; Univ Colo, PhD, 56. *Prof Exp:* Asst prof biol, Northland Col, 46-48; asst prof, Bradley Univ, 48-55; asst prof, Univ Colo, 55-60, chmn dept, 58-60; head dept biol sci, 68-74, PROF BIOL SCI, UNIV ARIZ, 61- *Concurrent Pos:* Inst dir, NSF, 58-60. *Mem:* Fel AAAS; Am Inst Biol Sci; Nat Asn Biol Teachers. *Res:* Cellular biology; biology education; slime mold physiology. *Mailing Add:* Dept of Biol Sci Univ of Ariz Tucson AZ 85721

YOUNGKEN, HEBER WILKINSON, JR, b Philadelphia, Pa, Aug 13, 13; m 42; c 2. SYNTHETIC INORGANIC CHEMISTRY. *Educ:* Bucknell Univ, AB, 35; Mass Col Pharm, BS, 38; Univ Minn, MS, 40, PhD, 42. *Prof Exp:* Asst biol & pharmacog, Mass Col Pharm, 35-39; asst pharmacog, Col Pharm, Univ Minn, 39-42; from instr to prof, Univ Wash, 45-57; prof pharmacog & dean, Col Pharm, Univ RI, 57-81, provost, Health Sci Affairs, 69-81. *Concurrent Pos:* Chmn, Plant Sci Seminar, 51; Nat Adv Coun Ed Health prof, 64- *Honors & Awards:* E L Newcomb Res Award, 53. *Mem:* Fel AAAS; Am Pharmaceut Asn; Soc Exp Biol Med; NY Acad Sci; Sigma Xi. *Res:* Plant chemistry and pharmacology of plant constituents; biosynthesis of drug plant glycosides and alkaloids; drugs from the sea. *Mailing Add:* Dept of Pharmacog Univ of RI Kingston RI 02881

YOUNGLAI, EDWARD VICTOR, b Trinidad, WI, July 15, 40; Can citizen; m 70; c 2. BIOCHEMISTRY, REPRODUCTIVE PHYSIOLOGY. *Educ:* McGill Univ, BSc, 64, PhD(biochem), 67. *Prof Exp:* Res asst biochem, McGill Univ, 64-67; asst prof, 70-75, ASSOC PROF OBSTET & GYNEC, McMASTER UNIV, 75- *Concurrent Pos:* Fel exp med, McGill Univ, 67-68; Med Res Coun Can fel vet clin studies, Cambridge Univ, 68-70; Med Res Coun Can scholar, 70-75 & res grants, McMaster Univ, 70- *Mem:* Endocrine Soc; Brit Soc Study Fertil; Brit Soc Endocrinol; Soc Study Reproduction; Can Biochem Soc. *Res:* Control of gonadal function; gonadal steroid biosynthesis and metabolism; secretion of hormones. *Mailing Add:* Dept of Obstet & Gynec McMaster Univ Health Sci Ctr Hamilton ON L8N 3Z5 Can

YOUNGLOVE, JAMES NEWTON, b Coleman, Tex, Dec 16, 27; m 49; c 3. MATHEMATICS. *Educ:* Univ Tex, BA, 51, PhD(math), 58. *Prof Exp:* Instr math, Univ Tex, 52-58; asst prof, Univ Mo, 58-65; assoc prof, 65-71, PROF MATH, UNIV HOUSTON, 71- *Mem:* Am Math Soc; Math Asn Am. *Res:* Point set topology. *Mailing Add:* Dept of Math Cent Campus 4800 Calhoun Houston TX 77004

YOUNGMAN, ARTHUR L, b Chicago, Ill, Oct 24, 37; m 63; c 2. BOTANY. *Educ:* Univ Mont, BA, 59; Western Reserve Univ, MS, 61; Univ Tex, PhD(bot), 65. *Prof Exp:* ASST PROF BIOL, WICHITA STATE UNIV, 65- *Mem:* Ecol Soc Am; Am Inst Biol Sci. *Res:* Physiological ecology of vascular plants; environmental impact of industrial activity on terrestrial ecosystems. *Mailing Add:* Dept of Biol Sci Wichita State Univ Wichita KS 67208

YOUNGMAN, EDWARD AUGUST, b Fresno, Calif, May 17, 25; m 47; c 3. ORGANIC CHEMISTRY, POLYMER CHEMISTRY. *Educ:* Univ Wash, BS, 48, PhD(chem), 52. *Prof Exp:* Chemist, Shell Develop Co, Calif, 52-58, res supvr, 58-66, head, Plastics & Resins Res Dept, 66-67, dir, Plastics Technol Ctr, Shell Chem Co, NJ, 67-69, dir phys sci, Biol Sci Res Ctr, 69-80; RETIRED. *Mem:* Am Chem Soc; Soc Chem Indust. *Res:* Physical science of biologically active molecules, especially their synthesis and application. *Mailing Add:* 300 Durham Lane Modesto CA 95350

YOUNGMAN, VERN E, b Valley, Nebr, Sept 11, 28; m 54. AGRONOMY. *Educ:* Univ Nebr, BS, 55, MS, 57; Washington State Univ, PhD(agron), 62. *Prof Exp:* Instr agron, Univ Nebr, 56-58; from instr to asst prof, Washington State Univ, 58-67; ASSOC PROF AGRON, COLO STATE UNIV, 67- *Mem:* Am Soc Agron; Soc Econ Bot; Asn Off Seed Analysts; Nat Asn Cols & Teachers of Agr. *Res:* Physiology, ecology and management of crop plants. *Mailing Add:* Dept Agron Colo State Univ Ft Collins CO 80523

YOUNGNER, JULIUS STUART, b New York, NY, Oct 24, 20; m 43; c 2. MEDICAL MICROBIOLOGY. *Educ:* NY Univ, AB, 39; Univ Mich, MS, 41, ScD(bact), 44; Am Bd Med Microbiol, dipl. *Prof Exp:* From asst to instr bact, Univ Mich, 41-44; asst path, Manhattan Proj, Univ Rochester, 45-46; instr, Univ Mich, 46-47; sr asst scientist, Nat Cancer Inst, 47-49; asst res prof virol & bact, Sch Med, 49-56, assoc prof microbiol, 56-60, PROF MICROBIOL, SCH MED, UNIV PITTSBURGH, 60-, CHMN DEPT, 66- *Concurrent Pos:* Vis prof, Nat Univ Athens, 63; mem virol & rickettsial study sect, NIH, 66-70; mem comn influenza, Armed Forces Epidemiol Bd, 70-73; mem bd sci counr, Nat Inst Allergy & Infectious Dis, 70-74; nat lectr, Found Microbiol, 72-73; mem study group, Immunol & Infectious Dis, Health Res & Serv Found, 79, Chmn, 78-79; mem clin A fel study sect, NIH, 79-80; mem microbiol & virol study group, Am Cancer Soc, 81-84. *Honors & Awards:* Lippard Mem lectr, Col Physicians & Surgeons, Columbia Univ, 80. *Mem:* AAAS; Am Acad Microbiol; Brit Soc Gen Microbiol; Am Soc Microbiol; Infectious Dis Soc Am. *Res:* Replication and properties of animal viruses; cellular and host resistance to virus infection; persistent viral infections. *Mailing Add:* Dept of Microbiol Univ of Pittsburgh Sch of Med Pittsburgh PA 15261

YOUNGNER, PHILIP GENEVUS, b Nelson, Minn, July 13, 20; m 47; c 4. PHYSICS. *Educ:* St Cloud State Col, BS, 44; Univ Wis, MS, 47, PhD(physics), 58. *Prof Exp:* Pub sch teacher, Minn, 39-41; radium technician, Wis Gen Hosp, 46-47; instr physics, Exten, Univ Wis, 47-49; from asst prof to assoc prof, 49-59, chmn dept, 60-80, PROF PHYSICS, ST CLOUD STATE UNIV, 59- *Concurrent Pos:* Pres, Ecostill Corp, 80- *Mem:* Am Phys Soc; Am Asn Physics Teachers. *Res:* Molecular spectra; solar energy; salt water conversion; atmospheric electricity. *Mailing Add:* Dept Physics St Cloud State Univ St Cloud MN 56301

YOUNGNER, VICTOR BERNARR, b Nelson, Minn, Apr 19, 22; m 44, 65; c 2. PLANT BREEDING, AGROSTOLOGY. *Educ:* Univ Minn, BS, 48, PhD(hort), 52. *Prof Exp:* Res asst hort, Univ Minn, 48-52; plant geneticist, Ferry Morse Seed Co, 52-55; from asst prof to assoc prof ornamental hort, Univ Calif, Los Angeles, 55-65; assoc prof agron, 65-68, chmn dept, 68-70, PROF AGRON, UNIV CALIF, RIVERSIDE, 68- *Mem:* AAAS; Soc Range Mgt; fel Am Soc Agron; Crop Sci Soc Am; Sigma Xi. *Res:* Genetics, breeding and ecology of grasses; ecology and physiology of chaparral plants; renovation and recycling of waste water; breeding and physiology of guayule (parthenium argentatum). *Mailing Add:* Dept of Bot & Plant Sci Univ of Calif Riverside CA 92521

YOUNGQUIST, MARY JOSEPHINE, b Fullerton, NDak, Oct 12, 30. PHOTOGRAPHIC CHEMISTRY. *Educ:* Univ Minn, BA, 57; Mass Inst Technol, PhD(org chem), 61. *Prof Exp:* Res fel org chem, Univ Minn, 61-63; sr chemist, 63-74, TECH STAFF ASST, EASTMAN KODAK CO, 75- *Res:* Technical editing; training coordinating. *Mailing Add:* Bldg 59 Eastman Kodak Co Res Labs Rochester NY 14650

YOUNGQUIST, RUDOLPH WILLIAM, b Minneapolis, Minn, Aug 10, 35; m 59; c 3. FOOD BIOCHEMISTRY. *Educ:* Univ Minn, BChem, 57; Iowa State Univ, MS, 60, PhD(biochem), 62. *Prof Exp:* RES BIOCHEMIST, PROCTER & GAMBLE CO, 62- *Mem:* AAAS; Am Chem Soc; Am Asn Cereal Chemists. *Res:* Starch and protein food biochemistry. *Mailing Add:* Procter & Gamble Co Miami Valley Labs PO Box 39175 Cincinnati OH 45239

YOUNGQUIST, WALTER, b Minneapolis, Minn, May 5, 21; m 43; c 4. GEOLOGY. *Educ:* Gustavus Adolphus Col, BA, 42; Univ Iowa, MS, 43, PhD(geol), 48. *Prof Exp:* Asst geol, Univ Iowa, 42-43; jr geologist, Groundwater Div, US Geol Surv, Iowa, Va & La, 43-44; asst paleont, Univ Iowa, 45-47; asst prof geol, Univ Idaho, 48-51; geologist, Int Petrol Co, Peru, 51-52, sr geologist, 52-53, chief spec studies sect, 53-54; prof geol, Univ Kans, 54-57; from assoc prof to prof, Univ Ore, 57-66; consult, Minerals Dept, Humble Oil & Refining Co, 66-73; GEOTHERMAL RESOURCES CONSULT, EUGENE WATER & ELEC BD, 73- *Concurrent Pos:* Mem, Geothermal Resources Coun. *Mem:* Fel AAAS; Geol Soc Am; Am Asn Petrol Geologists. *Res:* Geology and economics of mineral resources; petroleum geology; geothermal resources. *Mailing Add:* PO Box 5501 Eugene OR 97405

YOUNGS, CLARENCE GEORGE, b Didsbury, Alta, Oct 23, 26; m 51; c 3. FOOD PROCESSING. *Educ:* Univ Alta, BSc, 48; Univ Sask, MSc, 53, PhD(chem), 57. *Prof Exp:* RES OFFICER CROP UTILIZATION, PRAIRIE REGIONAL LAB, NAT RES COUN, CAN, 48- *Concurrent Pos:* Res award, Glycerine Producers Asn, 60. *Honors & Awards:* Can Award Merit, Am Oil Chemists Soc, 64. *Mem:* Can Inst Food Sci & Technol; Agr Inst Can. *Res:* Utilization of prairie crops for food and feed, particularly oilseeds and legumes. *Mailing Add:* Prairie Reg Lab 110 Gymnasium Rd Saskatoon SK S7N 0W9 Can

YOUNGS, ROBERT LELAND, b Pittsfield, Mass, Feb 10, 24; m 49; c 5. FORESTRY. *Educ:* State Univ NY, BS, 48; Univ Mich, MWT, 50; Yale Univ, PhD(forestry), 57. *Prof Exp:* Forest prod technologist, Forest Prod Lab, 51-66, proj leader fundamental properties, 58-64, chief div solid wood prod res, 64-66, dir div forest prod & eng res, 67-70, dir, Southern Forest Exp Sta, 70-72, assoc dep chief res, 72-75, DIR, FOREST PROD LAB, US FOREST SERV, 75- *Honors & Awards:* Wood Award, Forest Prod Res Soc, 57. *Mem:* AAAS; Soc Am Foresters; Soc Wood Sci & Technol (secy-treas, 58-59, vpres, 60-61, pres, 62-63); Forest Prod Res Soc; Am Forestry Asn. *Res:* Basic physical and mechanical properties of wood and related factors. *Mailing Add:* Forest Prod Lab PO Box 5130 Madison WI 53705

YOUNGSTROM, RICHARD EARL, b Durham, NC, Sept 11, 43; div; c 2. CHROMATOGRAPHY, RADIOCHEMISTRY. *Educ:* Duke Univ, BS, 65; Wash Univ, MA, 69. *Prof Exp:* From assoc scientist steroid chem to scientist radiochem, 69-70, sr scientist, 71-73, RES SECT LEADER, RADIOCHEM, SCHERING CORP, 77- *Mem:* Am Soc Testing & Mat; Am Chem Soc. *Res:* Systematic development/application of advanced chromatography methods for profiling organic mixtures and reactions; chromatographic profiles, reaction variables and isolation for overall product optimiation; improved liquid scintillation analytical procedures. *Mailing Add:* Natural Prod Res Dept Schering Corp 60 Orange St Bloomfield NJ 07003

YOUNKIN, LARRY MYRLE, b Markleton, Pa, Oct 16, 36; m 69; c 1. CIVIL ENGINEERING. *Educ:* Geneva Col, BS, 56; Univ Pittsburgh, BSCE, 59, MSCE, 62; Va Polytech Inst & State Univ, PhD(civil eng), 71. *Prof Exp:* Instr civil eng, Univ Pittsburgh, 56-59; asst prof, Geneva Col, 59-62; instr, Univ NMex, 62-64; asst prof, 66-72, ASSOC PROF CIVIL ENG, BUCKNELL UNIV, 72- *Concurrent Pos:* Consult engr, Pa Dept Transp, 71- *Mem:* Am Soc Civil Engrs; Am Geophys Union; Am Soc Eng Educ. *Res:* Open channel flow; hydraulic structures; sediment transport and yield from construction. *Mailing Add:* Dept of Civil Eng Bucknell Univ Lewisburg PA 17837

YOUNKIN, STUART G, b US, Jan 16, 12; m 43; c 5. PLANT PATHOLOGY. *Educ:* Iowa State Univ, BS, 36, MS, 39; Cornell Univ, PhD, 43. *Prof Exp:* From asst plant pathologist & geneticist to plant pathologist & geneticist, Campbell Soup Co, 43-52, asst to dir res, 52-53, dir agr res, 53-62, vpres agr res, 62-77, pres, Campbell Inst Agr Res, 66-77; RETIRED. *Concurrent Pos:* Mem agr bd, Nat Acad Sci-Nat Res Coun, 62-68, pres, Agr Res Inst, 64-65; mem panel world food supply, President's Sci Adv Comt, 66-67. *Mem:* Soc Econ Botanists; Am Soc Hort Sci; Am Phytopath Soc. *Res:* Virus diseases of potatoes; vegetable disease control; breeding of tomatoes and peppers. *Mailing Add:* 614 Elm Terr Riverton NJ 08077

YOUNOSZAI, RAFI, b Kabul, Afghanistan, June 13, 30; m 64; c 2. ANATOMY. *Educ:* Univ Calif, Berkeley, BSc, 57; Univ Minn, PhD(anat), 71. *Prof Exp:* Instr, Dept Anat, Univ Minn, 71-73, asst prof anat, 73-78; ASSOC PROF ANAT, COL OSTEOPATH MED OF THE PAC, 79- *Concurrent Pos:* Res coordr, Res Orgn Comt, Am Osteopathic Asn, Nat Osteopathic Found, 80-82. *Mem:* Am Asn Anatomists; Am Diabetes Asn. *Res:* Interacellular transport and release of insulin; effect of a low protein and high carbohydrate diet on insulin release; insulin release patterns of induced islet adenomas; electronyographic studies on patients with somatic dysfunctions before and subsequent to manipulative therapy. *Mailing Add:* Col Osteopathic Med of the Pac Pomona Mall East Pomona CA 91711

YOUNT, DAVID EUGENE, b Prescott, Ariz, June 5, 35; m 62, 75; c 4. ELEMENTARY PARTICLE PHYSICS. *Educ:* Calif Inst Technol, BS, 57; Stanford Univ, MS, 59, PhD(physics), 63. *Prof Exp:* From instr to asst prof physics, Princeton Univ, 62-64; NSF fel, Linear Accelerator Lab, Orsay, France, 64-65; res assoc, Stanford Linear Accelerator Ctr, 65-69; assoc prof, 69-72, PROF PHYSICS, UNIV HAWAII, HONOLULU, 72-, CHMN DEPT PHYSICS & ASTRON, 79- *Concurrent Pos:* 3M Co fel, Princeton Univ, 63; dir, Hawaii Topical Conf Particle Physics, 71. *Mem:* Am Chem Soc; Am Phys Soc; Undersea Med Soc. *Res:* Positron scattering, leptonic K-meson decay, hadronic photon absorption, photoproduction of mesons, positron-electron colliding beams, bubble nucleatron, and decompression sickness; instrumentation for particle beam monitors, spark chambers, streamer chambers and multiwire proportional chambers. *Mailing Add:* Dept of Physics & Astron Univ of Hawaii Honolulu HI 96822

YOUNT, ERNEST H, b Lincolnton, NC, Feb 23, 19; m 42; c 3. MEDICINE. *Educ:* Univ NC, BA, 40; Vanderbilt Univ, MD, 43. *Prof Exp:* Asst med, Univ Chicago, 45-48; from instr to assoc prof, 48-54, chmn dept, 52-72, PROF MED, BOWMAN GRAY SCH MED, 54- *Concurrent Pos:* Consult, Oak Ridge Inst Nuclear Studies, 50-58; mem dean's comt, Vet Admin Hosp, Salisbury, 54-63; mem, Nat Bd Med Exam, 58-61, chmn, 61. *Mem:* Am Fedn Clin Res; Am Soc Internal Med; Am Col Physicians; Am Diabetes Asn; Asn Prof Med. *Res:* Malaria; adrenal and thyroid function; diabetes. *Mailing Add:* Dept of Med Bowman Gray Sch of Med Winston-Salem NC 27103

YOUNT, RALPH GRANVILLE, b Indianapolis, Ind, Mar 25, 32; m 57; c 3. BIOCHEMISTRY. *Educ:* Wabash Col, AB, 54; Iowa State Univ, PhD, 58. *Prof Exp:* Res assoc enzymol, Brookhaven Nat Lab, 58-60; from asst prof chem & asst chemist to assoc prof & assoc chemist, 60-72, chmn biochem/biophys prog, 73-78, PROF BIOCHEM, WASH STATE UNIV, 72- *Concurrent Pos:* NIH spec fel, Sch Med, Univ Pa & vis prof, Johnson Found, 69-70. *Mem:* AAAS; Am Soc Biol Chemists; Am Chem Soc; NY Acad Sci; Biophys Soc. *Res:* Mechanism of enzyme action as it applies to contractile proteins. *Mailing Add:* Dept of Chem Wash State Univ Pullman WA 99163

YOUNTS, SANFORD EUGENE, b Lexington, NC, Aug 29, 30; m 54; c 1. SOIL SCIENCE, AGRONOMY. *Educ:* NC State Univ, BS, 52, MS, 55; Cornell Univ, PbD(agron), 57. *Prof Exp:* Asst prof soils, Univ Md, 57-58; agronomist, Am Potash Inst, 58-60; assoc prof soils, NC State Col, 60-64; regional dir, Am Potash Inst, 64-67, vpres, 67-69; assoc dean col agr & dir rural develop ctr, 69-72, VPRES SERV, UNIV GA, 72-, PROF AGRON, 69- *Mem:* AAAS; fel Am Soc Agron; Int Soc Soil Sci; fel Soil Sci Soc Am. *Res:* Soil fertility and crop physiology; root growth of field crops as influenced by fertilizer and lime placement; chloride nutrition of corn; potash requirements of forage crops; nitrogen sources for turf; copper nutrition of wheat, corn and soybeans. *Mailing Add:* Univ of Ga 300 Old College Athens GA 30601

YOURNO, JOSEPH DOMINIC, b Utica, NY, July 14, 36; m 60; c 2. MOLECULAR BIOLOGY, MICROBIAL GENETICS. *Educ:* Kenyon Col, AB, 58; Johns Hopkins Univ, PhD(biochem), 64; Univ Miami, MD, 74. *Prof Exp:* Geneticist, Brookhaven Nat Lab, NY, 65-72; instr & resident, 74-76, ASSOC PROF CLIN PATH, STATE UNIV NY, UPSTATE MED CTR, 76- *Res:* Gene-protein studies; effect of mutation on protein primary structure in bacteria; gene fusion; carcinogens as mutagens; diagnostic enzymology. *Mailing Add:* State Univ NY Upstate Med Ctr 750 E Adams St Syracuse NY 13210

YOURTEE, JOHN BOTELER, b Fredericksburg, Va, Dec 2, 46; m 68; c 1. CHEMICAL ENGINEERING, POLYMER CHEMISTRY. *Educ:* Univ Del, BS, 68; Mass Inst Technol, SM, 69; Univ Wis, PhD(chem eng), 73. *Prof Exp:* Res engr, Union Carbide Corp, 73-75, sr res engr plastics, 75-77; sr group leader, Merck & Co, Pittsburgh, 77-81; STAFF ENGR, EXXON CHEM CO, NJ, 81- *Mem:* Sigma Xi; Soc Plastics Engrs. *Res:* Product and process development of thermoplastic polymers and water-soluble polymers. *Mailing Add:* 3 Jefferson Dr Flanders NJ 07836

YOURTEE, LAWRENCE KARN, b Brunswick, Md, Mar 6, 17; m 41; c 1. ORGANIC CHEMISTRY. *Educ:* Washington Col, Md, BS, 37; Ga Inst Technol, MS, 39; Univ Tex, PhD(chem), 48. *Prof Exp:* Instr chem, Ga Inst Technol, 40-42 & Univ Tex, 46-47; asst prof, Univ Tenn, 47-48; assoc prof, 48-57, chmn dept, 57-71, Childs prof, 58-80, MCEWEN PROF CHEM, HAMILTON COL, 80- *Mem:* Am Chem Soc. *Res:* Synthesis and properties of heterocyclic nitrogen compounds; Pfitzinger reaction; use of ion-exchange resins in organic synthesis and separations. *Mailing Add:* Dept of Chem Hamilton Col Clinton NY 13323

YOUSE, BEVAN K, b Markle, Ind, Apr 5, 27; m 58; c 1. MATHEMATICAL ANALYSIS. *Educ:* Auburn Univ, BS, 49; Univ Ga, MS, 52. *Prof Exp:* Instr math, Memphis State Univ, 52-53 & Univ Ga, 53-54; asst prof, 54-67, ASSOC PROF MATH, EMORY UNIV, 67- *Concurrent Pos:* NSF fac fel, 60-61. *Mem:* AAAS; Am Math Soc; Math Asn Am. *Res:* Mathematical analysis. *Mailing Add:* Dept of Math Emory Univ Atlanta GA 30322

YOUSE, HOWARD RAY, b Bryant, Ind, May 22, 15; m 42. BOTANY. *Educ:* DePauw Univ, BA, 37; Ore State Col, MS, 42; Purdue Univ, PhD(bot), 51. *Prof Exp:* From instr to assoc prof, DePauw Univ, 40-55, head dept bot & bact, 73-78, prof bot, 55-80, chmn dept bot & bact, 78-80; RETIRED. *Mem:* AAAS; Bot Soc Am. *Res:* Pollen grains; seed germination. *Mailing Add:* PO Box 253 Greencastle IN 46135

YOUSEF, IBRAHIM MOHMOUD, b Egypt, Nov 20, 40; Can citizen; m 63; c 1. BIOCHEMISTRY, EXPERIMENTAL PATHOLOGY. *Educ:* Univ Ain Shams, Cairo, BSc, 61; Univ Col Wales, MSc, 65; Univ Edinburgh, PhD(biochem), 67. *Prof Exp:* Res assoc, Mich State Univ, 67-69; res assoc, Univ Toronto, 69-70, assoc pathol, 70-72, asst prof, 72-78; ASSOC PROF PEDIAT, UNIV MONTREAL, 78- *Concurrent Pos:* Fel med educ, Univ Toronto, 71; dir labs, Gallstone Study Can, 76-78; consult, Para-Med Educ Cols, Toronto, 74-78; dir, Liver Res Unit, Hosp She-Justine, Montreal, Can. *Mem:* Am Asn Study Liver Dis; Can Biochem Soc; Soc Exp Biol & Med; Am Oil Chemist Soc; Int Biochem Soc. *Res:* Bile formation and secretion; bile acid metabolism; cholestasis in adults and children; experimental cholestasis; fat absorption. *Mailing Add:* Res Ctr St Justine Hosp 3175 Cote Ste Catherine Montreal PQ H3T 1C5 Can

YOUSEF, MOHAMED KHALIL, b Cairo, Egypt, Aug 19, 35; US citizen; m 63; c 2. ENVIRONMENTAL PHYSIOLOGY. *Educ:* Ain Shams Univ, Cairo, BSc, 59; Univ Mo-Columbia, MS, 63, PhD(environ physiol), 66. *Prof Exp:* Res assoc environ physiol, Univ Mo-Columbia, 66-67; vis asst prof, Inst Arctic Biol, Univ Alaska, 67-68; asst prof, Lab Environ Patho-physiol, Desert Res Inst, Univ Nev, 68-70; from asst prof to assoc prof, 70-74, PROF BIOL & PHYSIOL, UNIV NEV, LAS VEGAS, 74-, COORDR HEALTH PREPROF PROG, 73-, DIR, DESERT BIOL RES CTR, 80- *Mem:* Int Soc Biometeorol; Am Physiol Soc; Soc Exp Biol & Med; Endocrine Soc; Am Col Sports Med. *Res:* Physiological adaptations to desert, mountain and arctic environments; role of the respiratory, cardiovascular and endocrine systems in adaptation; comparative thermoregulation during rest and exercise under different environments; comparative adaptations of organisms to various stressful environments; emphasis is on the role of cardiovascular, respiratory and endocrine systems. *Mailing Add:* Dept of Biol Sci Univ of Nev Las Vegas NV 89154

YOUSIF, SALAH MOHAMMAD, b Burin, Palestine, Nov 15, 38; m 68; c 3. ELECTRICAL ENGINEERING. *Educ:* Univ Alexandria, BSEE, 62; Mid East Tech Univ, Ankara, MSEE, 64; Ore State Univ, PhD(elec eng), 69. *Prof Exp:* Elec engr, Jordan Broadcasting Serv, 62-63 & Kuwait Broadcasting Serv, 64-65; instr elec eng, Mich State Univ, 66-68 & Ore State Univ, 68-69; asst prof, 69-72, assoc prof, 72-80, PROF ELEC ENG, CALIF STATE UNIV, SACRAMENTO, 80- *Mem:* Inst Elec & Electronics Engrs; Soc Indust & Appl Math; Pattern Recognition Soc. *Res:* Control, information and power systems; pattern recognition. *Mailing Add:* Dept of Elec Eng Calif State Univ 6000 J St Sacramento CA 95819

YOUSSEF, MARY NAGUIB, US citizen. SYSTEMS DESIGN, SYSTEMS SCIENCE. *Educ:* Univ Cairo, BS, 58; Columbia Univ, MA, 64; Stanford Univ, MS, 67; Ore State Univ, PhD(statist), 70. *Prof Exp:* Asst instr celestial mech, Cairo Univ, 58-61; mem tech staff & researcher, Oper Res Ctr, Inst Nat Planning, Cairo, 63-65; mem tech staff syst anal, Bell Tel Labs, 70-76, MEM TECH STAFF ECON & TIME SERIES FORECASTING, BELL LABS, 76- *Concurrent Pos:* Assoc prof oper res & comput info systs, Baruch Col, City Univ New York, 81-82. *Mem:* Sigma Xi; Am Statist Asn; Opers Res Soc Am.

Res: Modeling and analyzing queuing systems; development of approximate analytic solutions for unsolved queuing problems; methods for projecting telecommunication traffic in a special environment; economic and time series forecasting. *Mailing Add:* Bell Labs Crawfords Corner Rd Holmdel NJ 07733

YOUSSEF, NABIL NAGUIB, b Cairo, Egypt, Oct 19, 37; US citizen; m 63; c 3. MORPHOLOGY, CELL BIOLOGY. *Educ:* Ain Shams Univ, Cairo, BSc, 58; Utah State Univ, MS, 64, PhD(zool), 66. *Prof Exp:* Asst instr entom & zool, Ain Shams Univ, Cairo, 58-60; from res asst to res assoc, 64-68, asst prof, 68-75, ASSOC PROF ZOOL, UTAH STATE UNIV, 75- *Concurrent Pos:* USDA grant, 66-68. *Mem:* Sigma Xi; AAAS; fel Royal Entom Soc London; Entom Soc Am; Soc Protozoologists. *Res:* Fine structure of Protozoa and Insecta with special emphasis on morphogeneses of normal and abnormal tissues induced by drugs or pathogens. *Mailing Add:* Dept of Biol Utah State Univ Logan UT 84322

YOUSTEN, ALLAN A, b Racine, Wis, Nov 9, 36; c 2. MICROBIAL PHYSIOLOGY, MICROBIAL INSECTICIDES. *Educ:* Univ Wis, BS, 58; Cornell Univ, MS, 60, PhD, 63. *Prof Exp:* Microbial biochemist, Int Minerals & Chem Corp, 65-69; NIH spec fel, Univ Wis, 69-71; asst prof, 71-77, ASSOC PROF MICROBIOL, VA POLYTECH INST & STATE UNIV, 77- *Concurrent Pos:* Fulbright-Hays fel, Pasteur Inst, 80. *Mem:* AAAS; Am Soc Microbiol; Soc Indust Microbiol. *Res:* Physiology and structure of microorganisms; bacterial spore formation and germination; bacterial insect pathogens. *Mailing Add:* Dept Biol Va Polytech Inst & State Univ Blacksburg VA 24061

YOUTCHEFF, JOHN SHELDON, b Newark, NJ, Apr 16, 25; m 50; c 5. ASTROPHYSICS. *Educ:* Columbia Univ, AB & BS, 50; Univ Calif, Los Angeles, PhD, 54. *Prof Exp:* Dir test staff, US Naval Air Missile Test Ctr, 50-53; opers analyst, Advan Electronics Ctr, Gen Elec Co, 53-56, functional engr, Missile & Space Div, 56-60, consult engr, 60-63, mgr advan reliability concepts oper, 63-72; mgr reliability & maintainability, Litton Industs, 72-73; PROG DIR, US POSTAL SERV HQ, WASHINGTON, DC, 73- *Mem:* Fel AAAS; sr mem Inst Elec & Electronics Engrs; assoc fel Am Inst Aeronaut & Astronaut; Am Soc Mech Engrs; sr mem Am Astron Soc. *Res:* Operations analysis; advanced systems planning; aerospace and environmental systems. *Mailing Add:* 543 Midland Ave Berwyn PA 19312

YOUTSEY, KARL JOHN, b Chicago, Ill, May 6, 39; m 69; c 2. PHYSICS. *Educ:* Loyola Univ, Chicago, BS, 61; Ill Inst Technol, MS, 65, PhD(physics), 68. *Prof Exp:* Physicist, Physics Dept, UOP Inc, 61-64, physicist, Mat Sci Lab, 68-73, dir mat sci, Corp Res, 73-75, dir prod & process develop, Wolverine Div, 75-79, VPRES & GEN MGR, AUTOMOTIVE PROD DIV, UOP INC, 79- *Mem:* Sigma Xi; Am Phys Soc; Am Soc Metals. *Res:* Electronic and physical properties of ceramics; fuel cell technology; solar thermal energy systems; thin film technology; laboratory and industrial automation systems and design. *Mailing Add:* 1647 Riverside Ct Glenview IL 60025

YOUTZ, BYRON LEROY, b Burbank, Calif, Nov 10, 25; m 51; c 3. NUCLEAR PHYSICS, ENERGY STUDIES. *Educ:* Calif Inst Technol, BS, 48; Univ Calif, Berkeley, PhD(physics), 53. *Prof Exp:* Res physicist, Lawrence Radiation Lab, Univ Calif, 50-53; asst prof physics, Am Univ Beirut, 53-56, actg chmn dept, 55-56; from asst prof to prof, Reed Col, 56-68, actg pres, 67-68; prof physics & acad vpres, State Univ NY Col Old Westbury, 68-70; interim acad dean, 73-74, PROF PHYSICS, DIV SCI, EVERGREEN STATE COL, 70-, VPRES & PROVOST, 78- *Concurrent Pos:* Guest, Japanese Phys Educ Soc & Asia Found Physics Curricula, 61 & 66; mem steering comt, Phys Sci Study Comn, 61-; consult, Educ Serv Inc, Mass, 61-; prin lectr, Sem Sec Sch Physics Curricula, Salisbury, Fedn Rhodesia & Nyasaland, 63 & Sem Advan Topics in Phys Sci Study Comt Physics, Santiago, Chile, 64; mem adv comt, Boston Univ Math Proj, 73- *Mem:* AAAS; Am Phys Soc; Am Asn Physics Teachers; Int Solar Energy Soc; Sigma Xi. *Res:* Astrophysics; nuclear structures; energy sources. *Mailing Add:* 6113 Buckthorn Ct NW Olympia WA 98502

YOVANOVITCH, DRASKO D, b Belgrade, Yugoslavia, May 24, 30; US citizen; m 54; c 2. HIGH ENERGY PHYSICS. *Educ:* Belgrade Univ, BSc, 52; Univ Chicago, MSc, 56, PhD(physics), 59. *Prof Exp:* Res assoc physics, Enrico Fermi Inst, Univ Chicago, 59-60; asst physicist, Univ Calif, San Diego, 60-62; assoc physicist, High Energy Physics Div, Argonne Nat Lab, 62-72; PHYSICIST, NAT ACCELERATOR LAB, 72-, CHMN, PHYS DEPT, 79- *Mem:* Fel Am Phys Soc. *Mailing Add:* Nat Accelerator Lab PO Box 500 Batavia IL 60510

YOVITS, MARSHALL CLINTON, b Brooklyn, NY, May 16, 23; m 52; c 3. COMPUTER SCIENCES. *Educ:* Union Col, BS, 44, MS, 48; Yale Univ, MS, 50, PhD(physics), 51. *Prof Exp:* Physicist, Nat Adv Comt for Aeronaut, Langley Field, Va, 44-46; instr physics, Union Col, 46-48; instr, Yale Univ, 48-50; sr physicist, Appl Physics Lab, Johns Hopkins Univ, 51-56; physicist, Off Naval Res, 56, head info systs br, 56-62, dir naval anal group, 62-66; PROF COMPUT & INFO SCI & CHMN DEPT, OHIO STATE UNIV, 66-; DEAN, PURDUE SCH SCI, IND UNIV-PURDUE UNIV, INDIANAPOLIS, 80- *Concurrent Pos:* Ed, Adv Comput, 70-; chmn comput sci conf, NSF, Columbus Ohio, 73; mem biomed comt study sect, NIH, 70-74. *Honors & Awards:* Outstanding Performance Award, US Navy, 61, Superior Civilian Serv Award, 64. *Mem:* Sr mem Inst Elec & Electronics Engrs; Asn Comput Mach; AAAS; Sigma Xi; Comput Soc. *Res:* Information systems; management information; self-organizing systems; information science; development of a generalized theory of information flow analysis; relating information to its use in decision-making. *Mailing Add:* 1201 E 38th St PO Box 647 Ind Univ Purdue Univ Indianapolis IN 46223

YOW, FRANCIS WAGONER, b Asheville, NC, May 1, 31; m 49; c 2. EMBRYOLOGY. *Educ:* Western Carolina Univ, BS, 55; Emory Univ, MS, 56, PhD(protozool), 58. *Prof Exp:* Asst prof biol, Western Carolina Col, 58-60; from asst prof to assoc prof, 60-65, chmn dept, 63-74, PROF BIOL, KENYON COL, 65- *Concurrent Pos:* Consult-examr, NCent Asn Cols & Univs, 71- *Mem:* AAAS; Soc Protozoologists; Am Soc Zoologists; Soc Develop Biol. *Res:* Morphogenesis in ciliate protozoa; radiation biology and nutrition of invertebrates; nucleic acid synthesis; inhibition of cellular activities by radiation and chemical means. *Mailing Add:* Dept of Biol Kenyon Col Gambier OH 43022

YOW, MARTHA DUKES, b Talbotton, Ga, Jan 15, 22; m 44; c 3. PEDIATRICS. *Educ:* Univ SC, BS, 40, MD, 43; Am Bd Pediat, dipl. *Prof Exp:* Instr bact, 49-50, instr pediat, 50-52, from instr to asst assoc prof, 55-69, PROF PEDIAT, BAYLOR COL MED, 69-, DIR PEDIAT INFECTIOUS DIS SECT, 64- *Concurrent Pos:* Res fel pediat, Baylor Col Med, 50-52, Jones fel, 55-; NIH grant; mem bd sci coun, Nat Inst Allergy & Infectious Dis. *Mem:* Am Fedn Clin Res; Am Soc Microbiol; Soc Pediat Res; Infectious Dis Soc Am; Am Acad Pediat. *Res:* Infectious diseases; applied virology. *Mailing Add:* Dept of Pediat Baylor Col of Med Houston TX 77030

YOZWIAK, BERNARD JAMES, b Youngstown, Ohio, July 5, 19; m 43; c 4. MATHEMATICS. *Educ:* Marietta Col, AB, 40; Univ Pittsburgh, MS, 51, PhD(math), 61. *Prof Exp:* Clerk, Youngstown Sheet & Tube Co, 40-41; high sch prin & teacher, Ohio, 41-42; civilian instr, US Army Air Forces Tech Training Command, Ill & Wis, 42-44; clerk, Youngstown Sheet & Tube Co, 44-45; high sch prin & teacher, Ohio, 45-47; from asst prof to assoc prof, 47-63, chmn dept, 66-71, PROF MATH, YOUNGSTOWN STATE UNIV, 63-, DEAN COL ARTS & SCI, 71- *Mem:* Math Asn Am; Sigma Xi. *Res:* Summability methods. *Mailing Add:* 2080 S Schenley Ave Youngstown OH 44511

YPHANTIS, DAVID ANDREW, b Boston, Mass, July 14, 30; m 53; c 5. BIOPHYSICS, BIOCHEMISTRY. *Educ:* Harvard Univ, AB, 52; Mass Inst Technol, PhD(biophys), 55. *Prof Exp:* Am Cancer Soc fel, Mass Inst Technol, 55-56; from asst biophysicist to assoc biophysicist, Argonne Nat Lab, 56-58; from asst prof to assoc prof biochem, Rockefeller Univ, 58-65; prof biol, State Univ NY Buffalo, 65-68, prof biophys & chmn dept biol, 67-68; PROF BIOL, UNIV CONN, 68- *Concurrent Pos:* Consult, Argonne Nat Lab, 58-62 & NIH, 67- *Mem:* AAAS; Am Chem Soc; Biophys Soc; Am Soc Biol Chem. *Res:* Physical biochemistry; protein physical chemistry; ultracentrifugation. *Mailing Add:* Biol Sci Group Univ of Conn Storrs CT 06268

YU, ALBERT TZENG-TYNG, b Taiwan, June 22, 40; m 64; c 2. PLANT BREEDING. *Educ:* Nat Chung-Hsing Univ, Taiwan, BS, 63; Univ Calif, Davis, MS, 70, PhD(genetics), 72. *Prof Exp:* Res assoc plant breeding, Chung-Hsing Univ, 65-66; res geneticist, Univ Calif, Davis, 72; plant breeder, Niagara Seeds, FMC Corp, 72-74; PLANT BREEDER, PETOSEED CO, INC, GEORGE BALL CORP, 74- *Mem:* Sigma Xi. *Res:* Plant breeding programs for summer squash, melons and peppers, both hot and sweet, including disease resistance. *Mailing Add:* Petoseed Co Rte 4 PO Box 1255 Woodland CA 95695

YU, ANDREW B C, b Nov 24, 45; US citizen. PHARMACEUTICS, BIOPHARMACEUTICS. *Educ:* Albany Col Pharm, BS, 71; Univ Conn, PhD(pharmaceut sci), 76. *Prof Exp:* Asst prof pharm, Northeastern Univ, 76-80; SR RES PHARMACIST, STERLING WINTHROP RES INST, 79- *Concurrent Pos:* Investr, NIH biomed res support grant, 77-78; co-investr res contract, Dooner Labs, 78-79; monograph writer, Am Pharmaceut Asn, Pharmaceut Excipient Codex Comt, 78-79. *Mem:* Am Pharmaceut Asn; NY Acad Sci; Am Asn Col Pharm; Sigma Xi. *Res:* Pharmacokinetics of drugs in renal diseased patients; use of antibiotics in the treatment of bacterial endocarditis. *Mailing Add:* Sterling Winthrop Res Inst Rennselaer NY 12203

YU, BYUNG PAL, b Ham Hung, Korea, June 27, 31; US citizen; m 59; c 1. BIOCHEMISTRY, CELL PHYSIOLOGY. *Educ:* Mo State Univ, BS, 60; Univ Ill, PhD, 65. *Prof Exp:* From res instr to res asst prof, Med Col Pa, 65-68, from asst prof to assoc prof, 68-73; assoc prof, 73-78, PROF PHYSIOL, UNIV TEX HEALTH SCI CTR SAN ANTONIO, 78- *Concurrent Pos:* Am Diabetes Asn res & career develop award. *Mem:* Am Physiol Soc. *Res:* Biological membrane structure; biological aspects of aging. *Mailing Add:* Dept of Physiol Univ of Tex Health Sci Ctr San Antonio TX 78284

YU, CHANG-AN, b Taiwan, Oct 19, 37; US citizen; m 68; c 2. BIOCHEMISTRY. *Educ:* Nat Taiwan Univ, BS, 61, MS, 64; Univ Ill, PhD(biochem), 69. *Prof Exp:* Fel biochem, Univ Ill, 69-70; vis asst prof chem, State Univ NY, 70-75, res assoc prof, 76-80; ASSOC PROF BIOCHEM, OKLA STATE UNIV, 81- *Mem:* Am Soc Biol Chemists. *Res:* Membrane bioenergetic; biological oxidation; ubiquinone; protein interaction; photosynthesis. *Mailing Add:* Dept Biochhem Okla State Univ Stillwater OK 74078

YU, CHIA-NIEN, b Shanghai, China, Aug 5, 31; US citizen; m 66; c 3. ORGANIC CHEMISTRY. *Educ:* Univ Ill, Urbana, BS, 58; Univ Mich, MS, 59. *Prof Exp:* Res chemist, 59-67, RES SCIENTIST, NORWICH PHARMACAL CO, 67- *Res:* Synthesis of organic compounds for biological screenings. *Mailing Add:* Norwich-Eaton Pharmaceut Norwich NY 13815

YU, CHIA-PING, b Kiangsu, China, Aug 21, 34; m 61; c 2. AERONAUTICAL ENGINEERING. *Educ:* Taiwan Norm Technol, BS, 54; Purdue Univ, PhD(aeronaut eng), 64. *Prof Exp:* Instr aeronaut eng, Purdue Univ, 60-64; from asst prof to assoc prof aeronaut & eng sci, 67-70, PROF ENG SCI, STATE UNIV NY BUFFALO, 70- *Mem:* Am Inst Aeronaut & Astronaut; Am Phys Soc; AAAS; Am Geophys Union. *Res:* Cosmical and engineering magnetohydrodynamics; waves and instabilities of plasma; atmospheric dynamics; aerosol mechanics; physics of fluids. *Mailing Add:* Dept of Eng Sci State Univ of NY Buffalo NY 14214

YU, DAVID U L, b Hong Kong, Aug 27, 40; nat US; m 65; c 2. NUCLEAR PHYSICS, STRUCTURAL MECHANICS. *Educ:* Seattle Pac Col, BSc, 61; Univ Wash, PhD(theoret physics), 64. *Prof Exp:* Res assoc prof theoret physics, Stanford Univ, 64-66; Brit Sci Res Coun fel physics, Univ Surrey,

66-67; from asst prof to assoc prof, Seattle Pac Col, 67-73; mgr, Comput Sci Corp, Richland, Washington & El Segundo, Calif, 73-75; EXEC VPRES & DIR, BASIC TECHNOL, INC, 75- *Concurrent Pos:* Vpres, Int Inst Technol, 77-; assoc prof, Univ Washington, 68-72; fel, Ford Found, 62-63, NASA Jet Propulsion Lab, 69-70 & NSF fel, Ill Inst Tech, 72. *Mem:* Am Phys Soc; Am Asn Physics Teachers; Am Soc Mech Engrs. *Res:* Nuclear structure and reactions; elementary particle physics. *Mailing Add:* Basic Technol Inc 806 Manhattan Beach Blvd Manhattan Beach CA 90266

YU, FRANCIS T S, b Amoy City, China, Nov 12, 32; US citizen; m 62; c 2. ELECTRICAL ENGINEERING. *Educ:* Mapua Inst Technol, BSEE, 56; Univ Mich, MSE, 58, PhD(elec eng), 64. *Prof Exp:* Res asst, Commun Sci Lab, Univ Mich, 58-64, res assoc engr, 64-66, instr elec eng, 60-64, lectr, 64-65; from asst prof to prof elec eng, Wayne State Univ, 66-80; PROF ELEC ENG, PA STATE UNIV, 80- *Mem:* fel Inst Elec & Electronics Engrs; Optical Soc Am. *Res:* Ferroelectric storage and reproducing processes; optical communication and filtering; optical information processing; holography; information theory. *Mailing Add:* Dept Elec Eng Pa State Univ University Park PA 16802

YU, FU-LI, b Peking, China, May 2, 34; US citizen. CHEMICAL CARCINOGENESIS. *Educ:* Taiwan Chung-Shing Univ, BS, 56; Univ Ala, MS, 62; Univ Calif, San Francisco, PhD(biochem), 65. *Prof Exp:* Instr biochem, Univ NMex, 65-66; fel trainee, Inst Cancer Res, Columbia Univ, 66-69, res assoc, 69-73; asst prof, Jefferson Med Col, 73-79; asst prof, 79-80, ASSOC PROF BIOCHEM, COL MED, UNIV ILL, 80- *Mem:* Am Soc Biol Chemists; Am Asn Cancer Res; Am Chem Soc; Harvey Soc; NY Acad Sci. *Res:* Chemical carcinogenesis; hormone action; nucleic acid metabolism; RNA polymerase; gene regulation in mammalian cells. *Mailing Add:* Dept Biomed Sci Univ Ill Col Med 1601 Parkview Ave Rockford IL 61107

YU, GEORGE C S, b Hupei, China, Oct 30, 37; US citizen; m 62; c 2. STATISTICS. *Educ:* Univ Nebr-Lincoln, BS, 60; Univ Md, College Park, PhD(statist), 69. *Prof Exp:* Actuarial analyst, Metrop Life Ins Co, 62-65; asst prof math, State Univ NY Albany, 69-73; sr statistician, Hoffmann-La Roche, Inc, 73-75, asst dir, Res Statistics Dept, 75-78; DIR BIOMETRICS, REVLON HEALTH CARE GROUP, 78- *Concurrent Pos:* Fac fel, State Univ NY Albany, 70, NSF res grant, 71-72; res assoc, Univ Calif, Berkeley, 72-73. *Mem:* Am Soc Qual Control; Am Statist Asn; Biomet Soc. *Res:* Non-parametric methods; time series analysis; statistical quality control; biostatistics; biometrics. *Mailing Add:* Dept Biometrics One Scarsdale Rd Tuckahoe NY 10707

YU, GRACE WEI-CHI HU, b Feb 10, 37; US citizen; m 62; c 1. BIOLOGY, MOLECULAR BIOLOGY. *Educ:* Nat Taiwan Univ, BS, 59; Wash State Univ, MS, 63; Duke Univ, PhD(plant physiol), 67. *Prof Exp:* Res assoc plant physiol, Duke Univ, 66-68; lectr bot, Sch Med, Univ Calif, Los Angeles, 68, res assoc plant physiol, 68-71, asst res biologist, Neuropsychiat Inst, 71-72, ment health training prog fel, Brain Res Inst, 72-78, res assoc hemat & oncol, Dept Pediat, 75-78; ASST PROF PLANT PHYSIOL, DEPT BIOL, CALIF STATE UNIV DOMINGUEZ HILLS, 78- *Concurrent Pos:* Comput prog cert, Control Data Inst, 82; instr biol, bot, human anat & physiol, Los Angeles Commun Col & Compton Commun Col, 78- *Mem:* AAAS; Am Soc Plant Physiologists; Sigma Xi. *Res:* Plant physiology, especially ion transport; developmental biology. *Mailing Add:* 30303 Via Borica Rancho Palos Verdes CA 90272

YU, GRETA, b Canton, China, Jan 12, 17; nat US. PHYSICS, OPERATIONS RESEARCH. *Educ:* Sun Yat-Sen Univ, BS, 38; Univ Ill, Univ MS, 40; Univ Cincinnati, PhD(physics), 43. *Prof Exp:* Spectroscopist, Wright Aeronaut Corp, 43-45; physicist, US Naval Ord Plant, 45-49; res physicist, Cornell Aeronaut Lab, Inc, 50-56; sr tech specialist & tech staff, NAm Aviation, Inc, 56-57, sr mem tech staff, NAm Rockwell Corp, 67-71; tech consult econ res, State Ohio, 71-74; STAFF SCIENTIST, OHIO POWER SITTING COMN, 74-, MEM SITTING BD, 80- *Mem:* Am Phys Soc; Opers Res Soc Am; Sigma Xi. *Res:* Energy and environment research; nuclear and fossil power siting and evaluation; applied physics. *Mailing Add:* 601 Fairway Blvd Columbus OH 43213

YU, HWA NIEN, b Shanghai, China, Jan 17, 29; m 55; c 3. ELECTRICAL ENGINEERING. *Educ:* Univ Ill, BS, 53, MS, 54, PhD(elec eng), 58. *Prof Exp:* Assoc engr, Res Lab, Int Bus Mach Corp, 57-59, staff engr, Adv Systs Develop Div, 59-62, res staff mem semiconductor develop, Res Ctr, 62-80, MGR DEVICE & CIRCUIT TECHNOL, T J WATSON RES CTR, IBM CORP, 80- *Res:* Computer design; semiconductor devices; electronic computers; semiconductors. *Mailing Add:* 2849 Hickory Yorktown Heights NY 10598

YU, HYUK, b Kapsan, Korea, Jan 20, 33; m 63; c 3. PHYSICAL CHEMISTRY, BIOPHYSICS. *Educ:* Seoul Nat Univ, BS, 55; Univ Southern Calif, MS, 58; Princeton Univ, PhD(phys chem), 62. *Prof Exp:* Res chemist, Nat Bur Stand, 63-67; asst prof, 67-69, assoc prof, 69-77, PROF CHEM, UNIV WIS-MADISON, 78- *Concurrent Pos:* Res assoc, Dartmouth Col, 62-63; Fulbright lectr, 72; consult, Nat Bur Standards, DC, Eastman Kodak Co, NY & Tenn Eastman Co. *Mem:* AAAS; Am Chem Soc; Am Phys Soc; NY Acad Sci. *Res:* Structure and dynamics of biomembranes; polymer solution characterizations; syntheses of macromolecules; polymer dynamics in bulk and concentrated solutions. *Mailing Add:* Dept of Chem Univ of Wis Madison WI 53706

YU, JAMES CHUN-YING, b Hunan, China, Oct 14, 40; US citizen; m 65; c 2. ACOUSTICS, FLUID DYNAMICS. *Educ:* Nat Taiwan Univ, BSc, 62; Syracuse Univ, MSc, 68, PhD(mech eng), 71. *Prof Exp:* Instr mech eng, Syracuse Univ, 70-71; asst res prof, George Washington Univ, 71-75, assoc res prof, 75-76, assoc prof, 76-77; AEROSPACE TECHNOLOGIST ACOUST, NASA LANGLEY RES CTR, 77- *Concurrent Pos:* NASA res grant, Langley Res Ctr, 71- *Mem:* Am Inst Aeronaut & Astronaut; Acoust Soc Am. *Res:* Sound generation from fluid flows; acoustic measurements and instrumentation; turbulent flows. *Mailing Add:* NASA Langley Res Ctr MS-460 Hampton VA 23365

YU, JASON C, b Hupei, China, Feb 5, 36; m 65; c 3. TRANSPORTATION ENGINEERING, CIVIL ENGINEERING. *Educ:* Univ Taiwan, BS, 57; Ga Inst Technol, MS, 63; Univ WVa, PhD(civil eng), 67. *Prof Exp:* Traffic engr, WVa State Rd Comn, 64-65; res assoc civil eng, Univ WVa, 66-67; res specialist transp eng, Univ Pa, 67-68; from asst prof to assoc prof civil eng, Va Polytech Inst & State Univ, 68-74; PROF CIVIL ENG, UNIV UTAH, 74- *Concurrent Pos:* Mem tech comt parking & traffic control devices, Transp Res Bd, Nat Acad Sci-Nat Res Coun, 69-; ed, External Transp, Int Joint Comt Tall Bldg, 73-81. *Mem:* Am Soc Civil Engrs; Inst Traffic Engrs; Am Soc Eng Educ. *Res:* Transportation energy conservation strategies; development of generalized travel demand models; effects of transportation on land use development; transportation system planning, design and operation. *Mailing Add:* Dept Civil Eng Univ Utah Salt Lake City UT 84112

YU, KAI FUN, b Canton, China, July 19, 50; m 78. STATISTICS, MATHEMATICS. *Educ:* Dartmouth Col, AB, 73; Columbia Univ, PhD(statist), 78. *Prof Exp:* ASST PROF STATIST, YALE UNIV, 78- *Mem:* Am Statist Asn; Inst Math Statist. *Mailing Add:* Dept of Statist Yale Univ New Haven CT 06520

YU, KARL KA-CHUNG, b Shanghai, China, Aug 31, 36; m 62; c 2. SOLID STATE ELECTRONICS, MATERIALS SCIENCE. *Educ:* Carnegie-Mellon Univ, BS, 57, MS, 59, PhD(elec eng, mat sci), 66. *Prof Exp:* Assoc engr, Westinghouse Elec Corp, 59-61, sr engr, 66-78; prin staff engr, McDonnell Douglas Corp, 78-79; SR STAFF PHYSICIST, HUGHES AIRCRAFT CO, 79- *Mem:* Inst Elec & Electronics Engrs. *Res:* Research and development in the area of solid state semiconductor device physics with emphasis on memory devices. *Mailing Add:* 2105 N Mantle Lane Santa Ana CA 92701

YU, LEEPO CHENG, b Shanghai, China, June 25, 39; m 65; c 1. BIOPHYSICS. *Educ:* Brown Univ, BS, 63; Univ Md, PhD(physics), 69. *Prof Exp:* Res assoc muscle physiol, Brown Univ, 69-72; staff fel, 73-75, sr staff fel, 76-77, RES PHYSICIST MUSCLE X-RAY DIFFRACTION, NAT INST ARTHRITIS, METAB & DIGESTIVE DIS, 77- *Mem:* Am Phys Soc; Biophys Soc. *Res:* X-ray diffraction of striated vertebrate muscle; theoretical modelling of force generation. *Mailing Add:* Lab of Phys Biol Nat Inst of Arthritis Metab & Digestive Dis Bethesda MD 20014

YU, LINDA SHU-WAN CHANG, b Taiwan, China, Feb 7, 43; m 68; c 2. BIOENERGETICS. *Educ:* Nat Taiwan Normal Univ, BS, 65; Univ Ill, MS, 68, PhD(microbiol), 70. *Prof Exp:* Res asst prof bioenergetics, Chem Dept, State Univ NY at Albany, 76-81; ASSOC PROF BIOENERGETICS, DEPT BIOCHEM, OKLA STATE UNIV, 81- *Mem:* Am Soc Microbiol. *Res:* Bioenergetics; protein phospholipids; ubiquinone proteins. *Mailing Add:* Dept Biochem Okla State Univ Stillwater OK 74078

YU, MANG CHUNG, b Hong Kong, Mar 4, 39; US citizen; m 66. ANATOMY, NEUROANATOMY. *Educ:* St Edward's Univ, BS, 63, MS, 66, PhD(anat), 70. *Prof Exp:* Fels, State Univ NY Buffalo, 70-72; ASST PROF ANAT, COL MED & DENT NJ, 72- *Concurrent Pos:* Consult neuroanat, Vet Admin Hosp, East Orange, NJ, 72- *Mem:* Am Physiol Soc; Am Soc Neurosci; AAAS; Am Asn Anat. *Res:* Neurobiology; neuropathology. *Mailing Add:* Dept of Anat Col of Med & Dent of NJ Newark NJ 07103

YU, MASON K, b Canton, China, Aug 2, 26; US citizen; m 50; c 5. MECHANICAL ENGINEERING. *Educ:* Univ Mich, BSME, 50, MSME, 51. *Prof Exp:* Engr, Borg-Warner Corp, 51-53; res engr, Continental Aviation Eng Corp, 53-55; SR RES ENGR, EMISSIONS RES DEPT, GEN MOTORS RES LABS, 55- *Mem:* Am Soc Mech Engrs. *Res:* Computer application to gas turbine thermodynamic turbomachinery research and development. *Mailing Add:* Emissions Res Dept 12 Mile & Mound Rds Warren MI 48090

YU, MING LUN, b Hong Kong, Aug 21, 45; m 78; c 1. SOLID STATE PHYSICS. *Educ:* Hong Kong Univ, BSc, 67; Calif Inst Technol, MSc, 71, PhD(physics), 74. *Prof Exp:* Res assoc, Brookhaven Nat Lab, 73-74, asst physicist, 74-76, assoc physicist, 76-78; RES STAFF MEM, T J WATSON RES CTR, IBM CORP, 78- *Concurrent Pos:* Vis scientist, Physics Dept, State Univ NY, Stony Brook, 76-79. *Mem:* Am Phys Soc; Am Vacuum Soc. *Res:* Superconductivity; Josephson devices; secondary ion mass spectrometry. *Mailing Add:* IBM Res Ctr PO Box 218 Yorktown Heights NY 10598

YU, MING-HO, b Kaohsiung, Taiwan, May 22, 28; m 56; c 3. ENVIRONMENTAL HEALTH, NUTRITION. *Educ:* Nat Taiwan Univ, BS, 53; Utah State Univ, MS, 64, PhD(nutrit & biochem), 67. *Prof Exp:* Res asst agr chem, Taiwan Agr Res Inst, 54-55; asst res fel chem, Inst Chem Acad Sinica, 59-62; fel, Utah State Univ, 67 & Univ Alta, 67-68; vis asst prof plant biochem, 69-70, lectr environ biol, 70-71, asst prof, 71-74, assoc prof, 74-79, PROF ENVIRON BIOL, HUXLEY COL, WESTERN WASH UNIV, 79- *Mem:* AAAS; Am Pub Health Asn; Int Soc Fluoride Res. *Res:* Fluoride effects on the physiology and biochemistry of animals and plants; effects of pollutants on health; vitamin C metabolism. *Mailing Add:* Huxley Col Western Wash Univ Bellingham WA 98225

YU, MING-HUNG, plant cytogenetics, see previous edition

YU, NAI-TENG, b Pingtung, Formosa, Aug 19, 39; m 66. BIOPHYSICAL CHEMISTRY. *Educ:* Nat Taiwan Univ, BS, 63; NMex Highlands Univ, MS, 66; Mass Inst Technol, PhD(phys chem), 69. *Prof Exp:* Res chemist, Arthur D Little, Mass, 66; res assoc chem, Mass Inst Technol, 69-70; asst prof, 70-75, assoc prof, 75-80, PROF CHEM, GA INST TECHNOL, 80- *Concurrent Pos:* Res Corp res grant, Ga Inst Technol, 71-72, USPHS res grant, 71-82; res career develop award, NIH, 76-81. *Mem:* AAAS; Am Chem Soc; Biophys Soc; Asn Res Vision & Ophthal. *Res:* Laser Raman spectroscopy of biopolymers; temperature-jump relaxation kinetics; mechanisms of cataract lens formation. *Mailing Add:* Sch of Chem Ga Inst of Technol Atlanta GA 30332

YU, OLIVER SHUKIANG, b Chentu, China, July 8, 39; m 62; c 1. OPERATIONS RESEARCH, ELECTRICAL ENGINEERING. *Educ:* Nat Taiwan Univ, BSEE, 59; Ga Inst Technol, MSEE, 62; Stanford Univ, MS, 67, PhD(opers res), 72. *Prof Exp:* Res assoc civil defense study, Merrimack Col, 63-64; opers analyst, Opers Anal Dept, Stanford Res Inst, 64-68, res engr, Systs Eval Dept, 68-70, sr res engr, 70-74; proj mgr, Elec Power Res Inst, 74-77; planning specialist, Commonwealth Edison Co, 77; asst tech proj mgr, Res & Develop Planning & Assessment Dept, 78, tech mgr, Energy Study Ctr, 78-79, MGR PLANNING ANAL, ELEC POWER RES INST, 79- *Concurrent Pos:* Consult systs anal, SRI Int, 75; adj prof, Univ Calif, Berkeley, 80-81, Santa Clara Univ, 75-81, Calif State Univ, Hayward, 75-79 & San Jose State Univ, 79-81; Fulbright fel, 61-62. *Mem:* Sigma Xi; Inst Elec & Electronics Engrs; Opers Res Soc Am. *Res:* Planning, analysis and evaluation of large-scale systems program development and direction of systems analysis research. *Mailing Add:* Elec Power Res Inst PO Box 10412 Palo Alto CA 94303

YU, PAO-LO, b Shanghai, China, Feb 1, 24; US citizen; m 59; c 3. GENETICS, BIOSTATISTICS. *Educ:* Nanking Univ, BS, 47; Univ Minn, Minneapolis, MS, 54; NC State Univ, PhD(statist), 61. *Prof Exp:* Res asst exp statist, NC State Univ, 56-58; statistician, John L Smith Mem Cancer Res, Chas Pfizer & Co, 58-64; asst prof, 64-68, ASSOC PROF MED GENETICS, SCH MED, IND UNIV, INDIANAPOLIS, 68- *Mem:* Am Statist Asn; Biomet Soc; Am Soc Human Genetics. *Res:* Human gene mapping; determination of the genetics of quantitative traits; development of statistical methods for genetic study. *Mailing Add:* Dept of Med Genetics Ind Univ Med Ctr Indianapolis IN 46202

YU, PAUL N, b Kiangsi, China, Nov 17, 15; nat US; m 44; c 4. INTERNAL MEDICINE, CARDIOLOGY. *Educ:* Nat Med Col Shanghai, China, MD, 39; London Sch Trop Med & Hyg, 46, dipl, 47; Am Bd Internal Med, dipl, 56, cert cardiovasc dis, 57. *Prof Exp:* Instr med, asst resident & chief resident physician, Cen Hosp, Chunking, China, 40; asst resident physician, Hosp, 47, from instr to prof med, 48-69, SARA McCORT WARD PROF MED, SCH MED, UNIV ROCHESTER, 69-, HEAD CARDIOL UNIT & PHYSICIAN, HOSP, 63- *Concurrent Pos:* Hochstetter fel, Sch Med, Univ Rochester, 48-54; consult, State Depts Health & Social Welfare, NY, 55-, Genesee Hosp, Rochester, 57-, Vet Admin Hosp, Bath, 59-, Highland Hosp, Rochester, Frederick Thompson Mem Hosp, Canandaigua & Newark Community Hosps & St Mary's Hosp; from asst to sr assoc physician, Univ Rochester Hosp, 52-63, founding fel coun clin cardiol, Am Heart Asn; ed, Progress in Cardiol. *Mem:* Fel Am Col Physicians; sr mem Am Fedn Clin Res; Asn Am Physicians; Am Clin & Climatol Asn; Am Heart Asn (pres, 72-73). *Res:* Pulmonary circulation, hemodynamics; electrocardiography. *Mailing Add:* Dept of Med Univ of Rochester Sch of Med Rochester NY 14642

YU, PETER HAO, b Liaoning, China, May 26, 42; Can citizen; m 70; c 3. BIOCHEMISTRY, BIOLOGY. *Educ:* Nat Taiwan Univ, BSc, 64, MSc, 67; Univ Göttingen, DSc Agr(biol), 71. *Prof Exp:* Res scientist, Asn Molecular Biol Res, Ger, 71-73; assoc prof, Nat Taiwan Univ, 73-75; SR RES SCIENTIST, PSYCHIAT RES DIV, CAN DEPT HEALTH, 75- *Concurrent Pos:* Consult, Res Prog Directorate, Health & Welfare, Can, 77-; res assoc, Dept Psychiat, Univ Sask, 78- *Res:* Regulation of metabolism of catecholamine and the possible relationship to mental disorder. *Mailing Add:* Psychiat Res Div University Hosp Saskatoon SK S7N 0W8 Can

YU, PETER YOUND, b Shanghai, China, Sept 8, 44; m 71; c 1. EXPERIMENTAL SOLID STATE PHYSICS, SEMICONDUCTORS. *Educ:* Univ Hong Kong, BSc, 66 & 67; Brown Univ, PhD(physics), 72. *Prof Exp:* Fel, Univ Calif, Berkeley, 71-72, lectr physics, 72-73; res staff mem, Thomas J Watson Res Ctr, IBM Corp, 73-80; ASSOC PROF PHYSICS, UNIV CALIF, BERKELEY, 80- *Mem:* Am Phys Soc; Sigma Xi. *Res:* Optical properties and light scattering of semiconductors. *Mailing Add:* Phys Dept Univ Calif Berkeley CA 94720

YU, RILEY CHAOPING, neurobiology, genetics, see previous edition

YU, ROBERT KUAN-JEN, b China, Jan 27, 38; m 72. BIOCHEMISTRY, NEUROCHEMISTRY. *Educ:* Tunghai Univ, Taiwan, BS, 60; Univ Ill, Urbana, PhD(chem), 67. *Hon Degrees:* ScD, Toyko Univ, 80. *Prof Exp:* Res assoc neurol biochem, Albert Einstein Col Med, 68-69; from instr to asst prof, 69-75, ASSOC PROF NEUROL BIOCHEM, MED SCH, YALE UNIV, 75- *Concurrent Pos:* NIH fel, Albert Einstein Col Med, 67-68; Mary Fulton fel, William Randolph Hearst Found. *Honors & Awards:* Kitasoto Medal. *Mem:* AAAS; Am Chem Soc; Am Soc Neurochem; NY Acad Sci; Int Soc Neurochem. *Res:* Chemistry and metabolism of sphingolipids in the central nervous system, parasynpathetic nervous system and body fluids; sphingolipidosis; ionic properties of lipids in solution and membrane. *Mailing Add:* Dept of Neurol Yale Sch of Med New Haven CT 06510

YU, RUEY JIIN, b Hsin-chu, Taiwan, Mar 23, 32; m 59; c 3. CLINICAL PHARMACOLOGY. *Educ:* Nat Taiwan Univ, BSc, 56, MSc, 60; Univ Ottawa, PhD(org chem), 65. *Prof Exp:* Lectr chem, Nat Univ Taiwan, 61-62; Nat Res Coun Can fel, 65-67; asst prof, 67-73, ASSOC PROF DERMAT, SKIN & CANCER HOSP, TEMPLE UNIV, 73- *Mem:* Soc Invest Dermat. *Res:* Dermatopharmacology for skin disorders, such as psoriasis, acne and ichthyosis. *Mailing Add:* Skin & Cancer Hosp 3322 N Broad St Philadelphia PA 19140

YU, SHARON S M, b Taiwan; US citizen. BIOCHEMISTRY. *Educ:* City Univ New York, PhD(biochem), 75. *Prof Exp:* RES ASSOC, NEW YORK BLOOD CTR, LINDSLEY F KIMBALL RES INST, 75- *Res:* Biosynthesis of plasma proteins. *Mailing Add:* New York Blood Ctr 310 E 67th St New York NY 10021

YU, SHIH-AN, b Hupei, China, May 10, 27; m 55. BOTANY. *Educ:* Nat Taiwan Univ, BS, 50; Univ NH, MS, 56, PhD(hort), 59. *Prof Exp:* Res assoc forage breeding, Mich State Univ, 59-64; lectr bot, Univ Mich, Ann Arbor, 65-66, res assoc, 66-67; asst prof, 67-70, assoc prof, 70-75, PROF BIOL, EASTERN MICH UNIV, 75- *Res:* Fungal genetics and molecular genetics. *Mailing Add:* Dept of Biol Eastern Mich Univ Ypsilanti MI 48197

YU, SHIU YEH, b Formosa, China, June 1, 26; nat US; m 60. BIOCHEMISTRY, ORGANIC CHEMISTRY. *Educ:* Provincial Col Agr, China, BS, 51; Okla State Univ, MS, 56; St Louis Univ, PhD, 63. *Prof Exp:* Chemist & res assoc, Indust Res Inst, Formosa, 51-52; res asst, Okla State Univ, 52-56; res assoc, Inst Exp Path, Jewish Hosp, St Louis, 56-60; fel, Med Sch, St Louis Univ, 61-62; BIOCHEMIST, VET ADMIN HOSP, JEFFERSON BARRACKS, 63- *Concurrent Pos:* Clin biochem consult, St Louis State Hosp & Sch; res asst prof, Sch Med, Washington Univ, 72-; instr, Forest Park Community Col, 73- *Mem:* Geront Soc; Electron Micros Soc Am; Am Soc Exp Path; Am Heart Asn; Brit Biochem Soc. *Res:* Immunology; biochemistry of arteriosclerosis; structure of elastin and chemistry of elastase; mechanism of delayed hypersensitivity; mechanism of antibody formation. *Mailing Add:* Vet Admin Hosp Jefferson Barracks St Louis MO 63125

YU, SIMON SHIN-LUN, b Hong Kong, Mar 24, 45; US citizen; m 70. PHYSICS. *Educ:* Seattle Pac Univ, BSc, 67; Univ Wash, Seattle, MSc & PhD(physics), 70. *Prof Exp:* Res asst physics, Seattle Pac Univ, 64-67; fel, Univ Wash, 70-73; res assoc, Univ Pittsburgh, 73-77; PHYSICIST, LAWRENCE LIVERMORE LAB, 77- *Mem:* Am Phys Soc. *Res:* Theoretical physics. *Mailing Add:* Lawrence Livermore Lab Livermore CA 94550

YU, SIMON SHYI-JIAN, b Lotung, Taiwan, Sept 11, 35; US citizen; m 67; c 2. BIOCHEMICAL TOXICOLOGY, INSECTICIDE TOXICOLOGY. *Educ:* Nat Taiwan Univ, BS, 59; McGill Univ, MS, 65, PhD(entom), 68. *Prof Exp:* Res entomologist, Taiwan Sugar Co, 61-62; res asst toxicol, McGill Univ, 63-68; fel toxicol, Cornell Univ, 68-69; res assoc toxicol, Ore State Univ, 69-74, asst prof, 74-79; ASST PROF TOXICOL, UNIV FLA, 80- *Concurrent Pos:* Prin investr, Univ Fla, 81- *Mem:* Entom Soc Am; AAAS. *Res:* Biochemical toxicology of insects and related species, including detoxication mechanisms, enzyme induction, insecticide metabolism, insecticide resistance, insect-host plant interactions and purification of detoxifying enzymes. *Mailing Add:* Dept Entom & Nematol Univ Fla Gainesville FL 32611

YU, TS'AI-FAN, b Shanghai, China, Oct 24, 11; nat US. MEDICINE, METABOLISM. *Educ:* Ginling Col, China, BA, 32; Peiping Union Med Col, China, MD, 36. *Prof Exp:* From intern to chief resident med, Peiping Union Med Col, 35-40; instr med, Col Physicians & Surgeons, Columbia Univ, 50-56, assoc, 56-59, asst prof, 60-66; assoc prof, 66-73, RES PROF, MT SINAI SCH MED, 73- *Mem:* Am Physiol Soc; Am Soc Pharmacol & Exp Therapeut; Harvey Soc; Am Soc Nephrol; Am Rheumatism Asn. *Res:* Calcium and phosphorous metabolism in osteomalacia; purine metabolism and gout. *Mailing Add:* Mt Sinai Hosp 11 E 100th St New York NY 10029

YU, WEI WEN, b Shantung, China, July 10, 24; US citizen; m 53; c 3. STRUCTURAL ENGINEERING. *Educ:* Taiwan Norm Technol, BS, 50; Okla State Univ, MS, 55; Cornell Univ, PhD(struct eng), 60. *Prof Exp:* Teaching asst civil eng, Taiwan Norm Technol, 50-54; struct designer, T H McKaig & Assocs, NY, 55-56 & 59-60; res asst struct, Cornell Univ, 57-59; engr, Am Iron & Steel Inst, 60-67; staff engr, TRW, Inc, 67-68; assoc prof, 68-72, PROF CIVIL ENG, UNIV MO-ROLLA, 72- *Concurrent Pos:* Lectr, City Col New York, 64-65. *Mem:* Am Soc Civil Engrs; Am Concrete Inst. *Res:* Cold-formed steel structures; semi-rigid connection of steel framing; deflection of reinforced concrete beams; steel structures. *Mailing Add:* Dept of Civil Eng Univ of Mo Rolla MO 65401

YU, WEN-SHI, b Shanghai, China, Nov 17, 34; US citizen. CHEMICAL ENGINEERING. *Educ:* Nat Taiwan Univ, BS, 56; Pratt Inst, MS, 58; Polytech Inst Brooklyn, PhD(chem eng), 64. *Prof Exp:* ENGR, BROOKHAVEN NAT LAB, 61- *Mem:* Women Engrs; Sigma Xi. *Res:* Heat-transfer of forced-convection with liquid metals in the nuclear and space fields; heat transfer of single-phase and two-phase (boiling) flow; computer coding in applied science field; research development of hydrogen storage systems; thermal storage study and safety studies in the controlled thermal reactor program. *Mailing Add:* Brookhaven Nat Lab Upton NY 11973

YU, YI-YUAN, b China, Jan 29, 23; nat US; m 52; c 2. ENGINEERING MECHANICS, AEROSPACE ENGINEERING. *Educ:* Univ Tientsin, China, BS, 44; Northwestern Univ, MS, 50, PhD(eng mech), 51. *Prof Exp:* Res assoc, Northwestern Univ, 51; asst prof appl mech, Washington Univ, St Louis, 51-54; assoc prof, Syracuse Univ, 54-57; prof, Polytech Inst Brooklyn, 57-66; consult engr, Gen Elec Co, 66-71; distinguished prof aeronaut eng, Wichita State Univ, 72-75; mgr eng, Rocketdyne Div, Rockwell Int, 75-79, exec eng, Energy Systs Group, 79-81; DEAN, NEWARK COL ENG, NJ INST TECHNOL, 81- *Concurrent Pos:* Guggenheim fel, 59-60; consult, US Naval Appl Sci Lab, 63-69; lectr, Gen Elec Mod Eng Course, 63-73; adv, Mid East Tech Univ, Turkey, 66; mem ad hoc comt dynamic shock anal, US Navy, 67-68. *Mem:* Assoc fel Am Inst Aeronaut & Astronaut; Am Soc Mech Engrs; Am Soc Eng Educ; NY Acad Sci. *Res:* Stress and vibration analysis; theory of elasticity; theory of plates and shells; dynamics and control of structural and mechanical systems; laser dynamics. *Mailing Add:* NJ Inst Technol 323 High St Newark NJ 07102

YU, YUN-SHENG, b I-Hsing, Kiangsu, China, Nov 21, 26; US citizen; m 60; c 4. FLUID MECHANICS, WATER RESOURCES. *Educ:* Nat Taiwan Univ, BS, 53; Univ Iowa, MS, 56; Mass Inst Technol, ScD(civil eng), 60. *Prof Exp:* Res assoc hydraul, Iowa Inst Hydraul Res, 56-57; res assoc hydrodyn lab, Mass Inst Technol, 59-60; assoc prof fluid mech, 60-64, PROF FLUID MECH, UNIV KANS, 64- *Concurrent Pos:* Consult, US Army Tank-Automotive Ctr, 66; vis prof, Univ Mich, 67; vis prof, Qinghua Univ, Beizing, China, 80-81. *Mem:* AAAS; Am Soc Eng Educ; Am Geophys Union; Am Water Resources Asn. *Res:* Theoretical and applied hydrodynamics; water pollution; water resources systems analysis. *Mailing Add:* Dept of Civil Eng Univ of Kans 208 Learned Hall Lawrence KS 66045

YUAN, EDWARD LUNG, b China, July 2, 29; US citizen; m 54; c 2. PHYSICAL CHEMISTRY. *Educ:* Univ Calif, Berkeley, BS, 51; Univ Wis-Madison, PhD(phys chem), 54. *Prof Exp:* Res assoc high temperature kinetics, Univ Wis, 54-55; res chemist, 55-62, staff chemist, 63-68, res assoc, 68-72, RES FEL HIGH TEMPERATURE POLYMER APPLNS, E I DU PONT DE NEMOURS & CO, INC, 72- *Mem:* Am Chem Soc. *Res:* Electronics and high temperature materials; polymer chemistry; high temperature polymers; film formation mechanisms; electrical and electronics materials technology. *Mailing Add:* E I du Pont de Nemours & Co 3500 Grays Ferry Ave Philadelphia PA 19146

YUAN, JIAN-MIN, b Chungking, China, Aug 31, 44; m 71; c 2. CHEMICAL PHYSICS, LASER PHYSICS. *Educ:* Nat Taiwan Univ, BS, 66, MS, 68; Univ Chicago, PhD(chem physics), 73. *Prof Exp:* Fel scattering theory, Quantum Theory Proj, Univ Fla, 73-75; instr & res assoc laser interaction, Dept Chem, Univ Rochester, 75-78; ASST PROF PHYSICS, DEPT PHYSICS & ATMOSPHERIC SCI, DREXEL UNIV, 78- *Mem:* Am Phys Soc; Am Chem Soc; Sigma Xi. *Res:* Interaction of atomic and molecular dynamics with an intense laser field; molecular scattering theories; semiclassical approach and Faddeev equations approach; surface physics; nonlinear dynamics. *Mailing Add:* Dept of Physics & Atmospheric Sci Drexel Univ Philadelphia PA 19104

YUAN, LUKE CHIA LIU, b Changtehfu, China, Apr 5, 12; US citizen; m 42; c 1. PHYSICS. *Educ:* Yenching Univ, BS, 32, MS, 34; Calif Inst Technol, PhD(physics), 40. *Prof Exp:* Asst physics, Yenching Univ, 32-34; asst, Calif Inst Technol, 37-40, fel, 40-42; res physicist, RCA Labs, 42-46; res assoc, Princeton Univ, 46-49; SR PHYSICIST, BROOKHAVEN NAT LAB, UPTON, 49- *Concurrent Pos:* Guggenheim fel, 58; vis physicist, Europ Orgn Nuclear Res, 72-76. *Honors & Awards:* Achievement Award, Chinese Inst Elec Eng, 62. *Mem:* Fel Am Phys Soc; Acad Sinica; NY Acad Sci. *Res:* High energy physics; super energy accelerator and particle detection systems; cosmic rays; radio direction finding; frequency modulation radar systems. *Mailing Add:* 194 Bay Ave Patchogue NY 11772

YUAN, PAUL MIAU, b Canton, China, June 6, 49; m 74; c 2. BIOCHEMISTRY. *Educ:* Nat Cheng-Kong Univ, 72; NTex State Univ, PhD(biochem), 78. *Prof Exp:* Teaching & res asst enzyme & protein chem, Dept Chem, NTex State Univ, 74-78, fel, 78-80; res fel, 80-81, ASST RES SCIENTIST PROTEIN CHEM, DIV IMMUNOL, CITY OF HOPE RES INST, 81- *Mem:* Am Chem Soc. *Res:* Structural functional relationship of biological active proteins and peptides. *Mailing Add:* 2222 E Huntington Dr D41 Duarte CA 91010

YUAN, ROBERT L, b Nanking, China, US citizen; m 68; c 2. ENGINEERING, STRUCTURAL CONCRETE MATERIALS. *Educ:* Cheng Kung Univ, Taiwan, BS, 60; Univ Ill, Urbana, MS, 64, PhD(theoret & appl mech), 68. *Prof Exp:* Res assoc concrete res, Univ Ill, 67-68; asst prof, 68-74, assoc prof, 74-81, PROF CIVIL ENG, UNIV TEX, ARLINGTON, 81- *Mem:* Am Concrete Inst; Soc Exp Stress Anal; Am Soc Civil Eng. *Res:* Concrete and new building material research. *Mailing Add:* Dept Civil Eng PO Box 19308 Univ of Tex Arlington TX 76019

YUAN, SHAO WEN, b Shanghai, China, Apr 16, 14; nat US; m 50. AEROSPACE ENGINEERING. *Educ:* Univ Mich, BS, 36; Calif Inst Technol, MS, 37, PhD(aeronaut), 41; Stanford Univ, AE, 39. *Prof Exp:* Aero engr, Vultee Aircraft Corp, Calif, 37-38; chief struct engr, Timm Aircraft Co, 40-41; res engr, Vidal Res Corp, NJ, 41-42 & Glenn L Martin Co, Md, 42-43; chief vibration & res helicopter div, McDonnell Aircraft Corp, 43-45; res adv, Poly- tech Inst Brooklyn, 45-49, assoc prof aeronaut, 49-54, prof, 54-67; Hon Canadair Chair prof, Laval Univ, 57-58; prof aerospace eng, Univ Tex, 58-67; pres, Yuan Assocs, Calif, 67-68; chmn dept, 68-79, PROF MECH ENG & APPL SCI, GEORGE WASHINGTON UNIV, 68-; PRES, RESIDENTIAL & INDUST SOLAR ENERGY, INC, 79- *Concurrent Pos:* Consult, Aerojet Corp, Cornell Aeronaut Lab, US Dept Interior, Oak Ridge Nat Lab, NAm Aviation, Inc & Fairchild-Hiller Corp; hon adv, Nat Ctr Res China, Taiwan. *Mem:* Fel AAAS; assoc fel Am Inst Aeronaut & Astronaut; Am Soc Mech Engrs; Soc Eng Sci (pres, 77). *Res:* Solar energy earth storage and utilization; ground cold storage and utilization; airfold development; mass and heat transfer; fluid mechanics; magnetohydrodynamics; hypervelocity impact; Martin-Yuan low drag airfoil; Karman-Yuan helicopter rotor; jet circulation control rotor; high speed rotor; jet circulation control hydrofoil; vehicle control; wing-tip vortex control. *Mailing Add:* Sch of Eng & Appl Sci George Washington Univ Washington DC 20052

YUAN, SHAO-YUEN, b Shanghai, China, July 30, 29; US citizen; m 49; c 2. CHEMICAL ENGINEERING. *Educ:* Ill Inst Technol, BS, 50; Univ Louisville, MS, 51. *Prof Exp:* Res engr, E I du Pont de Nemours, 51-56; from res engr to sr res engr, Chevron Res Co, 56-66, supvr prod develop & tech serv, Chevron Chem Co, 66-69, sr proj engr, 69-75, staff engr, 75-78, sr staff engr, 78-81, REGIONAL EXEC, CHEVRON RES CO, STANDARD OIL CALIF, 81- *Mem:* Am Inst Chem Engrs; Am Chem Soc. *Mailing Add:* Chevron Res Co 525 Market St San Francisco CA 94105

YUAN, TZU-LIANG, b Ningpo, China, May 27, 22; nat US; m 60; c 2. SOILS. *Educ:* Nat Univ Chekiang, China, BSc, 45; Ohio State Univ, MSc, 52, PhD(agron), 55. *Prof Exp:* Asst instr soils, Nat Univ Chekiang, China, 45; instr, Nat Univ, Kweichow, 46-48; asst soils chemist, Taiwan Sugar Exp Sta, 48-51; res asst, Ohio Agr Exp Sta, 52-55; from asst prof to prof soil chem, 55-72, PROF SOIL SCI, UNIV FLA, 72- *Mem:* Fel AAAS; Soil Sci Soc Am; Clay Minerals Soc; NY Acad Sci; Int Soil Sci Soc. *Res:* Soil-forming processes; chemical nature of soils; soil properties in relation to plant nutrition. *Mailing Add:* Dept of Soil Sci Univ of Fla Gainesville FL 32611

YUAN, WILLIAM JEN CHUN, b Kiangsu Prov, Repub of China; US citizen. MATHEMATICAL STATISTICS, MEDICAL STATISTICS. *Educ:* Cheng Kung Univ, Taiwan, BA, 62; Wayne State Univ, MA, 66; Univ Calif, Berkeley, PhD(statist), 74. *Prof Exp:* Statistician & programmer, Texaco, Inc, 66-67; opers res analyst, Teknekron, Inc, 68-70; from teaching asst to teaching assoc statist, Univ Calif, Berkeley, 67-73; lectr statist, Univ Calif, Davis, 73-74; asst prof statist, State Univ NY, Stony Brook, 74-77; sr statistician, Comput & Info Sci, Schering Corp, 77-79; ASSOC DIR BIOSTATIST, IVES LABS, INC, 79- *Mem:* Sigma Xi; Inst Math Statist; Am Statist Asn. *Res:* Comparisons of statistical methods, nonparametric statistics, data analysis, biostatistics, analysis of categorized data, design of experiment, and sampling. *Mailing Add:* Ives Labs Inc 685 3rd Ave New York NY 10017

YUCEOGLU, YUSUF ZIYA, b Cesme, Turkey, Mar 28, 19; m 47. INTERNAL MEDICINE, CARDIOLOGY. *Educ:* Istanbul Univ, MD, 44. *Prof Exp:* Intern, Istanbul Univ Hosp, 43-44; resident internal med, Ankara Univ Hosp, 47-50, spec asst, 50-52; fel cardiol, Mt Sinai Hosp, New York, 53-55; res fel, Cardiopulmonary Lab, Maimonides Hosp, 55-57; NY Heart Asn fel, 55-57; from res assoc to assoc, Maimonides Hosp, 57-60, from asst attend physician to assoc attend physician, 61-67, dir cardiopulmonary lab, 66-67; ASSOC PROF MED, NEW YORK MED COL, 67- *Concurrent Pos:* From instr to asst prof med, State Univ NY Downstate Med Ctr, 55-67; asst attend physician, Kings County Hosp, 66-67; assoc attend physician, Flower & Fifth Ave Hosps, 67- & Metrop Hosps, 67- *Honors & Awards:* Cert Honor, Am Col Angiol & Int Col Angiol, 65. *Mem:* AMA; fel Am Col Cardiol; fel Am Col Angiol. *Res:* Cardiac physiology; vectorcardiography. *Mailing Add:* 330 E 33rd New York NY 10016

YUDELSON, JOSEPH SAMUEL, b Philadelphia, Pa, July 20, 25; m 52; c 4. POLYMER CHEMISTRY, PHOTOCHEMISTRY. *Educ:* Univ Pittsburgh, BS, 50; Ill Inst Technol, PhD(chem), 55. *Prof Exp:* Res chemist, 54-57, sr res chemist, 57-60, res assoc phys chem, 60-70, sr lab head, 70-80, SR RES ASSOC, SOLID STATE PHOTOSCI LAB, EASTMAN KODAK RES LAB, 80- *Mem:* Assoc Am Chem Soc; Soc Photog Scientists & Engrs. *Res:* Physical chemistry of hydrophilic polymers; photographic chemistry; nonaqueous solvents; inorganic photochemistry. *Mailing Add:* Eastman Kodak Co 1669 Lake Ave Rochester NY 14650

YUE, A(LFRED) S(HUI-CHOH), b Canton, China, Nov 12, 20; m 44; c 3. METALLURGY. *Educ:* Chao-Tung Univ, China, BS, 42; Ill Inst Technol, MS, 50; Purdue Univ, PhD(metall eng), 57. *Prof Exp:* Instr metall eng, Purdue Univ, 52-56; res metallurgist, Dow Chem Co, 56-62; res scientist, Lockheed Palo Alto Res Lab, 62-63, staff scientist, 63-66, sr mem, 66-69; PROF MAT SCI, UNIV CALIF, LOS ANGELES, 69- *Concurrent Pos:* Hon prof, Xian Jiao-tong Univ, China. *Mem:* Am Inst Aeronaut & Astronaut; Am Inst Mining, Metall & Petrol Eng; AAAS; NY Acad Sci; Am Soc Metals. *Res:* Development and characterization of semiconductor materials for energy conversion via the photovoltaic effect and detector application; preparation of p-n homo- and heterojunctions via the liquid- phase-epitaxial, chemical vapor deposition, close-space-vapor-transport and the directional solidification techniques. *Mailing Add:* 6532 Boelter Hall Univ Calif Los Angeles CA 90024

YUE, ON-CHING, b Macao, Apr 9, 47; US citizen; m 73; c 1. ELECTRICAL ENGINEERING. *Educ:* Cooper Union, BEE, 68; Rochester Inst Technol, MSEE, 71; Univ Calif, San Diego, PhD(info sci), 77. *Prof Exp:* Sr engr, Electronics Div, Gen Dynamics Corp, 68-77; MEM TECH STAFF, BELL LABS, 77- *Mem:* Inst Elec & Electronics Engrs. *Res:* Digital radio communication systems; communication theory; probability theory. *Mailing Add:* Bell Labs PO Box 400 Holmdel NJ 07733

YUE, ROBERT HON-SANG, b Canton, China, Sept 9, 37; US citizen; m 70; c 3. BIOCHEMISTRY. *Educ:* ETex Baptist Col, BS, 61; Univ Utah, PhD(biol chem), 68. *Prof Exp:* Res assoc biochem, Study Hereditary & Metab Dis, Univ Utah, 68-70; assoc res scientist, Inst Rehab Med, NY Univ Med Ctr, 70-72, res scientist, 72-73, res asst prof, 73-76, res assoc prof rehab med, 76-81; RES BIOCHEMIST, REVLON HEALTH CARE GROUP, 81- *Mem:* Am Chem Soc; AAAS; NY Acad Sci; Am Heart Asn. *Res:* Physical chemistry of the isolated proteins; mechanism of enzyme action; blood coagulation. *Mailing Add:* 259-15 86th Ave Floral Park New York NY 11001

YUEN, DAVID ALEXANDER, b Hong Kong, June 14, 48; US citizen. GEOPHYSICS, FLUID DYNAMICS. *Educ:* Calif Inst Technol, BS, 69; Scripps Inst Oceanog, Univ Calif, San Diego, MS, 73; Univ Calif, Los Angeles, PhD(geophys), 78. *Prof Exp:* Res geophysicist, Univ Calif, Los Angeles, 74-77; NSF fel geophys, Univ Toronto, 78-79; ASST PROF GEOPHYS, ARIZ STATE UNIV, 80- *Concurrent Pos:* NATO fel, Univ Toronto, 79-80. *Mem:* Am Geophys Union; Am Chem Soc; Am Phys Soc. *Res:* Earth's mantle; different time scales of instability mechanisms; rheology of the mantle; seismic attenuation processes in elastic-gravitational free oscillations; rotational dynamics; ice ages. *Mailing Add:* Dept Geol Ariz State Univ Tempe AZ 85287

YUEN, JACK K(WAN), b Honolulu, Hawaii, Apr 25, 19; m 42; c 3. CIVIL ENGINEERING. *Educ:* Univ Hawaii, BS, 51; Colo State Univ, MS, 65. *Prof Exp:* Civil engr, City of Santa Monica, Calif, 53-56; sr civil engr, Int Eng Co, Inc, 56-58; from asst prof to assoc prof civil eng, 58-71, PROF ENG, UNIV HAWAII, 71- *Mem:* Am Soc Civil Engrs. *Res:* Fluid mechanics; hydraulic structures. *Mailing Add:* Dept of Civil Eng Univ of Hawaii Honolulu HI 96822

YUEN, MAN-CHUEN, b Hong Kong, Aug 5, 33; nat US; m 58; c 3. FLUID DYNAMICS, HEAT TRANSFER. *Educ:* Purdue Univ, BS, 56; Mass Inst Technol, MS, 58; Harvard Univ Univ, PhD(eng), 65. *Prof Exp:* From asst prof to assoc prof mech eng & astronaut sci, 64-75, PROF MECH ENG, NORTHWESTERN UNIV, 75-, CHMN MECH ENG & ASTRONAUT SCI DEPT, 78- *Mem:* Am Inst Aeronaut & Astronaut; Am Soc Mech Engrs; Combustion Inst. *Res:* Multiphase and multicomponent fluid mechanics and heat transfer. *Mailing Add:* Dept of Mech Eng Technol Inst 2145 Sheridan Rd Evanston IL 60201

YUEN, PAUL C(HAN), b Hilo, Hawaii, June 7, 28; m 52; c 2. ELECTRICAL ENGINEERING. *Educ:* Univ Chicago, BS, 52; Ill Inst Technol, MS, 55, PhD(elec eng), 60. *Prof Exp:* Cyclotron technician, Univ Chicago, 50-52; engr, Standard Coil Prod, 53-54; assoc res engr, Armour Res Found, 54-57; res engr, Ill Inst Technol, 57-60, asst prof elec eng, 60-61; assoc prof, 61-65, actg dean, 69, assoc dean, Col Eng, 70-76, PROF ELEC ENG, UNIV HAWAII, 65-, DEAN, COL ENG, 81- *Mem:* Am Geophys Union; Am Soc Eng Educ; Inst Elec & Electronics Engrs; Int Union Radio Sci. *Res:* Radio wave propagation; satellite communications; ionospheric physics; renewable energy resources. *Mailing Add:* Col Eng 2540 Dole St Honolulu HI 96822

YUEN, TED GIM HING, b Canora, Sask, Dec 21, 33; m 58; c 4. EXPERIMENTAL PATHOLOGY. *Educ:* Andrews Univ, BA, 56; Univ Southern Calif, PhD(exp path), 69. *Prof Exp:* Fel exp path, Univ Southern Calif, 69-71; RES ASSOC NEUROPATH, HUNTINGTON INST APPL MED RES, 72- *Concurrent Pos:* Res assoc, Dept Path, Univ Southern Calif, 75-76. *Res:* Ultrastructural study of the effects of electrical stimulation of the brain; cerebrospinal fluid secretion, structure and function. *Mailing Add:* Huntington Inst of Appl Med Res 734 Fairmount Ave Pasadena CA 91105

YUHAS, JOHN M, b Passaic, NJ, Aug 10, 40; m 64; c 2. RADIOBIOLOGY, CANCER. *Educ:* Univ Scranton, BS, 62; Univ Md, MS, 64, PhD(radiation biol), 66. *Prof Exp:* Assoc staff scientist, Jackson Lab, 66-69; biologist, Oak Ridge Nat Lab, 69-76; ASSOC DIR, CANCER RES & TREATMENT CTR, UNIV NMEX, 76-, PROF RADIOL, SCH MED, 78- *Mem:* AAAS; Am Asn Cancer Res; Radiation Res Soc; Genetics Soc Am; NY Acad Sci. *Res:* Mammalian radiobiology; radioprotective drugs; experimental radiotherapy; toxicology; tumor immunology; carcinogenesis; oncogenic viruses. *Mailing Add:* Cancer Res & Treatment Ctr Univ of NMex Albuquerque NM 87131

YUHAS, JOSEPH GEORGE, b Cleveland, Ohio, Aug 26, 38; m 60; c 4. ANIMAL BEHAVIOR, ZOOLOGY. *Educ:* Ohio State Univ, BSc Agr, 60, BScEd & MSc, 62, PhD(zool), 70. *Prof Exp:* Res assoc wildlife, Ohio State Univ, 68-69; asst prof biol, Defiance Col, 69-75, chmn dept natural systs, 72-75; ASSOC PROF LIFE SCI & DIR, CTR FOR LIFE SCI, ST FRANCIS COL, 75- *Mem:* Animal Behav Soc; Am Inst Biol Sci. *Res:* Effects of environmental contamination on behavior; innate behavior and evolution; endocrine control of behavior; induced ovulation and delayed implantation. *Mailing Add:* Dept of Life Sci Univ of New Eng Biddeford ME 04005

YUILL, THOMAS MACKAY, b Berkeley, Calif, June 14, 37; m 60; c 2. VIROLOGY, ECOLOGY. *Educ:* Utah State Univ, BS, 59; Univ Wis, MS, 62, PhD(vet sci), 64. *Prof Exp:* Lab officer virol, Walter Reed Army Inst Res, 64-66, med biologist, SEATO Med Res Lab, 66-68; asst prof, 68-72, assoc prof vet sci, 72-76, chmn, Dept Vet Sci, 78-82, PROF VET SCI & WILDLIFE ECOL, UNIV WIS-MADISON, 76-, ASSOC DEAN RES & GRAD TRAINING, 82- *Concurrent Pos:* consult, NIH & Environ Protection Agency, 77-; pres, Orgn Trop Studies, 80-; hon prof vet microbiol, Univ Antioquia Fac Vet Med, Colombia, SAm. *Mem:* Am Soc Microbiol; Wildlife Soc; Wildlife Dis Asn (treas, 80-); Am Soc Trop Med & Hyg; Royal Soc Trop Med & Hyg. *Res:* Arbovirus epizootiology; wildlife diseases, especially duck plague in waterfowl; virus ecology. *Mailing Add:* Dept Vet Sci Univ Wis Madison WI 53706

YUKAWA, S(UMIO), b Seattle, Wash, Apr 25, 25; m 51; c 1. MECHANICAL METALLURGY. *Educ:* Univ Mich, BSE(chem eng) & BSE(metall eng), 51, MSE, 52, PhD(metall eng), 55. *Prof Exp:* Res assoc metall eng, Univ Mich, 53-54, instr, 54; METALLURGIST, GEN ELEC CO, 54- *Mem:* Fel Am Soc Metals; Am Inst Mining, Metall & Petrol Engrs; fel Am Soc Mech Engrs; Am Soc Testing & Mat. *Res:* Mechanical properties and engineering design criteria of metallic materials especially on deformation, fracture and fatigue behavior in power generation applications including steam and gas turbines, electrical generators and nuclear power equipment. *Mailing Add:* Mat & Processes Lab Gen Elec Co Schenectady NY 12345

YULE, HERBERT PHILLIP, b Chicago, Ill, Apr 17, 31; m 61; c 2. NUCLEAR CHEMISTRY, COMPUTER SCIENCE. *Educ:* Univ Chicago, PhD(nuclear chem), 60. *Prof Exp:* Res chemist, Calif Res Corp, 57-61; staff mem, Gen Atomic Div, Gen Dynamics Corp, Calif, 62-66; assoc prof activation anal, Tex A&M Univ, 66-69, assoc prof comput sci, 67-69; res chemist, Nat Bur Standards, 69-72; staff consult, 72-74, mgr comput serv, 74-78, MGR COMPUT FACIL, NUS CORP, 78- *Concurrent Pos:* Adj assoc prof biochem, Baylor Col Med, 67-69; lectr, Nat Bur Standards, 68 & NATO, 70; consult, Nat Bur Standards, 74- *Mem:* Am Nuclear Soc; Am Chem Soc. *Res:* Activation analysis, especially computer techniques; numerical analysis of data; computer and system programming. *Mailing Add:* NUS Corp 4 Research Pl Rockville MD 20850

YULE, THOMAS J, b Chicago, Ill, Nov 21, 40; m 66. NUCLEAR PHYSICS, REACTOR PHYSICS. *Educ:* John Carroll Univ, BS, 62; Univ Wis-Madison, MS, 64, PhD(physics), 68. *Prof Exp:* ASST PHYSICIST, ARGONNE NAT LAB, 68- *Mem:* Am Phys Soc. *Res:* Nuclear research instrumentation. *Mailing Add:* Div Reactor Physics Argonne Nat Lab Bldg 316 Argonne IL 60439

YUM, SU IL, b Seoul, Korea, June 25, 39; US citizen; m 68; c 2. CHEMICAL ENGINEERING, BIOMEDICAL ENGINEERING. *Educ:* Yonsei Univ, BS, 62; Univ Minn, MS, 67, PhD(chem eng), 70. *Prof Exp:* Res assoc biomat, Univ Utah, 69-71; develop engr, 71-72, co-proj leader, 72-74, proj leader, 74-75, area dir eng, 75-78, OTS PROG DIR, ALKA RES, ALZA CORP, 78- *Mem:* Am Chem Soc; Am Inst Chem Engrs. *Res:* Hydrodynamics of two-phase flow; diffusion in liquids and polymeric membranes; design of medical devices; stress analysis in plastic products. *Mailing Add:* Alza Res 950 Page Mill Rd Palo Alto CA 94304

YUN, KWANG-SIK, b Seoul, Korea, July 27, 29; m 60; c 1. PHYSICAL CHEMISTRY. *Educ:* Seoul Nat Univ, BS, 52; Univ Cincinnati, PhD(chem), 61. *Prof Exp:* Res assoc, Inst Molecular Physics, Univ Md, 60-63; Nat Res Coun Can fel, 63-65; scientist, Nat Ctr Atmospheric Res, Colo, 65-67; ASSOC PROF CHEM, UNIV MISS, 67- *Mem:* Am Chem Soc. *Res:* Kinetic theory of gases and liquids; gas phase chemical kinetics and chemical reactions of atmospheric gases. *Mailing Add:* Dept of Chem Univ of Miss University MS 38677

YUN, SEUNG SOO, b Korea, Mar 1, 31; US citizen; m 57; c 3. ACOUSTICS. *Educ:* Clark Univ, AB, 57; Brown Univ, MSc, 61, PhD(physics), 64. *Prof Exp:* Asst physicist, Ore Regional Primate Res Ctr, 63-65; res physicist, IIT Res Inst, 65-67; asst prof, 67-70, ASSOC PROF PHYSICS, OHIO UNIV, 70- *Mem:* Acoust Soc Am. *Res:* Physical acoustics and ultrasonics; absorption and dispersion of ultrasound in liquid and solid; critical phenomena. *Mailing Add:* Dept Physics Ohio Univ Athens OH 45701

YUN, SUK KOO, b Seoul, Korea, Nov 10, 30; US citizen; m 57; c 3. THEORETICAL HIGH ENERGY PHYSICS. *Educ:* Seoul Nat Univ, BS, 55; Univ Chicago, MS, 57; Boston Univ, PhD(physics), 67. *Prof Exp:* Instr, Clarkson Col Technol, 59-63; res assoc, Boston Univ, 66-67 & Syracuse Univ, 67-69; chmn natural sci div, 72-74, from asst prof to assoc prof, 69-78, PROF PHYSICS, SAGINAW VALLEY STATE COL, 78-, CHMN DEPT, 77- *Concurrent Pos:* NSF res grant, 68; res grant, Res Corp New York, 70-71; vis prof, Randall Lab, Univ Mich, 74 & 75, Syracuse Univ, 77 & Fermi Nat Accelerator Lab, 78, 79, 80 & 81; hon res assoc, Harvard Univ, 75 & 76; NSF travel grant to Japan, 78. *Mem:* Sigma Xi; Am Phys Soc. *Res:* Unified gauge theories of electromagnetic, weak and strong interactions. *Mailing Add:* Dept of Physics Saginaw Valley State Col University Center MI 48710

YUN, YOUNG MOK, b Chung Song Co, Korea, Sept 22, 31; m 66; c 2. ENTOMOLOGY. *Educ:* Wash State Univ, BS, 61; Ore State Univ, BS, 62; Mich State Univ, MS, 64, PhD(entom), 67. *Prof Exp:* ENTOMOLOGIST, AGR RES CTR, GREAT WESTERN SUGAR CO, 67- *Mem:* Entom Soc Am; Am Soc Sugar Beet Technologists. *Res:* Biology, ecology, and control of insects, nematodes, and diseases affecting sugar beets. *Mailing Add:* Agr Res Ctr Great Western Sugar Co Longmont CO 80501

YUND, E WILLIAM, b Pittsburgh, Pa, Feb 15, 14; m 66. NEUROPHYSIOLOGY, EXPERIMENTAL PSYCHOLOGY. *Educ:* Knox Col, BA, 65; Harvard Univ, MA, 67; Northeastern Univ, PhD(psychol), 70. *Prof Exp:* RES PSYCHOLOGIST, VET ADMIN MED CTR, MARTINEZ, CALIF, 73- *Concurrent Pos:* Res assoc psychol, Univ Calif, Berkeley, 72-; adj assoc prof neurol, Sch Med, Univ Calif, Davis, 78- *Mem:* Acoust Soc Am; Soc Neurosci; Asn Res Vision & Ophthal; Optical Soc Am; AAAS. *Res:* Binaural phenomena; pitch perception; auditory neurophysiology; color vision; spatial effects; visual neurophysiology, especially LGN, striate cortex and prestriate visual areas. *Mailing Add:* Neurophysiol-Biophys Res Lab 150 Muir Rd Martinez CA 94553

YUND, MARY ALICE, b Xenia, Ohio, Feb 12, 43; m 66. DEVELOPMENTAL BIOLOGY. *Educ:* Knox Col, BA, 65; Harvard Univ, MA, 67, PhD(biol), 70. *Prof Exp:* NIH fel, Univ Calif, Berkeley, 70-72, NIH trainee, 72-73, res geneticist, 73; asst prof biol, Wayne State Univ, 74-75; ASST RES GENETICIST, UNIV CALIF, BERKELEY, 75- *Concurrent Pos:* NSF res grant, 75; NIH res grant, 77. *Mem:* Sigma Xi; Soc Develop Biol; Genetics Soc Am; Am Soc Zoologists; AAAS. *Res:* Hormonal control of gene activity in differentiation of imaginal discs of Drosophila melanogaster; mechanism of steroid hormone action. *Mailing Add:* Dept of Genetics Univ of Calif Berkeley CA 94720

YUND, RICHARD ALLEN, b Ill, Dec 14, 33; m 57; c 2. MINERALOGY, GEOCHEMISTRY. *Educ:* Univ Ill, PhD(geol), 60. *Prof Exp:* Fel, Geophys Lab, Carnegie Inst, 60-61; from asst prof to assoc prof, 61-68, PROF GEOL, BROWN UNIV, 68- *Concurrent Pos:* Vis prof, Monash Univ, Melbourne, Australia, 73-; Fulbright sr res award, 73-74. *Honors & Awards:* Sr Scientist Award, WGer Gov, 78. *Mem:* Mineral Soc Am; Geochem Soc; Am Geophys Union. *Res:* Experimental study of the kinetics and mechanisms of solid state processes in minerals including coherent phase relations, exsolution, coarsening of precipitates, cation and oxygen diffusion and ductile deformation mechanisms. *Mailing Add:* Dept of Geol Sci Brown Univ Providence RI 02912

YUNE, HEUN YUNG, b Seoul, Korea, Feb 1, 29; US citizen; m 56; c 3. RADIOLOGY, SURGERY. *Educ:* Severence Union Med Col, MD, 56; Am Bd Radiol, dipl, 64; Korean Bd Radiol, dipl, 65. *Prof Exp:* Resident gen surg, Presby Med Ctr, Korea, 56-60; resident radiol, Vanderbilt Univ Hosp, 60-63, instr, Univ, 62-64; chief radiologist, Presby Med Ctr, Korea, 64-66; from asst prof to assoc prof radiol, Vanderbilt Univ, 66-71; PROF RADIOL, IND UNIV, INDIANAPOLIS, 71- *Concurrent Pos:* Consult radiologist, Indianapolis Vet Admin Hosp, 71 & Wishard Mem Hosp, Indianapolis, 75- *Honors & Awards:* Magna cum Laude Award, Radiol Soc NAm, 69; Silver Medal, Am Roentgen Ray Soc, 71, Bronze Medal & Cert Merit, 75. *Mem:* Radiol Soc NAm; Am Roentgen Ray Soc; Am Col Radiol; Asn Univ Radiol; Am Soc Head & Neck Radiol. *Res:* Vascular radiology; tumor angiography, angiography in trauma, angiography in endocrine disorder and lymphangiography; eye, ear, nose and throat radiology; head and neck tomography and contrast radiography in head and neck. *Mailing Add:* Dept of Radiol Ind Univ Med Ctr Indianapolis IN 46223

YUNGBLUTH, THOMAS ALAN, b Warren, Ill, Dec 12, 34. GENETICS, PLANT BREEDING. *Educ:* Univ Ill, BS, 56; Univ Minn, PhD(genetics), 66. *Prof Exp:* Asst prof, 66-72, assoc prof, 72-80, PROF BIOL, WESTERN KY UNIV, 80- *Mem:* Am Soc Agron; Crop Sci Soc Am; AAAS. *Mailing Add:* Dept Biol Western Ky Univ Bowling Green KY 42101

YUNGER, LIBBY MARIE, b East Cleveland, Ohio, Feb 20, 44. NEUROCHEMISTRY, PHARMACOLOGY. *Educ:* Earlham Col, BA, 66; Univ Iowa, MA, 71, PhD(physiol psychol), 74. *Prof Exp:* Res assoc, Univ Iowa, 73-74; Nat Inst Neurol Dis & Stroke fel, Univ Pittsburgh, 74-75; res biologist, Lederle Labs, Am Cyanamid Co, 75-78; ASSOC SR INVESTR, SMITH KLINE & FRENCH LABS, 78- *Mem:* Soc Neurosci. *Res:* Use of monoclonal and polyclonal antibodies to study physiological role of neurohormones and other mediators; binding and transport of putative neurotransmitters; hybridoma technology. *Mailing Add:* Smith Kline & French Labs 1500 Spring Garden St Philadelphia PA 19101

YUNGHANS, WAYNE N, b Lakewood, Ohio, Dec 10, 45; m 69; c 2. CYTOLOGY. *Educ:* Heidelberg Col, BS, 67; Purdue Univ, MS, 69, PhD(cytol), 74. *Prof Exp:* Res asst microbiol, US Army, 69-71; asst prof, 74-80, ASSOC PROF CYTOL, STATE UNIV NY COL FREDONIA, 80- *Honors & Awards:* State Univ NY Res Found Award, 75; NSF Award, 78. *Mem:* AAAS; Am Soc Plant Physiologists. *Res:* Isolation and purification of cellular membranes including plasma membranes, Golgi apparatus and endoplasmic reticulum; membranes characterized for enzyme activities and protein kinases and phosphoproteins. *Mailing Add:* Dept Biol State Univ Ny Col Fredonia NY 14063

YUNGUL, SULHI HASAN, b Ista[illegible] Turkey, Oct 20, 19; nat US; m 47; c 3. EXPLORATION GEOPHYSICS. *Educ:* Mont Sch Mines, BS, 43; Calif Inst Technol, MS, 44, GeophEngr, 45; Tex A&M Univ, PhD, 62. *Hon Degrees:* Geophys Engr, Mont Col Mineral Sci & Technol, Engr, 71. *Prof Exp:* From geophysicist to chief geophysicist, Mining Res & Explor Inst, Govt Turkey, 45-53, chief geophysicist, Etibank, 53-55; sr res assoc, Chevron Oil Field Res Co, 55-77, SR STAFF GEOPHYSICIST, CHEVRON RESOURCES CO, STANDARD OIL CO CALIF, 77- *Concurrent Pos:* Asst prof, Tex A&M Univ, 60-62; vis lectr, Univ Calif, Riverside, 72 & Calif State Univ, Fullerton, 75; adj prof, Univ Calif, Riverside, 76- *Mem:* Soc Explor Geophys; Am Geophys Union; Europ Asn Explor Geophys. *Res:* Solid earth exploration geophysics, especially gravity, magnetic and electrical; tectonophysics. *Mailing Add:* Chevron Resources Co PO Box 3722 San Francisco CA 94119

YUNICE, ANDY ANIECE, b Rahbeh-Akkar, Lebanon, Jan 2, 25; US citizen; m 59; c 3. BIOCHEMISTRY, ENVIRONMENTAL SCIENCE. *Educ:* Am Univ Beirut, BS, 49; Wayne State Univ, MS, 58; Univ Okla, PhD(environ health), 70. *Prof Exp:* Instr, Am Boys Sch Tripoli, Lebanon, 49-53; prin high sch, 53-54; res asst med, Wash Univ, 58-67, res instr, 67-70; RES BIOCHEMIST & DIR TRACE METAL RES LABS, VET ADMIN HOSP, 62- *Concurrent Pos:* Asst prof & mem grad fac, Sch Med, Univ Okla, 70-80, assoc prof physiol & biophys, 80-; hosp grant & co-prin investr, NIH grant, Vet Admin Hosp, 70- *Mem:* AAAS; Am Fedn Clin Res; Am Physiol Soc; Am Chem Soc; Sigma Xi. *Res:* Trace metal metabolism in post-alcoholic cirrhosis and cardiovascular diseases; nutrients interaction and alcoholism. *Mailing Add:* Vet Admin Med Ctr 151D Oklahoma City OK 73104

YUNICK, ROBERT P, b Schenectady, NY, Oct 27, 35; m 59; c 3. ORGANIC POLYMER CHEMISTRY. *Educ:* Union Col, NY, BS, 57; Rensselaer Polytech Inst, PhD(org chem), 61. *Prof Exp:* Res chemist, Olefins Div, Union Carbide Chem Corp, 61-63; mgr, 63-72, dir res, 72-76, vpres res, 76-80, VPRES CORP TECH, W HOWARD WRIGHT RES CTR, SCHENECTADY CHEM, INC, 80- *Mem:* Am Chem Soc; Am Ornithologists Union. *Res:* Organic synthesis of intermediates for resin synthesis; synthesis of phenolic, hydrocarbon, resorcinolic, polyester and polyesterimide resins; synthesis of high-temperature polymers. *Mailing Add:* Schenectady Chem Inc 2750 Balltown Rd Schenectady NY 12309

YUNIS, ADEL A, b Rahbeh, Lebanon, Mar 17, 30; m 59; c 3. INTERNAL MEDICINE. *Educ:* Am Univ Beirut, BA, 50, MD, 54. *Prof Exp:* Clin fel hemat, Washington Univ, 57-58, res fel, 58-59, res assoc biochem, 59-61, from instr to asst prof med, Med Sch, 61-64; from asst prof to assoc prof & dir hemat, 64-68, PROF MED & BIOCHEM, SCH MED, UNIV MIAMI, 68-, DIR DIV HEMAT, HOWARD HUGHES LABS HEMAT RES, 68- *Concurrent Pos:* Am Leukemia Soc scholar, 61-66; USPHS res career develop award, 66-71. *Mem:* Am Fedn Clin Res; Am Soc Hemat; Am Soc Exp Path; Asn Am Physicians; Am Soc Biol Chemists. *Res:* Colony stimulating factor and modulators of granulopoiesis; mechanism of action of bone marrow toxins and the pathogenesis of chloramphenicol-induced blood dyscrasias. *Mailing Add:* Univ of Miami Sch of Med PO Box 016960 Miami FL 33101

YUNIS, EDMOND, b Sincelejo, Colombia, Aug 8, 29; US citizen; m 65; c 1. MEDICINE, PATHOLOGY. *Educ:* Nat Univ Colombia, MD, 54. *Prof Exp:* Resident anat path, Univ Kans, 55-57; resident clin path, Univ Hosps, Univ Minn, Minneapolis, 57-59, from instr to prof lab med, 60-71, dir blood bank, 61-68, dir div immunol, 66-76, prof lab med & path, 71-76; CHIEF DIV IMMUNOGENETICS, SIDNEY FARBER CANCER INST & PROF PATH, HARVARD MED SCH, 76-; DIR HLA LAB, NORTHEAST REGIONAL RED CROSS BLOOD PROG, 76- *Mem:* Am Soc Exp Path; Am Asn Immunol. *Res:* Antigenicity in cells and animals; immunological capacity in animals related to thymus; transplantation immunology and immunogenetics. *Mailing Add:* Northeast Regional Red Cross Blood Prog Boston MA 02115

YUNIS, JORGE J, b Sincelejo, Colombia, Oct 5, 33; US citizen. GENETICS, PATHOLOGY. *Educ:* Inst Simon Araujo, Columbia, BS, 51; Cent Univ Madrid, MD, 56, Dr MD, 57. *Prof Exp:* Intern, Prov Hosp, Barranquilla, Colombia, 57-58, resident internal med, 58-59; resident clin & anat path, 59-62, from instr to assoc prof lab med, 62-69, dir grad studies lab med & path, 69-74, PROF LAB MED & PATH, HEAD DIV MED GENETICS, UNIV MINN, MINNEAPOLIS, 69-, DIR MED & PATH LABS, 77- *Concurrent Pos:* Fel lab med, Univ Minn, Minneapolis, 62-63; chmn human genetics comt health sci, Univ Minn, Minneapolis, 72- *Mem:* Am Soc Human Genetics; Am Soc Cell Biol; Am Asn Path & Bact; Acad Clin Lab Physicians & Sci; Am Soc Hemat. *Res:* Fine structure and molecular organization of chromosomes; chromosome defects in man. *Mailing Add:* Mayo & Univ of Minn Hosps Box 198 Minneapolis MN 55455

YUNKER, CONRAD ERHARDT, b Matawan, NJ, Dec 22, 27; m 58; c 4. ZOOLOGY, PARASITOLOGY. *Educ:* Univ Md, BS, 52, MS, 54, PhD, 58. *Prof Exp:* Staff mem med zool, US Naval Med Res Unit, Egypt, 55-57; res assoc zool, Univ Md, 58, asst prof, 58-59; entomologist, Entom Res Inst, Can Dept Agr, 59-60; scientist, Mid Am Res Unit, NIH, 60-61, SCIENTIST DIR, ROCKY MOUNTAIN LAB, NAT INST ALLERGY & INFECTIOUS DIS, 61- *Concurrent Pos:* Consult, Nat Inst Allergy & Infectious Dis, 59; mem, Bolivian Hemorrhagic Fever Comn, 63. *Honors & Awards:* Award, Inst Acarology, Ohio State Univ, 72; Sigrid Juselius Found, Helsinki, Finland, 75. *Mem:* Fel AAAS; Entom Soc Am; Tissue Cult Asn; Am Soc Parasitol; Am Soc Trop Med & Hyg. *Res:* Systematic acarology; medical entomology; arthropod tissue culture; arthropod-borne viruses. *Mailing Add:* Rocky Mountain Lab Hamilton MT 59840

YUNKER, MARK BERNARD, b Toronto, Ont, Dec, 48. ORGANIC CHEMISTRY. *Educ:* Univ Waterloo, BSc, 71, PhD(chem), 75. *Prof Exp:* Res assoc chem, Univ Hawaii, 75-77; lectr chem, Univ Victoria, 77-79; MEM STAFF, DOBROCKY SEA TECH LTD, 80- *Concurrent Pos:* Nat Res Coun Can fel, 75-77. *Mem:* Am Chem Soc; Chem Inst Can. *Res:* Synthetic chemistry of bioactive compounds; isolation and structure determination of marine natural products. *Mailing Add:* Dobrocky Sea Tech Ltd PO Box 6500 Sidney BC V8L 3S1 Can

YUNKER, MARTIN HENRY, b Milton Junction, Wis, Dec 28, 28; m 53; c 2. PHARMACY. *Educ:* Univ Wis, BS, 51, MS, 53, PhD(phys pharm), 57. *Prof Exp:* Tech asst to mgr pharmaceut prod, Merck, Sharp & Dohme Div, Merck, Inc, 57-58, supvr granulation dept, 58-59, supvr qual control, 59-61, res assoc pharmaceut res, 61-63; SR RES PHARMACIST, ABBOTT LABS, 63- *Mem:* Am Pharmaceut Asn. *Res:* Pharmaceutical research, including tablet formulations; biopharmaceutics; in vitro drug dissolution; preformulation characterization of drugs; parenteral formulations. *Mailing Add:* Dept 493 Abbott Labs North Chicago IL 60064

YUNKER, WAYNE HARRY, b Corvallis, Ore, Jan 8, 36. LIQUID SODIUM COOLANT TECHNOLOGY. *Educ:* Ore State Col, BS, 57; Univ Wash, PhD(chem), 61. *Prof Exp:* Res scientist chem, Gen Elec Co, 63-65; sr res scientist, Battelle Mem Inst, 65-70; sr res scientist chem, 71-77, FEL SCIENTIST CHEM, WESTINGHOUSE HANFORD CO, 78- *Mem:* Am Chem Soc; Sigma Xi. *Mailing Add:* Westinghouse Hanford Co PO Box 1970 Richland WA 99352

YURA, HAROLD THOMAS, b Buffalo, NY, Nov 20, 37; m 59; c 2. OPTICAL SIGNALS. *Educ:* Calif Inst Technol, BS, 59, PhD(physics), 62. *Prof Exp:* Staff scientist physics, Rand Corp, 62-70; SR SCIENTIST PHYSICS, AEROSPACE CORP, 70- *Concurrent Pos:* Adj prof, Univ Calif, Los Angeles, 75- *Mem:* Fel Optical Soc Am. *Res:* Wave propagation in random media and laser propagation phenomenology; strong optical scintellation effects; extension of the Huygens Fresnel principle to random media. *Mailing Add:* PO Box 92957 Los Angeles CA 90009

YURCHAK, SERGEI, b Butler Twp, Pa, Feb 11, 43. CHEMICAL ENGINEERING. *Educ:* Pa State Univ, BS, 64; Univ Wis, PhD(chem eng), 68. *Prof Exp:* Res chem engr, 69-72, sr res engr, 72-77, assoc engr, 76-80, RES ASSOC, MOBIL RES & DEVELOP CORP, 80- *Mem:* Am Inst Chem Engrs; Am Chem Soc; Sigma Xi. *Res:* Reaction kinetics and reactor design; metal catalysis; process development. *Mailing Add:* Mobil Res & Develop Corp Billingsport Rd Paulsboro NJ 08066

YURCHENCO, JOHN ALFONSO, b San Juan, Arg, Feb 22, 15; nat US; m 44; c 4. MEDICAL MICROBIOLOGY. *Educ:* Albion Col, BA, 41; Johns Hopkins Univ, ScD(bact), 49. *Prof Exp:* Chief div microbiol, Eaton Labs, Inc, 48-55; head dept chemother, Squibb Inst Med Res, 55-56; sr res scientist, Wyeth Labs, Inc, 56-82; RETIRED. *Res:* Chemotherapy bacterial infections; bacterial pathogenicity and virulence; low temperature stability of infectious bacterial pools; immunology. *Mailing Add:* 233 Sinkler Dr Radnor PA 19087

YUREK, GERALD G, b San Francisco, Calif, May 7, 35; m 59; c 1. BIOMEDICAL ENGINEERING, ELECTRICAL ENGINEERING. *Educ:* Calif Inst Technol, BS, 56; Stanford Univ, MS, 57, Engr & MS, 61, PhD(physiol), 64. *Prof Exp:* Elec engr, Instrument Sect, NIH, 57-59, develop engr, Instrument Eng & Develop Br, 61-63, SR INVESTR, LAB TECH DEVELOP, NAT HEART INST, 63- *Concurrent Pos:* Vpres, Joint Comt Eng in Med & Biol, 66, treas, 67-68, gen chmn ann conf, 70. *Mem:* AAAS; Asn Advan Med Instrumentation; Biomed Eng Soc. *Res:* Instrument and methods development for biochemical analysis; microchemical analysis instrumentation; cardiac anaphylaxis; microimmunochemistry; artificial circulatory support devices. *Mailing Add:* Lab of Tech Develop Nat Heart Inst Bethesda MD 20205

YURETICH, RICHARD FRANCIS, b Brooklyn, NY, Aug 30, 50. SEDIMENTOLOGY, GEOCHEMISTRY. *Educ:* New York Univ, BA, 71; Princeton Univ, MA, 76, PhD(geol), 76. *Prof Exp:* Res geologist, Gulf Res & Develop, Gulf Oil Corp, 76-77; ASST PROF GEOL, STATE UNIV NY COL ONEONTA, 77- *Mem:* Geol Soc Am; Soc Econ Paleontologists & Mineralogists; Int Asn Sedimentologists; Sigma Xi. *Res:* Lacustrine deposits; surface waters; rift valleys; processes of petroleum generation. *Mailing Add:* Dept of Earth Sci State Univ NY Oneonta NY 13820

YUREWICZ, EDWARD CHARLES, b Philadelphia, Pa, Feb 10, 45; m 67; c 2. GLYCOPROTEINS, ANTIGENS. *Educ:* Univ Del, BA, 66; Sch Med, Johns Hopkins Univ, PhD(physiol chem), 71. *Prof Exp:* Fel biochem, Univ Calif, Davis, 71-74; sr res biochemist, Merck Inst Therapeut Res, 74-75; ASST PROF GYNEC & OBSTET, SCH MED, WAYNE STATE UNIV, 75- *Mem:* AAAS; Am Soc Cell Biol; Am Soc Biol Chemists; Soc Complex Carbohydrates; Soc Study Reprod. *Res:* Structural characterization of cervical mucus glycoproteins; biochemical and immunochemical analysis of glycoprotein antigens in mammalian oocyte zona pellucida; biochemistry of sperm-egg interaction; glycoprotein biosynthesis in mouse blastocysts. *Mailing Add:* Dept Gynec & Obstet Sch Med Wayne State Univ CS Mott Ctr Detroit MI 48201

YURKIEWICZ, WILLIAM J, b Bloomsburg, Pa, Sept 21, 39; m 65; c 2. INSECT PHYSIOLOGY, BIOCHEMISTRY. *Educ:* Bloomsburg State Col, BS, 60; Bucknell Univ, MS, 62; Pa State Univ, PhD(entom), 65. *Prof Exp:* Asst entom, Pa State Univ, 63-65; res entomologist, USDA, Ga, 65-66; PROF BIOL, MILLERSVILLE STATE COL, 66- *Mem:* Entom Soc Am. *Res:* Insect flight physiology; neutral lipid and phospholipid composition and metabolism in insects; neural control of insect flight. *Mailing Add:* Dept of Biol Millersville State Col Millersville PA 17551

YURKOWSKI, MICHAEL, b Sask, Can, Sept 1, 28; m 57; c 3. BIOCHEMISTRY, NUTRITION. *Educ:* Univ Sask, BSA, 51, MSc, 59; Univ Guelph, PhD(nutrit), 68. *Prof Exp:* Anal chemist, Western Potash Corp Ltd, Sask, 51-52; indust chemist, Cereal & Oilseed Processing, Sask Wheat Pool, Can, 52-56; anal chemist, Plant Prod Div, Can Dept Agr, Ont, 59-60; food & drug directorate, Can Dept Nat Health & Welfare, Man, 60-62; res scientist marine lipid biochem, Halifax Lab, 62-65, RES SCIENTIST FISHERIES RES BD, CAN DEPT ENVIRON, NUTRIT BIOCHEM, FRESHWATER INST, FISHERIES SERV, 68- *Mem:* Chem Inst Can; Can Inst Food Sci & Technol. *Res:* Applied and basic nutrition of fish and freshwater organisms; lipid biochemistry of freshwater organisms; odours in freshwater and freshwater fish. *Mailing Add:* Freshwater Inst Fisheries Serv Can Dept Environ 501 Univ Crescent Winnipeg MB R3T 2N6 Can

YUROW, HARVEY WARREN, b New York, NY, Feb 14, 32; m 56; c 3. ANALYTICAL CHEMISTRY. *Educ:* Queens Col (NY), BS, 54; Pa State Univ, PhD(anal chem), 60. *Prof Exp:* Dept Defense fel, Rutgers Univ, 59-60; RES CHEMIST, EDGEWOOD ARSENAL, 60- *Mem:* Am Chem Soc; Sigma Xi. *Res:* Trace analysis of organic compounds via chromogen formation; structure-activity relationships for physiologically active compounds; organic analysis via chemiluminescence. *Mailing Add:* 3801 Maryland Ave Abingdon MD 21009

YUSHOK, WASLEY DONALD, b Woodbine, NJ, Mar 11, 20; m 50. BIOCHEMISTRY, CANCER. *Educ:* Rutgers Univ, BS, 41, MS, 43; Cornell Univ, PhD(chem embryol), 50. *Prof Exp:* Asst, Rutgers Univ, 41-43 & Cornell Univ, 46-49; asst to ed handbk biol data, Nat Res Coun, 50; res assoc, Univ Tex Med Br, 50-52; res biochemist, Biochem Res Found, 52-59, head div cancer biochem, 59-66; ASSOC MEM DIV BIOCHEM, INST FOR CANCER RES, 66- *Mem:* AAAS; Am Chem Soc; Am Asn Cancer Res; NY Acad Sci. *Res:* Regulation of metabolism and enzymes in cancer cells; nucleotide, protein and carbohydrate metabolism. *Mailing Add:* Inst for Cancer Res 7701 Burholme Ave Philadelphia PA 19111

YUSKA, HENRY, b Brooklyn, NY, Nov 7, 14; m 44; c 2. ORGANIC CHEMISTRY. *Educ:* City Col New York, BS, 35; Polytech Inst Brooklyn, MS, 39; Univ Ill, PhD(org chem), 42. *Prof Exp:* Res chemist, Jewish Hosp, Brooklyn, NY, 35-39; asst chem, Univ Ill, 41; res org chemist, Barrett Div, Allied Chem & Dye Corp, 42-43; resin group leader, Interchem Corp, 43-60, dir dept org chem, Cent Res Labs, 60-63; tech dir, Sun Chem Corp, 63-66; PROF CHEM, BROOKLYN COL, 66- *Concurrent Pos:* Instr, Eve Div, Hunter Col, 43-46. *Mem:* Am Chem Soc. *Res:* Synthetic resins; organic synthesis of monomers; biochemistry. *Mailing Add:* Dept of Chem Brooklyn Col Bedford Ave & Ave H Brooklyn NY 11210

YUSPA, STUART HOWARD, b Baltimore, Md, July 19, 41; m 65; c 2. CANCER. *Educ:* Johns Hopkins Univ, BS, 62; Univ Md, MD, 66; Am Bd Internal Med, dipl, 72. *Prof Exp:* Intern internal med, Hosp Univ Pa, 66-67; res assoc cancer, Nat Cancer Inst, 67-70; resident internal med, Hosp Univ Pa, 70-72; SR INVESTR CANCER, NAT CANCER INST, 72-, CHIEF, LAB CELLULAR CARCINOGENESIS & TUMOR PROM, 81- *Concurrent Pos:* Mem biol models segment, Carcinogenesis Prog, Nat Cancer Inst, 72-78. *Mem:* Am Asn Cancer Res; AAAS. *Res:* Determine mechanisms whereby chemicals initiate or promote malignant transformation of epithelial cells by using cell culture model systems. *Mailing Add:* Lab Cellular Carcinogenesis & Tumor Prom Nat Cancer Inst Bethesda MD 20205

YUST, CHARLES S(IMON), b Newark, NJ, Jan 21, 31; m 55; c 3. PHYSICAL METALLURGY. *Educ:* Newark Col Eng, BS, 52; Univ Tenn, MS, 60. *Prof Exp:* Metall engr, Oak Ridge Gaseous Diffusion Plant, 52-60; METALLURGIST, METALS & CERAMICS DIV, OAK RIDGE NAT LAB, 60- *Mem:* Am Ceramic Soc. *Res:* Theory of solid state sintering; deformation mechanisms in ceramics. *Mailing Add:* Oak Ridge Nat Lab PO Box X Oak Ridge TN 37830

YUSTER, PHILIP HAROLD, b Fargo, NDak, Nov 7, 17; m 47; c 2. RADIATION PHYSICS. *Educ:* NDak Col, BS, 39; Wash Univ, PhD(phys chem), 49. *Prof Exp:* Jr chemist, Panama Canal, 42-43; asst, Manhattan Dist, Univ Chicago, 43-44; asst, Los Alamos Sci Lab, 44-45; asst, Wash Univ, 45-49; assoc chemist, 49-58, SR CHEMIST, ARGONNE NAT LAB, 58- *Mem:* Am Phys Soc. *Res:* Mass spectroscopy; photochemistry; luminescence; color centers. *Mailing Add:* 9700 S Cass Ave Argonne IL 60439

YU-SUN, CLARE CHUAN-CHANG, b Nanking, China, Aug 16, 26. BIOLOGY. *Educ:* Seton Hill Col, BA, 50; Columbia Univ, BA, 51. *Prof Exp:* From asst prof to assoc prof, 57-64, PROF BIOL, UNIV ALBUQUERQUE, 64- *Mem:* Am Soc Microbiol; Environ Mutagen Soc. *Mailing Add:* Univ Albuquerque St Joseph Pl NW Albuquerque NM 87140

YUWILER, ARTHUR, b Mansfield, Ohio, Apr 4, 27; m 50; c 3. BIOCHEMISTRY. *Educ:* Univ Calif, Los Angeles, BS, 50, PhD(biochem), 56. *Prof Exp:* Asst chem, Univ Calif, Los Angeles, 50-51, asst physiol chem, 52-54, asst chem, 54-56, res biochemist, 57-59; res neurobiochemist, Vet Admin, Calif, 56-57; res assoc & dir labs & biochem sect, Schizophrenia & Psychopharmacol Res Proj, Ypsilanti State Hosp & Univ Mich, 59-62; asst prof biochem, 64-70, assoc prof, 70-76, PROF PSYCHIAT, UNIV CALIF, LOS ANGELES, 76-; CHIEF NEUROBIOCHEM RES, VET ADMIN BRENTWOOD HOSP, 62- *Concurrent Pos:* Res biochemist, Ment Health Res Inst, Univ Mich, 59-62; mem, Brain Res Inst, Univ Calif, Los Angeles, 65-; mem career develop award comt, MINH, 70-76 & Calif State Ment Health Adv Comt, 70-71; mem sci adv comt, Dystonia Found, 77- *Mem:* Am Soc Neurochem; Int Soc Neurochem; Am Col Neuropsychopharmacol; Soc Biol Psychiat; Am Soc Biol Chemists. *Res:* Amino acids and proteins; enzymes; biochemistry of schizophrenia; intermediary metabolism of neurohumors; stress. *Mailing Add:* 20620 Clarendon Woodland Hills CA 91364

Z

ZAALOUK, MOHAMED GAMAL, b Dessouk, Egypt, Aug 16, 35; m 63; c 2. NUCLEAR & CONTROL ENGINEERING. *Educ:* Cairo Univ, BS, 57; NC State Univ, MS, 62, PhD(nuclear eng), 66. *Prof Exp:* Engr, Egyptian Atomic Energy Estab, 57-60, asst prof reactor anal, 66-68; vis scientist, Inst Atomic Energy, Kjeller, Norway, 68-69; vis asst prof elec eng, NC State Univ, 69-72; prin engr nuclear/mech, Carolina Power & Light Co, 72-81; HEAD, DIV NUCLEAR ENG, HOUSTON LIGHTING & POWER, 81- *Concurrent Pos:* Lectr, Dept Nuclear Eng, Univ Alexandria, 66-68; Norweg Agency Res & Develop fel, Inst Atomic Energy, Kjeller, Norway, 68-69; AEC grants, NC State Univ, 69-71; mem staff proj mgt, Carolina Power & Light Co, 79-81. *Mem:* Am Nuclear Soc; Egyptian Soc Nuclear Sci. *Res:* Nuclear reactor analysis; control theory and systems; boiling dynamics; project management. *Mailing Add:* Houston Lighting & Power Box 1700 Houston TX 77001

ZABARA, JACOB, b Philadelphia, Pa, May 8, 32; m 70; c 2. PHYSIOLOGY, NEUROPHYSIOLOGY. *Educ:* Johns Hopkins Univ, BS, 53; Univ Pa, MS, 58, PhD(physiol), 59. *Prof Exp:* USPHS fel, Univ Pa, 59-60; instr pharmacol, Dartmouth Col, 60-61; instr pharmacol, Univ Pa, 61-63; USPHS spec fel biomath, 63-64; instr physiol, Univ Pa, 64-65, assoc pharmacol, 65-67, assoc physiol, 65-67; asst prof, 67-72, ASSOC PROF PHYSIOL, GRAD SCH, TEMPLE UNIV, 72- *Concurrent Pos:* Vis prof, Hadassah Med Sch, Hebrew Univ. *Mem:* Soc Neurosci; Biophys Soc; Undersea Med Soc; Am Asn Anat; Am Physiol Soc. *Res:* Neurophysiology and cybernetics. *Mailing Add:* Dept of Physiol & Biophys Temple Univ Grad Sch Philadelphia PA 19140

ZABARENKO, RALPH N, b Pittsburgh, Pa, Oct 16, 16. PSYCHIATRY. *Educ:* Univ Pittsburgh, BS, 37, MA, 39, MD, 43. *Prof Exp:* Psychiatrist, Staunton Clin, Univ Pittsburgh, 48-74; pvt pract, 49-74; PROF PSYCHIAT, ROCKFORD SCH MED, UNIV ILL, 74- *Concurrent Pos:* Clin assoc prof, Univ Pittsburgh, 49-74; mem fac, Pittsburgh Psychoanal Inst, 64-74. *Mem:* AMA; Am Psychoanal Asn; Soc Teachers Family Med. *Res:* Physician/psychiatrist education. *Mailing Add:* 1601 Parkview Dr Rockford IL 61101

ZABEL, CARROLL WAYNE, b Deer Creek, Minn, Oct 5, 20; m 43; c 3. PHYSICS. *Educ:* Lawrence Col, BA, 46; Mass Inst Technol, PhD(physics), 49. *Prof Exp:* Mem staff, Microwave Radar, Mass Inst Technol, 42-46; mem staff nuclear physics, Los Alamos Sci Lab, 49-65; assoc prof physics & assoc dean col arts & sci, 65-67, dir res & assoc dean grad sch, 67-71, PROF PHYSICS, UNIV HOUSTON, 70- *Concurrent Pos:* Secy nuclear cross sect adv group, AEC, 52-57, adv comt reactor safeguards, 65-69; mem, Atoms for Peace Mission, NZ, 58; corp vis comt, Dept Nuclear Eng, Mass Inst Technol, 63-66. *Mem:* AAAS; Am Phys Soc; Am Asn Physics Teachers; NY Acad Sci. *Res:* Nuclear engineering and physics. *Mailing Add:* Dept of Physics Univ of Houston Houston TX 77004

ZABEL, HARTMUT, b Radolfzell, WGer, Mar 21, 46; m 73; c 2. SOLID STATE PHYSICS. *Educ:* Univ Bonn, Vordipl, 69; Tech Univ Munich, Hauptdipl, 73; Univ Munich, PhD(physics), 78. *Prof Exp:* Fel physics, Univ Houston, 78-79; ASST PROF, UNIV ILL, URBANA-CHAMPAIGN, 79- *Mem:* Ger Phys Soc; Am Phys Soc. *Res:* X-ray and thermal neutron scattering studies of structural, thermal and lattice dynamical properties of solid solution systems, with main emphasis on hydrogen in metals and intercalated graphite. *Mailing Add:* Dept Physics Univ Ill 1110 W Green St Urbana IL 61801

ZABEL, ROBERT ALGER, b Boyceville, Wis, Mar 11, 17; m 44; c 5. FOREST PATHOLOGY. *Educ:* Univ Minn, BS, 38; State Univ NY, MS, 41, PhD(bot), 48. *Prof Exp:* Lab aide, Lake States Forest Exp Sta, US Forest Serv, 40; from asst prof to assoc prof forest path, 47-55, head dept bot & forest path, 55-65, assoc dean biol sci & undergrad instr, 65-66, vpres acad affairs, 70-73, PROF FOREST PATH, STATE UNIV NY COL ENVIRON SCI & FORESTRY, 55-, ASSOC DEAN BIOL SCI & INSTR, 66- *Mem:* AAAS; Soc Am Foresters; Am Soc Microbiol; Am Phytopath Soc; Am Inst Biol Sci. *Res:* Forest products deterioration; wood decays; lumber stains; evaluation of preservatives; root and heart rots; toxicants and fungicides. *Mailing Add:* State Univ NY Col Environ Sci Forestry Syracuse NY 13210

ZABETAKIS, MICHAEL GEORGE, flames, safety, see previous edition

ZABIELSKI, CHESTER V, b Schenectady, NY, July 19, 23. METALLURGY. *Educ:* Union Univ, NY, BS, 47; Columbia Univ, BS, 49; Rensselaer Polytech Inst, MS, 54 & 56; Univ Pittsburgh, PhD(metall), 65. *Prof Exp:* Chemist, Gen Aniline & Film Corp, 50-52; Olin Mathieson res asst, Rensselaer Polytech Inst, 52-54; metall engr, Westinghouse Elec Corp, Pa, 57-58; asst prof metall, Univ Pittsburgh, 58-67; SR PHYS METALLURGIST, US ARMY MAT RES AGENCY, 67- *Concurrent Pos:* Ford Found res grant, Univ Pittsburgh. *Mem:* Am Soc Metals; Am Inst Mining, Metall & Petrol Engrs; Am Inst Chem Engrs; Am Chem Soc; Nat Asn Corrosion Engrs. *Res:* Physical metallurgy; corrosion; metallurgy of uranium, steel, zirconium, titanium, copper and stainless steels; high temperature alloys; molten salt reactions; kinetics; thermodynamics; optical and x-ray spectroscopy. *Mailing Add:* Box 369 Cambridge MA 02238

ZABIK, MARY ELLEN, b Kendallville, Ind, Jan 20, 37; m 58; c 1. FOOD SCIENCE. *Educ:* Purdue Univ, BS, 59; Mich State Univ, MS, 61, PhD(food sci), 70. *Prof Exp:* Instr food res, 61-68 & 69-70, from asst prof to assoc prof food chem, 70-78, PROF FOOD CHEM, MICH STATE UNIV, 78- *Mem:* Inst Food Technologists; Am Oil Chemists Soc; Am Asn Cereal Chemists; Poultry Sci Asn. *Res:* Food chemistry and rheology; functionality of carbohydrates and proteins in food systems; reduction of environmental contamination from food systems. *Mailing Add:* Dept of Food Sci & Human Nutrit Mich State Univ East Lansing MI 48824

ZABIK, MATTHEW JOHN, b South Bend, Ind, Aug 22, 37; m 58; c 1. CHEMISTRY, TOXICOLOGY. *Educ:* Purdue Univ, Lafayette, BS, 59; Mich State Univ, MS, 62, PhD(org chem), 65. *Prof Exp:* From asst prof to assoc prof, 65-72, PROF ENTOM & ASSOC DIR PESTICIDE RES CTR, MICH STATE UNIV, 72- *Mem:* Am Chem Soc; Soc Environ Toxicol & Chem. *Res:* Photochemistry; environmental toxicology of xenobiotics. *Mailing Add:* Dept Entom Mich State Univ East Lansing MI 48824

ZABIN, BURTON ALLEN, b Chicago, Ill, Mar 18, 36; m 72. INORGANIC CHEMISTRY, ANALYTICAL CHEMISTRY. *Educ:* Univ Ill, BS, 57; Purdue Univ, PhD(inorg chem), 62. *Prof Exp:* Res assoc chem, Stanford Univ, 62-63; dir res, 63-72, DIV MGR CHEM, BIO-RAD LABS, 72- *Mem:* Am Chem Soc. *Res:* Separations chemistry, including ion exchange resins, gel filtration materials and other column chromatographic materials. *Mailing Add:* Bio-Rad Labs 32nd & Griffin Richmond CA 94804

ZABIN, IRVING, b Chicago, Ill, Nov 13, 19; m 42; c 3. BIOCHEMISTRY, MOLECULAR BIOLOGY. *Educ:* Univ Ill, BS, 40; Univ Chicago, PhD(biochem), 49. *Prof Exp:* Res assoc biochem, Univ Chicago, 49-50; res assoc biol chem, 50-51, from lectr to assoc prof, 51-64, PROF BIOL CHEM, SCH MED, UNIV CALIF, LOS ANGELES, 64- *Concurrent Pos:* Nat Multiple Sclerosis Soc scholar, 59-60; Guggenheim fel, 67-68; NATO sr fel sci, 75; vis prof, Pasteur Inst, Paris, 59-60 & 67-68 & Imp Col London, 75. *Mem:* AAAS; Am Soc Biol Chem; Am Soc Microbiol. *Res:* Protein structure, synthesis and control. *Mailing Add:* Dept of Biol Chem Univ of Calif Sch of Med Los Angeles CA 90024

ZABINSKI, MICHAEL PETER, b Haifa, Israel, May 30, 41; US citizen; m 64; c 1. SOLID MECHANICS, BIOMECHANICS. *Educ:* Univ Conn, BS, 62, MS, 63; Yale Univ, MS, 66, MPhil, 68, PhD(eng & appl sci), 69; Univ New Haven, MS, 77. *Prof Exp:* Sr engr, Olin Corp, 63-66; PROF ENG & PHYSICS, FAIRFIELD UNIV, 69- *Concurrent Pos:* Res grant, Fairfield Univ, 69-72; NIH grant internal med, Sch Med, Yale Univ, 72-76. *Mem:* Am Soc Mech Engrs; Am Soc Eng Educ. *Res:* Digital computing; computers in public school education; physical principles of peristaltic phenomena; mechanical properties of tissue. *Mailing Add:* Dept of Physics Fairfield Univ Fairfield CT 06430

ZABLOCKA-ESPLIN, BARBARA, b Warsaw, Poland, Jan 5, 25; m 64; c 4. NEUROPHARMACOLOGY, NEUROPHYSIOLOGY. *Educ:* Med Acad, Warsaw, dipl, 52, MD, 61. *Prof Exp:* Asst prof pharmacol, Med Acad, Warsaw, 52-55, sr asst prof, 55-61; Riker Int fel, Col Med, Univ Utah, 61-62, res assoc, 62-65, asst res prof, 65-68; asst prof, 68-77, ASSOC PROF PHARMACOL & THERAPEUT, McGILL UNIV, 77- *Mem:* Am Soc Pharmacol & Exp Therapeut; Can Pharmaceut Asn. *Res:* Central excitatory and depressant drugs; central transmitter substances. *Mailing Add:* Dept Pharm & Exp Therapeut McIntyre Med Bldg Montreal PQ M3G 1Y6 Can

ZABLOW, LEONARD, b New York, NY, Sept 3, 27; m 50; c 2. BIOPHYSICS, NEUROPHYSIOLOGY. *Educ:* Calif Inst Technol, BSc, 48; Columbia Univ, MA, 50. *Prof Exp:* Res worker biochem, Worcester Found Exp Biol, 51-52; res asst neurol, 52-60, res assoc neurol, 60-73, SR STAFF ASSOC NEUROL, COL PHYSICIANS & SURGEONS, COLUMBIA UNIV, 73- *Concurrent Pos:* Lectr, Polytech Inst Brooklyn, 59-66. *Mem:* Fel AAAS; Biophys Soc; Am Phys Soc. *Res:* Implications of scalp electroencephalograms for cortical source localization; spatial electroencephalogram analysis; focal generator size in clinical and experimental epilepsy; electromyography; source distributations in electroncephalography; computer analysis of the electroncephalogram and electromyogram; experimental epilepsy. *Mailing Add:* 5610 Post Rd Bronx NY 10471

ZABOROWSKI, LEON MICHAEL, environmental chemistry, see previous edition

ZABORSKY, OSKAR RUDOLF, b Neuwalddorf, Czech, Oct 6, 41; US citizen; m 68; c 2. BIOLOGICAL CHEMISTRY, BIOTECHNOLOGY. *Educ:* Philadelphia Col Pharm & Sci, BSc, 64; Univ Chicago, PhD(chem), 68. *Prof Exp:* NIH fel, Harvard Univ, 68-69; sr res chemist, Corp Res Labs, Esso Res & Eng Co, Linden, NJ, 69-74; PROG MGR ENZYME TECHNOL, RENEWABLE RESOURCES PROG, NSF, 74- *Mem:* AAAS; Am Chem Soc. *Res:* Modification of enzymes; immobilized enzymes; enzyme technology; biochemical engineering; fermentation technology; biomass fuels and chemicals; catalysis. *Mailing Add:* Renewable Resources Prog Nat Sci Found Washington DC 20550

ZABORSZKY, JOHN, b Budapest, Hungary, May 13, 14; nat US; m 59. ENGINEERING. *Educ:* Josef Nador Royal Hungarian Tech Univ, Budapest, dipl, 37, DSc, 42. *Prof Exp:* Chief engr in charge power syst eng, Munic Elec Works Budapest, 44-48; from asst prof to prof eng, Mo Sch Mines, 48-55; chmn dept systs, mech & aerospace eng, 64-68, chmn control systs sci & eng, 68-74, PROF ENG, WASH UNIV, 55-, CHMN SYSTS SCI & MATH DEPT, 74- *Concurrent Pos:* Docens, Royal Hungarian Tech Univ, 46-47; consult, Westinghouse Elec Co, 49-55, Babcock-Wilcox Co, 78, McDonnell Aircraft Co, Mo, Emerson Elec Co, Mo & Hi Voltage Equip Co, Ohio. *Mem:* Am Soc Mech Engrs; Soc Indust & Appl Math; fel Inst Elec & Electronics Engrs. *Res:* Control theory; optimal control; functional analysis approaches; identification adaptive control; estimation and filtering bilinear systems; controllability and observability; power systems dynamics, stability and control; switching phenomena; high voltage direct current. *Mailing Add:* 1925 S Signal Hills Dr St Louis MO 63122

ZABRANSKY, RONALD JOSEPH, b Little Ferry, NJ, Mar 18, 35; m 58; c 3. CLINICAL MICROBIOLOGY, CLINICAL BACTERIOLOGY. *Educ:* Rutgers Univ, BS, 56; Ohio State Univ, MS, 61, PhD(microbiol), 63; Am Bd Med Microbiol, dipl, 69. *Prof Exp:* Microbiologist, Battelle Mem Inst, 59-60; teaching asst med microbiol bact, Ohio State Univ, 60-61, res asst, 61-63; assoc consult microbiol, Mayo Clin, 63-64, consult, 64-69; DIR DIV MICROBIOL, MT SINAI MED CTR, MILWAUKEE, 69- *Concurrent Pos:* Asst clin prof, Dept Microbiol, Med Col Wis, 70-74; chmn, Nat Registry Microbiologists, 74-79; mem bd gov, Am Acad Microbiol, 74-79; assoc adj prof microbiol, Med Col Wis, 75-; asoc clin prof allied health, Univ Wis-Milwaukee, 78- *Mem:* Fel Am Acad Microbiol; Am Pub Health Asn; Am Soc Microbiol. *Res:* isolation and identification of anaerobic bacteria; invitro evaluation of antibiotics; antibiotic testing of anaerobic bacteria. *Mailing Add:* Div Microbiol Mt Sinai Med Ctr 950 N 12th St Milwaukee WI 53201

ZABRISKIE, FRANKLIN ROBERT, b New York, NY, Dec 21, 33. ASTRONOMY. *Educ:* Princeton Univ, BSE, 55, MSE, 57, PhD(astron), 60. *Prof Exp:* Asst prof astron, Wesleyan Univ, 60-66; assoc prof astron, Pa State Univ, University Park, 66-79; PRES, ASTRO COMPUT CONTROLS, INC, 80- *Mem:* Am Astron Soc; Int Astron Union; Am Geophys Union. *Res:* Design of instruments for optical telescopes; photoelectric stellar classification; studies of long period variable stars. *Mailing Add:* RD 1 Alexandria PA 16611

ZABRISKIE, JOHN LANSING, JR, b Auburn, NY, June 8, 39; m 63; c 2. ORGANIC CHEMISTRY. *Educ:* Dartmouth Col, BA, 61; Univ Rochester, PhD(chem), 66. *Prof Exp:* Sr chemist process res, Merck & Co, Inc, NJ, 65-68, tech asst to exec dir, animal sci res, 69-70, sr mgr pharmacol qual control, Merck Sharp & Dohme, 70-72, mgr pharmaceut mfg, 72-74, dir pharmaceut mfg, 74-79, secy new prod comt, 79-80, dir mkt planning, 80-81, DIR MGT ENG, MERCK SHARP & DOHME RES LABS, 81- *Res:* Organic synthesis and reaction mechanisms. *Mailing Add:* Merck Sharp & Dohme West Point PA 19486

ZABRONSKY, HERMAN, b Brooklyn, NY, April 5, 27; m 57; c 2. RELIABILITY, QUEUEING THEORY. *Educ:* City Univ NY, BS, 48; Univ Pa, MA, 51. *Prof Exp:* Assoc mathematician, Oak Ridge, 51-53; sr engr, Ford Instrument Co, 53-58 & RCA, 58-67; staff scientist, Computer Sci Corp, 67-73, Calculon, 78-79; SR STATISTICIAN, AM SYSTS CORP, 79- *Concurrent Pos:* Lectr math, Stevens Inst Technol, 59-65; consult econ, Int Bus Serv, 80-81. *Mem:* Math Asn Am. *Res:* Applied probability queveing reliability; econometrics; statistical theory of communications; partial differential equations; boundary value problems related to heat and mass transfer; reactors. *Mailing Add:* 10857 Bucknell Dr Wheaton MD 20902

ZABUSKY, NORMAN J, b New York, NY, Jan 4, 29; m 54; c 3. COMPUTATIONAL FLUID DYNAMICS. *Educ:* City Col New York, BEE, 51; Mass Inst Technol, MS, 53; Calif Inst Technol, PhD(physics), 59. *Prof Exp:* Res asst, Servo-Mech Lab, Mass Inst Technol, 51-53; mem tech staff, Missile & Radar Div, Raytheon Mfg Co, 53-55; NSF fel, Max Planck Inst Physics & Astrophys, 59-60; vis res assoc, Plasma Physics Lab, Princeton Univ, 60-61; mem tech staff, Bell Tel Labs, Inc, 61-63, supvr plasma & computational physics, 63-68, head computational physics res dept, 68-75; PROF MATH & ENG, UNIV PITTSBURGH, 76- *Concurrent Pos:* Dir, Int Sch Nonlinear Math & Physics, Ger, NATO, 66; mem comt support res in math sci, Nat Acad Sci, 66; J S Guggenheim fel, Oxford Univ, Math Inst & Weizmann Inst Sci, 71-72; vis prof, Lab Appl Math Physics, Tech Univ Denmark, 80; vis scientist, Nat Ctr Atmospheric Res, 80 & 81; consult, Exxon Res & Eng Co, Linden, NJ & Naval Res Lab, Washington, DC. *Mem:* AAAS; fel Am Phys Soc; fel NY Acad Sci. *Res:* Computer simulation approach for realistic nonlinear fluid, plasma and chemical dynamical systems. *Mailing Add:* Dept Math Univ Pittsburgh Pittsburgh PA 15260

ZACCARIA, ROBERT ANTHONY, b Philadelphia, Pa, May 29, 43; m 64; c 3. DEVELOPMENTAL BIOLOGY, VERTEBRATE ENDOCRINOLOGY. *Educ:* Bridgewater Col, BA, 65; Univ Va, PhD(biol), 73. *Prof Exp:* Asst prof, 73-80, ASSOC PROF BIOL, LYCOMING COL, 80- *Mem:* Am Soc Zool; AAAS; Am Inst Biol Sci; Sigma Xi. *Res:* Interaction among chromatophores in development of pigmentation in amphibians; limb regeneration in urodeles. *Mailing Add:* Dept Biol Lycoming Col Williamsport PA 17701

ZACCHEI, ANTHONY GABRIEL, b Philadelphia, Pa, Mar 31, 40; m 63; c 3. DRUG METABOLISM, MASS SPECTROMETRY. *Educ:* Villanova Univ, BS, 61, MS, 65; Univ Minn, Minneapolis, PhD(biochem), 68. *Prof Exp:* Res assoc pharmacol, 61-64, sr res pharmacologist, 68-70, res fellow, 70-73, sr res fellow drug metabolism, 73-78, DIR HUMAN DRUG METABOLISM, MERCK SHARP & DOHME RES LABS, 78- *Concurrent Pos:* Vis asst prof, Inst Lipid Res, Baylor Col Med, 72; adj asst prof med, Jefferson Med Col, 79; mem spec study sect, Nat Inst Gen Med Sci, NIH, 78. *Mem:* Am Soc Pharmacol & Exp Therapeut; AAAS; Am Chem Soc; Am Soc Mass Spectrometry. *Res:* Investigations into the physiological disposition of new drug products including absorption, excretion and metabolic studies. *Mailing Add:* Drug Metab Dept 805 Merck Sharp & Dohme Res Labs West Point PA 19486

ZACH, RETO, b Davos-Platz, Switz, Dec 27, 40; Can citizen; m 66; c 1. ZOOLOGY, ECOLOGY. *Educ:* Univ Alta, Edmonton, BSc, 72; Univ Toronto, PhD(zool), 77. *Prof Exp:* Fel zool, Univ BC, Vancouver, 77-78; RESEARCHER ECOL, ATOMIC ENERGY CAN, LTD, 78- *Mem:* Ecol Soc Am; Can Soc Zool; Cooper Ornith Soc; Am Ornithologists' Union. *Res:* Environmental impact of nuclear energy; ecological modelling; animal behavior; birds. *Mailing Add:* Atomic Energy of Can Ltd Environ Res Br Pinawa MB R0E 1L0 Can

ZACHARIAH, GERALD L, b McLouth, Kans, June 12, 33; m 53; c 3. AGRICULTURAL ENGINEERING. *Educ:* Kans State Univ, BS, 55, MS, 59; Purdue Univ, PhD(agr eng), 63. *Prof Exp:* Instr agr eng, Kans State Univ, 55-56 & 56-60 & Purdue Univ, 60-63; asst prof eng, Univ Calif, 63-65; from asst prof to prof agr eng, Purdue Univ, Lafayette, 65-75; chmn, Dept Agr Eng, 75-80, DEAN RESIDENT INSTR, UNIV FLA, 80- *Concurrent Pos:* Res grants, 55-; indust consult, 55- *Mem:* Am Soc Agr Engrs; Am Soc Eng Educ; Inst Food Technologists; Nat Soc Prof Engrs. *Res:* Automatic control; food engineering; processing of agricultural products. *Mailing Add:* 1001 McCarty Hall Univ of Fla Gainesville FL 32611

ZACHARIAS, DAVID EDWARD, b Philadelphia, Pa, May 16, 26; m 68; c 3. X-RAY CRYSTALLOGRAPHY, ORGANIC CHEMISTRY. *Educ:* Temple Univ, AB, 53, AM, 54; Univ Pittsburgh, PhD(x-ray crystallog), 69. *Prof Exp:* From jr chemist to sr chemist, Smith Kline & French Labs, Pa, 54-71; RES ASSOC, MOLECULAR STRUCT LAB, INST FOR CANCER RES, 71- *Mem:* AAAS; Am Crystallog Asn; Am Chem Soc; Royal Soc Chem. *Res:* Synthesis of heterocyclic compounds; single crystal x-ray structure determination of organic and biologically important compounds; x-ray powder diffraction. *Mailing Add:* Molecular Struct Lab Inst Cancer Res Philadelphia PA 19111

ZACHARIAS, JERROLD REINACH, b Jacksonville, Fla, Jan 23 05; m 27; c 2. PHYSICS, SCIENCE EDUCATION. *Educ:* Columbia Univ, AB, 26, AM, 27, PhD(physics), 32. *Prof Exp:* Tutor physics, City Col New York, 29-30; instr, Hunter Col, 31-36, asst prof, 36-40; staff mem, Radiation Labs, Mass Inst Technol, 41-45; head eng div, Los Alamos Sci Lab, 45; prof physics, 46-66, dir lab nuclear sci, 46-56, inst prof, 66-70, dir educ res ctr, 68-72, EMER INST PROF & EMER PROF PHYSICS, MASS INST TECHNOL, 70- *Concurrent Pos:* Dir, Sprague Elec Co; trustee, Educ Develop Ctr. *Mem:* Nat Acad Sci; fel Am Phys Soc; fel Am Acad Arts & Sci. *Res:* Electric and magnetic shapes of atomic nuclei; atomic clocks; military technology; education reform. *Mailing Add:* 32 Clifton St Belmont MA 02178

ZACHARIAS, LEONA RUTH, b New York, NY, Feb 6, 07; m 27; c 2. HUMAN DEVELOPMENT. *Educ:* Columbia Univ, AB, 27, MA, 28, PhD(anat, embryol), 37. *Prof Exp:* Asst, Am Mus Natural Hist, 28-30; asst neurol, Col Physicians & Surgeons, Columbia Univ, 29-32, instr anat, physiol & embryol, 36-45, instr, dept optom, Univ, 44-46; instr biol & vert embryol, Hunter Col, 32-33; lectr opthal res, 46-65, res assoc obstet & gynec, 65-69, PRIN ASSOC OBSTET & GYNEC, HARVARD MED SCH, 69- *Concurrent Pos:* Biologist, Mass Eye & Ear Infirmary, 46-65; assoc biologist, Vincent Mem Hosp, Mass Gen Hosp, 67-; res assoc, Mass Inst Technol. *Mem:* Am Asn Anat; Endocrine Soc. *Res:* Experimental embryology; pituitary innervation; blindness in premature infants; growth and sexual development of adolescent girls. *Mailing Add:* Dept of Gynec Mass Gen Hosp Fruit St Boston MA 02114

ZACHARIASEN, FREDRIK, b Chicago, Ill, June 14, 31; m 57. THEORETICAL PHYSICS. *Educ:* Univ Chicago, PhB, 50, BS, 51; Calif Inst Technol, PhD(physics), 56. *Prof Exp:* Instr physics, Mass Inst Technol, 55-56, jr res physicist, Univ Calif, 56-57; res assoc physics, Stanford Univ, 57-58, asst prof, 58-60; from asst prof to assoc prof, 60-65, PROF PHYSICS, CALIF INST TECHNOL, 65- *Concurrent Pos:* Consult, Rand Corp, 56-; Sloan Found fel, 60-64; consult, Los Alamos Sci Lab, 61-; Inst Defense Anal, 61-; Guggenheim Found fel, 70-71. *Res:* High energy particle physics. *Mailing Add:* Dept of Physics Calif Inst of Technol Pasadena CA 91109

ZACHARIASEN, K(ARSTEN) A(NDREAS), b Vardo, Norway, Mar 1, 24; div; c 3. CHEMICAL ENGINEERING. *Educ:* Inst Technol, Norway, Siv Ing, 50. *Prof Exp:* Lab engr, Vestfos Cellulose Works, Norway, 51-52; head, Process & Develop Lab, And H Kiaer & Co, Ltd, 52-55; process engr, Buckeye Cellulose Corp, 56-58, sect head, 59-63, mgr Memphis Plant, 64-68 & Foley Plant, 68-71, mgr, Grande Prairie Plant, Procter & Gamble Cellulose Ltd, 71-77, MGR CELL PROCESS DEVELOP, BUCKEYE CELLULOSE CORP, PROCTER & GAMBLE CO, 77- *Mem:* Tech Asn Pulp & Paper Indust; Norweg Chem Soc; Norweg Tech Asn Pulp & Paper Indust. *Res:* Cellulose research; pulping and bleaching. *Mailing Add:* Buckeye Cellulose Corp PO Box 8407 Memphis TN 38108

ZACHARIUS, ROBERT MARVIN, b New York, NY, Mar 21, 20; m 44; c 4. PLANT BIOCHEMISTRY, PLANT-PARASITE INTERACTIONS. *Educ:* NY Univ, BA, 43; Univ Colo, MA, 48; Univ Rochester, PhD(plant physiol), 53. *Prof Exp:* Asst chem, Univ Colo, 47-48; asst bot, Cornell Univ, 51-52; res chemist, Gen Cigar Co, Inc, Pa, 52-54; biochemist, Eastern Utilization Res Br, 54-57, res chemist, Eastern Utilization Res & Develop Div Pa, 57-71, res chemist, Plant Prod Lab, Eastern Regional Res Ctr, 71-74, RES CHEMIST, EASTERN REGIONAL RES CTR, AGR RES SERV, USDA, 74- *Concurrent Pos:* Lectr, St Joseph's Col, Pa. *Mem:* Int Asn Plant Tissue Cult; Am Phytopath Soc; Biochem Soc; Am Chem Soc; Am Soc Plant Physiol. *Res:* Non-protein nitrogen compounds of plants; plant proteins; nicotiana alkaloids; ion-exchange and chromatographic methods; electrophoresis; antimetabolites; plant metabolism; proteolytic inhibitors; plant-parasite interactions, stress physiology and phytoalexins; plant cell tissue culture. *Mailing Add:* USDA Sci & Educ Admin Eastern Regional Res Ctr Philadelphia PA 19118

ZACHARUK, R Y, b Yorkton, Sask, May 1, 28; m 52; c 2. INSECT MORPHOLOGY, INSECT PATHOLOGY. *Educ:* Univ Sask, BSA, 50, MSc, 55; Univ Glasgow, PhD(histochem, physiol), 61. *Prof Exp:* Res officer entom, Res Sta, Can Dept Agr, 50-63; assoc prof biol, 63-65, chmn dept, 65-67, PROF BIOL, UNIV REGINA, 67- *Concurrent Pos:* Agr Inst Can fel, 59-61. *Mem:* AAAS; Soc Invert Path; Electron Micros Soc Am; Can Soc Entom; Can Soc Zool. *Res:* Sense organ ultrastructure; neurophysiology; entomophagous fungi; histochemistry. *Mailing Add:* Dept of Biol Univ of Regina Regina SK S4S 0A2 Can

ZACHARY, LOREN WILLIAM, b Colfax, Iowa, Apr 26, 43; m 63; c 2. ENGINEERING. *Educ:* Iowa State Univ, BS, 66, MS, 74, PhD(eng mech), 76. *Prof Exp:* Asst eng, Aerospace Div, Martin Marietta Corp, 66-72; asst prof, 76-80, ASSOC PROF ENG MECH, IOWA STATE UNIV, 80- *Mem:* Soc Exp Stress Anal. *Res:* Experimental stress analysis; non-destructive testing. *Mailing Add:* 210 Lab of Mech Iowa State Univ Ames IA 50011

ZACHARY, NORMAN, b New York, NY, Sept 14, 26; m 54; c 3. COMPUTER SCIENCE, SYSTEMS ANALYSIS. *Educ:* NY Univ, AB, 47; Harvard Univ, PhD, 52. *Prof Exp:* Asst prof math, Univ Md, 51-52; mem, Inst Advan Study, 52-54; mem tech staff, Hughes Aircraft Co, 54-55; sect head, Sylvania Elec Prod, Inc, 55-57, lab mgr, Electronic Systs Div, 58-60; staff consult, Otis Elevator Co, 57-58; vpres, Gen Tel Co, Calif, Gen Tel & Electronics Corp, 60-63; dir commun & data systs, NAm Aviation, Inc, 63-64; dir, Harvard Comput Ctr, Mass, 64-71; EXEC V PRES & DIR, DATA ARCHITECTS, INC, 71- *Concurrent Pos:* Consult, banking, ins & financial industs. *Mem:* Am Math Soc; Asn Comput Mach. *Res:* Computers and systems analysis with application to the solution of engineering, administrative and management problems; real time systems; integrated business data processing. *Mailing Add:* 257 Prince St West Newton MA 02165

ZACHER, ALBERT RICHARD, high energy physics, see previous edition

ZACHMANOGLOU, ELEFTHERIOS CHARALAMBOS, b Thessaloniki, Greece, Mar 19, 34; US citizen. MATHEMATICS. *Educ:* Rensselaer Polytech Inst, BAeroE, 56, MS, 57; Univ Calif, Berkeley, PhD(appl math), 62. *Prof Exp:* From asst prof to assoc prof, 62-70, PROF MATH, PURDUE UNIV, LAFAYETTE, 70-, ASSOC HEAD DEPT, 81- *Concurrent Pos:* Fulbright res grant, Univ Rome, 65-66. *Mem:* Am Math Soc. *Res:* Partial differential equations; wave propagation. *Mailing Add:* Dept of Math Purdue Univ Lafayette IN 47907

ZACHOS, COSMOS K, b Athens, Greece, Sept 8, 51. PHYSICS. *Educ:* Princeton Univ, AB, 74; Calif Inst Technol, PhD(physics), 79. *Prof Exp:* Res fel in theoret, Calif Inst Technol, 79; res assoc, Univ Wis, Madison, 79-81; RES ASSOC PHYSICS, FERMI NAT ACCELERATOR LAB, 81- *Mem:* Sigma Xi. *Res:* Field theoretical model building involving supersymmetry and supergravity and the discovery of new field and group theoretical effects; discovery and illumination of the structure of voulocal symmetry in two dimensional models; asymptatic properties of magnetic monopoles. *Mailing Add:* Theory Div Fermi Lab Batavia IL 60510

ZACK, NEIL RICHARD, b Canton, Ohio, Apr 26, 47. INORGANIC CHEMISTRY, FLUORINE CHEMISTRY. *Educ:* Rensselaer Polytech Inst, BS, 69; Marshall Univ, MS, 70; Univ Idaho, PhD(chem), 74. *Prof Exp:* Fel chem, Utah State Univ, 74-75; fel, Univ Idaho, 75-76; sr chemist, Allied Chem Corp, 76-79; GROUP LEADER, EXXON NUCLEAR IDAHO CO, 79- *Mem:* Am Chem Soc; Sigma Xi; Inst Nuclear Mat Mgt. *Res:* Inorganic heterocyclics; fluorine containing derivatives of catenated sulfur compounds. *Mailing Add:* Rte 8 Box 356B Idaho Falls ID 83401

ZACKAY, VICTOR FRANCIS, b San Francisco, Calif, May 2, 20. PHYSICAL METALLURGY. *Educ:* Univ Calif, BS, 47, MS, 48, PhD(metall), 52. *Prof Exp:* Jr engr gen mech eng, San Francisco Ord Dist, 41-42; jr res engr glass metal wetting, Univ Calif, 49-50, instr phys metall, 51-52; asst prof, Pa State Univ, 52-54; res scientist, Sci Lab, Ford Motor Co, 54-57, supvr metall, 58-59, asst mgr metall, 60-62; lectr metall, Univ Calif, Berkeley, 62-66, asst dir, Inorg Mat Res Div, Lawrence Berkeley Lab, 64-75, prof, 66-80, assoc dean eng, 70-74. *Honors & Awards:* Howe Award, Am Soc Metals, 60, Albert Sauveur Achievement Award, 71. *Mem:* Fel Am Soc Metals; fel Am Inst Mining, Metall & Petrol Engrs. *Res:* Materials science and engineering; design of alloys for technology with emphasis on advanced energy conversion and storage devices. *Mailing Add:* 1014 West Rd New Canaan CT 06840

ZACKROFF, ROBERT V, b Philadelphia, Pa, Sept 14, 51. INTERMEDIATE FILAMENTS, MICROTUBULES. *Educ:* Temple Univ, AB, 73, MA, 75, PhD(biol), 79. *Prof Exp:* Res asst, Temple Univ, 73-75; fel, Carnegie-Mellon Univ, 79-81; SR RES ASSOC, MED SCH, NORTHWESTERN UNIV, 82- *Mem:* Am Soc Cell Biol. *Res:* Cell motility; biochemistry of the cytoskeleton; self assembly of cytoskeletal proteins; microtubules and intermediate filaments. *Mailing Add:* Dept Cell Biol & Anat Med Sch Northwestern Univ 303 E Chicago Ave Chicago IL 60611

ZACKS, JAMES LEE, b Iron Mountain, Mich, Mar 23, 41; m 66; c 2. VISON RESEARCH, NEUROSCIENCE. *Educ:* Harvard Univ, BA, 63; Univ Calif, Berkeley, MS & PhD(psychol), 67. *Prof Exp:* Asst prof psychol, Univ Pa, 67-71; assoc prof, 72-77, PROF PSYCHOL, MICH STATE UNIV, 77- *Concurrent Pos:* Prog dir, USPHS training grant, 70-76; prin investr, NSF res grant, 70-75; adj prof zool, Mich State Univ, 76-; vis prof, Dept Psychol, Northwestern Univ, 79-80. *Mem:* Fel Optical Soc Am; Fel Am Acad Optometry; Psychonomic Soc; Asn Res Vision & Ophthal; Soc Neurosci. *Res:* Basic visual capacities and peripheral visual mechanisms which might determine them. *Mailing Add:* Dept Psychol Mich State Univ East Lansing MI 48824

ZACKS, SHELEMYAHU, b Tel Aviv, Israel, Oct 15, 32; m 55; c 2. MATHEMATICAL STATISTICS, STATISTICAL ANALYSIS. *Educ:* Hebrew Univ, Israel, BA, 55; Israel Inst Technol, MSc, 60; Columbia Univ, PhD(indust eng), 62. *Prof Exp:* Sr lectr statist, Israel Inst Technol, 63-65; prof, Kans State Univ, 65-68; prof, Univ NMex, 68-70; prof math & statist, Case Western Reserve Univ, 70-79, chmn dept, 74-79; prof, Va Poly Tech, 79-80; PROF & CHMN, STATE UNIV NY BINGHAMTON, 80- *Concurrent Pos:* Fel statist, Stanford Univ, 62-63; consult, Inst Mgt Sci & Eng, George Washington Univ, 67- *Mem:* Fel Am Statist Asn; fel Inst Math Statist; Int Statist Inst. *Res:* Optimal design of sequential experiments; statistical adaptive processes; analysis of contingency tables; manpower forecasting for large military organizations; stochastic control. *Mailing Add:* Dept Math Sci State Univ NY Binghamton NY 13901

ZACKS, SUMNER IRWIN, b Boston, Mass, June 29, 29; m 53; c 3. PATHOLOGY. *Educ:* Harvard Univ, BA, 51, MD, 55; Am Bd Path, dipl, 61. *Hon Degrees:* MA, Univ Pa & Brown Univ. *Prof Exp:* From intern to asst resident path, Mass Gen Hosp, Boston, 55-58; from asst prof to prof path, Sch Med, Univ Pa, 62-76; PROF PATH & CHMN DEPT, SCH MED, BROWN UNIV, 76- *Concurrent Pos:* Neuropathologist, Pa Hosp, 61-76, assoc dir, Ayer Lab, 64-76; pathologist-in-chief, Miriam Hosp, 76- *Honors & Awards:* Hektoen Bronze Medal, AMA, 61. *Mem:* Histochem Soc (secy, 65-69); Am Soc Exp Path; Am Soc Cell Biol; Am Asn Neuropath; fel Col Am Path. *Res:* Fine structure of neuromuscular junctions, normal and in disease; fine structure pathology of muscle; molecular pathology of endotoxins. *Mailing Add:* Dept of Path 134 Summit Ave Providence RI 02906

ZACZEK, NORBERT MARION, b Baltimore, Md, Aug 15, 36; m 73; c 1. ORGANIC CHEMISTRY. *Educ:* Loyola Col, Md, BS, 58; Carnegie-Mellon Univ, PhD(org chem), 62. *Prof Exp:* From instr to assoc prof, 62-71, PROF CHEM, LOYOLA COL (MD), 71- *Mem:* AAAS; Am Chem Soc; Royal Soc Chem. *Mailing Add:* Dept Chem Loyola Col Baltimore MD 21210

ZACZEPINSKI, SIOMA, b Grodno, USSR, June 15, 40; US citizen; m 73; c 2. HYDROPROCESSING, RESEARCH MANAGEMENT. *Educ:* Univ Tenn, BS, 63. *Prof Exp:* Process engr, Exxon Res & Eng Co, 63-68, startup adv, 68-69; process adv, Esso Eng Ltd, Europe, 69-71; startup adv, Exxon Res & Eng Co, 71-72, proj leader, 72-74; tech mgr, Esso Thailand Standard, Ltd, 75-76, eng assoc, Europe, 77; sect head, 77-80, LAB DIR, EXXON RES & ENG CO, 80- *Res:* Direct coal liquefaction process. *Mailing Add:* PO Box 4255 Baytown TX 77052

ZADEH, L(OTFI) A, b Baku, Russia, Feb 4, 21; nat US; m 46; c 2. ELECTRICAL ENGINEERING. *Educ:* Teheran Univ, BS, 42; Mass Inst Technol, MS, 46; Columbia Univ, PhD(elec eng), 49. *Prof Exp:* From instr to prof elec eng, Columbia Univ, 46-59; chmn dept, 63-67, PROF ELEC ENG & COMPUT SCI, UNIV CALIF, BERKELEY, 59- *Concurrent Pos:* Chmn US comn, Int Union Radio Sci. *Mem:* Am Math Soc; Asn Comput Mach; Inst Elec & Electronics Engrs. *Res:* System theory; information processing; theory of fuzziness. *Mailing Add:* Dept of Elec Eng & Comput Sci Univ of Calif Berkeley CA 94720

ZADEH, NORMAN, operations research, see previous edition

ZADNIK, VALENTINE EDWARD, b Cleveland, Ohio, Feb 13, 34; m 58; c 4. GEOLOGY, ENGINEERING GEOLOGY. *Educ:* Western Reserve Univ, BA, 57; Univ Ill, MS, 58, PhD(geol, civil eng), 60. *Prof Exp:* Res geologist, Jersey Prod Res Co, 64-65; sr res geologist, Esso Prod Res Co, 65-66; res geologist, US Army Res Off, 66-74; STAFF GEOLOGIST, OFF ENERGY RESOURCES, US GEOL SURV, 74-, LIAISON GEOLOGIST, NAT PETROL RESERVE ALASKA, 77- *Concurrent Pos:* Fel int affairs, Princeton Univ, 70-71; mem comt rock mech & comt seismol, Nat Acad Sci. *Mem:* Asn Eng Geol; Sigma Xi. *Res:* Petroleum exploration; carbonate rock petrography; solid-earth geophysics, particularly seismology, gravity, geomagnetism and geodesy. *Mailing Add:* 105 S Park Dr Arlington VA 22204

ZADO, FRANK M, b Velika, Yugoslavia, Mar 28, 34; nat US; m 57; c 2. ELECTRONIC MATERIALS, ANALYTICAL CHEMISTRY. *Educ:* Univ Zagreb, BS, 57, PhD(inorg anal), 59. *Prof Exp:* Res chemist inorg chem, Rudjer Boskovic Inst, Zagreb, Yugoslavia, 59-64; Int Atomic Energy Agency fel, Univ Ill, 64-65, NSF res assoc, 65-66; res chemist anal chem, Rudjer Boskovic Inst, Zagreb, 67-69; MEM RES STAFF, WESTERN ELEC RES CTR, PRINCETON, NJ, 70- *Concurrent Pos:* Mem, Int Working Group on Soldering Flux Specif. *Mem:* Am Chem Soc. *Res:* Adsorption phenomena; trace gas analysis; environmental monitoring systems development; chemical characterization of soldering fluxes; electrochemical charge transfer mechanisms; manufacturing process optimization and control; electronic reliability; failure mechanism assessment. *Mailing Add:* Western Elec Res Ctr PO Box 900 Princeton NJ 08540

ZADOFF, LEON NATHAN, b Passaic, NJ, Aug 6, 23; m 44; c 2. PHYSICS. *Educ:* Cooper Union, BChE, 48; NY Univ, PhD(physics), 58. *Prof Exp:* Chem engr, Flintkote Co, 48; petrol chemist, Paragon Oil Co, 48-49; protein chemist, Botany Mills, Inc, 49; jr chem engr, City Fire Dept, New York, 49-52; physicist, NY Naval Shipyard, 52-54; proj supvr reactor physics, Ford Instrument Co, 54-58; assoc scientist, Repub Aviation Corp, 58-64, specialist physicist, Repub Aviation Div, Fairchild-Hiller Corp, NY, 64-72; CHIEF SCIENTIST, EMS DEVELOP CORP, FARMINGDALE, 72- *Concurrent Pos:* Lectr, Adelphi Col, 58-; adj assoc prof, NY Inst Technol, 72- *Mem:* AAAS; Am Phys Soc; Am Inst Aeronaut & Astronaut; NY Acad Sci. *Res:* Theoretical, plasma and reactor physics; electromagnetic wave propagation; quantum mechanics. *Mailing Add:* 17 Spruce St Merrick NY 11566

ZADUNAISKY, JOSE ATILIO, b Rosario, Arg, July 15, 32; m 54; c 2. PHYSIOLOGY, BIOPHYSICS. *Educ:* Univ Buenos Aires, MD, 56. *Prof Exp:* Instr, Inst Physiol, Med Sch, Univ Buenos Aires, 52-56; Arg Nat Res Coun estab investr, Dept Biophys, Med Sch, Univ Buenos Aires, 60-63; assoc prof physiol & dir res, Dept Opthal, Sch Med, Univ Louisville, 64-67; assoc prof ophthal & physiol, Sch Med, Yale Univ, 67-73; PROF PHYSIOL & EXP OPHTHAL, MED SCH, NY UNIV, 73- *Concurrent Pos:* Arg Res Coun fel biochem, Univ Col, Dublin, 58-59 & Inst Biol Chem, Copenhagen, 59-60; USPHS grants, 62-; exec ed, Exp Eye Res, 70-; consult, Visual Sci A Study Sect, USPHS, 76-80. *Mem:* Fel NY Acad Sci; Biophys Soc; Asn Res Vision & Ophthal; Am Soc Zoologists; Int Soc Eye Res (secy, 78-81). *Res:* Transport and permeability of biological membranes, especially epithelial tissues. *Mailing Add:* Dept of Physiol NY Univ Med Sch New York NY 10016

ZAEHRINGER, MARY VERONICA, b Philadelphia, Pa, May 27, 11. FOODS. *Educ:* Temple Univ, BS, 46; Cornell Univ, MS, 48, PhD(foods), 53. *Prof Exp:* Asst food res, Cornell Univ, 46-48, 51-53; from instr to asst prof home econ res, Mont State Col, 48-50; res prof home econ, 53-72, res prof food sci, 72-73, RES PROF BACT & BIOCHEM, AGR EXP STA, UNIV IDAHO, 73- *Concurrent Pos:* Res fel, Inst Storage & Processing Agr Produce, State Agr Univ, Wageningen, 67-68. *Mem:* Am Asn Cereal Chem; Am Chem Soc; Inst Food Technol; Potato Asn Am. *Res:* Potato texture; quality of food products. *Mailing Add:* 614 Ash St Moscow ID 83843

ZAERR, JOE BENJAMIN, b Los Angeles, Calif, Sept 9, 32; m 54; c 3. FOREST PHYSIOLOGY, GROWTH HORMONES. *Educ:* Univ Calif, Berkeley, BS, 54, PhD(plant physiol), 64. *Prof Exp:* Res assoc, Crops Res Div, Agr Res Serv, USDA, Md, 64-65; asst prof forestry, 65-71, assoc prof, 71-80, asst dean, Grad Sch, 77-80, PROF FORESTRY, ORE STATE UNIV, 81-; VPRES, PMS INSTRUMENT CO, CORVALLIS, 67- *Concurrent Pos:* vis res prof, Agr Univ, Warsaw, Poland, 73-74; Fulbright res scholar, WGer, 81-82. *Mem:* AAAS; Am Soc Plant Physiol; Soc Am Foresters; Scand Soc Plant Physiol. *Res:* Plant growth regulators; forest regeneration; bioelectrical potential in plants; root growth. *Mailing Add:* Forestry Sch Ore State Univ Corvallis OR 97331

ZAFFARANO, DANIEL JOSEPH, b Cleveland, Ohio, Dec 16, 17; m 46; c 6. NUCLEAR PHYSICS. *Educ:* Case Inst Technol, BS, 39; Ind Univ, MS, 48, PhD(physics), 49. *Prof Exp:* Tech liaison, Nat Carbon Co, 40-45; contract liaison, Appl Physics Lab, Johns Hopkins Univ, 45-46; from assoc prof to prof, 49-67, chmn dept physics, 61-71, DISTINGUISHED PROF PHYSICS, IOWA STATE UNIV, 67-, VPRES FOR RES & GRAD DEAN, 71- *Concurrent Pos:* Sci liaison officer, US Off Naval Res, London, 57-58. *Mem:* Fel Am Phys Soc. *Res:* Experimental nuclear physics. *Mailing Add:* 201 Beardshear Iowa State Univ Ames IA 50010

ZAFFARONI, ALEJANDRO, b Montevideo, Uruguay, Feb 27, 23; m 46; c 2. BIOCHEMISTRY. *Educ:* Univ Montevideo, BS, 41; Univ Rochester, PhD(biochem), 49. *Hon Degrees:* DSc, Univ Rochester, 72. *Prof Exp:* Dir biol res, Syntex SA, Mex, 51-54, dir res & develop, 54-56, vpres, 56-61, pres, Syntex Labs, Inc, exec vpres, Syntex Corp & pres, Syntex Res Ctr, Calif, 61-68; PRES & DIR RES, ALZA CORP, 68-; PRES, DYNAPOL, 72- *Concurrent Pos:* Hon prof, Univ Montevideo, 59. *Mem:* Am Chem Soc; Soc Exp Biol & Med; Endocrine Soc; Am Soc Biol Chemists; Am Soc Microbiol. *Res:* Biochemistry and pharmacology of steroid hormones. *Mailing Add:* Alza Corp 950 Page Mill Rd Palo Alto CA 94304

ZAFIRATOS, CHRIS DAN, b Portland, Ore, Nov 18, 31; m 57; c 4. NUCLEAR PHYSICS. *Educ:* Lewis & Clark Col, BS, 57; Univ Wash, PhD(physics), 62. *Prof Exp:* Res instr nuclear physics, Univ Wash, 62; staff mem, Los Alamos Sci Lab, 62-64; asst prof physics, Ore State Univ, 64-68; from asst prof to assoc prof, 68-72, chmn dept, 78-82, PROF PHYSICS, UNIV COLO, 72- *Concurrent Pos:* Chmn nuclear physics lab, Univ Colo, 74-76. *Mem:* Am Phys Soc. *Res:* Nuclear reactions; neutron and nuclear structure physics. *Mailing Add:* Dept of Physics Univ of Colo Boulder CO 80302

ZAFRAN, MISHA, b Berlin, Ger, Aug 10, 49; US citizen. MATHEMATICAL ANALYSIS. *Educ:* Univ Calif, Riverside, BS, 68, PhD(math), 72. *Prof Exp:* Mem math res, Inst Advan Study, 72-73; asst prof math, Stanford Univ, 73-79; mem staff, Inst Advan Study, 79-80; MEM STAFF, DEPT MATH, UNIV WASH, 80- *Mem:* Am Math Soc. *Res:* Interrelationships between harmonic analysis, spectral theory and interpolation of operators. *Mailing Add:* Dept of Math Univ Wash Seattle WA 98195

ZAGAR, WALTER T, b Brooklyn, NY, Oct 15, 28; m 51; c 4. PHYSICAL CHEMISTRY, POLYMER CHEMISTRY. *Educ:* Manhattan Col, BS, 50; Fordham Univ, MS, 55, PhD(phys chem), 58. *Prof Exp:* Chemist, Dextran Corp, 52-53; instr chem, Notre Dame Col, NY, 55-56; instr, Manhattan Col, 56-57; sr scientist, Polymer Chem Div, W R Grace & Co, 57-66; mgr plastics div, Allied Chem Corp, 66; mgr polymer develop, Chemplex Corp, 66-67; sr res chemist, Plastics Div, NJ, 67-72, La, 72-73, TECH SUPVR, ALLIED CHEM CORP, LA, 73- *Mem:* Soc Plastics Engrs; Am Chem Soc; NY Acad Sci. *Res:* Polymer development in area of polyethylene blends and additive systems for polymers, especially antioxidants, antistats and ultraviolet absorbers. *Mailing Add:* 5013 Parkhurst Dr Baton Rouge LA 70816

ZAGATA, MICHAEL DEFOREST, b Oneonta, NY, May 28, 42; m 81. NATURAL RESOURCES POLICY, ENVIRONMENTAL REGULATION. *Educ:* State Univ NY, Oneonta, BS, 64, MS, 68; Iowa State Univ, PhD(wildlife ecol), 72. *Prof Exp:* Teacher biol, Oneonta Consolidated Sch & Southampton Pub Schs, 64-69; asst prof wildlife ecol, Sch Forest Resources, Univ Maine, 72-75; field dir, Wildlife Soc, 76-77; dir fed rel, Nat Audubon Soc, 77-79; prog develop off, Bd Agr & Nat Resources, Nat Acad Sci, 79-80; MGR ECOL SCI, TENNECO, INC, 80- *Concurrent Pos:* Prin investr, US Forest Serv, 73-75; co-chmn, Pub Lands Task Force, Nat Asn Many Facturers; exec bd, Nat Resources Coun Am; mem, Waterfowl Feeding Adv Comm, US Fish & Wildlife Serv, 77-79; chmn, Conserv Affairs Comt, Wildlife Soc, 79-; mem, Nat Adv Comt Regional Plan Asn, 78 & Nat Comt Fish & Wildlife Res, 78- *Mem:* Wildlife Soc; Soc Petroleum Indust Biologists; NY Acad Sci; Am Fisheries Soc; Soc Wetland Scientists. *Res:* Impact of man-induced perturbations on fish and wildlife habitats and on the populations which occupy those habitats. *Mailing Add:* 1100 Milam Bldg PO Box 2511 Houston TX 77001

ZAGER, STANLEY E(DWARD), b Sheldon, Iowa, Mar 6, 21; m 49; c 2. CHEMICAL ENGINEERING. *Educ:* Iowa State Univ, BS, 43; Purdue Univ, PhD(chem eng), 50. *Prof Exp:* Jr chemist, Shell Develop Co, 43-46; lab asst, Purdue Univ, 46-47, asst instr, 47-50; res engr, Johns-Manville Corp, 50-57; sr res engr, Res Ctr, B F Goodrich Co, 57-60, sect leader, 60-63, corp task force secy, 64-65, mgr mgt & comput sci, 66-76; mgr process develop & licensing, H K Ferguson Co, 76-77; ASSOC PROF CHEM ENG, YOUNGSTOWN STATE UNIV, 77- *Mem:* Am Chem Soc; Am Inst Chem Engrs; Asn Comput Mach; Sigma Xi. *Res:* Application of computers and mathematics to scientific and business problems; process development, design, economics; improving energy recovery from fossil fuels, process and product development; heterogeneous catalysis; polymer processing. *Mailing Add:* 2874 Cedar Hill Rd Cuyahoga Falls OH 44223

ZAGON, IAN STUART, b New York, NY, Mar 28, 43; m 64. ANATOMY, DEVELOPMENTAL NEUROBIOLOGY. *Educ:* Univ Wis-Madison, BS, 65; Univ Ill, Urbana, MS, 69; Univ Colo, Denver, PhD(anat), 72. *Prof Exp:* Asst prof biol struct, Med Sch, Univ Miami, 72-74; asst prof, 74-78, ASSOC PROF ANAT, MILTON S HERSHEY MED SCH, PA STATE UNIV, 78- *Mem:* Soc Neurosci; Am Asn Anat; AAAS. *Res:* Developmental neurobiology, focusing on normal and abnormal brain and cerebellar development; effects of nitroso compounds and narcotic analgesics on CNS morphogenesis. *Mailing Add:* Dept of Anat Hershey Med Ctr Pa State Univ Hershey PA 17033

ZAHALSKY, ARTHUR C, b New York, NY, Oct 31, 30. BIOCHEMISTRY, PARASITOLOGY. *Educ:* McGill Univ, BSc, 52; NY Univ, PhD(microbiol), 63. *Prof Exp:* Res assoc & staff mem, Haskins Labs, 58-66; res collabr, Brookhaven Nat Labs, 68-74; asst prof microbiol, Queens Col (NY), 66-69; assoc prof biochem, doctoral prog, City Univ New York, 69-71; PROF LAB BIOCHEM, PARASITOL, SOUTHERN ILL UNIV, EDWARDSVILLE, 71- *Mem:* AAAS; Am Soc Parasitol; Biochem Soc; Royal Soc Trop Med Hyg. *Res:* Chemotherapy and immunology of African trypanosomiasis; mechanisms of action of trypanocides; host immune response to parasites. *Mailing Add:* Lab Biochem Parasitol Biol Sci Southern Ill Univ Edwardsville IL 62026

ZAHARKO, DANIEL SAMUEL, b New Westminster, BC, Nov 3, 30; US citizen; m 59; c 3. PHARMACOLOGY, PHYSIOLOGY. *Educ:* Univ BC, BPE, 53, dipl educ, 54; Univ Ill, MS, 55, PhD(physiol), 63. *Prof Exp:* Instr, Univ Sask, 55-57 & Univ Ill, 57-59; instr to asst prof pharmacol, Ind Univ, Bloomington, 63-68; USPHS res fel, 68-70, PHARMACOLOGIST, LAB CHEM PHARMACOL, NAT CANCER INST, 70- *Mem:* Am Asn Cancer Res; AAAS; Am Soc Pharmacol & Exp Therapeut. *Res:* Environmental physiology; biochemical pharmacology; cancer chemotherapy; pharmacokinetics. *Mailing Add:* Lab of Chem Pharmacol Nat Cancer Inst Bethesda MD 20205

ZAHL, PAUL ARTHUR, b Bensenville, Ill, Mar 20, 10; m 46; c 2. NATURAL SCIENCE, EXPERIMENTAL BIOLOGY. *Educ:* NCent Col, AB, 32; Harvard Univ, AM, 34, PhD(biol), 36. *Hon Degrees:* DSc, NCent Col, 72. *Prof Exp:* Asst comp anat & histol, Harvard Univ, 34-36, Parke Davis & Co res fel endocrinol, 36-37; staff physiologist, 37-46, assoc dir & secy corp, 46-58, RES ASSOC, HASKINS LABS, INC, NEW YORK, 58-; SR SCIENTIST, NAT GEOG SOC, 58- *Concurrent Pos:* Mem var expeds, 37-67; res assoc, Union Col, NY, 37-39; guest investr, Mem Hosp, New York, 39-41; res assoc, Am Mus Natural Hist, 51-64; adj prof biol, Fordham Univ, 64-; USPHS & Dept Health, Educ & Welfare grants. *Mem:* Am Soc Zoologists; Soc Exp Biol & Med; Ecol Soc Am; Radiol Soc NAm; Am Asn Cancer Res. *Res:* Experimental biology; natural history; exploration. *Mailing Add:* Nat Geog Soc 17th & M Sts NW Washington DC 20036

ZAHLER, RAPHAEL, medicine, see previous edition

ZAHLER, STANLEY ARNOLD, b New York, NY, May 28, 26; m 52; c 3. MICROBIAL GENETICS. *Educ:* NY Univ, AB, 48; Univ Chicago, MS, 49, PhD, 52. *Prof Exp:* Instr gen bact, Northern Ill Col Optom, 51; USPHS fel bact, Univ Ill, 52-54; instr microbiol, Univ Wash, 54-57, asst prof, 57-58; asst prof, Med Ctr, WVa Univ, 59; asst prof, 59-64, assoc prof, 64-79, assoc dir, Div Biol Sci, 75-78, PROF MICROBIAL GENETICS, CORNELL UNIV, 79- *Concurrent Pos:* Consult, Gen Elec Corp, 63-66, Sandoz, Inc, 80- & Dow Chem, 81-; USPHS spec fel, Scripps Clin & Res Found, 66-67. *Mem:* AAAS; Am Soc Microbiol; Genetics Soc Am; Brit Soc Gen Microbiol. *Res:* Bacteriophages; microbial genetics; developmental biology; metabolic controls; genetics of bacillus subtilis and other bacilli. *Mailing Add:* Sect of Genetics & Develop Cornell Univ Ithaca NY 14853

ZAHLER, WARREN LEIGH, b Springville, NY, June 28, 41; m 68; c 2. BIOLOGICAL CHEMISTRY. *Educ:* Alfred Univ, BA, 63; Univ Wis-Madison, MS, 66, PhD(biochem), 68. *Prof Exp:* NIH fel molecular biol, Vanderbilt Univ, 67-71, res assoc, 71-72; asst prof, 72-77, PROF BIOCHEM, UNIV MO-COLUMBIA, 77- *Mem:* Am Oil Chem Soc; Am Chem Soc; Soc Study Reproduction. *Res:* Isolation and characterization of sperm membranes. Study of the function of sperm membranes and membrane bound enzymes in reproduction. *Mailing Add:* Dept of Biochem Univ of Mo 105 Schweitzer Hall Columbia MO 65201

ZAHN, JOHN J, b Beaver Dam, Wis, May 8, 32; m 78; c 3. ENGINEERING MECHANICS, STRUCTURAL DESIGN. *Educ:* Univ Wis, BS, 54, MS, 59, PhD(mech), 64. *Prof Exp:* Instr eng mech, Univ Wis, 59-62, lectr, 62-64; ENGR, FOREST PROD LAB, FOREST SERV, USDA, 64- *Honors & Awards:* L J Markwardt Award, Forest Prod Res Soc, 78. *Mem:* Am Soc Civil Engrs; Forest Prod Res Soc. *Res:* Theory of elasticity; elastic stability; applied mathematics; probability. *Mailing Add:* Forest Prod Lab USDA Walnut St Madison WI 53705

ZAHND, HUGO, b Berne, Switz, May 16, 02; nat US; m 26; c 2. BIOCHEMISTRY. *Educ:* NY Univ, BS, 26; Columbia Univ, AM, 29, PhD(biochem), 33. *Prof Exp:* Tutor chem, 28-34, from instr to prof, 34-72, EMER PROF CHEM, BROOKLYN COL, 72- *Concurrent Pos:* Contrib, Acad Am Encycl, Arete Publ Co, Princeton, NJ, 80. *Mem:* Fel AAAS; Am Chem Soc; Hist Sci Soc; fel Am Inst Chem; NY Acad Sci. *Res:* Labile sulfur in proteins; quantitative inorganic and organic analysis; history of chemistry; chromatography as applied to the fields of alkaloids, amino acids and proteins. *Mailing Add:* 42 Herbert Ave Port Washington NY 11050

ZAHNLEY, JAMES CURRY, b Manhattan, Kans, Apr 16, 38; m 65; c 2. BIOCHEMISTRY. *Educ:* Kans State Univ, BS, 58; Purdue Univ, MS, 62, PhD(biochem), 63. *Prof Exp:* Res assoc enzym, Syntex Inst Molecular Biol, Calif, 63-64, assoc biochem, 64-65; asst res biochemist, NIH grant, 65-66; res chemist, Sci & Educ Admin Agr Res, 66-80, RES CHEMIST, WESTERN REGIONAL RES CTR, AGR RES SERV, USDA, 80- *Mem:* AAAS; Am Soc Biol Chemists; Am Chem Soc. *Res:* Enzymology; protein chemistry; food biochemistry. *Mailing Add:* Western Regional Res Ctr US Dept of Agr 800 Buchanan St Berkeley CA 94710

ZAHRADNIK, JOHN W(ALTER), b New Kensington, Pa, Jan 6, 28; m 50; c 5. AGRICULTURAL ENGINEERING. *Educ:* Pa State Univ, BS, 50; Iowa State Univ, MS, 51. *Prof Exp:* Agr engr, Near East Found, Iran, 51-54; asst res prof agr & food processing, 54-56, assoc res prof, 56-64, mem, Hokkaido exchange prog, Campus Coordr, Int Coop Admin, 57-60, prof biol process eng, 64-68, PROF AGR ENG, UNIV MASS, AMHERST, 68-, PROF MECH & AEROSPACE ENG, 67- *Concurrent Pos:* Consult engr, 57-; Danforth fel, 60-61. *Mem:* Am Soc Agr Engrs; Inst Food Technol; Am Soc Mech Engrs. *Res:* Heat and mass transfer in agricultural and food processing; Ruth processes in biology. *Mailing Add:* Dept Mech & Aerospace Eng Univ Mass Amherst MA 01002

ZAHRADNIK, RAYMOND LOUIS, b Ford City, Pa, Sept 18, 36; m 60; c 3. CHEMICAL ENGINEERING, ENERGY SCIENCE. *Educ:* Carnegie Inst Technol, BS, 59, MS, 61, PhD(chem eng), 63. *Prof Exp:* Sr engr res labs, Westinghouse Elec Corp, 61-65, fel engr, 65-66; from assoc prof to prof chem eng, Carnegie-Mellon Univ, 67-74; dir, Div Coal Conversion & Utilization, ERDA, 75-76; pres, Ray Zahradnik Consult, Inc, 76-77; DIR ENERGY RES, OCCIDENTAL RES CORP, 77- *Concurrent Pos:* Prog mgr energy res & technol, NSF, 72-74; mem res coord panel, Gas Res Inst, 77- *Res:* Energy research. *Mailing Add:* Occidental Res Corp PO Box 19601 Irvine CA 92713

ZAIDEL, ERAN, b Kibbutz Yagur, Israel, Jan 23, 44; US citizen; m 65; c 2. NEUROPSYCHOLOGY. *Educ:* Columbia Univ, AB, 67; Calif Inst Technol, MSc, 68, PhD(psychobiol), 73. *Prof Exp:* Res fel psychobiol, 73-76, sr res fel, 76-80, VIS ASSOC, DEPT BIOL, CALIF INST TECHNOL, 80- *Mem:* Soc Res Child Develop; Int Neuropsychol Soc; Acad Aphasia. *Res:* Neurolinguistics and psycholinguistics; cognitive and developmental psychology; epistemology and the philosophy of science, of mind and of language. *Mailing Add:* 156-29 Div of Biol Calif Inst Technol Pasadena CA 91125

ZAIDER, MARCO A, b Bacau, Romania, Jan 3, 46; Israeli citizen; m 68; c 3. NUCLEAR PHYSICS, RADIOLOGICAL PHYSICS. *Educ:* Bucharest Univ, MSc, 68; Tel Aviv Univ, PhD(nuclear physics), 76. *Prof Exp:* Teaching & res asst nuclear physics, Tel Aviv Univ, Israel, 71-76; fel, Los Alamos Sci Lab, 76-78, staff mem radiol physics, 78-79; RES ASSOC, COL PHYSICIANS & SURGEONS, COLUMBIA UNIV, 79- *Concurrent Pos:* Res grant, Los Alamos Sci Lab, 77-78. *Mem:* Am Asn Physicists Med; Radiation Res Soc. *Res:* Instrumentation; medical physics; biophysics. *Mailing Add:* Col Physicians & Surgeons Columbia Univ 630 W 168th St New York NY 10032

ZAIDI, SYED AMIR ALI, b Lahore, Pakistan, Apr 15, 35; m 62. NUCLEAR PHYSICS. *Educ:* Punjab Univ, BSc, 56; Univ Gottingen, 57-58; Univ Heidelberg, dipl physics, 60, PhD(physics), 64. *Prof Exp:* Vis res scientist, Max Planck Inst Nuclear Physics, 64-66; asst prof, 66-68, ASSOC PROF PHYSICS, UNIV TEX, AUSTIN, 68-, ASSOC DIR, CTR NUCLEAR STUDIES, 67- *Mem:* Fel Am Phys Soc. *Res:* Isobaric analogue resonances; nuclear structure studies using shell model description of reaction theory; heavy ion induced reactions; elementary particle physics. *Mailing Add:* Dept of Physics Univ of Tex Austin TX 78712

ZAIDMAN, SAMUEL, b Bucharest, Romania, Sept 4, 33; m 62; c 4. MATHEMATICS. *Educ:* Univ Bucharest, Lic, 55; Univ Paris, Dr d'Etat, 70. *Prof Exp:* Asst math, Univ Bucharest, 55-59; vis prof, Milan Polytech Inst, 61-64; PROF MATH, UNIV MONTREAL, 64- *Concurrent Pos:* Vis prof, Univ Geneva, 66-68. *Mem:* Am Math Soc; Can Math Soc. *Res:* Abstract differential equations; pseudo-differential operators; almost-periodic functions and equations. *Mailing Add:* Dept of Math Univ of Montreal Box 6128 Montreal PQ H3C 3S7 Can

ZAIKA, LAURA LARYSA, b Kharkow, Ukraine, June 23, 38; US citizen. FOOD CHEMISTRY. *Educ:* Drexel Inst Tech, BS, 60; Univ Pa, PhD(org chem), 64. *Prof Exp:* RES CHEMIST FOOD SAFETY, SCI & EDUC ADMIN-AGR RES, USDA, 64- *Mem:* Am Chem Soc; Inst Food Technologists; Asn Off Anal Chemists. *Res:* 2-aryl benzimidazoles; 1, 2, 3-benzotriazines; meat flavor investigations; chromatography; microbial metabolites; fermented meat products. *Mailing Add:* 5023 N Rosehill St Philadelphia PA 19120

ZAININGER, KARL HEINZ, b Endorf, Ger, Aug 3, 29; US citizen; m 52; c 3. SOLID STATE PHYSICS, PHYSICAL ELECTRONICS. *Educ:* City Col New York, BSEE, 59; Princeton Univ, MSE, 61, MA, 62, PhD(elec eng), 64. *Prof Exp:* Mem tech staff, David Sarnoff Res Ctr, RCA Labs, 59-68, group head solid state device technol group, 68-77; dir commercialization, Solar Energy Res Inst, 77-78; DIR MICROELECTRONICS, ELECTRONIC DEVICES & TECHNOL LAB, US ARMY, 78- *Concurrent Pos:* Vis prof, Hebrew Univ Jerusalem, 71-; mem comt electromagnetic radiation detection devices, Nat Mat Adv Bd. *Honors & Awards:* RCA Labs Achievement Award, 65. *Mem:* Inst Elec & Electronics Engrs. *Res:* Semiconductor devices; thin film physics; plasmas in solids; physical and electrical properties of SiO2; oxidation and optical properties of Si and GaAs; physics and technology of metal-insulator-semiconductor devices; radiation effects of metal-insulator-semiconductor structures. *Mailing Add:* ERADCOM Electronics Technol & Devices Lab Ft Monmouth NJ 07703

ZAISER, JAMES NORMAN, b Salem, NJ, Jan 23, 34; m 57; c 3. MECHANICAL ENGINEERING. *Educ:* Univ Del, PhD(appl sci), 64. *Prof Exp:* Instr mech eng, Univ Del, 58-63; res engr, Exp Sta, E I du Pont de Nemours & Co, 63; asst prof, 65-76, ASSOC PROF MECH ENG, BUCKNELL UNIV, 76- *Concurrent Pos:* NSF grant, Bucknell Univ, 66-67. *Mem:* Am Soc Mech Engrs; Am Soc Eng Educ. *Res:* Nonlinear analysis and dynamics of particles and rigid bodies; nonlinear analysis of systems described by ordinary and partial differential equations. *Mailing Add:* Dept of Mech Eng Bucknell Univ Lewisburg PA 17837

ZAITLIN, MILTON, b Mt Vernon, NY, Apr 2, 27; m 51; c 4. PLANT VIROLOGY. *Educ:* Univ Calif, BS, 49; Calif, Los Angeles, PhD(plant physiol), 54. *Prof Exp:* Res officer, Commonwealth Sci & Indust Res Orgn, Canberra, Australia, 54-58; asst prof hort, Univ Mo, 58-60; asst agr biochem, Univ Ariz, 60-62, from assoc prof to prof agr biochem & plant path, 66-73; PROF PLANT PATH, CORNELL UNIV, 73- *Concurrent Pos:* Guggenheim & Fulbright fels, 66-67; assoc ed, Virol, 66-71, ed, 72- *Mem:* Soc Gen Microbiol; fel Am Phytopath Soc; Am Soc Plant Physiologists; Am Soc Microbiol; Am Soc Virol. *Res:* Plant viruses; physiology of plant virus disease; molecular basis of plant-virus infections; viroids. *Mailing Add:* Dept of Plant Path Cornell Univ Ithaca NY 14853

ZAJAC, ALFRED, b Vienna, Austria, Feb 18, 17; US citizen; m 50; c 2. PHYSICS. *Educ:* Univ St Andrews, BSc, 46, Hons, 48; NY Univ, MS, 52; Polytech Inst Brooklyn, PhD(physics), 57. *Prof Exp:* From instr to assoc prof, 55-74, PROF PHYSICS & CHMN DEPT, ADELPHI UNIV, 74- *Concurrent Pos:* NSF res grant, 62-64. *Mem:* Am Phys Soc; Am Asn Physics Teachers; Am Crystallog Asn. *Res:* Crystal perfection, thermal motion and anomalous transmission of x-rays. *Mailing Add:* Dept of Physics Adelphi Univ Garden City NY 11530

ZAJAC, BARBARA ANN, b Fountain Springs, Pa, Mar 15, 37; m 57; c 1. INTERNAL MEDICINE, VIROLOGY. *Educ:* Univ Pa, BA, 58, PhD(microbiol), 67; Med Col Pa, MD, 79. *Prof Exp:* Assoc pediat/virol, Univ Pa, 69-70; from asst prof to assoc prof microbiol, Med Col Pa, 70-76; resident internal med, Abington Mem Hosp, 79-82; FEL INFECTIOUS DIS, HOSP UNIV PA, 82- *Concurrent Pos:* NIH fel, Div Virus Res, Children's Hosp Philadelphia, Pa, 67-69; grants, Res Corp & Anna Fuller Fund, 72-73, Damon Runyon Mem Fund, 73-75 & Nat Cancer Inst, 73-76. *Mem:* AMA; Asn Am Col Physicians; Int Asn Comp Res Leukemia. *Res:* Human tumor viruses, their host-parasite relationships and electron microscopic analysis. *Mailing Add:* 1040 Arthur Ave Huntingdon Valley PA 19006

ZAJAC, FELIX EDWARD, III, b Baltimore, Md, Dec 4, 41; m 62; c 2. NEUROPHYSIOLOGY, BIOMEDICAL ENGINEERING. *Educ:* Rensselaer Polytech Inst, BEE, 62; Stanford Univ, MS, 65, PhD(neurosci), 68. *Prof Exp:* Staff assoc, Lab Neural Control, Nat Inst Neurol Dis & Stroke, 68-70; asst prof elec eng, Univ Md, College Park, 70-73, assoc prof, 73-80, dir, Biomed Res Lab, 71-80; WITH ENG RES & DEVELOP CTR, VET ADMIN MED CTR, PALO ALTO, CALIF, 80- *Mem:* AAAS; Am Physiol Soc; Soc Neurosci; Inst Elec & Electronics Eng. *Res:* Neural control and biomechanics of animal movement with emphasis on cat locomotion and jumping. *Mailing Add:* Eng Res Develop Ctr 153 Vet Admin Med Ctr 3801 Miranada Ave Pala Alto CA 94304

ZAJAC, IHOR, b Lwiw, Ukraine, May 26, 31; US citizen; m 57; c 1. MEDICAL MICROBIOLOGY, VIROLOGY. *Educ:* Univ Pa, BA, 58; Hahnemann Med Col, MS, 60, PhD(microbiol), 64. *Prof Exp:* Asst microbiol, Hahnemann Med Col, 64-65, instr, 65; asst prof, Jefferson Med Col, 65-71; assoc sr investr, 71-75, SR INVESTR, SMITH KLINE & FRENCH LABS, 75- *Concurrent Pos:* Vis lectr, Med Col Pa, 72-78; vis assoc prof, Hahnemann Med Col, 81-; adj assoc prof, Jefferson Med Col, 81- *Mem:* Am Soc Microbiol; Tissue Cult Asn; Brit Soc Gen Microbiol; Soc Exp Biol & Med. *Res:* Enteroviruses; cell-virus interactions; cell membrane; interferon; bacterial and viral chemotherapy; anaerobic bacteria; bacterial receptors; neoplastic chemotherapy. *Mailing Add:* L-37 Res & Develop Smith Kline & French Lab Philadelphia PA 19101

ZAJAC, WALTER WILLIAM, JR, b Central Falls, RI, July 19, 34; m 59; c 6. ORGANIC CHEMISTRY, NATURAL PRODUCTS CHEMISTRY. *Educ:* Providence Col, BS, 55; Va Polytech Inst, MS, 57, PhD(chem), 60. *Prof Exp:* From asst prof to assoc prof, 59-72, PROF CHEM, VILLANOVA UNIV, 72- *Concurrent Pos:* Fel, Univ Alta, 65-66. *Mem:* Am Chem Soc; Royal Soc Chem. *Res:* Reduction of organic compounds; reactions of nitriles; synthesis, mechanism of ring closure reactions and conformation of homocyclic and heterocyclic systems; chemistry of alpha nitro ketones. *Mailing Add:* Dept of Chem Villanova Univ Villanova PA 19085

ZAJACEK, JOHN GEORGE, b Allentown, Pa, May 8, 36; m 64; c 3. ORGANIC CHEMISTRY. *Educ:* Lehigh Univ, BA, 58; Cornell Univ, PhD(org chem), 62. *Prof Exp:* MGR CHEM PROCESS RES & ANAL SERV, ARCO CHEM CO DIV, ATLANTIC-RICHFIELD CO, 62- *Concurrent Pos:* Instr, Drexel Inst Tech, 66- *Mem:* Am Chem Soc. *Res:* Oxidation of hydrocarbons; epoxidation of olefins; reactions of carbon monoxide; reduction of aromatic nitro compounds; metal catalyzed reactions; chemistry of selenium reactions, isocyanates, homogeneous and heterogeneous catalysis. *Mailing Add:* Res Dept Arco Chem Co 500 S Ridgeway Ave Glenolden PA 19087

ZAJIC, JAMES EDWARD, b Wichita, Kans, Mar 8, 28; m 52; c 3. MICROBIOLOGY, LAW. *Educ:* Univ Kans, BA, 51; Univ Wis, MS, 53; Univ Calif, PhD(microbiol), 56; Okla City Univ, JD, 67; FCIC. *Prof Exp:* Fel biochem, Argonne Nat Lab, 56-57; res microbiologist, Grain Processing Corp, Iowa, 57-61; group leader biochem, Kerr McGee Industs, 61-66; assoc prof biochem, Univ Western Ont, 67-70, asst dean fac eng sci, 72-75, prof biochem eng, 70-79; dean sci, 80-81, PROF MICROBIOL & GEOL, UNIV TEX, EL PASO, 80- *Mem:* Am Chem Soc; Soc Indust Microbiol; Am Soc Microbiol; Am Inst Chem Eng; Biomed Eng Soc. *Res:* Industrial fermentations; continuous fermentations and related engineering topics; environmental engineering; biochemistry of hydrocarbons; biogeochemistry. *Mailing Add:* Dept Microbiol & Geol Univ Tex El Paso TX 79968

ZAJONC, ARTHUR GUY, b Boston, Mass, Oct 11, 49; m 74; c 1. LASER PHYSICS, ATOMIC PHYSICS. *Educ:* Univ Mich, Ann Arbor, BSE, 71, MS, 73, PhD(physics), 76. *Prof Exp:* Fel atomic physics, Joint Inst Lab Astrophys, Nat Bur Standards & Univ Colo, 76-78; ASST PROF PHYSICS, AMHERST COL, 78- *Mem:* Am Phys Soc; Am Asn Physics Teachers; Hist Sci Soc. *Res:* Laser spectroscopy; radiative transfer; electron-atom collisions. *Mailing Add:* Dept of Physics Amherst Col Amherst MA 01002

ZAK, BENNIE, b Detroit, Mich, Sept 29, 19; m 46; c 3. CLINICAL BIOCHEMISTRY. *Educ:* Wayne State Univ, BS, 48, PhD(chem), 52. *Prof Exp:* Asst prof clin chem, 57-60, assoc prof path, 60-65, PROF PATH, SCH MED, WAYNE STATE UNIV, 65-, DIV HEAD CLIN CHEM, 80- *Concurrent Pos:* Res technician, Detroit Receiving Hosp, 50-51, med lab analyst & jr assoc prath, 51-57, head clin chem, 80- *Mem:* Am Chem Soc; Am Asn Clin Chem. *Res:* Spectrophotometric methods; rapid agar gel electrophoretic separations instrumentation in clinical chemistry; phosphate and phosphomonoesterase analysis and automation; problems in clinical laboratory spectrophotometry. *Mailing Add:* Dept Path Wayne State Univ Sch Med Detroit MI 48021

ZAK, RADOVAN HYNEK, b C Budejovice, Czech, June 15, 31; US citizen; m 63; c 2. BIOCHEMISTRY, PHYSIOLOGY. *Educ:* Prague Univ, Czech, BS, 52, Dr Nat Sci, 54; Czech Acad Sci, Prague, PhD(biomed sci), 61. *Prof Exp:* Instr org chem, Med Sch, Prague Univ, 51-53; res scientist physiol, Inst Physiol, Czech Acad Sci, 57-61; res fel physiol chem, Dept Med, Northwestern Univ, Chicago, 61-63; fel biochem, 63-65, instr, 65-67, from asst prof to assoc prof, 67-79, PROF, DEPT MED, UNIV CHICAGO, 79- *Honors & Awards:* Nat Award, Czech Acad Sci, 58. *Mem:* AAAS; Am Physiol Soc; Int Soc Heart Res; Am Soc Cell Biol. *Res:* Cardiac hypertrophy; protein synthesis and degradation; proliferation of cardiac myocytes; muscle proteins. *Mailing Add:* Dept of Med Box 407 950 E 59th St Chicago IL 60637

ZAKAIB, DANIEL D, b Montreal, Que, Apr 1, 25; m 48; c 2. PETROLEUM CHEMISTRY, ANALYTICAL CHEMISTRY. *Educ:* Montreal Tech Inst, dipl chem, 46; Sir George Williams Univ, BSc, 53. *Prof Exp:* Supvr, Montreal Refinery Lab, Brit Am Oil Co, 48-55, asst refinery chemist, 55-58, anal technologist, Head Off Toronto, 58-63, coordr, Anal Res Labs, Brit Am Res & Develop Co, 63-66; mgr anal & chem res, Res & Develop Dept, Gulf Oil Can, Ltd, 66-69, supvr petrol chem sect, Phys Sci Div, Gulf Res & Develop Co, 69-71, DIR TECH OPERS, RES & DEVELOP DEPT, GULF CAN, LTD, 71- *Mem:* Am Chem Soc; Am Soc Testing & Mat; Can Asn Appl Spectros; fel Chem Inst Can. *Res:* Technical administration of industrial research facility. *Mailing Add:* Gulf Can Ltd Res & Develop Dept 2489 N Sheridan Way Clarkson ON L5K 1A8 Can

ZAKARIJA, MARGITA, b Split, Yugoslavia, July 11, 37; Can citizen; m 66. ENDOCRINOLOGY. *Educ:* Univ Zagreb, MD, 65; McGill Univ, MSc, 71. *Prof Exp:* Res fel, 67-69, asst prof, 69-77, ASSOC PROF MED, McGILL UNIV, 77- *Concurrent Pos:* Assoc physician, Royal Victoria Hosp, 78- *Mem:* Endocrine Soc; Am Thyroid Asn; Europe Thyroid Asn; Can Soc Cell Biol. *Res:* Thyroid physio-pathology; the mode of action of thyrotropin and the thyroid-stimulating antibody (TSAb) of Graves' disease; immunochemical characteristics of TSAb. *Mailing Add:* Div Endocrinol & Metab 687 Pine Ave W Montreal PQ H3A 1A1 Can

ZAKETT, DONALD, b Tarrytown, NY, Aug 13, 51. MASS SPECTROMETRY. *Educ:* State Univ NY, Plattsburgh, BS, 76; Purdue Univ, PHD(chem), 81. *Prof Exp:* SR RES CHEMIST, DOW CHEM CO, 81- *Mem:* Am Chem Soc; Am Soc Mass Spectrometry. *Res:* Various aspects of mass spectrometric analysis as applied to organic analysis; ion-molecule collision processes. *Mailing Add:* 574 Bldg Anal Lab Dow Chem Co Midland MI 48640

ZAKHARY, RIZKALLA, b Assiut, Egypt, Sept 5, 24; m 66; c 2. HUMAN ANATOMY. *Educ:* Cairo Univ, BS, 49, MS, 54; Tulane Univ, PhD(anat), 64. *Prof Exp:* Technician & res asst biochem, US Naval Med Res Unit 3, Cairo, Egypt, 50-56; instr biol chem & gen sci, Am Univ Cairo, 57-60; asst prof anat & physiol, Sch Dent, Loyola Univ, La, 64-67; asst prof anat, 67-70, ASSOC PROF ANAT, SCH DENT, UNIV SOUTHERN CALIF, 70- *Concurrent Pos:* NIH grant, Tulane Univ, 65-67. *Mem:* AAAS; Am Asn Anatomists. *Res:* Hypothermia, academic and applied aspects; cryobiology; stress and hypothermia. *Mailing Add:* Dept Anat Sch Dent Univ Southern Calif Los Angeles CA 90007

ZAKI, ABD EL-MONEIM EMAM, b Cairo, UAR, Dec 18, 33; US citizen. HISTOLOGY, ORAL BIOLOGY. *Educ:* Cairo Univ, BChD, 55, DDR, 58; Ind Univ, MSD, 62; Univ Ill, PhD(anat), 69. *Prof Exp:* Dent surgeon, Demonstration & Training Ctr, Qualyub, UAR, 55-59; from instr to asst prof, Fac Dent, Cairo Univ, 62-67; res assoc, Col Dent, 67-70, asst prof histol, Col Dent & lectr, Col Med, 70-72, assoc prof histol, Col Dent & Sch Basic Med Sci, Med Ctr, 72-75, PROF HISTOL, COL DENT, UNIV ILL, 75- *Concurrent Pos:* UAR govt spec mission mem grad study, US, 59-62. *Mem:* AAAS; Am Asn Anat; Electron Micros Soc Am; Int Asn Dent Res. *Res:* Cellular control of mineralization using an amphibian odontogenic model and cytological aspects of odontogenesis. *Mailing Add:* 801 S Paulina St Chicago IL 60612

ZAKI, ATEF, b Cairo, Egypt, Jan 14, 35; US citizen; m 63; c 2. OBSTETRICS & GYNECOLOGY. *Educ:* Cairo Univ, MB, BCh, 59; Ain Shams Univ, Cairo, PhD(med), 63. *Prof Exp:* Clin res supvr, 66-67, med dir res, 67-74, DIR CLIN RES, SQUIBB INST MED RES, 74- *Concurrent Pos:* Pvt pract med, 63-70. *Res:* Pharmaceutical clinical research. *Mailing Add:* Squibb Inst for Med Res PO Box 4000 Princeton NJ 08540

ZAKI, MAHFOU H, b Cairo, Egypt, Apr 14, 24; US citizen; m 70. ENVIRONMENTAL MEDICINE, PUBLIC HEALTH. *Educ:* Cairo Univ, MB, ChB, 49; Univ Alexandria, MPH, 58; Columbia Univ, DrPH, 62. *Prof Exp:* Intern med & surg, Kasr-El-Eini Univ Hosp, Cairo, 50-51; med officer, Abu-Sidhom Health Ctr, Minia, 51-56; instr prev med, High Ints Pub Health, 57-59; staff mem edpidemiol, Sch Pub Health, Columbia Univ, 59-62; asst prof prev med, State Univ NY Downstate Med Ctr, 62-68, assoc prof environ med & community health, 68-76; ASSOC PROF ENVIRON MED & COMMUNITY HEALTH, KINGS COUNTY HOSP, 76- *Concurrent Pos:* Grants, Health Res Coun City New York, 64-68 & tuberc br, USPHS & Peace Corps; Peace Corps physician & prog tech adv, US State Dept, Afghanistan, 70-71; dir pub health, Suffolk County, New York; adj prof pub health, City

Univ New York, 73-; lectr, Sch Pub Health & Admin Med, Columbia Univ, 73- *Mem:* Fel Am Pub Health Asn; fel Royal Soc Trop Med & Hyg; Am Soc Trop Med & Hyg; fel Am Col Chest Physicians; Am Statist Asn. *Res:* Etiology of sarcoidosis; prevalence of infection with typical and atypical strains of Mycobacterium tuberculosis and of infection with Histoplasma capsulatum in Afghanistan. *Mailing Add:* Dept Environ Med & Community Health 451 Clarkson Ave Brooklyn NY 11234

ZAKIN, JACQUES L(OUIS), b New York, NY, Jan 28, 27; m 50; c 5. CHEMICAL ENGINEERING. *Educ:* Cornell Univ, BChem Eng, 49; Columbia Univ, MSc, 50; NY Univ, DEngSc, 59. *Prof Exp:* Chem engr res labs, Flintkote Co, 50-51; from res technologist to supvry technologist res dept, Socony Mobil Oil Co, 51-56 & 58-62; from assoc prof to prof chem eng, Univ Mo-Rolla, 62-77; PROF CHEM ENG & CHMN DEPT, OHIO STATE UNIV, 77- *Concurrent Pos:* Adj asst prof, Hofstra Col, 59-60 & 62; Am Chem Soc-Petrol Res Fund Int fel & vis prof, Israel Inst Technol, 68-69; vis scientist, Naval Res Lab, Washington, DC, 75-76. *Mem:* Am Inst Chem Engrs; Am Chem Soc; Rheology Soc; Am Soc Eng Educ. *Res:* Drag reduction inturbulent flow; mechanical degradation of high polymers; detailed structure of liquid turbulence; hot-wire anemometry; rheology of polymer solutions; lubricating greases. *Mailing Add:* Dept of Chem Eng Ohio State Univ Columbus OH 43210

ZAKKAY, VICTOR, b Baghdad, Iraq, Sept 8, 27; US citizen; m 52; c 2. FLUID MECHANICS, COMBUSTION. *Educ:* Polytech Inst Brooklyn, BAeronautEng, 52, MS, 53, PhD(aeronaut), 59. *Prof Exp:* Res asst, Polytech Inst Brooklyn, 52-55, res assoc, 55-58, res group leader, 58-59, from res asst prof to res assoc prof, 59-64; assoc prof aerospace eng, 64-65, prof aeronaut & astronaut, 65-73, asst dir Aerospace Lab, 70-76, actg chmn, Dept Appl Sci, 76-77, PROF APPL SCI, NY UNIV, 73-, DIR, ANTONIO FERRI AEROSPACE & ENERGETICS LABS, 76- & CHMN DEPT APPL SCI, 77- *Mem:* Am Inst Aeronaut & Astronaut. *Res:* Hypersonic and viscous compressible flow; heat transfer; experimental aerodynamics; combustion; turbulent mixing; fuel combustion fluidized bed coal combustion; hypersonic aerodynamics; wind tunnel technology; solar energy. *Mailing Add:* NY Univ 26-36 Stuyvesant St New York NY 10003

ZAKRAYSEK, LOUIS, b Conemaugh Twp, Pa, Dec 20, 28; m 52; c 3. METALLURGY, MATERIALS SCIENCE. *Educ:* Pa State Univ, BS, 52. *Prof Exp:* Mem staff, Chemet Training Prog, 52-53, metallurgist, 53-60, mgr metall & welding, 60-72, MGR PHYS METALL, GEN ELEC CO, SYRACUSE, 72- *Concurrent Pos:* Chmn joining tech comt, Inst Printed Circuits, 67-68; mem working group 9, Tech Comn 50, Int Electrotech Comn, 68-69. *Honors & Awards:* Cert of Achievement, Soc Automotive Engrs, Aerospace Coun, 67; President's Award, Inst Printed Circuits, 68. *Mem:* Fel Am Soc Metals; Metall Soc; Am Inst Mining, Metall & Petrol Engrs; Int Metallog Soc. *Res:* Development, selection, specification and application of materials and processes in commerical and military electronic equipment, especially as related to construction analysis, failure analysis, component assembly and electronic packaging. *Mailing Add:* 8432 Brewerton Rd PO Box 62 Cicero NY 13039

ZAKRISKI, PAUL MICHAEL, b Amsterdam, NY, July 12, 40; m 64; c 2. ANALYTICAL CHEMISTRY. *Educ:* Univ Rochester, AB, 62; Univ Cincinnati, PhD(org chem), 67. *Prof Exp:* Sr res chemist, 66-74, SECT LEADER, RES DIV, B F GOODRICH CO, BRECKSVILLE, 74- *Mem:* Am Chem Soc; Am Soc Mass Spectrometry. *Res:* Mass spectrometry for structure elucidation; high speed chromatography. *Mailing Add:* 8329 Wyatt Rd Broadview Heights OH 44147

ZAKRZEWSKI, RICHARD JEROME, b Hamtramck, Mich, Nov 5, 40; m 66; c 2. VERTEBRATE PALEONTOLOGY. *Educ:* Wayne State Univ, BS, 63; Univ Mich, MS, 65, PhD(vert paleont), 68. *Prof Exp:* NSF fel geol, Idaho State Univ-Los Angeles County Mus, 68-69; from asst prof to assoc prof earth sci, 69-78, PROF GEOL, FT HAYS KANS UNIV, 78-, DIR STERNBERG MEM MUS, 73- *Mem:* Soc Vert Paleont; Paleont Soc; Am Soc Mammal; Soc Syst Zool; Am Quaternary Asn. *Res:* Fossil mammals, particularly rodents; late Cenozoic stratigraphy. *Mailing Add:* Sternberg Mem Mus Ft Hays State Univ Hays KS 67601

ZAKRZEWSKI, SIGMUND FELIX, b Buenos Aires, Arg, Sept 15, 19; m 56; c 1. BIOCHEMISTRY. *Educ:* Univ Hamburg, MS, 52, PhD(biochem), 54. *Prof Exp:* Res asst, Sch Med, Western Reserve Univ, 52-53; res asst, Sch Med, Yale Univ, 53-56; sr cancer res scientist, 56-61, assoc cancer res scientist, 61-71, prin cancer res scientist, Dept Exp Therapeut, 71-76, PRIN CANCER RES SCIENTIST, DEPT CLIN PHARM & THERAPEUT, ROSWELL PARK MEM INST, 78- *Concurrent Pos:* Res prof, Dept Pharmacol, State Univ NY Buffalo, Roswell Park Div. *Mem:* AAAS; Am Asn Cancer Res. *Res:* Cancer chemotherapy; metabolism of folic acid and folic acid antagonist; pharmacokinetics of anticancer drugs in man. *Mailing Add:* Roswell Park Mem Inst 666 Elm St Buffalo NY 14263

ZAKRZEWSKI, THOMAS MICHAEL, b Jackson, Mich, Mar 13, 43; m 68; c 3. AEROSPACE SCIENCES, CHEMISTRY. *Educ:* Univ Mich, BS, 63. *Prof Exp:* Tech staff mem EO & IR sensors, Willow Run Labs, Inst Sci & Technol, Univ Mich, 63-69; tech staff mem IR sensors & systs, Gen Res Corp, 69-73; dir Washington opers IR systs & simulations, Mission Res Corp, 73-74; tech staff mem, Inst Res & Active Optics, 74-75, dir, Space Systs Dept, Gen Res Corp, 75-81, dir, Washington Opers, 78-81, DIR, EASTERN OPERS, TECHNOL APPLICATIONS GROUP & SPACE SYSTS DEPT, FLOW GENERAL, INC, 81- *Mem:* AAAS; Sigma Xi; Am Inst Aeronaut & Astronaut; Am Chem Soc; Nat Space Inst. *Res:* Electro-optical and infrared sensors, target signatures, and phenomenology; advanced offensive and defensive strategic systems; advanced space systems technology. *Mailing Add:* Flow General Inc 7655 Old Springhouse Rd McLean VA 22102

ZALAR, FRANK VICTOR, organic chemistry, polymer chemistry, see previous edition

ZALAY, ANDREW W(ILLIAM), b Budapest, Hungary, May 20, 18; m 46; c 3. ORGANIC CHEMISTRY. *Educ:* Budapest Tech Univ, dipl, 40, EMe, 42. *Prof Exp:* Res lab leader org chem, Chinoin Pharmaceut Works, Budapest, 51-56; res chemist, Textile Res Inst, NJ, 57-58; SR RES CHEMIST, STERLING-WINTHROP RES INST, 58- *Mem:* Am Chem Soc. *Res:* Pharmaceuticals. *Mailing Add:* Sterling-Winthrop Res Inst Columbia Turnpike Rensselaer NY 12144

ZALAY, ETHEL SUZANNE, b Budapest, Hungary, Sept 1, 19; m 46; c 3. ORGANIC CHEMISTRY. *Educ:* Univ Sci Budapest, Hungary, PhD, 44. *Prof Exp:* Owner, Dr Somody Lab, 45-51; org chemist, Fine Chem Producing Union, 51-54; owner, Dr Somody Lab, 54-56; org chemist, Textile Res Inst, 57; res chemist, Biol Res Lab, Philadelphia Gen Hosp, 57-58; res chemist, 58-69, assoc res chemist, 69-77, RES CHEMIST, STERLING-WINTHROP RES INST, STERLING DRUG, INC, 77- *Mem:* Am Chem Soc. *Res:* Fine organic chemicals; phospholipids; pharmaceuticals; heterocyclic chemistry. *Mailing Add:* Sterling-Winthrop Res Inst Columbia Turnpike Rensselaer NY 12144

ZALESAK, JOSEPH FRANCIS, b Fountain Hill, Pa, Jan 2, 42. UNDERWATER ACOUSTICS, TRANSDUCTION. *Educ:* LaSalle Col, BA, 63; Lehigh Univ, MS, 67, PhD(solid state physics), 72. *Prof Exp:* Physicist, 63-66, RES PHYSICIST, NAVAL RES LAB, 72- *Concurrent Pos:* Assoc prof, Univ Cent Fla, 80-81. *Mem:* Acoust Soc Am. *Res:* Underwater acoustic calibration techniques and development of calibration systems which implement the above techniques; acoustic radiation from vibrating structures; develop specialized underwater acoustic transducers. *Mailing Add:* Naval Res Lab Underwater Sound Reference Div Code 5983 PO Box 8337 Orlando FL 32856

ZALESKI, MAREK BOHDAN, b Krzemieniec, Oct 18, 36; US citizen. IMMUNOGENETICS, TRANSPLANTATION. *Educ:* Sch Med, Warsaw, MD, 60, Dr med sci, 63. *Prof Exp:* From res assoc to assoc prof, Dept Histol, Sch Med, Warsaw, Poland, 55-69; res asst prof, Dept Microbiol, State Univ NY, 69-72; asst prof anat & histol, Dept Anat, Mich State Univ, 72-74, assoc prof, 74-76; assoc prof, 76-79, PROF, DEPT MICROBIOL, STATE UNIV NY, 79- *Concurrent Pos:* Vis scientist, Inst Exp Biol & Genetics, Prague, 65; Brit coun scholar, Res Lab, Queen Victoria Hosp, 66-67; attend physician, Children Hosp, Poland, 60-66; mem, Witebski Ctr Immunol, 76-; prin invest, NIH res grant, 76- *Mem:* Transplantation Soc; Int Soc Exp Hemat; Am Asn Immunologists; NY Acad Sci. *Res:* Heterotopic bone tissue induction; cellular aspects of immune response; graft-verus-host reaction; immune response to alloantigens; genetic regulation of the immune response to alloantigens; author or coauthor of over 80 publications. *Mailing Add:* Dept Microbiol State Univ NY Buffalo NY 14214

ZALESKI, WITOLD ANDREW, b Pyzdry, Poland, Apr 4, 20; Can citizen; m 48; c 4. MEDICINE. *Educ:* Univ Edinburgh, MB, ChB, 46; Royal Col Physciians & Surgeons, Ireland, dipl psychol med, 52; Royal Col Physicians & Surgeons Can, cert psychiat, 62; Univ Sask, MD, adeundem, 64; FRCP(C), 72; Royal Col Psychiat, cert, 73. *Prof Exp:* Dep supt & consult psychiatrist, Ment Retardation Insts, Regional Hosp Bd Eng, Birmingham, 54-58; clin dir, Sask Training Sch, Mosse Jaw, Can, 58-67; assoc prof, 67-73, PROF PEDIAT & ASSOC PROF PSYCHIAT, UNIV SASK, 73-, DIR ALVIN BUCKWOLD CENT, UNIV HOSP, 67- *Concurrent Pos:* Vis consult psychiat, Univ Sask Hosp, 62-67. *Mem:* Fel Am Asn Ment Deficiency; Am Acad Ment Retardation; Can Med Asn; Can Psychiat Asn. *Res:* Etiology and prevention of mental retardation; inborn errors of metabolism; chromosomal anomalies; behavioral programs for the retarded; delivery of services in mental retardation. *Mailing Add:* Alvin Buckwold Ctr Univ of Sask Hosp Saskatoon SK S7N 0X0 Can

ZALEWSKI, EDMUND JOSEPH, b Schenectady, NY, July 23, 31; m 58; c 5. ORGANIC POLYMER CHEMISTRY. *Educ:* Union Col, BS, 64. *Prof Exp:* From technician polyester to group leader polymer, 50-67, MGR POLYMER, SCHENECTADY CHEM INC, 67- *Mem:* Am Chem Soc; Soc Plastics Engrs. *Res:* Development of organic and heterocyclic polymers exhibiting excellent mechanical properties coupled with chemical and thermal resistance for use as electrical insulation. *Mailing Add:* 2761 Maida Lane Schenectady NY 12306

ZALIK, SARA E, b Mex, May 23, 39; m 66; c 2. DEVELOPMENTAL BIOLOGY, CELL BIOLOGY. *Educ:* Nat Univ Mex, BS, 59; Univ Ill, PhD(anat), 63. *Prof Exp:* NIH int fel, Biol Div, Oak Ridge Nat Lab, 63-64; asst prof cell biol, Ctr Res & Advan Studies, Nat Polytech Inst, Mex, 64-66; from asst prof to assoc prof, 66-78, PROF ZOOL, UNIV ALTA, 78- *Mem:* AAAS; Can Soc Cell Biol; Am Soc Zool; Soc Develop Biol; Am Soc Cell Biol. *Res:* Cell differentiation and metaplasia; cell surface and its role in differentiation and early development. *Mailing Add:* Dept of Zool Univ of Alta Edmonton AB T6G 2E9 Can

ZALIK, SAUL, b Ratcliffe, Sask, May 11, 21; m 66; c 2. PLANT PHYSIOLOGY, BIOCHEMISTRY. *Educ:* Univ Man, BSA, 43, MSc, 48; Purdue Univ, PhD(plant physiol), 52. *Prof Exp:* Lectr plant sci, Univ Man, 48-49; from asst prof to assoc prof, 52-64, PROF PLANT PHYSIOL & BIOCHEM, UNIV ALTA, 64- *Mem:* AAAS; Am Soc Plant Physiol; Can Biochem Soc. *Res:* Metabolism of lipids; nucleic acids and proteins in relation to plant differentiation and development. *Mailing Add:* Dept of Plant Sci Univ of Alta Edmonton AB T6G 2E3 Can

ZALIPSKY, JEROME JAROSLAW, b Ukraine; US citizen; c 2. ANALYTICAL CHEMISTRY. *Educ:* St Joseph's Col, BS, 58, MS, 62; Univ Pa, PhD(anal chem), 70. *Prof Exp:* From chemist to group leader anal chem, Nat Drug Co, Richardson-Merrill Inc, 58-70; from sr scientist to group leader phys chem, 70-74, SECT HEAD PHYS & MICROANAL CHEM, WILLIAM H RORER INC, 74- *Mem:* Am Chem Soc. *Res:* Chemical structure elucidation of new drug substance; kinetics; characterization of hydrolysis products; analytical and physical profile of drug substance. *Mailing Add:* William H Rorer Inc 500 Virginia Dr Ft Washington PA 19034

ZALKAN, ROBERT LIBMAN, oceanography, nuclear engineering, see previous edition

ZALKIN, HOWARD, b New York, NY, Dec 31, 34; m 66; c 1. BIOCHEMISTRY. *Educ:* Univ Calif, Davis, BS, 56, MS, 59, PhD(biochem), 61. *Prof Exp:* Res assoc chem, Harvard Univ, 61-62; res assoc biochem, Pub Health Res Inst New York, 62-64; res assoc, Col Physicians & Surgeons, Columbia Univ, 64-66; from asst prof to assoc prof, 66-72, PROF BIOCHEM, PURDUE UNIV, LAFAYETTE, 72- *Concurrent Pos:* Fels, NSF, 61-63, USPHS, 63-64 & USPHS fel biol sci, Stanford Univ, 72-73. *Mem:* Am Soc Biol Chemists. *Res:* Regulation of enzyme activity, allosteric enzymes; structure and function of glutamine amidotransferases. Regulation of tryptophan biosynthesis. *Mailing Add:* Dept of Biochem Purdue Univ Lafayette IN 47907

ZALKOW, LEON HARRY, b Millen, Ga, Nov 27, 29; m 71; c 1. ORGANIC CHEMISTRY. *Educ:* Ga Inst Technol, BCE, 52, PhD(chem), 56. *Prof Exp:* Res fel, Wayne State Univ, 55-56, 57-59; res chemist, E I du Pont de Nemours & Co, 56-57; asst prof chem, Okla State Univ, 59-62, assoc prof, 62-65; assoc prof, 65-69, PROF CHEM, GA INST TECHNOL, 69- *Concurrent Pos:* Prof & head dept chem, Univ of the Negev, 70-72. *Mem:* AAAS; Am Chem Soc; The Chem Soc. *Res:* Natural products; conformational analysis; chemistry of bicyclic azides. *Mailing Add:* Dept of Chem Ga Inst of Technol Atlanta GA 30332

ZALL, LINDA S, b Nov 15, 50; US citizen. GEOLOGY. *Educ:* Cornell Univ, BS, 72, MS, 74, PhD(civil & environ eng), 76. *Prof Exp:* Instr photo-geol, Cornell Univ, 71-75; CONSULT ENVIRON & ENG REMOTE SENSING, EARTH SATELLITE CORP, 75- *Concurrent Pos:* Res engr, Calspan Corp, 71; eng geologist, Trans Alaska Oil Pipeline Proj, 73. *Mem:* Soc Econ Geologists; Am Soc Agron; Am Soc Photogram; Sigma Xi. *Res:* Photo-geology; various remote sensing techniques. *Mailing Add:* Earth Satellite Corp 7222 47th St Chevy Chase Washington DC 20015

ZALL, ROBERT ROUBEN, b Lowell, Mass, Dec 6, 25; m 49; c 3. FOOD SCIENCE. *Educ:* Univ Mass, BS, 49, MS, 50; Cornell Univ, PhD(food sci), 68. *Prof Exp:* Lab dir dairy prod, Grandview Dairies, Inc, NY, 50-51, mgr, Butter & Cheese Div, 51-53, mgr, Condensed Milks & Powder Div, 53-57, gen mgr corp, 57-66; dir res & prod, Crowley Food Co, 68-71; assoc prof, 71-76, PROF FOOD SCI, CORNELL UNIV, 76- *Concurrent Pos:* Environ Protection Agency pollution abatement demonstration grant, Whey Fractionation Plant, Crowley Foods Co, 69-72, proj dir, 71- *Honors & Awards:* Howard Marlatt Award Lab Technol, NY State Sanitarians, 79. *Mem:* Inst Food Technologists; Am Soc Agr Engrs; Int Asn Milk, Food & Environ Sanitarians. *Res:* Detergents as inhibitors in food; reusing cleaning fluids to reduce consumption of energy and chemicals; reclamation and renovation of food wastes; membrane filtration processing; utilization of whey fractions in foods. *Mailing Add:* Dept Food Sci Stocking Hall Cornell Univ Ithaca NY 14853

ZALLEN, EUGENIA MALONE, b Camp Hill, Ala, July 18, 32; m 59. FOOD SCIENCE. *Educ:* Auburn Univ, BS, 53; Purdue Univ, MS, 60; Univ Tenn, PhD(food sci), 74. *Prof Exp:* Dietetic intern, Med Ctr, Duke Univ, 53-54, assoc dietitian, 54-57; asst chief dietary, Univ Hosp, Emory Univ, 57-58; from instr to asst prof food & nutrit, Auburn Univ, 62-66; asst prof food, nutrit & inst admin, Univ Md, 67-72; researcher dairy sci, Okla State Univ, 72-73; researcher, Univ Tenn, 73-74; assoc prof & dir, Sch Home Econ, Univ Okla, 74-80. *Concurrent Pos:* Consult, Head Start Day Care Ctrs, Ala, 65-66; field reader, Bur Res, HEW, DC, 66-; consult, Univ Consult, Inc, Ala, 68 & Optimal Systs, Inc, Ga, 69-; pres, Acad World, Inc, Consults, 75- *Mem:* Am Home Econ Asn; Am Dietetic Asn; Inst Food Technologists; Sigma Xi; Soc Nutrit Educ. *Res:* Institution administration; quality factors in quantity food production; habits. analysis and automatic changes in food habits. *Mailing Add:* PO Box 4037 Greenville NC 27834

ZALLEN, RICHARD, b New York, NY, Jan 1, 37; m 64; c 2. CONDENSED MATTER PHYSICS. *Educ:* Rensselaer Polytech Inst, BS, 57; Harvard Univ, AM, 59, PhD(solid state physics), 64. *Prof Exp:* Res assoc, Res Div, Raytheon Co, 58-59; res asst solid state physics, Harvard Univ, 59-64, res fel, 64-65; STAFF MEM, XEROX RES LABS, 65- *Concurrent Pos:* Vis assoc prof, Israel Inst Technol, 71-72. *Mem:* Fel Am Phys Soc. *Res:* Experimental studies of optical properties of solids; vibrational and electronic structure of molecular solids, layer crystals, semiconductors, and amorphous solids; Raman scattering; optical effects in solids at high pressure; percolation theory; phase transitions; percolation; pressure effects; solid state theory. *Mailing Add:* Xerox Res Labs 800 Phillips Rd Bldg 114 Webster NY 14580

ZALOKAR, MARKO, b Ljubljana, Yugoslavia, July 14, 18; nat US; m 51; c 2. DEVELOPMENTAL GENETICS. *Educ:* Univ Ljubljana, dipl, 40; Univ Geneva, DSc(zool), 44. *Prof Exp:* Asst biol, Univ Geneva, 42-44, instr genetics, 46-47; fel, Calif Inst Technol, 47-49; asst prof, Univ Wash, 49-51; vis scientist, NIH, 52-54; res assoc, Wesleyan Univ, 54-55; vis scientist, Yale Univ, 55-61; assoc res biologist, Univ Calif, San Diego, 61-66, lectr biol, Univ Calif, Davis, 66-67 & Univ Calif, San Diego, 67-68; DIR RES, CTR MOLECULAR GENETICS, GIF-SUR-YVETTE, FRANCE, 68- *Mem:* AAAS; Genetics Soc Am; Soc Develop Biol. *Res:* Lens regeneration; anatomy and development of Drosophila; biochemical genetics of Neurospora; autoradiography; protein and ribonucleic acid biosynthesis; developmental genetics of Drosophila. *Mailing Add:* Centre de Genetique Molec Centre Nat de la Res Sci F 91190 Gif-sur-Yvette France

ZALOSH, ROBERT GEOFFREY, b New York, NY, Oct 10, 44; m 65; c 1. FLUID MECHANICS, HAZARD ANALYSIS. *Educ:* Cooper Union, BE, 65; Univ Rochester, MS, 66; Northeastern Univ, PhD(mech eng), 70. *Prof Exp:* Assoc scientist, Space Systs Div, Avco Corp, 66-67; sr scientist, Mt Auburn Res Assocs, Inc, 70-75; sr res scientist, 75-78, MGR EXPLOSION & ENERGETICS SECT, FACTORY MUTUAL RES CORP, 78- *Concurrent Pos:* Lectr mech eng, Northeastern Univ, 74-75. *Mem:* Am Soc Mech Engrs; Combustion Inst; Int Asn Hydrogen Energy. *Res:* Fire and explosion protection; explosion venting; vapor cloud dispersal; blast wave phenomena; advanced battery hazards. *Mailing Add:* Factory Mutual Res Corp 1151 Boston-Providence Turnpike Norwood MA 02062

ZALOUDEK, FRANK RICHARD, b St Louis, Mo, Nov 27, 32; m 57; c 2. MECHANICAL ENGINEERING. *Educ:* Wash Univ, BS, 54; Purdue Univ, MS, 55, PhD(eng), 59. *Prof Exp:* Sr engr, Hanford Atomic Prod Oper, Gen Elec Co, 59-64; res assoc, Pac Northwest Labs, Battelle Mem inst, 65-66, mgr thermal-hydraul anal, 66-70, vis fel, Seattle Res Ctr, 71, STAFF SCIENTIST, PAC NORTHWEST LABS, BATTELLE MEM INST, 72-; RESIDENT FAC & MECH ENG PROG COORDR, JOINT CTR GRAD STUDY, 72- *Concurrent Pos:* Lectr, Univ Wash Ctr Grad Study, Hanford, 54-70, assoc prof, Univ Wash, 71, affil assoc prof, 72- & Ore State Univ, 72- *Res:* Boiling heat transfer; dynamics of two-phase flows; nuclear reactor safety and heat removal systems. *Mailing Add:* Harrington Rd Richland WA 99352

ZALTZMAN, RAUL, civil & environmental engineering, see previous edition

ZALUBAS, ROMUALD, b Pandelys, Lithuania, July 20, 11; nat US; m 39; c 1. ASTROPHYSICS. *Educ:* Kaunas State Univ, MA, 36; Georgetown Univ, PhD(astrophys), 55. *Prof Exp:* Asst astron, Vilnius State Univ, 40-44; dir sec sch, Ger, 45-49; instr math, Nazareth Col (NY), 49-51; instr, Georgetown Univ, 52-57; PHYSICIST, NAT BUR STANDARDS, 55- *Mem:* AAAS; Am Astron Soc; Sigma Xi; Optical Soc Am. *Res:* Description and analysis of atomic spectra; thorium wavelength standards. *Mailing Add:* 908 Roswell Dr Silver Spring MD 20901

ZALUCKY, THEODORE B, b Beleluja, West-Ukraine, Apr 11, 19; US citizen; m 46; c 2. PHARMACY, PHARMACEUTICAL CHEMISTRY. *Educ:* Univ Vienna, MPharm, 42, DSc Nat(pharmaceut chem), 45; Ill, Chicago, BS, 52. *Prof Exp:* Anal chemist, Control Lab, Chicago Pharm Co, 52-53; res chemist, Foot Prod Lab, Scholl Mfg Co, Inc, 53-55; asst prof pharmaceut chem, 55-63, assoc prof pharm & pharmaceut chem, 63-72, PROF PHARM, COL PHARM, HOWARD UNIV, 72- *Concurrent Pos:* AEC grant, 62-63. *Mem:* Am Chem Soc; Am Pharmaceut Asn; Am Asn Cols Pharm; Acad Pharmaceut Sci; Shevchenko Sci Soc. *Res:* Chemistry of morphine alkaloids, epoxy ethers and some benzolypiperidines; structure-chromogenic activity relationship of phenolic compounds with Ehrlich reagent; isolation and structure of some new anhalonium alkaloids; spiro-compounds containing geranium and organo-metallic compounds. *Mailing Add:* Col of Pharm Howard Univ Washington DC 20059

ZALUSKY, RALPH, b Pawtucket, RI, Oct 11, 31; m 58; c 3. INTERNAL MEDICINE, HEMATOLOGY. *Educ:* Brown Univ, AB, 53; Boston Univ, MD, 57; Am Bd Internal Med, dipl, 64. *Prof Exp:* From intern to sr resident med, Duke Univ Hosp, 57-62; from asst prof to assoc prof, 66-77, PROF MED, MT SINAI SCH MED, 77-; CHIEF DIV HEMAT-ONCOL, BETH ISRAEL MED CTR, 76- *Concurrent Pos:* USPHS fel, Thorndike Mem Lab, Harvard Univ, 59-61; res assoc med, Mt Sinai Hosp, 64-65, asst attend hematologist, 65-66, actg chief hemat, 72-76, attend hematologist, 77- *Mem:* Am Fedn Clin Res; Am Soc Clin Nutrit; Am Soc Hemat. *Res:* Interrelationships between vitamin B-twelve and folic acid metabolism; sodium and potassium membrane transport; abnormal hemoglobins; erythropoietin physiology. *Mailing Add:* Div of Hemat-Oncol 10 ND Perlman Pl New York NY 10003

ZAM, STEPHEN G, III, b Toledo, Ohio, Nov 3, 32. PARASITOLOGY. *Educ:* Georgetown Univ, BS, 54; Catholic Univ, MS, 56; Univ Southern Calif, PhD(biol sci), 66. *Prof Exp:* Asst prof biol, Loyola Univ (Calif), 66; from asst prof parasitol to assoc prof zool, 66-77, ASSOC PROF MICROBIOL & CELL SCI, UNIV FLA, 77- *Concurrent Pos:* Consult, Marineland, 67- *Mem:* Am Soc Parasitol; Am Soc Trop Med & Hyg; Int Soc Parasitol. *Res:* Nematode physiology including biochemistry of nematode egg hatching and larval molting; immunology to helminth infections. *Mailing Add:* Div of Biol Sci Univ of Fla Gainesville FL 32611

ZAMBERNARD, JOSEPH, b Sept 5, 33; US citizen. CYTOLOGY. *Educ:* Univ Ala, AB, 53, MS, 56; Tulane Univ, PhD(cytol), 64. *Prof Exp:* Fel virol & immunol, Sch Med, Univ Colo, Denver, 64-66, asst prof anat, 66-72; assoc prof, Albany Med Col, 72-75; prof, 75-77, CHMN DEPT ANAT, SCH MED, WRIGHT STATE UNIV, 77- *Mem:* Electron Micros Soc Am; Am Soc Cell Biol; Am Asn Anatomists; Tissue Cult Asn. *Res:* Virology and immunology; ultrastructure. *Mailing Add:* Dept of Anat Wright State Univ Sch of Med Dayton OH 45401

ZAMBITO, ARTHUR JOSEPH, b Rochester, NY, Sept 7, 14; m 42; c 7. ORGANIC CHEMISTRY. *Educ:* Univ Mich, BS, 40, MS, 41, PhD(org chem), 47. *Prof Exp:* From res chemist to sr res chemist, 41-64, sect leader, Res & Develop Lab, 64-75, SR RES FEL, MERCK & CO INC, 75- *Mem:* Am Chem Soc. *Res:* Synthesis of pharmaceuticals; synthesis and isolation of amino acids; preparation of parenteral solutions and emulsions; synthesis of anticancer agents; antibiotics. *Mailing Add:* 75 Hillcrest Dr Clark NJ 07066

ZAMBONI, LUCIANO, b San Dona di Piave, Italy, Sept 6, 29; m 57; c 2. PATHOLOGY, ELECTRON MICROSCOPY. *Educ:* Univ Rome, MD, 55, dipl gastroenterol, 58. *Prof Exp:* Instr path, Univ Rome, 55-59; asst resident anat, Univ Calif, Los Angeles, 59-60; instr, McGill Univ, 60-61; asst resident path, Karolinska Inst, Sweden, 61-63; asst prof, 63-65, PROF PATH, UNIV CALIF, LOS ANGELES, 65-; CHIEF DEPT PATH & HEAD ELECTRON MICROS, LOS ANGELES COUNTY HARBOR-UCLA MED CTR, 63- *Mem:* Electron Micros Soc Am; Am Soc Cell Biol; Am Fertil Soc; Soc Study Reproduction; Ital Med Asn. *Res:* Reproductive biology; ultrastructural studies on embryogenesis, early reproduction and fertilization. *Mailing Add:* Dept of Path Harbor-UCLA Med Ctr Torrance CA 90509

ZAMBROW, J(OHN) L(UCIAN), b Milwaukee, Wis, Dec 9, 14; m 42; c 2. METALLURGY. *Educ:* Univ Wis, BS, 40, MS, 46; Ohio State Univ, PhD(metall), 48. *Prof Exp:* Mfg engr, Cutler-Hammer, Inc, 40-44; res engr, Battelle Mem Inst, 44-47; asst res prof metall, Ohio State Univ, 49; res engr, Sylvania Elec Prod, Inc, 49-53, mgr eng, 53-57; mgr eng, Sylvania-Corning Nuclear Corp, 57-59, dir eng, 59-62; mgr metall res, Res Ctr, 62-74, asst dir,

74-77, assoc dir, Res Ctr, 77-80, SR CONSULT, BORG-WARNER CORP, DES PLAINES, 80- *Mem:* Sigma Xi; Am Soc Metals; Am Nuclear Soc; Am Inst Mining, Metall & Petrol Engrs. *Res:* Physical and powder metallurgy; manufacturing process research and development. *Mailing Add:* 7 Yorkshire Dr Deerfield IL 60015

ZAME, ALAN, b New York, NY, Aug 16, 41. MATHEMATICS. *Educ:* Calif Inst Technol, BS, 62; Univ Calif, Berkeley, PhD(math), 65. *Prof Exp:* Assoc prof, 65-76, PROF MATH, UNIV MIAMI, 76- *Mem:* Am Math Soc; Am Math Asn. *Res:* Number theory; functional and combinatorial analysis. *Mailing Add:* Dept Math Univ Miami Coral Gables FL 33124

ZAME, WILLIAM ROBIN, b Long Beach, NY, Nov 4, 45. MATHEMATICS. *Educ:* Calif Inst Technol, BS, 65; Tulane Univ, MS, 67, PhD(math), 70. *Prof Exp:* Evans instr math, Rice Univ, 70-72; asst prof, State Univ NY Buffalo, 72-75; assoc prof, Tulane Univ, 75-78; ASSOC PROF MATH, STATE UNIV NY BUFFALO, 78- *Mem:* Am Math Soc. *Res:* Several complex variables; Banach algebras, C--algebras. *Mailing Add:* Dept of Math State Univ NY Buffalo NY 14215

ZAMECNIK, PAUL CHARLES, b Cleveland, Ohio, Nov 22, 12; m 36; c 3. MEDICINE. *Educ:* Dartmouth Col, AB, 33; Harvard Univ, MD, 36. *Hon Degrees:* Dr, Univ Utrecht, 66; DSc, Columbia Univ, 71. *Prof Exp:* Resident med, C P Huntington Mem Hosp, Boston, 36-37; intern, Univ Hosps, Cleveland, 38-39; Moseley traveling fel from Harvard Univ, Carlsberg Lab, Copenhagen, 39-40; Finney-Howell fel, Rockefeller Inst, 41-42; from instr to assoc prof, 42-56, Collis P Huntington prof, 56-79, EMER PROF ONCOL MED & DIR, J C WARREN LABS, HARVARD MED SCH, 79-; PRIN SCIENTIST, WORCESTER FOUND EXP BIOL, SHREWSBURY, MASS, 79- *Concurrent Pos:* Physician, Mass Gen Hosp, 56-79, sr physician, 79- *Honors & Awards:* James Ewing Award, 63; Borden Award, 65; John Collins Warren Triennial Prize, 46 & 50; Am Cancer Soc Nat Award, 68; Passano Award, 70. *Mem:* Nat Acad Sci; Asn Am Physicians; Am Acad Arts & Sci; Am Soc Biol Chemists; Am Asn Cancer Res (pres, 64-65). *Res:* Protein synthesis; cancer; nucleic acid metabolism; virology. *Mailing Add:* Huntington Labs Mass Gen Hosp Boston MA 02114

ZAMEL, NOE, b Rio Grande, Brazil, Apr 2, 35; m 59; c 3. RESPIRATORY PHYSIOLOGY. *Educ:* Col Med, Fed Univ Rio Grande do Sul, Brazil, MD, 58. *Prof Exp:* From instr to assoc prof med, Col Med, Fed Univ Rio Grande do Sul, Brazil, 62-70; assoc prof med & dir respiratory physiol, Col Med, Univ Nebr, Omaha, 70-72; asoc prof, 72-80, PROF MED, FAC MED & DIR RESPIRATORY PHYSIOL, TRIHOSP RESPIRATORY SERV, UNIV TORONTO, CN, 80- *Concurrent Pos:* Res fel respiratory physiol, Cardiovasc Res Inst, Univ Calif, San Francisco, 69. *Honors & Awards:* Miguel Couto Award, Col Med, Fed Univ Rio Grande do Sul, 58; Cecile Lehman Mayer Award, Am Col Chest Physicians, 69. *Mem:* Am Col Chest Physicians; Am Thoracic Soc; Am Fedn Clin Res; Can Soc Clin Invest; Am Physiol Soc. *Res:* Lung mechanics. *Mailing Add:* 207 Torresdale Ave Willowdale ON M2R 3E7 Can

ZAMENHOF, PATRICE JOY, b Santa Rosa, Calif, Apr 2, 34; m 61. MOLECULAR GENETICS. *Educ:* Univ Calif, Berkeley, AB, 56, PhD(microbiol), 62. *Prof Exp:* Res assoc biochem, Col Physicians & Surgeons, Columbia Univ, 62-64; asst prof, 64-71, ASSOC PROF BIOL CHEM, SCH MED, UNIV CALIF, LOS ANGELES, 71- *Concurrent Pos:* USPHS res grants, Univ Calif, Los Angeles, 65-68 & 70-, career develop award, Nat Inst Gen Med Sci, 67, mem cancer ctr, 75- *Mem:* Am Soc Microbiol; Genetics Soc Am; Am Soc Biol Chemists. *Res:* Mutagenic mechanisms; genetic instability in microorganisms; mutator genes; repair of genetic damage; functional interactions of inactive mutant proteins. *Mailing Add:* Dept of Biol Chem Univ of Calif Sch of Med Los Angeles CA 90024

ZAMENHOF, STEPHEN, b Warsaw, Poland, June 12, 11; nat US; m 61. BIOCHEMISTRY. *Educ:* Warsaw Polytech Sch, Dr Tech Sci, 36; Columbia Univ, PhD(biochem), 49. *Prof Exp:* Res assoc biochem, Columbia Univ, 50-51, from asst prof to assoc prof, 51-64; PROF MICROBIOL GENETICS & BIOL CHEM, SCH MED, UNIV CALIF, LOS ANGELES, 64- *Concurrent Pos:* Guggenheim fel, 58-59. *Mem:* Am Soc Biol Chem; Am Inst Nutrit; Soc Neurosci; Am Asn Anatomists; Am Soc Neurochem. *Res:* Microbial genetics; nucleic acids; prenatal brain development. *Mailing Add:* Dept of Microbiol & Immunol Univ of Calif Sch of Med Los Angeles CA 90024

ZAMES, GEORGE, b Lodz, Poland, Jan 7, 34; Can citizen; m 64; c 2. ELECTRICAL ENGINEERING. *Educ:* McGill Univ, BEng, 54; Mass Inst Technol, ScD(elec eng), 60. *Prof Exp:* Res assoc elec eng, Mass Inst Technol, 54-61, asst prof, 61-62, 63-65; res fel appl physics, Harvard Univ, 62-63; asst prof elec eng, Mass Inst Technol, 63-65; Nat Acad Sci res fel, Electronic Res Ctr, NASA, 65-67; Guggenheim fel, 67-68; sr scientist, Electronic Res Ctr, NASA, 68-72; vis prof elec eng, Technion, Haifa, 72-74; PROF ELEC ENG, McGILL UNIV, 74- *Mem:* Fel Inst Elec & Electronics Engrs; Sigma Xi. *Res:* Nonlinear systems; large systems; feedback hierarchies; control system theory; communication system theory; functional analysis. *Mailing Add:* Dept of Elec Eng 3480 University St Montreal PQ H3A 2A7 Can

ZAMICK, LARRY, b Winnipeg, Man, Mar 15, 35; m 66; c 2. NUCLEAR PHYSICS. *Educ:* Univ Man, BSc, 57; Mass Inst Technol, PhD(physics), 61. *Prof Exp:* Instr physics, Princeton Univ, 62-65, res assoc, 65-66; assoc prof, 66-70, PROF PHYSICS, RUTGERS UNIV, 70- *Mem:* Fel Am Phys Soc. *Res:* High energy deuteron-nucleus scattering; nuclear structure studies with the shell model. *Mailing Add:* Dept of Physics Rutgers Univ New Brunswick NJ 08903

ZAMIKOFF, IRVING IRA, b Toronto, Ont, Feb 13, 43; m 67; c 2. DENTISTRY, PROSTHODONTICS. *Educ:* Univ Toronto, DDS, 67; Univ Mich, MS, 70; Am Bd Prosthodont, dipl, 72. *Prof Exp:* ASSOC PROF PROSTHODONT, SCH DENT, LA STATE UNIV, NEW ORLEANS, 70- *Concurrent Pos:* Vis dentist, Charity Hosp, New Orleans, 70- *Mem:* Am Dent Asn; Int Asn Dent Res; Can Dent Asn; Am Col Prosthodont. *Mailing Add:* Dept of Prosthodont La State Univ Med Ctr New Orleans LA 70119

ZAMIR, LOLITA ORA, b Cairo, Egypt; Israeli & US citizen. BIO-ORGANIC CHEMISTRY, ORGANIC CHEMISTRY. *Educ:* Israel Inst Technol, MSc, 66; Yale Univ, PhD(bio-org chem), 73. *Prof Exp:* Teaching asst chem, Yale Univ, 68-73; res fel biochem, Harvard Univ, 73-74; sr res chemist, Merck Inst, 74-75; ASST PROF CHEM & ASSOC MEM CTR BIOCHEM RES, STATE UNIV NY, BINGHAMTON, 75- *Mem:* Am Chem Soc; Am Asn Women Sci; Am Asn Univ Prof. *Res:* Biosynthesis; fungal metabolites; natural products. *Mailing Add:* Dept of Chem State Univ of NY Binghamton NY 13901

ZAMORA, ANTONIO, b Nuevo Laredo, Mexico, Dec 6, 42; US citizen; m 67; c 1. COMPUTER SCIENCE, CHEMISTRY. *Educ:* Univ Tex, BS, 62; Ohio State Univ, MS, 69. *Prof Exp:* Med lab technician clin chem, US Army, 62-65; INFO SCIENTIST RES & DEVELOP, CHEM ABSTRACTS SERV, 65- *Mem:* Am Chem Soc; Asn Comput Mach; AAAS. *Res:* Automated language processing; artificial intelligence; information storage and retrieval. *Mailing Add:* Chem Abstracts Serv PO Box 3012 Columbus OH 43210

ZAMORA, CESARIO SIASOCO, b Marikina, Philippines, Nov 1, 38; US citizen; m 66; c 2. VETERINARY HISTOLOGY, VETERINARY GROSS ANATOMY. *Educ:* Univ Philippines, DVM, 59; Univ Minn, MS, 64; Univ Wis, Madison, PhD(vet sci), 72. *Prof Exp:* Instr vet anat, Univ Philippines, 59-62; res asst, Univ Minn, 62-64; instr to asst prof vet anat, Univ Philippines, 64-69; res asst, Univ Wis, 69-72; asst prof, 72-76, assoc prof, 76-81, PROF ANAT, WASH STATE UNIV, 81-, HEAD ANAT DIV, DEPT VET & COMP ANAT, PHARMACOL & PHYSIOL, COL VET MED, 81- *Mem:* Am Vet Med Asn; Am Asn Vet Anatomists; World Asn Vet Anatomists; Asn Am Vet Med Col. *Res:* Structure and function of the gastrointestinal tract of pigs; pathophysiology of gastric ulcers and enteric diseases of swine; structure and function of reproductive organs of domestic animals. *Mailing Add:* Dept Vet & Comp Anat Col Vet Med Wash State Univ Pullman WA 99164

ZAMRIK, SAM YUSUF, b Damascus, Syria, Dec 11, 32; US citizen; m 54; c 4. ENGINEERING MECHANICS. *Educ:* Univ Tex, BA, 56, BS, 57; Pa State Univ, MS, 61, PhD(eng mech), 65. *Prof Exp:* Design engr, Tex Pipe Line Co, 57-58; proj engr & consult, Gen Petrol Authority, 58-60; from instr to assoc prof eng mech, 60-75, PROF ENG MECH, PA STATE UNIV, UNIVERSITY PARK, 75- *Concurrent Pos:* Consult, Nat Forge Co, 68-72 & Gen Elec Co; fels, NASA & Ford Found; tech reviewer, NSF, NASA, Am Soc Mech Engrs & Soc Exp Stress Anal. *Mem:* Am Soc Testing & Mat; Am Soc Mech Engrs; Soc Exp Stress Anal; Sigma Xi. *Res:* Radiation effects on structural materials; fatigue and fracture mechanics; biaxial creep-fatigue interaction. *Mailing Add:* Dept of Eng Sci & Mech 121 Hammond Bldg University Park PA 16802

ZANAKIS, STELIOS(STEVE) H, b Athens, Greece, Nov 16, 40. MANAGEMENT SCIENCE, INDUSTRIAL ENGINEERING. *Educ:* Nat Tech Univ, Athens, Dipl, 64; Pa State Univ, MBA, 70, MA, 72, PhD(mgt sci), 73. *Prof Exp:* Engr aerodyn, Greek Res Ctr Nat Defense, 65-66; indust engr mgt consult, Greek Prod Ctr, 67-68; asst prof indust eng & systs anal, WVa Col Grad Studies, 72-76, prog dir, 73-80, assoc prof, 76-80; ASSOC PROF MAT & COORDR MGT SCI, FLA INT UNIV, 81- *Concurrent Pos:* Consult, Ashland Oil, 73, Union Carbide Corp, 75-76, WVa Dept Hwy, 76-77 & Charleston Area Med Ctr, 78-79; mem, WVa State Comprehensive Health Plan Comt, 73-74; prin, Mgt Systs Consults, 76- *Mem:* Am Inst Decision Sci; sr mem Am Inst Indust Engrs; Inst Mgt Sci; Am Prod & Inventory Control Soc; Hellenic Oper Res Soc. *Res:* Applications of operations research/ management science techniques to solve real management problems; production, inventory, distribution management; hospital management engineering; statistics/optimization interface; simulation and computer applications; prog evaluation and fund allocation under conflicting goals and objectives; forecasting and statistical analysis. *Mailing Add:* Sch Bus Mgt Dept Fla Int Univ Miami FL 33199

ZAND, ROBERT, b New York, NY, Jan 7, 30; m 52; c 3. BIOPHYSICAL CHEMISTRY, NEUROCHEMISTRY. *Educ:* Univ Mo, BS, 51; Polytech Inst Brooklyn, MS, 54; Brandeis Univ, PhD(chem), 61. *Prof Exp:* Res chemist, Irvington Varnish & Insulator, 53; assoc res biophysicist, 63-73, asst prof, 68-73, ASSOC PROF BIOCHEM & RES BIOPHYSICIST, UNIV MICH, ANN ARBOR, 73- *Concurrent Pos:* NIH fel, Harvard Med Sch, 61-63; fel, Brandeis Univ, 61-63; ODOL Found lectr, Univ Buenos Aires, 72; vis prof, Inst Venezolans-Italiano de Cultura, Caracas, Venezuela, 79. *Mem:* Am Chem Soc; Biophys Soc; Am Soc Neurochem; Am Soc Biol Chem; Int Soc Neurochem. *Res:* Conformation of proteins and small molecules by spectroscopic methods; use of amino acid analogs to determine stereochemical requirements of amino acid receptor sites; mechanism of the brain toxicity of bilirubin in the neonate; polymer analogs of biomembranes. *Mailing Add:* Biophys Res Div Univ of Mich Inst of Sci & Tech Ann Arbor MI 48109

ZAND, SIAVOSH MARC, b Tehran, Iran, Dec 9, 38. HYDROLOGY, ENVIRONMENTAL SCIENCES. *Educ:* Univ Tehran, BCE, 61; Univ Del, MCE, 66; Univ Calif, Berkeley, PhD(hydraul), 69. *Prof Exp:* Consult, Resources for Future, Inc, 67-68; systs hydrologist, Automated Environ Systs, Inc, NY, 68-69; RES HYDROLOGIST, US GEOL SURV, 69- *Mem:* Am Soc Civil Engrs; Am Geophys Union. *Res:* Hydraulics. *Mailing Add:* US Geol Surv 345 Middlefield Rd Menlo Park CA 94025

ZANDER, ANDREW THOMAS, b Chicago, Ill, Oct 27, 45; m 77; c 2. ANALYTICAL CHEMISTRY, SPECTROSCOPY. *Educ:* Univ Ill, Urbana, BS, 68; Univ Md, PhD(anal chem), 76. *Prof Exp:* Chemist, Chicago Bridge & Iron Co, 66; asst chemist anal chem, Standard Oil Co, Ind, 68-69; res assoc, Dept Chem, Ind Univ, 76-77; asst prof anal chem, Cleveland State Univ, 77-79; STAFF SCIENTIST, SPECTRA METRICS, INC, 79- *Mem:* Am Chem Soc; Soc Appl Spectros. *Res:* Design and development of single- and multi-element methods of atomic spectrometric analysis for trace metals; high resolution studies of spectral features in atomic absorption and atomic emission spectroscopy. *Mailing Add:* Spectra Metrics Inc 204 Andover St Andover MA 01810

ZANDER, ARLEN RAY, b Shiner, Tex, Dec 12, 40; m 64; c 3. NUCLEAR PHYSICS, ATOMIC PHYSICS. *Educ:* Univ Tex, Austin, BS, 64; Fla State Univ, PhD(nuclear physics), 70. *Prof Exp:* Res physicist, Phillips Petrol Co, 64-65; asst prof, 70-74, assoc prof, 74-79, PROF PHYSICS & EXTERNAL GRANTS COORDR, EAST TEX STATE UNIV, 79- *Mem:* Am Phys Soc; Am Asn Physics Teachers. *Res:* Direct nuclear reaction mechanisms; experimental fast neutron activation studies; x-ray fluorescence studies utilizing charged particle accelerators. *Mailing Add:* Dept Physics East Tex State Univ Commerce TX 75428

ZANDER, DONALD VICTOR, b Bellingham, Wash, Feb 15, 16; m 45; c 3. AVIAN PATHOLOGY, POULTRY NUTRITION & HUSBANDRY. *Educ:* Univ Calif, BS, 41, PhD(comp path), 53; Colo State Univ, MS, 45, DVM, 50. *Prof Exp:* Asst poultry husb, Univ Calif, 37-41, asst specialist & lectr vet med, 50-53, asst prof, 53-55; lab instr bact, Colo State Univ, 48; dir res lab, Heisdorf & Nelson Farms, Inc, 55-71, vpres, 61-72, DIR HEALTH RES, H&N INC, 72- *Mem:* Poultry Sci Asn; Am Vet Med Asn; Am Asn Avian Path (pres, 65-66); World Poultry Sci Asn; World Poultry Vet Asn. *Res:* Avian diseases; pathology, diagnosis and epizootiology; poultry husbandry and nutrition; pathogen-free poultry. *Mailing Add:* 18232 160th Ave NE Woodinville WA 90872

ZANDER, HELMUT A, b Bautzen, Ger, Oct 25, 12; nat US; m 42; c 4. DENTISTRY. *Educ:* Univ Würzburg, DMd, 34; Northwestern Univ, DDS, 38, MS, 40. *Hon Degrees:* Dr, Univ Zurich, 72. *Prof Exp:* Asst children's dent, Northwestern Univ, 38-40, res assoc, 40-42; asst prof clin dent, Dent Sch, Tufts Col, 42-47, from assoc prof to prof oral pediat, 47-51; prof periodont, Sch Dent, Univ Minn, 51-57; clin assoc prof dent, 66-72, PROF CLIN DENT & DENT RES, SCH MED & DENT, UNIV ROCHESTER, 72-; HEAD DEPT PERIODONT, EASTMAN DENT CTR, 57-, SR SCIENTIST, 77- *Mem:* Am Soc Dent for Children; Soc Exp Biol & Med; Am Dent Asn; Am Acad Periodont; Int Asn Dent Res. *Res:* Pulp pathology; caries etiology; preventive dentistry; dental histology; antibiosis; periodontology. *Mailing Add:* Eastman Dent Ctr 625 Elmwood Ave Rochester NY 14620

ZANDER, VERNON EMIL, b Toledo, Wash, Feb 3, 39; m 66; c 1. MATHEMATICS. *Educ:* Univ Wash, BS, 61; Catholic Univ, MS, 65, PhD(math), 69. *Prof Exp:* Mathematician, NIH, 61-66; asst prof math, West Ga Col, 68-72, assoc prof, 72-82; PRES, INTERCOASTAL DATA CORP, 82- *Mem:* Am Math Soc; Math Asn Am. *Res:* Development theory for integration of vector-valued functions on product spaces and integration of infinite products of vector-valued functions from Orlicz spaces. *Mailing Add:* Box 407 Rte 11 Carrollton GA 30117

ZANDI, IRAJ, b Teheran, Iran, June 30, 31; m 58; c 5. CIVIL ENGINEERING. *Educ:* Univ Teheran, BS, 52; Univ Okla, MS, 57; Ga Inst Technol, PhD, 59. *Hon Degrees:* MA, Univ Pa, 71. *Prof Exp:* Dir dept environ sanit, Ministry of Health, Govt Iran, 59-61; assoc prof eng, Abadan Inst Technol, Iran, 61-62; asst prof civil eng, Univ Del, 62-66; assoc prof, 66-69, actg dir nat ctr engergy mgt & power, 72-77, PROF CIVIL ENG, UNIV PA, 69- *Concurrent Pos:* Ed, J Pipeline, Am Soc Civil Engrs, 66-70. *Honors & Awards:* Soc Sigma Xi Ferst Award, Ga Inst Technol, 61. *Mem:* Am Soc Eng Educ; Am Soc Civil Engrs; Am Inst Chem Engrs. *Res:* Pipeline engineering; resource recovery; resources and energy analysis. *Mailing Add:* Dept Civil & Urban Eng Univ of Pa 220 S 33rd St Philadelphia PA 19104

ZANDLER, MELVIN E, b Wichita, Kans, Nov 28, 37; m 59; c 4. PHYSICAL CHEMISTRY. *Educ:* Friends Univ, BA, 60; Univ Wichita, MS, 63; Ariz State Univ, PhD(phys chem), 66. *Prof Exp:* Asst prof, 66-75, ASSOC PROF CHEM, WICHITA STATE UNIV, 75- *Concurrent Pos:* Petrol Res Fund res grant, 68-70; sabbatical leave, vis prof, Univ Calif, Berkeley, 78; NSF grant microcomput, 81-83. *Mem:* Am Chem Soc; Sigma Xi. *Res:* Theory of liquids and liquid mixtures; statistical thermodynamics; semi-empirical and ab-initio molecular orbital calculations; generation and optimization of reactive potential energy surfaces. *Mailing Add:* Dept of Chem Wichita State Univ Wichita KS 67208

ZANDY, HASSAN F, b Tehran, Iran, Mar 11, 12; US citizen; m 43; c 3. PHYSICS, SPECTROSCOPY. *Educ:* Univ Birmingham, BSc, 35, MSc, 49; Univ Tehran, PhD(physics), 53. *Hon Degrees:* PhD, Univ Tehran, 52. *Prof Exp:* Instr physics, Univ Tehran, 37-46, asst prof, 50-53; lectr, Univ Leicester, 47-50; Fulbright fel, Brooklyn Polytech Inst, 53-54; PROF PHYSICS, UNIV BRIDGEPORT, 54- *Concurrent Pos:* Mem vis scientist prog physics, NSF, 59-; NSF fac fel, 63-64, res grant plasma res, Univ Bridgeport, 72-73. *Mem:* Am Asn Physics Teachers. *Res:* High vacuum technique; measurement of temperature of hot plasmas by x-ray spectroscopy. *Mailing Add:* Dept of Physics Univ of Bridgeport Bridgeport CT 06602

ZANELLA, EUGENE F, b Framingham, Mass, Apr 17, 43; c 2. AQUATIC BIOLOGY. *Educ:* Boston Univ, BS, 65; Univ Mass, MS, 67. *Prof Exp:* Res fel aquatic biol, 70-77, asst prof, 77-80, RES ASSOC & GROUP LEADER BIO-RES GROUP, ENVIRON SCI DIV, INST PAPER CHEM, 77-, ASSOC PROF, 80- *Mem:* Am Fisheries Soc; NAm Benthological Soc; Tech Asn Pulp & Paper Indust. *Res:* Impacts of industrial effluents on aquatic organisms; toxicity of pulp and paper mill effluents to diverse aquatic communities. *Mailing Add:* 807 E Harding Appleton WI 54911

ZANEVELD, JACQUES RONALD VICTOR, b Leiderdorp, Neth, July 12, 44; US citizen; m 71. OCEANOGRAPHY. *Educ:* Old Dom Univ, BS, 64; Mass Inst Technol, SM, 66; Ore State Univ, PhD(oceanog), 71. *Prof Exp:* RES ASSOC PROF OCEANOG, ORE STATE UNIV, 71- *Mem:* Am Geophys Union; Optical Soc Am. *Res:* Theoretical and experimental relationships between light attenuation and scattering properties of the ocean and the dynamic properties of suspended and dissolved materials. *Mailing Add:* Sch of Oceanog Ore State Univ Corvallis OR 97331

ZANEVELD, LOURENS JAN DIRK, b The Hague, Netherlands, Mar 22, 42; US citizen; m 65. BIOCHEMISTRY, MEDICINE. *Educ:* Old Dom Col, BSc, 63; Univ Ga, DVM, 67, MS, 68, PhD(biochem), 70. *Prof Exp:* Res assoc biochem, Univ Ga, 69-71; asst prof obstet & gynec & res assoc, Univ Chicago, 71-74; sci adv & chief pop res ctr, IIT Res Inst, 74-75; assoc prof, 75-79, actg head, Dept Physiol & Biophysics, 79-81, PROF PHYSIOL, OBSTET & GYNECOL, UNIV ILL MED CTR, 79- *Mem:* Am Soc Exp Path; Am Soc Andrology; Soc Study Reproduction; Am Vet Med Asn; Perinatal Res Soc. *Res:* Reproduction; biochemistry and physiology of male and female genital tract secretions, speramtozoa and fertilization. *Mailing Add:* Dept of Physiol & Biophysics PO Box 6998 Chicago IL 60680

ZANGER, MURRAY, b New York, NY, May 5, 32; m 62; c 2. PHYSICAL ORGANIC CHEMISTRY. *Educ:* City Col New York, BS, 53; Univ Kans, PhD(org chem), 59. *Prof Exp:* Fel chem, Univ Wis, 59-60; res chemist, Marshall Lab, E I du Pont de Nemours & Co, 60-64; from asst prof to assoc prof org chem, 64-72, PROF CHEM, PHILADELPHIA COL PHARM & SCI, 72- *Concurrent Pos:* USPHS res grant phenothiazine chem, 66-69; consult, Sadtler Res Labs, 68- *Mem:* Am Chem Soc. *Res:* Organophosphorus compounds; cyclopropane and phenothiazine chemistry; carbenes; fluorcarbon and anionic polymers; sulfa drugs; organic mechanisms; electron spin resonance; nuclear magnetic resonance spectroscopy. *Mailing Add:* Dept of Chem 43rd St & Kingsessing Ave Philadelphia PA 19104

ZANINI-FISHER, MARGHERITA, b Como, Italy, Jan 5, 47; m 76; c 1. SOLID STATE PHYSICS, ELECTROCHEMISTRY. *Educ:* Univ Rome, PhD(physics), 71. *Prof Exp:* Res assoc physics, Italian Nat Res Coun, 71-74, staff scientist, 74-76; res assoc, Moore Sch Elec Eng, Univ Pa, 76-77; SCIENTIST, PHYSIC DEPT, SCI RES LAB, FORD MOTOR CO, 77- *Concurrent Pos:* Res assoc, Div Eng, Brown Univ, 74-76. *Mem:* Am Phys Soc. *Res:* New materials used for energy storage; electrochemistry; transport properties of solids. *Mailing Add:* Sci Res Lab Ford Motor Co Dearborn MI 48121

ZANJANI, ESMAIL DABAGHCHIAN, b Resht, Iran, Dec 23, 38; m 63; c 3. HEMATOLOGY, PHYSIOLOGY. *Educ:* NY Univ, BA, 64, MS, 66, PhD(hemat), 69. *Prof Exp:* From asst to res assoc exp hemat, NY Univ, 65-70; asst prof med & physiol, Mt Sinai Sch Med, 70-74, assoc prof physiol, 74-77; PROF MED & PHYSIOL, SCH MED, UNIV MINN, 77- *Mem:* AAAS; Harvey Soc; Am Soc Hemat; Am Soc Zool; NY Acad Sci. *Res:* Experimental hematology; hemopoietic stimulating factor; mechanisms of blood cell production and release; renal involvement in erythropoiesis; erythropoiesis in submammalian species; fetal erythropoiesis. *Mailing Add:* Vet Admin Hosp (151) 54 St & 48 Ave Minneapolis MN 55417

ZANKEL, KENNETH L, b New York, NY, Mar 29, 30; m 55; c 1. BIOPHYSICS, ENIVRONMENTAL SCIENCES. *Educ:* Rutgers Univ, BS, 51; Fla State Univ, MS, 55; Mich State Univ, PhD(physics), 58. *Prof Exp:* Asst res prof physics, Mich State Univ, 58-59; asst prof, Univ Ore, 59-63; Fulbright fel, Univ Heidelberg, 63-64; fel, Calif Inst Technol, 64-66; res fel, Sect Genetics Develop & Physiol, Cornell Univ, 66-69; scientist, Res Inst For Advan Studies, 69-75; MEM STAFF, ENVIRON CTR, MARTIN MARIETTA LABS RES & DEVELOP CTR, 75- *Mem:* Air Pollution Control Asn; fel, Acoust Soc Am. *Res:* Photobiology. *Mailing Add:* Martin Marietta Environ Ctr 1450 S Rolling Rd Baltimore MD 21227

ZANNONI, VINCENT G, b New York, NY, June 12, 28. BIOCHEMISTRY, PHARMACOLOGY. *Educ:* City Col New York, BS, 51; George Washington Univ, MS, 56, PhD(biochem), 59. *Prof Exp:* Biochemist, Goldwater Mem Hosp, New York, 51-54 & Nat Heart Inst, 54-56; res chemist, Nat Inst Arthritis & Metab Dis, 57-63; from asst prof to prof biochem pharmacol, Sch Med, NY Univ, 63-74; PROF PHARMACOL, MED SCH, UNIV MICH, ANN ARBOR, 74- *Mem:* AAAS; Am Soc Biol Chemists; Am Soc Pharmacol & Exp Therapeut; NY Acad Sci. *Res:* Inborn errors of metabolism; mechanisms of reactions; amino acid metabolism; enzymology; biochemical pharmacology. *Mailing Add:* Dept of Pharmacol Univ of Mich Med Sch Ann Arbor MI 48109

ZANONI, ALPHONSE E(LIGIUS), b Melrose Park, Ill, July 24, 34; m 60; c 6. ENGINEERING. *Educ:* Marquette Univ, BCE, 56; Univ Minn, MS, 60, PhD(civil eng), 64. *Prof Exp:* Consult engr, Toltz, King, Duvall, Anderson, Inc, Minn, 58-60; instr civil eng, 60-61, from asst prof to assoc prof, 64-76, chmn dept, 70-72, PROF CIVIL ENG, COL ENG, MARQUETTE UNIV, 76- *Concurrent Pos:* Consult water & waste water probs indust & munic. *Mem:* Am Soc Civil Engrs; Am Water Works Asn; Water Pollution Control Fedn; Sigma Xi; Asn Environ Eng Prof. *Res:* Water supply and pollution control. *Mailing Add:* Dept of Civil Eng Col of Eng 1515 W Wisconsin Ave Milwaukee WI 53233

ZANOWIAK, PAUL, b Little Falls, NJ, July 11, 33; m 57; c 4. PHARMACEUTICS. *Educ:* Rutgers Univ, BS, 54, MS, 57; Univ Fla, PhD(pharm), 59. *Prof Exp:* Instr pharm, Col Pharm, Univ Fla, 58-59; res & develop chemist, Noxell Corp, Md, 59-64; from asst prof to assoc prof pharmaceut, Sch Pharm, WVa Univ, 64-71; actg dean, 72-74, PROF PHARMACEUT & CHMN DEPT, TEMPLE UNIV, 71- *Concurrent Pos:* Am Found Pharm Educ fel; Mead-Johnson res grant; Lunsford Richardson Pharm Award. *Mem:* AAAS; Am Pharmaceut Asn; Acad Pharmaceut Sci; Am Asn Col Pharm. *Res:* Design and evaluation of dosage forms, especially those used in topical medication. *Mailing Add:* Dept of Pharm Temple Univ Sch of Pharm Philadelphia PA 19140

ZANZUCCHI, PETER JOHN, b Syracuse, NY, Apr 21, 41; m 67. ANALYTICAL CHEMISTRY. *Educ:* Le Moyne Col, NY, BS, 63; Univ Ill, Urbana, MS, 65, PhD(chem), 67. *Prof Exp:* STAFF CHEMIST, DAVID SARNOFF RES CTR, RCA CORP, 67- *Mem:* Electrochem Soc; Optical Soc Am; Am Soc Testing & Mat. *Res:* Measurement of the optical properties of inorganic materials, particularly semiconductor materials in the wavelength range 0.2 to 200 micrometers. *Mailing Add:* David Sarnoff Res Ctr RCA Corp Princeton NJ 08540

ZAO, ZANG Z, b Soochow, China, Aug 24, 16; US citizen; m 55; c 2. CARDIOLOGY. *Educ:* Med Col Düsseldorf, MD, 41. *Prof Exp:* Instr cardiol, Univ Tex Med Br, 57-58; instr med, Sch Med, Tulane Univ, 59-60; asst prof, Sch Med, Univ Miami, 60-62; dir vectorcardiogram lab, Degoesbriand Hosp, Col Med, Univ Vt, 62-67; head EKG & vectocardiogram labs, Cox Heart Inst, Ohio, 67-72; MEM STAFF, J ELECTROCARDIOL, 72- *Concurrent Pos:* Nat Heart Inst spec res fel, 59-61, res grant, 63-66; Vt Heart Asn res grant, 66; founder & first ed, J Electrocardiol; bd chmn & co-chmn dept res, Res in Electrocardiol, Inc, 68- *Honors & Awards:* 5th Interam Cong Cardiol Achievement Award. *Mem:* Sr mem Am Fedn Clin Res; fel Am Geriat Soc; fel Am Col Cardiol; Am Col Angiol. *Res:* Fundamental and clinical research in electrocardiology with special reference to electrocardiography and vectorcardiography. *Mailing Add:* Jour Electrocardiol PO Box 923-B Pac Beach Sta San Diego CA 92109

ZAPFFE, CARL ANDREW, b Brainerd, Minn, July 25, 12; m 37; c 8. METALLURGY, SPACE SCIENCES. *Educ:* Mich Technol Univ, BS, 33; Lehigh Univ, MSc, 34; Harvard Univ, ScD, 39. *Hon Degrees:* DEng, Mich Technol Univ, 60. *Prof Exp:* Metallurgist corrosion, Exp Sta, E I du Pont de Nemours & Co, Inc, 34-36; res assoc metall, Battelle Mem Inst, 38-43; asst tech dir stainless steel, Rustless Iron & Steel Corp, 43-45; CONSULT MAT ENG, 45- *Concurrent Pos:* Civilian scientist, Off Naval Res, 45-54. *Honors & Awards:* Procter Mem Award, Am Electroplaters Soc, 40. *Mem:* Hon life mem, Am Soc Metall; Am Chem Soc; Am Phys Soc; Am Geophys Soc; Int Soc Gravitation & Gen Relativity. *Res:* Stainless steels, superalloys and refractory metals; Pleistocene glaciation and Earth-moon evolution; relativistic physics and cosmology. *Mailing Add:* 6410 Murray Hill Rd Baltimore MD 21212

ZAPHYR, PETER ANTHONY, b Wheeling, WVa, Sept 4, 26; m 56; c 2. MATHEMATICS, MANAGEMENT INFORMATION SYSTEMS. *Educ:* Bethany Col, WVa, BS, 48; Univ WVa, MS, 49; Univ Pittsburgh, PhD(math), 57. *Prof Exp:* Instr math, Univ WVa, 49-50; asst, Ill Inst Technol, 50-51 & Univ Pittsburgh, 51-52; analyst, 52-61, mgr digital anal & comput sect, 61-65, asst to dir, Anal Dept, 65-69, mgr eng comput systs, Nuclear Energy Systs, 69-73, mgr, Eng Comput Serv, 73-80, DIR, POWER SYSTS COMPUT CTR, WESTINGHOUSE ELEC CORP, PITTSBURGH, 80- *Mem:* Asn Comput Mach. *Res:* Administration of industrial computing services and advanced applications of computers in engineering science, manufacturing and management. *Mailing Add:* 150 Morison Ave Greensburg PA 15601

ZAPISEK, WILLIAM FRANCIS, b Morris, NY, Mar 29, 35; m 59; c 3. BIOCHEMISTRY, DEVELOPMENTAL BIOLOGY. *Educ:* Syracuse Univ, BA, 60; Univ Conn, MS, 65, PhD(biochem), 67. *Prof Exp:* Fel biochem, Los Alamos Sci Lab, 67-68; asst prof, 68-72, assoc prof, 72-77, PROF BIOCHEM, CANISIUS COL, 77- *Mem:* AAAS; Am Chem Soc; Soc Develop Biol. *Res:* Characterization of low molecular weight methylated ribonucleic acid species; high pressure liquid chromatography analysis of organic pollutants of the aquatic environment; control of expression of mouse and fetoprotein gene. *Mailing Add:* Dept Chem Canisius Col Buffalo NY 14208

ZAPOL, WARREN MYRON, b New York, NY, Mar 16, 42; m 68; c 2. MEDICINE. *Educ:* Mass Inst Technol, BS, 62; Univ Rochester, MD, 66. *Prof Exp:* Res assoc, Nat Heart Inst, Bethesda, Md, 67-70; resident, 70-72, asst prof, 72-78, ASSOC PROF ANESTHESIA & DIR SPEC CTR RES ADULT RESPIRATORY FAILURE, HARVARD UNIV, 78- *Concurrent Pos:* Investr, US Antarctic Res Prof, 76-78 & 82- *Mem:* Am Physiol Soc; Am Soc Anethesiologists; Am Soc Artificial Internal Organs. *Res:* Circulation and gas exchange in animal models and man with acute lung injury; novel drug therapy in acute respiratory failure; diving seals in antarctica. *Mailing Add:* Dept Anesthesia Mass Gen Hosp Fruit St Boston MA 02114

ZAPOLSKY, HAROLD SAUL, b Chicago, Ill, Dec 24, 35; m 62; c 2. THEORETICAL PHYSICS. *Educ:* Shimer Col, AB, 54; Cornell Univ, PhD(physics), 62. *Prof Exp:* Nat Acad Sci-Nat Res Coun res assoc physics, Goddard Inst Space Studies, New York, 62-63; res assoc, Univ Md, College Park, 63-65, asst prof, 65-70; from assoc prog dir to prog dir theoret physics, NSF, 70-73; PROF PHYSICS & CHMN DEPT, RUTGERS UNIV, 73- *Mem:* Am Phys Soc; Am Astron Soc. *Res:* Quantum electrodynamics; astrophysics; general relativity. *Mailing Add:* Dept of Physics Rutgers Univ New Brunswick NJ 08903

ZAPP, JOHN ADAM, JR, b Pittsburgh, Pa, June 22, 11; m 34; c 2. TOXICOLOGY, INDUSTRIAL HYGIENE. *Educ:* Haverford Col, BS, 32; Univ Pa, MA, 34, PhD(physiol chem), 38. *Prof Exp:* Instr res med, Univ Pa, 38-43; regional gas officer, Civilian Defense Region, US Off Civilian Defense, 43-44; tech aide, Nat Defense Res Comt, 44-46; asst, E I DuPont de Nemours & Co, 46-48, asst dir, Haskell Lab, 48-52, dir Haskell Lab toxicol & indust med, 52-76; CONSULT TOXICOL & INDUST HYG, 76- *Concurrent Pos:* Porter fel, 40-43; Girvin fel, 41-42; consult res comt, Res Found, Univ Del, 49-, comt acceptable concentrations of toxic dusts & gases, Am Nat Stands Inst, 57-70, adv comt short-term inhalation limits, Commonwealth of Pa, 64-67, US Army Munitions Command Adv Group, 65-72 & panel biol & indust tech, Comt Res Life Sci, Nat Acad Sci-Nat Res Coun; mem bd trustees, Indust Health Found, 62-76 & Permanent Comt & Int Asn Occup Health, 64- *Mem:* AAAS; Soc Toxicol (pres, 67-68); Indust Hyg Asn; Am Soc Pharmacol & Exp Therapeut; Am Chem Soc. *Res:* Nitrogen extractives in mammalian muscle; chemical action of insulin; investigations of the toxic action of chemicals and techniques of industrial preventive medicine. *Mailing Add:* 318 Marshall St Kennett Square PA 19348

ZAPSALIS, CHARLES, b Lowell, Mass, Sept 22, 22; m 48. FOOD SCIENCE, CHEMISTRY. *Educ:* Springfield Col, BS, 52; Univ Mass, PhD(food sci, chem), 63. *Prof Exp:* Teacher, Jr High Sch, Mass, 52-53 & high, NY, 54-55; head sci dept high sch, Mass, 56-60; instrumental chemist, Beechnut Life Savers, Inc, 63, res mgr, 63-65; from asst prof to assoc prof, 65, PROF CHEM, FRAMINGHAM STATE COL, 65-, CHMN DEPT, 66- *Mem:* Am Chem Soc; Inst Food Technol. *Res:* Anthocyanins, chemical identification; pesticide methodology and characterization of tea components by gas chromatography; characterization of amino acids and polypeptides. *Mailing Add:* Dept of Chem Framingham State Col Framingham MA 01701

ZAR, JACOB L, b New York, NY, Mar 16, 17; m 39; c 2. MAGNETOHYDRODYNAMICS. *Educ:* City Col New York, BS, 38; Stevens Inst Technol, MSME, 43; NY Univ, PhD(physics), 51. *Prof Exp:* Proj engr, Thomas A Edison, Inc, 40-47; pres, Nat Radiac, Inc, 50-56; staff engr, Repub Aviation Corp, 56-57; dir exp develop, Airborne Accessories Corp, 57-59; sr staff scientist, Gen Precision, Inc, 59-60; res mgr, Schlumberger Well Surv Corp, 60-62; PRIN RES SCIENTIST, AVCO EVERETT RES LAB, 62- *Mem:* Am Phys Soc; Am Inst Aeronaut & Astronaut. *Res:* Superconductivity; laser applications; electron physics; electromechanical systems; superconducting magnets; solar energy; laser optical systems, windows and mirrors. *Mailing Add:* Avco Everett Res Lab Revere Beach Pkwy Everett MA 02149

ZAR, JERROLD HOWARD, b Chicago, Ill, June 28, 41; m 67; c 2. ECOLOGY, PHYSIOLOGY. *Educ:* Northern Ill Univ, BS, 62; Univ Ill, MS, 64, PhD(zool), 67. *Prof Exp:* Res assoc physiol ecol, Univ Ill, 67-68; asst prof, 68-71, assoc prof ecol & biostatist, 71-78, PROF BIOL SCI & CHMN DEPT, NORTHERN ILL UNIV, 78- *Concurrent Pos:* Staff consult, Argonne Nat Lab, 73-77 & US Environ Protection Agency, 74-; mem comt to rev methods ecotoxicol, Environ Studies Bd, Nat Res Coun, 79-81. *Mem:* AAAS; Ecol Soc Am; Am Physiol Soc; Int Asn Ecol; Biometric Soc. *Res:* Ecology; data processing; ecological animal physiology; environmental assessment; biostatistical analysis. *Mailing Add:* Dept Biol Sci Northern Ill Univ De Kalb IL 60115

ZARAFONETIS, CHRIS JOHN DIMITER, b Hillsboro, Tex, Jan 6, 14; m 43; c 1. INTERNAL MEDICINE. *Educ:* Univ Mich, BA, 36, MS, 37, MD, 41; Am Bd Internal Med, dipl, 50. *Prof Exp:* Externe, Simpson Mem Inst, Univ Mich, 40-41; intern, Boston City Hosp, 41-42; asst prof internal med & res assoc, Univ Mich, 47-50; assoc prof med, Sch Med, Temple Univ, 50-55, clin prof, 55-57, prof clin & res med, 57-60, chief hemat sect, Univ Hosp, 50-60; dir, 60-78, prof, 60-80, EMER PROF INTERNAL MED, SIMPSON MEM INST, MED SCH, UNIV MICH, ANN ARBOR, 80- *Concurrent Pos:* Res fel internal med, Med Sch, Univ Mich, 46-47; consult, Dept Defense, Directorate Res, Develop, Testing & Eval, Dept Army, Sci Adv Panel, Army Sci Bd, Vet Admin Hosp, Mich & hist unit, Dept Surgeon Gen, US Dept Army; mem bd, Med in Pub Interest, Inc & Gorgas Mem Inst, 81-; asst ed, Am J Med Sci, 51-60. *Honors & Awards:* Typhus Comn Medal, Legion of Merit, US; Order of Ismail, Egypt. *Mem:* Fel Am Col Physicians; Am Soc Clin Pharmacol & Therapeut (vpres, 65-66, pres, 68-69); fel Int Soc Hemat; hon mem Agr Med Asn; Am Therapeut Soc (pres, 68-69). *Res:* Histoplasmosis; infectious mononucleosis; lymphogranuloma and herpes viruses; rickettsial disease; potassium para-aminobenzoate acid in collagen and bullous disorders and conditions with excess fibrosis; blood dyscrasias; lipid mobilizer hormone and dyscrasias. *Mailing Add:* 2721 Bedford Rd Ann Arbor MI 48104

ZARATZIAN, VIRGINIA LOUISE, b Highland Park, Mich, Nov 15, 18. PHARMACOLOGY, TOXICOLOGY. *Educ:* Univ Mich, BS, 42 & 46, MS, 49; Wayne State Univ, PhD(Pharmacol), 56. *Prof Exp:* Res assoc neuropharmacol, Col Med, Univ Ill, 56-59; pharmacologist, US Food & Drug Admin, 59-61; res pharmacologist, USPHS, 61-63; survey pharmacologist, US Army, 63-66; pharmacologist, USDA, 66-68; pharmacologist, Psychopharmacol Res Br, NIMH, 68-78; PHARMACOLOGIST, FOOD SAFETY & INSPECTION SERV, USDA, 78- *Concurrent Pos:* Nat Acad Sci chem consult, Nat Adv Ctr Toxicol, 57-59; assoc prof, Univ Cincinnati, 62-63; vis prof, Sch Med, Tex Tech Univ, 72. *Mem:* AAAS; Am Chem Soc; Soc Toxicol; Pan Am Med Asn; Soc Pharmacol & Exp Therapeut. *Res:* Psychotropic drugs adverse reactions; environmental health; toxicology of economic poisons, food additives and air pollutants. *Mailing Add:* USDA PO Box 2217 Gaithersburg MD 20879

ZARCARO, ROBERT MICHAEL, b Springfield, Mass, Mar 4, 42; m 64; c 3. GENETICS, DEVELOPMENTAL BIOLOGY. *Educ:* Providence Col, BA, 64, MS, 66; Brown Univ, PhD(biol), 71. *Prof Exp:* Asst prof, 66-75, ASSOC PROF BIOL, PROVIDENCE COL, 75- *Mem:* AAAS. *Res:* Role of sulfhydryl compounds in mammalian pigmentation; genetic regulation of the multiple molecular forms of tyrosinase; role of protyrosinase in regulating melanogenesis. *Mailing Add:* 19 Bennington Rd Cranston RI 02910

ZARCO, ROMEO MORALES, b Caloocan, Philippines, Oct 7, 20; m 48; c 3. IMMUNOCHEMISTRY, PUBLIC HEALTH. *Educ:* Univ Philippines, MD, 43; Johns Hopkins Univ, MPH, 54. *Prof Exp:* Physician internal med, Philippine Gen Hosp, 43-44; from instr to prof microbiol, Univ Philippines, 46-67; assoc dir biochem res, Cordis Corp, 67-73, vpres opers, 77-80, DIR, CORDIS LABS, 73-, PRES OPERS, 80- *Concurrent Pos:* USPHS fel, 60-61; vis investr, Howard Hughes Med Inst, 61-62 & 64-67; asst prof, Univ Miami. *Honors & Awards:* Philippine Med Asn Res Award, 58. *Mem:* AAAS; Am Asn Immunol; NY Acad Sci. *Res:* Immunology of infectious diseases, including typhoid, cholera, leprosy and influenza; complement-anti-complementary factors from snake venom and immunosuppression and the separation and purification of the nine components of complement of human and guinea pig serum. *Mailing Add:* Cordis Labs 2140 N Miami Ave Miami FL 33127

ZARDECKI, ANDREW, b Warsaw, Poland, Aug 26, 42; m 66; c 1. QUANTUM OPTICS, ATMOSPHERIC OPTICS. *Educ:* Univ Warsaw, BSc, 64, MSc, 64; Polish Acad Sci, DSc, 68. *Prof Exp:* From asst to asst prof physics, Warsaw Tech Univ, 64-73; asst prof physics, Laval Univ, 73-79; STAFF MEM, LOS ALAMOS NAT LAB, 81- *Concurrent Pos:* Fel, Laval Univ, 70-72. *Mem:* Can Asn Physicists; Optical Soc Am; Am Phys Soc. *Res:* Functional techniques in the optical coherence theory; radiation theories, transport processes; atmospheric optics; pulse propagation in laser media; light scattering. *Mailing Add:* Los Alamos Nat Lab Loa Alamos NM 87545

ZARE, RICHARD NEIL, b Cleveland, Ohio, Nov 19, 39; m 63; c 3. CHEMICAL PHYSICS. *Educ:* Harvard Univ, BA, 61, PhD(chem physics), 64. *Prof Exp:* Fel, Harvard, 64; res assoc & fel, Joint Inst Lab Astrophys, Univ Colo, 64-65; asst prof chem, Mass Inst Technol, 65-66; asst prof physics, Univ Colo, 66-67, from asst prof to assoc prof physics & chem, 67-69; prof chem, Columbia Univ, 69-77; prof, 77-80, SHELL DISTINGUISHED PROF CHEM, STANFORD UNIV, 80- *Concurrent Pos:* Mem, Joint Inst Lab Astrophys, Univ Colo, 66-67, fel, 67-69, non-resident fel, 70; Alfred P Sloan res fel, 67-69; consult, Aeronomy Lab, Nat Oceanic & Atmospheric Admin, Radio Standards Physics Div, Nat Bur Standards, 68-77; Higgins prof nat sci, Columbia Univ, 75-77. *Honors & Awards:* Michael Polanyi Medal, 79; Earle K Plyler Prize, Am Phys Soc, 81. *Mem:* Nat Acad Sci; AAAS; fel Am Phys Soc; The Chem Soc; Am Acad Arts & Sci. *Res:* Problems associated with molecular photodissociation, molecular fluorescence and molecular chemiluminescence; application of lasers to chemical problems. *Mailing Add:* Dept Chem Stanford Univ Stanford CA 94305

ZAREM, ABE MORDECAI, b Chicago, Ill, Mar 7, 17; m 41; c 3. ELECTROOPTICS, ENGINEERING MANAGEMENT. *Educ:* Ill Inst Technol, BS, 39; Calif Inst Technol, MS, 40, PhD(elec eng), 44. *Hon Degrees:* LLD, Univ Calif, Santa Cruz, 67 & Ill Inst Technol, 68. *Prof Exp:* Group mgr elec eng, US Naval Ord Test Sta, 45-48; assoc dir, Stanford Res Inst, 48-56; pres & chmn bd, Electro-Optical Systems, Inc, Xerox Corp, 56-67, sr vpres & dir corp develop, 67-69, mgt & eng consult, 69-75, chmn & chief exec officer, 76-81. *Concurrent Pos:* Mem adv coun, Sch Eng, Stanford Univ, 66-78; mem comt 5 yr eng, Harvey Mudd Col, 67, mem eng clin adv bd, 69; mem vis comt, Div Eng & Appl Sci, Calif Inst Technol, 69- *Honors & Awards:* Sperry Award, Instrument Soc Am, 69. *Mem:* Fel Am Inst Aeronaut & Astronaut; fel Inst Elec & Electronics Engrs. *Res:* Determination of the role of socio-biological factors on the development of innovative attitudes, creative thinking and motivational behavioral patterns. *Mailing Add:* PO Box 11108 Beverly Hills CA 90213

ZAREM, HARVEY A, b Savannah, Ga, Feb 13, 32; m 58; c 3. PLASTIC SURGERY. *Educ:* Yale Univ, BA, 53; Columbia Univ, MD, 57. *Prof Exp:* Assoc prof surg, Univ Chicago, 66-73; PROF SURG & CHIEF DIV PLASTIC SURG, MED SCH, UNIV CALIF, LOS ANGELES, 73- *Concurrent Pos:* Markle scholar, Markle Found, 68. *Mem:* Plastic Surg Res Coun; Soc Univ Surgeons; Am Cleft Palate Asn; Soc Head & Neck Surgeons; Microcirc Soc. *Res:* Microvasculature; microsurgery. *Mailing Add:* Dept of Surg Univ of Calif Med Ctr Los Angeles CA 90024

ZAREMSKY, BARUCH, b Cleveland, Ohio, Sept 21, 26; m 51; c 3. ORGANOMETALLIC CHEMISTRY, PLASTICS CHEMISTRY. *Educ:* Western Reserve Univ, BS, 48, MS, 50, PhD(org chem), 54. *Prof Exp:* RES CHEMIST, FERRO CHEM DIV, FERRO CORP, BEDFORD, 53- *Mem:* Am Chem Soc. *Res:* Additives for polyvinyl chloride polypropylene, polycarbonates and polyesters; specialist in synthesis of organoten's. *Mailing Add:* Ferro Chem Div 7050 Krick Rd Bradford OH 44146

ZARET, THOMAS MICHAEL, b New York, NY, June 12, 45; m 73. FRESH WATER ECOLOGY. *Educ:* Univ Pittsburgh, BS, 66; Yale Univ, MPhil, 68, PhD(biol), 71. *Prof Exp:* Field technician hormone res, Boyce Thompson Plant Res Inst, 66; res assoc, 72-77, res asst prof, 77-81, RES ASSOC PROF ZOOL, UNIV WASH, 81- *Concurrent Pos:* NSF fel, 71-72, res award, 72-; consult, Panama Canal Co, 73-77, UNESCO, 75-76, Presidential Comn Sea-Level Canal, 77 & Govts Panama, Colombia & Venezuela, 72- *Mem:* AAAS; Am Soc Limnol & Oceanog; Am Soc Naturalists; Asn Trop Biol; Ecol Soc Am. *Res:* Ecology and evolutionary biology; freshwater community structure; ecology of fishes; tropical ecology. *Mailing Add:* Dept Zool FM-12 Univ Wash Seattle WA 98195

ZARGER, THOMAS GORDON, b Chambersburg, Pa, Oct 18, 18; m 47; c 1. FORESTRY, HORTICULTURE. *Educ:* Pa State Univ, BS, 40 & 49. *Prof Exp:* From jr forestry aide to forestry aide, Div Forestry, Fisheries & Wildlife Develop, Tenn Valley Authority, 40-43, from jr botanist to botanist, 43-48, staff forester, 49-65, forester, 65-66, staff forester, 66-80, PROG MGR LAND RECLAMATION, DIV LAND & FOREST RESOURCES, FISHERIES & WILDLIFE DEVELOP, TENN VALLEY AUTHORITY, 80- *Mem:* Am Soc Hort Sci; Soc Am Foresters. *Res:* Selection, propagation and testing of improved nut and other tree crop species; standing hardwood timber tree grades and vigor classes; forest tree improvement; coal surface mine reclamation techniques; wild land vegetation establishment. *Mailing Add:* Div Land & Forest Resources Tenn Valley Authority Norris TN 37828

ZARING, WILSON MILES, b Shelbyville, Ky, Nov 9, 26; m 50; c 2. MATHEMATICS. *Educ:* Ky Wesleyan Col, AB, 50; Univ Ky, MA, 52, PhD(math), 55. *Prof Exp:* From instr to asst prof, 55-63, ASSOC PROF MATH, UNIV ILL, URBANA, 63- *Honors & Awards:* Max Beberman Award, Ill Coun Teachers Math, 76. *Mem:* Am Math Soc; Math Asn Am. *Res:* Analysis. *Mailing Add:* Dept of Math Univ of Ill Urbana IL 61801

ZARISKI, OSCAR, b Kobrin, USSR, Apr 24, 99; nat US; m 24; c 2. MATHEMATICS. *Educ:* Univ Rome, Dr Math, 24. *Hon Degrees:* MA,l Harvard Univ, 47; DSc, Col Holy Cross, 49, Brandeis Univ, 65, Purdue Univ, 73, Harvard Univ, 81. *Prof Exp:* Int Educ Bd fel, Univ Rome, 25-27; Johnston scholar, Johns Hopkins Univ, 27-29, assoc math, 29-32, from assoc prof to prof, 32-45; vis prof, Univ Sao Paulo, 45; res prof, Univ Ill, 46-47; lectr, 40-41, prof, 47-61, Dwight Parker Robinson prof, 61-69, EMER DWIGHT PARKER ROBINSON PROF MATH, HARVARD UNIV, 69- *Concurrent Pos:* Vis mem, Inst Advan Study, 35-36, 39 & 60-61; lectr, Moscow, 36; Guggenheim fel, 39-40, Inst Hautes Etudes, Paris, 61 & 67. *Honors & Awards:* Cole Prize, Am Math Soc, 44, Steel Prize, 81; Nat Medal of Sci, 65. *Mem:* Nat Acad Sci; Am Acad Arts & Sci; AAAS; Am Math Soc (pres, 69-70); London Math Soc. *Res:* Algebraic geometry; modern algebra; topology. *Mailing Add:* 122 Sewall Ave Brookline MA 02146

ZARKOWER, ARIAN, b Tarnopol, Poland, Oct 10, 29; US citizen; m 60; c 2. VETERINARY MEDICINE, IMMUNOLOGY. *Educ:* Ont Vet Col, DVM, 56; Univ Maine, MS, 60; Cornell Univ, PhD(immunochem), 65. *Prof Exp:* Dist vet, NB Prov Vet Serv, 56-57; self-employed vet, 57-58; res asst animal path, Univ Maine, 58-70; res officer, Animal Dis Res Inst, Can Dept Agr, 60-62; res asst immunochem, Cornell Univ, 62-65; from asst prof to assoc prof vet sci, 65-77, PROF VET SCI, CTR AIR ENVIRON STUDY, PA STATE UNIV, 78-, MEM STAFF CTR, 70- *Mem:* Can Vet Med Asn; Am Soc Microbiol; Can Soc Immunol. *Res:* Experimental pathology; immune response and resistance in animals to infections. *Mailing Add:* Dept Vet Sci Pa State Univ University Park PA 16802

ZAROMB, SOLOMON, b Belchatow, Poland, Aug 15, 28; US citizen; m 76; c 2. PHYSICAL CHEMISTRY, ELECTROCHEMICAL ENGINEERING. *Educ:* Cooper Union, BChE, 50; Polytech Inst Brooklyn, PhD(chem), 54. *Prof Exp:* Res assoc light scattering, Mass Inst Technol, 53-55; assoc chemist semiconductors, IBM Corp, 56-58; res specialist electrochem devices, Philco Corp, 58-61; scientist res & develop monocrystalline thin films, Martin-Marietta Co, 62-63; pres electrochem & electro-optical systs & devices, Zaromb Res Corp, 63-81; ENVIRON SCIENTIST TOXIC GAS DETECTION, AGRONNE NAT LAB, 81- *Concurrent Pos:* Prin investr, Zaromb Res Found, grants from Nat Air Pollution Control Admin & Environ Protection Agency, 69-73. *Mem:* AAAS; Am Astron Soc; Am Chem Soc; Electrochem Soc. *Res:* Electrochemical and electro-optical systems, devices and techniques; aluminum batteries; processing of semiconductor crystals and thin films; solid solutions of ice; remote sensing of air pollutants; lidar spectroscopy; electrochemical and other toxic gas detectors or monitors. *Mailing Add:* 9700 S Cass Ave Argonne Nat Lab EES-362 Argonne IL 60439

ZAROSLINSKI, JOHN F, b Chicago, Ill, Sept 12, 25; m 51; c 2. PHARMACOLOGY, BIOCHEMISTRY. *Educ:* Univ Chicago, PhB, 49; Loyola Univ, Ill, PhD(pharmacol), 65. *Prof Exp:* Chemist, Armour Pharmaceut Co, 51-53; from pharmacologist to sr pharmacologist, Baxter Lab Inc, 53-58; sci dir, Arnar-Stone Labs, Inc, Div Am Hosp Supply Corp, 58-65, vpres res & develop, 65-75, vpres sci planning, 75-78; RETIRED. *Concurrent Pos:* Adj prof, Stritch Sch Med, Loyola Univ, Chicago, 65-; res consult, US Vet Hosp, Hines, Ill. *Mem:* British Pharmacol Soc; Am Chem Soc; NY Acad Sci; Am Soc Pharmacol & Exp Therapeut. *Res:* Pharmaceutical development; biochemical pharmacology; protein binding of drugs; evaluation of hypnotic drugs; pharmaceutical development and introduction of Intropin (dopamine) into therapy for treatment of shock in humans; supervised scientific and clinical studies leading to approval for use of dopamine in the treatment of shock. *Mailing Add:* 1202 Norman Lane Deerfield IL 60015

ZARRELLA, WILLIAM MICHAEL, physical chemistry, organic chemistry, deceased

ZARRUGH, LAURA HOFFMAN, medical anthropology, see previous edition

ZARTMAN, DAVID LESTER, b Albuquerque, NMex, July 6, 40; m 63; c 2. CYTOGENETICS, REPRODUCTION. *Educ:* NMex State Univ, BS, 62; Ohio State Univ, MS, 66, PhD(cytogenetics), 68. *Prof Exp:* Asst prof, 68-72, assoc prof, 72-78, PROF ANIMAL & RANGE SCI, NEW MEX STATE UNIV, 78- *Concurrent Pos:* NIH fel, 73; Fulbright-Hays fel, 76; pres, Mary K Zartman Inc, 78- *Mem:* Fel AAAS; Am Dairy Sci Asn; Sigma Xi; Animal Sci Soc Am; Am Inst Biol Sci. *Res:* Radiation genetics; sex and fertility control; reproduction; animal breeding; radio-telemetry of body temperature. *Mailing Add:* Animal Sci Dept Box 3-I NMex State Univ Las Cruces NM 88003

ZARTMAN, ROBERT EUGENE, b Lancaster, Pa, May 19, 36; m 75; c 7. GEOCHRONOLOGY. *Educ:* Pa State Univ, BS, 57; Calif Inst Technol, MS, 59, PhD(geol), 63. *Prof Exp:* Fel geol, Calif Inst Technol, 62; GEOLOGIST, ISOTOPE GEOL BR, US GEOL SURV, 62-, CHIEF, ISOTOPE GEOL BR, 81- *Concurrent Pos:* Vis assoc, Calif Inst Technol, 71-72; chmn working group on radiogenic isotopes, Int Asn of Volcanology & Chem of the Earth's Interior, 73-81. *Mem:* Fel Geol Soc Am; fel Mineral Soc Am; Am Geophys Union; Soc Econ Geol; Geochem Soc. *Res:* Determination of geologic age by the potassium-argon, rubidium-strontium and uranium-thorium-lead radiometric methods; study of geological processes by use of natural isotopic tracer systems. *Mailing Add:* Isotope Geol Br US Geol Surv STOP 963 Box 25046 Denver CO 80225

ZARWYN, B(ERTHOLD), b Austria, Aug 22, 21; nat US. ELECTRONIC ENGINEERING, OPERATIONS RESEARCH. *Educ:* Univ Lwow, ME, 46; Univ Munich, DrIng, 47; NY Univ, PhD(physics), 53; Columbia Univ, EngScD(mech eng), 64. *Prof Exp:* Asst prof mech eng, UNRRA, Univ Munich, 46-48; asst prof, Int Univ, Ger, 48-49; proj engr & dept head, Condenser Serv & Eng Co, NJ, 50-52; proj engr & head, Nuclear Aircraft Study Group, Curtiss-Wright Corp, 52-55; sr res engr, Am Mach & Foundry Co, NY, 55-57; chief physicist, Link Aviation Co, 57-58; dir basic res, Am Bosch-Arma Corp, NY, 58-64, corp consult, Airborne Instrument Lab, 63-65; chief engr, Bell Aerospace Corp, 65-66; sr consult, Mitre Corp, Mass, 66-68; actg chief engr, Hq, US Army Mat Command, 68-69, chief, Physics & Electronics Br, Res Div, 69-75, physical scientist, US Army Harry Diamond Labs, 75-77, chief, Syst Anal Br, 77-79, chief, Technol Div, 79-81, ASSIST TECH DIR, US ARMY ELECTRONIC RES & DEVELOP COMMAND, 81- *Concurrent Pos:* Mem staff, Columbia Univ, 54-55; vis physicist, Brookhaven Nat Lab & assoc prof, Univ Conn, 56-57; prof, Univ Hartford, 57; consult, Fairchild Engine & Airplane Co, 55-56 & Bendix Aviation Co, 57. *Mem:* Am Phys Soc; Inst Elec & Electronics Engrs; NY Acad Sci. *Res:* Nuclear physics and engineering; quantum electronics; solid state physics; propulsion; fluid flow; heat transfer; electronic computers and simulation; navigation and communication. *Mailing Add:* US Army Electronic Res & Develop Command 2800 Powder Mill Rd Adelphi MD 20783

ZARY, KEITH WILFRED, b Sask, Nov 28, 48; m 80. PLANT BREEDING. *Educ:* Univ Sask, BS, 71; Tex A&M Univ, MS, 78, PhD(hort), 80. *Prof Exp:* Res asst, Tex A&M Univ, 77-79; PLANT BREEDER, SUN SEEDS/AGRIGENETICS CORP, 80- *Mem:* Am Soc Hort Sci; AAAS; Sigma Xi. *Res:* Horticulturally superior pea (pisum satium) and bean (phascolus vulgaris) varieties for both processing and fresh market consumption. *Mailing Add:* Sun Seeds/Agrigentics Corp 1120-220th St West Farmington MN 55024

ZARZECKI, PETER, b Boston, Mass, Aug 29, 45. PHYSIOLOGY, NEUROPHYSIOLOGY. *Educ:* Univ Miami, BS, 68; Duke Univ, PhD(physiol & pharmacol), 74. *Prof Exp:* Res assoc neurophysiol, Rockefeller Univ, 74-77; ASST PROF PHYSIOL, QUEEN'S UNIV, ONT, 77- *Concurrent Pos:* Vis scientist physiol, Gothenburg Univ, 77; Med Res Coun Can res grant, 78-83, res develop award, 78-84. *Mem:* Soc Neurosci; Can Physiol Soc; Can Asn Univ Teachers. *Res:* Electrophysiological investigations into the control of the mammalian cerebral motor cortex. *Mailing Add:* Dept of Physiol Queen's Univ Kingston ON K7L 3N6 Can

ZASADA, ZIGMOND ANTHONY, b Schenectady, NY, May 1, 09; m 37; c 1. FORESTRY. *Educ:* State Univ NY, BS, 31. *Prof Exp:* Forester, Chippewa Nat Forest, US Forest Serv, 33-45, proj leader, Lake States Forest Exp Sta, 45-51, res ctr leader, 51-61, res forester, DC, 61-63, asst dir, NCent Forest Exp Sta, Minn, 63-67; res assoc, Cloquet Forestry Ctr, Col Forestry, Univ Minn, 67-76; FORESTRY CONSULT, 76- *Mem:* Fel Soc Am Foresters. *Res:* Economics of forest management and utilization; silviculture; mechanized timber harvesting. *Mailing Add:* 1015 Third Ave NW Grand Rapids MN 55744

ZASKE, DARWIN ERHARD, b Wadena, Minn, Mar 20, 49. CLINICAL PHARMACOLOGY. *Educ:* Univ Minn, BS, 72, PharmD, 73. *Prof Exp:* clin pharmacologist, St Paul-Ramsey Hosp & Med Ctr, 73-80; asst prof pharmacol, 75-80, MEM FAC, DEPT ADMIN & SOCIAL PHARMACOL, UNIV MINN, 80- *Concurrent Pos:* Instr pharmacol, Univ Minn, 73-74. *Mem:* Am Burn Asn; Am Soc Hosp Pharm. *Res:* Clinical application of drug-kinetic principles with the goal being patient individualization of drug therapy to provide more optimal patient therapy. *Mailing Add:* Dept Social Admin Pharmacol Univ Minn 115 & 128 Appleby Hall Minneapolis MN 55455

ZASLAWSKY, MAURICE, earthquake engineering, mechanics, see previous edition

ZASSENHAUS, HANS J, b Coblenz, Ger, May 28, 12, nat Can; m 42; c 3. MATHEMATICS. *Educ:* Univ Hamburg, Dr rer nat, 34, Dr habil, 38. *Hon Degrees:* MA, Glasgow Univ, 49; Dr, Univ Ottawa, 66 & McGill Univ, 74. *Prof Exp:* Asst instr, Univ Rostock, 34-36; asst, Univ Hamburg, 36-40; diaeten-docent math, Univ Hamburg, 40-47, assoc prof, 47-49; prof, McGill Univ, 49-59; prof, Univ Notre Dame, 59-64; RES PROF MATH, OHIO STATE UNIV, 64- *Concurrent Pos:* Vis prof math, Ctr Math Res, Montreal Univ, Univ Calif, Los Angeles, 70 & Warwick Univ, Eng, 72; Fairchild scholarship, Calif Inst Technol, 74-75. *Honors & Awards:* Jeffery-Williams Lect Award, Can Math Cong, 74. *Mem:* Math Asn Am; Am Math Soc; Can Math Cong; fel Royal Soc Can. *Res:* Group theory; Lie algebra; number theory; geometry of numbers; applied mathematics. *Mailing Add:* 942 Spring Grove Lane Worthington OH 43085

ZATKO, DAVID A, b North Tonawanda, NY, Nov 12, 40; m 66; c 1. INORGANIC CHEMISTRY. *Educ:* Colgate Univ, BA, 62; Univ Wis, PhD(chem), 66. *Prof Exp:* asst prof chem, Univ Ala, 67-74, assoc prof, 74-80; MEM STAFF, UNIVAC DIV, SPERRY CORP, 80- *Mem:* Am Chem Soc. *Res:* Analytic inorganic chemistry; coordination chemistry of silver II and silver III, palladium II, substituted ferrocenes; photoelectron spectroscopy; free radical ligands; oxidation-reductions in nonaqueous solvents. *Mailing Add:* Univac Div Sperry Corp PO Box 500 MS E8 134 Blue Bell PA 19422

ZATUCHNI, GERALD IRVING, b Philadelphia, Pa, Oct 5, 35; m 58; c 3. OBSTETRICS & GYNECOLOGY. *Educ:* Temple Univ, AB, 54, MD, 58, MSc, 65. *Prof Exp:* Instr obstet & gynec, Med Sch, Temple Univ, 65-66; dir family planning, Pop Coun, Inc, 66-69; adv, Govt of India, 69-71; Pop Coun, Inc consult family planning & obstet, WHO, 71-73; adv, Govt Iran, 73-75; PROF, DEPT OBSTET & GYNEC, NORTHWESTERN UNIV, 77-, DIR, PROG APPL RES FERTIL REGULATION, 77- *Mem:* AAAS; Am Fedn Clin Res; Am Fertil Soc; Am Col Obstet & Gynec. *Res:* Human reproductive research; contraceptive development; family planning; population study and research. *Mailing Add:* Northwestern Univ 303 E Superior St Chicago IL 60611

ZATUCHNI, JACOB, b Philadelphia, Pa, Oct 8, 20; m 45; c 4. INTERNAL MEDICINE, CARDIOVASCULAR DISEASE. *Educ:* Temple Univ, AB, 41, MD, 44, MS, 50. *Prof Exp:* Clin prof med, 61-65, PROF MED, SCH MED & HOSP, TEMPLE UNIV, 65-, DIR DEPT MED, 74-; CHIEF SECT CARDIOL, EPISCOPAL HOSP, PHILADELPHIA, 69- *Concurrent Pos:* Teaching chief med, Episcopal Hosp, 58-67; fel coun clin cardiol, Am Heart Asn, 63- *Mem:* AAAS; Am Thoracic Soc; AMA; fel Am Col Physicians. *Res:* Cardiovascular diseases. *Mailing Add:* 191 Presidential Blvd Bala Cynwyd PA 19004

ZATZ, JOEL L, US citizen. PHARMACEUTICS. *Educ:* Long Island Univ, BS, 56; St John's Univ, MS, 65; Columbia Univ, PhD(pharmaceut Sci), 68. *Prof Exp:* From asst prof to assoc prof, 68-79, PROF PHARMACEUT, RUTGERS UNIV, 79- *Concurrent Pos:* Consult, Merck & Co, 79- *Mem:* Am Pharmaceut Asn; Soc Cosmetic Chemists; Acad Pharmaceut Sci; Am Chem Soc; Am Asn Col Pharm. *Res:* Factors that influence transport of drugs through skin, including the physical chemistry of disperse systems and applications to pharmaceutical and cosmetic products. *Mailing Add:* Rutgers Col Pharm PO Box 789 Piscataway NJ 08854

ZATZ, LESLIE M, b Schenectady, NY, Nov 2, 28; m 53; c 3. RADIOLOGY. *Educ:* Union Col, NY, BS, 48; Albany Med Col, MD, 52; Univ Pa, MMS, 59. *Prof Exp:* Intern, Univ Chicago Clins, 52-53; resident radiol, Hosp Univ Pa, 55-58; from instr radiol to assoc prof, 59-72, actg dir diag radiol, 66-67, PROF RADIOL, SCH MED, STANFORD UNIV, 72- *Concurrent Pos:* NIH spec res fel, Postgrad Med Sch, Univ London, 65-66; consult, Vet Admin Hosp, Palo Alto, Calif, 60-72, chief radiol, 72- *Mem:* Am Col Radiol; Asn Univ Radiol; AMA; Am Soc Neuroradiol. *Res:* New diagnostic radiologic methods. *Mailing Add:* Dept of Radiol Vet Admin Hosp Palo Alto CA 94304

ZATZ, MARION M, b New York, NY, Feb 10, 45. IMMUNOLOGY. *Educ:* Barnard Col, BA, 65; Cornell Univ, PhD(immunol & microbiol), 70. *Prof Exp:* Fel immunol, Hosp Spec Surg, 70-71; Damon Runyan fel biochem, Albert Einstein Col Med, 71-72; instr microbiol, Sch Med, Yale Univ, 72-73, asst prof microbiol & path, 73-77, dir, Tissue Typing Lab, 72-74; guest worker, Immunol Br, Nat Cancer Inst, 74-79; ASSOC RES PROF BIOCHEM, SCH MED, GEORGE WASHINGTON UNIV, 78- *Concurrent Pos:* Asst clin prof med, Sch Med, Georgetown Univ, 78-81. *Mem:* Am Asn Immunologists. *Res:* Investigation of spontaneous leukemogenesis in AKR-J mice; investigation of genetic basis of resistance to growth of lymphoma. *Mailing Add:* 2300 Eye St NW George Washington Univ Sch Med Washington DC 20037

ZATZ, MARTIN, b 1944; US citizen. PHARMACOLOGY, PSYCHIATRY. *Educ:* Albert Einstein Col Med, PhD(pharmacol), 70, MD, 72. *Prof Exp:* Resident psychiat, Sch Med, Yale Univ, 72-74; res assoc, 74-76, staff fel, 76-78, MED OFFICER RES, SECT PHARMACOL, LAB CLIN SCI, NIMH, 78- *Res:* Circadian rhythms; cyclic nucleotides; regulation of receptor sensitivity; pineal gland. *Mailing Add:* Bldg 10 Rm 2D-47 9000 Rockville Pike Bethesda MD 20014

ZATZKIS, HENRY, b Holzminden, Ger, Apr 7, 15; nat US; m 51; c 2. THEORETICAL PHYSICS, APPLIED MATHEMATICS. *Educ:* Ohio State Univ, BS, 42; Ind Univ, MS, 44; Syracuse Univ, PhD(physics), 50. *Prof Exp:* Instr physics, Ind Univ, 42-44; instr, Univ NC, 44-46; instr math, Syracuse Univ, 46-51; instr, Univ Conn, 51-53; from asst prof to prof, 53-71, actg chmn dept, 59, DISTINGUISHED PROF MATH, NEWARK COL 71-, CHMN DEPT, 60- *Res:* Theory of relativity; heat conduction; acoustics. *Mailing Add:* 5 Elliott Pl West Orange NJ 07052

ZATZMAN, MARVIN LEON, b Philadelphia, Pa, Aug 6, 27; m 51; c 2. PHYSIOLOGY. *Educ:* City Col New York, BS, 50; Ohio State Univ, MS, 52, PhD(physiol), 55. *Prof Exp:* Asst prof physiol, Ohio State Univ, 55-56; asst prof, 56-61, assoc prof, 61-73, PROF PHYSIOL, MED CTR, UNIV MO-COLUMBIA, 73- *Mem:* AAAS; Biophys Soc; Int Soc Nephrology; Am Physiol Soc. *Res:* Renal, cardiovascular, hibernation. *Mailing Add:* Dept of Physiol Univ of Mo Med Ctr Columbia MO 65201

ZAUDER, HOWARD L, b New York, NY, Sept 13, 23; m 53; c 2. ANESTHESIOLOGY. *Educ:* Univ Vt, AB, 47, MS, 49; Duke Univ, PhD(physiol, pharmacol), 52; NY Univ, MD, 55. *Prof Exp:* Res assoc pharmacol, Univ Vt, 51-53; from asst prof to assoc prof anesthesiol, Albert Einstein Col Med, Yeshiva Univ, 58-67; prof anesthesiol & chmn dept, Univ Tex Med Sch San Antonio & prof pharmacol, Univ Tex Health Sci Ctr San Antonio, 68-78, assoc dean prof affairs univ, 77-78; PROF ANESTHESIOL & CHMN DEPT, STATE UNIV NY UPSTATE MED CTR, 78-, PROF PHARMACOL, 78- *Mem:* AAAS; Am Soc Pharmacol & Exp Therapeut; fel Am Col Anesthesiol. *Res:* Pharmacology of anesthetic agents; effects of radiation on response to anesthesia; pulmonary physiology; clinical application of gas chromatography. *Mailing Add:* Dept Anesthesiol State Univ NY Upstate Med Ctr Syracuse NY 13210

ZAUDERER, BERT, b Vienna, Austria, Mar 8, 37; US citizen; m 61; c 5. COAL TECHNOLOGY, ENERGY CONVERSION. *Educ:* City Col New York, BME, 58; Mass Inst Technol, SM, 60, ScD(mech eng), 62. *Prof Exp:* Res engr, Gen Elec Co, 61-67, group leader, 67-70; mgr magnetohydrodyn progs, Space Sci Lab, 70-79 & Energy Dept, 80-81; PRES, COAL TECHNOL CORP, 81- *Mem:* Am Inst Aeronaut & Astronaut; Am Phys Soc; Am Soc Mech Engrs. *Res:* Coal technology; advanced energy conversion. *Mailing Add:* PO Box 154 Merion Sta Philadelphia PA 19066

ZAUGG, HAROLD ELMER, b Chicago, Ill, Feb 27, 16; m 40; c 3. ORGANIC CHEMISTRY. *Educ:* Oberlin Col, AB, 37; Univ Minn, PhD(org chem), 41. *Prof Exp:* Asst org chem, Univ Minn, 38-40; res chemist, 41-56, res scientist, 56-59, res fel, 59-72, SR RES FEL, ABBOTT LABS, 72- *Concurrent Pos:* Fel, Purdue Univ, 58; chmn, Gordon Conf Org Reactions & Processes, 61; mem med study sect, NIH, 64-68; vis prof, Univ Southern Calif, 66; mem med chem study group, Walter Reed Army Inst Res, 77-81. *Mem:* Am Chem Soc. *Res:* Central nervous system drugs; organic syntheses and reaction mechanisms; solvent effects; chemistry of delocalized anions; amidoalkylations; medicinal chemistry of the cannabinoids. *Mailing Add:* 270 E Park Ave Lake Forest IL 60045

ZAUGG, WALDO S, b LaGrande, Ore, Dec 13, 30; m 53; c 4. BIOCHEMISTRY. *Educ:* Brigham Young Univ, BA, 58, PhD(biochem), 61. *Prof Exp:* Fel, Enzyme Inst, Univ Wis, 61-62; fel, Charles F Kettering Res Lab, 62-63, staff scientist, 63-65; biochemist, Western Fish Nutrit Lab, US Fish & Wildlife Serv, 65-76; operator, Mill-A Chem Lab, 76-78; BIOCHEMIST, NAT MARINE FISHERIES SERV, AQUACULT FIELD STA, 78- *Concurrent Pos:* Asst prof, Antioch Col, 63-65; USPHS grant, 64-65. *Mem:* Am Soc Biol Chemists. *Res:* Oxidation-reduction reactions and bioenergetics in photosynthetic bacteria, plants, mammals and poikilotherms; physiology and biochemistry of anadromous fishes. *Mailing Add:* Aquacult Field Sta Nat Marine Fisheries Serv Cook WA 98605

ZAUGG, WAYNE E, physical chemistry, see previous edition

ZAUKELIES, DAVID AARON, b Detroit, Mich, May 22, 25; m 56; c 2. PHYSICAL CHEMISTRY, MATERIALS SCIENCE ENGINEERING. *Educ:* Mich State Univ, BS, 46; Northwestern Univ, PhD(phys chem), 50. *Prof Exp:* Asst, Northwestern Univ, 46-49, res assoc phys chem, 49-50; res physicist, Dow Chem Co, 51-54; prof chem, Lee Col (Tenn), 54-55; res physicist, Chemstrand Corp, 55-60, Chemstrand Res Ctr, Inc, NC, 60-61, from assoc scientist to scientist, 61-70; scientist, 70-71, sci fel, Tech Ctr, 71-81, SR MONSANTO FEL, MONSANTO TEXTILES CO, 81- *Mem:* Am Chem Soc; Am Phys Soc. *Res:* Soiling of fibers and fabrics; spinning of petroleum and nylon yarns; continuous measurement of spun yarn properties and frequency analysis; measurement of fabric color variations and measurement of fabric hand; polyaromatic fibers, cords and composites; carpet fibers; optical properties of yarns and fabrics. *Mailing Add:* Tech Ctr Monsanto Textiles Co PO Box 12830 Pensacola FL 32575

ZAUNER, CHRISTIAN WALTER, b July 21, 30; m 57; c 3. EXERCISE PHYSIOLOGY, PULMONARY PHYSIOLOGY. *Educ:* West Chester State Col, BS, 56; Syracuse Univ, MS, 57; Southern Ill Univ, PhD(phys educ), 63. *Prof Exp:* Asst prof exercise physiol & res, Temple Univ, 63-65; assoc prof exercise physiol & res, 65-71, assoc prof med, 70-71, PROF EXERCISE PHYSIOL, RES & MED, UNIV FLA, 71- *Concurrent Pos:* Univ Fla fac develop grant & Thordgray Mem Fund, Dept Clin Physiol, Malmo Gen Hosp, Sweden, 71-72 & 78; consult cardiac rehab, Hosp Corp Am. *Honors & Awards:* Serv Citation, Coun Nat Coop in Aquatics, 72. *Mem:* Am Physiol Soc; Am Asn Health, Phys Educ & Recreation; Am Col Sports Med. *Res:* Lipid metabolism; exercise and training effects on lipids, work capacity, pulmonary and respiratory function; child athletes; exercise and training effects on circulation. *Mailing Add:* Col Phys Educ Univ Fla Gainesville FL 32611

ZAUSTINSKY, EUGENE MICHAEL, b Battle Creek, Mich, Oct 19, 26. GEOMETRY. *Educ:* Univ Calif, Los Angeles, AB, 48; Univ Southern Calif, AM, 54, PhD(math), 57. *Prof Exp:* Asst, Univ Southern Calif, 52-54, lectr, 54-57; asst prof math, San Jose State Col, 57; asst prof, Univ Calif, Santa Barbara, 58-61, asst prof, Univ Calif, Berkeley, 61-63; ASSOC PROF MATH, STATE UNIV NY STONY BROOK, 63- *Concurrent Pos:* Vis prof, Kent State Univ, 67 & Rockefeller Univ, 73. *Mem:* Am Math Soc; Math Asn Am; Math Soc France; Danish Math Soc; Swiss Math Soc. *Res:* Differential geometry and topology; synthetic differential geometry. *Mailing Add:* Dept of Math State Univ of NY Stony Brook NY 11794

ZAVALA, MARIA ELENA, b Pomona, Calif, Jan 9, 50. PLANT DEVELOPMENT. *Educ:* Pomona Col, BA, 72; Univ Calif, Berkeley, PhD(bot), 78. *Prof Exp:* Res assoc, Dept Biol, Ind Univ, 78-80; PLANT RES PHYSIOLOGIST, USDA, 80- *Concurrent Pos:* Lectr, Dept Bot, Univ Calif, Berkeley, 78. *Mem:* Bot Soc Am; Am Soc Cell Biol; Am Soc Plant Taxonomists; AAAS; Soc Advan of Chinese & Native Americans in Sci. *Res:* Plant anatomy and cell biology; development of pollen; cryogenic storage of plant cells; high resolution localization of plant compounds in situ. *Mailing Add:* Western Regional Res Ctr 800 Buchanan Ave Berkeley CA 94710

ZAVARIN, EUGENE, b Sombor, Yugoslavia, Feb 21, 24; nat US; m 56; c 5. ORGANIC CHEMISTRY. *Educ:* Univ Gottingen, dipl, 49; Univ Calif, Berkeley, PhD(org chem), 54. *Prof Exp:* Asst, Univ Calif, Berkeley, 52-53, sr lab technician, Forest Prod Lab, 52-54, asst specialist, 54-56, asst chemist, 56-62, assoc forest prod chemist, 62-68, PROF FORESTRY & FOREST PROD CHEMIST, FOREST PROD LAB, UNIV CALIF, 68- *Concurrent Pos:* NIH fel, Inst Org Chem, Gif-sur-Yvette, France, 63. *Mem:* Am Chem Soc; Forest Prod Res Soc; Phytochem Soc NAm; Int Acad Wood Sci; AAAS. *Res:* Chemosystematics; chemistry of natural products; polymer chemistry of lignocelluloses. *Mailing Add:* Forest Prod Lab Univ of Calif 1301 S 46th St Richmond CA 94804

ZAVECZ, JAMES HENRY, b Bethlehem, Pa, Dec 15, 46. PHARMACOLOGY. *Educ:* LaSalle Col, BA, 68; Ohio State Univ, PhD(pharmacol), 74. *Prof Exp:* Fel pharmacol, Med Col, Cornell Univ, 74-76, instr, 76-77; res pharmacologist, ICI Americas, Inc, 78-80; ASST PROF, DEPT PHARMACOL, EASTERN VA MED SCH, 80- *Mem:* NY Acad Sci; AAAS; Sigma Xi. *Res:* Effects of histamine on the heart; mechanism of action of cardiac glycosides. *Mailing Add:* Dept Pharmacol Eastern Va Med Sch PO Box 1980 Norfolk VA 23501

ZAVIST, ALGERD FRANK, b Chicago, Ill, July 2, 21; m 51; c 4. CHEMISTRY. *Educ:* Roosevelt Col, BS, 43; Univ Chicago, MS, 49, PhD(chem), 50. *Prof Exp:* Lab technician, Infilco, Inc, 40-41; plant chemist, W H Barber Co, 41-42; instr, Wilson Jr Col, 49; chemist, Res & Develop, Gen Elec Co, 50-54, supvr chem eng processes, 54-58, supvr chem eng & insulation develop, Mat & Processes Lab, NY, 58-62, mgr chem lab, Major Appliance Labs, 62-68, mgr, Major Appliance Labs, 68-79, MGR, APPL SCI & TECHNOL LAB, GEN ELEC CO, 80- *Mem:* Am Chem Soc; Soc Plastics Eng; Royal Soc Chem; Sigma Xi; Am Inst Chemists. *Res:* Reactions of free radicals in solution; physical organic and high polymer chemistry; relationships between molecular structure and electrical and physical properties. *Mailing Add:* Major Appliance Labs Gen Elec Co Bldg 35-1001 Appl Pk Louisville KY 40225

ZAVISZA, DANIEL MAXMILLIAN, b Hazardville, Conn, Nov 28, 38; m 63; c 3. PHYSICAL ORGANIC CHEMISTRY. *Educ:* Col of the Holy Cross, BS, 60; Clark Univ, PhD(phys org chem), 66. *Prof Exp:* Res chemist, 66-74, SR RES CHEMIST, AM CYANAMID CO, 74- *Res:* Organic polymer research and development; protein chemistry; condensation polymers. *Mailing Add:* Am Cyanamid Co W Main St Bound Brook NJ 08805

ZAVITSANOS, PETROS D, b Spartochori-Lefkas, Greece, July 26, 31; US citizen; m 57; c 4. PHYSICAL CHEMISTRY. *Educ:* Univ Calif, Berkeley, AB, 55; Univ Ill, Urbana, MS, 57, PhD(phys chem), 59. *Prof Exp:* Mem tech staff, Bell Tel Labs, Pa, 59-60; phys chemist, Space Sci Lab, Missile & Space Div, 61-66, group leader aerothermochem, 66-72, CONSULT-TECHNOL ENG, RE-ENTRY & ENVIRON SYSTS DIV, GEN ELEC CO, 72- *Mem:* Am Chem Soc. *Res:* Solid state chemistry and isotope effects; semiconductors; high temperature chemistry; mass spectrometry; heterogeneous reaction kinetics; chemi-ionization; laser applications; coal chemistry and cleaning techniques. *Mailing Add:* Re-entry & Environ Systs Div Gen Elec Co PO Box 8555 Philadelphia PA 19101

ZAVITSAS, ANDREAS ATHANASIOS, b Athens, Greece, July 14, 37; US citizen; m 59; c 1. PHYSICAL ORGANIC CHEMISTRY. *Educ:* City Col New York, BS, 59; Columbia Univ, MA, 61, PhD(chem), 62. *Prof Exp:* Res assoc chem, Brookhaven Nat Lab, 62-64; res chemist, Monsanto Co, Mass, 64-67; from asst prof to assoc prof, 67-73, grad dean, 75-79, PROF CHEM, LONG ISLAND UNIV, BROOKLYN CTR, 73- *Concurrent Pos:* Lectr, New Sch Soc Res, 61-64. *Mem:* Am Chem Soc; NY Acad Sci; fel Am Inst Chemists. *Res:* Organic free-radical chemistry; phenolic resin; electrochemical sensors. *Mailing Add:* Dept Chem Long Island Univ Brooklyn Ctr Brooklyn NY 11201

ZAVODNI, JOHN J, b Gallitzin, Pa, June 17, 43; m 65. PHYSIOLOGY. *Educ:* St Francis Col (Pa), BS, 64; Pa State Univ, PhD(physiol), 68. *Prof Exp:* Instr biol, St Francis Col (Pa), 64-65; asst prof, 68-75, ASSOC PROF ZOOL & CHMN DEPT SCI, PA STATE UNIV, MCKEESPORT CAMPUS, 75- *Mem:* NY Acad Sci; Am Asn Sex Educ & Coun; Sex Educ & Info Coun US. *Res:* Effects of exposure to increased oxygen tensions on the endocrine system; enforcement of water pollution. *Mailing Add:* Dept Zool Pa State Univ McKeesport PA 15132

ZAVODNI, ZAVIS MARIAN, b Prague, Czech, Aug 17, 41; US citizen; m 81. ROCK MECHANICS, GEOLOGICAL ENGINEERING. *Educ:* Princeton Univ, BSE, 64; Univ Ariz, MS, 69, PhD(geol eng), 71. *Prof Exp:* Instr math, Univ Sch, 64-66 & Am Sch Paris, 66-67; asst prof geol, Brooklyn Col, 71-74; mining engr, Kennecott Copper Corp, 74-80, MINING ENGR, KENNECOTT MINERALS CO, 80- *Concurrent Pos:* Geotech engr, Pincock, Allen & Holt, Inc, Tucson, Ariz, 72-74; appl res award, US Nat Comt Rock Mechanics, 79. *Mem:* Asn Eng Geologists; Can Inst Mining & Metall; Am Inst Mining, Metall & Petrol Engrs; Int Soc Rock Mechanics. *Res:* Slope stability; geomechanics; slope failure kinematics; mine waste dump design. *Mailing Add:* Kennecott Minerals Co PO Box 26813 Salt Lake City UT 84126

ZAVON, MITCHELL RALPH, b Woodhaven, NY, May 9, 23; m 47; c 4. MEDICINE. *Educ:* Boston Univ, MD, 49. *Prof Exp:* From asst prof to clin prof indust med, Kettering Lab, Col Med, Univ Cincinnati, 55-71; assoc dir, Huntingdon Res Ctr, 71-74; assoc dir, Med Div, Ethyl Corp, 74-76, med dir, 74-76; MED DIR, HOOKER CHEM CO, 76- *Concurrent Pos:* Dir occup health serv, Cincinnati Health Dept, 55-61, asst health comnr, 61-74; consult, USPHS, 57-59, 66-69, Joint Congressional Comt Atomic Energy, 58-59, Louisville-Jefferson County Health Dept, 59-60 & USDA, 63-69; exec coordr, Miami Valley Proj, Ohio, 68-71; mem staff, St Mary's & Niagara Falls Mem Hosp. *Res:* Radiation protection; biological effects of agricultural chemicals; occupational health. *Mailing Add:* Hooker Chem Co Box 728 Niagara Falls NY 14302

ZAVORTINK, THOMAS JAMES, b Ravenna, Ohio, May 27, 39. ENTOMOLOGY, BIOLOGY. *Educ:* Kent State Univ, BS, 61; Univ Calif, Los Angeles, MA, 63, PhD(zool), 67. *Prof Exp:* Asst res zoologist entom, Univ Calif, Los Angeles, 68-74; asst cur entom, Calif Acad Sci, San Francisco, 74-75; MEM FAC, DEPT BIOL, UNIV SAN FRANCISCO, 75- *Concurrent Pos:* Consult, Southeast Asia Mosquito Proj, Smithsonian Inst, 68-71. *Res:* Systematics and biology of mosquitoes and bees. *Mailing Add:* Dept Biol Univ San Francisco San Francisco CA 94117

ZAWACKI, BRUCE EDWIN, b Northampton, Mass, Dec 6, 35; m 61; c 3. SURGERY. *Educ:* Col Holy Cross, BS, 57; Harvard Med Sch, MD, 61. *Prof Exp:* Chief trauma study, US Army Inst Surg Res, 67-69; surgeon, Southern Calif Permanente Med Group, 69-71; asst prof, 71-74, ASSOC PROF SURG, SCH MED, UNIV SOUTHERN CALIF, 75-; HEAD PHYSICIAN BURN WARD, LOS ANGELES CO-UNIV SOUTHERN CALIF MED CTR, 71- *Concurrent Pos:* Consult, State Calif Comt Orgn & Delivery Burn Care, 78- *Mem:* Am Burn Asn. *Res:* Inhalation injury; doctor-patient relationship in life-threatening illnesses; burn depth. *Mailing Add:* Los Angeles Co-Univ 1200 N State St Rm 12-650 Los Angeles CA 90033

ZAWADZKI, JOSEPH FRANCIS, b Withee, Wis, May 30, 35; m 70; c 3. ORGANIC CHEMISTRY. *Educ:* Northland Col, BA, 57; Loyola Univ (Ill), MS, 60, PhD(org chem), 62. *Prof Exp:* Res assoc org chem, Univ Chicago, 62-64; RES INVESTR CHEM PROCESS RES, SEARLE LABS, 64- *Mem:* Am Chem Soc. *Res:* Synthetic organic chemistry; reaction mechanisms; molecular rearrangements. *Mailing Add:* G D Searle & Co PO Box 5110 Chicago IL 60680

ZAWADZKI, ZBIGNIEW APOLINARY, b Sosnowiec, Poland, July 23, 21; US citizen; m 47; c 2. MEDICINE. *Educ:* Univ Warsaw, Poland, MD, 47, DrSci, 51; Brown Univ, AM, 75. *Prof Exp:* Intern resident internal med, Dept Med, Univ Warsaw, Poland, 47-51; fel hemat, New Eng Med Ctr, Boston, Mass, 57-59; asst prof hemat, Dept hemat, Inst Hemat, Warsaw, 59-60; staff physician hemat & oncol, Vet Admin Hosp, Pittsburgh, Pa, 61-74; ASSOC PROF MED IMMUNOL & ONCOL, BROWN UNIV, 74- *Concurrent Pos:* Staff physician, Hosp Ministry Health, Warsaw, Poland, 47-60; adj asst prof hemat, Dept Hemat, Inst Hemat, Warsaw, Poland, 51-57; asst prof med, Polish Red Cross Hosp, Korea, 54-55; asst prof hemat & assoc prof oncol, Univ Pittsburgh, Pa, 67-74; dir Div Clin Immunol & Oncol, Mem Hosp, Pawtucket, RI, 74- *Mem:* Am Asn Immunologists; Am Soc Clin Oncol; AMA; Am Rheumatism Asn; Int Soc Hemat. *Res:* Paraproteinemias: the long-term studies of serum protein aberrations in myeloma and related disorders (macroglobulinemia, amyloidosis and heavy chain disease), in elderly, asymptomatic patients (idiopathic lanthanic paraproteinemia), and in patients with various chronic diseases, including connective tissue disorders, hepatopathies and myelopathies. *Mailing Add:* Mem Hosp Pawtucket RI 02860

ZAWESKI, EDWARD F, b Jamesport, NY, Nov 2, 33; m 65; c 4. ORGANIC CHEMISTRY. *Educ:* Fordham Univ, BS, 55; Iowa State Univ, PhD(org chem), 59. *Prof Exp:* Chemist, Res Labs, Ethyl Corp, 59-79; MGR LUBRICANT CRANKCASE DEVELOP & TECHNOL, EDWIN COOPER INC, 79- *Concurrent Pos:* Res assoc, 72. *Mem:* Am Chem Soc; Soc Automotive Engrs. *Res:* Formulation of lubricant blends for crankcase applications and the synthesis of new components for crankcase oils. *Mailing Add:* Edwin Cooper Inc 1525 S Broadway St Louis MO 63104

ZAWOISKI, EUGENE JOSEPH, b Plains, Pa, Aug 17, 27; m 49; c 5. PHYSIOLOGY. *Educ:* Temple Univ, AB, 49, MA, 51; Jefferson Med Col, PhD(physiol), 63. *Prof Exp:* Asst histol, Temple Univ, 49-50; res asst path, Sharp & Dohme, Inc, 51, res assoc toxicol, 51-55; res assoc gastrointestinal physiol, Merck Inst Therapeut Res, Pa, 55-62, res assoc toxicol & teratology, 62-65; from instr to asst prof physiol, 65-71, ASSOC PROF PHYSIOL, JEFFERSON MED COL, 71- *Concurrent Pos:* Co-adj lectr pharmacol, Cooper Hosp Sch Nursing, 67-74 & Rutgers Univ, physiol, 68, 70, 72. *Mem:* Am Physiol Soc. *Res:* Gastrointestinal physiology and pharmacology; teratology; mammalian physiology. *Mailing Add:* Dept of Physiol Jefferson Med Col Philadelphia PA 19107

ZAWORSKI, R(OBERT) J(OSEPH), b Portland, Ore, Jan 24, 26; m 48; c 5. MECHANICAL ENGINEERING. *Educ:* Mass Inst Technol, SB, 47, SM, 58, PhD, 66. *Prof Exp:* From mech engr to head planning develop sect, West Div Gen Eng, Creole Petrol Corp, 47-57; asst prof, 57-58, PROF MECH ENG, ORE STATE UNIV, 58- *Res:* Thermodynamics of irreversible processes. *Mailing Add:* Dept of Mech Eng Ore State Univ Corvallis OR 97731

ZAYE, DAVID FRANCIS, b Toledo, Ohio. INFORMATION SCIENCE, ANALYTICAL CHEMISTRY. *Educ:* Univ Toledo, BS, 62, MS, 64; Univ Hawaii, PhD(anal chem), 68. *Prof Exp:* From assoc ed to sr assoc ed anal chem, 68-74, SR ED, CHEM ABSTR SERV, AM CHEM SOC, 74- *Mem:* Am Chem Soc. *Res:* Scientific vocabulary management processes and information transfer techniques relating to numerical data. *Mailing Add:* Chem Abstr Serv Ohio State Univ Columbus OH 43210

ZBARSKY, SIDNEY HOWARD, b Vonda, Sask, Feb 19, 20; m 44; c 3. BIOCHEMISTRY. *Educ:* Univ Sask, BA, 40; Univ Toronto, MA, 42, PhD(biochem), 46. *Prof Exp:* Res officer, Biol & Med Res Br, Atomic Energy Proj, 46-48; asst prof physiol chem, Univ Minn, 48-49; assoc prof, Univ BC, 49-62, PROF BIOCHEM, UNIV BC, 62- *Concurrent Pos:* Killam sr fel, Univ BC, 72-73. *Mem:* AAAS; Am Chem Soc; Can Physiol Soc; Can Biochem Soc (vpres, 66-67, pres, 67-68); Am Soc Biol Chemists. *Res:* Detoxication mechanisms; metabolism of British anti-lewisite, purines and pyrimidines; nucleases and nucleic acid enzymes in the intestinal mucosa. *Mailing Add:* Dept Biochem Univ BC Vancouver BC V6T 1W5 Can

ZBORALSKE, F FRANK, b Fall Creek, Wis, Aug 2, 32; m 58; c 4. RADIOLOGY. *Educ:* Marquette Univ, MD, 58. *Prof Exp:* Intern, St Joseph's Hosp, Milwaukee, 58-59; resident, Milwaukee County Gen Hosp, 59-62; from instr to asst prof radiol, Sch Med, Marquette Univ, 62-65; actg asst prof, Med Ctr, Univ Calif, San Francisco, 64, from asst prof to assoc prof radiol & dir exp radiol lab, 65-67, chief sect gastrointestional radiol, 66-67; assoc prof radiol, 67-72, dir div diag radiol, 67-75, PROF RADIOL, SCH MED, STANFORD UNIV, 72- *Concurrent Pos:* Radiologist, Milwaukee County Gen Hosp, 62-65; James Picker Found scholar radiol, 62-65; attend physician & consult, Vet Admin Hosp, Wood, Wis, 65; co-dir NIH res training grants diag radiol, Med Ctr, Univ Calif, San Francisco, 65-67 & dir res training grant, Sch Med, Stanford Univ, 67-76; consult, Vet Admin Hosp, Palo Alto, Calif, 68 & Santa Clara Valley Med Ctr, San Jose, 68- *Mem:* Asn Univ Radiologists; assoc Am Gastroenterol Asn. *Res:* Esophageal motility; esophageal epithelial cell kinetics. *Mailing Add:* Dept of Radiol Stanford Univ Sch of Med Stanford CA 94305

ZBUZEK, VLASTA KMENTOVA, b Velka Losenice, Czech, Sept 6, 33; US citizen; m 65. ENDOCRINOLOGY, PHYSIOLOGY. *Educ:* Charles Univ, MS, 63, Cand Sci, 69, Dr rer nat(physiol), 69. *Prof Exp:* Res assoc exp endocrinol, Lab Endocrinol & Metab, Prague, 56-69; res fel reprod physiol, Pop Coun, Rockefeller Univ, 69-71; assoc res scientist physiol & endocrinol, Dept Path, NY Univ, 71-75, res scientist neuroendocrinol, Dept Anesthesiol, 75-78; res physiologist, Vet Admin Med Ctr, New York, 78-80. *Concurrent Pos:* adj asst prof, Dept Anesthesiol, Univ Med & Dent NJ, 80- *Mem:* Endocrine Soc. *Res:* Isolation and identification of TRH; gonado-thyroidal relationships; the effects of hormones on cholesterol metabolism; pathophysiology of vasopressin; vasopressin and aging; drugs and endogenous opiates neurochemical mechanisms. *Mailing Add:* 100 Manhattan Ave Apt 1314 Union City NJ 07087

ZBUZEK, VRATISLAV, b Prague, Czech, Mar 13, 30; US citizen; m 65. BIOCHEMISTRY, ENDOCRINOLOGY. *Educ:* Charles Univ, Czech, cert, 53, Cand Sci, 65, Dr rer nat, 67. *Prof Exp:* Res assoc biochem & physiol, Phys Cult Res Inst, Czech, 53-64; res assoc biochem & endocrinol, Lab Endocrinol & Metab, Charles Univ, 64-68; res fel physiol & endocrinol, Pop Coun, Rockefeller Univ, 68-70, res assoc biochem & endocrinol, 70-75, asst prof biochem & cell biol, 75-77; ASSOC BIOCHEM & ENDOCRINOL, UNIV MED & DENT NJ, 80- *Concurrent Pos:* Lectr, Fac Phys Cult & Sports, Charles Univ, 56-62; adj assoc prof, Col Staten Island, City Univ New York, 78- *Mem:* Harvey Soc; Am Chem Soc; NY Acad Sci. *Res:* Biochemistry and physiology of muscular activity; pituitary - thyrotropic function; ultrastructure of C-cells and bone cells; biochemistry of cytotoxic T-lymphocytes; drug and opiate neurochemical mechanisms. *Mailing Add:* 100 Manhattan Ave Apt 1314 Union City NJ 07087

ZDAN, WILLIAM, b New York, NY, June 9, 19; m 49; c 2. SYSTEMS & ELECTRONIC ENGINEERING. *Educ:* Cooper Union, BEE, 42; Polytech Inst Brooklyn, MEE, 55. *Prof Exp:* Proj engr, Western Elec Co, 41-51; proj mgr airborne naval guid control & display systs, Sperry Gyroscope Co, 51-59; sr engr, Arma Div, Am Bosch Arma Corp, 59-62; from mgr guid & control space vehicles to head systs anal deep submergence prog, Sperry Gyroscope Co, 62-67, sr res sect head, Sperry Systs Mgt Div, Great Neck, 67-71, PROG MGR & TECH DIR SHIP RES SIMULATORS, VESSEL TRAFFIC MGT SYSTS, VEHICLE MANEUVERING TRAINERS & COMPUT GENERATED IMAGES, DISPLAY SYSTS, SPERRY DIV, SPERRY CORP, 71- *Mem:* Am Inst Aeronaut & Astronaut; Inst Elec & Electronics Engrs Comput Soc; Asn Comput Mach. *Res:* Digital computer analysis and evaluation for use in large real-time simulation systems; design and development of vehicle simulators and ship handling trainers; system synthesis and design of vessel traffic management systems and computer generated images display systems. *Mailing Add:* 30 Appletree Lane East Hills NY 11576

ZDANIS, RICHARD ALBERT, b Baltimore, Md, July 15, 35; m 55; c 2. PHYSICS. *Educ:* Johns Hopkins Univ, AB, 57, PhD(physics), 60. *Prof Exp:* Res assoc physics, Princeton Univ, 60-61, instr, 61-62; from asst prof to assoc prof, 62-69, assoc provost 75-79, vpres admin serv, 77-79, PROF PHYSICS, JOHNS HOPKINS UNIV, 69-, VPROVOST, 79- *Mem:* Am Phys Soc; AAAS. *Res:* Experimental elementary particle research. *Mailing Add:* Garland Hall Johns Hopkins Univ Baltimore MD 21218

ZDERIC, JOHN ANTHONY, b San Jose, Calif, Jan 5, 24; m 49; c 1. PHARMACEUTICAL CHEMISTRY. *Educ:* San Jose State Col, AB, 50; Stanford Univ, MS, 52, PhD(org chem), 55. *Prof Exp:* Squibb fel, Wayne State Univ, 55-56; res chemist, Syntex Corp, 56-59, asst dir chem res, 59-61, dir labs, Syntex Inst Molecular Biol, 61-62, dir corp planning div, 64-66, vpres com develop, Syntex, Int, Mex, 66-70, asst corp vpres, Syntex Corp, 67-70, vpres, Syntex Labs, Inc, Calif, 70-73, VPRES ADMIN & TECH AFFAIRS, SYNTEX RES, 73- *Concurrent Pos:* Mem staff, Swiss Fed Inst Technol, 62-64; mem bd govs, Syva, 74- *Mem:* Am Chem Soc; Swiss Chem Soc. *Res:* Raney nickel catalyzed hydrogenolyses; macrocylic antibiotics; steroidal hormones; nucleocides and nucleotides. *Mailing Add:* Syntex Res 3401 Hillview Ave Palo Alto CA 94304

ZDUNKOWSKI, WILFORD G, b Driesen, Ger, May 4, 29; US citizen; m 51; c 2. PHYSICAL METEOROLOGY. *Educ:* Univ Utah, BS, 58, MS, 59; Univ Munich, DSc, 62. *Prof Exp:* Res asst atmospheric fluoride, Univ Utah, 57-58; res meteorologist, Intermountain Weather, Inc, 58-63; from asst prof to prof meteorol, Univ Utah, 63-77; PROF, UNIV MAINZ, GER, 77- *Concurrent Pos:* Res meteorologist, Univ Mainz, 59-61 & Meteorol Inst, Univ Munich, 61-62. *Mem:* Am Meteorol Soc; Am Geophys Union. *Res:* Atmospheric radiation; boundary laye theory. *Mailing Add:* Inst Meteorol Univ Mainz Mainz West Germany

ZEALEY, MARION EDWARD, b Augusta, Ga, Mar 26, 13; m 48; c 4. BIOCHEMISTRY, MICROBIOLOGY. *Educ:* Paine Col, AB, 34; Atlanta Univ, MS, 40; Univ Minn, PhD, 60. *Prof Exp:* Instr chem, Miles Col, 36-43; assoc prof, Paine Col, 43-44; assoc prof biochem, 48-59, USPHS fel, 63-65, PROF MICROBIOL, MEHARRY MED COL, 65- *Mem:* AAAS; Am Chem Soc. *Res:* Protein denaturation; x-ray effects; nucleic acids; cell biology. *Mailing Add:* Dept of Microbiol Meharry Med Col Nashville TN 37208

ZEBOLSKY, DONALD MICHAEL, b Chicago, Ill, Aug 20, 33; m 57; c 8. PHYSICAL CHEMISTRY. *Educ:* Northwestern Univ, BA, 56; Kans State Univ, PhD(phys chem), 63. *Prof Exp:* Chemist, Baxter Labs, 56-57; asst prof phys chem, Creighton Univ, 62-63; asst prof, Northern Ill Univ, 63-64; asst prof, 64-68, ASSOC PROF PHYS CHEM, CREIGHTON UNIV, 68- *Mem:* Am Chem Soc; NY Acad Sci. *Res:* Thermodynamics, kinetics and polarography of ionpairs and of transition metal-ion chelate formation with molecules related to imidazole; molecules containing sulfur as a ligand site. *Mailing Add:* Dept of Chem Creighton Univ Omaha NE 68178

ZEBOUNI, NADIM H, b Beirut, Lebanon, Apr 14, 28; m; c 2. SOLID STATE PHYSICS. *Educ:* Univ Paris, BS, 53; Nat Sch Advan Telecommun, France, MS, 55; La State Univ, PhD(physics), 61. *Prof Exp:* Eng del to Mid East, Co Gen TSF, 55-57; teaching asst, 57-58, asst prof, 60-65, ASSOC PROF PHYSICS, LA STATE UNIV, BATON ROUGE, 65-, ASTRON, 74- *Mem:* Am Phys Soc. *Mailing Add:* Dept of Physics La State Univ Baton Rouge LA 70803

ZEBOVITZ, EUGENE, b Chicago, Ill, Feb 24, 26; m 51; c 6. VIROLOGY. *Educ:* Roosevelt Univ, BS, 49; Univ Chicago, MS, 52, PhD(microbiol), 55. *Prof Exp:* Microbiologist, US Army Biol Labs, Ft Detrick, Md, 55-58; microbiologist, Universal Foods Corp, Wis, 58-62; microbiologist, US Army Biol Labs, 62-70; microbiologist, Naval Med Res Inst, Nat Naval Med Ctr, 70-74; HEALTH SCIENTIST ADMINR BIOL SCI, DIV RES GRANTS, NIH, 74- *Mem:* AAAS; Am Soc Microbiol; Sigma Xi; Soc Exp Biol & Med. *Res:* Mechanism of virus replication; molecular biology; viral genetics; health science administration. *Mailing Add:* Div Res Grants Rm 206 Westwood Bldg Nat Inst Health Bethesda MD 20205

ZEBROWITZ, S(TANLEY), b New York, NY, Nov 28, 27; m 53; c 2. ELECTRICAL ENGINEERING, COMMUNICATIONS. *Educ:* City Col New York, BEE, 49; Univ Pa, MS, 54; Temple Univ, MBA, 81. *Prof Exp:* Engr, Res Div, Philco Corp, 49-61, mgr tech staff, 62-65, mgr systs eng, 65-72, mgr design eng, Commun & Eng Div, Ford Aerospace & Commun, 72-81; PRES, STELCOM INT INC, 81- *Concurrent Pos:* Consult, Rome Air Develop Ctr, US Air Force, 62-; mem US comt for study group IX, Consult Comt on Int Radio, 66-72; exec comt, Int Solid Circuits Conf, 66-76. *Mem:* Fel Inst Elec & Electronics Engrs. *Res:* Communication systems; microwave and troposcatter propagation and system design; signal processing; integrated communication and computer networks. *Mailing Add:* Stelcom Int Inc PO Box 236 Oreland PA 19075

ZECH, ARTHUR CONRAD, b Julian, Nebr, Aug 24, 27; m 59; c 1. AGRONOMY, BIOCHEMISTRY. *Educ:* Univ Nebr, Lincoln, BS, 58; Kans State Univ, MS, 59, PhD(agron, biochem), 62. *Prof Exp:* Sr agronomist, 61-65, res scientist animal nutrit, 65-69, mgr agr sci res, 69-75, mgr plant sci res, 75-79, SR RES SCIENTIST, FARMLAND INDUSTS, INC, 79- *Mem:* Am Soc Agron; Am Soc Animal Sci; Poultry Sci Asn; Am Genetic Asn; Coun Agr Sci & Technol. *Res:* Animal nutrition; forage fertility and quality. *Mailing Add:* Farmland Industs Inc PO Box 7305 Kansas City MO 64116

ZECHIEL, LEON NORRIS, b Wilmington, Del, Sept 23, 23; m 46; c 4. ASTROPHYSICS, OPTICS. *Educ:* DePauw Univ, AB, 48; Ohio State Univ, MA, 51. *Prof Exp:* Res assoc, Res Found, Ohio State Univ, 53-58, assoc supvr & asst to dir, 58-59; sect head, GPL Div, Gen Precision, Inc, NY, 59-63, prin scientist, 63-68; mgr data mgt systs, Sanders Assocs, Inc, NH, 68-72; sr systs engr, NCR-Postal Systs Div, SC, 72-74; prog mgr, 74-75, MGR PROJ PLANNING, DAYTON RES DIV, HOBART CORP, 76- *Res:* Reentry and space vehicle guidance and navigation; aeronautical charting; optical and infrared instrumentation; stellar photography; air navigation; reconnaissance and surveillance techniques; computerized data management systems; postal systems automation; automated weighing and package labelling systems. *Mailing Add:* Hobart Corp 1555 Stanley Ave Dayton OH 45404

ZECHMAN, FREDERICK WILLIAM, JR, b Mar 16, 28; m 50; c 2. PHYSIOLOGY. *Educ:* Otterbein Col, BS, 49; Univ Md, MS, 51; Duke Univ, PhD, 56. *Prof Exp:* Asst zool, Univ Md, 49-51; biologist & asst to head biol br, US Off Naval Res, 51-53; instr physiol, Duke Univ, 53-57; from asst prof to assoc prof, Miami Univ, 57-61; from asst prof to assoc prof, 61-68, PROF PHYSIOL & CHMN DEPT PHYSIOL & BIOPHYS, MED CTR, UNIV KY, 68- *Concurrent Pos:* Consult biophys br, Aerospace Med Lab, Wright-Patterson AFB, 60-61. *Mem:* AAAS; Am Physiol Soc; Aerospace Med Asn; Soc Exp Biol & Med. *Res:* Respiratory regulation and mechanics; prolonged and periodic acceleration; effects of lower body negative pressure and posture change; mechanical, reflex and subjective responses to added airflow resistance; bedrest; exercise. *Mailing Add:* Dept of Physiol & Biophys Univ of Ky Med Ctr Lexington KY 40506

ZECHMANN, ALBERT W, b Sioux City, Iowa, Aug 21, 34; m 65; c 1. MATHEMATICS. *Educ:* Iowa State Univ, BS, 56, MS, 59, PhD(appl math), 61. *Prof Exp:* ASST PROF MATH, UNIV NEBR-LINCOLN, 61- *Mem:* Math Asn Am. *Res:* Solution of visco-elastic problems; unification of the theory of partial differential equations; study of Cauchy problem for elliptic equations. *Mailing Add:* 6710 Everett Lincoln NE 68506

ZEDECK, MORRIS SAMUEL, b Brooklyn, NY, Jan 25, 40; m 61; c 3. PHARMACOLOGY, BIOCHEMISTRY. *Educ:* Long Island Univ, BS, 61; Univ Mich, PhD(pharmacol), 65. *Prof Exp:* Asst prof pharmacol, Sch Med, Yale Univ, 67-68; assoc pharmacol, Sloan-Kettering Inst Cancer Res, 68-76; asst prof, 69-76, ASSOC PROF PHARMACOL, GRAD SCH MED SCI, SLOAN-KETTERING DIV, CORNELL UNIV, 76-; ASSOC MEM, SLOAN-KETTERING INST CANCER RES, 76- *Concurrent Pos:* Fel pharmacol, Sch Med, Yale Univ, 65-67. *Mem:* Am Asn Cancer Res; Am Soc Pharmacol & Exp Therapeut; Am Soc Prev Oncology; German Pharmacol Soc. *Res:* Effects of potential cancer chemotherapeutic agents upon the synthesis of nucleic acids, protein and induced enzymes; mechanism of action studies and preclinical toxicology studies of cancer chemotherapeutic agents; cellular control and regulation; chemical carcinogenesis. *Mailing Add:* Sloan-Kettering Inst for Cancer Res 410 E 68th St New York NY 10021

ZEDEK, MISHAEL, b Kaunas, Lithuania, July 16, 26; m 56; c 2. MATHEMATICS. *Educ:* Hebrew Univ, Israel, MSc, 52; Harvard Univ, PhD(math), 56. *Prof Exp:* Asst, Hebrew Univ, Israel, 52-53; asst, Harvard Univ, 53-55; instr math, Univ Calif, 56-58; from asst prof to assoc prof, 58-67, PROF MATH, UNIV MD, COLLEGE PARK, 68- *Mem:* Am Math Soc; Math Asn Am; London Math Soc. *Res:* Mathematical analysis; complex analysis; interpolation and approximation. *Mailing Add:* Dept of Math Univ of Md College Park MD 20742

ZEDLER, EMPRESS YOUNG, b Abilene, Tex, Nov 9, 08; m 28. SPEECH PATHOLOGY, PSYCHOLOGY. *Educ:* Univ Tex, Austin, BA, 28, MA, 48, PhD(speech path), 52. *Prof Exp:* Prof spec educ, 48-77, chmn dept, 64-77, PROF & DIR SPEECH, HEARING & LANG CLIN, SOUTHWEST TEX STATE UNIV, 77- *Mem:* Fel Am Speech & Hearing Asn; Am Psychol Asn; Acad Aphasia; fel Am Cong Rehab Med. *Res:* Language; learning disabilities. *Mailing Add:* PO Box 465 Luling TX 78648

ZEDLER, JOY BUSWELL, b Sioux Falls, SDak, Oct 15, 43; m 65; c 2. ECOLOGY. *Educ:* Augustana Col (SDak), BS, 64; Univ Wis, Madison, MS, 66, PhD(bot), 68. *Prof Exp:* Asst bot, Univ Wis, Madison, 64-66, fel, 66-67, res asst, 67-68; instr, Univ Mo, Columbia, 68-69; lectr, 69-72, asst prof, 72-77, assoc prof, 77-80, PROF BIOL, SAN DIEGO STATE UNIV, 80- *Mem:* Am Soc Limnol & Oceanog; Ecol Soc Am; Estuarine Res Fedn. *Res:* Coastal wetland structure and functioning, especially salt marsh ecology. *Mailing Add:* Dept of Biol San Diego State Univ San Diego CA 92182

ZEDLER, PAUL HUGO, b Milwaukee, Wis, June 22, 41; m 65; c 2. ECOLOGY, PLANT ECOLOGY. *Educ:* Univ Wis, Milwaukee, BS, 63, Univ Wis, Madison, MS, 66, PhD(bot), 68. *Prof Exp:* Arboretum botanist, Univ Wis, 64-68; fel forestry, Univ Mo, Columbia, 68-69; from asst to assoc prof, 69-78, PROF BIOL, SAN DIEGO STATE UNIV, 78- *Mem:* AAAS; Brit Ecol Soc; Ecol Soc Am. *Res:* Plant population ecology, fire ecology, successional studies, plant-substrate relationships. *Mailing Add:* Dept of Biol San Diego State Univ San Diego CA 92182

ZEE, ANTHONY, b China; m 71. THEORETICAL HIGH ENERGY PHYSICS. *Educ:* Princeton Univ, AB, 66; Harvard Univ, AM, 68, PhD(physics), 70. *Prof Exp:* Mem physics, Inst Advan Study, 70-72; asst prof, Rockefeller Univ, 72-73; asst prof physics, Princeton Univ, 73-78; assoc prof physics, Univ Pa, 78-80; PROF PHYSICS, UNIV WASH, 80- *Concurrent Pos:* A P Sloan Found fel, 73-78. *Res:* Unification of fundamental interactions; aspects of cosmology and gravity. *Mailing Add:* Dept Physics Univ Wash Seattle WA 98195

ZEE, DAVID SAMUEL, b Chicago, Ill, Aug 14, 44; c 2. NEUROLOGY, NEUROPHYSIOLOGY. *Educ:* Northwestern Univ, BA, 65; Johns Hopkins Univ, MD, 69. *Prof Exp:* Clin assoc neurol, NIH, 73-75; asst prof, 75-78, ASSOC PROF NEUROL, JOHNS HOPKINS UNIV, 78- *Concurrent Pos:* Nat Inst Neurol Dis & Stroke grant, 75-80, Nat Eye Inst res grant, 80-85; NIH res grant, 76-82. *Mem:* Asn Res Vision & Ophthal; Soc Neurosci; Am Acad Neurol; Am Neurol Asn. *Res:* Ocular motor disorders; ocular motor physiology; computer modelling; vestibular disorders. *Mailing Add:* Johns Hopkins Hosp Baltimore MD 21205

ZEE, PAULUS, b Amsterdam, Netherlands, July 2, 28; US citizen; m 57; c 4. PEDIATRICS, BIOCHEMISTRY. *Educ:* Univ Amsterdam, MD, 54; Tulane Univ, PhD(biochem), 65. *Prof Exp:* Resident pediat, Children's Mercy Hosp, Kansas City, Mo, 56-58; asst prof pediat & physiol, Univ Tenn, 64-68, ASSOC PROF PEDIAT & PHYSIOL, UNIV TENN, 68-; MEM, ST JUDE CHILDREN'S RES HOSP, 64- *Mem:* Am Oil Chem Soc; AMA; Am Acad Pediat; Am Inst Nutrit; Am Soc Clin Nutrit. *Res:* Lipid metabolism of the newborn; pediatric nutrition. *Mailing Add:* St Jude Children's Res Hosp PO Box 318 Memphis TN 38101

ZEE, YUAN CHUNG, b Shanghai, China, Aug 29, 35; m 66. VIROLOGY. *Educ:* Univ Calif, Berkeley, AB, 57, MA, 59, PhD(comp path), 66, Univ Calif, Davis, DVM, 63. *Prof Exp:* Res bacteriologist, Virol Div, Naval Biol Lab, Univ Calif, Berkeley, 63-66, from asst prof to assoc prof, 66-74, PROF VET MICROBIOL & CHMN DEPT, UNIV CALIF, DAVIS, 74- *Mem:* Am Vet Med Asn; Am Soc Microbiol. *Res:* Biological properties of animal viruses; mechanisms of virus replication and electron microscopy. *Mailing Add:* Dept of Vet Microbiol Univ of Calif Sch of Vet Med Davis CA 95616

ZEE-CHENG, ROBERT KWANG-YUEN, b Kashan, Chekiang, China, Sept 2, 25; m 49; c 4. ORGANIC CHEMISTRY, MEDICINAL CHEMISTRY. *Educ:* China Tech Inst, BS, 45; NMex Highlands Univ, MS, 57; Univ Tex, Austin, PhD(org chem), 63. *Prof Exp:* Res chemist & chem engr, Taiwan Pulp & Paper Corp, 46-56; asst org chem, NMex Highlands Univ, 56-57; res scientist & teaching asst, Univ Tex, Austin, 57-59; assoc chemist, Midwest Res Inst, 59-61; Welch Found fel, Univ Tex, Austin, 61-62; sr chemist, Celanese Corp Am, Tex, 62-65; sr chemist, Biol Sci Div, Midwest Res Inst, 65-71, prin chemist, 71-80; WITH MED CTR, UNIV KANS, 80- *Mem:* Am Chem Soc; Sigma Xi; AAAS. *Res:* Physical chemistry; chemical engineering; synthesis; identification; reaction mechanism of organic compounds; heterocyclic chemistry; cancer chemotherapy. *Mailing Add:* Univ Kans Med Ctr Rainbow Blvd & 39th Kansas City MO 66103

ZEEMAN, MAURICE GEORGE, b Rockland, Mass, Dec 1, 42; m 78. ZOOLOGY, COMPARATIVE IMMUNOLOGY. *Educ:* Calif State Univ, Northridge, BA, 69; Univ Calif, Los Angeles, MA, 72; Utah State Univ, PhD(zool), 80. *Prof Exp:* Teaching asst biol, Dept Zool, Univ Calif, Los Angeles, 69-70 & 71-72; res asst, Dept Biol, Utah State Univ, 75-80; ENVIRON TOXICOLOGIST, BUR VET MED, FOOD & DRUG ADMIN, 80- *Mem:* AAAS; Am Col Toxicol; NY Acad Sci; Soc Environ Toxicol Chem; Sigma Xi. *Res:* Effects of toxic agents on fish immune systems, environmental toxicology; fish physiology; pesticide effects of fish immunology and hematology. *Mailing Add:* Bureau Vet Med 5600 Fishers Lane Logan UT 84322

ZEEVAART, JAN ADRIAAN DINGENIS, b Baarland, Neth, Jan 5, 30; m 56; c 1. PLANT PHYSIOLOGY. *Educ:* State Agr Univ Wageningen, BSc, 53, MSc, 55, PhD(plant physiol), 58. *Prof Exp:* Asst plant physiol, State Agr Univ Wageningen, 55-58; res fel, Calif Inst Technol, 60-63; assoc prof, McMaster Univ, 63-65; assoc prof, 65-70, PROF PLANT PHYSIOL, MICH STATE UNIV, 70- *Concurrent Pos:* Guggenheim fel, Milstead Lab Chem Enzymol, Sittingbourne Res Ctr, 73-74. *Mem:* AAAS; Am Inst Biol Sci; Am Soc Plant Physiol; Soc Develop Biol; corresp mem Royal Dutch Acad Sci. *Res:* Physiology of flower formation; plant development as regulated by growth substances; gibberellins and abscisic acids; environmental physiology. *Mailing Add:* Dept Energy Plant Res Lab Mich State Univ East Lansing MI 48824

ZEFFREN, EUGENE, b St Louis, Mo, Nov 21, 41; m 64; c 2. BIO-ORGANIC CHEMISTRY. *Educ:* Wash Univ, AB, 63; Univ Chicago, MS, 65, PhD(org chem), 67. *Prof Exp:* Res chemist enzym, Procter & Gamble Co, 67-71, group leader, 71-74, sect head, 74-77, Aassoc dir, toilet goods div, Winton Hill Tech Ctr, 77-79; VPRES RES & DEVELOP, HELEN CURTIS, INC, 79- *Mem:* Am Chem Soc; Soc Socmetic Chemists. *Res:* Mechanism of enzyme action; model systems for enzymic catalysis; chemistry of hair keratins; protein structure. *Mailing Add:* 4401 W North Ave Helene Curtis Indust Inc Chicago IL 60639

ZEFTEL, LEO, b Providence, RI, Aug 7, 25; m 49; c 3. ORGANIC CHEMISTRY. *Educ:* Brown Univ, ScB, 49; Univ Rochester, PhD(chem), 51. *Prof Exp:* Chemist, Jackson Lab, Org Chem Dept, 51-57 & Plants Tech Sect, 57-59, supvr, 59-66, div head, Process Dept, 66-70, chief supvr chem-tech, 70-73, chief supvr prod, 73-75, SUPT, PROD CONTROL CHAMBERS WORKS, E I DU PONT DE NEMOURS & CO, INC, DEEPWATER, NJ, 75- *Mem:* Am Chem Soc. *Res:* Surfactants; intermediates; rubber chemicals; textile adjuvants; petroleum additives; polymers; dyes; ultraviolet absorbers; process development. *Mailing Add:* 4619 Sylvanus Dr Rockwood Hills Wilmington DE 19803

ZEGARELLI, EDWARD VICTOR, b Utica, NY, Sept 9, 12; m 39; c 4. DENTISTRY. *Educ:* Columbia Univ, AB, 34, DDS, 37; Univ Chicago, MS, 42; Am Bd Oral Med, dipl, 56. *Prof Exp:* Asst dent, 37-38, from instr to asst prof, 38-47, head diag & roentgenol, 47-57, prof, 57-58, dir, Div Stomatol, 58-77, Edwin S Robinson prof dent, Sch Dent & Oral Surg, 58-78, dean, 74-78, EMER PROF DENT & EMER DEAN, SCH DENT & ORAL SURG, COLUMBIA UNIV, 78-; DIR DENT SERV, COLUMBIA-PRESBY MED CTR, 74- *Concurrent Pos:* Dent alumni res award, Columbia Univ, 63; mem univ coun, Columbia Univ, 59-62, cancer coordr & chmn comt dent res, Sch

Dent & Oral Surg; mem coun dent therapeut, Am Dent Asn, 63-69, vchmn, 68-69, consult, 69-, consult, coun dent mat & devices, 70-; mem, NY Bd Dent Exam, 63-, pres, 70-71; attend dent surgeon & dir dent serv, Columbia-Presby Med Ctr & Delafield Inst Cancer Res; cent off consult & dentist in residence, Vet Admin, DC; police surgeon, New York Police Dept; chmn comt exam, NE Regional Bd Dent Examr, 69- & joint panel drugs in dent, Nat Acad Sci-Nat Res Coun-Food & Drug Admin; consult, EORange, Kingsbridge & Montrose Vet Admin Hosps, Grasslands, Phelps Mem & Vassar Bros Hosps & USPHS; consult, Nat Naval Dent Ctr, Bethesda, Md; dir dent serv, Columbia-Presby Med Ctr, 74-78; mem, NY State Health Res Coun, 75- *Honors & Awards:* Austin Sniffin Medal Honor, Dent Soc, NY, 61, Jarvie-Burkhardt Medal Honor, 70; Award of Merit, Am Asn Dent Exam, 71; Samuel J Miller Medal, Am Acad Oral Med, 76; Man Year, Am Asn Dent Examr, 78; William J Gies Medal, Am Col Dentists, 81. *Mem:* AAAS; Am Cancer Soc; fel Am Col Dent; hon mem Dent Soc Guatemala; hon fel Acad Gen Dent. *Res:* Diseases of the mouth and jaws, especially diagnosis; pharmacotherapeutics of oral diseases. *Mailing Add:* Sch Dent & Oral Surg Columbia Univ New York NY 10032

ZEGEL, WILLIAM CASE, b Port Jefferson, NY, Aug 4, 40; m 62; c 2. ENVIRONMENTAL ENGINEERING, PROJECT MANAGEMENT. *Educ:* Stevens Inst Technol, ME, 61, MS, 62, DSc(chem eng), 65; Environ Eng Intersoc, dipl, 76. *Prof Exp:* Instr chem, Newark Col Eng, 61-64; sr res engr, Allied Chem Corp, 64-68; develop mgr, Scott Res Labs, 68-72; sr res assoc, Ryckman, Edgerly, Tomlinson & Assocs, 72-75; vpres opers, Environ Sci & Eng Inc, 75-79; PRES, WATER & AIR RES INC, 79- *Concurrent Pos:* Vis lectr, Stevens Inst Technol, 65-68; tech consult, Environ Protection Agency Regional Air Pollution Study, 74-75. *Mem:* Am Inst Chem Engrs; Air Pollution Control Asn; AAAS; Nat Soc Prof Engrs; Sigma Xi. *Res:* Atmospheric chemistry; water chemistry; pollution control technology; environmental impact assessment; process analysis; project management. *Mailing Add:* 11011 NW 12 Place Gainesville FL 32601

ZEGURA, STEPHEN LUKE, b San Francisco, Calif, July 2, 43; div; c 1. HUMAN BIOLOGY, BIOLOGICAL ANTHROPOLOGY. *Educ:* Stanford Univ, BA, 65; Univ Wis-Madison, MS, 69, PhD(human biol), 71. *Prof Exp:* Asst prof anthrop, NY Univ, 71-72; asst prof, 72-77, ASSOC PROF ANTHROP, UNIV ARIZ, 77- *Concurrent Pos:* NY Univ career develop grant, Smithsonian Inst, 72. *Mem:* AAAS; Am Asn Phys Anthrop; Classification Soc; Am Anthrop Asn; Soc Study Human Biol. *Res:* Multivariate statistics; biological distance; Eskimology; population genetics; evolutionary theory. *Mailing Add:* Dept Anthrop Univ Ariz Tucson AZ 85721

ZEHNER, DAVID MURRAY, b Philadelphia, Pa, Aug 7, 43; m 67. SURFACE PHYSICS. *Educ:* Drexel Inst Technol, BS, 66; Brown Univ, PhD(physics), 71. *Prof Exp:* Res asst physics, Brown Univ, 67-71; res physicist surface physics, Oak Ridge Nat Labs, 71-80. *Mem:* Sigma Xi; Am Phys Soc; Am Vacuum Soc. *Res:* Investigation of surface properties of solids using surface sensitive spectroscopic techniques employing electrons, photons and ions as scattering probes; surface damage, chemisorption and catalytic phenomena. *Mailing Add:* 5 Brandywine Lenou City TN 37771

ZEHNER, LEE RANDALL, b Lansdowne, Pa, Mar 15, 47; m 73; c 2. ORGANIC CHEMISTRY. *Educ:* Univ Pa, BS, 68; Univ Minn, PhD(org chem), 73. *Prof Exp:* Res chemist org chem, Arco Chem Co, 73-75, sr res chemist, 75-78; group leader process develop, Ashland Chem Co, 78; res chemist, 78-79, SR RES CHEMIST, W R GRACE & CO, 79- *Mem:* Catalysis Soc; Am Chem Soc; Am Inst Chem Engrs. *Res:* Homogeneous and heterogeneous catalysis; carbonylation chemistry; vapor phase oxidation and hydrogenation; petrochemicals and specialty chemicals. *Mailing Add:* Res Div W R Grace & Co 7379 Rte 32 Colombia MD 21044

ZEHR, ELDON IRVIN, b Manson, Iowa, June 25, 35; m 57; c 3. PLANT PATHOLOGY. *Educ:* Goshen Col, BA, 60; Cornell Univ, MS, 65, PhD(plant path), 69. *Prof Exp:* From asst to assoc prof, 69-78, PROF PLANT PATH, CLEMSON UNIV, 78- *Mem:* Am Phytopath Soc; AAAS; Soc Nematologists. *Res:* Diseases of apples, peaches and grapes. *Mailing Add:* Dept of Plant Path & Physiol Clemson Univ Clemson SC 29631

ZEHR, FLOYD JOSEPH, b Lowville, NY, June 28, 29; m 57; c 4. EXPERIMENTAL PHYSICS. *Educ:* Eastern Mennonite Col, BS, 54; Goshen Col, BA, 57; Syracuse Univ, MS, 61 & 63, PhD(physics), 67. *Prof Exp:* Teacher jr high sch, PR, 54-56 & sr high sch, NY, 57-59; asst prof, 65-72, head dept, 69-71, ASSOC PROF PHYSICS, WESTMINSTER COL, PA, 72- *Concurrent Pos:* Researcher, Argonne Nat Lab, 71-72 & Oak Ridge Nat Lab, 79-80. *Mem:* Am Asn Physics Teachers. *Res:* Measurement of interatomic potential between lithium ions and helium atoms and lithium ions and hydrogen atoms; nuclear decay studies of LU-174 and Tm-174; neutron capture-gamma ray decay studies; residential solar space heating analyses. *Mailing Add:* Dept of Physics Westminster Col New Wilmington PA 16142

ZEHR, MARTIN DALE, b Carthage, NY, Sept 30, 50; m 77. NEUROPSYCHOLOGY. *Educ:* State Univ NY, Binghamton, BS, 72; Memphis State Univ, MS, 75, PhD(clin psychol), 79. *Prof Exp:* Grant coordr victimization, Correctional Res & Eval Ctr, 77-78; psychol intern, Vet Admin Med Ctr, Topeka, Kans, 78-769; NEUROPSYCHOLOGIST, VET ADMIN MED CTR, KANSAS CITY, MO, 79- *Concurrent Pos:* Adj asst prof, Dept Psychiat, Sch Med, Kans Univ, 80- *Mem:* Am Psychol Asn; Nat Acad Neuropsychologists; Am Asn Biofeedback Clinicians. *Res:* Relationship between structural or systemic damage to cortical tissues and disruption of behavioral and cognitive-intellectual functions. *Mailing Add:* 7645 Jarboe St Kansas City MO 64114

ZEHRT, WILLIAM H(AROLD), b Racine, Wis, June 9, 22; m 55; c 3. CIVIL ENGINEERING. *Educ:* Univ Wis, BS, 44, MSCE, 58, PhD(civil eng), 62. *Prof Exp:* Gen engr, Gen Eng Co, Wis, 47-48; bridge engr, Wis State Hwy Comn, 48-51; regional bridge engr, US Forest Serv, 51-55; br mgr bldg & related struct, Pub Works Off, Ninth Naval Dist, Ill, 55-57; instr civil eng struct, Univ Wis, 57-61; prof civil eng, Miss State Univ, 61-63; prof, Univ Ala, 63-66; PROF CIVIL ENG & CHMN DEPT, UNIV S ALA, 66- *Res:* Engineering structures; basic properties of wood as a structural material. *Mailing Add:* Div of Eng Univ of SAla Mobile AL 36688

ZEHRUNG, WINFIELD SCOTT, III, b Oil City, Pa, July 4, 31; m 57; c 3. ORGANIC CHEMISTRY. *Educ:* Allegheny Col, BS, 53, MS, 54; Univ Buffalo, PhD(chem), 57. *Prof Exp:* Instr chem, Allegheny Col, 54-57; res chemist, Yerkes Res Lab, E I du Pont de Nemours & Co, 57-62, lab supvr, Yerkes Film Plant, 62-65, staff scientist, Yerkes Res Lab, 65-67, tech rep venture develop sect, Film Dept, 67-71; plant mgr, Specialty Converters, Inc, 71-74, TECH DIR, SPECIALTY COMPOSITES CORP, 74- *Mem:* Am Chem Soc; Am Soc Qual Control; Soc Plastic Eng. *Res:* Nitrogen heterocycles; organic chemistry of cyanogen; vinyl polymers; pigmentation; color theory and applications; business analysis; urethane foam technology. *Mailing Add:* Specialty Composites Corp 650 Dawson Dr Newark DE 19713

ZEI, DINO, b Chicago, Ill, Aug 20, 27; m 49; c 2. EXPERIMENTAL PHYSICS, HISTORY OF SCIENCE. *Educ:* Beloit Col, BS, 50; Univ Wis, MS, 52, PhD, 57, MA, 72. *Prof Exp:* Physicist, Nat Bur Standards, 50; instr physics, Beloit Col, 52-53; asst prof, Milton Col, 53-54; assoc prof, St Cloud State Col, 55-57; prof physics, 57-78, WILLIAM HARLEY BARBER DISTINGUISHED PROF, RIPON COL, 78-, CHMN DEPT PHYSICS, 57- *Mem:* AAAS; Am Asn Physics Teachers; Am Phys Soc; Optical Soc Am; Hist Sci Soc. *Mailing Add:* Dept of Physics Ripon Col Ripon WI 54971

ZEIBERG, SEYMOUR L, b New York, NY, May 22, 34; m 57; c 2. AEROSPACE & SYSTEMS ENGINEERING. *Educ:* City Col New York, BME, 55; NY Univ, MME, 57, EngScD, 61. *Prof Exp:* Lectr mech eng, City Col New York, 55-61; asst prof, NY Univ, 61-62; proj scientist & group leader aerodyn, Gen Appl Sci Lab, Inc, 62-65; mgr gas dynamics, Aerospace Corp, 65-66, dir penetration aids systs, 66-67, dir prog definition, 67-68, group dir, Concepts & Plans, 68-72; dir systs planning group, R&D Assocs, Santa Monica, 72-77; assoc gen mgr, Advan Space Progs Div, Aerospace Corp, 77; dep undersecy of defense res & eng, Dept Defense, 77-81; VPRES ENG, MARTIN MARIETTA AEROSPACE, 81- *Honors & Awards:* Cert of Merit, US Air Force Systs Command, 72. *Mem:* Am Soc Mech Engrs; fel Am Inst Aeronaut & Astronaut. *Res:* Physics of reentry vehicles interaction with atmosphere; military reentry vehicle penetration aids; missile and reentry systems; strategic offence and defense systems. *Mailing Add:* 6138 Chesterbrook Rd McLean VA 22101

ZEIDE, BORIS, forest ecology, forest mensuration, see previous edition

ZEIDENBERGS, GIRTS, b Tukums, Latvia, Apr 5, 34; US citizen; m 55; c 3. ELECTRICAL ENGINEERING, SOLID STATE PHYSICS. *Educ:* Univ Conn, BS, 57; Syracuse Univ, MEE, 59, PhD(elec eng), 66. *Prof Exp:* Prog engr, Gen Elec Co, 57-59, engr, 59-63; res engr, Syracuse Univ, 63-67; develop engr, Systs Prod Assurance, 74-77, adv engr, Biomed Systs, 77-80, prod safety prog mgr, Info Records Div, 80-81, PROG MGR PROD SAFETY PROGS, IBM CORP, 81- *Mem:* Inst Elec & Electronics Engrs. *Res:* Network and circuit design; semiconductor devices; heterojunction; biomedical systems. *Mailing Add:* IBM Corp D644 Old Orchard Rd Armoric NY 10504

ZEIDERS, KENNETH EUGENE, b Sunbury, Pa, Aug 21, 20. PLANT PATHOLOGY, AGRONOMY. *Educ:* Pa State Univ, BS, 55, MS, 58. *Prof Exp:* Tech asst plant path, 57-59, plant pathologist, 59-75, RES PLANT PATHOLOGIST, US REGIONAL PASTURE RES LAB, AGR RES SERV, USDA, 75- *Concurrent Pos:* Plant pathologist, Dept Plant Path, Pa State Univ, 60- *Mem:* Am Phytopath Soc; Sigma Xi. *Res:* Diseases of forage grasses and legumes; inoculation methods; screening for disease resistance; environmental plant pathology. *Mailing Add:* US Regional Pasture Res Lab Sci & Educ Admin-Agr Res USDA University Park PA 16802

ZEIDLER, JAMES ROBERT, b Carlinville, Ill, Dec 1, 44; m 68; c 1. SONAR SIGNAL PROCESSING, ADAPTIVE SIGNAL PROCESSING. *Educ:* Macmurray Col, BA, 66; Mich State Univ, MS, 68; Univ Nebr, Lincoln, PhD(physics), 72. *Prof Exp:* Asst physics, Mich State Univ, 66-68; asst, Univ Nebr, Lincoln, 68-73, res assoc & instr optics, 73-74; physicist, Signal Processing Underwater Commun, Naval Undersea Ctr, 74-77, SUPVRY PHYSICIST, NAVAL OCEAN SYSTS CTR, 77- *Concurrent Pos:* Prin investr progs acoust detection, tracking & localiation & mem nat anal group, Navy Mobile Sonar Technol Comt. *Mem:* Inst Elec & Electronic Engrs. *Res:* Adaptive signal processing techniques; underwater acoustic communications; tracking and localization techniques; digital signal processing. *Mailing Add:* Code 6322 Naval Ocean Systs Ctr San Diego CA 92152

ZEIDMAN, BENJAMIN, b New York, NY, Oct 6, 31; m 56, 72; c 3. NUCLEAR PHYSICS. *Educ:* City Col New York, BS, 52; Washington Univ, PhD, 57. *Prof Exp:* SR PHYSICIST, ARGONNE NAT LAB, 57- *Concurrent Pos:* Ford Found fel, Niels Bohr Inst, Copenhagen, Denmark, 63-64; vis prof, State Univ NY, Stonybrook, 72, Max Plank Inst, Heidelberg, Ger, 75-76. *Honors & Awards:* Sr Scientist Awardee, Alexander von Humboldt Found, 75. *Mem:* AAAS; Am Phys Soc; Sigma Xi. *Res:* Intermediate energy; heavy ions; nuclear reactions, scattering, spectroscopy and structure. *Mailing Add:* Argonne Nat Lab Bldg 203 Argonne IL 60439

ZEIDMAN, IRVING, b Camden, NJ, Mar 17, 18; m 53; c 2. PATHOLOGY. *Educ:* Univ Pa, AB, 37, MD, 41. *Prof Exp:* From instr to assoc prof, 46-66, PROF PATH, SCH MED, UNIV PA, 66- *Res:* Cancer; chemical factors in cell adhesiveness; method of measuring surface area; effect of hyaluronidase on spread of tumors; transpulmonary passage of tumor cells; spread of cancer in lymphatic system. *Mailing Add:* Dept Path Sch Med Univ Pa Philadelphia PA 19104

ZEIGEL, ROBERT FRANCIS, b Washington, DC, June 22, 31; m 57, 77; c 3. VIROLOGY, CYTOLOGY. *Educ:* Eastern Ill Univ, BS, 53; Harvard Univ, AM, 55, PhD(biol), 59. *Prof Exp:* Res biologist, Nat Cancer Inst, 59-66; div rep, Roswell Park Mem Inst Div, Dept Microbiol, State Univ NY Buffalo, 70-72; ASSOC CANCER RES SCIENTIST, ROSWELL PARK MEM INST, 66-, ASSOC PROF MICROBIOL, ROSWELL PARK MEM INST DIV, STATE UNIV NY BUFFALO, 68-, REP, APP & PROM COMT, 76-, COORDR ELECTRON MICROS FACIL, CANCER CELL CTR, 80- *Concurrent Pos:* Consult, Nat Cancer Inst, 69-70; mem, Coun Asn Scientists, Roswell Park Mem Inst, 74-76. *Mem:* AAAS; Am Soc Cell Biol; Electron Micros Soc Am; Am Soc Zool. *Res:* Fine structural studies of mode of synthesis of oncogenic viral agents; search for viral agents and their association with human neoplasia; ultrastructure of picean tumors with possible environmental etiology; surface topography of maxillofacial protheses with relation to their ability to be adapted to various bio-environments. *Mailing Add:* Roswell Park Mem Inst Buffalo NY 14203

ZEIGER, ERROL, b New York, NY, Dec 11, 39; m 63; c 3. ENVIRONMENTAL MUTAGENESIS, MICROBIOLOGY. *Educ:* City Col New York, BS, 60; George Washington Univ, MS, 69, PhD(microbiol), 73. *Prof Exp:* Lab sci asst, Walter Reed Army Inst Res, 63-65; biologist, Lab Parasitic Dis, NIH, 65-66; fel, Dept Microbiol, George Washington Univ, 66-69; res microbiologist, Genetic Toxicol Br, Food & Drug Admin, 69-76; res microbiologist & head microbiol genetics sect, 76-78, RES MICROBIOLOGIST & HEAD ENVIRON MUTAGENESIS TEST DEVELOP PROG, CELLULAR & GENETIC TOXICOL BR, NAT INST ENVIRON HEALTH SCI, 78- *Mem:* AAAS; Am Soc Microbiol; Environ Mutagen Soc; Sigma Xi; Genetic Toxicol Asn. *Res:* Microbial systems for the detection of environmental mutagens; metabolism of mutagens to their genetically active forms; use of short-term test systems in evaluating the genetic toxicology of chemicals. *Mailing Add:* Cellualr & Genetic Toxicol Br NIEHS PO Box 12233 Research Triangle Park NC 27709

ZEIGER, H PAUL, b Niagara Falls, NY, Nov 12, 36; m 59; c 3. COMPUTER SCIENCE. *Educ:* Mass Inst Technol, SB, 58, SM, 60, PhD(elec eng), 64. *Prof Exp:* Ford Found fel elec eng, Mass Inst Technol, 64-65; asst prof elec eng, Univ BC, 65-66; asst prof aerospace eng, 66-71, ASSOC PROF COMPUT SCI, UNIV COLO, BOULDER, 71-, CHMN DEPT, 78- *Res:* Processing and transmission of information; automatic control; applied abstract algebra; art of computer programming; software engineering; formal methods for programmers. *Mailing Add:* Dept of Comput Sci Univ of Colo Boulder CO 80309

ZEIGER, HERBERT J, b Bronx, NY, Mar 16, 25; m 54; c 3. PHYSICS. *Educ:* City Col New York, BS, 44; Columbia Univ, MA, 48, PhD, 52. *Prof Exp:* Union Carbide & Carbon Corp fel, Columbia Univ, 52-53; RES PHYSICIST, LINCOLN LAB, MASS INST TECHNOL, 53- *Honors & Awards:* Townes Medal, Optical Soc Am, 81. *Mem:* Fel Am Phys Soc. *Res:* Solid state and molecular physics; masers and lasers. *Mailing Add:* 167 Pond Brook Rd Chestnut Hill MA 02167

ZEIGER, WILLIAM NATHANIEL, b Highland Park, Mich, Sept 7, 46; m 73. NATURAL PRODUCTS CHEMISTRY. *Educ:* Wayne State Univ, BA, 69; Univ Pa, PhD(chem), 72. *Prof Exp:* NIH trainee, 72-74, ASST MEM, MONELL CHEM SENSES CTR, 72- *Mem:* Am Chem Soc. *Res:* Food and flavor chemistry. *Mailing Add:* McCormick & Co Inc McCormick/Stange Flavor Div Hunt Valley MD 21031

ZEIGLER, A(LFRED) G(EYER), b Chambersburg, Pa, Nov 12, 23; m 54; c 2. INORGANIC CHEMISTRY, CHEMICAL ENGINEERING. *Educ:* Bucknell Univ, BSChE, 44; Pa State Univ, cert, 50. *Prof Exp:* Chief chem engr, Cochrane Corp, 46-52; tech dir, Am Water Softener Co, 52-63, gen mgr, 58-63, pres, 60-63, MGR, WATER CONDITIONING DIV, ENVIREX, INC, DIV, REXNORD CO, VALLEY FORGE, 63- *Concurrent Pos:* Consult, Elec Boat Div, Gen Dynamics Corp. *Mem:* Am Soc Testing & Mat; Am Chem Soc; Nat Asn Corrosion Engrs. *Res:* Industrial water conditioning; industrial waste treatment; decontamination of radioactive wastes. *Mailing Add:* RD 1 (303) Malvern PA 19355

ZEIGLER, JOHN MARTIN, b Greensburg, Ind, Dec 5, 51. ORGANOSILION CHEMISTRY, PHYSICAL ORGANIC CHEMISTRY. *Educ:* Wabash Col, BA, 74; Univ Ill, Urbana, PhD(org chem), 79. *Prof Exp:* Res chemist, Am Cyanamid Co, 79-81; MEM TECH STAFF, SANDIA NAT LABS, 81- *Mem:* Am Chem Soc; Sigma Xi; AAAS. *Res:* Synthesis, characterization and physical and electronic properties of organopolysilaus-a new class of highly promising materials; organometallic and synthetic organic chemistry. *Mailing Add:* Sandia Nat Labs Orgn 5811 Bldg 805 PO Box 5800 Albuquerque NM 87185

ZEIGLER, JOHN MILTON, b St Augustine, Fla, May 23, 22; m 46; c 3. GEOLOGY. *Educ:* Univ Colo, BA, 47; Harvard Univ, PhD(geol), 54. *Prof Exp:* Oil geologist, Calif Co, 48-50; assoc scientist, Woods Hole Oceanog Inst, 54-67; prof marine sci, Univ PR, Mayaguez, 67-71; assoc prof marine sci, Univ Va, 71-77; PROF MARINE SCI, COL WILLIAM & MARY, 71-, ASSOC DEAN, SCH MARINE SCI; ASST DIR & HEAD PHYS SCI, VA INST MARINE SCI, 71- *Concurrent Pos:* Lectr, Univ Chicago, 64-77; consult coastal processes & usage; mem bd trustees, Chesapeake Bay Consortium; assoc dir, Va Inst Marine Sci. *Res:* Beach processes; shallow water oceanography; coastal planning and management. *Mailing Add:* Va Inst of Marine Sci Gloucester Point VA 23062

ZEIGLER, ROYAL KEITH, b Kans, Dec 3, 19; m 43; c 4. MATHEMATICS, APPLIED STATISTICS. *Educ:* Ft Hays Kans State Col, BS, 41; Univ Nev, MS, 46; Univ Iowa, PhD(math statist), 49. *Prof Exp:* Assoc prof math, Bradley Univ, 49-51; statistician, AEC, 51-52; statistician, Theoret Physics Div, Los Alamos Sci Lab, 52-67, group leader statist serv, 68-75, mem staff, 75-79; CONSULT, 80- *Mem:* Fel AAAS; fel Am Statist Asn. *Res:* Sampling theory. *Mailing Add:* 165 Chamisa St Los Alamos NM 87544

ZEIKUS, J GREGORY, b Rahway, NJ, Oct 2, 45; m 67; c 2. MICROBIOLOGY. *Educ:* Univ SFla, BA, 67; Ind Univ, Bloomington, MA, 68, PhD(microbiol), 70. *Prof Exp:* NIH fel microbiol, Univ Ill, Champaign, 70-72; asst prof, 72-77, assoc prof, 77-80, PROF BACT, UNIV WIS-MADISON, 80- *Concurrent Pos:* Vis scientist & fel, Univ Marburg, Germany, 76-77 & Inst Pasteur, France, 81-82. *Mem:* Sigma Xi; Am Soc Microbiol; AAAS. *Res:* Microbial physiology and ecology; anaerobic bacterial metabolism; microbial methance formation; industrial fermentations. *Mailing Add:* Dept of Bact Univ of Wis Madison WI 53705

ZEILIK, MICHAEL, b Bridgeport, Conn, Sept 26, 46. INFRARED ASTRONOMY, BINARY STARS. *Educ:* Princeton Univ, BA, 68; Harvard Univ, MA, 69, PhD(astron), 75. *Prof Exp:* Instr astron, Southern Conn State Col, 69-72; instr astron, Harvard Univ, 74-75; asst prof, 75-79, ASSOC PROF ASTRON, UNIV NMEX, 79- *Concurrent Pos:* Vis assoc prof astron, Univ Calif, Berkeley, 80; prin investr, grant Res Corp & educ grant NSF, 80- *Honors & Awards:* Harlow Shapley Lectr, Am Astron Soc, 76. *Mem:* Int Astron Union; Royal Astron Soc; Am Astron Soc; Am Asn Physics Teachers; Am Asn Astron Educ. *Res:* Infrared photometry and polarimetry of star-formation regions in the Milky Way Galaxy; visual and infrared observations of peculiar binary star systems. *Mailing Add:* Dept Physics & Astron Univ NMex Albuquerque NM 87131

ZEINER, FREDERICK NEYER, b Finley, NDak, Mar 20, 17; m 42. ZOOLOGY. *Educ:* Univ Denver, BS, 38; Ind Univ, PhD(zool), 42. *Prof Exp:* Asst zool, Ind Univ, 38-40; from asst prof to prof, 46-74, EMER PROF ZOOL, UNIV DENVER, 74- *Concurrent Pos:* Res consult, Martin Co, 59 & 61; mem gov bd, Am Inst Biol Sci, 67-71. *Mem:* AAAS; Am Inst Biol Sci; Sigma Xi. *Res:* Pituitary-ovarian relationships during pregnancy; space physiology. *Mailing Add:* 1417 SElizabeth St Denver CO 80210

ZEINER, HELEN MARSH, b Big Timber, Mont, Oct 5, 12; m 42. BOTANY, ECOLOGY. *Educ:* Western Reserve Univ, AB, 33, MA, 35; Ind Univ, PhD, 44. *Prof Exp:* Teacher high sch, Ohio, 35-38; lectr bot, Ind Univ, 38-42; asst prof, Univ Denver, 46-49 & 58-65; CONSULT, DENVER BOT GARDENS, 65-, HON CUR HERBARIUM, 72- *Res:* Ecology; conservation. *Mailing Add:* 1417 SElizabeth St Denver CO 80210

ZEITLIN, JOEL LOEB, b Los Angeles, Calif, July 9, 42; m 72. MATHEMATICS. *Educ:* Univ Calif, Los Angeles, BA, 63, MA, 66, PhD(math), 69. *Prof Exp:* Asst prof math, Wash Univ, 69-72; prof, Cath Univ Valparaiso, 72-73; assoc prof, 73-80, PROF MATH, CALIF STATE UNIV, NORTHRIDGE, 80- *Concurrent Pos:* Fulbright Hays scholar, 72-73. *Mem:* Math Asn Am; Am Math Soc. *Res:* Lie groups; representation theory; special functions; geometry. *Mailing Add:* Dept of Math Calif State Univ Northridge CA 91324

ZEITZ, LOUIS, b Lakewood, NJ, Jan 22, 22; m 46; c 2. BIOPHYSICS, PHYSICS. *Educ:* Univ Calif, Berkeley, AB, 48; Stanford Univ, PhD(biophys), 62. *Prof Exp:* Res asst x-ray instrumentation, Appl Res Labs, Montrose, Calif, 51-52, res physicist, 52-56; res assoc physics, Univ Redlands, 56-58; res assoc, Biophys Lab, Stanford Univ, 58-59; res assoc, 62-63, ASSOC MEM BIOPHYS DIV, SLOAN-KETTERING INST, 69-; ASSOC PROF, SLOAN-KETTERING DIV, GRAD SCH MED, CORNELL UNIV, 69- *Concurrent Pos:* Nat Inst Child Health & Develop res grant, Sloan-Kettering Inst, 65-67; Dept Energy & NIH-Nat Cancer Inst grants. *Mem:* AAAS; Biophys Soc; Am Phys Soc; Radiation Res Soc; NY Acad Sci. *Res:* X-ray spectrochemical analysis; trace elements in living systems; mechanisms of radiation effects on cell development; in vivo bone mineral content measurement; radiological physics. *Mailing Add:* Biophys Div Sloan-Kettering Inst 410 E 68th St New York NY 10021

ZEIZEL, A(RTHUR) J(OHN), b Waterbury, Conn, Aug 17, 33; m 70. GEOLOGY, ENVIRONMENTAL SCIENCE. *Educ:* Univ Conn, BA, 56; Univ Ill, MS, 59, PhD(geol), 60. *Prof Exp:* Planning requirements officer, Off Metrop Develop, Dept Housing & Urban Develop, 67-68, dir, Dept Water Resources Res, 68-72, environ scientist, Off Asst Secy for Res & Technol, 72-79; PROG MGR WATER HAZARDS, FED EMER MGT AGENCY, DC, 79- *Concurrent Pos:* Mem comt water resources res, Fed Coun Sci & Technol. *Mem:* AAAS; fel Geol Soc Am. *Res:* Urban environmental planning; natural hazard reduction; water resources management; hydrogeology. *Mailing Add:* Off of the Asst Secy for Res Urban Develop 451 Seventh St SW Washington DC 20410

ZEIZEL, EUGENE PAUL, b Waterbury, Conn, Feb 26, 42. HYDROLOGY, WATER RESOURCES. *Educ:* Fla State Univ, BS, 64; Univ Nev, MS, 67; Va Polytech Inst & State Univ, PhD(civil eng), 74. *Prof Exp:* Res asst hydrol, Desert Res Inst, 67-68; scientist water resources, Hittman Assocs Inc, 73-75; PROJ DIR WATER POLLUTION, TETON COUNTY 208 PLANNING AGENCY, 75- *Mem:* Geol Soc Am; Am Water Res Asn. *Res:* Waste treatment management planning. *Mailing Add:* PO Box 1028 Jackson WY 83001

ZELAC, RONALD EDWARD, b Chicago, Ill, Jan 22, 41; m 61; c 2. RADIOLOGICAL HEALTH, RADIOLOGICAL PHYSICS. *Educ:* Univ Ill, Urbana, BS, 62, MS, 64; Univ Mich, Ann Arbor, MS, 65; Univ Fla, PhD(environ sci), 70; Am Bd Health Physics, cert, 71. *Prof Exp:* Res asst solid state physics, Coord Sci Lab, Univ Ill, Urbana, 63-64; chief health physicist, IIT Res Inst, 65-68; asst prof radiation biol, 70-80, ASSOC PROF RADIOL, TEMPLE UNIV, 80-, DIR RADIOL HEALTH & BIOHAZARDS CONTROL, 70- *Concurrent Pos:* Radiation physicist, Mercy Med Ctr, Chicago, 67-68; consult, Wyeth Labs, Pa, 71-, Presby-Univ Pa Med Ctr, 74-, Mobil Res & Develop Corp, NJ, 77- & Metropolitan Hosp, Philadelphia, 77-; adj assoc prof radiol, Univ Pa, 80- *Mem:* Health Physics Soc; Am Asn Physicists in Med; Sigma Xi. *Res:* Radiation dosimetry and radiological safety in research and health sciences. *Mailing Add:* Radiation Safety Off Health Sci Ctr Temple Univ Philadelphia PA 19140

ZELAZNY, LUCIAN WALTER, b Bristol, Conn, May 8, 42; m 62; c 4. SOIL MINERALOGY. *Educ:* Univ Vt, BS, 64, MS, 66; Va Polytech Inst, PhD(soil chem), 70. *Prof Exp:* Asst prof soils & asst soil chemist, Univ Fla, 70-75; ASSOC PROF SOIL MINERAL, VA POLYTECH INST & STATE UNIV, 75- *Concurrent Pos:* Nat Acad Sci-Nat Res Coun grant. *Mem:* Am Soc Agron; Clay Mineral Soc; AAAS. *Res:* The effect of deicing compounds on vegetation and water supplies; chemical, physical and mineralogical analysis of soils. *Mailing Add:* Dept of Agron Smyth Hall Va Polytech Inst & State Univ Blacksburg VA 24061

ZELBY, LEON W, b Sosnowiec, Poland, Mar 26, 25; US citizen; m 54; c 2. ELECTRICAL ENGINEERING, PHYSICS. *Educ:* Univ Pa, BS, 56, PhD(elec eng & physics), 61; Calif Inst Technol, MS, 57. *Prof Exp:* Res engr physics, RCA, NJ, 59-61; PROF ELEC ENG, UNIV OKLA, 67- *Concurrent Pos:* Consol Electrodyn Corp fel, Calif Inst Technol, 56-57; Minn-Honeywell Regulator Co fel, Univ Pa, 57-58, Harrison fel, 58-59; consult, RCA, 61-67 & Moore Sch Elec Eng, Univ Pa, 62-67; chief scientist energy anal, Inst Energy Anal, Oak Ridge, 75-76. *Mem:* Franklin Inst; AAAS; Inst Elec & Electronics Engrs; Am Inst Physics; Am Soc Eng Educ. *Res:* Energy analysis and policy; biomedical instrumentation; electromagnetic wave propagation; plasma diagnostics; effects of microwaves on organisms. *Mailing Add:* 1009 Whispering Pines Norman OK 73069

ZELDES, HENRY, b New Britain, Conn, June 11, 21; m 49; c 3. PHYSICAL CHEMISTRY. *Educ:* Yale Univ, BS, 42, MS, 44, PhD(phys chem), 47. *Prof Exp:* Res chemist, Sam Labs, Columbia Univ, 44-45, Carbide & Carbon Chem Corp, 45-46 & Clinton Labs, Monsanto Chem Corp, Tenn, 47; RES CHEMIST, OAK RIDGE NAT LAB, UNION CARBIDE CHEM CO, 48- *Mem:* Am Chem Soc; Am Phys Soc. *Res:* Radiochemistry; thermodynamics; electrolyte chemistry; nuclear and electron spin resonance. *Mailing Add:* 111 Lewis Lane Oak Ridge TN 37830

ZELDIN, ARKADY N, b Moscow, USSR, Aug 8, 39; m 67; c 1. POLYMER SCIENCE. *Educ:* Moscow Chem Technol Inst, MS, 62; Moscow Polytech Inst, PhD(chem eng), 70. *Prof Exp:* Engr polymer chem, All-Union Res Inst Petrol Refining, 62-67; scientist chem eng, All-Union Polytech Inst, 70-73; sr scientist chem, Sci Inst Fertilizers, 73-75; tech mgr plastics, Gibraltar Chem & Plastics Inc, 76; ASSOC CHEM ENGR POLYMER SCI, BROOKHAVEN NAT LAB, 76- *Res:* Polymer-concrete for high temperature and corrosion applications; high temperature polymer and copolymer systems for use in combination with inorganic compounds in geothermal applications. *Mailing Add:* Bldg 526 Brookhaven Nat Lab Upton NY 11973

ZELDIN, MARTEL, b New York, NY, Aug 11, 37; m 58; c 4. POLYMER CHEMISTRY, INORGANIC CHEMISTRY. *Educ:* Queens Col, NY, BS, 59; Brooklyn Col, MA, 62; Pa State Univ, PhD(chem), 66. *Prof Exp:* Chemist, Interchem Corp, 60-62; proj scientist, Union Carbide Corp, 66-68; asst prof chem, Polytech Inst Brooklyn, 68-72, assoc prof, 72-80; PROF & CHMN, IND UNIV & PURDUE UNIV, 81- *Concurrent Pos:* Consult, 72- *Mem:* Am Chem Soc. *Res:* inorganic and organometallic polymers; polymer degradation studies. *Mailing Add:* Dept of Chem Polytech Inst Brooklyn 333 Jay St Brooklyn NY 11201

ZELDIN, MICHAEL HERMEN, b Philadelphia, Pa, Mar 25, 38; m 61; c 3. CELL BIOLOGY, VISUAL PHYSIOLOGY. *Educ:* Franklin & Marshall Col, BS, 59; Temple Univ, MA, 61, PhD(biol), 65. *Prof Exp:* Res assoc biol, Brandeis Univ, 65-67; asst prof, Tufts Univ, 67-74; SR RES FEL, HARVARD UNIV, 74- *Concurrent Pos:* NIH fel, 65-67. *Mem:* AAAS; Am Chem Soc; Asn Res Vision & Ophthal. *Res:* Biochemistry and electrophysiology of the vertebrate retina; neurophysiology. structure and function of membranes. *Mailing Add:* 2 Clinton St No 37 Cambridge MA 02139

ZELEN, MARVIN, b New York, NY, June 21, 27; m 50; c 2. BIOMETRY, MATHEMATICAL STATISTICS. *Educ:* City Col New York, BS, 49; Univ NC, MA, 51; Am Univ, PhD(statist), 57. *Prof Exp:* Mathematician, Nat Bur Standards, 52-61; head math statist & appl math sect, Nat Cancer Inst, 63-67; prof statist, State Univ NY Buffalo, 67-77, dir statist lab, 71-77; PROF STATIST SCI, SIDNEY FARBER CANCER INST, SCH PUB HEALTH, HARVARD UNIV, 77-, CHMN, DEPT BIOSTATIST, 81- *Concurrent Pos:* Vis assoc prof, Univ Calif, Berkeley, 58; assoc prof math, Univ Md, 60-61; permanent mem math res ctr, Univ Wis, 60-63; sr Fulbright scholar, Imp Col & Sch Hyg & Trop Med, Univ London, 65-66; consult, Nat Cancer Inst. *Mem:* Biomet Soc; Am Statist Asn; Inst Math Statist; Royal Statist Soc; Am Soc Clin Oncol. *Res:* Probability and mathematical statistics; model building in biomedical sciences; statistical planning of scientific experiments; clinical trials in cancer. *Mailing Add:* Harvard Sch Pub Health 44 Binney St Boston MA 02115

ZELENKA, JERRY STEPHEN, b Cleveland, Ohio, Jan 27, 36; m 58; c 3. ELECTRONIC ENGINEERING, OPTICS. *Educ:* Univ Mich, Ann Arbor, BS, 58, MS, 59, PhD(elec eng), 66. *Prof Exp:* Engr, Res Div, Bendix Corp, 59-61; res engr radar & optics, Univ Mich, Ann Arbor, 61-72; res engr, Environ Res Inst Mich, 72-76; sr scientist, 76-80, ASST VPRES, SCI APPLN INC, 80- *Concurrent Pos:* Lab instr, Univ Mich, Ann Arbor, 58-59, lectr, 72; consult, Westinghouse Elec Corp, 69-72, Gen Motors Corp & IBM Corp, 71-76. *Honors & Awards:* M Barry Carlton Award, Sigma Xi. *Mem:* Inst Elec & Electronics Engrs; Optical Soc Am. *Res:* Systems analysis pertaining to coherent radars and to coherent optical processors. *Mailing Add:* Sci Appln Inc Suite A-214 Tucson AZ 85711

ZELENKA, PEGGY SUE, b Joplin, Mo, Oct 4, 42; m 66. DEVELOPMENTAL BIOLOGY. *Educ:* Rice Univ, BA, 64; Johns Hopkins Univ, PhD(biophys), 71. *Prof Exp:* Fel pediat, Johns Hopkins Sch Med, 71-72; staff fel develop biol, Nat Inst Child Health & Human Develop, 72-75; sr staff fel develop biol, 75-77, GENETICIST, NAT EYE INST, 77- *Mem:* Asn Res Vision & Ophthal; AAAS. *Res:* Biochemical mechanisms of cellular differentiation during embryonic development; specifically those changes occurring in membranes of developing embryonic chick lenses. *Mailing Add:* Nat Eye Inst Bldg 6 Rm 212 Bethesda MD 20014

ZELENY, RICHARD A(LAN), chemical engineering, deceased

ZELENY, WILLIAM BARDWELL, b Minneapolis, Minn, Mar 14, 34; m 60; c 2. THEORETICAL PHYSICS. *Educ:* Univ Md, BS, 56; Syracuse Univ, MS, 58, PhD(physics), 60. *Prof Exp:* Lectr physics, Univ Sydney, 60-62; asst prof, 62-65, ASSOC PROF PHYSICS, NAVAL POSTGRAD SCH, 65- *Concurrent Pos:* Consult, Data Dynamics, Inc, 65-67. *Mem:* Sigma Xi; Am Phys Soc. *Res:* Quantum field theory. *Mailing Add:* Dept Physics & Chem Naval Postgrad Sch Monterey CA 93940

ZELEZNICK, LOWELL D, b Milwaukee, Wis, Feb 1, 35; m 61; c 2. IMMUNOLOGY, ALLERGY. *Educ:* Univ Ill, Chicago, BS, 56, PhD(biochem), 61. *Prof Exp:* Res assoc biochem, Upjohn Co, 64-68; head biochem sect, 68-72, dir allergy dept, Alcon Labs Inc, 72-77; vpres sci & technol, Aerwey Labs, Inc, 77-78; MEM STAFF, CORP DEVELOP, ALLERGAN, 78- *Concurrent Pos:* Ciba fel microbiol, Ciba Pharmaceut Co, 60-63; fel molecular biol, Albert Einstein Col Med, 63-64; USPHS fel, 64-65; adj prof, Tex Christian Univ. *Mem:* AAAS; Am Chem Soc; Am Soc Biol Chem; Am Acad Allergy. *Res:* Drug metabolism; biosynthesis and structure of lipopolysaccharides and bacterial cell walls; immunology-allergy research; quality control and product development. *Mailing Add:* Corp Develop 2525 Dupont Dr Irvine CA 92713

ZELEZNIK, PAULINE, b Chicago, Ill, Jan 9, 29. INORGANIC CHEMISTRY, PHYSICAL CHEMISTRY. *Educ:* Nazareth Col, Mich, BS, 49; Marquette Univ, MS, 55; Univ Notre Dame, PhD(chem), 64. *Prof Exp:* From instr to assoc prof, 54-77, PROF CHEM, NAZARETH COL, 77- *Mem:* Sigma Xi; Am Chem Soc. *Res:* Radiation chemistry; bioinorganic chemistry. *Mailing Add:* Dept of Chem Nazareth Col Nazareth MI 49074

ZELEZNY, WILLIAM FRANCIS, b Rollins, Mont, Sept 5, 18; m 49. PHYSICAL CHEMISTRY. *Educ:* Mont State Col, BS, 40; Mont Sch Mines, MS, 41; Univ Iowa, PhD(phys chem), 51. *Prof Exp:* Chemist, Anaconda Copper Mining Co, 41-44; instr metall & phys chem, Univ Iowa, 48-49; aeronaut res scientist, Nat Adv Comt Aeronaut, 51-54; asst metallurgist, Div Indust Res, State Col Wash, 54-57; sr scientist, Atomic Energy Div, Phillips Petrol Co, Idaho, 57-66; asst metallurgist, Idaho Nuclear Corp, 66-70; mem staff, Los Alamos Sci Lab, 70-80; RETIRED. *Mem:* Am Chem Soc; Am Soc Metals; Am Inst Mining, Metall & Petrol Eng. *Res:* Kinetics of reaction at high temperatures; x-ray diffraction and spectroscopy; crystal structure; microprobe analysis of irradiated nuclear fuels. *Mailing Add:* PO Box 37 Rollins MT 59931

ZELIGMAN, ISRAEL, b Baltimore, Md, July 24, 13; m 43; c 3. DERMATOLOGY. *Educ:* Johns Hopkins Univ, AB, 33; Univ Md, MD, 37; Columbia Univ, MedScD, 42. *Prof Exp:* From instr to asst prof dermat, Univ Md, 46-56; asst, 46-50, from instr to asst prof, 50-63, ASSOC PROF DERMAT, SCH MED, JOHNS HOPKINS UNIV, 63- *Concurrent Pos:* Pvt pract. *Mem:* Soc Invest Dermat; AMA; Am Acad Dermat; Am Dermat Asn. *Res:* Relationship of porphyrins to dermatoses; dermalogic allergy. *Mailing Add:* 101 W Read St Baltimore MD 21201

ZELINSKI, ROBERT PAUL, b Chicago, Ill, Jan 13, 20; m 45; c 4. POLYMER CHEMISTRY, RUBBER CHEMISTRY. *Educ:* DePaul Univ, BS, 41; Northwestern Univ, PhD(org chem), 45. *Prof Exp:* Asst, Northwestern Univ, 41-42; from instr to prof chem & chmn dept, DePaul Univ, 43-55; group leader, Rubber Synthesis Br, 55-61, from sect mgr to mgr, 61-75, MGR, ENG PLASTICS BR, RES DIV, PHILLIPS PETROL CO, 75- *Concurrent Pos:* Asst, Northwestern Univ, 43-44. *Mem:* Am Chem Soc; Sigma Xi; Soc Plastics Engrs. *Res:* Synthesis of plastics and rubbers. *Mailing Add:* Rte 1 Box 517A Bartlesville OK 74003

ZELINSKY, DANIEL, b Chicago, Ill, Nov 22, 22; m 45; c 3. ALGEBRA. *Educ:* Univ Chicago, SB, 41, SM, 43, PhD(math), 46. *Prof Exp:* Instr math, Univ Chicago, 43-44; asst, Appl Math Group, Columbia Univ, 44-45; Nat Res Coun fel, Univ Chicago, 46, instr math, 46-47; Nat Res Coun fel, Inst Advan Study, 47-49; from asst prof to assoc prof, 49-60, chmn dept, 75-78, PROF MATH, NORTHWESTERN UNIV, EVANSTON, 60- *Concurrent Pos:* Mem exec comt, Nat Res Coun, 66-67; ed jour, Am Math Soc, 61-64. *Mem:* AAAS; Am Math Soc; Math Asn Am. *Res:* Rings; homological algebra. *Mailing Add:* Dept of Math Northwestern Univ Evanston IL 60201

ZELITCH, ISRAEL, b Philadelphia, Pa, June 18, 24; m 45; c 3. BIOCHEMISTRY, PLANT PHYSIOLOGY. *Educ:* Pa State Univ, BS, 47, MS, 48; Univ Wis, PhD(biochem), 51. *Prof Exp:* Nat Res Coun fel, Col Med, NY Univ-Bellevue Med Ctr, 51-52; asst biochemist, 52-54, assoc biochemist, 54-60, biochemist, 60-74, S W JOHNSON DISTINGUISHED SCIENTIST, CONN AGR EXP STA, 74-, HEAD, DEPT BIOCHEM & GENETICS, 63- . *Concurrent Pos:* Lectr & adj prof, Yale Univ, 58-; Guggenheim fel, Oxford Univ, 60; panel mem, NSF, 62-64 & Physiol Chem Study Sect, NIH, 66-70; Regents lectr, Univ Calif, Riverside, 71; Fulbright distinguished prof, Yugoslavia, 81. *Mem:* Am Chem Soc; Am Soc Biol Chem; Am Soc Plant Physiol; fel Am Acad Arts & Sci. *Res:* Plant biochemistry; photosynthesis; respiration; plant productivity. *Mailing Add:* Dept Biochem & Genetics Conn Agr Exp Sta PO Box 1106 New Haven CT 06504

ZELL, HOWARD CHARLES, b Philadelphia, Pa, Feb 11, 22; m 52. ORGANIC CHEMISTRY. *Educ:* St Joseph's Col, BS, 43; Univ Del, MS, 51; Univ Pa, PhD(org chem), 64. *Prof Exp:* Chemist, Publicker Industs, Inc, 43-47; res assoc org chem, Merck Sharp & Dohme Res Lab, 48-65; assoc scientist, Ethicon, Inc, 65-67, sr scientist, 67-69, prin scientist, 69-74; chemist, 74-81, SUPVY CHEMIST, FOOD & DRUG ADMIN, 81- *Mem:* AAAS; Am Chem Soc; Sigma Xi; NY Acad Sci; Pharm Asn Am. *Res:* Medicinal and polymer chemistry. *Mailing Add:* Food & Drug Admin HFD-534 Rockville MD 20857

ZELLER, ALBERT FONTENOT, b Oakland, Calif, Jan 10, 47; m 72; c 1. NUCLEAR PHYSICS, NUCLEAR CHEMISTRY. *Educ:* Univ Wash, BA, 71; Fla State Univ, MS, 73, PhD(nuclear chem), 74. *Prof Exp:* Res assoc nuclear physics, Fla State Univ, 74-75; res fel, Dept Nuclear Physics,

Australian Nat Univ, 75-78; res assoc nuclear physics, Cyclotron Inst, Tex A&M Univ, 78-79; SPECIALIST NUCLEAR PHYS, NAT SUPERCONDUCTING CYCLOTRON LAB, MICH STATE UNIV, 79- *Concurrent Pos:* Vis asst prof physics, Tex A&M Univ, 79- *Mem:* Am Phys Soc. *Res:* Heavy ion induced reactions. *Mailing Add:* Nat Superconducting Cycoltron Lab Mich State Univ East Lansing MI 48824

ZELLER, EDWARD JACOB, b Peoria, Ill, Nov 6, 25. GEOCHEMISTRY. *Educ:* Univ Ill, AB, 46; Univ Kans, MA, 48; Univ Wis, PhD(geol), 51. *Prof Exp:* Asst, State Geol Surv, Ill, 45-46; asst instr gen geol, Univ Kans, 45-46; proj assoc, USAEC contract, Wis, 51-56; prof geol & prin investr, USAEC res contract, 56-69, PROF GEOL, PHYSICS & ASTRON, UNIV KANS, 69- *Concurrent Pos:* Mem NSF US Antarctic Res Prog, 59-63; NSF sr fel, Physics Inst, Univ Berne, 60-61; guest scientist, Brookhaven Nat Lab, 65-66; US Air Force res contract, 67-68; prin investr, NASA contract, 72 & Oak Ridge Nat Lab contract, 72; del, 19th & 20th Int Geol Cong; Antarctic Int Radiomet Surv, NSF grant, 75-; co-dir, South Polar Ice Chem Proj, NSF grant, 78- *Mem:* AAAS; Geol Soc Am; Geochem Soc; Am Geophys Union; Int Asn Geochem & Cosmochem. *Res:* Thermoluminescence and electron spin resonance in geologic materials; radiation effects from nuclear waste; chemical interactions of fast protons in solid targets; lunar and asteroidal weathering; aerosols and planetary albedo; paleoclimatology. *Mailing Add:* Space Technol Labs Univ of Kans 2291 Irving Hill Dr-Campus W Lawrence KS 66044

ZELLER, FRANK JACOB, b Chicago, Ill, Dec 6, 27; m 52; c 3. REPRODUCTIVE ENDOCRINOLOGY. *Educ:* Univ Ill, BS, 51, MS, 52; Ind Univ, PhD(zool), 57. *Prof Exp:* Instr zool, Bryan Col, 52-53; asst, 53-56, res assoc, 56-57, from instr to assoc prof, 57-76, PROF ZOOL, IND UNIV, BLOOMINGTON, 76- *Mem:* Endocrine Soc; Soc Study Reproduction. *Res:* Reproduction in birds; effects of gonadotropins and sex hormones on the anterior pituitary gland and gonads. *Mailing Add:* Dept of Biol Ind Univ Bloomington IN 47401

ZELLER, MARY CLAUDIA, b Mansfield, Ohio, Dec 1, 10. MATHEMATICS. *Educ:* DePaul Univ, AB, 35; Univ Mich, MA, 40, PhD(math), 44. *Prof Exp:* From instr to asst prof math, Col St Francis, Ill, 41-50, dean, 53-69, assoc dir three year degree prog, 72-73, prof math, 50-76, dir grants & spec proj, 75-76, emer prof, 76-77. *Concurrent Pos:* Consult, Dept Higher Educ, Nat Cath Educ Asn, 71-72. *Mailing Add:* 4711 NE 28 Ave Ft Lauderdale FL 33308

ZELLER, MICHAEL EDWARD, b San Francisco, Calif, Oct 8, 39; m 60; c 2. HIGH ENERGY PHYSICS. *Educ:* Stanford Univ, BS, 61; Univ Calif, Los Angeles, MS, 63, PhD(physics), 68. *Prof Exp:* Res asst physics, Univ Calif, Los Angeles, 63-68, res fel, 68-69; from instr to asst prof, 69-75, ASSOC PROF PHYSICS, YALE UNIV, 75- *Mem:* NY Acad Sci; Am Phys Soc. *Res:* Polarization phenomena in the kaon-nucleon interaction; high energy, strong and weak interaction polarization phenomena. *Mailing Add:* J W Gibbs Lab Yale Univ New Haven CT 06520

ZELLEY, WALTER GAUNTT, b Camden, NJ, Oct 1, 21; m 46; c 3. ELECTROCHEMISTRY. *Educ:* Univ Pa, BS, 42. *Prof Exp:* Chemist, Lake Ont Ord Works, 42-43; chemist, Burlington Reduction Works, 43-44, res engr, Res Lab, 44-65, sr scientist, 65-67, eng assoc, 67-71, SECT HEAD, ALCOA TECH CTR, ALUMINUM CO AM, 71- *Mem:* Am Electroplaters Soc; Sigma Xi; Tech Asn Graphic Arts. *Res:* Chemical and electrochemical surface finishing of aluminum; application of aluminum in the graphic arts and packaging; organic coatings for aluminum. *Mailing Add:* Alcoa Tech Ctr Alcoa Center PA 15069

ZELLMER, DAVID LOUIS, b Portland, Ore, June 12, 42; m 66. ANALYTICAL CHEMISTRY. *Educ:* Univ Mich, BSChem, 64; Univ Ill, MS, 66, PhD(anal chem), 69. *Prof Exp:* From asst prof to assoc prof, 69-77, PROF CHEM, CALIF STATE UNIV, FRESNO, 77- *Mem:* Am Chem Soc; Meteoritical Soc. *Res:* Application of radiochemical and electrochemical techniques to the study of semiconducting electrode materials; analysis of extraterrestrial materials; instrumentation automation; computer assisted instruction. *Mailing Add:* Dept of Chem Calif State Univ Fresno CA 93740

ZELLNER, BENJAMIN HOLMES, b Forsyth, Ga, Apr 16, 42; m; c 3. ASTRONOMY. *Educ:* Ga Inst Technol, BS, 64; Univ Ariz, PhD(astron), 70. *Prof Exp:* Res assoc, Lunar & Planetary Lab, 70-76, res fel, 76-78, ASSOC RES PROF, UNIV ARIZ, 78- *Concurrent Pos:* Res fel, Observ Paris, Meudon, France, 72-73. *Mem:* Int Astron Union; Am Astron Soc. *Res:* Astronomical polarimetry; light scattering by circumstellar and interstellar material; physical properties of minor planets. *Mailing Add:* 1715 N Wagon Wheel Pl Tucson AZ 85705

ZELLNER, CARL NAEHER, b Brooklyn, NY, Mar 4, 10; m 36; c 1. ORGANIC CHEMISTRY. *Educ:* Princeton Univ, AB, 31, MA, 32, PhD(org chem), 34. *Prof Exp:* Res chemist, Merck & Co, Inc, 34-37, Tidewater Assoc Oil Co, 37-55 & Celanese Corp, NJ, 55-68; CHEM CONSULT, 68- *Mem:* AAAS; Am Chem Soc. *Res:* Conversion of petroleum hydrocarbons to industrial chemicals; exploratory polymer research. *Mailing Add:* Box 41 RD 2 River Rd New Hope PA 18938

ZELLWEGER, HANS ULRICH, b Lugano, Switz, June 19, 09; m 40; c 2. PEDIATRICS. *Educ:* Univ Zurich, MD, 34. *Hon Degrees:* MD, Univ Geneva. *Prof Exp:* Resident, Kanton Hosp, Lucerne, Switz, 34-37; mem staff, Albert Schweitzer Hosp, Lambarene, Gabun, 37-39; asst prof & resident pediat, Children's Hosp, Zurich, 40-51; prof & head dept, Am Univ Beirut, 51-57 & 58-59; res prof, 57-58, PROF PEDIAT, COL MED, UNIV IOWA, 59- *Concurrent Pos:* Gen secy, Int Cong Pediat, Zurich, 50; clin dir, Regional Genetic Consult Serv, Iowa, 77- *Mem:* Am Acad Neurol; Am Acad Cerebral Palsey (pres, 74-75); Am Pediat Soc; hon mem Austrian Pediat Soc; hon mem Swiss Pediat Soc. *Res:* Pediatric neurology; genetics; cytogenetics. *Mailing Add:* Dept Pediat Univ Hosps Iowa City IA 52240

ZELMAN, ALLEN, b Los Angeles, Calif, Feb 12, 38; m 72; c 2. BIOPHYSICS, BIOENGINEERING. *Educ:* Univ Calif, Berkeley, BA, 64, PhD(biophys), 71. *Prof Exp:* Asst prof biophys, Meharry Med Col, 72-75; asst prof biophys & biomed eng, 75-78, ASSOC PROF BIOPHYS & BIOMED ENG, RENSSELAER POLYTECH INST, 78-, DIR, MEMBRANE TRANSP LAB, 78- *Mem:* Biophys Soc; Am Inst Chem Engrs; Am Soc Artificial Internal Organs; Bioeng Soc; Filtration Soc. *Res:* Membrane technology in food processing, separation processes, water purification and blood banking; theoretical and experimental characterization & membrane transport processes. *Mailing Add:* Ctr for Bioeng Rensselaer Polytech Inst Troy NY 12181

ZELMANOWITZ, JULIUS MARTIN, b New York, NY, Feb 20, 41; m 62; c 1. MATHEMATICS, ALGEBRA. *Educ:* Harvard Univ, AB, 62; Univ Wis-Madison, MS, 63, PhD(math), 66. *Prof Exp:* Instr math, Univ Wis-Madison, 66; asst prof, 66-73, PROF MATH, UNIV CALIF, SANTA BARBARA, 73- *Concurrent Pos:* Vis asst prof, Univ Calif, Los Angeles, 69-70, vis assoc prof, 73-74; assoc prof, Carnegie-Mellon Univ, 70-71; vis prof, Univ Rome, 77 & The Technion, 79. *Mem:* Math Asn Am; Am Math Soc. *Res:* Algebra, rings and modules. *Mailing Add:* Dept of Math Univ of Calif Santa Barbara CA 93106

ZELNIK, MELVIN, b New York, NY, Sept 22, 28; m 62; c 2. DEMOGRAPHY. *Educ:* Miami Univ, BA, 55; Princeton Univ, PhD(sociol), 59. *Prof Exp:* Instr sociol, Pa State Univ, 58-59; demographic statistician, Pop Div, US Bur Census, 59-61; res assoc, Definitive Pop Res, Princeton Univ, 61-62; asst prof sociol, Ohio State Univ, 62-64; assoc prof, 66-69, PROF DEMOGRAPHY, JOHNS HOPKINS UNIV, 69- *Concurrent Pos:* Ford Found adv, Nat Inst Public Health, Indonesia, 72-73. *Honors & Awards:* Carl S Schultz Award, Pop Sect, Am Public Health Asn, 81. *Mem:* Pop Asn Am; Int Union Sci Study Pop. *Res:* Premarital sexual activity, use or nonuse of contraception, and reproductive behavior of adolescent females and males. *Mailing Add:* Dept Pop Dynamics Sch Hygiene & Public Health Johns Hopkins Univ Baltimore MD 21205

ZELSON, PHILIP RICHARD, b Long Beach, Calif, Sept 3, 45; m 67; c 2. BIOCHEMISTRY. *Educ:* Northwestern Univ, DDS, 70; Univ Rochester, PhD(biochem), 75. *Prof Exp:* ASST PROF ORAL MED, SCH DENT MED, UNIV PA, 74- *Concurrent Pos:* Res assoc biochem taste, Monell Chem Senses Ctr, 74-75, asst mem, 75-; res assoc biochem taste, Vet Admin, 75-78, staff dentist/res, 78- *Mem:* AAAS. *Res:* Etiologic and diagnostic factors in periodontal disease. *Mailing Add:* Monell Chem Senses Ctr 3500 Market St Philadelphia PA 19104

ZELTMANN, ALFRED HOWARD, b Brooklyn, NY, Dec 25, 21; m 51; c 3. PHYSICAL CHEMISTRY. *Educ:* State Col Wash, BS, 48; Univ NMex, PhD(chem), 52, MS, 61. *Prof Exp:* STAFF MEM PHYS CHEM, LOS ALAMOS SCI LAB, UNIV CALIF, 46- *Mem:* Am Chem Soc. *Res:* Chemical kinetics; radiation chemistry; high vacuum; preparation and chemistry of gaseous hydrides; nuclear magnetic resonance; complex ions; laser spectroscopy; laser isotope separation. *Mailing Add:* 393 Venado St Los Alamos NM 87544

ZELTMANN, EUGENE W, b Chicago, Ill, June 26, 40. PHYSICAL CHEMISTRY. *Educ:* Beloit Col, BA, 62; Johns Hopkins Univ, MA, 64, PhD(chem), 67. *Prof Exp:* Nuclear chemist, Knolls Atomic Power Lab, Gen Elec Co, NY, 67-70; Alfred E Smith fel in NY State, 70-71; asst to dir power div, NY State Pub Serv Comn, 71-72; mgr environ planning, Gas Turbine Div, 72-80, MGR, OPER PLANNING, GEN ELEC CO, 80- *Mem:* Am Chem Soc. *Res:* Chemical kinetics; fission track imaging analyses for purpose of determining presence of minute amounts of fissionable materials. *Mailing Add:* Indust Marine Stream Turbine Div Western Ave Bldg 60 Lynn MA 01910

ZEMACH, CHARLES, b Los Angeles, Calif, Sept 15, 30; m 58; c 3. ELEMENTARY PARTICLE PHYSICS. *Educ:* Harvard Univ, BA, 51, PhD(physics), 55. *Prof Exp:* Nat Sci fel, 55-56; instr physics, Univ Pa, 56-57; res assoc, Univ Calif, Berkeley, 57-58, from asst prof to prof, 58-71; officer & spec asst for technol, US Arms Control & Disarmament Agency, State Dept, 70-74, mem policy planning staff, 74-76; STAFF MEM, LOS ALAMOS NAT LAB, 76- *Concurrent Pos:* Alfred P Sloan Found fel, 59-63; Guggenheim Found fel, 66-67. *Mem:* Am Phys Soc. *Res:* Thermal neutron diffraction; quantum electrodynamics; strong interactions of elementary particles; fluid dynamics. *Mailing Add:* Los Alamos Nat Lab PO Box 1663 Los Alamos NM 87545

ZEMACH, RITA, b Paterson, NJ, Apr 3, 26; m 47; c 2. STATISTICS, PUBLIC HEALTH. *Educ:* Columbia Univ, BA, 47; Mich State Univ, MS, 61, PhD(statist, probability), 65. *Prof Exp:* Instr statist & probability, Mich State Univ, 65-66, asst prof systs sci, 66-72; assoc prof biostatist, Univ Mich, Ann Arbor, 72-73; CHIEF STATIST RES, MICH DEPT PUB HEALTH, 73- *Concurrent Pos:* Mem health care technol study sect, Dept Health, Educ & Welfare, 72-76; assoc adj prof, Col Human Med, Mich State Univ, 77- *Mem:* AAAS; Am Statist Asn; Am Pub Health Asn; Biomet Soc. *Res:* Health service and resource statistics; program evaluation and measurement methods. *Mailing Add:* Dept Pub Health 3500 North Logan St PO Box 30035 Lansing MI 48909

ZEMAITIS, MICHAEL ALAN, b York, Pa, Aug 21, 46; m 68; c 2. BIOCHEMICAL PHARMACOLOGY, TOXICOLOGY. *Educ:* Univ Pittsburgh, BS, 69; Pa State Univ, PhD(pharmacol), 75. *Prof Exp:* Instr, 75-76, asst prof, 76-80, ASSOC PROF PHARMACOL, UNIV PITTSBURGH, 80- *Mem:* Am Soc Pharmacol & Exp Therapeut; Soc Toxicol; NY Acad Sci; Am Asn Col Pharm. *Res:* Pathways of drug metabolism in man and laboratory animals; identification of metabolites of drugs and environmental chemicals. *Mailing Add:* 1014 Salk Hall Univ Pittsburgh Pittsburgh PA 15261

ZEMAN, FRANCES JUNE, b Cleveland, Ohio, Mar 5, 25. NUTRITION. *Educ:* Western Reserve Univ, BS, 46, MS, 57; Ohio State Univ, PhD(nutrit), 63. *Prof Exp:* Dietitian, Cleveland City Hosp, Ohio, 49-51, teaching dietitian, Sch Nursing, 51-57; asst prof home econ, Kent State Univ, 57-64; from asst prof to assoc prof, 64-74, PROF NUTRIT, UNIV CALIF, DAVIS, 74- *Mem:* AAAS; Am Physiol Soc; Am Inst Nutrit. *Res:* Nutrition in reproduction. *Mailing Add:* Dept of Nutrit Univ of Calif Davis CA 95616

ZEMANEK, JOSEPH, JR, b Blessing, Tex, Jan 1, 28; m 50; c 2. ACOUSTICS. *Educ:* Univ Tex, BS, 49; Southern Methodist Univ, MS, 57; Univ Calif, Los Angeles, PhD(physics), 62. *Prof Exp:* Test engr, Gen Elec Co, 49-50; jr technologist, Field Res Lab, Magnolia Petrol Co, 51-53, from res technologist to sr res technologist, 53-58, sr res technologist, 61-67, res assoc acoustic well logging, 67-81, SR RES ASSOC PETROL WELL LOG INTERPRETATION, MOBIL RES & DEVELOP CORP, 81- *Mem:* Sigma Xi; Acoust Soc Am; Soc Petrol Engrs; Soc Prof Well Log Analysts. *Res:* Acoustic wave propagation in isotropic media, attenuation and velocity measurements; acoustic well logging, development of instrumentation and methods; wave propagation in boreholes. *Mailing Add:* 936 Timber Dell Dallas TX 75232

ZEMANIAN, ARMEN HUMPARTSOUM, b Bridgewater, Mass, Apr 16, 25; m 58; c 4. APPLIED MATHEMATICS. *Educ:* City Col New York, BEE, 47; NY Univ, MEE, 49, Eng ScD, 53. *Prof Exp:* Tutor elec eng, City Col New York, 47-48; engr, Maintenance Co, 48-52; from instr to assoc prof elec eng, NY Univ, 52-62; chmn dept, 67-68 & 71-74, PROF ENG, STATE UNIV NY STONY BROOK, 62- *Concurrent Pos:* Res fel math inst, Univ Edinburgh, 68-69; consult, All-Tronics, Inc & Anaesthesia Assocs, NY; managing ed, Siam Rev, Soc Indust & Appl Math, 69-71, ed-in-chief publs, 70-74, vpres publ, 74-75; vis scholar, Food Res Inst, Stanford Univ, 75-76; NSF fac fel sci, 75-76. *Mem:* Soc Indust & Appl Math; fel Inst Elec & Electronic Engrs; Asn Am Geographers. *Res:* Mathematical systems theory; distribution theory; integral transforms; electrical network theory; agricultural marketing systems; transportation systems. *Mailing Add:* Dept Elec Eng State Univ NY Stony Brook NY 11794

ZEMBRODT, ANTHONY RAYMOND, b Covington, Ky, Jan 2, 43; m 66; c 3. ANALYTICAL CHEMISTRY, PHYSICAL CHEMISTRY. *Educ:* Thomas More Col, BA, 65; Ohio Univ, PhD(phys chem), 70. *Prof Exp:* scientist anal chem, 69-78, SECT MGR ANAL SERV, DRACKETT CO, BRISTOL MYERS CO, CINCINNATI, 78- *Concurrent Pos:* Lectr, NKy State Univ, 71-76 & Thomas More Col, 78. *Mem:* Soc Plastic Engrs; Cosmetics, Toiletry & Fragrance Asn; Chem Specialties Mfrs Asn; NAm Thermal Anal Soc; Am Chem Soc. *Res:* Thermal analysis of polymers; instrumental techniques for analyses and x-ray fluorescence of consumer products. *Mailing Add:* 1004 Park Lane Covington KY 41011

ZEMEL, JAY N(ORMAN), b New York, NY; m 50; c 3. ELECTRONIC ENGINEERING, ENGINEERING PHYSICS. *Educ:* Syracuse Univ, AB, 49, MS, 53, PhD, 56. *Hon Degrees:* MA, Univ Pa, 71. *Prof Exp:* Physicist, Naval Ord Lab, 54-58, chief surface & film group, Solid State Div, 58-66; chmn, Elec Eng & Sci Dept, 72-77, RCA PROF SOLID STATE ELECTRONICS, MOORE SCH ELEC ENG, UNIV PA, 66-, DIR, CTR CHEM ELECTRONICS, 79- *Concurrent Pos:* Guest lectr, Mat Lab, Imp Col, Univ London, 64; vis scientist, Zenith Radio Res Lab, Ltd, London, 64; coord ed, Thin Solid Films, 70-72, ed-in-chief, 72; vis prof, Ctr Invest & Advan Studies, Nat Polytech Inst, Mex, 71; mem comt predictive testing for mat performance, Nat Mat Adv Bd, 71-72; mem adv comt solidification metals & semiconductors, Univ Space Res Asn, 72-77; chmn, Gordon Conf on MIS Structures, 76; vis prof elec eng, Univ Tokyo, 78; dir, NATO Advan Study Inst on Non-Destructive Eval of Semiconductor Mat & Devices, 78. *Mem:* Am Phys Soc; fel Inst Elec & Electronics Engrs. *Res:* Chemically sensitive semiconductor devices. *Mailing Add:* Moore Sch Elec Eng Univ Pa 200 S 33rd St Philadelphia PA 19104

ZEMJANIS, RAIMUNDS, b Petrhoff, Russia, Sept 16, 18; US citizen; m 42; c 3. REPRODUCTIVE PHYSIOLOGY. *Educ:* Royal Vet Col Sweden, DVM, 48; Univ Minn, PhD, 57. *Prof Exp:* Teaching asst anat, Univ Latvia, 38-40; chief vet, A I Ctr Ostergotland, Sweden, 48-51; from instr to assoc prof, 52-59, PROF VET OBSTET, COL VET MED, UNIV MINN, ST PAUL, 59-, HEAD DEPT VET OBSTET & GYNEC, 71-, MEM STAFF, VET HOSP, 70- *Concurrent Pos:* US AID consult, Colombia, SAm, 62, Jamaica, 65 & Nigeria, 74 & 75; NIH spec fel, 68-69; assoc dean, Col Vet Med, Univ Minn, 76-78; For Agr Orgn consult, 78. *Mem:* Sigma Xi; Am Asn Vet Med Cols; Am Vet Med Asn; Soc Study Reproduction; Am Asn Vet Clinicians. *Res:* Animal reproduction and infertility; growth actors and enzyme inhibitors and growth of Vibrio fetus; histology and electron microscopy of the bovine endometrium and normal and degenerate monkey testes. *Mailing Add:* Col of Vet Med Univ of Minn St Paul MN 55108

ZEMKE, WARREN T, b Fairmont, Minn, Oct 9, 39; m 68; c 3. PHYSICAL CHEMISTRY, QUANTUM CHEMISTRY. *Educ:* St Olaf Col, BA, 61; Ill Inst Technol, PhD(chem), 69. *Prof Exp:* From instr to assoc prof, 66-80, PROF CHEM, WARTBURG COL, 80- *Concurrent Pos:* Vis assoc prof, Univ Iowa, 78-79. *Mem:* Sigma Xi; AAAS; Am Chem Soc; Am Phys Soc. *Res:* Molecular electronic wavefunctions; molecular spectroscopy and structure. *Mailing Add:* Dept of Chem Wartburg Col Waverly IA 50677

ZEMLICKA, JIRI, b Prague, Czech, July 31, 33; m 61; c 2. ORGANIC CHEMISTRY, BIOCHEMISTRY. *Educ:* Charles Univ, Prague, RNDr, 56; Czech Acad Sci, PhD(org chem), 59. *Prof Exp:* Res asst anal biochem, Inst Food Technol, Prague, 56; res scientist, Inst Org Chem & Biochem, Czech Acad Sci, 59-68; vis scientist, 68-69, res scientist, 70-80, ASSOC MEM, MICH CANCER FOUND, 80-; ASSOC PROF BIOCHEM, SCH MED, WAYNE STATE UNIV, 71- *Mem:* Am Chem Soc. *Res:* Chemistry of nucleic acids; protein biosynthesis. *Mailing Add:* Mich Cancer Found 110 E Warren Ave Detroit MI 48201

ZEMLIN, WILLARD R, b Two Harbors, Minn, July 20, 20; m 54; c 2. SPEECH & HEARING SCIENCES. *Educ:* Univ Minn, BA, 57, MS, 60, PhD(speech), 61. *Prof Exp:* Dir speech & hearing res lab, 61-76, PROF SPEECH & HEARING SCI, UNIV ILL, URBANA-CHAMPAIGN, 76- *Concurrent Pos:* Consult, Lincoln State Sch, 65-67. *Mem:* Am Speech & Hearing Asn; Acoust Soc Am. *Res:* Anatomy and physiology of normal and pathological speech and hearing mechanisms. *Mailing Add:* Speech & Hearing Res Lab Univ of Ill Champaign IL 61820

ZEMMER, JOSEPH LAWRENCE, JR, b Biloxi, Miss, Feb 23, 22; m 50; c 3. ALGEBRA. *Educ:* Tulane Univ, BS, 43, MS, 47; Univ Wis, PhD(math), 50. *Prof Exp:* From asst prof to assoc prof, 50-61, chmn dept, 67-70 & 73-76, PROF MATH, UNIV MO-COLUMBIA, 61- *Concurrent Pos:* Fulbright lectr, Osmania Univ, India, 63-64. *Mem:* Soc Indust Appl Math; Am Math Soc; Math Asn Am; Can Math Soc. *Res:* Projective planes and their coordinatizing algebraic systems, especially nearfields and Veblen-Wedderburn systems. *Mailing Add:* Dept of Math Univ of Mo Columbia MO 65211

ZEMON, STANLEY ALAN, b Detroit, Mich, June 16, 30; m 67. PHYSICS. *Educ:* Harvard Univ, AB, 52; Columbia Univ, AM, 58, PhD(physics), 64. *Prof Exp:* Res asst physics, Columbia Univ, 58-62, res scientist, 63-64, res assoc, 64-65; MEM TECH STAFF, GTE LABS, INC, 65- *Mem:* Am Phys Soc; Inst Elec & Electronics Engrs. *Res:* Superconductivity; low temperature physics; microwaves; acoustoelectric effect; ultrasonics; semiconductors; Brillouin scattering; lasers; acoustic surface waves; nonlinear acoustics; optical guided waves; nonlinear optics. *Mailing Add:* GTE Labs Inc 40 Sylvan Rd Waltham MA 02154

ZEMP, JOHN WORKMAN, b Camden, SC, Sept 28, 31; m 58; c 4. BIOCHEMISTRY. *Educ:* Col Charleston, BS, 53; Med Col SC, MS, 54; Univ NC, PhD(biochem), 66. *Prof Exp:* Asst prof biochem, Ctr Res Pharmacol & Toxicol, Sch Med, Univ NC, Chapel Hill, 67-69; from asst prof to assoc prof biochem, 69-73, actg dean, Col Med, 73-74, actg vpres acad affairs, 74-75, coordr res, 72-73, assoc dean acad affairs, 73-76, exec dir, Charleston Higher Educ Consortium, 77-81, PROF BIOCHEM, MED UNIV SC, 74-, DEAN, COL GRAD STUDIES & UNIV RES, 77- *Concurrent Pos:* NSF res fel, 66-67. *Mem:* AAAS; Am Chem Soc; Soc Neurosci; Soc Exp Biol & Med; NY Acad Sci. *Res:* Brain function and biochemistry; developmental neurobiology; nutrition; biochemical pharmacology. *Mailing Add:* Dept Biochem Med Univ SC Charleston SC 29401

ZEN, E-AN, b Peking, China, May 31, 28; nat US. GEOLOGY, PETROLOGY. *Educ:* Cornell Univ, BA, 51; Harvard Univ, AM, 52, PhD(geol), 55. *Prof Exp:* Res fel, Oceanog Inst, Woods Hole, 55-56, res assoc, 56-58; vis asst prof, Univ NC, 58-59; RES GEOLOGIST, US GEOL SURV, 59- *Concurrent Pos:* Vis assoc prof, Calif Inst Technol, 62, Crosby vis prof, Mass Inst Technol, 72 & Harry Hess Sr vis fel, Princton, 81. *Mem:* Nat Acad Sci; fel AAAS; fel Geol Soc Am; fel Mineral Soc Am; Mineral Asn Can. *Res:* Phase equilibrium of sedimentary and metamorphic rocks; stratigraphy and structure of NApplachians and NRockies; igneous petrology. *Mailing Add:* US Geol Surv Stop 959 Nat Ctr Reston VA 22092

ZENCHELSKY, SEYMOUR THEODORE, b New York, NY, July 6, 23. ANALYTICAL CHEMISTRY. *Educ:* NY Univ, BA, 44, MS, 47, PhD(chem), 52. *Prof Exp:* From instr to assoc prof chem, Rutgers Univ, New Brunswick, 51-64, prof, 64-80. *Mem:* AAAS; Am Chem Soc; Soc Appl Spectros; NY Acad Sci. *Res:* Instrumentation; nonaqueous titrations; spectrophotometry; atmospheric aerosols; organic aerosols. *Mailing Add:* 180 C Cedar Lane Highland Park NJ 08904

ZENDER, MICHAEL J, b Austin, Minn, Feb 27, 39. NUCLEAR PHYSICS. *Educ:* St John's Univ, Minn, BA, 61; Vanderbilt Univ, PhD(physics), 66. *Prof Exp:* From asst prof to assoc prof & chmn dept, 66-72, PROF PHYSICS, CALIF STATE UNIV, FRESNO, 73- *Mem:* Am Asn Physics Teachers; AAAS; Health Physics Soc; Am Asn Physicists Med. *Res:* Low energy nuclear, beta and gamma-ray spectroscopy; study of the Auger effect by using a post acceleration Geiger counter in conjunction with very thin counter windows; radiation safety; x-ray fluorescence analysis. *Mailing Add:* Dept Physics Fresno Shaw & Cedar Ave Fresno CA 93740

ZENER, CLARENCE MELVIN, b Indianapolis, Ind, Dec 1, 05; m 31; c 4. PHYSICS. *Educ:* Stanford Univ, AB, 26; Harvard Univ, PhD(physics), 29. *Prof Exp:* Sheldon traveling fel, Ger, 29-30; Nat Res Coun fel, Princeton Univ, 30-32; fel, Bristol Univ, 32-34; instr physics, Washington Univ, 35-37 & City Col New York, 37-40; assoc prof, State Col Wash, 40-42; from physicist to prin physicist, Watertown Arsenal, 42-45; prof physics, Univ Chicago, 45-51; assoc dir res labs, Westinghouse Elec Corp, 51-56, dir res labs, 56-62, dir sci, 62-65; dean col sci, Tex A&M Univ, 66-68; UNIV PROF PHYSICS, CARNEGIE-MELLON UNIV, 68- *Mem:* Nat Acad Sci; fel Am Phys Soc. *Res:* Theoretical physics and engineering, power from the ocean's thermocline. *Mailing Add:* Carnegie-Mellon Univ Pittsburgh PA 15213

ZENGEL, JANET ELAINE, b Baltimore, Md, Feb 21, 48; m 74; c 1. NEUROPHYSIOLOGY. *Educ:* Western Md Col, BA, 70; Univ Miami, PhD(physiol & biophysics), 73. *Prof Exp:* Res instr physiol & biophysics, Sch Med, Univ Miami, 74-78, res asst prof, 78-79; sr assoc anat, Sch Med, Emory Univ, 79-80; RES BIOLOGIST, VET ADMIN MED CTR, 80- *Concurrent Pos:* Adj asst prof neurosci & neurosurg, Col Med, Univ Fla, 80- *Mem:* Biophys Soc; Soc Neurosci; AAAS. *Res:* Neurophysiology; synaptic and neuromuscular transmission; role of calcium 2 in transmitter release; mechanisms of changes in efficacy; spinal cord physiology and anatomy. *Mailing Add:* Box J-244 JHM Health Ctr Col Med Univ Fla Gainesville FL 32605

ZENGEL, JANICE MARIE, b Baltimore, Md, Feb 21, 48; m 78; c 1. MOLECULAR GENETICS, BACTERIOL PHYSIOLOGY. *Educ:* Western Md Col, BA, 70; Univ Wis, PhD(genetics), 76. *Prof Exp:* Fel molecular genetics, Pharmacol Dept, Stanford Univ, 76-78, Neurol Dept, Baylor Col Med, 78-79; RES ASSOC MOLECULAR GENETICS, BIOL DEPT, UNIV ROCHESTER, 79- *Mem:* Am Soc Microbiol. *Res:* E coli molecular basis for the regulation of ribosome synthesis in E coli, using biochemical, genetic and recombinant DNA techniques. *Mailing Add:* Dept Biol Univ Rochester Rochester NY 14627

ZENGER, DONALD HENRY, b Little Falls, NY, July 27, 32; m 57; c 2. GEOLOGY. *Educ:* Union Col, NY, BS, 54; Dartmouth Col, MA, 59; Cornell Univ, PhD(geol), 62. *Prof Exp:* From instr to assoc prof, 62-73, PROF GEOL, POMONA COL, 73- *Concurrent Pos:* Grants, Geol Soc Am, 63 & Am Chem Soc, 66-74. *Mem:* Geol Soc Am; Int Asn Sedimentologists; Am Asn Petrol Geologists; Nat Asn Geol Teachers; Soc Econ Paleont & Mineral. *Res:* Silurian and Devonian stratigraphy, paleontology and carbonate petrology of New York and California. *Mailing Add:* Dept of Geol Pomona Col Claremont CA 91711

ZENISEK, CYRIL JAMES, b Cleveland, Ohio, Feb 6, 26; m 56; c 3. ZOOLOGY. *Educ:* Ohio State Univ, BSc, 49, MSc, 55, PhD(zool), 63. *Prof Exp:* From asst prof to assoc prof, 60-66, PROF BIOL, INDIANA UNIV PA, 66- *Mem:* Soc Syst Zool; Am Soc Ichthyol & Herpet; Ecol Soc Am; Soc Study Amphibians & Reptiles; Herpetologists League. *Res:* Taxonomy and distribution of amphibians. *Mailing Add:* Dept of Biol Ind Univ of Pa Indiana PA 15701

ZENITZ, BERNARD LEON, b Baltimore, Md, Mar 26, 17; m 56; c 2. MEDICINAL CHEMISTRY. *Educ:* Univ Md, BS, 37, PhD(pharmaceut chem), 43. *Prof Exp:* Sr res chemist, Frederic Stearns & Co, Mich, 44-47; sr res chemist & lab head, Sterling-Winthrop Res Inst, 47-81; RETIRED. *Honors & Awards:* Col Medal Gen Excellence & Pharmacog Prize, 37. *Mem:* Am Chem Soc. *Res:* Thymus gland extracts; sympathomimetic amines; quartenary ammonium salts; synthetic detergents; sterols; preparation of B-cyclohexylakylamines; halogen ring substituted propadrines; coronary dilators; local anesthetics; tranquilizers; antioxidants; antiinflammatory agents; antiobesity drugs; bronchodilators; analgesics. *Mailing Add:* 9 Bel Aire Dr Latham NY 12110

ZENKER, NICOLAS, b Paris, France, Dec 3, 21; nat US; m 52; c 4. PHARMACEUTICAL CHEMISTRY. *Educ:* Cath Univ Louvain, Cand, 48; Univ Calif, MA, 53, PhD(pharmaceut chem), 58. *Prof Exp:* Biochemist, Mt Zion Hosp, San Francisco, 53-60; asst prof pharmaceut chem, 60-63, assoc prof, 63-69, head dept, 69-79, PROF MED CHEM, UNIV MD, BALTIMORE, 69- *Mem:* Am Chem Soc. *Res:* Synthesis and mode of action of metabolic analogues; thyroadrenergic relationships. *Mailing Add:* Dept of Medicinal Chem Col of Pharm Univ of Md 636 W Lombard St Baltimore MD 21201

ZENONE, CHESTER, b Spangler, Pa, Dec 29, 40; m 69; c 2. GLACIO-HYDROLOGY. *Educ:* Purdue Univ, BS, 64; Mich State Univ, MS, 72. *Prof Exp:* Hydrologist, 68-82, SUPVRY HYDROLOGIST, WATER RESOURCES DIV, US GEOL SURV, 82- *Mem:* Nat Water Well Asn. *Res:* Snow and ice affected water resources in Alaska; author or coauthor of over 25 publications. *Mailing Add:* US Geol Surv WRD 733 W 4th Ave Suite 400 Anchorage AK 99501

ZENTILLI, MARCOS, b Santiago, Chile, May 31, 40; m 63; c 3. METALLOGENY. *Educ:* Univ De Chile, BS, 63; Queen's Univ, PhD(geol), 74. *Prof Exp:* Geologist mineral deposit, Inst Invest Geologicas, 63-68, exploration, Geophys Eng, Ltd, Toronto, 72; asst prof, 73-78, ASSOC PROF, DALHOUSIE UNIV, 78- *Res:* Regional metallogenic evolution of the Central Andes; geology of gold deposits of Nova Scotia; metallogenic evolution of Nova Scotia Appalachians; geological evolution of teritiary province of Eastern Iceland. *Mailing Add:* Dept Geol Dalhousie Univ Halifax NS B3H 3J5 Can

ZENTMYER, GEORGE AUBREY, JR, b North Platte, Nebr, Aug 9, 13; m 41; c 3. PHYTOPATHOLOGY. *Educ:* Univ Calif, Los Angeles, AB, 35; Univ Calif, MS, 36, PhD(plant path), 38. *Prof Exp:* Asst plant path, Univ Calif, 36-37; asst pathologist, Div Forest Path, Bur Plant Indust, USDA, 37-40 & Conn Exp Sta, 40-44; asst pathologist, 44-48, assoc plant pathologist, 48-55, fac res lectr, 64, chmn dept plant path, 68-73, PLANT PATHOLOGIST, UNIV CALIF RIVERSIDE, 55-, PROF PLANT PATH, 63- *Concurrent Pos:* Consult, Pineapple Res Inst, 61, Trust Territory, Pac Islands, 64 & 66, Rockefeller Found, Colombia, 67, Australian Govt, 68, US Agency Int Develop, Ghana & Nigeria, 69, NSF panel, 71- & SAfrican Govt & avacado growers, 80; Guggenheim fel, 64-65; mem, Nat Res Coun, 68-73; NATO sr sci fel, Eng, 71; mem var comts, Nat Acad Sci-Nat Res Coun; assoc ed, Annual Rev Phytopath, 70- *Honors & Awards:* Award of Merit, Am Phytopath Soc, Caribbean, 72. *Mem:* Nat Acad Sci; fel Am Phytopath Soc (secy, 59-62, pres, 65-66); Int Soc Plant Path; Mycol Soc Am; Asn Trop Biol. *Res:* Biology and physiology of root pathogens, especially Phytophthora; chemotaxis; chemotherapy; fungicides; diseases of avocado, cacao, other tropicals and subtropicals. *Mailing Add:* Dept Plant Path Univ Calif Riverside CA 92521

ZENTNER, THOMAS GLENN, b Rowena, Tex, Aug 6, 26; m 52; c 5. PULP CHEMISTRY, PAPER CHEMISTRY. *Educ:* Tex A&M Univ, BS, 48; Inst Paper Chem, MS, 50, Lawrence Col, PhD(chem), 52. *Prof Exp:* Mem staff, Gardner Div, Diamond Nat Corp, 52-59, dir res & develop, 59-60; dir forest prod oper, Olin Mathieson Chem Corp, 60-66; vpres res & develop, Olinkraft, Inc, La, 66-68, rep, Forest Prod Div, Olin Corp, West Monroe, 68-75, vpres res, Olinkraft, Inc, 74-79, VPRES RES, MANVILLE FOREST PROD, INC, 80- *Mem:* Am Chem Soc; corp mem Tech Asn Pulp & Paper Indust. *Res:* Paperboard manufacture; coating; converting for packaging; graphic arts. *Mailing Add:* Manville Forest Prod Inc PO Box 488 West Monroe LA 71291

ZENZ, CARL, b Vienna, Austria, Feb 1, 23; US citizen; m 47; c 3. OCCUPATIONAL MEDICINE. *Educ:* Jefferson Med Col, MD, 49; Univ Cincinnati, ScD, 57. *Prof Exp:* Intern, Ausbury Hosp, Minneapolis, Minn, 49-50; gen pract, Minn & Wis, 50-52; resident occup med, Allis-Chalmers Corp, 56-57, chief clin serv, 57-62, chief physician, 62-63, med dir, 63-65, dir med & hyg serv, 65-70, dir med serv, 70-80; CONSULT, 80- *Mem:* AAAS; Am Occup Med Asn; Am Indust Hyg Asn; fel Am Pub Health Asn; fel Am Acad Occup Med (past pres). *Mailing Add:* 2418 S Root River Pkwy Milwaukee WI 53227

ZENZ, FREDERICK A(NTON), b New York, NY, Aug 1, 22; m 49; c 4. CHEMICAL ENGINEERING. *Educ:* Queens Col, BS, 42; NY Univ, MChE, 50; Polytech Inst Brooklyn, DChE, 61. *Prof Exp:* Chem engr, M W Kellogg Co, 42-44, 46, develop engr, 53-56; chem engr, Kellex Corp, 44-45; res engr, Carbide & Carbon Chem Corp, Tenn, 45-46; process engr, Hydrocarbon Res, Inc, 46-53; mgr process dept, Assoc Nucleonics, Inc, 56-62; CONSULT, 62- *Concurrent Pos:* Lectr, NY Univ, 51-52; adj prof, Polytech Inst Brooklyn, 59-; prof, Manhattan Col, 69-; tech dir, Particulate Solid Res, Inc, 70-; dir, Process Equip Modelling & Mfg Co, 74-; vpres, The Ducon Co, 75- *Honors & Awards:* Tyler Award, Am Inst Chem Engrs, 58. *Mem:* Am Chem Soc; Am Nuclear Soc; Sigma Xi; Am Inst Chem Engrs. *Res:* Fluidization; two-phase flow; tower design; distillation; particle filtration; gas-solid reactions; nuclear power reactors; isotope separation; air fractionation; petroleum refining; ammonia. *Mailing Add:* Rte 9D PO Box 241 Garrison NY 10524

ZEOLI, G(ENE) W(ESLEY), b Los Angeles, Calif, Nov 9, 26; m 56; c 2. ELECTRICAL ENGINEERING. *Educ:* Univ Calif, Berkeley, BS, 48, MS, 49; Univ Calif, Los Angeles, PhD, 71. *Prof Exp:* Lectr elec eng, Univ Calif, 48-49; asst, Mass Inst Technol, 49-50, 51-52; mem tech staff radar systs res, Hughes Aircraft Co, 52-54, group head sensor syst anal, 54-57, sr scientist & head info processing staff, Signal Processing & Display Lab, 57-68, sr scientist, Staff Radar Systs & Signal Processing Lab, 68-76, chief scientist, Advan Progs Div, 76-81; PRES, GENE W ZEOLI, INC, 81- *Concurrent Pos:* Lectr, Univ Calif, Los Angeles, 54-55 & Loyola Univ, 71-72. *Mem:* Sigma Xi; Inst Elec & Electronics Engrs. *Res:* Communication and information theory. *Mailing Add:* 1405 Granvia Altamira Palos Verdes Estates CA 90274

ZEPF, THOMAS HERMAN, b Cincinnati, Ohio, Feb 13, 35. PHYSICS. *Educ:* Xavier Univ, Ohio, BS, 57; St Louis Univ, MS, 60, PhD(physics), 63. *Prof Exp:* From asst prof to assoc prof, 62-75, from actg chmn dept to chmn dept, 63-73, PROF PHYSICS, CREIGHTON UNIV, 75-, CHMN DEPT, 81- *Concurrent Pos:* Vis prof physics, St Louis Univ, 73-74. *Mem:* AAAS; Am Phys Soc; Am Asn Physics Teachers. *Res:* Surface physics; electron emission; x-ray diffraction; ultra-high vacuum techniques. *Mailing Add:* Dept of Physics Creighton Univ Omaha NE 68178

ZEPP, EDWIN ANDREW, b Orange, Calif, Sept 15, 45; m 79; c 1. ENDOCRINOLOGY, LIPID METABOLISM. *Educ:* WVa Univ, AB, 67, MS, 72, PhD(pharmacol), 76. *Prof Exp:* Res assoc, 76-78, ASST PROF BIOCHEM, KIRKSVILLE COL OSTEOPATH MED, 78- *Concurrent Pos:* Prin investr, Nat Cancer Inst, NIH, 78-; adj asst prof, Northeast Mo State Univ, 81- *Res:* Hormonal control of lipid metabolism and alterations by tumor-bearing and under conditions of dietary manipulation. *Mailing Add:* Dept Biochem Kirksville Col Osteopath Med Kirksville MO 63501

ZEPP, RICHARD GARDNER, b Brooklyn, NY, Nov 20, 41; m 68; c 1. ENVIRONMENTAL CHEMISTRY, PHYSICAL ORGANIC CHEMISTRY. *Educ:* Furman Univ, BS, 63; Fla State Univ, PhD(org chem), 68. *Prof Exp:* Res assoc photochem, Mich State Univ, 69-70; RES CHEMIST ENVIRON PHOTOCHEM, US ENVIRON PROTECTION AGENCY, 71- *Mem:* Am Chem Soc; Sigma Xi; Am Soc Limnol & Oceanog; AAAS. *Res:* Rates and products of chemical reactions of synthetic industrial chemicals, polycyclic aromatic hydrocarbons, and pesticides in water and soil; mathematical simulation of pollutant behavior in environment. *Mailing Add:* Environ Res Lab College Station Rd Athens GA 30613

ZEPPA, ROBERT, b New York, NY, Sept 17, 24; m 52; c 2. THORACIC SURGERY. *Educ:* Columbia Univ, AB, 48; Yale Univ, MD, 52. *Prof Exp:* Intern, Med Ctr, Univ Pittsburgh, 52-53; asst resident surg, Sch Med, Univ NC, 53-56, thoracic resident, 56-57, instr thoracic surg, 58-60, from asst prof surg to assoc prof, 60-65; co-chmn dept, 66-71, CHMN DEPT SURG, SCH MED, UNIV MIAMI, 71-, PROF SURG & PHARMACOL, 65- *Concurrent Pos:* USPHS career trainee, Sch Med, Wash Univ, 56-58; Markle scholar med sci, 59-64; assoc dir clin res unit, NC Mem Hosp, 61-65; chief surg serv, Vet Admin Hosp, Miami, Fla, 71- *Mem:* Am Col Surg; Am Surg Asn; Soc Surg Alimentary Tract; Soc Univ Surg. *Res:* Biologically active amines; portal hypertension; gastrointestinal physiology. *Mailing Add:* Sch Med Univ Miami PO Box 520875 Miami FL 33152

ZERBE, J(OHN) E(DWARD), b Chester, Pa, Dec 28, 23; m 46; c 2. MECHANICAL ENGINEERING. *Educ:* Swarthmore Col, BS, 44; Stanford Univ, MS, 47. *Prof Exp:* Mech engr, Ames Lab, Nat Adv Comt Aeronaut, 44-47; jr engr res lab, 47-48, from jr engr to sr engr, Bettis Atomic Power Lab, 48-54, supvry engr thermal & hydraul sect, 54, sect mgr, 55, mgr S5W reactor design, 55-58, mgr submarine reactor eng, 59-60, mgr surface ship reactor eng, 61-64, mgr large seed blanket reactor eng, 64-66, mgr light-water breeder proj, 66-73, mgr eng, Westinghouse Uranium Enrichment Opers, 74-75, mgr Tokomak Fusion Test Reactor Proj, Westinghouse Fusion Power Systs, 75-76, mgr reactor tecnol, 76-81, MGR TECHNOL PROGS, WESTINGHOUSE ADVAN REACTORS DIV, WESTINGHOUSE ELEC CORP, 81- *Mem:* Am Soc Mech Engrs. *Res:* Boiling heat transfer; fluid flow; nuclear core design. *Mailing Add:* Westinghouse Advan Reactors Div PO Box 158 Madison PA 15663

ZERBE, JOHN IRWIN, b Hegins, Pa, June 4, 26; m 51; c 3. WOOD SCIENCE, WOOD TECHNOLOGY. *Educ:* Pa State Univ, BS, 51; State Univ NY, MS, 53, PhD(wood technol), 56. *Prof Exp:* Asst wood technol, State Univ NY, 51-56; res asst prof housing res, Univ Ill, 56-58; mgr, Govt Specifications & Standards Dept, Nat Forest Prod Asn, 58-59, asst vpres, Tech Serv, 59-70; dir forest prod & eng res, 70-76, MGR ENERGY RES, DEVELOP & APPLICATION, FOREST SERV, USDA, 76- *Mem:* Forest Prod Res Soc; Soc Wood Sci & Technol; Soc Am Foresters. *Res:* Mechanical properties of wood. *Mailing Add:* 3310 Heatherdell Lane Madison WI 53713

ZERBY, CLAYTON DONALD, b Cleveland, Ohio, Jan 27, 24; m 49; c 3. PHYSICS, MECHANICAL ENGINEERING. *Educ:* Case Western Reserve Univ, BS, 50; Univ Tenn, MS, 56, PhD(physics), 60. *Prof Exp:* Engr, Oak Ridge Nat Lab, 50-54, group leader physics, 54-63, mgr physics & eng, Defense & Space Systs Dept, 63-66, mgr dept, 66-67, gen mgr, Korad Laser Dept, 67-71, pres, Ocean Systs, Inc, 71-73, Domsea Farms, Inc, 72-74, tech serv mgr, Nuclear Div, 74-76, dir off waste isolation, 76-78, PLANT MGR, PADUCAH GASEOUS DIFFUSION PLANT, UNION CARBIDE CORP, 78- *Concurrent Pos:* Lectr, Univ Tenn, 61-63 & Univ Ky, 80-81. *Mem:* Am Phys Soc; Am Nuclear Soc. *Res:* Theory of electromagnetic interactions; Monte Carlo methods; nuclear weapons effects; space vehicle radiation shielding; shielding against high energy particles; interaction of high energy particles with complex nuclei; nuclear waste terminal storage. *Mailing Add:* Union Carbide Corp PO Box 1410 Paducah KY 42001

ZEREN, RICHARD WILLIAM, b Baltimore, Md, June 3, 42; m 65; c 2. MECHANINCAL ENGINEERING, RESEARCH ADMINISTRATION. *Educ:* Duke Univ, BSME, 64; Stanford Univ, MS, 65, PhD(eng), 70. *Prof Exp:* Actg asst prof mech eng, Stanford Univ, 69; asst prof, Mich State Univ, 70-76; asst to dir, Fossil Fuel & Advan Systs Div, Elec Power Res Inst, 74-77, mgr prog integration & eval, 77-79; sr assoc, Booz-Allen & Hamilton, Inc, 80; DIR, PLANNING & EVAL DIV, ELEC POWER RES INST, 81- *Mem:* AAAS; Am Soc Mech Engrs; Int Asn Energy Economists. *Res:* Research and development administration. *Mailing Add:* 150 Corona Way Portola Valley CA 94025

ZERKLE, RONALD DALE, b Springfield, Ohio, Nov 3, 37; m 61; c 3. MECHANICAL ENGINEERING, THERMODYNAMICS. *Educ:* Univ Cincinnati, BS, 60; Northwestern Univ, MS, 62; Ga Inst Technol, PhD(heat transfer), 65. *Prof Exp:* From asst prof to assoc prof, 64-72, PROF MECH ENG, UNIV CINCINNATI, 72- *Mem:* Am Soc Mech Engrs. *Res:* Heat transfer; fluid mechanics; manufacturing technology. *Mailing Add:* 9047 Fontainebleau Terr Cincinnati OH 45231

ZERLA, FREDRIC JAMES, b Wheeling, WVa, Feb 23, 37; m 66; c 6. MATHEMATICS. *Educ:* Col Steubenville, BA, 58; Fla State Univ, MS, 60, PhD(math), 67. *Prof Exp:* Asst prof, 63-72, from asst chmn dept to actg chmn dept, 69-74, ASSOC PROF MATH, UNIV S FLA, 72-, UNDERGRAD ADV, DEPT MATH, 74- *Mem:* Math Asn Am. *Res:* Derivations in algebraic fields; field theory. *Mailing Add:* Dept of Math Univ of SFla Tampa FL 33620

ZERLIN, STANLEY, b New York, NY, Sept 15, 29; m 59; c 2. PSYCHOPHYSIOLOGY, ELECTROPHYSIOLOGY. *Educ:* City Col New York, BS, 51; Columbia Univ, MA, 53; Western Reserve Univ, PhD(audition), 59. *Prof Exp:* Asst proj dir, Cleveland Hearing & Speech Ctr, 57-58; proj dir, Auditory Res Lab, Vet Admin, 59-63, res scientist, 59-62, res dir, 62-63; res assoc auditory processes, Cent Inst for Deaf, 63-65; res assoc auditory evoked responses, Houston Speech & Hearing Ctr, 65-67; ASSOC PROF & RES ASSOC AUDITORY PROCESSES, OTOLARYNGOL LABS, UNIV CHICAGO, 67- *Mem:* Soc Neurosci; Acoust Soc Am; Am Speech & Hearing Asn; Int Soc Audiol. *Res:* Auditory electrophysiology, evoked response; cochlear processes; binaural interaction. *Mailing Add:* ENT Sect Dept of Surg Univ of Chicago 950 E 59th St Chicago IL 60637

ZERNOW, LOUIS, b Brooklyn, NY, Dec 27, 16; m 40; c 4. PHYSICS. *Educ:* Cooper Union, BChE, 38; Johns Hopkins Univ, PhD(physics), 53. *Prof Exp:* Mem staff, Ballistic Res Labs, Aberdeen Proving Ground, Ord Dept, US Dept Army, 40-51, chief, Rocket & Ammunition Br, 51-53 & Detonation Physics Br, 53-55; dir res & mgr ord res div, Aerojet-Gen Corp, 55-63; pres, Shock Hydrodynamics, Div Whittaker Corp, 63-81; PRES, ZERNOW TECH SERV INC, 81- *Concurrent Pos:* Consult, US Dept Army Gould Inc & Gen Dynamics. *Honors & Awards:* Meritorious Civilian Serv Award, US Dept Army, 44. *Mem:* Am Inst Aeronaut & Astronaut; Am Inst Mining, Metall & Petrol Eng; Soc Mfg Eng; Am Phys Soc; Acoust Soc Am. *Res:* Detonation and aerosol physics; explosives; high strain-rate behavior of materials; shock waves in solids; effects of super pressure on solids; ordnance systems and explosive metal forming. *Mailing Add:* 1103 E Mountain View Ave Glendora CA 91740

ZEROKA, DANIEL, b Plymouth, Pa, June 22, 41; m 67; c 2. THEORETICAL PHYSICAL CHEMISTRY. *Educ:* Wilkes Col, BS, 63; Univ Pa, PhD(theoret chem), 66. *Prof Exp:* NSF fel statist mech, Yale Univ, 66-67; asst prof, 67-74, ASSOC PROF CHEM, LEHIGH UNIV, 74- *Mem:* Am Phys Soc; Am Chem Soc. *Res:* Quantum chemistry; statistical mechanics; magnetic resonance. *Mailing Add:* Dept of Chem Lehigh Univ Bethlehem PA 18015

ZERONIAN, SARKIS HAIG, b Manchester, Eng, June 30, 32; m 70. TEXTILE CHEMISTRY. *Educ:* Univ Manchester, BScTech, 53, MScTech, 55, PhD(cellulose chem), 62. *Prof Exp:* Res officer cellulose chem, Brit Cotton Indust Res Asn, Manchester, Eng, 58-60; res fel, Inst Paper Chem, 62-63; sr res fel nonwoven fabrics, Manchester Col Sci & Technol, Eng, 63-66; res assoc cellulose chem, Columbia Cellulose Co, BC, Can, 66-68; from asst prof to assoc prof textile chem, 68-78, PROF TEXTILE SCI & CHMN, DIV TEXTILES & CLOTHING, UNIV CALIF, DAVIS, 78- *Mem:* Am Chem Soc; Am Asn Textile Chem & Colorists; fel Brit Textile Inst; Fiber Soc; Am Soc Testing & Mat. *Res:* Chemical and physical properties of natural and man-made fibers; properties of textile finishes. *Mailing Add:* Div of Textiles & Clothing Univ of Calif Davis CA 95616

ZERWEKH, CHARLES EZRA, JR, b Galveston, Tex, Aug 24, 22; m 50; c 3. ORGANIC CHEMISTRY. *Educ:* Univ Houston, BS, 44. *Prof Exp:* Chemist, Humble Oil & Refining Co, 44-45, from asst res physicist to res physicist, 45-49, from patent coordr to sr patent coordr, 49-55, supvry patent coordr, 55-57, head tech info sect, Res & Develop Div, 57-63; mgr, Records Mgt Div, Stand Oil Co, NJ, 63-66; tech info specialist, Esso Res & Eng Co, NJ, 66-67; MGR TECH INFO CTR, POLAROID CORP, CAMBRIDGE, 67- *Mem:* AAAS; Am Chem Soc; NY Acad Sci; Spec Libr Asn. *Res:* Technical information, especially patents, machine indexing, literature searching, technical files and information retrieval as applied to petrochemicals, petroleum processing, organic chemistry and photography. *Mailing Add:* 14 Herrick St Winchester MA 01890

ZERWEKH, ROBERT PAUL, b Peoria, Ill, Feb 25, 39; m 74; c 2. MECHANICAL METALLURGY, PHYSICAL METALLURGY. *Educ:* Univ Mo, Rolla, BS, 61; Univ Ill, Urbana, MS, 63; Iowa State Univ, PhD(metall), 70. *Prof Exp:* Sr engr mat, Elec Boat Div, Gen Dynamics Corp, 65-67; asst prof, 70-76, ASSOC PROF MECH ENG, UNIV KANS, 76-, ASSOC DEAN ENG, 80- *Concurrent Pos:* Sci grant, NASA/Langley Res Ctr, 76-78 & Gulf & Western Energy Prod Group, 79- *Mem:* Am Soc Metals; Metall Soc; Am Inst Mining, Metall & Petrol Engrs; Sigma Xi; Am Soc Eng Educ. *Res:* Deformation mechanisms; relationship between microstructure and properties; solid-state phase transformations. *Mailing Add:* Dept of Mech Eng Univ of Kans Lawrence KS 66045

ZETIK, DONALD FRANK, b Brenham, Tex, Nov 28, 38; m 69; c 2. PETROLEUM ENGINEERING, CHEMICAL PHYSICS. *Educ:* Tex A&M Univ, BS, 61; Univ Tex, Austin, PhD(phys chem), 68. *Prof Exp:* Engr petrol prod, Prod Res Lab, Humble Oil Co, 61-63; res assoc chem physics, Wash State Univ, 68-70; SR RES ENGR PETROL RESERVOIR PERFORMANCE, RES LAB, CITIES SERV CO, 70- *Concurrent Pos:* Adj prof, Univ Tulsa, 76-77. *Mem:* Soc Petrol Engrs; Asn Comput Mach; AAAS. *Res:* Numerical simulation of petroleum reservoir performance; development of new simulation techniques with emphasis on improved recovery processes. *Mailing Add:* PO Box 3908 4500 S 129 East Ave Tulsa OK 74134

ZETLER, BERNARD DAVID, b New York, NY, Aug 27, 15; m 40; c 2. OCEANOGRAPHY. *Educ:* Brooklyn Col, BA, 36. *Prof Exp:* Jr math scientist, Hydrography Off, US Dept Navy, Washington, DC, 38; computer, US Coast & Geod Surv, 38-39, mathematician, 39-53, oceanogr, 53-56, chief, Currents & Oceanog Br, 56-60 & Oceanog Anal Br, 60-63, res group off oceanog, 63-65, actg dir phys oceanog lab, Inst Oceanog, Environ Sci Serv Admin, Md, 65-68, dir phys oceanog lab, Atlantic Oceanog Labs, Fla, 68-72; RES OCEANOG, INST GEOPHYS & PLANETARY PHYSICS, UNIV CALIF, SAN DIEGO, 72- *Concurrent Pos:* Assoc prof lectr, George Washington Univ, 65-68; mem tsunami comt, Int Union Geod & Geophys; mem tides & mean sea level comt, Int Asn Phys Sci of the Ocean. *Mem:* Am Geophys Union. *Res:* Seismic sea waves; tides; currents; tsunami; earth tides. *Mailing Add:* Inst Geophys & Planetary Phys Univ Calif San Diego A-025 La Jolla CA 92093

ZETLMEISL, MICHAEL JOSEPH, b Baltimore, Md, Feb 26, 42; m 71; c 5. ELECTROCHEMISTRY. *Educ:* Spring Hill Col, BS, 66; Marquette Univ, MS, 67; St Louis Univ, PhD(chem), 71. *Prof Exp:* RES CHEMIST & PROJ LEADER CORROSION & ELECTROCHEM, PETROLITE CORP, 71- *Mem:* Am Chem Soc; Sigma Xi. *Res:* Electrochemistry of high temperature melts as related to corrosion of metals in gas turbines and boilers. *Mailing Add:* Petrolite Corp 369 Marshall Ave St Louis MO 63119

ZETTEL, LARRY JOSEPH, b Detroit, Mich, Sept 12, 44. COMPUTER SCIENCE EDUCATION. *Educ:* Univ Detroit, BS, 65; Mich State Univ, MS, 66, PhD(math), 70; Univ NMex, MS, 77. *Prof Exp:* Asst prof & chmn dept, Muskingum Col, 69-77, assoc prof math, 77-80; ASSOC PROF COMPUT SCI, LORAS COL, 80- *Mem:* Math Asn Am; Asn Comput Mach; Inst Elec & Electronics Engrs Comput Soc. *Res:* Non-associative algebras; computer usage in undergraduate instruction. *Mailing Add:* Dept of Math Loras Col Dubuque IA 52001

ZETTER, BRUCE ROBERT, b Providence, RI, Dec 23, 46. CELL BIOLOGY, VASCULARIZATION. *Educ:* Brandeis Univ, BA, 68; Univ RI, PhD(biol), 74. *Prof Exp:* Fel, Mass Inst Technol, 74-76; fel, Salk Inst, 76-77; asst res biochemist, Univ Calif Med Ctr, San Francisco, 77-78; ASST PROF, HARVARD MED SCH, 78- *Concurrent Pos:* Res assoc, Children's Hosp Med Ctr, Boston, Mass, 78- *Mem:* Am Soc Cell Biol. *Res:* Biology of the cells that comprise the vasculature, the vascular smooth muscle and endothelial cells; interactions of blood vessels with growing tumors with a special interest in the migration of capillary cells toward tumors. *Mailing Add:* Children's Hosp Med Ctr 300 Longwood Ave Boston MA 02115

ZETTL, ANTON, b Gakovo, Yugoslavia, Apr 25, 35; US citizen; m 64; c 2. MATHEMATICS. *Educ:* Ill Inst Technol, BS, 59; Univ Tenn, MA, 62, PhD(math), 64. *Prof Exp:* Assoc prof math, La State Univ, Baton Rouge, 68-69; assoc prof, 69-73, PROF MATH, NORTHERN ILL UNIV, 73- *Concurrent Pos:* NASA res grants, 65-67; res mem, Math Res Ctr, Univ Wis, 67-68; vis res fel, Univ Dundee, Scotland, 74-75; Brit Sci Res Coun res grant, 74-75; NSF res grants, 74-75, 75-76 & 76-77; vis res scientist appl math div, Argonne Nat Lab, 81-82. *Mem:* Am Math Soc; Soc Indust & Appl Math; Math Asn Am. *Res:* Differential equations; differential operators; norm inequalities for operators. *Mailing Add:* Dept of Math Northern Ill Univ De Kalb IL 60115

ZETTLEMOYER, ALBERT CHARLES, b Allentown, Pa, July 13, 15; m 40; c 5. COLLOID CHEMISTRY, SURFACE CHEMISTRY. *Educ:* Lehigh Univ, BS, 36, MS, 38; Mass Inst Technol, PhD(phys chem), 41. *Hon Degrees:* DSc, Clarkson Univ, 65; LLD, China Acad, Taiwan, 74. *Prof Exp:* Instr, Mass Inst Technol, 40-41; res chemist, Armstrong Cork Co, 41; from instr to prof, 41-60, res dir, Nat Printing Ink Res Inst, 46-68, vpres res & dir ctr surface & coatings res, 66-69, provost & vpres, 69-80, DISTINGUISHED PROF

CHEM, LEHIGH UNIV, 60-, UNIV DISTINGUISHED PROF, 80- *Concurrent Pos:* Chmn, Gordon Conf Chem Interfaces, 55, mem bd trustees, Gordon Conf, 60-63; co-ed, J Colloid & Interface Sci; ed, Advances in Colloid & Interface Sci. *Honors & Awards:* Mattiello Award, 57; Ault Award, 60; Bond Award, 61; Hillman Award, 66; Kendall Award, 68; Welch Lectr, 72. *Mem:* AAAS; Am Chem Soc (pres-elect, 80, pres, 81); Am Oil Chem Soc; fel Am Inst Chem; fel NY Acad Sci. *Res:* Surface chemistry and adsorption; gasses and liquids on solids; heterogeneous nucleation; flow properties of suspensions and molten resins; printability and printing quality of printing inks; heterogenous catalysis. *Mailing Add:* Sinclair Lab Lehigh Univ Bethlehem PA 18015

ZETTLER, FRANCIS WILLIAM, b Easton, Pa, Aug 13, 38; m 61; c 2. PLANT PATHOLOGY, ENTOMOLOGY. *Educ:* Pa State Univ, BS, 61; Cornell Univ, MS, 64, PhD(plant path), 66. *Prof Exp:* From asst prof to assoc prof, 66-75, PROF, UNIV FLA, 75- *Mem:* Am Phytopath Soc. *Res:* Transmission of plant viruses. identification, characterization and control of plant viruses; virus diseases of ornamental plants; research involving edible root crops in the family Araceae. *Mailing Add:* Dept of Plant Path Univ of Fla Gainesville FL 32601

ZETTNER, ALFRED, b Laibach, Yugoslavia, Nov 21, 28; US citizen; m 59; c 2. CLINICAL PATHOLOGY. *Educ:* Graz Univ, MD, 54. *Prof Exp:* Asst prof path & clin path, Yale Univ, 63-67, assoc prof clin path, 67-68, dir dept clin micros, 63-68; PROF PATH & HEAD DIV CLIN PATH, UNIV CALIF, SAN DIEGO, 68- *Concurrent Pos:* NIH trainee clin path, Yale Univ, 61-63. *Honors & Awards:* Gerald T Evans Award, 79. *Mem:* AAAS; Am Soc Clin Path; Am Fedn Clin Res; Acad Clin Lab Physicians & Sci; Am Asn Clin Chem. *Res:* Competitive binding assays; folates in human serum. *Mailing Add:* Univ Hosp Dept Path 225 W Dickinson St San Diego CA 92103

ZETTS, JOHN STEPHEN, b Youngstown, Ohio, June 14, 42. PHYSICS. *Educ:* Youngstown State Univ, BS, 64; Mich State Univ, MS, 66, PhD(physics), 71. *Prof Exp:* Asst prof physics, Youngstown State Univ, 70-73; ASST PROF PHYSICS & CHMN DEPT, UNIV PITTSBURGH, JOHNSTOWN, 73- *Mem:* Am Asn Physics Teachers. *Res:* Solid state physics; point defects in metals. *Mailing Add:* Dept of Physics Univ of Pittsburgh Johnstown PA 15904

ZEVNIK, FRANCIS C(LAIR), b Joliet, Ill, Jan 1, 22; m 45; c 4. CHEMICAL ENGINEERING. *Educ:* Univ Wis, BS, 43, MS, 47. *Prof Exp:* Chem engr, Sharples Chem, 43-44; chem supvr, E I du Pont de Nemours & Co, Inc, 47-53; sr engr, C F Braun & Co, 53-56; consult, E I du Pont de Nemours & Co, Inc, 56-65, sr res supvr, 65-69, sr design consult, 70-72; dir res eng, Kendall Co, 72-80; WITH FIBRE PROD LAB, COLGATE PALMOLIVE CO, 80- *Mem:* Am Asn Cost Engrs; Am Chem Soc; Nat Soc Prof Engrs. *Res:* Micro-porous structures and complex multi-component structures employing micro-porous materials; chemical engineering design; evaluations and economics; nonwoven and spunbonded textile sheet structures. *Mailing Add:* Colgate Palmolive Co Fibre Prod Lab West St Walpole MA 02081

ZEVOS, NICHOLAS, b Manchester, NH, June 24, 32; m 66; c 2. PHYSICAL CHEMISTRY. *Educ:* St Anselm's Col, BA, 54; Univ NH, PhD(chem), 63. *Prof Exp:* Instr chem, Univ NH, 63-64; res fel radiation chem, Sloan Kettering Inst, 64-66; fel, Cornell Univ, 66-68; asst prof, 68-75, chmn dept, 78-81, ASSOC PROF CHEM, STATE UNIV NY COL POTSDAM, 75- *Concurrent Pos:* Res assoc, Radiation Lab, Univ Notre Dame. *Mem:* AAAS; Am Chem Soc; Sigma Xi; InterAm Photochem Soc. *Res:* Gas phase kinetics; radiation and photochemistry. *Mailing Add:* Dept Chem State Univ NY Col Potsdam NY 13676

ZEWAIL, AHMED H, b Egypt, Feb 26, 46. LASERS, SOLAR ENERGY. *Educ:* Univ Alexandria, Egypt, BS, 67, MS, 69; Univ Pa, PhD(chem), 74. *Prof Exp:* Instr & researcher chem, Univ Alexandria, 67-69; res fel chem physics, Univ Calif, Berkeley, 74-75, IBM res fel, 75-76; asst prof, 76-78, ASSOC PROF CHEM PHYSICS, CALIF INST TECHNOL, 78- *Concurrent Pos:* Sloan Res Found fel, 78-; John van Geuns vis prof, Univ Amsterdam, 78; Camille & Henry Dreyfus teacher & scholar, 79-; vis prof, Univ Bordeaux, 81. *Mem:* Am Chem Soc; Am Inst Physics; Interam Photochem Soc. *Res:* Nonlinear laser spectroscopy; radiationless processes in molecules; energy transfer in solids; picosecond spectroscopy; solar photovoltaic conversion and laser-induced chemistry. *Mailing Add:* Dept of Chem Calif Inst of Technol Pasadena CA 91125

ZEY, ROBERT L, b California, Mo, Sept 19, 32; m 60; c 2. ORGANIC CHEMISTRY. *Educ:* Cent Methodist Col, AB, 54; Univ Nebr, MS, 59, PhD(chem), 61. *Prof Exp:* Res chemist, Mallinckrodt Chem Works, 61-65; from asst prof to assoc prof, 65-72, PROF CHEM, CENT MO STATE UNIV, 72- *Mem:* Am Chem Soc. *Res:* Cinnolines; aziridinones; x-ray contrast media. *Mailing Add:* Rte 1 Warrensburg MO 64093

ZEYA, HASAN ISMAIL, immunology, bacteriology, see previous edition

ZEYEN, RICHARD JOHN, b Mankato, Minn, Jan 17, 43. PLANT PATHOLOGY, HOST-PARASITE INTERACTIONS. *Educ:* Mankato State Univ, BS, 65, MS, 67; Univ Minn, St Paul, PhD(plant path & physiol), 70. *Prof Exp:* Asst gen biol, Mankato State Univ, 65-67; acad fel, 67-70, res assoc, 70-73, from asst prof to assoc prof, 73-82, PROF, DEPT PLANT PATH, UNIV MINN, ST PAUL, 82- *Concurrent Pos:* Consult, Minn Pollution Control Agency, 77; vis scientist, Imp Col Sci & Technol, London, 80-81 & Tel Aviv Univ, 81. *Mem:* Am Inst Biol Sci; Am Phytopath Soc; AAAS. *Res:* Electron optics; virus-vector relations; histopathology of plants; viral epidemiology; host-parasite relationships, physiology, in situ microanalysis of plant cell responses to parasite attack: fungi, bacteria, viruses, mycoplasma; electron optical facility director. *Mailing Add:* 304 Stakman Hall Dept Plant Path Univ Minn St Paul MN 55108

ZEZULKA, ALLISON YATES, nutrition, see previous edition

ZFASS, ALVIN MARTIN, b Norfolk, Va, Mar 30, 31; m 63; c 1. GASTROENTEROLOGY. *Educ:* Univ Va, BA, 53; Med Col Va, MD, 57. *Prof Exp:* Intern med, Bellevue-Cornell Med Ctr, 57-58; resident, Manhattan Vet Hosp, 58-60; mem, Sloan-Kettering Cancer Ctr, 60-61; from instr to assoc prof med, 63-77, PROF MED, MED COL VA, 77- *Concurrent Pos:* Fel gastroenterol, Manhattan Vet Hosp, 61-63; consult, McGuire Vet Hosp, 63-73, St Mary's Hosp, Richmond Mem Hosp & St Lukes Hosp. *Mem:* Am Gastroenterol Asn; Am Soc Gastroenterol Endoscopy. *Res:* Smooth muscle physiology of the esophagus; gastrointestinal hormones. *Mailing Add:* Med Col of Va Richmond VA 23298

ZGANJAR, EDWARD F, b Virginia, Minn, July 31, 38; m 60; c 4. NUCLEAR PHYSICS. *Educ:* St John's Univ, Minn, BS, 60; Vanderbilt Univ, MS, 63, PhD(physics), 66. *Prof Exp:* AEC fel, Vanderbilt Univ, 60-62 & 64-65, Nat Reactor Testing Sta, 65-66; from asst prof to assoc prof, 70-75, PROF PHYSICS, LA STATE UNIV, BATON ROUGE, 75- *Concurrent Pos:* Sabbatical leave, Oak Ridge Nat Lab, 73-74; chmn, exec comt, UNISOR, 73-75 & 79-80; mem syst nuclear energy comt & radiation safety comt, La State Univ, 75-; mem exec comt, Hollifield Heavy Iron Res Facility Users Groups; invited vis scientist, Brookhaven Nat Lab, 76 & 77 & GSI, Darmstadt, WGer. *Mem:* Am Phys Soc. *Res:* Low energy nuclear spectroscopy; beta and gamma ray spectroscopy. *Mailing Add:* Dept of Physics & Astron La State Univ Baton Rouge LA 70803

ZIA, PAUL Z, b Changchow, China, May 13, 26; m 51; c 2. STRUCTURAL ENGINEERING. *Educ:* Nat Chiao Tung Univ, BSCE, 49; Univ Wash, MSCE, 52; Univ Fla, PhD, 60. *Prof Exp:* Struct designer, Lakeland Eng Assocs, Inc, 51-52, proj engr, 53-54, secy & chief struct engr, 54-55, vpres & chief struct engr, 55; from instr to asst prof civil eng, Univ Fla, 55-61; assoc prof, NC State Univ, 61-64; vis assoc prof, Univ Calif, Berkeley, 64-65; assoc head dept, 67-79, PROF CIVIL ENG, NC STATE UNIV, 65-, HEAD DEPT, 79- *Honors & Awards:* Martin P Korn Award, Prestressed Concrete Inst, 74; T Y Lin Award, Am Soc Civil Engrs, 75, Raymond C Reese Award, 76; Western Elec Fund Award, Am Soc Eng Educ, 76. *Mem:* Fel Am Soc Civil Engrs; fel Am Concrete Inst. *Res:* Structural analysis and prestressed concrete structures. *Mailing Add:* Dept of Civil Eng NC State Univ PO Box 5993 Raleigh NC 27650

ZIA, ROYCE K P, b Shaoyang, China, Dec 1, 43; US citizen; m 71. THEORETICAL PHYSICS. *Educ:* Princeton Univ, AB, 64; Mass Inst Technol, PhD(physics), 68. *Prof Exp:* NATO fel physics, Europ Orgn Nuclear Res, Switz, 68-69; res fels, Univ Birmingham, Eng, 69-72, Rutherford High Energy Lab, 72-73 & Univ Southampton, 73-76; asst prof, 76-80, ASSOC PROF, VA POLYTECH INST & STATE UNIV, 80- *Concurrent Pos:* Danforth Assoc; Alexander von Humboldt fel. *Mem:* Sigma Xi. *Res:* Statistical and high energy physics; phase transitions and critical phenomena; applications of renormalization group analysis to interfacial properties; roughening transitions. *Mailing Add:* Dept of Physics Va Polytech Inst & State Univ Blacksburg VA 24061

ZIANCE, RONALD JOSEPH, pharmacology, see previous edition

ZIAUDDIN, SYED, b Mysore, India, Oct 25, 19; m 46; c 2. ATMOSPHERIC PHYSICS, SPACE PHYSICS. *Educ:* Univ Mysore, BSc, 41; Aligarh Muslim Univ, India, MSc, 45; Ill Inst Technol, MSEE, 49; Univ Sask, PhD(space physics), 60. *Prof Exp:* Lectr physics, Univ Mysore, 41-50, asst prof, 51-62; prof & chmn dept, Bangalore Univ, 63-66; ASSOC PROF PHYSICS, LAURENTIAN UNIV, 66-, CHMN, DEPT PHYSICS, 80- *Concurrent Pos:* Nat Res Coun Can fel, 61-62. *Mem:* Can Asn Physicists; Am Geophys Union; Am Asn Physics Teachers; Am Geog Soc; Inst Physics. *Res:* Atmospheric physics, especially the lower ionosphere; radio techniques; undergraduate teaching of physics. *Mailing Add:* Dept of Physics Laurentian Univ Sudbury ON P3E 2C6 Can

ZIBOH, VINCENT AZUBIKE, b Warri, Nigeria, Apr 21, 32; m 62; c 3. BIOCHEMISTRY. *Educ:* Doane Col, AB, 58; St Louis Univ, PhD(biochem), 62. *Prof Exp:* Res fel neurochem, Ill State Psychiat Inst, Chicago, 62-64; lectr chem path, Med Sch, Univ Ibadan, 64-67; res assoc dermat, 67-69, ASST PROF DERMAT & BIOCHEM, SCH MED, UNIV MIAMI, 69- *Concurrent Pos:* WHO fel clin chem, Bispebjerg Hosp, Copenhagen, Denmark, 66. *Mem:* AAAS; Brit Biochem Soc; Am Chem Soc; Soc Invest Dermat. *Res:* Biochemistry of lipids and steroids; regulation of lipogenesis from glucose in skin; biosynthesis and biochemical basis of prostaglandin action in the skin. *Mailing Add:* Dept Biochem Rosemsteel Sch Med Univ Miami Miami FL 33136

ZICCARDI, ROBERT JOHN, b New York, NY, Dec 25, 46; m 69. BIOCHEMISTRY, IMMUNOLOGY. *Educ:* Univ Conn, BA, 68; Univ Calif, Los Angeles, PhD(biochem), 73. *Prof Exp:* ASST MEM MOLECULAR IMMUNOL, SCRIPPS CLIN & RES FOUND, 73- *Res:* Complement protein structure, function and interaction with biological membranes. *Mailing Add:* Dept Molecular Immunol Scripps Clin & Res Found La Jolla CA 92307

ZICKEL, JOHN, b Munich, Ger, Feb 9, 19; US citizen; m 42; c 2. MECHANICAL ENGINEERING. *Educ:* Lehigh Univ, BS, 48, MS, 49; Brown Univ, PhD(appl math), 53. *Prof Exp:* Specialist, struct anal nuclear reactors, Knolls Atom Power Lab, 52-55, Gen Elec Atomic Power Dept, 55-58; mgr struct res rocket dept, Aerojet Gen Corp, 58-67; prof mech eng, 67-81, CHMN MECH ENG DEPT, CALIF STATE UNIV, SACRAMENTO, 81- *Honors & Awards:* Teeter Award, Soc Automotive Eng, 78. *Mem:* Fel Am Soc Mech Eng; Soc Exp Stress Anal; Sigma Xi; Am Soc Eng Educ; Soc Automotive Eng. *Res:* Flywheel technology; probabilistic design; product liability. *Mailing Add:* 6063 Ranger Way Carmichael CA 95608

ZICKER, ELDON LOUIS, b Milwaukee, Wis, Mar 12, 20; m 54; c 5. SOIL SCIENCE. *Educ:* Univ Wis, BS, 48, PhD(soils), 55. *Prof Exp:* Instr soil surv, Kans State Univ, 49; instr geol & soils, Yakima Valley Col, 59-64; dean, Sch Agr & Home Econ, 70-80, INSTR SOILS, DEPT PLANT & SOIL SCI, CALIF STATE UNIV, CHICO, 64-, PROF, 80- *Mem:* Am Soc Agron; Soil Sci Soc Am; Brit Soc Soil Sci; Sigma Xi; Am Chem Soc. *Res:* Soil genesis and development; world food and environment problems. *Mailing Add:* Dept Plant & Soil Sci First & Normal St Chico CA 95929

ZIDEK, JAMES VICTOR, b Acme, Alta, Sept 26, 39; m 61. MATHEMATICAL STATISTICS. *Educ:* Univ Alta, BSc, 61, MSc, 63; Stanford Univ, PhD(math statist), 67. *Prof Exp:* Lectr probability & statist, Univ Alta, 62-63; from asst prof to assoc prof probability & statist, 67-76, PROF, STATIST, UNIV BC, 76- *Concurrent Pos:* Hon res fel, Univ Col London, 71-82; vis sr res scientist, Commonwealth Sci & Indust Orgn, Australia, 76-77; sr assoc ed, Can J Statist, 80- *Mem:* Fel Inst Math Statist; Statist Soc Can; Royal Statist Soc; Am Statist Asn; Int Statist Inst. *Res:* statistical decision theory. *Mailing Add:* Dept Math 121/1984 Math Rd Univ BC Vancouver BC B6T 1W5 Can

ZIEBARTH, TIMOTHY DEAN, b Glendive, Mont, June 10, 46; m 66; c 2. ORGANIC CHEMISTRY, PHYSICAL ORGANIC CHEMISTRY. *Educ:* Mont State Univ, BS, 69; Ore State Univ, PhD(org chem), 73. *Prof Exp:* Fel org chem, Univ Colo, 72-74; CHIEF CHEMIST, HAUSER LABS, 74- *Mem:* Am Chem Soc. *Res:* Photochemistry of allylic amines; novel methods of polymer analysis; forensic chemistry. *Mailing Add:* Hauser Labs 5680 Central Ave Boulder CO 80302

ZIEBUR, ALLEN DOUGLAS, b Shawano, Wis, May 1, 23; m 49; c 2. MATHEMATICS. *Educ:* Univ Wis, PhD, 50. *Prof Exp:* From instr to assoc prof math, Ohio State Univ, 51-61; assoc prof, 61-63, PROF MATH, STATE UNIV NY BINGHAMTON, 63- *Mem:* Am Math Soc; Math Asn Am; Soc Indust & Appl Math. *Res:* Differential equations. *Mailing Add:* Dept of Math State Univ of NY Binghamton NY 13901

ZIEG, ROGER GRANT, b McCooke, Nebr, Aug 16, 39; m 70; c 2. PARASITOLOGY, PROTOZOOLOGY. *Educ:* Univ Nebr, BS, 61, MS, 63; Iowa State Univ, PhD(develop biol), 81. *Prof Exp:* In-charge res asst, Tissue Cult Collection, Am Type Cult Collection, 66-68, Protozoan Collection, 68-75; teaching asst biol & phys biochem, Iowa State Univ, 75-80; RES FEL CELL BIOL, UNIV MINN, 80- *Mem:* AAAS; Sigma Xi. *Res:* Corn and soybean tissue culture; morphogenesis in plant cell cultures; isolation of secondary products from plant tissue cultures; protoplast isolation and fusion. *Mailing Add:* 3656 S 40th Ave Minneapolis MN 55406

ZIEGEL, KENNETH DAVID, b Cleveland, Ohio, Mar 15, 35; m 60; c 2. PHYSICAL CHEMISTRY. *Educ:* Case Inst, BS, 56; Polytech Inst Brooklyn, PhD(polymer chem), 66. *Prof Exp:* Res engr, Esso Res & Eng Co, 56-60; res scientist, Radiation Appln Inc, 60-62; RES SCIENTIST, E I DU PONT DE NEMOURS & CO, INC, 62- *Concurrent Pos:* Exchange scientist, Slovak Acad Sci, Czech, 72. *Mem:* AAAS. *Res:* Diffusion of gases through polymeric membranes; radiation induced graft copolymerization to normally inert surfaces; adhesion; rheology of composites. *Mailing Add:* Elastomer Chem Dept Exp Sta E I du Pont de Nemours & Co Inc Wilmington DE 19898

ZIEGENHAGEN, ALLYN JAMES, b Wautoma, Wis, Sept 5, 35; m 80. CHEMICAL ENGINEERING, ECONOMICS ENGINEERING. *Educ:* Univ Wis, BS, 57, PhD(fluid mech, rheol, chem eng), 62; Mass Inst Technol, SM, 59. *Prof Exp:* Asst prof physics, Univ Wis, Milwaukee, 62-64; vis prof chem eng, Univ Valle, Colombia, 64-65; asst prof eng, Univ Wis, Milwaukee, 65-66; engr, Shell Develop Co, 66-70; sr res engr, 70-80, RES ASSOC, PROCESS DEVELOP DEPT, STAUFFER CHEM CO, 80- *Mem:* Am Inst Chem Engrs. *Res:* New process research and development in chlorinated hydrocarbons, agricultural chemicals and water pollution control; computer applications; catalyst development; food ingredient extraction from seaweed. *Mailing Add:* Process Develop Dept Stauffer Chem Co Richmond CA 94804

ZIEGER, HERMAN ERNST, b Philadelphia, Pa, May 17, 35; m 60; c 3. ORGANIC CHEMISTRY. *Educ:* Muhlenberg Col, BS, 56; Pa State Univ, PhD(org chem), 61. *Prof Exp:* Fulbright scholar, Univ Heidelberg, 60-61; from instr to assoc prof, 61-73, PROF CHEM, BROOKLYN COL, 73- *Concurrent Pos:* Vis assoc, Calif Inst Technol, 67-68; Alexander von Humboldt Found fel, 74-75; mem doctoral fac, City Univ New York. *Mem:* Am Chem Soc. *Res:* Organolithium chemistry; aryne chemistry; radical anion processes; kinetics and stereochemistry of carbanion coupling processes. *Mailing Add:* Dept of Chem Brooklyn Col Brooklyn NY 11210

ZIEGLER, ALAN CONRAD, b Galveston, Tex, Dec 10, 29; m 55; c 2. MAMMALOGY. *Educ:* Univ Calif, Berkeley, AB, 57, PhD(zool), 67. *Prof Exp:* VERT ZOOLOGIST, BISHOP MUS, 67- *Concurrent Pos:* Mem adv subcomt land vert, Hawaii Dept Agr, 68-; mammalogist mem, Hawaii Animal Species Adv Comn, 70-78; affil grad fac zool, Univ Hawaii, 71-, lectr, 73. *Mem:* Am Soc Mammal; Australian Mammal Soc. *Res:* Mammalian evolution; systematics and ecology of New Guinea land vertebrates; analysis of archaeological faunal remains. *Mailing Add:* 1355 Kalihi St PO Box 19000-A Honolulu HI 96819

ZIEGLER, ALFRED M, b Boston, Mass, Apr 23, 38; m 64; c 2. PALEONTOLOGY, STRATIGRAPHY. *Educ:* Bates Col, BSc, 59; Oxford Univ, DPhil(paleont), 64. *Prof Exp:* Fel paleont, Calif Inst Technol, 64-66; asst prof, 66-72, ASSOC PROF PALEONT, UNIV CHICAGO, 72-, PROF STRATIG, 76- *Concurrent Pos:* NSF grant, 72-74. *Mem:* Geol Soc Am; Brit Palaeontol Asn. *Res:* Paleontology, paleoecology and stratigraphy of the Silurian age deposits of the British Isles, Norway and eastern North America. *Mailing Add:* Dept of Geophys Sci Univ of Chicago Chicago IL 60637

ZIEGLER, DANIEL, b Quinter, Kans, July 6, 27; m 52; c 4. BIOCHEMISTRY. *Educ:* St Benedict's Col, Kans, BS, 49; Loyola Univ, Ill, PhD(biochem), 55. *Prof Exp:* Fel enzyme chem, Inst Enzyme Res, Univ Wis, 55-59, asst prof, 59-61; assoc prof, 61-68, PROF CHEM, UNIV TEX, AUSTIN, 68-, MEM STAFF, CLAYTON FOUND BIOCHEM INST, 61- *Concurrent Pos:* Estab investr, Am Heart Asn, 60-65. *Mem:* AAAS; Am Chem Soc; Am Soc Biol Chem. *Res:* Synthesis of protein hormones; mammalian mixed-function drug oxidases; flavoproteins of the electron transport system. *Mailing Add:* Clayton Found Biochem Inst Dept of Chem Univ of Tex Austin TX 78712

ZIEGLER, DEWEY KIPER, b Omaha, Nebr, May 31, 20; m 54; c 3. NEUROLOGY. *Educ:* Harvard Univ, BA, 41, MD, 45. *Prof Exp:* Assoc neurol, Col Physicians & Surgeons, Columbia Univ, 53-55; asst prof, Med Sch, Univ Minn, 55-56; assoc prof, 58-63, PROF NEUROL, UNIV KANS MED CTR, KANSAS CITY, 63-, CHMN DEPT, 73- *Concurrent Pos:* Consult, US Fed Hosp, Springfield, Mo & Vet Admin Hosp, Kansas City, Mo, 64-; clin prof neurol, Med Sch, Univ Mo-Kansas City; dir, Am Bd Psychiat & Neurol, 74-; mem comt stroke coun, Am Heart Asn, 81-83, mem exec comt. *Mem:* AMA; Soc Neurosci; Am Neurol Asn; fel Am Col Physicians; Am Epilepsy Soc. *Res:* Epidemiology and natural history of cerebrovascular disease; neurophysiological and biochemical basis of migraine. *Mailing Add:* Dept of Neurol Univ of Kans Med Ctr Kansas City KS 66103

ZIEGLER, EDWARD N, b Bronx, NY, Aug 15, 38; m 74; c 1. CHEMICAL ENGINEERING, ENVIRONMENTAL ENGINEERING. *Educ:* City Col New York, BChE, 60; Northwestern Univ, MS, 62, PhD(chem eng), 64. *Prof Exp:* Res assoc transport phenomena in fluidized solid systs, Argonne Nat Lab, 62-63; process res engr, Esso Res & Eng Co, 64-65; asst prof chem eng, 65-72, ASSOC PROF CHEM ENG, POLYTECH INST NEW YORK, 72- *Concurrent Pos:* Ed, Encycl Environ Sci & Eng, 75 & Advan Series Environ Sci & Eng, 79-80; consult, Brookhaven Nat Lab, 74-80; proj engr, Consol Edison Co, 80. *Mem:* Assoc mem Am Inst Chem Engrs; Sigma Xi; Air Pollution Control Asn. *Res:* Applied reaction kinetics; air pollution control; coal conversion; fluidization. *Mailing Add:* Dept Chem Eng 333 Jay St Brooklyn NY 11201

ZIEGLER, FREDERICK DIXON, b Waynesboro, Pa, Oct 14, 33. BIOCHEMISTRY, PHYSIOLOGY. *Educ:* Shippensburg State Col, BS, 57; Pa State Univ, MS, 60, PhD(zool), 62. *Prof Exp:* Res trainee virol, Pa State Univ, 62-63; res assoc biochem, State Univ NY Buffalo, 63-65; asst prof, McMaster Univ, 65-69; res scientist, 69-73, SR RES SCIENTIST, DIV LABS & RES, NY STATE DEPT HEALTH, 73- *Mem:* Am Chem Soc; Can Biochem Soc. *Res:* Metabolism; coagulation. *Mailing Add:* NY State Dept of Health Empire State Plaza Albany NY 12201

ZIEGLER, FREDERICK EDWARD, b Teaneck, NJ, Mar 29, 38; m 62; c 2. ORGANIC CHEMISTRY. *Educ:* Fairleigh Dickinson Univ, BS, 60; Columbia Univ, MA, 61, PhD(chem), 64. *Prof Exp:* Eugene Higgins fel, Columbia Univ, 60-61, NIH fel, 61-64; NSF fel, Mass Inst Technol, 64-65; from asst prof to assoc prof, 65-78, PROF CHEM, YALE UNIV, 78- *Honors & Awards:* Career Develop Awardee, NIH, 73-78. *Mem:* Am Chem Soc. *Res:* Organic synthetic methods and natural products synthesis. *Mailing Add:* Sterling Chem Lab Yale Univ New Haven CT 06520

ZIEGLER, GEORGE WILLIAM, JR, b Cleveland, Ohio, Oct 12, 16; c 2. PHYSICAL CHEMISTRY. *Educ:* Monmouth Col, BS, 39; Mass Inst Technol, cert, 44; Ohio State Univ, PhD, 50. *Prof Exp:* Asst physics, Monmouth Col, 37-39; analyst, Grasselli Chem Div, E I du Pont de Nemours & Co, 39-40, tech supvr, 40-42, asst to chief plant technologist, 42-43; leader high temperature calorimetry group, Res Found, Ohio State Univ, 46-50; group leader process develop, Int Resistance Co, 50-51, sect head, 51-53, head dept, 53; res chemist & mem staff, Mat Control Div, Curtis Pub Co, 53-55; dir spec projs lab, AMP, Inc, 55-60, from proj engr to sr proj engr, 60-70, mgr spec prod, 70-76; INDEPENDENT CONSULT, 76- *Concurrent Pos:* Assoc prof, Dickinson Col, 55-59. *Mem:* Am Chem Soc; Am Phys Soc; Am Soc Metals; Inst Elec & Electronics Eng; Inst Mgt Sci. *Res:* High temperature thermodynamics and kinetics; instrumentation; metallurgy; conducting films; heat transfer; color correction theory; photoengraving; radio frequency connectors; aluminum building wire connectors. *Mailing Add:* 17 Circle Dr Carlisle PA 17013

ZIEGLER, HANS K(ONRAD), b Munich, Ger, Mar 1, 11; nat US; m 37; c 3. ELECTRONIC ENGINEERING. *Educ:* Munich Tech Univ, BS, 32, MS, 34, PhD(electronic eng), 36. *Prof Exp:* Asst prof elec eng, Munich Tech Univ, 34-36; chief res & develop dept, Rosenthal Isolatoren, Inc, 36-47; sci consult, US Army Signal Res & Develop Lab, 47-56, asst dir res, 56-58, dir astroelectronics div, 58-59, chief scientist, 59-63, chief scientist & tech dir, 63-66, dep for sci & chief scientist, US Army Electronics Command, 66-71, dir, US Army Electronics Technol & Devices Lab, 71-76; RETIRED. *Concurrent Pos:* Consult, Kohler Co, Wis, 51-55; consult, 76- *Mem:* Fel Am Astronaut Soc; fel Inst Elec & Electronics Engrs. *Res:* Military electronics; communications; space science and technology; energy sources, conversion and transmission; solar energy; geophysics; meteorology; research management. *Mailing Add:* 32 E Larchmont Dr Colts Neck NJ 07722

ZIEGLER, JAMES FRANCIS, b Apr 20, 39; US citizen; m 69. NUCLEAR PHYSICS. *Educ:* Yale Univ, BS, 57, MS, 65, PhD(nuclear physics), 67. *Prof Exp:* Mem res staff, 67-69, DIR HIGH ENERGY ACCELERATOR LAB, RES CTR, IBM CORP, 69- *Mem:* Am Phys Soc. *Res:* Solid state analysis using nuclear physics techniques; ion-induced x-rays; nuclear backscattering; nuclear channeling; ion-implantation; optical microcircuits. *Mailing Add:* Res Ctr IBM Corp PO Box 218 Yorktown Heights NY 10598

ZIEGLER, JOHN BENJAMIN, b Rochester, NY, Jan 2, 17; m 46; c 3. SYNTHETIC ORGANIC CHEMISTRY, TAXONOMY OF LEPIDOPTERA. *Educ:* Univ Rochester, BS, 39; Univ Ill, MS, 40, PhD(org chem), 46. *Prof Exp:* Jr chemist, Merck & Co, Inc, NJ, 40-43; asst chem, Univ

Ill, 43-46; res chemist, J T Baker Chem Co, NJ, 46-48; assoc chemist, Develop Div, Ciba Pharmaceut Co, 48-52, supvr develop res labs, 52-62, mgr process res, 62-70, dir chem develop, Pharmaceut Div, Ciba-Geigy Corp, 70-75, dir process res, Pharmaceut Div, 75, sr staff scientist, 76-80; LAB & BUS ADMIN, DEPTS BIOL & CHEM PHYSICS, SETON HALL UNIV, 80- *Mem:* Am Chem Soc; Sigma Xi; Lepidop Soc (treas, 50-53); NY Acad Sci; fel Am Inst Chem. *Res:* Research and development of processes for synthesis of medicinal chemicals; taxonomic research in entomoloby, extra sensory perception and lepidoptera. *Mailing Add:* 64 Canoe Brook Pkwy Summit NJ 07901

ZIEGLER, JOHN HENRY, JR, b Altoona, Pa, Nov 10, 24; m 49; c 3. MEAT SCIENCE, ANIMAL SCIENCE. *Educ:* Pa State Univ, BS, 50, MS, 52, PhD(animal indust), 65. *Prof Exp:* Soil conservationist, USDA, 49; asst animal husb, Pa State Univ, 50-52; nutritionist, Near's Food Co, NY, 52-54; from instr animal indust to assoc prof meat sci, 54-76, PROF MEAT SCI, PA STATE UNIV, UNIVERSITY PARK, 76- *Mem:* Am Soc Meat Sci; Am Soc Animal Sci; Inst Food Technologists. *Res:* Meat animal carcass evaluation and utilization; basic adipose tissue anatomy and physiology; meat product development. *Mailing Add:* 15 Meats Lab Pa State Univ University Park PA 16802

ZIEGLER, MICHAEL GREGORY, b Chicago, Ill, May 12, 46. PHARMACOLOGY, MEDICINE. *Educ:* Loyola Univ, Chicago, BS, 67; Med Sch, Univ Chicago, MD, 71. *Prof Exp:* Residency med, Med Sch, Univ Kans, 73; pharmacol res assoc, NIMH, 73-75, pharmacologist, 75-76; attend physician med & consult, NIH, 74-76; asst prof med & pharmacol, Univ Tex Med Br Galveston, 76-80; ASST PROF MED, UNIV CALIF, SAN DIEGO, 80- *Res:* Clinical pharmacology; hypertension; sympathetic nervous system; neurotransmitters; catecholamines. *Mailing Add:* H-781-B Univ Hosp San Diego CA 92103

ZIEGLER, MICHAEL ROBERT, b York, Pa, Oct 31, 42; m 64; c 4. MATHEMATICAL ANALYSIS. *Educ:* Shippensburg State Col, BS, 64; Univ Del, MS, 67, PhD(math), 70. *Prof Exp:* Instr math, Univ Del, Georgetown Exten, 69-70; fel, Univ Ky, 70-71; ASSOC PROF MATH, MARQUETTE UNIV, 71- *Mem:* Am Math Soc; Math Asn Am. *Res:* Complex analysis; geometric function theory; univalent functions. *Mailing Add:* Dept of Math Marquette Univ Milwaukee WI 53233

ZIEGLER, MIRIAM MARY, b Gainesville, Fla, Dec 15, 45; m 78; c 2. PROTEIN CHEMISTRY, ENZYMOLOGY. *Educ:* Bucknell Univ, BS, 67; Harvard Univ, MA, 70, PhD(biochem), 72. *Prof Exp:* Res fel biol, Harvard Univ, 72-73, lectr, 73-75, res fel, 75-76; res fel biochem, Univ Ill, Urbana, 76-78, vis asst prof, 78-81; RES SCIENTIST, DEPT BIOCHEM & BIOPHYSICS, TEX A&M UNIV, COLLEGE STATION, 81- *Mem:* Biophys Soc; Am Soc Microbiol. *Res:* Enzymatic mechanism, structure, and subunit function of bacterial luciferase; chemical modification of proteins. *Mailing Add:* Dept Biochem & Biophys Tex A&M Univ College Station TX 77843

ZIEGLER, PAUL FOUT, b Baltimore, Md, Dec 3, 16; m 45; c 2. CHEMISTRY. *Educ:* Otterbein Col, BS, 39; Univ Cincinnati, MS, 47, PhD(chem), 63. *Prof Exp:* Analyst, Am Rolling Mills, Ohio, 39-40, chemist, 40-46; instr chem, Ala Polytech Inst, 49-52, asst prof, 52-58, ASSOC PROF CHEM, AUBURN UNIV, 58- *Mem:* Am Chem Soc. *Res:* Analytical and organic chemistry; synthesis and rearrangement. *Mailing Add:* Dept of Chem Auburn Univ Auburn AL 36830

ZIEGLER, PETER, b Vienna, Austria, Mar 26, 22; m 48. ORGANIC CHEMISTRY, BIOCHEMISTRY. *Educ:* Sir Geo Williams Col, BSc, 44; McGill Univ, PhD(biochem), 51. *Prof Exp:* Chemist, Frank W Horner, Ltd, 44-48; asst, McGill Univ, 48-51; group leader, 51-65, ASST DIR RES, CAN PACKERS, LTD, 66- *Mem:* Am Chem Soc; fel Chem Inst Can. *Res:* Fine chemicals; pharmaceuticals. *Mailing Add:* Res & Develop Labs Can Packers Ltd Toronto ON M6N 1K4 Can

ZIEGLER, RICHARD JAMES, b Norristown, Pa, May 30, 43; m 67. VIROLOGY. *Educ:* Muhlenberg Col, BS, 65; Temple Univ, PhD(microbiol), 70. *Prof Exp:* Instr microbiol, Med Sch, Temple Univ, 69; res assoc genetics, Rockefeller Univ, 70-71; asst prof microbiol, 71-77, ASSOC PROF MED MICROBIOL & IMMUNOL, MED SCH, UNIV MINN, DULUTH, 77- *Mem:* AAAS; Tissue Cult Asn; Am Soc Microbiol; Asn Am Med Cols. *Res:* Effects of neurotropic viral multiplication on central nervous system function and effects of herpes simplex virus replication on primary nerve tissue culture cells. *Mailing Add:* Dept of Microbiol Univ of Minn Med Sch Duluth MN 55812

ZIEGLER, ROBERT C(HARLES), b Buffalo, NY, Dec 11, 27. PHYSICS, ENVIRONMENTAL SCIENCES. *Educ:* Univ Buffalo, BA, 50, PhD(physics), 57. *Prof Exp:* Lectr physics, Univ Buffalo, 55-56; proj engr, Nucleonics Dept, Bell Aircraft Corp, 56-57; mem staff, Cornell Aeronaut Lab, Inc, 57-66, head remote sensing sect, 66-71, head environ sci sect, 71-73; consult, 74-75; tech staff environ sci dept, Calspan Corp, 75-81; CONSULT, 81- *Mem:* Am Phys Soc; Am Asn Physics Teachers; Optical Soc Am; Am Soc Photogram; Nat Soc Prof Engrs. *Res:* Geometrical and physical optics; nuclear physics; aerial remote sensing; environmental research. *Mailing Add:* 26 High Park Blvd Buffalo NY 14226

ZIEGLER, ROBERT G, b The Dalles, Ore, Apr 24, 24; m 53; c 3. INORGANIC CHEMISTRY. *Educ:* Ore State Univ, BA, 48, MS, 51; Univ Tenn, PhD, 69. *Prof Exp:* Control chemist, Barium Prod Ltd, 48-49; res chemist, Nitrogen Div, Allied Chem Corp, 52-57; from asst prof to assoc prof, 57-70, head dept, 69-74, PROF CHEM, LINCOLN MEM UNIV, 70- *Mem:* Am Chem Soc; Am Sci Affil. *Res:* Analytical and coordination chemistry; fertilizer technology. *Mailing Add:* Dept of Chem Lincoln Mem Univ Harrogate TN 37752

ZIEGLER, THERESA FRANCES, b Budapest, Hungary; nat US; wid; c 1. CHEMISTRY. *Educ:* Eotvos Lorand Univ, Budapest, BS, 46, PhD(phys chem), 49. *Prof Exp:* Res engr, State Biochem Res Inst, Hungary, 49-50; chemist, Steel Plant Lab, 53-56; radiochemist, Nat Health & Labor Inst, 56-57; RADIOCHEMIST, RADIATION SAFETY OFFICER, STAMFORD RES LABS, AM CYANAMID CO, 57- *Mem:* Am Chem Soc; Am Nuclear Soc; NY Acad Sci. *Res:* Radiosyntheses and radio-tacerwork in the following fields--agricultural and industrial chemicals, herbicides, pesticides and insecticides; pharmaceuticals; catalysts; technology of plastics, fibers and papers; surface coatings; biological membranes; industrial hygiene, toxicity studies; autoradiography, experience with sealed sources; radioactive semi-micro and micro syntheses. *Mailing Add:* 1937 W Main St Am Cyanamid Co Stamford CT 06904

ZIEGLER, WILLIAM ARTHUR, b St Louis, Mo, Feb 10, 24; m 51; c 2. ANALYTICAL CHEMISTRY. *Educ:* Univ Ill, AB, 48, MS, 49, PhD(anal chem), 52. *Prof Exp:* Teaching asst, Univ Ill, 48-52; chemist, Mallinckrodt Chem Works, 52, supvr, 52-55, asst mgr anal dept, Uranium Div, 55-60, mgr anal dept, 60-66, tech asst to dir qual control, 66-67; tech specialist, Nuclear Div, Kerr-McGee Corp, 67-69, mgr qual assurance, 69-70; mgr anal sect, Eastern Res Ctr, Stauffer Chem Co, 71-79; mgr, Anal Lab, 80, MGR SUPPORT GROUP, ADVAN MAT DIV, MAT RES CORP, 81- *Mem:* Am Chem Soc. *Res:* Sampling; uranium chemistry. *Mailing Add:* 61 Pocconock Trail New Canaan CT 06840

ZIEGRA, SUMNER ROOT, b Deep River, Conn, Feb 13, 23; m 45; c 2. PEDIATRICS. *Educ:* Univ Vt, BS, 45; Yale Univ, MD, 47; Am Bd Pediat, dipl, 57. *Prof Exp:* Fel pediat, Sch Med, NY Univ, 49-51; asst prof pediat, State Univ NY Downstate Med Ctr, 56-60; assoc prof, Jefferson Med Col, 60-63; from assoc prof to prof, Hahnemann Med Col, 63-70; prof, Col Med, Thomas Jefferson Univ, 70-72; PROF PEDIAT, MED COL PA, 73-, CHMN DEPT, 75- *Concurrent Pos:* Dir div B, Dept Pediat, Philadelphia Gen Hosp, 63-70, coordr, Hahnemann Div, 66-67; dir dept pediat, Lankenau Hosp, 70-72. *Res:* Infectious diseases. *Mailing Add:* Dept Pediat Med Col Pa Philadelphia PA 19129

ZIELEN, ALBIN JOHN, b Chicago, Ill, Dec 22, 25. SYSTEMS ANALYST, PHYSICAL CHEMISTRY. *Educ:* Miami Univ, BA, 50; Univ Calif, PhD(chem), 53. *Prof Exp:* Asst chem, Univ Calif, 51-52; chemist, Radiation Lab, Univ Calif, 52-53; ASSOC CHEMIST, ARGONNE NAT LAB, 53- *Mem:* Am Chem Soc. *Res:* Computer programming; neptunium solution chemistry; electrochemistry; reaction kinetics; complex ions. *Mailing Add:* Bldg 10 Argonne Nat Lab 9700 S Cass Ave Argonne IL 60439

ZIELEZNY, MARIA ANNA, b Kaczkowizna, Poland, Sept 20, 39; US citizen; m 69. BIOSTATISTICS. *Educ:* Univ Warsaw, MS, 62; Univ Calif, Los Angeles, PhD(biostatist), 71. *Prof Exp:* Res asst statist, Math Inst, Polish Acad Sci, Warsaw, 62-65; clin asst prof, 71-73, asst prof, 74-80, ASSOC PROF BIOSTATIST, DEPT SOCIAL & PREV MED, SCH MED, STATE UNIV NY BUFFALO, 80- *Mem:* Am Statist Asn; Am Pub Health Asn; Biomet Soc. *Res:* Statistical applications in particular to medicine, development of statistical methods in evaluation, discriminant analysis, measures of association, techniques for qualitative data. *Mailing Add:* Dept Social & Prev Med State Univ NY Sch Med 2211 Main St Buffalo NY 14214

ZIELEZNY, ZBIGNIEW HENRYK, b Knurow, Poland, Jan 11, 30; m 69. MATHEMATICAL ANALYSIS. *Educ:* Wroclaw Univ, Masters, 54, PhD(math), 59; Polish Acad Sci, docent, 64. *Prof Exp:* Adj math, Wroclaw Tech Univ, 58-61; adj, Polish Acad Sci, 61-64, docent, 64-69; vis prof, Univ Kiel, 69-70; assoc prof, 70-71, PROF MATH, STATE UNIV NY BUFFALO, 71- *Concurrent Pos:* Vis prof, Univ Kiel, WGer, 79. *Mem:* Am Math Soc. *Res:* Analysis, functional analysis; differential equations; existence and regularity of solutions of convolution equations in various spaces of distributions. *Mailing Add:* Dept of Math State Univ of NY 106 Diefendorf Hall Buffalo NY 14214

ZIELINSKI, ADAM, b Jaroslaw, Poland, Oct 2, 43; Can citizen; m 75; c 2. ELECTRICAL ENGINEERING, OCEAN ENGINEERING. *Educ:* Wroclaw Tech Univ, BEE & MEE, 67, PhD(elec eng), 72. *Prof Exp:* Res assoc, Wroclaw Tech Univ, 67-68, asst prof, 68-72; res fel, Tokyo Inst Technol, 72-74 & Univ NB, 74-75; asst prof, 75-80, ASSOC PROF ELEC ENG, MEM UNIV NFLD, 80- *Concurrent Pos:* Investr, Nat Res Coun Can operating grant, 76-77 & Natural Sci & Eng Res Coun Can strategic grant ocean eng, 78- *Mem:* Sr mem Inst Elec & Electronics Engrs; Marine Technol Soc. *Res:* Underwater acoustic communication in multipath environment; telemetry and instrumentation for investigation of ocean sediments; ocean electronic instrumentation; data acquisition and random signal processing. *Mailing Add:* Fac Eng Mem Univ Nfld St John's NF A1B 3X5 Can

ZIELINSKI, THERESA JULIA, b Brooklyn, NY. THEORETICAL CHEMISTRY. *Educ:* Fordham Univ, BS, 63, MS, 68, PhD(chem), 73. *Prof Exp:* ASST PROF CHEM, COL MT ST VINCENT, 72- *Mem:* Am Chem Soc. *Res:* Theoretical chemical study of purines and pyrimidines. *Mailing Add:* Apt 6 46 Raintree Island Tonawanda NY 14150

ZIELINSKI, WALTER L, JR, b Staten Island, NY, May 31, 32; m 71; c 2. ANALYTICAL CHEMISTRY. *Educ:* Wagner Col, BS, 54; NC State Univ, MS, 59; Georgetown Univ, PhD, 72. *Prof Exp:* Res chemist, Div Chem & Foods, Va Dept Agr, 59-61; res chemist, Hazleton Labs, 61-62; res chemist, Div Chem & Foods, Va Dept Agr, 62-63; res chemist, Res Ctr, Union Camp Corp, Ga, 63-64; staff scientist, Bionetics Res Labs, Inc, Va, 64-66, sr scientist, 67-68; sr chemist, Melpar, Inc, Va, 68; staff res chemist, Anal Chem Div, Nat Bur Standards, Washington, DC, 68-71, actg head, Separation & Purification Sect, 71-72; HEAD CHEM SECT, FREDERICK CANCER RES CTR, NAT CANCER INST, MD, 72-; LECTR, GEORGETOWN UNIV, 76- *Mem:* Am Chem Soc; AAAS. *Res:* Analytical methods in cancer research; method development in analytical gas chromatography; thermodynamics of solute-solvent interaction in gas chromatography;

development of ion-exchange and liquid chromatographic systems; structural analysis of copolymers and ion-exchangers by infrared spectroscopy; development of high-temperature liquid crystals for novel gas chromatographic separations; development of particle metrology. *Mailing Add:* Frederick Cancer Res Ctr PO Box B Frederick MD 21701

ZIELKE, HORST RONALD, b Pscinno, Poland, June 7, 42; US citizen; m 67; c 2. BIOCHEMISTRY, CELL BIOLOGY. *Educ:* Univ Ill, BS, 64; Mich State Univ, PhD(biochem), 68. *Prof Exp:* Res assoc, AEC Plant Res Lab, Mich State Univ, 68-71; res fel, Genetics Unit, Mass Gen Hosp, 71-73; asst prof, 73-81, ASSOC PROF PEDIAT RES, SCH MED, UNIV MD, 81- *Concurrent Pos:* Monsanto fel, 69; trustee, Am Type Culture Collection. *Mem:* Am Soc Cell Biol. *Res:* Metabolism and enzymology of cultured mammalian cells. *Mailing Add:* Dept of Pediat Res Sch of Med Univ of Md Baltimore MD 21201

ZIEMAN, JOSEPH CROWE, JR, b Mobile, Ala, June 9, 43; m 67. MARINE ECOLOGY, BIOLOGICAL OCEANOGRAPHY. *Educ:* Tulane Univ, BS, 65; Univ Miami, MS, 68, PhD(marine sci), 70. *Prof Exp:* Res asst thermal pollution, Inst Marine Sci, Univ Miami, 68-70; fel syst ecol, Inst Ecol, Univ Ga, 70-71; asst prof, 71-77, ASSOC PROF ENVIRON SCI, UNIV VA, 77- *Mem:* Ecol Soc Am; Am Soc Limnol & Oceanog; Sigma Xi; AAAS; Int Asn Aquatic Vascular Plant Biologists. *Res:* Comparative studies of tropical and temperate interface zones; seagrasses, coral reefs, mangroves and salt marshes; production, colonization, succession and recovery from disturbances; simulation modeling of growth and succession. *Mailing Add:* Dept Environ Sci Clark Hall Univ of Va Charlottesville VA 22903

ZIEMER, PAUL L, b Toledo, Ohio, June 28, 35; m 58; c 4. HEALTH PHYSICS. *Educ:* Wheaton Col, BS, 57; Vanderbilt Univ, MS, 59; Purdue Univ, PhD(bionucleonics), 62; Am Bd Health Physics, dipl, 65. *Prof Exp:* Physicist, US Naval Res Lab, Wash, 57; health physicist, Oak Ridge Nat Lab, 59; from asst prof to assoc prof health physics, 62-69, PROF HEALTH PHYSICS, PRUDUE UNIV, WEST LAFAYETTE, 69-, RADIOL CONTROL OFFICER, 59-, ASSOC HEAD BIONUCLEONICS, 71-, HEAD, SCH HEALTH SCI, 79- *Concurrent Pos:* Consult, Harrison Steel Castings Co, Ind, 62-66, satellite div, Union Carbide Corp, 66-67, Calif Nuclear, Inc, 66-68, Breed Radium Inst, 68-70, Detroit Diesel Allison Div, Gen Motors Corp, 69 & 77- Mobil Field Res Labs, 70- & Midwest Radiation Protection, Inc, 71-; mem panel examr, Am Bd Health Physics, 69-71; mem sci comt, Nat Coun Radiation Protection, Int Standards Orgn, Working Group 6 of Sci Comt on Radiation Protection, 76-81; ed, Health Physics J, 79-; vchmn comt N-13 radiation protection standards, Am Nat Standards, 81- *Honors & Awards:* Lederle Pharm Fac Award, 64; Elda E Anderson Award, Health Physics Soc, 71. *Mem:* Health Physics Soc (pres, 75); Int Radiation Protection Asn; AAAS. *Res:* Uptake, retention and excretion of inhaled radionuclides; radiation dosimetry. *Mailing Add:* Dept of Bionucleonics Purdue Univ West Lafayette IN 47907

ZIEMER, RODGER EDMUND, b Sargeant, Minn, Aug 22, 37; m 62; c 4. ELECTRICAL ENGINEERING. *Educ:* Univ Minn, BS, 60, MS, 62, PhD(elec eng), 65. *Prof Exp:* From asst prof to assoc prof elec eng, 68-73, grad coordr dept, 78-80, PROF ELEC ENG, UNIV MO-ROLLA, 73- *Concurrent Pos:* Consult, Electronics & Space Div, Emerson Elec Co, St Louis, 74-, govt electronics div, Motorola Inc, Scottsdale, Ariz, 80-; on leave, Motorola Inc, Scottsdale, Ariz, 80-81. *Mem:* Inst Elec & Electronics Engrs; Am Soc Eng Educ; Sigma Xi. *Res:* Statistical communication theory; digital signaling in impulsive noise; costas and phase lock loop performance in radio frequency environments; spread spectrum communication techniques; digital signal processing. *Mailing Add:* 1304 Highland Dr Rolla MO 65401

ZIEMER, WILLIAM P, b Manitowoc, Wis, Mar 26, 34; m 57; c 3. MATHEMATICS. *Educ:* Univ Wis, BS, 56, MS, 57; Brown Univ, PhD(math), 61. *Prof Exp:* Assoc prof, 61-77, PROF MATH, IND UNIV, BLOOMINGTON, 77- *Mem:* Am Math Soc; Math Asn Am. *Res:* Geometric analysis; area theory; surface theory; differential geometry. *Mailing Add:* Dept of Math Ind Univ Bloomington IN 47401

ZIEMINSKI, S(TEFAN) A(NTONI), b Zaleszczyki, Poland, Sept 4, 05; nat US; m 50; c 1. CHEMICAL ENGINEERING. *Educ:* Tech Univ, Poland, Chem eng, 27, Dr Tech Sci, 29. *Prof Exp:* Mgr, Chodorow Sugar Refinery, Poland, 34-38; dir, Chodorow Chem Works, 38-39; assoc prof chem eng, Polish Univ Col, Eng, 47-52; res assoc, Eng Res Inst, Univ Mich, 52-54; prof, 54-76, EMER PROF CHEM ENG, UNIV MAINE, ORONO, 76- *Mem:* Am Chem Soc; Am Inst Chem Engrs; Nat Soc Prof Engrs; Brit Inst Chem Engrs. *Res:* Mass transfer operations; beet sugar technology. *Mailing Add:* 16 Mainwood Ave Orono ME 04473

ZIEMNIAK, STEPHEN ERIC, b Rochester, NY, Mar 6, 42; m 70; c 2. AQUEOUS CHEMISTRY, COOLANT TECHNOLOGY. *Educ:* Rensselaer Polytech Inst, BChE, 64, PhD(chem eng), 68. *Prof Exp:* Fel, Los Alamos Sci Lab, 68-69; CHEM ENGR, KNOLLS ATOMIC POWER LAB, GEN ELEC CO, 70- *Res:* Establish principles of corrosion product transport in pressurized water reactor coolants, including thermodynamics of metal ion solubility behavior; hydrothermal crystallization mechanisms; fluid mechanics and numerical turbulence models. *Mailing Add:* 3 Crystal Lane Latham NY 12110

ZIENIUS, RAYMOND HENRY, b Montreal, Que, Nov 8, 34; m 70; c 2. ANALYTICAL CHEMISTRY. *Educ:* McGill Univ, BSc, 56, PhD, 59. *Prof Exp:* Asst chemist, Dom Tar & Chem Co, Ltd, 55; res chemist, Cent Res Lab, Can Industs Ltd, 59-67; asst prof, 67-72, ASSOC PROF CHEM, SIR GEORGE WILLIAMS CAMPUS, CONCORDIA UNIV, 72- *Mem:* Fel Chem Inst Can; Am Chem Soc. *Res:* Gas chromatography and other analytical methods. *Mailing Add:* Dept Chem Sir George Williams Campus Concordia Univ Montreal PQ H3G 1M8 Can

ZIENTY, FERDINAND B, b Chicago, Ill, Mar 21, 15; m 45; c 2. CHEMISTRY. *Educ:* Univ Ill, BS, 35; Univ Mich, MS, 36, PhD(pharmaceut chem), 38. *Prof Exp:* Res chemist, 38-40, res group leader, 40-47, from asst dir res to dir res, 47-60, adv org chem res, 60-64, mgr res & develop, food, feed & fine chem, 64-79, DIR RES & DEVELOP, HEALTH CARE DEVELOP, MONSANTO CO, 79- *Concurrent Pos:* Vpres res, George Lueders & Co, Subsid Monsanto Co, 68-70. *Mem:* Fel AAAS; Am Chem Soc; Am Pharmaceut Asn; Am Inst Chem Eng; fel NY Acad Sci. *Res:* Antispasmodics; sulfa drugs; ethylenediamine derivatives; organic heterocycles, including imidazole and thiophene chemistry; organic acids and anhydrides; nucleophilic substitutions; nucleophilicity of thiols; catalytic oxidations; flavors. *Mailing Add:* 850 Rampart Dr St Louis MO 63122

ZIENTY, MITCHELL FRANK, b Chicago, Ill, Feb 12, 13. ORGANIC CHEMISTRY. *Educ:* Univ Ill, PhC, 33; Univ Mich, BS, 38, MS, 39, PhD(org chem), 41. *Prof Exp:* Res chemist, Upjohn Co, 41-47; res chemist, Sumner Chem Co, Inc, 47-49, mgr labs, 49-52, asst res dir, Marschall Div, Miles Labs, Inc, 52-70, assoc res dir, 70-78; CONSULT, 78- *Concurrent Pos:* Mem adv coun, Western Mich Univ, 52-75. *Mem:* AAAS; Am Chem Soc; NY Acad Sci; Sigma Xi. *Res:* Organic syntheses; enzymes; polymers; catalysis. *Mailing Add:* 615 Liberty St Elkhart IN 46514

ZIERING, LANCE K, b New York, NY, May 17, 39; m 61; c 2. CHEMICAL ENGINEERING. *Educ:* City Col New York, BScChE, 62; Columbia Univ, MScChE, 63; Univ Conn, MBA, 69. *Prof Exp:* Chem engr, Am Cyanamid Co, 63-65, res chem engr, 65-67, group leader supvr, 67-69; asst prod mgr, 69-71, tech sales rep, 71-72, prod mgr films, 72-74, asst to vpres plastics, 74-76, tech serv mgr, 76-79, mkt mgr, 79-80, dir mkt, 80-81, VPRES & GEN MGR RUBICON, ICI AM INC, 81- *Res:* Process and product development of fuel cell and battery electrodes and components; cost estimating. *Mailing Add:* ICI Americas Inc Concord Pike & New Murphy Rd Wilmington DE 19897

ZIERLER, KENNETH LEVIE, b Baltimore, Md, Sept 5, 17; m 41; c 5. MEDICINE, PHYSIOLOGY. *Educ:* Johns Hopkins Univ, AB, 36; Univ Md, MD, 41. *Prof Exp:* Fel med, Sch Med, Johns Hopkins Univ, 46-48, from instr to assoc prof med, 48-64, prof med, 64-72, prof physiol, 69-72; dir, Inst Muscle Dis, Inc, 72-73; PROF PHYSIOL & MED, SCH MED, JOHNS HOPKINS UNIV & PHYSICIAN, JOHNS HOPKINS HOSP, 73- *Concurrent Pos:* Asst physician, Outpatient Dept, Johns Hopkins Hosp, 46-53, physician, 53-55, physician-in-charge phys ther dept, 50-57, chemist, 57-68, physician, 53-72, assoc prof environ med, Sch Hyg & Pub Health, Johns Hopkins Univ, 54-59; adj prof, Rockefeller Univ, 72-73; adj prof, Med Sch, Cornell Univ, 72-73; consult cardiovascular-B study sect, NIH, 72-76. *Mem:* Am Physiol Soc; Am Soc Clin Invest; Asn Am Physicians; Endocrine Soc. *Res:* Muscle metabolism and function; hormonal action; biomembranes; circulation; tracer kinetics; insulin, water and electrolytes. *Mailing Add:* Dept of Physiol Johns Hopkins Univ Sch of Med Baltimore MD 21205

ZIERLER, NEAL, b Baltimore, Md, Sept 17, 26. MATHEMATICS. *Educ:* Johns Hopkins Univ, AB, 45; Harvard Univ, AM, 49, PhD(math), 59. *Prof Exp:* Mathematician-physicist, Ballistic Res Labs, Aberdeen Proving Ground, Md, 51-52; mem staff, Instrumentation Lab, Mass Inst Technol, 52-54 & Lincoln Lab, 54-60; res group supvr, Jet Propulsion Lab, Calif Inst Technol, 60-61; sr scientist, Arcon Corp, Mass, 61-62; mem staff, Lincoln Lab, Mass Inst Technol, 62; sub-dept head, Mitre Corp, Mass, 62-65; MEM STAFF COMMUN RES DIV, INST DEFENSE ANAL, 65- *Mem:* Am Math Soc; Math Asn Am; fel Inst Elec & Electronics Engrs. *Res:* Algebra; mathematical foundations of quantum mechanics; coding and decoding of information; computer applications. *Mailing Add:* Inst for Defense Anal Thanet Rd Princeton NJ 08540

ZIETLOW, JAMES PHILIP, b Chicago, Ill, Dec 15, 21; m 52; c 3. PHYSICS. *Educ:* De Paul Univ, BS, 48; Ill Inst Technol, MS, 49, PhD(physics), 55. *Prof Exp:* Sr res physicist, Res & Develop Labs, Pure Oil Co, 51-56; prof physics & math, NMex Highlands Univ, 56-65, head dept physics & math, 56-63, grad dean, 63-64, head dept physics & math, 64-65; assoc dean, Col Arts & Sci, 69-78, PROF PHYSICS, WESTERN MICH UNIV, 65- *Mem:* Am Phys Soc; Coblentz Soc. *Res:* Infrared, Raman, ultraviolet and mass spectroscopies. *Mailing Add:* Dept of Physics Western Mich Univ Kalamazoo MI 49008

ZIEVE, LESLIE, b Minneapolis, Minn, Aug 6, 15; m 41; c 1. MEDICINE. *Educ:* Univ Minn, MA, 39, MD, 43, PhD(med), 52; Am Bd Internal Med, dipl, 51. *Prof Exp:* Resident med, Med Sch, Univ Minn, Minneapolis, 46-49, from instr to prof, 49-71; dir spec cancer lab, Vet Admin Hosp, Minneapolis, 61-72, staff physician, 49-77, assoc chief staff for res, 61-77, distinguished physician, 72-75; DIR RES, DEPT MED, HENNEPIN COUNTY MED CTR, 77- *Concurrent Pos:* Chief radioisotope unit, Vet Admin Hosp, Minneapolis, 50-72; mem exec comt, Grad Sch, Univ Minn, Minneapolis, 65-68; ed, J Lab & Clin Med, 67-70. *Honors & Awards:* Middleton Award, 62. *Mem:* Am Col Physicians. *Res:* Diseases of the liver and pancreas. *Mailing Add:* 2321 Parklands Rd St Louis Park MN 55416

ZIFF, MORRIS, b New York, NY, Nov 19, 13; m 40; c 2. INTERNAL MEDICINE. *Educ:* NY Univ, BS, 34, PhD(chem), 37, MD, 48. *Prof Exp:* Asst chem, NY Univ, 34-39; asst biochem, Col Physicians & Surgeons, Columbia Univ, 39-41, vis scholar, 41-44; instr & lectr, NY Univ, 44, adj asst prof, 48-50, from asst prof med to assoc prof, 54-58; PROF INTERNAL MED, SOUTHWEST MED CTR, UNIV TEX HEALTH SCI CTR, DALLAS, 58-, ASHBEL SMITH PROF, 81- *Concurrent Pos:* Instr, City Col New York, 41-44; from intern to asst resident, Bellevue Hosp, 48-50, chmn clin res sect study group rheumatic dis, 52-58; consult, USPHS, 55-63. *Honors & Awards:* Heberden Medal, Heberden Soc London, 64. *Mem:* Am Chem Soc; Harvey Soc; Am Soc Clin Invest; Am Rheumatism Asn (pres, 65-66); Am Col Physicians. *Res:* Chemistry of connective tissue; rheumatic diseases; immunology. *Mailing Add:* Dept Int Med Univ Tex Health Sci Ctr 5323 Harry Hines Blvd Dallas TX 75235

ZIFFER, HERMAN, b New York, NY, Feb 22, 30; m 55; c 3. ORGANIC CHEMISTRY. *Educ:* City Col New York, BS, 51; Ind Univ, MA, 53; Univ Ore, PhD(chem), 55. *Prof Exp:* Res chemist, Nat Aniline Div, Allied Chem Corp, 55-59; RES CHEMIST, NIH, 59- *Mem:* Am Chem Soc; Royal Soc Chem. *Res:* Photochemistry; asymmetric synthesis and the use of optical rotatory dispersion and other physical measurements for structure determination. *Mailing Add:* Bldg 2 Rm 120 NIH Bethesda MD 20014

ZIFFER, JACK, b New York, NY, Dec 2, 18; m 42; c 2. MICROBIOLOGY. *Educ:* Brooklyn Col, BS, 40; Univ London, PhD(biochem), 50. *Prof Exp:* Sr res microbiologist, Schenley Res Inst, 42-46; sr res fermentation chemist, A E Staley Co, 46-48; sr res microbiol chemist, Res Labs, Pabst Brewing Co, 50-55, head dept microbiol, Pabst Labs, 55-60, dir microbiol div, P-L Biochem, Inc, 60-67, vpres microbiol div, 67-76, vpres & tech dir, Premier Malt Prod, Inc, 69-76; prof microbiol, Tel-Aviv Univ, 76-77; PROF FOOD ENG & BIOTECHNOL, ISRAEL INST TECHNOL, HAIFA, 77- *Concurrent Pos:* Ed, Biotechnol Letters. *Mem:* Am Chem Soc; Am Phytopath Soc; Soc Invert Path; Soc Am Microbiologists. *Res:* Phytoactin; phytostreptin; penicillin; streptomycin; streptothricin; bacitracin; fungal amylase, glucoamylase, protease; bacterial amylase, gumase, protease; vitamin B12; riboflavin; gluconic acid; lactic acid; fungal anthraquinone pigments; cellulose decomposition; plant diseases; microbial insecticides; trans-N-deoxyribosylase; microbial rennet; industrial alcohol. *Mailing Add:* Dept of Food Eng & Biotechnol Israel Inst of Technol Haifa Israel

ZIFFREN, SIDNEY EDWARD, surgery, deceased

ZIGHELBOIM, JACOB, b Chernowitz, Rumania, Jan 2, 46; Venezuelan citizen; m 67; c 3. IMMUNOBIOLOGY, HEMATOLOGY. *Educ:* Col Moral & Luces, BS, 63; Univ Cent Venezuela, MD, 69. *Prof Exp:* From intern to resident internal med, Beilinson Hosp, Tel Aviv Sch Med, 70-72; fel immunobiol, Dept Microbiol & Immunol, 72-74, resident, Sch Med, 74-76, clin fel hematol & oncol, 76-81, asst prof microbiol, immunol & med, 81-82, ASSOC PROF, SCH MED, UNIV CALIF, LOS ANGELES, 82- *Mem:* Am Fedn Clin Res; Am Asn Immunologists; Am Soc Contemporary Ophthamol; Am Asn Cancer Res; Royal Entomol Soc. *Res:* Cellular and molecular analysis of regulation of cytotoxic immune responses to histocompatibility antigens; regulation on natural killer cell function; biologic approaches to the control of neoplastic disease. *Mailing Add:* Univ of Calif Sch of Med Le Conte Ave Los Angeles CA 90024

ZIGMAN, SEYMOUR, b Far Rockaway, NY, Nov 21, 32; m 54; c 1. BIOCHEMISTRY. *Educ:* Cornell Univ, BA, 54; Rutgers Univ, MS, 56, PhD(biochem), 59. *Prof Exp:* Fel biochem of the eye, Mass Eye & Ear Infirmary, 59-61, res assoc, 61-62; from instr to asst prof, 62-70, ASSOC PROF BIOCHEM OF THE EYE, SCH MED & DENT, UNIV ROCHESTER, 70- *Concurrent Pos:* Corp & investr, Marine Biol Lab, Woods Hole, Mass; res assoc, Mote Marine Lab, Sarasota, Fla; biol consult, Eastman Kodak Co. *Mem:* Am Chem Soc; Am Soc Biol Chemists; Am Soc Photobiol; Asn Res Vision & Ophthal. *Res:* Chemistry and metabolism of nucleic acids and proteins of the lens and cornea of the eye as related to ocular disorders; effects of near ultraviolet light on the eye lens and retina. *Mailing Add:* Univ Rochester Sch Med & Dent 601 Elmwood Ave Rochester NY 14642

ZIGMOND, MICHAEL JONATHAN, b Waterbury, Conn, Sept 1, 41. NEUROPHARMACOLOGY, PSYCHOPHARMACOLOGY. *Educ:* Carnegie-Mellon Univ, BS, 63; Univ Chicago, PhD(biopsychol), 68. *Prof Exp:* Teaching asst psychol, Carnegie-Mellon Univ, 62-63; res assoc, Mass Inst Technol, 67-69, instr, 69-70; asst prof, 70-75, assoc prof, 75-81, PROF BIOL & PSYCHOL, UNIV PITTSBURGH, 81- *Concurrent Pos:* Nat Inst Ment Health & Nat Inst Neurol & Commun Disorders & Stroke grantee, Univ Pittsburgh, 70-; mem, Neuropsychol Res Rev Comt, Nat Inst Ment Health, 74-78; Nat Inst Ment Health res career development awards, 75-; assoc dir basic res, Clin Res Ctr; assoc ed, J Neurosci, 80- & consult ed, Physiol Psychol, 81- *Mem:* AAAS; Am Soc Neurochem; Soc Neurosci; Am Soc Pharmacol & Exp Therapeut. *Res:* Interactions between brain neurochemistry, behavior and environment; control of biogenic amine metabolism; neuroplasticity; biological basics of recovery of function following brain damage. *Mailing Add:* Dept Biol Sci 571 Crawford Hall Univ Pittsburgh Pittsburgh PA 15260

ZIGMOND, RICHARD ERIC, b Willimantic, Conn, May 9, 44. NEUROBIOLOGY, NEUROENDOCRINOLOGY. *Educ:* Harvard Col, BA, 66; Rockefeller Univ, PhD(neurobiol), 71. *Prof Exp:* Fel physiol psychol, Rockefeller Univ, 71-72; fel neurochem, Univ Cambridge, 72-75; asst prof, 75-81, ASSOC PROF, HARVARD MED SCH, 81- *Concurrent Pos:* Tutor biochem sci, Harvard Col, 75-; lectr neurobiol course, Marine Biol Lab, 81-; lectr neurobiol & behav course, Cold Spring Harbor Lab, 79- *Mem:* Soc Neurosci; Brit Pharmacol Soc; Am Soc Pharmacol & Exp Therapeut; Sigma Xi. *Res:* Regulation of the levels of enzymes involved in the synthesis of neurotransmitters; recovery of function after sub-total neural damage; functional anatomy of the autonomic nervous system; identification and characterization of hormone-sensitive cells in the brain. *Mailing Add:* Dept of Pharmacol Harvard Med Sch Boston MA 02115

ZIHLMAN, ADRIENNE LOUELLA, b Chicago, Ill, Dec 29, 40. PHYSICAL ANTHROPOLOGY. *Educ:* Univ Colo, Boulder, BA, 62; Univ Calif, Berkeley, PhD(anthrop), 67. *Prof Exp:* Asst prof anthrop, 67-73, chmn dept, 75-77, assoc prof, 73-79, PROF ANTHROP, OAKES COL, UNIV CALIF, SANTA CRUZ, 79- *Concurrent Pos:* Wenner-Gren Found Anthrop Res grants, Transvaal Mus, Pretoria, SAfrica, Univ Witwatersrand, Anthrop Inst, Zurich & Med Sch, Makerere Univ, Uganda, 69, Nat Mus Kenya, Nairobi & Transvaal Mus, 74, Transvaal Mus, Univ Witwatersrand, 79. *Mem:* AAAS; Am Asn Phys Anthrop; Am Anthrop Asn; Am Soc Mammal; Int Primatol soc. *Res:* Locomotor behavior and anatomy of primates; reconstruction of behavior and anatomy of fossil hominoids; ape evolution and human origins; women in evolution. *Mailing Add:* Clark Kerr Hall Univ of Calif Santa Cruz CA 95064

ZIKAKIS, JOHN PHILIP, b Piraeus, Greece, Sept 16, 33; US citizen; m 58; c 1. BIOLOGICAL SCIENCES, BIOCHEMISTRY. *Educ:* Univ Del, BA, 65, MS, 67, PhD(biol, biochem), 70. *Prof Exp:* Res asst nutrit, Stine Lab, E I du Pont de Nemours & Co, Inc, 59-61; res assoc biochem genetics, 68-70, from asst prof to assoc prof, 70-81, PROF BIOCHEM GENETICS, UNIV DEL, 81- *Concurrent Pos:* Sci consult, Fedn Am Socs Exp Biol, 75; trustee, Riverside Hosp, 77-; Nat Oceanic & Atmospheric Admin grants, 77 & 78; indust & acad consult. *Honors & Awards:* Cert & Gold Medal, Univ Patra, Greece, 73. *Mem:* Am Chem Soc; Am Dairy Sci Asn; Am Inst Biol Sci; AAAS; NY Acad Sci. *Res:* Various studies with xanthine oxidase as it may relate to atherosclerosis; immunological and nutritional studies with xanthine oxidase; biochemical genetic studies on milk and blood protein; polymorphisms; animal product and by-product biochemistry; mammary metabolism and enzymology; marine sciences; author or coauthor of over 70 publications. *Mailing Add:* Dept Animal Sci & Agr Biochem Univ Del Newark DE 19711

ZILBER, JOSEPH ABRAHAM, b Boston, Mass, July 27, 23; m 54; c 3. MATHEMATICS. *Educ:* Harvard Univ, AB, 43, MA, 46, PhD, 63. *Prof Exp:* Instr math, Columbia Univ, 48-50 & Johns Hopkins Univ, 50-55; asst prof, Univ Ill, 55-56; lectr, Northwestern Univ, 56-57; res assoc, Brown Univ, 57-62; res assoc, Yale Univ, 62; asst prof, 62-64, ASSOC PROF MATH, OHIO STATE UNIV, 64- *Concurrent Pos:* Assoc ed, Math Rev, Am Math Soc, 57-62. *Mem:* AAAS; Am Math Soc; Math Asn Am. *Res:* Algebraic topology; category theory. *Mailing Add:* Dept of Math Ohio State Univ Columbus OH 43210

ZILCH, KARL T, b St Louis, Mo, Nov 14, 21; m 50; c 7. ORGANIC CHEMISTRY. *Educ:* Univ Mo, AB, 43, MA, 47, PhD(chem), 49. *Prof Exp:* Asst chem, Univ Mo, 47-49; res chemist, Northern Utilization Res Br, USDA, 49-55; res chemist & group leader, 55-59, res sect head, 59-61, TECH DIR, EMERY INDUSTS, INC, 61- *Concurrent Pos:* Instr chem, Bradley Univ, 50-51. *Mem:* Am Chem Soc; Am Oil Chem Soc; Swiss Chem Soc. *Res:* Synthesis and processing carboxylic acids; reactions and end use application of carboxylic acids. *Mailing Add:* 7682 Pine Glen Dr Cincinnati OH 45224

ZILCZER, JANET ANN, b New York, NY, Apr 30, 55. CRYSTALLOGRAPHY. *Educ:* George Washington Univ, BA, 76, MPhil, 79, PhD(geol), 81. *Prof Exp:* Teaching fel geol, George Washington Univ, 76-79; Smithsonian fel, Nat Mus Natural Hist, 79-81; LECTR GEOL, GEORGE MASON UNIV, 81- *Concurrent Pos:* Vis researcher, Nat Mus Natural Hist, Smithsonian Inst, 78. *Mem:* Mineral Soc Am. *Res:* Feldspar mineralogy; optical mineralogy; crystal physics and chemistry. *Mailing Add:* 2351 N Quantico St Arlington VA 22205

ZILE, MAIJA HELENE, b Latvia, Aug 3, 29; nat US; m 55; c 3. BIOCHEMISTRY. *Educ:* Univ Md, BS, 54; Univ Wis, MS, 56, PhD(biochem), 59. *Prof Exp:* Res fel biochem, Univ Wis, 59 & Harvard Univ, 59-61; res assoc biochem, Univ Wis, Madison, 61-76, assoc scientist, 76-81; ASST PROF, MICH STATE UNIV, 81- *Mem:* Sigma Xi; Am Inst Nutrit; Soc Exp Biol & Med. *Res:* Metabolism and function of vitamin A; function of vitamin A in cell proliferation and differentiation; cell cycle studies; function of vitamins and hormones at molecular level; anticarcinogenic properties of vitamine A; nutrition and cancer. *Mailing Add:* Dept Food Sci & Human Nutrit Mich State Univ East Lansing MI 48824

ZILINSKAS, BARBARA ANN, b Waltham, Mass, Sept 21, 47. BIOCHEMISTRY. *Educ:* Framingham State Col, BA, 69; Univ Ill, Urbana, MS, 70, PhD(biol), 75. *Prof Exp:* Lab technician biol, Univ Mass Environ Exp Sta, 68-69; NASA fel, Univ Ill, Urbana, 69-72, res & teaching asst, 73-74; fel, Smithsonian Radiation Biol Lab, 75; asst prof, 75-80, ASSOC PROF BIOCHEM, COOK COL, RUTGERS UNIV, 80- *Mem:* Am Soc Plant Physiologists; Biophys Soc; Am Soc Photobiol; AAAS; Sigma Xi. *Res:* Structure-function relationships of biological membranes, especially photosynthetic membranes; biochemistry and biophysics of the photosynthetic light reactions. *Mailing Add:* Dept of Biochem & Microbiol Cook Col Rutgers Univ New Brunswick NJ 08903

ZILKE, SAMUEL, b Chatfield, Man, Nov 4, 14. AGRONOMY, ECOLOGY. *Educ:* Univ Sask, BA, 48, BSEd, 49, BSAgr, 53, MS, 54; SDak State Univ, PhD(agron), 67. *Prof Exp:* Res officer & res asst plant ecol, Univ Sask, 50-55; res asst bot, SDak State Univ, 57-59 & agron & weed sci, 59-61; instr agr, Exten & Col Div, Alta Agr Col, 66-70; agr consult, 70-71; technician, Can Wildlife Serv, 71-72; AGR CONSULT, 72- *Concurrent Pos:* Lectr, Col Agr, Univ Sask, 52-55, consult fertilizers & herbicides, 66-71. *Mem:* Agr Inst Can; Ecol Soc Am; Can Soc Soil Sci; Am Inst Biol Sci; Agron Soc Am. *Res:* Ecological life histories of plants and their physiology under field conditions; effect of variable soil moisture and temperature on seeds; response of field and grass crops to fertilizer and herbicides; effect of aeration of soil on nitrification in late May and June; improvement of habitat for browsers such as Virginia deer, porcupine and rabbits. *Mailing Add:* Box 147 Springside Saskatchewan SK S0A 3V0 Can

ZILKEY, BRYAN FREDERICK, b Manitou, Man, Apr 14, 41; m 64; c 3. PLANT SCIENCE, BIOCHEMISTRY. *Educ:* Univ Man, BSA, 62, MSc, 63; Purdue Univ, Lafayette, PhD(plant physiol), 69. *Prof Exp:* RES SCIENTIST TOBACCO, RES BR, CAN DEPT AGR, 69- *Mem:* Can Soc Plant Physiol; Am Soc Plant Physiol; Can Fedn Biol Socs. *Res:* Lipid and carbohydrate metabolism and biosynthesis in germinating and developing castor bean endosperm; biochemistry and physiology of tobacco growth; tobacco smoke chemistry and biological properties. *Mailing Add:* Res Sta Can Dept of Agr Delhi ON N4B 2W9 Can

ZILL, LEONARD PETER, b Portland, Ore, Oct 9, 20; m 52; c 2. BIOCHEMISTRY. *Educ:* Ore State Col, BS, 42, MS, 44; Ind Univ, PhD(biochem), 50. *Prof Exp:* Asst chem, Ore State Col, 42-44; asst, Forest Prod Lab, US Forest Serv, 42-44; res assoc, Ind Univ, 47-50; biochemist, Oak Ridge Nat Lab, 50-57; sr biochemist, Res Inst Advan Studies, 57-63; chief biol adaptation br, 63-67, mem lunar sample anal planning team, 68-70, chief planetary biol div, 67-74, SR RES SCIENTIST, AMES RES CTR, NASA, 74- *Mem:* AAAS; Am Soc Photobiol; Am Soc Biol Chemists; Sigma Xi; Brit Biochem Soc. *Res:* Growth factors; wood and pulp chemistry; biochemistry of paramecia; chemistry and biochemistry of carbohydrates; photosynthesis; plant lipids. *Mailing Add:* Planetary Biol Div MS 239-4 Ames Res Ctr NASA Moffett Field CA 94035

ZILLER, STEPHEN A, JR, b Kansas City, Mo, Nov 2, 38; m 61; c 4. TOXICOLOGY, REGULATORY AFFAIRS. *Educ:* Rockhurst Col, BA, 61; St Louis Univ, PhD(biochem), 67. *Prof Exp:* Res biochemist, Res Div, 67-69, res nutritionist, 69-70, nutritionist, Food Prod Develop Div, 71-74, sect head food safety & nutrit, Food Prod Develop Div, 74-77, asst dir, 77-81, ASSOC DIR PROF & REGULATORY RELS, INDUST FOOD PROD DEVELOP DIV, PROCTER & GAMBLE CO, 81- *Mem:* AAAS; Am Chem Soc. *Res:* Metabolism of sterols and bile acids; drug metabolism; protein nutrition; food safety and nutrition. *Mailing Add:* Coffee Develop Div 6210 Center Hill Rd Cincinnati OH 45224

ZILVERSMIT, DONALD BERTHOLD, b Hengelo, Holland, July 11, 19; nat US; m 45; c 3. NUTRITIONAL BIOCHEMISTRY. *Educ:* Univ Calif, BS, 40, PhD(physiol), 48. *Hon Degrees:* Dr, Univ Utrecht, Neth, 80. *Prof Exp:* Clin demonstr, Dent Sch, Univ Calif, 46-48; from instr to prof physiol, Med Units, Univ Tenn, 48-66; PROF, DIV NUTRIT SCI & SECT BIOCHEM, MOLECULAR & CELL BIOL, DIV BIOL SCI, CORNELL UNIV, 66- *Concurrent Pos:* Consult, NIH, 55-; ed, J Lipid Res, 59-61; Am Heart Asn career investr, 59-; guest prof, State Univ Leiden, 61-62; vis fel exp path, Australian Nat Univ, 66; ed, Biochimica et Biophysica Acta, 69-80; NIH, Nat Heart, Lung & Blood Inst task forces arteriosclerosis, 70-71, 78-79, 80-82; vis prof biochem, Mass Inst Technol, 72-73; ed, Proceedings Soc Exp Biol & Med, 75- & adv bd, 77-; mem coun arteriosclerosis, Am Heart Asn. *Mem:* AAAS; Am Physiol Soc; Soc Exp Biol & Med; Am Soc Biol Chemists; Am Inst Nutrit. *Res:* Lipid metabolism; lipoproteins; membrane biochemistry; endocytosis; arteriosclerosis; use of isotopes in metabolic work. *Mailing Add:* Div of Nutrit Sci Cornell Univ Ithaca NY 14853

ZILZ, MELVIN LEONARD, b Detroit, Mich, Apr 15, 32; m 57; c 3. CELL BIOLOGY, BIOCHEMISTRY. *Educ:* Concordia Teachers Col, Ill, BS, 53; Univ Mich, Ann Arbor, MS & MA, 64; Wayne State Univ, PhD(biol), 70; Concordia Theol Sem, Ft Wayne, colloquy dipl, 78. *Prof Exp:* Teacher pvt sch, Ill, 53-57; instr high sch, Mich, 57-65, chmn dept sci, 58-65; asst prof biol, Concordia Sr Col, 65-72, chmn dept natural sci, 71-72, assoc prof biol & registr admis, 72-77, asst pres & assoc acad dean, 76-78, assoc prof pastoral ministry, 76-79, DEAN ADMIN, CONCORDIA THEOL SEM, 78-, PROF PASTORAL MINISTRY, 79- *Concurrent Pos:* Instr, Mich Lutheran Col, 62-63. *Mem:* AAAS; Nat Asn Biol Teachers. *Res:* Cellular research, especially cell division and the anaphase movement of chromosomes. *Mailing Add:* Concordia Theol Sem 6600 N Clinton Ft Wayne IN 46825

ZIMAR, FRANK, b Berlin, Wis, Apr 5, 18; m 43; c 3; m 57; c 4. CHEMISTRY, CERAMICS. *Educ:* Univ Wis, BS, 41; Univ Rochester, PhD(phys chem), 45. *Prof Exp:* Asst, Off Sci Res & Develop, Univ Rochester, 41-45; res chemist, 45-51, res assoc, 51-56, res supvr, 56-70, res assoc, 70-75, SR RES SCIENTIST, CORNING GLASS WORKS, 75- *Mem:* Am Ceramic Soc; Brit Soc Glass Technol. *Res:* Kinetics of heterogeneous reactions; surface chemistry of glass; thermal setting solder glass; glass redraw; application of films to glass; glass fiber technology; fiber optic waveguides; catalyst support ceramics. *Mailing Add:* Corning Glass Works Sullivan Park Painted Post NY 14870

ZIMBELMAN, ROBERT GEORGE, b Keenesburg, Colo, Sept 4, 30; m 52; c 4. REPRODUCTIVE ENDOCRINOLOGY. *Educ:* Colo State Univ, BS, 52; Univ Wis, MS, 57, PhD(endocrinol), 60. *Prof Exp:* Instr genetics, Univ Wis, 57-60; res assoc, Upjohn Co, 60-64, head vet biol res, 65, head reproduction & physiol res, Agr Prod Div, 65-71, res mgr reproduction & physiol res, Agr Prod Div, 71-76, RES MGR, EXP AGR SCI, UPJOHN CO, 77- *Mem:* Am Soc Animal Sci; Am Inst Biol Sci; Int Soc Ecotoxicol & Environ Safety; Soc Study Reproduction; Brit Soc Study Fertil. *Res:* Improving fertility and preciseness of breeding time in cattle with synchronization of estrus, improved mammary development and milk production by dairy cattle, endocrinology of growth of farm animals, new approaches to inhibition of estrus in pets, molecular biology in animals. *Mailing Add:* Exp Agr Sci Unit 9602-25-4 Upjohn Co Kalamazoo MI 49001

ZIMBRICK, JOHN DAVID, b Dickinson, NDak, Sept 18, 38; m 62; c 2. RADIATION BIOPHYSICS, RADIATION CHEMISTRY. *Educ:* Carleton Col, BA, 60; Univ Kans, MS, 62, PhD(radiation biophys), 67. *Prof Exp:* Asst physicist, IIT Res Inst, 62-64; chief environ studies sect, Health Serv Lab, US AEC, Idaho, 67-68; Nat Inst Gen Med Sci fel lab nuclear med & radiation biol, Univ Calif, Los Angeles, 68, US AEC fel, 68-69; from asst prof to assoc prof, 69-77, PROF RADIATION BIOPHYS, UNIV KANS, 77- *Concurrent Pos:* Consult mem, Radiation Study Sect, NIH, 78-82, chmn, 80-82; prog mgr radiobiol, US Dept Energy, 81-82. *Mem:* Health Physics Soc; Radiation Res Soc; Biophys Soc. *Res:* In vivo studies on DNA base damage induced by gamma radiation; electron spin resonance spectroscopy of radicals produced in biomolecules by radiation; application of electron spin resonance to cancer detection and treatment. *Mailing Add:* Dept of Radiation Biophys Univ of Kans Nuclear Reactor Ctr Lawrence KS 66045

ZIMDAHL, ROBERT LAWRENCE, b Buffalo, NY, Feb 28, 35; m 56; c 4. AGRONOMY, WEED SCIENCE. *Educ:* Cornell Univ, BS, 56, MS, 66; Ore State Univ, PhD(agron), 68. *Prof Exp:* Res assoc agron, Cornell Univ, 63-64; from asst prof to assoc prof, 68-77, PROF WEED SCI, COLO STATE UNIV, 77- *Concurrent Pos:* Vis prof, Univ Bologna, Italy, 76. *Mem:* Weed Sci Soc Am; Am Chem Soc; Am Soc Agron. *Res:* Herbicide degradation in soil; environmental pollution by pesticides. *Mailing Add:* Dept of Bot & Plant Path Colo State Univ Ft Collins CO 80521

ZIMERING, SHIMSHON, b Kishinev, Romania, July 6, 33; m 66; c 2. MATHEMATICAL ANALYSIS. *Educ:* Univ Geneva, BSc, 56, licence in math, 58; Free Univ Brussels, PhD(math, physics), 65. *Prof Exp:* Res asst, Weizmann Inst Sci, 58-59; res fel, Battelle Inst, Geneva, Switz, 61-66; hon res assoc math & Battelle Inst, Geneva, Switz fel, Harvard Univ, 66-67; mem advan studies ctr, Battelle Inst, Geneva, 67-68; ASSOC PROF MATH, OHIO STATE UNIV, 68- *Concurrent Pos:* Deleg, Int Conf Peaceful Uses Atomic Energy, Geneva, 64; NSF res grant, Ohio State Univ, 73-74. *Mem:* Am Math Soc. *Res:* Real analysis, summability and transform theory; boundary value problems; solid state physics. *Mailing Add:* Dept of Math Ohio State Univ Columbus OH 43210

ZIMM, BRUNO HASBROUCK, b Kingston, NY, Oct 31, 20; m 44; c 2. BIOPHYSICAL CHEMISTRY, POLYMER CHEMISTRY. *Educ:* Columbia Univ, AB, 41, MS, 43, PhD(chem), 44. *Prof Exp:* Asst chem, Columbia Univ, 41-44; res assoc & instr, Polytech Inst Brooklyn, 44-46; from instr to assoc prof, Univ Calif, 46-52; res assoc, Gen Elec Co, 51-60; PROF CHEM, UNIV CALIF, SAN DIEGO, 60- *Concurrent Pos:* Vis lectr, Harvard Univ, 50-51; vis prof, Yale Univ, 60. *Honors & Awards:* Leo Hendrik Baekland Award, Am Chem Soc, 57; Bingham Medal, Soc Rheol, 60; High Polymer Physics Prize, Am Phys Soc, 63; Chem Sci Award, Nat Acad Sci, 81; Kirlswood Medal, Yale Univ, 82. *Mem:* Nat Acad Sci; Am Chem Soc; Am Phys Soc; Soc Rheol; Am Soc Biol Chemists. *Res:* Theory of macromolecular solutions; properties and structure of high polymers and biological macromolecules. *Mailing Add:* B-017 Dept of Chem Univ of Calif La Jolla CA 92093

ZIMM, GEORGIANNA GREVATT, b Jersey City, NJ, Nov 5, 17; m 44; c 2. GENETICS. *Educ:* Columbia Univ, BA, 40; Univ Pa, MA, 42; Univ Calif, Berkeley, PhD(zool), 50. *Prof Exp:* Teaching asst biol, Univ Del, 40-42; teaching asst zool, Barnard Col, Columbia Univ, 43-45, lectr, 45-46; teaching asst, Univ Calif, Berkeley, 46-50; res asst genetics & bibliogr, 68-75, RES ASSOC BIOL, UNIV CALIF, SAN DIEGO, 75- *Mem:* AAAS; Genetics Soc Am. *Res:* Mutants and cytogenetics of Drosophila. *Mailing Add:* Dept of Biol Univ of Calif at San Diego La Jolla CA 92093

ZIMMACK, HAROLD LINCOLN, b Chicago, Ill, Feb 12, 25; m 56; c 3. INSECT PATHOLOGY. *Educ:* Eastern Ill Univ, BS, 51; Iowa State Univ, MS, 53, PhD(entom), 56. *Prof Exp:* Asst, Iowa State Univ, 51-56; prof biol, Eastern Ky Univ, 56-63; PROF ZOOL, BALL STATE UNIV, 63- *Concurrent Pos:* Sigma Xi & Ind Acad Sci res grants-in-aid, 67-68. *Mem:* Am Soc Zoologists; Entom Soc Am; AAAS; Soc Invert Path. *Res:* Rapid screening of potential insect pathogen through physiological studies. *Mailing Add:* Dept of Biol Ball State Univ 2000 University Muncie IN 47306

ZIMMER, ALBERT MICHAEL, b Salzgitter-Lebenstedt, Ger, Sept 29, 45; US citizen; m 62. NUCLEAR MEDICINE, BIONUCLEONICS. *Educ:* Univ of the Pac, BS, 68; Purdue Univ, MS, 72, PhD(bionucleonics), 74. *Prof Exp:* Pharmacist, Thrifty Drug Stores, Inc, 68-69; asst prof radiol & nuclear pharmacist, Med Col Wis, Milwaukee County Med Complex, 73-75; ASST PROF MED RADIOL & NUCLEAR PHARMACISTS, UNIV ILL MED CTR, 75- *Concurrent Pos:* Consult, Union Carbide, NY, Radiopharmaceuticals, 74-75; comt mem, Nuclear Pharm Sect Am Pharmaceut Asn, 75. *Mem:* Health Physics Soc; Am Pharmaceut Asn; Sigma Xi. *Res:* Development of new radiopharmaceuticals; the kinetics involved of current radiopharmaceuticals; quality control procedures of radiopharmaceuticals. *Mailing Add:* 6464 Coach House Rd Lisle IL 60532

ZIMMER, ARTHUR JAMES, b St Louis, Mo, May 12, 14; m 40; c 1. PHARMACEUTICAL CHEMISTRY. *Educ:* St Louis Col Pharm, BS, 40; Wash Univ, MS, 43, PhD(chem), 46. *Prof Exp:* From instr to prof, St Louis Col Pharm, 41-78, Charles E Caspari prof chem, 78-80. *Concurrent Pos:* Biochemist, Snodgras Lab, City Hosp, 60-; mem, US Pharmacopeial Conv, 70. *Mem:* Am Chem Soc; Am Pharmaceut Asn. *Res:* Instrumental analysis of pharmaceutical compounds. *Mailing Add:* 10038 Sheldon Dr St Louis MO 63137

ZIMMER, CARL R(ICHARD), b Syracuse, NY, July 10, 27; m 65. ELECTRICAL ENGINEERING. *Educ:* Cornell Univ, BEE, 49; Syracuse Univ, MEE, 50, PhD(elec eng), 58. *Prof Exp:* Res assoc elec eng, Syracuse Univ, 53-56, instr, 56-59; asst prof, 59-63, ASSOC PROF ENG, ARIZ STATE UNIV, 63- *Concurrent Pos:* Consult, Motorola Aerospace Ctr, 65-67. *Mem:* Inst Elec & Electronics Engrs. *Res:* Solid state devices; active networks. *Mailing Add:* Dept of Elec Eng Ariz State Univ Tempe AZ 85281

ZIMMER, DAVID E, b Neoga, Ill, Sept 25, 35; m 56; c 2. PLANT PATHOLOGY, PLANT BREEDING. *Educ:* Eastern Ill Univ, BS, 57; Purdue Univ, MS, 59, PhD(plant path), 61. *Prof Exp:* RES PLANT PATHOLOGIST, USDA, NDak State Univ, 61-, ADJ PROF PLANT PATH, RES LEADER & TECH ADV, 77- *Mem:* AAAS; Am Phytopath Soc; Crop Sci Soc Am. *Res:* Genetics of parasitism with special emphasis on obligate parasites; inheritance and nature of disease resistance in oilseed crops and the improvement of oil-seed crops through disease resistance breeding. *Mailing Add:* Dept Plant Path NDak State Univ Fargo ND 58102

ZIMMER, G(EORGE) A(RTHUR), b Chicago, Ill, Sept 11, 21; m 46; c 1. MECHANICAL ENGINEERING. *Educ:* Purdue Univ, BS, 47; Univ Del, MME, 53. *Prof Exp:* Engr, Fairbanks, Morse & Co, 47-48 & Aberdeen Proving Ground, US Dept Army, 48-54; res engr, Res Ctr, 54-61, res dir, 61-63, chief engr, 63-66, vpres eng, Morse Chaw Div, 66-80, GROUP VPRES ENG, TRANS COMP GROUP, BORG-WARNER CORP, 80- *Mem:* Am Soc Mech Engrs; Sigma Xi; Am Soc Metals. *Res:* Mechanics and materials; experimental stress analysis; mechanical power transmission design and development. *Mailing Add:* 101 Woolf Lane Ithaca NY 14850

ZIMMER, GEORGE P, biology, science education, deceased

ZIMMER, HANS, b Berlin, Ger, Feb 5, 21; m 46; c 1. ORGANIC CHEMISTRY. *Educ:* Tech Univ, Berlin, Cand, 47, Dipl, 49, DrIng, 50. *Prof Exp:* From asst prof to assoc prof, 54-61, PROF CHEM, UNIV CINCINNATI, 61- *Concurrent Pos:* Vis prof, Univ Mainz, 66-67, Univ Bonn, 67 & Univ Bern, 71; ed, Methodicum Chemicum; consult, Lithium Corp Am & Matheson, Coleman & Bell, 71-; ed, Ann Reports Inorg & Gen Syntheses, 72-78. *Mem:* Fel AAAS; Am Chem Soc; Ger Chem Soc. *Res:* Synthetic and metal organic chemistry. *Mailing Add:* Dept of Chem Univ of Cincinnati Cincinnati OH 45221

ZIMMER, JAMES GRIFFITH, b Lynbrook, NY, Apr 10, 32; m 71; c 3. PREVENTIVE MEDICINE, COMMUNITY HEALTH. *Educ:* Cornell Univ, BA, 53; Yale Univ, MD, 57; London Sch Hyg & Trop Med, dipl trop pub health, 66; Am Bd Internal Med, dipl, 65. *Prof Exp:* Intern internal med, Grace-New Haven Community Hosp, Conn, 57-58; resident, Strong Mem Hosp, Rochester, NY, 58-60; asst chief dermat, Walter Reed Army Inst Res, 61-63; from sr instr to asst prof prev med & community health, 63-67, actg chmn dept prev med, 68-69, ASSOC PROF PREV MED & COMMUNITY HEALTH, SCH MED & DENT, UNIV ROCHESTER, 68- *Concurrent Pos:* Milbank fac fel, Univ Rochester, 64-71; pres, exec dir, Med Serv Int, Inc, 68-70; pres, Genesee Valley Med Found, 70-; med dir, Regional Utilization & Med Rev Proj, 71- *Mem:* Am Fedn Clin Res; Am Pub Health Asn; Int Epidemiol Asn; fel Am Col Prev Med; Royal Soc Trop Med & Hyg. *Res:* Community health; medical care research, especially in areas of utilization and quality of care review and care of chronically ill and aged. *Mailing Add:* Dept of Prev Med Univ of Rochester Med Ctr Rochester NY 14642

ZIMMER, LOUIS GEORGE, b Marseilles, Ill, Nov 30, 26; m 48; c 2. GEOLOGY. *Educ:* Augustana Col, BA, 50; Univ Iowa, MS, 52. *Prof Exp:* Subsurface geologist, Ohio Oil Co, 52-57; dist geologist, J M Huber Corp, 57-62; PARTNER, MAGAW & ZIMMER, 62- *Res:* Petroleum geology. *Mailing Add:* Magaw & Zimmer Suite 404 Park/Harvey Ctr Bldg Oklahoma City OK 73102

ZIMMER, MARTIN F, b Metz, France, Apr 25, 29; US citizen; m; m; c 3. THERMODYNAMICS, EXPLOSIVES. *Educ:* Univ Munich, BS, 55, MS, 58; Munich Tech Univ, PhD(chem technol), 61. *Prof Exp:* Head fuel res lab, Ger Aeronaut Res Inst, Munich, 60-62; chemist, Naval Ord Sta, 62, head thermodyn br, 62-70; dir high explosive res & develop lab, Eglin AFB, Fla, 70-76; res prog mgr conventional munition, Air Force Off Sci Res, Bolling AFB, Washington, DC, 76-78; TECH DIR, MUNITIONS DIV, AIR FORCE ARMAMENT TECHNOL LAB, EGLIN AFB, FLA, 80- *Mem:* Combustion Inst. *Res:* Thermodynamics and combustion characteristics of energetic materials; detonation physics and explosive related phenomena; scientific and administrative management. *Mailing Add:* 124 Bayow Dr Niceville FL 32578

ZIMMER, RUSSEL LEONARD, b Springfield, Ill, Nov 7, 31. INVERTEBRATE BIOLOGY. *Educ:* Blackburn Col, AB, 53; Univ Wash, MS, 56, PhD(zool), 64. *Prof Exp:* Instr, 60-63, vis asst prof, 63-64, asst prof, 64-68, resident dir, Santa Catalina Marine Biol Lab, 68-76, ASSOC PROF BIOL SCI, UNIV SOUTHERN CALIF, 68- *Mem:* AAAS; Am Soc Zool; Soc Syst Zool; Marine Biol Asn UK. *Res:* Reproductive biology; larval development, metamorphosis and systematics of minor invertebrate phyla, especially Phoronida and other lophophorates. *Mailing Add:* Dept Biol Sci Univ Southern Calif Los Angeles CA 90007

ZIMMER, STEPHEN GEORGE, b Trenton, NJ, Oct 26, 42; m 67; c 2. VIROLOGY, MOLECULAR BIOLOGY. *Educ:* Rutgers Univ, AB, 64, MS, 66; Univ Colo, PhD(exp path), 73. *Prof Exp:* Fel molecular biol virol, Washington Univ, 74-76; ASST PROF PATH, UNIV KY, 76- *Mem:* Am Soc Microbiol; AAAS; Am Asn Cancer Res. *Res:* Regulation of viral gene expression; molecular mechanisms of viral transformation. *Mailing Add:* Div Biol Univ KY Lexington KY 40506

ZIMMER, WILLIAM FREDERICK, JR, b Glouster, Ohio, June 4, 23; m 44; c 6. ORGANIC POLYMER CHEMISTRY. *Educ:* Ohio State Univ, BSc, 48, MSc, 49, PhD(chem), 52. *Prof Exp:* Org chemist, Res Lab, Durez Plastics & Chems, Inc, 52-55; res supvr, Hooker Chem Corp, 55-59, mgr polymer res, 59-62; mgr fiber res, Behr-Manning Div, Norton Co, 63-64, group leader chem appln res & develop, 64-68, asst dir res, Grinding Wheel Div, 68-74, RES ASSOC GRINDING WHEEL DIV, NORTON CO, 74- *Mem:* Am Chem Soc. *Res:* Organofluorine chemistry; plastics and polymer chemistry and applications; fiber technology; abrasive systems and materials research; new product research and development. *Mailing Add:* 28 Walbridge Rd Paxton MA 01612

ZIMMERBERG, HYMAN JOSEPH, b New York, NY, Sept 7, 21; m 43; c 3. MATHEMATICS. *Educ:* Brooklyn Col, BA, 41; Univ Chicago, MS, 42, PhD(math), 45. *Prof Exp:* Instr math, Univ Chicago, 42-45 & NC State Col, 45-46; from instr to assoc prof math, 46-60, dir, NSF Undergrad Res Partic Prog, 62-69, 71-73, PROF MATH, RUTGERS UNIV, NEW BRUNSWICK, 60- *Mem:* Am Math Soc; Math Asn Am; Sigma Xi; Am Asn Univ Prof. *Res:* Boundary value problems; linear integro-differential-boundary-parameter problems. *Mailing Add:* Dept of Math Hill Ctr Rutgers Univ New Brunswick NJ 08903

ZIMMERER, ROBERT P, b Sheboygan, Wis, Dec 7, 29; m 56; c 3. PLANT PHYSIOLOGY, MICROBIOLOGY. *Educ:* Univ Wis, BS, 54; Cornell Univ, MS, 61; Pa State Univ, PhD(bot), 66. *Prof Exp:* Asst to sales mgr, Stauffer Chem Co, 55-56; asst plant mgr, Hopkins Agr Chem Co, 56-57; chemist, Marathon Div, Am Can Co, 57-59; asst bot, Cornell Univ, 59-61; from instr to assoc prof biol, 61-74, chmn dept, 74-77, DANA PROF BIOL, JUNIATA COL, 74- *Concurrent Pos:* Res assoc, Hershey Med Ctr, Pa State Univ, 70; vis prof, Univ Maine, 71; consult, USDA, 72-74 & J C Blair Mem Hosp, 74- *Mem:* Am Soc Plant Physiol; Bot Soc Am; Am Micros Soc; Am Soc Microbiol. *Res:* Biogenesis and function of biological membranes; biological regulatory mechanisms. *Mailing Add:* Dept Biol Juniata Col Huntingdon PA 16652

ZIMMERER, ROBERT W, b Brooklyn, NY, May 21, 29; m 60; c 2. EXPERIMENTAL PHYSICS, INSTRUMENTATION. *Educ:* Worcester Polytech Inst, BS, 51; NY Univ, MS, 55; Univ Colo, PhD(physics), 60. *Prof Exp:* Design engr, Hazeltine Electronics Corp, 51-55; asst physics, Univ Colo, 55-57, res assoc, 57-60; physicist, Nat Bur Stand, 60-66; chief scientist, Wm Ainsworth & Sons, Inc, Colo, 66-69; pres, Scientech, Inc, 69-72, vpres, 72-81; CONSULT, 81- *Concurrent Pos:* Dept Com sci fel, 65-66; phys sci consult, US Army Fitzsimons Gen Hosp, 69- *Mem:* Instrument Soc Am; Am Phys Soc; AAAS. *Res:* Microwave spectroscopy of gases; microwave generation and propagation at very short wavelengths; microwave power measurement; mass measurement by new methods; lung physiology; microcomputer modeling. *Mailing Add:* 131 W 2nd St Port Angeles WA 98362

ZIMMERING, STANLEY, b New York, NY, Apr 14, 24; m 51; c 3. GENETICS. *Educ:* Brooklyn Col, AB, 47; Columbia Univ, AM, 49; Univ Mo, PhD(zool), 53. *Prof Exp:* Lectr biol & res assoc, Univ Rochester, 53-55; asst prof, Trinity Col, Conn, 55-59; res exec zool, Ind Univ, 59-62; assoc prof biol, 62-66, PROF BIOL, BROWN UNIV, 66- *Res:* Segregation mechanisms; radiation genetics; chemical mutagenesis. *Mailing Add:* Div of Biol & Med Sci Brown Univ Providence RI 02912

ZIMMERMAN, ARTHUR MAURICE, b New York, NY, May 24, 29; m 53; c 3. PHYSIOLOGY, CELL BIOLOGY. *Educ:* NY Univ, BA, 50, MS, 54, PhD(cell physiol), 56. *Prof Exp:* Technician, NY Univ, 51-52; res assoc, NY Univ & Marine Biol Lab, Woods Hole, 55-56; Lalor res fel, Marine Biol Lab, Woods Hole, 56; Nat Cancer Inst res fel, Univ Calif, 56-58; from instr to asst prof pharmacol, Col Med, State Univ NY Downstate Med Ctr, 58-64; grad secy, Dept Zool, 70-75, assoc chmn grad affairs, 75-78, assoc dean, Div IV, Sch Grad Studies, 78-81, actg dir, Inst Immunol, 80-81, PROF ZOOL, UNIV TORONTO, 64- *Concurrent Pos:* Mem corp, Marine Biol Lab, Woods Hole; assoc ed, Can J Biochem, 80-; ed, Cell Biol Series, Acad Press; vis prof anat, Univ Tex Health Sci Ctr, San Antonio. *Mem:* Soc Gen Physiol; Am Soc Cell Biol (treas, 74-78); Can Soc Cell Biol (pres, 76). *Res:* Cell division; mechanism of cytokinesis and karyokinesis; nuclear-cytoplasmic interrelations; physiological effects of temperature and pressure; amoeboid movement; physicochemical aspects of protoplasmic gels; cell cycle studies and drug action on cells. *Mailing Add:* Dept of Zool Univ of Toronto Toronto ON M5S 1A1 Can

ZIMMERMAN, BARRY, b New York, NY, Jan 14, 38; m 62; c 3. ORGANIC CHEMISTRY. *Educ:* Brooklyn Col, BSc, 59, AM, 61; Fordham Univ, PhD(org chem), 67. *Prof Exp:* Lectr chem, Brooklyn Col, 59-61; instr, Bronx Community Col, 62-66; proj leader chem & plastics, Union Carbide Corp, New York, 66-72, mkt mgr cellular & elastomer mat, 72-76; mkt area sales mgr, Urethane Intermediates, 76-78; bus mgr urethane prods, 78-80, DIR RES & DEVELOP & MKT, GEN FELT INDUSTS, INC, SADDLE BROOK, 81- *Mem:* Am Chem Soc; Royal Soc Chem; NY Acad Sci. *Res:* Synthesis and application of new chemical species in rubber processing; cure accelerators; silanes; inorganic bonding in elastomer matricies; insecticide synthesis; microencapsulation; physiochemical properties of polyelectrolytes and other colloids; polyurethane synthesis and catalysis. *Mailing Add:* 5 Tara Dr Pomona NY 10970

ZIMMERMAN, BARRY, b Toronto, Ont, Nov 6, 41; m 64; c 2. IMMUNOLOGY. *Educ:* Univ Toronto, MD, 65; FRCP(Can), 80; Am Bd Pediat, dipl, 81. *Prof Exp:* Asst prof pediat & mem staff, Inst Immunol, Univ Toronto, 72-80; ASSOC PROF PEDIAT, DEPT PEDIAT & MEM STAFF, HOST RESISTANCE PROG, MCMASTER UNIV, 81- *Concurrent Pos:* Mem staff immunol, Hosp Sick Children & scientist, Res Inst, 71-80; grants, Med Res Coun Can, 71- & Nat Cancer Inst Can, 76-78; Med Res Coun Can scholar, 74-79. *Mem:* Am Asn Immunol; Am Asn Immunologists; Can Soc Immunol. *Res:* Immunochemistry of lymphocyte surface antigens and receptors; transplantation; homograft prolongation by antilymphocyte and enhancing sera; characterization of leukemic lymphocytes; cellular regulation of gamma globulin production; investigation of asthma. *Mailing Add:* Dept Pediat McMaster Univ Med Ctr 1200 Main St W Hamilton ON L8N 3Z5 Can

ZIMMERMAN, BEN GEORGE, b Newark, NJ, July 1, 34; m 60; c 2. PHARMACOLOGY. *Educ:* Columbia Univ, BS, 56; Univ Mich, PhD(pharmacol), 60. *Prof Exp:* Pharmacologist, Lederle Labs, Am Cyanamid Co, 60-61; res fel, Cardiovasc Labs, Col Med, Univ Iowa, 61-63; from asst prof to assoc prof pharmacol, 63-72, PROF PHARMACOL, UNIV MINN, MINNEAPOLIS, 72- *Concurrent Pos:* Mem coun high blood pressure res, Coun Circulation & Coun Basic Sci, Am Heart Asn. *Mem:* Am Soc Pharmacol & Exp Therapeut; Soc Exp Biol & Med. *Res:* Vascular effects of angiotensin and other pressor agents; influence of the sympathetic nervous system on various vascular beds; vascular role of prostaglandins. *Mailing Add:* 105 Millard Hall Univ of Minn Minneapolis MN 55455

ZIMMERMAN, C DUANE, b Mayville, Wis, Oct 23, 35. COMPUTER SCIENCE. *Educ:* Andrews Univ, BA, 57; Univ Minn, Minneapolis, MS, 60, PhD(comput sci), 69. *Prof Exp:* Instr math, Southern Missionary Col, 61-63; mathematician, Control Data Corp, 64-66; asst prof comput sci, Univ Minn, Minneapolis, 69-70; asst prof biomath, Loma Linda Univ, 70-80; DIR SYST DEVELOP, HBO & CO, 80- *Mem:* Asn Comput Mach; Inst Elec & Electronics Engrs Comput Soc. *Res:* Computer-medical applications. *Mailing Add:* HBO & Co 114 Airport Dr #105 San Bernadino CA 92408

ZIMMERMAN, CARLE CLARK, JR, b Winchester, Mass, Apr 25, 34; m 60; c 2. CHEMICAL ENGINEERING. *Educ:* Bucknell Univ, BS, 56; Cornell Univ, PhD(chem eng), 63. *Prof Exp:* Res engr process develop, 63-64, advan res engr, 64-70, sr res engr, 70-74, mgr anal dept, 74-77, mgr petrol chem dept, 77-81, MGR OIL SHALE PROJ GROUP, DENVER RES CTR, MARATHON OIL CO, 81- *Mem:* Am Inst Chem Engrs; Sigma Xi. *Res:* Development and design of new chemical processes. *Mailing Add:* PO Box 269 Marathon Oil Co Littleton CO 80160

ZIMMERMAN, CRAIG ARTHUR, b Painesville, Ohio, Mar 22, 37; m 62; c 2. BOTANY, PHYSIOLOGICAL ECOLOGY. *Educ:* Baldwin-Wallace Col, BS, 60; Univ Mich, MS, 62 & 64, PhD(bot), 69. *Prof Exp:* From instr to asst prof biol, Centre Col Ky, 67-74; environ specialist, Spindletop Res, Inc, 74-75; assoc prof, 75-80, PROF BIOL, AURORA COL, 80-, CHMN DEPT, 75- *Mem:* Am Inst Biol Sci; AAAS; Ecol Soc Am; Sigma Xi. *Res:* Causes, characteristics, and evolution of weed plants; comparing the biology of the weed with that of related cultivars and narrow endemics; biological indicators of stream pollution. *Mailing Add:* Dept of Biol Aurora Col Aurora IL 60507

ZIMMERMAN, DALE A, b Imlay City, Mich, June 7, 28; m 50; c 1. ORNITHOLOGY, ECOLOGY. *Educ:* Univ Mich, BS, 50, MS, 51, PhD, 56. *Prof Exp:* From asst prof to assoc prof, 57-72, PROF BIOL, WESTERN NMEX UNIV, 72-, CHMN DEPT, 77- *Concurrent Pos:* Mem expeds, Africa, 61, 63, 65 & 66. *Mem:* Am Ornith Union; Wilson Ornith Soc; Cooper Ornith Soc; Brit Ornith Union. *Res:* Taxonomy and ecology of birds and plants. *Mailing Add:* Dept of Biol Sci Western NMex Univ Silver City NM 88061

ZIMMERMAN, DANIEL HILL, b Los Angeles, Calif, June 3, 41; m 63; c 3. BIOCHEMISTRY, IMMUNOLOGY. *Educ:* Emory & Henry Col, BS, 63; Univ Fla, MS, 66, PhD(biochem), 69. *Prof Exp:* Jr staff fel biochem, Nat Inst Arthritis, Metab & Digestive Dis, 69-71, sr staff fel, 71-73; cellular immunologist, 73-77, sr res scientist, Res & Develop Dept, 77-80, PROG MGR CELL IMMUNOL, ELECTRO NUCLEONICS LABS INC, 81- *Mem:* Am Asn Immunol. *Res:* Synthesis and secretion of proteins; differentiation of antibody producing cells. *Mailing Add:* Electro Nucleonics Labs Inc 12050 Technical Rd Silver Spring MD 20904

ZIMMERMAN, DEAN R, b Compton, Ill, July 2, 32; m 53; c 2. ANIMAL NUTRITION. *Educ:* Iowa State Univ, BS, 54, PhD(swine nutrit), 60. *Prof Exp:* Res assoc nutrit, Univ Notre Dame, 60-62; asst prof biol, Wartburg Col, 62-65; assoc prof animal sci, Purdue Univ, 65-67; assoc prof, 67-73, PROF ANIMAL SCI, IOWA STATE UNIV, 73- *Mem:* Am Soc Animal Sci; Am Inst Nutrit. *Res:* Nutrition research, especially compensatory growth and development; nutrition-disease interrelationships; bioavailability of amino acids. *Mailing Add:* Dept of Animal Sci R337 Kildee Iowa State Univ Ames IA 50011

ZIMMERMAN, DON CHARLES, b Fargo, NDak, Feb 27, 34; m 58; c 1. BIOLOGICAL CHEMISTRY, PLANT PHYSIOLOGY. *Educ:* NDak State Univ, BS, 55, MS, 59, PhD(biochem), 64. *Prof Exp:* RES CHEMIST, SCI & EDUC ADMIN-AGR RES, USDA, 59-; ADJ PROF BIOCHEM, NDAK STATE UNIV, 69- *Concurrent Pos:* Asst prof, NDak State Univ, 64-69. *Mem:* AAAS; Am Chem Soc; Am Soc Plant Physiol. *Res:* Metabolism of unsaturated fatty acids; their oxidation by lipoxygenase and other enzymes during early plant growth. *Mailing Add:* Dept of Biochem NDak State Univ Fargo ND 58102

ZIMMERMAN, DONALD NATHAN, b Somerset, Pa, Dec 30, 32. PHYSICAL INORGANIC CHEMISTRY. *Educ:* Univ Md, College Park, BS, 61; Pa State Univ, MEd, 63; WVa Univ, PhD(chem), 69. *Prof Exp:* Teacher pub sch, Pa, 62-65; assoc prof, Ind Univ Pa, 69-73, prof chem, 73-78; MEM STAFF, ARGONNE NAT LAB, 78-81; MEM STAFF, DEPT PHYSICS & ASTRON, NORTHWESTERN UNIV, 81- *Mem:* AAAS; Am Chem Soc; Am Inst Physics; Royal Soc Chem. *Res:* Application of magnetochemical techniques to the determination of the structure of coordination compounds. *Mailing Add:* Dept Physics & Astron Northwestern Univ Evanston IL 60201

ZIMMERMAN, EARL ABRAM, b Harrisburg, Pa, May 5, 37; m 67. NEUROLOGY, NEUROENDOCRINOLOGY. *Educ:* Franklin & Marshall Univ, BS, 59; Univ Pa, MD, 63. *Prof Exp:* Resident & intern med, Presbyterian Hosp, 63-65; resident neurol, Neurol Inst, NY, 65-68; fel endocrinol, 70-72, asst prof neurol, 72-77, assoc prof, 78-81, PROF NEUROL, COL PHYSICIANS & SURGEONS, COLUMBIA UNIV, 81- *Concurrent Pos:* asst attending physician neurol, Presbyterian Hosp, 72-77, assoc attending physician, 78-81, attending physician, 81-; Lucy Moses Basic Res Prize neurol, Columbia Univ, 74. *Mem:* Am Neurol Asn; Am Acad Neurol; Endocrine Soc; Soc Neurosci; Histochem Soc. *Res:* Organization and evaluation of neuropeptide pathways in mammalian brain with an emphasis on hypothalmic systems. *Mailing Add:* Neurol Inst Col Physicians & Surgeons 710 W 168th St New York NY 10032

ZIMMERMAN, EARL GRAVES, b Detroit, Mich, Feb 15, 43; m 75; c 2. ECOLOGICAL GENETICS, POPULATION GENETICS. *Educ:* Ind State Univ, Terre Haute, BS, 65; Univ Ill, Urbana, MS, 67, PhD(zool), 70. *Prof Exp:* Asst mammal comp anat, Univ Ill, Urbana, 65-69, asst cytogenetics, 69-70; asst prof pop genetics, 70-75, fac res grant, 70-72, assoc prof pop genetics, 75-77, assoc prof biol sci, 77-81, PROF POP GENETICS, NORTH TEX STATE UNIV, 81- *Honors & Awards:* Jackson Award, Am Soc Mammal, 70. *Mem:* Am Soc Mammal; Genetics Soc Am; Soc Study Evolution. *Res:* Population genetics, biochemical variation and evolution of vertebrates. *Mailing Add:* Dept Biol North Tex State Univ Denton TX 76203

ZIMMERMAN, EDWARD JOHN, b Waynetown, Ind, July 12, 24; m 45; c 2. THEORETICAL PHYSICS, PHILOSOPHY OF SCIENCE. *Educ:* Univ Kans, AB, 45; Univ Ill, MS, 47, PhD(physics), 51. *Prof Exp:* Res assoc nuclear physics, Univ Ill, 50-51; from asst prof to assoc prof physics, 51-60, chmn dept, 62-66, PROF PHYSICS, UNIV NEBR-LINCOLN, 60- *Concurrent Pos:* Vis prof, Hamburg Univ, 57-58; NSF sci fac fel philos sci, Cambridge Univ, 66-67. *Mem:* Fel Am Phys Soc; Am Asn Physics Teachers; Philos Sci Asn; Brit Soc Philos Sci. *Res:* Foundations of physics; quantum mechanics. *Mailing Add:* Dept of Physics Univ of Nebr Lincoln NE 68588

ZIMMERMAN, ELMER LEROY, b Washington Co, Pa, Feb 5, 21; m 45; c 4. PHYSICS. *Educ:* Washington & Jefferson Col, AB, 42; Syracuse Univ, MA, 44; Ohio State Univ, PhD(physics), 50. *Prof Exp:* Physicist, Tenn Eastman Corp, 44-45, Oak Ridge Nat Lab, 50-55 & Nuclear Develop Corp Am, 55-58; supvr critical exp unit, Atomics Int Div, NAm Aviation, Inc, 58-60; vpres & tech dir, Solid State Radiations, Inc, 60-62; group leader radiation effects & reactor opers, Atomics Int Div, NAm Aviation, Inc, 62-64; asst mgr weapons effects dept, Solid State Physics Lab, TRW Systs, 64-67, mgr electronic & electro-magnetic effects dept, Vulnerability & Hardness Lab, 67-69, mem staff, Opers Res Dept, 69-77; NUCLEAR SURVIVABILITY MGT, GUID & CONTROL DIV, LITTON INDUSTS, INC, 77- *Mem:* Am Phys Soc; Inst Elec & Electronics Engrs; Am Nuclear Soc. *Res:* Nuclear spectroscopy and resonance; reactor physics and instrumentation; critical experiments; semiconductor radiation detectors; radiation effects and transport; ballistic and cruise missile systems engineering. *Mailing Add:* 22650 MacFarlane Dr Woodland Hills CA 91364

ZIMMERMAN, ELWOOD CURTIN, b Spokane, Wash, Dec 8, 12; m 41. ENTOMOLOGY. *Educ:* Univ Calif, BS, 36; Univ London, PhD(zool) & DIC, 56. *Hon Degrees:* DSc, Univ London, 80. *Prof Exp:* Field entomologist, Bishop Mus, Honolulu, Hawaii, 34-35, asst cur collections, 35-36, from asst entomologist to entomologist, 36-45, cur entom, 46-50, res assoc, 51-61, entomologist, 61-73; SR RES FEL, COMMONWEALTH SCI & INDUST RES ORGN, AUSTRALIA, 73-, CUR RHYNCHOPHORA, AUSTRALIAN NAT INSECT COL, 73- *Concurrent Pos:* Lectr, Univ Hawaii, 36-37, 40-41, entomologist, 58-61; assoc entomologist, Hawaiian Sugar Planters Exp Sta, 46-54; Fulbright adv researcher, Eng, 49, res & lectr, Eng, 49-51, Denmark & Sweden, 50; hon assoc, Brit Mus Natural Hist, 51- Entomologist, Mangarevan Exped Southeast Polynesia, 34, Lapham Fijian Exped, 38, Samoan Exped, 40 & NSF Eng, 54-56, 58, 66-67 & 69-73. *Mem:* AAAS; Australian Entom Soc; Entom Soc Am; Soc Syst Zool; Asn Trop Biol. *Res:* Systematic entomology; biogeography; evolution on islands; insular life; Curculionidae of Australia and Indo-Pacific; insects of Oceania and Hawaii. *Mailing Add:* CSIRO Box 1700 Canberra Australia

ZIMMERMAN, EMERY GILROY, b Los Angeles, Calif, June 23, 39; m 67; c 3. ANATOMY, MEDICINE. *Educ:* Pomona Col, BA, 61; Baylor Univ, MD, 67, PhD(anat), 71. *Prof Exp:* Intern med, Methodist Hosp, Houston, 68-69; instr anat, Col Med, Baylor Univ, 69-70; surgeon, Addiction Res Ctr, NIMH, Ky, 70-72; ASSOC PROF ANAT, SCH MED, UNIV CALIF, LOS ANGELES, 72- *Mem:* Am Physiol Soc; Endocrine Soc; Soc Exp Biol & Med; AMA; Am Soc Clin Pharmacol & Therapeut. *Res:* Neuroendocrinology, physiology, neuropharmacology. *Mailing Add:* Dept of Anat Univ of Calif Sch of Med Los Angeles CA 90024

ZIMMERMAN, ERNEST FREDERICK, b New York, NY, June 2, 33; m 57; c 3. TERATOLOGY, DEVELOPMENTAL BIOLOGY. *Educ:* George Washington Univ, BS, 56, MS, 58, PhD(pharmacol), 61. *Prof Exp:* Res asst pharmacol, George Washington Univ, 56-58; fel biol, Mass Inst Technol, 60-62; from instr to asst prof pharmacol, Sch Med, Stanford Univ, 62-68; assoc prof res pediat, 68-71, PROF RES PEDIAT, COL MED, UNIV CINCINNATI, 71-, ASSOC PROF RES PHARMACOL, 68-, DIR DIV CELL BIOL, INST DEVELOP RES, CHILDREN'S HOSP RES FOUND, 68-, DIR GRAD PROG DEVELOP BIOL, 71- *Mem:* AAAS; Am Soc Biol Chemists; Teratol Soc; Soc Cell Biol; Am Soc Pharmacol & Exp Therapeut. *Res:* Morphogenetic movement of palate; embryonic contractile proteins; eukaryotic chemotaxis; role of neurotransmitters in development and differentiation; molecular mechanisms of action of teratogenic drugs. *Mailing Add:* Inst Develop Res Elland & Bethesda Aves Cincinnati OH 45229

ZIMMERMAN, EUGENE MUNRO, b New Haven, Conn, June 27, 40. HEALTH SCIENCE ADMINISTRATION, VIROLOGY. *Educ:* Yale Univ, BA, 60; Wesleyan Univ, MA, 62; Univ Md, College Park, PhD(microbiol), 68. *Prof Exp:* Microbiologist, Ft Detrick, Md, 69-70; asst proj dir, Microbiol Assocs Inc, Md, 70-73; sr scientist, Litton-Bionetics Inc, 73-76; grants assoc, 76-77, asst prog dir carcinogenesis, Nat Cancer Inst, 77-78, exec secy, Review Br, 78-81, EXEC SECY, ALLERGY & IMMUNOL STUDY SECT, DIV RES GRANTS, NIH, 82- *Concurrent Pos:* Consult, Mt Sinai Sch Med, 75-76. *Mem:* AAAS; Tissue Cult Asn; Am Soc Microbiol. *Res:* Grant and contract review; biology of oncogenic herpesviruses and oncarnaviruses; treatment and prophylaxis of leukemia in animal models. *Mailing Add:* Allergy & Immunol Study Sect Div Res Grants NIH Westwood Bldg Rm 320 Bethesda MD 20205

ZIMMERMAN, GARY ALAN, b Seattle, Wash, Oct 19, 38; m 60; c 2. CLINICAL CHEMISTRY. *Educ:* Calif Inst Technol, BS, 60; Univ Wis, PhD(org chem), 65. *Prof Exp:* Asst prof chem, 64-68, assoc prof, 68-76, dean, Sch Sci & Eng, 73-80, vpres acad affairs, 80-81, DIR CLIN CHEM, SEATTLE UNIV, 68-, EXEC VPRES, 81- . *Concurrent Pos:* Lectr, Univ Wash, 65 & vis sci prog, Pac Sci Ctr, Seattle, 66-68; consult, Gordon Res Conf, 66-70 & Swed Hosp & Med Ctr, Seattle, 68-; vis prof chem, Univ Idaho, 73. *Mem:* AAAS; Am Chem Soc; Am Asn Clin Chemists (tres, 80-81, pres elect, 82, pres, 83); The Chem Soc; Soc Ger Chem. *Res:* Clinical applications of enzymatic assays; trace metal analyses; lipoproteins; isoenzymes. *Mailing Add:* Exec Vpres Seattle Univ Seattle WA 98122

ZIMMERMAN, GEORGE LANDIS, b Hershey, Pa, Aug 27, 20; m 53. PHYSICAL CHEMISTRY. *Educ:* Swarthmore Col, AB, 41; Univ Chicago, PhD, 49. *Prof Exp:* Res chemist sam labs, Manhattan Dist Proj, Columbia, 42-46; instr, Mass Inst Technol, 49-51; asst prof, 51-55, assoc prof, 55, PROF CHEM, BRYN MAWR COL, 55- *Mem:* Am Chem Soc. *Res:* Molecular spectroscopy. *Mailing Add:* Dept of Chem Bryn Mawr Col Bryn Mawr PA 19010

ZIMMERMAN, GEORGE OGUREK, b Katowice, Poland, Oct 20, 35; US citizen; m 64. LOW TEMPERATURE PHYSICS. *Educ:* Yale Univ, BS, 58, MS, 59, PhD(physics), 63. *Prof Exp:* Res asst physics, Yale Univ, 59-62, res assoc, 62-63; from asst prof to assoc prof physics, 63-73, assoc chmn dept, 72-73, PROF PHYSICS & CHMN DEPT, BOSTON UNIV, 73- *Concurrent Pos:* Vis scientist, Nat Magnet Lab, Mass Inst Technol, 65-; assoc physicist, Univ Calif, San Diego, 73; vis physicist, Brookhaven Nat Lab, 80. *Mem:* AAAS; NY Acad Sci; Am Phys Soc. *Res:* Low temperature phenomena, cryogenics, specifically pertaining to liquid and solid helium three; investigation of paramagnetic phenomena; investigation of phase transitions. *Mailing Add:* Dept of Physics Boston Univ 111 Cummington St Boston MA 02215

ZIMMERMAN, HARRY MARTIN, b Vilna Prov, Russia, Sept 28, 01; nat US; m 30. PATHOLOGY. *Educ:* Yale Univ, BS, 24, MD, 27. *Hon Degrees:* LHD, Yeshiva Univ, 58. *Prof Exp:* Ives fel, Sch Med, Yale Univ, 27-29, from asst prof path to assoc prof, 30-43; from assoc clin prof to prof, Col Physicians & Surgeons, Columbia Univ, 46-64; prof, 64-74, EMER PROF PATH, ALBERT EINSTEIN COL MED, 74- *Concurrent Pos:* Assoc pathologist, New Haven Hosp, Conn, 33-43; consult, Bristol Hosp, Conn, 38-43; consult, US Naval Hosp, St Albans, 46-49, Seton Hosp, 49-55, Beth Israel Hosp, 49-71, Armed Forces Inst Path, 49-71, Long Island Jewish Hosp, 54- & Vassar Bros Hosp, Poughkeepsie, NY, 61-; sr consult, Vet Admin Hosp, Bronx, 46-71; chief lab div, Montefiore Hosp, 46-73; Middleton Goldsmith lectr, NY Acad Med, 64. *Honors & Awards:* Golden Hope Chest Award, Nat Multiple Sclerosis Soc, 65; Max Weinstein Award, United Cerebral Palsy Found, 72. *Mem:* Fel Am Soc Clin Path; Am Asn Pathologists; Am Neurol Asn; Am Asn Neuropath (pres, 44); fel Col Am Path. *Res:* Neuropathology; demyelinating diseases; brain tumors. *Mailing Add:* Montefiore Hosp & Med Ctr 111 E 210th St Bronx NY 10467

ZIMMERMAN, HENRY B, b Brooklyn, NY, May 6, 17; m 43; c 2. CHEMISTRY, MATHEMATICS. *Educ:* Brooklyn Col, BA, 43; Polytech Inst Brooklyn, MS, 52. *Prof Exp:* Anal chemist, Coupland Labs, 41-43; res chemist, Seydell Chem Co, 46-50; pharmaceut res chemist, Schering Corp, 50-53; sr pharmaceut chemist, Ayerst Labs Div, Am Home Prod Corp, 53-55; dir pharmaceut develop, Nepera Chem Co, Warner-Lambert Pharmaceut Co, 55-57; coordr res & develop, 57-61, dir new prod develop, 61-66, dir tech serv, 66-68, vpres tech serv, 68-73, vpres regulatory affairs & new prod coord, 73-78, VPRES, REGULATORY AFFAIRS & INT LIAISON CARTER-WALLACE, INC, 78- *Mem:* Am Pharmaceut Asn; Drug Info Asn; Int Acad Law & Sci. *Res:* New product development; research administration; regulatory affairs. *Mailing Add:* Carter-Wallace Inc Cranbury NJ 08512

ZIMMERMAN, HOWARD ELLIOT, b New York, NY, July 5, 26; m 75; c 3. CHEMISTRY. *Educ:* Yale Univ, BS, 50, PhD(chem), 53. *Prof Exp:* Nat Res Coun fel chem, Harvard Univ, 53-54; from instr to asst prof, Northwestern Univ, 54-60; assoc prof, 60-61, PROF CHEM, UNIV WIS-MADISON, 61-, ARTHUR C COPE CHAIR CHEM, 75- *Concurrent Pos:* Mem grants comt, Res Corp, 66-72; chmn, 4th Int Union Pure & Appl Chem, Int Photochem Symp, Baden-Baden, Ger, 72; co-chmn org div, Inter Am Photochem Soc, 76-81, mem exec comt, 81-; fel, Japan Soc Prom Sci. *Honors & Awards:* Photochem Award, Am Chem Soc, 75 & James Flack Norris Award Phys-Org Chem, 76. *Mem:* Nat Acad Sci; Royal Soc Chem; Ger Chem Soc; Am Chem Soc. *Res:* Organic, physical-organic, synthetic organic chemistry; photochemistry; theoretical organic chemistry; photobiology; reaction mechanisms; stereochemistry; unusual organic phenomena and species. *Mailing Add:* Dept Chem Univ Wis Madison WI 53706

ZIMMERMAN, HYMAN JOSEPH, b Rochester, NY, July 14, 14; m 43; c 4. MEDICINE, HEPATOLOGY. *Educ:* Univ Rochester, AB, 36; Stanford Univ, MA, 38, MD, 42. *Prof Exp:* Intern, Stanford Univ Hosp, 42-43; resident med, Gallinger Munic Hosp & Med Div, George Washington Univ, 46-48, clin instr, Sch Med, 48-51; asst prof, Col Med, Univ Nebr, 51; chief med serv, Vet Admin Hosp, Omaha, 51-53; clin assoc prof med, Col Med, Univ Ill, 53-57; prof & chmn dept, Chicago Med Sch, 57-65; PROF MED, GEORGE WASHINGTON UNIV, 65- *Concurrent Pos:* Asst chief med serv, Vet Admin Hosp, DC, 48-49, dir liver & metab res lab, 65-68; chief med serv, Vet Admin West Side Hosp, Chicago, 53-65; chmn dept med, Mt Sinai Hosp, 57-65; prof, Sch Med, Boston Univ, 68-69; lectr, Sch Med, Tufts Univ, 68-69; clin prof med, Sch Med, Sch Med, Howard Univ, Georgetown Univ & Uniformed Serv Univ Health Sci; chief med serv, Vet Admin Hosp, DC, 68-78. *Mem:* Am Soc Clin Invest; Am Asn Study Liver Disease; Am Diabetes Asn; Am Fedn Clin Res; fel Am Col Physicians. *Res:* Physiology of the liver. *Mailing Add:* 7913 Charleston Ct Bethesda MD 20034

ZIMMERMAN, IRWIN DAVID, b Philadelphia, Pa, Oct 31, 31; m 57; c 4. NEUROPHYSIOLOGY, BIOPHYSICS. *Educ:* Univ Del, BA, 59; Univ Wash, PhD(physiol), 66. *Prof Exp:* Asst prof, 66-72, ASSOC PROF PHYSIOL & BIOPHYS, MED COL PA, 72- *Concurrent Pos:* NSF grant, 68-70; NIH grant, 72- *Mem:* Am Physiol Soc; Biophys Soc; Soc Neurosci. *Res:* Neural processing and coding of sensory information; membrane phenomena; development and aging of cental nervous system. *Mailing Add:* Dept Physiol & Biophys Med Col Pa Philadelphia PA 19129

ZIMMERMAN, IVAN HAROLD, b Orland, Calif, Nov 21, 43; m 75. CHEMICAL PHYSICS. *Educ:* Ore State Univ, BS, 66; Univ Wash, PhD(physics), 72. *Prof Exp:* Fel chem, Univ Rochester, 72-76, res assoc, 77-78; ASST PROF PHYSICS, CLARKSON COL, 78- *Mem:* Am Phys Soc; Am Chem Soc; NY Acad Sci; AAAS. *Res:* Atomic and molecular collisions; effects of intense laser radiation on molecular processes; ion-surface encounters; molecules near solid surfaces. *Mailing Add:* Dept of Physics Clarkson Col Potsdam NY 13676

ZIMMERMAN, JACK MCKAY, b New York, NY, Feb 4, 27; m 53; c 2. SURGERY. *Educ:* Princeton Univ, AB, 49; Johns Hopkins Univ, MD, 53; Univ Kansas City, MA, 63. *Prof Exp:* From intern to resident surg, Johns Hopkins Hosp, 53-59; assoc, Sch Med, Univ Kans, 59-60, asst prof, 60-65; ASSOC PROF SURG, JOHNS HOPKINS UNIV, 65- *Concurrent Pos:* Asst, Johns Hopkins Hosp, 54-59, surgeon, 65-, Halsted fel surg path, Univ, 55-56, instr, 58-59; staff surgeon, Vet Admin Hosp, Kansas City, 59-60, chief surg serv, 60-65; consult, Sch Dent, Univ Kans, 60; chief surg, Church Home & Hosp, 65-; consult, Vet Admin Hosp, Baltimore. *Mem:* Am Col Surg; Asn Am Med Cols; Soc Univ Surg. *Res:* Thoracic surgery; cardiovascular physiology, especially mechanisms of protection against cerebral injury following circulatory occlusion; wound healing and infections; care of advanced malignancy; medical education. *Mailing Add:* 100 N Broadway Baltimore MD 21231

ZIMMERMAN, JAMES JOSEPH, b Yankton, SDak, Feb 11, 33; m 61, 74; c 4. PHARMACY, PHARMACEUTICAL CHEMISTRY. *Educ:* Univ of the Pac, BS, 61; Univ Calif, San Francisco, PhD(pharmaceut chem), 69. *Prof Exp:* From asst prof to assoc prof, 68-78, PROF PHARMACEUTICS, SCH PHARM, TEMPLE UNIV, 78- *Concurrent Pos:* Res grant-in-aid, Temple Univ, 70-71 & 80-81. *Honors & Awards:* Lederle Award, Lederle Labs, 71. *Mem:* Am Asn Cols Pharm; Acad Pharmaceut Sci. *Res:* Substituent effects in alkaline and enzymatic hydrolysis of drug esters; linear free energy and isergonic relationships; drug stability; pharmacokinetics. *Mailing Add:* Dept of Pharm 3307 N Broad St Temple Univ Sch of Pharm Philadelphia PA 19140

ZIMMERMAN, JAMES KENNETH, b Nelson, Nebr, Aug 23, 43. BIOCHEMISTRY. *Educ:* Univ Nebr, Lincoln, BS, 65; Northwestern Univ, Evanston, PhD(biochem), 69. *Prof Exp:* NIH fel, Univ Va, 69-71; asst prof, 71-76, ASSOC PROF BIOCHEM, CLEMSON UNIV, 76- *Mem:* AAAS; Am Chem Soc; Am Soc Biol Chemists; Biophys Soc. *Res:* Associating protein systems; analytical gel chromatography by direct scanning; analytical ultracentrifugation; computer simulations. *Mailing Add:* Dept of Biochem Clemson Univ Clemson SC 29631

ZIMMERMAN, JAMES ROSCOE, b Norwood, Ohio, July 12, 28; m 50; c 3. ZOOLOGY, ENTOMOLOGY. *Educ:* Hanover Col, AB, 53; Ind Univ, MA, 55, PhD(zool), 57. *Prof Exp:* Asst prof zool, Univ Wichita, 57-58; assoc prof biol, Ind Cent Col, 58-61, actg chmn dept, 59-61; from asst prof to assoc prof, 61-68, head dept, 74-78, PROF BIOL, N MEX STATE UNIV, 68- *Concurrent Pos:* Vis prof, Escuela Sup De Agric'Herm Escob CD Juarez, 78-81. *Mem:* AAAS; Am Soc Zool; Entom Soc Am; Soc Systs Zool; Am Entom Soc. *Res:* Taxonomy of dytiscidae; parasitic hymenoptera. *Mailing Add:* Dept of Biol NMex State Univ Las Cruces NM 88003

ZIMMERMAN, JAY ALAN, b Philadelphia, Pa, Mar 1, 45; m 72. MAMMALIAN PHYSIOLOGY. *Educ:* Franklin & Marshall Col, AB, 67; Rutgers Univ, PhD(zool), 75. *Prof Exp:* ASST PROF BIOL, ST JOHN'S UNIV, NY, 75- *Mem:* Sigma Xi; Geront Soc; Soc Study Reproduction; AAAS. *Res:* Adaptive mechanisms of organ-system function and biochemistry during aging. *Mailing Add:* Dept of Biol St John's Univ Jamaica NY 11439

ZIMMERMAN, JOHN F, b Monticello, Iowa, June 22, 37; m 59; c 3. PHYSICAL CHEMISTRY, ANALYTICAL CHEMISTRY. *Educ:* Univ Iowa, BS, 59; Univ Kans, PhD(chem), 64. *Prof Exp:* Asst prof, 63-68, assoc prof, 68-79, PROF CHEM, WABASH COL, 79- *Res:* Use of personal computers in the chemistry lecture and laboratory; development of instrumentation for undergraduate laboratory instruction. *Mailing Add:* Dept of Chem Wabash Col Crawfordsville IN 47933

ZIMMERMAN, JOHN GORDON, b Brooklyn, NY, May 31, 16; m 39; c 4. PHYSICAL CHEMISTRY, INORGANIC CHEMISTRY. *Educ:* Univ Pa, BS, 37, MS, 39; Georgetown Univ, PhD(chem), 71. *Prof Exp:* Instr gen sci, Monmouth Jr Col, 38-42; shift supvr org chem prod, Ala Ord Works, 42-43; instr chem, Drexel Inst, 43-44; develop chemist org chem, Publicker Industs, Inc, 44-47; chmn sci div, St Helena exten, Col William & Mary, 47-48; asst prof, gen & phys chem, Westminster Col, 48-51; from asst prof to assoc prof, 51-72, PROF CHEM, US NAVAL ACAD, 72- *Mem:* Am Chem Soc. *Res:* Kinetics of substitution reactions of transition metal complexes. *Mailing Add:* Dept of Chem US Naval Acad Annapolis MD 21402

ZIMMERMAN, JOHN HARVEY, b St Paul, Minn, Feb 11, 45; m 69. MEDICAL ENTOMOLOGY. *Educ:* Concordia Col, MInn, BA, 67; Univ Del, Newark, MS, 69; Mich State Univ, E Lansing, PhD(entom), 75. *Prof Exp:* Entomologist, Navy Environ & Prev Med Unit, 75-77; mem staff, Navy Dis Vector Ecol Control Ctr, Naval Air Sta, 77-82; MEM STAFF, US NAVAL MED RES UNIT #3, CAIRO, EGYPT, 82- *Mem:* Sigma Xi; Entom Soc Am; Am Mosquito Control Asn. *Res:* The ecology, transmission and control of arthropod-borne diseases of medical and veterinary importance. *Mailing Add:* Navy Dis Vector Ecol Control Ctr Naval Air Sta Jacksonville FL 32212

ZIMMERMAN, JOHN LESTER, b Hamilton, Ont, Feb 17, 33; US citizen; m 55; c 3. ECOLOGY. *Educ:* Mich State Univ, BS, 53, MS, 59; Univ Ill, PhD(zool), 63. *Prof Exp:* Asst prof zool, 63-68, assoc prof biol, 68-76, PROF BIOL, KANS STATE UNIV, 76- *Concurrent Pos:* sci adv environ protection, Atlantic-Richfield Co, Calif, 74-75. *Mem:* Ecol Soc Am; Am Ornith Union; Wilson Ornith Soc; Cooper Ornith Soc; Sigma Xi. *Res:* Bioenergetics and niche requirements of birds, physiological ecology. *Mailing Add:* Div of Biol Kans State Univ Manhattan KS 66506

ZIMMERMAN, JOHN R(ICHARD), b Allentown, Pa, July 25, 25; m 54; c 2. MECHANICAL ENGINEERING. *Educ:* Yale Univ, BE, 46; Boston Univ, STB, 52; Lehigh Univ, MS, 60, PhD, 66. EPXAssoc prof mech eng, Pa State Univ, 66-71; prof, Clarkson Col Technol, 71-74; vis prof, Cornell Univ, 74-76; PROF MECH & AEROSPACE ENG, UNIV DEL, 76- *Mem:* Am Soc Mech Engrs; Am Soc Eng Educ; Am Asn Univ Prof; Sigma Xi; Am Soc Automotive Engrs. *Res:* Mechanical design; computer simulation; random vibrations; land transportation. *Mailing Add:* Dept of Mech & Aerospace Eng Univ of Del Newark DE 19711

ZIMMERMAN, JOSEPH, b New York, NY, Aug 9, 21; m 48; c 3. PHYSICAL CHEMISTRY, POLYMER CHEMISTRY. *Educ:* City Col New York, BS, 42; Columbia Univ, AM, 47, PhD(chem), 50. *Prof Exp:* Res chemist, Carothers Res Lab, 50-53, res assoc, 53-62, res fel, 62-64, res mgr, Carothers Res Lab, 64-71, res mgr, Indust Fibers Div, 71-78, RES FEL TEXTILE FIBERS DEPT, PIONEERING RES DIV, E I DU PONT DE NEMOURS & CO, INC, 78- *Mem:* Am Chem Soc; Sigma Xi. *Res:* Polymer and fiber research, especially polyamides, polyesters and aramids. *Mailing Add:* 906 Barley Dr Box 4042 Wilmington DE 19807

ZIMMERMAN, LEO M, surgery, deceased

ZIMMERMAN, LEONARD NORMAN, b Brooklyn, NY, Sept 13, 23; m 46; c 3. BACTERIOLOGY. *Educ:* Cornell Univ, BS, 48, MS, 49, PhD(bact), 51. *Prof Exp:* Asst, Cornell Univ, 48-51; from asst prof to assoc prof, 51-61, head dept microbiol & cell biol, 75-78, PROF BACT, PA STATE UNIV, UNIVERSITY PARK, 61-, ASSOC DEAN RES, COL SCI, 78- *Mem:* AAAS; Am Soc Microbiol. *Res:* Bacterial genetics and regulatory mechanisms. *Mailing Add:* 212 Whitmore Lab Pa State Univ University Park PA 16802

ZIMMERMAN, LESTER J, b Conway, Kans, July 16, 18; m 49; c 4. AGRONOMY, MATHEMATICS. *Educ:* Goshen Col, BA, 47; Purdue Univ, MS, 50, PhD(soil fertil), 56; Univ Ill, MA, 61. *Prof Exp:* Instr chem & math, 47-49, asst prof, 50-53, PROF MATH, GOSHEN COL, 55- *Concurrent Pos:* Soil survr, Soil Conserv Serv, USDA, 56-58; vis prof, Univ Zambia, 68-69 & 76-78. *Mem:* AAAS; Nat Coun Teachers Math; Soil Sci Soc Am; Soil Conserv Soc Am; Am Sci Affiliation. *Res:* Manganese; plant nutrition. *Mailing Add:* Dept of Math Goshen Col Goshen IN 46526

ZIMMERMAN, LORENZ EUGENE, b Washington, DC, Nov 15, 20; m 45, 59; c 6. PATHOLOGY. *Educ:* George Washington Univ, AB, 43, MD, 45; Am Bd Path, dipl, 52. *Hon Degrees:* DSc, Univ Ill, 81. *Prof Exp:* Assoc prof, 54-63, CLIN PROF OPHTHAL PATH, SCH MED, GEORGE WASHINGTON UNIV, 63-; CHIEF OPHTHAL PATH, ARMED FORCES INST PATH, 53- *Concurrent Pos:* Lectr, Johns Hopkins Univ, 59-; consult ophthal path, Washington Hosp Ctr, 75-; head, WHO Int Ref Ctr Tumors Eye & Ocular Adnexa, 72-; clin prof path, Uniformed Serv Univ Health Sci, 76- *Honors & Awards:* Ernst Jung Prize, Jung Found, Hamburg, WGer, 76; F C Donders lectr, Neth Ophthal Soc, Groningen, 78; Estelle Doheny mem lectr, Estelle Doheny Eye Found, Los Angeles, 78; Sir William Bowman lectr, Ophthal Soc UK, London, 80. *Mem:* Verhoeff Soc; Pan-Am Asn Ophthal; Asn Res Vision & Ophthal; Am Acad Ophthal & Otolaryngol. *Res:* Pathology of diseases of the eye and ocular adnexa. *Mailing Add:* 10016 E Bexhill Dr Kensington MD 20795

ZIMMERMAN, MARY PRISLOPSKI, b Bath, NY, Dec 3, 47; m 75. SYNTHETIC ORGANIC CHEMISTRY. *Educ:* State Univ NY Albany, BS, 70; Wesleyan Univ, MA, 73; Univ Rochester, MS, 74, PhD(org chem), 77. *Prof Exp:* Fel, Univ Rochester, 76-78, instr, 76-78; ADJ ASST PROF ORG CHEM, CLARKSON INST TEHCNOL, 78- *Mem:* Am Chem Soc; Sigma Xi. *Res:* Synthesis of natural products; synthetic methods; synthesis of morphinans. *Mailing Add:* 84 Market St Potsdam NY 13676

ZIMMERMAN, MORRIS, b New York, NY, June 22, 25; m 72; c 2. BIOCHEMISTRY. *Educ:* City Col New York, BS, 45; NY Univ, MA, 49; Ind Univ, PhD(chem), 55. *Prof Exp:* Res chemist, Lederle Labs, Am Cyanamid Co, 46-47; res chemist, Wyeth, Inc, 49-51; res asst, Purdue Univ, 51-52 & Ind Univ, 52-55; sr res chemist, R J Reynolds Tobacco Co, 55-57; res fel, 57-72, sr res fel, 72-82, SR INVESTR, MERCK SHARP & DOHME RES LABS, RAHWAY, 82- *Concurrent Pos:* Adj prof, Sch Med, NY Univ, 81- *Mem:* AAAS; Am Soc Biol Chem; Am Soc Cell Biol. *Res:* Antibiotics; protein chemistry; nicotine metabolism; cancer research; biochemical control mechanisms; tissue culture; cell biology; large scale enzyme isolation, enzyme chemistry and mechanisms; proteases, especially enzymology and role in disease. *Mailing Add:* 104 Johnston Dr Watchung NJ 07060

ZIMMERMAN, NORMAN, b New York, NY, May 6, 41; m 64. BIOCHEMISTRY, ENVIRONMENTAL SCIENCE. *Educ:* Univ Rochester, BA, 63; Brown Univ, ScM, 66; Univ Hawaii, PhD(biochem), 71. *Prof Exp:* Instr biol, Ripon Col, 68-69; fel cancer res, Univ Hawaii, 71-72; consult dir, Scientists Coop Industs, 72-75; mem tech staff environ sci, Mitre Corp, 75-78; SR REGULATORY ANALYST, OFF GEN COUN, AM PETROL INST, 78- *Concurrent Pos:* Dir sci res, Upper Conn Vally Hosp, 73-75; mem adj fac nursing, Cath Univ Am, 77; mem adj fac biol, Georgetown Univ, 77, adj res scientist, 77-79. *Honors & Awards:* Charlton Cancer Award, Am Cancer Soc, 59; Silver Medal Award, Am Chem Soc, 61; Rattigan Award-Third Prize, Am Soc Law & Med, 79. *Mem:* Sigma Xi; Am Soc Law & Med; Am Chem Soc. *Res:* Interaction of law and science, particularly as related to environmental/health science problems. *Mailing Add:* 4607 Barnes Rd Mason MI 48854

ZIMMERMAN, NORMAN H(ERBERT), b St Louis, Mo, May 12, 19; m 46; c 2. MECHANICS, MECHANICAL ENGINEERING. *Educ:* Wash Univ, BS, 42, MS, 50, DSc(appl mech), 56. *Prof Exp:* Instr & lectr, Wash Univ, 46-51; mech engr, Sverdrup & Parcel, Inc, 51; staff engr, White-Rodgers Elec Co, 51-53; proj dynamicist, 53-67, scientist, 67-70, br mgr, 70-75, BR CHIEF, MCDONNELL AIRCRAFT CO, MCDONNELL-DOUGLAS CORP, 76- *Concurrent Pos:* Mem, US Navy Aeroballistics Adv Comt, 68-72. *Honors & Awards:* Am Inst Aeronaut & Astronaut Award, 67. *Mem:* Am Inst Aeronaut & Astronaut. *Res:* Dynamics; aeroelasticity; fluid mechanics; vibration and flutter. *Mailing Add:* McDonnell Aircraft Co Dept 336 PO Box 516 St Louis MO 63166

ZIMMERMAN, PETER DAVID, b June 15, 41; US citizen; m 67; c 2. NUCLEAR PHYSICS, SCIENCE POLICY. *Educ:* Stanford Univ, BS, 63, PhD(physics), 69; Lund Univ, Sweden, Filosofie Licentiat, 67. *Prof Exp:* Res fel physics, Deutsches Electronen Synchrotron, 69-71; adj asst prof physics & planetary sci, Univ Calif, Los Angeles, 71-73; res assoc physics, Fermi Nat Accelerator Lab, 73-74; asst prof, 74-80, ASSOC PROF PHYSICS, LA STATE UNIV, 80- *Concurrent Pos:* Res affil, Mass Inst Technol, 75-; vis assoc res physicist, Univ Calif, San Diego, 81; consult, Inst Defense Anal, Off Technol Assessment. *Mem:* Am Phys Soc. *Res:* Electron scattering experiments from nuclei, principally at large energy loss; origin of stone meteorites; arms control, especially non-nuclear defense and nuclear test ban agreements; orbital mechanics of large manned satellites. *Mailing Add:* Dept of Physics & Astron La State Univ Baton Rouge LA 70803

ZIMMERMAN, RICHARD H(ORST), b Smithville, Ohio, Nov 6, 22; m 48; c 3. MECHANICAL ENGINEERING. *Educ:* Cleveland State Univ, BME, 43; Ohio State Univ, MS, 46. *Prof Exp:* Mech engr, Nat Adv Comt Aeronaut, 43-45; from instr to assoc prof, 46-57, PROF MECH ENG, OHIO STATE UNIV, 57- *Concurrent Pos:* Consult, Gen Elec Co, 56-59 & Rand Corp, 57-; exec dir univ planning, Ohio State Univ, 71-72, dean lower-div col for cent & outlying campuses, 67-71, actg vpres admin opers, 72-77. *Mem:* Am Soc Mech Engrs; Am Soc Eng Educ; Am Inst Aeronaut & Astronaut. *Res:* Thermodynamics; fluid dynamics; heat transfer. *Mailing Add:* Dept of Mech Eng Ohio State Univ Columbus OH 43210

ZIMMERMAN, RICHARD HALE, b Bowling Green, Ohio, Apr 11, 34; m 66; c 2. HORTICULTURE, PLANT PHYSIOLOGY. *Educ:* Mich State Univ, BS, 56; Rutgers Univ, MS, 59, PhD(hort), 62. *Prof Exp:* Silviculturist, Tex Forest Serv, 62-64; PLANT PHYSIOLOGIST, AGR RES CTR, USDA, 65- *Honors & Awards:* J H Gourley Award, Am Soc Hort Sci, 72, Stark Award, 78. *Mem:* Int Soc Hort Sci; Int Plant Propagators Soc; AAAS; fel Am Soc Hort Sci; Int Asn Plant Tissue Culture. *Res:* Tissue culture; juvenility and flower initiation in fruit trees and other woody plants; effects of growth regulators on plant growth and development. *Mailing Add:* Fruit Lab Agr Res Ctr USDA Beltsville MD 20705

ZIMMERMAN, ROBERT ALLAN, b Philadelphia, Pa, June 23, 38; m 60; c 2. RADIOLOGY. *Educ:* Temple Univ, BA, 60; Georgetown Univ Sch Med, MD, 64. *Prof Exp:* Intern, Georgetown Univ Hosp, 64-65; physician resident fel, Hosp Univ Pa, 65-69; radiologist, US Army, Europe, 69-72; asst prof, 72-77, assoc prof, 77-81, PROF RADIOL, HOSP UNIV PA, 81- *Concurrent Pos:* Chief sect neuroradiol, Hosp Univ Pa, 79-; assoc ed, J Comput Tomography, 77-82, Neuroradiol, 81- *Mem:* Am Soc Neuroradiol; Radiol Soc NAm; Asn Univ Radiologists; Am Soc Head & Neck Radiol. *Res:* Medical imaging of central nervous system trauma, using medical imaging in the diagnosis and management of pediatric brain tumors. *Mailing Add:* Dept Radiol Hosp Univ Pa 3400 Spruce St Philadelphia PA 19104

ZIMMERMAN, ROBERT LYMAN, b La Grande, Ore, Dec 30, 35; m 57; c 5. PHYSICS. *Educ:* Univ Ore, BA, 58; Univ Wash, PhD(physics), 63. *Prof Exp:* Physicist, Lawrence Radiation Lab, Univ Calif, Berkeley, 64-66; asst prof, 66-74, res assoc, 70-74, ASSOC PROF PHYSICS, UNIV & ASSOC PROF, INST THEORET SCI, UNIV ORE, 74- *Mem:* Am Phys Soc. *Res:* Quantum field theory; elementary particle physics; gravitation; astrophysics. *Mailing Add:* Dept of Physics Univ of Ore Eugene OR 97403

ZIMMERMAN, ROGER M, b Rehoboth, NMex, May 15, 36; m 56; c 2. CIVIL ENGINEERING, STRUCTURAL MECHANICS. *Educ:* Univ Colo, BS, 59, MS, 61, PhD(civil eng), 65. *Prof Exp:* Instr civil eng, Univ Colo, 59-63, res assoc, 63-64; from asst prof to assoc prof civil eng, NMex State Univ, 64-70, asst dean eng, 67-72, prof, 70-80, assoc dean, 72-74, actg dean, 74-75; WITH SANDIA CORP, 80- *Concurrent Pos:* Sr engr, Phys Sci Lab, NMex State Univ, 75- *Mem:* Am Concrete Inst; Am Soc Civil Engrs; Am Soc Eng Educ; Nat Soc Prof Engrs; Sigma Xi. *Res:* Multiaxial strength properties of plain concrete; deterioration of plain concrete; biomechanical aspects of simulated side and rear automobile impacts; safety aspects of school bus seats; evaluation of structures for seismic response. *Mailing Add:* Sandia Corp Albuquerque NM 87185

ZIMMERMAN, ROGER PAUL, b Oak Park, Ill, Sept 29, 46; m 74; c 1. NEUROBIOLOGY, VISUAL PHYSIOLOGY. *Educ:* Univ Ill, Chicago Circle, BS, 68; Yale Univ, MPhil, 69, PhD(biol), 77. *Prof Exp:* Res asst paleobot, Dept Biol Sci, Univ Ill, Chicago Circle, 65-68; teaching asst, Dept Biol, Yale Univ, 60 & 73; res fel, Biol Lab, Harvard Univ, 76 & 78; ASST PROF NEUROL SCI, RUSH-PRESBY-ST LUKES MED CTR, RUSH MED COL, 78-, ASST PROF PHYSIOL, 79- *Concurrent Pos:* Participant, NSF Summer Res Prog, Univ Ill, Chicago, 68; NSF fel, Yale Univ, 68-73; res asst, Walter Reed Army Inst of Res, US Army, 70-72; NIH fel, Harvard Univ, 76-78, teaching fel, Dept Biol, 78; course dir med neurobiol, Rush Med Col, 81- *Mem:* Asn Res in Vision & Ophthal; Soc Neurosci; AAAS; Sigma Xi. *Res:* Neurobiology of vision, including the physiology and ultrastructure of synaptic interactions in the vertebrate retina; physiology and pharmacology of glial cells; synaptic pharmacology of the insect compound eye and optic lobe. *Mailing Add:* Dept Neurol Sci & Physiol Rush Med Col 1753 W Congress Parkway Chicago IL 60612

ZIMMERMAN, SARAH E, b Indianapolis, Ind, Oct 29, 37. IMMUNOLOGY, BIOCHEMISTRY. *Educ:* Ind Univ, AB, 59, MA, 61; Wayne State Univ, PhD(biochem), 69. *Prof Exp:* Res asst biochem, Sch Med, Wayne State Univ, 68-69; res assoc chem, Ind Univ, Bloomington, 69-71; res assoc microbiol, 71-73, RES ASST, DEPT PATH, SCH MED, IND UNIV, INDIANAPOLIS, 73- *Mem:* Sigma Xi; Am Soc Microbiol; Am Asn Immunologists; Am Chem Soc. *Res:* Structure and specificity of antibody; relation of antibody specificity to genetic markers of antibody molecule; specific antibody class responses to selected pathogens; immunological diagnosis of viral, bacterial and fungal infections. *Mailing Add:* Dept Path Ind Univ Sch of Med Indianapolis IN 46223

ZIMMERMAN, SELMA BLAU, b New York, NY, Apr 1, 30; m 53; c 3. EMBRYOLOGY, CELL BIOLOGY. *Educ:* Hunter Col, BA, 50; NY Univ, MS, 54, PhD, 58. *Prof Exp:* Res asst, NY Univ, 53-55; res assoc pharmacol, Col Med, State Univ NY Downstate Med Ctr, 60-61; instr biol, Hunter Col, 61-64 & York Univ, Ont, 65-66; res assoc zool, Univ Toronto, 66-69; asst prof, 69-74, chmn, 74-75, coordr, 77-79, 81-82, PROF NATURAL SCI, GLENDON COL, YORK UNIV, 74- *Mem:* AAAS; Can Soc Cell Biol; Nutrit Today Soc; Can Asn Women Sci. *Res:* Pigment cell physiology; mechanisms of cell division; cell cycle studies and drug action on cells. *Mailing Add:* Natural Sci Div 2275 Bayview Ave Toronto ON M4N 3M6 Can

ZIMMERMAN, SHELDON BERNARD, b New York, NY, Nov 7, 26; m 50; c 1. MICROBIOLOGY. *Educ:* City Col New York, BS, 48; Long Island Univ, MS, 65; NY Univ, PhD(biol), 71. *Prof Exp:* Chemist pharmaceut, Vitamin Corp Am, 49-51; develop microbiologist pharmaceut, Schering Corp, 51-63; SECT HEAD PHARMACEUT, MERCK INST THERAPEUT RES, 63- *Mem:* Am Soc Microbiol; NY Acad Sci. *Res:* Discovery and mode of action of antibiotics; microbial physiology; microbial ecology; structure-activity relationships of antibiotics; Automated microbiological assays; microbial chemotherapeutics. *Mailing Add:* Merck Inst Therapeut Res PO Box 2000 Rahway NJ 07065

ZIMMERMAN, STANLEY WILLIAM, b Detroit, Mich, July 30, 07; m 32; c 4. ELECTRICAL ENGINEERING. *Educ:* Univ Mich, BS & MS, 30. *Prof Exp:* Asst, Res Dept, Detroit Edison Co, 29-30; test man, Gen Elec Co, NY & Mass, 30-32, test man, Pittsfield Works Lab, 32-34, res & develop engr, Lightning Arrester Dept, 35-45; in charge high voltage res lab, 45-58, prof, 45-76, EMER PROF ELEC ENG, SCH ELEC ENG, CORNELL UNIV, 76- *Concurrent Pos:* Mem staff, Eng Dept, Westinghouse Elec Corp, Pa, 52-, Ramo-Wooldridge, Inc, 59-60 & Lawrence Radiation Lab, Univ Calif, 61 & 66-67; mem, Int Conf Large Elec High Tension Systs; consult. *Mem:* Am Soc Eng Educ; sr mem Inst Elec & Electronics Engrs; Brit Inst Elec Engrs. *Res:* Circuit interruption and protection devices; lightning studies; single transient oscillography; wide band transformers; heavy machinery; electrical measurements and insulation; extra-high voltage apparatus design; ionization, pulsed radiation and partial discharge measurements; sulphur hexafluoride power transmission systems; dielectric stress analysis. *Mailing Add:* 102 Valley Rd Ithaca NY 14850

ZIMMERMAN, STEPHEN WILLIAM, b Ironton, Mo, Dec 27, 41. NEPHROLOGY, MEDICINE. *Educ:* Univ of Wis, BS, 63, MD, 66. *Prof Exp:* Chief nephrology Fitzsimmons Army Hosp, 70-72; fel, 69-70, fel nephropath, 72-74, asst prof, 74-80, ASSOC PROF MED, UNIV WIS, 80- *Concurrent Pos:* NIH grant, 77- *Mem:* Am Soc Nephrology; Int Soc Nephrology; Am Fedn Clin Res; Nat Kidney Found. *Res:* Effects of environmental toxins on the kidney; pathogenesis of renal disease. *Mailing Add:* Univ of Wis Hosp 600 Highland Ave Madison WI 53792

ZIMMERMAN, STEVEN B, b Chicago, Ill, June 5, 34; m 56. BIOCHEMISTRY. *Educ:* Univ Ill, BS, 56, MS, 57; Stanford Univ, PhD(biochem), 61. *Prof Exp:* Nat Found res fel, 61-62; RES CHEMIST, NAT INST ARTHRITIS, METAB & DIGESTIVE DIS, 64- *Mem:* Am Soc Biol Chem. *Res:* Nucleic acid synthesis and structure; mechanism of enzyme action. *Mailing Add:* Nat Inst Arth Metab & Kidney Dis 9000 Rockville Pike Bethesda MD 20205

ZIMMERMAN, STUART O, b Chicago, Ill, July 27, 35; m 59; c 1. MATHEMATICAL BIOLOGY. *Educ:* Univ Chicago, BA, 54, PhD(math biol), 64. *Prof Exp:* Res assoc, Univ Chicago, 63-65, from instr to asst prof math biol, 65-67; ASSOC PROF BIOMATH & ASSOC MEM, UNIV TEX DENT SCI INST HOUSTON, 67-, HEAD DEPT BIOMATH, UNIV TEX M D ANDERSON HOSP & TUMOR INST, 68-, PROF BIOMATH & BIOMATHEMATICIAN, 72-, HEAD, DIV BIOMED INFO RESOURCES, 81- *Concurrent Pos:* Consult, Ill State Dent Soc, 61- & Am Dent Asn, 66-; assoc mem, Univ Tex Grad Sch Biomed Sci Houston, 68-70, mem, 70-; actg dir common res comput facil, Univ Tex M D Anderson Hosp & Tumor Inst Houston, 68-73; chmn exec bd, Univ Tex Houston Educ & Res Comput Ctr, 73- *Mem:* AAAS; Am Statist Asn; Asn Comput Mach; Soc Math Biol. *Res:* Biomedical computing; mathematical modeling; image processing; computer karyotyping; information management systems; design and analysis of cancer and dental clinical trials. *Mailing Add:* M D Anderson Hosp 6723 Bertner Ave Houston TX 77030

ZIMMERMAN, THEODORE SAMUEL, b St Louis, Mo, May 3, 37; m 61; c 2. IMMUNOLOGY. *Educ:* Harvard Col, AB, 59; Harvard Med Sch, MD, 63. *Prof Exp:* Res fel hemostasis, Case Western Reserve Univ, 68-70; res fel, 70-72, assoc fel path, 72-74, ASSOC MEM MOLECULAR IMMUNOL, SCRIPPS CLIN & RES FOUND, 74-, CHIEF BLOOD COAGULATION LAB, GREEN HOSP, SCRIPPS CLIN, 72-; ASST PROF MED, UNIV CALIF, SAN DIEGO, 74- *Concurrent Pos:* Mem, Blood Dis & Resources Adv Comt, NIH, 74-77; mem-at-large exec comt, Coun Thrombosis, Am Heart Asn, 75-77; res career develop award, Nat Heart Lung & Blood Inst, 72-77, mem, Platelet Plasma-Protein Interaction, 72- *Mem:* Am Soc Clin Invest; Am Soc Hematol; Am Asn Immunol; Am Soc Exp Path; Am Col Physicians. *Res:* Immunochemistry of blood coagulation factors, especially Factor VIII; molecular basis of hemostatic mechanisms. *Mailing Add:* Scripps Clin & Res Found 10666 N Torrey Pines Rd La Jolla CA 92037

ZIMMERMAN, THOM J, b Lincoln, Ill, Oct 5, 42; m 70; c 1. OPTHALMOLOGY, OCULAR PHARMACOLOGY. *Educ:* Univ Ill, Champaign-Urbana, BS, 64, MD, 68; Univ Fla, PhD(pharmacol), 76; Nat Bd Med Examiners, dipl, 69; Am Bd Ophthal, dipl, 78. *Prof Exp:* Intern, Presbyterian St Lukes Hosp, Chicago, 68-69; resident, Dept Opthal, Col Med, Univ Fla, 71-74; glaucoma fel, Dept Ophthal, Washington Univ, St Louis, 76-77; actg chmn, Dept Ophthal, 77, assoc prof, 77-79, PROF OPTHAL, PHARMACOL & EXP THERAPEUTS & CHMN DEPT OPHTHAL, OSCHNER CLIN, LA STATE UNIV MED CTR, 79- *Concurrent Pos:* Heed Ophthalmic Found fel, 76-77; ophthalmic consult, glaucoma, US Pub Heath Hosp, New Orleans, 77-82; Robert E McCormick scholar, Res Prevent Blindness, Inc, 78; consult, Eye Adv Coun, Food & Drug Admin, 79; res career develop award, Nat Eye Inst, 78-; Flight for sight dept award, Ochner Clin, 79-80. *Mem:* Fel Am Col Clin Pharmacol; AMA; Asn Res Vision & Ophthal; Am Soc Clin Pharmacology; Am Soc Contemporary Ophthal. *Res:* Oscular pharamcology; pharmacology of the glaucoma drugs; clincial care of glaucoma medical and surgical. *Mailing Add:* Ochsner Clin 1514 Jefferson Hwy New Orleans LA 70121

ZIMMERMAN, THOMAS PAUL, b Plainfield, NJ, Sept 3, 42; m 66; c 2. BIOCHEMICAL PHARMACOLOGY. *Educ:* Providence Col, BS, 64; Brown Univ, PhD(biochem), 69. *Prof Exp:* Nat Inst Neurol Dis & Stroke res fel biol & med sci, Brown Univ, 69-71; res biochemist, 71-80, SR RES, WELLCOME RES LABS, BURROUGHS WELLCOME & CO, USA, INC, 80- *Mem:* Am Soc Pharmacol & Exp Therapeut. *Res:* Nucleic acids-purification, chemical and physical properties; purine metabolism and the mode of action of purine antimetabolites; cyclic nucleotide metabolism; biological methylation reactions; immunosuppression. *Mailing Add:* Dept Exp Ther Wellcome Res Labs 3030 Cornwallis Rd Research Triangle Park NC 27709

ZIMMERMAN, TOMMY LYNN, b Lima, Ohio, July 23, 43; m 67; c 2. SOIL & WATER CONSERVATION. *Educ:* Ohio State Univ, BS, 66; Pa State Univ, MS, 69, PhD(agron), 73. *Prof Exp:* From instr to asst prof agron, Delaware Valley Col, 71-75; consult soil scientist, 73-75; from asst prof to ASSOC PROF & TECH COORDR SOIL & WATER CONSERV & MGT TECHNOL, AGR TECH INST, OHIO STATE UNIV, 75- *Mem:* Am Soc Agron; Soil Sci Soc Am; Soil Conserv Soc Am; Coun Agr Sci Technol. *Mailing Add:* Agr Tech Inst Ohio State Univ Wooster OH 44691

ZIMMERMAN, WALTER BRUCE, b Evergreen Park, Ill, Nov 27, 33; m 55; c 3. SOLID STATE PHYSICS. *Educ:* Andrews Univ, BA, 55; Mich State Univ, MS, 57, PhD(physics), 60. *Prof Exp:* Asst physics, Mich State Univ, 58-60; sr physicist solar energy conversion, Gen Dynamics Astronaut, 60-62; from asst prof to assoc prof physics, Andrews Univ, 62-69; ASSOC PROF PHYSICS, IND UNIV, SOUTH BEND, 69-, CHMN DEPT PHYSICS, 74- *Mem:* Am Phys Soc; Am Asn Physics Teachers; Am Vacuum Soc. *Res:* Changes that occur in infrared absorption spectrum and lattice constant of lithium hydride as its isotopic composition is varied; magnetic effect in biological processes; agglutination of red blood cells in a magnetic field; solar energy conversion by cadmium sulfide films. *Mailing Add:* Dept of Physics Ind Univ 1825 Northside Blvd South Bend IN 46615

ZIMMERMAN, WILLIAM FREDERICK, b Chicago, Ill, July 7, 38; m 64; c 2. CELL BIOLOGY. *Educ:* Princeton Univ, BA, 60, PhD(biol), 66. *Prof Exp:* Instr biol, Princeton Univ, 64-66; asst prof, 66-72, ASSOC PROF BIOL, AMHERST COL, 72- *Concurrent Pos:* NSF res grants, 66-70; NIH spec fel, 69-70; Nat Eye Inst res grants, 70-83; vis res fel, Univ Nijmegen, 73-74 & Cambridge Univ, 79-80. *Mem:* AAAS; Asn for Res Vision & Ophthalmol. *Res:* Entrainment of circadian rhythms in insects; action spectra, carotenoid metabolism; cellular biochemistry of visual cycles, photoreceptor cell renewal and retinal pigment epithelium. *Mailing Add:* Dept of Biol Amherst Col Amherst MA 01002

ZIMMERMANN, BERNARD, b St Paul, Minn, June 26, 21; m 49; c 2. SURGERY. *Educ:* Harvard Univ, MD, 45; Univ Minn, PhD, 53; Am Bd Surg, dipl. *Prof Exp:* House officer, Boston City Hosp, Mass, 45-46; head surg res facil, Naval Med Res Inst, Nat Naval Med Ctr, Bethesda, Md, 46-48; fel surg, Med Sch, Univ Minn, 48-53, from instr to prof surg, 53-60; head dept, 60-73, PROF SURG, MED CTR, WVA UNIV, 60- *Concurrent Pos:* Am Cancer Soc scholar cancer res, 53-56; cancer coord, Sch Med, Univ Minn, 56-60; mem, USPHS Cancer Chemother Study Sect, 59-, interim comt, Orgn Cancer Coords, 57-60, bd dirs, St Paul Inst & Sci Mus, Minn, 56-60, adv comt inst res grants, Am Cancer Soc, 62-66 & prog proj rev comt, Inst Metab & Arthritis, 64-68. *Mem:* Endocrine Soc; Soc Exp Biol & Med; Soc Univ Surg; Am Soc Exp Path; Halsted Soc (secy-treas, 63-66, pres). *Res:* Surgical physiology; experimental diabetes; electrolyte balance in surgery; endocrine aspects of malignancy; adrenal function in surgery; experimental oncology. *Mailing Add:* Dept of Surg WVa Univ Med Ctr Morgantown WV 26506

ZIMMERMANN, CHARLES EDWARD, b Juneau, Wis, Nov 15, 30; m 56; c 4. PLANT PHYSIOLOGY. *Educ:* Univ Wis, BS, 53; Ore State Univ, MS, 62. *Prof Exp:* Technician, Wash State Univ, 56-59; res agronomist, USDA, Ore, 59-62, plant physiologist, Agr Res Serv, Ore State Univ, 62-70, res plant physiologist, Sci & Educ Admin-Agr Res, 70-80; EXEC VPRES, SUNNY HOPS INC, 80- *Mem:* Am Soc Plant Physiol; Am Soc Agron; Crop Sci Soc Am; Am Soc Brewing Chemists; Master Brewers Asn Am. *Res:* Production and quality of hops; relate gibberellins to morphogenic and physiologic changes in hops. *Mailing Add:* Sunny Hops Inc Box 838 Sunnyside WA 98944

ZIMMERMANN, EUGENE ROBERT CHARLES, b New York, NY, Mar 12, 24; m 47; c 3. ORAL PATHOLOGY, MICROBIOLOGY. *Educ:* Univ Md, DDS, 48; Am Univ, BS, 54; Univ Tex, MA, 62. *Prof Exp:* Intern dent, US Marine Hosp, Seattle, Wash, 48-49, clinician, 49-50; dent resident epidemiol & biomet, NIH, 50-54; instr oral diag, oral path & pub health, 54-55, asst prof histol, path & pub health, 55-57, assoc prof path & pub health, 57-59, PROF ORAL PATH & CHMN DEPT, BAYLOR COL DENT, 59- *Concurrent Pos:* Consult, Vet Admin Hosps, Dallas & Temple, Tex, US Army Hosps, Ft Bliss & Ft Hood, Tex & Ft Sill, Okla & USPHS Hosp, Ft Worth, Tex. *Mem:* Am Dent Asn; Am Pub Health Asn; Am Inst Oral Biol; Am Acad Oral Path; Royal Soc Health. *Res:* Fluoridation; ultrastructure of oral lesions; effect of geography and race upon gingival disease in children; role of adenoviruses in diseases of the mouth; adaptation of gingival epithelium to tissue culture technique; effects of aging and smoking habits on oral tissues. *Mailing Add:* 9830 Ash Creek Dr Dallas TX 75228

ZIMMERMANN, F(RANCIS) J(OHN), b Jersey City, NJ, Apr 21, 24; m 50; c 2. MECHANICAL ENGINEERING. *Educ:* Yale Univ, BE, 48; Mass Inst Technol, SM, 50, ME, 51, ScD(mech eng), 53. *Prof Exp:* Staff engr, Arthur D Little, Inc, 52-55; from asst prof to assoc prof mech eng, Yale Univ, 55-62; dir res & contract progs, 64-68, PROF MECH ENG, LAFAYETTE COL, 62-, HEAD DEPT, 78- *Concurrent Pos:* Asst prog dir eng sci prog, NSF, 61-62; consult, Arthur D Little, Inc, 55-61 & Air Prod & Chem, Inc, 63- *Mem:* AAAS; Am Soc Mech Engrs; Am Soc Eng Educ; Am Int Solar Energy Soc; Cryogenic Soc Am. *Res:* Thermodynamics; heat transfer; cryogenic engineering. *Mailing Add:* Dept Mech Eng Lafayette Col Easton PA 18042

ZIMMERMANN, H(ENRY) J(OSEPH), b St Louis, Mo, May 11, 16; m 45; c 4. ELECTRICAL ENGINEERING, ELECTRONICS. *Educ:* Wash Univ, BS, 38; Mass Inst Technol, SM, 42. *Prof Exp:* Instr, Wash Univ, 38-40; from instr to assoc prof, 40-52, assoc dir res lab electronics, 52-61, dir, 61-76, PROF ELEC ENG, MASS INST TECHNOL, 52- *Mem:* Fel Inst Elec & Electronics Engrs. *Res:* Electronic circuits; signal processing and perception. *Mailing Add:* 14 Russet Lane Lynnfield MA 01940

ZIMMERMANN, MARK EDWARD, b Weimar, Tex, Sept 29, 52; m 78. PHYSICS, APPLIED MATHEMATICS. *Educ:* Rice Univ, BA, 74; Calif Inst Technol, MS, 76, PhD(physics), 80. *Prof Exp:* Physicist, Inst Defense Analyses, 79-81; PHYSICIST, US GOVT, 81- *Mem:* Am Phys Soc. *Res:* Studies of developments in the physical sciences and emerging technologies. *Mailing Add:* 219 Dale Dr Silver Spring MD 20910

ZIMMERMANN, MARTIN HULDRYCH, b Bulach, Switz, Nov 27, 26; m 53; c 2. PLANT ANATOMY, PLANT PHYSIOLOGY. *Educ:* Swiss Fed Inst Technol, dipl, 51, DSc(biol), 53. *Hon Degrees:* MA, Harvard Univ, 70. *Prof Exp:* Asst plant physiol, Swiss Fed Inst Technol, 51-54; lectr forest physiol & forest physiologist, Cabot Found, 54-70, actg dir, Harvard Forest, 67-68, 69-70, CHARLES BULLARD PROF FORESTRY, HARVARD UNIV & DIR HARVARD FOREST, 70- *Concurrent Pos:* Mem, Orgn Trop Studies; Guggenheim fel, Swiss Fed Inst Technol, 68-69. *Mem:* AAAS; Am Soc Plant Physiol; Am Acad Arts & Sci; Int Asn Wood Anat; Int Acad Wood Sci. *Res:* Structure and physiology of trees and arborescent monocotyledons; translocation of nutrients in plants. *Mailing Add:* Harvard Forest Petersham MA 01366

ZIMMERMANN, R ERIK, b Newark, NJ, Oct 29, 41; m 71; c 4. ASTROPHYSICS. *Educ:* Pomona Col, BA, 63; Univ Calif, Los Angeles, MA, 66, PhD(astron), 70. *Prof Exp:* Asst prof astron, Mich State Univ, 68-71; assoc prof astron, Newark State Col, 71-74; DIR ROBERT J NOVINS PLANETARIUM, OCEAN COUNTY COL, 74- *Mem:* Int Planetarium Soc; Royal Astron Soc Can. *Res:* Stellar structure and evolution. *Mailing Add:* Robert J Novins Planetarium Ocean County Col CN 2001 Toms River NJ 08753

ZIMMERMANN, ROBERT ALAN, b Philadelphia, Pa, July 17, 37. PROTEIN SYNTHESIS, RNA STRUCTURE. *Educ:* Amherst Col, BA, 59; Mass Inst Technol, PhD(biophysics), 64. *Prof Exp:* Vis scientist biochem, Acad Sci USSR, 65-66; res fel microbiol, Med Sch, Harvard Univ, 66-69; res assoc molecular biol, Univ Geneva, 70-73; assoc prof microbiol & biochem, 73-77, PROF BIOCHEM, UNIV MASS, AMHERST, 77-, HEAD, BIOCHEM DEPT, 79- *Concurrent Pos:* Helen Hay Whitney Found fel, 68; sr fel, Europ Molecular Biol Orgn, 71; adv, WHO, 75-78; NIH res career develop award, 75. *Mem:* Am Chem Soc; Am Soc Biol Chemists; AAAS; Am Soc Microbiol; Sigma Xi. *Res:* Structure, function and biosynthesis of ribosomes in bacteria and yeast; RNA-protein interaction; primary and secondary structure of ribosomal RNA; photochemical labeling; properties of mutationally-altered ribosomes and their components. *Mailing Add:* Dept Biochem Univ Mass Amherst MA 01003

ZIMMERMANN, WILLIAM, JR, b Philadelphia, Pa, Oct 28, 30; m 62; c 3. PHYSICS. *Educ:* Amherst Col, AB, 52; Calif Inst Technol, PhD(physics), 58. *Prof Exp:* Fulbright fel, Neth, 58-59; lectr, 59-61, asst prof, 61-65, assoc prof, 65-70, PROF PHYSICS, UNIV MINN, MINNEAPOLIS, 70- *Concurrent Pos:* NSF sr fel, Finland, 67-68. *Mem:* Am Phys Soc; Am Asn Physics Teachers. *Res:* Low temperature physics; superfluid helium; liquid helium-3/helium-4 mixtures. *Mailing Add:* Sch of Physics & Astron Univ of Minn 116 Church St SE Minneapolis MN 55455

ZIMMERMANN, WILLIAM JOHN, b Mankato, Minn, May 7, 24; m 47; c 3. PARASITOLOGY. *Educ:* Mankato State Col, BS, 47; Iowa State Univ, MS, 52, PhD(parasitol), 55. *Prof Exp:* Asst zool, Iowa State Univ, 51-53, res assoc, Vet Med Res Inst, 54-55, from asst prof to assoc prof, 55-68, PROF PARASITOL PATH, VET MED RES INST, IOWA STATE UNIV, 68- *Mem:* Am Soc Parasitol; Conf Res Workers Animal Dis; Wildlife Dis Asn. *Res:* Epidemiology and control of trichinosis and toxoplasmosis; internal parasites of domestic animals. *Mailing Add:* Vet Med Res Inst Iowa State Univ Ames IA 50011

ZIMMON, DAVID SAMUEL, b Brooklyn, NY, Dec 2, 33; m 62; c 3. GASTROENTEROLOGY, LIVER DISEASE. *Educ:* Harvard Univ, MD, 58; Bd Internal Med, dipl, 66; Am Bd Internal Med, dipl, 68. *Prof Exp:* From intern to sr asst resident med, 2nd Med Div, Bellevue Hosp & Mem Ctr Cancer, 58-61; fel gastroenterol, 2nd Med Div, Bellevue Hosp, 61-62; res asst liver dis, Royal Free Hosp, London, 62-64; instr med, Med Col, 65, asst prof, 66-72, assoc prof, 72-79, PROF CLIN MED, SCH MED, NEW YORK UNIV, 79- *Concurrent Pos:* Instr med, Med Col, New York Univ, 65; chief, Gastroenterol Sect, New York Vet Admin Med Ctr, 65; asst vis physician, Bellevue Hosp, 69. *Mem:* Med Res Soc; Am Fedn Clin Res; Am Asn Study Liver Dis; Am Gastroenterol Asn; Am Soc Gastrointestinal Endoscopy. *Res:* Liver disease; hypertension; biliary and pancreatic disease; endoscopy; endoscopic surgery. *Mailing Add:* 36 7th Ave Suite 516 New York NY 10011

ZIMMT, WERNER SIEGFRIED, b Berlin, Ger, Sept 21, 21; nat US; m 47; c 3. POLYMER CHEMISTRY, POLLUTION CHEMISTRY. *Educ:* Univ Chicago, PhB & BS, 47, MS, 49, PhD(org chem), 51; Univ Penn, MS, 81. *Prof Exp:* Res chemist, E I du Pont de Nemours & Co, Inc, 51-60, chem assoc, Marshall Lab, 60-62, res assoc, 62-69, RES FEL, MARSHALL LAB, E I DU PONT DE NEMOURS & CO, INC, 69- *Honors & Awards:* George B Heckel Award, Nat Paint & Coatings Asn, 73. *Mem:* Am Chem Soc. *Res:* Free radical chemistry; synthesis and mechanism; paint technology; role of paint solvents in air pollution. *Mailing Add:* 418 Haverford Rd Wynnewood PA 19096

ZIMNY, MARILYN LUCILE, b Chicago, Ill, Dec 12, 27. ANATOMY. *Educ:* Univ Ill, BA, 48; Loyola Univ, Ill, MS, 51, PhD(anat), 54. *Prof Exp:* Asst anat, Med Sch, Loyola Univ, Ill, 51-53; from asst prof to assoc prof, 54-64, actg head dept, 75-76, PROF ANAT, LA STATE UNIV MED CTR, NEW ORLEANS, 64-, HEAD DEPT, 76- *Concurrent Pos:* Vis prof, Sch Med, Univ Costa Rica, 61 & 62; mem, Inst Arctic Biol, Univ Alaska, 66. *Mem:* Am Asn Anat; Am Physiol Soc; Electron Micros Soc Am; Orthop Res Soc; AAAS. *Res:* Orthopedic research. *Mailing Add:* Dept of Anat La State Univ Med Ctr New Orleans LA 70112

ZIMRING, LOIS JACOBS, b Chicago, Ill, Nov 19, 23; div; c 1. CHEMICAL PHYSICS. *Educ:* Univ Chicago, BS, 45, MS, 49, PhD(phys chem), 64. *Prof Exp:* Instr chem, Morgan Park Jr Col, 49-51; lectr phys sci, Univ Chicago, 59-61, instr, 61-64; asst prof chem, Univ Minn, 64-66; from asst prof to assoc prof natural sci, 66-72, PROF NATURAL SCI, MICH STATE UNIV, 72- *Mem:* Am Chem Soc. *Res:* Ultraviolet spectra of conjugated systems; crystal spectra of transition metal halides; solid state mixed alum systems; chirality of prebiotic molecules; changing cosmological views. *Mailing Add:* Dept Natural Sci Univ Col Mich State Univ East Lansing MI 48823

ZINDER, NORTON DAVID, b New York, NY, Nov 7, 28; m 49; c 2. MOLECULAR GENETICS. *Educ:* Columbia Univ, BA, 47; Univ Wis, MS, 49, PhD(med microbiol), 52. *Prof Exp:* Asst, 52-58, from assoc prof to prof, 58-76, JOHN D ROCKEFELLER, JR PROF MICROBIAL GENETICS, ROCKEFELLER UNIV, 76- *Honors & Awards:* Eli Lilly Award Microbiol, 62; US Steel Award Molecular Biol, 66; Sci Freedom & Responsibility Award, AAAS, 82. *Mem:* Nat Acad Sci; AAAS; Genetics Soc Am; Am Soc Microbiol; Am Soc Biol Chem. *Res:* Virology; protein biosynthesis; genetics. *Mailing Add:* Rockefeller Univ New York NY 10021

ZINDER, STEPHEN HENRY, b Madison, Wis, Oct 22, 50; m 76; c 1. MICROBIAL ECOLOGY, BIOGEOCHEMISTRY. *Educ:* Kenyon Col, BA, 72; Colo State Univ, MS, 74; Univ Wis, PhD(bacteriol), 77. *Prof Exp:* Trainee microbiol, Colo State Univ, 72-74; res asst bacteriol, Univ Wis, 74-77; scholar pub health, Univ Calif, Los Angeles, 77-79; ASST PROF MICROBIOL, CORNELL UNIV, 80- *Mem:* Am Soc Microbiol; AAAS; Sigma Xi. *Res:* Physiology and ecology of methanogenic and other anaerobic bacteria; microbial biogeochemistry of elements especially sulfur and selenium. *Mailing Add:* Dept Microbiol 410 Stocking Hall Cornell Univ Ithaca NY 14853

ZINDLER, RICHARD EUGENE, b Benton Harbor, Mich, Mar 5, 27; m 58; c 2. MATHEMATICS, OPERATIONS RESEARCH. *Educ:* Mich State Univ, BS & MS, 49, PhD(math), 56. *Prof Exp:* Asst math, Mich State Univ, 49-52; asst prof, 52-57, assoc prof, 57-63, PROF ENG RES, PA STATE UNIV, 63- *Mem:* AAAS; Am Math Soc; Acoust Soc Am; Opers Res Soc Am; Asn Comput Mach. *Res:* Weapon system analysis and synthesis; primate behavior. *Mailing Add:* Dept of Indust & Mgt Systs Eng Pa State Univ State College PA 16802

ZINGARO, JOSEPH S, b Mt Morris, NY, Mar 5, 28; m 52; c 4. SCIENCE EDUCATION, CHEMISTRY. *Educ:* State Univ NY Col Geneseo, BS, 51; Syracuse Univ, MS, 55 & 62, PhD, 66. *Prof Exp:* Teacher & chmn dept sci, Vernon-Verona-Sherrill Cent Sch, 51-58; PROF CHEM & CHMN DEPT, STATE UNIV NY COL BUFFALO, 58- *Concurrent Pos:* NSF inst grants, 66-81. *Mem:* AAAS; Am Chem Soc. *Res:* Science teaching, especially chemistry teaching; electrical conductance and thermodynamic functions as they relate to solutions. *Mailing Add:* Dept of Chem State Univ of NY Col Buffalo NY 14222

ZINGARO, RALPH ANTHONY, b Brooklyn, NY, Oct 27, 25; m 50; c 2. INORGANIC CHEMISTRY. *Educ:* City Col New York, BS, 46; Univ Kans, MS, 49, PhD, 50. *Prof Exp:* Sr res chemist, Eastman Kodak Co, 50-52; asst prof, Univ Ark, 52-53; res chemist, Am Cyanamid Co, 53-54; from asst prof to assoc prof, 54-64, PROF CHEM, TEX A&M UNIV, 64- *Concurrent Pos:* NIH spec fel, 68-69; Fulbright lectr, Univ Buenos Aires, 72. *Mem:* Am Chem Soc; NY Acad Sci. *Res:* Chemistry and biochemistry of selenium and arsenic. *Mailing Add:* Dept of Chem Tex A&M Univ College Station TX 77843

ZINGESER, MAURICE ROY, b Birmingham, Ala, Mar 17, 21; m 47; c 3. ANATOMY, ORTHODONTICS. *Educ:* New York Univ, AB, 42; Columbia Univ, DDS, 46; Tufts Univ, MS, 50; Am Bd Orthod, dipl, 63. *Prof Exp:* Intern surg, New York Polyclin Hosp, 46-48; clin assoc orthod, Tufts Univ, 48-50; dent surgeon, USPHS, 50-52; res assoc growth & develop, Dent Sch, Univ Ore, 54-55; vis scientist anthrop, Ore Regional Primate Res Ctr, 63-80; RES ASSOC, DEPT ANAT, DENT SCH, ORE HEALTH SCI UNIV, 80- *Concurrent Pos:* Guest lectr, Tufts, Boston & Georgetown Univs, 60-69; contrib, Int Cong Anthrop & Ethnol Sci, 68; chmn craniofacial biol sect, Int Cong Primatol, 72; guest lectr, Hebrew Univ & Univ London, 72. *Mem:* AAAS; Am Dent Asn; Am Asn Orthod; Int Asn Dent Res; Am Asn Phys Anthrop. *Res:* Primate odontology, craniofacial embryology and craniology. *Mailing Add:* Ore Health Sci Univ 611 Campus Dr Portland OR 97201

ZINGESSER, LAWRENCE H, b Portchester, NY, Dec 27, 30; m; div; c 3. RADIOLOGY. *Educ:* Syracuse Univ, AB, 51; Chicago Med Sch, MD, 55. *Prof Exp:* From intern med to resident, Grad Hosp, Univ Pa, 55-57; resident radiol, Grace-New Haven Hosp, Yale Univ, 59-62; from asst prof to prof radiol, Albert Einstein Col Med, 73-77; CHIEF NEURORADIOL & ATTEND PHYSICIAN, ST VINCENT'S HOSP, NEW YORK, 77- *Concurrent Pos:* NIH spec fel neuroradiol, Albert Einstein Col Med, 62-64, Nat Inst Neurol Dis & Stroke grant cerebral blood flow, 66-69, clin prof radiol, 77-79; asst attend, Bronx Munic Hosp Ctr, NY, 63-65; clin prof radiol, NY Med Col, 80- *Mem:* Am Soc Neuroradiol; Radiol Soc NAm; Am Col Radiol; French Soc Neuroradiol. *Res:* Regional cerebral blood flow in neurologic disease states; neuroradiology. *Mailing Add:* Dept of Radiol 153 W 11th St New York NY 10011

ZINGG, WALTER, b Kloten, Switz, Mar 29, 24; Can citizen; m 49; c 4. SURGERY, BIOENGINEERING. *Educ:* Univ Zurich, MD, 50; Univ Man, MSc, 52; FRCS(C), 58. *Prof Exp:* Lectr physiol, Univ Man, 56-57, lectr surg, 57-61, asst prof, 61-64; from asst prof to assoc prof, 64-78, mem inst biomed eng, 72-75, PROF SURG & HON PROF DENT, UNIV TORONTO, 78-, PROF & ASSOC DIR INST BIOMED ENG, 75- *Concurrent Pos:* Assoc scientist, Hosp Sick Children, 64-68, sr scientist, 68-80, head, Div Surg Res, 80-; consult, Ont Crippled Children's Ctr, Toronto, 65- & Ont Vet Col, Univ Guelph, 70- *Mem:* Am Soc Artificial Internal Organs; Can Physiol Soc; Can Biomet Soc (pres, 78-80); fel Am Col Surg; fel Am Col Cardiol. *Res:* Surgical research; biomaterials; artificial pancreas. *Mailing Add:* Hosp for Sick Children 555 University Ave Toronto ON M5G 1X8 Can

ZINGMARK, RICHARD G, b San Francisco, Calif, July 4, 41; m 62; c 6. ALGOLOGY. *Educ:* Humboldt State Col, BA, 64, MA, 65; Univ Calif, Santa Barbara, PhD(biol), 69. *Prof Exp:* NSF fel, Marine Lab, Duke Univ, 69-70; ASSOC PROF BIOL & MARINE SCI, UNIV SC, 76-, RES ASSOC MARINE SCI, BELLE W BARUCH COASTAL RES INST, 70- *Concurrent Pos:* Consult, James H Carr & Assoc, 76- *Mem:* Phycol Soc Am; Int Phycol Soc; Brit Phycol Soc; Am Soc Limnol & Oceanog; Western Soc Naturalists. *Res:* Sexual reproduction of dinoflagellates; effects of toxic materials on the growth and reproduction of phytoplankton; phytoplankton ultrastructure; phytoplankton life histories. *Mailing Add:* Dept of Biol Univ of SC Columbia SC 29208

ZINGULA, RICHARD PAUL, b Cedar Rapids, Iowa, May 31, 29; m 53; c 2. PALEONTOLOGY. *Educ:* Iowa State Univ, BS, 51; La State Univ, MS, 53, PhD(geol), 58. *Prof Exp:* Assoc geologist, Humble Oil & Refining Co, 54-60, supvry paleontologist, 60-69, sr prof geologist, 69-72; res paleontologist, Imp Oil Ltd, 72-74; sr prof geologist, Exxon Co USA, 74-76, SR EXPLOR GEOLOGIST, EXXON CO USA, 76- *Mem:* Geol Soc Am; Paleont Soc Am; Soc Econ Paleontologists & Mineralogists; Am Asn Petrol Geologists. *Res:* Micropaleontology; stratigraphy. *Mailing Add:* Exxon Co USA PO Box 4279 Houston TX 77001

ZINK, FRANK W, b Pullman, Wash, June 17, 23; m 46; c 2. PLANT BREEDING. *Educ:* Univ Calif, Davis, BS, 47, MS, 48. *Prof Exp:* Asst specialist, 48-53, assoc specialist, 54-60, specialist, 61-69, RES SPECIALIST VEG CROPS, CALIF AGR EXP STA, UNIV CALIF, DAVIS, 69-, LECTR, COL AGR, 74- *Concurrent Pos:* Shell Develop grant, 60-61; Veg Growers Asn grant, 60-67; Melon Growers Asn grant, 72-75. *Mem:* Am Soc Hort Sci; Am Phytopath Soc; Am Soc Agron; Int Soc Hort Sci. *Res:* Lettuce breeding, disease resistance; melon breeding for mechanization and disease resistance. *Mailing Add:* Dept Veg Crops Univ Calif Davis CA 95616

ZINK, GILBERT LEROY, b Wheeling, WVa, Aug 14, 42; m 63; c 4. IMMUNOGENETICS. *Educ:* Ohio State Univ, BSc, 65, MSc, 67, PhD(immunogenetics), 71. *Prof Exp:* Res assoc, Ohio State Univ, 67-71, res assoc immunogenetics lab, Dept Dairy Sci, 72; res assoc lectr dept biol sci, 72-75, asst prof, 75-80, ASSOC PROF BIOL SCI, PHILADELPHIA COL PHARM & SCI, 80- *Concurrent Pos:* Co-investr, NIH res grant, 77-80. *Mem:* AAAS; Int Soc Animal Blood Group Res. *Res:* Determination of the significance of the weak histocompatability antigens in mice with regard to tumor immunity and cell differentiation; also a project to develop an invitro technique; predict weak sensitizers in medications and cosmetics. *Mailing Add:* Dept of Biol Sci 43rd St & Kingsessing Mall Philadelphia PA 19104

ZINK, JEFFREY IRVE, b Milwaukee, Wis, Jan 8, 45; m 68. INORGANIC CHEMISTRY, PHOTOCHEMISTRY. *Educ:* Univ of Wis, BS, 66; Univ Ill, PhD(chem), 70. *Prof Exp:* Teaching asst chem, Univ Ill, 66-67, res asst chem, 67-68; asst prof, 70-76, assoc prof, 76-82, PROF CHEM, UNIV CALIF, LOS ANGELES, 82- *Concurrent Pos:* Camille & Henry Dreyfus teacher/scholar, 74-79. *Honors & Awards:* Alexander von Humboldt Award, 78. *Mem:* Am Chem Soc; Interam Photochem Soc; Nat Audubon Soc. *Res:* Photochemistry, triboluminescence; solar energy conversion and storage; structure and bonding transition metal compounds. *Mailing Add:* Dept of Chem Univ of Calif Los Angeles CA 90025

ZINK, ROBERT EDWIN, b Minneapolis, Minn, Nov 16, 28; m 50; c 3. MATHEMATICS. *Educ:* Univ Minn, BA, 49, MA, 51, PhD(math), 53. *Prof Exp:* Asst math, Univ Minn, 49-53; instr, Purdue Univ, 53-54; lectr, George Washington Univ, 55-56; from asst prof to assoc prof math, 56-66, asst head dept, 65-69, asst dean grad sch, 69-72, PROF MATH, PURDUE UNIV, LAFAYETTE, 66- *Concurrent Pos:* Vis prof, Wabash Col, 61-62 & dept math, Univ Calif, Irvine, 68-69. *Mem:* Am Math Soc; Math Asn Am. *Res:* Theory of measure and integration; theory of functions of a real variable. *Mailing Add:* Div of Math Sci Purdue Univ Lafayette IN 47907

ZINK, SANDRA, b Dodge City, Kans, Sept 17, 39; c 2. PHYSICS, COMPUTER SCIENCE. *Educ:* Univ NMex, BS, 66, MS, 68, PhD(physics), 73. *Prof Exp:* Assoc Western Univs fel molecular physics, Los Alamos Sci Lab, 71-73, staff mem solar physics, 73-75; guest scientist, Max-Planck Inst Extraterrestrial Physics, 75-76; STAFF MEM MED PHYSICS & COMPUT TREATMENT PLANNING, LOS ALAMOS SCI LAB, 77- *Mem:* Am Asn Physicists in Med. *Res:* Biophysics and medical physics with computer applications. *Mailing Add:* MS 809 PO Box 1663 Los Alamos NM 87545

ZINKE, OTTO HENRY, b Webster Groves, Mo, Aug 13, 26; m 55; c 3. PHYSICS. *Educ:* Wash Univ, AB, 50, AM, 53, PhD, 56. *Prof Exp:* Salesman, Nuclear Consults Corp, 52-53; mem res staff, Linde Co Union Carbide Corp, 56-57; asst prof physics, Univ Mo, 57-59; from asst prof to assoc prof physics, Univ Ark, Fayetteville, 59-69, prof, 69-80. *Res:* Transient phenomena in plasmas and metals. *Mailing Add:* 817 N Jackson Fayetteville AR 72701

ZINKE, PAUL JOSEPH, b Los Angeles, Calif, Nov 10, 20; m 47; c 2. FORESTRY. SOIL SCIENCE. *Educ:* Univ Calif, BS, 42, MS, 52, PhD(soil sci), 56. *Prof Exp:* Forester, Tongass Nat Forest, US Forest Serv, 42-43, res forester, Calif Forest & Range Exp Sta, 46-56; ASSOC PROF FORESTRY & SOIL SCI, UNIV CALIF, BERKELEY, 57- *Concurrent Pos:* In charge, Calif Soil Veg Surv, USDA-US Forest Serv, 59-61; adv, Appl Sci Res Corp Thailand, 67-; adv, Radar Nat Resource Inventory Amazon Basin, Brazil, 71-; mem comt study defoliation effects in SEAsia, Nat Acad Sci, 71- *Mem:* AAAS; Soc Am Foresters; Soil Sci Soc Am; Soil Conserv Soc Am; Soc Range Mgt. *Res:* Forest influences and environment; forest soils; soil morphology; soil-vegetation relationships; plant ecology. *Mailing Add:* Sch of Forestry & Conserv 145 Mulford Hall Univ of Calif Berkeley CA 94720

ZINKEL, DUANE FORST, b Manitowoc, Wis, Aug 11, 34; m 61; c 5. ORGANIC CHEMISTRY. *Educ:* Univ Wis, BS, 56, PhD(biochem), 61. *Prof Exp:* RES CHEMIST, FOREST PROD LAB, US FOREST SERV, 61- *Mem:* Am Chem Soc; Sigma Xi. *Res:* Softwood extractives and derived products; structure determination; analytical development and analysis; biosynthesis. *Mailing Add:* Forest Prod Lab US Forest Serv PO Box 5130 Madison WI 53705

ZINKHAM, ROBERT EDWARD, b Rochester, Pa, Jan 19, 23; m 56; c 3. MECHANICAL METALLURGY. *Educ:* Geneva Col, BS, 49; Carnegie-Mellon Univ, BSME, 49; Univ Pittsburgh, MS, 56. *Prof Exp:* Develop engr, Jones & Laughlin Steel Corp, 49-57; supvr mech testing, Allegheny Ludlum Steel Corp, 57-60; res engr drilling methods, Gulf Res & Develop Co, 60-63; res scientist mech metall, 63-68, DIR MECH METALL, REYNOLDS METALS CO, 68- *Concurrent Pos:* Chmn subcomt fracture toughness, Metal Prop Coun, Inc, 72- *Mem:* Am Soc Mech Engrs; fel Am Soc Metals; Am Soc Testing & Mat. *Res:* Mechanical metallurgy, specializing in fracture mechanics, fatigue, mechanical testing and residual stresses involving aluminum. *Mailing Add:* 9204 Westmoor Dr Richmond VA 23229

ZINKHAM, WILLIAM HOWARD, b Uniontown, Md, May 23, 24; m 52; c 2. PEDIATRICS. *Educ:* Johns Hopkins Univ, AB, 44, MD, 47; Am Bd Pediat, cert pediat, 56, cert hemat-oncol, 74. *Prof Exp:* From instr to prof, 56-77, DISTINGUISHED SERV PROF PEDIAT, SCH MED, JOHNS HOPKINS UNIV, 77- *Mem:* Am Pediat Soc; Soc Clin Invest; Soc Pediat Res. *Res:* Hematology; metabolism of normal and abnormal erythrocytes. *Mailing Add:* Dept of Pediat Johns Hopkins Univ Sch of Med Baltimore MD 21218

ZINKL, JOSEPH GRANDJEAN, b Albuquerque, NMex, Aug 30, 39; m 69; c 2. CYTOLOGY, TOXICOLOGY. *Educ:* Univ Calif, Davis, BS, 64, DVM, 66, PhD(comparative path), 71. *Prof Exp:* Sr fel, Nat Inst Environ Health, 71-74; Pathologist, US Fish & Wildlife Serv, 74-76; ASSOC PROF CLIN PATH, SCH VET MED, UNIV CALIF, DAVIS, 76- *Mem:* Am Col Vet Pathologists; Wildlife Dis Asn; Am Soc Vet Clin Path. *Res:* Brain cholinesterase activity in forest birds after aerial application of insecticides; phagocytic, bacteriocidal and chemotactic ability of neutrophils of domestic animals; clinical cytology of diseases of domestic animals. *Mailing Add:* Dept Clin Path Sch Vet Med Univ Calif Davis CA 95616

ZINMAN, WALTER GEORGE, b New York, NY, Nov 9, 29; m 55; c 2. CHEMISTRY. *Educ:* Rensselaer Polytech Inst, BChE, 51; Harvard Univ, PhD(chem), 55. *Prof Exp:* Res chemist missile & space vehicle div, Gen Elec Co, 56-59; prin res & develop engr, Repub Aviation Corp, 59-65; res group leader, Polytech Inst Brooklyn, 65-66; propulsion engr, Grumman Aircraft Eng Corp, 66-70, consult, 70-72; asst to dir res, Surface Activation Corp, NY, 72-73; CHEM CONSULT, 73- *Mem:* Am Chem Soc; Am Phys Soc. *Res:* Reaction of dissociated gases with solids; gaseous detonations; homogeneous kinetics; fluid mechanics and reacting flows; foundations thermodynamics. *Mailing Add:* 8 Coventry Rd Syosset NY 11791

ZINN, BEN T, b Tel-Aviv, Israel, Apr 21, 37; US citizen; c 2. COMBUSTION, FLUID MECHANICS. *Educ:* NY Univ, BS, 61; Stanford Univ, MS, 62; Princeton Univ, MA, 63, PhD(aerospace & mech sci), 66. *Prof Exp:* Asst res combustion instability, Princeton Univ, 64-65; from asst prof to prof, 65-74, REGENTS PROF AEROSPACE ENG, GA INST TECHNOL, 74- *Concurrent Pos:* Consult, Lockheed Ga Res Labs, Naval Weapons Ctr, Calif & adv group aerospace res & develop, NATO; consult, Brazilian Space Res Inst, 77-; ed measurements in combustion systs, Am Inst Aeronaut & Astronaut Progress in Aeronaut & Astronaut J, 77-78; mem bd vis, Nat Acad Fire Prevention & Control, 78-80; assoc ed, Am Inst Aeronaut & Astronaut. *Honors & Awards:* NASA Cert of Recognition, 74; Sustained Res Award, Sigma Xi, 76. *Mem:* Assoc fel Am Inst Aeronaut & Astronaut; Combustion Inst. *Res:* Combustion in energy and propulsion generating devices; fire safety; acoustics. *Mailing Add:* Sch of Aerospace Eng Ga Inst of Technol Atlanta GA 30332

ZINN, DALE WENDEL, b Parkersburg, WVa; m 54; c 2. ANIMAL HUSBANDRY. *Educ:* WVa Univ, MS, 56; Univ Mo, PhD, 53. *Prof Exp:* Asst prof animal husb, NMex State Univ, 57-61; from assoc prof to prof animal sci, Tex Tech Univ, 61-75, chmn dept, 69-74, asst dean, Col Agr Sci & dir div agr serv, 74-75; DEAN COL AGR & FORESTRY & DIR AGR & FORESTRY EXP STA, WVA UNIV, 75- *Mem:* Am Soc Animal Sci; Am Meat Sci Asn; Sigma Xi. *Res:* Production and quality factors affecting quantity and quality of meat and meat products. *Mailing Add:* Col of Agr & Forestry WVa Univ Morgantown WV 26506

ZINN, DONALD JOSEPH, b New York, NY, Apr 19, 11; m 41; c 2. INVERTEBRATE ZOOLOGY. *Educ:* Harvard Univ, SB, 33; Univ RI, MS, 37; Yale Univ, PhD(zool), 42. *Prof Exp:* Dir, Bass Biol Lab, Fla, 33-35; tech asst, Ro-Lab, Conn, 38-39; asst, Osborn Zool Lab, Yale Univ, 40-41; naturalist, Marine Biol Lab, Woods Hole, 45-46; from instr to prof zool, 46-74, actg chmn dept, 60-62, chmn dept, 62-65 & 73-74, EMER PROF ZOOL, UNIV RI, 74- *Concurrent Pos:* Chief mosquito control proj, Pine Orchard Asn, Conn, 40; dir, Agassiz Mem Exped, Penikese Island, 47; res assoc, Narragansett Marine Lab, 55-74; deleg, Int Cong Zool, London, 58; co-ed, Psammonalia, 66-69; mem, President's Adv Panel Timber & The Environ, 71-74; mem aquatic ecol sect, Int Biol Prog; ecol consult, US Plywood-Champion Papers; mem corp, Bermuda Biol Sta & Marine Biol Lab, Woods Hole Oceanog Inst; pres, Nat Wildlife Fedn, 68-71; trustee, New England

Natural Resources Ctr, 72-; mem shore erosion adv panel, US Army Corps Engrs, 74-80; mem, Falmouth, Mass, Conserv Comn, 77-; pres, Cape Cod Mus Natural Hist, 80- *Mem:* Fel AAAS; Am Inst Biol Sci; Ecol Soc Am. *Res:* Ecology and taxonomy of marine beaches intertidal interstitial fauna and flora; littoral benthos and fouling organisms; tunicate and entomostracan taxonomy; histological techniques with micrometazoa; conservation education; conservation of natural resources. *Mailing Add:* PO Box 589 Falmouth MA 02541

ZINN, GARY WILLIAM, b Oxford, WVa, Sept 20, 44; m 67; c 2. FOREST ECONOMICS, FOREST MANAGEMENT. *Educ:* WVa Univ, BS, 66; State Univ NY Col Forestry, Syracuse Univ, MS, 68, PhD(forest econ), 72. *Prof Exp:* Instr forestry econ, State Univ NY Col Forestry, Syracuse Univ, 71; asst prof, 72-77, ASSOC PROF FOREST MGT, WVA UNIV, 77- *Mem:* Soc Am Foresters; Southern Econ Asn; Am Foresty Asn. *Res:* Economic contributions of forest-based activity to regions; regional development; forest and natural resource policy; forest land use and management planning. *Mailing Add:* Div Forestry WVa Univ Morgantown WV 26506

ZINN, JOHN, b Brooklyn, NY, Feb 28, 28; m 54; c 3. APPLIED PHYSICS. *Educ:* Cornell Univ, AB, 49; Univ Calif, Berkeley, PhD(phys chem), 58. *Prof Exp:* Chemist, Catalin Corp Am, 49-50 & M W Kellogg Co, 52-54; assoc chem, Univ Calif, 55-56, MEM STAFF, LOS ALAMOS SCI LAB, UNIV CALIF, 57- *Concurrent Pos:* Asst prof dept aeronaut eng, Univ Colo, 67-68. *Mem:* Am Phys Soc. *Res:* Theoretical research in atmospheric physics and chemistry; atmospheric effects of nuclear explosions. *Mailing Add:* 600 Barranca Rd Los Alamos NM 87544

ZINN, RICHARD AVERY, nutrition, physiology, see previous edition

ZINN, ROBERT JAMES, b Chicago, Ill, Aug 4, 46. ASTRONOMY. *Educ:* Case Inst Technol, BS, 68; Yale Univ, PhD(astron), 74. *Prof Exp:* Fel astron, Hale Observs, Carnegie Inst Washington, 74-80; ASST PROF ASTRON, YALE UNIV OBSERV, 80- *Mem:* Am Astron Soc; Int Astron Union. *Res:* Stellar evolution; the chemical compositions of globular cluster stars, variable stars, and the stellar populations of the galaxies of the Local Group. *Mailing Add:* Yale Univ Observ 260 Whitney Ave New Haven CT 06511

ZINN, WALTER HENRY, b Kitchener, Ont, Dec 10, 06; nat US; m 33, 66; c 2. PHYSICS. *Educ:* Queen's Univ, Ont, BA, 27, MA, 29; Columbia Univ, PhD(physics), 34. *Hon Degrees:* DSc, Queen's Univ, Ont, 57. *Prof Exp:* Asst physics, Queen's Univ, Ont, 27-28; asst, Columbia Univ, 31-32; from instr to asst prof, City Col New York, 32-41; physicist, Metall Lab, Manhattan Dist, Univ Chicago, 42-46; dir, Argonne Nat Lab, 45-56; vpres, Combustion Eng, Inc, 59-71; RETIRED. *Concurrent Pos:* Spec consult, Joint Cong Comt Atomic Energy, 56; spec mem, President's Sci Adv Comt; pres, Gen Nuclear Eng Corp, 56-64. *Honors & Awards:* Spec commendation, US AEC, 56, Enrico Fermi Award, 69; Cert of Merit, Am Power Conf, 57; Atoms for Peace Award, 60. *Mem:* Nat Acad Sci; Nat Acad Eng; AAAS; fel Am Phys Soc; Am Nuclear Soc (pres, 55). *Res:* Nuclear physics and reactor development. *Mailing Add:* 2940 Bay Meadow Ct Clearwater FL 33519

ZINNER, STEPHEN HARVEY, b New York, NY, Apr 29, 39; m 66; c 2. INFECTIOUS DISEASES, EPIDEMIOLOGY. *Educ:* Northwestern Univ, BA, 61; Sch Med, Univ Pa, MD, 65; Am Bd Internal Med, cert internal med, 72, cert infectious dis, 74. *Prof Exp:* Res fel bacterio & immunol, Channing Lab, Med Sch, Harvard Univ, 67-68, res assoc med, 68-69, res fel, Thorndike Lab, 61-71, instr med, Med Sch, 71-72; asst prof biol & med sci, 72-76, assoc prof, 76-81, PROF MED, MED SECT, BROWN UNIV, 81- *Concurrent Pos:* Field officer, Nat Cancer Chronic Dis Control, USPHS, 67-69; clin instr med, Med Sch, Harvard Univ, 72-; consult infectious dis, RI Hosp, Women & Infants Hosp & Vet Admin Hosp, 72-, Miriam Hosp, Providence, 76-; head, Div Infectious Dis, Roger Williams Gen Hosp & Brown Univ, 72- *Mem:* Infectious Dis Soc Am; Am Soc Microbiol; Am Fedn Clin Res; Soc Epidemiol Res. *Res:* Epidemiology of blood pressure in infants and children; infections in the immunosuppressed patient; antibiotic combinations; new methods for in vitro antibiotic activity determinations; reactive antibodies to Gram-negative infecting organisms. *Mailing Add:* Dept Med Roger Williams Gen Hosp 825 Chalkstone Ave Providence RI 02908

ZINNES, HAROLD, b New York, NY, Apr 7, 29; m 53; c 3. ORGANIC CHEMISTRY. *Educ:* Rutgers Univ, BS, 51; Univ Mich, MS, 52, PhD, 55. *Prof Exp:* Res assoc, E R Squibb & Co, 56-58; scientist, 58-63, sr scientist, 63-68, sr res assoc, Warner-Lambert Res Inst, 68-77, DIR PHARMACEUT TECH DEVELOP, WARNER-LAMBERT INT, 77- *Mem:* Am Chem Soc; Am Pharmaceut Asn. *Res:* Medicinals; natural products; antibiotics; heterocycles; indoles; benzothiazines; anti-inflammatory agents; international pharmaceutical development. *Mailing Add:* Warner-Lambert Int 201 Tabor Rd Morris Plains NJ 07950

ZINS, GERALD RAYMOND, b New Ulm, Minn, Oct 23, 32; m 81; c 3. PHARMACOLOGY. *Educ:* SDak State Univ, BS, 54; Univ Chicago, PhD(pharmacol), 58. *Prof Exp:* Res assoc & instr, Univ Chicago, 58-59; res scientist, Upjohn Co, 59-66; vis assoc prof, State Univ NY Upstate Med Ctr, 66-67; sr scientist, 67-68, head, 68-81, MGR CARDIOVASC RES, UPJOHN CO, 81- *Mem:* AAAS; Am Soc Pharmacol & Exp Therapeut; Am Soc Nephrol. *Res:* Renal and cardiovascular pharmacology; renal prostaglandins; drug metabolism; hypertension; intermediary carbohydrate metabolism. *Mailing Add:* Upjohn Co 301 Henrietta St Kalamazoo MI 49001

ZINSER, EDWARD JOHN, b Toronto, Ont, Mar 13, 41; m 66; c 2. ANALYTICAL CHEMISTRY. *Educ:* Univ Toronto, BSc, 65, PhD(anal chem), 69. *Prof Exp:* Asst, Univ Toronto, 65-68; fel, Queen's Univ, Ont, 69-70; res chemist, Marshall Lab, Pa, 70-71, res chemist, Exp Sta, Wilmington, Del, 72, sr prod specialist, Wynnewood, Pa, 72-73, tech objectives mgr, Finishes Div, Wilmington, Del, 73-74, RES SUPVR, MARSHALL RES & DEVLOP LAB, E I DU PONT DE NEMOURS & CO, PHILADELPHIA, PA, 74- *Concurrent Pos:* Nat Res Coun Can scholar, Univ Toronto, 68-70. *Mem:* Am Chem Soc; Chem Inst Can; Fedn Soc Coatings Technol. *Res:* Environmental analytical chemistry; electrochemistry; atomic absorption; spectroscopy; pigment dispersion; organic coatings; fluorocarbon coatings. *Mailing Add:* 865 Goshen Rd Newton Square PA 19073

ZINSMEISTER, GEORGE EMIL, b Huntington, NY, Dec 27, 39; m 65. MECHANICAL ENGINEERING, HEAT TRANSFER. *Educ:* Rensselaer Polytech Inst, BME, 61; Purdue Univ, MSME, 63, PhD(mech eng), 65. *Prof Exp:* Res engr, E I du Pont de Nemours & Co, Inc, Del, 65-66; asst prof, 66-69, ASSOC PROF MECH ENG, UNIV MASS, AMHERST, 69- *Concurrent Pos:* NSF res grants, 67-70 & 72-73. *Mem:* Am Soc Mech Engrs. *Res:* Heat transfer in composite materials; prediction of thermal processing conditions in foods; engineering education. *Mailing Add:* Dept of Mech Eng Univ of Mass Amherst MA 01003

ZINSMEISTER, PHILIP PRICE, b Columbus, Ohio, May 15, 40; m 68; c 1. DEVELOPMENTAL BIOLOGY. *Educ:* Wittenberg Univ, BS, 62; Univ Ill, MS, 66, PhD(zool), 69. *Prof Exp:* Master biol, US Peace Corps, Ghana, 62-64; lectr, Univ Sci & Technol, Kumasi, Ghana, 70-72; vis asst prof, Univ Ill, 72-73; assoc prof, 73-80, PROF BIOL, OGLETHORPE UNIV, 80-, CHMN, DIV SCI & MATH, 73- *Concurrent Pos:* Asst prof biol, Northeast Mo State Col, 70. *Mem:* Am Inst Biol Sci; Soc Develop Biol. *Res:* Insect oogenesis and development; nerve cell development. *Mailing Add:* Oglethorpe Univ 4484 Peachtree Rd NE Atlanta GA 30319

ZINSMEISTER, WILLIAM JOHN, b Nogales, Ariz, May 6, 43. PALEOBIOGEOGRAPHY, INVERTEBRATE PALEONTOLOGY. *Educ:* Calif State Col, Long Beach, BS, 69; Univ Calif, Riverside, MS, 73, PhD(geol), 74. *Prof Exp:* Fel, 74-75, res assoc paleont, 75-80, SR RES ASSOC, INST POLAR STUDIES, OHIO STATE UNIV, 80- *Concurrent Pos:* NSF grant, 74-76 & 77-; Nat Geog Soc grant, 76-77. *Mem:* Paleont Soc; Int Paleont Asn; Sigma Xi. *Res:* Changes in the distribution of shallow-water marine faunas in the southern hemisphere in response to the final fragmentation of Gondwanaland during the late Cretaceous and early Tertiary. *Mailing Add:* Inst of Polar Studies Ohio State Univ Columbus OH 43210

ZINSSER, HARRY FREDERICK, b Pittsburgh, Pa, May 1, 18; m 43; c 4. CARDIOLOGY. *Educ:* Univ Pittsburgh, BS, 37, MD, 39. *Prof Exp:* Teaching fel internal med, Sch Med, Univ Pittsburgh, 40-42, asst instr, 46-47; fel, 47-48, from asst instr to assoc, 48-51, asst prof clin med, 51-53, asst prof med, 53-55, assoc prof clin med, 55-58, assoc prof med, 58-68, prof cardiol, Div Grad Med, 63-68, dir cardiol, Grad Hosp, 63-78, chmn, Dept Med, 70-79, PROF MED, SCH MED, UNIV PA, 68- *Concurrent Pos:* Secy, Subspecialty Bd Cardiovasc Dis, 79-; vpres, Am Heart Asn, 79-80. *Mem:* Am Fedn Clin Res; Am Soc Clin Invest; Am Clin & Climat Asn; Asn Univ Cardiol. *Res:* Cardiovascular diseases. *Mailing Add:* 1112 Woodmont Rd Gladwyne PA 19035

ZINTEL, HAROLD ALBERT, b Akron, Ohio, Dec 27, 12; m 38; c 5. SURGERY. *Educ:* Univ Akron, BS, 34; Univ Pa, MD, 38, DSc(med), 46. *Hon Degrees:* DSc, Univ Akron, 56. *Prof Exp:* Asst biol, Univ Akron, 33-34; asst path, Med Sch, Univ Pa, 35-36, asst chief med officer, Hosp, 39-40, from asst instr surg to instr, Med Sch, 40-47, asst prof, Med Sch & Grad Sch Med, 47, lectr, Grad Sch Nursing, 47-48, asst prof, Grad Sch Med, 50-54, assoc prof, Med Sch, 51-52, prof clin surg, 52-54; clin prof, Col Physicians & Surgeons, Columbia Univ, 54-69; prof, 70-81, EMER PROF SURG, MED SCH, NORTHWESTERN UNIV, CHICAGO, 81-; DIR, DEPT SPEC EDUC PROJ, AM COL SURGEONS, 81- *Concurrent Pos:* Consult, Camden Munic Hosp, 48-54, Children's Hosp of Philadelphia, 51-54 & Vet Admin Hosp, Philadelphia, 53-54; attend surgeon & dir surg, St Luke's Hosp Ctr, 54-69; consult, Off Surgeon Gen, US Army, 58-67; asst dir, Am Col Surgeons, 69-80; trustee, Comn Prof Hosp Activities, 69- *Mem:* AAAS; Soc Vascular Surg; Soc Univ Surgeons (pres, 55-56); Am Geriat Soc; Am Cancer Soc. *Res:* Antibiotics; wound healing; peripheral vascular hypertension; antiseptics; carcinoma of head of pancreas; nutrition; portal hypertension; trauma; computers in medicine; allied health manpower; continuing medical education. *Mailing Add:* Col of Surgeons 55 E Erie St Chicago IL 60611

ZIOCK, KLAUS OTTO H, b Herchen, Ger, Feb 4, 25; nat US; m 52; c 4. EXPERIMENTAL PHYSICS. *Educ:* Univ Bonn, Dipl, 49, Dr rer nat, 56. *Prof Exp:* Physicist, E Leybold's Nachfolger, Ger, 50-55; res assoc, Univ Bonn, 56-58; res assoc physics, Yale Univ, 58-60, asst prof, 60-62; assoc prof, 60-72, actg dir, Va Assoc Res Ctr, 62-64, PROF PHYSICS, UNIV VA, 72- *Concurrent Pos:* Vis scientist, Europ Orgn Nuclear Res, 69-70. *Honors & Awards:* Alexander von Humboldt Award, 77. *Mem:* Am Phys Soc. *Res:* Nuclear physics; physics of elementary particles; atomic physics. *Mailing Add:* Dept of Physics Univ of Va Charlottesville VA 22901

ZIOLO, RONALD F, b Philadelphia, Pa, Aug 16, 44; m 67; c 3. CHEMISTRY. *Educ:* Univ Calif, Los Angeles, BS, 66; Temple Univ, PhD(chem), 70. *Prof Exp:* Res fel chem, Calif Inst Technol, 71-72; assoc scientist, 73, scientist, 74-78, SR SCIENTIST, XEROX CORP, 78- *Mem:* AAAS; Am Chem Soc; Sigma Xi; Am Crystallog Asn. *Res:* Inorganic and organometallic chemistry; x-ray crystallography; structure and bonding; magnetic and optical properties; chemistry of high surface area materials. *Mailing Add:* Webster Res Ctr Bldg 114 Xerox Corp Webster NY 14580

ZIONY, JOSEPH ISRAEL, b Los Angeles, Calif, Apr 6, 35; m 61; c 3. GEOLOGY. *Educ:* Univ Calif, Los Angeles, AB, 56, MA, 59, PhD(geol), 66. *Prof Exp:* Geologist, Mil Geol Br, DC, 57-59, Fuels Br, Calif, 59-60, Southwestern Br, 65-69 & Eng Geol Br, 69-73, dep chief, Off Earthquake Studies, 73-76 & Earthquake Hazards Br, Menlo Park, 76-77, reg geologist, Western Region, Reston, Va, 77-81, GROUND MOTION & FAULTING BR, US GEOL SURV, MENLO PARK, CALIF, 77- *Mem:* Geol Soc Am; Seismol Soc Am; Asn Eng Geol. *Res:* Earthquake hazards assessment; delineation of active faults in southern california; evaluation of their relative activity using late quaternary slip histories; estimation of their earthquake potential. *Mailing Add:* US Geol Surv 345 Middlefield Rd Menlo Park CA 94025

ZIPF, ELIZABETH M(ARGARET), b Barrington, NJ, Nov 17, 27. BIOLOGY, INFORMATION SCIENCE. *Educ:* Univ Va, BA, 50, PhD(biol), 59; Univ Pa, MA, 52. *Prof Exp:* Res biologist cancer res, Med Sch, Univ Va, 55; res asst biol, Princeton Univ, 56-57; assoc ed, 57-62, sr assoc ed, 62-63, actg supvry ed, biol & bio-med subj, Biol Abstracts, 63-64, supvry ed, 64-71, head, Ed Dept, 71-80, actg dir, Sci Div, 80-81, TECH CONSULT TO PRES, BIOSCI INFO SERV, 81- *Concurrent Pos:* Fel, Univ Pa, 62-63; consult in prep Water Resources Thesaurus, Off Water Resources Res, US Dept Interior, 66; mem Z-39 comt, Am Standards Asn, 66-67 & Nat Fed Sci Abstracting & Indexing Serv. *Mem:* Fel AAAS; Am Inst Biol Sci; Coun Biol Ed; Am Soc Zool. *Res:* Biological research in invertebrate and vertebrate embryology; teratoma formation in salamanders; information science in biology and biomedical fields. *Mailing Add:* Bio Sci Info Serv 2100 Arch St Philadelphia PA 19103

ZIPFEL, CHRISTIE LEWIS, b Detroit, Mich, Oct 2, 41; m 64. LOW TEMPERATURE PHYSICS. *Educ:* Vassar Col, AB, 63; Univ Mich, MS, 65, PhD(physics), 69. *Prof Exp:* Instr physics, State Univ NY Stony Brook, 69-72; asst prof, Towson State Col, 72-74; RES ASSOC PHYSICS, BELL LABS, MURRAY HILL, 74- *Mem:* Am Phys Soc. *Res:* Electrons on the surface of liquid helium. *Mailing Add:* Bell Labs 1d-209 Murray Hill NJ 07974

ZIPFEL, GEORGE G, JR, b Richmond, Va, Dec 23, 38; m 64. ACOUSTICS. *Educ:* Mass Inst Technol, BS, 60, BEE, 61; Univ Fla, MSE, 62; Univ Mich, PhD(physics), 68. *Prof Exp:* Res assoc, Inst Theoret Physics, State Univ NY Stony Brook, 68-71; Nat Res Coun res assoc, US Naval Res Lab, 71-73; MEM TECH STAFF, BELL LABS, 73- *Mem:* AAAS; Acoust Soc Am; Am Phys Soc. *Res:* Statistical field theory; scattering theory; particle physics; applied classical field theory; statistical field theory; piezoelectric devices. *Mailing Add:* Bell Labs Whippany Rd Whippany NJ 07981

ZIPP, ADAM PETER, b Baltimore, Md, Nov 19, 47; m 74. BIOPHYSICAL CHEMISTRY, BIOPHYSICS. *Educ:* Loyola Col, BS, 69; Princeton Univ, MA, 71, PhD(chem), 73. *Prof Exp:* NIH fel biophys, dept pharmaceut chem, Univ Calif Med Ctr, San Francisco, 74-77; mem staff, Blood Chem Lab, 77-81, DIR RES & DEVELOP, AMES DIV, MILES LABS, 81- *Mem:* Sigma Xi; AAAS; Biophys Soc; Am Chem Soc; Am Asn Clin Chemists. *Res:* Physical chemistry of proteins; application of physical chemical techniques to the study of biomedical problems; physical chemical studies of normal and diseases erythrocytes; clinical chemistry; solid phase technology for the clinical laboratory. *Mailing Add:* Ames Co Div Miles Labs 1127 Myrtle St Elkhart IN 46514

ZIPP, ARDEN PETER, b Dolgeville, NY, July 14, 38; c 2. PHYSICAL INORGANIC CHEMISTRY. *Educ:* Colgate Univ, AB, 60; Univ Pa, PhD, 64. *Prof Exp:* Asst prof chem, Drew Univ, 64-66; from asst prof to assoc prof, 66-73, PROF CHEM, STATE UNIV NY COL CORTLAND, 73- *Mem:* Am Chem Soc; Sigma Xi. *Res:* Transition metal complexes with sulfur containing ligands; oxidation reduction reactions of transition metal ions. *Mailing Add:* Dept Chem State Univ NY Col Cortland NY 13045

ZIPPIN, CALVIN, b Albany, NY, July 17, 26; m 64; c 2. BIOSTATISTICS, EPIDEMIOLOGY. *Educ:* State Univ NY, AB, 47; Johns Hopkins Univ, ScD(biostatist), 53. *Prof Exp:* Res asst statist, Sterling-Winthrop Res Inst, 47-50; res asst biostatist, Johns Hopkins Univ, 50-53; instr, Sch Pub Health, Univ Calif, Berkeley, 53-55, from asst res biostatistician to res biostatistician, Cancer Res Inst, 55-67, asst prof prev med, 58-60, lectr, 60-67, lectr path, 61-67, PROF EPIDEMIOL, CANCER RES INST, DEPT EPIDEMIOL & INT HEALTH & DEPT PATH, SCH MED, UNIV CALIF, SAN FRANCISCO, 67- *Concurrent Pos:* Consult, US Naval Biol Lab, 55-66 & Letterman Gen Hosp, 58-; vis assoc prof, Stanford Univ, 62; NIH spec fel, London Sch Hyg & Trop Med, 64-65; temporary adv, WHO, 69, 72 & 74; Eleanor Roosevelt Int Cancer fel, Univ London, 75. *Mem:* AAAS; fel Am Statist Asn; Am Asn Cancer Ed; Biomet Soc; fel Royal Statist Soc. *Res:* Identification of environmental and other factors associated with the risk of cancer as well as study of patient and disease characteristics which influence pattern of survival following diagnosis of a malignancy; biometry and epidemiology in cancer research. *Mailing Add:* Cancer Res Inst Univ of Calif San Francisco CA 94143

ZIPSER, DAVID, b New York, NY, May 31, 37; m 65; c 2. MOLECULAR GENETICS. *Educ:* Cornell Univ, BS, 58; Harvard Univ, PhD(biochem), 63. *Prof Exp:* Prof biol, Columbia Univ, 65-69; INVESTR GENETICS, COLD SPRING HARBOR LAB, 70- *Res:* Lactose operon function in bacteria. *Mailing Add:* 34 Spring Cold Spring Harbor NY 11724

ZIRAKZADEH, ABOULGHASSEM, b Isfahan, Iran, Feb 7, 22; m 51; c 1. MATHEMATICS. *Educ:* Univ Teheran, BS, 44; Univ Mich, MS, 49; Okla State Univ, PhD(math), 53. *Prof Exp:* Instr math, Okla State Univ, 52-53, Univ Colo, 53-54 & Wash State Univ, 54-55; asst prof, Univ Teheran, 55-56; asst prof, 57-64, ASSOC PROF MATH, UNIV COLO, BOULDER, 64- *Mem:* Am Math Soc; Math Asn Am. *Res:* Geometry; convexity. *Mailing Add:* Dept of Math Univ of Colo Boulder CO 80302

ZIRIN, HAROLD, b Boston, Mass, Oct 7, 29; m 57; c 2. ASTRONOMY. *Educ:* Harvard Univ, AB, 50, MA, 51, PhD(astrophys), 53. *Prof Exp:* Physicist, Rand Corp, 52-53; instr astron, Harvard Univ, 53-55; mem sr res staff, High Altitude Observ, Univ Colo, 55-64; PROF ASTROPHYS, CALIF INST TECHNOL, 64- *Concurrent Pos:* Sloane fel, 58-60; Guggenheim fel, 61; dir, Big Bear Solar Observ, 69-; mem staff, Hale Observ, 64-80; dir, Aura, 78- *Mem:* Am Astron Soc; Am Geophys Union. *Res:* Solar physics; stellar spectroscopy; interstellar matter; geophysics. *Mailing Add:* Dept of Astrophys Calif Inst of Technol Pasadena CA 91125

ZIRINO, ALBERTO, b Berlin, Ger, Jan 7, 41; m 64; c 3. CHEMICAL OCEANOGRAPHY, POLAROGRAPHY. *Educ:* Univ Calif, Los Angeles, BS, 63; San Diego State Col, MS, 66; Univ Wash, PhD(oceanog), 70. *Prof Exp:* Res assoc oceanog, Univ Wash, 67-70; OCEANOGRAPHER, NAVAL UNDERSEA CTR, 70- *Concurrent Pos:* Nat Res Coun assoc, 70; instr, Grossmont Col, 70-75. *Res:* Voltammetric detection of trace metals in seawater; speciation of zinc, cadmium, lead, copper seawater; electrochemistry. *Mailing Add:* 5327 Bragg San Diego CA 92122

ZIRKER, JACK BERNARD, b New York, NY, July 19, 27; m 51; c 3. SOLAR PHYSICS. *Educ:* City Col New York, BME, 49; Harvard Univ, PhD(astron), 56. *Prof Exp:* Mech eng labs, Radio Corp Am, 49-53, astrophysicist, Sacramento Peak Observ, 56-64; astrophysicist & prof physics, Univ Hawaii, 64-78, ACTG DIR, SACRAMENTO PEAK OBSERV, 76-78, DIR, 78- *Concurrent Pos:* Consult, NASA, 68-; mem, Astron Adv Panel, NSF, 73-76 & mem comt, Solar-Terrestrial Res, Nat Res Coun, 81-82. *Mem:* Am Astron Soc. *Res:* Physics of the outer atmosphere of the sun. *Mailing Add:* Sacramento Peak Observ Sunspot NM 88349

ZIRKIND, RALPH, b New York, NY, Oct 20, 18; m 40; c 3. PHYSICS. *Educ:* City Col New York, BS, 40; Ill Inst Technol, MS, 46; Univ Md, College Park, PhD(physics), 59. *Hon Degrees:* DSc, Univ RI, 68. *Prof Exp:* Tech asst metall, Naval Inspector Ord, US Dept Navy, 41-42, physicist, 42-45, physicist, Bur Aeronaut, 45-52, chief physicist, 52-60; physicist, Advan Res Projs Agency, US Dept Defense, 60-64; prof, Aerospace Eng, Polytech Inst Brooklyn, 64-70; prof elec eng, Univ RI, 70-72; physicist, Advan Projs Res Agency, US Dept Defense, 72-74; prin scientist, Gen Res Corp, McLean, Va, 74-81; CONSULT, 81- *Concurrent Pos:* Consult, Jet Propulsion Lab, 64-; prof, Univ RI, 73- *Mem:* Am Phys Soc. *Res:* Optical and radiation physics; atmospheric sciences; optical physics; lasers, atmospheric physics. *Mailing Add:* 820 Hillsboro Dr Silver Spring MD 20902

ZIRKLE, LARRY DON, b Wheeler, Tex, Nov 11, 36; m 57; c 3. MECHANICAL ENGINEERING. *Educ:* Okla State Univ, BS, 59, MS, 60; Univ Tex, Austin, PhD(eng mech), 69. *Prof Exp:* Assoc engr, Tex Instruments Inc, 60-61; asst prof eng mech, Univ Tex, Austin, 69-70; asst prof, 70-74, assoc prof mech eng, 74-77, DIR STUDENT SERV, ENG, TECHNOL & ARCHIT, OKLA STATE UNIV, 77- *Mem:* Am Soc Mech Engrs; Am Soc Eng Educ; Inst Elec & Electronics Engrs; Soc Prof Engrs; Nat Soc Prof Engrs. *Res:* Random vibrations with particular interest in nonlinear systems; application of engineering to biomedical problems; control theory; nonlinear analysis; dynamics; student counceling and advisement, academic student affairs; co-op education. *Mailing Add:* EN101 Okla State Univ Stillwater OK 74074

ZIRKLE, RAYMOND ELLIOTT, b Springfield, Ill, Jan 9, 02; m 24; c 2. BIOPHYSICS. *Educ:* Univ Mo, AB, 28, PhD(bot), 32. *Prof Exp:* Asst bot, Univ Mo, 28-30, instr, 30-32; Nat Res Coun fel, Johnson Found, Univ Pa, 32-34, Johnson Pound fel med physics, 34-38, lectr biophys, 36-38, instr exp radiol, 37-38, assoc, 38-40; asst prof biol, Bryn Mawr Col, 38-40; prof bot, Ind Univ, 40-44; prof, 44-48, prof radiobiol, 48-59, prof biophys, 59-67, dir inst radiobiol & biophys, 45-48, chmn comt biophys, 54-64, chmn dept biophys, 64-66, EMER PROF BIOPHYS, UNIV CHICAGO, 67- *Concurrent Pos:* Prin biologist, Manhattan Dist, Metall Lab, Chicago & Clinton Labs, Tenn, 42-46; Hitchcock prof, Univ Calif, 51. *Mem:* Nat Acad Sci; AAAS; Am Philos Soc; Biophys Soc; Radiation Res Soc (pres, 52-53). *Res:* Mechanisms of mitosis; irradiation of small fractions of individual cells; comparative biological effects of ultraviolet and various ionizing radiations. *Mailing Add:* 4675 W Red Rock Dr Perry Park SWDC Larkspur CO 80118

ZISCHKE, JAMES ALBERT, b Sioux Falls, SDak, Sept 18, 34; m 61; c 1. INVERTEBRATE ZOOLOGY, AQUATIC ECOLOGY. *Educ:* Univ Wis, BS, 57; Univ SDak, MA, 60; Tulane Univ, PhD(parasitol), 66. *Prof Exp:* Instr, 63-65, from asst prof to assoc prof, 66-78, PROF BIOL, ST OLAF COL, 78- *Concurrent Pos:* Partic, AEC Res Prog, PR Nuclear Ctr, 67; Duke Univ res fel, Cent Univ Venezuela, 67-68; NSF fac fel, Univ Miami, 71-72 & Argonne Nat Lab, 76; aquatic biologist, US Environ Protection Agency, 76-79 & Oak Ridge Nat Lab, 78-79. *Mem:* Am Soc Zool; Ecol Soc Am. *Res:* Trematode taxonomy, life histories and reproduction; schistosome dermatitis; molluscan physiology; marine littoral ecology; stream ecology; parasitology. *Mailing Add:* Dept of Biol St Olaf Col Northfield MN 55057

ZISK, STANLEY HARRIS, b Boston, Mass. RADAR ASTRONOMY, MASER AMPLIFIER DESIGN. *Educ:* Mass Inst Technol, SB & SM, 53; Stanford Univ, PhD(elec eng & radio astron), 65. *Prof Exp:* Res assoc elec eng, 65-68, MEM SCI STAFF, HAYSTACK OBSERV, MASS INST TECHNOL, 68- *Concurrent Pos:* Prin investr, Haystack Observ, 69-; vis scientist, Ltapetinga Radio Observ, Brazil, 74- *Mem:* Am Astron Soc; Am Geophys Union; Union Radio Int Sci; Inst Elec & Electronics Engrs. *Mailing Add:* Haystack Observ Mass Inst Technol Westford MA 01886

ZISKIN, MARVIN CARL, b Philadelphia, Pa, Oct 1, 36; m 60; c 3. BIOMEDICAL ENGINEERING. *Educ:* Temple Univ, AB, 58, MD, 62; Drexel Inst, MSBmE, 65. *Prof Exp:* Intern, West Jersey Hosp, Camden, 62-63; NIH fel, Drexel Inst, 63-65; NASA fel theoret biophys, 65; instr radiol & res assoc diag ultrasonics, Hahnemann Med Col, 65-66; from asst prof to assoc prof radiol & med physics, 68-76, PROF RADIOL & MED PHYSICS, MED SCH, TEMPLE UNIV, 76-, CHMN COMT BIOPHYS & BIOENG, 74- *Concurrent Pos:* Lectr biomed eng, Drexel Univ, 65-71, adj assoc prof, 71-; NSF fel analog & digital electronics, 72; mem comt on sci & arts, Franklin Inst, 72-; mem bd dirs, Inst Ultrasonics in Med. *Mem:* Inst Ultrasonics in Med; Am Heart Asn; Inst Elec & Electronics Eng; Soc Photo-Optical Instrument Eng; NY Acad Sci. *Res:* Biomathematics; diagnostic ultrasonics; thermography; image processing; vision; hearing; information processing in the nervous system. *Mailing Add:* Dept of Radiol Temple Univ Med Sch Philadelphia PA 19140

ZISMAN, WILLIAM ALBERT, b Albany, NY, Aug 21, 05; m 35; c 1. PHYSICAL CHEMISTRY. *Educ:* Mass Inst Technol, BS, 27, MS, 28; Harvard Univ, PhD(physics), 32. *Hon Degrees:* DSc, Clarkson Col Technol, 65. *Prof Exp:* Res assoc geophys, Harvard Univ, 31-33; statistician, Div Econ & Statist, Pub Works Admin, 33-35; mgt div, Resettlement Admin, 35-38; vis res scientist, Carnegie Inst Geophys Lab, 38-39; physicist, Naval Res Lab, Washington, DC, 39-42, head lubrication br, 47-53, surface chem br, 53-57, supt chem div, 56-68, chair of sci in chem physics, 69-75; RETIRED. *Concurrent Pos:* Lectr, Am Univ & Georgetown Univ. *Honors & Awards:* Carbide & Carbon Award, Am Chem Soc, 55, Kendall Award, 63; Am Soc Lubrication Eng Nat Award, 61; Mayo D Hersey Award, Am Soc Mech Eng, 69; Matiello Award, Fedn Socs Paint Technol, 71. *Mem:* Am Chem Soc; Am Phys Soc; Am Soc Lubrication Eng; NY Acad Sci. *Res:* Surface and colloidal chemistry; monomolecular films; surface potentials; friction, lubrication, adhesion, corrosion inhibition, adsorption, wetting and surface properties of polymers. *Mailing Add:* 200 E Melbourne Ave Silver Spring MD 20901

ZISON, STANLEY WARREN, b Philadelphia, Pa, Oct 9, 44; m 68; c 3. ENVIRONMENTAL ENGINEERING, STATISTICS. *Educ:* Drexel Univ, BSc, 69, MSc, 70, PhD(environ eng), 74. *Prof Exp:* Lab chemist water qual anal, Drexel Univ, 70-72; environ specialist III, Iowa Dept of Environ Qual, 72-74; assoc biochemist, Water Resources Engrs, 74-75; PRIN ENGR ENVIRON ENG, TETRA TECH, INC, 75- *Concurrent Pos:* Consult engr, US Fish & Wildlife Serv, 78- *Mem:* AAAS; Water Pollution Control Fedn; Am Statist Asn; Royal Statist Soc. *Res:* Non-point pollution; mathematical modeling of surface waters; statistical analysis of environmental data; computer applications to environmental problems. *Mailing Add:* 3932 Balsa St Irvine CA 92714

ZISSIS, GEORGE JOHN, b Lebanon, Ind, Dec 31, 22; m 54; c 4. OPTICS. *Educ:* Purdue Univ, BS, 46, MS, 50, PhD(physics), 54. *Prof Exp:* Instr eng physics, Purdue Univ, 46-50, 52-54; assoc scientist, Atomic Power Div, Westinghouse Elec Corp, 54-55; mem spec air defense study, Off Naval Res, 57; alt head infrared lab, Inst Sci & Technol, 57-64, head lab, 64-69, chief scientist, Willow Run Labs & Tech Mgr, Infrared & Optics Div, Inst Sci & Technol, 69-73, CHIEF SCIENTIST, INFRARED & OPTICS DIV, ENVIRON RES INST MICH, UNIV MICH, 73- *Concurrent Pos:* Vis lectr, Univ Mich, 61-62, lectr, Dept Elec Eng, 70-72, adj prof elec & comput eng, 73-; mem staff, Res Eng, Support Div, Inst Defense Anal, DC, 62-64, consult, 64-72; consult, Army Res Off, 64-72; mem comt space prog earth observ, Nat Res Coun-Nat Acad Sci, chmn, 69-72; adv, Div Earth Sci, US Geol Surv; ed-in-chief, J Remote Sensing of the Environ, 71-78. *Mem:* Fel AAAS; fel Optical Soc Am; Am Soc Photogram; Sigma Xi; Soc Photo-Optical Instrumentation Engrs. *Res:* High resolution spectroscopy; infrared; radiometry; optical radiation physics; precision measurements. *Mailing Add:* 1549 Stonehaven Rd Ann Arbor MI 48104

ZITARELLI, DAVID EARL, b Chester, Pa, Aug 12, 41; m 66. MATHEMATICS. *Educ:* Temple Univ, BA, 63, MA, 65; Pa State Univ, PhD(math), 70. *Prof Exp:* asst prof, 70-77, ASSOC PROF MATH, TEMPLE UNIV, 77- *Mem:* Am Math Soc; Math Asn Am. *Res:* History of mathematics; algebraic theory of semigroups. *Mailing Add:* Dept of Math Temple Univ Philadelphia PA 19122

ZITNAK, AMBROSE, b Bratislava, Czech, Dec 30, 22; nat Can; m 50; c 3. PLANT BIOCHEMISTRY, FOOD TECHNOLOGY. *Educ:* Slovak Inst Tech, Czech, BSA, 46; Univ Alta, MSc, 53, PhD, 55. *Prof Exp:* Res officer, Agr Res Inst, Czech, 46-47; asst forage chem, Agr Exp Sta, Swiss Fed Inst Technol, 47-48; asst plant biochem, Univ Alta, 51-55, chief analyst feed & soil chem, 55-57; ASSOC PROF HORT BIOCHEM, UNIV GUELPH, 57- *Mem:* Can Inst Food Technol; Can Soc Plant Physiol; Can Soc Hort Sci; Can Geog Soc; Agr Inst Can. *Res:* Solanaceous glycoalkaloids; plant growth substances; technology of fruit and vegetable preservation; heat-browning of potato products; physiology of the potato tuber; cyanogenic glucosides. *Mailing Add:* Dept of Hort Sci Univ of Guelph Guelph ON N1G 2W1 Can

ZITOMER, FRED, b Chicago, Ill, Oct 19, 33; m 57; c 3. ANALYTICAL CHEMISTRY. *Educ:* Park Col, BA, 58; Kans State Univ, MS, 60, PhD(anal chem), 63. *Prof Exp:* Asst org synthesis, Park Col, 56-58; asst anal chem, Kans State Univ, 58-63; anal chemist, Res Lab, Celanese Corp, NJ, 63-64; res chemist, Agr Res Ctr, Dow Chem Co, Mich, 64-66; res chemist, Res Lab, 66-67, anal group leader, 67-71, supvr anal dept, 71-74, MGR ANAL CHEM & PHYS TESTING, CELANESE RES CO, 74- *Mem:* Am Chem Soc; Am Soc Mass Spectrometry. *Res:* Mass spectrometry; gas chromatography; trace analysis; analytical methods development; flammability, nonwovens, rubber, polymer degradation mechanisms; nuclear magnetic resonance; infrared; electron spectroscopic chemical analysis; liquid chromatography; electron spin resonance; thermal analysis. *Mailing Add:* Celanese Res Co PO Box 1000 Summit NJ 07901

ZITOMER, RICHARD STEPHEN, b New York, NY, Sept 29, 46; m 69; c 4. MOLECULAR BIOLOGY. *Educ:* Univ Pa, BA, 68, PhD(biol), 72. *Prof Exp:* Fel, Dept Biochem, Univ Pa, 72-73 & Dept Genetics, Univ Wash, 73-75; asst prof, 76-81, ASSOC PROF GENETICS, DEPT BIOL SCI, STATE UNIV NY, 81- *Concurrent Pos:* Res career develop award, NIH, 81-86. *Res:* Regulation of the expression of the cytochrome c genes of yeast. *Mailing Add:* Dept Biol Sic State Univ NY Albany NY 12222

ZITRIN, ARTHUR, b NY, Apr 10, 18; m 42; c 2. PSYCHIATRY. *Educ:* City Col New York, BS, 38; NY Univ, MS, 41, MD, 45. *Prof Exp:* Instr physiol, Hunter Col, 48-49; from clin asst psychiat to clin instr, 49-54, from asst clin prof to assoc prof, 54-67, PROF PSYCHIAT, SCH MED, NY UNIV, 67- *Concurrent Pos:* Pvt pract; sr psychiatrist, Bellevue Hosp, 50-, asst dir psychiat div, 54-55, dir, 55-69. *Mem:* Am Psychiat Asn; Am Psychoanal Asn; Asn Res Nerv & Ment Dis. *Res:* Physiological psychology; psychoanalysis; clinical psychiatry. *Mailing Add:* 56 Ruxton Rd Great Neck NY 11023

ZITRON, NORMAN RALPH, b New York, NY, May 22, 30. APPLIED MATHEMATICS. *Educ:* Cornell Univ, AB, 52; NY Univ, MS, 56, PhD(math), 59. *Prof Exp:* Lab asst physics, NY Univ, 52-53, res asst, Courant Inst Math Sci, 54-58; tech assoc appl physics, Harvard Univ, 58-59; res assoc eng, Brown Univ, 59-60; asst prof eng sci, Fla State Univ, 60-61; asst prof math, Res Ctr, Univ Wis, 61-62; ASSOC PROF MATH, PURDUE UNIV, 62- *Concurrent Pos:* Fulbright sr res scholar, Tech Univ Denmark, 64-65; assoc res mathematician, Radiation Lab, Univ Mich, 65-66; sr res fel, Univ Surrey, 68; res assoc, Univ Calif, Berkeley, 71; vis scholar, Stanford Univ, 72 & 78-79. *Mem:* Am Math Soc. *Res:* Propagation, diffraction and scattering of electromagnetic, acoustic and elastic waves; asymptotoic solutions of partial differential equations; optimization. *Mailing Add:* Div of Math Sci Purdue Univ Lafayette IN 47907

ZITTER, ROBERT NATHAN, b New York, NY, Oct 3, 28; m 64. SOLID STATE PHYSICS, QUANTUM ELECTRONICS. *Educ:* Univ Chicago, BA, 50, MS, 52 & 60, PhD(physics), 62. *Prof Exp:* Mathematician, US Naval Proving Grounds, 52; res physicist, Chicago Midway Labs, 52-60; mem tech staff, Bell Tel Labs, 62-67; PROF PHYSICS, SOUTHERN ILL UNIV, CARBONDALE, 67- *Mem:* Am Phys Soc. *Res:* Semiconductors and semimetals; photoconductivity; gaseous lasers; infrared detection. *Mailing Add:* Dept of Physics Southern Ill Univ Carbondale IL 62901

ZITTER, THOMAS ANDREW, b Saginaw, Mich, Dec 30, 41; m 66; c 3. PLANT VIROLOGY. *Educ:* Mich State Univ, BS, 63, PhD(plant path), 68. *Prof Exp:* Asst prof & asst plant pathologist, Agr Res & Educ Ctr, Univ Fla, 68-74, assoc prof, 74-79; MEM STAFF, DEPT PLANT PATH, CORNELL UNIV, 79- *Mem:* Am Phytopath Soc; Entom Soc Am; Asn Appl Biologists. *Res:* Isolation and identification of vegetable viruses; establishment of plant-vector-virus relationships; determination of epidemiology and control of virus diseases. *Mailing Add:* Dept Plant Path Cornell Univ Ithaca NY 14853

ZITZEWITZ, PAUL WILLIAM, b Chicago, Ill, June 5, 42; m 66; c 2. EXPERIMENTAL ATOMIC PHYSICS. *Educ:* Carleton Col, BA, 64; Harvard Univ, AM, 65, PhD(physics), 70. *Prof Exp:* Scholar physics, Univ Western Ont, 70-72; res fel & sr physicist, Corning Glass Works, 72-73; asst prof, 73-78, ASSOC PROF PHYSICS, UNIV MICH, DEARBORN, 78- *Mem:* Am Phys Soc; Am Asn Physics Teachers; Sigma Xi; Int Soc Study Origins Life. *Res:* Positrons; positron interactions in solids; positronium; atom-surface interactions; atomic spectroscopy; fundamental constants; origins of biological optical activity. *Mailing Add:* Dept of Natural Sci Univ of Mich Dearborn MI 48128

ZIVI, SAMUEL M(EISNER), b St Louis, Mo, June 4, 25; m 49; c 3. MECHANICAL ENGINEERING, NUCLEAR ENGINEERING. *Educ:* Iowa State Univ, BSME, 46; Wash Univ, MSME, 48. *Prof Exp:* Mech engr, Kennard Corp, 48-52; sr mech engr, Midwest Res Inst, 52-55, sect head, 55-56; staff engr, Atomic Energy Div, Am-Standard Corp, 56-57; develop engr, Kennard Div, Am Air Filter Co, Inc, 57-58; mem tech staff, Ramo-Wooldridge Div, TRW Inc, 58-60, proj mgr, TRW Space Technol Labs, 61-64; mgr appl thermodyn dept, TRW Systs, 64-70, mgr laser prod, TRW Inc, 70-71; staff, Agronne Nat Lab, 71-80. *Concurrent Pos:* Lectr, Kjeller, Norway, 62. *Mem:* Am Soc Mech Engrs; Inst Nuclear Engrs; Sigma Xi. *Res:* Thermodynamics; heat transfer; energetics; fluid mechanics. *Mailing Add:* 2016 Euclid-4 Santa Monica CA 90405

ZIVNUSKA, JOHN ARTHUR, b San Diego, Calif, July 10, 16. FOREST ECONOMICS, ACADEMIC ADMINISTRATION. *Educ:* Univ Calif, Berkeley, BS, 38, MS, 40; Univ Minn, St Paul, PhD(agr econ), 47. *Prof Exp:* Instr forestry, Univ Minn, 46-47; from instr to assoc prof , Sch Forestry & Conserv, Univ Calif, Berkeley, 48-59; dean, 65-74, PROF FORESTRY, SCH FORESTRY & CONSERV, UNIV CALIF, BERKELEY, 59- *Concurrent Pos:* Fulbright lectr, Agr Col Norway, Vollebekk, 54-55; consult, Econ Comn Asia & Far East, 57; mem forestry res adv comt, USDA, 64-70, mem agr res policy adv comt, 71-72; pres, Asn State Cols & Univ Forestry Res Orgns, 71-72. *Mem:* Soc Am Foresters. *Res:* Demand for timber; economics of forest industries; forest taxation; international forestry. *Mailing Add:* 145 Mulford Hall Univ of Calif Berkeley CA 94720

ZLATKIS, ALBERT, b Pomorzany, Poland, Mar 27, 24; nat US; m 47; c 3. ANALYTICAL CHEMISTRY, ORGANIC CHEMISTRY. *Educ:* Univ Toronto, BASc, 47, MASc, 48; Wayne State Univ, PhD(chem), 52. *Prof Exp:* Demonstr chem eng, Univ Toronto, 47-48; instr, Wayne State Univ, 49-52, res assoc, 52-53; res chemist, Shell Oil Co, Tex, 53-55; from instr to assoc prof chem, 54-62, chmn dept, 58-62, PROF CHEM, UNIV HOUSTON, 62- *Concurrent Pos:* Adj prof, Baylor Col Med, 72- *Honors & Awards:* Award Chromatog, Am Chem Soc, 73; Technol Award, 75 & 80. *Mem:* Am Chem Soc. *Res:* Gas chromatography and mass spectrometry of biological metabolites; clinical chemistry; environmental studies; chemistry of flavors and natural products; reactions of thermal electrons with organic compounds. *Mailing Add:* Dept of Chem Univ of Houston Houston TX 77004

ZLETZ, ALEX, b Detroit, Mich, Mar 28, 19; m 48; c 4. PHYSICAL CHEMISTRY, ORGANIC CHEMISTRY. *Educ:* Wayne Univ, BS, 40, MS, 48; Purdue Univ, PhD(chem), 50. *Prof Exp:* Electroplating chemist, Auto City Plating Co, 41; res chemist, Stand Oil Co, 50-54, group leader, 54-61; group leader, Am Oil Co, 61-79; MEM STAFF, AMOCO CHEM CORP, 79- *Concurrent Pos:* Guest scientist, Free Radicals Proj, Nat Bur Stand, 57. *Mem:* Am Chem Soc; Royal Soc Chem. *Res:* High vacuum; extreme pressure; aryl borons; polyolefins; liquid rocket fuels; free radical and hydrocarbon chemistry; catalysis; fluids and lubricants; greases; railway diesel lubricating oil; hydrocarbon oxidation; homogeneous and heterogeneous oxidation of hydrocarbons to chemical intermediates. *Mailing Add:* 1004 Mill St Apt 106 Naperville IL 60540

ZLOBEC, SANJO, b Brezicani, Yugoslavia, Nov 16, 40; m 65; c 2. APPLIED MATHEMATICS. *Educ:* Univ Zagreb, BSc, 63, MSc, 67; Northwestern Univ, PhD(appl math), 70. *Prof Exp:* Res engr, Northwestern Univ, 68-69, lectr math, 69-70; Nat Res Coun Can grant, 70-81, asst prof, 70-76, ASSOC PROF MATH, MCGILL UNIV, 76- *Concurrent Pos:* Vis asst prof, Univ Zagreb, 71-72; vis prof, Univ Del, 78; vis scientist, Coun Sci Indust Res, Pretoria, 78-79. *Mem:* Soc Indust & Appl Math; Am Math Soc. *Res:* Optimization theory and applications; applied functional analysis; numerical analysis. *Mailing Add:* Dept of Math McGill Univ 805 Sherbrooke W Montreal PQ H3A 2K6 Can

ZLOCHOWER, ISAAC AARON, b New York, NY, Mar 10, 38; m 65; c 5. PHYSICAL CHEMISTRY. *Educ:* Brooklyn Col, BS, 59; Columbia Univ, MA, 63, PhD(chem physics), 66. *Prof Exp:* Res asst, Sch Mines, Columbia Univ, 65-67, res assoc, 67; chemist, Esso Res & Eng Co, NJ, 67-68, res chemist, 68-70, sr res chemist, 70-74, RES ASSOC FIBER GLASS DIV, PPG INDUSTS, INC, 74- *Concurrent Pos:* Lectr chem eng, Univ Pittsburgh, 75. *Res:* Surface chemistry of glass fibers, reinforced cements, leached fiber catalysts; automobile exhaust conversion; characterization of liquid membranes. *Mailing Add:* 2205 Shady Ave Pittsburgh PA 15217

ZLOT, WILLIAM LEONARD, b New York, NY, June 20, 29; m 56; c 2. MATHEMATICS. *Educ:* City Col New York, BS, 50; Columbia Univ, MA, 52, MBA, 53, PhD(math educ), 57, MA, 59. *Prof Exp:* Lectr math, City Col New York, 53-57, instr, 57-59; assoc prof, Paterson State Col, 59-61; from asst prof to assoc prof math educ, Yeshiva Univ, 61-67; assoc prof math, City Col New York, 67-69; PROF MATH EDUC, DIV SCI & MATH EDUC, SCH EDUC, NY UNIV, 69- *Mem:* Am Math Soc; Math Asn Am. *Mailing Add:* Div Sci & Math Educ Sch of Educ NY Univ 32 Washington Pl New York NY 10003

ZLOTNICK, MARTIN, b New York, NY, Feb 16, 28; div; c 4. AERONAUTICAL ENGINEERING. *Educ:* NY Univ, BAeroE, 48; Univ Va, MAeroE, 51. *Prof Exp:* Aeronaut res scientist, Nat Adv Comt Aeronaut, Va, 48-53; prin aerodynamicist, Repub Aviation Corp, NY, 53-55; 53-55; prin staff scientist, Avco Res & Adv Develop, Mass, 55-62; mem prof staff, Hudson Inst, NY, 62-65; prin res scientist, Heliodyne Corp, Calif, 65-66 & Avco Everett Res Lab, Mass, 66-68; phys scientist, US Army Advan Ballistic Missile Defense Agency, 68-75; proj officer, 75-80, BR CHIEF ADVAN CONCEPTS, DEPT ENERGY, 80- *Concurrent Pos:* Consult, Hudson Inst, 66-68. *Mem:* Am Inst Aeronaut & Astronaut; Sigma Xi. *Res:* Interaction of technology with political-strategic problems; aerospace weapon-system analysis; applied research in energy technology. *Mailing Add:* Dept of Energy Washington DC 20545

ZMESKAL, OTTO, b Chicago, Ill, July 16, 15; m 40; c 3. PHYSICAL METALLURGY. *Educ:* Ill Inst Technol, BS, 36, MS, 38; Mass Inst Technol, ScD(phys metall), 41. *Prof Exp:* Apprentice, Carnegie-Ill Steel Corp, 36; from instr to asst prof metall, Ill Inst Technol, 36-43, prof metall eng & dir dept, 46-54; asst metall, Mass Inst Technol, 38-41; res metallurgist, Universal-Cyclops Steel Corp, 43-45, dir res, 45-46; res prof metall eng, Univ Fla, 54-58; dean col eng, 58-70, PROF CHEM ENG, UNIV TOLEDO, 70- *Honors & Awards:* Am Soc Metals Award, 53. *Mem:* Am Soc Metals; Am Soc Eng Educ; Am Inst Mining, Metall & Petrol Engrs; Nat Soc Prof Engrs; Brit Iron & Steel Inst. *Res:* Kinetics of formation of sigma phase; tempering of high alloy steels; development of high temperature alloys; powder metallurgy. *Mailing Add:* Dept of Chem Eng Univ of Toledo Toledo OH 43606

ZMIJEWSKI, CHESTER MICHAEL, b Buffalo, NY, June 3, 32; m 54; c 4. IMMUNOLOGY. *Educ:* Univ Buffalo, BA, 55, MA, 57, PhD(immunol), 60; Millard Fillmore Hosp, cert med tech, 55. *Prof Exp:* Asst bact & immunol, Sch Med, Univ Buffalo, 55-58, instr & res fel, 60-61; asst prof clin path & dir blood bank, Med Col Va, 61-63; from asst prof immunol to assoc prof, Sch Med, Duke Univ, 63-70; dir transplantation immunol, Ortho Res Found, 70-73; ASSOC PROF PATH, SCH MED, UNIV PA, 75-, DIR CLIN IMMUNOL, WILLIAM PEPPER LAB, UNIV PA HOSP, 73- *Concurrent Pos:* Lectr, Approved Sch Med Technol, 59-61; consult blood bank & serol labs, Millard Fillmore Hosp, Buffalo, 60-61; mem ad hoc subcomt stand adv panel collab res in transplantation & immunol, NIH, 64; immunologist, Yerkes Regional Primate Res Ctr, 65; assoc res prof, Sch Med, State Univ NY Buffalo. *Mem:* Affil Royal Soc Med; Am Asn Immunol; NY Acad Sci; Int Soc Blood Transfusion; Am Asn Blood Banks. *Res:* Immunohematology; immunogenetics; histocompatibility testing for human allo-transplantation; cancer research and tissue culture. *Mailing Add:* William Pepper Lab Hosp Univ Pa Philadelphia PA 19104

ZMOLA, PAUL C(ARL), b Chicago, Ill, Nov 21, 23; wid; c 1. ENGINEERING. *Educ:* Purdue Univ, BS, 44, MS, 47, PhD(eng), 50. *Prof Exp:* Mfg engr, Western Elec Co, 44-45; instr mech eng, Purdue Univ, 45-48; sr develop engr, Oak Ridge Nat Lab, 50-55; mgr reactor eng, Small Submarine Reactor Proj, Combustion Eng, Inc, 56-59, mgr adv develop, Combustion Div, 59-66, mgr thermal design, 67-71, mgr res & develop prod sales, Power Systs Group, 72-76, dir, Tech Liaison Corp, Group, 77-80; CONSULT, 81- *Mem:* AAAS; Am Soc Mech Engrs; Am Nuclear Soc. *Res:* Nuclear reactor design and development; heat transfer; thermodynamics; fluid mechanics. *Mailing Add:* 5409 Newington Rd Bethesda MD 20816

ZMOLEK, WILLIAM G, b Toledo, Iowa, July 3, 21; m 45; c 5. ANIMAL SCIENCE. *Educ:* Iowa State Col, BS, 44, MS, 51. *Prof Exp:* County exten dir, 44-47, PROF ANIMAL SCI, AGR EXTEN SERV, IOWA STATE UNIV, 63-, EXTEN LIVESTOCK SPECIALIST, 48- *Concurrent Pos:* Agr rep, Newton Nat Bank, 48. *Honors & Awards:* Outstanding Educ Accomplishments Extension Award, Am Animal Sci Asn, 78. *Mem:* Am Soc Animal Sci. *Mailing Add:* Kildee Hall 109 Iowa State Univ Ames IA 50010

ZOBEL, BRUCE JOHN, b Calif, Feb 11, 20; m 41; c 4. FOREST GENETICS. *Educ:* Univ Calif, BS, 43, MF, 49, PhD(forest genetics), 51. *Prof Exp:* Asst to logging engr, Pac Lumber Co, 43-44; sr lab asst, Univ Calif, 46-49; silviculturist, Tex Forest Serv, 51-56; assoc prof forest genetics, 56-58, prof, 58-62, Edwin F Conger distinguished prof forestry, 62-80, EMER PROF & CONSULT, NC STATE UNIV, 80- *Honors & Awards:* Biol Res Award, Am Soc Foresters, 68; Res Award, Tech Asn Pulp & Paper Asn, 73, Gold Medal, 75; Oliver Max Gardner Award, 72; Outstanding Exten Serv Award, NC State Univ, 73 & Forest Farmer Award, 78. *Mem:* Fel Am Soc Foresters; fel Tech Asn Pulp & Paper Asn; fel Int Acad Wood Sci. *Res:* Silviculture. *Mailing Add:* Sch of Forest Resources NC State Univ Raleigh NC 27607

ZOBEL, CARL RICHARD, b Pittsburgh, Pa, Aug 29, 28; m 55; c 2. MOLECULAR BIOPHYSICS, BIOPHYSICAL CHEMISTRY. *Educ:* Purdue Univ, BS, 51; Univ Rochester, PhD(phys chem), 54. *Prof Exp:* Res assoc physics, Univ Mich, 54-56; asst prof chem, Am Univ Beirut, 56-59; res assoc biophys, Johns Hopkins Univ, 59-62; asst prof, 62-68, ASSOC PROF BIOPHYS SCI, SCH MED, STATE UNIV NY BUFFALO, 68- *Concurrent Pos:* Du Pont fel infrared spectros, 55-56. *Mem:* AAAS; Electron Micros Soc Am; Biophys Soc; Am Soc Cell Biol. *Res:* Electron microscopy, particularly of macromolecules and ordered complexes of macromolecules; development of staining methods for electron microscopy; structure and function of motile systems, particularly striated muscle; physico-chemical studies of macromolecules and their interactions. *Mailing Add:* Dept of Biophys Sci Sch of Med State Univ NY 118 Cary Hall Buffalo NY 14214

ZOBEL, DONALD BRUCE, b Salinas, Calif, July 17, 42; m 66; c 2. PLANT ECOLOGY. *Educ:* NC State Univ, BS, 64; Duke Univ, MA, 66, PhD(bot), 68. *Prof Exp:* Asst prof, 68-74, ASSOC PROF BOT, ORE STATE UNIV, 74- *Mem:* Ecol Soc Am; AAAS. *Res:* Physiological plant ecology; water relations of plants. *Mailing Add:* Dept Bot & Plant Path Ore State Univ Corvallis OR 97331

ZOBEL, EDWARD C(HARLES), b Manistee, Mich, Oct 5, 21; m 45; c 3. ENGINEERING MECHANICS. *Educ:* Univ Mich, BS, 48, MS, 50. *Prof Exp:* Spec instr aeronaut eng, Wayne State Univ, 48, instr eng mech, 48-51; mat rev engr, Aircraft Div, Kaiser Corp, Mich, 51-52; field engr, Div Indust Serv, Wash State Univ, 52-54; asst prof, 54-59, ASSOC PROF ENG MECH, WAYNE STATE UNIV, 59- *Concurrent Pos:* Consult, Army Tank Automotive Command, 61-; prin investr, Mich Dept State Hwy & Fed Hwy Admin, 70-72. *Mem:* Soc Exp Stress Anal; assoc Am Inst Aeronaut & Astronaut. *Res:* Vibrational and structural theory; transverse vibration theory. *Mailing Add:* Dept of Mech Eng Sci Wayne State Univ Detroit MI 48202

ZOBEL, HENRY FREEMAN, b Ft Scott, Kans, Mar 13, 22; m 44; c 3. PHYSICAL CHEMISTRY, ANALYTICAL CHEMISTRY. *Educ:* Univ Ill, Champaign, BS, 50, MS, 51. *Prof Exp:* Chemist, Northern Regional Lab, Ill, 51-67; SECT LEADER STRUCT PROPERTIES, MOFFETT TECH CTR, CPC INT, INC, 67- *Concurrent Pos:* Corn Industs res fel, Northern Regional Lab, Ill, 65-67; mem sci adv comt, Am Inst Baking. *Mem:* Am Chem Soc; Am Asn Cereal Chem. *Res:* Physical properties and structure of natural polymers such as granular starches, starch derived products and synthetic polymers. *Mailing Add:* Moffett Tech Ctr CPC Int Inc Box 345 Argo IL 60501

ZOBELL, CLAUDE E, b Provo, Utah, Aug 22, 04; m 30, 46; c 2. MICROBIOLOGY. *Educ:* Utah State Univ, BS, 27, MS, 29; Univ Calif, PhD(bact), 31. *Hon Degrees:* DSc, Utah State Univ, 80. *Prof Exp:* Prin pub sch, Idaho, 24-26; asst bact, Exp Sta, Utah State Univ, 27-28, instr col, 28-29; asst, Hooper Found, 30-31, from instr to prof microbiol, 32-72, in charge biol prog, 36-37, asst dir, 37-48, chmn div marine biol, 57-60, EMER PROF MICROBIOL, SCRIPPS INST OCEANOG, UNIV CALIF, 72- *Concurrent Pos:* Assoc, Univ Wis, 38-39; assoc oceanog, Inst Woods Hole, 39; spec fel, Rockefeller Found, 47-48; consult chmn, Comt Geomicrobiol, Nat Res Coun, 46-56; lectr, Princeton Univ, 48; mem polar microbiol comt, Am Soc Microbiol-Nat Res Coun, 57-72; founder & ed-in-chief, Geomicrobiol J, 78-82. *Mem:* AAAS; Am Soc Microbiol; Am Soc Limnol & Oceanog (pres, 49); Brit Soc Gen Microbiol; Soc Indust Microbiol. *Res:* Biofouling; marine microbiology; petroleum microbiology; barobiology; microbial modification of petroleum; effects of deep-sea pressure on microbial activities; attachment of bacteria to solid surfaces; the functions of microorganisms as geochemical agents. *Mailing Add:* Scripps Inst of Oceanog A-002 Univ of Calif San Diego La Jolla CA 92093

ZOBRIST, GEORGE W(INSTON), b Highland, Ill, Feb 13, 34; m 55; c 3. ELECTRICAL ENGINEERING, COMPUTER SIMULATION. *Educ:* Univ Mo, BSEE, 58, PhD(elec eng), 65; Wichita State Univ, MSEE, 61. *Prof Exp:* Electronic scientist, US Naval Ord Test Sta, Calif, 58-59; assoc engr, Boeing Co, Kans, 59-60; res assoc radar, Res Dept, Wichita State Univ, 60-61; from instr to assoc prof elec eng, Univ Mo-Columbia, 61-69, undergrad prog dir, 68-69; assoc prof elec & electronic systs, Univ SFla, 69-70; prof elec eng & chmn dept, Univ Miami, 70-71; prof elec & electronic systs, Univ SFla, 71-76; prof elec eng & chmn dept, Univ Toledo, 76-79; DIR COMPUT SCI & ENG, SANBORN, STEKETSE, OTIS & EVANS, 79- *Concurrent Pos:* Lectr, Stevens Inst Technol, 67; NASA res grant, 67-68; sr vis res fel, Univ Edinburgh, 72-73, res prof, 73-74; elec engr & consult, US Naval Ord Test Sta, Calif, 65; consult, Wilcox Elec, Mo, 66-69, M Jones Assoc, Calif, 67-68, Med Serv Bur, Fla, 69-73, Defense Commun Agency, 71-72, US Naval Res Lab, 71-72, NASA Kennedy Space Ctr, Fla, 73-76 & Prestolite Co, Toledo, 77- *Mem:* Inst Elec & Electronics Engrs; Nat Soc Prof Engrs. *Res:* Radar circuitry design; electronic countermeasure research; topological analysis of networks; electrical engineering education; computer-aided circuit design; DC motor design. *Mailing Add:* Sanborn Steketse Otis & Evans 1001 Madison Ave Toledo OH 43624

ZODROW, ERWIN LORENZ, b Deutsch Krone, Ger, Jan 5, 34; Can citizen; m 63; c 1. MATHEMATICAL GEOLOGY, SULFATE MINERALOGY. *Educ:* St Francis Xavier Univ, BSc, 62; Pa State Univ, MSc, 67; Univ Western Ont, PhD(geol), 73. *Prof Exp:* Asst party chief geol, Que Cartier Mining Co, 61; field engr, Algoma Ore Properties, 62-63; mem staff mine & develop, Iron Ore Co Can, 64-68; lectr & asst prof, Xavier Col, 70-78; ASSOC PROF GEOL, COL CAPE BRETON, 78- *Concurrent Pos:* Res assoc, NS Mus, 77- *Mem:* AAAS; Mineral Asn Can; Am Inst Mining, Metall & Petrol Engrs; Can Inst Mining & Metall; Mineral Soc Am. *Res:* Mathematical geology such as sampling designs for minerals, factor analysis, lognormal distributions of percentages and methodology; sulfate mineralogy, paragenesis and products of pyrite; paleobotany, especially Pennsylvanian fossil flora of Sydney Coalfield, Nova Scotia, Canada; trace elements in coal. *Mailing Add:* Dept of Geol Col of Cape Breton Sydney NS B1P 6L2 Can

ZOEBISCH, OSCAR CORNELIUS, b Albany, Minn, Dec 16, 19; m 45; c 4. PLANT GENETICS, PLANT PHYSIOLOGY. *Educ:* Univ Minn, BS, 46, MS & PhD(plant genetics), 50. *Prof Exp:* Asst prof agr & asst agronomist, Univ Hawaii, 50-52; asst lab mgr pineapple div, Libby, McNeill & Libby, 52-56, asst plantation mgr, 56-57, asst dir res, Fla Citrus Div, 57-58, mgr agr res, Eastern Div Labs, 58-60, asst dir agr res, Eastern & Can Div & mgr cent agr res, 60-65; dir develop & serv, New England States, biol dept, 65-79, SR RES BIOLOGIST, EXP STA, E I DU PONT DE NEMOURS & CO, INC, 79- *Mem:* Am Soc Agron; Am Entom Soc; Am Phytopath Soc; AAAS. *Res:* Research and development of pineapple, citrus and vegetable crops. *Mailing Add:* E I du Pont de Nemours & Co Inc 308 E Lancaster Ave Wynnewood PA 19096

ZOELLER, GILBERT NORBERT, b St Louis, Mo, Sept 30, 31; m 53; c 3. DENTISTRY. *Educ:* St Louis Univ, BS, 53, DDS, 57. *Prof Exp:* Instr pedodontics, St Louis Univ, Sch Dent, 57-62, assoc prof prosthodontics, 66-70; assoc prof & dir clin, Dent Fac, 74-76, PROF & DIR GEN PROG DENT, SCH DENT MED, SOUTHERN ILL UNIV, 78-; HOSP STAFF DENT, ST ANTHONY'S MED CTR, 75-; PVT PRACT GEN DENT, ST LOUIS, 57- *Concurrent Pos:* Several USPHS grants, 68-70. *Mem:* Int Asn Dent Res; Sigma Xi. *Res:* Dental materials; in vitro penetration of acid etchant into dentin; biomedical bases for dental therapy; effect of x-rays upon fetal rat calvarial bone cells. *Mailing Add:* 10004 Kennerly Rd St Anthony's Med Ctr St Louis MO 63128

ZOELLNER, JOHN ARTHUR, b Ames, Iowa, July 27, 27; m 51; c 3. STATISTICS. *Educ:* Iowa State Col, BS, 51, MS, 53. *Prof Exp:* Mgr statist methods, Gen Elec Co, 56-61; supvr anal & prog, IIT Res Inst, 61-63, mgr opers dept, 63-66, asst dir opers, 66-69, dep dir opers, 69-75; DEP & TECH DIR, ELECTROMAGNETIC COMPATIBILITY ANAL CTR, DEPT OF DEFENSE, 76- *Mem:* Inst Elec & Electronics Engrs; Asn Comput Mach; Opers Res Soc Am. *Res:* Analytical engineering; operational and statistical analysis. *Mailing Add:* Electromagnetic Compat Anal Ctr Bldg 120 North Severn Annapolis MD 21402

ZOGG, CARL A, b Belleville, Ill, Feb 9, 27; m 52; c 6. MEDICAL PHYSIOLOGY, NUTRITION. *Educ:* Univ Ill, BS, 49, MS, 60, PhD(nutrit in dairy sci), 62. *Prof Exp:* Milk sanitarian, Dressel Young Dairy, 49-58; asst dairy sci, Univ Ill. 58-62, res assoc physiol reprod, 62-63; asst prof physiol, 63-71, assoc prof physiol & pharmacol, 71-78, PROF PHYSIOL, SCH MED, UNIV N DAK, 78- *Res:* Ruminant nutrition and physiology; male reproductive physiology; physiology of lactation of simple stomached animals; hyperbaric physiology, nutrition and microbiology; nutritional studies conducted on subjects exposed to hyperbaric helium-molecular oxygen environmental conditions; cecal function in monogastric animals and gastrointestinal motility. *Mailing Add:* Dept of Physiol Univ of NDak Sch of Med Grand Forks ND 58201

ZOGLIO, MICHAEL ANTHONY, b Providence, RI, June 27, 36; m 59; c 3. PHARMACEUTICAL CHEMISTRY. *Educ:* Univ RI, BSc, 58; Univ Minn, PhD(med chem), 66. *Prof Exp:* Mgr pharm res, Sandoz Wander Inc, 64-70; dir pharmaceut develop, Hoechst Pharmaceut Inc, 70-72; dir pharmaceut res & develop, Merrell Nat Labs, 72-81, RES ASSOC, MERRELL-DOW, PHARMACEUT, 81- *Concurrent Pos:* Adj asst prof biopharmaceut, Col Pharm, Univ Cincinnati, 74-; vis prof pharm, Univ Wis, 75- *Mem:* Fel Am Pharmaceut Asn; AAAS; Am Asn Col Pharm. *Res:* Drug stability; drug absorption; physicochemical characterization of pharmaceuticals; physical aspects of dosage form processing. *Mailing Add:* Merrel Dow Pharmaceut Inc 2110 E Galbraith Rd Cincinnati OH 45215

ZOGORSKI, JOHN STEWARD, b Trenton, NJ, Mar 5, 46; c 4. ENVIRONMENTAL SCIENCE, WATER RESOURCES. *Educ:* Drexel Univ, BS, 69; Rutgers Univ, MS, 72, PhD(environ sci), 75. *Prof Exp:* Hydrologist water resources div, US Geol Surv, 65-79; proj mgr, Rice Univ, 73-74; asst prof civil & environ eng, Univ Louisville, 74-77; ASSOC PROF ENVIRON SCI, IND UNIV, 77-, DIR, ENVIRON SYSTS APPLN CTR, 79- *Concurrent Pos:* Co-prin investr, NJ Water Resources Res Inst, Rutgers Univ, 72-73 & Clark Maritime Proj, Sverdrup & Parcel & Assocs, Univ Louisville, 74-75; proj dir & prin investr, Colgate-Palmolive, Inc, 75; proj dir & prin investr, Louisville Water Co, 74-77 & Ky Water Resources Res Inst, 77-78; co-prin investr, Ohio State Univ & Ind Univ, 77-78, Indianapolis Water Co, 78-80, Ind State Bd Health, 78-80, Ind Dept Natural Resources, 78-79 & 80-81, US Geol Surv, 80-81 & City Columbus, Ind, 80-81; prin investr, US Environ Protection Agency, 81-82; consult, Union Carbide Corp, 80 & US Environ Protection Agency, 81. *Mem:* Am Water Works Asn; Water Pollution Control Fedn; Int Asn Water Pollution Res; Am Water Resources Asn; Int Water Resources Asn. *Res:* Environmental sciences and environmental engineering with emphasis on water resources and water quality assessment; applied hydrology; management of river basins; water and wastewater treatment; aquatic chemistry; impacts of surface mining; removal of trace organics from drinking water. *Mailing Add:* Sch of Pub & Environ Affairs 400 E Seventh St Bloomington IN 47405

ZOGRAFI, GEORGE, b New York, NY, Mar 13, 36; m 57; c 3. PHARMACEUTICAL CHEMISTRY, SURFACE CHEMISTRY. *Educ:* Columbia Univ, BS, 56; Univ Mich, MS, 58, PhD(pharmaceut chem), 61. *Hon Degrees:* DS, Columbia Univ, 76. *Prof Exp:* Asst prof pharm, Columbia Univ, 61-64; from asst prof to assoc prof, Univ Mich, 64-72; PROF PHARM, UNIV WIS-MADISON, 72-, DEAN, 75- *Concurrent Pos:* Am Found Pharmaceut Educ Pfeiffer Mem res fel, Utrecht Univ, 70-71. *Mem:* AAAS; Am Pharmaceut Asn; fel Am Acad Pharmaceut Sci; Am Chem Soc. *Res:* Physical chemical basis for therapeutic activity of drugs; interfacial activity of drugs; lipids and proteins emphasizing structure and function of biological membranes. *Mailing Add:* Sch of Pharm Univ of Wis-Madison Madison WI 53706

ZOLBER, KATHLEEN KEEN, b Walla Walla, Wash, Dec 9, 16; m. NUTRITION. *Educ:* Walla Walla Col, BS, 41; Wash State Univ, MA, 61; Univ Wis, PhD(food systs admin), 68. *Prof Exp:* Food serv dir, Walla Walla Col, 41-50, mgr col store, 51-59, from asst prof to assoc prof foods & nutrit, 59-64; dir dietetic internship, 67-71, PROF NUTRIT, LOMA LINDA UNIV, 64-, DIR DIETETIC EDUC, 71-, DIR NUTRIT SERV, MED CTR, 72- *Mem:* Am Dietetic Asn (pres-elect, 81-82, pres, 82-83); Am Mgt Asn; Am Pub Health Asn; Am Home Econ Asn; AAAS. *Res:* Productivity in food service systems; role of technicians in heath care professions; health and nutrition. *Mailing Add:* Box 981 Loma Linda CA 92354

ZOLLA-PAZNER, SUSAN BETH, b Chicago, Ill, Feb 25, 42. IMMUNOLOGY. *Educ:* Stanford Univ, BA, 63; Univ Calif, San Francisco, PhD(microbiol), 67. *Prof Exp:* NIH fel, 67-69, asst prof, 69-78, ASSOC PROF PATH, MED SCH, NY UNIV, 78-, RES MICROBIOLOGIST, MANHATTAN VET ADMIN HOSP, 69-, CHIEF CLIN IMMUNOL, 79- *Mem:* AAAS; Am Asn Immunol. *Res:* Regulation of the immune response; effects of malignoncies on immune function. *Mailing Add:* Dept of Path NY Univ Sch of Med New York NY 10016

ZOLLARS, RICHARD LEE, b Minneapolis, Minn, Nov 9, 46; m 68; c 1. POLYMERS, STABILITY THEORY. *Educ:* Univ Minn, BChe, 68; Univ Colo, MS, 72, PhD(chem eng), 74. *Prof Exp:* Sr engr, Union Carbide Corp, 74-77; asst prof chem eng, Univ Colo, 77-78; asst prof, 78-81, ASSOC PROF CHEM ENG, WASH STATE UNIV, 81- *Mem:* Am Inst Chem Engrs; Am Chem Soc; Am Soc Eng Educ; AAAS. *Res:* Fundamental aspects of hetero phase polymerizations and how they affect and are affected by reactor conditions; interfacial phenomenon; stability analysis; particulate systems. *Mailing Add:* Dept Chem Eng Wash State Univ Pullman WA 99164

ZOLLER, PAUL, b Lucerne, Switz, Nov 23, 39; nat US; m 67; c 2. POLYMER PHYSICS. *Educ:* Swiss Fed Inst Technol, dipl phys, 65; Univ Wis-Madison, MSc, 67, PhD(physics), 68. *Prof Exp:* Res assoc physics, Univ Wis, 68-69; res physicist polymers, Film Dept, E I du Pont de Nemours & Co, 69-72; prof polymer sci, Neu-Technikum Buchs, Switz, 72-77; MEM STAFF POLYMER SCI, CENT RES & DEVELOP DEPT, E I DU PONT DE NEMOURS & CO, INC, 77- *Mem:* Am Phys Soc. *Res:* Pressure, volume and temperature relationships of polymers; polymer rheology; characterization and low-temperature properties of polymers; polymer processing. *Mailing Add:* Cent Res & Develop Dept E I du Pont de Nemours & Co Inc Wilmington DE 19898

ZOLLER, WILLIAM H, b Cedar Rapids, Iowa, Mar 3, 43; m 69; c 4. NUCLEAR CHEMISTRY. *Educ:* Univ Alaska, BS, 65; Mass Inst Technol, PhD(nuclear chem), 69. *Prof Exp:* Tech asst, Inst Geophys, Univ Hawaii, 65; res asst, Arthur A Noyes Nuclear Chem Ctr, Mass Inst Technol, 65-69, res assoc, 69; res assoc, Inst Geophys, Univ Hawaii, 69-70; asst prof nuclear & environ chem, 70-74, assoc prof nuclear & environ chem, 74-79, PROF NUCLEAR & ANAL CHEM, UNIV MD, COLLEGE PARK, 79- *Mem:* AAAS; Am Phys Soc; Am Meteorol Soc; Am Chem Soc; Am Geophys Union. *Res:* Nuclear phenomenon and environmental chemical problems, especially with respect to air and water pollution; instrumental neutron and photon activation analysis of air pollutants; atmospheric chemical studies in Antarctica the Arctic and Hawaii. *Mailing Add:* Dept Chem Univ Md College Park MD 20742

ZOLLINGER, JOSEPH LAMAR, b Salt Lake City, Utah, July 9, 27; m 52; c 7. ORGANIC CHEMISTRY. *Educ:* Univ Utah, BS, 51, PhD(chem), 54. *Prof Exp:* Res org chemist, M W Kellogg Co, 54-57; res specialist, 57-77, sr res specialist, 77-79, SR PATENT LIAISON, 3M CO, 79- *Mem:* Am Chem Soc. *Res:* Organic fluorine compounds; elastomers; fluoronitrogen compounds; polymers; silicon compounds; abrasion resistant coatings. *Mailing Add:* 3M Com Chem Div 3M Ctr 236-GC-01 St Paul MN 55144

ZOLLMAN, DEAN ALVIN, b Kendallville, Ind, Oct 13, 41; m 74; c 2. PHYSICS EDUCATION. *Educ:* Ind Univ, BS, 64, MS, 65; Univ Md, PhD(physics), 70. *Prof Exp:* Asst prof physics, Kans State Univ, 70-75; staff physicist, Am Asn Physics Teachers, 75-77; ASSOC PROF PHYSICS, KANS STATE UNIV, 77- *Concurrent Pos:* Film repository ed, Am Asn Physics Teachers, 76-; vis assoc prof physics, Univ Utah, 81-82. *Mem:* Am Asn Physics Teachers; Nat Asn Res Sci Teaching; Nat Sci Teachers Asn. *Res:* Instructional strategies to teach physics effectively to college students; problem solving and reasoning abilities of college students; applications of videodise and computer technologies to physics instruction. *Mailing Add:* Dept Physics Kans State Univ Manhattan KS 66506

ZOLLO, RONALD FRANCIS, b Brooklyn, NY, Sept 13, 41. CIVIL ENGINEERING, MATERIALS SCIENCE. *Educ:* Carnegie Inst Technol, BS, 63, MS, 66; Carnegie-Mellon Univ, PhD(civil eng), 71. *Prof Exp:* Lectr civil eng, City Col New York, 69, asst prof, 70-72; ASSOC PROF CIVIL ENG, UNIV MIAMI, 72- *Concurrent Pos:* Consult, Roman Stone Construct Co, Inc, 71-76; res fel, Battelle Mem Inst, 72-76; NSF res grant, City Col New York & Battelle Mem Inst, 72-76; consult prof engr. *Mem:* Am Soc Civil Engrs; Am Soc Eng Educ; Am Concrete Inst. *Res:* Hybrid computer techniques applied to civil engineering problems; structural and solid mechanics; fiber reinforced concrete; ferro cement. *Mailing Add:* 3050 SW 21st St Miami FL 33145

ZOLLWEG, JOHN ALLMAN, b Rochester, NY, July 3, 42; m 67; c 2. PHYSICAL CHEMISTRY. *Educ:* Oberlin Col, AB, 64; Cornell Univ, PhD(phys chem), 69. *Prof Exp:* NSF fel, Mass Inst Technol, 68-70; asst prof, 70-76, ASSOC PROF CHEM, UNIV MAINE, ORONO, 76- *Concurrent Pos:* Vis res fel, Cornell Univ, 80-81. *Res:* Optical mixing spectroscopy; experimental and theoretical study of fluids, including simulation of fluid systems on a digital computer; fluids, including simulation of two dimensional systems on a digital computer and excess enthalpies of mixtures at cryogenic temperatures. *Mailing Add:* Dept of Chem Aubert Hall Univ of Maine Orono ME 04469

ZOLLWEG, ROBERT JOHN, b Medina, NY, Aug 1, 24; m 46; c 2. EXPERIMENTAL PHYSICS. *Educ:* Northwestern Univ, BS, 49, MS, 50; Cornell Univ, PhD(physics), 55. *Prof Exp:* Asst, Cornell Univ, 50-54; sr physicist, 54-68, adv physicist, 68-80, CONSULT PHYSICIST, RES LABS, WESTINGHOUSE ELEC CORP, 80- *Mem:* Am Phys Soc. *Res:* Solid state optics; photoemission and optical absorption; electron reflection from metal surfaces; optical properties of plasmas; thermionic energy conversions; arc discharges. *Mailing Add:* Westinghouse Res Labs Pittsburgh PA 15235

ZOLMAN, JAMES F, b Dayton, Ohio, Aug 1, 36; m 56; c 3. NEUROPSYCHOLOGY, PSYCHOPHARMACOLOGY. *Educ:* Denison Univ, BS, 58; Univ Calif, Berkeley, PhD(psychol), 63. *Prof Exp:* NIMH fel, Dept Psychiat & Brain Res Inst, Univ Calif, Los Angeles, 62-64; asst prof, 64-69, assoc prof, 69-79, PROF PHYSIOL & BIOPHYS, MED CTR, UNIV KY, 79- *Concurrent Pos:* Found Fund fel res psychiat, Inst Psychiat, London, Eng, 71-72; Fogarty sr int fel, Dept Animal Behaviour, Cambridge, Eng, 79-80. *Mem:* AAAS; Am Psychol Asn; Psychonomic Soc; Soc Neurosci; Int Soc Develop Psychobiol. *Res:* Developmental psychopharmacology. *Mailing Add:* Dept Physiol & Biophys Univ Ky Med Ctr Lexington KY 40536

ZOLNOWSKI, DENNIS RONALD, b Buffalo, NY, Mar 9, 43; m 71. NUCLEAR PHYSICS. *Educ:* Canisius Col, NY, BS, 64; Univ Notre Dame, PhD(physics), 71. *Prof Exp:* Res assoc, 71-73, RES SCIENTIST PHYSICS, CYCLOTRON INST, TEX A&M UNIV, 74- *Concurrent Pos:* Welch Found fel, 71-72. *Mem:* Am Phys Soc. *Res:* Heavy-ion reactions; structure; in-beam gamma ray and conversion electron experiments; isomeric states; radioactivity. *Mailing Add:* Cyclotron Inst Tex A&M Univ College Station TX 77840

ZOLOTOR, LAURENCE ARTHUR, b Kansas City, Mo, Nov 30, 41; m 60; c 4. VIROLOGY. *Educ:* Univ Mo-Kansas City, BS, 64, MS, 66; Kans State Univ, PhD(virol), 70. *Prof Exp:* Fel virol, Baylor Col Med, 70-72; res assoc chem carcinogenesis; Vet Admin Hosp, Univ Minn, 72-74; MICROBIOLOGIST VIROL, NAT CTR TOXICOL RES, 74- *Mem:* Am Soc Microbiol; Tissue Cult Asn. *Res:* Development of cell transformation bioassay systems involving the interaction of agents (physical, virial or chemical carcinogens). Validated systems will be used to evaluate agents as to their potential for producing or enhancing neoplasia and to study their toxicity level for cultured mammalian cells. *Mailing Add:* 6001 Pecan Lake Rd Little Rock AR 72204

ZOLOTOROFE, DONALD LEE, b Bronx, NY, Sept 5, 46. CHEMICAL ENGINEERING, POLYMER CHEMISTRY. *Educ:* Cornell Univ, BS, 67, MS, 69, PhD(chem eng), 71. *Prof Exp:* CHEM ENGR, ROHM AND HAAS CO, 71- *Res:* Physical properties of polymeric systems; bulk solution and emulsion polymerization processes (product and process development); high pressure process development; monomer process engineering. *Mailing Add:* Monomer & Fluid Process Eng 727 Norristown Rd Spring House PA 19477

ZOLTAI, TIBOR, b Gyor, Hungary, Oct 17, 25; m 50; c 3. MINERALOGY, CRYSTALLOGRAPHY. *Educ:* Univ Toronto, BASc, 55; Mass Inst Technol, PhD(mineral), 59. *Prof Exp:* From asst prof to assoc prof, 59-64, chmn dept geol & geophys, 63-71, PROF MINERAL, UNIV MINN, MINNEAPOLIS, 64- *Mem:* Geol Soc Am; Mineral Soc Am; Am Crystallog Asn; Mineral Asn Can. *Res:* Crystal structures and crystal chemistry of minerals. *Mailing Add:* Dept of Geol & Geophys Univ of Minn Minneapolis MN 55455

ZOLTAN, BART JOSEPH, b Budapest, Hungary, Dec 26, 46; US citizen; m 80; c 1. INSTRUMENTATION, ELECTRO-OPTICS. *Educ:* Fairleigh Dickinson Univ, BS, 69, MS, 73. *Prof Exp:* Sr engr, Kearfott Div, Singer Co, 69-77; SR RES ENGR, MED RES DIV, AM CYANAMID, 77- *Mem:* Inst Elec & Electronic Engrs; Instrument Soc Am. *Res:* Development of instrumentation in support of biomedical and pharmacological research; use of electro-optical techniques for measurements or analysis. *Mailing Add:* 152 De Wolf Rd Old Tappan NJ 07675

ZOLTANI, CSABA KALMAN, b Hungary, Jan 28, 37. GAS DYNAMICS, NUMERICAL ANALYSIS. *Educ:* Mass Inst Technol, BS, 59; Swiss Fed Inst Technol, ScD(mech eng), 73. *Prof Exp:* RES PHYSICIST, BALLISTIC RES LAB, ABERDEEN PROVING GROUND, 66-68, 70- *Mem:* Am Math Soc; Asn Comput Mach; Am Inst Aeronaut & Astronaut. *Res:* Combustion theory. *Mailing Add:* Ballistic Res Lab AMD Aberdeen Proving Ground MD 21005

ZOLTEWICZ, JOHN A, b Nanticoke, Pa, Dec 5, 35; m 65; c 3. ORGANIC CHEMISTRY. *Educ:* Princeton Unib, AB, 57, PhD(org chem), 60. *Prof Exp:* NATO fel, Univ Munich, 60-61; Shell Corp Fund fel, Brown Univ, 61-62, NIH fel, 62-63; from asst prof to assoc prof chem, 63-73, PROF CHEM, UNIV FLA, 73- *Mem:* Am Chem Soc. *Res:* Heterocyclic chemistry; kinetics; rates and mechanism of hydrogen-deuterium exchange in heterocycles; radical-anion heteroaromatic nucleophilic substitution; thiamine model studies; covalent amination. *Mailing Add:* Dept of Chem Univ of Fla Gainesville FL 32611

ZOLTON, RAYMOND PETER, b Jersey City, NJ, May 21, 39; m 60; c 3. HEMATOLOGY. *Educ:* Newark Col Eng, BS, 63; Univ Del, MS, 67; Purdue Univ, PhD(biochem), 72. *Prof Exp:* Engr dyes, E I du Pont de Nemours & Co, Inc, 63-68; res assoc, Wayne State Univ, 72-74; SR SCIENTIST COAGULATION, ORTHO DIAG INC, 74- *Concurrent Pos:* Mem thrombosis coun, Am Heart Asn. *Mem:* Am Soc Coagulation. *Res:* Development of diagnostic test for coagulation and fibrinolysis parameters. *Mailing Add:* 70 Cedar Grove Rd Sommerville NJ 08876

ZOMBECK, MARTIN VINCENT, b Peekskill, NY, Aug 14, 36; m 63; c 2. PHYSICS. *Educ:* Mass Inst Technol, BS, 57, PhD(physics), 69. *Prof Exp:* Observer, Smithsonian Astrophys Observ, 61-64; res asst physics, Mass Inst Technol, 64-69; proj scientist, Am Sci & Eng, Inc, 69-73; head physics & instrumentation, Damon Corp, 73-74; res assoc, Harvard Col Observ, 74-78; PHYSICIST, SMITHSONIAN ASTROPHYS OBSERV, 78- *Mem:* Am Phys Soc; Am Astron Soc; Int Astron Union. *Res:* Solar and stellar x-ray astronomy from rockets and space observatories; x-ray imaging instrumentation; x-ray optics; x-ray spectroscopy. *Mailing Add:* Ctr for Astrophys 60 Garden St Cambridge MA 02138

ZOMPA, LEVERETT JOSEPH, b Lawrence, Mass, May 31, 38; m 66; c 6. INORGANIC CHEMISTRY. *Educ:* Merrimack Col, BS, 59; Col Holy Cross, MS, 60; Boston Col, PhD(inorg chem), 64. *Prof Exp:* Asst prof chem, Boston Col, 64-65; fel, Mich State Univ, 65-66; from asst prof to assoc prof, 66-77, PROF CHEM, UNIV MASS, BOSTON, 77- CHMN DEPT, 73- *Mem:* Am Chem Soc; The Chem Soc; Sigma Xi. *Res:* Transition metal complexes of stereorestrictive amines and amino acids; complexes of anions-structive, bonding and selectivity. *Mailing Add:* 6 Kathleen Dr Andover MA 01810

ZOMZELY-NEURATH, CLAIRE ELEANORE, b Newark, NJ, July 4, 24; m 63. NEUROBIOLOGY. *Educ:* Columbia Univ, BS, 50; Harvard Univ, MS, 56, PhD(biochem, nutrit), 58. *Prof Exp:* Res technician, Columbia Univ, 50-53; res technician obstet & gynec, Sch Med, NY Univ, 53-54; Fulbright fel, Lab Comp Biochem, Col France, 58-59; res assoc med, Sch Med, NY Univ, 59-60; res biochemist, Monsanto Chem Co, Mo, 60-62; asst res biochemist, Sch Med, Univ Calif, Los Angeles, 62-70; mem biochem, Roche Inst Molecular Biol, 70-80; RES DIR, DEPT RES, QUEEN'S MED CTR, HONOLULU, HAWAII, 80- *Concurrent Pos:* Adj prof, Col Med & Dent NJ; adj prof biochem, Dept Physiol, John A Burns Sch Med, Univ Hawaii, 80- *Mem:* AAAS; Am Physiol Soc; Am Soc Biol Chem; Am Soc Neurochem; Int Soc Neurochem. *Res:* Regulation of cerebral protein synthesis; effects of environmental and behavioral factors on cerebral protein and nuclei acid synthesis during development and aging. *Mailing Add:* PO Box 861 Dept Res Queen's Med Ctr Honolulu HI 96808

ZON, GERALD, b Buffalo, NY, Apr 3, 45. ORGANIC CHEMISTRY. *Educ:* Canisius Col, BS, 67; Princeton Univ, PhD(org chem), 71. *Prof Exp:* Res assoc chem, Ohio State Univ, 71-72, NIH fel, 72-73; ASSOC PROF CHEM, CATH UNIV AM, 73- *Concurrent Pos:* Sr res assoc, Andrulis Res Corp, 75- *Mem:* Am Chem Soc; Fedn Am Supporting Sci & Technol. *Res:* Synthesis, stereochemistry and mechanism of anticancer drugs; novel reactions of organometalloid systems. *Mailing Add:* Dept of Chem Cath Univ of Am Washington DC 20064

ZONIS, IRWIN S(AMUEL), b Boston, Mass, June 22, 30; m 55; c 3. CHEMICAL ENGINEERING. *Educ:* Rensselaer Polytech Inst, BChE, 50; Mass Inst Technol, MS, 52. *Prof Exp:* Proj mgr, Nat Res Corp, 51-57; chief process engr, Columbia-Nat Corp, 57-59; supvr chem eng, Dixon Chem & Res Inc, 59-62; plant mgr, 62-63, opers mgr, 63-64, vpres opers, chem div, 64-69, GEN MGR CHEM DIV & V PRES, ESSEX CHEM CORP, 69- *Concurrent Pos:* Mem, NJ State Air Pollution Control Comn, 66-67 & NJ State Clean Air Coun, 68, vchmn, 70, 71, chmn, 72- *Mem:* AAAS; Am Chem Soc; Am Inst Chem Engrs; Air Pollution Control Asn. *Res:* Heavy inorganic chemicals; production management; air quality control; extractive metallurgy. *Mailing Add:* 71 Crestmont Rd West Orange NJ 07015

ZOOK, ALMA CLAIRE, b Los Angeles, Calif, June 27, 50. SPECTROSCOPY OF DIATOMIC MOLECULES. *Educ:* Pomona Col, Calif, BA, 72; Univ Calif, Berkeley, PhD(astron), 79. *Prof Exp:* Asst prof physics, Hamilton Col, 78-82; ASST PROF PHYSICS, POMONA COL, 82- *Mem:* Am Astron Soc; Astron Soc Pac; Optical Soc Am; Am Women Sci; AAAS. *Res:* Optical spectroscopy of peculiar red giants; laboratory spectroscopy of astronomically interesting molecules. *Mailing Add:* Dept Physics Pomona Col Claremont CA 91711

ZOOK, BERNARD CHARLES, b Beach, NC, Nov 1, 35; m 55; c 3. RADIATION PATHOLOGY, CONGENITAL DISEASES. *Educ:* Colo State Univ, BS, 62, DVM, 63; Am Col Vet Pathologists, cert, 68. *Prof Exp:* Res fel path, Med Sch, Harvard Univ, 63-67, asst, 67-69, res fel electron micros, Sch Pub Health, 67-68; res fel path, Angell Mem Animal Hosp, 63-67, assoc pathologist, 67-69; asst prof, 69-74, DIR, ANIMAL RES FACIL, MED CTR, GEORGE WASHINGTON UNIV, 72-, ASSOC PROF PATH, 74- *Concurrent Pos:* Res assoc, Smithsonian Inst, 69-; pathologist, Litton Bionetics, 76- *Mem:* Am Vet Med Asn; Am Col Vet Pathologists; Radiation Res Soc; Am Asn Pathologists; Nat Soc Med Res. *Mailing Add:* Med Ctr George Washington Univ 2300 Eye St NW Washington DC 20037

ZOOK, HARRY DAVID, b Milroy, Pa, Feb 8, 16; m 37; c 2. ORGANIC CHEMISTRY, ACADEMIC ADMINISTRATION. *Educ:* Pa State Col, BS, 38, PhD(org chem), 42; Northwestern Univ, MS, 39. *Prof Exp:* Asst org chem, Northwestern Univ, 38-39; asst chem, 39-41, from instr to assoc prof, 41-60, asst to vpres res, 65-70, PROF CHEM, PA STATE UNIV, UNIVERSITY PARK, 60-, ASST VPRES RES & ASSOC DEAN GRAD SCH, 70- *Concurrent Pos:* Vis lectr, Stanford Univ, 62. *Mem:* Am Chem Soc; Royal Soc Chem. *Res:* Kinetics and mechanism of organic reactions. *Mailing Add:* Pa State Univ 128 Willard University Park PA 16802

ZOOT, ROBERT MARTIN, research administration, see previous edition

ZORDAN, THOMAS ANTHONY, b Rockford, Ill, Nov 21, 43. PHYSICAL CHEMISTRY. *Educ:* Northern Ill Univ, BS, 65; Univ Louisville, PhD(phys chem), 69. *Prof Exp:* Res chemist, Gulf Res & Develop Co, 69-72; sr engr, Nuclear Ctr, Westinghouse Elec Corp, 72-74, mgr safeguards eval, 74-77, mgr reliability & safety, 77-78, mgr standard plant eng, 78-80; PROJ MGR, D'APPOLONIA CONSULT ENGRS, 80- *Mem:* Am Chem Soc; AAAS; Am Inst Chem Engrs. *Res:* Thermodynamics of solutions and pure substances; theory of the liquid state; calorimetry of chemical reactions; nuclear power reactor safety; nuclear power plant design. *Mailing Add:* 10 Duff Rd Pittsburgh PA 15235

ZORN, BICE SECHI, b Cagliari, Italy, May 20, 28; m 55. HIGH ENERGY PHYSICS. *Educ:* Univ Cagliari, Sardinia, PhD(physics), 52. *Prof Exp:* Asst physics, Padova, 52-56; physics assoc, Brookhaven Nat Lab, 56-62; res asst prof physics, 62-65, asst prof, 65-68, res assoc prof, 68-72, ASSOC PROF PHYSICS, UNIV MD, COLLEGE PARK, 72- *Mem:* Am Phys Soc; Ital Phys Soc. *Res:* High energy experimental particle physics using nuclear emulsions, bubble chambers, counter wire chambers, spark chambers and other existing techniques as detetors of particles. *Mailing Add:* Dept of Physics Univ of Md College Park MD 20740

ZORN, GUS TOM, b Ada, Okla, June 18, 24; m 55. HIGH ENERGY PHYSICS. *Educ:* Okla State Univ, BS, 48; Univ NMex, MS, 52; Univ Padua, PhD(physics), 54. *Prof Exp:* Res assoc physics, Brookhaven Nat Lab, 54-56, assoc physicist, 56-62; assoc prof physics, 62-72, PROF PHYSICS, UNIV MD, COLLEGE PARK, 72- *Concurrent Pos:* Vis scientist, Max Planck Inst Physics, 58. *Mem:* Fel Am Phys Soc; Ital Phys Soc. *Res:* Collective ion acceleration; electron ring accelerator for heavy ions; experimental high energy and elementary particle physics, using nuclear emulsions, bubble chambers, counters and spark chambers. *Mailing Add:* Dept of Physics & Astron Univ of Md College Park MD 20742

ZORN, JENS CHRISTIAN, b Halle, Ger, June 19, 31; US citizen; m 54; c 2. ATOMIC PHYSICS. *Educ:* Miami Univ, AB, 55; Yale Univ, MS, 57, PhD(physics), 61. *Prof Exp:* Engr, Sarkes Tarzian, Inc, Ind, 53-54; res asst physics, Univ Tubingen, 55-56; consult, Sch Med, Yale Univ, 59-61, instr, 61-62; from asst prof to assoc prof, 62-69, PROF PHYSICS, UNIV MICH, ANN ARBOR, 70- *Concurrent Pos:* Vis prof, Univ Puebla, 64-65; Phoenix fac fel, Univ Mich, 65-66. *Mem:* Fel Am Phys Soc; Am Asn Physics Teachers. *Res:* Atomic and molecular structure; atomic beams; microwave spectroscopy; laboratory astrophysics; space physics; scientific manpower administration. *Mailing Add:* Randall Lab of Physics Univ of Mich Ann Arbor MI 48104

ZORNIG, JOHN GRANT, b Davenport, Iowa, Apr 22, 44. COMMUNICATIONS ENGINEERING, DIGITAL SYSTEMS. *Educ:* Yale Univ, BS, 66, MS, 72, PhD(eng), 74. *Prof Exp:* Lectr, 74-75, assoc prof, 75-79, ASSOC PROF ELEC ENG, DEPT ENG & APPL SCI, YALE UNIV, 79- *Concurrent Pos:* Consult, Xybion Corp, 76-77, Periphonics Inc & Allied Corp, 81. *Mem:* Inst Elec & Electronics Engrs; Acoust Soc Am. *Res:* Sound propagation in the ocean for application to communication and detection systems by physical scale modelling; vehicular robotics. *Mailing Add:* 2157 Yale Sta 15 Prospect St New Haven CT 06520

ZOROWSKI, CARL F(RANK), b Pittsburgh, Pa, July 14, 30; m 54; c 3. MECHANICAL ENGINEERING. *Educ:* Carnegie Inst Technol, BS, 52, MS, 53, PhD(mech eng), 56. *Prof Exp:* From instr to assoc prof mech eng, Carnegie Inst Technol, 54-62; from assoc prof to prof mech & aerospace eng, 62-69, assoc head dept, 66-72, head dept, 72-79, R J REYNOLDS PROF MECH & AEROSPACE ENG, NC STATE UNIV, 69-, ASSOC DEAN, SCH ENG, 79- *Concurrent Pos:* Orgn Europ Econ Coop sr vis fel, Brit Iron & Steel Res Asn, Sheffield, Eng, 62; consult, Army Res Off, Durham, 71 & Monsanto Co, 63- *Honors & Awards:* Sigma Xi Res Award, 67; Westerm Elec Award, Am Soc Eng Educ, 68; Fiber Soc Res Award, 70; Charles Russ Richards Award, Am Soc Mech Engrs, 75. *Mem:* Am Soc Mech Engrs (vpres, 80-83); Am Soc Eng Educ; Fiber Soc; Soc Rheology. *Res:* Applied mechanics and mechanical design with emphasis on fibers, textile and composite property characterization and deformation mechanics; mechanical system and component design and dynamic response analysis; metal forming mechanics. *Mailing Add:* Dept of Mech & Aerospace Eng NC State Univ Raleigh NC 27650

ZORY, PETER S, JR, b Syracuse, NY, Oct 9, 36; m 61; c 2. LASERS. *Educ:* Syracuse Univ, BS, 58; Carnegie-Mellon Univ, PhD(physics), 64. *Prof Exp:* Physicist, Gyroscope Div, Sperry Rand Corp, 64-66, sr physicist, 66-68; mem prof staff, T J Watson Res Ctr, IBM Corp, 68-78; SR SCIENTIST, OPTICAL INFO SYSTS INC, 78- *Mem:* Inst Elec & Electronics Eng; Optical Soc Am. *Res:* Laser research. *Mailing Add:* Optical Info Systs Inc 350 Executive Blvd Elmsford NY 10523

ZORZOLI, ANITA, b New York, NY, Dec 27, 17. BIOCHEMISTRY, PHYSIOLOGY. *Educ:* Hunter Col, AB, 38; Columbia Univ, AM, 40; NY Univ, PhD(biol), 45. *Prof Exp:* Asst zool, Columbia Univ, 40-42; asst instr biol, NY Univ, 44-45; res asst path, Sch Med, Wash Univ, 45-46, instr biochem, Sch Dent, 46-48, res assoc pharmacol, Sch Med, 48-49, asst prof biochem, Sch Dent, 48-52; asst prof, Southern Ill Univ, 52-55; from assoc prof to prof biol, 55-73, PROF BIOL, JOHN GUY VASSAR CHAIR, VASSAR COL, 73- *Concurrent Pos:* Mem corp, Marine Biol Lab, Woods Hole. *Mem:* Fel AAAS; fel Geront Soc (vpres, 65-66); Am Physiol Soc; Int Asn Geront; Am Aging Asn. *Res:* Biochemistry of aging in mice. *Mailing Add:* Dept of Biol Vassar Col Poughkeepsie NY 12601

ZOSS, ABRAHAM OSCAR, b South Bend, Ind, Feb 17, 17; m 39; c 3. INDUSTRIAL CHEMISTRY. *Educ:* Univ Notre Dame, BSChE, 38, MS, 39, PhD(org chem), 41. *Prof Exp:* Asst, Univ Notre Dame, 39-41; res chemist, Gen Aniline & Film Corp, NJ, 41-43, Pa, 43-47, dept chemist, NJ, 47-49, area supt, 49-51, prod mgr, 51-54, tech mgr, 54-55, plant mgr, 55-57; mgr mfg admin, Chem Div, Minn Mining & Mfg Co, 57-58, div prod mgr, 58-60; vpres, Photek, Inc, 60-62; asst corp tech dir, Celanese Corp, 62-65, corp tech dir, 65-66, corp dir com develop, 66-69, vpres, Tenneco Chem, Inc, NY, 69-71, vpres corp dev, Universal Oil Prod Co, 71-72; group vpres, Engelhard Minerals & Chem Corp, 72-77; VPRES, CPS CHEM CO, INC, 77- *Concurrent Pos:* Mem field info agency, Off Tech Serv, US Dept Com, Ger, 46; mem, Textile Res Inst Centennial of Sci Award, Univ Notre Dame, 65. *Mem:* AAAS; Am Chem Soc; Am Inst Chem Engrs; Com Develop Asn; NY Acad Sci. *Res:* Acetylene and high polymer chemistry; petrochemicals; synthetic fibers; plastics; metal carbonyls and powders; coatings; forest products; catalytic chemistry; specialty monomers; polymers. *Mailing Add:* Claridge House I Verona NJ 07044

ZOSS, LESLIE M(ILTON), b Lockport, NY, Nov 23, 26; m 49; c 4. MECHANICAL ENGINEERING. *Educ:* Purdue Univ, BS, 49, MS, 50, PhD(mech eng), 52. *Prof Exp:* Instr mech eng lab, Purdue Univ, 49-50; res engr, Taylor Instrument Co, 52-55, tech training dir, 55-58; from asst prof to prof, 58-66, head dept, 65-76, RES PROF MECH ENG, VALPARAISO UNIV, 66- *Concurrent Pos:* Consult, Esso Res & Eng Co, 59-65, Am Oil Co, 66-68, Shell Chem Co, 69-70 & Eli Lilly & Co, 71- *Honors & Awards:* Donald P Eckman Educ Award, Instrument Soc Am, 68. *Mem:* Am Soc Mech Engrs; Am Soc Eng Educ; fel Instrument Soc Am. *Res:* Instrumentation for automatic control. *Mailing Add:* Dept of Mech Eng Valparaiso Univ Valparaiso IN 46383

ZOTOS, JOHN, b Brockton, Mass, Jan 12, 32; m 58; c 3. MATERIALS SCIENCE, METALLURGY. *Educ:* Northeastern Univ, BSChE, 54; Mass Inst Technol, MSMet, 56, Metall Engr, 67. *Prof Exp:* Eng asst metall, Raytheon Mfg Co, 54; proj metallurgist, Watertown Arsenal's Rodman Lab, 55-56, asst chief exp foundry br, 56-60; asst prof, 60-66, ASSOC PROF MECH ENG, NORTHEASTERN UNIV, 66- *Concurrent Pos:* Mat & metall consult & lectr to indust, 60-; consult & mem bd dir, Indust Magnetics, Inc, Mass, 63-70; NSF sci fac fel, 63-70; Welding Res Coun study grant, 69; consult & mem tech adv vd, Thermo Magnetics, Inc, Mass, 70- *Honors & Awards:* Adams Mem Award, Am Welding Soc, 72. *Mem:* Am Foundrymen's Soc; Am Defense Preparedness Asn; Am Inst Mining, Metall & Petrol Engrs; Am Inst Chem Engrs; Am Soc Metals. *Res:* Development of mathematical models which describe the chemical, mechanical and physical properties of both ferrous and non-ferrous casting alloys; use of electromagnetic solid state joining for bonding similar and dissimilar metals and alloys; the role and responsibilities of the professional person in his civic and religious communities. *Mailing Add:* 28 Old Coach Rd Cohasset MA 02025

ZOTTOLA, EDMUND ANTHONY, b Gilroy, Calif, June 25, 32; m 60; c 4. FOOD SCIENCE. *Educ:* Ore State Univ, BS, 54, MS, 58; Univ Minn, St Paul, PhD(dairy tech), 64. *Prof Exp:* Res asst food sci, Ore State Univ, 56-58; res fel food sci & industs, Univ Minn, St Paul, 58-64; bacteriologist, Nat Dairy Prod Corp, Ill, 64-65; microbiologist, Nodaway Valley Foods, Iowa, 65-66; assoc prof food sci & industs, 66-72, PROF FOOD SCI & NUTRIT, UNIV MINN, ST PAUL, 72-, EXTEN FOOD MICROBIOLOGIST, 66- *Mem:* Inst Food Technologists; Am Dairy Sci Asn; Int Asn Milk, Food & Environ Sanitarians. *Res:* Spoilage and pathogenic microorganisms in food; thermal destruction of microorganisms; airborne microorganisms; food plant and equipment sanitation; detection of microorganisms in raw and processed foods; attachment of microorganisms to food and food contact surfaces; microorganisms involved in cheese manufacturing and the technology of cheese manufacture. *Mailing Add:* Dept of Food Sci & Nutrit Univ of Minn St Paul MN 55108

ZOTTOLI, ROBERT, b Boston, Mass, Apr 17, 39; c 1. INVERTEBRATE ZOOLOGY. *Educ:* Bowdoin Col, BA, 60; Univ NH, MS, 63, PhD(zool), 66. *Prof Exp:* Asst biol, Univ NH, 61-63; from asst prof to assoc prof, 65-75, PROF BIOL, FITCHBURG STATE COL, 75- *Mem:* AAAS; Sigma Xi; Am Soc Limnol Oceanogr; Am Soc Zool. *Res:* Natural history of polychaetous annelid worms; polychaete family ampharetidae. *Mailing Add:* Fitchburg State Col Fitchburg MA 01420

ZOTTOLI, STEVEN JAYNES, b Boston, Mass, Aug 28, 47; c 2. NEUROBIOLOGY. *Educ:* Bowdoin Col, BA, 69; Univ Mass, Amherst, MS, 72, PhD(zool), 76. *Prof Exp:* Lectr cell physiol, Col Our Lady of the Elms, 73-74; NAT INST NEUROL & COMMUN DIS & STROKE FEL, RES INST ALCOHOLISM, NIH, 75- *Concurrent Pos:* Grass fel, 78. *Mem:* Soc Neurosci; Am Soc Zoologists. *Res:* Neurophysiological, morphological and behavioral studies of Mauthner cell function in teleosts. *Mailing Add:* Dept of Physiol State Univ NY Buffalo NY 14214

ZOUMALAN, SARKISS, b Tehran, Iran, Oct 28, 48; m 75; c 2. MATERIAL SCIENCE ENGINEERING. *Educ:* Univ Nancy, France, PhD(solid state chem), 75. *Prof Exp:* Quality control supvr, Res & Develop, Atomic Energy Orgn, France & Iran, 77-78; quality control supvr, Res & Develop, Organon Teknik, 78-80; RES SCIENTIST, RES & DEVELOP, ARCO SOLAR INDUST, 80- *Mem:* Am Chem Soc; Am Hydrogen Soc. *Mailing Add:* 5145 N Douglas Fir Rd Calabasas CA 91302

ZOUMAS, BARRY LEE, nutrition, food science, see previous edition

ZOUROS, ELEFTHERIOS, b Lesbos, Greece, Aug 31, 39; m 68; c 2. POPULATION GENETICS. *Educ:* Agr Col Athens, BSc, 63, PhD(biol), 68; Univ Chicago, PhD(biol), 72. *Prof Exp:* Res assoc biol, Agr Col Athens, 65-68; fel pop biol, Univ Chicago, 69-73; ASSOC PROF BIOL, DALHOUSIE UNIV, 73- *Concurrent Pos:* Scholar, Greek Nat Found Scholars, 66; Ford Found fel, 69. *Mem:* Genetics Soc Am; Am Soc Naturalists; Genetics Soc Can; Soc Study Evolution. *Res:* Genetic basis of the evolutionary process. *Mailing Add:* Dept Biol Dalhousie Univ Halifax NS B3H 4S1 Can

ZRAKET, CHARLES ANTHONY, b Lawrence, Mass, Jan 9, 24; m 61; c 4. ELECTRICAL & SYSTEMS ENGINEERING. *Educ:* Northeasterm Univ, BS, 51; Mass Inst Technol, SM, 53. *Prof Exp:* Tech staff mem, Digital Comput Lab, Mass Inst Technol, 51-53 & Lincoln Labs, 53-54, sect leader, 54-56, group leader, 56-58; dept head systs design, 58-61, tech dir systs planning & res div, 61-67, vpres & tech dir, 67-69, vpres, 69-74, sr vpres, 75-78, EXEC VPRES, MITRE CORP, 78- *Concurrent Pos:* Consult, Dept Defense, Inst Comput Sci & Nat Bur Standards. *Mem:* AAAS; fel Inst Elec & Electronics Engrs; Am Mgt Asn; Am Inst Aeronaut & Astronaut; NY Acad Sci. *Res:* Digital computers; digital computer programming; electronic control systems for large-scale, real-time use; information systems; communications systems; transportation systems; environmental control; energy; educational technology; law enforcement. *Mailing Add:* MITRE Corp Westgate Res Park McLean VA 22102

ZRUDSKY, DONALD RICHARD, b Cedar Rapids, Iowa, Apr 4, 34; div; c 2. SOLID STATE PHYSICS, ELECTRICAL ENGINEERING. *Educ:* Iowa State Univ, BS, 56, MS, 59; Univ Iowa, PhD(physics), 68. *Prof Exp:* Asst engr, Rockwell Corp, 56-57; res helper physics, Ames Lab, 57-59; res staff, Rockwell Corp, 59-62, assoc engr, 62-65; NASA trainee physics, Univ Iowa, 65-68; asst prof elec eng, Univ Toledo, 68-71, assoc prof, 71-80. *Concurrent Pos:* Dir NSF grant, 70-71; consult, Keithley Instruments Corp, 73 & Los Alamos Sci Lab, 78. *Mem:* Am Phys Soc; Inst Elec & Electronics Engrs. *Res:* Solid state materials, specifically, magnetic alloys, magnetic compounds and semiconductors; solid state devices; integrated circuits; field effect devices; stirling cycle magnetic heat engines; electronic circuits; instrumentation. *Mailing Add:* 7201 Wood Hollow Dr Apt 406 Austin TX 78766

ZSCHEILE, FREDERICK PAUL, JR, b Burlington, Kans, May 11, 07; m 33; c 3. PLANT PHYSIOLOGY, PHYTOPATHOLOGY. *Educ:* Univ Calif, BS, 28, PhD(plant physiol), 31. *Prof Exp:* Nat Res Coun fel biol, Univ Chicago, 31-33, asst pediat, 33-34, res assoc chem, 34-37, res assoc bot, 44-46; from asst prof agr chem & asst chemist to assoc prof & assoc chemist, Purdue Univ, 37-44; from assoc prof to prof, 46-74, from assoc biochemist to biochemist, Exp Sta, 46-74, EMER PROF AGRON, COL AGR, UNIV CALIF, DAVIS, 74- *Concurrent Pos:* Guggenheim fel, 58-59. *Mem:* AAAS; Am Chem Soc; Am Soc Plant Physiol; fel Am Inst Chem; Am Phytopath Soc. *Res:* Spectrophotometry of plant pigments; preservation of carotene and vitamin A; biochemical nature of disease resistance in plants; phytotron design; gas chromatography of amino acids; lysine in food plants. *Mailing Add:* 236 B St Davis CA 95616

ZSIGMOND, ELEMER K, b Budapest, Hungary, May 16, 30; US citizen. ANESTHESIOLOGY. *Educ:* Univ Budapest, MD, 55. *Prof Exp:* Intern med, Clins, Med Sch, Univ Budapest, 54-55; resident internal med, Sztalinvarosi Korhaz, Hungary, 55-56; cardiol res, Balatonfüred, Hungary, 56-57; intern med, Allegheny Gen Hosp, Pittsburgh, Pa, 60-61, resident anesthesiol, 61-63, dir anesthesiol res lab, 66-68; rpof anesthesiol, Med Ctr, Univ Mich, Ann Arbor, 68-79; PROF ANESTHESIOL, MED CTR, UNIV ILL, 79- *Concurrent Pos:* Res fel anesthesiol, Allegheny Gen Hosp, Pittsburgh, Pa, 63-66. *Mem:* Am Soc Anesthesiol; Int Anesthesia Res Soc; NY Acad Sci; Am Soc Clin Pharmacol. *Res:* Plasmacholinesterase studies to determine susceptibility to drugs used in anesthesia; malignant hyperpyrexia determinations. *Mailing Add:* Univ Hosp Univ Ill Med Ctr 1740 W Taylor St Chicago IL 60612

ZSIGRAY, ROBERT MICHAEL, b Glen Rogers, WVa, Mar 22, 39; m 70; c 4. MICROBIOLOGY. *Educ:* Miami Univ, AB, 61; Georgetown Univ, MS, 67, PhD(biol), 69. *Prof Exp:* Microbiologist, Wis State Lab Hyg, 61; res technologist genetics, US Army Biol Lab, Ft Detrick, 62-64, Nat Res Coun res assoc, 68-70; asst prof, 70-76, ASSOC PROF MICROBIOL, UNIV NH, 76- *Mem:* AAAS; Am Soc Microbiol. *Res:* Entry of exogenous DNA into cells. *Mailing Add:* Dept of Microbiol Univ of NH Durham NH 03824

ZSOTER, THOMAS, b Budapest, Hungary, Dec 27, 22; m 53; c 2. INTERNAL MEDICINE. *Educ:* Univ Budapest, MD, 47; FRCP(C). *Prof Exp:* Resident med, Univ Budapest, 47-49, instr internal med, 49-51; asst prof, Univ Szeged, 50-54, assoc prof med, 54-57; head circulation lab, Ayerst, McKenna & Harrison, Ltd, 57-60; ASSOC PROF PHARMACOL, UNIV TORONTO, 66-, ASSOC PROF MED, 68- *Concurrent Pos:* French Govt fel, Paris, 48-49; staff mem, Div Clin Pharmacol, Toronto Western Hosp, Ont, 66-, dir, 73-75. *Mem:* Fel Am Col Physicians; Can Pharmacol Soc; Can Fedn Biol Soc. *Res:* Circulation; pathophysiology; congestive heart failure; hemodynamics in experimental valvular defects; microscopic circulation; cardiovascular pharmacology; hypertension; calcium autopanistic drugs. *Mailing Add:* Dept of Pharmacol Univ of Toronto Toronto ON M5S 1A8 Can

ZUBAL, I GEORGE, b Lorain, Ohio, July 9, 50. MEDICAL IMAGING, THERAPY PLANNING. *Educ:* Ohio State Univ, BS, 72, MS, 74; Uni des Saarlandes, WGer, PhD(biophysics), 81. *Prof Exp:* ASST PROF, STATE UNIV NY, 81-; FEL, BROOKHAVEN NAT LAB, 81- *Mem:* Inst Elec & Electronics Engrs. *Res:* Development of software programs for analyzing medical patient pictures and application of these results to the radio therapy planning with nonconventional radiation. *Mailing Add:* Med Dept Bldg 490 Brookhaven Nat Lab Upton NY 11973

ZUBALY, ROBERT B(ARNES), b Philadelphia, Pa, Apr 20, 33; m 56; c 3. NAVAL ARCHITECTURE, MECHANICAL ENGINEERING. *Educ:* Webb Inst Naval Archit, BS, 55; Columbia Univ, MS, 59. *Prof Exp:* From instr to assoc prof, 55-66, PROF ENG, STATE NY MARITIME COL, 66- *Concurrent Pos:* Res engr, Davidson Lab, Stevens Inst Technol, 57-61; res assoc, Webb Inst Naval Archit, 61- *Mem:* Soc Naval Archit & Marine Engrs; Am Soc Eng Educ. *Res:* Ship design; ship response to sea; ocean transportation; naval architecture, hydrodynamics. *Mailing Add:* Dept Eng State Univ of NY Maritime Col Bronx NY 10465

ZUBAY, GEOFFREY, b Chicago, Ill, Nov 15, 31. BIOLOGY. *Educ:* Univ Chicago, PhB, 49, MS, 52; Harvard Univ, PhD(phys chem), 57. *Prof Exp:* NSF res fel molecular biol, King's Col, Univ London, 57-59, NIH fel, 59-60; res assoc, Rockefeller Inst, 60-61; asst biochemist, Brookhaven Nat Lab, 61-63; assoc prof, 63-71, PROF MOLECULAR BIOL, COLUMBIA UNIV, 72- *Res:* Physics; molecular biology of gene regulation. *Mailing Add:* Dept of Biol Sci Columbia Univ New York NY 10027

ZUBECK, ROBERT BRUCE, b Minneapolis, Minn, Oct 12, 44; m 69. LOW TEMPERATURE PHYSICS, APPLIED PHYSICS. *Educ:* Univ Minn, BPhys, 66; Stanford Univ, MS, 68, PhD(appl physics), 73. *Prof Exp:* Consult, Stanford Res Inst, 69-70, res assoc appl physics, Stanford Univ, 73-77; STAFF ENGR, IBM CORP, 77- *Res:* High resolution low temperature calorimetry; magnetic flux pinning in high field superconductors; electronbeam co-deposition techniques; growth morphology and crystallographic ordering of A-15 superconductors; synthesis of new superconductors; thin film magnetics; process reliability. *Mailing Add:* Gen Prod Div IBM Corp San Jose CA 95193

ZUBECKIS, EDGAR, b Latvia, Dec 27, 02; nat Can. FOOD TECHNOLOGY. *Educ:* Acad Agr Jelgava, DrAgr, 44. *Prof Exp:* Pvt docent, Fruit Tech, Univ Riga, 36-38; docent, Acad Agr Jelgava, 40-44; prof agr & fruit tech, Univ Bonn, 47-49; res scientist, Ont Res Coun, 53-55 & Hort Res Inst, Ont Dept Agr, 55-68; CONSULT, 68- *Mem:* NY Acad Sci; AAAS; Can Inst Food Sci & Technol. *Mailing Add:* Apt 406 185 Stephen Dr Toronto ON M8Y 3N5 Can

ZUBER, B(ERT) L, b Houston, Tex, Oct 27, 38; div; c 2. BIOENGINEERING. *Educ:* Univ Pa, BA, 60, BS, 61; Mass Inst Technol, MS, 63, PhD(bioeng), 65. *Prof Exp:* From asst prof to assoc prof bioeng & physiol, 65-73, actg head bioeng prog, 70-71, prof physiol, Med Ctr, 73-78, PROF BIO ENG, UNIV ILL, CHICAGO CIRCLE, 73- *Concurrent Pos:* Consult, Biosysts, Inc, Mass, 65-66, Aerospace Med Res Lab, Wright-Patterson AFB, Ohio, 71, Pollution Monitors, Inc, Chicago, 71, Dept Psychiat, Univ Chicago, 76-77, Manteno Mental Health Ctr, Ill, 7-79 & Eng Design Assocs, San Francisco, 76-79; asst attend, Presby-St Luke's Hosp, 65-69, assoc attend, 69-76; dir, Biomed Eng Consult Serv, 66-67; USPHS res grant, 68-73; NSF res grant, 74-76; mem bd dir, Nat Asn Bioengrs, 72-75; vis scientist, Bell Labs, NJ, 75; consult, Chicago Habits Clin, Ltd, Evanston, Ill, 79- & Rehab Eng Res & Design Ctr, Hines Vet Admin Hosp, Hines, Ill, 80-; lectr, Dept Orthopedics, Stritch Sch Med, Loyola Univ, Maywood, Ill, 80- *Mem:* Am Physiol Soc; Inst Elec & Electronics Engrs; Biomed Eng Soc; Asn Res Vision & Ophthal; Int Brain Res Orgn. *Res:* Physiological control systems; neurophysiological and control systems aspects of visual and oculomotor function; bioinstrumentation; bioengineering education; information processing in reading; reading aids for the blind. *Mailing Add:* Bioeng Prog Univ of Ill at Chicago Circle Chicago IL 60680

ZUBER, MARCUS STANLEY, b Gettysburg, SDak, Jan 10, 12; m 41; c 1. AGRONOMY. *Educ:* SDak State Univ, BS, 37; Iowa State Univ, MS, 40, PhD(plant breeding), 50. *Prof Exp:* Agent corn invests, Div Cereal Crops & Dis, Mo Agr Exp Sta, USDA, 37-42, assoc agronomist & in charge corn breeding, Div Cereal Crops, 46-50, res agronomist & in charge, 50-73, res leader, Corn Breeding, Div Cereal Crops, 73-76; PROF AGRON, UNIV MO-COLUMBIA, 56- *Mem:* AAAS; Am Soc Agron. *Res:* Corn breeding and genetics; physiology; insect and disease resistance; cereal chemistry. *Mailing Add:* Dept of Agron 109 Curtis Hall Univ of Mo-Columbia Columbia MO 65201

ZUBER, NOVAK, b Belgrade, Yugoslavia, Dec 4, 22; nat US; m 58. ENGINEERING. *Educ:* Univ Calif, Los Angeles, BS, 51, MSc, 54, PhD(eng), 59. *Prof Exp:* From asst res engr to assoc res engr, Univ Calif, Los Angeles, 51-58; mem tech staff, Res Lab, Ramo-Wooldridge Corp, 58-60; thermal engr, Gen Eng Lab, Gen Elec Co, 60-62, sr thermal engr, Adv Tech Labs, 62-65, consult engr, Res & Develop Ctr, 65-67; prof mech eng, NY Univ, 67-69; Fuller E Callaway Prof, Ga Inst Technol, 69-77; SR REACTOR ANALYST REACTOR SAFETY RES, NUCLEAR REGULATORY COMN, 77- *Concurrent Pos:* Consult, Mech Div, Off Sci Res, US Air Force, 63 & Los Alamos Sci Lab, 67. *Honors & Awards:* Mem Award, Am Soc Mech Engrs, 62. *Mem:* Am Inst Aeronaut & Astronaut; Am Inst Chem Engrs; Am Soc Mech Engrs. *Res:* Heat transfer; fluid dynamics; thermodynamics; transport phenomena in multi-phase systems. *Mailing Add:* 703 New Mark Esplonade Rockville MD 20850

ZUBER, WILLIAM HENRY, JR, b Memphis, Tenn, Sept 26, 37; m 59; c 3. PHYSICAL CHEMISTRY. *Educ:* Memphis State Univ, BS, 60; Univ Ky, PhD(phys chem), 64. *Prof Exp:* Asst prof chem, Murray State Univ, 64-66; asst prof, 66-70, ASSOC PROF CHEM, MEMPHIS STATE UNIV, 70- *Mem:* Am Chem Soc. *Res:* Nonaqueous solution chemistry. *Mailing Add:* Dept of Chem Memphis State Univ Memphis TN 38152

ZUBERER, DAVID ALAN, b Paterson, NJ, Feb 9, 47; m 68; c 1. SOIL MICROBIOLOGY, MICROBIAL ECOLOGY. *Educ:* WVa Univ, AB, 69, MS, 71; Univ SFla, PhD(biol), 76. *Prof Exp:* Res scientist microbiol, Univ Fla, 76-78; ASST PROF BOIL MICROBIOL, TEX A&M UNIV, 78- *Mem:* Am Soc Microbiol; Am Soc Agron; Soil Sci Soc Am; AAAS. *Res:* Biological nitrogen fixation, including associative N2-fixation in grasses and N2-fixation by legumes; use of beneficial microorganisms to enhance plant nutrient uptake; mycorrhizae and reclamation microbiology. *Mailing Add:* Dept Soil & Crop Sci Tex A&M Univ College Station TX 77843

ZUBIETA, JON ANDONI, b New York, June 16, 45; m 69; c 2. INORGANIC CHEMISTRY. *Educ:* Fordham Univ, BS, 66; Columbia Univ, PhD(chem), 71. *Prof Exp:* Res assoc chem, Univ Sussex, 71-73; asst prof, 73-80, ASSOC PROF CHEM, STATE UNIV NY, ALBANY, 80- *Concurrent Pos:* NIH fel, 72-73; NATO travelling fel, 81-82. *Mem:* Am Chem Soc. *Res:* Inorganic models for molybdoenzymes; electroanalytical chemistry; structure and reactivity of cluster compounds. *Mailing Add:* Dept Chem State Univ NY Albany NY 12222

ZUBIN, JOSEPH, b Raseiniai, Lithuania, Oct 9, 00; nat US; m 34; c 3. EXPERIMENTAL PSYCOPATHOLOGY, EXPERIMENTAL EPIDEMIOLOGY. *Educ:* Johns Hopkins Univ, AB, 21; Columbia Univ, PhD(educ psychol), 32; Am Bd Prof Psychol, dipl, 50. *Hon Degrees:* MD, Univ Lund, 72; ScD, Univ Rochester, 76. *Prof Exp:* Asst educ psychol, Teachers Col, Columbia Univ, 30-31, instr psychomet, Col Physicians & Surgeons, 32-33; instr educ psychol, City Col New York, 34-36; asst psychologist, Ment Hosp Surv Comt, Nat Comt Ment Hyg, 36-38; assoc res psychologist, 38-56, prin res scientist biomet, 56-60, dir biomet res unit, 56-75, chief psychiat res, 60-75, ATTEND BIOMETRICIAN, NY STATE PSYCHIAT INST, 78-; EMER PROF PSYCHOL & SPEC LECTR PSYCHOL & PSYCHIAT, COLUMBIA UNIV, 69- *Concurrent Pos:* From instr to asst prof psychiat, Col Physicians & Surgeons, Columbia Univ, 39-50, adj prof, 50-56, prof, Univ, 56-69; co-ed, publ, Am Psychopath Asn, 44-71; instr, Postdoctoral Inst, Am Psychol Asn, 50, 53, 55, 56, 60, 61, 64, 65 & 67; mem study sect psychopharmacol, NIMH, 62-65; mem study sect develop behav sci, NIH, 66-70; adj prof, Queens Col, 70-; prof lectr, NY Sch Psychiat, Manhattan State Hosp, 71-75; assoc ed, J Abnorm Psychol, 73-; consult, Vet Admin & NIMH; Distinguished res prof psychiat, Univ Pittsburgh Med Sch, 79-; res career scientist, Vet Admin Hosp, Pittsburgh, 79- *Honors & Awards:* Paul H Hoch Lectr Award, 68; Stanley R Dean Award, Am Col Psychiatrists, 74; Distinguished Scientist Award, Am Psychol Asn, 75; Behavioral Sci Award, NY Acad Sci, 81. *Mem:* fel Am Psychol Asn; Am Psychopath Asn (pres, 51-52); Am Col Neuropsychopharmacol (pres, 71-72). *Res:* Experimental psychopathology; vulnerability to schizophrenia for the identification of vulnerability and episode markers, triggering stressors needed to elicit latent vulnerability, and buffering factors (social networks, premorbid personality and ecological niches); authored or coauthored over 200 articles and seven books. *Mailing Add:* Vet Admin Hosp 151R Highland Dr Pittsburgh PA 15206

ZUBKO, L(EONARD) M(ARTIN), b Bridgeport, Conn, July 8, 20; m 41; c 1. MECHANICAL ENGINEERING. *Educ:* Rutgers Univ, BSME, 42; Rensselaer Polytech Inst, MME, 49. *Prof Exp:* Instr mech eng, Rensselaer Polytech Inst, 46-49; assoc prof, Univ Ill, 49-51 & 52-55; proj engr, Sverdrup Parcel Consult Engrs, 51-52; mgr propulsion appl res, Flight Propulsion Lab Dept, 55-60, mgr adv eng, 60-73, MGR USSR PROGS, GEN ELEC CO, 73- *Concurrent Pos:* Mem subcomt combustion, NASA, 56-58; adj assoc prof, Univ Vt, 64-71. *Mem:* Am Soc Mech Engrs; Am Inst Aeronaut & Astronaut; Am Ord Asn; Nat Soc Prof Engrs. *Res:* Gas dynamics; fluid mechanics; heat transfer; combustion; mechanisms. *Mailing Add:* Gen Elec Co Gas Turbine Div Bldg 500 Schenectady NY 12345

ZUBKOFF, PAUL LEON, b Niagara Falls, NY, Nov 24, 34; m 60; c 2. BIOLOGICAL OCEANOGRAPHY, BIOCHEMISTRY. *Educ:* Univ Buffalo, BA, 56; George Washington Univ, MS, 58; Cornell Univ, PhD(biochem), 62. *Prof Exp:* Res asst biochem, George Washington Univ, 56-58; res asst, Cornell Univ, 58-61; res biol chemist, Univ Calif, Los Angeles, 61-63; NIH trainee & res assoc biophys, Mass Inst Technol, 63-66; asst prof biochem, Ohio State Univ, 66-70; SR MARINE SCIENTIST & HEAD ENVIRON PHYSIOL, VA INST MARINE SCI, 70-; ASSOC PROF MARINE SCI, COL WILLIAM & MARY & UNIV VA, 70- *Mem:* Atlantic Estuarine Res Soc; Am Chem Soc; Am Nuclear Soc; Am Soc Limnol & Oceanog; Int Asn Great Lakes Res. *Res:* Dynamics of aquatic ecosystems; comparative biochemistry of mass molecular and metabolism of marine invertebrates. *Mailing Add:* Dept of Environ Physiol Va Inst of Marine Sci Gloucester Point VA 23062

ZUBLER, EDWARD GEORGE, b Lackawanna, NY, Mar 12, 25; m 50; c 3. PHYSICAL CHEMISTRY. *Educ:* Canisius Col, BS, 49; Univ Notre Dame, PhD(phys chem), 53. *Prof Exp:* Res phys chemist, 53-65, tech leader, 65-72, RES ADV, GEN ELEC CO, 72- *Concurrent Pos:* Lectr, Fenn Col, 60-65 & Cleveland State Univ, 65-66. *Honors & Awards:* Elenbaas Award, Philip's Gloeilampenfabrieken-Netherlands, 81. *Mem:* Am Chem Soc. *Res:* Gas chemistry; high temperature gas-metal reactions; mass spectrometry; high and ultra high vacuum techniques. *Mailing Add:* Lighting Res & Tech Serv Oper Lab Gen Elec Co Number 1310 Nela Pk Cleveland OH 44112

ZUBRISKI, JOSEPH CAZIMER, b Goodman, Wis, July 7, 19; m 46; c 3. SOIL SCIENCE. *Educ:* Univ Wis, BS, 47, MS, 48, PhD(soils), 51. *Prof Exp:* From asst prof to assoc prof, 51-63, PROF SOILS, NDAK STATE UNIV, 63- *Mem:* Soil Sci Soc Am; Am Soc Agron. *Res:* soil fertility; effect of plant population and fertilizers on yield and quality of sunflower seeds; soil phosphorus; fertilizer and water management of irrigated crops. *Mailing Add:* Dept of Soils NDak State Univ Fargo ND 58102

ZUBROD, CHARLES GORDON, b New York, NY, Jan 22, 14; m 40; c 5. CANCER. *Educ:* Col of the Holy Cross, AB, 36; Columbia Univ, MD, 40. *Hon Degrees:* DSc, Col of the Holy Cross, 69. *Prof Exp:* Intern, Cent Islip State Hosp, NJ, 40-41 & Jersey City Hosp, NY, 41-42; intern & asst resident med, Presby Hosp, New York, 42-43; instr med, Sch Med, Johns Hopkins Univ, 46-49, asst prof med & pharmacol, 49-53; assoc prof med & dir res, Dept Med, St Louis Univ, 53-54; chief gen med br, Nat Cancer Inst, 54-55, clin dir, 55-61, chmn med bd, 57-58, dir int res, 61-65, sci dir chemother, 65-72, dir div cancer treatment, 72-74; PROF ONCOL & CHMN DEPT, PROF MED & DIR COMPREHENSIVE CANCER CTR, SCH MED, UNIV MIAMI, 74- *Concurrent Pos:* Roche res fel chemother bact dis, Johns Hopkins Hosp, 46-49; mem, Mt Desert Island Biol Lab; mem & mem exec comt, Lerner Marine Lab, Bimini. *Honors & Awards:* Lasker Award, 72. *Mem:* Am Soc Clin Invest; Am Soc Pharmacol & Exp Therapeut; Am Asn Cancer Res (pres, 77); Am Asn Cancer Insts (pres, 78); Asn Am Physicians. *Res:* Pharmacology, especially of cancer chemotherapeutic agents; marine biology. *Mailing Add:* Univ of Miami Comp Cancer Ctr PO Box 016960 Miami FL 33101

ZUBRZYCKI, LEONARD JOSEPH, b Camden, NJ, Feb 25, 32; m 54; c 1. MEDICAL MICROBIOLOGY. *Educ:* Temple Univ, AB, 53, PhD(med microbiol), 58. *Prof Exp:* Sr scientist, Wyeth, Inc, 58-61; ASSOC PROF MICROBIOL, SCH MED, TEMPLE UNIV, 61- *Mem:* AAAS; Am Soc Microbiol; Brit Soc Gen Microbiol. *Res:* Bacterial genetics. *Mailing Add:* Dept Microbiol Temple Univ Philadelphia PA 19122

ZUCCARELLI, ANTHONY JOSEPH, b New York, NY, Aug 11, 44; m 68; c 1. MOLECULAR BIOLOGY, MOLECULAR GENETICS. *Educ:* Cornell Univ, BS, 66; Loma Linda Univ, MS, 68; Calif Inst Technol, PhD(biophys), 74. *Prof Exp:* Fel molecular biol, Am Cancer Soc, 74-76; ASST PROF MICROBIOL, LOMA LINDA UNIV, 76- *Mem:* Am Soc Microbiol. *Res:* Investigation of the early stages of infection with the single-stranded DNA bacteriophage--X174, particularly the mechanisms of initiation and synthesis of the complementary strand in parental replicative forms; isolation and characterization of-X174 deletion mutants to determine funcational overlapping between viral cistrons. *Mailing Add:* Dept of Biol Loma Linda Univ Loma Linda CA 92350

ZUCCARELLO, WILLIAM A, b Trenton, NJ, July 29, 28; m 66. ENDOCRINOLOGY, BIOCHEMISTRY. *Educ:* Rutgers Univ, BS, 50, MS, 51; Univ Wis, PhD, 57. *Prof Exp:* Pharmacologist, Carroll Dunham Smith Pharmacol Co, 58-60, head pharmacol dept, NJ, 60-63; sr endocrinologist, 63-67, sr investr biochem, 67-74, CLIN DATA COORDR, SMITH KLINE & FRENCH LABS, 74- *Res:* Adrenal and reproductive physiology; anti-inflammatory agents; diuretic-anti hypertensive agents; neuropharmacology; medical applications of enzymes; anesthetic drugs; adrenal-thyroid-gonadal interrelationships; inhibitors of adrenal steroid biosynthesis; immunological aspects of arthritis; hypothalamic releasing factors. *Mailing Add:* Smith Kline & French Labs 1500 Spring Garden St Philadelphia PA 19101

ZUCCHETTO, JAMES JOHN, b Brooklyn, NY, Mar 11, 46; m 78; c 1. SYSTEMS ECOLOGY, ENVIRONMENTAL SCIENCE. *Educ:* Polytech Inst Brooklyn, BS, 66; NY Univ, MS, 69; Univ Fla, PhD(syst ecol), 75. *Prof Exp:* Mem tech staff, Bell Tel Labs, Inc, 68-71; asst syst ecol, Univ Fla, 72-75, assoc eng energy in transp, 75-76; guest researcher environ, Univ Stockholm, 76-78; ASST PROF REGIONAL SCI, UNIV PA, 78- *Concurrent Pos:* Researcher, Rockefeller Found, 77 & Univ Pa, 78-79; consult, US Nat Res Coun, 76 & Fed Energy Admin, 75. *Mem:* Regional Sci Asn; Sigma Xi. *Res:* Ecological models; regional energy-ecological-economic interactions; energy analysis; general systems; environmental impact evaluation; systems analysis. *Mailing Add:* Dept of Regional Sci 3718 Locust Walk Philadelphia PA 19104

ZUCHELLI, ARTLEY JOSEPH, b Alexandria, Va, Nov 3, 34. PHYSICS. *Educ:* Univ Va, BA, 55, PhD(physics), 58. *Prof Exp:* NSF fel, Univ Birmingham, 58-59; assoc prof physics, Univ Miss, 59-63; assoc prof, 63-67, PROF PHYSICS, GEORGE WASHINGTON UNIV, 67- *Res:* Theoretical, classical and quantum fields. *Mailing Add:* Dept of Physics George Washington Univ Washington DC 20052

ZUCK, DONALD ANTON, b Hafford, Sask, Dec 27, 18; m 44, 58; c 3. PHARMACEUTICAL CHEMISTRY. *Educ:* Univ Alta, BSc, 48; Univ Wis, MS, 50, PhD(pharm), 52. *Prof Exp:* Lectr, Sch Pharm, Univ BC, 48-50; from pharmaceut chmeist to sr pharmaceut chemist, Eli Lilly & Co, 52-65; PROF PHARM, COL PHARM, UNIV SASK, 65- *Concurrent Pos:* Examr, Pharm Exam Bd Can, 72-77; sci ed, Can J Pharmaceut Sci, 72-82; mem, Drug Qual Assessment Comt, 74- *Mem:* Am Pharmaceut Asn; fel Am Found Pharm Educ; Can Pharm Asn; Am Asn Cols Pharm; Asn Fac Pharm Can. *Res:* Physical chemistry as applied to pharmaceutical problems. *Mailing Add:* 103 Baldwin Crescent Saskatoon SK S7H 3M5 Can

ZUCK, ROBERT KARL, b Rochester, NY; m 38; c 4. BOTANY. *Educ:* Oberlin Col, AB, 37; Univ Tenn, MS, 39; Univ Chicago, PhD(bot), 43. *Prof Exp:* Asst plant pathologist, Exp Sta, Univ Tenn, 38-41; asst bot, Univ Chicago, 41-43; instr biol, Evansville Col, 43-44; plant pathologist, Bur Plant Indust, Soils & Agr Eng, USDA, Md, 44-46; from asst prof to assoc prof bot, 46-55, chmn dept, 47-77, prof, 55-80, EMER PROF BOT, DREW UNIV, 80- *Concurrent Pos:* Adj prof dept bot & cur, Florence & Robert Zurk Arbortum, Drew Univ, 80- *Mem:* Fel AAAS; Am Phytopath Soc; Bot Soc Am; Mycol Soc Am; Asn Trop Biol. *Res:* Mycology; plant evolution. *Mailing Add:* Dept of Bot Drew Univ Madison NJ 07940

ZUCKER, ALEXANDER, b Zagreb, Yugoslavia, Aug 1, 24; nat US; m 53; c 3. NUCLEAR PHYSICS. *Educ:* Univ Vt, BA, 47; Yale Univ, MS, 48, PhD(physics), 50. *Prof Exp:* Res asst physics, Yale Univ, 48-50; physicist, Oak Ridge Nat Lab, 50-53, sr physicist, 53-70, assoc div dir, 60-70; prof physics, Univ Tenn, 68-72; exec dir, Environ Studies Bd, Nat Acad Sci-Nat Acad Eng, 70-72; dir heavy ion proj, 72-74, ASSOC DIR, OAK RIDGE NAT LAB, 73- *Concurrent Pos:* Guggenheim fel & Fulbright res scholar, 66-67; del, Pugwash Conf, 71; mem comt nuclear sci & nuclear physics panel, Physics Surv, Nat Res Coun; US del peaceful uses of atomic energy, USSR; mem res coord panel, Gas Res Inst, 78-; mem, Nuclear Physics Deleg to People's Repub China, Nat Acad Sci, 79; ed, Nuclear Sci Applications, 80- *Mem:* Fel AAAS; fel Am Phys Soc. *Res:* Nuclear reactions with heavy ions; medium energy nuclear physics, including scattering and polarization of protons; few-nucleon interactions; high-current electronuclear machines; AVF and heavy ion cyclotrons; environment and public policy; managing physical research programs related to energy. *Mailing Add:* Oak Ridge Nat Lab Oak Ridge TN 37830

ZUCKER, GORDON L(ESLIE), b Providence, RI, Nov 24, 29; m 51; c 3. METALLURGY. *Educ:* Mass Inst Technol, SB, 51; Univ Wis, MS, 54; Columbia Univ, Dr Eng Sci, 59. *Prof Exp:* Engr, Semiconductor & Mat Div, Radio Corp, Am, 58-59; mem tech staff, Cent Res Labs, Tex Instruments Inc, 59-62; sr scientist, Sperry Rand Res Ctr, 62-64; group mgr, Res Div, Cadillac Gage Co, 64-66; dept head, Electronics Div, Union Carbide Corp, 66-70; tech dir, Tansitor Electronics Inc, 70-72; mgr engr, Dickson Electronics Corp, 73-75; tech dir, Mineral Res Ctr, Mont Tech Alumni Found, 76-79, PROF MINERAL PROCESSING ENG, MONT COL MINERAL SCI & TECHNOL, 75- *Mem:* Am Chem Soc; Electrochem Soc. *Res:* Fine particle technology; electronic materials; electrochemistry; surface chemistry. *Mailing Add:* Mont Col Mineral Sci & Technol Butte MT 59701

ZUCKER, IRVING, b Montreal, Que, Oct 2, 40; m 63; c 2. BIOLOGICAL RHYTHMS, NEUROENDOCRINOLOGY. *Educ:* McGill Univ, BSc, 61; Univ Chicago, PhD(biopsychol), 64. *Prof Exp:* Res assoc reprod physiol, Ore Regional Primate Res Ctr, 64-65; vis scientist, Sch Med, Univ Wis, 65; res assoc reprod physiol, Ore Regional Primate Res Ctr, 66; from asst prof to assoc prof psychol, 66-74, PROF PSYCHOL, UNIV CALIF, BERKELEY, 74- *Mem:* AAAS; Animal Behav Soc; Am Soc Mammalogists; Neurosci Soc. *Res:* Seasonal reproductive cycles; Circadian clocks; behavioral endocrinology. *Mailing Add:* Dept of Psychol Univ of Calif Berkeley CA 94720

ZUCKER, IRVING H, b Bronx, NY, July 13, 42; m 70; c 3. PHYSIOLOGY. *Educ:* City Col New York, BS, 65; Univ Mo-Kansas City, MS, 67; New York Med Col, PhD(physiol), 72. *Prof Exp:* USPHS fel, 72-73, asst prof, 73-76, ASSOC PROF PHYSIOL, UNIV NEBR MED CTR OMAHA, 76- *Concurrent Pos:* Estab investr, Am Heart Asn, 77-82; mem, Great Planes regional rev group, Am Heart Asn; Masua Honor lectr, 81. *Mem:* Am Physiol Soc; Am Heart Asn; Soc Exp Biol & Med. *Res:* Cardiovascular receptors and the neural control of blood volume. *Mailing Add:* Dept of Physiol & Biophys Univ of Nebr Med Ctr Omaha NE 68105

ZUCKER, JOSEPH, b New York, NY, Apr 11, 28; m 53; c 3. SOLID STATE PHYSICS. *Educ:* Univ Miami, BS, 51; NY Univ, MS, 55, PhD(physics), 61. *Prof Exp:* Res assoc elec eng, Res Div, Col Eng, NY Univ, 51-55; engr, Sylvania Elec Prod, Inc, 55-57, sr engr, 57-59, res engr, 59-63, adv res engr, 63-65, eng specialist. 65-66, adv eng specialist, 66-68, MEM TECH STAFF, GEN TEL & ELECTRONICS LABS, 68- *Concurrent Pos:* Lectr, Polytech Inst Brooklyn, 60-65, adj prof, 65-72; adj prof, Hofstra Univ, 65-68. *Honors & Awards:* IR 100 Award, Indust Res Mag, 65. *Mem:* AAAS; NY Acad Sci; Am Phys Soc; Inst Elec & Electronics Eng; Sigma Xi. *Res:* Transport properties of bulk semiconductors; optical probing of acoustoelectric interactions in piezoelectric semiconductors; microwave detectors, modulators and harmonic generators; photoelastic and electrooptic effect; acoustic surface wave devices; light emitting diodes; integrated optical devices; optical communication systems. *Mailing Add:* 182 Puritan Rd Swampscott MA 01907

ZUCKER, MARJORIE BASS, b New York, NY, June 10, 19; m 38; c 4. PHYSIOLOGY, HEMATOLOGY. *Educ:* Vassar Col, AB, 39; Columbia Univ, PhD(physiol), 44. *Prof Exp:* Instr physiol, Col Physicians & Surgeons, Columbia Univ, 42-44, res asst, 45-49; from asst prof to assoc prof, Col Dent, NY Univ, 49-55; assoc mem, Sloan-Kettering Inst Cancer Res, 55-63; assoc prof path, 63-71, PROF PATH, SCH MED, NY UNIV, 71- *Concurrent Pos:* Asst res dir, Eastern Div Res Lab, Am Nat Red Cross, 63-70; mem hemat study sect, NIH, 70-74, Int Comt Haemostasis & Thrombosis, 70-76 & review comt B, Nat Heart, Lung & Blood Inst, 76-80. *Mem:* Am Physiol Soc; Soc Exp Biol & Med; Am Soc Hemat; Int Soc Hemat; Int Soc Thrombosis & Haemostasis. *Res:* Platelets and blood coagulation. *Mailing Add:* Dept of Path NY Univ Med Ctr New York NY 10016

ZUCKER, MARTIN SAMUEL, b New York, NY, Mar 15, 30; m 58; c 3. PLASMA PHYSICS, RADIATION PHYSICS. *Educ:* Cornell Univ, BEngPhys, 52; Univ Wis, MSc, 53, PhD(nuclear physics), 61. *Prof Exp:* Asst physicist, 58-62, consult, Radiation Div, Nuclear Eng Dept, 61-63, ASSOC PHYSICIST, BROOKHAVEN NAT LAB, 63- *Mem:* AAAS; Am Phys Soc; Am Asn Physics Teachers; Am Nuclear Soc. *Res:* Fast neutron polarization; electrical effects of nuclear radiations on matter; direct conversion of energy to electricity; statistical mechanics; chemical physics; accelerator development; scientific applications of computers. *Mailing Add:* Brookhaven Nat Lab Upton NY 11973

ZUCKER, MELVIN JOSEPH, b Charleston, SC, May 6, 29; div; c 2. SOLID STATE PHYSICS. *Educ:* Brooklyn Col, BS, 51; Rutgers Univ, PhD(physics), 57. *Prof Exp:* Physicist, Airborne Instruments Lab, Cutler-Hammer, Inc, 57-59; mem tech staff, Semiconductor Div, Hughes Aircraft Co, 58-62; mem tech staff, Am-Standard Corp, NJ, 62-68; chmn dept math & physics, 69-77, ASSOC PROF, MERCER COUNTY COMMUNITY COL, NJ, 69- *Concurrent Pos:* Consult, Off Promoting Tech Innovation, State NJ. *Mem:* Am Phys Soc. *Res:* Impurities in superconductors; semiconductor devices; paramagnetic resonance; peizoresitivity studies in semiconductors. *Mailing Add:* Dept of Math & Physics PO Box B Mercer Community Col Trenton NJ 08690

ZUCKER, OVED SHLOMO FRANK, b Jerusalem, Isreal, June 24, 39; US citizen; m 60; c 3. ELECTRICAL ENGINEERING, PLASMA PHYSICS. *Educ:* City Univ NY, BEE, 65. *Prof Exp:* Mem tech staff elec eng, Lawrence Livermore Lab, 65-78; STAFF PHYSICIST, PHYSICS INT CO, 78- *Concurrent Pos:* Consult physics, Lawrence Livermore Lab, 78-79 & La Jolla Inst, 79; ed, Energy Storage Compression & Switching Conf & Proceedings, 74. *Mem:* Am Phys Soc. *Res:* Relativistic electron beam; space-time energy compression; solid state physics. *Mailing Add:* Physics Int Co 2700 Merced St San Leandro CA 94577

ZUCKER, PAUL ALAN, b New York, NY, Nov 20, 44; m 73; c 1. PHYSICS, THEORETICAL PHYSICS. *Educ:* Univ Chicago, BS, 66; Stanford Univ, MS, 67, PhD(physics), 71. *Prof Exp:* Res assoc physics, Univ Ore, 70-72 & Univ Minn, 72-75; SR PHYSICIST, APPL PHYSICS LAB, JOHNS HOPKINS UNIV, 75- *Mem:* Am Phys Soc; AAAS; Inst Elec & Electronics Engrs. *Res:* Electroproduction and weak production of nucleon resonances; signal processing; Kalman filtering; system identification; estimation; model validation. *Mailing Add:* Johns Hopkins Appl Physics Lab Johns Hopkins Rd Laurel MD 20810

ZUCKER, ROBERT ALBERT, b New York, NY, Dec 9, 31; m 79; c 3. CLINICAL PSYCHOLOGY, PSYCHOPATHOLOGY. *Educ:* City Col New York, BCE, 56; Harvard Univ, PhD(clin psychol), 66. *Prof Exp:* Asst prof psychol, Rutgers Univ, 63-68; asst prof, 68-70, assoc prof, 70-75, PROF CLIN PSYCHOL, MICH STATE UNIV, 75- *Concurrent Pos:* Consult ed, J Studies Alcohol, 64-, Asn Journalists, 69-; prin investr grants adolescent drinking, Nat Inst Mental Health, 66-71; consult, Vet Admin Hosp, Battle Creek, Mich, 74-76; vis prof, Univ Tex, Austin, 75-; bd dir, Nat Coun Alcoholism, 78-81; vis scholar alcohol problems, Nat Alcohol Abuse & Alcoholism 80-81. *Mem:* Fel Am Psychol Asn; Soc Life Hist Res Psychopath. *Res:* Longitudinal development of psychopathology with special interest in alcohol and drug abuse; personality influences on behavior; personality theory; psychotherapy. *Mailing Add:* Dept Psychol Mich State Univ East Lansing MI 48824

ZUCKER, ROBERT MARTIN, b New York, NY, May 13, 43. BIOPHYSICS, BIOLOGY. *Educ:* Univ Calif, Los Angeles, BS, 65, MS, 66, PhD(biophys), 70. *Prof Exp:* Res scientist hematol, Univ Calif, Los Angeles, 66-70; res, Max Planck Inst Protein & Leather Res, 70-72; ASSOC SCIENTIST BIOPHYS & BIOL, PAPANICOLAOU CANCER RES INST, 72- *Concurrent Pos:* Asst prof med, Univ Miami, 74- *Mem:* Am Chem Soc; Am Soc Cell Biol; NY Acad Sci; Am Asn Cancer Res. *Res:* Differentiations of leukemia cells using biophysical and biochemical parometers; differential hemoglobin production during differentiation. *Mailing Add:* 1155 NW 14th St PO Box 016188 Miami FL 33101

ZUCKER, ROBERT STEPHEN, b Philadelphia, Pa, Apr 18, 45; m 68; c 1. NEUROPHYSIOLOGY. *Educ:* Mass Inst Technol, SB, 66; Stanford Univ, PhD(neurol sci), 71. *Prof Exp:* Asst prof, 73-80, ASSOC PROF PHYSIOL, UNIV CALIF, BERKELEY, 80- *Concurrent Pos:* Hon asst res assoc dept biophys, Univ Col, Univ London, Eng, 71-73; temp investr, Cellular Neurobiol Lab, France, 73-74; res fel, Alfred P Sloan Found, 76-80. *Mem:* Soc Neurosci; AAAS; Biophys Soc. *Res:* Synaptic transmission; synaptic plasticity; excitable membrane biophysics; neurophysiological basis of behavior; neuronal calcium metabolism; egg fertilization and activation. *Mailing Add:* Dept of Physiol & Anat Univ of Calif Berkeley CA 94720

ZUCKER, STEVEN MARK, b New York, NY, Sept 12, 49. MATHEMATICS. *Educ:* Brown Univ, ScB, 70; Princeton Univ, PhD(math), 74. *Prof Exp:* Asst prof math, Rutgers Univ, 74-80; MEM FAC, MATH DEPT, PRINCETON UNIV, 80- *Concurrent Pos:* NSF grant, 76- *Mem:* Am Math Soc. *Res:* Analytic methods in algebraic geometry; Hodge theory and the cohomology of projective varieties; differential geometry. *Mailing Add:* Dept Math Princeton Univ PO Box 37 Princeton NJ 08540

ZUCKERBERG, HYAM L, b New York, NY, Dec 5, 37; m 64; c 1. MATHEMATICS. *Educ:* Yeshiva Univ, BA & BHL, 59, MA, 61, PhD(math), 63. *Prof Exp:* Res mathematician, Davidson Lab, Stevens Inst Technol, 63-80; PROF MATH, LONG ISLAND UNIV, 80- *Mem:* Am Math Soc. *Res:* Conformal mapping; potential theory; Hilbert spaces; topology; Bergman kernel function. *Mailing Add:* Dept of Math Long Island Univ Brooklyn Ctr Bedford Ave & Ave H Brooklyn NY 11201

ZUCKERBROD, DAVID, b Brooklyn, NY, Aug 27, 54; m 79. ELECTROCHEMISTRY. *Educ:* Rensselaer Polytech Inst, BS, 75, PhD(inorg chem), 82. *Prof Exp:* SR ENGR, WESTINGHOUSE ELEC CORP, 80- *Mem:* Am Chem Soc. *Mailing Add:* 5706 Beacon St Pittsburgh PA 15217

ZUCKER-FRANKLIN, DOROTHEA, b Berlin, Ger, Aug 9, 29; US citizen; m 56; c 1. CELL BIOLOGY. *Educ:* Hunter Col, BA, 52; New York Med Col, MD, 56. *Prof Exp:* Intern med, Philadelphia Gen Hosp, Pa, 56-57; resident, Montefiore Hosp, New York, 57-59, USPHS res fel hemat, 59-61; USPHS res fel electron micros, 61-63, from asst prof to assoc prof, 63-74, PROF MED, SCH MED, NY UNIV, 74- *Concurrent Pos:* Attend physician, Bellevue Hosp, New York, 63-; attend physician, Univ Hosp, New York, 63-; spec consult path training comt, Nat Inst Gen Med Sci; USPHS res career scientist award, 66-76; Nat Inst Arthritis & Metab Dis res grant; assoc ed, Blood, 64-75 & 81, J Reticuloendothelial Soc, 65-73, Am J Path, 78-, Am J Med & J Hemat Oncol; mem blood prod comt, Food & Drug Admin, 81. *Mem:* Am Fedn Clin Res; Am Soc Hemat; Am Soc Exp Path; Am Soc Clin Invest; Am Asn Physicians. *Res:* Hematology, including white blood cells, coagulation of blood, and platelets; immunology; electron microscopy. *Mailing Add:* Dept of Med NY Univ Sch of Med New York NY 10016

ZUCKERMAN, BENJAMIN MICHAEL, b New York, NY, Aug 16, 43; m 68. ASTRONOMY. *Educ:* Mass Inst Technol, SB & SM, 63; Harvard Univ, PhD(astron), 68. *Prof Exp:* Asst prof, 68-71, From asst prof to assoc prof, 68-76, PROF PHYSICS & ASTRON, UNIV MD, COLLEGE PARK, 76- *Concurrent Pos:* Alfred P Sloan res fel, 72-74; consult, Jet Propulsion Lab; Guggenheim Found fel, 77. *Honors & Awards:* Helen B Warner Prize, Am Astron Soc, 75. *Mem:* Int Astron Union; Int Union Radio Sci; Am Astron Soc. *Res:* Interstellar medium and radio astronomy, especially spectral line radio astronomy. *Mailing Add:* Dept of Physics & Astron Univ of Md College Park MD 20742

ZUCKERMAN, BERNARD, b Camden, NJ, Aug 18, 31; m 51; c 2. PHOTOGRAPHIC CHEMISTRY. *Educ:* Drexel Inst Technol, BS, 60; Univ Pa, MS, 63. *Prof Exp:* Res physicist, Atlantic Ref Co, 60-61; chemist, Missile & Space Div, Gen Elec Co, 61-63; scientist, 63-71, sr scientist, 71-77, mgr, Emulsion Addenda Labs, 77-81, MGR PROD PLANNING, POLAROID CORP, 81- *Mem:* Soc Photog Sci & Eng. *Res:* Structural analysis of organic compounds and catalysts; solid state properties of electroluminescent materials; spectral sensitization processes in silver halides; photographic materials and systems. *Mailing Add:* Polaroid Corp 575 Technol Square Cambridge MA 02139

ZUCKERMAN, ISRAEL, b St Louis, Mo, Oct 10, 24; m 54; c 2. MATHEMATICS. *Educ:* City Col New York, BBA, 46; Brooklyn Col, MA, 58; Rutgers Univ, PhD(math), 63. *Prof Exp:* Instr math, Brooklyn Col, 56-58 & Rutgers Univ, 59-63; asst prof, Queens Col, 63-65 & Vassar Col, 65-66; assoc prof, 66-77, PROF MATH, LONG ISLAND UNIV, BROOKLYN CTR, 77- *Mem:* Math Asn Am; Am Math Soc. *Res:* Differential algebra; ring theory. *Mailing Add:* Dept of Math Long Island Univ Brooklyn Ctr Brooklyn NY 11201

ZUCKERMAN, JEROLD J, b Philadelphia, Pa, Feb 29, 36; m 59; c 5. INORGANIC CHEMISTRY, ORGANOMETALLIC CHEMISTRY. *Educ:* Univ Pa, BS, 57; Harvard Univ, AM, 59, PhD(chem), 60; Cambridge Univ, PhD(chem), 62, ScD, 76. *Prof Exp:* USPHS fel, 60-62; asst prof chem, Cornell Univ, 62-68; assoc prof, State Univ NY Albany, 68-72, dir res, 72-73, prof chem, 72-76; chmn dept, 76-80, PROF CHEM, UNIV OKLA, 76- *Concurrent Pos:* NIH res grants, 63-68; NSF grants, 64-; Advan Res Proj Agency res grants, 65-68; consult, Union Carbide Corp, 65-67; Res Corp res grant, 68-72; State Univ NY Res Found res grant, 69-75; Am Chem Soc Petrol Res Fund res grant, 69-72; sr fel award, Alexander von Humboldt Found, 73; vis prof, Tech Univ, Berlin, Ger, 73; mem int adv bd, Int Comn Appln Mossbuaer Effect, 75; pres bd trustees, Brunswick Common Sch Dist, Rensselaer County, NY, 71-76; regional ed, Inorg & Nuclear Chem Letters, 70-81; chmn ad hoc panel, Mossbauer Spectros, Nat Res Coun-Nat Acad Sci; prof assoc, Univ d Aix Marseille III, France, 79 & 82; consult various industs. *Mem:* Fel AAAS; Am Chem Soc; Royal Soc Chem; Sigma Xi; Am Asn Univ Professors. *Res:* Fourth group organometallic chemistry; structure by x-ray diffraction, infrared, nuclear magnetic resonance, mass and Mossbauer techniques; application of tin-119 Mossabauer spectroscopy to chemical problems. *Mailing Add:* Dept Chem Univ Okla Norman OK 73019

ZUCKERMAN, LEO, b Brooklyn, NY, July 3, 17; m 42; c 3. LABORATORY MEDICINE, TECHNICAL MANAGEMENT . *Educ:* Brooklyn Col, BA, 42. *Prof Exp:* Foreman blood fractionation, E R Squibb & Sons, 42-44, res assoc group leader, 44-52; res assoc, Ortho Res Found, 52-58, supvr blood prod & biol mfg, Ortho Pharmaceut Corp, 58-62, mgr fractionation dept, Ortho Diag, 62-72, mfg dir biochem prod, 72-73, mfg dir serol prod, 73-76, dir mfg serv int, 76-78, dir tech serv int, 78-82, DIR REGULATORY COMPLIANCE, ORTHO DIAG INC, 82- *Mem:* Am Chem Soc; Am Inst Chem; Am Asn Clin Chem; Soc Cryobiol; NY Acad Sci. *Res:* Coagulation; immunology; serology; chromatography; electrophoresis; lyophilization; protein isolation and characterization; clinical chemisty; cryobiology; blood fractionation. *Mailing Add:* Tech Serv Int Ortho Diagnostic Systems Raritan NJ 08869

ZUCKERMAN, MARTIN MICHAEL, b Brooklyn, NY, June 27, 34; m 60. MATHEMATICAL LOGIC. *Educ:* Brandeis Univ, BA, 55; Brown Univ, MA, 60; Yeshiva Univ, PhD(math), 67. *Prof Exp:* Mathematician, Int Elec Co, 61-63; instr math, NY Univ, 63-66; asst prof, Hunter Col, 67-68; asst prof, 68-72, ASSOC PROF MATH, CITY COL NEW YORK, 72- *Mem:* Am Math Soc; Asn Symbolic Logic; Math Asn Am. *Res:* Set theory. *Mailing Add:* Dept of Math Convent Ave & 138th St City Col of New York New York NY 10031

ZUCKERMAN, SAMUEL, b New York, NY, Oct 22, 15; m 38; c 2. ORGANIC CHEMISTRY. *Educ:* City Col, BS, 37; Polytech Inst Brooklyn, MS, 42, PhD, 50. *Prof Exp:* Chemist, 36-50, tech dir & plant mgr, Brooklyn Div, 50-60, V PRES & DIR, H KOHNSTAMM & CO, INC, 59- *Honors & Awards:* Medal Award, Soc Cosmetic Chem, 70. *Mem:* Am Chem Soc; Soc Cosmetic Chem. *Res:* Organic synthesis of dyestuffs; chemical microscopy; cosmetic colors for camouflage; certified food, drug and cosmetic colors. *Mailing Add:* H Kohnstamm & Co Inc 161 Ave of the Americas New York NY 10013

ZUCKERMANN, MARTIN JULIUS, b Berlin, Ger, July 7, 36; m 60; c 4. PHYSICS. *Educ:* Oxford Univ, BA, 60, PhD(phyiscs), 64. *Prof Exp:* Fel, Univ Chicago, 64-65; asst prof physics, Univ Va, 65-67; lectr, Imp Col, Univ London, 67-69; assoc prof, 69-80, PROF PHYSICS, MCGILL UNIV, 80- *Mem:* Am Inst Physics. *Res:* Theoretical solid state physics; investigation into superconductivity and magnetism in disordered systems; weather physics. *Mailing Add:* Dept of Physics Eaton Lab McGill Univ 3600 Univ St Montreal PQ H3A 2T5 Can

ZUDKEVITCH, DAVID, b Hadera, Israel, Jan 15, 30; US citizen; c 1. CHEMICAL ENGINEERING. *Educ:* Israel Inst Technol, BSc, 53, Dipl Ing, 54; Polytech Inst Brooklyn, MChE, 58, PhD(chem eng), 59. *Prof Exp:* Plant engr, Fertilizers & Chem Co, Israel, 53; lab dir, Alliance Tire & Rubber Co, 53-55; engr, Exxon Res & Eng Co, 59-62, eng assoc & consult thermodyn, 62-75; SR ENG ASSOC, ALLIED CHEM CORP, 75- *Concurrent Pos:* Adj prof, Newark Col Eng; mem comt tech data, Am Petrol Inst; mem, Nat Acad Rev Panel for Nat Bur Standards Heat Div, 76-77. *Mem:* Am Chem Soc; Am Inst Chem Engrs; Am Petrol Inst; Gas Processors Asn. *Res:* Development of correlations for physical and thermodynamic properties, especially phase equilibria; evaluation and development of separation and transport processes; evaluation and design of pollution abatement processes and energy utilization. *Mailing Add:* Allied Chem Corp Morristown NJ 07960

ZUECH, ERNEST A, b Frontenac, Kans, Nov 17, 34; m 56; c 3. ORGANIC CHEMISTRY. *Educ:* Kans State Col, Pittsburg, BS, 55, MS, 56; Iowa State Univ, PhD(org chem), 60. *Prof Exp:* Asst org chem, Ohio State Univ, 60-61; chemist, 61-68, sect mgr, 68-78, br mgr, 78-80, DIR PETROL RES, PHILLIPS PETROL CO, 80- *Mem:* Am Chem Soc. *Res:* Organometallic chemistry. *Mailing Add:* Phillips Petrol Co 4th & Keeler Bartlesville OK 74004

ZUEHLKE, CARL WILLIAM, b Bonduel, Wis, Oct 28, 16; m 44; c 2. ANALYTICAL CHEMISTRY. *Educ:* Univ Wis, BS, 38; Univ Mich, MS, 40, PhD(anal chem), 42. *Prof Exp:* Chief chemist, Methods Lab, Gen Chem Div, Allied Chem & Dye Corp, 42-45, E St Louis Works, 45-46, asst mgr, Chem Control Div, 46-48; res assoc, Eastman Kodak Co, 48-61, asst head chem div, Res Labs, 61-68, head anal sci div, Res Labs, 68-79; RETIRED. *Concurrent Pos:* Chmn, Gordon Res Conf Anal Chem, 67. *Mem:* AAAS; Am Mgt Asn; Am Chem Soc. *Res:* Analytical chemistry of germanium; analysis for micro amounts of mercury. *Mailing Add:* 92 Skyview Lane Rochester NY 14625

ZUEHLKE, RICHARD WILLIAM, b Milwaukee, Wis, June 17, 33; m 55; c 3. PHYSICAL CHEMISTRY, MARINE CHEMISTRY. *Educ:* Lawrence Col, BS, 55; Univ Minn, PhD(chem), 60. *Prof Exp:* From instr to asst prof chem, Lawrence Univ, 58-68; chmn dept chem, Univ Bridgeport, 68-73, acad liaison officer, 73-74, Remington prof, 68-80; ASSOC MARINE SCIENTIST, GRAD SCH OCEANOG, UNIV RI, 80- *Concurrent Pos:* Consult, Kimberly-Clark Corp, 60-62; NSF fac fel, Univ Pittsburgh, 66-67; consult, United Illum Co, 69-71 & Wooster Davis & Cifelli Chem Specialties Corp, 70-73; consult, Oxford Univ Press, 74-76 & Sperry Remington Co, 76-77; vis prof oceanog, Univ RI, 76-77. *Mem:* AAAS; Am Geophys Union; Am Chem Soc; fel Am Inst Chem. *Res:* Chemical education; computer simulation and modeling; marine surface chemistry. *Mailing Add:* Grad Sch Oceanog Univ RI Kingston RI 02881

ZUG, GEORGE R, b Carlisle, Pa, Nov 16, 38; m 60; c 2. HERPETOLOGY, MORPHOLOGY. *Educ:* Albright Col, BS, 60; Univ Fla, MS, 63; Univ Mich, PhD(zool), 68. *Prof Exp:* Instr zool, Univ Mich, 68; asst cur herpet, 69-73, CUR HERPET, MUS NATURAL HIST, SMITHSONIAN INST, 73-, CHMN, DEPT VERT ZOOL, 77- *Mem:* Soc Study Evolution; Soc Study Amphibians & Reptiles; Soc Syst Zool; Am Soc Ichthyol & Herpet. *Res:* Systematics and evolution of reptiles and amphibians, particularly chelonians; morphology of reptiles and amphibians and functional relationships; locomotion of vertebrates. *Mailing Add:* Div of Reptiles & Amphibians US Nat Mus Smithsonian Inst Washington DC 20560

ZUGIBE, FREDERICK T, b Garnerville, NY, May 28, 28; m 51; c 7. FORENSIC MEDICINE, CARDIOVASCULAR DISEASES. *Educ:* St Francis Col, BS, 52; Univ Chicago, MS, 59, PhD(anat), 60; WVa Univ, MD, 68; Am Bd Path & Family Practice, dipl. *Prof Exp:* Res histologist, Lederle Labs, Am Cyanamid Co, 50-52, chemist, 53-55; asst ophthal, Col Physicians & Surgeons, Columbia Univ, 55; res histochemist in chg atherosclerosis sect, Vet Admin Hosp, Downey, Ill, 56-60; dir cardiovasc res, Vet Admin Hosp, Pittsburgh, 61-69; CHIEF MED EXAMR, ROCKLAND COUNTY, NY, 69- *Concurrent Pos:* Adj prof, Duquesne Univ; asst res prof, Sch Med, Univ Pittsburgh, 61-69; adj assoc prof path, Columbia Univ, 69-; consult path, ABC Labs; consult, Vet Admin Comt Connective Tissue, Skeletal & Muscles, dir, Angelus Path Lab; consult path, Police Surgeon & Ambulance Corp, physician; fel coun arteriosclerosis & coun thrombosis, Am Heart Asn; continuing educ award path, Am Soc Clin Path & Am Col Path, 75-77, 77-80 & 81-84. *Honors & Awards:* Physicians Recognition Award, AMA, 71-74, 74-77, 77-80 & 81-84; Shields Law Enforcement Award, 73; Distingusihed Serv Award, Rockland County & Am Legion Award for Serv in Nicaragua During Earthquake, 73; Am Heart Asn Serv Recognition Award, 74. *Mem:* Histochem Soc; fel Am Heart Asn; NY Acad Sci; fel Am Acad Forensic Sci; fel Am Col Cardiol. *Res:* Atherosclerosis and aging research; carbohydrate, lipid and enzyme histochemistry; ultramicrohistochemistry; cardiovascular research; histochemistry and forensic pathology research. *Mailing Add:* One Angelus Dr Garnerville NY 10923

ZUHR, RAYMOND ARTHUR, b New York, NY, May 20, 40; m 82; c 2. PLASMA-MATERIAL INTERACTIONS, SURFACE PHYSICS. *Educ:* Rensselaer Polytech Inst, BME, 62, MS, 72, PhD(physics), 74. *Prof Exp:* Assoc, Rensselaer Polytech Inst, 74-76; res assoc, State Univ NY, Albany, 76-77; MEM STAFF, OAK RIDGE NAT LAB, 77- *Mem:* Am Phys Soc; Am Vacuum Soc. *Res:* Plasma-wall interactions in magnetic confinement fusion devices using Rutherford backscattering and nuclear reaction analysis; single surfaces using Rutherford backscattering and electron spectroscopy. *Mailing Add:* Oak Ridge Nat Lab Bldg 3003 PO Box X Oak Ridge TN 37830

ZUIDEMA, GEORGE DALE, b Holland, Mich, Mar 8, 28; m 53; c 4. SURGERY. *Educ:* Hope Col, AB, 49; Johns Hopkins Univ, MD, 53; Am Bd Surg, dipl. *Hon Degrees:* DSc, Hope Col, 69. *Prof Exp:* Intern surg, Mass Gen Hosp, 53-54, asst resident, 54 & 57-58, chief resident, 59; from asst prof to prof, Med Sch, Univ Mich, 60-64; PROF SURG & DIR DEPT, SCH MED, JOHNS HOPKINS UNIV & SURGEON-IN-CHIEF HOSP, 64- *Concurrent Pos:* Fel, Harvard Med Sch, 59; attend surgeon, Ann Arbor Vet Admin Hosp, 60-64; USPHS sr res fel, 61, career develop award, 63; Markle scholar acad med, 61-66; consult, Walter Reed Army Med Ctr, Sinai & Baltimore City Hosps & clin ctr, NIH; asst ed, J Surg Res, 60, ed, 66-, mem, Inst Med, Nat Acad Sci. *Honors & Awards:* Russel Award, Univ Mich, 63; hon fel, Royal Col Surg, Ireland, 72. *Mem:* Fel Am Col Surgeons; Asn Am Med Cols; Soc Univ Surgeons; Am Surg Asn; Am Soc Clin Surg. *Res:* Cardiovascular and acceleration physiology; space medicine; gastrointestinal and hepatic physiology. *Mailing Add:* Dept of Surg Johns Hopkins Hosp Baltimore MD 21205

ZUK, WILLIAM, b New York, NY, July 6, 24; m 48; c 4. STRUCTURAL ENGINEERING. *Educ:* Cornell Univ, BSc, 44, PhD(struct mech), 55; Johns Hopkins Univ, MSc, 47. *Prof Exp:* Asst prof civil eng, Univ Denver, 50-52; from assoc prof to prof civil eng, 55-64, PROF ARCHIT & DIR ARCHIT TECHNOL, UNIV VA, 64- *Concurrent Pos:* Consult, Martin Aircraft Co, 55 & Va Hwy Res Coun, 56- *Mem:* Am Soc Civil Engrs; Am Concrete Inst. *Res:* Structural dynamics; suspension structures; thermal behavior of structures; kinetic structures; systems design. *Mailing Add:* Campbell Hall Univ of Va Charlottesville VA 22903

ZUKEL, WILLIAM JOHN, b Northampton, Mass, June 8, 22. CARDIOVASCULAR DISEASES. *Educ:* Univ Mass, BS, 43; Hahnemann Med Col, MD, 47; London Sch Hyg & Trop Med, dipl pub health, 61. *Prof Exp:* Intern & resident med, Newton-Wellesley Hosp, Newton, Mass, 47-49; from asst med officer in chg to med officer in chg, Newton Heart Prog, USPHS, Mass, 49-51, from asst chief to actg chief, Heart Dis Control Prog, DC, 51-52, asst med, Mass Gen Hosp, 52-53, asst med, Albany Med Col, 53-55, chief oper res, Heart Dis Control Prog, DC, 55-57, asst dir, Nat Heart Inst, 57-58, prog asst, Off Surgeon Gen, 58-60, assoc dir collab studies, Nat Heart Inst, 62-67, assoc dir epidemiol & biomet, 67-69, assoc dir clin appln & prev, 69-79, assoc dir prog coord & plan, 79-81, ASSOC DIR SCI PROGS, DIV HEART & VASCULAR DIS, NAT HEART & LUNG INST, 81-

Concurrent Pos: USPHS fel cardiol, NY State Dept Health, 53-55; assoc clin prof prev med & community health, Sch Med, George Washington Univ, 63-72, assoc clin prof epidemiol & environ health, 72-80. *Mem:* AMA; fel Am Heart Asn; fel Am Pub Health Asn; fel Am Col Cardiol; fel Int Soc Cardiol. *Res:* Clinical trials, prevention and epidemiological studies. *Mailing Add:* Rm 4C10 Fed Bldg 7550 Wisconsin Ave Bethesda MD 20205

ZUKER, MICHAEL, b Montreal, Que, Apr 1, 49. BIOMATHEMATICS. *Educ:* McGill Univ, BSc, 70; Mass Inst Technol, PhD(probability theory), 74. *Prof Exp:* asst res off biomath, 74-80, ASSOC RES OFF BIOMATH, NAT RES COUN CAN, 80- *Concurrent Pos:* Sessional lectr, Carleton Univ, 75-76. *Mem:* Am Math Soc. *Res:* Mathematics, including modeling and statistical analysis of biological systems and computer algorithms applied to problems in molecular biology. *Mailing Add:* Nat Res Coun 100 Sussex Dr Ottawa ON K1A 0R6 Can

ZUKOSKI, CHARLES FREDERICK, b St Louis, Mo, Jan 26, 26; m 53; c 3. SURGERY. *Educ:* Univ NC, AB, 47; Harvard Med Sch, MD, 51. *Prof Exp:* From intern surg to resident, Roosevelt Hosp, New York, 51-52; resident, Univ Ala Hosp, 55-58, instr, Univ, 58-59; res fel, Med Col Va, 59-61; from asst prof to assoc prof, Sch Med, Vanderbilt Univ, 61-68; assoc prof, Univ NC, Chapel Hill, 68-69; PROF SURG, COL MED, UNIV ARIZ, 69- *Concurrent Pos:* Nat Inst Neurol Dis & Blindness spec trainee, 59-61; Nat Inst Allergy & Infectious Dis spec fel, 66-67; Josiah Macy Jr sr fac fel, 76-77. *Mem:* Am Col Surg; Soc Univ Surg; Am Surg Asn; Am Soc Exp Path; Transplantation Soc. *Res:* Homotransplantation; renal allografts; experimental and clinical research. *Mailing Add:* Dept of Surg Univ of Ariz Col of Med Tucson AZ 85724

ZUKOSKI, EDWARD EDOM, b Birmingham, Ala, June 29, 27; m 60; c 3. FLUID MECHANICS, COMBUSTION. *Educ:* Harvard Univ, BS, 50; Calif Inst Technol, MS, 51, PhD(aeronaut), 54. *Prof Exp:* Sr res engr, Jet Propulsion Lab, Calif Inst Technol, 54-57, from asst prof to assoc prof eng, 57-66, PROF JET PROPULSION & MECH ENG, CALIF INST TECHNOL, 66- *Concurrent Pos:* Mem fire res comt, Nat Acad Sci, 65-71. *Mem:* Fel Am Inst Aeronaut & Astronaut; Int Combustion Inst. *Res:* Combustion of air-fuel mixtures; interaction of transverse jets with supersonic flows; separation of turbulent boundary layers; electrical phenomena in high density seeded plasma; uncontrolled fires in buildings. *Mailing Add:* Calif Inst of Technol 1201 E California St Pasadena CA 91125

ZUKOTYNSKI, STEFAN, b Warsaw, Poland, Feb 26, 39; m 68. SOLID STATE PHYSICS, ELECTRICAL ENGINEERING. *Educ:* Univ Warsaw, Mag, 61, PhD(physics), 66. *Prof Exp:* Nat Res Coun Can fel, Univ Alta, 66-68; asst prof, 68-72, assoc prof, 72-81, PROF ELEC ENG, UNIV TORONT0, 81- *Concurrent Pos:* Consult, Elec Eng Consociates Ltd, 71-; resident vis, Bell Labs, 77-78. *Mem:* Can Asn Physicists; Am Phys Soc; Inst Elec & Electronics Eng. *Res:* Electrical and optical properties of semiconductors. *Mailing Add:* Dept of Elec Eng Univ of Toronto Toronto ON M5S 1A4 Can

ZUKOWSKI, LUCILLE PINETTE, b Millinocket, Maine, Nov 2, 16; m 55; c 1. MATHEMATICS. *Educ:* Colby Col, BA, 37; Syracuse Univ, MA, 43. *Prof Exp:* Assoc prof, 45-71, PROF MATH, COLBY COL, 71-, CHMN DEPT, 70- *Concurrent Pos:* Teaching fel math, Univ Mich, 54-55; vis prof, Robert Col, Istanbul, 65-66 & Iranzamin Col, Tehran, Iran, 72-73. *Mem:* Soc Indust & Appl Math; Math Asn Am. *Res:* Algebra; analysis; geometry. *Mailing Add:* 16 Cherry Hill Dr Waterville ME 04901

ZULALIAN, JACK, b New York, NY, Apr 21, 36. METABOLISM. *Educ:* Queens Col, NY, BS, 57; Purdue Univ, Lafayette, PhD(chem), 62. *Prof Exp:* Res assoc natural prod biosynthesis, Korman Res Labs, Albert Einstein Med Ctr, Philadelphia, 62-66; SR RES CHEMIST, METAB, AGR DIV, AM CYANAMID CO, 66- *Mem:* Am Chem Soc. *Res:* Organic synthesis; metabolism of organic compounds designed for use in agriculture as herbicides; pesticides and animal health; radiotracter synthesis. *Mailing Add:* Metab Agr Div Am Cyanamid Co PO Box 400 Princeton NJ 08540

ZULL, JAMES E, b North Branch, Mich, Sept 29, 39; m 61, 68; c 3. BIOCHEMISTRY, CELLULAR BIOLOGY. *Educ:* Houghton Col, BA, 61; Univ Wis, MS, 63, PhD(biochem), 66. *Prof Exp:* Fel biochem, Univ Wis, 65-66; from asst prof to assoc prof, 66-77, PROF BIOL, CASE WESTERN RESERVE UNIV, 77- *Concurrent Pos:* NIH career develop award, 71-76. *Mem:* Am Chem Soc; Am Soc Biol Chemists; AAAS. *Res:* Membrane-hormone interactions; structure and function of biomembranes; hormone mechanisms; peptide structure; lysosome function. *Mailing Add:* Dept of Biol & Biochem Case Western Reserve Univ Cleveland OH 44106

ZULLO, VICTOR AUGUST, b San Francisco, Calif, July 24, 36; m 72. INVERTEBRATE PALEONTOLOGY, ZOOLOGY. *Educ:* Univ Calif, AB, 58, MA, 60, PhD(paleont), 63. *Prof Exp:* Fel systs-ecol prog, Woods Hole Marine Biol Lab, 62-63, resident systematist, 63-67, asst dir prog, 64-66; assoc cur, Dept Geol, Calif Acad Sci, 67-70, chmn, 68-70; dir prog environ sci, 71, PROF GEOL, UNIV NC, WILMINGTON, 71- *Concurrent Pos:* Res assoc, Los Angeles County Mus Natural Hist; adj prof, Univ NC, Chapel Hill. *Mem:* AAAS; Geol Soc Am; Sigma Xi; Paleont Soc; Paleont Res Inst. *Res:* Systematics, evolution and biogeography of Cirripedia; paleontology and biostratigraphy of Cenozoic marine deposits. *Mailing Add:* Dept of Earth Sci Univ of NC Wilmington NC 28403

ZUMAN, PETR, b Prague, Czech, Jan 13, 26; m 51; c 2. ELECTROCHEMISTRY, PHYSICAL ORGANIC CHEMISTRY. *Educ:* Charles Univ, Prague, RNDr(chem), 50; Czech Acad Sci, DrSc, 62; Univ Birmingham, DSc, 68. *Prof Exp:* Head org polarography div J Heyrovsky Inst Polarography, Czech Acad Sci, Prague, 50-68; PROF CHEM, CLARKSON COL TECHNOL, 70- *Concurrent Pos:* Sr vis fel, Univ Birmingham, 66-70; distinguished vis prof, Brooklyn Polytech Inst, 67; co-chmn org div, Int Electrochem Soc, 67-71; assoc mem comn electroanal chem, Int Union Pure & Appl Chem, 71; Theophilus Redwood lectureship, The Chem Soc, 75; consult, Xerox Corp, 72-76, Technicon, 74- & IBM Corp, 75-76 & 81-; vis prof, Univ Amsterdam, 77, Free Univ Brussels, 77 & Univ Utrecht, 79. *Honors & Awards:* Benedetti-Pichler Award, Am Microchem Soc, 75; Gold Medal Award, Am Electroplaters Soc, 76. *Mem:* Am Chem Soc; Sigma Xi; The Chem Soc; Electrochem Soc; Int Electrochem Soc (secy/treas, 81-). *Res:* Use of polarography and other electrochemical and optical methods for study of reactivity, equilibria, kinetics and mechanisms of reactions of organic compounds. *Mailing Add:* Dept of Chem Clarkson Col of Technol Potsdam NY 13676

ZUMBERGE, JOHN EDWARD, b Minneapolis, Minn, Aug 3, 48; m 74. GEOCHEMISTRY, ORGANIC CHEMISTRY. *Educ:* Univ Mich, BS, 70; Univ Ariz, MS, 73, PhD(geosci), 76. *Prof Exp:* Res assoc geochem, Univ Ariz, 76-79; MGR ORG GEOCHEM RES, CITIES SERV CO, 81- *Mem:* Geochem Soc; Am Asn Petrol Geologists. *Res:* Organic geochemistry of Precambrian sedimentary rocks; amino acid biogeochemistry; petroleum geochemistry. *Mailing Add:* 533 Space Sci Bldg Univ Ariz Tucson AZ 85721

ZUMBRUNNEN, CHARLES EDWARD, b Grafton, WVa, Oct 29, 21. DENTISTRY. *Educ:* WVa Wesleyan Col, BS, 43; Northwestern Univ, Chicago, DDS, 45; Univ NC, Chapel Hill, MPH, 64. *Prof Exp:* Pvt dent pract, Huntington, WVa, 48-51 & 54-63; DIR, BUR DENT PUB HEALTH, NH DEPT HEALTH & WELFARE, 64- *Concurrent Pos:* Instr, Sch Dent Med, Tufts Univ, 69-; prof, NH Tech Inst, Concord, 70-71 & 80- *Mem:* Asn State & Territorial Dent Dirs; Am Col Dent; Am Dent Asn. *Res:* Dental health education methodology in elementary schools. *Mailing Add:* NH Dept of Health & Welfare Hazen Dr Concord NH 03301

ZUMMO, NATALE, b Independence, La, Nov 10, 31; m 54; c 3. PLANT PATHOLOGY. *Educ:* Southeastern La Col, BS, 56; La State Univ, MS, 58, PhD(plant path), 60. *Prof Exp:* Res plant pathologist, Sugar Cane Field Sta, 60-66, RES PLANT PATHOLOGIST, US SUGAR CROPS FIELD STA, USDA, 66- *Concurrent Pos:* Sr res fel, Inst Agr Res, Ahmadu Bello Univ, Zaria, Nigeria & cereals pathologist, Orgn African Unity, Sci & Tech Res Comn Joint Proj 26, USAID, 74-76; adj prof plant path, Miss State Univ, 80- *Mem:* Am Phytopath Soc. *Res:* Diseases of sugar cane and sweet sorghum; insect transmission of virus diseases. *Mailing Add:* USDA Sugar Crops Field Sta Rte 13 Box 14 Meridian MS 39301

ZUMOFF, BARNETT, b Brooklyn, NY, June 1, 26; m 51; c 3. MEDICINE, MEDICAL RESEARCH. *Educ:* Columbia Univ, AB, 45; Long Island Col Med, MD, 49. *Prof Exp:* Res fel, Sloan-Kettering Inst, 55-57, from asst to assoc, 57-61; from asst prof to prof med, Albert Einstein Col Med, 65-82; ATTEND PHYSICIAN & CHIEF DIV ENDOCRINOL & METAB, BETH ISRAEL MED CTR, 81-; PROF MED, MT SINAI SCH MED, 82- *Concurrent Pos:* Mem coun arteriosclerosis, Am Heart Asn; asst dir, Clin Res Ctr, Montefiore Hosp, 61-76, dir, 76-81, attend physician, 61- *Mem:* Am Soc Clin Invest; Am Physiol Soc; Aerospace Med Asn; Asn Mil Surg US; Am Fedn Clin Res. *Res:* Human steroid metabolism; cholesterol metabolism and atherosclerosis; radioisotope tracer studies in man; hormones in breast and prostate cancer; obesity; reproductive biology; hormonal chronobiology. *Mailing Add:* Div Endocrinol & Metab Dept Med Beth Israel Med Ctr New York NY 10003

ZUMSTEG, FREDRICK C, JR, b Mansfield, Ohio, Apr 24, 43; m 68. EXPERIMENTAL SOLID STATE PHYSICS. *Educ:* Univ Ill, BS, 64; Univ Rochester, PhD(physics), 72. *Prof Exp:* Res assoc, Cornell Univ, 71-73; RES PHYSICIST, E I DU PONT DE NEMOURS & CO, INC, 73- *Mem:* Am Phys Soc. *Res:* Development and characterization of new electrooptic and nonlinear optic materials. *Mailing Add:* Cent Res Dept Exp Sta E I du Pont de Nemours & Co Inc Wilmington DE 19898

ZUMWALT, GLEN W(ALLACE), b Vinita, Okla, Apr 21, 26; m 52; c 5. AERONAUTICAL ENGINEERING. *Educ:* Univ Tex, BS, 48 & 49, MS, 53; Univ Ill, PhD(mech & aeronaut eng), 59. *Prof Exp:* Instr eng mech, Univ Tex, 53-55; res assoc mech eng, Univ Ill, 55-59; from asst prof to prof aeronaut eng, Okla State Univ, 59-68; DISTINGUISHED PROF AERONAUT ENG, WICHITA STATE UNIV, 68- *Concurrent Pos:* Fel, Inst Aerophys, Univ Toronto, 62; consult various industs. *Mem:* Assoc fel Am Inst Aeronaut & Astronaut; Am Soc Eng Educ; Am Soc Eng Educ. *Res:* Gas dynamics; aerodynamics; wind tunnel test and design. *Mailing Add:* 6311 Marjorie Lane Wichita KS 67208

ZUMWALT, LLOYD ROBERT, b Richmond, Calif, Sept 4, 14; m 60, 78; c 2. PHYSICAL CHEMISTRY. *Educ:* Univ Calif, BS, 36; Calif Inst Technol, PhD(phys chem), 39. *Prof Exp:* Asst, Calif Inst Technol, 36-39, Noyes fel, 39-41; res chemist, Shell Develop Co, 41-42; sr chemist, Oak Ridge Nat Lab, 46-48; dir, Western Div, Tracerlab, Inc, 48-56; vpres, Nuclear Sci & Eng Corp, 56-57; res staff mem, Gen Atomic Div, Gen Dynamics CorP, 57-60; sr res adv, 60-67; prof, 67-80, EMER PROF NUCLEAR ENG, NC STATE UNIV, 80- *Concurrent Pos:* Consult, Gen Atomic Co, 67-79, Los Alamos Sci Lab & Brookhaven Nat Lab, 73-78 & Oak Ridge Nat Lb, 81. *Mem:* Am Chem Soc; fel Am Nuclear Soc. *Res:* Fission product and tritium diffusion and sorption in materials; high temperature and nuclear reactor chemistry; effect of radiaiton on materials; nuclear fuel recycle. *Mailing Add:* Dept of Nuclear Eng NC State Univ Box 5636 Raleigh NC 27650

ZUND, JOSEPH DAVID, b Ft Worth, Tex, Apr 27, 39. MATHEMATICS, MATHEMATICAL PHYSICS. *Educ:* Agr & Mech Col Tex, BA & MS, 61; Univ Tex, PhD(math), 64. *Prof Exp:* Res assoc, Southwest Ctr, Advan Studies, Tex, 64 & 65; from asst prof to assoc prof math, NC State Univ, 65-69; assoc prof, Va Polytech Inst, 69-70; assoc prof math sci, 70-71, PROF MATH & MATH SCI, N MEX STATE UNIV, 72- *Concurrent Pos:* Res assoc, Inst Field Physics, Univ NC, Chapel Hill, 64-65, vis lectr, Dept Math, 65; vis prof, Cambridge Univ, 68-70. *Mem:* Tensor Soc; Am Phys Soc; Ital Math Union; London Math Soc. *Res:* Differential and projective geometry; general relativity; electromagnetic theory. *Mailing Add:* Dept of Math Sci NMex State Univ Las Cruces NM 88003

ZUNDE, PRANAS, b Kaunas, Lithuania, Nov 26, 23; US citizen; m 45; c 5. INFORMATION SCIENCE, SYSTEMS ENGINEERING. *Educ:* Hannover Tech Univ, MS, 47; George Washington Univ, MS, 65; Ga Inst Technol, PhD(indust eng), 68. *Prof Exp:* Consult info systs, Europe, 47-61; syst analyst, Document Inc, Washington, DC, 61-63; proj mgr info systs, 63-64, dep head mgt systs, 64-65; sr res scientist, 65-68, assoc prof info sci & indust eng, 68-72, PROF INFO SCI & INDUST ENG, GA INST TECHNOL, 72- *Concurrent Pos:* Consult, Document, Inc, 65-66, Lockheed-Ga Co, 66-67, Ga State Govt, 71 & Nat Inst Technol, Quito, Ecuador, 72; prin investr, HEW, 69-71 & NSF, 72-; Fulbright prof, Nat Acad Sci, 76; vis prof, Univ Simon Bolivar, Caracas, Venezuela, 78 & J Kepler Univ, Lina, Austria, 81. *Mem:* Sigma Xi; Am Soc Info Sci; Semiotic Soc Am. *Res:* Design of information and communication systems; human factors in systems design; control and socioeconomic systems; operations research; systems theory; design of educational systems; foundations of information science. *Mailing Add:* 1808 Timothy Dr NE Atlanta GA 30329

ZUNG, JOSEPH T, physical chemistry, quantum chemistry, deceased

ZUNG, WILLIAM WEN-KWAI, b Shanghai, China; US citizen. PSYCHIATRY, PSYCHOPHARMACOLOGY. *Educ:* Univ Wis, BS, 49; Union Theol Sem, NY, BD, 52; Trinity Univ, MS, 56; Univ Tex Med Br Galveston, MD, 61. *Prof Exp:* Instr, 65-66, assoc, 66-67, from asst prof to assoc prof, 67-72, PROF PSYCHIAT, MED CTR, DUKE UNIV, 73- *Concurrent Pos:* Clin investr, Vet Admin Hosp, Durham, NC, 65-67; NIMH res career develop award, 67-72; consult, Ctr Studies Suicide Prev, NIMH, 70-71, Career Develop Rev Div, Vet Admin Cent Off, 72- & Res Task Force, NIMH, 72-; consult pub health serv, Bur Drugs, Food & Drug Admin, 73-75 & mem geriat adv panel, 73-75. *Honors & Awards:* Award for Excellence, Am Acad Gen Pract, 69. *Mem:* Asn Psychophysiol Study Sleep; Am Asn Suicidol; Am Psychiat Asn; Acad Psychosom Med; fel Int Col Psychosom Med. *Res:* Affective disorders, especially depressive disorders, anxiety disorders and suicide; psychopharmacology of depression, neurophysiological aspects, including sleep disturbances in psychiatric disorders; biometric approach to psychopathology; mathematical models of psychiatric illness. *Mailing Add:* Vet Admin Hosp 508 Fulton St Durham NC 27705

ZUNKER, HEINZ OTTO HERMANN, b Berlin, Ger, May 27, 24; m 63; c 2. PATHOLOGY. *Educ:* Free Univ Berlin, MD, 54; Am Bd Path, cert, 66. *Prof Exp:* From intern to resident internal med, Free Univ Berlin, 54-56; head pharmacol res, Pharmaceut Co, 57-59; res assoc pharmacol, Columbia Univ, 60-61, assoc path, Col Physicians & Surgeons, 65-68, asst prof, 68; chief path & dir labs, Deaconess Hosp, Evansville, Ind, 68-73; assoc prof path & dir clin path, Col Med, Univ S Fla, 74-75; CHIEF PATHOLOGIST & DIR LABS, BEAUMONT MED SURG HOSP, BEAUMONT, 75- *Concurrent Pos:* Vis fel path, Columbia-Presby Med Ctr, 62-65; asst attend pathologist, Presby Hosp & consult pathologist, Harlem Hosp, New York, 66-68; assoc prof allied health sci, Univ Evansville & Ind State Univ, Evansville, 72-73. *Mem:* Col Am Path; Am Soc Clin Path; NY Acad Sci. *Res:* Pharmacology; experimental pathology; electron microscopy; clinical chemistry. *Mailing Add:* Beaumont Med Surg Hosp PO Box 5817 Beaumont TX 77702

ZUPKO, ARTHUR GEORGE, b Yonkers, NY, Nov 22, 16; m 47; c 1. PHARMACOLOGY. *Educ:* Univ Fla, BS, 42; Purdue Univ, MS, 48, PhD(pharmacol), 49. *Prof Exp:* Malariologist, CZ Authority, 34-36; res assoc biophys & chem, Burroughs-Wellcome & Co, 36-37; asst pharmacol, Purdue Univ, 46-48; from asst prof to prof, St Louis Col Pharm, 49-55; from assoc dean to dean, Long Island Univ, 55-56, provost, 60-75, pres, Brooklyn Col Pharm, 75, pres, Arnold & Marie Schwartz Col Pharm & Health Sci, 75-79; RETIRED. *Concurrent Pos:* Consult, various drug firms. *Honors & Awards:* H H Schaefer Award, Am Pharmaceut Asn, 78. *Mem:* AAAS; Am Pharmaceut Asn; NY Acad Sci; Am Geront Soc. *Res:* Anticholinergics on sweating; insecticide toxicology; hypertension; alcohol metabolism; drug interactions. *Mailing Add:* Arnold & Marie Schwartz Long Island Univ 75 DeKalb Ave Brooklyn NY 11201

ZUPPERO, ANTHONY CHARLES, JR, b Lakewood, Ohio. PHYSICS, SYSTEMS ENGINEERING. *Educ:* Case Western Reserve Univ, BS, 65, PhD(physics), 70. *Prof Exp:* Staff mem systs eng, Albuquerque, NMex, 70-74, staff mem physics, Livermore, Calif, 74-77, mem tech staff systs eng, 77-79, REAL-TIME COMPUT ALGORITHM DESIGN, SANDIA NAT LABS, ALBUQUERQUE, 79- *Mem:* AAAS. *Res:* Laser photochemistry; information systems; pulse power systems; applied engineering; laser strain seismometry; energy research and development. *Mailing Add:* 2435 Jaycox Rd Albuquerque NM 87111

ZURAWSKI, VINCENT RICHARD, JR, b Irvington, NJ, June 10, 46; m 68; c 2. BIOCHEMISTRY, IMMUNOLOGY. *Educ:* Montclair State Col, BA, 68; Purdue Univ, PhD(chem), 73. *Prof Exp:* Res assoc biochem, Purdue Univ, 74; res fel med virol, immunochem & cell biol, Harvard Med Sch, 75-78, instr path, 78-79; VPRES & TECH DIR, CENTOCOR, 79- *Concurrent Pos:* Res fel med virol, immunochem & cell biol, Cardiac Biochem Lab, 75-78, res fel, Cell & Molecular Res Lab, Mass Gen Hosp, Boston, 78-79. *Mem:* AAAS; Am Chem Soc. *Res:* Immunochemical and immunobiological research aimed at producing large amounts of monoclonal antibody of predetermined specificity both in vivo and in vitro for structural studies; therapeutic applications and applications to cellular immunology. *Mailing Add:* Centocor 244 Great Valley Parkway Malvern PA 19355

ZURIER, ROBERT B, b Passaic, NJ, Feb 19, 34; m 62; c 1. CELL BIOLOGY. *Educ:* Rutgers Univ, BS, 55; Southwestern Med Sch, Univ Tex, MD, 62; Univ Pa, MA, 82. *Prof Exp:* Asst, assoc & prof med, Sch Med, Univ Conn, 73-80; PROF MED & CHIEF RHEUMATOLOGY SECT, SCH MED, UNIV PA, 80- *Mem:* Am Soc Clin Invest; Am Rheumatism Asn; Am Asn Immunologists. *Res:* Role of prostaglandins in immune responses and inflammatory reactions. *Mailing Add:* Rheumatology Sect Box 630 Hosp Univ Pa 3400 Spruce St Philadelphia PA 19104

ZURMUHLE, ROBERT W, b Lucerne, Switz, Nov 27, 33; US citizen. NUCLEAR PHYISCS. *Educ:* Univ Zurich, PhD(physics), 60. *Prof Exp:* Res assoc, 61-63, asst prof, 63-67, assoc prof, 67-76, PROF PHYSICS, UNIV PA, 76- *Mem:* Fel Am Phys Soc. *Res:* Nuclear structure and nuclear reactions. *Mailing Add:* Dept of Physics Univ of Pa Philadelphia PA 19104

ZUSI, RICHARD LAURENCE, b Winchester, Mass, Jan 27, 30; m 53; c 3. ZOOLOGY. *Educ:* Northwestern Univ, BA, 51; Univ Mich, MS, 53, PhD(zool), 59. *Prof Exp:* Lab asst dendrol, Univ Mich, 52-53; instr zool, Univ Maine, 58-61, asst prof, 61-63; RES SCIENTIST, DIV BIRDS, NAT MUS NATURAL HIST, SMITHSONIAN INST, 63- *Mem:* AAAS; Cooper Ornith Soc; Wilson Ornith Soc; Am Ornithologists Union; Brit Ornithologists Union. *Res:* Ornithology, especially functional anatomy, behavior, evolution and classification of birds. *Mailing Add:* 4770 Edgefield Rd Bethesda MD 20014

ZUSMAN, FRED SELWYN, b Boston, Mass, July 24, 31; m 54; c 2. MATHEMATICS. *Educ:* Harvard Univ, AB, 52, MA, 55. *Prof Exp:* Analyst, Nat Security Agency, 52-54; sr mathematician appl physics lab, Johns Hopkins Univ, 55-61; sr scientist, Opers Res Inc, 62; dir comput lab, Nat Biomed Res Found, 63; dir comput ctr, Opers Res Inc, 63-67, sr scientist, 67-69; vpres, Sci Mgt Systs, Inc, 69-72, pres, 72; EXEC SCIENTIST & DIR COMPUT SCI, OPERS RES INC, 72- *Concurrent Pos:* Lectr, Sch Hyg & Pub Health, Johns Hopkins Univ, 60-63. *Mem:* Asn Comput Mach; Opers Res Soc Am. *Res:* Operations research; computer technology; system simulation; medical applications of computers. *Mailing Add:* 200 E Indian Spring Dr Silver Spring MD 20901

ZUSMAN, JACK, b Brooklyn, NY, Jan 6, 34; m 55; c 4. PSYCHIATRY, PUBLIC HEALTH. *Educ:* Columbia Univ, AB, 55, MPH, 66; Ind Univ, MA, 56; Albert Einstein Col Med, MD, 60. *Prof Exp:* Intern, USPHS Hosp, New Orleans, La, 60-61, epidemic intel serv officer, Communicable Dis Ctr, 61-62, ment health career develop officer, NIMH, 62-66, staff psychiatrist, Epidemiol Studies Br, 66-67, chief, Ctr Epidemiol Studies, 67-68; assoc prof psychiat, State Univ NY Buffalo, 68-71, dir div community psychiat, 69-74, prof, 71-75; PROF PSYCHIAT, UNIV SOUTHERN CALIF, 75- *Concurrent Pos:* Trainee community psychiat, Columbia Univ, 64-66; adj prof law & psychiat, 74-75 & Univ Southern Calif, 79- *Mem:* AMA; Am Acad Psychiat & Law; Am Psychiat Asn. *Res:* Social factors which influence the course of mental illness and methods of their control; interaction of law and psychiatry; methods of organizing and providing medical care. *Mailing Add:* Univ Southern Calif 1934 Hosp Pl Los Angeles CA 90033

ZUSPAN, FREDERICK PAUL, b Richwood, Ohio, Jan 20, 22; m 43; c 3. OBSTETRICS & GYNECOLOGY. *Educ:* Ohio State Univ, BA, 47, MD, 51. *Prof Exp:* Chief dept obstet & gynec, McDowell Mem Hosp, Ky, 56-58, chief clin serv, 57-58; asst prof obstet & gynec, Sch Med, Western Reserve Univ, 59-60; prof & chmn dept, Med Col Ga, 60-66; Joseph Bolivar DeLee prof & chmn dept, Univ Chicago, 66-74; CHMN DEPT OBSTET & GYNEC, OHIO STATE UNIV, 74- *Concurrent Pos:* Oglebay fel obstet & gynec, Sch Med, Western Reserve Univ, 58-60; assoc examr & dir, Am Bd Obstet & Gynec, 65-80; gynecologist-in-chief, Chicago Lying-In Hosp, 66-74; pres, Barren Found, 74-76; founding ed, J Reprod Med; ed, Am J Obstet & Gynec & Current Concepts in Obstet & Gynec; consult ed, Acta Cytologica, Exerpta Medica, Obstet & Gynec Surv, Hypertension, J Obstet & Gynec (Mex) & J Reprod Med; maternal-fetal medicine. *Res:* Human reproductive physiology; epinephrine and norephinephrine in the obstetric patient. *Mailing Add:* Dept of Obstet & Gynec Ohio State Univ Columbus OH 43210

ZUSPAN, G WILLIAM, b Richwood, Ohio, Mar 24, 26; m 48; c 5. METALLURGICAL ENGINEERING. *Educ:* Ohio State Univ, BMetE & MS, 51. *Prof Exp:* Plant metallurgist, E I du Pont de Nemours & Co, 51-53; res metallurgist, Battelle Mem Inst, 53-54; asst prof metall eng, 54-67, dean freshmen, 67-80, ASSOC PROF ENG, DREXEL UNIV, 67-, ASST VPRES STUDENT AFFAIRS, 72- *Mem:* Am Soc Metals; Am Soc Eng Educ; Nat Asn Corrosion Engrs. *Res:* Chemical metallurgy and corrosion. *Mailing Add:* Drexel Univ 32nd & Chestnut Philadelphia PA 19104

ZUSY, DENNIS, b Milwaukee, Wis, Dec 21, 28. ECOLOGY, PHILOSOPHY OF SCIENCE. *Educ:* Aquinas Inst, MA, 52 & 56; Northwestern Univ, MS, 64, PhD(biol), 67. *Prof Exp:* Asst prof philos, St Xavier Col, Ill, 56-62; from asst prof to prof biol, Clarke Col, 71-81; PROF PHILOS & RELIGION, AQUINAS INST THEOL, 67- *Concurrent Pos:* Vis asst prof biol, Concordia Teachers Col, Ill, 67-71. *Mem:* AAAS; Ecol Soc Am; Sigma Xi. *Res:* Biological rhythms; freshwater ecology; philosophical implications and history of scientific concepts. *Mailing Add:* Aquinas Inst Theol 3642 Lindell Blvd St Louis MO 63108

ZUZACK, JOHN W, b St Louis, Mo, Sept 24, 38; m 62; c 2. ORGANIC CHEMISTRY. *Educ:* St Louis Univ, BS, 61, MS, 64, PhD(org chem), 67. *Prof Exp:* Lab instr freshman & org chem, St Louis Univ, 61-65, res asst med chem, 65-66; ASSOC PROF MED CHEM, ST LOUIS COL PHARM, 66- *Mem:* Am Chem Soc. *Res:* Leukemia chemotherapy; structure activity relationships in rickettsiostatic and analgesic agents. *Mailing Add:* Dept of Chem & Pharmaceut Chem St Louis Col of Pharm St Louis MO 63110

ZUZOLO, RALPH C, b Italy, Sept 5, 29; US citizen. CELL PHYSIOLOGY. *Educ:* NY Univ, BA, 56, MS, 60, PhD(biol), 65. *Prof Exp:* Assoc prof biol, 64-74, supvr, Dept Biol, Sch Gen Studies, 72-74, INSTR, ROBERT CHAMBERS LAB CELLULAR MICROSURGERY, CITY COL NEW YORK, 74-, LAB CO-DIR, 80-; RES SCIENTIST, GUGGENHEIM INST DENT RES, NY UNIV, 78- *Concurrent Pos:* NASA grant, NY Univ, 66, adj asst prof, 74-78, adj assoc prof, 78-; vis scientist, Boyce Thompson Inst Plant Res, 77-78. *Mem:* AAAS; Am Inst Physics; Soc Appl Spectros; Sigma Xi. *Res:* Microsurgery, the application of the laser as a microsurgical tool and the effect of lasers irradiation on cells; effect of chemical carcinogens and bisulfite on nucleic acid in living cells; the effect and detection of insect nuclear polyhedrosis virus after microinjection into early vertebrate embryos. *Mailing Add:* Robert Chambers Lab Microsurgery Marshak Bldg City Col New York New York NY 10031

ZVAIFLER, NATHAN J, b Newark, NJ, Nov 26, 27; m 52; c 3. MEDICINE, IMMUNOLOGY. *Educ:* Haverford Col, BS, 48; Jefferson Med Col, MD, 52. *Prof Exp:* Resident med, Univ Mich, 55-58, instr, Med Sch, 58-59; from instr to prof, Georgetown Univ, 60-70; PROF RHEUMATOL, UNIV CALIF, SAN DIEGO, 70- *Concurrent Pos:* NIH fel arthritis, Univ Mich, 58-60. *Res:* Arthritis. *Mailing Add:* Dept of Med Univ of Calif Hosp 225 W Dickinson St San Diego CA 92103

ZVEJNIEKS, ANDREJS, b Rauna, Latvia, Jan 6, 22; m 51. ORGANIC CHEMISTRY. *Educ:* Latvia Univ, BS, 43, MS, 44; Royal Inst Technol, Sweden, PhD, 55. *Prof Exp:* Res engr, Liljeholmens Stearinfabriks, AB, Sweden, 45-48, sect leader, 48-56; qual control supvr, Conn Adamant Plaster Co, 56; tech adv to plant mgr, Chem Div, Gen Mills, Inc, 57-58, tech dir, Petrol Chem Dept, 58-60, dir appln res, 60-62, sr scientist, 62; pres, AZ Prod, Inc, Fla, 62-72; PRES & CHIEF EXEC OFF, AZS CORP, 72- *Concurrent Pos:* Mem, Hwy Res Bd, Nat Acad Sci-Nat Res Coun, 59- *Mem:* Am Chem Soc. *Res:* Organic ammonium compounds; ore flotation reagents; petroleum chemicals. *Mailing Add:* 2337 Christopher Walk Atlanta GA 30327

ZVENGROWSKI, PETER DANIEL, b New York, NY, Sept 8, 39. MATHEMATICS. *Educ:* Rensselaer Polytech Inst, BS, 59; Univ Chicago, MS, 60, PhD(math), 65. *Prof Exp:* Asst prof math, Univ Ill, Urbana, 64-70; asst prof, 70-72, chmn div pure math, 72-74, ASSOC PROF MATH, UNIV CALGARY, 72- *Res:* Algebraic topology and homotopy theory. *Mailing Add:* Dept of Math Univ of Calgary Calgary AB T2N 1N4 Can

ZVEREV, A(NATOL) I(VAN), b Moscow, Russia, Nov 20, 13; nat US; m; c 3. ENGINEERING. *Educ:* Electrotech Inst Leningrad, Russia, MS, 38; Russian Acad Transp, PhD, 41. *Prof Exp:* Sr engr, Ministry Transp, Russia, 38-39, chief commun engr, 39-40, mil engr, 41-42; design engr, Siemens & Halske Co, Ger, 43-45; prof & dir, Int Prof Sch, Munich, 45-47; sr design engr, Elec Construct Co of Charleroi, Belg, 47-53; sr engr, Electronics Div, 53-56, fel eng, 56-58, sect mgr network synthesis, 58-66, consult engr, Advan Technol Lab, 66-70, ADV ENGR, ADVAN TECHNOL LAB, WESTINGHOUSE ELEC CORP, BALTIMORE, 70- *Mem:* Fel Inst Elec & Electronics Engrs. *Res:* Communications; microwave acoustic nuclear radiation; radar; millimeter waves, parametric devices, filter networks, antennas. *Mailing Add:* Hillcrest Rd Hanover MD 21076

ZWAAN, JOHAN, b Gorinchem, Neth, Sept 28, 34; m 60; c 2. OPHTHALMOLOGY, HUMAN ANATOMY. *Educ:* Univ Amsterdam, MedDrs, 60, Dr(embryol), 63. *Prof Exp:* From asst anat to head asst, Lab Anat & Embryol, Univ Amsterdam, 58-63; fel pediat, Sch Med, Johns Hopkins Univ, 63-64; from asst prof to assoc prof, Sch Med, Univ Va, 64-71; assoc prof anat, 71-78, ASST PROF OPHTHAL, HARVARD MED SCH, 78- *Concurrent Pos:* Lectr, Acad Phys Educ, Amsterdam, 62-63; res assoc ophthal, Children's Hosp Med Ctr, Boston, 71-75; assoc prof anat & resident ophthal, Albany Med Col, 75-78; asst ophthal, Mass Eye & Ear Infirmary, 78-, dir pediat & ocular motility serv, 81-; res assoc, Mass Inst Technol, 81- *Mem:* AAAS; Am Asn Anatomists; Soc Develop Biol; Asn Res Vision & Ophthal; Am Acad Ophthal. *Res:* Chemical and morphological changes in differentiation of vertebrate cells (model system; eye lens); developmental genetics; ophthalmic genetics; teratology; normal and abnormal development of the visual system. *Mailing Add:* Mass Eye & Ear Infirmary 243 Charles St Boston MA 02114

ZWADYK, PETER, JR, b Kansas City, Kans, Apr 3, 41; m 63; c 4. MICROBIOLOGY. *Educ:* Univ Kans, BS, 62; Univ Iowa, MS, 66, PhD(microbiol), 71. *Prof Exp:* Microbiologist, Sci Assocs, 62-63; scientist microbiol, Mead Johnson & Co, 66-69; asst prof path & microbiol, 71-75, asst prof microbiol, 71-76, ASSOC PROF MICROBIOL, DUKE UNIV, 76-, ASSOC PROF PATH, 75-; CHIEF MICROBIOL, VET ADMIN HOSP, DURHAM, 71- *Mem:* Am Soc Microbiol; Sigma Xi; Southeastern Asn Clin Microbiol. *Res:* Mechanism of pathogenecity; antibiotics. *Mailing Add:* Vet Admin Hosp Fulton St & Erwin Rd Durham NC 27705

ZWANZIG, FRANCES RYDER, b South Amboy, NJ, Oct 22, 29; m 53; c 2. CHEMISTRY. *Educ:* Columbia Univ, BA, 51; Yale Univ, MS, 53, PhD(chem), 56. *Prof Exp:* Res asst physiol chem, Sch Med, Johns Hopkins Univ, 55-58; asst ed, Rev Mod Physics, Am Phys Soc, Washington, DC, 69-73; asst ed, Transp Res Bd, 77-81, staff officer, Off Chem & Chem Technol, 80-81, ASSOC ED PROCEEDINGS, NAT ACAD SCI, WASHINGTON, DC, 81- *Mem:* Am Chem Soc. *Mailing Add:* 5314 Sangamore Rd Bethesda MD 20016

ZWANZIG, ROBERT WALTER, b Brooklyn, NY, Apr 9, 28; m 53; c 2. CHEMICAL PHYSICS. *Educ:* Polytech Inst Brooklyn, BS, 48; Univ Southern Calif, MS, 50; Calif Inst Technol, PhD(chem), 52. *Prof Exp:* Res fel theoret chem, Yale Univ, 51-54; asst prof chem, Johns Hopkins Univ, 54-58; phys chemist, Nat Bur Stand, 58-66; res prof, 66-79, DISTINGUISHED PROF, INST PHYS SCI & TECHNOL, UNIV MD, COLLEGE PARK, 79- *Concurrent Pos:* Sherman Fairchild scholar, Calif Inst Technol, 74-75. *Honors & Awards:* Peter Debye Award Phys Chem, Am Chem Soc, 76. *Mem:* Nat Acad Sci; Am Chem Soc; Am Phys Soc; Am Acad Arts & Sci. *Res:* Theoretical chemical physics; statistical mechanics; theory of liquids and gases. *Mailing Add:* Inst Phys Sci & Technol Univ of Md College Park MD 20740

ZWANZIGER, DANIEL, b New York, NY, May 20, 35. THEORETICAL PHYSICS. *Educ:* Columbia Univ, BA, 55, PhD(physics), 60. *Prof Exp:* NSF fel physics, Univ Calif, Berkeley, 60-61, lectr, 61-62; scientist, Univ Rome, 62-63; vis, Saclay Ctr Nuclear Studies, France, 63-65; vis scientist, 65-67, assoc prof physics, 67-74, PROF PHYSICS, NY UNIV, 74- *Concurrent Pos:* Assoc, Europ Orgn Nuclear Res, Switz, 80; vis prof, Ecole Normale Superieure, France, 81. *Mem:* Am Phys Soc; Fedn Am Scientists. *Res:* Quantum field theory; quantum electordynamics; mathematical physics. *Mailing Add:* Dept of Physics NY Univ 4 Washington Pl New York NY 10003

ZWARICH, RONALD JAMES, b Kamloops, BC, Apr 26, 36. PHYSICAL CHEMISTRY. *Educ:* Univ BC, BSc, 63, PhD(chem), 69. *Prof Exp:* Asst prof chem, State Univ NY Albany, 71-75; asst prof, 75-80, ASSOC PROF CHEM, UNIV PETROL & MINERALS, SAUDI ARABIA, 80- *Mem:* Am Chem Soc. *Res:* Molecular spectroscopy; vibrational structure and electronic properties of aromatic and heterocyclic compounds. *Mailing Add:* Box 146 Univ Petrol & Minerals Dhahran Saudi Arabia

ZWARUN, ANDREW ALEXANDER, b Pidvolochyska, Ukraine, Feb 9, 43; US citizen; m 67; c 2. MEDICAL DEVICE DEVELOPMENT, STERILIZATION. *Educ:* Ohio State Univ, BSc, 65, MSc, 67; Univ Ky, PhD(soil microbiol), 70. *Prof Exp:* Asst prof agron, Univ Md, Eastern Shore, 70-71; chief microbiologist, Johnston Labs, Inc, 71-74; res microbiologist, Betz Labs, Inc, 74-76; DIR RES, PROPPER MFG CO, 77- *Mem:* Am Soc Microbiol; Health Indust Mfg Asn; Sigma Xi. *Res:* Automation of microbial and biochemical procedures; trace metal toxicities; microbial activity in soils and water; industrial water treatment. *Mailing Add:* Propper Mfg Co 36-04 Skillman Ave Long Island City NY 11101

ZWEBEN, CARL HENRY, b Albany, NY. COMPOSITE MATERIALS & STRUCTURES. *Educ:* Cooper Union, BCE, 60; Columbia Univ, MS, 61; Polytech Inst, Brooklyn, PhD(appl mech), 66. *Prof Exp:* Res engr, Space Sci Lab, Gen Elec Co, 66-69; sr res engr, Jet Propulsion Lab, 69-70; prog mgr, Mat Sci Corp, 70-72; res assoc, E I du Pont de Nemours & Co, Inc, 72-78; mech technol mgr, 78-80, STAFF ENGR, COMPOSITE MAT & STRUCT, SPACE DIV, GEN ELEC CO, 80- *Concurrent Pos:* Consult, Nat Mat Adv Bd, Nat Acad Sci, 69 & 81-82 & Ctr Composite Mat, Univ Del, 78-; lectr, Univ Calif, Los Angeles, 73- & Univ Cambridge, Eng, 79-; consult, Metal Matrix Composites Info Anal Ctr, US Dept Defense. *Honors & Awards:* Tech Brief Award, NASA, 72. *Mem:* Am Soc Test & Mat; Am Soc Mech Eng; Am Soc Civil Eng; Soc Aerospace Mat & Process Engrs; Am Inst Aeronaut & Astronaut. *Res:* Properties and application of polymer, metal and ceramic matrix fibrous composite materials including, design and analysis, development of test methods, micromechanics, fatigue, fracture, impact, failure mechanics, material development, structured test. *Mailing Add:* Gen Elec Co PO Box 8555 Philadelphia PA 19101

ZWEBEN, STUART HARVEY, b New York, NY, Apr 21, 48; m 71; c 1. COMPUTER SCIENCE. *Educ:* City Col NY, BS, 68; Purdue Univ, MS, 71, PhD(comput sci), 74. *Prof Exp:* Syst analyst comput sci, IBM Corp, 69-70; instr, Purdue Univ, 74; asst prof, 74-80, ASSOC PROF COMPUT & INFO SCI, OHIO STATE UNIV, 80- *Concurrent Pos:* Prin investr res grant, Ohio State Univ, 75, Dow Chem Co, 78-79, US Army Res Off, 80- & Nat Sci Found, 81-; dept coordr grants, Dept Health, Educ & Welfare, 77-79. *Mem:* Asn Comput Mach; Inst Elec & Electronics Engrs. *Res:* Software engineering; programming methodology; analysis of algorithms; data structures. *Mailing Add:* Dept of Comput & Info Sci 2036 Neil Ave Mall Columbus OH 43210

ZWECKER, WILLIAM R, b Vienna, Austria, Apr 19, 12; US citizen; m 46; c 2. ORGANIC CHEMISTRY. *Educ:* Vienna Tech Univ, MChemE, 34; Dresden Tech Univ, PhD(cellulose chem), 37. *Prof Exp:* PRES & CONSULT ENGR, ULTRA CELLULOSE INC, 46- *Concurrent Pos:* Chmn war conf paper & packaging, US Army & Navy, 42. *Mem:* Soc Am Mil Eng. *Res:* Cellulose chemistry; new products; domestic and overseas market analysis; commercial cigarette papers; aircraft insulation and plastic helmet lines. *Mailing Add:* 101 Main St Bethany WV 26032

ZWEIBEL, ELLEN GOULD, b New York, NY, Dec 20, 52. THEORETICAL ASTROPHYSICS. *Educ:* Univ Chicago, BA, 73; Princeton Univ, PhD(astrophys sci), 77. *Prof Exp:* Vis mem, Inst Advan Study, 77-78; STAFF MEM SOLAR PHYSICS, HIGH ALTITUDE OBSERV, NAT CTR ATMOSPHERIC RES, 78- *Mem:* Am Astron Soc. *Res:* Plasma astrophysics, especially cosmic rays and solar and interplanetary physics. *Mailing Add:* Dept Astro-Geophysics Univ Colo Boulder CO 80309

ZWEIFACH, BENJAMIN WILLIAM, b New York, NY, Nov 27, 10; m 37; c 3. PHYSIOLOGY, BIOENGINEERING. *Educ:* City Col New York, BS, 31; NY Univ, MS, 33, PhD(anat), 36. *Prof Exp:* Asst biol, NY Univ, 31-33, asst anat, Col Med, 35-36, res assoc, 38-45; res assoc med, Med Col, Cornell Univ, 45-47, asst prof physiol, 47-52; assoc prof biol, NY Univ, 52-55, from assoc prof path to prof, Sch Med, 55-66; PROF BIOENG, UNIV CALIF, SAN DIEGO, 66- *Concurrent Pos:* Charlton res fel, Med Sch, Tufts Col, 37-38; ed, Josiah Macy, Jr Found Conf Factors Regulating Blood Pressure, 48-53; mem cardiovasc study sect, USPHS & subcomt shock, Nat Res Coun; estab investr, Am Heart Asn, 55-60; career investr, Health Res Coun, New York, 60-66. *Honors & Awards:* Landis Award, 71; Malpighi Gold Medal, 80. *Mem:* Am Physiol Soc; Soc Exp Biol & Med; Histochem Soc; Microcirc Soc (pres, 79-80); fel NY Acad Sci. *Mailing Add:* Dept Bioeng Univ Calif San Diego La Jolla CA 92093

ZWEIFEL, GEORGE, b Rapperswil, Switz, Oct 2, 26; m 53; c 2. ORGANIC CHEMISTRY. *Educ:* Swiss Fed Inst Technol, Dr sc tech, 55. *Prof Exp:* Res asst carbohydrate chem, Univ Edinburgh, 55-56; res fel, Univ Birmingham, 56-58; res assoc boron chem, Purdue Univ, 58-63; assoc prof chem, 63-72, PROF CHEM, UNIV CALIF, DAVIS, 72- *Mem:* Am Chem Soc. *Res:* Chemistry of natural products; utilization of organoboranes and organoalanes in organic syntheses. *Mailing Add:* Dept of Chem Univ of Calif Davis CA 95616

ZWEIFEL, PAUL FREDERICK, b New York, NY, June 21, 29; m 50, 60, 67; c 4. MATHEMATICAL PHYSICS, NUCLEAR SCIENCE. *Educ:* Carnegie Inst Technol, BS, 48; Duke Univ, PhD, 54. *Prof Exp:* Asst physicist, Chem Lab, Am Brake Shoe Co, 48; teacher, Malcom Gordon Sch, NY, 48-49; asst, Duke Univ, 50-52; res assoc, Knolls Atomic Power Lab, Gen Elec Co, 53-56, mgr theoret physics, 56-57; consult physicist, 57-58; assoc prof nuclear eng, Univ Mich, Ann Arbor, 58-60, prof, 60-68; from prof to univ prof, 68-75, DISTINGUISHED UNIV PROF PHYSICS & NUCLEAR ENG, VA POLYTECH INST & STATE UNIV, 75- *Concurrent Pos:* Fel Duke Univ,

52-53; mem adv comt reactor physics, Atomic Energy Comn, 57-64; vis prof, Middle East Tech Univ, Ankara, 64-65; consult, indust orgns & govt labs; vis prof, Rockefeller Univ, 73, 74-75; fel, J S Guggenheim Mem Found, 74-75; vis prof, Univ Florence, 75, vis prof, Univ Ulm, WGer, 78, Univ Milan, 78; consult, Los Alamos Sci Lab, 75- & Nuclear Regulatory Comn, 76. *Honors & Awards:* E O Lawrence Award, 72. *Mem:* Am Phys Soc; Am Nuclear Soc; Fedn Am Sci (secy, 57-58); Am Math Soc; Int Asn Math Physics. *Res:* Mathematical physics; neutron transport theory and nuclear energy; foundations of quantum mechanics. *Mailing Add:* Dept of Physics Va Polytech Inst & State Univ Blacksburg VA 24061

ZWEIFEL, RICHARD GEORGE, b Los Angeles, Calif, Nov 5, 26; m 56; c 3. HERPETOLOGY. *Educ:* Univ Calif, Los Angeles, BA, 50, PhD(zool), 54. *Prof Exp:* From asst cur to assoc cur, 54-65, chmn dept, 68-80, CUR HERPET, AM MUS NATURAL HIST, 65- *Mem:* Am Soc Ichthyol & Herpet; Soc Study Evolution; Ecol Soc Am; Soc Study Amphibians & Reptiles. *Res:* Ecology and systematics of amphibians and reptiles. *Mailing Add:* Dept of Herpet Am Mus of Natural Hist Cent Park W at 79th St New York NY 10024

ZWEIFLER, ANDREW J, b Newark, NJ, Feb 2, 30; m 54; c 5. INTERNAL MEDICINE. *Educ:* Haverford Col, AB, 50; Jefferson Med Col, MD, 54. *Prof Exp:* Intern, Mt Sinai Hosp, New York, 54-55; resident internal med, 57-60, Nat Heart & Lung Inst fel, 60-63, from instr to assoc prof, 60-72, PROF INTERNAL MED, MED CTR, UNIV MICH, ANN ARBOR, 72- *Concurrent Pos:* Vis prof, Meharry Med Col, 67-68; fel coun arteriosclerosis & coun thrombosis, Am Heart Asn. *Mem:* Am Fedn Clin Res. *Res:* Thrombosis; vascular disease; hypertension. *Mailing Add:* Dept of Internal Med Univ of Mich Med Ctr Ann Arbor MI 48104

ZWEIG, ARNOLD, physical organic chemistry, deceased

ZWEIG, FELIX, b Ft Wayne, Ind, Sept 25, 16; m 45; c 3. ELECTRICAL ENGINEERING. *Educ:* Yale Univ, BE, 38, PhD(elec eng), 41. *Prof Exp:* From asst prof to assoc prof, 43-55, chmn dept, 61-66, PROF ENG & APPL SCI, YALE UNIV, 66- *Concurrent Pos:* Res assoc, Mass Inst Technol, 46; consult, Gen Elec Co, 46-48, Gen Precision, Inc, 51-59, Burroughs Corp, 53, Bristol Co, 60-61 & Autonetics Div, NAm Aviation, Inc, 61. *Mem:* Inst Elec & Electronics Engrs. *Res:* Feedback control systems and inertial navigation. *Mailing Add:* Dept of Eng & Appl Sci Yale Univ New Haven CT 06520

ZWEIG, GEORGE, b Moscow, USSR, May 20, 37; US citizen; c 2. HIGH ENERGY PHYSICS, NEUROSCIENCES. *Educ:* Univ Mich, BS, 59; Calif Inst Technol, PhD(physics), 63. *Prof Exp:* Nat Acad Sci-Nat Res Coun fel high energy physics, Europ Orgn Nuclear Res, 63-64; from asst prof to assoc prof physics, 64-67, PROF PHYSICS, CALIF INST TECHNOL, 67- *Concurrent Pos:* Sloan Found fel, 66-68, 74-78; mem staff, Los Alamos Nat Lab, 81-82; MacArthur fel, 81. *Mem:* Am Phys Soc. *Mailing Add:* Lauritsen Lab Calif Inst Technol Pasadena CA 91125

ZWEIG, GILBERT, b New York, NY, Apr 5, 38; c 2. ENGINEERING PHYSICS, PHOTO-OPTICS. *Educ:* NY Univ, BA & BME, 60, MS, 65. *Prof Exp:* Res staff mem, IBM, T J Watson Res Ctr, 61-63; supvr advan res, Pitney-Bowes, Inc, 63-73; vpres & cofounder, Imtex, Inc, 73-74; dep tech dir, TWT Labs Inc, Div Arkwright Inc, 74-78, dir tech bus develop, 78-81; VPRES, MCI OPTONIX INC, SUBSID MITSUBISHI CHEM INDUSTS AM, 81- *Mem:* Sigma Xi; Soc Photog Sci & Eng; Am Asn Physicists Med; Optical Soc Am; Soc Photo-Optical Instrument Eng. *Res:* imaging systems of non-silver classification; including electrophotographic diazo and radioluminescent image technologies. *Mailing Add:* TWT Labs Inc Main St Fiskeville RI 02823

ZWEIG, GUNTER, b Hamburg, Ger, May 12, 23; nat US; m 49; c 2. PESTICIDE CHEMISTRY. *Educ:* Univ Md, BS, 44, PhD(biochem), 52. *Prof Exp:* Lab instr, Univ Md, 48-50; biochemist, Borden Co, 51-53 & C F Kettering Found, 53-57; from assoc chemist to supv chemist, Pesticide Residue Res Lab, Univ Calif, Davis, 57-64, lectr entom, Univ, 57-65; dir life sci div, Syracuse Univ Res Corp, 65-72, dir, Int Indust Develop Ctr, 72-73; chief, Environ Fate Br, Hazard Eval Div, Off Pesticide Progs, Environ Protection Agency, 73-80; VIS SCHOLAR & LECTR, UNIV CALIF, BERKELEY, 80- *Concurrent Pos:* Rothschild fel, Weizmann Inst, 63-64. *Mem:* AAAS; Am Chem Soc. *Res:* Methods of residue analysis of pesticides; metabolism and mechanism of action of pesticides; regulation of pesticides. *Mailing Add:* 25 Mozden Lane Pleasant Hill CA 94523

ZWEIG, HANS JACOB, b Essen, Ger, Jan 10, 27; US citizen; m 69; c 3. MATHEMATICAL STATISTICS, OPERATIONS RESEARCH. *Educ:* Univ Rochester, AB, 49; Brown Univ, MA, 51; Stanford Univ, PhD(statist), 63. *Prof Exp:* Res phys, Eastman Kodak Co, 51-60; mgr optics technol, IBM Corp, 64-68; vpres res & develop, Credit Data, TRW Inc, 68-70; assoc prof opers res, Naval Postgrad Sch, 70-76; MEM STAFF, ESL, INC, 76- *Concurrent Pos:* Consult opers res, Systs Explor, 72-73. *Mem:* Fel Optical Soc Am; Inst Math Statist; NY Acad Sci. *Res:* Optical physics; systems analysis, especially computers and communications. *Mailing Add:* ESL Inc 495 Java Dr Sunnyvale CA 94086

ZWEIG, JOHN E, b Poestenkill, NY, June 24, 36; m 66; c 3. MECHANICAL ENGINEERING. *Educ:* Rensselaer Polytech Inst, BME, 57, MSE, 60, PhD(mech eng), 70. *Prof Exp:* Instr mech eng, Rensselaer Polytech Inst, 57-59; mech engr, 60-64, chief exp mech & thermodynamics lab, 64-71, chief appl math & mech div, 71-77, CHIEF DEVELOP ENGR, WATERVLIET ARSENAL, 77- *Mem:* Am Soc Mech Engrs; Soc Exp Stress Anal. *Res:* Fluid dynamics; heat transfer; experimental mechanics. *Mailing Add:* US Army Benet Lab Watervliet Arsenal Watervliet NY 12189

ZWEIG, RONALD DAVID, b Gary, Ind, Apr 14, 47. BIOLOGY, LIMNOLOGY. *Educ:* Univ Calif, Berkeley, BA, 71. *Prof Exp:* Staff res assoc plant path, Univ Calif, Berkeley, 72; res asst neurophysiol, Boston Univ, 74-75; co-prin investr, Ecol Modeling, 77-80, prin investr, Aquacult, 80-81, DIR AQUATIC STUDIES, NEW ALCHEMY INST, 75- *Concurrent Pos:* Task force mem, US Cong Off Technol Assessment, 78 & 79; adj fac, Ramapo Col, Dartmouth Col, Univ Calif, Santa Cruz, Skidmore Col & Univ New Hampshire; Aquacult res & training adv, Fac UN, Wuxi, China, 82- *Honors & Awards:* Sarah Lawrence lectr, Lowell Lectr Series, New Eng Aquarium. *Mem:* Am Fisheries Soc. *Res:* Tropical biology; aquatic biology; marine biology; aquaculture; agriculture; hydroponics; integrated systems; ecological village design and architecture. *Mailing Add:* New Alchemy Inst 237 Hatchville Rd East Falmouth MA 02536

ZWEIMAN, BURTON, b New York, NY, June 7, 31; m 62; c 2. MEDICINE. *Educ:* Univ Pa, AB, 52, MD, 56. *Prof Exp:* Assoc med, 63-67, from asst prof to assoc prof, 67-75, co-chief allergy & immunol, 69-74, CHIEF ALLERGY & IMMUNOL SECT, UNIV PA SCH OF MED, 74-, PROF MED, 75- *Concurrent Pos:* Chmn, Weather and Air Pollution Comt, Am Acad Allergy, 71-72; mem bd dirs, Am Bd Allergy & Immunol, co-chmn, 79-80. *Mem:* Am Bd Allergy & Immunol (treas, 76-78); Am Acad Allergy; Am Asn Immunol; Am Col Physicians; Am Fedn Clin Res. *Res:* Cellular inflammatory reactions in allergic diseases; immunologic mechanisms in demyelinating disease and systemic lupus erythematosus. *Mailing Add:* Univ Pa Sch of Med 36th & Hamilton Walk Philadelphia PA 19104

ZWEMER, THOMAS J, b Mishawaka, Ind, Mar 23, 25; m 49; c 3. ORTHODONTICS. *Educ:* Univ Ill, DDS, 50; Northwestern Univ, MSD, 54. *Prof Exp:* Instr pedodont, Marquette Univ, 50-52, from asst prof to assoc prof oral rehab, 52-58; from asst prof to assoc prof orthod, Sch Dent, Loma Linda Univ, 58-66, chmn dept, 60-66; PROF DENT & ASSOC DEAN CLIN SCI, SCH DENT, MED COL GA, 66- *Concurrent Pos:* Mem attend staff, Wood's Vet Admin Hosp, 54-56; consult, Cerebral Palsy Clin, 54-58; chief dent serv, Milwaukee Children's Hosp, 55-58. *Mem:* Am Asn Orthod; Am Dent Asn; Am Col Dent; Int Asn Dent Res. *Res:* Health care delivery systems; physical anthropology. *Mailing Add:* Sch of Dent Med Col of Ga Augusta GA 30902

ZWERDLING, SOLOMON, b New York, NY, Jan 31, 22; m 44; c 3. SOLID STATE PHYSICS, PHYSICAL CHEMISTRY. *Educ:* Drew Univ, BA, 43; Johns Hopkins Univ, MA, 44; Columbia Univ, MA, 47, PhD(chem), 52. *Prof Exp:* Instr chem, Johns Hopkins Univ, 43-44; asst prof naval sci & tactics, Columbia Univ, 46, asst chem, 46-49; sr res chemist, Lever Bros Co, 51-52; asst group leader & div staff physicist, Lincoln lab, Mass Inst Technol, 52-63, staff physicist, Div Sponsored Res, Ctr Mat Sci & Eng, 63-68; res scientist, Douglas Advan Res Labs, Calif, 68-70, mgr res, Solid State Sci Dept, McDonnell Douglas Res Labs, 70-74; dir solar energy prog, Argonne Nat Lab, 75-77; mgr res & develop, Northeast Solar Energy Ctr, 77-79; SUPVR ADVAN PHOTOVOLTAIC DEVELOP GROUP, JET PROPULSION LAB, 79- *Concurrent Pos:* Mem bd dir, A D Jones Optical Co Inc, Burlington, Mass. *Mem:* Fel Optical Soc Am; Int Solar Energy Soc; sr mem Inst Elec & Electronics Engrs; sr mem Inst Elec & Electronic Engrs; Am Phys Soc. *Res:* Infrared absorption of solids; infrared magneto-optical effects in semiconductors at liquid helium temperature; physics of semiconductor electronic energy band structure; excitons in semiconductors; far infrared spectroscopy and detectors; metal physics, strength and corrosion; general solar energy conversion; photovoltaic solar cells; chemical vapor deposition technology for thin film electronic devices. *Mailing Add:* Jet Propulsion Lab MS 512-103 4800 Oak Grove Dr Pasadena CA 91109

ZWERLING, ISRAEL, b New York, NY, June 12, 17; m 40; c 2. PSYCHIATRY. *Educ:* City Col New York, BS, 37, MS, 38; Columbia Univ, PhD(psychol), 47; State Univ NY, MD, 50. *Prof Exp:* High sch instr, NY, 39-42; instr psychol, City Col New York, 47-49 & Hunter Col, 49-50; from asst prof to prof psychiat, Albert Einstein Col Med, 54-73, exec chmn psychiat, 68-71; dir, Bronx State Hosp, 66-73; PROF MENT HEALTH SCI & CHMN DEPT, HAHNEMANN MED COL, 73- *Concurrent Pos:* Lectr & psychiatrist-in-chg alcohol clin, State Univ NY, 54-55. *Mem:* Am Psychosom Soc; Am Psychol Asn; Am Psychoanal Asn. *Res:* Social and community psychiatry. *Mailing Add:* Dept Ment Health Sci Hahnemann Med Col Philadelphia PA 19102

ZWERMAN, PAUL JOSEPH, b Kimball, Ohio, Apr 26, 11; m 35; c 1. CONSERVATION. *Educ:* Ohio State Univ, BS, 31, MS, 38, PhD(soils), 49. *Prof Exp:* Soil scientist, Soil Conserv Serv, USDA, 34-50; from assoc prof to prof soil & water conserv, 50-76, EMER PROF SOIL CONSERV, CORNELL UNIV, 76- *Concurrent Pos:* Dist soil scientist, Bur Land Mgt, 76- *Mem:* Soil Sci Soc Am; Am Soc Agr Eng; Soil Conserv Soc Am; Sigma Xi; fel Am Soc Agron. *Res:* Environmental quality; relating soil and management to the problem of waste disposal; soil and water conservation; drainage and tillage. *Mailing Add:* Dept of Agron Cornell Univ Ithaca NY 14850

ZWERNER, ROBERT KENT, b Terre Haute, Ind, Oct 3, 43; m 77; c 4. MICROBIOLOGY. *Educ:* Ind Univ, BA, 65; Ind State Univ, MA, 67; Purdue Univ PhD(immunol), 73. *Prof Exp:* Res fel, Dept Microbiol, 73-74, res fel, Nat Cancer Inst, 74-76, res assoc, 76-79, assoc coordr, Tissue Culture Core Fac, Univ Ala Tumor Inst, 77-81, ASSOC SCIENTIST, DIABETES RES & TRAINING CTR, UNIV ALA MED CTR, 77-, ASST RES PROF, DEPT MICROBIOL, 79-, DIR, CELL CULTURE CTR, 79- *Res:* Large scale mammalian cell culture-growing suspension cell lines in fermenters and developing new methods of growth and harvesting products from cultures; endocrine effects on the immune system: the influence of hormones on ability of the immune system to respond to antigenic stimulus. *Mailing Add:* Rm 820 Diabetes Hosp Univ Ala Med Ctr Birmingham AL 35294

ZWICK, DAAN MARSH, b New York, NY, July 28, 22; m 48; c 3. PHOTOGRAPHIC CHEMISTRY, PHYSICS. *Educ:* Univ Vt, BSChem, 43. *Prof Exp:* Instr physics, Univ Vt, 43-44; res chemist photog chem, 44-56, res assoc photog sci, 56-73, sr lab head color physics, 73-78, SR RES ASSOC, EASTMAN KODAK CO RES LABS, 78- *Honors & Awards:* Kalmus Gold Medal, Soc Motion Picture & TV Engrs, 72, AGFA Geuaert Gold Medal, 75. *Mem:* Fel Soc Motion Picture & TV Engrs; Soc Photog Scientists & Engrs. *Res:* Problems in the image structure of photographic materials; color reproduction with photographic materials. *Mailing Add:* 25 Boulevard Pkwy Rochester NY 14612

ZWICK, EARL J, b Canton, Ohio, May 20, 31. MATHEMATICS. *Educ:* Kent State Univ, BS, 53, MS, 57; Ohio State Univ, PhD(math ed), 64. *Prof Exp:* Teacher pub schc, Ohio, 53-61; instr math, Ohio State Univ, 62-63; assoc prof, 63-72, PROF MATH, IND STATE UNIV, TERRE HAUTE, 72- *Mem:* Nat Coun Teachers Math. *Res:* Teaching methods. *Mailing Add:* Dept of Math Ind State Univ Terre Haute IN 47809

ZWICK, ROBERT WARD, b Seattle, Wash, Sept 22, 22; m 48; c 2. ENTOMOLOGY. *Educ:* Univ Wash, BS, 47; Wash State Univ, MS, 51, PhD(entom), 62. *Prof Exp:* Res biologist, Fisheries Res Inst, 47-50; entomologist, 10th Naval Dist, San Juan, PR, 53-57 & Eng Sect, US Army Caribbean, CZ, 57-59; asst entomologist, Wash State Univ, 59-62; entomologist, Pan Am Sanit Bur Jamaica, 62-63; asst prof entom, 64-69, ASSOC PROF ENTOM, MID-COLUMBIA EXP STA, ORE STATE UNIV, 69- *Mem:* Entom Soc Am. *Res:* Control and management of insect and mite pests of deciduous tree fruit crops. *Mailing Add:* Mid-Columbia Exp Sta 3005 Exp Sta Dr Hood River OR 97031

ZWICKEL, FRED CHARLES, b Seattle, Wash, Dec 18, 26; m 51; c 3. WILDLIFE ECOLOGY, ZOOLOGY. *Educ:* Wash State Univ, BSc, 50, MSc, 58; Univ BC, PhD(zool), 65. *Prof Exp:* Biologist, State Dept Game, Wash, 50-61; asst prof wildlife ecol, Ore State Univ, 66-67; asst prof zool, 67-71, assoc prof, 71-77, PROF ZOOL, UNIV ALTA, 77- *Concurrent Pos:* Nat Res Coun Can-NATO overseas res fel natural hist, Aberdeen Univ, 65-66; sabbatical study, Inst Appl Zool, Univ Hokkaido, Sapporo, Japan, 73-74 & Wau Ecol Inst, Papua, New Guinea, 80-81. *Honors & Awards:* Roberts Award, Cooper Ornith Soc, 65. *Mem:* Am Ornith Union; Cooper Ornith Soc; Wildlife Soc; Am Soc Mammal; Can Soc Zool. *Res:* Population ecology; general biology of gallinaceous birds and land mammals. *Mailing Add:* Dept of Zool Univ of Alta Edmonton AB T6G 2E9 Can

ZWICKER, BENJAMIN M G, b Pendleton, Ore, July 11, 15; m 42; c 2. CHEMISTRY. *Educ:* Whitman Col, AB, 35; Univ Wash, MS, 38, PhD(phys chem), 40. *Prof Exp:* Res chemist, B F Goodrich Chem Co, 40-43, mgr, Akron Exp Sta, 43-50, dir new prod planning, 50-60, dir planning, 60-78, incharge environ sci, 58-78; res assoc, Scripps Inst Oceanog, Univ Calif, San Diego, 79-81; RETIRED. *Concurrent Pos:* Mem tech & res comts, Off Rubber Reserve, 43-50; consult indust chem & toxicol, 78- *Mem:* Am Chem Soc; Soc Chem Indust; Am Inst Chem Eng. *Res:* Analytical, physical and organic chemistry; academic oceanography; geology; microscopy; polymer chemistry; industrial chemistry and economics; research, development and business management toxicology, biodegradation. *Mailing Add:* 8581 Tulane St San Diego CA 92122

ZWICKER, WALTER KARL, b Vienna, Austria, Sept 5, 23; US citizen; m 56. SOLID STATE CHEMISTRY. *Educ:* Univ Vienna, PhD(mineral chem), 54. *Prof Exp:* Res fel chem, Harvard Univ, 54-55; res chemist, Metals Res Labs, Union Carbide Corp, 55-59, & Res Ctr, Union Carbide Nuclear Co, 59-64; sr res chemist, Thiokol Chem Corp, 64-65; SR PROJ LEADER, PHILIPS LABS, N AM PHILIPS CORP, 65- *Mem:* Sr mem Am Chem Soc; Electrochem Soc; fel Am Mineral Soc. *Res:* Solid state science; crystal growth; mineral synthesis and phase equilibria; thin films; semiconductors and dielectrics. *Mailing Add:* Philips Labs NAm Philips Corp Briarcliff Manor NY 10510

ZWICKEY, ROBERT EARL, veterinary medicine, deceased

ZWIEBEL, IMRE, chemical engineering, see previous edition

ZWIEP, DONALD N, b Hull, Iowa, Mar 18, 24; m 48; c 4. MECHANICAL ENGINEERING. *Educ:* Iowa State Univ, BS, 48, MS, 51. *Hon Degrees:* DE, Worcester Polytech Inst, 65. *Prof Exp:* From asst prof to assoc prof mech eng, Colo State Univ, 51-57; PROF MECH ENG & HEAD DEPT, WORCESTER POLYTECH INST, 57- *Concurrent Pos:* Chief consult, Aviation Div, Forney Mfg Co, 56-57; chmn trustees, James F Lincoln Arc Welding Found, 76- *Mem:* Am Soc Mech Engrs; Am Soc Eng Educ; Am Welding Soc. *Res:* Design and mechanics. *Mailing Add:* Dept of Mech Eng Worcester Polytech Inst Worcester MA 01609

ZWIER, PAUL J, b Denver, Colo, Oct 24, 27; m 51; c 6. MATHEMATICS. *Educ:* Calvin Col, AB, 50; Univ Mich, MA, 51; Purdue Univ, PhD(math), 60. *Prof Exp:* Instr math, Purdue Univ, 58-60; from asst prof to assoc prof, 60-74, chmn dept, 77-80, PROF MATH, CALVIN COL, 74- *Mem:* Math Asn Am; Am Math Soc. *Res:* Non-associative rings. *Mailing Add:* Dept of Math Calvin Col Grand Rapids MI 49506

ZWILLING, BRUCE STEPHEN, b Brooklyn, NY, Jan 16, 43; m 67; c 2. IMMUNOBIOLOGY. *Educ:* Fairleigh Dickinson Univ, BS, 65; NY Univ, MS, 68; Univ Mo, PhD(microbiol), 71. *Prof Exp:* Guest worker immunol, Biol Br, Nat Cancer Inst, 72-73; asst prof, 74-79, ASSOC PROF MICROBIOL, COL BIOL SCI, OHIO STATE UNIV, 79- *Mem:* AAAS; Am Soc Microbiol; Am Asn Cancer Res; Am Asn Immunol. *Res:* Tumor immunology and immunotherapy including the effects of chemical carcinogens on immunity and the role of the macrophage in neoplasia. *Mailing Add:* Dept of Microbiol Ohio State Univ Col Biol Sci Columbus OH 43210

ZWILSKY, KLAUS M(AX), b Berlin, Ger, Aug 16, 32; US citizen; m 56; c 2. METALLURGY, MATERIALS SCIENCE. *Educ:* Mass Inst Technol, BS, 54, MS, 55, ScD(metall), 59. *Prof Exp:* Dir metall res, New Eng Mat Lab, Inc, 59-62; sr res assoc metall, Pratt & Whitney Aircraft Div, United Aircraft Corp, 62-63; sr scientist solid state, Melpar, Inc, Westinghouse Air Brake Co, 63-64; head alloy develop br, Annapolis Div, Naval Ship Res & Develop Ctr, 64-67; phys metallurgist, AEC, Dept of Energy, 67-73, chief mat & radiation effects br, Off of Fusion Energy, 73-81; EXEC DIR, NAT MAT ADV BD, NAT ACAD SCI, 81- *Mem:* Fel Am Soc Metals; Am Nuclear Soc; Sigma Xi. *Res:* Physical and nuclear metallurgy including high temperature, composite, and powder metallurgy; nuclear materials for fission reactors and materials for fusion reactors; administration of studies on strategic materials; materials policy and materials science and engineering. *Mailing Add:* Nat Mat Adv Bd 2101 Constitution Ave Washington DC 20418

ZWISLOCKI, JOZEF JOHN, b Lwow, Poland, Mar 19, 22; nat US; m 54. AUDITORY BIOPHYSICS, PSYCHOPHYSICS. *Educ:* Swiss Fed Tech Inst, EE, 44, DTech Sci, 48. *Prof Exp:* Res asst & head electroacoustical lab dept otolaryngol, Univ Basel, 45-51; res fel, Psychoacoustics Lab, Harvard Univ, 51-57; res assoc prof audiol, 57-62, from assoc prof to prof elec eng, 60-74, dir, Lab Sensory Commun, 63-74, PROF SENSORY SCI & DIR INST SENSORY RES, SYRACUSE UNIV, 74- *Concurrent Pos:* Assoc res prof, State Univ NY Upstate Med Ctr, 61-67, res prof, 67-; mem comt hearing & bio-acoustics, Nat Res Coun, 53-, mem exec coun, 64-68; mem rev panel commun sci, NIH, 66-70, chmn, 69-70, mem communicative disorders rev comt, 71-75; Sigma Xi fac res award, 73; Amplifon Prize, Int Ctr Res & Study, Milan, Italy, 76. *Mem:* AAAS; fel Acoust Soc Am; Soc Neurosci; NY Acad Sci; Asn Res Otolaryngology. *Res:* Sound transmission in middle and inner ear; psychoacoustics; mathematical analysis of auditory system; audiological diagnostic methods; acoustic instruments. *Mailing Add:* Inst Sensory Res Syracuse Univ Syracuse NY 13210

ZWOLENIK, JAMES J, b Cleveland, Ohio, Dec 31, 33. SCIENCE POLICY. *Educ:* Western Reserve Univ, AB, 56; Yale Univ, PhD(phys chem), 61; Univ Cambridge, PhD, 64. *Prof Exp:* NSF fel, Queens Col, Univ Cambridge, 60-62; res chemist, Fundamental Res Group, Chevron Res Co, 63-67; assoc prog dir chem dynamics, Chem Sect, 67-70, staff assoc, Off Policy Studies, 70-71, Spec Anal Sect, Div Sci Resources Studies, 71-74, off div dir, Div Sci Resources Studies, 74-75, staff dir & exec secy, Comt Eighth Nat Sci Bd, 75-76, spec asst, Nat Sci Bd, 76-79, STAFF ASSOC, OFF AUDIT & OVERSIGHT, NSF, 79- *Concurrent Pos:* Instr, Exten Div, Univ Calif, Berkeley, 65-67; collabr, Smithsonian Radiation Biol Lab, 68-70; vpres, Higher Educ Group, Wash, DC, 76-77, pres, 77-78. *Mem:* Am Chem Soc; Am Phys Soc; AAAS; Am Asn Advan Humanities. *Res:* Photochemistry; kinetic spectroscopy; science policy; higher education. *Mailing Add:* Nat Sci Found 1800 G St Northwest Washington DC 20550

ZWOLINSKI, BRUNO JOHN, b Buffalo, NY, Nov 4, 19; m 52; c 3. PHYSICAL CHEMISTRY. *Educ:* Canisius Col, BS, 41; Purdue Univ, MS, 43; Princeton Univ, AM, 44, PhD(phys chem), 47. *Prof Exp:* Instr chem eng, sci & mgt war training, Purdue Univ, 42; asst, Princeton Univ, 43-44; res scientist, Manhattan Proj, Columbia Univ, 44-45; Am Chem Soc fel, Univ Utah, 47-48, asst prof chem, 48-53; sr physicist, Stanford Res Inst, 53-57; prin res chemist & dir res projs chem & petrol res lab & lectr chem, Carnegie Inst Technol, 57-61; dir, Thermodyn Res Ctr, 61-78, PROF CHEM, TEX A&M UNIV, 61- *Concurrent Pos:* Asst dir chem prog, NSF, 54-57; mem adv bd off critical tables, Nat Res Coun. *Mem:* Fel NY Acad Sci; fel Am Inst Chemists; fel AAAS. *Res:* Compilation of selected values of physical, thermodynamic and spectral data of chemical compounds; dynamic properties of liquids; charge or electron transfer phenomena in chemical kinetics; statistical thermodynamics. *Mailing Add:* Thermodyn Res Ctr Tex A&M Univ College Station TX 77840

ZWOLINSKI, MALCOLM JOHN, b Winchester, NH, Oct 23, 37; m 59; c 2. FOREST HYDROLOGY, FOREST FIRE MANAGEMENT. *Educ:* Univ NH, BS, 59; Yale Univ, MF, 61; Univ Ariz, PhD(watershed mgt), 66. *Prof Exp:* Res assoc watershed mgt, 64-65, from asst prof to assoc prof, 66-72, PROF WATERSHED MGT, UNIV ARIZ, 72-, ASSOC DIR SCH RENEWABLE NATURAL RESOURCES, 75- *Mem:* Fel AAAS; Soc Am Foresters; Soil Conserv Soc Am. *Res:* Watershed hydrology; effects of forest management practices on water yields, including infiltration, soil erosion, interception by vegetation and soil moisture changes; prescribed burning in natural forest ecosystems; forest fire management. *Mailing Add:* Sch Renewable Natural Resources Col of Agr Univ of Ariz Tucson AZ 85721

ZWORYKIN, VLADIMIR KOSMA, b Mourom, Russia, July 30, 89; nat US; m 16, 51; c 2. PHYSICS. *Educ:* Inst Technol, Petrograd, Russia, EE, 12; Univ Pittsburgh, PhD(physics), 26. *Hon Degrees:* DSc, Polytech Inst Brooklyn, 38 & Rutgers Univ, 72. *Prof Exp:* Res engr, Westinghouse Elec & Mfg Co, 20-29; dir electronic res, RCA Mfg Co, 29-42, assoc res dir, RCA Labs, RCA Corp, 42-45, dir electronic res, 46-54, vpres & tech consult, 47-54, consult, 54-78, hon vpres, 54-; RETIRED. *Honors & Awards:* Liebmann Prize, 34; Overseas Award, Brit Inst Elec Eng, 39, Faraday Medal, 65; Modern Pioneer Award, Nat Mfrs Asn, 40; Rumford Medal, Am Acad Arts & Sci, 41; Cert Appreciation, US War Dept, 45; Potts Medal, Franklin Inst & Cert Commendation, US Dept Navy, 47; Chevalier Cross, Legion of Honor, France, 48; Gold Medal Achievement, Poor Richard Club, 49; Progress Medal, Soc Motion Picture & TV Engrs, 50; Lamme Award, Inst Elec & Electronics Engrs, 48, Medal of Honor, 51, Edison Medal, 52; Gold Medal, French Union Inventors, 54; Cristoforo Colombo Award, 59; Order of Merit, Italian Govt, 59; Trasenster Medal, Univ Liege, 59, Med Electronics Medal, 63; Broadcast Pioneers Award, 60. *Mem:* Nat Acad Sci; AAAS; Nat Inventors Hall Fame; Asn Russian-Am Engrs; Japan Soc Med Electronics. *Res:* Electronics; television; electron optics; electron microscope. *Mailing Add:* RCA Labs RCA Corp Princeton NJ 08540

ZWOYER, EUGENE, b Plainfield, NJ, Sept 8, 26; m 46; c 3. STRUCTURAL ENGINEERING. *Educ:* Univ NMex, BS, 47; Ill Inst Technol, MS, 49; Univ Ill, PhD(eng), 53. *Prof Exp:* Assoc prof civil eng, Univ NMex, 48-61, res prof civil eng & dir Eric H Wang Civil Eng Facil, 61-70; EXEC DIR & SECY, AM SOC CIVIL ENGRS, 72- *Concurrent Pos:* Res assoc, Univ Ill, 51-53, consult engr, Eugene Zwoyer & Assocs, 53-72; mem, Interprof Coun Environ Design, 72-, secy, 72 & 78; trustee, People-to-People Int, 74 & Small Bus Res Corp, 76-79; mem, Engr Joint Coun Int Comn, 75-79, Cert Comn, 75-79 & Finance Comt, 75-79, dir, Coun, 77-79, chmn, Sub-Comt for 1979 UN Conf Sci & Technol for Develop, 78-80; dir, Eng Socs Comn Energy, 77-, secy, treas & mem exec comt, 78. *Mem:* AAAS; Am Soc Civil Engrs; Nat Soc Prof Engrs; Am Concrete Inst; Am Soc Eng Educ. *Res:* Ultimate strength of structures, particularly on structures to resist effects of nuclear weapons. *Mailing Add:* Am Soc Civil Engrs 345 E 47th St New York NY 10017

ZYCH, ALLEN DALE, b Cleveland, Ohio, Apr 8, 38; m 75; c 2. ASTROPHYSICS. *Educ:* Case Inst Technol, BS, 61, MS, 65; Case Western Reserve Univ, PhD(physics), 68. *Prof Exp:* Fel physics, Case Western Reserve Univ, 68-70, asst prof, 70-77, ASSOC PROF PHYSICS, UNIV CALIF, RIVERSIDE, 77- *Mem:* Am Phys Soc; Am Geophys Union; Am Astron Soc; Inst Electronics & Elec Engrs. *Res:* Experimental high energy astrophysics. *Mailing Add:* Dept of Physics Univ of Calif Riverside CA 92502

ZYGMONT, ANTHONY J, b Philadelphia, Pa, Sept 16, 37. SYSTEMS ENGINEERING. *Educ:* Villanova Univ, BEE, 59; Drexel Univ, MSEE, 63; Univ Pa, PhD(elec eng), 71. *Prof Exp:* Jr engr commun systs, Philco Corp, 59-62; engr, Radio Corp Am, 62-63; sr engr radar systs, Philco Corp, 63; ASSOC PROF ELEC ENG SYSTS, VILLANOVA UNIV, 63- *Concurrent Pos:* Educ consult, Philadelphia Elec Co, 70- *Mem:* Inst Elec & Electronics Engrs; Instrument Soc Am; Am Soc Eng Educ. *Res:* Application of systems engineering to large scale problems, especially the problems of identification and optimization. *Mailing Add:* Dept of Elec Eng Villanova Univ Villanova PA 19085

ZYGMUND, ANTONI, b Warsaw, Poland, Dec 26, 00; nat US; m 25; c 1. MATHEMATICS. *Educ:* Univ Warsaw, PhD(math), 23. *Hon Degrees:* DSc, Wash Univ, 72, Univ Torun, Poland, 73, Univ Paris, 74, Univ Upsala, 77. *Prof Exp:* Instr math, Warsaw Polytech Sch, 22-30; privat docent, Univ Warsaw, 26-30; prof, Wilno Univ, 30-39; vis lectr, Mass Inst Technol, 39-40; from asst prof to assoc prof, Mt Holyoke Col, 40-45; prof, Univ Pa, 45-47; prof, 47-67, SWIFT DISTINGUISHED SERV PROF MATH, UNIV CHICAGO, 67- *Concurrent Pos:* Rockefeller fel, Oxford Univ & Cambridge Univ, 29-30; Guggenheim fel, 53-54. *Honors & Awards:* Prize, Polish Acad Sci, 39. *Mem:* Nat Acad Sci; Am Acad Arts & Sci; fel Am Math Soc (vpres, 54-); hon mem London Math Soc; Polish Acad Sci. Spanish Acad Sci. *Res:* Fourier series; real variables. *Mailing Add:* Dept of Math Univ of Chicago Chicago IL 60637

ZYGMUNT, WALTER A, b Calumet City, Ill, Mar 24, 24; m 52; c 2. MICROBIOLOGY, BIOCHEMISTRY. *Educ:* Univ Ill, BS, 47, MS, 48, PhD(bact), 50. *Prof Exp:* Res microbiologist res labs, Merck & Co, Inc, 50-53; res microbiologist & biochemist, 53-75, ASSOC DIR BIOL RES, MEAD JOHNSON RES CTR, 75- *Mem:* Fel AAAS; Am Chem Soc; Am Soc Microbiol; fel Am Acad Microbiol; Soc Indust Microbiol. *Res:* Microbial chemistry; chemotherapy; amino acid antagonists; immunology; pulmonary biochemistry; metabolic diseases. *Mailing Add:* Mead Johnson Res Ctr 2404 Pennsylvania St Evansville IN 47721

ZYGMUNT, WARREN W, b Toledo, Ohio, June 24, 09. GEOLOGY. *Educ:* Ohio State Univ, BA, 30, MA, 34, PhD(geol), 40. *Prof Exp:* Asst prof geol, Ohio Univ, 41-55; geologist, US Geol Surv, 55-74; RETIRED. *Concurrent Pos:* Vis prof, Ariz State Univ, 63-64, lectr, 64-68; consult, Salt River Proj, 64-67. *Mem:* Geol Soc Am; Am Asn Petrol Geologists. *Res:* Structural and petroleum geology; stratigraphy; geomorphology. *Mailing Add:* 6107 E Rose Circle Dr Phoenix AZ 85018

ZYSK, E(DWARD) D(ENNIS), b New York, NY, Oct 9, 21; m 54. METALLURGY, THERMOMETRY. *Educ:* Polytech Inst Brooklyn, BMetE, 49, MMetE, 53, MS, 64. *Prof Exp:* Tech asst to smelting supt, Phelps Dodge Refining Corp, 49-51; supvr chlorination, Titanium Metals Corp Am, 51-52; asst, Polytech Inst Brooklyn, 52-53; proj engr, Tube Reducing Corp, 53-55; res metallurgist, 55-58, head metall develop sect, 58-77, head res, Sect Metall, 77-78, TECH DIR, RES & DEVELOP CTR, CORTERET OPER, ENGELHARD INDUSTS DIV, ENGELHARD CORP, 78- *Concurrent Pos:* Chmn, comt 96 thermocouples, Am Nat Standards Inst; tech adv thermocouples, US Deleg, Int Orgn Legal Metrology; lectr precious metal metall, Polytech Inst NY, 80. *Mem:* Fel Am Soc Testing & Mat; Am Inst Mining, Metall & Petrol Engrs; Sigma Xi; Am Soc Metals. *Res:* Reclaiming, melting, processing, fabrication of precious metals and development of industrial applications; development of high temperature properties of precious metals and testing of precious and refractory metals; high temperature and cyrogenic thermometry, compatibility of precious and refractory metals. *Mailing Add:* Engelhard Indust Div Menlo Park Edison NJ 08817

ZYTKUS, EUGENE HENRY, b Toledo, Ohio, Aug 1, 18; m 42; c 1. CHEMICAL ENGINEERING. *Educ:* Univ Toledo, BS, 41; Univ Mich, MS, 48. *Prof Exp:* Engr, Plaskon Div, Libbey-Owens-Ford Co, 48-49; engr, Eng Dept, 49-56, res engr, Polychems Dept, 56-59, res supvr, 59-62, res assoc, Plastics Dept, 62-72, res assoc, Polymer Intermediates Dept, 72-78, RES ASSOC, PETROCHEM DEPT, E I DU PONT DE NEMOURS & CO, INC, 78- *Mem:* Am Chem Soc; Am Inst Chem Engrs. *Res:* New plastics and plastic products; new manufacturing processes for monomers and synthetic polymers; new fabrication techniques for plastics; new process evaluation, development and plant design; including environmental and personnel protection. *Mailing Add:* Res & Develop Div E I du Pont de Nemours & Co Inc Wilmington DE 19898